All Music Guide to

Classical MUSIC

THE DEFINITIVE GUIDE

TO CLASSICAL MUSIC

Edited by

Chris Woodstra

Gerald Brennan

Allen Schrott

AMG
All Media Guide

Backbeat Books

All Media Guide has created the world's largest and most comprehensive information databases for music, videos, DVDs, and video games. With coverage of both in-print and out-of-print titles, the massive AMG archive includes reviews, plot synopses, biographies, ratings, images, titles, credits, essays, and thousands of descriptive categories. All content is original, written expressly for AMG by a worldwide network of professional staff and freelance writers specializing in music, movies, and games. The AMG databases—**All Music Guide®**, **All Movie Guide®**, and **All Game Guide™**—are licensed by major retailers, Internet sites, and other entertainment media providers and are available to the public through its websites (www.allmusic.com, www.allmovie.com, www.allgame.com) and through its published works: *All Music Guide, All Music Guide to Rock, All Music Guide to Country, All Music Guide to Jazz, All Music Guide to the Blues, All Music Guide to Electronica, All Music Guide to Soul, All Music Guide to Hip Hop* and *All Music Guide to Classical Music.*

All Media Guide, LLC, 1168 Oak Valley Drive, Ann Arbor, MI 48108
T: 734/887-5600. F: 734/827-2492
www.allmediaguide.com, www.allmusic.com, www.allmovie.com, www.allgame.com

Published by **Backbeat Books**
600 Harrison Street, San Francisco, CA 94107
www.backbeatbooks.com
Email: books@musicplayer.com
An imprint of the Music Player Network
Publishers of *Guitar Player, Bass Player, Keyboard, EQ,* and other magazines
United Entertainment Media. Inc.
A CMP Information company

CMP
United Business Media

AMG
All Media Guide

Distributed to the book trade in the US and Canada by
Publishers Group West, 1700 Fourth Street, Berkeley, CA 94710

Distributed to the music trade in the US and Canada
by Hal Leonard Publishing, P.O. Box 13819, Milwaukee, WI 53213

Cover design: Wagner Design, Ann Arbor, Michigan
Text composition: Interactive Composition Corporation

ISBN: 0–87930–865–6

Library of Congress Cataloging-in-Publication Data

All music guide to classical music : the definitive guide to classical music / edited by Chris Woodstra, Gerald Brennan, and Allen Schrott.
p. cm.
Includes index.
ISBN-13: 978-087930-865-0
ISBN-10: 0-87930-865-6 (alk. paper)
1. Sound recordings—Reviews. 2. Music—Discography. I. Woodstra, Chris. II. Brennan, Gerald. III. Schrott, Allen.
ML156.9.A385 2005
016.78026'6—dc22

2005023988

Printed in the United States of America
05 06 07 08 09 5 4 3 2 1

Contents

How to Use This Book

Performer entries:

ARTIST NAME

VITAL STATISTICS: Date and place of birth (**b.**) and death (**d.**), if known. Groups and ensembles have dates and places of formation (**f.**) and disbanding (**db.**), if known.

OCCUPATION: The musical activity for which the artist is best known.

BIOGRAPHY: An overview of the artist's life and musical career.

ALBUM RECOMMENDATIONS: Selected recordings highlighting the artist's best work. For widely recorded artists, the selections represent an introduction to their work, and a starter list for collectors.

ALBUM TITLE: The name of the album, if one is given on the package. Albums without proper titles have been assigned one based on their contents (e.g., "Beethoven: Symphonies 5 & 7").

PERFORMERS: Contributing musicians, listed by last name. Opera casts and other long lists have been truncated. Conductors are labeled with the abbreviation "(cond.)." Common ensemble types have also been abbreviated, including: Symphony Orchestra ("SO"), Philharmonic Orchestra ("PO"), Chamber Orchestra ("CO"), and String Quartet ("SQ").

YEAR: Publication year of the album, if known. Not to be confused with the date of the original recording (not given).

LABEL: The label and catalogue number of the album, if known. Deutsche Grammophon, Harmonia Mundi, and Deutsche Harmonia Mundi have been abbreviated for space ("DG," "HM," and "DHM" respectively).

Luciano Pavarotti

b. October 12, 1935, Modena, Italy

Tenor

One of the most successful and admired opera singers of all time, Luciano Pavarotti was king among tenors from the late 1960s through the 1990s. His voice was noted for its exciting upper register, and tailor-made for the operas of Verdi, Bellini, Donizetti, and Puccini, and, as it darkened slightly over the years, for the verismo composers as well. His vocal longevity, which kept him singing youthfully well into his 60s, and still beautifully after that, is a credit to his commanding technique and artistry, and remarkable considering his nearly 40 years of performing.

Pavarotti's father was a baker, and his mother worked in a cigar factory. As a boy, he sang alto in the cathedral choir, and when his voice changed he joined the Modena city choir. He had brief careers as a schoolteacher and an insurance agent; during that time, his major extracurricular activity was not music but soccer, and his play made him a local star. However, increased involvement in the choir (which took prizes in international competitions) led him to pursue vocal studies, and he eventually settled on singing as his aspiration.

Pavarotti studied voice with Arrigo Polo in Modena, then with Ettore Campogalliani in Mantua. His operatic debut was as Rodolfo in *La Bohème* in Reggio Emilia (April 19, 1961), and soon increasing success led to a debut in Amsterdam on January 18, 1963, as Edgardo in *Lucia di Lammermoor.* After singing the same role with Joan Sutherland in Miami in 1965, he was engaged to travel with her in the Sutherland Williamson International Grand Opera Company, touring Australia. In 1966 he appeared at Covent Garden as Tonio in *La Fille du régiment*, where his seemingly effortless handling of the nine successive high Cs in the aria "Pour mon âme" sent his career into high orbit. He repeated the feat at the Metropolitan Opera in 1972, and for more than two decades after that he was a fixture on the operatic scene, appearing in nearly every major European and American house, and even in China, where he performed Puccini's *La Bohème* in the 1980s.

Pavarotti appeared in the first "Live from the Met" broadcast on the PBS network and has been the most consistent draw on that series for years. His outstanding catalogue of recordings on the London (Decca) record label preserves nearly every role he ever performed and will be hard to match for its quality and scope. His charity work has included AIDS benefit concerts and world hunger gala events, as well as his "Pavarotti and Friends" concerts to benefit children, especially in the former Yugoslav states. He also founded a quadrennial contest to identify talented young singers and boost their careers. And, as one of the "Three Tenors," he has brought operatic singing to a wider popular audience than previously might have been thought possible. In 2003 he released his first solo crossover CD, *Ti adoro,* and in March 2004 he said farewell to the world of fully staged opera with performances of Puccini's *Tosca* at the Met. *–AMG*

Recommended:

- ○ **Puccini: La Bohème** / Karajan (cond.), Freni, Pavarotti, Ghiaurov, Panerai, BPO / 1987 / London 421049
- ○ **Donizetti: La Fille du régiment** / Bonynge (cond.), Pavarotti, Sutherland, Sinclair, Garrett, Covent Garden Royal Opera House Orch. / 1986 / London 414520
- ○ **Verdi: Rigoletto** / Bonynge (cond.), Pavarotti, Sutherland, Milnes, London SO / 1985 / London 414269
- ○ **Mascagni: Cavalleria Rusticana; Leoncavallo: Pagliacci** / Gavazzeni, Patane (conds.), Pavarotti, Freni, Cappuccilli, Varady / 1988 / London 414590
- ○ **Pavarotti: The Early Years** / Pavarotti, etc. / 1994 / BMG 62541
- ○ **Luciano Pavarotti** / Pavarotti, etc. / 2001 / Decca 467920
- ○ **Pavarotti Edition** / Pavarotti, etc. / 2001 / Decca 470000
- ○ **Ti Adoro** / Pavarotti, etc. / 2003 / Decca 000109602

Composer entries:

COMPOSER NAME

VITAL STATISTICS: Date and place of birth (**b.**) and death (**d.**), if known.

GENRES: Genres listed after the occupation "Composer" represent types of works selected for individual discussion in the WORKS section below.

BIOGRAPHY: An overview of the composer's life and musical career.

WORKS: Each composer entry includes selected works, broken down into genres (Chamber Music, Opera, etc.) where appropriate. Less familiar composers, or those who are known more for their bodies of work as a whole than for individual compositions, may have only an "Overview of Works." Likewise, individual genres may have overview entries.

GENRE

WORK TITLE

DATE(S) OF COMPOSITION: Dates of revision are also given, if known.

WORK DESCRIPTION: A brief discussion of the work's genesis, stylistic elements, musical content, and historical significance. Opera and selected ballet entries also include a plot synopsis.

ALBUM RECOMMENDATIONS: Each work entry will include one or more recommended recordings unless the work has never been released on CD. For frequently recorded works, the recommendations may be considered reliable introductions to the music at hand and samplings, as diverse as possible, of the excellent performances available. For less familiar works with fewer recordings to choose from, the recommendations may be the only choices on the market.

Igor Stravinsky

b. June 17, 1882, Orianenbaum, Russia **d.** April 6, 1971, New York, NY
Composer: Ballet, Symphonic, Orchestral, Chamber Music, Music for Band, Keyboard Music, Concerto, Choral, Opera, Musical Theater, Vocal

Igor Stravinsky was one of music's truly epochal innovators; no other composer of the twentieth century exerted such a pervasive influence or dominated his art in the way that Stravinsky did during his five-decade musical career. Aside from purely technical considerations such as rhythm and harmony, the most important hallmark of Stravinsky's style is, indeed, its changing face. Emerging from the spirit of late Russian nationalism and ending his career with a thorny, individual language steeped in 12-tone principles, Stravinsky assumed a number of aesthetic guises throughout the course of his development while always retaining a distinctive, essential identity.

Although he was the son of one of the Mariinsky Theater's principal basses and a talented amateur pianist, Stravinsky had no more musical training than that of any other Russian upper-class child. He entered law school, but also began private composition and orchestration studies with Nicolai Rimsky-Korsakov. By 1909, the orchestral works *Scherzo fantastique* and *Fireworks* had impressed Sergei Diaghilev enough for him to ask Stravinsky to orchestrate, and subsequently compose, ballets for his company. Stravinsky's triad of early ballets—*The Firebird* (1909–10), *Petrushka* (1910–11), and most importantly *The Rite of Spring* (1911–13)—did more to establish his reputation than any of his other works; indeed, the riot which followed the premiere of *The Rite* is one of the most notorious . . .

BALLET MUSIC

***Pulcinella* (1920; revised 1965)**

Before World War I, Serge Diaghilev's Ballets russes had enjoyed a tremendously rewarding relationship with Igor Stravinsky, both financially and artistically. In the aftermath of World War I, however, Stravinsky was struggling to adjust to his exile in Switzerland and could think of nothing he wanted to compose or adapt for Diaghilev's use. Enterprisingly, Diaghilev presented Stravinsky with the work of the Baroque composer Giovanni Battista Pergolesi, with the idea that the composer could adapt the tunes into a ballet. When Stravinsky proved amenable to the idea, Diaghilev presented him with an old manuscript of Italian commedia dell'arte episodes featuring a heroine named Pulcinella, and suggested Stravinsky base the action on one of these stories. To sweeten the deal, Diaghilev assured Stravinsky that no less an artist than Pablo Picasso would design the sets, and that Léonide Massine, whom Stravinsky respected greatly, would choreograph. These inducements proved overwhelming, and Stravinsky completed *Pulcinella* in 1920; its premiere was given that May by the Ballets russes in Paris, conducted by Ernest Ansermet.

The actual plot Stravinsky chose, involving jealous lovers, mistaken identities, and resuscitating magicians, is complicated and busy enough that Stravinsky himself admitted that the resulting work as more of an *action dansante* than a ballet, although it is subtitled "ballet avec chante" ("ballet with singing"). Stravinsky chose movements from numerous Pergolesi works (and works perhaps mistakenly ascribed to Pergolesi) to illustrate the action, and scored them for a small eighteenth century orchestra: no clarinets or percussion, and concerto and ripenio groups in the strings. Three vocal soloists form part of the orchestra, without portraying individual characters.

Although he distorted phrases and chord patterns in adapting Pergolesi's music, Stravinsky left much of the basic melodic and rhythmic content unaltered; Pergolesi, and his stock of bright, engaging melodies, therefore deserve much of the credit for the success of *Pulcinella.* But Stravinsky's contribution is equally engaging: *Pulcinella* is brilliantly scored, using modern string textures that would not sound out of place in Bartók, and engaging combinations like flute, oboe and pizzicato strings or (in an especially witty moment) trombone and double bass. A sense of carefree play never lets up through the score's bustlings and scurryings, and Stravinsky takes care to make sure that the instrumentation remains varied, and that the movements cohere to form a larger formal design. The result sounds characteristic of both Stravinsky and Pergolesi: eighteenth century music living in a twentieth century world.

While *Pulcinella* was a success for Diaghilev, it proved even more fruitful for Stravinsky: it eventually paved the way for his neo-Classical style. As he was to write later, "*Pulcinella* was my discovery of the past, the epiphany through which the whole of my late work became possible. It was a backward look, of course, but it was a look in the mirror, too." *—Andrew Lindemann Malone*

Recommended:

- ○ **Stravinsky: Pulcinella; Octet; Renard; Ragtime** / Salonen (cond.), Kenny, Aler, Tomlinson, London Sinfonietta / 1991 / Sony 45965
- ○ **Stravinsky: Pulcinella; Petrushka** / Chailly (cond.), Antonacci, Shimell, Ballo, Concertgebouw / 1995 / London 443774
- ○ **Stravinsky: Le Sacre du printemps; L'Oiseau de feu; Jeu de cartes; Petrouchka; Pulcinella** / Abbado (cond.), London SO / DG 453085

Contributors

All Music Guide

Chris Woodstra, Vice President of Content Development
Gerald Brennan, Director of Content, Classical Music
Allen Schrott, Senior Managing Editor, Classical Music

Classical Editors

Patsy Morita, Associate Editor
James Manheim, Assistant Editor
David N. Lewis, Assistant Editor

Editorial Contributions

Zoran Minderovic
Michael Rodman
Mark Kirschenmann
Dean McFarlane-Parrott
Mark Knoll

Technical Editors

Mark Donkers, Director of Data Processing
Maeve K. Sullivan, Classical Data Processing Supervisor
Suky Morita
Ryan Sult
Corwin Moore
Eileen Donis-Forster
Terrina Anderson

Copy Editors

Rachel Sprovtsoff-Mangus
Karen Paik

Contributors

Robert Adelson
Jason Ankeny
Robert Barefield
Peter Bates
Hector Bellman
Michael Blostein
"Blue" Gene Tyranny
Natalie Boisvert
Chris Boyes
Gerald Brennan
David Brensilver
Roy Brewer
Seth Brodsky
Rachel Campbell
Neil Cardew-Fanning
Norbert Carnovale
Alexander Carpenter
David Cashman
Eugene Chadbourne
Steven Coburn
Adrian Corleonis
Dawn Culbertson
Robert Cummings
Mona DeQuis
Roger Dettmer
Timothy Dickey
John Dobson
Bruce Eder
Erik Eriksson
Ann Feeney
Meredith Gailey
Margaret Godfrey
Robert Gold
Eric Goldberg
Jeremy Grimshaw
Kristen Grimshaw
Jennifer Hambrick
James Harley
Craig Harris
Sean Hickey
D. J. Hoek
Michael Jameson
Blair Johnston
John Keillor
David Kent
Stephen Kingsbury
Robert Kirzinger
Roberta Klarreich
Caroline Kovtun
Rita Laurance
Richard LeSueur
James Leonard
Uncle Dave Lewis
James Liu
Bruce Lundgren
Andrus Madsen
Tim Mahon
Andrew Lindemann Malone
Donato Mancini
James Manheim
David A. McCarthy
Todd McComb
Zoran Minderovic
Edward Moore
Patsy Morita
Chris Morrison
Michael Morrison
Theresa Muir
Meredith Murphy
Brian Olewnick
Graham Olson
Thomas Oram
John Palmer
Russell Platt
Umberto Posarelli
Douglas Purl
Aaron Rabushka
James Reel
Wayne Gerard Reisig
Brian Robins
Michael Rodman
Mark Satola
Allen Schrott
Sol Louis Siegel
Walter Simmons
DJ Sparr
Corie Stanton Root
Joseph Stevenson
Emily Stoops
Franklin Stover
Virginia Sublett
Sylvia Typaldos
Rachael Unite
Nemesio Valle
Lynn Vought
Tod Whitesel
Bob Williams
Brian Wise
Darren Wong
Ron Wynn
James Zychowicz

Introduction

Defining "classical music" is a bewildering task. On one hand, the word "Classical" refers to a specific time period (ca. 1735–1820), with the music of Haydn, Mozart, and the young Beethoven at its center. And there is a wider body of music that is generally *recognized* as classical music, specifically music written between the Renaissance era and the early decades of the twentieth century that you'd be likely to hear at a symphony concert, in an opera house, in a recital hall, or on a classical radio station (this is the "know it when you hear it" approach). But taking into account the full, true variety of music that falls under the classical umbrella means grappling with a host of contradictions and extremes: ancient music and music written yesterday, music for traditional instruments and music for computers and electronics, music in miniature and music on the grandest of scales, music that soothes and music that assaults the ears with agonizing cacophony, music you could dance to and music with no discernible rhythmic pulse, serious music and comedy, music for one performer and music for groups of hundreds, rigorously organized music and music generated randomly, and much more. In other words, to understand classical music you must leave behind preconceptions about sound, source, and materials, and embrace the uncertainty.

The bulk of what we consider classical music is indeed old music. The classical "greatest hits," like Handel's *Messiah*, Beethoven's *Ninth Symphony*, and Tchaikovsky's *1812 Overture*, are mostly from the period between 1700 and 1900. Sometimes we even consider music to be classical simply *because* it is old. John Dowland, the Lennon-McCartney of his day who penned popular songs in sixteenth century London, is considered a classical composer today. That's because we still play and sing his music, albeit in a different context. (Lennon-McCartney songs may be considered classical music 400 years from now.)

Classical music also tends to work within a basic set of forms: the symphony, the concerto, the string quartet, and opera, to name but a few. These traditional formats have changed over time, sometimes getting stretched beyond recognition, but their essential qualities are compelling enough that they have persisted for centuries. They are *archetypes*, and essential expressions of what it means to be human. Consider the symphony, in which all the tribes gather to sing together as one; or the concerto, in which an individual by turn sings with and is pitted against a larger group. Consider the compelling rightness and economy of the string quartet—four points of sound that define a musical space.

Opera's appeal is obvious: an entire fabulous singing universe that stands in stark contrast to the mundane one we live in. It summons the deepest passions of listeners and collectors, and is in a way the apotheosis of all art, because (to paraphrase Hazel Morley) it creates a world of divine singing, beautiful music, intense drama, great literature, seductive lighting, breathtaking dress and scenery, innovative directing, sensitive conducting, and convincing acting. When it succeeds, it is the stuff of legends–also fistfights, stinging invective, and endless argument. Nothing in the entire world of music rouses more rapture (and antagonism) than the subject of opera singers. They are the divas; the Western world hails them throughout as goddesses, and their male counterparts as idols of legend. Princes and princesses bow to *them*.

Focusing on age and traditional forms still cannot account fully for the category of classical music, most obviously because many of its greatest composers and musical works belong to the twentieth, and now twenty-first, centuries; often these composers and works represent fundamental breaks from established forms, materials, and schools of thought. But contemporary composers working in the classical tradition consciously connect and interact with the established traditions of the genre. John Cage's infamous *4'33"*, for instance, a three-movement piece made of nothing but silence with no intentional sounds at all, at first seems to break entirely new ground. But in actuality it points backward to the progressively brief and sparse scores of the modernist Anton Webern, and even to the five minutes of silence that the great symphonist Gustav Mahler insisted upon between the first two movements of his second symphony. Once considered an avant-garde novelty, *4'33"* is now a hallmark of twentieth century composition and thought. The bottom line is: classical music evolves, and our concept of what it includes must evolve right along with it. That's why in this book you'll find information on many living composers—most with a clear orientation towards the classical tradition (John Adams and Thomas Adès, for instance), but also a few, like Brian Eno and The Who's Pete Townshend, who are better known in other spheres and who don't often come to mind when one thinks of classical music. Eno is here because he pretty much invented ambient music, which in turn influenced the minimalist movement and the modern spiritualists like Arvo Pärt and John Tavener. Mr. Townshend is included because his "rock opera" *Tommy* is a full-fledged opera that changes the way we think about what an opera can be, as well as amazing rock music.

One of the things keeping classical music from becoming a mere museum (or worse, a morgue) is each generation's tendency to reinterpret the classics. Composers are limited in the accuracy with which they can relate their conversations with the Muses, for in order to preserve and communicate them, they have to write them down in scores using a small set of symbols. It's amazing how different two performances of the same work can sound without breaking the letter of the law. A few controversial performers even manage to play fast and loose with the letter while bringing forth so much of the genuine spirit of a work that no one gets too upset; indeed, some of these scofflaws are highly celebrated.

So, it's not just the greatest music that has lasted for generations; the greatest performances live on as well. Listen and discover for yourself why Arturo Toscanini's legendary version of Beethoven's *Missa Solemnis* has never been out of print despite being more than 60 years old. Did you know that there are eight separate recordings still available of Wilhelm Furtwängler conducting Beethoven's *Ninth Symphony*, and that each one is different, and in its way great? Is your favorite pianist doing justice to that Rachmaninov piano concerto? Well, you can always listen to Sergey Rachmaninov play it himself and then judge for *yourself*. You can hear Béla Bartók, Sergey Prokofiev, and Dmitry Shostakovich play their own pieces, or hear Edward Elgar conduct his symphonies and cello concerto. You won't get state-of-the-art sound quality, but what you do get dwarfs the sonic shortcomings.

Today, we can't even imagine a world without recorded music. But even a century ago, music lovers who wanted to hear great concert music had to save up their coins for tickets and an elegant night on the town. The home stereo was a piano, where brother and sister could play four-hand reductions of the newest symphonies. Though the sounds they made were pale in comparison to our fine stereo and surround-sound setups (not to mention the concert hall experience), the level of amateur musicianship was much higher then, with a larger percentage of people taking part. Except for the last century, to have music in one's home meant that family members had to be musically creative, or at least re-creative. These days we plug in and press a button.

In many ways our dependence on recordings for our musical diet is unfortunate. In classical music especially, a recording is only a *copy* of the original performance. Though the buzzings of a loudspeaker are a fine proxy for the acoustic presence of real instruments and voices, they cannot be mistaken for the real experience any more than a picture of a landscape can be confused with an actual one.

But without great recordings, we are lost, since without them none of us could encounter even a fraction of the music they offer in our lifetimes. And so this volume is devoted to the wealth of music those recordings offer us. In these pages, you'll find biographies of every significant classical composer whose music has been recorded, and hundreds of notable recording artists and ensembles. There are succinct and informative essays devoted to the major periods and genres of the art to help orient you. From there you can explore nearly 4,000 detailed descriptions of important pieces of classical music, more than 12,000 recommended recordings, and hundreds of opera and ballet synopses. And, for the first time ever, you can have all of this in a single handy and affordable volume.

There is much fine music that has been unjustly forgotten, but there is no music that has lasted for centuries that has been unjustly remembered. We invite you to explore the rich world of classical music with us. The expert will find the solid and reliable reference one has come to expect from the All Music Guide series, and newcomers will find an introduction to a musical journey that may last a lifetime.
—Gerald Brennan

A

A Sei Voci

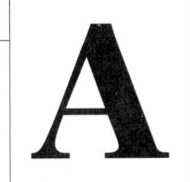

f. 1977, Sablé-sur-Sarthe, France
Ensemble
The vocal ensemble A Sei Voci is based in the French city of Sablé-sur-Sarthe and was founded in 1977. The name, naturally, is so given as the group uniformly consists of six regular member voices, although other singers and instrumentalists are added as each project they undertake may require. A Sei Voci was founded with the purpose of recovering vocal works from the Baroque and Renaissance periods that were not yet revived or otherwise known to the public.

Early on, A Sei Voci established itself as a force to be reckoned with through a series of concerts, held mainly in continental Europe, in which the "visual" show proved of equal interest to that given in the music. A Sei Voci also became known through a number of outstanding recordings made for the French company Erato, where the group was often identified as "Ensemble a sei voci." In 1991, A Sei Voci was reorganized with original member Bernard Fabré-Garrus named as leader, and at that time the shortened form of the name became permanent. Under Fabré-Garrus' leadership, the group flourished and soon found itself in a position to negotiate a new recording contract with Auvidis Astrée. Thankfully, this arrangement managed to survive Auvidis Astrée's absorption by the French media giant Naïve.

A Sei Voci has recorded works by Gesualdo, Josquin Desprez, Charles d'Helfer, Janequin, Monteverdi, Jommelli, and many others, and its trophy case is filled with multiple awards and citations of distinction, including the Choc de Musique, Diapason d'Or, and the Grand Prix du Disque of the Académie de Charles Cros, to name just a few. A Sei Voci is no longer just limited to Renaissance and Baroque literature, but is now known for its performances in works of Mahler and Brahms. Since the beginning of Fabré-Garrus' directorship, A Sei Voci has likewise reached out to contemporary composers as well and has given premieres of new works by composers such as Thierry Escaich and Jean-François Zygel. *—Uncle Dave Lewis*

Recommended:
- ○ **Monteverdi: Selva Morale** / Fabré-Garrus (cond.), A Sei Voci / 2000 / Astrée 8815
- ○ **Une messe imaginaire** / Fabré-Garrus (cond.), A Sei Voci / 1999 / Astrée 8677
- ○ **Josquin Desprez: Messes de L'Homme Armé** / Fabré-Garrus (cond.), A Sei Voci / 2001 / Astrée Naïve 8809

Claudio Abbado

b. Jun. 26, 1933, Milan, Italy
Conductor
Claudio Abbado is one of the leading conductors of the late twentieth and early twenty-first centuries. He has held a number of prestigious posts, any one of which would be a crowning achievement for a conductor, and his musical presence in both concert and recordings has left an undeniable legacy of excellence.

His family traces its roots to a prominent Moorish family expelled from Spain in 1492, and is said to include the architect of the Alhambra. His father was Michelangelo Abbado, a violinist and teacher who gave both Claudio and his brother, Marcello Abbado, their first piano and music lessons (Marcello has gone on to become a pianist and composer).

Claudio was educated at the Milan Conservatory, graduating in 1955 with a certificate in piano. While a student there, he also studied conducting with Antonio Votto. In 1955, he studied piano with Friedrich Gulda in Salzburg, and then (from 1956 to 1958) attended Hans Swarowsky's conducting classes at the Vienna Academy of Music.

In 1958, he made his conducting debut in Trieste, and won the Koussevitsky Competition at Tanglewood. This led to his engagement in several provincial opera houses and orchestras, as well as a teaching position at Parma Conservatory. After winning the 1963 Dimitri Mitropoulos Prize, he was awarded a five-month position on the staff of the New York Philharmonic, with which he made his American professional debut on April 7, 1963. The year 1965 marked his debut with the Vienna Philharmonic at the Salzburg Festival, as well as his return to his home town of Milan to conduct at La Scala. He would conduct there again in 1967, become the company's resident director in 1968, and be named music director in 1971.

Abbado was credited with raising the performing standards at La Scala, and for broadening its repertory. He also organized its orchestral players into the Orchestra della Scala, whose performances of works by such composers as Schoenberg, Nono, Ligeti, Stockhausen, and Berio brought Abbado special acclaim as an interpreter of modern works.

In 1971, he was appointed principal conductor of the Vienna Philharmonic. Soon after, he formed a relationship with the London Symphony Orchestra, of which he became principal conductor in 1979, and finally music director, a post he retained until 1988. Other activities during this period included the founding of the European Community Youth Orchestra, the Chamber Orchestra of Europe, and the Gustav Mahler Youth Chamber Orchestra.

For the period 1982–86 Abbado served as principal guest conductor at the Chicago Symphony Orchestra, after which he was appointed music director of the Vienna State Opera. The Viennese further honored him by appointing him General Music Director of the City. During his tenure, he founded (1988) the Wien Modern music festival, which has now grown to encompass all forms of contemporary art.

Abbado succeeded Herbert von Karajan as music director of the Berlin Philharmonic in 1989. In 1991, he relinquished his position at the Vienna State Opera, but he has maintained a presence in the city by founding the annual Vienna prize for young composers. In 1994, he succeeded to another post once held by Karajan, namely the directorship of the Salzburg Easter Festival.

Abbado is an exciting conductor who relishes the beauty of tone. His extensive discography includes the complete symphonic works of Mahler, Schubert, Ravel, Tchaikovsky, Mendelssohn, and Beethoven, and dozens of other recordings. *—Joseph Stevenson*

Recommended:
- ○ **Brahms: Tragic Overture; Song of Destiny; Symphony 3** / Abbado (cond.), Berlin PO / DG 429765
- ○ **Mozart: Symphonies 25 & 31; Masonic Funeral Music; Posthorn Symphony** / Abbado (cond.) / 2004 / Sony Classical 93079
- ○ **Nono: Il canto sospeso; Mahler: Kindertotenlieder** / Abbado (cond.), Bonney, Lipovšek, Otto, Torzewski / 1993 / Sony 53360
- ○ **Claudio Abbado Conducts Mussorgsky** / Abbado (cond.), London SO / 1981 / RCA 61354

Maurice Abravanel

b. Jan. 6, 1903, Thessaloniki, Greece, **d.** Sep. 22, 1993, Salt Lake City, UT
Conductor
The state of Utah became a flourishing classical music scene thanks to the efforts of Maurice Abravanel, who served as music director of the Utah Symphony for 32 years starting in 1947. Although his peers might have looked at a posting in Utah as death in the boondocks, to Abravanel it was an opportunity to accomplish his dream of building up a permanent symphony orchestra of his own in a part of the world that was sorely lacking such a resource. Doing this meant turning down a lucrative contract with Radio City Music Hall, and even working without pay during the orchestra's most extreme periods of financial struggle.

Born of Spanish and Portuguese parents (and a descendant of Queen Isabella of Spain), Abravanel spent his early years in Switzerland. He studied in Germany under Kurt Weill, who was a major influence both technically and philosophically. Abravanel conducted an orchestra for the first time as a teenager in Switzerland, and his abilities soon put him in front of the orchestras of the Berlin State Opera and the Paris Opera. He went to Australia for several years, the first indication of his dedication toward hands-on musical involvement outside the geographical mainstream. When he was 33, he was hired as the youngest-yet conductor of the Metropolitan Opera in New York City. He took on an incredibly busy schedule, at one point conducting seven performances of five different operas over a period of nine days. While in the Big Apple, he shifted his talents to Broadway, renewing his relationship with Weill to become the conductor of all of the composer's American productions.

A few years later came the first one-year contract to conduct the nearly amateurish Utah Symphony. The Western scenery may have balanced out the sour notes, however, and Abravanel decided to stay put. He retired from the orchestra in 1979, but he remained active in Utah's cultural community, as well as internationally, until his death. Under his guidance, the Utah Symphony developed a superb international reputation, which Abravanel accomplished not by importing players from outside the area, but by working diligently with the local musicians in order to make them competent full-time players. The symphony made four world tours and recorded with Vanguard, Vox, Angel, and CBS. Abravanel championed contemporary music, programming compositions by Edgard Varèse as well as Utah composers such as Leroy Robertson and Crawford Gates.

Other Abravanel activities outside of Mormon territory included directing the Music Academy of the West in Santa Barbara, CA, from 1956 through 1979. In 1981 he was appointed an artist-in-residence for life at Tanglewood. He served on the National Council of the Arts from 1970 through 1976, and received the American Symphony Orchestra League's Golden Baton Award in 1981. In 1970, he became a member of the first music panel of the National Endowment for the Arts. He received a Tony Award for *Regina* and Grammy nominations for some of the more than 100 recordings with the Utah Symphony, many of which are considered classics. *—Eugene Chadbourne*

Recommended:

- ○ **Mahler: Symphonies 7 & 8** / Abravanel (cond.), Utah SO / 2003 / Artemis 1222
- ○ **Honegger: Judith; Milhaud: La Création** / Abravanel (cond.), Utah SO / 1995 / Vanguard 8088
- ○ **Milhaud: Pacem in Terris; L' Homme et son désir** / Abravanel (cond.), Utah SO / 1993 / Vanguard 8067
- ○ **Vaughan Williams: Symphony 6; Dona Nobis Pacem** / Abravanel (cond.), Utah SO / 1995 / Vanguard 7

Academy of Ancient Music

f. 1973, London, England
Ensemble

Keyboardist Christopher Hogwood established the Academy of Ancient Music in 1973, using as his model an ensemble that had been founded in 1726 to perform music that was at least 150 years old. Thus, Hogwood's orchestra was one of the first in modern times to perform Baroque works on Baroque instruments. Hogwood chose members who were not only masters of their instruments, but also scholars of performance style of the period. The orchestra quickly gained recognition for its authentic performances and recordings, and stirred up musicological debate. In 1978, it expanded its repertory to include the works of Mozart and Haydn and their contemporaries. The orchestra has recorded or taken on recording the complete symphonies of Mozart (the first such cycle on period instruments), Haydn, and Beethoven, and the complete piano concertos of Beethoven and Mozart. Recorded for Decca, these were under the direction of Hogwood, who also led recordings of Mozart's *La Clemenza di Tito*, Haydn's *Orfeo ed Euridice* and Handel's *Rinaldo*, all of which were prize-winners and featured famed mezzo-soprano Cecilia Bartoli.

In 1996, Andrew Manze was named associate director, and Paul Goodwin was named associate conductor, allowing the Academy to expand its performance schedule and begin recording for the Harmonia Mundi label. The Academy also began extending invitations to others, such as Stephen Cleobury with the Choir of King's College, Cambridge; Edward Higginbottom with the Choir of New College, Oxford; Stephen Layton with Polyphony; and Masaaki Suzuki with the Japan Bach Collegium to be guest directors, furthering the Academy's vocal and choral repertoire. Instrumentalists Giuliano Carmignola, Richard Egarr, and Pavlo Beznosiuk also were asked to guest direct.

Paul Goodwin began commissioning new works specifically for the distinctive instruments of the Academy, the first being 1997's *Eternity's Sunrise* for voice and Baroque ensemble by John Tavener. Other commissioned works came from David Bedford; John Woolrich, whose *Arcangelo* for the group commemorated the 350th birthday of Arcangelo Corelli; and Thea Musgrave.

Andrew Manze stepped down from his post in 2003, as the Academy celebrated its 30th anniversary. The ensemble marked the year by also celebrating the Corelli anniversary and the 60th birthday of John Tavener in special concerts, and by beginning an exploration of the music of Mendelssohn, once again expanding its musicological horizons. *—Patsy Morita*

Recommended:

- ○ **Vivaldi: 6 Cello Concertos** / Hogwood (cond.), Coin / 1989 / L'Oiseau-Lyre 421732
- ○ **Handel: Rinaldo** / Hogwood (cond.), Bartoli, Daniels / 2000 / Decca 467087
- ○ **Handel: Water Music; Fireworks Music; Concerto a due cori 3** / Hogwood (cond.) / 1997 / L'Oiseau-Lyre 455709
- ○ **Pergolesi: Marian Vespers** / Higginbottom (cond), Birchall, Daneman / 2002 / Erato 46684
- ○ **Bach: 7 Harpsichord Concertos; Triple Concerto** / Manze (cond.), Egarr / 2002 / HM 907283/84
- ○ **J.C. Bach: Overture, Adriano in Siria; 3 Symphonies; Sinfonia Concertante** / Standage (cond.), Brown, Watkin, Bruine / 1993 / Chandos 540
- ○ **Vivaldi: Magnificat RV610; Gloria RV589; Vivaldi: Dixit Dominus RV594** / Cleobury (cond.), King's College Choir / 2002 / EMI 57265
- ○ **Tavener: Total Eclipse; Agraphon** / Higginbottom, Goodwin (cond.), Rozario, Harle / 2001 / HM 907271
- ○ **Handel: Messiah** / Hogwood (cond.), Preston, Elliott, Kirkby, Watkinson, Nelson / 1991 / L'oiseau-Lyre 430488

Academy of St. Martin-in-the-Fields

f. 1959, London, England
Ensemble

In 1958, violinist Neville Marriner invited a dozen of his colleagues to form an ensemble which would focus on playing Baroque music. Taking the meaning of ensemble playing to heart, the group decided to work without a conductor, as did many chamber orchestras of the Baroque period. In this cooperative spirit, the ensemble worked toward the brilliantly energetic sound and high standard of musicianship which have become its hallmarks. The group performed its premier concert on the auspicious date, Friday, November 13, 1959, in the Church of St. Martin-in-the-Fields from which the ensemble takes its name.

Unable to generate sufficient interest in concerts, the ensemble sought recognition in the recording studio; Louise Hanson Dyer, wealthy founder of the L'Oiseau-Lyre Company, gave the Academy its first recording contract in 1961. Other contracts soon followed, including a five-year contract with Argo in 1965. In addition, the ensemble became popular in other venues with appearances on the BBC Proms program and in performances of Vivaldi's *Four Seasons* and Wagner's *Siegfried Idyll* for BBC television films.

Incorporated in 1970 under the management of Marriner and four other founding members, the Academy rapidly developed into a highly popular ensemble. With no permanent concert venue of its own, the Academy toured widely between short seasons at the Royal Festival Hall and the Church of St. Martin-in-the-Fields; a tradition that has continued throughout the history of the group. The ensemble also expanded its repertoire to include music from the Baroque to the present day; the ensemble took three different forms to accommodate this variety of music. The largest of these was a group of about 45 musicians lead by Marriner, who, reluctantly, had taken on the role of conductor. The second group was the Chamber Ensemble, which was originally formed in 1967 for the specific purpose of performing large-scale string chamber music. The third form is a small group similar in size to the original ensemble, which is responsible for most of the touring and has, at various times, been lead from the concert master's chair by Neville Marriner, Iona Brown and Kenneth Sillito. The Academy's fluidity of form is made practical by the fact that the musicians are not full-time employees; instead, they are hired as needed for specific engagements.

An association with the Philips company, which began in 1971, set the ensemble on a course toward its establishment as a world-class orchestra. In 1975, Philips offered separate recording contracts to the Academy and to Marriner. Another milestone in the Academy's history, also in 1975, was the formation of the Chorus of the Academy of St. Martin-in-the-Fields under the direction of Laszlo Heltay. Initially created to perform Bach's *B minor mass* on an Academy tour, the Chorus became a regular addition to the ensemble.

Between concert tours, the ensemble has recorded a wide variety of works including symphony cycles of Schubert and Beethoven. The orchestra has more than 300 recordings to its credit, and it is estimated that an average of 30 minutes of the Academy's work is broadcast on each classical music radio station in the U.S. every day of the year. The Academy has also continued its film work, performing the score for the movie *Amadeus* in 1984.

Throughout its long and illustrious history, the Academy of St. Martin-in-the-Fields has upheld a consistently high standard of virtuosity and ensemble playing. Still under the direction of Kenneth Sillito and principal guest conductor Murray Perahia, this group, with its broad repertoire and structural flexibility continues to be one of the most distinguished and sought-after ensembles in the world of classical music. *—Corie Stanton Root*

Recommended:

- ○ **Mozart: Horn Concertos 1–4** / Marriner (cond.), Tuckwell / 2001 / EMI 74967
- ○ **Bach: Orchestral Suite 2 & 3; Concerto for 2 Violins** / Marriner (cond.), Szeryng, Hasson / 2003 / Decca 473847
- ○ **Vivaldi: La Cetra** / Brown (cond.) / 1996 / London 448110
- ○ **Vaughan Williams: Orchestral Works** / Marriner, Boult, Wordsworth (conds.) / 1999 / Decca 460357
- ○ **Mozart: Sextet in F; Eine kleine Nachtmusik; Divertimento K. 136** / Marriner (cond.) / Philips 412269

Salvatore Accardo

b. Sep. 26, 1941, Turin, Italy
Violinist

Salvatore Accardo is an outstanding Italian violin virtuoso, best known as a master of the works of Niccolò Paganini, but equally accomplished across a wide variety of repertory for the instrument. His playing is characterized by a taut, visceral tone and a disciplined musical approach that avoids self-indulgence. Having also established himself as a successful conductor, chamber musician, and teacher, Accardo may be considered one of the most accomplished and influential musicians of his generation.

Accardo was born in the northern Italian town of Turin, but as a teenager he went to Naples to study violin at the Conservatorio di San Pietro a Majella; it was there, at the age of 13, that he gave his first performance of the devilish Caprices of Paganini, beginning a lifelong association with that music. He later studied in Siena, at the Accademia Musicale Chigiana. After winning the 1956 Geneva Competition and the 1958 Paganini Competition in Genoa, Accardo began a performing career that has kept him busy ever since, both as a soloist with major orchestras and as a recitalist. His repertory includes all of the violin music of Paganini, the solo partitas of J.S. Bach, virtually every mainstream violin concerto from the Classical, Romantic, and Modern eras, and a number of contemporary works. Works composed specifically for Accardo include Walter Piston's *Fantasia for Violin and Orchestra*, Iannis Xenakis' *Dikhthas*, and Franco Donatoni's *Argot*. The most notable entries in Accardo's extensive discography include his complete cycle of Paganini concertos (the first of its kind), Max Bruch's complete music for violin and orchestra, and the complete sonatas and partitas of Bach.

In 1968, he founded the Italian Chamber Orchestra and became its first conductor. He later conducted the ensemble I Musici, and in 1994 he was appointed conductor of the Orchestra del Teatro San Carlo in Naples. He is a founding member of the Accardo String Quartet and of the Walter Stauffer Academy, where he routinely gives master classes, and also of the Cremona Academy for string players. In 1987, he published a book, *L'arte del violino* (The Art of the Violin). *—Allen Schrott*

Recommended:

- ○ **Accardo Plays Paganini: Complete Recordings** / Dutoit (cond.), Accardo (violin), London PO / DG 463754
- ○ **Mozart: Violin Concertos 1 & 2; Rondo in C** / Accardo (violin & cond.), Prague CO / 1998 / Fone 98F03
- ○ **Beethoven: Violin Sonatas 1 & 9** / Accardo (violin), Lessona / 1997 / Fonit Cetra 116
- ○ **Chausson: Concert; Saint-Saëns: Sonata Op75** / Accardo (violin), Canino / 1993 / Dynamic 44
- ○ **Vivaldi: Op.7–12** / Accardo, I Musici / 1997 / Philips 456186
- ○ **Bach: 3 Violin Concertos** / Mutter, Accardo (violin & cond.), English CO / 1991 / EMI 47005

Adam de la Halle

b. ca. 1245, Arras, France, **d.** ca. 1288, Naples, Italy (?)
Composer: Vocal

Adam de la Halle occupies a unique position astride two trends in music history. On the one hand, he was the "last of the Trouvères," bringing to a close the brilliant early flowering of Old French lyric poetry; the large body of his facile and conventional courtly chansons stand perfectly in line with the traditions fostered by Eleanor of Aquitaine, Thibault de Champagne, King of Navarre, and the eloquent Gace Brulé. On the other hand, Adam mingled this traditional monophonic composition with the more esoteric form of the thirteenth century motet, and performed the first experiments in polyphonic secular song. In this respect, he placed himself squarely in the middle of stylistic trends that would come to greatest fruition in the next century, with the Ars Nova of Philippe de Vitry and preeminently in the figure of Guillaume de Machaut.

Sadly, for a poet and musician of such versatility and prowess, not a single piece of datable documentation for his life survives. The form of his name (and later manuscript attributions) tell of his birth in the city of Arras—a positive hotbed of literary culture—80 miles north of Paris. (Another form of his name, "le Boscu," suggests a handicap or even a hunchback, but Adam in a late poem denies this disability!) His father Henri was well educated, and probably a cleric and civic employee who died in 1290; Adam's wife, named Maroie, may have died in Arras in 1287.

Adam himself is often described as "Maistre," indicating his completion of some advanced studies; these took place either at Vauchelles Abbey, or more likely, in Paris. Adam also certainly participated in the lively activities of Arras' literary societies, the *Confrérie des jongleurs* (Guild of Artesian Jongleurs) and the renowned *Puy d'Arras*. This latter association chose a king who would judge poetic competitions among the members; God Himself was rumored to attend the festivities to hear their poetry. In 1282, Adam apparently traveled as poet and musician in the retinue of Robert II, Count of Artois, on a campaign to Naples to aid his uncle Charles d'Anjou after the massacre of the Sicilian Vespers. Adam died in Italy, sometime between 1285 (the death of Charles and the occasion for his poem *Le roi de Secile*) and 1289.

As noted above, Adam de la Halle produced a remarkably versatile body of works. And unlike the majority of the Trouvère poets, whose songs survive in large anthologies, several manuscripts attempt to collect music only of his; one manuscript in Paris even presages Machaut by sorting Adam's "collected works" by genre. He composed 36 chansons in the Trouvère tradition—a comparatively prolific number. Seventeen jeux-partis (stanzaic dialogues between two poets) contain his wittily phrased (if conventional) contributions on the subject of courtly love. His longer works include an epic *Chanson de geste* about the King of Sicily, a satiric drama (*Le jeu de la Feuillée*), and a pastoral drama with music—*Le jeu de Robin et de Marion*—which is often dubbed the "first comic opera."

In addition, he completed at least five essays in the genre of the polytextual French motet, and a set of 16 dance-based refrain songs of various forms called Rondeaux. This last set, called *Le Rondel Adam* in a manuscript copy of his works, contains probably the first polyphonic settings of vernacular song in Europe. *—Timothy Dickey*

Overview of Works (ca. 1270–1300)

Adam de la Halle was a primary musical and literary figure in thirteenth century France. Copies of Adam's works are plentiful in thirteenth century manuscript sources, but a single volume located in the Bibliothèque Nationale in Paris (fr.25566) contains nearly all of his works, and is obviously copied with great care; this is considered the primary source for his music.

Adam's *Le Jeu d'Adam ou de la feuille* is considered an early masterwork of both French lyric poetry and theater, but it is *Le jeu de Robin et de Marion* that stands as the most significant of his musical efforts. Created as an entertainment for Charles, the Duke of Anjou, in 1283, *Le jeu de Robin et de Marion* is like a medieval mini-opera with its mixture of songs, dialogue and dramatic action. It is based on the troubadour form of the Pastourelle, and superficially resembles the pastoral intermezzo common in the seventeenth century, but there is likely no historical connection—it appears that Adam's successors failed to follow the model he provided.

Among his monophonic works there are 36 chansons and 18 works classified as jeux-partis. These take the form of a dialogue between Adam and another poet, in all but one case identified as Jehan Bretel. As Bretel usually initiates the correspondence, it is generally believed that he is responsible for most of the melodies, rather than Adam. However in some instances some differences may be found in the melodic shape between Adam's verses and those of his colleague.

Adam de la Halle is one of a very small number of thirteenth century composers who wrote both monophonic and polyphonic music. The larger group of polyphonic pieces consists of 14 works that are described as Rondeaux. Laid out in three voices, these are not true "rondos" in that most are not written in a closed form which endlessly repeats. Rather, the first phrases of most rondeaux simply return to answer succeeding lines of text, in the manner of a ritornello. The polyphonic voicing of the rondeaux is technically primitive, with the three voices seldom exceeding the range of a tenth. But in his ballade, *Dieus soit en cheste maison*, Adam achieves colorful dissonances through use of cross relations in his voicing. A true rondo is achieved in *Fines Amourettes ai*, which is in the form of a virelai; it is very short, consisting of only seven measures of music.

Five three-voice motets round out the known musical work of Adam de la Halle. Six other motets have been ascribed to him as they contain melodies that occur in his authenticated works, but there is no definitive word on the true authorship of these pieces. There are several works of Adam de la Halle which exist as text only with no musical setting extant. *—Uncle Dave Lewis*

Recommended:

- ○ **Le Roman de la Rose** / Alla Francesca / 2001 / Opus 111 30303

VOCAL

Le jeu de Robin et de Marion (The Play of Robin and Marion) (ca. 1280)

Adam de la Halle (born Adan le Bossus, and also known as Adan de la Hale and Adan d'Arras) was the thirteenth century genius who united the polyphonic composition of the Notre Dame school with the various popular and liturgical expressions of dramatic poetry in music, and who perfected the form of the motet. By his time, religious works had moved from the staging of simple texts performed around the church altar (e.g., the *Quem quaeritis* mentioned by Saint Ethelwood, ca. 970) to the development of miracle and mystery plays staged publicly outside the churches. And in popular music, the troubadours and trouvères had developed a high lyricism and subtlety in the expression of knightly love. Within this historical context, Adam de la Halle, famed also as a playwright, established the roots of comic opera with *Le jeu de Robin et de Marion* (in medieval French, *Le Jeu de Robechon et Marote*), composed ca. 1282.

The basic plot is simple: A knight, Auber, while out hunting with a falcon, interrupts the young shepherdess Marion as she is daydreaming of her betrothed in the village. She manages to rebuff his advances—mostly by saying she's not interested in him even if he is a horseman and a knight, his horse makes her afraid, and she loves Robin—and then she asks Robin and his friends (Gautier, Baudon, and Péronelle, who join in a jolly song making jest of the knight) for protection from the knight. However, Auber comes back, carries Marion away as Robin and his friends hide (!), but Marion uses her wiles to get rid of the knight by herself. Afterward, Marion, Robin, and the rest celebrate with Huars the piper who organizes parodies ("Le jeu du Saint"—The Saint's Play, and "Le Jeu du Roi"—The King's Play) for the festivities.

The piece is organized in nine scenes, with distinct music for each character—often with Marion's reflections and daydreams accompanied by gentle guitar and winds in Asian modes with free melisma, the knight by strident percussion, Robin echoing Marion's sentiments, and jolly dance rhythms taking over when the two are together. The direct emotions of this work still speak to us today—there are foot tapping rhythms, a lot of humor, and lovely lyricism. *—"Blue Gene" Tyranny*

Recommended:

- ○ **Adam de la Halle: Le jeu de Robin et de Marion** / Binkley, Schola Cantorum Basilienses / Focus 913
- ○ **Adam de la Halle: Le jeu de Robin et de Marion** / Perceval Ensemble / 1981 / Arion 68162

Adolphe Adam

b. Jul. 24, 1803, Paris, France, **d.** May 3, 1856, Paris, France

Composer: Ballet, Vocal, Opera

Best known today for his ballet *Giselle* and for the Christmas carol *Cantique de Noël*, Adolphe Adam, born in 1803, was a prolific composer of ballets, vaudeville, incidental music, and comic opera, and one of the most popular of his day.

His father was a pianist and teacher, but was firmly set against the idea of his son following in his footsteps. Adam was determined, however, and studied and composed secretly under the tutelage of his older friend Ferdinand Hérold, a popular composer of the day. When Adam was 17, his father relented, and he was permitted to study at the Paris Conservatoire—but only after he promised that he would learn music only as an amusement, not as a career. He came to the notice of Boieldieu, who became his mentor and encouraged him to write for the theater. His first opera, *Le mal du pays*, was premiered at the Gymnase-Dramatique (where he played in the orchestra), and was followed in 1829 by *Pierre et Cathérine*, at the Opéra-Comique. Paired with Auber's *La fiancée*, it was a great success. In 1830, Adam left Paris for London, escaping political turmoil; in England, he wrote mostly ballet music. (His brother-in-law was the manager of the King's Theater.) Though he returned to France in 1832, his work remained popular across the Channel, and he premiered his *Faust* in London in 1833.

The comic opera *Le Chalet*, in 1834, was the greatest success of his career: popular in France throughout the nineteenth century, it was later forgotten. *Le Postillon de Lonjumeau* (1836) and *Giselle* (1841) were also successful, but his attempt at grand opera, *Richard en Palestine* (1844), was given only polite attention.

By 1847, Adam was wealthy and influential enough to open his own opera house, the Opéra-National. However, during the political turmoil of 1848 ("the year of revolutions"), he had to close down—only four months after its opening, losing not only his own investments but the capital he had borrowed. While greatly burdened by these debts, he was still popular enough that his old royalties and new compositions, including *Le Toréador* (1849) and *Si j'étais roi* (1852) enabled him to pay the debt off steadily while he supported himself with musical journalism. In 1849, Adam also became a composition professor at the Conservatoire, and by 1852, his debts were paid off. He died in 1856.

Adam's music is characterized by a Gallic charm, whether filtered through the wistful lyricism of *Giselle* or the worldly wit of *Le Postillon de Lonjumeau* (in which he satirized the world of opera). Often accused of superficiality, he admittedly had no great desire to produce innovative, deeply felt, or especially sophisticated works, and focused his energies on giving his audiences the tuneful, graceful music and vivid theatrical entertainment that they wanted. *—Ann Feeney*

BALLET

Giselle (1841)

The ballet *Giselle*, although generally identified with the name of composer Adolphe Adam, was the creation of French poet and novelist Théophile Gautier (1811–70). Gautier was inspired by a poem in Heinrich Heine's book *De l'allemagne* that recounted an eastern European legend of the Wili (or "wally"), the soul of an unmarried girl who has died before her wedding day and who dances in the forest for all eternity and drags unfortunate men to their doom. Gautier immediately envisaged the work as a ballet but had no experience in plotting one. For this he turned to dramatist Vernay de Saint-Georges, who worked out a proper scenario from Gautier's ideas.

Rather than presenting the work cold to the director of the Paris Opéra, Gautier showed it first to Jules Perrot, then mentor to a ballerina, Carlotta Grisi, who had made her Paris Opéra debut just weeks before. Grisi liked the scenario, and both she and Perrot lobbied successfully to have it produced, but on the condition that it be ready by June 1841—in less than a month. Fortunately, Perrot had already contacted composer Adolphe Adam, known for his ability to cook up a quick score in a short time. Adam had begun work on April 11, before the ballet was approved. The work was finished on June 8, 1841, a mere 20 days before the production was launched.

Giselle was more than a mere success; it is credited with "inventing" Romantic ballet as we know it. Its tragic theme of the heroine doomed to dance forever was re-created subtly in countless ballets afterward. The very stage costumes of the Wilis—tutus and tights—marked the introduction of standard ballet apparel. Adam's music is serious in nature and not frivolous; even played uncut with all the repeats intact, *Giselle* is anything but monotonous. The first act sparkles with charm and grace, and is packed with strong, memorable melodies. The second act, with its more sober dramatic content, is often brooding and mysterious, yet still maintaining the rhythmic lilt of the first. It is Adam's finest theatrical creation outside of his opera *Le Postillon de Lonjumeau.*

Grisi gave performances of *Giselle* at the Opéra for years afterward, and the ballet was staged in Paris as late as 1868. By then Perrot had moved to St. Petersburg and was choreographer for the Imperial Ballet Theater. He made *Giselle* a staple of the Russian company, and after Perrot's retirement Marius Petipa retooled the choreography, creating the basis for the standard *Giselle* that is seen today. The most celebrated *Giselle* given under Petipa's direction was his last revival of the work in 1903, featuring the dynamic and now-legendary ballerina Anna Pavlova.

Some additions to the score are considered standard. Léon Minkus may have added the waltz variation that replaces Adam's original in the first act, and no one knows how another waltz variation of the first act's love music wound up added to the second act. However, these changes are strictly observed in present-day performances. *—Uncle Dave Lewis*

Synopsis:

Act One. (The story is set in a medieval Rhineland village in vineyard country.) Hilarion, the village gamekeeper, is in love with Giselle, who is also the object of the affections of the youthful Albrecht, Duke of Silesia. The latter, however, is in disguise as a peasant using the name Loys. Giselle's mother, Berthe, wants her to marry Hilarion, but when Loys expresses his love for her, she succumbs to his charms, much to the dismay of Hilarion, who, after being rejected by her and driven off by Loys, decides he will take revenge against the young peasant.

It is wine harvest time and the peasants are celebrating. Giselle takes part in the festivities, having been warned by Berthe that too much dancing can be dangerous for young girls—some have died and become Wilis, ghost-like beings that roam the forest in the night in pursuit of young men, who dance under their spell until they fall dead from exhaustion. The Prince of Kurland and his beautiful daughter Princess Bathilde arrive amid the festivities, and Giselle dances for her. Bathilde is betrothed to Albrecht and she now departs. Loys arrives and by now Hilarion has learned of his true identity, having discovered a special sword he had hidden away. He reveals the peasant youth is really Duke Albrecht and summons the Princess. Albrecht, ignoring Giselle and explaining his disguise as a harmless amusement, takes the Princess arm-in-arm to the utter shock of Giselle. She goes mad and dances spellbound before the crowd, which includes Berthe. Giselle picks up the sword belonging to Albrecht and plunges it into her heart, her mother clutching her in her arms as she dies. A contrite Albrecht stands aghast at the scene.

Act Two. It is midnight and Hilarion wanders about Giselle's gravesite. Myrta, the Queen of the Wilis, appears and summons her ghostly sister spirits, among whom now is Giselle, who hovers above her tomb. Hilarion wanders off as Albrecht approaches carrying lilies for the grave. He sees Giselle's image and is entranced by it, following it into the woods. Hilarion returns and is encircled by a throng of Wilis, who induce him to dance wildly until he falls dead. Albrecht now reenters the scene and is condemned to the same fate as that of Hilarion by the Wilis' Queen, but Giselle intercedes, using a cross to protect him. Still, the two are forced to dance, but Albrecht is inspired by her love and survives the marathon event until dawn arrives, at which time the spirits return to the kingdom of shadows, Giselle among them. Albrecht is left alone to grieve. *—Robert Cummings*

Recommended:

- ○ **Adam: Giselle** / Bonynge (cond.), Covent Garden / 1996 / Decca 452185

VOCAL

Cantique de Noël ("O Holy Night"), for voice & orchestra (1847)

Adam, as a composer of both ballet and vocal music, knew how to showcase the artistry of his performers—dancers or singers. While his greatest showpiece for the voice is perhaps the Postillon aria from *Le Postillon de Lonjumeau*, the *Cantique de Noël* is by far his best known, familiar to both classical and popular audiences. When it was first published, many religious leaders felt that the *Cantique* was too theatrical, making a showpiece out of a text that demanded a more contemplative treatment. Audiences, however, disagreed, and the song is still popular both in the original French version, "Minuit, Chrétiens," and the English-language version, "O Holy Night." The rising vocal line builds slowly, further intensifying at the exclamatory "Peuple, à genoux," and then climaxing on a high B flat at the triumphant "Noël!" Although he performed it in Swedish rather than the original French (perhaps sacrificing some of the nuances of Adam's text setting), Jussi Björling's recording is a standard rendition of this work. *—Ann Feeney*

Recommended:

○ **Sumi Jo: The Christmas Album** / Jo / 2001 / Erato 85819

OPERA

Le Postillon de Lonjumeau (1836)

Adolphe Adam (1803–56), son of pianist and teacher Louis Adam, applied his early studies at the Paris Conservatoire to the writing of vaudeville beginning before he had reached his 21st birthday. His father had strongly opposed his following music as a career, and not until 1817 was Adolphe finally permitted to attend the Conservatoire. There, composer Adrien Boieldieu greatly assisted Adam in discovering that his gift lay with the writing of light music. Immensely popular in his time, Adam eventually managed no less than 33 operettas and three more serious works. While the latter were not well received, most of his lighter works became favorites with Parisian audiences, some gaining a place in the repertory elsewhere in Europe as well.

Le Postillon's successful premiere followed by two years that of another operetta which had greatly pleased its audiences, *Le Chalet* (1834). In *Le Postillon*, Adam had a subject that offered him a range of color and plot ready-made for a work both humorous and musically substantive. Set in the time of Louis XV, the libretto by Adolphe de Leuven and Léon Levy permits the composer to observe the world of opera during the fading years of the *ancien régime*, especially the opera management of that time. His Postillon (the coachman who rides the left-hand lead horse in a coach horse team), Chapelou, is discovered singing in a public market by the manager of the Paris Opéra, who forthwith offers him a contract to sing at his theater. Dazzled by his prospects, Chapelou abandons his new bride, Madeleine. In Paris, the singer becomes Saint-Phar, gains celebrity, is invited to visit a certain Madame de Latour, falls in love with her, discovers she is actually his wife (now well-to-do owing to an inheritance), and is finally reunited with her.

The music thrives on the contrast of Chapelou's village life and the heady atmosphere of the Opéra, and on the enormous changes the Postillon's life undergoes after his achievement of celebrity. Chapelou's "Mes amis, écoutez l'histoire" has been a showpiece for many tenors with its high D. Adam parodies the music of the earlier period with the "Aria di Bravoura" at the opening of Act II. Here, trills, staccati, and elaborate runs replicate (and then some) the over-ornamented music of Louis XV's time. Madeleine ruminates on the love she still feels for the husband who abandoned her on her wedding night with music redolent of grand opera.

Altogether remarkable are Adam's gift for near infallible pacing and for providing effervescent music that lifts, sustains, and delights, that fits his characters impeccably—and never outstays its welcome. While Adam's entertainments were conceived with the Parisian populace in mind, *Le Postillon* seems to have found a more permanent hold on the affections of Germans and Austrians. With little doubt, this operetta offers the best introduction to Adam's seldom cloying confections. *—Erik Eriksson*

Synopsis:

Act One. The setting of the first act of *Le Postillon de Lonjumeau* is the French village of Lonjumeau in 1766. Chapelou, post-horse rider of Lonjumeau, has just married Madeleine, proprietress of the village tavern. After their friends have left the wedding ceremony and celebration, Chapelou and Madeleine reveal to one another that they have both been to consult the oracles of soothsayers to divine the future of their union; Madeleine to a hunchbacked shepherd, and Chapelou to an old witch. The results on both sides predict disaster for the marriage, but under the circumstances they agree to ignore this advice. Madeleine goes off to attend to her patrons, and Biju, a fellow rider and a rival to Chapelou for Madeleine's affections, enters. A testy conversation ensues between Chapelou and Biju, but they are interrupted by the arrival of the Marquis de Corcy. He is the director of the Royal Opera in Paris and is having a bad day: he is both short a singer for a production of *Castor and Pollux* and in need of a wheelwright, as one of the wheels has fallen off his carriage. As he waits, peasants encourage Chapelou to sing his song of the mail carriage. It is a difficult number that requires a high tenor, and Chapelou carries it off with ease and aplomb. The Marquis is elated by Chapelou's performance and offers to make him a singing star in Paris, but makes it a condition that he leave immediately. Chapelou resists, but the Marquis is not prepared to take no for an answer. Chapelou departs with the Marquis, and when Madeleine finally appears, Biju gleefully informs her that Chapelou has just abandoned their union on their wedding night.

Act Two. The business of the second act takes place ten years later in Paris, and everyone's name changes, with the exception of the Marquis. Madeleine has come into a considerable fortune, thanks to the bequest of a wealthy aunt. She is no longer called Madeleine but is now Madame de Latour, and the action is set in her spacious Paris apartment. Despite Biju's intrigue, she is still in love with Chapelou, who is now known as Saint-Phar, a famous singer at the Opera. Biju, now Alcindor, is the leader of the Opera chorus. An opera rehearsal is to be held shortly in the apartment, and Madame de Latour indicates that she is about to play a trick on the celebrated "widower" Saint-Phar. As the Marquis arrives to lead the rehearsal, Madame de Latour departs.

Saint-Phar reluctantly sings a romance that turns out so well that everyone in the company decides to leave for dinner, save Alcindor, who steps forward to sing a number of his own after the rest are gone. Saint-Phar begs Alcindor to leave, however, for he is desperately in love with Madame de Latour and plans to throw himself at her feet. He notes the resemblance between her and Madeleine but is too dim to make the connection. When she appears, Saint-Phar professes his love for her, and she confronts him with a letter from his "wife" Madeleine. He protests that he is unmarried, and she offers to marry him later that evening. He agrees, but the Marquis overhears Saint-Phar's plot to have the wedding carried out by one of the boys in the chorus, rather than a priest, just to be on the safe side. The Marquis relays the plot to Madame de Latour, who merely arranges to have a real priest substituted for the fake, eating her revenge cold.

Act Three. The first scene of Act Three takes place in a wedding chamber. Alcindor lays the whole story out to the Marquis, who can't wait to see Saint-Phar hang for bigamy. Saint-Phar sings happily of his triumph with Madame de Latour in the aria "A la noblesse, je m'allie," and then Alcindor arrives with the bad news. Saint-Phar is thunderstruck and becomes virtually apoplectic when "Madeleine" (Madame de Latour in her peasant garb) enters to accuse him of marrying another. Saint-Phar drops his torch, plunging the stage into darkness. In the dark, Madame de Latour carries on a conversation between herself and "Madeleine" by disguising her voice, convincing Saint-Phar that the two women are having an argument. The lights come up, and the Marquis arrives with soldiers to take the unlucky Saint-Phar to his doom. At this point Madame de Latour reveals the ruse and tells the soldiers that the crime Saint-Phar has committed is not one of bigamy, but of marrying the same woman twice. The Marquis storms out in a blind rage, and Saint-Phar pledges to Madame de Latour that he will leave the stage for her, just as he had left her for the stage at their initial wedding.*—Uncle Dave Lewis*

Recommended:

○ **Adam: Le Postillon de Lonjumeau** / Fulton (cond.), Aler, J. Anderson, Monte Carlo PO / 2001 / EMI 574106

Theo Adam

b. Aug. 1, 1926, Dresden, Germany

Bass

Born in 1926, Theo Adam is one of the leading bass singers of the post–World War II era, particularly well known for his Wagnerian roles. He joined the boys' choir of the Dresden Kreuzchor in 1937, a traditional starting point for singers of that city. He began studying music in his hometown and in Weimar. He was called for military service in 1944 but resumed musical studies when the war ended.

His professional debut was at the Dresden State Opera in 1949, which led to a guest appearance in the Bayreuth Festival of 1952, which was also the year he joined the Berlin State Opera. Despite the handicap of living in the Soviet bloc, Adam was selected in 1963, after a few appearances in smaller roles, to sing the role of Wotan in Wagner's *Ring* operas at the Wagnerian shrine of Bayreuth in 1963. He later sang the other major bass roles in Wagner's operas: Hans Sachs, King Mark, Amfortas, and the Dutchman. Adam is also well known for the non-Wagnerian roles of Baron Ochs (Strauss's *Rosenkavalier*), Pizzaro (Beethoven's *Fidelio*), *Wozzeck* (Berg), King Philip (Verdi's *Don Carlos*), La Roche (Strauss' *Capriccio*), *Don Giovanni* (Mozart), and several other important parts.

Adam appeared at the world's most prestigious venues, including the Metropolitan in 1963, Covent Garden in 1967, and the *Salzburg Festival* in 1972, He is also a highly esteemed oratorio singer. In addition to singing the Bach Passions and several cantatas, he is exceptional in the title role of Mendelssohn's *Elijah*.

Adam's interpretations are intelligent and dramatic, his voice robust. Beginning in 1977, Adam made regular television appearances on his show "Theo Adam lädt ein" (An Invitation from Theo Adam). The author of several books, Adam is the laureate of numerous awards, including the Schumann Prize of the City of Zwickau, the National First Prize of the German Democratic Republic, and the title of "Chamber Singer of Austria." *—Joseph Stevenson*

Recommended:

○ **Wagner: Der fliegende Holländer** / Klemperer (cond.), Adam, Silja, Talvela, Burmeister, New Philharmonia / 2000 / Angel 67405B

○ **Mendelssohn: Elias** / Sawallisch (cond.), Ameling, Schreier, Rotzsch, Adam, LGO / 1993 / Philips 438368

○ **Wagner: Tannhäuser** / Gerdes (cond.), Nilsson, Fischer-Dieskau, Adam, Windgassen, Orchester des Deutschen Opern / 2002 / DG 471708

○ **D'Albert: Tiefland** / Schmitz (cond.), Adam, Hoppe, Vogel, Kuhse, Dresden Staatskapelle / 1997 / Berlin Classics 0091082

○ **Dessau: Einstein** / Suitner (cond.), Buchner, Adam, Garduhn, Suss, Orchestra of the Florence May / 2003 / Opera d'Oro 1371

○ **Strauss: Lieder** / Adam, Suitner (cond.), Shetler, Dresden Staatskapelle / 1996 / Berlin Classics 0091212

John Adams

b. Feb. 15, 1947, Worcester, MA

Composer: Orchestral, Chamber Music, Opera, Concerto, Keyboard, Vocal, Choral

Born in Massachusetts in 1947, composer John Adams was raised in Vermont and New Hampshire, surrounded by the active cultural life of New England. At the age of ten he began studying clarinet, musical theory, and composition. His main clarinet teacher was Felix Viscuglia of the Boston Symphony Orchestra. He later attended Harvard University, studying composition with Leon Kirchner, David Del Tredici, and Roger Sessions, while substituting as a clarinetist in the Boston Symphony. In 1971, he was appointed head of the composition department at the San Francisco Conservatory, a position he held until 1981. Adams founded a series of "New and Unusual Music" concerts with the San Francisco Symphony Orchestra, which lead to his appointment as its composer-in-residence (1983–85), making him the first composer to hold such a post with the SFSO.

Adams emerged in the last decades of the twentieth century as one of the most influential and widely performed American composers since Copland. In early works, such as *Phrygian Gates* (1977) for piano, and *Common Tones in Simple Time* (1979) for orchestra, Adams' musical language is most heavily influenced by the stripped-down harmonic palette and motoric pulse of minimalism. Nevertheless, even in these works, Adams' trademark rhythmic vigor and sense of large-scale architecture are already in evidence. In the 1980s, Adams' affinity with the orchestra came into full effect with *Harmonielehre* (1985), a work that fuses motoric repetitions, harmonic conciseness, and lush, textured emotionalism. Also important during this time are the exhilarating overture *Short Ride in a Fast Machine* (1986), and the chugging, machine-like *Fearful Symmetries* (1988). However, it is Adams' stage works that have emerged as his most important contributions to musical literature. The "reality-based" operas *Nixon in China* (1987) and *The Death of Klinghoffer* (1990–91) elicited both praise and controversy. His large-scale song, *The Wound-Dresser* (1988), set to Walt Whitman's poetry, demonstrated great emotional depth and development. *I Was Looking at the Ceiling and Then I Saw the Sky* (1995), inspired by the 1994 Northridge earthquake, represents Adams' first foray into the realm of musical theater. Through the 1990s, Adams continued to draw on increasingly diverse sources of musical inspiration, from the electronics of *Hoodoo Zephyr* (1992), to cartoon music *Chamber Symphony* (1992), to the bluegrass of *John's Book of Alleged Dances* (1994). In 1995, Adams received music composition's most lucrative honor, the Grawemeyer Prize, for his Violin Concerto. He is frequently recorded, with Nonesuch Records releasing most of his music. Adams is also active as a conductor, distinguishing himself—particularly with the Ensemble Moderne—as a champion of challenging twentieth century works by composers such as Conlon Nancarrow and Frank Zappa. *—AMG*

ORCHESTRAL

The Chairman Dances, foxtrot (1985)

John Adams' *The Chairman Dances* is a "foxtrot for orchestra" that emerged as an offshoot of the composer's 1986 opera *Nixon in China* and has become one of the composer's most popular works. The opera, which presents a fanciful account of the 1972 visit to China by President Richard Nixon and his entourage (including wife Pat and National Security Advisor Henry Kissinger), made a profound, lingering impression upon audiences that few operas of the late twentieth century ever had. Certainly one important contributor to this response is the peculiar immediacy of the work. The faces one sees onstage are both real and familiar. Even as the opening-night crowd gasped with delight as the mock-up of Air Force One descended to the stage, the real Richard Nixon continued the post-Watergate rehabilitation of his image, wearing his elder statesmanship like a pair of battered, comfortable slippers and lunching on the terrace at San Clemente with Pat. Henry Kissinger enjoyed a similar status, while Madame Mao, thousands of miles away, considered her role in the Cultural Revolution from her prison cell. A like familiarity and intimacy informs the opera's third act—which is the direct source of *The Chairman Dances*—in which protocol and ceremony are forgotten as the audience is led into the apparent privacy of the characters' bedrooms to hear their intimate discussions. Each sings of his or her current personal concerns, while at some level the couples (Dick and Pat, Chairman and Madam Mao) connect with each other on the emotional plane of nostalgia. The Nixons reminisce about their early, pre-public married lives: a time of groceries and slipcovers for Pat, of five-card stud and military service for Dick. The Maos look back to their youthful idealism and budding romance, and foxtrot together, for old times' sake, to the wistful tune that forms the basis of this composition. The chugging and coloristic flashes that begin the work give way to the dance theme proper in the strings, the piano eventually emerging both as participant in and a source of commentary upon the proceedings. The work "runs out" instead of ending, as though in imitation of the hand-wound gramophone which had accompanied the dancing of the Maos in earlier, and perhaps less complicated and foreboding, times. *—Michael Rodman*

Recommended:

- ○ **Adams: The Chairman Dances; Grand Pianola Music; Fearful Symmetries** / Adams (cond.), San Francisco SO / 1999 / Nonesuch 79453
- ○ **American Classics** / Gershwin, Adams, Ellington & Bernstein / Mauceri (cond.), Hollywood Bowl SO / 1993 / Philips 438663

Chamber Symphony (1992)

Arnold Schoenberg surprised some contemporaries by citing both Wagner and Brahms, two composers seen by many as overseeing opposing musical camps, as influences on his compositional style. How then would the leader of the Second Viennese School react upon learning that he was one of two even more contradictory inspirations for John Adams' Chamber Symphony—his counterpart being the delightfully frenzied music that accompanied 1950s cartoons? As Adams tells the story, he was studying the score of Schoenberg's *Chamber Symphony*, Op. 9, while his seven-year-old son watched cartoons in the next room. This odd combination resulted in one of Adams' most adventurous works, one that helped set a new musical trajectory that would distance Adams farther than ever before from his minimalist counterparts Steve Reich and Philip Glass. In fact, by the time the *Chamber Symphony* was composed, Adams' musical language had evolved into one much too free in rhythm, harmony, and melody to still be called minimalist. This trend would continue a year later with his rhapsodic and exploratory *violin concerto*.

The *Chamber Symphony*'s frantic beginning, with its absurdly insistent percussion and caricatural accompaniment, somehow recalls both Schoenberg and *Looney Tunes*. Perhaps these two aesthetics are not that far apart. Composed in 1907, Schoenberg's *Chamber Symphony*, Op. 9 emerged at the end of his initial thrust towards atonality, but before his codification of dissonance into the twelve-tone system. Thus the work retains some remnants of traditional harmony, almost ending some phrases with tonal cadences, while maintaining an overall melodic angularity. On the other hand, the cartoon music of mid-century American television used increased dissonance as a comic tool, with dizzying chromatic runs and deliberately odd harmonies exaggerating the slapstick action on the screen. In the final analysis, the two worlds are not so far apart.

Adams proves this, composing his *Chamber Symphony* for an ensemble identical to the one called for in Schoenberg's Op. 9, but adding a jazz combo of sorts, including drum set, synthesizer, trombone, and trumpet. Schoenberg's obtuse lines are blended with the musical pyrotechnics that could set a cartoon land chase scene, and is done in such a way that the two elements are indiscernible at any given moment. Adams also acknowledges other influences in this amalgam, namely Milhaud's *La Création du monde*, Stravinsky's *L'Histoire du Soldat*, and Hindemith's *Kleine Kammermusik*. Occasionally, the motoric patterns and static harmonies of Adams' earlier works re-emerge in the *Chamber Symphony*, but by and large this piece reflects and engenders a compositional style that becomes increasingly distanced from those of Steve Reich, Philip Glass, and Terry Riley, and increasingly difficult to describe as minimalist. *—Jeremy Grimshaw*

Recommended:

- ○ **Adams: Chamber Symphony; Grand Pianola Music** / Adams (cond.), London Sinfonietta / 1994 / Nonesuch 79219
- ○ **Adams: Chamber Symphony; Shaker Loops; Phrygian Gates** / S. Edwards (cond.), Ensemble Modern / 1997 / BMG 68674

Fearful Symmetries (1988)

Adams has commented frequently on the two sides of his compositional persona. The "serious" side is exemplified by somber works like *The Wound-Dresser* (1989) and grand statements like *Harmonielehre* (1984–85) and the opera *The Death of Klinghoffer* (1990). Then there is the "trickster" side, in which Adams indulges his sense of humor and irony; *Fearful Symmetries* is written in this vein. It was written in 1988, and premiered that year by the Orchestra of St. Luke's conducted by Adams himself.

Fearful Symmetries was written in the wake of the first performances of Adams' notorious opera *Nixon in China*. It uses much the same orchestration as the opera, with prominent roles for saxophones and synthesizer, as well as a large complement of brass. Adams has in fact noted some similarities in sound between *Fearful Symmetries* and what is perhaps the best-known excerpt from *Nixon in China*, the "foxtrot for orchestra," *The Chairman Dances*.

Fearful Symmetries takes its title from William Blake's *The Tyger*—Adams liked what he called the "combination of passion and precision" of the title, although there is no further connection with the Blake poem. The music is symmetrical in some respects, with its regular four- and eight-bar phrases. Within that framework Adams incorporates many of his typical stylistic elements: a regular and prominent pulse, big band and boogie-woogie riffs, and all sorts of polyrhythmic and polyphonic play. Something of the process of minimalism remains, but Adams' take on minimalism is very dynamic and fast-moving here. A "lounge lizard" saxophone quartet, augmented by English horn and bassoon, helps keep the tone light and humorous. The synthesizer, which has become a mainstay in the Adams orchestra, is featured prominently, sometimes imitating a cheesy organ, sometimes providing swirling, shimmering, Philip Glass-like arpeggios. Every time the music threatens to become pompous or self-important, the boogie-woogie rhythm returns or the brass instruments blast forth to lighten the tone again. With all its complex, and exciting, rhythmic activity, it is no surprise that *Fearful Symmetries* has been choreographed over a dozen times. A more lyrical approach emerges toward the middle of the piece, but even then the propulsive rhythm lurks just beneath the surface. Ultimately, the piece ends on a surprisingly quiet note, as the texture gradually lightens and the rhythmic activity spends itself. *—Chris Morrison*

Recommended:

○ **Adams: Fearful Symmetries; The Wound-Dresser** / Adams (cond.), Sylvan, St. Luke's CO / 1989 / Nonesuch 79218

Harmonielehre (1984–1985)

Towards the end of his tenure (from 1982 to 1985) as composer-in-residence of the San Francisco Symphony, John Adams endured a composer's block that lasted for over a year. Then he had a dream. In the dream, while driving over the San Francisco Bay Bridge, he saw a huge tanker in the bay, and the tanker ascended into the sky. This dream image translated itself musically into a series of loud, pounding E minor chords. With this as his beginning, Adams' block was gone, and over the succeeding three months, he quickly created his orchestral work *Harmonielehre*, a symphony in all but name which Adams defined as "a kind of allegory about [the] quest for grace." The work's title refers to the famous 1911 book *Die Harmonielehre* by Arnold Schoenberg. While studying at Harvard in the late 1960s and early 1970s, Adams had worked with composer Leon Kirchner, who had been a student of Schoenberg's in Los Angeles in the 1940s. As a student, Adams was more interested in the Beatles and Miles Davis than in Schoenberg, who was lionized in the academic world, and he had to work very hard to shake Schoenberg's influence. Some of that struggle is evident in *Harmonielehre*, which combines some of the sound and procedures of minimalism with music very reminiscent of the late nineteenth and early twentieth centuries (Adams cites Schoenberg, along with Gustav Mahler, Jean Sibelius, and Claude Debussy, as important influences on this piece).

Those pounding E minor chords, blasted out by the orchestra, open Part I of the work, and the anger implicit in those chords lurks below the shimmering surface that emerges. A lush, slightly dissonant tune takes over, and the music becomes slow and languid even though the tension level remains high. The pounding chords return to close the movement. According to Adams, Part II, "The Anfortas Wound," is a meditation on "sickness and infirmity," both spiritual and physical. Taking the wounding of the Grail King Anfortas as its inspiration, the movement is slow and unsettled, and very dark. The music builds to a couple of angry crescendos, but the sense of malaise remains. That malaise is dispelled in Part III, "Meister Eckhardt and Quackie." Adams's image here is of the famed medieval mystic, floating through the air with the composer's daughter Emily (nicknamed Quackie as a child) and whispering to her the secret of grace and redemption. Here the textures are bright and shimmering, with Adams' characteristically transparent orchestration coming to the fore. Tuned percussion, swirling strings, and a brass-drenched climax close the work. *—Chris Morrison*

Recommended:

○ **Adams: Harmonielehre** / de Waart (cond.), San Francisco SO / 1985 / Nonesuch 79115

Naïve and Sentimental Music (1997–1998)

Naïve and Sentimental Music seems at first like a glib, almost self-deprecating title for a large-scale orchestral work. But that would be beneath John Adams, who has a knack for infusing his appealing soundscapes with weight and philosophy. In fact, Adams uses the word "sentimental" here to convey self-awareness, even self-consciousness. And so the title—and indeed, the entire piece—is a deliberate study in the balance and integration of opposites: innocence with perspective, spontaneity with design, and beauty with rhetoric.

Adams actually took the title from Friedrich von Schiller's essay, *"Über naïve und sentimentalische Dichtung"* (On Naïve and Sentimental Poetry), in which was laid out the contrast that is central to Adams' musical argument: "naïve" refers to creation directly from within, without self-analysis or historical reference; "sentimentality" involves second-guessing and reference to the past. It could be said that Adams has always been a "sentimental" composer; even the simplicity of his early minimalist style was a deliberate departure from the prevailing post-serialism that had come before. And so, in this work Adams appears to be on a personal quest to find and incorporate more of Schiller's naïveté.

The first movement, sharing the title of the whole work and taking 18 minutes of the 45-minute work, starts with a beautiful theme for flute above plucked harp and guitar. It has popular accents and a gentle, lightly swinging gait. Throughout the course of the movement, it goes through all sorts of emotional and dramatic changes, soaring and roaring. Its tendency to make sudden, wide leaps keeps it fresh and often draws it into breathtakingly high registers in the strings. As Adams' friend and colleague Ingram Marshall wrote in the Nonesuch Records liner notes, "it's a trip." Adams calls the second movement "Mother of the Man." Earlier, he had made an orchestral arrangement of the *Berceuse élégiaque* by Ferruccio Busoni, which that composer subtitled "Cradle Song of the Man at the Coffin of His Mother." The movement casts the voice of a lone electric guitar against the world of the orchestra; the integration of the two sounds is an achievement in itself, and a striking dramatic effect. The finale, "Chain to the Rhythm," is in fact an essay in gathering rhythmic force that is ultimately released in an explosive coda. It is built from very small interlocking rhythmic cells and has a large percussion section delicately used for color until the earthquake of the final bars. *—AMG*

Recommended:

○ **Adams: Naïve and Sentimental Music** / Salonen (cond.), Los Angeles PO / 2002 / Nonesuch 79636

Short Ride in a Fast Machine, fanfare (1986)

Composing one half of John Adams's orchestral set *Two Fanfares*, *Short Ride in a Fast Machine* exhibits an unbound rhythmic energy and spectacular, kaleidoscopic color. Commissioned by the Pittsburgh Symphony to mark the 1986 opening of the Great Woods Summer Festival, the work is appropriately celebratory. The composer notes that his work reflects the exhilaration he felt as a passenger in a very fast sports car; indeed, unbridled kineticism is what literally "drives" this work. Thrust forward by the insistent woodblock and the perpetual motion of the excited winds, the strings and brass engage in a four-minute adventure in percussive polyrhythms and increasingly frenzied exclamations. Because of this composition's aural thrills and intrinsic programmability (it has become a staple of the "opener" repertoire), it became the most frequently performed orchestral work by a living American composer in the last decade of the twentieth century. *—Jeremy Grimshaw*

Recommended:

○ **Adams: Harmonielehre; The Chairman Dances** / Rattle (cond.), City of Birmingham SO / 1994 / EMI 55051

○ **Adams: The Chairman Dances** / de Waart (cond.), San Francisco SO / 1999 / Nonesuch 79453

CHAMBER MUSIC

John's Book of Alleged Dances, for string quartet & sampler (1994)

These dances, says Adams, are "alleged" because "the steps for them have yet to be invented." They were written for the Kronos Quartet. Adams "prepared" a piano in the fashion of John Cage: he attached screws, bolts, rubber erasers, weather stripping, and other material to the strings of the piano. The key playing that string would then produce a given percussive sound rather than a note. Then Adams sampled the prepared piano sounds, organized them into loops, and set them up as short rhythm tracks. The idea was that, as called for in six of the dances, a member of the quartet would trigger these loops to perform them "live." This idea proved to be too complicated, so Adams just recorded them. In those six numbers the quartet plays with the prerecorded prepared piano loops. The order of movements is that used in a recording of the work supervised by the composer. However, essentially there is no fixed order. The exuberance, one could even call it rowdiness, of these dances, makes for a score that is technically extremely demanding. Interestingly, the composer supplies highly entertaining notes to explain all the titles, also mentioning the musical contents of some of the pieces. "Judah to Ocean," for example, is the route of streetcar that Adams could from hear his window. "Toot Nipple" (the name is from the novel *Postcards* by E. Annie Proulx), features "furious chainsaw triads on the cello." "Dogjam" is a demon fiddle piece, "in twisted hillbilly chromatics." Other movements include a tender song for a young teenager, a scat-like song, a portrait of an aging Cuban dictator, a portrait of two housing contractors hired by the composer, a sluggish escalator in a local Macy's, and a serenade in unclear rhythms. The overall effect is humorous, attractive, and sometimes quite wild. *—Joseph Stevenson*

Recommended:

○ **Adams: Gnarly Buttons; John's Book of Alleged Dances** / Adams (cond.), London Sinfonietta, Kronos Quartet / 1999 / Nonesuch 79453

Shaker Loops, for 7 strings or string orchestra (1978; revised 1983)

From 1972 to 1982, John Adams worked at the San Francisco Conservatory of Music. As head of their new music program, he conducted the Conservatory orchestra and new music ensemble and taught various classes. Adams found the constant interaction with musicians stimulating, particularly his students' reactions to his compositional ideas. To create *Shaker Loops*, which he regards as one of his first truly characteristic pieces—and one of the first in which he used the repetitive style known as minimalism—he used some material he had created for a string quartet called *Wavemaker*. Dissatisfied with the material, Adams rewrote the music for septet (three violins, one viola, two cellos, and one bass), creating what he called a "modular" score. The loops mentioned in the title are melodic patterns of different lengths that are distributed among the seven instruments and that interact and overlap in various ways. Changes in the patterns are signaled by a conductor. In this form, *Shaker Loops* was premiered in 1978, by the San Francisco Conservatory's New Music Ensemble under Adams' own direction. He eventually created a through-composed version of the work that doesn't require a conductor. In 1982 and 1983 he also adapted the work for a full string orchestra.

The Shakers referred to in the title are the members of the United Society of Believers, the famed New England-based religious community known for their ecstatic dances of worship (or "shaking"). Adams grew up near an old Shaker community in New Hampshire, and he drew a connection between the shaking and a quick movement of bow across string that marks much of this composition. The work is in four movements, played without pause. The propulsive, almost locomotive-like motion of the first movement, "Shaking and Trembling," forms quite a contrast to the almost static second, "Hymning Slews," with its long slides (or glissandi) over a bed of longer, sustained tones. The mood here is hushed, and the third movement, "Loops and Verses," extends this mood with its simple yet haunting cello lines leading the way. But more agitated music emerges and gains momentum, culminating in what Adams has called a "wild push-pull section" of considerable force. A cloud of pulsating harmonics leads to the energetic fourth movement, "A Final Shaking." *Shaker Loops* has become one of Adams' most frequently performed pieces. It has also been choreographed several times, and a portion of the first movement was used, albeit briefly, in the 1987 film *Barfly*. *—Chris Morrison*

Recommended:

○ **Adams: Violin Concerto; Shaker Loops** / Adams (cond.), Kremer, St. Luke's CO / 1996 / Nonesuch 79360

○ **Minimalist** / Warren-Green (cond.), London CO / 1994 / Virgin 61121

OPERA

The Death of Klinghoffer (1989–1991)

John Adams' second opera is in some ways similar to its successful predecessor, *Nixon in China*—each is written to a libretto by Alice Goodman, each takes actual historical events and figures as its point of departure, and each envisions its characters taking introspective approaches to the events that unfold before them. There are important differences, however, attributable to both the dramatic content and the creative approach adopted by Adams, Goodman, and director Peter Sellars. Whereas the events of *Nixon in China* play out in the dramatic "present"—evolving through revealing exchanges between characters and personalities—those of *The Death of Klinghoffer* (centered around the murder of Leon Klinghoffer during the hijacking of the *Achille Lauro* in 1985) are musically "recounted," much like those surrounding the death of Jesus in Johann Sebastian Bach's Passion oratorios; each character presents his or her reflections on the events leading up to Klinghoffer's murder in a manner that assumes the outcome is already a matter of record. The connection to Bach's Passions (acknowledged by the composer himself) not only gives the work a somewhat dreamlike stasis but also lends a messianic quality to the central character of Leon Klinghoffer—a man whose tragic murder was the result of a seemingly irreconcilable and profoundly tragic conflict. In this case the underlying conflict is that between Arabs and Jews, here represented via allusion to the biblical story of Hagar (mother of Ishmael, supposed progenitor of the Arab people). Adams' characteristic slow-moving harmonies and inexorable rhythm are present here, but there is more of a tendency to invoke chromaticism and contrapuntal devices than in his earlier opera. Often the bass line becomes unexpectedly active. The characters still resemble icons more than warm-blooded people, but there is considerably more range of emotion used in their music. There are individual outbursts of emotion that do much to humanize the characters, such as Klinghoffer's angry retort to a propagandistic speech by a Palestinian, or Mrs. Klinghoffer's confrontation with the ship's captain after learning that he has misled the passengers (including her) regarding Leon's death for purposes of keeping up morale. *—AMG*

Synopsis:

The Middle East in early October 1985.

Act One. In the prologue, both Palestinians and Jews sing of how they have been exiled from their homes. When Act One opens, the ship's captain recalls how the chain of events began. Most of the passengers were on shore to see the pyramids, while the older ones had stayed on board. The captain was told that the ship had been taken over by terrorists and went to the restaurant, where the terrorists had gathered. The first officer, in turn, remembers how he helped a wounded man to the sick bay, and the Swiss grandmother also remembers the events in "My grandson, Didi." Molqi, with "Give these orders," takes command of the ship, saying the passengers will be safe. The scene closes with an Ocean Chorus. In the next scene, Mamoud tells the captain of the events that propelled him, including his family's expulsion from its home and the death of his brother. The captain wishes that if only the two sides could share such stories, peace might come from it, but Mamoud answers that that would be the end of their hopes. The captain declares, "I have often reflected that this is no ship," saying that every ship is a kind of self-contained prison. The Austrian woman sings of how she locked herself in her cabin in "I kept my distance," eating the fruit and chocolate there, and Mamoud sings of freedom: "Those birds flying above us." The Night Chorus closes the act, singing of the miseries of persecution and ending on a note of fear.

Act Two. In a prologue to the second act, the chorus tells the story of how Hagar was exiled from Abraham's house after Sarah became jealous. As she and her son Ishmael were dying in the desert, an angel provided them with water. (This story is a vital one in both the Islamic and Judaic traditions; Jews consider themselves Abraham's descendants by his son Isaac, while Muslims consider Ishmael a prophet and ancestor of Mohammed.) Molqi wonders what will happen if their demands are not met, and the captain enters with a message that he has received no response. Mamoud announces that they will kill the hostages, and Klinghoffer, in his wheelchair, responds, denouncing them for their anger and hate, saying that they just want to see people die: "I've never been a violent man." Rambo responds with insults—"You are always complaining of your suffering"—and Omar sings of his people's exile and longs to die a martyr: "It is as if our earthly life." He and Molqi fight, and Molqi silently wheels Klinghoffer offstage. Marilyn, believing that Klinghoffer has been taken to the sick bay, tries to distance herself from the situation, pretending to herself that it isn't happening. Meanwhile, he is killed offstage. Molqi enters and coldly hands her Klinghoffer's passport, saying just "American kaput." Mamoud announces that the killing will continue, and the captain asks to be the next one to die. Depicting the body being thrown overboard, a dancer, dressed as Klinghoffer's double, dances with the body. The scene ends with a Day Chorus. The captain tries to console Marilyn, but she is furious at him for having sympathized with the terrorists: "You embraced them." Disconsolate, she thinks back on their happy marriage, concluding that she wishes they had killed her instead. *—Ann Feeney*

Recommended:

○ **Adams: The Death Of Klinghoffer** / Nagano (cond.), Hampson, Sylvan, Maddalena, Lyon Opera Orchestra / 1992 / Nonesuch 79281

El Niño, a Nativity Oratorio (1999–2000)

El Niño tells the story of Jesus' birth and simultaneously pulls the listener out of that story, relating it to more contemporary happenings and providing a more general meditation on the mystery of birth itself. Adams' score—which includes soprano, mezzo-soprano, and baritone soloists, countertenors, chorus, children's chorus, and orchestra—sets texts from many sources, including familiar passages from the Bible as well as portions of the Apocrypha and poetry by several Hispanic authors. The music brings together all the stylistic elements Adams has explored in his previous work: pop and other vernacular musics, jazz, minimalism, and a variety of other twentieth century innovations, along with some of the monumentality of Handel's *Messiah* (one of Adams' main influences here). *El Niño* originated in commissions from the San Francisco Symphony and Paris' Châtelet Theater, where it was premiered under Kent Nagano's direction on December 15, 2000.

Part One begins with "I Sing of a Maiden," with its aggressive opening (reminiscent of the dramatic first theme of Adams' *Harmonielehre*) and exciting polyrhythms. The Annunciation is then addressed in "Hail, Mary, Gracious!" and the mysterious "La Anunciación," one of the lengthier portions of the oratorio, in which Mexican author Rosario Castellanos' poem depicts the joys and difficulties of the birth process in moving terms. The lovely, lyrical "Magnificat" features the solo soprano and women's chorus. Joseph's anger at the news of Mary's pregnancy, as related in the *Apocryphal Gospel of James* and depicted in "Now She Was Sixteen Years Old," is calmed with an angel's appearance in "Joseph's Dream." In the dramatic "Shake the Heavens," with words from *Haggai* familiar from Handel's *Messiah*, the baritone sings a vigorous, heavily embellished aria. "The Christmas Star," which closes Part One, contrasts the intensity of Chilean poet Gabriela Mistral's evocation of the ecstasy of religious revelation with the calm of Hildegard of Bingen's *O quam preciosa*.

Part Two moves from the sadness of "Pues mi Dios ha nacido a penar" (Because My Lord Was Born to Suffer), with words by the seventeenth century Mexican nun Sor Juana Inés de la Cruz, to the sardonic boogie-woogie rhythms of "When Herod Heard." The quiet chorale "And When They Were Departed" leads into the joyous "Dawn Air," a love song by Chilean writer Vicente Huidobro. Herod's slaughter of the innocents, depicted in three separate numbers, is given a modern perspective in the dark, despairing "Memorial De Tlatelolco," where Castellanos' poem is used to relate it to the Aztecs' defeat by the conquistadors and a violent 1968 confrontation between Mexican police and civilians. The oratorio closes on a fanciful note with settings of two stories from the *Apocryphal Pseudo-Matthew*. "Jesus And The Dragons" is followed by "A Palm Tree," which tells of the infant Jesus causing a palm tree to bend and a stream to appear, providing nourishment for the Holy Family. The music ends peacefully with the children's chorus and gentle guitar accompaniment. *—Chris Morrison*

Synopsis:

In the original Peter Sellars production of *El Niño*, while on-stage singers portray Mary, Joseph, and various commentators using texts drawn from the Bible and Latin American poets, an overhead screen displays a video counterpoint-narrative, sometimes showing dancers in a desert setting and sometimes following a young pregnant woman and her boyfriend through a Hispanic community in modern Southern California. This synopsis relates only to the main stage developments.

Countertenors and chorus sing an anonymous early English poem praising Mary: "I sing of a maiden, a matchless maiden, king of all kings for her son she's taken." The angel Gabriel brings word to a cautious but willing Mary that she is about to conceive the Son of God. Mary comes to terms with this unexpected manifestation of a previously invisible God in her Annunciation scene, a setting of Rosario Castellanos' poem "Because from the start you were fated to be mine." The chorus declares, "For with God nothing shall be impossible."

In "The Babe Leaped in Her Womb," Mary goes into hiding during her pregnancy in the hills of Judea, and Mary's God-engendered fetus fills the hostess, Elisabeth, with the Holy Spirit. The ensemble performs a short Magnificat, in which Mary proclaims "My soul doth magnify the Lord." Joseph confronts Mary angrily over her pregnancy, sure that he has been cuckolded, but an angel comes to him in a dream and clears up the confusion.

Joseph and Mary travel to Bethlehem. Mary is ambivalent about her pregnancy, singing another Castellanos poem: "Like all guests my son got in the way, taking up a space that was my space," but later, "through the wound of his departure, through the hemorrhage of his breaking free, the last I ever felt of solitude, of myself looking through a pane of glass, also slipped away." Upon the birth of Jesus, the world becomes calm, and the Christmas star appears.

Mary insists that Jesus be allowed to sleep now, for he will suffer enough later as an adult. Meanwhile, Herod learns of the birth, and sends wise men to find the child on the pretext of wanting to worship him himself. These "three kings" do so, introduce themselves, and deliver gifts. Joseph, realizing the benefits of his situation, sings in happiness the Vicente Huidobro poem "Dawn Air": "My soul's above the sea and whistling a dream." But Herod orders that all children in Bethlehem be slaughtered, and Mary, in warning, delivers the Castellanos "Memorial de Tlatelolco": "Darkness engenders violence and violence demands darkness to coagulate in crime." This is followed by a Sor Juana Inès de la Cruz poem in which the elements are invoked to come to the aid of the threatened Jesus (Love).

Finally comes a story of how the baby Jesus pacifies dragons menacing Mary, Joseph, and their traveling companions, and another in which the child miraculously causes a palm tree to feed his mother and a pure spring to gush forth, the final words drawn from a related Castellanos poem. *—James Reel*

Recommended:

○ **Adams: El Niño** / Nagano (cond.), Marco, Upshaw, Hunt, White, Berlin German SO / 2001 / Nonesuch 79634

Nixon in China (1985–1987)

The brainchild of famed director Peter Sellars, and first performed in 1987, *Nixon in China* remains one of John Adams' best-known compositions. Like works by Philip Glass and others, it represents an attempt to reconcile the theatrical demands of opera with the seemingly incompatible musical language of minimalism. The resulting work, rich in subtext and color, caused quite a stir at the time of its premiere. Looking back, it seems clear that the resurgence of interest in new opera seen in the late 1980s and early 1990s can be partially attributed to the success of *Nixon in China.*

The opera is based on Richard Nixon's famous visit to communist China in 1972. President Nixon and his wife, Pat, were the first official American visitors to the People's Republic since Mao Tse-tung's communist takeover in 1949. The visit, which yielded no immediate political gains, nevertheless was a first step in the reestablishment of formal diplomatic relations between China and the United States. Alice Goodman's libretto, written entirely in rhymed couplets, is tightly focused on the main characters: Richard Nixon, Pat Nixon, Chou En-lai, Mao Tse-tung, and Chiang Ch'ing (Mao's fourth wife). A smaller though not insignificant role is given to Henry Kissinger, who accompanied the Nixons on their historic visit. The differences among the main characters—particularly Nixon, Chou En-lai, and Chairman Mao—emerge as the dramatic emphasis of the piece, creating a picture of each as both a person and a public figure. The work is decidedly sympathetic to the Chinese, who display the greater breadth of thought and understanding. Pat Nixon also emerges as a very personable and sensitive heroine. Nixon himself comes off as a self-conscious, but effective, statesman—perhaps an attempt at historical accuracy. Adams' music, especially his skillful text setting and use of orchestral colors, adapts easily to the requirements of Goodman's characters. Each person "speaks" with his/her own melodic contour (especially Nixon, whose stilted delivery remains clichéd) and occupies a unique musical sphere, in much the same way as characters are associated with leitmotifs in the operas of Wagner.

The large-scale architecture of scenes, and of the piece as a whole, succeeds in creating a complete picture of the historic visit, as well as the effect of that visit on the main characters. Perhaps the opera's biggest handicap is that Adams' musical vocabulary of the time—slow in harmonic rhythm and highly repetitive—limits the possibilities for realistic action and expression. Everything seems to happen in slow motion, and characters are forced to engage in passages of self-explanation—announcing their worldviews and feelings instead of being allowed to interact naturally. On the other hand, the subject matter brings with it a measure of formality, and Adams' music magnifies that quality without ever becoming stuffy. *—Allen Schrott*

Synopsis:

Act One. Act One opens as Chinese soldiers and Chou En-lai wait for President Nixon's plane to arrive; the soldiers sing a song in praise of China and the revolution, "Soldiers of Heaven Hold the Sky." Nixon disembarks, and he and Chou share inconsequential pleasantries, and Nixon then contemplates the historic nature of his mission and the way it is making news in "News Has a Kind of Mystery." He compares his landing in China to the Apollo mission landing on the moon and happily reflects that it is being broadcast in prime time in the United States. In Mao's study, the Chairman quotes his own sayings and makes obscure jokes, echoed by his sycophantic secretaries, and Nixon and Kissinger both try to turn the conversation to practical matters. But Mao continues to control the situation, even after he pretends to doze off. During a state banquet, the conversations are more normal, and Chou proposes a toast, "Ladies and Gentlemen, Comrades and Friends." Nixon declares that his former enmity toward China was wrong, and more toasting ensues.

Act Two. In Act Two, Pat Nixon is taken on tours highlighting various aspects of China's cultural and economic development, meets a group of school children and reacts to them with her own, straightforward, "I Don't Daydream and Don't Look Back." She hopes that their rapport is a sign of things to come. At a performance of a Chinese revolutionary ballet, "The Red Detachment of Women," written by Madame Mao, Pat Nixon is perturbed by the brutal depiction of prerevolutionary abuse of workers, including a young woman. Madame Mao castigates the performers, criticizing them on nearly every point, and displays her almost pathological egocentrism in her aria "I Am the Wife of Mao Tse-tung."

Act Three. Act Three takes place on the last night of the visit. Mao dances with Madame Mao ("The Maos' Dance"), and as they lie in bed that night, each character continues in the same vein in which they began the opera. Mao continues to play mind games by means of his seemingly aimless and yet pointed remarks; Nixon thinks, not always to the point, about the war and remembers his hamburger stand; Pat Nixon converses with him; Madame Mao speaks in revolutionary slogans; and Chou wonders, "How much of what we did was good?" *—Ann Feeney*

Recommended:

○ **Adams: Nixon in China (complete opera)** / de Waart (cond.), Hampson, Sylvan, Maddalena, Craney, St. Luke's CO / 1988 / Nonesuch 79177

○ **Adams: Music From Nixon In China** / de Waart (cond.), Hampson, Sylvan, Maddalena, Craney, St. Luke's CO / 1987 / Nonesuch 79193

CONCERTO

Violin Concerto (1993)

John Adams' *Violin Concerto* (1993) represents something of an aesthetic shift for the composer, perhaps reflecting a "post-post-modernist" world view. Continuing in a direction suggested in the early 1990s by the increasingly ambiguous harmonies and rhythms of works such as the opera *The Death of Klinghoffer* and the *Chamber Symphony,* the Violin Concerto's unceasing melody and immediate—rather than cumulative—expressivity strike a sharp contrast with the motoric mysticism of Adams' early works. The work follows a traditional three-movement plan: a lengthy, dramatic first movement is followed by a chaconne that is both staid and warmly intimate, which in turn leads into a bustling, high-energy finale. The most prominent remnant of Adams' minimalist beginnings is the use of textural blocks that serve as background for the solo part. The textures, however, are built upon instrumental color and varying figures used in the accompaniment rather than on the steady rhythmic flow and glacial harmonic rhythm typical of the composer's early works. The first movement, titled simply with a metronomic designation (quarter note = 78), begins with a series of eerily rising legato lines in the strings. The soloist enters almost immediately and will hardly find a moment of rest during the course of the work. As the violin explores different modes of melody and figuration, certain ideas are picked up and tossed around by the orchestra, while the initial succession of rising parallel chords in the strings spreads its increasing tension to the winds and brass. The use of synthesizers—a hallmark of Adams' orchestral music—contributes to the overall color spectrum while providing distinctive color. As the movement progresses, the rising lines shift from legato to pizzicato as the solo line grows more and more urgent. The accompaniment becomes sparser, completely dissolving with the arrival of the violin's extended cadenza. The cadenza melts into the long, sustained tones of the chaconne. With its subterranean ground bass, this movement exudes a tranquil yet troubled aura akin to fusion of Salvador Dali's "The Persistence of Memory" and Pachelbel's *Canon in D* (the use of which as source material Adams acknowledges in his notes). Again, electronic sounds provide an ethereality to the familiar bass line, while the orchestra and soloist play both with and against the ear's expectations; some figures are foreign, others similar to Pachelbel's original. As though in contrast to the principle of repetition embodied in Pachelbel's canon, an unobtrusive pattern on the marimba cycles in the background. After the final sustained tones of the second movement evaporate, the Toccata begins with a sudden burst of aggressive energy. Frenzied patterns that appear in defined blocks suddenly break into colorful fragments, creating a variety of gestures and textures that, borne upon the movement's unflagging rhythmic and metric flow, carry the work to its close. This work was composed, as the composer states, "always with the goal of making the musical idea and the reality of its execution one and the same thing." In this sense, the exploratory yet expressive nature of the solo part makes it a work both for and about the violin. *—Jeremy Grimshaw*

Recommended:

- ○ **Adams: Violin Concerto; Shaker Loops** / Nagano (cond.), Kremer, London SO / 1996 / Nonesuch 79360
- ○ **Adams, Glass: Violin Concertos** / Eschenbach (cond.), McDuffie, Houston SO / 1999 / Telarc 80494

KEYBOARD

Phrygian Gates (1977)

John Adams, who once described himself as "a minimalist bored with minimalism," wrote *Phrygian Gates* (1977) in an effort to "convolute and enrich" the style. One of the composer's earliest forays into the minimalist aesthetic, *Phrygian Gates* is centered around a shift from the Lydian mode to the Phrygian, with its contiguous sections divided according to tonal center. The first section, in A, is predominantly in the Lydian mode; following a fleeting dip into the Phrygian mode, the work moves to a new tonal center, D. In this section the Lydian is used for a slightly shorter time, and the Phrygian gradually gains dominance. This pattern is followed through fully half of the cycle of tonal centers until, by the end, the Phrygian mode has established complete dominance. This process is indeed the motivation behind the "gate" of the title; the "gate" that denotes a precise moment of change in electronic music here applies to the motion from one mode to another. *Phrygian Gates* has a generally shimmering, wave-like texture, but, as in conventional tonal music, every tonal center has its own effect: some sections are heavy and crass, others lilting and peaceful. *—Graham Olson*

Recommended:

- ○ **American Piano Music of Our Time** / Oppens / 1991 / Music & Arts 604
- ○ **O'Riley, Piano** / O'Riley / 1990 / Albany 038

VOCAL

The Wound-Dresser, for baritone & orchestra (1988)

The Wound-Dresser is a setting of most of the poem of the same name by Walt Whitman. Scored for baritone and orchestra, the work was written in 1989 and premiered that year by Sanford Sylvan and the St. Paul Chamber Orchestra under the direction of the composer. Whitman's poem is part of the series "Drum-Taps," which treated Civil War themes. The poet visited hospitals during the war, nursing and otherwise helping and consoling the wounded. The horror of what he encountered there, and the compassion and selflessness with which he went about his frequently disturbing duties, are embodied in the poem. While he was composing his setting, Adams' own father was dying of Alzheimer's disease. Having watched his mother devote herself to caring for him, Adams was struck by the bond that develops between a caretaker and a dying person. Therefore, there is a particularly personal aspect to Adams' response to the poem. This profoundly moving work begins in an almost matter-of-fact fashion, as the speaker (presumably Whitman) goes about his business of tending to the wounded. Quiet, pulsating chords accompany, with a solo violin soaring over all. The anxiety level rises briefly as the protagonist looks directly into the eyes of one of the wounded. The text then becomes more specific about particular injuries and infections. Broken and missing limbs, deep wounds, gangrene—he sees them all, and deals with them as impassively as he can, only briefly giving way to his revulsion. The music moves unrelentingly, but with an understated tone, through the horrible imagery. It is occasionally dissonant, but mostly calm and restrained, almost preternaturally so given the grim subject matter. The tones are muted—strings, trumpet, flute, and synthesizer. The baritone inhabits a fairly narrow range, mirroring the emotional restraint of the piece. Only in a couple of places does the emotion burst forth more dramatically. Toward the end, a solo trumpet sums up the somber military mood. The work ends peacefully with an extended chord, perhaps reflecting Whitman's (and Adams') compassion and sense of hope. *—Chris Morrison*

Recommended:

- ○ **Adams: The Wound-Dresser; Christian Zeal and Activity; Five Songs; Eros Piano** / Adams (cond.), Sylvan, St. Luke's / 1999 / Nonesuch 79453
- ○ **John Adams: Shaker Loops; The Wound-Dresser; Short Ride in a Fast Machine** / Alsop (cond.), Gunn, Bournemouth SO / 2004 / Naxos 8559031

CHORAL

Harmonium, for chorus & orchestra (1980–1981)

Composed in 1981, at the point when minimalism was moving toward audience-pleasing ethereality and away from the audience-alienating repetition of the 1960s and 1970s that gave birth to the genre, John Adams' *Harmonium* was, in fact, already looking ahead to the "post-minimalist" style that Adams would forge with works such as *The Death of Klinghoffer* (1991) and the *Violin Concerto* (1993). With its alternating passages of throbbing minimal textures and dramatic lyricism, *Harmonium* hinted at a more exploratory vein. The piece sets three texts, one by the English poet John Donne and the other two by Emily Dickinson. The Donne piece, entitled *Negative Love or The Nothing*, is set to music that begins with simple repeated tones sung on single syllables. As the tones expand into chords, the syllables expand into the opening lines of the text. The polyrhythmic juxtapositions of twos against threes and threes against fours, stock elements of the minimalist palette, suddenly become even more obtuse, in order, paradoxically, to emphasize the declamation of the text. This situation creates a free space in which varied rhythms add new drama to the blocks of harmony and webs of accompaniment.

The middle movement sets Dickinson's pensive *Because I Could Not Stop for Death*. The suspension of time implicit in the poem is portrayed musically by long-suspended harmonies in the strings. The impetus, then, is no longer the rhythm of the text so much as the mood conjured up by the poetic discourse, a mood expressed by blocks of harmonies and slight dissonances suspended long enough to succumb to any resolution. As the poem progresses, so do the rhythmic tension and activity, carrying the work boldly and without pause into the final movement. The sensuality that—except in the title—is largely implicit in the third text, *Wild Nights*, is made explicit in the music. A sudden metric shift marks the movement's beginning, which brims with the sort of grandiose melodic-rhythmic complexes for which Adams is best known. As in the first movement, the declamation of the text lends rhythmic variety to the lines sung above the accompanying web. The exclamatory passages in the text provide opportunity for corresponding orchestral emphases and bursts of instrumental color. The first two stanzas of the poem, full of anticipation and Romantic anxiety, give way to more tranquilly sensual imagery: "Rowing in Eden—Ah, the sea!" Rhythmic energy is reined in, and undulating incantations of "rowing" flow underneath the remainder of the text, drawing it to an idyllic close. *—Jeremy Grimshaw*

Recommended:

- ○ **Adams: Harmonium** / de Waart (cond.), San Francisco SO / 1984 / ECM 821465
- ○ **Adams: Harmonium; Rachmaninov: The Bells** / Shaw (cond.), Fleming, Atlanta SO / 1996 / Telarc 80365

Thomas Adès

b. Mar. 31, 1971, London, England

Composer: Orchestral, Opera

Thomas Adès is among the brightest young stars in contemporary composition, and a musician of broad achievement and influence. His complex and appealing music exhibits a flair for drama, humor, and personal expression, and is notable for the creative use of instrumental color. Also active as a pianist and conductor, Adès divides his time between composition and a busy performing schedule, as well as teaching at the Royal Academy of Music and serving as artistic director of the Aldeburgh Festival.

Having studied at the Guildhall School of Music, Adès took second prize in piano at the 1989 BBC Young Musician of the Year competition. Further studies at King's College, Cambridge, confirmed a move towards composition as his primary vocation, and his first works were written there. After his graduation in 1992, Adès moved quickly into the professional world with a performance of his *Chamber Symphony* by the BBC Philharmonic (in 1993 under Matthias Bamert). Further performances came during his tenure as Composer in Association with the Halle Orchestra, for which he wrote *The Origin of the Harp* (1994), and *These Premises are Alarmed* (1996). Other works composed during this period include *Still Sorrowing*, Op. 7, and *Traced Overhead*, Op. 15 for solo piano; *... but all shall be well*, Op. 10 for orchestra; *Arcadania*, Op. 12 for string quartet; and *Living Toys*, Op. 9 for chamber ensemble, which was commissioned by the London Sinfonietta under Oliver Knussen. Adès' reputation was secured by his chamber opera, *Powder Her Face*, Op. 14, a commission from Almeida Opera for the 1995 Cheltenham Festival. Its premiere, as well as productions in Germany and the United States attracted enormous critical attention and praise, and led to a commission for the 2004 season at Covent Garden (*The Tempest*, an adaptation of Shakespeare). His first large-scale orchestral work, *Asyla*—which was premiered by Simon Rattle and the Birmingham Symphony Orchestra in 1997—established Adès' reputation as a composer of lasting value and individuality. *—Allen Schrott*

ORCHESTRAL

Asyla, Op. 17 (1997)

Asyla (a plural of the word asylum) was commissioned by the City of Birmingham Symphony Orchestra and first performed by that ensemble in October 1997, under the direction of Sir Simon Rattle (who subsequently recorded the work with the CBSO). Set in four movements and lasting approximately 22 minutes, it employs a very large orchestra and features two pianists (one of whom plays both a concert grand and upright piano, while the other performs on an upright piano tuned a quarter-tone flat) and a battery of six percussionists. The ambivalence of the title suggests the possibilities of both sanctuary and madhouse, and both are woven into the substance of the work.

The first movement, indicated simply as "I," suggests a free-floating expansiveness. It begins with rising splashes of cowbells and percussion. The horns then announce a darting figure soon taken up by the strings and later, the winds. Gradually increasing in presence is a restless rhythmic figure. A solo violin appears and the music broadens. Over very low brass, high brass sound an insistent, punctuating motive, buzzing like wasps. Interjections from the rest of the orchestra whirl about and the movement ends with crisp snaps of percussion.

Movement II opens somewhat hesitantly with muted cowbells. A plaintive descending figure is voiced by the English horn, as a rising, threatening figure emerges from the low brass, the upper theme constantly folding over the lower as it passes to the strings. Over increasingly active and chiming percussion, the high theme is taken up by the horn, a bass clarinet growls menacingly in its bottom register, and the section ends quickly.

Movement III begins with a quiet wash of percussion and piano. Soon a high rhythmic figure of almost spastic insistence is conjured over a growing marching theme sounded vigorously by the side drum. An ascending pizzicato figure is heard from the upper strings over the ever more insistent pulse as the movement lurches toward its end.

The final movement is introduced by glowering low voices, over which high wind figures hurtle hither and yon like lightning in a threatening summer sky. Brief moments of serenity offer themselves amidst a flowing, measured theme sounded by the strings, even as the lower orchestral voices sound their crawling motive from the depths. The movement gathers energy and, at less than four minutes into the section, the orchestra erupts briefly in full voice, then recedes as the strings wander searchingly toward a quiet conclusion.

The effect of this work is quite spectacular, with a virtuoso handling of the extensive complement of instruments called for by the score. Adès is unerringly apt in his choice of color, his employment of broad range (from very low to very high), his use of imaginatively assembled percussion sounds, and his firm sense of structure. *Asyla* also evidences an enveloping sense of depth and mystery, not revealing all of its secrets on first listening. *—Erik Eriksson*

Recommended:

○ **Adès: Asyla** / Rattle (cond.), City of Birmingham SO / 1999 / EMI 56818

OPERA

Powder Her Face, Op. 14 (1995)

Written for the Almeida Opera Company and premiered at the 1995 Cheltenham Festival, *Powder Her Face* helped put Thomas Adès on the musical map. Full of brash instrumental textures and imaginative vocal writing, the racy chamber opera showed a degree of creativity and compositional sure-handedness that prompted comparisons with Benjamin Britten and Henry Purcell, among others. The libretto, by Phillip Hensher, is loosely fashioned after events in the life of Margaret, Duchess of Argyll—a famous beauty whose social renown turned to infamy during a scandalous divorce trial (largely focused on her sexual infidelities, which were graphically depicted in her own collection of Polaroid snapshots). The judgment in the case was scathing, and the Duchess never recovered from the disgrace.

Powder Her Face is in two acts, the first beginning in the year 1990, and the second ending in the same year; the intervening scenes take place at different times during the Duchess's life. It is never made clear whether we are witnessing events as they unfold or seeing them through the filter of the Duchess's memory. This ambiguity is enhanced by the fact that Adès assigns multiple roles to the supporting singers, all of whom are first seen as employees of the hotel where the Duchess lives. Is she merely populating her memories with the faces at hand, or are there deeper connections between the people that affect her life? The first and last scenes of the opera are essentially the same scene, interrupted by the intervening flashbacks. The inner scenes trace the events leading up to her marriage to the Duke, their divorce, and her final collapse into poverty and despair.

Powder Her Face requires four singers and a chamber ensemble of 15 players, and demands virtuosity from all. The vocal parts—lyric soprano (the Duchess), coloratura soprano (the Maid/Confidant), tenor (Electrician/Lounge Lizard), and bass (the Duke/Judge)—require extremes of range and expression, and the instrumental parts, the most striking of which is a bravura accordion part, are intricate and rhythmically complex. However, the overall musical effect is clear and deceptively simple, often incorporating popular styles from the 1920s through the 1950s. *—AMG*

Synopsis:

Act One. Scene One—1990

A hotel Maid and an Electrician are playing around in the room of Margaret, formerly the Duchess of Argyll; egged on by the Maid, the Electrician dresses in the Duchess' clothes and sings a raunchy parody of an old song written about her. When the Duchess returns and catches them mocking her, they treat her with open disrespect, knowing that the manager is on his way to evict her from the hotel.

Scene Two—1934

The soon-to-be Duchess awaits her fiancé, the Duke, along with two friends, a Confidant (Maid) and a Lounge Lizard (Electrician). Impatient for the Duke's arrival, she laments her extreme boredom, and sings longingly of his virtues. Meanwhile, the Confidant and Lounge Lizard trade vicious gossip; they see a juicy disaster in the upcoming marriage. The Lounge Lizard performs a song, and the Duke (Hotel Manager) finally arrives.

Scene Three—1936

Stealing a few minutes before the big wedding, and vicariously enjoying the food and gifts assembled, an acid-tongued Maid sings an aria in praise of wealth and excess.

Scene Four—1953

The Duchess is alone in her hotel—bored, hungry, and wanting "room service." She dials, ritualistically, slowly, and requests claret and sandwiches. Beef sandwiches. When the waiter (Electrician) arrives—aware of his true purpose in this transaction—she enacts an elaborate seduction charade before finally performing oral sex on him.

Scene Five—1953

The Duke (Hotel Manager) comes home to his mistress (Maid), having left the Duchess at a party where she is still enjoying her admirers and "pashes." The mistress toys with the Duke, dropping not-so-subtle hints about the Duchess' infidelities while the two of them play at "jumpies." Eventually he becomes enraged, and the two of them tear the Duchess' room apart looking for evidence.

Act Two. Scene Six—1955

Rubberneckers (Maid and Electrician) gawk and comment on the Duke and Duchess' divorce trial. The Duchess appears, and the Judge (Hotel Manager) delivers a lengthy judgment against her, gradually becoming overcome with emotion as he recounts the salacious facts of the trial. The Duchess attempts to salvage her dignity as she leaves.

Scene Seven—1970

A journalist (Maid) conducts an awkward interview with the Duchess, having been admonished not to discuss "certain things." A large collection of hat boxes is delivered while they stick to safe topics, like beauty and "hostessing." Soon, however, the Duchess erupts with a hateful and irrational diatribe against the vulgarity of modern society, and chases the reporter from the room. She is left with the last of her packages—the hotel bill.

Scene Seven—1990

The Hotel Manager appears and attempts to inform the faded Duchess of her eviction as gently as possible. She is resistant, however, and eventually makes a clumsy offer of sexual favors in return for his consideration. After he leaves in disgust, she recounts memories from her childhood, when she was cared for and fawned over by faithful servants, her maid in particular. The Manager returns to announce the arrival of her car, and she leaves in silence. *—Allen Schrott*

Recommended:

○ **Adès: Powder Her Face** / Ades (cond.), J. Gomez, V. Anderson, Bryson, A. Morris, Almeida Ensemble / 1998 / EMI 56649

John Mark Ainsley

b. Jul. 9, 1963, Crewe, Cheshire, England

Tenor

John Mark Ainsley is a leading British tenor especially associated with repertory from the Classical era and earlier. He studied at Oxford, where his teacher was Diane Forlano. In his earliest professional appearances, he established himself as a Mozart tenor, including the role of Idomeneo at the Welsh National Opera and as Don Ottavio (*Don Giovanni*) at the Aix-en-Provence and Glyndebourne Festivals. His first American appearances were in concerts in New York and Boston, and in 1992 he debuted with the Berlin Philharmonic Orchestra.

His first Viennese appearances were in performances of both the *St. Matthew* and *St John Passions* by Bach with the Musik Verein in 1992. The conductor on those occasions was Peter Schreier, who is also one of the era's finest lieder and Bach tenors. Among his other leading roles are the title part of Gluck's *Orfeo* (his debut role at the Netherlands Opera, 1966), Tito in Mozart's *La Clemenza di Tito* (for his first appearance in Sydney, 1997), Fenton in Verdi's *Falstaff*, Lensky in Tchaikovsky's *Eugene Onegin*, and Jonathan in Nielsen's *Saul and David*. He has sung and recorded the role of Lysander in Britten's *A Midsummer Night's Dream*.

He is also an active recitalist and concert artist who has appeared with Les Musiciens du Louvre, the New York Philharmonic, the Berlin Philharmonic, L'Orchestre de Paris, the London Symphony, the Vienna Philharmonic, the San Francisco Symphony, and the Boston Symphony. He records for several labels, but is most closely associated with Hyperion, which has selected him to appear on six discs of its great series of the complete Schubert songs. His repertory for that company includes music of Stravinsky, Vaughan Williams, Warlock, William Lloyd Webber, Grainger, Britten, Ireland, Finzi, and Quilter. *—Joseph Stevenson*

Recommended:

○ **Songs by Peter Warlock** / Ainsley, Vignoles / 1994 / Hyperion 66736

○ **Rameau: Dardanus** / Minkowski (cond.), Ainsley, Gens, Kozena, Courtis, Les Musiciens du Louvre / 2000 / Archiv 463476

○ **Vaughan Williams: Along the Field and other songs** / Ainsley, Nash Ensemble / Hyperion 67168

○ **Goldschmidt: Der gewaltige Hahnrei; Mediterranean Songs** / Knothe, Zagrosek (conds.), Alexander, Ainsley, Kraus, Wottrich, Berlin RSO, LGO, Berlin RSO / 1994 / London 440850

Roberto Alagna

b. Jun. 7, 1963, Clichy-sur-Bois, France
Tenor

Born in France of Sicilian parents, Roberto Alagna studied music in Paris. He gained notoriety by winning first prize in the 1988 Luciano Pavarotti Competition and soon made his stage debut as Alfredo in *La Traviata* with the Glyndebourne Touring Opera Company, soon to be followed by debuts in Montpellier, Monte Carlo, and the Teatro alla Scala in Milan (also in *La Traviata*). His *Teatro alla Scala* debut came at the invitation of Riccardo Muti in a fabled production with Tiziana Fabbricini which was telecast. In 1990 he sang Rodolfo in Puccini's *La Bohème*—a role that has become one of his most popular; it was also the role of his Covent Garden Opera debut in 1992 and his Metropolitan Opera debut in 1996. Another role which was very important during the early part of his career was the title role in Gounod's *Romeo et Juliette*, which he has sung with great success in Paris, London, and New York.

This role proved to be even more important for his personal life, as he met his second wife, Angela Gheorghiu, while they were performing this opera together. His first wife had died after a lengthy illness, and this new romance brought a renewed warmth and passion to his performances. Their performances of *L'elisir d'amore*, *La Bohème* and *Werther* are greatly admired, and together the two have become one of opera's few genuine double attractions. Alagna is known to introduce acrobatic tricks into productions of *L'Elisir d'amore* which few other tenors would attempt. His appearances in 1996 at the *Theatre-Chatelet Paris* and Covent Garden Opera, London, as Don Carlo in the original French version of Verdi's opera has helped bring the French edition back to the fore. Other operas which have proved successful for Alagna are *Rigoletto*, *Macbeth*, *Lucia di Lammermoor*, *Roberto Devereux*, *L'amico Fritz*, *Carmen*, and *La Rondine*.

Alagna is a self-taught tenor who learned his craft by listening to recordings to pick up ideas and find those that work for him. He usually mentions two of his predecessors when asked whose recordings were most influential; these are Beniamino Gigli and Nicolai Gedda. He feels his voice is like Gedda's in its brightness and timber. His recordings of *La Bohème* on Decca and *Romeo et Juliette* on EMI display some attempts at the vocal refinements which characterized Gedda's singing. Alagna's willingness to step beyond the standard score is displayed in the use of an alternative version of "Una furtiva lágrima" in his London recording of *L'Elisir d'amore*, using the new critical edition of *La Bohème* in the Decca recording with Chailly, as well as singing the original French version of *Don Carlo*. His voice is a very fine lyric tenor with a bright and ringing upper register, but when it is put under pressure it tends to turn harsh. With the assumption on stage and on recording of Verdi's *Don Carlo* and both *Werther* and *Manon* of Massenet, Alagna moved into more dramatic roles, and in his recordings of the early 2000s he moved easily around the heart of the operatic repertory. *—Richard LeSueur*

Recommended:

- ○ **Donizetti: L'Elisir d'Amore** / Viotti (cond.), Alagna, Devia, Spagnoli, Pratico, English CO / Erato 98483
- ○ **Donizetti: Lucie de Lammermoor** / Pido (cond.), Dessay, Alagna, Cavallier, Tezier, Lyon National Opera Orch. / 2002 / Virgin 45528
- ○ **Nessun Dorma** / Edwards, Elder (cond.), Alagna / 2003 / EMI 57627
- ○ **Duets & Arias** / Armstrong (cond.), Alagna, Gheorghiu, Royal Opera House Orch. Covent Garden / 1996 / EMI 56117
- ○ **Offenbach: Les Contes d'Hoffmann** / Nagano (cond.), Jo, Van Dam, Dessay, Ragon, Alagna, Lyon National Opera Orch. / 1996 / Erato 14330

Jehan Ariste Alain

b. Feb. 3, 1911, St. Germain-en-Laye, France, **d.** Jun. 20, 1940, Saumur, France
Composer: Keyboard

Jehan Ariste Alain was born in St. Germain-en-Laye to a musical family headed by his father Albert, who was an organist, composer and organ builder. The elder Alain had built an organ into his own living room and home schooled three of his children (Jehan, Olivier, and Marie-Claire) in the art of playing the "King of Instruments." At age 16, Jehan Alain enrolled in the Paris Conservatoire, where he continued his organ studies with Marcel Dupré, taking composition with Roger-Ducasse and Paul Dukas, and fugue with Georges Caussade. It is Caussade who is said to have had the deepest impact on Alain's own musical personality. Alain studied at the Conservatoire for the next 12 years, taking First Prize in Harmony and Fugue in 1934, and following it with a First Prize in Organ and Improvisation in 1939.

In 1935 he married, and from that time on he made his living playing at two places of worship: the Church of Saint-Nicolas de Maisons-Lafitte, and the synagogue at the Rue Notre-Dame-de-Nazareth. Like his father, Alain had an organ built into his home; this one had a rank of pedals that split at the center between a pair of divisions: 16' and 8' stops on the first half, and smaller stops on the second. It was on this instrument that he conceived his major mature works: the *Trois Danses*, *Le Jardin suspendu*, *Litanies*, and the *Fantasies*.

Jehan Alain's short life was difficult. He served in the French Army in 1933 and 1934, during which time he contracted a near-fatal case of pneumonia. His sister Odile was killed in a mountain climbing accident in 1937. At the end of 1939, Alain was mobilized again—this time in the Eighth Motorized Armored Division—and he died fighting the Germans in Petit-puy (outside Saumur) on May 20, 1940, at age 29. The manuscript pages of his final work, a full symphonic orchestration of the *Trois Danses*, were sucked out of the window of a moving train as Alain rode on to his final rendezvous.

In spite of the brevity of his life, Alain produced approximately 120 works. As a whole, his output is strikingly consistent and complete unto itself; scholars of Alain's music have difficulty developing precise dates for many of the works since telltale signs of stylistic development are practically absent from his music. His works sound with one voice, varied, but mature. Alain's music makes extensive use of the church modes, as well as coloristic dissonance. A somewhat rhapsodic approach to rhythm creates an ecstatic building up of bold, colorful and phantasmagoric sections in the *Litanies* and the *Trois Danses* that can be tremendously exciting to hear. In *Le Jardin suspendu* and short works such as the lovely *Choral dorien* he created smooth, mysterious textures that suggest an otherworldly, even divine, presence.

With his death, France immediately appreciated what she had lost; the first book-length study on Alain's music was published in 1941. In the early 1970s, Alain's sister Marie-Claire made the first complete recording of his organ music, and in the digital era, further complete sets have been issued with Kevin Bowyer (Nimbus) and Eric Lebrun (Naxos). Lesser known is a considerable body of Alain's piano music, in addition to some choral music, including two masses, chamber music, and songs. *—Uncle Dave Lewis*

KEYBOARD

Trois Danses, Op. 81 (1937–1939)

Jehan Alain's *Trois Danses* (*Three Dances*) for organ are most prominent among the ill-fated composer's 120 works. Alain undertook the *Three Dances* as piano pieces in 1937 and scored them out fully for organ in 1939. In 1940 he began an orchestration of this set, and he attempted to continue the work even though he was mobilized into the French army. However, the manuscript pages were sucked out of the window of a moving train into an open field as Alain moved toward his final engagement in battle. An attempt was made after his death to recover the manuscript, but none of it was found even though children in the countryside recalled that they had played with the "funny pages that came with the rain." Composer Raymond Gallois-Montbrun subsequently completed an orchestration, but it is primarily as an organ piece that the *Three Dances* are known.

The opening movement, "Joies" (Joys), begins with a nebulous rising figure that subsequently becomes the basis for all transitional material in the work. Most of "Joies" is centered on a nervous, insistent figuration in 7/8 time, and this pattern goes through a number of transformations. Before the big climax near the end of the piece, there is an amazing section in which Alain pits an uneven rhythmic figure in the middle of the organ's range against some very rapid patterns in higher registers, played pianissimo. Fans of metal and gothic rock music, take note—there is something for you here.

The middle movement, "Deuils" (Mourning), is a piece that expresses deep grief, and it may have some connection with Alain's loss of his younger sister Odile in a mountain-climbing accident. It begins slowly and mysteriously, and about midway through there is a section based on an ostinato pattern in 6/8, subjected to novel variations. This settles down to a quiet, somber solo melody by the conclusion of the movement.

Finally, in "Luttes" (Struggles), Alain reprises much of the rhythmic character of "Joies." While the overall texture is brighter in color, it is also more aggravated in content, indeed indicative of "struggle" without clear resolution of the conflict by the work's close. *—Uncle Dave Lewis*

Recommended:

- ○ **Jehan Alain: Complete Organ Works Vol. 2** / M.C. Alain / 2001 / Erato 85773
- ○ **Alain: Organ Works Vol. 2** / Lebrun / 1997 / Naxos 553633

Litanies, Op. 79 (1937)

Litanies was composed in 1937 and remains the best-known and most-often-played organ work of French composer Jehan Alain. This short composition is based on a snatch of chant-like melody, given as an incipit at the start of the work. *Litanies* is improvisational in nature and takes this melodic idea through a variety of guises, ranging from joyous, gentle, and reflective expressions through more troubled, apprehensive and generally serious passages. The motif is placed in contrast with a two-chord progression that likewise is subjected to some interesting transformations. The work concludes with an impressive downward chordal passage based on a whole-tone scale, finally resolving in a large complex of notes that is neither predominantly major or minor.

Alain left an explanatory postscript that appears at the end of the published score stating his intent: "When the Christian soul in its distress finds no new words with which to implore God's mercy, it repeats endlessly the same invocation with strong faith. Reason having attained its zenith, Faith alone reaches on high." *—Uncle Dave Lewis*

Recommended:

- ○ **Jehan Alain: Complete Organ Works Vol. 1** / M.C. Alain / 2000 / Erato 80214
- ○ **Hans Fagius Plays Organ Favourites** / Fagius / 1987 / Bis 365

Marie-Claire Alain

b. Aug. 10, 1926, St. Germain-en-Laye, France
Organist

Marie-Claire Alain was the youngest child in a family of distinguished musicians, born August 10, 1926, in St. Germain-en Laye, a Paris suburb. Her father, Albert Alain, a composer and amateur organ builder, had been a pupil of Guilmant and Fauré. Her sister Odile was a promising soprano and pianist who lost her life early in a mountaineering accident; her older brother, Olivier, was a composer, pianist, and musicologist. Her oldest brother was the renowned Jehan Alain, a composer and organist whose teachers included Dupré, Dukas, and Roger-Ducasse. He numbered Messiaen and Poulenc among his closest friends and his works for organ—*Litanies*, in particular—established him as one of the brightest stars among rising French composers in the decade before his battlefield death in 1940, at 29. A twin sense of loss and inheritance informed her studies and career.

With the allied liberation of Paris in August 1944, she entered the Paris Conservatoire, studying with Dupré for organ, Pié-Caussade for counterpoint and fugue, and Maurice Duruflé for harmony. Duruflé composed one of the finest of his small but masterly group of organ works as an *hommage* to Marie-Claire's brother, the *Prélude et fugue sur le nom d'Alain*, Op. 7 (1942). She studied with Duruflé from 1944 until 1950, schoolwork being augmented by private lessons. During her Conservatoire years, she carried off four Premier Prix. After the inauguration of her career in 1950, she took a prize for organ at the Geneva International Competition and gave her first public recital. The Amis de Orgue awarded her the Bach Prize in 1951. After a further two years of study with Gaston Litaize, she took up her career in earnest, giving well over 2,000 recitals worldwide. Her recordings number in the hundreds, and she has twice recorded the complete organ works of Bach. By the 1980s, she had become known as a specialist in seventeenth and eighteenth century music, with numerous recordings of works by Couperin, Grigny, Daquin, Vivaldi, Buxtehude, Pachelbel, Handel, C.P.E. Bach, Haydn, and Mozart—among many others—to her credit. But she has also made distinguished recordings of Romantic repertoire with albums of works by Mendelssohn, César Franck, Liszt, Widor, Vierne, Poulenc, and Jehan Alain—whose punctilious execution is suffused with passion—carrying into the twenty-first century living traditions extending to the middle of the nineteenth. She is much in demand as a teacher. *—Adrian Corleonis*

Recommended:

- ○ **French Christmas Carols for Organ** / Alain / Erato 45455
- ○ **Buxtehude: Organ Works** / Alain / Erato 12979
- ○ **Jehan Alain: Complete Organ Works Vol. 1** / Alain / 2000 / Erato 80214
- ○ **Bach: Complete Works for Organ** / Alain / Erato 96358
- ○ **Bach: Complete Works for Organ Vol. 1** / Alain / Erato 96718
- ○ **Famous Music for Organ** / Alain / Erato 45976

Alban Berg Quartet

f. 1971, Vienna, Austria
Ensemble

The Alban Berg Quartet was founded in 1971 and within a decade was established as one of the finest string quartets in the world. It is known for its large recorded sets of the complete quartets of many masters of the genre.

Its founding members were all part of a Viennese chamber orchestra, who, while getting together to play chamber music, discovered the musical rapport essential to founding a great quartet. Deciding to honor a Viennese composer in their choice of names, they selected Alban Berg, one of the members of the group of atonal composers known as the Second Viennese School. According to violist Thomas Kakuska, the choice reflects Berg's position as a member of this revolutionary group of composers, but also his status as the most traditional-minded of them. Kakuska said, "We have chosen our name to show that we want to make a balance between the Romantic repertoire and also to play contemporary music."

The Quartet achieves its interpretations by consensus, not by the domination of any individual member. In addition to the given qualities of excellent ensemble, clean intonation, and a sense of unanimity of purpose, the qualities most often mentioned by reviewers, one may note the remarkable uniformity of tone among its four members. The group's sound is a warm one, although it can be rhythmically incisive when called for.

Its highly acclaimed recordings include complete sets of the quartets of Beethoven, Brahms, and Bartók and the string quartet works of Berg and Anton Webern. The group has also recorded substantial amounts of the quartet repertory of Mozart, Haydn, Dvořák, both Janáček quartets, and works by Ravel, Schumann, Debussy, Stravinsky, and Berio. Its repertoire of more recent music has acclaimed recordings of quartets by von Einem, Haubenstock-Ramati, Rihm, Schnittke, and Urbanner, many of them composed for and dedicated to the Quartet. In 1977, they paid tribute to Franz Schubert by playing only his music during his 200th anniversary year.

The members of the quartet (which include violinists Günter Pichler and Gerhard Schulz, violist Kakuska, and cellist Valentin Erben, of whom Schulz and Erben are founding members) are all faculty members of the Wiener Hochschule für Musik and also teach master classes on German chamber music regularly at the Musikhochschule in Cologne. They have won 30 major international recording awards, representing virtually every top prize of note. *—Joseph Stevenson*

Recommended:

- ○ **Strauss & Lanner: Waltzes** / Alban Berg Quartet / 1994 / EMI 54881
- ○ **Schubert: String Quartets 10 & 14** / Alban Berg Quartet / 1997 / EMI 56470
- ○ **Haydn: String Quartets Op. 76 2–4** / Alban Berg Quartet / 1996 / EMI 56166
- ○ **Mozart: String Quintets, KV 515 & 516** / Alban Berg Quartet, Wolf / EMI 49085
- ○ **Bartók: Complete String Quartets** / Alban Berg Quartet / 2002 / EMI 575652
- ○ **Beethoven: Complete String Quartets** / Alban Berg Quartet / 1999 / EMI 73606
- ○ **Beethoven: String Quartets 14 & 15** / Alban Berg Quartet / 1997 / EMI 69793
- ○ **Lutosławski: Streichquartett; Urbanner: Streichquartett 4; Berio: Notturno** / Alban Berg Quartet / 1997 / EMI 56363

Isaac Albéniz

b. May 29, 1860, Camprodón, Spain (Catalonia), **d.** May 18, 1909, Cambô-les-Bains, France
Composer: Keyboard, Opera

Born in 1860, Isaac Albéniz is best known for piano music that brilliantly evokes the spirit of Spain. As a composer-virtuoso, Albéniz successfully melded together composition and performance to create a bravura style reminiscent of the music of Franz Liszt, seasoned with Spanish folk idioms. The work that most convincingly represents this synthesis of virtuosity and tradition is the enchantingly colorful and atmospheric *Iberia*, a suite of 12 pieces recalling Spanish (particularly Andalusian) places and dances. Albéniz used folklore as his inspiration, but created a singular melodic style, which eventually influenced Debussy and Ravel. Believing that artistic originality and an interest in one's national musical tradition do not exclude each other, Albéniz likewise was largely the creator of the Spanish musical idiom that would be adopted and developed by Granados and de Falla.

A child prodigy, Albéniz was accepted, at the age of seven, as a private pupil by Antoine-François Marmontel, the celebrated piano pedagogue whose students included Bizet and Debussy. Back in Spain within a year, he gave a concert tour and eventually entered the Madrid Conservatory. He soon ran away, concertized around Spain, and in 1872 stowed away on a ship sailing for Latin America. Upon his return to Europe the following year, he entered the Leipzig Conservatory, where he briefly studied with Carl Reinecke. Soon thereafter, a patron enabled him to enter Brussels Conservatory to study piano and composition. Albéniz won the conservatory's first prize in 1879; the following year, he obtained an audience with Franz Liszt in Budapest; for a while he joined the master's entourage and continued to work on his technique as a pianist. After more wandering through Europe and South America, he settled in Barcelona in 1883, married, and began a family.

By that time, Albéniz already had a reputation as a composer of brilliant salon music for the piano. Around 1890, he met Felipe Pedrell, a prominent musicologist, composer, and collector of folk songs. Following the encounter with Pedrell, Albéniz re-examined his work as a composer, deciding to seek new inspiration in the rich musical traditions of Spain. Not yet satisfied with his craftsmanship, Albéniz moved to Paris to study with Paul Dukas and Vincent d'Indy. The restless Albéniz somehow hung on to a job teaching piano at Paris' Schola Cantorum from 1893 to 1900; then he undertook further peregrinations, all the while working on his masterpiece, *Iberia*. An immensely popular work, *Iberia* has also been transcribed for orchestra; successful orchestral versions include Leopold Stokowski's orchestration of "Fête-Dieu à Seville." Another work which gained wide popularity as an orchestral transcription is the *Tango for piano in D major*. Albéniz also wrote for the stage; his lyric comedy *Pepita Jiménez* and several other works were produced in the 1890s. He died in 1909. *—AMG*

KEYBOARD

España, Op. 165 (1890)

Albéniz's popular set of six album leaves, *España*, is the acme of his salon piano compositions. None of the pieces is longer than approximately four minutes, and none has the technical challenges and intricate textures of his masterpiece *Iberia*. The rhythms, modal harmonies, and subtle dramatics of its simple lines so completely evoke Spain that anything more would be gilding the lily. Together, the six pieces could be viewed as Albéniz's take on the traditional keyboard suite, made up as it is of a prelude followed by dances with a couple of non-dance movements thrown in. The prelude is really an introduction in the sense that its opening phrases sound like a ceremonial fanfare announcement. In between these are phrases where the changing harmonies of triplets split between the hands foreshadow what's to come in the Malagueña later. The second album leaf is the famous *Tango in D*, Albéniz's most recognized melody, frequently transcribed for other instruments. The Malagueña places the fandango rhythm in the right hand and the melody in the left hand. The fourth piece, *Serenata*, alternates playful staccato phrases with more legato, song-like melodies while frequently changing harmonies color its expressions. Fifth is the Capricho Catalan, a delicate song played almost entirely in parallel thirds over a constant offbeat accompaniment. The last piece is a Basque dance in 5/8 meter, the Zortzico. It has a distinctive, dotted-rhythm device that covers the second and third beats of each measure, and often the fourth and fifth also, normally beat out on a drum. *—Patsy Morita*

Recommended:

- ○ **Albéniz: Iberia Books 1 & 2 / España** / Barenboim / 2001 / Teldec 81703
- ○ **Favourite Spanish Encores** / de Burgos (cond.), de Larrocha, Royal PO / 2001 / Decca 467687
- ○ **Albeniz: España/Granada/Tango** / Kyriakou / 1993 / ZYX 4183

Iberia Suite (1905–1909)

This collection of 12 pieces is generally regarded as Albéniz's most important compositional effort. The works are divided among four books, each containing three pieces, the whole having a duration of nearly 90 minutes. In this colorful suite the composer depicts a different region of Spain in all but the first work—hence, his choice of the collective title *Iberia*, Spain's ancient name. The first piece, "Evocación," which serves as a sort of introduction to the set, is not concerned with offering an impression of a specific geographical locale, though it evokes images of Spain in general. It is dark and serene in the outer sections, passionate in the central panel, and tinged with a gentle exoticism throughout. "El Puerto" refers to the seaport of Cadiz, and its music is lively and colorful, full of Spanish playfulness, stomping rhythms, and a sense of mischief. The ensuing "Fête-Dieu à Seville" begins mysteriously and hesitantly, as if trying to generate momentum. When it does get going, it deftly moves from playful innocence to brilliant drama and on to lyrical warmth, one reason why it has inspired orchestral transcriptions, including one by Leopold Stokowski. But then the whole suite has enjoyed several transcriptions for orchestra. "Seville"'s middle section, like most in the series, is a lovely, peaceful interlude. *Book II*'s opening work, "Rondena," is another playful, jaunty piece featuring a range of keyboard colors in its imaginative writing. "Almeria" has expressive depth in its overall reflective character, while "Triana" is playful and bright and full of color, even in its few subdued moments. "El Albaicin" leads off *Book III* with an almost Rachmaninovian busyness that soon yields to a more reflective manner, after which these moods are deftly juxtaposed. "El Polo" is a sheer delight in its hiccup-like rhythms and sometimes sour, almost drunken chords. The ensuing "Lavapies" splashes notes about in the upper ranges, then settles into a suavely playful middle section. "Málaga" opens the final book in a mysterious, rhythmic way, then evolves toward a nervous, busy manner whose few moments of respite always quickly yield back to the more impetuous dominating side. The aforementioned "Jerez" is largely subdued, but lively in its mixture of playfulness and nocturnal exoticism. The concluding "Eritana" brims with energy and sunshine, apparently divulging the happiness the composer associated with the tavern near Seville that he depicts here. *—Robert Cummings*

Recommended:

- ○ **Albéniz: Iberia; Granados: Goyescas** / de Larrocha / 1996 / London 448191
- ○ **Albéniz: Iberia Books 1–4** / G. Gonzalez / 1998 / Naxos 554311
- ○ **Alicia de Larrocha I** / de Larrocha / 1998 / Philips 456883

Piezas características, Op. 92 (1888–1889)

Isaac Albéniz composed nearly 250 published works, mostly for the piano, during his three decades or so of active professional life before his untimely death at age 49, but today he is remembered almost exclusively as the composer of the famous *Iberia Suite* (1905–09). Aside from the occasional concert test-drive of one odd individual salon miniature or another, one might go many seasons without hearing any Albéniz music other than that grand set of 12 pieces. Still, there is Spanish treasure to be found within the piano scores aside from *Iberia*, and some of the best of it is contained in the *Doce piezas características* for piano, Op. 92 (B 29), otherwise known as the *12 Character Pieces*. The collection was composed in 1888 and 1889 and released to the public at the same time by Albéniz's usual publisher, Madrid's Antonio Romero.

The *12 Character Pieces* are just that: 12 short or shortish works of light piano entertainment, dance-oriented for the most part and filled with easygoing, syrupy tunes and a certain amount of transcendental technicality (Albéniz was, after all, much influenced by Liszt throughout the 1880s). Contrary to what we might normally assume about Albéniz's music, these pieces are not necessarily specifically Spanish in nature—certainly the gavotte, minuet, barcarolle, polka, waltz, polonaise, and mazurka dance forms, each of which is represented in Op. 92, have nothing innately to do with Andalusia or Spain in general.

The *Doce piezas características* are: 1) Gavotte, 2) Minuetto (*A Sylvia*), 3) Barcarola (*Cielo sin nubes*), 4) *Plegaria*, 5) *Conchita* (Polka), 6) *Pilar* (waltz), 7) *Zambra*, 8) Pavana, 9) Polonesa, 10) Mazurka, 11) Staccata (Capricho), and 12) *Torre Bermeja* (Serenata). *—Blair Johnston*

Recuerdos de viaje, Op. 71 (1887)

The seven *Recuerdos de viaje*, Op. 71 (B 18) of Isaac Albéniz were written in 1886 and 1887, shortly after the composer and his young family moved to Madrid. The composer's life during the mid-1880s included a series of promising professional ups and heartbreaking private downs. In January 1886 he gave a now-famous recital at the salon of his publisher Antonio Romero, a recital that more than any other single performance launched his career as a pianist-composer of national and international note, but just three months later his infant daughter Blanca died. The event was made all the more bitter by the fact that Albéniz had named the child in honor of his deceased sister, who had perished by her own hand some time before. Albéniz soon learned, however, that the first biography of him had appeared in print (he was still just 25), and his spirits were lifted somewhat. The *Recuerdos de viaje* (Travel Reminiscences) in no way capture the swells and collapses of these tumultuous months; they are, instead, seven individual miniatures in a light but passion-filled vein, meant entirely for salon entertainment and virtuoso display purposes.

The seven *Recuerdos de viaje* are: 1) *En el mar (Barcarola)* (also published separately in London, ca. 1892, as "On the Water"), 2) *Leyenda (Barcarola)*, 3) *Alborada*, 4) *En la Alhambra*, 5) *Puerta de tierra (Bolero)* (also published separately in London as *Andalucía (Bolero)*, 6) *Rumores de la caleta (Malagueña)*, and 7) *En la playa*. The Malagueña (No. 6, "Murmurs of the Cove"), with its guitar-like figurations and standard Spanish cross rhythms (three against two, or, more properly, 3/4 time against 6/8), is the best known of the lot. *—Blair Johnston*

Recommended:

- ○ **Albéniz: Recuerdos de viaje** / E. Sánchez / 1997 / Ensayo 9740
- ○ **Favourite Spanish Encores** / de Burgos (cond.), de Larrocha, Royal PO / 2001 / Decca 467687

Suite española No. 1, Op. 47 (1886)

This popular set of eight pieces is a fairly early composition, quite different from the mature works, such as *Iberia*, for which Albéniz is principally known. Each piece represents a specific region of Spain and is cast as a dance, song, or musical form characteristic of that place. Without exception, they are technically easier than *Iberia*, but the writing often imitates guitar figurations rather than pianistic ones, making for some interesting interpretive problems. In spite of its early place in the chronology of Albéniz's output, the entire suite is highly effective and subtly evocative. Although playable as a suite, the various pieces are often heard separately, frequently in one of the orchestral versions done by Arbós and others.

"Granada" (Serenata) is a graceful serenade evoking the strumming of the guitar in simple tonic-dominant harmonies against a characteristic melody. "Cataluña" (Curranda), a Spanish-style courante, is a lively dance in 6/8 time, recalling an early Romantic hunting song. "Sevilla" (Sevillanas) is a flamenco-style dance of Andalusian origin, and here Albéniz creates one of particular grace. The typical flamenco rhythm underlies a lyrical melody in the main sections, while the two hands play a recitative-like melody an octave apart for the contrasting sections. This is one of the best-known pieces from the suite. "Cadiz" (Saeta) is another type of song of Andalusian origin, primarily religious in nature and usually sung at Lent to accompany outdoor penitential activities. Once again, Albéniz evokes typical guitar figurations in the accompaniment, while the right hand plays a lyrical melody.

"Asturias" (Legend), more famous in its guitar transcription, is in three parts. The first has a hypnotic melody emerging from a repeated single-note ostinato and building to a climax, while the second is a dramatic and haunting recitative, evoking the narrative of a legend. The third part is an exact repetition of the first part, with a short coda added. This number is equally as well known as "Sevilla." "Aragón" (Fantasía) is the longest and most pianistically virtuosic piece of the suite. It alternates a rhythmic dance with a slower central stanza that imitates, once again, typical guitar figurations. At one point, before the brilliant presentation of the main material, Albéniz recalls the opening piece of the suite, creating a cyclic link, musically and emotionally, with "Granada." "Castilla" (Seguidillas) evokes a seguidilla, a song and dance of southern Spain that alternates sung lines with guitar interludes. This alternation is brilliantly evoked in the contrasts of piano figuration in this rhythmic dance. "Cuba" (Notturno) is more a dance than a nocturne, its main section suggesting the African-inspired rhythms of the Western hemisphere with its gentle hemiola cross-rhythms. The central section is more lyrical and nostalgic, in keeping with the title. *—Steven Coburn*

Recommended:

○ **Granados: Goyescas; Albéniz: Iberia** / M. Jones / 1999 / Nimbus 5595

○ **Albeniz: Iberia** / de Larrocha / 1992 / EMI 64504

OPERA

Merlin (1898–1902)

Isaac Albéniz's three-act opera *Merlin* was undertaken in 1898 as the first part of a proposed trilogy of operas based on the legend of King Arthur written by Albéniz's librettist Francis Burdett Money-Coutts. Money-Coutts' idea was to raise a cycle of English-language operas on the scale of Richard Wagner's tetralogy *Der Ring des Nibelungen*, and Albéniz, also a Wagner enthusiast, originally welcomed the notion with enthusiasm. But the work proved slow going, and although the score of *Merlin* was completed by 1902, at Albéniz's death in 1909 only two-thirds of *Lancelot*, the second opera in the trilogy, were scored out. The third opera, *Guinevere*, was never even begun by Albéniz, and none of the music to this cycle of three operas was heard in Albéniz's lifetime.

An attempt to stage *Merlin* was held in 1960 by a cultural group belonging to the Junior Football Club of Barcelona, but it was unable to make full use of the score, as part of it was missing. It wasn't until June 1998, 100 years after Albéniz first began the opera, that a complete performance of *Merlin* was given under the baton of José de Eusebio, who also rehabilitated the score from the remaining manuscripts. It was an effort well worth it, as *Merlin* contains some truly glorious music, both in its generous writing for the singers and its magnificent orchestral prelude. Where *Merlin* is dragged down is in Money-Coutts' ponderous libretto, which is chock full of Chatterton-esque English archaisms that never really existed in English usage and clumsy, pretentious lines of dialogue that do not lend themselves to musical setting with ease. In the days when the opera was yet unedited and unavailable for performance, knowledge of Money-Coutts' verbal extravagance was enough for many critics to deride and discourage its revival; the 1998 production was such an extraordinary success that it has reversed this view and paved the way for the 2003 revival of Albéniz and Money-Coutts' earlier English-language effort *Henry Clifford*. *—Uncle Dave Lewis*

Synopsis:

Act One. (The story is set in mythological medieval England, beginning at around the year 500.) The opening act presents the familiar account of the youthful Arthur, withdrawing the sword from the stone, thus elevating himself to the throne as King of England. Merlin, a prophet and magician who carries a magic wand giving him great powers, serves as counsel to King Arthur. As the act progresses Arthur draws opposition from Morgan le Fay, his fairy half-sister, and from Mordred, his nephew.

Act Two. This act begins at Tintagel Castle where Arthur, in love with Guinevere, confides in Merlin about his feelings for her. The latter sees Guinevere as a potential threat and decides he must somehow tarnish her image. An insurrection against Arthur, led by Mordred and supported by Morgan le Fay and Sir Pellinore, fails, and the three are brought in to face the King's justice. But the forgiving Arthur pardons them. Nevertheless, the evil Morgan begins to scheme against him immediately, concluding that Merlin must first be dealt with in order to overthrow Arthur.

Act Three. Determined to sabotage the relationship between Arthur and Guinevere, Merlin seeks out the gnomes to obtain gold, which he needs to carry out his plan. He summons Nivian, a Saracen slave girl, who, with her group of gnomes, dances for him. Her seductive movements enchant Merlin and when she asks him to let her hold his magic wand, he hands it over to her. He then enters the gnomes' cave to capture their gold. But Nivian, hoping to obtain freedom from the gnomes, strikes a rock with the wand and unintentionally closes the entrance to the cave, thereby trapping Merlin inside. Morgan is happy with the outcome. (The abrupt ending here is explained by the fact that Albéniz intended to compose two more installments on the Arthur legend, but was never able to complete them.) *—Robert Cummings*

Recommended:

○ **Albéniz: Merlin** / De Eusebio (cond.), Domingo, C. Alvarez, A.M. Martinez, Henschel, Madrid SO / 2000 / Decca 467096

Tomaso Albinoni

b. Jun. 14, 1671, Venice, Italy, **d.** Jan. 17, 1751, Venice, Italy

Composer: Concerto, Orchestral, Opera

Not much is known about the life of Tomaso Albinoni. He was the eldest son of a wealthy Venetian paper merchant. The family was very well off, and in his adult life Tomaso was financially independent. He thought of himself as an amateur musician. Although completely trained in his art, he did not seek professional employment in music. He was a fine performer on the violin, and one of the most prolific writers of the violin concerto in the high Baroque. Initially Albinoni attempted to compose church music, but did not meet with much success. However in 1694, with the publication of 12 trio sonatas and the production of his opera *Zenobia, Regina de Palmireni*, Albinoni had found his milieu. For the rest of his life he would compose cantatas, operas, instrumental sonatas and concerti. His operas were popular throughout Italy, and are very original, although not well known today. In 1705, he married the soprano opera singer Margherita Rimandi. Together they had six children, while she continued with her singing career. Tomaso Albinoni meanwhile had inherited a portion of his father's estate, and began a singing school. In 1722, he published a collection of 12 concerti. He also was invited to Munich where a production of his opera *I veri amici* was given as part of the festivities honoring the marriage of the Prince Elector to the daughter of the Emperor. This occurred at perhaps the height of Albinoni's fame.

Albinoni was extremely prolific and is said to have composed over 80 operas, 40 solo cantatas, 79 sonatas, 59 concerti, and 8 sinfonias. He composed oboe concertos, treating the oboe as a lyrical, melodic instrument, much as the voice would have been treated. His compositions are extremely individual, and he possessed great gifts as a melodist. His compositions were much admired by Johann Sebastian Bach, who used themes of Albinoni's in several of his keyboard fugues. Two of these themes come from Albinoni's work *Opera Prima*. Bach also used to practice realizing the continuo harmonies using bass lines of Albinoni, and pieces of Albinoni's were used by Bach for teaching. Albinoni was at one time accorded a place in the history of music next to Arcangelo Corelli and Antonio Vivaldi. At the beginning of the twentieth century, editions of his works were published, and his violin music is still performed. *—Rita Laurance*

CONCERTO

Concerti à cinque, Op. 7 (before 1715)

Dedicated to an amateur musician and patron, Giovanni Donato Correggio, the *Concerti a cinque*, Op. 7 consist of four concertos with one oboe, four with two oboes, and the remaining for strings and continuo alone. These pieces are significant for a number of reasons. They are believed to have been the first concertos of this kind to be published by an Italian. Also important is the fact that Albinoni designated them as concertos "with" oboe rather than "for" oboe, bolstering the role of the strings and emphasizing the chamber music aspect.

Albinoni is credited with having firmly established the three-movement concerto form (fast-slow-fast). This form found its origin in the vocal da capo aria structure ("A" section followed by "B" section in a contrasting mood and key, usually in a slower tempo, followed by a return of the "A" section). Some of the concertos hint at the ritornello form later perfected by Vivaldi. The outer movements, as a rule, are in an ABA form. Many of the final movements are often in 3/8 or 6/8 meter, and there is frequent use of hemiola, a rhythmic device that implies changing meters of three into two and vice versa by shifting accents and note duration. Fugal writing in the third movements is also a favorite device employed by Albinoni, which can be viewed as a throwback to an older style. The concertos are lively and sunny, with more gravitas in the middle movements. *Op. 7, No. 6 in D major*, with one oboe, follows the typical form for the outer movements: 1) tutti statement in the strings; 2) abbreviated statement in the oboe built on the same material; 3) short string interlude; 4) opening material again in the oboe part, but longer, more elaborate with thinner accompaniment underneath; 5) sequential passagework; and 6) return of the beginning. The Adagio is in a contrasting minor key, with longing expressed through a simply spun-out oboe line. The final Allegro dances in a triple meter, made all the more interesting with hemiola used at the cadences. One is struck by the vocal nature of the writing for the oboe. It is a more idiomatic approach than the string-like model used by Vivaldi for his winds, with room to breathe. The *Op. 7, No. 2 in C major*, with two oboes, is atypical in that its first movement is in a triple meter rather than its final movement. The Allegro opens with an energetic unison in the strings followed by the usual abbreviated statement by the oboes, back to unison strings, then again to the oboes for a complete statement of their solo material. The oboes usually appear together in thirds, never individually or in counterpoint. The writing, as is typical with the Baroque style, is sequential in nature, but not as virtuosic as Vivaldi. The Adagio features a single oboe line over sustained strings and seems to be conceived more harmonically, rather than melodically. As in many of the slow movements, there is a feeling of suspension in anticipation of the final movement, another Allegro. Scored for strings only, *Op. 7, No. 4 in G major* offers no surprises in terms of form, but is an absolute delight. The basic format, again, is faithfully observed. *—Mona DeQuis*

Recommended:

○ **Albinoni: Concerti Op7; Sonatas Op2** / I Musici, Holliger, Bourgue / 1992 / Philips 432115

Concerti à cinque, Op. 9 (before 1722)

In the preface to his first published work, the *Sonata a tre*, published in 1684, Albinoni describes himself as "musico di Violino dilettante Veneto." Throughout his life, Albinoni remained a dilettante (although he later dropped the word when describing himself), the necessity or earning a living as a musician obviated by the inheritance of a large family business. His passionate devotion to music and determination to be ranked as professional resulted in an output that played a major part in the development of the Venetian concerto and chamber forms. Originally coming to prominence as an opera composer at the end of the seventeenth century,

Albinoni subsequently made a substantial contribution to the concerto repertoire. This includes five sets of published works (Opp. 2, 5, 7, 9, and 10), each of which includes 12 concertos (in the instance of Op. 2, six are termed "sinfonie"), the standard number for published sets in the eighteenth century.

Of these, Op. 9, first published in Amsterdam by Le Cène in 1722, is arguably the finest and probably the best known today. The set is divided into three groups: Concerto Nos. 1, 4, 7, and 10 are scored for solo violin, strings, and continuo, Nos. 2, 5, 8, and 11 have a solo part for one oboe, while the remainder (Nos. 3, 6, 9, and 12) feature solo parts for two oboes. All are in the standard three-movement form, with an opening allegro followed by a slow movement, usually an adagio, and a another allegro to conclude. In general terms more loosely constructed than the contemporary concertos of Vivaldi, the concertos of Op. 9 reveal in abundance the melodic gifts which gained Albinoni his considerable renown as an opera composer. The flowing lyricism of the ravishingly beautiful central Adagio of the *Oboe Concerto in D minor, Op. 9, No. 2* provides an excellent example, a movement in which the long lyrical lines drawn by the oboe over a bed of gentle string arpeggiations evokes the loveliest of operatic arias. Particular attention might also be drawn to the Adagio (non troppo) of the *Concerto for two oboes, Op. 9, No. 6*, which is full of rich harmony and Corellian suspensions. Although Albinoni's opening allegros are energetic, they lack the pace and forward momentum of those of Vivaldi, showing a preference for longer thematic material and a generally more lyrical approach. The finales often have a lightness and urbane gaiety coupled with many felicitous rhythmic subtleties, as for example the final Allegro of the *Concerto in C for two oboes, Op. 9, No. 9.* Long overshadowed by Vivaldi and the totally unjustified fame of the ubiquitous, spurious *Adagio*, it is in this fine set of concertos that the listener has an opportunity to discover some of the best of the real Albinoni, a composer who, in the words of Arthur Hutchings, is "ridiculously undervalued." *—Brian Robins*

Recommended:

- ○ **Albinoni: The Complete Concertos Op 9; Adagio For Organ And Strings** / Holliger, Garatti, Bourgue, Ayo, I Musici / 1997 / Philips 456333

ORCHESTRAL

Adagio, for violin, strings & organ in G minor (1945)

Many composers have attained fame through a single work which has gone on to become an international favorite, and Tomaso Albinoni would have belonged to that category if it were not for the fact that the famous Albinoni *Adagio* was not written by him. This soulful and elegiac work was in fact created by the Italian musicologist Remo Giazotto, who came across a tiny manuscript fragment (consisting of just a few measures of the melody line and basso continuo part) among relics in a library collection in Dresden, shortly after the end of World War II. After considering the evidence, Giazotto concluded that he had unearthed a portion of a church sonata (sonata da chiesa) which he presumed had been composed by Albinoni, possibly as part of his Op. 4 set, around 1708.

On the basis of these findings, Giazotto proceeded to construct a complete single-movement work around the fragmentary theme he had ascribed to the Venetian master. The scoring, for organ and strings, and indeed the key of G minor, lend themselves to a mood of great solemnity, and the melody is a magnificent one no matter who composed it, with outbursts of quasi-improvised melancholy that suggests the tragic passion of an opera. All in all, this hybridized (some would say fraudulent) work is one of the most popular examples of music attributed to the Italian Baroque, and if (as is widely thought) Giazotto was canny enough to secure copyright to the piece, the Albinoni-Giazotto *Adagio* must have brought him wealth. New recordings of the work continue to appear every year. *—Michael Jameson*

Recommended:

- ○ **Mozart: Eine kleine Nachtmusik Albinoni: Adagio** / Marriner (cond.), Brown, Academy of St. Martin-in-the-Fields / EMI 47391

OPERA

Pimpinone, comic intermezzo (1708)

In the early years of the eighteenth century, Apostolo Zeno and other dramatic poets began reforming the way serious operas were presented. It had been common practice to include comic scenes within a serious opera and to provide lavish entertainments known as intermedi between the acts. With the reforms, opera librettos were purged of comic scenes or characters, and extraneous spectacle was discouraged. However, the tradition of interweaving the acts of a smaller work of a contrasting genre between the acts of a larger, more serious work persisted, and the result was the emergence of the comic intermezzo. Albinoni's setting of *Pimpinone* is one of the earliest of the Venetian intermezzi to survive from this time period. It consists of three intermezzi with a linking plot. The first two were performed after the first and second acts, while the third was placed somewhere within the final act of the serious opera, as a respite during a scene change. The librettist of *Pimpinone* was Pietro Pariati. His text sparkles with wit, humor, repartee, and comic wrangling. The story contrasts two stock characters of Italian comedy, the guileful young female servant girl and the gullible old member of the Italian nobility. The themes are of social conflict between the classes, and the comedy satirizes everyday Venetian life. Albinoni's setting is marked by brief arias and duets, delightful, simple melodies, playful counterpoint, and a parlando style that looks forward to the buffo writing that emerged later in the century. The original performance of *Pimpinone* was given at the premiere of *Astarto*, a serious opera by Albinoni, at the Teatro S. Cassiano of Venice, in 1708. *Pimpinone* quickly became a standard work in the operatic repertoire and was performed internationally, as far away as Moscow and Ljubljana. Performance traditions grew up around pairs of players, such as Rosa Ungarelli and Antonio Ristorini, who specialized in comic roles and took the intermezzi from city to city and from theater to theater as they traveled. *—Rita Laurance*

Synopsis:

Pimpinone has enjoyed a successful entrepreneurial career and amassed considerable wealth, but has no sweetheart to spend it on. The young lady Vespetta, who is more attracted by Pimpinone's money than she is repelled by his old age, schemes to curry his favor by first gaining employment in his house as a maid. She succeeds in getting herself hired, and in fact executes her job so well that Pimpinone becomes dependent on her. To keep her around he asks for her hand in marriage and even promises to provide her with a dowry himself, as long as she promises to be faithful and obedient (he is cognizant, after all, of the disparity in age and the possibility of her straying). She soon tires of the considerable restrictions her husband places on her freedom, however. She wants the liberty to go to the theater, dances, and masquerades, and to visit friends and receive guests freely, and threatens to leave him (taking with her a substantial alimonial bounty, of course). Pimpinone, in turn, threatens to cut off her support. The argument escalates in their alternating arias and final duet, until in the end Vespetta wins out, securing both her freedom and her fortune. *—Jeremy Grimshaw*

Recommended:

- ○ **Albinoni: Vespetta e Pimpinone; 6 Balletti a Cinque** / Nemeth (cond.), Karoly, Savaria Baroque Orchestra / Hungaroton 32006
- ○ **Albinoni: Pimpinone, Barcello: 3 Sonatas** / Trimarchi, Zilio, I Soloisti Veneti / Fonit Cetra Italia 40

Alfonso X (El Sabio)

b. Nov. 23, 1221, Toledo, Spain, **d.** Apr. 4, 1284, Seville, Spain

Composer: Vocal

Alfonso X, the thirteenth century Spanish King of Castile and León, has been called a Renaissance man before the Renaissance. As a warrior prince, he led fierce Spanish armies against the Moorish occupation. As a politician on the European stage, he contended for the crown of the Holy Roman Empire. At the same time, he made his court a multicultural haven for artists, scientists, and musicians—Jews, Muslims, and Christians alike. The king himself composed poetry and learned treatises, and left an enduring cultural legacy that continues to this day.

Alfonso achieved the unified throne of Castile and León in 1252 upon the death of his father, Fernando III "the Saintly." He immediately embarked upon an ambitious program of military and political campaigns that would last throughout the 30 years of his reign. By the end of his life, his contemporaries were disillusioned by his ambition; modern historians have repeated their accusation that he dealt too harshly with his own family members and risked the political stability of the entire realm. However, he unquestionably fostered within the Spanish court a cultural and intellectual renaissance. His sobriquet "el Sabio" means both the Learned and the Wise, reflecting Alfonso's support of both learning and the wisdom that results from it. Alfonso was the first king to codify the Castilian language in both written and spoken courtly records; he himself composed a history of the world in that language, as well as codes of law and treatises on astronomy. For lyric poetry, Alfonso favored Galician-Portuguese. Both that language and his court's poetry are related to the Provençal lyrics of the Troubadors, many of whom took refuge in Alfonso's court during the Albigensian Crusade. Alfonso was buried in Seville Cathedral. His will bequeathed the Cantigas de Santa Maria to the Cathedral for singing on Marian feasts; this custom still takes place in the twenty-first century.

The Cantigas represent Alfonso's most enduring cultural contribution. Four sumptuous manuscripts preserve a collection of over 400 Galician songs to the Virgin Mary compiled in Alfonso's court between 1250 and 1280. Most of the Cantigas relate miracles the Virgin performed for Compostela pilgrims; every tenth poem lauds her outright. Alfonso himself probably wrote a number of the elegant poems. The manuscript illuminations preserve his physical portrait for posterity, and also document the vibrant musical life of his court: its images record some 40 different musical instruments played by nobles and commoners, women, Jews, and Muslims. *—Timothy Dickey*

VOCAL

Cantigas de Santa Maria (ca. 1270–1290)

The thirteenth century monarch of the unified Castile and León, Alfonso X earned the sobriquet "el Sabio" (Alfonso the Wise, or the Learned) for his vast erudition and cultural sophistication. He endowed university chairs, including one in music. He first adopted the Castilian language for all court records, and wrote learned treatises on law, astronomy, and the history of the world. He both composed lyric poetry in Galician Portuguese and made his court a haven for poets. Not only did troubadours and trouveres pass through his lands in the retinue of their traveling masters, some spent long periods in his court—especially as a refuge during the Albigensian Crusade. Over the span of many years, Alfonso composed, compiled, and arranged a massive collection of poetry and music in honor of the Virgin Mary, the *Cantigas de Santa Maria.* The volume is an enduring testament to his devotion and skill.

The *Cantigas de Santa Maria* contains more than 400 Galician songs, many of which must have come from Alfonso's pen. Many contemporaries credit him with the making or finding of songs to the Virgin, and several individual pieces in the collection speak in the first person (notably the first Prologue song, and numbers 357, 400, and 401). Alfonso also gave the collection its rigorous and systematic structure. Throughout the collection, nine songs about the Virgin's miraculous intercession (*cantigas de miragres*) are followed by a single general song in praise of Her (*cantigas de loor*); the enormous collection thus reads just like the "decades" of the Marian Rosary prayers. The poetry most commonly follows a refrain form (A bba A bba A, the foundation of the later French virelai and the Italian ballata and lauda). Its texts portray the Virgin's grace and assistance to innumerable medieval folk in all walks of life: clergy, pilgrims, nobles, warriors, craftsmen, wives, and husbands. Musically, each poem arrives in the guise of a simple modal melody. Dorian and mixolydian modes predominate, and both triple and duple mensural meters appear. The melodies are simple and often completely syllabic, with clear cadences and phrase structures reminiscent of popular dances. The sumptuous miniatures illustrating the texts in several manuscript editions of the *Cantigas* yield precious clues to their performance: many show individuals and groups singing to the accompaniment of a bewildering variety of over 40 types of musical instruments. These images document the rich musical life of his court. *—Timothy Dickey*

Recommended:

- ○ **Alfonso X El Sabio: Cantigas de Santa Maria** / Savall (cond.), Hesperion XX, Capella Reial de Catalunya / 1993 / Astrée 8508

Hugo Alfvén

b. May 1, 1872, Stockholm, Sweden, **d.** May 8, 1960, Falun, Sweden

Composer: Orchestral, Symphonic

The Swedish composer Hugo Alfvén holds a position in the history of his country's music somewhat analogous to that of Edvard Grieg in Norway or Jean Sibelius in Finland: Alfvén informed his essentially Romantic style with a regard for the history and folk culture of his homeland. His five symphonies, three *Swedish Rhapsodies,* and numerous cantatas and patriotic works evoke the land of Sweden and make extensive use of Swedish folk songs and dances; most of them have an explicit extramusical program or theme. In addtion to composing music, Alfvén was also a painter.

After studies at the Stockholm Conservatory, Alfvén played violin in the *Hovkapellet,* the Swedish court orchestra, from 1890 to 1897. His first compositions date from those years. The success of his *Symphony No. 2 in D,* Op. 11 (premiered under Wilhelm Stenhammar's direction in 1899), led to Alfvén's being awarded the Jenny Lind stipend, which allowed him to study in France and Germany for three years. Shortly after his return from that trip, he wrote perhaps his best-known work, the *Swedish Rhapsody No. 1* (1903–04). Subtitled "Midsommarvaka" (Midsummer Vigil), this portrait of a Swedish summer makes use of several Swedish folk songs; it was among the first compositions by a Swedish composer to do so. Two further *Swedish Rhapsodies,* equally tuneful works, followed in 1907 and 1937.

In 1908, Alfvén was elected to Sweden's Royal Academy of Music. Two years later he became the music director of the Royal University of Uppsala; among his duties there was directing the student choir. Choral conducting was always a large part of Alfvén's life: he was also the conductor of the Siljan Choir, a sort of mega-choir, for over 50 years, and directed the Initiates of Orpheus, a choral group with which Alfvén toured Europe over 20 times during the period 1910–47. A significant number of Alfvén's 225 compositions are in fact for chorus, many of them designed for amateur groups. The composer himself believed his five symphonies to be among his best works; the fourth includes two textless voice parts. Among his other well-known pieces are the incidental music for Ludwig Nordstrom's play *Gustav II Adolf,* Op. 121 (1932), the Elegy of which is often used as funeral music; and one of his last works, the 1957 ballet *The Prodigal Son,* Op. 217. He was also called on frequently to write cantatas and other works for festive and patriotic occasions. *—Chris Morrison*

Overview of Works (1884–1957)

Swedish composer Hugo Alfvén was one of the three principal composers of that country's late Romantic period (Peterson-Berger and Stenhammar were the other two). Peterson-Berger was more typical of Sweden's sweetness and light, Stenhammar of its sternness and power, but Alfvén was by far the most emotional, the most sensual, and the most structurally radical of any Swedish composer of the period. Alfvén wrote in all the major late Romantic forms except opera and chamber music. Best-known for his cheerful and atmospheric *Three Swedish Rhapsodies*—the *Second,* Op. 58 (1907) is perhaps his most popular composition—Alfvén's most characteristic works are his four completed symphonies, works clearly in the Romantic tradition of autobiographical orchestral works. In listening to them, one gets a picture of Alfvén at each stage of his compositional life. His *Symphony No. 1 in F minor,* Op. 24 (1897) is an intensely serious work from the Grave that opens it to the melodramatic finale that concludes it. But despite this seriousness, the 25-year-old Alfvén relaxes in the songlike Andante and the rollicking Allegro molto scherzando. His *Symphony No. 2 in D major,* Op. 28 (1897–98) starts with an Allegro that is a far less earnest and far more brilliant work than the *First.* But the grim Andante and the grotesque Scherzo are far deeper than the *First* and the concluding Preludium and Fugue with choral conclusion is the most impressive movement in all early Alfvén. His *Symphony No. 3 in E major,* Op. 54 (1905) is a warmer, more relaxed, and more conventionally Swedish work than either of its predecessors. But the *Symphony No. 4,* Op. 93 (1918–19) is the most radical work Alfvén ever composed. A single-movement work scored for large orchestra with obbligato wordless soprano and tenor, the *Fourth* bears the subtitle "From the outskirts of the archipelago" and is cast in a single, dramatic movement. The drama of the piece—indeed, the whole of the piece from its themes to its orchestration—is entirely rooted in the sexual love represented by the soprano and tenor. An extremely evocative and overwhelmingly powerful work, Alfvén's *Fourth* is generally considered to be his symphonic masterpiece. Alfvén himself considered his choral-orchestral *Herrans bon* (The Lord's Prayer), Op. 39, (1899–1901) to be his masterpiece. With its passionately devotional tone, its lush chromatic harmonies, its ardently towering themes, its huge formal structure, and its crowning quadruple fugue, it may well be his greatest work and a work that rivals the choral-orchestral aspirations of other similar works of the *fin de siècle.* *—James Leonard*

Recommended:

- ○ **Hugo Alfvén conducts Hovkapellet** / Westerberg (cond.), Alfven (cond.), Stockholm PO / 1994 / Swedish Society 1003

ORCHESTRAL

Midsommarvaka (Midsummer Vigil), Swedish Rhapsody No. 1, Op. 19 (1903)

This acclaimed work is a typical Romantic-era folk-based rhapsody. The familiar opening tune for clarinet over pizzicato strings introduces a carefree, almost flippant, mood. As the tempo slows down, a longer section features an English horn solo, eventually leading to a succession of dances which suggest considerable revelry. In Sweden, Midsummer Night, or St. John's Eve, is "midsommar," a celebration fraught with powerful symbolism. Revelers stay up late to celebrate the shortest night—with virtually no darkness—of the year. Composed in 1904, this piece became so popular that Alfvén later expanded it into ballet score called *St. John's Eve.* *—Joseph Stevenson*

Recommended:

- ○ **Swedish Orchestral Favourites** / Kamu (cond.), Helsingborg SO / 1995 / Naxos 553115
- ○ **Grieg: Peer Gynt, Suites 1 & 2; Symphonic Dances** / Berglund (cond.), Bournemouth Sinfonietta / 2001 / EMI 74731
- ○ **Alfvén: Swedish Rhapsodies; A Legend of the Skerries** / Sakari (cond.), Iceland SO / 1994 / Chandos 9313

SYMPHONIC

Symphonies (1896–1953)

The four symphonies of composer Hugo Alfvén are his greatest single set of works and arguably the greatest contribution of Sweden to the European symphony between Berwald and Pettersson. As symphonies, they are on a level with those of Denmark's Carl Nielsen and Finland's Jean Sibelius. But unlike those of the more objective Nielsen or Sibelius, Alfvén's symphonies are highly expressive and deeply personal works that make use of the full late Romantic orchestra and the heavy rhetoric of late Romantic music.

Alfvén's *Symphony No. 1 in F minor,* Op. 7 (1897) is an immensely serious and enormously ambitious work in four movements from the opening Grave to the concluding melodramatic Finale. But Alfvén's ambitions are outstripped by the lovingly lyrical Andante and the relaxed and rollicking Allegro molto scherzando, and the work is more memorable for its tender intimacy than its grand and glorious apotheosis. Alfvén's *Symphony No. 2 in D major,* Op. 11 (1897–98) is an enormous autobiographical Romantic program symphony depicting a young man's coming of age. The opening Allegro is earnest, enthusiastic, and excitable. The following Andante is grim, glowering, and grandiose, and the Scherzo after that is grotesquely grandiloquent. The closing magniloquent Preludium and extravagant Fugue, with its almost overdone choral conclusion, concludes a late Romantic symphony on a level with Mahler's *First* or Rachmaninov's *Second.*

Alfvén's *Symphony No. 3 in E major,* Op. 23 (1905) is a more warmly colored and more lyrically relaxed work and thus a more conventionally Swedish work, a cozier symphony whose only ambition is to beguile and charm. But in his *Symphony No. 4,* Op. 39 (1918–19) Alfvén returned to the grand ambitions of the autobiographical Romantic progam symphony with a single-movement work scored for gargantuan late Romantic orchestra with obbligato wordless soprano and tenor. Subtitled "From the outskirts of the archipelago," Alfvén's *Fourth* is the musical representation of a love affair with its passionate ecstasies, its rapturous blisses, and its voluptuous despairs. Alfvén's *Symphony No. 5,* Op. 54 (1942–53) is a single-movement torso that the composer described as "both technically and in other respects the least terrible thing I have produced." *—James Leonard*

Recommended:

- ○ **Hugo Alfvén: Midsommarvaka; Symphony 2** / N. Järvi (cond.), Stockholm PO / 1987 / Bis 385
- ○ **Hugo Alfvén: Dalarapsodi; Symphony 3; Den förlorade Sonen** / N. Järvi (cond.), Mannberg, Lanzky-Otto, Nilsson, Johansson, Stockholm PO / 1989 / Bis 455
- ○ **Hugo Alfvén: Symphony 5; Bergakungen Suite; Elegy from Gustav II Adolf** / N. Järvi (cond.), Stockholm PO / 1992 / Bis 585

Charles-Valentin Alkan

b. Nov. 30, 1813, Paris, France, **d.** Mar. 29, 1888, Paris, France

Composer: Keyboard, Choral

Charles-Valentin Alkan was one of the great composer-pianists of the nineteenth century and a major influence on many subsequent musicians. He wrote some of the most unusual and technically difficult music of his time, an output that no less an authority than Ferruccio Busoni called "the greatest achievement in piano music after Liszt."

Alkan was an extraordinary prodigy: he entered the Paris Conservatoire when he was six years old and won first prizes for solfège at age seven, for piano at 11, for harmony at 14, and for organ at 21. He quickly made a name for himself in the Paris salons as a gifted young pianist and played some London concerts in 1833 to great acclaim. From 1829 to 1836 he was a part-time teacher at the Paris Conservatoire, but he never joined the regular staff.

Alkan was well known in intellectual circles—he counted among his friends Victor Hugo, George Sand, and Fryderyk Chopin—but he was always something of an introvert and misanthrope; at age 25 he dropped out of society, the first of his frequent and sometimes lengthy withdrawals. Over the next 35 years he appeared in public only rarely; not very much is known about his life in those years. Only in 1873 did he make a return to the concert stage, playing a series of *Petits concerts* at the Salle Erard (where he also taught classes in the afternoons).

Alkan was devoted to his Jewish faith and was quite a scholar on the subject. One curious, but untrue, legend has it that he died when, as he reached for a copy of the *Talmud* on top of a large shelf, the bookcase fell over and he was crushed to death.

Alkan published his first music at age 14; ultimately his catalog extended to 76 opus numbers, most of them works for solo piano. The earliest of his compositions were in the familiar forms of the day: opera paraphrases and collections of studies that showed off his unusual facility. His compositions started to get more ambitious in the 1840s—the harmonies bolder, the rhythms more irregular—and many of the works called for extravagant, nearly superhuman technique. These works range from larger works like the *Grande sonate "Les quatre âges,"* Op. 33 (1848), to shorter pieces like *Le chemin de fer,* Op. 27 (1844), the first musical portrait of the railroad, and the humorous and peculiar *Funeral March for a Dead Parrot.*

Perhaps his most ambitious opus is the set of *Twelve Études in all the minor keys,* Op. 39 (1857). The 12 pieces aggregate to form (in order) a four-movement Symphony, a three-movement Concerto, a set of variations, an overture, and three independent pieces. They are very demanding of a performer—pianist Raymond Lewenthal has called them "a ride in Hell." The first movement of the "Concerto" alone contains 1,343 measures (more than the entirety of Beethoven's *Hammerklavier Sonata*) and lasts half an hour.

Alkan played his own works very rarely in public. He did however play a range of music unusual for his time, including the then-unfashionable late Beethoven sonatas, various Schubert sonatas, and much Baroque music. His playing style was noted for its clarity, its restraint in rhythm and dynamics, and its intellectual quality.

Alkan and his music were largely neglected during his lifetime, and he was nearly forgotten upon his death. But with the attention of Ferruccio Busoni, Kaikhosru Sorabji, Egon Petri, and other giants of the early-to-middle twentieth century, as well as the later advocacy via recordings of Petri, Lewenthal and Ronald Smith, Alkan's position in music history has been assured. *—Chris Morrison*

KEYBOARD

Concerto for solo piano in G sharp minor, Op. 39/8–10 (1846–1857)

Alkan might be dismissed as a mordant satirist, a miniaturist of genius, and a freakish rival of Liszt's in fashioning a transcendental keyboard technique were it not for a handful of works looming as an avenue of astounding, colossal, enigmatic sphinxes. Those works include "Quasi-Faust" (from the *Grande Sonate*); the late, misleadingly named *Impromptu,* Op. 69, for *pédalier;* the *Symphonie for solo piano;* or that comic masterpiece *Le festin d'Ésope.* Towering above them—and above nearly all of the piano literature of the nineteenth century—the *Concerto for solo piano* staggers the listener as much by its proportions as by its richness of invention, every rift filled with ore. Failure to secure a post as chief professor of piano at the Paris Conservatoire in 1848 deeply embittered Alkan, exacerbating his already reclusive nature. In the almost wholly undocumented years following, he realized the utmost throw of his genius in works furnishing a single player with technical and expressive resources expressly designed to rival those of an orchestra, including an ambitious *Overture,* the four movements of the *Symphonie,* and the three of the concerto, all published by Richault in 1857 in the collection of *12 Études dans les tons mineurs,* Op. 39, thus dispensing with orchestra, conductor, audience, critics, and other noisome nuisances. For good or ill, he also dispensed with all but the most resourceful performers for the concerto; it is rife with the most cruelly taxing demands before the works of Busoni and Sorabji. The monumental opening movement expands the classical sonata form to a Beethovenian architectonic grandeur and it plays for nearly half an hour, with solo and tutti passages alternating effusive lyricism with sweeping power. The work's central Adagio is Alkan's pithiest, darkest nocturne, brooding and mysterious, beset by the suggestion of distant drums. And the Allegretto alla-barbaresca, a majestically skirling polonaise, crowns the concerto's cascading splendors with a viscerally compelling *fiat.* Alkan evidently had doubts about the first movement's length, for he authorized an ill-advised cut of 40 of the score's 72 pages to make "un morceau de concert, d'un durée ordinaire." It was probably in this truncated form that he performed this single movement at one of his *Petits Concerts* in the 1870s. Thus, it remained for Egon Petri to give the concerto its proper premiere as part of a series of BBC commemorative broadcasts over 1938–39, 50 years after Alkan's death. *—Adrian Corleonis*

Recommended:

- ○ **Charles-Valentin Alkan: Concerto For Solo Piano** / Hamelin / Music & Arts 724
- ○ **Ronald Smith plays Alkan** / R. Smith / 1996 / APR 7031

Les diablotins, Op. 63/45 (1861)

Published by Richault in 1861—the same year as the misleadlingly titled *Sonatine*—the *Esquisses* make a constantly startling index to Alkan's suavest fantasy and his most peccant humor. Drawn from the latter, *Les diablotins* (imps, little devils) captures the imagination with a pungent immediacy quite unlike any of those other great Romantic evocations of the creatures of air, such as the Arimanes of Schumann's *Manfred,* the gossamer Sylphs of Berlioz's *La damnation de Faust,* Liszt's *Feux-follets,* or the Gnomes of his *Gnomenreigen.* The only comparable vignette, perhaps, is Alkan's own *Esprits follets* from Book 3 of *Chants,* Op. 65. *Les diablotins* opens with strident fanfares, fortissimo et sonore, that are in unison and then in thirds, and finally in vehemently exasperated chords spanning the keyboard. This is met with the aural equivalent of "raspberries" (or Bronx cheers), which led Raymond Lewenthal and Ronald Smith, the two superlative writers and pianists responsible for the 1960s Alkan revival, to invoke the name of experimental modernist Henry Cowell. "These tone clusters," Lewenthal noted, "can easily enough be explained as triads with single and double acciaccaturas, such as terrified editors of Scarlatti so much for a century and a half that they expurgated them as if they were four-letter Anglo-Saxon words. . . . " Alkan included Scarlatti in his concert programs throughout his reluctant virtuoso career, though he was sufficiently audacious to have hit upon this grating device without prompting and never shied away from the most grinding dissonances (as in the Allegramente of the *Sonatine*), provided they arose through pure musical logic. Momentarily quelled, the imps—their tone clusters muted—parade a stifled strut until a chorale-like voice from the choir, so to speak, marked *Quasi-Santo,* is greeted derisively. Another, *Quasi-Santa,* is an attempt at exorcism tentatively met before it provokes an animated fracas and sudden disappearance. Though the *Esquisses* are a compilation that must have been years in the making, and the precise dating of Alkan's compositions is often impossible, it is difficult to reconcile the (what else!) impish humor of *Les diablotins* with the self-portrait that emerges in letters from the early 1860s to his friend, Ferdinand Hiller, of a cranky, dyspeptic, frail old man. Alkan would turn 48 in the year of *Les diablotins'* publication! *—Adrian Corleonis*

Recommended:

- ○ **Raymond Lewenthal: The Concerto Recordings** / Lewenthal, Mackerras, de Carvalho (conds.), London SO / 1999 / Elan 82284

Études dans tous les tons majeurs, Op. 35 (1847–1848)

Overshadowed somewhat by his stupendous Op. 39 set of *Etudes in Minor Keys,* Alkan's dozen *Etudes in Major Keys,* Op. 35, nevertheless display a startlingly original individuality. Published in 1848, these etudes explore and consolidate a technique—requiring absolute finger independence, superhuman rapidity, and a paradoxical ability to cover the entire keyboard simultaneously—for wringing from the mid-nineteenth century piano, with its weak sustaining power, a piquancy of detail etched upon a canvas of orchestral richness. Moreover, as an apostle of the *style sévère*, Alkan designed these etudes to be played in a light, sec, rhythmically precise manner antithetical to the heavily pedaled, rubato-dimpled Lisztian style which had begun to supplant it at the time of composition. Liszt is alluded to in the first etude, an Allegretto in A, which Alkan scholar and pianist Ronald Smith has suggested calling "Wallenstadt revisited"—"one cannot resist the impression that *Au lac de Wallenstadt* from the first book of Liszt's *Années de pèlerinage* might have been lurking somewhere in the back of Alkan's mind." The resemblance to the "Églogue" from the same collection is even more pronounced and may, indeed, constitute parody. In pointed contrast to Liszt's purling lushness, Alkan's piece requires deft voicing (amid a swirl of scalar and broken-chord figures) and a prim, rhythmically steady élan to come off. The varieties of staccato demanded throughout the set—against the rival claims of a genuine (that is, finger-held) legato—reveal the forgotten face of Romantic pianism. This preoccupation reaches its apogee in the A flat etude, where a single hand must sustain an eloquent legato melody while providing a staccato accompaniment ranging over an octave and a half without resorting to the pedal! Observing that this is by no means a mere technical freak, Alkan's authoritative expositor, Raymond Lewenthal, declared: "This is a perfect work, perfect as music, perfect as the etude it sets out to be. It is an exquisite garden scene, a love duet accompanied by softly plucking lutes—or théorbes if you must be *recherché*—in a fabled land of griffins, fountains and unicorns." In contrast to this exquisite delicacy, fullness of texture is often achieved by rapid octaves in both hands, as in the mighty Contrapunctus in C sharp, a two-part invention relieved by a trio in thirds, or the piston-like Allegro barbaro in F, which may have prompted Bartók's like-titled piece. The final Etude in E, with its rapid octaves against a what would retrospectively be called a stride accompaniment—the parts changing hands Godowsky-style—is notable for its giddy effervescence. Another sort of texture is essayed in the Etude in C, which Smith calls "the most testing exercise in tremolando ever devised." Yet another is found in the widely spaced writing of the B flat etude, alternating the extreme reaches of the hand in a way later used by Brahms. With these resources in hand, so to speak, Alkan treats the listener to a quaint yet titanic parody of the popular parlor pieces of his day in the E flat "L'Incendie au village voisin"—"fire in the neighboring village"—which manages to be simultaneously hilarious and what the critic and composer Bernard van Dieren described as "an exquisite tone painting like one of the movements of *Harold in Italy*" by Berlioz.—*Adrian Corleonis*

Recommended:

○ **Alkan: 12 Etudes, Op35** / Ringeissen / 2001 / Naxos 555495

Études dans tous les tons mineurs, Op. 39 (1846–1857)

Alkan's etudes—in particular the Op. 39 *Minor-Key Etudes*—are the preserve of pianistic supermen. It is at once their bane and their glory that only when animated by the few pianistic wizards of each generation—Busoni, Petri, John Ogdon, Marc-André Hamelin—do their unique qualities come into focus. For the adventure of the *Minor-Key Etudes* is to achieve by means of ten fingers on a keyboard a power and magnificence rivaling that of a full orchestra, and to do so, moreover, within the constraints of the exceedingly sec, rhythmically precise *style sévère*. Four of the Etudes comprise a substantial symphony in which the formal procedures of Classical sonata form are knowingly wrought by an eminently Gothic sensibility, including a second-movement "Marche funèbre," which evokes funeral marches by Beethoven, Berlioz, and Chopin. Three more etudes make a Concerto in which alternations of "solo" and "tutti" are cunningly suggested. Playing nearly 30 minutes, and wrought in a veritable fury of invention, the Concerto's first movement is arguably the most resplendent pianistic creation of the nineteenth century. Technical matters explored in previous etudes are subsumed in the momentum of the Symphony and the Concerto, as well as in that of the penultimate number, an ambitious "Ouverture," as studies in the projection of vast and subtly inwrought designs embracing a colossal range of expression. Examples of this projection are the Concerto's tensely brooding second-movement nocturne, and the mordant, skirling majesty of its third movement polonaise. Capping the *Minor-Key Etudes*, the 25 racily succinct variations of "Le Festin d'Ésope" ("Aesop's feast") index the technical keys to Alkan's unique pianistic universe as they highlight his often puzzling vein of bizarre humor. The set was published in 1857, not quite a decade after the *Major-Key Etudes* and six years after Liszt's final recension of his *Transcendental Etudes*, to which the *Minor-Key Études* are, in a sense, a reply. Nothing in Liszt's pianistic *oeuvre*, and only the first movement of his *Faust Symphony*, approaches the seemingly sprawling but tightly integrated and triumphantly powerful architecture of Alkan's Concerto's first movement. A consummate virtuoso and peer of Chopin and Liszt, Alkan seems to have performed only a drastically cut version of this movement on a single occasion in 1876, followed by the "Marche funèbre" and misleadingly titled "Minuet" ("a real *Hexen minuett*, complete with broomsticks," Raymond Lewenthal called it) from the Symphony. Thus, it was left for Egon Petri, to give the Symphony and Concerto their proper premieres in a series of BBC commemorative concerts of 1938 and 1939, a half century after Alkan's death. —*Adrian Corleonis*

Recommended:

○ **Ronald Smith plays Alkan** / R. Smith / 1996 / APR 7031

Préludes dans tous les tons majeurs et mineurs, Op. 31 (1847)

Published in 1847, Alkan's 25 *Preludes, Op. 31*—one each in all major and minor keys, returning at last to C major—are less a collection than a miscellany, unlike those of his friend Chopin. They were probably put together to please a publisher. The impression is reinforced by the specification of each prelude "for piano or organ," though, as Alkan scholar and pianist Ronald Smith has noted, several of them are ineffectual on the organ and others impossible. With a pedal part occasionally noted on a third staff, the instrument Alkan probably had in mind was the *pedalier*—a piano equipped with an organ-like pedal board, of which he became an apostle and for which he wrote a number of other works (including his last large-scale composition, the awesome and misleadingly titled *Impromptu sur le choral de Luther—Un fort rempart est notre Dieu*, Op. 69). In any case, all are playable (with some minor adjustments) on the piano, and the set is catalogued with his piano works. A preponderance of bland devotional numbers (e.g., "Prière," "Prière du matin," "Prière du soir") is relieved by the triumphant affirmation of "Psaume 150me" ("Hallelujah. Praise God in His sanctuary; praise him in the sky, His stronghold") and the strangely archaic "Ancienne mélodie de la synagogue." Genre pieces—"Romance," "Rêve d'amour," "Le Temps qui n'est plus"—lighten this mixed bag with facile charm and, occasionally, weight it with an eerie darkness, as in the haunting "Chanson de la folle au bord de la mer" (Song of the Madwoman by the Shore). Interleaved throughout are deft demonstrations of how such time-honored, purely musical devices as fugue, modulation, pedal points, and the like, can yield fresh, unique, audacious expression in the hands of a master. Finally, several numbers draw from that mysterious well of pristine poetry which overflows unmixed from time to time in Alkan's music—for instance "Anniversaire," described by Smith as "an impressive elegy equal to the finest of Mendelssohn's *Songs without Words*," and, above all, the exquisite "J'étais endormie, mais mon coeur veillait. ..." ("I was asleep, But my heart was wakeful" from the Song of Solomon 5:2). In sum, while Alkan's Preludes, taken together, make an uneven, heterogeneous impression, they nevertheless contain some of his most characteristic and inspired invention. —*Adrian Corleonis*

Recommended:

○ **Alkan: Preludes Op31** / L. Martin / Marco Polo 223284

CHORAL

Marcia funèbre, sulla morte d'un Papagallo (Funeral March for a Dead Parrot) (1858)

One of Alkan's first and most discerning twentieth century admirers, Bernard van Dieren, looking over his scattered, enigmatic, often bizarre oeuvre, with only rumor to draw upon for clues to the man behind it, ventured that "The best one could do to 'make something' of his life would be to suggest that it was wrapped in mystery." Despite the discovery of a cache of letters to his friend, Ferdinand Hiller, which throws some light on his day-to-day existence, the most avid research has failed to flesh out Alkan's shadowy remains and nearly everything about him must be inferred from circumstantial evidence. Some of the most revealing circumstances surrounding his *Marcia Funèbre sulla Morte d'un Pappagallo*—Funeral March for a Dead Parrot—published by Richault in 1859, are that Rossini's 1817 comic opera hit, *La gazza ladra* (The Thieving Magpie), enjoyed a revival of five performances in Paris in 1858, and that Alkan's closest pupil (and probably his natural son), Elie Miriam Delaborde (1839–1913), as a refugee from the Franco-Prussian War, arrived in London in 1870 with 121 cockatoos and parrots. If Alkan, that *rara avis*, was not himself a bird fancier, he was close to one who was. In any case, the allusions, verbal and musical, to Rossini's opera semiseria are compelling. A footnote near the beginning of the score tells us, tongue-in-cheek, "This reminiscence is due solely to an ornithological accident. I pray you, connoisseurs of *La gazza ladra*, do not attribute the slightest impertinence to the deceased parrot's song." And the score's title page, comically strutting, casts the composer as an Italian—"Parole e Musica del Cittadino C° Vino Alkan (primogenito)."

In *La gazza ladra*, the servant girl, Ninetta, has been condemned to death for stealing various valuables which, in fact, a thieving pet magpie has spirited away. The funereal march to which she is led to the gallows is parodied in Alkan's score by a melancholy bassoon and three oboes laconically imitating the parrot's squawk. A tenor enters to ask, in recitative, "As-tu déjeuné, Jaco"—the French equivalent for "Polly want a cracker?" or "Who's a pretty Polly?"—repeated by the bass and leading to the lugubrious march in which tenor and bass are joined by two sopranos mournfully declaiming together, "As-tu déjeuné, Jaco? Et de quoi? Ah." From this spare material Alkan wrings some pithy and compellingly concise developments, including a fugato of strangely wailing melismas on "Ah," to an effect at once grotesque, suggestive of operatic hurly-burly, and, in its compositional cunning, sublime. The composer specifies that the reed stops of a harmonium—an instrument which Berlioz had been pushing since the 1840s and which was catching on by 1859—could be substituted for bassoon and oboes. It has been suggested—on the merest circumstantial speculation—that Alkan's *Marcia Funèbre* may have been inspired by, or even figured in, the programs chez the retired Rossini at which the latter's *péchés de vieillesse* (sins of old age), delightful musical parodies and audacities, were heard. —*Adrian Corleonis*

Recommended:

○ **Raymond Lewenthal: The Concerto Recordings** / Lewenthal, Mackerras, de Carvalho (conds.), London SO / 1999 / Elan 82284

John Alldis

b. Aug. 10, 1929, London, England
Conductor

Best known as founder of the London choir that bore his name, John Alldis was one of England's most prominent and peripatetic choral directors, working with a number of ensembles in music ranging from the Renaissance to the present. In 1967, for example, Alldis prepared his choir for the first European performance of Stravinsky's *Requiem Canticles*, conducted overall by Pierre Boulez. Alldis studied at King's College, Cambridge, from 1949 to 1952, working as a choral scholar under Boris Ord. He later obtained a master's degree there in 1957. In 1962, he founded the professional, 16-member John Alldis Choir, which launched itself with the world premiere of Alexander Goehr's *A Little Cantata of Proverbs*. Contemporary music would continue to figure importantly in Alldis' repertory. Alldis quickly became so highly regarded as a choral conductor that in 1966, the London Symphony Orchestra hired him to form and direct its first standing choral group. Alldis switched to the London Philharmonic Chorus in 1969, with which he remained until 1982. Meanwhile, the John Alldis Choir participated in several studio recordings of opera for such major labels as Decca and RCA. During this period, Alldis also taught at London's Guildhall School of Music and Drama (1966–79), served as joint chief conductor of Radio Denmark (mainly leading its Danish State Radio Chorus, 1971–77), and conducted the Groupe Vocal de France (1979–83). After a relatively fallow period through much of the 1980s, Alldis was a music consultant to the Israel Chamber Choir from 1989 to 1991; Israel's notoriously tough music critics gave him mixed notices. He was more highly regarded in England, where in 1992 he became chorus master of Manchester's Hallé Choir (although, oddly, he was dropped from the 2001 edition of the nationalistic *New Grove*) and in France, where in 1994 he was named a *chevalier de l'Ordre des Arts et des Lettres*. In the mid-1990s he guest-conducted the Tokyo Philharmonic Chorus and the Central Philharmonic Society of China in Beijing. —*James Reel*

Recommended:

○ **Vaughan Williams: Sinfonia Antarctica; The Wasps** / Boult (cond.), Alldis (cond.), London PO / 1991 / EMI 64020

○ **Handel: Messiah** / Alldis (cond.), Langridge, Lott, Hodgson, Cold, London PO / 2002 / Sparrow 51560

Gregorio Allegri

b. 1582, Rome, Italy, **d.** Feb. 7, 1652, Rome, Italy
Composer: Choral

Born in 1582, Gregorio Allegri, an Italian priest, singer, and composer in the tradition of the *stile antico*, is primarily known for his *Miserere*, a nine-part setting of Psalm 51. He spent much of his life working in Roman churches, joining the papal choir in 1629 and eventually becoming its choirmaster. According to a legend, Mozart wrote out the full score of this work after hearing it only once, thus effectively circumventing the rule which prohibited anyone from removing any parts of the score from the Sistine Chapel, where it was guarded.

During the Romantic period, when composers and literary figures embraced the ideals of the *stile antico*, Allegri's *Miserere* was much admired. Allegri's other works include motets and instrumental concertini. He died in 1652. —*Zoran Minderovic*

CHORAL

Miserere mei Deus (Psalm 51), motet (1630s)

It is Holy Week in Rome, the heart of christendom. Dusk has fallen and the solemn service of *Tenebrae* is concluding. One by one the candles are snuffed, leaving the congregation in darkness. For hundreds of years, the papal choir—one of the most conservative musical establishments in the world—observed the entire service in plainchant, from the *Lamentations of Jeremiah* to the Responsories that narrate Christ's suffering and death. Then, at the very end of the day, the full choir breaks into parts for one piece: Gregorio Allegri's *Miserere*.

The Medici Pope Leo X first mandated the silent recitation of *Psalm 51* at the conclusion of Tenebrae. Each Catholic soul across the world considers, then, David's desperate poetic plea for God's mercy. The Pope's own singers, however, quickly adopted the practice of a fully polyphonic performance of the *Psalm* (later in the fifteenth century, Palestrina contributed a setting). Allegri joined the papal choir in 1629, serving for the rest of his life. In the 1630s he composed a setting of *Miserere mei* for Holy Week that eventually became his greatest musical legacy. The papal choir sang it every year from the seventeenth century until the choir collapsed in 1870. Louis Spohr knew the piece, and the young Felix Mendelssohn heard it sung once. The penalty for copying its music, which the papal choir considered its exclusive property, was excommunication.

Allegri's musical structure follows what by then was common practice for the singing of this *Psalm*: alternation between plainchant verses and different choral elaborations of the chant. His *Miserere* opens with a five-voiced choir that harmonizes the first *Psalm* verse, with the chant melody known as the *tonus peregrinus*. Allegri's music uses the conservative and balanced *stile antico*, the classic ancient style of Palestrina. Some imitation is present, and Allegri spices the harmonies with rich, dissonant suspensions. A simple chanted verse follows, then a verse sung by a distant choir of four soloists. Each solo verse over the years of its performance became gradually encrusted with a rich oral tradition of *abbellimenti*, the characteristic traceries of vocal ornamentation by the best singers in the Catholic Church. The great castrati (male sopranos) added an angelic leap to high C at the crux of each solo verse. The very final solo verse leads not into the expected chant, but instead a choral refrain that includes the full nine-voiced texture; gradually, though, the dynamic recedes into the shadows. —*Timothy Dickey*

Recommended:

○ **Allegri: Miserere** / Phillips (cond.), Tallis Scholars / 2001 / Gimell 339

○ **Allegri: Miserere** / Cleobury (cond.), King's College Choir / 2003 / EMI 75877

Nancy Allen

b. New York, NY
Harpist

Nancy Allen is well respected by many not only as a harpist, but also as a teacher. She grew up in New York City, dividing her studies among the harp with Pearl Chertok, the piano, and the oboe. She was fortunate enough to spend the summer of 1972 learning from Lily Laskine in France, before enrolling at Juilliard, where she studied under Marcel Grandjany. In 1973 she won the Fifth International Harp Competition in Israel. She made her New York recital debut in 1975, and her early career included touring with flutist Ransom Wilson. Since then, she has also worked closely with Kathleen Battle, Richard Stolzman, Manuel Barrueco, and Carol Wincenc on recital projects. She regularly performs with the New York-based Orpheus Chamber Orchestra and the Chamber Music Society of Lincoln Center and signed on as principal harpist with the New York Philharmonic in 1999, which allowed her to stay close to her young family. However, she also appears internationally with ensembles such as the English Chamber Orchestra, St. Paul Chamber Orchestra, Los Angeles Chamber Orchestra, and the Royal Philharmonic. Allen joined the faculty of Juilliard in 1985 and now heads the harp program there, as well as at Yale, where she joined the faculty in 1992, and at the Aspen Music Festival and School. Many of her students now hold positions in well-known orchestras around the world. Her recording of Ravel's *Introduction and Allegro* with the Tokyo String Quartet, Wilson, and clarinetist David Shifrin was nominated for a Grammy award. Allen's other recordings can be found on a variety of labels, covering a variety of music from Bach to Ives to Takemitsu. —*Patsy Morita*

Recommended:

○ **A Celebration For Harp** / Allen / 1987 / EMI 69070

○ **Ravel & Debussy** / Schwarz (cond.), Allen, Shifrin, Wilson, Tokyo SQ, LACO / 1983 / EMI 47520

○ **Rodrigo Concertos** / Allen / EMI 47869

Sir Thomas Allen

b. Sep. 10, 1944, Seaham Harbour, England
Baritone

Recognized as much for his acting ability as for his fine singing, baritone Thomas Allen brings a strong sense of style and character to all types of music; his broad repertory includes Monteverdi, Mozart, Tchaikovsky, the lighter Wagner roles, Britten's *Billy Budd*, Prokofiev's *War and Peace*, and Janáček's *The Cunning Little Vixen*. Allen grew up in a mining community in the north of England where his father ran a glee club and a dance band, provided accompaniment for a local choir, and collected musical instruments. As a boy, Allen learned both piano and organ from his father, and sang in various local choirs. By the age of 16, he was singing baritone solos in the school choir, and even participating as a soloist in various local recitals, as well as continuing his organ lessons and studying music at school.

He successfully auditioned for the Royal College of Music in 1964, where he intended to focus his energies on lieder and oratorio, but by 1967 he had already made his first operatic appearance as a substitute singer in Benjamin's *The Prima Donna*.

In 1968, before graduating, he won the Queen's Prize, an award which included lessons with James Lockhart, the new Music Director of the Welsh National Opera. Lockhart encouraged him to audition for the WNO, and he was engaged in 1968 to join the company the next year. Between that time and the beginning of his engagement, he sang in the Glyndebourne Festival Chorus.

At the Welsh National Opera, Lockhart continued to act as a coach and mentor, and Allen made his debut as Figaro in Rossini's *Il Barbiere di Siviglia* in 1969. He made his Covent Garden debut as Donald in *Billy Budd* in 1971 (he also took on the title role for the WNO the same year) and his Glyndebourne debut in 1973 as Papageno, sang his first Wagner role (Melot in *Tristan and Isolde*, at Covent

Garden), and created the role of the Count in Musgrave's *The Voice of Ariadne* in 1974 at the Aldeburgh Festival. During this period he gave special attention to the major Mozart baritone roles, and, in 1977, sang his first *Don Giovanni* at the Salzburg Festival, to great acclaim for both his singing and his acting. He garnered even more attention as the Count in a performance of *Figaro* a few months later at Covent Garden, and made his Met debut as Papageno in 1981. In 1980, he sang Tchaikovsky's *Eugene Onegin* for the first time at the Welsh National Opera, and this role soon joined Don Giovanni as one of his signature roles. During the 1980s, he started adding a few Verdi roles to his repertoire, such as Posa in *Don Carlo* and Ford in *Falstaff*, though he was wary of the heavier roles. In 1999, he was knighted in Queen Elizabeth's Birthday Honors.

He recorded two equally fine performances of Don Giovanni—one based on a Glyndebourne performance with Haitink (EMI CDS7 47037-8), the other on Philips with Marriner. His *Eugene Onegin*, conducted by Levine (Deutsche Grammophon), captures him in magnificent form in a memorable role. *—Ann Feeney*

Recommended:

- ○ **Tchaikovsky: Eugen Onegin** / Levine (cond.), Otter, Freni, Allen, Lang, Dresden Staatskapelle / DG 423959
- ○ **Mozart: Le Nozze Di Figaro** / Solti (cond.), Te Kanawa, Ramey, Von Stade, Allen, London PO / 1983 / Decca 410150
- ○ **On the Idle Hill of Summer** / Allen, Parsons / 2001 / EMI 67428
- ○ **Fauré, Ravel, Poulenc: Melodies** / Allen, Vignoles / 1994 / Virgin 545053
- ○ **Janáček: The Cunning Little Vixen** / Rattle (cond.), Allen, Tear, Montague, Howell / 2003 / Chandos 3101
- ○ **Barber: Dover Beach** / Allen, Vignoles, Endellion SQ / 1994 / Virgin 45033

Ambrosian Singers

f. 1951, London, England

Ensemble

The Ambrosian Singers are one of the best-known London choral groups, particularly esteemed for their wide variety of recorded repertory. The group's founding was connected to the beginnings of the post-World War II early music movement in England. One of its co-founders was Denis Stevens (b. 1922), a British musicologist and viola player who joined the BBC Music Department in 1949 and developed programs of Renaissance and early Baroque music. The other was John McCarthy (b. 1919), a professional tenor soloist.

They organized the Ambrosian Singers as a small, professional chorus in 1951. The group's aim was to give authentic, accurate performances of the complex polyphonic choral music of the medieval and Renaissance eras. Its first professional engagement involved the musical illustrations for the BBC Series *The History of Western Music*, which was primarily Stevens' production. In so doing, the group sampled a wide repertory in addition to its primary area of interest.

Stevens left the BBC and went to Cornell University in the U.S. in 1955, ending his formal ties with the group. In 1956, a group of six solo singers from the choir founded the Ambrosian Consort. Since then, the organization of the Ambrosian Singers has evolved into a talent pool of some 700 professional singers available for work in concerts, operas, recording, and films and television. Groups drawn from the 700 perform under the original name, The Ambrosian Opera Chorus, the John McCarthy Singers, and others. While John McCarthy was choral director for the London Symphony Orchestra (1961–66), the group called the "London Symphony Orchestra Chorus" was, in fact, the Ambrosian Singers.

The organization is considered ideal for specific recording projects, for it can provide a choir of experienced studio singers of the needed size and type of experience for anything from Baroque operas to film scores. It participated in the great RCA *Classic Film Scores* series. Aside from purely classical work, it has participated in numerous Christmas albums and appeared in albums with such pop and rock artists as Neil Diamond, Grace Jones, Van Morrison, and Julie Andrews.

Its original film score credits include *Brainstorm, Krull, Chariots of Fire, Sphinx*, and *The Secret of NIMH*, and in such film score excerpt albums as *Cinema Italiano: Film Scores of Ennio Morricone and Nino Rota* (conducted by Henry Mancini, collections of Miklos Rozsa scores, and original scores from MGM *Classic Musicals*). *—Joseph Stevenson*

Recommended:

- ○ **The Christmas Album** / Meakins (cond.), Royal PO, Ambrosian Singers / 1995 / Tring 083
- ○ **Cherubini: Messes pour les cérémonies royales** / Muti (cond.), Ambrosian Singers, London PO / 2003 / EMI 585258

Elly Ameling

b. Feb. 8, 1933, Rotterdam, Netherlands

Soprano

Elly Ameling is a Dutch soprano renowned for her performances of art song and oratorio. She is among the few singers to gain worldwide fame without being an operatic star. In fact, though she did sing one staged role (Ilia in Mozart's *Idomeneo* in 1973 and 1974), she avoided opera almost entirely during her more than 40-year performing career, choosing to focus instead on concert and recital repertory.

Ameling began her vocal studies with Jo Bollekamp and Jacoba Dresden Dhont in Rotterdam, and later coached French song literature with the renowned singer Pierre Bernac. She first came to attention by winning the 1956 Hertogenbosch and 1958 Geneva competitions. Debut recitals in Amsterdam (1961), London (1966), and New York (1968) were important milestones in a developing career that eventually took her all over the world. She found special favor with the Japanese public.

As a concert artist, Ameling was especially noted for her Bach and Mozart interpretations. At the same time, her performances in works such as the oratorios of Haydn and Mendelssohn and the Fourth Symphony of Mahler are justly admired. Her concerts also included performances of Alban Berg's *Sieben frühe Lieder* and *Altenberg Lieder*, as well as Berlioz's *Les nuits d'été* and Ravel's *Shéhérazade*. Always interested in new music, she sang in the premiere of Frank Martin's *Mystère de la Nativité* in 1959. She had the honor of singing during the wedding of Princess Christina of the Netherlands in 1975, as well as during the Royal Crowning Ceremony of Princess Beatrix of the Netherlands in 1980.

Ameling's vast repertory includes songs in German, French, Dutch, English, Italian, Spanish, and Japanese. She was most strongly associated with the songs of Franz Schubert, but she was an equally accomplished interpreter of Mozart, Schumann, Brahms, and Hugo Wolf. Her outstanding feel for the French *mélodie* is on display in EMI's complete recordings of the songs of Debussy, Fauré, Poulenc, and Ravel, with Dalton Baldwin at the piano. Other notable career highlights include a recording of the complete songs of the Dutch Baroque composer Constantijn Huygens (with the baritone Max van Egmond), recital performances of songs by Joaquin Rodrigo and Xavier Montsalvage (they do not often appear on her recordings), and performances of Frank Martin, Samuel Barber, and Benjamin Britten. Ameling occasionally gave cabaret evenings in intimate settings, including the Stratford Festival in Canada.

Elly Ameling's voice is a light soprano of great purity, with a wonderful command of the entire dynamic range and a wide variety of expressive colors. She moved very little on stage, and so even the slightest hand gesture carried great meaning. Having been an audience favorite for over thirty years, Ameling retired from the recital stage in the mid-1990s, following a series of farewell recitals in her favorite cities. However, she continues to share her love of song by giving master classes for young singers. *—Richard LeSueur*

Recommended:

- ○ **The Artistry of Elly Ameling** / Ameling / 2003 / Philips 000121702
- ○ **Elly Ameling: The Early Recordings Vol. 1** / Ameling / 1995 / DHM 26613
- ○ **Schubert & Schumann: Lieder** / Ameling, Demus / 1990 / DHM 77085
- ○ **Bach: Sacred Masterworks** / Munchinger (cond.), Ameling, Wunderlich, Pears, Krause / London 455783
- ○ **Mozart: Lieder & Notturni** / Ameling, Baldwin, Cooymans, Vanderbilt, Ludemann / 1991 / Philips 422524

American Brass Quintet

f. 1960

Ensemble

The American Brass Quintet made its debut in 1960, when brass chamber music was relatively unknown to concert audiences. This necessitated building a repertoire almost from scratch—in stark contrast to the modern-day string quartet, which has some 300 years of literature to choose from. The ABQ has since given over 100 premieres of new works for brass while amassing a discography of over 40 recordings. This is the largest body of serious brass music ever recorded by a single ensemble.

While many brass quintets have prospered by performing arrangements of popular, jazz, and rock styles in pops concert settings, the ABQ is known for its serious, thoughtful approach to the genre. The ensemble's core literature consists of contemporary works, their own editions of Renaissance and Baroque music, and rediscoveries of forgotten nineteenth century brass repertoire. The many composers who have been commissioned by the ABQ over the years include Jan Bach, William Bolcom, Elliott Carter, Jacob Druckman, Eric Ewazen, William Schuman, Ralph Shapey, Gunther Schuller, Virgil Thomson, and Melinda Wagner.

Having toured throughout Europe, Asia, South and Central America, the Middle East, Australia, and the United States, the ABQ has been hailed as "the high priests of brass" by *Newsweek*, "positively breathtaking," by the *New York Times*, and "of all the brass quintets, this country's most distinguished" by the *American Record Guide*. The Quintet has never wavered in its dedication to serious brass music, as evidenced by its ongoing residencies at the Juilliard School (since 1987) and the Aspen Music Festival (since 1970). *—Brian Wise*

Recommended:

- ○ **American Visions** / American Brass Quintet / 2003 / Summit 365
- ○ **Fyre & Lightning** / American Brass Quintet / 1995 / Summit 181
- ○ **American Brass Quintet** / 1989 / New World 80377
- ○ **Classic American Brass** / American Brass Quintet / 2000 / Summit 275

Géza Anda

b. Nov. 19, 1921, Budapest, Hungary, **d.** Jun. 14, 1976, Zürich, Switzerland
Pianist
Since his death in 1976 at the age of 55, Géza Anda's considerable reputation has faded somewhat from view. But in his heyday he was widely regarded as a transcendent pianist, possessed of a natural technique that gave his performances an intimate quality—even when he was scaling the Himalayan heights of his signature Brahms B flat major concerto. It was with that work that he made his debut in 1939 in Budapest under Willem Mengelberg.

Anda was born in 1921 in Budapest; after studying with Imre Stefaniai and Imre Keeri-Szanto, he became a piano pupil of Ernst von Dohnányi at the Royal Music Academy. A stipend allowed him to travel to Berlin, where he performed Franck's *Symphonic Variations* under Furtwängler. Anda remained in Berlin during the first years of World War II, but in 1942 he fled to Switzerland, where he encountered the great pianist and teacher Edwin Fischer. Fischer was a proponent of performing the Mozart piano concertos while conducting from the keyboard, and Anda would later adopt this practice, adding bench-led performances of all the concertos (even the early ones) to his repertoire. Anda was among the first to explore the whole range of Mozart's concertos, at a time when only the "greatest hits" were heard in concert halls; his outstanding 1960s recordings of the complete cycle with the Camerata Academica of the Salzburg Mozarteum remain a milestone in the history of recorded music.

Anda's style was noteworthy for its transparency of texture and its singing qualities, which led Furtwängler to dub him a "troubadour" of the piano. His flawless technique allowed him to invest his performances with considerable individuality: his readings of Schumann, for instance, were breathtakingly multidimensional, full of asides and highly appropriate introspective commentary conveyed from within Schumann's notes. He was especially influenced by his artistic partnership with the great Romanian pianist Clara Haskil, with whom he played two-piano repertoire from 1953 to 1958. Her moral commitment to conveying music's essence deepened Anda's own musical insight; his subsequent performances reflected a new harnessing of Anda's strong musical personality to the service of the music's meaning.

Although his repertoire was wide and ranged across core Classical-Romantic territory, it is likely that Anda will be most remembered for his interpretations of the music of his countryman Béla Bartók, whose three piano concertos he recorded in 1959 and 1960. These performances are masterpieces of technical ease and artistic mastery, and remain available in commercial release. A few months before the end of his too-brief life, Anda went into the studio and left a final testament of waltzes by Chopin, interpreted in an astonishing otherworldly manner. Anda allows the rhythmic impulse of Chopin's triple-time to hover almost motionlessly, as if contemplated from a distant and ethereal height. *—Mark Satola*

Recommended:
- ○ **Mozart: The Piano Concertos** / Anda, Salzburg Mozart Camerata Academy / DG 469510
- ○ **Mozart: Piano Concertos 6, 17 & 21** / Anda, Salzburg Mozart Camerata Academy / 1995 / DG 447436
- ○ **Géza Anda** / Anda, Fricsay (conds.), Salzburg Mozart Camerata Academy, Berlin RSO / 1999 / Philips 456772

Marian Anderson

b. Feb. 27, 1897, Philadelphia, PA, **d.** Apr. 8, 1993, Portland, OR
Contralto
A legendary African-American interpreter of both operatic and concert repertoire, Marian Anderson was possessed of one of the finest contralto voices in living memory. Her career was notable not only for her artistic achievements—which were many—but also for a dignified tenacity in the face of discrimination. She opened doors for subsequent generations of black American singers.

Having sung since childhood, and subsequently studied with a number of teachers in her native Philadelphia, Anderson first rose to prominence when she appeared with the New York Philharmonic Orchestra in 1925. In the early 1930s she made a successful concert tour of Europe, and solidified her growing reputation with further appearances in New York and London.

In 1939, Anderson scheduled an appearance at Constitution Hall in Washington, D.C., but was denied the use of the building by its owners, the Daughters of the American Revolution, who objected to the presentation of a black performer. Eleanor Roosevelt resigned her membership in the DAR in protest of this decision and then scheduled an appearance for Anderson at the Lincoln Memorial on Easter Sunday. The resulting concert, attended by thousands and broadcast nationwide, forever established Anderson as an ambassador for racial progress—a role she embraced with great pride and success for the remainder of her career. Fittingly, Anderson's 1955 appearance at the Metropolitan Opera marked the first by an African-American singer, preparing the way for such future stars as Leontyne Price and Shirley Verrett.

Marian Anderson's voice was dark, rich, and possessed of great power and agility. Her repertory ranged from opera and concert material to Negro spirituals, and she brought to all things a great sense of commitment and integrity. Arturo Toscanini is noted to have remarked that a voice like hers only appears "once in a hundred years." Her extraordinary range extended all the way down to the D below middle C—as displayed in her performances of Schubert's song *Death and the Maiden* (*Der Tod und das Mädchen*)—as well as upwards into soprano territory (as an exercise, she even sang the devastatingly difficult "Casta diva" from Bellini's *Norma*). While her voice was most distinctive in the lower range, she was also capable of lightening it almost to leggiero proportions—as she did in works of Handel and other Baroque composers—and of bringing a near-ideal combination of classical training and folk-like spontaneity to the spirituals that were an integral part of her concert and recording repertoire. *—AMG*

Recommended:
- ○ **The Lady from Philadelphia** / O'Connell (cond.), Anderson, Victory SO / Pearl 9069
- ○ **Marian Anderson** / Collingwood, O'Connell (conds.), Anderson / Pearl 9318
- ○ **Softly Awakes My Heart** / Bourdon, Collingwood (conds.), Anderson / 2001 / Naxos 120566
- ○ **Schubert & Schumann Lieder** / Anderson, Rupp / 2000 / RCA 63575
- ○ **Marian Anderson** / Anderson / 1989 / BMG 7911

Piotr Anderszewski

b. Apr. 4, 1969, Warsaw, Poland
Pianist
Pianist Piotr Anderszewski has developed into an artist seemingly with a taste for highly structured works, most particularly Beethoven's *Diabelli Variations*. But that does not mean his performances are dry, academic readings of the piano repertoire's great works. Rather, he has been praised for his sensitivity and imaginative interpretations.

Warsaw-born Anderszewski studied piano at the Lyon and Strasbourg conservatories, the Chopin Academy of Music in Warsaw, and the University of Southern California in Los Angeles. He also attended master classes in Italy with Fou Ts'ong, Murray Perahia, and Leon Fleisher. The 1990 Leeds Piano Competition was the beginning of his career. There, he performed the *Diabelli Variations*, then followed that with Webern's *Variations*. However, in the middle of the Webern, he suddenly walked offstage, forfeiting the competition. He was not having an artistic fit of pique, but rather felt that the Beethoven performance spoke well enough for him. In fact, that Beethoven performance resulted in two important invitations: one to perform a solo recital at Wigmore Hall, the other to record the *Variations* for Teldec. He decided to turn down the offer from Teldec, feeling at the time that a studio recording would lose the spontaneity of a live recording. He began touring in Europe, most frequently appearing in London, but maintaining a home base in Paris, and for a time he toured the world with violinist Viktoria Mullova, also making his first recording with her. His first solo recordings were of Bach, Beethoven, and Webern. In 2000, he made his American debut and was given the Karol Szymanowski Award for his interpretations of that composer's works. The next year Anderszewski signed a recording contract with Virgin Classics. Finally, he was ready to record the *Diabelli Variations*, and filmmaker Bruno Monsaigneon documented the process and Anderszewski's thoughts on the work, much in the same way he had documented Glenn Gould performing the *Goldberg Variations*. The recording itself received high praise and several awards. Anderszewski's next project was performing and recording Mozart piano concertos while conducting from the piano. In 2002, he was awarded the prestigious Gilmore Prize, hoping to use some of the prize monies to record his favorite Szymanowski pieces. *—Patsy Morita*

Recommended:
- ○ **Chopin: Ballades; Mazurkas; Polonaises** / Anderszewski / 2003 / Virgin 45620
- ○ **Beethoven: Diabelli Variations** / Anderszewski / 2001 / Virgin 545468
- ○ **Bach: Partitas 1, 3 & 6** / Anderszewski / 2002 / Virgin 45526

Maurice André

b. May 21, 1933, Alès, France
Trumpeter
Maurice André has rightly earned a reputation as one of the finest trumpet virtuosos of the twentieth and twenty-first centuries. He has made numerous concert appearances and recordings and has inspired composers like Blacher, Jolivet, and Tomasi to write major works for his instrument.

André was born in the Cévennes district of southern France. Young Maurice began taking vocal instruction (solfeggio) at age ten, but two years later, influenced by his father—a miner, but also an excellent amateur trumpeter—began playing the cornet and eventually the trumpet. But he also followed his father's occupation, becoming a miner at age 14. It was not long until the elder André realized the depth of his son's talent and arranged lessons for him with local teacher Léon Barthélémy. Because his father's wages were meager, André could not consider study at the Paris Conservatory, but through Barthélémy's clever plan, he gained admittance, tuition-free, by first joining a military band. At the age of 18, André began studies at the conservatory under Raymond Sabarich. He quickly demonstrated his immense talents, winning first prizes there for both cornet and trumpet playing in his first two years. In 1953, he began playing professionally in two ensembles, the Lamoureux Concert Association Orchestra and the Radio France Philharmonic Orchestra. André captured first prize in trumpet at the 1955 Geneva International Competition. He left the two orchestral posts in 1960 and 1962, respectively, joining the orchestra of the Opéra Comique in the latter year. In 1963, André was asked to sit on the jury of the Munich International Competition, but entered as a candidate instead and captured first prize, thus establishing himself at the age of 30 as one of the leading young trumpeters in the world. He immediately launched a solo career, which was eventually managed by his wife Liliane. He began making his first recordings around this time, most with the French label Erato. Many of his most important and popular later ones, however, were done for EMI. He has also recorded for Deutsche Grammophon, Philips, and smaller labels. Because the repertory for the trumpet was relatively small, he began transcribing—or engaged others to transcribe—works for oboe, violin, and other instruments. The Tartini *Violin Concerto in D major* was one such example, the transcription being done by Jean Thilde. André also began commissioning works from some of the leading composers of the day. Throughout the 1960s and 1970s, André maintained a heavy concert schedule, playing with many of the leading orchestras and conductors in Europe and the United States and making numerous recordings. In a 1978 interview, André estimated that he typically played a 180-concert schedule and had made over 220 recordings up to that time. By 2003, André had appeared on over 300 recordings, though he had significantly reduced his concert schedule. While he has recorded music from most periods, he has tended to focus on Baroque repertory, such as works by Bach, Telemann, Handel, Torelli, and Albinoni. On many of his concert tours, André's younger brother Raymond, also a trumpeter of some renown, has accompanied him. In 1979, the first Maurice André Trumpet Competition was held. Subsequent events in the series took place in 1988, 1997, and 2000. André usually serves as chairman of the jury. *—Robert Cummings*

Recommended:

- ○ **The Trumpet Shall Sound** / André / 2003 / DG 000019302
- ○ **Virtuoso Trumpet** / André and other soloists / 2000 / DG 469229
- ○ **Concertos by Mozart, Vivaldi, Telemann & Hummel** / Karajan (cond.), André, Berlin PO / 1998 / EMI 66961
- ○ **Maurice André** / André, Bilgram / 1992 / EMI 54330
- ○ **Baroque Trumpet Concertos** / Marriner, Wallez (conds.), André / 1999 / Angel 73423

Louis Andriessen

b. Jun. 6, 1939, Utrecht, Netherlands

Composer: Orchestral, Vocal

Composer Louis Andriessen was born in Utrecht into a musical family headed by his father Hendrik Andriessen, one of the recognized pioneers of modern Dutch music. Louis Andriessen began his musical studies with his father, and then studied in The Hague with Kees van Baaren, and later in Milan with Luciano Berio. Early Andriessen works are serial, but by 1963 he was working with graphic notation, as in the piano piece *Registers*, using a combination of fixed and non-fixed elements to facilitate improvisation. In 1969, Andriessen participated in his first large-scale theatrical "happening," *Reconstructie*, at the Holland Festival in collaboration with Ton de Leeuw, Misha Mengelberg, Peter Schat, and Jan van Vlijmen. In 1970, Andriessen swore off writing music for standard symphonic ensembles for good, a decision which was to profoundly impact his development. For a time, he worked in electronic music; and he then first ventured into theater on his own with *Il Principe*. Andriessen experienced a creative breakthrough in 1976, with *De Staat*, a large choral work based on Plato's *Republic* sung in the original Greek, combining ancient Greek scales, Stravinskian rhythms, repetition, and hocket. *De Staat* earned Andriessen the coveted Kees van Baaren Prize, and since then he has garnered numerous awards, citations, and commissions. The unusual instrumentation of *De Staat* deserves mention: four women's voices, four oboes, four horns, four trumpets, four trombones, two electric guitars, bass guitar, two pianos, two harps, and four violas.

"All that whining about textural sonorous fields and special instrumental effects bores me," Andriessen has said. "Instrumentation must correspond to the structure of the music." Andriessen often uses rock instruments, such as electric guitar, bass, and synthesizer to augment his ensembles. Andriessen also composes music designed to challenge the talents of specific performers; *Forget-Me-Not* requires an oboist to also play piano, and in *TAO* there is a part for a pianist who speaks and also plays the koto. Andriessen is regarded to some extent as an ensemble builder; Orchestra de Volharding is a group he formed to play the same-named Andriessen work, and the ensemble came together afterward to program and commission other repertoire. In the United States, performing groups such as the California Ear Unit and Bang On A Can have eagerly programmed and recorded Andriessen works such as *Workers Union* and *Hoketus*. Younger composers view the work of Andriessen as an alternative to academic serialism and American minimalism, and aspiring composers from many nations have come to Holland to study with him at the Royal Conservatory at The Hague. After *De Staat*, Andriessen's major works have included *De Tijd*, *Facing Death* for the Kronos Quartet, and *Trilogy of the Last Day*. He collaborated with stage director Robert Wilson on the four-part *De Materie* in 1989. In the 1990s, a fruitful collaboration with film director Peter Greenaway led to several works, including the films *M is for Man, Music, Mozart*; *Rosa: The Death of a Composer*; and the opera *Writing To Vermeer*, which premiered in 1999. Sometimes didactic in his defense of his progressive political views, Andriessen is nevertheless far from humorless. His penetrating insight as an essayist on topics such as Stravinsky may be read in his book *The Apollonian Clockwork*, published in 1989. Andriessen has said "I don't feel comfortable with composers like Schoenberg who always push ahead in one direction. I prefer the jacks-of-all-trades: the Purcells and Stravinskys, who are at home anywhere, borrowing here, and stealing there." His popularity with young listeners and presence on the scene has provided an unprecedented boost to the prominence of contemporary Dutch music throughout the world. *—Uncle Dave Lewis*

Overview of Works

The works of Louis Andriessen would seem to exemplify musical postmodernism—born in the first generation of composers for whom crossing boundaries between new and old, high and low, was no longer a novelty, Andriessen draws on the gamut of Western music history and the full stylistic breadth of music in the twentieth century. Of course, all too often the term "postmodern," when applied to music, suggest connotations such as "unorganized," "soulless," or even "sloppy." Such notions hardly apply to Andriessen's oeuvre; transcending traditionally institutionalized musical forms and sonorities (often using keyboards, electric guitars, etc.) and applying the process-oriented ideals of minimalism not only to notes and rhythms but to borrowings and allusions, Andriessen's works do not ironically elevate the trivial, but rather utilize a wide array of approaches in exploring some of the fundamental dimensions of existence. Andriessen manifests his interest in musical historicism in several of his early works for orchestra and large ensemble, such as his *Introspezione II* and *III* (1963–65), *Anachronie I* and *II* (1967, 1969), and *Contra Tempus* (1968). These works draw on various influences, from jazz and pop, to the high serialism of Boulez, to the indeterminism of Cage, resulting in heterogeneous collages that have elicited comparisons to Charles Ives. In *Contra Tempus*, Andriessen acknowledges the historic influence of Stravinsky in particular, ending the piece on the harmony with which Stravinsky had begun his neo-Classicist masterwork *Symphony of Psalms*. The 1970s are generally regarded as the beginning of Andriessen's "maturity," largely due to his abandonment of the traditional orchestral ensemble in such important works as *De Staat* (for voices and large ensemble). Andriessen further established his reputation for instrumental distinctiveness with *De volharding* ("Perseverance") from 1972 and *Hoketus* in 1977, both of which called for unusual instrumentations and both of which produced ensembles by the same names. Andriessen also demonstrated a strong social consciousness during this time: *Volkslied*, from 1971, transforms the Dutch national anthem into that of the (now former) Soviet Union; in 1975, he composed *Worker's Union*, "for any loud-sounding group of instruments." These works, along with other chamber pieces from the period such as *Mausoleum* from 1981, also demonstrate the influence of American minimalism on Andriessen's style. Throughout the 1970s and early 1980s, Andriessen concerned himself with the methodical application of composition ideas to a limited pool of compositional resources. This attention to fundamental ideas is reflected with particular clarity in both the substance and subject matter of works such as *De Tijd* (Time), a work for vocal forces and large ensemble based on a text by St. Augustine and composed in 1981. Also, the large-scale stage work *De Materie* ("Matter") from 1989 is a piece using both minimalist concepts and complex musical allusions, for which Andriessen collaborated with director Robert Wilson. In the 1990s, however, some sensed Andriessen listing in the direction of neo-Romanticism with the more operatically oriented *Rosa, A Horse Drama* (1994) and the large-scale choral and instrumental work *Trilogie van de laatste Dag* (1997). *—Jeremy Grimshaw*

Recommended:

- ○ **L. Andriessen: Zilver** / California EAR Unit / 1997 / New Albion 094

ORCHESTRAL

Hoketus, for 2 ensembles (1975–1977)

Louis Andriessen's *Hoketus* is one of the few works in the literature that manage to be irritating and completely fascinating at the same time. It was composed between 1975 and 1977 for a minimalist music project at the Royal Conservatory of the Hague, where Andriessen taught. Like many minimalist compositions, it offers very little actual music, preferring instead to rhythmically manipulate and extend a small amount of material. Andriessen's primary method for this manipulation and extension is the eponymous hocket—a medieval technique in which consecutive notes of a rhythmic or melodic motif are alternated between instruments or voices.

The ancient nature of this method is somewhat undermined by the work's instrumentation, which calls for two groups, each containing panpipes, alto saxophone, piano, electric piano, bass guitar, and conga drums. *Hoketus* begins with two nearly identical chords separated by pauses, and with each chord played only by one of the two groups. These two chords are then grouped into three-chord groups, then groups of four, then six chords; the piece moves onwards from there, without changing the chords, the instrumentation, or who's playing what. It is all hypnotically spare and lucid. Finally, the composer introduces rhythmic accents, which had been absent for the first part of the work, and eliminates the pauses, providing more opportunities for rhythmic manipulation.

Andriessen then introduces another set of two somewhat brighter-sounding chords, which are run through the same gamut of changes and variations. These two chords are replaced a few times until finally a melody emerges; this is also divided up between the two groups of instruments. At this point, the music has been going nonstop for so long that it is actually stunning when Andriessen introduces a pause, just before the music's final elaboration, which crescendos into one last solid chord. These machinations may seem cold and sterile from a schematic description, but even as it annoys, *Hoketus* commands attention. *—Andrew Malone*

Recommended:

- ○ **Gigantic Dancing Human Machine** / Bang On A Can / 2002 / Cantaloupe 21012
- ○ **Andriessen: Mausoleum; Hoketus** / Hoketus Ensemble / Donemus 20

VOCAL

De Staat, for female chorus & ensemble (1972–1976)

De Staat (*The Republic*) by Louis Andriessen is a mixed choral and instrumental work scored for four women's voices, four oboes, four horns, four trumpets, four trombones, two electric guitars, bass guitar, two pianos, two harps, and four violas. The text is sung in ancient Greek and is taken from those parts of Plato's *Republic* that deal specifically with matters of mode and music. Plato sought to suppress musical modes that tended to intoxicate the listener, and he proposed to restrain craftsmen who made "many-keyed" instruments such as the harp and dulcimer which were capable of playing in these modes. As Plato states, "any alteration in the modes of music is always followed by alteration in the most fundamental laws of state." Andriessen uses Plato's text as a mixed metaphor for the relationship between politics and music. Andriessen doesn't agree that the basic working materials of music have a political connotation, i.e., "there is no such thing as a fascist dominant seventh"—however, once a composer puts those materials together into a work, a type of social order is achieved. Conversely, Andriessen doesn't believe that musical innovation poses a real threat to the State; as he once wrote, "I regret the fact that Plato was wrong! If only it were true."

The grouping of instruments into units of four relates directly to the musical material itself, which is based on tetrachords, or groups of four notes each. Andriessen claims that "*De Staat* has nothing to do with Greek music," but some of the long passages scored in rushing unison sixteenths for the whole ensemble have an unmistakably Greek modal flavor—perhaps unavoidable, given the subject. Another external similarity in *De Staat* is to the music of Stravinsky and in particular the rhythmic profile of *Le sacre du printemps*. For most of the 36 minutes that constitute *De Staat*, the ensemble plays at a loud volume, and many passages are aggressive in character. But it never wears out its welcome; the work has an entirely satisfying dramatic plan in which one section moves breathlessly into the next. Just before the final choral section the ensemble divides into pairs, and the work concludes with a startlingly complex hocket which is played in the horns, finally merging into a near unison texture.

While Andriessen since has written several works on a larger scale that, perhaps, elucidate his intentions more clearly than *De Staat*, this remains his best-known and most-programmed work. It is certainly one of the most exciting and original compositions to come out of the 1970s, a period dominated on one hand by academic serialism and by faddish minimalism, on the other. *—Uncle Dave Lewis*

Recommended:

- ○ **L. Andriessen: De Staat** / De Leeuw (cond.), Arnold Schoenberg Choir / 1991 / Nonesuch 79251

Leif Ove Andsnes

b. 1970, Karmoy, Norway

Pianist

One of the most successful pianists of the generation that came of age at the end of the twentieth century, Leif Ove Andsnes is particularly known for his attention to the music of his native Norway. "I always played a lot of Grieg from my childhood," he has said. "I always loved Grieg and I don't know if it's only because I'm Norwegian."

He entered Bergen Conservatory in 1986 and studied with Jiri Hlinka, a well-known Czech piano professor. Andsnes made his U.S. debut in 1989, appearing in New York and Washington, then traveling to Canada. In the same year he appeared with great acclaim at the Edinburgh Festival where he played with the Oslo Philharmonic Orchestra under the direction of Mariss Jansons.

Since then he has undertaken frequent touring. He debuted with the Berlin Philharmonic in 1992, and in the same year he made his first appearance at the BBC's *Henry Wood Proms* in London, playing Britten's piano concerto. He has returned to the *Proms*, playing in Beethoven's second piano concerto and Rachmaninov's *Concerto No. 3*.

His first trip to Japan came in 1993, where he played in Tokyo with the Bergen Philharmonic, and he gave his first concerts in Australia in 1994. Among the other orchestras with which he has collaborated are the Danish Radio Symphony Orchestra, the London Symphony Orchestra, and the Leipzig Gewandhaus Orchestra. He joined the Danish Radio Orchestra, the Oslo Philharmonic, the Boston Symphony, the Cleveland Orchestra, and the Detroit Symphony Orchestra on major tours.

Andsnes also performs frequently as a solo recitalist, accompanist, and chamber music participant. He tours as part of a piano trio with the violinist and cellist brother-and-sister team of Christian and Tanja Tetzlaff.

He is an exclusive recording artist with the EMI Classics label, on which he has presented a repertory with an unusual mix of well-known and lesser-known music. "I had a teacher who was always very conscious that one should play things that people don't normally hear as well and I find often that pianists are very conventional in their repertoire thinking. I like to explore new things that are not often done," Andsnes says. Alongside Rachmaninov's third concerto and works of Brahms and Schumann, he has made discs of piano music of Grieg, Janáček, and Nielsen, as well as a recital disc of Norwegian piano music.

Andsnes is a winner of the Hindemith Prize (1987), the Norwegian Music Critics Prize (1988), the Grieg Prize (1990), the Dorothy B. Chandler Performing Arts Award (1992), the Gilmore Prize (1997), the Choc de la Monde de la Musique (a coveted French magazine award) (1998), and, in the year 2000, a Royal Philharmonic Society award for best instrumentalist. His recording activities have won two German Record Critics' awards. *—Joseph Stevenson*

Recommended:

- ○ **A Portrait** / Andsnes / 2001 / EMI 74789
- ○ **Debussy, Janáček, Nielsen, Ravel, Schumann, Brahms: Violin & Viola Sonatas** / Andsnes, Tetzlaff (violin & viola) / 2002 / Virgin 562016
- ○ **Janáček: Piano Music** / Andsnes / 2000 / Virgin 61839
- ○ **Haydn: Piano Sonatas** / Andsnes / 1999 / EMI 56756
- ○ **Grieg: Lyric Pieces (Performed on Grieg's Piano)** / Andsnes / 2002 / EMI 57296
- ○ **Liszt: Piano Recital** / Andsnes / 2001 / Angel 57002

Anonymous 4

f. 1986

Ensemble

The female vocal quartet called Anonymous 4 has become one of the most popular and respected small vocal groups specializing in early music. The group has attained the elusive combination of popularity and respect through its unique blend of creativity and scholarly/historical depth.

The name "Anonymous 4" comes from a scholarly convention for designating anonymous medieval writers and scribes with numbers; working with a particular manuscript by the scribe known as Anonymous 4, they found it an ideal name for their new quartet. The group was formed in 1986. Its purpose was to experiment with the sound of medieval music (both chant and polyphony) as sung by higher voices. Its four members are all singers of considerable beauty of tone, range, and flexibility, but all of them had nontraditional backgrounds to one extent or another. Marsha Genensky, originally a folk singer, earned an M.A. in Folklore and Folklife from the University of Pennsylvania. She is an expert in traditional American shape-note singing, and experimented with different vocal techniques for the different strains of British-American folksong. Susan Hellauer, a native of New York City, was a trumpeter with a B.A. in music from Queens College. She had always been fascinated by vocal music of the medieval and Renaissance eras, leading her to become a singer and to earn advanced musicology degrees at Queens College and Columbia University. Jacqueline Horner, of Belfast, Northern Ireland, is the only non-American in the group. She attended Queen's University, earning a B.A. with joint honors in music and English. In London, she studied performance practice at City University and the Guildhall School of Music and Drama. Like many other medieval-oriented performers, she is interested in both early and modern music, and has performed with Pierre Boulez's Ensemble InterContemporain, the Ensemble for Early Music, Ensemble Moderne, and Continuum. She moved to New York, which she calls her "favorite city in the universe." Johanna Maria Rose has a broad background in several of the arts. She earned an M.A. in Early Music Performance at Sarah Lawrence College.

Anonymous 4 is renowned for the depth of its scholarship. Hellauer does the primary music research, and when needed prepares the group's repertory by transcribing it into modern notation from original sources. Genensky and Rose are in charge of language research and study of literary sources, and adapting readings for their concerts. The teamwork results in concerts that avoid presenting the music in a vacuum. Anonymous 4's programs are innovative and entertaining, relating the music to its time and milieu through narrative and poetry interwoven with the music. Sometimes they fill out groups of chants or fragmentary pieces of polyphony with music of their own composition in order to make convincing wholes, but the new music they create is done accurately enough to blend seamlessly with the medieval originals.

Beyond such historical considerations, the group's astonishingly beautiful and pure vocal blend has made it one of the leading acts in classical music recording. Despite being involved in what may seem a narrowly specialized academic area of music, they have sold about a million copies of their recordings on the Harmonia Mundi Label. Among these were *On Yoolis Night*, a medieval Christmas album that won the prestigious French Diapason d'Or award. Their first disc, *An English Ladymass*, was *CD Review's* Classical Early Music Disc of the Year, and their fourth, *The Lily and the Lamb*, was *Classic CD's* Disc of the Year for 1996. Tower Music reported that its *11,000 Virgins* disc of music by Hildegard von Bingen was one of the top 100 Independent Label releases in 1997–98. In 2003 the group turned to early American religious traditions with its *American Angels* album. *—Joseph Stevenson*

Recommended:

- ○ **1000: A Mass for the End of Time** / Anonymous 4 / 2000 / HM 907224
- ○ **An English Ladymass** / Anonymous 4 / 1992 / HM 907080
- ○ **On Yoolis Night** / Anonymous 4 / 1993 / HM 907099
- ○ **Love's Illusion** / Anonymous 4 / 2003 / HM 2907109
- ○ **Hildegard: 11,000 Virgins** / Anonymous 4 / 2003 / HM 807200

Ernest Ansermet

b. Nov. 11, 1883, Vevey, Switzerland, **d.** Feb. 20, 1969, Geneva, Switzerland
Conductor

For 50 years he directed an orchestra that was second-rate in tone and technique, yet Ernest Ansermet drew performances from it that cut right to the heart of the music. A musician of catholic taste, Ansermet was a reliable, insightful interpreter of composers from Mozart to Martin. His recordings in the 1950s and 1960s with the Suisse Romande Orchestra, which he founded, retain strong interest for collectors who value nuance over tonal sheen. These recordings are of especial interest as they provide a link to composers active in Paris in the early twentieth century, with whom Ansermet was closely associated.

As a child, he studied math with his father, a teacher, and music with his mother. Ansermet's early training seemed to add up to a career in mathematics; he specialized in that subject at Lausanne University, graduating in 1903. Ansermet served as a professor of mathematics from 1905 to 1909. But during this time his interest in music only increased; he kept an eye trained on the technique of local conductors, and took courses in music with Alexandre Denéréaz, Otto Barblan, and Ernest Bloch. Ansermet sought further advice on conducting from Felix Mottl in Munich and Artur Nikisch in Berlin, then concentrated mainly on teaching himself the art of the baton.

His first professional efforts were leading the summer Kursaal concerts in Montreux (1912–14), and conducting symphonic concerts in Geneva (1915–18). In 1918 he organized the Orchestre de la Suisse Romande in Geneva, from the start performing a substantial amount of contemporary French and Russian music. Ansermet befriended many of the great progressive composers of the time, especially Claude Debussy, Maurice Ravel, and Igor Stravinsky. Through Stravinsky, Ansermet met Serge Diaghilev and was appointed principal conductor of the latter's ballets russes, touring with the company to Paris, London, Italy, Spain, South America, and the United States. During a 1916 tour Ansermet made his first recordings with the ballets russes orchestra—the beginning of a half century of making intriguing records with less-than-stellar ensembles. Through his association with the ballets russes, Ansermet was able to premiere many of the period's most important dance scores, including Falla's *Three-Cornered Hat*, Prokofiev's *The Buffoon*, Satie's *Parade*, and Stravinsky's *Pulcinella*. As an extra-curricular wartime diversion, on September 28, 1918, Ansermet premiered Stravinsky's *L'Histoire du soldat* in Geneva.

He developed the reputation of—in the words of Nicholas Slonimsky—"a scholarly and progressive musician capable of fine interpretations of both classical and modern works." Although the Suisse Romande Orchestra, with which he recorded for Decca in the 1950s and 1960s, could be criticized for its wiry strings and sour woodwinds, the group delivered to Ansermet highly accurate performances notable for their clear textures and delicate timbral balances.

Ansermet was, not surprisingly, a gifted conductor of Classical-era music, but he had little opportunity to record it. He is best remembered for his *sui generis* recordings of the music of his French contemporaries Debussy, Ravel, and Roussel, and his Swiss compatriots Honegger and Martin. But Ansermet was also a strong champion of such other contemporary composers as Bartók and Britten, premiering the latter's opera *The Rape of Lucretia*. He retired from conducting in 1967, to the end performing and committing to disc such rarities as Magnard's *Symphony No. 4*.

Ansermet's compositions include a symphonic poem, *Feuilles de printemps*; he also orchestrated Debussy's *Six épigraphes antiques*, among other pieces. His publications include *Le Geste du chef d'orchestre* (1943) and *Les Fondements de la musique dans la conscience humaine* (1961), in which he used mathematics to discredit 12-tone and other advanced compositional techniques. *—James Reel*

Recommended:

- ○ **Ernest Ansermet** / Ansermet (cond.), Suisse Romande Orchestra / EMI 75094
- ○ **Ansermet Conducts Chabrier** / Ansermet (cond.), Suisse Romande Orchestra / 1997 / London 452890
- ○ **Stravinsky: Ballets, Stage Works, Orchestral Works** / Ansermet (cond.), Suisse Romande Orchestra / 2001 / Decca 467818
- ○ **Debussy, Dukas, Saint-Saëns (Orchestral Works)** / Ansermet (cond.), Suisse Romande Orchestra / 2003 / Testament 1324

George Antheil

b. Jul. 8, 1900, Trenton, NJ, Feb. 12, 1959, New York, NY
Composer: Keyboard, Chamber Music, Orchestral, Symphonic

George Antheil was the first American composer of the twentieth century to gain international attention. Following musical studies in his teens in the U.S. with composers Constantin von Sternberg and Ernest Bloch, Antheil made his first splash as a touring concert pianist in Europe and soon attracted attention for his extraordinary athleticism and mettle. The latter quality served him particularly well as he presented programs that included his own jazzy, jittery, percussive piano works (with evocative titles like *Airplane Sonata*, *Jazz Sonata*, *Sonata Sauvage*, *Mechanisms*, and *Death of Machines*), as well as those by equally thorny modernist Arnold Schoenberg.

As one of the first wave of American expatriates who flocked to Paris in the 1920s, Antheil associated with many of the most important cultural figures of the day, including William Butler Yeats, Ezra Pound, James Joyce, Pablo Picasso, and Igor Stravinsky. While in Europe, Antheil composed his most famous work, *Ballet mécanique*, a clangorous sonic essay requiring an extensive battery of percussion instruments including a siren, electric bells, airplane propellers, an alarm clock and eight grand pianos. It created a sensation at its initial performance in Paris (1926), but the work fell flat at its Carnegie Hall premiere in 1927, cementing Antheil's lasting reputation as the "Bad Boy of Music," a designation he would live to regret.

Spurred on by the boom in contemporary opera in Germany, Antheil wrote the score and libretto to *Transatlantic*, a period piece, full of jazzy rhythms and popular song parodies. His first opera to be performed in America, *Helen Retires* (based on the legendary Helen of Troy) failed to generate similar critical success. From the mid-1930s to his death in 1959, two interrelated currents within Antheil's output reflected the further evolution of his style. While the rhythmic vitality and harmonic tang of his early works continued to take a central role, Antheil's increasing involvement with film work and his "rediscovery" of the symphonic tradition embodied in the works of Beethoven and Mahler signaled new stylistic concerns and brought his works to an entirely new audience. His symphonies from this period are infused with a newly melodic, even Romantic breadth, and Antheil came under the spell of the pervasive "American" sound that dominated the music of his fellow countrymen in the 1930s and 1940s. Following in the steps of composers such as Copland, Thomson, and Harris, he began to incorporate folk-like elements and aural "wide-open landscapes" into his concert works and film scores like *The Plainsman* (1936) and *The Fighting Kentuckian* (1949). While he continued to produce a string of other film scores and keyboard, instrumental, and symphonic works, Antheil's interest in opera was reawakened after two decades with a string of operas in the early 1950s, the most successful of which was *Volpone*. After a long period of indifference toward his music, audiences began to rediscover Antheil's idiosyncratic talent via an increasing stream of recordings beginning in the 1970s.

George Antheil managed to sustain a productive musical career despite his involvement in an astonishing range of other endeavors. At various times, he supported the composition of "legitimate" music with more lucrative film-scoring work; wrote columns and articles for *Esquire* on topics ranging from war predictions to endocriminology (the study of the human glands and their relation to criminal behavior); created a syndicated romantic advice column; penned a vastly entertaining, shamelessly name-dropping autobiography, *Bad Boy of Music* (1947); and co-invented, with Hollywood actress Hedy Lamarr, a radio-directed torpedo that presaged by 50 years the development of digital cellular telephony. *—Michael Rodman*

KEYBOARD

Works for Piano (1912–1956)

If we are to overlook George Antheil's notable talent for self-mythologizing (he audaciously wrote an autobiography at the age of 35, entitled *Bad Boy of Music*) and take him at his word, the following anecdote sheds considerable light on Antheil's style as a pianist and, consequently, his early compositions for piano. As the story goes, Antheil had heard that a well-connected music agent was looking for a fiery new pianist to replace keyboard maverick Leo Ornstein. A month before auditioning for the agent, Antheil bought two fishbowls, filled them with water, and sat between them on the piano bench. During the next several weeks, Antheil practiced for up to 20 hours a day, alternately soaking one swollen, bloody hand in the water while practicing with the other.

In fact, it was precisely during this time that Antheil wrote some of his most infamously difficult works, some of which find few rivals for uninhibited physicality and relentless gesture; listening to their thick blocks of sound and crashing rhythms, one is inclined to accept the fishbowl story as accurate. It is certainly the sort of visual image summoned by his *Sonata Sauvage* from 1923. The opening and closing movements of the piece juxtapose brief, tranquil, Debussyesque pastiche with noisy, ham-fisted hammerings so thick in their scoring as to obscure any sense of melody or harmonic trajectory; indeed, the last few bars of the first movement consist of nothing but furious pounding at the extremes of the keyboard. The *Second Sonata* (subtitled "The Airplane") begins with a grotesquely graceful glissando, and in its first few episodes feigns friendliness. A mysterious and mechanistic ostinato develops in the left hand, however, that is soon answered by insistent telegraphic chords in the treble. Here again, an unexpected cinematic cutaway to a faux impressionist Elysium is shattered abruptly by a barrage of violent, primal tone clusters. The goal here seems to be to put the listener ill at ease: Antheil repeats the same clunky chord just a few more times than he knows he should, a little louder than he should. This, of course, makes his genuinely mellow moments all the more dramatic, and the more playful passages (such as the parade of keyboard styles in the *Jazz Sonata* from 1922) even more exuberant.

After the burst of brash piano works from the early 1920s, Antheil spent much of his time in subsequent decades composing for ballet, stage, and film, eventually arriving at something like a neo-Romantic style. The lesser-known piano works that emerged in later years, though energetic, are tempered somewhat by stylistic maturity and a stronger sense of form. The *Sonata No. 4* (1948), for example, channels the rhythmicality of the *Sonata Sauvage* into a more discernible structure. *Sonata No. 5* from 1950 is given over to lyricism in the first two movements (though there is always the specter of irony close by), with a glimpse of the younger Antheil in the driving finale. *—Jeremy Grimshaw*

Recommended:

- ○ **Bad Boy of Music** / Verbit / 1994 / Albany 146
- ○ **Antheil Plays Antheil** / Antheil, F.C. Adler (cond.), Vienna PO, Roger Wagner Chorale / 2002 / Other Minds 1003

CHAMBER MUSIC

Ballet mécanique, for 4 pianos, 2 electric bells, 2 airplane propellers & percussion (May 25, 1953)

A signal work in the history of American music, George Antheil's *Ballet mécanique* (1923–25) is notable not only for its early use of massed percussion, but also for spawning the first great "scandal" of American music—a singular honor in the atmosphere of early twentieth century avant-gardism. Antheil, who was among the first wave of American expatriates in Europe in the early 1920s, took a profound interest in rethinking traditional conceptions of musical form. Rather than delineating the form of a work by the manipulation of harmonic and melodic materials, Antheil postulated, it might be possible to sculpt music using a "time-space" principle—that is, using time (via rhythm) as a canvas for which tones merely provide coloration. Taking the music of Stravinsky as his point of departure, Antheil produced a number of works that made particular use of rhythm and percussive effects, most notably in a series of piano works with titles like *Airplane Sonata* (1921), *Sonata Sauvage* (1922–1923), and *Death of Machines* (1923).

With *Ballet mécanique*, however, Antheil took this aesthetic to new extremes. The results, in fact, caused a sensation when the work was first unleashed upon audiences in the mid-1920s. *Ballet mécanique* began as an accompaniment to an experimental film (this was, it must be remembered, the period before synchronous soundtracks) by painter/filmmaker Fernand Léger. The ethos of the film, which is composed of abstract, repetitive, even absurd images of machinery, household objects, geometric shapes, and human faces, is aptly echoed in Antheil's score. Ultimately, however, technical limitations prevented the marriage of sound and image. Antheil's score called for the synchronization of a number of Pianolas (a type of player piano), a feat that required a level of mechanical precision impossible in precomputer days. (It wasn't until 1999, in fact, that the score—through the aid of computer-controlled pianos—was first realized according to Antheil's original vision.) Still, Antheil fashioned *Ballet mécanique* into a clangorous concert work that calls for multiple keyboards and a battery of percussion "instruments" that includes a siren, electric bells, and airplane propellers.

When the work was first performed in Paris at a private function in 1926, it created a genuine sensation. "A number of persons instantly fell over from the gigantic concussion!" Antheil proudly recounted. (He also reported audience members hanging from the chandelier and women being tossed into the air from stretched blankets, among other examples of Roaring Twenties misbehavior.) When the work was introduced to America in a 1927 Carnegie Hall premiere, it fell flat (largely through the ill-considered meddling of a zealous promoter) but caused a riotous response and cemented Antheil's reputation as the "Bad Boy of Music." Though Antheil went on to produce a sizable (albeit toned-down) body of operas, film scores, and other works, *Ballet mécanique* remains his best-known effort and a remarkable sonic artifact of its time and place. *—Michael Rodman*

Recommended:

- ○ **Fighting the Waves: Music of George Antheil** / H.K. Gruber (cond.), Ensemble Modern / 1996 / BMG 68066
- ○ **Antheil: Ballet Mécanique** / D. Spalding (cond.), Philadelphia Virtuosi CO / 2001 / Naxos 559060

ORCHESTRAL

A Jazz Symphony, for piano & jazz orchestra (1925; 1955)

George Antheil composed *A Jazz Symphony* in 1925, in anticipation of a commission from jazz bandleader Paul Whiteman. Whiteman had taken a chance on George Gershwin's *Rhapsody in Blue* in the "Experiment in Modern Music" concert held at Aeolian Hall on March 9, 1924, and his gamble paid off handsomely. Whiteman was looking to repeat his success and spread the word among composers that he was looking for a major-league work, either a concerto or a symphony, to present at a follow-up Carnegie Hall concert of December 29, 1925.

Unfortunately for Antheil, then resident in Paris, Whiteman did not take interest in *A Jazz Symphony*, possibly since it was difficult to read and ultramodern in style. Antheil instead programmed *A Jazz Symphony* for his own Carnegie Hall debut scheduled for April 10, 1927. Antheil found an ally in the form of bandleader, composer, and publisher W.C. Handy, who agreed to lead his own orchestra in the work. In the course of some 25 rehearsals held on behalf of *A Jazz Symphony*, Handy found its intricacies beyond his means and handed leadership of the concert over to Allie Ross, an associate conductor of the Harlem Symphony.

At the Carnegie Hall concert, *A Jazz Symphony* received an ovation, and critical notices describing Antheil's notorious Carnegie Hall debut that bothered to mention *A Jazz Symphony* were entirely favorable. George Gershwin was present at the concert and remarked, "I really can't compare Antheil's jazz with mine. He deals in polytonalities and dissonance and follows (the sympathies of) Stravinsky and the French." Had the 13-minute *Jazz Symphony* alone been the major work programmed for this Carnegie Hall concert, then Antheil's reputation might well have been assured in New York. But this was not to be; the main work presented was *Ballet mécanique*, which came close to precipitating an in-concert brawl at Carnegie Hall. So while *A Jazz Symphony* was a success, the concert itself was a disaster, and Antheil's *Jazz Symphony* was forgotten.

In 1954, Antheil undertook a major overhaul of *Ballet mécanique*, and the following year he similarly turned his attention to *A Jazz Symphony*. He streamlined the original Whiteman-styled orchestration down to a basic wind band with piano and removed a number of improvised solos included in the original. *A Jazz Symphony* is not set in any kind of symphonic form; rather, it is a patchwork collage of jazz-inspired rhythms and gestures. Antheil greatly reduced the number of "patches" used and eliminated several bars of repetition, much as he had in his 1954 *Ballet mécanique*. In the end, the 13-minute work was reduced by more than half to six minutes, and it was in this form that the work was finally published and, for three decades, programmed. The music starts with a kind of Afro-Cuban jazz, alternating with a dissonant dance somewhere between a "stomp" and ragtime. There are quick changes of time signatures, asymmetrical combinations of duple and triple meter, Harlem stride piano solos with tone cluster chords, and an ending that suddenly goes into a wild and crazy kind of sliding and swooping waltz with sentimental harmonies and dissonant harmonics above.The original version, which included prerecorded airplane propeller sounds, was revived for the first time under Maurice Peress with the New Palais Royale Orchestra at the 92nd Street Y Summer Jazzfest in New York in June 1986. *—Uncle Dave Lewis*

Recommended:

- ○ **Fighting the Waves: Music of George Antheil** / H.K. Gruber (cond.), Ensemble Modern / 1996 / BMG 68066

SYMPHONIC

Symphony No. 4 ("1942") (1942)

The four-movement *Symphony No. 4* was written while Antheil was a reporter for the *Los Angeles Daily News* during World War II. The mood, intent, orchestration, and even rhythmic approach are extremely reminiscent of the style of Dmitry Shostakovich. From the militaristic feeling of the Moderato to the counterpoint in the bitterly ironic Scherzo, the neo-Romantic influence of the Russian composer is strongly felt. The piece is traditionally tonal and rich with memorable melodies. On an emotional level, it is a far cry from the music of the self-proclaimed "bad boy" of modern music (the title of Antheil's autobiography) who led the avant-garde of the 1920s. Virgil Thomson heard the piece as filled "with every kind of joke, acrobatic turn, patriotic reference and glamorous monstrosity." Antheil's friend Leopold

Stokowski premiered the work on an NBC Symphony Orchestra broadcast in 1944, and it reportedly was one of the works that led to the parting of the ways between Stokowski and NBC. *—Mona DeQuis*

Recommended:

○ **Antheil: Symphonies 4 & 6** / Kuchar (cond.), National SO of Ukraine / 2000 / Naxos 559033

○ **Antheil: Symphonies 4 & 5** / H. Wolff (cond.), Frankfurt Radio SO / CPO 999706

Jacques Arcadelt

b. 1505, Liège, Belgium, **d.** 1568, Paris, France

Composer: Vocal

While the madrigal is thought of as an Italian and later an English style, it grew from Franco-Flemish polyphonic roots as much as from Italian chordal song styles such as the frottola. Arcadelt from the Netherlands, Philippe Verdelot from France, and Costanzo Festa from Italy are appropriately enough considered the three fathers of the form. Arcadelt's *Il bianco e dolce cigno* (The White, Sweet Swan) is considered by many to be the epitome of the early Italian four-part madrigal, with its rich harmonies, sophisticated details, and sensual textures. The madrigal was also viewed in Italy (much less so in England) as a way of joining text and music to enhance and illustrate the text, and like many of the Italian madrigalists, Arcadelt was particularly inspired by Petrarca's writing; almost half of his settings are to texts by Petrarca.

Very little is known about Arcadelt's early life in his homeland. In 1538 he left Liège for the musical courts of Florence, where his first book of madrigals was a great success. It was followed by his second, third, and fourth books, published in 1539, the year he moved to Rome. He wrote almost exclusively for four voices, but even after five-voice writing became dominant his madrigals still remained popular, with even his first book being reprinted over thirty times. The popularity and influence of his techniques also showed in the work of Monteverdi and Palestrina.

In 1555 he moved to France, where he served Charles, the Duke of Guise, as chapel master, and also served in the royal court. Following the French tastes he wrote chansons rather than madrigals. During this period, the two styles were fairly closely linked, as many madrigals were more or less harmonic enrichments of the top vocal line. Most of Arcadelt's chansons are chordal, with the occasional polyphonic piece, such as *Souvent amour.* He often used rhythmic changes to emphasize the structure of a chord or a critical word in the text. *—Ann Feeney*

Overview of Works (1530–1568)

Born in Liège, Jacques Arcadelt (1505–68) became one of the most important composers involved with the early development of the Italian madrigal. Much of the earlier part of his creative life was spent in Italy. Arriving in Florence in 1538, he was attached to the Papal Chapel in Rome from 1544 to 1545. Along with another Franco-Flemish musician, Philippe Verdelot, Arcadelt was instrumental in establishing the madrigal as a serious form. This effort was part of a literary movement that was a conscious reaction against such lighter forms of secular polyphonic vocal music as the frottola. The hero of this high-minded reform was Petrarch, many of whose poems were set by Arcadelt. At this stage of its development, the madrigal was an unaccompanied (a cappella) contrapuntal piece nearly always scored for four solo voices. The structure is free, the music eschewing repetition in favor of maintaining the natural flow of the text until the final lines are worked into a concluding epigrammatic structure. Virtually all Arcadelt's madrigals, over 200 published in five books between 1538 and 1544, conform to such a design. The principal topic of the madrigals is love—idealized and usually unrequited. Praise and longing for the unattainable loved one sometimes gives way to recrimination. Painting of particularly potent words is common, as is the use of metaphor. The latter is employed by Arcadelt in his most famous madrigal *Il bianco e dolce cigno* (The White, Sweet Swan), a piece whose widespread popularity ensured its appearance in many collections during the sixteenth century and beyond. Unlike the contemporary French chanson, erotic imagery is relatively rare in Arcadelt's madrigals, as are religious topics.

In 1555, Arcadelt returned north, settling in Paris. It is during this period that the chanson starts to play an increasingly important role in his output. While still generally maintaining the four-part texture of the madrigal, the chanson was a lighter form, less concerned with contrapuntal writing and often embracing earthier topics. Those by Arcadelt, however, are more refined than many, being composed with the same elegance and melodic grace that characterize his madrigals. He composed some 120 chansons, many of them appearing in the collections of Le Roy & Ballard, the leading Parisian publishers. Sacred music forms a smaller but not insignificant part of Arcadelt's output. A book of four-part motets was published in Venice in 1545, and a collection of four- and five-part masses appeared in Paris in 1557. *—Brian Robins*

Recommended:

○ **French Chansons** / Scholars of London / 1994 / Early Music 550880

L'Archibudelli

Ensemble

The name of this internationally renowned group means bow and gut strings. In its almost decade-long existence, its membership has continually changed from two to eight string performers with several constant players: Vera Beths, Jürgen Kussmaul, and Anner Bylsma. This continuous regrouping allows the musicians to present a wide repetoire of pieces and also fits their desire to enjoy performing with a variety of musician friends, rather than attempting to maintain a fixed form as a string quartet or quintet. The group emphasizes the authentic presentation of works of the eighteenth, nineteenth, and twentieth centuries, and prefers to play on gut strings in order to realize the older timbres in performance. *—"Blue Gene" Tyranny*

Recommended:

○ **Brahms: String Sextets** / Archibudelli / 1996 / Sony 68252

○ **Mozart: Divertimenti K334 & 247** / Archibudelli / 1991 / Sony 46494

○ **Mendelssohn & Gade: Octets for Strings** / Archibudelli / 1992 / Sony 48307

○ **Haydn: The Last 3 String Quartets** / Archibudelli / 1997 / Sony 62731

○ **Mendelssohn: String Quintets** / Archibudelli / 2000 / Sony 60766

Arditti Quartet

f. 1974, London, England

Ensemble

Founded by violinist Irvine Arditti in 1974 while he was a student at the Royal Academy of Music in London, the Arditti Quartet has established itself as one of the world's foremost chamber ensembles dedicated to contemporary music. Literally hundreds of new works have been written for the quartet, and the group has made it a priority to work closely with the composers it commissions. Among the very long list of composers who have written for the quartet are: Harrison Birtwistle, John Cage, Elliott Carter, Brian Ferneyhough, Sofia Gubaidulina, Mauricio Kagel, György Ligeti, Conlon Nancarrow, Wolfgang Rihm, Karlheinz Stockhausen, and Iannis Xenakis. In addition, the Arditti Quartet has performed and recorded most of the major string quartet repertoire of the twentieth century.

With an interest in new music, the young violinist Irvine Arditti began working with like-minded colleagues. One of those was the talented cellist Rohan de Saram, the other pillar of the quartet, who joined in 1979, remaining through occasional personnel changes in the second violin and viola positions. Second violinist Graeme Jennings began with the group in 1994, and violist Dov Scheindlin joined in 1997. As the quartet became established, they were invited to perform at contemporary music festivals throughout the world. The Arditti Quartet has contributed greatly to the revitalization of the string quartet as a relevant musical genre to new audiences and musicians. The ensemble was awarded the 1999 Ernst von Siemens Music Prize for lifetime achievement, one of the most prestigious prizes in Europe. The group has been honored with many other awards, particularly for its recordings.

The Arditti Quartet has released over 100 recordings. The major collection is found on the French label, Auvidis Montaigne, which now numbers nearly 40 discs. These include important historical works from composers such as those of the Second Viennese School (Schoenberg, Berg, Webern), the collected works of prominent composers such as Carter, Pascal Dusapin, Ferneyhough, Toshio Hosokawa, Kagel, and Xenakis, and sets of pieces from different countries and regions, including Germany, Italy, Scandinavia, and the U.S.

In 1982, the members of the quartet were signed on as tutors at the prestigious Darmstadt Summer Course for New Music, returning for each bi-annual session until 1996. Master classes, workshops, and a busy touring and recording schedule continue to be the primary components of the quartet's activities.

While the quartet has remained extremely active for over 25 years, the individual members continue to pursue other musical activities. Irvine Arditti and Rohan de Saram, in particular, have had a number of solo works written for them by some of the composers who have written for the group. The close relation established between the quartet and particular composers has led to a proliferation of different chamber combinations. Carter and Xenakis, for example, have written piano quintets, and Ferneyhough's Fourth String Quartet includes a part for soprano. Electronics have also been incorporated into compositions by Roger Reynolds and Gerard Pape. It is safe to say that through all of its activities and steadfast dedication to the music of our time, the Arditti String Quartet has established itself as a vital force in the world of contemporary chamber music. *—Jim Harley*

Recommended:

○ **Kurtág, Lutosławski & Gubaidulina: Works for String Quartet** / Arditti SQ / 2001 / Naïve 782147

○ **Lachenmann: Reigen seliger Geister; Tanzsuite mit Deutschlandlied** / Henzold (cond.), Arditti String Quartet, Berlin German SO / 2000 / Montaigne 782130

○ **Berio: The String Quartets** / Arditti SQ / Montaigne 782155

○ **Rihm: String Quartets 1, 8 & 5** / Arditti SQ / 2000 / Montaigne 782134

○ **Kagel: Pan; String Quartets 1–3** / Arditti SQ / 2000 / Montaigne 782129

○ **Henze: Streichquartetten 1–5** / Arditti SQ / 1986 / Wergo 60114

Irvine Arditti

b. Feb. 8, 1953, London, England

Violinist

Irvine Arditti is the first violinist and leader of the Arditti Quartet, an ensemble that he co-founded as a student of the Royal Academy of Music in London in 1974. From 1978 to 1980, Arditti served as co-concertmaster for the London Symphony Orchestra, a position he voluntarily left in order to devote more time to the quartet. This turned out to be the right choice, as since then the Arditti String Quartet has become an institution in the realm of contemporary chamber music. The list of new works by contemporary composers commissioned over the years by the Arditti Quartet is of staggering size and comprehension, but among the many figures who have written specifically for the Arditti Quartet are John Cage, Philip Glass, Helmut Lachenmann, Sofiya Gubaidulina, and Wolfgang Rihm. From 1982 to 1996 the Arditti Quartet gave annual master classes at the Darmstadt Summer Courses for New Music.

Irvine Arditti is also widely recognized as a leading soloist and interpreter of contemporary concerto literature for the violin. One of his most famous recordings is for Mode Records containing John Cage's *Freeman Etudes*, a solo violin work Arditti also premiered. Arditti has also given first performances of concertos by composers Luciano Berio, Brian Ferneyhough, and Iannis Xenakis. Both the Arditti Quartet and its leader have recorded for a wide variety of labels, but most frequently for Disques Montaigne, which was ultimately merged with Naïve Classical. The Arditti Quartet actively performs entire quartet cycles, including those of Elliott Carter, Hans Werner Henze, and Arnold Schoenberg. The group has won numerous recording prizes, including the Deutsche Schallplatten and the Gramophone Awards, both landing in the winner's circle multiple times in these honors. *—Uncle Dave Lewis*

Recommended:

○ **Cage: Freeman Etudes Books 1 & 2** / Arditti / 1993 / Mode 32

○ **Recital For Violin** / Arditti / 1990 / Montaigne 789003

○ **Berio, Xenakis, Mirafornes** / Nott (cond.), Arditti, Moscow PO / 1995 / Bis 772

Anton Arensky

b. Jul. 12, 1861, Novgorod, Russia, **d.** Feb. 25, 1906, Terioki, Russia

Composer: Chamber Music, Orchestral

Little known today, Anton Arensky was one of the brightest stars of the late nineteenth century Russian music scene. Arensky was born in 1861 to a pair of devoted amateur musicians under whose guidance he began his training. After private studies (piano and composition) with Zikke in St. Petersburg, Arensky entered that city's conservatory in 1879, taking lessons from Rimsky-Korsakov. He scored consistently high marks with conservatory faculty during his three years as a student, eventually graduating with a gold medal; upon the completion of his studies in 1882 Arensky became one of the youngest professors ever hired by the Moscow Conservatory.

Arensky's years at Moscow were fruitful; between 1882 and his resignation from the Conservatory's faculty in 1895 he completed most of his larger works (including the early *Piano Concerto* of 1882 and both Symphonies: B minor 1883; A major 1889). In 1891 his first opera, *Son na Volge* (A Dream on the Volga)—which he had worked on intermittently since his student days—was successfully premiered in Moscow. His next operatic endeavor, however, fared rather worse than the first; *Rafael* was an immediate failure at its 1894 premiere.

Asked to replace Balakirev as director of the imperial chapel in St. Petersburg, Arensky returned to his home city in 1895; save for occasional national and international tours, he remained there for the rest of his life. By the mid-1890s Arensky's somewhat diminished stature as a composer was replaced by an increased public awareness of his gifts at the keyboard and on the podium. Having served as director of the Russian Choral Society (1888 to 1895) during his Moscow days, Arensky was no stranger to the baton, and in 1901 he resigned his position at the imperial chapel to pursue a fuller schedule of conducting and performing appearances. Death came prematurely in 1905 when Arensky, after decades of hard living and overindulgence, succumbed to tuberculosis.

Save for the well-known *Variations on a Theme of Tchaikovsky* for string orchestra, little of Arensky's substantial output has maintained a place on contemporary concert programs. He was essentially a miniaturist, and his finest music is to be found in the shorter works for solo piano and his melodious songs (which seem to have influenced Rachmaninov's conception of Russian song). Arensky's style, especially in such early works as the *Piano Concerto* and *First Symphony*, is too inconsistent to bear witness to a strong musical personality, and instead presents as a pastiche of stylistic traits borrowed from a variety of influences, such as Chopin and Tchaikovsky (though rarely Arensky's own teacher Rimsky-Korsakov). However, his influence as a teacher—to such future luminaries as Rachmaninov and Scriabin—has earned him a place of distinction in the history of Russian music. *—Blair Johnston*

Overview of Works (1882–1905)

Although he studied with Rimsky-Korsakov, Arensky did not become a nationalist composer. His cosmopolitan (that is, looking to Europe more than Russia) works more resembled those of Tchaikovsky. Arensky had a surer sense of structure and compositional technique than Tchaikovsky, but only a middling gift for melody, so his music is basically appealing, but rather generic. It's obviously late Romantic Russian, but it lacks a unique personality. Arensky was more likely to use Russian nationalist material in his early compositions, such as the opera *A Dream on the Volga* (1888), when he was still under the influence of Rimsky-Korsakov. He would later pick up a folk tune now and then for very specific use, such as in his 1899 *Fantasia on a Russian Folk Song for piano and orchestra.* Short, abstract pieces dominate his instrumental catalog, particularly large series of piano etudes, preludes, and caprices. He also wrote a fair number of character pieces for keyboard, the sort of thing popular at the time among amateur pianists.

More substantial works in this vein are his four suites for two pianos; these are more technically challenging and exuberant, but quite different from one another. The first suite is a standard trio of salon-like pieces, including a waltz that has become one of the composer's few enduring items; the second is a series of character sketches; the third is a hefty set of variations; and the fourth applies a more advanced, chromatic style to salon forms. Arensky was also a prolific writer of songs, many of which have become standard fare for Russian singers, but are seldom performed by others.

His chamber works are lyrical, varied, and emotionally direct, but again don't quite set Arensky apart from other secondary Russian composers of the period. His two substantial piano trios, particularly the first, hover just outside the standard repertory. His other chamber works, including two string quartets and a Schumann-esque piano quintet, tend to emphasize lyricism over drama. His second quartet, which substitutes a second cello for second violin, is the source of the *Variations on a Theme by Tchaikovsky*, more often heard transcribed for string orchestra.

Arensky's orchestral output includes a single ballet, the pseudo-Oriental *Egyptian Nights*; a rather Chopin-esque piano concerto; and two melodic but undistinctive symphonies in the Taneyev mold. For voice and orchestra, there exist three operas (now banished to the encyclopedias) and a colorful, delicate setting for chorus and orchestra of Pushkin's *The Fountain of Bakhchisarai.* *—James Reel*

Recommended:

○ **Arensky: Piano Music** / Coombs / 1998 / Hyperion 67066

○ **Arensky: Symphony 1** / Polyansky (cond.), Russian State SO / 2003 / Chandos 10086

CHAMBER MUSIC

Piano Trio No. 1 in D minor, Op. 32 (1894)

Arensky's *Piano Trio, Op. 32* was composed in memory of cellist Karl Davidov, friend of both the composer and Tchaikovsky, as well as director of the St. Petersburg Conservatory during Arensky's studies. The cello plays a prominent role in the trio, at times matching or surpassing the violin in importance. In fact, many sections of the piece sound like a piano and cello duet, perhaps honoring not just Davidov but also Arensky's cellist father. The piece opens with a soaring, lyrical movement which interrupts the warm, flowing sections with sudden, passionate outbursts containing playful traces of Mendelssohnian charm. As a whole, the first movement exudes remarkable power and energy. Even the lyrical passages are accompanied by a pulsating accompanying figure in the piano, resulting in a feeling of constant motion and energy. The second movement is a light-hearted, ear-tickling scherzo which entices the listener to join in the dance. This light-hearted movement is followed by a tender, reflective "Elegia," with the muted cello introducing the melancholy theme. Even the passages which evoke a happier mood seem to be only memories. The dreamlike third movement is abruptly answered by the more forceful, dramatic opening of the finale, which serves to pull together fragments from the preceding movement in a summarizing final paragraph. *—Kristen Grimshaw*

Recommended:

○ **Arensky: Piano Trios 1 & 2** / Borodin Trio / 1997 / Chandos 7048

○ **Tchaikovsky, Arensky: Piano Trios** / Bronfman, C.L. Lin, G. Hoffman / 1994 / Sony 53269

ORCHESTRAL

Variations on a Theme of Tchaikovsky, Op. 35a (1894)

Although composer Anton Arensky studied under Rimsky-Korsakov, his heartfelt and deeply lyrical music owes more to Tchaikovsky. In the slow movement of his *String Quartet No. 2*, Op. 35, from 1894, Arensky wrote a tribute to the recently deceased Tchaikovsky in a set of variations based on a theme taken from

Tchaikovsky's children's song *A Legend*, Op. 54/5. But the slow movement proved so popular at the string quartet's premiere that Arensky transcribed it later that same year for string orchestra as his *Variations on a Theme of Tchaikovsky*, Op. 35a, and it has been his most popular piece ever since. The work is, like all of Arensky's music, essentially lyrical. After a statement of the theme, Moderato, the piece moves through seven variations and a coda that alternate between fast and slow music: Variation I, Un poco più mosso; Variation I, Allegro non troppo; Variation III, Andantino tranquillo; Variation IV, Vivace; Variation V, Andante; Variation VI, Allegro con spirito; Variation VII, Andante con moto; and a Moderato coda. While not the deepest work of the Russian Silver Age, Arensky's *Tchaikovsky Variations* offer well-composed and affecting music. —*James Leonard*

Recommended:

○ **Tchaikovsky: Symphonies 1–3; Arensky: Variations** / Dorati (cond.), London SO / 1997 / Mercury 434391

○ **A Russian Mosaic** / Rachlevsky (cond.), Kremlin CO / 2001 / Claves 509909

Dominick Argento

b. Oct. 27, 1927, York, PA

Composer: Opera, Vocal, Choral

American composer Dominick Argento is known for music for the voice: opera, choral music, art song. Long associated with the University of Minnesota, he has attracted commissions from singers and ensembles from all over the U.S. and Europe. After serving in World War II, Argento studied composition with Nicolas Nabokov at the Peabody Conservatory and with Baltimore composer Hugo Weisgall. At Peabody, he finished undergraduate studies in 1951 and took a Master of Music degree in 1954, studying, with Henry Cowell among others. Argento also studied in Florence on three Fulbright fellowships, working with Dallapiccola, who influenced his use of 12-tone techniques. He had a lifelong affection for the city and wrote much of his music there. Argento completed a Ph.D. at the Eastman School of Music under Howard Hanson and Alan Hovhaness in 1957. The two strands of Argento's education, stressing American extensions of Romanticism and postwar European formalism, would mix in his mature compositions.

Argento's early works include the one-act operas *Sicilian Limes* (1954, based on a play by the Italian absurdist writer Pirandello) and *The Boor* (1957, after Chekhov's *The Bear*). In the 1950s Argento served as music director of Baltimore's Hilltop Opera; there he met stage director John Olon-Scrymgeour, who became Argento's librettist for these and many later works. Over his entire career Argento showed a flair for drawing on diverse text sources and constructing a unique musical world for each new work while maintaining a distinct musical personality. Argento was hired as professor of theory and composition at Minnesota in 1958.

After settling in the upper Midwest, Argento gained commissions from the top ensembles and organizations in the region. Argento presented an unusually accessible version of the reigning serialist orthodoxy of the day, introducing tonal centers into the flow of the music, and his works began to gain attention beyond Minnesota. The operas *Christopher Sly* (1963, based on Shakespeare's *The Taming of the Shrew*), *The Masque of Angels* (1964, on an original libretto), and *The Shoemaker's Holiday* (1967, after a play by Shakespeare's contemporary Dekker), all moved from Minnesota to New York stages. The Saint Paul Chamber Orchestra commissioned the suite *Royal Invitation* (1964), and the Civic Orchestra of Minneapolis commissioned *Variations for Orchestra (The Mask of Night)* (1965). Argento's close association with Sir Tyrone Guthrie and Douglas Campbell, directors of the Minnesota Theatre Company, led to commissions for incidental music for several Guthrie productions. Argento and Olon-Scrymgeour also created the Center Opera Company (now Minnesota Opera), which opened with *The Masque of Angels*.

The eclectic opera *Postcard from Morocco* received national attention in 1971, and four years later Argento received the Pulitzer Prize for Music for his song cycle *From the Diary of Virginia Woolf*. He was elected to the American Academy of Arts and Letters in 1979. As he received these honors, Argento launched his first full-length opera, the critically acclaimed *The Voyage of Edgar Allan Poe*. Its intense, freely atonal vocal language aptly portrays the end of the desperate poet's life. In 1979 the New York City Opera premiered *Miss Havisham's Fire*, with soprano Rita Shane in the title role. The epilogue of this opera became the monodrama *Miss Havisham's Wedding* (1981). He then wrote his own librettos for the highly theatrical *Casanova's Homecoming* (1983), an opera buffa based on Casanova's memoirs, and *The Aspern Papers* (1988, after Henry James), an opera that mixes traits of bel canto with 12-tone techniques. Argento has also examined fame and the immigrant experience in *The Dream of Valentino* (1984), set in the early days of Hollywood.

The 1970s and 1980s saw the composer working increasingly often in the song cycle form. Among his major song cycles are *To Be Sung Upon the Water* (1973), *I Hate and I Love* (1982), and *The Andree Expedition* (1983). The song cycle *A Few Words About Chekhov*, was given its premiere in 1996 by Frederica von Stade, Håkan Hagegård, and accompanist Martin Katz at the Ordway Theater in St. Paul. At the turn of the century he wrote his first piece for young voices, *Orpheus*, which also marked the first time he composed on a computer. In 1997 Argento was honored with the title of Composer Laureate to the Minnesota Orchestra, a lifetime appointment. His association with Minnesota's Dale Warland Singers culminated in the release of *Walden Pond*, a CD featuring three of Argento's choral works that was nominated for a Grammy award in 2003. —*AMG*

Overview of Works

Among twentieth century American composers associated with opera—Menotti, Moore, Barber, Bolcom, Glass—Dominick Argento must be ranked among the most important. But his songs, choral works, instrumental, and orchestral works have also left their mark. Argento generally employs a post-Romantic expressive language—replete with lush strings and rich, powerful brass-writing—often using elements of jazz and even serial techniques, all to yield a quite approachable style. His first attempt at opera came in 1954 with *Sicilian Limes*, which he withdrew. In 1955, he completed *Songs About Spring* (texts by e.e. cummings), which he began in 1950. These and the other early operas—*The Boor* (1957), *Colonel Jonathan the Saint* (1958–61), *Christopher Sly* (1962–63), *The Masque of Angels* (1964), and *The Shoemaker's Holiday* (1967)—divulged skill, but it was not until *Postcard From Morocco* (1971) that Argento scored a major success. This one-act opera exhibits the composer's more eclectic side in its music, as well as his sense for drama and contrast. *The Voyage of Edgar Allan Poe* (1975–76) and *Miss Havisham's Fire* (1977–78) were further successes, the former yielding a quite effective concert suite entitled *Le tombeau d'Edgar Poe*, for tenor and orchestra. It is a beautiful, atmospheric work in four connected sections that is, in its own realm, as compelling as the opera in capturing the innocence, twistedness, and bizarre fantasy world of the famous American poet/writer. *Casanova's Homecoming* (1980–84) and *The Aspern Papers* (1988) were also successful, as was his opera *The Dream of Valentino* (1993), which again divulges the composer's versatility in presenting music of different styles. Argento extracted a suite from this opera, *Valentino Dances* (1994), using three original tangos. The work, employing a large percussion section and accordion, effectively conveys the glamorous character of the silent film era of 1920s Hollywood. Argento's orchestral compositions have generally been offshoots from his operas, but there have been several successful independent works in the genre too. His *A Ring of Time* (1972–73) is a four-movement effort depicting the four seasons and carrying the subtitle "Preludes and Pageants for Orchestra and Bells." It is an apt description of this powerful, atmospheric composition that features masterful orchestration and bell-rich sonorities. In the realm of song, his Pulitzer Prize–winning cycle *From the Diary of Virginia Woolf* represents Argento's grandest achievement, portraying the growing psychological torment in the life of the British writer, who committed suicide in 1941. Among his choral works, Argento's beautiful and profound *Te Deum* is considered his most important. —*Robert Cummings*

Recommended:

○ **Valentino Dances: Music of Argento** / Oue (cond.), Schimmel, Shelton, Minnesota O / 2000 / Reference 91

○ **Casa Guidi: Frederica von Stade Sings Argento** / Oue (cond.), Von Stade, Hara, Minnesota O / 2002 / Reference 100

○ **Argento: Walden Pond** / Warland (cond.), Dale Warland Singers, Lark Quartet / 2003 / Gothic 49217

OPERA

Postcard from Morocco (1971)

Dominick Argento's one-act chamber opera *Postcard from Morocco* (1971) is a distinctive combination of surrealist fancy and psychological drama, abstraction and reflection. It shows Argento at his most adventurous, and remains one of the most challenging works in the composer's output. The seventh of Argento's 14 operas, it was the first since *The Boor* (1957) to achieve much notoriety, and it marked the beginning of a decade-long string of stage works that would culminate with the highly successful *Miss Havisham's Fire* (1979). Like all of Argento's operas, *Postcard* is stylistically unique, tailored harmonically and structurally to the specific needs of its libretto. In this case, eclecticism is the order of the day, including everything from Wagnerian quotations and dance music to astringent modernism. The use of almost every available classification of singer—seven in all, from high coloratura soprano to low bass, each of which requires a different vocal treatment—only emphasizes that variety. But there is still a discernible compositional voice that those familiar with Argento's music will recognize as his. *Postcard* was premiered at the Cedar Village Theater in Minneapolis on October 14, 1971, conducted by Philip Brunelle, and directed by the librettist, John Donahue.

Donahue's inventive libretto is focused on the fears and protective social mechanisms that alienate people from each other. He created a group of travelers in a train station (presumably in Morocco), each of which carries something of symbolic importance in his or her luggage. Their relative eagerness or reluctance to share what they carry, as well as their curiosity about each other's secrets, forms the plot, such as it is. In the kind of self-expository format that can easily fall flat, but which here fuels a startlingly personal drama, each traveler sings about his or her baggage, profession, or personal fixation. These metaphorical items—shoes, cake boxes, musical instruments—become the defining characteristics of their owners; yet, the way in which each person sings about his or her own item fleshes out a surprisingly complex and human world of feeling and experience. In the end, there is no real interaction between the characters, and listeners who require conflict development and resolution will not find it here. Rather, the successive exposure to the characters' worlds and memories forms the substance of the drama.

The lyric soprano's aria, which begins: "I keep my lover in a box," is a particularly striking episode. The music is hauntingly lyrical, and the grotesque image quickly gives way to a sense of deep longing and regret. It bears a resemblance to the final song of Argento's Pulitzer Prize-winning song cycle, *From the Diary of Virgina Woolf.* Equally affecting is the "Puppets" aria, sung by the bass. Melodically jagged and unforgiving, and creepily detailed in its depiction of the puppet-master's complete control over each and every detail of his creations, it challenges listeners' notions of free will and independence. *—AMG*

Synopsis:

The time and place are indistinct; perhaps it is 1914, a railway station in Morocco. Passengers without names populate the lounge, each with closely guarded baggage. According to librettist John Donahue, "We see each one trying hard to protect whatever small part of himself he has in his suitcase, the symbol of his secret or lack of secret, his dream or lack of dream. It is through the actions of these waiting creatures that we see our own fears and anxieties along with the fierce way in which man protects himself from the stranger, his probing wish for company and comfort. The ultimate defense for this group is to discover a waiting creature (like Mr. Owen) vulnerable enough to reveal the real contents of his suitcase."

The action opens with a babble of passengers identified only by their belongings: a lady with a cake box, a man with a paint box (eventually revealed to be Mr. Owen), a man with a cornet case, a lady with a hatbox, a man with old luggage, a man with shoe samples, a lady with a hand mirror. At the side of the room, a puppet show is underway; some of the puppets are cardboard, but others seem human.

The Mirror Lady explains that she never travels without a mirror, which helps her see around things, spy on lovers, and frighten old men with their own reflections. Meanwhile, two puppets cavort at building a ship, descending into a fight. Next a foreign singer performs in a made-up language while the passengers continue to chatter. The Old-Luggage Man explains to onlookers that he always carries old suitcases lest they be stolen, and never travels with anything important to him; then he inadvertently suggests that he may have stolen this baggage from someone else.

The Cornet Man sings of the instrument in his case, admitting that he's not a professional, and refusing to show anyone his cornet. The Hat Lady reluctantly reveals to interlocutors that she makes hats, but shows nothing. The shoe man praises his merchandise, but refuses to display it without an appointment.

Two operetta singers perform a Viennese number while the passengers continue to chat. The Cake Lady claims that she keeps her lover in her box, but disputes Mr. Owen's claim that he once saw and sketched the two of them. The two drift into an odd love duet, after which Mr. Owen confesses that in his youth he imagined seeing a magical ship sailing through the forest, but he was unable to board it. The passengers quiz Mr. Owen on the contents of his box and press him to paint their group portrait; he refuses, the passengers jostle him and he drops his box, which opens to reveal—emptiness. After a moment, the passengers resume their individual arias, then shift their attention to the violent puppet show. They board a train, leaving Mr. Owen behind on the puppet stage. The puppet ship materializes; Mr. Owen becomes its captain and he and a puppet sail into the distance. *—James Reel*

Recommended:

○ **Argento: Postcard From Morocco** / Brunelle (cond.), Hardy, Bailey, Brandt, Busse, Minnesota Opera / 1992 / CRI 614

VOCAL

From the Diary of Virginia Woolf (1974)

As the title implies, *From the Diary of Virginia Woolf* is a cycle of eight songs based on excerpts from the diary of the writer Virginia Woolf. It was written for the great English mezzo-soprano Janet Baker, and it earned Argento the Pulitzer Prize for composition in 1975. The choice of a prose, rather than poetic, source for a text is a common theme for Argento, who did the same thing in his cycles *Letters from Composers, The Andrée Expedition,* and *Casa Guidi.* In each case, he captures the cadence and flow of these more free-form writings without sacrificing musical structure or melodic interest. The composer's original intention was to use excerpts from Woolf's novel *The Waves* as the basis for his cycle. But in reading her newly published diaries he discovered a source much richer in musical and expressive possibilities. The highly confessional diary texts illuminate Woolf's inner world in a more immediate way than do her literary works, but there is no attempt on Argento's part to depict the author's character or personality—her voice—in his music. Rather, he sets each song based solely on the emotional and declamatory content of the text itself. Because of the fluid vocal writing—flowing, sinuous, and never really tuneful—Argento relies on the piano to dictate structure and mood. The result is a set of surprisingly tight-knit songs that feel more concise than they are, and which amplify Woolf's sentiments without ever overshadowing her words. Argento's distinctive blend of tonal harmony and expressive dissonance runs through *From the Diary,* as does his talent for walking the difficult line between speech-like declamation and more lyrical vocal writing. The result is one of the finest song cycles yet written by an American composer. *—AMG*

Recommended:

○ **Argento: From The Diary of Virginia Woolf / Benson: Songs For The End Of The World** / Dupuy, Welcher (cond.), Garvey, Bacon, Howard, Russell, Sills / 1989 / Gasparo 273

○ **Dominick Argento: From the Diary of Virginia Woolf** / Baker, Isepp / 1997 / D'Note 1019

CHORAL

Peter Quince at the Clavier, for chorus & piano (1979)

Dominick Argento's 1979 work *Peter Quince at the Clavier* might at first glance seem a very peculiar thing—Argento describes it as a "Sonatina for Mixed Chorus and Piano Concertante"—but one realizes after getting to know the Wallace Stevens poem of the same name that that peculiar description is in fact perfectly appropriate for the subject. The poem takes music itself as its subject (woven in and around a tale of a specific human soul), takes a "four-movement shape," and specifically mentions a piano. Argento's decision to fashion his 20-minute setting of this verse as a four-movement sonatina was an insightful, but also seemingly inevitable one.

The first movement is marked *Poco maestoso ma piacevole* (there are some later fluctuations of tempo) and is begun by the piano alone. The piano inspires the choir, when it comes in a few bars later, to draw a parallel between the fingers making music on the piano and the sounds of the piano making music in the soul. Through most of the movement the piano continues with the firm dotted rhythms of the opening, while the choir maintains a smooth melodic character.

Cascading chromatic arpeggios from the piano begin the second movement, painting in music the green, clear water of the text. But the end of the movement is anything but lush, and certainly not gentle, as the singers, with the percussive help of the pianist, imitate the sounds of a crashing cymbal and raucous horns. The third movement is a scherzo with a running tambourine-like background, while the Adagio assai final movement ends in a C major "sacrament of praise."

Argento's *Peter Quince at the Clavier* was commissioned by The Institute for the Arts and Humanistic Studies for the Pennsylvania State University Choirs, in commemoration of the tercentenary of the founding of Pennsylvania by William Penn. *—Blair Johnston*

Recommended:

○ **Argento: An American Romantic** / Brunelle (cond.), O'Riley, Plymouth Music Series Orchestra / 1998 / Collins 15232

Martha Argerich

b. Jun. 5, 1941, Buenos Aires, Argentina

Pianist

Born in Buenos Aires, Martha Argerich was enrolled for piano study at the age of five by her mother, with piano teacher Vincenzo Scaramuzza. He stressed lyricism and feeling: "When the sound is empty," he said to her, "it sounds like a pair of pants walking into the room with nothing inside them." She made her debut playing a Mozart concerto when she was eight, mentally preparing herself for the concert by making herself believe that, "if I missed a single note, I would explode." She did not miss a single note. In 1955 her family moved to Europe, where she studied in Switzerland with Madeleine Lipatti, then with Nikita Magaloff and eventually with Friedrich Gulda, an early idol.

In 1957, at the age of 16, she won the Geneva International Competition and the Ferruccio Busoni International Competition within three weeks. At the Bolzano Competition she met Arturo Benedetti Michelangeli. When she was about 20 and in the throes of an artistic crisis, she sought him out for lessons regarding her approach to music.

In 1965 she became the first pianist from the Western Hemisphere to win first prize at the Chopin Competition in Warsaw, and the following year, she made her U.S. debut in Lincoln Center's Great Performers Series. Her long association with the Deutsche Grammophon label began in 1967.

Although she plays Haydn, Mozart, Beethoven, and Schumann, her repertoire centers on composers such as Rachmaninov, Ravel, and Prokofiev, and more modern composers, including Lutosławski and Messiaen. After the first few years of her career she gave up playing solo recitals, preferring collaborative musical work. Only her first two albums were solo.

She first publicly played chamber music when she was 17, accompanying violinist Joseph Szigeti. Especially known as a chamber-music player and as a graceful musical collaborator, she has performed with pianists Stephen Kovacevich, Nicolas Economou, Nelson Freire, and Alexandre Rabinovich, violinist Gidon Kremer, and cellist Mischa Maisky.

Among her standout recordings are those of Messiaen's *Visions de l'Amen*, the Piano Concerto No. 1 of Tchaikovsky, and the third concertos of Prokofiev and Rachmaninov. The Deutsche Grammophon coupling of the Tchaikovsky and Prokofiev, conducted by her then-husband, Charles Dutoit, is considered among the great classics of recorded piano concerto repertory. *—Joseph Stevenson*

Recommended:

- ○ **Martha Argerich: Live From The Concertgebouw** / Argerich / 2000 / Angel 57101
- ○ **Debut Recital** / Argerich / DG 447430
- ○ **Beethoven: Violin Sonatas 9 & 10** / Argerich, Kremer (violin) / 1995 / DG 447054
- ○ **Chopin: Piano Concertos 1 & 2** / Dutoit (cond.), Argerich, Montreal SO / 1999 / EMI 56798
- ○ **Bartok: Concerto 3; Prokofiev: Concertos 1 & 3** / Dutoit (cond.), Argerich, Montreal SO / 1998 / EMI 56654
- ○ **Rachmaninov: Concerto 3; Tchaikovsky: Concerto 1** / Chailly (cond.), Kondrashin (cond.), Argerich, Berlin RSO, Bavarian RSO / 1995 / Philips 446673

Thomas Arne

b. Mar. 12, 1710, London, England, **d.** Mar. 5, 1778, London, England

Composer: Vocal, Opera

Thomas Arne was born in London to an upholsterer. He attended Eton College to study law, but also undertook violin with Michael Festing against the objections of his father. This disobedience was eventually uncovered, but Arne's father eventually withdrew his opposition and allowed his son to pursue a musical career. Arne got started by providing singing lessons to his brother Richard and sister Susannah; the three of them would present Arne's first masque, *Rosamond*, at Lincoln's Inn Fields in 1733 (the sister, under her married name of Mrs. Susannah Cibber, would become the most admired dramatic actress of her age).

Arne married singer Cecelia Young in 1736. Establishing himself as house composer at Drury Lane, in 1737 Arne produced *Comus*, a masque which introduced, in Dr. Burney's words, "an era in English Music." This was followed by the masque *Alfred* in 1740, including *"Rule, Britannia!"*—destined to become one of England's most popular patriotic songs. In 1745, Arne unveiled his arrangement of the English tune "God Save our Noble King" at Drury Lane. As *"God Save the King,"* Arne's setting would be adopted as the national anthem of Britain. 1745 also witnessed the opening of the pleasure gardens of Vauxhall, and Arne was a major contributor of popular songs performed there for nearly two decades.

Owing to a salary dispute with impresario David Garrick, Cibber defected to Covent Garden in 1750, and Arne likewise followed. This led to a bitter competitive battle between the two theaters. In 1755, Cibber would return to Drury Lane, but Arne was out of favor with Garrick, and left for Dublin with his wife and a student, Miss Charlotte Brent. Arne became involved romantically with Brent, and returned to London, leaving his wife behind in Dublin. The difficulty with Garrick still proving an obstacle, Arne took up residence at Covent Garden. There in 1759–62, Arne produced four works that would set stylistic standards in English theater for generations; first, a revamping of Gay's *The Beggar's Opera*, and in 1760 *Thomas and Sally*, the first English comic opera based on an Italian model. *Artaxerxes*, a grand opera and Arne's crowning artistic achievement, followed in 1762, as did his greatest commercial success, *Love in A Village*, which introduced pasticcio opera to England.

In 1766, Susannah Cibber died, and Charlotte Brent departed to marry the violinist Thomas Pinto. A revival of *Artaxerxes* given at Drury Lane in 1768 failed against a competing production at Covent Garden starring Mrs. Pinto. Though mortally wounded in a professional sense, Arne would continue to write and produce a few more stage works, including his lost valedictory effort *Caractacus* (1776). Arne's fortunes foundered, and by 1770, his wife was petitioning for support. In October 1777, after two decades of separation, Arne and Cecilia were reconciled, but by that time, his health was failing, and he died the following March at age 67.

Outside of *Thomas and Sally*, the patriotic tunes and some songs, Arne's music went into total eclipse for two centuries, and much of it burned in the Drury Lane fire of 1809. Of Arne's stage works, which numbered over a hundred, only fourteen survive. In surviving songs and cantatas, Arne achieves an exquisitely light transparency of texture, and often his orchestration is striking in its boldness and color. His vocal writing is difficult but not showy; it flows naturally, and the frame in which it resides is ordered and direct. He also left some odes, the oratorio *Judith*, sacred music, four symphonies, several overtures, six keyboard concerti, chamber music, and many fine songs, particularly those on texts of Shakespeare. *—Uncle Dave Lewis*

Overview of Works (1733–1777)

For most in the classical music community (and for many even beyond), Thomas Arne is known for one work, *"Rule, Britannia!,"* with its text by James Thomson and its perhaps premature assertion that "Britons never will be slaves." But the commonly known *"Rule, Britannia!"* melody is only a refrain of an ensemble song with six verses, and the song itself is the finale of a larger work, a masque entitled *Alfred* commissioned by Frederick, Prince of Wales and first performed at his country estate in 1740. *"Rule, Britannia!"* was a hit from the start, and Arne, who knew a valuable property when he saw one, revised *Alfred* twice to take advantage of it. But an English theatergoer of the middle eighteenth century would have known much more of Arne than just one catchy song. Arne's career, in an era of rapid change, lasted more than 40 years, from the early 1730s until his death in 1778.

One reason Arne's works have fallen into obscurity is that many of them are written in genres that are relatively unfamiliar today. He was a man of the theater in a time when dramas might use music in various ways, and he composed not only operas of several kinds but also burlesques, masques, pantomimes, and a great deal of incidental music for plays. *Alfred* was a masque, a genre that, with its mixture of music, dance, and stage and costume design, would seem ideally suited to revival by early music specialists. By Arne's time, however, these genres were losing ground to the fascinating new world of Italian opera. In a way, then, Arne was old-fashioned, but he was also alert to new trends: he was ahead of the game in creating English-language versions of contemporary Italian styles. His 1762 comic opera *Thomas and Sally*, one of his most famous works aside from *Alfred*, was an especially successful piece that sparkled with the light new Italian musical language. Arne's few instrumental works, many influenced by the London style of Johann Christian Bach, are worthy of more frequent performances as well, and his solo cantatas have been wonderfully revived by soprano Emma Kirkby. *—James Manheim*

Recommended:

- ○ **Arne: The Six Organ Concertos** / R.B. Willams, A. Shepherd (cond.), Cantilena / 1988 / Chandos 8604
- ○ **Arne: Four Symphonies** / A. Shepherd (cond.), Cantilena / 1985 / Chandos 8403
- ○ **Arne: Complete Trio Sonatas** / Standage (cond.), Collegium Musicum 90 / 2001 / Chandos 0666
- ○ **Arne: Eight Sonatas or Lessons for the Harpsichord** / Demeyere / Accent 21145

VOCAL

Rule, Britannia! (1740)

Thomas Augustine Arne (1710–78) was the son of a well-to-do artisan from Covent Garden in London. The future composer received legal training and began to practice that profession, but found that he preferred music instead. He started studying and attending musical events in disguise and managed enough early success to survive the explosion that came when his father found out.

Arne had his breakout year as a composer in 1740 with two major state-sponsored hits. The first was his musical setting of a masque written by Congreve, *The Judgment of Paris*. The success of this work led to Arne's being engaged by Frederick, Prince of Wales, to write music for a new masque, *Alfred*, that the Prince wished to stage to honor the accession of his father, King George I, to the British throne and to celebrate the birthday of Princess Augusta. *Alfred* was performed at Cliveden House in Maidenhead, the residence of Prince Frederick, in 1740. "Rule, Britannia!" was the stirring finale of the masque, and it was acclaimed from the start. The text was written by James Thompson (1700–48).

"Rule, Britannia!" was not heard in London until 1745, but from its first performance there it became nearly universally known and loved. The Jacobite opponents of the Hanoverian dynasty even attempted to co-opt the song by writing their own words to its infectious, Handelian tune. In practice, the song is known primarily through its rousing refrain—the part that actually begins with the words *"Rule, Britannia!"* The late Peter Pears once recorded the whole melody with all its several verses, revealing that in toto this famous song is actually pretty tedious.

But the good bits are still beloved by patriotic Britons who like to remember when the Royal Navy really did rule the waves. *"Rule, Britannia!"* still maintains its status as the favorite patriotic air of the British people and as an unofficial second national anthem. *—Joseph Stevenson*

Recommended:

- ○ **Unforgettable Classics: Great British Music** / Groves (cond.), A. Collins, Royal Liverpool PO / 1997 / EMI 72433
- ○ **English National Songs** / J. Barlow (cond.), J. Potter, Skeaping, Broadside Band / 1993 / Saydisc 400

OPERA

Thomas and Sally, or The Sailor's Return (1760)

Between 1733 and 1776, English composer Thomas Arne wrote music for about 90 stage works, including plays, masques, pantomimes, and opera. Many of his dramatic scores are now lost, probably in the disastrous fire at Covent Garden in 1808. One that has survived is the pastoral opera *Thomas and Sally*, which was first produced at Covent Garden in 1760. Cast in two acts, it was described as a dramatic pastoral and served as an appendix, so to speak, to the main play of the evening. The librettist was Isaac Bickerstaff, who provided Arne with a slight plot revolving around four characters: Sally, her sailor lover Thomas, a squire who tries to woo Sally while Thomas is away at sea, and Dorcas, a matron who encourages the Squire. *Thomas and Sally* is of particular note for being the first English comic opera to be sung throughout, most previous (and many subsequent) examples having spoken dialogue. The nautical flavor of the libretto gave Arne the opportunity to introduce a sturdy score that also includes a rousing hunting song for the Squire. Sally's songs are cast in simple buffo style, although the role was originally created by Arne's protégée, Charlotte Brent, who boasted a formidable range of coloratura, which Arne fully employed in his English opera seria *Artaxerxes*, two years later. *—Brian Robins*

Synopsis:

A timeless Arcadian love story in a English setting. The Thomas of the title is a sailor, roaming the seas in service of King George and the motherland. Sally, his sweetheart, waits anxiously for her love to return to port.

Act One. The opera opens with a lively hunting song from the Squire, a wealthy bachelor with an eye for Sally's beauty. His praise for the hunt expresses his overall worldview (and his later pleas to Sally): "Since life is no more than a passage at best, let's strew the way over with flowers." Meanwhile, a sullen Sally waits at her doorway, spinning (a universal symbol of psychological turmoil) as she pines for Thomas. Her matronly confidant, Dorcas, encourages her to abandon her naïve devotion; after all, she says, who's to say Thomas doesn't have a girl in every port? Go for the Squire, she urges, and make a comfortable life with his riches. Sally remains undeterred. Later, walking through the woods, Sally happens upon the Squire. She tries to leave, but her suitor stops her. There's no one around, he says, "but Cupid, you, and I." She invokes her lower social status, but the Squire knows very well her resistance owes to Thomas, not to her low birth. He tempts her with his riches, but she resists: "The heart's not worth gaining that has to be bought."

Act Two. At sea, Thomas guides his ship and men toward port. They're all looking forward to chasing women, but Thomas insists he'll remain as true to his girl as to the Crown. Meanwhile, Dorcas and the Squire are found in the meadow, conspiring to bend Sally's will. Dorcas disappears as Sally approaches with her milk pails, while the Squire hides in the bushes. Sally sings as she walks, clutching the token of fidelity from Thomas that she wears and praying to the Spirits to help her remain faithful herself. The Squire emerges and tries to woo her once again, but is interrupted by Thomas, who drives his rival away. Defeated, the Squire now invokes Sally's low social status and bids her good riddance. With Thomas at last, Sally begs him not to leave again. He must answer the King's call, Thomas replies, but offers another oath instead: he wishes to marry Sally before leaving on his next mission. Their final duet, preceding the series of lively dances depicting the wedding celebrations with which the opera concludes, provides the lighthearted moral of the story: "Ye British youths, be brave, you'll find/The British virgins will be kind: protect their beauty from alarms/And they'll repay you with their charms." *—Jeremy Grimshaw*

Arnold Schoenberg Choir

f. 1972, Vienna, Austria

Ensemble

The Arnold Schoenberg Choir (Arnold Schoenberg-Chor) is one of the leading choral ensembles of Vienna, particularly known for a series of Baroque music recordings. It was founded in 1972 by Erwin Ortner. Ortner, a Viennese who had been a member of the Vienna Boys' Choir, graduated from the Vienna Academy of music and Performing Arts, having studied musical pedagogy, sacred music, and orchestral conducting with Hans Swarowsky and choral conducting with Hans Gillesberger.

Ortner and the chorus chose their name to honor Arnold Schoenberg (1874–1951) as a great Viennese-born composer. While Schoenberg was known as one of the leaders in musical modernism in the twentieth century, use of his name was not intended to indicate a musical predilection. In fact, the chorus has a wide-ranging repertoire that extends from Renaissance to contemporary music.

The choir is a fully professional organization made up of experienced singers, all of whom are students or graduates of the Vienna University of Music and Performing Arts. The choir has performed in operatic productions, including operas by Mozart, the rarely-heard *Fierabras* by Franz Schubert, and Olivier Messiaen's *Saint-François diAssise.* They frequently perform in the Salzburg Festival, Corinthian Summer, the Vienna Festival Week, Wien Moderne, and the Styriarte Graz.

The Arnold Schoenberg Choir formed a close working relationship with the conductor and early music pioneer Nikolaus Harnoncourt. Together with Harnoncourt's *Concentus Musicus Wien* they have participated in many recordings of Classical and Baroque masterworks, including the complete sacred music of Mozart, Bach's *Mass in B minor*, Haydn's *Creation*, Beethoven's *Missa Solemnis* and *Symphony No. 9*, Purcell's *Dido & Aeneas*, operas by Handel, and Monteverdi's *Vespers.*

In 1996 Ortner directed the choir in the complete secular choral music of Franz Schubert on seven discs, a release that won the German *Schallplattenkritik* prize, the French *Diapason d'or*, and the Japanese recording academy's grand prize. *—Joseph Stevenson*

Recommended:

- ○ **Lieder & Romanzen: Secular Choruses** / Ortner, Keiding, Korondi, Mossyrsch, Widihofer, Arnold Schoenberg Choir / 1994 / Teldec 92058
- ○ **Mozart: Sacred Music** / Harnoncourt (cond.), Hampson, McNair, Bonney, Pregardien, Magnus, Margiono, Vienna Concentus Musicus, Arnold Schoenberg Choir / 1995 / Teldec 98928
- ○ **Haydn: Seven Last Words** / Harnoncourt (cond.), Ortner, Holl, Johnson, Nielsen, Arnold Schoenberg Choir, Vienna Concentus Musicus / 1992 / Teldec 46458
- ○ **Bach: Johannes Passion** / Harnoncourt (cond.), Holl, Johnson, Lipovšek, Scharinger, Arnold Schoenberg Choir, Vienna Concentus Musicus / 1995 / Teldec 48622

Malcolm Arnold

b. Oct. 21, 1921, Northampton, England

Composer: Film Music, Chamber Music, Orchestral, Symphonic

Sir Malcolm Arnold's 60-year career has shown him to be perhaps the most versatile and prolific of the many British composers who emerged in the post-World War II era. Born in Northampton in 1921, Arnold was trained as a composer and trumpeter at the Royal College of Music from 1938 to 1941 (under Gordon Jacob for composition and Ernest Hall for trumpet), after which he won a trumpet position with the London Philharmonic Orchestra. After a promotion to principal trumpet in 1942, Arnold's career there was interrupted by two years of military service (1944–45) and a year with Sir Adrian Boult and the BBC Symphony (during the 1945–46 season). Arnold returned to the London Philharmonic in 1946, but soon found that composition was exercising an increasingly strong hold over his musical attention. Upon receiving the Mendelssohn scholarship in 1948 (which, in addition to prestige, provided the young composer with funds to spend a year in Italy), Arnold resigned from the orchestra to devote himself to composition (and, later, conducting) on a full-time basis.

Arnold's output over the next 50 years was prodigious: nine symphonies, 20 concertos, five ballets (including a version of *Sweeney Todd* in 1959), and a seemingly inexhaustible supply of smaller pieces for all kinds of ensembles. A successful secondary career as a film composer resulted in over 80 scores, including the Academy Award-winning *Bridge on the River Kwai.* Arnold has been the recipient of many public and academic honors, including honorary doctorates from the universities of Exeter, Durham, and Leicester, and the Ivor Novello Award for "Outstanding Services to British Music" in 1986. Named Commander of the British Empire in 1970, he was further honored in 1993 when his name appeared among those selected as Knights of the British Empire.

His resistance to identification with any of the various and ubiquitous "schools" of composition during the latter half of the twentieth century earned him the unbridled displeasure of many critics and fellow composers. On the surface, his music seems more intended to welcome audiences than to put his formidable technical skills on display, or to make musical or artistic "progress." While at times the overly accessible surface contours of his work (particularly the large-scale orchestral pieces) obscure the fundamental tensions that drive the music at a deeper level, Arnold's sense of craftsmanship—an aristocratic pride that prohibits him from engaging in what he sees as vulgar twentieth century techniques, while also perhaps causing his music-making to fall short of its deeply expressive potential—has resulted in an enviable consistency of output. Arnold named Berlioz as an inspiration; influence also came from a composer who provided England with its wartime anthem and who was always more popular in England than on the Continent—the similarly anti-modernist and individualist Jean Sibelius. *—Blair Johnston*

Overview of Works

The compositions of English composer Sir Malcolm Arnold can be divided into three groups: his symphonies, the most important and representative body; his film scores, the largest corner of his output with nearly 120 scores; and the remainder of his catalog, which contains other orchestral works, operas, songs, concertos, instrumental compositions, and chamber works. Stylistically, Arnold was a conservative, but his music never sounded stale and rarely derivative.

Arnold's *Symphony No. 1* (1949) is a charming, three-movement work that displayed talent, if not genius. The fairly popular *Second* (1953) in four movements (all of Arnold's symphonies feature three or four movements) offers a lovely Lento third movement and is at least a minor masterpiece. *Symphony No. 3* (1957) is less compelling, but with the *Fourth* (1960) and *Fifth* (1960–61), Arnold's expressive language is deeper, the latter symphony an especially gripping work in its Mahlerian grimness and exotic sonorities. The *Symphony No. 6* (1967) is a successful if somewhat understated work featuring jazz and popular music elements. *Symphony No. 7* (1973) may be Arnold's greatest. Again, Mahler comes to mind, and also the *Symphony No. 4* of Vaughan Williams, especially in the shattering first movement that is perhaps the composer's most profoundly unsettling creation. The *Eighth* (1978) carries over some of the tension from its predecessor, but is less powerful though still compelling. The *Ninth* (1986), the longest in the set at about 48 minutes, is effective and has an exaugural air about it.

Arnold's film scores have generally been neglected, but there are many gems among them, including the justly praised effort for David Lean's *The Bridge on the River Kwai* (1957). Arnold won an Academy Award for this heroic and colorful score and perhaps should have done so for other worthy efforts, like those for *The Sound Barrier* (1952), *Hobson's Choice* (1953), *The Inn of the Sixth Happiness* (1958), and *Whistle Down the Wind* (1961).

Arnold's other works include 20 concertos, among them the bluesy *Concerto for Guitar and Chamber Orchestra* (1959) written for Julian Bream. The *Fantasy on a Theme of John Field*, for piano and orchestra (1975), is really a one-movement concerto that features some highly imaginative writing with a titanic and dramatic struggle between piano and orchestra. Speaking of works entitled "Fantasy," Arnold consecutively wrote a spate of them in 1966 for bassoon, clarinet, horn, flute, and oboe. Three years later, he wrote more fantasies, one each for trumpet, trombone, and tuba. His two operas, *The Dancing Master* (1952) and *The Open Window* (1956), are short, charming works that suggest that with the right libretto, Arnold might have turned out a masterful full-length opera. *—Robert Cummings*

Recommended:

- ○ **Arnold: The Collection** / Handley (cond.), Howarth (cond.), M. Arnold (cond.), various orchestras & performers / 2001 / RCA Red Seal 88392
- ○ **Arnold: Dances** / Penny (cond.), Brisbane Queensland SO / 1996 / Naxos 553526
- ○ **Arnold: Sinfoniettas 1–3; Oboe & Flute Concertos** / Pople (cond.), London Festival O / 1997 / Arte Nova 46503
- ○ **Arnold: Complete Music for Solo Piano** / Firth / Koch 7162
- ○ **Arnold: Chamber Music Vol. 1** / Nash Ensemble / 2001 / Hyperion 55071

FILM MUSIC

Bridge on the River Kwai (1957)

Arnold reportedly did not care much for the score he composed for David Lean's epic film. He was not given what he considered adequate time to do a good job. In a bit of irony, he won his Academy Award for this score.

The story is essentially an allegory about the senselessness of war. Based on a historical event, the story concerns a Japanese prisoner-of-war camp where a group of captured British officers are forced to build a railroad bridge intended to allow the Japanese to ship troops and military equipment to the Burmese coast of the Indian Ocean. This was doubly a violation of the laws of war: officers are not supposed to be subject to performing labor as POWs, and no POW is supposed to be forced to perform actions in direct aid of the military efforts of his own country's enemy. Once the senior British officer (Alec Guinness) capitulates to Japanese coercion and orders his men to build the bridge, he gains an emotional investment in completing the momentous project (in effect, rooting for the enemy). Meanwhile, an escaped prisoner (William Holden) gets word of the construction back to British headquarters on Ceylon. He leads a demolition team back to the site, where they destroy it just as the first troop train is passing over it.

The score is a piece with strong, violent contrasts, with passages depicting the brutality of the prison camp guards as well as the sweeping grandeur of the location settings. It includes, of course, the famous "Colonel Bogey" march, which was written in 1914 by Sir Kenneth Alford. The British troops whistle it as a token of their defiance as they are marched into the camp; by 1942 this jaunty tune had acquired a set of lyrics, known to all British servicemen, that disparage the masculine equipment of various enemy leaders. The original soundtrack recording of the score (aside from revealing sonic weaknesses of the original studio recordings) also confirmed Arnold's sense that there were weaknesses and repetitions in the complete score. A later concert suite serves the salutory purpose of showing that even so, there was a considerable amount of first-rate music in it. *—Joseph Stevenson*

Recommended:

- ○ **Film Music of Sir Malcolm Arnold Vol. 1** / Hickox (cond.), London SO / 2002 / Chandos 9100

CHAMBER MUSIC

Sonatina for clarinet & piano, Op. 29 (1951)

Completed in January 1951, the same month that produced Arnold's *Oboe Sonatina* (Op. 28), the *Clarinet Sonatina* was given its first performance on March 20 of that year at the Gallery of the Royal Society of British Artists in London. The accompanying pianist was Geoffrey Corbett, and the clarinetist none other than a young Colin Davis, before his worldwide renown as a conductor.

The *Clarinet Sonatina* is in three brief movements, totaling some nine minutes. Three themes dominate the first movement, Allegro con brio. The first is a bit wild, with several wide leaps and chordal punctuations from the piano, the second hints at jazz rhythms, and the third provides a quiet interlude before the concluding return of the opening theme. The second-movement Andantino is gentle and lovely, and the third, appropriately marked Furioso, is a breathless dance in triple meter that provides quite a workout for both instrumentalists. *—Chris Morrison*

Recommended:

- ○ **English Music for Clarinet & Piano** / de Peyer, Pryor / 1987 / Chandos 8549
- ○ **Arnold: Chamber Music Vol. 2** / Nash Ensemble / 2001 / Hyperion 55072

ORCHESTRAL

Four Scottish Dances, Op. 59 (1957)

Appearing in the wake of the extremely successful *English Dances*, the *Four Scottish Dances* were composed early in 1957 for the *BBC Light Music Festival*. They were first performed by the BBC Concert Orchestra, under Arnold's direction, at London's *Royal Festival Hall* on June 8, 1957. A popular arrangement of the *Dances* for brass band was made by Ray Farr in 1984.

Parts of the opening dance, a strathspey, are in a swinging, moderately slow tempo. The other parts, in a quicker tempo, are enlivened by some fast tonguing by the trumpets and trombones. A lighthearted reel follows; with a main theme derived from a Robert Burns song, this dance began life as part of Arnold's score for the 1949 film *The Beautiful Country of Ayr*. The third dance is something of a nature portrait, its lovely slow tune played by the flute over a wash of strings and decorations from the harp. Featuring a drone-like the first dance, the finale is brief but lively, in the manner of a highland fling, with a busy side drum contributing to the excitement with which the set ends. *—Chris Morrison*

Recommended:

- ○ **Arnold: Four Scottish Dances; Symphony 3** / M. Arnold (cond.), London PO / 1988 / Phoenix USA 102
- ○ **Malcolm Arnold: Dances** / B. Thomson (cond.), Philharmonia O / 1990 / Chandos 8867

SYMPHONIC

Symphony No. 3, Op. 63 (1957)

One of the most popular of Arnold's nine symphonies, the *Symphony No. 3* was commissioned by, and is dedicated to, the Royal Liverpool Philharmonic Society. John Pritchard conducted the Royal Liverpool Philharmonic in the work's premiere performance at London's Royal Albert Hall on December 2, 1957.

Arnold has cited the music of Jean Sibelius as being an important influence on his own compositions, and the thematic relationships between the three movements of Arnold's *Third Symphony* are reminiscent of similar processes in some of the Finnish composer's larger works. The first movement of the symphony, starting at an Allegro tempo, opens with a lyrical theme played by the violins and violas, with woodwind support and nervous pizzicati underneath. Ideas pass mercurially from instrument to instrument. Then a lovely new theme is introduced by the oboe, followed by other solo winds. This new theme is juxtaposed with the more anxious setting of the first, leading to the development section. These same two themes reappear as the movement abruptly speeds to a stormy Vivace concluding section. The second movement, marked Lento, has been described by the composer as "elegiac in character." It is a passacaglia, a set of 20 variations on a slow, dissonant chorale-like theme. More overtly tuneful than either of its predecessors, the third-movement finale opens with playful woodwinds and a humorous "oompah" accompaniment. Starting at a brisk Allegro con brio, the music speeds to Presto for the forceful coda. *—Chris Morrison*

Recommended:

- ○ **Arnold: Four Scottish Dances; Symphony 3** / M. Arnold (cond.), London PO / 1988 / Phoenix USA 102
- ○ **Arnold: Symphonies 3 & 4** / Hickox (cond.), London SO / 1994 / Chandos 9290

Symphony No. 4, Op. 71 (1960)

This symphony is unusual in several respects: it features catchy, pop-oriented themes; its scoring requires an exotic array of percussion instruments, including tom-toms, bongos, and marimbaphones; and it has a genuine sense of humor, an element often missing from large orchestral scores from the latter half of the twentieth century. Moreover, it is quite accessible for the listener throughout all of its 40-minute or so length.

The first movement, marked Allegro—Poco più mosso—Tempo primo, opens with ascending and descending scales played in opposite motion, making up an important element here and later in the symphony. The main theme is a leisurely, simple, somewhat Stravinskian creation of neo-Classical character. A second theme, lively and pop-like, is played to exotic, jazzy accompaniment. The central part of the movement features imaginative thematic development and much conflict, with passages of rhythmic, jabbing brass and insistent, pounding drums. There follows a reprise, but with considerable changes, and the movement quietly ends.

The ensuing Scherzo (Vivace ma no troppo) is largely subdued and lightly scored in its humorous, often playfully menacing music. Lasting about five minutes, it is reminiscent of the spirit, though not style, of the Scherzo of compatriot Vaughan Williams' war-era *Symphony No. 5.* The third movement, Andantino, exudes a rich sense of lyricism in its two themes, but exoticism surfaces again in the percussion writing. Tension accrues and the music works up to a powerful climax before returning to the generally serene mood dominating the movement.

The Rondo finale features a busy, playful fugal main theme and a slower, more sedate alternate one. The ascending/descending scale from the first movement also reappears here. After the themes are developed, a boisterous, somewhat Ivesian march seems to come out of nowhere to disrupt the proceedings. But the fugal theme returns to triumphantly close out the symphony. *—Robert Cummings*

Recommended:

○ **Arnold: Symphony 4** / M. Arnold (cond.), London PO / 1990 / Lyrita 200

○ **Arnold: Symphonies 3 & 4** / Penny (cond.), National SO of Ireland / 1998 / Naxos 553739

Claudio Arrau

b. Feb. 6, 1903, Chillán, Chile, **d.** Jun. 9, 1991, Mürzzuschlag, Austria
Pianist

A patrician artist whose matinee-idol appearance was as elegant as his playing, Claudio Arrau achieved a major reputation for his performances of Brahms and Liszt. Indeed, few Romantic-period composers, from Beethoven onward, were beyond his grasp. In addition to that repertory, his Debussy was regarded by many connoisseurs as exemplary. Arrau believed that his abiding interest in psychoanalysis aided him in probing the intent of those whose works he performed. Certainly, Arrau's performances were marked by a balance between heart and intellect.

Arrau was born in Chillán, Chile, on February 6, 1903. He received piano instruction from his mother at an early age, making his debut performance in Santiago at the age of five playing Mozart, Beethoven, and Chopin. At the age of ten the Chilean government sent him to Berlin, where he enrolled in the Stern Conservatory of Music. His teacher there was Martin Krause. While studying he entered competitions, and won the Ibach Prize and the Gustav Holländer Medal. He also began giving recitals in Germany and Scandinavia, earning excited comment over the excellence of his technique, and the maturity of his interpretations. In 1918 he made a major European tour, giving concertos accompanied by illustrious conductors such as Nikisch, Furtwängler, and Mengelberg. He returned to South America in 1921, and made a triumphal tour beginning in Santiago de Chile. He made his first North American tour in 1924, appearing with the Boston Symphony Orchestra and the Chicago Symphony Orchestra. He joined the faculty of the Stern Conservatory in 1924. He won the Grand Prix Internationale des Pianistes in Geneva in 1927, and toured in the Soviet Union in 1929, and again in 1930.

He continued a notable concertizing career throughout the 1930s, including a famous series in 1935 and 1936 in Berlin, in which he played the complete keyboard works of J.S. Bach followed by the complete keyboard works of Mozart. He then announced that he would no longer play Bach, asserting that his music was not conceived for the modern grand piano. In 1938 he played all of the Beethoven piano sonatas and five piano concertos in a series of recitals in Mexico City, and repeated the feat during the next two years in Buenos Aires and Santiago. When World War II broke out he ended his association with the Stern Conservatory and returned to Chile, founding a piano school there. But the next year, after a tour of the United States where he received the highest critical acclaim, he and his family moved permanently to New York. He devoted himself to concertizing, teaching, and recording. His complete Beethoven cycles became legendary; in 1952 he performed such a series, in which each recital was broadcast live by the BBC.

After World War II his concert tours included Australia, Czechoslovakia, Romania, India, South Africa, Israel, and Japan. In the 1960s he made definitive recordings of the complete Beethoven piano sonatas; he also supervised the editing and publication of an Urtext edition of the same sonatas. In the 1970s, Chile, which had enjoyed a record as one of South America's most democratic nations, fell to the military government of Pinochet. In protest, Arrau gave up his Chilean citizenship in 1978, and became a naturalized citizen of the U.S. Despite this, or perhaps because of it, he continued to be a revered figure in Chile; in 1983 he was awarded the Chilean National Arts Prize. He returned at the age of 81 to tour Chile in 1984, his first performances there in 17 years. He died in Mürzzuschlag, Austria, on June 9, 1991. *—AMG*

Recommended:

○ **Chopin: The Nocturnes** / Arrau / 2001 / Philips 464694

○ **Liszt: Trancendental Etudes** / Arrau / Philips 416458

○ **The Early Recordings** / Arrau / Pearl 0070

○ **Claudio Arrau** / Haitink (cond.), Arrau, Concertgebouw / 1998 / Philips 456706

○ **Arrau Plays Beethoven** / Arrau / Philips 416145

Juan Crisóstomo Arriaga

b. Jan. 27, 1806, Rigoitia (near Bilbao), Spain, **d.** Jan. 17, 1826, Paris, France
Composer: Chamber Music, Symphonic

The remarkable career of composer Juan Crisóstomo Arriaga, dubbed the "Spanish Mozart" by musicians of the late nineteenth century, was cut tragically short by his death just ten days before his 20th birthday. Today his fame rests as much on brilliant potential as it does on his actual output of music (of which there is, sadly, quite little).

Arriaga was born on January 27, 1806 (50 years to the day after Mozart) in the Basque town of Bilbao. An account of his life by musicologist and composer Francois Fétis (with whom Arriaga would later study) indicates that young Juan Crisóstomo received almost no childhood training in music, though it is quite possible that this account (like many later ones, including those that claim Arriaga was born two years later than he actually was) is slanted so as to make Arriaga's already exceptional precociousness even more pronounced. One way or the other, the pieces composed by Arriaga in Bilbao, while not as finely crafted as the music from just a few years later, show no lack of formal understanding. He was, in addition, a skilled violinist as a youth, though whether his ability derived solely from innate talent or was in part the result of study with some nameless violinist remains unknown.

At 15 Arriaga enrolled at the Paris Conservatoire, where he studied violin with the legendary Pierre Baillot and was trained in counterpoint and harmony by Fétis. In 1823 he earned the Conservatoire's second prize in fugue and counterpoint and shortly thereafter was hired as an assistant for one of the Conservatoire's harmony courses. During 1824 he published three string quartets (D minor, A major, and E flat major). For the remaining two years of his life Arriaga focused his creative energies on vocal and choral music (both sacred and secular, including such large-scale works as the *Stabat Mater*, a mass which has since been lost, and several cantatas/dramatic "scenes"), though he found time to complete the large *Symphony in D major* as well. His death may have been due to a lung infection.

Arriaga was essentially a conservative composer whose innate personality was strong enough to manifest itself despite the rigid academic constraints maintained by the Paris Conservatoire at that time. The Italian influence which saturates Arriaga's earliest music (including the *Overture for orchestra*, Op. 1 and the opera *The Happy Slaves*, produced in Bilbao in 1820) was discarded almost immediately upon entering the Conservatoire, where Arriaga's developing contrapuntal and harmonic skills enabled him to forge an elegant style which owes much to the aristocratic, formal (but nevertheless very flexible) outlines of the Viennese Classical masters.

Once a forgotten figure in the history of music, Arriaga was brought back into the concert hall during the late nineteenth century, and a publishing campaign was begun in his native Bilbao during the middle twentieth century. The comparatively meager size of Arriaga's contribution to the concert repertory, however, has ensured that he remains a little-known, undervalued musical gem. *—Blair Johnston*

Overview of Works (1817–1826)

In his 19 years, "The Spanish Mozart" Juan Crisóstomo Arriaga produced a prodigious amount of vocal and instrumental music. Just how many works remains in doubt; modern scholarship, which only began to turn its attention to Arriaga in the 1980s, estimates the figure at 30–35 pieces based on extant documentation. The actual output was likely higher, but in the present century only about 20 Arriaga works exist, with additional pieces extant in the form of fragments.

Of his vocal music, the major work is unquestionably his opera, *Los esclavos felices* (*The Happy Slaves*, 1819). Today only the overture and bits and pieces of 14 numbers remain. The overture is a highly energetic, even electrifying piece, demonstrating a fresh approach to instrumentation within a lively, folk dance inspired idiom. In the last year of his life, Arriaga refined this overture, and while the second version is more conventional in approach, it is also more skillful as an orchestral work, losing little of the original's freshness and verve.

Arriaga also composed two cantatas based on Prix de Rome texts, *Agar dans le désert* and *Herminie*. The finale of *Agar* is tremendously exciting, with a bright orchestration underscoring exceedingly difficult writing for the solo soprano in a high register. Two recitative/aria combinations also exist, *Hymen* and *Helás, helás*, modeled after settings by Sacchini and Cherubini. Of Arriaga's choral settings only two three-voice motets remain.

Arriaga's main instrumental work is his masterpiece, the *Symphony in D* (1825)—probably also his last completed work. This is a full-scale, dramatic, 40-minute symphony inspired by Beethoven and well within the emerging style and spirit of Romanticism. The orchestration is assured and stylistically at the leading edge of the era. An *Overture, Nonetto*, Op. 1 (1818), shows the 12-year-old composer already had a command of part writing and an original approach to developing ideas. Thematic development is central to the *Three String Quartets* (1824) which, although not as engaging as his works for larger forces, contain some of the harmonic turns and twists characteristic of Arriaga's work in general. In the first two quartets, the first violin part takes the lead and the others follow; in the third we see a more integrated approach to quartet writing.

Arriaga played guitar and probably keyboard, four short works being extant for the latter. However, Arriaga's main instrument was the violin, and two sets of virtuosic variations provide some clue as to his own playing. The *Tema variado en cuarteto*, Op. 17, takes a simple tune and subjects it to thick and highly chromatic variations. Another set; the Op. 22 *Variations on "La Hungara"* exists in two versions, the first consisting of florid violin variations over a simple figured bass. Arriaga rescored this piece for string quartet in order to present it at the Madrid court in 1822. Arriaga's earliest piece, *Nada y mucho*, is scored for three violins over a ground bass, and was written when he was 11. *—Uncle Dave Lewis*

Recommended:

○ **Arriaga: L'Oeuvre Orchestrale** / Savall (cond.), Capella Reial de Catalunya, Le Concert des Nations / 1995 / Astrée 8532

CHAMBER MUSIC

String Quartets (before 1824)

Arriaga's three quartets were published in Paris when he was 18, only two years after his coming to the Paris Conservatoire to study and the same year he was appointed by the school as an assistant. They are works ensconced in the late Classical tradition, both in sound and structure, certainly old-fashioned at the time of their composition. Devices such as unison voices, a minuet as the third movement, and slow introductions are all references to the chamber music of Haydn and Mozart. The youthfulness of the works is occasionally revealed in rigid cadences and awkward transitions, but also in the inventive themes, often built of rhythmic cells that are used effectively in development sections.

The first violin, Arriaga's instrument, dominates the *String Quartet No. 1 in D minor*, although the other instruments are not merely drones. The opening Allegro recalls Mozart, alternating unison figures and those in harmony, and alternating between D minor and D major, finally choosing to end in the major. The Adagio con espressione is slightly Schubertian with the lower strings playing repeated-note accompaniment to the first violin's solo filled with long runs. The third movement is a Menuetto worthy of Haydn. The final movement begins with a *Sturm und Drang* Adagio before a galloping Allegretto that again switches back and forth between minor and major.

The *String Quartet No. 2 in A major* begins with a lively Allegro, followed by an Andante and variations. The pizzicato variation hints at Mendelssohn, while the final one has touches of canon. The Menuetto is subtitled Scherzo, giving away its playful nature. A quiet but dashing Andante introduces the final Allegro, a Rossinian, enthusiastic romp.

The last quartet is the most sophisticated, showing a greater balance between instruments and more dramatic use of dynamics and harmonies. Just like the first quartet, the Allegro theme alternates unison and non-unison figures. The Pastorale, marked Andantino, is very reminiscent of Boccherini, with a delicate theme flavored with grace notes and harmonies in parallel thirds. An episode in the minor brings to mind the storm in Beethoven's *"Pastoral" Symphony*. The C minor third movement is a minuet in name only, being rather more like a scherzo in nature, while its C major Trio seems frivolous in comparison. The Presto agitato finale is in sonata form with an extended development section that skillfully switches between major and minor, contrasting the two themes: one with dotted rhythm, the other with running triplets. *—Patsy Morita*

Recommended:

○ **Arriaga: Three String Quartets** / Arriaga Quartet / 2000 / ASV 1012

○ **Arriaga: Cuartetos** / Cuarteto Casals / HM 987038

SYMPHONIC

Symphony in D major (ca. 1825)

Arriaga died at the age of 19, and yet his output included an opera, cantatas, chamber, and orchestral works, and many shorter pieces. At 18—when this, his first and only symphony, was written—he was already an assistant professor at the Paris Conservatoire. This work shows no trace of youthful immaturity; indeed, the long, slow introduction has an almost Beethovenian authority and leads to an equally powerful faster section that sustains the mood of high seriousness. The sorrowful slow movement contains expressive writing for woodwind, and the flute also has an important part in the brief, syncopated minuet and trio. The final scherzo is far from being an anticlimax. Marked Allegro con moto, it has all the melodic and rhythmic drive of the earlier movements. Other echoes of the earlier movements include passages in minor keys casting chilling shadows over the musical narrative. The smoothly classical grace that marks many of Arriaga's other works is replaced in the symphony by music as dramatic and compelling as anything that followed it in early Romantic period. *—Roy Brewer*

Recommended:

○ **Arriaga: L'Oeuvre Orchestrale** / Savall (cond.), Capella Reial de Catalunya, Le Concert des Nations / 1995 / Astrée 8532

○ **Sinfonias Españolas** / Concerto Köln / Capriccio 10488

Martina Arroyo

b. Feb. 2, 1937, New York, NY

Soprano

Martina Arroyo was one of the major American singers who suddenly appeared on the international vocal scene in the 1950s and 1960s. She was also a leader in a pioneering generation of black American singers who followed the example of Marian Anderson in breaking barriers on the opera and concert stages.

She attended Hunter College in New York, taking a Bachelor of Arts in Romance Languages. She won the 1958 Metropolitan Opera Auditions (sharing first prize with the similarly illustrious Grace Bumbry). Arroyo was immediately invited to participate in a Carnegie Hall concert performance of Ildebrando Pizzetti's *L'Assassinio nella cattedrale*, a new opera based on T.S. Eliot's play about the murder of St. Thomas à Beckett. This was followed by a period of singing minor roles at the Metropolitan Opera.

She went to Europe, which at that time was better disposed to ignore the skin color of singers portraying nominally "white" roles in operas, and immediately took the leading roles in operas in Vienna, Düsseldorf, Berlin, Frankfurt, and Zurich, accepting a contract to join the company of the Zurich Opera from 1963 to 1965.

She was a classic spinto soprano, tailor-made for the most powerful Verdi roles, yet was able to handle Mozart parts with the necessary lightness and flexibility. Among her best-known roles were Gioconda, Santuzza, Donna Anna, Butterfly, Liù (*Turandot*) and Wagner's Elsa, and most of the major roles of Strauss, Verdi, Mozart, and Puccini.

She was invited to sing her first leading role at the Metropolitan in 1965, as a last-minute substitute for Birgit Nilsson as *Aïda*. She went on to become one of the favorite stars of the Metropolitan, where she sang all the major Verdi parts. She was asked to sing in the season opening performance at the Met three times. She remains associated with the Metropolitan as a frequent participant on the "Singer's Roundtable" feature on Metropolitan Saturday matinee broadcasts and sang over 20 times on the popular *Tonight Show* on America's NBC television.

She made her debut in Britain at a concert performance of Meyerbeer's *Les Huguenots* in 1968 as Valentine and in the same year made her operatic debut in that country at Covent Garden, singing Aïda. Her Paris Opéra debut was in 1973. Arroyo also appeared regularly on the concert platform in a wide variety of repertory that ranged from Handel oratorios such as *Judas Maccabeus* and *Samson* to Beethoven's *Ninth Symphony* and *Missa Solemnis*, Rossini's *Stabat Mater*, the requiems of Verdi and Fauré, and such modern compositions as Barber's *Andromache's Farewell* (which she premiered), Karlheinz Stockhausen's *Momente*, William Bolcom's *Simple Stories*, and *African Oratorio* by Carlo Franci.

Arroyo has taught at Louisiana State University in Baton Rouge, the University of California at Los Angeles, the University of Delaware, Wilberforce University, and the International Sommerakademie-Mozarteum in Salzburg. She is now a Distinguished Professor of Voice at the School of Music at Indiana University, Bloomington, Indiana. She is co-author (with Dr. Willard Boyd) of the National Endowment of the Arts' Task Force Report of Music Education in the United States.

Arroyo was appointed by President Gerald Ford as a member of the National Endowment of the Arts, served twenty years as a member of the Board of Trustees of Carnegie Hall (and was subsequently named a lifetime Honorary Trustee), is a member of the Board of Trustees of Hunter College of the City of New York University, and won honors from the Licia Albanese-Puccini Foundation. She made over 50 recordings in a wide variety of repertory from oratorio to spirituals. *—Joseph Stevenson*

Recommended:

○ **Verdi: Requiem** / Bernstein (cond.), Oldham, Domingo, Arroyo, Raimondi, London SO / 1993 / Sony 47639

○ **Meyerbeer: Les Huguenots** / Bonynge (cond.), Sutherland, Te Kanawa, Augér, Bacquier, Arroyo, New Philharmonia Orch. / 1991 / Decca 430549

○ **Verdi: Aida** / Abbado (cond.), Domingo, Ghiaurov, Arroyo, Cossotto, La Scala Theater Orchestra / 1998 / Opera d'Oro 1167

○ **Meyerbeer: L'Africaine** / Albrecht (cond.), Milnes, Arroyo, Rydl, Hermann, Bavarian Radio Orch. / 2001 / Myto 11235

Les Arts Florissants

f. 1979, Paris, France

Ensemble

Founded by the eminent harpsichordist William Christie in 1979, Les Arts Florissants is one of the world's most acclaimed ensembles performing Baroque and Classical vocal and instrumental music. The group was named after a one-act opera by the French Baroque composer Marc-Antoine Charpentier. An extraordinary musician and scholar, Christie immersed himself in the French Baroque, rediscovering numerous forgotten masterpieces in the Bibliothèque Nationale in Paris, editing, and performing works by a number of important French composers, including Charpentier, Campra, Couperin, and Rameau. In addition to rediscovering, editing, and producing many neglected French works, Christie and his ensemble have also performed much standard, and lesser-known, Baroque repertoire, particularly music for the stage, including works by English and Italian composers. In 1983, Les Arts Florissants produced Purcell's Dido and Aeneas and Monteverdi's *Ballo delle ingrate*. Two years later, the group performed Rameau's *Anacréon* and Charpentier's *Actéon*. As a central figure of the French Baroque, Charpentier, a versatile and profound composer, as well as Molière's collaborator, attracted Christie's interest, and Les Arts Florissants produced several of this composer's forgotten works. In 1987, the ensemble received the Grand Prix de la Critique for the production of Lully's *Atys*, and this work was presented with great success in Madrid, Florence, and New York. The group received another Grand Prix de la Critique, in 1989, for their production of *The Fairy Queen* by Purcell. Molière's *Le Malade imaginaire*, with incidental music by Charpentier, was produced in 1990. Three years later, Les Arts Florissants performed Charpentier's *Médée*. In 1996, the ensemble presented a highly acclaimed production of Rameau's *Hippolyte et Aricie*. Featured for the 2000–01 season were works by Rameau (*Les Indes galantes* and *Zoroastre*), Charpentier, Couperin, Brossard, Cesti, and Handel. The extensive discography of Les Arts Florissants includes more than 40 discs for the Harmonia Mundi label. Since 1994, however, the group has recorded exclusively for Erato/Warner Classics. Their award-winning recordings include Purcell's *King Arthur* and Rameau's *Hippolyte et Aricie*, which both received the Grammophone Award, *Early Opera category*, and Rameau's *Grands Motets*, which received the Grammophone Award, Baroque Vocal category. Other critically acclaimed recordings include Handel's *Alcina*, *Acis* and *Galatea*, and *Orlando*, Mozart's *Great Mass in C minor* and Requiem, *Purcell's Dido* and *Aeneas*, Charpentier's *Les Plaisirs de Versailles*, *La Descente d'Orphée aux Enfers*, and *Medée*, Monteverdi's *Vespro della beata Vergine*, Rameau's *Les Fêtes d'Hébé*, Mondonville's *Grands Motets*, Landi's *Sant'Alessio*, and Couperin's *Leçons de Ténèbres*. *—AMG*

Recommended:

- ○ **Rameau: Hippolyte et Aricie** / Christie (cond.), Agnew, Hunt, Padmore, Berg, Les Arts Florissants Orchestra & Chorus / Erato 063015517
- ○ **Mozart: Die Zauberflöte** / Christie (cond.), Dessay, Blochwitz, Scharinger, White, Les Arts Florissants / 1996 / Erato 12705
- ○ **Monteverdi: Il Combattimento di Tancredi e Clorinda** / Christie, Arts Florissants Orchestra & Chorus / 1998 / HM 7901426
- ○ **Lully: Atys** / Christie (cond.), Fouchecourt, Laurens, Deletre, Gardeil, Les Arts Florissants / HM 90125759
- ○ **Mozart: Requiem; Ave Verum Corpus** / Christie (cond.), Pregardien, Stutzmann, Berg, Panzarella, Les Arts Florissants Orchestra & Chorus / Erato 10697
- ○ **Rameau: Les Grands Motets** / Christie (cond.), Agnew, Daneman, Rime, Rivenq, Les Arts Florissants Orchestra & Chorus / Erato 96967

Vladimir Ashkenazy

b. Jul. 6, 1937, Gorki, Russia
Pianist, Conductor

Vladimir Ashkenazy's parents were both professional pianists; they taught him piano beginning at age six. His father was a non-observant Russian Jew, and his mother was a Russian of Eastern Orthodox faith. After his debut in Moscow at the tender age of eight, Ashkenazy was subsequently put on track for a musical career and enrolled in Moscow's Central Music School. His regular piano teacher there was Anaida Sumbatian.

In 1955 he entered the Moscow Conservatory, studying with the great pianist Lev Oborin. In the same year he won second prize in the Fifth Warsaw International Chopin Competition. The following year he won the Gold Medal in the Brussels Queen Elizabeth International piano competition and then toured the United States in 1958. In 1961 he married an Icelandic pianist who was studying in Moscow, Sofia Johannsdottir. He won first prize in the Second Tchaikovsky Competition in Moscow in 1962, sharing that honor with British pianist John Ogden. In 1963 Ashkenazy and his wife, travelling on their Soviet passports, went to London, where he made his debut in an orchestral concert at Festival Hall, a great success. He stayed on in England and centered his life and career there, beginning a long association with England's Decca (London) records. He quickly made a reputation as one of the most brilliant pianists in the Russian tradition. In 1971 he moved with his family to Reykjavik, where he was awarded Iceland's Order of the Falcon. In 1972 he took Icelandic citizenship and later established a home base in Switzerland.

He took up the conductor's baton in the 1970s and increased his activity in that sphere steadily, becoming principal guest conductor of the Philharmonic Orchestra of London (1981), music director of the Royal Philharmonic of London (1987), principal guest conductor of the Cleveland Orchestra (1987) and chief conductor of the Berlin Radio Symphony Orchestra (1989). Between 1998 and 2003, he was the Czech Philharmonic's chief conductor, and he took up leadership of Japan's NHK Symphony Orchestra in the 2004–05 season, while continuing as music director of the European Union Youth Orchestra. With the end of the Soviet Union, he has made triumphant return concerts in Russia.

His piano playing is bright and incisive, with clear articulation and intellectual depth that does not interfere with the production of warm feeling. He has exceptional control over tone color. Although he possesses a considerable degree of sheer strength, his excellent playing in delicate passages creates the dominant impression. His repertoire is wide-ranging, and he has recorded most of it, from Haydn to the works of the first half of the twentieth century. He has made particularly valuable recordings of the complete piano works of Chopin, Rachmaninov, and Scriabin. Other excellent series include music of Brahms, Liszt, and the complete Prokofiev concertos. As a conductor, he is highly effective in Russian music, particularly in Prokofiev, and has made the leading recording of that composer's *Romeo and Juliet*. He has made his own orchestration of Musorgsky's *Pictures at an Exhibition* and recorded the work in that highly effective version, in Gortchakov's orchestration, and in its original form as a piano solo. He remains active in both careers. *—Joseph Stevenson*

Recommended:

- ○ **Chopin: 4 Ballads; 4 Scherzi** / Ashkenazy / 1999 / Decca 466499
- ○ **Sibelius: Symphonies 3, 5, 6 & 7** / Ashkenazy (cond.), London PO / 1997 / London 455405
- ○ **Rachmaninov: Symphonies 1–3** / Ashkenazy (cond.), Concertgebouw / 1996 / London 448116
- ○ **Beethoven: Piano Sonatas 14, 23 & 8** / Ashkenazy / 2003 / Decca 473845
- ○ **Schumann: The Works for Solo Piano** / Ashkenazy / 2002 / Decca 470915
- ○ **Rautavaara: Piano Concerto 3** / Ashkenazy (piano & cond.), Helsinki PO / Ondine 950
- ○ **Shostakovich: 24 Preludes & Fugues** / Ashkenazy / 1999 / Decca 466066
- ○ **Rachmaninov: Piano Concertos 1–4** / Previn (cond.), Ashkenazy, London SO / 1995 / London 444839

Bob van Asperen

b. Oct. 8, 1947, Amsterdam, Netherlands
Harpsichordist, Conductor

The Dutch performer Bob van Asperen is a recognized specialist in the realm of performance on period keyboard instruments. Born and raised in Amsterdam, Asperen completed a conventional university course of study in music before embarking on lessons with harpsichord master Gustav Leonhardt starting in 1967; Asperen made his debut in Haarlem in 1968. Also in 1968 Asperen joined the group Quadro Hotteterre, of which he was a member until 1984. Asperen completed his studies in 1972 after finishing a course in organ at the Amsterdam Conservatory given by Albert de Klerk. Afterward he accepted a teaching post at the Royal Conservatory in The Hague, which he held until tapped to replace the departing Gustav Leonhardt at the Sweelinck Conservatory, prompting Asperen's return to Amsterdam. His teaching duties in the Netherlands have not restrained him from touring internationally; Asperen has given master classes elsewhere in Europe and also Canada, the United States, and Australia.

Asperen's repertoire on harpsichord, organ, and clavichord is expansive and ranges from the music of John Bull to that of Antonio Soler, whose works Asperen has recorded in their entirety. Asperen has also recorded the complete published keyboard output of Carl Philipp Emanuel Bach and Jan Pieterszoon Sweelinck. Among the record labels that Asperen has recorded for are EMI, Sony, Virgin, Teldec, Deutsche Harmonia Mundi, N.M. Classics, and Astrée; his recordings have won many awards, including the Deutsche Schallplattenpreis. As a musicologist, Asperen has prepared many editions and reconstructions of works by composers from the Low Countries, particularly on behalf of Dutch Baroque composer Cornelis Thymanszoon Padbrué, but also members of the van Noordt family and naturally, Sweelinck . Asperen has also rehabilitated a few works of Johann Sebastian Bach that were not previously known; he has recorded the multiple keyboard concerti of Bach with his former professor Gustav Leonhardt. *—Uncle Dave Lewis*

Recommended:

- ○ **C.P.E. Bach: Hamburg Concertos** / Asperen (cond.), Melante Amsterdam / Virgin 61913
- ○ **Bach: Sonatas for Violin & Harpsichord Vol. 1** / Asperen, van Dael / 2000 / Naxos 554614
- ○ **Bach: Concertos for 3–4 Harpsichords** / Asperen (hpschd & cond.), Klapprott, Lohff, Bussi, Melante Amsterdam / 1996 / Virgin 724354520426
- ○ **Frescobaldi: Works for Harpsichord** / Asperen / 1987 / Teldec 843774

Atlanta Symphony Orchestra

f. 1947, Atlanta, GA
Ensemble

One of the youngest of America's major orchestras, the Atlanta Symphony Orchestra began in 1945 as the Atlanta Youth Symphony, created by members of the Atlanta Music Club to give high-quality performance opportunities to young musicians in the Atlanta area. Over its history, the ensemble has grown from a community orchestra of volunteers and part-time employees to a world-class ensemble with a reputation for musical excellence.

Under the direction of the gifted conductor and teacher Henry Sopkin, the Atlanta Youth Symphony became the Atlanta Symphony Orchestra (ASO) in 1947. Although still in its fledgling years, the Orchestra flourished under Sopkin's leadership: expanding its repertoire, increasing its programs for young players, and improving the level of musicianship among its members. As it grew, the Orchestra was able to attract world-renowned soloists such as Glenn Gould and Isaac Stern, which further enhanced its reputation as a top-notch regional orchestra. In 1964, the ASO, still an organization of part-time musicians, became a founding member of the Atlanta Arts Alliance which later became the internationally acclaimed Woodruff Arts Center.

When Henry Sopkin announced his retirement in 1966, an arduous search began to find a replacement for this talented and visionary conductor. The job was offered to Robert Shaw, who initially turned down the position because he felt that he was not well-versed enough in orchestral repertoire to "stay ahead of the musicians." When he finally accepted the music director's position in 1967, it was obvious that he was equal to the challenge. Shaw immediately expanded the ASO to 87 full-time musicians, created the 200-voice Atlanta Symphony Orchestra Chorus, and raised the expected level of musicianship to a new and highly professional standard. He also began to organize significant tours for the ASO which brought national recognition and recording opportunities to the group. Under Shaw's leadership, the ASO performed for the inauguration of President Carter in 1977 and released the first commercial digital orchestral recording for Telarc.

With its national reputation for excellence of musicianship well established, the ASO made numerous recordings, won 15 Grammy Awards and toured internationally under Shaw's direction. In 1988, Shaw retired from his position as ASO music director although he continued to hold the positions of director emeritus and conductor laureate until his death in 1999. Following Shaw's retirement, Yoel Levi became the third music director in ASO history. A conductor of international reputation, Levi has continued the tradition of musical excellence for which the ASO has become known. He led the ensemble on its second European tour in 1991 to enthusiastic audiences. In 1995, the ASO celebrated its 50th anniversary season with two nationwide television broadcasts and a successful tour of the northeastern United States, and performed for the opening ceremony of the Olympic Games in 1996 which was viewed by more than 3.5 billion people worldwide. In 2001, Robert Spano became music director, with Donald Runnicles as principal guest conductor. *—Corie Stanton Root*

Recommended:

- ○ **Orff: Carmina Burana** / Runnicles (cond.), MacKenzie, Hong, Olsen, Patriarco, Atlanta SO & Chorus / 2001 / Telarc 60575
- ○ **Berlioz: Requiem; Boito: Prologue to Mefistofeles** / Shaw (cond.), Aler, Cheek, Atlanta SO & Chorus / Telarc 80109
- ○ **Choral Masterpieces** / Shaw (cond.), Baughman, Brown, Atlanta SO & Chorus / 1985 / Telarc 80119
- ○ **Vivaldi: Gloria; Bach: Magnificat** / Shaw (cond.), Upshaw, Simpson, Gordon, Stone, Jensen, Atlanta SO, St. Petersburg Chamber Choir / 1989 / Telarc 80194

Daniel Auber

b. Jan. 29, 1782, Caen, Normandy, France, **d.** May 12, 1871, Paris, France

Composer: Opera

A dominant figure in nineteenth century French opera, Auber was born to a royal huntsman in the Normandy region. Auber demonstrated facility at the keyboard as a child, and by 1799 he had produced a string quartet that demonstrated his awareness of emerging Romantic styles. Auber's first one-act stage work, *Julie*, reached the stage in an amateur performance in 1805; in 1811, Italian composer Luigi Cherubini saw a revised version and agreed to take Auber under his wing. A string of failures led Auber to abandon composition around 1813, but in 1819, Auber's father died bankrupt, and Auber turned back to composition as means of self-preservation. The following year, Auber enjoyed his first hit, *Le bergère châtelaine*.

In 1823, Auber met playwright Eugène Scribe, and their joint reign may be compared with that of Gilbert and Sullivan in England. Their first major hit, *Le Maçon*, appeared in 1825, and with it began "the golden age of the *Opéra comique*." In 1828, Auber and Scribe fulfilled a commission from the Académie Royale de Musique with *La muette de portici*, known in English-speaking lands as *Masaniello*. This grand opera, dealing with a seventeenth century Neapolitan revolt, was so effective that it provided a catalyst for a successful Belgian insurrection against Dutch occupation in 1830. That year, Auber and Scribe introduced *Fra Diavolo*, with its comic tale of banditry; this touched off an entire subgenre of comic bandit operas. In 1833, the partnership launched another grand opera, *Gustave III*; an Italian translation of Scribe's libretto later served as the basis for Verdi's *Un Ballo in Maschera*. *Le Domino Noir* of 1837 was the Auber/Scribe work most frequently revived in its own century, achieving 1,209 performances by 1909.

In 1842, Auber was named head of the Paris Conservatoire. He helped to build up this institution considerably over his 30-year tenure, enlarging the composition, piano and orchestral instrument departments. In 1861, Scribe died, and Auber produced only two more operas afterward. The second of these, *Rêve d'amour*, was his final hit, produced in 1869 when Auber was 87 years old. In 1870, the Franco-Prussian War broke out, and Auber resigned from his post at the Conservatoire so that its building might be converted into a hospital. The aged composer did not long survive the horrors and privations of the Paris Commune, and died at age 89 in the midst of the German occupation.

For the next four decades, several of Auber's operas held the stage in Paris and elsewhere. Even early phonograph records testify to his tremendous popularity; witness Ellen Beach Yaw's recording of "C'est l'histoire amoureuse" (*Manon Lescaut*), made for the Gramophone & Typewriter company in London in 1898. By 1910, however, Auber's work was dropping from even the French repertory, with only *Fra Diavolo* keeping a tenuous hold. Changing times and tastes led to the neglect of Auber's music, with the exception of some of his overtures, in particular that for *Les Diamants de la couronne* (The Crown Jewels). Rossini accurately evaluated Auber's compositions as "little music, but by a great musician" Auber was the recipient of praise from kings, emperors, and eminent men of learning, and five biographies of him appeared during his own lifetime. *—Uncle Dave Lewis*

OPERA

Fra Diavolo (1830)

Although Daniel Auber gave birth to French grand opera with the premiere of his *La Muette de Portici*, he was mostly known during his career as a composer of fine opéras comiques; in these works, his energetic orchestral textures, spicy harmonies, and tuneful melodies all found their ideal outlet. Of his comic operas, *Fra Diavolo* was among the biggest successes, and it lasted in the repertoire of Paris' *Opéra Comique* until the beginning of the twentieth century. Some of the songs remained in the popular repertoire long after the complete opera had fallen out of fashion, and Eugène Scribe's plot was even parodied in a 1933 movie starring Laurel and Hardy.

The drama was inspired by the historical figure of Fra Diavolo—an Italian rebel whose real name was Michele Pezza—who waged bitter warfare against the occupying French forces in his native Naples around the turn of the nineteenth century. However, Scribe's libretto has little, if any, of history in it; in this comedic treatment, the character of Fra Diavolo, already legendary in both France and Italy for his fearsome and bloodthirsty character, becomes a charismatic hero. Romantic revisions of history were popular in the early part of the nineteenth century, as can be seen in the incredible popularity of Rossini's opera *Le Comte Ory*; however Auber and Scribe's new work, full of amorous intrigue, rascally henchmen, and earthy humor, was a dramatic masterstroke.

As well as an excellent libretto, *Fra Diavolo* has a lively score with brilliant, deftly textured vocal characterizations. The overture and ensembles are skillfully written and the action of the drama quickly paced. The opera premiered in 1830, the same year as *La Muette de Portici*, and it became an instant sensation in Paris. *—Rita Laurance*

Synopsis:

Act One. Inside Matheo's inn, the *carabinieri* are drinking to the reward they hope to win when they capture the bandit chief Fra Diavolo. Lorenzo, however, is miserable, as Matheo has determined to marry his daughter to Francesco, a rich farmer. They quietly pledge their love, when from outside, Lady Pamela and Lord Cockburn are heard calling for help. They rush in ("Ah! quel voyage"), disillusioned with travel. They had just eloped, with all her jewels and wardrobe, and have been robbed by a highwayman. Lorenzo leads his men out, and Pamela and Cockburn start to quarrel. She blames him for taking a shortcut, and he says he did it to avoid the elegant Marquis who has been following them and flirting with her. He'll be complaisant in anything but that, and she answers that she'll do anything but take orders, they declare in their duet, "Je voulais bien." Another carriage pulls up, and out comes the Marquis himself (Fra Diavolo in disguise.) He and Pamela are delighted by the coincidence, but the Marquis is less pleased. Zerline sings him a song about the bandit, "Voyez sur cette roche," describing his handsome appearance and many amorous conquests. He jokingly adds a verse suggesting that perhaps Diavolo is blamed for some conquests that were not his own doing. Beppe and Giacomo come in, disguised as pilgrims, and Diavolo pays for their lodging. They whisper to him that the theft went off perfectly, except for a box of gold that was supposed to be with the travelers. When the others leave, Diavolo sings a love song to Pamela, "Le gondolier fidèle," and notices she is wearing a miniature portrait of herself, framed with diamonds. When she shows it to him, he declares his passion and refuses to return it. When Cockburn comes back, Diavolo resumes his song, much to the husband's displeasure. Lorenzo and the soldiers return, bringing news that they have killed several of the bandits and found a jewel case in their camp. Pamela joyfully recognizes it as hers and has Cockburn give Lorenzo 10,000 francs, enough money that he can marry Zerline after all. Diavolo, Beppe, and Giacomo fume while the others rejoice in the finale.

Act Two. Act Two opens with Zerline, caught between rushing about to serve the guests and telling herself how much she loves Lorenzo ("Ne craignez rien"). Pamela and Cockburn enter, quarreling again, and he notices the portrait is missing, though she distracts him. When the three of them leave, Diavolo sings another song, "Agnès la jouvencelle," as a signal to his men. They hide when Zerline comes back and sings as she undresses, "Oui, c'est demain," much to their gratification, especially when she pauses to admire her figure. She says her prayers ("O Vierge sainte") and goes to bed. The bandits get ready to enter the Cockburns' room to resteal the treasure, but Beppe suggests killing Zerline to keep her from raising an alarm. They briefly quarrel, finally agreeing to do it, but there is a loud knocking from outdoors from Lorenzo and the *carabinieri.* When they come in, Beppe and Giacomo hide while Diavolo nonchalantly emerges, and when asked to explain his presence so near the ladies' bedrooms, declares he came by invitation, from not just one, but both. He suggests discreet silence, but Lorenzo insists upon a duel, which Diavolo accepts, hoping to avenge his losses. When the women come in, Zerline is brokenhearted and Pamela furious at being accused of infidelity, to the glee of Diavolo and his men ("Voila donc sa constance").

Act Three. Act Three opens the next day, Palm Sunday, with Diavolo relishing his plan for revenge and way of life ("J'ai revu nos amis"). All the rich travelers he robs, a poor pilgrim receives both gold and bread, and women are relieved of nothing except what they might choose to give. He anticipates his men ambushing Lorenzo while he returns to the inn and steals the jewels, gold, and perhaps, if she accepts his invitation, Pamela. He leaves a note for Beppe and Giacomo, and exits. Zerline is to marry Francesco after all, and the wedding procession passes by ("C'est grand fête"), followed by Beppe and Giacomo, and after the procession stops to pray, and leaves, they read the note. They are to alert Diavolo when the coast is clear by ringing the hermitage bell. Beppe is briefly troubled by scruples about theft on a holy day, but Giacomo assures him a crime against an Englishman won't count. Lorenzo returns, wishing he could forget Zerline, whom he loved so much ("Pour toujours, toujours"). He intends to avenge himself by letting Diavolo kill him. Zerline and Matheo come out of the inn, and she asks him to explain his behavior. He doesn't answer, and the *carabinieri* return, urging him to lead them on. He tells them to wait for him, intending to keep the appointment for the duel; Zerline becomes desperate as the peasants urge her to come to the wedding and Lorenzo's men urge him to come fight the bandits ("Allons, allons, jeunes filles"). Beppe and Giacomo drink and become tipsy, and repeat the phrases Zerline used when undressing, and she realizes that they must have been hiding and listening. She tells Lorenzo of her suspicions, and he has them searched. When he reads the note, Pamela and Cockburn are reconciled. Lorenzo orders Giacomo taken to the hermitage to ring the bell, Beppe is set up as bait to draw Diavolo out. When he enters, he is quickly arrested, to general rejoicing: "Grand Dieu, je te rends." *—Ann Feeney*

Recommended:

○ **Auber: Fra Diavolo** / Soustrot (cond.), Gedda, Mesple, Berbie, Bastin, Monte Carlo PO / 2002 / EMI 575251

La Muette de Portici (1828)

With *La Muette de Portici,* Daniel-François-Esprit Auber and Eugène Scribe created a new genre of nineteenth century opera. It was to become known as French grand opera, and other practitioners of the genre would include Meyerbeer, Rossini, and Halévy. Eugène Scribe was the literary genius behind the form who wrote many of the texts for these composers, including *La Juive, Les Huguenots,* and *Robert le Diable,* three of the biggest hits of the nineteenth century Paris Opéra. Grand opera contained lavish sets, large crowd scenes, choruses, processions, ballets, huge *tableaux,* extravagant scenic effects, and sensational stories with often revolutionary themes. The political fervor of the story and music of *La Muette* made it instantly popular throughout Europe. It became associated with revolutionary ideas after it inspired an uprising in Brussels which led to the creation of an independent Belgian state, and it is thought to have spurred unrest in France itself in 1830. In accordance with the sensationalist tendencies of grand opera, Scribe has the revolutionary leader Masaniello go mentally insane after he has been poisoned, and has his sister Fenella hurl herself into Mount Vesuvius, just as it begins to erupt.

The libretto to *La Muette,* written by Germain Delavigne, was originally in three acts. The censors demanded changes to the text, and Scribe rewrote it several times before coming up with a dramaturgically successful solution. In accordance with the censor's demands, he suppressed much of the revolutionary material. But he also expanded the work into a five-act creation and added the main character of Fenella. She is a mute girl who expresses herself only through pantomime acted out against dramatic orchestral accompaniments. She is the sister to the fisherman Masaniello, and she has been betrayed and seduced by a member of the Spanish ruling class. It is Masaniello who will later become, partly because of the fate of his sister, the leader of the revolutionaries who take back the city of Naples from the Spanish. The fates of Masaniello and his mute sister are delicately intertwined throughout the opera. She is driven to suicide by the violent events of the revolution and the tragedy of her own betrayal, while he is eventually murdered by the very men whom he led to victory against the Spanish nobility. The story of Masaniello was set several times in the nineteenth century. He was an actual historical figure, and did lead a popular revolt against the Spanish in Naples in 1647. The character of Fenella was taken from an 1822 Walter Scott novel called *Peveril of the Peak.* The tradition of pantomime was taken from the French *melodramme,* and added an effective touch of pathos and dramaturgical balance to the violence of the story. *—Rita Laurance*

Synopsis:

Act One. The opera opens at the palace of the Spanish viceroy of Naples. Preparations are being made for the wedding of the viceroy's son Alphonse to the Spanish princess Elvire. Alphonse has recently seduced and abandoned a local Neapolitan girl named Fenella. He expresses his remorse and his concern over her having been arrested by his men, for she is helpless and mute. Elvire, meanwhile, contemplates her love for Alphonse. Her happiness is interrupted by the arrival of a mute girl, pursued by Alphonse's men. It is Fenella. She rushes in and asks the princess in pantomime for her protection. She then joins the procession to the chapel where the wedding is to take place. After the ceremony, however, she tells the princess that it was Alphonse who betrayed her, and Elvire is horrified. Fenella rushes quickly away into the crowds.

Act Two. Back at the seaside town of Portici, Masaniello tells the other fishermen that the right time will come for open revolt against Spanish rule, and that the time is coming soon. He and his friend Pietro worry about the fate of Fenella and swear to gain vengeance against whoever wronged her. Fenella returns and refuses to tell them the identity of her attacker, but tells them that he is married. Masaniello rallies the other fishermen around him and incites them to rebellion.

Act Three. In the main square of Naples, Alphonse pleads with Elvire. He tells her that he loves her and repents for all his wrongs. Finally they are reconciled, and he tells his men to find Fenella. The business of the bustling city goes on, and Fenella enters the crowded square. When Alphonse's soldiers attempt to arrest her, Masaniello steps forward and calls for his men. Rioting breaks out, and Masaniello and the other fishermen take the city from the Spanish.

Act Four. Masaniello has returned to his home in Portici. There he despairs of the effects of revolution. The men have taken to looting and plundering, and there is widespread bloodshed. Fenella is terrified of all the violence, and he rocks her and sings her to sleep. Masaniello's men enter, asking him to lead them against the Spanish again, but he refuses, saying that he doesn't want any more violence. Alphonse and Elvire come to the house and ask Fenella for her protection against the revolutionary forces. She agrees, and Masaniello offers them hospitality. When Pietro and the other fishermen see that Masaniello is protecting a Spanish noble, they begin to plot against his life, saying that he is just as much a tyrant as any of the Spanish.

Act Five. Pietro has given Masaniello poison and tells the others that soon their former leader will go mad from its effects. One of the revolutionary leaders enters to say that Alphonse is bringing more Spanish troops to fight against them. They ask Masaniello to save them, and he staggers forth, already insane from the drugs that he has taken. Fenella calms him, and he exits with his troops. But his men kill him when he once again saves Elvire from being murdered by them. The Spanish defeat the revolutionaries, and Fenella commits suicide by leaping into the mouth of Mount Vesuvius, just as it begins to erupt. *—Rita Laurance*

Recommended:

○ **Auber: La Muette de Portici** / T. Fulton (cond.), A. Kraus, J. Anderson, Aler, Lafont, Monte Carlo PO / 2002 / EMI 575257

Arleen Augér

b. Sep. 13, 1939, Los Angeles, CA, **d.** Jun. 10, 1993, Leusden, Netherlands

Soprano

Augér performed in the fields of opera and art song, but as her career evolved she began to focus her musical energies on the latter, preferring the intimacy of recitals to the bustle involved in staged operatic performances. Her voice was sweet-toned and pure, but also capable of a good deal of warmth and expressiveness. She was much loved as a teacher. Renée Fleming, who was one of her students, said that had she lived longer, she would undoubtedly have become one of the great lieder teachers. Her early death cut her career short, but she left a wide recorded legacy.

Born near Los Angeles, she graduated from the University in California in 1963, having studied not only voice but piano and violin. After graduating, she moved to Chicago, where she studied with Ralph Errole. Returning to Los Angeles, she won the I. Victor Fuchs Competition, and with it, an audition for the Vienna State Opera, where Josef Krips, the director, offered her a contract despite her lack of stage experience. She made her operatic debut in 1967 there, as the Queen of the Night in Mozart's *Die Zauberflöte,* and made her Salzburg Festival debut in 1969. In 1970, Erik Werba invited her to perform the soprano part of Hugo Wolf's *Italienisches Liederbuch* in a series of performances which he was producing at Wolf's own summer house. She began to focus more and more of her attention on song, oratorio, and church music, and she left the Vienna State Opera in 1974. By that point her 1975 La Scala and 1978 Met debuts were almost afterthoughts, for she was clearly turning away from the operatic world. She came to worldwide fame when she sang Mozart's *Exsultate, jubilate* at the wedding of the Duke and Duchess of York in 1986, which was seen by an estimated television audience of 300 million. (The couple left the selection of music and performers up to Simon Preston, director of music at Westminster Abbey.) In 1993, she died of cancer.

Fortunately, she made a number of recordings during her career, of art song, sacred music, and opera. She made an excellent Constanze in the Böhm *Die Entführung aus dem Serail*, and also recorded a very fine sampling of Handel and Bach arias (Delos 3026). Her collection of Schumann lieder on Berlin Classics (0021862BC) shows her sensitvity to nuance and emotional expressiveness. *—Ann Feeney*

Recommended:

○ **Arleen Augér: American Soprano** / Augér, various / 1992 / Delos 3712

○ **Schubert: The Complete Songs Vol. 9** / Augér, Johnson / 1990 / Hyperion 33009

○ **Love Songs** / Augér, Baldwin / 1992 / Delos 3029

○ **Mahler: Symphony 2** / Rattle (cond.), Baker, Augér, Birmingham SO / 1991 / EMI 47962

Georges Auric

b. Feb. 15, 1899, Lodève, Hérault, France, **d.** Jul. 23, 1983, Paris, France

Composer: Film Music, Ballet, Chamber Music

More than the other members of the group of French composers known as "Les Six," Georges Auric made his mark as a composer of incidental and dramatic music. His early encounter with ballet impresario Serge Diaghilev resulted in commissions for a number of dance scores. Among them were the slightly acerbic, mock-Romantic confections *Les Fâcheux* (1924) and *Les Matelots* (1925). The bulk of his ballet work, for Diaghilev and others, was produced between 1924 and 1934, and then between 1949 and 1952. Auric was also an early specialist in music for movies, a pursuit that occupied him primarily between his two ballet phases. His first film score was for Jean Cocteau's notorious 1930 Surrealist opus *Le Sang d'un poète*, and his score for the 1932 film *A Nous la liberté* also gained currency as a symphonic suite. Film fanciers will have certainly encountered Auric's scores for the 1949–50 Cocteau creations *Les Parents terribles* and *Orphée*. And his *Moulin Rouge*, music for the popular 1952 film about Toulouse-Lautrec, even produced a pop hit, "Where Is Your Heart?"

Born in 1899, Auric began his studies at the Montpellier Conservatory, then went on to the Paris Conservatory and the Schola Cantorum, where he studied with d'Indy and Roussel. By the time he was 16, he had written *Gaspard et Zoé*, music for a magic lantern show, as well as some 300 songs and piano pieces; at 18 came the ballet *Les Noces de Gamache*. He turned to comic opera at 20, with *La Reine de coeur*, a work he later destroyed. As part of the disillusioned young generation that survived World War I, he joined the anti-Romantic movement that was forming around Satie and Cocteau. The ideal was the new, the innovative, the urban, the American (in the rather limited and romanticized French understanding of America), and Satie's concept of music as something that should produce "auditory pleasure without demanding disproportionate attention from the listener." Auric found himself lounging around Satie in the company of five other young composers: Poulenc, Milhaud, Honegger, Durey, and Tailleferre. The group was initially called "Les nouveaux jeunes"; in 1920, critic Henri Collet dubbed them "Les Six," although each member followed a largely independent aesthetic path. Overall, there is much musical irony in Auric's works, in which popular tunes are combined with advanced harmony. Because his music is most easily described by what it is not—not as lighthearted and tender as Poulenc's, not as dour as Honegger's, not as exuberant with polyrhythmy and polytonality as Milhaud's—Auric, like Durey and Tailleferre, never gained the popularity and respect of his three more famous compatriots. Nevertheless, as critic Boris de Schloezer remarked in 1926, Auric's conscious, self-ironic efforts to create the impression of superficiality, may conceal a profound musical impulse. In fact, in 1930, the year he composed the score for *Le Sang d'un poète*, Auric wrote his Sonata for piano in F, a serious, lyrically expressive work which may seem at odds with the composer's public image. In his later years, Auric assumed a number of administrative responsibilities. From 1962 to 1968, he was the general administrator of the Opéra and Opéra Comique in Paris. This was right in the middle of his tenure, from 1954 to 1977, as president of the French Union of Composers and Authors. He also wrote music criticism for *Marianne*, *Paris-Soir*, and *Nouvelles Littéraires*. Auric died in 1983. *—James Reel*

FILM MUSIC

La Belle et la bête (1945–1946)

Of the members of France's notorious Les Six, Georges Auric (along with Arthur Honegger) had the most notable film scoring career. In addition to scoring several major films for French cinema, Auric wrote the scores to Audrey Hepburn's star-making *Roman Holiday* (1953), *Moulin Rouge* (1952), *The Lavender Hill Mob* (1951), and *The Innocents* (1961). Jean Cocteau and Auric worked together on films from 1930, when the poet turned his hand to cinema; notable collaborations included *Le Sang d'un poète* (Blood of a Poet), *Orphée*, *Le Testament d'Orphée*, *L'Aigle à deux têtes*, and *Les Parents terribles*.

Nazi occupation of France (1940–44) put the French film industry on hold. But directly after the war Auric composed what is probably his best-known score, that to Cocteau's *La Belle et la bête* (The Beauty and the Beast). Cocteau had begun filming it in August of that year, using as his literary source the famous original fairy-tale by Jeanne-Marie Leprince de Beaumont (1711–80). The production was troubled; the budget was minuscule, and Cocteau had health problems which made the assistance he received from Réné Clément in shooting and directing it invaluable. Cocteau also had an inflexible schedule and the film had to be finished in April 1946.

Auric scored the film for a full symphony orchestra and a wordless mixed chorus. Writing and orchestrating the score, which comprises 24 cues, consumed so much time that it was not possible to synchronize the score to the film, but merely to record it in free time along with the film. Paradoxically, this added to the remarkable, timeless fairy-tale atmosphere of the film, which slowly gained a reputation as an international cinematic masterpiece.

The score to *La Belle et la bête* was thought lost, but after the composer's death it was discovered in a mass of manuscripts he had stored in boxes. The conductor Adriano edited it and made the first good recording of it, released by Marco Polo records in 1994. The unsynchronized nature of the original score should make it possible to substitute Adriano's (or someone else's) modern stereophonic recording for the original soundtrack. *—Joseph Stevenson*

Recommended:

○ **Auric: La Belle et la bête** / Adriano (cond.), Moscow SO / 1996 / Marco Polo 223765

Moulin Rouge (1952)

Georges Auric seems to be remembered for two things: his film music and having been part of Les Six. Of the former, the "Song From Moulin Rouge," with its quintessential French waltz style, became his most famous piece of music, even an international hit.

There have been at least four different films with the title *Moulin Rouge*. The 1953 film could have been called "Lautrec," as it is essentially a biopic of Toulouse-Lautrec. It is perhaps fitting that Auric composed the score for this film, as there are many points of similarity between the composer and the artist, who died less than two years after Auric's birth. Both could be charming, impudent, sardonic, and emotionally detached. Both were more at ease and less bored by the worlds of cabaret and music hall than more elevated social strata. Auric's music from his early days as a member of Les Six (of which, in actuality, he was probably the best representative) was more than a little influenced by the popular music of the cabaret. It is no surprise that the dances and popular music from 1890s Paris in the film have such a ring of authenticity. Thanks to both director and composer, music is never intrusive and appears only where it needs to be. Indeed, compared to the typical Hollywood film score, one is rather amazed with how relatively little music there is in *Moulin Rouge*, particularly of the non-integral sort (i.e., "mood" music not being shown performed on screen). There also is no bloated orchestration or melodramaticism to be found in Auric's score.

It is all the more ironic, then, that "April Again," the song Jeanne Avril (unfortunately played by Zsa-Zsa Gabor, but sung by Muriel Smith) sings at the *Moulin Rouge*, and probably the most sentimental item in the score, became the film's most memorable piece. This "Song from Moulin Rouge" quickly found itself re-arranged many times for various instrumental combinations. The melody became even more popular with a new set of lyrics, "Where is Your Heart?" by William Enquick. *—Neil Cardew-Fanning*

Recommended:

○ **Auric: Film Music** / R. Gamba (cond.), BBC PO / 1999 / Chandos 9774

Orphée (1949)

In a classic director-composer partnership, Georges Auric composed the score for Jean Cocteau's fifth film as both writer and director, *Orphée* (1949), based on his 1926 play. In many ways the score is similar to Auric's score for Cocteau's classic *La belle et la bête*. The mood, while not as fantastical as the earlier film, is still otherworldly. The woodwinds and reed instruments are used to carry much of the melody in the score, adding a pastoral tone, but also in keeping with the overall style of the music of Les Six, the group of French composers, friends of Cocteau, which included Auric. The score includes a heroic main theme, eerie strings, and throbbing drums to represent the underworld, and a love theme that is moving, yet shadowed by tragedy. Auric also made a nod to an earlier French version of the Greek myth by including his own lush orchestral arrangement of the "Complaint of Eurydice" from Gluck's opera *Orphée et Eurydice*. *—Patsy Morita*

Recommended:

○ **Classic Film Music of Auric Vol. 2** / Adriano (cond.), Slovak Radio SO / 1999 / Marco Polo 8225066

BALLET

Les Matelots (1924)

Georges Auric, a talented but lesser-known member of the group of young, early twentieth century composers known as Les Six, composed his ballet *Les Matelots* for a performance by Diaghilev's famous ensemble in 1924. It was the second of Auric's ballets for Diaghilev, who, one year earlier, had been so impressed by Auric's incidental music for a presentation of Molière's *Les fâcheux* that he enlisted Auric to collaborate on a ballet version. The collaboration continued with *Les Matelots*, presented with choreography by Massine, and another ballet, *La pastorale*, both of which were considered successful at the time but have since been somewhat neglected. The story of the *Les Matelots* (*The Sailors*), like the music, is lighthearted, playful, and uncomplicated. Three sailors, about to embark on a sea voyage, pay a visit to a pair of young ladies. During their visit, one of the sailors (originally played by the famous dancer Serge Lifar) becomes enamored with one of the girls and asks to marry her upon his return from sea. She agrees and bids a sad farewell to the sailors. Her friend also bids adieu, leaving the girl alone to pine for her lover. When the sailors return to shore, they decide to test the girl's faithfulness by donning disguises and posing as suitors. Their efforts thwarted by the girl's unfailing fidelity, the lover reveals his true identity and embraces his bride-to-be. The suite drawn from the music for the ballet presents the drama and romance of the story in gentle caricature. The plaintive melody representing the girl's solitude is tempered in its longing by the lilting accompaniment and occasional chromatic meandering in the bass—a subtle polytonal shading characteristic of Auric's style and of Les Six in general. Auric's careful attention to orchestration plays a central role in painting the shifting moods of the melodrama, the brass and percussion evoking a charming and slightly awkward regality, the nimble string lines conveying the nervous anticipation of the fresh-faced lovers. The set of variations associated with the sailors at once depicts the young men's bravado as well as their humor, with strutting fanfares alternating with a restlessly fast bassoon line or slapstick chromatic inflections in the upper winds and strings. Perhaps most appealing is Auric's ability to move smoothly from the comic to the earnest, as if telling the story with a knowing wink and a nod. *—Jeremy Grimshaw*

CHAMBER MUSIC

Trio for oboe, clarinet & bassoon (1938)

Through much of this lighthearted woodwind trio, Auric thinks in terms of three interdependent melodic lines rather than a dominant theme supported by subservient harmonic accompaniment. In this respect, he seems strongly influenced by the insistence of Nadia Boulanger, the leading French composition teacher of Auric's time, that music should be conceived vertically in the manner of Renaissance madrigals, rather than horizontally in the tune-and-chord manner of the eighteenth and nineteenth centuries. Yet there's nothing archaic or even intellectual in the sound of this trio; it's breezy entertainment in the wry style for which the music of Auric's circle, Les Six, is best-known. The first movement, "Décidé," is in what might be called anal-retentive sonata-allegro form; Auric thoroughly develops the whimsical first theme before even introducing the second, with which he briefly toys before returning to the initial material. The melodies never stray far from the music hall and remain perky through the entire course of the movement. The Romance movement employs a spacious theme that constantly shifts among the three players, while whatever instruments aren't playing the melody do their best to tangle it in wandering subsidiary lines, like a boy swinging his feet impatiently while watching a mushy scene in some movie. Gallic insouciance returns in the generically named "Final," a rondo-variation flirtation with a cheeky waltz that clucks, swirls, loses its balance, and hobbles back toward equilibrium. *—James Reel*

Recommended:

- ○ **French Wind Music** / Pro Arte Wind Quintet / 1992 / Nimbus 5327
- ○ **Poulenc; Koechlin; Milhaud; Auric; Satie** / Hexagon Ensemble / 2000 / Arsis 99031

Emanuel Ax

b. Jun. 8, 1949, Lwow, Poland

Pianist

From a string of early career successes in the 1970s, Emanuel Ax has emerged as one of the most versatile, brilliant, and universally respected pianists on the international concert scene.

Ax's father was a coach at the Lwow Opera House. Emanuel's talent and interest in music manifested itself early; his first instrument was actually the violin, though he eventually took up piano lessons with his father. After living for a time in Warsaw, then Winnipeg, Canada, the family moved to the United States in 1961, and Ax began studies with Mieczyslaw Munz at the Juilliard School. He made his first concert tour, to South Africa, in 1969; in the following year he became an American citizen.

Ax is the rare musician who was able to parlay exposure via the competition circuit into a lasting and truly successful international career. After disappointing finishes in high-profile events like the Chopin Competition and the Queen Elizabeth Competition, Ax withdrew from competing for a time to make his New York debut, at Alice Tully Hall, on March 12, 1973. In the following year, he at last took top prize in an event of some importance, the Rubinstein Piano Master Competition. It was with this success—which included an American concert tour—that Ax's star began to rise toward international superstardom. In 1979 he was awarded the coveted Avery Fisher Prize, which led to a recording contract with RCA Victor.

As a soloist Ax has demonstrated a particular affinity for the Romantics; nonetheless, his repertoire is among the most diverse of any pianist on the scene today and ranges from the music of Haydn, Mozart, and Beethoven to important twentieth century figures like Tippett, Henze, and Hindemith. He is also a particular champion of contemporary music, and has played and commissioned works from such composers as Joseph Schwantner, John Adams, and Christopher Rouse. He is considered by players and audiences alike to be a chamber musician *par excellence*; his frequent partners in this endeavor include Isaac Stern, Jaime Laredo, and Richard Stolzman. His regular collaborations with cellist Yo-Yo Ma have netted the pair three Grammy Awards. Ax has also demonstrated an interest in "authentic" performance; he recorded the Chopin concerti on an 1853 Erard piano very similar to Chopin's own instrument. Ax maintains a busy recording and recital schedule and frequently appears with the world's leading orchestras and at the major music festivals. He resides with his wife, pianist Yoko Nozaki, and their two children in New York City. *—Joseph Stevenson*

Recommended:

- ○ **Ax Plays Brahms** / Ax / 1992 / Sony 48046
- ○ **Ax Plays Haydn Sonatas** / Ax / 1994 / Sony 53635
- ○ **Rachmaninoff, Prokofiev: Cello Sonatas** / Ma, Ax / 2003 / Sony 90397
- ○ **Brahms, Mozart, Beethoven: Trios** / Ax, Ma, Stoltzman (clarinet) / 1995 / Sony 57499

Milton Babbitt

b. May 10, 1916, Philadelphia, PA
Composer
Revered for his pioneering work in serial organization and in musical electronics, Milton Babbitt (b. 1916) is a major American composer, theorist, and teacher. Born in Philadelphia and raised in Jackson, MS, he began his study of the violin at age four. He later learned to play clarinet and saxophone, exhibiting an early interest in jazz and popular song.

Despite his gift for music, he attended the University of Pennsylvania to pursue a career in mathematics. He then decided to attend New York University, studying music with Marion Bauer and Philip James. Babbitt was attracted to the epochal discoveries of Schoenberg, at a time when 12-tone and serial techniques were still relatively new. After receiving a B.A. from NYU in 1935, he studied composition with Roger Sessions, at first privately, and then later at Princeton University, where he received a Master of Fine Arts in 1942. During World War II he worked as a mathematical researcher and taught mathematics at Princeton. At this time he developed the complex ramifications of Schoenberg's 12-tone compositional method into what came to be known as total serialism. In a nutshell, what this meant was that he expanded Schoenberg's 12-tone system, wherein compositional structure is determined by manipulation of a constant sequence of the 12 pitches of the chromatic scale—to other aspects of music: rhythm, dynamics, timbre, and other parameters were structured according to fixed sequences that acquired structural importance both in being manipulated on their own and in interaction with other serial parameters. He succeeded Sessions on Princeton's music faculty in 1948 and later taught also at the Juilliard School in New York.

Babbitt is credited with writing the first serial work, *Three Compositions for Piano,* in 1947, at least one year before Messiaen's studies. Babbitt's important early works in his rigorously organized serial style include the first two string quartets (1948, 1954), the jazz-influenced *All Set* (1957) and *Partitions* for piano (1957). Babbitt is also responsible for developing and classifying such important serialist concepts as combinatoriality, partitioning, arrays, pitch class, pitch set, and the time-point system. In extending the challenging language of Schoenberg, Babbitt's "new complexity" continually met with incomprehension from audiences and musicians alike. This led Babbitt to seek means of composing and performing outside of traditional settings and formats. He found what he was looking for in the emerging analog technology of the RCA Mark II synthesizer and the Columbia-Princeton recording studio, which he co-founded with Otto Luening and Vladimir Ussachevsky in 1959. One year later, Babbitt completed his first entirely synthesized work, *Vision and Prayer. Philomel* (1964) shows his use of the human voice as an essential part of his conception; it was one of the earliest pieces to combine tape playback with a live performance, in this case one by Babbitt's wife, soprano Bethany Beardslee.

Later works such as *Post-Partitions* for piano (1966) and *Relata II* for orchestra (1968), show Babbitt's increasingly dense modes of musical significance, achieved through close connections between pitch and rhythmic organization, and through the use of every possible musical parameter in delineating structure. The *String Quartet No. 3* (1970) includes metronomic stability, changes of velocity engineered by changes in metrical density, sectional form, and the use of many other musical parameters—including the distinction between arco and pizzicato string playing—to integrate the polyphony. Performances of these works have rarely been successful, if even possible.

In addition to his degrees from NYU and Princeton, Babbitt has received a lifetime Pulitzer Prize in composition for his contributions to 12-tone and electronic music. He has also been recognized by numerous universities for his contributions. Babbitt, who once named Jerome Kern as the composer with whom he would most like to have traded places, is a member of the American Academy of Arts and Letters and a Fellow of the American Academy of Arts and Sciences.—*AMG*

Overview of Works
"I want a piece of music," composer Milton Babbitt has said, "to be literally as much as possible." Indeed, each piece of his large and varied body of compositions seems to aspire to exhaust its own possibilities, to begin a very clearly defined task and carry it to its full fruition. Though this rigor has certainly translated into a musical language that many listeners find indecipherable and inaccessible, it has also served to expand for subsequent generations of composers the palette of musical possibilities, and blurred the boundary between what is theoretically engaging and what is aurally appealing.

Babbitt, a trained mathematician, compares his compositional interests to the theoretical sciences, in which explorations of the furthest abstract reaches of a field (such as physics or math) yield results that may not trickle down to practical experience in a very discernible way. His musical experiments, he insisted, plumbed similar depths of musical possibilities. His fundamental method of exploration throughout his career was the 12-tone method as developed by Schoenberg and the Second Viennese School; he would extrapolate this method in various ways. In his *Partitions* from 1957, multiple tone rows develop simultaneously on the horizontal plane, while their constituent segments create new vertical 12-tone relationships. His *Relata I,* a work for orchestra from 1965, maps a dauntingly complex matrix of intersecting 12-tone systems onto various divisions and subdivisions of the instrumental groups in the orchestra.

One of Babbitt's most important innovations (in company with French composer Pierre Boulez) was to project the serial principles of 12-tone method onto other parameters of composition, such as duration and articulation. Early in his career, for example, his *Three Compositions for Piano* (1947) mapped the same numerical sequence (5-1-4-2) to determine pitches as well as the length of their groupings. Other works realized this in different ways: his *String Quartet No. 3* (1970), for example, maps 12-tone sequences onto 12 divisions within each measure of the piece; this and other pieces use similar methods to determine register, articulation, timbre, and dynamics as well.

The complexity of Babbitt's compositional procedures challenges the abilities of even the most accomplished performers, and some of his ideas simply cannot be realized by human players. Thus, while continuing to compose for a wide range of instrumental and vocal combinations, Babbitt also established himself as one of the twentieth century's foremost composers of electronic music. His *Philomel,* a work for electronics and voice from 1964, is a stunning integration of theoretical apparatus and emotional expression. Other important electronic works include *Composition for Synthesizer* (1961), *Vision and Prayer* (1961), and *Ensembles for Synthesizer* (1964). His works of the 1970s and 1980s demonstrate both an increasing complexity of method as well as an increasing ability to render those methods for performance by instruments or voices, as seen in *A Solo Requiem* (for solo and two pianos, 1977), *Transfigured Notes for String Orchestra* (1986), and a number of other works for a variety of media and instrumentation. —*Jeremy Grimshaw*

Recommended:

- ○ **Milton Babbitt: Philomel** / Beardslee, L. Webber, R. Miller, Kuderna / 1995 / New World 80466
- ○ **Babbitt: Piano Works** / R. Taub / HM 905160
- ○ **Babbitt: Concerto for Piano & Orchestra; The Head Of The Bed** / A. Feinberg, Korf & Wuorinen (conds.), Bettina, American Composers Orchestra, Parnassus / 1987 / New World 80346
- ○ **Milton Babbitt: Soli e Duettini; Swan Song No 1** / Milarsky (cond.), Cygnus Ensemble / 2003 / Bridge 9135
- ○ **Milton Babbitt: Occasional Variations** / M. Babbitt, Composers Quartet, Sherry Quartet / 2003 / Tzadik 7088

Carl Philipp Emanuel Bach

b. Mar. 8, 1714, Weimar, Germany, **d.** Dec. 14, 1788, Hamburg, Germany
Composer: Keyboard, Symphonic, Chamber Music, Choral
The second surviving son of J.S. Bach, Carl Philipp Emanuel was the most innovative and idiosyncratic member of an extremely talented musical family. His music, unlike that of his father or that of the master he influenced, Haydn, did not define an era so much as reveal a deeply personal response to the musical conventions of his time.

C.P.E. Bach could play his father's technically demanding keyboard pieces at sight by the time he was seven. Also an exceptional student in areas other than music, he enrolled at the University of Leipzig in 1731 to study law, then transferred to the University of Frankfurt an der Oder. He graduated in 1734, but remained in that backwater town giving keyboard lessons, involving himself in public concerts, and learning the composer's craft.

By 1740 Bach was in Berlin as harpsichordist to Frederick the Great of Prussia. Here he was first exposed to Italian opera seria, and its dramatic style infiltrated his instrumental music. Little of this was heard at court, where Bach accompanied the flutist-king in one reactionary concerto after another by Quantz. He made several attempts to find a new position, but the stress of the king's disfavor was partially relieved in 1756, when Frederick became distracted by the Seven Years' War and was frequently away from the court. Bach found a select audience for his remarkable and experimental series of keyboard works such as the so-called "Prussian" and "Württemberg" sonatas (composed in the early 1740s) and the *Sonatas with Varied Repeats* (1760).

Bach finally got himself released from Frederick's service in 1768 in order to succeed Telemann as cantor at the Johanneum in Hamburg, also serving as music director for the city's five major churches; he held this post until his death.

Stylistically distant from his father's rigorous polyphony, C.P.E. Bach was something of a proto-Romantic; he was the master of *Empfindsamkeit*, or "intimate expressiveness." The dark, dramatic, improvisation-like passages that appear in some of Mozart's and Haydn's works are due in part to his influence; his music in time became known all over Europe. His impulsive works for solo keyboard, which lurch into unexpected keys, change tempo and dynamics abruptly, and fly along with wide-ranging themes, are especially compelling. One account of Bach's after-dinner improvisations described the sweaty, glazed-eyed musician as "possessed," an adjective that would be applied to equally intense and idiosyncratic musicians in the Romantic age. Many of his symphonies are as audacious as his keyboard pieces.

In the area of chamber music, Bach pulled the keyboard out of its subsidiary Baroque role and made it a full partner with, or even leader of, the other instruments. Yet here he fashioned the music to the public's conservative expectations, as he did with his church music. He composed prolifically in many genres, and much of his work awaits public rediscovery.

Bach also produced an important account of performance practice in the second half of the eighteenth century, translated into English as *Essay on the True Art of Playing Keyboard Instruments*. —*James Reel*

KEYBOARD

Works for Keyboard (1731–1788)

The most gifted son of Johann Sebastian Bach, the highest embodiment of the German *Aufklarung* in music, and the greatest keyboard composer of his generation, Carl Philipp Emanuel Bach (1714–88) essentially wrote his keyboard works in three periods. The works of C.P.E. Bach's youth, his *Two Marches and Two Polonaises* from 1725, were part of the *Notebuch für Anna Magdalena Bach* and thus still part of the basic musical childhood of anyone who learns the piano. The works of Bach's Berlin period are best represented by the three groups of sonatas: the *Sechs Sonaten fur Cembalo* from 1742 dedicated to Friedrich the Great of Prussia, the *Sechs Sonaten per Cembalo* from 1744 dedicated to Carl Eugen of Württemberg, and the sonatas and sonatinas of his "Versuch über die wahre Art das Clavier zu spielen" (Essay on the True Art of Playing the Keyboard) from 1753. In all three sets, Bach's music is virtuosic and soulful and capricious and fantastic and ecstatic. The intellectual wit and the emotional depth of Bach's sonatas is the apogee of the *empfindsamer Stil* in German music and was an enormous influence on Haydn, Mozart, and the young Beethoven. The works of Bach's Hamburg period are gathered together in the *Sechs Sammlunghen von Sonaten, Freien Fantasien und Rondos für Kenner und Liebhaber* (Six Collections of Sonatas, Free Fantasies and Rondos for Amateurs and Connoisseurs) from 1779 through 1787. In these collections, Bach's fantasy and imagination are set loose, and the works are among the most expressive and most profound ever composed for the keyboard. —*James Leonard*

Recommended:

- ○ **C.P.E. Bach: For Connoisseurs & Amateurs** / Antalffy / CPO 999100
- ○ **C.P.E. Bach: Complete Keyboard Fantasias** / E. Garvey / 1988 / Elan 2214
- ○ **C.P.E. Bach: Sonatas & "Petites Pièces" Vol. 1** / Spanyi / 2002 / BIS 1087

SYMPHONIC

Sei sinfonie ("Hamburg"), H. 657–662 (1773)

C.P.E. Bach composed the six *"Hamburg" Sinfonias* to fulfill a commission by Baron Gottfried van Swieten (the noted eighteenth century Austrian diplomat who was a patron of Mozart and Beethoven, and who wrote the texts for Haydn's *Creation* and *The Seasons*). Van Swieten gave Bach free reign to compose these works as he wished, so the result is one of startling originality. The sinfonias are all in the more "conservative" three-movement form (some composers, such as the Mannheim school's Johann Stamitz, were already adding a fourth movement to their sinfonias, which became the standard for Haydn, Mozart, and Beethoven); but, they are far from conservative or restrained in terms of harmonic, thematic, and emotional invention.

Already in the first couple of measures of the *Sinfonia No. 1* we find the dramatic shifts of mood and dynamics that are perfect examples of the *empfindsamer Stil*, or sensitive style, prevalent in northern Germany at this time (a direct challenge to the Baroque ideal of one consistent emotion throughout the movement). The sinfonias are marked by the same restless, passionate, impetuous, and humorous quality that is also evident in the early works of Haydn. Grace and elegance coexist with unpredictability and the willingness to surprise.

Sudden shifts in key and an asymmetry of phrasing make these works all the more engaging. The wonderfully abrupt ending of the first movement of *Sinfonia No. 2*, Allegro di molto, is a case in point. Many sections culminate in theatrically conceived unisons, a favorite device of Bach's, and better yet are the abrupt transitions whereby one movement simply elides into the next without preparation. Examples of this are found at the end of the first movements of both *Sinfonias Nos. 3* and *5*.

There is no strict formula for the structure of the outer fast movements in terms of meter, tempo, or mood. The slow movements rely heavily on chromaticism and ornamental devices such as the appoggiatura (stress of a dissonant note on a strong part of the beat, resolving on the weaker part of the beat creating the feeling of a "sigh"). The second movement of *Sinfonia No. 6*, Poco andante, contains a beautifully meandering and tonally ambiguous middle section. —*Mona DeQuis*

Recommended:

- ○ **Bach: Six Symphonies Wq 182** / Pinnock, English Concert / Archiv 415300

Orchester-sinfonien, H. 663–666 (1775–1776)

The second of Johann Sebastian Bach's many sons, Carl Philipp Emanuel Bach, was a major force in the development of the Classical symphonic form. The Sinfonias, W. 183 (1780), dedicated to the Crown Prince of Prussia, demonstrate a greater familiarity with the work of Joseph Haydn than do Emanuel Bach's earlier symphonies, especially in regard to the expansion of the genre's scope and form. Unlike the composer's previous set of six symphonies, written for four-part string ensemble and continuo, the four works at hand are for "twelve obbligato parts," indicating the inclusion of woodwinds. They are further marked by a greater length and variety of expressive content than was then conventional in a three-movement format. Sudden dissonances emerge and tonalities becomes clouded at key moments, echoing the influence of Haydn during his "Sturm und Drang" (Storm and Stress) period but also developing the vocabulary of Bach's own keyboard music. The second work in the set, the Sinfonia in E flat major, is remarkably forward looking in the importance and length of its final movement. While the Sinfonias have enjoyed more frequent performances by early music ensembles than by symphony orchestras, they are fine, imaginative, and well-crafted works that clearly express the powerful artistic personality of this composer. —*Joseph Stevenson*

Recommended:

- ○ **C. P. E. Bach: 4 Symphonies** / G. Leonhardt (cond.), Orch. of the Age of Enlightenment / 1994 / Virgin 61182
- ○ **C. P. E. Bach: Symphonies; Concerto** / Mai, Akademie für Alte Musik, Berlin / 1998 / HM 901622

CHAMBER MUSIC

Flute Sonatas (1735–1786)

The second son of Johann Sebastian Bach, Carl Philipp Emanuel spent a substantial part of his career in the service of the flute-loving (and playing) Frederick the Great at his court in Potsdam. Unlike Mozart, Emanuel Bach liked the flute as an instrument and composed a number of concertos and sonatas for the instrument. The earliest of these is a group of sonatas composed while Bach was still working in Frankfurt, where he attended university and subsequently taught and directed concerts. These include a *Sonata in G*, Wq 134, probably composed by 1735, and a group of seven sonatas, Wq 123–129, composed between 1735 and 1740, two years after Bach moved to Berlin. All are three-movement works in fast-slow-fast format and are cast in the old Baroque continuo sonata style, with the harpsichord (and cello) providing a bass accompaniment. After Bach had taken up his post with Frederick, he composed three more continuo sonatas, but increasingly turned to the more modern style of accompanied sonata pioneered by his father in the violin and flute sonatas. In these, the harpsichord enters more closely into dialogue with the flute, becoming more of an equal partner than mere supporter. Although these sonatas were composed during Bach's earlier years at Potsdam (the mid-1740s), it seems unlikely that they were composed with the king in mind. Although an enthusiastic amateur, the Prussian king was unlikely to have been sufficiently skilled to play some of the more demanding passages in Bach's music. Moreover, Frederick was no great admirer of Bach, preferring the easygoing, mellifluous music of his concertmaster Johann Quantz to Bach's more expressive, at times turbulent writing. The dissonant harmony of a movement like the Adagio di molto of the *Sonata in E*, probably composed around 1749, would not have been at all to Frederick's taste. Late in life, Bach surprisingly returned to the continuo style of sonata with an isolated work, the *Sonata in G*, Wq 133, completed in 1786, just two years before his death. —*Brian Robins*

Recommended:

- ○ **C.P.E. Bach: Sonatas for Flute & Harpsichord Wq 83–87** / Drahos, Pertis / 1991 / Naxos 550513

CHORAL

Auferstehung und Himmelfahrt Jesu, oratorio, H. 777 (1774–1780; revised 1788)

Carl Philipp Emanuel Bach is perhaps best known to modern audiences for his keyboard sonatas, which exemplify the spirit of the *empfindsamer stil* (sensitive style) of the middle 1700s. This compositional style is usually described in terms of its Mannerist harmonic expression, elegant figuration, dramatic dynamic shifts, and overall diversity. While these are all fair assessments, they tend to draw attention away from some of Bach's own favorite compositions, particularly the sacred works he composed after accepting an appointment as music director for the five largest churches in Hamburg. Prior to this, his three decades of employment in the Berlin court of Frederick the Great had provided him with ample opportunities to develop his intimate and subtle approach to musical gesture and to nurture the affinities his music shared with literary and philosophical trends of the day (the court being a hub of intellectual activity); the demand for sacred music, however, was slim. During Bach's 20 years in Hamburg, he composed a number of remarkable sacred vocal works, which received performances in public as well as church venues. Among the composer's own favorites was his oratorio *Die Auferstehung und Himmelfahrt Jesu* (The Resurrection and Ascension of Jesus), which received its first performance in 1778.

Although the shift in style concomitant to his change in employment was rather drastic, there is a continuity and evolution of style readily apparent in *Die Auferstehung*. C.P.E. Bach's innovative and unexpected harmonic turns are still present, as are his almost cinematic shifts of mood. Now, though, these devices are not focused with the microscopic intensity of solo keyboard music, but rather enhanced and highlighted through their application to a dramatic medium. Some scholars have observed that Bach's score lends its saving grace to an otherwise mediocre text by Karl Wilhelm Ramler, whose Passion texts nonetheless enjoyed considerable popularity in their settings by a number of composers. It would seem that even the most gripping and effective text would be overshadowed by C.P.E. Bach's setting, which heightens the drama of each poetic nuance and exaggerates the emotional trajectories of the most intense passages. The fluidity of recitatives such as the bass' "Judäa zittert" (Judea trembles) allows an interplay of soloist and orchestra that never loses its momentum; the aria that follows, "Mein Geist, voll Furcht und Freuden, bebet" (My spirit quakes with fear and joy), is marked by the lush and lengthy melismas that accompany the words "Die Glorie der Gottheit strahlt" (The glory of God shines forth). The choruses likewise magnify the surface idiosyncrasies of Bach's style—for example, rendering the gracefully angular melody in "Tod! Wo Ist dein Stachel" (Death, where is thy sting) in jubilant counterpoint. The work's lone duet, "Vater deiner schwachen Kinder" (O Father of Thy feeble children), perhaps best exemplifies Bach's skill at subtle inflection—a gift perhaps developed at the keyboard, but integrated convincingly into his sacred music. *—Jeremy Grimshaw*

Recommended:

- ○ **C.P.E. Bach: Die Auferstehung und Himmelfahrt Jesu** / S. Kuijken (cond.), Schwabe, C. & S. Genz, La Petite Bande / Hyperion 67364
- ○ **C.P.E. Bach: Die Auferstehung und Himmelfahrt Jesu** / Herreweghe (cond.), Martinpelto, Pregardien, P. Harvey, Orch. Of the Age of Enlightenment / 1992 / Virgin 59069

Johann Christian Bach

b. Sep. 5, 1735, Leipzig, Germany, **d.** Jan. 1, 1782, London, England
Composer: Symphonic

Johann Christian Bach had more fame in his lifetime than his father, the illustrious Johann Sebastian Bach, ever enjoyed. One of the leading composers of the Classical era, he is no longer eclipsed entirely by Haydn, Mozart, and Beethoven. He was the youngest son of Johann Sebastian Bach, who presumably gave the boy solid musical instruction but died when Johann Christian was 15. He was sent to Berlin to live and study with his well-established half-brother Carl Philipp Emanuel Bach.

Johann Christian gained a desire to write opera, and at the age of 19, he disregarded his brother's advice and set off for Italy. After some time writing church music, he was commissioned to write an opera to Metastasio's libretto *Artaserse* in 1760. It was the first in a string of three successful operas, which resulted in a call from London to write operas for the new king's theater. His first London effort, *Orione*, was produced on February 19, 1763. It won considerable praise and was transformed into a sensation when King George III and Queen Sophie Charlotte returned to see it again the next night.

The 20-year-old queen was German, homesick, and happy to hire a young German as her household musician and teacher for herself and her children. He was also an on-call accompanist for whenever King George decided to play flute. He met the Mozart family when they visited in 1764 and became a strong influence on the talented young Wolfgang.

A new impresario broke the king's theater contract with Bach, who then founded (in 1765) the Bach-Abel concerts with notable composer Carl Friedrich Abel. This became the leading concert series in London, initially held at Carlisle house in Soho Square, but later moving to Almack's Assembly Rooms on King Street. The series ran through 1782 and Bach soon found his operas back in favor. In 1768, Bach made history by becoming the first person to give a solo piano performance in London.

Bach also wrote music for notable political occasions on the Continent as well as in Britain. In the late 1770s, his fortunes declined. His music lost its popularity, and his steward embezzled practically all his wealth. His health declined, and he died in 1782 in considerable debt. Queen Sophie met the immediate expenses of the estate and established a life pension for Bach's widow, Cecilia. *—Joseph Stevenson*

Overview of Works (1758–1781)

Johann Christian Bach (1735–1782), the youngest son of Johann Sebastian Bach by his second wife, was the epitome of the cosmopolitan composer of the eighteenth century. He wrote for the market: liturgical music for Milan; operas for Naples, London, Mannheim, and Paris; orchestral music for concert halls in London, Mannheim, and Amsterdam; keyboard music for his pupils and his own public performances.

Taught first by his father and then by his brother Carl Philipp in Berlin after the death of his father, Johann Christian moved to Italy in 1754, converted to Catholicism in 1757, and, as the organist at Milan Cathedral, wrote austere music in the style of Palestrina. In 1760, Bach's opera seria *Artaserse* was premiered in Turin. Its success was followed by his second opera premiered in Naples in 1761 and his third opera in 1762. In 1763, Bach moved to London where *Orione* premiered in February, followed by the premiere of *Zanaida* in May. Bach's London operas are serious, conservative works written in the dominant *styl galant*. His *Temistocle*, written for and premiered in Mannheim in 1772, is more extravagant, demanding greater virtuosity of the singers and the orchestra. His last opera, and only French opera, *Armidis de Gaule*, was premiered in Paris in 1779 and withdrawn after three performances.

Bach's orchestral music grew out of his operas and his first set of *Concertos*, Op. 1, are essentially opera overtures. But Bach quickly developed a separate orchestral manner with more interesting themes and more extended developments. His two sets of *Symphonies*, Opp. 6 and 8, are on a level with the best symphonies of the time. His last set of orchestral works, the *Grand Overtures*, Op. 18, published in 1779, incorporate themes and music from his opera, but developed in a powerful symphonic manner. Bach's feel for the orchestra is also evident in his *Sinfonia Concertante* composed from the 1770s onward. *—James Leonard*

Recommended:

- ○ **Johann Christian Bach: Symphonies & Concertos** / Akademie für Alte Musik, Berlin / 2004 / HM 901803
- ○ **Johann Christian Bach: Woodwind Concertos Vol. 1** / Halstead (cond.), Robson, Brown, Ward, Hanover Band / CPO 999346
- ○ **Johann Christian Bach: Berlin Harpsichord Concertos Vol. 1** / Halstead (cond.), Hanover Band / CPO 999393

SYMPHONIC

Symphonies, Op. 3 (1765)

After seven years of work and study in Milan, the young J.C. Bach permanently moved to London, where he was ensconced as an expert on Italian opera. He was soon dividing his time between the stage and the concert hall; in 1764, he and composer Carl Friedrich Abel began promoting "symphony concerts," first in private residences and ultimately in the Hanover Square Rooms, in which Bach had a financial interest. Bach contributed about 90 symphonies to the series; some 60 survive. The six works published as his Op. 3 stand among his earliest efforts in the genre and reflect Bach's background in Italian opera; each is in the old three-movement, fast-slow-fast format of the Italian overture or sinfonia. They lack the storm-and-stress elements that would soon characterize the works of Haydn and C.P.E. Bach and avoid the special orchestral effects that would shortly be *de rigeur* in Mannheim and Paris. These sunny, well-balanced examples of the galant style strongly influenced the eight-year-old Mozart, who wrote his first symphonies during a trip to London when these works were first being played. Bach employed the same format for each little symphony. Happily turbulent outer movements embrace an Andante or Andantino of elegance and repose. The first movement is always a lively and compact sonata-allegro form, with a couple of themes (not highly contrasted, the more lyrical melody usually little more than a brief phrase) put through a short development before being restated. The other movements are usually in ABA form, or are rudimentary rondos—again, contrasting material tends to make very short appearances. Third movements evoke the minuet or gigue, though they are not so marked. Eighteenth century publishers typically front-loaded a publication with the most arresting compositions, pushing the more routine music to the back. So it is with Bach's Op. 3, dedicated to the Prince of York, brother of King George III. *Symphony No. 1* in D provides a festive beginning. The opening of *Symphony No. 2* in C is more jittery, but the Andante is memorably serene with a suggestion of melancholy. The fast movements of *No. 3 in E flat* begin to show more restraint, although the Andantino is notable for its bucolic use of flutes. High spirits return to *No. 4 in B flat. No. 5 in F* and *No. 6 in G* are more formulaic, except for the expressive Andante of the Sixth, and the finale of the *Fifth,* where a few patches of elegance interrupt the lighthearted music. *—James Reel*

Recommended:

- **J.C. Bach: Symphonies Op 3** / Pople (cond.), London Festival O / 1995 / Arte Nova 30488

Johann Christoph Friedrich Bach

b. Jun. 21, 1732, Leipzig, Germany, **d.** Jan. 26, 1795, Bückeburg, Germany

Composer

Johann Christoph Friedrich Bach was one of four J.S. Bach sons who attained renown in classical music. He is generally ranked behind Carl Philipp Emanuel in importance, but stands about on equal footing with Wilhelm Friedemann and Johann Christian. Johann Christoph Friedrich (generally referred to as "Friedrich") is known as the "Bückeburg" Bach, since he served at the court there from 1750, when he was just 18, until his death in 1795. His early music reflected the style of his father, while his mature compositions began showing Italian influences, offering a sort of cross between the German and Italian schools. His late works began to exhibit Classical characteristics. To clear up matters about the large Bach family and his position within it, Friedrich was the oldest surviving son of J.S. Bach and his second wife Anna Magdalena, and was the third oldest of the four Bach sons who attained musical prominence: Wilhelm Friedemann was the oldest, born 1710, followed by Carl Philipp Emanuel (b. 1714) (their mother being Maria Barbara Bach), and the last was Johann Christian (b. 1735).

Friedrich was given his first music lessons by his father and later by a cousin of his father, Johann Elias Bach. When he was about 17 Friedrich enrolled at the University of Leipzig in preparation for a career in law, but left after a year, apparently because his father had become seriously ill. (The elder Bach died in July 1750.) Friedrich must have decided that not only would funds for his education be lacking, but that he must choose a career in music since this was where his greatest talents lay. After all, he was by now a keyboard player of virtuoso rank. Moreover, he was offered an attractive post in the chamber orchestra at the Bückeburg court, under Count Wilhelm of Schaumberg-Lippe.

In 1759 he was appointed concertmaster of the orchestra, though he had, in effect, already served in that capacity for three years. While his position was secure and his work with the highly-respected chamber ensemble more than satisfactory to the Court, his music seems not to have been highly regarded or performed often.

With arrival at Court in 1771 of Johann Gottfried Herder, Friedrich's creative juices seems to have been stimulated, as the two collaborated on several successful choral and dramatic compositions, including the cantata *Michaels Sieg* and the oratorio *Die Kindheit Jesu.* Herder's departure five years later was a blow to the composer, and in 1778 he took leave of his post for a trip to England to visit his brother Johann Christoph. It was in London that he grew fond of Mozart's music from the many concerts he attended.

After his return to Bückeburg, that same year, Friedrich continued to compose at a fairly prolific pace, his music divulging a more Classical bent. The Court was now under the rule of Count Philipp Ernst (Count Wilhelm died in 1777), but still enjoyed high musical standards. Friedrich wrote his last symphony in 1794, remaining active until his last days. *—Robert Cummings*

Overview of Works (1760–1794)

Johann Christoph Friedrich Bach (1732–95) was the fifth son of Johann Sebastian Bach to survive to adulthood. After studying law at the University of Leipzig, he took up a post at the small German court of Bückeburg in 1750, remaining in service there for the rest of his life. For this reason he is generally referred to as the "Bückeburg Bach."

His output covers most of the popular genres of the latter half of the eighteenth century, and includes 20 symphonies, some half dozen keyboard concertos, a body of chamber music and keyboard works, oratorios and sacred cantatas, dramatic works, and secular cantatas and songs. Most of the symphonies, generally cast in three-movement form, are in the easygoing, mellifluous *galant* style, but the last of them, dating from 1794 is a more ambitious four-movement work that shows clear indications of the style of Haydn and Mozart. Bach was a renowned keyboard player, and in addition to his concertos, a number of his chamber works feature the piano. Worthy of particular note is a Cello Sonata in A, composed in 1789, which effectively exploits the cello's lyrical qualities in some fine cantabile writing. A number of Bach's dramatic works (both secular and sacred) have librettos by the outstanding poet Johann Gottfried von Herder, but unfortunately the music of his two major secular dramas, *Brutus* and *Philoktetes* has been lost. However, a recent recording of his extended solo dramatic cantata *Cassandra* shows Bach to have possessed a keen dramatic instinct. The dominant style at the Bückeburg court, as at many German courts during this period, was Italian, an influence clearly apparent in Bach's *Cassandra,* an early work dating from around 1769, which is set to an anonymous Italian text. In its depiction of the emotions of the Trojan princess who foresees the destruction of Troy, the cantata maintains a level of intensity that suggests further exploration of his dramatic works may affect the standard assessment of Bach as being an agreeable, but not particularly profound, composer. *—Brian Robins*

Recommended:

- **J. C. F. Bach: Symphonies** / Glaetzner (cond.), New Bach Collegium Musicum Leipzig / Brilliant 99785/7
- **J. C. F. Bach: Die Kindheit Jesu, Wachet Auf** / H. Max (cond.), Meens, van der Kamp, Schlick, Helling, Das Kleine Konzert / Capriccio 10292

Johann Sebastian Bach

b. Mar. 21, 1685, Eisenach, Germany, **d.** Jul. 28, 1750, Leipzig, Germany

Composer: Keyboard, Choral, Chamber Music, Concerto, Orchestral, Vocal

Johann Sebastian Bach was better known as a virtuoso organist than as a composer in his day. His sacred music, organ and choral works, and other instrumental music had an enthusiasm and seeming freedom that concealed immense rigor. Bach's use of counterpoint was brilliant and innovative, and the immense complexities of his compositional style—which often included religious and numerological symbols that seem to fit perfectly together in a profound puzzle of special codes—still amaze musicians today. Many consider him the greatest composer of all time.

Bach was born in Eisenach in 1685. He was taught to play the violin and harpsichord by his father, Johann Ambrosius, a court trumpeter in the service of the Duke of Eisenach. Young Johann was not yet ten when his father died, leaving him orphaned. He was taken in by his recently married oldest brother, Johann Christoph, who lived in Ohrdruf. Because of his excellent singing voice, Bach attained a position at the Michaelis monastery at Lüneberg in 1700. His voice changed a short while later, but he stayed on as an instrumentalist. After taking a short-lived post in Weimar in 1703 as a violinist, Bach became organist at the Neue Kirche in Arnstadt (1703–07). His relationship with the church council was tenuous as the young musician often shirked his responsibilities, preferring to practice the organ. One account describes a four-month leave granted Bach, to travel to Lubeck where he would familiarize himself with the music of Dietrich Buxtehude. He returned to Arnstadt long after was expected and much to the dismay of the council. He then briefly served at St. Blasius in Mühlhausen as organist, beginning in June 1707, and married his cousin, Maria Barbara Bach, that fall. Bach composed his famous *Toccata and Fugue in D minor* (BWV 565); and his first cantatas while in Mühlhausen, but quickly outgrew the musical resources of the town. He next took a post for the Duke of Sachsen-Weimar in 1708, serving as court organist and playing in the orchestra, eventually becoming its leader in 1714. He wrote many organ compositions during this period, including his *Orgel-Büchlein.* Owing to politics between the Duke and his officials, Bach left Weimar and secured a post in December 1717 as Kapellmeister at Cöthen. In 1720, Bach's wife suddenly died, leaving him with four children (three others had died in infancy). A short while later, he met his second wife, soprano Anna Magdalena Wilcke, whom he married in December 1721. She would bear 13 children, though only five would survive childhood. The six *Brandenburg Concertos* (BWV 1046–51), among many other secular works, date from his Cöthen years. Bach became Kantor of the Thomas School in Leipzig in May 1723 and held the post until his death. It was in Leipzig that he composed the bulk of his religious and secular cantatas. Bach eventually became dissatisfied with this post, not only because of its meager financial rewards, but also because of onerous duties and inadequate facilities. Thus, he took on other projects, chief among which was the directorship of the city's Collegium Musicum, an ensemble of professional and amateur musicians who gave weekly concerts, in 1729. He also became music director at the Dresden Court in 1736, in the service of Frederick Augustus II; though his duties were vague and apparently few, they allowed him freedom to compose what he wanted. Bach began making trips to Berlin in the 1740s, not least because his son Carl Philipp Emanuel served as a court musician there. In May 1747, the composer was warmly received by King Frederick II of Prussia, for whom he wrote the gloriously abstruse *Musical Offering* (BWV 1079). Among Bach's last works was his 1749 *Mass in B minor.* Besieged by diabetes, he died on July 28, 1750. *—Robert Cummings*

KEYBOARD

Canonic Variations on "Vom Himmel hoch da komm ich her," for organ, BWV 769 (Jun., 1747)

A canon is a composition based on a tune that starts in one voice and then is picked up in turn by other voices; a simple example is "Row, Row, Row your Boat." The simple melody "Vom Himmel hoch" (From Heaven on High) is an Advent hymn in the Lutheran church calendar. In representation of God's manifestation of Himself on earth, the tune mostly descends by simple steps down the scale. Bach first presents the tune in its original form, and it makes an elegant canon. Then he sets to work spinning out several minutes of exquisite variations on it, each time setting the variations canonically; hence the "canonic variations" title. The simplicity of the tune makes Bach's complex counterpoint unusually transparent, and the combination of counterpoint and variation makes for an attractive mix of intellect and decorative display. This work, unusually ingenious even for Bach, dated from the last years of his life. It was written for a composers' society that Bach joined briefly, and was probably intended as a virtuoso demonstration of the possibilities of the canonic procedure. It is of a piece with the other towering intellectual achievements of Bach's final years, the *Art of Fugue* and the *Musical Offering*. Igor Stravinsky made a sparkling setting of this work for small chorus and instrumental ensemble. Without adding or subtracting a note, merely by the placement of new instruments and accents, Stravinsky imposed a delicious overlay of his own rhythmic style in this tribute paid to one great composer by another. *—Joseph Stevenson*

Recommended:

○ **Bach: Great Organ Works** / G. Leonhardt / 1997 / Sony 63185

○ **Bach: Great Organ Works** / Walcha / DG 453064

○ **Bach: The Organ Works Vol. 9** / Walcha / Archiv 463721

Canons on the first 8 bass notes of the aria to the Goldberg Variations, BWV 1087 (1742)

In 1975, the Bibliothèque Nationale in Paris acquired a unique and unusual copy of the first edition of the *Goldberg Variations* (BWV 998) of Johann Sebastian Bach. Published in 1742 as the fourth part of the *Clavier-Übung*, this copy of the work popularly known as the *Goldbergs* had been Bach's own; such sources are highly valued as they frequently contain markings and corrections in the composer's hand. In this case, there was an added bonus in the form of a hitherto unknown Bach composition, *Verschiedene Canones über die ersteren acht Fundamental Noten vorheriger Arie von J.S. Bach* (Divers Canons Upon the First Eight Notes of the Preceding Aria by J.S. Bach). At the time of their discovery, the *Verschiedene Canones* were the first major new Bach works found in generations.

The 14 canons are rendered in puzzle notation and range from two to six unspecified voices. All of the individual canons are open-ended, with "infinite" repeat signs placed at the end. At the conclusion of the source, Bach adds the marking "et cetera," indicating that he could have continued further had he not ran out of pages to write the music on. Two slightly revised versions of these canons were already known from other sources. No. 11 "Canon duplex" appears as the canon Bach inscribed in an album for Johann Gottfreid Fulde (BWV 1077, dated October 15, 1747). No. 13 "Canon triplex" is seen as the canon included in the portrait painted of Bach by Elias Gottlieb Haussmann in 1746 (BWV 1076). All 14 canons first appeared in print published by Bärenreiter in 1976, and the Neue Bach Ausgabe assigned this group a collective number of BWV 1087.

Although the *Goldberg* ground is the point of departure for these canons, only numbers 12, "Canon duplex über besagte Fundamental-Noten à 5," and 14, "Canon à 4 per Augmentationem et diminutionem" bear any outward resemblance to the texture of the *Goldbergs*. The enigmatic scoring of these short pieces provides quite a challenge to performers aspiring to interpret them. The first published edition contains proposed solutions to the puzzles, but in practical performance, approaches vary considerably. In the Marlboro recording from 1975, which was the first, Pablo Casals and his group treated all the canons as separate pieces, bringing each to an end with an added fermata. By comparison, in a recording made two decades later, the musicians from Aston Magna under Daniel Stepner string the canons together in a continuous fabric. The aleatoric aspect of the *Verschiedene Canones* may suggest to some that Bach dropped this little nugget into a time continuum, emerging only to confound twentieth century musicians. However, the energy and verve of these short pieces suggest that Bach was perhaps having a bit of fun within the context of his craft. The *Verschiedene Canones* also provides an invaluable key to understanding the hidden canonic art so seamlessly employed by Bach in his late works. *—Uncle Dave Lewis*

Recommended:

○ **Bach Trio Sonatas** / Palladian Ensemble / 1996 / Linn 5036

○ **Bach: Keyboard Works Vol. 2, Goldberg Variations** / M. Suzuki / 1997 / Bis 819

○ **Bach: Musical Offering; Canons** / G. von der Goltz, K. Kaiser, Behringer / 1999 / Haenssler 92133

Chorale preludes

As organist at Weimar, Johann Sebastian Bach was charged with providing a harmonic underpinning for the singing of Lutheran chorale tunes chosen for each day. Bach wrote out many of these harmonizations, in part as instruction for younger composers (they are still used for this purpose). A derivation of this practice, Bach's conception of the organ chorale, as manifested in the chorale preludes, dates from 1713–14, about the time he became familiar with Vivaldi's concertos.

Bach's *Orgelbüchlein* (Little Organ Book) contains chorale preludes for the church year written during the composer's service at Weimar (1708–17). In about 1713, Bach began assembling the *Orgel-Büchlein*, and his earliest entries seem to be *Herr Christ, der ein'ge Gottes-Sohn*, BWV 601, *In dulci jubilo*, BWV 608, *Christ ist erstanden*, BWV 627, and *Heut' triumphieret Gottes Sohn*, BWV 630. These were very original compositions, highly expressive miniatures based on a chorale melody, supported with refined counterpoint, and featuring highly condensed motivic writing.

Bach's *Orgelbüchlein* was essentially complete by 1716. Only the fragment *O Traurigkeit* and the chorale prelude, *Helft mir Gottes Güte preisen*, BWV 613, were added later. "Complete" is used with some reservation here, because Bach originally projected 164 pieces but completed fewer than 50. In Bach's manuscript, pages with finished pieces alternate with blank ones intended for other chorale preludes. The later pieces differ from Bach's earlier chorale elaborations, in that they contain only one statement of the melody and are intended to demonstrate how to accompany a chorale with contrapuntally proper figurations that support the meaning of the text.

In the early 1740s Bach assembled a number of chorale preludes, possibly with the intention of publishing them as a set. These *Achtzehn Choräle (Eighteen Chorales)* BWV 651–668 were almost certainly written before 1723 and revised later. The *Fantasia super Komm, heiliger Geist*, BWV 651), is an especially impressive, extended elaboration of the chorale melody, which is in the pedal. The tune is treated in a less ornate fashion in the next prelude of the set (BWV 652). The highly convoluted *Von Gott will ich nicht lassen*, BWV 658, also contains the chorale melody in the pedal.

The six *Schübler chorales* (BWV 645–650) are derived from Bach's cantatas and contain one of his most popular chorale preludes, on the melody *Wachet auf, ruft uns die Stimme*, BWV 645.

The third part of Bach's Clavier-Übung, published in Leipzig in 1739, contains 21 chorale preludes (not all appear in every publication), many of which are for manuals only. Nine of these are meant for use during the Mass, while the others are for the catechism. Among the most impressive is *Kyrie, Gott heiliger Geist*, BWV 671, which is in five voices with the chorale melody in the pedal. More complex is the first of two preludes on *Aus tiefer Not schrei ich zu dir*, BWV 686, which is in six parts, including two pedal parts. *—John Palmer*

Recommended:

○ **Bach: Leipzig Chorales** / Bowyer / 1998 / Nimbus 5573

Chromatic Fantasia and Fugue in D minor, BWV 903 (before 1723)

Much of J.S. Bach's keyboard music has, over the course of the last several decades, been transplanted from its nineteenth century home in the piano repertoire back to the care of harpsichordists, its original interpreters. There are really just a few Bach keyboard works that are still widely and actively performed by the world's pianists: the *Well-Tempered Clavier* and the *Goldberg Variations*, certainly, and the *English* and *French Suites*—and the *Chromatic Fantasia and Fugue in D minor*, BWV 903, a work of such color and vitality that it would be foolish to ever expect pianists to completely let it go (even if that nature of the writing, especially in the Fantasia portion, makes for a piece that works better on a plucked keyboard instrument such as the harpsichord).

The *Chromatic Fantasia and Fugue* survives in several slightly different versions. BWV 903a dates from some time before 1720; the version we know as BWV 903 dates from about 1720, when Bach was living and working in Cöthen; and around 1730, after having moved to Leipzig, Bach revised the piece again. The work's name is not a random one: there is indeed chromaticism in profusion throughout both the wild, flowing arpeggiations and rich recitative-like passagework of the Fantasia and the comparatively lean counterpoint of the following fugue, whose subject is built around a sequential chromatic ascent. The work is a sizable one—79 measures for the Fantasia, 161 for the Fugue—and one that takes strong, dexterous fingers to articulate clearly. *—Blair Johnston*

Recommended:

○ **Bach: Fantasia in C minor; Two- and Three-Part Inventions** / A. Hewitt / 1994 / Hyperion 66746

○ **Glenn Gould Plays Bach and Scarlatti** / G. Gould / 2002 / Sony 87753

○ **Bach: Chromatic Fantasy and Fugue** / A. Schiff / Hungaroton 11690

○ **Bach: Fantaisies, Toccatas & Fugues** / Verlet / 1995 / Astrée Auvidis 8565

Clavier-Übung

The four volumes of Bach's *Clavier-Übung* (Keyboard Practice or Keyboard Exercise) were his only works published during his lifetime. Containing some of his most well-known keyboard works, they are highly representative of his didactic and contrapuntal skills and of his intellect and personality. *Clavier-Übung I* (published in 1731) contains the *Six Partitas for keyboard* (BWV 825–830). Johann Kuhnau, Bach's predecessor in Leipzig, had written suites, or "parties," each one in a different key of the diatonic scale. Bach picked up where Kuhnau left off, with one in B flat major, but stopped short of a final one in F. He did not follow Kuhnau's standard order of prelude, allemande, courante, sarabande, and gigue, instead using different forms such as a fantasia to begin a suite and reordering the dances or substituting his own highly imaginative, stylized dances, even throwing in a cunning, not-quite-dance "Burlesca" in the middle.

Clavier-Übung II (published in 1735) consists of just two works: the *Italian Concerto* (BWV 971) and the *French Overture* (BWV 831). Both were Bach's interpretation of the fashions of the time. The *Italian Concerto*, sometimes thought to be the missing F major work in the set of *6 Partitas*, is specifically written for a two-manual harpsichord and, according to Bach's introduction, is "for lovers of music, for their enjoyment." One performer carries out both the virtuosic soloist and ripieno parts of an Italianate concerto in the typical fast-slow-fast three movements. The *French Overture* is an adaptation of a Baroque French orchestral suite in ten movements, beginning with an extensive overture that is followed by dances. The suite is noble and self-possessed, somewhat like the stereotypical French personality. *Clavier-Übung III* (published in 1739), sometimes referred to as the "German Organ Mass," is specifically for organ. It contains a total of 27 pieces: settings of the German Kyrie and Gloria, (BWV 669–677), settings of six catechism chorales (BWV 678–689), and four duets (really Inventions) (BWV 802–805), all framed by the *Prelude and Fugue in E flat major* (BWV 552). The number of pieces and settings are just some of the references to the Trinity and dualism found throughout the book, signs of Bach's devotional nature. *Clavier-Übung IV* (published in 1741) contains a single work, the *Goldberg Variations*. Many consider it the *ne plus ultra* of Bach's keyboard writing. Beginning with the simple yet sophisticated aria, each subsequent variation demonstrates Bach's skill at technically complex but aurally sublime music. *—Patsy Morita*

Concertos & transcriptions for organ

In his youth, Johann Sebastian Bach transcribed for organ six concertos by other composers as a means of educating himself. Probably accomplished before 1714, these six include three concertos by Vivaldi, two by Duke Johann Ernst of Saxe-Weimar and one by an unknown composer: *Concerto No. 1 in G major* (BWV 592) after Duke Johann Ernst's *Concerto in G major; Concerto No. 2 in A minor* (BWV 593) after Vivaldi's *Concerto No. 8 in A minor for Two Violins*, Op. 3; *Concerto No. 3 in C major* (BWV 594) after Vivaldi's *Concerto No. 11 in D major for Violin* and *Orchestra*, Op. 7, called "Il Grosso Mogul"; *Concerto No. 4 in C major* (BWV 595) after the first movement of Duke Johann Ernst's *Concerto in C major; Concerto No. 5 in D minor* after Vivaldi's *Concerto No. 11 in D minor for Violin and Orchestra*, Op. 3; and *Concerto No. 6* (BWV 597) after a concerto by an unknown composer. All are in the standard three-movement form, except the single-movement *Concerto No. 4*. For the most part, Bach's concertos are direct transcriptions of the original works, although there are instances of Bach adding further lines of counterpoint. Also, in *Concerto No. 3*, Bach replaced Vivaldi's Grave central movement with a recitative-like Adagio, whether an original composition or a transcription of a movement from an unidentified concerto is uncertain. But despite the strictness of Bach's transcriptions, his six concertos are so cunningly arranged for the organ that they almost sound as if they were written for the instrument. *—James Leonard*

Recommended:

- ○ **Bach: Transcriptions** / van Dijk / 1999 / Haenssler 92095

English Suites for keyboard (ca. 1715)

Bach's so-called *Six English Suites for harpsichord* (BWV 806–811) are simultaneously a puzzle and a paradigm of Baroque suite writing. The puzzle is in the name; Bach's own manuscripts have not survived, but an early copy bears the designation "fait pour les Anglois," or made for the English. That is, there's nothing at all English about the music itself, merely its recipients. Yet Bach seems to have written these works in the 1720s, possibly just before the *Six French Suites* and *Six Partitas*, and most likely for the private use of his students and friends—the suites were never published in his lifetime, but exist in several contemporary copies. Any attempts to connect these works to a specific Englishman—for example, some visitor to Cöthen, where Bach was then Kapellmeister—are purely speculative, and there is no evidence that the suites even reached England before Johann Christian Bach settled in London with them after his father's death. A wag might suggest that "Anglois" is a misprint for "Angoisses," or anguishes, given the difficulty of many of the movements. Those movements are, in fact, French dances arranged in a specific, unvarying pattern common to Baroque dance suites. First is an Allemande, a supposedly German dance in quadruple meter and binary form. Next comes a Courante (two in the first suite), in slow triple meter and binary form. The succeeding movement, the Sarabande, is closely related to the Courante in pulse and meter, but is even more solemn. The suites always end with a Gigue, usually a bit faster than what has come before, with dotted rhythms and duple meter. This setup effectively unites western Europe in music, the movements originating in or evoking Germany, France, Spain, and England, respectively. Bach expanded this format by launching each suite with a Prélude, another binary movement at a measured pace. And he inserted an extra pair of linked, lighter dances before the Gigues. In the first two suites, he chose Bourrées, moderately quick pieces in duple meter. In the third and sixth suites are Gavottes, more gracious and slightly slower but still simple dances. The fourth suite holds a pair of triple-meter Minuets, and the fifth features Passepieds, also in triple meter. Bach Germanicizes all these French dance movements by making them exercises in counterpoint, especially thick in the elaborate Préludes, moderately complex in the "core" dances, and fairly rudimentary in the "extra" dances preceding the Gigues. *—James Reel*

Recommended:

- ○ **Bach: 6 English Suites** / Parmentier / 2000 / Wildboar 9302

Fantasia and Fugue, for organ in G minor ("Great"), BWV 542 (before 1725)

Evidence suggests that J.S. Bach completed and revised the *Fantasia and Fugue in G minor for organ*, BWV 542 (the "Great" G minor, as opposed to BWV 578, the "Little" G minor), as an audition for an organist position in Hamburg in 1720. Bach didn't get the job, but, happily enough, posterity did get the piece; generations of organists since then have considered it one of their repertoire's crown jewels. The two parts of BWV 542 (the fantasia—sometimes titled Prelude instead—and the fugue) are thought to have been composed separately: the fugue is assigned Bach's Weimar years (1708–17) and the fantasia to his time in Cöthen (1717–23, but, if the audition theory is correct, not later than 1720).

The fantasia opens spaciously and in recitative-like style, but as it unfolds Bach finds room for dense passages in upper-voice imitation. There are five more or less balanced sections to this fantasy; intensely dramatic sections are interwoven with quieter, more even passages. The wide tonal scope of the fantasia has been a subject of fascination for two centuries of musicians: just when some kind of harmonic stability seems to arrive, Bach shoots off on a mock-improvised cadenza that jolts the music into a whole new pitch realm. Thus the fantasia both lives up to its name and contains quite a bit of contrapuntal rigor, and then, on top of that, more than one worthy mind has deemed the fugue to be Bach's ultimate accomplishment in the field of organ counterpoint. The task of selecting a king from that noble crowd, however, is not an enviable one. Though it provides the sense of a stable answer to the fantasia in its predominantly even sixteenth note rhythms, it is similarly ambitious harmonically: Bach makes two revolutions through the entire circle of fifths. The fugue makes a fine contrast with the later music of the fantasia while nevertheless seeming of a piece with it. *—Blair Johnston*

Recommended:

- ○ **The 'Great' Fantasias, Preludes & Fugues** / C. Herrick / 1999 / Hyperion 44122
- ○ **Bach: Toccata & Fugue in D Minor & Other Favorite Organ Works** / Rogg / 1999 / EMI 73568
- ○ **Essential Classics: Bach Organ Music** / Biggs / 1991 / Sony 46551

French Suites for keyboard

Bach's *Six French Suites* aren't particularly French, and there are actually eight of them. The standard set consists of BWV 812–817, but the freestanding suites in A minor, BWV 818, and E flat major, BWV 819, contended for inclusion in this group during Bach's lifetime, probably in place of the standard fifth and sixth suites. Bach never published any of this music; he revised it heavily throughout his life and seemed particularly dissatisfied with BWV 818 and 819. Not until Bach biographer Johann Forkel prepared an edition in the early nineteenth century did BWV 812–817 become widely available and known by the collective title "French." True, Bach gave each of the dance movements a French title, but only a few of these are really French dances. It was Forkel who declared that they were "written in the French taste," by which he meant an emphasis on tunefulness and consonant harmony rather than good German structure and counterpoint. Although the suites offer some technical challenges, they are easier to play than much of Bach's other keyboard music and they soon became favorites of piano teachers. Ignoring the two "outsider" suites, each of the works adheres to the same basic format. First comes a fairly solemn Allemande, a German dance, followed by an Italian courante and a Spanish sarabande. Each suite ends with a quasi-English gigue. Yet Bach does more than merely plug a new tune into a standard dance rhythm; each piece employs a different texture or metrical scheme. Between the sarabande and gigue fall several other dances, usually at least a pair of minuets. That's the pattern established by *Suite No. 1 in D minor. Suite No. 2 in C minor* varies only by inserting a hummable air after the sarabande; the same spot is occupied in *Suite No. 3 in B minor* by a so-called Anglaise, which is actually a gavotte. *Suite No. 4 in E flat major* synthesizes the patterns of its two immediate predecessors; the central movement is now explicitly called gavotte, and the first minuet is replaced by an air (these airs, by the way, are much livelier than the famously serene air from Bach's *Orchestral Suite No. 3*). *Suite No. 5 in G major* also includes a gavotte and replaces the minuets with a highly French pairing of bourrée and loure. The widely traveled *Suite No. 6 in E major* separates the gavotte from the final gigue with a polonaise, minuet, and bourrée. *—James Reel*

Recommended:

- ○ **Bach: The French Suites** / G. Gould / 2001 / Sony 87764

Fugue, for organ in G minor ("Little"), BWV 578 (1707)

Let there be no confusion about it: J.S. Bach's *Fugue in G minor for organ*, BWV 578, is known as the *"Little" G minor* not because it is a work of small importance or even because it is an unusually short work in its own right, but simply so that it and the much longer and later *"Great" G minor Fantasia and Fugue*, BWV 542, might not be mistaken for one another. Bach probably composed the *"Little" G minor Fugue* sometime between 1703 and 1707, when he was a young, up-and-coming organist in the city of Arnstadt.

The *"Little" G minor's* four-and-a-half-measure subject is one of Bach's most widely recognized tunes. It is worked out in four voices, the pedal voice being honored as the full equal of the three manual voices—even to the extent that the feet are required, in one electrifying passage late in the Fugue, to have a go at a sixteenth note figuration of the countersubject. During the episodes, Bach employs one of Corelli's most beloved sequential gestures: imitation between two voices on an eighth note upbeat figure that first leaps up a fourth and then falls back down one step at a time. And those who love to find precise, mathematical structural divisions and markers in Bach's music will enjoy noting that it is in the 33rd measure—one measure shy of the exact midpoint of BWV 578—that Bach first introduces the subject in a key outside the tonic-dominant loop of the exposition. *—Blair Johnston*

Recommended:

- ○ **Bach: Great Organ Favorites** / Biggs / 1988 / CBS 42644
- ○ **Bach: Organ Works Vol. 4** / G. Weinberger / CPO 999653

Goldberg Variations, BWV 988 (ca. 1741)

Johann Sebastian Bach completed the *Goldberg Variations*, BWV 988, for keyboard in 1741. The work consists of an aria and 30 variations. Scholars at the end of the twentieth century were still debating the exact details of the work's origin, but many accept that J.G. Goldberg commissioned it. His job was to perform for Count Keyserkingk, a chronic insomniac who needed music to lull him to sleep. Many records suggest that Bach once taught Goldberg, a famed virtuoso, who would have easily been able to play the variations. It is also believed that the technical wizardry required to play the variations comes directly from Bach's study of Domenico Scarlatti's *Essercizi* for keyboard from 1739, itself a daunting piece for exceptional players only.

The aria that Bach used is of unknown origin; it was probably not the composer's own, but was related to a now-untraceable French keyboard dance. The basic harmonies and structures of the variations are all the same as the theme's. The work exemplifies Bach's quest for the greatest amount of diversity within relentless unity. The *Goldberg Variations* are among the most sophisticated works ever written for keyboard, but the work does not sound like the awesomely complex compendium that it is. The music is deceptively simple and heartfelt, with a noble calm even when the performer is obliged to cross hands at lightning speeds. It never seethes or gets gritty, and is, of course, never boring. The aria theme is subjected to ever-new means of contrapuntal manipulation. Every third variation is a different kind of canon. The final variation breaks with this trend in order to offer up a quodlibet which uses well-known tunes for a humorous effect. The tunes, "Cabbage and beets have driven me away" and "I have so long been away from you," were a rousing, popular tune and an end-of-the-evening dance number respectively.

This work is sublime and compassionate, graceful, warm, and relentlessly intricate, a demonstration of unmatched craft in music history and genuine, poetic imagination. The *Goldberg Variations* is a work that still engages scholars hundreds of years after its publication and is equally valuable for attracting new listeners to this sort of music. *—John Keillor*

Recommended:

- ○ **Bach: Goldberg Variations** / Leonhardt / 2004 / DHM 60146
- ○ **Glenn Gould: A State of Wonder** / G. Gould / 2002 / Sony 87703
- ○ **Bach: Variations Goldberg** / K. Gilbert / HM 1951240
- ○ **Bach: Goldberg Variations** / Zhu / 1999 / Mandala 4950
- ○ **Bach: Goldberg Variations; Beethoven: Diabelli Variations** / Barenboim / 2000 / Teldec 82138

Partita for keyboard No. 1 in B flat major, BWV 825 (1726–1731)

The six *Partitas* (BWV 825–830) are part of Bach's *Clavier-Übung*, but were published singly, beginning in 1726 with this B flat major effort. A new partita appeared each year thereafter until 1731, when the whole collection was issued. Each of the six is a suite containing allemandes, sarabandes, minuets, and various other dances and numbers. The *B flat major Partita* consists of seven short movements, the first being a praeludium, a moderately paced piece so typical of Bach's music in its stately confidence, serene joy, and deftly wrought contrapuntal writing. There follow an allemande, corrente (courante), sarabande, and gigue which comprise the standard sequence of dances that make up a partita. Actually, Bach inserted two brief minuets between the sarabande and gigue.

The allemande is lively and brimming with thematic activity, contrapuntal elements abounding in subtle detail, the music racing by breathlessly under beams of sunshine. The corrente is a bit shorter than the two previous movements. It too, is lively, but lighter in mood and more carefree than the allemande. The ensuing sarabande is gentle in its serenity, graceful in its slow pace, and ultimately mesmerizing in the near-transparency of its subtly crafted textures. At nearly four minutes, this is the longest of the seven movements. The two lively minuets that ensue are light and playful, the second following the first without pause. They are imaginatively wrought pieces and serve as a kind of interlude before the arrival of the gigue. Each lasts a bit under a minute. The gigue is rhythmic and fast-paced, breathless in its graceful drive and bouncy manner. It is an eventful minute-and-a-half and the perfect crown to this suite. *—Robert Cummings*

Recommended:

- ○ **Bach: Partita 1; English Suite 3 & French Suite 2** / Pires / DG 447894
- ○ **Bach: 6 Partitas; Goldberg Variations; French Overture & Italian Concerto** / Pinnock / 2003 / DG 000048502
- ○ **Dinu Lipatti: Bach, Mozart, Scarlatti, Schubert** / Lipatti / 1999 / EMI 6700321
- ○ **Bach: The Six Partitas** / Parmentier / 1992 / Wildboar 9101
- ○ **J. S. Bach: Partitas** / K. Gilbert / 1985 / HM 90114445
- ○ **Bach: The Six Partitas** / A. Hewitt / 1997 / Hyperion 69191

Partita for keyboard No. 2 in C minor, BWV 826 (1726–1731)

While this partita and the four that followed appeared after 1726, all were written during that year, a year that saw publication of the B flat major piece first. Bach published a new partita each year until 1731, when all six appeared together. Each of these works consists of dances—typically an Allemande, Courante, Sarabande, and Gigue—and other pieces, forming a whole that could just as easily have been called a suite. They generally show Bach's lighter side, though there is a fair share of serious music here, too. All the partitas have seven movements except for this C minor effort, which comprises six. Another unusual aspect is its exclusion of a Gigue at the close, where Bach substituted a Rondeau and Capriccio.

This suite opens with a Sinfonia which, speaking of serious music, achieves a depth of expression to rival much of Bach's more profound keyboard music. It is in three sections, the first ponderous and dramatic, the succeeding two having progressively faster tempos. The theme in the second section has a soothing serenity in its animated nonchalance, while the final part is lively and light in its variant of this theme, and brims with Bach's deft counterpoint and rhythmic subtlety.

The Allemande that follows is somewhat subdued but features an undercurrent of contrapuntal activity with many delicious details that often come refreshingly to the foreground. The remaining four numbers are much shorter and lighter in expressive content. Best among them may be the ensuing Courante, a sunny, graceful piece whose contrapuntal elements seem to blend rather than conjure, imply rather than articulate.

The ensuing Sarabande is slow, almost hymn-like in its solemn yet soothing manner. The lively Rondeau that follows is jumpy and full of playfulness, while the closing Capriccio is meatier, both in its muscular first section and in the inversion of material from the opening that comes in the latter half. It is also quite a challenging finale for the performer.

This partita will have a duration of about 15 minutes, excluding repeats, a longer one than the slighter first, third, and fifth, but shorter than the fourth and sixth partitas. *—Robert Cummings*

Recommended:

- ○ **Bach: 6 Partitas; Goldberg Variations; French Overture & Italian Concerto** / Pinnock / 2003 / DG 000048502
- ○ **Live from the Concertgebouw 1978 & 1979** / Argerich / 2000 / EMI 56975B
- ○ **Bach: Complete Partitas For Harpsichord** / Verlet / 1994 / Philips 442559
- ○ **J. S. Bach: Partitas** / K. Gilbert / 1985 / HM 90114445

Partita for keyboard No. 3 in A minor, BWV 827 (1726–1731)

Johann Sebastian Bach probably completed his *Partita for keyboard No. 3 in A minor*, BWV 827 in 1725. It is the third of six works that the composer released on three separate occasions in 1726, 1730, and 1731. This final publication was called "Opus 1" and was dedicated to the delight of music lovers. It was also called *Keyboard Practice*, one of four books of keyboard study he published in his lifetime. These partitas can also be regarded as suites, with an opening piece that is followed by a collection of dances. His predecessor at St. Thomas in Leipzig, Johann Kuhnau, had published similar books of keyboard suites he called "Partie" in 1689 and 1692. Each partie represented a different degree of the diatonic scale. Bach chose to do the same thing, picking up where Kuhnau left off, at B flat. He then made six of the seven partitas necessary to make up all seven degrees of the scale.

Just as the names of forms were not fixed in the Baroque era, Bach was not bound by fixed structures either. Kuhnau followed a standard plan of Praeludium, Allemande, Courante, Sarabande, and Gigue, whereas none of Bach's partitas are the same; he omits certain dances, substitutes others, and presents them in orders that please him. The opening of the third partita in A minor is not a prelude, or overture, but rather a Fantasia. It is a marvelous and extremely difficult movement. Bach did not let the traditions of instrumental music restrict his imagination in the slightest. The idea of including a movement entitled Burlesca in *Partita No. 3* is striking insofar as it is not really a dance at all. The idea of following the opening movement with a non-dance was uncommon, if not unheard of. The ribald title of the movement is also an aside for the man himself, a staunch Lutheran. This partita is also dedicated to Bach's second wife, Anna Magdalena. Her own copy of the work substituted the word "Burlesca" with "Menuet." One common quality to these partitas is the extent to which the composer sounds as though he is having a wonderful time composing these pieces. There is a lightness of spirit to them that is not heard frequently in his other works, which overwhelm and stupefy much of the time. His *Orchestral Suites* are similar in spirit, but they lack the rigorous counterpoint of the partitas. The partitas were well received and did bring in additional cash and notoriety, but they were later seen as too difficult for amateur pianists. Listeners who are beginning their study of this composer would do well to begin here, with these partitas. They are inviting and an honest representation of the composer. *—John Keillor*

Recommended:

- ○ **Bach: The Six Partitas** / A. Hewitt / 1997 / Hyperion 69191
- ○ **Bach: The Six Partitas** / Rampe / 2000 / Virgin 545404
- ○ **Bach: Partitas 1, 3, 6** / Anderszewski / 2002 / Virgin 45526

Partita for keyboard No. 4 in D major, BWV 828 (1726–1731)

Bach composed the six partitas in 1726, but issued only the first that year, publishing the others individually, one each year until 1731, when all were issued as a set. These brilliant half-dozen works are easily among Bach's most significant keyboard efforts. Comprised of dances (Allemande, Courante, Sarabande, and Gigue) and other pieces, each partita is a suite divulging much color and often requiring a good measure of virtuosity from the performer. This fourth partita and the sixth are the two longest, each lasting over well over 20 minutes when repeats are ignored, and thus a half-hour or likely more when they are observed.

The D major partita opens with a brilliant and lengthy Overture (or Ouverture in the French spelling used by Bach). Its character has been likened to the style of French operatic overtures of the period, not least because of its slow, dramatic opening and succeeding fast section. That section is the heart of the piece—light and colorful at the outset, then turning more substantive and muscular as thematic development grows amid much deft contrapuntal activity.

The ensuing Allemande is no less substantial in size (the first two movements, in fact, comprise over half the length of the entire suite). But the music of the Allemande also contains a good measure of expressive depth in its largely subdued and serene manner. The ensuing Courante is light and jovial, the perfect foil for the serious yet calm character of the preceding piece. The fourth movement features a jaunty Aria, whose counterpoint has a muscularity in its rippling digital flow.

The ensuing Sarabande is sweet and gentle in its slow pacing and augurs a kind of melting lyricism that will flower in the Classical and Romantic periods. A relatively brief Menuet follows, beaming its sunny rays in a graceful and lively but unhurried way. The Gigue, as usual, closes out this partita with fast, brilliant writing. Here the music seems busily to be working its way downward or upward, always with a sense of glee and industriousness, subtly crafted counterpoint abounding. *—Robert Cummings*

Recommended:

- ○ **Bach: 6 Partitas, BWV 825–830** / Pinnock / 1999 / Haenssler 92115
- ○ **Bach: 6 Partitas; Goldberg Variations; French Overture & Italian Concerto** / Pinnock / 2003 / DG B000048502
- ○ **Bach: Partitas 4, 5, 6** / G. Gould / 2001 / Sony 87768
- ○ **Bach: The Six Partitas** / Parmentier / 1992 / Wildboar 9101

Partita for keyboard No. 5 in G major, BWV 829 (1726–1731)

This partita is probably the briefest of the six in the set, though Nos. 1 and 3 are also slight works, and in a given performance, with repeats observed in one piece and ignored in another, may have a marginally shorter timing. That said, the diminutive fifth is a fine work even if it lacks the grander scales of the D major fourth and E minor sixth. Comprised of the usual seven movements and featuring the more or less requisite Allemande, Courante (the Italian Corrente here), Sarabande, and Gigue, it is a light, buoyant work of such brilliance and subtlety as to stand alongside its more grandiose siblings.

The opening Praeambulum ripples with buoyancy and joy as notes cascade seemingly in all directions with breathless energy. The music here has been called Haydnesque, and while it may augur that master's style, it is still pure Bach in all his inventive genius. The ensuing Allemande, by contrast, is subdued and playful, delightfully graceful, too, in its moderate pacing. The brief Courante bustles with the same kind of energy heard in the Praeambulum, but ultimately divulges a somewhat more subdued character.

The Sarabande follows, a serene yet at times playful piece whose relatively lengthy duration and gentleness are a sort of island of restraint amid all the bustle and brightness surrounding it. The music is quite transparent here in its slow pacing, thus allowing Bach's deft contrapuntal writing to emerge in all its subtlety. The ensuing Tempo di Minuetto is light and graceful, full of energy right up to its suddenly subdued close. A hearty Passepied follows, introducing a sort of muscular manner, with much writing in the middle and lower registers.

As usual a Gigue closes this work, bringing energy and a sense of near-ecstasy in its joy. Here, the contrapuntal writing is full of subtle details, the ear noticing something delightfully different on each subsequent hearing. Moreover, this colorful music is quite a virtuosic challenge to the performer, the fugue-like section midway through especially taxing the fingers. *—Robert Cummings*

Recommended:

- ○ **Bach: 6 Partitas BWV 825–830** / Pinnock / 1999 / Haenssler 92115
- ○ **Bach: Chromatic Fantasy & Fugue** / A. Schiff / Hungaroton 11690
- ○ **Bach: Partitas 4, 5, 6** / G. Gould / 2001 / Sony 87768
- ○ **Bach: Partitas** / K. Gilbert / 1985 / HM 90114445

Partita for keyboard No. 6 in E minor, BWV 830 (1726–1731)

This is the last of the partitas in this set, which as a group were published in 1731, but appeared individually, one each year, beginning with the B flat major first in 1726. Preceded by the diminutive fifth partita in G major—about half its size—the sixth is probably the longest of the partitas, though different combinations of observing or ignoring repeats could make the fourth in D major longer. The sixth is not only grand in length, however, but in depth of expression as well, its opening toccata one of the more profound movements in any of the partitas.

Speaking of size, this toccata is also the longest movement found in any of the six. It opens with a somber introduction of dramatic character and moves onto a livelier section of serious demeanor, whose music both alternates, and is heard simultaneously, with the powerful theme from the opening. Bach's contrapuntal writing here imparts a sense of the profound, suggesting both serenity and a conflicting undercurrent. This movement bears more than a vague resemblance to Bach's famous *Toccata and Fugue for organ*, though the more contemplative ending here sets it apart from that great work.

The ensuing Allemande is elegant and lighter in its moderate pacing, but not without its subtleties and profundities. The music turns more animated and even somewhat dark in a variant that appears midway through. The Corrente (or Courante, in French) follows, a livelier piece, generally light and energetic. A brief Air comes next, bringing a celebratory bustle and colorful virtuosity.

The gentle Sarabande has a disrupted flow and sense of yearning throughout, but never allows these darker undercurrents to overtake the mostly serene manner. The Tempo di gavotta that follows is lively but subdued in its jaunty character. The concluding Gigue, written in 8/4 meter—not a proper Gigue time—is muscular and lively in its outer sections, but dark and ominous at the beginning of the brilliant fugal buildup that starts midway through. The music swells to triumphant heights at the end. This may well be the finest of the *Six Partitas* in the set. *—Robert Cummings*

Recommended:

- ○ **Bach: The 6 Partitas** / A. Hewitt / 1997 / Hyperion 69191
- ○ **Bach: 6 Partitas BWV 825–830** / Pinnock / 1999 / Haenssler 92115
- ○ **Bach: Partitas 4, 5, 6** / G. Gould / 2001 / Sony 87768
- ○ **Bach: The Six Partitas** / Rampe / 2000 / Virgin 545404

Passacaglia and Fugue for organ in C minor, BWV 582 (1708–1712)

Even though he was one of music's great conservatives, it is often (and rightly) remarked that J.S. Bach was a great cosmopolitan—in his music, the north countries meet southern Germany, France, and Italy in striking ways previously almost unknown. In the *Passacaglia and Fugue in C minor*, BWV 582, Bach joins together elements from distinct nations and traditions in ways that may be heard very close to the musical surface indeed. The eight-bar ground bass upon which the Passacaglia is based (and also the Fugue, which is actually not marked by Bach as a distinct and separate piece, but rather as just another use of the passacaglia ground bass, "Thema fugatum") seems to have been extracted from a sacred work by an obscure contemporary French composer named Alain Raison. There are, leading up to the fugue portion, 21 statements of the ground bass in all, starting with the unharmonized bass solo at the very opening and growing ever more active until at last a full-blown frenzy of imitative sixteenth notes in the upper voices leads the way to the fugue; during a few of the middle variations, the ground bass moves up into the soprano and then into the alto voice. The fugue makes use only of the first four bars of the French ground bass, transforming it into a subject upon which Bach can, over the course of 124 bars, exercise the full glory of his wholly northern-learned contrapuntal genius. Since the fugue is not really separate in the manner of, for example, Bach's preludes and fugues, the work is sometimes known simply as the Passacaglia. *—Blair Johnston*

Recommended:

- ○ **Bach: Great Organ Favorites** / Biggs / 1988 / CBS 42644
- ○ **Bach: Organ Recital** / K. Richter / 1997 / London 455291

Pastorale for organ in F major, BWV 590 (after 1720)

Very little is known of the precise origins of this Bach organ work in the key of F major, BWV 590, which is usually known as the *"Pastorale" in F*, and sometimes "*Pastorella*" in some sources. It comprises four sections, and is thought by most scholars to have been written for performance during the Christmas services held at the main Leipzig churches with which Bach was closely associated. The work was therefore written presumably around the year 1720. No autograph copy has survived, nor is there any plausible indication of how the work might have fitted into the Christmas liturgy, though it is now regarded as definitely Bach's work, having been long-disputed due to lack of clearly attributable material.

Without question, however, the emergence of certain galant-style features places the *Pastorale* late in Bach's career. The most interesting attribute is the use (in each of the first two sections) of "Piffero" or "piping" style, based on the drone bass line and skirling bagpipe melodies widely encountered in Italian Christmas folk music. Even in the late twentieth century, the ancient traditions of bagpipe-playing shepherds processing through small towns have been upheld at Christmas, the idea being that the ritual recalls the shepherds' journey to Bethlehem. Traditional Piffero music usually offers two melodies in canon, normally heard against a drone bass line and entirely based on tonic, subdominant, and dominant harmonies. Interestingly, there are also examples of Piffero technique to be found in the *Christmas Oratorio*, notably in the Sinfonia preceding Part II, and also in a small number of other Bach works.

The third movement is far more sophisticated and its aria-like theme has a special symbolism. The three-flat key signature and triple meter were often used to represent angels, and the assumption is that here Bach intended to depict the appearance of the angels to the shepherds as recorded in Luke's gospel (2:8–15). The concluding section of the work is a gigue in fugal form, the melody of which has been traced by Christoph Wolff to an early Medieval hymn-tune *"Resonet in laudibus,"* itself often sung at Christmas to portray the shepherds' rejoicing upon finding the infant Jesus. *—Michael Jameson*

Recommended:

- ○ **Bach: Toccata & Fugue; Preludes & Fugues** / Biggs / 2002 / Sony 89955
- ○ **Bach: Complete Works for Organ Vol. 12** / Alain / 1994 / Erato 96745

Prelude and Fugue for organ in A minor, BWV 543 (after 1715)

J.S. Bach's *Prelude and Fugue in A minor for organ*, BWV 543 (an alternate version is numbered BWV 543a) is probably a product of his years as court organist to the Duke of Saxe-Weimar (1708–17). It is the final incarnation of music first tried out by Bach in the harpsichord *Fugue in A minor*, BWV 944, of 1708 or earlier. Not as famous as some other Bach organ works, it is the equal of the best of them. The Prelude is a massive, dramatic thing with a weighty, chromatically descending subject, made all the weightier when it is thrust into the pedals midway through the piece. A master organist can shape this into one of the most compelling of all Bach's fugue introductions. At the end of the fugue itself there is an electrifying passage of freewheeling, utterly unfugal organ virtuosity. Some observers contend that the chromatic, toccata-like prelude bears the marks of Bach's early, north German-influenced style, while the fugue could be a later product of his maturity. It was not uncommon for Bach to adapt or join together previously composed music to form new pieces. *—Blair Johnston*

Recommended:

- ○ **Bach: Toccata & Fugue; Preludes & Fugues** / Biggs / 2002 / Sony 89955
- ○ **Bach: Complete Works for Organ Vol. 12** / M. C. Alain / 1994 / Erato 96745

Prelude and Fugue, for organ in D major ("Little"), BWV 532 (1713)

Bach composed most of his organ works in Weimar, where he worked between 1708 and 1717; after he left that city, his duties did not involve the composition of works for the organ. His years as organist there witnessed important stylistic developments in his freely composed preludes and fugues. Bach had not yet codified the clear two-section prelude and fugue of the type we find in the *Well-Tempered Clavier*. Instead, the *D major prelude and fugue*, BWV 532, features a lengthy, complex, self-contained fugue preceded by a multisectional prelude. The prelude opens with a rhapsodic passage initiated by a rising scale in the pedals. Busy figurations for the manuals proceed over sustained pedal tones as the passage moves away from D major and comes to a stop. When the ensuing Alla breve section begins, we realize that all that has come before is introductory, and the prelude continues in D major. Harmonic sequences and block chords dominate the texture of this, the most substantial part of the prelude, which closes with new material in an adagio tempo that emphasizes E major before a final cadence on the tonic.

After seven complete entries of the subject that remain in the tonic and dominant, the Fugue in D major becomes one of the most interesting of Bach's fugues in terms of harmony. Bach takes his subject, eight measures long and consisting of tight figurations that encompass an entire octave, through first the relative minor and mediant minor (not unusual) and then, at about the middle of the piece, the minor harmony built on the leading tone (C sharp) and the major harmony on the supertonic (very unusual). After these adventurous excursions we hear an extended episode with a flurry of figures on the dominant and then a welcome, full entry of the subject on the tonic that is so powerful in its resolution of the preceding tension that the coda has the nature of an afterthought. As in the prelude, block chords are prominent in this unusual fugue. *—John Palmer*

Recommended:

- ○ **Bach: Toccata & Fugue in D minor; Concerto 2 in A minor** / Michael Murray / 1983 / Telarc 80088
- ○ **Bach: Complete Works for Organ Vol. 10** / M. C. Alain / 1994 / Erato 96743
- ○ **Bach: L'Oeuvre d'orgue** / Rogg / HM 290772

Prelude and Fugue for organ in E flat major ("St Anne"), BWV 552 (1739)

Johann Sebastian' Bach's Prelude and Fugue in E flat major, owes its nickname "St. Anne" to the close similarity between the theme of the fugue itself, and the eponymous hymn tune by William Croft (1678–1727), to which the words of Isaac Watts' great hymn "O God our help in ages past" is normally sung. There is, however, no evidence whatever to suggest that Bach might have known Croft's hymn tune "St. Anne," which was not known to be sung outside of the British Isles. This work was included in Part III of Bach's *Clavier-Übung* (literally "Keyboard-Practice") which was first published in September 1739. It was Bach's first major published edition devoted to new organ pieces, and was issued with the rather cumbersome subtitle of *Dritter Theil der Clavier Übung bestehend in verschieden Vorspielen über die Catechismus—und andere Gesaenge, vor die Orgel* (Third Part of the Keyboard Studies Comprising Various Preludes on the Catechism and other Hymns for Organ). The complete volume was made up of multiple settings of the German Kyrie and Gloria, pairs of settings of each of the six catechism chorales, and four duets. Surmounting all these was the superb and majestic *E flat Prelude and Fugue*, the "St. Anne." It is not possible to determine whether or not Bach wrote these pieces with any particular occasion in mind, although some authorities have suggested that he may well have played some or perhaps all of the set in a recital he gave on the newly installed organ of the Frauernkirche, in Dresden, on December 1, 1736. Others have opined that the occasion of the first performance may have been the celebrations held throughout Lutheran Germany on August 12, 1739 to commemorate the bicentenary of the Confession of Augsburg. However, possibly the most likely impulse for these works was Bach's newly rekindled interest in the church chorale, which had been occasioned by his work for the Schemelli Hymnal project of 1736. Gregory Butler, a noted authority on the original manuscripts of Bach's organ works, has written that "*Clavier-Übung III* represents a landmark in Bach's oeuvre. In it are forecast many of the preoccupations which dominate the works of his last decade; a concentration on the techniques of fugue and canon... an interest in highly abstract, recherché musical thought; and a preoccupation with saying the last word in a given genre with an attendant monumentality of conception." The "St. Anne" Prelude and Fugue attests powerfully to Bach's attainments in each of these areas, and stands as one of the most noble and eloquent utterances among his many organ compositions. *—Michael Jameson*

Recommended:

- ○ **Bach: The Great Fantasias, Preludes and Fugues** / C. Herrick / 1993 / Hyperion 66791/2
- ○ **Bach: Complete Works for Organ Vol. 7** / M. C. Alain / 1994 / Erato 96724
- ○ **Bach: L'Oeuvre d'orgue** / Rogg / HM 290772

Prelude and Fugue for organ in E minor ("Wedge"), BWV 548 (ca. 1725; revised 1727)

This massive work, requiring a good 15 minutes in performance, is one of Bach's most important and flamboyant organ compositions. Unlike most of his other preludes and fugues, this one seems to be a mature work written after Bach settled in Leipzig in 1723. Unexpectedly, it's the prelude that displays the most severe musical architecture, while the fugue is comparatively freewheeling (and harder to play). The grand prelude is cast in a verse and refrain structure, but employs three related thematic elements—two for the verses. The refrain initially arches across 18 bars of the score; after the first verse, it returns in the dominant, establishing the tonality for the second verse. Here, Bach introduces the third theme, a dotted figure linked to the themes of both the refrain and the first verse. After this second verse, the refrain returns, modulating into the subdominant, where the third verse develops the themes presented in the first two. The refrain returns one last time; under the influence of the dominant pedal note that introduces it, the refrain avoids returning to the tonic until its very last chord. Despite its strict melodic structure, the prelude is a great harmonic adventure.

Now comes the fugue, which manages to fall into ternary form while following the usual fugal conventions. The first of the three sections is a self-contained fugue, complete with its own exposition, modulations, and episodes. The fugue theme is something of a chromatic wedge expanding around a tonic point, this wedge giving the work its nickname. The theme picks up two chromatic countersubjects during the first exposition. After the harmonic tension and surprise of this first section, the fugue's second section settles into the principal key. This portion is a 100-measure toccata, full of extremely virtuosic runs. The fugue theme pops up now and then and is also echoed in the pedal material, but doesn't fully reassert itself until the third panel of this triptych, which until near the end is a note-for-note repetition of the first section. The work ends, however, in a resplendent Picardy third, concluding this otherwise minor-mode fugue in a blaze of E major. *—James Reel*

Recommended:

- ○ **Bach: The Great Fantasias, Preludes & Fugues** / C. Herrick / 1993 / Hyperion 66791/2
- ○ **Bach: Great Organ Works** / G. Leonhardt / 1997 / Seon 63185

Prelude and Fugue for organ in G major, BWV 541 (after 1712; revised ca. 1724)

This work was probably written during Johann Sebastian Bach's service at Weimar (1708–17), most likely in 1712. Sometime after 1740, Bach revised the piece. At one time, J.P. Kellner, an organist, copied out the work, adding the first 13 measures of the Andante from Bach's *Organ Sonata No. 4 in E minor* as a kind of an intermezzo between the prelude and fugue. Bach's obsession with repeated notes and chords in this work seems to be an attribute of his "Weimar style." Repeated notes are a salient feature not only of the fugue (a characteristic associated by some with the north German school), but of the prelude as well, where the repetition of entire chords plays a significant role. Repetition to this degree is somewhat unusual in works of the time, found in little organ music and almost no harpsichord works. A graceful passage consisting of a single line elegantly opens the triple meter prelude, filling in harmonies and providing no hint of the thicker texture to come. When the other voices enter, the device of repetition begins immediately, alternating measures of repeated chords with the fluid line of the opening. At times, the chords become very thick, while only the pedal part maintains the constant sixteenth note movement. As a motif of six repeated eighth notes moves from voice to voice, Bach passes through numerous chromatic alterations of the melodic material. Unlike some of his later works, which employ repetition to prepare suspensions, the reiteration of notes and chords here is for its own sake, creating rhythmic drive.

The fugue subject is built principally of repeated notes with little melodic contour. Beyond this and the key of G major, there is little relationship to the prelude, for the repeated notes do not grow into repeated chords. In an unusual move, Bach takes some of the middle entries of the subject through the tonic minor, and a Neapolitan cadence near the end is striking. Although there is only one extended episode, this and the other, shorter, episodes amount to half of the fugue. This work is a dense, motivically intense piece that is more a study in compositional rigor and harmonic adventurousness than in the presentation of tuneful material. *—John Palmer*

Recommended:

- ○ **Bach Organ Blaster** / Michael Murray / 1995 / Telarc 80316
- ○ **Albert Schweitzer Plays Bach Vol. 1** / Schweitzer / Pearl 9959
- ○ **Bach: Complete Works for Organ Vol. 14** / M.C. Alain / 1994 / Erato 96747
- ○ **Bach: L'Oeuvre d'orgue** / Rogg / HM 290772

Toccata and Fugue for organ in D minor ("Dorian"), BWV 538 (1712–1723)

According to the obituary printed after his death, Johann Sebastian Bach composed most of his organ works in Weimar, where he worked between 1708 and 1717. This is not surprising, since after his appointment at Weimar his duties did not involve the composition of works for the organ. His years as organist there witnessed a tremendous development in his compositional style, particularly in the realm of freely composed preludes and fugues.

Scholars believe Bach began this work while in Weimar, and completed it probably in 1723. Bach's omission of the B flat from the key signature (it appears instead as an accidental) has prompted the nickname "Dorian," but it is clearly minor, not truly Dorian. The lively toccata is, as one would expect, a great vehicle for the demonstration of digital dexterity, but its square rhythms mark it as an early work. Bach seems to have been influenced by the north German school in his use of two manuals for the toccata. The fugue is the real prize of this work; its weight makes the preceding toccata seem superfluous. Striking stylistic contrasts abound in the fugue, with an Italianate, vocal-style subject and numerous repeated chords, another nod to the north German school. At 222 measures, it is one of the composer's longest fugues, over half of it being dedicated to intense episodic development. In the exposition, we hear four entries of the subject, a seven-measure, syncopated theme, each paired with one of two countersubjects. A counter-exposition follows, reversing the order of the entries, placing the dominant-level answers before the tonic entries as the counterpoint loosens a bit. The four entries in the developmental segment, the first and third of which initiate brief canons, explore various harmonies. In the recapitulation, three more entries also introduce canons and, as with earlier subject entries, maintain a dense contrapuntal structure. With one exception, episodes are not built on new material, but derive from a canonic sequence that follows the first answer in the exposition. These episodes also are canonic, but the nature of the material makes the passages sound less contrapuntal than the subject entries and emphasizes cross rhythms. Even after the final entry, with its full pedal, Bach begins another episode, this one functioning as a coda. *—John Palmer*

Recommended:

- ○ **Bach: Four Great Toccatas and Fugues** / Biggs / 2003 / Sony 87983
- ○ **Bach: Toccatas and Passacaglia** / C. Herrick / 1990 / Hyperion 44124
- ○ **Bach: Great Organ Works** / Hurford / 1994 / London 443485

Toccata and Fugue for organ in D minor, BWV 565 (1708)

Johann Sebastian Bach's most famous organ piece is notable for its rhythmic drive as well for as its arresting opening motif. Considered the epitome of scary organ music by the many who associate it with melodramatic silent-film scenes, it has been transcribed in various ways. Through much of the twentieth century it was often heard in an orchestral arrangement by Leopold Stokowski. The romanticized, roaring registration often used in organ performances is still effective, although interpretations aiming for historical accuracy tend to give the work a lighter touch. It is difficult to establish a chronology of Bach's organ works, for most of their autograph manuscripts (except for those from the end of his career) have been lost. Works such as this one have come down to us only in copies made by his students. In the absence of clues provided by the composer's handwriting, the paper he wrote on, inscriptions that appear on the manuscript, and so forth, scholars have tried to guess the date of this work based on stylistic considerations. Because of its most salient structural aspect—the interpenetration of the toccata material and the contrapuntal fugue—the work has been assigned to the beginning of Bach's career, before his 1708 move to Weimar. It is perhaps the very earliest among Bach's well-known masterpieces. The alternation of quasi-improvisatory and contrapuntal sections was characteristic of the works of the north German organist Dietrich Buxtehude, whom Bach walked some two hundred miles to hear in 1704, taking a leave of absence from his post as organist at the Neukirche in Arnstadt. By fully realizing the dramatic potential inherent in this technique, Bach created a timeless work. *—Joseph Stevenson*

Recommended:

- ○ **Bach: Toccata & Fugue in D minor; Concerto 2 in A minor** / Michael Murray / 1983 / Telarc 80088
- ○ **Bach: Toccata & Fugue; Preludes & Fugues** / Biggs / 2002 / Sony 89955
- ○ **Bach: Toccata & Fugue in D minor & Other Favorite Organ Works** / Rogg / 1999 / Seraphim 73568
- ○ **Bach: L'Oeuvre d'orgue** / Rogg / HM 290772

Toccata and Fugue for organ in F major, BWV 540 (before 1731)

Most of Bach's works for the organ date from his years in Weimar (1708–17). This period witnessed a tremendous development in his compositional style, particularly in the realm of the freely composed preludes or toccatas and fugues—those not based on preexisting chorales.

The fugue and toccata of BWV 540 were each published individually during the eighteenth century; many believe the toccata to have been written apart from, and probably after, the fugue—a possibility that has led many to perform the pieces alone. This is not difficult to justify, for each is a self-contained masterwork. Together, they form what many believe to be Bach's best composition in the prelude and fugue genre, and they have both enjoyed great popularity.

It is possible the toccata was written for an organ other than the one Bach used in Weimar; the highest pedal pitch in the piece was not available on that organ. It was, however, to be found in Weissenfels and at one of the churches in Köthen. The piece is immense and, at 450 measures in length, can hardly be heard as a "prelude." Bravura passages for both the hands and feet take the listener through various harmonic areas in this expansive work, which derives its rhythmic drive from a persistent, Italianate figure. Neapolitan sixths, averted cadences, and sequences contribute to the tension of a sustained climax in the second half of the toccata.

The fugue is actually a double-fugue that presents a stark contrast to the preceding toccata. Harmonic daring characterizes the piece: an unresolved dissonance in the second measure sets the precedent for numerous other such instances, including accented non-harmonic tones. After the four-voice exposition—with both a subject and countersubject—has run its course, a complete counterexposition begins. Instead of continuing with an independent episode, Bach writes another fugal section, with a new, lively subject, featuring entries that move through minor keys, including the dominant minor. Throughout this second fugue, the pedal is absent, infusing the succession of entries and episodes with a sense of anticipation, or preparation, of something to come. This turns out to be just the function of the section when the first subject and its countersubject return, almost stealthily, in the midst of the contrapuntal texture. The return of the first fugue does not assert itself, however, until its first answer, which is accompanied in the pedal (finally) by the subject of the second fugue. Bach truncates and distorts this second subject as six more entries of the first subject float around the tonic before a final statement, with a powerful pedal entry, closes the piece. *—John Palmer*

Recommended:

- ○ **Bach: Toccatas & Fugues** / C. Herrick / 1990 / Hyperion 66434
- ○ **Bach: Four Great Toccatas & Fugues (SACD)** / Biggs / 2003 / Sony 87983
- ○ **Bach at Zwolle** / Michael Murray / Telarc 80385

Toccata, Adagio, and Fugue for organ in C major, BWV 564 (ca. 1712)

During his early days as a professional organist, Bach tinkered and toyed with all shapes, sizes, and kinds of non-chorale organ music, eventually perfecting the species of two-part toccata and fugue or prelude and fugue form so well known through such famous examples as the *Toccata and Fugue in D minor,* BWV 565 (ca. 1708). Only a single surviving work bears witness to the composer's passing interest in a three-part subspecies of that form: the *Toccata, Adagio and Fugue in C major,* BWV 564, which has been attributed both to Bach's years in Weimar (1708–17) and to the preceding period.

After a substantial, seemingly improvised (but of course carefully constructed) opening, the Toccata blossoms into wonderfully rich counterpoint in a pseudo-Baroque concerto style; some have heard Vivaldi's influence here, which would indicate a date of about 1713 or shortly thereafter). The Adagio is more often than not performed as a freestanding piece, both by organists and in a famous arrangement for cello. It is at its essence a melody with steadily plodding accompaniment. The Fugue takes up a long, multi-limbed subject with patches of broken triads and the same kind of quick, upper-pedal-point oscillation that characterizes the subject of the famous Fugue in BWV 565. Unlike that more famous work, however, this Fugue has no grandiose cadenza at the end, instead running its course in pure contrapuntal fashion with just slight embellishment at the cadence, followed by a brief coda. *—Blair Johnston*

Recommended:

○ **Bach: Toccata & Fugue in D minor & Other Favorite Organ Works** / Rogg / 1999 / Seraphim 73568

○ **Bach: Four Great Toccatas & Fugues** / Biggs / 2003 / Sony 87983

○ **Bach: Toccatas & Fugues** / C. Herrick / 1990 / Hyperion 66434

Trio sonata for organ No. 1 in E flat major, BWV 525 (ca. 1727)

Many of J.S. Bach's most beloved keyboard compositions were intended partly as instructional material. The six *Trio Sonatas for Organ,* BWV 525–530, may be such pieces; they are thought to have been incorporated into the lessons that Johann Sebastian gave to his son Wilhelm Friedemann. The six sonatas were composed close to the beginning of Bach's life in Leipzig. Unlike some of the others, which make use of genuine trio sonata music earlier composed for three players, the first of them, the *Trio Sonata No. 1 in E flat major* for organ, BWV 525, is apparently a wholly original work.

The process of condensing the by-then venerable trio sonata medium into music for a single keyboard player—with the three original voices assigned to two manuals and the pedals—was not accomplished in a single bold step. Bach's *Three-Part Inventions* of the early 1720s draw heavily on trio sonata idioms, as do several other keyboard works (the B minor Prelude in the first volume of the *Well-Tempered Clavier* being a key example). And we must also remember that while living in Cöthen in the early 1720s Bach had condensed the trio sonata texture for two players (e.g. the *Six Sonatas for Violin and Harpsichord,* BWV 1014–1019). Still, BWV 525 is something striking and new: a full-fledged chamber sonata for a single player, and probably the first of the organ trio sonatas to be composed.

Even so, there is very little else that is truly new about the music of BWV 525—the score might easily be played by two instruments and basso continuo, and very few listeners would be aware that it is in fact not an authentic trio sonata. The opening of the first movement is built by way of the normal upper-voices imitation, to which the bass voice adds "walking" eighth notes. The astute listener or player will certainly notice that the manner of the movement's active sixteenth notes owes as much to the Baroque concerto as to the Baroque sonata (as, indeed, does the late Italian Baroque three-movement format of BWV 525), but the fusion of sonata and concerto styles is something that we notice time and again throughout Bach's chamber sonatas.

The C minor Adagio is in a true binary form whose rhythms occasionally make quasi-siciliano shapes. The Allegro finale jumps forth in 3/4 time; the movement again falls into two halves, and at the start of the second half Bach turns the main subject of the movement—a series of leaping eighth notes and some consequent sixteenth note runs—upside down. *—Blair Johnston*

Recommended:

○ **Bach: Complete Works for Organ Vol. 13** / M. C. Alain / 1994 / Erato 96746

○ **Bach Trio Sonatas** / Palladian Ensemble / 1996 / Linn 5036

Trio sonata for organ No. 5 in C major, BWV 529 (ca. 1727)

It was once thought that all six of J.S. Bach's trio sonatas for organ (BWV 525–530) were composed in or about 1727; now, however, the period during which he is believed to have worked on these fascinating pieces has been expanded, and a composition date as late as 1731 has been assigned to the *Trio Sonata for organ No. 5 in C major,* BWV 529. It is, like the others of the set, a work in three movements in which the traditional three voices of the Baroque trio sonata are all assigned to a single keyboard player—one upper instrument voice for each hand and the basso continuo to the feet (pedals). And so, in typical Johann Sebastian fashion, something very new is created from something very old—and this process represents an important, if not widely known, step in the evolution of the sonata as it is now generally understood.

Freshness of instrumentation and layout aside, the music of BWV 529 is representative of the Baroque chamber sonata tradition. The normal sonata-style imitative gesture is made to open the Allegro first movement; here a bit of invertible counterpoint is used, the second voice entering before it properly "should," to add a little interest to the standard technique. The main subject of the movement has two distinct elements to it: sixteenth notes that oscillate around a fixed internal pedal point and a follow-up idea in bouncy eighth notes. Precious little material is added as the movement moves forward—what we have is essentially an ingenious 155-bar working-out of just two contrasting thoughts.

The following Largo is as florid a movement as is to be found in the organ sonatas; the two highly ornamented upper voices weave in and around one another atop a steady bass line. The Allegro finale is the most typical trio-sonata movement in BWV 529; one can indeed imagine the opening bars having been penned by Arcangelo Corelli, though the following compact and elaborate working-out of this basic contrapuntal cell would have been entirely beyond the scope of the Roman master. *—Blair Johnston*

Recommended:

○ **Bach: Complete Works for Organ Vol. 13** / M. C. Alain / 1994 / Erato 96746

○ **Bach: Trio Sonatas** / Musica Pacifica / 1996 / Virgin 45192

Two-Part Inventions (15) for keyboard (ca. 1720; revised 1723)

"A proper guide, by which lovers of the harpsichord, and especially those who crave instruction, are shown a clear way of learning not only to play cleanly in two voices but also, after further progress, to deal correctly with three obbligato voices, and also to create and properly develop good musical ideas; but, above all else, to acquire a true cantabile style of playing, and, with it, to get a good foretaste of the art of composition."

Thus reads J.S. Bach's own description, provided in a paragraph-long preface to the volume that contains the final 1723 versions of the pieces, of his *Two-* and *Three-Part Inventions* for keyboard. His purpose in writing them could not be made more plain—and, indeed, it was not as instructional material in some general sense that he first conceived the pieces, but rather as exercises specifically designed for his 12-year-old son Wilhelm Friedemann (the first versions of the pieces are to be found in the 1722 *Clavier-Büchlein* for Wilhelm Friedemann). There are 30 pieces altogether, 15 *Inventions* in two voices and 15 *Sinfonias* in three.

The 15 *Two-Part Inventions* are written in the 15 keys that were at the time considered to be standard for keyboard use (remember that the *Well-Tempered Clavier,* which explores all 24 keys, was a novelty made possible only by the advent of more sophisticated tuning systems). The original order of the pieces was rather different than is the order in which one today finds them—it was Bach himself, however, and not modern editors, who rearranged the pieces. The final key scheme is as follows: 1. C major, 2. C minor, 3. D major, 4. D minor, 5. E flat major, 6. E major, 7. E minor, 8. F major, 9. F minor, 10. G major, 11. G minor, 12. A major, 13. A minor, 14. B flat major, 15. B minor.

The *Two-Part Inventions* are perfectly suited for the development and maintenance of finger dexterity (they are often used specifically as preparation for the *Well-Tempered Clavier*), and one will find them on the pianos of not only young students and their teachers, but also many accomplished pianists who have realized that simpler is not always easier. But these 15 short pieces—only a few break the 30-bar mark by an appreciable amount—are also phenomenally well-composed; they are miniature specimens of ingenious motivic development. *—Blair Johnston*

Recommended:

○ **Bach: Fantasia in C minor; Two- & Three-Part Inventions; Chromatic Fantasia & Fugue** / A. Hewitt / 1994 / Hyperion 66746

○ **Great Pianists of the 20th Century: András Schiff** / A. Schiff / 1999 / Philips 456925

○ **Bach: Inventions & Sinfonias** / Koopman / Capriccio 10210

Well-Tempered Clavier, Book 1 (1722)

Many consider the two books of the *Well-Tempered Clavier* Bach's finest keyboard collection. He completed the first volume in Cöthen in 1722 and the second around 16 years later in Leipzig. Both books consist of 24 preludes and fugues going through all the keys, a total of 48 pieces in each volume, though some recordings give 24 tracks, one for each key covered. Book 1 opens with a prelude and fugue in the following sequence: C major, C minor, C sharp major, C sharp minor, D major, D minor, etc.

The *First Book* is more focused in its greater stylistic unity than its successor. Most of the preludes deal with a specific technical feature, while the fugues are more varied in style and form and often seem to express a whole world of developmental possibilities for the music. The *First Book*'s opening prelude is soothing and serene in its scalar writing, its manner of thematic flow seeming to augur the more intimate character of the first movement of Beethoven's *Moonlight Sonata,* written three-quarters of a century later. The succeeding fugue is also somewhat subdued in its more animated pacing and deft contrapuntal activity. The prelude and fugue that follow are livelier, the latter quite playful and charming.

But there are such vast riches in this monumental set, too many even for lengthy analysis. The *E major Fugue,* for example, has a delightful carefree manner in its colorful sixteenth note passages and its consistently inventive keyboard writing. The *Prelude in F sharp minor* has a subtlety that may not be grasped upon first or second hearing. There are sinister elements here, as well as a sense of yearning and frustration. The four-voice *G minor Fugue* has a muscular and heroic character, Bach's contrapuntal writing again divulging his utter mastery. The gentle *G sharp minor Prelude* is a beautiful piece, mixing sunshine and sadness. The *A major Fugue* has a jaunty, exhilaration about its lively music, its first part comprised of eighth notes, the latter of sixteenth notes. The *B flat major Fugue* has a sense of joy and humor in its lively manner, yet manages to achieve an expressive depth one would not normally associate with that kind of description.

Analysis of Bach's music here often runs into controversial areas, with a few musicians tailoring their interpretation according to religious symbolism they believe to be present in the score. For example, a passage in the *F minor Fugue* has been interpreted as representing Christ's crucifixion, owing to its descending chromatic manner and other features. In the end, this view, as well as the idea that certain numbers (representing tones or other compositional elements) symbolize other religious events, must be assessed as highly dubious speculation. The music though, regardless of how one hears it, is masterful from first prelude to last fugue. *—Robert Cummings*

Recommended:

- ○ **Bach: Le Clavier Bien Tempéré** / Moroney / HM 3901285
- ○ **Bach: The Well-Tempered Clavier, Book 1** / Aldwell / 1992 / Nonesuch 79272
- ○ **Bach: The Well-Tempered Clavier Book 1** / G. Gould / 1994 / Sony 52600
- ○ **Bach: Das Wohltempierte Klavier Teil 1,1** / Jaccottet / 1989 / Pilz 160121

Well-Tempered Clavier Book 1, No. 1 in C major, BWV 846 (1722)

The prelude in C major that opens the first volume of Bach's *Well-tempered Clavier* may well be his most universally recognized piece of music—and yet, as fate would have it, many of those who know it have never heard the fugue for which it is a prelude, and might in fact have no idea that it is part of a larger work that counts among the most significant and groundbreaking musical efforts ever penned. Because of the mathematics involved, the tuning, or temperament, of a keyboard instrument must necessarily be only an approximation of intervallic perfection. Various methods of arriving at a satisfying approximation were tried out during the Renaissance and Baroque, but none was really successful—none produced a tuned instrument that could play in more than a small handful of keys without the result sounding grossly out of tune—until the late seventeenth century, when several satisfying methods came into general use. Now a harpsichordist could play to good effect in each of the 24 keys, and around 1722 Bach decided to compose a prelude and a fugue in each of them. Historical considerations aside, the pages of the *Well-tempered Clavier* are felt by many to be the most flawlessly crafted, brilliantly designed music ever composed.

The C major prelude is on the surface a most simple piece of music: a series of chords unfolds, each arpeggiated in exactly the same way. But the cleverness by which that exact series of harmonies in that exact spacing with that exact arpeggiation was devised cannot be overestimated. In fact, Bach spent a great deal of effort on this seemingly effortless miniature, and it took him more than one try to get it right—it is one of just a few *Well-tempered Clavier* pieces that exist in more than one version. The fugue is in four voices, and, interestingly enough, its subject is ever-present, which means that there are no episodes in the ordinary sense of the word, only a continuous contrapuntal elaboration of the subject (which is set against itself in the fugue's second half in a stretto of supreme elegance). *—Blair Johnston*

Recommended:

- ○ **Passion for Piano** / W. Kempff / 2000 / DG 469232
- ○ **Anna Magdalena Bach Notebook (Highlights)** / McGegan / 2001 / HM Classical Express 3957042
- ○ **Sviatoslav Richter: In Memoriam** / S. Richter / DG 457668
- ○ **Busoni and His Legacy** / Busoni / 2002 / Arbiter 134

Well-Tempered Clavier, Book 2 (ca. 1740)

The first book of Bach's *Das Wohltemperierte Klavier* (The Well-Tempered Clavier) was complete by 1722. Bach gave the present title to the work, which was composed "for the use and practice of musical youth eager to learn and for the amusement of those already skilled in this study." Bach composed a paired Prelude and Fugue in each of the 24 keys to demonstrate the viability of the new "equal-temperament" system, which allows one to play in all keys without producing out-of-tune intervals, as happened with Pythagorean and "mean tone" tunings. Furthermore, the pieces are as much compositional studies as keyboard works.

Twenty years later, Bach assembled another set of preludes and fugues. The title page is missing from the manuscript, but its similarity to the "first" book of *The Well-Tempered Clavier* led editors to entitle it "Book II." Bach worked on the second book over a long period of time, even reworking pieces he had written for other purposes, as he had in the first book. Some of the preludes and fugues date from the 1720s. Possibly the most substantial revision for the second book was to No. 3, in C sharp major, which was originally in C major. Fugues Nos. 15 and 17 survive in earlier versions in which they are connected with different preludes than we find in The Well-Tempered Clavier.

There are many musical differences between the works of Book II and those of Book I. The preludes in the second group explore a greater range of forms and styles than do the earlier examples. Most striking are the experiments in the style of the Italian bipartite keyboard sonata, codified by Domenico Scarlatti. Like earlier dance movements, these consist of two repeated sections. Some of the "sonata" preludes in Book II, such as Nos. 5, 12, and 21, feature a recapitulation of the opening material, while others (Nos. 10 and 15) have parallel closing sections. Prelude No. 17 is an Italian concert-ritornello movement; Nos. 13 and 23 also display concerto traits. The tenth is a two-part invention and Nos. 4 and 14 are ariosos. Those that are clearly derived form dance forms—No. 5 from the gigue and No. 8 from the allemande—lack the traditional binary form.

Like the fugues of Book I, those of Book II employ every device of formal fugue writing. In terms of compositional economy, No. 2 of the second Book is a masterpiece—in the first 28 measures there are 24 statements of the one-measure subject, producing almost painfully dense counterpoint. Fifteen of the fugues are in three voices; nine are in four. Four of these (Nos. 4, 17, 18 and 23) are double fugues and No. 14 is a triple fugue, the third subject of which recalls a subject from the C sharp minor Fugue of Book I. In general, the fugues of Book II are thematically more restrained than those of Book I. Instead, Bach seems to experiment with the contrapuntal potential inherent in each of the fugue subjects. *—John Palmer*

Recommended:

- ○ **Bach: The Well-Tempered Clavier II** / G. Gould / 1993 / Sony 52603
- ○ **Bach: The Well-Tempered Clavier Book II** / Aldwell / 1989 / Nonesuch 79200
- ○ **Bach: The Well-Tempered Clavier Book II** / Nikolayeva / 1982 / MK 418043

CHORAL

Also hat Gott die Welt geliebt, cantata, BWV 68 (May 21, 1725)

Johann Sebastian Bach completed his *Cantata No. 68, "Also hat Gott die Welt geliebt,"* BWV 68 in 1725. It was composed for Whit-Monday, and it was part of the second cycle of cantatas that Bach wrote as the cantor for the School of Saint Thomas in Leipzig. The cantata uses different movement forms to create an effective palindrome: chorus, aria, recitative, aria, and chorus. Its texts are from disparate sources, including the local poet Christiane Mariane von Ziegler; this cantata is one of nine by Bach to feature her words prominently.

Ziegler took John 3:16–21 as her point of departure to create a text specifically intended for the occasion of Whit-Monday, demonstrating the possibility of redemption through faith, opening with "God so Loved the World." A hymn by Salamo Liscow from 1675 opens with the same words, and Bach weaves this into the opening chorus as well, as well as the cantus firmus hymn melody by Gottfried Vopelius (1682). The orchestration of this opening chorale is rich, featuring a four-part chorus with the upper parts thickened with doubling oboes and oboe da caccia.

The soprano melody of the first aria is among the most popular melodies of Bach's catalog. It is airy and well-proportioned, enough so to be reminiscent of the period phrasing style of melodic writing to come into its own later in the century. The cello answers the soprano; the two are effectively paired. In the second aria, the bass is coupled with answering oboes and oboe da caccia. Bach actually wrote both of these arias years before this cantata, while he was still working at Weimar. They were originally presented to Duke Christian of Saxe-Weißenfels. Other than a few adjustments, they are the same pieces.

The final movement is a double-fugue motet. In addition to the already bountiful textures of the opening movement, trombones are added to strengthen the lines of the altos, tenors, and basses. The symmetry of this work is delightful for its understatement. It is strikingly cohesive for a work that draws from earlier work by the composer and others, as well as scripture and the words of other poets. This is one of the cantatas that listeners should go out of their way to become acquainted with; it is invulnerable to exhaustion. *—John Keillor*

Recommended:

- ○ **Bach: Cantates BWV 41, 6, 68** / Coin (cond.), B. Schlick, A. Scholl, Pregardien, G. Schwarz, Ens. Baroque de Limoges / 1996 / Astree 8555
- ○ **Bach: Cantatas BWV 68 -70** / Rilling (cond.), Stuttgart Gachinger Kantorei, Stuttgart Bach Collegium, / 1970 / Haenssler 92022

Aus der Tiefen rufe ich, Herr, zu dir, cantata, BWV 131 (1707–1708)

This profoundly felt work provides the best possible evidence that Bach composed no immature cantatas. One of his earliest essays in the form, BWV 131 ("Out of the deep have I called") was composed in 1707 or 1708 in Mühlhausen, where Bach served as organist during that period. One of relatively few autograph scores of the cantatas to survive, BWV 131 includes the notation that it was "set to music at the request of Heern D. Georg: Christ: Eilmar." Eilmar was archdeacon of St. Mary's in Mühlhausen, a man with whom Bach had developed a particular friendship—Eilmar later stood as godfather to the composer's firstborn son, Wilhelm Friedemann.

The Bach scholar Christoph Wolff has also suggested that Eilmar may have been the author of the text. Like many other early cantata texts, it is largely based on a biblical source, Psalm 130. Juxtaposed with the entire setting of the psalm are two strophes from the chorale "Herr Jesu Christ" by Bartholomäus Ringwaldt, employed in the arias for bass and tenor. No precise liturgical occasion for this profoundly penitential cantata has been established, although it may have been used at a commemorative service of penitence following a great fire that devastated Mühlhausen in May 1707, shortly before Bach took up his post. In spite of the predominantly sober mood, the work is illuminated by the flashes of word painting characteristic of Bach's earlier cantatas. Also consistent with the early type of cantata are the opening orchestral sinfonia and lack of closed forms; the work falls into interconnected blocks rather than individual numbers. Thus the sinfonia leads directly into the opening chorus, which is itself divided into sections, a slow introduction and quicker fugal continuation. This is followed by a through-composed bass arioso-like passage with oboe obbligato in which the plaint-like words of the psalm alternate with those of an ornamented version of the chorale intoned by solo soprano. The note of hope brought by the chorale is maintained by the chorus ("I wait for the Lord") that stands at the center of the work. The succeeding tenor aria returns to the minor as the text speaks of the soul's long wait for morning. Again a stanza of the chorale, this time sung by the alto, is superimposed. The final chorus begins with a dramatic stroke, a threefold invocation on the word "Israel," before proceeding to conclude this remarkable cantata with a fugue. *—Brian Robins*

Recommended:

- ○ **Bach: Kantanten, Aus der Tiefen** / Herreweghe (cond.), B. Schlick, Lesne, H. Crook, Kooy, Collegium Vocale, Ghent / 1992 / Virgin 59237
- ○ **Bach: Cantatas BWV 130–132** / Rilling (cond.), Stuttgart Bach Collegium / 1977 / Haenssler 92041
- ○ **Bach: Early Cantatas from Mühlhausen & Weimar** / J. Thomas, J. Baird, Minter, B. Butterfield, American Bach Soloists / 1995 / Koch 7235

Christ lag in Todesbanden, cantata, BWV 4 (before 1708)

The style of this famous cantata clearly places it in the early part of Bach's career; it was probably composed for the Easter celebration in Mühlhausen in either 1707 or 1708, when Bach was in his early twenties. During Bach's early years as cantor at the Thomaskirche in Leipzig, he presented the church with nearly five complete cycles of music for the weekly Sunday worship service, and the cantata, based on Martin Luther's Easter hymn *"Christ lag in Todesbanden,"* was recopied and revived for this Leipzig repertory. Despite what would have been a decidedly old-fashioned style by the time of Bach's arrival in Leipzig, the composer seems to have surmised that it would make the same powerful impression at that time as it still does in ours.

Christ lag in Todesbanden shows no signs of the simplifying reforms and stylistic internationalization (as advanced by Erdmann Neumeister) so prevalent in this genre of Lutheran church music around the beginning of the eighteenth century. Nor is there evidence of Italianate operatic recitatives and arias. Rather, the successive movements stolidly expound the successive strophes of Luther's chorale.

Luther's 1524 melody (with echoes of the Gregorian hymn "Pange lingua gloriosi") permeates the musical substance of each movement. In the Lutheran service, the cantata would have been performed immediately following the weekly Gospel text, understood as an element of the worship immediately pertinent to its theological content, and perhaps even commenting upon it like the sermon that followed.

After an opening sinfonia (which contains strong motivic echoes of the chorale), Bach sets the first verse of text in the form of an extended chorale prelude, with passages of imitation crowned by the chorale melody sung as a cantus firmus in the highest voice. Though this austere, even archaic, structure produces a somber tone, the movement closes (as does each verse) with an exuberant Allelujah. The second verse, which describes the ancient power of death, adopts an appropriately forceful tone derived from octave leaps in the melody. The third chorale verse, sung as a cantus firmus by a tenor solo, has an accompaniment for obbligato violin.

The structure of the cantata is based on a symmetrical layout, Chorale-Duet-Solo-Chorale-Solo-Duet-Chorale, and the central fourth movement becomes the focal point of the whole work. This vibrant contrapuntal movement depicts the "wondrous battle" between life and death which Luther's text asserts was won by Christ's death. There follows a bass aria replete with rhetorical gestures, such as a famous melodic leap down a diminished twelfth when the vanquishing of Death occurs. Verse six invites all present in the worship service to celebrate the holy festival of this victory; the phrases of this duet dance above a festive dotted-rhythm in the accompaniment. The final verse is set homophonically, in hymn style, appropriate for congregational participation. *—Timothy Dickey*

Recommended:

- ○ **Bach: Christ lag in Todesbanden; Oster-Oratorium** / A. Parrott (cond.), Taverner Consort & Players / 1994 / Virgin 91765
- ○ **Bach: Cantatas BWV 4, 150, 196** / M. Suzuki (cond.), Kurisu, Tachikawa, Katano, Kooy, Bach Collegium Japan / 1995 / Bis 751
- ○ **Bach: Cantatas BWV 4, 56 & 82** / F. Lehmann (cond.), Krebs, Jung, Frankfurt am Main State Music School Choir / Archiv 449756

Der Himmel lacht! die Erde jubilieret, Ccantata, BWV 31 (Apr. 21, 1715)

Cantata No. 31 ("Heaven laughs, the earth rejoices") is a jubilant and lavishly scored work composed in Weimar, where it was first performed on April 21, 1715. Following his promotion to concertmaster at the Weimar court at the end of 1713, Bach was required to prepare and perform one cantata every month in the ducal chapel. BWV 31 is one of approximately 20 extant cantatas composed between 1714 and 1716 to fulfill these duties. One of only two extant cantatas by Bach composed for Easter Day (the other is BWV 4), it was also used the following year, and the composer is known to have revived it with minor alterations in Leipzig at least twice: in 1724, and again in 1731. Like almost all of Bach's Weimar cantatas composed after 1713, the text is by the Weimar court librarian Salomo Franck. The orchestral scoring includes parts for three trumpets, timpani, three oboes, oboe da caccia, strings, and continuo.

The cantata opens, as do many from this period, with an instrumental movement featuring a prominent trumpet motif; its dance-like character and festive mood introduce the following chorus. The long recitative for bass that follows announces Christ's resurrection ("Awaited day"). "Prince of life, strong warrior," the text of the following bass aria might lead one to expect further celebratory pomp, but instead Bach scores it with only a vigorously articulated continuo accompaniment. Two further pairs of recitative and short arias follow—the first for tenor, the second allotted to the soprano. The tenor aria is lively, as befits words that bring faith in the true believer's own resurrection. The soprano's recitative and aria become more reflective; the soloist's radiant expectation of life after death is sympathetically supported by an obbligato oboe, while the strings play the melody of Nicolaus Herman's "Wenn mein Stündlein vorhanden ist" (1575). The same hymn provides the material for the closing four-part chorale setting, which is augmented by obbligato trumpet and violin parts that ascend high above the choral texture. *—Brian Robins*

Recommended:

- ○ **Bach: Cantatas Vol. 6; BWV 21 & 31** / M. Suzuki (cond.), Turk, Frimmer, Kooy, Bach Collegium Japan / 1997 / Bis 851

Ein feste Burg ist unser Gott, cantata, BWV 80 (1727–1731)

The Reformation Festival is one of the major annual events in the Lutheran calendar; it is celebrated on October 31, the day on which Martin Luther nailed his 95 theses to the door of the castle church at Wittenburg in 1517. BWV 80 ("A mighty fortress is our God"), one of Bach's most famous cantatas, is one of two that Bach composed for the Festival. Unlike BWV 79, its companion, BWV 80 has a highly complex history. It appears to have started life as a Lenten cantata (BWV 80a) composed during Bach's period in Weimar, probably in 1715; in 1723, his first year in Leipzig, Bach expanded the work for use at the Festival that year, in the process dropping the great chorus based on Luther's famous hymn in favor of a simple four-part harmonization. At some later date Bach again revised the cantata, replacing the opening chorale with a chorus in the old polyphonic style. Confusion over the instrumentation of BWV 80 is exacerbated by the loss of Bach's original score and parts; the version known today comes from a copy made by Bach's pupil and son-in-law, Johann Christoph Altnickol. Further confusion resulted when trumpet and timpani parts composed by Bach's eldest son, Wilhelm Friedemann Bach, found their way into the first printing of the work; although spurious, they are still included in many of the performances heard today.

Luther's well-known hymn dominates the work; aside from its prominence in choral movements, it serves as a cantus firmus in a duet for soprano and bass (No. 2). A second soprano aria with only continuo accompaniment follows the succeeding bass recitative; its small scale and reflective character provide relief from the prevailing grandeur of the work. The other solo number is a duet for alto and tenor (No. 7) with an obbligato part for oboe da caccia (an oboe in the original Weimar version). The concluding chorale returns to Luther's hymn, setting the final strophe as a simple four-part harmonization. *—Brian Robins*

Recommended:

- ○ **J. S. Bach: Magnificat BWV 243** / Herreweghe (cond.), B. Schlick, Mellon, Lesne, H. Crook, Collegium Vocale, La Chapelle Royale / 1990 / HM 901326
- ○ **Bach: Cantatas BWV 80–82** / Rilling (cond.), Fischer-Dieskau, Auger, Hamari, Huttenlöcher, Gachinger Kantorei, Württemberg CO Heilbronn / Haenssler 92026

Er rufet seinen Schafen mit Namen, cantata, BWV 175 (May 22, 1725)

First performed on the third day of Pentecost (Whit Tuesday), May 22, 1725, BWV 175 ("He calleth his sheep by name") belongs to a group of nine cantatas composed that year to texts by Christiane Mariane von Ziegler (1695–1760). She was a Leipzig-born poet who enjoyed the support of the literary reformer Johann Christoph Gottsched. The series marks the end of the so-called "chorale cantatas" that dominate Bach's second annual cantata cycle (Jahrgang) composed during 1724–25. Each of Ziegler's texts follows the same structure; a Biblical text followed by alternating recitatives and arias, and a concluding chorale. The instrumental scoring is unusual; it includes two trumpets, three recorders, violoncello piccolo (a smaller cello with range and sonority somewhere between a viola and cello), strings and basso continuo.

The cantata opens with a short accompanied recitative for tenor, the text drawn from the Gospel of the day, the parable of the good shepherd (John 10:3). The pastoral sentiment is underlined by the lyrical accompaniment provided by the three recorders. The beautiful da capo alto aria which follows retains both the recorders and the mood, the gently rocking continuo line of the first part mirroring the spirit's desire to be led by the shepherd to green pastures. In the central section, the yearning of the "languishing heart" is supported by the first recorder's chromatic lines.

The following tenor recitative brings a greater sense of drama as the singer agitatedly asks "Where do I find thee?" The answer comes in the succeeding lively aria (also for tenor) with its ornamental obligato part for violoncello piccolo. This aria is a parody, having originally been composed for a cantata written in honor of the birthday of Prince Leopold of Cöthen during the period Bach was employed there (1717–23).

The third aria, for bass, follows a simple alto recitative taken from the Gospel of John (10:6). The text of the aria is Ziegler's commentary on the foregoing recitative, "Open your ears"; the singer is given the support of two trumpets in a sturdy movement that stands in marked contrast to the pastoral peacefulness of most of the cantata. The final chorale, a four-part setting of "Komm, heiliger geist," was borrowed from Cantata No. 59, with new words taken from Johann Rist's hymn "O Gottes Geist, mein Trost und Rath" (1651). *—Brian Robins*

Recommended:

- ○ **Bach: Cantates BWV 85, 183, 199 & 175** / Coin (cond.), B. Schlick, A. Scholl, Pregardien, G. Schwarz, Concerto Vocale, Ens. Baroque de Limoges / 1995 / Astree 8544
- ○ **Bach: Cantatas BWV 172–175** / Rilling (cond.), Gachinger Kantorei, Stuttgart Bach Collegium / 1984 / Haenssler 92052

Erschallet, ihr Lieder, cantata, BWV 172 (May 20, 1714)

Bach's appointment as organist to the ducal court at Weimar in 1708 made no formal demands on him to compose cantatas; during his early years there he produced only a few occasional works. Following his promotion to concertmaster in the spring of 1814, he was required to compose and perform one cantata each month. Cantata No. 172 ("Ring out, ye songs"), for Whit Sunday (the feast of Pentecost), was the third of these works, first performed in the ducal chapel on May 20, 1714. Although Bach composed three other cantatas for Pentecost (Nos. 59, 74, and 34), BWV 172 seems to have been a particular favorite of the composer's, being revived and revised by him several times after he took up his cantorship in Leipzig.

The text, like those of the majority of the cantatas Bach composed in Weimar, is probably the work of the Weimar court librarian and poet Salomo Franck. Formally it departs from the older style of through-composed Biblical cantatas Bach had written in his pre-Weimar days, introducing closed forms such as the recitative and da capo aria.

In keeping with the festive spirit of the day, the cantata opens with a brilliantly joyous four-part chorus with trumpets and timpani. A short bass recitative—the only one in the cantata—leads to a da capo aria in which the bass asks the Holy Trinity to "enter into us." The powerful plea is supported by three obligato trumpets; Bach takes this trinity symbolism a step further by writing the vocal part mainly in intervals of a third. This leads to another aria, this time for tenor, and in a completely contrasting mood. Here, gently flowing strings create a mood of tranquility, "wafting the soul" on the breath of the Holy Spirit. The following duet for soprano and alto takes the form of a dialogue between the impatient Soul and the Holy Spirit. It employs the kind of neo-erotic language often used in such duets, its "purified happiness" (as described by Albert Schweitzer) counterpointed by an ornamented version of Martin Luther's chorale "Veni creator Spiritus," heard first on the oboe, later on the organ. The cantata concludes with a strophe from Philip Nicolai's beautiful chorale "Wie schön leuchtet der Morgenstern." *—Brian Robins*

Recommended:

- ○ **Bach: Whitsun Cantatas** / J. E. Gardiner (cond.), Monteverdi Choir, English Baroque Soloists / 2000 / DG 463584
- ○ **Bach: Cantatas BWV 172–175** / Rilling (cond.), Frankfurt Kantorei, Stuttgart Bach Collegium / 1984 / Haenssler 92052
- ○ **Bach: 3 Weimar Cantatas** / Rifkin (cond.), The Bach Ens. / 2001 / Dorian 93231

Geist und Seele wird verwirret, cantata, BWV 35 (Sep. 8, 1726)

J. S. Bach composed the cantata *Geist und Seele wird verwirret*, BWV 35 (*Cantata No. 35*) in 1726 for use on Trinity XII (the 12th Sunday after Trinity): September 8 that year. It is one of a handful of cantatas composed during the summer and autumn of 1726 for alto soloist and instrumental ensemble (*Vergnügte Ruh, beliebte Seelenlust*, BWV 170 is probably the most famous of these alto cantatas). The text of *Geist und Seele wird verwirret* was authored in 1711 by Georg Christian Lehms of Darmstadt, a librarian whose work Bach used in several other cantatas of the mid-1720s and also in a few of Bach's Weimar cantatas. The Scripture for Trinity XII is from Mark 7:31–37, and relates the tale of Jesus healing the deaf man; the cantata text is closely-knit with the story, reflecting on and responding to it in two Parts.

The alto soloist of *Cantata No. 35* is supported by an ensemble made up of the usual strings and basso continuo, a pair of oboes, oboe da caccia, and the kind of organ obbligato that starts creeping into Bach's cantatas during the mid-1720s. The organ obbligato of BWV 35 is particularly interesting, in that it allows us to draw a connection between the cantata and a work that, were it not for the cantata, would be hopelessly lost to us: the *Harpsichord Concerto in D minor*, BWV 1059. Just a few measures of that harpsichord concerto survive; they happen, however, to be identical with the opening measures of the Sinfonia that begins Part I of *Cantata No. 35*, and that has allowed scholars to make reconstructions of that first movement of the harpsichord concerto. Furthermore, some musicologists believe that the Sinfonia at the opening of Part II is really the finale of the lost concerto in disguised form, and that the second aria might be the second movement.

There are three arias for the alto to sing: No. 2 "Geist und Seele wird verwirret" (Spirit and soul are bewildered), No. 4. "Gott hat alles wohl gemacht!" (God has crafted everything so well!), and No. 7 "Ich wünsche mir, bei Gott zu leben" (I wish now only to live by God). *—Blair Johnston*

Recommended:

- ○ **Cantatas pour alto; BWV 35, 54 & 170** / Herreweghe (cond.), A. Scholl, Orch. du Collegium Vocale / 1998 / HM 901644
- ○ **Bach: Cantatas for Alto** / Rappé, Concerto Avenna / 1995 / CD Accord 033
- ○ **Bach: Cantates pour alto; BWV 35, 53, 82** / Banchini (cond.), R. Jacobs, Ens. 415 / HM 1951273

Geschwinde, ihr wirbelnden Winde, cantata, BWV 201 (1729)

In 1729, Bach took up the musical directorship of a series of concerts in Leipzig known as the Collegium Musicum, a generic term employed in Germany for (generally) semiprofessional and often informal concerts normally founded on student music making. Two such organizations existed in Leipzig in Bach's day, the one he became involved with having been founded by Telemann in 1702. Such concerts generally involved the performance of instrumental works (Bach's keyboard concertos were intended for performance at the Collegium Musicum) and small-scale secular vocal works. For the occasional special concert, larger works were sometimes given; it is into this category that Bach's secular *Cantata No. 201*, ("Haste, haste, you whirling winds" or "The Dispute between Phoebus and Pan") falls. It was composed in the same year that Bach took up the directorship, a time when he would obviously want something new for the Collegium. The text, an adaptation of an episode in Ovid's *Metamorphosis*, is by Picander, the pseudonym of the poet Christian Friedrich Henrici.

Bach enjoyed a fruitful period of collaboration with Picander around this time, the partnership producing not only the *St. Matthew* and *St. Mark Passions* but also both sacred and secular cantatas. The designation of the work as a *dramma per musica* is revealing, since that was a rubric frequently applied to operas during the eighteenth century. Indeed, in common with a number of Bach's other secular cantatas, "Phoebus and Pan" might be regarded as a miniature opera, the closest the composer came to a genre he otherwise never explored. The plot, probably rich in contemporary allusions, involves a thinly veiled satire on poor music making and singing. Phoebus and Pan each anger the other with claims of vocal superiority. Their quarrel is interrupted by Momus (soprano), who pokes fun at Pan. Eventually Mercurius (alto) suggests a singing contest, which is opened with a beautiful aria for Phoebus. Pan, in contrast, makes a fool of himself thanks to Bach's employment of stock clichés and popular, low style that alludes to the simple galant music gaining popularity at the time. The two judges who have seconded the contestants (Tmolus for Pheobus, Midas for Pan) both find in favor of their principals. Midas' obviously absurd decision earns him a pair of asses' ears (and a wonderful bray in the accompaniment!) to join his champion's fools' cap. The work opens and closes with large da capo choruses. Sharply characterized and wittily inventive, "Phoebus and Pan" reveals a side of Bach too little familiar to those who know him only by his instrumental and sacred vocal works. *—Brian Robins*

Recommended:

- ○ **Bach: Der streit zwischen Phoebus & Pan** / R. Jacobs (cond.), Akademie für Alte Musik Berlin / HM 901544
- ○ **Bach: The Contest Between Phoebus & Pan** / Rilling (cond.), Rubens, Danz, Goerne, Odinius, Gächinger Kantorei, Stuttgart Bach Collegium / 1997 / Haenssler 92061

Gott der Herr ist Sonn und Schild, cantata, BWV 79 (Oct. 31, 1725)

BWV 79 ("God is a light and a shield") is one of two cantatas Bach composed for the *Reformation Festival*, an important event in the Lutheran calendar celebrated annually on October 31. It dates from 1725 and, although less well-known than its companion, BWV 80, "Ein fest Burg," it is a work whose splendor befits the ceremonial occasion. It is lavishly scored for two horns, timpani, two flutes (added for a later performance which took place at some time between 1728 and 1731), two oboes, strings, and continuo in addition to the normal four-part chorus and vocal soloists. The text is anonymous, but may be the work of Erdmann Neumeister, an important figure in the development of the Lutheran cantata.

The cantata opens with a resplendent sinfonia; its pounding drum beats and obbligato horn parts lead directly into the choral entry, a setting of a verse from Psalm 84. The second part of this magnificent opening chorus is a dynamic four-part fugue. The alto aria which follows is a paraphrase of the same psalm verse, but the triumphant mood of the chorus is here replaced one of devotion. The third movement is an elaborate chorale setting of the famous hymn *"Nun danket alle Gott"* by Martin Rinkart (1636); both the timpani and the horn join their voices with that of the chorus. The succeeding bass recitative introduces an animated duet for the soprano and bass soloists calling on God to maintain his support. The cantata concludes with a simple four-part choral harmonization of the hymn *"Nun lasst uns Gott, dem Herrn"* by Gustav Helmbold. Three of the movements were later parodied in Bach's *Lutheran Masses*–BWV 234 (the alto aria) and BWV 236 (the opening chorus and the duet). *–Brian Robins*

Recommended:

- ○ **Bach: Kantaten BWV 79, 80, 192, 50** / Rotzsch (cond.), Auger, Schreier, Adam, Wenkel, Neues Bach Collegium Musicum Leipzig / 1994 / Berlin Classics 0021762
- ○ **Bach: Cantatas BWV 77–79** / Rilling (cond.), Gächinger Kantorei, Stuttgart Bach Collegium / 1983 / Haenssler 92025

Gott fähret auf mit Jauchzen, cantata, BWV 43 (May 30, 1726)

One of six extant works Bach composed for Ascensiontide, BWV 43, *God is gone up with a merry noise*, was first performed on May 30, 1726, which falls within the period of Bach's third annual cantata cycle or *Jahrgang*. It was a time during which he had largely broken off from composing and performing cantatas of his own in favor of those of his cousin, Johann Ludwig Bach of Meiningen. The text is in fact taken from the same source as those employed in the cantatas of Johann Lugwig that Bach had been performing in Leipzig since February 1726. Often attributed to the Rudolstadt cantor and pastor Christoph Helm, later research suggests they are more likely to be the work of Duke Ernst Ludwig of Saxe-Meiningen, an important innovator of the new style of freely constructed cantatas that emerged in the early years of the eighteenth century. The cantata has 11 numbers and is divided into two parts, one of which would have prefaced the sermon, with the second part succeeding it. In keeping with most of Bach's cantatas for celebratory feasts, the scoring includes trumpets and tympani in addition to the customary two oboes, strings, and continuo bass. The full panoply is heard in the opening and closing choruses that frame the work, the first of which, a complex contrapuntal structure, is based on Psalm 47:5–6. The final chorale, "Du Lebensfürst, Herr Jesu Christ," is an unaltered four-part setting dating from the seventeenth century by Christoph Peter. Between these two choral movements, Bach introduces a sequence of alternating recitatives and arias divided between the four soloists. Because of the large number of movements, the arias are all short, in particular those in Part 1 for tenor (the third) and soprano (the fifth), both of which are cast in two-part (binary) form rather than the da capo arias of the Leipzig period. The texts of the recitatives and arias are concerned more with Christ's triumph over death than the events of the ascension, the bass aria in particular being a triumphant celebration accompanied by a brilliant trumpet obbligato. The final aria for alto, "In spirit yet I see him," is more devotional, with the oboes providing blissfully intertwining support. Bach's autograph score is in the Staatsbibliothek, Berlin. *–Brian Robins*

Recommended:

- ○ **Bach: Himmerfarhts-Oratorium** / Herreweghe (cond.), Schlick, Patriasz, Pregardien, Kooy, Collegium Vocale / HM 901479
- ○ **Bach: Cantatas for Ascension** / J. E. Gardiner (cond.), Chance, Varcoe, Argenta, Monteverdi Choir, English Baroque Soloists / 2000 / Archiv 463583

Gott soll allein mein Herze haben, cantata, BWV 169 (Oct. 20, 1726)

Like so many composers of his day, J.S. Bach was not at all afraid to reuse good musical material. Sometimes he plundered the same source more than once; this is the case with the music from which he drew the *Cantata No. 169, Gott soll allein mein Herz haben*, BWV 169, of 1726–a now-lost oboe (or possibly viola) concerto. It is the source not only for two of the numbers in BWV 169 but also for the *Harpsichord Concerto in E major*, BWV 1053 from about ten years later. *Gott soll allein mein Herz haben* was composed for the eighteenth Sunday after Trinity (which fell on October 20 in 1726) and is a setting of an anonymous text.

Bach uses a medium-sized ensemble in BWV 169: solo alto, two oboes (really oboes d'amore), oboe da caccia (or taille), strings, organ obbligato, and four-part chorus. The opening sinfonia and No. 5, the aria "Stirb in mir" ("Die in me"), are the two portions of music extracted from the lost oboe/viola concerto; each is a whole step lower than its counterpart in the later *Harpsichord Concerto* (E and C sharp minor in the harpsichord work are D and B minor, respectively, in the cantata). In the sinfonia, the organ obbligato is honored with the task of reproducing the original solo part. In "Stirb in mir," things are not quite so simple: the organ and the alto soloist offer, simultaneously, slightly different versions of the original solo line–sometimes their two versions line up note-by-note, but sometimes, usually so that the alto might better carry the text, they diverge and become counterpoints to one another. Bach sets a new text to an old melody, that of the Lutheran hymn *"Nun bitten wir den Heiligen Geist,"* in the final chorale, "Du süsse Liebe." *–Blair Johnston*

Recommended:

- ○ **Bach: Cantatas 54; 169 & 170** / R. King (cond.), J. Bowman, King's Consort / 1989 / Hyperion 66326
- ○ **Bach Alto Cantatas** / Kangas (cond.), Groop, Ostrobothnian CO / 1997 / Finlandia 25325

Gottes Zeit ist die allerbeste Zeit, cantata ("Actus Tragicus"), BWV 106 (ca. 1707)

One of the best known of Bach's earlier cantatas, No. 106 ("God's time is the best of all times") was almost certainly composed as a funeral work, possibly for the obsequies of Bach's uncle Tobias Lämmerwirt, who died in August 1707. Frequently referred to as the "Actus tragicus," it was probably written in Mühlhausen, the Thuringian town in which Bach served as organist in 1707–08. The text consists of a group of Bible verses and chorale strophes, brought together by an unknown compiler; they form a continuous sequence of eight sections in performance. The vocal scoring is for the usual four-part chorus, with solo ariosos for tenor (No. 3), bass (No. 4) alto (No. 6), and bass and alto (No. 7). The unusual instrumental scoring of two recorders (an instrument associated with death), two violas da gamba, and continuo underlines the serious nature of the work; the prevailing dark-hued texture is established from the outset in the somber but peaceful beauty of the opening instrumental sonatina, a format also adopted in the roughly contemporaneous *Cantata No. 4*. The sonatina leads into a chorus propounding the theme that life and death come to all in God's own good time. The chorus develops into a lively fugal section as man's days on earth are considered, but again takes on a darker resonance as the text refers to his mortality. To a halting arioso the tenor soloist laments the brevity of man's life on earth, only to be emphatically reminded by the bass that it is God's law that all men must die. The superb chorus that stands at the center of the cantata at first elaborates on this theme, but then tranquilly welcomes the thought of death with the words "Yes, come Lord Jesus." The idea of the repose of death is then picked up in the sole aria for alto with an obbligato part for viola da gamba. The bass then follows with the words of Christ to the sinner on the cross, before the chorale hymn "In dich hab ich gehoffet, Herr" (composed by Adam Reusner in 1533) and a fugue on the word "Amen" bring this short, but intensely moving cantata to an unexpectedly exuberant conclusion. *–Brian Robins*

Recommended:

- ○ **Bach: Cantatas Vol. 2; BWV 71, 131 & 106** / M. Suzuki (cond.), Kooy, Turk, Mera, Yanagisawa, Bach Collegium Japan / 1995 / Bis 781
- ○ **Bach: Actus Tragicus** / Junghanel, Cantus Cölln / HM 901694
- ○ **Bach: Peace Be With You** / Patterson (cond.), Gloria Dei Cantores / 2000 / Gloria Dei Cantores 28

Herz und Mund und Tat und Leben, cantata, BWV 147 (Jul. 2, 1723)

Johann Sebastian Bach's sacred *Cantata No. 147 "Herz und Mund und Tat und Leben"* (BWV 147) (Heart and Mouth, Deeds and Life), was written for the feast of the Visitation of the Virgin Mary and first performed in its final definitive form in Leipzig to mark the feast day, July 2, 1723. Much of the work originated during the composer's tenure as *Konzertmeister* in Weimar, where upon his appointment in 1714 he also assumed responsibility for the provision of a new cantata each month for services held in the Duke's chapel. In its earliest form (BWV 147a), this cantata was intended to be given on the fourth Sunday of Advent, 1716. This version contained four main arias and an opening chorus, but no recitative sections, three of which were added later, along with the great chorale, which brings each of the main sections to its close. The autograph of the Leipzig version survives intact, but all except the opening movement of the first version has perished. Interestingly, the composer's original design for the Advent feasts at Weimar would have been considered entirely unsuitable by the church authorities in Leipzig, who had forbidden the performance of all concert music during this period of the liturgical year. Bach managed to overcome this restriction by incorporating references to the "Magnificat" (*Luke 1: 39–56*) into the score, thus tailoring the cantata specifically to the Feast of the Visitation.

The final version begins with an elaborate chorus in C major, in which the celebratory tone is established by the fanfare-like opening section for orchestra. The vocal parts are in fugal form, with the entries staggered from the upper register to the lowest in succession, and later this ordering is skillfully reversed when the bass voices are heard first of all at reprise. A tenor recitative accompanied by strings alone is followed by an alto aria in the key of B minor, in which the oboe d'amore has a prominent obbligato role. The major aria of Part I is given to the solo soprano. As Nicolas Anderson has written, "Bereite dir, Jesu, in D minor with violin obbligato constitutes a lyrically expressive high point in the work. There is a beguiling innocence about the vocal line, while that of the violin, predominately in triplets, provides an ecstatic accompaniment." Part I concludes with the famous chorale known in English as *"Jesu, Joy of Man's Desiring."* The second part of this cantata begins with a muscular and powerful aria in F major for the tenor soloist, accompanied by the continuo group consisting of cello, violone, and organ. There follows an accompanied recitative section for alto, in which the texture is punctuated by interjections from a pair of oboes da caccia in a manner reminiscent of similar sections in the *Passions*. The final solo aria for the bass is again in the triumphant key of C major, with important parts for trumpet, oboes, and supporting strings. According to Anderson, "this resonant piece, with passages of vocal coloratura, proclaims Christ's wonders. The melodic contours of the vocal line at times seem to foreshadow the middle section of the alto aria 'Es is vollbracht' in the *St. John Passion*." This cantata concludes with a further setting of material from the hymn text by Martin Jahn, which had brought the first section of the work to its close in a virtually identical orchestral setting. *—Michael Jameson*

Recommended:

- ○ **Bach: Magnificat** / Cleobury (cond.), King's College Choir / 2000 / EMI 56994
- ○ **Bach: Cantatas Wachet auf & Herz und Mund** / J. E. Gardiner (cond.), Chance, Varcoe, Holton, Monteverdi Choir, English Baroque Soloists / 1992 / Archiv 463587
- ○ **Bach: Favourite Cantatas** / Antal (cond.), Kertesi, Hungarian Radio Chorus, Falloni CO / 1997 / Naxos 554042

Himmelskönig, sei willkommen, cantata, BWV 182 (Mar. 25, 1714)

In March 1714, Bach, who had been organist at the ducal chapel in Weimar since 1708, was promoted to the post of concertmaster. Among the additional duties that came with the new post was the obligation to provide a church cantata each month. The Cantata, BWV 182 ("King of heaven, be thou welcome"), was composed for the Feast of the Annunciation or Palm Sunday, which in 1714 fell on March 25. Given that the Lutheran church did not allow cantatas during Lent (the exception being when, as in 1714, the Annunciation fell on a Sunday), it is almost certain that BWV 182 represents the first work Bach composed as part of his new post. Compared to most of the composer's earlier cantatas, it is particularly extensive (comprising eight sections) and elaborate, suggesting that the composer set out to provide something special for his first effort in the service of Duke Wilhlem Ernst. The author of the texts has not been positively identified, but was most likely Salomo Franck, the Weimar court librarian and poet whose texts Bach is known to have begun to setting upon assuming his new duties.

The text has three sources: Psalm 40:8–9, the Palm Sunday Gospel (Matthew 21:1–9) recounting Christ's entry into Jerusalem, and a strophe from the hymn "Jesu Leiden, Pein und Tod" (1633) by Paul Stockmann. Like the majority of Bach's earlier cantatas, BWV 182 opens with an instrumental movement, in this instance marked "sonata" rather than the more usual "sinfonia." It is scored for solo recorder and violin with a pizzicato accompaniment by violins, divided violas, cello and bass continuo. The second movement, a lively da capo chorus, uses the words of the welcoming crowds in Jerusalem as Jesus enters the city. The succeeding bass recitative, the only one in the cantata, uses Jesus' words as He prepares to submit to his father's will; here Bach makes use of the arioso style that he later adopted in setting the words of Christ in his Passions. Three other arias follow: the first, for bass, has words that might be taken to allude to the Assumption as well as the forthcoming Passion; the next, for alto, is a meditative call for submission to the Savior, supported by obbligato recorder; finally, a dramatic, declamatory aria for tenor evokes the agony of the road to the Cross. The last two movements are choral: The first is a chorale fantasia based on Stockmann's hymn, the second a lightly dancing chorus that returns to the rejoicing mood of the opening. *—Brian Robins*

Recommended:

- ○ **Bach: Early Cantatas from Mühlhausen & Weimar** / J. Thomas (cond.), American Bach Soloists / 1995 / Koch 7235
- ○ **Bach: 3 Weimar Cantatas** / Rifkin (cond.), The Bach Ens. / 2001 / Dorian 93231
- ○ **Bach: Psalm 51; Kantate "Himmelskönig sei Willkommen"** / Letzbor (cond.), Ars Antiqua Austria / Symphonia 95139
- ○ **Bach: Cantatas Vol. 3; BWV 12, 54, 162 & 182** / M. Suzuki (cond.), Kooy, Kurisu, Mera, Sakurada, Bach Collegium Japan / 1996 / Bis 791

Ich habe genug, cantata, BWV 82 (Feb. 2, 1727)

Composed for the Feast of the Purification of Mary, which fell on February 2, 1727, Bach's Cantata No. 82 *"Ich habe genug"* (It is enough) (BWV 82) sets an anonymous text on the Gospel of Luke 2, 22–32. Like *Christ lag in Todesbanden* (BWV 4) and *"Ich will den Kreuzstab gerne tragen"* (BWV 56), it is not a chorale cantata, but a cantata for bass soloist, solo oboe, strings, and basso continuo. Severely dark in tone and extremely restrained in execution, "Ich habe genug" is one of the bleakest of Bach's cantatas. The text of its closing aria sums up its message: "With joy I greet my death; would that it were here already; then I shall escape the distress which afflicts me here on earth." "Ich habe genug" is resolutely in C minor with its first, fourth, and fifth movements in the tonic and its second movement ending in the dominant of the third movement's relative major of E flat major. The organizational plan of the work is an alternation of aria and recitative with the first, third, and fifth movements being arias and the second and fourth movement's being recitatives. Both recitatives begin secco and end with more lyrical lines, a very brief Andante in the first and only a slightly longer Adagio arioso in the second. The opening aria is slow and dismal, with a keening obbligato oboe above the strings and the anguished bass below. The central aria is slightly faster with a tender melody in the strings to comfort the sighing, disconsolate bass; the closing aria, marked Vivace in triple time with an elaborately embellished bass melody, is nearly a dance of death as befits the text. *—James Leonard*

Recommended:

- ○ **Bach: Mein Herze schwimmt in Blut & others** / von der Goltz (cond.), Kirkby, Freiburg Barockorchester / 1999 / Carus 83302
- ○ **Bach: Cantates pour basse** / Herreweghe (cond.), Kooy, La Chapelle Royale / HM 1951365
- ○ **Bach: Ich habe genug; Hunt Cantata; Wedding Cantata** / Parrott (cond.), R. Goodman (cond.), Kirkby, D. Thomas, Taverner Consort & Players; The Parley of Instruments / 2000 / Hyperion 22041
- ○ **Bach: Cantatas for the Feast of the Purification of Mary** / Gardiner (cond.), Monteverdi Choir, English Baroque Soloists / Archiv 463585

Ich hatte viel Bekümmernis, cantata, BWV 21 (Jun. 17, 1714)

One of the glories among the canon of Bach's cantatas, BWV 21 ("I was sore afflicted") is one of the earliest composed by Bach for Duke Wilhelm Ernst in Weimar. Although composed for the third Sunday after Trinity in 1714 (June 17), scholars believe it to be an expanded version of a cantata composed in the previous year and designed for more general use. Whatever its genesis, it is a deeply moving work revealing the greatness and dazzling technical virtuosity of the young composer. Bach's own high regard for the work is demonstrated by the fact that he almost certainly performed it in a revised version when applying for a post in Hamburg in 1720, further revising the cantata when it was given on June 13, 1723, in Leipzig, shortly after Bach's appointment as cantor. It is planned on a grand scale, with an opening orchestral sinfonia (a common feature of the Weimar cantatas) succeeded by no less than ten succeeding vocal sections divided into two parts, one preceding and one following the sermon. The scoring of the original version is for soprano, tenor, and bass soloists, four-part chorus, trumpets, timpani, oboe, bassoon, strings, and bass continuo. Bach's revisions involve differing dispositions of the solo vocal parts. The text is by Salomon Franck, the Weimar court librarian and poet responsible for the librettos of the majority of the cantatas Bach composed at the ducal court between 1714 and 1716. It takes as its basis the Gospel for the day, the parable of the lost sheep as narrated in Luke 15:1–10. The opening sinfonia for oboe and strings is informed by the sorrowing mood that characterizes most of the cantata. It leads to a magnificent three-part chorus, a fugal opening section succeeded by a lively central section whose major mode briefly lifts the prevailing sorrowing mood before returning to end in contemplation. The first aria for tenor (later soprano), "Sighs, tears, troubles and distress" expresses these grief-stricken sentiments with an anguish emphasized, contrapuntally, by the poignant lines of an obbligato oboe. The long tenor recitative that follows is a direct address from the sinner asking God not to turn away from him. It prefaces a "simile" aria for tenor, the words comparing the torrents of "salty tears" shed in the opening section to the vividly illustrated power of stormy seas in the central part. The first part concludes with an uplifting and consolatory chorus taken from the opening words of Psalm 42, "Why troublest thou, my soul?" Part II opens with a recitative and aria in dialogue form between the soul (soprano) and Jesus (bass), a form of dramatization frequently employed by Bach, particularly in the earlier cantatas. Here the lost soul calling out to Jesus in its darkest moments is answered by the promise of light and salvation, full of warmth in the accompanied recitative and fervent acceptance in the aria. The following chorus (initially conceived as the cantata's concluding movement) employs two strophes of Georg Neumark's hymn *"Wer nur den lieben Gott lässt walten,"* the first in long held notes by the tenors, the second similarly sustained by the sopranos. The final soprano aria brings about the long awaited move from darkness to light—"Rejoice, O soul, rejoice O heart"—as the singer rejoices in the thought of the comfort of God. The final chorus brings this superb cantata to a dazzling peroration, the use of trumpets and drums for the first time in the work underlining the text's concentration on "honor, glory and power." *—Brian Robins*

Recommended:

- ○ **Bach: Ich hatte viel Bekümmernis** / Herreweghe (cond.), Schlick, Lesne, La Chapelle Royale, Collegium Vocale, / HM 1951328
- ○ **Bach: Magnificat; Cantata BWV 21; Motet[s]** / Fasolis (cond.), Coro della Radio Svizzari Lungano, Ens. Vanitas / 1994 / Arts 47374

Ich liebe den Höchsten von ganzem Gemüte, cantata, BWV 174 (Jun. 6, 1729)

Bach's early years as cantor in Leipzig witnessed an extraordinary output of cantatas for weekly Sunday use at the Thomaskirche and the Nicolaikirche, the two principal churches in the city. The vast majority of these date from between 1723 and 1726; thereafter his productivity seems to have fallen dramatically, although a full accounting is made difficult by the fact that so many have been lost. BWV 174

("I love the highest with my whole heart") belongs to one of these later, probably incomplete cycles. Composed for Whit Monday in 1729, it was first performed on June 6, 1729. The cantatas of this period, Bach's fourth annual cycle (or Jahrgang), are notable for the settings of texts by Picander, the pseudonym of the poet Christian Friedrich Henrici. Bach's collaboration with Picander was particularly fruitful, producing not only the *St. Matthew* and *St. Mark Passions*, but a number of his secular cantatas. The poet suggested that Bach set an entire cycle of his cantata texts during the course of 1729, but this was either left incomplete or lost.

The text, drawn from the Gospel of the day (John 3:16–21), is short, consisting of only two expansive da capo arias separated by a recitative for tenor and a final chorale strophe. The reason may well have been practical, since Bach would also have had to prepare a festive cantata for performance the previous day, the feast of Pentecost. To give BWV 174 greater substance, Bach prefaced it with an expanded version of the opening movement of the *Brandenburg Concerto No. 3*, adding two horns, three oboes and bassoon to the concerto's nine-part string scoring, in the process producing one of his most richly textured instrumental movements.

The opening alto aria employs the oboes, whose intertwining lines support the gently expressed sentiments (the words from which the cantata takes its name) and give the aria something of a pastoral quality. The succeeding tenor recitative takes advantage of the concerto's string scoring by employing an accompaniment of three violins and three violas. The aria for bass which follows is suitably more robust; in it the call to the faithful to take the "opportunity of salvation" is underpinned by busy violins and violas. The cantata concludes with a four-part harmonization of the first strophe of Martin Schalling's hymn "Herzlich lieb hab ich dich" (1569). *—Brian Robins*

Recommended:

- ○ **Bach: Cantatas BWV 172–175** / Rilling (cond.), Gachinger Kantorei / 1984 / Haenssler 92052

Ich steh mit einem Fuss im Grabe, cantata, BWV 156 (Jan. 23, 1729)

Bach's *Cantata No. 156, "Ich steh' mit einem Fuss im Grabe"* ("I stand with one foot in the grave") is thought to have been first performed on January 23, 1729. The cantata, to a text by Christian Friedrich Henrici (otherwise known by his pseudonym Picander) was intended for performance during church services on a third Sunday following epiphany.

The work opens with a sinfonia in F, for oboe and strings, which originated in a concerto movement (now lost) which Bach subsequently recast as the slow movement of his harpsichord concerto in F minor. In the cantata, however, the solo oboe line is considerably less florid in style, and ends on the dominant so as to provide a link with the tenor aria which follows. The aria itself is notable because of the tenor voice's interaction with a chorale, sung by the soprano, whose melody is attributed to Johann Schein, one of Bach's predecessors at Leipzig. The chorale is accompanied by a unison string theme, and its first section is written in such a way as to facilitate a different continuation for each subsequent reprise. The string melody opens with a sustained note corresponding with the tenor's line "Ich steh'" ("I stand"), but Bach ingeniously ensures that the links between the contorted, anguished phrase-end (always in C minor) and the words sung by the tenor in the second repeated line, "kranke Leib" ("sick body"), are impressed upon the listener. Of all the infinitely varied methods by which Bach weaves chorales into the fabric of his cantatas, this work displays one of the most subtle.

Now, a bass recitative follows, to the words "no longer here on earth." This leads in turn to an alto aria in B flat major, "Herr, was du willt" ("Lord, according to thy will"), set in modified da capo style. At this point, the atmosphere is lightened considerably by the three-part contrapuntal accompaniment for solo oboe, violins, and continuo, but there are still telling pauses at every utterance of the word "Sterben" ("death") in the central episode of this A-B-A construction. Finally a second solo bass recitative takes us to a setting in four parts of the chorale "Herr, wie du willt" by Kaspar Bienemann (1582), whose opening phrase has already been anticipated by the recitative which precedes it. *—Michael Jameson*

Recommended:

- ○ **Bach: Cantatas BWV 156–159** / Rilling (cond.), Gächinger Kantorei, Stuttgart Bach Collegium / 1973 / Haenssler 92048
- ○ **Bach: Cantatas for the 3rd Sunday in Epiphany** / J. E. Gardiner (cond.), Varcoe, Mingardo, Monteverdi Choir, English Baroque Soloists / Archiv 463582

Ich will den Kreuzstab gerne tragen, cantata, BWV 56 (Oct. 27, 1726)

Composed for the nineteenth Sunday after Trinity, which fell on October 27, 1726, Bach's *Cantata No. 56 "Ich will den Kreuzstab gerne tragen"* (I will gladly carry the cross) (BWV 56) sets a text by an unknown author based on the *Gospel* according to *Matthew:* 1–8) and concludes with the chorale by Johann Franck from 1653. Like the slightly later "Ich arme Mensch, ich Sundenknecht" (BWV 55), "Ich will den Kreuzstab gerne tragen" is written for solo voice, in this case a bass-baritone, and begins in gloomy G minor as befits its text, which dwells on "affliction, trouble, and distress." The soloist is accompanied by a pair of oboes and taille, strings, and basso continuo. The Kreuzstab was a navigational tool, a precursor to the sextant, and the text is filled with nautical references. "Kreuz" means both cross and sharp, and Bach made use of the pun, sharpening notes noticeably in the first aria. "Ich will den Kreuzstab gerne tragen" starts in G minor with its first movement in the tonic, its second and third movements in the relative major of B flat, and its fourth and fifth in the subdominant of C minor with a picardy third on the final cadence. The first movement is a large-scale da capo aria for soloists and full orchestra, with the oboes and taille doubling the strings. The second movement is an in-tempo recitative for soloist and continuo with an obbligato solo cello playing arpeggios, imitating undulating waves, for all but the last five bars where the text indicates arrival into port. The third movement is a hearty da capo aria in the form of a trio sonata for soloist, oboe, and continuo. The fourth movement is a restrained recitative for soloist, strings, and continuo. The cantata concludes with a hushed and hopeful harmonization of Franck's chorale for the otherwise tacit chorus and full orchestra. *—James Leonard*

Recommended:

- ○ **Matthias Goerne: Bach Cantatas** / Norrington (cond.), Goerne, Camerata Academica Salzburg / 1999 / Decca 466570
- ○ **Bach, Buxtehude: Kantaten** / K. Richter (cond.), Fischer-Dieskau, Munchener Bach-Orchester / 2000 / DG 463517

Jauchzet Gott in allen Landen, cantata, BWV 51 (Sep. 17, 1730)

One of the most enduringly popular of Bach's solo cantatas, *Jauchzet Gott in allen Landen*, BWV 51 (for soprano, trumpet, strings and continuo), was originally written for the fifteenth Sunday after Trinity. It is thought to have been composed around 1730, during Bach's seventh year as Kantor of the Thomaskirche in Leipzig. Bach may have written the cantata text himself; it does not correspond closely to the readings for its appointed Sunday, which speak of vanity and faithlessness, hence his addition of "et in ogni tempo" (at any time) to the designation for its use.

The four movements are structured in the traditional chorale cantata form. The opening da capo aria, in ritornello form, features brilliant passagework for both soloists, with a forthright, unison C major arpeggio announcing the initial, somewhat Vivaldian, theme. The intricate counterpoint between trumpet and soprano throughout the first movement is an outstanding example of Bach's writing for voice and obbligato instrument. Each of the solo lines interlocks with the other in a finely balanced duet, and abundantly illustrates the call to "praise God in every nation."

The second movement is a recitative that begins with a clear, restrained chordal accompaniment in the upper strings coupled with a bass ostinato. The soprano melody is gentle and mostly syllabic until the eighth bar, when the bassline "walks" underneath a highly ornate, melismatic vocal line. At the word "lallen" (stammer) Bach displays his interest in word-painting with a particularly elongated phrase that is both meandering and jagged.

The ensuing dal segno aria, in an expansive 12/8 meter, accompanied by continuo, features a largely stepwise bassline that constantly flows upward. Although it is nominally in A minor, no hint of melancholy intrudes. The text, a prayer for God to bestow his mercies every new day, is set to a complex, wide-ranging melodic line that has an instrumental quality. Offbeats and weak beats are given particular stress in an unusual section where the bassline abruptly drops away as the vocal phrases become suddenly rapturous and quite independent of the occasional continuo punctuation.

The final movement starts as a violin duet, while the soprano sings the chorale tune "Nun Lob', mein Seel', den Herren," exhorting all to "give praise, glory, and honor to Father, Son, and Holy Ghost." In a gracious 3/4 meter, its long instrumental sections are both playful and confident, making much of imitative passages for the violins that tumble against and tease each other. The lengthy, concluding "Alleluja," rejoined by trumpet, is a noteworthy example of the virtuosic demands Bach often places on soloists. Its rollicking exuberance lends a particularly joyous tone to the cantata's conclusion. *—Virginia Sublett*

Recommended:

- ○ **Bach: Cantatas** / Huggett (cond.), Argenta, Sonnerie Ens. / 1994 / Virgin 45038
- ○ **Bach: Cantatas & Arias** / Gelhorn (cond.), Schwarzkopf, Philharmonia Orch. / 1999 / EMI 67206
- ○ **Bach: Magnificat; Jauchzet Gott in allen Landen** / J. E. Gardiner (cond.), Kirkby, English Baroque Soloists / Philips 411458

Jesu, der du meine Seele, cantata, BWV 78 (Sep. 10, 1724)

One of the greatest of the so-called "chorale cantatas" that dominate Bach's second annual cycle of Leipzig cantatas, BWV 78 ("Jesus, Thou of my soul"), was composed for the 14th Sunday after Trinity in 1724, and first performed on September 10 of that year. The anonymous librettist based his text on the Johann Rist hymn (1641) from which the cantata takes its name. Deeply penitential in nature, the text bears little relationship to the appointed Gospel of the day (Luke 17:11–19), the story of the healing of the ten lepers. The scoring is for horn, flute, two oboes, strings, and continuo in addition to four-part chorus and soloists.

The cantata opens with a choral passacaglia that unfolds with majestic spaciousness over a descending chromatic bass line; Bach often used this device to illustrate sin—or, in the words of the chorus, "grievous spiritual woe." The chorale melody is heard in the soprano line, which is supported by the horn and flute; only in the central section is the darkly expressive mood alleviated. The succeeding duet for soprano and alto is a wonderful example of Bach's word painting; the canonic vocal writing and forward-pressing continuo accompaniment provide a vivid illustration of hastening "with feeble but eager steps." The following recitative for tenor is long and dramatic, and the acute anguish of the text is sustained throughout; at times the recitative gives way to arioso. With the following tenor aria, the mood of the cantata starts to change, and the text begins to focus on the cleansing properties of Christ's blood. The final solo numbers, a recitative and aria for bass, take up this theme of redemption; the aria is a virtuosic movement that includes a demanding obbligato part for solo oboe. The final stanza of Rist's hymn forms the text of the concluding chorale, the hymn melody now treated to a simple, but moving four-part harmonization. *—Brian Robins*

Recommended:

- ○ **Bach: Trauerode** / Herreweghe (cond.), Schmithusen, C. Brett, H. Crook, Kooy, La Chapelle Royale / HM 901270
- ○ **Bach: 6 Favourite Cantatas** / Rifkin (cond.), The Bach Ens. / 1997 / L'Oiseau-Lyre 455706
- ○ **Bach: Cantatas Vol. VI; Favorite Cantatas** / J. Thomas (cond.), American Bach Soloists / 1996 / Koch 7234

Lass, Fürstin, lass noch einen Strahl, cantata, BWV 198 (Oct. 17, 1727)

Bach's *Cantata No. 198 "Lass, Fürstin, lass noch einen Strahl"* (Let, Princess, let one more tear) (BWV 198) is a grim and gloomy funeral ode. The text by Johann Christoph Gottsched, one of the leaders of the German Enlightenment, is arguably the best cantata text Bach ever set. Written for the funeral of Queen and Electress Christiane Eberhardine on October 17, 1727, "Lass, Fürstin, lass noch einen Strahl" is one of Bach's greatest mourning works, ranking just below the great *Passion* in its musical and emotional depth. The cantata is richly and darkly scored for soprano, alto, tenor, and bass soloists and chorus, pairs of transverse flutes, oboes doubling oboe d'amores and viola da gambas, strings, and a basso continuo that includes lute, harpsichord, cello, and bass. "Lass, Fürstin, lass noch einen Strahl" is in two unequal parts of seven and three movements, the first part coming before the ceremony and the second after. The first part opens with a massive and mournful chorale fantasia for chorus and full orchestra. This is followed by a grief-stricken recitative and aria for soprano soloist and strings. Then there is a remarkable recitative and aria for alto soloist in which the sobbing recitative is accompanied by ringing transverse flutes and oboe d'amores above viola da gambas, lute, strings, and continuo and the aria is a slow and heartfelt trio sonata with obbligato viola da gambas. This is followed by a lyrical recitative for tenor soloist, oboe d'amores, and continuo. The first part closes with a dour chorale fugue with full orchestra colla parte. The second part opens with an anguished aria for tenor soloist, obbligato transvere flute, oboe d'amore, viola da gambas, strings, lute, and cello continuo. This is followed by a three-part movement for bass soloist and continuo: a resolute recitative, a more flowing adagio, and a brokenhearted arioso accompanied by pairs of transverse flutes and oboes. "Lass, Fürstin, lass noch einen Strahl" concludes with a slow, stately, and deeply sorrowful dance in 6/8 for chorus and full orchestra. *—James Leonard*

Recommended:

- ○ **Heart's Solace** / Parrott (cond.), Taverner Consort and Players / 1998 / Sony 60155
- ○ **Bach: Cantate Trauerode BWV198; Cantate BWV 78** / Herreweghe (cond.), Brett, Kooy, H. Crook, La Chapelle Royale / HM 901270
- ○ **Bach: Cantatas; Actus tragicus** / J. E. Gardiner (cond.), Chance, Varcoe, Argenta, Johnson, Monteverdi Choir, English Baroque Soloists / Archiv 463581

Lobe den Herren, den mächtigen König der Ehren, cantata, BWV 137 (Aug. 19, 1725)

Composed in Leipzig, BWV 137 ("Praise the Lord, the almighty king") is a cantata for the twelfth Sunday after Trinity, August 19, 1725. Although standing outside the second annual cycle Bach composed for Leipzig during the liturgical year of 1724–25, it conforms stylistically to many of the so-called "chorale cantatas" that dominate that period. The Bach scholar Christoph Wolff suggests that BWV 137 was explicitly designed to fill one of the gaps in the second cycle. It has no particular liturgical connections with the twelfth Sunday after Trinity, and Bach may also have had the Leipzig Town Council election service (which occurred around this time) in mind. Certainly the festive character of the work, with its scoring for three trumpets and timpani, would have made it suitable for performance on a ceremonial occasion. The work, in fact, is a rarity among Bach's cantatas in that it makes no use of either biblically derived recitative or poetic aria texts, being based solely on the five stanzas of the hymn (chorale) from which it takes its name. The text, written by Joachim Neander in 1680, has an associated melody known in the English-speaking world as "Praise to the Lord, the almighty, the king of creation." Bach uses this melody in all five movements of the cantata. The opening movement is typical of the fantasia type employed in the chorale cantatas; following a lively orchestral introduction (with trumpets, timpani, two oboes, and strings) the lower voices (alto, tenor, and bass) enter to a theme based on this sinfonia while the melody of Neander's hymn is sung by the sopranos in short notes, rather than the customary long ones. The second stanza of the hymn is set as a trio; the tune is embellished by the alto soloist and supported by solo violin and continuo. This movement was later transcribed by Bach to form the sixth of the well-known *Schübler Chorales* for organ. In the third stanza, the hymn is heard in an imitative dialogue for the soprano and bass soloists, accompanied by the two oboes. Trio texture returns for the fourth verse, where the tune is given principally to a solo trumpet, leaving the tenor soloist the freedom for ornamental flourishes. The brilliant final chorus is a four-part setting of the hymn tune embellished by trumpets and timpani. It was later reused in the wedding cantata *"Herr Gott, Beherrscher aller Dinge,"* BWV 120a (1729). The original parts of BWV 137 were preserved in the library of the Thomasschule in Leipzig until its demolition in 1902. They are now housed in the Staatsbibliotek, Berlin. *—Brian Robins*

Recommended:

- ○ **Bach: Cantatas, BWV 136–139** / Rilling (cond.), Auger, Kraus, Schreckenbach, Heldwein, Stuttgart Bach Collegium / 1977 / Haenssler 92043
- ○ **Bach: Sacred Cantatas** / Rotzsch (cond.), Auger, Wenkel, Schreier, Neues Bachsiches Collegium Musicum / 1994 / Berlin Classics 91765

Lobet Gott in seinen Reichen, cantata ("Ascension Oratorio"), BWV 11 (May 19, 1735)

There are four extant works by Johan Sebastian Bach for the Feast of the Ascension, part of the liturgical cycle for Easter. Three are cantatas belonging to the cantata cycles composed in 1723–1724 (BWV 37), 1724–1725 (BWV 128), and 1725–1726 (BWV 43). Although often designated as a cantata, the present work is more accurately described as a short oratorio, including as it does a narrative role for the Evangelist. It was composed in 1735, and first performed in one of the principal Leipzig churches on May 19 of that year. The Evangelist's narration was drawn by an unknown librettist from the Gospels of Luke and Mark, and the Acts of the Apostles. These sections plus two recitatives and the chorale placed at the center of the work are the only original parts of the oratorio, the opening and closing choruses, and the two arias all being drawn from previously written cantatas, now lost. The two choruses are planned on a grand scale, with the same brilliantly festive scoring (including three trumpets and drums) Bach had employed in Parts I, III, and IV of the *Christmas Oratorio* of 1734–1735. The closing chorus is chorale-based, using the hymn *"Von Gott will ich nicht lassen"* as a choral cantus firmus around which the orchestra weaves a joyously dance-like fantasia. "Ach bleibe doch," the alto aria is an extensive revision of an aria originally found in a lost wedding cantata, the same source the composer drew upon for the Agnus Dei of the *Mass in B minor.* The soprano aria "Jesu, deine Gandenblicke" is remarkable for the scoring of two flutes, oboe, violins, and violas without bass, the lightly translucent texture reflecting the text's allusion to Christ leaving his body to ascend to Heaven. The central section of recitative includes a telling piece of dramatization at the appearance of the angels, "two men in white apparel," whose words are addressed to the amazed onlookers as a duet. *—Brian Robins*

Recommended:

- ○ **Bach: Himmelfahrts-Oratorioum** / Herreweghe (cond.), Schlick, Patriasz, Pregardien, Kooy, Collegium Vocale / HM 901479
- ○ **Bach: Magnificat; Easter Oratorio** / Parrott (Cond.), Taverner Consort & Players / 1999 / Virgin 61647
- ○ **Bach: Ascension** / J. E. Gardiner (cond.), Chance, Varcoe, Argenta, Monteverdi Choir, English Baroque Soloists / 2000 / Archiv 463583
- ○ **Bach: Easter & Ascension Oratorios** / Rilling (cond.), Augér, Cuccaro, Hamari, Gachinger Kantorei, Wurttemberg CO Heilbronn / 1980 / Haenssler 92077

Mein Herze schwimmt im Blut, cantata, BWV 199 (Aug. 12, 1714)

Bach joined the ducal court at Weimar as organist in 1708, being promoted to concertmaster at the end of 1713. Prior to this appointment, there were no demands on him to compose church cantatas. Recent research has shown that *Cantata No. 199, "Mein Herze schwimmt im Blut* (My Heart Swims in Blood) provides one of the few exceptions, having been first given at Weimar on August 27, 1713, the 11th Sunday after Trinity. It was also performed in the ducal chapel on the equivalent Sunday the following year, by which time Bach's new duties as concertmaster called for the preparation and performance of one church cantata every month. The cantata is the earliest extant cantata by Bach for solo voice, in this instance, soprano. The vocal parts are technically demanding, containing challenges that Weimar's accomplished professional singers could meet. In fact, the work may have been composed for one such singer, falsettist Johann Friedrich Weldig. The composer later revived the work in Cöthen (where it may have been sung by his second wife, Anna Magdalena, a highly accomplished singer) and in Leipzig. The text by Darmstadt court poet Georg Christian Lehms draws on the Gospel for the day

(*Luke 18:9–14*), which relates the parable of the proud Pharisee and the humble tax collector. The theme is that of humility and repentance. Bach casts the cantata in eight sections alternating between recitative and aria, the only deviation being the interpolation of a stanza from the hymn *Wo soll ich fliehen hin* by Caspar Stieler (1679), the singers' intonation of the chorale supported by obbligato viola. With the exception of this typically Lutheran gesture, the scheme thus closely conforms to that of the Italian cantata, a form Bach is known to have studied with considerable interest. Unusually for Bach, the cantata opens with a deeply felt accompanied (strings alone) recitative, establishing from the outset the penitential mood of the work. The first aria is a grief-stricken supplication of great beauty accompanied by solo oboe, while the second is a broadly conceived plea to God to retain patience with the sinner. The final aria is cast in the form of a gigue, the dance-like rhythms underpinning the singers' joyful acceptance of God's forgiveness. *—Brian Robins*

Recommended:

- ○ **J.S. Bach: Mein Herze Schwimmt im Blut** / Goltz (cond.), Kirkby, Arfken, Freiburg Baroque Orch. / 1999 / Carus 83302
- ○ **Bach: Cantates BWV 85, 183, 199, 175** / Coin (cond.), Schlick, A. Scholl, Pregardien, Concerto Vocale de Lepizig, Ens. Baroque de Limoges / 1995 / Astree 8544
- ○ **Bach: Cantatas & Arias** / Dart (cond.), Schwarzkopf, Sutcliffe, Philharmonia Orch. / 1999 / EMI 67206
- ○ **Bach: Cantatas BWV 113; 179 & 199** / J. E.Gardiner (cond.), Monteverdi Choir, English Baroque Soloists / Archiv 463591

Mer hahn en neue Oberkeet, cantata ("Peasant Cantata"), BWV 212 (Aug. 30, 1742)

Along with the *Coffee Cantata* (BWV 211), the *Peasant Cantata* reveals Bach's rich but little-known comedic vein. The occasion of its composition was the appointment in 1742 of the Leipzig chamberlain Carl Heinrich von Dieskau as Provost (ruler) of a number of villages in the immediate vicinity of Leipzig, where Bach was based as cantor. To celebrate the event (and Dieskau's birthday), a *fête* was held, probably in the village of Klein-Zschocher, at which the principal entertainment was a firework display and the performance of Bach's cantata. The idea for a musical contribution came from Picander, the pseudonym of poet Christian Friedrich Henrici, himself a government official in Leipzig. Bach had enjoyed a particularly fruitful collaboration with Picander during the 1730s, the partnership producing not only the *St. Matthew Passion* and *St. Mark Passion*, but a number of sacred and secular cantatas. There are two rustic characters in this cantata, a courting couple sung by soprano and bass, Picander accordingly setting parts of the text in Saxon dialect (the title is an example). It is now also known that Bach's music drew heavily, perhaps exclusively, on popular tunes of the day, giving the cantata a deliberately bucolic character unique in his music. The opening sinfonia, a potpourri of dance tunes, is followed by a duet based on a rustic bourrée in which the couple celebrate the arrival of a new lord of the manor who gives them beer—"real strong stuff." In the succeeding accompanying recitative (in which Bach introduces the tune of the "Quodlibet" from the *Goldberg Variations*) the peasant flirts with his girl, who responds with an aria in polonaise style expressing the excitement of love. Dance, in fact, dominates the musical numbers, among them the famous "La Folia," which Bach uses for the accompaniment to the aria (No. 8), in which the soprano sings the praises of the new chamberlain. Most maintain the same rustic quality, the sole exception being the more courtly minuet as the soprano sings of the sweetness of life in Klein-Zschocher (No. 14). These simple sentiments of courtship and fealty are rounded off with another delightful duet in which the couple announce their intention to leave for the tavern "where the bagpipes drone." It has been suggested that Bach, the highly sophisticated urban musician and master of counterpoint, was simply making ironic comment on the crudity of popular music in the *Peasant Cantata*. True or not, the work remains one of his most infectiously enjoyable. *—Brian Robins*

Recommended:

- ○ **Bach: Secular Cantatas** / K. McMillan, Roschmann, Les Violons du Roy / 1994 / Dorian 90199
- ○ **Bach: Cantatas BWV 211 & 213** / M. Antal (cond.), Kertesi, Mukk, Failoni CO / 1992 / Naxos 550641

Non sa che sia dolore, cantata, BWV 209 (after 1729)

While Bach is primarily associated with the sacred cantata, he also composed a number of secular works in the form. BWV 209 ("He does not know what it is to suffer") is unique among the extant works of this type in being the only one set to an Italian text. The principal source is a copy made around 1800 by Bach's first biographer, Johann Nikolaus Forkel, and its authenticity has been doubted by some scholars. The date of composition is unknown, but the anonymous poet's specific address to the town of Ansbach has led Bach experts to believe that it may have been composed in honor of Johann Matthias Gesner, a native of Ansbach who was rector of the Thomasschule in Leipzig between 1730 and 1734. The court at Ansbach was strongly inclined toward Italian culture, not only performing operas by such composers as Cesti and Alessandro Scarlatti but also employing Italian musicians, most notably the famous instrumental composer Giuseppe Torelli. Bach's cantata for solo soprano closely follows the model of those of Scarlatti in its adherence to alternating recitative and aria. In addition to newly written poetry, the text also draws on passages from such famous writers as Giovanni Battista Guarini (his *Rime* of 1598) and Pietro Metastasio. The subject is apparently concerned with the departure of a young man to sea to enter military service. The cantata is prefaced by a lively sinfonia for flute and strings in the form of a concerto. The following accompanied recitative is concerned with the pain of departure, a topic taken up in the succeeding aria, "Go then, and with pain leave to us the suffering heart," an expressive movement embellished by a highly ornamental part for the solo flute. The central section is more lively, with a vocal line suggestive of the rocking motion of the sea while the continuo intimates the prospect of military glory. After a brief secco recitative, the second aria takes up the sea metaphor, pointing up the relief felt by the steersman when he regains control of his ship after experiencing stormy weather. *—Brian Robins*

Recommended:

- ○ **Bach: Cantatas** / Huggett (cond.), Argenta, Sonnerie Ens. / 1999 / Virgin 61644
- ○ **Bach: Geschwinde, Geschwinde** / Leitner (cond.), Poulenard, Cappella Coloniensis / Capriccio 10615
- ○ **Elly Ameling: The Early Recordings Vol. 2** / Ameling, Aureum Collegium / 1995 / DHM 26614
- ○ **Bach: Secular Cantatas BWV 208 & 209** / Rilling (cond.), Gachinger Kantorei, Stuttgart Bach Collegium, / 1999 / Haenssler 92065

Nun komm, der Heiden Heiland, cantata, BWV 62 (Dec. 3, 1724)

This is the second of two cantatas Bach based on Martin Luther's Advent hymn (*"Come now, Savior of the heathen"*), the other being an early Weimar cantata, BWV 61, dating from 1714. The present work was composed for Advent Sunday, 1724, and was given its first performance in Leipzig on December 3. It thus belongs to the second annual cycle (*Jahrgang*) of Leipzig cantatas and conforms to the type of so-called "chorale cantata" that dominates the 1724–1725 cycle. In keeping with such chorale-based works, Luther's hymn is used throughout, the opening and closing choruses incorporating the first and last verses, while the alternating arias and recitatives framed by the choruses are free poetic paraphrases of verses 2–7 of the hymn. The librettist has not been identified. It is scored for the customary four-part vocal ensemble, with an orchestra consisting of two oboes, bassoon, "corno" (usually taken to mean a horn, but possibly a type of slide trumpet), strings, and continuo. The lively opening chorus is of the chorale fantasia type favored by Bach, the chorale melody appearing first in the continuo, and subsequently the upper strings and oboes before being intoned by the choral sopranos. The tenor aria that follows is a joyful anticipation of the coming of the Christ, "Marvel, O man." This is followed by a recitative and majestic aria for bass, the last line "O bright radiance" being transformed into an awestruck arioso. A delicate accompanied recitative for soprano and alto precedes the final chorus, a simple four-part harmonization of the hymn melody. *—Brian Robins*

Recommended:

- ○ **J.S. Bach: Adventskantaten BWV 36, 61 & 62** / Herreweghe (cond.), Rubens, Pregardien, Kooy, Collegium Vocale / HM 901605
- ○ **Bach: Cantatas; Advent** / Gardiner (cond.), Argenta, A. R. Johnson, Bär, P. Lang, English Baroque Soloists / 1992 / Archiv 463588

Schweigt stille, plaudert nicht, cantata ("Coffee Cantata"), BWV 211 (1732–1734)

It is neither the lessons of the Lutheran faith nor the depth of his own spiritual beliefs that J.S. Bach explores in his 211th cantata, *Schweige stille, plaudert nicht*, BWV 211; rather, it is a simple, earthly pleasure that had recently taken hold of European society, moving poets first to extoll and then, as in the case of Christian Friedrich Menrici Picander's text for BWV 211, to satirize: namely, coffee. The citizens of Leipzig, the city that Bach called home from 1723 on, were by all accounts especially enamored of this new, stimulating, and as some people of the time felt, dangerous beverage; in the *Coffee Cantata*, a concerned Leipzig father seeks to break his daughter from her addiction to it. Finally, by threat of preventing her from marrying, he succeeds in doing so; but after he leaves to find a husband for her, she turns full circle and proclaims that no suitor need bother her unless he is willing to insert a clause into the marriage contract that she can make coffee whenever and however she pleases!

This most secular and comical work, which was probably composed sometime in the mid-1730s, is indeed a far cry from the Bach cantata as most people understand it. The *Coffee Cantata* has ten musical numbers (five of them recitatives) and three characters. Schlendrian, the father, is a bass; Lieschen, his daughter, is a soprano; and there is a tenor narrator. The orchestra is made up of strings, basso continuo and a single flute. The narrator sets the stage with a few brief measures of recitative (No. 1), and then Schlendrian grumbles his way through a D major aria, the strings twitching happily, the bass plodding steadily (No. 2). Schlendrian confronts his "naughty daughter" in No. 3. Lieschen sings lovingly of her favorite beverage in her first aria (No. 4), but tension arises between father and daughter again in No. 5. Then Schlendrian seems to get an idea (No. 6), and in the recitative of No. 7 he unleashes his secret weapon: she's grounded from going on any more dates until she gives up coffee forever. Lieschen, excited at the prospect of really getting a husband, sings a bouncing G major aria (No. 8); and then comes the punch line: the tenor narrator tells, in recitative (No. 9), that Lieschen is only playing a game with her father. An absurd final "chorus" (really just the three singers) in G major comments that if all the old maids and mothers and grandmas drink coffee, how can the daughters refuse it? *—Blair Johnston*

Recommended:

- ○ **Bach: The Coffee Cantata** / Somary (cond.), Monoyios, Oosting, Amor Artis Chorale & Baroque Orch. / 1999 / Lyrichord 8039
- ○ **Bach: Secular Cantatas** / D. Roschmann, Les Violons du Roy / 1994 / Dorian 90199
- ○ **Bach: Secular Cantatas** / Suzuki (cond.), Bach Collegium Japan, Schreckenberger, Sampson / 2004 / BIS 1411

Schwingt freudig euch empor, cantata, BWV 36 (Dec. 2, 1731)

BWV 36 ("Soar joyfully aloft") has a particularly complex history. The version under consideration here represents Bach's reworking of a work that started life in 1725 as a secular cantata of the same name (BWV 36c). Composed to a libretto by the Leipzig civil servant and poet Picander (the pseudonym of the poet Christian Friedrich Henrici), the cantata was written as a birthday tribute to an unidentified Leipzig academic. The following year, Bach revived the work with a new text by Picander for the birthday of the wife of his old employer, Prince Leopold of Anhalt-Cöthen, with whom he maintained close contact after moving to Leipzig. This version, now lost, bears the name *Steigt freudig in die Luft*, BWV 36a. At some point between this second secular version and 1730, Bach decided to turn the work into a sacred cantata for Advent Sunday, adding a chorale and adapting it to a new text by an unknown author. In 1731, he returned to the work yet again, expanding it from five numbers to eight, while further restructuring and revising the existing numbers. Finally, in 1735, Bach returned the work to its secular origins using yet another new text, *Die Freude reget sich* (BWV 36b), probably also by Picander. According to the Bach scholar Christoph Wolff the occasion may have been the inauguration of the Leipzig professor Andreas Florens Rivinius as rector of the Thomasschule. The whole history of BWV 36 provides an interesting insight into the working methods of Bach, who, throughout his composing life, constantly reworked and refined material he considered to be of value.

The 1731 sacred cantata is a large-scale work divided into two parts, the first of which would have been performed before the sermon, the second afterwards.

The scoring of the cantata is the usual SATB vocal disposition, with solo arias for soprano, tenor, and bass; the instrumental forces are a pair of oboes d'amores, strings, and continuo. A particular feature of the 1731 version was the addition of three stanzas of Martin Luther's great Advent hymn "Nun komm der Heiden Heiland" (Nos. 2, 4, and 6), previously used in the two Advent cantatas which bear its name, BWV 61 and 62. For the final chorale Bach retained a strophe he had added in 1730 from another beautiful Advent hymn, Philip Nicolai's "Wie schön leuchtet der Morgenstern" (1599).

The opening chorus, as befits the season and its original secular celebratory origins, is a joyous affair; each part enters in imitation, but the writing involves both contrapuntal and homophonic passages. The only aria in the first part is for tenor; it is a dance-like movement in da capo form with an obbligato part for oboe d'amore, the text casting Jesus in the familiar role of bridegroom of the enraptured soul. Part two opens with a spirited aria for bass ("Welcome precious treasure"), the text calling on Jesus to enter the "pure heart." The final soprano aria is a delicately textured movement with muted string accompaniment. *—Brian Robins*

Recommended:

- ○ **Bach: Cantatas; Advent** / J. E. Gardiner (cond.), Argenta, P. Lang, A. R. Johnson, Bär, Monteverdi Choir, English Baroque Soloists / 1992 / DG 463588
- ○ **J.S. Bach: Adventskantaten BWV 36, 61 & 62** / Herreweghe (cond.), Rubens, S. Connolly, Pregardien, Collegium Vocale / HM 901605

Vergnügte Ruh, beliebte Seelenlust, cantata, BWV 170 (Jul. 28, 1726)

During his years as Kapellmeister at Cöthen (1717–22), J.S. Bach was given a respite from the task, central to any Lutheran church musician, of composing sacred cantatas; but when he was appointed Cantor in the city of Leipzig in 1723, he immediately set about composing cantatas at an astonishing rate. The job demanded that he produce a cantata for every Sunday and for each important feast day in the liturgical year. Bach didn't always find time to write completely new cantatas, but still, the ink spent between 1723 and 1729 on cantatas would fill several vats. One of the highlights of the third "cycle" of Leipzig cantatas, which Bach worked on between 1725 and 1727, is the chamber cantata *Vergnügte Ruh, beliebte Seelenlust*, BWV 170, a setting of texts by G.C. Lehms (a Lutheran poet who was born one year before Bach and died at the age of 33, nine years before Bach wrote BWV 170) scored for just a single contralto soloist and small orchestra.

Vergnügte Ruh, beliebte Seelenlust, which translates as Pleasant Rest, Beloved Soul's Joy and was composed for use on the sixth Sunday after Trinity, is essentially three large arias for contralto, between which are placed two "Rezitativs." The first aria, "Vergnügte Ruh, beliebte Seelenlust," is in da capo form, and tells, by way of rich music that throbs with inner passion (just listen to the string rhythms, which resemble those used at the start of Jean Sibelius' warm *Symphony No. 2*), that "pleasant rest" can be attained only through union with Heaven.

The second aria, "Wie jammern mich doch die verkehrten Herzen" (How I Lament for Those Whose Hearts Have Gone Wrong), inhabits a world utterly different from that of the first; it is thinly textured and full of pointed, sharp articulations—and, most importantly, there is no real bass line, this absence indicating, according to some, the lack of a guiding force in the lives of the poor lost souls spoken of in the text.

In "Mir ekelt mehr zu leben" (Life Disgusts Me), the third and final aria (again a da capo aria), the contralto asks to be released from the bonds of life so that she might know everlasting life at "the dwelling-house in which [she] can find peace." *—Blair Johnston*

Recommended:

- ○ **Cantates pour alto** / Herreweghe (cond.), A. Scholl, Orch. du Collegium Vocale / 1998 / HM 901644
- ○ **Bach: Cantatas BWV 169–171** / Rilling (cond.), Stuttgart Bach Collegium / 1983 / Haenssler 92051
- ○ **René Jacobs: Portraits** / Pregardien (cond.), R. Jacobs, Linde Consort / 1997 / Virgin 61397
- ○ **Bach Cantatas 54; 169 & 170** / R. King (cond.), J. Bowman, The King's Consort / 1989 / Hyperion 66326

Wachet auf, ruft uns die Stimme, cantata, BWV 140 (Nov. 25, 1731)

This is one of the best-known and most theatrical of Bach's sacred cantatas. It was written in 1731 as part of Bach's series of five cantatas for every Sunday and special feast day in the Lutheran calendar. This particular cantata was written for a rarely occurring date, the 27th Sunday after Trinity. This day occurs only in years when Easter comes unusually early. Since this was a rare event (it happened only twice during Bach's 26 years in Leipzig), Bach used an unusually large ensemble and wrote the cantata on a large scale.

The chorale used in the cantata (and the work's title) comes from a 1599 hymn tune by Philipp Nicolai. Literally, the title translates as "Wake up, the voices are calling us." To fit the three syllables of the German, the more commonly found translation "Sleepers Wake" is used, and it is by this name that it is best known in English.

The text is a treatment of Jesus' parable of the Wise and Foolish Virgins (or, as some translations have it, Wise and Foolish Bridesmaids). What is foolish about these young women of Jesus' story is that through inattention they don't notice that the bridegroom has arrived, so they miss the wedding and the wedding feast. In fact, they don't even make it into Bach's cantata, for it only mentions the wise bridesmaids, who do not sleep through the Bridegroom's arrival and, hence, witness the wedding and partake in the feast. The Bridegroom is allegorical for Jesus; his bride is the Christian soul. And these two allegorical figures have an ardent, even operatic, love duet assigned to soprano and bass.

The opening chorus is bustling, depicting crowds in Jerusalem waiting for the Bridegroom. A tenor recitative represents the night watchmen giving word of the arrival. Then follows the duet between Jesus and the soul. The Bridegroom welcomes the bride into his abode, and there is a chorus of thanksgiving and glory. *—Joseph Stevenson*

Recommended:

- ○ **Bach: 6 Favourite Cantatas** / Rifkin (cond.), J. Baird, Minter, J. Thomas, The Bach Ens. / 1997 / L'Oiseau-Lyre 455706
- ○ **Bach: Magnificat** / Cleobury (cond.), King's College Choir, Academy of Ancient Music (UK) / 2000 / EMI 56994
- ○ **Bach: Cantatas BWV 140 & 147** / J. E. Gardiner (cond.), Chance, Varcoe, Holton, A. R. Johnson, Monteverdi Choir, English Baroque Soloists / 1992 / Archiv 463587

Was mir behagt, cantata ("Hunting Cantata"), BWV 208 (Feb. 23, 1713)

Known in its original German diminutive as the "Jagdkantate," the full title of Johann Sebastian Bach's *Cantata No. 208, Was mir behagt, (Hunting Cantata)* in English translation is "The cheerful hunt is all that gives me pleasure." It is likely that Bach wrote the work, one of his best-know secular cantatas, in 1713, for the birthday of Duke Christian of Saxe-Weisenfels on February 23 of that year. At this point, Bach had been commissioned to stage a series of concerts at Weisenfels, and one of the works he composed especially was this, arguably his first "modern" cantata, to texts by Salomon Franck. According to Bach scholar Konrad Küscher, "courtly celebration always takes precedence over classical accuracy" in Bach's secular cantatas, "but the use of mythological names for the solo voices at least guarantees some slight dramatic action." In this allegorical setting, four solo voices are employed. The roles of Diana (a goddess associated with, among many other things, the moon and hunting) and Pales (a divinity associated with cattle), were given to sopranos; Endymion is sung by the tenor, and the bass singer takes the role of Pan. Duke Christian apparently had a great love for hunting, and Diana sings that hunting was indeed the favored recreation of gods and heroes of antiquity. Endymion appears, only to find that he is rejected by Diana, his lover, who seems interested only in the progress of the hunt; Endymion sings of his remorse in two linked arias with recitatives. As the pair join for a short dialogue, it becomes clear that Diana's action is not a deliberate attempt to spurn Endymion. Rather, as she sings, since today is the birthday of a great hunter, the Duke Christian, she has focused her energies temporarily on the celebrations, in which she is now joined by Endymion himself. A similar pattern of arias and recitatives now follows the appearance of the other principal voices, in the roles of Pan and Pales, who also join in unreserved Ducal praises, before they are joined by Diana and Endymion, who serenade the Duke in duet. Pan and Pales each sing a further aria, before the cantata ends with a rousing chorus. It is interesting to note that in this work, the principal singers were equipped with props, reflecting their allegorical and mythological characteristics. Diana, for example, carried a hunter's spear, and later on, Pan presented his shepherd's crook to the Duke, laying it at his feet, suggesting that the work was performed, originally at least, in a semi-staged fashion. This highly stylized antique characterization was further heightened by details of Bach's imaginative orchestration. A pair of hunting horns provides an obbligato part for Diana's aria, and the first aria sung by Pales features accompaniment from two recorders. This is the familiar "Schafe können sicher weiden" or "Sheep may safely graze," the subtext of which was designed to show the Duke's beneficence and kindness to his subjects. Certain numbers found their way into later cantatas by Bach, and, as Küscher concludes, "the Hunt cantata was an example of Bach's early vocal music, that he was pleased to draw on throughout his further career." *—Michael Jameson*

Recommended:

- ○ **Bach: Ich habe genug; Hunt Cantata; Wedding Cantata** / R. Goodman (cond.), J. Smith, Kirkby, S. Davies, M. George, Parley of Instruments / 2000 / Hyperion 22041
- ○ **Bach: Secular Cantatas BWV 208 & 209** / Rilling (cond.), Gachinger Kantorei, Stuttgart Bach Collegium, / 1999 / Haenssler 92065

Weichet nur, betrübte Schatten, cantata ("Wedding Cantata"), BWV 202 (before 1730)

The links between J.S. Bach and those offices that required from him the production of church music—sacred cantatas, organ music, etc.—were, if not broken altogether, very much weakened during his years as Kapellmeister at Cöthen (1718–23) (where the Prince loved chamber music and was bored by sacred music); not surprisingly, Bach produced very little such music during those years. There is, however, a body of secular cantatas from Cöthen which shows that, although separated from liturgical necessity, the composer still cultivated an interest in the musical genre that would later characterize his religious works. One of these, *Cantata No. 202, Weichet nur, betrübte Schatten*, BWV 202 (the *Wedding Cantata*), showcases the occasional, dramatic quality of these works.

BWV 202 is actually one of three secular cantatas designed for use at wedding celebrations (the others are *Cantatas Nos. 210 and 216*, the latter of which has only partially survived); but its fame is such that it alone has earned the popular name *Wedding Cantata*. The author of the cantata's text remains unknown; it might have been Salomon Franck, or possibly C.F. Hunold. The nine musical numbers—four arias (all but one of which are da capo arias), three recitatives, one recitativo and arioso, and a final, happy Gavotte—are scored for solo soprano, oboe, strings, and basso continuo, and celebrate the dawning of both spring and love.

It is principally the text that distinguishes this cantata from Bach's sacred cantatas for solo voice; formally, the arias and secco recitatives are structured identically to their liturgical fellows. The first aria opens with a series of diminished harmonies; these paint a sensuous picture of spring's lazy pleasures as the singer invites the depressing shades of winter to depart. The contrast between the upward arpeggios of the A section and the bustling, lively B section underscores the textual change from shadow to sunlight, from winter's cold to spring's bursting flowers. The second aria, with its bustling continuo accompaniment, is a vividly melismatic depiction of warm breezes hurrying through the reborn world. The third, in ritornello form with solo violin, is the only aria without da capo, as well as the only one in a minor key. The fourth aria, "Sich üben in Lieben," features a delightful oboe melody; its form is ritornello da capo. The text remarks that love's pleasantries are better than the fleeting joys of spring. The concluding gavotte presents a stately little wedding march with tutti, which the soprano's line then gracefully ornaments.*—Blair Johnston*

Recommended:

- ○ **Bach: Cantatas & Arias** / Klemperer (cond.), Schwarzkopf, Amsterdam Concertgebouw / 1999 / EMI 67206
- ○ **Bach: Hochzeitskantaten** / R. Goebel (cond.), C. Schäfer, Musica Antiqua Köln / DG 459621
- ○ **Bach: Ich habe genug; Hunt Cantata; Wedding Cantata** / A. Parrott (cond.), Kirkby, D. Thomas, Taverner Consort & Players / 2000 / Hyperion 22041

Weinen, Klagen, Sorgen, Zagen, cantata, BWV 12 (Apr. 22, 1714)

Bach was appointed court organist at Weimar in 1708, a position that made no specific demands on him to compose cantatas. However, after he was promoted to the post of concertmaster in March 1714 his duties expanded. "Wienen, klagen, sorgen, zagen" (Weeping, Wailing, Lamenting, Fearing") was one of the first fruits of Bach's new status, a cantata composed for the third Sunday after Easter (April 22, 1714). It is among the early cantatas later revived for use in Leipzig, where it was performed on April 30, 1724. The text, which describes the afflictions of the Christian and exhorts hearers to remain firm in faithfulness, is believed to be the work of the Weimar court poet Salomo Franck, who furnished the texts of most of Bach's Weimar cantatas. The work is scored for SATB chorus, alto, tenor, and bass soloists, and an orchestra including oboe, "tromba" (trumpet), strings and continuo.

As is typical of Bach's early cantatas, the work includes an introductory instrumental sinfonia, here marked Adagio assai. With its plangent oboe solo, the sinfonia is reminiscent of the slow movement of a concerto. The opening chorus is built over a repeated chromatic bass pattern, with each of the words of the title pronounced in turn and overlapping the next. This chorus was later arranged by Bach to form the Crucifixus of the great Mass in B minor. The early style of BWV 12 is confirmed by the inclusion of only one very short passage of recitative. It is given to the alto, and leads straight into an aria (also for alto) via an ascending scale depicting entry into the "Kingdom of God," the words of the final line of the recitative. It is the first of the three successive arias. The text, based upon a passage from Acts, reminds Christians that despite tribulation "their comfort is Christ's wounds." The resolute bass aria that follows also features a rising scale, this time to emphasize the singer's determined "I will follow Christ." The final aria for tenor adds two instrumental voices (symbolizing the Holy Trinity), an ostinato bass, and trumpet, which intones the chorale melody "Jesu, meine Freude." This highly original cantata, which served Bach so well for later recycling, comes to a close with a four-part chorale setting of the hymn "Was Gott tut, das ist wohlgetan" by Samuel Rodigast (1674). *—Brian Robins*

Recommended:

- ○ **Bach: Cantatas Vol. 3** / M. Suzuki (cond.), Kurisu, Mera, Sakurada, Kooy, Bach Collegium Japan / 1996 / Bis 791
- ○ **Bach: Complete Cantatas Vol. 2** / Koopman (cond.), Mertens, Pregardien, Schlick, Wessel, Amsterdam Baroque Orch & Choir / 1995 / Erato 12598
- ○ **Bach: Actus Tragicus** / Junghanel (cond.), Cantus Colln / HM 901694
- ○ **Bach: Easter Cantata** / Richter (cond.), Schreier, T. Adam, A. Reynolds, Eliscu, Münchner Bach Orch & Chor / 1976 / Archiv 439374

Widerstehe doch der Sünde, cantata, BWV 54 (Mar. 4, 1714)

The exact date of composition for BWV 54 ("Stand firm against sin") has not been established, but most authorities believe it was composed around 1714, shortly after Bach was promoted to the post of concertmaster at the Weimar court. Bach, who had joined the Weimar court as organist in 1708, had no duties in Weimar that formally involved the composition of sacred cantatas until 1714; only BWV 21 has been firmly assigned an earlier date. The libretto of BWV 54 is drawn from a collection by Georg Christian Lehms first published in 1711, and intended for the two Kapellmeisters at Darmstadt, Gottfried Grünewald and Christoph Graupner. From the libretto we learn that the cantata was intended for the third Sunday in Lent. It is one of only a dozen among Bach's 200 or so extant cantatas to call for a single voice (three of which, BWV 199, BWV 35, and BWV 170 are also settings of texts by Lehms), in this instance an alto.

The formal scheme is simple: two arias separated by a recitative; there is no concluding chorale. It therefore shows the influence—especially in its clear division of da capo aria and recitative—of the secular Italian cantata and opera seria. The theme, a warning to resist the wiles of Satan, is clearly inspired by the Gospel for the day (Luke 11:14–28) which relates the story of the casting out of devils by Jesus. The expansive and harmonically rich opening aria exhorts the Christian not to let "venom seize you" in the shape of the wiles of Satan. After a recitative warning that those "wed with" sin will not enter God's kingdom, comes a second aria in which Bach's colorful symbolism is fully in evidence. Formally it is a three-part fugue between voice, unison violins and violas, the sinuous chromatic subject of which paints an ever-present of picture of sin in its many statements. The text again makes reference to the presence of the devil in sinners. *—Brian Robins*

Recommended:

- ○ **Bach: Cantatas Vol. 3** / M. Suzuki (cond.), Mera, Bach Collegium Japan / 1996 / Bis 791
- ○ **Salve Regina: Vivaldi, Telemann, Bach & Pergolesi** / R. King (cond.), J. Bowman, The King's Consort / 2002 / Meridan 84479

Wir danken dir, Gott, wir danken dir, cantata, BWV 29 (Aug. 27, 1731)

BWV 29 ("We thank thee, O God, we thank thee") is one of a number of cantatas J.S. Bach composed for the ceremonies attending the installation of new members of the Leipzig city council (other examples are cantatas Nos. 119 and 120). An important part of these ceremonies, which traditionally took place at the end of August, was the church service held at St. Nicholas'. The present work was composed for the event in 1731, the service taking place on August 27 that year. In keeping with the festive and ceremonial pomp of the occasion, Bach's cantata is lavishly scored for an orchestra including three trumpets, timpani, two oboes, strings, and continuo bass, and vocal forces including the usual four-part chorus, and soprano, alto, tenor, and bass soloists. An unknown librettist provided the text glorifying the power of God and extolling him to protect "town and palaces." This cantata opens with a sinfonia in the form of a remarkable arrangement of the Prelude from the *Violin Partita in E major,* BWV 1006. The violin part is given to obbligato organ, the material largely imitated in the orchestral parts to produce a concerto-like structure. Many listeners will recognize the fugal opening chorus, since it is a reworking of what would eventually become the "Gratias agimus tibi" and "Dona nobis pacem" sections of the monumental *Mass in B minor,* BWV 232. The text is drawn from Psalm 75:1. Three arias interspersed by recitatives follow. The first aria, for tenor, has a violin obbligato, and Bach returns to its A section, a setting of the words "Hallelujah, strength and might," for the alto aria that forms the penultimate number. In between comes a soprano aria in gentle siciliano rhythm with an obbligato part for oboe. The final number is a four-part setting of the fifth stanza of Johann Gramann's hymn *"Nun lob, mein Seel, den Herren"* (1549), the trumpets and drums adding their magnificence and splendor to this jubilant work. *—Brian Robins*

Recommended:

- ○ **Bach: Wir danken dir, Gott** / Herreweghe (cond.), D. York, Danz, Padmore, Kooy, Collegium Vocale / HM 901690

Wir müssen durch viel Trübsal, cantata, BWV 146 (May 12, 1726)

It was a lifelong habit for Bach to borrow musical material from his previous works for use in new compositions. BWV 146 ("We must through much tribulation enter the kingdom of God") offers an interesting example of this procedure; it includes a reworking of the first two movements of a lost violin concerto which also appeared later in the D minor *Harpsichord Concerto,* BWV 1052.

Cantata No. 146 was composed for the third Sunday after Easter, and was first performed on either May 12, 1726 or April 18, 1728. In the gospel for the day (John 16:16–22) the resurrected Christ tells the disciples he will shortly leave them, but that sorrow will turn to joy. As with the superb *Cantata No. 12,* composed many years earlier for the same Sunday, it is the theme of a journey from darkness to light that Bach takes up. This is little apparent in the lively opening sinfonia (which corresponds to the first movement of the concerto), an example of the sort of organ obbligato movement that prefaces a number of Bach's later cantatas (the *Cantata No. 188, of ca. 1728,* uses the final movement of the same D minor Concerto, adapted in the same way). The opening chorus is superimposed onto the deeply moving slow movement of the concerto, with the anguish of the repeated (ostinato) bass line ideally underlining a text concerned with the tribulation that must be endured before the kingdom of heaven is attained. The choral writing, in long sustained notes, is rhythmically independent of the orchestra, which again features a concerto-like obbligato part for organ. As in the *Cantata No. 12,* Bach uses a rising scale to illustrate the ascent to heaven in the long alto aria that follows. A long accompanied recitative and aria for soprano follow, the former pervaded by anguished dissonance. The text of the aria (taken from Psalm 126, "They that sow in tears") is perhaps better illustrated by the affective flute and oboe d'amore solos than by the vocal line. The lively penultimate number, "How shall I myself rejoice," is a duet for tenor and bass in da capo form; it includes exuberant runs for the two singers. The text and instrumentation for the concluding chorale, Johann Schop's "Werde munter, mein Gemüte" is missing in the surviving sources for the work, all of which postdate Bach's death. *—Brian Robins*

Recommended:

- ○ **Bach: Cantatas Vol. 15** / Koopman (cond.), Amsterdam Baroque Orch & Choir / 2004 / Challenge 72215

Chorale settings for 4 voices

From the start of the Protestant Reformation in Germany, the congregational chorale, or hymn melody, occupied a place at the heart of the newly established Lutheran liturgy. Martin Luther himself valued music highly, and was an accomplished musician. Under his auspices the Lutheran church rapidly established a substantial collection of chorale texts and music; many of the melodies employed were adapted from existing sacred and secular sources (often from the vast Roman Catholic heritage). During the course of the seventeenth century, the number of chorales increased substantially, entering every aspect of religious life. It was also during this time that composers started to incorporate chorale melodies into both sacred vocal compositions and instrumental music.

By the time Bach began his compositional career early in the eighteenth century, the chorale was thus firmly embedded within musical life in Lutheran Germany. Bach's use of the chorale falls broadly into two categories: chorales are incorporated into his cantatas and passion settings, and are used as a foundation for instrumental compositions, mostly for organ. Universal congregational knowledge of chorale tunes meant that Bach could employ them to point to a didactic message that would be clearly understood. One or more chorales appear in virtually every one of the cantatas, either in simple four-part harmonizations or woven into complex contrapuntal structures. Bach's most concentrated use of the chorale can be found in his second annual cycle of cantatas composed in Leipzig during 1724 and 1725. In these so-called "chorale cantatas" every movement is based on a hymn text or a paraphrase of it, with the associated melody also appearing in a variety of guises to give the cantata a strong sense of structural integration. In the great passion settings, the chorale performs a rather different function: the simple harmonizations act to furnish moments of reflection over the course of the unfolding drama. The most memorable example in this context is the fivefold use of the famous "Passion Chorale" (known in the English-speaking world as *"O sacred head"* and itself based on a secular melody) in the *St. Matthew Passion.* Bach's use of chorale melodies in his instrumental works also varies between relatively straightforward transcription in some of the chorale preludes and highly skilled polyphonic structures in which the tune is intricately embedded in fantasia-like structures.

Bach himself composed relatively few chorale melodies, but he did edit a collection published in Leipzig in 1736 known as the *Schemelli Songbook,* after its publisher Georg Christian Schemelli. It includes the texts of nearly 1,000 hymns, with melodies for 69 of them. Of these Bach is known to be the composer of 19, forming his most extensive single contribution to the genre. Beyond these, four original tunes appear in the second of the two instructional books Bach prepared for his second wife, Anna Magdalena, and Part Four of the *Christmas Oratorio* and the final chorale of the motet *Komm, Jesu, komm* provide rare examples of Bach's incorporating a melody of his own composition into a larger work. *—Brian Robins*

Recommended:

- ○ **Bach: Ein Choralbuch** / Rilling (cond.), S. Rubens, A. Schmidt, Pregardien, Stuttgart Bach Collegium / 1999 / Haenssler 92085
- ○ **Bach: A Book of Chorale Settings for Advent & Christmas** / Rilling (cond.), S. Rubens, A. Schmidt, Behringer, Stuttgart Bach Collegium / Haenssler 92078
- ○ **Bach: Motets, Chorales & Songs** / Harnoncourt & others (conds.), Vienna Concentus Musicus / 1999 / Teldec 25712

Christmas Oratorio, BWV 248 (1734–1735)

Although German composer Johann Sebastian Bach entitled his work *Weihnachtsoratorium* (Christmas Oratorio), it is in fact closer to a cantata cycle than an oratorio. Composed and compiled for the Christmas season as celebrated in Leipzig in 1734 and early 1735, the six parts of the *Christmas Oratorio* were intended to be performed on the six major feast days over that 13-day period from December 25 through January 6: the "First Day of Christmas," the "Second Day of Christmas," the "Third Day of Christmas," the "Feast of the Circumcision," the "First Sunday of the New Year," and the "Feast of the Epiphany." Furthermore, each part of the work is designed to function as an independent musical unit; each part (except the second, which starts with a "Pastoral Symphony") begins and ends with choruses in the tonic key, and each part tells a separate part of the Christmas story.

However, Bach also clearly intended the music to be heard as a unified work: Not only does the oratorio tell a single story based on Biblical texts, but it is musically organized around the key of D major. The musical content of the oratorio is, for the most part, drawn from three secular cantatas: *Herkules auf dem Scheidewege* (BWV 213), *Tönet, ihr Pauken! Erschallet, Trompeten!* (BWV 214), and *Preisse dein Glücke, gesegnetes Sachsen* (BWV 215). In addition, portions of the music were drawn from the lost *St. Mark Passion,* and the sixth part of the oratorio was later given an independent existence as a separate cantata (BWV 248a).

So skillful is Bach's adaptation that listeners at the time would have been unlikely to be disturbed by Bach's self-plagiarism (which was a common procedure for him anyhow). In the manner of Bach's *Passions,* the text of the *Christmas Oratorio* is drawn from the *Gospel* interspersed with meditations on the meaning of the *Gospel* texts. While scholars conjecture that these meditations were written by Bach's usual collaborator, Christian Friedrich Henrici (known as Picander), some also suspect that Bach might have written or rewritten many of them himself because Picander did not include the text of the oratorio among his collected works. A joyfully celebratory work, the *Christmas Oratorio* is one of the peaks in Bach's compositional oeuvre.

The story is related in recitative by an Evangelist, or narrator, thus placing the work within the long-established tradition of religious drama. However, unlike earlier oratorios and unlike Bach's own settings of the Passion story, there is virtually no dramatic dialogue, The only named characters are the Angel in Part Two and Herod in Part Six. Scored for the usual four-part vocal forces, the oratorio is given is own distinctive character through the varied orchestration featured in each section. Thus Part One, largely a joyous celebration of Christ's birth, is adorned by brilliantly festive trumpets and timpani. The following cantata stands in complete contrast, its gentle pastoral mood reflected in scoring that includes pairs of oboes d'amore and their more rustic cousin, the oboe da caccia. Bach then gives symmetry to the first three cantatas by bringing the trumpets and timpani back for Part Three, which opens with an exultant chorus before proceeding to the arrival of the shepherds at the manger. Part Four introduces a pair of horns into the orchestra; their resplendent tones dominate an opening chorus celebrating the glory of God. Part Five, for the lesser feast of the Sunday after New Year, calls for smaller orchestral forces—just a pair of oboes supporting the usual strings and continuo, perhaps as a counterpart to the second cantata. Finally the full majesty of trumpets and drums returns in Part 6, the topic of which is God's power over evil, here personified by Herod and his dealings with the three Magi. *—James Leonard*

Recommended:

- ○ **Bach: Weihnachtsoratorium** / K. Richter (cond.), Wunderlich, C. Ludwig, Janowitz, Munchener Bach-Orchester / Archiv 427236
- ○ **Bach: Oratorio de Noël** / R. Jacobs (cond.), Roschmann, A. Scholl, Akademie für Alte Musik Berlin / HM 2908113/15
- ○ **Bach: Weihnachts-Oratorium** / Koopman (cond.), L. Larsson, von Magnus, Pregardien, Mertens, Amsterdam Baroque Orchestra / 1996 / Erato 14635
- ○ **Bach: Weihnachtsoratorium** / Harnoncourt (cond.), Esswood, Equiluz, Nimsgern, Vienna Concentus Musicus / 1991 / Teldec 74893

Magnificat in D major, BWV 243 (ca. 1732)

Johann Sebastian Bach became director of music in the city of Leipzig and cantor at St. Thomas Church there in May 1723. By December he had already composed 30 cantatas, and on Christmas day his choir presented three newly written works: the *Cantata No. 63,* Christen ätzet diesen Tag, a Sanctus in C for the morning service, and a *Magnificat in E flat* for Vespers.The last of these pieces was the original draft of the *Magnificat in D major,* BWV 243, which, in its final form, has become one of Bach's best-loved and most frequently performed choral works. Revisions, completed between 1728 and 1731, included the addition of flute and trumpet parts, which explains the transposition to the more trumpet-friendly key of D and the excision of four interpolated movements that were not part of the canticle text.

The Marian canticle "Magnificat" had been part of the evening service from the earliest days of the church. In Luke's infancy narrative, when Gabriel informed Mary that she was to bear the son of God, all she could say was, "I am the servant of the Lord. Do with me what you will." It was not until she visited her cousin Elisabeth that she allowed her elation to overflow and sang, "My soul magnifies the Lord, and my spirit has rejoiced in God my savior." Composers have always found this joyous text a rich inspiration, and Bach's setting is one of his finest choral works. Bach divides the text into 11 parts, roughly corresponding to the ten verses of the canticle (with a separate setting for "all generations shall call me blessed," the second half of verse three), and adds the Gloria Patri (lesser Doxology), as was (and is still) traditional. The work is scored for five-part chorus, soprano, alto, tenor and bass soloists, two flutes, oboe, oboe d'amore, oboe da caccia, bassoon, three trumpets, timpani, strings, and continuo. A sense of exultation is evident throughout, tempered with modesty and awe. The two festive outer movements mingle imitative elements with emphatic rhythmic impetus.The brilliant vocal counterpoint above pedal points in the "Gloria," twice rising, then falling in triplets through the sections blurs the perception both of harmonic and metric structure, swirling and rushing like the restless wings of the heavenly host. The excitement of "et exultavit," set in a bouncy triple meter and replete with rippling passagework, is countered by the broad peacefulness of "quia respexit," with its plaintive oboe d'amore obbligato. In contrast to "et exultavit," where the lines leap upward, here the melodic phrases tend downward in humility. A lengthy fughetta for full chorus is followed by a bass aria, with its repetitive, bold insistence on strength. A duet section suggests yearning, while the character of the next two movements is undeniably martial, especially reinforced in the tenor aria by a unison string accompaniment. "Esurientes" is lazy and humorous, and the ensuing trio is exquisite, with a wandering melody played by unison oboes, the voices twining around it in slow counterpoint. The piece ends as it began, with trumpets and kettledrums blazing. *— Virginia Sublett*

Recommended:

- ○ **The Symphony of Harmony & Invention** / Christophers (cond.), The Sixteen / 2000 / Linn 148
- ○ **Vivaldi: Gloria; Ostro picta; Bach: Magnificat** / Hickox (cond.), Kirkby, Bonner, Chance, Ainsley, Collegium Musicum 90 / 1991 / Chandos 0518
- ○ **Bach: Magnificat; Easter Oratorio** / A. Parrott (cond.), Taverner Consort & Players / 1999 / Virgin 61647
- ○ **Bach: Magnificat** / Herreweghe (cond.), B. Schlick, Lesne, A. Mellon, H. Crook, La Chapelle Royale / 2003 / Harmonia Mundi 3001326

Mass in B minor, BWV 232 (ca. 1748)

In 1733, Bach wrote a letter petitioning Friedrich August II, the Catholic Elector of Saxony, to grant him a courtly title that might be of value to him in getting his due respect from the powers in Leipzig. To warm up the sovereign to his cause, he enclosed two pieces of music as special proof of his dedication to the composition of church music; these pieces were the Kyrie and Gloria of the Mass in B minor, a juggernaut of religious music that Bach didn't complete until the very end of his life. Why a composer who must have normally worked at blinding speed took 15 years with a single mass is not known, since there was no opportunity for its performance. As a mass, it's far too vast for liturgical use, and earnest religious music couldn't have been welcomed in secular, courtly programs. It definitely wasn't entirely performed while Bach lived, but it seems possible he didn't intend it to be performed that way at all. Many movements are highly effective revisions of past works, often cantatas, spanning much of his career, and the others were composed expressly for the mass. These facts, and the wide differences in style the work contains, suggest it was intended as a summation of his whole oeuvre, but that can never be known.

Of course, the mystery of its purpose and origins have fed the fire of enthusiasm that surrounds the mass. For once, the hype is mostly worth believing. Commentators stumble over each other to praise it, treating it like a St. Peter's of music for good reasons; the Mass in B minor positively crackles with energy, and almost everything that is good about Bach is found in it. Hearing even the brooding Kyrie for the first time can be like having of a pair of jumper cables applied to the heart. Unfortunately, the size, scale, and historical importance of the mass, taken together, seems to confuse certain interpreters into performing it with the overblown orchestral forces and exaggerated expression of late Romantic music. It becomes an overstated banality when treated that way; smaller orchestras can bring out of it an amazing, galvanized lyricism and mechanical power. The range and depth of moods is itself incredible enough; listeners almost prefer to hear the movements discretely to be able to properly take them in. From the most ecstatic, trumpeting orchestral jubilation of the start of the Gloria, to the tender, pained longing in the soprano and tenor duet of the *Laudamus te,* or the unstoppable fugue of the *Cum sancto Spiritu,* the Mass in B minor is as exhilarating to the listeners as it is exhausting to performers. Some lighter, simpler choral movements, like the *Gratias agimus tibi,* have a minor function of granting needed rest, but there don't seem to be quite enough of them to make it really functional as a concert piece. For the highly trainable medium of the compact disc, however, it's just right. *—Donato Mancini*

Recommended:

- ○ **Bach: Messe In H-Moll** / Harnoncourt (cond.), Hansmann, Iiyama, H. Watts, Equiluz, Concentus Musicus Wien / 1994 / Teldec 95517
- ○ **Bach: Mass in B minor** / Klemperer (cond.), Giebel, J. Baker, Gedda, Prey, New Philharmonia Orch. / EMI 63364
- ○ **Bach: Mass In B Minor** / J.E. Gardiner (cond.), English Baroque Soloists / Archiv 415514

Motets (1726–1749)

Johann Sebastian Bach's motets have never left the repertory of the Thomarenchor that Bach led at Leipzig. The idea of these masterpieces being preserved through the years at Leipzig, as Bach's reputation in the wider world faded and then rose again, may have influenced the belief that Bach's motets had all been composed at Leipzig, starting around 1723. As it so often does, modern scholarship has ruined the good story. Besides adding at least two works, BWV Anh. 159 and 160, to the six, BWV 225 through 230, that had been previously deemed the complete Bach motets, researchers have also determined that two of the motets were almost certainly composed in the mid-1710s, years before Bach took up his post at the Thomaskirche. Doubt has also been cast on the very authenticity of BWV 230. Scholars had also assumed that all of Bach's motets had been composed for funerary purposes, but this too has fallen out of favor in some circles. Controversy has touched the motets' performance practice as well. For many years, it was assumed that the motets were meant to be heard a cappella. The discovery of instrumental parts for BWV 226, *Der Geist hilft unser Schwachheit auf,* led some to argue that it must be the exception that proves the rule, while others maintain that it only shows Bach conforming to the practice of using instruments in colla parte with voices, then common in motets. Bach worked within the specific demands of the motet form, setting Biblical and chorale texts, using the dependent instrumentation, and writing counterpoint for choir—actually, mostly double choir—both complex and treacherous to perform. But his motets continually show the ambition and innovation that marked Bach's use of other forms. Even in his early, more conventional motets, BWV Anh. 159 ("Ich lasse dich nicht") and BWV 228 ("Furchte dach nicht"), Bach raised the contrapuntal bar with imitative writing far more sophisticated than that in his contemporaries' motets. Later motets have striking structures; BWV 226 opens with a section of exquisite word-painting—a fluttering of eight notes for the Holy Ghost and repeated, exotic intervals for "unutterable"—then settles into a rock-solid fugue to state the doctrine at its core. BWV 227, "Jesu, meine Freunde," is a lengthy, impassioned, shatteringly powerful profession of faith in the minor mode. Bach alternates between a hymn and a passage from the epistles of St. Paul to achieve both cyclic unity and complementary dissimilarity with the texts alone; he mirrors it in the music, which finds its core in a central fugue that is both imposing and uplifting at once. *—Andrew Lindemann Malone*

Recommended:

- ○ **Bach: The Six Motets BWV 225–30; Jesu, Meine Freude Fantasia** / A. Mackay, The Sarum Consort / 2001 / ASV 218
- ○ **Bach 2000 Vol. 7: Motets, Chorales & Songs** / Harnoncourt (cond.), Concentus Musicus Wien / 1999 / Teldec 25712

St. John Passion (Johannes-Passion), BWV 245 (Apr. 7, 1724; revised 1725)

J.S. Bach's *Johannes-Passion*, or *St. John Passion*, BWV 245—one of just two surviving Bach Passion works out of an original four or five—is, simply put, a headache for editors and performers wishing to recreate the authentic, stamped-and-approved original work. There is no such beast: the work was performed at least four times during Bach's lifetime, and for each new presentation he overhauled the music, adding numbers, deleting numbers, changing numbers, so that today we really have four different *St. John Passions* through which to pick and choose our way. Happily enough, however, Bach misses the mark in not a single one of those numbers, and the director can hardly go wrong selecting from such a wealth of fine material. The *St. John Passion* was first heard on April 7, 1724 (Good Friday), and then reproduced for Leipzig churchgoers in 1725, sometime in the early 1730s (perhaps 1732), and then again in 1749. Perhaps in part because of its sometimes bewildering compositional history and the fact that its texts were not really conceived as a single entity (Bach seems to have arranged the texts himself from a number of disparate sources, and sometimes his efforts—which seem to have been hasty ones—are not altogether graceful), the *St. John Passion* has never been a sweepingly popular work like the *St. Matthew Passion*, BWV 244. But it is a monumental work that must have made quite an impression indeed at its first performance, early on in Bach's tenure as Cantor of Leipzig.

The *St. John Passion* calls for four vocal soloists, four-part chorus, and a large orchestra including not only the now-usual string instruments, flutes, oboes, and basso continuo, but also oboes d'amore, oboes da caccia, and violas d'amore; and there is even the possibility of letting a lutenist into the ensemble! Although the work perhaps lacks the scope of its cousin the *St. Matthew Passion*, it has an immediate, dramatic quality. Bach enacts, as a kind of musical equivalent of the Passion Play, an episode from the story detailing the arrest, trial, and crucifixion, with the words of the historical persons—Christ, Pilate, Peter, and John as Evangelist—set in recitatives, followed by a solo commenting on the emotional and spiritual meaning of the event described. The chorus portrays the crowd—soldiers, priests, and populace—in addition to singing chorales, based on familiar themes. By contrast, the arias are special events (there are just three in the whole of the first part) during which the course of the Passion drama is paused and room is made for profound reflection *—Blair Johnston*

Recommended:

- ○ **Bach: St. John Passion** / J.E. Gardiner (cond.), Chance, Rufus Muller, Varcoe, Argento, English Baroque Soloists / 1975 / Archiv 419324
- ○ **Bach: Johannes-Passion** / Harnoncourt (cond.), Blasi, Lipovsek, Holl, Rolfe Johnson, Concentus Musicus Wien / 1995 / Teldec 48622
- ○ **Bach: St. John Passion** / A. Parrott (cond.), Taverner Consort & Players / 2002 / Virgin 62019

St. Matthew Passion (Matthäus-Passion), BWV 244 (Apr. 11, 1727)

It is unclear exactly how many Passion settings Bach wrote: perhaps but not likely five, possibly three or four. Only two survive today; the second of these, the *St. Matthew Passion* dates from 1729. The Passions, Biblical texts set as large-scale musical works, were performed on Good Friday and told the story of Christ's Crucifixion, according to the Gospels.

The *St. Matthew Passion* is a work very different in character from its extant predecessor, the *St. John Passion*: the former is deeply devotional, introspective, and meditative in character, while the latter is more intensely dramatic, with more action in its narrative. The *St. Matthew Passion* is often compared with Bach's monumental *Mass in B minor* in terms of both scope and piety. Performed at St. Thomas' Church in Leipzig, the work sets a text by Christian Picander (who may have been the author of a hypothetical, now-lost 1725 Bach Passion). Another significant difference between the St. John and St. Matthew works lies in their respective texts: the St. John text is very short, beginning with Judas' betrayal of Christ, and focusing on Christ's trial before Pilate; the St. Matthew text, on the other hand, is very long, containing almost twice as many verses as the St. John text.

The *St. Matthew Passion* is also much grander musically, with its two four-part choirs and large orchestra of strings, flutes, oboes, harpsichord, and organ. Bach makes particularly poignant and varied use of his two choirs in this piece; they are heard representing the voices of different communities of believers, and also of the clamorous, derisive crowds at the Crucifixion. One celebrated aspect of the work is the way Bach uses the instrument groups to achieve various text-painting effects; a halo around Christ is suggested, for example, by the soft, sustained chords of a string ensemble, and Bach depicts the weariness of Christ on the road to Calvary with a deep pedal point. Like the *St. John Passion*, the *St. Matthew Passion* contains both Gospel text and hymn text, and both employ recitatives, arias, and choruses.

The similarities between Bach's Passions and the Catholic oratorio genre are striking. The Passions are, like the oratorio, a kind of religious opera; as in that more overtly dramatic genre, arias serve as a vehicle for lyrical expression and recitatives to advance the textual narrative. The central figure, both musically and dramatically, in the *St. Matthew Passion* is the Evangelist (a tenor), who narrates the story. The nature of his purely narrative, non-participatory, role is made clear through his confinement to passages of recitative; he is never afforded the opportunity for more expansive lyricism. This mode of expression falls to the other vocal soloists, who adopt the personae of those involved in the drama and give them voice.

The score is best appreciated as a whole, in which context the dramatic sweep and spiritual conviction of the work are abundantly clear. However, there are a number of notable highlights that are frequently excerpted. These include the soprano aria "Blute nur, du liebes Herz," the alto aria "Erbarme dich," which incorporates an obbligato violin, and the bass aria "Mache dich, mein Herze, rein." *—Alexander Carpenter*

Recommended:

- ○ **Bach: St. Matthew Passion** / Klemperer (cond.), Fischer-Dieskau, Schwarzkopf, Pears, C. Ludwig, Philharmonia Orch. / 2001 / EMI 67542
- ○ **Bach: Matthaüs-Passion** / Furtwängler (cond.), Dermota, Fischer-Dieskau, Grümmer, Höffgen, Vienna PO / 1995 / EMI 65509
- ○ **Bach: Matthaüs-Passion** / Harnoncourt (cond.), Pregardien, Goerne, C. Schafer, Röschmann, Concentus Musicus Wien / 2001 / Teldec 81036
- ○ **Bach: Matthäus-Passion** / Brueggen (cond.), van der Meer, Sigmundsson, Bostridge, van der Kamp, Orch. of the 18th Century / 2002 / Philips 473263

CHAMBER MUSIC

Cello Suite No. 1 in G major, BWV 1007 (ca. 1720)

It is thought that Bach wrote his six suites for unaccompanied cello between 1717 and 1723, while he was in the employ of Prince Leopold of Anhalt-Cöthen and had two superb solo cellists, Bernard Christian Linigke and Christian Ferdinand Abel, at his disposal. However, the earliest copy of the suites dates from 1726, and no autographs survive. Thus a chronological order is difficult to prove, though one guesses that these suites were composed in numerical order from the way that they gradually evolve and deepen, both technically and musically.

A Baroque suite is typically a collection of dance movements, usually in binary form with each half repeated. Common elements of the suite were the Allemande (German dance), a moderately slow duple-meter dance; the Courante, a faster dance in triple meter; the Sarabande, a Spanish-derived dance in a slow triple meter with emphasis on the second beat; and a Gigue (Jig), which is rapid, jaunty, and energetic. Bach took these typical dance forms and abstracted them, and then added a free-form, almost improvisatory Prelude which sets the tone for each suite, and a galanterie, an additional dance interposed between Sarabande and Gigue. (In the first two suites, Bach uses a pair of Minuets.) With these dances, Bach experimented and created the first, and arguably still the finest, solo works for a relatively new instrument.

The first suite, in G major, gives the feel of innocent simplicity, and serves as a marvelous opening to these extraordinary works. The Prelude recalls the C major Prelude which opens Book One of the *Well-Tempered Clavier*. Each piece sets a remarkable atmosphere with no melodies, only strong rhythmic patterns, cunningly evolving harmonies, and evocative textures. Bach uses short, arpeggiated phrases to build larger-scale crescendos and decrescendos, and these phrases in turn aggregate into still larger structures, evoking an endlessly more complicated fractal pattern. This quality would become a characteristic of Bach's cello writing, along with a distinctive rhythmic quality far removed from the character of the original dances. Bach's suiite may have been inspired by viol writing in France and cello writing in Italy, but there was nothing like it before the first suite, and little like it after, except for the five suites that followed. *—James Liu*

Recommended:

- ○ **Bach: Suites for Violoncello Solo** / Bylsma / 1992 / Sony 48047
- ○ **Bach: Suites for Solo Cello Complete** / Starker / 1991 / Mercury 432756
- ○ **Bach: 6 Cello Suites** / Casals / 1997 / EMI 66215
- ○ **Bach: Cello-Suiten** / Rostropovich / 1995 / EMI 55363
- ○ **Bach: Suite 1 in G, Veress: Sonata for violoncello** / Demenga / 1993 / ECM 437440

Cello Suite No. 2 in D minor, BWV 1008 (ca. 1720)

The *Suite in D minor* is one of two minor-key suites among the six for solo cello. With this suite, Bach seems to aspire to an almost Beethovenian mixture of tragedy and defiance, all within his usual framework of strict procedures. There are six movements: a Prelude, Allemande, Courante, Sarabande, double Minuet, and Gigue.

The Prelude reminds this listener of a great Bach organ toccata (and some observers, indeed, have speculated on links between Bach's organ improvisations and his string writing). Bach uses a simple arpeggio figure to build phrases of ever-increasing complexity, as in the parallel passage in the first suite. But here the minor-key arpeggio that sets the tone for the work is used to gradually build tension as it climbs through the cello's range in a series of rising waves. The movement builds to a high-pitched, tense climax, followed by an improviser's silence while the echoes die out. Finally we return to the low strings for a coda that sums up the movement in small, intimate terms.

Each of the movements that follow offers its own take on tragedy and defiance, but the moments that best characterize this suite include the unusual and dramatic double Minuet and the resigned Sarabande. Mstislav Rostropovich memorably described the latter movement as an essay in "white-hot solitude," and its stylized dirge and ringing open fifths recall the laments of the great masters of the French viol tradition. This suite, perhaps above all the others, compels the listener's attention through the contrast between the graceful and courtly language of the French dances that constitute the suite form and the dark, sinewy meat of Bach's own compositional thinking. At the end the Gigue wraps things up with angular rhythms and violent, unrelenting passions. But Bach isn't done with us yet; this movement prepares for the sunniness of the next suite in the set. *—James Liu*

Recommended:

- ○ **Bach: Suites for Violoncello Solo** / Bylsma / 1992 / Sony 48047
- ○ **Bach: Suites for Solo Cello Complete** / Starker / 1991 / Mercury 432756
- ○ **Bach: The 6 Unaccompanied Cello Suites** / Ma / 1983 / Sony 37867
- ○ **Bach: Cello Suites 1–6** / Casals / 2000 / Naxos 110915-16
- ○ **Jacqueline du Pré: Early BBC Recordings 1961 - 1965** / Du Pré / 1999 / EMI 73377

Cello Suite No. 3 in C major, BWV 1009 (ca. 1720)

The *Suite in C major* is probably the most popular of Bach's six suites for solo cello, among cellists and listeners alike. How could one resist the work's mix of nobility, exuberance, and relative contrapuntal simplicity? Casals, who more than any other performer brought these suites to the forefront of the cello repertory, found in it a heroic quality. Yet this suite also has close ties to its brethren. The Prelude recalls the discursive improvisatory flavor of the second suite, but opens with a descending figure and a mood of bright sunshine instead of the study in tragedy and tension that the second suite undertakes from the beginning. The Prelude also makes brilliant use of a mighty pedal point; a single note is held in the bass register while a series of progressively richer and richer figures build tension, pushing harder and harder for resolution. A similar figure is used to heighten a sense of pathos in the Prelude to the *St. John Passion.* Here, however, the pedal point develops instead into an expression of great warmth and happiness.

After the Prelude come a lively Allemande, a Courante, a Sarabande, a double Bourrée, and a Gigue. The Sarabande proceeds in a series of triple and quadruple stops that offer the cellist plenty of room for gutsy expressiveness and at the same time outline the implied polyphony that so fascinates those who hear these works. For this suite, as in the fourth suite, Bach uses a pair of Bourrées for the galant element. These reinforce the sense of buoyant optimism that pervades the work, though a sudden minor-key turn in the second Bourrée reminds us that no triumph is ever complete. But the final Gigue restores the lightness of this bouncy, virtuosic suite, perhaps the most idiomatic to the cello of all six suites. *—James Liu*

Recommended:

- ○ **Bach: Suites for Violoncello Solo** / Bylsma / 1992 / Sony 48047
- ○ **Bach: Suites for Solo Cello Complete** / Starker / 1991 / Mercury 432756
- ○ **Bach: 6 Cello Suites** / Casals / 1997 / EMI 66215
- ○ **Bach: Cello-Suiten** / Rostropovich / 1995 / EMI 55363
- ○ **Bach: 6 Cello Suites BWV 1007–1012** / ter Linden / 2002 / Harmonia Mundi 2907346/47

Cello Suite No. 4 in E flat major, BWV 1010 (ca. 1720)

The six Bach suites for solo cello may be arranged according to their modern, galant dance movements into three pairs (Nos. 1 and 2 use Minuets, Nos. 3 and 4 Bourrées, and Nos. 5 and 6 Gavottes). They also form two sequences of three in terms of key and mood (major-minor-major), and the *Suite in E flat major* opens the second group of three. This second group goes beyond the first group of three in its contrapuntal density and in its sense of untrammeled imagination. So we encounter in the opening movement the use of a repetitive arpeggio to build complex phrases, as in the first suite. But here the sense of improvisatory fantasy is stronger: the arpeggio descends in a gradual figure and varies negligibly as it explores a range of keys. Bach alternates this descending arpeggio pattern with three wave-like cadenzas that rise and fall in a faster rhythm and gradually begin to sound more and more like the arpeggio figures, until both emerge in a triumphant E flat major. The broken-up texture and the structural ambition remind one of Bach's large, quasi-improvisatory organ pieces.

This extension and stretching of ideas from the earlier suites pervades the remainder of the fourth suite. The Allemande and Courante have simple lines, like those in the first suite, and the stately Sarabande seems like an optimistic take on its counterpart in the second suite. The Sarabande is noteworthy for its startlingly consistent maintenance of the texture of melody line with harmonic accompaniment—on a single cello! The main section of the double Bourrée seems to implement a call-and-response illusion with a single line, while the second section offers a lovely contrast with a limpid, quiet succession of quarter notes and textural simplicity. The quirky rhythms of the Gigue confirm that this is new ground, deeper in its multi-instrument contrapuntal illusions, more ambitious in scope and depth. And this finale in turn prepares us for the glories of the final two suites. *—James Liu*

Recommended:

- ○ **Bach: Suites for Violoncello Solo** / Bylsma / 1992 / Sony 48047
- ○ **Bach: Suites for Solo Cello Complete** / Starker / 1991 / Mercury 432756
- ○ **Bach: The Unaccompanied Cello Suites** / Ma / 1983 / Sony 37867
- ○ **Bach: Cello-Suiten** / Rostropovich / 1995 / EMI 55363
- ○ **Bach: Cello Suites** / Rosen / 1994 / John Marks Records 06
- ○ **Bach: 6 Suites per violoncello solo senza basso** / Wispelwey / 1998 / Channel Classics 12298

Cello Suite No. 5 in C minor, BWV 1011 (ca. 1720)

Bach's fifth cello suite, in C minor, continues the experiments with texture, style, and counterpoint undertaken in the first four works in the set of six. It calls for the top string of the cello to be played scordatura, in this case tuned down from A to G. This affects the sonority of the open string and the overtones produced when played with other strings, creating a distinctive effect. Some cellists disregard the unusual tuning specification, but doing so adds to the work's already formidable technical challenges.

The fifth suite's Prelude replaces the toccata-like movements of the rest of the set with an overture in the French style, beginning with a slow, moody Adagio introduction with dense chords and irregular rhythms. These lead into an Allegro section where a fugue-like counterpoint is implied but not explicitly played.

The Allemande and Courante have a mournfulness reminiscent of their counterparts in the second suite, but feature richer, denser chording. But as much as Bach explores the contrapuntal possibilities of the cello here, his truly sublime achievement is the Sarabande. It offers some 100 notes of one-voice, single-line playing, with no chords and an unchanging rhythmic pattern. And yet its mix of great leaps and leading tones convey a lifetime of sorrow and wisdom. The harmonic structure is haunting, providing one point of tension after another with little resolution until the very end. The Gavotte galanterie is chordal and anguished again despite its name, but the final Gigue closes on a much more ambiguous, hushed note than does its D minor relative. *—James Liu*

Recommended:

- ○ **Bach: Suites for Violoncello Solo** / Bylsma / 1992 / Sony 48047
- ○ **Bach: Suites for Solo Cello Complete** / Starker / 1991 / Mercury 432756
- ○ **Bach: 6 Suiten für violoncello** / Casals / 1997 / EMI 66215
- ○ **Bach: The 6 Unaccompanied Cello Suites** / Ma / 1993 / Sony 37867

Cello Suite No. 6 in D major, BWV 1012 (ca. 1720)

As unique and extraordinary as each of Bach's other five cello suites are, the *Suite No. 6* is perhaps the most ambitious, strangest, richest of all. For this suite, Bach chose the key of D major, the triumphant key of his *Magnificat* and the "Dona nobis pacem" which concludes the *Mass in B minor.* He also calls for a five-stringed variant on the cello, though the work is playable on a conventional (four-stringed) cello. With these resources, Bach calls for resounding joy, carefully implied harmonies, and a rich, dense counterpoint that tests the cellist's skills to the maximum.

The Prelude, in a steady triple meter, is the only place in the set where Bach employed the dynamic markings (forte and piano), to simulate the effect of a Vivaldi-like echo sonata with phrases calling, responding, and gradually growing and developing into a fast-moving and playful cadenza and an untroubled recapitulation. With each suite Bach continues his progression away from simple dance-like structural roots. Melodic leaps are introduced in the fourth suite, chords in the fifth suite, and a subtle mix of chords, leaps, and implied harmonies, which become as important as the melodies, in the sixth suite. Indeed, this suite comes close in its technical challenges to the polyphonic simulations that Bach created in the partitas and sonatas for solo violin.

Joy takes many forms in this suite, from the echo-sonata textures of the Prelude to the stately grace and implied bass harmonies of the Allemande and Sarabande, and the homophonic march-like Courante. But the most unusual movement here must be the double Gavotte, where the subsections call for wide chords and melody over a ground bass, almost resembling a hurdy-gurdy playing at a peasant celebration. Its like wouldn't be heard again until Zoltán Kodály took up solo cello writing some 200 years later. The Gigue culminates this suite, and this great cycle, with a duet for solo cello, where the two interlocking voices gradually climb the scale, ascending to a high climax and sweeping back down to finish. *—James Liu*

Recommended:

- ○ **Bach: Suites for Violoncello Solo** / Bylsma / 1992 / Sony 48047
- ○ **Bach: Suites for Solo Cello Complete** / Starker / 1991 / Mercury 432756

○ **Bach: 6 Cello Suites** / Casals / 1997 / EMI 66215

○ **Bach: Cello-Suiten** / Rostropovich / 1995 / EMI 55363

○ **Hosokawa, Bach, Yun** / Demenga / 2002 / ECM 461862

Flute Sonatas (ca. 1724–1741)

In Bach's day, two quite distinctive instruments had the generic name of "flute": the transverse flute (today's normal orchestral flute), and the recorder, or "block flute." Bach composed extensively for both in his orchestral and choral works, but his sonatas were all written for the transverse flute. There are four authenticated sonatas. Two, in B minor (BWV 1030) and A (BWV 1032) are scored for flute and obbligato keyboard, while the other two, in E minor (BWV 1034) and E (BWV 1035) were composed for flute and continuo. In addition there are two further sonatas, BWV 1031 in E flat, and BWV 1033 in C, attributed to Bach, but now considered to be of doubtful authenticity. Of these, BWV 1031 is a reworking of a trio by the Berlin flutist and composer Quantz. BWV 1020 in G minor is definitely spurious; it is probably the work of Bach's eldest son, Carl Philipp Emanuel. Most scholars are agreed that in their relatively simple structure and content these three works fall in some way short of the quality found in the four authenticated sonatas.

Although these four works are believed by some authorities to date from Bach's years as Kapellmeister in Cöthen (1717–23), a period when his duties called for new instrumental and orchestral works, their date of composition is by no means certain. They may indeed date from the later Leipzig period. Like the accompanied violin sonatas, both of the sonatas with obbligato keyboard (i.e., with the keyboard part fully written out, as opposed to written out in continuo harmonies) involve a greater degree of integration between the solo instrument and harpsichord than is customary in Baroque sonatas. Both these two works and the continuo *Sonata in E minor* are in concerto form, with the opening quick Allegro cast in the ritornello form familiar from the concertos of Vivaldi. The finest of all these works, the B minor, has a beautiful opening Andante which is among the most expansive and finely wrought of all Bach's movements of this kind. In this sonata Bach reverses the usual order of the succeeding movements, following the Andante with a Largo in siciliana rhythm before concluding with a fugal Presto that demands considerable agility from both flutist and harpsichordist. The *A Major Sonata* extends the concerto form even further, both first and last movements being in ritornello form. The more modern galant style of the *E major Sonata* has led to suggestions that it may have been the last to be composed, possibly during one of Bach's trips to the Berlin court of the flute-playing monarch Frederick the Great. *—Brian Robins*

Recommended:

○ **Bach: Flute Sonatas** / B. Kuijken, Demeyere / Accent 22150

Die Kunst der Fuge (Art of the Fugue), BWV 1080 (ca. 1749)

Johann Sebastian Bach never completed *The Art of Fugue*, BWV 1080. It is a collection of contrapuntal movements with no definite order of presentation or instrumentation. Movements have been added and taken away from the final score over the years. Since the revival of popular interest in Bach's music in the 1850s, historians have narrowed the margin of error regarding the history and performance of *The Art of Fugue* with impressive efficiency. What is certain is that it is among the most gripping instrumental works that exists, demonstrating practically every composing technique available to Bach.

The work was among his estate; he probably did not discuss the work with anyone, or there would have been more pressure to have its mysteries settled before his passing. His son, Carl Philipp Emanuel, found and published the work as he found it in 1751, still incomplete. It did not sell well. Originally it was thought that Bach had been working on it and died in a race to finish it. Research has proven that he began the piece in the early 1740s (he died in 1750) and returned to work on it further over the years. It has also intrigued alert listeners to hear the final, unfinished movement trail off with B flat, A, C, B natural, which in German musical terminology translates to the word "BACH." This poignant accident of history has done wonders for the general interest in the piece, though in its day the public considered this just shoddy, and C.P.E. Bach attempted to compensate purchasers with the inclusion of a well-known chorale prelude, which was not related to the rest of the work.

Listening to *The Art of Fugue* is hearing everything available to the composer of fugues, woven together better than any other composer has done, and rife with a sublime poetic energy. Throughout the twentieth century, a tenuously agreed upon arrangement of 22 movements makes up a most likely reliable incarnation of what the composer had in mind. It is slightly longer than 80 minutes in duration and alternates between keyboard and small ensemble as required. Most of it can be played on the keyboard, but exact instrumentation was not necessarily as specific in the early eighteenth century as it would be later on. The theme is not obscured at any point, though he sometimes reverses it, turns it upside down, or both, or combines these variations with the theme's original form, all performed concurrently. Simply writing a good canon takes skill, and what Bach manages with *The Art of Fugue* cannot be matched by anything in this regard, except perhaps a few of his other works, such as *The Musical Offering*. In spite of the technical/theoretical maelstrom *The Art of Fugue* leaves for scholars to wade into, there is nothing about its character to deter the casual listener. The opposite is true; it is almost impossible to find a more benevolent piece of music. One can listen to it for years with only a casual grasp of the greatness that lays amid the scintillating arabesques that pervade the material. Once entered into the world of this work, it will gradually reveal itself to maintain potency greater than most people expect music to be able to contain. *—John Keillor*

Recommended:

○ **Bach: Die Kunst der Fuge** / Savall (cond.) / 2001 / Alia Vox 9818

○ **Bach: The Art of Fugue** / Emerson SQ / 2003 / Deutsche Grammophon 000090802

○ **Bach: The Art of Fugue/Music Offering** / Marriner (cond.) / 1994 / Philips 442556

○ **Bach: Die Kunst der Fuge** / Moroney / Harmonia Mundi 1951169/70

Musikalisches Opfer (Musical Offering), BWV 1079 (1747)

Johann Sebastian Bach's *The Musical Offering*, BWV 1079, consists of 16 movements and is slightly longer than 50 minutes in duration, resulting from a challenge to develop a theme played for the composer by Frederick the Great. The meeting took place on May 7, 1747, and Bach's son, Carl Philipp Emanuel, who often accompanied Frederick in performances of chamber music, arranged for the two men to meet. By then, J.S. Bach, "the old Bach of Leipzig," was considered as a writer of old-fashioned music, but his improvising skills were still legendary. Frederick, the King of Prussia, did not approve of overly complicated music, clearly preferring the fashionable galant style to the complicated fugues of high Baroque music. In an apparent attempt to confound the old master, the monarch offered an awkward chromatic subject for the elderly composer to improvise upon, and was amazed by Bach's handling of this "Royal Theme." Afterward, the improviser insisted that he still had not done the theme justice, and that he would endeavor to do so. Later that year, *The Musical Offering* appeared in print, dedicated to Frederick the Great, and published at the composer's own expense. It demonstrates the full arsenal of the Baroque composer of fugues and does it with more fluency than any other composer of the time would have been able to provide. Of course, it takes into account the monarch's passion for flute playing and offers a prominent part for the instrument.

Unfortunately, this gesture of respect and reverence more or less backfired. The flute part is fiendishly difficult, and there is no allowance for the monarch's clear preference for galant music; it is as Baroque as anything else Bach wrote, except where he takes galant ideas and makes them more Baroque. For example, instead of performing a simple "sigh" gesture in the flute sonata movement, a descending interval that sounds like a sigh, Bach sequences it in different pitches until it is as difficult and Baroque as anything as he had written before. Galant music is meant to be simple, a return to melody over harmony, and is the first step toward the Classical music of Haydn and Mozart. Furthering the conflict between Bach's offering and Frederick's goodwill was the theological inferences imbedded in the music. Much of it is in a holy code that was clearly derivative of church music and Frederick, a man of the enlightenment, had little use for anything liturgical. In the centuries that divide the composer's world-view and the current millennium, the many Lutheran inferences of the music have lost the impact they once had.

The Musical Offering can be compared to *The Art of Fugue* for its thorough handling of the theme. The quality of the music is diverse, heavenly, and inexhaustible. It stands as one of the finest pieces of chamber music from the Baroque era, and is a favorite among musicians who enjoy a challenge. *—John Keillor*

Recommended:

○ **Bach: L'Offrande musicale** / Moroney, M. Cook, See, Holloway, ter Linden, / HM 1951260

○ **Bach: Musikalisches Opfer** / Savall (cond.), Le Concert des Nations / Alia Vox 9817

○ **Bach: Musical Offering** / Harnoncourt (cond.), Concentus Musicus Wien / 2000 / Teldec 81223

○ **Bach: Musical Offering** / S. Kuijken, W. Kuijken, G. Leonhardt, Kohnen, B. Kuijken, M. Leonhardt / 1997 / Seon 63189

Partita for solo violin No. 1 in B minor, BWV 1002 (ca. 1720)

Of Bach's three partitas for solo violin, the first is the most old-fashioned in its choice of dance movements. The work is structurally unusual among Bach's sonatas and partitas for solo instruments in that it consists of four pairs of movements, the second of each pair offering a variation (or, employing the French term *double*) on the first. Another nod to older forms is the overall layout of the movements; the pairs fall into the slow-fast-slow-fast pattern of the church sonata or sonata da chiesa. To complicate matters, each *double* is much faster than the movement it varies. The work is technically challenging, generally more difficult than the third partita but not as tough as the second, the famous *Chaconne* of which is clotted with double and triple stops.

The opening Allemanda announces that it's not for sissy violinists with an immediate series of double stops (which were easier to play in Bach's time than today, thanks to the convex Baroque bow). This is a typical example of the allemanda (or allemande), a slow, serious German dance in quadruple meter and binary form, its improvisational-seeming melodies refusing to conform to the expected phrases. Its "Double" is faster and in 2/2, following the same contours as the original melodies, but now filling them in with even runs of notes. The "Correnta" is the Italian version of the dance form known in French as courante: fairly fast, in 3/4, sawing up and down the scale. Its 'Double," marked Presto, again rolls all over the staff, but the notes now fly by almost as fast as possible. The mood becomes somber with the Sarabande, the only movement in this partita to receive the French version of its title. Indeed, unlike the common Italian model, this French Sarabande is slow (in 3/4 meter) and expressive, its second half almost entirely in double stops. Its "Double" switches to 9/8 and increases the tempo, but the mood remains questioning and unsettled; at least Bach now eases off the multiple stops. Finally comes a movement in *Tempo di Borea* (related to the bourée), fast and sharply accented in a meter marked 2/4 but really feeling more like 2/2; again, Bach employs multiple stops through most of this movement. Its "Double" is in 12/4, the shape of the original melody obscured by the fast, nonstop passagework. *—James Reel*

Recommended:

- ○ **Bach: Sonatas & Partitas for Solo Violin** / Szeryng / DG 453004
- ○ **Bach: Complete Sonatas & Partitas for Solo Violin** / Grumiaux / 1993 / Philips 438736
- ○ **Bach: Sonatas & Partitas BWV 1001–1006** / S. Kuijken / 1990 / DHM 77043
- ○ **Works for Solo Violin** / Mullova / Philips 420948
- ○ **Leonid Kogan Legacy Volume XIII** / L. Kogan / Arlecchino 46
- ○ **Bach: Sonatas and Partitas BWV 1001–1006** / S. Vegh / 1997 / Auvidis Valois 4427

Partita for solo violin No. 2 in D minor, BWV 1004 (ca. 1720)

Alongside Paganini's *24 Caprices for solo violin* and Bach's six cello suites, his Partitas and Sonatas (three apiece) for solo violin stand out among their comparatively few siblings as magnificent music written for an unaccompanied stringed instrument. And while they also represent the zenith of polyphonic writing for a non-keyboard instrument, Bach's Sonatas and Partitas were also crucially important in the development of violin technique. With their colossal scope, huge technical demands, and musical complexity, and notwithstanding their awesome intellectual intensity, these creations greatly transcended anything that had preceded them, including the Partitas for solo violin by von Westhoff (1696), and various comparable solo works by Biber, Pisendel, and others. It seems most probable that either the Dresden virtuosi Pisendel or Volumier, or even more likely the Cöthen Konzertmeister Spiess, would have been the first players to attempt these exceptionally challenging works, all of which sound as if they were written for an age of instrumental virtuosity that still lay far in the future.

The sonatas are restricted to four movements (slow-fast-slow-fast, as with the early sonata da chiesa), one of which is a fugue. The Partitas are generally more extended, and of unorthodox formal design (as perhaps is implied by their more wide-ranging generic title), and by the more exploratory, improvisatory feel of the music even as they consist of sequences of Baroque dances. The awesome and eloquent *Partita No. 2 in D minor,* BWV 1004, seems for the most part to follow the conventional outline of the Baroque suite, opening with an earnest and purposeful Allemanda unexpectedly free of chordal multiple-stopping. There follow a Corrente and a Sarabanda, whose brief coda furnishes the link with the succeeding Giga.

However, this work concludes with the most labyrinthine and intellectually powerful single movement ever devised for an unaccompanied string instrument. This is Bach's famous Chaconne (originally "Ciaccona"), a colossal arched series of 64 stunning variants upon the stark, open-ended four-measure phrase heard at the beginning. Two monumental outer sections in the minor enclose a major-key central episode, and this great structure encompasses every aspect of violin-playing technique and contrapuntal ingenuity that would have been known in Bach's day. The Chaconne, whose duration exceeds 15 minutes (and is thus longer than the rest of the work put together) is often performed as a free-standing movement and has also been widely transcribed for other instruments. *—Michael Jameson*

Recommended:

- ○ **Bach: Sonatas & Partitas BWV 1001–1006** / S. Kuijken / 1990 / DHM 77043
- ○ **Bach: Sonaten & Partiten** / Milstein / DG 457701
- ○ **Bach: Complete Sonatas & Partitas for Solo Violin** / Grumiaux / 1993 / Philips 438736
- ○ **Bach Works for Violin Solo** / L. St. John / 1996 / Well-Tempered 5180
- ○ **Bach: Sonatas and Partitas for Solo Violin** / E. Wallfisch / 1997 / Hyperion 22009

Partita for solo violin No. 3 in E major, BWV 1006 (ca. 1720)

Although J.S. Bach described his six sonatas and partitas for solo violin as *Libro primo* (Book 1), he never followed them up with a second volume; so the *Partita for solo violin No. 3 in E major,* BWV 1006 (Cöthen, 1720), stands as the composer's last utterance in the unlikely medium of the unaccompanied violin. There were some solo violin works that predate Bach's efforts—Biber's *Passacaglia,* Westhoff's *Six Partitas*—but they cannot compare.

This *Partita* is perhaps the most exuberant and cheery of the three in the book; while it is no picnic in the park for the violinist, it offers easier going than the chaconne in the second partita with its strings of double and triple stops. The work consists of dance movements that are mostly French in origin and that diverge from those in the other two: Preludio, Loure, Gavotte en Rondeau, Menuet I and II, Bourrée, and Gigue. The Preludio, which was adapted by Bach for use in two of his cantatas, proceeds almost entirely in brilliant sixteenth notes. A Loure is a slow subspecies of French jig, usually (as is the case here) in 6/4 time; Bach's is perhaps a less heavy dance than the average loure. The Gavotte is, as the name suggests, set up as a kind of rondo, with restatements of the opening material surrounding contrasting episodes; the happy gavotte tune is played five times in all (six if one counts the repeat of the opening eight bars). The two Menuets are traditionally played da capo with the end result: Menuet I—Menuet II—Menuet I. The Bourrée is short and rapid. A gigue can be either French in style or Italian; Bach selects the quicker, snappier Italian variety to close the *E major Partita.*

Bach at some point transcribed the entirety of this *Partita* for solo lute; that version is known as BWV 1006a. *—Blair Johnston*

Recommended:

- ○ **Bach: Sonatas & Partitas BWV 1001–1006** / S. Kuijken / 1990 / DHM 77043
- ○ **Bach: Sonaten & Partiten** / Milstein / DG 457701
- ○ **Bach: Complete Sonatas & Partitas for Solo Violin** / Grumiaux / 1993 / Philips 438736
- ○ **Bach: Sonatas and Partitas for Solo Violin** / E. Wallfisch / 1997 / Hyperion 22009
- ○ **Bach 2000 Vol. 124: Sonatas and Partitas BWV 1004–1006** / Zehetmair / 2000 / Teldec 81229

Sonata for solo violin No. 1 in G minor, BWV 1001 (ca. 1720)

The first work in J.S. Bach's *Sei Solo a Violino senza Basso accompagnato, Libro Primo* (Six Solos for violin without accompaniment, Book 1, all composed in 1720—pity that he never fashioned a "Book 2") is also the most frequently played of the lot: the *Sonata No. 1 in G minor,* BWV 1001. Of the three sonatas in the volume (there are three sonatas and three partitas), the G minor is technically the simplest and also the shortest, making it a good entry-point for the violinist looking to tackle this magnificent volume of music. However, its greater accessibility vis-à-vis the other two sonatas in no way implies that it is somehow a less sophisticated piece of music—indeed, its riches run as deep as those of any of the other pages in the volume, the great *Chaconne* of BWV 1004 included. Each of the three sonatas for solo violin is set in the slow-fast-slow-fast four-movement pattern of the sonata da chiesa, and in each the second movement is a fugue. In BWV 1001 the movements are: Adagio, Fuga, Siciliana, and Presto.

The Adagio is a wildly, but very elegantly, embellished progression of harmonies. All the embellishments, and embellishments mean not only little turns, appoggiaturas, and the like, but also whole melodic gestures, scales, and small arpeggios, are written out quite carefully by Bach—the result is a work that might sound improvised but is most definitely not. The G minor Fuga is the most compact of the three fugues in the volume (and note that these are not in fact fugues in the proper sense of the word, but rather a kind of fugue/Baroque-concerto hybrid form). It was transcribed for lute by Bach at some later time (BWV 1000). The Siciliana is a gentle thing in B flat major; the main melody is played in the lowest register of the instrument while a warm commentary unfolds in the upper register. The Presto finale is a moto perpetuo in sixteenth notes whose 3/8 meter has at times a hint of cross-rhythm to it. *—Blair Johnston*

Recommended:

- ○ **Bach: Sonatas & Partitas BWV 1001–1006** / S. Kuijken / 1990 / DHM 77043
- ○ **Bach: Complete Sonatas & Partitas for Solo Violin** / Grumiaux / 1993 / Philips 438736
- ○ **Bach: Sonatas & Partitas for Violin** / Szeryng / DG 453004
- ○ **Bach: Sonatas & Partitas** / J. Heifetz / 1994 / RCA 0902661748

Sonata for solo violin No. 2 in A minor, BWV 1003 (ca. 1720)

According to the manuscripts of Bach's *Sonatas and Partitas for Solo Violin* BWV 1001–06, the six pieces were completed in 1720, while the composer was employed at the Cöthen court. At Cöthen, Bach devoted himself primarily to the composition of instrumental music; this period saw the composition of the *Brandenburg Concertos,* the violin and keyboard concertos, the orchestral suites and the first part of the *Well-Tempered Clavier,* among other works. Often Bach composed works of each genre in cycles, with six works in each.

In the case of the *Sonatas and Partitas for Solo Violin,* Bach alternated three sonatas with three partitas. The partitas consist of between five and eight dance movements, while the sonatas are in four movements, none of which is a dance except the third movement of the first sonata, in G minor, which is a Siciliana. Throughout these six works there is evidence of not only Bach's knowledge of the technical capabilities of the violin, but also of his ability to create dense counterpoint and effective harmony with one stringed instrument. The solo violin sonatas were first published between 1817 and 1828.

A rhapsodic Grave opens the second Sonata, in A minor, (BWV 1003). At such a slow tempo, the highly ornamented melody seems to meander at will, navigating a course of highly contrasting rhythms and decorative flourishes that release the melodic potential of the minor mode. The overall "free" nature of the Grave makes it sound like a prelude to the ensuing movement. As in all three of the violin sonatas, the second movement, the central point of the piece, is a fugue. Daunting in both size and complexity, the Fugue pushes forward relentlessly, creating a dense contrapuntal web. Bach sets the third movement apart from the others through both an Andante tempo and contrasting key. The writing is more homophonic here, with a calm melody that provides a needed foil to the harsh energy of the preceding Fugue. A lively, lighthearted Allegro, rich with rhythmic and melodic variations, returns to A minor and closes the piece. *—John Palmer*

Recommended:

- ○ **Bach: Sonatas & Partitas BWV 1001–1006** / S. Kuijken / 1990 / DHM 77043
- ○ **Bach: Complete Sonatas & Partitas for Solo Violin** / Grumiaux / 1993 / Philips 438736
- ○ **Bach: Sonates & Partitas for Solo Violin** / S. Vegh / 1999 / Auvidis 4865
- ○ **Bach Sonatas for Unaccompanied Violin** / Milstein / 2001 / EMI 66869
- ○ **Bach 2000 Vol. 123: Sonatas & Partitas BWV 1001–1003** / Zehetmair / 2000 / Teldec 81230

Sonata for solo violin No. 3 in C major, BWV 1005 (ca. 1720)

The first two sonatas and the three partitas of J.S. Bach's six sonatas and partitas for solo violin make considerable demands on performers. However, the *Sonata for solo violin No. 3 in C major,* BWV 1005 is in a class by itself; it is so challenging a piece on every front that even the usually unflappable Jascha Heifetz used to break out in a cold sweat and suffer nervous bow-shakes when playing it, and it is a work of such consummate mastery, so perfectly planned and balanced, that any flaw in the performance sticks out like a sore thumb. In all fairness, Bach has gone beyond the bounds of reason in this grand *Sonata*—the violinist is asked to play music that might give a harpsichordist a headache (indeed, Bach arranged the *Sonata's* first movement for harpsichord)—but the music is so rewarding that all the toil is worth it in the end. Surely this satisfaction comes in part from the unreal, some have even said mystical, effect of a single string instrument producing such rich, dense music without the benefit of any real bass capability. Like each of the other two sonatas in the solo violin volume, the *C major Sonata* has four movements. They are: Adagio, Fuga, Largo, and Allegro assai.

Whereas the opening movements of the previous two solo violin sonatas are written in highly embellished, mock-improvisational style, that of the third sonata lacks ornamentation altogether. Instead it evolves from a single, repeating dotted rhythm—one harmonic layer is added and then another, the steady pulsation being interrupted only twice (once near the beginning and once near the end) for the purpose of expanded and enriching major cadences. The Fuga, which, like all the solo violin fugues, is actually a fugue/Baroque concerto hybrid, ranks among the longest fugues, measure-wise, ever created by any composer for any instrument or ensemble. The subject is derived from the chorale *"Komm, heiliger Geist"* and is turned upside-down midway through the fugue. The splendid Largo in F major has achieved some fame outside the *Sonata,* while the Allegro assai finale is the same kind of fleet-footed binary-form piece that closes each of the other two solo violin sonatas. *—Blair Johnston*

Recommended:

- ○ **Bach: Sonatas & Partitas BWV 1001–1006** / Kuijken / 1990 / DHM 77043
- ○ **Bach: Complete Sonatas & Partitas for Solo Violin** / Grumiaux / 1993 / Philips 438736
- ○ **Sonatas and Partitas Vol. 2** / Podger / 1999 / Channel Classics 14498
- ○ **Bach Sonatas for Unaccompanied Violin** / Milstein / 2001 / EMI 66869

Sonatas for violin & keyboard (1717–1723)

Johann Sebastian Bach's six sonatas for violin and harpsichord were written while the composer was working for Prince Leopold of Cöthen, between 1717 and 1723. This was Bach's only fully secular position, and the modest amount of chamber music that survives from this period was presumably, considering the Prince's enthusiasm for music and Bach's generally prolific rate of production, the tip of a veritable iceberg. The violin sonatas, like the *Brandenburg Concertos* of roughly the same time, follow Italian models (with a melodic idiom and an alternation of fast and slow movements), but at many junctures add touches of contrapuntal density so characteristic of the composer. Their most notable feature is the active role taken by the harpsichord, which instead of simply providing chordal continuo support enters into melodic and contrapuntal dialogue with the violin. They are, in effect, trio sonatas, with the harpsichord's right hand becoming a second solo "instrument," and the left hand taking the usual continuo role. In this respect Bach, normally considered a conservative composer, seemed far ahead of his time. In addition to the six works (BWV 1014–1019) known as sonatas for violin and harpsichord, there are two works (BWV 1021 and 1023) designated sonatas for violin and basso continuo; these were probably composed slightly earlier. Several other such sonatas are of dubious authenticity. *—AMG*

Recommended:

- ○ **Bach: Complete Sonatas for Violin & Obbligato Harpsichord** / Podger, Pinnock / 2000 / Channel Classics 14798

Viola da gamba Sonata No. 1 in G major, BWV 1027 (ca. 1720)

Johan Sebastian Bach's appointment as Kapellmeister at the city of Cöthen was basically a happy one, not because of any great esteem inherent in the title but because the Prince of Cöthen was a true music lover with a voracious appetite for the kind of pure instrumental music that the composer had had little time for in his previous position. This work is in fact an arrangement of the *Trio Sonata for two flutes and basso continuo in G major,* BWV 1039, composed around the same time, a process of musical reevaluation that bears witness to what is arguably Bach's most important contribution to the development of eighteenth century chamber music: the elevation of the harpsichord from subordinate, partly improvised basso continuo to equal (sometimes superior), fully written-out musical partner in the duo sonata style.

The process in reality was simple, requiring only that the right hand of the harpsichord assume the role of the missing third instrument; in the case of this sonata, the flute part not taken over by the keyboardist is moved down to a register more congenial to the viola da gamba. The normal four-movement mold of the Baroque sonata da chiesa is at work in this piece: Adagio, Allegro ma non tanto, Andante, Allegro moderato. The strong movement-to-movement connection is most easily seen and heard in the way that the opening Adagio, in luxuriantly flowing 12/8 time, has no final cadence of its own but rather connects directly to the following Allegro via a half cadence (cunningly, the opening movement winds down to G minor, the major mode appearing only as the next movement begins). Both these first two movements open in the traditional imitative style of the Baroque trio sonata. A third of the way into the Allegro ma non tanto movement, Bach turns the melody upside down and proceeds to give it a new contrapuntal treatment; two-thirds of the way in, the original form of the subject returns over a dramatic dominant pedal. Far less energetic and outgoing is the languid Andante, whose ever-repeating sixteenth note mini-arpeggios and broken bass octaves cover a wide and colorfully chromatic harmonic distance in just 18 bars of music. A wonderful moment, radiant within the movement's languid E minor tonality, is achieved when Bach arrives at D major at the exact midpoint. Once the eighth notes of the final Allegro moderato begin, they hardly ever rest. Bach seems to be thoroughly enjoying his contrapuntal prowess here, even in the very first measure, when the opening gesture of the harpsichord right hand is used, in inverted fashion, to initiate the bass line. *—Blair Johnston*

Recommended:

- ○ **Bach: Sonatas for Viola da Gamba** / Savall, Koopman / 2002 / Virgin 562065
- ○ **Bach: Three Gamba Sonatas; Brandenburg Concerto 4** / Casals, Baumgartner / 1994 / Sony 66572
- ○ **Bach: Sonates pour viole de gambe et clavecin** / Pandolfo, Alessandrini / HM 1955218

CONCERTO

Brandenburg Concerto No. 1 in F major, BWV 1046 (ca. 1717)

The *Brandenburg Concerto No. 1 in F major,* BWV 1046, is the first of six great concertos which, taken in combination, add up the most complex and artistically successful failed job application in recorded history. They were written around 1721 and dedicated to Christian Ludwig, Margrave of Brandenburg in March of the same year. Bach's position at Cöthen was becoming less desirable to him; his wife had died in 1720 while Bach accompanied his employer, Prince Leopold of Anthalt-Cöthen, to Carlsbad. The prince was also reallocating funds from music to his palace guard, no doubt because the prince's new wife was not a music lover.

Christian Ludwig probably heard Bach perform in 1719, or perhaps earlier at the spas in Carlsbad, where Prince Leopold would have Bach accompany him. Bach sent a beautifully rendered score of the concertos to the Margrave in 1721, suspecting that the royal might be interested in giving him a job, but there is no known response to Bach's political overture.

The first concerto is, like all of Bach's concertos, indebted to the methods of the Italians. Vivaldi was particularly attractive to the German composer, who eagerly copied out Vivaldi's scores in order to understand his use of contrast, rhythmic propulsion, and orchestration. The *Brandenburg Concertos* were not as unusual as was once thought; Italian composers created concertos for widely varying combinations of instruments, and Bach's shifting textures have their parallels in works by other composers. But the handling of the Italian concerto material went unmatched throughout the Baroque era. One unique, perhaps non-Italian idea in the *Brandenburg Concerto No. 1* is Bach's use of hunting horns. The concerto also calls for three oboes and a bassoon, as well as continuo strings and the violino piccolo. The sound of the horns stands out, but the composer manages to make them blend into the ensemble through the use of multiple winds.

Though the first movement does not have a tempo marking, performances of the four-movement work are about 20 minutes in duration. Each movement has a brisk pace and extraordinary counterpoint that inventively shades and blurs the contrast between the small concertino group and the tutti ensemble. Along with the horn, the violino piccolo seems to have been included in order to draw more attention to the innovative qualities of the music. The *Brandenburg Concertos* contain some of Bach's most brilliant counterpoint, and the attention-grabbing orchestration of the first concerto has not diminished the work's value at all. It is among Bach's best works. *—John Keillor*

Recommended:

- ○ **Bach: Brandenburg Concertos 1–3; Oboe Concertos** / Pinnock (cond.), English Concert / Archiv 471720
- ○ **Bach: Brandenburg Concertos; Orchestral Suites; Chamber Music** / R. Goebel (cond.), Musica Antiqua Köln / Archiv 471656
- ○ **Bach: Brandenberg Concertos** / Savall (cond.), Capella Reial de Catalunya, Le Concert des Nations / 2000 / Astree 9948

Brandenburg Concerto No. 2 in F major, BWV 1047 (ca. 1717)

Between 1719 and 1721, Bach assembled six concertos for Christian Ludwig, the Margrave of Brandenburg, either on commission or as a job application. The *Brandenburg Concerto No. 2* may have been one of the last to be written, and it certainly seems like a special-occasion piece. It's a concerto featuring four prominent instruments—trumpet, recorder, oboe, and violin—against a foundation of strings and continuo. The writing is virtuosic and brilliant; the high trumpet part, in particular, brings many fine players to grief. The work basically follows the Italian concerto grosso pattern, punctuating the solo group's music with tutti outbursts for the strings, although here the soloists are often more integrated into the musical fabric than in the Italian model. The strongly rhythmic first movement, lacking a tempo indication, deploys the soloists both as members of the overall ensemble and as out-front players, in varying combinations. The orchestra introduces an energetic eight-bar theme, then, two at a time and separated by restatements of the opening melody, the soloists jump in with their own two-bar motif. From this point on, the soloists rarely recede completely, constantly toying with their short motif and picking up fragments of the initial theme as well. The trumpet retires from the plaintive Andante, leaving the other three soloists, with bare continuo accompaniment, to focus on a sighing phrase. One instrument's entrance overlaps another's last notes in a sort of counterpoint that, despite several efforts, never gets off the ground. Revamping a theme from the first movement, the Allegro assai takes counterpoint more seriously. In the earlier movements, Bach had passed a melody from one instrument to another, fully exploiting their contrasting colors. Now, in this final movement, the soloists each provide different voices in a full-fledged fugue, with the string orchestra merely reinforcing key moments. This fugue is no academic exercise; the music is bright and festive, clearly intended to show how a learned structure could be incorporated into popular entertainment at the margrave's court. *—James Reel*

Recommended:

- ○ **Bach: Brandenburg Concertos 1–3; Oboe Concertos** / Pinnock (cond.), English Concert / Archiv 471720
- ○ **Bach: Brandenburg Concertos; Orchestral Suites; Chamber Music** / R. Goebel, Musica Antiqua Köln / Archiv 471656
- ○ **Bach: Brandenberg Concertos** / Savall (cond.), Capella Reial de Catalunya, Le Concert des Nations / 2000 / Astree 9948

Brandenburg Concerto No. 3 in G major, BWV 1048 (1721)

In 1721, J.S. Bach dedicated six orchestral pieces to Margrave Christian Ludwig of Brandenburg, ostensibly in response to a commission, but more likely as a sugar-coated job application. These pieces display a variety of styles, influences, and musical preoccupations and were probably not conceived of as a set. However, all of them share in Bach's great talent for absorbing new styles (among them the Italian concerto grosso) and then expanding and improving upon them. At any rate, the Margrave never thanked Bach, paid him a fee, staged a performance of the works, or offered him a position. Such was life, even for Bach.

The *Concerto No. 3 in G major* may have been written while Bach was at Weimar, given that it (along with Nos. 1 and 6) is reminiscent of the Italian concerto, a genre with which Bach was fascinated at the time. The motoric rhythm, clear melodic outline, and motivic construction owe a lot to the comparable works of Vivaldi, but the clarified harmony and more interesting counterpoint are unmistakably Bach's. The work's two main sections, both in G major (one alla breve, the other in 12/8 time), are separated by a brief Adagio which may be realized as a short violin cadenza. The concerto is written for three violins, three violas, and three cellos, with bass and continuo. The relationship between the instruments is subjective to the listener; as the positioning of the parts fluctuates, it may appear that there are no soloists, that the players are all soloists, or that the violins, violas, and cellos occupy their own solo groups. The Italian concerto grosso's distinction between concertino (a small group of soloists) and ripieno (the full ensemble) becomes in Bach's hands, and especially distinctively in the *Brandenburg Concerto No. 3*, a kaleidoscopic range of colors and shades. *—Allen Schrott*

Recommended:

- ○ **Bach: Brandenburg Concertos 1–3; Oboe Concertos** / Pinnock (cond.), English Concert / Archiv 471720
- ○ **Bach: Brandenburg Concertos 1–3** / Pinnock (cond.), English Concert / Archiv 410500
- ○ **Bach: Brandenberg Concertos** / Savall (cond.), Capella Reial de Catalunya, Le Concert des Nations / 2000 / Astree 9948

Brandenburg Concerto No. 4 in G major, BWV 1049 (ca. 1720)

It has been supposed that Johann Sebastian Bach composed this and five more *Brandenburg Concertos* between 1717 and 1721, at Cöthen, although work may have begun on some of them at Weimar after 1708. *No. 4* is scored for a concertino of solo violin and two *flûtes à bec* (i.e. recorders) and a ripieno of violins, violas, cellos, and continuo. We can be sure only that the concertos predated March 24, 1721, when he dedicated them collectively to Christian Ludwig, Margrave of Brandenburg, whom Bach probably met on his 1719 trip to Berlin to select a new harpsichord. Christian Ludwig may not have heard any, however; the composer's meticulously hand-copied score, fulsomely dedicated according to custom, eventually came into the possession of Frederick the Great's sister, Princess Amalie, who bequeathed it to a school library in Berlin.

The diversified character of these six concertos implies random composition. It was common practice in the Baroque era to use whatever instruments were available at any given time. Only the third and sixth concertos have no wind instruments (No. 6, indeed, has no violins, only lower strings). Bach carefully listed the "beak flute," or recorder, as a concertino instrument in concertos two and four; only in the Concerto No. 5 did he specify a flute. But flutists have appropriated both works since their rediscovery. Indeed, the emergence of the recorder from obscurity is so recent that few anywhere have been trained to perform Bach's demanding solo parts.

Like its companion works, *No. 4* is contrapuntally intricate and tightly argued; what sets it apart is a lightness of scoring that produces transparent textures. There is a prevailing gentleness, too—even in the swift fugal finale—that befits flutes (or recorders), although the solo violin part is ornately difficult. Indeed, the first movement's challenging violin part embodies a sort of dramatic confrontation between solo and orchestra that stands out as one extreme in the continuum of solo-orchestra relationships that these concertos so thoroughly explore. Both the first and second movements are in triple meter (3/8 in the opening Allegro; 3/4 in the gently melancholic, E minor Andante that follows), while the finale is alla breve (2/2). Despite a double bar, the Andante prepares us harmonically for the fugal games one is tempted to call antics in the finale. *—Roger Dettmer*

Recommended:

- ○ **Bach: Brandenburg Concertos 4–6; Triple Concerto** / Pinnock (cond.), English Concert / Archiv 474220
- ○ **Bach: Brandenburg Concertos; Orchestral Suites; Chamber Music** / R. Goebel (cond.), Musica Antiqua Köln / Archiv 471656
- ○ **Bach: Brandenberg Concertos** / Savall (cond.), Capella Reial de Catalunya, Le Concert des Nations / 2000 / Astree 9948

Brandenburg Concerto No. 5 in D major, BWV 1050 (ca. 1720)

Johann Sebastian Bach most likely completed his *Brandenburg Concerto No. 5 in D major*, BWV 1050, in 1721. This work is the fifth of six concertos the composer dedicated to Christian Ludwig, Margrave of Brandenburg. The offering was likely a sort of application for employment; Bach got no response, but these pieces have become some of his best-known material. Every one of the concertos is distinct, as are the composer's sets of suites and partitas. Hearing the fifth concerto in the context of the rest of the set makes it clear that, apart from Bach's inimitable strength as a contrapuntist, the key to his ability to make music that is both sublime and entertaining lies in the fact that in his hands, everything is elastic. No other composer of the Baroque era could write through the constraints of form as if it was not there at all. Bach saw more options than anyone else, in form and in influence. The way he blended the Italian sound into his own in these concertos ennobled both Italian and German music. The scope of his vision and his relentless invention, making everything he wrote new, frustrates any attempt at comparison.

This fifth concerto is scored for flute, solo violin, obbligato harpsichord, and strings. It is the only one of the six pieces to have any solo material given to the harpsichord, which is part of the continuo throughout the other works, filling out the harmonies. What is quite bizarre and beautiful about the opening movement is the way the solo instruments and string ensemble seem to be muscling in on each other's musical functions. More specifically, the ritornello is almost carried away by the soloists although it is normally the territory of the tutti ensemble. The harpsichord seems to be holding the work together, and there are episodes in the second half of the movement where everything has ground to a halt except for the harpsichord. At the end of the movement, the other soloists actually support the free-flowing harpsichord line. It is a sort of divide-and-conquer movement, with tutti versus soloists, and also soloists against soloists. The harpsichord wins. No one wrote music with this sort of free play of function before Bach.

The following two movements, briefer than the first, form an admirable contrast. The second movement is for soloists only, somber and cooperative. Though it is intimate and free of the first movement's tension, it is the most concerto-like movement in the traditional sense. This is a colossal irony, considering how the tensions of the concerto form were exploded in the first, which is as much a departure from the form as it is an adherent. The final movement is a charming dance, a lively gigue with fugal powers. *—John Keillor*

Recommended:

- ○ **Bach: Brandenburg Concertos 4–6; Triple Concerto** / Pinnock (cond.), English Concert / Archiv 474220
- ○ **Bach: Brandenburg Concertos; Orchestral Suites; Chamber Music** / R. Goebel (cond.), Musica Antiqua Köln / Archiv 471656
- ○ **Bach: Brandenberg Concertos** / Savall (cond.), Capella Reial de Catalunya, Le Concert des Nations / 2000 / Astree 9948

Brandenburg Concerto No. 6 in B flat major, BWV 1051 (ca. 1709)

Johann Sebastian Bach's *Brandenburg Concerto No. 6 in B flat major,* BWV 1051 is the final concerto in a set of works dedicated to Christian Ludwig, Margrave of Brandenburg. (It may actually have been the first composed, however.) They were intended as a job application, but the job did not appear.

Bach's sonic imagination was seemingly limitless, and for this final concerto he chose to limit the work's instrumentation to strings and continuo, meaning that the only non-bowed instrument heard is the harpsichord. Every other concerto in the set made extensive use of contrasting timbres, balancing the strings with the winds, often in unprecedented ways. This limitation of timbre is also extended to register; there are no violins, just two violas, two violas da gamba, a cello, and the violone, which is near the cello range and is from the gamba family. The overall effect of this decision is a spirit of repose and conclusion. There are no visceral contrasts in the music, though the final Allegro is faster than the other two movements; the concerto, whenever it was actually composed, makes a splendid way to end the overall set.

Bach's writing for these instruments was unconventional for the time. In the early eighteenth century the lower members of the violin family were considered orchestral instruments with supporting roles. They were given comparatively easy parts to play, while the gamba and its relatives were regarded as chamber instruments and necessarily received more difficult lines. Bach chose to reverse the level of difficulty, giving the viola and cello the tough solo parts, while the gamba players were free to cruise along in the supporting roles. In the second-movement Adagio, they are completely silent.

The form of the three-movement work is also filled with reversals. The opening movement sounds initially like a freely composed fugal arrangement, free of the stark contrasts normally associated with concerto form. Its ritornello, normally a focused bit of recurring melody, rambles along without drawing much attention to itself, while the music that is supposed to be spun out of the ritornello is concise and sharp. Compounding the irregularities further, the second movement (lovely and languid) ends in a different key from the one it starts in. The final movement assumes the character of a fugal gigue, but reveals itself to be a set of variations based on the initial ritornello, which is a much freer demonstration than the traditional spinning-out of the initial material.

Overall, these surprises result in what is in many ways is the most various and striking among the *Brandenburg Concertos*. Its beauty is equal to its invention. *—John Keillor*

Recommended:

- ○ **Bach: Brandenburg Concertos; Triple Concerto** / Pinnock (cond.), English Concert / Archiv 474220
- ○ **Bach: Brandenburg Concertos; Orchestral Suites; Chamber Music** / R. Goebel (cond.), Musica Antiqua Köln / Archiv 471656
- ○ **Bach: Brandenberg Concertos** / Savall (cond.), Capella Reial de Catalunya, Le Concert des Nations / 2000 / Astree 9948

Concerto for flute, violin, harpsichord & strings in A minor ("Triple"), BWV 1044 (ca. 1730)

Each of Bach's harpsichord concertos, save perhaps one, is really a new arrangement made by him of a concerto conceived for another solo instrument (invariably violin or oboe). A similar origin can be ascribed to the *Concerto for flute, violin, harpsichord, and strings in A minor,* BWV 1044 (the *Triple Concerto,* as it is known), though in the case of this most unusual of all Baroque concertos it is not another concerto, but rather two separate keyboard works that Bach plundered. The occasion for which Bach crafted the *Triple Concerto* is unknown, but it very likely falls among those works composed for performance by the Leipzig Collegium Musicum; a tentative composition date of ca. 1730–35 is usually assigned. Whereas in most of the harpsichord concertos Bach remains relatively true to his sources—the original solo part is of course fleshed out in wholly new ways and the tutti scoring is sometimes adapted to suit, but the course of the music usually remains largely untouched—in BWV 1044, Bach treats his two sources very freely indeed, so much so that one cannot really call the work a transcription or arrangement; it is, rather, a new composition "after" the other two. The two sources are: for the first and last of the *Concerto's* three movements, the *Prelude and Fugue in A minor for harpsichord,* BWV 894; and for the middle movement, the middle movement of the *Organ Sonata in D minor,* BWV 527. Throughout the triplet-driven opening *Allegro,* which takes its material only from the prelude half of BWV 1044, the harpsichord is utterly superior to the flute and the violin, who spend most of their time working out countermelodies to and brief commentaries on the harpsichord's often dense oratory (the *Concerto* is properly called a concerto for "harpsichord, flute, and violin," though one will hardly ever find the soli listed in that order). In the Adagio, ma non tanto, e dolce second movement, however, the flute and violin come to the fore, the former engaging in a pleasant pastoral dialogue with the harpsichord while the latter accompanies them with strolling pizzicati. Bach converts the fugue of BWV 1044 into an Alla breve movement, throughout which the harpsichordist again reigns supreme. *—Blair Johnston*

Recommended:

- ○ **Bach: Brandenburgische Konzerte** / R. Goebel (cond.), Musica Antiqua Köln / Archiv 423116
- ○ **Bach: Violin Concertos** / E. Wallfisch (cond.), C. MacIntosh, P. Nicholson, Orch. of the Age of Enlightenment / 1999 / Virgin 61558

Harpsichord Concerto No. 1 in D minor (or for 2 oboes & organ or for violin) BWV 1052 (1738–1739)

This concerto, composed during Johann Sebastian Bach's Cöthen period, is thought to be based on a lost violin concerto. It is clear from the manuscript notation that the concerto was composed for the two manuals of the harpsichord, but it is frequently performed on the single keyboard of the modern piano. The piece is composed in three movements; the first one was later used by Bach as an organ prelude, and the slow movement became the first chorus of his *Cantata No. 146, "Wir müssen durch viel Trübsal."*

Like most of Bach's instrumental concertos, this work employs the Italian ritornello form. The ritornello of the first movement is a driving six-bar unison theme whose opening five notes form the foundation for the majority of the movement. The theme's power stems from its ever-expanding leaps and its emphatic closing cadence. Most of the soloist's passages are derived from this theme, but Bach later introduces a chromatic, toccata-like secondary theme for effect. The ritornello immediately gives way to a carefully mapped progression through the neighboring keys, using the dominant minor, the relative major, the relative major of the dominant minor, and so forth. The soloist leads the concerto through sections of contrapuntal and harmonic exploration, interspersed with several varied restatements of the ritornello by the strings. Following an elaborate cadenza by the soloist, the first movement closes with a unison restatement of the ritornello. The slow second movement is in G minor, which is unusual in that most of Bach's concertos and sonatas that begin in a minor key have a second movement in a major key, and vice-versa. Like Bach's two violin concertos, the movement is built on a foundation of a solemn basso ostinato which also serves as the ritornello. The movement's structure is symmetrical, with the first half progressing from G minor to C minor, and then to a B flat major cadence; the progression then retraces its steps, through C minor and again back to G minor. Similarly, the opening and closing statements of the ritornello are both in unison. Throughout the piece, the soloist weaves an increasingly florid melody over the ground bass, adding a lyrical quality to the somber character of the movement. The Allegro finale movement is constructed in a similar manner to the opening movement. In 3/4 time, its opening 12-bar ritornello begins with a downward scale and has a recurring rhythmic figure consisting of two sixteenth notes and an eighth note. In parts of the ritornello, the melody is traded between the bass and treble. The first solo section is a toccata-like figure. The final statement of the ritornello is preceded by a short but elaborate cadenza, as in the first movement. *—David Kent*

Recommended:

- ○ **Bach: Harpsichord Concertos** / van Asperen (cond.), Melante Amsterdam / 1999 / Virgin 561716
- ○ **Bach: Complete Harpsichord Concertos** / Pinnock (cond.), English Concert / Archiv 471754
- ○ **Bach:Piano Concertos Nos. 1–5 & 7** / L. Bernstein (cond.), G. Gould, Columbia SO / 2002 / Sony 87760
- ○ **J. S. Bach: Keyboard Concertos & French Suite No. 5** / Marriner (cond.), Gavrilov, Academy of St. Martin-in-the-Fields / 1999 / EMI 73641

Harpsichord Concerto No. 2 in E major (or for oboe d'amore in F major) BWV 1053 (1738–1739)

While Johann Sebastian Bach is credited with many harpsichord concertos, it should be noted that most of these works are arrangements of works for other instruments, often by other composers. When, during the late 1730s, the Leipzig Collegium Musicum, of which he was director, put together some ad-hoc performances of music for harpsichord and orchestra, Bach's contribution was an arrangement of an old work. The *Harpsichord Concerto No. 2,* arranged in 1738 or 1739 and scored for the usual ensemble of soloist, strings, and basso continuo, is almost certainly derived from a concerto—now lost—for oboe or oboe d'amore and orchestra in F major, possibly composed by Bach during his tenure in Cöthen two decades earlier. It is a splendid work in the then-modern three-movement pattern, cheerful and gregarious. The concerto opens with the same kind of lengthy da capo Allegro movement that begins the *Violin Concerto in E major* and a handful of the *Brandenburg Concertos* (a kind of allegro that would have been rather old-fashioned by the late 1730s and early 1740s). The middle section of the movement is of the continuously developmental fortspinnung type, taking the basic melody of the tutti's ritornello and setting it up against one or another of several mock-improvisational digressions from the harpsichord; a strong close to C sharp minor is made, complete with dramatic grand pause, before the reprise of the opening ritornello. The second movement is a deliciously affected Siciliano in C sharp minor; the dotted rhythm melody as laid out by the violins in the opening bars of the movement and supported by some lush chromaticism in the parts below. Soon enough the harpsichord takes over the melodic thought, elaborating at great length against a transparent chordal background. The opening tutti is called upon once more to provide a finish. Bach casts the third movement, Allegro again, in a three-part da capo design very similar to the one used in the first movement. Here, however, a joyous 3/8 meter is at work, and one catches a hint of a gigue from time to time. A nice rising chromatic idea in eighth notes pops up during the less stable middle portion and is set up sequentially against some strong unison cadential gestures in the strings; soon the ritornello melody begins to sneak back in bits and pieces. Again, Bach makes a powerful cadence to the minor mode (this time G sharp) before conjuring up the reprise of the happy opening ritornello. *—Blair Johnston*

Recommended:

- ○ **Bach: Harpsichord Concertos BWV 1053–1057** / G. Leonhardt (cond.), Leonhardt Consort / 2000 / Teldec 81219
- ○ **J. S. Bach: Keyboard Concertos & French Suite 5** / Marriner (cond.), Gavrilov, Academy of St. Martin-in-the-Fields / 1999 / EMI 73641
- ○ **Bach: Keyboard Concertos 2, 3 & 7** / Golschmann (cond.), G. Gould, Columbia SO / 2001 / Sony 87761

Harpsichord Concerto No. 3 in D major, BWV 1054 (1738–1739)

Johann Sebastian Bach's *Harpsichord Concerto No. 3 in D major,* BWV 1054, is an adaptation of his own *Violin Concerto in E major,* BWV 1042. He made it sometime during the 1730s for performance by the Leipzig Collegium Musicum—a large ensemble made up of the city's music enthusiasts that played in taverns and coffee shops a few times a week. Bach, since 1729, had been director. Most, if not all, of Bach's harpsichord concertos are transcriptions of concertos for other instruments, but only in a few cases have those source pieces survived. A piece like BWV 1054 provides us with a wonderful opportunity to examine just how Bach went about recasting the old material into a new and very individual work for harpsichord.

The most obvious change by far is the transposition from E major down to D major (the second movement is moved from C sharp minor down to B minor accordingly)—standard operating procedure for the harpsichord transcriptions, in this case especially fortunate because the highest notes of the solo part in the violin version go a whole tone above what was possible on the normal harpsichord of the day. The course of the music remains unchanged, but the solo part cannot claim the same thing: the basic shapes in the part remain the same (they are filled out to exploit the harpsichord's polyphonic capabilities, naturally), but some of the figurations have changed to the point that wholly new melodic lines are sometimes drawn. Bach makes a couple of very slight tempo alterations, or perhaps just omissions: Allegro is indicated in the violin version, while the first movement has no indication at all in the harpsichord version (Allegro would be assumed); and the original Allegro assai marking at the head of the third movement is now simply Allegro. *—Blair Johnston*

Recommended:

- ○ **Bach: Harpsichord Concertos BWV 1052, 1054 & 1056** / Hogwood (cond.), Rousset, Academy of Ancient Music (UK) / 1997 / L'Oiseau-Lyre 448178
- ○ **Bach: Harpsichord Concertos Vol. 1** / R. Wooley, P. Nicholson, Purcell Quartet / 1996 / Chandos 0595
- ○ **J. S. Bach: Keyboard Concertos & French Suite 5** / Marriner (cond.), Gavrilov, Academy of St. Martin-in-the-Fields / 1999 / Angel 73641
- ○ **Bach: Piano Concertos 1–5 & 7** / Golschmann (cond.), G. Gould, Columbia SO / 2002 / Sony 87760
- ○ **Bach: Harpsichord Concertos BWV 1053–1057** / G. Leonhardt (cond.), Leonardt Consort / 2000 / Teldec 81219

Harpsichord Concerto No. 4 in A major (or for oboe d'amore) BWV 1055 (1738–1739)

Music history records that the world's first harpsichord concertos were the product of J. S. Bach's pen; yet, while Bach did come up with about fourteen concertos featuring one or more harpsichordists in solo roles, it is important to note that as far as we can tell, Bach never once actually *composed* a concerto for harpsichord and ensemble—he only arranged them from already existing instrumental concertos (usually, but not exclusively, his own). Why, precisely, this is so remains a bit unclear; perhaps the entrenched role of the harpsichord as a continuo instrument made it difficult for the composer to conceive of it combined with an ensemble in any other way. Or, perhaps even the ingenious Bach was unsure of what an actual harpsichord concerto would be like and so—having effectively plundered his own and other composers' music so many times in the past—he simply proceeded to do so again when, during the late 1730s, the Leipzig Collegium Musicum put together some ad-hoc performances of music for harpsichord and orchestra.

Although the source work upon which Bach drew when writing the *Concerto No. 4 in A major* for harpsichord, strings, and continuo, BWV 1055, has not survived, it seems to have been a concerto for oboe d'amore originally composed by Bach sometime during his years as Kapellmeister at Cöthen (1717–23). BWV 1055 is a rich three-movement piece, the detailed harpsichord textures and seamless design of which have lead many musicologists to believe that it is in fact one of the last of Bach's seven complete concertos for single harpsichord to have been arranged, showing how quickly and how well he was able to absorb the promising new genre into his own personal idiom.

The ritornello design of the opening Allegro is firmly in the Corelli-Vivaldi tradition that Bach knew so well. The ritornello theme, given to the tutti and reinforced at times by harpsichord obbligato (but never actually played by the harpsichord, as per tradition) is made to alternate with the more elaborate gestures of the soloist. An exact reprise of the opening version of the ritornello draws a conclusion.

There is something of the chaconne or passacaglia to the descending bass-line idea of the Larghetto in F sharp minor, though as the movement unfolds it takes an entirely different course than either of those two hyper-repetitive forms would allow. An almost obsessive long-short-long rhythm in the upper voices of the string background reinforces the luscious harpsichord obbligato.

The borders of the ritornello theme used in the final Allegro ma non tanto are perhaps even clearer than those of the opening Allegro; it appears in alternation with the less firmly entrenched, even occasionally pseudo-improvisational extravagances of the soloist. After a firm move to E major during the central portion of the movement, the ritornello creeps around in the key of F sharp minor for a while, temporarily dispelling the exuberance that has hitherto been the movement's only tone. *—Blair Johnston*

Recommended:

- ○ **Bach: Brandenburg Concertos 1–3; 2 Oboe Concertos** / Pinnock (cond.), Reichenberg, English Concert / Archiv 471720
- ○ **Bach: Harpsichord Concertos 1053–1057** / G. Leonhardt, Leonhardt Consort / 2000 / Teldec 81219
- ○ **Bach: Harpsichord Concertos Vol. 3** / P. Nicholson, L. Cummings, Purcell Quartet / 1999 / Chandos 0636
- ○ **Bach: Piano Concertos 1–5 & 7** / Golschmann (cond.), G. Gould, Columbia SO / 1992 / Sony 52591

Harpsichord Concerto No. 5 in F minor (or for oboe or violin in G minor) BWV 1056 (1738–1739)

Like Johann Sebastian Bach's better known *Concerto in D minor,* this work is thought to be a transcription of a lost concerto. While some scholars have attributed the violin composition to Vivaldi or to a minor German composer, the counterpoint and structure of the clavier seem indicative of Bach's idiom. Written during Bach's Cöthen period, the concerto is in three movements; all three are in ritornello form, in which each movement is based upon a single theme restated in various orchestrations at the opening, the closing, and after each exploratory section.

The first movement, an Allegro, has hints of the form that would later be described as a sonata-rondo. It begins with a tutti exposition of a 14-bar ritornello, characterized by a firmly stated bass figure and a recurring sixteenth note triplet in the upper voice. Even in the solo episodes, the bass figure from the ritornello is frequently restated. Once the ritornello is introduced, the soloist elaborates on the triplet figure with light accompaniment. After the tutti restates the ritornello in A flat, the soloist embarks upon a sonata-like development, firmly rooted in the tonic, to build up momentum. Midway through this section, the tutti briefly suggests the ritornello, then gives way to the soloist for a full 24 bars of triplet figures. In the equivalent of a sonata's recapitulation, the ritornello and the soloist's triplets are restated, finally concluding in a compressed eight-bar ritornello. The main sense of contrast in the first movement is conveyed not by variation of keys or of a primary and secondary theme, but by the distinction between the soloist's triplets and the orchestra's sturdy ritornello.

The slow movement, in the relative major of A flat, begins with a lengthy and elaborate 21-bar arabesque, lightly accompanied by a sparse bass figure of eighth notes. The frequent and extensive ornamentation in the melody make this movement somewhat rococo in character. The F minor finale is a vigorous, flowing movement in triple time that gives it an air of constant motion. The ritornello is 24 bars in length and can be divided into two distinct parts. In the first section, a scalar passage of sixteenth notes is traded between the upper and lower voices against a more triadic accompaniment of eighth notes. The second section consists of a series of contrary and parallel scale passages, leading to a firmly declared cadence. The soloist next develops the ritornello, without introducing any substantially new material. After the ritornello is restated in A flat, there is an episode based on a figure of descending trills. Included in this passage is a curious passage in which crashing chords—alternating between the tutti and the soloist—build up tension which is finally released in a decisive C major cadence. The soloist recapitulates the first main solo in C, but there is no definitive restatement of the ritornello as a whole until the final recapitulation at the close of the concerto. *—David Kent*

Recommended:

- ○ **Bach: Harpsichord Concertos BWV 1052, 1054 & 1056** / Hogwood (cond.), Rousset, Academy of Ancient Music (UK) / 1997 / Decca 448178
- ○ **Bach: Harpsichord Concertos BWV 1055–1058** / Rilling (cond.), R. Levin, Stuttgart Bach Collegium / 1999 / Haenssler 92128
- ○ **J. S. Bach: Keyboard Concertos & French Suite 5** / Marriner (cond.), Gavrilov, Academy of St. Martin-in-the-Fields / 1999 / Angel 73641
- ○ **Bach: Keyboard Concertos 1, 4 & 5** / Golschmann (cond.), G. Gould, Columbia SO / 2002 / Sony 87760

Harpsichord Concerto No. 6 in F major, BWV 1057 (1738–1739)

Like each of J.S. Bach's other harpsichord concertos, excepting perhaps one, the *Harpsichord Concerto No. 6 in F major,* BWV 1057 is actually a transcription of an earlier concerto conceived for one of the more traditional concerto solo instruments. When Bach made these transcriptions in the 1730s, the keyboard was a newcomer to the concerto scene. Many of the original source works for the harpsichord concertos have been lost, but the one arranged for keyboard use in BWV 1057 is alive and quite well—for it is none other than the *Brandenburg Concerto No. 4 in G major* that Bach has reused, transposing the music down a whole step and recasting the original solo violin part for keyboard. The structure of the music remains unchanged in the harpsichord version (and the two important obbligato recorders are still present), but Bach has done much more than simply adapt the solo violin part to make it better fall under the keyboardist's fingers—he has completely rewritten the part. A great deal of music exists in the solo part where none existed before (the harpsichordist must play where, in the *Brandenburg Concerto,* the violinist rests), and the textures and figurations of the part are, quite naturally, a great deal richer. In the second movement, *Andante,* the scoring has been changed noticeably to allow the harpsichordist to take over music originally given to the two recorders; where, in *Brandenburg No. 4,* the recorders were part of the solo group, here they are members of the ripieno. The finale, marked Presto in *Brandenburg No. 4,* is now an Allegro assai. *—Blair Johnston*

Recommended:

- ○ **Bach: Harpsichord Concertos** / V. Neumann (cond.), Ruzickova, Prague Chamber Soloists / 2001 / Supraphon 3569
- ○ **Bach: Harpsichord Concertos Vol. 3** / R. Woolley, Purcell Quartet / 1999 / Chandos 636
- ○ **Bach: Harpsichord Concertos BWV 1053–1057** / G. Leonhardt (cond.), Leonhardt Consort / 2000 / Teldec 81219
- ○ **Bach: Keyboard Concertos & French Suite No 5** / Marriner (cond.), Gavrilov, Academy of St. Martin-in-the-Fields / 1999 / Angel 73641

Harpsichord Concerto No. 7 in G minor, BWV 1058 (1738–1739)

In only four cases do the concertos upon which J.S. Bach based his harpsichord concertos of the 1730s survive (there was no such thing as a harpsichord concerto until Bach began transcribing old violin and oboe concertos for performance by the Leipzig Collegium Musicum), and three of them are the famous three violin concertos (BWV 1041, 1042, and 1043, the last for two violins, and likewise for two harpsichords in the adaptation). It is the first of those violin concertos, the *Concerto in A minor,* BWV 1041, that Bach reshaped into the *Harpsichord Concerto No. 7 in G minor,* BWV 1058.

The harpsichord version of the concerto, which is, of course, transposed down a whole tone, offers perhaps the most stunning solo part of all the Bach harpsichord concertos. In each of the concertos, the harpsichord solo part is less an arrangement of the original solo line than it is a newly composed part that simply takes the original as a starting point, but in BWV 1058, and especially in the outer movements (which retain the original tempo indications; none in the case of the first movement, Allegro assai in the case of the finale), the depth and richness of Bach's new take on the solo part are wonderful. The harpsichord's status as tame continuo instrument is left behind altogether during the electrifying virtuoso passagework that begins to creep into the finale just past its midpoint and never leaves. *—Blair Johnston*

Recommended:

- ○ **Bach: Keyboard Concertos BWV 1054, 1055, 1058, 1063 & 1064** / Koopman (cond.), Mathot, Marisaldi, Amsterdam Baroque Orch. / 1990 / Erato 16167
- ○ **Bach: Keyboard Concertos & French Suite 5** / Marriner (cond.), Gavrilov, Academy of St. Martin-in-the-Fields / 1999 / EMI 73641
- ○ **Bach: Keyboard Concertos 2, 3 & 7** / Golschmann (cond.), Gould, Columbia SO / 2002 / Sony 87761
- ○ **Bach: Concertos BWV 1054 & 1058; Mozart: Piano Concerto 25** / Bashmet (cond.), S. Richter, Orch. di Padova e del Veneto / 1996 / Teldec 194245

Harpsichord Concerto No. 8 in D minor, BWV 1059 (1738–1739)

To say that J.S. Bach's *Harpsichord Concerto No. 8 in D minor,* BWV 1059, is incomplete doesn't really begin to explain the real state of affairs. Just nine bars of the piece—the first nine bars—have survived. Because of Bach's practice of reusing and reshaping his own material, however, it is possible to reconstruct at least the first movement of the concerto with reasonable accuracy, and several such reconstructions do exist.

The situation is a complicated one and needs some explaining. We know that BWV 1059, like nearly all of Bach's harpsichord concertos, is (or perhaps was—it very nearly qualifies as a "lost" work) an adaptation of a concerto written for another instrument, in this case oboe. That work is completely lost. Before he ever got around to making the harpsichord version (which probably dates from the mid- to late 1730s), however, Bach adapted the first movement of the oboe concerto for use as the opening sinfonia of *Cantata No. 35, Geist und Seele wird verwirret,* BWV 35, of 1726—we know this because the surviving nine bars of the harpsichord version are identical to the opening of BWV 35's opening sinfonia. As that sinfonia has an obbligato organ part, it is not an impossible task to fashion a rough cut of the first movement of the *Harpsichord Concerto No. 8 in D minor.*

Furthermore, it may well be the case that the remaining two movements of the concerto, seemingly lost altogether, are to be found in that same cantata. The very first solo alto aria of the cantata also has an obbligato organ part and may be the slow movement "in disguise" (of course, we know from other examples of Bach adapting his concerto slow movements as arias that the music sometimes takes very different shapes to accommodate two soloists—the singer and the obbligato—and reconstruction by working backwards is a risky business), and the second half of the cantata begins with another sinfonia that some feel to be a new form of the oboe concerto finale.

Because the work does not actually exist in a proper sense, performances and recordings of BWV 1059 are understandably few and far between. But there is value in a reconstruction such as Igor Kipnis' well-known one, enough to give us a taste, perhaps, of the lost ambrosia. *—Blair Johnston*

Recommended:

- ○ **Rosalind Tureck Collection V: Bach & Mozart** / Tureck (cond.), Tureck Bach Players / 2000 / VAI Audio 1192–2
- ○ **Bach: Harpsichord Concertos** / Leonhardt, Leonhardt Consort / 1995 / Teldec 97452
- ○ **Bach: Keyboard Concertos BWV 1054,1055,1058,1063 & 1064** / Koopman (cond.), Mathot, Marisaldi, Amsterdam Baroque Orch. / 1990 / Erato 16167

Concerto for 2 harpsichords & strings in C minor (or for oboe & violin in D minor), BWV 1060 (ca. 1736)

Bach's "first" *Concerto for Two Harpsichords in C minor* from approximately 1730 is a transcription of a now lost concerto for two solo instruments and string orchestra. Scholars conjecture that the earlier concerto was intended for violin and oboe soloists and it has been reconstructed in this form (also BWV 1060).

As in all of Bach's concertos for solo instruments and orchestra, this concerto is laid out in three movements: two fast outer movements here marked Allegro enclosing a central slow movement here marked Adagio. With its echo effects between the two soloists in the outer movements and its long cantabile lines in the central movement, the C minor concerto is skillfully written for two soloists. However, like Bach's later transcription of his *Concerto for Two Violins in D minor* as another *Concerto for Two Harpsichords in C minor,* some critics question the effectiveness of substituting two keyboard instruments for two melodic instruments and point out the thicker textures of the two-harpsichord concerto as demonstrating the inferiority of this version of the concerto. Other critics assert that, when performed on lighter instruments by players with more supple technique, the two-harpsichord concerto is in no way a lesser work than the proposed violin and oboe concerto version. *—James Leonard*

Recommended:

- ○ **Bach: Harpsichord Concertos** / G. Leonhardt (cond.), van Asperen, Melante Amsterdam / 1999 / Virgin 561716
- ○ **Bach: The Orchestral Suites** / Hogwood (cond.), Rousset, Academy of Ancient Music (UK) / 1998 / London 458069
- ○ **Bach: Harpsichord Concertos BWV 1060–1062, 1061a** / Rilling (cond.), R. Levin, Kahane, Oregon Bach Festival CO / 1999 / Haenssler 92129

Concerto for 3 harpsichords & strings in D minor, BWV 1063 (ca. 1730)

There are two different scholarly explanations of the origin of Bach's *Concerto for Three Harpsichords in D minor.* One holds that the work is a transcription or arrangement of works by other composers in the manner of Bach's adaptation of the violin concertos for organ. Given the originality and the expressivity of the D minor concerto, this explanation seems unlikely to other scholars, who assert instead that the work was composed by Bach for domestic musicmaking between himself and his two eldest sons, Wilhelm Friedemann and Carl Philip Emanuel. These scholars point to the dominance of the first harpsichord part, especially to its two cadenzas in the opening movement, and to the Germanic gravitas of the unison theme that permeates the opening movement like the unison theme of the *Harpsichord Concerto in D minor* (BWV 1052). Whichever explanation is correct (and at this point, it is unlikely that conclusive proof will ever be found), all scholars agree that the *Concerto for Three Harpsichords in D minor* is one of Bach's finest concerted works. The weight and power of the fast outer movements, the pathos of the central Alla Siciliano, the beauty of the work's melodies, and the contrapuntal skill with which they are developed all place this concerto among Bach's best harpsichord concertos. *—James Leonard*

Recommended:

- ○ **Bach: Harpsichord Concertos BWV 1052, 1061, 1063 & 1064** / G. Leonhardt (cond.), A. Curtis, Tachezi, Uittenbosch, E. Muller, Leonhardt Consort / 2000 / Teldec 81218
- ○ **Bach: Concertos for Three & Four Harpsichords** / Rilling (cond.), E. Levin, Behringer, Videla, B. Kleiner, Stuttgart Bach Collegium / 2000 / Haenssler 92130
- ○ **Bach: Harpsichord Concertos** / G. Leonhardt (cond.), A. Curtis, Tachezi, Uittenbosch, E. Muller, Leonhardt Consort / 1995 / Teldec 97452

Concerto for 3 harpsichords & strings in C major (or for 3 violins in D major), BWV 1064 (ca. 1730)

The great Bach scholar Philipp Spitta called the *Concerto for Three Harpsichords in C major* "one of Bach's most impressive compositions." Despite critics' objections that Bach's other concertos for multiple harpsichords are frequently overwritten and over-dense, few have brought this charge against the C major concerto. Part of the reason for this is that the orchestra is frequently treated soloistically, so the solo harpsichordists' lines stand out more clearly. Part of the reason is that the soloists' left hands often play the same bass line, thereby making the three upper lines seem more melodic. And part of the reason is that, except in the third and final movement, the three soloists are treated as a single musical unit, entering simultaneously and developing the same thematic material. The three movements of the C major concerto are built on a more expansive and inclusive scale than most of Bach's other harpsichord concertos, and they have a corresponding expressivity and depth. The opening Allegro is broadly built on several themes; the central A minor Adagio is a solemn, even melancholy piece with the three soloists' lyrical lines floated over an ostinato bass; and the closing Allegro is a fugato with three separate cadenzas for each of the soloists.

This concerto is believed to be a transcription by Bach of a concerto for three violins, now lost, but the work is sometimes played in a three-violin reconstruction that was made for the *Neue Bach-Ausgabe* edition of Bach's works. *—James Leonard*

Recommended:

- ○ **Bach: Complete Harpsichord Concertos** / Pinnock (cond.), Gilbert, Mortensen, English Concert / Archiv 471754
- ○ **Bach: Concertos for 2, 3 & 4 Harpsichords** / van Asperen (cond.), Klapprott, Lohff, Melante Amsterdam / 1996 / Virgin 724354520426
- ○ **Bach: Concertos for Three & Four Harpsichords BWV 1063–1065** / Rilling (cond.), Levin, Videla, Stuttgart Bach Collegium / 2000 / Haenssler 92130

Concerto for 4 harpsichords & strings in A minor, BWV 1065 (ca. 1730)

Bach's *Concerto for Four Harpsichords and String Orchestra in A minor* is an adaptation from around 1730–33 of Vivaldi's *B minor Concerto for Four Violins and String Orchestra in B minor* No. 10, Op. 3. Bach had gotten to know Vivaldi's Op. 3 while an organist at Weimar, where he transcribed ten of them for solo harpsichord and six of them for organ. This later adaptation is far more ambitious. In it, Bach has both tightened and expanded Vivaldi's counterpoint, enriched his harmonies with lusher harmonies, and expanded the solo parts with greater complexity and greater clarity. The result is a work that not only avoids the criticism of being too thickly textured, but actually improves on the original work. Written in the standard three-movement concerto form of the Baroque period, Bach's *Concerto for Four Harpsichords* is a brilliant virtuoso piece for the soloists. *—James Leonard*

Recommended:

- ○ **Bach: Harpsichord Concertos Vol. 2** / R. Woolley, P. Nicholson, L. Cummings, Toll, Purcell Quartet / 1998 / Chandos 0611
- ○ **Bach: Concertos for 3 & 4 Harpsichords** / van Asperen (cond), Klapprott, Lohff, Bussi, Melante Amsterdam / 1996 / Virgin 72435452042
- ○ **Bach: Concertos for 3 & 4 Harpsichords BWV 1063–1065** / Rilling (cond.), R. Levin, Videla, Behringer, B. Kleiner, Stuttgart Bach Collegium / 2000 / Haenssler 92130

Italian Concerto for solo keyboard in F major, BWV 971 (ca. 1735)

Johann Sebastian Bach's "Italian" Concerto is featured in his *Clavierübung, Part 2.* The preface to the first published edition of 1735 (issued by Christoph Weigl of Nuremberg) made it clear that this "Übung" (or "exercise") was written exclusively for a two-manual harpsichord or Clavicymbal, and was, according to the composer himself, intended "for lovers of music, for their enjoyment," and not solely for the purposes of their technical advancement. The prescribed two-manual instrument was quite clearly a deliberate choice on Bach's part, since its use enabled the player and indeed the composer to explore new timbral contrasts and dynamic gradations that had been hitherto unavailable to keyboard players. Bach's early exploitation and championship of the expanded potentialities of the harpsichord partly accounted for the phenomenal growth in the popularity of the instrument, especially toward the end of Bach's life.

Described by J.A. Scheibe as "a perfect model of a well-designed solo concerto," Bach's "Concerto after the Italian Style" is not, as was once supposed, a reduction of a full keyboard concerto with orchestra, but rather an attempt at recreating the elements of concerto style in microcosm in a brilliant work for a solo instrument. This work manages to capture and sustain the fundamental principle of dialogue and exchange between concertino and ripieno groups found in any conventional concerto. Using a fascinating and intellectually rigorous alternation between solo and tutti passagework, Bach manages to assign the normal tutti function of the absent orchestra to the more powerful principal manual of the harpsichord, giving the virtuoso writing normally reserved for the soloist to the second manual. It would be reasonable to call the Italian Concerto a compendium-style work. In this regard at least, it has but one equal in the entire literature, this being the *Concerto for Orchestra* by Bartók.

In its ordering of movements, the work follows the standard Baroque concerto pattern, in which a central slow movement (Andante) is framed by two faster ones. Only in the central movement does the music take the form of a highly ornamented melody line for the right hand heard above a straightforward chordal accompaniment. Remarkably, however, the left hand part (in thirds) actually takes up the main melody of the brilliant opening movement (without tempo marking), already remarkable for its élan and bravura craftsmanship and for the way in which the music echoes contemporary orchestral technique so masterfully. The tonal scheme of the Presto finale is very simple, hardly veering away from tonic and dominant harmonies. The payoff here, however, is the tremendous vitality and dynamism of the music, based on nothing more complex than an F major ascending scale from which Bach crafts his essential materials. As one would expect from a master contrapuntist, the theme is heard in augmentation and diminution, in inversion and contrary motion, and indeed in a whole panoply of spectacular concatenations that leave the listener marveling by the close at the fact that this is a work for just one player, two hands, and two manuals! *—Michael Jameson*

Recommended:

- ○ **Bach: Italian Concerto; Chromatic Fantasy; Various Pieces** / G. Gould / 2001 / Sony 87753
- ○ **Bach: French Overture; Italian Concerto; 4 Duets & 2 Capriccios** / A. Hewitt / Hyperion 67306
- ○ **Bach: 6 Partitas; Goldberg Variations; French Overture & Italian Concerto** / Pinnock / 2003 / DG B000048502
- ○ **Bach: Italian Concerto; French Overture** / Moroney / Virgin 59272

Oboe Concerto in D minor, BWV 1059r (1738–1739)

In 1729, Bach took over the directorship of the Collegium Musicum in Leipzig, one of two concert organizations in the city that met during the winter months. The society Bach became involved with had originally been founded by Telemann in 1702, and held its meetings at Zimmerman's coffeehouse on Friday evenings. It was for the Collegium Musicum that Bach composed many of his concertos, many of them adapted from existing works composed during his Cöthen days (1717–23) and already reused in cantata movements. Many thus involve considerable problems of reconstruction, the *Oboe Concerto in D minor* being a particularly difficult example. It takes as its basis an oboe concerto Bach started but abandoned after the first few bars, presumably because he was not happy with it. As heard today, the outer movements are reconstructed from the sinfonias, known to be part of a lost concerto, which open each part of a cantata for solo alto, *Geist und Seele wird verwirret,* BWV 35 (1726). It is also possible that the cantata's first aria, a da capo movement in siciliana rhythm, formed the original central slow movement. Since this presents special reconstruction difficulties, the movement is therefore adapted from the opening sinfonia of the cantata *Ich steh mit einem Fuss im Grabe,* BWV 156 (1729), also familiar as the slow movement of the *Harpsichord Concerto in F minor,* BWV 1056. *—Brian Robins*

Recommended:

- ○ **Bach: Complete Orchestral Works** / I. Brown (cond.), H. Holliger, Academy of St. Martin-in-the-Fields / 1997 / Philips 456377

Violin Concerto No. 1 in A minor, BWV 1041 (ca. 1730)

The court of young Prince Leopold at Cöthen was the penultimate step on Bach's professional ascent from organist at Arnstadt, in 1703, to Kantor at Leipzig, from 1723 to the end of his life. He had been Konzertmeister at Weimar (1708–17) before his appointment as Kapellmeister at Cöthen, where he remained for six years. He wrote much instrumental (rather than liturgical) music in this secular position, although most of it has been lost. Among the survivors were the *Brandenburg Concertos* and three other concertos for one or more solo violins with string and continuo accompaniment: the A minor and E major concertos for his concertmaster at Cöthen, Joseph Spiess, and the *D minor Concerto for Two Violins.*

Formally, he cast all but *Brandenburg No. 3* in three movements—quick, slow, quick—modeled on the Italian Baroque concertos of Vivaldi. Bach's genius was the ability to individualize as well as transcend the style of that older and admired contemporary who was indirectly his mentor. In the *Violin Concerto No. 1 in A minor,* BWV 1041, as in the other two violin concertos, the central movement is an aria without words—lyrical, expressively warm, ever gentle, yet inescapably melancholic in case of the A minor, perhaps the most inherently somber key in the tonal lexicon. On either side, an implicit although unmarked Allegro leads off in 2/4 time, with ritornello structure. As usual in Bach's concertos, the soloist's relationship with the full-ensemble passages hangs in a fascinating balance between competition and cooperation. A jig concludes in 3/8 time, marked Allegro assai and foreshadowing the rondos that Haydn and Mozart developed after Bach's death. *—Roger Dettmer*

Recommended:

- ○ **Bach: Solo & Double Violin Concertos** / Manze (cond.), Podger, Academy of Ancient Music (UK) / HM 907155
- ○ **Bach: Violin Concertos** / Harnoncourt (cond.), A. Harnoncourt, Vienna Concentus Musicus / 2000 / Teldec 81221
- ○ **Bach: Violin Concertos** / Standage (cond.), Comberti, M. Golding, Collegium Musicum 90 / 1996 / Chandos 0594
- ○ **Bach: Concertos for 1, 2 & 3 Violins** / E. Wallfisch (cond.), Orch. of the Age of Enlightenment / 1993 / Virgin 59319

Violin Concerto No. 2 in E major, BWV 1042 (before 1730)

This work, along with Bach's other surviving violin concerto, was composed during his stint in the service of the Prince of Anhalt-Cöthen. J.N. Forkel, Bach's original biographer, describes the concerto as being "full of an unconquerable joy of life, that sings in the triumph of the first and last movements." By the time Bach composed this concerto he had long been familiar with Antonio Vivaldi's influential works in the same medium. In the concerto's scintillating and ebullient first movement (Allegro), Bach takes the basic idea of ritornello form (around which Vivaldi's and almost all other Baroque concertos are composed), employs the essential motivic processes involved in that kind of composition, and shapes the whole into a superb da capo-form dialogue between soloist and accompanying ripieno group in which neither has supremacy over the other. While a certain balance between the soloist and the accompaniment is maintained, the basic content of the movement, defined by a powerful arpeggiated triad motif (reminiscent of Vivaldi's violin concerto "Il favorito"), becomes a springboard for continuous invention and subtly virtuosic embellishment. In the central Adagio, a deeply mournful instrumental aria of unique beauty, the violin's intricate musings are woven in and around a quiet ostinato in the bass instruments. The Allegro assai rondo finale is a dance-like movement of an extraordinary exuberance. Each successive contrasting passage exploits the violin's bravura capabilities more and more, until at last the final refrain swoops in on the wings of wild 32nd notes. The *Harpsichord Concerto in D major,* BWV 1054, is a transcription made by Bach, probably during the late 1730s, of this *E major Violin Concerto. —Blair Johnston*

Recommended:

- ○ **Bach: Violin Concertos** / R. King (cond.), C. MacIntosh, E. Wallfisch, King's Consort / 1989 / Hyperion 66380
- ○ **Bach: Violinkonzerte** / S. Kuijken (cond.), Van Dael, La Petite Bande / 1989 / DHM 77006
- ○ **Bach: Violin Concertos** / Harnoncourt (cond.), A. Harnoncourt, Concentus Musicus Wien / 1994 / Teldec 95518

Concerto, for 2 violins & strings in D minor ("Double"), BWV 1043 (1730–1731)

This music was composed at Cöthen between 1717 and 1723, and very likely first played by Joseph Spiess and Martin Friedrich Marcus with Prince Leopold's court orchestra. At Cöthen, Bach had no organ to play, despite his pan-German reputation as a virtuoso on that behemoth among Baroque instruments. However, he was proficient as well on the violin, the viola da gamba, and of course the clavier. Without his first choice available, or church duties such as Leipzig demanded later on, Johann Sebastian concentrated on instrumental music in various combinations—much of it subsequently lost. Along with the *Brandenburg Concertos* as a set, only two more concertos for solo violin and the D minor for two violins survived out of who knows how many, beyond the ones Bach rewrote at Leipzig after 1729 for one, two, three, and four claviers. All of his concertos, *Brandenburgs* included, had Vivaldi as their point of departure, and some were even transcriptions of the Italian master's works. Bach's genius was, of course, that he could individualize as well as transcend the music of a man indirectly his mentor. His works hadn't the sensuality or esprit of Vivaldi's; Bach was German Lutheran, bound beyond climate and environment by a religion that denounced the secular excesses in which Roman Catholicism (as Luther viewed it from within) had wallowed since the Middle Ages.

While opera had no place in Bach's education, life, or music, he was nonetheless sublimely capable of lyricism, warmth, and gentleness, never more so than in the Largo ma non tanto middle movement of this *Double Concerto,* with its 12/8 Siciliano rhythm and solo lines that seem to caress one another as they overlap and intertwine. On either side of this blissful dialog, however, the Baroque contrapuntist displays his mastery of synthesis and organization. The concerto opens with a fugal exposition of two contrasting themes, and their "development" in the ritornello style through G minor and C minor before the orchestra "reprises" the opening theme one last time. The allegro finale, in triple meter, likewise features imitation and repetition with the soloists front and center. Even more than in the first movement, there is a feeling of sonata form in embryo, with the charming surprise of a reprise in G minor instead of the tonic D minor. *—Roger Dettmer*

Recommended:

- ○ **Bach: Violinkonzerte** / S. Kuijken (cond.), Van Dael, La Petite Bande / 1989 / DHM 77006
- ○ **Bach: The Violin Concertos / Concerto for Violin and Oboe** / R. King (cond.), MacIntosh, E. Wallfisch, King's Consort / 1989 / Hyperion 66380
- ○ **Bach: Violin Concertos** / Manze (cond.), Podger, Academy of Ancient Music (UK), / 1995 / Harmonia Mundi 907155
- ○ **Bach: Violin Concertos** / Standage (cond.), Comberti, Golding, Collegium Musicum 90 / 1996 / Chandos 0594

ORCHESTRAL

Orchestral Suites, BWV 1066–1069 (ca. 1725–1739)

Bach wrote only four suites for orchestra, yet of his nearly 1,100 compositions they stand among his most popular. That is primarily true of the second and third suites, but since the advent of the CD allowed all four to be recorded on a single disc, listeners have become familiar with the entire set. They are hardly anomalies in his catalog; their structure is very much like that of his three partitas for solo violin, his six suites for solo cello, and, for harpsichord, his six partitas and six *English Suites.* In all of these works, an abstract introduction is followed by a series of light dance pieces. What sets the orchestral suites apart from these other works, aside from their instrumentation, is the form and weight of their introductions.

In Germany and France, the suites are usually called ouvertures, which is also the designation of the first movement. This practice dates to a habit established in France around 1660, when Lully began deriving orchestral suites from overtures and dances drawn from his operas. It should also be noted that "orchestral" is a loose term; the ensemble may consist of as little as a string quartet and one to three woodwinds, plus trumpets and timpani in the last two suites.

Bach's suites are freestanding works, although the first movement of the fourth suite was later recycled in a cantata (BWV 110). Some scholarly conjecture holds that they date from Bach's years in Cöthen (1717–23), judging especially from the old-fashioned style of the first suite. But no performance parts date from before Bach's Leipzig period; the first and fourth suites must have been written by 1725, and the second and third may be substantially later; we know that Bach led the Collegium Musicum, his coffeehouse band, in the third in 1731 and the second around 1738.

The first movement of each suite is an ouverture, a hefty movement in the French style propelled by dotted rhythms; when played in the Baroque manner, the music lopes along in a series of "ta-dahs." The first of the three sections is stately, and repeated immediately. The second section is faster and contrapuntal; the third returns to material from the opening, and then the second and third sections are repeated as a pair.

The ouverture is followed by four or six dance movements, always in binary form with both sections repeated. Sometimes, especially in the first suite, two dances of the same type are linked to make an ABA structure. Of the several dance forms Bach employs, the gavotte, bourrée, and minuet occur most often. The gavotte and bourrée are both in 2/2 time; the gavotte skips along gently, while the bourrée has a much faster pulse. The minuet, in 3/4 time with a strong first beat, would survive into the symphonies of Haydn and Mozart. *—James Reel*

Recommended:

○ **Bach: Les Quatre Ouvertures** / Savall (cond.), Capella Reial de Catalunya, Le Concert des Nations / 2000 / Astree 9958

VOCAL

Komm, süsser Tod, for voice & continuo, BWV 478 (1736)

J.S. Bach's *Komm, süsser Tod*, BWV 478, is one of the 60 or so sacred songs that Bach, then chapel master and director of choral music in Leipzig, provided for inclusion in the 1736 *Musicalisches Gesang-Buch von Georg Schmelli*, a practical volume of songs published in Leipzig (by Bernhard Christian Breitkopf, founder of the famous and still-extant publishing house that bears his name) for use in the city. For most of these sacred songs, Bach had only to devise bass lines and figured bass indications—the melodies selected were old and famous Lutheran tunes. *Komm, süsser Tod*, however, is an exception. Its melody is known in no other source than the *Schmelli Gesang-Buch*, and it is generally believed that Bach wrote the piece from scratch. (There are two or three other entries in the *Gesang-Buch* that seem also to have been newly composed.) Those familiar with ordinary German chorales will find themselves on familiar ground with *Komm, süsser Tod*, but its solo vocal line seems especially to exemplify Bach's supremely confident devotional side.

Schmelli's *Gesang-Buch* is partitioned by topic, so that the devout Lutheran might have a song for any and every occasion. There are songs for morning, evening, Advent and Good Friday (and also for all other times in the liturgical year), and there are songs for Death, of which *Komm, süsser Tod* is one. The song has five verses, written around 1724 by some unknown poet, each of which begins which the text "Komm, süsser Tod, komm selige Ruh" (Come, sweet death; come, blessed rest), and each of which is set to the same eight short phrases of triple-meter music. A beautiful orchestral version of this piece was made by Leopold Stokowski in 1946; it opens with all the strings muted except for a solo cello that "sings" the melody. *—Blair Johnston*

Recommended:

○ **Bach: Zehemelli-Gesangbuch** / K. Mertens, B. Schlick, W. Moller / CPO 999407

Wilhelm Friedemann Bach

b. Nov. 22, 1710, Weimar, Germany, **d.** Jul. 1, 1784, Berlin, Germany
Composer: Keyboard

Admirers of Wilhelm Friedemann Bach consider him in many ways the most original and interesting of the composer-sons of the great Johann Sebastian. His music fell generally into the transitional period between Baroque and Classical styles, but it was distinctive and personal.

Naturally, he was taught by his father, who also sent him to study violin with J.G. Graun and saw to it that W.F. Bach's great successes in general education at Leipzig's Thomasschule and the University of Leipzig (where he studied philosophy, law, and mathematics) did not interfere with his music. After graduation he worked as a musical assistant for his father. He left home at the age of 23 to become organist of the Sophienkirche in Dresden. This was a part-time position, allowing him time for more math studies, and composition of operas and ballets for the local Court.

In 1746, he became the organist at the Liebfrauenkirche in Hallé, a better position involving not only playing organ in that church, but organizing orchestral performances in the city's three main churches. He became known for his brilliant organ improvisations and is generally listed as the last great German Baroque organist. He ran into trouble due to his interests in modern enlightenment philosophy and his inability to take seriously the very pious style of the town's rulers. Chafing at their attempts to restrict him, he applied for various jobs elsewhere as they opened up, further irritating the town fathers.

In 1751 he married Dorothea Elisabeth Georgi. In 1756, with the coming of the Seven Years' War, Hallé became an open city and Bach and his family suffered depredations from the various armies that went through. Despite inflation, the town fathers turned down his request for a raise in 1761. In 1762, he received an appointment as Kapellmeister in Darmstadt, seemingly a congenial position. But Bach delayed leaving Hallé and lost the job. He finally walked off the job in Hallé in 1764, setting himself up as a teacher in the town. He lived precariously after that, often sabotaging himself in attempts to get new jobs. He also earned the undying enmity of generations of music historians by losing many of the manuscripts of his father that had come into his care, receiving pages of bad press from them as a result. He treated his own music as carelessly, and much of it is also lost. He died in poverty in 1784 from a pulmonary disease. *—Joseph Stevenson*

Overview of Works (1784–1822)

Wilhelm Friedemann Bach (1710–84), the eldest son of Johann Sebastian and Maria Barbara, was the least of any of Bach's composer sons. His talent was arguably the greatest of any of Bach's sons and his intensely contrapuntal training under his father was probably the best any composer could have. But like his life, Wilhelm Friedemann's music is eccentric, emotional, extravagant, and essentially unclassifiable. Wilhelm Friedemann's 20 church cantatas composed between 1746 and 1764 are a hodgepodge of musics with movements in the expressive *empfindsamer stil*, movements in the austere style of his father, and even movements that parody other composers' cantatas. His keyboard music moves from the proto-Romantic polonaises of 1765 to the archaic fugues of 1778. His orchestral music can move from a French overture to *empfindsamer stil* Andante in the same work to full-blown suites for orchestra in the height of the late Baroque style. Although he spent the last ten years of his life working on it, Wilhelm Friedemann's only opera remained unfinished at his death. *—James Leonard*

Recommended:

○ **W. F. Bach: Concerti** / G. von der Goltz (cond.), Freiburg Barockorchester / Carus 83304

○ **W. F. Bach: Orchestral Works** / Haenchen (cond.), C. P. E. Bach CO / Brilliant 99785/6

○ **W. F. Bach: Das Orgelwerk** / Baumgratz / 1999 / Christophorus 4006

KEYBOARD

12 Polonaises, F. 12 (ca. 1765; revised ca. 1775)

The first and in many ways the worst of the sons of Johann Sebastian Bach, Wilhelm Friedemann Bach (1710–1784) was a disgrace to the family name. After a lifetime of frittering away his immense compositional gifts on works that can be described as conservatively Baroque, sensitive in a modern fashion, and—to put it bluntly—unfinished, Wilhelm Friedemann ended his career by selling off his father's music and selling his own music forged with his father's name. And yet when he was good, Wilhelm Friedemann was very, very good—a composer of formidable contrapuntal skills combined with deep expressivity—and he was rarely better than he was in his *12 Polonaises for keyboard* (a 13th Polonaise in C major was also composed at about the same time, but was clearly conceived as a separate work). Composed around 1765 (the dating of Bach's works is nearly impossible to know owing to the carelessness of his life), the *12 Polonaises* were written in Halle, while Bach was throwing away the last, best chance he had to obtain a solid, permanent place in Darmstadt. They are exquisitely sensitive works that are wonderfully well formed and harmonically and melodically expressive. Based on the Polish dance form that Chopin later made his own, Bach's *Polonaises* are among the very best works he wrote, and were highly esteemed by the first generation of Romantic composers. The first 12 were written in parallel major and minor keys ascending from C–C major, C minor, D major, D minor, E flat major, E flat minor, F major, F minor, G major, G minor—thus pointing to an organization beyond the haphazard organization of most of his other music. Although some of Bach's smaller character pieces for keyboard are equally fine, the *12 Polonaises* are certainly his best set of works for keyboard and arguably his best works in any genre. *—James Leonard*

Recommended:

○ **W. F. Bach: Polonaises** / Rousset / 1996 / Virgin 61295

Wilhelm Backhaus

b. Mar. 26, 1884, Leipzig, Germany, **d.** Jul. 5, 1969, Villach, Austria
Pianist

Wilhelm Backhaus was born in Leipzig, Germany, on March 26, 1884. He made a concert debut there at the age of eight, and studied at the Leipzig Conservatory with Reckendorf. In 1899 he left Leipzig to study with Eugen d'Albert in Frankfurt am Main. He made a major debut tour in 1900 and quickly gained a fine reputation as a player and as a teacher. His American debut was on January 5, 1912, in New York, playing the Beethoven *Piano Concerto No. 5* with Walter Damrosch and the New York Symphony Orchestra. In 1930 he moved to Lugano and acquired Swiss citizenship. Backhaus established a teaching career there and continued to make concert tours throughout his long life. His last U.S. appearance was in New York in 1962, at age 78; reviews judged that his powers were undiminished. He died on July 5, 1969, in Villach, Austria, where he had gone to make a concert appearance.

Especially during the later phase of his career, he had a remarkably high reputation as a pianist whose devotion to the composer's intentions was total and unselfish. His performances were in the classic line of those that strove to present the music in one broadly viewed arc of concept and logic, embracing not just single movements but entire works. His recorded output ranges from Mozart through the main Classical and Romantic repertoire. It is not surprising that his work was particularly excellent when he encountered those composers who built large-scale, logically constructed classical works, such as Beethoven and Brahms; in reference to his recordings of such works, terms like "magisterial," "exemplary," and "direct" have often been employed by reviewers. Late in his life he came to be regarded as a Beethoven specialist, and he recorded virtually the entire corpus of keyboard works of that master, as well as extensive groups of Brahms and Mozart, and works by Schumann, Grieg, Chopin, and Liszt, including concertos and solo works. He also made some chamber music recordings, notably of Brahms' cello sonatas with Pierre Fournier, and a notable account of the Schubert *"Trout" Quintet*. —*Joseph Stevenson*

Recommended:

- ○ **Beethoven: 4 Piano Sonatas** / Backhaus / 1992 / Orfeo 300921
- ○ **Wilhelm Backhaus plays Chopin, Moszkowski & Brahms** / Boult, Barbirolli, Ronald (conds.), Backhaus, BBC SO / 2001 / Andante 2996–2999
- ○ **Concertos: Brahms 2; Mozart 27** / Bohm (cond.), Backhaus / 1999 / Decca 466380

Paul Badura-Skoda

b. Oct. 6, 1927, Vienna, Austria

Pianist

Austrian pianist Paul Badura-Skoda is one of the most honored and frequently recorded concert artists of the second half of the twentieth century. Badura-Skoda studied in the master class of Edwin Fischer in Lucerne and made his debut in Vienna in 1948. Word quickly spread about Badura-Skoda's artistry, and in 1949 he appeared in concertos partnered by conductors Herbert von Karajan and Wilhelm Furtwängler. Badura-Skoda has seldom been idle since, and his concert tours have taken him around the world many times. Badura-Skoda made his New York debut in 1953.

Badura-Skoda has performed a wide range of piano music and was a close friend to Swiss composer Frank Martin, who dedicated his *Piano Concerto No. 2* to Badura-Skoda, in addition to some smaller works. But Badura-Skoda's name is most closely related to the Viennese classicists, Mozart, Beethoven, and Schubert, whose keyboard works, including whole cycles of sonatas, he has recorded, in some cases multiple times. Beginning in the 1950s, Badura-Skoda began to quietly make the case for the use of late eighteenth and early nineteenth century keyboards in the interpretation of this literature, anticipating the period instrument boom by decades. In this respect, Badura-Skoda was helped and to some degree influenced by the work of his wife, musicologist Eva Badura-Skoda. Paul Badura-Skoda has also played in a four-hand piano duet with fellow countryman Jörg Demus, and the pair collaborated on a book, *Die Klaviersonaten von Ludwig van Beethoven*, which was published in 1970.

Badura-Skoda's recording career encompasses an enormous number of recordings. He began with a justly famous series of discs on the Westminster label in the early 1950s and since then has recorded for Deutsche Grammophon, Astreé, Arcana, Music & Arts, Sanctuary Classics, Jecklin-Disc, Harmonia Mundi, and many others. In 2003 Badura-Skoda embarked on a world tour to celebrate the occasion of his 75th birthday. Badura-Skoda also composes; among his works are a *Mass in D*. —*Uncle Dave Lewis*

Recommended:

- ○ **Mozart: Sonatas K332; 333; 457; 475** / Badura-Skoda / 2001 / Astree 8868
- ○ **Mozart: Pieces for Piano** / Badura-Skoda / 2001 / Astree 8864
- ○ **Schubert: Works for Solo Piano** / Badura-Skoda / MCA 29844

Julianne Baird

b. Dec. 10, 1952, Statesville, North Carolina

Soprano

Julianne Baird is an accomplished early music singer who brings scholarly expertise and a clear soprano voice to bear on a wide repertory of music, primarily from the sixteenth, seventeenth, and eighteenth centuries. She has made dozens of solo recordings for the Dorian, Koch, L'Oiseau-Lyre, and Albany labels, among others, and appears as a soloist on some of the best complete recordings of Baroque opera and oratorio available in the catalog.

Baird began her career singing with the Waverly Consort and other ensembles. Her first major engagement was in the world premiere of Steve Reich's *Tehillim* with the New York Philharmonic in 1983—a foray into contemporary music that, while not especially relevant to the rest of her work, nevertheless gave her career a boost. Throughout the rest of the 1980s and 1990s, Baird solidified her reputation as one of early music's most charismatic young performers, appearing internationally in works of Handel, Bach, Purcell, and Monteverdi. In concert, she also explored the lute song repertory, French, Italian, and German solo cantatas, and Renaissance vocal works.

Her extensive musicological education (including a Ph.D. from Stanford University) has allowed her to combine her natural musicality and vocal gifts with an uncommon degree of stylistic knowledge and understanding. The results, thankfully unacademic in sound and feeling, have made her popular with conductors and audiences alike. She has been particularly successful as an interpreter of Handel in general and of the *Messiah* in particular, where her clear sound and judicious ornamentation always seem right at home.

On occasion, Baird has ventured into eighteenth and nineteenth century works. Her recording of Mozart songs for Dorian captures the composer's crisp style, if not always his warmth and humor. Her performances of Schubert include a unique recording of the 18-song version of the *Winterreise* song cycle.

Since 1989, Baird has served on the faculty of New Jersey's Rutgers University, where she has earned a reputation as a committed and capable teacher. She is also in demand nationwide for master classes and recitals. —*AMG*

Recommended:

- ○ **The English Lute Song** / Baird, McFarlane (lute) / 1988 / Dorian 90109
- ○ **Glorious Handel Soprano Arias** / Baird / 1999 / Newport 85646
- ○ **A Collection of English Lute Songs** / Baird, McFarlane (lute) / 1989 / Dorian 90126
- ○ **Monteverdi: L'Orfeo** / Gardiner (cond.), Otter, Chance, Dawson, Baird, English Baroque Soloists / Archiv 419250

Dame Janet Baker

b. Aug. 21, 1933, Hatfield, England

Mezzo-Soprano

While mezzo-soprano Janet Baker was best known for her performances of British music, especially that of her compatriot Benjamin Britten, she was also a fine performer of art song, sacred music, and Classical and pre-Classical opera. Her repertoire, as well as her background frequently, overlapped that of her great predecessor, Kathleen Ferrier; and though her career was mostly centered in England, and she always had a special place in the regard of English audiences, her fame was international.

In 1956, she won the second prize in the Kathleen Ferrier Competition; that year also saw her operatic debut as Roza in Smetana's *The Secret*, in an Oxford University Opera Club performance. In 1962, she first sang with the English Opera Group, as Polly in Benjamin Britten's famous production of *The Beggar's Opera* at Aldeburgh. She later credited the leading spirits of that group, Britten and tenor Peter Pears, as giving the ensemble and its singers the highest possible standards, as well as raising the reputation of British singers internationally. In 1966, she made her Covent Garden debut as Hermia in Britten's *A Midsummer Night's Dream*, and her Glyndebourne debut as Purcell's Dido. In 1971, Britten wrote the role of Kate Julian for Baker in his opera *Owen Wingrave*, written for BBC television.

As her operatic career progressed, Baker focused on pre-Classical and Classical works such as Gluck's *Orfeo ed Euridice*, Handel's *Giulio Cesare*, the title role of Gluck's *Alceste*, Dido in Purcell's *Dido and Aeneas*, Ottavia in Monteverdi's *L'incoronazione di Poppea*, and Dorabella in Mozart's *Cosi fan tutte*. However, she also performed Romantic and twentieth century roles such as Dido in Berlioz's *Les Troyens a Carthage*; Donizetti's *Maria Stuarda*; Charlotte in Massenet's *Werther*, and Octavian in Richard Strauss' *Der Rosenkavalier*. Much of her recital repertoire was drawn from the standard works of Fauré, Schumann, Schubert, Duparc, Haydn, and Mahler, and the British masters such as Purcell and Elgar; however, she also drew from the works of lesser-known composers, particularly from the pre-classical period, taking special pleasure in bringing their works to public attention. In 1982, she gave her farewell performances as Orfeo in London and at Glyndebourne.—*Ann Feeney*

Recommended:

- ○ **The Very Best of Janet Baker** / Baker / 2002 / EMI 75069
- ○ **Baker Sings Haydn, Schumann, Schubert, Wolf, R. Strauss** / Baker / 2000 / BBC Legends 4049
- ○ **Gluck: Orfeo ed Euridice** / Leppard (cond.), Baker, Gale, Nolan, Speiser, Mallandaine, London PO / Erato 45864
- ○ **Handel: Ariodante** / Leppard (cond.), Baker, Garcia, Baker, Ramey, English CO / 2003 / Philips 000087602
- ○ **Janet Baker sings Berlioz** / Barbirolli, Gibson (conds.), Baker / 2004 / EMI 62789

Mily Balakirev

b. Jan. 2, 1837, Nizhny-Novgorod, Russia, **d.** May 29, 1910, St. Petersburg, Russia

Composer: Keyboard, Orchestral

Mily Balakirev learned his craft from local musicians. Conductor Karl Eisrich introduced Balakirev to the music of Chopin, Glinka, and Alexander Ulybyshev, a music loving landowner who maintained a vast library of musical scores. In 1855, Balakirev composed his *Piano Fantasia on Themes from Glinka's A Life For the Tsar*, and Ulybyshev took Balakirev to St. Petersburg to meet Glinka himself. Glinka appreciated Balakirev's talent, and offered advice and encouragement. Balakirev enjoyed a brilliant debut as a pianist in St. Petersburg, and in 1858 performed Beethoven's *Piano Concerto No. 5* in the presence of the Tsar. In April 1858, Balakirev fell ill with "brain fever"; although he recovered, he would suffer from lifelong headaches, nervousness, and depression. With the deaths of both Glinka and Ulybyshev, Balakirev decided to carry on their ideas of a style reflective of the Russian national spirit. Balakirev wrote incidental music to Shakespeare's play *King Lear* in 1859–61, and its resulting popularity enhanced his reputation. In 1861, Balakirev established the Free School of Music with Gabriel Lomakin, with the support of Tsar Nicolas. At the Free School's concerts, Balakirev programmed his own music and that of his students— Cui, Rimsky-Korsakov, Mussorgsky, and

Borodin. This last-named group, along with Balakirev himself, were dubbed the "Mighty Handful" in the Russian press, and recognized as the standard bearers of a new form of Russian musical art.

When Lomakin resigned from the Free School in November 1867, Balakirev assumed its directorship. Along with his prestige came an increased lack of sensitivity and overbearing personality traits; by the late 1860s, Mussorgsky and Rimsky-Korsakov were exchanging letters complaining about Balakirev's "interference." Likewise, St. Petersburg audiences were protesting the lack of light, familiar fare on the Free School concert programs. Balakirev stepped down from the directorship of the Free School in April 1869, but bounced back with his most famous work, the brilliant piano fantasy *Islamey*, premiered by Nicholas Rubinstein in December. Rubinstein played the work at concerts in Paris and elsewhere, and it achieved great popularity in the West. In addition, Balakirev met and encouraged Tchaikovsky, who composed his *Romeo and Juliet Fantasy Overture* under the older composer's watchful eye. The Free School's concert season of 1871–72 was a disaster; as a result, Balakirev lapsed into a depression lasting five years, and Rimsky-Korsakov overtook the direction of the institution. Friends helped revive Balakirev's spirits, and he returned as an instructor in 1877, but began to match temperaments with Rimsky-Korsakov, who resigned in 1880. Balakirev returned to the post of director, and in 1883 premiered his finest work, the symphonic poem *Tamara*. Well received in Russia, *Tamara* was a true revelation for musicians in France, who were amazed by the textures of Russian orchestral color.

In 1883, Balakirev accepted the position of Music Director of Imperial Chapel, naming Rimsky-Korsakov as his assistant. Three years later, Balakirev quarreled with his publisher, Jurgenson, and was dropped from their roster. In 1890, Rimsky-Korsakov held a gala in honor of his own 25th anniversary as a composer; Balakirev refused to attend, occasioning the final break in their relations. Having retired from the Imperial Chapel in 1894, Balakirev made his final public appearance conducting his *First Symphony* at the Free School in 1898. On the strength of this symphony Balakirev acquired a new publisher, and resumed composition, including the *"Glinka" Cantata* (1904) and a *Second Symphony* (1909). Unfortunately, these later works were received with complete indifference. As he had offended practically everyone in his social circle, few friends were left to comfort Balakirev in his last years. He died at the age of 73. *—Uncle Dave Lewis*

Overview of Works (1852–1909)

Mily Balakirev (1835–1914) was the dominant figure in Russian music in the later part of the nineteenth century. His influence on Borodin, Mussorgsky, Rimsky-Korsakov, Tchaikovsky, and Liapunov is inestimable and his advocacy of European avant-garde music, along with ardent nationalism, was decisive in determining the course of Russian music through the Communist Revolution. Balakirev's own compositions, however, are few in number and almost all are compromised by his inability to complete works. Only his magnificent *Piano Sonata in B flat minor* from 1855–56 was finished in a single burst. His dark *King Lear Incidental Music* was first written from 1858–61 and later rewritten from 1902–05. His sensual symphonic poem *Tamara* took him from 1867–82 to complete. His monumental *Symphony in C major* was begun and large sections of it finished between 1864–66, but set aside for a quarter century and finally completed from 1893–97. Even his superb *Symphony in D minor*, based on a Scherzo composed in the 1860s, took from 1900–08 to complete. And *Islamey*, his virtuoso fantasy for solo piano and still his most popular work, was written in 1869 and then rewritten in 1902. Despite these disjunctures, Balakirev's music is completely compelling, essentially organic, and quintessentially Russian. It has tremendous strength, enormous energy, voluptuous colors, and an overwhelming sense of soulfulness that puts it among the greatest Russian music of the nineteenth century. *—James Leonard*

Recommended:

- ○ **Balakirev: Piano Music** / N. Walker / 1999 / ASV 1048
- ○ **Balakirev: Symphonies 1 & 2; Russia; Tamara; Overture on 3 Russian Themes** / Svetlanov (cond.), London PO / 1998 / Hyperion 22030

KEYBOARD

Islamey, oriental fantasy (1869; revised 1902)

Many examples of Russian music were inspired by Russia's nineteenth century conquest of Caucasian territories between the Black and Caspian Seas and the conquest of Turkic kingdoms between the states which are now known as Iran and Afghanistan. This resulted in a rise of interest in all forms of arts and literature of these newly incorporated regions, and these people's musics were quickly imitated in Russian concert music. Mily Balakirev's 1862 work *Islamey* is supreme among piano works with such a genesis. It is a large-scale fantasy incorporating three themes from Islamic regions of the Caucasus area, decked out with rich harmonies and developed into one of the most flashy virtuoso pieces for the instrument. In 1909, one year before Balakirev's death, the Italian Alfredo Casella introduced his orchestration of the piece, which is suitably dazzling and colorful. The two versions are a little off the beaten track of the standard repertoire, yet they are popular when played because of their color and great vigor. *—Joseph Stevenson*

Recommended:

- ○ **Great Pianists of the 20th Century: Andrei Gavrilov** / Gavrilov / 1999 / Philips 456787
- ○ **Simon Barere: Live Recordings at Carnegie Hall Vol. 3** / Barere / 2001 / APR 5623
- ○ **Emil Gilels Legacy Vol. 5: First Recital in the West** / Gilels / 2002 / Doremi 7795
- ○ **Great Pianists of the 20th Century: Julius Katchen I** / Katchen / 1998 / Philips 456856
- ○ **Rimsky-Korsakov: Scheherazade** / Gergiev (cond.), Kirov Orch. / 2002 / Philips 470840

ORCHESTRAL

Tamara, symphonic poem (1867–1882)

Russian composer Mily Balakirev's symphonic poem *Tamara*, or *Thamar*, today one of his best-known works, was the result of 15 years of thought. One of the leaders of the famed Mighty Handful, Balakirev produced a colorful orchestral work that affected not only his fellow Russian composers, especially Rimsky-Korsakov and Ippolitov-Ivanov, but also the generation following, including Sibelius and Ravel.

Tamara was based on a ballad by the poet Mikhail Lermontov, himself inspired by an ancient local legend while exiled to the Caucasus. Balakirev initially saw the work as a possible symbol of the recent political unification of the Caucasus under Russian rule. The poetic style and romantic language of the poem are as important to an understanding of the work as its plot, which describes a beautiful but evil princess (Tamara) whose songs lure travelers to her enchanted castle in the Caucasus by the river Terek. After a night of passion, the princess murders the traveler, whose body is borne away by the river.

Balakirev began the work in 1867; work progressed sporadically. In the mid-1870s, during a four-year battle with depression, his friends confiscated his sketches fearing what he might do to them. Yet in 1876 it was Balakirev's friends who helped rekindle his interest in music again by returning the score to him and begging him to resume its composition. Three years later, he performed *Tamara* on piano to an enthusiastic audience of friends, but when two more years went by without orchestration or performance, it was a gently nagging letter from Stasov which provided the final impetus. In March 1883, a year later, it was premiered with the composer conducting, and the 15-year odyssey, of which perhaps only three years total were spent intensively working on *Tamara*, was finally completed.

Dedicated to Franz Liszt, originator of the tone poem, *Tamara* bears his influence in form and language, which sometimes embraces an Oriental exoticism, but remains distinctively Russian in the vast scope of its orchestration. Liszt asked for a four-hand arrangement of the work, which Balakirev later provided. In 1912 Diaghilev and Fokine produced a ballet to Balakirev's score.

The slow and soft introduction (and conclusion) to *Tamara*, the rest of which is noticeably faster, is a characteristic of Balakirev's mature orchestral works. The work opens with rippling figures in the strings and low brass, representing the river, which establish the impressively pervasive feeling of foreboding; the key is an ominous B minor. Lyrically supple woodwind melodies abound in the work, and the first few notes of what will later be identified as Tamara's love song are heard from the English horn. After a few more notes of the love song are heard, the rippling returns. The bulk of the piece is then taken up with the two love themes of Tamara. Balakirev develops these melodies from seductive lyricism to driving passion to the murderous climax, after which they ironically assume their original form, and the river music returns. A surprisingly sweet-sounding codetta frames the fairy tale. *—Thomas Oram*

Recommended:

- ○ **Balakirev: Symphonies 1 & 2; Russia; Tamara; Overture on 3 Russian Themes** / Svetlanov (cond.), London PO / 1998 / Hyperion 22030
- ○ **Balakirev: Symphonies 2; Tamara; Piano Concerto** / Sinaisky (cond.), BBC PO / 1999 / Chandos 9727

Dalton Baldwin

b. Dec. 19, 1931, Summit, NJ
Pianist

Accompanist Dalton Baldwin began his musical training at the Juilliard School of Music and then went to the Oberlin Conservatory of Music where he earned his B.Mus. He continued his studies in Paris with Nadia Boulanger and Madeleine Lipatti and in 1954 he began his long and successful partnership with Gérard Souzay. While maintaining his partnership with Souzay, Baldwin began to perform and record on a regular basis with Elly Ameling in 1970. In the mid-1970s, he began an association with Jessye Norman both on stage and in the recording studio. He accompanied Arleen Augér's first New York recital in 1984 and recorded an award winning disc of *Love Songs* with her. Concentrating primarily on the song repertoire, Baldwin was coached by composers Poulenc, Sibelius, Martin, and Barber. He has played in many world premieres, notably of Rorem's *War Scenes* in 1969 with Souzay. Baldwin has accompanied many singers including Mady Mesple, Edda Moser, Jennie Tourel, Marilyn Horne, Frederica von Stade, Nicolai Gedda, José van Dam, William Parker, and Steven Kimbrough. Touring with these artists has brought Baldwin to all of the major music capitals of the world. Baldwin gives lectures on the art of the accompanist and has served as artistic director for art song festivals at Westminster Choir College (Princeton, NJ), University of Wisconsin-Milwaukee, Cleveland Institute of Music, and University of Colorado (Boulder). He and Souzay give master classes in Geneva every summer for young professional singers and accompanists from around the world. He also teaches at the Manhattan School of Music and in Princeton.

Dalton Baldwin has made over one hundred recordings of song recitals and has won numerous prizes for his work with Elly Ameling and Gérard Souzay. In 1987, he was awarded the *Croix de Commandant de l'Ordre des Arts et Lettres* by the French government. He is best known for his playing of the French repertoire and he has recorded the complete songs of Debussy, Fauré, Poulenc, Ravel, and Roussel with various artists. His recordings of Schubert and of Schumann with Ameling and Souzay are highly regarded also. Although best known in partnership with singers, Baldwin has worked with violinist Henryk Szering and cellist Pierre Fournier.

Dalton Baldwin's playing is characterized by subtle changes of tonal color and sensitivity to the needs of the performer. He has a wonderful control of dynamics and never allows the piano to overshadow the singer. Whenever possible, Baldwin returns to the Himalayas and the wildlife preserves of Africa to replenish his need for natural beauty. *—Richard LeSueur*

Recommended:

- ○ **Debussy: Mélodies** / Ameling, Von Stade, Souzay, Command, Mesplé, Baldwin (piano) / EMI 64095
- ○ **Poulenc: Mélodies** / Ameling, Souzay, Gedda, Parker, Sénéchal, Baldwin (piano) / EMI 64087
- ○ **Ave Maria – Ameling sings Schubert** / Ameling, Baldwin (piano) / Philips 420870
- ○ **Fauré: Intégrale des Mélodies** / Ameling, Souzay, Baldwin (piano) / EMI 64079

Baltimore Symphony Orchestra

f. Feb. 11, 1916, Baltimore, MD

Ensemble

The Baltimore Symphony Orchestra was established as a municipal ensemble with funding from local government agencies. The orchestra's first concert took place at the Lyric Theatre on February 11, 1916; its players were mostly local musicians joined by a few members of the Philadelphia Orchestra. Gustav Strube was appointed the group's first musical director in 1917. During his 13-year tenure, the number of concerts gradually increased, children's concerts were established in 1924, and several famous artists and guest conductors were attracted, including Siegfried Wagner, son of the composer. Strube's departure in 1930 resulted in a period of uncertainty for the orchestra, worsened by the national depression. His successor was George Siemonn, who worked vigorously for increased municipal funding and for the introduction of new compositions at concerts. He also conducted the orchestra's historic first radio broadcast concerts. Ernest Schelling was appointed music director in 1935 and became the first BSO conductor to lead a performance of Handel's *Messiah* during Christmas week. Following Schelling, Werner Janssen was appointed music director in 1937. He would become well-known for his film scores, which included Jean Renoir's 1945 *The Southerner* and the Marx Brothers' 1946 comedy *A Night in Casablanca.* He was succeeded by Harold Barlow in 1939, but neither of these two conductors could overcome the financial and morale problems plaguing the orchestra. In 1942, the director of Baltimore's Peabody Conservatory, Reginald Stewart, was appointed music director of the BSO. A talented pianist and conductor, the Scottish-born Stewart initiated many changes. By 1945, with the help of Eleanor Roosevelt and Met star Rosa Ponselle, the orchestra's size was increased to 90 members, its schedule of concerts expanded, and its repertory broadened. By the early 1950s, however, deficits and other problems precipitated Stewart's resignation and the departure of several orchestra members. Italian conductor Massimo Freccia took the reins in 1952 and immediately set diligently to work for solutions to the many difficulties facing the orchestra. He often presented concert versions of operas and conducted other large-scale works, drawing in sizable audiences. Peter Herman Adler succeeded Freccia in 1959. Under his directorship, regular subscription concerts and youth and children's concerts substantially increased and numerous new compositions were presented or premiered. In 1964, the orchestra began performing with the Baltimore Civic Opera Company. Romanian-born Sergiu Comissiona was appointed music director in 1968 by philanthropist Joseph Meyerhoff, who had become president of the symphony orchestra organization three years earlier. These two figures guided the orchestra to some of its greatest artistic triumphs, as well as to financial stability over the next decade and a half. Comissiona made numerous recordings with the orchestra and led many successful tours abroad. Meyerhoff donated $10.5 million toward the construction of a new hall, covering nearly half its final cost. The orchestra gave its first concert in *Meyerhoff Symphony Hall* on September 16, 1982. American David Zinman, previously conductor of the Rochester Philharmonic Orchestra, was appointed music director in 1985 and maintained the high standards set during the Comissiona era. He also made numerous recordings, and the orchestra began regular radio broadcasts in 1986. Zinman and the BSO won several Grammy awards, the first in 1987 in a collaborative effort with Yo-Yo Ma featuring cello concertos by Britten and Barber. Russian conductor Yuri Temirkanov succeeded Zinman in 1999. Temirkanov and the orchestra are frequently heard on NPR's Performance Today and regularly make recordings. *—Robert Cummings*

Recommended:

- ○ **Piano Concertos of Gershwin & Ravel** / Zinman (cond.), Grimaud (piano), Baltimore SO / 1997 / Erato 19571
- ○ **Schumann: Symphonies 2 & 3** / Zinman (cond.), BSO / 1991 / Telarc 80182
- ○ **Rouse:Symphony 1; Phantasmata** / Zinman (cond.), BSO / 1989 / Nonesuch 79230

Adriano Banchieri

b. Sep. 3, 1568, Bologna, Italy, **d.** 1634, Bologna, Italy

Composer: Vocal

Born Tomaso Banchieri in Bologna, Banchieri was named "Adriano" when he started his novitiate in the Olivetian (Benedictine) monastic order in 1589. Banchieri studied with Gioseffo Guami and was best known as an organist. From 1592 to 1609, he held posts at monasteries and in churches in Lucca, Imola, Venice, and Verona. He settled in 1609 at the monastery of San Michele, in Bosco, on the outskirts of Bologna. In 1610, Banchieri participated in the canonization celebrations in Milan held in honor of San Carlo Borromeo. In 1615, Banchieri founded an early society for instrumental music, the Academia del Floridi; Claudio Monteverdi joined in 1620. As his health failed, Banchieri left Bosco and resettled in Bologna, where he died in 1634.

Banchieri's output consists of almost equal amounts of sacred and secular music; nearly all of it was published during his own lifetime. The sacred music, consisting of 12 mass settings, psalms, motets and other works, has elicited mixed reviews by scholars. Some note the conservatism of the masses, said to be in concord with the recommendations of the Council of Trent. However, others write that Banchieri's greatest innovations are to be found in his sacred music. From a middle-ground perspective, it's worth noting that Banchieri's *Concerti ecclesiastici* of 1599 are set for two four-part choirs with a figured bass, placing them among the earliest known examples of sacred music with a fully functional instrumental part.

Banchieri' s first publication is a collection of canzonas that appeared in 1596; he subsequently published works (a small part of his output) intended for instruments alone. Banchieri was also a prolific author of treatises that have proved invaluable in studies of seventeenth century performance style. In his theoretical writings, he describes methods of realizing figured-bass accompaniment, executing vocal ornaments, and introduces elements of notation such as the use of the "modern tie," barlines and accenting within a bar. He was also one of the first composers to make use of expression marks.

Banchieri's most influential works are his "Madrigal Comedies," which, like the masses, are 12 in number; spanning from the popular *La pazzia senile* of 1599 to *Trantiniamenti da villa* in 1630. Banchieri's madrigal books are arranged within the context of a related theme, and are meant to be performed as a whole evening's entertainment, somewhat akin to musical comedy revue. Banchieri was thoroughly in touch with the often coarse and bawdy secular humor of his day; as his pseudonymous popular novella, *The Nobility of the Ass* (1595) demonstrates. This jocose quality is encountered everywhere in Banchieri's Madrigal Comedies. *Il Festino del Giovedi Grasso* contains a number entitled "Contrappunto bestiale alla mente" in which his singers cuckoo, hoot, meow and woof. Banchieri was an expert on the dialects of northern Italy, and a veritable Tower of Babel of these dialects may be found in his *Barca di Venetia per Padova* of 1605. Appreciated by seventeenth century audiences, the earthiness of Banchieri's madrigals has remained appealing throughout the centuries.

Banchieri fits the true designation of a "renaissance man," given his interests in the sacred and secular, music theory, literature, linguistics, and architecture. In music, Banchieri foresaw trends that were leading toward Baroque style, but never composed opera, preferring instead to cultivate the Madrigal Comedy to its highest degree of artistic achievement, irreverence, and popular appeal. *—Uncle Dave Lewis*

VOCAL

Barca di Venetia per padova, madrigals, Op. 12 (1605; revised 1623)

Adriano Banchieri was a monk, but that didn't temper his explosive musical style or stop him from earning a reputation as one of the bad boys of late Renaissance music (he was described at various times as "L'enfant terrible," "The Dissonant One," etc.). Banchieri also had a wonderful secular sense of humor, and it shows in such madrigal comedies as *Barca di Venetia per Padova* ("Venetian Boat bound for Padua"), a set of 20 madrigals for five voices composed in 1605 and then revised somewhat in 1623.

The story is simple: several Italians and one German are traveling on a boat from Venice to Padua. Banchieri's treatment of this plain story, however, is full of wit (and also much graceful music). The characters all speak in their own dialects/languages, and often the text runs in several simultaneous and barely-related strands, much like a real-life conversation does. The text, incidentally, was apparently written entirely by Banchieri.

Near the beginning of the journey, the boatman recommends to the travelers that they decide on a pastime of some kind to make the voyage more pleasurable, and one of the passengers (specifically, a bookseller from Florence) suggests that the five best singers from their number entertain the others by singing songs by the composer Banchieri! So, for most of the work, the singers—who are selected by an audition held in the sixth madrigal of the set—sing madrigals. [Note that Banchieri has composed all of the "Banchieri madrigals" sung in *Barca di Venetia per Padova* from scratch—he doesn't reuse earlier material.] They finish some, but reject others as "too boring" (a wonderful touch of self-mockery). Banchieri uses the in-story madrigal singing as a chance to compose some madrigals in other composers' styles: Madrigals 9 and 10 are in the style of Gesualdo, Madrigal 14 imitates Marenzio, and Madrigal 15 is as Spano might have composed it.

Light touches abound. The German, who is now drunk, wanders off once into music of his own after the others have stopped singing (Madrigal 8). A lute string breaks in Madrigal 17 (the "lute music" is actually provided by the singers using empty syllables, and the string breaks when the first soprano makes a squawking sound). Two Jews enter the scene (Madrigal 13), and Banchieri provides some faux-Hebrew texts. As the travelers arrive in Padua (Madrigal 19), they give three cheers for Banchieri!

In 1623, for a new publication, Banchieri added an instrumental bass line to the original a cappella score. *—Blair Johnston*

Recommended:

- ○ **Banchieri: Barca di Venetia per Padova** / Ensemble Clement Janequin / HM 901281
- ○ **Adriano Banchieri: Il Zabaione Musicale** / F. Lombardo (cond.), L' Homme Arme Ensemble / 1995 / Arts 47258

Festino nella sera del giovedì grasso avanti cena, madrigals, Op. 18 (1608)

The Benedictine monk Adriano Banchieri occupies an important place in early seventeenth century Italian music. As a composer of sacred music, he was a great innovator and experimenter, playing a major role in the development of continuo bass. Banchieri was also an important theorist and organizer of musical life in his native Bologna, where he settled after residencies in various Italian monasteries. Somewhat surprisingly for a composer at the forefront of the seminal musical developments that took place in Italy around 1600, he never attempted an opera, the most revolutionary new form to emerge during that period. Instead, Banchieri preferred to remain faithful to the madrigal, now in the last stages of its development at the hands of Monteverdi. Banchieri seems to have had a particular predilection for comic madrigals, frequently combining them into an entertainment known as the madrigal comedy. The most famous of such works is the *Festino nella sera del giovedì grasso avanti cena* (Fete for the Evening of Carnival Thursday Before Supper). Rather like Boccaccio's *The Decameron*, it takes the form of an entertainment given before the guests and introduced in a prologue by Pleasure, who relates to other members of the party how he met an old man downstairs called Antique Rigour, an allegory for the old, polyphonic music or prima prattica. The *Festino*, then, is an entertainment about music, Pleasure being the representative of the modern, or seconda prattica style. Having bid Antique Rigour to "cast his old papers to a grocer," Pleasure then introduces the entertainment: a series of madrigals in between four and seven parts accompanied by continuo. They vary widely, ranging from an absurd onomatopoeic "improvised animal counterpoint," the calls of a street cryer headed "Foolish nonsense (but great fun)," to the mock-serious "The Lovers Sing a Little Song." Various madrigal styles are caricatured ("a madrigal full of conceits," for example) during the course of the comedy, which is by no means all buffoonery. For Banchieri, comedy was a serious business, as it was for his immediate forerunner, Orazio Vecchio, who spoke for composers of the madrigal comedies when he claimed that "just as much grace, talent, and naturalness is required to portray a comic part as to endow an old man with prudence and wisdom." *—Brian Robins*

Recommended:

- ○ **Banchieri, Striggio: Madrigalkomodien** / R. Alessandrini, Concerto Italiano / 1995 / Opus 111 30137
- ○ **Banchieri: Il festino del giovedi grasso** / Ottetto Polifonico Patavino / 1993 / Rivo Alto 9204

Chiara Banchini

b. Lugano, Switzerland
Violinist, Conductor

Swiss violinist Chiara Banchini is the co-founder and leader of the period instrument group Ensemble 415, which takes its name from the pitch recommended in old Baroque-era treatises for the note A below middle C: 415 cycles per second.

Banchini was born in Lugano, Switzerland and graduated from the Geneva Conservatory. Afterwards, Banchini studied with violinist Sandor Végh, but in the meantime had developed an interest in Baroque violin techniques and decided to further her studies with Belgian violinist Sigiswald Kuijken at the Royal Conservatory in The Hague. Upon earning her diploma, Banchini accepted a teaching post at the Centre for Early Music in Geneva, and at this time she began to appear on the concert circuit as a solo artist. After Banchini relocated from Geneva to the Schola Cantorum in Basel in 1981, in her own words she "felt the need to fill a vacuum in the Swiss musical vista" and formed Ensemble 415, her period instrument orchestra playing at Baroque pitch, rather than at the modern A of 440 cycles per second. The band attracted an immediate following as a live group, but did not develop an international reputation until it reached an exclusive recording agreement with the French label Harmonia Mundi in 1989. In 1992 Banchini and Ensemble 415 scored a critical and commercial hit with their recording of Arcangelo Corelli's *Concerti grossi*, Op. 6. Even more popular, and to date the most famous of Ensemble 415's recordings, was the 1996 release of the *Stabat Mater* of Antonio Vivaldi with guest vocalist Andreas Scholl, who later toured with Ensemble 415 in this work and became a star in his own right.

Banchini has also recorded for the labels Erato, Deutsche Harmonia Mundi, Virgin, Accent, Astreé, and for the Zig Zag Territories label. Banchini plays a Nicola Amati violin, which was hand crafted in Italy in 1674. *—Uncle Dave Lewis*

Recommended:

- ○ **Boccherini: Symphonies** / Banchini (cond.), Ensemble 415 / HM 1901291
- ○ **Corelli: Sonatas Op5** / Banchini (violin), Contini, Gohl, Christensen / 2000 / HM 1951307
- ○ **Tartini: Concerti** / Banchini (cond.), Ensemble 415 / 1995 / HM 901548
- ○ **Vivaldi: Stabat Mater** / Banchini (cond.), Ensemble 415 / HM 801571

Samuel Barber

b. Mar. 9, 1910, West Chester, PA, **d.** Jan. 23, 1981, New York, NY
Composer: Orchestral, Concerto, Vocal, Keyboard, Chamber Music, Opera

An open-hearted yet tough romantic, Samuel Barber was one of the few twentieth century American composers to fight for the primacy of lyricism. In his last decades he seemed to be losing the battle, but by the end of the century Barber had posthumously become one of America's most widely performed and recorded composers. In particular, his emotive *Violin Concerto* and *Adagio for Strings* have gained a popularity exceeded only by certain works of Aaron Copland.

Barber entered the Curtis Institute of Music in Philadelphia in 1924, where he met future opera composer Gian Carlo Menotti; the two would become lifelong lovers. Barber was an able pianist and a baritone of some talent, but he was an even more precocious composer. His 1933 Curtis graduation piece, the spirited *School for Scandal Overture*, has become a beloved concert opener.

Barber developed into America's most enduring composer of art songs; most popular is his tender setting for soprano and chamber orchestra of James Agee's *Knoxville: Summer of 1915*. Barber had unerring taste in texts, and his literary interests led him to compose some allusive short orchestral pieces. Yet he was particularly adept at writing abstract works, such as *Music for a Scene from Shelley*. Many of these are in large forms: two symphonies, one string quartet (from which was drawn the *Adagio for Strings*, first popularized by Arturo Toscanini), an ambitious piano sonata, and one concerto each for violin, cello, and piano. While following traditional formats, they are propelled by a dramatic expressivity that hadn't been fashionable since Sibelius. Equally direct in their emotional content are his three *Essays for Orchestra*, the second being the best crafted and most acclaimed.

Barber would have seemed an ideal composer for the stage, but he had limited success in that realm. *Medea*, a 1947 dance score for Martha Graham, has found greater longevity in orchestral excerpts. His 1958 *Vanessa* garnered him the first of two Pulitzer Prizes (the second was for his *Piano Concerto*), but, like most other American operas, it quickly dropped out of sight. Barber wrote *Anthony and Cleopatra* to open the new Metropolitan Opera House in 1966, but critical reaction was so hostile that he produced very little during his remaining 15 years. Barber was too conservative to be fashionable; his harmony could be astringent, but his tonality remained secure, his rhythms were strong and clear, and he was not above writing a good melody. *—James Reel*

ORCHESTRAL

Adagio for strings, Op. 11 (1936)

The *Adagio*, now almost invariably played in its orchestral version, comes from the slow movement of Barber's *String Quartet No. 1*, Op. 11 (1936), and must be counted among the most familiar pieces of American concert music; it has become a popular classic and even exists in a choral version. The music has something of the archaic dignity of Renaissance polyphony; a rhapsodic ascending phrase is repeated, inverted, expanded and embellished before rising to a brittle climax, then fading into silence. The gradual build-up and slow release of tension—the archetypical "arch" form—gives the work an inexorable quality. In the quartet it serves the work well, giving point and focus to its neighboring movements, though somewhat upstaging them by its eloquence.

The orchestral version, first performed in 1938 by the NBC Symphony Orchestra and Arturo Toscanini (on the same occasion as Barber's *First Essay for Orchestra*), conveys both tranquillity and grief, and has frequently been chosen to mark occasions of public mourning; it was, for instance, played at the funerals of F.D.R., J.F.K. and Princess Grace, and has appeared in the scores to a number of poignant films, including *The Elephant Man* and *Platoon.* Since then it has frequently been heard all over the world, and was one of the few American works to be played regularly in the Soviet Union during the cold war. It is, however, not necessary to regard the *Adagio* as a lament. The work is an intense meditation by a composer who, in his 26th year, already possessed the confidence and craftsmanship to make a powerful personal statement with clarity and sincerity. Its poignancy, simplicity, and dignity have been praised by such composers as Ned Rorem, Roy Harris, William Schuman and Aaron Copland. *—Roy Brewer*

Recommended:

- ○ **Thomas Schippers Conducts Barber, Menotti, Berg & D'Indy** / Schippers (cond.), New York PO / 1996 / Sony 62837
- ○ **Classic Performances: Bernstein's America** / L. Bernstein (cond.), Los Angeles PO / 1999 / DG 463465

Essay, Op. 12 (1937)

Samuel Barber's *First Essay for Orchestra* (1938), along with his extremely well-known *Adagio for Strings* of the same year, brought Barber worldwide recognition after being premiered by maestro Arturo Toscanini and the New York Symphony Orchestra on November 5, 1938. Toscanini was known for not championing the composers of the time or American composers and their works. Yet, in Barber, he heard music that matched the beauty and emotion of previous masters.

Barber, along with Gian Carlo Menotti, a fellow composer and lifelong friend, visited Toscanini for the first time approximately five years before the famous premiere concert. Here, Toscanini informed Barber that he intended to conduct one of his works. In spring of 1938, Barber sent to Toscanini the score for the *First Essay for Orchestra* along with the *Adagio for Strings,* hoping that one of them would be chosen for performance. Within months, Toscanini returned the scores to Barber. Toscanini included no comments about the works or plans for performance. Barber was bothered by this and did not visit Toscanini that summer as scheduled. Menotti did visit, though, and here Toscanini informed him that he intended to conduct both of Barber's compositions.

The form of this piece was inspired by the essay of the literary world. In the written essay, one main idea is presented at the beginning and then expanded upon. The brevity of the essay form and its focus upon a single idea attracted Barber. He first experimented with his derived essay form for music in his *Three Essays for Piano* (1926).

The first section of the *Essay for orchestra No. 1* has an elegiac character. The strings begin in a somber mood. The intensity increases toward a first climax and then descends to a desolate fanfare followed by a restatement of the first theme. A scherzo-like section follows in which the rhythm of the lower piano strings plays a prominent part. The tension mounts to reach an intense climax that winds down amidst murmurations of the piano. A new crescendo brings a powerful restatement of the initial theme. Then the music dies out to the lament of distant trumpets. *—AMG*

Recommended:

- ○ **Music of Samuel Barber** / L. Slatkin (cond.), St. Louis SO / EMI 49463
- ○ **Barber: Adagio; Symphony 1** / Zinman (cond.), Baltimore SO / 1992 / Argo 436288

Music for a Scene from Shelley, Op. 7 (1933)

Barber completed this work in August 1933, and Werner Janssen led the first performance with the New York Philharmonic on March 24, 1935. It is scored for triple winds, trumpets and trombones, four horns, tuba, timpani plus one percussionist, harp, and strings. Barber wrote the *School for Scandal Overture,* his first work for orchestra, in 1931 while still a student at the Curtis Institute of Music. Despite Fritz Reiner's refusal to conduct it with the Curtis Orchestra, the music won a prize that enabled the composer to revisit Europe in 1933 for 18 months. At the home of Gian-Carlo Menotti in Cadegliano, Italy, he created his second orchestral work—*Music for a Scene From Shelley.* Barber would later write: "In the summer of 1933, I was reading *Prometheus Unbound.* The lines in Act II, Scene V, where Shelley indicates music (quoted on the title page of the score), suggested the composition. It is really incidental music for this scene, and has nothing at all to do with the figure of Prometheus...." However, to his beloved uncle and father-like champion, Sidney Homer, "the new piece sounds like Prometheus struggling against his bonds. Not like Shelley but still like Prometheus."

Barbara B. Heyman, the composer's foremost biographer and critic, has written that Barber "moved away from Brahms and toward Debussy" in search of an orchestral style. She calls Shelley a "tone poem... in an AB form with a coda," adding that "what is striking is the way Barber has supported tone painting through orchestral color."

The music begins very softly with muted strings, horns, and trumpets, Adagio, ma non troppo in triple meter (9/8 time). The first subject is a four-note theme that descends chromatically. The second is marked "a little less slowly," to be played "exultantly" at triple-forte level by violins and violas. There is a memorable trumpet solo further on, followed by an increase in speed and intensity that prepares the way for a "pesante, fortissimo" climax. What Heyman identifies as a coda recalls the spirit of the opening, if not the letter. *Music for a Scene From Shelley* concludes softly on a muted brass chord. *—Roger Dettmer*

Recommended:

- ○ **Barber: Adagio; Symphony 1** / Zinman (cond.), Baltimore SO / 1992 / Argo 436288
- ○ **Samuel Barber: Medea's Meditation & other works** / N. Järvi (cond.), Detroit SO / 2001 / Chandos 9908

The School for Scandal, overture, Op. 5 (1931–1933)

With the stunning success of his first orchestral work, *Overture to The School for Scandal* (1931–33), Samuel Barber was recognized as one of the most promising talents of his generation. Over the following four decades, he emerged as one of the signal personalities in American music and produced a body of works that have become staples—orchestral, chamber, vocal, operatic—of the concert repertoire. Richard Sheridan's play *The School for Scandal* (1777) is a comedy of manners that contains plenty of wit and amorous intrigue. Barber's overture is not so much incidental music as it is a sophisticated tone poem; while it wasn't written for any particular production of the play, it deftly captures the atmosphere of Sheridan's work. Characterized by the composer's trademark lyricism and effervescent, frolicsome orchestral color, the music convincingly reflects the play's general tone. The overture is a miniature rondo in which themes and fragments of themes are intertwined with all the ingenuity of Sheridan's complicated story. The splashy, hectic opening is followed by a pastoral theme for oboe, repeated by lushly scored strings. The slyly twisted tonality of the middle section provides subtle allusion to the scheming and duplicity that make up the play's tortuous plot. Barber makes ingenious use of the children's game-song, "I sent a letter to my love," while harmonic conflicts and rhythmic eccentricities maintain the buoyant mood. A thoroughly modern work with no concessions to eighteenth century pastiche, this composition possesses all the glitter and panache of a true theater piece and remains a firm favorite with concert audiences. *—Roy Brewer*

Recommended:

- ○ **Thomas Schippers Conducts Barber, Menotti, Berg, D'Indy** / Schippers (cond.), New York PO / 1996 / Sony 62837
- ○ **Bernstein, Barber & Gershwin** / G. Schwarz (cond.), Seattle SO / 1990 / Delos 3078

CONCERTO

Capricorn Concerto, for flute, oboe, trumpet & strings, Op. 21 (1944)

Samuel Barber's *Capricorn Concerto* (1944) is named after the house in Mount Kisco, NY, where the composer lived with his partner and collaborator Gian-Carlo Menotti from 1943 to 1974. The work's instrumental forces—flute, oboe, and trumpet in soloistic roles, accompanied by string orchestra—suggest a kinship with the Baroque concerto grosso. However, the connection is deceptive; instead of interacting with the orchestra in the same musical realm, as leading instruments do in the concerto grosso, the soloists here seem to exist on an altogether different emotional plane from that of the orchestra, navigating from an extroverted, Bernstein-like breeziness into a meditative world of their own. There is no difficulty in recognizing the nervous energy of the dancing polyrhythms and jazzy syncopations as distinctly American, while the more lyrical passages at once recall the noble pathos of the composer's string quartets. The flute is the prima donna of the ensemble, assuming a place of prominence with both ardent songs and fluid trills, while the oboe takes on a more expressive, calming role. In the first movement, the trumpet is treated almost like another woodwind instrument; its brassier moments are reserved for later. The movement is in three sections: a short introduction for the strings is followed by a supple melody played by each of the solo instruments in turn, leading to a driving Allegro. The thematic material of the entire movement is derived, in various permutations, from the introduction. The second movement, Allegretto, is a demure scherzo with new thematic material. The trumpet plays muted and staccato throughout; here, the soloists unite as a concertato, lightly accompanied by the strings. What follows is a short, poetic interlude and an Allegro con brio finale that does not seem to posses a true "brio" quality. The carnival spirit of the trumpet's opening invitation is swiftly followed by an intense episodic development of earlier themes. Some fans of Barber's other music find this work a bit on the dry side. But it is imaginative, entertaining, and very skillfully composed music. —*Roy Brewer*

Recommended:

○ **Howard Hanson Conducts Barber, Piston, Griffes and others** / Hanson (cond.), Eastman-Rochester Orch. / 1992 / Mercury 434307

○ **Barber: Violin, Cello & Capricorn Concertos** / L. Slatkin (cond.), Takezawa, Isserlis, St. Louis SO / 1996 / RCA 68283

Cello Concerto in A minor, Op. 22 (1945)

Barber was a corporal on inactive duty in the U.S. Army Air Force when he undertook the *Cello Concerto,* in January 1945, commissioned by John Nicholas Brown of Providence, RI, for the Russian-born cellist Raya Garbousova. Serge Koussevitzky, celebrating his 20th season as music director of the Boston Symphony Orchestra, masterminded the project, even facilitating Barber's discharge from the military. The new concerto enjoyed a greater success on tour in Carnegie Hall than in its premiere on April 5, 1946, in Boston's Symphony Hall. New York City critics were lavish in their praise, and later that spring gave the work their Fifth Annual Award as "exceptional among orchestral compositions performed for the first time [here] during the concert season." Yet Barber was not fully satisfied by the work and—as with many of his pieces—made numerous changes between 1947 and publication in 1950, most of them in the opening Allegro. Three decades later he considered simplifying the solo part, to encourage more performances, but prolonged illness prevented any further changes. If the *Cello Concerto* may never rival the popularity of his 1939 *Violin Concerto,* it has come abreast of the 1962 *Piano Concerto,* well ahead of the *Capricorn Concerto* which immediately preceded it.

The sonata-form Allegro moderato in D minor is half again longer than either succeeding movement, yet all of its thematic materials are encapsulated in the first 25 measures, introduced by the orchestra. It begins with a jagged, metrically irregular, two-bar motif (2/4 + 3/4) that not only recurs but dominates the development section. Immediately after, flute and English horn play a principal theme whose salient feature is a descending scale. This is followed by a triplet figure for bassoon that also takes on structural significance later. Next, violins play a lyrical second theme before the triplets return, then the inaugural motif slightly altered. The soloist enters with a short, not-showy cadenza before the second exposition in which thematic materials are developmentally extended, all of this before the development section proper. The latter ends with a more elaborate solo cadenza, followed by the recapitulation and a coda based on the opening motif.

As Barbara Heyman wrote in *The Composer and His Music,* the Andante sostenuto slow movement, in C sharp minor, "spins a sad and romantically tender siciliana in canon between the cello and orchestra in a set of free variations." Cello and oboe introduce the principal subject over muted strings, after which the oboe yields to a variety of echoing instruments.

For Heyman the concluding Molto allegro e appassionato, "centering around A minor, [is] a kind of rondo-fantasy [with] a restless theme characterized by a persistently reiterated, descending semitone and an arpeggiated seventh chord." She also notes "interjections of a somber, dirge-like theme (in C minor) over a ground bass." The movement begins and ends as the first did, with a jagged new motif for full orchestra, ending in A major. —*Roger Dettmer*

Recommended:

○ **Samuel Barber: Orchestral Works Vol. 2** / Alsop (cond.), W. Warner, Scottish National Orch. / 2001 / Naxos 559088

○ **Barber: Violin, Cello & Capricorn Concertos** / L. Slatkin (cond.), Isserlis, St. Louis SO / 1996 / RCA 68283

○ **Barber: Symphony No 2; Cello Concerto; Medea** / Barber (cond.), Nelsova, New SO of London / Pearl 0151

Piano Concerto, Op. 38 (1962)

Samuel Barber's *Piano Concerto* (1960–62) served as the composer's final masterpiece, and arguably the zenith of his professional life. For its composition he received his second Pulitzer Prize (1963) and, one year later, the Music Critics' Circle Award; during this period, Barber was among the most honored and respected living American composers, both at home and abroad.

The concerto was commissioned in 1959 by G. Schirmer, Inc.—Barber's publisher for most of his career—in honor of the company's upcoming 100th anniversary. The work was to be among the first performed at Lincoln Center's new *Philharmonic Hall,* which was under construction at the time; John Browning, Barber's favorite pianist at the time, would be the soloist with the Boston Symphony Orchestra under the direction of Erich Leinsdorf.

The concerto is notable as an instance of the composer's self-borrowing; for the work's second movement, he orchestrated and elaborated upon the *Elegy for Flute and Piano* (1959). This movement, as well as the concerto's first, was complete by 1960, but the last movement was not completed until two weeks prior to the premiere, on September 24, 1962. Work was partly delayed by Barber's lengthy depression following the death of his sister; also, in the spring of 1962, Barber became the first American composer to attend the Congress of Soviet Composers.

As he had done in previous compositions intended for a soloist, Barber worked closely with Browning to shape the work around his style and technical skills—apparently listening to three days worth of the pianist's repertoire in the process (similar partnerships were formed during the composition of the *Cello Concerto* (1945), with Raya Garbousova, and the *Piano Sonata* (1949), with Vladimir Horowitz).

The resulting masterwork incorporates Barber's natural affinity for flowing melody and rather traditional compositional demeanor into an imposing structure. Eschewing any need for an orchestral introduction, the first movement ends with a declamatory recitative for the soloist—substantial enough to accommodate three distinct themes—that gradually gives way to a more lyrical strain in the full orchestra. Over the course of the movement, which is roughly in sonata form, these two elements—declamation and impassioned lyricism—are ever more intricately entwined.

The previously mentioned second movement is considerably calmer in mood, very much like a song; true to its origins, it features the solo flute as a main protagonist, while the piano occasionally assumes an accompanimental role. The finale, much more rhythmic and active, seizes obsessively on an ostinato figure in the piano that, within the movement's persistent 5/8 meter, takes on a sinuous, ambiguous quality. —*Chris Boyes*

Recommended:

○ **Samuel Barber: Symphony No 1; Piano Concerto** / L. Slatkin (cond.), J. Browning, St. Louis SO / 1991 / RCA Victor 60732

○ **Barber: Concertos for Violin & Piano** / Y. Levi (cond.), J. K. Parker, Atlanta SO / 1997 / Telarc 80441

Violin Concerto, Op. 14 (1939)

Given the lush, lyrical, Romantic propensities of Samuel Barber's music, it should come as no surprise that the composer achieved great success in that most Romantic of genres, the solo instrumental concerto. Indeed, Barber wrote a concerto for each of the "Big Three" concerto instruments: piano, violin, and cello, producing a trio of works that have earned a secure place in the standard repertoire. With an extensive timbral palette and the opportunity for virtuosic display at his disposal, Barber made full use of the concerto's possibilities, from exquisitely colored, tender lyricism to splashy, breathless pyrotechnics.

Excepting a now-lost piano concerto the composer wrote at the age of 20, the *Violin Concerto* was Barber's first essay in the genre. Unfortunately for the composer, the *Violin Concerto's* creation was affected by meddling and interference on the part of the commissioning parties. Soap tycoon Samuel Fels offered a substantial fee to Barber to write a work for the young Russian-born violinist Iso Briselli. After seeing the first two movements, Briselli insisted that the finale be a flashy showpiece that would allow him to display his technical prowess. Barber complied, producing a brief moto perpetuo of under four minutes' duration—less than half as long as either of the other movements. However, Briselli objected to the final movement. According to early accounts, Briselli found the finale, in which the violinist is required to produce near-constant torrents of notes, impossible to play. The violinist later claimed that he objected purely on artistic grounds, and that the movement simply did not fit with the other two. Whatever the reason, Briselli refused to play the piece, and Fels asked Barber to return the advance that he had been paid. Nevertheless, the work was successfully premiered on February 7, 1941, by Albert Spalding and the Philadelphia Orchestra conducted by Eugene Ormandy.

Although the Concerto's Allegro is marked by a predominantly lyrical, even vernal, quality, the movement is hardly free of the conflict and high drama typifying the concerto tradition. The flowing, organic material that opens the movement is contrasted by a short, distinctive iambic rhythmic figure which recurs in various guises throughout. The characteristically lyrical Andante, which, like so many of Barber's slow movements, possesses a melancholic, elegiac quality, is tinged with a certain mercurial moodiness. The final perpetual-motion Presto is a breathless, nonstop whirlwind that races by in a steady, virtually uninterrupted rhythmic flow illuminated by brilliant flashes of color. —*AMG*

Recommended:

○ **Barber, Walton: Violin Concertos; Bloch: Schelomo** / Zinman (cond.), J. Bell, Baltimore SO / 1997 / London 452851

○ **Barber, Maxwell Davies: Violin Concertos** / Bernstein (cond.), I. Stern, New York PO / 1995 / Sony 64506

VOCAL

Hermit Songs, for voice & piano, Op. 29 (1952–1953)

This cycle of ten songs was commissioned by the Elizabeth Sprague Coolidge Foundation and completed during 1952 and 1953. The texts are anonymous writings from Irish monastic sources of the eighth through the thirteenth centuries—most notably marginalia of hand-copied manuscripts—that embrace every possible sentiment, from the devout to the obscene. Barber responded with sympathetic settings that greatly amplify the humor, wisdom, and piety of the various texts. Leontyne Price gave the first performance of the *Hermit Songs,* with the composer at the piano, in Washington, D.C., October 30, 1953.

The first song, *At Saint Patrick's Purgatory*, is a prayer to God asking for protection on an upcoming voyage. The speaker also asks for forgiveness for his sins. This first song is musically similar to the other songs of the cycle. Occurrences in this song such as mixed meter, a lack of time signature, and the extraordinary presence of open fourths and fifths continue throughout *Hermit Songs*. The second song, *Church Bell at Night* is a short, calm song, claiming that the company of a bell is better than that of a "light and foolish woman." The third song is a beautiful recitative aria titled *St. Ita's Vision*. The aria section is a beautiful lullaby sung to the baby Jesus. *The Heavenly Banquet* is the title of the fourth song. It is festive and describes the speaker's wish to feed and entertain biblical figures. The fifth song of the cycle, *The Crucifixion*, is a tender lament highlighted by dissonance. Barber does well in bringing out the suffering entailed by the speaker. *Sea-Snatch*, the sixth song, is frantic and describes a ship lost to a storm at sea. The seventh song, *Promiscuity*, is short and mischievous. The next song, *The Monk and his Cat*, has a relaxed mood and compares the daily lives, eyes, and joys of the two figures in the title. *The Praises of God* is the ninth song. This song points to the foolishness of those who do not enjoy singing. The final song, titled *The Desire for Hermitage*, is calm, yet dissonant, and contemplates hermitage and death. Barber had an interest in the idea of reclusion and hermitage throughout his career. *—AMG*

Recommended:

○ **Leontyne Price Sings Barber** / L. Price, Barber / 1994 / RCA Victor 61983

○ **Secrets of the Old: Complete Song of Barber** / Studer, J. Browning / 1994 / DG 435867

Knoxville: Summer of 1915, for high voice & orchestra, Op. 24 (1947; revised 1950)

In the latter half of the twentieth century, the ravages and long, painful aftermath of World War II were undoubtedly the most potent catalyst in changing the face of artistic thought. Certainly, World War II affected many composers of divergent inclinations, resulting in changing aesthetics and modes of musical expression. This war was in part responsible for music newly and especially concerned with and informed by technology and tragedy, rationality and remorse.

While never explicitly explained as such by the composer, it is tempting to view Samuel Barber's *Knoxville: Summer of 1915* (1947) as an expression of one facet of his reactions to World War II. While portions of Barber's wartime *Symphony No. 2* (1944–47) are clearly cast in an overtly patriotic mode, *Knoxville* finds at its center an urgently intense, almost overwhelming nostalgia, free of unrest though characterized by a pervasively sensuous immediacy.

This latter aspect of both music and text is a crucial element in the dynamics of the work. It is an ardent and sincere—rather than merely sentimental—nostalgia Barber evokes, informed by a sense and realization of loss. Much of the appeal that James Agee's text (which Barber had discovered in an anthology drawn from *Partisan Review*) must have had for the composer came not only from the inherent qualities of the prose, but also in the similarity in the ages of author and composer as well as the shared experience of the idyllic childhood expressed in Agee's warm, vivid tones. "It has become that time of evening," begins Barber's setting, characterized in its most serene moments by supple, liquid vocal lines, uncomplicated, often diatonic harmony, and the regular lilt of triplet rhythms. The pictorial sense of Barber's orchestration is fully equal to that of the text, emerging in subtle instrumental characterizations of both the more languid aspects of the Knoxville twilight—nocturnal insects, the gentle spray of a garden hose, the subdued rocking of "parents on porches"—and momentary disturbances such as a passing streetcar, its overhead spark "crackling and cursing... like a small malignant spirit set to dog its tracks." *—Michael Rodman*

Recommended:

○ **Knoxville: Summer of 1915** / Zinman (cond.), Upshaw, St. Luke's CO / 1989 / Nonesuch 79187

○ **Knoxville: Summer of 1915; Essay 1 & 2; Adagio** / Y. Levi (cond.), S. McNair, Atlanta SO / 1992 / Telarc 80250

○ **Leontyne Price Sings Barber** / Schippers (cond.), L. Price, New Philharmonia Orch. / 1994 / RCA Victor 61983

KEYBOARD

Excursions, Op. 20 (1942–1944)

Although Barber is not known for his piano compositions, he nevertheless wrote a few works of importance for the instrument. His *Piano Concerto*, Op. 38 (1962), and *Piano Sonata*, Op. 26 (1949), come to mind, but the *Excursions* are also high-quality compositions. Indeed, they are among his most popular instrumental works, with a dozen or so recordings available by 2002. Vladimir Horowitz premiered the set, minus *No. 3*, on January 4, 1945, at the Academy of Music in Philadelphia. The third piece was unplayed because Barber's publisher Schirmer initially left it out of the set. All the *Excursions* are short, the entire set lasting about 12 to 15 minutes. Each is based on a folk tune or idiom and captures some slice of Americana. The first piece, marked Un poco allegro, depicts the hustle and bustle of the city with catchy, tricky rhythms, jazzy playfulness, and motoric drive. The second piece, "In Slow Blues Tempo," has a bluesy manner to be sure, but is not imitation-Gershwin or beholden to other popular composers of the day. The music is sassy and spiky, confident in its nonchalance and stop-and-start gait. The third *Excursion* (Allegretto), a set of variations on *The Streets of Laredo*, is mainly a lullaby. The slow, quasi-Romantic manner of the theme is interrupted by jazzy, energetic variants throughout that are both playful and touching. The final piece (Allegro molto) is a barn dance, somewhat in the spirit of Copland's from *Rodeo*, but jazzier and more amusingly mischievous, not least to the soloist who must tackle Barber's tricky rhythms. *—Robert Cummings*

Recommended:

○ **Barber: Solo Piano Music** / D. Pollack / 1998 / Naxos 559015

○ **Barber: Complete Works for Solo Piano** / Parkin / 1993 / Chandos 9177

Piano Sonata, Op. 26 (1949)

Samuel Barber's *Piano Sonata* (1947–49) was hailed upon its premiere as a masterpiece of American musical literature and the newest landmark work for the piano. The instant importance of the work was highlighted by its having been first performed by the internationally known pianist Vladimir Horowitz; Barber's sonata was the first large-scale American piano work to be premiered by such a prestigious figure. Horowitz himself pronounced the sonata "the first truly great native work in the form."

The piece was commissioned in the fall of 1947 by Irving Berlin and Richard Rodgers to commemorate the 25th anniversary of the League of Composers. Barber set to work almost immediately and finished the first movement quickly, despite multiple projects that occupied his energies. Soon these other engagements drew Barber away from the sonata, and work stalled. The second movement was not completed until eight months later, with the third finished soon after. Barber originally had a three-movement sonata in mind, but Horowitz convinced him that the piece needed a "very flashy last movement." This last movement caused Barber much frustration. After months with no progress, Horowitz telephoned Barber and, hoping to inspire him, called him a "constipated composer." Barber became angry and wrote the entire fourth movement the next day. This was in June 1949, nearly two years after the work was commissioned.

This piece was composed in the middle of Barber's long career, during which much of his music fused his lyrical, elongated melodic style with new compositional devices. The sonata has levels of chromaticism and dissonance not approached in earlier works. There is even some use of 12-tone techniques in the first three movements, significant because of prior criticism that Barber's music represented a throwback to the Romantic period.

Barber chose to set all movements in conventional forms; the first is cast in sonata form. This movement is fast-moving and energetic. A noticeable aspect is the contrast heard between sections with fragmented, dotted rhythms and sections characterized by sweeping, lyrical melodies and smooth accompaniment. The second movement is a nimble and delicate scherzo, set in rondo form. The third movement, languorous and expressive, is the most demonstrative of Barber's encounter with the innovations of the early twentieth century. Chromaticism and melodies using all 12 tones are abundant. A four-voice fugue, formally similar to those of Bach (much loved by Barber) serves as the finale. Though conventional in structure, this movement also contains complicated syncopated rhythms and jazz harmonies. *—Chris Boyes*

Recommended:

○ **Horowitz Plays Prokofiev, Barber & Kabalevsky Sonatas** / Horowitz / 1990 / RCA Victor 60377

○ **Earl Wild: 20th & 21st Century Piano Sonatas** / E. Wild / 2000 / Ivory 71005

○ **Barber: Solo Piano Music** / D. Pollack / 1998 / Naxos 559015

CHAMBER MUSIC

String Quartet in B major, Op. 11 (1936)

Samuel Barber's first and only string quartet didn't end up the way he intended it to, for the second movement eventually overshadowed the entire opus when he transcribed it for string orchestra as the *Adagio for Strings*. In addition, a projected last movement never really came together, and the piece as a whole became marked as a vehicle for bringing the *Adagio* to life. The first movement has merit, however, in that it shows Barber experimenting with a style somewhat removed from his usual hyper-melodic idiom. Barber composed the piece in the summer of 1936 at St. Wolfgang, Austria, a small mountain town near Salzburg, where he and Gian Carlo Menotti had rented a cottage. It was premiered at the American Academy in Rome by the Pro Arte Quartet in December of the same year. The finished work has two movements. The first, Molto allegro e appassionato, is structured in a loose sonata form. Reminiscent of Beethoven and unlike, in terms of rhetoric, most of Barber's works, it is structured around rhythmic motifs rather than on the basis of a central, emotionally charged melody. The second movement, Molto adagio; molto allegro, begins with one of the most famous melodies in history, the slow, sensitive cantilena which became the *Adagio for Strings*. The second half of the movement, Molto allegro (originally intended to be the last movement) is a rather unexciting and perfunctory recapitulation of first-movement material. *—Graham Olson*

Recommended:

- **American Originals** / Emerson SQ / 1992 / DG 435864
- **Barber: Dover Beach; Songs; String Quartet; Serenade** / Endellion SQ / 1994 / Virgin 45033

OPERA

Vanessa, Op. 32 (1956–1957; revised 1964)

Samuel Barber's *Vanessa* (1958) is widely considered to be the first operatic masterpiece by an American composer. Dimitri Mitropoulos, who assisted Barber with the orchestration for *Vanessa*, proclaimed, "At last, an American grand opera!" The composer was nearly 50 years old at time of the premiere, and some wondered why Barber had waited so long to compose an opera. Barber responded by stating that he needed "long-term preparation for the job," citing the combined challenges of "how to write for orchestra, how to write for chorus and ballet, [and] how to write for solo voice and orchestra," as the difficulties of the genre.

Barber's biggest challenge in composing an opera was finding a high-quality libretto. The composer had been attempting to find one since as far back as 1934, but began searching in earnest during the early 1940s. Communications with literary figures, such as Thornton Wilder and James Agee, came to nothing, and so, in the spring of 1952, Barber turned to Gian Carlo Menotti, his partner in life and fellow composer. Having fashioned the libretti for many of his own operas, Menotti was well prepared for the task, and the two eventually settled on Isak Dinesen's *Seven Gothic Tales* as a suitable inspiration. Menotti immediately drafted a first scene for Barber, and by the end of that summer the scene's music was composed. However, Menotti's work on his own compositions kept him from completing the libretto for two further years; he was finally prompted to act by Barber's refusal to compose another note of music until he had the entire drama in hand. By the end of the summer of 1955 the libretto was complete.

Vanessa is the story of a mother (Vanessa) and daughter (Erika) whose experiences with love are tragically parallel. Having waited many years in self-imposed solitude for the return of her lost love, Anatol, Vanessa meets, and falls in love, with his son (also named Anatol). Unfortunately, Erika also falls for the young man, and the opportunistic visitor seduces and impregnates her. Not returning Erika's love, Anatol instead marries (for suspicious reasons) the elder Vanessa—who knows nothing of the affair—leaving Erika to begin her own long period of loneliness.

Vanessa was premiered on January 23, 1958, at the Metropolitan Opera. The opera received stellar reviews, and Barber was hailed as a national hero. Much credit belongs to the renowned American soprano, Eleanor Steber, who stepped into the title role at relatively short notice (Sena Jurinac, the original choice, had taken ill); her performance was a triumph. Unfortunately, the European premiere was less successful, and its harsh reception on the continent has surely hindered its place in the repertory since. Barber made slight revisions to the work in 1964, eliminating some sections he felt to be dramatically stagnant, and removing one especially difficult section (the coloratura "skating" aria). *—AMG*

Synopsis:

Act One. The story takes place at a rural gothic manor around 1905 in an unspecified northern country. Middle-aged, attractive Vanessa is withdrawn, obsessed with thoughts of the lover she has not seen for 20 years, Anatol, the lover for whom she is ever in waiting. Her aging mother, the Baroness, assails her daughter's self-imposed exile with her own form of withdrawal, her chilling silence. Anatol's look-alike son, also named Anatol, arrives at the manor and Vanessa at first mistakes him for his father, inquiring whether he still loves her. Erika, Vanessa's beautiful niece, asks the young Anatol to leave, but he is determined to stay.

Act Two. The action in this panel takes place about a month later. Erika goes to the Baroness and confides she was seduced by the charming young Anatol on his first night at the manor. She recounts her refusal to accept his subsequent marriage proposal because he would not promise faithfulness. Cryptically, the Baroness warns her granddaughter to have suspicions of love when it seems to perfectly fit our preconceived idea of it. Vanessa and Anatol, fresh from an ice-skating junket (and obviously in love), tell the alcoholic Old Doctor of their plans for a grand ball for the coming New Year's Eve. Erika, aware of her aunt's feelings for Anatol and still harboring strong ones of her own for him, tells the young philanderer she will have nothing to do with him.

Act Three. The Old Doctor announces the engagement of Anatol and Vanessa at the ball. Erika, pregnant with Anatol's child, is disheartened at the news and hurries outside to attempt to induce an abortion. When she is missed, Anatol goes in search of her and finds her unconscious in a ravine. After she regains consciousness back at the manor she indicates to the Baroness that Anatol's child has been aborted.

Act Four. Vanessa, unsuspecting of Erika's affair with Anatol, as well as the reasons behind her recent troubles, marries Anatol. She announces they will live in Paris, and informs Erika that she is giving her the manor. She asks her to explain the recent strange incident, but Erika withholds the true account of the events. After the newlyweds depart, Erika, who has become reclusive now, explains to her grandmother that now is the time to begin her own period of waiting. *—Robert Cummings*

Recommended:

- **Barber: Vanessa** / Mitropoulos (cond.), Steber, Gedda, Tozzi, Elias, Resnik / 1957 / RCA 7899
- **Barber: Vanessa** / Slatkin (cond.), Graham, Brewer, Burden / 2004 / Chandos 5032

Sir John Barbirolli

b. Dec. 2, 1899, London, England, **d.** Jul. 29, 1970, London, England
Conductor

Sir John Barbirolli studied cello as a boy, making his debut public appearance at the age of twelve. He received a formal education at Trinity College of Music and the Royal Academy of Music, from which he graduated in 1916. Upon graduation, he found a position in the Queen's Hall Orchestra, becoming its youngest member. He made his professional solo debut as a cellist in Aeolian Hall, London, in 1917.

During World War I he joined the British Army; while in the service he got his first taste of conducting by leading an all-volunteer orchestra. After his service ended in 1919, he returned to the Queen's Hall Orchestra. He also resumed performances as a cello soloist, appearing with the Bournemouth Municipal Orchestra. He joined and toured with the International String Quartet beginning in 1923. Soon after, he organized and conducted a chamber orchestra in Chelsea.

The British National Opera Company engaged him to conduct on tour. On December 12, 1927, he attracted attention by successfully substituting as conductor of the London Symphony Orchestra when Sir Thomas Beecham was indisposed; during the 1928 season he began to conducting opera regularly in London at both Sadler's Wells and Covent Garden.

In 1933 he was appointed permanent conductor of the Scottish Orchestra, remaining in that position for three seasons. At the same time he was the conductor of the Leeds Symphony Orchestra, and guest-conducted several orchestras at home and abroad. During the 1936–37 season he accepted a ten-week position as guest conductor of the New York Philharmonic. This led to an invitation to assume the principal conductorship of that orchestra, in which capacity he succeeded Arturo Toscanini. Barbirolli remained with the Philharmonic through 1942. During his tenure in New York, he gave the world premieres of the *Violin Concerto* and the *Sinfonia da Requiem* of Benjamin Britten, then resident in New York. While in the United States, Barbirolli also appeared with various American and Canadian orchestras.

By the end of his fifth season in New York, an uneasy relationship with the New York Philharmonic and declining enthusiasm from critics and audiences (who preferred a style more flamboyant than his objective approach) led him to return to England. In 1943 he began his long tenure as conductor of the Hallé Orchestra in Manchester; in 1958 he reduced the number of yearly concerts he performed with them when he took the title "Conductor-in-Chief," and in 1968 he retired from the Hallé with the title "Conductor Laureate for Life."

Meanwhile he had returned to America; recruited by the Houston Symphony Orchestra's indefatigable patroness Ima Hogg to succeed Leopold Stokowski, he became their conductor from 1961–67. The 1960s were also marked by many guest and touring appearances with the Philharmonia Orchestra, the BBC Symphony Orchestra, and the Hallé. He was knighted in 1949 and was made a Companion of Honour in 1969.

His repertoire centered on the late Romantic era, and on British composers Elgar, Vaughan Williams, and Delius; he led the first performances of Vaughan Williams' *Symphony No. 7* and *Symphony No. 8*. Aside from the music of Britten, he showed little interest in music of modern tendencies; late in his career, though, he developed a particular affinity for Gustav Mahler. Barbirolli left a notable recorded legacy that extends well into the stereo LP era. *—Joseph Stevenson*

Recommended:

- **Barbirolli Conducts Sibelius** / Barbirolli (cond.), Halle Orchestra / 1988 / EMI 769205
- **Mahler: Symphony 9** / Barbirolli (cond.), Berlin PO / 2002 / EMI 67926
- **Barbirolli Conducts Elgar & Vaughan Williams** / Barbirolli (cond.), Allegri SQ, City of London Sinfonia / 2000 / Angel 67264
- **Vaughan Williams: Symphony 5; Bax: Tintagel** / Barbirolli (cond.), Philharmonia Orch., London SO / 1994 / EMI 65110
- **Maestro Gentile** / Barbirolli (cond.) / 2001 / Past Perfect 205633
- **BBC Legends: Barbirolli** / Barbirolli (cond.), Harper, Halle Orch., BBC SO / 1996 / BBC 4401

Daniel Barenboim

b. Nov. 15, 1942, Buenos Aires, Argentina
Conductor, Pianist

Daniel Barenboim was born in Buenos Aires on November 15, 1942, into a family of Ukrainian Jewish descent. Daniel's mother was his first piano teacher; he later studied with his father, Enrique Barenboim, who was an eminent music professor.

After playing for the noted violinist Adolph Busch, who was impressed by his talent, Daniel made his debut recital at the age of seven. In 1951, he played at the *Mozarteum* in Salzburg and observed Igor Markevitch's conducting class. The family moved to Israel in 1952; two years later, Daniel went back to Salzburg for a conducting course with Markevitch, piano studies with Edwin Fischer, and chamber music performance with Enrico Mainardi. In the same year, he enrolled in the Accademia di Santa Cecilia in Rome, becoming, in 1956, one of the Academy's youngest graduates. He studied conducting with Carlo Zecchi at the Accademia Musicale Chigiana in Siena, also attending Nadia Boulanger's music theory and composition class at Fontainebleau. After recitals in Paris in 1955, he made his London debut in 1956, playing a recital in Festival Hall as part of the Mozart bicentennial celebrations. His U.S. debut was at New York's Carnegie Hall on January 20, 1957, in Prokofiev's *Piano Concerto No. 1,* with Leopold Stokowski conducting the Symphony of the Air. Later that year, he made his conducting debut in Haifa, Israel. His first North American recital was on January 17, 1958, in New York. Barenboim played his first cycle of the complete 32 piano sonatas of Beethoven in Tel Aviv in 1960 and then in New York. As a frequent conductor of the English Chamber Orchestra from 1964, he often appeared as soloist-conductor in concertos, touring with the ECO in Latin America and the Far East. Debuts with leading orchestras included the London Symphony Orchestra (New York, 1968), Berlin Philharmonic (1969), and New York Philharmonic (1970). Since then he has guest conducted virtually all of the world's leading orchestras. He led London's South Bank Summer Music Festival from 1968 to 1970. His first appearance conducting opera was at the Edinburgh Festival in 1973; his debut opera was *Don Giovanni.*

In 1967, Barenboim married the brilliant cellist Jacqueline Du Pré, with whom he made several exceptional recital recordings. The couple also participated in a number of excellent concert and documentary films for television directed by Christopher Nupen. Unfortunately, this partnership ended when Du Pré contracted multiple sclerosis, which forced her to end her playing career in 1972. (She died in 1987.)

Barenboim became music director of the Orchestre de Paris in 1975. In 1988, the French Minister of Culture announced Barenboim's appointment as artistic director of the new Bastille Opéra in Paris. Sadly, following political squabbles, which included disputes over money and artistic policy, a new Minister of Culture dismissed Barenboim in January 1989. However, that same month he was named as Sir George Solti's successor as music director of the Chicago Symphony Orchestra. In 1992, Barenboim became music director of the Berlin State Opera, then named chief conductor for life by its orchestra in 2002. He has also received awards for his efforts to bring together and mentor young Israeli and Palestinian musicians.

Barenboim has a rich recorded repertoire as a conductor, pianist, accompanist, and chamber music player. Interestingly, as a pianist, he tends to focus on Mozart, Beethoven, and the early Romantics, while as a conductor he favors later Romantic music, particularly Brahms and Bruckner (he has won a medal from the Bruckner Society of America). With German baritone Dietrich Fischer-Dieskau he has played acclaimed recitals of lieder, notably those of Hugo Wolf. In 2004 he resigned his position in Chicago, citing stress brought on by the numerous nonmusical activities conductors of American orchestras are expected to undertake.*—Joseph Stevenson*

Recommended:

○ **Wagner: Overtures, Preludes & Great Scenes** / Barenboim (cond.), Jerusalem, Meier, Salminen, Lipovsek, Botha, Struckmann, Chicago SO, Berlin PO, / 2000 / Teldec 81791

○ **Mozart: Piano Concertos 20–27** / Barenboim (piano & cond.), Berlin PO / 1990 / Teldec 72024

○ **Bruckner: Symphony 7** / Barenboim (cond.), Berlin PO / 1995 / Teldec 77118

○ **Bach: Goldberg Variations; Beethoven: Diabelli Variations** / Barenboim / 2000 / Teldec 82138

○ **Chopin: Complete Nocturnes** / Barenboim / DG 453022

Manuel Barrueco

b. Dec. 16, 1952, Santiago de Cuba, Cuba

Guitarist

Manuel Barrueco is admired for his masterful and eloquent guitar playing, his deep musicianship, and his versatility in programming. He did his early studies at the Esteban Salas Conservatory in Cuba. When he was a teenager, his family moved to the United States, and he went on to study at the Peabody Conservatory with Aaron Shearer. He made his Carnegie Hall recital debut in 1974, the same year he won the Concerto Artists Guild Competition. He has performed with orchestras in Europe and Asia, as well as North America. Not only have his performances been broadcast on national networks in Japan, Germany, and Spain, but he has also appeared on the American television shows *CBS Sunday Morning, Breakfast with the Arts,* and *Mr. Roger's Neighborhood.*

His concert and recital programs reveal his commitment to expanding the repertory for the classical guitar and working with other highly skilled performers. His own transcriptions of Bach's *Violin Sonatas* are widely acclaimed. Barrueco has premiered works by Toru Takemitsu and Roberto Sierra and collaborated with Steven Stucky and Arvo Pärt. He has toured with jazz guitarist Al di Meola and released an album of duets, *Nylon and Steel,* with di Meola, rock guitarist Steve Morse, and Andy Summers, formerly of the rock group the Police. His recordings, primarily found on the EMI label, also reflect this versatility. The traditional guitar repertoire of Spanish composers Albéniz, Rodrigo, Turina, and de Falla is represented, but you also find Latin and South American composers such as Chavez, Piazzolla, and Barrios-Mangoré, and Cuban composers Lecuona and Brouwer and many others on his albums.

Barrueco's other great commitment is to teaching. He helped establish the guitar program at the Manhattan School of Music right after his own graduation, and now teaches at the Peabody Conservatory, annually presenting a master-class seminar for students from around the world. *—Patsy Morita*

Recommended:

○ **Cuba** / Barrueco / 1999 / EMI 56757

○ **Albéniz & Turina** / Barrueco / 1997 / EMI 66574

Rudolf Barshai

b. Oct. 1, 1924, Krasnodarsk, Russia

Conductor

Initially best known to Western audiences for his work with the Moscow Chamber Orchestra, an ensemble he founded, Rudolf Barshai later turned to directing many of the Soviet Union's leading orchestras in repertory beyond the chamber works that brought him his first recognition. Immigration to Israel in the 1970s led to several other Western engagements before the breakdown of Communism encouraged him to return to Russia in 1993 for several important performances. He brought to both his chamber and full symphony interpretations a scrupulous musicianship and attention to tonal subtleties, as well as dynamic contrasts some found too keenly emphasized. Barshai trained as a violinist at the Moscow Conservatory with Lev Zeitlin, a pupil of Leopold Auer. Barshai then pursued study of the viola at the conservatory under the tutelage of Vadim Borisovsky, celebrated as an uncommonly astute violist and chamber player. Barshai, too, moved in the direction of chamber music, founding the Philharmonic Quartet (later reorganized as the Borodin Quartet) and making a reputation as a solo player as well. Barshai subsequently cofounded the Tchaikovsky Quartet, finding himself also included in chamber ensembles led by violinist Leonid Kogan and performing often with such luminaries as Emil Gilels, Sviatoslav Richter, David Oistrakh, and Mstislav Rostropovich. Having harbored a not-yet-satisfied urge to direct, Barshai took up conducting studies with Ilya Musin in Leningrad, a move that led to his formation of the Moscow Chamber Orchestra in 1955. With this ensemble, Barshai was able to implement his ideas about chamber performance, foremost among them being firm, supple tone and clarity in execution. Both his Beethoven and Mozart symphony cycles were noteworthy in their day, embracing performance ideas that would be carried further during the growth of the period performance movement, then just beginning. With the MCO, Barshai was able to tour extensively in Western countries, becoming one of the Soviet Union's most widely recognized conductors as he also began undertaking recording projects with Western artists. In the late 1960s, Barshai began to conduct other, larger orchestras in the Soviet Union. In 1969, he was assigned the premiere of Shostakovich's *Symphony No. 14,* whose concentrated orchestration was ideally suited to the Moscow Chamber Orchestra. In 1976, Barshai immigrated to Israel and began active participation in the nation's musical life. His leadership of the Israel Chamber Orchestra began with his arrival and continued until 1981; during that period he also directed the New Israel Orchestra. From 1982 until 1988, he was engaged as artistic adviser of the Bournemouth Symphony Orchestra, also serving the Vancouver Symphony Orchestra as music director from 1985 to 1988. Barshai was also principal guest conductor of the Orchestre National de France beginning in 1987. He has guest-conducted a number of the world's other leading orchestras. Barshai's return to Russia in 1993 was the result of an invitation to lead the Russian National Orchestra in a performance of Mahler's *Symphony No. 9.* In May 1999, a group of 20 Swiss musicians established the Camerata Rudolf Barshai, having chosen Barshai to direct their ensemble. Aside from his conducting and viola performances, Barshai has significantly added to the chamber music literature with a number of transcriptions and arrangements, in particular the several derived from Shostakovich's string quartets. *—Erik Eriksson*

Recommended:

○ **Shostakovich: Symphonies 5 & 6** / Barshai (cond.) / Brilliant 6275-3

○ **Shostakovich: Symphonies** / Barshai (cond.), Aleksashkin, Vaneev / Brilliant 6275

Béla Bartók

b. Mar. 25, 1881, Nagyszentmiklós, Hungary, **d.** Sep. 26, 1945, New York, NY

Composer: Keyboard, Chamber Music, Concerto, Orchestral, Ballet, Opera

Pianist

Through his far-reaching endeavors as composer, performer, educator, and ethnomusicolgist, Béla Bartók emerged as one of the most forceful and influential musical personalities of the twentieth century. Born in Nagyszentmiklós, Hungary (now Romania) on March 25, 1881, Bartók began his musical training with piano studies at the age of five, foreshadowing his lifelong affinity for the instrument. Following his graduation from the Royal Academy of Music in 1901 and the composition of his first mature works—most notably, the symphonic poem *Kossuth* (1903)—Bartók embarked on one of the classic field studies in the history of ethnomusicology. With fellow countryman and composer Zoltán Kodály, he traveled throughout Hungary and neighboring countries, collecting thousands of authentic folksongs. Bartók's immersion in this music lasted for decades, and the intricacies he discovered therein, from plangent modality to fiercely aggressive rhythms, exerted a potent influence on his own musical language.

In addition to his compositional activities and folk music research, Bartók's career unfolded amid a bustling schedule of teaching and performing. The great success he enjoyed as a concert artist in the 1920s was offset somewhat by difficulties that arose from the tenuous political atmosphere in Hungary, a situation exacerbated by the composer's frank manner. As the specter of fascism in Europe in the 1930s grew ever more sinister, he refused to play in Germany and banned radio broadcasts of his music there and in Italy. A concert in Budapest on October 8, 1940, was the composer's farewell to the country which had provided him so much inspiration and yet caused him so much grief. Days later, Bartók and his wife set sail for America.

In his final years Bartók was beleaguered by poor health. Though his prospects seemed sunnier in the final year of his life, his last great hope—to return to Hungary—was dashed in the aftermath of World War II. He died of leukemia in New York on September 26, 1945. The composer's legacy included a number of ambitious but unrealized projects, including a seventh string quartet; two major works, the *Viola Concerto* and the *Piano Concerto No. 3,* were completed from Bartók's in-progress scores and sketches by his pupil, Tibor Serly.

From its roots in the music he performed as a pianist—Mozart, Beethoven, Chopin, Brahms—Bartók's own style evolved through several stages into one of the most distinctive and influential musical idioms of the first half of the twentieth century. The complete assimilation of elements from varied sources—the Classical masters, contemporaries like Debussy, folk songs—is one of the signal traits of Bartók's music. The polychromatic orchestral textures of Richard Strauss had an immediate and long-lasting effect upon Bartók's own instrumental sense, evidenced in masterpieces such as *Music for Strings, Percussion, and Celesta* (1936) and the *Concerto for Orchestra* (1945). Bartók demonstrated an especial concern with form in his exploitation and refinement of devices like palindromes, arches, and proportions based on the "golden section." Perhaps above all other elements, though, it is the ingenious application of rhythm that gives Bartók's music its keen edge. Inspired by the folk music he loved, Bartók infused his works with asymmetrical, sometimes driving, often savage, rhythms, which supply violent propulsion to works such as *Allegro barbaro* (1911) and the *Sonata for Two Pianos and Percussion* (1937). If a single example from Bartók's catalogue can be regarded as representative, it is certainly the piano collection *Mikrokosmos* (1926–39), originally intended as a progressive keyboard primer for the composer's son, Peter. These six volumes, comprising 153 pieces, remain valuable not only as a pedagogical tool but as an exhaustive glossary of the techniques—melodic, harmonic, rhythmic, formal—that provided a vessel for Bartók's extraordinary musical personality. *—Michael Rodman*

Recommended:

○ **Bartók Plays Bartók** / Bartók, Pasztóry / Pearl 9166

○ **József Szigeti & Béla Bartók** / Bartók, Szigeti (violin) / 2001 / Hungaroton 12330

KEYBOARD

Allegro barbaro, Sz. 49 (1911)

Allegro barbaro for solo piano is one of Bartók's most famous pieces, and one of his most frequently performed compositions. This piece typifies Bartók's early compositional esthetic in many respects, most obviously in its use of folk elements drawn from Hungarian, Romanian, and Slovak folk music traditions. This combination of Eastern European folk tunes results in interesting melodic and harmonic textures, especially in the blending of Hungarian and Romanian scales: the former are largely pentatonic or whole tone, while the latter are more chromatic. Bartók also uses modal scales in this piece. The work is quite long—over 200 measures—and is comprised of a number of contrasting sections. The rhythmic repetition of the accompaniment is reflected in the melody, which features repeating motives surrounding a single pitch.

Bartók's discovery of Eastern European folk music, and his use of it in his compositions, parallels the musical development of one of his contemporaries, Igor Stravinsky. Like Bartók, Stravinsky began employing dance rhythms and folk tunes in the first decades of the twentieth century. In Bartók's *Allegro barbaro,* the use of pounding ostinatos suggest a number of Stravinsky's contemporaneous compositions. While it is not known how well Bartók knew Stravinsky's music around 1910–11, by the early 1920s it is almost certain that Bartók was familiar with many of Stravinsky's works, and this familiarity is more immediately evident in the former's piano music of the 1920s.

Bartók's *Allegro barbaro* is an example of what could be called integrated folkstyle; that is, like Stravinsky, Bartók's knowledge and understanding of folk music traditions became highly developed, so much so that both composers were able to construct "authentic" folk material as part of their own compositional idiom. Neither Stravinsky nor Bartók could be said to be simply borrowing or quoting folk material; instead, they created their own. Bartók himself wrote that, in using folk music, the composer's goal should be "to assimilate the idiom of folk music so completely that he is able to forget all about it." Useful parallels may be drawn between the *Allegro barbaro* and two of Stravinsky's works: *The Rite of Spring* and *The Wedding.* Bartók's piece is similar to the "Rite" in that the "primitive" is strongly evoked, particularly in the forceful rhythmic figures. In *The Wedding,* which was completed some years after the *Allegro barbaro,* the difficulty in distinguishing between authentic and new folk material recalls Bartók's accomplished integration of folk material. Many scholars see the *Allegro barbaro* as a pivotal moment in Bartók's stylistic development: after it, his music began to display the characteristics of his mature works, including complex, carefully crafted structure, percussive piano timbres, clear, spare textures, and harmonic color employed with confidence. *—Alexander Carpenter*

Recommended:

○ **Bartók: Works For Piano Solo** / Kocsis / 1995 / Philips 446368

○ **Kocsis Plays Bartók** / Kocsis / Denon 7813

○ **Bartók Plays Bartók** / Bartók / Pearl 9166

Mikrokosmos, progressive pieces in 6 volumes, Sz. 107 (1926–1939)

Mikrokosmos was originally designed as a collection of pieces for the beginning pianist, but over time it took on grander proportions, comprising 153 individual pieces that spanned the range of technical difficulty. Dividing into six volumes, it begins with pieces for beginners and progresses to those that challenge even the most accomplished pianist. That *Mikrokosmos* has become a viable progressive method is demonstrated by its ubiquity in the repertories of modern piano students, but its reputation rests on more than its technical and pedagogical applications; Bartók's work represents a varied and finely crafted catalog of twentieth century musical idioms. In Bartók's own words, it "appears as a synthesis of all the musical and technical problems which were treated and in some case only partially solved in the previous piano works." Perhaps chief among these musical problems was Bartók's attempted synthesis of Eastern and Western European musical traditions, particularly Eastern folk music with the Germanic tradition (as represented by Bach and Beethoven) and with the progressive harmonies of Claude Debussy.

The first 66 pieces in *Mikrokosmos* (volumes one and two) are dedicated to Bartók's son, Peter, for whose use they were originally intended. Many of these pieces are technical exercises, useful for developing finger and hand independence, as well as hand span; however, they are also of interest for their musical language. Hungarian folk tunes, pentatonic, whole-tone and modal harmonies, as well as more adventurous octatonic chromatic scales all form the basis for these short pieces.

Volumes three and four comprise numbers 67 through 121. These pieces display increased harmonic complexity and technical demands. Bartók employs more polymodes (the use of different modes, or keys, simultaneously), along with octatonic and diatonic scale fragments to construct these pieces. The compositions in the third and fourth volumes are also important because they betray the influence of Franz Liszt, particularly in terms of tone color; Bartók wrote of his desire, in these pieces, to "poetically color the piano tone."

The final volumes of the *Mikrokosmos,* five and six, were intended as concert pieces for professional pianists. They differ from the preceding pieces in many respects: their contrapuntal texture is more dense (four parts), the melodic and harmonic material is more characteristic of Bartók's non-pedagogical works, and rhythmic structures are much more complicated and include vigorous syncopations and Bulgarian dance rhythms.

While Bartók's intention to synthesize Bach, Beethoven, and Debussy was perhaps not fully realized, *Mikrokosmos* nonetheless compares well with some of Bach and Debussy's ostensibly pedagogical keyboard works. Like Bach's *Inventions* or Debussy's *Études,* for example, *Mikrokosmos* is not merely a work of practical value, but also a work of art with much purely musical substance. *—Alexander Carpenter*

Recommended:

○ **Bartók: Mikrokosmos** / Sandor / 1992 / Sony 52528

○ **Bartók: Mikrokosmos** / Bartók-Pásztory / 2000 / Hungaroton 31993/4

Piano Sonata, Sz. 80 (1926)

After three years of relative inactivity as a composer, Béla Bartók returned to writing music with a vengeance in 1926, producing a variety of works in what has come to be known as his "piano year." In June, he sent his family to the country and began working on a series of short piano pieces that evolved into his *Piano Sonata* and the suite *Out of Doors.* At the time, Bartók did not know how the individual pieces would eventually coalesce into finished works. His primary concern was nothing less than a radical revision of his piano style. Bartók's expanding concert schedule throughout Europe and America provided further impetus to create new works for his own use as a performer. The *Piano Sonata* is one manifestation of the composer's retooled keyboard idiom. The sonata's language is direct, polytonal, and frequently very dissonant. Its polyphony is clear, its melodic development essentialized: instead of themes, Bartók develops motivic cells, which he subjects to extension and variation. The material itself is folk-derived, reflecting Bartók's interest in Hungarian and Romanian folk music. The sonata opens in heavy stamping rhythm, jolly enough but a bit fearsome for its dissonances and the occasional tone cluster. The first motif, a dotted hop into a repeated, hammering note, is heard immediately; the second, a brusque three-note ascending figure on a minor third, follows quickly. Although the movement centers on E major, there is much play with remote keys in either hand. Bartók embellishes his material with coloristic devices new to his style, including fast, blurred glissandi and tone clusters. These effects tend to erode the tonality in ways different from the atonalism of his violin sonatas of a few years earlier. The hammering rhythms are almost relentless throughout, and the movement ends emphatically. The second movement, Sostenuto e pesante, features bell-like chords in the left hand, answered by a tolling melody of narrow scope in the right. The musical rhetoric here is primarily harmonic, building up an argument of anguished dissonance from the sustained rhythm of the tolling figures. A pentatonic motif in octaves, answered by heavy open-fifth chords in the left hand, launches the concluding compact rondo, in which Bartók explores various folk styles in three episodic sections. Originally there were four such episodes, but Bartók excised the evocation of bagpipe music (which he incorporated into the *Out of Doors* suite as "Musettes"), leaving three picturesque representations of folk singing, peasant flutes, and Romanian fiddlers. The pentatonic ritornello motif brings the work to a driving conclusion. *—Mark Satola*

Recommended:

- ○ **Kocsis Plays Bartók** / Kocsis / Denon 7813
- ○ **Live from the Concertgebouw 1978 & 1979** / Argerich / 2000 / EMI 56975

Romanian Folk Dances (Román népi táncok), Sz. 56 (1915)

As many listeners are aware, Bartók was not only a devotee of folk music, but was one of the foremost experts of his time in Eastern European folk music, collecting over 6,000 folk melodies and arranging many of them for various instruments and ensembles. His *Six Romanian Folk Dances* are fairly straightforward renderings of their folk tune derivatives. Thus, as he did in his large collection for piano, *For Children* (1908–10), Bartók elaborated little on the source materials, fashioning each piece to be a simple miniature of a half-minute to a minute in length. For the Folk Dances, Bartók used seven melodies from fiddle tunes (though the score is divided into only six sections). The tunes were collected between 1910 and 1912 in Maros-Torda, Bihar, Torda-Aranyos, and Torontal. Bartók was drawn to Romanian folk music, instrumental music in particular, because of its timbral diversity—Romanian folk dance tunes are often performed by ensembles comprised of diverse instrument combinations—and its variety and quality of tunes. For Bartók in 1915, these Romanian instrumental tunes offered greater possibilities than the instrumental folk tunes from his own native Hungary, as attested by the number of his works based on Romanian themes.

The first of the *Romanian Folk Dances* is "Stick Dance," a colorful, lively piece whose infectious buoyancy and carefree gait exude delightful Romanian flavors. The ensuing "Sash Dance" has a start-and-stop manner throughout its half minute, the bouncy music pausing to catch its breath after each phrase. The third item, "In One Spot," combines a simple pulse in the bass with an exotic theme in the upper register, the whole yielding a gypsy-like character of striking quality.

Number four in the collection is "Horn Dance," a slow piece whose childlike simplicity (both in rhythm and theme) conveys an innocence in its pastoral, somewhat wistful melody. The next piece, "Romanian Polka," brims with ethnic color and merrymaking in its lively rhythm and peasant-like dance theme. The only regret the listener might have here is that the composer did not go on a bit longer than the mere half-minute he spent, in light of the colorful and utterly infectious foot-stomping material. The last of the pieces in the set is "Fast Dance, which features two themes, each of similar character. They are both breathless in their pacing, each conveying a sense of unbridled celebration. *—Robert Cummings*

Recommended:

- ○ **Kocsis Plays Bartók** / Kocsis / Denon 7813
- ○ **Bartók: Romanian Folk Dances; Dance Suite; Improvisations; Sonatina** / Jandó / 2002 / Naxos 554718

Sonatina, Sz. 55 (1915; revised after 1930)

In print, Béla Bartók always proclaimed the superiority of Hungarian folk music over Romania's indigenous music; still, the latter was a direct source of inspiration for some of his own works, including this *Sonatina for piano* (1915). Less than four minutes long, the Sonatina explores a succession of Romanian folk songs and dances in Bartók's most attractive and accessible style, at the same time placing before the performer a number of technical challenges. Of particular interest is the depiction of peasant bagpipes in the first movement, with its droning open fifths in the left hand and widely-spaced grace note figurations in the right. *—Mark Satola*

Recommended:

- ○ **Béla Bartók: Works For Piano Solo 1** / Kocsis / 1992 / Philips 434104
- ○ **Géza Anda: Liszt: Piano Sonata & others; Bartók, Delibes-Dohnányi** / Anda / 1995 / Testament 1067
- ○ **Bartók: Piano Concerto 3, 3 Burlesques, Allegro barbaro, Suite Op. 14** / Ránki / Hungaroton 31036

Suite, Sz. 62 (Op. 14) (1916)

While Bartók had spent a number of years prior to 1916 collecting and compiling folk tunes from Eastern Europe, the *Suite for piano* solo does not directly reflect this. Other pieces composed by Bartók around this time include a large number of Romanian, Slovak, and Hungarian folk songs; the suite however, is one of only a few works from this time not to use folk song-derived material. Bartók's strong affinity for folk music is still evident in the suite, as some of the movements have a distinctly Romanian folk flavor, while others reflect Bartók's interest in Arab peasant music. The suite is one of Bartók's most significant and substantial works for piano, with the only other comparable work in his oeuvre being the *Piano Sonata,* composed in 1926.

Though it appears that Bartók had intended for the suite to have five movements, in the end he abandoned a short Andante and published the suite as a four-movement work. The opening movement has a decidedly folk-like character, sounding rhythmically like a Romanian peasant dance. Its thematic material is derived from the Lydian mode, but also from whole tone scales, which are prevalent in this movement. On close inspection, it is clearly a very Bartókian work. This is most obivous in the movement's complex harmonic structure, which juxtaposes chromaticism and non-traditional harmonic procedures with the simple harmonies associated with folk tunes. Scholars have noted this juxtaposing in the melody as well, where Bartók combines perfect and diminished fifths, thereby comingling tonally stable structures with tension-ridden, unstable ones. This technique continues into the second movement, a quick Scherzo in which further tonal instability—bordering on atonality—is created though the use of nonfunctional augmented chords. The third movement, an Allegro molto that is even faster than the preceding Scherzo, continues the trend of acceleration through successive movements. The Allegro was, as Bartók admitted, influenced by the music of Arabic North Africa, which accounts for the movement's vigorous ostinato figures and chromatic musical language. The most interesting part of this entire work, arguably, is the final movement. From the very beginning of the suite, the tempo accelerates, and by the time the fourth movement begins, the expectation is that it will continue to gain speed and momentum, and will propel the work to a breathless conclusion. This, however, is not the case. Bartók subverts the listener's expectations by suddenly slowing down, a profoundly dramatic gesture. Not only does the tempo change in the fourth movement, but also the character of the work, as this final movement consists of soft, gentle, and even mournful music. The rambunctious repeating rhythmic figures of the preceding movement are gone, replaced by halting rhythms. The tonal ambiguity introduced early in this work continues in the fourth movement, but Bartók's bitonal music is softened by a reduced tempo and dynamics: semitones are still clashing, but here in the context of music expressing sorrow and tragedy. *—Alexander Carpenter*

Recommended:

- ○ **Bartók Plays Bartók** / Bartok / Pearl 9166
- ○ **Kocsis Plays Bartók** / Kocsis / Denon 7813

CHAMBER MUSIC

Contrasts, for clarinet, violin, & piano, Sz. 111 (1938)

Violinist Joseph Szigeti motivated this work, asking pianist/composer Bartók for something the two of them could play with clarinetist Benny Goodman. Szigeti even sent Bartók some of Goodman's jazz trio records to provide an idea of the clarinetist's style. Szigeti and Goodman were hoping for a two-movement piece in the Hungarian lassù-friss format (like Bartók's two rhapsodies for violin and piano and Liszt's *Hungarian Rhapsodies*), music that would fit on a single 78 rpm record. Bartók instead provided a three-movement work, twice the expected duration. His piano writing here is uncharacteristically restrained, merely supporting the other two instruments, which enjoy some brilliant if strenuous material. The title *Contrasts* indicates that Bartók explores the timbral differences between the instruments rather than reconciling and blending them.

The first movement, "Verbunkos" (Recruiting Dance), in moderate tempo, follows an ABA structure, but a complicated one. The marching first theme, featuring violin pizzicatos inspired by the Blues movement of Ravel's *Violin Sonata,* is angular and playful, and undergoes some variation before a second, folk-like meno mosso theme arrives and submits to its own development. The movement's third section initially seems like further development, the opening theme returning in fragmented and tonally unhinged form. The clarinet takes a cadenza; it will be the violin's turn in the finale.

The second movement, "Pihenö" (Relaxation), marked Lento, is a slow interlude characteristic of Bartók's "night music," mingling mystery with repose, and even suggesting gamelan music in the piano part. Finally comes the "Sebes" (Fast Dance). Here, the clarinetist switches from an instrument in A to a B flat clarinet, and the violinist picks up a deliberately mistuned instrument, sawing away in the beginning like a village fiddler. (The conventional instruments return in the movement's gentler central section.) Although Bartók employs Hungarian-style themes, he seems not to quote any authentic folk tunes. The violinist takes a cadenza going into the third section, and the highly virtuosic movement ends with a grotesque, shrill, comic coda. *—James Reel*

Recommended:

○ **Benny Goodman Collector's Edition** / B. Goodman, Szigeti, Bartók / 1986 / CBS 42227

○ **Bartók: Rhapsodies, Contrasts, Sonata for Solo Violin** / Kocsis, Berkes, Szenthelyi / 2000 / Hungaroton 31038

○ **Bartók: Sonata for unaccompanied violin; 2 Rhapsodies & others** / Osostowicz, Tomes, M. Collins / 1993 / Hyperion 66415

44 Duos for 2 violins, Sz. 98 (1931)

Béla Bartók composed his *44 Duos* (1931) at the request of Erich Doflein, a German violinist and teacher. In 1930, Doflein had asked Bartók for permission to arrange some of the pieces from the composer's piano collection *For Children* for violin duo, intending to use them as graded pieces for young violinists. Bartók instead decided to compose some original duos, and during the following year worked in close consultation with Doflein to produce them.

Like many of Bartók's pedagogical works, the Duos' purpose was twofold: first, to provide young musicians with structured technical studies, and second, to introduce young players to folk music. The Duos are comprised entirely of folk-inspired music whose geographical and cultural compass includes Ukraine, Serbia, Hungary, and other Slovak regions, as well as music from the Arabic world.

Though Bartók, like Stravinsky, had such a familiarity with the folk music of his native country that he could create original folk tunes without recourse to "authentic" source materials, the Duos are actually based on pre-existing ethnic melodies. While they share with works like *For Children* and *Ten Easy Pieces* a folk music-based pedagogical purpose, they perhaps have more in common with *Mikrokosmos* (1926–39) in that above and beyond their practical use, both are possessed of undeniable musical interest and value. Like some of the pieces in *Mikrokosmos*, the Duos are constructed with considerable harmonic and contrapuntal sophistication, and, despite their use of folk tunes, are written in a distinctly modern idiom. Bartók fragments, develops, and manipulates his chosen folk tunes in the Duos, placing them within the context his own harmonic sense. The result is a collection suitable for young players—the textures are simple, double stops are used only occasionally, and aside from some pizzicato passages, no special bowing or other playing techniques are required. Nonetheless, they are rife with aurally challenging bitonal passages, polyrhythms, and plenty of brash dissonances.

In 1932, Doflein published 32 of the Duos in his first-level book of violin pieces for students. Inspired by his pedagogical collaboration with Doflein, Bartók continued work on his own collection of graded pieces for piano, culminating in his monumental *Mikrokosmos*. *—Alexander Carpenter*

Recommended:

○ **Bartók: 44 Duos pour Deux Violins** / S. Végh, Lysy / Astrée Auvidis 7720

○ **Bartók: 44 Duos for two violins** / A. Kiss, Balogh / 1991 / Hyperion 66453

○ **Bartók: 44 Duos, Shostakovich: 3 Violin Duets, Prokofiev: Sonata** / I. Perlman, P. Zukerman / 1996 / EMI 65994

Sonata for 2 pianos & 2 percussion, Sz. 110 (1937)

In 1925, Béla Bartók told interviewer Dezso Kosztolanyi that his first instrument was not, as might have been expected, the piano, but a drum he was given at the age of two. At the age of four, he was attracted to the piano, picking out Hungarian folk songs with one finger. These twin instrumental influences converged in one of the composer's most remarkable works, the *Sonata for Two Pianos and Percussion* (1937), composed on a commission from the Basle chapter of the International Society for Contemporary Music. Bartók had previously explored similar instrumental combinations: the middle movement of the *Piano Concerto No. 1*, for instance, is a dialogue between the soloist and percussion. In this work, however, Bartók decided that, for purposes of balance, the percussion section was better offset by two pianos. The first movement begins with a long introduction over a soft timpani roll, the two pianos alternately presenting a twisting, chromatic theme punctuated by sharp bursts from the cymbal and startling trills and glissandi from the keyboards. A looming accelerando launches the main Allegro, a barbaric but high-spirited affair whose theme is uttered by the pianos in short-breathed phrases. The keyboard parts are characterized by much interplay and cross-counterpoint, while the xylophone and side drum provide vigorous propulsion. A second theme in quick, limping rhythm is presented in an episode framed by brief passages of drifting chords and timbres. A fugitive figuration in the pianos, highlighted by the triangle, leads to a grim, motoric march in 9/8. A climax featuring big, hieratic chords from the keyboards proceeds to a fugato treatment of the second theme, bringing the movement to an emphatic conclusion. The second movement is a characteristic example of Bartók's "night music," the dark nocturnal weft evoked by pointillistic use of cymbal, triangle and a soft, steady beat from side drum. The pianos present an inward, highly chromatic theme. In the ominous middle section, one piano plays dark, looming octaves while the other presents an urgent six-note motif based on a minor third (a recurrent figure in Bartók's music), joined by xylophone. The nocturnal atmosphere returns, this time colored by sharp cries from pianos and percussion and the return of the minor-third motif. The finale, marked by supremely intricate interplay among pianists and percussionists, features some of Bartók's wildest music. The harmonies become veritably woozy, reeling up and down chromatically as the pace quickens through a series of dance episodes in the composer's burlesque style. As the rhythmic impulse drives toward a climax, the music begins to fragment. Instead of the expected tutti ending, the movement quietly winds down to a final, limpid arpeggiated chord, a pure C major sonority, and an almost inaudible finger tap on the cymbal. *—Mark Satola*

Recommended:

○ **Bartok: Sonata for 2 Pianos & Percussion; 2 Pictures** / Kocsis, Ranki, Cser, Racz / Hungaroton 12400

○ **Sir Georg Solti & Murray Perahia: Bartók & Brahms** / Solti, Perahia, Corkhill, Glennie / 1988 / CBS 42625

Violin Sonata No. 1 in C sharp minor, Sz. 75 (Op. 21) (1921)

Béla Bartók wrote both of his violin sonatas for the Hungarian violinist Jelly d'Aranyi. Of the two works, the *Sonata No. 1, Op. 21* is more traditional, both in structure and temperament; its three clearly delineated movements are marked by a character that is alternately rhapsodic and violent, but always virtuosic. Despite any appearance of conventionality, however, the sonata represents one of Bartók's most radical statements in its expressionistic rhetoric and its near-atonal harmonic and melodic language (notwithstanding the nominal indication that it is in the key of C sharp minor). The arresting opening bars are underpinned by fast, dissonant arpeggios from the piano that evoke the sounds of the cimbalom, a dulcimer-like instrument from Bartók's native Hungary. The violinist's first statement is broad and chromatic, a passionate declamation in a setting of nocturnal fantasy. Both harmonically and melodically, these opposing elements recall Bartók's contemporaneous stage pantomime *The Miraculous Mandarin*, completed in piano score two years previously. The movement is discursive and often impulsive; while there is confluence and cooperation between the two instruments throughout, thematic material is rarely shared. In this highly dissonant context, the occasional consonance sounds peculiar. A subsidiary theme, for instance, features the interval of a major sixth; often perceived as almost cloyingly sweet, it here emerges in an entirely different light. A searching cadenza-like solo passage for the violin opens the second movement. The piano eventually joins in with a series of ascending chords, no less unsettled for their limpid, impressionistic sonority; even in the turbulent setting of this work, Bartók's debt to the music of Debussy and Ravel is evident. A middle section is ominous and imposing, with frightening, arpeggiated octaves in the piano, increasing in volume as if some catastrophe were imminent; the violin, meanwhile, cries out in double stops and chords. The octaves recede, giving way to the desolate air of the opening. The finale is a series of increasingly wild dances, folk-like in style but wholly expressionistic. Bartók here makes his greatest demands upon the players' virtuosity and stamina as he leads them through a series of episodes that, however abstract in nature, arrange themselves roughly into a rondo form. Midway through is a grotesque pesante section marked by a thick and heavy stamping tread in the piano and detached skirlings from the violin in diffident response. The frenetic dance rhythms return, bringing the work to a grim conclusion. The *Sonata No. 1* was premiered in Vienna by violinist Mary Dickenson-Auner and pianist Eduard Steuermann; d'Aranyi and Bartók first performed it at a private recital in London's Hungarian Legation in March 1922. *—Mark Satola*

Recommended:

○ **Isabelle Faust, Bartók: Sonates** / Faust, Kupiec / HM 911623

○ **David Oistrakh Edition** / D. Oistrakh, S. Richter / 1997 / Melodiya 40710

Violin Sonata No. 2 in C major, Sz. 76 (1922)

Despite their conventionally accepted numbering, Béla Bartók's first and second violin sonatas were actually the composer's fourth and fifth works in that genre. Bartók's three earlier sonatas, composed during his student years, are in a Romantic, almost Brahmsian, vein, and show few signs of the bold strides the composer was to make more than two decades later. During the years preceding the first and second sonatas, Bartók, an accomplished pianist, often performed with violinists. He dedicated these two sonatas to one such musician, Jelly d'Arányi, a Hungarian-born violinist living in London. Performances of these works with d'Arányi and others quickly spread Bartók's reputation throughout Europe and garnered praise from Stravinsky, Ravel, Szymanowski, Poulenc, and Milhaud. In this work, which was composed between July and November 1922, Bartók abandoned the traditional three-movement form of the *Sonata No. 1*, creating, instead, a more unified, two-movement composition. Nevertheless, the two works share some common features: their assimilation of Schoenberg's extreme chromaticism, and their finales, where the influence of dance music from Eastern European folk traditions comes to the fore. Of course, these movements are not actual folk music, but instead, a highly stylized treatment of folk-like material that prompted Bartók to warn a fellow Hungarian pianist: "We must be careful to avoid any attempt to put on such works as my two Sonatas for violin... in places where the level of music appreciation is as low as it is in Hungarian country towns. Such works would merely rouse antagonism in an audience which has not been trained to listen." The structure of this Sonata, for which the composer himself expressed a preference, can be considered a metaphor for the development of folk song as a natural outgrowth of improvisation. The work opens with a long melody in the style of a hora lunga—a free improvisation found in Romanian peasant music—that uses a small group of motivic patterns. This theme returns twice: once in an agitated guise at the end of the first movement, and then once again at the end, the climax of the sonata. In this final appearance, played in the violin's high register, the theme takes on a more stabilized shape in the context of the movement's dance rhythm. Bartók scholar László Somfai concludes that this plan reveals a hidden program to the Sonata: "Bartók recreated the evolution of peasant music... in miniature, from the improvisatory 'ur-form' (using his own themes) to the crystallized stanzaic formation of lyric songs." *—Robert Adelson*

Recommended:

- ○ **Anne-Sophie Mutter, Penderecki: Violin Concerto 2** / Mutter, Orkis / DG 453507
- ○ **Bartók: Sonatas for Violin and Piano** / G. Kremer, I. Smirnov / Hungaroton 11655

Sonata for solo violin, Sz. 117 (1944)

This piece came at a time when Bartók was writing more direct, less aurally challenging compositions like the *Third Piano Concerto* (1945) and *Concerto for Orchestra* (1943; rev. 1945). Moreover, any work for solo violin is reduced to certain limitations of sound, no matter how complex a scale it is conceived on, no matter how lofty the composer's goals are. In this sonata, perhaps more than in any other chamber work of his, Bartók relies on melody and turns away from complex rhythms, fully aware that this kind of solo genre must be built upon essentials.

He gradually reduced the level of complexity in the work as it proceeded from movement to movement. Not that it is substantially complex at the outset; indeed, even the first movement is relatively straightforward, though it is formally elaborate and the longest of the four panels. Inspired by Bach's great chaconne from *Partita for Violin No. 2*, BWV 1004, it begins in a serious vein and carries the marking Tempo di ciaccona. A solemn chaconne theme is presented at the outset and another melody, this one played in sixths, is next introduced. A third one, of a more flowing nature than the previous two, ensues. There follow a fairly elaborate development section and a varied reprise.

The second movement is marked Fuga: Risoluto, non troppo vivo. Obviously this is a fugue, but not the kind one would expect for an essentially monodic instrument, for here we have a four-part fugue! Bartók presents a theme and its inversion in various episodes, often simultaneously. While this description might suggest a complex listening experience, the music is quite easily grasped throughout.

The third movement, marked Melodia: Adagio, presents an attractive, if somewhat sober theme with no harmonies. Its beauty and effectiveness are undeniable in this relatively simple scheme. The middle section is brief and breaks with the monodic character of the main material. The overall mood of this movement is one that contains a mixture of serenity and ethereality.

The finale, marked Presto, begins with a theme played in *perpetuum mobile* style. But the mood is mysterious, the violin making gossamer sounds in its rush forward. This material alternates with a couple of high-spirited dance tunes throughout the movement. The structure of the finale resembles that of a Rondo, and can loosely be classed as such. While the first movement offers many challenges to the soloist, the finale contains its share of difficulties, too, and visually strikes audiences as the most virtuosic.

A typical performance of Bartók's *Solo Violin Sonata* lasts from 20 to 24 minutes. The work was commissioned by Yehudi Menuhin, who premiered it. *—Robert Cummings*

Recommended:

- ○ **Références: Yehudi Menuhin, Bartók** / Yehudi Menuhin / EMI 74799
- ○ **Andre Gertler: Bach, Bartók. Berg** / Gertler / Hungaroton 31635
- ○ **Bartók: Violin Sonatas** / Tetzlaff / Virgin 45668

String Quartet No. 1 in A minor, Sz. 40 (Op. 7) (1908)

In a letter to violinist Stefi Geyer, Bartók described the opening movement of this quartet as his "funeral dirge." The quartet's first four notes—two descending minor sixths played imitatively by the first and second violins—are nearly identical to the opening motif of the second, giocoso, movement of the *Violin Concerto No. 1* (1908), Bartók's musical portrait of Geyer, with whom he was unrequitedly in love. Bartók dealt with the rejection of his love in a series of autobiographical works, of which this quartet is the culmination. Kodály called this quartet a "return to life," and its three accelerating movements (Lento, Allegretto, and Allegro vivace) plainly trace a course from the Liebestod-like anguish of the convoluted first movement to the heady, forceful finale. The Lento is marked by a hyper-chromatic Romantic mood characteristic of many works written around the turn of the century. Sadness and despair are the prevailing sentiments in this work, with wistful nostalgia expressed in passing episodes of Impressionistic delicacy that are quickly subsumed by the darker mood. After the first theme is explored, (the counterpoint is reminiscent of Beethoven's late string quartets), a funereal element is introduced with forceful, bell-like fifths on the cello, over which sounds a sobbing second theme, on viola and second violin harmonized in thirds, while the first violin muses detachedly in the upper register. The mood and style are reminiscent of the first violin concerto's opening movement. A hesitant bridge passage accelerates gradually to the next movement, which presents a delicate and witty theme, a stepwise motif that is subjected to a series of explorations in various settings suggestive of variation technique. The mood is ambiguous, despite light-hearted interplay among the instruments; when a distinct mood finally manifests itself toward the end of the movement, it is one of anger, driven by an insistent pulsing ostinato on a single note that begins as an ominous pizzicato on the cello and grows to fist-shaking open fifths arco. The mood is not resolved by movement's end. Another bridge passage leads to the finale, an accelerating Allegro vivace that is the longest of the three movements. In the first movement, there was only a brief suggestion of Hungarian folk music in the cello's soulful melody during the Impressionistic episode; here the character of folk music is more pronounced. Its use here, though not as organic as in later works, nevertheless seems central to the young composer's "return to life" after a period of despair. The main theme, which has a "scolding" quality (and is intervallically related to the descending sixths of the first movement), is developed through a series of episodes, one of which parodies European café music, after which it is treated, fugato-style, in a grotesque, scherzando section. The coda is fast and propulsive, the final, emphatic chords of open fifths barely able to block its momentum. *—Mark Satola*

Recommended:

- ○ **Bartók: 6 String Quartets** / Takacs SQ / Hungaroton 12502
- ○ **Bartók: 6 String Quartets** / Emerson SQ / DG 423657

String Quartet No. 2 in A minor, Sz. 67 (Op. 17) (1915–1917)

Bartók was living in seclusion outside Budapest during the years of the First World War, and some of this isolation may have made its way into his *String Quartet No. 2*, which was composed between 1915 and 1917. Nevertheless, unlike its predecessor, this quartet is possessed of a classical detachment and Apollonian poise that sets it apart from the intense emotionality of Bartók's pre-war compositions.

The second quartet is in three movements, an Allegro molto capriccioso framed by two slow movements, marked Moderato and Lento, a disposition that seems to anticipate the arch forms that would later fascinate the composer. The first movement opens with soft murmuring from second violin and viola on the close interval of the minor second; major and minor seconds will play an important role throughout in the harmonic profile of the work. The main theme is pensive, a rising fillip on an augmented fourth setting the unsettled tone. As in other works from the era, especially the yet-to-come violin sonatas, Bartók here approaches a type of atonality, a "pseudo-atonality" that is partly a function of his radical, harmonically advanced polyphony, wherein melodies that have clear and easily comprehended shapes intertwine with each other in ways that produce great intervallic and harmonic tensions; yet these same processes also yield gem-like moments of diatonic triads, all the more beautiful for their rarity. A moment of exquisite and limpid beauty occurs midway through when a folk-like theme emerges from the polyphony, accompanied with music of Ravelian refinement; after a more serious development section, this theme returns, its triple time gently counterbalanced by double-time pizzicato chords that suggest the strumming of a guitar.

By contrast, the second movement is wild and driving. Its main theme, a relentless ostinato emphasizing the minor third, is evocative of the primitive Arabian tunes Bartók had heard and collected in North Africa a few years previously (Biskra, 1913). The accompaniment is even more primitive, a one-note ostinato punctuated by pizzicato notes, giving the effect of Arabian drumming. Although the near-claustrophobic quality of the music's limited scale gives it a grim sound, the treatment is clearly playful. Midway there is a slower section, a sort of diffident serenade that quickly gives way to a return of the driving main theme, which is subjected to increasing expansion and variation within a rondo-like structure. The coda is fast and light, swirling through briefly and then disappearing.

Where the opening moderato is perhaps the most sonically ravishing music Bartók ever wrote, the concluding Lento is the strangest and most desolate. The instruments do not so much play themes or motives as muse on fragments of themes, more intervallic phrases than melodies, like unrelenting sighs uttered in a landscape of despairing major and minor seconds. The material slowly coalesces into longer shapes as the movement proceeds, but cannot sustain any lengthy argument; after a brief but intense chordal climax, the music sinks back into the Slough of Despond from which it emerged: there are a few more sighs, then two quiet pizzicato notes from the cello draw the curtain. *—Mark Satola*

Recommended:

○ **Bartók: Quatuors 1 & 2** / Quatuor Végh / Astrée Auvidis 7717

○ **Bartók: 6 String Quartets** / Takacs SQ / Hungaroton 12502

String Quartet No. 3 in C sharp major, Sz. 85 (1927)

Bartók's *String Quartet No. 3* shared first prize with a quartet by Alfredo Casella at the 1927 Musical Fund Society of Philadelphia Competition. Its striking qualities could not have escaped the judges' notice. Of Bartok's six quartets, the third is the most concentrated in thematic material and structure. In this quartet, Bartók subjected folk-style themes and motifs to a technique he called "expansion in range," wherein melodic shape and intervallic relations were stretched to produce themes that develop freely without compromising musical unity. Bartók scholar Elliott Antokoletz suggests that this new approach was partly due to the Treaty of Trianon, signed in 1920 by the Allied forces and Hungary. The Treaty's punitive partition of Hungary effectively moved much of Bartók's folk-music hunting grounds outside the borders of Hungary (which in fact lost two-thirds of its land and population under the Trianon terms). With his primary source cut off, Bartók integrated folk material into a more cosmopolitan style, such as he had encountered during his tours of post-war Europe.

The *String Quartet No. 3* is in a single movement, lasting a little more than a quarter of an hour. It is divided into two main parts, marked respectively Moderato and Allegro, plus a recapitulation of the first part and a short coda that reprises material from the second part. While the structural integration is inherited from Liszt's Piano Sonata in B minor, the contrapuntal technique is a legacy from the late string quartets of Beethoven. The "Prima parte" begins with a short-breathed parlando-style theme on violin over a tightly-spaced, dissonant chord centered around C sharp. The mood is desolate, though the folk-like themes are clear and immediately comprehensible. Subsequent development extends the short motives in length and explores the tightly integrated counterpoint in increasingly arduous rhetoric. A technical feature that will grow into an important dramatic device first appears here; glissandi that function as stylized portamenti add an inquisitive quality to the proceedings.

A return of the initial parlando motif, now on the cello, launches the "Seconda parte" where the folk-like material drives the proceedings into a wild episodic dance. Here Bartók employs unusual techniques that would subsequently become regular features of his string writing, including sul ponticello (playing close to the bridge), jeté (bouncing the bow off the strings), col legno (playing with the wood of the bow), and the so-called "Bartók pizzicato," in which the string snaps back audibly on the fingerboard. Bartók uses these devices for more than color; they underscore the expression of the movement's high spirits and punctuate the proceedings in a percussive way. Toward the end of the second part there is a nervous fugato that is brought to a full stop by a series of glissando chords, followed by a vigorous stretto of double and triple-stopped chords. The recapitulation of the first part is, if anything, even more desolate than the original, with a Pierrot-like sadness created by the glissandi, which recur like question marks. A tender lament from the violin leads to an anguished outcry of dissonant chords before the coda swirls in, ghostly and fugitive at first, then with full force and vigor. Some precipitous, downward swooping glissandi in the lower strings lead to a fierce stretto on the first violin in primitive open fifths. Brutal chords end the work brusquely. *—Mark Satola*

Recommended:

○ **White Man Sleeps** / Kronos Quartet / 1987 / Nonesuch 79163

○ **Bartók: 6 String Quartets** / Takacs SQ / 1998 / London 455297

○ **Bartók: 6 String Quartets** / Emerson SQ / DG 423657

String Quartet No. 4 in C major, Sz. 91 (1928)

Bartók's String Quartet No. 4 was written in the summer of 1928 and premiered that fall by the Kolisch Quartet, led by Arnold Schoenberg's brother-in-law, Rudolf Kolisch. The work represents both an intensification and relaxation of elements present in Bartók's previous quartet, completed a year before the fourth. While the radically dissonant harmonic language and rigorous motivic development found in the third string quartet are intensified in the fourth quartet, the third's tightly interwoven single-movement structure is, in the fourth, "opened out" into a more easily comprehended, five-movement span arranged in Bartók's characteristic "arch" form. The composer did point out, however, that the five movements functioned collectively according to the template of sonata form.

Earlier commentators suggested that Bartók had ventured into a personal style of serialism or even complete atonality with this work, a conclusion that while not entirely accurate is understandable. The first movement presents in rapid succession three motive-groupings, small melodic cells that are expanded and embellished. The first is a dissonant giusto phrase in counterpoint, the second an emphatic, six-note declamation that twists upward a minor third and brusquely drops back down, and the third a longer, lyrical phrase that is related in shape to the second. These Ur-melodies are intervallically related to primitive Magyar folk music, but their setting is more dissonant, abstract and expressionistic. Bartók makes effective use of such effects as insistent glissandi and the noisy Bartók pizzicato. A dark, nocturnal mood is established here and prevails through the entire work.

The second movement is a ghostly scherzo, played almost entirely with mutes. The players must execute fast shifts from arco to pizzicato throughout as they negotiate compressed and fragmented themes that are derived primarily from the second motivic cell of the first movement. The movement disappears in a series of fast, rising glissandi.

The keystone of the "arch" is the third movement, "Non troppo lento," a night-song. Over a quiet, tightly-voiced chord suggesting the drone of bagpipes, the cello sings a rhapsodic Magyar-style melody which is answered by the violin in a lengthy variation. The central portion is limned with high, squeaking notes from the upper instruments, suggesting the sounds of nocturnal insects, before the cello and violin return in counterpoint with the parlando melody. The movement closes with a fragmented reprise of the curious middle section, very quiet and with mutes on.

The second scherzo is entirely pizzicato, and the dissonant harmonies are relaxed. A modal theme, again related to the second, scalar "cell" and its more consonant accompaniment, is treated in a subtly burlesque manner. There is the suggestion of Arabian music in the sinuous nature of the theme, as well as the drumming and strumming effects in the accompaniments, liberally punctuated by the snapping "Bartók" pizzicato.

Shrill, double-stopped chords and driving motoric rhythms launch the finale, whose intense main theme refers to the opening giusto cell of the first movement. The other thematic cells are also evoked in this furious Allegro molto, the third lyrical cell expanded to a long-breathed arching melody. The second, brusque cell is inverted in the middle section, and grows in importance until it brings the work to an angry conclusion. *—Mark Satola*

Recommended:

○ **Bartók: 6 String Quartets** / Takacs SQ / 1998 / London 455297

○ **Bartók: 6 String Quartets** / Emerson SQ / DG 423657

○ **Bartók: String Quartets 1–6** / Alban Berg Quartet / 2002 / EMI 575652

String Quartet No. 5 in B flat major, Sz. 102 (1934)

In the six years separating the fourth and fifth string quartets, Bartók wrote comparatively little music, but the works he did complete pointed to his mature style of the 1930s and 1940s, in which directness of compositional technique is coupled with a new concern for clear communication. The *Cantata Profana* (1930) and *Piano Concerto No. 2* (1931) demonstrated a new linear style that incorporated elements of unabashed triadic harmony; while the *44 Duos for 2 violins,* Sz. 98 (1931) were pivotal to a number of artistic roads Bartók would shortly travel. As teaching pieces they rekindled Bartók's interest in creating learning material based on Eastern European folk music, and as explorations of string technique, they paved the way for the *String Quartet No. 5,* easily Bartók's most virtuosic essay in the form.

For his fifth string quartet, Bartók again used the five-movement arch form, this time employing a more distinctive variation technique in which the first and fifth movements, and the second and fourth, closely mirror each other. The opening movement presents its three ideas in rapid succession: the first is a series of unison repeated notes from which rockets a querulous, chromatic melody, the second features a trilling figuration, and the third is rhythmically irregular with many double-stops. The development is introduced by a quiet, sinuous passage based on the first theme in imitative counterpoint, after which the theme turns into a Fugue. A dance-like passage emerges as the third theme, which then becomes an accompaniment for the second theme. The structure of the movement is loosely palindromic, and the themes are subjected to numerous variations. The inverted first theme brings the movement to an emphatic close.

The second movement begins in "night music" mode, with evanescent trills leading to a prayerful chorale in simple triadic harmony, and short-breathed sighs in unrelated keys from the violin. The nocturnal atmosphere takes over in the middle section, extending the sense of unease from the movement's introduction, with trills and pizzicati evoking the sounds of unseen birds and strange insects. After a restrained climax, the chorale resumes, but the triads are now chromatically tinged and anxious.

The keystone of the quartet's arch form is the middle movement, a scherzo in which ten eighth notes per bar are subdivided according to the formula 5+2+3. A short arpeggiated theme is answered by a lively, irregular dance melody. In the middle section, the arpeggiated theme is intervallically compressed to become a high, skirling ostinato on the violin, against which a simple tune is sounded alternately by the other instruments. The dance tune returns with even higher spirits, though the ending is quiet and droll.

The fourth movement harks back to the second, and varies its material expressively. Desolate night music elements are now laced with a touch of humor, glissando pizzicati and short tremolando chords filling in for the second movement's prayerful sighs. The movement rises to an angry climax before closing with a series of glissando pizzicato chords from the cello that rise like question marks.

The finale, a variant of the first movement, modifies the original themes and sets them to a vigorous dance rhythm of serious intensity. The demands on the players are great, and the movement's propulsion is interrupted only by a short, satiric episode in which the violin plays a banal scale a half-tone higher than its accompaniment. A fast coda abruptly ends the work. *—Mark Satola*

Recommended:

○ **Bartók: Six String Quartets** / Juilliard SQ / 1997 / Sony 63234

○ **Bartók: String Quartets 1–6** / Alban Berg Quartet / 2002 / EMI 575652

○ **Bartók: Six String Quartets** / Emerson SQ / DG 423657

String Quartet No. 6 in D major, Sz. 114 (1939)

Bartók's last completed quartet exemplifies the composer's continuing search for new forms, even as he sought to distill and clarify his mode of expression. The form he devised for the *String Quartet No. 6* is ingenious: each movement is preceded by an introductory section marked "Mesto" ("sadly"), with increasing complexity at each appearance. The "mesto" theme functions both as a motto and as the source of much of the quartet's thematic substance. In the fourth movement, rather than giving way to a lively finale (the original plan as indicated by Bartók's sketches), the motto continues on to become the conclusion itself.

The sad introductory theme is played first by solo viola, whose last notes are the germ for a unison statement by all four instruments in peremptory three-note phrases that will return later, as a sort of subsidiary motto. The first theme is in quick triplets that are chromatically sinuous. The second theme is a folk-like melody, with a prominent "Scotch snap" rhythm. The first theme dominates the development, which is fairly strenuous and darker in mood. After a brief appearance of the second theme, the movement ends simply with a reprise of the first theme, now detached and musing.

The "mesto" introduction to the second movement is in two-part counterpoint, the cello stating the melody accompanied by upper strings in a tremolando counter-melody. The subsequent Marcia is bitter and ironic, and the "Scotch snap" rhythm is prominent. The appearance of the second theme is ingenious: the march rhythm continues as an accompaniment to the rising glissandi of the new tune. The middle section suspends the propulsive march as the cello rhapsodizes, cadenza-like, on a variation of the second theme. This is accompanied by high trills from the violins and harsh, guitar-like strumming on the viola. The return of the march is bizarre, with extremely high octave doubling from the first violin and a filling out of the implied triadic harmonies which create an ironic, hallucinatory effect.

For its third appearance, the "mesto" ritornello is in three-part harmony; it leads to a rude "Burlesca," with vulgar stamping rhythms and a melody reminiscent of the "teasing songs" prevalent in Eastern European folk music. The second theme moves within a narrow intervallic range, evoking the Arabic melodies Bartók collected in North Africa. In the central part, the "Scotch snap" theme from the first movement is mused upon before the burlesque returns, this time entirely in pizzicato. At the conclusion, an attempt to sound the "Scotch snap" theme is shouted down by angry chords.

In the slow finale, the "mesto" melody, now in four parts, continues on to become the entire movement, and the second theme recalls the unison motto of the first movement. The triplet theme is also recalled, now in a setting of profound desolation, and the "Scotch snap" tune makes a wistful appearance. Ghostly tremolandi accompany the return of the "mesto" theme; there is a moment of half-hearted protest that dwindles to resignation. The cello ends it all with a question mark, plucked chords based on the "mesto" motto. *—Mark Satola*

Recommended:

○ **Bartók: String Quartets** / New Budapest Quartet / 1996 / Hyperion 22003

○ **Bartok: 6 String Quartets** / Takacs SQ / Hungaroton 12502

○ **Bartók: 6 String Quartets** / Emerson SQ / DG 423657

○ **Bartók: String Quartets 1–6** / Alban Berg Quartet / 2002 / EMI 575652

CONCERTO

Concerto for Orchestra, Sz. 116 (1943; revised 1945)

In 1943, after a year of precipitously declining health, Bartók was diagnosed with leukemia. He had been in the United States for nearly three years, a period in which he had to endure financial hardship, artistic isolation and separation from the source of his inspiration, Hungary, and its wealth of folk music. What income and recognition he did receive came mostly from his appearances as a pianist (or sometimes as duo-pianist with his wife Ditta Pasztory), but poor health prevented him from performing after January 1943. It seemed as if his life had come to a standstill when he received a commission for a large orchestral work from Serge Koussevitzky, music director of the Boston Symphony Orchestra. The funds for the commission came, unbeknownst to Bartók, from his close friends and fellow Hungarian émigrés Joseph Szigeti and Fritz Reiner. Bartók traveled to Saranac Lake, New York, and worked on the *Concerto for Orchestra* between August and October, 1943. The work was first heard in 1944, and though Bartók was unable to attend the Boston premiere, he did hear a subsequent performance in New York City.

Like the fourth and fifth string quartets (1928 and 1934), the *Concerto for Orchestra* is in five movements, arranged in what is called an "arch" form, in which the first and fifth movements are related, as are the second and fourth, with the third movement functioning as the keystone of the arch. The Concerto's opening bars present a theme of rising fourths in cellos and basses, answered by tremolando strings and fluttering flutes in Bartók's characteristic "night music" style. Trumpets, pianissimo, chant a pungent, short-phrased chorale on which the theme of the main Allegro vivace is based. A lyrical second theme is introduced by the oboe, but the mood remains dark as the material is developed. Only when brass erupt in a modal fugato section is there the suggestion that things may lighten. Bartók noted that the progress of the Concerto was toward light from initial darkness, and that the thematic material of the fugato will return in modified form as the basis of the joyous moto perpetuo finale.

The second movement is titled "Games of Couples," and presents woodwinds in successive pairs, with close intervallic relationships derived from Dalmatian folk music. The syncopated rhythm that accompanies these games—performed by side drum without snares—carries over into the middle section, a soft chorale for brass. Bartók described the keystone third movement, "Elegia," as a "lugubrious death-song," in which unsettled "night music" effects alternate with intense, prayerful supplications (again related to the chorale-like material that pervades the first half of the work). The subsequent "Interrupted Intermezzo" presents the first real carefree moments of the work, with its satiric treatment of the march theme from Shostakovich's *"Leningrad" Symphony,* which Bartók heard in a radio broadcast. Bartók scholar Elliott Antokoletz notes that the movement's warm, cantabile melody for violas quotes a popular song by Zsigmond Vincze, "You are Lovely, You are Beautiful, Hungary," bringing an unmistakable note of homesickness to the music. The finale opens with a leaping call to order for all four horns unison, followed by a wild moto perpetuo dance, in which the succeeding episodes hardly stop for breath. Bartók provided two endings, the first rather abrupt, the second more traditionally climactic, and making use of the upward-moving minor third motif that served as an intervallic motto for Bartók in many works. The alternate ending is the one that is usually played. *—Mark Satola*

Recommended:

○ **Bartók: Concerto for Orchestra** / F. Reiner (cond.), Chicago SO / 1993 / RCA 61504

○ **Bartók: Concerto for Orchestra; Music SPC, Kodály: Hary Janos Suite** / Karajan (cond.), London Philharmonia Orch. / 1998 / EMI 66596

○ **Bartók: Concerto for Orchestra; 3 Village Scenes; Kossuth** / I. Fischer (cond.), Budapest Festival Orch. / 1998 / Philips 456575

Piano Concerto No. 1 in A major, Sz. 83 (1926–1929)

The culmination of Béla Bartók's so-called "piano year," 1926, was his *Piano Concerto No. 1,* which he premiered in Frankfurt, in July 1927, with Furtwängler conducting. The work was at best cautiously received; at worst, it met with incomprehension and derision, especially in the United States. Bartók had spent the summer of 1926 reworking his entire approach to composition, abandoning the traditional concept of theme. Instead, he sought to attain a more basic level of expression, working with motifs or note-cells, with narrow range and simple rhythmic impulses. As he demonstrated in this concerto, however, the reduction was accomplished in order to bring about a new type of elaboration that was both independent of the post-Romantic compositional procedures of the recent past and fully participant in the modern spirit of musical innovation. This composition's close relation to the other major piano works of 1926, exemplified by the *Out of Doors* piano suite, is immediately evident in the first movement's repeated hammering notes in the lowest register of the piano. Percussion immediately comes to the fore in these introductory bars, where it collaborates with the piano (underscoring Bartók's recent thoughts on the percussive nature of the instrument), while horns blast a fortissimo theme so primitive that it seems less than a theme. Indeed, it is one of two note-cells from which the entire work grows with ever-greater elaboration. The driving pulse is unceasing throughout, while the themes themselves, augmented and extended through variation-style technique, remain somewhat neutral in their emotional cast. Bartók employs a range of piano effects including glissandi that are not anchored in any tonality, as well as whole-tone scales and tight clusters based on the interval of the minor second (sometimes spaced over an octave). The strings are used sparingly, mostly for textural variety, playing in unison (occasionally in canon), with most of the harmonic work done by the winds. A ritornello of polyphonic fanfares in brass and winds is particularly striking, and its final appearance triggers the brief and uncompromising coda. The strings are silent during the second movement, which is scored for piano, winds, and percussion alone. The ever-present primitive rhythmic pulse is halved here, with piano and percussion opening the movement in stark harmonic black and white. Winds doubled at the octave state a gloomy theme in canon, which expands organically and is answered by the piano in sharp dissonance. Midway through the Andante, the piano slips into a dissonant ostinato in slow 3/8 (soft percussion accompanying), while the winds slowly weave a fine texture based on the main theme. The episode expands and fades, with percussion having the last, nearly inaudible, word. The frenzied finale is launched by loud percussion, picking up almost attacca from the slow pulse of the preceding movement. Here, the strings join the pulse with a fast, primitive-sounding ostinato (open fifths) over which the martellato theme is pounded out by the piano. The percussive character of the movement, exemplified by a short, insolent trumpet solo, may indicate Bartók's awareness of some of the jazz-influenced works of the 1920s; however, the movement is essentially a wild Hungarian dance. The brass fanfares return, with "night music" (reminiscent of the "Musiques nocturnes," the *Out of Doors* piano suite), glissandi played by flutes and piano, and the concerto rushes to a spirited conclusion. *—Mark Satola*

Recommended:

- ○ **Bartók: Piano Concertos 1 & 2; Stravinsky: 3 Movements from Petrushka** / Abbado (cond.), Pollini, Chicago SO / 2001 / DG 471360
- ○ **Bartók: Piano Concertos 1–3** / Salonen (cond.), Y. Bronfman, Los Angeles PO / 2001 / Sony 89732
- ○ **Bartók: Piano Concertos; Violin Concerto; Concerto For Orchestra** / C. Davis (cond.), Kovacevich, London SO / 1993 / Philips 438812

Piano Concerto No. 2 in G major, Sz. 95 (1930–1931)

Bartók's Second Piano Concerto (1930–31) is one of the composer's more accessible compositions for performers and audiences alike, yet tough-rhythmed and toccata-like. His previous effort in the genre, the *Piano Concerto No. 1* (1926), is somewhat thornier in its idiom and technical demands, and had not to that point enjoyed much popularity. Since Bartók wrote most of his piano music for his own use as a performer throughout Europe and the United States, it seems natural that he would have wanted a work with more universal appeal. Though Bartók completed the *Second Concerto* in October 1931, it was not premiered until January 23, 1933—an especially notable event, since this marked the last time he ever appeared in soon-to-be Nazified Germany.

In approaching the composition of his *Second Concerto,* Bartók made a conscious effort to limit the difficulty of the solo and the orchestral parts. The latter aspect had proven particularly troublesome in the *First Concerto*—so much so, in fact, that the New York Philharmonic, which was to have given the premiere, could not master it in time, and another work had to be substituted on the program. The composer himself acknowledged that the piano part was arduous and later said that the concerto "is a bit difficult—one might even say very difficult!—as much for orchestra as for audience." He evidently learned the lesson well, since the *Second Concerto* has enjoyed both critical acclaim and worldwide popularity.

The overall form of the *Second Concerto* is symmetrical—the tempo structure is fast-slow-fast-slow-fast—in the Bartókian manner which has come to be identified as arch form. The first movement, marked Allegro, is highlighted by the active, punctuating piano solo. The piano's quick, rhythmic pace and fragmentary scalar movement suggest the influence of Stravinsky, and the ballet *Petrushka* (1910–11) in particular. The concerto's instrumentation similarly betrays Bartók's affinity with Stravinsky, as the string section remains silent for the entire first movement—a characteristic which also reflects an increasing emphasis on the wind and percussion sections of the orchestra in the early decades of the twentieth century. Sections of neo-Bachian counterpoint may also reflect Stravinsky's influence.

The strings make their entrance at the beginning of the Adagio second movement. Markedly different from its predecessor, this central movement begins with a slow chorale stated by the strings in stacked perfect fifths. After this first chorale section, the piano enters, accompanied only by timpani— a striking, unusual instrumental pairing that readily illustrates Bartók's frequent employment of the piano as an extension of the percussion family. The middle section of this movement, signalled by a change to a Presto tempo, is extremely quick and light. The movement is rounded out by a return to the original slow tempo and the reappearance of motives from the beginning of the movement. The third movement is a free variation of the first and is similar in pace and melodic shape. *—Chris Boyes*

Recommended:

- ○ **Bartók: Klavierkonzerte 1–3** / Fricsay (cond.), Anda, Radio SO Berlin / DG 447399
- ○ **Bartók: Piano Concertos 1, 2 & 3** / Salonen (cond.), Bronfman, Los Angeles PO / 2000 / Sony 89732
- ○ **Gyorgy Sandor Plays Bartók** / Gielen (cond.), Sandor, Vienna SO / 1992 / Vox 5506
- ○ **Bartók: Piano Concertos Nos. 1 & 2; Stravinsky** / C. Abbado (cond.), Pollini, Chicago SO / 2001 / DG 471360

Piano Concerto No. 3 in E major, Sz. 119 (1945)

Bartók composed the *Piano Concerto No. 3* in the United States. It differs radically from his first two piano concertos in its lack of overt virtuosity, its lack of conspicuous modernism, and its greater adherence to traditional models and forms. Even the Hungarian melodic and rhythmic elements, while still present, are not as pronounced as in his earlier concertos. The *Third* is a warmer and more melodic work with a more popular appeal that does not in any way compromise its musical integrity. Bartók wrote the concerto for his wife, Ditta Pasztory. He completed all but the final 17 bars, which were left in his musical shorthand. His friend Tibor Serly finished the work and it was premiered on February 8, 1946, by György Sándor with Eugene Ormandy conducting the Philadelphia Orchestra.

The *Third* is in three movements: Allegretto, Andante religioso, and Allegro vivace. The Allegretto is in sonata form with two subjects: a rhythmic opening theme and a lyrical second melody. These are developed and recapitulated in a more or less conventional fashion and the movement is rounded off with an elegiac coda of quiet beauty. The Andante religioso is one of Bartók's most heartfelt and heart-warming pieces, a three-part movement with the outer sections being a chorale for piano and orchestra with almost Bachian counterpoint and a central section of gloriously expansive Bartókian night music with bird calls and insect noises. The Allegro vivace that follows attaca is a much more boisterous movement in the form of a rondo with two contrasting episodes and an extended coda. With its angular themes, its spiky rhythms, its contrapuntal developments, its aggressive orchestration with a large part for percussion, and its bravura piano writing, the Allegro vivace is by far the most Bartókian movement of the *Third. —James Leonard*

Recommended:

- ○ **Martha Argerich: Prokofiev, Bartók** / Dutoit (cond.), Argerich, Montreal SO / 1998 / EMI 56654
- ○ **Monique Haas Plays Bartók, Debussy & Ravel** / Fricsay (cond.), M. Haas, Berlin RIAS-SO / 1993 / DG 439666
- ○ **Références: Dinu Lipatti** / Sacher (cond.), Lipatti, Orchester der SWR / 2001 / EMI 67572
- ○ **Bela Bartók: Piano Concertos, Violin Concerto; Concerto for Orchestra** / C. Davis (cond.), Kovacevich, London SO / 1993 / Philips 438812

Viola Concerto, Sz. 120 (1945)

While the nature of musical composition most often involves a state of artistic solitude and independence, the untimely death of a composer has at times made necessary the unexpected aid of a collaborator. Indeed, the list of compositions that were completed by others after the death of the composer is surprisingly varied. The most famous examples are those of Mozart's *Requiem* and Mahler's *Tenth Symphony,* but other composers—including Puccini, Berg, and Elgar—also left behind unfinished works that were later brought to a more complete state with varying degrees of success. Béla Bartók was surely aware of his own impending demise as he worked feverishly in order to complete his last two major works, the *Piano Concerto No. 3* and the *Viola Concerto,* in 1945. Although the *Third Piano Concerto* was fully realized except for the orchestration of the final 17 bars, the Viola Concerto presented a somewhat more complex problem. Bartók's friend and pupil, Tibor Serly, was entrusted with the completion of this work, which he discussed in a 1969 interview with David Dalton: "Bartók never worked in a reduced score or a piano reduction. He did not like to make piano reductions; he always refused to do that. Bartók was one of those rare composers who thought orchestrally. He tried to put down the orchestration as best he could so that it would be visible and possibly playable. He did not think in terms of just writing down the harmonic content, then the melody, and then going on from there. This manuscript is not a reduced sketch in any sense of the term. Where it was completed, every single instrumental part, every single particle has been put in. However, he did not mark the instruments; he made very few designations. If you could once decipher those parts, the orchestration was complete as it is. I had to clearly decipher the sketches so that everything went into place: skipped bars, additions, and other alterations. Now there are a few little places, for instance in the slow movement, where he knew exactly what he wanted to do, but put in only touches of orchestration. There are other parts, as in the last movement, where only the melodic line comes up, but he knew what was going on there; he had just not put it in."

The work, which had been commissioned by violist William Primrose in 1945, was finally premiered in 1950 by Primrose with Antal Dorati and the Minneapolis Symphony Orchestra. The Concerto is divided into three movements, each linked to the next by seamless transitions of mood. The first, Moderato, begins with the first theme lightly accompanied by pizzicato cellos and basses, followed by a cadenza-like passage that leads to the entrance of the full orchestra. The movement contains three main themes, which are treated in a manner not unlike that of a Classical sonata-allegro movement. The second movement, Adagio religioso, begins with a suggestion of the work's first theme and unfolds into a more lyrical statement incorporating a rather brief moment of agitation in its center. In the final movement, Allegro vivace, Bartók makes characteristic use of dance rhythms, evoking the folk-like atmosphere and simplicity that were particular hallmarks of his earlier style. *—Michael Rodman*

Recommended:

- ○ **Concertgebouw Series: Mozart, Mahler, de Falla, Bartók** / Klemperer (cond.), Primrose, Concertgebouw / Audiophile 547
- ○ **Bartók: Concerto for viola; Movement for viola & orchestra** / Eötvös (cond.), Kashkashian, Netherlands Radio CO / 2000 / ECM 465420
- ○ **Bartók: 4 Pieces, Rhapsodies, Concerto for viola** / Korodi (cond.), Németh, Budapest PO / Hungaroton 31050

Violin Concerto (No. 2) in B minor, Sz. 112 (1937–1938)

Bartók's lifelong interest in variation as a compositional stratagem found its fullest expression in this Concerto, which he completed in 1938. Bartók had been at work on the *Music for Strings, Percussion and Celesta* when his close friend, violinist Zoltán Székely, asked him for a concerto. Bartók initially planned a large-scale theme-and-variations work, but Szekély indicated a preference for a traditional, three-movement work. Bartók's response was ingenious, preserving his own plan for variations within the framework of three movements. The middle movement, Andante tranquillo, follows a traditional theme-and-variations plan, while the finale is a large-scale variant of the first movement. Szekély gave the first performance in Amsterdam in 1939, with the Amsterdam Concertgebouw Orchestra conducted by Willem Mengelberg. That premiere was recorded on 78 rpm shellac discs; the recording has been released to the public, and while its sound quality can at best be called poor, it preserves Bartók's own tempo and balance preferences. Over measured B major chords from the harp, punctuated by pizzicato low strings (which sound the five-note motif, B-F sharp-A-E-B, that is the foundation of all the concerto's thematic material), the soloist launches a noble theme in verbunkos rhythm, a long-breathed melody of forthright optimism that immediately places the concerto in Olympian altitudes. In keeping with the Apollonian poise of this Allegro non troppo, the accompaniment is often light and sparing, achieving maximum coloristic effects with minimal scoring (despite the fact that the orchestra is fairly large, with woodwinds in pairs, four horns, three trombones, and a large percussion section). The second theme, marked risoluto, is playful but highly chromatic, with chattering woodwinds accompanying. The main theme returns more than once, like an informal ritornello, in the course of the movement, which Bartók shapes palindromically. Toward the end there is a difficult cadenza almost entirely in double stops and chords. Given the importance of variation technique to Bartók's musical rhetoric, it's interesting to note that aside from a few piano pieces, this concerto's second movement is his only large-scale essay in theme-and-variations form. With soft taps from the timpani beneath, the soloist brings forth the tender and limpid theme which is then treated to six highly differentiated variations. The brusque unison string phrases that open the finale are related to the five-note motif heard at the work's outset. They are answered by the soloist's capricious variant of the opening theme. The themes of the first movement have been, in Bartók's characteristic fashion, elaborated and extended, but their relationship to the first movement is always clear, not least because the structure of the finale closely follows that of the Allegro non troppo. Particularly charming is a waltz-like version of the theme that occurs before the final rush to climax, in which the five-note motif is transformed into the more emphatic four-note phrase (B-A-D-B) that ends the work. Bartók's original ending, in which the soloist was silent during the concluding tutti, was rejected by Szekély, who wanted a finish that was more like a concerto instead of a symphony. Bartók obliged with an alternate ending, which is the one generally used, but he appended the original ending to the published score. It features some fearsome forte arpeggios for the three trombones. *—Mark Satola*

Recommended:

- ○ **In Memorian: Yehudi Menuhin** / Ansermet (cond.), Yehudi Menuhin, SRO / Music & Arts 1053
- ○ **Strauss, Bartók: Violin Concertos** / Rozhdestvensky (cond.), I. Oistrakh, Moscow State SO / 1996 / Audiophile 101519
- ○ **Références: Yehudi Menhuin, Bartók** / Furtwängler (cond.), Yehudi Menuhin, London Philharmonia Orch. / EMI 74799
- ○ **Bartók: Violin Concerto 2; Rhapsodies** / Boulez (cond.), G. Shaham, Chicago SO / DG 459639

ORCHESTRAL

The Miraculous Mandarin, pantomime, Sz. 73 (Op. 19) (1918–1919; revised 1926)

Béla Bartók's pantomime *The Miraculous Mandarin* stands at the head of a group of works (including the *Four Orchestral Pieces,* the two violin sonatas, and ballet *The Wooden Prince*) that effectively bring to a close the first half of his career. A defining in Bartók's early career was the experience, in 1903, of hearing Richard Strauss' *Also Sprach Zarathustra.* Consequently, the most important orchestral scores of Bartók's early years feature striking coloristic effects and a highly complex internal counterpoint inherited from Strauss, though with Bartók's own stylistic and rhetorical profile. This work represents the zenith of this stylistic trend. Based on a play by Menyhert (Melchior) Lengyel, *The Miraculous Mandarin* tells the sordid (but "beautiful," to use Bartók's term) story of three urban toughs who force a girl to lure men to their lair, where they will then be attacked and robbed. Among those ensnared is a wealthy and otherworldly Mandarin, whose desire for the girl inures him against the robbers' attempts to kill him by using a variety of methods. Only when the girl submits to the Mandarin's desires is he finally able to die from his wounds. Writing to his first wife, Bartók described the unforgettable opening bars as "an awful clamor, clatter, stampeding and blowing of horns." Swirling strings and blaring winds depict the chaotic urban street scene, from which we are transported into the robbers' lair. Bartók is at his most dissonant here, his expressionistic chromaticism pushing close to the border of atonality. The girl's seductive call is represented by a snaky clarinet theme, which is answered first by a poor student, then a shabby old man. The robbers toss both of the unlikely prospects down the stairs. The appearance of the Mandarin is underscored by an imposing wall of timbres over a low pedal point, with frightening emphasis from the organ. The girl hesitantly dances with the Mandarin to a sinuous and unsettling waltz, but his lust turns the pas de deux into a frantic chase. Bartók here translates his *Allegro Barbaro* style into an expressionistic sequence of impressive skill and excitement (the concert suite ends with the climax of the chase). The robbers' attempts to kill the Mandarin are graphically depicted, with low, muffled music for the smothering and sharp orchestral sforzandi accompanying each stab of the sword. When the girl takes pity on the Mandarin, her gestures are accompanied by an eerie variant of the waltz theme. The death of the Mandarin is among the most terrifying music ever written: an offstage chorus keens wordlessly on a rocking minor third, while a cold cantabile in the strings is punctuated by dissonant clusters from winds and percussion depicting the Mandarin's horrible death spasms. Bartók's original version of the score was tied closely to the dramaturgy of pantomime, with long sections of recitative-style music to mirror the stage action. Subsequent revisions brought the score into a more symphonic shape. *—Mark Satola*

Recommended:

- ○ **Bartók: Concerto for Orchestra; The Miraculous Mandarin** / Chailly (cond.), Royal Concertgebouw Orch. / 2001 / Decca 458841
- ○ **Bartók: Orchestral Works; Bluebeard's Castle** / Dorati (cond.), London SO / 2004 / Mercury 4756255

Music for Strings, Percussion, & Celesta, Sz. 106 (1936)

Bartók wrote some of his finest music for the Swiss conductor Paul Sacher, in whom he found a particularly sympathetic champion. *Music for Strings, Percussion and Celesta,* written for Sacher in 1936, explores with great refinement and mastery the musical concepts that Bartók had been developing since the mid-1920s. In the *Piano Concerto No. 1,* Bartók explored the percussive elements of the piano, coupling it effectively with percussion only in the introduction to the concerto's slow movement. In *Music for Strings, Percussion and Celesta,* Bartók ingeniously sets the piano with the percussion instruments, where its melodic and harmonic material functions in support of the two string choirs.

Since the early 1930s, Bartók had also incorporated elements of Baroque music into his compositions, inspired partly by his exploration of pre-Classical keyboard composers such as Scarlatti, Rameau and Couperin. In reflection of this, *Music for Strings, Percussion and Celesta* evokes the Baroque concerto grosso, with its two antiphonal string orchestras separated by a battery of tuned and untuned percussion instruments. The work's prosaic title was actually just a working title which was subsequently allowed to stand.

The opening movement, Andante tranquillo, is a slow fugue on a chromatic melody that springs from a five-note cell, each subsequent phrase growing in length and elaborating on its predecessor. At this point, the two string orchestras play together. As the string voices accumulate, the fugue's texture increases in complexity and the chromatic implications of the theme are brought to a rigorously dissonant fulfillment. The fugue climaxes at its apogee with an ominous rumble from the timpani and a loud stroke on the tam-tam. As the fugue folds in upon itself the celesta makes its first entrance with an arpeggiated chord, mysterious and remote. The work subsequently grows from the motivic material explored in this first movement.

Bartók deploys (antiphonal) string choirs for the second movement, a fast, fugitive piece in which the two orchestras chase each other through a breathtaking series of elaborations on the main theme. In the percussion section, piano, xylophone, and harp take the lead while two side drums (with and without snares) provide emphatic punctuation. The third movement is one of Bartók's most accomplished "night music" pieces, with cricket-like notes from the xylophone, eerie timpani glissandi, fragmentary murmurs, and frightened exclamations from the strings, along with the always-mysterious notes of the celesta floating clear and sphinx-like over the nocturnal weft. The finale, a dance of energy and abandon, restores the antiphonal deployment of the strings and juxtaposes the diatonic aspects of the work's main theme with its chromatic elements. There are also some striking touches like the furious, strummed four-note chords in the violins, violas and cellos that opens the movement, a theme midway through that is based on a repeated note first hammered out on piano and xylophone, and then a grand peroration of the initial fugue theme, now with its intervals doubled and richly harmonized. In the quick coda there is a brief, suspended moment ("a tempo allargando") before the work tumbles to a conclusion in unabashed A major. *—Mark Satola*

Recommended:

- ○ **Bartók: Konzert für Orchester** / Fricsay (cond.), Berlin RIAS-SO / 1996 / DG 447443

○ **Evgeny Mravinsky in Prague** / Mravinsky (cond.), Leningrad PO / Praga 256016/19

○ **Bartók: Music SPC; Hungarian Sketches** / F. Reiner (cond.), Chicago SO / 2001 / JVC 12

Romanian Folk Dances (Román népi táncok), Sz. 68 (1917)

This is the orchestral version of the composer's 1915 *Romanian Folkdances for piano*, Sz. 56. They are, in either version, very short, light pieces, and while their quality is fairly high (what folk music of Bartók's is not?), they are ultimately less significant works in the output of the composer.

The first of the seven dances, "Stick Dance," is played at a leisurely tempo, and though the general pacing is lively, the music has a restrained quality. The theme is attractive and Bartók's approach is straightforward in presenting the ethnic elements, as it is throughout the set. The second item, "Round Dance," less than a minute in duration, is playful and subtle. The next, "In One Spot," is colorful in its mysterious character, having an exotic upper-register melody with all the flavor and allure of Gypsy music. The fourth entry, the "Horn Dance," is wistful in nature and borders on the reflective, though it remains essentially light and colorful. At nearly two minutes, it is the longest of the dances in the set. The ensuing "Romanian Polka" is lively and colorful, lasting about a half-minute. The last two dances are both entitled "Short and Sweet." The first is, indeed, quite short and the closing number, though longer, lasts less than a minute. Both are rollicking, joyous dances whose celebration perfectly caps this colorful set of folk-inspired pieces.

A typical performance of these dances would last about seven minutes. The piano version is more popular in the concert halls and has also received substantially more recordings. *—Robert Cummings*

Recommended:

○ **Bartók: The Miraculous Mandarin Complete Ballet** / I. Fischer (cond.), Budapest Festival Orch. / 1997 / Philips 454430

○ **Antal Dorati Conducts Kodály & Bartók** / Dorati (cond.), Minnesota Orch. / 1990 / Mercury 432005

BALLET

The Wooden Prince, Sz. 60 (Op. 13) (1914–1917)

While the least successful artistically (and the most difficult to stage) of Bartók's three dramatic works, the ballet *The Wooden Prince* was nevertheless a great success with the audience at its premiere in Budapest in May 1917. No doubt this was due in part to the happy circumstances under which it was first produced. Unlike many of Bartók's previous works, whose earliest performances had suffered from insufficient preparation, the original production of *The Wooden Prince* enjoyed the benefit of an unprecedented 30 rehearsals under conductor Egisto Tango.

Much of the problem posed by *The Wooden Prince* lies with its dramatic component. The story was written by Hungarian dramatist Béla Balázs, who had previously supplied the libretto for *Bluebeard's Castle* (1911). In the ballet, the simple tale of a Prince's attempts to woo and win a reluctant Princess through the use of a broomstick dummy of himself was complicated by Balázs' introduction of a Fairy who plays both sides of the game, initially hindering the Prince in his ardor but later taking pity on him and helping him to win the hand of his beloved. The Fairy's almost perverse change of heart seems inexplicable in the rudimentary fairy tale context, and the other characters are entirely one-dimensional, in stark contrast to the deep psychological portraits Balázs provided (via Maeterlinck) for *Bluebeard's Castle*. Further, none of the characters is granted specific identification with a distinctive musical motif, as was notably the case in Bartók's following stage work, the ballet-pantomime *The Miraculous Mandarin* (1918–19).

The score calls for one of the largest orchestras Bartók ever summoned, including woodwinds, horns, and trumpets in fours, pairs of saxophones and cornets, and a large complement of tuned and non-pitched percussion. The opening, based on a long-held C major triad, has been compared to that of Wagner's *Das Rheingold*; fully three minutes elapse before the curtain rises. In *The Wooden Prince*, Bartók expresses his musical ideas in a unique style of impressionism similar to that which distinguishes the *Images, op. 10* (1910) and the *Four Orchestral Pieces, op. 12* (1912). While the sound world is ravishing, the shape of the piece is somewhat diffuse. Notable exceptions include the billowing music that accompanies the episode in which the Fairy causes the river to rise against the Prince as he seeks the Princess; the grotesque episode when the Fairy enchants the stick figure the Prince has fashioned, causing it to dance, is similarly striking. This music, the most focused in the piece, looks forward to the direction Bartók would take in subsequent decades, while much of the score represents a valedictory for the composer's style up to that point.

Despite subsequent stagings, notably the Cubism-influenced Budapest production of 1935 and that at the Bartók Festival of 1948, *The Wooden Prince* has not entered the repertory as a stage work; it remains known primarily in the form of a concert suite arranged by the composer in 1921 and expanded in 1931–32. *—Mark Satola*

Synopsis:

The story takes place in an enchanted land where a handsome, lovelorn Prince, who has wandered the countryside, arrives in a magical forest near a brook. In a picturesque flower garden he observes a Princess, whose striking beauty immediately captivates him. She is, however, taken back to her palace by the Fairy of Nature, and when the Prince attempts to pursue her, he is stymied by the protective actions of the forest and brook.

The Prince decides to use a ruse to draw the Princess back out of her palace and into the flower garden. He constructs a wooden puppet, dresses it with his princely garments and even adorns it with plentiful locks of his hair. He also places his crown on the wooden effigy. Soon the Princess observes the figure and departs her palace. She quickly finds she is enamored of this regal-looking handsome prince. When she moves away from him for a moment, the Prince confronts her in his now-simple garb, forlorn and unimposing in his appearance.

The Princess is startled and repulsed by him and hurries back to her wooden prince. The Nature Fairy then brings the handsome puppet to life, and he begins to dance. The Princess joins him, but the dance is frenzied in its hectic pacing and begins tiring her. Meanwhile, the Prince stands alone, dispirited, watching their wildly animated movements. The Nature Fairy takes pity on the forlorn Prince and directs the trees and plants to pay him homage. They bend low before him and present the Prince with a crown made of flowers. By now the Princess has become exhausted from the wild dance and the wooden prince has stumbled to the ground.

The Princess finally becomes attracted to the "human" Prince, who is now alluring to her in his newfound, simpler glory. But when she attempts to go to him, it is she this time who is held back by the trees and plants. She soon realizes she must renounce her crown to merit the Prince's love. She does so, and the two embrace and kiss. *—Robert Cummings*

Recommended:

○ **Bartók: The Wooden Prince; Music SPC** / Dorati (cond.), London SO / 1995 / Mercury 434357

○ **Bartók: The Wooden Prince Suite; 2 Portraits** / Adam Fischer (cond.), Hungarian State SO / 1993 / Nimbus 5362

OPERA

Duke Bluebeard's Castle (A kékszakkallú Herceg Vára), Sz. 48 (Op. 11) (1911; revised 1912)

The year 1911 was, from one perspective, exactly the wrong time for a young, albeit respected, composer to be making his initial foray into opera. As Bartók labored on his first and only essay in the genre, he must have been aware that entertainment-seeking European audiences were then enjoying the efforts of a formidable cadre of established, wildly successful operatic composers. Still active as *Bluebeard's Castle* took shape were crowd-pleasers Puccini, Giordano, and Mascagni in Italy and Humperdinck and Richard Strauss in Germany, among others. It is not too surprising, then, to learn that when Bartók submitted the imaginatively dark-hued *Bluebeard* to the Hungarian Fine Arts Commission, the opera was rejected for a prize with a time-honored dismissal: "unplayable." It took another seven years for *Bluebeard's Castle* to receive its first staging; the work was finally premiered with much success by the Royal Hungarian Opera in May 1918. Its promising reception was, however, curtailed by the political intrigues of wartime Hungary. Librettist Béla Balázs (1884–1949) was inclined toward political views contrary to those of the government. After Bartók, whether out of loyalty or personal conviction, refused to suppress Balázs' name at subsequent performances, he himself withdrew the work, and it remained unperformed in Budapest for another 20 years.

While at the time of *Bluebeard*'s composition Bartók was continuing to absorb the influence of other composers (including Liszt, Wagner, Strauss, and, then very recently, Debussy), the composer was also engaged with other, more deeply rooted musical concerns. The best-known and perhaps most important of these was his long-standing interest in the folk songs of his native Hungary and surrounding lands, which he spent several years collecting and transcribing together with his associate Zoltán Kodály. Particularly attractive to the composer were this music's exotic modes and scales and flexible, speech-inflected rhythms.

This latter aspect in particular proved central to Bartók's conception of *Bluebeard's Castle* at a time when his experience as a vocal composer had been limited largely to concise forms such as those he had observed in his travels to peasant villages. "I wanted to magnify," he later wrote of the opera, "the dramatic fluidum of [composer] Székely's folk ballads for the stage. And I wanted to depict a modern soul in the primary colors of folk song." Bartók uses mostly pentantonic scales as Bluebeard's wife Judith opens the doors of his castle and comes to the realization that she is one of his gruesome prizes. The climax of the arch form of the work is achieved in tension, volume, orchestration, and lighting at the opening of the fifth door, where the tonality changes to a new chromatic scale that stands in sharp contrast to all that has gone before. The score uses only one musical motif: a movement of a semitone symbolizing the omnipresent blood.

The composer was further attracted to the project by the story of Bluebeard itself, which had already attained several incarnations by the time of Bartók's setting.

Originally recounting the crimes against children perpetrated by the fifteenth century Marshal of France Gilles de Retz, the story was spun into a fairy tale by Charles Perrault and later fashioned into a play/libretto (for Paul Dukas) by Maurice Maeterlinck. Bartók employed Balázs' symbolist version, in which fantastic elements provide metaphorical associations with Bluebeard's entrapment in loneliness and his wife's ultimately unsuccessful attempts to free him from this fate. The plot is totally allegorical and lacks action. *—Michael Rodman*

Synopsis:

The drama of Bluebeard and Judith is preceded by a spoken introduction in which a "minstrel" admonishes the audience to look beyond the surface of the unfolding events in order to determine their true meaning. From the top of a staircase, Bluebeard and Judith make their entrance, he solemn, she apprehensive in the dismal atmosphere. Nearly indistinguishable in the gloorn are seven doors, all of them locked. Judith's curiosity leads her to implore Bluebeard to open the doors; though he initially resists, he gives in to her wishes by handing her the key to the first. Upon opening the door, a shaft of red light pours out. Inside, Judith can see various instruments of torture: shackles, daggers, branding irons, and the like. As Bluebeard explains that this is his torture chamber, Judith notices that the dampness of the walls comes not from mildew but from blood. The orchestra sounds the "blood motive"—a minor second in various permutations—which recurs with the revelation of the horror within each room.

Bluebeard, again hesitant at first, consents to give Judith the key to the second door, which opens to a yellowish red light. Stockpiled within are battle weapons and other armaments, all stained with blood. The third door is opened to reveal a golden light, which emanates from Bluebeard's treasury. The radiance of the jewels and coins is reflected in the bright flourishes of the celesta amid the D major background of the orchestra—but only until Judith sees the blood on these treasures. The fourth door opens to blue-green light as a spectacular garden is revealed. This time the specter of blood is seen upon the stems of the roses and on the ground itself. The opening of the fifth door is heralded by a dazzling light accompanied by the rich sonority of consecutive major chords in a manner that suggests Bartók's debt to Debussy. The majestic vista that is revealed is the whole of Bluebeard's kingdom, which Judith regards with awe until she is finally pressed to move on by the bloody shadow cast by the clouds. As the sixth door is opened, the stage unexpectedly grows darker. A mysterious body of water—a lake of tears, Bluebeard reveals—captures Judith's attention.

Presently, Bluebeard decrees that the last door must remain closed forever. At this point Judith tells him that she has guessed his secret, making the accusation that he has murdered all of his former wives. In order to see for herself, she demands that he open the last door, and he gives her the key. As she opens the door, she sees that there are indeed three women inside, but they are not dead. Richly bedecked, they slowly and solemnly process from the room as Bluebeard explains that they are his former wives. After paying homage to them he takes similarly grand vestments from the third room and slowly places them on Judith. As she realizes that she must share the fate of these women, the three wives proceed back into the room and are followed by Judith. As the door closes after them, the lights dim and the grave chords in the low strings that introduced the opera return, now accompanied by filaments of the blood motive and transformed into an expression of Bluebeard's resignation and despair. *—Michael Rodman*

Recommended:

- ○ **Bartók: Duke Bluebeard's Castle** / Kertesz (cond.), C. Ludwig, W. Berry, London SO / 1999 / Decca 466377
- ○ **Bártok: Bluebeard's Castle** / Dorati (cond.), Szönyi, M. Szekely, London SO / 1992 / Mercury 434325
- ○ **Béla Bartók: Bluebeard's Castle, Op. 11** / Eötvös (cond.), Kallisch, P. Fried, Stuttgart SWR Radio-SO / 2001 / Haenssler 93070

Cecilia Bartoli

b. Jun. 4, 1966, Rome, Italy

Mezzo-Soprano

During the final decade of the twentieth century, Cecilia Bartoli emerged as perhaps the public's favorite concert singer, with no sign in the twenty-first that her singular mix of vocal pyrotechnics, physical attractiveness, intelligent musicianship, and audience seduction would decline. Only Luciano Pavarotti sold more discs for Decca in the same period. Bartoli has been winning awards globally every year since 1992. She sings opera, of course, but for only part of each season, and by choice in a limited number of congenial venues. Although Monte Carlo is her home, Zürich audiences are frequent beneficiaries of her operatic activity, where Nikolaus Harnoncourt, one of the two most influential conductors in her career, regularly presides. She sang Cherubino in Mozart's *Figaro* there in 1989, officially the first year of her career, and later on, Susanna. She also sang her first Zerlina, then Donna Elvira in *Don Giovanni*, and Fiordiligi in *Così*, not, from reports, a vocal triumph. But that feat means she has sung all three of the opera's women: Dorabella for the first time in 1990, and the maid Despina, her debut role at the Met, in 1996. Bartoli made her New York debut, however, in 1990 at a *Mostly Mozart* concert, returning in 1992 for three sold-out performances, followed by a U.S. tour. Her other Mozart roles include Cecilio in *Lucio Silla*, Idamante in *Idomeneo*, Sesto in *La clemenza di Tito*, and Sifare in *Mitridate*.

She made her U.S. opera debut at Houston in 1993 in Rossini's *Il barbiere di Siviglia*, the other most prominent composer in her stage career to date. Not counting the Shepherd Boy at age nine in *Tosca* at Rome, where her father was a career chorister, or an appearance at Catania in 1987—just a year after she began intensive vocal training under her mother—Rossini was initially predominant: *La pietra del paragone* in 1988, then *La scala di seta* at Pesaro, and *The Barber* at Ludwigsburg in 1989. She made her La Scala debut in 1991 as Isolier in *Le comte Ory*, and in 1992 added Angiolina, aka La Cenerentola, at Bologna. Otherwise, she has appeared in two Haydn operas, *Armida* and *L'anima del filosofo*—the latter at Vienna in 1995, and her debut role at London's Royal Opera in October 2001. The only other stage role to date has been Paisiello's Nina. Bartoli characterizes herself as "a child of the eighteenth century"—increasingly reflected in recordings that now include CDs of Vivaldi and early operatic arias by Gluck (issued as *Dreams and Fables*). Of the more than 20 releases by 2002, ten have been operas, all by Mozart and Rossini. Although her mother remains Bartoli's only teacher (and traveling companion, as Renata Tebaldi's mother used to be), the Italian musicologist Claudio Osele became a valued consultant on the Vivaldi project.

Bartoli trained formally at Rome's Santa Cecilia Conservatory—choosing the trombone paradoxically, but then she also wanted to be a flamenco dancer before emerging as a coloratura mezzo with a high C. In recital, pianists have included Daniel Barenboim (who also conducted her first Berlioz's *Nuits d'été*), Myung-Whun Chung, and regularly since 1995, Jean-Yves Thibaudet. The question becomes, however, after half a lifetime of singing, where does she go from here? Her on-stage slapstick in Rossini's operas (with *L'italiana in Algeri* still untried) does not befit the direction she is taking musically. But Bartoli has brains as well as charm, and celebrity once experienced is unslakable. *—Roger Dettmer*

Recommended:

- ○ **Rossini: La Cenerentola** / Chailly (cond.), Bartoli, Corbelli, Matteuzzi, Pertusi, Bologna Community Theater Orch. / 1993 / London 436902
- ○ **Mozart: Arias** / Fischer (cond.), Bartoli, Vienna CO / 1991 / London 430513
- ○ **If You Love Me: 18th Century Italian Songs** / Bartoli, Fischer / 1992 / London 436267
- ○ **The Salieri Album** / Fischer (cond.), Bartoli, Orch. of the Age of Enlightenment / 2003 / Decca 000109702
- ○ **The Vivaldi Album** / Antonini (cond.), Bartoli, Il Giardino Arminico / 1999 / Decca 466569
- ○ **The Art of Cecilia Bartoli** / Bartoli / 2002 / Decca 473380
- ○ **Dreams and Fables: Gluck Italian Arias** / Forck (cond.), Bartoli, Berlin Academy for Early Music / 2001 / Decca 467248

Yuri Bashmet

b. Jun. 2, 1953, Rostov-on-Don, Russia

Violist

Professional violists are often limited by a scarcity of repertoire for their instrument, but Yuri Bashmet has successfully surmounted this challenge and enjoys a flourishing international solo career. Born in 1953 in Rostov-on-Don in Russia and raised in Lvov in the Ukraine, he began studies at the Moscow Conservatoire at age 18. Barely out of his teens, he became the youngest person ever to be appointed to a professorship at that same institution. In 1976, Bashmet won the first prize at the International Viola Competition in Munich, which effectively launched his career.

Bashmet has been the first violist ever to give a solo recital in a number of major concert halls, including La Scala in Milan and the Concertgebouw in Amsterdam. Today he is widely regarded as the finest viola player on the international circuit, and has brought newfound status to this somewhat unsung orchestral instrument. He has inspired many composers to write for him, notably fellow Russian, Alfred Schnittke. In 1986, he premiered the composer's now-ubiquitous *Viola Concerto* at the *Concertgebouw* in Amsterdam.

Other works written for Bashmet include Georgian composer Giya Kancheli's *Mourned by the Wind*, which the violist premiered at the Berlin Festival, *The Myrrh Bearer* by John Tavener, and Sofia Gubaidulina's *Viola Concerto*, which he premiered with the Chicago Symphony Orchestra and Kent Nagano in April 1997. Bashmet also gave the world premiere of Benjamin Britten's recently edited *Double Concerto for violin and viola* with Gidon Kremer and the Hallé Orchestra conducted by Kent Nagano in Manchester in 1998.

The year 1992 marked the beginning of Bashmet's partnership with the Moscow Soloists, which he directs himself. Comprised of musicians nominated by professors at the Moscow Conservatoire, it features some of the brightest new talent from the Russian school of string playing. In recent seasons, the group has appeared in Moscow, Athens, Amsterdam, Paris, and at the *BBC Promenades*.

Bashmet has appeared with all the world's leading orchestras, including the Berlin Philharmonic, Royal Concertgebouw, Boston Symphony, Chicago

Symphony, Montreal Symphony, Los Angeles Philharmonic, and London's Philharmonia Orchestra. In 1993, the London Symphony Orchestra presented a four-concert Yuri Bashmet festival at the Barbican. Chamber music collaborators over the years have included Gidon Kremer, the Borodin Quartet, Viktoria Mullova, Mstislav Rostropovich and Maxim Vengerov. *—Brian Wise*

Recommended:

○ **Bashmet Plays Schubert, Schumann, Bruch & Enesco** / Bashmet, Muntian (piano) / 1990 / RCA 60112

○ **Kancheli: Styx; Gubaidulina: Viola Concerto** / Gergiev (cond.), Bashmet, Mariinsky Theater Orchestra / DG 471494

○ **Bashmet Plays Shostakovich, Hindemith & Britten** / Bashmet / Mezhdunarodnaya Kniga 418015

Mattia Battistini

b. Feb. 27, 1856, Contigliano, Italy, **d.** Nov. 7, 1928, Colle Baccaro, Italy

Baritone

Baritone Mattia Battistini was born on February 27, 1856 in Contigliano, near Rome. In Rome, he studied voice with Eugenio Terziani and later with Vencesleo Persichini. In 1878, he made his professional debut at the Teatro Argentina in Donizetti's *La Favorita* on less than a day's notice. He was a great success, and over the next several years sang throughout northern Italy in *Il Trovatore, La Forza del Destino, Rigoletto, Les Huguenots, L' Africaine, I Puritani, Lucia di Lammermoor, Ernani*, and many other operas. In 1881, he travelled to South America and on his return stopped at Madrid and Seville to sing Figaro in *The Barber of Seville*. In 1883, he sang at Covent Garden in London and had a mild success, but how could such a young singer expect to steal headlines from the likes of Sembrich, Marconi, and Edwuard de Reszke? In 1888, he returned to South America, but the voyage was very difficult—that was the last time Battistini crossed the Atlantic. He felt that crossing the English Channel was as long as he wanted to be on a ship again. Massenet was so beguiled by his voice that he rewrote the tenor role of *Werther* so that Battistini could sing it. Beginning in 1893, he spent long periods of time each season in Russia. The opera house at St. Petersburg included on its roster Marcella Sembrich, Fernando de Lucia, Adamo Didur, and many other great singers from the turn of the century. From this point on, his career was a succession of triumphs matched by few singers in the history of opera. He sang several Russian operas including *Russlan and Ludmilla* by Glinka, *The Demon* by Rubinstein, and *The Queen of Spades* and *Eugene Onegin* by Tchaikovsky. He would sing in Italian while his colleagues sang the original Russian text. His last opera performances were in Padua, 1921, when he repeated his *Rigoletto*. He continued to perform in recitals and concerts until 1927, an astonishing 49 years after his debut. He died on November 7, 1928 at Colle Baccaro near Rieti.

Battistini had one of the most beautiful baritone voices ever recorded. It was not the largest voice but, because of his exemplary control, it had a commanding presence. His voice was quite agile and he could crescendo and/or diminuendo with ease in any range. If his voice had any weakness, it was in the lower register which, at least on recording, does not carry well. On several recordings, he transposed the lower notes up an octave as in his recording of "Eri tu" from Verdi's *Un Ballo in Maschera*.

Battistini was already 45 years old when he made his first recordings in 1902, and he continued to record until 1924 when he was 67. In all, he recorded over 100 items, and each one has examples which we would want every singer to listen to and to understand. His earliest recordings are prime examples of great singing (Romophon 82008-2), with the aria from *Eugene Onegin* representing the pinnacle of vocal performance. He ends the aria on an unwritten high F which proceeds to swell and then diminish away into nothingness. He recorded many arias several times during his career, and while the voice was more secure in the earlier recordings, the later ones show little loss of technical prowess. The consistency of his artistry is the most truly remarkable aspect of this "King of the Baritones." *—Richard LeSueur*

Recommended:

○ **Mattia Battistini** / Battistini / 1997 / Symposium 1210

○ **Battistini** / Sabajno (cond.), Corsi, Sillich, Colazza, Mokrzycka, La Scala Theater Orch. / 1992 / Nimbus 7831

Kathleen Battle

b. Aug. 13, 1948, Portsmouth, OH

Soprano

One of the most famous African-American sopranos, Kathleen Battle received her vocal training at the Cincinnati College Conservatory, where she studied voice with Franklin Bens and also worked with Italo Tajo. While at Cincinnati she came to the attention of conductor Thomas Schippers who brought her to the Spoleto Festival in South Carolina to sing the Brahms *Requiem* in 1972. She made her stage debut in Rossini's *Il barbiere di Siviglia* as Rosina with the Michigan Opera Theater in Detroit in 1975. Susanna in Mozart's *Le nozze di Figaro* was her New York City Opera debut role in 1976. During this time, she also sang orchestral concerts in New York, Los Angeles and Cleveland. James Levine brought her to the Metropolitan Opera in New York as the Shepherd in Wagner's *Tannhäuser* in 1978, and she appeared frequently at the Met in important roles until 1994. She first appeared in Europe in 1978 at the Italian Spoleto Festival, and in 1979 debuted at the Glyndebourne Festival.

Her first appearance at Salzburg was in 1982 at an all-Mozart concert, and she often returned in concert, recital and opera. Her important opera roles at Salzburg were Susanna, Zerlina and Despina, three Mozart roles with which she has been associated at many opera houses around the world. She has appeared at most of the major opera houses of the world including San Francisco, Chicago, Covent Garden, London, Geneva, Vienna, and Berlin. In 1985, she was the soprano soloist in Mozart's *Coronation Mass* at St. Peter's Cathedral at the Vatican, in a performance conducted by Herbert von Karajan. She sang Handel's *Semele*,in a highly acclaimed performance in 1985 at Carnegie Hall and later recorded the role. In 1990 she was joined by Jessye Norman for a concert of spirituals which was conducted by James Levine at Carnegie Hall. Although best known for roles in the operas of Mozart and Strauss (Zdenka, Sophie and Zerbinetta), Battle has also had great success in Massenet's *Werther*, Donizetti's *L'elisir d'amore, Don Pasquale*, and *La fille du regiment*, Verdi's *Un ballo in maschera* and *Falstaff* and Rossini's *Il barbiere di Siviglia* and *L'Italiana in Algeri*. Battle has maintained an active recital career, and her Schubert interpretations are very fine. Her recital programs have also featured songs by Mozart, Strauss, Fauré and Rodrigo.

Kathleen Battle's voice is a high, very pure soprano with great charm. She has excellent technical control, which has allowed her to sing the difficult coloratura roles of Rosina and Zerbinetta though her approach is always more lyric that that of most coloratura sopranos. She is an excellent actress and tries to give full characterization to each of her roles. Several of her best roles were televised live from the Metropolitan Opera, New York and later released on video.

A perfectionist in her own work, Battle became more and more difficult to deal with as her career moved forward. Some felt that her demands were becoming unreasonable, and her behavior became erratic. These difficulties came to public attention when she was dismissed from the Metropolitan Opera in 1994 for "unprofessional conduct." Battle has continued to appear in concert and recital and remains a favorite of the public. *—Richard LeSueur*

Recommended:

○ **The Best of Kathleen Battle** / Battle, various artists / 2004 / DG 000349502

○ **Kathleen Battle in Concert** / Battle, Levine (cond.) / DG 445524

○ **Kathleen Battle Sings Mozart** / Battle, Previn (cond.), Royal PO / 1986 / EMI 47355

○ **Pleasures of Their Company** / Battle, Parkening / 1986 / Angel 47196

Bavarian Radio Symphony Orchestra

f. 1949, Munich, Germany

Ensemble

Of the three major orchestras based in Munich, the Bavarian Radio Symphony Orchestra is probably the most prominent and arguably the finest. It has been by far the most heavily recorded of the three and one of the most often-recorded ensembles in the world, its LPs and CDs appearing on a variety of major and minor labels over the years. Moreover, all of its music directors have been internationally acclaimed as among the leading conductors of their time.

The Bavarian Symphony Orchestra was established in 1949 and from that time to the present, has functioned under the financial and organizational auspices of the Bavarian Radio of Munich. Eugen Jochum was appointed the ensemble's first music director and he immediately proceeded to build the orchestra into one of Germany's finest. Its initial recordings were made under his baton in 1950. The orchestra's reputation in concert developed even more quickly under Jochum: several critically acclaimed tours of Europe throughout the 1950s, reaching from Austria to Great Britain, established its prominence early on. Igor Stravinsky led the ensemble in performances of his own works in 1951 and four years later, Paul Hindemith conducted a program featuring his music. Other prominent artists and conductors also appeared in the 1950s, including the orchestra's next music director Rafael Kubelik, who succeeded Jochum in 1961. Kubelik's notable recordings with BRSO include several of the Mahler symphonies and Schoenberg's *Gurrelieder*. Kubelik was a conservative in matters of repertory, largely focusing on Classical and Romantic works. He also made a number of successful concert tours of Europe and North America with the BRSO in both the 1960s and 1970s. The BRSO continued to attract major artists and guest conductors, including Carlo Maria Giulini, Bernard Haitink, Zubin Mehta, and Leonard Bernstein, who made regular appearances with the ensemble beginning in 1976. Kubelik resigned in September 1979 and Kiril Kondrashin, a recent defector from the Soviet Union and one of the world's most-respected conductors, was chosen to become his successor. He was never officially named music director—though he functioned in that capacity—and when he suddenly died of a heart attack in 1981, the orchestra was left without a director until 1983, when Sir Colin Davis took the podium. During his tenure, many successful tours were undertaken, including ones to Japan in 1984 and to the United States in 1986. Davis's critically acclaimed recordings with the BRSO include CD issues of the Mendelssohn symphonies and Beethoven's only opera, *Fidelio*. Lorin Maazel succeeded him in 1993 and continued the tradition of conducting and recording many choral and vocal works. The BRSO's CD issues under Maazel's direction include compelling performances of several Mahler works with Waltraud Meier. Maazel's tenure with the orchestra ended in 2002. His successor was Mariss Jansons, music director of the Pittsburgh Symphony Orchestra.

The orchestra, which has regularly broadcast concerts over Bavarian Radio throughout its existence, consists of 115 members and performs in *the Philharmonie Munich am Gasteig* and *the Herkulessaal of the Munich Residenz*. Sometimes known outside Germany as the Munich Symphony, in addition to the full orchestra, several smaller ensembles including the Koeckert-Quartet, the Bach Collegium Munich and the Munich Brass Ensemble have been established by members of the larger group. The popularity and critical acclaim given these smaller ensembles reflects the high standard of musicianship present within the full orchestra. —*Robert Cummings*

Recommended:

- ○ **Mahler: Symphony 6** / Kubelik (cond.), Bavarian RSO / 2001 / Audite 95480
- ○ **Mahler: Symphony 1; Songs of a Wayfarer** / Kubelik (cond.), Fischer-Dieskau, Bavarian RSO / 1999 / DG 460654
- ○ **Beethoven: Symphonies 4 & 7** / C. Kleiber (cond.), Bavarian RSO / Melodram 40047

Bavarian State Opera Orchestra

f. 1653, Munich, Germany
Ensemble

The Bavarian State Opera has one of the longest and most honored histories of any opera house in the world. Its orchestra also serves the Bavarian State Ballet and gives concerts as the Bavarian State Orchestra.

From the fifteenth century, Munich's major force in music was the Electoral court. The enthusiasm of Henriette Adelheid of Savoy (wife of the Elector's son) expedited the building of an opera house, which hosted its first performances in 1653. The Court Kapellmeister, Kerll, rapidly built the opera into the equal of any in Europe.

But the Electoral court moved to Brussels when Maximilian II Emmanuel was appointed governor of the Netherlands, taking the opera company with him. He returned in 1725. His successors Karl Albrecht (1726–45) and Maximilian III Joseph (1745–77) restored the opera to its earlier sumptuousness. A Residenztheater (also called the Cuvilliéstheater) was built in the electoral palace in 1753. In 1787 Elector Carl Theodor (1778–99) banned Italian opera, which drastically lessened the activities and standards of the opera. It was not until 1805 that this ban ended.

In the aftermath of the Napoleonic Wars, the rulers of Bavaria were elevated to the rank of King. The Residenztheater saw the world premieres of Weber's *Abu Hassan* (1811) and Meyerbeer's first opera, *Jephthas Gelübde* (1812). King Ludwig I approved the construction of a *Hof- und Nationaltheater* (Court and National Theater). Designed by Karl von Fisher, it was finished in 1818, destroyed by fire in 1823, and rebuilt the same year. The appointment of Franz Lachner as conductor brought the Bavarian Court Opera back up to its rank among the top of European companies.

When the young Irish dancer Lola Montez appeared on the *Hof- und Nationaltheater* stage in 1846, King Ludwig became infatuated. He made her a countess, showered her with gold and jewelry, and let her control governmental decisions. This sparked the populace revolt of 1848, forcing Ludwig's abdication in favor of his son, Maximilian.

The next king, Ludwig II, had his own historic operatic infatuation—with the music of Richard Wagner, who had been exiled for his role in the 1848 Revolution in Leipzig. Ludwig brought Wagner back to Germany in 1864, and his Opera gave the premieres of *Tristan und Isolde* and *Die Meistersinger*. Extravagant living and a notorious extramarital affair compelled Wagner to leave Munich. Ludwig had the Opera stage the two completed parts of *Das Ring der Nibelungen* against Wagner's will in 1869 and 1870. The angered Wagner built his Festival Theater in Bayreuth instead of Munich, but well after Ludwig's mysterious death in 1876. Munich built the Prinzergententheater, modeled after Bayreuth.

The Munich Opera maintained its reputation throughout the twentieth century. It was renamed the Bavarian State Opera, and the house became simply the Nationaltheater after 1918. Hans Knappertsbusch and Clemens Krauss were leading conductors up to World War II, during which the Cuvilliés and the Nationaltheater were both destroyed. After the war, the company moved to the Prinzregententheater. The two houses were rebuilt and reopened in 1958 and 1963 respectively. The immediate post-War years saw the tradition of great conductors continue, with Georg Solti, Ferenc Fricsay, Rudolf Kempe, and Joseph Keilberth on the podium. In 1971 Wolfgang Sawallisch began a long reign, stepping down in 1998. The Prinzregententheater was renovated in 1996, and is now used by the State Opera for some events. Zubin Mehta became music director of the Bavarian State Opera and State Orchestra in 1998. —*Joseph Stevenson*

Recommended:

- ○ **Orff: Antigonae** / Solti (cond.), Hafliger, Schech, Kuen, Kusche, Bavarian State Opera Orch. / 1995 / Orfeo 4079521
- ○ **Strauss: Der Rosenkavalier** / Kleiber (cond.), Popp, Fassbaender, Moll, Dernesch, Bavarian State Opera Orch. / Living Stage 1040
- ○ **Beethoven: Symphonie 6** / Kleiber (cond.), Bavarian State Opera Orch. / 2003 / Orfeo 600031

Arnold Bax

b. Nov. 8, 1883, Streatham, England, **d.** Oct. 3, 1953, Cork, Ireland
Composer: Orchestral, Chamber Music, Symphonic

Born of cultured and wealthy parents, Bax was insulated from the loss of direction that many composers felt during, and immediately after, the First World War. For him the prewar world of Debussy, Ravel, and Stravinsky was still alive in all its myth and mystery. He described himself as "a brazen romantic," and in many respects could be considered the last of the European post-Romantic school of composers.

During his five years at the Royal Academy of Music, Bax was deeply impressed by the poetry of W.B. Yeats, founder of the *Irish National Theater*, an influence that led to a close association with Celtic culture and legend for the rest of his life. He wrote poetry under the pseudonym Dermot O'Byrne, and assisted his brother, the playwright and critic Clifford Bax, in editing a magazine called *Orpheus*, dedicated to the mystical arts.

His first mature work, *In the Fairy Hills*, is typical of the fantastic and exotic nature of his orchestral writing, chromatic and opulent, with a broad melodic sweep and luminous harmonies. *The Garden of Fand* (1916), an imaginative evocation of an ancient legend of sea gods and goddesses, is similarly impressionistic, though less naturalistic, than Debussy's *La Mer*. *Tintagel*, a tone poem inspired by traditional English stories of King Arthur and his Knights of the Round Table was composed in 1919 after a holiday in Cornwall and quickly became Bax's most frequently performed work.

Living in the shadow of composers of the stature of Elgar and Vaughan Williams, Bax received little public recognition until late in life. Up to the late 1930s, his songs, choral works, and chamber music were rarely heard, and, had it not been for a broadening of his style and the championship of Sir Adrian Boult, conductor of the BBC Symphony Orchestra, Bax would probably be remembered, if at all, for his comparatively youthful works. Even in the 1960s the English music critic Burnett James was moved to call this neglect "myopic and moronic."

On a visit to Scandinavia in 1932, Bax met Sibelius and the two composers became friends; while Sibelius' influence is not obvious in Bax's symphonic style, he is clearly indebted to the Finnish master in *Winter Legends* and *The tale the pine trees knew*.

The symphony, a form to which he turned again and again between 1922 and 1939, provided an outlet for a more taut, structured and contrapuntal approach that nevertheless retains elements of fantasy and mysticism. *Symphony No. 1*, the only one recorded in his lifetime, was first performed in 1922, and followed by six more. The fifth is dedicated to Sibelius and the sixth contains a theme from Sibelius' tone poem *Tapiola*.

Bax did not take well to approaching old age. He became withdrawn and dependent on alcohol. In 1943, he wrote a bitterly nostalgic memoir of his earlier years called *Farewell to my youth* (edited by Lewis Foreman; Scolar [sic] Press (Now Ashgate); 1992). In 1942, he was appointed Master of the Kings' Music and received a knighthood. His last work, written to celebrate Queen Elizabeth II's coronation in 1953, is a set of madrigals called *What is it like to be young and fair*. He died while on holiday in Cork, Ireland. —*Roy Brewer*

ORCHESTRAL

Tintagel, tone poem (1917–1919)

Tintagel is an ancient ruined castle on the North Cornish coast, the sort of wild meeting place between the land and the Atlantic that often inspired Bax. He wrote the work in piano score in October of 1917, ostensibly creating pictorial music about the castle and its historical, artistic, and musical associations. He wrote that "[I]t is intended to evoke... the castle-crowned cliff of Tintagel, and more particularly the wide distances of the Atlantic as seen from the cliffs of Cornwall on a sunny but not windless summer day." Among the castle's historical distinctions is its legendary connection with King Arthur and with the cast of one of the greatest of medieval love legends, that of King Mark and Tristam and Iseult. Hence, Bax makes effective use of an important motive from Wagner's opera on the latter subject. This tale of a pair made helpless by love to resist infidelity and betrayal points to the underlying emotion of the piece: in 1912 Bax had met pianist Harriet Cohen and over the next five years was inexorably drawn to her. While wrestling with the decision whether to leave his wife and children to live with her, he vacationed with her at Tintagel for six weeks in August and September of 1917. (He did leave his family the following March.) The music is marked by this agony and passion. When he finally orchestrated the work in 1919, he dedicated it to Harriet under her nickname, Tania. It is exceptional music, requiring a conductor capable of great subtlety in orchestral balances. *—Joseph Stevenson*

Recommended:

○ **Vaughan Williams: Symphony 5; Bax: Tintagel** / Barbirolli (cond.), London SO / 1994 / EMI 65110

○ **Bould Conducts Bax** / Boult (cond.), London PO / 1992 / Lyrita 231

CHAMBER MUSIC

Elegiac Trio, for flute, viola & harp (1916)

In 1916, one of the most prototypically English of twentieth century composers, Arnold Bax, horrified by the two-edged sword slicing through the British Empire—there was the continental war, later dubbed World War I, and there was the escalating tension between Britain and Ireland, which erupted in the Easter Rising in spring of 1916—began a series of gripping, emotionally intense concert pieces that many feel represent him at his best as a musician. Among these important compositions is the aptly named *Elegiac Trio* (1916) for flute, viola, and harp.

It may or may not be coincidence that the Bax *Elegiac Trio* was written in such close proximity to Debussy's more famous *Trio* for the same instrumental combination (Debussy finished his *Trio for flute, viola, and harp* in late 1915, Bax wrote his *Trio* in April and May of the following year); there simply is no evidence that Bax did or did not know of Debussy's recent work when he began his. On the one hand, the two pieces are very similar in nature—any two works for so texturally striking an instrumental group must necessarily share many traits—but on the other hand, the Bax *Elegiac Trio* is, for all the silken texture of the flute and the sonorous wash of the harp, a much "edgier" piece than Debussy's. Its deeply lyric manner seems to bear the scars of some just-healed wound; each glowing moment is more like a wish than a reality.

The *Elegiac Trio* is in one continuous movement, marked Moderate Tempo and given the character indication "Smooth and flowing." It begins with wavelike rushes from the harp, which seem to invoke G minor and D minor at the same time (the key signature has just one flat, but, as happens in so much J.S. Bach music, it is G rather than D that is the fundamental tone—a throwback to the days of modal music). Inspired, the violist sings a melody that is equal parts sustain and quick ornamentation; soon the flute takes over, and then wind- and string-player join in counterpoint. A sweet tune in chromatically modified E major serves as a second theme. As if to dispel any remaining uncertainty of key-frame, the piece finishes in shiny G major.

The *Trio*, which runs about nine and a half minutes in performance, was first played on March 26, 1917, at a concert organized by the Oriana Madrigal Society, and it was published in 1920 by Chester. *—Blair Johnston*

Recommended:

○ **Meditations** / Järvi, Cortese, Langlamet / 1995 / Chandos 9395

Fantasy Sonata, for viola & harp (1927)

In 1926 Bax made the acquaintance of the Russian Countess and Count Benckendorff, who had settled in Ipswich. The Countess was the virtuoso harpist Maria Korchinska and her husband was a fine flautist. Bax drew inspiration from Korchinska's excellent technique. It was for her that he composed the *Fantasy Sonata for viola and harp* in April 1927. Korchinska's ability is clear in her two recordings of the piece. Korchinska, with Raymond Jerry, gave the first performance of the *Fantasy Sonata* in London's Wigmore Hall in October 30, 1927. In general, response to the first performance was positive, but, like all of Bax's chamber works, it has failed to find a place in the repertoire.

The egalitarian nature of the work is evident in Bax's switching between describing the work as "for viola and harp" and "for harp and viola." The harp does participate as an equal partner and exposes and develops much of the material. The first three movements proceed without pause in this relaxed work. Although there are no actual Irish folk song melodies in the piece, Bax's frequent use of modal melodies and dance rhythms gives it an Irish character.

Opening with a theme in the viola, the first movement, Allegro molto—Andante, is a sonata-form structure. The viola's melody, in the Dorian mode, provides the fundamental material from which other themes are drawn, and it reappears as a transitional passage between movements and one last time at the end of the last movement. Thus, the viola theme is the driving force behind the entire piece. The second movement, Allegro moderato, continues the level of energy of the first but presents new themes, both derived from the first-movement viola melody. A hearty, waltz-like melody gives the movement the feeling of a scherzo.

The transparent Lento espressivo provides welcome contrast in tempo and atmosphere, as does the full stop before the finale. Chords reminiscent of Debussy support a modal theme, played on the harp, that sounds almost improvised because of its loose construction. The secondary theme, however, is a soaring melody on the viola above harp arpeggios. Bax distributes the return of the first theme elegantly between viola and harp, emphasizing the equality of the two instruments.

Marked Allegro moderato, the last movement renews the energy of the first and is filled with dance rhythms and melodic turns that evoke Irish folk music. Some have found in the scheme of the *Fantasy Sonata* a narrative in which a character—the opening melody for the viola—introduces more characters, the separate movements in between appearances of the theme. *—John Palmer*

Recommended:

○ **Bax: Quintet for harp & strings; Elegiac Trio** / Mobius / 2000 / Naxos 554507

Harp Quintet (1919)

Bax completed the *Quintet for Harp and Strings* in 1919, but its first performance did not occur until February 1921. Written about a year after the *First Quartet*, the score is dedicated to Raymond Jerry, violist for the Philharmonic Quartet, the ensemble that gave the premieres of both the *First Quartet and the Harp Quintet*, the latter with harpist Gwendolen Mason.

Bax once described himself as "a brazen Romantic—by that I mean [he added] that my music is the expression of emotional states. I have no interest whatever in sound for its own sake or in any modernist 'isms' or factions." In the *Quintet for Harp and Strings*, Bax's musical stance is clear in both the music and the expressive markings such as "veiled and mysterious." The harp was one of Bax's favorite instruments to use in chamber works, and his writing for it is usually demanding. As in other Bax works for harp, the quality of sound is the most striking feature.

In a single, compact movement that requires about 12 minutes to perform, the *Quintet for Harp and Strings* has the formal sections of sonata form. Its straightforward structure, however, disguises complexities of texture and harmony. Bax's harmonic idiom is diatonic, with chromaticism acting chiefly as a decorative element and providing the "Romantic" edge we hear in most of his music. Harmonic variation is the driving force in the work, especially in the development section, although melodic figurations evolve constantly. The themes are broad, singing, and expansive, while harmonies are used as much for their individual sonorities as for structural direction.

Compositional economy and thematic transformation mark the *Quintet*. The first four notes of the first theme are incorporated into the second and act as a recurring motive. The exposition takes up the greater portion of the piece and contains the dramatic climax of the work, marked Molto vivace, when the harp steps into the foreground as the strings play tremolando, creating an effect of symphonic grandeur. Quite a different effect results during the passage marked "veiled and mysterious," which ushers in the recapitulation with muted strings supporting the harp, which occasionally has harmonics. *—John Palmer*

Recommended:

○ **Bax: Nonet; Oboe Quintet; Elegiac Trio** / Nash Ensemble / 1996 / Hyperion 66807

Clarinet Sonata in D major (1934)

The Arnold Bax *Sonata for clarinet and piano* (composed June 1934) is one of those odd musical items that comes along once or twice a century that, being accidentally misnamed in a major reference, somehow never manages to shake off the shackles of its happenstance misnomer. You see, despite being called "Sonata in B flat major" in catalogs and lists and databases around the world, it is in fact a work in D major. (The mistake is easy enough to trace: the work is a sonata for B flat clarinet and piano, and the "B flat"—which of course describes the transposition of the clarinet part, not the key of the piece—simply got moved over a few syllables.) Beyond this musicological speed bump, the sonata has had an ordinary life; it is neither very famous nor hopelessly obscure. The occasion of its first performance on June 17, 1935, at a London Contemporary Music Centre concert was, however, one that at least two people remembered very well for the rest of their lives: first, Bax, because the sonata was played twice, and second, composer Lennox Berkeley, whose own piece was supposed to get played in the concert but, having been lost in the mail, was replaced by a second go at the Bax sonata.

The *Clarinet Sonata* is in two movements, which together last something under 15 minutes; it is clearly the work of a middle-aged composer who, perhaps having lost some of the edge that drove his music to fame early on in his career, can boast of having replaced that edge with a sure, solid, beautifully balanced lyric technique.

The first movement is Molto moderato. Clarinet and piano begin together—fitting, as their activities are very equal in importance throughout the sonata. In fact, considering that the clarinet is a woodwind and its player needs air to survive, there are relatively few spots at which the piano is heard alone—a measure here, a measure there. The movement is in the usual two-theme sonata shape; both tunes are smooth and supple, a far cry indeed from the days of old when major contrast between first and second themes was a must.

Perhaps because of that very smoothness, the fact that the first movement is really quite tricky to perform may well go unnoticed by most listeners; not so of the difficulties of the second movement, Vivace. Sixteenth notes are flung around from clarinet to piano in vintage moto perpetuo style, foiled only by a sharp-pointed repeated dotted figure. But, quite contrary to expectation, Bax does not throw in an explosive virtuosic close; instead, he lets things slow down and provides a brief, dolcissimo reprise of the first movement's downward-floating main theme at the very end. *—Blair Johnston*

Recommended:

○ **Bax: Nonet; Oboe Quintet; Elegiac Trio** / M. Collins, I. Brown / 1996 / Hyperion 66807

SYMPHONIC

Symphonies (1922–1939)

Sir Arnold Bax's symphonic music, while never really imitative or lacking in innovation, divulges a kinship with the styles of Vaughan Williams, Rachmaninov, and Korngold. But it is tarter, not as sweet as many of the orchestral works of these last two composers. One unusual aspect about Bax's symphonies is that all are in three movements and all but one (*Symphony No. 2*) have Lento markings for the middle panel. His first movements tend to have a mixture of slow and fast music, usually opening with a slow, mysterious introduction, then moving onto intense conflicts later to be resolved. Except for the half-hour-plus *First*, all last around 40 to 43 minutes. *Symphony No. 1* (1921) is remarkably mature in its assured orchestration and sense of development. The work is dominated by a militaristic five-note motif, which transforms throughout, bringing conflict and sadness and finally grand triumph. The dark second movement (Lento solenne) is perhaps the best of the three. The gritty *Symphony No. 2* (1925) is one of Bax's more complex creations, featuring deft motivic ties between the outer movements and a lyrical second movement whose opening also recalls a motif from the first movement. This is a strong work, perhaps among his greatest symphonic efforts, but far less popular than the *Symphony No. 3* (1928–29), probably Bax's most often-performed of the seven. It is an exotic symphony (are there echoes of Rimsky-Korsakov and early Stravinsky here?). In any event, it is a colorful, thoroughly well-crafted composition that features a lovely, pastoral second movement and a lovely, serene ending to the colorful finale. The *Symphony No. 4* (1930) has been assessed with contradictory opinions. Called episodic and structurally loose, its music is powerful and very communicative, with a lovely second movement Lento—which some consider among his finest symphonic creations—and a vigorous, attractive finale. If the *Third* can be called Bax's Russian symphony, then the *Fifth* (1931) is his northern symphony. The composer himself referred to its craggy northern character, which one hears mostly in the colorful first movement, particularly in the Poco lento introduction and in the vague echoes of Sibelius in the finale, a movement that opens with an attractive string theme of liturgical aspect. *Symphony No. 6* (1934), considered by some to be the composer's finest orchestral work, features two vehement outer movements and a haunting central panel of Delian mystery and darkness. If this can be called Bax's most ferocious and dynamic symphony, then one might observe that the 1939 *Seventh* is his most dignified, especially in the theme and variations finale. Again, the central Lento is quite touching and the first movement brilliant and colorful. *—Robert Cummings*

Recommended:

○ **Bax: The Symphonies** / Handley (cond.), BBC PO / 2003 / Chandos 10122

BBC Philharmonic Orchestra

f. 1922, Manchester, England

Ensemble

The BBC Philharmonic, based in Manchester, is one of the most important orchestras in the United Kingdom, distinguishing itself through sheer visibility and through a solid commitment to contemporary British music that has included the establishment of a composer/conductor position.

The orchestra's history is rather checkered, for it has had to endure numerous crises. In 1922, prior to the official establishment of the British Broadcasting Corporation, Manchester had a radio station known as 2YZ, housed on the premises of the Metropolitan Vickers Electrical Company. Early on, a small orchestra was established for broadcasts, concentrating mainly on light music, but expanding on occasion for performances of symphonic repertoire and opera. The station gained a reputation for broadcasting British music, including first radio performances of music by Edward Elgar, Gustav Holst, and William Walton. When the BBC was established, in 1927, the 2YZ orchestra was renamed the Northern Wireless Orchestra; later it became the BBC Northern Orchestra. Its existence was always precarious, but the group's size and repertoire increased. During World War II, the orchestra gave concerts in various communities around the region, bringing it a wider public. The Northern Orchestra continued to gain a strong reputation for performing and broadcasting British music, particularly works by living composers who were often invited to conduct the orchestra themselves.

In 1961, the BBC Northern Orchestra made its first appearance at the Henry Wood Promenade Concerts under the direction of George Hurst. The regional identity of the ensemble began from that point to evolve into a national and international one. After a difficult strike in 1980, the BBC made the commitment to support a full orchestra in Manchester, and, in 1982, the ensemble was given its current name. Its principal conductor at that time was Sir Edward Downs, who was succeeded in 1991 by Yan Pascal Tortelier. In 2002 Gianandrea Noseda was named principal conductor.

The ensemble's reputation for adventurous programming has expanded to international scope as well, as composers from various countries have come to Manchester to conduct the orchestra. In 1991, the post of composer/conductor was created, with Sir Peter Maxwell Davies being the first appointment. Davies composed a number of works for the orchestra, including several symphonies culminating with *Symphony No. 7*, premiered in 2000. Along the way, he has also recorded a number of his orchestral works for CD release. Scottish composer James MacMillan was named his successor in 2001.

The people of Manchester and the north of England are rightly proud of their radio orchestra. With so much British culture and finance administered in London, there is an independent spirit driving the culture of the north. The BBC Philharmonic has not only survived, but has thrived. It has developed a character distinct from that of the larger BBC Symphony Orchestra, based in London, more populist, perhaps, but also more adventurous and, with the orchestra's large recording catalogue, generous outreach programs, and international tours, more entrepreneurial. *—Jim Harley*

Recommended:

○ **Britten** / Hickox (cond.), Wright, Hill, Varcoe, Stephen, BBCPO / 1996 / Chandos 9487

○ **Music of Yoshimatsu** / Fujioka (cond.), BBCPO / 2003 / Chandos 10070

○ **Bax: The Symphonies** / Handley (cond.), BBCPO / 2003 / Chandos 10122

○ **Gliere: Symphony No. 3** / Downes (cond.), BBCPO / 1991 / MHS 514454

BBC Singers

f. 1930, London, England

Ensemble

Although Britain is a land with a rich choral tradition, the BBC Singers bill themselves as Britain's only full-time, fully professional choir. It was founded at the same time the British Broadcasting Corporation founded its Symphony Orchestra, and for the same purpose: to be available for broadcast work of a wide range of musical repertory.

Over their history, the BBC Singers have been particularly noted for their revivals of great British music from the Renaissance through the age of Purcell, and for its commitment to newer music, particularly by British composers. It has sung world premieres of such notable works as Britten's *A Boy was Born* and *Hymn to St Cecilia*, Poulenc's *Figure Humaine*, Henze's *Orpheus Behind the Wire* and numerous other works.

Under its conductor, Stephen Cleobury and his predecessors, it has made numerous recordings, including choral works of Charles Ives and Richard Strauss, and became the first choir to sing an a cappella selection as a part of one of the traditional *Proms Concerts*.*—Joseph Stevenson*

Recommended:

○ **Stainer: The Crucifixion** / Kay (cond.), BBC Singers, George, Hill, Phillips, Leith Hill Festival Singers / 1997 / Chandos 9551

○ **Ikons: Choral Music of John Tavener** / Joly (cond.), BBC Singers / 1994 / United 88023

○ **Poulenc: Gloria; Stabat Mater** / Tortelier (cond.), Watson, BBC Singers, BBCPO / 1995 / Chandos 9341

BBC Symphony Orchestra

f. 1930, London, England

Ensemble

Funded and administered by the British Broadcasting Company, the BBC Symphony Orchestra has, since its establishment in 1930, enjoyed freedom from the financial concerns that often plague independent orchestras. Because of this, it has been able to engage in more adventurous programming than many other major orchestras, focusing on new or lesser-known compositions. In addition to its full schedule of broadcast performances for BBC Radio 3, the BBCSO performs more than 70 public concerts a year. With its affinity for contemporary compositions, this ensemble of approximately 100 musicians has earned its reputation as one of the foremost broadcasting orchestras in Europe.

Although not officially established until 1930, plans for a BBC Orchestra were hatched in 1927. Negotiations delayed the fruition of these plans until Adrian Boult was appointed director of music in January 1930. The orchestra offered its first performance in October 1930 at Queen's Hall playing Wagner, Brahms, and Ravel to enthusiastic reviews. During its early years, the orchestra established its commitment to new and unusual repertoire by programming works by such contemporary composers as Schoenberg, Bartók, and Alban Berg; many of which were conducted by the composers themselves. Boult insisted that music by British composers be prominently represented in the orchestra's repertoire; to that end, the BBCSO presented broadcasts of works by Constant Lambert, Edward Elgar and Ralph Vaughan Williams.

In 1935 administrators began to express concern over the organization's programming policies; the ensuing tensions between the BBC and the artistic directors of the orchestra boiled over in 1936, and Edward Clark, who was a primary figure in forming the BBC's musical policy, angrily resigned. For the next 25 years, the orchestra's repertoire became considerably more focused on the works of Romantic and post-Romantic composers, temporarily leaving behind the ensemble's penchant for more contemporary music.

After Boult's retirement in 1950, Sir Malcolm Sargent was appointed chief conductor. His otherwise unremarkable tenure included the establishment of the *Henry Wood Promenade Concerts* at Queen's Hall (and later at the Royal Albert Hall), and the opening of the *Royal Festival Hall* which was to become one of the orchestra's permanent concert venues. Sargent was succeeded in 1957 by Rudolf Schwarz who began once again to broaden the orchestra's repertoire. The BBC commissioned and premiered several pieces by composers such as Roberto Gerhard during the 1960s in an effort to elevate the international status of the orchestra. Unfortunately, financial constraints did not allow the BBC Symphony to blossom as was hoped, but the changes made by Schwarz helped the orchestra recover some of its former glory. Antál Doráti replaced Schwarz as chief conductor of the orchestra in 1963 and organized the ensemble's first American tour in 1965. Sharing the podium with Pierre Boulez, Doráti's adventurous choice of repertoire focused on works by distinguished contemporary composers, and this highly successful tour brought the orchestra its long-sought international recognition. Boulez's affiliation with the BBC Symphony was instrumental in bringing the orchestra's concert repertoire back to its original focus on new works.

Following Boulez were Rudolf Kempe, Gennady Rozhdestvensky, John Pritchard, Andrew Davis, and Leonard Slatkin, who was named chief conductor in 2000. While the principal orchestra is based in London, regional BBC orchestras are resident in Manchester (BBC Philharmonic), Glasgow (BBC Scottish Orchestra) and Cardiff (BBC National Orchestra of Wales).—*Corie Stanton Root*

Recommended:

- ○ **Lutosławski: Partita; Chain 2; Piano Concerto** / Lutosławski (cond.), Mutter, Zimerman, Moll, BBCSO / 2002 / DG 471588
- ○ **Delius: Orchestral Works** / Davis (cond.), BBCSO / 2001 / Teldec 89084
- ○ **Schoenberg: Gurre-Leider; 4 Songs Op22** / Boulez (cond.), BBC Singers, Minton, Nimsgern, Bowen, Thomas. BBCSO / 1993 / Sony 48459

Amy Marcy Cheney Beach

b. Sep. 5, 1867, Henniker, NH, **d.** Dec. 27, 1944, New York, NY

Composer: Chamber Music, Choral Music, Concerto, Symphonic

Composer Amy Beach began her musical training early, singing over 40 tunes accurately at the age of one, improvising harmonic lines before age two, and composing at four. A child prodigy on the piano, Amy began lessons at age six and gave her first public recitals at age seven, including works by Handel, Beethoven, and Chopin. Enrolled in a private school in Boston, Amy studied piano, theory, and composition, and taught herself orchestration and fugue. Her earlier development was admired by several, including Longfellow, Oliver Wendell Holmes, William Mason, and Henry Harris Aubrey Beach (her future husband).

Embarking on her professional performing career in 1883, Beach debuted in a concerto performance with an orchestra conducted by Adolf Neuendorff. She performed with the Boston Symphony Orchestra in March 1885 in the first of several performances. After marrying Dr. Beach, Amy lessened the number of public performances, out of respect for her husband's wishes, and turned her concentration to composition. Her first published work, *The Rainy Day* (1880), was a setting of a Longfellow poem. Beach's compositional style was that of the late Romantics, rich in lyricism, chromaticism, thick textures, and frequent modulation. She was disciplined in her composition, often producing massive amounts of music in a matter of days. The works written during the period of her marriage (1885–1910) include the *Mass in E flat*, Op. 5, *Eilende Wolken*, Op. 18, the *Symphony*, Op. 32, and the *Piano Concerto*, Op. 45, all of which were premiered by the important performing groups of Boston. The significance of this honor lies in the fact that seldom did orchestras perform works of "local" composers, and even less often did they perform works composed by a woman.

Several of Beach's compositions were commissioned for significant events and organizations, including the dedication of the Women's Building of the World's Columbian Exposition in Chicago (*Festival Jubilate*, Op. 17, 1893), the Trans-Mississippi Exposition in Omaha (*Song of Welcome*, Op. 42, 1898), the International Exposition in San Francisco (*Panama Hymn*, Op. 74, 1915), and the San Francisco Chamber Music Society (*Theme and Variations for Flute and String Quartet*, Op. 80). The range of commissions indicates that interest in Beach's music was not limited to the Boston area. In fact, many consider her to be the most successful American woman composer.

After the death of her husband in 1910, Beach traveled to Europe to establish her performing career, to spread her recognition as a composer, and to promote the sale of her published works. She received favorable reviews of both her compositional and performance ability. Beach returned to the United States at the beginning of World War I to a busy touring schedule. She continued to perform and compose, working to promote young musicians, and serving as leader of several organizations. She served in the Music Teachers National Association and the Music Educators National Conference, and was president and cofounder of the Association of American Women Composers. Her recognition did not wane, and honors included two retrospective concerts in 1942, in honor of Beach's 75th birthday. She died in 1944 of heart disease. —*Kristen Grimshaw*

Overview of Works (1885–1944)

It is a curious irony that, had Amy Beach disregarded her husband's request that she curtail her performance career, the demanding schedule of a touring pianist may not have allowed her to produce the magnificent works for which she is now revered. Likewise, had she followed the advice of some and gone to Europe to study, rather than undertaking a self-guided study of the musical canon at home, she may not have acquired the careful combination of individuality and inherited wisdom that characterizes her oeuvre.

Though making up a relatively small portion of her output, Beach's orchestral works have proven to be among her most impressive and enduring. The *Piano Concerto* from 1899 reflects the keen idiomatic knowledge of a virtuoso performer, while the *Gaelic Symphony* (1896), her only offering in that genre, exhibits the composer's rare balance of lyricism and craftsmanship. Her chamber works are few but fine: the *Piano Quintet* (1907) exhibits a Brahmsian sensitivity, while the *String Quartet* (1929) subjects borrowed Inuit melodies to deeply chromatic, nearly atonal harmonies. As a pianist, Beach produced a wealth of keyboard works, many of them borrowing folk melodies and/or bearing evocative titles or programs; these include the *Variations on Balkan Themes* (1904), *Eskimos: Four Characteristic Pieces* (1907), *Hermit Thrush at Eve, Hermit Thrush at Morn* (1921), and *From Grandmother's Garden* (1922). While Beach often leans toward the picturesque, folksy, and even Arcadian in her narrative subject matter, her grasp of more tumultuous emotion is clearly evinced in her setting for orchestra and soprano of the Biblical tragedy *Jephthah's Daughter* (1903).

By far Beach was most prolific in the genre of the solo song. She composed some 65, a number of which attained considerable fame, including *Ecstasy*, on her own text (1893), and her setting of Robert Browning's *The Year's at the Spring* (1900). *Cabildo* (1932) remained her only operatic effort, but she composed extensively for vocal ensembles, in both sacred and secular veins. Her settings of Shakespeare (*Three Shakespeare Choruses*, 1897) and Tennyson (*The Sea Fairies*, 1904), stand out among her three dozen or so choral concert pieces. In addition to the *Mass in E flat*, a highly ambitious work for voices and orchestra that approaches 90 minutes in length, Beach wrote numerous other sacred choral works that reflected her own religious devotion, and which enjoyed continued church performances even while her instrumental works were still awaiting rediscovery in the late twentieth century. —*Jeremy Grimshaw*

Recommended:

- ○ **Amy Beach: Chanson d'amour** / Kirkby, Romantic Chamber Group of London / 2000 / Bis 1245
- ○ **Amy Beach: "Gaelic" Symphony; Piano Concerto** / Schermerhorn (cond.), Feinberg, Nashville SO / 2003 / Naxos 8559139
- ○ **Amy Beach: Music for Violin, Viola & Piano** / Klugherz-Timmons Duo / 1997 / Centaur 2312

CHAMBER MUSIC

Violin Sonata in A minor, Op. 34 (1896)

A very fine concert pianist, Amy Marcy Cheney Beach's (or Mrs. H.H.A. Beach as she was also known) compositions are well within the traditional European vein, despite the fact that she was one of the first Americans fully trained in the United States. Unlike some of her contemporaries (Arthur Foote) and the next generation of composers (Arthur Farwell and Charles Ives) who started to incorporate folksongs and elements of African-American and Native American music, Beach was not interested in creating a nationalistic American style. Her work is close to Johannes Brahms, Franz Liszt, Robert Schumann, and Fryderyk Chopin.

Along with her *Gaelic Symphony*, *Quintet*, and *Mass in E flat*, the *Sonata for Piano and Violin* is considered one of Beach's most important works. It was first performed in 1897 with the composer at the piano and violinist Franz Kniesel, concertmaster of the Boston Symphony. Comparisons with Brahms are inevitable: the music is autumnal, serious, and conceived within the "classical" four-movement sonata form with no descriptive titles or programmatic references (I. Allegro moderato, II. Scherzo: molto vivace, III. Largo con dolore, IV. Allegro con fuoco). This is pure music for music's sake. The two instruments are true partners, sharing the material in equal measure. Richly lyrical and emotional, Beach's sonata at times contains the same rhythmic ambiguity prevalent in Brahms.

The first movement starts with an ominous passage in octaves on the piano, setting a dark, somber tone. A second movement, light in mood, is a playful scherzo with a lovely contrasting middle section. An extended piano solo begins the highly emotional third movement. The final movement's momentum surges forward dramatically, with brief interludes of repose and one little "token" contrapuntal passage. This is music that impresses with its musicality and lyricism rather than with technical display. Anyone familiar with the violin sonatas of Brahms, Cesar Franck, and Schumann will find the neglect of this work inexplicable. *—Mona DeQuis*

Recommended:

- ○ **Amy Beach: Sonata Op34; Corigliano: Sonata** / Macomber, D. Walsh / 1995 / Koch 37223
- ○ **Arturo Delmoni: Sonatas Of Brahms & Beach** / Delmoni, Funahashi / 1996 / John Marks 02

Beaux Arts Trio

f. 1955, Lenox, MA

Ensemble

Long recognized as the leading piano trio in a competitive field, the Beaux Arts Trio is known for precise, straightforward performances and recordings of everything in the standard Central European trio literature. In concert, the group makes frequent forays into contemporary and non-mainstream music, but this is hardly evident in its conservative discography.

The trio made its debut July 13, 1955, having been assembled by French violinist Daniel Guilet; his inclination was to name the ensemble after himself, but he settled on a French name that would outlast the group's initial personnel. Guilet, born in France in 1899, had concertized as a soloist and chamber musician (notably with the Calvet Quartet) before moving to the U.S. in 1941. He joined the NBC Symphony in 1944 and became its concertmaster in 1951. Guilet had performed and recorded chamber music with cellist Bernard Greenhouse and pianist Menahem Pressler in studio recordings. The three first came together in a recording for MGM of *Carnival of the Animals*, were mutually impressed with the grouping, and soon formed the trio.

Greenhouse, born in New Jersey in 1916, was principal cellist in the CBS Symphony and a member of the Dorian Quartet. Pressler, born in 1923 in Magdeburg, Germany, had fled with his family to Palestine when Hitler came to power. He had been an international soloist from his early twenties. The group embarked on a 45-city American tour in late 1955, playing mostly low-profile community concerts. For the first several seasons, the middle of each concert would be a potpourri of well-known, flashy, or sentimental pieces for violin and piano or cello and piano.

The trio's interpretations were initially fairly free, but upon Guilet's retirement in 1969, new violinist Isidore Cohen urged the group to take musical markings more literally. Cohen, born in Brooklyn in 1922, had been a founding member of the Schneider String Quartet and had played second violin with the Juilliard Quartet. The Cohen-Greenhouse-Pressler combination became known for scrupulous performances that balanced expansiveness with zest.

The personnel began to change more frequently starting in 1987, when the retiring Greenhouse was replaced by cellist Peter Wiley. In 1992, Cohen left and was replaced by Ida Kavafian, an American born in Istanbul in 1952. Kavafian had helped form the hip chamber group Tashi in 1973. Like cellist Greenhouse, Kavafian was unafraid of contemporary music and the trio's performances of new works increased during her tenure, a period when the group took on a hard-driving elegance.

Pressler, reportedly a difficult personality, found himself with two new partners in 1998: violinist Young Uck Kim, born in South Korea in 1947, known principally as a soloist except for tours and recordings with pianist Emanuel Ax and cellist Yo-Yo Ma; and cellist Antonio Meneses, born in Brazil in 1957, a soloist who had won the 1982 Tchaikovsky International Competition. This incarnation of the trio was initially criticized for Pressler's uneven technique and the strings' occasional intonation trouble.

The Beaux Arts Trio enjoyed a long-term recording contract with Philips from the late 1950s. Its first project was a Beethoven cycle, and the ensemble went on to record all of the trios—and, with guest artists, piano quartets, and quintets—of the major Classical and Romantic composers. The group's most remarkable project was recording the complete trios of Haydn in the 1970s. The group began digitally re-recording much of its repertory in the 1980s, but new CDs dwindled in the 1990s and the post-Cohen era is poorly documented on disc.

British violinist Daniel Hope, a founding member of the London International Quintet, replaced Kim in early 2002. At 27, Hope was the youngest violinist to join the trio, and arrived as a champion of twentieth century and contemporary music. He vowed to persuade his new partners to "incorporate some element of contemporary music into every future program." *—James Reel*

Recommended:

- ○ **Beethoven: Trios** / Beaux Arts Trio / 2001 / Philips 464683
- ○ **Dvořák: Complete Piano Trios** / Beaux Arts Trio / 1996 / Philips 454259
- ○ **Philips Recordings, 1967–1974** / Beaux Arts Trio / 2003 / Philips 000150602

Sir Thomas Beecham

b. Apr. 29, 1879, St. Helens (near Liverpool), England, **d.** Mar. 8, 1961, London, England

Conductor

Conductor Sir Thomas Beecham was born into wealth; his father, Sir Joseph Beecham, was the manufacturer of "Beecham's Pills," an all-purpose remedy very popular in Britain. More importantly, though, Sir Joseph was also a lover of music and exposed his son to it from an early age; happily, he raised no objection to Thomas' pursuit of a musical career.

After both formal and audidactic training, Beecham made his professional debut as a symphony conductor in 1905 with members of the Queen's Hall Orchestra. When he wanted an orchestra to conduct full time, he simply used the resources of the family fortune to start one, which he led for a number of years. In 1910 Beecham began producing operas as a private impresario; he brought to the stage the British premieres of Strauss' shocking *Salomé* and *Elektra* (under the composer's baton) and of operas by Delius. He founded the Beecham Opera Company, comprised mainly of British singers, in 1915.

However, even a fortune the size of his could not keep pace with the expenses of such activities. He was declared bankrupt in 1919 and withdrew from music to put his financial affairs into order. Having recovered by 1923, he returned to the podium, and his conducting career soon flourished. In 1928 he made his American debut with the New York Philharmonic; characteristic of his championing of Delius, he founded a festival dedicated to the music of that composer in 1929.

In 1932 Beecham, dissatisfied with the standards of the orchestral scene, founded the London Philharmonic Orchestra, staffing it with the finest players. It quickly became a top-rank ensemble and successfully toured the Continent. He became artistic director at Covent Garden in 1932, and ruled there in his customary autocratic manner. When the war began, Beecham toured the United States and Australia. He was appointed music director and conductor of the Seattle Symphony Orchestra (1941–43) and was a frequent guest conductor at the Metropolitan Opera Company until he returned to England in 1944.

Upon his arrival in England, Beecham discovered that the orchestras there weren't overly enthusiastic at the prospect of working permanently in proximity to his withering tongue and dictatorial manner. Even the London Philharmonic Orchestra, with a new charter that permitted it to make some of its own decisions, showed little interest in having him at the helm full-time. So, typically, Beecham founded a new orchestra in 1946—the Royal Philharmonic Orchestra—and maintained his relationship with this group for the remainder of his career.

Beecham had already made a notable number of recordings before World War II. With the coming of the LP record after the war, and into the beginning of the stereo era, he recorded frequently. His recordings of Mozart, Haydn, Handel (he did not like Bach), Delius, Mendelssohn, Berlioz, and Sibelius are particularly esteemed; his recordings of *Carmen* and *Madama Butterfly* remain classics. *—Joseph Stevenson*

Recommended:

- ○ **Delius: Orchestral Works** / Beecham (cond.), Royal PO / 2001 / EMI 67553
- ○ **Haydn: Symphonies 99–104** / Beecham (cond.), Royal PO / 2003 / EMI 85513
- ○ **Delius: Orchestra Works Vol. 1** / Beecham (cond.), Royal PO, London PO / 2000 / Naxos 110904
- ○ **Sir Thomas Beecham: Rossini; Dvořák; Wagner** / Beecham (cond.), Widdop, Patriss, Garside, Herrmann, London PO, Royal PO / EMI 75938
- ○ **Beecham: Maestro Tempestoso** / Beecham (cond.), Szigeti, Laskine, Roy, London PO, Royal PO / 2000 / History 205224

Ludwig van Beethoven

b. Dec. 16, 1770, Bonn, Germany, **d.** Mar. 26, 1827, Vienna, Austria

Composer: Symphonic, Keyboard, Chamber Music, Concerto, Orchestral, Choral, Opera, Vocal, Ballet

The events of Beethoven's life are the stuff of Romantic legend, evoking images of the solitary creator shaking his fist at Fate and finally overcoming it through a supreme effort of creative will. Born in the small German city of Bonn on or around December 16, 1770, he received his early training from his father and other local musicians. As a teenager, he earned some money as an assistant to his teacher, Christian Gottlob Neefe, then was granted half of his father's salary as court musician from the Electorate of Cologne in order to care for his two younger brothers as his father gave in to alcoholism. Beethoven played viola in various orchestras, becoming friends with other players such as Antoine Reicha, Nikolaus Simrock, and Franz Ries, and began taking on composition commissions. As a member of the court chapel orchestra, he was able to travel some and meet members of the nobility, one of whom, Count Ferdinand Waldstein, would become a great friend and patron to him. Beethoven moved to Vienna in 1792 to study with Haydn; despite the prickliness of their relationship, Haydn's concise humor helped form Beethoven's style. His subsequent teachers in composition were Johann Georg

Albrechtsberger and Antonio Salieri. In 1794, he began his career in earnest as a pianist and composer, taking advantage whenever he could of the patronage of others. Around 1800, Beethoven began to notice his gradually encroaching deafness. His growing despondency only intensified his antisocial tendencies. However, the *Symphony No. 3* ("Eroica") of 1803 began a sustained period of groundbreaking creative triumph. In later years, Beethoven was plagued by personal difficulties, including a series of failed romances and a nasty custody battle over a nephew, Karl. Yet after a long period of comparative compositional inactivity lasting from about 1811 to 1817, his creative imagination triumphed once again over his troubles. Beethoven's late works, especially the last five of his 16 string quartets and the last four of his 32 piano sonatas, have an ecstatic quality in which many have found a mystical significance. Beethoven died in Vienna on March 26, 1827.

Beethoven's epochal career is often divided into early, middle, and late periods, represented, respectively, by works based on Classic-period models, by revolutionary pieces that expanded the vocabulary of music, and by compositions written in a unique, highly personal musical language incorporating elements of contrapuntal and variation writing while approaching large-scale forms with complete freedom. Though certainly subject to debate, these divisions point to the immense depth and multifariousness of Beethoven's creative personality. Beethoven profoundly transformed every genre he touched, and the music of the nineteenth century seems to grow from his compositions as if from a chrysalis. A formidable pianist, he moved the piano sonata from the drawing room to the concert hall with such ambitious and virtuosic middle-period works as the *"Waldstein"* (No. 21) and *"Appassionata"* (No. 23) sonatas. His song cycle *An die ferne Geliebte* of 1816 set the pattern for similar cycles by all the Romantic song composers, from Schubert to Wolf. The Romantic tradition of descriptive or "program" music began with Beethoven's "Pastoral" *Symphony No. 6*. Even in the second half of the nineteenth century, Beethoven still directly inspired both conservatives (such as Brahms, who, like Beethoven, fundamentally stayed within the confines of Classical form) and radicals (such as Wagner, who viewed the *Ninth Symphony* as a harbinger of his own vision of a total art work, integrating vocal and instrumental music with the other arts). In many ways revolutionary, Beethoven's music remains universally appealing because of its characteristic humanism and dramatic power. *—AMG*

SYMPHONIC

Symphony No. 1 in C major, Op. 21 (1800)

The year 1800 marked a watershed in Beethoven's development. On April 2 in Vienna, he made his debut as a composer of symphonies during a concert he had arranged and financed himself. Beethoven began to work intensively on the symphony in 1799, completing the work the following year. The symphony, though enthusiastically received at its premiere, already carried portents of the composer's coming radicalism. At the time, some observers commented upon the work's prominent use of wind instruments, but few noted the first symphony's masterstroke; it opens with the "wrong" chord—a dominant seventh of the subdominant key of F major, and not the expected tonic chord of C major. The English musicologist Sir Donald Francis Tovey dubbed this work "a comedy of manners." It is, in some sense, a skit on the deeply engrained style and vocabulary of Classicism itself, though the humor is unquestionably Beethoven's own. The opening movement begins with the celebrated discord mentioned above, which ushers in the slow introduction, questioning and insistent. It leads to the start of the exposition, again interrogatory in character. Fanfares add a martial flavor to the music, which is offset by the more lyrically inclined second subject group. The exposition is repeated, according to Classical convention, and the development which follows is terse and far more acerbic in manner, and does not allow the same contrast between songful and martial elements. Already extremely mature and "studied," this austere development is relieved only when the recapitulation arrives, now with great forcefulness. The imitative dialogues between wind and strings are predictably Classical in style, as is the jubilant coda. The Andante seems more subdued and relaxed, but the manner in which it preserves the latent drama associated with symphonic form is particularly subtle and entertaining. It begins with a fugal motif, derived from the rising tonic triad heard at the start of the first movement's exposition, and used so emphatically in its coda. An ingenious piece of orchestration occurs at the close of the Andante's exposition. Triplet figures in the violins and flute and off-beat accompanying chords are supported by regular drum-taps, perhaps pointing forward to the start of the *Concerto for Violin and Orchestra*, Op. 61, and to the closing bars of the *Concerto for Piano and Orchestra, No. 5* ("Emperor"), Op. 73. The third movement's marking raises the question of whether Beethoven could have intended this to be a stately Haydn minuet before he increased the tempo indication. The incisive rhythmic energy suggests something wholly new, and the movement already has the manner of Beethoven's later scherzi—it is one in all but name. While a more static episode in D flat follows the main material, and the central trio section is more reserved, it is significant, surely, that several Beethoven manuscripts (including that of his "Eroica" *Symphony No. 3* in E flat) contain similar third-movement tempo markings. Tovey likened the explosive start of the finale to the release of "a cat from a bag." The whole orchestra plays a unison fortissimo chord of G, the dominant, an effect that recalls the slow introduction of the first movement. The main motif is derived from nothing more complex than a rising scale on the tonic, but throughout the movement, Beethoven's use of scalar figures becomes increasingly obsessive, as the theme is heard in a variety of keys, and is often heard in inversion when various instruments are in dialogue. The development features a daring harmonic treatment of the scale theme, and Beethoven employs much dense counterpoint before the work ends in a positive and triumphant reassertion of C major. *—Michael Jameson*

Recommended:

- ○ **Beethoven: Symphonies 1 & 3 "Eroica"** / Harnoncourt (cond.), CO of Europe / 1992 / Teldec 75708
- ○ **Beethoven: Symphonies 1 & 2** / B. Walter (cond.), Columbia SO / 2004 / Sony 93087
- ○ **Beethoven: Symphonies 1 & 3, Creatures of Prometheus** / Norrington (cond.), London Classical Players / 1997 / Virgin 61374
- ○ **Beethoven: The 9 Symphonies & Overtures (Box Set)** / Szell (cond.), Cleveland Orch. / 1992 / Sony 48396
- ○ **Beethoven: Symphonies 1 & 2** / Wand (cond.), NDR SO / 1993 / RCA Victor 68057
- ○ **Beethoven: 9 Symphonien** / Karajan (cond.), Berlin PO / DG 429036
- ○ **Beethoven: Symphonies 1 & 2** / C. Abbado (Cond.), Berlin PO / 2000 / DG 471487

Symphony No. 2 in D major, Op. 36 (1801–1802)

Measured against the hot-wired *First Symphony*, the heroic *Third*, and the heaven-storming *Fifth*—all of them written between 1799 and 1808—Beethoven's Second is a relaxed work in greater part, akin to the *Fourth* and *Sixth* symphonies. This has prompted music listeners ever since to wonder how he could have created a work as buoyant as *No. 2* at a time when his worsening deafness had been diagnosed as incurable and irreversible.

The work came to term in 1802 from sketches organized the previous year. Likelier than not, it reflects several happy months in the rural retreat of Heiligenstadt, on the recommendation of an otologist. From one window in his isolated cottage he could see eastward to the Danube, and beyond. Outside, he roamed the fields and surrounding woods freely, yet his mood was "morose" according to Ferdinand Ries, the devoted pupil who visited him there.

Beethoven introduced the new symphony at Vienna on April 5, 1803, at a mammoth Akademie in the Theater an der Wien, along with the *Third Piano Concerto* (completed in 1800), a new oratorio, *Christ on the Mount of Olives*, and a repeat performance of the *First Symphony* from 1800. In the third movement of No. 2, the word scherzo appeared symphonically for the first time, although it retained a song and trio form, and was built on the sudden juxtapositions of loud and soft, with changes in their patterns just when he'd seemed to settle on one. The scoring, however, continued to employ traditional pairs of winds and brass, timpani, and strings.

An Adagio molto introduction anticipates the soft-loud contrasts that explode like Chinese firecrackers two movements later, although the sound and shape of it recall Haydn. The exposition begins in measure 35, with a main subject of Mozartian levitation, but thereafter Beethoven asserts his own less courtly and more confrontational personality.

As in the *First Symphony*, he wrote the first, second, and fourth movements in sonata form. The longest of them is this A major Larghetto in triple meter, if all the repeats are observed. Finding an accommodating tempo can pose problems: largo, after all, means "broad," the slowest tempo in music. Larghetto is a diminutive form—i.e., not as slow—but how slow (or not slow) remains the conductor's call.

After Beethoven's surprises in (as well as of) the scherzo, he chortles throughout a finale marked Allegro molto, mostly at his own syncopated jokes. They begin in the first measure and don't let up till the double-bar. Many of his contemporaries were shocked, and several reviled him in print. One Viennese critic, after a repeat performance in 1804, called *Symphony No. 2* "a crass monster, a hideously writhing, wounded dragon that refuses to die and, though bleeding in the finale, furiously thrashes about with its stiffened tail." One should always keep posterity in mind whenever a spiky new piece tempts us to dismiss it without a trial (whereas easy-listening pieces tend to spoil as quickly as unrefrigerated seafood, and most should). *—Roger Dettmer*

Recommended:

- ○ **Beethoven: Symphonies 1 & 2** / C. Abbado (cond.), Berlin PO / 2000 / DG 471487
- ○ **Beethoven: Symphonies Nos. 1–9; Overtures** / C. von Dohnányi (cond.), Cleveland Orch. / 2001 / Telarc 61943
- ○ **Beethoven: Sinfonie Nr 2 D-dur op 36** / K. Sanderling (cond.), Leningrad PO / 2004 / DG 474983
- ○ **Beethoven: Symphonies 2 & 5** / Szell (cond.), Cleveland Orch. / 2002 / Sony 89844
- ○ **Beethoven: Symphonies 1 & 2** / Walter (cond.), Columbia SO / 2004 / Sony 93087

○ **Great Conductors of the 20th Century: Otto Klemperer** / Klemperer (cond.), Berlin RSO / EMI 75465

○ **Beethoven: 9 Symphonien** / Karajan (cond.), Berlin PO / DG 429036

Symphony No. 3 in E flat major ("Eroica"), Op. 55 (1803)

Beethoven completed this work in 1804; it was introduced privately in Vienna, chez Prince Lobkowitz, to whom it is dedicated. Beethoven also conducted the public premiere on April 7, 1805, in the Theater an der Wien. Despite everything written to the contrary, the *Sinfonia eroica* was never a "portrait" of Napoleon Bonaparte, although Beethoven did plan to dedicate it to the charismatic Corsican "First Consul of France." He went into a rage, however, when a pupil, Ferdinand Ries, brought news in May 1804 that Napoleon had crowned himself Emperor. According to Ries, Beethoven shouted that the General was only "an ordinary human being, [and] went to the table, took hold of the title page, tore it in two, and threw it on the floor."

A different story posits that Beethoven erased the Napoleonic dedication from a copy made in August 1804 and entitled *Sinfonia grande*. In fact, *Sinfonia eroica* did not appear as the work's title until publication in 1806.

What Beethoven never told Ries was that Prince Lobkowitz, before May 1804, had proffered a handsome fee in exchange for the dedication, which Napoleon's subsequent arrogance made possible. Or that Beethoven realized the advantage in bringing with him a *Sinfonia Bonaparte* when a Parisian trip was proposed later on (but never materialized). It was conductor Arturo Toscanini who put everything into perspective 50-odd years ago: "Some say Napoleon, some say Hitler, some say Mussolini; for me it is Allegro con brio."

The sheer length of the *Eroica*'s first movement was revolutionary—an opening movement of 691 measures, plus an exposition repeat of 151 measures. No less revolutionary was Beethoven's jarring C sharp at the end of a main theme in E flat major—indeed it is an E flat arpeggio. Not until the recapitulation does that C sharp become D flat enharmonically. It is in this movement that the long-range harmonic connections explored over the course of the Romantic era have their real start; the movement is heroic mainly in the vastness of its reach.

A "Funeral March" slow movement was hardly revolutionary, but the span of his C minor slow movement, in rondo form, was unprecedented, and so was its range of emotions from outright grief to C major solace. Although "hunt" music in the third-movement Trio may have startled the *Eroica*'s first audience after funerary tragedy on an unprecedented scale, hunting music in Beethoven's time was even more modish than funeral marches. However, he used it for more than mere surprise in the midst of an onrushing and sometimes raucous scherzo (thereby banishing minuets and Ländlers until the symphonies of Bruckner and Mahler). Psychologically he needed sunshine after so much weighty, solemn music.

He was also setting up a racy finale—a set of variations including a fugue that detractors ever since have called a falling-off of inspiration. This kind of argument ignores, however, not only what preceded the *Eroica* historically—Bach's *Goldberg Variations* for example—but also Beethoven's own ennoblement of the form. He had already used the legato second theme of his *Eroica* finale in *The Creatures of Prometheus* (ballet music of 1800), in an 1802 *Contredanse*, and as the subject of 15 keyboard variations that same year (Op. 35), subtitled *Eroica* once the symphony had been published. A never-ending wonder is the viability of this subject after so much use. Beethoven's range of invention in the symphonic finale of 1804—from hymnody to humor, from fugue to dance, culminating in a Presto coda—successfully freed the listener from the gripping, even shocking drama that has stalked his first and second movements. *—Roger Dettmer*

Recommended:

○ **Beethoven: Symphony 3; Overtures** / Muti (cond.), Philadelphia Orch. / 1999 / Seraphim 73424

○ **Beethoven: Symphony 3 "Eroica"; How a Great Symphony Came to Be Written** / L. Bernstein (cond.), New York PO / 1999 / Sony 60692

○ **Beethoven: Symphonies 1 & 3 "Eroica"** / Norrington (cond.), London Classical Players / Virgin 471488

○ **Beethoven: Symphonies 3, 5 & 7** / Solti (cond.), London Philharmonia Orch. / 2001 / Decca 467679

○ **Beethoven: Symphony 3 "Eroica"; Overtures "Leonore" 1 & 2** / Klemperer (cond.), Philharmonia Orch. / EMI 67741

○ **Beethoven: 9 Symphonien** / Karajan (cond.), Berlin PO / DG 429036

Symphony No. 4 in B flat major, Op. 60 (1807)

Robert Schumann described this symphony as "a slender Greek maiden between two Norse giants," and started the long-standing tradition which holds that somehow Beethoven's even-numbered symphonies are less profound than the odd-numbered ones. This may seem true at first glance, but there is much that Schumann's analysis leaves unsaid. While the lambent beauty of the Adagio might suggest the kind of Classicism that the Eroica transcended, one should remember that, in many senses, the Fourth, emerging from an intensely foreboding, and even tragic, introduction, is no less heroic than either the Eroica or the Fifth. Dark-hued and intensely chromatic strivings pull the music from B flat minor toward the unison F which heralds the beginning of the sunny Allegro vivace exposition. While Weber criticized the deliberately sparse-sounding introduction, Tovey sensed its immense stature, writing of the "sky-dome vastness" of its harmonic progression. The Adagio, a sonata structure minus development, begins with an insistent rhythm which recurs several times. At the start, the violins sing out the sublimely reflective principal motif, a tenderly lyrical utterance which stands in direct contrast to the opening figure. These two contrasting elements are always at the hub of the movement, the expressive violin theme later becoming the subject of variations. The reprise of the second group then leads to the highly atmospheric coda. What follows is the Scherzo; a bucolic main theme suggests the rustic folk-dance idioms that Beethoven knew well; nevertheless, the movement surpasses the Eroica's Scherzo in power and dynamism. It should be noted that this is the first of Beethoven's symphonic scherzos to feature a repeat of the trio section, which is significant, given the massive nature of the surrounding material. The scherzo is heard one last time, now abridged, before the shattering final coda with its three-bar horn solo. Expanded scherzos also figure in several of Beethoven's later symphonies (the exception is the Eighth), and sketches suggest the technique was originally envisaged for the Fifth. Opening with a series of mercurial sixteenth note fragments from which the first subject group is derived, the final movement is "perpetuum mobile." As the movement unfolds, the oboe's second theme provides contrast with the initial statement, the relentless development section posing serious technical challenges to the lower instruments: bassoon, cellos, and basses. In the coda, surely one of Beethoven's most humorous inventions, the theme is passed around at half speed after a "false" ending has been reached, and finally brushed aside dramatically as cellos and basses plummet down the scale before the striking final bars for full orchestra. *—Michael Jameson*

Recommended:

○ **Beethoven: Symphonies 1, 2, 4 & 5** / Böhm (cond.), Vienna PO / 1993 / DG 439681

○ **Beethoven: 9 Symphonien** / Karajan (cond.), Berlin PO / DG 429036

○ **Beethoven: Symphonies 3 "Eroica" & 4** / C. Abbado (cond.), Berlin PO / 2000 / DG 471488

○ **Beethoven: Symphonies 3 & 4** / Zinman (cond.), Tonhalle Orch. Zurich / 1998 / Arte Nova 59214

○ **Beethoven: Symphonies 4 & 7; King Stephen Overture** / Szell (cond.), Cleveland Orch. / 1992 / Sony 48396

○ **The Klemperer Legacy: Beethoven Symphonies 4 & 5** / Klemperer (cond.), Bavarian RSO / 1998 / EMI 66865

○ **Wilhelm Furtwängler: Recordings 1942–1944 Vol. 1** / Furtwängler (cond.), Berlin PO / 2001 / DG 471289

Symphony No. 5 in C minor ("Fate") Op. 67 (1808)

Beethoven worked on the *Fifth Symphony* for more than four years, completing it in 1808, and introducing it on December 22 of that year at what must have been one of the most extraordinary concerts in history. The marathon program included the *Fifth* and *Sixth Symphonies;* the *Choral Fantasy*, Op. 80; the *Fourth Piano Concerto;* and parts of the *Mass in C*. Vienna was in the grip of exceptionally cold weather, the hall was unheated, and the musicians woefully under-prepared. As Schindler noted, "the reception accorded to these works was not as desired, and probably no better than the author himself had expected. The public was not endowed with the necessary degree of comprehension for such extraordinary music, and the performance left a great deal to be desired."

Following early indifference, the public only gradually began to come to terms with the *Fifth*. One of its earliest proponents, the poet and composer E.T.A. Hoffmann wrote, "How this magnificent composition carries the listener on and on in a continually ascending climax into the ghostly world of infinity!... the human breast, squeezed by monstrous presentiments and destructive powers, seems to gasp for breath; soon a kindly figure approaches full of radiance, and illuminates the depths of terrifying night." In his *Howard's End*, E.M. Forster writes of the work, suggesting that it satisfies "all sort and conditions." The characters of Helen and Tibby know the work well, the latter even describing "the transitional passage on the drum" before the finale. That Forster dwelt at such length on the work shows the extent to which it had become absorbed into the Romantic consciousness.

Hermann Kretzschmar wrote of the "stirring dogged and desperate struggle" of the first movement, one of the most concentrated of all Beethoven's symphonic sonata movements. It is derived almost exclusively from the rhythmic cell of the opening, which is even felt in the accompaniment of the second subject group. There follows a variation movement in which cellos introduce the theme, increasingly elaborated and with shorter note values at every reappearance. A second, hymn-like motif is heard as its counterfoil.

The tripartite scherzo follows; the main idea is based on an ominous arpeggio figure, but we hear also the omnipresent "Fate" rhythm, exactly as it is experienced in the first movement. The central section, which replaces the customary trio, is a pounding fugato beginning in the cellos and basses, and then running through the rest of the orchestra. Of particular structural interest is the inter-linking bridge passage which connects the last two movements. Over the drum-beat referred to by

Forster's Tibby, the music climbs inexorably toward the tremendous assertion of C major triumph at the start of the finale. The epic grandeur of the music, now with martial trombones and piccolo added (the *Fifth* also calls for contrabassoon), has irresistible drive and sweep, though that eventual victory is still some way off is suggested by the return of the ominous scherzo figure during the extended development. *—Michael Jameson*

Recommended:

- ○ **Beethoven: Symphonien 5 & 7** / C. Kleiber (cond.), Vienna PO / 1995 / DG 447400
- ○ **Beethoven: 9 Symphonien** / Karajan (cond.), Berlin PO / DG 429036
- ○ **Beethoven: Symphonies 2 & 5** / Szell (cond.), Cleveland Orch. / 1992 / Sony 48396
- ○ **Beethoven: Symphonies 5 & 7** / Klemperer (cond.), Philharmonia Orch. / 2002 / EMI 67852
- ○ **Wilhelm Furtwängler: Recordings 1942–1944 Vol. 1** / Furtwängler (cond.), Berlin PO / 2001 / DG 471289
- ○ **Beethoven: Symphony 5; Egmont** / Masur (cond.), New York PO / 2001 / Apex 89078
- ○ **Beethoven: Symphonies 5 & 6 "Pastorale"** / C. Abbado (cond.), Berlin PO / 2000 / DG 469000
- ○ **Guido Cantelli: The NBC Braodcast Concerts, 1950** / Cantelli, NBC SO / 2003 / Testament 1317

Symphony No. 6 in F major ("Pastoral") Op. 68 (1808)

For roughly 175 years, the music appreciation racket has told us that Beethoven composed symphonies in contrasting odd-even pairs after 1803, none more startling than the heaven-storming *Fifth* and bucolic *Sixth*. Originally, however, he assigned the designation of "No. 5" to the *Pastoral* for their shared debut on surely the most historic night in Western music, December 22, 1808. Beginning at 6:30 p.m. in the unheated Theater an der Wien, he premiered both symphonies, the *Fourth Piano Concerto, "Choral" Fantasy, "Ah! perfido!"* (a concert aria from 1796), and introduced a Viennese audience to excerpts from the *C major Mass*, an Esterházy commission of 1807 that Prince Nicolaus II disliked when he heard it.

Beethoven began making specific notes for a "Sinfonia pastorale" in 1806, but didn't complete the work until 1808, in the village of Heiligenstadt northwest of Vienna. If this had been an unlikely hatchery in 1807 for the fist-brandishing *Fifth Symphony*, it perfectly suited—as he noted in his sketchbook—"recollections of country life... more the expression of feeling than of painting" in his ensuing woodwind-drenched symphony (although violins get first crack at nine of its 12 significant themes).

"Cheerful impressions wakened by arrival in the country" (Allegro ma non troppo, in F major, 2/4) is the first movement. It is in sonata form, pretty much by the book, with violins introducing all themes. The second-movement "Scene by the brook" (Andante molto moto, in B flat major and 12/8 time) is a Sonata structure again, but more relaxed, with a limpid main theme for violins and a bassoon subtheme. In the coda, the flute impersonates a nightingale, the oboe a quail, and the clarinet a cuckoo. The third movement, "Merry gathering of country folk" (Allegro, 3/4 time, F major), is an expanded song-and-trio, with a 2/4 section in "tempo d'Allegro" that creates the effect of an ABCABCA structure, leading without pause to the fourth movement, "Thunderstorm; tempest" (Allegro; F minor, 4/4). From the first raindrop to last, this is purely depictive music. It is followed by a ten-bar chorale that segues the final "Shepherd's song; glad and grateful tidings after the storm" (Allegretto; F major, 6/8), a sonata-rondo, whose C-section some have called a development section. The fun includes a sly parody of amateur musicians before the long, progressively tranquil coda that ends with a pianistic gesture: two fortissimo chords. *—Roger Dettmer*

Recommended:

- ○ **Beethoven: Symphonies 5, 6, 7 & 8** / Ormandy (cond.), Philadelphia Orch. / Sony 63266
- ○ **Beethoven: Symphonies 4 & 6 "Pastorale"** / Walter (cond.), Columbia SO / 1995 / Sony 64462
- ○ **Beethoven: Symphonies 6 & 8** / Furtwängler (cond.), Vienna PO / 1989 / EMI 63034
- ○ **Beethoven: Symphonien 6 "Pastorale" & 8** / C. Abbado (cond.), Vienna PO / DG 445542
- ○ **Beethoven: Symphonies 3 & 6** / Scherchen (cond.), Vienna State Opera Orch. / 2001 / Westminister 471241
- ○ **Classic Performances: Bernstein in Vienna** / L. Bernstein (cond.), Vienna PO / 1999 / DG 463468

Symphony No. 7 in A major, Op. 92 (1812)

Ludwig van Beethoven completed this work in 1812, but withheld the first performance until December 8, 1813, in Vienna. It is scored for pairs of flutes, oboes, clarinets, bassoons, horns, and trumpets, plus timpani and string choir.

1812 was an eventful year for the very famous, seriously deafened Beethoven. July was especially noteworthy. At Teplitz he finally met Goethe (1749–1832), but was disappointed to find (he felt) an aging courtier who was no longer a firebrand or kindred democrat; worse yet, a musical dilettante. A week before that only meeting of German giants, Beethoven had written the letter to his mysterious "immortal beloved" that was discovered posthumously in a secret drawer. Then, toward the end of the year, he meddled unbidden in the affairs of his youngest brother, Johann, who was cohabiting contentedly with a housekeeper. Somehow, he found time to compose the last of his ten sonatas for violin and piano and to complete a new pair of symphonies—the *Seventh* and *Eighth*—both begun in 1809. He introduced the *Seventh* at a charity concert for wounded soldiers, and repeated it four nights later by popular demand.

Richard Wagner called *Symphony No. 7* "the apotheosis of the dance," meaning of course to praise its Dionysian spirit. But this oxymoron stuck like feathers to hot tar, encouraging irrelevant and awkward choreography (by Isadore Duncan and Léonide Massine among others) and licensing the music appreciation racket to misinterpret Beethoven's intent as well as his content. Wholly abstract and utterly symphonic, the *Seventh* was his definitive break with stylistic conventions practiced by Mozart, Haydn, and a legion of lesser mortals who copied them. He stretched harmonic rules, and gave breadth to symphonic forms that Haydn and Mozart anticipated. If, in his orchestral music, Beethoven was the last Austro-German Classicist, he did point those who followed him to the path of Romanticism.

While the poco sostenuto introduction begins by observing time-honored rules of harmony, within 62 measures it modulates from A major to the alien keys of C and F major, then back again! The transition from solemn 4/4 meter to 6/8 for the balance of an evergreen vivace movement (in sonata form) further exemplifies Beethoven's conceptual stretch.

Coming from the 20-minute funeral march of his earlier *Eroica Symphony*, Beethoven created an allegretto "slow" movement. He established a funerary mood (without its being specifically elegiac) through the repetition of a 2/4 rhythmic motif in A minor, the most somber key of the tempered scale. A minor serves more than an expressive function, moreover; it readies us for the reappearance of F major in a tumultuous five-part Scherzo marked Presto. Two trios go slower (assai meno presto), in D major—a long distance harmonically in 1812 from the work's A major tonic. The beginning of a third trio turns into a short coda capped by five fortissimo chords.

A major finally returns in the final movement. Here more than anywhere else in his orchestral music, Beethoven became a race-car driver. As in the "slow" movement, the rhythm is 2/4, but sonata-form replaces ABA. And there's a grand coda longer than the exposition, the development, or the reprise, which, furthermore, begins in B minor! But modulations bring it back to A major in time for a heart-pounding final lap with the accelerator pressed to the floor. *—Roger Dettmer*

Recommended:

- ○ **Beethoven: Symphonies 5 & 7** / C. Kleiber (cond.), Vienna PO / 1995 / DG 447400
- ○ **Beethoven: 9 Symphonien** / Karajan (cond.), Berlin PO / DG 429036
- ○ **Beethoven: Symphonies 5–8** / Toscanini (cond.), NBC SO / 1998 / RCA 55836
- ○ **Beethoven: Symphonies 5 & 7** / Thielemann (cond.), Philharmonia Orch. / DG 449981
- ○ **Beethoven: Symphony 7; Overtures** / Dorati (cond.), London SO / 1992 / Mercury 462958
- ○ **Beethoven: Symphonies 7 & 8** / Muti (cond.), Philadelphia Orch. / 1999 / Seraphim 73569
- ○ **Beethoven: Symphonies 5 & 7** / Vladimir Ashkenazy (cond.), Philharmonia Orch. / 1998 / Penguin Classics 460603

Symphony No. 8 in F major, Op. 93 (1812)

Beethoven completed this work in 1812, and conducted the first performance at Vienna on February 27, 1814. The year 1812 was both eventful and productive for the very deaf but very famous Beethoven. In July, at Teplitz spa, he finally met the great Goethe (1749–1832), but was disappointed to find (in his opinion) an aging courtier who was neither a firebrand nor a fellow democrat, and furthermore a musical dilettante. In turn, Beethoven's power both as a person and as an artist impressed Goethe, but the old poet-playwright was fatigued by his high-pitched intensity and offended by a lack of manners bordering on rudeness.

Withal, Beethoven somehow made time in 1812 to compose a final violin and piano sonata (Op. 96), and to complete a new pair of symphonies. *Nos. 7* and *8*, begun in 1809 (the year of the *Emperor Concerto*), were related in much the way his *Fifth* and *Sixth* symphonies had been. In 1813 he conducted the Dionysian Seventh to great acclaim, but saved the elfin *Eighth* for an 1814 concert where it was fatally sandwiched between the *Seventh Symphony* and *Wellington's Victory, or the Battle of Vittoria*. This last was adored by the audience in direct proportion to its awfulness, but they only sniffed at the *Eighth*.

Compared to the *Seventh, No. 8* is benign as well as brief. There are four movements, in all of which the old Classical forms are clearly delineated but somehow thrown out of balance by a constant barrage of curiously humorous distortions. Were the work not such an essentially lyrical joy, one might divine hints of the creative crisis to come for its maker. Its metronomic second movement (which is perhaps an actual tweaking of the recently invented metronome) has only 81 bars—the fewest in Beethoven's symphonic canon. The composer asked that the third movement be played Tempo di minuetto (in fact it is a Ländler), rather than at scherzo speed. The movement's heavy, graceless accents seem to poke fun at the courtly world only recently passed.The first and final movements are both written in sonata form, both marked Allegro vivace—con brio, too, in the first.

Beethoven reserved for the finale a leviathan-length coda, by then one of his musical signatures—236 bars, only 30 fewer than the combined exposition, development, and reprise! The movement wears its complexity so lightly that its true subtlety may all too easily pass unnoticed. Sudden loud interruptions in a very remote key herald still more radical explorations in the development. Here, the main rondo theme is debated in counterpoint, with cross rhythms and unexpected harmonic twists. But the giant coda is only the last joke in a work of cloudless skies and merriment. As John N. Burk summed the work up in his evergreen *Life and Works of Beethoven*: "[His] humor seems to consist of sudden turns in the course of an even and lyrical flow, breaking in upon formal, almost archaic periods. It is a sudden irregularity, showing its head where all [had been] regular—an altered rhythm, an explosion of fortissimo, a foreign note or an unrelated tonality... like divine play in that pure region of tonal thinking [where] melody and invention pour forth... and fancy is furiously alive." Beethoven himself thought it one of his best symphonies, while Robert Schumann praised its "profound humor" and wrote that the second movement particularly filled him with "tranquility and happiness." *—Roger Dettmer*

Recommended:

- ○ **Beethoven: Symphonies 6 "Pastoral" & 8** / Leibowitz (cond.), Royal PO / 1992 / Chesky 69
- ○ **Beethoven: Symphonien 6 "Pastorale" & 8** / C. Abbado (cond.), Vienna PO / DG 445542
- ○ **Beethoven: Symphonies 7 & 8** / Rattle (cond.), Vienna PO / 2003 / EMI 57570
- ○ **Beethoven: Symphonies 1–9; Grosse Fuge; Egmont Overtures (Box Set)** / Böhm (cond.), Vienna PO / 2004 / Universal Classics B000217402

Symphony No. 9 in D minor ("Choral") Op. 125 (1824)

On May 7, 1824, Ludwig van Beethoven experienced what must certainly have been the greatest public triumph of his career. The audience which gathered at the Hoftheater adjacent to the Vienna Kärtnertor heard not only the abridged local premiere of Beethoven's *Missa Solemnis* (the Kyrie, Credo, and Gloria were given) and Op.124 *Overture*, but also the first performance of the composer's 'Choral' Symphony. The event was a rousing success; indeed, one of the most moving accounts of Beethoven's final years describes how the profoundly deaf composer, unable to hear the colossal response of his admirers, had to be turned around by one of the soloists so that he could see the hundreds of clapping hands!

Beethoven's *Symphony No. 9* started life as two separate works—a symphony with a choral finale, and a purely instrumental work in D minor. He labored on these sporadically for almost ten years before finally deciding (in 1822) to combine the two ideas into one symphony, with Friedrich von Schiller's *Ode an die freude* (Ode to Joy)—a text he had contemplated setting for a number of years—as the finale.

The finished work is of visionary scope and proportions, and represents the apogee of technical difficulty in its day. There are passages, notably a horn solo in the slow movement, which would have been almost impossible to play on the transitional valveless brass instruments of Beethoven's time. As Dennis Matthews writes: "As with other late-period works, there are places where the medium quivers under the weight of thought and emotion, where the deaf composer seemed to fight against, or reach beyond, instrumental and vocal limitations."

The Ninth also personifies the musical duality that was to become the nineteenth century—the conflict between the Classic and Romantic, the old and new. The radically different styles of Brahms and Liszt, for instance, both had their precedents in this work. On one hand, there was the search for a broader vocabulary (especially in terms of harmony and rhythm) within the eighteenth century framework; on the other, true Romanticism, embracing the imperfect, the unattainable, the personal and the extreme—qualities that violate the very nature of Classicism. When viewed individually, the first three movements still have their roots distinctly in the eighteenth century, while the fourth—rhapsodic, and imbued with poetic meaning—seems to explode from that mold, drawing the entire work into the realm of program music, a defining concept of musical Romanticism.

Beethoven's Ninth represents a fitting culmination to the composer's symphonic ouvre—a body of work that is still unmatched in its scope and seminal ingenuity—and remains a pillar of the modern symphonic repertoire. *—AMG*

Recommended:

- ○ **Beethoven: Symphonie 9; Ouvertüre "Coriolan"** / Karajan (cond.), W. Berry, Janowitz, Kmentt, Rossl-Majdan, Berlin PO / DG 447401
- ○ **Beethoven: Symphonie Nr 9** / C. Abbado (cond.), Eaglen, W. Meier, Heppner, Terfel, Berlin PO / 2004 / Sony 93011
- ○ **Great Conductors of the 20th Century: Wilhelm Furtwängler** / Furtwängler (cond.), E. Berger, W. Ludwig, Pitzinger, Watzke, Berlin PO / 2000 / EMI 62875
- ○ **Beethoven: Symphony 9; Schoenberg** / Leinsdorf (cond.), J. Marsh, Veasey, Domingo, Milnes, Boston SO / RCA Victor 63682
- ○ **Beethoven: Symphony 9 "Choral"** / Klemperer (cond.), C. Ludwig, Hotter, Kmentt, Nordmo-Loevberg, Philharmonia Orch. / 1999 / Testament 1177

KEYBOARD

Andante in F major ("Andante favori"), WoO 57 (1804)

Originally intended as the slow movement of the *"Waldstein" Sonata*, this piece was excised and left to exist on its own. It is lovely but diffuse music, and has gone through alternating periods of affection and neglect. Its opening theme consists basically of a simple phrase repeated a few intervals apart with increasing (but still slight) elaboration toward the end. After its first statement, it receives a short, more ornamented variation, then appears again as before. Another variation ensues, more wayward and slipping into the minor mode before the original theme returns. This variation sequence sets the basic pattern for the piece: a sort of rondo in which the intervening episodes are variations on the refrain, which recurs in abbreviated form. The variations include a playful, skipping, staccato section, a two-part invention alluding vaguely to Johann Sebastian Bach, and a staccato treatment in the right had over wandering figurations in the left. The movement ends in quietly resonating meditation, an interesting experiment in piano sonority that Beethoven carried out more aggressively in the *"Waldstein" Sonata*. *—James Reel*

Recommended:

- ○ **Beethoven: Bagatelles & Dances Vol. 3** / Jando / 2001 / Naxos 553799
- ○ **Great Pianists of the 20th Century: Sviatoslav Richter II** / S. Richter / 1998 / Philips 456949

Bagatelle in A minor ("Für Elise"), WoO 59 (1810)

Among enthusiasts of Beethoveniana, the identity of the "Elise" in the title of the composer's most famous piano miniature, *Für Elise*, is almost as much of an enigma as that of the "Immortal Beloved." (One of the most popular theories is that "Elise" is actually "Therese"—that is, Therese Malfatti, the longtime object of the composer's affections.) Given the modest technical demands of this work—it has long been a favorite of keyboard novices—it is reasonable to conclude in any case that "Elise" was a beginning piano student.

Though usually designated a bagatelle, *Für Elise* has the form of a compact rondo (ABACA). In spite of its brevity, the work bears the distinctive stamp of its creator. There is a slight hint of brooding in the Slavic-tinged A minor refrain; the B episode, in F major, possesses the yearning, songlike character of so many of Beethoven's slow movements. In the C episode, a very effective modulation from D minor to B flat major is achieved via a simple but very characteristic half-step shift in the bass. Like a tiny cut gem, *Für Elise* is flawless; even in an effort of such petite proportions, one is reminded of Leonard Bernstein's observation of the "sense of rightness" which pervades all of Beethoven's works. *— Wayne Gerard Reisig*

Recommended:

- ○ **Für Elise: Romantic Piano Music** / Szokolay / 1999 / Naxos 553795
- ○ **Beethoven: Bagatelles Op. 33, 119, 126** / Brendel / 1997 / Philips 456031
- ○ **Favourite Beethoven** / Vladimir Ashkenazy / 1992 / Philips 436380

Seven Bagatelles, Op. 33 (1802)

Beethoven wrote this, his first set of *Bagatelles*, at a time when his style was rapidly evolving. He would turn out his watershed *Symphony No. 3 "Eroica"* the following year and thereafter regularly strike out new paths in the symphonic, keyboard, choral, and chamber genres. These seven *Bagatelles*, however, while well-crafted and quite attractive, are light and relatively unadventurous works. The E flat major *First*, marked Andante grazioso—quasi allegretto, is a charming piece, jaunty and playful in its catchy main theme and slightly weightier in its brief middle section. The *Bagatelle No. 2 in C major* is a Scherzo marked Allegro. Its main part features a light, jumpy theme followed by a serious second subject. The trio section features a vibrant theme of mostly ascending sonorities based on the second subject. The ensuing *Bagatelle in F major "Allegretto"* is short at about two minutes and quite mellow in its mostly middle-register playfulness. The Andante *Fourth*, in A major, begins gently and gracefully enough, but coarsens its manner a bit in later contrasting episodes. The ensuing *Bagatelle in C major "Allegro ma non troppo"* is colorful in its ascending arpeggiations and lively, stop-and-start theme. *No. 6*, in D major (Allegretto—quasi andante), is gentle and upbeat in its leisurely pacing and graceful manner. The concluding *Bagatelle in A flat major "Presto,"* at just under two minutes, is the shortest and most driven *Bagatelle*. It is also filled with that characteristic Beethovenian mischief and restlessness, shifting from one idea to the next, then back to an earlier one, but now showing imaginative development. *—Robert Cummings*

Recommended:

- ○ **Beethoven: Bagatelles** / D. Matthews / 1994 / Vanguard 8073
- ○ **Beethoven: Bagatelles** / Brendel / 1997 / Philips 456031

11 Bagatelles, Op. 119 (1822)

The date of composition of the *Bagatelles*, Op. 119 given in the headnote (1822) refers to the date of their completion. It is generally believed that a few of them date back to the 1790s, perhaps to as early as 1793. Some of these Bagatelles in their original sketch form may have been intended as movements for a piano sonata, while others may have had roots in other projected keyboard compositions before Beethoven shelved them. Most of the pieces are worthwhile, even if as a group they seem an odd assemblage.

The first *Bagatelle*, marked Allegretto, is a charming minuet, possibly originally dating back to the beginning of the nineteenth century. No. 8 is also a minuet, but of a less lively, more subtle character. It is among the more compelling items in the set. The second Bagatelle (Andante con moto) features an attractive, lyrical melody that might have started out as a song. The same might also be said about No. 4, also an Andante (cantabile). The Sixth is a lighthearted Scherzo (after an opening Andante) that might have fit well in one of the earlier sonatas. No. 7, marked Allegro ma non troppo, features a colorful display of the use of trills, and the Ninth (Vivace moderato) is a somewhat unsettled, if not unsettling, waltz. The Eleventh, marked Andante ma non troppo, sounds like a late work. Its straightforward thematic and harmonic wares reveal subtlety and simple charm, as well as a maturity and mastery of form. This piece provides a most effective close to this varied collection.

Because Nos. 7 through 11 were published in 1821, two years before the entire set, one might surmise that Beethoven favored them over those in the first half of the collection. Indeed, the latter five are the better compositions, and offer the potential listener a more rewarding experience. *—Robert Cummings*

Recommended:

- ○ **Beethoven: Bagatelles** / Brendel / 1997 / Philips 456031
- ○ **Beethoven: Piano Sonatas Opp. 81a & 106** / Kovacevich / 2003 / EMI 57520

Six Bagatelles, Op. 126 (1823)

This is the last and probably finest of the three sets of *Bagatelles* Beethoven wrote. In general, the six works comprising the collection are not as light as those in the earlier sets and the three lone *Bagatelles* without opus numbers. That said, the opening piece in Op. 126 is decidedly pleasant and light. Marked Andante con moto, it is a mostly serene work whose joyous main theme exudes a sense of self-confidence. Textures lighten in the latter part of the work, as the music takes on an almost angelic glow, heralding the incandescent close of the composer's last piano sonata. The *Bagatelle No. 2 in G minor* contrasts with the opening work in both its livelier Allegro tempo and somewhat anxious mood. Still, the ambivalent main theme here never tilts toward the dark side in its mixture of the stormy and playful, of the anxious and the delicate. The *Bagatelle No. 3 in E flat major,* marked Andante, is tranquil in its serenity and grandeur, its theme noble and clearly looking toward the nascent Romantic movement. Does this work augur the mood, perhaps even the keyboard writing, in the middle movement of Brahms' *Piano Concerto No. 1?* The *Bagatelle No. 4 in B minor* is a Presto filled with angst in its driving rhythms and heroic, stormy main theme. An alternate melody in the upper register, also lively and energetic, exhibits a measure of calm and gracefulness, and on its second appearance closes out this anxious piece in a relatively subdued mood. The G major *No. 5,* marked Quasi Allegretto, provides stark contrast to the preceding *Bagatelle* in its serene, dreamy, and consistently gentle manner. While it offers few technical challenges to the pianist, it will present sufficient interpretive ones. The concluding *Bagatelle in E flat major* is marked Presto—Andante amabile e con moto, and begins with a surge of swirling currents that quickly turn tame for the introduction of the dreamy main theme. The music gradually becomes more animated, prodded by elements from the opening, and the theme exhibits a deeper expressive manner in its mixture of heroism and serenity. The opening surge mischievously returns to close out this masterpiece. *—Robert Cummings*

Recommended:

- ○ **Beethoven: Piano Sonatas Opp. 26, 49, 109** / Kovacevich / 1996 / EMI 56148
- ○ **Beethoven: Bagatelles** / Brendel / 1997 / Philips 456031
- ○ **Artur Schnabel: Beethoven Piano Sonatas Vol. 9** / A. Schnabel / Piano Library 295

Diabelli Variations, Op. 120 (1819)

In 1819, the music publisher Anton Diabelli decided to raise money for the family members of soldiers killed in recent wars. He wrote a theme in hopes of inducing some of the leading composers of the day to contribute variations, planning to publish the entire set. In all, he sent his melody to fifty-one composers in Austria, one of whom was Beethoven (another was Schubert). Beethoven's initial inclination was to turn down the project, though eventually he submitted a variation. But the composer soon became intrigued at the prospect of writing a larger set of variations on Diabelli's theme. In the end, he turned out a nearly hour-long work with more variations than any other of his works in the form. This composition makes a worthy companion piece for Bach's mighty *Goldberg Variations*.

Diabelli's theme is lively and rather simple, and while many have derided it as bland and even stupid, it does have a rather naive charm, with its little turns and its rhythmic drive. This was just the kind of simple theme that had inspired the composer's variation thinking in the past. One example is Beethoven's *Seven Variations on "Kind, willst du schlafen"*, WoO 75, from 1799. He seemed to regard such weak or trite melodic creations as skeletal outlines whose notes begged to be infused with personality and color.

There are several key features to the method Beethoven used in fashioning the *Diabelli Variations.* For one thing, he tended to retain in each variation some aspect of the previous one. Some have argued that each item is arranged almost randomly, that they could be reordered to make the work more effective. Yet one finds both delightful commentaries on the variation just gone by and an overarching structure to the whole set. The first variation, marked Alla Marcia is a deliberately pompous and parodistic take on the theme. It is in a slow tempo; the succeeding variations, with a mixture of fast and slow, work gradually toward a climactic release reached in Variation Ten. After that, the music relaxes for a time. Other patterns of peaks and valleys are discernible, with the greatest of the climactic episodes occurring with the fugue near the end of the work.

The work's final moments share, in Joseph Kerman's words, the "visionary aura" of the variations that concude the Piano Sonata No. 32 in C minor. Other noteworthy variations include No. 14, marked Grave e maestoso, a most profound entry and one of the longest, lasting around four minutes. Both Variations 23 and 24 are powerful panels, too, the former a brilliant, energetic creation and the latter divulging a somewhat Bach-like character. Several times Beethoven explores chromatic harmonies that seem far beyond even Schubert's prescient works of the 1820s.

For all its inspired artistry the work has typically proven difficult for listeners. Like the *"Hammerklavier" sonata, No. 29,* it is both long and extremely concentrated. Some publishers and pianists have tampered with the score in an effort to make it more listenable, but their efforts tend to weaken what is a somewhat intellectual masterpiece.

This work was first published in 1823 in Vienna, bearing a dedication to Antonie Brentano (sometimes believed to be the "Immortal Beloved" of an earlier phase of the composer's life). A typical performance of this composition lasts about 50 to 58 minutes. *—Robert Cummings*

Recommended:

- ○ **Beethoven: Diabelli: Variations** / Kinderman / 2002 / Helios 55082
- ○ **Beethoven: Diabelli Variations** / Pollini / 2000 / DG 459645
- ○ **Great Pianists of the 20th Century: Alfred Brendel II** / Brendel / 1999 / Philips 456730
- ○ **Great Pianists of the 20th Century: Artur Schnabel** / A. Schnabel / 1998 / Philips 456961

Eroica Variations, Op. 35 (1802)

Often referred to as the *Eroica Variations,* Beethoven's *15 Variations and Fugue on an Original Theme,* Op. 35 (1802) might more aptly be called the *Prometheus Variations.* The theme upon which the variations are based was first heard by the public in the finale of Beethoven's ballet *The Creatures of Prometheus,* Op. 43 (1800–01), and it also appears as the seventh of his *12 Contredanses,* WoO 14 (1800–02); still later, and most prominently of all, it plays a central role in the finale of the *Symphony No. 3 (Eroica),* Op. 55 (1803). As the composer indicated in a letter to the publisher Breitkopf & Härtel, the variations are "written in quite a new style and . . . in an entirely different way."

Beethoven was almost certainly alluding to the overall layout of the set. First, the theme's bass line appears alone, and then in a series of introductory variations of two, three, and four voices. By beginning with this basso del tema Beethoven emphasizes its comic aspects, especially the three fortissimo octaves in its second half. When the actual theme finally appears, together with the bass, three variations have already unfolded; it is only at this point, however, that Beethoven commences "counting" the variations. Though the final fugue opens with a subject derived from the basso del tema, by its close it reasserts the prominence of the main theme. Beethoven's compositional technique here is markedly more sophisticated than in his earlier essays in the genre; still, the harmonic scheme never ventures far afield from the prevailing E flat major tonality. The relative minor (C minor) emerges in No. 6, the parallel minor (E flat minor) in No. 14, and most refreshingly, the major mediant (G major) at the close of No. 15. The most striking feature of the Variations is the infusion of fugues, canons, ground basses and other characteristically Baroque elements into a work firmly grounded in the high Classical style. The particular importance Beethoven grants the bass line anticipates the precedence of harmonic progressions over melodic material in one of the most monumental accomplishments in the theme-and-variations genre, the *33 Variations on a Waltz by Diabelli,* Op. 120 (1819–23). *—John Palmer*

Recommended:

- ○ **Beethoven: Eroica-Variations** / Jandó / 1992 / Naxos 550676

○ **Beethoven: Piano Concerto 5 "Emperor"; Variations & Fugue** / Curzon, Vienna PO / 1996 / Decca 452302

Piano Sonata No. 1 in F minor, Op. 2/1 (1793–1795)

Though this sonata is obviously an early piece, it still sounds very much like Beethoven in its driving rhythms, muscularity and overall sonic world. It is a fairly serious piece, too, but does not contain much that anyone would assess as profound or innovative. Still, it is a strong composition, even though it shows outside influences: for all the composer's stylistic traits throughout the work, it cannot be denied that the voice of Mozart is present, most notably in the first movement. Beethoven was still evolving his style at this point in his career and had not yet even written an important work for orchestra. For whatever flaws one might point out in this composition, it nevertheless fully deserves to be in the company of the other sonatas comprising the mighty canon of 32. Beethoven dedicated this sonata to composer Joseph Haydn. A typical performance of it lasts from 16 to 20 minutes.

The first movement begins with a bouncy theme that hints at seriousness but remains rather bright and energetic. It must be noted that it seems to have been lifted from the finale of the Mozart Symphony No. 40, whose main theme only differs significantly in its key of G minor. Two more themes appear, the former a bit more serious and darker. The development section turns more intense, focusing on the drive and darker aspects of the thematic material. Ultimately this Allegretto con brio is solidly constructed, if unadventurous, and its thematic similarity to the Mozart Symphony serves in the end to illustrate the quite different ways the two composers treated the same material.

The ensuing Adagio derives its main theme from the slow movement of Beethoven's Piano Quartet, No. 3, WoO 36. The melody is serenely joyful in its pristine Classicism, and while it is rather simple and direct, it is also effective in capturing a mood of ecstasy and bliss.

The Menuetto third movement (Allegretto) is robust and not intended to sound danceable. It is full of color and features an attractive trio, after which the main material is reprised.

The finale (Prestissimo) may be the most Beethovenian movement here. It begins with a manic rush of energy, the theme seemingly in frantic pursuit of something elusive. The alternate subject is playful and comparatively dainty, featuring upper register sonorities that could hardly offer greater contrast. This movement is in sonata form, and so after the reappearance of the main theme, there is a quite effective development section, which ends as it sort of grows back into the recapitulation. *—Robert Cummings*

Recommended:

○ **Beethoven: Piano Sonatas Op 2, Nos. 1, 2 & 3** / Perahia / 1995 / Sony 64397

○ **Beethoven: 4 Sonatas on Period Instruments** / Bilson / 2001 / Claves 502104

○ **Beethoven: Piano Works Vol. 1** / A. Schnabel / 2002 / Naxos Historical 110693

○ **Beethoven: Complete Piano Sonatas Vol. 1** / Nakamichi / RCA Victor 57688

Piano Sonata No. 2 in A major, Op. 2/2 (1794–1795)

Beethoven dedicated the three sonatas of Op. 2 to Franz Joseph Haydn, with whom he studied composition during his first two years in Vienna. All three borrow material from Beethoven's *Piano Quartets,* WoO 36, *Nos. 1 and 3,* possibly of 1785. The sonatas were premièred in the fall of 1795 at the home of Prince Carl Lichnowksy, with Haydn in attendance, and were published in March 1796 by Artaria in Vienna.

The sonatas of Op. 2 are very broadly conceived, each with four movements instead of three, creating a format like that of a symphony through the addition of a minuet or scherzo. The second movements are slow and ponderous, typical of this period in Beethoven's career. Scherzos appear as third movements in Nos. 2 & 3, although they are not any faster than earlier minuets by Haydn. They are, however, longer than their precursors.

Beethoven's experimentation with tonal material within Classical-era frameworks begins with his earliest published works, as the first movement of the Op. 2, No. 2 sonata clearly demonstrates. After establishing the key of A major through a fragmentary, disjointed theme, Beethoven begins the transition to the dominant. When the second theme arrives, however, it is on the dominant minor (E minor), implying the keys of G major and C major. This implication is realized at the beginning of the development section, which is on C major. In the recapitulation, one would expect the transition to lead to the tonic, but here it suggests, again, C major through its dominant. At the moment the second theme arrives, Beethoven creates a deceptive cadence by moving to A minor, thus resolving the second theme to the tonic.

Sustained chords over a pizzicato-like bass part at the opening of the second movement could have been realized only on the most recent pianos of the time. In this movement, Beethoven borrowed material from the *Piano Quartet,* WoO 36, *No. 3.*

Beethoven retains the formal principles of the minuet for his third movement, an Allegretto Scherzo. There are, however, distinctly Beethovenian features, such as the second theme of the Scherzo being only a slight modification of the first theme, as well as the extension of the second section. In a reference to the key relationships of the first movement, Beethoven sets the Trio in A minor.

In the Rondo finale Beethoven applies some sonata-form procedures to the traditional rondo format and flexes his variation muscles. The overall structure is ABACAB'AC'A. Episode B touches on the dominant to such a degree that its return is rewritten to stress the tonic, while episode C is set in A minor, a key which is abandoned in favor of A major on its return. *—John Palmer*

Recommended:

○ **Great Pianists of the 20th Century: Wilhelm Kempff III** / W. Kempff / 1999 / Philips 456868

○ **Beethoven: Piano Sonatas 28, 6 & 2** / Ciccolini / Bongiovanni 110693

○ **Beethoven: Piano Works Vol. 1** / A. Schnabel / 2002 / Naxos Historical 63765

Piano Sonata No. 3 in C major, Op. 2/3 (1794–1795)

This is the last of the three sonatas from the Op. 2 group that Beethoven, more or less, composed simultaneously. Like the *First Piano Sonata,* the Third draws on material from his youthful work, *Piano Quartet No. 3,* and, like the *Second,* it contains some significant innovations. The first movement, marked Allegro con brio opens with a witty, impish theme, initiated by a figuration in double-thirds, which dominates the movement. Additional motifs generated from the initial theme complete the first theme group, and while all the general mood remains light-hearted, the music is also dramatic and replete with characteristic Beethovenian drive and assertiveness, this energy exemplified by brilliantly ascending arpeggiated chords. The second main theme, based on material from the aforementioned Piano Quartet, is lyrical, combining an air of graceful nonchalance and elegant spontaneity. What follows is a remarkable passage that begins with the opening theme and goes on to feature three ascending arpeggiated chords, the last of which, an augmented triad that sounds at first like a bold misstep, is both mischievous and unexpected, not to mention absolutely daring for its time. In the development section, Beethoven deftly moves through several modulations and then briefly suspends all development, indeed, all thematic activity. Suggesting the despair of a traveler who is lost, this static moment ends when the main theme reappears in a more assertive form. The movement ends with a coda, which Beethoven enlarges to monumental proportions, in violation of any traditional conception of a coda. The Adagio second movement features a lovely, somewhat ponderous, theme that seems to hesitate as it moves along. It is played twice the same way, then is heard boldly and in a different key. After this restatement, it returns, more or less, to its original form, but is heard now mostly in the upper register. The brief third movement Scherzo (Allegro) begins with a confident, impish theme, whose rhythms and melodic fragments spray the movement with much color and delight. There is a brief trio section, which is rather athematic, but creates a contrast with its rich arpeggios and stormy atmosphere. The finale, marked Allegro assai, is a rondo with a sparkly theme which moves rapidly upward, then tumbles humorously down. This arched pattern dominates the movement even as thematic transformations occur. A second theme appears that is dreamy and lyrical, providing effective contrast. There are many transitions and episodic passages throughout, imparting a range of color, illuminating the joyful mood. The Sonata concludes with a recapitulation and a lengthy, brilliant coda. Like the other sonatas in the Op. 2 group, this work is dedicated to Joseph Haydn. *—Robert Cummings*

Recommended:

○ **The Art of the Fortepiano** / van Buskirk / 2000 / Lyrichord 8042

○ **Rubinstein Collection Vol. 55: Beethoven, Schubert** / Arthur Rubinstein / 1999 / RCA 63055

○ **Beethoven: Piano Works Vol. 1** / A. Schnabel / 2002 / Naxos Historical 110693

Piano Sonata No. 4 in E flat major ("Grand Sonata") Op. 7 (1796–1797)

This early piano sonata, his fourth, is the longest example of the genre in Beethoven's catalog except for the massive "Hammerklavier" sonata of 20 years later. Much is made of Beethoven the revolutionary, and it is too easy to claim that this sonata's symphonic scope is another mark of the young man's daring genius. However, this composition, although unusually long, is a fairly straightforward work which observes the conventions of its day. The first movement, Allegro molto e con brio, begins with throbbing chords full of anticipation, but quickly gives way to a bright, confident melody that wanders up and down the scale; it wouldn't be out of place in a Mozart sonata. Beethoven does insert a few brusque chords to introduce the jaunty second subject, and is in the habit of suddenly lightening the mood in mid-tune, but this is nothing compared to the mercurial sonatas Emanuel Bach had written a few decades earlier. Most of the thematic elements closely resemble each other, and they are even harder to differentiate over Beethoven's insistent, energetic 6/8 rhythm. The development section makes much of a strongly syncopated version of the second subject, then drops back to toy a while with the first subject and all the other miscellaneous material Beethoven packed into the exposition. Beethoven's treatment of this theme is a bit too sequential and level-headed for a good development section, but far too free for a serious recapitulation.

Leaving this issue undecided, Beethoven eventually draws the movement to a close. The Largo con gran espressione is an early example of the stately slow movements which Beethoven would later bring to extraordinary poetic heights. The measured main theme is as arresting for its pauses as for its arrangement of notes; as the accompaniment becomes more elaborate, these pauses provide the melody with an aura of grandeur. Beethoven never loses sight of this theme during the course of the movement; he merely varies it by filling in the silences with a more legato melodic treatment, even while making the accompaniment (which shifts from bass to treble) more staccato.The Allegro third movement doesn't stray too far from the old minuet style, although Beethoven, characteristically, creates a melody full of hesitations and little deviations from the expected harmonic path. The mood becomes more serious in the central trio section, churning as it does through E flat minor, but the passage is too brief to alter the movement's essentially light-hearted character. A light mood also characterizes the concluding rondo (Poco allegretto e grazioso). This is not the manic sort of finale that Beethoven would later indulge in, but a gentle frolic interrupted by a single stormy episode a quarter of the way through. Admittedly, this is an otherwise uneventful rondo, with the main subject and its variants dominating the remainder of the movement. But it does offer many passages of something rarely found in Beethoven's music: an appealing sweetness. *—James Reel*

Recommended:

- **Brahms: 4 Balladen; Schubert: Sonate; Beethoven: Sonate Op 7** / Michelangeli / 1999 / DG 457762
- **Beethoven: Piano Sonatas Op. 7, 22 & 27, No. 1** / O'Conor / 1994 / Telarc 80363
- **Beeethoven Piano Sonatas Complete Vol. 8** / A. Fischer / Hungaroton 31633
- **Beethoven: Piano Works Vol. 2** / A. Schnabel / 2002 / Naxos Historical 110694

Piano Sonata No. 5 in C minor, Op. 10/1 (1795–1797)

Beethoven began the other two sonatas comprising the Op. 10 group in 1796, but may have started this work toward the end of 1795. Marked Allegro molto e con brio the first movement opens with a probing theme, based on a C minor chord, which introduces a questing, questioning mood, not unlike the opening of the *"Pathetique" sonata*. Here, however, the initial tempo is brisk and the inital utterance appears more direct. However, as the musical discourse unfolds, the straightforward beginning yields to unexpected developments. For example, in the first theme group, Beethoven introduces an interesting element: a mysterious descending phrase bringing what seems as both consolation and triumph. After the initial material is restated, certain differences become apparent: for instance, the "question" phrase is not followed by an "answer," this absence introducing a general feeling of ambiguity and uncertainty. The development section is unusual, for, despite some expansion of previously stated themes, most of the music here is new, thereby violating the conventional rules of sonata form. The recapitulation presents an abridgement of the exposition and an effective transformation of the second theme. In the second movement (Adagio molto), one hears two themes, the first a flowing melody that becomes inwardly agitated as it rises, and the latter a somewhat hesitant invention that seems to seek serenity, but is hampered at times by figurations played by the left hand. The stormy transition separating the two themes is quite interesting—seemingly a harbinger of darkness that never arrives. After the reappearance of the thematic material, in slightly altered form, there is a coda based on the opening melody. The finale is a vibrant Prestissimo, essentially driven by a mood of typical Beethovenian anxiety yearning for joy. This movement's first theme is a decidedly ominous six-note figure, possibly a precursor to the famous "fate" motto of the *Fifth Symphony*. A variant of the first, the second theme is nevertheless its opposite in effect, expressing a spirit of joy and humor. A brief development section leads to a recapitulation, and the movement is completed by a coda. *—Robert Cummings*

Recommended:

- **Beethoven: The Op 10 Piano Sonatas** / R. Goode / 1991 / Nonesuch 79213
- **Beethoven: Piano Sonatas Vol. 5** / Jandó / 1988 / Naxos 550161
- **Beethoven: Piano Works Vol. 2** / A. Schnabel / 2002 / Naxos Historical 110694

Piano Sonata No. 6 in F major, Op. 10/2 (1796–1797)

This is the shortest of the three sonatas from the Op. 10 group and generally regarded as the least important. Still, it is hardly without significance and features many masterful strokes. The finale, for example, is one of Beethoven's most attractive creations among his early piano sonatas. The composer himself was quite fond of the work, probably relishing its humor and quirkiness.

The work is cast in three movements: Allegro, Allegretto, and Presto. It was not unusual for Beethoven to exclude a slow movement. The first movement begins with two emphatic chords answered by a triplet figure that contains a mischievous turn, which literally invites the next statement. It comes, though this time the first chord is lower. After this opening banter, another short theme is introduced, and it easily, despite its lyrical nature, joins the playful scene. A second theme group now appears, headed by a happy but brash melody: rising in a hurry, it proceeds to generate other busy ideas. The material is repeated, after which comes the development section, launched unexpectedly by the triplet figure that appeared after the opening pair of chords. Fairly complex, this section is based less on previous materials and more on new ideas. The recapitulation follows, but, surprisingly, in the remote key of D. The movement ends without a coda, its thematic material being exploited colorfully and brilliantly right up to the close. The second movement is actually a scherzo, though Beethoven did not designate it so. It begins with emphatic chords treading upward ominously from the lower ranges. When the higher register is reached, the mood reaches a somewhat higher plateau. The theme is immediately repeated, then appears two octaves higher, lighter in texture but deeper in feeling. A brief trio section is presented: it is both jovial and comforting and contrasts well with the more serious tone of the previous section. The finale may be the most attractive movement of the entire work. It begins with one of those memorable, frantic humorous themes, so typical of Beethoven. The melody seems to build upward with several turns along the way, the left hand beginning, the right hand entering to suggest fugal properties. Playful and roguish, driven by tremendous energy, the musical narrative proceeds with gusto, the main theme generating subsidiary ideas and second thoughts. Toward the end of this process, chords in the bass register suggest an entirely new idea, but the narrative momentum is maintained by a fragment of the initial theme, eventually leading, following a repetition, to a variation of the theme. After an elaborate development section and a reprise, a brief but brilliant coda closes the work. *—Robert Cummings*

Recommended:

- **Bach: English Suite; Chopin: Nocturnes; Beethoven: Sonata** / Horszowski / 1990 / Elektra Nonesuch 79232
- **Beethoven: Piano Sonatas Vol. 3** / Taub / 1996 / Vox 7532
- **Beethoven: Piano Works Vol. 2** / A. Schnabel / 2002 / Naxos Historical 110694

Piano Sonata No. 7 in D major, Op. 10/3 (1797–1798)

The timing of Beethoven's early publications was shrewdly calculated. Beethoven performed some of these works often enough for them to become familiar, and people encouraged him to publish them (the Trios, Op. 1, are an example). That his publications would be a success was almost a given, especially since the early ones involved the instrument on which he was an acknowledged virtuoso, the piano. It is also significant that his first publications were not symphonies, operas or string quartets, genres associated with Haydn and Mozart. That his first ten piano sonatas, as well as the two of Op. 49, were composed before Beethoven attempted a symphony or string quartet suggests that the piano was something of an experimental medium for the young composer, who was coming to grips with organizing large forms.

The three works of Op. 10 are in C minor, F major and D major. The first was begun in 1795 and the third completed by July 1798. Published in September 1798, by Eder in Vienna, the set is dedicated to Countess Anna Margarete von Browne, whose husband, Count Johann von Browne (1767–1827), was one of Beethoven's chief early patrons. The Countess also received the dedications of the Variations, WoO 76 and WoO 71. An early critic praised the *Sonatas* of Op. 10, noting that they were composed in "an earnest, manly style."

Already in the opening Presto of the third sonata, Beethoven expands the traditional sonata form movement, but not the expository sections. It is true that the main theme is ten measures long and followed by a six-measure contrasting phrase, but this was less striking to Beethoven's contemporaries than a transition that is twice as long as the theme. There is such a wealth of material that it is best to discuss the work in terms of "theme groups," not merely themes. The second theme and closing groups have 11 contrasting ideas among them, and the momentary shift to the minor mode in the second theme group is more than just a colorful device; it has long-range implications. When this material returns in the recapitulation, it does so on the tonic minor (D minor), the relative minor of F major and the key of the second movement. This brief appearance of a "flat" key in the recapitulation is anticipated by the "flat" key areas of the development section.

Marked Largo e mesto and in 6/8, the second movement is cast in D minor. Beethoven explores the full range of the keyboard in this emotive sonata-form structure before it dissolves in the manner of the "Funeral March" of the *Third Symphony*.

The Minuet returns to D major. In a move somewhat unusual for Beethoven, the second theme of the minuet is very different from the first, providing the same contrast typical of a Haydn minuet. The trio, in G major, does not follow the traditional format and gives the pianist a chance to do some fancy hand crossing.

The Rondo finale is a showcase for Beethoven's variation technique. The rondo theme is altered upon return, as is the material of the first episode, which is spliced to the beginning of a new episode later in the movement. Fragments of the rondo theme tease the listener in this high energy movement. *—John Palmer*

Recommended:

- ○ **Beethoven: Piano Sonatas Op. 10, No. 3 & 57; Beethoven-Liszt: Symphony 1** / E. Wild / 1999 / Ivory Classics 70905
- ○ **Beethoven Piano Sonatas** / A. Pratt / 1996 / EMI 55290
- ○ **Beethoven: Piano Works Vol. 3** / A. Schnabel / 2002 / Naxos Historical 110695

Piano Sonata No. 8 in C minor ("Pathétique") Op. 13 (1797–1798)

This was the earliest of Beethoven's piano sonatas to reach warhorse status. The work is cast in three movements: the first is marked Grave—Allegro di molto e con brio; the second, Adagio cantabile; and the finale, Rondo (Allegro). Beethoven opens this composition with a slow, meditative introduction, using this feature for the first time in a sonata. Seemingly posing a question, or struggling to overcome a dilemma, the music seeks resolution and relief, which appears in the exposition proper, when the movement, driven by tremolando octaves in the left hand, quickens, and theme transforms itself into deeply anxious utterance, introducing, once again, a questing, uncertain mood, without excluding forceful utterances, possibly indicating a desire to transcend the feeling of uncertainty. During the brief development section, a sense of dramatic tension predominates, but the general tone changes in the recapitulation, leading to a coda, which closes the movement. The second movement begins with a soothing, languid, melancholy melody of an autumnal beauty. Dominating the entire movement, this initial theme eclipses both the subdued second theme and the moment of dramatic tension in the middle section of the movement. The Rondo finale is really the second Rondo in the sonata, since the middle movement possesses the structural features of that form. This movement opens with a gracefully eloquent theme accompanied by arpeggiated figures played by the left hand. Although the mood seems bright, the music is tinged by melancholy, notwithstanding the playful second theme. Following repetition and thematic development, the first theme surfaces as simultaneously more agile and more delicate. A lengthy, brilliant coda completes the movement. Dedicated to Prince Lichnowsky, this composition was first published in Vienna in 1799. *—Robert Cummings*

Recommended:

- ○ **Beethoven: Piano Sonatas Opp. 13, 14 & 22** / Kovacevich / 1998 / EMI 56586
- ○ **Beethoven: Piano Sonatas** / A. Schnabel / EMI 63765
- ○ **Beethoven: Piano Sonatas Opp. 13, 27 No. 2, 90, 81a** / Moravec / 2001 / Supraphon 3582
- ○ **Beethoven: 2 Sonatas, 6 Bagatelles, Choral Fantasy** / S. Richter / 1995 / Melodiya 29462
- ○ **Beethoven par Gieseking** / Gieseking / 2000 / Tahra 394/400

Piano Sonata No. 9 in E major, Op. 14/1 (1798)

By the time Beethoven wrote this Sonata, his ninth, he was already displaying a strongly individual voice in his piano works and would shortly embark on his *First Symphony* (1800) and other large works. Perhaps less compelling than its predecessor, the celebrated *"Pathétique,"* this Sonata is an immensely interesting work, containing many subtle turns, surprises, and fresh ideas. Cast in three movements—Allegro, Allegretto, Rondo (Allegro comodo)—this composition begins with a lively, optimistic theme, against repeated chords in the left hand which accompany, and goad, the main narrative line. Initially a harbinger of light and joy, the main theme, introduces some tension when repeated, and the mood slightly darkens. In Beethoven's musical narrative, it seems, an initial mood, or impression, often leads to unexpected developments, creating a richly-textured poetic substance. Thus, for example, when the second subject appears, its four descending notes transform the musical canvas into a space ruled by different varieties of doubt and mystery, considerably expanding the emotional and intellectual range of the narrative. Eventually, this episode proceeds to a triumphant ending, and the exposition material is repeated. The development section begins with the main theme transformed, but then a new idea comes to the fore. Somewhat derivative, this idea ushers in a rather atypical development episode. Although this is quite surprising from an intellectual standpoint, the appearance of this theme seems utterly natural, a logical outgrowth of a remember discourse. In the reprise, which follows this brief excursion, the main theme occurs with new accompaniment—ascending scales in the left hand—which imparts an ecstatic character to the music. A brief, brilliant coda concludes the movement. The ensuing Scherzo, though it carries the normally lively marking of Allegretto, operates as the slow movement. There is much tension in its restless main theme, and even the brighter music of the trio sections is not free of a sense of struggle. The finale begins with a rush of energy which traces a downward-moving trajectory. Despite the downward motion, the mood is one of wit, playfulness, and humor. While the second theme introduces some calm, the narrative line is driven by fast rhythms. Interestingly, there is some thematic development in this Rondo, which sounds almost symphonic. *—Robert Cummings*

Recommended:

- ○ **Beethoven: Moonlight Sonata; Pathétique; Sonatas 9, 10 & 13** / Gieseking / Seraphim 69019
- ○ **Beethoven: Piano Sonatas Vol. 6** / Jandó / 1988 / Naxos 550162
- ○ **Brahms: Piano Concerto No. 2 & others** / Bachauer / 1994 / Mercury 434340

Piano Sonata No. 10 in G major, Op. 14/2 (1799)

This work has an unusual structure in its three movements: Allegro, Andante, and Scherzo (Allegro assai). A Scherzo, of course, is usually an inner movement, but Beethoven was never one to follow convention. He makes the pattern work well here and the piece sounds perfectly logical even at first hearing. The sonata begins with an invigorating burst of fresh air—springtime country air, in this case. It should be mentioned here that the composer may have started this work in late 1798, even though its mood would suggest at least late winter, if not spring, of the following year as its gestating point. Of course, Beethoven's inspiration was hardly limited by the time of year or other such external factors. There are three main themes in the first movement, all heard in rapid succession and all ecstatic in their joy and sense of merriment. The exposition is repeated and a fairly elaborate development section ensues. Here, there is some tension, but the thematic transformations and subtle interlacing of the various materials are of greater significance. The recapitulation presents all the themes from the exposition once more, but with some minor changes. The middle movement Andante begins with a proud, march-like theme, quite lively considering the slow tempo. Three variations follow, without any significant change of mood. The second variation emphasizes the rhythmic aspects of the theme, while in the third the left hand takes up the main line, the right supplying the accompaniment. The movement ends with a brief restatement of the theme given in chords by both hands. The finale begins with a lively theme of considerable keyboard range, with direction changing and movement often hesitant. An alternate theme, a bit less colorful but warmer, appears and provides fine contrast. There is much humor in this high-spirited three-minute movement. *—Robert Cummings*

Recommended:

- ○ **Beethoven: Piano Sonatas Op. 6, 7 & 14** / Lortie / 1998 / Chandos 9347
- ○ **Liszt: The Piano Concertos; Beethoven: Sonatas 10, 19 & 20** / S. Richter / 2001 / Philips 464710
- ○ **Beethoven: Piano Works Vol. 3** / A. Schnabel / 2002 / Naxos Historical 110695

Piano Sonata No. 11 in B flat major, Op. 22 (1800)

With the *Eleventh Piano Sonata,* Beethoven moves closer to the more far-reaching expressive worlds of the Op. 31 group of sonatas. Cast in four movements: Allegro con brio, Adagio con molto espressione, Menuetto, and Rondo (Allegretto), the sonata starts off almost as if it were beginning in the middle of a passage. A vigorous, but seemingly incomplete, theme is presented. As the material immediately starts to repeat itself, the opening motif is abbreviated and then the vigorous theme is heard again, but fuller now, expanding its range of color and reaching a triumphant chordal passage. Other thematic material sprouts delightfully and the exposition is completed. In the ensuing development section, the opening idea appears in altered form, and a second theme follows. As the themes are developed, a mysterious statement (based on the second theme) is heard in the bass, and its hypnotic fade-out completes the development section in a most imaginative manner. The recapitulation presents the material from the exposition, but with some attractive changes. The opening melody of the second movement has often been viewed as a foreshadowing of Chopin's more intimate rhetoric. Certainly, this theme has a Romantic flavor: accompanied by repeated chords in the left hand, it proceeds with grace, creating an atmosphere of gentle yearning. A second melody intrudes, without breaking the delicate mood. As the main theme is further developed, through original thematic twists and much colorful writing, the listener is tempted to imagine the music as an orchestral or chamber piece. The Menuetto, the shortest movement, features a theme which seemingly lacks substance. However, as the movement progresses, Beethoven substantially enriches this theme by imaginatively adding color. The brief trio section is turbulent and unsettled, providing splendid contrast to the brighter world of the dance melody. The Rondo finale opens with a somewhat long-winded, lively theme that seems in search of a more joyous sonic space. A second, less distinctive, theme appears, maintaining a general atmosphere of joyous haste. After a new idea, based on the opening theme, is presented, the main material reappears, but with several deft alterations and transformations. After many fireworks, including some beguiling rhythmic antics, the sonata closes with a brilliant coda. *—Robert Cummings*

Recommended:

- ○ **Beethoven: Piano Sonatas 11, 13 & 31** / Ohlsson / 2003 / Arabesque 6773
- ○ **Great Pianists of the 20th Century: Wilhelm Kempff III** / W. Kempff / 1999 / Philips 456868
- ○ **Beethoven: Piano Works Vol. 4** / A. Schnabel / 2003 / Naxos Historical 110756

Piano Sonata No. 12 in A flat major ("Funeral March") Op. 26 (1800–1801)

Beethoven's *Piano Sonata No. 12 in A flat major,* Op. 26 (1800–01) was especially popular among the Romantics; even Chopin, who rarely performed Beethoven's music in public, included it in his repertoire. The work reflects Beethoven's ongoing experimentation with the form of the piano sonata; in place of the more conventional sonata-allegro movement, he begins the sonata with a theme and variations, a still-novel innovation that Mozart had introduced a few decades earlier. The opening Andante theme is faintly ceremonial, decorated with a few well-placed turns. The first variation merely uses arpeggios to fill in the spaces between the notes of the theme. The second is more of a surprise, the melody falling to the left hand for a bumptious treatment while the right hand provides accompaniment with rapid syncopated chords. The third variation is almost a minor-mode inversion of the second, slowing down considerably and moving the syncopated accompaniment into the bass. The fourth variation is a capricious treatment of theme with a sputtering accompaniment; the fifth compensates by smoothing out the melody, though it retains a busy triplet rhythm in the left hand. The movement closes with a brief, dignified restatement of the melody. With its surging theme, the short Allegro molto Scherzo is a near-twin to the corresponding movement in the composer's slightly earlier *Symphony No. 1 in C major,* Op. 21 (1799–1800). The abbreviated Trio has something of the character of a chorale, but Beethoven sweeps all this away so he can get on with the movement that lends the sonata its familiar moniker. The full title of the "Funeral March" movement is "Marcia funebre sulla morte d'un Eroe"; the dead hero is never identified and is likely a mere literary device. Here, the obvious symphonic parallel is the second movement of the composer's not-too-distant *"Eroica" Symphony* (1803), right down to the irregularly palpitating rhythmic figure. Left-hand drum rolls dominate the contrasting middle section, but the more subdued march proper returns for another statement. This leads unexpectedly and almost without pause into the brisk, bright Allegro, an impetuous little ABA movement with the middle section offering a taste of drama but steering clear of anything too serious. With its perpetual-motion left-hand figures, the music can do little else than simply wind down at the end. *—James Reel*

Recommended:

- **Beethoven: Piano Sonatas Opp. 26, 27 & 49** / Kovacevich / 2001 / EMI 57131
- **Beethoven: Erioca Variations; Bagatelles Op 126; Sonata 12** / Pontinen / 1986 / Bis 353
- **Beethoven: Sonaten Opp. 22, 26 & 53 "Waldstein"** / Pollini / DG 435472
- **Alfred Brendel: Beethoven Piano Sonatas Vol. 4** / Brendel / 1992 / Vox 5060
- **Beethoven: Piano Works Vol. 4** / A. Schnabel / 2003 / Naxos Historical 110756
- **Great Pianists of the 20th Century: Sviatoslav Richter II** / S. Richter / 1998 / Philips 456949

Piano Sonata No. 13 in E flat major ("Quasi una fantasia") Op. 27/1 (1800–1801)

While Beethoven's *Sonata,* Op. 27, *No. 2,* the familiar *Moonlight,* may get the publicity and the performances, it's the Op. 27, *No. 1, in E flat* that represents a radical breakthrough for the composer. It's also fun to listen to. Subtitled *Sonata quasi una Fantasia* like its opusmate, this work's closely-connected sections do in fact form something resembling a free fantasia. The opening movement is not a fast movement in sonata form, but a song-like Andante in a playful slow-dance rhythm; this is abruptly interrupted by a free and virtuosic Allegro, which in turn reverts to the original Andante as if nothing had happened. A brief, stormy Scherzo (Allegro molto e vivace), in which the hands play three-note patterns in opposition to each other, is contrasted with a trio in syncopated "hunting" rhythm—an eccentric movement that would have fit in nicely with the Op. 33 *Bagatelles.* A lovely, largely chordal Adagio con espressione is in fact an introduction to the Allegro vivace finale, an elaborately worked-out rondo with a good deal of contrapuntal passagework. At its climax, the music comes to a sudden halt, and the Adagio theme returns for a beautiful moment before a Presto coda brings the sonata to a brilliant conclusion. *—Sol Louis Siegel*

Recommended:

- **Moonlight: Beethoven Sonatas "Quasi una Fantasia"** / Pires / 2001 / DG 453457
- **Beethoven: Piano Sonatas 14, 23 & 13** / A. Watts / 1999 / Seraphim 73285
- **Beethoven: Piano Works Vol. 4** / A. Schnabel / 2003 / Naxos Historical 110756

Piano Sonata No. 14 in C sharp minor ("Moonlight"), Op. 27/2 (1801)

Beethoven billed each of the two works published under Op. 27 as a *sonata quasi una fantasia,* presumably a hint that he was trying to meld the formal conventions of the eighteenth century sonata with a newer, freer, more Romantic style. Many musicians consider the first of this pair, the *Piano Sonata No. 13 in E flat major* (1800–01), to be the superior work, but the *Piano Sonata No. 14 in C sharp minor* (1801) is by far more popular; in fact, it is one of Beethoven's most beloved works, and its first movement takes a place among the most widely and instantly recognizable music the composer ever penned. The familiar appellation *Moonlight* is not the composer's own, but the invention of German music critic Ludwig Rellstab, who compared the first movement's rippling texture to the moonlight shimmering on Lake Lucerne.

The first movement is marked Adagio sostenuto, a virtual invitation to draw out the music to such an extent that the slight, probing melody becomes difficult to follow, leaving listeners to be hypnotized by the undulating arpeggios that serve as an introduction and then (theoretically) recede into accompaniment. The right tempo is key to the effectiveness of this movement. Played too fast, the music sounds mechanical; perhaps more frequently, though, it is played with with funereal slowness. A tempo between these extremes brings out the music's yearning character, particularly in the portion in which slow sighs rise and fall in the treble, with a weary echo in the bass.

The first movement is not really in sonata form; it essentially lays out thematic material—a brooding opening, the "sighing" passage, and a regretful little hymn—with some poignant modulations along the way, then repeats everything. The second movement, Allegretto, is a short, delicate interlude with a syncopated tune in the treble that is interrupted by slightly darker ruminations in the bass during the central section. The Presto transforms the first movement's contemplative arpeggios into a frantic, obsessive figure whose upward ripple that even infects the melody, investing the finale with a character that looks forward to the *"Waldstein" Sonata.* This movement, rather than the first, is the one that assumes a sonata-allegro form, though Beethoven breaks with tradition by making all the thematic units equally agitated. If the Adagio was a reflection of private, inner thought, the Presto is high public drama, an unexpected and effective contrast to the sonata's intimate beginning. *—James Reel*

Recommended:

- **Beethoven: Moonlight; Appassionata; Waldstein** / Vladimir Ashkenazy / 1998 / Penguin Classics 460602
- **Beethoven Piano Sonatas: Pathetique; Moonlight; Waldstein** / Cliburn / 1996 / Arabesque 6677
- **Rudolf Serkin Plays Beethoven** / R. Serkin / 2003 / Sony 90395
- **Beethoven: Sonatas** / Schnabel / 1989 / RCA Victor 60356
- **Ivan Moravec, Beethoven: Sonatas Opp. 13, 27 No. 2, 90, 81a** / Moravec / 2001 / Supraphon 3582

Piano Sonata No. 15 in D major ("Pastoral") Op. 28 (1801)

Compared to the groundbreaking sonatas of Op. 27, Beethoven's *Piano Sonata in D major,* Op. 28 is something of a retrospective work in terms of form: clearly, the composer still had something to say in the "standard" four-movement scheme of his earlier sonatas. A remarkable feature of this work is that each movement establishes its own insistent, dominating rhythm at its outset. The first measure of the opening Allegro, for example, is simply three quarter notes on the tonic note D, a figure that both establishes the work's 3/4 meter and commences the first subject. The flowing, carefree second subject, based on the same rhythmic pattern, derives from a series of rocking chords in both hands. The overall effect is one of cheerful contentment, though the development builds to a considerably dramatic climax.

The second movement, Andante is a not-very-slow slow movement in ABA song form. Here, Beethoven creates a serious, lyrical theme in D minor from a series of chords over an insistent left hand in sixteenth notes. The middle section, in the major mode, alternates syncopated chords with descending right-hand triplets, material that makes a plaintive minor-mode return in the coda.

The Allegro vivace Scherzo, again in 3/4, rises from a sardonic series of descending single notes, one to a measure and an octave apart, after which the right hand jumps both above and below the left with the theme. The Trio section, reviving the minor mode, is a series of rocking triplet figures.

Like the first movement, the Allegro, ma non troppo finale at once establishes a rhythm and commences with the main theme. The movement is in 6/8; the alternation of quarter note and eighth note rhythms provides a syncopated "rambling" feel. Beethoven finds fresh variants for every repeat of this theme, all the way to the brilliant coda. *—Sol Louis Siegel*

Recommended:

- **Beethoven: Piano Sonatas, Op 7 & Op 28 "Pastoral", Op. 49, No. 2** / Brendel / 1996 / Philips 446624
- **Beethoven: Piano Sonatas Vol. II** / G. Gould / 1994 / Sony 52642
- **Beethoven: Piano Sonatas Vol. 3** / Sherman / 1998 / GM 2057

Piano Sonata No. 16 in G major, Op. 31/1 (1802)

After completing his Op. 28 piano sonata, Beethoven told his friend Krumpholz that he was dissatisfied with what he had written and was setting out to compose in a new way. However, the Op. 31 sonatas don't seem to indicate any radical changes. In the first of the three sonatas, one gesture really stands out: in the first movement's recapitulation, where traditional sonata form requires the music to appear in the dominant key (in this case, D major), Beethoven slips instead into the submediant, a vaguely unsettling place, suggesting that the music still has some distance to travel before it reaches its harmonic home. Beethoven would often employ this trick later in life. The opening Allegro vivace begins in a flurry of notes, which gives way to a theme consisting of curt, impatient chords. A longer version of the flurry is followed by the quick chordal theme again. Then a new, impetuous subject bursts in, briefly venturing into the minor mode. The succinct development is devoted entirely to the "flurry" material, and barely before it's begun, the opening section is recapitulated. Near the end it loses melodic direction and, as mentioned, drifts into the "wrong" key before lurching into an abrupt G major conclusion. The Adagio grazioso is based on a trilling melody that rumbles when it moves to the keyboard's lower register. The tune flies about capriciously before offering a leaner, plainer version of itself. The initial version returns, seeming more than ever like a self-centered ballerina twirling over a clumsy Ländler rhythm. Throbbing chords dominate the next section and allow the music to descend into a hazy minor-mode region. The opening melody returns focus to the movement and is shortly displaced by a gently pealing, bell-like section. The principal subject comes back in one of its most frivolously ornamented guises yet and surrenders to a section that is little more than trills competing with a hypnotic repetition of chords, before flitting up toward the top of the keyboard and away. Beethoven displayed subtlety in the concluding rondo, a good-natured Allegretto whose first contrasting section alludes to the previous movement's penchant for trills. By and large, this rondo is really a series of short variations on the primary theme, almost all of them turning the left hand into a perpetual motion machine; the right-hand material, in contrast, is quite easy-going. The theme becomes slow and coy as the coda arrives, but ultimately whirls toward a conclusion that turns out to be a string of muttered little afterthoughts. *—James Reel*

Recommended:

- **Beethoven: Sonatas & Bagatelles** / Mia Chung / 1994 / Channel Classics 7195
- **Beethoven: Klaviersonaten Op 31** / Kovacevich / 1995 / EMI 55226
- **Beethoven Piano Sonatas 29, 16** / Ohlsson / 2000 / Arabesque 6737

Piano Sonata No. 17 in D minor ("Tempest"), Op. 31/2 (1802)

Written in 1802, the three sonatas of Beethoven's Op. 31 probably coincide with the drafting of his famous "Heiligenstadt Testament," in which he expresses despair at his enroaching deafness. If any of the composer's works from this year indicate that he had embarked on a new path, it is the *Piano Sonata No. 17 in D minor,* Op. 31/2. The composer famously dismissed an inquiry about the "meaning" of this work with the advice to read Shakespeare's *The Tempest*; given the music's overtly dramatic character, it is easy to see how Beethoven might have drawn parallels to, or even inspiration from, the Bard's famous tragedy.

The first six measures present two vastly different ideas: an ascending Largo arpeggiation of the dominant chord, juxtaposed against a frenetic repeated-note Allegro figure that descends and halts abruptly on another dominant chord. It is this passage, and not the ascending forte arpeggios in the bass that appear a few measures later, that forms the main substance of the movement's first theme group. This becomes clear when, in the recapitulation, Beethoven dispenses with the forte passage, connecting the main and secondary themes with new material, which in itself is not an unusual sonata-form procedure. The whole represents the most concentrated, motivically conceived movement Beethoven had yet composed.

The second movement, Adagio, is in B flat major; the movement's tonality is worthy of comment here, since it plays an important modulatory role in the third movement. Like the first movement, the second is a sonata-allegro and opens with a broken triad; unlike the first movement, however, it lacks a development section, and has clearly articulated first and second themes.

The D minor finale is again a sonata-allegro. The first theme outlines the tonic triad, while the contrasting second theme moves in almost completely stepwise fashion. In the development section Beethoven employs the first theme exclusively, using repetition and prolonged harmonies to create an overpowering sense of anticipation. Portentously, Beethoven provides further development in a coda that is as long as the exposition.*—John Palmer*

Recommended:

- **Beethoven Piano Sonatas: Moonlight; Pathétique & others** / Pires / 2001 / Erato 89225
- **Beethoven: Favourite Piano Sonatas** / Vladimir Ashkenazy / 1997 / London 452952
- **Beethoven: Piano Sonatas 17, 18, 21 Waldstein & 22** / Solomon / 2000 / Testament 1190
- **Great Pianists of the 20th Century: Sviatoslav Richter 2** / S. Richter / 1998 / Philips 456949

Piano Sonata No. 18 in E flat major ("Hunt") Op. 31/3 (1802)

This was the third of a group of piano sonatas with which Beethoven took another large step forward in the genre he ultimately revolutionized. This one was last of the 32 works to have a minuet movement, clearly a holdover from the eighteenth century that the composer subsequently felt compelled to abandon. The so-called *"Hunt" Sonata*'s first movement, marked Allegro, begins with a three-note motif which seems to gently demand the listener's attention. From this fragment and the vigorous bass response of four chords, Beethoven ingeniously builds the first theme group. A fast, jaunty melody launches the second subject and keeps the mood light and relatively calm. The material is repeated and the development ensues, based mainly on the themes in the first group, though Beethoven uses all the previous material. The rhythmic appeal at the outset of the development section owes much to the composer's deft transformation of the bass response to the opening motif. The recapitulation follows and a brief coda closes the movement. The second movement is an unorthodox Scherzo marked Allegro vivace. It is unorthodox because it lacks a trio section, features substantial thematic development, and is in 2/4 (instead of triple) time. The main theme is fast-paced and optimistic, forming a double-arch pattern. A secondary idea here sounds almost like humorous commentary on the main material. Another theme, frantic and breathless, turns the mood toward the manic and ecstatic. The material is then developed, with much humor emerging as the music slides and slips via colorful glissando-like effects. The recapitulation features ingenious changes in the themes, and the movement closes with a brilliant, short coda. The third movement (Menuetto: Moderato e grazioso) is charming and without doubt the most traditional panel in the sonata. Clearly it hearkens back to the previous century, and perhaps, after the rather "modern" Scherzo, the composer intended it as a contrast. An elegant main theme leads to vigorous, almost disruptive, secondary material. The themes are repeated and a coda closes the movement. Beginning with a rush of energy, the finale Presto con fuoco features a spry descending melody with left-hand accompaniment. Another theme, likened by some to a "horn call" (thus giving this sonata its rather inappropriate nickname) appears, and the narrative unfolds unrelentingly. There is much playfulness in this rhythmic music: the "horn call" theme, for instance, seems to bounce all over the sonic landscape and the energetic, buoyant mood never flags. After the exposition repeat, there is some development of the materials, and a new theme appears. After the reprise, a brief coda closes the sonata. *—Robert Cummings*

Recommended:

- **Great Pianists of the 20th Century: Artur Rubinstein III** / Artur Rubinstein / 1999 / Philips 456967
- **Hommage á Werner Haas** / W. Haas / 2001 / MDG 6421086
- **Great Pianists of the 20th Century: Clara Haskil II** / Haskil / 1999 / Philips 456829

Piano Sonata No. 19 in G minor, Op. 49/1 (ca. 1797)

While this Sonata comes numerically just after the three from Op. 31 (Nos. 16–18), it predates them chronologically by at least five years. Beethoven, ever the perfectionist, suppressed many of his early works, sometimes revising them before finally sending them to the publisher or deciding after close examination that they were fit for print after all. Of course, in many cases, he simply withheld the work from publication for life, apparently never satisfied with it. He seems to have written his *Piano Sonata No. 19* around 1797, making it roughly contemporary with Sonatas Nos. 4 through 7. The other sonata from Op. 49, No. 20, is also an early composition, probably begun a year or so before this one. Beethoven's brother Caspar is the party responsible for the sudden appearance of this composition in Vienna, in 1805. He took it upon himself, against his brother's wishes, to send this and its sibling sonata to the publisher, although both works might have surfaced after the composer's death anyway, as did a great many others without opus numbers. Still, it is possible these sonatas might never have survived had it not been for Caspar van Beethoven. The reason the composer was unsure of the artistic worth of this sonata must have had to do with its modest proportions. As for its quality, he must eventually have come to realize that this was a worthy creation. The work is cast in two short movements: Andante and Rondo—Allegro. The first movement, unusual for Beethoven, begins slowly with a rather simple, somber theme. This Andante's second subject group is livelier and brighter the first. The exposition material is repeated, and then the development section begins, focusing on the second theme. It is brief, and like most of the movement, delicate and subtle. There follows a reprise, with some ingenious changes, and then the movement closes quietly. The Rondo second movement is brief and also simply constructed. The main theme is vigorous and probably the most muscular-sounding music in the work. It is a happy but somewhat nervous melody that transforms to a more mellow character in the closing moments. The second theme is a bit more energetic and colorful. This sonata is not difficult to play and its generally uncomplicated and genial nature suggest that the composer might have intended to call this work a "sonatina." *—Robert Cummings*

Recommended:

- **Liszt: The Piano Concertos; Beethoven: Piano Sonatas 10, 19 & 20** / S. Richter / 2001 / Philips 464710
- **Beethoven: Piano Sonatas Vol. 8** / Jandó / 1988 / Naxos 550167
- **Beethoven: Piano Works Vol. 2** / A. Schnabel / 2002 / Naxos Historical 110694

Piano Sonata No. 20 in G major, Op. 49/2 (1795–1796)

The *Piano Sonata No. 20* was probably written around the time Beethoven composed the *Third* and *Fourth* sonatas, but because it was published in Vienna in 1805, nearly a decade after it was written, it was assigned then-current opus and sonata numbers, placing it amid works from the composer's middle period. Similar circumstances caused Beethoven's *B flat Piano Concerto* to appear as his Second, even though it predated the *First.* Owing to his perfectionist tendencies, Beethoven often suppressed works in his early years, either revising them later for publication, or determining after reflection that they in fact did meet his high standards. Still, he withheld many early works from publication for life, apparently never satisfied with them. In the case of this sonata and its immediate predecessor (No. 19), it was Caspar van Beethoven, the composer's brother, who decided they were worthy of publication. Against the composer's will, he presented them to a publishing house, thus allowing posterity to hear works that might otherwise have gotten lost or destroyed. It is believed that, had Beethoven himself released this sonata for publication, he would have called it a sonatina, owing to its modest proportions.

The 20th Piano Sonata is cast in two movements, Allegro ma non troppo and Tempo di menuetto. It is a straightforward work, featuring little of the sophistication evident in most of the other piano sonatas. The first movement features an aristocratic theme, delicate yet stately. It, and a more playful second theme undergo only minimal development before recapitulating at the end, making for a simplified sonata form.

The second movement of the *Piano Sonata No. 20* shares a melodic theme with the Minuet of the Op. 20 Septet. Because the Septet was the later piece (1799–1800), Beethoven's suppression of the sonata and reuse of one of its themes suggests that he perhaps planned to scrap the piano work altogether. But the composer was known to recycle melodies, in some instances several times. This Minuet features a charming melody that, along with its accompanying material, is repeated several times, varying somewhat in appearance, but remaining simple and unsophisticated. *—Robert Cummings*

Recommended:

- ○ **Beethoven: Piano Sonatas Vol. 5** / Sherman / GM 2068
- ○ **Liszt: The Piano Concertos; Beethoven: Piano Sonatas 10, 19 & 20** / S. Richter / 1994 / Philips 438486
- ○ **Beethoven: Piano Works, Vol. 2** / Schnabel / 2002 / Naxos Historical 8110694

Piano Sonata No. 21 in C major ("Waldstein") Op. 53 (1803–1804)

Following the acquisition of an Erard fortepiano in 1803, Beethoven was inspired to write this sonata, one of the finest among his 32. The composer had known for about two years that he was losing his hearing, but he was far from complete deafness. The crisper tones of the new instrument were much more appealing to him than his old Walter piano. This sonata, dedicated to the composer's patron and friend Count Ferdinand von Waldstein, came on the scene as a great challenge for pianists. The first movement, marked Allegro con brio, begins with a rhythmic, driving, obsessive theme that creates an enormous sonic space and a veritable energy field between the hammering chords in the left hand and the right hand's completion of the phrase, several octaves higher. Reiterated, starting from a slightly lower register, the theme seems less energetic, but the effect is deceptive. While the energy level remains high, additional ideas are developed, and the second subject is introduced as each of these ideas strives to dominate the composition's discourse. This second subject, in E major, introduces a moment of tranquillity, but calm quickly dissipates, moving toward a brilliant, triumphant finish with the underlying rhythmic intensity of the main theme. The development section begins with a darker cast to the main theme, which then goes off into a new direction. The previous materials become interlaced and developed, and this process generates considerable tension. In the reprise that follows, Beethoven ingeniously avoids a mere restatement by expanding on the phrase at the end of the main theme's first reappearance. There are many other deft touches here, including the brilliant coda based on the main theme. The second movement, bearing the marking Introduzione (Adagio molto), is short, serious, and introspective, drawing its immense dramatic power from the many figurative transformations of the initial three-note utterance spanning the interval of a sixth. Significantly, the mysterious, contemplative mood of the opening is enriched by the expressive lyricism of the melody appearing in the middle part. This counterpoint of pure lyricism and contemplation constitutes the essence of the movement. Originally, Beethoven wrote what is now known as the *Andante favori* as the second movement, but decided not to include a movement he considered too long. Without pause, the music emerges from the philosophical atmosphere of the Adagio and blossoms into the brilliant main theme of the finale, marked Rondo (Allegretto moderato). This melody, appearing as seven notes then repeating all but the last, has a pastoral quality in its quieter moments at the beginning. However, Beethoven transforms this tranquil mood into one of ecstatic celebration, spelled out by colorful sprays of notes that establish a harmonic base. As the theme develops and new ideas are introduced, the dramatic intensity of the movement, reinforced by a repetitive octave-figuration in the left hand, yields to moments of fatigue. However, the main theme returns, imposing a triumphant and joyous sense of order, and a scintillating coda completes the composition. With its mighty rhythmic drive, harmonic inventiveness, thematic incandescence, and wealth of ideas, this sonata is one of the great works of the piano repertoire. *—AMG*

Recommended:

- ○ **Beethoven Piano Sonatas: Pathetique; Moonlight; Waldstein** / Ohlsson / 1996 / Arabesque 6677
- ○ **Beethoven: Piano Sonatas 21, 23 & 26** / Tan / 1994 / Virgin 61160
- ○ **Beethoven: Sonaten Opp. 22, 26 & 53 Waldstein** / Pollini / DG 435472
- ○ **Horowitz: The Complete Masterworks Recordings Vol. VI** / Horowitz / 1993 / Sony 53467
- ○ **Great Pianists of the 20th Century: Walter Gieseking II** / Gieseking / 1999 / Philips 456790

Piano Sonata No. 22 in F major, Op. 54 (1804)

This brief work falls right between Beethoven's monumental *"Waldstein"* and *"Appassionata"* sonatas, with the *"Eroica" Symphony* lurking nearby. Playable on a five-octave keyboard, this little sonata lures amateurs and then snares them in unexpected technical complications. Billed as minuet, the first movement takes a measured, deliberate tempo, the simple, pleasant, ruminative theme lifting up from the bass. However, just when the student pianist starts enjoying the somewhat complacent mood of this beginning, the trio storms through with nasty octaves in both hands. This development, which really feels like a strange interruption, seems inexplicable. Returning in a slightly more ornate form, the stately opening utterance leads, once again, to the ill-tempered trio, then appears again, goes through transformations which include some dissonant chords, and ends. The second of the two movements, an Allegretto, is one of Beethoven's typical perpetual-motion rondos. This one has a dark edge to it, veering into the minor and keeping up the flood of sixteenth notes, thus seriously limiting the individuality of the various episodes. Amateurs generally must give up entirely by the time they reach the strenuous coda, in which the two hands race each other to the final bar. *—James Reel*

Recommended:

- ○ **Beethoven: Piano Sonatas 14–17, 21–23, 24, 32** / Gulda / 1994 / London 443012
- ○ **Beethoven: Sonatas Opp. 54, 57, 78 & 90** / Pollini / 2003 / DG B000005902

Piano Sonata No. 23 in F minor ("Appassionata") Op. 57 (1804–1805)

From the writing of his Heiligenstadt Testament in 1802 up to the composition of the *"Appassionata"* in 1804–05, Beethoven produced some of his most pivotal works, music that foreshadows and heralds the arrival of what is commonly identified as the "second" period of his creativity. Beethoven, it seemed, had turned inward and begun to produce music only he could fully understand. If he had resigned himself to the futility of his cosmic anger, he also determined to thrust his immense genius in the face of God and Man alike, accepting no limitations upon the magnitude or trajectory of his creativity. It was the Beethoven of these works who unleashed the *"Appassionata" Sonata* in 1805.

Opening with a dark, enigmatic theme—one of the most striking curtain-raisers in any of Beethoven's sontatas—the work abruptly explodes with what some have called shrieks of rage. The work makes immediate, fearsome demands upon the pianist, calling both for percussive handfuls of chords and accompanimental figuration demanding the utmost delicacy. The movement is driven forward with a demonic intensity and a daring harmonic sense; the opening phrase, as one example, is repeated a half-step higher in the second phrase, momentarily shrouding the tonal center in a strange, unsettling ambiguity. Prefiguring the dot-dot-dot-dash motive of the *Fifth Symphony* among its rhythmic materials, the *"Appassionata"* unfolds with a volatile, start-and-stop rhythmic scheme that lends it a particular sense of conflict and urgency. In one of the classic examples of Beethoven's organic motivic sense, the second theme of the first movement makes clear reference to the first; while the genesis of its rhythm and contour is obvious, Beethoven here transforms it into a lyrical and yearning if brief moment of respite.

The second movement, a relaxed andante, is a set of variations on a simple, chorale-like theme that retains a shade of the dotted rhythms of the first movement. The variations gradually increase in activity; a sudden reprise of the more sedate original theme and leads without pause to a savage, impassioned finale. Here, Beethoven makes formidable demands upon both instrument (especially the pianos of his own day) and player; the Presto finale is nothing so much as a pounding blur of fury.

The sonata's "Appassionata" subtitle is not Beethoven's own; it was first applied by a Hamburg publisher in 1838. *—Michael Morrison*

Recommended:

- ○ **Rudolf Serkin Plays Beethoven** / R. Serkin / 2003 / Sony 90395
- ○ **Beethoven: Sonatas Opp. 54, 57, 78 & 90** / Pollini / 2003 / DG B000005902

- ○ **Glenn Gould Edition: Beethoven Piano Sonatas Vol. II** / G. Gould / 1994 / Sony 52642
- ○ **Great Pianists of the 20th Century: Sviatoslav Richter II** / S. Richter / 1998 / Philips 456949
- ○ **Ivan Moravec Plays Beethoven Vol. 2** / Moravec / 1994 / VAI Audio 1069

Piano Sonata No. 24 in F sharp major ("A Thérèse") Op. 78 (1809)

Beethoven took a nearly five-year break from piano sonata composition after finishing the earth-shaking *"Appassionata" sonata* of 1804–05. He returned to the genre only in May 1809, when the departure of his friend Archduke Rudolph prompted him to begin the *"Les Adieux" Sonata* (No. 26, Op. 81a). Before that piece was finished, however, Beethoven wrote, signed, and affixed opus numbers to two other piano sonatas (both relatively brief works), so that, according to the numbering scheme, the *Piano Sonata No. 24 in F sharp major*, Op. 78, is the immediate successor to the *"Appassionata" Sonata*. Op. 78 was a work for which Beethoven had considerable affection; the tendency of posterity to assign nicknames to the works of major composers has resulted in Op. 78 occasionally being called "A Thérèse," by reason of its having been dedicated to Countess Therese von Brunsvik.

This composition seems the work of a man who has finally exorcised all his demons. It is a light piece in two movements. The first bears a serene Andante cantabile introduction, really just a single phrase. The main Allegro ma non troppo material flows effortlessly from the opening in one long, undulating theme that gradually breaks into more fragmentary components, then pulls itself together again. This is a matter of gentle examination rather than disintegration; Beethoven employs all these elements in a mild variation of the theme, then eases into a development section that maintains the same mood except for one fairly agitated passage near the end. Things return to the tranquil norm with the recapitulation.

The compact second movement, Allegro vivace, is a frisky rondo that trades in sudden contrasts in dynamics, major and minor modes, and texture; Beethoven sometimes strips the music down to one-part writing that sounds thick only because of its fleetness. *—AMG*

Recommended:

- ○ **Beethoven: Piano Sonatas 14, 23, 24 & 26** / R. Casadesus / 2003 / Sony 87285
- ○ **Beethoven: Piano Concerto 3; Piano Sonatas Nos 21 & 24** / Pommier / 2002 / Apex 48994
- ○ **Beethoven Piano Sonatas Vol. 4** / Brendel / 1992 / Vox 5060

Piano Sonata No. 25 in G major ("Cuckoo") Op. 79 (1809)

Like the *Sonata No. 24* in F sharp major, Op. 78, Beethoven's little *G major Piano Sonata*, Op. 79, was written in 1809. Both works share several instantly discernible features. Firstly, both sonatas are surprisingly undemonstrative in tone, revealing a pronounced avoidance of bravura showiness, unwarranted rhetoric, and above all, extravagant emotionalism. Where they differ markedly, however, is in their respective number of movements, since the *G major Sonata* has three self-contained movements, conforming to established architectural principles, whereas in the earlier opus, sonata allegro and slow movements are effectively linked together thanks to the substantial Adagio cantabile preface offered before, and leading, without a break, to the main first allegro.

The *G major Sonata, No. 25,* comprises an opening Presto, an Andante slow movement, and a finale marked Vivace. The first movement also has the qualifying term alla Tedesca, or "in the German style." From the outset, the work arouses a strong and positive impression, as a result of its sharply chiselled rhythmic formulae and a certain direct (if not to say at times abrupt) candor and spontaneity. That feeling of directness and clarity of expression also informs the following movement, a brief but eloquent Andante in 9/8 meter and simple ternary form. This not only reaffirms Viennese tastes, both in terms of the directness already referred to, but also in the pronounced feeling of "naturalness," at times approaching pastoral straightforwardness which is an unmistakable characteristic here. Simplicity and directness are also crucial in the brief and witty finale, a fully formed Vivace rondo, lasting fractionally under two minutes. This sonata is sometimes given the nickname "The Cuckoo," because of the distinctive pattern of falling intervals and repeated note groupings which permeate the score at various points, never more obviously than during the final movement. *—Michael Jameson*

Recommended:

- ○ **Beethoven: Complete Piano Sonatas, Vol. 9** / A. Fischer / Hungaroton 31634
- ○ **Daniel Pollack, Pianist: The Legendary Moscow Recordings** / D. Pollack / 2002 / Cambria 1133
- ○ **Great Pianists of the 20th Century: Wilhelm Backhaus I** / W. Backhaus / 1998 / Philips 456718

Piano Sonata No. 26 in E flat major ("Les Adieux") Op. 81a (1809–1810)

Ludwig van Beethoven's *Piano Sonata No. 26 in E flat major ("Les Adieux")*, Op. 81a, would seem to be a programmatic or semi-programmatic piece of music, but there is some disagreement over the authenticity of that program—or at least over the degree to which Beethoven desired that program to be publicly known. In the spring of 1809, the French army attacked Vienna, and Beethoven's friend, patron, and pupil Archduke Rudolph was forced to flee the city for many months. It is known that on May 21, 1809, Beethoven inscribed the words "On the departure of His Majesty the revered Archduke Rudolph" (originally in French) at the head of the score of his latest project, Op. 81a; but the first published edition of the sonata (1811) goes a step further, assigning to the sonata's three movements the titles "Les adieux," "l'absence," "et le retour" (the farewell, the absence, and the return), respectively. According to some, this assignment of a movement-by-movement program was at Beethoven's express directions; but other sources maintain that Beethoven was absolutely beside himself with fury that his publisher took such a liberty with his music. Whatever the case may be, there can be no doubt that *Les Adieux* is real and touching evidence of one friend's care for another, and it comes as no real surprise that the piece is far better known for its titles than for its superb music.

If the programmatic titles of the three movements are authentic, then it must be said that the idea of focusing the sorrow of farewell (the first movement, Adagio-Allegro) into an E flat major vessel is a brilliant one; for, against so warm a tonal background, the resigned falling chromaticisms introduced in the slow, 16-bar introduction and then taken up with a vengeance at the start of the symphonically-conceived Allegro pull the heartstrings far better and more believably than a melodramatic, minor-mode dirge could. The central movement is a slender Andante espressivo through the cracks of whose grim, dissonant C minor occasionally bursts a glimmer of brightness (the hope for reunion, or perhaps a warm memory, if one is following the program): twice a shimmering left-hand figuration provides the right hand with enough courage to come up with a lovely cantabile melody, first in G major, then later in F. A transition passage makes the way directly into the rousing third movement, Vivacissimamente. *—Blair Johnston*

Recommended:

- ○ **Hommage á Rachmaninov** / Pletnev / DG 459634
- ○ **Beethoven: Piano Sonatas Opp. 81a & 106** / Brendel / 1996 / Philips 446093
- ○ **Ivan Moravec, Beethoven: Sonatas Opp. 13, 27 No. 2, 90 & 81a** / Moravec / 2001 / Supraphon 3582
- ○ **Great Pianists of the 20th Century: Leopold Godowsky** / Godowsky / 1999 / Philips 456805

Piano Sonata No. 27 in E minor, Op. 90 (1814)

The *Piano Sonata No. 27 in E minor*, Op. 90 (1814) is one of Beethoven's shorter sonatas, but its relatively modest proportions belie an emotional complexity that looks forward to his imminent valedictory works in the genre. By this time Beethoven had begun to provide tempo indications in German rather than Italian, perhaps acknowledging that his music had come to represent an especially personal, Romantic form of expression. The composer had for a time considered titling this work "Struggle Between Head and Heart" or "Conversation with the Beloved," the latter alluding to a love affair between Count Moritz Lichnowsky, the sonata's dedicatee, and an opera singer he later married.

The first movement's marking, "Mit Lebhaftigkeit und durchaus mit Empfindung und Ausdruck," calls for "Vivacity and continuous sentiment and expressivity." It begins with powerful chords that could be a muscular updating of a Renaissance dance; these are answered by more subdued material. The music alternates between fast, impulsive gestures and gentle, bereft sighs, almost always in the minor mode. All this falls into two rather similar theme groups, each a mixture of emotions. Oddly, Beethoven bases the movement's curt development section on a tiny lyrical idea from the first group, building it into music restless and declamatory as that in the opening bars.

The count's future wife would seem to be a bad match, judging from the first movement, but with the Rondo the affair seems to have settled into naive, mutual submissiveness. Marked "Nicht zu geschwind und sehr singbar vorgetragen" (Not too fast, and highly songful), the music revolves around themes constructed from repeated notes, an idea echoed in the quite literal repetitions of the cantabile main subject. The music is not quite as simple as it seems; contrasting episodes introduce fleeting minor-mode shadows, and even some subtle polyphony. Unlike the count's marriage, the sonata ends peacefully. *—James Reel*

Recommended:

- ○ **Moonight Sonata; Sonata in e minor; Sonata in E Major** / Nagai / 1984 / Bis 281
- ○ **Beethoven: The Late Piano Sonatas** / W. Kempff / DG 453010
- ○ **Ivan Moravec Plays Beethoven** / Moravec / 1992 / VAI Audio 1021
- ○ **Alfred Brendel Plays Beethoven Piano Sonatas Vol. 1** / Brendel / 1991 / VoxBox 5028

Piano Sonata No. 28 in A major, Op. 101 (1816)

Beethoven's *Sonata No. 28* is a generally subdued work, like its immediate predecessor. Unlike that piece, however, it foreshadows the styles and trends of the future and, though sometimes overlooked, deserves the attention of pianists and listeners.

According to Schindler, who was not always a reliable source, Beethoven described the first movement of this sonata as containing "impressions and reveries." The latter word appears to fit the generally dreamy and peaceful mood of this movement. It is short and carries the description "Etwas lebhaft, und mit der innigsten Empfindung" (Somewhat lively, and with the most ardent perception). Obviously, the composer was hoping to draw the pianist's attention to the many subtleties of the piece. The work begins with a peaceful but hesitant theme (Allegretto ma non troppo), whose character suggests that there is a sense of insecurity even in moments of tranquillity. The melody also seems to augur the mellow and quirky side of Brahms' artistic persona. As the movement progresses, the theme varies, intensifying somewhat in the middle section, as well as suggesting a mood of sadness. Serenity returns towards the end of the movement, but now transformed and darker, as if reconciled to a tragic fate. The second movement, bearing the description "Lebhaft, marschmässig" (Lively, restrained march), clearly foreshadows the piano music of Schumann. The mood is joyful, but there are moments of both tranquility and tension in this Vivace alla marcia. It is as if the dual nature of the first movement is expanded here to show a wider gulf, greater extremes of feelings. Still, the movement's mood is predominantly high-spirited. The next movement, marked Adagio ma non troppo, con affetto, bears the description "Langsam und sehnsuchtvoll; (Slowly and longingly). The main theme is solemn and mournful, but remains serene and untroubled throughout the movement. The music seems a meditation on some past disappointment or loss, but never utters a cry, always sounding at peace, even if there is the suggestion of yearning. The finale begins without pause after the third movement. Marked Allegro, it proclaims joy at the outset with its all-conquering, chipper main theme. This movement carries the description "Geschwind, doch nicht zu sehr und mit Entschlossenheit" (Quickly, but not rushed and with determination). Yet, the subdued and reflective nature of most of the previous music emerges, too. It is as if the composer is rejoicing, but not too vigorously in the expectation that the next of life's inevitable vicissitudes might bring tragedy. The masterstroke here is the development: it contains a brilliant fugue, fitting well in this well-constructed sonata-form movement. There follow the usual reprise and coda to close this fine composition. While this work immediately preceded the famous and imposing *Piano Sonata No. 29* ("Hammerklavier") and was itself preceded by several better-known works, it is a masterpiece. *—Robert Cummings*

Recommended:

- ○ **Beethoven: Die späten Klaviersonaten** / Pollini / DG 449740
- ○ **Beethoven: The Late Sonatas** / Goode / 1988 / Nonesuch 79211
- ○ **Horowitz Complete Masterworks Recordings Vol. V: A Baroque & Classical Recital** / Horowitz / 1993 / Sony 53466
- ○ **Beethoven: Piano Sonatas 7, 14 Moonlight & 28** / Anda / 1996 / Testament 1070

Piano Sonata No. 29 in B flat major ("Hammerklavier") Op. 106 (1817–1818)

To English speakers, the term "Hammerklavier" suggests pounding at the keyboard. Beethoven's *"Hammerklavier" Sonata* may have its percussive moments, but this title is simply the German word for pianoforte. In other words, the composer was simply specifying that this work absolutely had to be played on the modern keyboard with hammered strings, and that the old plucked-string harpsichord was not an option. In fact, Beethoven's last five piano sonatas all had this designation, but it became the nickname only for the mighty Op. 106. The first movement, Allegro, bursts in with a heroic proclamation, a series of grand, double-dotted chords in the manner of a Baroque overture. Soon, light cascades of notes attempt a resolution into a pretty music-box figure before the opening chords are evoked again. Beethoven lays out his basic material for this large movement in just the first couple of minutes. Almost immediately he runs through it all again with greater harmonic displacement. What follows is a contrapuntal treatment of the opening theme, prefiguring the massive fugue that will end the sonata. Beethoven's further development of his subjects runs through episodes that are alternately sparkling and pounding, punctuated by an increasingly fearsome motto of those opening chords. Halfway through the recapitulation the harmonic framework melts, and the music lands in the distant key of B minor. The sonata requires another half-hour to recover from this jolt. The ensuing Scherzo is a miniature; starting with a hunting-call figure, it falls into a minor-mode whirlpool of a trio, the effect of which the A section can't quite shake off upon its return. The gargantuan slow movement, Adagio sostenuto, drifts through a haze of harmonic instability. Beethoven marks it Appassionato e con molto sentimento, requiring an intense emotional connection between the pianist and the score. The themes, as in many of Beethoven's late slow movements, suffer from smudged outlines; rather than following a tune, one has the impression of deep stillness, a few moments of flowing but aimless movement, stillness again, and so forth. Beethoven carefully alternates fuller-sounding sections with passages marked una corda, indicating the use of the soft pedal to produce shadowy, distant musical scenes. Although the movement is officially in F sharp minor, the music wanders through the keys, placing the subsidiary idea in D major. This is the key Beethoven generally reserved for religious sentiment, and here it implies the possibility of spiritual enlightenment even in the most confusing circumstances. The last movement grows out of a Largo, a gradual return to life that slowly pulls fragmentary phrases together before erupting into a dramatic three-voice fugue. Earlier generations of pianists dismissed the fugue as unplayable (not just because of the tempo), but that is clearly an unfair assessment. True, the counterpoint is exceedingly complex, but Beethoven's mastery of the texture is supreme. At times, the music is dense and angry, even threatening (twice) to dissolve into wrathful trills. Uneven, the forward motion thins out and slightly relaxes, without, however, really flagging. When the fugue suddenly turns into a quiet, meditative canon, the contrast is tremendous. Nevertheless, it regains the original momentum, and the movement concludes with an imposing series of grand, resounding chords.*—James Reel*

Recommended:

- ○ **Richter, Beethoven: Sonatas 29 & 3; Bagatelles Op 126** / S. Richter / 2000 / BBC Legends 4052
- ○ **Beethoven: Die späten Klaviersonaten** / Pollini / DG 449740
- ○ **Beethoven: The Late Piano Sonatas** / Brendel / 1993 / Philips 438374

Piano Sonata No. 30 in E major, Op. 109 (1820)

By the time Beethoven composed this work, his output had declined substantially, perhaps owing to his deafness and disappointments in life. The only complete works to emerge from the period of 1820–23 were the last three piano sonatas, the *Missa Solemnis* and the *Ninth Symphony.* Even when compared to these imposing works, the *E major Piano Sonata* retains its status of a masterpiece. It is a remarkable work in several respects. The first movement has a nearly unique structure: it opens with theme marked Vivace ma non troppo that almost immediately slows to an Adagio espressivo. Thereafter, the two contrasting tempos and utterances alternate. Scarlatti and Mozart had used such a scheme before, but never in such a bold and innovative fashion. On the surface, this short movement has a serene, almost angelic quality, but, like many other works written during this period, the composition's surface is merely one dimension among many. Indeed, nothing about this sonata is one-dimensional. Thus, for example, the subdued, brightly lit realm suggested by the beginning of the works eventually leads the listener to sections where the narrative slows down, conjuring up dark shadows which intimate feelings of longing and doubt. The second movement, given its sonata form structure would be typical of a Beethoven first movement if it were not for its terse development and extreme brevity. There are two subject groups in this Prestissimo, with the first led by an assertive theme that more than vaguely suggests Schumann's piano style. More subdued at the outset, the second subject generates tension and energy as it progresses. Following a brief development, an interesting reprise leads to a concise coda. The finale is twice as long as the previous two movements put together. It is a theme-and-variations scheme, whose main theme is marked Andante molto cantabile ed espressivo. The melody is beautiful, in style looking toward the Romantic movement that was then in its infancy. It is tranquil yet melancholy, pleased but valedictory. Some of the six variations generate further variations either through development (the third variation), or as a result of a two-tiered layout (the second variation). While the finale contains many lively moments, it is predominantly slow-to-moderate in tempo and generally subdued, gaining in confidence as the narrative proceeds. This movement concludes with the main theme played slowly and serenely. While the ending suggests a certain peaceful resolution of life's struggles and conflicts, it also reveals a feeling of resignation which is free of conflict and fear. *—Robert Cummings*

Recommended:

- ○ **Moonlight: Beethoven Sonatas "Quasi una Fantasia"** / Pires / 2001 / DG 453457
- ○ **Beethoven: Piano Sonatas 21, 23, 30 & 31** / Gieseking / 2001 / EMI 67586
- ○ **Beethoven: Pianos Sonatas 8, 14, 23 & 30** / R. Serkin / 2003 / Sony 512868
- ○ **Great Pianists of the 20th Century: Artur Schnabel** / A. Schnabel / 1998 / Philips 456961

Piano Sonata No. 31 in A flat major, Op. 110 (1821–1822)

Beethoven's piano sonatas grew in complexity and depth as the cycle of 32 progressed. The last dozen or so could be called absolute masterpieces of piano music, with the latter half of that group rising to a level that often inspires awe and wonderment. This work, though sometimes overshadowed by the mighty *"Hammerklavier" Sonata,* and the last, the C minor, Op. 111, seems quite as impressive as these better-known works. This unusual work, thematically threadbare at the outset, is a great and deeply profound composition, whose fugal finale achieves the highest keyboard art. This composition opens with a gentle, slow idea of strong spiritual character, the music sounding mesmeric, tranquil, chorale-like, intimate. Its fabric consists of many threads, but on the surface there is little of actual substance, at least from the standpoint of musical analysis. Yet this lovely but seemingly unpromising opening contains the seeds of this movement's rich thematic and harmonic material. The latter half of the first subject is borrowed from the Largo second movement of Haydn's *Symphony No. 88,* in G major. At the time

Beethoven was writing this Sonata, he was suffering the first bouts of the illness that would take his life six years later. The serene, rather valedictory mood of the first movement (Moderato cantabile, molto espressivo) may reflect his sense of mortality, of an impending doom. The second subject is lively, but in all its elements seems to be on the descent, expressing, perhaps the end of a journey. The development introduces some tension and subtly disrupts the serenity, without, however, essentially altering the general mood of tranquility.

The second movement (Allegro molto) is short and jovial. Or is it? It certainly starts off with a happy demeanor, but that temperament is periodically interrupted by a ponderous ritardando, which finally overtakes the direction and character of the piece. The third movement, marked Adagio ma non troppo, is somber, bordering on the funereal. This ponderous, dark music may reflect the composer's deepest doubts and disappointments. The finale begins without pause after the Adagio. Its theme, almost Bach-like in its contentedness and fugal character, sounds serene, expressing, perhaps, the composer's acceptance of his fate. This is a movement of great subtlety and beauty, and its structure is masterful and original. The middle section is quiet and dark, its mood looking back to the darkness of the Adagio. Suddenly the piano unleashes ten fateful chords in a slow crescendo. The main theme then reappears and struggles for a time with the dominant mood of darkness. Eventually it gains strength, transforming the movement into a triumphant, ecstatic, radiant utterance. *—Robert Cummings*

Recommended:

- ○ **Beethoven: Piano Sonatas Opp. 109, 110, 11** / F. Kempff / 2000 / Bis 1120
- ○ **Beethoven: The Final Piano Sonatas** / Kuerti / Analekta 23182
- ○ **Beethoven: The Last Three Piano Sonatas** / Kinderman / 2002 / Helios 55083
- ○ **Great Pianists of the 20th Century: Myra Hess** / Hess / 1999 / Philips 456832

Piano Sonata No. 32 in C minor, Op. 111 (1821–1822)

Without doubt, this is one of the greatest piano sonatas ever written. While there are quite a few of Beethoven's own that are more popular, perhaps only one or two of them rival this one in sheer profundity. This Sonata's stormy first movement and its ensuing lengthy Arietta, which comprises the theme-and-variations second panel, take the listener into sound-worlds previously unexplored by other composers, making this work one of the most influential musical creations ever. Not only did it help shape the course of piano music, it influenced the orchestral compositions of Franck, Wagner, Mahler, and many others. Prokofiev modeled the structure of his *Symphony No. 2* directly on the sonata—an Allegro followed by a long theme-and-variations second movement. The sonata begins with a grim introduction (Maestoso), typical of the composer's serious style, because it starts the narrative with a question, or dilemma, with dark, emphatic chords followed by trills, which introduce an added element of uncertainty. One might wonder whether the remainder of the movement will search out some answer to the apparent question, as in the *"Pathétique,"* but that does not happen. It seems that a lack of a resolution reflects the composer's realization that vicissitudes of life may inspire questions which cannot be answered. The main body of the first movement, marked Allegro con brio ed appassionato, begins in a sinister vein on the bass notes with the appearance of the main theme, itself a dark, hesitant creation. After it is presented in full, the tempo slows, ushering in another idea. Tranquil and reassuring, this new idea is short-lived, and the main theme returns. After the narrative is repeated, with some alterations, the development section begins. Here, in the midst of much brilliant contrapuntal writing, the mood darkens, and an element of dramatic tension is introduced as the main theme goes through several transformations. When the alternate theme appears after a climactic episode, the atmosphere changes from somber to mysterious. There is no reprise as such, since the main material is not repeated, but rather is reviewed in partial form before reaching a final climax, after which the music fades slowly.

The second movement (Adagio molto semplice e cantabile) opens with one of the composer's most serene creations in any genre. The theme sounds peaceful and angelic, but almost static, too, in its glacial pacing. It strikes one as not the kind of melody that might yield variations of sundry character. This theme and the first three variations form the first section of the movement, wherein the atmosphere and character of the music change from the sublime to the almost giddily joyous and back to the sublime. It is the fourth variation that marks the second half of the movement, the most profound music in this work. After a series of trills, this section begins with the variation slowly emerging from a haze and transporting the listener to the highest levels of musical experience. Some view this long closing section as a "farewell" by the composer. Indeed, Beethoven seems to fashion a musical language transcending terrestrial constraints, and the notes appear to be ascending into the heavens as the ending approaches. *—Robert Cummings*

Recommended:

- ○ **Glenn Gould Edition: Beethoven Piano Sonatas Vol. II** / G. Gould / 1994 / Sony 52642
- ○ **Great Pianists of the 20th Century: Alfred Brendel II** / Brendel / 1999 / Philips 456730
- ○ **Beethoven: Die Späten Klaviersonaten** / Pollini / DG 449740
- ○ **Great Pianists of the 20th Century: Sviatoslav Richter II** / S. Richter / 1998 / Philips 456949
- ○ **Egon Petri: His Recordings 1939–1942** / E. Petri / 1993 / APR 7024

Rondo a Capriccio in G major ("Rage Over a Lost Penny"), Op. 129 (1795–1798)

Though Beethoven's *Rondo a capriccio in G major,* Op. 129 is today a recital favorite, it was apparently unknown in the composer's own lifetime. Indeed, the incomplete manuscript, dating to 1795, came to light only at an auction of Beethoven's personal effects following his death in 1827. The work was first published in 1828 by Beethoven's colleague, the publisher Anton Diabelli, today best remembered for his association with Beethoven's monumental set of *33 Variations,* Op. 120. It has been suggested that Diabelli himself completed the Rondo, although the original edition gives no indication that the work was incomplete and had been significantly rearranged. The manuscript disappeared for many years and was considered lost until it turned up in the United States just after World War II. From the original manuscript, musicologist Erich Hertzmann prepared a new edition, published in 1949.

The title on Beethoven's manuscript of the work is "Alla ingharese quasi un capriccio"; the familiar subtitle "Rage over a Lost Penny" was later added by Anton Schindler. Marked Allegro vivace and in 2/4, the Rondo a capriccio combines a familiar rondo scheme with Beethoven's singular variation technique. The Rondo theme itself has two parts, each consisting of an eight-measure antecedent-consequent phrase. The statements of this darting, quicksilver theme are separated by episodes that are just as frenetic. In one of the Rondo's most distinct features, each return of the main theme is different from its initial presentation. Such alterations range from graceful ornamentation of the melodic line to changes of mode from major to minor. During one statement, the tune appears in the left hand, while in the lengthy coda, Beethoven's treatment of the material becomes conspicuously developmental. It is possibly this departure from a more conventional conception of the rondo that led Beethoven to use the expression "quasi un capriccio" (like a fantasy). *—John Palmer*

Recommended:

- ○ **Complete Beethoven Edition Vol. 3** / W. Kempff / DG 453700
- ○ **Beethoven: Bagatelles & Dances Vol. 3** / Jandó / 2001 / Naxos 553799

Variations in F major on an original theme, Op. 34 (1802)

The *Variations in F Major,* Op. 34, were dedicated to Princess Barbara Odescalchi, one of Beethoven's pupils and a very capable pianist. The set was begun in May, 1802, at about the same time Beethoven started work on the *Variations in E flat,* Op. 35. Both sets of variations were offered to Breitkopf & Härtel in October 1802.

The *Variations,* Op. 34, were innovative in that each of the six variations is in a different key. Beethoven directed his publisher to point out this novelty in the printed edition of the work. Furthermore, the fact that he gave the work an opus number attests to Beethoven's belief in the importance of the piece, in part because the theme was original. Overall, the set is an excellent example of the "improvisatory" side of Beethoven's variation technique. However, this characteristic of the piece does not necessarily indicate that variations are "written-out" improvisations, as opposed to compositionally "worked-out" ideas.

Beethoven's theme exhibits the typical Classical-era rounded (ABA') structure, although the central, contrasting melody is only six measures in length. The simple theme is in Beethoven's best "singing" style, marked cantabile and with an overall arch; turns and trills add a light, Mozartean delicacy to a relaxed atmosphere. Relaxation ceases at the beginning of the first variation, in D major (distant from F major). Beethoven seems to fill spaces in the original theme with as many notes as possible in this highly decorative variation. The central part of the theme is extended before the return of the first theme. A change of tempo signals the arrival of the second variation, set in B flat (much closer to F major) and 6/8 meter. Beethoven hacks the tune into pieces, placing one part in a low register and having the next skyrocket into a much higher register. Rapid movement is juxtaposed with nearly motionless chords as Beethoven, oddly, chooses to repeat the "B" and "A'" segments of the theme as a unit. The constant eighth note motion of the third variation thinly disguises the shape of the theme, now set in G major. A shift to E flat major brings with it the fourth variation and its more easily recognizable rendition of the theme, despite the triple meter. The central part of the theme appears simultaneously in octaves in the right hand and in fragments in the left. The key (C minor) and march tempo of the fifth variation look forward to the soon-to-be-composed second movement of the *Third Symphony.* At the end of this variation Beethoven moves from C minor to C major, creating the dominant of F major and preparing the way for the sixth and final variation. Beethoven's coda returns to the original Adagio tempo, the virtuosic writing enhancing his developmental presentation of the stepwise motion from the first two measures of the theme. The last few measures feature a return of the theme. *—John Palmer*

Recommended:

○ **Beethoven: Eroica-Variations** / Jandó / 1992 / Naxos 550676

○ **Sviatoslav Richter Vol. 9** / S. Richter / Olympia 339

CHAMBER MUSIC

Cello Sonata No. 3 in A major, Op. 69 (1807–1808)

Completed in 1808, the same year as his Fifth and Sixth Symphonies, Beethoven's *Cello Sonata No. 3 in A Major*, Op. 69 bears the heading *Inter Lacrimas et Luctum*, (Amid Tears and Sorrow). While this richly melodic work does not immediately strike the listener as doleful, there is some melancholy behind its reflective lyricism. True, the first movement, Allegro ma non tanto, is darkly shaded, but for the most part it is characterized by the pensive, cantilena melody that the cello introduces in the beginning. This theme veers into a more aggressive episode, then makes way for the second subject, which is also in two parts. Again, the first is highly lyrical while the second surges forward energetically. The development section breaks these themes into their component parts and gives each a brief elaboration, alternating the contentious material with the more reflective passages, often in the lower registers of the instruments. The recapitulation allows all the basic material to reappear without incident.

The Scherzo, marked Allegro molto, finds the two instruments trading fragments of a syncopated melody, lurching from A minor to E minor and C major until tripping into a more songlike trio section featuring arresting dynamic contrasts and a bass drone. This whole structure is repeated, with the final appearance of the scherzo proper sneaking away on cello pizzicati.

The Adagio cantabile is technically only the introduction to the last movement, but it could almost stand alone on its 18 bars of gentle lyricism for the cello. An Allegro vivace breaks in; it's a sonata-form movement, with the first subject a happy whirl and the second a reminiscence of the cantabile material from the first movement. The development provides a virtuosic workout for both instruments, especially the piano, but the gentler coda ends the sonata on a note of noble jubilation. *—James Reel*

Recommended:

○ **Beethoven: Complete Music for Cello & Piano** / Rostropovich, S. Richter / 1994 / Philips 442565

○ **Beethoven: Complete Sonatas for Pianoforte & Violoncello** / Bylsma, van Immerseel / 1999 / Sony 60761

○ **Complete Beethoven Edition Vol. 8: Cello Sonatas** / Maisky, Argerich / DG 453748

Cello Sonata No. 4 in C major, Op. 102/1 (1815)

Beethoven's composition of sonatas for cello and piano was unprecedented; he had no models in the works of Haydn or Mozart. Only recently had the instrument begun to liberate itself from its role in the traditional basso continuo. Also, Beethoven was the first to completely write out the keyboard parts for large-scale cello and keyboard works.

Large temporal gaps appear in Beethoven's composition of sonatas for cello and piano. The first two, Op. 5, were composed in 1796, while Beethoven was in Berlin. He would not embark on another such project until 1807, when he composed the *Sonata*, Op. 69. Eight years later he would return to the idiom to write a pair of sonatas that appeared as Op. 102.

Published in March 1817 by Simrock in Bonn, the *Sonatas for Cello and Piano*, Op. 102, were dedicated to the Countess Marie von Erdödy (1779–1837), although only in a later, Vienna publication. The Countess had been friends with the composer since about 1803. Beethoven actually lived with her and her husband, Count Peter Erdödy, for a time in 1808. The Countess, who after leaving Vienna in 1815 continued to correspond with Beethoven, also received the dedication of the Trios, Op. 70. During the last year of the Erdödys' residence in Vienna, they spent the summer at Jedlersee with Beethoven. Because Count Rasumovsky's palace had burned down earlier in the year, his resident cellist, Joseph Linke, also spent the summer at Jedlersee with the Erdödy family. Beethoven's close contact with the cellist provided the inspiration for the composition of the Op. 102 cello sonatas.

The sonatas of Op. 102 developed during the period of Beethoven's withdrawal from society, perhaps explaining the intimacy of the works. His self-imposed distance from his fellow Viennese was probably in large part due to an increasing deterioration in his hearing—the Conversation Books date from 1818 onward. The overall construction of each of the sonatas reveals Beethoven's continuing quest to create a fluid, "total sonata" that was more than a sum of its movements.

In his autograph score, Beethoven referred to Op. 102, No. 2 as a "free" sonata. It is easy to understand why Beethoven used such a term. The work is in two fast movements, each with a slow, introductory segment. As in the *"Waldstein" piano sonata*, Op. 53, the slow introduction to the finale acts somewhat like an intermezzo, replacing a proper slow movement. A reminiscence of the slow introduction to the first movement before the finale also occurs, as also occurs in the *Piano Sonata No. 28*, Op. 101. Although Op. 102, No. 2 ends in C major, the first movement is in A minor, the relative minor of C major. In an unusual move, Beethoven moves from the tonic in the first-movement slow introduction to the relative minor for the remainder of the movement, effectively creating a huge deceptive cadence that dominates the proceedings until the finale. Beethoven used similar plans in his *Piano Quartets*, WoO. 36, of 1785. *—John Palmer*

Recommended:

○ **Beethoven: The Cello Sonatas** / Harrell, Vladimir Ashkenazy / 2000 / Decca 466733

○ **Beethoven: Music for Cello & Piano** / Fournier, W. Kempff / DG 453013

○ **Beethoven: Complete Music for Cello & Piano** / Rostropovich, S. Richter / 1994 / Philips 442565

Cello Sonata No. 5 in D major, Op. 102/2 (1815)

Beethoven's composition of sonatas for cello and piano was unprecedented; he had no models in the works of Haydn or Mozart. Only recently had the instrument begun to liberate itself from its role in the traditional basso continuo. Also, Beethoven was the first to completely write out the keyboard parts for large-scale cello and keyboard works.

Large temporal gaps appear in Beethoven's composition of sonatas for cello and piano. The first two, Op. 5, were composed in 1796, while Beethoven was in Berlin. He would not embark on another such project until 1807, when he composed the *Sonata*, Op. 69. Eight years later he would return to the idiom to write a pair of sonatas that appeared as Op. 102.

Published in March 1817 by Simrock in Bonn, the *Sonatas for Cello and Piano*, Op. 102, were dedicated to the Countess Marie von Erdödy (1779–1837), although only in a later, Vienna publication. The Countess had been friends with the composer since about 1803. Beethoven actually lived with her and her husband, Count Peter Erdödy, for a time in 1808. The Countess, who after leaving Vienna in 1815 continued to correspond with Beethoven, also received the dedication of the Trios, Op. 70. During the last year of the Erdödys' residence in Vienna, they spent the summer at Jedlersee with Beethoven. Because Count Rasumovsky's palace had burned down earlier in the year, his resident cellist, Joseph Linke, also spent the summer at Jedlersee with the Erdödy family. Beethoven's close contact with the cellist provided the inspiration for the composition of the Op. 102 cello sonatas. The sonatas of Op. 102 developed during the period of Beethoven's withdrawal from society, perhaps explaining the intimacy of the works. His self-imposed distance from his fellow Viennese was probably in large part due to an increasing deterioration in his hearing—the Conversation Books date from 1818 onward.

The final work written by the composer for solo instrument and piano, Beethoven's *Sonata for cello and piano No. 5* traverses the terrain covered by the composer in his late string quartets. The overall construction of the sonata, Op. 102 No. 2, reveals Beethoven's continuing quest to create a fluid, "total sonata," that was more than a sum of its movements. Except for Bach's solo suites, this sonata is regarded as the most technically and spiritually taxing major work for cello before the twentieth century.

Opening without a slow introduction, the first movement of Op. 102, No. 2, marked Allegro con brio, is a diminutive sonata-form structure with a harmonically adventurous development section and a modified recapitulation. Unlike all other of Beethoven's cello sonatas, No. 2 contains a fully-fledged slow movement. Nevertheless, it is joined to the finale through a harmonic device: the final chord of the Adagio is a dominant seventh chord that tends to resolve toward the tonic; the finale, in D major, begins immediately. The most interesting feature of the sonata is the fugue in the last movement. Its harsh-sounding, relentless counterpoint looks ahead to the *"Hammerklavier" sonata* and the *Grosse Fuge*. The subject of the cello sonata fugue is obviously derived from Baroque models; this is especially evident in the large leap downward from B natural to C sharp. The return of first-movement themes in the finale seems to function more as reminiscence than as recapitulation. *—John Palmer*

Recommended:

○ **Beethoven: Complete Cello Sonatas** / Casals, R. Serkin / Sony 58985

○ **Beethoven: Music for Cello & Piano** / Fournier, W. Kempff / DG 453013

○ **Beethoven: Complete Music for Cello & Piano** / Rostropovich, S. Richter / 1994 / Philips 442565

Fugue for string quartet in B flat major ("Grosse Fuge"), Op. 133 (1825)

Beethoven's *Grosse Fuge* was originally to have served as the finale to the *String Quartet No. 13 in B flat major*, Op. 130 (1825); in fact, that work was first performed with this monumental creation as its sixth and concluding movement. However, the *Grosse Fuge*, a complete entity in its own right, proved too difficult for the performers and for some members of the audience. Moreover, it seemed an outsized finale for the relatively modest quartet. Beethoven subsequently produced a new final movement for the quartet, an attractive Rondo more in keeping with the spirit of the entire work.

The *Grosse Fuge*, eventually published as an independent work, is one of Beethoven's crowning achievements in the medium of chamber music. The work opens with an introduction, or "overtura." Here the mood is dramatic, effectively setting the stage for the whole work. The main theme—heroic and defiant, powerful and self-confident—is presented in four different versions. First, it is played fortissimo, in an emphatic, assertive manner, which will reemerge as its definitive guise in the coda. The subsequent accounts of the theme gradually become calmer and quieter.

The first fugal section is a double fugue marked Allegro. Here the main theme competes against another subject, which is also fiery and assertive. Their struggle, which includes substantial development, continues fortissimo. The second section, marked Meno mosso e moderato, is also a double fugue, its lyricism providing effective contrast to its predecessor. Here a new theme emerges from the counterpoint of the main melody. The third section, marked Allegro molto e con brio, features further struggle in which the theme eventually falters and seems to disintegrate. The second subject from the first fugal section emerges and appears to take control. Eventually, the main theme is rejuvenated in a passage marked Meno mosso moderato, and the signs of struggle fade in the two Allegro subsections that follow. The coda features the main theme in its original version, but now expanded and clearly triumphant. The mood turns reflective and mysterious, and suddenly the second subject appears, supported by the main theme. The work ends powerfully and magnificently. *—Robert Cummings*

Recommended:

○ **Beethoven: Les Quatuors 7** / Quatour Végh / Valois 4407

○ **Beethoven: Complete String Quartets** / Alban Berg Quartet / 1997 / EMI 66408

○ **Beethoven: Complete String Quartets** / Vegh Quartet / 2000 / Naive 4871

Kakadu Variations for piano trio in G major, Op. 121a (1803)

Beethoven's Piano Trio, Op. 121a, is a set of variations on "Ich bin der Schneider Kakadu," from *Die Schwestern von Prag*, a singspiel by Wenzel Müller (1767–1835) that premièred in Vienna in 1794. The variations were probably composed in 1803, and may have been offered for publication at that time. Evidently, they were offered to Breitkopf & Härtel in 1816 and rejected, nonetheless eventually printed in May 1824 by both Steiner in Vienna and Chappell in London, incorporating Beethoven's revisions of 1816–1817. Steiner's print carries simply "Op. 121." A year later Schott published the *Opferlied* with the same opus number, requiring later publishers to append an "a" to the Trio and "b" to the *Opferlied*. It seems difficult to believe that Beethoven's *Kakadu variations* were composed in the same year as the "*Waldstein*" *Sonata*, Op. 53. The variations show none of the harmonic exploration or motivic manipulation characteristic of the sonata, and are quite conventional. This is most certainly because he wrote the piece hoping it would sell widely, which is why he chose a popular theme. He did, however, give the work an opus number.

The Adagio introduction begins in G minor with a unison descending figure. A new motive appears when the repeated chords begin in the piano, after which Beethoven touches on B flat major, but does not commit, preferring to head back to G minor. The opening and secondary motives mingle as the dynamic level grows, stopping on the dominant of G minor/major. Müller's theme perfectly fits traditional Classical-era proportions. In two parts, the first tune consists of two four-measure segments that each carry an arching melody, while the second part contains two eight-measure sections. Variation No. 1 is entirely the property of the piano. Beethoven closely follows the original patterns of repetition and harmony, except for the addition of a dominant chord at the very end of the fourth measure—a subtle change that appears in every variation but the third, ninth and tenth. Marked leggiermente (light, nimble), the second variation proceeds without cello, the rapid violin part moving in triplets over the duple rhythm of the piano part. The cello takes center stage in the third variation, maintaining the basic shape of the theme but none of its details, while triplets return in the piano part of variation No. 4, in which the theme is easily recognizable. In contrast to the previous variation, the violin and cello dominate the fifth variation, the piano occasionally decorating and doubling. The melodic material here actually sounds more like that of the introduction than the theme. Flashy octaves in the piano obscure the theme in variation No. 6, while the more delicate seventh variation gives the pianist a rest. Syncopated lines characterize the eighth variation, as segments of the theme are traded between the strings and piano. Finally, Beethoven changes key, somewhat, setting the ninth variation in G minor, the key of the introduction, and emphasizing the relationship between the two sections by marking the variation "Adagio." The slow tempo allows this to be the most decorated variation of the set. The major mode returns in variation No. 10, in 6/8 meter. The coda consists of two more variations, the first of which revisits G minor; the second returns to both G major and 2/4 meter. *—John Palmer*

Recommended:

○ **Issac Stern Collection: Trio Recordings Vol. 2** / I. Stern, L. Rose, Istomin / 1990 / Sony 46738

○ **Beethoven: The Complete Cycle of Trios Vol. 1** / Kalichstein-Laredo-Robinson Trio / 2003 / Arabesque 6758

○ **Complete Beethoven Edition Vol. 9** / Fournier, W. Kempff, Szeryng / DG 453751

○ **Great Chamber Music Recordings: Thibaud, Casals & Cortot** / Thibaud, Casals, Cortot / 2002 / Naxos 8110188

Piano Trio in E flat major, Op. 1/1 (1794–1795)

While some members of the nobility kept full orchestras or opera companies on their estates, most were content with (or could afford only) much smaller ensembles. Prince Karl von Lichnowsky was among the latter, maintaining a string quartet to perform in his home. At one of Lichnowsky's weekly soirées Beethoven's three piano trios later published as Op. 1 received their first performance. The Op. 1 *Trios* were composed in 1794–95, although Douglas Johnson has shown that the first of the set may have been written in Bonn and then revised in 1793. In May 1795 Beethoven negotiated a contract with Artaria to have the trios published in Vienna and dedicated to Prince Lichnowsky, who secretly subsidized the printing. These were the first works to which Beethoven gave an opus number. Evidently, Beethoven planned to make the trios popular among connoisseurs through performances before publication in order to increase sales. This strategy worked, for advertisements attracted 123 subscribers, who requested 241 scores.

The *Trios*, Op. 1, reveal Beethoven's complete assimilation of the high-Classic style, as well as his use of the style in a very personal manner. Beethoven's later, masterful manipulation of the tonal system is already evident in his *Trio in E flat major*. A brief hint of A flat major in the opening measures of the first movement anticipates the importance of that key in the development. Motives from the first theme group dominate the development, which runs headlong into a recapitulation that truncates the first and second themes but extends and develops the closing material. The writing for cello in this movement does not represent a major break from tradition, for it generally parallels the piano bass part. Only a few measures of "development" separate the exposition and recapitulation of the second movement, marked Adagio cantabile and in A flat major. The recapitulation does not present the exposition themes in their original forms, but ornamentally varied. The scherzo falls into the traditional pattern of repetition found in the classical-era minuet and trio. However, Beethoven greatly expands the second part of the scherzo section, basing his material on motives from the first section. The trio section is in A flat major, a key that permeates the entire piece. The leap of a tenth, from G to B flat, that opens the finale is reminiscent of the arpeggio rising to the same B flat at the beginning of the first movement. Marked Presto, the finale is set in sonata form, and the first theme is divided between piano and violin, the leaps and falling arpeggios of the former contrasting with the stepwise motion of the latter. The second theme, on the dominant, also begins with a falling arpeggio, while a frenetic closing section wraps up the exposition. Opening with the first theme, the development section passes through several keys, gradually growing quieter until coming to rest on a sustained dominant-seventh chord. Beethoven differentiates the recapitulation from the exposition by developing the second theme and by again emphasizing A flat major. *—John Palmer*

Recommended:

○ **Beethoven: Piano Trios Op 1; Piano Trio WoO 38; 14 Variations Op 44** / Stern, Rose, Istomin / 1995 / Sony 64510

○ **Casals Edition: Schubert, Beethoven** / Casals, Istomin, J. Fuchs / 1993 / Sony 58988

○ **Beethoven: The Piano Trios** / Beaux Arts Trio / 2001 / Philips 468411

○ **Beethoven: Ten Trios for Piano, Violin & Cello** / Borodin Trio / 1987 / Chandos 8352/3/4/5

Piano Trio in G major, Op. 1/2 (1794–1795)

Some critics have noted "symphonic ambitions" in the three trios of Beethoven's Op. 1, citing their uncharacteristic four-movement format. As do many of Haydn's symphonies, the second *Trio in G major* opens with a slow introduction. An Allegro tempo marks the beginning of the sonata form proper, and soon is heard evidence of Beethoven's early predilection for lengthy transitions. The second theme is on the dominant, and references to the first theme close the exposition. Brief ventures into flat-key areas characterize the development, while the recapitulation begins an octave higher than expected, and Beethoven includes some new transitional material.

In the E major second movement Beethoven employs tonal procedures similar to those he would use in his late works. After the first theme appears in the piano and violin, a modulation ushers in the second theme, played in the piano on the dominant. A second modulation prepares the closing theme, an arpeggiated figure on G major, a third above the tonic. The recapitulation of both the first and second themes is on the tonic; however, an unexpected modulation moves to C major for the closing theme, now a third below the tonic, achieving a kind of tonal balance we find in many of the late quartets and piano sonatas.

The G major scherzo is a lively movement that bears Beethoven's stamp particularly in the use of the same motivic material in both parts of the scherzo section while still producing an easily recognizable formal structure. Harmonically, the trio rocks back and forth between D major and B minor.

One of the most peculiar aspects of the Presto finale is its extended transition, which spends an almost unbearable amount of time on the dominant of the dominant. The development section is a tour de force of motivic manipulation that Beethoven would not surpass until his *String Quartet*, Op. 18, No. 1. The recapitulation begins surreptitiously as the violin states the opening theme over a piano figure that continues from the development. *—John Palmer*

Recommended:

- ○ **Beethoven: Piano Trios Op 1; Piano Trio WoO 38; 14 Variations Op 44** / I. Stern, L. Rose, Istomin / 1995 / Sony 64510
- ○ **Beethoven: Complete Piano Trios Vol. 1** / Trio Parnassus / 2001 / MDG 3031051
- ○ **Beethoven: The Piano Trios** / Beaux Arts Trio / 2001 / Philips 468411

Piano Trio in C minor, Op. 1/3 (1794–1795)

Legend has it that Haydn was present at one of Lichnowsky's weekly soirées when Beethoven's three piano trios, later published as Op. 1, received their first performance supposedly in late 1793, and he praised all three works highly, although he recommended against the publication of the final one, the *Trio in C Minor*. Recent scholarship shows clearly that Haydn must have heard the pieces upon his return from London in August 1795, after they had been published.

The *Trios*, Op. 1, reveal Beethoven's complete assimilation of the high Classical style. Some critics have heard "symphonic ambitions" in the three trios, especially in the slow introduction to *No. 2* and the uncharacteristic four-movement format of all three. Haydn's *Symphony No. 95 in C Minor* may have influenced Beethoven's composition of Op. 1, *No. 3*, also in C minor. Still considered the finest of the three Op. 1 trios, the C minor exhibits writing on a grand scale with tightly controlled, long-range tonal implications and generation of forward momentum, especially in the first movement. The trio seems to be the first evidence of Beethoven's predilection for writing dramatic, tempestuous works in C minor. We also find Beethoven creating links between movements. In both the first and last movements of the C minor there is an emphasis on the interval C-E flat.

In the slow movement Beethoven begins to distance himself from the superficial variation technique of the Classical style and work toward more complex principles. In variation III, for example, rapid scales and melodic fragments maintain the harmonic contour of the theme, but the theme itself is unrecognizable. Beethoven retains the traditional repetitions of an eight-measure, antecedent-consequent theme, as well as the obligatory minor-key variation, in this case, variation IV.

Unlike the third movements of the E flat and G major trios, that of the C minor trio is labeled Menuetto, not Scherzo. Similar to the E flat and G major trios, however, is the construction of the second part of the minuet from material of the first part. The trio section is in C major, anticipating a key relationship that would appear in the Scherzo of the *Fifth Symphony*. The first theme of the finale is built on the interval of a minor third; this theme eventually becomes accompaniment to the leaping second theme—a technique borrowed from Haydn. *—John Palmer*

Recommended:

- ○ **Beethoven: Complete Music for Piano Trio Vol. 4** / Florestan Trio / 2004 / Hyperion 67466
- ○ **Beethoven: 10 Trios for Piano, Violin and Cello** / Borodin Trio / 1987 / Chandos 8352
- ○ **Beethoven: The Piano Trios** / Beaux Arts Trio / 2001 / Philips 468411
- ○ **Beethoven: Trios** / Coin, Cohen, Hobarth / HM 7901475
- ○ **Beethoven: Piano Trios Op 1; Piano Trio WoO 38; 14 Variations Op 44** / Stern, Rose, Istomin / 1995 / Sony 64510

Piano Trio in D major ("Ghost") Op. 70/1 (1808)

The two piano trios of Ludwig van Beethoven's Opus 70 were both composed in 1808 during the composer's stay at the house of the Countess Marie von Erdödy; out of gratitude for her hospitality, he dedicated both works to her. The Op. 70 trios inaugurated a period during which Beethoven wrote a great deal of chamber music both dense and wonderfully intimate. The *Piano Trio No. 5 in D major*, Op. 70, No. 1, has three movements, an old-fashioned scheme that Beethoven endows with new concision. Because of its strangely scored and undeniably eerie-sounding slow movement it was dubbed the *"Ghost" Trio*. The name has stuck with the work ever since. The ghostly music may have had its roots in sketches for a *Macbeth* opera that Beethoven was contemplating at the time.

But one mustn't listen for ghosts in the other two movements—they positively sparkle with life, from the wonderfully boisterous metric obfuscation that opens the Allegro vivace e con brio first movement (the movement is in 3/4 time, but in the first few measures the eighth notes, after a single group of three, are grouped in fours), through the swinging scales that underscore that same movement's second theme, and finally to the humorous, scampering Presto finale and its occasional comic fermatas. And yes, one should chuckle as the pianist, violinist, and cellist try desperately not to step on each other's toes when, near the close of both the exposition and the recapitulation of the finale, the piano takes off with a rapid-fire little right-hand cadenza that moves to a completely ridiculous key and the strings have no choice but to help the piano find its way back by spinning out a chromatically ascending sequence in octaves that does manage to arrive at the proper key but, unfortunately, manages to get the downbeats all out of sync!

More serious structural thinking is on display as well—consider the elaborate modulation from tonic to dominant in the first movement's exposition, forecast by a quick shading, as in the *Symphony No. 3*, within moments of the beginning of the piece. The harmonic scheme of the work as a whole is elaborate, with references and interconnections between movements. As much as any other work Beethoven ever wrote, the *"Ghost" Trio* invites and challenges listeners to appreciate it at a variety of levels. *—Blair Johnston*

Recommended:

- ○ **Beethoven: Piano Trios & Cello Sonatas** / P. Zukerman, Barenboim, Du Pre / 2001 / EMI 74834
- ○ **Beethoven: The Piano Trios** / Beaux Arts Trio / 2001 / Philips 468411
- ○ **Complete Beethoven Edition Vol. 9** / Fournier, W. Kempff, Szeryng / DG 453751
- ○ **Beethoven: Ten Trios for Piano, Violin & Cello** / Borodin Trio / 1987 / Chandos 8352/3/4/5

Piano Trio in E flat major, Op. 70/2 (1808)

Composed in the same year as the *Fifth* and *Sixth Symphonies*, the *Trios* of Op. 70 represent a return to the traditional intimacy of chamber music that Beethoven had put aside in favor of composition on a grand, symphonic scale. In contrast to works of the previous five years, the *Trios*, Op. 70, are more lyrical and seemingly freer harmonically. Beethoven dedicated the *Trios*, Op. 70, to Countess Marie Erdödy, in whose home the composer had recently taken lodgings and who hosted their first performance in December 1808.

The trios are highly intricate and imbued with subtle implications that have large-scale realizations, sometimes in another movement. The motivic manipulation and harmonic exploration that are hallmarks of Beethoven's mature style are evident throughout these works. Of the *Trio in E flat*, Donald Francis Tovey noted that Beethoven had achieved an "integration of Mozart's and Haydn's resources, with results that transcend all possibility of resemblance to the style of their origins...." While Tovey's assessment is arguably a slight exaggeration, the first movement of the *Trio in E flat* gives an idea of what he meant. Beginning with a slow introduction, a practice generally associated with Haydn, the 4/4 time signature shifts to 6/8 for the sonata form proper. An abrupt modulation ushers in the second theme group, the first part of which is on the dominant minor. The development section passes quickly through numerous harmonies while developing fragments of the first theme, after which the recapitulation sneaks in almost imperceptibly and in the "wrong" key. Beethoven sets the second theme group in the tonic minor but reaffirms the tonic major through an extended closing group and, strikingly, the return of the slow introduction. Although the *Trio in E flat* is a four-movement work, there is no slow movement. An Allegretto set of variations, in C major, appears in its place. The movement features two themes, one in the tonic and the second in C minor, both of which are varied. An extended scherzo fills the third spot in the work. Beethoven's format departs from tradition in that some of the repeats are not literal. Furthermore, the movement is arranged so that the trio section appears twice. The overall lyricism of the movement sets it apart from most of Beethoven's previous scherzos. Virtuosic in conception, the finale resembles the first movement of Beethoven's *Piano Sonata in C Major, "Waldstein,"* Op. 53, in that the second theme is in the major mediant (in the case of the *Trio*, G major) instead of the dominant. When the second theme group appears in the recapitulation it is set in C major, not the tonic. Beethoven thereby creates "tonal balance" by writing the second theme first a third above, then below, the tonic. Such harmonic relationships are abundant in Beethoven's late works. *—John Palmer*

Recommended:

- ○ **Issac Stern Collection: The Trio Recordings Vol. 2** / I. Stern, L. Rose, Istomin / 1990 / Sony 46738
- ○ **Complete Beethoven Edition Vol. 9** / Fournier, W. Kempff, Szeryng / DG 453751

Piano Trio in B flat major ("Archduke"), Op. 97 (1810–1811)

Beethoven himself, looking back at his life's work, considered the *Piano Trio in B flat major*, Op. 97, of 1810–11, to be among his very finest creations. (The work is universally known as the *"Archduke" Trio* because, like many Beethoven works, it is dedicated to the composer's patron Archduke Rudolph; less justifiable is its place in the catalog as the *Piano Trio No. 7*—for, while there are piano trios to which the numbers 8 through 12 have been assigned, the *"Archduke"* is actually Beethoven's last finished utterance in the medium.) Generations of performing pianists and string players have agreed with Beethoven's judgment, and the work has, perhaps to the unjust neglect of Beethoven's many other piano trios, cornered the market for late Classical piano trios. In the *"Archduke" Trio*, for really only the second or third time in piano trio history, both the violin and cello achieve a status truly equal to that of the piano.

The reason that this work, of all the work's Beethoven dedicated to Archduke Rudolph, should acquire the nickname *"Archduke"* is really very simple: the word fits the music, and if there never had been a Rudolph or if he should never have taken an interest in Beethoven, the nickname would still fit perfectly. There is, from the very first bars of the opening Allegro moderato, a nobleness to the work that cannot but impress; and that nobleness is made all the more potent and believable by being very frequently understated, as during the solo piano phrase that introduces the first movement's main theme—piano, dolce, supremely lyrical. When the strings enter, six bars into the piece, they do so by sneaking in during the piano's cadence and then offering a lush little duet that easily falls back into the main theme. Even when things grow more heated later on in the exposition there is never the sense of anything particularly urgent—everything is under perfect control, and smooth songfulness, not dramatic physicality, is paramount.

The second of the *"Archduke" Trio's* four movements is a light-footed Scherzo started by the cello and violin alone; the slithering chromaticism of the trio section is strange and mysterious. The Andante cantabile ma però moto third movement is a set of variations on a very serious (but semplice) D major theme; and the Allegro moderato finale, which follows the Andante without break, is a rollicking rondo in which our happy noble indulges in a bit of refined *Trinklied.* —*Blair Johnston*

Recommended:

- ○ **Beethoven: Piano Trios "Archduke;" "Ghost"** / Beaux Arts Trio / 1986 / Philips 412891
- ○ **Issac Stern Collection: Trio Recordings Vol. 2** / I. Stern, L. Rose, Istomin / 1990 / Sony 46738
- ○ **Richter Authorized Recordings: Beethoven II** / S. Richter, Kopelman, Berlinsky / 1994 / Philips 438624
- ○ **Beethoven: Trios 6 & 8** / Rostropovich, Gilels, Kogan / Monitor 62010

Quintet for piano, oboe, clarinet, horn & bassoon in E flat major, Op. 16 (1796)

Written in the mid-1790s, when Beethoven still toiled in the shadow of Mozart and Haydn, the *Quintet for Piano and Winds* shows the strong influence of the two elder composers, as do the six string quartets of Op. 18 he was composing at about the same time. Yet Beethoven was already beginning to assert his own personality here through the occasional violent contrast in dynamics. The writing for winds strongly recalls Mozart's woodwind serenades, but the sometimes rumbling and ever forceful piano style anticipates Beethoven's later keyboard works. And unlike Mozart, Beethoven sets the piano in opposition to the block of woodwinds. He also made an alternate quartet version with the same opus number, replacing the winds with violin, viola, and cello.

The first movement begins with a placid introduction, marked Grave; it's like a distant hunting call for winds answered lyrically by the piano, then approaching nearer (and louder). The piano takes charge as the movement's main matter, Allegro ma non troppo, gets underway. It starts with a charming, antique tune immediately repeated by the winds and then used as the basis for rapid, keyboard-roaming passagework on the piano. There's a rustic dance-like melody, and eventually the keyboard introduces a third, more placid but rhythmically decisive theme, soon shouted out by the winds. Beethoven puts these themes through the standard sonata-form development, but when it's time for the recapitulation, the jokester Beethoven brings back the themes in the "wrong" key, according to the classical formula.

The second movement, Andante cantabile, balances lyricism with counterpoint. It's a rondo, with the serene main theme increasingly ornate in its second and third appearances. The first contrasting episode is a dialogue between oboe and bassoon, answered by canonic figures in the other winds. The second contrasting episode features a minor-key horn solo. The final return of the main theme, however florid it becomes, ends with quiet scale passages in contrary motion.

The finale, Allegro ma non troppo, is also a rondo, but one that develops the primary thematic material—another hunting tune, gently called out first by the piano—almost as fully as in a sonata-allegro format. The first contrasting episode is all arpeggios, first in the piano and then in the winds, elements that will return through the rest of the movement. Indeed, the work ends in a string of joyful, rustic arpeggios and hunting calls.—*James Reel*

Recommended:

- ○ **Barenboim Chicago - Berlin: Beethoven, Mozart Quintets** / Barenboim, Clevenger, H. Schellenberger, L. Combs, Damiano / Erato 96359
- ○ **Netherlands Wind Ensemble: Beethoven** / Netherlands Wind Ensemble, Donohoe / 1996 / Chandos 9470
- ○ **Complete Beethoven Edition Vol. 14: Chamber Works** / J. Levine, Ensemble Wien-Berlin / 1997 / DG 453772
- ○ **Richter Authorized Recordings: Beethoven II** / S. Richter, Quintette Moragues / 1994 / Philips 438624

Septet for strings & woodwinds in E flat major, Op. 20 (1799–1800)

One of the last works Beethoven wrote before he became aware of his encroaching deafness, the Septet is a lighthearted work in the spirit of the eighteenth century serenade. Beethoven had it premiered in the same concert in which he unveiled his *Symphony No. 1.* The Septet was an immediate success, and the composer later expressed a certain resentment toward this work, remarking that it's popularity eclipsed more deserving compositions. Nevertheless, the Septet is an interesting work, filled with youthful energy and containing engaging and attractive solos for the instrumentalists. The first of the work's six movements is a slow and deliberate introduction prefacing a fresh and energetic Allegro con brio. The first subject is carried initially by the violin, then by the clarinet. The second theme brings several other instruments into a dialogue, but is essentially ignored in the development section; after an elaboration of a fragmented version of the first theme, the development section closes in the right key but without a true recapitulation. In the Adagio cantabile, Beethoven shifts to the key of A flat, introducing a tranquil, swaying melody, which the clarinet and violin each play. The other instruments are generally limited to colorful support, except when the horn takes a tentative melodic lead. The Minuet borrows its main theme from Beethoven's *Piano Sonata in G major,* Op. 49/2 (an earlier work despite its higher opus number). It's a spry tune over a tick-tock accompaniment. As is common in Beethoven's works of this period, the minuet contains two trios, the second pulling its insistent rhythm from the opening material. The fourth movement, an Andante, is a set of variations on the Rhenish folk song *"Ach Schiffer, lieber Schiffer."* It's yet another lighthearted, bouncy tune, though a curiously unmemorable one; it merely provides Beethoven a suitably-shaped frame on which to hang his own busy melodic excursions and showcase the various instruments of the ensemble. The Scherzo, marked Allegro molto e vivace, is a vigorous piece with a hint of the hunt about it, thanks to the little figure played by the horn at the beginning. The contrasting trio is essentially a tuneful cello solo accompanied by the other strings and bassoon. In the final movement, a slow introduction (Andante con moto alla marcia) sounds almost ominous, with anticipatory material for the horn and violin. Soon this mood is dispelled by an exuberant Presto, in which the forward motion is occasionally interrupted by calm interludes. The movement also features fanfares, prominent solo material, and even a full cadenza for the violin. —*James Reel*

Recommended:

- ○ **Beethoven In New York** / D. Shifrin (cond.), Chamber Music Society of Lincoln Center / 1996 / Delos 3177
- ○ **Complete Beethoven Edition Vol. 14: Chamber Works** / Vienna PO Chamber Ensemble / 1997 / DG 453772

String Quartet No. 1 in F major, Op. 18/1 (1798–1800)

Although the whole Op. 18 set of string quartets was dedicated to Prince Lobkowitz, a loyal and enthusiastic patron of Beethoven's, an earlier version of the Op. 18, No. 1 quartet existed and was dedicated to Beethoven's friend, Karl Amenda. Amenda was a theologian and violinist who made Beethoven's acquaintance in Vienna. Apparently, Beethoven was unhappy with his first version of the quartet and wrote Amenda a letter requesting that the piece not be shown to or played by anyone. He added that he had a lot to learn about quartet writing and had finished a new version of the piece.

The No. 1 quartet exists in four movements, the first of which is an Allegro con brio. Although there are parts that are quick and spirited, they are mixed with many lyrical qualities as well. The opening motive, centering in on the pitch of F with a melodic turn, is an important one, as it returns in various ways throughout the movement. The music takes on a more fiery character in the development where the key turns to minor before working itself back into the opening motive and its various inventive (and sometimes surprising) manifestations to bring the movement to a close.

Beethoven's sketches show that he composed the second movement, an Adagio, with the intention to depict the tomb scene from Shakespeare's *Romeo and Juliet.* Beethoven's markings for the movement read Adagio affetuoso ed appassionato, and this emotion comes to the fore immediately with the opening violin melody which sings out over a pulse of moving triplets in the other instruments. The melody returns again in the cello and is developed in a bittersweet manner, moving for a time from the minor key into major. There is a stormy development before the melody returns, this time over a much more agitated accompaniment. Beethoven's use of silence between high-tension chords is original and has great dramatic appeal.

The third movement is a clever and playful Scherzo whose uneven phrase structures and boisterous accents provide a feeling of surprise and jocularity. In the trio section the first violin is kept busy with numerous brilliant passages.

The final movement is a pleasant Allegro that, similarly to the first movement, develops the opening motive in many creative ways. This motive, which is introduced by the violin, is built on a sequence of fast-moving triplets, the effect of which is especially virtuosic. —*Emily Stoops*

Recommended:

- ○ **Beethoven: The Early String Quartets Op 18** / Smithsonian SQ / 1988 / Smithsonian 322

○ **Beethoven: Complete String Quartets** / Quatour Végh / 1996 / Auvidis Valois 4400

○ **Beethoven: The Complete String Quartets** / Alban Berg Quartet / 1999 / EMI Classics 73606

String Quartet No. 2 in G major ("Compliments") Op. 18/2 (1798–1800)

Beethoven wrote his Op. 18, No. 2 string quartet in G major between the years of 1798–1800. Although this piece is numbered as second in the Op. 18 set, it is generally believed to be the third in Beethoven's chronological order of composition. He put off writing in the quartet form for a long time in his compositional life, and numerous sketches and revisions show that it was not an easy task for the young composer.

The second quartet, like all the others in the Op. 18 set, is comprised of four movements. It has earned the nickname *"Compliments"* because it is so polite and graceful in nature. The first movement is an Allegro that opens with a charming violin melody that leads to a quick cadence. Overall, this movement is pleasant, has many points of resolution (predictable cadences), and simple phrase structures. The melody, usually in the violin, is a combination of sweet lyric phrases and bright, playful fragments. During the lyrical parts the accompaniment is light and playful. It is easy to hear the influence of Haydn in the way Beethoven reuses and builds upon the opening melodic material throughout the movement. Even while heavily influenced by Haydn's compositional methods, however, Beethoven adds his own delightful musical invention.

Adagio cantabile marks the character of the second movement, which begins with a melody that is sweet but also formal, almost courtly in nature. What makes this movement highly unusual is the subsequent Allegro section that boisterously interrupts halfway through. The allegro is as brief as it is unexpected, and the movement ends with the same adagio feel in which it began.

The third movement is, predictably, a light and playful Scherzo that dances along with the good nature of any Scherzo. Unlike many of Beethoven's other Scherzos, however, this one does not contain any of the musical surprises that often bring a humorous or boisterous feel to the movement. It is, instead, lively but very polite in character.

The final movement is an Allegro with a Quasi Presto marking. It is quite energetic and quick from the start and, similarly to the first movement, the opening motif returns and is developed in many inventive ways. Most of the melodic motion is scalar, though it is combined with short lyrical melodies. The close of the movement is exuberant and in keeping with the good nature of the piece. *—Emily Stoops*

Recommended:

○ **Beethoven: The Opus 18 Project** / Brodsky Quartet / Challenge Classics 72009

○ **Beethoven: The Early String Quartets Op 18** / Smithsonian SQ / 1988 / Smithsonian 322

○ **Beethoven: Complete String Quartets** / Quatour Végh / 1996 / Auvidis Valois 4400

○ **Beethoven: The Complete String Quartets** / Alban Berg Quartet / 1999 / EMI 73606

String Quartet No. 3 in D major, Op. 18/3 (1798–1800)

Before turning to the composition of string quartets, Beethoven devoted his first years in Vienna to mastering the genres popular in that city: piano sonatas, string trios, duo sonatas for piano and violin or cello, and short songs and opera arias. No doubt Beethoven's apparent trepidation when approaching the string quartet medium was a result of the immense shadow cast by Haydn, whose Opp. 71 and 73 were composed in 1793, the year Beethoven began to study with the older master. Haydn published his six *"Erdödy" Quartets*, Op. 76, in 1797, and his two quartets of Op. 77 in 1799. To prepare himself for his eventual foray into the genre, Beethoven studied the works of others. In particular, he copied Haydn's Op. 20, No. 1 in 1793–94, and Mozart's K. 387 and 464 while he was beginning work on Op. 18 The quartets were published 1801 in Vienna, in two sets of three by Mollo & Co. They were not written in their published order, but rather Nos. 3, 1, 2, 5, 4, and 6.

The number of quartets comprising his Op. 18 is but one of Beethoven's nods to tradition, for sets usually included six works. Also, in Nos. 2 and 5, Beethoven seems to confront his predecessors directly, and as a result, moves to another level of composition. In his Op. 18 quartets we find Beethoven both mastering the styles of his predecessors and forging into new territory. For instance, the independence of the four parts is much greater than in the works of his predecessors, which may be attributable to the fact that Beethoven developed his skills during a time freed from the hitherto ubiquitous basso continuo. Despite the numerous recent models, and despite the fact that the *String Quartets*, Op. 18, are clearly a product of their time, they could not have been written by any composer other than Beethoven. Dedicated to Prince Franz Joseph von Lobkowitz, the six quartets of Op. 18 constitute Beethoven's most ambitious project of his early Vienna years.

The quartet in D major (No. 3) was the first composed. Its opening, with nearly all of the motion in the first violin supported by sustained harmonies, resembles the beginning of Haydn's *Quartet*, Op. 50, *No. 6*, also in D major. The first movement begins with an emphasis on the dominant-seventh chord, while the second theme group flirts with the minor dominant, allowing an unusual excursion into C major. The rest of the quartet comprises a conventional movement pattern, but the Presto finale is a sonata, not a rondo. Although it is not labeled as such, the third movement is a minuet, albeit with some unusual, forward-looking touches. For example, the return of the minuet after the trio is not the standard da capo repeat, but is completely written out, with additional repetitions of and variations on the original material. *—John Palmer*

Recommended:

○ **Beethoven: Quatours Op 18** / Quatuor Turner / HM 911540.41

○ **Beethoven: Complete String Quartets** / Quartet Végh / 1996 / Auvidis Valois 4400

○ **Beethoven: The Complete String Quartets** / Alban Berg Quartet / 1999 / EMI 73606

String Quartet No. 4 in C minor, Op. 18/4 (1798–1800)

The only quartet from Beethoven's Opus 18 set to be cast in a minor key, this was also, despite its number, the last of the six to be completed. C minor would come to be a key Beethoven reserved for highly dramatic works, including most famously the *Fifth Symphony.* Before this quartet, though, he'd used C minor without any special sense of tragedy; now, for the first time, he invests his C minor music with a special emotional depth, particularly in the sonata form Allegro ma non tanto. This opening movement immediately spins forth a worried violin theme over agitated accompaniment, interrupted by a series of jagged chords. The violins continue with lyrical, minor mode material, still with a restless accompaniment in the viola and cello. The exposition continues through several brief episodes in the same vein, ending with an odd sequence of quiet chords, a soft allusion to the jagged chords heard earlier. In the development section, Beethoven heightens the anxiety through key modulations while essentially repeating the structure of the exposition; apparently he felt little need to wrench the thematic components apart and recombine their fragments. By the time the recapitulation arrives, the thematic pattern has been clarified.

The surprise comes with the structure of the inner movements. There's no traditional slow movement; instead, Beethoven offers a scherzo followed by a minuet, both in moderate tempos. The scherzo is not the raucous joke Beethoven would favor in his symphonies. It feels more like a traditional minuet, with a fairly capricious character (the key is now C major). The structure could be considered a sonata form, with the central section being a largely polyphonic development of the themes Beethoven has already introduced.

The minuet proper, Allegretto, returns to C minor. If the scherzo seemed more like a minuet, this minuet has the character of a scherzo, fairly quick and unsettled. The trio features a jittery eighth note figure in the first violin, under which the second violin trades two-bar phrases with the viola and cello.

The concluding C minor Allegro is a rondo that begins with an impassioned theme dominated by the first violin. The second section is more placid, and the next contrasting episode features humorous triplets rising from the cello up through the ensemble. The third contrasting episode picks up more of the agitation of the rondo theme, so when the latter returns one last time it can make its full effect only if played, as Beethoven indicates, as quickly as possible.*—James Reel*

Recommended:

○ **Beethoven: String Quartets Op 18** / Vlach Quartet / 2000 / Supraphon 3490

○ **Beethoven: Complete String Quartets** / Quatour Végh / 1996 / Valois 4400

○ **Beethoven: The Complete String Quartets** / Alban Berg Quartet / 1999 / EMI 73606

String Quartet No. 5 in A major, Op. 18/5 (1798–1800)

Despite its numbering, this quartet was probably the fourth of the six that comprise Beethoven's Op. 18 set, dedicated to Prince Lobkowitz. The composer reordered the entire group upon its completion in 1800. The musicologist Brandenburg claimed that the chronological order of the six works was 3, 1, 2, 5, 4, and 6. Beethoven's rearranging was logical, based apparently on the character of the quartets. In general, the first three (in the final numbering) are fairly faithful to Classical forms, while the second three tend to be unorthodox and somewhat experimental. In certain respects, the latter trio of quartets might be viewed as a significant part of the composer's transition to the methods and styles of his so-called middle period.

The *String Quartet No. 5*'s first movement, marked Allegro, opens with a theme that is more than vaguely Mozartean. But much of the music here is also reminiscent of parts of Beethoven's own *Sonata for Violin & Piano No. 2 in A major*, Op. 12/2 (1797–98), written in the same key. The main theme is joyous and the mood optimistic, though the second subject contains material that is a bit more serious. The development section is noteworthy for what it mostly lacks—development. Only the latter half contains substantive development, but in a manner that looks backward in style, or, rather, aims toward the simple. The recapitulation includes some delightful changes in the material.

The second-movement Menuetto features an attractive, lively dance theme whose simplicity is beguiling for its grace and subtle character. If the first movement stands as the least progressive panel in this work, then the trio of this Menuetto may be the most advanced. Yet, it too, is rather simple, and more than one commentator has heard in it a foreshadowing of the music of Schubert. Beethoven puts on display some interesting canonic writing when the main dance melody returns. The next movement is marked Andante cantabile, and its Mozartean character has often been noted. Mozart's *Quartet in A, K. 464*, has been cited as the work Beethoven chose as a model, and the corresponding movements in that work divulge many similarities with the third and fourth movements here. Beethoven presents a simple slow theme and follows with five variations. As suggested above, the finale, too, is indebted to Mozart. Indeed, Beethoven borrows a theme, placing it near the end of the development section. But "imitation" would be too strong a word to use in describing the relationship between the two composers' music in the finale. In fact, the main themes clearly come from the pen of Beethoven, and the development section, muscular and anxious, is also easily recognized as his, despite the thematic foray into Mozart's world. This Allegro movement features a recapitulation and closes with an attractive coda.

A typical performance of the quartet lasts around a half hour. *—Robert Cummings*

Recommended:

- ○ **Beethoven: Complete Quartets Vol. III** / Orford SQ / 1994 / Delos 3033
- ○ **Beethoven: Quatuors Op 18 5 & 6** / Mosaiques Quartet / 1995 / Astree 8541
- ○ **Beethoven: Complete String Quartets** / Quatour Végh / 1996 / Auvidis Valois 4400
- ○ **Beethoven: The Complete String Quartets** / Alban Berg Quartet / 1999 / EMI 73606

String Quartet No. 6 in B flat major, Op. 18/6 (1798–1800)

This was the last written of the group of six quartets comprising the Op. 18 set. Especially in its second and fourth movements it offers glimpses of the mature Beethoven.

The first movement is marked Allegro con brio, and while it hardly introduces anything innovative it does present some musical merrymaking. The joyful main theme contains that already characteristic Beethovenian urgency. The second theme is less driven and takes on an almost stately character at the outset, but eventually turns effervescent and manic. The material is repeated, after which the development section ensues. Here, the music becomes a little more serious, even tense. There is a clever little joke that occurs in the latter part, when the music stops dead unexpectedly, suddenly capturing the attention of the listener. After the development concludes the main material is heard again and the movement ends.

The second movement is an Adagio of great beauty and simplicity. Yet, as was so often the case with this composer, his simplicity has a sophistication. It comes across as pure music, clothed in instrumentation that is perfectly appropriate for its innocent character. The alternate melody is also simple and lovely. The main theme returns and there follows a brief coda. While this is the least sensational movement in the work, it may be the most effective.

The Scherzo ensues. Marked Allegro, it is a busy, talkative movement, full of joy and humor and presents such a contrast to the Adagio that one feels its playfulness and humor more strongly. The finale, subtitled "La Malinconia" and marked Adagio at the outset and later Allegretto quasi allegro, presents probably the most complex music in the work. It begins with a dark, slow introduction, quite unlike anything else in the quartet. The mood is mysterious and intense throughout the first third of the movement. When the Allegretto section begins, Beethoven does not take us back to the backward-looking delight of the first movement, but rather to a more modern sound of joy. The character of the themes is decidedly less rooted in the language of Mozart and Haydn here, more foretelling of Beethoven's own style-to-come. All six quartets from the Op. 18 set were dedicated to Prince Lobkowitz and were first published in Vienna in 1801. *—Robert Cummings*

Recommended:

- ○ **Beethoven: String Quartets Vol. 2** / Le Quatour Talich / 1986 / Calliope 9634
- ○ **Beethoven: Quatuors Op 18 Nos. 5 & 6** / Quatour Mosaïques / 1995 / Astree 8541
- ○ **Beethoven: Complete String Quartets** / Quatour Végh / 1996 / Auvidis Valois 4400
- ○ **Beethoven: The Complete String Quartets** / Alban Berg Quartet / 1999 / EMI 73606

String Quartet No. 7 in F major ("Rasumovsky 1") Op. 59/1 (1806)

Beethoven wrote three quartets in 1806 and dedicated them to Russian nobleman Count Rasumovsky. This F major effort is generally regarded as the greatest of the trio, as well as one of the composer's finest chamber works. A lot has been made of the fact that it was one of the compositions that heralded his second period. The *"Eroica" Symphony*, coming slightly earlier, is generally viewed as the starting point. All three quartets are lengthy works and considerably difficult to execute. That they were all written in a six-month period beginning in April 1806 divulges the speed and mastery Beethoven possessed. The *String Quartet No. 7* was first performed in February 1807, and published in Vienna the following year.

The first movement is marked Allegro and begins on the cello with one of those powerful themes by Beethoven that seem to encompass the world. One senses its greatness and growth potential almost immediately, as it emerges from the depths. The second subject consists of an attractive theme for cello and a lyrical melody. When the lengthy and profound development section begins, one is reminded of the corresponding section in the *"Eroica" Symphony*. Both are massive and full of developmental ideas. Here there is much contrapuntal activity in the manner of a massive double fugue. This is the heart of the movement, full of drama and divulging much brilliant writing. The recapitulation is not in any way a mere restatement of the exposition, but itself a section that involves further thematic transformations. The extended coda, triumphant and powerful in contrast to the tragedy suggested in the recapitulation, is also deftly conceived.

The second movement is nearly as brilliant and complex as the first. It is marked Allegretto vivace e sempre scherzando. It has a sonata-like structure, and Beethoven seems to fashion the movement from a rhythmic scrap. The form of this movement is quite unique: after the first scherzando section, Beethoven follows, not unexpectedly, with a brilliant trio, after which comes development of the themes. But then there ensues a second scherzando section, trio, and finally a third scherzando.

The movements that follow are also on a high artistic plane, but may seem anticlimactic by comparison. The third, marked Adagio molto e mesto, is dark and tragic, profoundly so. One is reminded of the second movement of the *"Eroica"* here, even though its character is more funereal and less tragic. This Adagio is emotional, too, with its main theme of sadness, maybe even pity. The second subject does not break the dark atmosphere that grips the movement.

The finale is marked Allegro and subtitled "Thème Russe." Its use of a Russian theme is in deference to its dedicatee, who was the Russian ambassador. This cheerful melody appears at the outset and is based on a folk song. There is some canonic and contrapuntal activity surrounding it almost from the beginning. The finale also features a development section and recapitulation. In general, this movement is light and not quite as complex as the others. Some have found that it does not fit the character of the quartet. In a sense, it is the least persuasive panel in the work, not because of some intrinsic weakness, but owing to its more genial nature. *—Robert Cummings*

Recommended:

- ○ **Beethoven: The Complete String Quartets** / Alban Berg Quartet / 1999 / EMI 73606
- ○ **Beethoven: The Complete String Quartets** / Végh Quartet / Music & Arts 1084
- ○ **Beethoven: The Middle String Quartets** / Juilliard SQ / 1983 / CBS 37869
- ○ **Beethoven: Complete String Quartets** / Quartetto Italiano / 1996 / Philips 454062

String Quartet No. 8 in E minor ("Rasumovsky 2"), Op. 59/2 (1806)

Beethoven's second set of quartets, Op. 59, inhabit a very different universe from that of his first set, Op. 18. Although only six years had passed since the publication of the Op. 18 quartets, Beethoven's style changed immensely. The Op. 59 quartets were composed in the wake of the *"Eroica" Symphony*, and the vastness of the individual movements; the symphonic, orchestral character of the string writing; and the stretched formal boundaries led some critics to dub the first of the set an *"Eroica"* for string quartet.

The Bureau des Arts et d'Industrie in Vienna published the three Rasumovsky quartets in 1808 with a dedication to the Russian Ambassador in Vienna, Count Andreas Kirillovich Rasumovsky (1752–1836), who had commissioned them. Rasumovsky would also receive, with Prince Lobkowitz, the dedications of the *Symphony No. 5 and No. 6*. The Russian Ambassador was one of Beethoven's principal supporters until a fire destroyed much of his wealth in December 1814. More important to Beethoven was Rasumovsky's maintenance involved in the premieres of numerous works by Beethoven, including the quartets Opp. 18, 59, 95, 127, 130, 132, and 135; the *"Archduke" Trio*; and the *Symphony No. 9*.

Beethoven began drafting the score of the first of the Op. 59 quartets on May 26, 1806, although there is evidence that he started to sketch them in the fall of 1804; by November 1806, all three were complete. Because Rasumovsky was to have exclusive rights to the pieces for a year, their publication was delayed until January 1808. Beethoven sold the rights to not only the Bureau des Arts et d'Industrie in Vienna, but also to Clementi and Co. in London. As a tribute to Rasumovsky's heritage, Beethoven planned to use Russian folk themes in each of the three quartets, but did so only in the finale of the first and the slow movement of the second. All three are in four movements, the third augmented by a slow introduction to the first movement.

The opening of the first movement of the *String Quartet in E minor* is actually more evocative of the *Symphony No. 3* than it is the beginning of Op. 59/1. Two widely spaced chords introduce the piece, which immediately begins a presentation of the theme. However, the movement lacks the expansiveness of its two siblings, creating a very tight, nervous atmosphere and calling for a traditional repeat of the development section. The prominence of the Neapolitan, both the pitch F natural and the harmony of F major, creates a palpable pathos. The large coda takes a path as harmonically adventurous as the development section. Carl Czerny (1791–1857), a former student of Beethoven, noted that the composer was inspired to write the slow movement of Op. 59/2, in E major, while contemplating a starry sky. The chorale-like opening of the movement looks forward to the *Heiliger Dankgesang* of Op. 132. The recapitulation of the hymn-like theme features an active cello line and a second violin part that sails above the first violin's melody. As in the first movement, the E minor scherzo emphasizes the Neapolitan F major. The Russian theme appears in the E major Trio, where it is given extensive contrapuntal treatment, appearing first in the viola, followed by the second violin, cello, and lastly, first violin. The finale again flirts with F major, this time primarily through C major (the dominant of F), which is found throughout the first 50 measures. Marked Presto, it is generally light and jovial, featuring a carefree main theme, rather atypical of the composer's style at this time. The second subject leads to a development section, after which the themes reappear to suggest a Rondo. Overall, this movement has much charm and rather parallels in spirit the finale in the previous quartet. This one, however, seems to fit in better with the character of its preceding three movements. *—John Palmer*

Recommended:

- ○ **Beethoven: String Quartets Op 59 1–3 'Rasumovsky'** / Lindsay SQ / 1994 / ASV 207
- ○ **Beethoven: Complete String Quartets** / Quartetto Italiano / 1996 / Philips 454062
- ○ **Beethoven: The Complete String Quartets** / Alban Berg Quartet / 1999 / EMI 73606
- ○ **Beethoven: Complete String Quartets** / Quatour Végh / 1996 / Valois 4400

String Quartet No. 9 in C major ("Rasumovsky 3") Op. 59/3 (1806)

The C major quartet, the final quartet of Op. 59, opens with a strange introduction—its first harmony is a diminished chord built on F sharp. After a suspenseful decrescendo, the chord moves to the dominant of B flat. This does not lead where we expect it, and the ensuing measures seem directionless until we hear the dominant of C major. However, the tonic is not confirmed until after the exposition has begun. In the development, Beethoven takes the harmony as far afield as the Neapolitan, D flat, creating a similar relationship to the one found in the first movement of the E minor quartet. Although the sonata-form second movement is not marked *Thème russe,* its melancholy melody does sound eastern European in origin, and the pizzicato playing on the cello lends the movement a folk-music quality. The third movement is a minuet, Beethoven's first since the *Piano Sonata,* Op. 31, *No. 3* of 1802. The Trio's tonality of F major looks back both to the key of the first quartet and to that harmony's presence in the second. Beethoven directs that the coda is to move without break into the finale. The blistering finale, in 2/2 meter, is one of Beethoven's most important fugal movements. Until the fourth voice enters (the first violin), it seems that Beethoven intends to compose an actual fugue. Beethoven embarks on a wide exploration of harmonies in this combination of sonata-form and fugue. *—John Palmer*

Recommended:

- ○ **Beethoven: String Quartets; String Quintet Op 29** / Budapest SQ / 1997 / Sony 62870
- ○ **Beethoven: The Complete String Quartets** / Alban Berg Quartet / 1999 / EMI 73606
- ○ **Beethoven: Complete String Quartets** / Quatour Végh / 1996 / Auvidis Valois 4400
- ○ **Beethoven: Complete String Quartets** / Quartetto Italiano / 1996 / Philips 454062

String Quartet No. 10 in E flat major ("Harp"), Op. 74 (1809)

This quartet is contemporary with Beethoven's unsettled *Symphony No. 5* and *"Les Adieux" Sonata* and is less troubled than those works. Even so, it opens with a hesitant Poco adagio introduction that is twice interrupted by jolting chords. The main Allegro material begins with a confident little fanfare followed by a thin yet stimulating theme managed predominantly by the first violin, amid the contrapuntal lines of the other instruments. Pizzicati notes (which give this "Harp" Quartet its nickname) with an agitated accompaniment lead to a short round of rough chords, and then a swirling phrase traded among the instruments that metamorphoses into a violin melody similar to that of the first subject. The thorough development section combines all the effects Beethoven has deployed so far: fretting accompaniment figures supporting the long melodies, then the short phrases, and ultimately the pizzicato material. This section, despite its wayward harmony and sense of urgency, is more stirring than worrisome. The movement closes with an extremely truncated overview of the original themes rather than a full recapitulation.

The Adagio ma non troppo is a typical Beethoven slow movement, paradoxically full of uneasy serenity. Even the many extended hymn-like sections are troubled by the cello's restless, ascending line when the theme is carried by the violins, or by the upper instruments' fidgety figures when the cello takes the melody.

Next comes the Presto movement, an intense scherzo. Its first trio offers no relief, starting as it does with the cello's buzz saw motif, which infects the entire brief section. After a repeat of the A material, a second trio, thematically linked to the first, hints at a fugue. After one more appearance of the A section, the music subsides and, without a break, segues into a demure Allegretto theme. This forms the basis of six variations. Jagged treatments alternate with flowing elaborations, culminating in a swirling little coda that unexpectedly takes its leave with three soft chords. *—James Reel*

Recommended:

- ○ **Beethoven: Complete String Quartets** / Alban Berg Quartet / 1997 / EMI 66408
- ○ **Beethoven: The Complete String Quartets** / Vegh Quartet / Music & Arts 1084
- ○ **Beethoven: String Quartets Opp. 74 & 95** / Cleveland Quartet / 1994 / Telarc 80351
- ○ **Beethoven: String Quartets Opp. 59 & 74** / Quatuor Turner / HM 905252

String Quartet No. 11 in F minor ("Serioso"), Op. 95 (1810)

Composed in late 1810, this work from the end of Beethoven's middle period is unique in his output and indeed in the entire repertoire of chamber music. Within its compact and extraordinarily violent course, it includes harmonic experiments that look far forward into the Romantic era—its third movement, for example, progresses from the home key of F minor through B minor, the most distant key relationship of all. Yet in the stark conciseness of its angry gestures it is anything but Romantic. The first movement, the shortest one in the entire corpus of the Beethoven quartets, exceeds even the parallel movement of the composer's familiar *Symphony No. 5* in concentration. Its main thematic area contains three distinct elements: an abrupt five-note gesture, an ominous silence, and a lurching octave figure. The contemplative second movement, features dense contrapuntal passages that travel through mysterious harmonic shifts. The third movement, which follows the second without pause, returns to the unsettled mood of the opening with thematic material drawn from it, and its middle section is an odd and extremely melancholy march that probably gave the work its title (which is Beethoven's own). Only at the very end of the jittery finale does the mood brighten, and even that brightening seems merely to occur for convention's sake. *—AMG*

Recommended:

- ○ **Beethoven: String Quartets 15 & 11** / Guarneri Quartet / 1990 / Philips 422388
- ○ **Beethoven: The Complete String Quartets** / Alban Berg Quartet / 1999 / EMI 73606
- ○ **Beethoven: Complete String Quartets** / Quatour Vegh / 1996 / Auvidis Valois 4400

String Quartet No. 12 in E flat major, Op. 127 (1823–1824)

This work may well be the most mild-mannered and conventional of Beethoven's late quartets. It is ironic that he originally had more grandiose ideas for it, intending it to contain six movements, including one subtitled "La gaieté" and an Adagio apparently of darker character. In any event, Beethoven settled on this less ambitious, but still effective scheme of four movements, with an Adagio theme and variations second movement, followed by a scherzo and a jovial finale.

What is unusual about this quartet, however, is not its traditional qualities—rare enough in Beethoven—but its lack of muscularity and conflict in the first movement. One hears little nervous energy and angst here, but plenty of lyricism in the main Allegro section that makes up the bulk of the movement. The introduction is marked Maestoso and presents a fanfare that builds up, imparting some expectation of drama and drive, if not of Beethovenian heroic fury. What follows is a lively theme of gentle, lyrical character. In fact, all the thematic material in this movement is nearly free of tension and grit. There is some contrapuntal activity in the fabric of the main theme (and its variants), and the fanfare of the opening returns just before the development, but merely yields once more to the cheerful main material. If there is anything unusual about this movement, it is the development, which resembles a succession of variations. The recapitulation maintains the generally peaceful tenor of the movement, and the coda turns sweet and caressing.

The aforementioned second movement theme-and-variations (Adagio ma non troppo e molto cantabile) presents a lovely, songful melody and six variations. Yet the movement has a thematic structure similar to a typical ABA scheme, with the third variation comprising the middle section. But one may hear it as separate variations as well. It has been asserted that the main theme does not appear conducive to thematic offshoots, owing to its mellifluous character and seeming uniqueness (and lush beauty), but Beethoven manages to mine its depths to find the six very attractive variations and a coda. The third variation's prayerful character imparts a religiosity that seems to highlight, if not define, the mood of the entire Adagio.

The third movement Scherzando vivace breaks with the gentler moods of the music thus far. It begins, like the first movement, with a fanfare, but here on pizzicato strings. The main theme appears on the cello, and is bandied about amid a fugal treatment that starts, stops, and starts again. The middle section is colorful in its dance-like music and constantly changing ideas. On the whole, this movement offers splendid contrast to the lyricism of the preceding pair.

The finale returns to the mood of the first two movements, with lively but unhurried music that shows no sign of that Beethovenian nervous energy. This is music of folk character, with the main theme sounding a bit oafish, but cleverly so. Its slightly odd character and husky rhythmic accompaniment impart a rural air to the proceedings. The thematic material of the second subject is in much the same mode. There is a short development section, followed by a reprise (which comes after a deftly wrought false reprise). This quartet was first published in Mainz in 1826. The composer dedicated it to Prince Nikolai Golitsin, who had commissioned him to write it and the two quartets that followed. *—Robert Cummings*

Recommended:

- ○ **Beethoven: The Complete String Quartets** / Alban Berg Quartet / 1999 / EMI Classics 73606
- ○ **Beethoven: The Late String Quartets** / Emerson SQ / 1996 / DG B000048402

String Quartet No. 13 in B flat major ("Lieb"), Op. 130 (1825–1826)

This effort is among Beethoven's final works and is the last of the three quartets composed to meet the commission of Prince Nikolai Golitzin. No. 12, Op. 127, was written in the period 1823–24 and was followed by the *15th*, Op. 132, in 1825. This 13th Quartet was completed in early January 1826, but its original finale was replaced by a new one finished in late November 1826. This second finale is said to be Beethoven's last completed compositon. The composer agreed to replace the original, the so-called *Grosse Fuge*, Op. 133, at the behest of his publisher. It is a rather self-contained composition anyway, and proved quite difficult for the performers and audience who heard the work at its premiere on March 21, 1826. But Beethoven probably also recognized that the *Grosse Fuge* was a rather outsized piece, too grand to serve as the finale for the B flat Thirteenth, a great piece in its own right, but a work whose character in the preceding five movements is less epic-sounding.

This work obtained the nickname "Lieb" (dear) from Beethoven himself, who referred to it that way in some of his writings. It consists of six movements and may be looked upon as similar to a divertimento or suite, in the older sense of those forms. The first movement alternates slow and fast music throughout, bearing the markings Adagio ma non troppo and Allegro. It moves from the somber to the playful, from the contemplative to the joyous. Beethoven's treatment of the thematic material and his handling of the sonata-allegro form is quite innovative here.

There follows a short Scherzo, one of the composer's best in any genre. The writing in this Presto movement is brilliant and full of color; the mood is light and witty. The ensuing Andante con moto ma non troppo is bright and quite lively, despite its marking; indeed, Beethoven also included the direction here of poco scherzando.

The next movement is marked Alla danza Tedesca (dance in the German style). The music here is again light but also a bit dry. The following passage, marked Cavatina, Adagio molto esspressivo, is somber and melancholy, and also quite profound. The composer himself spoke of the effect this music had on his emotional state, of its ability to draw an occasional tear. The main theme, as its marking suggests, is songlike and quite lovely.

As mentioned above, the finale is the last completed piece Beethoven wrote. Its happy mood does not betray the composer's health problems and emotional state. Although he had just recovered from a serious illness, he was still not well and would live only a few months more. Moreover, Beethoven wrote this finale during a reluctant stay at his brother Johann's residence in Gneixendorff (in the Danube Valley) where he had traveled with his troubled nephew, Karl. The composer did not get along with his sister-in-law, and one can only imagine that the uncomfortable circumstances under which he wrote this music were hardly conducive to composition, especially composition of a happy cast. In any event, this finale provides a brilliant close to the work, quite a different one than that of the original rather complex fugue. This Quartet was first published in Vienna in 1827, carrying a dedication to Prince Golitzin. The premiere of the final version took place on April 22, 1827, a month after the composer's death. *—Robert Cummings*

Recommended:

- ○ **Beethoven: The Late String Quartets** / Emerson SQ / DG B000048402
- ○ **Beethoven: Complete String Quartets** / Quatour Végh / 1996 / Valois 4400
- ○ **Beethoven: The Complete String Quartets** / Alban Berg Quartet / 1999 / EMI 73606

String Quartet No. 14 in C sharp minor, Op. 131 (1826)

Despite its opus number, this quartet came after the 15th (1825), one of three composed to meet a commission from Prince Nikolai Golitzin. The others were Nos. 12 and 13. Like the 13th and 15th, this C sharp minor Quartet consists of more than the usual three or four movements. There are, in fact, seven movements to this massive work, and its form, as one might suspect, is also most unusual.

The Quartet begins with a fugue, marked Adagio ma non troppo e molto espressivo. The mood throughout is somber, but with a religiosity and tenderness that seem to suggest the composer's sense of his own mortality (Beethoven would die in March 1827). Near the end of this movement the music fades, then leads directly into the second movement, marked Allegro molto vivace, which seems as if it could be a more typical first movement. It begins at a pianissimo level with a theme that might seem more suited to a Rondo finale. A transitional theme appears next, and eventually we arrive at a second subject. The material is reprised but afterward there follows no actual development section. Instead, an expanded coda develops the transitional theme. At this juncture, the traditional sonata-allegro form seems obscured.

The third movement begins without pause, and actually serves as a brief interlude to the long slow movement, which is marked Andante ma non troppo e molto cantabile. It consists of a theme and six variations, most of which involve harmony rather than the essence of the melody itself. This movement is one of the most profound and complex Beethoven ever fashioned in the chamber genre. Each variation is played in a different tempo, thus creating a true "variety" that, to some ears, may seem at first to impart a disjointed quality. Yet, Beethoven's invention and cleverness are present everywhere. The fifth variation, for instance, with its deftly-wrought syncopation, is wonderfully mysterious and the coda slyly starts off as if it will become yet another variation, but it subtly returns to the main themes, then brings the movement to a close with a gentle fade.

The Presto fifth movement is brimming with energy and charm. It is an attractive, humorous Scherzo with a trio section and may be, despite a few innovative touches by Beethoven, the most traditional of the movements comprising this quartet. Its rather abrupt and harsh ending leads to a brief interlude-like Adagio quasi un poco andante. The sixth movement, like the third, is very brief.

The finale begins with a gruff theme, that is immediately followed by a less fierce but darker theme. A third melody is introduced shortly afterward, closer in character to the last, but expressing sadness and melancholy. The themes reappear, with the form thus far seeming to suggest the movement could be a Rondo. But Beethoven veers toward thematic development, as if to say he has finally found his way to the sonata-allegro form. There follows a recapitulation but with many highly imaginative changes in the previous material. A powerful and tragic coda closes what many consider Beethoven's greatest quartet. It was first published in Mainz in 1827 and was dedicated to Baron Joseph von Stutterheim. *—Robert Cummings*

Recommended:

- ○ **Beethoven: The Complete String Quartets** / Alban Berg Quartet / 1999 / EMI Classics 73606
- ○ **Beethoven: The Late String Quartets** / Emerson SQ / DG B000048402

String Quartet No. 15 in A minor ("Heiliger Dankgesang"), Op. 132 (1825)

This was the second of the three quartets Beethoven completed to satisfy the commission from Prince Nikolai Golitzin. No. 12, Op. 127 (1823–24), was the first to be finished, followed by this A minor effort, with the 13th (1826) coming last. The work carries the nickname "Heiliger Dankgesang" because of the note written in the score (actually in French) by Beethoven that pertains to the third movement.

From this note, as well as from the time of the work's composition, one can safely deduce that the crisis one clearly hears in the music is related to the lengthy illness Beethoven suffered from April of 1825 until August of that year. The composer makes no attempt to depict his feelings during the illness; rather, he reflects on them and gives thanks in this score for his recovery, for the vanquishing of the pain and suffering that he must surely have felt were symptoms of a life-threatening illness.

The first movement, marked Assai sostenuto, Allegro, has an odd but ingenious structure: Beethoven presents a four-note motif that proves to be the central force throughout, developing it in between three separate expositions. There are two main theme groups, the first of which apparently represents the composer's physical suffering, the latter his sense of hope to overcome it. These subjects transform brilliantly as the movement progresses, with the theme of suffering finally appearing as a joyous hymn at the close.

The second movement is a Scherzo marked Allegro ma non tanto. While the mood of the music here is happy, its slightly restrained character suggests the recovering composer is a bit leery about venturing into too much activity. The third movement, marked Molto adagio, is the work's emotional centerpiece. A slow, hymn-like theme of religious character dominates the proceedings, appearing in different guises throughout, in the end arriving at its definitive, celestial version. The form of this movement is unusual, consisting of five sections and progressing from depictions of the sick composer's hopes, to his feelings of recovery and returning strength, and finally to his recovery and thankfulness to God.

The fourth movement is comprised of a short march, marked Assai vivace. In certain ways, this is a rather puzzling chapter in the overall scheme of the music, the slightly martial nature of the theme seeming out of focus with the rest of the work. Yet, the music here serves as an effective contrast to the preceding movement, as if to suggest a return from the heavens back to the reality of earth.

The finale is a Rondo marked Allegro appassionato. There is nothing innovative in the form here, Beethoven apparently content to suggest that a return to routine can bring sufficient rewards for his purposes, as it may symbolize that a return to health can make one appreciate the simple things in life. Here the mood is joyous throughout and full of color and sunshine. The composer clearly conveys that the crisis is behind him, that the music does not celebrate triumph here, but rather expresses joy and thankfulness. This work was first published in Paris and Berlin in 1827 and was dedicated to Prince Nikolai Golitzin. *—Robert Cummings*

Recommended:

- **Beethoven: String Quartets Opp. 59. 1 & 3, 95, 132** / Borodin Quartet / 1998 / Virgin 61406
- **Beethoven: String Quartets Opp. 131 & 132** / Alban Berg Quartet / 1997 / EMI 69793
- **Beethoven: Complete String Quartets** / Végh Quartet / 1996 / Valois 4400

String Quartet No. 16 in F major, Op. 135 (1826)

Beethoven wrote the bulk of this, his final quartet, in a two-month burst of activity amid health problems and shortly after his nephew Karl attempted to commit suicide. But there's not a hint of self-pity or anguish in this compact, good-natured work. For Beethoven's valedictory composition, this quartet is surprisingly small-scaled, finding inspiration in the quartets of Beethoven's one-time teacher Haydn. The first movement, Allegretto, takes standard sonata form. Its principal theme in 2/4 hints at a march; this, the light textures, and Beethoven's reliance on very short phrases give the movement a playful nature that is emphasized by Beethoven's abrupt melodic and harmonic shifts and frequent interruptions in mid-phrase.

Beethoven carries this unpredictability over to the second movement, Vivace, which is a scherzo and trio. Again, the overall format is traditional, but the movement abounds in rhythmic asymmetry disrupting the basic 3/4 meter, as well as suddenly modulating chromatic harmonies and melodies being gagged at inopportune moments. It's one of the most comic creations in Beethoven's chamber music. In deep contrast is the slow movement, Lento assai cantante e tranquillo. This is a D flat major theme with four variations; variety and development come more through harmonic coloring than motivic manipulation. The second variation slips into a dark C sharp minor, the only spot in this work where listeners obsessed with music as autobiography might find a reflection of Beethoven's troubled life. The third variation returns to the major key for a quiet treatment of the theme in canon between the first violin and cello, and the fourth toys with rhythmic details without disrupting the music's serenity.

The finale initially seems to be a great, tragic utterance; Beethoven casts the introduction, Grave ma non troppo tratto, in F minor. At the head of the score Beethoven has written, in German, "The difficult decision," and next to the tempo indication are the words "Muss es sein?" (Must it be?). The cello and viola seem to be asking that question in the introduction, but soon the music breaks into an F major Allegro; here, Beethoven has written "Es muss sein!" (It must be!). Those three syllables form the rhythmic basis of the main theme, and seem to be inspired by an exchange between Beethoven and a friend regarding payment of money. The movement proceeds according to sonata structure, spirits remaining high right through the whimsical pizzicato passage that leads to the affirmative final bars. *—James Reel*

Recommended:

- **Beethoven: The Late String Quartets** / Hollywood SQ / 1996 / Testament 3082
- **Beethoven: The Late String Quartets** / Vermeer Quartet / 1993 / Teldec 91496
- **Beethoven: The Complete String Quartets** / Alban Berg Quartet / 1999 / EMI 73606
- **Beethoven: Complete String Quartets** / Végh Quartet / 1996 / Valois 4400

Trio for clarinet, cello & piano in B flat major ("Gassenhauer"), Op. 11 (1798)

For his earliest publications, Beethoven avoided the genres in which his predecessors Haydn and Mozart had garnered their greatest respect: the symphony, string quartet, and opera. Most of Beethoven's chamber music for winds dates from his early years; the popularity of such ensembles did not survive the end of the eighteenth century. It seems Beethoven did not consider his works for winds very important and may have looked upon such compositions as preliminary studies for the use of winds in his symphonies.

The finale, a set of variations, is based on the theme of the trio *Pria ch'io l'impegno*, from Joseph Weigl's opera *L'amor marinaro* of 1797. Weigl (1766–1846) was a composer and conductor at the *Kärntnertor Theater* in Vienna. The most sensible tale of the origins of the *Trio*, Op. 11, is found in Thayer, who suggests that a local clarinetist asked Beethoven to employ the Weigl theme in the finale of the work, as the tune was very popular at the time. The publication, in 1798 by Mollo in Vienna, is dedicated to Countess Maria Wilhelmine von Thun, the mother-in-law of Prince Karl Lichnowsky, one of Beethoven's chief patrons. A contemporary review of the trio notes Beethoven's "unusual harmonic knowledge."

Differences between the clarinet and optional violin part are few: descending lines in the clarinet are altered in the violin part when they would pass below its range, and some of the single notes in the clarinet part are written in double- or triple-stops for the violin. The most striking feature of the Allegro con brio first movement is the transition between the first and second themes. After a convincing modulation to the dominant, F major, what sounds like a second theme begins, but on D major. This quickly dissolves into fragments of the first theme and leads to the actual second theme, appearing first in the piano in F major. Beethoven forgoes the D major episode in the recapitulation. Beethoven sets the central Adagio in E flat major. In sonata form with a brief development, the movement's recapitulation is highly decorated. The finale is as much a vehicle for Beethoven's piano virtuosity as it is an example of his variation technique. The first variation is for piano alone and features detached runs and tremolo technique. The fourth variation, on the tonic minor, brings with it a moment of reflection before the piano, in another flamboyant outburst, abruptly changes the mood with a fortissimo entrance at the beginning of the fifth variation. The theme is most clearly perceptible in the sixth variation, while the aggressive seventh variation, again on the tonic minor, is built of rhythmic fragments of the theme in true Beethovenian fashion. Only the broad outline of the theme remains in the elegant eighth variation. The final variation again clearly articulates the theme before slipping momentarily into G major and 6/8 meter for a developmental coda that eventually moves back to the tonic and opening meter. *—John Palmer*

Recommended:

- **Beethoven: The Complete Music for Piano Trio Vol. 4** / Florestan Trio / 2004 / Hyperion 67466
- **Beethoven: Piano Trios** / Chung Trio / 1994 / EMI 55187
- **Beethoven: Kammermusik** / Drolc Quartet / 1997 / DG 453772

Variations on Handel's "See, the Conqu'ring Hero comes" for cello & piano in G major, WoO 45 (1796)

By the end of his life, Beethoven had composed nearly 70 sets of variations. Most of the early ones were based on themes by other composers and were not given opus numbers, which Beethoven reserved for what he felt to be his more substantial, important works.

In May–July 1796, Beethoven was in Berlin as part of a concert tour. While there, he composed, or at least began, a number of important works, including the *Cello Sonatas*, Op. 5, and the *Variations for cello and piano in G major* on *"See the conqu'ring hero comes"* from Handel's oratorio, *Judas Maccabaeus*, WoO 45. The variations are dedicated to Princess Christiane von Lichnowsky, wife of Prince Karl von Lichnowsky, one of Beethoven's most important patrons in Vienna, in whose home Beethoven lived between 1793 and 1795. *The Variations*, WoO 45, were published in 1797 by Artaria in Vienna. As Handel's oratorios were not performed in Vienna at this time, it is likely that the suggestion of the theme came from Baron Gottfried van Swieten (1733–1803), a champion of the works of both Bach and Handel and one of Beethoven's early patrons.

The variations of WoO 45 are in the decorative, high-Classical style and maintain the harmonic movement of the theme. We find none of the probing of tonal relationships as in the *Variations in F major*, Op. 34, and none of the multiplicity of material to be varied as in the *Variations in E flat*, Op. 35. What we do find is a virtuosity and control unparalleled in Beethoven's earlier works. Also, the variations are notable in that Beethoven had few examples on which to model his compositions for the unusual combination of cello and piano.

Handel's theme is rounded binary structure with a central section that emphasizes the relative minor, E minor, a harmony Beethoven stresses from the first variation. The cello makes its first appearance in the second variation, exaggerating the leaps in the theme over a repeated-note accompaniment in the piano. Leaps are the salient feature of the cello part in Variation No. 3; the busy piano part fills any and all melodic gaps created by the cello. Variation No. 4, the first of the two minor variations, returns to a more recognizable form of the theme while probing the pathetic possibilities of the minor mode. In the fifth and sixth variations, Beethoven divides material between the two instruments, perhaps preparing for the very active cello part of Variation No. 7. The shape of the theme all but disappears in No. 8, the second minor variation, in which phrase lengths are delineated by rising and falling scales in the piano. After a calm, contrasting ninth variation that reduces the theme to its bare bones, an agitated tenth variation erupts that features a soaring, cello part. The 11th variation is technically difficult and highly ornamental, and is followed by a meter change to 3/8, which drastically alters the rhythmic aspects of the theme. *—John Palmer*

Recommended:

- **Beethoven: Cello Sonatas and Variations** / Kalish, Krosnick / 1995 / Arabesque 6656

- ○ **Beethoven: The Music for Cello and Piano** / Fournier, W. Kempff / DG 453013
- ○ **Beethoven: Sonates pour violoncelle et piano** / Tortelier, Heidsieck / 1994 / EMI 569422

Violin Sonata No. 5 in F major ("Spring") Op. 24 (1800–1801)

This, Beethoven's fifth violin sonata, was the first to break away from the Classical three-movement sonata format. It was a tentative breach, though; the new Scherzo is barely more than a minute long. The work breaks with the eighteenth century in other ways, particularly in the relaxed lyricism that suffuses each movement.

The opening Allegro begins with one of those generously lyrical themes, sung by the violin over delicate keyboard accompaniment. A second theme group is busier and more clouded, but the soft sunlight soon returns in the curvaceous opening melody. In the development section, Beethoven uncharacteristically gives equal attention to all his themes, but he casts the opening tune in a minor key, maintaining an unsettled (though never violent) feeling throughout the section. The slow movement, Adagio molto espressivo, shifts to the key of B flat and a deeply pensive mood. The piano first presents the nostalgic melody, upon which the violin then meditates for a while. The two instruments then engage in a gentle dialogue based on this theme. The witty third movement, Scherzo and Trio, Allegro molto, begins and ends with a brief stop-and-start tune, with the violin deliberately out of sync with the piano. In the middle comes a very brief, skittering passage for both instruments. The final movement is far more substantial. A rondo marked Allegro ma non troppo, it begins in a pleasant, rather courtly Mozartean style. This refrain returns in various guises, though never significantly altered; in between are minor mode passages of some agitation and modest drama, although the sunny disposition of the main theme wins out in the end. *—James Reel*

Recommended:

- ○ **Beethoven: Complete Violin Sonatas** / Dumay, Pires / 2002 / DG 471495
- ○ **Beethoven: The Sonatas for Piano & Violin** / D. Oistrakh, Oborin / 2001 / Philips 468406
- ○ **Beethoven: Violin Sonatas 5 "Spring" & 9 "Kreutzer"** / Nishizaki, Jandó / 1991 / Naxos 550283

Violin Sonata No. 9 in A major ("Kreutzer") Op. 47 (1802–1803)

Although the *"Kreutzer" Sonata*, Op. 47, is dedicated to Rodolphe Kreutzer, the original dedication was to George P. Bridgetower (1779–1860), for whom the piece was written. Bridgetower, an African-Polish violinist who lived in London, toured Europe in 1802 and 1803. Upon his arrival in Vienna he was introduced by Prince Lichnowsky to Beethoven, who set about fashioning two movements to precede a finale he had originally intended for the Op. 30, No. 1 sonata. Because the date for Bridgetower's concert had been set, Beethoven had to work quickly to complete the virtuosic piece before its first performance by Bridgetower and the composer on May 24, 1803.

Rodolphe Kreutzer (1766–1831) was a French violinist of great renown whom Beethoven met in Vienna in 1798. Beethoven's decision to dedicate the sonata to Kreutzer instead of Bridgetower was probably related to his intended move to Paris and a wish to ingratiate himself with French musical luminaries. (Beethoven was also considering "Bonaparte" as a title for his *Third Symphony*.) Legend has it that Beethoven changed the dedication because he and Bridgetower quarreled over a woman. Kreutzer most likely never knew of the dedication, and it is almost certain that he never played the piece.

The *"Kreutzer" Sonata* was published in 1805 by Simrock in Bonn and Birchall in London. Beethoven described the piece as "written in a very concertante style, like that of a concerto," explaining the internal conflict generally associated with his larger works. Furthermore, the piano writing is much more powerful than in preceding works, anticipating the piano sonatas Opp. 53 and 54.

Beethoven's "new path" is everywhere evident in the first movement of the *"Kreutzer" Sonata*. The only slow introduction Beethoven ever wrote for a violin sonata is actually the only portion of the movement in A major, which gives way to A minor at the beginning of the Presto sonata-form section. Although thematic material is very abundant, Beethoven focuses on one theme from the closing group throughout the development, which spirals progressively deeper into flat-key territory, realizing the implications of B flat major's brief appearance early in the exposition. Development of the first theme does not occur until the lengthy, weighty coda, which is much more symphonic than chamber-style in conception. The vast dimensions and free formal treatment of Beethoven's great middle-period works are not far away.

More light-hearted than the preceding movement, the central Andante, in F major, is a set of variations. The third of the four variations is in the tonic minor. In each variation, Beethoven stretches the melodic aspect of the theme nearly beyond recognition while maintaining the harmonic progression and pattern of repetition of the original.

A tarantella rhythm and 6/8 time contribute to the finale's atmosphere of interminable forward motion, which is enhanced by the introduction of the first theme in a fugal treatment. The sonata-form movement features a second theme on the dominant and in 2/4, which shifts immediately back to 6/8 for the closing material. Because it was originally intended for the *Sonata in A major*, Op. 30, No. 1, the finale was extant months before Beethoven composed the first two movements. The prominence of F major in the development section of the finale may have prompted Beethoven to compose the Andante in that key, as well as to touch on flat keys in the first movement.

In Tolstoy's novella *The Kreutzer Sonata*, the work symbolizes the ultimate in the powerful sensuous appeal of music. *—John Palmer*

Recommended:

- ○ **Beethoven: Violin Sonatas; Kreutzer; Spring** / I. Perlman, Vladimir Ashkenazy / 1983 / London 410554
- ○ **Kreisler Plays Beethoven Vol. 3** / Kreisler, Rupp / 2000 / Biddulph 80203
- ○ **Beethoven: The Sonatas for Piano & Violin** / D. Oistrakh, Oborin / 2001 / Philips 468406
- ○ **Beethoven: Sonatas 1 & 9** / Accardo, Lessona / 1997 / Fonit Cetra 116
- ○ **Complete Beethoven Edition Vol. 7: Violin Sonatas** / G. Kremer, Argerich / DG 453743

Violin Sonata No. 10 in G major ("The Cockcrow") Op. 96 (1812; revised 1814)

Beethoven composed the Violin Sonata in G major, Op. 96, just before a near cessation of serious music composition in 1813. The gradual reduction in output after 1812 may have been related to Beethoven's unsuccessful search for a woman with whom to share his life, which apparently reached its apex in the fall of 1812 with the "Immortal Beloved" crisis. The year 1812, however, saw the completion of the Seventh and Eighth Symphonies and the Op. 96 Violin Sonata, as well as an expansion of Beethoven's fame and reputation both at home and abroad. By this time his works appeared on concert programs as frequently as those of Mozart and Haydn.

The Sonata in G major was written for celebrated French violinist Pierre Rode and dedicated to Archduke Rudolph, a patron and student of Beethoven. Rode and the Archduke gave the first public performance of the sonata on December 29, 1812, four years before the work was published in Vienna by Steiner. Sketched in early- or mid-1812, the sonata was completed in November, just after Beethoven had returned from visiting his brother in Linz, where he had finished the *Eighth Symphony*. The Op. 96 sonata features none of the tempestuousness of the *"Kreutzer" Sonata*, and Sydney Finkelstein has written that "the mood [of op. 96] is one of gentle lyricism, with but glimpses of the profound depths of experience and conquest of pain that had made possible the achievement of this serenity." The work provides an unexpected close to Beethoven's so-called "middle" period.

From the outset of the first movement it is clear that the symphonic energy of the *"Kreutzer" Sonata* is nowhere to be found. Beethoven forgoes the slow introduction and the tempo Presto intensity, creating a more contemplative atmosphere. However, we still find an abundance of material, with numerous thematic elements in the exposition, in the middle of which a hint of B flat major anticipates the "flat key" passages in the recapitulation and the E flat major key of the second movement. The falling, sighing segment of the second closing theme dominates the development section, which subtly trills its way into the recapitulation. As in the first movement of the Op. 47 sonata, developmental treatment of the first theme occurs only in the extended coda. The hymn-like harmonic movement of the opening theme creates a sense of repose in the second movement. Marked Adagio espressivo, the sonata-form structure lacks a development section, a typical attribute of slow-movement sonata form. Beethoven indicated there be no break between the Adagio and the ensuing Scherzo. Beethoven cast the Scherzo in G minor, followed by a Trio in E flat major. The Scherzo section, with its detached melody and accompaniment, ends in such a way that the transition to G major in the coda is almost imperceptible. The only surprise is that the movement ends in the major, not the minor. Pastoral qualities permeate the finale, a set of variations on a simple, eight-measure theme. The variations proceed without interruption, at one point changing from 2/4 to 6/8 meter for a slow lyrical segment that pushes toward E flat major and a literal statement of the theme before moving on to the next variation. A G minor variation that resembles the first theme of the first movement precedes a return to the finale theme on the tonic key. Beethoven closes with a witty, Adagio-Presto coda. *—John Palmer*

Recommended:

- ○ **Références: Beethoven Violin Sonatas** / Yehudi Menuhin, Kentner / 2001 / EMI 74804
- ○ **Beethoven: The Sonatas for Piano & Violin** / D. Oistrakh, Oborin / 2001 / Philips 468406
- ○ **Complete Beethoven Edition: Violin Sonatas** / G. Kremer, Argerich / DG 453743

CONCERTO

Piano Concerto No. 1 in C major, Op. 15 (1795; revised 1800)

Confusingly, Beethoven's *Piano Concerto No. 1* (1795–1800) actually follows the *Concerto No. 2* in order of composition. The confusion is explained by the fact that the composer withhheld what is now known as the *Second Concerto* from publication in order to make substantial revisions (including an all-new rondo), in the meantime proceeding to complete and publish the present work. There are distinct Mozartean moments in the *First Concerto*, particularly in the quiet, strings-only introduction to the opening Allegro con brio. With the entrance of the orchestra (complete with brass and timpani), however, the music takes on a more martial character and a distinctive vigor peculiar to Beethoven's style. The second subject, played by violins and woodwinds over a restless bass accompaniment, unfolds in longer, more lyrical phrases. When the piano finally enters, it's with material that can be heard as a variant of either of the themes already presented; a recurring rhythmic figure, though, clearly links it to the music that opens the work. Throughout the remainder of the movement, Beethoven employs light, rapid passagework no doubt intended to display the composer's own virtuosity. Further opportunity for pianistic display arises at the cadenza, which is followed by a brief coda. The Largo second movement begins with a vocally expressive, lyrical melody, an almost prayerful moment that forecasts the profound slow movements of Beethoven's final period. The orchestra answers with a more forthright theme, then eases into a variant of the piano's melody. The soloist returns with further comments in this vein, highly ornamented and subtly supported and commented upon by the strings and woodwinds. After a poignant episode in which the keyboard adopts for the first time a thin, unassuming texture, the piano reintroduces the opening theme, soon joined by the orchestra. The movement closes in a hushed atmosphere. The Allegro scherzando rondo is typical of much of Beethoven's music of the period: full of high spirits, rhythmic syncopations, and irregular phrasings. The piano presents a comically sputtering theme, soon echoed by the full ensemble. Several of the succeeding episodes have a quirky urgency and comic almost melodrama of the sort that inspired silent film scores more than a century later. The work draws to a conclusion in a spirit of both boldness and mischief. *—James Reel*

Recommended:

- ○ **Beethoven: Piano Concerto 1; "Les Adieux" Sonata** / Ormandy (cond.), R. Serkin, Philadelphia Orch. / 1983 / Sony 37807
- ○ **Complete Beethoven Edition Vol. 2** / Jochum (cond.), Pollini, Vienna PO / DG 453707
- ○ **Sviatoslav Richter à Prague** / Bakala (cond.), S. Richter, Brno State PO / Praga 356020–34

Piano Concerto No. 2 in B flat major, Op. 19 (1788–1798)

For almost two centuries, the original version of the *Piano Concerto No. 2* was assigned to the year 1794, when Beethoven was 23 and needed a showpiece for his public debut in Vienna. He did introduce it in the Court Theater on March 29, 1795, during the Lenten season when Hapsburg Catholicism banned all theatrical activity. But latter-day scholarship has determined that most of the *B flat Concerto*—certainly the first two movements—were written at Bonn in 1789 and 1790, three years after his curtailed first visit to Vienna, but three before his return in November 1792, with a letter of introduction from Count Ferdinand Waldstein and an invitation to study with Haydn. In other words, he was as young as Chopin when the latter composed his first concerto (which, further in common with Beethoven's *B flat*, was published out of sequence as *No. 2*). Whether or not Haydn saw it during the 14 contentious months that Beethoven was his pupil, we don't know.

Beethoven revised the concerto to include a new finale during his study year with Haydn. This was this version he introduced in 1795 and then further revised in 1798 for Prague, giving it still another finale. (The "official" *First Concerto, in C*, published as Op. 15, wasn't composed until 1797.) To keep the *B flat* for his own use, he left the solo part un-notated until the Leipzig publisher Hoffmeister agreed to buy the work in 1801, for half the price of a new sonata. The composer didn't haggle: "I really don't give [it] out as one of my best.... Still, it will not disgrace you in any way to publish it."

Although the *B flat* has come down to us as one of the two runts in Beethoven's concerto litter (along with the "*Triple*"), it is nonetheless a work of substantial charm and considerable elegance, with several Haydn-like surprises including an abundance of themes. In the opening Allegro con brio movement, however, he followed Classical rules, concentrating on the two principal subjects of a double exposition (by the orchestra first, next by the soloist), then a development section, and finally a recapitulation. The main themes in their cheerful confidence are distinctly Beethoven's, though their working-out is clearly influenced not only by Haydn but also by the recently departed Mozart. The middle movement—Adagio, in E flat major—hints at the slow movement of the *Fourth Concerto* to come a decade later. It is, in effect, an accompanied fantasia that resembles a carefree theme and variations, with an attention-getting solo recitative-like passage at the end. The twice-rewritten finale, Molto allegro, combines sonata and rondo forms, with perhaps the nicest surprise of all saved for last: a brief solo rumination which the orchestra brusquely interrupts with a terminal tantara. *—Roger Dettmer*

Recommended:

- ○ **Beethoven: Piano Concertos 1–4** / Szell (cond.), Gilels, Cleveland Orch. / 196 / EMI 69506
- ○ **Beethoven: Piano Concertos 2 & 3** / Abbado (cond.), Argerich, Mahler CO / 2004 / DG 000339802
- ○ **Beethoven: Piano Concertos 2 & 5** / Levine (cond.), Kissin, Philharmonia Orch. / 1997 / Sony 62926
- ○ **Beethoven Complete Edition: Concertos Vol. 2** / Jochum (cond.), Pollini, Vienna PO / DG 453707
- ○ **Beethoven: The Piano Concertos** / Bernstein (cond.), Zimerman, Vienna PO / DG 435467

Piano Concerto No. 3 in C minor, Op. 37 (1800–1803)

Beethoven composed this work in 1799–1800, and introduced it at Vienna on April 5, 1803. The first sketches go back to 1797—after he'd composed the *B flat Piano Concerto* (published as No. 2), but before composition of the *C major Concerto* (in 1798, published as No. 1). Although Beethoven played the first performance of *No. 3* in 1803 from a short score—no one was going to steal it from him!—he'd actually completed the music prior to April 1800, apart from a few last-minute adjustments. In other words, before he wrote the *Second Symphony* (Op. 36), the *Moonlight Piano Sonata* (Op. 27/2), or the Op. 31 triptych for keyboard.

The model for this startlingly dramatic concerto was Mozart's *C minor* (K. 491), which Beethoven played in public concerts. But "model" does not mean he merely imitated; indeed, the orchestra's traditional first exposition is so extensively developed that the soloist's repetition risks sounding anticlimactic. Otherwise, as Charles Rosen has written with formidable insight in *The Classical Style*, "There are many passages in the first movement, Allegro con brio, which allude to Mozart's concerto in the same key... particularly the role of the piano after the cadenza. But the striking development section, with [a] new melody half-recitative [and] half-aria, is entirely original, as is the new sense of weight to the form." Beethoven wrote down that cadenza several years later, to preserve the work's character and momentum, when implacable deafness seriously disadvantaged his public appearances at the keyboard.

To his contemporaries the slow movement came—still can come—as a shock. Not only did he mark it Largo (which is to say very slowly), in 3/8 time, but chose the remote key of E major (four sharps, vs. *C minor*'s three flats). Alone, the piano leads off for 11 measures, introducing both the main theme and ornamentation that accompanies it throughout. Here Beethoven anticipated the solo opening of his *G major Fourth Concerto* five years down the road, although in that work he dispensed with thematic decorations, beautiful as they were (and are) in the Largo of *No. 3*.

Characteristically, the finale is a rondo Allegro, again in tonic *C minor*, with a pair of principal themes introduced by the soloist. This movement is rich in humor yet also dramatic, with a passage midway in E major to remind us where we've been. Following another (but brief) cadenza, Beethoven switches to C major, accelerates the tempo to Presto, and gives the orchestra the last word. *—Roger Dettmer*

Recommended:

- ○ **Beethoven: The Piano Concertos** / Haitink (cond.), Schiff, Dresden Staatskapelle / 1997 / Teldec 13159
- ○ **Beethoven: Piano Concertos 2 & 3** / Abbado (cond.), Argerich, Mahler CO / 2004 / DG 000339802
- ○ **Beethoven: Piano Concerto 3; Mozart: Piano Concerto 22** / Muti (cond.), Richter, London Philharmonia Orch. / 1993 / EMI 64750
- ○ **Beethoven: Piano Concertos** / Toscanini (cond.), Rubinstein, NBC SO / 2001 / Andante 1995
- ○ **Beethoven: The Five Piano Concertos** / Levine (cond.), Brendel, Chicago SO / Philips 456045
- ○ **Schnabel Plays the Beethoven Piano Concertos** / Sargent (cond.), Schnabel, London PO / Pearl 9063

Piano Concerto No. 4 in G major, Op. 58 (1805–1806)

Beethoven's famously copious notebooks confirm that he only composed after an indeterminate period of inspiration, followed by a period of experimentation, followed by a period of gestation: in other words, an evolutionary process. While we know in most cases when works were premiered and published, we don't know when exactly he conceived them, or what chain of change preceded their first public performance. We remain in the dark, for example, on what days of which months—or for that matter in what year—he concentrated on the *Fourth Piano Concerto* to the exclusion of all else.

Not that we need to know. It suffices to recognize its revolutionary (as well as evolutionary) nature, beginning with the very first chord. No concerto before, by Beethoven or anyone else, began as the G major does, with the solo instrument playing unaccompanied—not only that but playing both dolce and softly! The miracle, however, is that Beethoven introduces the main theme and rhythm of the entire first movement within five sweet, soft, solo measures ending on a D major (dominant) chord, which the orchestra answers in B major before modulating to the tonic G. There is none of Beethoven's characteristic vehemence, not even at a crescendo to forte with sforzando punctuation in measures 20–22, although he composed the *Fourth Concerto* and *Appassionata Sonata* concurrently, all the while the *Fifth Symphony* was incubating in his other-consciousness.

Fascinatingly, principal themes in the opening movements of the *Fourth Concerto* and *Fifth Symphony* share a rhythmic motto: three short notes of equal value followed by a longer fourth note. (In the concerto, all of these are the same note; in the symphony, the last one is a third lower.) Noteworthy, too, was the premiere of both works on the same Vienna program—that storied four-hour marathon of December 22, 1808, in the unheated Theater an der Wien, which also introduced the *Pastoral Symphony* and *"Chorale" Fantasie* with an orchestra that refused to rehearse with the composer present. Apropos of the *G major Concerto*: while a traditional double-exposition follows its trailblazing start, Beethoven's instrumental textures, tonal weight, subtleties of harmony, and especially the illusion he creates of improvisation were seven-league strides.

The slow movement is even more revolutionary, despite the brevity of only 72 measures and its indebtedness to the middle, Romanza movement of Mozart's *D minor Concerto* (K. 466), which Beethoven played publicly with outstanding success. However, in his own concerto, the juxtaposition of implacable strings playing both forte and staccato, and the piano's conciliatory legato response with the "soft" pedal down throughout, was unprecedented. Such palpable confrontation was not the norm in concertos. Neither was the orchestra's eventual capitulation, followed without pause by a rondo-finale marked vivace, whose presto coda is as scintillant as any music Beethoven ever wrote.

Even so, solo pianists and their audiences were slower to take up the *Fourth* than Beethoven's other concertos. But Mendelssohn—a general who savored caviar—loved it best, and played it at his last London concert, in 1846: a program that also featured his own music for *A Midsummer Night's Dream* and the *Scottish Symphony*. *—Roger Dettmer*

Recommended:

- ○ **Beethoven: Piano Concertos 2 & 4** / S. Simon (cond.), A. Newman, New York Philomusica / 1988 / Newport Classic 60081
- ○ **Beethoven: Piano Concertos** / (two versions included) / Bohm (cond.), Gieseking, Zecchi (cond.), Haskil / 2001 / Andante 1995
- ○ **Beethoven: Complete Piano Sonatas & Concertos (Box)** / Haitink (cond.), Arrau, Concertgebouw / 1998 / Philips 462358
- ○ **Beethoven: Concertos 3 & 4** / Abbado (cond.), Pollini, Berlin PO / 2001 / DG 471352

Piano Concerto No. 5 in E flat major ("Emperor"), Op. 73 (1809)

As is true of many of the composer's works with nicknames—e.g. the *"Moonlight" Sonata*, the *"Spring" Sonata*—the "Emperor" moniker attached to Beethoven's *Piano Concerto No. 5 in E flat major*, Op. 73 (1809) is not the composer's own. Still, there is hardly an adjective that could more aptly evoke the work's impressive scale and majesty. Despite its considerable technical demands, the *"Emperor" Concerto* handily transcends the typical role of the concerto as a mere virtuoso vehicle. Indeed, it is virtually symphonic in conception; its E flat major key (the same as that of the *"Eroica" Symphony*), expansive form, and sometimes martial, always grand, character grant the concerto a place among the defining works in the composer's heroic vein. The first performance of the Concerto was likely that given by Friedrich Schneider in Leipzig on November 28, 1811.

The *Concerto No. 5* is Beethoven's final essay in the concerto genre. He may have lost interest in concertante works at least in part because of his advancing deafness, which brought an end to his own career as a pianist. Tellingly, he himself never publicly played the *Concerto No. 5*, though he had written his four previous piano concerti for his own use on the concert stage. Moreover, the athletic, virtuoso ideal rarely fit the language of Beethoven's late works, even though some of the last piano sonatas are punishingly difficult.

In the *Piano Concerto No. 4*, Beethoven made a striking break with convention in commencing the work with a piano solo. In the opening Allegro of No. 5, he takes this idea to an extreme, providing the soloist with an extended cadenza, punctuated by tutti chords from the orchestra, that outlines in miniature the entire 20-minute movement. The main theme is marchlike and assertive; the somewhat more relaxed second theme first appears cloaked in mystery, in a minor-key version that soon gives way to the expected statement in the dominant major. The grandeur of the movement is colored by excursions to remote keys that, however, never fully thwart the powerful forward drive.

The lyrical and idyllic second movement, Adagio un poco moto, is one of Beethoven's most tender and intimate statements. The piano predominates here—not in a virtuoso context, but in a manner and texture that prefigure the nocturnes of Chopin. A long dominant pedal underpins a muted, even ethereal transition to the Rondo. In contrast to the noble magnificence of the opening Allegro, the Rondo is a movement of jubilant affirmation, evidenced at once by the upward-surging, dance-like main theme. Though the ambitious conception of the Concerto remains ever at the fore in the Rondo, *Beethoven* nevertheless does not shy away from providing the soloist with passages of exceptional brilliance. *—Michael Rodman*

Recommended:

- ○ **Beethoven: Piano Concerto 5 "Emperor"** / Rattle (cond.), Brendel, Vienna PO / 2001 / Philips 468666
- ○ **Références; Edwin Fischer, Beethoven: Piano Concerto 5** / Furtwängler (cond.), E. Fischer, London PO / EMI 74800
- ○ **Arturo Benedetti Michelangeli (8-CD set)** / Giulini (cond.), Michelangeli, Vienna SO / DG B000001602
- ○ **Beethoven: Piano Concerto 5; Dvořák: Symphony 8** / Szell (cond.), Gilels, Cleveland Orch. / 1996 / EMI 69509
- ○ **Beethoven: Complete Piano Sonatas & Concertos (Box)** / Haitink (cond.), Arrau, Concertgebouw / 1998 / Philips 462358
- ○ **Beethoven: The Piano Concertos** / C. Abbado (cond.), Pollini, Berlin PO / 1994 / DG 439770

Romance for violin & orchestra No. 1 in G major, Op. 40 (ca. 1801)

Beethoven's reputation as a pianist often obscures the fact that he was a very capable violinist. Although not an accomplished master, he possessed a profound love for and understanding of the instrument, evident in his ten violin sonatas, the violin concerto, and numerous quintets, quartets, and other chamber works. The two *Romances* for violin stand out because they are single-movement works in concerto settings. The *Romance in G major* was published in 1803 by Hoffmeister & Kühnel in Leipzig; the date of its first performance is not known. Despite the lower opus number, it was composed at least five years after the *Romance in F*, Op. 50, which was published in 1805. He retained the early Classical orchestra he employed for his earlier *Piano Concerto in B flat*, Op. 19: one flute, two oboes, two bassoons, two horns, and strings. Often described as a "preparation" for the *Violin Concerto*, Op. 61, of 1806, the *Romance in G* stands as a fine work in its own right, clearly demonstrating Beethoven's mastery of the high-Classical style of Mozart and Haydn. Furthermore, Beethoven creates subtle connections between disparate sections of a work.

Cast in a two-episode rondo format (ABACA coda), the *Romance in G* is not imbued with sonata-form characteristics, as are many of Beethoven's later rondo movements. The rondo theme (A) is in two parts, each performed first by the soloist then repeated by the orchestra. Descending sixteenth notes in the solo part mark the beginning of B, in which the orchestra is relegated to a purely accompanimental role, creating unity by including figures from the rondo. Section B spends a significant amount of time on the dominant (D major); however, this does not represent a modulation but a preparation for the return of the rondo in G major. Again, the soloist performs both segments of the A section alone, this time including a running eighth note accompaniment under each of the literally repeated themes. Beethoven set the second episode, C, in E minor. The minor mode, dotted rhythms, and staccato passages give the section a "gypsy" music tinge. The foray into a new key area ends with the return of the G major rondo theme, again played by the soloist, but with accompaniment by the orchestra. Beethoven forgoes the repetition of each of the two parts of the rondo and ends the work with a brief coda featuring a lengthy trill in the solo violin. The three fortissimo chords that close the piece seem oddly, possibly comically, out of place in this generally quiet work, but they do resemble the orchestral string parts at the end of each rondo section. *—John Palmer*

Recommended:

- ○ **Beethoven: Violin Concerto; Violin Romances** / Haitink (cond.), Grumiaux, Concertgebouw / 1989 / Philips 426064
- ○ **David Oistrakh: The Essential** / Rozhdestvensky (cond.), D. Oistrakh, Moscow PSO / 2000 / RCA Victor 72914
- ○ **Beethoven: Violin Concerto, Romances** / Masur (cond.), Mutter, New York PO / DG 471349
- ○ **Berliner Sinfonie-Orchester: Kurt Sanderling** / K. Sanderling (cond.), Oistrakh, Berlin SO / 2002 / HM 2905255/59
- ○ **Beethoven: Complete Concertos Vol. 1** / Haitink (cond.), Grumiaux, Concertgebouw / 1994 / Philips 442577

Romance for violin & orchestra No. 2 in F major, Op. 50 (1802)

Not published until 1805 (Bureau des Arts et d'Industrie, Vienna), the *Romance in F* was probably first performed in November 1798; so, although it bears the designation, "Romance No. 2," and a later opus than its G major sibling, it is actually the earlier of the two compositions. The orchestral scoring Beethoven chose for the Romance in F major is the same as that for his early *Piano Concerto in B flat*, Op. 19: 1 flute, 2 oboes, 2 bassoons, 2 horns and strings. Possibly because of its early conception, the *Romance in F* is less adventurous in conception than the later *Romance in G*, Op. 40, and still includes lengthy transitions between sections. However, the *Romance in F* contains a richer harmonic vocabulary than its later counterpart.

As he would for his *Romance in G*, Beethoven chose a two-episode rondo format (ABACA coda) for the brief, lyrical *Romance in F*. The rondo section (A) features an antecedent-consequent theme performed first by the soloist, with orchestral string accompaniment, then by the entire orchestra. The melody itself is highly decorated, with numerous trills, turns and grace notes. A forceful, dotted-rhythm figure that closes each appearance of the rondo acts as a transition to the ensuing episode.

Episode B maintains the lyric character of the rondo theme, adding large, dramatic leaps followed by descending scales and arpeggios. A glimpse of F minor precedes a literal return to the rondo, this time performed with a lighter accompaniment. The minor mode at the end of episode B proves to be portentous, as episode C begins in the tonic minor. Beethoven makes full use of the "flat" key area by presenting the rondo theme on D flat major, initiating an extended transition back to F major for the final return of the rondo theme. The coda, while never venturing from the tonic, acts as something of a summation when the soloist borrows the triplet motion prominent in episode C and performs a dramatic, trilled figure from the end of episode B. *—John Palmer*

Recommended:

- ○ **Beethoven: Violin Concerto; Violin Romances** / Haitink (cond.), Grumiaux, Concertgebouw / 1989 / Philips 426064
- ○ **Beethoven: Violin Concerto; Violin Romances** / Smetacek (cond.), Josef Suk, Prague S / 1999 / Supraphon 3164
- ○ **Beethoven: Violin Concerto; Romances** / Mutter, Masur (cond.), New York PO / DG 471349
- ○ **David Oistrakh: The Essential** / Rozhdestvensky (cond.), D. Oistrakh, Moscow PSO / 2000 / RCA Victor 72914

Triple Concerto for piano, violin, cello & orchestra in C major, Op. 56 (1803–1804)

Beethoven's *"Triple" Concerto* is often treated as the less brilliant sibling of the more imposing works composed around the same time: *Fidelio*, the *Fourth Piano Concerto*, the *Violin Concerto*, and the *Fourth Symphony*. It is important to note that this work was written with an amateur pianist in mind: the relatively simple piano part was designed for Beethoven's patron, the Archduke Rudolf; nevertheless, professional musicians are required for the brutal cello part and the less difficult—but still quite challenging—violin part. The work was not premiered until 1808, failed to go over well, and has received limited attention ever since. The themes do tend to wander, their development is rather haphazard, and there are no showy cadenzas; in the work's favor, the subtle effects for the soloists and their imaginative interplay with the orchestra must be noted. The concerto follows all the expected patterns. The first movement, Allegro, is in sonata form, with the principal themes laid out by the orchestra before the soloists put in an appearance. The first theme is optimistic, elegant, mildly striving, but completely unpretentious: almost a German walking tune. The two string soloists come in with their version of the first theme, which is soon taken up by the piano with the strings playing a subsidiary role. The soloists develop this material sometimes individually, sometimes the strings alternating with the piano, and sometimes in conjunction with various components of the orchestra. In general, though, only one soloist takes the spotlight at a time, if only for a few bars. This polite turn-taking stretches the movement beyond the point its thematic material merits, the inventive dialogue among the instruments almost compensating for the thin content. The second movement, Largo, is far more compact. Written in A flat major, this movement is highly cantabile and poetic, with the cello first singing out the theme at some length. The piano offers some atmospheric support, while the two string soloists handle most of the lingering, effusive lyricism. Clouds pass over during a minor mode episode imposed by the orchestra near the end, but the soloists modulate back to the major for a seamless transition into the finale, a Rondo alla Polacca. The "Polish" designation has to do with the rhythm rather than any appropriations of folk tunes. The movement begins sweetly enough, though with some tough turns for the string players. Spirits rise through the remainder of the rondo, with a light but distinctly pulsing rhythm (there is nevertheless an obvious polonaise right in the middle of it all) and several instances of rapid passagework for the string soloists. The trio rushes through a penultimate breakneck episode, but slows down for its last, dance-like section while the orchestra keeps trying to cut in with a big, affirmative conclusion. *—James Reel*

Recommended:

- ○ **Face To Face With Beethoven** / Karajan (cond.), Mutter, Ma, Zeltser, Berlin PO / 1998 / DG 457861
- ○ **Beethoven: Triple Concerto; Brahms: Double Concerto** / Karajan (cond.), D. Oistrakh, S. Richter, Rostropovich, Berlin PO / 1998 / EMI 66954
- ○ **Mendelssohn: Violin Concerto; Beethoven: Triple Concerto** / Ivanov (cond.), Oistrakh, Oborin, Knushevitsky, USSR State SO / 1991 / Multisonic 0104

Violin Concerto in D major, Op. 61 (1806)

Beethoven wrote his Violin Concerto in D major, Op. 61 (1806) at the height of his so-called "second" period, one of the most fecund phases of his creativity. In the few years leading up to the Violin Concerto, Beethoven had produced such masterpieces as the *Symphony No. 3*, Op. 55 (1803), the *Piano Concerto No. 4*, Op. 58 (1805–06), and two of his most important piano sonatas, *No. 21 in C major*, Op. 53 ("Waldstein," 1803–04), and *No. 23 in F minor*, Op. 57 ("Appassionata," 1804–05). The Violin Concerto represents a continuation—indeed, one of the crowning achievements—of Beethoven's exploration of the concerto, a form he would essay only once more, in the *Piano Concerto No. 5* (1809).

By the time of the Violin Concerto, Beethoven had employed the violin in concertante roles in a more limited context. Around the time of the first two symphonies, he produced two romances for violin and orchestra; a few years later, he used the violin as a member of the solo trio in the *Triple Concerto* (1803–04). These works, despite their musical effectiveness, must still be regarded as studies and workings-out in relation to the *Violin Concerto*, which more clearly demonstrates Beethoven's mastery in marshalling the distinctive formal and dramatic forces of the concerto form.

Characteristic of Beethoven's music, the dramatic and structural implications of the Concerto emerge at the outset, in a series of quiet timpani strokes that led some early detractors to dismiss the work as the "Kettledrum Concerto." Striking as it is, this fleeting, throbbing motive is more than just an attention-getter; indeed, it provides the very basis for the melodic and rhythmic material that is to follow. At over 25 minutes in length, the first movement is notable as one of the most extended in any of Beethoven's works, including the symphonies. Its breadth arises from Beethoven's adoption of the Classical ritornello form—here manifested in the extended tutti that precedes the entrance of the violin—and from the composer's expansive treatment of the melodic material throughout. The second movement takes a place among the most serene music Beethoven ever produced. Free from the dramatic unrest of the first movement, the second is marked by a tranquil, organic lyricism. Toward the end, an abrupt orchestral outburst leads into a cadenza, which in turn takes the work directly into the final movement. The genial Rondo, marked by a folk-like robustness and dancelike energy, makes some of the work's more virtuosic demands on the soloist.

At the prompting of Muzio Clementi—one of the greatest piano virtuosi of the day aside from Beethoven himself—Beethoven later made a surprisingly effective transcription of the Violin Concerto as the unnumbered *Piano Concerto in D major*, Op. 61a, famously adding to the first movement an extended cadenza that employs timpani in addition to the piano. *—Michael Rodman*

Recommended:

- ○ **Mendelssohn, Beethoven: Violin Concertos** / Norrington (cond.), Bell, Camerata Salzburg / 2002 / Sony 89505
- ○ **Beethoven: Violin Concerto; Romances (Hybrid SACD)** / Mutter, Masur (cond.), New York PO / DG B000010236
- ○ **Beethoven: Violin Concerto** / Giulini (cond.), Perlman, Philharmonia Orch. / 1998 / EMI 66952
- ○ **Favourite Violin Concertos** / Davis (cond.), Grumiaux, Concertgebouw / 1994 / Philips 442287
- ○ **Kreisler Plays Beethoven** / Barbirolli (cond.), Kreisler, London PO / 1995 / Biddulph 100
- ○ **Beethoven: Concerto per violino e orchestra** / Gui (cond.), D. Oistrakh, Milan Radio SO / Fonit Cetra 2028

ORCHESTRAL

Coriolan Overture, Op. 62 (1807)

Shakespeare's *Coriolanus* was not the direct inspiration for Beethoven's overture of the same name; instead, the work was written to accompany Heinrich Joseph von Collin's all-but-forgotten drama *Coriolan*, which was revived in Vienna's Burgtheater in 1807. Beethoven's music depicts the story of Coriolanus in an often stormy essay whose evolution mirrors the action in the drama.

In the drama, Coriolanus is a Roman patrician who has been banished from his native city as a result of his lack of concern for the starving people there. After taking up with the Volscians and plotting revenge, the proud and disgraced Coriolanus leads their armies against Rome. Upon reaching the border of his former city, he is approached by emissaries who plead with him to abandon his intentions to invade. Coriolanus, who has long waited for the day on which he will finally avenge his eviction and humiliation, sends them away and prepares for attack. A last effort to save Rome comes when his mother and his wife plead with him to desist. He is at last dissuaded from carrying out his plans, realizing they are now abhorrent to him. In Collin's play, he determines that he must regain his honor, which can only be effected by death at his own hand.

The sonata-allegro-form overture begins darkly, Allegro con brio, the strings thrice playing an intense unison C, each time answered by a single emphatic chord from the orchestra that rises higher with each response. The strings then take up a rhythmic, agitated figure which makes up the main part of the first subject. This music represents Coriolanus' proud character, his defiance and unsettled nature; it longs, half cries out, but manages to sound subdued, as though ruled by some dark inner constraint. A second theme appears, a memorable creation of great lyrical beauty that also possesses an unmistakably heroic element—a trait nearly ubiquitous in Beethoven's middle-period works. A brief development follows, focusing mainly on the two-note motive that appears at the close of the second subject.

The recapitulation might almost be regarded as a second development, since the thematic material is presented quite differently this time and the key switches from C minor to F minor. The expansive coda makes use of the second theme group at its outset, then turns intense and grim. The music from the opening returns, but dissolves quickly into a dark haze, fading to uneasy silence. Many believe that this ending is a depiction of the actual death of Coriolanus; it may be, however, that it merely reflects his realization that he must die by his own hand to restore his tarnished honor.

The *Coriolan Overture* is one of the most frequently performed and recorded of Beethoven's orchestral works. It was premiered in March 1807 and first published in Vienna in the following year. The work is about nine minutes in duration. *—Robert Cummings*

Recommended:

- ○ **Beethoven: Symphony 6 "Pastoral"** / Klemperer (cond.), Philharmonia Orch. / 2003 / EMI 67966
- ○ **Beethoven: Symphony 3 "Eroica"; Overtures (SACD)** / Szell (cond.), Cleveland Orch. / 2000 / Sony 89341
- ○ **Recordings 1942–1944 Vol. 1** / Furtwängler (cond.), Berlin PO / 2001 / DG 471289

Egmont, incidental music, Op. 84 (1809–1810)

When a commission to provide a music score for Goethe's *Egmont* was offered, Beethoven eagerly snatched up the opportunity. The subject matter of *Egmont* appealed to him: the struggle for freedom. This general theme had already been explored, albeit in a quite different story and venue, in the opera *Fidelio.*

Goethe's play depicts the Spanish persecution of the people of the Netherlands in 1567–68 via an inquisition. Count Egmont, a Catholic loyal to the Spanish, pleads for tolerance from the Spanish King, who instead dispatches the malevolent Duke of Alva to command the forces to maintain order. Egmont is eventually arrested by Alva and sentenced to death. His love, Clara (a fictional character—the real Egmont was married and the father of 11 children), plots his escape but fails. She poisons herself, and Egmont is executed, but with the knowledge that the rebellion is in progress and that the people will be free.

Egmont opens with its justly famous overture, for years a staple in the concert hall. It begins in a somber, serious mood, marked *Sostenuto ma non troppo.* The music seems to portray oppression and darkness, the opening motif revealed to represent the tyrant, but when the tempo picks up with a vigorous Allegro, the mood shifts to one of heroic defiance with a theme which seems descending into the depths to do battle. The tyrant's motif evolves throughout the overture and near the end becomes rhythmic and dark and brings on Egmont's execution. The mood of the piece then turns triumphant and celebratory, providing a glorious close.

Next is one of Clara's two songs, "Die Trommel gerühet." She mixes feelings about love and the military, longing to be with Egmont, marching in his army. Entr'actes Nos. 1 and 2 follow, the former maintaining the sweet mood from Clara's song, then turning agitated, while the latter, marked Larghetto, is very touching. Clara's second song follows, "Freudvoll und leidvoll," a quite moving outpouring of love.

Entr'acte No. 3 ensues, wherein the theme from the love song is developed at the outset, with the mood tranquil and bright. The music turns martial then to depict the rebellious forces. The fourth entr'acte, marked Larghetto, begins with a wail of pain, then presents a melancholy and beautiful melody. Clara's death is portrayed by sad, touching music, in another Larghetto tempo.

The Melodrama is next. With soft, soothing music, Egmont falls asleep and dreams of Clara. He sees her as a spirit of liberty, who tells him that the Netherlands will have freedom. He then ponders his imminent execution, but revels in thoughts of the freedom his people will soon enjoy. In the last section, *Siegessymphonie,* Beethoven reprises the heroic and triumphant music from the close of the overture.

This score was unusual for Beethoven in the large amount of slow music he composed. The first performance of the play with the music came on June 15, 1810. A performance of it (apart from Goethe's drama) lasts about 40 to 45 minutes. *—Robert Cummings*

Recommended:

- ○ **Beethoven: Complete Overtures** / Masur (cond.), Leipzig Gewandhaus Orch. / 1993 / Philips 438706
- ○ **Beethoven: Egmont Op 84** / Szell (cond.), Lorengar, Vienna PO / 1996 / Decca 448593
- ○ **Complete Beethoven Edition Vol. 3** / Abbado (cond.), Studer, Berlin PO / DG 453713

Fidelio, overture, Op. 72c (1814)

The première of *Fidelio,* at the Theater an der Wien on the evening of 20 November 1805, took place only seven days after Napoleon's army had entered Vienna. Members of the Austrian nobility, who typically supported Beethoven, had fled the city, which means that not many people attended the first performance. Poor attendance and unfavorable reviews led to the withdrawal of the opera after only three performances. Beethoven's subsequent revision, combining the first two acts into one (resulting in a two-act format), premièred on 29 March 1806, but there was only one performance. However, Napoleon's subsequent losses throughout Europe in 1812–14 emboldened the Viennese, and in this atmosphere of triumph the Kärntnertor-Theater in Vienna requested a revival of the opera. Beethoven made numerous changes to the score and composed a new overture. Beethoven's third version of *Fidelio* was first performed May 23, 1814; however, the overture would not be heard until the second performance on May 26. This overture, the fourth that Beethoven composed for the opera, has remained as the standard overture since its composition. *The Leonore Overture No. 2,* performed for the first version of the opera, is a successful curtain raiser, but its anticipation of the climax of the second act proved destructive to the drama. *Leonore Overture No. 3* is a revision of *No. 2,* while the overture *Leonore No. 1,* Op. 138 was found among Beethoven's papers after his death; it is not linked to either of the first two productions, and may have been written for a projected Prague performance of 1807. Unlike *Leonore Overtures 2* and *3,* this work does not anticipate the music of the drama.

Cast in sonata form, it opens with a fortissimo outburst that is a fragment of the first theme. This gives way to the main theme, played by the horn, a moment later. The secondary theme, for a combination of horn and strings, is even more forceful than the first, and the exposition moves to the development without repeat. Brief and intense, the development section almost imperceptibly becomes the recapitulation, and the return of the opening measures marks the beginning of a triumphant coda. The choice of E major for the overture of an opera in C major may seem curious, especially when all three Leonore overtures are in C major. But E major is a bright key, anticipating the liberation of Florestan without actually quoting the music, and it is the same key as Leonore's aria, "Komm, Hoffnung" ("Come, hope"). *—John Palmer*

Recommended:

- ○ **Beethoven: Symphony 8; Overtures** / Karajan (cond.), Berlin PO / DG 439005
- ○ **Otto Klemperer (7 CD Box)** / Klemperer (cond.), Philharmonia Orch. / 1993 / EMI 68057

Leonore Overture No. 3 in C major, Op. 72b (1805–1806)

There are no fewer than four separate overtures for Beethoven's only opera *Fidelio.* This unusual state of affairs can be attributed to the extremely long and convoluted evolution of the opera, which actually began life as *Leonore,* the first version of which was staged in 1805, when Napoleon's troops were overrunning Vienna.

The work concerns the Spanish nobleman Florestan, who has been wrongfully imprisoned by his enemy Don Pizarro. Leonore, Florestan's wife, is keen to help, and disguises herself as Fidelio, and wins the trust of the jailer Rocco, who employs her (believing Fidelio to be a man) as his assistant. Also unaware of the subterfuge, and entirely convinced by the disguise, Rocco's daughter Marzelline falls in love with Fidelio, and their match is encouraged by Rocco, though her real suitor Jaquino is understandably confused. In any event, Fidelio wins the confidence of her employer, and is finally allowed to see the imprisoned Florestan. Pizarro arrives at the jail, resolved to kill Fidelio, but he is prevented and all the prisoners are freed.

It is not clear when the first two *Leonora* overtures were written, but Beethoven quickly suppressed *No. 1*; it was not published until 1838, long after his death. *Leonora No. 2* (1805) is much longer, and like *No. 3,* it conveys the themes of the opera, and suggests its overall dramaturgy in microcosm. The *Leonora Overture No. 3,* Op. 72, was composed in 1806, and is much the most successful of the three Leonora overtures. One important distinction between the *Leonora* overtures and the *Fidelio* overture of 1814 is that the later work makes no attempt at a précis of the whole opera, but instead it provides the powerful curtain-raiser that Beethoven by now sensed was needed to properly complete the piece. Mendelssohn was the first conductor to program all four overtures together, during a concert at the Leipzig Gewandhaus given in 1840.

Leonora No. 3 opens with a solemn slow introduction, entirely fitting given the lofty themes of personal freedom under review in the opera. The main C major allegro begins softly, in unison on the strings, but develops into a magnificent heraldic hymn to liberty. Further points to note are the two off-stage trumpet fanfares heard in the central development section, the second sounding closer, thus signifying the moment of approaching release. The coda begins with a spectacular rising passage for the violin section, a virtuoso ensemble device that was again designed to make the climax of the overture prefigure the ultimate outcome of the opera as decisively as possible. *—Michael Jameson*

Recommended:

- ○ **Karel Ancerl: Celebrated Overtures** / Ancerl (cond.), Czech PO / 1999 / Supraphon 011
- ○ **Beethoven: Complete Overtures** / Masur (cond.), Leipzig Gewandhaus Orch. / 1993 / Philips 438706

○ **Beethoven: Complete Symphonies & Selected Overtures** / Furtwängler (cond.), Vienna PO / Music & Arts 942

○ **Complete Beethoven Edition Vol. 20** / Klemperer (cond.), Berlin State Opera Orch. / 1997 / DG 453804

Ruins of Athens, incidental music, Op. 113 (1811)

In 1811 Beethoven was commissioned to provide incidental music to August von Kotzebue's *Prologue (König Stephan) and Epilogue (Die Ruinen von Athen)*, which were to be performed at the opening of the new imperial theater in Pest on February 10, 1812. Because the occasion was patriotic, the works are filled with flattery for the current emperor, Franz. Both works were well received at their premieres; the *Overture to Die Ruinen von Athen* was published in 1823 by Steiner in Vienna, but the complete piece was not printed until 1846.

Die Ruinen von Athen (The Ruins of Athens) tells the story of Minerva, who, after sleeping for 2,000 years, awakens to find the Parthenon destroyed and Athens occupied by the Turks. Culture and reason have disappeared from what was the ancient Greek world, but these human qualities have been preserved in Pest by the enlightened Emperor Franz.

In addition to solo soprano and bass, four-part chorus, and a full orchestra with paired woodwinds and four horns, Beethoven calls for piccolo and percussion—instruments associated by the Viennese with Turkish Janissary bands. This instrumentation would reappear in Beethoven's Ninth Symphony, in the Turkish March variation of the finale.

Beethoven constructed the *Overture to Die Ruinen von Athen* in an unusual manner: the key relationships follow the sonata-form pattern, but the treatment of the melodic material does not. Marked Andante con moto, a slow introduction begins with a brief gesture, in G minor, stated first by the string basses and then moving through the rest of the orchestra. An arching tune in the strings gives way to the first theme, Allegro ma non troppo, set in G major and played on the oboe. Transitional material modulates to the dominant, where the second theme, more angular than the first, also appears in the oboe. A diminutive development refers to the introduction by briefly touching on the minor mode with melodic material drawn from the transition—not the first or second theme (this is the main deviation from standard sonata form). After the return to the tonic, we hear neither the first or second themes, but rather a recapitulation built almost entirely on transitional material, which closes the overture in G major. To Beethoven, key relationships—not an ordered repetition of melodic material—were the crux of the Classical style.

Aside from the overture, the "Chorus of the Dervishes" and the "Marcia alla Turca" remain the most effective and appealing selections from the incidental score, composed in a popular "Turkish" style.—*John Palmer*

Recommended:

○ **Complete Beethoven Edition Vol. 3** / B. Klee (cond.), C. Abbado (cond.), Auger, Crass, Hirte, B. Ganz, Berlin PO / DG 453713

○ **Beethoven: Mass in C; Ruins of Athens** / Beecham (cond.), Beecham Choral Society, Royal PO / EMI 64385

Wellington's Victory, Op. 91 (1813)

Few works by great composers are as famously infamous as Beethoven's *Wellington's Victory*, Op. 91 (1813). This most dubious of Beethoven's accomplishments is a hodgepodge, a potboiler, and a special-effects extravaganza that hardly ranks with the composer's greatest works; still, its melodramatic, gaudy bombast lends it a certain charm and appeal that has allowed it to retain greater popularity than a mere curiosity would merit. The popular success of *Wellington's Victory* in Beethoven's own lifetime is suggested both by the lucre it brought the composer—in terms of financial return, it was one of his most rewarding efforts—and by the variety of editions in which it was published, including one for two pianos and offstage cannons. The composer himself defended the work against critics as one might protect a child from bullies; in response to one critic's negative assessment, he wrote that "what I sh*t (scheisse) is better than anything you could ever think up!"

The work had its genesis in a commission from Johannes Maelzel, best remembered for his role in the development of the metronome. Maelzel asked Beethoven to write a piece for a contrivance of his own invention, the *Panharmonicon*. This "mechanical orchestra" worked on the same principle as a barrel organ, using various types of organ pipes to recreate the sounds of brass and woodwinds, while a pneumatic system powered actual percussion instruments like triangles, cymbals, and drums. Beethoven filled Maelzel's request with *Wellington's Victory*, a work commemorating the then-recent British victory over the French at the Battle of Victoria. Soon after, Beethoven made a version for orchestra, touching off a battle of its own between the composer and Maelzel over ownership rights to the work. In any event, the more extensive instrumental palette offered by the orchestra spurred the composer to even greater heights of veracity, including the addition of an entirely new section in which the conflict itself is played out in you-are-there sonic detail. Beethoven's only "battle" piece belongs to a genre characterized mainly by the recreation of the sounds of warfare; such works typically include antiphonal effects (representing opposing forces), patriotic tunes, military tattoos, fanfares, and marches, and even the boom of actual artillery. *Wellington's Victory* is amply equipped with such features, arranged into a loosely structured sonic tableau. Strains of "Rule, Brittania" and "God Save the King" celebrate the British triumph and provide Beethoven a source of thematic and motivic material, while the French are represented by "Malbrouk s'en va-t-en guerre," whose tune is perhaps more familiar as "For He's a Jolly Good Fellow." The showy, extensive use of brass and percussion lends a martial atmosphere throughout. But the crowning touch of realism is the use of real ordnance, supplementing the instrumental volleys with gunfire and cannonades. Because of this last feature—which hardly falls within the usual means of an orchestra—*Wellington's Victory* is often paired with Tchaikovsky's similarly armed *1812 Overture* on concert programs and recordings. —*Michael Rodman*

Recommended:

○ **Tchaikovsky: 1812 Overture; Capriccio Italien, Beethoven** / Dorati (cond.), H. Lawrence (cond.), London SO / 1996 / Philips 434360

CHORAL

Choral Fantasy, for piano, chorus & orchestra, Op. 80 (1808; revised 1809)

Beethoven composed this work in the autumn of 1808 and played as well as conducted the first performance on December 22 of that year in Vienna. In addition to pairs of winds and brass plus timpani and strings, it calls for solo voices and mixed chorus.

Although a hybrid work without precedent, emulated only twice since (by Ferruccio Busoni and Ralph Vaughan Williams), the "*Choral Fantasy*," as it has come to be called, was composed hurriedly as a crowd-pleasing endpiece for a pre-Christmas Akademie concert. A great deal went wrong during that four-hour marathon in the Theater an der Wien, yet it was destined to become one of the most famous evenings in all of musical history.

A soprano soloist had been engaged to sing the concert aria *Ah! Perfido*, but quarreled with Beethoven during rehearsal and withdrew in a rage; her replacement was a teenager, not only intimidated but uncontrollably tremulous. The orchestra, which had had trouble previously with their famously irascible composer, who had badmouthed them in the bargain, refused to rehearse until he left the room. Choral parts for the *Fantasie* came from the copyists still wet. The old theater's primitive heating system, taxed by a cold wave that year, broke down before the concert. To cap the litany of misadventures, Beethoven forgot to tell the orchestra to ignore a repeat in the A major Adagio section of the *Fantasie*; thus, while he went forward on the keyboard, they went backward until the performance broke down, and had to resume *in medias res*. Beethoven, to his credit, accepted the blame.

Before that debacle, an intrepid audience had shivered through the world premieres of the fifth and sixth symphonies, the first public performance of *Piano Concerto No. 4*, and half of the recent *Mass in C* (Op. 86, for Haydn's patron, Esterházy), as well as the works already mentioned. As for the bedeviled "*Choral Fantasy*," it proved to be a prototype, in effect, of the choral finale to come 15 years later in the Ninth Symphony. Even the theme of its mainly amiable variations in C-related keys resembles the more celebrated one he would compose for Schiller's *"Ode to Joy"* in 1823. Its original form, however, goes all the way back to 1795 (a year before *Ah! Perfido*)—to a song, with verses by Gottfried August Bürger, entitled *Gegenliebe* (Mutual Love).

Despite the rapid composition (for Beethoven) of his "*Choral Fantasy*," sketches in the storied *Notebooks* reveal that he had first thoughts about the substance and treatment in 1800. Remarkably, he published it in 1811 exactly as written three years before—except for the solo introduction in C minor, which he had improvised at the premiere. It has never been determined definitively if the author of the text was Beethoven's friend, Christoph Kuffner. In the event, it is sung first by six solo voices—two sopranos and alto, then two tenors and baritone—after that by the chorus. Surely only a curmudgeon could fail to be charmed by the work's overall insouciance, just as only someone stone-deaf would fail to recognize it as stylistically authoritative, middle-period Beethoven. —*Roger Dettmer*

Recommended:

○ **Beethoven: Symphony 9 "Choral"** / L. Bernstein (cond.), R. Serkin, New York PO / 1997 / Sony 63240

○ **Beethoven in Berlin** / C. Abbado (cond.), Kissin, Berlin PO / 1992 / DG 435617

○ **Beethoven: 2 Piano Sonatas; 6 Bagatelles, Choral Fantasy** / K. Sanderling (cond.), S. Richter, USSR Radio & TV SO / 1995 / Melodiya 29462

Christus am Ölberge (Christ on the Mount of Olives), oratorio, Op. 85 (1803; revised 1804)

The oratorio *Christus am Ölberg* (Christ on the Mount of Olives) is the earliest of Beethoven's three major choral works. Beethoven likely began work on the piece in late 1802 or early 1803, not long after he described the personal crisis brought on by his encroaching deafness in the Heiligenstadt Testament; indeed, many have observed a parallel between Christ's suffering, as depicted in Franz Xaver Huber's text, and his condition. *Christus* also falls within Beethoven's ongoing series of ruminations on "the death of the hero," which first emerged in the *Cantata on the Death of the Emperor Joseph II*, WoO 87 (1790), and, along with the oratorio, continued with the *Symphony No. 3* in E flat major ("Eroica," 1803), and the opera *Fidelio* (1805). Because *Christus* was Beethoven's first major work on a religious subject, some have asserted that it represents the awakening of religious impulses in the composer. This view, however, must be tempered by the fact that a composition of this type fit well with Beethoven's plans to hold a Holy Week concert for his own benefit.

Christus received its first performance at Beethoven's "Akademie" concert of April 5, in the Theater-an-der-Wien. Reviews were mixed, possibly prompting the revisions that followed in 1804. While in Teplitz in August 1811, Beethoven revised the work a second time, in anticipation of its publication by Breitkopf & Härtel in Leipzig later that year. Although the work received frequent performances throughout the nineteenth century, modern performances are rare.

The work is scored for soprano, tenor, and bass soloists (Seraph, Christ, and Peter, respectively), a four-part chorus representing soldiers and disciples, and a large orchestra. The three episodes in Huber's text—Christ's prayer on the Mount of Olives, arrest, and glorification—naturally suggested to Beethoven a three-part structure while providing room for a variety of expressive devices.

Horns open the Grave introduction, set in the minor mode. In the following recitative, Christ describes his readiness to be judged in place of humanity. He goes on to describe the torment of his soul in an aria, set to a pulsing accompaniment, that exhibits traits of the operatic da capo form. In the opening recitative of the second section, Seraph, the intermediary between Christ and God, announces to the world that Christ will die so they may live. In her aria, Seraph tries to increase humanity's guilt when she informs the world that Christ will die out of love for them. Tension increases after this gentle beginning, when the chorus of angels participates in what is essentially the second half of Seraph's aria. The addition of trombones builds the dramatic effect, reaching a climax as the choir explains what will happen to those who do not honor the blood of Christ: "Verdammung ist ihr Los!" ("Damnation is their lot!).

Musically, the most interesting segment of *Christus* is the final section, which features Christ and the choruses of soldiers and disciples in combination, followed by the chorus of angels. As the soldiers announce firmly that Christ must be taken away for judgment, the disciples sing timidly, fearing for their lives. They are repeatedly interrupted by outbursts from the soldiers before both choruses give way to Christ, who looks forward to the end of the affair. After much of the section is repeated, Christ finally proclaims his victory over Hell. The triumph is confirmed by the ensuing chorus of angels, who exclaim, "Worlds sing of thanks and honor" in the major mode, providing a fitting contrast to the somber atmosphere of the introduction and opening recitative. *—John Palmer*

Recommended:

- ○ **Choral Masterpieces** / R. Shaw (cond.), Atlanta SO / 1985 / Telarc 80119
- ○ **Complete Beethoven Edition Vol. 19** / B. Klee (cond.), Harwood, J. King, Crass, Vienna SO / DG 453798

Mass in C major, Op. 86 (1807)

Each year, in honor of his wife's name-day (September 8), Prince Nikolaus Esterházy II commissioned a new mass setting to be sung at his residence in Eisenstadt, Austria. In 1807, the commission fell to Beethoven, whose fame, already firmly established in Vienna, had begun to spread throughout Europe. Still, the commission caused the composer some anxiety, for between 1796 and 1802, his former teacher, Franz Joseph Haydn, had composed six such masses for Esterházy, and Beethoven dreaded the inevitable comparison between his efforts and those of the older master. Nevertheless, he spent part of the summer working on the mass in Baden, and completed it in Heiligenstadt at the same time that he worked on his *Fifth* and *Sixth* Symphonies.

The *Mass in C Major* was first performed on September 13, 1807, under the composer's direction. While Beethoven seems to have been quite pleased with the work, his first effort in the genre, Prince Esterházy was not, describing it as "unbearably ridiculous and detestable." The composer was undeterred, however, and the mass received a more positive response after an 1812 performance at Prince Karl Lichnowsky's residence near Troppau. (Sections had also been performed at Beethoven's legendary Akademie concert on December 22, 1808.) At the time of the work's publication, Beethoven considered dedicating it to Napoleon, but finally decided upon Prince Ferdinand Kinsky—possibly as an intentional snub to the ungrateful Esterházy.

That Beethoven wished to set the mass text "in a manner in which it has rarely been treated" is evident right from the opening of the Kyrie, which begins with unaccompanied bass voices. A passage in the Sanctus, scored for voices and tympani only, must have been equally startling to contemporary audiences. Much like Haydn before him, Beethoven further divided main sections of the mass into smaller units, allowing for a symphonic progression of keys and tempi.

Beethoven reduces the choral texture to unison or octave singing for particularly profound passages of text, including "Quoniam tu solus sanctus" (Thou alone are holy), "Deum verum de Deo vero" (True God from true God) and "sub Pontio Pilato" (under Pontius Pilate). As in the *Fifth Symphony*, the contrast between C major and C minor is a salient feature. The texts associated with these keys imbue the contrast with particular meaning: C minor implies anguish, C major, relief. This is especially evident in the Agnus Dei, where the C minor of "miserere nobis" (Have mercy on us) gives way to a "dona nobis pacem" (Grant us peace) in C major. *—John Palmer*

Recommended:

- ○ **Beethoven: Missa Solemnis** / Giulini (cond.), Ameling, J. Baker, Altmeyer, Rintzler, New Philharmonia Orch. / EMI 62693
- ○ **Complete Beethoven Edition Vol. 3** / J. E. Gardiner (cond.), Robbin, Kendall, Miles, Margiono, Orch. Revolutionnaire et Romantique / DG 453700

Missa Solemnis in D major, Op. 123 (1819–1823)

Past 50, Beethoven found himself deaf, eluded by true love, rejected by the nephew for whom he had assumed a paternal role, plagued by myriad illnesses. And yet, at that point in his life, the composer wrote on the score of his *Missa Solemnis*, "to my God, who has never deserted me." What inner state brought humility forth from this Promethean figure, a recognition and awe of one's place in the cosmos from this fervent, defiant advocate of the dignity of humankind? In his faith he was as unshakable as Bach or Bruckner, but it was a faith forge-tempered by this inner state and fed by nature more so than scripture and spire. It was reflected in this opus 123 mountain-cathedral from the last great period which also saw the *Ninth Symphony* and the last quartets. Ironically, the disposition of the great mass was as earthbound as any promotional process, with the composer touting it as "the greatest work which I have composed thus far" to lure back publishers who had become wary of some of Beethoven's less ethical dealings. Here, it would seem, his word is genuine. With the "Alle Menschen" of the *Ninth Symphony*, the twin summits of the two mighty late works form a yin-yang of the composer's deeply held beliefs.

The composition of the great mass occupied Beethoven from 1818 to 1823, taking it well past the occasion for which it was composed, the installation of the Archduke Rudolph as Archbishop of Olmütz. To prepare, Beethoven immersed himself in church music history for one year. The result was the essence of the composer, reverently looking back while forging ahead. In addition to soloists and chorus, the mass utilizes an organ and expanded orchestra. The five main sections of the ordinary of the Roman Catholic mass are subdivided. The opening Kyrie is marked by dramatic ebb and flow, the interaction of chorus and soloist thoroughly integrated. This is followed by the jubilant Gloria, its unbridled ecstasy initially considered unsuitable for service, with virtual shouts of Gloria forming the coda. In the Credo, this core of the Catholic faith, Beethoven utilizes old church modes in harness with his own then-modern music idiom and employs these for vivid tone painting. A warmer ecstasy pervades the Sanctus; here is Man, childlike, reaching for the Creator; perhaps the most beautiful moment occurs in its Benedictus; the effect of the solo violin is like that of a long-sought peace, descending upon and infusing the soul like balm. The Agnus Dei commences dark and brooding, later becoming, ironically, martial in the Dona nobis pacem and the listener is reminded that nearly two decades of continental war had but recently came to a close. The soloists have the final impassioned word, Beethoven ending his mass with an affecting plea for universal peace. *—Wayne Reisig*

Recommended:

- ○ **Beethoven: Missa Solemnis** / L. Bernstein (cond.), Moser, H. Schwarz, Kollo, Moll, Concertgebouw / DG 469546
- ○ **Beethoven: Missa Solemnis** / Bohm (cond.), M. Price, C. Ludwig, Ochman, Talvela, Vienna PO / DG 437925
- ○ **Beethoven: Missa Solemnis** / Giulini (cond.), H. Harper, J. Baker, Tear, Sotin, London PO / 1990 / EMI 69440
- ○ **Beethoven: Symphony 9** / Toscanini (cond.), L. Marshall, N. Merriman, Conley, Hines, NBC SO / 1998 / RCA Victor 55837

Meeresstille und glückliche Fahrt (Calm Sea and Prosperous Voyage), cantata for chorus & orchestra, Op. 112 (1814–1815)

In the summer of 1814 the crowned heads of Europe made their way to Vienna to participate in a Congress, the intent of which was to restore order to the post-Napoleonic continent. It was in this context that Beethoven composed *Meerestille und glückliche Fahrt* (Calm Sea and Happy Voyage), Op. 112. The cantata was first performed on December 25, 1815, at a benefit concert for the Hospital Fund, along with a revival of Beethoven's oratorio *Christus am Ölberge* (The Mount of Olives), Op. 85, and the Overture in C major, *Zur Namensfeier*, op. 115. When it was published in 1822, by Steiner in Vienna, Beethoven dedicated the cantata to Goethe and sent the poet a copy of the score. Goethe, however, never replied to the composer, possibly because he was very ill at the time of Beethoven's communication.

Meerestille und glückliche Fahrt is most notable for the way Beethoven both weds and contrasts Goethe's two poems, *"Tiefe Stille herrscht im Wasser"* ("A deep calm reigns over the water") and *"Die Nebel zerreissen"* ("The fog breaks up"). Also, this brief gem contains some of the composer's most expressive choral writing. In the era of sailing vessels "Meerestille" meant "dead calm" in a menacing or threatening sense. Beethoven conveys this intimidation by incorporating very few chord changes in the first measures of the piece, which move in a plodding, hesitant tempo. Text painting continues as the choir sings breathlessly, "Keine Luft von keiner Seite!" ("No air from any side!"), the words separated by quarter- and half-note rests, while "Fürchterlich" (frightful) is set to a sustained, accented outburst. Beethoven conveys the "ungeheuren Weite" ("vast expanse") of the ocean by combining an extremely wide range in both the chorus and orchestra with a triplet rhythmic motion.

Music of the first two lines returns before the shift to "Glückliche Fahrt," signaled by a rising scale in the strings. The triumphant atmosphere looks forward to passage of the *Ninth Symphony.* Especially effective is the rapid interplay of voices and instruments on "Geschwinde! Geschwinde!" ("Swiftly! Swiftly!") and the excitement of a sailor sighting land, conveyed through the manifold repetitions of "das Land!" *—John Palmer*

Recommended:

- ○ **Beethoven Late Choral Music** / Tilson Thomas (cond.), Ambrosian Singers, London SO / 1975 / Sony 33509
- ○ **Complete Beethoven Edition Vol. 3** / J.E. Gardiner (cond.), Monteverdi Choir, Orch. Revolutionnaire et Romantique / DG 453700

OPERA

Fidelio, opera, Op. 72 (1804–1806; revised 1814)

Fidelio, Ludwig van Beethoven's only opera, takes as its subject a theme close to the composer's heart: the defeat of tyranny through man's innate desire for liberty. The first version of the opera, premiered in 1805 under the title *Leonore* (the name of the heroine), was staggeringly unsuccessful. This was largely the result, however, of circumstances beyond Beethoven's control: Vienna was then occupied by Napoleon's troops, who made up a large part of the audience. It seems likely that the Beethoven-loving but troubled Viennese had more pressing concerns than attending such an entertainment. And the members of Napoleon's army might not have appreciated the opera's themes, which ran counter to the soldiers' very presence in Vienna.

Beethoven retooled the opera in 1806, shuffling certain sections and making cuts. In this form *Leonore* was revived with considerable success, although Beethoven withdrew the opera from performance because of suspicions that he was not receiving his full share of the proceeds. In 1814 Beethoven revised the opera yet again, changing its name to *Fidelio.* This final version was a success, both in the theater and in the composer's own esteem, and it is this version that is generally regarded as the "definitive" incarnation of the opera. Each of the three "Fidelios" featured a different overture: the first version used what is now called the *Leonore Overture No. 2*; the second, *Leonore No. 3*; and the final used the *Fidelio Overture.* (Beethoven composed *Leonore No. 1* for a Prague staging which never took place.) Though rarely heard in performances of the complete opera, each of the "Leonore" overtures has retained a place in the concert repertory.

The original libretto was fashioned by Joseph Sonnleithner after Jean Bouilly's *Leonore* (1798). The text for the final version was reworked by the Leipzig-born playwright and poet Georg Friedrich Treitschke, whom Beethoven had met in 1811. The story concerns Leonore, who is trying to free her political-prisoner husband, the Spanish nobleman Florestan, from the prison of the evil Pizarro by disguising herself as a man, Fidelio, and working in the prison.

Highlights from the score include the Act One quartet "Mir ist so wunderbar," which is certainly the most famous excerpt from the opera; Marcellina's Act One aria, "O wär' ich schon mit dir vereint," in which she discloses her burgeoning love for Fidelio; Florestan's Act One aria, "In des Lebens Frühlingstagen," which he sings in his cell thinking of his wife; and the lovely "O namenlose Freude," a moving duet between Florestan and Leonore that follows her foiling of the murder plot. There is much spoken dialogue throughout *Fidelio*; some have cited this aspect in criticism, saying that it robs the work of its momentum. That view is a minority one, however, and *Fidelio* has generally been held in high critical esteem; despite its sometimes shaky plot, the music is unassailably great and blazes with Beethoven's steadfast commitment to liberty and humanity. *Fidelio* makes explicit the strand of political idealism that seems to simmer beneath the surfaces of many of his other works, and if it does not have the universal appeal of some of his better-known orchestral classics, it nevertheless seems very close to Beethoven's own heart.*—AMG*

Synopsis:

Act One. The story is set in eighteenth century Spain. At a prison near Seville, Leonora suspects her husband Florestan is being held on orders from his arch enemy, prison governor Don Pizarro. She has disguised herself as a young man named Fidelio and obtained employment at the prison under the chief jailer Rocco. He is greatly impressed by Fidelio's work, and his daughter Marcellina begins falling in love with the cleverly disguised Leonora. Rocco, in fact, pledges that his daughter will marry Fidelio, instead of her other suitor, his assistant Jacquino. This announcement pleases Marcellina, but understandably alarms Leonora. At her request, Rocco allows her to take on more duties, but he warns that she must stay away from a certain prisoner in a dungeon below—a prisoner Leonora is convinced is Florestan.

In Scene Two, Don Pizarro is warned of an impending visit by Don Fernando, Minister of State and friend of Florestan, who has heard that the prison governor often incarcerates his enemies. Pizarro quickly calculates that Florestan must die, but cannot convince Rocco to perform the awful deed. The chief jailer does, however, agree to dig Florestan's grave. Leonora overhears the murder plans and begins a scheme of her own. After Pizarro's departure she reminds Rocco to allow the prisoners to take their customary walk outside, since it is due on this particular day. As the prisoners enter into the sunlight, Leonora searches in vain for Florestan among them. Rocco tells her that Pizarro has approved of the marriage of Marcellina to Fidelio, then asks her to go to the dungeon with him, where they will dig the grave.

Act Two. The first scene opens in the dungeon where the malnourished, partly delirious Florestan is held. Rocco and Leonora enter and begin digging, the latter not able to determine for certain if her husband is the prisoner she sees. She decides she will thwart the murder plans, no matter who he is. Finally, when she takes food to him, she recognizes him. Florestan, however, is unaware of her identity and becomes even more demented when Rocco refuses his request to send word to his wife that he is alive. She attempts to comfort him in his growing torment. Pizarro enters with a knife, intent on killing Florestan. Leonora divulges her true identity and brandishes a pistol, threatening to shoot Pizarro. Jacquino enters to announce the arrival of Don Fernando, bringing on the opera's biggest climactic moment: Pizarro now realizes his plot is thwarted and he is ruined.

Scene Two opens with Don Fernando seeing his friend Florestan, whom he had assumed was dead owing to false accounts issued by Pizarro. Leonora frees her husband from his restraints and the story ends happily. *—Robert Cummings*

Recommended:

- ○ **Beethoven: Fidelio** / Klemperer (cond.), Ludwig, Vickers, W. Berry, Frick, Philharmonia Orch. / 2000 / EMI 67361

VOCAL

Adelaide, song, Op. 46 (1794–1795)

Adelaide, the most famous of Beethoven's lieder, was composed in 1794 or 1795. Indeed, the song was apparently one of his own favorites; he identified it as such in a letter to the poet Friedrich von Matthisson, and he himself played the accompaniment in an 1815 concert in celebration of the Empress of Russia's birthday.

The song is structured like a sonata in miniature, with a middle passage that goes through several keys. While at first consideration the text seems to call for a strophic setting, Beethoven's through-composed treatment imbues the words and descriptions in the poem with an extra measure of color and expressivity. The first verse of the setting, for example, in which the poet describes wandering in a garden during a spring night, is tranquil; in the second, when he describes seeing the face of his beloved in the grandeur of nature, the music is far more stately; in the third, the piano vividly depicts both rushing waves and the song of the nightingales. Throughout, however, the overall tone, one of ecstatic contemplation, is the same. One of the song's most important unifying elements is the tender repetition of the name "Adelaide." *—Ann Feeney*

Recommended:

- ○ **Salzburg Festival Live, 1957–1965, Vol. 5 Beethoven** / Fischer-Dieskau, Moore / 1985 / Orfeo 140501
- ○ **Schumann: Dichterliebe, etc.** / Wunderlich, Giesen / 1997 / DG 449747
- ○ **Beethoven Lieder** / Fischer-Dieskau, Klust / 1995 / Testament 1057

Ah! perfido!... Per pieta, non dirmi addio, scena and aria for soprano & orchestra, Op. 65 (1796)

Ah, perfido! is an early Beethoven work, immersed in eighteenth century operatic tradition. The reason it bears an opus number high in relation to its date of composition is that, though it was written in 1796, it was not published until 1805. The piece was probably written for its first performer, the then-celebrated soprano Josepha Duschek. Composed in Prague and modeled on Mozart's *Bella mia fiamma,* which was also written for Duschek, this has generally been one of the composer's more popular vocal pieces down through the years. A decade or so after composing the work, Beethoven reflected that it was suited more to a theater setting than to the concert hall. He was unusually emphatic in stipulating that it needed "a curtain," or similar environs, to achieve its proper effect. The work is a setting of verses by Pietro Trapassi, a Roman who was court poet in Vienna (1729–82) and who wrote under the name of Metastasio.

The text deals with a young woman betrayed by her lover, expressing the rage she experiences. At first, she pleads with the gods to punish him, but then asks for mercy for him. Then she offers to die for him, instead. After bewailing her fate, she asks for mercy. The music begins dramatically with the soprano intoning the words, "Ah, perfido! spergiuro, barbaro traditor, tu parti? ("Ah, unfaithful liar! vile deceiver, you leave me?") The music then slows, and the young woman's emotions for a time seem contained, but tension quickly develops. Still, for all the rage she expresses, she does not erupt with a potent outburst to vent her feelings, but instead maintains an intensity that seems to border on just such an outburst. When the aria, "Per pieta, non dirmi addio" ("For pity's sake, do not leave me") is reached, the spirit of Mozart appears. (The character of the theme in the third movement of Mozart's *"Gran Partita" Serenade No. 10*, K. 361, is not unlike that of the attractive melody here.) The aria music, marked Adagio, is most moving and effective in its heartrending beauty. Even if it is strongly reminiscent of Mozart, it is it charming enough not to seem derivative. The tempo returns to Allegro as the soprano lashes out at her cruel treatment at the hands of fate. There is a brief return to an Adagio tempo before the Allegro conclusion.

The orchestral writing is effective throughout, even if it, too, owes something to Mozart. While some may feel the music sounds less agitated in places than the text might seem to call for, Beethoven captures the spirit of Metastasio's verses. The range of emotions that he depicts in the music, together with the ebb and flow of tension, are remarkably well balanced. The work, known for its immense vocal difficulty, was premiered on November 21, 1796, in Leipzig. A typical performance of it lasts about from about 12 to 15 minutes. *—Robert Cummings*

Recommended:

- ○ **Références: Elisabeth Schwarzkopf** / Karajan (cond.), Schwarzkopf, London Philharmonia Orch. / EMI 63201
- ○ **Beethoven: Messe in C** / J. E. Gardiner (cond.), Margiono, Orch. Revolutionnaire et Romantique / Archiv 435391
- ○ **Karita Mattila: German Romantic Arias** / C. Davis (cond.), Mattila, Staatskapelle Dresden / 2002 / Erato 42141
- ○ **Complete Beethoven Edition Vol. 3** / C. Abbado (cond.), Studer, Berlin PO / DG 453700

An die ferne Geliebte, song cycle, Op. 98 (1816)

An die ferne Geliebte ("To the distant beloved") is an important song cycle, not just for its musical value, but because it stands as a significant turning point in Beethoven's style and career. It is a work which carved out a new path in many respects for the composer: the heroism and splendor of the past are missing here; the extroverted persona becomes muted, giving way to a more ponderous, inward expressiveness; and, on a personal level, the music symbolized Beethoven's realization that he would likely never marry, and that his youth, with all its bitter disappointments, had passed. Yet, the music, while reflecting the composer's pain, never suggests any self-pity; in fact, the mood remains rather sober, even bright in mood at times, and always accepting of fate. "Yearning," rather than "suffering," would actually be a better word to associate with these six songs, composed to texts by Alois Jeitteles, then a medical student, who seems to have written the words especially for these settings. This song cycle is also important because it was the first major effort written in a through-composed style, eventually exerting a great influence on the lieder of Schumann and many later composers. The individual songs share some thematic relationships and are linked via the piano accompaniment, which delivers a sort of connecting interlude between songs. Beethoven thus excludes the option of performing just one song or a selection from the entire work. The first song, "Auf dem Hügel sitz ich spähend" ("On the hill sit I, peering"), features subdued music that is rather bright, considering the longing and yearning for the "beloved" mentioned in the text. Clearly, this is music expressing the composer's acceptance of sorrow and loss. The next song, "Wo die Berge so blau" ("Where the mountains so blue"), is a bit darker and more somber in mood, but the yearning remains. "Leichte Segler in den Höhen" ("Light veils in the heights") is quite playful at the outset, departing from the more melancholy atmosphere of the previous songs. The ensuing item, "Diese Wolken in den Höhen" ("These clouds in the heights") is also somewhat cheerful, but, like the last song, seems essentially dominated by a mood of longing. In fact, while these middle songs seem brighter, their apparent lightness brings the underlying sense of loss into sharper focus. The penultimate song, "Es kehret der Maien, es blühet die Au" ("May returns, the meadow blooms"), maintains an animated mood. The touching "Nimm sie hin denn, diese Lieder" ("Take, then, these songs"), which powerfully closes the cycle, includes a nostalgic reiteration of the first song's melody. *—Robert Cummings*

Recommended:

- ○ **Beethoven, Berlioz, Franz, Grieg & others: Songs** / Hampson, G. Parsons / 2002 / EMI 575187
- ○ **The Unforgettable Voice of Peter Anders** / Anders, Raucheisen / 1998 / Tahra 201/2
- ○ **Complete Beethoven Edition Vol. 3** / Schlusnus, Peschko / DG 453700

BALLET

Die Geschöpfe des Prometheus (The Creatures of Prometheus), Op. 43 (1800–1801)

Beethoven's ballet score *Die Geschöpfe des Prometheus* (The Creatures of Prometheus) was created in collaboration with choreographer Salvatore Viganò. Commissioned in 1800, the ballet was the composer's first major work for the stage. Premiered in Vienna's Burgtheater on March 28, 1801, *Prometheus* was initially a great success, and within a few years it had been peformed dozens of times. Still, it was criticized by a contemporary as "fragmentary" and "too learned for a ballet," and the score, save for the overture, has since been generally neglected as little more than an historical curiosity. The work's opus number is somewhat problematic. In June 1801, Artaria published Beethoven's piano arrangement of the score, dedicated to Prince Lichnowsky, as Op. 24. In the same year, the firm of Mollo intended to publish a pair of violin sonatas as Op. 23; likely because of a printing error, the second of these, now familiar as the "Spring" Sonata, was issued separately as Op. 24, necessitating a change in opus number for *Prometheus*. Three years later, Hoffmeister published the full score of the overture only as Op. 43, lending the false impression that the work was composed some years later than it actually was.

Aside from a few interesting aspects of its orchestration, the most important part of the ballet, musically speaking, is the sixteenth and final number. This section shares its key, main theme, and bass line with the seventh of the *Twelve Contredanses*, WoO 14, composed at intervals between 1791 and 1802. It is certain that the material of this particular dance dates from about the time of the ballet, though scholars disagree on which work was the first to take shape; considering the composer's working method, it is entirely possible that the two developed simultaneously. In any event, this workhorse of a theme came to even greater prominence through its use in Beethoven's *15 Variations and Fugue for piano*, Op. 35, and in the finale of his epochal *Symphony No. 3 in E flat major* ("Eroica"), Op. 55. *—John Palmer*

Recommended:

- ○ **Beethoven: Die Geschöpfe des Prometheus** / Harnoncourt (cond.), COE / 1995 / Teldec 90876
- ○ **Complete Beethoven Edition Vol. 3** / Orpheus CO / DG 453713

Joshua Bell

b. Dec. 9, 1967, Bloomington, IN

Violinist

Joshua Bell, one of the top young violinists of our time, was born in 1967, in Bloomington, Indiana. Fortuitously, the small city in the limestone district of Indiana is the home of the Indiana University School of Music, which eventually assumed a decisive role in Bell's musical development. Bell was exposed to music from an early age and began his violin studies with Mimi Zweig. Bell's talents developed rapidly; he made his debut as a soloist in performance with the Bloomington Symphony Orchestra at the age of seven. The eminent violin teacher Josef Gingold, a member of Indiana University's music faculty, took an interest in him and became his teacher; eventually Bell entered the University as a student. Bell's studies with Gingold were supplemented by additional studies and master classes with Ivan Galamian and Henryk Szeryng. Bell came to wide national attention as a grand prize winner in the first annual *Seventeen* Magazine/General Motors National Concerto Competition in Rochester, New York. He soon appeared as a soloist with the Philadelphia Orchestra under Riccardo Muti on September 24, 1982—the youngest person ever to appear with the orchestra as a soloist on a subscription concert. Bell's 1985 Carnegie Hall debut with the St. Louis Symphony Orchestra was greeted with the kind of enthusiastic reviews that were a bellwether of his successful concert and recording career.

By the mid-1990s Bell had recorded much of the standard violin repertoire, exhibiting a musically informed and winning personal style. His playing is lyrical and bright, marked by a high-minded approach and a smooth, silvery tone. In the late 1990s Bell's eclectic tastes and multifaceted talents found voice in a wide range of projects outside the realm of the traditional violin repertoire. Bell's playing on John Corigliano's score to *The Red Violin* (1998) was singled out as one of the film's more memorable elements, while in 1999 he collaborated on a well-received CD of bluegrass-influenced music by composer Edgar Meyer. By the early 2000s, Bell was seen on numerous television programs and was even named one of *People* magazine's "50 Most Beautiful People." He continued to work with musicians outside the classical realm, such as Chick Corea and James Taylor, meanwhile performing with the world's top orchestras and conductors. Other collaborations led to Bell's establishing chamber music recital series in both London and Paris. Artists such as Steven Isserlis, Pamela Frank, Jean-Yves Thibaudet are his partners in these recitals and in recordings. *—AMG*

Recommended:

- ○ **Violin Concertos of Barber, Walton & Bloch** / Zinman (cond.), Bell, Baltimore SO / 1997 / London 452851
- ○ **Gershwin Fantasy** / Williams (cond.), Bell, London SO / 1998 / Sony 60659
- ○ **The Red Violin** / Salonen (cond.), Bell, Knowles, Wright, Ricotti, London PO / 1999 / Sony 63010
- ○ **Bernstein: West Side Story Suite** / Zinman (cond.), Bell, London PO / 2001 / Sony 89358

Vincenzo Bellini

b. Nov. 3, 1801, Catania, Sicily, Italy, **d.** Sep. 23, 1835, Puteaux, France
Composer: Opera

Vincenzo Salvatore Carmelo Francesco Bellini was one of the most important composers of Italian opera in his time. He was born in 1801 in Catanina, Sicily, to a family already steeped in music; his father and grandfather were both career musicians. He began composing before receiving any formal music education. Bellini developed a reputation for fine craftsmanship, particularly in the way he forged an intricate relationship between the music and the libretto. To perform one of his operas, singers required extremely agile voices. His abilities and talent earned him the admiration of other composers, including Berlioz, Chopin, and even Wagner, and his flowing, exquisitely sculpted vocal lines represent the epitome of the *bel canto* ideal.

Bellini entered the Royal College of Music of San Sebastiano, now the Naples Conservatory, in 1819. Although he started off in elementary classes, he progressed rapidly and was granted free tuition by 1820. He soon developed into a teacher, becoming a *primo maestrino* in 1824. Bellini's first opera, *Adelson e Salvini*, was chosen to be performed by the conservatory's students. After the initial performance in February 1825, it was performed repeatedly throughout the year. This particular work was never performed outside of the conservatory, but it did serve as a source of material for at least five other operas Bellini composed. Shortly thereafter, Domenico Barbaja of the San Carlo Opera offered Bellini his first commission for an opera, which resulted in *Bianca e Gernando* (1826). That first commission was followed by a second from Barbaja, *Il pirata* (1827), and led to a long-term collaboration between Bellini and librettist Felice Romani. The premiere of *Il pirata* on October 27, 1827, at La Scala, Milan, established Bellini as an internationally acclaimed opera composer.

As Bellini gained experience and recognition, he settled into a working method that stressed quality instead of quantity. He composed fewer operas, for which he commanded higher prices. He was not, however, immune to the pressures of production. His opera *Zaira* (1829), written with Romani for the inauguration of the Teatro Ducale at Parma, was hurriedly completed; the opera was a notable failure and was never produced again. He rebounded, though, with *I Capuleti e i Montecchi* (based on Shakespeare's *Romeo and Juliet*) in 1830.

The year 1831 proved most successful for Bellini as two of his most famous operas, *La sonnambula* and *Norma*, were produced. Although *Norma* was unenthusiastically received, many critics and Bellini himself believed it to be his finest work. Its aria "Casta diva" is one of the evergreens of the classical vocal repertory. These two operas were followed by a less successful composition, *Beatrice di Tenda*. This opera was premiered at La Fenice, Venice on March 16, 1833, a month later than scheduled; the failure led to the falling out of Bellini and Romani.

Bellini spent the summer of 1833 in London directing performances of his operas. He then moved to Paris, where he composed and produced his last opera, *I puritani*, which premiered on January 24, 1835. The libretto for this particular opera was written by the exiled Italian poet Count Carlo Pepoli. Unlike Bellini's previous two operas, *I puritani* was enthusiastically received. At the height of his career and only 33 years old, Bellini died of a chronic intestinal ailment on September 23, 1835, in a small town near near Paris. *—Bruce Lundgren*

OPERA

Beatrice di Tenda (1833)

Having scored a huge success with *I Capuleti e i Montecchi*, Bellini was asked to compose another work for La Fenice, the Venetian opera house most famous for having "risen" from its own ashes on several occasions. The result, *Beatrice di Tenda*, would mark Bellini's final collaboration with his longtime librettist, Felice Romani—and would fail to repeat the achievements of his earlier work. It was premiered at La Fenice on March 16, 1833. From the beginning, Bellini intended his new opera to feature Giuditta Pasta, the star prima donna of the day, in the leading role. In fact, Bellini allowed the diva to choose her own topic, the story of the powerful noblewoman *Beatrice di Tenda* who becomes ensnared in a net of romantic intrigues. This caused friction between the composer and Romani, who had always been free to choose his own topics.

Their relationship worsened during the composition process, and they ended their collaboration on poor terms when Romani issued a written apology for the poor quality (in his opinion) of the finished product. The arguments between Romani and Bellini went public, with both men and their supporters entering into a paper war in the newspapers and musical publications. Each blamed the other for the lateness of the production, and both accused each other of behaving unprofessionally. Romani blamed Bellini's philandering and lack of commitment, and Bellini called Romani the King of Sloth. Much of *Beatrice* was written quite hurriedly, due both to the late receipt of libretto portions from Romani and the last-minute substitution of Orazio Cartagenova into the role of the Count. As a result, the piece did not hold together as well as some of Bellini's other works, and the opening run of performances was not well received. However, there is much beautiful music in *Beatrice*, and the opera was produced on several occasions in the years following Bellini's death.

No major opera company staged *Beatrice di Tenda* during the late nineteenth or early twentieth centuries until 1959, during the heart of the bel canto revival. That resulted in a critical reappraisal which vindicated Bellini's claims that *Beatrice* was the equal of any of his more successful works. Contemporary audiences have proven forgiving toward the plot's similarities to *Anna Bolena* and have admired the many genuinely lovely passages in the opera. The most popular of these is the trio for Beatrice, Agnese, and Orombello in the last act, which Bellini in fact adapted from his other failure, *Zaira*, though he made it simpler and more memorable in this presentation. He also gave a particularly effective scene to Filippo, as well as several show-stopping scenes for the soprano. On the whole, it is not an innovative work, either for Bellini as a composer or for the developing bel canto genre, but it does have considerable power to please audiences with its constant flow of melodic arias, duets, and ensembles. *—AMG*

Synopsis:

Act One. The opera opens in the courtyard of the castle of Binasco near Milan, the home of Filippo Maria Visconti and Beatrice de Lascari. Beatrice is the Countess of Tenda and the widow of Facino Cane. She has married the dissolute Filippo Visconti and secured his position as Duke. Beatrice is much older than he is however, and he has already begun looking over her lady-in-waiting Agnese del Maino. A party is going on at the palace, and Filippo exits from it, upset. When asked why, he replies that he cannot tolerate the idea that Beatrice is still the ruler, that she still has more power than he does, and that all the vassals pay her homage instead of him. He hears Agnese singing from inside the festival hall and his passion is aroused. He resolves to break with Beatrice and pursue the woman he loves. But Agnese, unknown to him, loves Orombello, Lord of Ventimiglia. Orombello in turn is drawn to Beatrice, even though they are related. Agnese sends for him, inviting him to her rooms, and he thinks that the letter is from Beatrice.

Later that night, when Orombello shows up at Agnese's quarters, he is surprised to learn that his secret admirer is not Beatrice but one of her attendants. He confesses his love for Beatrice to the impassioned Agnese, and Agnese becomes jealous. She decides to be revenged against Beatrice by spreading the rumor that she having is an adulterous affair. The next day Beatrice is sitting in the garden trying to understand her husband's hostilities towards her. Filippo, having heard Agnese's rumor, thinks that now he has evidence against Beatrice and can sue for divorce. He accuses her of trying to deprive him of his ducal powers and rights, and she is justly upset. She proclaims her innocence to no avail.

Beatrice goes off to pray before a statue of her dead husband. She hopes that his spirit will lend her guidance in her hour of need. However, Orombello finds her and begins protesting his love for her. He has been followed by Filippo's men and the two are quickly discovered. Both are taken and thrown into prison, even though Beatrice continues to protest her innocence.

Act Two. The act opens in a great hall of the castle, where preparations for a legal hearing have been made. Orombello has been cruelly tortured by the Duke's men and has confessed his guilt and implicated Beatrice along with him. It seems that Beatrice's fate is sealed. She faces the jurors and calmly denies each of the accusations against her. When Orombello is brought in, he also retracts his confession, which was made under duress, and vows to die rather than betray Beatrice. Agnese is filled with remorse. She sees their nobility and is moved to beg for their lives to Filippo. He also is moved and almost refuses to sign the death sentence. But, again enraged at the deference paid to his wife, who he thinks has more power than he does, he signs away their lives.

All of the castle is in mourning. Beatrice is in a castle cell where she, too, has been cruelly tortured. After a night of prayer, she emerges crippled, barely able to walk, but with a transfiguring light infusing her face. All around her are moved to pity, but she announces to them proudly that even under torture, she said nothing. She tells her ladies not to mourn her but to deny her slanderers and uphold her good name. Upon hearing her words, Agnese is overcome by feelings of guilt and remorse, and she casts herself at her mistress' feet in repentance. Beatrice is at first enraged when she understands the extent of Agnese's complicity, but Orombello exhorts her to be forgiving. The three sing in harmonious thirds of forgiveness, and then Beatrice and Orombello march in noble procession to their deaths. *—Rita Laurance*

Recommended:

- ○ **Bellini: Beatrice di Tenda** / P. Steinberg (cond.), Gruberova, Kasarova, Bernardini, ORF SO / Nightingale 70560
- ○ **Bellini: Beatrice Di Tenda** / Rescigno (cond.), J. Sutherland, Horne, Sordello, Kabaivanska, American Opera Society / 1996 / Bella Voce 7226

I Capuleti e i Montecchi (1830)

Shakespeare's play Romeo and Juliet has inspired literally hundreds of opera composers, and each setting has cast a light not only on the original work, but also on the composer and his or her era. Bellini's treatment, the most notable from the bel canto era, emphasizes the poignancy of the story—further enhanced by his choice of a mezzo-soprano trouser role for Romeo (a device that by then was considered slightly old-fashioned for a romantic lead), which emphasizes the youth and vulnerability of the lovers. While there are fiery moments, particularly the various martial declarations in the first scene (for both Tebaldo and Romeo), most of the opera spins out extended threads of wistful and longing song, in passages that count among the best of the bel canto elegiac style.

This opera actually has very little in common with Shakespeare's *Romeo and Juliet*, retaining only the names of the protagonists and the faked death/missed messages debacle. It sets the story into a more historical perspective, changing the feud between the Capulets and Montagues into that of the Guelphs (Capulets) versus Ghibellines (Montagues) from Italian history. It also trims characters out of the story line—we see only Romeo, Juliet (Giulietta), Juliet's father, Friar Lawrence, and Tebaldo (who is now the Capulet engaged to Juliet), and when the opera opens, Romeo and Juliet have already met and fallen in love.

"Oh, quante volte," Giulietta's opening aria in which she longs for Romeo to return to her, is the opera's best-known aria and is highly typical of the entire work. Romeo has one martial cabaletta after the Capulets reject an offer of peace, but otherwise his music, too, mostly expresses the vulnerability and pathos of the two lovers. However, Bellini's mastery is not just in the beauty of the music for the lovers, but in the way it is set against the bloodthirsty music of the chorus, showing both families in the grip of war fever. Bellini used something of the same technique later, in Norma; there the stark contrast is largely limited to the first act, rather than being a focal point of the entire opera.

Bellini was only 29 when he began his setting, but he had already enjoyed two major critical successes (*Il Pirata* in 1827 and *La straniera* in 1829) as well as three other operas and numerous songs and pieces of sacred music. For many, the work opens Bellini's mature period as a composer, displaying a powerful grasp on musical structure and harmony. His characteristic blending of arioso and aria and intensely melodic setting of recitative (which at times almost becomes indistinguishable from arioso) is already present in many moments, most notably in the final ensemble, and this is a style he was to bring to much fuller fruition in *La sonnambula*, *Norma*, and *I Puritani*. While much of the opera contains reworked materials, the reworkings were generally improvements on their originals.

Romeo and Juliet was Bellini's first opera to premiere in Venice at La Fenice, where it enjoyed an enormous success. In 1833, it premiered in London at the King's Theater in the spring (where Bellini was present to witness this new triumph) and at the Paris Opera in the fall, where once again it was very successfully received. Bellini enjoyed some secret personal satisfaction from these successes: the opera included reworked versions of several melodies from *Zaira*, which Bellini believed had been unjustly labeled a failure.

In the later part of the century, the work dropped in critical opinion, though it retained some popularity on the stage. Franz Liszt, Berlioz, and Wagner all condemned it as hopelessly old-fashioned, although even such musical progressives could not deny the appeal and richness of the melodies. It was revived in 1935, the centenary of Bellini's death, and during the bel canto revivals of the later twentieth century it was a regular if not frequent item in the repertoire of both opera houses and recording studios. In 1966, Claudio Abbado even created a version assigning Romeo to a tenor, but it was not widely adopted: almost without exception, Romeo remained a trouser role. *—Ann Feeney*

Synopsis:

Act One. (The story takes place in thirteenth century Verona.) Capellio's supporters (Guelph party) assemble in a gallery in the Capuleti palace. They fear an attack from the Montecchi followers, members of the so-called Ghibelline party. Tebaldo, who is betrothed to Giulietta, daughter of Capellio, announces he will take revenge on Romeo, the Montecchi leader and slayer of Capellio's son. Posing as a Ghibelline ambassador, Romeo enters and proposes a truce between the warring parties, offering his regrets for the "accidental" demise of Capellio's son. He also sets forth a proposal of marriage between his leader Romeo and Giulietta. The offer is rejected and he is informed that Tebaldo is to marry Giulietta anyway.

In Giulietta's quarters, Romeo enters with Lorenzo, one of his lieutenants. The young Romeo urges her to elope with him. Emotionally torn between loyalties to her family and her love for him, she insists she cannot flee with him and implores Romeo to abandon further attempts to dissuade her.

Romeo poses as a Guelph and enters a courtyard in the Capuleti palace, just as wedding plans are being made for Giulietta and Tebaldo. The Montecchi forces commence an attack now, and during the melee and resultant confusion Romeo finds Giulietta and again pleads with her to elope with him. Capellio and Tebaldo enter and recognize Romeo, still believing him to be the Ghibelline envoy though. But he divulges his actual identity, and his forces then arrive to protect him, while Giulietta is separated from him by Guelph partisans.

Act Two. In Capellio's palace Giulietta worries over the fate of Romeo as Lorenzo enters to offer her a drug that he claims will emulate death. He explains that when she awakens from its deep sleep, Romeo will be at her side. But she is hesitant to take it, concerned about the drug's powers. Capellio enters and orders Lorenzo to be put under watch.

Outside Capellio's palace, Romeo worries about Lorenzo, who has failed to rendezvous with him as planned. Suddenly, Tebaldo appears and the two prepare for a duel. But they hear the song of a lament in the distance and soon find out it is for Giulietta.

The Montecchi mourn the death of Giulietta at the gravesite of the Capuletti. Her tomb is opened by Romeo's supporters and he bids her a tearful farewell. In his dark anguish he drinks poison. Giulietta wakes up moments later, sees Romeo and reveals to him that she had taken the drug given her by Lorenzo. But her resurrection is too late: Romeo gradually weakens and falls dead. The bereft Giulietta then collapses and dies on top of his lifeless body. The horrified Capuleti and Montecchi hurry toward the scene, surrounding the corpses of the deceased young lovers. *—Robert Cummings*

Recommended:

○ **Bellini: I Capuleti e i Montecchi** / R. Abbado (cond.), Kasarova, Mei, Vargas, Chiummo, Munich Radio Orch. / 1998 / RCA Victor 68899

○ **Bellini: I Capuleti e i Montecchi** / Runnicles (cond.), Larmore, H-K. Hong, R. Lloyd, P. Groves, Scottish CO / Teldec 21472

Norma (1831)

Bellini followed up the success of his tender comedy *La Sonnambula* with this grand and exotic tale. In its keen characterization and its dramatic conflict between love and patriotic duty it anticipates the major themes of several Verdi operas. The conflict in the opera is between the native Druids of Britain and the Roman soldiers who are occupying the country. The Druid leaders are Oroveso (the High Priest) and Norma (the High Priestess), and the main Romans are the Proconsul Pollione and his centurion Flavio. *Norma* was Vincenzo Bellini's eighth opera and the one that completely secured his fame and fortune as a composer. Although, according to some contemporary reviews, the audience responded coolly to some aspects of *Norma* at its first performance at Milan's La Scala opera house on December 26, 1831, the public soon warmed to it and made it a popular success. In the nineteenth century, musicians as diverse as Richard Wagner, Giuseppe Verdi, Johannes Brahms, and Gustav Mahler, regarded *Norma* as a pivotal work. Today *Norma* is accepted as Bellini's most successful tragic opera.

Felice Romani based the libretto on Alexandre Soumet's play of the same name, which had premiered in Paris in April 1831 to great critical acclaim. In 1998, David Kimbell noted that, despite this immediate literary source, the opera's plot and the nature of its title character have an earlier source in the Greek myth of *Medea*. Kimbell has also noted the distinct similarities between Romani's *Norma* and his text for Giovanni Pacini's opera *La sacerdotessa d'Irminsul* (1820).

The music of *Norma* is laden with all of the conventions of Italian opera in the first half of the nineteenth century, including solo vocal arias and duets, some of which follow the prototypical Rossinian crescendo into full-fledged end-of-act choruses. After the introduction, Pollione's cavatina ("Meco all'altar di Venere") foreshadows the events of the opera. Its form is essentially ternary, with the C minor tonality, nervous violin tremolo, and rhythmically active lower strings of the B section contrasting with the C major tonality of the A section. But Bellini avoids a complete reprise of the A section, returning ultimately to the disturbing minor-mode inflections and nervous instrumental texture of the B material. Pollione's cavatina is paired with a cabaletta ("Me protegge, mi defende"), in which he sings of the protective power of love, in the heroic key of E flat major and triumphant dotted rhythms. Norma's famed cavatina, "Casta diva," a prayer to the moon goddess, is introduced by a silvery flute solo over undulating violin arpeggios. Rather than independently, as previously in "Va crudele, al Dio spietato"/"E tu pure, ah! tu non sai!," Pollione and Adalgisa together in their duet "Vieni in Roma"/"Ciel! Così parlar l'ascolto sempre" complete musical phrases: once Adalgisa agrees to go to Rome with Pollione, she is under his musical control. A similar concept governs the Act II duet between Adalgisa and Norma ("Mira, o Norma"/"Ah! perchè la mia costanza"), in which Norma's weakening resolve to allow Adalgisa to beg for Pollione's return is mirrored in her willingness to adopt Adalgisa's musical language. The finale of Act I consists of a trio in which Norma is musically pitted against Pollione and Adalgisa, and in that of Act II, Oroveso and the chorus of druids punctuate Norma's central aria ("Deh! Non voleri vittime") as she ascends her funeral pyre. *—Jennifer Hambrick*

Synopsis:

Act One. In the forest of the Druids in the first century B.C., Oroveso summons the order ("Ite sul colle") for the ceremony at which Norma will cut the sacred mistletoe. They hope she will bring them victory over the occupying Roman forces. When they leave, Pollione and Flavio enter cautiously. Pollione tells him that though Norma is his lover and the mother of his children, he loves another priestess, Adalgisa. He narrates a dream in which he and Adalgisa were in Rome, exchanging their marriage vows, and Adalgisa disappeared with a terrible cry. He heard his children weeping, and then a voice triumphantly proclaiming that Norma has avenged herself ("Meco all'altar di Venere"). Flavio urges him to flee as the Druids approach, and Pollione declares that his love will protect him ("Me protegge, me difende"), and that he will defy any god that tries to take Adalgisa away from him. They leave, and the Druids return, followed by Norma. She chastises them for speaking of war near the altar, before their gods have announced the time, and assures them that Rome will fall through its own vices, not their swords. As she cuts the mistletoe, she prays to the moon goddess ("Sediziose voci … Casta diva"). The Druids sing that Pollione will fall, and she prays, aside, for him to return to her as loving as before ("Ah! bello a me ritorna"). They leave, and Adalgisa comes to pray, torn between love and duty. Pollione enters, and she orders him to leave her. But he pleads with her ("Va, crudele, al Dio spietato"). When he tells her he has been recalled to Rome and asks her to come with him, she first says she cannot, but wavers as he continues to plead ("Vieni in Roma, ah, vieni, o cara"), and she agrees to meet him later and leave with him. In Norma's dwelling, she is troubled by the sight of her children, a painful reminder of Pollione's possible infidelity. He has told her he has been recalled to Rome, but has not spoken of bringing her with him. Clotilde leaves with the children, and Adalgisa enters. Norma greets her kindly, and Adalgisa confesses that she wishes to renounce her vow of chastity, as she is in love ("A pie dell'ara ov'io pregava"). She describes falling in love, and Norma, aside, remembers the same emotions. Aloud, she tells Adalgisa she will release her, and asks her who the man is. Adalgisa says he is a Roman, and Pollione appears. Norma is furious and he begs her to be merciful towards the innocent Adalgisa. Norma assures Adalgisa she is the victim of a seducer ("Oh! Di qual sei tu vittima")/ Pollione turns to leave, and Adalgisa refuses to accompany him, calling him a traitor. Norma scornfully tells him to forget his promises, his children, and his honor ("Vanne, si, mi lascia, indegno"), and he angrily responds while Adalgisa laments. Outside, they hear the Druids gathering, and he leaves.

Act Two. The second act opens in Norma's bedroom, where she plans to stab her sleeping children, both out of hate and to protect them from the vengeance of the Druids or slavery in Rome, but she cannot bring herself to kill them. She sends for Adalgisa, and when she arrives, Norma asks her to take the children when she leaves with Pollione ("Deh! con te, li prendi"). She asks only that they not be abandoned or enslaved; Adalgisa can retain honors and riches for her own children. Adalgisa refuses, saying she will plead with Pollione to return to Norma, and when Norma refuses to countenance this, Adalgisa begs her to think of her children ("Mira, o Norma"). Norma agrees, and the two swear eternal friendship ("Si, fino all'ore estreme"). The Druid warriors gather, wondering why Pollione has not left yet. Oroveso enters and tells them Pollione will replaced by a far more fearsome proconsul, and that Norma has not responded to this new situation. They must keep their hate hidden until their gods call for war. Inside the temple, Norma, now hopeful, waits for Pollione, but Clotilde reports that Adalgisa was unsuccessful and that Pollione threatened to steal her from their gods' very altar. Norma furiously summons the Druids to declare war ("Guerra, Guerra!"), saying she will indicate the appropriate sacrificial victim. Clotilde reports that a Roman was caught entering the temple, and Pollione is brought in. They question him, but he refuses to answer. Norma takes a dagger to kill him, but hesitates, then sends everyone away, saying she must interrogate him. When they are alone ("In mia man alfin tu sei"), she offers to let him escape if he renounces Adalgisa and leaves, but he refuses. When she threatens to take her revenge not on him but on Adalgisa and their children, he is horrified and pleads with her to kill him or let him kill himself, but she says she intends to make him as unhappy as she is ("Nel suo cor ti' vo ferire"). She calls for the Druids to return and tells them that a priestess who has defiled her vows must be burnt alive. Pollione begs her to be silent, but after keeping him in suspense, she declares that she herself is the one. She turns to him and says a cruel god, stronger than they, wanted them united in life and death ("Qual cor tradisti, qual cor perdesti"). He tells her his remorse has reawakened his love for her. Oroveso and the Druids plead with her to say she was raving, but she is steadfast. She pleads with Oroveso to protect her children, and he finally agrees ("Deh! Non volerli vittime"). Pollione and Norma both say they can die contented, and as Oroveso prays that his grief will be forgiven, she and Pollione are taken to the stake to be burnt. *—Ann Feeney*

Recommended:

○ **Bellini: Norma** / Serafin (cond.), Callas, Filippeschi, Stignani, Orch. del Teatro La Scala / 1997 / EMI 56271

○ **Bellini: Norma** / Serafin (cond.), Callas, C. Ludwig, F. Corelli, Zaccaria, Orch. del Teatro La Scala / 1997 / EMI 66428

Il Pirata (1827)

It is difficult for modern listeners to imagine a time when a mad scene and a fallen hero weren't standard fare, but when Bellini composed his *Il Pirata* these plot elements were novelties. The Gothic novel, with its Byronic heroes, virtuous, sensitive heroines, and stormy plots was becoming a major literary form, and *Il Pirata* parlayed this trend into a triumphant run of performances at La Scala. The music reflects the mood of the original play (*Bertram, ou Le pirate* by J.S. Taylor), though with the softer edges that Bellini and his librettist, Felice Romani decided would make it more appropriate for the operatic stage.

Imogene, the heroine, has music that reflects her emotional tumult and ever-growing fragility. Her music is generally languid, but occasionally becomes fevered. Gualtiero, the hero, reflects rather more of the self-pitying than the fiery, dangerous side of the gothic hero (his original character in the play is far more violent and bitter), but the music in which he declares his despair over what he perceives as Imogene's betrayal is lovely enough to make him relatively sympathetic. There is more pathos than fire in his voluntary surrender to justice (compare it, for example, to another hero turned bandit, Verdi's Ernani, or I Masnadieri), but the music is moving and effective. The most famous scene in the opera is Imogene's mad scene. The fiery runs and trills and vocal leaps vividly depict the way that her mind has become disconnected from all reality and is focused only on Gualtiero's impending execution. While later composers were to write more vocally beautiful mad scenes, such as Donizetti in his Lucia di Lammermoor or Linda di Chamounix, this was the first great example of the device and one of the most convincing. *—AMG*

Synopsis:

Act One. Act One opens during a storm on the coast. Some fishermen and Godfredo are rescuing the sailors of a wrecked ship. Gualtiero and Itulbo come ashore, and Godfredo greets Gualtiero affectionately. He tells him that since Gualtiero's banishment, he himself has been deprived of his home and possessions and has become a hermit. Gualtiero tells him that in his suffering, he was sustained only by his thoughts of Imogene ("Nel furor delle tempeste"). The fishermen return and say that Imogene is coming in person to help, and Godfredo urges Gualtiero to hide so she will not recognize him. He declares that he lives only for his love of her ("Per te di vane lagrime"), but he agrees to hide. When Imogene enters, she questions Itulbo, asking in particular about the fate of the pirate leader in the region they just traveled, and when Itulbo answers that he is probably imprisoned or dead, she tries to hide her despair, remembering a dream in which she was lamenting over his bloodied corpse ("Lo sognai ferito, esangue"). She confides to Adele ("Quando a un tratto") that she also dreamt that her husband accused her of causing his death. Gualtiero briefly emerges and recognizes her, but Godfredo makes him return to hiding, as the chorus comments on her sadness, and she determines to help the stranger she glimpsed.

On the castle terrace, the pirates are celebrating their rescue ("Evviva! allegri!"), and Itulbo warns them to leave before Imogene enters for fear that she might guess their real identity. Adele tells her that she invited the stranger to ask for her help, and he followed her in silence. Gualtiero enters. Refusing her offered gift of money, he tells her he has suffered losses which cannot be recovered, and that fate has robbed him of his family and homeland. She finds herself strangely frightened and turns to leave, telling him to pray for one even more unhappy than he. He reveals his identity and she runs into his arms, but then tears herself away. He asks why she is living in Ernesto's court, and she unhappily tells him that to save her father, she was forced to marry Ernesto. He bursts out in rage ("Pietosa al padre! e meco"), and she defends her action. Her ladies enter with her son, and Gualtiero is ready to kill him. But at her pleas, he instead embraces him ("Bagnato dalle lagrime"). He leaves, and Adele tells her Ernesto is on his way. His soldiers sing of his victories ("Piu temuto, piu splendido nome"), but he shares the glory with them ("Si, vincemmo"). Imogene sadly greets him, and he asks why she sheltered the strangers. He suspects them of being pirates and questions Itulbo. Imogene dissuades him from imprisoning them, but Gualtiero can barely restrain his anger and keep his identity concealed. He quietly tells Imogene to meet him that night so he can speak to her one last time, threatening her with her family's deaths if she does not agree. Ernesto is still suspicious, and Itulbo, Godfredo, Imogene, and Adele express their dismay. Only Imogene's collapse keeps Gualtiero from attacking Ernesto then and there.

Act Two. Adele and her ladies comment on Imogene's continued distress. She enters, followed by Ernesto, who is angry over her continued sorrow. He accuses her of still loving Gualtiero ("Tu m'appristi in cor ferita"). She responds that he knew of that love when he forced her to marry him, but he tells her that now, with all hope of her affection gone, he will find pleasure only in making her as unhappy as he is. A messenger brings him news that Gualtiero is hidden in his own court, and despite Imogene's warnings that it will mean his death, he is determined to seek his enemy out. On the terrace, Itulbo tries to persuade Gualtiero to leave without seeing Imogene, but he is adamant. When she arrives, he tells her he will leave if she comes with him; otherwise, he will seek revenge or death. At her tears, he tries to comfort her with the thought that they will find a peaceful refuge somewhere ("Per noi tranquillo un porto"), but she says she could not escape her remorse. Ernesto approaches, and, recognizing Gualtiero, is overjoyed at the thought that he is in his power. Gualtiero bitterly says he does not wish to live ("Cedo al destin orribile"). He rushes out from hiding and he and Ernesto go off to fight, though she frantically begs them to kill her instead. When Adele and her ladies come in and urge her to leave, she instead runs to try to stop the duel.

Inside, ladies and knights lament Ernesto's death ("Lasso! perir cosi") and condemn Gualtiero as a traitor. He himself enters and tells them that though he arranged for his followers to escape and could have escaped himself, he will surrender. They are unwillingly moved at his courage. He tells Adele ("Tu vedrai la sventurata") that he hopes Imogene will forgive and pray for him and tells the knights that he hopes his memory will not be always hated, and that his tomb will speak of his suffering ("Ma non fia sempre odiata"), though they declare it will speak only of his crimes. He and the knights leave for the trial, and Imogene enters with her son. She is insane with grief and relives Ernesto's death. She briefly recognizes her son ("Col sorriso d'innocenza") but thinks the sound of the trumpet announcing Gualtiero's death sentence is that of the Last Judgement. Recognizing it for what it is, she cries out in horror for the sun to hide itself ("Oh, Sole! ti vela"). She imagines the scaffold prepared for Gualtiero's execution, and collapses. *—Ann Feeney*

Recommended:

- ○ **Bellini: Il Pirata** / Gavazzeni (cond.), Caballé, Marti, Cappuccilli, Raimondi, Orch. RTV Italiana, Rome / 1999 / EMI 67121
- ○ **Bellini: Il Pirata** / Rescigno (cond.), Callas, Caballé, Ferraro, Sarfaty, American Opera Society Orch. / Verona 28014

I Puritani (1835)

This "melodramma serio" in three acts, with a libretto by Count Carlo Pepoli after the play *Têtes Rondes et Cavaliers* (Roundheads and Cavaliers) by Ancelot and Xavier, was premiered in Paris at the Théâtre Italien on January 24, 1835. The title was chosen because of the popularity of Scott's novel *Old Mortality* (1816), titled in French *Les puritains d'Ecosse* (1817) and in Italian *I puritani di Scozia* (1825). This popular work broke new ground in its unusual rhythmic phrase lengths, its extended time scale in the Wagnerian manner, its bel canto style that was modified to fit the dramatic action, and its spectacular stage effects and orchestrations. It was Bellini's final opera.

There is no overture, but Bellini creates the perfect atmosphere and foreshadows events to come with a minimum of means—tympani rolls, a long series of sforzando chords, frequent change between parallel major and minor keys—as the sunrise illuminates the courtyard of a fortress near Plymouth with turrets, battlements, and drawbridges in the scene. It is the time of war between the Royalists and the Puritans. Soldiers sing "Arise!" and there are morning prayers. Riccardo (Sir Richard Forth) hopes to marry Elvira, daughter of governor Lord Walton, but she loves Arturo (Lord Arthur Talbot). Bellini's deliberate blurring of closed and open forms is exemplified here when Riccardo's aria expressing grief ("Ah! per sempre io ti perdei") seems to begin earlier in the arioso "O Elvira, o mio sospir."

Elvira learns from her uncle Giorgio (Sir George) that Lord Walton has agreed to let her marry Arturo. Her happiness is expressed in the cabaletta "A quel nome." In the Hall of Arms a chorus welcomes Arturo, whose cavatina turns into a quartet. Walton has a prisoner who discloses to Arturo that she is Queen Henrietta Maria, a Royalist. Arturo disguises her in Elvira's wedding veil and smuggles her out of the castle with Riccardo's secret complicity. The escape is discovered and Arturo is declared a traitor.

Act II presents Elvira's emotional suffering. The chorus "Cinta di fiori e col bel crin disciolto" describes, in 11-syllable lines most often employed in recitatives and some serenades, her "disheveled hair" and "garland of flowers." Riccardo agrees with Giorgio that, out of concern for Elvira, Arturo must be saved. The chorus sings "Suoni la tromba...": "To die in war is glorious, we cry 'liberty'!"... with "lealtà" (loyalty!) and "fedeltà" (fidelity!) substituted in Italy.

In Act III, Arturo is chased through a furious storm but loses the armed men. In a wooded garden near Elvira's rooms, he hears her sing a song he taught her and sings the melody along with her. He explains why he had to flee; Elvira has a relapse at the sound of drums, and her cries bring guards who arrest Arturo. He is saved moments before his execution by Cromwell's declaration of amnesty (announced by a hunting horn). Calls for death from the soldiers are changed to cries of joy for the lovers by the people. *—"Blue Gene" Tyranny*

Synopsis:

Act One. The action takes place during the English Civil War (1642–48). The first scene opens at the fortress of Lord Gualtiero Walton. Festivities begin in celebration of the marriage of Elvira, Walton's daughter, to Lord Arturo Talbo, a Stuart sympathizer. Riccardo, a Puritan Colonel, confides in Bruno, a Puritan officer, that he had wanted to marry Elvira, but that she had never showed any interest in him. In Elvira's quarters, she stews over fears she may have to marry Riccardo, but her uncle, Sir Giorgio Walton, tells he has already convinced her father to give her hand to Arturo.

Arturo arrives in the Hall of Arms and is informed by Walton that he cannot attend the couple's wedding, since he must accompany a young female prisoner, believed to be a Stuart spy, to London. The suspect is brought in and confesses her identity to Arturo—she is Charles I's widow, Queen Henrietta Maria, known in the opera as Enrichetta. Realizing a death sentence awaits her once her identity becomes known, Arturo decides to help her. Elvira enters and, assuming the strange woman is an attendant, lays a bridal veil on her head to examine its appearance. She departs, leaving the veil and, unwittingly, a disguise for Enrichetta to use for escape. Riccardo enters to challenge Arturo to a duel, but recognizing the prisoner agrees to allow her to flee with his rival. But when Elvira reenters, the plan falters amid confusion and orders are issued for the apprehension of Arturo and Enrichetta. Elvira now begins losing her sanity.

Act Two. Giorgio, the deranged Elvira, and many attendants are in a hallway in the fortress. Riccardo enters to announce that Arturo will be captured and executed. Elvira hallucinates, seeing and hearing Arturo, while Giorgio and Riccardo pity her in her madness. The former convinces Riccardo that Elvira could not survive news of Arturo's death and that he must be spared. Riccardo agrees, leaving provision for his execution in the event Arturo takes part in any attack with Cavalier forces on the fortress.

Act Three. Outside Elvira's quarters Arturo is pursued by Puritan soldiers. After he eludes them, Elvira appears and recognizes him. The sight temporarily restores her sanity and the two declare their love for each other. Arturo also explains the circumstances of his relationship to Enrichetta. Elvira is jolted back to madness, however, by the sound of a drum, and she calls out in fear. Arturo is captured by Giorgio, Riccardo, and a group of soldiers. He is then condemned to death, but when Elvira hears the grim sentence pronounced, she regains her sanity once more and insists she will die with him. A messenger enters to bring news of Cromwell's victory and that amnesty for all has been declared. Arturo and Elvira are now celebrated and free to marry. *—Robert Cummings*

Recommended:

- ○ **Bellini: I Puritani** / Bonynge (cond.), J. Sutherland, Pavarotti, Cappuccilli, Ghiaurov, London SO / London 417588

La sonnambula (1831)

La sonnambula, a light, romantic opera in which romantic difficulties arise from the misinterpretation of the heroine's sleepwalking activities, was one of Bellini's finer triumphs. Exquisite vocal lines, asymmetrical but beautiful in their spontaneity and originality, are the hallmarks of this opera. The libretto was by Felice Romani. The basis for his story line was a ballet by Eugène Scribe, which in turn was based on a comédie-vaudeville of two acts that had been staged in Paris in 1819. Somnambulism was a common theme in nineteenth century opera, but none of the other stories is quite the same as that of Bellini's opera. The premiere was at the Teatro Carcano of Milan, on March 6, 1831. It was very well received by critics and public alike, and the work helped to cement Bellini's reputation as one of the compositional stars of nineteenth century bel canto opera.

Originally Romani and Bellini had contracted with the Carcano theater to produce an opera based on Victor Hugo's *Hernani*, which at that time had caused a furor in revolutionary France, but the Hugo story did not get past the conservative Milanese censors. The Carcano was attempting to establish itself as competition to the great La Scala theater of Milan, and Bellini and Romani were hired in hopes that they could produce a work to rival the opulent productions of La Scala. The city was at that time controlled by Austria, and the government in power was in no mood to encourage rebellion or revolution. So Bellini and Romani chose a less controversial subject.

Bellini began work on *La sonnambula* in January of 1831. Still recovering from a serious illness, the convalescing Bellini stayed at the home of the Contessa Giuseppina Appiani, a cultured woman known for the sophistication of her salon. Also a friend of Donizetti and Verdi, she was not unacquainted with the world of opera and gave Bellini a creative work environment. The prima donna Giuditta Pasta had already been hired to sing the title role in the Ernani project, and it was a simple matter to convince her to take the lead role of *La sonnambula.* Bellini had a singer of virtuosic technical capabilities, and a musician of incomparable talent, to help him create the romantic role of Amina. He particularly suited the music to Pasta's strengths, and her performance conquered the Milanese public completely.

The original work on which *La sonnambula* was based was a ballet, and its pastoral and sentimental qualities were accentuated in the libretto. It was left up to Bellini to bring out these qualities and exploit them. The opening music is joyful, celebrating, and rustic. The beginning scenes establish the ambiance of the story, and the dramatic development proceeds apace thanks to Bellini's incredible vocal writing. One of the highlights of the drama comes in the first act, as the villagers recount the story of a phantom (who is actually Amina) said to be haunting their village. She walks at night, dressed in a long white gown, and even the animals turn away and howl. The chorus is set syllabically to give it an ominous feel, and as the ghost passes by, there is a sudden brightening of the tonality from E flat to D major. Another highlight is Amina's solo "Ah! Non giunge!," which has survived as one of the all-time favorites of Italian opera. The bright, tender, gentleness of the aria aptly portrays Amina's personality, and the recitatives throughout are handled with the same dramatic and musical sympathy; in many ways, they pave the way for the fusion of recitative and aria that came to opera later in the nineteenth century. Amina's famous sleepwalking scene, ending with its brilliant and demanding cabaletta, has made the tole a favorite with coloratura sopranos including such historic divas as Adelina Patti, Luisa Tetrazzini, and Jenny Lind in the nineteenth century to to Galli-Curci, dal Monte, Callas, and Sutherland in the twentieth. —*AMG*

Synopsis:

Act One. The opera takes place during the early nineteenth century in a Swiss village. As the curtain rises, one sees a set with mountains in the distance, a water mill in the background, and the village inn in the foreground. The villagers are celebrating the engagement of Amina, an orphan raised by the owner of the village mill, and a wealthy landowner named Elvino. They are preparing for the wedding, which is to be celebrated that week. Lisa, owner of the inn, is madly in love with Elvino, and her heart is filled with jealousy at the thought that he will soon marry someone else. But Alessio has been flirting with her recently, and her vanity is somewhat gratified by this. Amina's guardian Theresa enters with Elvino on her arm. Next the village notary arrives, and the engagement is certified. Elvino places the ring of his mother on Amina's waiting finger, and there is general rejoicing.

Just then a stranger enters the village and requests that his horses be given water and food. He is counseled to spend the night at the inn rather than journey on to the castle during dark. It is Count Rodolpho, the owner of the castle, although the villagers don't recognize him. When told that Amina is soon to be a bride, he showers her with gallant compliments, and Elvino becomes jealous. Theresa tells all assembled of a strange phantom that wanders the village in a white gown during the night. The villagers join in the hue and cry, and all are urged to get to bed before nightfall. The Count laughs off the story, and all retire to bed.

Back at Rodolpho's rooms, Lisa is flirting with the Count. She tells him that the villagers know his true identity and soon will send him a welcome party. A noise is heard, and Lisa quickly hides, but drops her handkerchief as she flees. It is Amina, walking in her sleep. The Count immediately realizes that she is sleepwalking, and that it is she whom the villagers have mistaken for a phantom during the night. When Amina begins talking in her sleep as well, the Count tactfully leaves, locking the door behind him, so that she can get some rest. She lies down on the Count's couch and falls fast asleep. But Lisa has seen everything, and she brings the already jealous Elvino and the other villagers to the scene. Amina wakes in confusion, and all suspect her of infidelity. Elvino immediately repudiates her, although she insists that she is innocent of any wrongdoing.

Act Two. Between the village and the castle the villagers have gathered, hoping to convince the Count to intercede on Amina's behalf. But Elvino takes back his mother's ring and again rejects Amina. He even has gone so far as to promise to marry Lisa instead. Even though the Count tells Elvino that Amina is a somnambulist, plans are being made for the new wedding—Elvino has never heard of somnambulism. In an effort to convince Elvino that Lisa, too, was unfaithful, Theresa shows him the handkerchief that she found in the Count's room. The Count again tries to explain about sleepwalking, and just then, right before their eyes, all the villagers behold Amina walking along the roof of the mill. She crosses over a decrepit old bridge which spans the quickly turning mill wheel. She is fast asleep, and one false step would mean her death! But she finishes her dangerous crossing and joins the villagers, although still fast asleep. She begins lamenting the ways of the merciless Elvino, speaking of the ring he so recently took back from her. She carries some dried flowers that he had given to her a few days before, and she weeps over them. Unable to bear her sorrow any longer, Elvino kneels before her. Gently he replaces the ring on her finger, and the rejoicing of the villagers awakens her to a scene of joy. The original wedding ceremony can now go forward. —*Rita Laurance*

Recommended:

- ○ **Bellini: La Sonnambula** / Bonynge (cond.), Sutherland, Pavarotti, Ghiaurov, National PO / 1987 / London 417424
- ○ **Bellini: La Sonnambula** / Votto (cond.), Callas, N. Monti, Zaccaria, Orch. del Teatro La Scala / 1997 / EMI 56278

Gabriela Beňačková

b. Mar. 25, 1944, Bratislava, Czechoslovakia

Soprano

While best known for her accomplishments in Czech music, particularly that of Dvořák and Smetana, Beňačková has performed in nearly all the lirico-spinto soprano roles in the Italian repertoire. She has earned equal praise for her musicianship and vocal beauty, though she is occasionally accused of bringing a non-Italianate coolness to those roles. She has also sung the more lyric Wagner roles, including Eva and Senta.

Her opera debut was at the National Theater in Prague, as Natasha in Prokofiev's *War and Peace*, in 1970. In 1975, she sang her first Jenufa there; like Dvořák's *Rusalka*, that role has since become one of her signatures. Jenufa was also the vehicle for her 1978 Vienna State Opera debut. In 1979, she made her Covent Garden debut as Tatyana in Tchaikovsky's *Eugene Onegin*. She sang the title role of Smetana's *LibuS̆e* for the re-opening of the National Theater in Prague in 1983. Her Met debut was as Kát'a Kabanová in 1991, which she also recorded with Sir Charles Mackerras in 1997. She also continued her career as a concert artist in works by Dvořák, Janáček and Mahler. Beňačková has been involved in the restoration of Gustav Mahler's birthplace at Kaliste in the Czech Republic. —*Ann Feeney*

Recommended:

- ○ **Janáček: Jenufa** / Jilek (cond.), Beňačková, Barova, Pribyl, Berman, Brno Janáček Opera Chorus & Orch. / Supraphon 102751
- ○ **Smetana: The Bartered Bride** / Kosler (cond.), Beňačková, Dvorsky, Novak, Jindrak, Czech PO & Chorus / Supraphon 103511
- ○ **Gabriela Beňačková - Operatic Recital** / Neumann, Gregor (conds.), Beňačková, Czech PO / Supraphon 112239

Franz (František) Benda

b. Nov. 22, 1709, Alt-Benatek, Czechoslovakia, **d.** Mar. 7, 1786, Neuendorf, Germany

Composer

Franz Benda was one of the leaders in a generation of Bohemian musicians who entered Austrian and German musical life, filling important roles in the development of late Baroque and early Classical music.

František Benda (later Germanized to Franz) was the oldest of five musical children of a linen weaver and village musician who had married Dorota Brixi, an offspring of another major Bohemian music family. This was the foundation of a dynasty of musicians that continues to this day, when one can readily obtain compact discs performed by a family group called the Benda Musicians.

František, the eldest, became a choirboy at St. Nicholas church in Prague when he was nine, giving him the opportunity for musical studies. However, he ran away from its discipline at 11 to Dresden, Germany, where he got a similar position and learned violin. He returned to Prague in 1723, becoming alto soloist in a Jesuit seminary, where he received a good general and musical education, remaining there until his voice changed and he then returned home and resumed violin studies.

When he got a little older, he fell in love with a baker's daughter and petitioned the local count for permission to learn the secrets of Bohemian gingerbread. The count offered as an alternative to pay Benda's way to Prague for more violin studies. After ten weeks, his teacher there, Konicek, pronounced him a fully trained professional. Benda later said he learned more by following around a Jewish street musician named Lebel.

The 16-year-old Benda escaped Bohemia without permission and got work in Poland. Benda formed a house orchestra for Governor Suchaczewski that was so good he was hired away by the King of Poland, Augustus II the Strong, in 1732. The king died a year later, leaving Benda unemployed. He went to Dresden, got a job, and came to the attention of King Frederick the Great of Prussia, who hired him in 1740 to a job Benda kept for life. He even accompanied Frederick (who was a flute player) on his military campaigns. He had six children, among whom four (two boys and two girls) became professional musicians. His main compositional legacy is an assortment of violin sonatas written at the Prussian court, in which he influenced the future development of violin playing. These manuscripts also contain many observations about style and ornamentation of the period, valuable to research in the "authentic" performance movement. —*Joseph Stevenson*

Overview of Works (1735–1786)

Franz (or František) Benda was one of the leading members of a family of Bohemian musicians, of whom Franz and his brother Georg (Jirí Antonín) were the most notable. Trained as chorister, he subsequently gained renown as a violinist, a talent which was first brought to the notice of the future Frederick the Great, who took him into his service. His life spans the important changes in music which took place during the eighteenth century, a period during which the late Baroque forms of Handel and Bach were replaced by a variety of transitional styles which eventually lead to the fully-fledged Classical works of Haydn and Mozart. The Berlin of Frederick the Great was a melting pot of these advanced styles, the flute-playing king (himself a composer) being fond of the modern, graceful galant style exemplified by his Kapellmeister, Johann Quantz. Also employed by Frederick at the Berlin court was Bach's eldest son, Carl Philipp Emanuel, whose deeply expressive and often agitated music (known as the *Empfindsamer Stil*) may have pleased the king less, but became synonymous with north German music of the mid-century. Benda's compositions, which include symphonies, violin and other concertos, and solo and chamber works for violin, reflect elements of both the galant and *Empfindsamer Stil*, both of which had similar objectives in mind—the simplification of music from counterpoint in favor of a more natural mode of expressivity, a musical philosophy closely tied to the growth of Enlightenment. The restless, dynamism of the *Empfindsamer Stil* can clearly be heard in the opening Allegro con brio of the *Flute Concerto in E minor* by Benda. Here the music is characterized by restless energy, disruptions, and wide leaps typical of the north German style. Another *Flute Concerto in G* has a long, brooding Largo equally typical of the extreme expressivity sought by composers such as Benda and C.P.E. Bach, while the final Presto of the same concerto more closely approaches the lighter, more elegant galant writing. Unlike his brother Georg, who was primarily a dramatic composer, Franz Benda paid virtually no attention to vocal music. *—Brian Robins*

Recommended:

- ○ **F. Benda: 10 Sinfonie** / Munclinger (cond.), Ars Rediviva / 2002 / Supraphon 3646
- ○ **F. Benda: Flute Concertos** / Munclinger (cond.), Adorjan, Ars Rediviva / Orfeo 151101

Cathy Berberian

b. Jul. 4, 1928, Attleboro, MA, **d.** Mar. 6, 1983, Rome, Italy
Mezzo-Soprano

A much-respected artist, mezzo-soprano Cathy Berberian won her reputation as an interpreter of difficult contemporary scores, but left an exemplary recorded performance in an opera by Monteverdi as a centerpiece of her rarefied art. In fact, Berberian was an accomplished performer in a great many musical styles, performing works from the pre-Baroque era up to contemporary times. Married between 1950 and 1966 to Italian composer Luciano Berio, the singer moved in circles that encouraged her to explore the music of her own age. She turned out to be the most persuasive advocate many a modern composer could desire.

Cross-discipline and cross-cultural training aided Berberian in the formation of her own broad tastes. At Columbia University and New York University, she exposed herself to literature, mime, and the dances of Iberian, Armenian, and Middle East cultures, among other subjects. Following voice training with Giorgina del Vigo in Milan, she made her debut in 1957 at a concert of contemporary music in Naples. Identified as a musical and technically secure interpreter of vocally treacherous works of the day, she was invited to Rome to perform on a program of music by John Cage the next year. Her first American appearance as a professional singer took place at the Tanglewood festival in 1960; she perfomed in Berio's *Circles*, one of a series of works written to take advantage of her remarkable technical brilliance and her riveting presence on the concert stage. Fame overtook her quickly, and she became the preferred interpreter of works written specifically for her by the likes of Sylvano Bussotti, Hans Werner Henze, and Igor Stravinsky. Many such works proved all but unperformable by anyone else.

Tragically short-lived, Berberian left a recorded legacy that displays her all-encompassing interests. In addition to the expected works by Berio and Cage, she recorded a number of folk songs, "Summertime" from Gershwin's *Porgy and Bess*, and a powerfully affecting Ottavia in Nikolaus Harnoncourt's edition of Monteverdi's *L'incoronazione di Poppea*. Her anguished farewell to Rome holds both great feeling and poised vocalism and is one of the high moments in the performance.

In addition to her performing skills, Berberian was a composer of some note. Her *Stripsody*, written in 1966, reveals both humor and the ability to exploit her own virtuosity as a performer. *—Erik Eriksson*

Recommended:

- ○ **MagnifiCathy: The Many Voices of Cathy Berberian** / Berberian / 1988 / Wergo 60054
- ○ **Berio: Circles; Sequenzae I, III, V** / Berberian, Casadesus, Nicolet, Globokar, Drouet / 1991 / Wergo 6021
- ○ **Cathy Berberian Sings Monteverdi** / Harnoncourt (cond.), Berberian, Esswood, Rogers, Kozma, Theuring, Vienna Concentus Musicus / 1995 / Teldec 10032
- ○ **Berberian Sings Berio** / Berberian / RCA 62540
- ○ **Berio: Point on the Curve to Find...** / Bernasconi, Berio (conds.), Holliger, Berberian, Castellani, Schwartz, Contrechamps Ensemble, Swiss-Italian Radio Orchestra / 1999 / Aura 0171

Alban Berg

b. Feb. 9, 1885, Vienna, Austria, **d.** Dec. 24, 1935, Vienna, Austria
Composer: Opera, Orchestral, Concerto, Chamber Music, Vocal, Keyboard

Alban Maria Johannes Berg is one of the central figures of twentieth century musical composition. As one of the triumvirate of the Second Viennese School, Berg produced a rather small body of work that is nonetheless distinguished by a strongly Romantic aesthetic and a distinctive dramatic sense.

Berg's father was an export salesman, his mother the daughter of the Austrian Imperial jeweler. The young Alban's musical training consisted mainly of piano lessons from his aunt. By his teenage years, however, he had composed dozens of songs without the benefit of formal compositional studies. Berg was a dreamy youth and an indifferent student. In 1903, he endured the end of a passionate (if adolescent) love affair, failed his school finishing exams, and became despondent over the death of his idol, composer Hugo Wolf, all of which led to a suicide attempt. However, he survived to repeat his final year of school and went to work as an apprentice accountant. In 1904 Berg's brother, Charley, took Alban's compositions to Arnold Schoenberg, who accepted Berg as a student. In 1907 Berg met the singer Helene Nahowski, overcame her parents' objections over his poor health (he had severe asthma) and lack of prospects, and married her in 1911.

The composer was drafted into the Austrian army in 1915, served for 11 months, and was discharged for poor health. The army experience led him to revisit *Woyzeck*, Georg Büchner's tragedy about a horribly brutalized private. In 1917, Berg began an operatic adaptation of the play, which occupied him for the next five years. When the Austro-Hungarian empire collapsed in the wake of World War I, Berg found work as business manager of Schoenberg's Society for Private Musical Performances, an organization which allowed Vienna's musical avant-garde to enjoy professionally prepared performances before friendly, critic-free audiences.

After a number of interruptions related to personal and familial affairs, Berg completed *Wozzeck* in 1922. Though initially savaged by critics, the opera eventually gained momentum, enjoying performances throughout Europe and recognition as a masterpiece. Berg's next major work, the *Chamber Concerto* (1923–25) was among his first to demonstrate the influence of Schoenberg's 12-tone method, though the work does not make rigorous, consistent use of 12-tone practices. In 1925 and 1926, Berg wrote the *Lyric Suite* for string quartet, parts of which systematically employ 12-tone principles. The *Lyric Suite* remains one of the composer's most often performed works; George Gershwin, it is said, had a particular admiration for this music. Years after Berg's death, scholars confirmed that the composer had originally included a sung text in the last movement, a tribute to his "secret" lover, Hanna Fuchs-Robertin. The Suite is now sometimes performed with this restored text.

The last of Berg's works are among his most important. The *Violin Concerto* (1935) is dedicated "to the Memory of an Angel," a reference to the daughter of Alma Mahler (a close ally) and Walter Gropius, Manon, who had died at the age of 19. The work is particularly striking in its lyrical expressiveness and for the incorporation of tonal elements into its 12-tone idiom. At the time of his death from blood poisoning in 1935, Berg was in the middle of work on his opera *Lulu*, a sexual horror story, which he had begun in 1929. The opera's unfinished third act was completed by Friedrich Cerha in 1976, after 12 years of work. *—AMG*

OPERA

Lulu (1929–1935)

On May 29, 1905, Karl Kraus staged Frank Wedekind's play *Büchse der Pandora* (Pandora's Box) in Vienna. Among those in attendance was the 20-year-old Alban Berg, who found in Wedekind's dramas "the really new direction—the emphasis on the sensual in modern works!" 23 years later the composer began work on *Lulu* (1929–35), an opera based on Wedekind's tragedies. Unlike Georg Büchner's *Wozzeck*, Wedekind's plays presented Berg with complete plots and stylized dialogue. The composer fashioned the seven acts of two Wedekind plays into the seven scenes of his opera, developing a tight, cyclic structure not present in Wedekind's original. As with *Wozzeck*, Berg found himself drawn to the mundane realities represented in Wedekind's work.

Berg composed *Lulu* according to his unique application of 12-tone principles, and, as in his *Violin Concerto* (1935), chose row forms that yielded diatonic sonorities. Furthermore, while a single row dictates the thematic material, Berg freely manipulates the row to produce the melodic shapes he associates with his characters. Berg complements these Wagnerian leitmotifs with instrumental associations: the saxophone for Alwa and the piano for Rodrigo. Each character has his or her own row, and Berg uses other musical gestures to represent characters further; the coarseness of the athlete Rodrigo is depicted in pentatonic scales, as well as in forearm and fist clusters on the piano.

The story is a sordid one, concerning sex, seduction, degradation, and betrayal. The title character is in many ways the ultimate representation of the familiar Romantic-era figure of the femme fatale, the woman whose sexuality brings men to their doom. A physician falls in love with her, discovers her with a painter, and dies of a heart attack from the shock. She marries the painter, who commits suicide when she becomes unfaithful. She finds an old lover and marries him after seducing him away from his fiancée. He then discovers her in an illicit relationship with his son and gives her a pistol with which to kill herself out of shame. She shoots him instead. She does a term in jail, and after her release runs off to London with the son and with a Countess who has a passion for her. She becomes a prostitute and is then murdered by Jack the Ripper. The opera is introduced by a cynical prologue in which the characters are presented by a ringmaster as a menagerie of animals.

The hinge between Lulu's rise and fall is the "Film Music" between the first and second scenes of Act Two, which depicts Lulu's trial and imprisonment. The "Film Music" also splices together the two Wedekind plays, for the action of *Büchse der Pandora* begins in the second scene of Act Two. Both the scenario of the film and the accompanying music are palindromes—the events and music move forward to the halfway point, then reverse direction for the same number of measures—and the second half of the three-minute segment is a mirror image of the first. Lulu's existence is that of a purely sensual creature made manifest in the eyes of men. She is molded by them in their imaginations to be what they think she is, which is why all of her husbands call her by different names. When speaking to one another of Lulu, they generally speak of her body, how it looks, and how she uses it; for the most part they do not even use her real name. There is no mention of her existence apart from men, and she herself expresses a wish to be a man in the second scene of Act Two. Her physical existence enables her rise to the top of the social ladder and is similarly responsible for her downfall and eventual death.

Although Berg had completed all of the music and libretto for *Lulu* before he died, he never finished the orchestration of Act Three. The path the opera took to its premiere was highly unusual. The Nazi German Arts Ministry had banned the opera as "degenerate" before it was even complete. The director of the Berlin State Opera, Erich Kleiber, had been intending to perform it. He responded to the ban with an act of defiance: he asked Berg to prepare a suite from the opera, which Berg did, including two mainly orchestral sections of the unfinished final act. Kleiber presented the suite despite the anger of Nazi officials, and promptly left the country. Later, working from Berg's manuscripts, Viennese composer Friedrich Cerha orchestrated Act Three over a period of more than a decade. The first performance of the "complete" opera was given in Paris on February 24, 1979. *—John Palmer*

Synopsis:

Prologue. An Animal Tamer comes on-stage and recites an introduction to the opera, couching the action in terms of animal characteristics. Lulu, in a pantomime costume, is carried out by a stage hand at the tamer's call: "Go and fetch our serpent out!"

Act One, Scene One. Lulu, in the same costume as before, but now in an artist's studio, is having her portrait painted. She is the wife of Dr. Goll and mistress of Dr. Schön, who is present with his son Alwa. When the pair leave, the Painter makes amorous advances on Lulu, who playfully makes him chase her. She is kneeling on the floor, clasping the painter's legs, when Dr. Goll arrives. He is so shocked by what he sees that he dies.

Scene Two. Time has elapsed; Lulu is married to the painter, who remains powerfully infatuated with her. The decrepit old Schigolch pays her a visit; it's clear that he knows her character and her past, but their relationship is never spelled out. Dr. Schön also comes. Although his is betrothed to another, he can't break the hold Lulu has on his passions. He reveals that Lulu lived under his "protection," as well as many more ambiguous details about her past. The young painter is so disturbed that he locks himself in the bathroom and commits suicide. It's all the same to Lulu.

Scene Three. Again, time has elapsed. Lulu is working as a theatrical dancer; she is in her dressing room with Alwa when the call comes to take to the stage. When she sees that Dr. Schön is in the audience with his fiancée, she faints on-stage, then refuses to perform. Dr. Schön bursts into the dressing room. She forces him to write a letter renouncing his future wife, then gets ready for her performance.

Act Two, Scene One. Lulu and Dr. Schön are married, but he is tormented by jealousy toward her many admirers—even toward the Countess Geschwitz, who has a homosexual crush on Lulu. Dr. Schön goes out to the stock exchange for awhile, returning to find his wife surrounded by drooling male admirers, including Schigolch and, to his horror, his own son Alwa. He pulls a revolver on the party, then hands the gun to Lulu, urging her to commit suicide. She shoots him, then pleads with Alwa for protection. But he can do nothing and the police carry her away.

Interlude—Film. A silent film is shown, depicting Lulu's life throughout the next year, from arrest, to trial, imprisonment, medical council, the isolation ward, and the route toward her liberation.

Act Two, Scene Two. The setting is the same as that of Scene One, but now Lulu's worshippers are planning her escape. The Countess goes off to infiltrate the prison and take Lulu's place. Rodrigo, one of the admirers of Scene One, intends to take her on tour as a circus performer, but when she arrives he finds that she has grown so weak and useless that he threatens to turn her in. Lulu and Alwa, made rich by his inheritance, make plans to run away together. "Isn't this the couch your father bled to death on?" she whispers as they embrace.

Act Three, Scene One. There is a dinner party going on at the sumptuous Parisian home of Lulu and Alwa. The guests include Schigolch, Rodrigo, a Marquis, a Banker, the Painter, and the Countess. They're boasting of their wealth, which is tied up in Jungfrau railway shares. Rodrigo and the Marquis turn on Lulu, using the fact that she remains wanted in Germany to blackmail her; the Marquis wants to sell her to a brothel in Cairo for 1,200 marks. Then they learn that Jungfrau shares have crashed, and the party turns into a nest of hostilities. Lulu swaps clothes with a young man and rushes out with Alwa, narrowly escaping capture by the police.

Scene Two. Lulu now lives in a dismal London apartment with Alwa and Schigolch, so poor that she has been driven into prostitution. Tonight is her "debut." Lulu brings home her first client, a tight-lipped professor. Soon after he leaves, the Countess arrives unexpectedly, bearing a surprise. It's the portrait of the young Lulu from the first scene, which the men hang, making happy, nostalgic statements, marveling at her past beauty. An angry black client of Lulu's gets into a scuffle with her, and Alwa winds up getting killed. Later, Lulu disappears into the bedroom with her next client, Jack the Ripper, as the Countess makes resolutions to start a new life. Lulu's scream of death pierces the air. As the killer leaves the apartment, he stabs the Countess, who dies even as she proclaims her devotion to Lulu. *—Donato Mancini*

Recommended:

○ **Berg: Lulu** / Boulez (cond.), Stratas, Minton, H. Schwarz, Mazura, Paris Opera Orch. / 2000 / DG 463617

***Wozzeck*, Op. 7 (1917–1922)**

This is the first great atonal opera. Its story is a grim one—a poverty-stricken soldier struggles to support his illegitimate son and the boy's mother while enduring victimization and humiliation from virtually everyone he encounters, until finally he discovers that his girlfriend has been unfaithful. He murders her, and then, crazed with guilt and apprehension, he drowns while trying to recover the murder weapon from a lake. The final scene is chilling: we see tragedy beginning anew as the orphaned toddler, still unaware of what has happened, hops off innocently to where the older children have found the mother's corpse.

Berg saw the Vienna premiere of Georg Büchner's play *Woyzeck* in May 1914 and decided immediately to set it to music. It was three years, though, before he was able to begin work on the opera due to required military service; the experience heightened Berg's identification with the story's main character, the soldier Wozzeck. A family crisis and two serious intervals of bronchial asthma further delayed composition, but the work was finally completed in the spring of 1922. By 1923, the vocal score (published at Berg's own expense) had received critical praise, prompting Universal Edition to accept the publication of the full score. *Wozzeck* was premiered on December 14, 1925; despite opposition from right-wing factions in Berlin, it immediately became an unqualified critical and popular success.

Preliminary sketches of Büchner's play were recovered, faded and nearly indecipherable, 38 years after Büchner's death (at the age of 23) in 1837; the novelist K.E. Franzos painstakingly reconstructed them, and finally arranged for the drama's performance on November 8, 1913. The story centered around a true incident in which a poverty-stricken soldier, Woyzeck (Franzos misread the name in the poorly preserved manuscript), stabbed his mistress and was later executed. Büchner gathered the specific details and even some of Woyzeck's explicit verbal phrases from a report by the court-appointed physician who concluded that Woyzeck could stand trial.

Berg used the second edition of the play for his libretto, reducing the number of scenes from 26 to 15 but otherwise preserving most of the original dialogue. This reduction involved a reordering of the scenes into a coherent structure of three acts of five scenes each. Act One is expository, showing Wozzeck in relationship to various environments and people in his life. In the developmental second act, Wozzeck gradually becomes aware of Marie's infidelity, and in Act Three comes the catastrophe of Marie's murder, Wozzeck's drowning, and the epilogue.

Musically, Wozzeck is in the same freely atonal style Berg had developed in the *Three Orchestral Pieces*, Op. 6, although there are many pseudo-tonal and tonal passages interspersed, almost always for dramatic effect. In order to reflect the unique character of the scenes, Berg felt it necessary to construct a separate, musically closed form for each one. This device does not seem to evoke the number operas of the past, but rather lends the work a very modern cohesion and concision that focus its grim, violent subject matter. Each scene is part of a larger multi-movement form that covers an entire act.

Act One, with its focus on the divergent aspects of Wozzeck's personality, needed a loosely constructed form. Its five scenes are set as five character pieces—Suite, Rhapsody, Military March and Lullaby, Passacaglia, and Quasi-Rondo. The developmental Act Two called for a more dramatic and organic form; hence its Symphony-Sonata, Fantasy and Fugue, Largo, Scherzo, and Rondo con introduzione movements. In Act Three, the inevitability of the catastrophe and epilogue is characterized musically by six inventions on ostinato ideas—inventions, respectively, on a theme, a note, a rhythm, a hexachord, a key, and on a regular eighth note figure. The fourth and fifth scenes are separated by an important interlude, which receives its own invention (thus there are six inventions rather than five).

Berg himself thought the opera to be very successful; the listener could be completely unaware of the complex web of musical and dramatic form while being completely absorbed by the human and social elements. Indeed, this has proven *Wozzeck*'s most enduring quality; it stands as a landmark achievement in both music and music drama, and is one of the elite few among twentieth century operas to enjoy repertory status. *—Steven Coburn*

Synopsis:

Act One. Scene One. Wozzeck is shaving his Captain in his room, while the Captain chatters nonstop about his strange obsessions regarding life and the passage of time. He proceeds to chastise Wozzeck's morals, reminding him of his bastard child. Wozzeck responds with a vehement statement about the rich and how virtue is a luxury and not for "us poor people." The Captain, taken aback, tries to mollify him.

Scene Two. Wozzeck and Andres, another soldier, are cutting firewood for the Captain in an open field in the late afternoon. Wozzeck begins to have strange hallucinations, which for the audience stand in sharp contrast to Andres' relative sanity.

Scene Three. Marie and her neighbor Margaret watch a military band pass by, and Marie admires the Drum Major. Later, she sings her child a lullaby. Wozzeck now arrives and becomes caught up in descriptions of his hallucinations, which he calls "visions." Marie is disturbed that he ignores their child. Wozzeck rushes off as Marie, fearing for his sanity, repeats the motivically important phrase "we poor people."

Scene Four. Wozzeck is in the Doctor's study, where he regularly submits himself to weird experiments to earn some extra money. In this bizarre scene, it is not clear whose sanity is in greater danger.

Scene Five. Marie and the Drum Major are on the street in front of her house. They flirt with one another. Then, after rejecting a first advance, Marie succumbs, and they rush inside together.

Act Two, Scene One. Marie is alone in her room, admiring the earrings given her by the Drum Major. Wozzeck arrives and asks her where they came from. Marie lies, saying that she found them. He hands his meager wages to her and leaves. Marie is seized with despair.

Scene Two. The Captain and the Doctor are talking together on the street about the Captain's ludicrous ailments. As Wozzeck passes by, they taunt him with allusions to Marie's infidelity with the Drum Major.

Scene Three. Wozzeck and Marie are on the street, and he confronts her with his suspicions. She admits her infidelity as Wozzeck flies into a rage and nearly assaults her physically. She cries, prophetically, "better a knife in my body than a hand on me!" She haughtily leaves, as Wozzeck repeats to himself, "better a knife...."

Scene Four. Two drunk Journeymen are entertaining the crowd in a beer garden. Wozzeck enters and sees Marie and the Drum Major dancing together. He is about to attack them when the music stops. Later, as he broods on a bench, a fool approaches him and says, "I smell blood." Wozzeck has a vision in which everything is covered in a red mist.

Scene Five. The Drum Major enters the barracks where Wozzeck and the soldiers sleep. He brags about his seduction of Marie and then beats Wozzeck.

Act Three, Scene One. Marie is alone in her room reading the story of Mary Magdalene from the Bible.

Scene Two. It is dusk on a path near a pond, and Marie and Wozzeck are walking together. Although Marie is nervous and wants to leave, Wozzeck makes her sit with him and reminisce about their life together. As she tries to escape, he draws a knife and murders her.

Scene Three. Wozzeck, in a daze, enters a tavern where Margaret sees blood on his hands and clothing. He becomes panicked and rushes out.

Scene Four. Wozzeck has returned to the pond to search for the knife so he can hide it. Confused and scared, he wades into the water to wash away the blood. The Doctor and Captain hear him drown as they are passing by. They panic and run off.

Scene Five. Children are playing on the street the next morning. They callously tell Marie's child that his mother is dead, but he plays on, uncaring, and follows them offstage as the curtain falls. *—Steven Coburn*

Recommended:

- ○ **Berg: Wozzeck; Schoenberg: Erwartung** / C. von Dohnányi (cond.), Silja, Waechter, Zednik, Laubenthal, Vienna PO / London 417348
- ○ **Alban Berg: Wozzeck** / C. Abbado (cond.), Grundheber, H. Behrens, Haugland, Langridge, Vienna PO / 1988 / DG 423587
- ○ **Wozzeck** / Mitropoulos (cond.), E. Farrell, Harrel, Mordino, R. Herbert, New York PO / Sony 62759

ORCHESTRAL

Three Pieces, Op. 6 (1913–1929)

This is Berg's first work for orchestra alone, but follows his *Altenberg Songs*, his first orchestral work of any kind, by three years. In that time, Berg's style became less consciously extravagant, yet the *Three Pieces* retain the powerful expressionistic style of the earlier songs, as well as the mammoth orchestra. Another difference here is the abandonment of the highly concentrated forms of the *Altenberg Songs* and a greater focus on more traditional large-scale motivic development. This development in Berg's style was a conscious gesture to impress Schoenberg, who had been critical of the aphoristic *Altenberg Songs*.

The three movements—Praeludium (Prelude), "Reigen" (Round Dances), Marsch (March)—were intended by Berg to be played as a continuous set. The form is inspired by the traditional symphony, with the central, dance-like "Reigen" filling the role of both dance movement and slow movement. Here, more than anywhere else, the influence of Mahler on Berg can be seen, particularly in the Marsch with its emotional similarity to the Finale of Mahler's *Symphony No. 6*. Both seem to depict a tragic march of fate leading to a catastrophic conclusion, expressed in both works by percussive hammer strokes. The movement is also dominated by linear counterpoint similar in style to Mahler's *Symphony No. 9*, the premiere of which Berg had heard in 1912. The Praeludium also looks to Mahler, with its percussive opening (anticipated in Mahler's *Third*) and its powerful central climax. The Reigen movement is a strangely transformed Viennese waltz framed by an introduction and slow conclusion. Berg later said it was a study for the Inn scene of *Wozzeck* (Act Two, Scene Four). All three movements are linked by complex and intricate thematic relationships as an organizing factor in lieu of a discernible tonality. But the work is further buttressed by Berg's reliance on traditional formal organization, as well, a tendency that was to receive its most thorough expression seven years later in *Wozzeck*. *—Steven Coburn*

Recommended:

- ○ **Berg: Lulu-Suite; Altenberg-Lieder; 3 Orchesterstücke** / C. Abbado (cond.), Price, London SO / 1997 / DG 449714
- ○ **Webern: Passacaglia; Schoenberg: Variations; Berg: 3 Pieces from the Lyric Suite** / Karajan (cond.), Berlin PO / 1999 / DG 457760
- ○ **Vienna: Schoenberg, Webern & Berg** / Dorati (cond.), London SO / 1990 / Mercury 432006

CONCERTO

Chamber Concerto, for piano, violin, and 13 wind instruments (1923–1925)

Alban Berg's *Chamber Concerto* (1923–25) followed on the heels of the composer's greatly successful opera *Wozzeck* (1917–22). Dedicated to Berg's teacher, mentor, and friend Arnold Schoenberg, the *Chamber Concerto* is a transitional work, marking the near-end of the composer's freely atonal period and approaching Schoenberg's 12-tone technique. The Concerto, in fact, actually features a number of 12-note rows, though they are not yet used in a thoroughly systematic fashion. In the year following the Concerto's completion, Berg finished the well-known *Lyric Suite* (1925–26), his first extended work in the 12-tone idiom. The *Chamber Concerto* is remarkable for the thoroughness of its organization; that is, it was composed with rigorous attention to minute details, and its structure is derived from a series of complex mathematical relationships. This is evident, for example, in the number of measures in each of the work's three movements. The first movement consists of variations that appear in alternating sets of 30 and 60 measures, totalling 240 measures; the second movement is exactly 240 measures long; and the number of measures in the final movement is equal to the sum of the measures in the first two (480). The work is both motivically and thematically highly integrated, with material from the first two movements returning in the final movement. The Concerto is thus symmetrical and balanced in a manner associated less often with Berg than with Anton Webern, Berg's fellow Schoenberg disciple. The Concerto has been described as a manifestation of Berg's early "constructivist" tendencies and is notable for the manner in which Berg combines atonal and 12-tone music in the same work with ease. *—Alexander Carpenter*

Recommended:

- ○ **Berg: Violin Concerto; Chamber Concerto** / Sinopoli (cond.), Lucchesini, K. Watanabe, Staatskapelle Dresden / Teldec 18155
- ○ **Berg: Chamber Concerto; Three Orchestral Pieces Op 6; Violin Concerto** / Boulez (cond.), Barenboim, Gawriloff, BBC SO / 1995 / Sony 68331
- ○ **Berg: Chamber Concerto; Stravinsky: Concerto in E-flat** / Boulez (cond.), Barenboim, P. Zukerman, Ensemble Intercontemporain / 1982 / DG 447405

Violin Concerto (1935)

When Berg received a commission for a concerto from the violinist Louis Krasner in January 1935, he was busy working on *Lulu* and set the commission aside. On April 22 of that year, the beloved daughter of his friend Alma Mahler, Manon Gropius, died at the age of 18, and Berg ceased work on the opera to compose his *Violin Concerto* as a memorial. Working at an unusually fast pace, Berg completed the score by August 11, though did not live to hear its premiere in April 1936. Some commentators have lamented the fact that work on the *Violin Concerto* prevented Berg from completing *Lulu*, which many view as his most important work. Yet the *Violin Concerto* has become Berg's single most popular and regularly programmed work. Beyond the firmly tonal works of his youth, the *Violin Concerto* is also Berg's most accessible score in its compelling combination of both tonal and atonal idioms.

As with many of Berg's pieces, the concerto follows a program governed by a strict formal design. The four movements are may be grouped into two parts of two movements each, with only a short break between movements two and three. The first two movements are structured like a Classical sonata-allegro and dance movement, respectively, and together form a musical portrait of the girl. The second part reverses the typical pattern of the Classical symphony, placing an Allegro, in this case an intense and elaborate cadenza-like movement first, followed by an Adagio, a set of variations after the Bach chorale *It Is Enough*. These movements represent the catastrophe of death and, ultimately, the sublimity of transfiguration.

Berg's use of tonality in the Violin Concerto is unique. The tone row upon which the work is constructed begins on a string of thirds that alternately outline minor and major triads, lending a distictive tonal element to passages that are apparently otherwise atonal. The work's tonal aspect is futher embodied in Berg's incorporation of a Carinthian folk song in the second movement and the aforementioned use of Bach's chorale, with Bach's own harmonization, in the third. (The last four notes of Berg's row, in fact, "coincide"—certainly by design—with the first four of Bach's chorale. Throughout, Berg's juxtaposition of tonal and atonal elements, as well as the alternation of richly lyrical, even Romantic passages with more formalized, deterministic sections, create a musical analogy for the more general theme of lost youth. *—Steven Coburn*

Recommended:

- ○ **Berg: Violin Concerto; Rihm: Time Chant** / J. Levine (cond.), Mutter, Chicago SO / DG 437093
- ○ **Bach, Bartók, Berg** / Kletzki (cond.), Gertler Philharmonia Orch. / Hungaroton 31635
- ○ **Webern conducts Berg Violin Concerto** / A. Webern (cond.), Krasner, BBC SO / 1991 / Continuum 1004

CHAMBER MUSIC

Lyric Suite, for string quartet (1925–1926)

Berg's *Lyric Suite* abounds in secret messages. In purely musical terms, Berg here for the first time employs Schoenberg's 12-tone system, basing some of the third and fifth movements on rows using all 12 notes of the chromatic scale. (And in one row, Berg proudly told Schoenberg, he used not only all available notes, but all available intervals.) Also, the fourth movement carries a quotation from the *Lyric Symphony* of Zemlinsky, to whom the suite is dedicated. In more personal terms, the music documents the course of Berg's extramarital affair with Hanna Fuchs-Robettin. Not only do the movement titles suggest an all-too-familiar sequence (from jovial through amorous and ecstatic to gloomy and sorrowful), but Berg incorporates his and Fuchs-Robettin's initials into the melodies and ties the metronome markings to numerological associations with their names. The sixth movement's quotation of Wagner's *Tristan und Isolde* is a clear reference to illicit love.

The first movement, though freely atonal, lives up to its designation of Allegretto gioviale; it's a short, perky piece. Things become quieter and more intimate with the sensuous Andante amoroso, although the mood is still sometimes rather capricious, despite an elegiac interlude at its center. Intensity builds with the Allegro misterioso, which opens with nocturnal insect music, liberally employing pizzicato and other effects. This is, effectively, the work's scherzo movement, and at its center is a Trio estatico—still keeping a fairly quick tempo, but now using mostly conventional bowing for longer-lined phrases. The scherzo music reappears, running in reverse to the movement's end.

The fourth movement, Adagio appassionato, forms the quartet's emotional center, with something tense and foreboding about much of the music's passion. A thrashing, dissonant climax gives way to a long passage of relative, but not quite settled, repose. The ensuing Presto delirando-Tenebroso alternates frantic music with quiet, dark, tense passages. The concluding Largo desolato maintains these moods at a much slower tempo, the music gradually dying away. *—James Reel*

Recommended:

- ○ **Alban Berg: Lyric Suite** / Upshaw, Kronos Quartet / 2003 / Nonesuch 79696
- ○ **Berg: Streichquartet Op 3; Lyrische Suite** / Arditti SQ / 2000 / Disques Montaigne 782119

VOCAL

Altenberg Lieder, Op. 4 (1912)

Berg's *Altenberg Lieder*, Op.4 (1912) effectively mark the end of his career as a composer of songs. Near the beginning of his career, Berg wrote dozens of lieder, most of which remained unpublished during his lifetime. His earliest successes under the tutelage of Arnold Schoenberg also included a number of songs, most notably the four of Op. 2. The *Altenberg Lieder*, though composed after Berg's formal studies with Schoenberg had ended, nonetheless bear the mark of the elder composer's powerful influence. Though Schoenberg discouraged Berg from writing songs, he is probably at least partly responsible for the nature and character of the *Altenberg Lieder*, since they were written as Berg was also occupied with the orchestration of Schoenberg's massive song cycle *Gurrelieder* (1901–11). The orchestral richness of Gurrelieder is certainly evident in Berg's songs, but so is the influence of Gustav Mahler, whose *Das Lied von der Erde* (1908–09) had made such a lasting impression on Berg when he first heard the work in 1911.

The *Altenberg Lieder* are sensitively and masterfully executed and reveal the composer's adroitness at orchestration and the inherently lyrical expressivity of his musical language. Berg no doubt could have continued composing songs with great success but was devastated by Schoenberg's initial response to the *Altenberg Lieder* and by the scandal that attended their first performance. After hearing some of the songs, Schoenberg wrote to Berg, "they bother me." At their first public performance on a program that included the *Six Pieces for Orchestra*, Op. 6 (1909) of fellow Schoenberg disciple Anton Webern, as well as Mahler's *Kindertotenlieder* (1901–04), the audience rioted.

The *Altenberg Lieder* are drawn from the whimsical, somewhat eccentric poetry of Peter Altenberg, a "coffeehouse" poet and friend of Berg and his wife. According to musicologist Mark DeVoto, Altenberg often sent "epigrammatic... scurrilous poems in blank verse" on postcards to his friends, five of which Berg chose for the present cycle; Berg's full title for the work, in fact, is *Five Orchestral Songs on Picture-Postcard Texts of Peter Altenberg.* Each of the songs is symmetrically conceived; that is, each begins and ends with similar, if not identical, harmonic or motivic gestures. The songs make considerable use of canon, passacaglia, and variation form. Berg also employs an expanded tonal language that includes the use of whole-tone scales, total chromaticism, and, as DeVoto notes, a proto-12-tone system of pitch organization that prefigures Schoenberg's method by more than a decade. After composing the *Altenberg Lieder*, Berg turned primarily to instrumental music, and later, to opera. It was, in fact, Berg's operas and works like the *Lyric Suite* for string quartet (1925–26) and the *Violin Concerto* (1935) that would assure him a place in musical history. Still, Berg might have achieved similar success as a composer of songs had the *Altenberg Lieder* been greeted with less derision from both Viennese concertgoers and his influential teacher. *—Alexander Carpenter*

Recommended:

- ○ **Jessye Norman; Alban Berg** / Boulez (cond.), J. Norman, London SO / 1995 / Sony 66826
- ○ **Berg: Altenberg-Lieder; Lulu-Suite; Lyrische Suite** / C. Abbado (cond.), Banse, Vienna PO / DG 447749
- ○ **Berg: Lulu-Suite; Altenberg-Lieder; 3 Orchesterstücke** / Abbado (cond.), M. Price, London SO / 1997 / DG 449714

Four Songs, Op. 2 (ca. 1909–1910)

Alban Berg's set of *Four Songs*, Op. 2 (ca. 1909–10) was the composer's second published work, appearing between the *Piano Sonata*, Op. 1 (1907–08) and the *String Quartet*, Op. 3 (1910). The songs were likely composed at roughly the same time as the Quartet, a significant point since the songs represent Berg's work as a pupil of Arnold Schoenberg, while the Quartet marks the end of Berg's student years.

Berg wrote a large number of songs both prior to and during his apprenticeship with Schoenberg. It was through the composition of songs, in fact, that Berg—like Schoenberg himself as well as Berg's fellow pupil, Anton Webern—came to terms with the formal problems that accompanied the dissolution of functional harmony in their respective musical languages. As musicologist Mark DeVoto notes, Schoenberg shepherded Berg towards instrumental works rather than songs. While the Quartet clearly satisfied Schoenberg in this respect, Op. 2 suggests that Berg was at the same time still interested in exploring song rather than giving his efforts over completely to composing in the larger forms.

The songs of Op. 2 share a common poetic theme: death. The first of the four songs, "Schlafen, schlafen," is a setting of a text by Friedrich Hebbel. Though Berg assigns it the key signature of D minor, a clear sense of tonality is present only at the beginning and end of this symmetrical song. The opening and end of the song are also related thematically: the end is the opening in retrograde. The middle of the song is harmonically ambiguous and characterized by pervasive chromaticism, "skyscraper" (13th) chords, and quartal sonorities. In his essay on Berg's songs, De Voto points out the use of chords related by a semitone in this song, coining the term "creeping" to describe this tendency in Berg's music. The other three songs in the cycle, "Schlafend trägt man mich in mein Heimatland," "Nun ich der Riesen Stärksten überwand," and "Warm die Lüfte," are all based on texts by Alfred Mombert. The second and third songs are similar to the first in their employment of key signatures, chromaticism, an unusual application of functional harmony, and symmetrical structure. The fourth song differs from the first three in one important respect: it is considered Berg's first successful attempt at writing atonal music. It is the longest song of the cycle and, significantly, carries no key signature; musicologists have noted, however, that despite its atonal language, "Warm die Lüfte" still contains a number of clear tonal implications. *—Alexander Carpenter*

Recommended:

- ○ **Berg: Lieder (1900–1925)** / Shirai, Höll / Capriccio 10419
- ○ **Schoenberg: Cabaret Songs; Berg: Lieder; Webern: 7 Early Songs** / Dorow, Crone / 1988 / Etcetera 1051
- ○ **Fischer-Dieskau sings Schoenberg, Berg, Webern Songs** / Fischer-Dieskau, A. Reimann / 2002 / Classica d'Oro 4015

KEYBOARD

Piano Sonata, Op. 1 (ca. 1907–1908)

Berg's Piano Sonata, Op. 1 (1908) was the composer's first published work. To the dismay of his most important mentor, Arnold Schoenberg, Berg had a great affinity with the lied; before beginning his studies with Schoenberg in 1904, the self-taught young Berg had already written dozens of songs. However, Schoenberg directed Berg toward instrumental composition, and under Schoenberg's tutelage Berg composed the *Piano Sonata*, the *12 Variations on a Theme* (1908–09) for piano, and the *String Quartet*, Op. 3 (1910).

The sonata represents a major stylistic leap for Berg. As musicologist Bruce Archibald notes, the composer's earlier piano music is "in the language—tonal, textural, and gestural—of Brahms and Schumann." The sonata, on the other hand, is in a newer idiom, exhibiting the strong influence of the iconoclastic Schoenberg. Berg employs a traditional sonata form for his Op. 1. The work's single movement consists of an exposition that includes two contrasting themes, a development section in which the themes are expanded, and a recapitulation, in which the themes are restated. The harmonic language is profoundly Schoenbergian, and parallels may be drawn between this work and Schoenberg's *Chamber Symphony No. 1*, Op. 9, with its whole-tone and quartal harmonies. The sonata also makes use of a three-note motivic cell—consisting of a perfect fourth plus an augmented fourth, spanning a major seventh—often found elsewhere in the early atonal music of Schoenberg, Berg, and Webern. The influence of Wagner is also evident in the sonata, especially in Berg's use of unresolved tonal suspensions.

Completed in 1908, the sonata was not published until 1910 (at the composer's own expense). Though Berg publicly performed a number of his own piano works, the sonata was never a part of his repertoire. *—Alexander Carpenter*

Recommended:

○ **Debussy: 12 Etudes, Berg: Sonate** / Pollini / DG 423678

○ **Schoenberg: Piano Concerto; Klavierstücke, Berg: Sonata, Webern** / Uchida / 2001 / Philips 468033

○ **Glenn Gould: Berg, Krenek, Webern, Debussy, Ravel** / G. Gould / 1995 / Sony 52661

Teresa Berganza

b. Mar. 16, 1935, Madrid, Spain

Mezzo-Soprano

Mezzo-soprano Teresa Berganza's career always had something of a Spanish flavor to it, even though she excelled in Mozart and Rossini roles and other elements of the traditional repertory. She consistently championed Spanish music, from zarzuela (the Spanish musical theater genre), to the songs of Granados and Falla. She also sang the title role of *Carmen* frequently, bringing her own unique sense of the character (as well as extensive research, much of it in Spain, observing Spanish gypsy women) to both stage and recordings. A musician of unusual breadth and ability, Berganza was an accomplished pianist and organist, and even studied conducting and composition. Her voice, which had an impressive upper extension, managed to cross boundaries as well: in 1960 she was offered the role of Violetta—a mainstay of the soprano repertory—in Verdi's *La Traviata* at La Scala in Milan.

Berganza studied at the Madrid Conservatory, under Lola Rodriguez Aragon, who herself studied with Elisabeth Schumann. She credits her teacher with the complete process of her development, from a raw talent to a polished artist; throughout her career, she continued to study with Aragon, developing interpretations or working out minor vocal problems. Berganza made her professional debut in 1956 at the Madrid Athenaeum in Schumann's song cycle *Frauenliebe und -Leben*, and made her operatic debut at the Aix-in-Provence Festival as Dorabella in *Così fan Tutte*. She made her Glyndebourne debut in 1958 as Cherubino.

In the same year, she made her U.S. debut in Dallas, singing the comprimario role of Neris in a production of Medea. The Medea was Maria Callas, and Berganza later declared that she never learned as much about musical drama and stage discipline as from Callas, who treated her "like a younger sister," even insisting that Berganza be allowed to portray Neris as a young woman close to Medea's own age, rather than an older, matronly figure, as was customary. Berganza made her Covent Garden debut as Rosina in 1960; throughout the 1960s and early 1970s she sang mostly Rossini and Mozart. She made her Met debut as Cherubino in 1967.

Berganza first sang *Carmen* in 1977, and described it later as a deeply liberating experience—personally as well as musically. In preparing the role, she visited Seville to observe gypsy women, read the original novel by Prosper Merimee, and studied the score deeply. She developed her own perceptions of Carmen: she was a free spirit within a restrictive culture, but far from being a prostitute or a tramp, and even possessing a certain sweetness. While many critics applauded her presentation, others found it lacking in blood and guts—too "ladylike." (Berganza countered this with her observation that, far from being the flamboyant, hand-on-the-hip, promiscuous creatures of popular thinking, real Spanish gypsy women in fact follow a fairly rigid standard of decorum.) She brought the same kind of original thinking to the role of Zerlina in *Don Giovanni*, and in the famous Joseph Losey film, she sang her as a fully mature and sensual young woman, rather than a simple and bedazzled girl.

Berganza was also a prominent recitalist, specializing in Spanish song. Among her recordings, her Rosina (one of the most beautiful on record), and her collection of Spanish songs on Claves are both outstanding.*—Ann Feeney*

Recommended:

○ **Una voce poco fa: A Portrait of Teresa Berganza** / Berganza / 2004 / Decca 000233502

○ **Teresa Berganza** / Gibson, Pitchard (conds.), Berganza, de Peyer, Parsons, Lavilla, London SO / 2001 / Decca 467905

○ **Teresa Berganza: Zarzuela Recital** / Asensio (cond.), Berganza, English CO / 1997 / Ensayo 9707

○ **The Barber of Seville** / Varviso (cond.), Ghiaurov, Corena, Berganza, Benelli, Rossini Orch. & Chorus / 1999 / London 452591

Carlo Bergonzi

b. Jul. 13, 1927, Polisene

Tenor

Tenor Carlo Bergonzi, for many, epitomized Verdian grace and style, not only for his generation, but for the entire twentieth century. His parents were great opera lovers and took him to see *Il trovatore* when he was just six. Bergonzi responded enthusiastically: the next morning, his parents found him in the kitchen, singing "Di quella pira" as best he could, and staging the scene with kitchen implements. He performed under slightly more formal auspices, in church choirs and in child roles in the Busseto Opera. When he was 14, he auditioned for Edmondo Grandini. Grandini decided that Bergonzi was a baritone and offered him lessons. Bergonzi moved to Brescia to study with him, though his studies were interrupted by the war and later by his imprisonment for anti-Nazi activities in a German prisoner-of-war camp. When the war ended, he returned to Italy and began studies at the Boito Conservatory in Parma.

At the conservatory, he was still considered a baritone. He studied with Ettore Campogalliani and after graduation, made his professional debut as Schaunard in *La bohème* in 1947, his debut in a lead as Rossini's *Figaro* in 1948 at Lecce, and continued to sing leading baritone roles there, even at one point replacing Tito Gobbi as Rigoletto. However, he himself remained convinced that he was a tenor. Finally, having used what he had learned at the conservatory and recordings of other tenors, particularly Caruso, Schipa, Gigli, and Pertile, and what he remembered from singing on stage with Schipa and Gigli, he made his debut as a tenor at Bari as Andrea Chenier in 1951 and soon sang two major Verdi tenor roles: Riccardo (*Un ballo in maschera*) and Alvaro in *La forza del destino*. To keep his voice flexible, he also sang lighter roles, such as Nemorino and even Nero in Monteverdi's *L'incoronazione di Poppea*. In 1953 he made his La Scala debut creating the role of Mas'Aniello in Napoli's opera and his London debut as Alvaro, his American debut at the Lyric Opera of Chicago in 1955, and his Met debut the following year. His Covent Garden debut, again as Alvaro, was not until 1962. He became a regular performer at nearly all of the great opera houses, renowned not only for his singing, but for consistency. He kept his versatility throughout his career, alternating lyric and spinto roles and even some verismo roles. He was never a great stage actor, nor did he have the matinee-idol looks of some of his contemporaries, but was an excellent vocal actor, singing each role with the colors he felt it demanded, rather than a "one voice fits all" approach. During the 1980s he began to focus more on recitals and concert performances and also became a well-known teacher, concentrating on technique. He created a voice school in Busseto, and was instrumental in the "Concorso internazionale di voci verdiane," a competition for aspiring Verdi singers.

He recorded all of his major Verdi roles. He often referred to his 1976 recording on Philips of 31 major arias from every Verdi opera, which won the *Deutscher Schalplattenpries, Premio della critica discographica italiana*, and the Stereo Review Record of the Year awards, as the recording of which he was proudest. His complete recording of *Pagliacci* on Deutsche Grammophon for von Karajan shows him thoroughly at home in the verismo style. On Sony, he made an exemplary recording of Italian songs. *—Ann Feeney*

Recommended:

○ **Carlo Bergonzi** / Queler (cond.), Bergonzi, Wustman, New York Opera Orch. / 1998 / Sony 60785

○ **The Sublime Voice** / Bergonzi / 2001 / Decca 467023

○ **Verdi: La Traviata** / Pitchard (cond.), Sutherland, Bergonzi, Merrill, Palma, Maggio Musicale Fiorentino Orch. & Chorus / 2002 / Decca 470440

Luciano Berio

b. Oct. 24, 1925, Oneglia, Italy, **d.** May 27, 2003, Rome, Italy

Composer: Avant-garde, Chamber Music, Vocal

Luciano Berio was one of the most important Italian composers of the second half of the twentieth century, a leader of the international avant-garde who has managed to write music that is communicative and pleasing to audiences. He received musical instruction from his father and grandfather, organists in Oneglia, and continued musical training through his school years. After World War II he went to Milan to study law but also became a composition pupil with Ghedini, a composer known for his interest in many styles. He passed that interest on to Berio, who started his career as a neo-Classicist.

Whie in school Berio met met a remarkable American singer, Cathy Berberian. They married and went to the U.S. on their honeymoon. At Tanglewood, he met his famous countryman Luigi Dallapiccola, who was teaching there. From him, Berio learned to work with the 12-tone system and also absorbed an interest in working with sound as a musical parameter. He met the electronic music pioneers Ussachevsky and Luening, which furthered his interest in sound. This led him, on his return to Europe, to seek out Bruno Maderna, Henri Pousseur, and Karlheinz Stockhausen, leaders of the European avant-garde who were also interested in electronic music.

In 1955 Berio and Bruno Maderna founded a *Studio di Fonologia* at a Milan radio station; it was the first electronic music studio in Italy. Berio became very active there, organizing concerts and also publishing a new music journal, both under the name *Incontri musicali*. He resigned his position with the studio in 1961, worn out by overwork, red tape, and political infighting.

Berio explored the frontiers of sound, particularly vocal sound, thanks to his association with Berberian. She was willing and able to produce a remarkable variety of extended techniques with her voice, which she did with the utmost musicianship. But Berberian was also able to win audiences with her superior showmanship. Representative of Berio's vocal writing is *Sequenza III* for solo voice, which portrays 44 emotional states in seven and a half minutes and includes conventional singing, coughs, sighs, sobs, and a sound Berio called "girl-bird." The work *Omaggio a Joyce* used Berberian's voice as the source sounds for a tape music piece. The more traditional *Folk Songs* was a display piece for her facility with languages. Berio's noteworthy, ongoing series of solo instrumental works—many in the*Sequenza* series—have often explored the timbral possbilities of a particular instrument.

In the 1960s Berio taught at Tanglewood, Dartington, Darmstadt, Harvard, Juilliard, and Mills College, Oakland, California. By the end of the decade, his marriage to Berberian had ended, and he returned to Europe. One of his most remarkable "American" compositions was *Sinfonia* (1969), a striking work built on the principles of quotation and collage. Back in Italy, he produced a series of television programs to popularize modern music. He was appointed to the board of IRCAM in Paris and wrote other notable works, such as *Voci* and *Coro*. In 1987 he founded Tempo Reale, a research institute in Milan. One of his many important later works is *Renderings*, which utilizes the fragmentary posthumous sketches of *Schubert*'s *Tenth Symphony* with clouds of sound that eventually coalesce into syntactic units. Berio died in Rome in 2003. —*Joseph Stevenson*

AVANT-GARDE

Visage, for tape (1961)

On the subject of faces (or "visages"), there's a fascinating moment in an interview between Berio and himself where he speaks of "an expressivity which is like that of a human face which can at times be happy, sad, joyful, tired and in the end lifeless." At first, the notion that the human face can express certain emotional states seems necessarily distinct from the state of "lifelessness." But in fact that distinction might be the most spinal tension in all of Berio's music—the tension between a material which is essentially inanimate and infinitely flexible, and the burning, glowing humanity which can at any moment be breathed into it, if only temporarily. Voice—in this case Cathy Berberian's voice—is often the life-breath, with what Berio calls its "excess of connotations." But often Berio chooses to deal with voice the way Flaubert was said to deal with words—surgically; and works like *Thema (Omaggio a Joyce)*, *Sequenza III*, and *Visage* radiate from the friction between the intimacy of vox humana and the elastic, obliterating force of Berio's deconstructive techniques.

The inimitable tautness and unease that results from this conflict of means and materials is stretched into an epic span in *Visage*; Berberian's prerecorded voice—performing all manner of vocal and expressive gestures, almost entirely without actual words—becomes a kind of Shakespearean soliloquist in gibberish-land, and she's surrounded by a vast sound scape of electronic sounds which provide her a proscenium—and which also play a spying ear, receiving, and giving from the other side.

The kind of wordless vocal theater which unfolds is as equally Berberian's accomplishment as Berio's; at moments, Berberian's performance suggests some kind of onomatopoeic Ur-language, its cries, sighs, grunts, and burbles dissolving all polite speech and flooding into the realm of the immediate and pre-civilized. Orgasms and post coital murmurings violently cut into wailing laments and fearful shouts, then into smug small talk. But at almost all moments, this vocality is tinged with a great strangeness, even danger: the electronic house and linguistic nonsense which passes through it are wildly at odds, and do not harmonize comfortably.

The sublime coda to *Visage* is one of twentieth century music's holy moments: the gibberish of Berberian, inflected by a kind of enlightenment (or the aping of enlightenment), gradually cedes to an electronic hive of sound, swirling with the buzz of cybernetic bees; the body seems to have entirely passed into an automated ether, aerates into nothing via studio technology. It is indeed a moment of death, acoustically distinct from but expressively identical to those later moments of mortal darkening in Berio's music, as in *Coro* or *Un Re in Ascolto*. And it is perhaps in this moment most of all that the life in the face, its sense of imploring presence, becomes most moving—as it leaves. The shock of the human, Berio seems to hint, won't hit us until it's flanked by the in-, non-, and super human. —*Seth Brodsky*

Recommended:

○ **Berio: Many More Voices** / Berberian / 1998 / RCA 68302

○ **Berio: Visage, Passaggio** / E. Ross / Musica d'Oggi 1017

CHAMBER MUSIC

34 Duetti, for 2 violins (1979–1983)

Berio began his 34 Duets (1979–83) as a set of exercises in the spirit of Bartók's *Mikrokosmos*, i.e. pieces that would offer an opportunity for inexperienced players to perform music in a contemporary idiom while unhindered by undue technical difficulty. While some of the Duets fall within this scope, Berio's focus broadens in a number of the pieces to include personal, social, and cultural commentary. Each of the Duets is named for one of one of Berio's musical friends, "Pierre" (Boulez), for example, or predecessors, as in "Béla" (Bartók). The pieces, however, are not caricatures, but rather represent changing musical perspectives filtered through Berio's stylistic approaches. Although each of the Duets has a particular musical character, Berio's reference points for the pieces' namesakes seem to be more private than public. As a group, the Duets tie in with Berio's longstanding aesthetic concerns: the juxtaposition of folk-like with serially influenced melodies, allusion and connotation, and constant awareness of the violin's performance tradition. The last of these connects the Duets with Berio's *Sequenza* series for solo instruments, particularly *Sequenza VIII* (1976) for solo violin, written just prior to the Duets and the most historically "aware" entry of the *Sequenza* series.

Each of the Duets has a tonal center and may be described as essentially a melody with accompaniment. Many are about 30 seconds long; most are between 30 and 75 seconds. The longest, "Edoardo," is not a duet but an ensemble piece, to be performed (presumably) by an entire class of beginners. Each Duet may be breifly described as follows:

1. Béla (Bartók): simple modal melody, essentially two-pitch accompaniment.
2. Shlomit (Almog): melody; three-pitched accompaniment of different phrase length.
3. Yossi (Pecker): very active, repeated-note figures set against one another; a basic melody based on a five-pitch rising and falling scale.
4. Rodion (Shchedrin): contemplative melody; simple countermelody.
5. Maja (Pliseckaja): slow, intense, rising three-pitch figure developing into a two-octave scale.
6. Bruno (Maderna): a charming, almost naïve, quick waltz with double stops and strummed chords in the subordinate part.
7. Camilla (Adami): asymmetrical scale with a nervous two-pitch figure.
8. Peppino (di Giugno): Romantic, contrapuntal song.
9. Marcello (Parmi): melody of half-steps plus fifth, repeating phrase and antecedent.
10. Giorgio Federico (Ghedini): lyric adagio; pizzicato accompaniment.
11. Valerio (Adami): short melodic phrase transforming texturally.
12. Daniela (Rabinovitch): two complementary scales in contrary motion, straightforward rhythm.
13. Jeanne (Parmi): grating multi-stops, melody like a brutal children's tune.
14. Pierre (Boulez): crossing scales, skittering ponticello texture.
15. Tatjana (Globokar): naïve tune and counterpoint, in harmonics.
16. Rivi (Pecker): lamenting chromatic tune, arpeggiated counterpoint.
17. Leonardo (Pinzauti): major-scale exercise against active modal part.
18. Piero (Farulli): martial double stops; modal melody.
19. Annie (Neuberger): surreal carnival waltz; double stopped accompaniment.
20. Edoardo (Sanguinetti): for the whole ensemble with two "soloists," aggressive tremolos.
21. Fiamma (Nicolodi): exercise-like passages superimposed at different pitch ranges.
22. Vinko (Globokar): ebbing and flowing repeated-note accompaniment under arpeggiated melody.
23. Franco (Gulli): interfering parts in similar range; scalar melodies.
24. Aldo (Bennici): lovely Italian folk-like tune, contrary motion counterpoint.
25. Carlo (Chiarappa): odd-sounding arpeggiated rising and falling tune, development.
26. Henri (Pousseur): folk-like tune with repeated-note pizzicato.
27. Alfredo (Fiorenzani): quiet skittering ponticello accompaniment; slow tune.
28. Igor (Stravinsky): stolid Russian folk-like tune, simple background.
29. Alfred (Schlee): manic, staccato, tune with accompaniment.
30. Massimo (Mila): slow, expressionistic; short outbursts of emotion.
31. Mauricio (Kagel): two sections, major mode phrase reprised with intervals skewed.
32. Maurice (Fleurer): double-stop main motif developing into freer scales, returning.
33. Lorin (Maazel): aggressive, petulant low part, faster commentary above.
34. Lele (d'Amico): light ponticello high accompaniment, melancholy minor-mode tune. —*Robert Kirzinger*

Recommended:

- ○ **Berio: Duetti, Denisov: Sonata** / Bulov, Gringolts / 2001 / Bis 1047
- ○ **Berio: Duetti; Sequenza VIII; Due Pezzi; Corale** / Accademia Bizantina / Denon 75448

Sequenza I-XIV (1958–2002)

For those whose only exposure to the music of Luciano Berio has been the frenetic collage and pastiche that comprises the famous second movement of his *Sinfonia* (from 1969), the *Sequenzas* may seem expressively disciplined and texturally stark. This open-ended series of works began with the *Sequenza for flute* in 1958 and, over the course of the subsequent four decades, numbered into the mid-teens. Each sequenza subjects given collections of pitches to various melodic and harmonic "experiments," conducted in each case within the context of a different solo instrument. The wide variety of instruments involved hearkens back to Hindemith's exhaustive instrumental studies, in which he composed a sonata for virtually every instrument in the orchestra. Berio's series differs from Hindemith's, however, both in scope and concept. Berio's pieces are generally quite short, most of them between eight and ten minutes (although *Sequenza XII* for bassoon runs nearly half an hour). Also, his collection of instruments is somewhat more varied, with *Sequenzas* for saxophone (No. IXb, 1981), guitar (No. XI, 1988), and even accordion (XIII, 1996). Likewise, his approach to each instrument is rather more ambitious, attending not only to the physicality of the instrument but to its sense of history and character—which is to say that the accordion *Sequenza*, for example, contains gestures and moods that would sound ill-at-home if performed by some other instrument. This is not to say that the players remain in their comfort zone. Quite the opposite: in exploiting each instrument's possibilities, Berio attempts to shatter the boundary between extreme virtuosity and uninhibited expression.

The "experimentational" nature of the compositional process in the *Sequenzas* finds a corollary in the technological "research and development" that Berio undertakes for each instrument. Berio uses a stunning array of "extended techniques" to exploit the most extreme timbral possibilities of each instrument. In *Sequenza X* for trumpet (1984), the performer turns and projects a burst of sound into the belly of an open piano with the pedal depressed, thus setting some of the strings into vibration and creating a ghostly resonance. The singer performing *Sequenza III* (1965–66) produces all manner of noises, including busy chattering, scat-singing, and disconcerting yelps. *Sequenza V* (1966) combines the trombone's inherent pitch fluidity with a seemingly endless battery of articulatory tricks and muting techniques. *Sequenza VI* for viola (1967) consists more prominently of stretches of relentless tremolos.

While the *Sequenzas* should be considered on their own terms, each providing a dizzying terrain of sound possibilities, they have served Berio as a kind of musical laboratory. Berio crafted an entire series of pieces constructed basically as tropes on the *Sequenza* material. In *Chemins I*, the harp from *Sequenza II* (1963) is joined by an ensemble, while both *Chemins II* and *Chemins III* add layers of sound to the viola's material in *Sequenza VI*. The *Sequenzas* for saxophone, guitar, oboe, trumpet, and violin have also been subjected to elaborations in later pieces. *—Jeremy Grimshaw*

Recommended:

- ○ **Berio: Sequenzas** / Ensemble Intercontemporain / DG 457038

VOCAL

Folk Songs, for soprano & 7 instruments (1964)

The appearance of Luciano Berio's *Folk Songs* in 1964 caused notice because of their simplicity and tonal harmonic palette. Listening to the arrangements, however, elucidates how novel and even radical the harmonizations are. The settings are for mezzo-soprano and small orchestra and were written for the composer's then-wife, the American singer Cathy Berberian. Her extraordinary musicianship, vocal control, and interest in the latest music (and the earliest, for she was also a leader in the rediscovery of Renaissance and early Baroque music) made her the international vocal star of avant-garde music.

In this cycle, Berio took advantage of her great gift for tone color and language. There are nine languages and dialects among the 11 songs, and in each of them Berberian was capable of projecting the sound and diction of an authentic, indigenous singer. One of the most striking changes in vocal coloration comes in the final song, which has one verse in Russian. Berberian seamlessly switches from a Turkic sound to a Russian and then back again.

The first song is a lover's description of a loved one; the second is a Christmas song in tones of awe. The Armenian song describes the rising moon, and the French one is a playful song about how to win a fair maiden's heart. The Sicilian song is sung by fishermen's wives as they await their men's return from the sea. The two Italian songs were written by Berio when he and Berberian were both students together. The Sardinian song is a sad song sung to a nightingale. The two Avergnac songs were found in Cataloube's collections *Songs of the Auvergne*, but re-harmonized by Berio.

The final song was found by Berberian on a 78-rpm Soviet recording. She sang it phonetically, and it was then noted down and harmonized by Berio. A professor of Uralic and Altaic languages was able to determine (a tribute to the accuracy of Berberian's ear for sounds in unfamiliar languages) that it is a song about two young lovers plotting an after-dark rendezvous: "You go by this path, and I'll go by that path, and thus we will confound our enemies," went the translation of one verse; the two appear to be planning to meet in a garden where roses can bloom. —Joseph Stevenson

Recommended:

- ○ **Dagmar Pecková: Mahler, Berio** / Belohlavek (cond.), Pecková, Prague Chamber PO / Supraphon 3264
- ○ **Cathy Berberian Sings Berio & Weill** / Berio (cond.), Berberian, Julliard Ensemble / RCA Victor 62540
- ○ **Berio: Folk Songs; Sequenza VI, Boulez** / M. Ceccanti (cond.), L. Castellani, Contempoartensemble / 1997 / Arts 47376

Circles, for female voice, harp & 2 percussionists (1960)

Luciano Berio's *Circles* (1960) is an exploration of sound and meaning, bringing together two threads of the composer's aesthetic concerns of the time. Berio had previously explored instrumental timbre in such works as *Différences for tape and ensemble* (1959) and textual meaning in works like *Thema (Omaggio a Joyce)* for taped voice (1958). Berio's work reflected the avant-garde's fascination with the purely sonic potential of text and timbre. Stockhausen had temporarily removed spoken and sung text from its semantic context in the tape work *Gesang der Jünglinge* (1956); Boulez considered similar questions in his massive *Pli selon pli* (1957–62), based on texts by Mallarmé. In *Circles*, two percussionists are each encircled by instruments of three families: metal, skin, and wood. Pitched (vibraphone), semi-pitched (temple blocks) and unpitched (tam-tam) instruments correspond to three types of sound produced by the singer: exact sung pitch, approximate pitch, and speech. Berio sets three poems (two of them twice) of e.e. cummings; the fragmentary semantic structure of the poems enables the composer to provide musical parallels and commentary, while the sound of the words, often onomatopoeic, provides material for imitation. For example, the first word, "sting," is immediately followed by the plucked strings of the harp. Indeed, the harpist is a kind of mediator, at times supporting or following the voice, at other times the percussion. The many layers of interaction among meanings and sound lead to some very complex structural situations. The pitch organization is serial, while the presentation of the text (often considerably fragmented) allows for repetition, a circular return of different facets of the material. As the piece progresses, there is gradual loss of structure. Initially, the most straightforward of the poems is sung without fragmentation, and the musical material is mostly pitch-based. However, semantically obscure poems, which even in their original form seem fragmented, become further fractured, spoken without pitch, and accompanied by unpitched percussion instruments. In keeping with the cyclical idea, the music eventually returns to its initial state of relative structural cohesion. *—Robert Kirzinger*

Recommended:

- ○ **Berio: Circles; Sequenzas I, III, V** / Berberian, J-C. Casadesus, Drouet, Pierre / 1991 / Wergo 6021

O King, for voice & ensemble (1967–1968)

Italian composer Luciano Berio composed *O King* in two versions: a chamber version for voice, flute, clarinet, violin, cello, and piano and a symphonic version for eight amplified voices and full orchestra, the latter being incorporated into Berio's *Sinfonia* (1968) as the second movement. *O King* is a threnody for the civil rights leader who was assassinated while Berio was teaching at the Juilliard School in New York. A work harmonically based on two whole-tone scales, the vocalist or vocalists of *O King* "discover" the name "Martin Luther King" first through its vowels then adding consonants until the whole name is sung completely only in the final bars of the piece. A mysterious and mournful piece in which the voice blends uncannily with the instruments and the texture is essentially a veil of slow, shimmering sounds, *O King* is one of Berio's most immediately appealing and affecting works. *—James Leonard*

Recommended:

- ○ **Berio: Chamber Music** / Ensemble Avantgarde / 1998 / MDG 6130754

Sinfonia, for 8 amplified voices & orchestra (1968–1969)

Luciano Berio's *Sinfonia* (1968–69) premiered in its initial four-movement version under the composer's direction in 1968; Berio later added the fifth movement as a summation. Dedicated to Leonard Bernstein, this work was commissioned on the occasion of the 125th anniversary season of the New York Philharmonic. The vocal parts in *Sinfonia* were composed for the Swingle Singers, famous for their a cappella renditions of many instrumental classics. *Sinfonia* is the first of Berio's pieces to directly engage the ghosts of music history, exemplified by Gustav Mahler, whose *Second Symphony* Berio's appropriates. *Sinfonia* uses a large, relatively traditional orchestra, and the eight voices of the Swingle Singers. Berio's use of the Mahler Scherzo and other appropriated material (including music of Bach, Boulez, Berg, Stravinsky, Stockhausen, and many others), does not, as the composer makes it clear, amount to the technique of collage. For example, the Mahler movement forms the philosophical and structural armature for the third movement of *Sinfonia*, at least partly as a basis for commentary on music history in general. Specifically, the distinctive characteristics of the Scherzo serves as catalysts for the proliferation of musical references with similar traits. The depth and extent of interconnectivity among these references parallels Berio's use of Beckett's narrative *The Unnameable* and the threads spun off from that text. One can hear Beckett throughout the movement, just as one can hear Mahler—blurred or momentarily obliterated by other sounds, other meanings, but always returning.

The first movement of *Sinfonia* begins with a wash of sound from a tam-tam followed by an open chord in the voices. The vocal texts come primarily from structural anthropologist Claude Levi-Strauss' *Le cru et le cuit* (The Raw and the Cooked). The piano plays an especially prominent role in this movement. The second movement demonstrates a technique of harmonic construction common in Berio's work from this period onward. Clearly stated is the initial, whole-tone-based chord that only in retrospect seems to grow in complexity as the movement progresses. Berio modified the harmonic density of this work in order to bridge the first and third movements. Once again, Berio manages to tie together a purely musical process and an extramusical reference. The sung text consists of syllables of the phrase "O Martin Luther King," which, in addition to honoring the human rights leader, allows Berio to use every vowel sound as an individual sonic element. The building up of the semantic entity of the phrase via the basic cells of language mirrors the similar process of generating harmonic cohesion from a basic collection of notes. The fourth movement disperses the energy of the third movement. The sung text centers on the phrase "Rose de sang" (rose of blood), a transformation of the text found in the fourth movement of Mahler's *Second Symphony*. Berio became convinced of the necessity of the fifth movement only after *Sinfonia*'s initial performances. The complex fifth movement acts as a commentary on the entire piece, much as the third movement "analyzed" the Mahler Scherzo. *Sinfonia* also contains an encyclopedic store of technical and philosophical approaches to the problems of late twentieth century music. Not only does *Sinfonia* function effectively as a way to approach the music of the past, but it also seems to illuminate the future. *—Robert Kirzinger*

Recommended:

- ○ **Berio: Sinfonia; Eindrücke** / Boulez (cond.), New Swingle Singers, Orch. National de France / Erato 45228

Sir Lennox Berkeley

b. May 12, 1903, Boars Hill, Oxford, England, **d.** Dec. 26, 1989, London, England
Composer

Though his profile outside the United Kingdom was overshadowed somewhat by the illustrious careers of Walton, Tippett, and Britten, Sir Lennox Berkeley left an indelible mark on British music in the twentieth century. A student of Nadia Boulanger with an ear for songlike lyricism, Berkeley established a style that combined French melodic elegance with English triadic sonority and neo-Classical clarity.

Berkeley was born into an aristocratic family, but lost out on his inheritance because his birth had preceded his parents' marriage. He nonetheless enjoyed a relatively comfortable childhood and eventually arrived at Oxford, where he studied French. (This academic background lent his later songs on French texts a particularly elegant contour.) Ravel, upon examining some of Berkeley's student compositions, encouraged him to focus on musical studies and recommended him for study with Nadia Boulanger. Berkeley was well-suited to Boulanger's infamously methodic, craft-like approach, and thrived under her tutelage. Works such as his *Serenade*, Op. 12, and the *Divertimento*, Op. 18, which remain in the British orchestral repertoire, resonate with Boulanger's influence; Peter Dickinson has described the Finale of the latter piece as "a cross between Haydn and Poulenc." Berkeley's piano works and chamber pieces demonstrate a similar disposition. Also, during his time in Paris, he converted to Catholicism, a decision that would infuse his later vocal and choral works, such as the Missa brevis, with a particular spiritual fervor. As a young composer he maintained his friendship with Ravel, and also made the acquaintance of Poulenc; in fact, much of his music betrays the influence of Les Six.

Berkeley was employed for a time as a programmer for the BBC during World War II, then in 1946 took a position at the Royal Academy of Music, where he remained on the faculty for over two decades and mentored a number of important figures in the subsequent generation, including Bennett, Maw, and, most familiar to non-Brits, John Tavener. Berkeley counted Britten among his closest friends, and, following Britten's revival of British opera, he wrote a number of operatic works as well, including the successful *A Dinner Engagement*. A subsequent opera, *Faldon Park*, remained incomplete in the composer's later life. In fact, his faculties gradually deteriorated over the course of several years preceding his death in 1989. His last years were spent, rather, receiving the honors due him; subsequent to his knighthood in 1974, he received numerous accolades and an honorary degree from the international musical community. *—Jeremy Grimshaw*

Overview of Works (1924–1983)

Lennox Berkeley has more in common with the internationalist English composers William Walton and especially Benjamin Britten than he does with the nationalist composers Gustav Holst and Vaughan Williams. Part of this comes from Berkeley's heritage—his mother was French—and part of it comes from his training—he spent the years 1927–32 studying composition with Nadia Boulanger in Paris. Although essentially a lyrical composer, he wrote successfully in all the major forms of vocal and instrumental music. His tonal language began in modernist tonality, but shifted in the late 1950s toward a more dissonant language, eventually incorporating atonal and serial compositional traits. His early style was understandably French neo-Classical—Ravel and Stravinsky were his models and Poulenc his lifelong friend—but he developed an independent style much harder-edged and tougher in the later 1930s. Among Berkeley's best and most characteristic works are the grand opera *Nelson* (1953); two symphonies (1940 and 1956–58); the well-known guitar concerto written for Julian Bream (1974); the song settings of *Auden* (1958) for voice and piano, and *St. Teresa of Avila* (1947) for voice and strings; and the religious choral works *Domini est terra* (1937) and the late *Magnificat and Nunc Dimittis* (1980). Although not as individualistic a composer as Britten, Berkeley's music has great craftsmanship and integrity. *—James Leonard*

Recommended:

- ○ **Lennox Berkeley Centenary Album** / retrospective anthology, various artists / 2003 / EMI 585138
- ○ **Sir Lennox Berkeley: A Centenary Tribute** / Nash Ensemble / 2003 / Hyperion 55135
- ○ **Berkeley Conducts Berkeley** / Berkeley (cond.), London PO / 1992 / Lyrita 226

Berlin Radio Symphony Orchestra

f. 1946
Ensemble

There may be more confusion over the identity of this orchestra than any other major ensemble in the West, not least because it has had three names over the years. Founded in 1946 in the American sector of Berlin, the orchestra was formed while Berlin (and most of Germany) was emerging from the destruction of the war. The ensemble was given the name of RIAS Symphony Orchestra, the initials standing for "Radio in the American Sector." Later the ensemble adopted the name of Berlin Radio Symphony Orchestra, by which many concertgoers and record collectors still know them.

In 1993, the orchestra was renamed Deutsches Sinfonie-Orchester Berlin. In part the change was necessary to avoid confusion with another Berlin ensemble, the Radio Symphony Orchestra of Berlin, often listed on recordings and in catalogs in German as Rundfunk-Sinfonieorchester Berlin. And here is where the confusion worsens: this latter group is often now mistakenly listed at Internet sites, in reference works and in catalogs as the Berlin Radio Symphony Orchestra. Actually, such a translation of their German name would normally be quite acceptable.

In any event, the new Deutsches Sinfonie-Orchester Berlin is led by music director Vladimir Ashkenazy and has as its principal guest conductor Gunter Wand. The former became music director in 1989 when he succeeded Riccardo Chailly. The orchestra plays subscription series at both the Philharmonie in Berlin and at the Konzerthaus, located in the former East Berlin. Eliahu Inbal, Gerd Albrecht, Lothar Zagrosek and other distinguished conductors have frequently led the orchestra. Zagrosek has made several important recordings with the Deutsches Sinfonie-Orchester Berlin for Decca Records. The group has also recorded for Denon, Orfeo, Capriccio, and cpo. They are probably the most significant orchestra in Berlin after the Berlin Philharmonic. *—Robert Cummings*

Recommended:

- ○ **Music of Rimsky-Korsakov** / Jurowski (cond.), Berlin RSO / 1999 / Capriccio 10833
- ○ **Pettersson: Symphony 8** / Sanderling (cond.), Berlin RSO / CPO 999085
- ○ **Strauss: Violin Concerto; Oboe Concerto** / Ashkenazy (cond.), Hunt, Walker, Belkin, Berlin RSO / 1993 / Decca 436415

Berlin Philharmonic Orchestra

f. 1862, Berlin, Germany
Ensemble

In a city of rich cultural and artistic history, the Berlin Philharmonic Orchestra is one of Berlin's three excellent orchestras. A democratic, self-governing organization, members choose the resident conductor, orchestra manager and new orchestra members (after a one-year probation) by vote of the membership at large. Members with ten years' seniority are eligible for pension benefits. Performing approximately 100 concerts a year, the Berlin Philharmonic tours internationally and generates most of its operating capital through ticket sales and revenue from its extensive broadcasting and recording contracts. Several significant ensembles including the Brandis and Westphalian string quartets, the Philharmonic Octet, and the Twelve Philharmonic Cellists are made up from the Berlin Philharmonic's 114 members, internationally acclaimed for their polished performances and high standards of musicianship.

Founded in 1862 by Benjamin Bilse under the name Bilsesche Kapelle (Bilse's Band), the original 60-member ensemble gained popularity. It was renamed and reorganized under the financial management of Hermann Wolff in 1882. Hans von Bülow set the ensemble on its course of artistic excellence, beginning as principal conductor in 1887. He insisted on the highest musical standards, attracted world-renowned guest conductors such as Tchaikovsky, Brahms, and Strauss, and supervised the renovation of the orchestra's home venue, a converted roller skating rink. Due to ill health, von Bülow resigned his position in 1892. The Philharmonic played at his funeral ceremony in February 1894.

Over the next several years, Wolff engaged a series of popular guest conductors including Hans Richter and Richard Strauss. Then in 1895, Hungarian-born Arthur Nikisch was chosen as resident conductor and led the Berlin Philharmonic to its well-earned reputation as the most respected touring orchestra in Europe. He brought out the lyrical qualities for which this ensemble became famous.

Soon after Nikisch's death in 1922, the reins of leadership were given to Berliner Wilhelm Furtwängler. Over the next two decades, Furtwängler debuted works by the likes of Debussy, Stravinsky, Prokofiev, and Schoenberg. Important soloists were a regular feature during this period and included such luminaries as Paul Hindemith and Yehudi Menuhin.

Difficult economic times came after the worldwide financial crash in 1929 but the ensemble was able to survive through subsidies from the city of Berlin, the German government, and the Berlin Radio Network. Further hardship came when its home venue was destroyed by a bomb in January 1944. Performing in borrowed spaces, the orchestra continued even after the beloved Furtwängler was detained during the political vindication proceedings which took place after Hitler's fall in 1945. Leo Borchard was named resident conductor in May 1945, but was shot and killed by an Occupation soldier three months later. Sergiu Celibidache was chosen to follow Borchard and was widely acclaimed for his inclusion of contemporary repertoire, much of which had been banned during Hitler's reign. When Furtwängler was finally released in 1947, he and Celibidache shared the Berlin Philharmonic's podium until Furtwängler's death in 1954.

The members of the Philharmonic chose Herbert von Karajan as resident conductor in 1955. Under his leadership, the orchestra gained worldwide recognition. The Philharmonic began construction of a new concert hall in 1963. Designed by architect Hans Scharoun, the orchestra's home venue near Berlin's Brandenburg Gate seats 2,000 audience members and contains an impressive Schuke organ. Von Karajan also began the orchestra's tradition of committing five performances each season to twentieth century music.

Late in that 1989, following von Karajan's death, Claudio Abbado was chosen to continue the Berlin Philharmonic's tradition of musical excellence and polished performance and lead this world-renowned orchestra into the twenty-first century. *—Corie Stanton Root*

Recommended:

- ○ **Kempe Conducts Strauss** / Kempe (cond.), Tortelier, Cappone, Berlin PO / 2003 / Testament 1249
- ○ **Bruckner: Symphony 8** / Jochum (cond.), Berlin PO / DG 431163
- ○ **Beethoven: Symphony 3 & 9** / Furtwängler (cond.), Anders, Hongen, Briem, Watake, Berlin PO / Documents 919/20
- ○ **Beethoven: Symphonies 7 & 8** / Furtwängler (cond.), Berlin PO / DG 427401
- ○ **Beethoven: Symphonies 5, 6 & 9** / Karajan (cond.), Schreier, Van Dam, Tomowa-Sintow, Baltsa, Berlin PO / DG 000005202
- ○ **Recordings 1942–1944 Vol. 1** / Furtwängler (cond.), Berlin PO / 2001 / DG 471289

Hector Berlioz

b. Dec. 11, 1803, La Côte-St.-André, Isère, France, **d.** Mar. 8, 1869, Paris, France
Composer: Symphonic, Opera, Orchestral, Vocal, Choral, Concerto

Berlioz, the passionate, ardent, irrepressible genius of French Romanticism, left a rich and original oeuvre which exerted a profound influence on nineteenth century music. Berlioz developed a profound affinity toward music and literature as a child. Sent to Paris at 17 to study medicine, he was enchanted by Gluck's operas, firmly deciding to become a composer. With his father's reluctant consent, Berlioz entered the Paris Conservatoire in 1826. His originality was already apparent and disconcerting—a competition cantata, *Cléopâtre* (1829), looms as his first sustained masterpiece—and he won the Prix de Rome in 1830 amid the turmoil of the July Revolution. Meanwhile, a performance of *Hamlet* in September 1827, with Harriet Smithson as Ophelia, provoked an overwhelming but unrequited passion, whose aftermath may be heard in the *Symphonie fantastique* (1830).

Returning from Rome, Berlioz organized a concert in 1832, featuring his symphony. Harriet Smithson was in the audience. They were introduced days later and married on October 3, 1833.

Berlioz settled into a career pattern which he maintained for more than a decade, writing reviews, organizing concerts, and composing a series of visionary masterpieces: *Harold en Italie* (1834), the monumental *Requiem* (1837), and an opera, *Benvenuto Cellini* (1838), a crushing fiasco. At year's end, the dying Paganini made Berlioz a gift of 20,000 francs, enabling him to devote nearly a year to the composition of his "dramatic symphony," *Roméo et Juliette* (1839). And, to commemorate the tenth anniversary of the July Revolution, came the *Symphonie funèbre et triomphale* (1840).

Iridescently scored, an exquisite collection of six Gautier settings, *Les nuits d'été*, opened the new decade. This was a difficult time for Berlioz, as his marriage failed to bring him the happiness he desired. Concert tours to Brussels, many German cities, Vienna, Pesth, Prague, and London occupied him through most of the 1840s. He composed *La Damnation de Faust*, en route, offering the new work to a half-empty house in Paris, December 6, 1846. Expenses were catastrophic, and only a successful concert tour to St. Petersburg saved him.

He sat out the revolutionary upheavals of 1848 in London, returning to Paris in July. The massive *Te Deum*—a "little brother" to the *Requiem*—was largely composed over 1849, though it would not be heard until 1855. *L'Enfance du Christ*, scored an immediate and enduring success from its first performance on December 10, 1854. Elected to the Institut de France in 1855, he started receiving a members' stipend, and this provided him with a modicum of financial security. Consequently, Berlioz was able to devote himself to the *summa* of his career, his vast opera, *Les Troyens*, based on Virgil's *Aeneid*, the Roman poet's unfinished epic masterpiece. The opera was completed in 1858. As he negotiated for its performance, he composed a *comique* adaptation of Shakespeare's *Much Ado About Nothing*, which met with a rapturous Baden première, on August 9, 1862. Unfortunately, only the third, fourth, and fifth acts of *Les Troyens* were mounted by the Théatre-Lyrique, a successful premiere, on November 4, 1863, and a run of 21 performances notwithstanding. This lopsided production stemmed from a compromise (bitterly regretted by the composer) that Berlioz had made with the Théâtre-Lyrique.

Though frail and ailing, Berlioz conducted his works in Vienna and Cologne in 1866, traveling to St. Petersburg and Moscow in the winter of 1867–68. Despondent and tortured by self-doubt, the composer received a triumphant welcome in Russia. Back in Paris in March 1868, he was but a walking shadow as paralysis slowly overcame him. *—Adrian Corleonis*

SYMPHONIC

Symphonie fantastique, H.48 (Op. 14) (Apr. 1830)

Berlioz composed this work in 1830 and conducted the first performance in Paris on December 5 of that same year. He revised it in 1832 and added two cornets to the instrumentation in 1845.

Berlioz the composer was a full-blown Romantic, whose infatuation-at-first-sight with a pretty British ingénue named Harriet Smithson influenced his *Fantastic Symphony*. Miss Smithson came to Paris to play Shakespeare, Berlioz's hero (along with Virgil, Goethe, Gluck, Beethoven, Lord Byron, and Victor Hugo). Harriet was "The Beloved" of his *programme fantastique*. "A young musician of morbid sensibility . . . in a paroxysm of lovesick despair" attempts suicide, but takes only enough laudanum to induce hallucinations, in which his Beloved appears as a recurring melody with several personalities, finally as a bacchante at a satanic ritual. Despite the lurid scenario, Berlioz's five-movement structure owes more to Beethoven's *Pastoral Symphony* than anyone seems to have noticed at the time, or, for that matter, since. Where Beethoven whipped up a storm, Berlioz created a mob scene that concludes with the protagonist's death: his decapitated head bounces into a waiting basket pizzicato. In the finale, Berlioz went far beyond Beethoven's merrymaking peasants; he created a witches' sabbath, without precedent in music before 1830. Along with liberating orchestral color, he overthrew the tyranny of bar-lines, downbeat accents, and academic dogma.

"Dreams, Passions" begins with the hero's despair, a Largo introduction in C minor that leads to the main body of the movement in C (and later G) major, marked Agitato ed appassionato assai. The Beloved's signature melody is the main theme of a sonata structure with exposition repeat; she returns in the development, in the recap, and in a grand coda of notable length and contrapuntal éclat.

"A Ball" (Allegro non troppo, A major) is the waltz without a trio, although a contrasting section in F major has unison flute and oboe playing the Beloved's theme.

"Scene in the Fields" is an Adagio that begins and concludes with an antiphonal shepherds' duet on oboe and English horn. Near the end of a free-form central section, the Beloved appears. Four timpanists playing very softly—a Berlioz signature—imitate a distant storm before the two shepherds lead their flocks homeward.

The G minor "March to the Scaffold" recreates a scene from the Revolution, Allegretto non troppo, with a repeat usually ignored in twentieth century performances. The protagonist dreams he's been condemned to die for killing his Beloved, who appears briefly as a clarinet, and he is guillotined as the crowd shouts approval.

"Dream of the Witches' Sabbath" features a four-part structure after an eerie introduction in E flat. The Beloved's melody is the main theme of Part I, now, however, distorted and vulgarized by clarinets. Distant bells introduce Part II, in which bassoons and tuba play the Gregorian *Dies irae*. Part III is the Witches' Dance, a fugue that Berlioz called a ronde. Part IV combines the *Dies irae* and Witches' Dance until the latter triumphs, electrifyingly. *—Roger Dettmer*

Recommended:

○ **Berlioz: Symphonie Fantastique** / Muti (cond.), Philadelphia Orch. / 1999 / Seraphim 73554

○ **Berlioz: Symphonic Fantastique** / Norrington, London Classical Players / 1997 / Virgin 61379

OPERA

Béatrice et Bénédict, H. 138 (Aug. 1860–Feb. 1862)

Berlioz at the end of the 1850s was in the midst of protracted negotiations for the production of the opera *Les Troyens*—his *summa*, testament, and grandest work—and miserably in the grip of a variously diagnosed intestinal complaint which could keep him in bed for days. Wagner arrived in Paris in the autumn of 1859 to present concerts of his music which Berlioz, as critic of the *Journal des débats*, was obliged to review. With the Prelude to *Tristan und Isolde*, Romanticism confronted its post-Romantic successor—and was perplexed. "I have read and reread this curious work several times," Berlioz wrote in his otherwise generally laudatory notice. "I have listened to it with the most careful attention and a keen desire to understand, but I must confess that I still have no idea what the composer was trying to do." To his young friend, the Belgian composer Adolphe Samuel, he wrote frankly that "...I found it a painful experience, even while admiring the vehemence of his musical feeling in particular instances. But the diminished sevenths, the dissonances, the brutal modulations, threw me into a fever, and I have to say I hate that style of music—it revolts me."

Rumors that Wagner's *Tannhäuser* was to be mounted at the Opéra, in preference to *Les Troyens*, understandably embittered him. In March 1860 his favorite sister and confidante, Adèle, died suddenly. Amazingly, he found respite in the composition of an opéra comique, *Béatrice et Bénédict*, based upon Shakespeare's *Much Ado About Nothing*. Early in 1859, illness had forced him to abandon a commission for an operetta for the annual festival at Baden-Baden, but during Berlioz's visit in August of the following year, Edouard Bénazet, director of the Baden festival, agreed to stage the new work-in-progress. Berlioz's second wife, Marie, died on June 13, 1862, and *Béatrice et Bénédict* received a rapturous Baden premiere the following August 9. The work's zesty richness and wealth of invention are well represented in its overture, which has become a popular concert piece. Its fleet verve and mercurial brilliance reflect the spirited banter of the antagonistic main characters, who are destined to become lovers and spouses. Their interplay is set off by candid sentiment and a luminous Mediterranean serenity soaring hand in hand. It is appropriate, too, to note that Berlioz's winsome, brimming melody and brisk, Mozartian linearity stand in the sharpest possible contrast to the harmonically based, chromatically laced eroticism of Wagner's *Tristan und Isolde*. Berlioz here casts a last, lingering, light, and lovingly sardonic look at Romantic love—close in spirit to his mélodie *L'île inconnue*, from *Les nuits d'été*—before casting his magic wand, Prospero-like, away, for *Béatrice et Bénédict* was to be his last major work. Berlioz's own description of its overall effect, epitomized in the *Béatrice et Bénédict* overture, is still the most apt: "a caprice written with the point of a needle." The score is dedicated to Bénazet. *—Adrian Corleonis*

Synopsis:

Act One. The first act opens with the people celebrating news of Don Pedro's victory over the Moorish fleet ("Le More est en fuite") and dancing. A messenger tells Léonato and his family that Pedro, Bénédict, and Claudio are on their way back. Béatrice immediately pours scorn on the messenger's praise of Bénédict, but Léonato hurries to assure the messenger that it is just part of a game between the two. Héro is delighted at the thought of Claudio's return ("Je vais le voir"). The men arrive and Béatrice and Bénédict immediately begin sparring verbally ("Comment le dédain pourrait-il mourir?"), each finding an unusual pleasure in their battle of wits. Bénédict declares his refusal to marry, particularly when a blonde like Béatrice is involved, and she in turn responds that she has no intention herself of marriage, especially not to a man with a beard like Bénédict. (And if you don't see the rest of the plot coming from here...) Pedro offers to ask for Héro's hand on Claudio's behalf, and the wedding is arranged for that very evening. Pedro offers to make arrangements for Bénédict, who refuses, laughing at the very notion. Claudio and Pedro describe matrimonial bliss, accusing him of matrimonophobia, and he in turn accuses them of matrimonomania ("Me marier? Dieu me pardonne!") Bénédict goes so far as to say that if he ever does entangle himself, they can put a sign on his house declaring, "Here you may see Bénédict, the married man." Pedro takes this as a challenge and enlists Héro's help. Sommarone presents a wedding song he has composed himself ("Mourez, tendres epoux"), though the general opinion is that he shouldn't have. Bénédict sits reading and, pretending not to notice his presence. Pedro, Claudio, and Léonato discuss Béatrice's deep, tormenting love for Bénédict, but agree not to tell him, for fear that he would just mock her. When they leave, Bénédict thinks this over and finds it not difficult to persuade himself to love her ("Ah! Je vais l'aimer"). Héro and Ursule perform the same maneuver on Béatrice. Afterwards, Héro and Ursule go into the garden; reflecting on the beauty of the night, which at times makes even Héro melancholy, they sing a nocturne ("Nuit paisable et sereine).

Act Two. The next act takes place later that evening. Sommarone improvises a drinking song ("Le vin de Syracuse"). Béatrice thinks over what she has heard ("Dieu! Que viens-je d'entendre?") and remembers how anxious she was when Bénédict left with the army, and how she had a nightmare about Bénédict dying in battle. She had laughed at her fears then, but now she remembers that she woke up in tears and realizes she loves him. Héro and Ursule come in, and Héro comments on her agitation, pretending she thinks Béatrice has just had another quarrel with Bénédict. Béatrice insists on changing the subject, and the three reflect on Héro's impending marriage ("Je vais, d'un coeur amant"). Héro and Ursule comment on the unusual romantic turn of Béatrice's comments. Béatrice remains behind as Héro and Ursule go to dress, and after a chorus sings a wedding song behind the scenes, Bénédict comes in. The two of them are remarkably awkward, and after the rest of the wedding party appears ("Dieu qui guidas"), Claudio and Héro sing a brief prayer for their love. The notary announces that he has been told to prepare two contracts, and finally Béatrice and Bénédict openly admit their love in their own feigned offhand way. The sign saying "Here you may see Bénédict the married man" is duly unveiled, and in their light love duet "L'amour est un flambeau," the two agree to declare a truce that night and resume hostilities on the morrow. *—Ann Feeney*

Recommended:

○ **Hector Berlioz: Béatrice et Bénédict** / J. Nelson (cond.), S. Graham, Viala, S. McNair, C. Robbin, Lyon Opera Orch. / Erato 45773

○ **Berlioz: Béatrice et Bénédict** / C. Davis (cond.), Veasey, Mitchinson, Cantelo, H. Watts, London SO / 1996 / London 448113

○ **Berlioz: Béatrice & Bénédict** / C. Davis (cond.), Wilson-Johnson, Gritton, Mingardo, London SO / LSO Live 0004

Les Troyens, H. 133a (1858)

"It was Virgil who first found the way to my heart and opened my budding imagination, by speaking to me of epic passions for which instinct had prepared me," Berlioz confided in his *Memoirs*. But only near the end of his career did the doomed city of Troy and the inexorable passion of Dido and Aeneas take hold. On a quiet stopover in Weimar to visit Liszt in the spring of 1854, the latter's mistress, Princess Carolyne Sayn-Wittgenstein, broached the subject of a "vast opera"; with the complicity of his friends, Berlioz's resistance thus dissolved. He began the libretto in the spring of 1856 and completed it on June 26; the work was interrupted only by an irresistible urge to compose the sublime fourth-act love duet, "Nuit d'ivresse."

Though he took his story from Virgil's *Aeneid*, Berlioz almost wholly invented Cassandra, prophetess of the fall of Troy, and took some useful cues from Shakespeare. He not only adapted lines (e.g., "On such a night as this" from *The Merchant of Venice* for Dido and Aeneas' duet) but also drew some notable *coups de théâtre* as well: the apparition of the shades of Hector, Priam, and Cassandra, for instance, prompting Aeneas to fulfill his destiny, owes something to the tormenting ghosts near the end of *Richard III*. And the cynical reluctance of Berlioz's Trojan sentries to leave the comforts of Carthaginian wine and women for that dubious Italian glory—sandwiched between moments of tremendous tension—is Shakespearean to the core.

On June 21, 1854, Berlioz was elected a member of the Institute (an elite honorary academy, representing the five major academic disciplines), conferring recognition as one of the "immortals" as well as an annual stipend of 1,500 francs. Assured of financial security at last, he devoted himself without constraint to his vast legend, substantially completing the score on April 12, 1858. Thus, *Les Troyens* became an ideal grand opera, fraught with superhuman requirements, including two great singing actresses and a lyric tenor who can rise *commandingly* to B flat, B natural, or C above the staff—a creature nearly as legendary as Aeneas, the demigod he is to portray. Unusual virtuosity is demanded of the chorus, too. While the work is hardly unperformable, as glib Parisian *boulevardiers* quipped, the peculiar constellation of forces required to bring *Les Troyens* persuasively to the stage is sufficiently unusual that one may expect to hear it (in E.J. Dent's apt phrase) "only at rare and solemn intervals." *Les Troyens* matches its subject with a richness and repletion unparalleled in Berlioz's oeuvre—its five acts playing some four hours—and rivaled for sheer creative reach by a mere handful of operatic works in any century.

After protracted negotiations, Berlioz allowed the Théâtre Lyrique to produce the third, fourth, and fifth acts under the title *Les Troyens à Carthage*. Despite stellar casting, the enthusiasm of the performers, and glowing press, cuts made to the already truncated score after its premiere on November 4, 1863, made its run of 21 performances an increasingly embittering experience for the composer. "It finished him," Gounod would write of *Les Troyens*. "Like his namesake, Hector, he died beneath the walls of Troy." Not until decades later was the work performed in its entirety.

The opera contains two major numbers that are often played as orchestral excerpts. The first is the "Trojan March," which is heard in different versions in both parts of the opera, and the other is the "Royal Hunt and Storm." The latter is a brilliant orchestral movement, with striking and original off-stage effects; it opens with a section including exuberant hunting horns, a pastoral episode, and a gathering and then brilliantly evocative thunderstorm. The storm occurs as Dido and Aeneas take refuge in a cave, and the rising excitement and the outbreak of the storm also musically symbolize their passion and lovemaking. *—AMG*

Synopsis:

Part One. The first part of the opera, "The Capture of Troy," opens on the plains below the ancient citadel of Troy. A carnival atmosphere pervades the deserted camp of the Greek army. Amid dancing, games, and delirious revelry the Trojans are celebrating the departure of the Greeks after a decade-long siege. In the distance can be seen the huge wooden horse which the revelers assume to have been deserted or left behind as an offering. Only the clairvoyant Princess Cassandra is apprehensive. She is coaxed by her fiancé, the soldier Choroebus, into joining her parents, King Priam and Queen Hecuba, at the thanksgiving ceremony. Andromache, widow of slain hero Hector, arrives with their son Astyanax and presents him to the king. The crowd offers condolences and lauds the sacrifice of Hector, but Cassandra warns that greater peril awaits the general populace.

The veteran Aeneas arrives in great agitation and relates that the high priest Laocoon has been strangled to death by two sea serpents after he had hurled a javelin at the wooden horse. Amid the horror of the Trojans, Priam, fearing the incident is a sign of displeasure from the gods, orders that the horse be hauled through a breach in the city's wall and therein be offered as a sacrifice. A parade assembles, and the horse is wheeled in amid a mood of great triumph until an ominous sound of clashing metal is heard, seemingly from within the huge timber beast. The Trojans, initially taken aback, convince themselves that it is a good omen and proceed forward. Cassandra, sick at heart, knows otherwise and turns away in despair.

That night, the ghost of Hector appears to Aeneas in his tent and warns him of the imminent doom of Troy. It is too late to save the city, but the spirit admonishes Aeneas to take as many people as he can take and set sail for Italy; there they will found a great city that will become the hub of a great empire. As the phantom fades, the wounded priest Pantheus brings news that Grecian soldiers have emerged from inside the huge horse and have begun to lay waste to the city. Hard on his heels are Choroebus and his soldiers, who rally Aeneas and vow to fight to the death for the city of Troy.

The scene shifts to the temple of the goddess Vesta as the grieving Trojan women implore the gods to intervene. But Cassandra, who shares the same vision of the ghost of Hector, tells them that it is too late—but that Aeneas and the many others who will flee the fall of the city will build a new Troy on far shores. Heartened and resolved to die proudly, the women rally around Cassandra (also aware that her beloved Choroebus has fallen in battle), who has seized a lyre. As they lift their voices in a hymn of praise, the Greeks enter and are astonished at the stoic bravery of the women. As they steel themselves and storm forward to demand treasure, the women begin to kill themselves, some flinging themselves from the battlements, others stabbing themselves. The last words heard from Cassandra and her dwindling circle are "Save Troy her sons, Aeneas! To Italia! To Italia!"

Part Two. The second part of the opera, "The Trojans at Carthage," opens as Queen Dido receives homage from the people of Carthage. Aeneas, posing as a sailor, arrives with the emigrant Trojans, and all are cordially and heartily welcomed. At this point, Narbal the prime minister arrives and notifies Dido of the city's besiegement by the Numidians. Aeneas reveals his identity, and the Trojans and army of Carthage join ranks to defeat the invaders. Dido, taken with Aeneas' bravery, falls in love with him. This causes concern on the part of her sister Anna and likewise of Narbal, for the queen now spends more time and attention on her newfound love than on her duties as monarch. Likewise in love, Aeneas has lost sight of his goal, and as he and the queen are locked in a lovers' embrace, the god Mercury appears with the stern reminder "To Italia!" This admonition is carried over into the entr'acte, "Royal Hunt and the Storm." Depicted is a cave where Dido and Aeneas take refuge, their leisurely hunt having been interrupted by a severe and fiery thunderstorm. Amidst the tempest can be heard supernatural voices chanting "Italia! Italia!"

The tempest subsides and gives way to a scene at the harbor of Carthage. All the pleasures of the city, provided by a grateful populace, have created a paradise for the Trojans. But Aeneas, now resolute, rallies his men to the task that lies before them. Emphasis comes from the ghosts of King Priam, Cassandra, Hector, and Choroebus, and the Trojans, with renewed and steely resolve, prepare to leave. When Aeneas bids her farewell, Dido is enraged and inconsolable. She sends him off and assembles her priests to assist her in ritual suicide. She stabs herself, cursing her former beloved and the city he will found, "eternal Rome," prophetically invoking the name of Hannibal. She dies, and her subjects vow to take up the vendetta in a future age. *—Wayne Reisig*

Recommended:

- ○ **Berlioz: Les Troyens** / Dutoit (cond.), Lakes, Pollet, D. Voight, SO de Monreal / 1994 / Decca 443693
- ○ **Berlioz: Les Troyens** / C. Davis (cond.), Vickers, Veasy, B. Lindholm, Orch. of Covent Garden Royal Opera House / Philips 416432

ORCHESTRAL

Le carnival romain, ouverture caractéristique, H.95 (Op. 9) (Jan. 1844)

Berlioz's most popular and most virtuosic overture is actually an independent concert piece, but it has close ties to an opera. After the premiere of his opera *Benvenuto Cellini*, based on the autobiography of the famous Italian Renaissance sculptor, Berlioz never forgave the conductor for his lifeless delivery of the second act's saltarello finale. So ten years later he used the saltarello as the opening of his *Roman Carnival Overture*, and took the trouble to conduct the work himself in its first performances. But even before the strings and winds can really launch the revelry, the solo horn and clarinet introduce some harmonic ambiguity, and the English horn slips in with the rapturous love-duet theme from the opera's first act. Suddenly, three swirling woodwind passages suggest that fireworks are being set off on the Piazza Colonna, and the saltarello takes over, eventually incorporating the love theme into the festivities.

Berlioz was so pleased with this overture, and with its reception as well, that he advocated using it as the prelude to the second act of *Benvenuto Cellini*. This practice is usually followed to this day. After the overture's publication in full score, Johann Peter Pixis arranged it for two pianos, eight hands. This arrangement received a performance by the pianistic luminaries Franz Liszt, Charles Hallé, Ferdinand Hiller, and Pixis himself—full testimony to its status as one of the hits of its day. *—James Reel*

Recommended:

- ○ **Berlioz: Overtures** / Munch (cond.), Boston SO / 1993 / RCA Victor 61400
- ○ **Berlioz: Overtures** / C. Davis (cond.), Staatskapelle Dresden / 1998 / RCA Victor 68790

Le Corsaire, overture, H. 101 (Op. 21) (1846; revised before 1852)

Although Berlioz was one of the greatest proponents of music that adhered to a detailed program, this concert overture actually has nothing to do with Lord Byron's narrative poem about the pirate Jean Lafitte, from which the title comes. Berlioz sketched this work during a visit to Nice in 1844, and called its first version *The Tower of Nice*, having written it in the ruined fortification on the city's coastline. Berlioz provided this description: "I discovered the ruins of a tower built on the edge of a precipice: in front of it is a tiny level spot where I stretch myself in the sun and watch, at my ease, the approach of the distant ships; I count the fishing-boats and gaze with admiration on the sparkling, gleaming tracks, which (as Moore says) should lead to some happy and peaceful isle."

The overture turns out not to be an entirely placid seascape, though. When Berlioz rewrote it for an 1851 performance in London he called it *Le Corsair rouge*, after James Fenimore Cooper's *The Red Rover*, in which a cliff-side tower figures prominently. But Berlioz soon felt this title was misleading, so he deleted the adjective—giving rise to the misconception that the music is based on Byron's work. The final title fits well, though, for the overture is particularly swashbuckling. The brilliant opening is a rushing passage for the strings (no fewer than 59, Berlioz specified), punctuated by syncopated wind chords. The ensuing string-caressed Adagio is far more serene, apparently representing the sea as viewed from Berlioz's tower on a summer day. The initial Allegro material bursts back onto the scene, and the themes are rapidly developed up to a coruscating finale. *—James Reel*

Recommended:

- ○ **Berlioz: Overtures** / Talmi (cond.), San Diego SO / 1991 / Naxos 550999
- ○ **Berlioz: Symphonie fantastique** / Beecham (cond.), Royal PO / 2003 / EMI 67972

Marche de Rákóczy (Rákóczy March), H. 109 (Feb. 1846)

At the beginning of 1846, Berlioz was in Vienna. Following a farewell concert on January 11th, with the virtuoso Heinrich Wilhelm Ernst taking the viola solo in *Harold en Italie*, the intendant of the Hungarian National Theater, Count Ráday, suggested to Berlioz that if he wished to score a success in Pesth, which Berlioz was to visit, he should arrange the national Hungarian air, *Rákóczy-induló*, or *Rákóczy march*. Locked into the forced marriage of the Austro-Hungarian empire, Hungarians were seething with anti-Austrian sentiment, and Berlioz was, after all, from a nation which had seen two revolutions within living memory and was, moreover, widely regarded—if in a somewhat different sense—as the most revolutionary of living composers.

He sketched the march the evening before leaving Vienna and completed it upon his arrival in Pesth. It was included in his first concert there, given on February 15, a Sunday morning, with the *Roman Carnival Overture*, movements from the *Symphonie fantastique*, and *Harold en Italie*. Wisely, Berlioz reserved it for last. An open letter to his friend, Humbert Ferrand, included in his *Memoirs*, describes with inimitable verve one of the most stupendous successes of his career. Before the concert, a newspaper editor, one M. Horváth, after examining Berlioz's arrangement of the *Rákóczy air* as it lay beneath the hand of the copyist, presented himself to the composer. "Well?" Berlioz asked. "Well—I'm nervous... You state the theme piano. We, on the contrary, are accustomed to hearing it played fortissimo." With the serene assurance of the great master depicted in August Prinzhofer's pair of oft-reproduced engravings, made just weeks before, Berlioz replied, "Don't worry, you shall have such a forte as you have never heard in your life." Indeed, after a fanfare, the theme is announced by flutes and clarinets, set off by string pizzicati, and repeated several times with suspenseful alternations of loud and soft until, as Berlioz writes, "a long crescendo... with fragments of the theme reintroduced fugally, broken by the dull thud of the bass drum, like the thump of distant cannon...." The excitement was palpable and electric, and "as the orchestra unleashed its full fury and the long-delayed fortissimo burst forth, a tumult of shouting and stamping convulsed the theater...." The piece had to be repeated, to even greater excitement. During his central European tour, Berlioz had begun the composition of *La Damnation de Faust*. With his arrangement of the *Rákóczy air* such a superbly accomplished fact, he did not hesitate to designate its opening scene as "the plains of Hungary," and to have Faust, like Hamlet, view troops passing to the strains of the *Rákóczy March*, for which he added a more elaborate coda. The autograph score was purchased by Count Casimir Batthianyi for 500 francs. *—Adrian Corleonis*

Recommended:

- ○ **Colours of the Orchestra** / Fricsay (cond.), Berlin Radio SO / 2000 / DG 469238
- ○ **Wilhelm Furtwängler Conducts Romantic Music** / Furtwängler (cond.), Berlin PO / Opus Kura 2036

Rob Roy Overture, H.54 (Jul. 1831)

A rollicking tribute to the Scottish warrior Rob Roy, this concert overture was composed in Nice and Rome, around the same time Berlioz was writing the "Scène aux champs" for his Symphonie fantastique. The overture has much more in common, though, with his later *Harold en Italie*, sharing several themes with the larger work.

The sonata form overture opens with a jig-like Scottish tune in the horns that is soon echoed by the rest of the orchestra. The lower strings and bassoon introduce a vigorous, slightly militant melody that is answered by a more playful passage for violins and woodwinds. A great deal of fragmentary Scottish folk-like material is passed around, and eventually the English horn and harp present the long, lyrical theme that would later represent the hero of *Harold en Italie*; this is one of the overture's most extended passages. All the themes then undergo a rollicking development and finale. The hostile reaction of the audience at the Parisian premiere led Berlioz to destroy the score (though not without setting a duplicate aside), thus explaining why this piece, unlike most of his other well-known compositions of the period, lacks an opus number.*—James Reel*

Recommended:

- ○ **Berlioz: Overtures** / Talmi (cond.), San Diego SO / 1994 / Naxos 550999
- ○ **Great Conductors of the 20th Century: Sir Adrian Boult** / Boult (cond.), London PO / EMI 75459

VOCAL

La Mort de Cléopâtre, scène lyrique for soprano & orchestra, H.36 (Jul. 1829)

La Mort de Cléopâtre (The Death of Cleopatra) was Berlioz's third attempt to win the Prix de Rome from the Academie des Beaux-Arts. His first attempt in 1827 was *La Mort d'Orphée*, which failed to place. His second attempt in 1828 was *Herminie*, which took second place. Berlioz called *La Mort de Cléopâtre* "a lyric scene" for soprano and orchestra, setting a text by P.A. Vieillard. The vocal writing is extremely dramatic, but it ignores distinctions between recitative and aria, which infuriated the jury. The orchestral writing is lush and full, with extraordinary harmonies that likewise alienated the jury. *La Mort de Cléopâtre* was judged such a failure in the eyes of the Academie that it gave no first place prize that year. The following year, Berlioz won the Prix de Rome with his conservative *La Mort de Sardanapale*, but, having already composed his wildly experimental and incredibly wild *Symphonie fantastique*, he found that he no longer cared all that much about the Academie. *—James Leonard*

Recommended:

- ○ **Berlioz: La Mort de Sardanapale** / J.-C. Casadesus (cond.), Lagrange, Orch. Nationale de Lille / HM 901542
- ○ **Berlioz 5-CD Box** / Gibson (cond.), J. Baker, London SO / 2002 / EMI 575570

Les Nuits d'été, song cycle, H. 81 (Op. 7) (Sep. 1841)

This is a cycle of six settings of poems written by Théophile Gautier. Though their subjects have little direct connection, each possesses the sultry, scented charm implied by Berlioz's title. The songs were composed in 1832 and published in 1841. Except for "Absence," which was orchestrated in 1843, the orchestral versions of the remaining songs were completed in 1856.

Aside from their immediate appeal, they suggest that, before the rise of a new school of composers such as Fauré, Duparc, Debussy, and Ravel, Berlioz was reacting to a demand for songs of a distinctively French character, compared with the then-widely popular German lied. However, the American musicologist Alfred Einstein's assertion that Berlioz "sowed the seeds for the entire musical lyricism of the nineteenth century in the French language" is surely an exaggeration: he was too much an admirer of German music to do such a thing. Indeed, the first song "Villanelle" is almost strophic, only the third stanza showing any real harmonic or melodic changes in the vocal line, a device which makes it reminiscent of Schubert.

Singers tend to pick and choose among the songs performed but, since all easily stand on their own merits, this does not matter a great deal. "Absence," a call for the return of the beloved, would, for example, make an impressive opening to the cycle. "Le spectre de la rose" ("I am the ghost of the rose you wore at the ball") is operatic in character and avoids the obvious waltz rhythms used in the ballet music which was also inspired by this poem. "Sur la lagunes," a lament for a dead lover, was also set by Fauré under the title *Chanson de pêcheur*. Berlioz makes it into a barcarolle, with a flowing accompaniment and echoes of Spain and Italy. "Au cimetiere" (the churchyard where the beloved lies) is a lament, with the added dimension of modern-sounding semitone changes and enharmonic modulations—evidence of Berlioz's constant search for ways to distance himself from conventional tonality. The final song, "L'ile inconnue," a light serenade, ("where will you go, fair one in my magic boat") is—apart from one rather awkward cadence just before the lady replies—similarly progressive in its tonality. The tenderly expressive qualities of these settings makes one wish that Berlioz had continued his dedication to French poetry. *—Roy Brewer*

Recommended:

- ○ **Berlioz: Les Nuits d'été; Mélodies** / J. Levine (cond.), von Otter, Berlin PO / DG 445823
- ○ **Berlioz: Les Nuits d'été; Ravel: Shéhérazade** / Ansermet (cond.), Crespin, SRO / 1999 / Decca 460973

CHORAL

La Damnation de Faust, légende dramatique, H. 111 (Op. 24) (Nov. 1845–Oct. 1846)

Despite the hurly-burly and mixed reviews attending the dedication of Beethoven's statue in Bonn in August 1845, organized by his friend Liszt, Berlioz's imagination was stimulated by the journey. His thoughts turned to Goethe's *Faust*, and, taking the *Huit Scènes de Faust*—which he had published in 1829 as his Opus 1 only to recall and destroy every copy he could lay hands on—as his starting point, he began to flesh out a new musical form. The resulting "légende dramatique," often called a cantata, is in the nature of a concert opera, similar to the "symphonie dramatique" *Roméo et Juliette*—salient moments from familiar literary works projected as vocal scenes or by the expressive power of music alone, with plot complications and baneful recitatives elided, to be seen in the mind's eye, thus dispensing with the requirements of staging. This "open" dramaturgy had been one of the revelations of *Faust*, which Berlioz recalled in the *Memoirs*—"The marvelous book fascinated me from the first. I could not put it down, I read it incessantly, at meals, at the theater, in the street." It was what Liszt and Berlioz had spoken of at their first meeting, on the eve of the *Symphonie fantastique*'s premiere in December 1830. *Faust*, the tormented, suicidal philosopher who suddenly seeks the meaning of life in life itself—not only in love but in the immense solitude of nature—struck a chord, so to speak, with the Romantic generation. But reverence for a classic did not prevent Berlioz from finding the "hero" contemptible in his abandonment of the village girl he has, with Mephistopheles' help, seduced. The startlingly vivid, non-Goethean, cinematic Ride to the Abyss—impossible to stage in Berlioz's day and awkward in ours—is capped by Faust's screaming plunge into Hell as the soul of his lover, Marguerite, is welcomed by a choir of angels. *La Damnation de Faust* is dedicated to Liszt, whose own greatest symphonic work, *Eine Faust Symphonie*, would follow in 1854. Berlioz gave his work, at his own expense, before a half-empty house on December 6, 1846, and again on the 20th with the same result. "Nothing in my career as an artist wounded me more deeply than this unexpected indifference," Berlioz wrote. He was, to boot, financially ruined. *—Adrian Corleonis*

Recommended:

- ○ **Berlioz: La Damnation De Faust** / C. Davis (cond.), Veasey, Gedda, Bastin, Van Allan, London SO / Philips 416395
- ○ **Berlioz: La Damnation De Faust** / M-Y. Chung (cond.), von Otter, B. Terfel, K. Lewis, von Halem, Philharmonia Orch. / 1998 / DG 453500
- ○ **Berlioz: La Damnation De Faust** / Solti (cond.), Riegel, Von Stade, Van Dam, M. King, Chicago SO / London 414680

L' Enfance du Christ, oratorio, H. 130 (Op. 25) (Oct. 1850–Jul. 1854)

This is one of the rare Berlioz compositions which was a rousing, noncontroversial success from its first full performance. But it was preceded by a curious episode. As is the case of many Berlioz works, this gentle and popular oratorio was developed by incorporating and expanding upon an earlier composition. In 1850, Berlioz conducted a work he described as "The Flight into Egypt." This, he said, was a mystery play by a composer named "Pierre Ducre," written in 1679. This was a scam, and it worked. The music was his own, and he presented it under this ruse to see what reaction would occur among the critics who habitually attacked anything from his pen. Sure enough, some critics took the occasion to express their insincere "hopes" that Berlioz would learn something from this music about how to write sincere, devout music.

Berlioz retained "The Flight into Egypt" as the centerpiece of the larger work. In it the shepherds arrive to worship and say farewell to the Baby Jesus, Mary, and Joseph, who have already been warned by the angels to flee towards Egypt. The central section ends with the lovely "Sleep of the Holy Family." The new opening section, "Herod's Dream" which begins with Jesus' birth, transitions to Jerusalem to Herod's dream that a new king has been born, and the King's bloody determination to secure his throne for his own line by slaughtering all newborns, and closes with the aforementioned angelic warning. The final part depicts the Holy Family having arrived in Sais, where the Romans and Egyptians turn them away, but they are given safe haven, finally, by the Ishmaelites.

This tender and lovely music—scored with the skill and imagination for which Berlioz is famous but not employing sensational orchestral effects—was an instant success and went on to growing fame. It was an age of interest in the form of the religious oratorio; Handel's were being revived, as was Haydn's *The Creation*; Mendelssohn wrote *Elijah* and *Paulus*, and a host of lesser composers attempted their own. Berlioz's stands somewhat apart from these in its general sense of intimacy; in few if any works of this general character do we get such a sense of the humanity of the main characters. The Holy Family is presented as a baby, loving and concerned parents, and husband and wife.

The December 10, 1854, premiere was so successful that a Christmas Eve performance was quickly laid on, and repeated again about a month later. Berlioz conducted it in several cities, once receiving a laurel wreath from a rapturous audience. *—Joseph Stevenson*

Recommended:

- ○ **Berlioz: L'Enfance du Christ** / Herreweghe (cond.), Agnew, Gens, Orch. des Champs Elysées / HM 2901632/33
- ○ **Berlioz: L'Enfance Du Christ** / Dutoit (cond.), S. Graham, Le Roux, Ainsley, OS de Montreal / 2000 / Decca 458915

Lélio, ou Le retour à la vie, monodrame lyrique, H. 55 (Op. 14bis) (Jul. 1831–1832; revised 1854)

Berlioz wrote *Symphonie Fantastique* partly as an expression of his obsessive love for Harriet Smithson. *Lelio, or The Return to Life*, is a sequel to that work, more directly and overtly autobiographical, depicting the hero's awakening from the drugged dream and his subsequent thoughts and actions. The piece daringly combines narration and music in six movements, ranging from a simple song with piano accompaniment to two large-scale choral works, with dramatic monologues in between them. Many of the musical portions are directly taken from or inspired by earlier works or fragments of ideas. The narration itself is a chance for Berlioz to speak directly to his audiences and critics. One of the monologues is an attack on a Parisian music critic, Fétis (who was given to demanding "good taste" in everything and often adapted the works of other composers, such as Beethoven, to reflect this taste). The narrator even mimicked Fétis' voice during this monologue, and the critic was outraged by the laugher and applause from both audience and orchestra. In another section, the narrator longs for "this Juliet, this Ophelia, whom my heart is always seeking." Berlioz was expressing his obsession not only with Harriet Smithson, who had inspired the murderous fantasies of *Symphonie Fantastique*, but also Camille Moke, his "Ariel, that enchanting fairy," a piano instructor who had married another man. The music dwells on many of the subjects which consumed Berlioz's attention. In the first, a nymph's song lures a fisherman to follow her into the waters. The music has a light surface charm, but hints at darker things, as her call becomes more alluring and the music more disturbed. The "Chorus of Shades," written originally as part of his *La Mort de Cleopatre*, is powerful and mysterious, as the spirits of the dead remind the living that they, too, shall perish. As the narrator longs to be freed of civilization, a chorus of brigands sings a rousing, rollicking song about the joys of a free life, with the pleasures of their female prisoners. A more tender note is drawn as Lélio's own voice (sung by a singer, rather than the narrator) longs for the bliss of love, and in arching, passionate phrases, calls for his beloved to come to him. An instrumental harp interlude follows, and the work ends with the narrator himself conducting a chorus in which the spirits of the island (from Shakespeare's *The Tempest*) bid a sad farewell to Miranda, and finally falling back into despair. *—Ann Feeney*

Recommended:

- ○ **Berlioz: Lélio; Symphonie fantastique; Tristia** / Dutoit (cond.), OS de Montreal / 2001 / Decca 458011
- ○ **Berlioz: La Mort d'Ophélie; Œuvres pour chœur** / Tetu (cond.), Lee, Courtis, Orch. Nationale de Lyon / HM 1951293

Requiem (Grande Messe des morts), H. 75 (Op. 5) (Jun. 1837; revised 1852)

The instrumental forces alone demand that we step back and look at Hector Berlioz *Grand Messe des morts*, Op. 5 (*Requiem*) a little differently than we might look at another composition—even another large-scale, theatrical composition—from the 1830s: in addition to the usual large orchestra and chorus, Berlioz calls for no fewer than 16 timpani and four extra brass choirs! When the French ministry of the interior commissioned a requiem mass from Berlioz in 1837 and decreed that the conservative conductor Francois-Antoine Habeneck would lead the December 5 first performance of the work, they can hardly have had such a thing in mind (nobody had yet ever even conceived of an instrumentation like that before, certainly not for indoor use); but Berlioz, through all his many ups and downs as a composer, was never one to suppress his fiery sense of the dramatic (as fiery as his bright red hair, so the stories go), and, in the end, even Habeneck—who, according to a not impartial Berlioz, tried his best to ruin the *Requiem*'s premiere—had to admire the spark of genius and the sheer spunk that it took to put that thing on paper. Today the *Requiem* is Berlioz's second-most famous work, behind the *Symphony Fantastique*, though, as one might imagine from its performance requirements, it is not his second-most frequent visitor to the concert hall (or the cathedral, as the case might be).

Berlioz' *Grand Messe des morts*, scored for orchestra, tenor soloist, and SSTTBB chorus plus the extra forces listed above, is in ten sections and runs in excess of an hour and a quarter. Not all of its music is massive (the extra forces explode onto the scene in the Tuba mirum portion of the Dies irae sequence in No. 2 and then disappear), and indeed much of it is quite intimate—for example the slender No. 3 Quid sum miser, which immediately follows the outburst in No. 2, or the opening of No. 9 Sanctus, which features the solo tenor. And the *Requiem* ends in absolute tenderness, the Lamb of God (No. 10 Agnus Dei) having taken away the sins of the world and accepted the dead into a new world, of which we mortals can hear only vague echoes—timpani strokes left over from the explosive Last Judgment held earlier in the mass, now distant and gentle. *—Blair Johnston*

Recommended:

- ○ **Berlioz: Requiem; Te Deum** / C. Davis (cond.), London SO / 2001 / Philips 464689
- ○ **Berlioz: Requiem & 5 Pieces Sacrées** / Dutoit (cond.), Ainsley, OS Montreal / 1999 / Decca 458921

Roméo et Juliette, symphonie dramatique, H.79 (Op. 17) (Sep. 1839)

Roméo et Juliette employs orchestra, chorus, and vocal soloists and lasts more than 90 minutes. Yet it is by no means an opera; Berlioz tends to musicalize the mood of each scene rather than set the details. He sometimes makes much of minor episodes (notably the famous "Queen Mab" scherzo), and interpolates scenes not found in Shakespeare. Berlioz devised the text himself, engaging Emile Deschamps to set it to verse. The work falls into three large sections subdivided into smaller numbers.

Part I consists of an introduction ("Fighting; Tumult; Intervention of the Prince") followed by a prologue. The fast introduction, starting in the violas and building through the orchestra, depicts the combat between the Montagues and Capulets. The prologue begins with a choral recitative (with contralto) briefly describing the conflict between the families and offering a plot synopsis up through Romeo's arrival at Juliet's balcony, complete with previews of melodies that will be more fully developed later. Next, the contralto, accompanied by harp, woodwinds, and eventually cellos, describes the lovers' rapture. This section ends with a brief scherzo in which Mercutio (solo tenor) and the chorus tease Romeo about his infatuation.

Part II, widely excerpted for orchestral concerts and recordings, begins with a depiction of Romeo's solitude and erotic yearning at the Capulets' ball ("Romeo alone; Sadness; Distant noises of music and dancing; Great feast at the Capulets'"). The oboe, with assistance from the clarinet, is prominent in this passionate music over a restless bass line, competing with waltzing dance music. Next, a long movement in which the chorus enacts the end of the Capulets' feast on a peaceful night is followed by a love scene without voices ("Love Scene: Serene night; The Capulets' garden silent and deserted; The young Capulets pass"). The section ends with the quicksilver, Mendelssohnian scherzo "Queen Mab, or the dream fairy."

Part III skips ahead to the play's tragic conclusion, beginning with a slow fugue representing Juliet's funeral procession, and a brief choral contribution. "Romeo at the Capulet's Tomb" presents the hero's frantic arrival, with cold chords leading to a bleak if sometimes convulsive last scene between the dying lovers, including bereft wind and brass chorales and recollections of Romeo's oboe music and Juliet's clarinet theme. The chorus returns for the finale, as in the prologue commenting on the action, but now representing the Montagues and Capulets, who learn the full truth from Friar Laurence (a bass); appalled, they work toward reconciliation. —*James Reel*

Recommended:

○ **Berlioz: Roméo & Juliette; Les Nuits d'été** / Muti (cond.), J. Norman, Aler, Estes, Philadelphia Orch. / 1998 / EMI 72640

Te Deum, H. 118 (Op. 22) (1849)

Berlioz never believed in doing things on a small scale—witness his *Les Troyens*, almost unstageably long—but his *Te Deum* is probably the largest of all, particularly in comparison to the typical jubilant but far less theatrical settings of other composers. The first performance, in 1855, had almost 1,000 performers, including a 600-voice children's choir. The scale of the work is so huge that Berlioz himself called it "apocalyptic." It was originally conceived as a thanksgiving for a military occasion, probably the return of Napoleon from his Italian campaigns, and so includes an extra-liturgical prelude and final "Marche pour la presentation des drapeaux" (March for the presentation of the flags), which are generally omitted from contemporary performances. By the time Berlioz was able to publish and perform the work, he chose to dedicate it to Prince Albert (the husband of Queen Victoria), who was about as mild-mannered and untheatrical a prince as can be imagined!

Its unabashed theatricality speaks of both Berlioz's own general lack of religious sentiments and to the original political and public nature of his original conception of the piece. Berlioz composed a good deal of religious music, certainly, and many of his musical dramas are based on religious themes, but it was the sweeping emotion of these stories, rather than the spiritual content, that drew his attention. In the Te Deum text, a hymn of praise to God and a plea for God's protection, he found a scope for this kind of dramatic sense.

The Te Deum is ambitious both in scale and in musical complexity; the choral writing in particular is dense, but nonetheless coherent and well-structured, especially in the first section. The work employs frequent contrasts. The first section, a hymn setting of the first part of the *Te Deum* text, begins with huge chords from the winds, brass, and organ, and are followed by a dense choral fugue from both of the three-part choirs. The second also begins with the organ, but here it is lyrical, rather than thunderous, as is the choral writing, which begins with the women's voices, supported by the winds. The work rises to a lyrical climax, but as the text begins to describe how "heaven and the earth are full of your praises," the texture again becomes heavier and louder with the introduction of the percussion. The third and fourth sections follow this same pattern of periods of quiet followed by huge climaxes, with only the fifth section, a passage for solo tenor and women's voices, remaining hushed throughout. The excitement here is conveyed by the rising of the voices, rather than an increase in volume. The last section is the most church-like, beginning with a stately organ passage, but this, too, is overwhelmed by the dramatic instrumental and choral writing, before it ends to the sound of thundering brasses. —*Ann Feeney*

Recommended:

○ **Berlioz: Requiem; Te Deum** / C. Davis (cond.), London SO / 2001 / Philips 464689

CONCERTO

Harold en Italie (Harold in Italy), symphony for viola & orchestra, H. 68 (Op. 16) (Jul. 1834)

Though the work was originally intended as a vehicle for the virtuoso violinist Nicolo Paganini to exhibit his considerable skill on the viola, Berlioz's *Harold in Italy* (1834) eventually became a four-movement symphony which Paganini, who wanted to be "playing all the time," eventually declined to perform. Somewhat akin to the *Symphonie fantastique* (1830) in its quasi-autobiographical cast and employment of a unifying idée fixe, *Harold* finds Berlioz imagining himself in the role of Byron's Harold for the purpose of recounting his own experiences in Italy.

The first movement, entitled "Harold in the Mountains," outlines a progression from melancholy into happiness and ultimately, into joy. The sobering fugato which opens the movement soon gives way to an uncertain melody in the woodwinds, which blossoms until the viola presents it in full as Harold's theme, the idée fixe. The movement continues its ascent into joy with an effervescent, unrelenting allegro which eases up only to allow the viola to restate the idée fixe, now fitted into another fugato, before the accelerating momentum brings the movement to an end.

Like Mendelssohn, Berlioz made the second movement of his "Italian" symphony a "Pilgrim's March." Essentially restricted to a strophic march structure, the movement is notable for its daring modulations, each marked by the tolling of two bells. The viola enters again in the middle section, lyrically presenting the idée fixe in the periphery of the passing march before taking on an accompanying role as the procession moves off into the distance.

The third movement, "Serenade of an Abruzzi Mountaineer," begins with an accurate replication of Italian bagpipes, or piferari. The rustic affect is made complete with the introduction of the serenade's main melody by the English horn. The viola restates the melody in conjunction with the idée fixe, and the movement develops as Berlioz expounds upon the counterpoint between the two melodies. A somewhat resigned coda, comprising all three elements, ends the movement on a misleadingly peaceful tone.

"The Orgy of Brigands," as the finale is titled, opens with the viola revisiting several thematic ideas from prior movements before it is unceremoniously interrupted by the brash, rhythmic power of the orgy itself. Following this brass-fueled, slightly demented fury, the viola briefly returns with the "Pilgrim's March" and a final statement of Harold's theme as the composer's nostalgic reminiscence comes to a close. —*Graham Olson*

Recommended:

○ **Berlioz: Harold en Italie H68, Op 16, Bruch: Scottish Fantasy** / Oistrakh (cond.), Tolpygo / 1997 / Russian Revelation 10051

○ **Berlioz: Harold en Italie H68, Op 16, Berlioz: Troyens H133a, Berlioz: Tristia H119, Op 18** / Davis (cond.), Imai / Philips 416431

○ **Berlioz: Harold en Italie H68, Op 16, Berlioz: Mort de Cléopâtre H36** / Bernstein (cond.) / 1999 / Sony 60696

Pierre Bernac

b. Jan. 12, 1899, Paris, France, **d.** Oct. 17, 1979, Avignon, France

Baritone

The baritone Pierre Bernac was one of the most important French singers of the twentieth century. His singing was characterized by a refined, high, and light baritone voice with impeccably clear and gentle enunciation and a sensitive and flexible approach to phrasing. His close relationships to several major composers, most notably Francis Poulenc, made him the definitive interpreter of a large repertoire of mélodies.

After early studies with André Caplet and Yvonne Gouverné, Bernac made his recital debut in Paris in 1925. In 1926, he gave his first Poulenc premiere with *Chansons gailliardes*. In the early 1930s, he also studied lieder with Reinhard von Wahrlich. Bernac met Poulenc in 1934 when he asked Poulenc to accompany him for some Debussy mélodies, and on April 3, 1935, they gave their first recital together, which included the first performance of Poulenc's *Cinq poèmes de Paul Eluard*. They toured the world together until Bernac's retirement in 1960. Poulenc wrote 90 songs for Bernac and Bernac's interpretations of these works with the composer at the piano have been recorded on disc (his complete recordings were reissued in 1999) and discussed in his two books: *The Interpretation of French Song* (London, 1970) and *Francis Poulenc: The Man and His Songs* (London, 1977). Bernac also collaborated with other important composers of the twentieth century, including Hindemith, Berkeley, Barber, Jolivet, Sauguet, and Françaix. He turned to teaching in later life; his most famous student was Gérard Souzay. Bernac's only performances on the opera stage were in the role of Pelléas in Debussy's *Pelléas et Mélisande* (in 1933 at the Théâtre des Champs-Elysées and in 1936 in Geneva under the baton of Ernest Ansermet). —*Robert Adelson*

Recommended:

○ **The Essential Pierre Bernac** / Bernac, Beydts (cond.), Moore, Johnson, Poulenc / Testament 3161

○ **Poulenc: Mélodies** / Bernac, Poulenc (piano) / Ades 20293

○ **Poulenc: Mélodies** / Bernac, Poulenc (piano) / Ades 20294

Leonard Bernstein

b. Aug. 25, 1918, Lawrence, MA, **d.** Oct. 14, 1990, New York, NY

Composer: Musical Theater, Opera, Symphonic, Orchestral, Concerto, Choral, Vocal, Ballet

Conductor

As composer, conductor, and educator, Leonard Bernstein (1918–90) emerged as one of a handful of figures in the twentieth century who truly changed the face of music. As a composer, Bernstein left a far-reaching legacy that includes three symphonies, a film score of singular distinction, (*On the Waterfront*), and an important body of stage works, including one of the cornerstones of American musical theater, *West Side Story* (1957). The first American-born conductor to attain international superstardom, Bernstein made a profound impression on audiences; his podium manner was dynamic, even flamboyant, to an extent never before witnessed. Bernstein's extroverted manner attracted much criticism from those who dismissed him as a mere exhibitionist; his advocates, however, far outnumbered his detractors.

Born in Lawrence, MA, Bernstein made his mark first as a composer. He attended Harvard University, where he studied with Walter Piston among other distinguished figures. Occasionally he wrote popular songs on the side using the pseudonym Lenny Amber ("amber" being the English translation of the word "Bernstein"). His works of the 1940s, both weighty and light, brought him considerable acclaim; the single year of 1944 saw the premieres of two especially well-received scores, the *Symphony No. 1, "Jeremiah"*, and the ballet *Fancy Free*. During his sometimes rocky tenure (1958–69) as music director of the New York Philharmonic, Bernstein brought that ensemble to a new level of prestige and popularity: every

Bernstein concert and recording became a much-anticipated event. Through his association with the New York Philharmonic and a never-ending stream of guest engagements worldwide, Bernstein became particularly renowned as an interpreter of Mahler and Copland; he did much to carve out the prominent place in the orchestral concert repertory that both composers now maintain. Already well-known by the time he took over the New York Philharmonic, Bernstein became truly famous in 1958, with the first of his series of televised Young People's Concerts, fondly remembered by many as their introduction to the world of classical music. Among the first group of students to receive training at the Berkshire Music Center at Tanglewood, Bernstein soon became the institution's guiding light, serving as teacher and mentor for generations of musicians. Though he remained a giant of the podium until the very end, Bernstein curtailed his conducting activities in later years in order to spend more time composing. Little of Bernstein's music from the 1970s on has attained the same level of popularity achieved by his earlier works; still, it comprises a distinguished, substantial body of work that includes the *Mass* (1971), the opera *A Quiet Place* (1983) and the song cycle *Arias and Barcarolles* (1988). *—AMG*

Recommended:

- ○ **Bernstein Conducts Copland** / Bernstein (cond.), New York PO / 2003 / Sony 87327
- ○ **Bernstein Conducts Bernstein** / Bernstein (cond.) / DG 000001402
- ○ **Beethoven: Symphonies 6 & 8; King Stephen Overture** / Bernstein (cond.), New York PO / 1998 / Sony 60557
- ○ **Schumann: The 4 Symphonies** / Bernstein (cond.), Vienna PO / DG 453049
- ○ **Mahler: Symphony 6; Kindertotenlieder** / Bernstein (cond.), Hampson, Vienna PO / 1986 / DG 427697

MUSICAL THEATER

West Side Story (1955–1957)

On January 9, 1949, Leonard Bernstein entered this into his log: "Jerry R. [Robbins] called today with a noble idea: a modern version of *Romeo and Juliet* set in slums at the coincidence of Easter-Passover celebrations. Feelings run high between Jews and Catholics. Former: Capulets; latter: Montagues. Juliet is Jewish." The newly formed State of Israel and the resultant war made the idea topical, and Bernstein, of Jewish descent, was familiar with Catholicism.

From the beginning, Robbins suggested that Arthur Laurents write the book, which was to be called *East Side Story.* However, other projects forced them to put off work until 1955. In the late summer of that year, while in Los Angeles with Laurents, Bernstein saw a newspaper article about fights between Mexican and Anglo gangs on Olivera Street. The two decided that recently arrived Puerto Ricans and first-generation Americans born of European immigrants would be a more accessible alternative to the Capulets and Montagues than would Jews and Catholics, and Latin American rhythms began to take shape in Bernstein's head. Neither Laurents nor Bernstein wanted to compose the lyrics for the songs, and they enlisted the 26-year-old Stephen Sondheim in October 1955. The title was changed to *West Side Story* when the creators realized that gang warfare in New York had moved from the East Side to the West. *West Side Story* opened at New York's Winter Garden Theater on September 26, 1957, and has remained in the repertory ever since. The film version of 1961 was a smashing success, earning ten Oscars, including Best Picture. *West Side Story* is one of Bernstein's most impressive achievements in any style of composition. Its mixture of Latin American rhythms, big band jazz harmonies and instrumentation, contrapuntal writing, and colloquial language is handled with such skill and sensitivity that the result makes it seem as though these elements had always coexisted.

Arthur Laurents' book for *West Side Story* is not really a retelling or paraphrase of Shakespeare's *Romeo and Juliet,* but rather uses the play as a point of departure. Feuding families become rival gangs of different ethnic backgrounds, and Tony (Romeo) kills Maria's (Juliet's) brother, but the "star-crossed" lovers do not have the chance to commit suicide. The most powerful and musically complex moment in the show occurs at about the midpoint, as Tony and Maria sing of their love in a reprise of "Tonight," Anita anticipates her upcoming date with Bernardo, and Riff and Bernardo, with their respective gangs, prepare for the rumble that evening. The result is a quintet with moments of dense rhythmic and melodic polyphony, conveying musically the meaning of the simultaneous but unrelated lines of text. Other highlights include the energetic "America," with its alternating 6/8 and 3/4 time signatures, while "Tonight" and "Maria" boast some of the most memorable melodies from the American stage. "Somewhere," in its opening phrase, features a melodic line borrowed from the slow movement of Beethoven's *Piano Concerto No. 5,* Op. 73.

Another factor contributing to the musical's success was its strong dance element, evident in songs such as "America" as well as in confrontations between the rival gangs. The setting for the gangs' "neutral turf" negotiations, for example, is a gymnasium dance at which a distinctive mambo serves as the musical backdrop. Bernstein, even as he broke new ground, drew on a tradition of Broadway choreography that was reaching its high point as the work took shape, and the result was a work that combined rhythmic energy, kinetic appeal, romance, and compositional sophistication. The action on stage may seem a bit dated in this day of the modern gangster, but the work's virtues are undimmed. It may well be a strong candidate for an innovatively updated production. *—AMG*

Synopsis:

During the Prologue, two rival gangs dance antagonistically, conveying the tension that exists between them. The Jets, a group of boys of European extraction, are led by Riff, while the Sharks, Puerto Rican boys, are led by Bernardo. Police officers make the two gangs disperse. In the next scene, we learn that Riff is determined to rid the streets of Sharks as he leads the gang in a song of loyalty, "Jet Song." Riff decides that later that evening, at a dance, he will challenge the Sharks to a "rumble" over territory. He leaves to enlist his friend and former Jet, Tony, to help with the fight. Tony is at work at Doc's drugstore when Riff meets him. Tony has left behind the gang, looking for other things in life. In "Something's Comin'," he talks of an unknown but exciting future. Eventually, however, he agrees to join in the rumble.

Maria, Bernardo's sister, has just come to New York from Puerto Rico in order to marry Bernardo's friend, Chino. While she is at the dance ("Dance at the Gym") she meets Tony and, despite the hatred between the two gangs, she falls in love with him, and he with her. On the street afterward, Tony muses on his new love ("Maria"). Later, Tony meets Maria on the fire escape of her apartment building, and they sing of their mutual love in "Tonight." While Tony and Maria are together, the gangs prepare to meet at Doc's drugstore to make plans for the rumble, choosing weapons and a location. While the boys head to their meeting at the store, their girlfriends are at home, where Bernardo, Anita and two of her friends argue over the relative merits of Puerto Rico and the United States ("America"); Anita tries to convince the homesick ones that life is better in the U.S.A. Bernardo remains skeptical.

Riff and the rest of the Jets wait at the drugstore for the Sharks. They are nervous, but Riff tries to calm them down ("Cool"). After the Sharks arrive, the group discuss possibilities, and it is decided, according to Tony's suggestion, that the two best members in the group should fight, using only bare fists, under the highway the next evening. Bernardo thinks the pair will be himself and Tony, and he threatens him. Lieutenant Schrank enters the drugstore and is pleased to see the boys "getting along." After kicking the Sharks out of the store, Schrank asks the Jets where the rumble will be, telling them he is on their side. When they don't answer, he berates the boys, calling them children of "immigrant scum."

Tony arrives at the bridal shop where Maria works, and Maria convinces Tony that he must stop the rumble. They then create a mock wedding, pledging their love ("One Hand, One Heart"). A powerful quintet results when Anita sings in anticipation of the upcoming evening; Tony and Maria once again declare their love; and Riff and Bernardo discuss with their gangs their expectations for the rumble.

After the gangs meet under the highway, Ice and Bernardo, the chosen representatives, begin to fight. Keeping his promise to Maria, Tony rushes in and tries to convince them all to leave peacefully. Bernardo knows that Tony has been seeing his sister and attacks Tony. Knives appear everywhere as Bernardo and Riff square off. Eventually, Bernardo stabs Riff, and Tony is so furious that he takes Riff's knife and stabs Bernardo. All the gang members begin a large fight, which is broken up by approaching police cars. Everyone runs off, except the dead Bernardo and Riff.

Maria waits in her room for Tony, singing happily ("I Feel Pretty"). Chino rushes into her room to tell her what has happened. At first she insists there was no rumble, because Tony promised it wouldn't happen. Once she realizes it did indeed take place, she asks Chino if Tony was hurt. Chino informs Maria that Tony killed her brother, then grabs a gun and leaves to find Tony. Maria, stunned by the news of her brother's death, is confused when Tony climbs up the fire escape to see her. She cannot stop loving Tony, especially when she learns Bernardo first killed Riff, and the two of them wish they could find a place where their love would be possible ("Somewhere"). Gang members run through the streets, trying to escape from the police. Action and Snowboy, two of the Jets, are questioned by Officer Krupke and tell the Officer how they relate to their parents and other adults ("Gee, Officer Krupke").

When the distraught Anita comes to Maria's room, Tony quickly leaves through the window and finds his way to Doc's drugstore, hiding there. Anita scolds Maria for associating with Tony ("A Boy Like That"). However, in "I Have a Love," Maria convinces Anita that she and Tony are genuinely in love, after which Anita consents to go to the drugstore and warn Tony that Chino is after him. When she arrives at Doc's, the assembled Jets mock her for being Puerto Rican, making her furious. Out of spite she tells them to deliver to Tony a message: Chino, as an act of vengeance, has killed Maria.

After Doc gives Tony Anita's message, Tony comes out of hiding and wanders the streets, dazed. He is stunned and pleased when he comes across Maria at midnight, but moments later Chino appears and shoots Tony, who dies. The gang members gather round his body. Confused and weary of the pointless, destructive rivalry, they join in a final reprise of "Somewhere" and carry Tony's body away. *—John Palmer*

Recommended:

- ○ **West Side Story (Original Broadway Cast)** / Goberman (cond.), Kert, C. Lawrence / Sony Broadway 62704

OPERA

Candide, operetta in 2 acts (1973)

The history of Leonard Bernstein's comic operetta *Candide* is nearly as involved as its plot. Originally conceived in 1956, the work underwent several layers of change to score and libretto before the creation of the composer's "final revised version," which Bernstein himself conducted in concert form in 1989. The plot, though altered rather substantially along the way by multiple librettists, still retained the basic shape of the story as originally adapted from Voltaire. The various versions tend alternately toward the hazy poles of "musical" and "operetta," with the final work leaning in the latter direction.

The underlying optimism of the story is conveyed musically through an eclectic collection of styles, whose diversity seems to reflect the myriad circumstances in which Candide finds himself. Often the musical numbers become stylized dance caricatures, lending the work as a whole a vaguely vaudevillian tone (somewhat comparable to—but rather less darkly ironic than—Kurt Weill's *Love Life*, from only eight years previous). At several points the work goes out of its way to spoof operatic conventions, but Bernstein and his collaborators are careful to make sure that the self-consciously melodramatic tone does not supplant entirely the underlying poignancy at the story's heart. (The original 1956 production was slightly more straight-faced, while a 1973 version, some say, emphasized the frivolous to a fault; the final version drew from both.) The overture to the work is one of the most familiar in American musical theater, with its rowdy motives and strident bursts of orchestrational and rhythmic color juxtaposed with its metrically odd but endearingly lyrical main theme.

Although Bernstein's compositional style is distinctive, his collaborators contributed indelibly to the tone of the work. The original libretto was adapted from Voltaire by Lillian Hellman and reworked extensively for subsequent productions by Hugh Wheeler (after Hellman retracted her version). Lyrics were penned by several different authors, including the esteemed American poet Richard Wilbur and, for the 1973 version, Stephen Sondheim. Some of the changes imposed at various stages were substantial: one character disappeared entirely in 1973, while Voltaire himself appeared as narrator. Several new songs supplanted old ones in that version, and some characters of little consequence in the original version took part in more substantial subplots in Wheeler's libretto as well. In 1988, under Bernstein's supervision, some of Wheeler's additions were affixed to Hellman's outline, and various numbers previously used only in particular revivals (as well as some music cut before opening night in 1956) were brought together to make the final and most comprehensive version. *—Jeremy Grimshaw*

Synopsis:

Act One. Act One begins in Westphalia, where everybody is blissfully happy. Candide informs the audience that "Life is happiness indeed," and Maximilian and Cunegonde find that their matchless beauty means that "Life is absolute perfection." Dr. Pangloss explains that this is because all is for the best in "The best of all possible worlds." In the castle park, Candide and Cunegonde see Pangloss giving Paquette some private lessons; then they themselves declare their mutual love ("Oh, happy we"), though he dreams of pastoral simplicity and she of the social whirl. However, when he asks to marry her, Candide is cast out for his presumption. He tries to comfort himself with Pangloss' philosophy ("It must be so"), but things change for the worse when he is press-ganged into the Bulgar army and is brutally whipped for attempting to desert.

The Bulgar and the Abar armies fight in Westphalia, where the Baron and his entire family are killed; Cunegonde is raped by an entire regiment before she is bayoneted. Candide searches unsuccessfully for her corpse ("Cunegonde! Cunegonde, is it true?"). He wanders through the countryside as a beggar and gives his few coins to a man rotting from syphilis, who turns out to be Pangloss. His own troubles have not shaken his belief that all is for the best, he explains ("Dear boy"). They go to Lisbon and witness an earthquake that kills 30,000 people, but Pangloss is undeterred. He and Candide are thus arrested for heresy and at an auto-da-fé, which the chorus happily witnesses ("What a day, what a day"), Candide is again whipped and Pangloss is hanged. Candide decides that since he cannot see the loving-kindness of people and the goodness of the world, the problem must be his ("It must be me"). In Paris, Cunegonde, having survived, is the mistress of both a Bishop and a wealthy Jew. She determines to bravely hide her sense of shame by taking all the jewels and pleasure she can get ("Glitter and be gay"). Candide's wanderings take him to Paris, and they are reunited ("You were dead, you know"). The Old Lady, Cunegonde's companion, warns them that both of Cunegonde's patrons are on their way, and Candide ends up killing them both, accidentally. The three flee to Cadiz, and the Old Lady recounts her own story of misfortune, rape, slavery, and having a buttock cut off for food during a siege. She tells the chorus that "I am easily assimilated." Candide joins the army, and the three of them leave for the New World.

Act Two. The second act opens in Buenos Aires, with the chorus asking the audience whether they have understood the lesson of "Universal good." They discover Paquette and Maximilian (both of whom survived) disguised as slave girls. The Governor falls in love with Maximilian, but upon learning his true gender instead suggests to Cunegonde that they briefly enjoy the fleeting pleasure of love ("My love"). She insists that, as a virgin, she will consent only to marriage. He agrees, a Jesuit discreetly disappears with Maximilian, and the Old Lady tells Candide that the police from Paris are on his trail. He goes to hide in the jungle. The Old Lady and Cunegonde celebrate the power of their feminine wiles ("We are women"). Candide and a companion, Cacambo, stumble across a Jesuit camp, where they find that the Father and Mother Superior are actually Maximilian and Paquette ("Come, heathen of America"). Candide tells Maximilian that Cunegonde is alive and that he plans to marry her, and when Maximilian is affronted at the unsuitable match, Candide accidentally (again) stabs him to death and flees.

Three years later, back in Buenos Aires, Cunegonde demands that the Governor finally marry her, and the Old Lady finds comfort and boredom even worse than painful excitement ("Quiet"). In the jungle, Candide and Cacambo find themselves in Eldorado, a peaceful Utopia. However, as much as he appreciates its beauties ("The Ballad of Eldorado"), Candide is miserable without Cunegonde. As a parting gift, the residents of Eldorado present Candide with a flock of golden sheep, but only two survive the trip back. Afraid of being arrested in Buenos Aires, he gives one to Cacambo, to ransom Cunegonde from the Governor, with a message to meet him in Venice. On his way, he stops in Surinam, where Martin, showing him a mutilated slave from a sugar plantation, tries to explain to Candide that life is not perfect and laughter is the only way to survive ("Words, words, words"). Candide thinks his own philosophy is vindicated when he sells the other sheep to the villainous Vanderdendur in exchange for a ship heading to Venice ("Bon voyage"). The ship sinks, and Candide escapes on a raft, where he meets five kings rowed by a galley slave, Pangloss. The kings plan to leave their pomp for the simple life ("The Kings' Barcarolle"). In Venice, the kings start the simple life by gambling in the Casino, where the Old Lady, her employer, Maximilian (who survived), and a crook wonder about the futility of their endeavors ("What's the use"). The Old Lady and Cunegonde, masked, ask Candide for help, which he gladly offers, while Pangloss, who has won, revels in the attention of the ladies ("Millions of rubles"). He recognizes Cunegonde and is disillusioned ("Nothing more than this"). For several days, he is unable to speak. They have just enough money left to purchase a small farm, where none of them is happy. The chorus comments that ("Life is neither good nor bad"), and Candide finally rouses himself to propose marriage to Cunegonde and resolves to "Make our garden grow." The others join in this aspiration in the finale. *—Ann Feeney*

Recommended:

- ○ **Bernstein Conducts Candide** / Bernstein (cond.), Hadley, J. Anderson, C. Ludwig, London SO / DG 449696
- ○ **Candide (Opera House Version, 1982)** / Mauceri (cond.), D. Eisler, Lankston, New York City Opera Orch. / 1986 / New World 80340
- ○ **Candide (Broadway Cast Recording)** / Bernstein (cond.), B. Cook, Rounseville, New York PO, Candide Pit Orch. / 2003 / Sony 86859

SYMPHONIC

Symphony No. 1 ("Jeremiah") (1942)

The *"Jeremiah" Symphony* (1942) represents Leonard Bernstein's first foray into the realm of large-scale orchestral composition. The work began life as the single-movement *Lamentation* for soprano and orchestra, sketched out by the composer in the summer of 1939. Bernstein worked it into its final form three years later, at which point it became the final movement of his symphony-in-progress. The completion of the first two movements was soon undertaken amid a frantic burst of activity, as Bernstein hoped to finish the work in time to enter it in a competition sponsored by the New England Conservatory of Music. Biographer Meryle Secrest details the frenetic scene that accompanied the last-minute completion of the work:

"He tore into the project, finishing the piano score in the space of ten days.... [The orchestration] took three days and nights, working around the clock. Even so, it was too late to mail the manuscript to meet the competition deadline of December 31, 1942. True to form, Bernstein got on a train for Boston and delivered his work in person, just two hours before midnight."

Though the symphony did not win the New England Conservatory Prize, it was selected by the New York Critic's Circle as the best new symphonic work for 1943–44. Bernstein himself conducted the premiere on January 28, 1944, leading the Pittsburgh Symphony Orchestra.

Though *Jeremiah* is cast in the traditional multi-movement shape of a symphony, Bernstein greatly alters and expands the more usual context of each movement as it relates to the entire work. The opening "Prophecy" serves as a dark and somber evocation of biblical seer Jeremiah's warning of the destruction of Jerusalem and its temple. The scherzo-like second movement, "Profanation," employs irregular and constantly changing meter to represent the chaos that accompanied the destruction of the temple, drawing its thematic material in part from the traditional Sabbath service. The final movement is a "Lamentation" in which the orchestra accompanies a mezzo-soprano soloist in passages (in Hebrew) from the *Book of Lamentations* that reflect upon the demise of Jerusalem. *—Michael Rodman*

Recommended:

- **Bernstein: Symphonies 1 & 2** / Bernstein (cond.), New York PO / 1999 / Sony 60697

Symphony No. 2 ("The Age of Anxiety") (1949; revised 1965)

This fiery and dramatic work, which is at the same time both a symphony and a dazzling piano concerto, is one of the most often played and most important orchestral compositions of the immediate post-World War II period.

After his sensational debuts of the 1943–44 season (as a last-minute replacement at the New York Philharmonic, and as a Broadway, ballet, and symphony composer), Leonard Bernstein's biggest professional problem was how to balance his triple-threat talents as pianist, composer, and conductor—he could have had a splendid full-time career as any one of the three. As a "serious" composer Bernstein was preoccupied with questions concerning the emptiness of modern life, particularly among disaffected middle-class Americans. The loss of and search for personal and spiritual meaning is a theme in his music as recurrent and important as Benjamin Britten's well-known preoccupation with the subject of the loss of innocence.

W.H. Auden's long poem *"The Age of Anxiety"* addresses Bernstein's theme so strongly that one almost suspects the poem defined certain ideas for Bernstein in artistic terms. The poem is a narrative that follows a woman and three men, all lonely, who meet in a bar and form a drinking friendship for that night because of their common insecurities and needs. They party (if one can use the word for their desperate search for what one of them calls the "colossal Dad"—no less than a central meaning for life) through the night.

Bernstein wrote the piece while pursuing his increasingly hectic conducting career. The work was written in airplanes and hotels around the world, including the historic year of 1948, while he was in Palestine as it became Israel and immediately was attacked by all its neighbors.

The symphony is in a unique two-movement form, all instrumental but programmatically following the stages of Auden's poem fairly closely. The first movement begins with a Prologue, followed by a large set of 14 variations on it, grouped into two seven-part sections called "The Seven Ages" and "The Seven Stages." This is a serious and dramatic discourse.

Part Two is itself in three parts. "The Dirge," the work's slow movement, depicts the group's cab ride to the woman's apartment for a nightcap. The eclectic Bernstein bases this part on a 12-tone row, letting atonal music depict both their emotional low point and (when it suddenly turns lush and romantic) suggest what they are lacking. In "The Masque" (the scherzo of the piece) the orchestra drops out except for the percussion and the piano, which suddenly plays white-hot piano jazz, including a blues theme Bernstein had written earlier. After a sudden four-measure outburst from the jazz "audience," the jazz music jumps offstage to an upright piano. The party is over. The guests have gone home.

A slow Epilogue (originally without piano but rewritten because potential soloists hated having to sit the last four minutes on stage without playing) ponders the lessons of the night, and seems to find the way to faith and meaning. *—Joseph Stevenson*

Recommended:

- **Bernstein: Symphony 2; Serenade** / Bernstein (cond.), Foss, New York PO / Sony 60558

Symphony No. 3 ("Kaddish") (1963–1977)

Originally intending to present the work for the 75th anniversary of the Boston Symphony Orchestra in 1955, Bernstein did not turn his attention to his *Symphony No. 3* until 1961. Its 1963 premiere took place not in Boston, however, but in Tel Aviv, perhaps a more fitting location considering its subject matter: the work's text (in English, Aramaic, and Hebrew), delivered by a woman, deals with issues of faith, declaring that man averts destruction via his identification with God through work and through art. The work's subtitle, "Kaddish," means Sanctification in Aramaic and is a prayer offered for the Jewish dead.

The first movement ("Invocation") opens with the narrator addressing God and offering prayers. The music that ensues is filled with conflict, but often restrained and deferring to the narrator. Choral passages have a dramatic, rhythmically jazzy character, mixing both a sense of austerity with the Broadway side of Bernstein's colorful musical persona.

The second movement ("Din-Torah") seethes with tension and at times borders on despair, as the narrator questions whether God hears her pleas, thus raising a crisis of faith. Again, especially at the outset, the music steps to the background for the narrator's dramatic cries, but when it takes center stage, it is filled with dissonance and austerity, percussion rumbling, the chorus seemingly disjointed. In the latter half the soprano delivers a lovely though quite anguished lullaby, with the chorus joining in later on for one of the symphony's most touching passages. Here tonality is restored, too, Bernstein seeming to signal rejection of atonality, even though he employs serial techniques throughout the symphony, particularly in the second movement.

The final movement (Scherzo and Finale) opens with the narrator questioning God's purposes, accompanied by menacing, almost diabolical music. But soon the narrator urges all to believe and the music becomes hopeful, with a heroic, epic theme that divulges the influence of Copland. Eventually, however, a faith crisis arises and the music turns dark. The narrator then reaffirms faith and the music exudes a sense of celebration; at the end the belief theme is presented in triumph, crowning the restoration of faith. The *"Kaddish" Symphony*, lasting about 45 minutes, exists in a version for piano and voices, a less effective scoring that has the advantage of allowing the work to be performed by groups with limited resources. *—Robert Cummings*

Recommended:

- **Bernstein: "Kaddish" Symphony 3; Chichester Psalms** / Bernstein (cond.), Tourel, Montealegre, New York PO / 1998 / Sony 60595

ORCHESTRAL

Serenade (after Plato: Symposium) (1954)

Bernstein's own notes for the *Serenade for violin and orchestra* (1954) stress, a bit disingenuously, that the work has no "literal program," but was inspired by a rereading of *Symposium*, Plato's celebrated dialogue on the nature of love. Still, the composer provides a detailed description of each movement "for the benefit of those interested in literary allusion." For the most part, Bernstein indeed eschews an obvious programmatic approach in his setting of the dialogue, resisting the temptation to translate into music Aristophanes' onset of hiccoughs or Apollodorus' delight in the rhythm of the syllables of Pausanias' name. (Or, for that matter, using a pausane—a trombone—to portray Pausanias.) As a result, some critics have argued that Bernstein's invocation of Plato's work constitutes little more than a sign of intellectual elitism, a remnant of the composer's years at Harvard. There is, however, more to the work's relationship to the *Symposium*: what the composer derives from Plato is a model for relating the parts of a large-scale work through a process of continuous variation.

In the *Symposium*, as in other Platonic dialogues, each successive speaker takes as a starting point the virtues or deficiencies of the previous speaker's remarks. In this way, new ideas are introduced while at the same time serving to refine, delimit, or expand upon earlier ideas. In Bernstein's Serenade, similarly, the intervals and contours of the opening theme reappear and are examined from new angles and in new contexts throughout the remainder of the work. There is also a second, hidden program embedded in the Serenade. Woven into the fabric are three complete movements from Bernstein's *Anniversaries*, short piano pieces the composer wrote throughout his life as birthday gifts or memorial tributes to intimates—a particularly appropriate "borrowing," perhaps, for a work about the power of love.

The Serenade's first movement, "Phaedrus; Pausanius" (Lento; Allegro), is cast as a slow fugato introduction followed by a sonata-allegro. Bernstein compares the movement to a "lyrical oration in praise of Eros" and an expression of "the duality of lover and the beloved." The second movement, "Aristophanes" (Allegro), assumes, in Bernstein's words, the role of "bedtime storyteller, invoking the fairy-tale mythology of love." "Eryximachus" (Presto), a brief fugato, echoes the work's contrapuntal opening. "Agathon" (Adagio), in three-part song form (ABA), "embraces all aspects of love's powers, charms, and functions." The final movement, "Socrates; Alcibiades" (Molto tenuto; Allegro molto vivace), begins with a slow reflection based on a section of the previous movement, giving way to a rondo marked by the festive high spirits of a bacchanalian celebration.

Serenade calls for an orchestra composed of strings, harp and percussion. The work was premiered at the 1954 Venice Festival with Isaac Stern as soloist and Bernstein as conductor, and was later choreographed, most notably as Jerome Robbins' ballet *Serenade for Seven*. *—Robert Adelson*

Recommended:

- **Bernstein: Serenade; Dutilleux: Violin Concerto "L'Arbre des Songes"** / Bernstein (cond.), I. Stern, Symphony of the Air / 1995 / Sony 64508
- **Glass, Rorem: Violin Concertos, Bernstein: Serenade** / Bernstein (cond.), G. Kremer, Israel PO / DG 445185

CONCERTO

Prelude, Fugue & Riffs (1949)

Leonard Bernstein's *Prelude, Fugue and Riffs* were written for Woody Herman's Band. By 1945 Herman had adopted a small number of "progressive" set pieces into his band's book, among them Stravinsky's *Ebony Concerto*. However when Bernstein put the finishing touches on *Prelude, Fugue and Riffs* in late 1949, the Herman organization had disbanded. Bernstein later adapted some of its music for use in the 1952 show *Wonderful Town*. The original was finally heard for the first time in an episode of the CBS television show *Omnibus*, hosted by Bernstein and entitled *What Is Jazz*, that aired October 16, 1955. Benny Goodman played the clarinet lead intended for Herman. Bernstein's first recording of the work, also made with Goodman, would appear on the Columbia album *Meeting at the Summit* in 1966.

Prelude, Fugue and Riffs is scored for a standard dance-band instrumentation of solo clarinet, saxes and trumpets in fives, four trombones, piano, string bass, and drums, to which Bernstein adds a second percussion part. It is one of the most frequently performed of Bernstein's shorter concert works, and has been widely embraced by wind ensembles in particular. While it was intended as a sort of crossover piece that combines jazz and classical elements, the material in *Prelude, Fugue and Riffs* leans more heavily in favor of the jazz aspect. Stravinsky's jazz-inspired music is an obvious point of reference for this work, and the similarity is felt most strongly in the opening Prelude, scored for the brass. This is followed by the Fugue for the saxes. In the Riffs section the solo clarinet is heard over the whole ensemble, which concludes with a riff reminiscent of Count Basie and of Kansas City-style ensemble jamming.

Bernstein's overall organization is mostly cellular, and the piece lacks a strong central theme. However, at individual points within *Prelude, Fugue and Riffs*, some of Bernstein's best and most characteristic ideas appear in miniature—for example, the tough, dissonant blues section in the Prelude that perks up your attention like a strong cup of coffee. Rhythmically, the piece has a lot of verve, and there is a fair amount of intricate pointillism scored in the sax parts. The section that precedes the final Count Basie-like riff looks forward to the approach Bernstein employed in the "Rumble" music from *West Side Story*.

Prelude, Fugue and Riffs works as a jazzy showstopper in symphonic band concerts. By 1949 Bernstein had already gained a tremendous amount of experience scoring for dance bands in a popular vein. His attempt to carry this experience over into a "serious" context differs from the approach of Stravinsky, Milhaud and others, who were coming from the classical end of the spectrum and largely developing their own, more obviously "composed" requirements for jazz ensembles. In this respect, Bernstein's *Prelude, Fugue and Riffs* "swings" more effectively than other pieces of its kind, and is absolutely faultless in practical terms in its orientation as a dance band "chart." *—Uncle Dave Lewis*

Recommended:

- ○ **Classic Performances: Bernstein's America** / Bernstein (cond.), P. Schmidt, Vienna PO / 1999 / DG 463465
- ○ **Netherlands Wind Ensemble: Bernstein; Gershwin** / Dufallo (cond.), DeBoer, Netherlands Wind Ensemble, / 1993 / Chandos 9210

CHORAL

Chichester Psalms (1965)

During his 12 years as music director of the New York Philharmonic (1958–69), Leonard Bernstein turned away from composition for the most part, completing just two new works. One was the Symphony No. 3, *"Kaddish"* (1963), which coincided with a period in which Bernstein was carrying on a debate with himself on the future of music—specifically the "conflict" between melodic, accessible music and a more experimental, avant-garde approach. Bernstein took a sabbatical from the Philharmonic during the 1964–65 season and spent a few months writing 12-tone music. But he was dissatisfied with the result, writing that "It just wasn't *my* music; it wasn't honest." So he abandoned that work and started writing what he later called "the most accessible, B flat majorish piece I've ever written." This was the *Chichester Psalms*, composed mostly during the spring of 1965 on a commission by the Dean of Chichester Cathedral in Sussex, England, who wanted a new work for a festival featuring the combined cathedral choirs of Winchester, Salisbury, and Chichester. That festival performance, featuring all male singers (Bernstein's preference for the composition), took place at Chichester on July 31, 1965, two weeks after the work's official premiere in New York on July 15, 1965, with alto John Bogart, the Camerata Singers, and the New York Philharmonic, all under Bernstein's direction.

Each of the three movements of the *Chichester Psalms* features a setting, in Hebrew, of one complete psalm, along with a verse or more of a second. Some of the musical material was taken from an aborted Broadway musical, *The Skin of Our Teeth*, which was one of the pieces Bernstein worked on during his sabbatical year. The first movement opens dramatically with a chorale-like setting of a portion of Psalm 108 ("Awake, psaltery and harp!"), followed by a lively, almost jazzy, Psalm 100 ("Make a joyful noise unto the Lord"). The second movement begins with a lovely lyrical tune, sung initially by a boy soprano soloist, for Psalm 23 ("The Lord is my shepherd, I shall not want"). That melody is taken up by the chorus, but the mood is suddenly interrupted by an aggressive setting of the opening of Psalm 2 ("Why do the nations rage"). The lyrical tune eventually appears in counterpoint with this more aggressive music, and Psalm 2 gives way to a peaceful return of the boy soprano. A passionate theme for the strings opens the final movement. The mood calms as the chorus intones a peaceful setting of Psalm 131 ("Lord, my heart is not haughty"), including one variation sung wordlessly. A group of soloists from the chorus explores this melody further, in preparation for a quiet and haunting setting of the opening of Psalm 133 ("Behold how good, and how pleasant it is") and a final Amen. *—Chris Morrison*

Recommended:

- ○ **Bernstein: Chichester Psalms** / Alsop (cond.), Bournemouth SO & Chorus / 1998 / Naxos 60595

Mass (1971)

Leonard Bernstein's *Mass*, a "theater piece for singers, players and dancers," was commissioned to open the new John F. Kennedy Center for the Performing Arts in Washington, D.C., on September 8, 1971. On February 16, 1981, Bernstein's *Mass* became the first work by an American-born composer performed at the Vienna State Opera.

The text of *Mass* consists of the Roman Catholic mass with additional material written by Bernstein and Stephen Schwartz, who wrote *Godspell*. Pit forces include strings, percussion, and organ, while on the stage are a blues combo and rock band with a "Street Chorus." Bernstein wanted to appeal to young people, and his inclusion of rock and blues elements and the abundance of young performers on stage in *Mass* were certainly influenced by the recent successes of *Hair* and *Jesus Christ Superstar*, as well as Schwartz's own *Godspell*. The composer described *Mass* as "an entirely new concept. It has all the qualities of a dramatic work, catastrophe and climax . . . all those terms out of Aristotle." Bernstein's amalgam of church chorales, show-tune melodies, folk song, rock, and blues, requiring over 200 performers, irritated some critics and pleased others.

"Eclectic" hardly describes the assemblage of styles and idioms in Bernstein's *Mass*. After a four voice Kyrie, the Celebrant—the main character of the drama—enters and accompanies himself on the electric guitar as he sings "A Simple Song," a hymn-like piece praising God. A psalm, "I Will Sing to the Lord a New Song," follows. Pre-recorded music plays a large part in the work, particularly a six-part "Alleluia" during which dancing acolytes dress the denim-clad Celebrant in ceremonial robes. Shortly afterward, a brass band enters the floodlight-filled auditorium, marching through the audience and performing music from Bernstein's abandoned musical, *The Skin of Our Teeth*. The Street Chorus joins the band, as do a boys' chorus and mixed chorus. Among the 31 numbers in *Mass* are rock and blues solos and a gospel-style, revivalist segment for the Preacher. As the piece progresses, Bernstein and Schwartz confront such topics as the role of religion in the face of violence, the Vietnam War, the assassinations of John and Robert Kennedy and Martin Luther King Jr., and the persecution of the pacifist Berrigan brothers.

As the piece approaches the celebration of the Eucharist (the high point of the Catholic mass), acolytes adorn the Celebrant with increasingly elaborate robes and other vestments, superficially symbolizing his duties and creating a chasm between him and the congregation. Eventually the Celebrant goes mad, smashes the Communion vessels, and interrupts the mass. After this, as Bernstein notes, "It then remains for each individual on the stage to find a new seed of faith within himself through painful Meditation." Once it is found, the participants pass peace to one another and into the audience, "and hopefully into the world outside." The piece closes with a recording of the composer's voice, speaking, "The mass is ended. Go in peace," the traditional closing of the Catholic mass. *—John Palmer*

Recommended:

- ○ **Bernstein: Mass** / Bernstein (cond.), Titus, Norman Scribner Choir, Berkshire Boy Choir / 1997 / Sony 63089
- ○ **Bernstein: Mass** / Nagano (cond.), Frischling, Berliner Rundfunkchor, Soloists of the Pacific Mozart Ens. / HM 801840/41

VOCAL

Arias & Barcarolles (1988)

After a 1960 White House performance by Bernstein, President Eisenhower declared, "I like music with a theme, not all those arias and barcarolles." Snagging his title from Eisenhower's remark, Bernstein concocts a song cycle that veers from dodecaphony to scat singing to klezmer. But the texts, mostly written by Bernstein, assuredly do have a theme: love. The song cycle was premiered in 1988 in a version for four voices and piano duet; within a year, Bernstein had reduced the vocal requirement to one mezzo-soprano and one baritone. In 1989, Bright Sheng expanded the piano part to strings and percussion, and by 1993, Bruce Coughlin had made a full orchestration.

In the Prelude, the vocalists sing "I love you" over a rhythmically jagged, nearly atonal accompaniment. Obviously, love is more complicated than the singers admit, as is discovered in the following "Love Duet," in which the subject is the song itself ("Is it art or minimal music or classical or popular song?"); the restless song symbolizes the singers' relationship.

"Little Smary," for mezzo, sets a bedtime story often told by Bernstein's mother (who is credited as author), in which Little Smary loses and then finds her "wuddit" (rabbit). At the moment of loss, the music becomes distressed and atonal, although there is a flourish of hard-won Straussian triumph at the end. "The Love of My Life," for baritone, is a largely 12-tone piece with moments of tonality and even allusions to the blues; the singer is realizing that great love may be anticlimactic. "Greeting," for mezzo, is an adaptation of a song Bernstein wrote in 1955 upon the birth of his son, Alexander. It's a moment of repose before the baritone launches into "Oif Mayn Khas'neh" (At My Wedding), a Yiddish text by Yankev Yitsshok Segal. This is a slightly surreal Jewish wedding scene; the music, based on a tone row, is a savage dismemberment of klezmer style, with a slow, cantorial cadenza giving way to a frenzied conclusion. Quiet returns in the duet "Mr. and Mrs. Webb Say Goodnight," a bedtime conversation between Charles Webb, dean of the Indiana School of Music, and his wife, Kenda. The music briefly surveys mid-twentieth century pop styles. The pianists (or orchestral musicians) quietly sing scat, representing boys who refuse to go to sleep, while their parents wish they themselves could nod off. Finally, the two soloists merely hum throughout the serene, waltz-like but elegiac "Nachspiel (Postlude) (In memoriam ...)." —*James Reel*

Recommended:

○ **Bernstein: Arias & Barcarolles** / Bernstein, Tilson Thomas (cond.), Hampson, Von Stade, London SO / 1996 / DG 439926

BALLET

Fancy Free (1944)

Fancy Free was Leonard Bernstein's first foray into the world of the ballet, and it immediately became extremely popular. The work's timing was significant. It had its premiere on April 18, 1944, just weeks after the successful premiere of the "Jeremiah" symphony and shortly after his appearance with the New York Philharmonic on a nationwide concert broadcast late in 1943. This triple shot of Bernstein established him once and for all as a major player in the musical world.

The story of the ballet is a simple one, devised by Jerome Robbins. It takes place in New York City, where three sailors are on shore leave. While in New York, they meet three girls in a bar, dance with them, fight over them, and then realize how stupid it is to let women come between friends. The plot line was reused by Bernstein in *On The Town*, his popular first Broadway musical.

The music in *Fancy Free* is based to a considerable degree on popular styles of the day. This is heard at the beginning with "Big Stuff," a popular hit Bernstein recorded as a single later, made famous by Billie Holiday. The jazzy style of the piece was relatively new to both Bernstein's writing and to concert music in general—it had only been about 20 years since *Rhapsody in Blue* broke many of the boundaries between jazz and classical music. Bernstein continued to explore this influence in many of his subsequent works.

The structure of the work is designed with dance in mind; there is little connective tissue between the sections, which are bridged with solo piano music. The sections include music derived not only from jazz, but also from styles ranging from Stravinsky to vaudeville. This kind of combining of styles is pervasive in Bernstein's writing; it continues in his later works, such as *Facsimile*, *Candide*, and the *Mass*. The music from the ballet was made into a concert suite for orchestra by Bernstein. The suite has six movements: "Dance of the Three Sailors," "Scene at the Bar," "Pas de Deux," "Pantomime," "Three Variations" (Gallop, Waltz, Danzón), and "Finale." It was premiered on January 14, 1945, by the Pittsburgh Symphony under Bernstein's own baton. —*Michael Blostein*

Synopsis:

Scene—In and outside of a Manhattan neighborhood bar

Three American sailors burst in, full of youthful energy and mischief. They play about, tricking one another into buying the drinks and generally raising hell. A pretty girl walks in and they drag her into the action, playing purse-snatching games. The girl stalks off and two of the sailors follow. The remaining sailor bumps into a nice girl, buys her a drink, and they dance romantically. The two sailors return with the other girl, and the two girls recognize one another. They chatter happily and want to remain together, but the boys decide that there are one too many of them for the pair of ladies. They decide to dance for the girls, then the girls can pick the loser. They dance, but the girls refuse to judge them. The boys brawl and the girls walk out in disgust. The lads make up, take their leave of the bar, and immediately fall under the influence of a passing girl, and one by one they break away to follow her around the corner. —*Gerald Brennan*

Recommended:

○ **Bernstein Conducts Bernstein (SACD)** / Bernstein (cond.), New York PO / 2000 / Sony 89043

Michel Béroff

b. May 9, 1950, Epinal, France

Pianist

Not every musician can deal with the music of French avant-garde composer Olivier Messiaen very easily. After all, it isn't every composer that bases one entire set of solo piano pieces on the songs of birds, or creates as intense and as difficult a composition to play as the *Quartet for the End of Time*. Michel Béroff has established a reputation as one of the premier interpreters of this composer's music, but is also known for superior performances of composers such as Beethoven, Brahms, Bartók, Prokofiev, Mozart, Debussy, Mussorgsky, Stravinsky, Schumann, and Schubert.

He undertook his studies beginning with the conservatory in Nancy and later switched to the larger CNSM in Paris where he immediately stood out as one of the best pianists. He gave his first recital in Paris in 1966 for which he won the first prize in the Olivier Messiaen International Piano Competition. Since then his career has taken him all over the world. He has performed as a piano soloist under the baton of most of the great conductors including Daniel Barenboim, Leonard Bernstein, Pierre Boulez, Seiji Ozawa, Andre Previn, and many others. He collaborates with many other performers in the context of recitals or chamber music, including Pierre Amoyal, Jean-Philippe Collard, Augustin Dumay, Barbara Hendricks, and Lynn Harrell. He has also conducted detailed studies of the theories of conducting as well as the left-handed piano repertoire. Southpaws everywhere can delight in his recording of the Ravel *Concerto for the Left Hand*, done with the London Symphony Orchestra and Claudio Abbado for Deutsche Grammophon. The former interest led to him beginning another career as an orchestra conductor, which continues to be overshadowed by his busy schedule as a pianist. He has however established himself as an educator in the conducting field. He returned to his student haunts at CNSM in 1989 to teach conducting, and has also taught the fine art of baton waving at Freiburg's Music University (Musikhochschule) since 1994.

In 1996 he toured Japan extensively, performing the works of Debussy and recording these compositions for the Japanese Denon label. The resulting five albums won an equal number of Grand Prix du Disques awards. During this tour he also worked with the NHK Symphony and Shinsei Japan Philharmonic. Received with much enthusiasm in Japan, he returned later the same year for recitals and the recording of Debussy's *Le Bal Masqué* with Seiji Ozawa and Wolfgang Holzmair for Philips Classics. He then undertook a period of concentration on the works of Stravinsky, presenting an orchestral and recital project with the Residentie Orchestra of the Hague. In 2000 he toured England and Spain with the London Philharmonic Orchestra conducted by Kurt Masur.

The Béroff discography is immense. His EMI output includes the complete works for piano and orchestra by Prokofiev, Stravinsky, and Liszt, as well as other works by Messiaen, Schumann, Brahms, and Debussy. —*Eugene Chadbourne*

Recommended:

○ **Debussy: Complete Solo Piano Works** / Béroff / 1996 / Denon 78847

○ **Messiaen: Vingt Regards sur l'Enfant Jésus** / Béroff / 1987 / EMI 569668

○ **Prokofiev: The 5 Piano Concertos** / Masur (cond.), Béroff, Portal, LGO, Parrenin Quatuor / 1992 / EMI 62542

Walter Berry

b. Apr. 8, 1929, Vienna, Austria, **d.** Oct. 20, 2000, Vienna, Austria

Bass

Bass Walter Berry grew, by measured and steady advancement, into one of the leading artists of his time. Beginning at the Vienna Staatsoper at the early age of 21, he progressed through the major Mozart baritone and bass roles to such weightier challenges as Beethoven's Pizarro and Wagner's Kurwenal, Telramund, and even Wotan. He was able to transmute the sunny, rounded, very Viennese sound of his wide-ranging instrument into something more potent, more incisive for his Wagner roles and he became one of the most celebrated Wozzecks of his day. His musicianship and sturdy voice made him a welcome guest at many of the world's leading opera venues and he was regarded as an affecting recitalist as well.

Originally intending to pursue a career in engineering, Berry switched to vocal study and trained with Hermann Gallos at the Vienna Musical Academy. He made his debut as a soloist in Honegger's *Jeanne-d'Arc* and soon thereafter joined the Staatsoper. As early as 1953, he was singing Masetto at Salzburg, the first of an outstanding gallery of Mozart characterizations. At the festival, he also participated in the premieres of Gottfried von Einem's *Prozess* (1953), Rolf Leibermann's *Penelope* (1954), and Werner Egk's *Irische Legende* (1954).

America heard Berry for the first time when he presented his genial Mozart Figaro at Chicago's Lyric Opera in 1957. Three years later, he returned to Chicago as part of a more stellar cast (Schwarzkopf, Streich, his then-wife Christa Ludwig, and Eberhard Wächter) to offer a Figaro unchallenged by any other than Cesare Siepi's. Berry subsequently sang Leporello, Don Alfonso, Fernando (*Fidelio*), and Baron Ochs in Chicago.

On October 2, 1966, Berry made his debut at the Metropolitan Opera in a production of Strauss' *Die Frau Ohne Schatten* conducted by Karl Böhm. Together with James King's Emperor, Leonie Rysanek's Empress and Christa Ludwig's Dyer's Wife, Berry's Barak was hailed as a magnificent accomplishment and an immense popular success. A live recording with that same quartet of principals, captured in Salzburg in 1974, reveals each singer performing at such a pitch of vocal and interpretive splendor as to have made the collaboration legendary. Although his marriage to Ludwig had ended in 1971, Berry was still the partner of choice for the mezzo-soprano's intense and soaring Dyer's Wife. Berry made his Covent Garden debut as Barak in 1976 and sang the role in San Francisco that same year.

Berry's increasingly powerful voice tended toward the lower end of bass-baritone spectrum and his Baron Ochs managed the bottommost notes with authority. His recording with Bernstein is both substantially sung and interpreted with Viennese lightness. Berry had accumulated an extensive discography by the time of his death, remaining in good voice until the very end of his life (he participated in a Renée Fleming Strauss recital shortly before his death). His hearty and endearing Papageno was recorded twice. His Pizarro in the 1961 Klemperer recording of *Fidelio*, despite the conductor's slow pacing, served notice that his was an art destined for more than Mozart. His singing of the bass arias in Klemperer's recording of *Bach's St. Matthew Passion* is fluent and deeply felt, notwithstanding, once again, some glacial tempi.

Though never quite viewed as a star personality, Berry crafted his own unique spot among the great singers who reigned in the twentieth century's second half. *—Erik Eriksson*

Recommended:

- ○ **Mendelssohn, Wolf, Pfitzner & Mahler: Lieder** / Berry, Buchbinder / 1999 / Orfeo 520991
- ○ **Mozart: Così fan tutte** / Böhm (cond.), Schwarzkopf, Ludwig, Kraus, Taddei, Berry, Schmidt, Steffek / 2000 / Angel 67379
- ○ **Mozart: Die Zauberflöte** / Klemperer (cond.), Gedda, Janowitz, Berry, Unger, Ludwig, Popp, Frick, Schwarzkopf, Crass, Hoffgen / 2000 / Angel 67385B

Franz Berwald

b. Jul. 23, 1796, Stockholm, Sweden, **d.** Apr. 3, 1868, Stockholm, Sweden
Composer: Symphonic, Orchestral

Franz Berwald was one of the seminal composers of the first half of the nineteenth century, a precursor of the Scandinavian symphonic school which would come to fruition a half century later. Yet as a musician in his native Sweden he labored in obscurity and was forced to make a living in such nonmusical fields as glass blowing, lumbering, orthopedics, and physical therapy.

Berwald was born in Stockholm. His father, a German orchestral violinist, imparted some training on his son, but Franz was largely self-taught. At 16 he joined the Royal Opera Orchestra and began to compose. His *Grand Septet for Clarinet, Bassoon, Horn and String Quartet* was premiered in 1828; already a pattern was set, for that idiosyncratic work met with indifference from Swedish audiences.

Berwald spent some time in Norway, then went to Berlin to study music further. From there he went to Vienna where he found an audience for his work. There his opera *Estrella di Soria* was performed to acclaim. In 1841 he married in that city and the following year produced his *First Symphony, "La Serieuse."* That same year he returned to Sweden only to find that his reputation had not preceded him. Nonetheless he continued to compose, turning out operas and three more symphonies: *No. 2 ("La Capricieuse"), No. 3 ("La Singuliere")*, and *No. 4*.

Failed performances induced Berwald to go abroad again, unsuccessfully to Paris where he received no performances, and to Vienna where once again he found an appreciative audience for his opera *A Swedish Country Betrothal*. It was ironic then that in his homeland he obtained neither the post of music director at Uppsala University nor that of court conductor.

Thwarted in his first career, the composer was often forced to turn to other endeavors such as glass blowing and running a sawmill. But Berwald, a kindly and humanistic man, seemed to find his nonmusical niche in orthopedics and in blazing trails in its accompanying physical therapy, specializing in congenital spinal deformities of children. Here would seem to be a rarity among creative artists, one to put the inner urge and ego on hold sublimating these in tending to the external needs of humankind.

Finally, in his sixties, musical breaks came his way in Sweden. His first Vienna-period opera *Estrella di Soria* was performed and earlier instrumental works began to appear in print. He was accepted in the Swedish Academy and made a professor of composition in 1867. But, sadly, Berwald succumbed to pneumonia the following year.

Like his contemporary Berlioz, Berwald was a visionary. He preferred to use established forms to contain a unique mode of thought. His four symphonies (1842–1945) are especially significant as they are precursors of Sibelius and Nielsen in their streamlined contours and unexpected harmonic and melodic devices. As such, he was one of the most important of the early Romantics. *—Wayne Gerard Reisig*

SYMPHONIC

Symphony No. 1 in G minor ("Sinfonie Sérieuse") (1842)

Franz Berwald's *Sinfonie sérieuse* was premiered on December 2, 1843, in Stockholm, conducted by Johan Fredrik Berwald, the composer's cousin. The performance was not what it should have been. In addition to not helping the composer's reputation, it became the only performance of any of his symphonies during his lifetime. Given that Berwald spent a number of years in Berlin and Vienna, the *Sinfonie sérieuse* is comparable in style and structure to those of his contemporaries Felix Mendelssohn and Robert Schumann.

The first movement Allegro con energia, is in the traditional sonata-allegro form. Without any introduction, the first theme group begins its passionate journey with a loud chord, and then quickly drops to piano. Berwald presents an abundance of motivic fragments, but as with Beethoven, his transitions seem to be just as significant as the primary themes. The more lyrical second theme calls to mind the earlier Romantic composer Carl Maria von Weber. A development section follows with bits of counterpoint utilizing transitional material from the first theme group. Prior to the "official" recapitulation, Berwald sneaks in a statement of the second theme that, this time, is much more bold in character. The "real" recapitulation unfolds in typical fashion, but unlike the serious opening in minor, the movement concludes with an exuberant flourish in major.

As with most slow movements, the Allegro maestoso is in a ternary form (ABA). When hearing the solemn lyricism of the A section, with its chromatic lines and sustained pedal points, it is difficult not to think of the future works of Johannes Brahms and Carl Nielsen. In contrast, the B section is bolder and more dramatic. This leads into a development of sorts, before returning to the nobility of the opening.

While not as facile and mercurial as many of Mendelssohn's scherzos, the third movement, Stretto, is, in essence, the typical scherzo movement: fast tempo, a meter of three, and the ABA form. Its themes drive it toward the more serene middle section. However, the second presentation of the A section dissipates rather than giving a sense of finality to the movement.

Thematic material from the second movement serves as an introduction to the first theme group of the final movement. Again, sonata-allegro form is the large-scale structural determinant. The surging fervor of the second theme in the strings is contrasted and answered in the woodwinds. The development section has some truly contrapuntal moments using material from the first theme group to prepare the way for the recapitulation. From out of the wilderness, a valiant solo trombone signals the end of the muscular, energetic work. *—AMG*

Recommended:

- ○ **Berwald: Symphonies 1 & 2** / Kamu (cond.), Helsingborg SO / 1995 / Naxos 553051
- ○ **Berwald: The Four Symphonies** / Ehrling (cond.), Malmö SO / 1996 / Bis 795/796

Symphony No. 3 in C major ("Sinfonie Singulière") (1845)

Although Swedish composer Franz Berwald's *Symphony No. 3, "Sinfonie singulière"* was completed in 1845, it did not receive its first performance until 1905. In fact, only one of Berwald's four symphonies was performed during his lifetime. Considered by many to be the first great Scandinavian composer, he has been described as a cross between Felix Mendelssohn, an acquaintance of Berwald's, and Finland's Jean Sibelius, born three years before Berwald's death.

Not only is it widely held that the *Sinfonie singulière* is Berwald's finest work, but that it may be the first great Scandinavian orchestral work. The symphony is unique for this time period in that it has only three movements rather than the traditional four. While Berwald's earlier symphonies are right at home in the German Romantic school of Schumann and Mendelssohn (Berwald lived in Berlin and Vienna at various times), this piece looks forward with the robust and rustic quality one associates with later Nordic composers such as Edvard Grieg, Sibelius, and Carl Nielsen or Nationalists such as Antonín Dvořák.

The first movement, Allegro fuocoso, is in the traditional mid-nineteenth century sonata-allegro form. But, Berwald combines the organic compositional technique of Beethoven with one resembling tone painting to establish an atmosphere. Starting quietly, there is a feeling of great anticipation. Utilizing the interval of a fourth in various guises, Berwald uses motivic development and transformation rather than long, spun-out melodies, creating a sense of transition and evolution. This is a section of "gestation" rather than introduction in the traditional sense. The middle movement, in ternary form (ABA), begins with a heartfelt, Brahmsian Adagio. With a startling thump in the tympani about four minutes in, Berwald breaks into a scherzo that would have made Mendelssohn envious. Playful exchanges between winds and strings show Berwald's skill as an orchestrator and his mastery of manipulating thematic fragments. His not so subtle harmonic sequences are very much like Bruckner's in that they do not always advance the tonal scheme, but are, nonetheless, terrifically appealing. After a few minutes, the Adagio returns as abruptly as it disappeared. The final movement is highly charged and dramatic. Another Brucknerian moment occurs with a soft woodwind chorale over pizzicato strings, which flowers into a grand statement of this same theme. There is a quotation of the middle movement's Adagio melody about five minutes in, followed by a new lyrical theme that precedes a recapitulation of the beginning of this movement. A quiet return of the woodwind chorale in minor explodes into a joyfully victorious final statement, back in major, bringing this richly Romantic symphony to an end. In Franz Berwald's *Sinfonie singulière* one can hear some of the stylistic qualities that anticipate later composers such as Brahms, Bruckner, Sibelius, and Dvořák. *—Mona DeQuis*

Recommended:

- ○ **Schubert: Symphonie 4 "Tragische"; Berwald: Symphonien 3 & 4** / I. Markevitch (cond.), Berlin PO / 1998 / DG 457705

○ **Berwald: Sinfonies Naïve, Singulière** / Salonen (cond.), Radiosymfonikerna / 1988 / Musica Sveciae 421

○ **Berwald: Sinfonie Singulière; Symphony in E Flat** / Ehrling (cond.), London SO / 1991 / Bluebell 37

Symphony No. 4 in E flat ("Sinfonie Naïve") (1845)

Berwald spent the early part of the year 1842 in Vienna, where his music was very well-received and where he wrote his first two symphonies, those with the nicknames *"Sérieuse"* and *"Capricieuse"*. Later that year he returned to his native Sweden hoping to continue his string of successes. But his music didn't make much of an impression there. Nevertheless he continued his composing, completing his other two symphonies—the so-called *"Singulière"* and *"Naïve"*—in the year 1845. He went to Paris in 1846, hoping to interest composer-conductor Daniel-François Auber in premiering the *Sinfonie Naïve*. Nothing came of that, though, and the symphony, now sans title (by Berwald's choice) and simply known as the *Symphony No. 4*, waited until April 9, 1878, for its first performance. That premiere was conducted by Ludvig Norman, who did more than anyone else to keep Berwald's music before the public in the decades after the composer's death.

Whether called *Sinfonie Naïve* or *Symphony No. 4*, the work radiates a feeling of contentment and lightheartedness. The first movement, somewhat misleadingly marked Allegro risoluto, begins in a rather relaxed mood. A playful staccato figure leads into the peaceful second idea, which becomes the basis of the following development. This movement, and the work as a whole, displays Berwald's distinctive, pungent harmonic sense and melodic freshness. The noble, pastoral second-movement Adagio leads without pause into an energetic scherzo, whose elfin quality calls the music of Felix Mendelssohn to mind. Rhythmic playfulness marks the Finale, an Allegro vivace that concludes with a sudden acceleration and exciting coda. *—Chris Morrison*

Recommended:

○ **Berwald: Symphonies 3 & 4; Piano Concerto** / Kamu (cond.), Helsingborg SO / 1995 / Naxos 553052

○ **Berwald: Sinfonie Singulière; Symphony in E Flat** / Ehrling (cond.), London SO / 1991 / Bluebell 37

ORCHESTRAL

Estrella de Soria, overture to the opera (1841)

Berwald started his opera *Estrella di Soria* around 1838 but, busy with traveling and other musical projects, he only completed the work in 1841 in Vienna. A private performance of the opera took place that year, but it didn't receive its first public hearing until April 9, 1862, when Stockholm's Royal Opera presented it to great acclaim. It has been revived on occasion—particularly in Sweden—in the twentieth century, including for the 150th anniversary of Berwald's birth in 1946.

The opera's overture, sometimes referred to as a tragic overture, has become one of Berwald's best-known compositions. The portentous slow introduction leads into a stormy Allegro. The slower, graceful second theme quotes Estrella's main aria from the opera's first act. A third folksy theme also makes an appearance. After the three themes are repeated and worked over a bit, a new idea in the clarinet leads into the peaceful coda. Normally this would lead into the opera's first act, but several different concert endings have been created to allow for separate performance of the overture. *—Chris Morrison*

Recommended:

○ **Berwald: Symphonies 1 & 2** / Kamu (cond.), Helsingborg SO / 1995 / Naxos 553051

○ **Berwald: Overtures & Symphonies** / R. Goodman (cond.), Swedish Radio Orch. / 1996 / Hyperion 67081

Heinrich Ignaz Franz von Biber

b. Aug. 12, 1644, Wartenberg, Bohemia (Czech Rep.), **d.** May 3, 1704, Salzburg, Austria

Composer: Chamber Music, Choral

Heinrich Ignaz Franz von Biber may have been the finest violinist of the seventeenth century. He was also a highly innovative composer whose works—most notably his sonatas for violin—are gaining new prominence in the performing repertory.

Biber was born in the Bohemian town of Wartenberg (now in the Czech Republic). Little is known of his background or education, although he is believed to have studied in Vienna with the eminent German violinist Johann Heinrich Schmelzer. He began his career playing violin and gamba in the aristocratic courts of Moravia, and is known to have assumed a post in the band belonging to Count Karl of Liechtenstein-Castelcorno at Kromeriz. In 1670, he abandoned this position without permission, and joined the Kapelle in Salzburg, being named Kapellmeister there in 1684. His brilliance and virtuosity on the violin made Biber one of the most renowned soloists in Europe, and in 1690 Emperor Leopold I added the aristocratic prefix "von" to his name. He died at age 59 in Salzburg.

Biber's compositions stand as some of the most startlingly advanced music of the Baroque era. Biber's manuscripts and publications record violin improvisations in unprecedented detail; in his *Sonata Representativa*, one will find Biber's instrumental impressions of cuckoos, frogs, cats, and marching musketeers. These are supplied with a simple ground bass that provides plenty of room for the soloist to stretch out and show off, but are written at such a high level of difficulty that few violinists attempt to master them. In his *"Mystery"*, or *"Rosenkranz"* sonatas, Biber makes extensive use of scordatura, violin re-tunings that change the tonal character of the instrument and make "impossible" figurations possible.

Biber was clearly influenced by the *Musurgia Universalis*, a theoretical work written by German Jesuit scientist and mathematician Athanasius Kircher. First published in 1650, Kircher draws parallels between musical tones, planetary motion, and psychological states of being. Biber's music is strongly effective emotionally, and in works of a programmatic character, such as his orchestral piece *Battalia*, he attempts to combine both a literal and subjective listening experience. In *Battalia*, the orchestra is required to play several marching songs in different keys at once—in a manner similar to the music of Charles Ives—to indicate eager soldiers of various regiments leading off to battle. A soft, hushed passage at the end of the work represents the result, a somber tableau of battlefield dead.

Biber also composed a number of sacred vocal works; most of these reside easily within the required strictures of the Church. A standout piece is his 15-part requiem, an expressive and harmonically adventurous mass that eschews the sobriety of the text in favor of glorious antiphonal choral textures. Along those same lines, musicologists have established that the anonymous, huge 54-part *Missa Salisburgensis* is also likely the work of von Biber. *—Uncle Dave Lewis*

CHAMBER MUSIC

Mystery (Rosary) Sonatas, for violin & continuo (1676)

After working in Moravia and Styria, Bohemian-born Heinrich Ignaz von Biber (1644–1704) was appointed Kapellmeister to the court of the Prince-Archbishop of Salzburg in either 1670 or 1671. By that time he was the most famous violin virtuoso in Europe, particularly renowned for his mastery of the art of scordatura, a method which involved tuning the violin to different notes to obtain unusual chords or alter the tonal color of the music.

It was for his own instrument that Biber composed his greatest instrumental work, the so-called *"Mystery"* or *"Rosary" Sonatas*. A beautifully prepared presentation copy shows that the sonatas were dedicated to the archbishop, Biber adding that he has consecrated them to the 15 sacred mysteries "which you promote so strongly." This is a reference to the recently installed archbishop's espousal of the influential Salzburg Confraternity of the Rosary. The mysteries are divided into three sections, "The Five Joyful Mysteries," concerned with the events of the birth of Christ, "The Five Sorrowful Mysteries," which cover the Passion, and "The Five Glorious Mysteries" dealing with the Resurrection, and Assumption and coronation of the Virgin. Each of these 15 topics was set by Biber as a sonata for violin and bass continuo consisting of from three to five movements. As was common practice with groups of sonatas in the seventeenth century, the whole is concluded by a large-scale passacaglia which stands outside the sonatas as a separate movement. In common with other instrumental works of Biber's, the music is programmatic, with Biber using scordatura technique in all but the opening sonata and the final Passacaglia (which are tuned in the normal way, G, D, A, E) to produce a range of striking coloristic effects. Thus in the opening sonata, "The Annunciation," the fluttering of Gabriel's wings as he appears to Mary is vividly evoked high in the violin's register, while the Praeludium of Sonata 10, "The Crucifixion" (tuned G, D, A, D) features not only harsh chords depicting the hammer blows of the nails into the Cross, but a contrasting theme of ineffable bittersweetness expressive of the suffering before redemption. Another extraordinary piece of scordatura tuning (A flat, E flat, G, D) is responsible for the veiled sound given to the violin in Sonata 6, "The Sweating of Blood," which deals with Christ's agonizing in the nocturnal setting of the Garden of Gethsemane. The *"Mystery" Sonatas* represent a unique contribution to the violin repertoire, works that in their technical and interpretative demands still represent a formidable challenge to even today's finest players. *—Brian Robins*

Recommended:

○ **Biber: Mystery Sonatas** / J. Holloway, D. Moroney, Tragicomedia / Virgin 62062

○ **Biber: Mystery Sonatas** / Demeterova, Tuma / Supraphon 3155

Sonata representativa, for violin & continuo in A major (1669)

Sometime in the middle of the 1660s, Heinrich Biber entered the service of Count Karl von Liechtenstein-Kastelkorn, who established his residence in the city of Kromeriz in Moravia and maintained an orchestra for performances in his castle. Between the beginning of his tenure at Kromeriz and his departure for Salzburg in 1670 against the Count's wishes, Biber composed a great number of instrumental works, the manuscripts of which are still housed at the Kromeriz Castle. Count Karl had a predilection for programmatic music and this was surely the impetus behind's Biber's composition of the *Sonata representativa*, for violin and continuo in A major, of 1669 (according to Jiri Sehnal).

Biber's *Sonata representativa* is not programmatic in the nineteenth century sense, rather, the sonata "represents" the sounds of several animals. Biber took these imitative passages directly from the *Musurgia Universalis*, written by the musicologist Athanasius Kircher. Kircher was the first to develop a "Doctrine of Affections," which directly related psychological states to various musical devices and expressions. In *Musurgia Universalis*, Kircher attempted to transcribe in musical notation the sounds of animals. Biber's sonata is for solo violin with continuo, often realized with a theorbo, harpsichord, or organ, or a combination of these. Each movement runs into the next without pause.

Biber opens his *Sonata representativa* with a not-so-programmatic Allegro that is in AB form with a slow introduction. A dotted figure in the opening melody becomes increasingly prominent at the climax of the movement. The "Nachtigal" movement begins with an extended, cadenza-like segment for violin alone in which the instrument imitates a nightingale through falling thirds and trills. In "CuCu" we hear the familiar sound of the cuckoo played beneath a rapid tremolo on the violin. This high-energy movement lasts only about half a minute before moving into the next section, "Fresch" (Frog), in which Biber conveys the croaking of a frog by writing harmonic seconds and out-of-tune glissandos mixed with some tuneless scraping of the strings. A lyric slow passage closes the movement. "Die Henn und der Hann" (The Cock and Hen) is a very fast, brief movement also featuring glissandos and clashing semitones. "Die Wachtel" (Quail) provides contrast with its slow tempo and *pp* dynamic as it presents a reiterated dotted figure. "Die Katz" (Cat) has a rising tune, the last note of which slides downward, evoking a cat's "meow." The eighth movement, "Musquiter Mars" (Musketeer's March) also appears in Biber's later *Battalia* (1673), although somewhat altered and with the title, "Der Mars." Its drone accompaniment and percussive interjections, supporting rapid violin figurations, set it apart from the rest of the sonata. Biber closes the sonata with a slow Allemande, in ternary form, and devoid of imitative noises. *—John Palmer*

Recommended:

- ○ **Biber: Violin Sonatas** / Romanesca / 2002 / HM 2907344/45

CHORAL

Missa Salisburgensis (1682–1696)

The *Missa Salisburgensis* is the largest piece of polychoral sacred music ever written. Unfortunately, there is no knowing who actually wrote it. The only copy of the music that survives is in the hand of an anonymous copyist, and no credit is given to the composer. Although most commentators guess that the *Missa* is by Heinrich Biber because of certain harmonic and melodic formulas, it is just a guess. The work could have been by Biber, by his rival Georg Muffat, by a younger colleague, or even by a committee of composers. While this might seem odd to post-Baroque audiences, the anonymity of the composer wholly suits the work itself. Premiered for the 1682 celebration of the 1,100th anniversary of the founding of Salzburg as a center of Catholicism, the *Missa Salisburgensis* is the *ne plus ultra* of Baroque celebratory music. Written in 53 parts and scored for six choruses stationed throughout Salzburg Cathedral with each chorus having its own instrumental group associated with it; plus two sets of distant trumpets, trombones, and tympani; and two (and possibly six) organs, the *Missa Salisburgensis* must have taken the talents of virtually every musician in Salzburg to perform. As the title states, the work sets the Latin text of the ordinary of the mass: Kyrie, Gloria, Credo, Sanctus-Benedictus, and Agnus Dei. Interspersed between these movements are three instrumental sonatas, one after the Gloria, another after the Credo, and the last after the Agnus Dei. After the third sonata, the work concludes with a motet "Plaudite tympana" (Sound the drums). The melodies are often liturgically based or occasionally drawn from folk songs. Because of the near-constant use of natural trumpets tuned in C throughout the work, most of it is in celebratory C major. And because it was performed in the cavernous acoustics of the Salzburg cathedral, it was relatively structurally simple (any complications would have been lost in the acoustic haze). But for all its relative simplicity, the effect is literally overwhelming. *—James Leonard*

Recommended:

- ○ **Biber: Missa Salisburgensis** / R. Goebel (cond.), Musica Antiqua Köln, Gabrieli Consort & Players / 1998 / Archiv B000010036

E. Power Biggs

b. Mar. 29, 1906, Westcliff, England, **d.** Mar. 10, 1977, Boston, MA
Organist

E. Power Biggs studied music at the Royal Academy of Music, emigrating to the U.S. in 1930 and becoming a citizen in 1937. He concertized widely, eventually broadcasting a weekly radio program from 1942–58 on a classic Aeolian-Skinner organ from the Musch-Reisinger Museum at Harvard University. This program alone brought the sound of organ music, particularly that of the Baroque, to an unprecedented large audience.

Biggs' inexhaustible energy as a performer was instrumental to the popularization of both the organ and Baroque music, and his activities extended well beyond these broadcasts. He toured and recorded widely, playing a huge variety of modern and historic organs and the music best suited for them, eventually expanding his repertory into every period of music. A series of LPs Biggs recorded for Columbia in the 1960s did much to make Bach's organ masterpieces familiar to a variety of listeners that ranged well beyond the traditional classical audience. Biggs also courted crossover listeners with a recording of Scott Joplin rags made on the pedal harpsichord.

He also worked with a number of contemporary composers on commissions, including Walter Piston and Roy Harris. After the onset of arthritis, which led to a forced retirement, Biggs concentrated on editing and publishing early organ music. By the time of his death in 1977, the name E. Power Biggs had become synonymous with the organ for several generations of music lovers. *—Steven Coburn*

Recommended:

- ○ **Scott Joplin Super Hits** / Biggs / 2000 / Sony 89267
- ○ **Bach: Toccata & Fugue; Preludes & Fugues** / Biggs / 2002 / Sony 89955
- ○ **Music of Saint-Saëns** / Ormandy, Entremont (conds.), Biggs, Ma, Tortelier, Marion, etc., Philadelphia Orch. / 1991 / Sony 47655
- ○ **Copland: Symphony for Organ & Orchestra, Copland: Symphony 3** / Bernstein (cond.), Biggs, New York PO / 1997 / Sony 63155

Malcolm Bilson

b. Oct. 24, 1935, Los Angeles, CA
Fortepianist

The sound of a fortepiano in Mozart performances is familiar enough nowadays that many listeners consider it simply an equal alternative to conventional performances. But it wasn't always this way: for many years, Malcolm Bilson labored almost alone in the field. Born in California in 1935, Bilson attended Bard College and majored in piano—conventional piano. He spent three years in Europe after graduating, gained degrees from the Vienna State Academy and the Ecole Normale de Musique in Paris, completed doctoral studies at the University of Illinois, and joined the faculty at Illinois in 1962. Taking home the Rudolf Ganz Biennial Award for piano performance in 1963, Bilson seemed well on the way to a strong piano career in the academic world.

In 1968, however, Bilson was hired at Cornell University, where he met antique instrument builder Philip Belt. Belt introduced Bilson to the fortepiano, the instrument for which Mozart's sonatas and concertos were written. Quieter and less resonant but more agile than a modern grand, the instrument bowled Bilson over musically. "It was the first time I'd been able to play every note Mozart had written," he explained. "The modern piano develops the tone slowly and is ideal for long, gradually unfolding lines but poor for phrases containing frequent changes in stress." He began performing on the fortepiano, at first mostly in university settings, and then, as the authentic performance movement grew to encompass music of the Classical era, on the concert stages of the world. He toured with cellist Anner Bylsma and made numerous recordings, including a complete set of Mozart's piano concertos on which he was accompanied by the English Baroque Soloists and conductor John Eliot Gardiner, for the Deutsche Grammophon label.

Like other period instrument performers, Bilson in the 1990s and 2000s became interested in music of the early nineteenth century. In 1994 he and his students presented all 32 of Beethoven's piano sonatas in concert in New York, perhaps the first time they had been played together in public on instruments of Beethoven's time since they were composed. In the estimation of *The New York Times*, "what emerged in these performances was an unusually clear sense of how revolutionary these works must have sounded in their time." Freely giving his time to chamber music and vocal performances as well as his own solo career, he often worked with Gardiner's Orchestre Révolutionnaire et Romantique. Bilson's activities in 2004 included a group of appearances at Hungary's *Sopron Early Music Days* festival. *—James Manheim*

Recommended:

- ○ **Mozart: Concertos 20 & 21** / Gardiner (cond.), Bilson, English Baroque Soloists / 1987 / Archiv 419609
- ○ **Scubert: Piano Sonatas** / Bilson / Hungaroton 31588
- ○ **Mozart: Sonatas Vol. 1** / Bilson / Hungaroton 31009
- ○ **Mozart: Complete Piano Concertos** / Gardiner (cond.), Bilson, Tan, Levin, English Baroque Soloists / Archiv 463111
- ○ **Beethoven: 4 Sonatas on Period Instruments** / Bilson / 2001 / Claves 502104

Gilles Binchois

b. 1400, Mons, Hainaut, Belgium, **d.** Sep. 20, 1460, Soignies (near Mons), Belgium
Composer

Destined to become one of the most influential composers of the early fifteenth century, Gilles Binchois was born sometime around 1460, probably in Mons, to a well-placed bourgeois family. His father, Jean de Binche, was a councillor to Duke Guillaume IV of Hainaut and his daughter Jaqueline of Bavaria. His son may thus have received his first training at the court of Mons, with its ties to royal France and Burgundy. The earliest surviving documents of his life relate his service to the church of Ste.-Waudru in Mons, as organist from December 8, 1419, until July 28, 1423; it is likely that he also trained as a chorister. Duchess Jaqueline fled to England in 1423 and married Duke Humphrey of Gloucester; this may explain Binchois' early contacts with the English nobles occupying northern France. For some time around 1424, Binchois was in Paris, apparently lending courtly service to William de la Pole, Earl of Suffolk.

Two lines in Ockeghem's lament on Binchois' death suggest the possibility of military service in the composer's youth. The "honorable worldliness" in this poem, however, could as easily refer to his courtly service to Suffolk and, from the late 1420s, the court of Burgundy. Gaps in the surviving payment lists prevent certain dating of his arrival in the Burgundian court chapel, but by 1431 he was fifth in seniority. In this year, he composed his single isorhythmic motet, for the baptism of Duke Philip the Good's son.

Unlike the majority of fifteenth century musicians, Binchois never became a priest nor did he take a university degree. This did not prevent his service as chaplain the Burgundian Dukes, however, with a long list of lucrative prebend incomes *in absentia* in Bruges, Mons, Cassel, and Soignies. In addition to his choir service, Binchois composed a great deal of sacred music, continued to compose widely in the courtly chanson genres, and likely performed his own songs to harp accompaniment. Around 1437 he was awarded an honorary secretariat. He travelled little during the decades of his Burgundian service, but was in Mons in 1449—with Guillaume Dufay.

A provostship at St.-Vincent in Soignies from 1452 led to Binchois' retirement there in February 1453. He continued to receive the income from his benefices there until his death in 1460. His musical contacts apparently also still throve in retirement, as the composers Guillaume Malbeque and Johannes Regis both worked in Soignies at this time. Upon Binchois' death, both Guillaume Dufay and Johannes Ockeghem composed moving laments in music: the one alluding to two specific chansons of Binchois, the other to his general style. Already in 1442, the Burgundian poet Martin le Franc had credited Binchois (and Dufay) with a rejuvenation of the art of music on the Continent; his chansons would serve composers throughout the century as models for elaboration and parody. A portrait of the legendary musician "Tymotheus" by Jan van Eyck may perserve the serious countenance of Binchois for posterity, while a number of important Continental music manuscripts offer his chansons to a later age. *—Timothy Dickey*

Overview of Works (ca. 1430–1450)

Though cited by fifteenth century poet Martin le Franc as a peer of Dufay in the art of fresh, modern music, Binchois is more often slighted in our own time. His style underwent less change than Dufay's, and the surviving manuscripts of the time do not preserve his music as widely. But such accidents of transmission and taste should not cloud his accomplishment. Writing in Northern lands, he encountered the novel *contenance* of English music earlier than Dufay, and quickly adopted its sweetness and harmonic fullness. In fact, two songs of his at least were well-known in England, and through the century his music was mistaken as English. Above all, Binchois was a superb melodist, crafting shapely, rhythmically balanced, and elegant tunes, and vivifying them with harmonic cross-relations.

This melodic gift is displayed most clearly in his over 50 surviving songs, the fruit of his long association with Burgundian court society. Over half survive in a single collection, the (Venetian) Canonici manuscript—a fact that demonstrates both the wide popularity of his songs and the tantalizing probability of lost works. Nearly all the surviving songs are in triple time (with certain small rhythmic "fingerprints" evident in his style), and all set texts in the fixed Rondeau form. The charming and elegant melodic arches fall quite often into structures which are completely balanced at the poetic midpoint of a stanza; the effortless character suits the restraint of many of his texts of courtly love. But the guileless melody of *Amoureux suy*, for example, is heavily spiced with delayed cross relations in the harmony (heard also in the sublime *Ay douloureux*). *De plus en plus*, whose later fame included a mass based upon it by Ockeghem, demonstrates another aspect of his harmonic practice: the surprising twists that playfully frustrate the listener's sense of tonal coherence. Binchois' literary taste seems to have been highly developed; his chosen texts include those by the three greatest poets of his age: Christine de Pizan (*Dueil angoisseus*), Charles d'Orléans (*Mon cuer chante*), and Alain Chartier (*Tristre plaisir*).

Unfortunately, his surviving sacred music is somewhat more sparse, though scholars are optimistic about locating more traces of the *absconditus* Binchois. The pieces discovered so far include a variety of service music for three (and occasionally four) voices, in a surprising diversity of style. A number of mass movements, some of them apparently composed in pairs, display an extroverted vitality of textural changes. One incomplete isorhythmic motet survives, *Nove cantum melodie*, composed for the baptism of Philip the Good's son in 1431. In comparison with the towering sacred compositions of Dufay, however, his surviving sacred music is simple and homophonic in texture, serving the daily worship needs of the Ducal chapel (many pieces paraphrase chants specific to the Rite of Paris, in primary use in Burgundy). Six settings of the Magnificat, all helpfully in different "tones" (modes), a number of hymns and antiphons, other items for the mass, a fauxbourdon psalm (*In exitu Israel*), and a Te Deum fill out an eminently functional catalog. *—Timothy Dickey*

Recommended:

○ **Mon Souverain Desir** / Ens. Gilles Binchois / 1998 / Virgin 45285

Thomas Binkley

b. Dec. 26, 1931, Cleveland, OH, **d.** Apr. 28, 1995, Bloomington, IN

Conductor

Though he would later claim a burning childhood desire to become a dancer, a life of music beckoned to Thomas Binkley from an early age. He enjoyed playing folk music on his guitar, as well as trombone in a local band (an arm injury forced him to abandon the latter). He took lessons from lutenist Joseph Iadone and proceeded to study music at the University of Illinois under Dragan Plamenac and Claude Palisca. While there, he performed on lute and early woodwind instruments in the Collegium pioneered by George Hunter. After graduating with honors in 1954, Binkley pursued graduate work in musicology at the university and then at the University of Munich. The expatriate life suited him well at first and he founded the Munich-based performance ensemble Studio für Alte Musik in 1959 with Nigel Rogers, Sterling Jones, and Estonian singer Andrea von Ramm. The group, later known as the Studio für Frühen Musik, brought him to worldwide musical attention. Binkley made more than 40 recordings with the Studio für Frühen Musik, earning numerous European prizes, including the Preis der deutschen Schallplattenkritik and the French Grand Prix du Disque; the ensemble also toured up to nine months out of the year. In 1972, Wulf Arlt asked them to transfer from Munich to Basle for residency at the Schola Cantorum Basiliensis. The ensemble disbanded in 1976 and Binkley returned to the States, first fulfilling a dream of homesteading in California and then teaching at Stanford University. In 1979, Indiana University offered (apparently at the behest of two students of Binkley's) to create an Early Music Institute under his directorship. He served in this capacity for 15 years until his January 1995 retirement, teaching a generation of early music performers, producing a further 45 recordings, establishing and acting as general editor for two series of scholarly publications, and creating the Thomas Binkley Early Music Recordings Archive. He began his own early music recording label (Focus Records, part of the EMI group), made wine, and gardened. The heart of Binkley's philosophy of performance was a marked distinction between the paper record of a piece of music and the sounding event. "The work is not the performance"; "The document [i.e. the musical score] is not the sound." Believing that, as with American jazz, medieval musics were notated as only scant mnemonic indicators of the musical sound, which was always different when enacted in performance, he sought a richer performance context than the reproduction of the mere notes on the page. Theoretical, rhetorical, and literary sources lent him such evidence. Binkley further admonished his singers to completely know their texts (which he was known for performing in full) and to memorize them in keeping with an oral tradition. Finally, he imaginatively wove the instruments and practices of folk music—notoriously the traditions of Arabic music that the studio musicians encountered by accident while on tour in North Africa—into a rich tapestry of instrumental improvisation around a singer's lyric performance. *—Timothy Dickey*

Recommended:

○ **Troubadours, Trouvères, Minstrels** / Binkley (cond.), Studio der frühen Musik / 1995 / Teldec 97938

○ **Hildegard of Bingen: The Lauds of Saint Ursula** / Binkley (cond.), Musicians of the Early Music Institute / Focus 911

○ **Dufay: Missa Se La Face Ay Pale** / Binkley (cond.), Pro Arte Singers / Focus 934

○ **Halle: Le Jeu de Robin et Marion** / Binkley (cond.), Musicians of the Schola Cantorum Basiliensis / Focus 913

Idil Biret

b. Nov. 21, 1941, Ankara, Turkey

Pianist

Turkish pianist Idil Biret is a fixture of the Naxos catalog and its completist enterprises, having recorded the collected piano works of Chopin and Brahms for the label. In 2004 she was at work on a cycle of Beethoven's 32 piano sonatas for her own IBA (Idil Biret Archives) label. She has appeared with most of the world's major orchestras and presented recitals in many countries, with a notable high point being a complete performance of Liszt's brutally difficult transcriptions of Beethoven's nine symphonies at the 1986 Montpellier Festival in France. Studio performances of those transcriptions were recorded for EMI and are also slated for release on the IBA label. Biret was, in short, one of the world's top-rank pianists, not a star whose name was familiar even to casual listeners, but a versatile virtuosa whose capabilities were well known to enthusiasts.

Born November 21, 1941, in Ankara, Turkey, Biret was a classic child prodigy. Turks called her the Turkish Mozart, and when she was eight the financially strapped Turkish Parliament voted a special appropriation to make possible her musical education in Europe. Hypersensitive to music as a baby, she gained the ability to hear a tune and reproduce it on the piano when she was only two. She had an uncanny ability to learn music in her mind without practicing it at the keyboard, delivering it perfectly formed to the amazement of onlookers. Biret's first teacher in France was the famed pedagogue Nadia Boulanger, under whose tutelage she blazed through the curriculum at the Paris Conservatory. She took three first prizes there at 15 and began her professional career the following year. Biret later studied with German pianist Wilhelm Kempff, who called her his favorite disciple.

One major event of her early career was a series of concerts she gave in Moscow in 1960, organized by Russian pianist Emil Gilels. She would go on to play over 100 concerts in Russia. In 1963 Biret made her U.S. debut with the Boston Symphony in Rachmaninov's *Piano Concerto No. 3*, a trademark work in her repertoire. However, in addition to her Chopin and Brahms cycles, Biret was known for performing and recording contemporary music. She recorded extremely adventurous music for composer Ilhan Mimaroglu's label Finnadar in the 1970s, and her 1995 Naxos disc of Pierre Boulez's three sonatas won France's Golden Diapason award. *—James Manheim*

Recommended:

- ○ **Chopin: Piano Favourites** / Biret / 1997 / Naxos 554046
- ○ **Boulez: Sonatas 1–3** / Biret / 1995 / Naxos 553353
- ○ **Brahms: Variations** / Biret / 1991 / Naxos 550350
- ○ **Rachmaninov: Concertos 2 & 3** / Wit (cond.), Biret, Katowice Polish Radio Orch. / 2000 / Naxos 554376

Harrison Birtwistle

b. Jul. 15, 1934, Accrington, England

Composer

Sir Harrison Birtwistle started taking clarinet lessons as a youth and was composing by age 11. In 1952 he won a scholarship to the Royal Manchester College of Music, where he studied with Richard Hall. There he encountered a group of like-minded young musicians—Peter Maxwell Davies, Alexander Goehr, John Ogdon, and Elgar Howarth—with whom he formed the New Music Manchester group, which specialized in performances of modern music. Birtwistle continued his studies at the Royal Academy of Music in London with clarinetist Reginald Kell, and made his living as a professional clarinetist for a time. His earliest surviving composition, *Refrains and Choruses* (1957), and other early works like the *Monody for Corpus Christi* (1959), show a certain debt to the music of Igor Stravinsky, and feature a combination of serialism and Medieval techniques.

From 1962 to 1965 Birtwistle served as Director of Music at the *Cranborne Chase School* in Dorset. In 1966 he won a Harkness International Scholarship which enabled him to spend two years in the United States, the first of which was spent as a visiting fellow at Princeton University. While there, he wrote his one-act opera *Punch and Judy* (1966–67). Back in England in 1967, Birtwistle formed the Pierrot Players with Peter Maxwell Davies. The group specialized in new musical works with a theatrical element, and Birtwistle wrote several works for them, the last of which was *Medusa* (1969, rev. 1970 and 1978). After Davies took over the Pierrot Players in 1970 and reformed them as the Fires of London, Birtwistle and clarinetist Alan Hacker formed a similar group, Matrix. Through the 1960s Birtwistle became known as one of the leading avant-garde composers in England.

In 1973, Birtwistle served as Cornell Visiting Professor at Swarthmore College in Pennsylvania. Two years later he was appointed musical director of the new National Theatre on the South Bank in London. Compositionally he devoted much of the 1970s and early 1980s to his opera *The Mask of Orpheus* (1974–77, rev. 1984). It and works like *The Triumph of Time* (1972) examine one of Birtwistle's favorite themes, the cyclic nature of time and how this idea can be conveyed in music. Three further operas, *Gawain* (1991, rev. 1994), *The Second Mrs. Kong* (1993–94), and *The Last Supper* (2000), followed.

Birtwistle received his knighthood in 1988. By this time, he was exploring larger sounds and gestures in his music, as in the orchestral work *Earth Dances* (1985–86). His music continued to attract attention in the 1990s. On the last night of the 1995 *BBC Proms*, his work *Panic* for saxophone, drummer, and orchestra was premiered and broadcast to a worldwide audience of some 100 million people. The festival Secret Theatres: The Harrison Birtwistle Retrospective was held at London's Royal Festival Hall in April and May 1996; the festival was named after his composition *Secret Theatre* (1984). The latter was written for the London Sinfonietta, for which Birtwistle has written often, starting with *Verses for Ensembles* (1969) and including the oft-performed *Silbury Air* (1977).

At the end of 2000 Birtwistle served as Director of Composition at London's Royal College of Music, was the Henry Purcell Professor of Composition at King's College London, and was Composer in Residence with the London Philharmonic Orchestra. *—Chris Morrison*

Overview of Works (1959)

The varied works by British composer Harrison Birtwistle exhibit a unique combination of inheritances. Scholars trace his gestural directness and structural sturdiness to Stravinsky, his use of rigorous processes to Webern, Messiaen, and Boulez, his orchestrational sense to Varèse, and his underlying formalistic tendencies to a fascination with antiquity (an eclectic mix shared somewhat by his colleague, Peter Maxwell Davies). These various influences, manifested through Birtwistle's own highly personalized musical language, create music that is highly dialectical: in the textural and formal aspects of his instrumental works as well as in the unwieldy dramatic structures of his stage pieces, there is a constant balance between articulating boundaries and transgressing them; there is always a system in his works, one of the composer's former students has observed, and Birtwistle invariably seeks to set to set it slightly off kilter.

Although his first "acknowledged" work, a wind quintet from 1957 entitled *Refrains and Choruses*, followed no overall formal plan, Birtwistle soon developed an affinity for highly structured, often ritualized musical systems. *Tragoedia*, a mixed chamber work from 1965, borrowed concepts that would prove a rich source of inspiration for Birtwistle: the conventions of Greek drama. The composer would take the idea of ritual and method even further in *Verses for Ensembles* (1969), in which combinations of reiterated musical gestures would find complement in specific stage movements for the instrumentalists. (He would pick this concept up again in later pieces, such as the chamber piece *Secret Theatre* from 1984.) Even when stage movement isn't required of his performers, Birtwistle's instrumental pieces still convey a sense of obsessive choreography or motion: the textural countercurrents in the orchestral work *The Triumph of Time* (1971) seek to evoke the tension between the temporal (mortality) and the eternal (the unchanging periodicities of the universe); *Silbury Air* (for chamber ensemble, 1977) places a melody in perpetual asynchrony with the piece's interlocking structural cycles; in the orchestral work *Earth Dances* (1986), instrumental layers rub against each other like subterranean strata; *Carmen arcadiae mechanicae perpetuum* (chamber ensemble, 1977) depicts the whimsical machinery of a Paul Klee painting.

The realization of formalist structure as musical ritual is even more marked in Birtwistle's operatic works. In *Punch and Judy*, an opera comprised in part of musical materials from *Tragoedia*, Birtwistle developed a method of compartmentalizing exchanges and expressions into discrete musical units; in fact the opera contains over 100 distinct numbers that resist coalescing into a coherent plot line in the traditional sense. Birtwistle took a similar tack in the less-successful *Monodrama* (1967), a theatrical work for a single singer and chamber ensemble, and *Bow Down* (1977), a theatrical work inspired by Japanese Noh drama. He fully realized his ideas about structure and expression in the monumental *Mask of Orpheus*, begun in 1973 but not premiered until 1986. His ritualized dramatic and musical elements would cede somewhat to a more narrative style in subsequent operas, such as *Gawain* (1991), *The Second Mrs. Kong* (1994), and *The Last Supper* (1999). *—Jeremy Grimshaw*

Recommended:

- ○ **Birtwistle: The Woman and the Hare** / Nash Ens. / 2002 / Black Box 1046
- ○ **Birtwistle: Secret Theatre** / Boulez (cond.), Whittlesey, Ens. InterContemporain / DG 439910
- ○ **Birtwistle: Refrains and Choruses** / Galliard Ens. / 2001 / Deux-Elles 1019

Georges Bizet

b. Oct. 25, 1838, Paris, France, **d.** Jun. 3, 1875, Bougival, France

Composer: Opera, Orchestral, Keyboard, Symphonic

Known for one of the world's most popular operas, *Carmen*, Georges Bizet deserves attention as well for other works of remarkable melodic charm. Many of his works received cool receptions on their premieres but are now considered central to the repertory of classical music.

Bizet was born in Paris on October 25, 1838 and grew up in a happy, musical family that encouraged his talents. He learned to read music at the same time he learned to read letters, and equally well. Entering the Paris Conservatory before he was ten, he earned first prize in solfège within six months, a first prize in piano in 1852, and eventually, the coveted *Prix de Rome* in 1857 for his cantata *Clovis et Clotilde*. His teachers had included Marmontel for piano and Halévy for composition, but the greatest influence on him was Charles Gounod, of whom Bizet later said "You were the beginning of my life as an artist." Bizet himself hid away his *Symphony in C*, written when he was 17, feeling it was too much like its models, Gounod's symphonies. The two years spent in Rome after winning his prize, would be the only extensive time, and a greatly impressionable one, that Bizet would spend outside of Paris in his brief life. When he returned to Paris, he lost confidence in his natural talents and began to substitute dry Germanic or academic writing for his own developing idiom. He composed a one-act opera for production at the Opéra-Comique, but the theater's director engaged him to write a full-length opera instead, *Les pêcheurs de perles* (The Pearl Fishers). It was not a success at the time, but despite a few weaknesses, the work was revived in 1886, and its sheer beauty has earned it a respected position among the lesser-played operatic repertory. In

1863 Bizet's father bought land outside Paris where he built two bungalows, one of which Bizet frequently used as a compositional retreat. He began a friendship (apparently not a physical one) with a neighbor-woman named Céleste Mogador, a former actress, author, courtesan, circus rider, and dance-hall girl. She is said to have been the model for his masterpiece's title role of *Carmen*. Bizet earned his living as an accompanist and publishing house arranger. Meanwhile, he poured his creative efforts into an immense five-act opera in the grand tradition, *Ivan IV*, but it was never performed. This proved to be a pattern for the rest of his career. Bizet would work hard to get an opera produced, and even if he did, it would usually receive only a handful of performances. Bizet's corpus of unfinished works is large, and testifies to his unsettled existence and his difficulty in finding a place in France's notoriously hierarchical and conservative musical world. In 1869 Bizet married Geneviève Halévy, daughter of his teacher. The marriage did not turn out to be a happy one, primarily due to her family's history of mental illness. In 1872, Bizet's splendid incidental music for the play *L'arlèsienne* was poorly received, but when the composer assembled the music into an orchestral suite for a November performance, it found great acclaim. At last confident of his creative vision, Bizet was able to steer his final masterpiece through various obstacles, including the objections of singers and theater directors who were shocked by *Carmen*'s subject matter. When the opera had its premiere on March 3, 1875, it was received barely well enough to hang on for future productions. Although it took audiences only a few weeks to catch on, Bizet died convinced it was a failure. *—AMG*

OPERA

Carmen (1873–1874)

The reception history of Georges Bizet's final dramatic work, *Carmen*, is rife with ironies. Although almost unanimously condemned by Parisian critics after its first performances in 1875 for its overt sexuality and graphic final scene, *Carmen* intrigued a number of sophisticated minds and ultimately reached the public in a way that perhaps no other opera has. Bizet's aim in composing *Carmen* had been to transform the flaccid, moralistic bourgeois genre of opéra comique into a more sophisticated type of staged work. With a libretto by Ludovic Halévy and Henri Meilhac, *Carmen* survives in no single authoritative version despite its enormous popularity and influence. Guiraud converted the original sections of spoken dialogue into recitative for the 1875 Vienna performances. In recent years the original version has made a striking comeback, and one can argue that it is far more telling dramatically than the traditional version with the recitatives. There is also a popular orchestral suite drawn from the opera, and several violin and piano fantasies on its themes also exist. *Carmen* is cornerstone item in any opera collection. It is ironic that Bizet composed one of music's most evocative landscapes of Spain without ever having been there.

Bizet based his opéra comique on Prosper Mérimée's story, *Carmen*, which had appeared in October 1845. Librettists Halévy and Meilhac emphasized the exotic characters of Mérimée's story and retained the themes of social class distinctions, overt sexuality, and misogyny that emerge so forcefully in Mérimée's model. Bizet gave musical expression to the libretto using recurring motives, a distinctive melodic style, and manipulations of genre conventions to give each character a musical significance and a unique expressive idiom. The opera's prelude introduces some of the most important themes, including Escamillo's toreador music and an exotic and sinewy chromatic motive that permeates the opera as a musical symbol for both Carmen's character and the insurmountable power of fate. The gypsy fortune-teller Carmen sings in dance numbers, such as the habanera ("L'amour est un oiseau rebelle") and the seguidilla ("Près des ramparts de Seville") of Act One, and the Gypsy song ("Les tringles des sisters tintaient") of Act Two. Traversing boundaries of diatonic harmony, the sultry chromaticism of Carmen's habanera theme underscores her status as both ethnic outsider and sexually adventuresome female. In this she stands in sharp contrast to Micaëla, whose Act Three aria ("Je sais que rien ne m'épouvante") is set in the ternary form of the elevated bel canto French grand opera aria. The bullfighter Escamillo announces his trade and masculine prowess in the rollicking Act Two toreador song ("Toréador, en garde!"), which carries the musical suggestion of battle in its fanfare opening and insistent march rhythm. Don José's musical styles reflect different levels in his descent from dutiful soldier to the underworld of obsession. In Act One, Don José sings in a duet with Micaëla ("Ma mère, je la vois"), adopting her elevated lyrical vocal style. In Act Two, after his imprisonment, Don José sings a more popular march-like tune ("Halte-là! Qui va là? Dragon d'Alcala"), reflecting his lower social status. His angst-ridden wailings in the opera's final scene defy clear formal arrangement and convey the psychological turmoil of an obsessed and defeated individual. Thus did Bizet forge a work that both summed up the musical resources available to him and had enough color and sheer melodic attractiveness to insinuate itself permanently into the public mind. *Carmen*, indeed, has been the subject of several popular-music adaptations over the years. *—AMG*

Synopsis:

Act One. The opera is set in Spain in the 1830s. As Act One begins, some soldiers are idly people-watching. When Micaëla timidly approaches, asking for Don José, they happily offer to keep her company while she waits, but she thanks them and darts away. Boys march in, imitating the changing of the guard, and when José comes in with the new squad, Morales tells him of Micaëla's visit. Zuniga questions José about whether the girls in the cigarette factory are attractive; José has no idea. The girls themselves come out on their break, smoking ("Dans l'air, nous suivons des yeux"). The men ask where Carmen is and a moment later, she makes her entrance. They demand to know when she will fall in love with them, and she teases them with her philosophy that love is an untamed bird that approaches when you stop pursuing it ("L'amour est un oiseau")—the famous Habanera. Piqued that José pays no attention, she throws him a flower. The girls return inside, and José picks up the flower, musing that if there are such things as witches, Carmen must certainly be one. Micaëla returns, and in their nostalgic duet, "Parle-moi de ma mère," she tells José the news of his mother and gives him a kiss from her, which he considers protection from the demon who was about to entrap him. When she leaves, he reads his mother's letter, which advises him to marry Micaëla. But just as he decides to do so and to throw Carmen's flower away, a tumult bursts out. Carmen and another girl have gotten into a fight and Carmen has slashed her opponent's face. She is insolently unconcerned, and Zuniga puts her under arrest, ordering José to watch her while he fills out the papers. Alone with her, José is not long able to resist her, especially when she sings the sensual Seguidilla telling how she intends to join her lover ("Près des remparts de Séville"), a position which is now open. As they leave for prison, she escapes, and José is arrested in her stead.

Act Two. The second act opens in the tavern where Carmen had planned to meet José a month later. She, Frasquita, and Mercédès entertain the soldiers with a song, "Les triangles des sistres tintaient," but refuse to leave with them. Escamillo, the famous bullfighter, enters and regales them with the macho Toreador Song ("Votre toast"). Though he approaches her, Carmen is not interested, at least for the moment. When the soldiers go, Remendado and Dancairo narrate their plan to smuggle contraband ("Nous avons en tête une affaire"), but Carmen refuses to go—she is waiting for José. They suggest that she persuade José to join them, and he is heard singing as he approaches ("Halte-là! Qui va là"), and they leave. Things progress nicely between them, especially when Carmen dances for him, until he hears the retreat to the barracks. Carmen is furious that he would think of leaving her, and he tells her that he loves her, saying that in prison he kept her flower and thought of nothing but her ("La fleur que tu m'avais jetée," the Flower Song). She insists that if he really loved her, he'd join her for a life of freedom with the smugglers ("Là-bas, là-bas dans les montaignes"), but he refuses. When Zuniga comes in in pursuit of Carmen, and José draws his sword when Zuniga orders him away, he has no choice but to desert. Carmen assures him of a life of liberty.

Act Three. In Act Three, the smugglers and José are carrying contraband ("Ecoute, écoute, compagnon, écoute"). José and Carmen quarrel over his jealousy. Frasquita and Mercédès read their fortunes in cards ("Melons! Coupons!"), finding predictions of wealth and love, but when Carmen does so, she sees only death, first for her, then for José ("En vain pour éviter"). She accepts death as fate. Over José's objections, she, Frasquita, and Mercédès go to persuade the customs officials to turn the other way ("Quant au douanier"), and José is left guarding the goods. Micaëla comes up quietly, praying for God's protection, trying to fight her fear ("Je dis que rien ne m'épouvante"). José sees movement and fires, and she hides, but it is Escamillo who comes out. He cheerfully tells José that he is in search of a gypsy he is madly in love with, and when José learns it is Carmen, he insists that they fight over her. Escamillo has the advantage, but refuses to strike to kill, a compunction José does not feel when Escamillo stumbles. Carmen returns and stops José, and Escamillo gallantly thanks her and distributes tickets for the next bullfight, telling Carmen that "One who loves me will come." He leaves, and José turns on Carmen, but Micaëla is found, interrupting the scene. She tells José his mother needs him ("Là-bas est la chaumiere"), but José refuses to leave Carmen ("Dut-il m'en couter la vie"). When Micaëla tells him his mother is dying, he turns to go, but warns Carmen they will meet again. As they leave, Escamillo is heard singing in the distance.

Act Four. The fourth act takes place outside the bullring, where merchants, soldiers, and the crowd all gather ("A deux cuartos!"). Escamillo makes his grand entrance, Carmen on his arm. When he goes into the ring, Frasquita and Mercédès warn Carmen that they have seen José, and advise her to leave. She says that she is not afraid and remains behind to talk to him ("C'est toi?"). He first begs and then threatens her to make her leave with him, but she refuses, saying not even death will make her surrender her freedom. Showing her contempt of his threats, she throws his ring at him, and he stabs her. As the crowd returns, celebrating Escamillo's triumph, José confesses and surrenders, calling Carmen's name. *—Ann Feeney*

Recommended:

- ○ **Bizet: Carmen** / Beecham (cond.), de los Angeles, Gedda, Micheau, Blanc, Orch. National de la RTF / Angel 67353
- ○ **Bizet: Carmen** / Karajan (cond.), Baltsa, Carreras, Van Dam, Ricciarelli, Berlin PO / DG 410088
- ○ **Bizet: Carmen** / Maazel (cond.), Migenes, Domingo, Raimondi, Esham, Orch. National de France / Erato 45207

Les Pêcheurs de perles (1863)
Despite its exotic setting, this early opera stubbornly refuses to abandon the stage and enter the heart, as *Carmen* undoubtedly did. What conviction there is comes mainly from the 25-year-old composer's melodic fluency and subtle treatment of the orchestra, as in the beautiful tune of the *Prelude*.

The scene is set in Ceylon and concerns the love of Zurga, king of the pearl fishers, and his friend Nadir for a priestess, Leïla. In the first act, the two men meet and have apparently recovered from their infatuation; but the priestess is appointed by the pearl fishers to protect them from the wrath of the Hindu god Brahma during the fishing season. Despite her veil, Nadir recognizes Leïla, again falls in love with her, and his affection is returned. Despite Leïla's vow of chastity, they are found in the sanctuary of the temple. The High Priest Nourabad tears off her veil and Zurga, in a jealous fury, condemns her to death. But, it appears, Zurga once showed his gratitude to a girl who helped him when he was being attacked by robbers by giving her a necklace, and he notices that Leïla is wearing the necklace. He decides to free her, starts a fire in the pearl fishers' tents, and the prisoners escape. (In later productions, Zurga is usually killed, but this does not happen in the printed libretto of the original vocal score).

The plot is mawkish, the characters weakly drawn, and much of the music derivative (mainly of Gounod and Massenet, though there is also a considerable debt to Verdi). The best (and worst) parts are the concerted choruses and ensembles, though Zurga and Nadir's duet "Au fond de la Temple," which returns again and again in the manner of a leitmotif, has to some extent proved an insurance against the eclipse of *Les Pêcheurs*. Leïla's oath of chastity, "Je le jure" in Act One, is also treated in this episodic way. Bizet received few favors from his librettists (Carré and Piestre) and highlight discs are usually more impressive than complete performances. *—Roy Brewer*

Synopsis:

Act One. (The action takes place in ancient Ceylon.) The first scene opens near a seashore, with an ancient Hindu temple seen in ruins in the background. Fishermen drink and celebrate, or cast their nets in the water for the next catch. One of them, Zurga, is chosen as the leader (and later king) of the fishermen by the assembly. A friend of his, Nadir, arrives amid continued celebrations.

When Zurga and Nadir are alone, they reminisce about the recent past, when both had fallen in love with the same woman, a woman they found an emotional drain. They had promised to avoid further contact with her and to retain their own friendship for life. Nourabad, high priest of Brahma, arrives on the island with a mysterious young woman, who is to lead the fishermen in prayer and initiate their yearly tradition of searching for pearls. She is, as one may have already guessed, Leïla, the woman whom Zurga and Nadir had once loved. Nadir recognizes her veiled face, but Zurga fails to. She enters the temple with Nourabad for prayer. Nadir privately reveals he has long desired and pursued her. Later, he and Leïla have an encounter and renew their love for each other.

Act Two. At night, amid the ruins of the temple, Leïla reveals to Nourabad how she saved the life of a stranger, who, grateful for her action, gave her a beautiful necklace. Leïla and Nadir have another passionate rendezvous, but shortly after his departure a gunshot is heard. An angry crowd stirs and at the behest of Nourabad, guards search for the culprit and bring back Nadir. The crowd demands the execution of both Nadir and Leïla. But Zurga intervenes and orders them set free. Nourabad, however, unveils Leïla's face to the horror of Zurga, who now recognizes her. He withdraws his clemency for them and commands they both be put to death.

Act Three. While Zurga agonizes over his decision, Leïla is brought to him under guard. She pleads for Nadir's life, asserting his innocence. But Zurga sees her deep love for Nadir and becomes enraged. As Leïla is taken away she gives her necklace to a fisherman with instructions to deliver it to her mother. Zurga, however, seizes it from him.

Leïla is taken by Nourabad and attendants to Nadir, so the pair can be prepared for execution. As Nourabad and several others are about to stab them before a crowd, Zurga enters and halts their action by telling them their camp is in flames. The crowd is suddenly alarmed and disperse to extinguish the fire, set by Zurga as a subterfuge. Zurga shows Leïla the necklace, gives the lovers his blessing, then implores them to flee. Nourabad overhears, and orders an attack on Zurga as the lovers escape. *—Robert Cummings*

Recommended:

- ○ **Bizet: Les Pêcheurs De Perles** / Plasson (cond.), Hendricks, Aler, Quilico, Courtis, Orch. de Capitole de Toulouse / EMI 49837

ORCHESTRAL

L'Arlésienne, suite No. 1 from the incidental music (1872)
Both *L'Arlésienne* suites are taken from the incidental music Bizet wrote for Alfred Daudet's play of the same name, a melodrama about the love of the hero, Frédéri, for a girl from Arles in Provence, France. In a little over six weeks, and limited to an orchestra of 26 players, Bizet produced 27 numbers, some no more than a few bars long. Taken together, they are an orchestral *tour de force*. The orchestra includes a saxophone in E flat, tambourine, piano, and harmonium, with the addition of a small chorus. A few passages are for string quartet alone. The overall effect is of a fully developed, closely integrated set of movements that, as concert performances of the original version have shown, easily stand on their own, and benefit from being freed from the dialogue that accompanied them in the play.

A month after the first production Bizet rescored the four extracts that form the first suite for full orchestra, with the equally sunny and melodious second suite arranged by his friend, the composer Ernest Guiraud, after Bizet's death. Both have proved more durable than the play. Lyrical and spirited by turns, the melodies are rooted in Provençal folk songs and dances, yet have all the color and drama associated with the composer of *Carmen*.

The first suite comprises four movements: Prelude, Intermezzo (with its title changed to Minuet), Adagietto, and Carillon. Apart from the scoring, the Prelude and Adagietto are unchanged from the original. The latter, a calm reverie for strings, has some magical effects that could not have been conveyed by the original small orchestra. Brass chords set against exultant strings vividly suggest the sound of bells in the Carillon.

Guiraud was closely associated with Bizet's music, having supplied recitatives for *Carmen*. The choral sections make a satisfying whole when the two suites are played consecutively. Guiraud uses almost the same orchestra as Bizet, though in places with less subtlety. A Pastorale and its following chorus are treated in a similar way to Bizet's Carillon. The Intermezzo, with some fine woodwind passages in the trio section, reinstates the Minuet from the first suite. A second Minuet imported from Bizet's opera *The Fair Maid of Perth* is pleasant, but sounds rather odd in this context. Guiraud's version of the Farandole (slightly altered from Bizet's) captures the exhilarating nature of this moderately fast traditional "chain" dance. *—Roy Brewer*

Recommended:

- ○ **Bizet: L'Arlésienne Suites 1 & 2, Carmen Suite 1** / Abbado (cond.), London SO / DG 423472
- ○ **Bizet: Carmen Suites; L'Arlésienne Suites** / Ormandy (cond.), Philadelphia Orch. / 1992 / Sony 48159
- ○ **Paul Paray Conducts French Orchestral Music** / Paray (cond.), Detroit SO / 2004 / Mercury 4756268

KEYBOARD

Jeux d'enfants (Children's Games), for piano, 4 hands, Op. 22 (1871)
Like Schumann's *Kinderszenen* and Debussy's *Children's Corner*, Bizet's *Jeux d'enfants* for piano duet is more about children than for children to play. It's a suite of a dozen miniatures, each a minute or two long, evoking the simple games and interests of very young children. Most of Bizet's piano works are miniatures and mood pieces, and *Jeux d'enfants* stands out from this oeuvre only in its special vivacity and tunefulness. "L'Escarpolette" (The Swing) is a slow, graceful opening number that mimics the movement of a swing with gentle arpeggios and brief, "push-off" melodic gestures. "La Toupie" (The Top) maintains a spinning figure in the background of a scampering main theme. Offering contrast with the top's energy is a berceuse called "La Poupée" (The Doll), a sweet, gently rocking lullaby. Galloping through the nursery now are "Les Chevaux de bois" (The Wooden Horses), in which Bizet revisits the spinning figure from "La Toupie" and now uses it, along with a quick march tune, to depict a little equestrian stampede. "Le Volant," with its sequence of tiny rising and falling phrases, portrays a shuttlecock being knocked back and forth in a game of badminton. "Trompette et tambour" (Trumpet and Drum) is a perky miniature march suitable for toy soldiers (and looking ahead to the "Children's March" in *Carmen*). "Les Bulles de savon" sounds as if it might accompany the progress of rabbits or grasshoppers across a field, but it actually concerns soap bubbles popping in the air. In "Les Quatre coins," it's the children themselves who take to the field, the music following them as they run to the playing area's four corners, a game that begins slowly but ends up rather frantic. The hesitant music of "Colin-maillard" depicts a game of blind man's bluff, while the more vigorous "Saute-mouton" engages in musical leapfrog. "Petit Mari, petite femme" offers the suite's greatest emotional depth, a slow, tender movement inspired by children playing at being husband and wife; the music includes a rapturous little climax almost worthy of one of Bizet's operatic love duets. Finally, "Le Bal" is an effervescent galop, an exuberant music-hall finale. Bizet arranged five of these movements for orchestra, calling it either *Jeux d'enfants* like the original or *Petite Suite*. *—James Reel*

Recommended:

- ○ **French 4-Hand Piano Music** / W. Klien, B. Klien / 1967 / VoxBox 5078

SYMPHONIC

Symphony in C major (1855)
Though Bizet's *Symphony in C major* (1855) today enjoys regular performances, the mature composer regarded the work as a youthful indiscretion and suppressed it. Indeed, the symphony remained unperformed until 1935, two years after it turned up in a bundle of manuscripts donated to the Paris Conservatory by

composer Reynaldo Hahn. Bizet, whose reputation rests on a mere handful of works, always attached greater importance to his later *Symphony in C major* (1871), subtitled "Roma." Nonetheless, the decidely less inspired "Roma" remains eclipsed in the shadow of its ebullient predecessor.

The 1855 symphony, written when Bizet was 17, was strongly influenced by the two symphonies of Gounod, which in turn owe something to Schubert and Mozart. The opening Allegro vivo commences with a short, inquiring rhythmic figure, a three-note motive that recalls the terseness of the material from which Beethoven spins the first movement of his *Fifth Symphony.* The second subject, in which the oboes and flutes figure prominently, is far more relaxed and linear. It is this subject that dominates the energetic development, though the first subject maintains a regular presence in one guise or another.

The Adagio begins with an introductory passage accompanied by a motive derived from the main rhythmic figure of the first movement. The oboe takes up a haunting, Oriental-inflected cantilena, the strings answering with a warm, serene theme of their own, no doubt inspired by bel canto opera. Bizet interrupts this lyrical, luxuriant expanse with a slow fugal section based on the motive that accompanied the introduction. A transition back to the oboe melody carries the movement to a gentle close.

The Scherzo begins with a Scottish tinge, a lively jigging rhythm. Bizet employs this first tune as counterpoint for the broad second subject, a string melody that recalls the soaring lines of Mendelssohn's *"Italian" Symphony.* The first subject pops up again, this time over a rustic drone bass, as the main substance of the movement's central Trio.

The fourth movement, a nimble, breathless Allegro vivo, opens with a whizzing workout for the strings, which take a few bars' rest as the brass and woodwinds play a cheerful march. A third melody affords a moment of lyricism for the strings, though they soon resume the scurrying pace of the opening. The symphony ends in a blaze of colorful virtuosity, an apt conclusion for a work so thoroughly infused with the composer's youthful exuberance. *—James Reel*

Recommended:

- ○ **Bizet: Symphony in C major; Smetana: The Moldau** / Stokowski (cond.) / 1992 / Sony 48264
- ○ **Ravel: Ma Mère L'oye, Bizet: Symphony in C** / Saraste (cond.), Scottish CO / Virgin 790744
- ○ **Bizet: Symphony in C; Patrie; Jeux d'enfants; Carmen Suites 1 & 2** / Ozawa (cond.), Orch. National de France / 2004 / EMI Classics 86089

Jussi Björling

b. Feb. 5, 1911, Stora Tuna, Sweden, **d.** Sep. 9, 1960, Stockholm, Sweden
Tenor

Jussi Björling was one of the most admired tenors of the twentieth century. He was never an effective actor on stage nor was he particularly handsome, but his excellent technique, scrupulous musicianship, and beautiful voice, with its powerful and focused top, made him one of the most-demanded stars of his day. Those with a fondness for such comparisons consistently called him "the second Caruso" or "the Swedish Caruso." Some found his rather smooth timbre inexpressive, particularly those used to Gigli's frequent use of sobs and other extra-musical effects, but others found that its directness, combined with his sensitivity to phrasing, made the music all the more expressive. At times he did have a tendency to sing slightly sharp, but to listeners without an acute sense of pitch it was almost undetectable.

Björling came from a musical family and began his career early—his singing debut came at the age of five. His father, David, was a fine singer who formed the Björling Male Quartet with the older three boys, Olle, Jussi, and Gosta. They performed worldwide, made some recordings for American Columbia (including Jussi's first solo recordings), and settled in the United States in 1920. While they were wildly popular, they had financial problems, and when David Björling died in 1926, the quartet broke up.

In 1928, Jussi succeeded in getting an audition with Karl-Martin Oehmann. Oehrmann was so impressed that he recommended Björling to the Royal Opera in Stockholm, where he was given a stipend for room, board, studies at the conservatory, and a new suit. Two years later, Björling made his operatic debut as the Lamplighter in Puccini's *Manon Lescaut* and took on his first leading role a month later as Don Ottavio in Mozart's *Don Giovanni.* In 1933, he first sang the role of Romeo in Gounod's *Romeo et Juliette,* a role with which he would later become strongly associated. He met Anna-Lisa Berg, a lyric soprano, while at the Swedish Music Academy and Royal Opera school, and their marriage lasted until his death, despite the alcoholism that troubled his entire adult life.

He made his Vienna debut in 1936, his United States debut in a Carnegie Hall concert in 1937 (his United States operatic debut was a short time later that same year, as the Duke of Mantua, in Chicago), and his Salzburg debut as Don Ottavio in *Don Giovanni.* In 1936, he also began a long recording association with HMV. He made his Met debut in 1938 in *La Bohème* and in 1939 his Covent Garden debut as Manrico. Like those of most other opera singers, his international career was limited by World War II, but when the war was over, he again sang all over the world. In 1950, he took the title role in the famous Met production of Verdi's *Don Carlo* that inaugurated Rudolf Bing's administration. As his career expanded and he was able to be more selective about his stage roles, he began to limit his repertoire to the major Italian and French lyric roles, with a few forays into the lyrico-spinto repertoire. However, he recorded and performed in concert excerpts from many roles he had never explored on stage, as well as lieder and his beloved Swedish songs.

In March of 1960, Björling had a heart attack before a performance at Covent Garden. While he chose to finish the performance, his symptoms became still more serious, and he and his family returned to Sweden, where he died that September. *—Ann Feeney*

Recommended:

- ○ **Jussi Björling Ultimate Collection** / Björling / 1999 / RCA 634682
- ○ **Madama Butterfly** / Santini (cond.), Björling, Los Angeles, Sereni, dePalma, Rome Opera Orch. & Chorus / 1990 / EMI 63634
- ○ **The Very Best of Jussi Björling** / Björling, various artists / 2003 / EMI 75900
- ○ **Leoncavallo: Pagliacci** / Cellini (cond.), Björling, Los Angeles, Warren, Merrill, RCA Victor Orch. & Chorus / 1998 / Angel 66778
- ○ **Jussi Björling at Carnegie Hall** / Björling, Schauwecker / 1991 / BMG 60520

Judith Blegen

b. Apr. 27, 1941, Missoula, MT
Soprano

Judith Blegen, a successful lyric coloratura soprano, was known for singing the high-flying, sparkling roles, like Musetta in *La bohème,* Sophie in *Der Rosenkavalier,* and Blondchen in *Die Entführung aus dem Serail*; she also excelled in oratorio and recital repertory. Her career began in 1963, while still a student at the Curtis Institute in Philadelphia, when she was engaged to perform at Gian Carlo Menotti's Spoleto festival. (The composer would create the role of Emily in his opera *Help! Help! The Globolinks!* for Blegen in 1969). Blegen spent the next several years cultivating an operatic career in Europe, first in Nuremburg, and then in Vienna and Salzburg. During that time she established herself as a top-notch performer in a wide variety of roles, including Zerbinetta (*Ariadne auf Naxos*), Susanna (*The Marriage of Figaro*), Olympia (*The Tales of Hoffmann*), Rosina (*The Barber of Seville*), and Papagena (*The Magic Flute*).

From 1969 on, Blegen sang frequently at New York's Metropolitan opera, where she added Zerlina (*Don Giovanni*), Adele (*Die Fledermaus*), Sophie, Blondchen, and Gilda (Rigoletto) to her repertory, as well as many other leading roles. Covent Garden engaged her for a production of *Cosi fan tutte* in 1975, and in 1977 she made her debut at the Paris Opera, further cementing her international reputation.

The best examples of Blegen's singing preserved on record include an *Exultate Jubilate* of Mozart and Haydn's *Lord Nelson Mass* on Sony, a *La bohème* on RCA with Plácido Domingo and Sherill Milnes, and Orff's *Carmina Burana* with Michael Tilson Thomas on CBS. *—AMG*

Recommended:

- ○ **Orff: Carmina Burana** / Shaw (cond.), Hagegård, Blegen, Brown, Atlanta SO / 2000 / Telarc 60056
- ○ **Puccini: La Bohème** / Solti (cond.), Alldis, Burgess, Domingo, Caballe, Milnes, Blegen, London PO / 1998 / BMG 1394962
- ○ **Mahler: Symphony 4** / Levine (cond.), Blegen, Chicago SO / 2004 / RCA Red Seal 59413

Sir Arthur Bliss

b. Aug. 2, 1891, London, England, **d.** Mar. 27, 1975, London, England
Composer: Film Music, Symphonic, Ballet

Although outspoken in his support of the post-World War I Parisian avant-garde during his youth, English composer Arthur Bliss ended his long career as a dedicated proponent of a more conservative, neo-Romantic musical aesthetic. Educated at Pembroke College, Cambridge and at the Royal College of Music (where he found his studies with Charles Stanford too stifling), Bliss' earliest music (all later withdrawn and subsequently destroyed by the composer) shows a strong knowledge of and interest in the music of Edward Elgar.

After service with the Royal Fusiliers (and later the Grenadier Guards) during the War, however, Bliss' musical aesthetic changed dramatically, and he quickly became known as a thoroughly "modern" composer, owing more allegiance to the exciting happenings on the continent than to the musical life of his own country. His music from the 1920s (such as the *Rhapsody for two voices and chamber ensemble*) is characterized by unusual vocal techniques, jazz influence, and striking harmonic procedures (not to mention occasionally exotic ensembles—e.g. the incidental music to *The Tempest,* 1921, scored for two male voices, trumpet, trombone, piano, gong, and five percussionists!)

Bliss' notable career as a conductor began in 1921 with his appointment as conductor of the Portsmouth Philharmonic Society. Invited to compose a work for the Three Choirs Festival in 1922, Bliss created one of his best-known works, the

Colour Symphony; this adventuresome work had the unwelcome side effect of causing a strain in the relationship between Bliss and Elgar, a dedicated conservative through whom the actual commission for the work had come. After two years in California with his brother and father (1923–25) (during which time Bliss lived in semi-retirement from the musical world and married Trudy Hoffmann), the composer returned to Great Britain and resumed his active composing career with the *Introduction and Allegro* of 1926 (commissioned and premiered by Leopold Stokowski).

Over the course of the 1920s Bliss began to re-evaluate his heritage as a composer and found him veering away from the "modernist" tendencies of the post-War years in favor of a richer melodic approach in which sound musical rhetoric and construction occasionally suffer in favor of expression and clarity of dramatic purpose. The five-movement *Morning Heroes*, a choral symphony dedicated to the victims of World War I and premiered in 1930, is a fine example of Bliss' new outlook.

The first years of World War II were spent in the United States teaching at Berkeley, but Bliss returned to England to take over as director of music at the BBC from 1942 to 1944. Knighted for services to British music in 1950, Bliss served as Master of the Queen's Music from 1953 to until his death in 1975 at the age of 83. *—Blair Johnston*

FILM MUSIC

Things to Come (1934–1935)

Sir Arthur Bliss' score for the movie *Things to Come* (1936) was a landmark in film music: it was the first time in the sound era that a major composer from the concert hall had contributed a score to a dramatic (i.e. non-musical) feature film. Bliss was reluctant to take the assignment until he received the reassurances of H.G. Wells, whose writings were to serve as the basis for the movie, that the music would be well treated. He accepted and wrote his score based on what was presumed to be the final shooting script of the movie. After that point, however, sections of the script were dropped or rewritten. Bliss was left in a quandry, as he had prepared a concert suite from the music as he'd written it. He felt obliged to conform the suite to the content of the film, and so some sections of the music were lost. During the late 1960s, scholar/editor Christopher Palmer received Bliss' permission to prepare an expanded version of the suite, but even that missed some of the lost music. Finally, in the 1990s, Philip Lane prepared a 32-minute suite entitled *Things to Come: Concert Music From the Film* that assembled all of Bliss' music that survived, from autograph score and recording sessions. The resulting 11-movement work opens with a profound "Prologue" played maestoso, highlighted by a dark part for the strings and intermittent trumpet flourishes. The charming second movement, the "Ballet for Children," played allegro moderato, is the most characteristic of Bliss' style, a light, faux-French piece evocative of the late 1920s, with beautiful wind parts all capturing the playful spirit of the film's innocent opening section. The third movement, "March," is the most-famous section of the score, an ominous rush to doom punctuated by the trumpets. The fourth movement, "Attack," played allegro con fuoco, is heavy on the brass, horns, and percussion, representing the fury of battle. The fifth, "The World in Ruins," done lento doloroso, is a darkly atmospheric piece dominated by the horns and percussion; the sixth movement, "Pestilence," done molto sustenuto, is an extension of the previous movement in mood and tone. The seventh, "Excavation," played moderato e pesante, may be the greatest showpiece for the percussion section of an orchestra this side of "The Anvil Chorus," though the sweeping parts for horns, brass, and strings hold their own. The eighth movement, "The Building of the New World," allegro moderato molto deciso, is a sweeping, rushed showcase for the whole orchestra with special movements for the winds, horns, and brass; "Machines," the ninth movement, done moderato, is a gorgeous workout for the flutes and reeds. "Attack on the Moon Gun," molto allegro fuoco, is similar in character to "Attack"; finally, the "Epilogue," done maestoso, gathers together the most noble and uplifting parts of Bliss' score, including a ravishing horn and string fanfare depicting the entry of the airmen that was "lost" for 60 years, all ending on a note of triumph. *—Bruce Eder*

Recommended:

- ○ **The Film Music of Sir Arthur Bliss** / R. Gamba (cond.), BBC PO / 2001 / Chandos 9896

SYMPHONIC

A Colour Symphony (1921–1922; revised 1932)

A Colour Symphony, dedicated to legendary conductor Sir Adrian Boult, was British composer Sir Arthur Bliss' first major work for orchestra. Completed in 1922, it shares the full-blooded Romantic style of his teachers at the Royal College of Music in London (Charles Stanford, Gustav Holst, and Ralph Vaughan Williams), but is laced with a more progressive twentieth century edge. No less a musical figure than Sir Edward Elgar encouraged the Gloucester Three Choirs Festival to commission the work, along with pieces by two other promising young English composers: Eugene Goossens and Herbert Howells. Its premiere in Gloucester Cathedral in 1922, conducted by the composer, was marred by a badly prepared performance. Some, including Elgar, found it disconcertingly "modern." Bliss revised large portions of the symphony in 1932, and it is that version that is popular today.

Bliss found his inspiration for *A Colour Symphony* in a book about the symbolic associations of the primary colors in heraldry. The four movements, episodic in nature, each characterize a particular color. The composer contended that the intent behind the work was to evoke or imply certain feelings and moods rather than to dictate a specific program or scenario. This work is marked with vivid orchestration and a tuneful accessibility. The first movement, "Purple" (Andante maestoso), captures the noble dignity Bliss associated with "... Pageantry, Royalty, and Death." A feeling of ceremony is established through a processional-like quality, while the martial aspect is reinforced by bold trumpet fanfares. "Red" (Allegro vivace) embodies fire, energy, and impetuosity. Exciting contrasts exist between a lilting lyricism in the strings and brilliant passages in the brass. These latter moments bring Igor Stravinsky to mind. "Blue" (Gently flowing) is the most introspective and perhaps most evocative movement. The composer referred to the obvious association of this color, "... Deep Water, Skies. ..." Indeed, its imagery and tonality border on the impressionistic. The final movement, "Green" (Moderato), is the most "modern" sounding with its angular melodic line that initiates the first of two fugues. Bliss described the color green as "... Hope, Youth, Joy, Spring, and Victory." Again, there are moments of Stravinsky-like vitality and ritualistic repetition, similar to his *Firebird* ballet. After a somewhat academic opening, the movement launches into a triumphant affirmation. A second fugue section leads to an explosive climax featuring six thundering tympani, eventually ending on an almost jazzy sounding sixth chord. *—Mona DeQuis*

Recommended:

- ○ **Bliss: A Colour Symphony; Adam Zero** / Lloyd-Jones (cond.), English Northern Phil. / 1996 / Naxos 553460
- ○ **Bliss: A Colour Symphony; The Enchantress; Cello Concerto** / Handley (cond.), Ulster Orch. / 1997 / Chandos 7073
- ○ **Bliss Conducts Bliss** / Bliss (cond.), London SO / 1995 / Dutton 2501

BALLET

Checkmate (1937)

English composer Arthur Bliss first conceived the idea for his ballet *Checkmate* at a dinner party in 1922. Among those present was the lead female dancer in Diaghilev's ballets russes, Tamara Karsavina. Bliss recalled she had danced the role of the murderous Queen Thamar in the first Diaghliev ballet he ever saw and that memory and her presence gave him the idea of "the pitiless queens in chess ... to become the starting point of the ballet *Checkmate*." The ballet was composed years later and premiered in 1937 at the Théâtre des Champs Elysees in Paris under the musical direction of Constant Lambert.

Composed in Bliss' lightly rhythmic, intensely colorful and highly dramatic modernist style, the ballet is in six sections: "Prologue—The Players," "Dance of the Four Knights," "Entry of the Black Queen," "The Red Knight's Mazurka," "Ceremony of the Red Bishops," and "Finale—Checkmate." The opening shows the two players, Love and Death playing for the lives of their subjects. The next four sections introduce the various main pieces in the game and are all relatively brief. The Finale depicts the actual game and climaxes with the Black Queen killing the Red King from behind. *Checkmate* proved a turning point in British ballet and resulted in many more ballet commissions for Bliss. *—James Leonard*

Synopsis:

As the curtain rises two players sit with a chessboard between them. The Golden Player is Love; the Black Player is Death. Love wins the first move and raises a red pawn to his heart. The curtain closes.

The curtain rises again and the stage has become a giant chessboard. The Red Pawns enter and dance a cheerful number. The two Red Knights enter followed by the two Black Knights, who challenge one another in dance. The Black Queen enters and dances seductively. One of the Red Knights is infatuated by the Red Queen and as she leaves the stage, she throws him a rose. The Red Knight dances an energetic solo. Three Red pawns then enter carrying the banners of the Red Knights and prepare to receive the two Red Bishops. The two Red Castles enter, symbolizing military force. The weak and feeble King enters accompanied by the Queen. The game begins when all are settled.

The stage erupts with the action of the attack and eventually the Black Queen puts the Red King into check. The King summons aid from the Red Bishops, but the Black Queen thwarts this plan. The Red Queen pleads to the Black Queen to spare the King's life, but the Black Queen summons her Knights, who carry the Red Queen away. The only piece who can now save the King is the Red Knight.

He and the Black Queen duel, though this Red Knight is torn between his love for the Black Queen and the duty to kill her. The Knight beats her down, but hesitates to kill her. He turns his back to the Queen and kneels before the Red King confessing that he could not kill her. As he kneels, the Queen strikes and slays him. Love and Death reappear as all the pieces except the Black Queen gather around the dead Knight and raise him onto their shoulders and the funeral procession begins. The Red King and Black Queen are now alone. The Black Queen dances while the Red King looks on with fascination, dread, and fear. The Queen hates the old King's weakness and quits the stage triumphantly.

The Red King is now alone. He thrice tries to escape, but a growing hoard of black pieces thwart him, building to a frenzy as the final onslaught begins. As his death becomes certain, he has a vision of himself as the vital and strong King of his youth. The Black Queen enters and puts his last hopes to rest as she strikes the King with a spear. She seizes the crown from his head as the King falls dead. Checkmate. *—Gerald Brennan*

Recommended:

○ **English Ballet Suites: Lambert, Bliss & Walton** / Lloyd-Jones (cond.), English Northern Phil. / 2003 / Helios 55099

Marc Blitzstein

b. Mar. 2, 1905, Philadelphia, PA, **d.** Jan. 22, 1964, Fort-de-France, Martinique
Composer: Opera, Musical Theater

In the first half of the twentieth century, no one successfully fused classical and popular music styles or convincingly fit American vernacular speech to music as well as composer-pianist Marc Blitzstein. Blitzstein composed primarily for the musical stage, using his own librettos, though he also wrote non-dramatic vocal and instrumental music as well. From experimental and polytonal beginnings, Blitzstein's music changed as he rejected the idea of art for art's sake in the 1930s and turned instead to a socially oriented aesthetic that had been embraced by Bertolt Brecht and the rest of the scattered or destroyed German avant-garde.

Exposed to music as a young child, he attended the University of Pennsylvania, losing a scholarship after he flunked a physical education class, but persisting with studies in piano and composition. In 1926 he appeared as solo pianist with the Philadelphia Orchestra, soon after which he left for further compositional studies in Europe. He major mentors for the next two years were Nadia Boulanger and Arnold Schoenberg. Afterwards, he made his first two major New York appearances in 1928: as a composer-pianist performing his Sonata for Piano (1927) and as a music critic in the periodical *Modern Music*. His criticism was better received than his composition, and he returned to Europe in 1929, continuing to compose and write.

Blitzstein's first operas were short avant-garde works; they included *Triple Sec* (1928) and *Parabola Circula* (1929). However, with *The Condemned*, a 1932 work on the subject of the Sacco-Vanzetti trial, Blitzstein began to take up the social themes common to most of his later work. In the mid-1930s he attended Hanns Eisler's lectures on the social responsibilities of musicians and took them to heart. *The Cradle Will Rock* (1936) was the most important of Blitzstein's works of this period, which lasted through 1941. The work was originally intended for the Federal Theatre Project, but it was considered too controversial (the plot dealt with a revolutionary labor uprising), and it ended up as a production of Orson Welles's Mercury Theater (and eventually as subject matter for the Tim Robbins film *Cradle Will Rock* of 1999).

While serving in the U.S. Air Force in London from 1942 to 1945, Blitzstein wholeheartedly supported the war effort with his music. After the war he returned to writing for the stage, though somewhat less militantly than previously. A Koussevitsky Foundation commission led to the opera *Regina* (1946–49), originally intended as a Broadway musical and based on Lillian Hellman's *The Little Foxes*. Stage works of the 1950s included *Reuben Reuben* (1950–55) and *Juno* (1957–59), based on Sean O'Casey's play *Juno and the Paycock*, two unsuccessful attempts at Broadway musical theatre. On the other hand, his adaptation of Brecht's *Die Dreigroschenoper* as *The Threepenny Opera* was an off-Broadway hit and has become the standard English version. In the 1960s Blitzstein received a Ford Foundation/Metropolitan Opera commission to return to the Sacco and Vanzetti story. *Sacco and Vanzetti*, and two more one-act operas on stories by Bernard Malamud, were never completed: Blitzstein died after being beaten up by three sailors he met in a bar while on vacation on Martinique.*—AMG*

OPERA

Regina (1946–1948; revised 1953)

Marc Blitzstein (1905–64) came to national notoriety in 1937 when the Federal Theatre Project canceled its planned production of his pro-union play *The Cradle Will Rock*. Producers Orson Welles and John Houseman led a celebrated march from the previously scheduled theater to a new venue with a bare stage, where the work was performed in concert, with the composer at the piano. Blitzstein was one of the leading New York Depression-era leftist artists, adept at Broadway music and classical styles alike. He is also known for preparing the best-known English translation of Kurt Weill's *Die Dreigroschenoper* (The Threepenny Opera) and its most famous song, "Die Moritat von Mackie Messer" (Mack the Knife). Lillian Hellman was also a leading leftist author of the time. One of her best-known plays, *The Little Foxes*, became the basis for the Blitzstein's own libretto for this opera. Hellman was surprised when she was asked to permit its use as an opera and did not take part in its adaptation.

The Little Foxes is a searing dramatic portrayal of a wealthy American family whose members scramble to get more than their fair share of the wealth. Blitzstein named his opera *Regina*, after the main character.

The protagonists are mainly members of the wealthy Hubbard family, symbols of greed and corruption. The story is set in Alabama in 1900, allowing Hellman and Blitzstein to use African Americans and other common folk of the region to represent the proletarian ideal, and the social and financial system of the Deep South to represent the decaying stages of capitalism. The plot concerns the conclusion of a business deal and the rapacious struggle of various family members to get the best part of its spoils. Regina is the most ruthless, and the person who acts or sings her role enjoys the opportunity to portray one of the most savage acts towards a presumed loved one in the whole history of American theater.

The work was written to be played on Broadway, although it is a through-composed opera. Blitzstein found it perfectly natural to tailor his music so as to mix classical structures, harmonies, and procedures with indigenous American musical forms such as field songs, spirituals, blues, ragtime, minstrel tunes, early Dixieland jazz, and gospel elements. Following the typical path of a Broadway musical, *Regina* was first given at the Shubert Theater in New Haven, CT, on October 6, 1949. This represented its out-of-town "try out." It was then given its official opening at the 46th Street Theater in the Broadway district of New York on October 31. The production was successful, considering its operatic form. The drama is intense and perfectly served by the music. Blitzstein expanded the orchestration to that of a standard operatic ensemble for a new production at the New York City Center in 1953. A revival at City Center in 1958 is credited with revealing the opera as an American masterpiece. It has continued to be performed, and gains strength, it seems, with each new production. *—Joseph Stevenson*

Synopsis:

Bowden, AL, 1900. The main characters are three siblings: Benjamin Hubbard, Regina Giddens, and Oscar Hubbard. Regina's husband is Horace Giddens, and they have a daughter, Alexandra (Zan). Oscar's wife is Birdie Hubbard, and they have a son, Leo.

Prologue. Addie and Cal, Regina's housekeeper and houseman, sing African-American gospel music and ragtime as they serve breakfast to Alexandra. Regina angrily interrupts, demanding that they stop their "music hall" singing.

Act One. In the Giddens' living room, after dinner, Birdie enters, quite taken with a northern visitor, Mr. Marshall, because of his manners and his knowledge of music. She offers to get out a music album and play, but Oscar forbids it. Birdie comes from traditional Southern aristocracy, from the Lionnett Plantation. Ben Hubbard puts it insultingly: "Twenty years ago we took over their plantation, their cotton, and their daughter."

Marshall and the Hubbards have agreed to build a new cotton mill in town. Marshall is to return next week to formalize the handshake deal, in which each Hubbard will put up 75,000 dollars. But Marshall, Oscar, and Ben point out that Regina has not yet gotten her husband to join the deal; without his 75,000 dollars it will fall through, and Horace is in Johns Hopkins Hospital in Baltimore for a heart condition.

Regina guarantees his presence next Friday, but only if his share is worthwhile. The brothers realize that Regina is holding out for a larger cut. To Oscar's distress, Ben and Regina agree to boost her portion to 40 percent. The new money is to come out of Oscar's share, but they mollify him with a plan to marry Leo to Alexandra (even though they are first cousins). Regina calls in Alexandra and informs her that she is to go to Baltimore to bring her father home. Although Alexandra does not want to go, she readily submits. This angers Regina, who reflects, "When I was young I loathed and despised anyone, when they obeyed so easily."

Later, Birdie warns Alexandra that the family intends to marry her to Leo. Alexandra says she will refuse, but Birdie warns, "They'll make you, and I couldn't stand that." Alexandra leaves. But Oscar has heard her disclosing the plans to Alexandra. As she passes him on the way out, he slaps her hard across the face.

Act Two. A week later, in the living room, Regina is getting a dinner party together for Marshall's return; she is very tense because Zan has not returned yet with Horace. She goes off to the kitchen. Leo enters and starts searching through the room, looking for cigars. Oscar, his father, catches him. Leo wonders whether Horace is absent because he doesn't want to invest in the plan, and he tells Oscar that Horace has 88,000 dollars' worth of bearer bonds hidden in a box in the room.

Horace and Alexandra arrive. He is exhausted from his voyage, and Alexandra carefully puts his two bottles of medicine where they can quickly be retrieved: one upstairs and one downstairs. Horace is shocked to hear from Addie that Regina is planning to pair Leo and Alexandra. He calls for Regina.

Despite his exhaustion, she insists on talking business. Although they both profess not to want any fighting, Regina begins to chide him about his past unfaithfulness. That, he responds, came after ten years without sex from her, and he concludes that since she's trying to make him feel guilty, she wants something from him. As the party goes on, Horace asks his lawyer to come the next day to draw up a new will. Regina asks whether he is ready to do business and, when he declines, shamelessly flirts with her old beau John Bagtry in order to make him jealous. Meanwhile, Leo succeeds in finding the box with the bonds and making off with them.

As the party winds down, Regina is shocked to hear Oscar and Ben assuring Marshall that they have raised the whole sum. This starts an argument after the guests are gone between herself and Ben, which Horace says he gets a great kick out of watching. He also mentions that he is going to change his will. The vocal ensemble grows complex, but above it all Regina can be heard exclaiming, "I hope you die soon. I'll be waiting!"

Act Three. In the living room the next afternoon, Horace gives Addie money to help Alexandra get away after he is dead. Then he confronts Regina. He informs her that Leo has stolen 88,000 dollars in bonds from him, enabling Oscar and Ben to make the deal without them. Regina realizes she can prove the theft and exults that it puts the brothers in her power. But Horace says he has changed his will; it now declares that he loaned the bonds, and leaving only the bonds for Regina.

Furious, Regina attacks Horace with the most demeaning and murderous words she can think of, including the fact that there was never a doctor's diagnosis that she should not have sex; she made it up because of her loathing for him. Horace has a heart attack. Reaching for the medicine, he drops the bottle, which shatters. Regina stands immobile when he begs her to get the upstairs bottle and tries to rush upstairs to get it himself. He collapses on the fourth step. She calls for him to be taken upstairs and has the doctor called for.

Now she reveals to her brothers that she knows the truth about the bonds and can prove it. They are to give her a 75 percent share of the enterprise, or she will go to the prosecutor. They submit when wailing from upstairs informs them that Horace, the only person who can gainsay Regina's accusations, is dead.

But Alexandra has heard some of that scene. Together with the fact that her father died on the stairs, what she has heard tells her all that happened, and why. She coldly informs her mother that she is going away. Regina disappears up the stairs. *—Joseph Stevenson*

Recommended:

○ **Blitzstein: Regina** / Mauceri (cond.), Ciesinski, Ramey, etc.; / London 433 812

MUSICAL THEATER

The Cradle Will Rock (1936)

Marc Blitzstein's *The Cradle Will Rock* is regarded as one of the seminal works in the history of American theater. The circumstances of the work's creation and premiere are legendary, indeed, the original production mirrored the real-life struggles of the story itself. As the premiere of the pro-union play neared, political machinations forced the withdrawal of Federal Theater Project funding, and the theater was locked. The cast literally took their cause to the streets, performing selections outside the theater until the producers found a temporary location. In order to circumvent union rules, only the piano was onstage for the performance; the actors sang and delivered their lines from their seats in the theater.

The play's setting is Steeltown, USA. Most of the action takes place during a drive to organize against the oppressive forces of wealth and privilege. The first scene, set on a street corner, opens with "Moll's Song." Moll sings about working two days a week for little pay at the steel mill; for the rest of the time she is forced to hustle on the streets. "Moll and Gent" depicts an unsuccessful pickup. In "Moll and Dick," a policeman takes a bribe not to arrest the Gent, telling Moll about the union meeting that day and trying to pick her up.

Scene Two unfolds in the night court, where several members of the anti-union Liberty Committee are mistakenly arrested. They shout for Mr. Mister, who apparently owns everything in Steeltown, to spring them in "Oh, What a Filthy Night Court!".

Scene Three, set at a mission, explores the relationship between money and religious influence.

Scene Four takes place on the lawn of Mr. Mister's home. Editor Daily is revealed as a "procurer" who reports the news in a manner favoring "whatever side will pay the best" in the song "The Freedom of the Press." "Croon-Spoon," sung by Junior Mister and Sister Mister, concerns the barely troubled dreamlands of the rich.

In Scene Five, union member Gus Polock and his wife Sadie get blown up at the drugstore by Mr. Mister's thugs, and Harry Druggist is warned that he better say that Gus set the bomb himself.

Scene Six, set in a hotel lobby, introduces various apolitical artists who show deference to the rich while secretly holding them in contempt.

Scene Seven returns the action to the night court. The song "Nickel Under the Foot" reminds one to always have some money around to fall back on. Larry Foreman, a union organizer, is arrested for "inciting to riot" (i.e. passing out leaflets). He sings the title song and delivers an inspiring oration about closed shops and mutually supportive unions.

Scene Eight takes place in the faculty room, whose atmosphere Blitzstein evokes with fragments of collegiate songs. Mr. Mister, a trustee, seeks a professor to get the college boys interested in military training in order to put down union organization.

In Scene Nine, Doctor Specialist cooperates in saying that Joe Worker was "drunk," although he has a bad stomach and cannot drink, when strikebreaking thugs pushed him into machinery. Joe's wife sings about her husband's plight.

Scene Ten again returns to the night court. Mr. Mister tries to get Larry Foreman to sell out the union. Larry tells Mister to use his money to buy a big piece of toast, because to "me and my Aunt Jessie you're a poached egg." The Finale is a reprise of the title song as the union marches outside. *—"Blue Gene" Tyranny*

Recommended:

○ **Blitzstein: Cradle Will Rock** / LuPone, The Acting Company / 1999 / Jay 1300

○ **Blitzstein: Musical Theatre Premières** / Original Cast - 1938 Broadway Production / 1998 / Pearl 0009

Ernest Bloch

b. Jul. 24, 1880, Geneva, Switzerland, **d.** Jul. 15, 1959, Portland, OR

Composer: Chamber Music, Concerto

A highly individual composer, Ernest Bloch did not pioneer any new style in music but spoke with a distinctive voice into which he could assimilate folk influences, 12-tone technique, and even coloristic quarter tones. In a stylistically atomized century his interests were universal, and his music was both beloved by the public and inspirational for a younger and more academically oriented generation.

His father was the quintessential Swiss, a well-off manufacturer of watches and clocks, including cuckoo clocks. Ernest had a diverse musical training that included advanced violin training, study of eurhythmics with Émile Jacques-Dalcroze; he traveled from Switzerland to Belgium, Munich, and Paris in due course. Bloch wrote prolifically in his student years but did not publish any of his works. He is not related to his contemporary Ernest Bloch (1885–1977), a German philosopher interested in musical issues.

Bloch married Margarethe Schneider in 1904; one of their children, Suzanne, became a well-known lute player. His music began to attract interest, and in 1910 his opera *Macbeth* was staged in Paris to a mostly uncomprehending audience. About this time he began writing music with specifically Jewish aspects in subject matter, reflected by orientalisms in the melodies—often derived from Jewish worship chants and folk music. Some of the best known compositions of this series are the violin work *Baal-Shem*, an *Israel Symphony*, and *Schelomo*, a tone poem that also is one of the great cello concertos.

In 1916 he traveled to the U.S. as conductor for the Maud Allan dance company. The outfit went broke, stranding him in Ohio. The composer was thus forced to remain in America, but he soon found success as a composer, conductor, and music school administrator and teacher. In 1924 he took American citizenship. He became director of the San Francisco Conservatory in 1925 and in 1927 won first prize in a contest sponsored by *Musical America* with his composition *America, an Epic Rhapsody*.

He returned to Switzerland in 1930, and mostly lived there for the next decade. He composed and traveled widely in Europe to conduct his works. The rise of Nazism in Germany and a desire to retain his U.S. citizenship prompted a return to that country before World War II broke out. He settled at scenic Agate Beach, OR, and was appointed a professor at the University of California in Berkeley, teaching summer courses until he retired in 1952.

During both of his American teaching careers he shaped the early careers of an enviable list of successful students, including Antheil, Kirchner, and Sessions. Bloch died of cancer in 1959. *—Joseph Stevenson*

CHAMBER MUSIC

Baal Shem, for violin & piano (1923)

Ernest Bloch composed his *Baal Shem, Three Pictures from Hassidic Life* in 1923, the year in which he procured American citizenship. Along with his most familiar work, *Schelomo, Rhapsody for cello and orchestra*, his three pieces *From Jewish Life*, the *Méditation hébraïque*, and the *Sacred Service* of 1930, the triptych *Baal Shem* belongs to a distinctive and unmistakable genus of pieces, in which Bloch's personal voice was now powerfully established as being "Jewish" in utterance above all else. But as the critic Erik Levi suggests, it is important to remember that "Bloch's Jewishness derived from an inner impulse, not through a conscious absorption of Hebraic folk elements." To this we could also add Bloch's own assertion: "it is neither my purpose nor desire to attempt a reconstruction of Jewish music, nor to base my work on more or less authentic melodies . . . I am not an archaeologist; for me the most important thing is to write good and sincere music."

Baal Shem continues the process of thought. "What interests me," wrote Bloch, "is the Jewish soul, the enigmatic, ardent, turbulent soul that I feel vibrating throughout the Bible . . . it is all this that I endeavour to hear in myself and to transcribe into my music; the venerable emotion of the race that slumbers way down in our souls." Bloch's *Baal Shem* comprises I. "Vidui" (Contrition)—Un poco lento; II. "Nigun" (Improvisation)—Adagio non troppo; III. "Simchas Torah" (Rejoicing)—Allegro giocoso. As Erik Levi writes, "*Nigun* is the most extrovert composition.

Here, Bloch attempts to recreate the feeling of ecstatic religious chanting through a highly charged and ornate melodic line that rises to a fever pitch of spiritual intensity before dying away to a gentle close. Before this comes *Vidui* in which the fervour of a sinner returning to God is evoked by cantilena writing of considerable nobility. The final section of *Baal Shem, Simchas Torah,* inspired by the moment when Moses handed down the torch to the children of Israel, is a lively, optimistic and exhilarating piece." The trilogy was originally intended for violin and piano; however, Bloch also produced an edition with orchestral accompaniment in 1939; *Baal Shem* is also occasionally performed by cellists, with either form of accompaniment. —Michael Jameson

Recommended:

○ **Bloch: Baal Shem; 2 Violin Sonatas** / L. Friedman, A. Schiller / 1996 / ASV 714

○ **Isaac Stern: A Life in Music Vol. 28; Hindemith, Copland & Bloch** / I. Stern, Zakin / 1996 / Sony 64533

From Jewish Life, for cello & piano (1924)

Ernest Bloch composed his three pieces *From Jewish Life* in 1924 and dedicated the set to Hans Kindler, solo cellist of the New York Philharmonic, who had previously given the successful premiere of the *Hebraic Rhapsody for cello and orchestra "Schelomo" (Solomon)*, Bloch's best known work. Along with the suite *Baal Shem* (1923), and the *Méditation hébraïque* (1924), the triptych *From Jewish Life* belongs to a distinctive and unmistakable genus of pieces, in which Bloch's personal voice was now powerfully established as being "Jewish" in utterance above all else. But as the critic Erik Levi suggests, it is important to remember that "Bloch's Jewishness derived from an inner impulse, not through a conscious absorption of Hebraic folk elements." To this we could also add Bloch's own assertion: "it is neither my purpose nor desire to attempt a reconstruction of Jewish music, nor to base my work on more or less authentic melodies... I am not an archaeologist; for me the most important thing is to write good and sincere music."

But as Erik Levi continues to suggest, "In essence Bloch's Jewish music is emotional in feeling and colored by an exotic atmosphere. The melodic lines are declamatory, emphasizing intervals of an augmented second, and are often supported by impressionist harmonies." These qualities are felt especially powerfully in *From Jewish Life*; the three pieces are titled: 1. "Prayer" (Andante moderato); 2. "Supplication" (Allegro non troppo); 3. "Jewish Song" (Moderato). The overall atmosphere is one of intense sadness and introspection, and the series is concerned far less with virtuosity than with the peculiar power of expression that invariably distinguished such archaic and timeless themes as Bloch chose to employ in this work. *—Michael Jameson*

Recommended:

○ **The Cantorial Voice Of The 'Cello** / Bloemendal, Tryon / 1995 / Dorian 90208

○ **Bloch: Meditations Hebraïques** / Bruns, Ishay / 1999 / Opus 111 30232

CONCERTO

Schelomo, rhapsody for cello & orchestra (1915–1916)

The *Hebraic Rhapsody* for cello and orchestra *Schelomo* ("Solomon") is the best-known work of Ernst Bloch's "Jewish Cycle." It was composed in the space of two months, between December 1915 and February 1916, and dedicated to the Russian cellist Alexander Barjansky. The Carnegie Hall premiere, by the New York Philharmonic under Artur Bodanzky, with the orchestra's principal cellist Hans Kindler taking the solo role, occurred during a concert including the entire Jewish Cycle. Bloch himself is known to have directed the work only once, when Barjansky performed *Schelomo* at the Rome Augusteo in 1933.

In his program notes, Bloch explained "for years I've had sketches for the book of Ecclesiastes that I wanted to put into music... if you will, the cello can be imagined to be the reincarnated voice of King Solomon, while the orchestra's more complex voice belongs to his time, his world... to his experience. The cello represents a meditative voice, tragically alone." Although in free rhapsodic form, *Schelomo* can be subdivided into three sections, preceded by the cello's opening soliloquy. The work begins with Solomon's lamentation ("vanity... all is vanity.") before we hear a succession of languorous slow dances and luminous reflective figures (the celesta takes a very important part here) punctuated by occasional outbursts of anger from the brass, paraphrasing motifs from the Hebrew Shofar. In each of these, Solomon abandons himself to the seductive and voluptuous atmosphere, while the dense counterpoint evokes a near Tower of Babel of tortured complexity, before a gigantic climax is reached.

Now, Solomon's initial protestations of disgust return, as oboe and bassoon solos invoke the synagogue chant *"Asher kidshonu."* At first, the cello resists the cantor's voice, but then becomes progressively intertwined with its texture as the mounting liturgical chant approaches a second major climax. In the concluding episode, again the mood is one of bitter despair and resignation, though a fleeting heavenly vision interposes, only to be denied in another frenetic orchestral outburst, which soon disintegrates, leaving the lone and desolate voice of the cello reflecting again on Solomon's conviction that "all is vanity." *Schelomo* ends in a mood of dark, unmitigated pessimism, darker, surely, than even its opening utterances would have intimated. Bloch added "this is my only work that culminates in a total negation—but the subject demanded it." *—Michael Jameson*

Recommended:

○ **Pierre Fournier, Violoncello** / Wallenstein (cond.), Fournier, Berlin PO / 1999 / DG 457761

Suite hébraïque, for viola or violin & orchestra (1951)

Bloch really started to musically reflect on his Jewish heritage once he had moved to the United States in 1916. The "Jewish Cycle" of large-scale works was the main fruit of these reflections, and Bloch regularly returned to Jewish themes in later phases of his career, as in the *Suite hébraïque*, which has become popular among both violinists and violists in both orchestra- and piano-accompanied versions. The suite draws on traditional Jewish sources, as well as melodic and timbral inspirations, such as the sound of the shofar's call. The opening Rapsodie's languorous main theme contains some Hebraic inflections. Most of the movement is forceful, with barely repressed emotion and a few telling dissonances. A march rhythm and a passionate theme from the viola characterize the second movement, titled "Processional." The finale, "Affirmation," opens and closes with a full-throated theme over a dance-like, lilting rhythm, framing a sweet, graceful central section. *—Chris Morrison*

Recommended:

○ **Bloch: Schelomo; Violin Concerto, Suite hébraïque** / J. Rohan (cond.), Bress, Prague SO / 1999 / Supraphon 3169

Violin Concerto (1937–1938)

Bloch's full-bodied, large-scale, colorfully scored violin concerto has never caught on in the concert hall, despite early championing by the soloist who commissioned it, Joseph Szigeti. Bloch had studied with Ysaÿe, but he hadn't touched the violin in years until this commission arrived; he took it up again in an effort to write as idiomatically for the instrument as possible.

The work's original program notes stated that Bloch quotes Native American themes (Bloch had spent the 1920s in the United States), but this is not quite correct; he does allude to American Indian music without using authentic melodies, but for that matter he also alludes to the same cantorial sort of eastern European and eastern Mediterranean music that suffused his more popular *Schelomo*. Indeed, the Hebraic influence seems especially strong here, particularly in the third movement, but Bloch insisted, "I can only say that in it there is neither Jewish inspiration nor intention."

The first of the three movements, Allegro deciso, begins with a horn call whose first measure might have been plucked straight from *Schelomo*, but which settles into an ominous rhythmic figure that would become a cliché in later cowboy-and-Indian movies. This and two brief, more singing melodies provide the basic material for the movement, which subjects the themes to a series of transformations. The music is highly rhapsodic with frequent tempo changes, yet Bloch praised Szigeti for not pulling the music around too much.

The brief, dreamlike Andante alludes even more strongly to Bloch's earlier Hebraic-Impressionist style. The music is dark and exotically modal, with the soloist frequently pulling out of the movement's basic processional plod and leading the orchestra into freer, more restless rhythmic and harmonic material. The final movement, "Deciso," arrives with a confident yet dour orchestral introduction, whereupon the violin arrives with melodic and rhythmic echoes of the first movement, and soon introduces new thematic material. Again, Bloch favors a rhapsodic, transformational approach to his themes, shifting from lyrical episodes to playful interludes, ending with a grand, extroverted passage into which the quotation from the first movement insinuates itself one last time. *—James Reel*

Recommended:

○ **Bloch: Schelomo; Violin Concerto; Suite hébraïque** / Rohan (cond.), Bress, Prague SO / 1999 / Supraphon 3169

Karl-Birger Blomdahl

b. Oct. 19, 1916, Växjö, Sweden, **d.** Jun. 14, 1968, Kungsängen, Sweden

Composer: Symphonic, Opera

Remembered most vividly for his 1958 "space opera" *Aniara*, composer and educator Karl-Birger Blomdahl was a leader in the Monday Group, a gathering of Swedish composers who met regularly to discuss contemporary music. Well trained, Blomdahl moved from a style rooted in traditional Scandinavian music to a Hindemith-derived contemporary approach to composition, encompassing extended melismas, choral motives, electronic music, and even elements of jazz. At age 18, Blomdahl traveled to Stockholm intending to major in biochemistry. An abiding interest in music derailed his original purpose, however, and he began studies with Hilding Rosenberg, whose interest in motivic composition is reflected in Blomdahl's *Woodwind Trio* from 1938 and both the *Symfoniska Danser* and *String Quartet No. 1* from the following year. Following service during World War II, Blomdahl resumed his training at the Royal Academy of Music, studying conducting with Tor Mann and pursuing work on music of the Baroque period with Danish conductor Mogens Wøldike, an early specialist in that field. Even before his work with Wøldike, Blomdahl conjured the essential character of the Baroque age with his 1944 *Concerto Grosso*, and from 1945, his *Three Polyphonic Pieces for piano* and his *String Trio*. His *Symphony No. 2*, written in 1947, is further evidence of this interest. During the 1940s, Blomdahl's participation in and eventual leadership of the Monday Group fed his growing interest in contemporary music. Meeting in Blomdahl's apartment, the members—composers, musicologists, and players—were intrigued by Paul Hindemith's compositional theories as outlined in his *Unterweisung in Tonsatz*. Aside from compositional techniques, topics of interest ranged from instructional methodologies to the popular media and its role in the country's musical life. A focused and proactive core from the group later assumed leadership of the chamber music association Fylkingen and, once more following Blomdahl's lead, moved to positions of controlling authority in the Swedish contingent of the International Society for Contemporary Music. The 1950s brought in new directions to Blomdahl's music, one of them encircling mythology. With choreographer Birgit Åkesson and poet Erik Lindegren, Blomdahl composed two striking ballets, *Sisyphos* and *Minotauros*, in 1954 and 1958, respectively. At the same time, he was writing *Aniara*, an opera set in space and described by the composer as "a revue of man in time and space." Like the aforementioned ballets, *Aniara* represents the first phase of Blomdahl's mature period. Here, shifts occur within a diverse collection of musical forms, moving among choral music, extended wordless arioso, the so-called "Mina tapes," (electronic interjections), and jazzy moments conjuring mindless frivolity. Undoubtedly the work's novelty attracted the attention of the popular press after its Stockholm premiere in 1959 and afforded it a notoriety beyond that given other modern works, but its examination of man's prospects in a cold and distant new environment remains compelling and Blomdahl's musical language entirely apt for the text. A second opera, *Herr von Hancken*, first heard in 1965 at the Royal Opera House, was a mind-twisting tragedy couched in opera buffa form; it failed despite a credible libretto by Lindegren. The lyric interest of *Aniara* and the earlier operas' variety of expression were replaced by continuous recitative punctuated by a few moments of arioso form. A professor at the Swedish Royal Academy of Music from 1960 to 1964, Blomdahl was director of music for Swedish Radio at the time of his death in 1968. —*Erik Eriksson*

SYMPHONIC

Symphony No. 3 ("Facetter") (1950)

This, Blomdahl's *Third Symphony*, is regarded as his first real masterpiece and is among the greatest of Scandinavian symphonies. It also manifests the first signs of the composer's interest in 12-tone composition: although Blomdahl never fully embraced serialism, this work is nevertheless built from segments of a 12-tone row. It is in a single movement comprising five sections, and lasts between 20 and 25 minutes in performance. The opening introduction is, Blomdahl said, "cold" and "desolately lyrical." The second part is a lament for the victims of Warsaw during World War II. The third movement is the fastest portion of the symphony, a two-part scherzo in shifting accents. The fourth movement is introduced with timpani and military drum with a "machine-like, inexorable" flow of counterpoint. This builds to a masterly climax, by which time it gains a dance-like character. The final section is a varied recapitulation of the opening. —*Joseph Stevenson*

Recommended:

○ **Blomdahl: Symphonies 1–3** / Segerstam (cond.), Swedish Radio SO / 1991 / Bis 611

OPERA

Aniara, Space Opera of 2038 (1957–1958)

Often billed as the first "science-fiction opera," the action of this opera by one of Sweden's most important composers takes place upon a spaceship named Aniara, filled with refugees from a ravished home planet named Dorisland. Their link with the outside is a device called the Mima, a kind of cosmic television which gathers images of wonders of the universe, but, having a soul, it returns in grief to the destruction of Dorisland. The ship is under the rule of Chefone and his enforcers, called "Space Cadets," while the human element is provided by the lovely dances of the woman pilot, Isagel, and the tender song of the officer called only the "Mimarobe." The Mima itself has a voice in some of the first electronic music to be heard in any opera. The story is pageant-like, showing highlights of over 20 years spent on the ship, for early in the voyage a harsh maneuver meant to avoid an asteroid left them without propellant to return to a proper course, so the entire shipboard society is doomed to wander off in the wrong direction, dying during an endless journey. The music is often radical: basses pulse with the rhythm of "SOS, Aniara" in Morse code. Sometimes there is 12-tone music, sometimes a harsh jazz idiom. Isagel's music and the Mimarobe's song in adoration of her has a rare, crystalline beauty. Very rarely encountered in the repertoire, there is nevertheless a strange fascination in this widely varied score and its parade of hopeless characters. —*Joseph Stevenson*

Synopsis:

Act One. Aniara is a spaceship carrying 8,000 people, most of them refugees from the lethally radioactive Earth (called "Doris" or "Douris" in the opera); they, like thousands of others on other spaceships, intend to begin life anew on Mars.

A chorus of emigrants fills in this background together with Mimarobe, the ship's chief engineer, who also has an oracular apparatus called Mima. This is a sort of hourglass that gathers and sifts thoughts and memories from throughout time and the universe, and conveys them to passengers who seek consolation from the emptiness and terror of space. Next, people gather in the assembly hall for the midsummer dance, presided over by a carefree dancer named Daisi Doody. As the sole survivor of Dorisburg, the city of joy, Daisi sings in a language nobody can understand, although the people happily mimic it. The ship's high comedian, Sandon, also joins the festivities; he proclaims the might of sheer zaniness to overcome sorrow and fear.

Sorrow, fear, and full-scale panic break out, however, when the ship is flung off course by a "swarm of leonids," presumably asteroids, and is sent hurtling into deep space. Chefone, the ship's commander, and three technicians explain the disaster; Chefone declares that the passengers are privileged, for even though they are forever lost in space, at least they are still alive, rather than having been annihilated in the collisions. The dance resumes, first hesitantly, then desperately.

In a long solo passage, the first Chief Technician philosophizes that space is actually God's spirit, and likens Aniara to "a tiny bubble in the glass of God." Next, the Mimarobe ponders the power of Mima to soothe the troubled passengers with images of exotic planets; he also implies that all is not well with the ship's pilot, a woman named Isagel. Meanwhile, Mima displays images of the home planet to comfort the people, but then shows the planet exploding. The people react with anguish, but Sandon reminds them that they are safe, exiled as they are from the solar system.

Act Two. Mima "dies" of grief, or perhaps of the same radiation that has destroyed Douris. Chefone holds the Mimarobe accountable for Mima's breakdown, and consigns him and Isagel, who represents pure thought or abstract beauty, to the brig. Daisi Doody and several others respond by performing a lascivious, life-affirming dance, while the Chief Technicians oversee a Mass of Repentance.

After two decades, Chefone gathers the people in the ship's Hall of Light Years to celebrate their journey's twentieth anniversary by launching the body of the deceased chief engineer in an Urn of Rescue. The passengers, space cadets, and a blind poetess ruminate on death, heaven, and the possibility that Chance and Miracle share a source. In the final scene, Isagel dances "the disintegration of her soul," the poetess dies, and the Mimarobe observes that the ship's inhabitants have all died, one by one. Although they ranged through the universe, they were forever immobile prisoners in Aniara. —*James Reel*

Recommended:

○ **Blomdahl: Aniara, Space Opera of 2038** / S. Westerberg (cond.), Hoel, Andenberg, Haugan, Parkman, Radiosymfonikerna / 1985 / Caprice 22016

Herbert Blomstedt

b. Jul. 11, 1927, Springfield, MA

Conductor

Herbert Thorson Blomstedt is a leading conductor, especially famed for his early twentieth century symphonic repertory. He was born in the United States of Swedish parents who moved back to Sweden in 1929. His mother was a pianist who gave him his first music lessons. He took general education courses at the University of Uppsala and music studies at the Royal College of Music in Stockholm. He went to Paris for conducting lessons with Igor Markevitch, inheriting something of that maestro's brisk, clear presentation of the music. He continued conducting studies with Jean Morel at the Juilliard School in New York and with Leonard Bernstein at the Berkshire Music Center in Tanglewood, where in 1953 he won the Koussevitzky Conducting Prize.

His professional conducting debut was the next year with the Stockholm Philharmonic. The same year, he was appointed music director with the Norrköpping Symphony Orchestra, a well-respected Swedish orchestra. In 1955, he took first prize in the Salzburg conducting competition. He remained in his position with Norrköpping through the 1961 season, following that with the post of first conductor of the Oslo Philharmonic (1962–68) and frequently conducting the Royal Danish Symphony Orchestra in Copenhagen. In 1967, he began a long tenure as music director of that orchestra until the end of the season in 1977.

In 1975, Blomstedt was invited by the musicians of the Dresden State Orchestra (Staatskapelle) to become their music director. In that position, he frequently recorded for Western companies as well as the East German state recording company, making especially notable recordings of symphonies of Nielsen and Berwald. During his ten years at the helm, he led the orchestra on well-received international tours.

He was appointed music director of the San Francisco Symphony Orchestra in 1985 and spent ten years in that position. His time there included a period when the orchestra had to be quickly rebuilt after many of its musicians were split off to form the San Francisco Performing Arts Orchestra, which plays for the opera and ballet. This reorganization took place with no appreciable drop in quality and soon the orchestra was recognized as better than ever. Blomstedt made several notable recordings with it on the London label and he remains conductor laureate of the orchestra.

In 1995, he took a two-year term as chief conductor of the NDR Symphony in Hamburg and in 1998 became music director of the Leipzig Gewandhaus Orchestra. He has guest conducted many of the world's leading orchestras and his recordings have won some of the leading prizes, including the French Grand Prix du Disque and Belgian Caecilia Prize for his San Francisco recording of Nielsen's *Fourth* and *Fifth* symphonies and a German Record Critics award for Best Recording of 1995 for Mahler's *Symphony No 2*. His Grammy Awards include Best Choral Recording for Orff's *Carmina Burana* and Brahms' *German Requiem* and Best Classical Engineered Recording for Bartók's *Concerto for Orchestra*. *—Joseph Stevenson*

Recommended:

- **Hindemith: Orchestral Works** / Blomstedt (cond.) / Decca 000201102
- **Nielsen: Symphonies 1–4** / Blomstedt (cond.), Schultz, Rasmussen, Danish RSO / 2000 / EMI 74188
- **Norgard: Luna; Symphony 3; Twilight** / Blomstedt, Joergensen, Latham-Koenig, Veto, Schultz (conds.), Rummel, Nybye, Danish RSO / 1996 / Dacapo 224041

John Blow

b. Feb. 23, 1649, Newark-on-Trent, Nottinghamshire **d.** Oct. 1, 1708, Westminster, England

Composer: Vocal

John Blow was the most important Baroque English composer before Henry Purcell. His organ compositions, court odes, songs, and single opera, *Venus and Adonis*, are his most important works.

Blow was born in February 1649 and was baptized on the 23rd of that month. He became a choirboy in the Chapel Royal at an early age and must therefore already have served in that capacity in another church, perhaps in Newark. Blow studied with the chorus master Henry Cooke, and later with Christopher Gibbons, the son of Orlando Gibbons and a composer of lesser rank. In December 1668, Blow was given the post of organist at Westminster Abbey, a prestigious position indicating his considerable keyboard skills. A month later he was taken into the royal court to serve as a performer on the virginal. His first works seem to date from this period, with the 1670 anthem, *O Lord, I Have Sinned*, for vocal soloists, chorus, and organ, perhaps his earliest surviving effort. Around this time Blow took on the young Henry Purcell as a student and was given the post of composer-in-ordinary for voices, an indication his vocal works had already found much favor.

Blow was taken into the service of the Chapel Royal in March 1674, and in July he procured a post there as children's chorus master. During this period Purcell began a more intense regimen of studies with Blow, and a friendship between the two arose. In 1674 Blow married Elizabeth Braddock. She would bear him five children, of whom two would die before reaching adulthood. Elizabeth herself lived for only nine years after their marriage. Blow was appointed organist (he was one of three) at the Chapel Royal in 1676, but despite his apparent successes and later affluence, he seems to have had some financial struggles during his married years, if one can judge by the family's modest living quarters.

During this time and until 1685—the year of James II's coronation—Blow composed most of his anthems and his opera *Venus and Adonis*. In the late 1670s he began composition of a large group of songs, which appeared in anthologies from 1679 through 1684. Blow also began writing many odes during this period. His *Begin the Song* (1684), the first of the *St. Cecilia's Day Odes*, for vocal soloists, chorus, and instrumental ensemble, is a masterpiece and one of his greatest works.

Blow continued composing at a fairly prolific rate in the latter years of the seventeenth century and garnered further posts, including master of choristers at St. Paul's Cathedral, in 1687. The death of Henry Purcell on November 21, 1695, was a devastating loss for Blow. He was moved by the event to write one of his finest masterworks in 1696, *An Ode, on the Death of Mr. Henry Purcell*, for two countertenors and two recorders.

In 1700 Blow was appointed composer of the Royal Chapel, virtually designating him England's greatest living composer. Ironically, his output slowed to a trickle in the succeeding years, and what little he did produce was not necessarily new: the 1702 anthem, *The Lord God Is a Sun and Shield*, for vocal soloists, chorus, instrumental ensemble, and organ, for instance, is based on the 1686 effort of the same title. Blow died on October 1, 1708, in London. *—Robert Cummings*

Overview of Works (1670–1702)

John Blow's professional appointments and his personal beliefs both influenced the music he composed. Blow began his musical career as a chorister in the English Royal Chapel, quickly obtaining positions as Master of the Children (on the death of his mentor Pelham Humfrey), Organist of the Chapel Royal, and eventually Composer of the King's Music. The responsibilities of these positions dictated an emphasis on music for the church, as well as frequent celebratory pieces and an undercurrent of keyboard music. Throughout his oeuvre, Blow synthesized the current styles of English, French, and Italian music; throughout, he also composed in his own idiosyncratic and daring harmonic idiom. His harmonic panache, sadly, earned Blow the deep disparagement of Charles Burney, a prominent early music historian. Later criticism, however, justly reinstated Blow's music alongside that of his better-known contemporary Henry Purcell.

Blow himself thought his most important contribution was to the church, in writing various types of anthems for the seventeenth century Anglican church. The most splendid examples are his "symphony anthems," scored for choir (the Chapel Royal) and string consort. Typically, these grandiose pieces begin with an instrumental French overture and feature careful alternation between instrumental ritornelli, choral passages, and vocal solo ensembles. Perhaps the grandest of all are the symphony anthems Blow composed for the highest occasions of state, including three coronations (James II, William and Mary, and Queen Anne) and the consecration of St. Paul's Cathedral. He also wrote significant numbers of more modest "verse" anthems without instruments, and old-style "full" anthems for choir alone, and an exceptionally large number of Services for the Anglican morning and evening worship.

Though his secular music sometimes falls below the high level of polish he reserved for the Royal Chapel's music, Blow also significantly wrote in a number of courtly genres. He composed extensively (over 100 pieces) for keyboard and wrote an influential keyboard treatise. He set over 100 secular songs, catches, and solo works, as well as 15 years' worth of court odes for New Years and royal birthdays. Last, but certainly not least, Blow wrote and produced the first true English opera, *Venus and Adonis*. The 1683 production starred the king's former mistress and their child Mary Tudor. Blow's *Venus and Adonis* expertly blended elements of Lullian French drama (the overture and dances) with the Italian cantata and the rich tradition of the English masque; it exercised a great influence on Purcell's *Dido and Aeneas*. *—Timothy Dickey*

Recommended:

- **Blow: Anthems** / Hill (cond.), Holman (cond.), Winchester Cathedral Choir, Parley of Instruments / 1995 / Hyperion 67031
- **Blow: Fairest work of happy Nature** / Ainsley, T. Roberts, Chateauneuf / 1993 / Hyperion 66646
- **Blow: Venus & Adonis** / Jacobs (cond.), Joshua, Finley, Blaze, Orch. of the Age of Enlightenment / HM 2901684

VOCAL

Ode on the Death of Mr. Henry Purcell (ca. 1695)

The commemoration of the death of a fellow creative artist by the writing of an ode was a long and well-established practice by the time of Purcell's premature death in 1695. The brilliant young master was widely mourned, and many shared the sentiments expressed in John Dryden's tribute to the composer: "So ceas'd the rival crew when Purcell came, They sung no more, or only sung his fame." Few were more affected by Purcell's than John Blow, who not only taught the youthful Purcell, but became his close friend. (Blow's esteem for Purcell was such that he resigned from the post of organist of Westminster Abbey so that it could be assumed by Purcell.) It was therefore entirely fitting that Blow would not only set Dryden's ode to music, but do so in a manner that places it among the composer's most affecting works.

Ode on the Death of Mr. Henry Purcell is scored for two male altos, accompaniment by a pair of alto recorders, viol, and bass continuo. Blow's most extended work for solo voices, it is structured as a continuous sequence of arias and duets, with a central recitative. The sense of loss reflected in the work climaxes with the eloquent setting of the final lines, "The Gods are pleas'd alone with Purcell's Layes, Nor know to mend their Choice." *—Brian Robins*

Recommended:

- **Blow: An Ode on the Death of Mr. Henry Purcell** / Lesne, Dugardin, La Canzona / 2000 / Virgin 545342
- **Blow: Ode on the Death of Mr Henry Purcell** / Deller (cond.), Deller Consort / HM 190201

Luigi Boccherini

b. Feb. 19, 1743, Lucca, Italy, **d.** May 28, 1805, Madrid, Spain

Composer: Chamber Music, Concerto

Franz Joseph Haydn may be the father of the string quartet, but Luigi Boccherini might be considered one of its uncles. Born on February 19, 1743, Boccherini was the son of a professional musician who was the first double bassist to perform solo concerts. The elder Boccherini started to give his son cello lessons when the boy was five years old. Luigi continued his studies from the age of nine with Abbé Vanucci, music director of the cathedral at San Martino. When the boy made his first public appearance it was conceded that he had already surpassed his teacher's skills. He was sent to Rome, where he trained with G. B. Costanzi, music director of St. Peter's Basilica. After one year in Rome, Luigi and his father were summoned to Vienna, where they were hired by the Imperial Theater Orchestra.

Boccherini's compositions were first published when he was 17 years old. In 1765 Boccherini and his father went to Milan, which at the time was a magnet for talented musicians. It was there that he wrote his first string quartet. In the same year, the ill health that would plague Boccherini all his life began to take its toll. The composer endured a further blow in 1766 when his father died. He formed a new partnership with the violinist Filippo Manfredi; they toured Italy in 1767 and made their way to Paris, where they became a sensation. In Paris Boccherini published a number of notable works, including a set of six string quartets. Following his successes there, Boccherini began writing and publishing prolifically.

In 1769 Boccherini and Manfredi journeyed to Spain, where the composer enjoyed great acclaim. Boccherini then took up another new genre, the string quintet. He in fact became best known for these works, written for string quartet with an additional cello. Now enjoying the benefits of a steady job, Boccherini married in 1771.

Boccherini's wife died of a stroke in 1785. That year his Spanish patron, Archbishop Don Luis, also died, leaving Boccherini without a position. He petitioned King Charles, asking to be retained in some musical position. Charles granted him a pension and assigned him various musical duties. There was an upturn in Boccherini's fortunes in 1786 when he was commissioned as "Composer of Our Chamber" by Friedrich Wilhelm, who was soon to become King of Prussia. Though he wrote most of his new music for Friedrich Wilhelm, Boccherini remained in Spain, where he wrote his only opera, a zarzuela called *La clementina*.

In 1787 Boccherini remarried. In 1796 he entered into an arrangement with publisher, composer, and piano manufacturer Ignaz Pleyel, who both praised and published Boccherini's works while cheating him of income. In February 1803, Boccherini was reported as living in "distress," but this is as likely from emotional depression as financial hardship, for in 1802 two of his daughters died from an epidemic within a few days of each other. In 1804 both his wife and his only living daughter died. It seems clear that Boccherini, although he continued to compose up to the end, had little interest in living, and died on May 28, 1805 of what was described as "pulmonary suffocation." He was buried in the Church of San Justo in Madrid. In 1927 his remains were disinterred and he was reburied in the Basilica of San Francesco in his hometown of Lucca. *—AMG*

Overview of Works (1760–1804)

One of the most important contemporaries of Haydn and Mozart, the Italian composer and cellist Luigi Boccherini (1743–1805) spent much of his life in Spain. He worked in the service of the Infante, and enjoyed the patronage of several noble families. He also, while remaining in Spain, was appointed composer to Friedrich William II, King of Prussia. Boccherini's extensive output is dominated by chamber music, in particular string quartets and string quintets; he composed over a hundred works in each of those genres alone. In the string quintets he overwhelmingly favored the form employing two violins, viola, and two cellos, unlike Mozart whose quintets are scored for two violas and one cello; Boccherini used that instrumentation in only 12 of his 125 string quintets. In the quintets employing two cellos, Boccherini frequently creates unique sonorities by writing for the first cello in a high register, at times reaching the tessitura of the violin.

Always interested in using color to expressive purpose, his scores are littered with such instructions as "amoroso" (lovingly). It is this concentration on elegance and gentle sweetness that led to the aphorism that "Boccherini is the wife of Haydn," the implication being that his music lacks the intellectual depth of the Viennese master's. It is an impression unfortunately not contradicted by the composer's most famous piece, the Minuet from his *String Quintet*, Op. 11, No. 5. This is to overlook not only the very differing character of their music, but a bittersweet ambivalence in Boccherini's music that is frequently exceptionally affecting. This quality is also apparent in Boccherini's best known sacred work, the *Stabat Mater*, G. 532 (G = Gérard, the cataloguer of Boccherini's works), a work whose gentle poignancy places it in a direct line of descent from Pergolesi's even more famous setting of the text.

In addition to his large output of chamber music, which also includes 16 sextets for various instruments, some 60 string trios, and violin and cello sonatas, Boccherini also composed 33 symphonies, four cello concertos, and a single dramatic work, *La Clementina*, G. 540—a zarzuela in two acts, first performed in Madrid in 1786. The symphonies were mostly published in sets, of which the most important is Op. 37, a group of four fine works written in 1786 and 1787. Each contains splendid examples of Boccherini's colorful orchestration, in addition to the unexpected harmonic twists which so often leave his music hovering uncertainly between major and minor modes. Also remarkable is his *Symphony in D minor*, Op. 12, No. 4 (G. 506), *"La casa del diavolo"* (The House of the Devil), an uncharacteristically stormy work employing material from Gluck's ballet *Don Juan*. Of the cello concertos, the best-known to concertgoers is that in B flat, in fact an arrangement by the nineteenth century cellist Friedrich Grützmacher that owes little to Boccherini's style. *—Brian Robins*

Recommended:

- ○ **Boccherini: Symphonies Opp. 35, 41 & 42** / Akademie für Alte Musik, Berlin / HM 1951597
- ○ **Boccherini: Concerti per violoncello** / Czarnecki (cond.), J. Berger, SW German CO, Pforzheim / EBS 6058
- ○ **Boccherini: The Guitar Quintets** / I. Brown (cond.), P. Romero, Academy of St. Martin-in-the-Fields CO / 1993 / Philips 438769
- ○ **Boccherini: Cello Sonatas Vol. 1** / C. Benda, S. Benda / 1999 / Naxos 554324
- ○ **Boccherini: Sei Sonate di Cembalo e Violino Obbligato** / Ogg, E. Moreno / 2000 / Glossa 920306
- ○ **Boccherini: Sei duetti per due violini Op 5** / Rogliano, Iannetta / Tactus 740204

CHAMBER MUSIC

Cello Sonata in A major, G. 4

Boccherini's cello sonatas are not mentioned in the catalog he kept of his own compositions. It has been speculated that this was because he may never have intended them to be published, viewing them either as immature works (they were written sometime before he was 25) or as too difficult for amateur performers. It is uncertain if the manuscripts are autographs, but it is certain that the music is his and that he performed them in his concerts. They are all are scored for cello and basso, not a full continuo, because there is no figured bass in the score, but probably another string instrument. Most modern performances do, however, fill this out like a traditional basso continuo.

The *Sonata in A major*, G. 4, has a peculiar and confusing history, which accounts for the various forms found in performances and recordings. It is one of a set of six sonatas that was published (unauthorized by Boccherini) three times in London between 1770 and 1816, and in more modern editions, some of which have a piano part added, not to mention the versions transcribed for violin. All the editions of this sonata place the slow movement first, giving the order Adagio-Allegro-Affetuoso, although it is in the manuscript traditionally with a fast-slow-fast structure. One particular edition has only the first two movements, which is why some recordings feature two movements and some, three. And finally, to confuse things further, there is a manuscript version that has an entirely different Allegro movement (and which does place the Adagio first). The Allegro that is normally used in performance is based on an aria, *Se d'un amor tiranno*, G. 557, for soprano and cello, which Boccherini composed for Metastasio's *Artaserse*. (The same aria is used again in Boccherini's *Sextet for flute and strings*, Op. 16/6.) It is a Baroque-sounding song, about the constancy of love, filled with florid and virtuosic passages, played in the upper register of the cello. The Adagio is also very lyrical and organic in its ornamentation and in the way phrases are linked together. The final Affetuoso is a minuet, elegantly stated with the soloist at times echoing itself, using a drone, or throwing off a showy fillip. Overall, the sonata is characteristic of the *Empfindsamkeit* fashion of the day. *—Patsy Morita*

Recommended:

- ○ **Boccherini: String Quintets Op 29; Cello Sonatas** / Bylsma, W. Kuijken, H. Smith / 1997 / Seon 63190
- ○ **Boccherini: Cello Sonatas Vol. 1** / C. Benda, S. Benda / 1999 / Naxos 554324

Guitar Quintet in E major, G. 446 (1798)

It may seem inevitable that the prolific Luigi Boccherini, an Italian working in Spain and thus drawing inspiration from two guitar-crazed countries, would eventually write music for the guitar. And so he did, near the end of his career, but his eight surviving guitar quintets (the numbering goes up to nine, but *No. 8* has been lost) are merely afterthoughts, transcriptions of earlier non-guitar works. His *Guitar Quintet No. 2* is a straightforward arrangement of his *Piano Quintet No. 4*, Op. 57, yet it is perfectly idiomatic for the guitar. The opening movement, Maestoso assai, keeps the guitar well-integrated into the instrumental texture, providing a rippling undercurrent for a musical argument dominated by the first violin. A noble, processional figure launches the sonata-form movement that subjects its pleasant but not especially memorable themes to an array of unexpected modulations. In the second movement, an Adagio section leads from what initially seems to be a dotted rhythm Baroque "ouverture" into a sweetly lyrical passage; this is all a set-up for the main Allegretto, which skips and trills from the major mode to the minor and back again without casting any deep shadows along the way. The finale is a minuet that Boccherini designated "Polacca," because of the outer sections' eastern European syncopations and readiness to slip between major and minor. The central section initially seems like more generic, Classical-era minuet material, but before this has a chance to develop, the dark-hued syncopations take over, smoothly leading back into the A-section music. *—James Reel*

Recommended:

- ○ **Boccherini: Guitar Quintets, Vol. 2** / R. Savino, Artaria Quartet / 1991 / HM Classical Express 3957039

- ○ **Boccherini: Quintets with Guitar I-VI** / J. Lindberg, Drottningholm Baroque Ens. / 1992 / Bis 597
- ○ **Boccherini: The Guitar Quintets** / I. Brown (cond.), P. Romero, Academy of St. Martin-in-the-Fields CO / 1993 / Philips 438769

Guitar Quintet in D major ("Fandango"), G. 448 (1798)

This quintet for guitar and string quartet is one of a dozen that Boccherini arranged from earlier works in 1798 and 1799 for François de Borgia, Marquis of Benavente. The earlier works in this instance are the *String Quintet in D major,* Op. 10/6 (G. 270) of 1771 and the *String Quintet in D major,* Op. 40/2 (G. 341) of 1788. The opening two movements of the guitar quintet come from the opening movements of the earlier string quintet. The first, Pastorale, features muted strings playing a delicate, sweet, flowing melody with the guitar rippling along with them. The livelier second movement, Allegro maestoso, gives the guitar a secondary role, while the cello, Boccherini's own instrument, takes the lead, contrasting soloistic outbursts with more lyrical passages. The remainder of the quintet is taken from the later *String Quintet* and is not really two separate movements, but an introduction marked Grave assai and a Fandango, from which the quintet takes its nickname. The introduction is serious, beginning in the major mode, the same as the first two movements, but it ends in the minor, the mode of the final dance. The Spanish dance's rhythm repeats continually as the instruments trade the melody, the complexity of layers builds, and the speed gradually increases. Halfway through, Boccherini throws in the sistrum and castanets to provide percussive accents as the players rush toward the end. *—Patsy Morita*

Recommended:

- ○ **Boccherini: Guitar Quintets Vol. 1** / R. Savino, Artaria Quartet / HM 3957026
- ○ **Boccherini: Quintets with Guitar I-VI** / J. Lindberg, Drottingholm Baroque Ens. / 1992 / Bis 597
- ○ **Boccherini: The Guitar Quintets** / I. Brown (cond.), P. Romero, Academy of St. Martin-in-the-Fields CO / 1993 / Philips 438769

Guitar Quintet in C major ("La Ritirata di Madrid"), G. 453 (1798)

Boccherini's quintets for guitar and strings originally existed in two separate sets of six pieces. The first set exists in its entirety today, but unfortunately, only two of the second set have survived. Of the two remaining pieces, the *Quintet No. 9 in C major,* titled "La Ritirata di Madrid," was written late in the composer's career, probably around 1798. This piece stands out for its imaginative and pictorial fourth movement, which is based on Madrid, Boccherini's home during much of his life.

The first movement of the *Quintet No. 9,* Allegro Maestoso assai, is built on a march-like melody in C major that is good-natured and festive. It contains frequent contrasts between the playful first theme and more lyrical later themes. The guitar plays a virtuosic role, as do the first violin and the cello. The cello soars into the upper register at several points, which would seem unusual were it not for the fact that Boccherini himself was a virtuoso cellist. The various instruments are really of equal importance, because the melody (often heard in the violin or cello) is supported by active and playful inner parts. Boccherini uses syncopation throughout, which is a trademark of his style and helps sustain the energy and motion throughout this relatively long movement.

The second movement, Andantino, begins in the morose-sounding key of A minor and moves quickly back to C major. This alternation between major and minor creates a duel of sorts between the musical representations of joy and sorrow. Even the extensive cello solo that spends most of its time in major is eventually pulled into minor. A rhythmic pulse in the minor sections creates an undercurrent that is almost like a heartbeat. Toward the end of piece, the opening minor theme returns and comes to rest in the final key of A minor.

The carefree energy and playfulness of the third movement, Allegretto, exist in direct contrast to the sorrow of the previous movement. Played by the guitar and passed to the violin, the main theme dances along, complemented by light offbeats in the other voices. The simple melodies become more elaborate with Boccherini's use of trills and other ornamentation. The middle of the movement takes a foray into minor, echoing the mood of the previous movement, but this section is somewhat brief and moves back into the playful first theme to finish.

"La Ritirata di Madrid" (Retreat From Madrid) is the final movement, and is a theme and set of variations that Boccherini used in several of his earlier chamber works, including the *Piano Quintet,* Op. 57/6. Boccherini's intent was to create the image of a military troop approaching and retreating from Madrid. The movement opens at a very soft dynamic level and is almost imperceptible to the listener. The theme is simple, and rhythmically it resembles a military march, evoking memories of the march-like quality of the first movement. In the 11 variations that follow, each one grows slightly in dynamic level until the middle of the movement, Variation 6, where it reaches a dynamic high point. Boccherini's instructions for this variation are to imitate a drum, which the guitar does by strumming very strong rhythmic chords. The other instruments have fast, excited moving notes and the effect is that of a military parade passing by. From this midpoint, each of the following variations drops in volume until the music is once again imperceptible, evoking the image of the troop retreating and finally fading away in the distance. *—Emily Stoops*

Recommended:

- ○ **Boccherini: Guitar Quintets** / R. Savino, Artaria Quartet / 2002 / HM Classical Express 3957069
- ○ **Boccherini: The Guitar Quintets** / I. Brown (cond.), P. Romero, Academy of St. Martin-in-the-Fields / 1993 / Philips 438769

String Quintet (Quintettino) in C major ("La musica notturna delle strade di Madrid"), G. 324

This quintet is both very much a characteristic piece of Boccherini and at the same time not a characteristic piece. Its title is usually translated as "Night Music in the Streets of Madrid," but it really is a musical representation of life in Madrid's evenings in Boccherini's day, quoting music of the locals and also replicating other sounds with music. He often incorporated Spanish musical idioms into his own music, using the fandango and other dances in other works, and he even composed musical paintings, such as in the *String Quintet,* Op. 11, *No. 6 "The Aviary."* Here, each movement of this quintet represents a different scene, and none really have a traditional Classical-period form, as his other quintets do. The work is so unusual that Boccherini himself did not want it published, feeling that it would be incomprehensible to anyone not familiar with the city life of Madrid. The opening movement is in two sections: "Ave Maria" and "Minuetto di Ciechi." The "Ave Maria" opens with quiet pizzicatos representing the tolling of church bells, followed by a monotone monolog by the first violin. The"Minuet of the Blind" features the cellos being strummed like guitars to accompany the street singer. The second movement, "Rosario," is a prayerful duet, punctuated by faint, bell-like pizzicatos from the second violin. This is interrupted by a fanfare-like passage for the full quintet. The prayer is restated, the first cello joining in with a more ornamented line, almost like the ancient florid organum. The fanfare is heard again, followed by the final verse of the prayer. The third movement is known by several names: "Passacalle," "Los Manolos," or "I spagnoli si divertono per la strade." It again uses the instruments as guitars to accompany the animated dance melody of the cello. It also features an interlude with one of the violins playing the harmony theme in arpeggios. The interlude is repeated at the end of the movement, fading off into the distance, and followed by the violin monolog heard in the first movement. Finally, the night watch is heard passing by, a light march over a drone that also fades away as they go on their rounds. The melody of this movement was re-used by Boccherini for variations in the *Guitar Quintet,* G. 453. The entire quintet was orchestrated in 1903 by Max Schoenherr. *—Patsy Morita*

Recommended:

- ○ **Hidden Masterpieces of the Baroque Vol. 2** / N. Jenkins, Clarion Music Society / Newport Classic 60076
- ○ **Respighi: Fontane di Roma; Pini di Roma; Antiche Danze ed Arie Suite III** / Karajan (cond.), Berlin PO / 1997 / DG 449724

String Quintet in E major, G. 275 (1771)

Boccherini began writing string quintets after he became court composer in Aranjuez for Don Luis, the brother of King Carlos III of Spain. Don Luis also employed the Font String Quartet, a father and three sons, whom Boccherini would join as a second cello. Having an extra cello allowed him to use the cello as more than just the traditional continuo bass line. He used both cellos more fully, as much as part of the melody and harmony as the violins and viola. His first set of six quintets was written in 1771 as his Op. 11. It was published four years later, which was when it was also given the Op. 13 designation. This final quintet in E major from the set includes Boccherini's most famous melody, the Minuet. The Amoroso that opens the quintet is not a typical first movement for the period. It is not in the sonata-allegro form, and it is slower than Allegro, being marked Andantino mosso. It is a smooth, luxurious dialogue between the muted instruments. Often the two violins are paired, as are the viola and first cello, moving in parallel thirds over a gently pulsing bass. Approximately two-thirds of the way through there is a rapid, Italianate duet between the cellos, a brief interlude in the otherwise serene movement. The Allegro con spirito that follows is more like what is traditionally expected as a first movement. In true sonata form, it uses simple harmonies and call and response between instruments to create a lively, almost celebratory or regal disposition. Third is the famous Minuet, with examples of all Boccherini's favorite melodic tricks: repetition of short motives, triad or scalar figures, rhythmic symmetry, and delicate ornaments. The violins play with mutes on, while the other instruments play pizzicato. The second violin provides the pulse under the first violin's syncopated melody. In the Trio section, scalar figures make up the melody, which is passed between all the instruments, still with the offbeat feel of the Minuet. The rondo finale has a main subject in much the same spirit as the second movement. During the intervening episodes, all the performers have a chance to use trills, double stops, and more to show off their skills. The episodes also provide Boccherini the opportunity to more fully explore shifts in tonality. The final statement of the theme is played resolutely, ending with a decisive series of chords. *—Patsy Morita*

Recommended:

- ○ **Boccherini: Quintetti per archi** / Quintetto Boccherini / 1997 / Ensayo 9703
- ○ **Boccherini: Cello Quintets** / R. Lester, Vanbrugh Quartet / Hyperion 67287

CONCERTO

Cello Concerto in B flat major, G. 482 (1770–1772)

One of the greatest cellists of the eighteenth century, Boccherini was also a prolific composer, who masterfully incorporated the cello into works representing genres which has traditionally used the cello for harmonic support. While some of Boccherini's cello concertos remained within the technical confines of the late Baroque idiom, several works fully exploit the instrument's technical and sonic capabilities, featuring double stops, the thumb position, and brilliant runs in the highest register. This work is Boccherini's most famous concerto, and it is easy to understand why this work is so popular when one thinks of the sheer beauty of the music. Opening with a concisely effective orchestral introduction, the first movement, with its richly expressive themes, rewards the soloist with a score in which virtuosity is clearly sublimated to create a musical narrative of exceptional elegance and charm. Boccherini allows the soloist to display a rich variety of sonorities, including the cello's entrance chord, as well as the mellifluous legato arpeggiation figure centered on a ostinato open A string. A certain melancholy aura that haunts the first movement blossoms into a poetically phrased lament in the extraordinary second movement. Dispelling the sadness of the second movement, the final movement celebrates the spirit of play, inviting the soloist to delight in a manifestation of lightness and pure energy.

Interestingly, however, this concerto owes much to the nineteenth century German cellist Friedrich Grützmacher, who used the original manuscript to create what some scholars regard as a profoundly altered work in 1895. The first and third movements of this concerto as we know it are, in fact, Grützmacher's amalgamation of of Boccherini's original version and the *Cello Sonata in B flat major*, G. 565. Significantly, the second movement of Grützmacher's version comes from the second movement, without the ritornello, of Boccherini's *Cello Concerto in G major*, G. 480. The ritornello that Grützmacher includes in this movement is of mysterious origin, possibly his own work. While the musical ideas in this work are undoubtedly Boccherini's, the work may owe much of its popularity to Grützmacher's creative orchestration and phrasing. *—AMG*

Recommended:

- ○ **Boccherini: Cello Concertos; Cello Sonatas** / Kangas (cond.), Isserlis, Ostrobothnian CO / 1991 / Virgin 59015
- ○ **Boccherini: Concerti per Violoncello** / Czarnecki (cond.), J. Berger, SW German CO Pforzheim / EBS 6058
- ○ **Boccherini: Concertos pour Violoncello; Aria Accademica** / C. Coin (cond.), Ensemble Baroque de Limoges / 1993 / Astrée 8517
- ○ **János Starker: Artist Profile** / Starker, Giulini (cond.), London Philharmonia Orch. / 1996 / EMI 68745

Andrea Bocelli

b. Sep. 22, 1958, Lajatico, Tuscany, Italy
Tenor

Andrea Bocelli has been called "the fourth tenor"; the blind, Tuscan-born, vocalist has emerged as one of the most exciting voices in the arena of light classical vocals and has made inroads into the world of opera as well. His participation in Pavarotti's 1992 hit *Miserere* album and Zucchero Fornaciari's 1993 world tour brought him international attention. Bocelli has been most successful as a pop ballad singer, having recorded duets with Celine Dion, Sarah Brightman, and Eros Ramazzotti. Al Jarreau, who sang with Bocelli during "The Night Of Proms" in November 1995, praised Bocelli with these words: "I have had the honor to sing with the most beautiful voice in the world."

Bocelli grew up on farm in Lajatico, a rural village in Tuscany. Beginning piano lessons at the age of six, he later added flute and saxophone to his talents. Born with poor eyesight, he became totally blind at the age of 12 following a soccer accident. Despite his obvious musical talents, Bocelli did not consider a career in music until he had studied law at the University of Pisa and had earned a Doctor of Law degree. Inspired to pursue music, he studied with the famed tenor Franco Corelli, supporting himself by peforming in piano bars.

Bocelli's first break as a singer came in 1992 when Fornaciari auditioned tenors to record a demo tape of *Miserere*, which he had co-written with Bono of the Irish rock group U2. Successfully passing the audition, Bocelli recorded the tune as a duet with Pavarotti. After touring with Fornaciari in 1993, Bocelli performed as a guest star in the Pavarotti International festival held in Modena in September 1994. In addition to performing solo and in a duet with Pavarotti, Bocelli sang with Bryan Adams, Andreas Vollenweider, and Nancy Gustavsson. In November 1995, Bocelli toured Holland, Belgium, Germany, Spain, and France on the pop "Night of Proms" bill, which also featured Al Jarreau, Bryan Ferry, Roger Hodgson of Supertramp, and John Miles.

Bocelli's first two albums—1994's *Andrea Bocelli* and 1996's *Bocelli*—showcased his operatic singing. His third effort, *Viaggio Italiano* (Italian Journey), featured famous arias and traditional songs from Naples. Although released only in Italy, the album sold more than 300,000 copies. With his fourth album, *Romanza*, released in 1997, Bocelli turned to pop music. The album included the hit "Time To Say Goodbye," recorded as a duet with Sarah Brightman. Bocelli continued to focus on pop balladry with his fifth album, *Sogno*, released in 1999, which featured a duet with Celine Dion on the David Foster and Carole Bayer Sager-penned tune, "The Prayer"; it sold more than ten million copies, received a Golden Globe award and led to Bocelli being nominated for a Grammy as best new artist.

The early 2000s saw Bocelli making an attempt to win credibility in the world of mainstream opera, touring in a series of operatic appearances and releasing the album *Verdi* and taking lead roles in recorded versions of *Tosca*, *La bohème*, and *Il trovatore*. Some opera fans pointed to deficiencies in his partially microphone-formed technique, while others lauded his ability to bring new audiences to opera. Neither the admirers nor the detractors could ignore the sheer charisma that drew ordinary listeners to this genuine, unassuming vocal star. *—Craig Harris*

Recommended:

- ○ **Romanza** / Groslot (cond.), Bocelli, Corti, Malavasi, Amoruso, etc. / 1996 / Philips 539207
- ○ **Verdi** / Mehta (cond.), Bocelli, Israel PO / 2000 / Philips 464600
- ○ **Verdi: Il Trovatore** / Mercurio (cond.), Bocelli, Colombara, Villarroel, Zaremba, etc., Orchestra del Teatro Massimo / 2004 / Decca 000262902

Karl Böhm

b. Aug. 28, 1894, Graz, Austria, **d.** Aug. 14, 1981, Salzburg, Austria
Conductor

Karl Böhm was one of the greatest conductors of the twentieth century in the German tradition. He studied music as a child and continued to work and study in music while serving in the Austrian Army during World War I—and while completing a doctorate in law. He coached singers at the Graz Opera and was permitted to conduct a performance of Nessler's *Der Trompeter von Sackingen*. He never had conducting lessons, but made close studies of the work of both Bruno Walter and Carl Muck.

In 1921 he was hired by the Bavarian State Opera in Munich, and then he became Generalmusikdirektor in both Darmstadt (1927) and Hamburg (1931–33). He gained a reputation for his fine performances of Mozart, Wagner, and Richard Strauss, as well as his championing of modern German music, including operas by Krenek and Berg. Böhm debuted in Vienna in 1933, leading Wagner's *Tristan und Isolde*. In 1934 he became Director of the Dresden State Opera, Richard Strauss's favorite theater. There, Böhm conducted premieres of Strauss's *Die schweigsame Frau* (1935) and *Dafne* (1938). He remained at the helm in Dresden through 1943, at which point he became director of the Vienna State Opera (1943–45). Richard Strauss was not in official favor, and Joseph Goebbels banned any recognition of the great composer's 80th birthday in 1944. However, Böhm participated in a de facto observance, as a large number of Strauss's orchestral and operatic works "just happened" to be played about the time of the birthday.

After the war, Böhm was forbidden to perform until he underwent "de-Nazification," a procedure whereby prominent Austro-Germans were investigated for complicity in Nazi crimes. He was eventually cleared of any suspicion, and was permitted to resume work in 1947.

Böhm oversaw the German repertory at the Teatro Colón in Buenos Aires (1950–53), and again served as director of the Vienna State Opera (1954–56). He debuted in the USA at New York's Metropolitan Opera with Mozart's *Don Giovanni* in 1957, and took prominent German orchestras and opera companies on tour. The Vienna Philharmonic bestowed on him the title "Ehrendirigent," and he was proclaimed Generalmusikdirector of Austria. He left a legacy of many great recordings, including a complete Wagner *Ring* cycle considered by many critics to be the best. While his Wagner and Strauss were sumptuously Romantic, his Mozart was scrupulously Classical in approach. *—Joseph Stevenson*

Recommended:

- ○ **Great Conductors of the 20th Century** / Bohm (cond.) / 2003 / EMI 75944
- ○ **Böhm: Maestro Decente, Disc 1** / Bohm (cond.) / 2002 / Documents 220825-303
- ○ **Mozart: Symphonies 40 & 41** / Bohm (cond.), Berlin PO / DG 469620

François-Adrien Boieldieu

b. Dec. 16, 1775, Rouen, France, **d.** Oct. 8, 1834, Jarcy, France
Composer: Opera, Concerto

Perhaps the most significant composer in France in the early decades of the nineteenth century, François-Adrien Boieldieu wrote comic operas that were among the best-known and most-performed of his day. His felicitous melodic sense led his contemporaries to dub him "the French Mozart."

Boieldieu's first music teacher was Urbain Cordonnier, the children's choirmaster at Rouen Cathedral. Even before he learned to read music, Boieldieu was taking part in church music performances, learning the music by ear. Later Boieldieu studied organ and piano with Charles Broche. In 1791, he was appointed organist at the church of St. André in Rouen. At about this time he also started composing, and in 1793 his first opera *La fille coupable*—with a libretto by his father—was performed in Rouen. Before long he was also appearing as a pianist, including some of his own works in his programs.

In the summer of 1796 Boieldieu moved to Paris, where he wrote several well-received operas over the next few years, including his first great success *Le Calife de Bagdad* (1800). Legend has it that Luigi Cherubini, one of the most influential musicians of that time, heard *Le Calife de Bagdad* and, thinking its composer musically ignorant, offered Boieldieu music lessons.

In 1802 Boieldieu married dancer Clotilde Mafleurai. The marriage fell apart after just a few months, and Boieldieu left Paris for Russia in 1803, taking a post as conductor of the Imperial Opera. (Boieldieu remained separated from Clotilde until her death in 1827, at which point he married the singer Jeanne Phillis-Bertin, with whom he had been carrying on a long-standing affair.)

Boieldieu's contract in Russia called for him to write three operas a year. He didn't quite live up to that expectation, but during his seven years in Russia he managed to produce ten operas. On his return to France in 1811, Boieldieu composed his opera *Jean de Paris* (1812), which reestablished his fame with the Paris audience. Three years later he was appointed court composer and accompanist, and in 1817 he took over Étienne Nicolas Méhul's position as professor of composition at the Paris Conservatoire, a post he held until 1826.

In the late 1810s and early 1820s Boieldieu didn't compose much due to ill health, but he was named a Chevalier of the Legion of Honor in 1821. During that time, the operas of Gioacchino Rossini became the rage in Paris. Rossini himself moved to Paris in 1823, and much French music of that time took on elements of the Rossini sound. Remaining true to his own style, Boieldieu composed what is perhaps his masterpiece, *La dame blanche* (1825), as a kind of response to the Rossini enthusiasm. *La dame blanche* was a massive success, in France and internationally, and remained in the European repertoire for many decades. Boieldieu's next opera, *Les deux nuits* (1829), didn't fare so well.

By this time, he was much afflicted by health problems, particularly the consumptive laryngitis which led to the loss of his voice. He also had financial problems, but eventually received a pension from the French government. Unable to compose, Boieldieu turned to painting; some of his paintings still can be seen at the Rouen Museum. Five days after his death in 1834, Boieldieu was given a state funeral, and was buried in the cemetery in Rouen. *—Chris Morrison*

OPERA

La Dame Blanche (1825)

La Dame Blanche (The White Lady) was among the most popular French comic operas of the nineteenth century; it had over 1,000 performances at Paris' *Opéra-Comique* alone. Although it has since faded into the annals of operatic history, it shows its composer, Adrien Boieldieu and the very genre it inhabits at their best. *La Dame Blanche* also demonstrates that even such a staunchly French composer as Boieldieu—who struggled to uphold traditional French musical values against the rising tide of Italian opera—was unable to resist the dramatic and musical appeal of Italian forms, especially in his writing for vocal ensembles. Also notable are the many folk-like tunes and dances that allude to the story's Scottish setting.

Eugène Scribe's libretto for *La Dame Blanche* was drawn from three separate novels of Sir Walter Scott: *Guy Mannering, The Monastery,* and *The Abbott.* The merging of these three sources into a unified dramatic structure marks this as one of Scribe's finer efforts. The plot revolves around a struggle for ownership of a Scottish castle, the rightful owners of which, the Count and Countess Avenel, are both deceased; their opportunistic and greedy steward attempts to claim the castle, and the noble title, for himself, but he is opposed by the Count and Countesses orphan daughter, who invokes the legend of the White Lady, the Avenel's guardian spirit, in her plans. In the process, Anna is reunited with her long-lost sweetheart, the unknowing rightful heir to the title and castle, Julien (introduced as George Brown, a military officer). Scribe's treatment of the haunting White Lady subject matter was especially ripe for musical invention, and is surely one of the primary reasons for the opera's success.

Boieldieu's score is notable for a group of particularly memorable numbers—especially the "Ballad of the White Lady," sung by the peasant girl, Jenny, in the first act, and the young Brown's first aria. However, neither of these surpasses the skill, wit, and thorough inventiveness of the central auction scene, during which the rival parties bid for the castle. More than any other number in the opera, it betrays Boieldieu's digestion of the best qualities of Rossini and thge other Italians, for whom the climactic ensemble was a dramatic mainstay. *—AMG*

Synopsis:

In the Scottish highlands lies a village overshadowed by the castle of the Count of Avenel. But there is no count; the heir to the title disappeared mysteriously as a child some years before. It's possible that the rightful heir will someday return, but meanwhile the estate is in danger of falling into the hands of its unpleasant steward.

Act One. The villagers gather for a baptism, celebrating even though the ceremony can't take place; the public official who was to act as godfather has fallen ill. A stranger named Georges Brown ambles onto the scene, noting that he is a royal officer, and sings of the joys of being a soldier. A villager named Jenny realizes that he is qualified to serve as godfather for the baptism; Georges agrees to her request, to the delight of the villagers. Amid the festivities, Jenny sings a song about La Dame Blanche, or the White Lady, an unearthly but beneficent creature who haunts the castle and protects women from unfaithful husbands and errant lovers. Georges thinks this just an amusing story, but the villagers, especially Jenny's husband, are unnerved by it. Alone, Jenny complains to Georges that her husband is chronically afraid, and praises Georges' bravery. Georges claims to feel fear in the presence of pretty women, and solicits a fortifying kiss from Jenny. He then offers to intercede for Dikson, a tenant farmer on the castle estate who has been summoned to a meeting with the White Lady.

Act Two. Gaveston, steward of the estate of the missing Count Avenel, plots to obtain the castle for himself in an upcoming auction. Anna, his ward, opposes this plan. Georges arrives at midnight; finding himself alone in a part of the castle, he implores the White Lady to appear, vowing to work in her best interests. It's Anna who actually appears, persuading Georges to act on her behalf to interfere in Gaveston's nefarious schemes (presumably she had planned to ask this of Dikson). The next day, all assemble for the auction. Amid great excitement among the crowd, Georges outbids Gaveston for the estate, Anna/the White Lady having promised to provide him the necessary 100,000 francs.

Act Three. Anna is rejoicing over this turn of events, and the tenant farmers are paying homage to their new landlord. Anna's anticipation of moving into the castle with Georges—having found money to pay for the property in an Avenel treasure chest—is dashed by news from Marguerite, a retainer of the noble family, that the long-lost young count Julien is about to return and take charge. Before long, Georges is threatened with arrest if he doesn't come through with full payment for the estate; just in time Anna arrives, dressed as the White Lady, with the funds. Furious, Gaveston rips off the White Lady's veil, revealing Anna's identity. But it soon also becomes clear that Georges and Julien are one and the same. The young count takes his place as Avenel heir, simultaneously taking Anna as his bride. *—James Reel*

Recommended:

○ **Boieldieu: La Dame Blanche** / Minkowski (cond.), R. Blake, Massis, Delunsch, Fouchecourt, Ens. Orch. de Paris / 1997 / EMI 556355

CONCERTO

Harp Concerto, Op. 77 (1801)

Boieldieu's output of instrumental music was initially meager, and virtually ceased once he became one of the most popular opera composers in Paris, starting around 1797 (when he was only 22 years old). In his youth, he did write enough piano pieces to get himself appointed professor of piano at the new Paris Conservatory in 1798, and into the very beginning of the nineteenth century he also wrote regularly for the harp; when he moved from Rouen to Paris in 1795, he roomed with Sebastian Erard, the inventor of the double-action harp. Boieldieu's *Harp Concerto in C,* Op. 77, also redundantly known as *Concerto in Three Tempi,* is an appealing, tuneful work that retains a firm if not central place in the harp repertory.

The first movement, Allegro brillante, is about as long as the next two combined. It opens with a festive and somewhat ceremonial fast theme, which is followed by a flowing but restless melody and some busy, more generic material, all in the late Classical style employed in the 1790s with more individuality by the likes of Mozart and Beethoven. After the orchestra's presentation of the themes, the harp takes them up with a great deal of passagework, several trills, and a few glissandos tossed in for "brillante" effect. The soloist remains in the forefront for the remainder of the movement, with the orchestra providing rudimentary accompaniment and the occasional, requisite tutti declamation. The solo writing is especially intricate through much of the development section, but the harpist is denied a cadenza here.

The brief second movement, marked either Andante lento or Largo, depending on the edition, begins with an imposing, almost threatening minor-mode statement by the orchestra, with the harp then taking up a plaintive melody. The movement's second section is a sad but determined air that wouldn't be out of place in one of Boieldieu's operas. A transition leads directly into the final movement, aptly designated Allegro agitato. It's a rondo bouncing off an urgent, hyperactive primary theme. The intervening episodes become increasingly extroverted and brighter, with a brief, darkly sparkling cadenza just before the main theme's first return and another glissando-graced little cadenza just before the final episode. *—James Reel*

Recommended:

○ **Romantic Harp Concertos** / Rampal (cond.), Nordmann, Franz Liszt CO / 1995 / Sony 58919

○ **Harp Concertos: Handel, Boieldieu & Dittersdorf** / Brown (cond.), M. Robles, Academy of St. Martin-in-the-Fields / 1990 / London 425723

Arrigo Boito

b. Feb. 4, 1842, Padua, Italy, **d.** Jun. 10, 1918, Milan, Italy

Composer: Opera

Poet, novelist, and composer, Boito is known for the single opera he completed, *Mefistofele.* Like Rossini, who wrote three dozen operas by his mid-thirties and spent the next 40 years of his life unable or unwilling to complete another, Boito underwent some kind of crisis early, and worked for 54 years, unsuccessfully, at completing his second opera.

Arrigo Boito was born Enrico Boito in Padua, Italy, on February 24, 1842. His father was Silvestro Boito, a minor painter, and his mother was Josephine Radolinska, a Polish noblewoman. Silvestro abandoned the family while his son was still a small boy. When Enrico showed musical ability, his mother encouraged it, then, partly by telling her tale of poverty and desertion, managed to get him into the Milan Conservatory on scholarship. As a student at the Milan Conservatory, Boito was awarded a stipend after winning composition prizes that enabled him to travel and study abroad for two years. He took advantage of the prize to visit Poland, his mother's birthplace, as well as England, Germany, and France. He was much impressed during these sojourns with the dramatic power of the operas of Beethoven and especially of Wagner. Boito had a brilliant and wide-ranging mind, with a devouring appetite for classical literature. He changed his name to Arrigo about the time he received a scholarship for study in Paris. He wrote numerous cantatas, some operas, and other music, and he conceived plans for operas based on Nero and Goethe's Faust.

In 1868 he premiered his *Mefistofele* at La Scala. The highly literary and literate Boito also wrote the work's libretto. At its premiere performance (more than six hours long), a pious contingent, objecting to the thematic modernism of Boito's version of the Faust legend, demonstrated angrily. After the second performance was likewise ill-received, Boito withdrew the opera and undertook modifications to appease criticism. *Mefistofele* has become a staple of the repertoire, one of the most exciting and compelling of all operas. Later in life he came close to completing another opera, *Nerone.* The conductor Toscanini championed the work, but it has not found a secure foothold in the repertory. Dry as his font of musical inspiration became, Boito nevertheless retained his literary powers in full. He wrote librettos for Ponchielli's *La Gioconda* and for Verdi's great late-life Shakespearean operas, *Falstaff* and *Othello.* Boito's poetry has never fallen out of favor, and his letters reveal unusual gifts as well. Seldom, if ever, has anyone else secured a seemingly imperishable niche in musical history with so little output. *—Douglas Purl*

OPERA

Mefistofele (1868; revised 1875)

Arrigo Boito was an author and poet of the nineteenth century known for his literary works, which included the librettos to Verdi's *Otello* and *Falstaff.* He was also a composer, and initially one of the few admirers of Richard Wagner on the Italian operatic scene. For the opera *Mefistofele,* Boito both wrote the libretto and composed the score—the first time that had happened at La Scala. His initial conception was highly ambitious; he hoped to change the face of Italian opera forever. His was one of the many musical works of the time which sought to capture the essence of Goethe's *Faust* on the operatic stage. Perhaps more than any other musician of the day, Boito understood the spirit of Goethe's text, and he remains quite true to much of it throughout the opera. The premiere took place on March 5, 1868 at Milan's Teatro alla Scala. It was not well received by the conservative Milanese public, who had been given advance notice in the press that Boito hoped to change Italian opera traditions. They loved the opening, which is a poetic prologue set in heaven, and contrasts demonic declamatory writing for Mefistofele with the hymn-like intoning of the heavenly hosts. However, the opera was unwieldy in its first version; after the prologue came five more monumental acts. The exhausted audience rejected it almost completely.

For the revival of his opera at Bologna's Teatro Communale in 1875, Boito completely rewrote the score. The length of the work was greatly reduced and much of the music changed. Anything that had offended the audience, such as the battle symphony and the emperor's court scene, was completely cut. Some of the more massive numbers were given smaller settings, and the amount of dialogue was lessened. The second performance also had the advantage of a very fine cast; the initial cast at La Scala hadn't been equal to the complexities of Boito's opera. But the singers in Bologna triumphed, and the public applauded the new work. A year later, Boito made further revisions, and it is this version which is usually performed and considered the definitive work. *Mefistofele* was often revived in the twentieth century (memorably with Caruso and Chaliapin in 1901), and it has become a part of the standard operatic repertoire.

The original version of the opera, although massive, was carefully conceived, and contains many structural and musical unifying elements. The heavenly chorus of the opening prologue returns both at the prison scene, the highlight of the opera, and at the close, as Faust is redeemed. Boito transforms entire pieces into new, contrasting numbers, in order to emphasize changes of contexts and highlight dramatic tensions in the story. He also organizes the entire structure through his selection of keys for different emotional contexts. Overall, though there are many Germanic touches, evoking Beethoven as well as Wagner, it is the French models of Meyerbeer that define the music more strongly. Boito's *Mefistofele,* although lesser in stature than Berlioz's *Damnation of Faust* and less popular than Gounod's version of the tale, is probably the most faithful to the original conception of Goethe's poetics. *—Rita Laurance*

Synopsis:

Prologue—Heaven. The opera opens with music for instruments and three choruses: the Cherubim, the Celestial Host, and the Chorus Mysticus (the choruses replace the words of God in Goethe's original text). The first voices we hear are those of the Celestial host as they intone a hymn of praise to the Lord: "Ave Signor degli angeli e dei santi!" (Hail Lord of angels and of saints). Mephistopheles appears. Though Mephistopheles, too, begins with the words "Ave Signor," the tone of his address clearly comes through in his sardonic melody. After all, he is not of the same ilk as the Celestial Host, and, seemingly proud of this, he apologizes for his "lowly idiom." Mephistopheles goes on to complain that the human race has become so base and idiotic that he no longer derives any pleasure from tempting any of them—it is simply too easy. The Chorus Mysticus asks whether he knows Faust. He does, and he wagers that he will ensnare the "strange madman." The bet is accepted. The appearance of the Cherubim, whom Mephistopheles loathes, prompts his disappearance (indeed, the sight of thousands of winged babies would frighten even the bravest of souls). The choruses resume their hymn of praise to close the Prologue.

Act One—Frankfurt. As the curtain rises, we find Faust and his pupil, Wagner, strolling through Frankfurt on Easter Sunday. Weaving in and out of the holiday crowd is a gray friar, arousing curiosity in some but fear in others. During the celebrations, Faust and Wagner watch from a distance. When evening descends, the festivities come to an end and the gray friar reappears. Faust believes he sees tongues of fire and smoke spurting from the friar's feet, and that the mysterious gray-robed figure is encircling them. Wagner sees nothing of the sort and suggests that the two of them leave. In Goethe's Faust, there is no friar, but rather a poodle.

The scene changes to Faust's study, wherein Faust prepares to read the Gospels. As he opens the book, a cry rings out from a dark corner of the room, and the friar appears. Now certain that he confronts a supernatural being, Faust demands the identity of the intruder. Mephistopheles explains that he is the "Spirit who constantly denies everything."

The grim, bragging harangue provokes Faust's curiosity rather than fear, and he agrees to a pact by which Mephistopheles will serve Faust in this life, in exchange for a reversal of roles in the next. Faust imposes a condition, however: his soul will not be forfeit unless Mephistopheles can satisfy the craving of his spirit to the extent that he will say to the fleeting moment, "Arrestati, sei bello" (Remain, for you are beautiful). The condition accepted, Faust is whisked away with the help of the devil's cloak.

Act Two—A village. Faust and Mephistopheles stroll around a cottage garden. Faust, going by the name of Heinrich, is courting Margareta while Mephistopheles walks with Marta, telling her that he has never experienced love. Faust/Heinrich makes an assignation with Margareta, and when he discovers that she sleeps in the same bed as her mother, he gives her a potion which will deepen the older woman's slumber, making their night of love possible. Then, in a breathless, syncopated quartet, the two couples proclaim their contrasting approaches to love until finally the women begin shouting "Away, away," and the men alternate with the women, crying "Stay, stay!"

We are then transported to a craggy mountainscape, eerily lit by a blood-red moon. Faust and Mephistopheles climb the mountainside to join the witches and warlocks in the celebration of the Witches' Sabbath. Once at the top, Mephistopheles becomes the centerpiece at a grotesque dinner party whose guests are his subjects and Faust. Mephistopheles seizes a balloon and proceeds to tell Faust of the earth's vileness. The orchestra's triangle conveys the delicate nature of the orb, and Mephistopheles's rising and falling line mockingly illustrates the rising and declining of the earth as it passes around the sun. As the Witches and Warlocks continue their revel, Faust, exclaiming "Stupor, stupor," sees a vision of Margareta with a blood-red line around her neck.

Act Three—A prison cell. Act Three opens with Margareta imprisoned, accused of poisoning her mother and drowning her infant. Mephistopheles has led Faust to her, and Faust pleads with her to escape with them. The two lovers imagine fleeing to an enchanted isle in a duet.

Mephistopheles interrupts the duet when he enters and asks the couple to make haste, as dawn is rapidly approaching. Margareta immediately recognizes Mephistopheles as the devil and realizes that Faust's love is tainted with evil. She therefore rejects Faust and turns to heaven to beg for forgiveness. The Celestial Hst then announces her redemption.

Act Four—Ancient Greece. Mephistopheles has delivered Faust to Classical Greece. On the banks of the River Peneus, Helen of Troy greets the full moon. She withdraws as Faust and Mephistopheles enter. Mephistopheles, bored, decides to return to the Witches Mountain. Faust leaves the scene, enchanted with Helen and the fact that he is in ancient Greece. Helen returns, obsessed with the burning of Troy. Faust enters, and Helen is pleased by the elegant rhyme and sound of his song. The two are immediately mutually smitten and sing of their rapture in a duet. Faust and Helen then retire to the grotto.

Epilogue—Faust's study. Many years later, in his study, the aged Faust thinks of the emptiness of his experience. He dwells on what is to be his final dream: to rule over a prosperous populace in peace. As Faust clasps the gospels, praying for salvation, Mephistopheles, employing the melody of Faust's duet with Helen, tempts Faust to new adventures. The Celestial Host breaks in on Mephistopheles' futile attempt, and Faust, upon hearing the angelic voices, finally utters the words "Arrestati, sei bello" (Remain, for you are beautiful). The Celestial voices, with their music from the Prologue, welcome Faust's soul to heaven. *—John Palmer*

Recommended:

○ **Boito: Mefistofele** / Fabritiis (cond.), Ghiaurov, Pavarotti, Freni, Caballé, National PO / 1985 / London 410175

○ **Boito: Mefistofele** / J. Rudel (cond.), Treigle, Domingo, Caballé, London SO / 1997 / EMI 66501

○ **Boito: Mefistofele** / Patané (cond.), Ramey, Marton, Domingo, Hungarian State Orch. / 1990 / Sony 44983

William Bolcom

b. May 26, 1938, Seattle, WA

Composer: Keyboard, Vocal, Opera, Choral

William Bolcom (b. 1938) has been one of the most versatile American composers of modern times, writing in a wide variety of media including chamber music, piano works, song cycles, opera, and symphonies, all the while displaying a mastery of many different styles. Although not given to radical experimentation, he consciously avoids blindly following European styles, whether old or contemporary. He describes Charles Ives as his greatest influence, and in his operas and stage works he chooses to set pieces about American characters by American authors and includes idioms such as ragtime and jazz in his works. In addition to this wide stylistic diversity, his works often display a trenchant sense of humor, on display in works such as the song *Lime Jello Marshmallow Cottage Cheese Surprise.*

Bolcom studied composition at the University of Washington with John Verrall at the age of eleven, and upon obtaining his bachelor's degree at twenty, began to study with Darius Milhaud at Mills College. In 1960, Milhaud took Bolcom to Paris, where he also worked with Messiaen. In 1961 Bolcom went on to study with Leland Smith at Stanford. After earning his doctorate in composition there in 1964, he won the Marc Blitzstein Award from the American Academy of Arts and Letters for *Dynamite Tonite* (1960), a piece that shows the influence of Milhaud and the Parisian cabarets. His *Casino Paradise,* written in 1990, while still cabaret-style, shows more of an individual voice. He returned to the Paris Conservatoire in 1964, and graduated in 1965, winning the second prize in that year's composition competition, as well as his first of two Guggenheim Fellowships. Bolcom won two Koussevitzky Foundation Awards in 1976 and 1993, for the *First Piano Quartet,* and the *Lyric Concerto for Flute and Orchestra,* respectively. He has been commissioned by many of America's greatest musical institutions, including the orchestras of Philadelphia, St. Louis, Seattle, New York, Baltimore, Boston, and the Lyric Opera of Chicago.

He is also a noted performer, and in 1973, his recording of the complete piano music of Gershwin was released, and named Stereo Review's Record of the Year. In 1988, he won the Pulitzer Prize in music for his *12 New Etudes for Piano.* One of his most ambitious undertakings was a setting of William Blake's *Songs of Innocence and of Experience,* for soloists, chorus, and orchestra, which premiered at the Stuttgart Opera in 1984, after 25 years of work. The popular Concerto in D for Violin and Orchestra was premiered in Saarbrucken by Sergiu Luca and Dennis Russell Davies. The *Fantasia Concertante* for viola, cello, and orchestra was premiered in 1986 by James Levine and the Vienna Philharmonic in Salzburg. Bolcom's *Fifth Symphony* was premiered by in 1990 by Davies and the Philadelphia Orchestra. Bolcom has written two major operas, both commissions for the Lyric Opera of Chicago, *McTeague* (1992) and *A View from the Bridge* (1999), for which Arthur Miller was also the librettist. The *McTeague* premiere—again conducted by Davies—starred Ben Heppner in the title role and Catherine Malfitano as his wife.

Since 1973, Bolcom has taught at the University of Michigan. He became a full professor there in 1983, and in 1994 he was named the Ross Lee Finney Distinguished University Professor of Music. Bolcom also holds honorary doctorates from the San Francisco Conservatory of Music and Albion College. He is married to, and has made over 20 recordings with mezzo-soprano Joan Morris. *—Ann Feeney*

KEYBOARD

Three Ghost Rags (1970–1971)

In the late 1960s, there arose a renewed interest in the music of the greatest ragtime composer, Scott Joplin. The exploration of this master's oeuvre spurred several American composers to write rags of their own, including William Bolcom. His *Ghost Rags* of 1970, which were named as a set by the pianist Paul Jacobs, have become the best-loved of his ragtime explorations, and Bolcom invests these essays in old-time music with style and wit. Bolcom wrote the first of these rags, *Graceful Ghost,* in memory of his father, and it has become his single most famous work. The ghost who stalks these pages is indeed a graceful and welcome presence. An elegant melodic curve, gentle minor-mode harmonies, and an expert use of the flowing syncopations of ragtime rhythm make the piece feel wistful and noble at the same time. Bolcom has also prepared a very effective transcription for violin and piano of this rag. The second Ghost Rag, titled *Poltergeist (Rag Fantasy),* does not make an outward show of being haunting but nevertheless sounds more ghostly, with suspended appogiaturas, unexpected harmonies, and syncopations that snap a bit more than those of *Graceful Ghost.* The music takes several entertaining jaunts down long hallways to dead ends before reluctantly coming to a conclusion. *Dream Shadows* concludes the *Ghost Rags.* One writer has described it as a "white telephone rag," and of the three rags in the set this one is the most redolent of the old-time serials. Slower and sweeter than the other two, it still comes with surprising harmonies, tricky syncopations, and langorous melodies that might provide numerous opportunities for some smoky-eyed heroine to toss her hair. Bolcom's *Ghost* rags are charming and thorougly idiomatic, not exercises at all but tributes, of the highest order, to a neglected American music. Their musical language subtly updates that of Joplin without in the least sacrificing its character. *—Andrew Lindemann Malone*

Recommended:

○ **Bolcom: The Complete Rags for Piano** / J. Murphy / 1998 / Albany 325

VOCAL

Cabaret Songs (1977–1996)

The collaboration between poet Arnold Weinstein and composer William Bolcom dates back to the 1960s when the two worked together to write the musical theater piece *Dynamite Tonite.* In the late 1970s, the two renewed their working partnership again to produce, over the next two decades, four successful volumes of *Cabaret Songs.* Bolcom had long been performing in this elusive, problematic genre, accompanying his wife, Joan Morris, whose voice heavily inspired and affected these songs. The authors made clear the artistic heritage they were claiming, identifying a heavily German cabaret lineage from Kurt Weill and Bertolt Brecht back through Arnold Schoenberg all the way to Franz Schubert. These 24 songs' fascinating blend of sophisticated rhetoric and seeming unrefinement have led to their frequent inclusion in both vocal recitals and theatrical revues. Rarely predictable but always pleasing, the songs tread a most delicate balance between pathos and bathos.

The first set of six was composed between late 1977 and mid-1978. "Over the Piano," the first song, encapsulates the entire cycle. Over a harmonically florid, heavily rubato accompaniment, an engaging melodic line, alternating between lyricism and parlando, tells an intriguing tale with a wry final twist. The set continues with the personable "Fur" through the grandiose "He Tipped the Waiter" and resignedly simple "Waitin" to end with two of the most popular songs: the "Song of Black Max" and "Amor." The former is something of a through-composed "Mack the Knife," while the latter is a charming melody to a lively Latin rhythm that brings the set to a delightful close.

The companion second volume, the most cohesive cycle of the three, contains more reflective songs—music for the morning after the celebration. The gracefully rhythmic "Places to Live" yields to one of the more striking songs, the jazzy and forthright "Toothbrush Time," the jagged melodic line of which both belies and reaffirms the disenchantment of the singer. "Surprise," a chromatic enigma, gives way to "The Actor" which in turn leads to "Oh Close the Curtain," a ballad reminiscent of Sondheim. Again the set closes with a calculated audience-pleaser, "George"—a darkly humorous tale which references both Puccini and ragtime music, among others.

Notable in the third set, which combines late 1970s and mid-1990s compositions, are the touching though satirical "Love In the Thirties" and the darkly philosophical "Miracle Song"—another number with highbrow and lowbrow allusions side by side, as evidenced by the performance marking "Mahlerian Jazz Waltz." The final song, "Radical Sally" is a languidly honest female counterpart to "Black Max." Prominent in the fourth set, which dates from the mid-1990s, are the cheeky "Poet Pal of Mine," the mysterious lullaby "Can't Sleep," and the syncopated dirge "At the Last Lousy Moments of Love." The cycle concludes with "Blue," a freely melodic, simply accompanied summation of its predecessors: its phrase "awf'ly smart people are often awful dumb!" can be read as touching acknowledgment of the unpretentious and unselfconscious manner in which both poet and composer have drawn from all ends of the artistic spectrum. *—Thomas Oram*

Recommended:

○ **Songs of America** / de Gaetani, Kalish / 1988 / Nonesuch 79178

OPERA

A View From the Bridge (1997–1999)

By the 1999 premiere of *A View From the Bridge* at Lyric Opera of Chicago, William Bolcom had become a skilled chameleon, drawing from any number of stylistic sources to generate a coherent if eclectic style of his own. *A View From the Bridge* is highly accessible without pandering to a "pops" audience, as if the Carlisle Floyd of *Of Mice and Men* had used some contemporary techniques to spice up a Richard Rodgers show. Bolcom has said he was partly inspired by tuneful old Broadway musicals and while this opera could never be confused with *Carousel*, it does often indulge in big, smooth vocal lines and, in the orchestra, immediately identifiable motifs. This is no pastiche, but the score does, in two places, make important use of Johnny Black's 1915 pop song "Paper Doll." The first occurrence is where the song appears in Miller's original play. It gets a Neapolitan, even Puccini-esque, treatment from the Sicilian character Rodolfo, who uses it to prove he can sing what he thinks is "jazz." The song returns later in a 1950s-style, early rock & roll arrangement when the characters put a recording of it on the turntable. Otherwise, Bolcom's score veers from pitched speech to bel canto singing to a recitative in which only the rhythms, not the pitches, are notated. For the text, Bolcom and librettist Arnold Weinstein, working with Arthur Miller, employed an early, seldom-performed version of Miller's play *A View From the Bridge*. This 1955 script is shorter than the 1957 revision and is written in what Bolcom has described as "blank verse" able to be set to music with minimal revamping. The story takes place in 1950s Red Hook, Brooklyn, amid Italian-American longshoremen and their families. At the center is Eddie Carbone, who, distracted by his blossoming young niece Catherine, has gradually become sexually estranged from his wife Beatrice. Two of Beatrice's cousins, Rodolfo and Marco, have just arrived illegally from Sicily and are being sheltered in the Carbone home. Tensions between the men rise and eventually lead to tragedy. This is prime verismo material and in his preference for lyrical declamation rather than self-contained arias, Bolcom carries on both a twentieth century tradition of vocal writing and shows how the gritty, red-blooded verismo approach of Leoncavallo and his contemporaries can be revamped for the twenty-first century. *—James Reel*

Synopsis:

In the Red Hook district of Brooklyn in the 1950s, a lawyer named Alfieri recounts the sad tale of longshoreman Eddie Carbone; it's a story well known in the area, for several neighbors join in the telling.

Act One. Two stevedores tell Eddie that a ship has docked with his wife's two Sicilian cousins, who are smuggling themselves into the United States. They'll be brought to Eddie's house that night. Arriving home, Eddie finds his niece Catherine, whom he has raised as a daughter, looking disturbingly grown up, a notion intensified when Catherine announces her success at stenography school and a job offer. Perturbed that he is about to lose her, Eddie gives Catherine stern advice about entering the world of work. Then he urges Catherine and his wife, Beatrice, to keep mum about the cousins; the chorus adds its own anecdote about how the community punished another man who betrayed confidences to Immigration.

The cousins, Marco and Rodolpho, arrive, complain of the poverty in Sicily, and reveal their dreams of wealth in America. The charming Rodolpho begins to annoy Eddie as he breaks into opera arias and a Neapolitanized version of "Paper Doll" to show what a fine singer he is.

Weeks later, Eddie is fed up with Rodolpho's flashy, sassy manner, but his real problem is his lack of a sex life with his wife, about which Beatrice confronts him. Eddie is also dismayed by Rodolpho's popularity with the neighbors. In front of his house, Eddie finds Rodolpho and Catherine returning from a stroll. Privately, he warns Catherine that Rodolpho will try to marry her only for the sake of getting legal immigration papers; Beatrice then takes Catherine aside and warns her that Eddie subconsciously wants the girl for himself.

Eddie consults the lawyer Alfieri on how to keep Catherine safe from Rodolpho; Alfieri responds that the only sure method would be to turn him in to Immigration. Later, tension is running high in the Carbone home; Catherine puts on a recording of "Paper Doll" and invites Rodolpho to dance. Furious, Eddie forces Rodolpho into a fight, but Marco puts Eddie in his place.

Act Two. Eddie is drinking heavily among his longshoreman friends. At home, Rodolpho and Catherine engage in a love duet that leads them to the bedroom. The drunken Eddie barges in, tries to throw Rodolpho out, gives Catherine a violent kiss, then gives Rodolpho a kiss even more brutal to shame him.

After an unfulfilling conversation with Alfieri, Eddie resolves to call Immigration. The resulting raid nets the Sicilian brothers and two other immigrants; the Carbone women and the neighbors suspect that Eddie has turned them in. In jail, Marco expresses his frustration over not being able to get a satisfactory apology from Eddie. But he is released to attend the wedding of Rodolpho and Catherine. The neighbors are shunning Eddie; his marriage is in ruins. Now Marco shows up to force Eddie to his knees in apology; Eddie pulls a knife, but Marco forces Eddie to stab himself. *—James Reel*

Recommended:

○ **Bolcom: A View from the Bridge** / D. R. Davies (cond.), K. Josephson, C. Malfitano, Turay, Rambaldi, Chicago Lyric Opera Orch / 2001 / New World 80588

CHORAL

Songs of Innocence and Experience (1956–1981)

Composer William Bolcom's famously broad tastes include a passion for the poetry of English transcendentalist poet William Blake; like many before and since, Bolcom decided to set Blake's mystical visions to music. Few composers, however, have made it a lifelong project. As a teenager, Bolcom first picked up the poet's work and became inspired to compose, putting away his finished settings into a large envelope. Twenty-five years later the envelope was full of 46 songs blending styles ranging from the popular (rock and reggae) to folk (ballad and dance forms) to modern classical. The three-hour result, *Songs of Innocence and Experience*, premiered in Stuttgart on January 8, 1984, has become perhaps Bolcom's most famous and most acclaimed composition, having since received several performances in the world's major musical centers. To see it as a summa of his life's work, however, as some have, is to underestimate his efforts since then. Nevertheless, the work is perhaps the composer's most successful effort in breaking boundaries of genre with powerful, illustrative music that can more accurately be assessed as an amalgam of styles than as a series of studies in different areas.

Orchestrated between 1981 and 1982, the work calls for nearly three hundred performers, including an orchestra, chorus, children's chorus, madrigal group, and rock band. Soloists required include not only tenor, baritone, soprano, contralto, and mezzo-soprano, but also boy soprano, coloratura soprano, country singer, and rock singer as well.

Songs are grouped into symphony-like movements. The first third of the work is the "Songs of Innocence"; the first of its three movements begins with a spirited tenor "Introduction." Other highlights include Blake's famous "The Lamb," set here as a chromatic, string-accompanied soprano solo. The movement concludes with the rock singer's "The Little Black Boy," a touching plea for tolerance. The second part includes the madrigal group's "Laughing Song" and the Brittenesque tenor solo "Spring." The final part of the "Songs of Innocence" begins with a "Nocturne" for percussion, and includes a dissonant, highly-charged "The Little Boy Lost," which yields to the soothing rock ballad "The Little Boy Found."

The "Songs of Experience" comprise the final two thirds. After a brief first movement, the second includes a rhythmic, parlando choral setting of Blake's famous "The Tyger." In the third movement, Bolcom betrays his penchant for popular song with a foxtrot setting of "The Little Vagabond," which gives way to a pathos-filled "Holy Thursday" for soprano. The final third, also in three movements, includes the joyful "The Lilly" for tenor and chorus, a voluptuous "The Garden of Love," and a Messiaen-like "Vocalise." The work concludes with an intensely dramatic final movement, which culminates in the grandiose finale "A Divine Image."

Neither an opera nor an oratorio, Bolcom's *Songs of Innocence and Experience* nevertheless possesses a strong dramatic quality, as both poet and composer wrestle with fundamental questions of human nature throughout what might best be termed a "song cycle." Bolcom himself summed up the thrust of his "musical illumination" of Blake's poetry as "in truth, there is joy." *—Thomas Oram*

Recommended:

○ **Bolcom: Songs of Innocence and of Experience** / Slatkin (cond.), soloists, choirs, University of Michigan SO / 2004 / Naxos 8559216-18

Jorge Bolet

b. Nov. 15, 1914, Havana, Cuba, **d.** Oct. 16, 1990, Mountain View, CA

Pianist

Virtuoso pianist Jorge Bolet began his keyboard studies at the age of nine. His progress excited his local teachers and he received a scholarship at the age of 12 to study in the United States, at the Curtis Institute of Music in Philadelphia. There his piano teacher was David Saperton. Beginning in 1932 he studied with Leopold Godowsky and Moritz Rosenthal, and, briefly, with Rudolf Serkin. He won the Naumburg Prize in 1937 and the Josef Hofmann Award in 1938. He became Rudolf Serkin's teaching assistant at the Curtis Institute in 1939. In 1942 he joined the United States armed forces. After the end of the war he was a part of the U.S. cccupying forces in Japan. There, he conducted the first performance in that country of Gilbert and Sullivan's *The Mikado*. He resumed his piano career after taking private lessons with Abram Chassins. Over a period of a few years he developed a reputation as a virtuoso player of astonishing power, able to play the most difficult works by Liszt with an impression of natural ease that left the feeling that there was no limit to his pianistic range. He became the head of the piano faculty at Curtis, and also was on the piano faculty of Indiana University at Bloomington. While in the United States he preferred the pronunciation "George" for his first name.

Until nearly the end of his life he maintained a major performing and recording career. His recordings were primarily for the Decca (London) company. He produced many estimable performances, notably those of the major piano works by Franz Liszt, as well as concertos and other works. As exciting as some of these recordings were, he was an artist whose full range of brilliance was not caught by the microphone. *—Joseph Stevenson*

Recommended:

- ○ **Liszt: Favourite Piano Works** / Bolet / 1995 / London 444851
- ○ **Liszt: Études d'exécution transcendante** / Bolet / 1997 / Ensayo 9711
- ○ **Liszt: Paraphrases** / Bolet / 2002 / Ensayo 9742

Claude Bolling

b. Apr. 10, 1930, Cannes, France

Pianist

Claude Bolling (b. 1930) treads a fine line between the disciplines of jazz and classical music. Initially Bolling gained a reputation as a jazz pianist and a bandleader working in the tradition of Duke Ellington, but he also made a thorough investigation of classical technical resources through his study with composer Maurice Duruflé. In 1969 Bolling's dual interests bore fruit in the form of his Sonata for Two Pianists, which he played with Jean-Bernard Pommier. Through the balance of the 1970s Bolling continued to write highly popular and tasty jazz-styled *Suites* for various instrumental combinations, the most popular of which was the "Suite for Flute and Jazz Piano Trio" (1975) written for classical flutist Jean-Pierre Rampal. He went on to collaborate with other top classical musicians. Bolling is credited in some circles for helping spur on the concept of a classical musician applying his or her talents to jazz and other types of improvised music. *—Uncle Dave Lewis*

Recommended:

- ○ **Bolling: Suite for Chamber Orchestra** / Bolling (cond.), English CO / 1983 / CBS 37798
- ○ **Bolling: Suite for Flute and Jazz Piano Trio** / Rampal, Bolling, Sabiani, Hediguer / 2002 / Fremeaux 443

Barbara Bonney

b. Apr. 19, 1956, Montclair, NJ

Soprano

Barbara Bonney is one of her generation's most versatile singers, having achieved equal success with art song, oratorio, modern vocal music, and opera, and on top of all that having become a highly proficient cellist. Her smallish but well-projected voice is especially suited to Mozart, the lighter Richard Strauss operas, and all but the heaviest lieder, and she has been careful in her choice of repertoire; even in her forties, she could still call forth a fresh, girlish timbre when it was needed.

Her family was not a musical one, and it was only by chance that her parents discovered she had perfect pitch and a sense of music—when she was three, they noticed that she could perfectly imitate musical noises, such as the melody that one of the household clocks chimed. When she was older, she started piano, but found that she preferred the more songful tones of the cello. It was an interest in German that led to her singing career—as a college student at the University of New Hampshire she decided to spend a year in Germany, studying at the University of Salzburg. She worked a wide variety of jobs to support herself, including cooking, selling produce at a vegetable stand, and copying music, and one day a friend suggested that she audition for the famed Mozarteum orchestra there. She hadn't brought her cello overseas with her, since the costs of shipping were prohibitive, so instead she prepared a song for her audition, and was offered a position as a lieder student. Spurred on by this success, she auditioned for the Darmstadt Opera (knowing only two arias out of the entire operatic repertoire), and was given the ingenue role of Anna in Nicolai's *Die Lustigen Weiber von Windsor* (The Merry Wives of Windsor). During her years with the company, she learned over 40 operatic roles.

In 1984, she made her Vienna State Opera debut as Sophie in Richard Strauss's *Der Rosenkavalier*, a role which was to become one of her most famous. Another characteristic role, that of Pamina in Mozart's *Die Zauberflöte*, she first undertook in her 1985 La Scala debut. In 1987, she sang Sophie at Monte Carlo, which brought her to the attention of conductor Carlos Kleiber. Lucia Popp, too, greatly admired her Sophie, and when Popp relinquished the role, moving on to the Marschallin, she declared that she was passing it on to Bonney. Her Met debut was in 1988, as Naiad in Strauss's *Ariadne auf Naxos*. During the 1990s, increasingly able to pick and choose what roles and repertoire she would sing, she began to reduce her operatic roles to a few of her special favorites, such as Pamina, Susanna (in Mozart's *Le nozze di Figaro*), and Ilia (in his *Idomeneo*), and adding a few new roles, such as Zdenka in Strauss's *Arabella* and Hanna Glawari (in Lehár's *Die lustige Witwe* [The Merry Widow]). Like Popp, she chose to drop the role of Sophie, leaving it for younger singers. This would allow her to spend more time singing lieder performances, and also to teach.

She was briefly married to baritone Hakan Hagegård. Among her recordings, her Mozart arias (London) and Schubert lieder (Teldec) capture her voice and singing quite well.*—Ann Feeney*

Recommended:

- ○ **Barbara Bonney Sings Mozart** / Hogwood (cond.), Bonney, Academy of Ancient Music / 1998 / London 460571
- ○ **Franz Schubert: Lieder** / Bonney, Parsons (piano) / 1994 / Teldec 90873
- ○ **Diamonds in the Snow: Nordic Songs** / Bonney, Pappano / 2000 / Decca 466762
- ○ **Im Chambre séparée: The Operetta Album** / Bonney, Schneider / 2003 / Decca 000047402

Giovanni Bononcini

b. Jul. 18, 1670, Modena, Italy, **d.** Jul. 9, 1747, Vienna, Austria

Composer

Giovanni Battista Bononcini was the most prominent figure from the Bononcini family of composers and musicians, whose other members included his father Giovanni Maria (1642–78), and his brothers Giovanni Maria II (1678–1753), and Antonio Maria (1677–1726). Giovanni Battista was one of the leading composers of his day, spending much of his career in Vienna and London. In the latter locale he was a rival of Handel for a time, despite religious and political opposition to his works. Bononcini's operas and cantatas were widely performed and highly acclaimed throughout Europe and England during his day.

While Bononcini's first known formal musical education came in Bologna after 1678, he likely had training as a choirboy, as well as taking lessons on cello in his early childhood. Orphaned when he was eight, he was sent to Bologna, where he studied cello and composition with G.P. Colonna, probably from 1680–85. Near the end of this period of instruction he began writing his first compositions, his Opp. 1 and 2 (1685) being sets of 12 pieces each for two violins and continuo. There followed three sinfonie (1685–87), as well as oratorios and masses. The masses were written for San Giovanni Cathedral, in Monte, where he had become *maestro di cappella* in 1687.

In 1692 Bononcini accepted a post with Filippo Colonna in Rome, for whom he composed operas, serenatas, and an oratorio. The young composer had one great success during this Roman period, the opera *Il trionfo di Camilla* (1696), which was especially well received in Naples. In 1697 Bononcini traveled to Vienna to accept a highly-paid post in the Court of Leopold I. He was quite productive throughout his eight years under the emperor, who died in 1705. Bononcini was retained at Court by Leopold's successor, Joseph: indeed, by 1705 he was regarded by many as the leading composer in Europe.

Bononcini composed a dozen dramatic works during Joseph's reign (1705–11), but seems to have fallen somewhat out of favor with Charles VI, who became Emperor in 1711. Bononcini traveled back to Italy and took a position in 1714 in Rome with Charles VI's ambassador there, Johann Wenzel. The ambassador died five years later, after which Bononcini was taken on at London's Royal Academy of Music in 1720. His first works, especially the opera *Muzio Scevola*, were extremely successful there.

Because of his Catholic background and associations with politically unpopular figures, however, Bononcini found the situation in England increasingly difficult, and thus departed in 1732 for Paris. He might have left as early as 1724, had there not been an offer from the Duchess of Marlborough, whose substantial stipends gave sufficient incentive to him to stay on and conduct private concerts for her until 1731. Oddly, he had many successes during his years in England, probably as many as Handel for the same period. But several intolerant factions eventually drove him off.

In the early 1730s he performed before the Court at Lisbon, but returned to Vienna in 1736. There he composed two operas, performed the following year with acclaim. The composer's last significant work was a *Te Deum*, commissioned, probably in 1740, by Empress Maria Theresa. It was premiered in February 1741. Bononcini was apparently not very active in his last years, perhaps because of the death of his daughter in Vienna in 1743. Also, his wife Margherita, may have been separated from him during his last years. *—Robert Cummings*

Overview of Works (ca. 1690–1741)

At the heart of a large body of compositions by Giovanni Bononcini lies some 60 operas, a substantial number of largely unpublished secular chamber cantatas, and sacred works that include oratorios and smaller scale pieces for solo voices. His operas were immensely successful in their day. Long before he arrived in England his *Camilla* (1698) had been given 64 performances at the Queen's (later Kings') Theatre, becoming the first Italian opera to achieve popularity on the English stage, albeit in translation. He arrived in England in 1719 to join Handel as a composer for the Royal Academy of Music, newly-established to promote lavishly staged Italian opera performed by some of the greatest Italian singers of the day. In 1720, a revised version of *Astarto* (originally first performed in Rome in 1715) achieved an enormous success which was quickly supplemented by works such as *Griselda* (1722). Indeed, at this point of his career Bononcini's operas were considerably more to the public taste than those of Handel. Distinguished by lyrical, memorable melodies, they tapped a sentimental vein very different from the heroic operas of the latter. The eponymous heroine of *Griselda*, for example, is not a member of royalty or the aristocracy, but a simple shepherdess. The eighteenth century English historian Sir John Hawkins summed up Bononcini's greatest attribute when he wrote that "his genius was adapted to the expression of tender and pathetic sentiments. His melodies are the richest and sweetest that we know of...." This ability to express gently affecting melancholy is also carried over to Bononcini's exquisite chamber cantatas for one or two voices, refined, cultivated works reflecting the subtle ideals of the Arcadian Academy in Rome. A typical piece like "Misero pastorello" readily reveals why its composer's cantatas were accorded such high status. Assessment of Bononcini's sacred music is more difficult, there being few modern editions or recordings, but in general terms it reflects the more conservative approach to sacred music taken by Italian masters of this period. While progressive ideas appeared in opera, older-style polyphony continued to dominate church music. In addition to vocal music, Bononcini also composed chamber music, principally trio sonatas or sonatas for his own instrument, the cello. One such sonata, in A minor, shows the composer successfully translating the tuneful cantabile writing of his operatic arias to the lyrical capabilities of the instrument. *—Brian Robins*

Recommended:

- ○ **Bononcini: Amarilli** / Lesne, Il Seminario Musicale / 1993 / Virgin 45000
- ○ **Bononcini: Arie, Correnti, Sarabande, Gighe & Allemande** / Iannetta, Priori / Tactus 640201
- ○ **Bononcini: Divertimenti da Camera** / Tripla Concordia / 2000 / Stradivarius 33578

Richard Bonynge

b. Sep. 29, 1920, Sydney, Australia
Conductor

Conductor Richard Bonynge began his studies at the New South Wales Conservatorium in Sydney as a piano student of Lindley Evans, a former accompanist of renowned Australian soprano Nellie Melba. At 14, Bonynge performed the Grieg piano concerto, an impressive beginning to an even more magical career. He later continued his studies at the Royal College of Music with pianist Herbert Fryer, in London. This institution frowned upon his desire to add conducting to his course load as, effectively, a second major area of study. Consequently, Bonynge forfeited his scholarship and continued his education privately. Also, having developed a serious interest in vocal technique, Bonynge began serving as accompanist to soprano Joan Sutherland. This relationship led to the couple's marriage in 1954, perhaps the most remarkable such professional union to date. It was at this point that the young musician transferred his attention to research of the bel canto operatic repertoire.

His debut on the podium in 1962 was uniquely sudden: the conductor of the Saint Cecilia Orchestra in Rome cancelled due to illness and his replacement was struck by an automobile, leaving only Bonynge to take the podium. He began, still without formal training, to conduct Sutherland's performances, beginning with Gounod's *Faust* in Vancouver and Bellini's *La Sonnambula* in San Francisco, both in 1963. After his Covent Garden debut in 1964 with a performance of Bellini's *I Puritani*, Bonynge and his wife returned to Australia the next year. There he assumed the position of music director of the Sutherland-Williamson International Grand Opera Company.

In 1966, Bonynge had his Metropolitan Opera debut with Sutherland performing the title role in Donizetti's *Lucia di Lammermoor*. As his reputation and career blossomed, the conductor enjoyed continued success when he was named artistic director of the Vancouver Opera, a position he held from 1974–78. Concurrently, Bonynge acted as music director of the Australian Opera from 1975–86. In 1977, he was awarded the Commander of the British Empire. In 1983 he was given the same honor in his native Australia, and in 1989 the French government gave him the rank of Commandeur de l'Ordre National de Mérite.

Bonynge championed a revival of the vocal ornamentation that had been customary during the late eighteenth and early nineteenth centuries. This period was dear to Bonynge, who has carefully studied the operas of Bellini as well as French opera of the period, and has composed cadenzas used by many singers (including Sutherland). One of the world's premier opera conductors, Bonynge has directed the masterpieces of the genre at the leading opera houses worldwide. His list of recorded operas is no less impressive and includes many works (including a number of nineteenth century ballet scores) previously not familiar to opera connoisseurs, such as those by Delibes, Graun, and Massenet. Most of these recordings feature Sutherland.

At Joan Sutherland's last performances, Bonynge conducted in front of audiences in the United States, Great Britain, and Australia. After she had left the stage for the last time, Bonynge continued his acclaimed career without pause. He remains one of opera's most important figures and is an important supporter of Australian singers and of the young artists' program at the Australian Opera, established during his tenure as music director. Richard Bonynge, with unquestionable devotion, gives his full attention to the world of opera. Bonynge has said, "I did not choose music, music chose me." One might observe, then, that opera chose a tireless and devoted champion. *—David Brensilver*

Recommended:

- ○ **Delibes: Lakmé** / Bonynge (cond.), Sutherland, Bacquier, Berbie, Sinclair, Monte Carlo National Opera Orch. & Chorus / 1989 / London 425485
- ○ **Tchaikovsky: The 3 Ballets** / Bonynge (cond.), National PO / 1999 / Decca 460411
- ○ **Donizetti: La Fille Du Régiment** / Bonynge (cond.), Pavarotti, Sutherland, Sinclair, Garret, Covent Garden Royal Opera House Orch. / 1986 / London 414520
- ○ **Verdi: La Traviata** / Bonynge (cond.), Pavarotti, Sutherland, Jones, Tomlinson, National Philharmonic Orch. / 1991 / London 430491

Alexander Borodin

b. Nov. 12, 1833, St. Petersburg, Russia, **d.** Feb. 27, 1887, St. Petersburg, Russia
Composer: Opera, Chamber Music, Orchestral, Symphonic, Keyboard

Though far from prolific as a composer—by day he was a scientist noted for his research on aldehydes—Alexander Borodin nevertheless earned a secure place in the history of Russian music. As a creative spirit, Borodin was the most accomplished of the Russian nationalists composers. He had a particular gift for the distinctive stripe of exoticism so evident in his most frequently performed work, the *Polovtsian Dances* from the opera *Prince Igor*.

The illegitimate son of a Georgian prince and a doctor's wife, Borodin enjoyed a comfortable upbringing. As a child he learned to play several instruments and tried his hand at composing, but other aptitudes directed his formal education. He studied chemistry at St. Petersburg's Medico-Surgical Academy, obtaining his doctorate in 1858 and pursuing further studies in Europe until 1862. Upon his return to Russia, he became a professor at his alma mater; but even as an academic career apparently loomed before him, he maintained a devotion to music.

Under the influence of Mily Balakirev, whom he met in 1862, Borodin became interested in applying elements of Russian folk music to works for the concert hall and stage. He joined a circle of like-minded composers—Balakirev, Rimsky-Korsakov, Mussorgsky, and Cui—famously dubbed "The Five" or "The Mighty Handful." The influence of Balakirev in particular is at once in evident in the *Symphony No. 1 in E flat major* (1867). Borodin began the much craggier *Symphony No. 2 in B minor* in 1869, the same year he commenced labor on his most important work, the opulent four-act opera *Prince Igor*. While it took Borodin more than five years to complete the symphony, work on *Prince Igor* dragged on for decades. Borodin, who had in the meantime completed a number of other works, left the opera unfinished at the time of his death. It was completed posthumously by Rimsky-Korsakov, a skillful craftsman and a particularly apt match for Borodin's colorful musical character, and Alexander Glazunov. Glazunov also completed the *Symphony No. 3 in A minor*, which the composer had been working on until the time of his death.

Aside from teaching chemistry and conducting research, Borodin helped found a series of medical courses for women in 1872. Such activities, as well as the poor health that plagued him in the 1880s, drained the energy that he might have devoted to composition. Still, as a part-time composer, Borodin jeft a significant oeuvre: more than a dozen worthy songs, miscellaneous piano pieces, two string quartets (the second of which contains a ravishing Nocturne often performed in an arrangement for string orchestra), and the popular tone poem *In the Steppes of Central Asia* (1880). He died while attending a ball in St. Petersburg on February 27, 1887. *—James Reel*

OPERA

Prince Igor (1869–1887)

Alexander Borodin was a chemist by profession, but is more readily remembered as among the finest of nineteenth century Russian composers. Borodin's dual life prevented him from completing a number of important musical works, among them the opera *Prince Igor*. The composer labored on the score (and text) intermittently for nearly 20 years, intending to create a great historical tableau based on an ancient ballad about a hero in Russia's struggles against the tribes of Central Asia. The Polovtsy tribe took Igor prisoner for a time, and this episode provides much of the dramatic impetus for the opera. *Prince Igor*—later completed by Rimsky-Korsakov, Glazunov, and others—remains one of the most important works in the history of Russian opera, though it is only rarely staged outside of its native land. Various reconstructions of Borodin's original intentions have been made, and the vast dimensions of the work pose problems. The work combines influences from French grand opera (rarely staged much anymore either) with, especially in its depiction of the "exotic" Polovtsy, the typically Russian harmonic daring also associated with Mussorgsky.

The most famous music from the opera is a set of dances, the *Polovtsian Dances*, that accompany a banquet put on by the Khan of the Polovtsy. These are overwhelmingly brilliant and irresistibly barbaric in the best Romantic crowd-pleasing manner, particularly when performed with the original choral parts. The Dances gained an unexpected popular currency when one of the more memorable tunes was transformed into the song "Stranger in Paradise" as part of the Broadway musical *Kismet* (1953). *—Joseph Stevenson*

Synopsis:

Prologue. (The story is set in 1185 in and around the city of Poutivl, Russia.) Igor, Prince of Seversk, and his son Vladimir (by his first wife) leave Poutivl to pursue the enemy Tartar tribe Polovtsy. Their departure comes at the time of an eclipse of the sun, said to be a bad omen, but one the Prince ignores.

Act One. Prince Vladimir Galitzky, Igor's wanton brother-in-law, is decreed ruler of Poutivl in his absence. Two tipsy gulok players, Skoula and Yeroshka, praise Galitzky in his court and recount his most recent dissolute adventure, the abduction of a maiden. A group of maidens enter to object to the kidnapping, but Galitzky orders them away.

In the quarters of Yaroslavna (Galitzky's sister and Igor's wife), the Princess longs for her husband's return. The maidens enter to tell her of the abduction. Galitzky suddenly appears and agrees to release the girl at the behest of his headstrong sister. After his departure, a group of boyars enter to deliver news of the capture of Igor and his son by the Polovtsy. Suddenly an alarm is heard to announce that Poutivl is under siege by a Polovtsian army led by the Khan Gzak.

Act Two. In the camp of the warring Polovtsians, Konchakovna, daughter of the Khan Konchak, reflects on her love for Vladimir. As Russian prisoners march past, Konchakovna directs a group of women to give them water. Vladimir sneaks into her tent and the two renew their declarations of love for each other. They quickly depart when they hear Igor approaching. The Prince yearns for freedom and for Yaroslavna, and is soon approached by the Polovtsian Ovlur, who offers a plan of escape. Igor refuses at first, but then begins weighing his proposal. After Ovlur departs, Khan Konchak appears and offers Igor his freedom in return for a promise of peace. He further proposes the two might even become allies. Igor steadfastly rejects his offers. Konchak admires the principled Igor, however, and orders entertainment, even offering a maiden to his prisoner.

Act Three. Khan Gzak arrives at the encampment a victorious commander, bringing prisoners and booty from Poutivl to the dismay of the already-captured Russians. Konchak initiates festivities that include drinking and dancing. After the two Khans depart to assess and divide the plunder, the other Polovtsians overindulge, most becoming drunk. Ovlur meets with Igor, but Konchakovna, aware of the escape plan, pleads for Vladimir to remain. She causes a disturbance and Igor must flee without his son. Afterward, some Polovtsy threaten Vladimir, but Konchak intervenes on his behalf and even gives approval of his marriage to Konchakovna.

Act Four. At the wall of Poutivl, the dejected Yaroslavna suddenly becomes overjoyed at the sight of her husband riding toward the city. He dismounts his horse and the two share a rapturous reunion. Skoula and Yeroshka appear, tipsy and gainsaying Prince Igor. But they quickly decide that supporting him is better than political exile. They ring the bell and announce their loyalty to him. The opera ends with a chorus of welcoming for Prince Igor. *—Robert Cummings*

Recommended:

- ○ **Borodin: Prince Igor** / Gergiev (cond.), Borodina, Gorchakova, Gassiev, Kit, Kirov Opera & Orch. / 1995 / Philips 442537
- ○ **Borodin: Prince Igor** / Ermler (cond.), I. Petrov, Tugarinova, Atlantov, Eisen, Orch. of the Bolshoi Theater, Moscow / 1996 / Melodiya 29346
- ○ **Borodin: Prince Igor** / Semkov (cond.), Chekerliiksi, Christoff, Winer-Chenisheva, Todorov, Sofia National Opera Orch. / EMI 66814

CHAMBER MUSIC

String Quartet No. 1 in A major (1874–1879)

When Borodin began sketching out his first string quartet in 1873, he wanted to produce something identifiably Russian, rather than follow German traditions slavishly. Yet he was not fully committed to the musical nationalism of Mussorgsky and other members of the Mighty Handful. The resulting quartet contains many Slavic touches, written as it was during the long gestation of Borodin's opera *Prince Igor*, but it takes a predominantly Classical (yes, German) form. Borodin had the quartet sketched out by 1875, did substantial work on it in 1877, and completed it in 1879.

The first movement is in sonata form, prefaced by a Moderato introduction that could almost pass for a Russian folk song, although the melody seems to be original. From the beginning, Borodin is willing to use all four instruments melodically, although he tends to relegate the cello to a supporting role that enriches the group's sonority. The movement's main portion, Allegro, begins with a flowing theme drawn from the finale of Beethoven's *String Quartet in B flat*, Op. 130. It sounds like full-fledged Borodin, though, with its mid-phrase grace notes. The theme is passed among the violins and the cello in little variants on its basic form. The second subject flows just as freely if slightly more urgently, often over a drone bass. It's all light and good-natured, only occasionally building much tension. Things do get exciting early in the development when the cello leads the way into a little fugue, but the rest of the development simply maintains the varied-repetition format Borodin established early in the exposition, breaking into separate sections of mildly contrasting character. After the full recapitulation, the movement ends with a long, hushed coda.

The Andante con moto begins with a slightly folk-like melody. Its viola counterpoint is derived directly from a Russian folk tune, "The Song of the Sparrow Hills" (this song also found its way into *Prince Igor*). The movement becomes a series of mild variants on this and the opening, original melody. In the song, an eagle holds a crow in its talons; the crow, in mortal danger himself, tells the eagle of having seen a young hero lying dead, over whom hovered three songbirds representing the hero's mother, sister, and wife. Borodin may have patterned his movement after the song's subject matter. The first portion, laying out the themes, would be associated with the eagle and the crow; the fugato in the middle depicts the hero and the distraught songbirds; and the ending, an impassioned rephrasing of the opening material, deals with their grief.

Borodin leaves all this behind when he launches the Scherzo, an almost perpetual-motion presto that remains light-hearted, never threatening. The middle trio section stretches out and employs some striking instrumental effects, notably violin harmonics. The music alternately evokes a glass harmonica and, with a busier accompaniment, a music box.

The finale is another sonata-form movement, again with a slow, haunted introduction. The main Allegro risoluto material bursts in with a driving, nervous, sharply accented theme. This subsides long enough for Borodin to introduce a second subject of repeated, hesitant little phrases. These themes develop through Borodin's technique of varied repetition, the second subject becoming more assertive when it reappears and the first subject binding the movement together with its urgent momentum, which culminates in a frenzied yet uplifting coda. Hints of the second movement lend the work an overall unity. *—James Reel*

Recommended:

- ○ **Borodin: String Quartets 1 & 2** / Borodin Quartet / 2001 / Chandos 9965

String Quartet No. 2 in D major (1881)

Borodin's *String Quartet No. 2 in D major* differs from many of the composer's other works in two ways: it was completed quickly, during August 1881, and it lacks a published program. These two factors may be related; Borodin dedicated the quartet to his wife Ekaterina, and it was written as an evocation of when they met and fell in love in Heidelberg 20 years earlier. The composer seems to have represented himself in this quartet with the cello (he was an amateur player), while Ekaterina is portrayed by the first violin. Each of the movements is warm and blissful, the whole suggesting the depiction of a growing, deepening love. The first movement opens with a sweet, sighing melody, traded between first violin and cello in an almost conversational manner. Borodin and Ekaterina dominate the rest of the movement with a beguiling discourse; even the development brings effortless, serene reshapings of the exposition's melodies, and the luminous coda rounds out the movement nicely. A Scherzo, written in a free sonata form, follows. The light first subject skips along gracefully, while the second subject is reminiscent of a waltz; both are gentle dances, gently handled. The development is in more decisive duple rhythm, but the recapitulation soon brings back the triple rhythm and its attendant character. Borodin and Ekaterina reappear in the famous Nocturne which follows. Over a luminous gauze of accompaniment from the second violin and viola, the cello introduces a long, tender, ardent melody marked cantabile ed espressivo. This melody soon passes to the first violin, which plays it over commentary from the cello. A more decisive second theme enters on both instruments, which develop it before playing the first theme in an intimate canon. The first theme lingers until the end of the movement, when in a long coda it ascends until the violin and cello play it together in a silvery thread of tone. The finale begins with an Andante introduction, as if unwilling to come down from the emotional heights of the previous movement, soon leading into a quicksilver, energetic Vivace, whose long coda provides a fittingly joyous conclusion to the entire work. As love letters go, Borodin's *String Quartet No. 2* is unsurpassed; as string quartets go, it is deservedly loved. *—Andrew Lindemann Malone*

Recommended:

- ○ **Dvořák: "American" Quartet; Tchaikovsky: Quartet 1; Borodin: Quartet 2** / Emerson SQ / 1994 / DG 445551

ORCHESTRAL

In the Steppes of Central Asia (V sredney Azii) (1880)

In 1880, as part of the celebrations for the 25th year of Tsar Alexander II's reign, two producers were supposed to contribute a series of small dramas glorifying Alexander's successes. Twelve Russian composers were contacted to provide incidental music for these scenes. The producers dropped out of sight before the festival, and *Borodin* seems to have been the only composer who responded to the call. The musical picture he wrote for the occasion, *In the Steppes of Central Asia*, became famous in its own right almost immediately, both at home and elsewhere.

The work is dedicated to Franz Liszt, master of the programmatic orchestral tone poem, a form to which Borodin brings a distinctly Russian slant. The program depicts a caravan of Central Asian traders, escorted across the desert by Russian soldiers. A quiet, bare high E on the violins, suggesting the desolation of the landscape, opens the work. A Russian folk song representing the military guard plays as if from a distance, first on clarinet, then on horn. The English horn then plays a lilting, oriental-inflected theme representing the native merchants, while a chromatic pizzicato accompaniment in the strings suggests the tread of camels across the desert. Each theme becomes more elaborate and louder as the trading party approaches, until finally the two tunes interweave in counterpoint, representing (in Borodin's words) "the peace-loving songs of the conquered and their conquerors join[ed] in harmony." After this climax, both themes recede, leaving the high E alone in the desert. Borodin's original program, particularly the part quoted above and a reference to the "terrible fighting force" of the Russian army, was considerably altered by the time of an 1882 performance in Moscow, as the tsar's government was ill disposed to discussing its colonial designs on Central Asia. To modern listeners, however, *In the Steppes of Central Asia* is simply a charming, well-crafted, exotically inflected sonic portrait. *—Andrew Lindemann Malone*

Recommended:

- ○ **Alexander Borodin: Symphonies 1 & 2** / Vladimir Ashkenazy (cond.), Royal PO / 1994 / London 436651
- ○ **Ancerl Gold 4: Mussorgsky, Borodin, Rimsky-Korsakov** / Ancerl (cond.), Czech PO / 2002 / Supraphon 3664
- ○ **Tchaikovsky: Marche Slav** / L. Slatkin (cond.), St. Louis SO / 1982 / Telarc 80072

Nocturne (1881–1885)

Alexander Borodin's most famous piece of music, the *Notturno*, or *Nocturne for string orchestra*, is really an arrangement of the identically-titled slow movement of Borodin's *String Quartet No. 2 in D major* of 1881; it is a fresh and wonderfully self-indulgent piece of chamber music which deserves wider familiarity in its original guise. There is arguably much lost in Sargent's adaptation for string orchestra: the *Notturno* is thought to be a musical reminiscence of Borodin's first meeting with his wife, and there is an appropriate intimacy to the original quartet version that is obscured by even the best of larger ensembles. Similarly, the work's passionate climax is all the more potent and rich when four individuals must struggle to produce a dramatic, full sound; what is electrifying when played by four can become ordinary when played by four dozen. That said, Sargent's arrangement is perhaps the most successful of the many that have appeared over the years, and the nature of the piece is essentially unaltered. Borodin knew the capacities of string instruments well; the *Nocturne* is clearly and brilliantly designed to work as chamber music. In contrast, the famous Barber *Adagio* is a far better piece in its string orchestra version than in its original string quartet form, largely because Barber's feel for the string quartet was not as healthy as Borodin's. Compared, for instance, to Rimsky-Korsakov's version for violin and orchestra, Sargent's string orchestra arrangement seems downright authentic. *—Blair Johnston*

Recommended:

- ○ **Greatest Hits: The Tsar** / Ormandy (cond.), Philadelphia Orch. / 1996 / Sony 62683
- ○ **Masters of the Bow: Cello** / Judd (cond.), J. Lloyd Webber, Royal PO / 2003 / DG B000020902

SYMPHONIC

Symphony No. 2 in B minor (1869–1876)

Alexander Borodin's *Symphony No. 2* in B minor took a long while to compose, as Borodin fit it in between labors on other works and his efforts as a scientist to ensure that women had access to chemistry courses. It was begun in 1869, but the piano score was not complete until 1875, and the orchestral version was not performed until 1877. That version was revised in 1879 after a poorly received premiere. Yet posterity has made the Symphony No. 2 not only Borodin's most popular symphony, but the most popular symphony written by any member of the nationalist Mighty Handful (Nikolay Rimsky-Korsakov, César Cui, Modest Mussorgsky, Mili Balakirev, and Borodin), because of its vividly rugged harmonies, deft orchestration, and a seemingly inexhaustible fund of energetic, passionate, and, above all, Russian themes.

A program for all but the second movement of the symphony has survived, as Borodin told it to critic Vladimir Stassov. The sonata-form first movement depicts a gathering of Russian knights; it opens with a strong, noble theme played on unison strings, as brasses and winds provide dark color and essay a chivalric-sounding contrasting theme. After a few repetitions of the opening music, a second theme enters, based on motifs from the folk songs "The Terrible Tsar" and "The Nightingale" and distinguished by its easy lyricism. The development section introduces a gallop rhythm which affects fragments of the themes and lends a knightly feel to the proceedings, leading into a recapitulation whose longer notes and thicker orchestration make it even more emphatic than the exposition. The Prestissimo scherzo which follows uses a sustained brass chord to modulate from B minor to F major (a remote key), and then launches into a succession of quick, bright, lightly scored melodies. The Trio takes a graceful, winding theme (also derived from the abovementioned folk songs) and runs it through various keys. The Andante third movement portrays a legendary minstrel named Bayan, and evokes the sound of his zither in the opening bars with harp and pizzicato strings. At first, a warm horn melody dominates, but soon a struggle develops between a nervous, minor-mode motive introduced on the woodwinds and the opening melody. Finally, the opening melody enters triumphantly in the strings, and leads into a coda which brings back the minstrel evocation; this in turn leads directly into the Allegro finale. This finale depicts a jubilant crowd, using an appropriately buoyant main theme (decorated with generous percussion) and a second theme which begins as a quiet lyric, but soon expands into a celebration itself. A new development theme recalls the symphony's opening music, but this soon yields to a supremely joyous, unstoppable elaboration of the two main themes, whose momentum propels the music through the recapitulation and the coda. Borodin's *Symphony No. 2* deserves its exalted position in the annals of the Mighty Handful's orchestral music. *—Andrew Lindemann Malone*

Recommended:

- ○ **Borodin: Symphony 2; Petite Suite** / Svetlanov (cond.), State SO of Russia / 1994 / RCA Victor 62505
- ○ **Borodin: Symphony 2; Prince Igor Orchestral Music** / R. Kubelik (cond.), Vienna PO / 2001 / Seraphim 74276
- ○ **Rimsky-Korsakov: Scheherazade; Borodin: Symphony 2** / Kondrashin (cond.), Concertgebouw / 2001 / Philips 464735

KEYBOARD

Petite Suite (1885)

Borodin wrote little enough—an opera, a couple of symphonies, a tone poem for orchestra, a couple of string quartets, a string quintet for chamber musicians, and a handful of songs for voice and piano—and next to nothing of any substance for the piano alone. The largest of his piano works is the *Petite Suite*, seven brief movements composed over a period of five years, dedicated to the Countess Louise de Merci d'Argenteau and published in 1885. Following Borodin's death in 1887, Glazunov edited and orchestrated a number of his works, including the *Petite Suite*. In Borodin's autograph, the score bears the dedication "Petit poeme d'amour d'une jeune fille" (Little poems on the love of a young girl). Each movement of the work also has a brief explanation following it. The austerely liturgical first "Au couvent" (At the Convent), "The Church's vows foster thoughts only of God"; the shyly charming second Intermezzo, "Dreaming of Society Life"; the grandly joyous "Mazurka I," "Thinking only of dancing"; the lyrically romantic "Mazurka II," "Thinking both of the dance and the dancer"; the voluptuously lyrical "Reverie" (Dreams), "Thinking only of the dance"; the sensually chaste Serenade, "Dreaming of love"; and the closing romantic Nocturne, "Lulled by the happieness of being in love." Clearly, Borodin had a specific program for the whole work, a work that is part dance, part dream, and all love. *—James Leonard*

Recommended:

- ○ **Tchaikovsky: The Seasons; Borodin: Petite Suite** / Edlina / 1995 / Chandos 9309

Willi Boskovsky

b. Jun. 16, 1909, Vienna, Austria, **d.** Apr. 20, 1991, Visp, Switzerland

Conductor

Willi Boskovsky was a major figure twice over in classical music, first as the concertmaster of the Vienna Philharmonic Orchestra from 1936 until his retirement in 1979, and for 25 years (1954–79) as conductor of the orchestra's renowned New Year's concerts. The latter, principally devoted to the music of Johann Strauss II, made Boskovsky into a star at the podium and resulted in recordings, mostly of Strauss, but also of Mozart, Liszt, and Dvořák, among other composers.

Boskovsky entered the Vienna Academy of Music at nine as a violin student. He graduated in 1927 and pursued a career as a soloist and with his own chamber group, the Boskovsky Trio, over the next five years. In 1933, he joined the Vienna Philharmonic and became the orchestra's concertmaster in 1936. Over the next 18 years, he remained in the violin section and also organized the Vienna Octet.

In 1954, Boskovsky succeeded Clemens Krauss at the podium for the orchestra's New Year's concerts, thus beginning a quarter century of these performances, which were broadcast internationally on radio and later on television. Boskovsky's approach to the waltzes, polkas, and quadrilles that made up these programs proved immensely popular, bringing out their lyricism without sacrificing their more majestic qualities. In 1958, the violinist-turned-conductor made the first of dozens of LPs of Viennese waltz music for Decca Records. His timing was impeccable, as these were among the earliest stereo recordings of the repertory and appeared just as stereo was sweeping into homes. They became some of the biggest and steadiest sellers in Decca's classical catalog over the next two decades, even topping the classical charts in England. In the early 1960s, Boskovsky's appearances in America as a guest conductor with the New York Philharmonic and the Los Angeles Philharmonic orchestras were considered major musical events. He surprised audiences and critics alike by reviving a custom from Strauss' own performances, bringing his violin to the podium and using both it and his bow as batons, almost waltzing to the music as he conducted, and occasionally playing along as well.

During the 1960s, Boskovsky branched out in his recordings, most notably with a landmark nine-volume series of Mozart dances, marches, and minuets for Decca; meanwhile, for EMI, he recorded a series of Viennese operettas, including Strauss' *Fledermaus* and *Wiener Blut*, Zeller's *Der Vogelhandler*, Lehár's *Paganini*, and Suppé's *Boccaccio*. Peter G. Davis, writing in *The New York Times* in 1972, praised Boskovsky's recording of *Fledermaus* for its "razor-sharp precision," "lean sonorities," and "muscular thrust," remarking that "he can kick up his heels when called for and still preserve the undercurrent of warmth." Boskovsky remained active following his 1979 retirement from the Vienna Philharmonic and recorded well into the digital era with the Johann Strauss Orchestra of Vienna. His best recordings of the Viennese repertory, in orchestral music and operetta, remain highly prized and in print on CD. *—Bruce Eder*

Recommended:

- ○ **Mozart: Dances & Marches** / Boskovsky (cond.), Vienna Mozart Ensemble / 1991 / London 430634
- ○ **The Strauss Family** / Boskovsky (cond.), Vienna PO / London 455254
- ○ **J. Strauss II: Waltzes** / Boskovsky (cond.), Vienna Johann Strauss Orch. / 2001 / EMI 74311
- ○ **Lehár: Waltzes** / Boskovsky (cond.), Vienna Johann Strauss Orch. / 2001 / EMI 74735
- ○ **Overtures, Marches, Polkas & Waltzes** / Boskovsky (cond.), Vienna Johann Strauss Orch. / 2002 / EMI 575676

Boston Camerata

f. 1954, Boston, MA

Ensemble

The Boston Camerata is one of the oldest early music ensembles in the United States. It is known for the innovative programming of its director, Joel Cohen, and for taking on various eras and styles of music in an effort to discover links among them.

The Boston Camerata was founded in 1954 as an organization associated with the Boston Museum of Fine Arts. It began a new direction after the appointment of Joel Cohen as its director in 1968, the same year it made its first commercial recording. Cohen was a graduate of Harvard University in composition and had been a student of Nadia Boulanger in Paris; he was known as a conductor, lute player, and researcher into early music. Cohen's musicianship and research into Medieval and Renaissance sources were highly praised in the 1970s when he made a number of recordings and appearances with the great French tenor Hughes Cuénod.

In 1974, the Boston Camerata ended its association with the Museum and began the international touring that has made it a major name in the worldwide original instruments movement. It has performed in Canada, England, Spain, France, Germany, Italy, Portugal, the Netherlands, Singapore, Israel, and Mexico. It made its first Japanese tour in 1995 and its first trip to Scandinavia in 1996.

In 1981, the Boston Camerata began a series of appearances at the biennial Boston Early Music Festivals that lasted through the 1993 Festival. It also has appeared at Tanglewood, festivals in Berkeley and San Antonio, and at the Kalamazoo Medieval Institute.

Boston Camerata has recorded for the labels Erato, Harmonia Mundi, Nonesuch, Telefunken, and Glissando. In 1989, Cohen and the Camerata won the Grand Prix du Disque award of the Academie Charles Cros, Paris, for its compact disc *The Legend of Tristan et Iseult*, which used original musical and poetic sources of the Medieval age to recount the Arthurian legend of the two lovers, and tracing threads and development of the legend over the years and in different places. At the same time they developed a concert production of the same project, which is still often requested by major European festivals. A similar project was based on another great Medieval legend, the *Roman de Fauvel*, which was recorded and broadcast on the French national television network. In 1993 the Camerata provided the music track for *The Guardian of Memory*, a TV project for the Library of Congress. Boston Camerata has also participated in television productions for British, German, Swiss, Norwegian, Swedish, and Canadian radio, and produced a U.S. nationally syndicated radio series.

The compact disc *An American Christmas* traced Christmas music found in North American folk music to sources in the British Isles and western Europe, and its 1993 recording of Jean Gilles' *Requiem* was a best seller on the European classical charts.

In 1996, the Camerata traveled to Sabbathday Lake in Maine, the site of the only remaining functioning community of the religious sect known as the Shakers, and lived there while recording several of their hymns and songs for the disc *Simple Gifts*. The ensemble went on to explore the history of American spiritual song from the famous *Federal Songbook* and the shaped-note hymnbooks of the American South. Another notable recorded production is *Cantigas*, music of King Alfonso X el Sabio. Since the music was written at a time when Moorish influence was strong in Spain, the Camerata traveled to Fez, Morocco, to make the recording, which they did with the participation of a leading Arabic music ensemble of that country directed by Mohammed Briouel. This disc won the prestigious Holland Edison Prize. *—Joseph Stevenson*

Recommended:

- ○ **A Medieval Christmas** / Cohen (cond.), Boston Camerata / 1975 / Nonesuch 71315
- ○ **An American Christmas** / Cohen (cond.), Boston Camerata / Erato 92874
- ○ **Le Roman de Fauvel** / Cohen (cond.), Fleagle, Azema, Collver, Visse, Boston Camerata / 1995 / Erato 96392
- ○ **Tristan et Iseult** / Cohen (cond.), Douglass, Hargis, Hite, Ledroit, Boston Camerata / 1987 / Erato 98482

Boston Pops Orchestra

f. Jul. 11, 1885, Boston, MA

Ensemble

Banker Henry Lee Higginson established Boston's first full-time resident orchestra. An unprecedented one-million-dollar grant endowed the Boston Symphony Orchestra, which, since its debut on October 22, 1881, has established itself as one of the great orchestras of the world.

In order to give orchestra members summer employment, and to recapture the ambience of the Bilse Orchestra's beer-hall concerts in Berlin where Higginson had been a music student, Higginson established a second BSO season in the spring, played by a reduced orchestra initially called the Music Hall Promenade Orchestra. The "Pops," as it became known informally and later officially, was also an audience hit. The Boston Pops remains, essentially, the Boston Symphony Orchestra minus its first chair players.

In 1930 Arthur Fiedler, a BSO member who had already founded his own orchestra of fellow BSO members and initiated (in 1929) a popular concert series at the outdoors waterfront area called the Esplanade, was engaged as the Pops' full-time conductor. He devised an innovative format comprising three parts: a popular symphony or concerto flanked by lighter music. Fiedler, a flamboyant, camera-loving personality, soon gathered a huge personal following among record-buyers in North America, also making the Pops a household word and one of RCA Red Seal Records' best-selling acts.

In 1969, Boston television station WGBH began televising the *Evening with Pops* series, making the organization even more of a household word. The live broadcasts of the spectacular Fourth of July concerts on the Esplanade are a regular holiday event for large numbers of American music lovers.

After Fiedler's 50 years at the helm, he was succeeded in 1980 by John Williams, the famous film score composer. Williams' programs, frequently including a composition of his own (for which he was sometimes criticized), altered the content of Pops concerts somewhat, but maintained the tradition of three parts, with the heaviest music in the middle. Following Williams' retirement in 1993, the young conductor and Carnegie Mellon University alumnus Keith Lockhart (the same age as Fiedler when he was appointed), was named Pops maestro in 1995. He returned the orchestra to its previous association with RCA (Williams had recorded on Philips and Sony), and as the twentieth century ended, his engaging personality and handsome good looks were building a personal following similar to Fiedler's. *—Joseph Stevenson*

Recommended:

- ○ **Pops Stoppers** / Fiedler (cond.), Boston Pops Orch. / 1999 / BMG 63304
- ○ **Encore!** / Williams (cond.), Boston Pops Orch. / 2004 / Philips 000260602
- ○ **American Classics** / Williams (cond.), Boston Pops Orch. / Philips 468156
- ○ **Gershwin: Orchestral Works** / Fiedler (cond.), Wild, Cardillo, Boston Pops Orch. / 2001 / RCA 68019
- ○ **Arthur Fiedler & Boston Pops at the Movies** / Fiedler (cond.), Boston Pops Orch. / 2003 / BMG 47947

Boston Symphony Orchestra

f. Oct. 22, 1881, Boston, MA

Ensemble

As befits a city which figures so prominently in American history, Boston is also home to one of the oldest surviving orchestras in the United States, and one of the finest in the world. The Boston Symphony Orchestra came into existence through the influence—and deep pockets—of Henry Lee Higginson, a banker who sought to establish a permanent, world-class orchestra in a city whose instrumental ensembles to that point had consisted mainly of ad hoc and amateur groups. The BSO, consisting mainly of German-born musicans and led by George Henschel, gave its first performance in a season of 22 pairs of concerts on October 22, 1881.

The fledgling orchestra thrived in the last decades of the nineteenth century under the leadership of Wilhelm Gericke (1884–89), Arthur Nikisch (1889–93), and

Emil Paur (1893–98); Gericke assumed the podium again in 1898 and led the orchestra for another several seasons. In 1900 the BSO moved from its original home, the Music Hall (now the Aquarius Theater), into the brand-new, acoustically magnificent Symphony Hall. Karl Muck assumed leadership of the BSO in 1906, but returned to his native Germany in 1908 to become the Generalmusikdirektor in Berlin. Muck returned in 1912, replacing Max Fiedler. With America's entry into World War I, Muck, an unapologetic German nationalist, found his position in jeopardy. Despite the intervention of Higginson, now 84, Muck was arrested in 1918 and detained as an enemy alien until the end of the war.

Henri Rabaud was engaged for one season in 1918 and was succeeded by Pierre Monteux, a brilliant and capable conductor whose resumé included leading the infamous premiere of Stravinsky's *Le sacre du printemps* in Paris in 1913. The dynamic Serge Koussevitzky helmed the BSO from 1924 to 1949, ushering in what many consider the orchestra's golden age. Koussevitsky both brought the BSO to its highest standard and demonstrated an uncommon interest in new music; for the orchestra's anniversary season in 1931, he oversaw a commissioning series that yielded an outstanding body of works, including Stravinsky's *Symphony of Psalms* and works by Copland, Prokofiev, Respighi, Honegger, and Hindemith. Since Koussevitsky's tenure, the orchestra has maintained a tradition of podium stability under the batons of luminaries like Charles Munch (1949–63), Erich Leinsdorf (1963–68), William Steinberg (1968–73), Seiji Ozawa (1973–2002), and James Levine (2002–present). Since the founding of the annual Tanglewood Music Festival in 1940, the BSO has served as the official resident orchestra of that institution.

In 1885 the BSO established a series of summertime "Promenade Concerts"; by 1900 these concerts had come to be identified by their famous Boston Pops moniker. The Pops became a solid institution after 1930 when Max Fiedler's son, Arthur, became their conductor; he led the group for an unprecedented 50 years. Fiedler was succeeded in 1980 by the Academy Award-winning composer John Williams; in 1995, the 35-year-old Keith Lockhart became the Pops' music director. Both the BSO and the Boston Pops are amply represented on recordings that range from repertoire staples to works commissioned and premiered by the ensembles to film scores. *—AMG*

Recommended:

- ○ **Berlioz: Symphonie Fantastique; Roméo et Juliette** / Munch (cond.), Varon, Valletti, Tozzi, Elias, BSO / 1997 / RCA 34168
- ○ **Ives, Ruggles & Piston** / Tilson Thomas (cond.), BSO / 2001 / DG 463633
- ○ **Sergei Koussevitzky Conducts Sibelius** / Koussevitzky (cond.), BSO / AS Disc 558
- ○ **Koussevitzky: Maestro Risoluto** / Koussevitzky (cond.), Heifetz, BSO / History 205259

Ian Bostridge

b. Dec. 25, 1964, London, England
Tenor

Ian Bostridge is perhaps the best-known English tenor to emerge since the death of Peter Pears. He has become closely associated with the art song repertory, as well as with the music of Benjamin Britten.

Before becoming a singer, Bostridge obtained his Ph.D. in history and philosophy from St. John's College of Oxford. However, reaching the finals of both the Kathleen Ferrier and Richard Tauber competitions and winning the 1991 National Federation of Music Societies/Esso Award proved decisive in moving him towards a career in singing. The Young Concert Artists Trust gave him a financial grant to develop his career, and he debuted at Wigmore Hall in London in 1993. One of his most important early recitals was in 1994 at the Purcell Room, where he gave a highly acclaimed performance of Schubert's *Winterreise*. In the same year, he made his first appearance at the Aldeburgh Festival. Since then he has become strongly associated with the music of the Festival's founder, Benjamin Britten. He made his first New York appearances in 1998 at the Frick Collection and in 1999 at Alice Tully Hall. In 1998 he debuted at the Munich Festival as Nerone in *L'Incoronazione di Poppea*. His debut with the Vienna Philharmonic Orchestra was in 1999.

His operatic debut was in 1994 at the Covent Garden Festival's production of Britten's *A Midsummer Night's Dream* as Lysander. In 1995, he sang his first solo recital at Wigmore Hall and increased his European recital presence with appearances in Lyon and Cologne. His debut with the English National Opera was as Tamino in Mozart's *The Magic Flute* in 1996, and he was acclaimed for his seductive portrayal of the ghost Quint in Britten's *The Turn of the Screw* at the Royal Opera House, Covent Garden.

His operatic recordings include *A Midsummer Night's Dream* (as Francis Flute), as Belmonte in Mozart's *Die Entführung aus dem Serail*, and Tom Rakewell in Stravinsky's *The Rake's Progress*.

He is in much demand as a recital singer and in that capacity has sung on several volumes of Hyperion's epochal complete Schubert song collection (including the recording of *Die schöne Müllerin*). He has also issued recordings of Robert Schumann's *Dichterliebe*, songs of Reynaldo Hahn, a program of little-known Britten songs, and one volume of Jecklin-Disc's set of the complete songs of Othmar Schoeck.

His concert repertory recordings include Bach's *Magnificat* and *St. Matthew Passion*, Handel's *Israel in Egypt*, Stravinsky's *Cantata*, most of the Britten orchestral song cycles for tenor voice, the Mozart *Requiem*, Finzi's *Die natalis*, Rossini's *Petite Messe Solennelle*, and Michael Nyman's *Noises, Sounds, & Sweet Airs*. *—Joseph Stevenson*

Recommended:

- ○ **Schubert Lieder Vol. 1** / Bostridge, Drake / 1998 / Angel 56347
- ○ **The English Songbook** / Bostridge, Drake / 1999 / Angel 56830B
- ○ **Schumann: Dichterliebe; Liederkreis Op24; Lieder** / Bostridge, Drake / 1998 / EMI 56575
- ○ **Monteverdi: L'Orfeo** / Haim (cond.), Dessay, Bostridge, Agnew, Gens, Maltman, Le Concert D'Astree / 2004 / Virgin 45642

Catherine Bott

b. Sep. 11, 1952, Leamington Spa, England
Soprano

Catherine Bott is one of the leading London-based sopranos, particularly renowned among those participating regularly in early music performances. She studied with Arthur Reckless at the Guildhall School of Music. The early music movement was burgeoning in England at the time of her graduation, and she found that the music appealed to her sensibilities. Her interpretations and performances are frequently noted for their intelligence.

Her recordings include Purcell's *The Fairy Queen* (Erato), the part of Drusilla in *L'Incoronazione di Poppea* on Deutsche Grammophon, Herodiade Figlia in Stradella's *San Giovanni Battista* (Erato), Venus in John Blow's *Venus and Adonis*, a recording of Monteverdi's *Vespers*, Monteverdi's *Orfeo*, and a recital of "mad songs" and scenes from English Restoration theater, all the latter on Decca.

She has appeared with Marc Minkowski and Les Musiciens du Louvre; the Amsterdam Baroque Orchestra; Christopher Hogwood and the Academy of Ancient Music; Stephen Layton and Polyphony; the New London Consort under Philip Pickett; the Australian Brandenburg Orchestra; and the American Bach Soloists. Works she has sung include Mozart's *Requiem*, *Regina Coeli*, and *Exsultate Jubilate*; programs of vocal music by Handel and Vivaldi, Handel's *Messiah*, Bach's *B Minor Mass*, and Carissimi's *Historia de Jepthe*.

However, her activities are not limited to Classical and Baroque music. Romantic era works include Fauré's *Requiem*, Nielsen's Third Symphony, and Mahler's *Das Klagende Lied*. Her modern repertory includes Berio's *Laborintus II*; Michael Nyman's *Noises, Sounds, and Sweet Airs*; Nicolai Korndorf's *Hymnus III*; John Harle's *Silencium*; and Michael Torke's *Four Proverbs*. She also sang on the soundtrack of the film *The Emerald Forest*.

She has appeared at the Brixen and Spitalfield's Festivals, the Kilkenny Arts Week, and the Lunchtime Concert Series at St. John's, Smith, Square. She has made 40 broadcast recordings for BBC Radio 3. *—Joseph Stevenson*

Recommended:

- ○ **Haydn: Arianna a Naxos; Scots Songs; English Canzonettas** / Bott, Tan, Kelly, Beznosiuk, Pleeth, Bury / 2002 / Meridian 84495
- ○ **Elizabethan & Jacobean Consort Music** / Pickett (cond.), New London Consort, Bott, George / 1993 / Linn 11
- ○ **Fairest Isle: A New National Songbook** / Holman (cond.), Bott, Cornwell, Parley of Instruments / Hyperion 67115

Pierre Boulez

b. Mar. 26, 1925, Montbrison, France
Composer: Keyboard, Chamber Music, Vocal, Avant-Garde
Conductor

Pierre Boulez (b. 1925), French composer, conductor, and music theorist, is regarded as a leading composer of the post-Webern serialist movement who also embraced elements of aleatory and electronics. As a child Boulez demonstrated a formidable aptitude in mathematics, but left for Paris in 1942 to enroll in the Paris Conservatoire. His studies there often ran into difficulties, as he was rapidly developing revolutionary—"Praise be to amnesia"—attitudes towards all things traditional. But two decisive influences during those years helped to shape his musical personality. The first was Messiaen's famous analysis course, the other was René Leibowitz, who introduced him to serial music, where Boulez found "a harmonic and contrapuntal richness and a capacity for development an extension of a kind I have never found anywhere else."

By the late 1940s, Boulez began using a technique known as total serialization. A work which soon gave Boulez public notice was his Second Piano Sonata (1948), following a much publicized concert in Darmstadt in 1952 by Yvonne Loriod, Messiaen's wife. The piece from the 1950s that sealed his reputation was *Le Marteau sans Maître* from 1954 (revised in 1955), for singer and chamber ensemble. The instrumentation gives prominence to exotic percussion, extended vocal techniques, and textures that are often brittle but also lyrical. Rigorously organized, *Le Marteau* nonetheless goes beyond strict serialism to a more personal style. The premiere took place in Germany in 1955 under *Hans Rosbaud*. The Südwestfunk Radio underwrote an astounding 50 rehearsals in order that the piece be properly performed. During the latter 1950s he began allowing greater freedom for the performer in works like *Improvisations sur Mallarmé* for soprano and chamber ensemble. In his Third Piano Sonata (1957), the pianist can reorder the five movements in a variety of ways, and certain passages within the movements offer alternate paths, thereby making the artist select which to play and which to omit. In 1957, Boulez embarked on *Pli Selon Pli*, a work in five movements for soprano and orchestra to texts by Mallarmé, making use of a more restrained open-form technique. The middle movements are scored for sub-groups of the orchestra, balancing the larger forces of the outer movements. Boulez is also known for withdrawing and rewriting his compositions, making nearly everything he writes "a work in progress." For instance, *... explosante-fixe ...*, first sketched in 1971 has engendered a number of works and transitory phases over approximately twenty five years, including a 1996 version for Solo MIDI Flute and Chamber Ensemble. In 2000, he also received the prestigious Grawemeyer Award in Composition for his forty minute chamber piece *Sur Incises* for three pianos, three harps, and three percussionists.

Boulez is also one of the twentieth century's most influential conductors, known for extraordinarily precise performances of contemporary works by Bartok, Ligeti, Messiaen, and Varése, among many others. In 1968 he was named Music Director of both the BBC Symphony Orchestra and New York Philharmonic. In 1969, the Cleveland Orchestra named him Principal Guest Conductor. In 1970 French President Pompidou announced the experimental electronic music institute, Institut de Recherche et de Coordination Acoustique/Musique (IRCAM) to be under Boulez's administration, eventually causing him to withdraw from the BBC and New York posts. In 1975, he formed the Ensemble Inter Contemporain, an ensemble devoted entirely to the performance of new music, including his own *Repons* (1980). He was also appointed Principal Guest Conductor of the Chicago Symphony Orchestra in 1995. As a conductor, Boulez has made many notable recordings; in 1996 he won a Grammy for his recording of Debussy's *La Mer* with the Cleveland Orchestra. *—Joseph Stevenson*

Recommended:

- ○ **Boulez: Répons; Dialogue de l'ombre double** / Boulez (cond.), Cambreling, Cerutti, Vassilakis, Boffard, InterContemporain Ensemble / 1998 / DG 457605
- ○ **Debussy: Pelléas et Mélisande** / Boulez (cond.), Soderstrom, Minton, Wicks, McIntyre, Royal Opera House Orchestra & Chorus / 1991 / Sony 47265
- ○ **Varèse** / Boulez (cond.), Yakar, Beauregard, New York PO, InterContemporain Ensemble / 1990 / Sony 45844
- ○ **Complete Webern** / Boulez (cond.), Kremer, Zimerman, Oelze, Finley, Berlin PO, Emerson SQ / DG 457637
- ○ **Messiaen** / Boulez (cond.), Cleveland Orch. / 1995 / DG 445827
- ○ **Boulez: Pli Selon Pli; Livre Pour Cordes** / Boulez (cond.), Lukomska, D'Alton, Bergmann, Stingl, BBCSO, Strings of the New Philharmonia / 1995 / Sony 68335

KEYBOARD

Piano Sonata No. 3 (1955–1957; revised 1963)

With his *Piano Sonata No. 2* (1948), Pierre Boulez began expanding his use of serial techniques beyond the realm of pitch to other musical elements such as rhythm and dynamics. This led him to the notion of "perpetual expansion," a sort of open form in which works might vary extensively from performance to performance and exist in a constant state of revision. He derived this concept from the great French poet Stéphane Mallarmé, whose *Livre* was such a free-form collection, begun in the early 1870s but left unfinished at the poet's death in 1898.

The *Sonata No. 3* is the first such open form work, begun in the mid-1950s, revised in 1963, but never completed in the usual sense. The sonata is usually described by the composer and other commentators as having five movements or "formants" ("Antiphonie," "Trope," "Constellation," "Strophe," and "Séquence"); however, only two, Formant 2: "Trope" and Formant 3: "Constellation-Miroir," have been published. The other three are regarded as "works in progress." Boulez gave the Sonata its premiere on September 26, 1957, at Darmstadt, where he regularly taught in the late 1950s and early 1960s. There remains some controversy as to whether Boulez or Karlheinz Stockhausen—whose *Klavierstücke XI*, also an open form work, was likewise premiered at Darmstadt in July 1957—was the real revolutionary in this area.

Boulez described his Sonata's form and inspiration in the article "Sonata, que me veux-tu?" (Sonata, What Do You Want Of Me?). The "Trope" movement, which appeared in print in the form of a spiral booklet, consists of four sections: "Texte," "Parenthèse," "Commentaire," and "Glose." These can be played in several different orders. "Texte," probably the simplest of the four sections, is often featured first, whereas "Commentaire," with its scherzo-like playfulness and dramatic chords (including a particularly long-held one at its end), sounds most like a normal conclusion.

The sheet music of "Constellation-Miroir" consists of nine large sheets in six "constellations"—three of "Points" (structures concentrating on single notes, printed in green), two of "Blocs" (structures based on chords and arpeggios, printed in red), and a short "Mélange" (featuring both single notes and chords). "Constellation-Miroir" would normally be played in the order "Mélange"—"Points 3"—"Blocs II"—"Points 2"—"Blocs I"—"Points 1," as opposed to an unpublished version of the movement which is played in reverse order. Elements within each of the six sections can be arranged in several different ways. Boulez likens the structure to a map of an unknown city in which the performer "must direct himself through a tight network of routes." The music of "Constellation-Miroir" alternates between spare, delicate passages and more assertive, granitic sections; it is a remote and enigmatic movement, with considerable space between its gestures. *—Chris Morrison*

Recommended:

- ○ **Boulez: Piano Sonatas 1–3** / Biret / 1995 / Naxos 553353

CHAMBER MUSIC

Eclat, for 9 percussionists & 6 instrumentalists (1965)

Eclat is a kind of work in progress, a small but self-contained part of a larger whole, *Eclat/Multiples*. *Eclat* itself is a short work for chamber ensemble, composed in 1965. It is scored for an eclectic and colorful group of instruments: guitar, piano, celesta, harp, glockenspiel, vibraphone, mandolin, bells, and cimbalom, along with a sextet of wind and strings. The opening gestures of the piece delineates the work's harmonic spectrum; intervals are subsequently drawn from the opening chords to build other chords and melodic structures. Following an improvisatory piano cadenza, the ensemble begins a process of timbral layering, combining free and strict time as the work develops into a kaleidoscope of color. Throughout *Eclat*, the question of music time is central, and there is constant tension between moments of free time, time controlled by pulse, and a combination of the two. The piece essentially builds to a climax of color and instrumental contrast by the midpoint, then turning around and working backwards through and developing material from the opening sections. The jagged first half of the piece gives way to a more homogenous musical discourse as the work moves toward its conclusion.

Eclat/Multiples represents an expansion of the original *Eclat*, exploring small rhythmic cells and instrument combinations, in essence "multiplying" the various possible motivic combinations, which are exchanged between small, soloistic ensembles and the larger ensemble. *—Alexander Carpenter*

Recommended:

- ○ **Boulez: Rituel; Eclat; Multiples** / Boulez (cond.), Ens. InterContemporain / 1990 / Sony 45839

Sur Incises, for 3 pianos, 3 harps, 2 vibes & marimba (1995–1998)

Pierre Boulez completed *Sur Incises* in 1998. It is scored for three pianos, three harps, and three percussionists. The composer chose to divide the work into Moment I and Moment II, which add up to a total of 37 minutes in duration. Based on an earlier work for solo piano, entitled *Incises*, *Sur Incises* spins out in directions in a new and arresting manner that is bristling with energy, exploding the context of the original piece. Originally, the idea was to write a sort of piano concerto, but the composer could not find instruments to match that instrument's speed for certain types of melody. What he ended up writing was a testament to the nature of the instrument instead. The piano as an instrument generates its sound though a complex operation, and *Sur Incises* seems to deconstruct that sound and reassemble it so that all the components of its system of aural delivery are laid bare for the listener. Everything about the piano's sound quality is amplified; the harp brings the piano's strings into the foreground, while the percussion brings out the soundboard and the attack of the player's hands upon the keyboard. The composer is revealing fresh ideas here, in his fifth decade of professional composing. *Sur Incises* careens into uncharted territories of monochrome color. It is dense yet fluid, majestic yet immediate. Some moments will remind alert listeners of Boulez's *Le Marteau sans maître* of the 1950s, but no rehashing of old ideas is detectable. There is a similar correlation with his work *Derive* from the 1980s. The manner in which ideas spin out of the fabric of *Sur Incises* is comparable. However, it is the way the composer has built on the discoveries of these works that stands out. With each new composition, he has continued to build his vocabulary. Previously unheard nuances assert themselves in *Sur Incises*. When one of the pianos performs a solo line, it reveals itself as the core of the work's sound. The full ensemble sounds like one enormous instrument, to which the piano is the primary component. Yet it is also a many-headed hydra, often featuring several voices churning out melody in compelling counterpoint. There are cadenzas that will challenge versatile performers, adding an edge of rawness to a soundscape of otherwise fiery and organic elegance.

This work was dedicated to Paul Sacher on his 90th birthday. Sacher was a friend of the composer and a generous sponsor of avant-garde music throughout the bulk of the second half of the twentieth century. His institute in Basil, Switzerland holds the score sketches from many great works, including those of Boulez, Webern, and others. *—John Keillor*

Recommended:

○ **Boulez: Sur Incises; Messagesquisse; Anthèmes 2** / Boulez (cond.), Ens. InterContemporain / 2000 / DG 463475

VOCAL

Le marteau sans maître (1953–1955)

Pierre Boulez completed *Le marteau sans maître* (The Hammer Without a Master) in 1955, soon after he had abandoned the strict tenets of serialism. It is one of three pieces that Boulez wrote using texts by surrealist poet René Char. Three of his poems are used here, "L'Artisanat furieux," "Bourreaux de solitude," and "Bel édifice et les pressentiments." The ensemble consists of soprano and chamber group, with the soprano singing in only some of the nine movements. This work was partially inspired by Schoenberg's *Pierrot Lunaire*, and Boulez has written about how these works resemble each other. He combined them in many concert programs. Taken together, these works exemplify the twentieth century avant-garde; both works are indicative of genius, sincerity, and rigor. Furthermore, they are works of sublime beauty, though the first listen often proves daunting for many. As it progresses it becomes more complex, but like Joyce's *Finnegans Wake*, it is the beginning that seems strangest. Once past this point, the comprehensibility of the whole work becomes increasingly apparent. By the end of the piece, listeners with an open heart will already be looking forward to another hearing.

The three poems included in the work are also indicative of three different ways of combining instruments. They are staggered and absorbed by the final movement. The soprano becomes part of the ensemble, singing lines without text, and no more prominent than any other player. Again, aspects resemble *Pierrot Lunaire*, which does not utilize the entire ensemble until the end. There is a train of aesthetic thought in progress here, which begins with Schoenberg's writing cabaret songs for extra income from around the turn of the century. Then, in 1912, Schoenberg's *Pierrot Lunaire* was a comment on the cabaret aesthetic, bringing that style of song into the realm of avant-garde rigor. Boulez continued this direction; *Le marteau sans maître* is much more complex than Schoenberg's 1912 masterpiece, and equally musical, though when the work was first premiered even the most well-disposed musicians were hesitant to embrace it. During the rehearsals for the American premiere, a player asked the composer where the poetry was, the warmth, in the piece. Boulez replied "Oh, it's there." About 35 minutes long, its nine movements build upon nuances of mystery and sensation that do not exist anywhere else in Western music. Yet there is never a sense of grandness that often pervades such an original work. Business as usual pervades the flow of the movements, and the modesty of that effect, that complete absence of redirecting the listener's interest to the composer, is likewise unique. It is a tenet of modernism that the self-aggrandizing of the romantic artist should be dismissed, but this idea seems rarely possible. Even in the chance operation works of Cage, specifically intended to eliminate the intentions of the composer, one cannot forget for an instant that it is Cage's work being performed. If the artist puts effort into his or her work, it is usually inevitable that something of the artist's ego will make its presence felt. Somehow, Boulez avoided this in *Le marteau sans maître*. It is one of the finest and most enduring chamber works of the twentieth century. Exotic and immediate, this work has been dismissed out of fear, resentment, and misunderstanding. Listeners need not be afraid; this is beautiful music. *—John Keillor*

Recommended:

○ **KammarensembleN Live** / B. T. Andersson (cond.), KammerensembleN / 1997 / Caprice 21581

○ **Boulez: Le Marteau Sans Maître; Sonatine; Messiaen: 7 Haïkaï** / Boulez (cond.), Deroubaix / Adès 20290

Pli selon pli, for soprano & orchestra (1957–1962)

Pierre Boulez's masterpiece *Pli selon Pli* is a kind of musically self-fulfilling prophecy. Taking its title from a poem by Stephane Mallarmé, in which "folds upon folds" of mist gradually dissipate to reveal the stone walls of Bruges, the piece itself has unfolded in a similar manner: it began as a set of three "Improvisations on Mallarmé" composed at intervals during the late 1950s, was expanded with the composition of a "Tombeau" in 1959, and reached near-completion with the prefatory "Don [du poème]" added in 1960. Boulez's accretions and adjustments didn't stop there. In 1962, he adjusted the orchestration by expanding the "Don" from a simple soprano/piano duo to a large ensemble and enlarging the instrumentation used in the first Improvisation, as well, in order to give the overall orchestration of the whole five-movement structure a double hairpin form: from large to small (in the second, central Improvisation) to large. Finally in 1989, Boulez made one last set of alterations, solidifying the structural ordering of sections in certain movements that had originally been left structurally variable in performance.

The work's long and tenuous gestation reflects the elusiveness that characterizes the poetry by Mallarmé that it sets. Mallarmé's symbolisms are as rich with meaning as they are ambiguous and intractable—that is, meaning whose presence and breadth can often be sensed, but whose actual content remains hard to apprehend. Boulez seeks a musical analogy to this quality. Every gesture and sonority seems utterly precise and deliberately crafted, yet the work as a whole remains fluid and diaphanous, with a sense of flow more than form. The "Don" begins with a sudden, strident bang, exploiting from the first moment the work's enormous percussion battery, but then immediately turns willowy and veiled. Likewise, after the initial utterance of the opening line ("Behold, the child of an Idumaean night!"), the voice becomes a ghost, haunting the varied orchestral landscape with intermittent textual foreshadows of the Improvisations to follow. Even though the poetry of the central movements proceeds in a more discernible fashion, with more lyrical contours in the voice, occasionally the angularity of line and exaggeration of articulation strains against the bounds of the grammatical and seeks transcendence in the purely acoustic. The *Tombeau*, growing slowly from its initial pianistic mumblings into a frenetic orchestral jumble, concludes the piece with a shimmering setting of a most Mallarméian sentiment: "A trickling stream we vilify as death." *—Jeremy Grimshaw*

Recommended:

○ **Boulez: Pli selon pli; Livre pour cordes** / Boulez (cond.), Lukomska, D'Alton, Bergmann, Stingl, BBC SO / 1995 / Sony 68335

AVANT-GARDE

. . . explosante-fixe . . . , for midi-flute, orchestra & electronics (1991–1993)

In 1971, Pierre Boulez was asked to contribute a short musical tribute to Igor Stravinsky, who had died that year. Boulez created what amounted to a musical puzzle, a page of seven musical fragments labeled Originel and Transitoires II-VII. The notes are written out, but the instrumentation is left open, moving from a single line in the Originel, introducing the seven-note cell that underlies all the material, to two lines in Transitoire II, to three in Transitoire III, and so on. There are instructions given for going from one fragment to another, elaborating the form, and so on.

This compositional schematic was published in 1972, and Boulez worked that year and the next on a "realization" of the music for an ensemble of flute, seven other instruments, and an electroacoustic component for spatializing and manipulating the instrumental sounds. Performances at that time were not completely successful, due primarily to the instability of the halaphone, the electronic element developed by German engineer Hans-Peter Haller. Boulez put the piece aside to work on other projects, but the music was never far from his mind. In fact, the seven-note cell underlying . . . *explosante-fixe* . . . was used in 1974 for *Rituels*, and in *Repons* in 1981.

In the late 1980s, with new technology available to him at IRCAM, the research institute he founded in Paris, Boulez returned to . . . *explosante-fixe* . . . once more. The expanded version of . . . *explosante-fixe* . . . consists of (as of 1993) Transitoire VII, Transitoire V, and Originel, with two entirely electronic transitional passages, Interstitiel 1 and 2. The solo flute is "shadowed" by two other flutes as well as transformed versions of its music processed live by computer. The supporting ensemble is a mixed group almost identical to that used in *Repons*, six keyboard/percussion soloists.

As one might expect from a piece featuring the flute, the music is bright. It is also dramatic. The amplification of the soloist ensures that it will be heard even when the ensemble is playing full out. The seven-note cell underlying the score ensures a degree of harmonic coherence, and this is apparent from close listening. Each of the three main sections uses a different transposition of this cell, and Boulez has taken care to feature the main pitch of each prominently, providing tonal anchors. As the title might suggest (taken from a poem by André Breton), the music proceeds in fragments, in fits and starts, alternating between flurries of activity and more reflective passages. The electronics are very well-integrated into the instrumental textures, enhancing the instrumental palette rather than opposing it. *—Jim Harley*

Recommended:

○ **Boulez Conducts Boulez: Explosante-Fixe** / Boulez (cond.), Ens. InterContemporain / 1995 / DG 445833

Joseph Boulogne, Chevalier de Saint-Georges

b. Dec. 25, 1745 (?), Basse Terre, Guadeloupe (?), **d.** Jun. 10, 1799, Paris, France

Composer

Composer and virtuoso violinist Joseph Bologne, better-known as the Chevalier de Saint-Georges, was unique in the eighteenth century musical world for his unusual background and multiple talents. Born in Guadalupe to a planter and his African slave, Saint-Georges settled in Paris in 1747. An expert fencer, he was made a chevalier and *Gendarme de la Garde du Roi* at the age of 19. Living on a comfortable annuity provided by his father, he enjoyed great popularity in Paris society. In 1766, the Italian fencer Faldoni came to Paris to challenge Saint-Georges. Although Faldoni won, he called Saint-Georges the finest swordsman in all of Europe. Saint-Georges probably studied composition with Gossec and violin with Lolli, but little information about his musical studies exists. In 1769, he became a violinist in a new orchestra founded by Gossec, the Concert des Amateurs, which performed at the Hôtel de Soubise. Soon, Saint-Georges became concertmaster of the Concert des Amateurs and performed his pair of violin concertos, Op. 2, with the orchestra in 1772. In 1773, when Gossec left the Amateurs to direct the Concert Spirituel, Saint-Georges was appointed musical director. In the following few years, this orchestra developed a reputation as the best in Paris and one of the best on the continent. In 1774, Saint-Georges' father died, leaving him without an annuity. In order to support himself, he began publishing a great deal of music, much of which featured the violin. Among these works were two sets of string quartets (a genre rarely practiced in France at that early date), a dozen violin concertos, and at least ten symphonies concertantes. In 1776, a scandal erupted when Saint-Georges was proposed as the next music director of the Opéra de Paris. His candidacy was challenged by several prominent singers at the Opéra, who complained to Queen Marie Antoinette about the prospect of having to follow orders from a mulatto. Saint-Georges presented his first opera, *Ernestine*, at *the Comédie-Italienne* in 1777. Although Saint-Georges' music was well-received, the libretto was criticized and it never had a second performance. His second opera, *La chasse*, did not fare much better, with only four performances. Despite the response to these, Saint-Georges decided to compose nothing but operas, giving up instrumental music. He became music director at the private theater of Mme de Montesson, morganatic wife of the Duke of Orléans, who also named him *Lieutenant de chasse* of the Duke's hunting chateau at Raincy. Saint-Georges' third opera, *La partie de chasse*, was performed at Raincy in 1778, and his fourth, *L'amant anonyme* was performed at Mme de Montesson's theater in 1780. When the Concert des Amateurs disbanded in 1781, Saint-Georges, under the sponsorship of the Masonic lodge *la Loge Olympique*, established the Concert de la Loge Olympique. Saint-Georges commissioned Haydn to write his Paris symphonies for this orchestra. When the Duke of Orléans died in 1785, Saint-Georges found himself without patronage in Paris. In 1787, he decided to travel to London, where the fencing master Angelo invited him to give fencing exhibitions. When he returned to Paris, he composed his most successful opera, *La fille-garçon*, and continued to lead the orchestra at *la Loge Olympique*. After becoming involved in revolutionary politics and the French National Guard, he completed his final opera, *Guillaume tout coeur*, for the theater in Lille. In 1793, during the terror, he spent 18 months in the military prison. He was presumed killed during the 1795 slave revolt on Saint Domingue (Haiti), but reappeared in France in 1797 to direct one more orchestra, at the Masonic lodge *Cercle de l'Harmonie*, before his death in 1799. *—Robert Adelson*

Overview of Works (ca. 1770–1799)

Joseph Boulogne, Chevalier de Saint-Georges, thought to be the first composer of African descent who worked within the European classical tradition, is sometimes referred to as *Le Mozart Noir* or the Black Mozart. In fact, since the prime years of Saint-Georges' activity as an instrumental composer were in the middle and late 1770s, just before and during Mozart's extended stay in Paris, the influence likely went in the other direction. Saint-Georges was the toast of Paris at the time, a champion fencer, a star violinist, a noted womanizer, and the object of brewing but veiled racial controversy. A top student of Gossec, perhaps the most influential French composer of the day, he should be remembered not so much as a black pioneer (he founded no school of Creole composition), but as one of the architects of the Parisian style that did much to shape Mozart's music and that today offers buried riches of its own.

Saint-Georges' compositional career falls into two phases. Most of his instrumental music was written, and published with great success, in the 1770s. Three genres predominate in his works of this period: the symphonie concertante, the string quartet, and the violin concerto. In focusing on the first two of these, Saint-Georges was well ahead of the curve; his 10 or more symphonies concertantes, along with several similar mixed quartets, were sterling examples of that sprightly genre that rapidly spread eastward into German-speaking lands. Unlike Mozart's and Haydn's famous examples, those by Saint-Georges had two movements. His string quartets were among the first composed in Paris, and his facility in that new genre suggests that he was conversant with wider European trends.

Saint-Georges' roughly ten violin concertos were written for his own use, and it was with his first two that he kicked off his performing career in 1772. They are not explosively virtuosic in the Italian manner but are full of elegant melody and reveal the composer's gifts as a violinist in their frequent flights to the very top of the instrument's range. The opening movements of several of the concertos are unusually expansive, with the orchestral expositions unfurling a large canvas for the soloist to fill in. Their central movements possess what has several times (notably in the *New Grove Dictionary*) been described as Creole nostalgia or melancholy, whatever that might be. In fact these movements are attractive examples of the sweet sentimentalism common to Parisian instrumental music of the era, the musical counterpart of the lush and slightly frivolous art of Fragonard and his friends.

Later in life, Saint-Georges devoted himself primarily to opera. His operatic works, unfortunately, have mostly been lost. Especially tantalizing is a work called *Le droit du seigneur* to which Saint-Georges' name was attached, but that is now thought to have been written mostly by someone else. It may have been drawn from the same source material that produced Mozart's subversive *Le nozze di Figaro*—material that would have had special resonance in the hands of a man who was the son of a French colonial lord and his African slave. *—James Manheim*

Recommended:

- ○ **Le Mozart Noir** / Lamon, Melsted, Gilardeau, Tafelmusik Baroque Orch. / 2003 / CBC 5225
- ○ **Saint-Georges: Sonatas for violin & harpsichord** / Haudebourg, Kantorow / 1999 / Arion 55445
- ○ **Saint-Georges: String Quartets** / Coleridge SQ / Afka 557

Sir Adrian Boult

b. Apr. 8, 1889, Chester, England, **d.** Mar. 24, 1983, Farnham, England
Conductor

Neither as colorful a public figure as fellow Briton Sir Thomas Beecham, nor as stormy and commanding on the podium as some of his better-known international contemporaries, Sir Adrian Boult nevertheless was one of Britain's foremost conductors for nearly 70 years. He championed contemporary music, introducing Holst's *The Planets* and Berg's *Wozzeck* to the British public, but his pioneering work with the BBC Orchestra, which he created and directed for 20 years, is often regarded as his signature achievement.

Born to a wealthy shipowner, Boult spent his grammar school days in London at Westminster School and took to music early. At Christ Church, Oxford, Boult flourished under the guidance of conductor Hugh Allen. In addition, Boult worked with Artur Nikisch during a stay at the Leipzig Conservatory (1912–13). Boult also studied with composer Max Reger, but a serious illness that kept him out of World War I cut his continental sojourn short.

Boult made his debut at Queen's Hall with the London Symphony Orchestra in 1918. From that first concert Boult demonstrated support for British music, including Vaughn Williams' then virtually unknown *"London" Symphony* on the program. The concert led to an invitation from Holst to conduct the premiere of *The Planets* at a private concert at Queen's Hall. In 1919 Boult joined faculty of the Royal College of Music.

In the years following World War I, Boult conducted both orchestral music and opera. He served as principal conductor for Diaghilev's ballets russes during their London stay in 1919, and in 1926 rejoined the staff at Covent Garden. In 1924 Boult accepted the directorship of the recently formed City of Birmingham Symphony Orchestra, which he molded into a first-rank ensemble.

In 1930 Boult received an invitation to organize and direct the newly formed BBC Symphony Orchestra. Boult took the group on numerous international tours and began its long, distinguished recording career. During the Second World War Boult and the orchestra took up residence in Bristol, but German raids drove them to Bedford. In 1950 Boult passed the BBC baton to Malcolm Sargent and assumed directorship of the London Philharmonic Orchestra, which he took on a politically significant tour of the USSR in 1956. Following his retirement from the LPO in 1957, Boult rejoined the City of Birmingham Symphony Orchestra for one year, and returned to the Royal College to teach a new generation of conductors from 1962 to 1966. He ceased conducting altogether in 1979, after several years of occasional appearances. According to most accounts, Boult's conducting was unimpaired even at the ripe age of 90. He died in 1983, just two weeks shy of his 94th birthday.

Boult felt that it was the conductor's duty to present as much music as possible to the listening public without regard for the conductor's own personal tastes, leaving it to posterity to preserve particular pieces. Describing himself as a musical "purist," Boult believed that everything necessary for a successful performance was to be found within the printed score. Although some critics complained that Boult's musical persona lacked the colorful quality of true greatness, his gentlemanly conduct on the podium earned him respect from his musicians that hours of tirades might not have. On his "off nights," Boult's music-making perhaps came across as dull or workmanlike, but often his clarity of approach and fidelity to the score produced electrifying results.

Boult's autobiography, *My Own Trumpet*, was published in 1973. He was knighted in 1937, and made a Companion of Honour in 1969. *—Blair Johnston*

Recommended:

- ○ **Holst: The Planets; Elgar: Enigma Variations** / Boult (cond.), London SO, London PO / 2002 / EMI 67749
- ○ **Vaughan Williams** / Boult (cond.), London PO / 1991 / EMI 64022
- ○ **Sir Adrian Boult** / Boult (cond.) / EMI 75459
- ○ **Elgar: Cockaigne Overture; Symphony 2** / Boult (cond.), London PO / 1991 / EMI 764014

James Bowman

b. Nov. 6, 1941, Oxford, England
Countertenor

James Bowman has been a model for an entire generation of countertenors. A fixture on the operatic and concert stages of Europe since the late 1960s, he has made more than 130 commercial recordings. His distinctive voice—highly expressive and colorful, if not conventionally beautiful—is well-suited to the music of Handel, Purcell, and Benjamin Britten, all of whom have been pillars of his prolific career.

Bowman began singing as an alto chorister in the choirs of Ely Cathedral and Oxford's New College, where he received degrees in education and history. His solo career began with a successful audition for Benjamin Britten's English Opera Group in 1967. The composer offered him the role of Oberon in his *A Midsummer Night's Dream*, as well as a concert at London's Queen Elizabeth Hall. Bowman continued to sing Oberon throughout his career, and made an excellent recording of the role for Hyperion in 1990. His association with Britten would continue, as well; the composer wrote the role of Apollo in *Death in Venice* for him, and also dedicated his *Canticle No. 4* to Bowman.

In 1970, Bowman became the first countertenor to sing at Glyndebourne, in a production of Cavalli's *La calisto*. By 1972, he had also debuted with the English National Opera and Covent Garden in operas of Handel (*Semele*) and Peter Maxwell Davies (*Taverner*). He would eventually sing most of the great Handelian operas, including *Xerxes*, *Giulio Cesare*, *Orlando*, and *Rinaldo*.

Bowman has premiered a number of contemporary works, aside from those already mentioned. He was the first to sing the role of Astron in Michael Tippett's opera *The Ice Break*, in 1977; he sang Alan Ridout's *Phaeton* for BBC Radio; Michael Nyman wrote his *Self-Laudatory Hymn of Inanna and Her Omnipotence* for Bowman; and Bowman was the first to record John Tavener's *Akathist of Thanksgiving* and a number of works by Geoffrey Burgon.

As an oratorio singer, Bowman has been successful in standard roles, like Handel's *Messiah* and *Chandos Anthems*, Vivaldi's *Salve Regina*, Orff's *Carmina Burana*, and Henry Purcell's *Birthday Odes*. Purcell's music has been a particular focus of his recordings on the Hyperion label, most of which have been in collaboration with Robert King and the King's Consort.

Paris has been almost a second home to Bowman during his career, and in recognition of his contribution to Parisian culture, the government made him *Chevalier de l'Ordre des Arts et des Lettres* in 1992. He also presented a sold-out 25th anniversary concert at the Palais Garnier that same year. *—AMG*

Recommended:

- ○ **The James Bowman Collection** / King (cond.), Bowman, Tubb, King's Consort / 1996 / Hyperion 3
- ○ **Handel: Heroic Arias** / King (cond.), Bowman, Goodwin, MacIntosh, Ward, Clark, King's Consort / 1991 / Hyperion 66483
- ○ **Mr. Henry Purcell's Most Admirable Composures** / King, Bowman, King's Consort / 1989 / Hyperion 66288

William Boyce

b. Sep. 1, 1711, London, England, **d.** Feb. 7, 1779, London, England
Composer: Symphonic

The leading native-born composer of eighteenth century England (save perhaps for Thomas Arne), William Boyce was born in London in 1711. He received his primary musical training as a boy soprano at St. Paul's Cathedral. When his voice changed, Boyce necessarily left the choir and began to study organ with the church's organist and composer, Maurice Greene. In 1734, Boyce accepted his first professional position as organist at the Oxford Chapel, where he remained for two years, also spending time teaching at a variety of nearby schools. From that position, Boyce moved on to serve in the same capacity at St. Michael's, and concurrently assumed a court composer position at the Chapel Royal. He was, a year later, named director of England's Three Choirs Festival, an annual celebration that was the first such endeavor of its kind and continues today in London.

Boyce's profile began to rise in the 1750s. In 1749, Boyce accepted employment as organist at the All Hallows Church, but also began a relationship with the Drury Lane Theater; he composed a wealth of incidental music over the next three years for that establishment. When, in 1755, the flourishing musician's former teacher Maurice Greene died, Boyce assumed the position "Master of the King's Music," an appointment widely considered the apex of his artistic career; in this post he reached the height of his celebrity in London. In this capacity, Boyce composed music (primarily odes) to be performed at specific royal occasions. Boyce also was named conductor at St. Paul's Cathedral's Sons of Clergy Festival.

In 1758, the Royal Chapel, who had already employed Boyce as court composer, hired him as chief organist. Boyce was rapidly losing his hearing, however, and was forced to resign his posts at both St. Michael's and All Hallows Church. His deafness had developed early in his life but did not handicap him until it worsened considerably in his later years. In forced retirement, Boyce committed himself to editing and organizing a collection of English church scores by numerous composers, including William Byrd and Henry Purcell. This compilation, entitled *Cathedral Music*, had been a project started by his teacher Maurice Greene many years prior to his death. Much of its remains prominent in the Anglican Church repertoire today.

Boyce produced a generous quantity of music during his career, and is most widely recognized for his symphonies, anthems, and overtures. His eight symphonies, all in three movements, combine Baroque style with forward looking elements; like other early "symphonies" in Italy, these were closely linked to the theatrical overture form; indeed, these symphonies were essentially collations of pieces borrowed from Boyce's own catalog of music for theater. Boyce composed music for keyboard, as well as chamber music for varied ensembles; a group of 12 trio sonatas in the Italian manner, published in 1747, proved particularly successful.

The music essayist Charles Burney recognized an essential English quality in Boyce's works, but the composer fell into obscurity in the nineteenth century. It was not until the 1930s that a quantity of his music (specifically his symphonies, overtures, and three concerti grossi) was rediscovered. Prominent in the revival of his works was the English conductor Constant Lambert, who edited scores of his music and programmed it repeatedly. *—David Brensilver*

SYMPHONIC

Eight Symphonies, Op. 2

William Boyce's *Eight Symphonies* were first published in 1760, the title doubtless a reflection of the increasing popularity of the form at the time. In truth, they are not true symphonies at all, rather being overtures (the two terms were interchangeable in the eighteenth century) composed for a variety of occasional dramatic works written between 1739 and 1756. As such they differ little from the subsequent issue of *Twelve Overtures*, works drawn from similar sources, and so old-fashioned by the time of publication (1770) that the edition's failure caused the modest Boyce to refrain from publishing more of his own works. The *Eight Symphonies* however had met with greater success, enjoying a popularity that has been revived in modern times. In common with his English contemporaries, long saddled as being merely a clone of Handel, Boyce's music in fact displays all the best qualities of English music of the period. This may be characterized as owning to a tuneful, breezily open-air quality, often (as in the case of Boyce) incorporating an easy mastery of counterpoint that is always worn lightly, never academically. Such qualities typify these delightful little "symphonies." Three, *No. 1 in B flat (Ode for New Year,* 1756), *No. 2 in A (Ode for the King's Birthday, 1756)*, and *No. 5 in D (Ode for St. Cecilia's Day, 1739*), have their origination in occasional works, the first two dating from the period just before Boyce took over from Maurice Greene as Master of the King's Musick and was already fulfilling some of the ailing Greene's duties. Three further works, *No. 3 in C minor (The Chaplet)*, *No. 4 in F (The Shepherd's Lottery)*, and *No. 6 in F (Solomon)*, started life as overtures to dramatic works, while *No. 7 in B flat* is the overture to the splendid Pindaric Ode of 1740. The provenance of the final work, *No. 8 in D minor*, is not known. It is also known as *The Worcester Overture*. With the exception of the two-movement No. 6, which concludes with an elegant Larghetto, all the symphonies have three movements, the last usually a stylized dance movement. As would be expected with works drawn from a variety of sources, the scoring varies. Nos. 1, 2, 3, 6, 7, and 8 call for forces including pairs of oboes and bassoons, strings, and harpsichord continuo. In Nos. 1, 7, and 8, flutes replace the oboes in the slow movement (they were played by the same performers in the eighteenth century). *No. 4* adds a pair of horns to this combination, while *No. 5* is the most grandly scored of the collection, with trumpets and drums adding a ceremonial pomp especially in the splendid opening Allegro ma non troppo. *—Brian Robins*

Recommended:

- ○ **William Boyce: 8 Symphonies** / Pinnock (cond.), English Concert / 1987 / Archiv 419631

Liona Boyd

b. Jul. 11, 1949, London, England
Guitarist

Billed by her promoters as the "First Lady of the Guitar," Liona Boyd has fully lived up to that accolade and more: Since the early 1980s, she has been one of the most popular classical guitarists, male or female. She also performs music in other genres, placing several of her recordings in the crossover realm.

Born in London, Boyd spent the latter half of her childhood in Toronto, where her family had twice settled, the first move there ending in a brief return to England. She began studying guitar at age 13 with Eli Kassner in Toronto and later with Narciso Yepes, Andrés Segovia, and with her early idol, Julian Bream. She received a degree in music from the University of Toronto, then took further instruction from Alexandre Lagoya in Nice and Paris. In 1974, she made her first recording, a collection of pieces entitled *The Guitar*, issued on the Boot/London label. Her second effort was issued shortly afterward, *The Guitar Artistry of Liona Boyd*. By now, her career as a recitalist was in full bloom: radio interviews and a story about her in *Time* magazine led to her critically successful debut at Carnegie Hall in March 1975. Shortly afterward, she performed several classical works at a Gordon Lightfoot concert to an enthusiastic reception and subsequently joined his troupe for a highly successful tour. Much concert activity in Canada and numerous appearances on Canadian television followed. Owing to the efforts of country guitarist Chet Atkins, who was impressed by her skills at a Nashville concert, she appeared on the American television program *Today*, which featured an interview with her by Gene Shalit. She continued giving concerts in nonclassical venues, as well as performing traditional recitals in the world's most-respected concert halls. Her concert tours, covering the Americas, Europe, and Asia, were numerous and generally garnered positive notices; her 1980 tour of Japan was especially successful. Further recordings appeared, including her CBS album *The First Lady of the Guitar* and a collection of Baroque works performed with Andrew Davis and the English Chamber Orchestra. Some of her albums during this period had mixed results in the market place: The 1982 LP *The Best of Liona Boyd* was a best-seller, while the ensuing *Virtuoso* (1983), her first digital recording that contained some of her finest performances of "serious" music (compositions by Villa-Lobos, Berkeley, and others) achieved only mediocre sales.

Throughout the latter twentieth century and into the 2000s, Boyd's career continued to thrive. By 2002, she had recorded about 20 albums for some of the largest labels, including RCA, Sony, and Polygram. Moreover, her numerous concert appearances throughout the world were generally major events of critical acclaim. Even her personal life had attracted attention, not least because of her eight-year romance with Canadian Prime Minister Pierre Trudeau, which ended in 1983. She commented candidly on that relationship in her 1998 autobiography, *In My Own Key*, which presents interesting accounts of her concert and personal life, featuring anecdotes about encounters with Queen Elizabeth, actors Roger Moore and Robert Redford, and musicians Andrés Segovia, Alexandre Lagoya, Chet Atkins, Oscar Peterson, and many more. Boyd relocated to Beverly Hills in 1992 when she married John Simon, a successful California real estate developer. Her later recordings include *Whispers of Love* (2000) and *Camino Latino* (2002), the former containing some of Boyd's own compositions and the latter divulging a mixture of Latin styles and employing several jazz musicians. *—Robert Cummings*

Recommended:

- ○ **The Romantic Guitar of Liona Boyd** / Robertson (cond.), Boyd / 2001 / Moston 570042
- ○ **Liona Boyd – The Spanish Album** / Boyd / 1998 / Moston 8014
- ○ **Miniatures for Guitar** / Boyd / 1996 / Moston 8003

Johannes Brahms

b. May 7, 1833, Hamburg, Germany, **d.** Apr. 3, 1897, Vienna, Austria

Composer: Symphonic, Orchestral, Chamber Music, Concerto, Keyboard, Vocal, Choral

The stature of Johannes Brahms among classical composers is well illustrated by his inclusion among the "Three Bs" triumvirate of Bach, Beethoven, and Brahms. Of all the major composers of the late Romantic era, Brahms was the one most attached to the Classical ideal as manifested in the music of Haydn, Mozart, and especially Beethoven; indeed, Hans von Bülow once characterized Brahms' *Symphony No. 1* (1855–76) as "Beethoven's Tenth." As a youth, Brahms was championed by Robert Schumann as music's greatest hope for the future; as a mature composer, Brahms became for conservative musical journalists the most potent symbol of musical tradition, a stalwart against the "degeneration" represented by the music of Wagner and his school. Brahms' symphonies, choral and vocal works, chamber music, and piano pieces are imbued with strong emotional feeling, yet take shape according to a thoroughly considered structural plan.

The son of a double bassist in the Hamburg Philharmonic Society, Brahms demonstrated great promise from the beginning. He began his musical career as a pianist, contributing to the family coffers as a teenager by playing in restaurants, taverns, and even brothels. Though by his early twenties he enjoyed associations with luminaries like violinists Eduard Reményi and Joseph Joachim, the friend and mentor who was most instrumental in advancing his career was Schumann, who all but adopted him and became his most ardent partisan, and their esteem was mutual. Following Schumann's death in 1856, Brahms became the closest confidant and lifelong friend of the composer's widow, pianist and composer Clara Wieck Schumann. After a life of spectacular musical triumphs and failed loves (the composer was involved in several romantic entanglements but never wed), Brahms died of liver cancer on April 3, 1897.

In every genre in which he composed, Brahms produced works that have become staples of the repertory. His most ambitious work, the *German Requiem* (1863–67), is the composer's singular reinterpretation of an age-old form. The four symphonies—lushly scored, grand in scope, and deeply expressive—are cornerstones of the symphonic literature. Brahms' concertos are, similarly, in a monumental, quasi-symphonic vein: the two piano concertos (1856–59 and 1881) and the *Violin Concerto* (1878) call for soloists with both considerable technical skill and stamina. His chamber music is among the most sophisticated and exquisitely crafted of the Romantic era; for but a single example, his works that incorporate the clarinet (e.g. the *Trio in A minor*, Op. 114 and the two *Sonatas*, Op. 120), an instrument largely overlooked by his contemporaries, remain unsurpassed. Though the piano sonata never held for Brahms the same appeal it had for Beethoven (Brahms wrote three to Beethoven's 32), he produced a voluminous body of music for the piano. He showed a particular affinity for variations—notably, on themes of Schumann (1854), Handel (1861), and Paganini (1862–63)—and likewise produced a passel of national dances and character pieces such as ballades, intermezzi, and rhapsodies. Collectively, these constitute one of the essential bodies of work in the realm of nineteenth century keyboard music. *—AMG*

SYMPHONIC

Symphony No. 1 in C minor, Op. 68 (1855–1876)

Brahms composed this work between 1855 and 1876. Otto Dessoff led a "tryout" first performance in Karlsruhe, Germany, on November 4, 1876. At Düsseldorf in 1854–56 (where he helped Clara Schumann with her seven children while terminally mad Robert, her husband, wasted away in an asylum) the young Brahms undertook on two separate occasions to sketch a symphony. By the end of 1858, one set of sketches had been assimilated into the *First Piano Concerto*, that gargantuan "serious" piece with Baroque underpinnings, in the tradition of Beethoven's *Grosse Fuge* and *"Hammerklavier" Sonata*. Sketches for a C major Allegro movement, in sonata form and 6/8 time, were saved for subsequent expansion and development. When, in 1862, he showed the results to now-widowed Clara, she expressed admiration but also concern that it ended too abruptly. For the next 12 years, Brahms kept this music close at hand. Finally, in 1874, he willed himself to complete the First Symphony that friends and admirers (beginning with Schumann in 1853, shortly after their first meeting) had been urging him to compose.

He polished the Allegro of 1855–62, now in C minor, then wrote a solemn introduction hinting at themes already 12–20 years old. These included a recurring motto of three ascending semitones, repeated in the slow movement. Having created a horse to pull the cart, Brahms addressed the middle movements: one slow (Andante moderato, in E major, then C sharp minor), the other quasi-scherzoid (Un poco allegretto e grazioso, pleasant and graceful, in A flat, F minor, and finally B major), respectively in triple and duple meters. Certain kinds of performance can make the central movements sound out-of-place, which is not meant, however, to impugn their intrinsic quality. Both exemplify a master of musical art in his time, who had reached a rarefied synthesis of conflicting creative forces. Their substance and style bespeak maturity no less than the monumental finale created to trump them. There an ominous preface in C minor leads to a C major Allegro non troppo ma con brio (not too quickly but spiritedly), which remains in 4/4 time until a climactic alla-breve acceleration into the coda.

Brahms' decade of residence in Vienna had smoothed as well as ripened him: the middle movements could be called Schubertian, by way of Schumann. The finale, however, pays homage to the Germany's Baroque masters: Scheidt, Froberger, Buxtehude, Bach, and expatriated Handel. Simultaneously it honors the symphonic architectonics of Beethoven without regressing. Although he belonged to the generation that succeeded Chopin and Schumann, Brahms liberated music as much as they from the traditional Germanic tyrannies of bar-lines, four- and eight-bar phrasing, downbeat accents, and rhythmic squareness. While none of the music by his colleagues sounded richer (not even Bruckner's with augmented winds and brass), Brahms achieved his ends with astonishingly simple means—the basic Beethoven orchestra, sans bass drum, cymbals, or piccolo—plain to the point of abstemiousness on paper, but inimitably sonorous in performance. *—Roger Dettmer*

Recommended:

- ○ **Brahms: Symphony 1; Gesang der Parzen** / C. Abbado (cond.), Berlin PO / DG 431790
- ○ **Brahms: Symphony 1** / Celibidache (cond.), SWR Stuttgart Radio SO / DG 459636
- ○ **Brahms: The Four Symphonies** / Szell (cond.), Cleveland Orch. / 1992 / Sony 48398
- ○ **Bruno Walter The Edition: Brahms Symphony 1** / Walter (cond.), Columbia SO / Sony 66248
- ○ **Brahms: Sinfonien** / Furtwängler (cond.), Vienna PO / 1995 / EMI 65513

Symphony No. 2 in D major, Op. 73 (1877)

Johannes Brahms composed his *Symphony No. 2* in the summer of 1877, less than a year after the premiere of his *Symphony No. 1* (Op.68 in C minor)—an astonishing fact given that the former had taken him 15 years to complete. Finally confident in his abilities as a symphonist, and less troubled by the looming shadow of Beethoven, Brahms created a much more spontaneous work that was well received by both critics and audiences. When compared with the works of his contemporaries, this piece is conservative in both orchestration and formal structure. But it is by no means reactionary. Rather, Brahms revised and expanded upon the eighteenth century model, largely replacing thematic contrast with transformation and variation, and adding his distinctive richness of harmony and rhythm.

There is both unity and variety in this symphony: Brahms manages to combine the light and dark, the lyrical and forceful, the extroverted and introspective—all the while growing the piece organically from the "seed" of the very first three notes (D-C sharp-D, heard in the cellos and the double basses). This compositional economy is instinctively apparent to the ear, and helps to make the entire work intelligible without sacrificing interest or spontaneity.

Brahms's orchestration is full, rich, and often ingenious. He chooses to make the ensemble one unified voice, and has introduced his entire spectrum of instrumental colors after only 40 bars; however, one never gets the sense that he is overusing the orchestra. Instead he creates a texture in constant flux, shifting the focus of the ear, and extracting individual colors to great effect.

The piece opens with the three-note germinating cell and a simple horn melody; we are then introduced to two subjects in turn, the first announced by the violins, and the second by the cellos and violas in a luxurious duet. After developing both themes, Brahms creates an interesting recapitulation by briefly combining the initial horn melody and the first subject, and then dwelling extensively on the second subject. A short coda is attached to the end.

Two bassoons color the second movement's opening cello theme with a dark counterpoint, creating an immediate contrast to the first movement. It is here that we begin to see the more introspective side of Brahms, although this is by no means a brooding movement; there a surprising variety of expression within the slow prevailing tempo.

With the third movement, Brahms for the first time departs from a string-dominated texture, and allows a solo oboe to introduce the opening theme, while pizzicato cellos and a woodwind choir provide accompaniment. Full of rhythmic interest, this movement has frequent meter changes, expectant fermatas, and Brahms' distinctive cross-rhythms.

The moody and unpredictable finale oscillates between manic energy and somberness; Brahms is constantly changing direction, sometimes so abruptly as to pull the rug out from beneath your feet. The motion never stops, and when the final D major fanfare arrives, one has the sense of having been on a wild ride.—*Allen Schrott*

Recommended:

- ○ **Brahms: Symphony 2** / Solti (cond.), Chicago SO / Penguin Classics 460623
- ○ **Brahms: Symphony 2; Academic Festival Overture; Alto Rhapsody** / C. Abbado (cond.), Berlin PO / 1998 / DG 459054
- ○ **Brahms: The Four Symphonies** / Szell (cond.), Cleveland Orch. / 1992 / Sony 48398
- ○ **Brahms: Symphonies 2 & 3** / B. Walter (cond.), Columbia SO / Sony 66248
- ○ **Brahms: Sinfonien** / Furtwängler (cond.), Vienna PO / 1995 / EMI 65513

Symphony No. 3 in F major, Op. 90 (1883)

The time when performers and composers had personal mottoes—Wieniawski's "Il faut risquer" (I must risk it), Joachim's "Frei aber einsam" (Free but lonely), Brahms' "Frei aber froh" (Free but happy)—is long since past, but still such mottoes are more than just biographical curiosities: there are at least two very well-recognized musical encryptions of those mottoes. Schumann, Albert Dietrich, and Brahms put their collective talents together to compose the *"F-A-E" Sonata* as a gift for Joachim, and, when Brahms came up with his own motto, he decided to use the pitches of its initials (F-A-F) as the motto theme for his *Symphony No. 3* in F, Op. 90.

Brahms composed the *Symphony No. 3* in the summer of 1883 after a five year long sabbatical from symphonic work. It is often considered the other three symphonies' "poor sister"—a prominent feature, yes, on any symphonic season calendar, but not quite the same stunning pinnacle of symphonic achievement that each of the other three is. How wrong that notion is!

If mass consumption has less taste for the *Third Symphony*'s odd mix of overt heroism and dense formal logic than it has for the apparently more sensuous, even voluptuous, music of the second or fourth symphonies, or the Beethovenian spiritual journey of the *First Symphony*'s outer movements, that is hardly evidence of a shortcoming on the composer's part. And indeed there is something heroic about the *Symphony No. 3*, enough to prompt Hans Richter, who conducted the premiere of the piece, to suggest that Brahms give it the subtitle "Eroica" (a suggestion that Brahms didn't take). It is a heroism utterly unlike the kind brought to mind by the composer of the actual *"Eroica" Symphony*, however. How could a symphony that begins with a musical manifestation of the bittersweet words "free but happy" approach Beethoven's *Third* or *Fifth* in raw grittiness?

The symphony is in four movements: Allegro con brio, Andante, Poco allegretto, and Allegro. The winds open the first movement with a three-chord rendition of F-A-F (actually A flat), after which a tempestuous first theme, also outlining F-A-F, takes over. The second theme is as beautiful a melody, pulsating with warmth, as one might hope for.

The melody of the Andante is rather like that of the *First Symphony*'s third movement, and not just because it is first given by a clarinet; it also has the same initial rhythm and the same gentle intervallic circle. Poco allegretto is hardly a scherzo; it is almost mournful.

The finale rekindles some of the first movement's dramatic fire. The quiet, unison theme of the opening is like the long-lost twin of the quiet, unison theme at the opening of the *Second Symphony*'s finale, except that what is in the *Second Symphony* a joyous occasion is in the *Third Symphony* intense and shadowed. The F-A-F motto appears again in the final bars, this time winding downward towards the final serene F major chord by way of luxurious string tremolandos. —*Blair Johnston*

Recommended:

- ○ **Brahms: Symphony 3; Tragische Ouvertüre; Schicksalslied** / C. Abbado (cond.), Berlin PO / DG 429765
- ○ **Brahms: The 4 Symphonies** / Szell (cond.), Cleveland Orch. / 1992 / Sony 48398
- ○ **Brahms: Sinfonien** / Furtwängler (cond.), Vienna PO / 1995 / EMI 65513
- ○ **Bruno Walter: The Edition, Vol. 3 (Box Set)** / B. Walter (cond.), Columbia SO / Sony 66248

Symphony No. 4 in E minor, Op. 98 (1884–1885)

That Brahms initially approached the symphonic form with trepidation is fairly evident from the chronology of his works. It wasn't until the age of 43 that he completed his *First Symphony*. Indeed, the composer's output to that point suggests a conscious process of self-education. A number of smaller-scale orchestral works, including the *Variations on a Theme of Haydn* and the proto-symphonic *Piano Concerto No. 1*, suggest preparation for what Brahms clearly saw as the elusive of compositional enterprises. He was to meet the challenge with a skill and individual spirit, one of Classicism refracted through the prism of high Romanticism, that led many to pronounce him heir to Beethoven.

Brahms' *Fourth Symphony* (1885), his last, provides with its serious tone, striking complexities, and inspired construction a fitting valedictory to his work in this genre. That its impact was immediate if initially puzzling is clear from the account by the biographer Max Kalbeck of its first run-through (at two pianos) for a small and distinguished audience: "After the wonderful Allegro...I expected that one of those present would break out in a loud 'Bravo.' Into his blond beard [conductor Hans] Richter murmured something that from afar would be taken as an expression of approval....The others remained persistently quiet....Finally Brahms grumbled, "So, let's go on!" and gave a sign to continue; whereupon [eminent critic Eduard] Hanslick heaved a sigh and quickly exploded, as if he had to relieve his mind and yet feared speaking up too late: 'For this whole movement I had the feeling that I was being given a beating by two incredibly intelligent people....'"

Each of the movements bears the distinct stamp of the composer's personality. The first begins with a theme in E minor based upon the interval of a third, which also provides a structural and motivic foundation for the remainder of the work. There is a notable sense of unrest from beginning to end, and the tragic, even fatalistic atmosphere is further and stunningly underlined by the final, minor-key plagal (IV-I) cadence. The second movement, which opens with a brief, melancholy sort of fanfare, gives way to the quietly accompanied winds in perhaps one of the loveliest of any of the composer's themes, granted particular plangency through the use of the flat sixth and seventh scale degrees borrowed from the minor mode. This material is gradually developed into soaring, tutti lyricism that fades into ethereal quiet. The third movement, a lusty, stomping, duple dance, proved so popular in Brahms' lifetime that audiences constantly demanded that it be repeated. The last movement is perhaps most notable of all, cast as it is in the "archaic" Baroque form of a chaconne—variations over a ground bass. The chaconne's subject is in fact a slight modification of that used by Bach in his *Cantata No. 150*; though deceptively simple—essentially an ascending minor scale segment from the tonic note to the dominant, then a leap back to the tonic—Brahms uses this skeleton as the basis for an increasingly elaborate and thematic harmonic framework. From its first presentation, which is not as a bass line, but as a theme in the winds, Brahms gradually weaves some 34 variations that steadily build in intensity, as though in defiance to the oppressive, insistent rotation of the ground. The final variations lead directly into an ending which reconfirms the weight of tragedy and pathos borne by the first movement.—*Michael Rodman*

Recommended:

- ○ **Brahms: Symphony 4** / C. Kleiber (cond.), Vienna PO / 1981 / DG 457706
- ○ **Brahms: Symphonie 4; Haydn-Variationen; Nänie** / C. Abbado (cond.), Berlin PO / DG 435349
- ○ **Brahms: The 4 Symphonies** / Szell (cond.), Cleveland Orch. / 1992 / Sony 48398
- ○ **Bruno Walter The Edition: Brahms Symphony 4; Tragic Overture; Shicksalslied** / B. Walter (cond.), Columbia SO / Sony 66248
- ○ **Brahms: The 4 Symphonies; Haydn Variations; Piano Concerto 2** / Furtwängler (cond.), Berlin PO / Music & Arts 804
- ○ **Bernstein Century: Brahms Symphony No 4; Overtures** / Bernstein (cond.), New York Philharmonic / 2000 / Sony 61846

ORCHESTRAL

Academic Festival Overture, Op. 80 (1879)

Brahms composed this work and the *Tragic Overture* in the summer of 1880 in Bad Ischl, Austria, and conducted the first *Academic Festival* performance in Breslau on January 3, 1881. Despite Brahms' catalogue of 122 numbered works and at least 40 more works without, he wrote only 14 for orchestra: four symphonies, two early serenades, two piano concertos, two string concertos, two concert overtures, the *Haydn Variations*, and transcriptions of three *Hungarian Dances* from the 21 composed for four-hand piano between 1868 and 1880. No opera, though, or ballet or incidental theater music. Furthermore, from 1859 to 1874, he limited his orchestral writing to seven choral pieces (which, however, included *A German Requiem*, his longest work in any form).

On March 11, 1879, the University of Breslau—Wroclaw today, in Poland—awarded him an honorary doctorate, for which he thanked them on a postcard. A friend replied that the University expected "a doctoral symphony ... at the very least a solemn ode" quid pro quo. What they received 19 months later was this ten-minute *Academic Festival Overture*. To start the New Year, Brahms himself premiered it in the Silesian capital.

This music is arguably the crusty composer's most ebullient, scored for the largest orchestra in his oeuvre: piccolo, contrabassoon, a third trumpet, tuba, bass drum, triangle, and cymbals, in addition to the usual wind pairs, four horns, two trumpets, three trombones, timpani, and strings. For subject matter to fill a flexible sonata structure, he chose four student drinking songs. In the order of their appearance, these are "What comes therefrom on high" (staccato triads and off-center accents in C minor), "We have built a stately house" (three trumpets, solemnly in C major), "Der Landesvater" (The Sovereign; legato violins in E major), and finally, after the seriatim reprise of one, two, and three in tonic C major, the most famous song of all, the medieval student song "Gaudeamus igitur" (Let us therefore rejoice), in the coda. This may not have been what Breslau expected, but for global audiences ever since, the *Academic Festival Overture* ranks alongside the keyboard *Waltz*, Op. 39, No. 16, as Brahms' most beloved instrumental music. *—Roger Dettmer*

Recommended:

- ○ **Brahms: Symphony 2** / Solti (cond.), Chicago SO / Penguin Classics 460623
- ○ **Brahms: Symphony 2; Academic Festival Overture; Alto Rhapsody** / Abbado (cond.), Berlin PO / 1998 / DG 459054
- ○ **Brahms: Symphony 1; Haydn Variations; Academic Festival Overture** / Walter (cond.), Columbia SO / 1995 / Sony 64470

Serenade No. 1 in D major, Op. 11 (1858)

Brahms composed this work in 1858, during his three-year tenure in the principality of Detmold as choir conductor and court pianist. With court services requiring only three months a year of his time, at a modest but regular salary (including piano lessons for the princess), Brahms had plenty of time to concertize, study, and extend himself creatively. Although his musician-father had begun by teaching him the violin and cello, the boy Johannes was fascinated by the piano, which his loving parent encouraged. Not surprisingly, most of Brahms' early music was written for those three instruments, the piano in particular. Schumann, however, wasted no time in urging his new (and last) protégé to compose for orchestra, a symphony no less. What Brahms labored to create without success during a three-year period after the master's mental collapse—when he was living chez Schumann in Düsseldorf to help Clara raise her seven children—found its way into the *First Piano Concerto* (1856–58), and later on into the *German Requiem*.

The *Serenade No. 1* likewise evolved—from a nonet for winds and strings, written at Detmold in 1858, but recast for chamber orchestra during the next year (both versions have been lost, or were destroyed by the composer). He gave this material its final and surviving form in 1859, adding two more movements to the original four before publishing it in 1860 as his first orchestral work. Odd as it may seem today, both this and a second *Serenade in A*, Op. 16, written in 1860 (without violins, only lower strings, winds, and brass) were considered avant-garde, on the cutting edge of modernism!

Posthumous analysts have enumerated the influences of Haydn, Mozart, Schubert, Beethoven—even Schumann—in this sweetly bucolic work. But its uniquely Brahmsian sound, even early on, renders derivation hypotheses irrelevant. Among German-speaking composers of the nineteenth century, only the teenage Mendelssohn and 20-year-old Mahler revealed comparably distinctive voices early on.

Although Brahms employed sonata-form in the opening Allegro molto and the Adagio third movements of the *Serenade No. 1*, it is basically a dance work. The jaunty, dotted main subject sets a mood that recurs several times before its apotheosis in a rondo-finale, one that virtually cries out for choreography.

In between, we find plenty of diversions and surprises. Both the second and the fifth movements are scherzos. The first of them is marked Allegro non troppo (that modifying "not-too-much" remained a Brahmsian caution throughout his lifetime). Song sections are cast dramatically in D minor, but the slightly-faster trio inhabits sun-dappled B flat major.

The third movement, Adagio non troppo, is the work's emotional fulcrum; this too is in B flat major. A full-blown development section does not cramp or curb the movement's soaring melodism.

A minuet within a minuet follows—the first one in G major, the second one in G minor with an espressivo, legato theme played the violins over plucked violas. The second scherzo comes next, an unqualified Allegro in D major, with a rio in C. The shortest movement in the piece, it pays overt homage to Beethoven.

The concluding rondo in 2/4 time is another unmodified Allegro in D major. Clarinets and bassoons an octave apart, playing in thirds, announce the principal subject. While concert-hall decorum forbids our dancing in the aisles, there's really no way to keep one's feet from tapping in time with the music. *—Roger Dettmer*

Recommended:

- ○ **Brahms: Symphonies 3 & 4; Serenade 1** / Kertesz (cond.), London SO / 1968 / London 448200
- ○ **Brahms: Serenades; Haydn Variations; Academic Festival Overture & others** / Boult (cond.), London PO / 1995 / EMI 68655

Serenade No. 2 in A major, Op. 16 (1857–1860)

Johannes Brahms was somewhat less naturally inclined towards orchestral music than he was towards other varieties of instrumental composition; whereas he seems to have been born with a feel for chamber and piano shapes and textures, we find that he felt compelled to test the orchestral waters a little bit at a time and avoid—avoid for a very long time indeed, as any who knows the history of his *First Symphony* can attest—plunging headlong into a full-scale symphonic challenge. When Brahms accepted the post of choral director at the court of Lippe-Detmold in the late 1850s, he found that, for the first time in his life, he had access to an orchestra. He put that access to good use, composing two orchestral serenades and continuing work on the piano concerto he had begun in 1854. With the completion of the *Serenade No. 2 in A major*, Op. 16, in 1859, Brahms counted this first period of development as an orchestral composer as finished. Except for the occasional bit of work on the not-soon-to-be-completed *Symphony No. 1*, he didn't write another note for orchestra until the *Haydn Variations* of 1873.

Brahms revised the *Serenade No. 2* twice. In 1860, he rescored the work for a small orchestra without violins, and in 1875 he tinkered with some of the superficial markings. The final scoring is more "serenade-like" than that of the *Serenade No. 1*, with winds and low strings. This lends the work a certain mellow quality and creates an outdoor-evocative, wind-band sound. The work is built around the traditional (or, as Brahms' critics would have it, outdated) multi-movement suite model. The five movements are: 1. Allegro moderato, 2. Scherzo, 3. Adagio non troppo, 4. Quasi menuetto, 5. Rondo. The first movement opens with one of the most relaxed and effortless-sounding woodwind tunes one will ever hear, and continues in that easy-going vein—only during the development section does Brahms brew any real anxiety, and only in that same section do the strings assert themselves. The Scherzo is an energetic Vivace, the Adagio non troppo a rich and serious essay; and the quasi-minuet movement is absolutely undanceable and peculiarly stoic. By comparison, the Rondo finale (Allegro) is joyous and sunny, and very near at times to a rollicking peasant dance. *—Blair Johnston*

Recommended:

- ○ **Johannes Brahms: Symphonies 1 & 2, Serenade 2; Haydn Variations** / Kertesz (cond.), London SO / 1996 / London 448197
- ○ **Brahms: Serenades 1 & 2; Haydn Variations; Academic Festival Overture & others** / Boult (cond.), London PO / 1988 / EMI 69203
- ○ **Brahms: Symphony 2; Serenade 2** / Rahbari (cond.), BRT PO, Brussels / 1990 / Naxos 550279

Tragic Overture, Op. 81 (1880–1881)

Brahms composed this work on holiday during the summer of 1880, and Hans Richter led the first performance with the Vienna Philharmonic on December 26 of that year. In two different editions of *Essays in Musical Analysis*, Sir Donald Francis Tovey pontificated at length about the tragedy Brahms had in mind for this companion piece to the jolly *Academic Festival Overture*. From Ischl in the Austrian Alps the composer wrote to his publisher, "I could not refuse my melancholy nature the satisfaction of composing an overture for a tragedy." To his friend the conductor Carl Reinecke he said of the pair that "one of them weeps, the other one laughs," as with the comic and tragic masks in Greek and Roman theater.

Brahms did not, however, give any further hint of a specific "tragedy," nor had he suffered any recent private loss or given any indication of uncommon sadness. He wasn't, in truth, very fond of the title *Tragic*, referring to the work at one point as the "Dramatic Overture" although a canvass of his friends failed to produce an alternative that anyone liked better. Interestingly, 64 measures at the end of the exposition appeared in a sketchbook from the year 1869, which was principally concerned with the working-out of his *Alto Rhapsody* and *Liebeslieder Waltzes*. By then, inward grief over his mother's death had been sublimated in *A German Requiem*, and he had made the pleasant decision to live permanently in Vienna.

A melancholy streak in Brahms' personality that dated from childhood surfaced regularly in his later music, but "Melancholy Overture" wouldn't have sounded half so well as *Tragic*, although it more nearly fits the mood of Op. 81. In the event, this structurally traditional work (unlike the *Academic Festival*) opens with a pair of Beethovenian chords used thematically later on to set up the gloomy and agitated

D minor main subject in 2/2 time. This is developed considerably before we hear a more lyrical second subject in F major. A third subject (the one from his 1869 sketchbook, with dotted rhythm and horn punctuation) adds a further element of contrast before the development proper begins Molto più moderato—much slower than the exposition tempo. This development is brief, however, after which the three subjects are recapitulated in reverse order, as Beethoven's did in the *Coriolan Overture*, and Wagner's in the *Flying Dutchman*. —*Roger Dettmer*

Recommended:

- **Brahms: Symphony 3; Tragische Ouvertüre; Schicksalslied** / C. Abbado (cond.), Berlin PO / DG 429765
- **Brahms: Symphony 1; Tragic Overture** / Masur, New York PO / 1991 / Apex 439887
- **Brahms: Symphony 1; Tragic Overture; Academic Festival Overture** / Haitink (cond.), Concertgebouw / 2003 / Philips B000054702

Variations on a Theme of Haydn in B flat major ("St. Anthony Variations"), Op. 56a (1873)

In Brahms' earliest sets of variations, especially those of Op. 9, the melody is of primary importance. His later studies of Beethoven, however, led to a new variation approach, in which he adhered instead to a theme's basic phrase structure and harmonic pattern. As with the *Händel Variations*, Op. 24, the eight *Variations on a Theme of Haydn*, Op. 56a, are bound by a consistent harmonic motion; at times, this is the only perceptible remnant of the original theme. Since its first performance in Vienna, on November 2, 1873, this has been among Brahms' most popular compositions—a sprawling masterwork based on the simplest of thematic germs, very much in the tradition of Bach's *Goldberg Variations* and Beethoven's *Diabelli Variations*.

Brahms composed both the orchestral and two-piano versions of the *Variations on a Theme of Haydn* in the summer of 1873, while at the Starnberger See near Munich; during the same months, he completed the *String Quartets*, Op. 51. The piano variations, Op. 56b, were published first, in 1873 by Simrock in Berlin; the orchestral setting in 1874, also by Simrock.

Commonly referred to as the "St. Anthony" variations, the piece is based on a theme from the first of a set of six Divertimenti (Feldparthien)—for many years thought to be by Haydn, but now thought to be by Haydn's pupil, Ignace Pleyel—the second movement of which is based on an old Burgenland (an Austrian state that abuts Hungary) chant entitled, "Chorale St. Anthony."

Brahms shatters the stately atmosphere of the theme with a pulsating horn passage in the first variation, in which the melodic aspect of the theme has all but disappeared. A great outburst from the strings accents the second variation, while the third returns to the character of the theme, if not the original rhythm and pitches. A climbing woodwind tune traces the general shape of the theme in the quiet fourth variation, while the fifth takes off at lightning speed, emphasizing the falling intervals in the original theme. Brass and winds initiate the martial sixth variation, in which the theme is easily recognized. The seventh variation has some of the character of a Strauss waltz, while slithering contrapuntal lines noodle their way through the eighth. The work closes with a passacaglia in which the theme, gently articulated at first by the woodwinds at the opening, returns with the force of the full orchestra. The repeated, five-measure bass line of the passacaglia is derived from the main theme; because the bass line provides the variation material in this last segment, what we have are variations on a variation of the original theme. —*John Palmer*

Recommended:

- **Brahms: Symphonie 4; Haydn-Variationen; Nänie** / Abbado (cond.), Steinberg (cond.), Berlin PO / DG 435349
- **Brahms: Symphony 1; Haydn Variations; Tragic Overture** / Sawallisch (cond.), London PO / Seraphim 73555
- **Brahms: Symphony 3; Haydn-Variationen** / Bernstein (cond.), Vienna PO / DG 445507

CHAMBER MUSIC

Cello Sonata No. 1 in E minor, Op. 38 (1862–1865)

Brahms' *First Cello Sonata* is a product of the same period (1862–65) as the *Piano Quintet*, Op. 34 and is cut from much the same musical cloth—it is moody, powerful, and grandly structured. The opening movement (Allegro non troppo), with a long exposition repeat, takes up more than half the 25- to 30-minute playing time. Its long, elaborate opening theme establishes the nocturnal and introspective tone of the entire work. The second subject group expands the scope of the work by introducing a great, soaring theme in the minor between two calmer ones in the major. The development builds to a great climax in which it is the cello that accompanies the piano, reminding us that the work is titled *Sonate für Klavier und Violoncello* rather than the other way around. The coda somehow finds its way to a hard-won peace in the major. In this imposing movement, which obviates the need for a slow movement, might be found the origin of the great slow opening-movement structures of Mahler and Shostakovich. The second movement (Allegretto quasi Menuetto) is a wistful, melancholy minuet; its Trio is marked by the repeated halting and restarting of the music. The emotions that Brahms has held back up to now are unleashed in the closing Allegro, a powerful and passionate fugue that works its way into rondo form and closes, like the *Quintet*, with a breathless coda. —*Sol Louis Siegel*

Recommended:

- **Brahms: Die Cellosonaten** / Rostropovich, R. Serkin / DG 410510
- **Brahms: Cello Sonatas 1 & 2; Bruch: Kol Nidrei** / Du Pré, Barenboim / 2002 / EMI 57293

Cello Sonata No. 2 in F major, Op. 99 (1886)

After his first cello sonata, Brahms wrote all four of his symphonies before turning to a second sonata. Although it's a product of his middle years, this F major work is marked by a youthful boldness and symphonic approach to the piano writing, while never sacrificing a generous, easy lyricism.

The first movement, Allegro vivace, sends the cello leaping around the staff over the piano's tremolo notes. It's the piano that introduces the ardent second subject, soon falling into cross rhythms that undermine the music's 3/4 pulse. The dramatic development is comparatively dark, often hovering in the minor, but youthful assurance returns in the recapitulation.

The slow movement, Adagio affetuoso, ventures into the distant key of F sharp major with the cello providing a mere pizzicato accompaniment as the piano introduces the noble first theme. The more impassioned middle section falls into F minor and the lower reaches of the cello, then it gives way to the urgent return of the first section.

Again, the piano takes the lead at the beginning of the scherzo, Allegro passionato, a quietly gathering storm that breaks when the cello soon enters in full voice. The piano part in this movement is especially complex, but the atmosphere becomes more serene in the central trio section, which glides from F minor to major. Last comes a rondo, Allegro molto, that initially seems too light to cap such a substantial, serious sonata. The first section, soft, gentle, and songlike, punctuates episodes that are in turn march-like, ardent, and stern. The principal melody's final return, however, is sunny, and the cellist may optionally revive it with pizzicato rather than bowed notes. —*James Reel*

Recommended:

- **Brahms: Die Cellosonaten** / Rostropovich, R. Serkin / DG 410510
- **Brahms: Cello Sonatas 1 & 2; Mendelssohn: Cello Sonata 2** / Starker, Sebok / 1996 / Mercury 434377

Clarinet Quintet in B minor, Op. 115 (1891)

When Clara Schumann first heard this quintet, she wrote: "It is a really marvelous work, the wailing clarinet takes hold of one; it is most moving. And what interesting music, deep and full of meaning!" These poignant words by Brahms' closest female friend belie Brahms' disingenuous comparison of the work with his earlier *Clarinet Trio*: "[It is] a far greater piece of foolishness." From the first movement, the music pulsates with yearning. In its opening measures are the seeds that germinate in the rest of composition, which is equally perfect in its power of evocation and its structural rigor. The autumnal mood of the work results in part from the subtle shifts throughout between the closely related keys of D major and B minor.

Most notable is the second movement Adagio, a tender love song whose wistfulness seems to reflect the entire decline of the late Romantic musical ethos. Of course there is more to this piece than its dreamlike evocations. Listen to the Presto, with its Hungarian folk-dance style and the finale's intriguing variations, the last of which returns full circle to the opening theme of the first movement. "Foolishness" indeed! —*Peter Bates*

Recommended:

- **Brahms, Weber: Clarinet Quintets** / Stoltzman, Tokyo SQ / 1995 / RCA Victor 68033
- **Mozart & Brahms: Clarinet Quintets** / de Peyer, Melos Ens. / 2001 / Seraphim 74520
- **Brahms: Clarinet Quintet; Clarinet Trio** / T. King, Gabrieli Quartet / 1986 / Hyperion 66107
- **Brahms & Yun: Clarinet Quintets** / S. Meyer, Wiener Streichsextett / 1991 / EMI 754304

Clarinet Sonata No. 1 in F minor, Op. 120/1 (1894)

In an Indian summer of creativity near the end of his career, Johannes Brahms wrote the two Sonatas, Op. 120 (1894), the *Trio for Clarinet, Cello and Piano*, Op. 114 (1891), and the *Quintet for Clarinet and Strings*, Op. 115 (1891) especially for Richard Mühlfeld, a clarinetist he much admired. The *Clarinet Sonata No 1 in F minor*, Op. 120, opens with a tense Allegro appassionato that makes full use of the clarinet's higher register and eventually winds down to a tenderly expressive coda. The following Andante sustains the sweetly reflective mood, and after a dancelike Allegretto led by the clarinet—a tune that could easily have come from one of the *Liebeslieder Waltzes*—the work ends with a high-spirited Vivace.

Brahms transcribed both this sonata and its companion, Op. 120, *No. 2, for viola*, in which arrangement they are widely performed. Many feel, however, that it is only in the original versions that the full scope of the sonatas' expressive and coloristic nuances can be realized. *—Roy Brewer*

Recommended:

○ **Brahms Clarinet Sonatas** / T. King, C. Benson / 1986 / Hyperion 66202

○ **Brahms: Sonatas for Clarinet & Piano** / de Peyer, G. Pryor / 1987 / Chandos 8563

○ **William Kapell: Heifetz, Primrose, Kurtz** / Primrose (viola), Kapell / 1998 / RCA Victor 902668996

Clarinet Sonata No. 2 in E flat major, Op. 120/2 (1894)

After finishing the *Violin Sonata No. 3 in D minor*, Op. 108 in 1888, Johannes Brahms returned to the duo sonata just once more; in 1894, in quick succession, he composed a pair of sonatas for clarinet (or viola) and piano that were published together the following year as Op. 120. The dedicatee of these two works was the clarinettist Richard Mühlfeld, whose playing had been an inspiration to the aging Brahms. The two Op. 120 sonatas, the first of which is in F minor, the second of which is in E flat major, are as like to one another as peas in a pod: rich-textured; songful, indeed, more truly songful than any of the string sonatas, partly by reason of the clarinettist's need to breathe; and not at all filled with the kind of hair-raising drama that has made the *D minor Violin Sonata* so famous. Because of their opposite modalities, they complement one another as perfectly as do the *Tragic Overture* and the *Academic Festival Overture* of 15 years earlier.

The *Sonata No. 2 in E flat major*, Op. 120 has three movements: *Allegro amabile, Allegro appassionato-sosteneto*, and *Andante con moto-Allegro-Più tranquillo*. The wealth of long-limbed, lyrical melody in the opening and closing movements led Brahms to abandon the idea of a slow movement in favor of a scherzo-type middle movement in E flat minor; the central trio section, a B major Sostenuto ("ma dolce e ben cantando"), serves nicely to fill the gap left by that missing slow movement. The finale is a theme and variations in which the clarinet and piano join together to spin yard after yard of silken, overlapping, arpeggiated spiderwebs. *—Blair Johnston*

Recommended:

○ **Brahms: Sonaten für Viola und Klavier** / Kashkashian, R. Levin / 1997 / ECM 457068

○ **Brahms: Sonatas for Clarinet & Piano** / de Peyer, G. Pryor / 1987 / Chandos 8563

○ **Brahms: Clarinet Sonatas** / T. King, C. Benson / 1986 / Hyperion 66202

Piano Quartet No. 1 in G minor, Op. 25 (1861)

Johannes Brahms completed his *Piano Quartet No. 1* in G minor in 1861. Though this work received mixed reviews by friends and critics alike, it has remained alive in the concert world. Throughout the twentieth century, its popularity continued to grow as the listening public came to recognize Brahms as perhaps the quintessential master of Romantic chamber music. His first quartet for piano, violin, viola, and cello harkens back to the music of Schubert, one of Brahms' favorite composers, as well as forward with inventiveness that inspired composers in the next century, especially Schoenberg. While his contemporaries were writing music that was an obvious break with the past, particularly Wagner, Brahms wrote in the old forms, which hung together with a pleasing and deceptive looseness, as did the works of Schubert. Scratching the surface of Brahms' first piano quartet reveals that the themes and textures do not hang together loosely at all. Everything is built out of thematic material, which is without precedent in chamber music. It is the kernel of what Schoenberg described as "developing variation" and prepares the way for atonality, which coheres only when all the material is in reference to itself. The G minor quartet is pure clarity in a way that did not exist before Brahms. This quartet was also the first chamber work of Brahms' that he played in public.

The first movement of the G minor quartet has the sweetness of heroic themes in repose, but it also simmers, at least in a good performance. In bad renditions of this work, the tension is ignored in favor of an empty niceness, which is certainly to be avoided. The second movement, an Intermezzo, is introspective and full of musical inquiry among the strings. Themes spread out searching for something, with a beautiful and mysterious effect. The Andante third movement has a dreamy grandness, which is normally an effect reserved for orchestral forces. The Hungarian, Rondo finale is pure fire, blasting through rousing themes with a concerted vigor.

Many generations after the work's inception, it has withstood the public's initial reservations. It should also be pointed out that other influential musicians thought it was pure genius. One great violinist regarded it as proof that Brahms was Beethoven's musical heir. There were many such reactions. Schoenberg liked it enough to orchestrate it. He gave his reasons for doing so as follows: "1. I like the piece. 2. It is seldom played. 3. It is always played very badly; the better the pianist, the louder he plays and you hear nothing from the strings. I wanted to hear everything...." *—John Keillor*

Recommended:

○ **Johannes Brahms: Klavierquartett; Balladen** / Gilels, Amadeus Quartet / DG 447407

○ **Brahms: Piano Quartets** / Domus / 1999 / Virgin 61615

○ **Brahms: Piano Quartets** / Borodin Trio, Golani / 1989 / Chandos 8809

○ **Brahms: Intermezzo** / Perahia, Amadeus Quartet / 2001 / Legacy 89856

Piano Quartet No. 2 in A major, Op. 26 (1861)

Johannes Brahms completed his *Piano Quartet No. 2 in A*, Op. 26 in 1861. It is the companion piece to the composer's first piano quartet, Op. 25, which was written in the same year. This second quartet is a testament to the composer's love of Schubert's music and Vienna, the city that Brahms was fated to adopt. By the time Brahms had relocated to Vienna from Hamburg there was a revival of interest in Schubert's instrumental music and chamber music in general. Earlier in the century there was no chamber music being performed because the leader of the only professional string quartet had died in 1830. Nearly twenty years later, the Hellmesberger Quartet was founded, focusing on Schubert's unpublished chamber works. Brahms' first two piano quartets made a large impression on the ensemble, which premiered both of them.

Brahms made Schubert's chamber music the focus of several years of careful study in the second half of the 1850s. This is audible in the Op. 26 piano quartet insofar as the phrases hang together with a loose ease that builds upon the music's overall form with a deceptive effortlessness. What Brahms brings to the table is a concentration of incident; there is a broader palette of variety in his music, more new ways of presenting the material so that it continues to be fresh and reinforced concurrently. The opening is "polychoral": the piano and the trio each make statements separately and then together, which sets the stage for two separate musical bodies to play against each other. And like Schubert, Brahms does not shy away from including popular references in his music, including a burst of schmaltzy waltz music in the quartet's second movement, a Romanze featuring an overall discipline that allows for the occasional glimpse into camp without lowing the music's overall standard. The composer labeled this movement "Night Piece," and it takes strange risks such as the one described, remaining afloat as only Schubert or Brahms could. (Schoenberg in his String Quartet No. 1 continued this tradition of including possibly disastrous popular themes to a sublime effect.) Brahms was in many ways the conduit between the First Viennese School of Haydn, Mozart, Beethoven, and Schubert, and the Second Viennese School of Schoenberg, Berg, and Webern. His historical importance could not be more real, and his music is worth every bit of fuss attributed to it. *—John Keillor*

Recommended:

○ **Complete Piano Quartets** / Beaux Arts Trio, Trampler / 1996 / Philips 454017

○ **Brahms: Piano Quartets** / Domus / 1999 / Virgin 61615

Piano Quartet No. 3 in C minor ("Werther"), Op. 60 (1875)

Brahms composed the first version of the work that would eventually become his *Third Piano Quartet*, Op. 60 (to which the subtitle *"Werther"* is often attached), in Dusseldorf in 1855–56. The first version had emerged concurrently with first drafts for the first two piano quartets, Op. 25 and Op. 26, all received enthusiastically by his close friends, including Albert Dietrich and Joseph Joachim. At this point, No. 3 was in the key of C sharp minor. Even when (a year later) Joachim wrote to Brahms concerning the piece it still comprised three movements only, an opening Allegro, an Andante, and what Brahms' termed a "concise" finale. While its two sister works were completed in 1859 and 1861, Op. 60 was put aside, since neither Brahms nor his associates were satisfied with it. By 1869, he returned to it again and contemplated its publication as his Op. 54. But further extensive revisions followed and the quartet assumed its final shape in the winter of 1873–74 in Vienna, with minor revisions the following summer. A letter from Brahms, sent with the manuscript to Theodor Billroth includes the following enigmatic comment: "the quartet has communicated itself to me only in the strangest ways... For instance, the illustration to the last chapter of the man in the blue frock and yellow waistcoat." This refers, somewhat obliquely, to Goethe's *Werther*, which Brahms admired. Meanwhile, he remained deeply dissatisfied with the work, and wrote to his publisher Fritz Simrock "you may attach a picture on the title page, i.e. a head with the pistol before it."

The definitive version is comprised of the 1855–56 score's opening movement, a scherzo from 1856–61, and an Andante and finale (allegro commodo) from 1875. The work, now in the general key of C minor, reflects the turbulent and vacillating self-doubts that Brahms felt so deeply. Indeed, little more darkly oppressive movements than the first exist anywhere else in Brahms' chamber output, while the "new" andante in E major is certainly one of the most beautiful. Above all, however, the work fully deserves its Goethe connections, for neither Brahms nor *Werther* enjoyed a contented course en route to their respective destinies.

The *C minor Piano Quartet* was first performed in Vienna on November 18, 1875, with Brahms himself at the piano, and members of the Hellmesberger Quartet. *—Michael Jameson*

Recommended:

○ **Brahms: Piano Quartets 1 & 3** / Heimbach Chamber Music Festival / 2002 / EMI 557377

- ○ **Brahms: Piano Quartets** / Turovsky, Dubinsky, Edlina, Golani, Borodin Trio / 1989 / Chandos 8809
- ○ **Brahms: Piano Quartets** / Domus / 1999 / Virgin 61615

Piano Quintet in F minor, Op. 34a (1861)

This youthful work had a difficult birth. Brahms introduced it as a string quintet in 1862, but violinist Joseph Joachim found the music too weighty to be supported by strings and suggested recasting it for piano. So Brahms fashioned it into a sonata for two pianos, but this version didn't satisfy pianist Clara Schumann, who persuaded Brahms to bring strings back into the picture. The final transformation, for piano and string quartet, was finished in the fall of 1864; Brahms published it with a dedication to Princess Anna of Hesse—not unusual for a young composer seeking patronage, but also perhaps something of a slight to Joachim and Clara Schumann, who had had such a hand in its multi-stage genesis. The piano quintet displays young Brahms at his least risk-averse; the overall effect is often brash despite episodes of generous lyricism, and the use of themes and whipcrack changes in harmony seem impulsive, although Brahms is careful to thread certain motivic elements, particularly descending semitones, through all the movements in an effort to achieve structural unity. (This was an idea Brahms picked up from Beethoven's *Appassionata sonata.*) Cunningly, Brahms begins by lulling listeners into complacency with a restrained statement of the first movement's initial theme. Soon, though, the theme erupts with energy, whereupon the music slips into the unexpected key of C sharp minor for the second subject. Brahms subjects this material to a wayward development, and in the recapitulation he shifts the second theme into F sharp minor. The second movement, Adagio, is an episode of serenity, although it is always open to harmonic instability; it's based on a faintly Slavic melody with a wistful harmonization. The Scherzo begins with low pizzicato cello notes, a launching pad for the syncopated main theme that creeps up through the strings and soon explodes into a robust, minor-key march. The contrasting trio section is in the comforting key of C major and manages to create a flowing, lyrical interlude out of what is essentially a fanfare figure. After an ominous introduction, the finale builds into a fast rondo with the arrival of an impetuous but quiet theme over a nervous, almost galloping accompaniment. The first violin ushers in a second subject, slower and somewhat pleading. Brahms knocks these themes back and forth rather than supplying a formal development section, and then overlaps many of the movement's—and the entire quintet's—principal motifs in a Presto coda. *—James Reel*

Recommended:

- ○ **Brahms: Klavierquintett; Schoenberg: Kammersymphonie arr. Webern** / Hagen Quartett, P. Gulda / DG 437804
- ○ **Brahms: The Three String Quartets; Piano Quintet** / New Budapest Quartet, P. Lane / 1997 / Hyperion 22018
- ○ **Brahms: Piano Quintet; String Quintet** / Takács Quartet, A. Schiff / 1991 / London 430529
- ○ **The Busch Quartet: Brahms, Schumann** / Busch Quartet, R. Serkin / Pearl 9275

Piano Trio No. 1 in B major, Op. 8 (1853; revised 1889)

It is well known that Brahms was in the habit of destroying those of his works which did not please him, and this fate befell not only youthful experiments, but entire mature works. So great was his insecurity that perhaps even great symphonies and concertos, which might have warmed all humankind, produced instead only a few moments of warmth from the composer's fireplace. A youthful work which escaped such a dire fate is Brahms' *First Piano Trio.* Completed in early 1854, it was the first of the composer's chamber works to be published. This occurred in spite of criticism from none other than Clara Schumann, whom Brahms adored and respected as friend and musician. Some 34 years later, Brahms accepted the invitation of his publisher, Simrock, to revise some of his early works, including this trio. Uncharacteristically, Brahms permitted both versions of the work to exist, and even suggested the two be promoted together. A century later, it is the revised version that is most often performed and recorded.

Like Brahms' other piano trios, and unlike those of Mozart, the work is in four movements, with a second-movement scherzo added to the usual three movements. This gives the work a near-symphonic scope; a performance can run to nearly 40 minutes. The work begins pensively. After a brief piano introduction comes a marvelous cello solo theme which migrates to the entire ensemble. Rather than developing in the manner of Mozart's trios, the work then unfolds more like the first movement of a symphony, rich in themes and ideas. This long first movement, in fact, was that which Brahms most extensively revised in the later version of the work.

The Scherzo features a whispered, skipping minor theme which quickly bursts into a major key and becomes positively exuberant. A second, bucolic theme, still in the major mode, builds to grand proportions before the first theme returns, develops in startling directions, and ends the movement dramatically but quietly.

The work becomes mysterious in the Adagio. A passage of soft, stepping piano chords beneath singing phrases in the violin leads to an extended and very warm cello passage. In spite of its overall darkness, the movement is serene, almost meditative. It ends, as it began, with stepping piano chords.

The final movement is the most expansive of all, as Brahms once again makes use of the piano's power to create a symphonic sweep. A once-repeated passage of syncopation is strangely distracting, but the movement builds to a satisfying finish. As a piano trio, the work is notably enormous in scope and sound. Reflecting in its two versions both early and mature Brahms, it is a virtual blueprint of the composer's stylistic development. *—Michael Morrison*

Recommended:

- ○ **Brahms: Complete Trios** / Beaux Arts Trio / 1993 / Philips 438365
- ○ **Brahms: Trios** / Eroica Trio / 2002 / EMI 57199
- ○ **Rubinstein Collection Vol. 72: Paino Trios 1 & 2** / Artur Rubinstein, Szeryng, Fournier / 1999 / RCA 63072

Piano Trio No. 2 in C major, Op. 87 (1880–1882)

It seems to have taken Brahms over two years to complete the opus 87 trio, but the result evidently pleased him and he boasted of the work to his publisher, Simrock. Brahms' close friend Clara Schumann pronounced the piece "a splendid work" and "a great musical treat." A generously proportioned work in four movements, it features a second movement andante and third movement scherzo, an arrangement common in his symphonies but reversed in his other piano trios. He had first mentioned it and a companion work, an E flat trio, in a letter to a friend in the summer of 1880, but did not reveal it to Simrock until July 1882. By then, the E flat work had disappeared.

The piece opens thickly, with strange dissonances and a heavy feel, and seems to proceed sluggishly. It is nonetheless dynamically, rhythmically, and chromatically challenging and gives the sense of being a major work, and the first movement ends with symphonic grandeur. The slow movement is similarly heavy of texture, and Brahms makes considerable use of double-stopping as a way of making the two stringed instruments sound like four or even more. The scherzo, a four-minute presto, is begun and ended by a fluttering figure which generates momentum and contains a lyrical passage of some tenderness. The finale is the most adventuresome of the four movements and contains puzzling transitions and modulations which resolve to produce powerful effects. The final dénouement of the work is positively huge, proving that, in the hands of Brahms, even the tiny piano trio can be a large and imposing work. His boasts of the piece would seem to have been true. *—Michael Morrison*

Recommended:

- ○ **Brahms: Trios 1 & 2** / Eroica Trio / 2002 / EMI 57199
- ○ **Rubinstein Collection Vol. 72: Brahms Piano Trios 1 & 2** / Artur Rubinstein, Szeryng, Fournier / 1999 / RCA 6260
- ○ **Brahms: Complete Trios** / Beaux Arts Trio / 1993 / Philips 438603

Piano Trio No. 3 in C minor, Op. 101 (1886)

Of Brahms' three known piano trios, plus one other which is attributed to him, this is by far the shortest and most compact work. By the summer of 1886, Brahms had finished and seen to the premiere of the last of his four symphonies, and he would not produce another large-scale orchestral work. During an extended stay at Thun, Switzerland, Brahms perhaps turned inward and was beginning to distill his musical thoughts down to purer forms. Always expansive, Brahms had been known for employing large four-movement structures in his piano concertos and trios. Although still a four-movement work containing a three-minute presto as second movement, the C minor trio is terse. And even though it has much to say, it is, by Brahmsian standards, positively taut and pithy. From the opening, the first movement in particular is a no-nonsense statement in short phrases and simple rhythmic patterns. Opening with a sort of "sit down and shut up" statement, the work is intense and even quickly hurls pizzicato notes from the strings to quell any last-second bustlings. The movement flows without becoming fulsome, and ends dramatically. The brief presto non assai is positively delicate—a term not generally applied to the music of Brahms. A third-movement andante is nearly as brief but more lyrical in tone and texture. The finale begins insistently and marches through a series of short riffs before pushing to an aggressive finish. While the work is powerful and even muscular, it does not give the impression, as do the earlier trios, of a symphony masquerading as a chamber work. *—Michael Morrison*

Recommended:

- ○ **Johannes Brahms: Complete Trios** / Pressler, Greenhouse, Guilet, Beaux Arts Trio / 1993 / Philips 438365
- ○ **Johannes Brahms: The Three Piano Trios** / Borodin Trio / 1983 / Chandos 8334
- ○ **Kalichstein, Laredo & Robinson Trio Plays Brahms, Mendelssohn & Dvořák** / Kalichstein, Laredo & Robinson Trio / 1993 / VoxBox 3029

String Quartet No. 1 in C minor, Op. 51/1 (1866–1873)

Brahms' attitude toward the importance of the string quartet as the ultimate expression of the composer's craft can be understood when it is considered that he reputedly sketched and destroyed some 20 quartets before creating one worthy of publication. Also, when it is considered that Haydn produced 68, Mozart 23 and Beethoven 16 quartets, Brahms' three quartets stand as a testament to his own harsh standards. The publication of the *Quartets*, Op. 51, then, represented for Brahms a milestone in his career similar to the publication of his *First Symphony*: he had taken on the masters of the past and now deemed himself worthy of comparison.

These first two quartets were completed just before Brahms seriously embarked upon his almost exclusive engagement with orchestral works and as such represent not only a culmination of everything he had learned to this point, but as models for all that was to follow. Brahms' greatest accomplishment as a composer was his "developing variation" technique in which an entire work was generated from a single motive or group of motives. In the two quartets of Op. 51, Brahms' gives no clearer nor more pervasive an example of this technique.

This quartet is so pervaded by the motives of the first movement, that it can be considered cyclic (a multi-movement work that uses recurring passages or themes throughout). The close tonal relationships and integrated key structure of the four movements add to the overall coherence. In the opening Allegro, a bold and rising arpeggio over a throbbing accompaniment sets the epic tone for the movement. It is in the strictest sonata form, with each subsequent theme developing and expanding logically and methodically out of the last. The Romantic character of the Romanze (Poco Adagio) movement belies its complex and highly organized structure. Its themes are all derived from the opening motive of the first movement. Third is the Allegretto molto moderato e comodo. Un poco più animato. This is a scherzo and trio in regular form. The main theme of the Scherzo, in an unusual duple rather than triple meter, is derived not from the opening of the quartet, but from the middle section of the first theme. The Trio is in Brahms' Ländler style, imitating an Austrian peasant dance. In the energetic Finale (Allegro), Brahms brought together all the motives and structural elements of the quartet. In addition, he used a section of the first movement's main theme as a recurring motto to articulate the movement's large-scale form. *—Steven Coburn*

Recommended:

- ○ **Brahms: String Quartets** / Alban Berg Quartet / 1993 / EMI 54829
- ○ **Brahms: String Quartets Op 51** / Takacs SQ / 1990 / London 425526
- ○ **Brahms: Die Streichquartette; Dvořák: "Amerikanisches"-Quartett** / Amadeus Quartet / DG 457707

String Quartet No. 2 in A minor, Op. 51/2 (1865)

Johannes Brahms' first two string quartets, the two works of Op. 51, were released for public consumption in 1873. These are not actually his first efforts in the genre—we know that he tried his hand at well over a dozen string quartets as a younger man (none of which met with his approval and all of which were eventually scrapped)—and yet, Brahms spent the better part of a decade working on Op. 51. We know that Op. 51, No. 1, in C minor was begun all the way back in 1865, and while the date that Brahms began incubating material, privately or on paper, for the *String Quartet No. 2 in A minor*, Op. 51, No. 2, is less clear, it is unlikely that he would spend eight years on Op. 51, No. 1, and then dash Op. 51, No. 2, off in a matter of days. If he did work on them simultaneously for any great length of time, the achievement becomes perhaps even greater, for the two works are really as different from one another as night and day. The C minor work is as rhythmically compact, note efficient, and, in its outer movements, forward-driven as anything Brahms ever wrote. The A minor quartet, which Brahms dedicated to his friend the Viennese surgeon and amateur string player Dr. Theodor Billroth, is, on the other hand, composed along altogether more lyric lines (but by no means less dramatic lines).

The four movements of Op. 51, No. 2, are: 1. Allegro non troppo, 2. Andante moderato, 3. Quasi Minuetto, moderato—Allegretto vivace, and 4. Allegro non assai. There is a spaciousness to parts of the opening Allegro non troppo that would have had no place in the first movement of the C minor quartet. The opening of the first theme, with its four espressivo, even perhaps wistful, half notes in the first violin (the pitches are A-F-A-E, probably a reference to Joseph Joachim's motto "FAE: Frei aber einsam" [freely, but solitary]), certainly has plenty of room—both rhythmically and intervallically, in it; and the C major second theme, with its mezza voce, grazioso parallel thirds, is *gemütlichkeit* (sociable warmth), if ever chamber music has known it.

After the rich A flat major Romanze first movement of Op. 51, No. 2, Brahms provides the A minor quartet with an Andante moderato slow movement in A major that is, by comparison, gossamer-textured. In a central episode, heated tremolos and firm, marcato declarations from the first violin and cello move the movement strangely close to the idioms of opera for a short time. The minuet is quietly—and mostly homophonically—scored (the open fifth drone in the cello is a wonderful and peculiar touch); the Allegretto vivace music runs along in happy sixteenth notes.

The finale is more graceful than headstrong, and even the strong hemiola pattern of the main tune sounds almost as if borrowed from the dance hall. *—Blair Johnston*

Recommended:

- ○ **Brahms: String Quartets** / Alban Berg Quartet / 1993 / EMI 54829
- ○ **Brahms: String Quartets Op51** / Takacs SQ / 1990 / London 425526
- ○ **Brahms: String Quartets Op51** / Janâcek Quartet / 2001 / Supraphon 3562

String Quartet No. 3 in B flat major, Op. 67 (1876)

By the late 1870s, Brahms had grown very confident of his ability to manage the major genres of instrumental music, and whereas works like his *First Symphony* and the first two string quartets are the products of many years of drafting and revising, he tackled his *String Quartet No. 3* in B flat major, Op. 67—his last string quartet—in just a single year: 1876. It is often lamented that Brahms left posterity just three string quartets; but they make for a perfectly complementary trio. Each is in a position nearly equidistant from the other two around the dramatic wheel. There are the headlong plunges into raw physical drama and even gritty (for Brahms) pathos in the *C minor Quartet* (Op. 51 No. 1), and then the gentler, more lyric but still minor-mode strains of the *A minor Quartet* (Op. 51, No. 2). To round the threesome out, Brahms composed a bright and sunny work in B flat major that happens also to be one of the most flawlessly-crafted items in the repertoire. Brahms dedicated the *String Quartet No. 3* to his friend Professor Th. W. Engelmann, and it was premiered in Berlin in October of the same year he composed it.

The first of the quartet's four movements is a Vivace in 6/8 time. Brahms seems to be having great fun throwing accents and sforzandos into the "wrong" parts of the measure throughout the spiccato first theme. The second theme is similarly fun-loving—it moves into 2/4 time leaps around on a little dactylic rhythm (long/short-short) and sounds, at least until the legato second strain of the theme arrives, uncannily like a famous children's folk song. An Andante in F major serves as the slow movement; it has in the middle of it two measures of 5/4 time—an unusual thing for Brahms. An Agitato (Allegretto non troppo) fills the scherzo position and is written in true da capo form. The glory of Op. 67, many feel, is the extraordinary final theme and variations movement (Poco Allegretto), at the end of which the theme of the first movement makes an encore appearance. *—Blair Johnston*

Recommended:

- ○ **Johannes Brahms: String Quartets** / Alben Berg Quartet / 1993 / EMI 54829
- ○ **Brahms: Piano Quintet; String Quartet** / Takács SQ / 1991 / London 430529
- ○ **Brahms: String Quartet 1–3; Clarinet Quintet** / Léner SQ / 1997 / EMI 566422

String Quintet No. 1 in F major ("Spring"), Op. 88 (1882)

At the time Brahms wrote his *String Quintet No. 1 in F major* (1882), the models for the genre were exemplified in the works of Schubert and Mozart. Schubert calls for a configuration of two violins, one viola, and two cellos; Mozart calls for two violins, two violas, and one cello, the instrumentation adopted by Brahms for his *First Quintet*.

The three-movement Quintet is generated entirely from ideas contained in the central Grave ed appassionato movement, which in turn evolved from a long-aborted piano work. In the mid-1850s Brahms had written a sarabande and gavotte for piano in a neo-Baroque style, the manuscripts of which Brahms eventually burned (along with a great quantity of other material). What the composer did not count on, however, was that a number of his friends and professional acquaintances retained copies of the same work. It was not until the twentieth century that scholars unearthed the original piano pieces and discovered their connection to the *String Quintet*.

In neither the piano works nor the Quintet's middle movement is the Baroque influence difficult to hear. With the original tempi intact, the middle movement functions in much the same manner as a scherzo and trio. Brahms creates further tension by casting the two dances in the keys of A major and C sharp major, respectively, creating conflict and ambiguity as to which tonal center will prevail; ultimately, the A major sarabande/scherzando emerges victorious.

The entire Quintet is a bizarre collection whose very nature would seem to defy cohesion; still, it does indeed hold together, a testament to the composer's masterful handling of its diverse elements. The thoroughly Romantic opening movement is not particularly unusual for Brahms, and there is little in it to betray the work's "Baroque" origins. The third movement is more forthright in its presentation of the source material, here treated with distinctive humor as a collection of Baroque textures that fall all over one another in a sort of organized chaos. It begins with a fugal subject, or fragment of a subject, that attempts to unfold but cannot get to the point of establishing rhythmic surety. Despite the fugal subject's by-the-book opening in a pattern of tonic-dominant entrances, the accompanying chords that are supposed to provide a propulsive rhythmic edge keep coming in at the "wrong" time, diluting the flow. This continues until the accompaniment assumes a greater normalcy; by then, however, it is too late and the fugue has given up. The music assumes a homophonic, fully nineteenth century guise that clearly embodies the music of Brahms' own time. The work as a whole seems to be the composer's humorous retraction of his musical revivalism, a flight of historical fancy that ends as he is finally wrenched back into his own century. *—John Keillor*

Recommended:

- ○ **Brahms: String Quintets** / Raphael Ens. / 1994 / Hyperion 66804
- ○ **Brahms: String Quintets 1 & 2** / Juilliard SQ, Trampler / 2001 / Sony 89737

String Quintet No. 2 in G major, Op. 111 (1890)

The piano was the instrument with which Brahms felt most comfortable, and he hesitated to publish chamber music for strings, with or without piano, for many years. He generally asked violinist Joseph Joachim (1831–1907) for assessments of his works for strings before they were printed. The failure of a string quintet version of the *Piano Quintet*, Op. 34, rekindled his anxieties and he avoided writing for such forces until 1882, when he finished the *Quintet*, Op. 88. His second quintet, the *Quintet for two violins, two violas and cello in G major*, Op. 111, composed in the summer of 1890, was first performed in Vienna on November 11, 1890. Simrock in Berlin published the work in 1891.

Brahms intended the *Quintet in G major*, Op. 111, to be his last work. In December 1890 Brahms sent Simrock an alteration to the finale of the quintet, including this instruction: "With this note you can take leave of my music, because it is high time to stop." The following spring he wrote out his will and decided to concentrate only on unpublished works he deemed worthwhile, dispensing with the others and with composing anew. Brahms, however, did not stick to his resolution. Nevertheless, permeated with an Austrian vivacity, the Op. 111 quintet gives no hint of being planned as a valedictory work.

The opening of the first movement, the cello tune included, derives from sketches Brahms had made in Italy for a fifth symphony. Laboring under a tremolo accompaniment from the other four instruments, the cello is entrusted with the arpeggiated, leaping main theme. As the sonata-form movement progresses, the theme dissolves into a transition to the dominant, D major, and the second group of themes, the first of which consists of a three-note figure that evokes the air of a Viennese waltz. The development section, beginning on B flat major, initially stresses the opening arpeggio of the main theme, but quickly moves on to develop segments of the second group and the transition. As is often the case with Brahms, the entrance of the recapitulation is disguised through new instrumentation, beginning with the third measure of the theme. Whereas the cello plumbed the warm depths of its register at the beginning of the movement, here the violin soars high above the tremolo accompaniment. All the material of the second group is resolved to the tonic before the movement closes with a developmental coda.

Brahms' favorite stringed instrument, the viola, introduces the theme of the ensuing Adagio, cast in variation form in D minor. The variation technique is used more freely than in Brahms' earlier such movements. Wistful and transparent, the Adagio is marked by unexpected shifts between major and minor and finally closes on D major. The composer's long-time friend Elisabeth von Herzogenberg found the Adagio and the Minuet much to her liking, recognizing in them "such perfect unity of emotion, vigor and effect." Fragments of first-movement themes appear in the opening melody of the minuet-like third movement, set in G minor, while the coda revisits the G major trio. The fourth movement is peppered with a Hungarian csárdás flavor, especially its animated coda. *—John Palmer*

Recommended:

- ○ **Brahms: String Quintets** / Raphael Ens. / 1994 / Hyperion 66804
- ○ **Brahms: Quintettes Op 111 & 115** / Melos-Quartett Stuttgart, Causse, Portal / HM 1951349

String Sextet No. 1 in B flat major, Op. 18 (1860)

Johannes Brahms completed his *String Sextet in B flat Major No. 1*, Op. 18, in 1860. It is in four movements and slightly less than 40 minutes in duration. The composer was still in his 20s when he wrote this work, and while it clearly bears his artistic stamp, it also betrays the strength of his early influences, including Haydn, Mozart, Beethoven, and Schubert. Early works such as these make it sometimes difficult to determine the true direction of Brahms' musical vision except that he loved the music that had been coming out of Vienna for the last hundred years. However, it is also true that the full Romantic writing of the generation directly preceding his own, that of Schumann, who discovered and promoted him, is absent in Brahms' compositions. This first sextet reveals an especially acute understanding of Schubert's later writing. There is as much Classical order in this sextet as there are Romantic leanings. The use of a string sextet as an ensemble was comparatively new. Spohr provided the only notable precedent. Brahms is also partial to certain Baroque conventions, such as the fugato in the Andante second movement.

The first *String Sextet* was written in the summertime, while Brahms was vacationing on the banks of the Elbe. Its ineluctable, Viennese strains seem to come through in spite of his pride in being a tough kid from Hamburg. The sweetness of Vienna's indigenous sound comes through in this work, which is perhaps why it keeps reconfiguring its textures, resisting the urge to bathe in the loveliness of the city's soundscape, which can reduce itself to alkaline desolation in a matter of moments. That was the bizarre danger about Vienna that this sextet works with; it is a city that loves music, especially its waltzes and its famous composers. Becoming part of that scene can easily reduce a musician to an imitator, making it undesirable, yet it is ironically a mecca for composers. While Wagner and Schumann broke with its expectations, Brahms worked with them, loved the city's paradox, and never allowed musical sleaze to get the upper hand. His music is so eventful because he does not want to be pinned onto a dance floor laden with waltzing Viennese locals. It is a strange risk to take but it resulted in wonderfully enduring music. *—John Keillor*

Recommended:

- ○ **Brahms: String Sextets** / Raphael Ens. / 2000 / Hyperion 20276
- ○ **Brahms: String Sextets** / L'Archibudelli / 1996 / Sony 68252
- ○ **Brahms: String Sextet No 1; Theme and Variations in D minor** / Kocian Quartet / 2001 / Praga 250166

String Sextet No. 2 in G major, Op. 36 (1864–1865)

After Brahms' successful *Sextet No. 1 in B flat Major*, Op. 18 was published in 1862, he embarked on a second in September 1864, which was completed the following May. It was published in 1866, and the first performance followed on February 3, 1867, in Vienna. Quieter and more reflective than the first sextet, the second did not achieve the immediate success enjoyed by its predecessor. During the composition of the *Second Sextet*, Brahms kept the work to himself. Brahms' relationship with Agathe von Siebold, a singer in Göttingen for whom he had composed the Lieder, Opp. 14 and 19, had reached a point of such intensity that both she and her friends assumed an engagement was imminent. Brahms was intent on continuing to see Siebold, although he did not wish to "wear fetters," as he put it in a letter to her. Siebold broke off the relationship, leaving Brahms despondent. The *Sextet*, Op. 36, is really dedicated to her. Three times near the end of the first-movement exposition the first and second violins, together, spell "Agathe" by playing the pitches A-G-A-D-H-E ("H" is the German designation for B natural). After the composition of the *Sextet*, Brahms noted to a friend, "Here I have freed myself from my last love."

The themes of all four movements are related. The first opens with a rising fifth that proceeds up a half step, only to leap up another fifth. The theme of the Adagio third movement follows the same pattern except the leaps are fourths separated by a whole step. The tremolo opening of the fourth movement includes leaps of fourths and fifths and movement by whole steps, while these same intervals permeate the ensuing thematic material. Leaps of fourths and fifths are buried in the accompaniment of the Scherzo, while the Trio theme features the original pattern in the opposite direction.

From the beginning, the ambivalent main theme of the Allegro ma non troppo first movement shifts between G major and E flat major, a repeated G–F sharp tremolo in the first viola providing the only anchor in the nebulous first 30 measures. The tremolo permeates the entire development section of the lengthy movement, the coda of which presents the main theme fully in G major, without the E flat inflections.

Instead of placing a slow movement second, Brahms follows the Allegro with a somewhat gloomy, minor mode Scherzo in 2/4 meter. A jocular central section, shifting to the major and a 3/4 meter, provides a foil to the mood of the Scherzo. The pensive Adagio, a set of five variations with a coda, contains some of the most dense contrapuntal layering of the sextet. The stormy finale is a combination of rondo and sonata forms. The opening six measures reappear several times on different harmonies, dominating the texture of the movement. *—John Palmer*

Recommended:

- ○ **Brahms: String Sextets** / L'Archibudelli / 1996 / Sony 68252
- ○ **Brahms: String Sextets** / Raphael Ens. / 2000 / Hyperion 20276
- ○ **Brahms: Quintette; Sextette** / Amadeus Quartet / DG 419875

Trio for clarinet, cello & piano in A minor, Op. 114 (1891)

The *Clarinet Trio* is the first of four chamber works inspired by the principal clarinetist of the Meiningen Court Orchestra, Richard Mühlfeld. Brahms had been aware of Mühlfeld's artistry since the 1880s, for the Meiningen Orchestra had played his *Second Piano Concerto* and premiered his *Fourth Symphony*. It was in 1891, however, that Brahms, while on a week-long stay at the Meiningen court in March, asked Mühlfeld to perform privately for him. Apparently Brahms was impressed, and in November he returned to Meiningen with two new works in hand—the *Trio for clarinet, cello and piano*, Op. 114, and the *Quintet for clarinet and strings*, Op. 115.

The *Trio* is a typical example of the restrained and concentrated style of Brahms' later works. It is in the typical four-movement form, and offers nothing remarkable or unusual except in its polished workmanship and Romantic warmth. There is no question that this work, as with the later sonatas for clarinet, was written with that instrument in mind—the alternative of the viola was added by the first publisher. Regardless, the clarinet plays almost a subordinate role to the cello, weaving contrapuntal inner parts as often as it takes the main melodic material.

In the first movement, Allegro a fairly straightforward sonata form grows out of a simple rising arpeggio and descending scale that grow into a complex contrapuntal web that is sustained throughout. A particularly sensitive use of color and registral combinations between the instruments characterizes the second-movement Adagio; the entire movement is constructed of subtle rearrangements of two basic ideas. The third movement is marked Andantino grazioso. The main section of this typical dance form is a lovely and nostalgic Viennese waltz, while the trio section is an Austrian Ländler, the forerunner of the waltz, replete with yodeling clarinet. This short and exciting rondo finale (Allegro is in Brahms' typical gypsy idiom, with its mixture of three-against-four rhythms and colorful minor-mode harmonies. It is the only movement of the *Clarinet Trio* that could be considered virtuosic, and it ends the work decisively. *—Steven Coburn*

Recommended:

- ○ **Brahms: Clarinet Quintet; Clarinet Trio** / T. King, C. Benson, Georgian / 1986 / Hyperion 66107
- ○ **Ax, Stolzman & Ma: Brahms, Beethoven & Mozart** / Ax, Stoltzman, Ma / 1995 / Sony 57499

Trio for horn, violin & piano in E flat major, Op. 40 (1865)

This Trio comes at the end of Brahms' early chamber compositions and in many ways looks back nostalgically to his youth. First of all, the specification for "natural horn" (without valves) as opposed to the modern and more familiar valved horn was for Brahms a keen reminder of his childhood. His father had been a professional natural horn player and had instructed the young Brahms on that instrument. Second, Brahms quotes the folk song "Dort in den Weiden steht ein Haus" (There in the Willows Stands a House) in the Adagio movement, one of his childhood favorites, learned from his mother. There is some evidence that this entire, deeply emotional movement was an elegy in her memory. And last, the entire mood and tone of the piece, aided in no small part by the scoring, is evocative of nature and hunting, two of the most important themes of the Romantic movement to which Brahms was closely allied, via Schumann, in his youth. Also, mainly because of the scoring and its allusions to "occasional" rather than "serious" music, this Trio stands somewhat apart from Brahms' other chamber works. It is unique in his output, yet remains a deeply personal statement.

Instead of the usual sonata movement, Brahms opens the Trio with an expanded ternary-form Andante movement (ABABA) that alternates a longing and nostalgic melody with a faster, yearning passage. Again Brahms avoids the usual form and puts the principal section of the Scherzo into an abbreviated sonata form. It is a rousing hunting song, full of energy and good spirits. The central Trio is a Ländler, an Austrian folk dance, which adds to the rustic flavor of the entire movement. Introspective and deeply personal, the third movement Adagio is in a simple ternary (ABA), yet is complicated by Brahms' use of a fugal exposition to present the principal material. It is in the emotionally charged reprise that Brahms quotes the aforementioned folk song, to great rhetorical effect, one of Brahms' most intense compositions. As if to compensate for the Adagio, Brahms concludes the Trio with as light and rollicking an Allegro as he was capable of writing. Again the horn's hunting qualities are featured, and the Trio ends in a virtuosic tour de force for all three instruments. *—Steven Coburn*

Recommended:

- ○ **Franck: Violin Sonata; Brahms: Horn Trio** / Vladimir Ashkenazy, Perlman, Tuckwell / 1997 / London 452887
- ○ **Brahms & Beethoven: Music for Horn** / L. Greer, S. Lubin, S. Chase / 1991 / HM Classical Express 3957037

Violin Sonata No. 1 in G major ("Regen"), Op. 78 (1878–1879)

Composed in the high summer of his creative career after the completion of the *Symphony No. 1* and the *Violin Concerto*, Brahms' *Violin Sonata in G major* is a gloriously lyrical work with long-breathed melodies rather than terse themes, and expansive extrapolations rather than concise developments. It is also one of Brahms' most tightly structured and cogently argued works, with a degree of formal integration rare in his works. The dotted rhythm of the opening movement's first theme dominates the second theme of the central movement and all of the closing movement, and the second theme of the central movement returns in the central section of the closing movement. The sonata is in three movements: Vivace ma non troppo, Adagio, and Allegro molto moderato. The opening Vivace, significantly slowed by its modifying ma non troppo, is a sweet-tempered movement in sonata form with two lyrical themes. The central Adagio is in ternary form, with a heartfelt main theme full of double and triple stops in the violin. The closing Allegro molto moderato starts with a direct quotation from the opening of Brahms' *Regenlied*, Op. 59/3 (Rain Song), a melancholy minor-keyed song recalling the long-lost days of youth. In the *Violin Sonata*, Brahms likewise starts it in the minor, but with the return of the theme of the Adagio, he returns the music to the consoling tonic major of the sonata. The work ends with a warm, sunset coda of great beauty. *—James Leonard*

Recommended:

- ○ **Brahms: Violin & Viola Sonatas** / P. Zukerman, Barenboim / 1998 / DG 453121
- ○ **Brahms: The Violin Sonatas** / Suk, Katchen / 2001 / Decca 466393
- ○ **Brahms: Violin Sonatas 1–3** / K.-W. Chung, Frankl / 1998 / EMI 56203
- ○ **Sonatas of Brahms & Beach** / Delmoni, Funahashi / 1995 / John Marks 2

Violin Sonata No. 2 in A major ("Thun"), Op. 100 (1886)

While on vacation in Thun during August 1886, Johannes Brahms found himself so refreshed and musically invigorated that he proclaimed the area to be "so full of melodies that one has to be careful not to step on any." Indeed, during his time there Brahms composed three of his most beloved chamber works in just a matter of days. Op. 99 is the second of Brahms' two cello sonatas, and Op. 101 the great C minor piano trio; in between these is Op. 100, the *Sonata for piano and violin No. 2 in A major* (the order in which the instruments are listed—piano first and then violin—is Brahms' own indication; he was following in the footsteps of Mozart and Beethoven by giving the keyboardist top billing). The *Sonata* was premiered in Vienna a few weeks before Christmas 1886 by Brahms and then-famous violinist Joseph Hellmesberger.

The A major sonata is both the shortest and the most immediately ingratiating of Brahms' three violin sonatas; not for a single moment is the radiant, happy mood ever put in real jeopardy (even during the fractured contrapuntal passages in the first movement's development), and the tunes are of the long-spun, heart-warming variety that sticks in the mind's ear. Brahms achieves a three-movement plan by combining slow movement and scherzo into one—in this central movement, passages of sweet and simple Andante tranquillo alternate with fleet-footed Vivace episodes during which Brahms introduces hemiola and off-beat rhythmic accents. The Allegro amabile first movement is aptly summed up by that word, "amabile"—one hardly expects that the second theme could possibly outdo the first in terms of sheer lyric beauty, but somehow Brahms manages it. In the Allegro grazioso (quasi Andante) last movement Brahms builds a relaxed rondo around a main theme whose contours are so deep and velvety that it has become customary for violinists to play the entire theme on the instrument's rich G string. *—Blair Johnston*

Recommended:

- ○ **Brahms: Violin Sonatas 1–3** / K.-W. Chung, Frankl / 1997 / EMI 40710
- ○ **Brahms: The Violin Sonatas** / Suk, Katchen / 2001 / Decca 466393
- ○ **Brahms: Violin & Viola Sonatas** / P. Zukerman, Barenboim / 1998 / DG 453121
- ○ **Brahms: Violin Sonatas 1–3** / Perlman, Vladimir Ashkenazy / 1998 / EMI 66945

Violin Sonata No. 3 in D minor, Op. 108 (1886–1888)

Johannes Brahms began his *Sonata for piano and violin No. 3 in D minor*, Op. 108, almost immediately after finishing the *Sonata No. 2 in A major*, Op. 100, during a vacation in Thun in the summer of 1886, but he set the work aside for two years and completed it only when he returned to Thun in 1888 for another vacation. The two works are in fact utterly different from one another: the *A major Sonata* is easygoing and radiates with warm melody from start to finish, while the *D minor Sonata* is an athletic, fibrous, and at times even nervous affair that offers drama of a far more epic nature. Brahms dedicated the *Sonata No. 3* to Hans von Bülow, pianist, conductor, friend, and champion of the composer; it was first performed by Brahms and violinist Jenö Hubay in Budapest on December 22, 1888.

Brahms returns to the four-movement sonata design in the *D minor Violin Sonata* (he had combined two movements into one in the *A major Sonata* to make a three-movement piece). At the *Sonata*'s opening a lean violin melody rides atop sinister (or nearly so) syncopated broken octaves in the piano; both that theme and those octaves will generate nearly everything that we hear in the Allegro first movement—even the warmer second theme owes its identity to the recurring dotted figure of the first theme. The development of the movement is nothing short of astonishing: the entire thing unfolds over a dominant pedal that seems to grow ever more ominous but then, in one of the work's truly shining moments, suddenly grows incandescent to lead the way into the recapitulation.

The Adagio in D major is truly a lied without words, deeply resonant and richly melodic. The scherzo movement—Un poco presto e con sentimento—is an ingenious piece of workmanship, elegantly scored and flawlessly balanced but of a somewhat mysterious character: Clara Schumann described it as "like a lovely girl playing with her lover," while others have heard melancholy or even bitterness in it. The *Sonata*'s most turbulent and obviously dramatic music is reserved for the final Presto agitato movement. *—Blair Johnston*

Recommended:

- ○ **Brahms: Violin & Viola Sonatas** / P. Zukerman, Barenboim / 1998 / DG 453121
- ○ **Brahms: The Violin Sonatas** / Suk, Katchen / 2001 / Decca 466393
- ○ **Brahms: Violin Concerto; Violin Sonata 3: 5 Hungarian Dances** / Yehudi Menuhin; H. Menuhin / 2004 / EMI 62822
- ○ **Brahms: Violin Concerto; Violin Sonata 3** / Oistrakh, Yampolsky / 2003 / EMI 67974

CONCERTO

Double Concerto for violin, cello & orchestra in A minor, Op. 102 (1887)

Brahms wrote this work during the summer of 1887, and conducted the premiere himself on October 18 in Cologne, with Joseph Joachim and Robert Hausmann as, respectively, the violin and cello soloists. Brahms had just turned 20 when he met Joseph Joachim (1831–1907), already a celebrated violinist at 22 and destined to be acclaimed also as a composer, conductor, and educator. It was Joachim who commended his new friend to Robert and Clara Schumann, thereby assuring his celebrity. For 30 years the two were fast friends despite the distance usually separating their power bases: Joachim's in Berlin, Brahms' in Vienna finally. "Jussuf," however, had a weakness—obsessive jealousy of his wife Amalie, whom he accused of adultery in 1881 with his (and Brahms' and Dvořák's) publisher, Fritz Simrock. Brahms disbelieved, and said so in a consolatory letter to Frau Joachim. During divorce hearings she produced this letter in court, and the judge agreed publicly with its contents.

As a result, Joachim cut off communications with Brahms for six years, although he continued to play the composer's music. Finally, seeking to repair the damage, Brahms composed the *"Double" Concerto* as a peace offering; the effort was successful, although their camaraderie of former years was never fully restored. In addition to composing the "Thun" sonatas of 1886 for violin and cello, Brahms had been studying Baroque concerti grossi, so the sound of string instruments was in his ear. This concerto would be his last orchestral work.

From the Swiss vacation resort of Hofstetter on Lake Thun, he wrote to several persons about his "strange flight of fancy... for fiddle and cello." But first he sent a postcard to Joachim, received on July 19, 1887, by which time Brahms had completed the work and was copying solo parts. When Joachim responded enthusiastically by return mail, Brahms asked him to arrange a play-through with Robert Hausmann, who had introduced the Op. 99 *Cello Sonata* a few months prior; Brahms himself would accompany on the piano. This took place at Clara Schumann's home in Baden-Baden in September (her diary notes that "Brahms and Joachim have spoken to one another again after years of silence"). Although neither the Cologne premiere nor the first Vienna performance was a success, the concerto finally entered the repertory, even if it never enjoyed the success of his violin concerto or the two for piano.

The opening Allegro (A minor; 4/4) begins with the kernel of the main theme, then a cello "recitative," and finally the kernel of a more lyrical second theme. Next, the violin has a turn, though the cello intrudes after five bars, following which the orchestra finally gets to play a 44-bar exposition of themes already previewed. Soloists perform the traditional second exposition, but there is not, in the development or recapitulation, a lot of unison playing. Thoughout, the soloists are not stars with a supporting cast, but merely leading characters in a primarily orchestral drama. Unison passages appear in the A and A' sections of the sweetly autumnal, folk-flavored, song-form Andante in D major (3/4 time). The solo instruments dovetail or briefly overlap in an F major middle section, until a magical enharmonic transition leads back to unison playing.

The lighthearted but "not too lively" rondo (vivace non troppo) has repeating A sections with a staccato-marcato rhythm that wrong-headed playing can accelerate and by so doing adulterate. The B section is broader, with chords on the cello that the violin echoes. The C section, in F major, is similarly broad but longer, before the A material returns one more time, with a jaunty tilt of the cap and a kind of jig—all the more entertaining in light of Brahms' short stature, bushy beard and, by then, Santa-like corpulence. —*Roger Dettmer*

Recommended:

- ○ **Great Violinists—Heifetz: Brahms, Bruch, Glazunov** / Ormandy (cond.), Heifetz, Feuermann, Philadelphia Orch. / 2000 / Naxos 110940
- ○ **Beethoven: Triple Concerto; Brahms: Double Concerto** / Szell (cond.), D. Oistrakh, Rostropovich, Cleveland Orch. / 1998 / EMI 66954
- ○ **Brahms: Double Concerto; Beethoven: Triple Concerto** / B. Walter (cond.), Francescatti, Fournier, Columbia SO / 1995 / Sony 64479

Piano Concerto No. 1 in D minor, Op. 15 (1854–1859)

Johannes Brahms was 20 years old when, in 1853, he first made the acquaintance of Robert Schumann through a letter of recommendation provided by the famous violinist Joseph Joachim. It was Schumann's unabashed praise of the music that Brahms showed him that, more than anything else, provided the young composer with the courage necessary to begin work on a full-scale symphony the next year. That courage, however, fell short in the end—Brahms felt himself too inexperienced and was too haunted by the "footsteps of a giant" (Beethoven) to begin fruitful symphonic work—and Brahms reorganized the material he had written as a sonata for two pianos. By 1858, this sonata for two pianos had itself been reborn as the *Piano Concerto No. 1 in D minor*, Op. 15.

The *Piano Concerto No. 1* as we know it today is a complete reworking of the ideas and themes of the original duo-sonata source; much of it is completely new music. The premiere of the piece in January 1859 was not the failure that it is sometimes portrayed to have been, but the cold response at a follow-up performance in Leipzig left a bitter taste in Brahms' mouth that he never forgot—Leipzig remained an enemy for the rest of his life.

The concerto is in three movements: Maestoso, Adagio, and Allegro non troppo. The orchestral exposition to the giant Maestoso is mighty, epic, and tragic in no small portion; much later, a radiant, chorale-like second idea is offered by the soloist, who Brahms provides with the kind of rich, deep sonorities so characteristic of his piano writing. At the recapitulation, which is ushered in by a massive climax in which the pianist is forced to use all his/her strength to compete with the massive orchestral bursts, the pianist boldly takes over the mighty utterances that began the movement.

Brahms wrote the words "Benedictus qui venit in nomine Domini" at the head of the slow movement, but whether the words are an homage to Robert Schumann (whom Brahms sometimes called Domini), a portrait of Clara Schumann (the most popular interpretation, and one seemingly supported by a letter from Brahms to Clara), or some other reference is unknown.

The rondo-theme of the finale is introduced by the piano alone, and, later on, the soloist gets his/her one and only chance to impress the audience with a cadenza—though it is dramatic necessity, not garish virtuosity, that demands the cadenza in the first place. —*Blair Johnston*

Recommended:

- ○ **Brahms: Die Klavierkonzerte** / Jochum (cond.), Gilels, Berlin PO / DG 447446
- ○ **Brahms: Piano Concerto 1; Schumann: Introduction & Allegro** / Szell (cond.), R. Serkin, Cleveland Orch. / 1992 / Sony 48166
- ○ **Brahms: Piano Concerto 1; Piano Sonata & others** / Konwitschny (cond.), W. Kempff, Staatskapelle Dresden / 1992 / DG 437374
- ○ **Brahms: Klavierkonzert; Violinkonzert; Doppelkonzert** / L. Bernstein (cond.), K. Zimerman, Vienna PO / DG 431207
- ○ **Brahms: Klavierkonzert 1** / C. Abbado (cond.), Pollini, Berlin PO / DG 447041

Piano Concerto No. 2 in B flat major, Op. 83 (1881)

Portly, grey-bearded, and a celebrity, on the eve of his 45th birthday, he began sketching themes for the *Second Piano Concerto* following the first of eight trips to Italy. He put these aside, however, to compose the *D major Violin Concerto*. Still in a symphonic mode after his *Second Symphony*, he added a scherzo to the *B flat Piano Concerto*'s otherwise traditional three-movement form. Brahms finished composing it on July 7, 1881.

Before the Budapest premiere on November 9, however, he tried the music at Meiningen with Hans von Bülow's orchestra, during closed rehearsals of other repertory. He returned there after Budapest for a public performance on November 27, conducted by Bülow, who talked up the work to his former father-in-law, Franz Liszt. Liszt requested a score, and later on wrote to Brahms, "At first reading this work seemed to me a little gray in tone; I have, however, come gradually to understand it. It possesses the pregnant character of a distinguished work of art, in which thought and feeling move in noble harmony." Praise indeed from an acknowledged old master, whose 1853 invitation to join his "New German Music Verein" Brahms had cursorily declined.

Brahms incorporated several quite daring (for him) changes in procedure. He jettisoned the usual orchestral exposition in the opening movement; after the solo horn plays a wistfully expansive first theme with piano arpeggios, extended by the strings, the soloist unleashes a virtuosic cadenza that propels us into the exposition. Additional themes pour forth as if from a cornucopia, always paced by the piano, leading to a tempestuous development section that never loses sight of the opening horn theme. Its formal restatement signals a mostly benign reprise. There's a brilliant close, though, which poses a serious structural problem for soloist and conductor: how do you keep the ensuing scherzo from sounding anti-climactic, or worse yet, superfluous?

Without appearing to understate or rein-in the opening Allegro non troppo movement, it dare not be played to the hilt. The entire work's structural fulcrum has to be the end of the scherzo, an Allegro appassionato in D minor with a soft-grained second theme; otherwise, the remaining two movements risk outstaying their welcome. Helpfully, the scherzo boasts a brilliant D major trio section, and a tempestuous close. But it must sound harrowing in order for the ensuing Andante to work its calming charm.

The solo cello begins and ends the third movement with a poignant B flat melody that Brahms recalled five years later in his song "Immer leiser wird mein Schlummer." The middle portion, however, grows expressively high-strung until the clarinets restore calm with a piano-accompanied duet of russet beauty.

Brahms marked his sonata-rondo finale Allegretto grazioso, although it accelerates later on as the solo writing becomes more and more brilliant, but this never becomes threateningly powerful. Some have claimed to hear "gypsies" in the string writing; but even if so, it would be what Hungarians call *Verbunkos*, subliminally remembered from Brahms' teenage tours with the violinist Reményi, who first introduced him to Liszt. —*Roger Dettmer*

Recommended:

- ○ **Rubinstein Collection Vol. 71: Brahms; Schumann** / Ormandy (cond.), Artur Rubinstein, Philadelphia Orch. / 1999 / RCA Victor 63071

- ○ **Brahms: Die Klavierkonzerte** / Jochum (cond.), Gilels, Berlin PO / DG 447446
- ○ **Brahms: The Piano Concertos** / C. Abbado (cond.), Pollini, Vienna PO / DG 453067

Violin Concerto in D major, Op. 77 (1878)

Brahms composed this music during the summer of 1878, and led the first performance, with its dedicatee Joseph Joachim as soloist, in Leipzig on January 1, 1879.

In the 1860s, Brahms toured as Joachim's pianist. Despite the kilometers separating them otherwise—the violinist lived in Berlin, while Brahms settled permanently in Vienna after 1867—their mutual regard as well as affection flourished. Until 1881, that is, when "Jussuf," a pathologically jealous husband, accused his wife of adultery, naming his and Brahms' publisher, Fritz Simrock, as correspondent. Knowing Joachim's mania, Brahms consoled the lady privately in a letter that she made public during divorce proceedings—one that the judge agreed with publicly, adding injury to insult in the fiddler's mind. For the next six years there was silence between them. Brahms, atypically, broke the ice by writing his *"Double" Concerto* in 1887 for Joachim and a cellist of choice—the composer's last work for orchestra, although he lived a decade longer. Even so, Joachim was never as close as in 1878, when Brahms put aside sketches for a new piano concerto (the B flat, Op. 83, finished later) to make one for him instead.

A summer composer, he wrote the music in Pörtschach, a small resort community on the Wörther-see in south-central Austria that he found both charming and congenial (until "lady admirers" annoyed him beyond tolerance in 1879). Brahms created a large work, in the Beethoven tradition, though he gave up the idea of two movements in the middle; in their place he put an F major Adagio, with a seraphic oboe solo but a stormier central section in F sharp minor before calm returns.

The opening movement, marked not too fast, has a sonorous orchestral introduction in 3/4 time amounting to a first exposition of the main theme. When the violin enters, it is with an extended display over horns in octaves and a timpani roll before playing the main theme and a "secondary" group, from which one melody is outright gorgeous. Brahms begins his development section in A minor; a cadenza that Joachim contributed comes after the recapitulation.

Next comes the filigreed Adagio already discussed, then a rondo-finale with a "Hungarian" main theme (marked joyous but not too lively). Most agree that Brahms was saluting Joachim's origin; he was born near Pressburg, later called Poszony—today Bratislava in the Czech Republic. The music teems with challenges yet never becomes the circus-piece that so many nineteenth century fiddle concertos were. *—Roger Dettmer*

Recommended:

- ○ **Brahms, Tchaikovsky: Violin Concertos** / F. Reiner (Cond.), J. Heifetz, Chicago SO / 1989 / RCA Victor 61742
- ○ **Brahms: Violin Concerto; Violin Sonata 3** / Szell (cond.), D. Oistrakh, Cleveland Orch. / 2003 / EMI 67974
- ○ **Kreisler: Violin Concertos** / Barbirolli (cond.), Kreisler, London PO / Pearl 9362

KEYBOARD

Ballades, Op. 10 (1854)

These four works operate as a set and should be played that way. Even though the first Ballade has an inscription that it is based on Herder's translation of the Scottish ballad *Edward*, no one has found proof that the other three are linked to this story in any way. Whether there was an underlying literary connection in Brahms' mind hardly matters though, as the four Ballades are linked into a dramatic narrative in so compelling a manner that some commentators consider this an unlabeled sonata. Stylistically it is rather more advanced than the earlier sonatas, and anticipates the *First Piano Concerto*. The first Ballade, Andante, in D minor, opens with a slow and grim march, which is followed by a bold and dramatic central Allegro and concludes with a variation of the opening. The second Ballade, Andante, in D major, is structured much the same way. The opening though, is lyrical while the central episode is substantially longer and more varied than in the first Ballade. Brahms labeled the third Ballade in B minor Intermezzo. The three-part plan is reversed, with the faster music surrounding a slower central section. The tone of this scherzo-like piece is fantastic and lugubrious, but in spite of this, it seems to bridge the gap emotionally between the heroic and epic tone of the first two Ballades to the lyrical and wistful final Ballade. This concluding piece in B major is more complex structurally than its predecessors, although the principal tone is lyrical rather than dramatic. The entire set is an early masterpiece, entirely original and effective. *—Steven Coburn*

Recommended:

- ○ **Great Pianists of the 20th Century: Wilhelm Kempff I** / W. Kempff / 1998 / Philips 456862
- ○ **Great Pianists of the 20th Century: Arturo Benedetti Michelangeli II** / Michelangeli / 1999 / Philips 456904
- ○ **Emil Gilels: Von Weber, Brahms** / Gilels / Praga 250039

Fantasias, Op. 116 (1892)

Until 1865, a significant percentage of Brahms' published work was for piano solo. After this time, he concentrated on vocal music, not publishing a major work for piano until the *Eight Piano Pieces*, Op. 76, of 1878 and the *Two Rhapsodies*, Op. 79, of 1879. Brahms would take another break from the piano until the composition of Opp. 116–119 in the early 1890s. Thus, works for piano open and close his career as a composer. Although the late piano works are brief, they are among the most complex, dense, and reflective works composed for the instrument.

A month before publication, the *Fantasias, Op. 116*, encompassed five rather than seven pieces, and Brahms suggested to his publisher that the five be printed in one volume. In the end, Brahms added two pieces to the set, which was published in two volumes. Despite the division, aspects of the works themselves create some coherence for the whole. The first and last pieces are Capriccios in D minor and Nos. 4, 5 and 6 are in E major (No. 5 begins in minor but ends in major). Furthermore, there exist thematic links, the most obvious of which occurs in the opening measures of the third and seventh pieces and at the return of the first theme in the fifteenth measure of No. 4.

The *Fantasias, Op. 116*, do not require the technical facility necessary to perform many of Brahms' earlier works, but an incisive musicality is paramount for a proper understanding of these musical miniatures. Composed mostly in the summer of 1892, the pieces were published that year by Simrock in Berlin. Nos. 1–3 were first performed at a concert of January 30, 1893; No. 7 received its premiere on February 18 of the same year. Contrary to his usual practice, Brahms gave the set a descriptive rather than a generic title.

A fiery work in D minor, the first Capriccio is marked Presto, and requires a technique that is nearly Lisztian. The A minor Intermezzo obscures its triple meter in its outer sections, while the central episode shifts to a clearly articulated 3/8. The third piece, a Capriccio in G minor, returns to the fiery atmosphere of the first piece. Set in the Neapolitan E flat major, the central section falls into a trio format, its quarter note triplets creating a sense of rhythmic freedom.

The format of No. 4, an Intermezzo, is unusual, and is in part the result of Brahms' predilection for developing variation. The first half of the piece alternates between two themes (A and B), which return in varied forms. After the diminutive third variation of A, a new idea (C) begins on the dominant. The ensuing variation of A returns to the tonic, but what seems to be a typical ternary construction is thwarted by a return of C, now on the tonic, sandwiched in the middle of the "reprise," which does not behave at all like the first half of the piece. Symmetry is the salient feature of the fifth piece, an Intermezzo. In the opening measures, the material is vertically symmetrical. The motive, at first a half-step, moves upward in the uppermost voice and downward in the lowest, a process reversed on the next beat. The chords, too, are vertically symmetrical, with the narrowest intervals at the outermost extremes. The sixth piece, again marked Intermezzo, brings to mind some of the characteristics of a courtly minuet, while the initial charge of the final D minor Capriccio halts at its more fluid central section before the return of the opening, which ends on D major. *—John Palmer*

Recommended:

- ○ **Brahms: The Late Piano Music** / Kovacevich / 1994 / Philips 442589
- ○ **Yevgeny Kissin: Schubert; Brahms; Liszt** / Kissin / DG 445562
- ○ **Brahms: Die Klavierkonzerte** / Gilels / DG 447446
- ○ **Wilhelm Kempff: Complete 1950s Solo Recordings; Schumann; Brahms** / Kempff / 2003 / DG B000085502

Hungarian Dances for piano, 4 hands, WoO 1 (1858–1879)

Brahms completed these 21 dances for piano, four hands, in 1869. They are divided into four books, the first two of which were completed by 1868, at which time Brahms and Clara Schumann premiered them at a private gathering, on November 1. Each contained five dances, while Books III and IV were comprised of five and six dances, respectively. These were first performed in 1880, also by the composer and Clara Schumann.

Brahms used Hungarian Gypsy folk material in these pieces, having been introduced to it around 1850 by Hungarian violinist Ede Remenyi. However, some of the themes were Brahms' own, but retained Hungarian Gypsy flavors. Joachim claimed that Nos. 11, 14, and 16 were strictly of the composer's own devising. In 1872, Brahms arranged the first ten dances for solo piano, calling them simply *Ten Hungarian Dances*. A year later he adapted three of the dances for orchestra, Nos. 1, 3, and 10. Other arrangers later transcribed the dances for orchestra and various ensembles, as the music grew more popular.

The First Dance, in G minor, certainly has a Gypsy flavor in its lively exoticism. But, like many, it is also Brahmsian: the composer took so well to this idiom because it was not alien to his nature, as evidenced by his G minor *Piano Quartet* and *Violin Concerto*, both of which seem to incorporate these folkish elements naturally into their fabric.

The playful No. 3, in F major, is another gem, both for its subtlety and vibrant colors. No. 5, in F sharp minor, is one of the most famous in the set, containing one of those themes that virtually every man and woman on the street has heard in one guise or other. The humor and lively style of No. 7, in A major, make it attractive, but it sounds less the product of folk influence. The ensuing dance, in A minor, sounds somewhat the product of a Lisztian treatment. Book II's closing item, No. 10 in E major, is vibrant and joyous, full of color and rhythmic appeal. No wonder Brahms was moved to orchestrate it.

Brahms felt that the latter two books were superior to the first pair. Most musicologists would probably agree. The very first item, No. 11, in A minor, has a more subtle expressive manner than most in the previous books. It is less overtly folkish, as are Nos. 12 and 14, both in D minor. On average the 11 pieces in the final two books are also shorter and less colorful, though they possess greater depth.

That said, the B flat major No. 15 returns to the style of the earlier books, showing more color and brighter moods. The rollicking F minor dance that follows is quite attractive and also sounds less Gypsy-influenced. No. 17, in F sharp minor, shows an array of colors and moods. The remaining four are fairly short, but all quite worthwhile. *—Robert Cummings*

Recommended:

- ○ **Brahms: Hungarian Dances** / I. Fischer (cond.), Budapest Festival Orch. / 1999 / Philips 462589
- ○ **Brahms: 21 Hungarian Dances** / C. Abbado (cond.), Vienna PO / 1984 / DG 410615
- ○ **Brahms: Danses Hongroises; Valses** / Duo Crommelynck / 1987 / Claves 508710

Three Intermezzos, Op. 117 (1892)

Occasionally unsure what title, if any, he should give a piece, Brahms came to use the term intermezzo as a rubric under which he could file anything that was not especially whimsical or fiery. The *Three Intermezzi*, Op. 117, do not require the technical facility necessary to perform many of his earlier works, but an incisive musicality is paramount for a proper understanding of these musical miniatures. The fact that they are all marked Andante also presents a problem for the performer, who must probe the details of each work and stress the contrasting elements. All three Intermezzi of Op. 117 were written in the summer of 1892, the year of their publication. This is one of the rare cases in which Brahms gave a specific title for an entire set of pieces. Two of the three Intermezzi received their first performances shortly after they were written: No. 1 on February 18, 1893, and No. 2 on January 30 of the same year.

Prefaced by lines from Herder's translation of *Lady Anne Bothwell's Lament*, a Scottish lullaby, the first Intermezzo is in E flat major and cast in ABA' form. The central section, on E flat minor, obscures the 6/8 meter before returning to the major mode for the modified reprise of the first section.

A sonata-form movement in B flat minor, the second Intermezzo provides an excellent example of thematic transformation. The first theme, traced by the uppermost thirty-second notes in the arpeggios of the first two measures, becomes the second theme, played in the top notes of block chords 30 measures later. Because the rhythmic movement from note to note is changed and the textures of the two passages are very dissimilar, it takes a perceptive pianist to locate and bring out the transformed melody. Brahms chooses the relative major, D flat, for the second theme while the development section is built around the fluid arpeggios of the first theme. In the recapitulation, the second theme, truncated and transformed, vacillates between the tonic major and minor.

Brahms once referred to the third Intermezzo of Op. 117 as "the lullaby of all my grief." In C sharp minor, the piece is in ternary form (ABA), with a central section on A major. Section A consists of two ideas, the first stated in parallel octaves. The entire complex is repeated, although the melodies are accompanied differently and some segments appear in a higher register. The move to A major for the B section creates a sense of relaxation as the leaping theme, again with right-hand octaves, provides a stark contrast to the linear, opening idea. A brief transition leads to the return of section A, re-harmonized and in a form more akin to its second half than to the beginning. *—John Palmer*

Recommended:

- ○ **Great Pianists of the 20th Century: Radu Lupu** / Lupu / 1999 / Philips 456895
- ○ **Brahms: 4 Ballades; 2 Rhapsodies, Intermezzi** / G. Gould / 1992 / Sony 52651
- ○ **Brahms: The Late Piano Music** / Kovacevich / 1994 / Philips 442589
- ○ **Wilhelm Kempff: Complete 1950s Solo Recordings; Schumann; Brahms** / Kempff / 2003 / DG B000085502

Piano Sonata No. 1 in C major, Op. 1 (1852)

On September 30, 1853, the 20-year-old Brahms played a number of his keyboard works for Robert Schumann. Among these were both the First and Second Piano Sonatas, which Schumann hailed as "veiled symphonies." Although published as Op. 1, the *Sonata No. 1 in C major* is actually the fourth piano sonata Brahms is known to have composed; the third was published as Op. 2, and the first two were evidently destroyed. The enormous scale and breadth of this sonata were probably what Schumann had in mind in drawing his symphonic analogy. Cast in four long movements, the *Sonata No. 1* is a remarkably cohesive and effective work for so young and inexperienced a composer.

Aside from the sonata's scope, another feature that Schumann might have found particularly attractive is the folk flavor of the Andante second movement, a set of variations on what Brahms believed to be an old German minnelied. (The authenticity of the song has since been brought into question.) Schumann was also almost certainly struck by Brahms' early mastery of large-scale sonata form, a particular concern of Schumann's throughout his own compositional career.

The first movement is in a fairly conventional sonata-allegro form, but uses the technique of thematic transformation pioneered by Liszt and Berlioz. Here, the movement's main themes are altered in character and rhythm as the music proceeds, as opposed to a Classical fragmentation and recombination of motives. The following movement is a Beethovenian scherzo based on a motive from the final bars of the Andante, a derivation that creates a sense of union between the central movements. This technique is continued in the Rondo finale, whose opening is derived from a transformation of material from the first movement. In this sonata Brahms foreshadows many of the characteristics of his mature piano works, including formal mastery, thematic development and transformation, and a distinctive if somewhat thick virtuoso keyboard scoring that owes surprisingly little to Liszt and Chopin. *—Steven Coburn*

Recommended:

- ○ **Brahms: Piano Sonatas 1 & 2** / Biret / 1991 / Naxos 550351
- ○ **10th Van Cliburn International Piano Competition** / Nakamatsu / 1997 / HM 907218

Piano Sonata No. 2 in F sharp minor, Op. 2 (1852)

Composed in November 1852 and published in 1853 by Breitkopf & Härtel in Leipzig, the *Piano Sonata No. 2 in F sharp minor*, Op. 2, is dedicated to Clara Schumann. Although it is the first piano sonata Brahms completed, it may have been first performed in public only as late as February 2, 1882, in Vienna.

The F sharp minor sonata is a study in contrasts between passages of ebullient, youthful passion and moments imbued with the delicacy of folk song. Thematic relationships exist between the different movements, notably the Andante and Scherzo, the main idea of which also forms part of the main themes of the first movement and Finale.

Developmental fragmentation of the first movement's main theme takes place already in the exposition of the first movement, as the transition to the second theme group begins. Numerous appearances of the opening measures of the main theme in the development section make the entrance of the recapitulation difficult to spot, as it begins not on the tonic, but a diminished harmony and proceeds a half step lower than it "should." It is only in the fifth measure of the recapitulation that the theme finds its proper harmonic track.

Brahms tended to compose the slow, central movements of his sonatas before outer ones. The Andante of Op. 2, in B minor, consists of three variations on *"Mir ist leide,"* a German Minnesang; it is one of Brahms' first attempts at variation form. The variations are free, particularly the second, which grows to a powerful climax on the relative major (D major).

Brahms follows Beethoven's example by writing a theme for the second part of the Scherzo that is a variant of the first part, the main idea of which is a 6/8 meter variant of the Andante theme. The D major Trio contrasts with the B minor Scherzo both through the key change and the static nature of the Trio's theme. With the return of the Scherzo, Brahms gives free reign to his developmental tendencies. In a personal copy of the sonata, the composer gives alternate renderings of passages that require a large hand.

Brahms prefaces the Finale with a sostenuto introduction. Dominated by the kind of flourishes he would abandon later in his career, the introduction itself is a fantasy-like elaboration of the theme of the more strictly constructed sonata-form Finale. The theme resembles in shape the main idea of the first movement, though disguised by a greater note values. After modulating to the relative major in the aggressive exposition, Brahms begins the development with harmonically adventurous broken chords that mimic the close of the exposition. The athletic coda is heavily fortified with flashy runs and wide leaps. *—John Palmer*

Recommended:

- ○ **Brahms: Fantasies, Piano Pieces, Sonata 2** / Ax / 1995 / Sony 69284
- ○ **Brahms: Piano Sonatas 1 & 2; Scherzo** / Vogt / EMI 557392

Piano Sonata No. 3 in F minor, Op. 5 (1853)

At the age of 20, on his third and final try, Brahms established himself as a master of a genre that, decades earlier, Beethoven infused with a new level of personal expression and, indeed, epochally transformed: the solo piano sonata. In terms of both form and expression, Brahms' *Piano Sonata No. 3 in F minor* is conceived on a grand scale. The first movement, marked Allegro maestoso (though many pianists seem to play it Adagio maestoso), indeed opens majestically, with a theme marked by great solid chords that range across the entire keyboard. The second subject begins lyrically, but it, too, swells in grandeur, and the whole movement builds to a triumphant climax in the bright major mode. The slow movement, Andante, is one of the great love poems in music, its two lyrical themes combining at last in a magnificent expression of rapturous passion. The Scherzo is a dark and dramatic waltz for which the grandly solemn, chordal Trio provides welcome relief. A haunting Intermezzo, a disturbing movement with ghostly echoes of the Sonata's opening, is followed by the Finale, in which a dark, gnarly dance of death is contrasted with a broad, confident chordal second subject. In contrast to conventional sonata practice, the second theme ultimately prevails, bringing this youthful masterwork to a triumphant conclusion. *—Sol Louis Siegel*

Recommended:

- ○ **Brahms: Sonata; 4 Ballades** / Hough / Hyperion 67237
- ○ **Brahms: Sonata 3; Klavierstücke** / Grimaud / Denon 79782

Eight Pieces, Op. 76 (1871–1878)

This is the first set of miniature masterpieces that were to comprise the remaining output of Brahms' solo piano music. It is not known precisely why Brahms quit producing large-scale piano works after the Paganini *Studies*, Op. 35, but the small size of the remaining works in no way lessens either their complexity or musical significance. They are all imbued with Brahms' now fully matured technique of "developing variation" in which the entire musical fabric is spun from germinal motives, often a single one for an entire piece. The intense and strict organizational principles, however, in no way detract from the emotional warmth and romantic color of these works. On the contrary, they serve to enhance and distill the emotional power in a way that gives these short works a gravity and sophistication that belies their small scale. The Capriccio in F sharp minor is restless and impassioned, alternating sweeping arpeggios with lyrical interludes. Playful is the best description of the Capriccio in B minor. In Brahms' best gypsy style, this piece subjects a wistful theme to a series of figurative transformations. The Intermezzo in A flat major consists merely of two ideas, played in succession twice. The first is legato syncopated chords against a gentle staccato accompaniment, and the second a lyrical rising melody. Darkly lyrical is the mood of the next Intermezzo in B flat major. The relaxed figuration and singing melody are in contrast to the chromatic and unsettled harmony. As the emotional center of the set, the Capriccio in C sharp minor is also the largest work. Full of complex rhythms and surging passages, this work is passionate and powerful. The Intermezzo in A major is an emotional respite from the previous Capriccio. It is comprised of two contrasting lyrical ideas, and is gentle and restive. The opening and closing refrains of the Intermezzo in A minor are somewhat reminiscent of the tone of the opening of the first of the Op. 10 *Ballades*. The reminder of the piece is a sadly wistful melody over a flowing accompaniment. The final Capriccio in C major is one of Brahms' most difficult short piano works. A whirling figuration leads to an exhilarating climax. The rhythm is highly complex and demands mature musicianship for an effective interpretation. *—Steven Coburn*

Recommended:

- ○ **Brahms: Piano Pieces; 2 Rhapsodies; Fantasies** / Biret / 1990 / Naxos 550353

Six Pieces, Op. 118 (1892)

In these six pieces, in contrast to the Op. 116 or Op. 117 sets, there is little in the way of commonality or connection, nor are there the problems of consecutive performance offered by Op. 117. The pieces are simply arranged to work effectively as a set. As with all the later piano pieces, these miniatures are ternary in outward form, yet full of the motivic density and complexity typical of Brahms' later style. They are also infused with the introspective melancholy shared by most of the composer's late works. The Intermezzo in A minor that opens the set is in a concentrated sonata form. Its restless introductory quality and ambiguous harmony render the piece ineffective when performed alone. The following Intermezzo in A major is a large ternary Nocturne. Brahms displays his contrapuntal genius in some effective and effortless canons in the central section. Deeply lyrical and moving, it is one of Brahms' loveliest creations. For the first time since his youth, Brahms used the title Ballade for the next piece in G minor. Unlike the Op. 10 *Ballades*, though, there is nothing that can be construed as narrative in this tightly organized yet passionate piece; it could as easily been called a Capriccio. The following Intermezzo in F minor offers some complicated contrapuntal writing in its restless outer sections. The central section is really a chorale, but spread over the lower half of the keyboard in alternating chords. For the next piece, Brahms turns to another unique title: Romanze in F major. The outer section is a true chorale with the melody doubled at the octave in the inner voices. The central section is also unique in that it is a Berceuse—a lullaby consisting of varied statements of the melody over an ostinato accompaniment. The obvious model here is Chopin. The final work is an Intermezzo in E flat minor. There is some evidence that this piece was conceived orchestrally, perhaps for a new symphony, but eventually converted to piano form. Its tragically grand and epic tone supports this theory. The outer section is a plaintive melody accompanied by ambiguous diminished harmony, while the central section is a broad and nobly tragic march. *—Steven Coburn*

Recommended:

- ○ **Brahms: The Late Piano Music** / Kovacevich / 1994 / Philips 442589
- ○ **Brahms: 2 Rhapsodies; 3 Intermezzos; 6 Piano Pieces; 6 Piano Pieces** / Lupu / 1987 / London 417599
- ○ **Brahms: Piano Sonata 3; Brahms: 6 Klavierstücke** / Grimaud / Denon 79782

Four Pieces, Op. 119 (1892)

Until 1865, a significant percentage of Brahms' published work was for piano solo. After this time, he concentrated on vocal music, not publishing a major work for piano until the *Eight Piano Pieces*, Op. 76, of 1878, followed immediately by the *Two Rhapsodies*, Op. 79, of 1879. Brahms would take another break from the piano until the early 1890s, when he released Opp. 116 through 119. Thus, works for piano open and close his compositional career. Unity seems not to have been an issue with Brahms in the late sets of piano pieces, except in the case of the *Fantasias*, Op. 116. Although the late piano works are brief, they are among the most complex, dense, and reflective works ever composed for the instrument. Most likely composed in the summer of 1893, the *Klavierstücke* (*Piano Pieces*), Op. 119, were published in Berlin by Simrock in 1893. They were first performed in London in January 1894.

Brahms was uncomfortable with descriptive titles for his pieces, and often resorted to the noncommittal "Klavierstücke." Occasionally unsure as to what title, if any, he should give an individual piece, Brahms came to use the term "intermezzo" as a rubric under which he could file anything that was not especially whimsical or fiery. Thus, the three Intermezzi of Op. 119 are not all constructed alike. The Op. 119 pieces do not require the technical facility necessary to play many of his earlier works, but an incisive musicality is paramount for a proper performance of these musical miniatures.

Brahms disguises the bar line in a masterful fashion at the beginning of the first piece, an Intermezzo in B minor. Described by Walter Frisch as a B minor triad that is "embedded in a chord that looks, but cannot be said to function, like a E minor ninth," the first three notes (a B minor triad) really function as an upbeat to what follows. Thus, the second half of each measure belongs, harmonically, with the first half of the next. Such an analysis reveals a circle of fifths progression into the fourth measure, at which point the real bar line becomes meaningful. After the central section, which is less linear than the opening material, the beginning of the piece returns, but with touches of the tonic major. The strongest cadence, on B minor, occurs at the end of what is the most harmonically rich, yet harmonically ambivalent, of Brahms's works.

Agitated repeated notes characterize the E minor Intermezzo, whose first section consists of varied presentations of the opening theme. The waltz-like central section, itself in two parts, uses the same melody as the opening measures, disguised by the different tempo, rhythm, and accompaniment. The reprise of the first section skips little material, and the piece ends with a reminiscence of the waltz.

The Intermezzo in C major is a frivolous, humorous romp with the melody in the thumb of right hand, accompanied both above and below. The piece has the feel, though not the form, of a scherzo; its middle segment is set off more by harmony than by new melodic material.

The fourth and final piece of the set, a Rhapsody in E flat major, is the longest of Brahms's late piano works. A passage built of triplets sets off the harsh opening from the more lyrical central episode, which features a stepwise melody over broken chords. A varied form of the main theme appears before the literal reprise. The Rhapsody's firm close on E flat minor is very unusual, and looks back to the second of Schubert's *Four Impromptus*, D. 899. *—John Palmer*

Recommended:

- ○ **Brahms: 2 Rhapsodies; 3 Intermezzos; 6 Piano Pieces; Four Piano Pieces** / Lupu / 1987 / London 417599
- ○ **Van Cliburn: My Favorite Brahms** / Cliburn / 1999 / BMG 0902663566
- ○ **Brahms: The Late Piano Music** / Kovacevich / 1994 / Philips 442589

Two Rhapsodies, Op. 79 (1879)

The two *Rhapsodies*, Op. 79 are strong, dramatic works that date from Brahms' full compositional maturity. They differ from each other in their formal layouts much more than in their expressive mode, for which reason they are rarely performed together. The first of the pair, in B minor, is in the ABA form of a scherzo; indeed, there is a palpable affinity between the Rhapsody and Chopin's *Scherzo in B minor*, Op. 20. As in Chopin's work, the main section of the Rhapsody is an emotional cry for which the much quieter middle section provides needed relief; here, Brahms invests the harmonies with a particular subtlety. The second Rhapsody, in G minor, is one of the composer's most popular and effective piano works, tautly written and darkly dramatic. It is cast in a sonata-allegro form; the cascading chords of the first subject cloud the work's tonality in ambiguity, while the second subject, which unfolds in the piano's lower registers, provides a dramatic contrast rather than a lyrical one. This six-minute work, only half as long as its predecessor, foreshadows the tragic but proud mode of larger-scale works like the Symphony No. 4 in E minor, Op. 98 (1884–85). *—Sol Louis Siegel*

Recommended:

- ○ **Martha Argerich: Debut Recital** / Argerich / 2003 / DG 447430
- ○ **Brahms: Piano Pieces; 2 Rhapsodies; Fantasies** / Biret / 1990 / Naxos 550353

Variations and Fugue on a Theme of Handel, Op. 24 (1861)

Brahms' works for piano open and close his career as a composer. In his earliest sets of variations, especially those of Op. 9, the melody is of primary importance, and Brahms clings to it while freely changing the harmony. His later studies of Beethoven, however, led to his transformation of the melody into something new, adhering to the theme's basic phrase structure and harmonic pattern. As had Bach in his *"Goldberg" Variations* and Beethoven in the *"Diabelli" Variations*, Brahms, in the *Variations and Fugue on a Theme of Handel*, Op. 24, constructed a sprawling masterwork based on a very simple idea. Brahms' intended his earlier variations, such as Opp. 9, 21, and 23, for private audiences, but composed the *Handel Variations* and the later *Paganini Variations*, Op. 35, with the concert hall in mind. Composed in 1861 and published in 1862 by Breitkopf & Härtel in Leipzig, the *Händel Variations* were first performed by Brahms in Hamburg on December 7, 1861. The set is also one of the works with which Brahms introduced himself to Vienna in a concert of November 29, 1862.

Brahms may have been attracted by the utter simplicity of Handel's theme and the challenge it posed. The melody is the Air from the third movement of the first suite in B flat major of Handel's *Suites de pièces de clavecin* of 1733. (Handel himself wrote a set of variations on this same Air.) Brahms certainly recognized the harmonic potential suggested by the theme's sequential structure, re-harmonizing recurrent notes. At several points, Brahms pairs the variations such that the second "varies" the material of the first. Donald Francis Tovey recognizes a larger grouping in variations 14–18, which he describes as "aris[ing] one out of the other in a wonderful decrescendo of tone and crescendo of Romantic beauty." Brahms did not at all abandon the past in his *Handel Variations*. A strict canon forms the basis of variation 6, and variations 5, 6 and 13 constitute the traditional ventures into the tonic minor. We hear a Hungarian rhapsody in No. 13 and a fast Siciliana in 12/8 in No. 19. Such distinct character is also to be found in the "music box" variation (No. 22) and the chromatic fantasia atmosphere of No. 20. The closing fugue, with a subject derived from the original Air, is a study in the free use of Baroque counterpoint. *—John Palmer*

Recommended:

- ○ **Brahms: Handel Variations; Six Piano Pieces; Rhapsodies** / Ax / 1992 / Sony 48046
- ○ **Brahms: Piano Concertos 1 & 2; Handel Variations; Waltzes** / L. Fleisher / 1997 / Sony 63225

Variations on a Theme of Paganini, Op. 35 (1862–1863)

With this set of pieces, Brahms placed himself squarely in the tradition of nineteenth century piano étude composition. His use of Paganini's *Twenty-Fourth Caprice* as inspiration is telling because both Liszt and Schumann had made arrangements of Paganini caprices for the purpose of piano studies. For Brahms, this was a political statement. First of all, the Caprice he chose to set had its own set of variations attached that Liszt had transcribed literally. But, by writing two new sets of *Variations*, Brahms set himself up as opposed to the virtuosic school represented by Liszt. Second, by choosing a Caprice that Schumann did not transcribe, by creating two separate books (Schumann's Paganini transcriptions were published as two separate sets), and by using the designation Studien (like Schumann) rather than Études (like Liszt) Brahms showed himself to be allied to both Schumann and a continuation of his aesthetic.

The inspiration for the *Paganini Variations* came from lengthy conversations on piano technique with the great virtuoso Carl Tausig. Brahms jokingly referred to these Studies as his "finger exercises," but in fact, he created a unique and formidably difficult style of piano playing that he never again approached in his pianistic output. From the technical standpoint, the principal problems are those of double-note technique and rhythm. Brahms seemed less interested in fluent finger work than in complex arpeggiations and difficult chord configurations. In a way, Brahms technique is more a technique of the wrist, arm, and back than of the fingers. Musically, the principal problem arises in the division into two books. Both sets begin with a statement of the theme and have full-blown Finales. Also, both sets are similar enough in organization and style to become musically (if not technically) monotonous when played back-to-back. Unfortunately the best of the Studies are strewn between the books; therefore, a performance of one or the other inevitably leaves out some of the most interesting material. There is no clear-cut solution to this dilemma, and most pianists simply play both books, eliminating the statement of the theme for Book II. These two books of variations are neither as complex nor sophisticated as the *Handel* or *Schumann Variations*, but are still magnificent creations, and create an idiomatically Brahmsian piano style that has never been surpassed in difficulty or originality. *—Steven Coburn*

Recommended:

- ○ **Great Pianists of the 20th Century: Arturo Benedetti Michelangeli II** / Michelangeli / 1999 / Philips 456904
- ○ **Great Pianists of the 20th Century: Claudio Arrau** / Arrau / 1998 / Philips 456706

Waltzes for piano, 4 hands, Op. 39 (1865)

Composed in January 1865, the *Waltzes*, Op. 39 are dedicated to Dr. Eduard Hanslick (1825–1904), a famous Viennese music critic who championed the music of Schumann and Brahms and was pleased to find, "no narcissistic affectation" in Brahms' piano music. Publication of the *Waltzes* was by J. Reiter-Biedermann in both Leipzig and Winterthur, the four-hand version appearing first (1866), the two-hand version second (1867).

At the time Brahms composed the *Waltzes*, Op. 39, he had taken up residence in Vienna, but still hoped to obtain a permanent position in Hamburg. The *Waltzes* are a tribute to both the dance form for which Vienna had become famous and the music of Schubert, one of Vienna's native sons. Not long before composing his *Waltzes*, Brahms had begun editing and arranging Schubert's dance music.

The limitations of the waltz form forced Brahms' creativity to find other means of expression, particularly in harmonic manipulation, making each of the sixteen *Waltzes* a gem. However, nearly all of them possess a few common characteristics, such as a rounded binary form in which the first half moves to a new key and the "recapitulating" second half begins with a quasi-developmental segment before returning to the main theme and the home key. Many display the harmonic invention and subtlety that mark Brahms' later piano works as well as the large-scale structures of the 1860s.

Most of the *Waltzes* are in "sharp" keys (No. 6 is in C sharp major, as "sharp" as possible), which Brahms then colors by venturing into "flat" harmonies. Neighboring *Waltzes* are generally in keys a third or fifth apart, and are sometimes related through parallel major or minor, such as Nos. 6 and 7.

It is enlightening to examine one of the *Waltzes* in detail. In No. 12, in E major, the four-measure main theme consists of a descending step in the highest voice. The next few measures are really a variation of this tune, nestled in a middle voice and developed in an eighth note turning figure that moves to the dominant before a full repetition. What seems like a return to the opening in the second half is actually developmental because it is in E minor and consists of repetitions of the first two measures, not the entire theme. After modulating to F major (the Neapolitan, a powerfully expressive harmony in E minor), Brahms stealthily makes his way back to the major mode and the second half of the theme, although when E major appears it acts as the dominant of A major-the wrong key. There is no cadence on E major until the last few beats of the piece.

Brahms employs a similar harmonic procedure in the recapitulation of No. 1, in which the entire theme returns, literally, in the wrong key. Here however, the developmental portion of the second half is clearly so, repeating the theme's eighth note turning figure over several harmonies. Perhaps most peculiar is No. 9, which begins in D minor, moves to D major and closes on A major. *—John Palmer*

Recommended:

- ○ **Brahms: Danses Hongroises; Valses** / Duo Crommelynck / 1987 / Claves 508710
- ○ **Brahms: Walzer; Liebeslieder-Walzer** / Backhaus / 1997 / EMI 566425

VOCAL

Liebeslieder Waltzes for vocal quartet & piano, 4 hands, Op. 52 (1868–1869)

In May 1863, Johannes Brahms accepted the directorship of the Vienna Singakademie, followed in September 1872 by the directorship of the Vienna Gesellschaftskonzerte. During his tenure in both positions, Brahms produced numerous works for chorus, both accompanied and a cappella. Many of these works are for vocal quartet, although they are occasionally performed by larger ensembles. Among these are the *Liebeslieder Waltzes*, Op. 52 and the *Neue Liebeslieder Waltzes*, Op. 65.

Brahms' *Liebeslieder* [Love Songs] *Waltzes* consist of eighteen poems arranged for two pianos and vocal quartet, setting texts from George Friedrich Daumer's *Polydora*. Brahms' sketches suggest that he conceived the shape of the entire cycle before completing individual waltzes.

Published in 1869, the *Liebeslieder* were first performed on January 5, 1870, in Vienna. After Brahms received a copy of the first edition he wrote to the publisher, Simrock, in Berlin, "I must confess that it was the first time I smiled at the sight of a printed work of mine!" The original publication is for two pianos and voice ad libitum, indicating that the voices are optional. This direction, made possible by the fact that the vocal lines are present in the piano part, was evidently inserted by the publisher, who hoped to increase sales. Brahms, of course, realized that this removed some of the most charming aspect of the pieces, and the direction was omitted from the second set of *Liebeslieder*, Op. 65. In the winter of 1869–70, Brahms orchestrated a suite of waltzes taken from the *Liebeslieder* for a Berlin performance. He chose Nos. 1, 2, 4, 5, 8, 9, and 11, and composed a new piece, which became No. 9, in the *Neue Liebeslieder* set of waltzes.

Brahms' *Liebeslieder* represent the mingling of the folk music of northern Germany (the composer's former homeland) and the waltzes and Ländler of Upper

Austria (his new homeland). In effect, Brahms' *Liebeslieder* are stylized Viennese waltzes. Nearly all of Daumer's poems are pastoral verses on both the positive and negative attributes of love. Brahms' settings tends toward folk music in their melodic characteristics, with none of the text painting that a lesser composer may have employed. A few numbers, however, stand out from the rest. Those that are concerned with different expressions receive appropriate treatment. For instance, No. 12, "Schlosser auf, und mache Schlösser," (Get up locksmith, and make me locks) finds the narrator in a moment of anger as he asks a locksmith to make innumerable locks for him, claiming, "Then the wicked, wicked mouths / Shall I shut forever!" The intensity of Brahms' setting conveys the urgency of the request in this, the shortest of the 18 songs. In the ninth song, a man notices a pink-faced girl peering out of a house on the bank of the Danube. Ten iron bars protect the doors of the house, but the man explains he could easily tear them down. The calm atmosphere is shattered as the man explains his intention of breaking through the bars, after which the first lines return with their fluid music. The 16th poem, "Ein dunkler Schacht ist Liebe," (Love is a pit of despair), receives the most fiery setting of all. *—John Palmer*

Recommended:

- ○ **Brahms: Liebeslieder-Walzer** / E. Mathis, Fassbaender, Schreier, Fischer-Dieskau, K. Engel & Sawallisch / DG 423133
- ○ **Brahms & Schumann: Liebeslieder** / Bonney, von Otter, Streit, Bär, H. Deutsch & Forsberg / 1995 / EMI 55430

Neue Liebeslieder Waltzes for vocal quartet & piano, 4 hands, Op. 65 (1874)

The 1868 *Liebeslieder Waltzes* were an immense success, as popular in their own time as they remain in ours. Brahms decided to tap into the same vein six years later with these "New Love Song Waltzes," scored, as before, for four voices (soprano, alto, tenor, bass) and piano duet. Like those of the earlier set, these texts originated with folk songs of various languages; they were translated into German by Georg Friedrich Daumer (1800–75) in his *Polydora: A World-Poetic Songbook*. The 1868 set drew mostly on Russian, Polish, and Hungarian folk poetry, but here the provenance of the texts ranges as far afield as Turkey (No. 1) and Malaysia (No. 10). Overall, the tone of the poetry is serious, and Brahms fashioned the music to suit their often somber moods.

There are 14 waltzes in this set, plus an epilogue entitled "Zum Schluss: Nun, ihr Musen, genug!" The epilogue, a setting of the final verse of Goethe's *Alexis und Dora*, stood apart from the 14 exotic texts and forms a conclusion with an intriguing relationship to the whole. Brahms divided the 14 waltz songs into two groups of seven and ordered them in a logical manner. Each set opens and closes with a song for vocal quartet, and key relationships within each group follow a pattern. There are thematic, harmonic, and rhythmic interrelationships among the various numbers as well. For example, Nos. 1, 3, and 7 share a motivic idea, while Nos. 1, 4, 5, and 10 have rhythmic elements in common. Also, though their melodies are unrelated, Nos. 10 and 11 initially use identical harmonies.

No. 1, "Verzicht,' O Herz, auf Rettung," is lively and muscular, while the ensuing "Finstere Schatten der Nacht" is subdued and nocturnal—its title translates to "Dark Shadows of the Night." The lovely melodies given to the soprano soloist in Nos. 6, "Rosen steckt mir an die Mutter," and 9, "Nagen am Herzen," are touching, and the effervescence of No. 11 is delightful. The tenor part in No. 10, "Alles, Alles in den Wind," is deftly fashioned by Brahms. The ensemble writing in No. 14, "Flammenauge, dunkles Haar," is full of color and reaches nearly ecstatic outpourings.

All in all, this is a masterful work that remains widely performed by vocal quartets of various abilities, even if it perhaps lacks some of the freshness of the Op. 52 *Liebeslieder Waltzes*. *—Robert Cummings*

Recommended:

- ○ **Brahms and Schumann: Liebeslieder** / Bonney, von Otter, Streit, Bär, H. Deutsch & Forsberg / 1995 / EMI 55430
- ○ **Johannes Brahms: Liebeslieder Waltzes** / R. Shaw (cond.), Robert Shaw Festival Singers / 1993 / Telarc 80326

Songs (1853–1896)

Johannes Brahms composed 212 songs, spanning virtually the length of his career, beginning with the *Six Songs*, Op. 3, from 1851, and ending with the *Four Serious Songs*, Op. 121, from 1896, the year of his death. These were all written for solo voice and piano accompaniment; he also composed 25 vocal duets and 70 quartets. Brahms wrote both strophic and through-composed songs, and certain peculiarities of his style sometimes stand in the way of full appreciation of his immense talent. His long-breathed themes, for example, can sometimes seem to wander off course and end oddly. Aside from those in the folk mode, relatively few Brahms songs are miraculously limpid miniatures in comparison with the many of Schubert's. But in general they are as masterful as those of any other composer in the German lied tradition.

While Brahms' Op. 3 songs divulge the strong influence of Schumann and the Op. 6 and Op. 7 sets are likewise best regarded as early works, his *Eight Lieder and Romances*, Op. 14 (1858) reveal the composer evolving in new directions, using folk sources and embracing a popular style of love song in No. 1 ("Outside the Window"), No. 4 ("A Sonnet") and No. 7 ("Serenade"). The use of folk material continued in the *Five Poems*, Op. 19 (1858).

The songs of Brahms' full maturity are for the most part ambitious affairs, often with concentrated harmonies and piano parts that go far beyond mere accompaniment. Brahms' one song cycle came with the *Romances from Ludwig Tieck's Magelone*, Op. 33 (1861–68). While the 15 songs that comprise this effort are generally neglected, the lullaby, No. 9, "Rest, Sweetheart", is quite popular. The four other sets completed in 1868, Opp. 46, 47, 48, and 49, are strong collections, with "Wiegenlied," Op. 49, No. 4 (the so-called "Brahms lullaby") without doubt the most famous lullaby ever written.

Brahms' *Eight Lieder und Gesänge of G.F. Daumer*, Op. 57 (1871) shows the composer's mastery in the handling of texts that concern unrequited love and veiled eroticism. (At several points during his career, Brahms became interested in the works of specific poets and responded to that interest with song composition.) The Opp. 58 and 59 sets (1868–73) feature both variety and high quality, while the *Nine Lieder und Gesänge*, Op. 63 (1874) comes close to the features of a song cycle, despite use of texts by three different poets. The 23 songs comprising the Opp. 69 through 72 sets came in the period 1875 to 1877 and are somewhat uneven in quality. "An den Mond" (text by Simrock), from the *Five Gesange*, Op. 71, is one of the more popular items here.

Brahms' next song sets, Opp. 84, 85, and 86 (1877–82), feature many fine efforts, including the immensely popular "Feldeinsamkeit" (text by Allmers), from Op. 86. The later song collections, Opp. 91, 94, 95, 96, and 97 (29 total), feature many interesting songs, with the Op. 94 collection featuring subject matter dealing with lost youth and death. The first song here, "With 40 Years", is a profound and powerful fusing of words (those of Rückert) and music. Brahms' final sets, Opp. 105, 106, 107, and 121, saw the composer delving into a variety of moods, from the folkish "Mädchenlied," Op. 107 ([1886–88] text by Heyse), to the Biblically-sourced fatalism of "Denn gehet dem Menschen", from the Four Serious Songs, Op. 121. This dark set, inspired by the imminent death of the composer's lifelong friend Clara Schumann, proved his own swan songs. *—Robert Cummings*

Recommended:

- ○ **Brahms: Lieder** / Groop, Lubimov / Ondine 896
- ○ **Brahms: Lieder** / von Otter, Forsberg / 1990 / DG 429727
- ○ **Brahms: Meine Mädel hat einen Rosenmund: 31 Deutsche Volkslieder** / Prey, P. Coburn, Parsons / Capriccio 10199
- ○ **Lieberabende Salzburger Festspiele Live Vol. 2** / Fischer-Dieskau, G. Moore / 1985 / Orfeo 140201

Vier ernste Gesänge (Four Serious Songs), Op. 121 (1896)

On March 26, 1896, Brahms' lifelong friend and champion, Clara Schumann, suffered a stroke. Brahms, who considered Clara to be the "greatest wealth" in his life, was deeply shocked and forced to confront the fact that she might soon die. To cope, he immersed himself in work, completing the *Vier ernste Gesänge* (Four Serious Songs), Op. 121, by his birthday, May 7, 1896.

Brahms compiled the texts for the *Vier ernste Gesänge* from Martin Luther's translation of the Bible—mostly passages from the apocryphon, Ecclesiastes. The four songs represent a progression of thought about, and reaction to, death, and by virtue of their subject hardly require the adjective, "serious." Appearing after a decade in which the composer wrote no original songs, these four songs are truly unique in Brahms' output: they show no trace of folksong influence, they are not in strophic form, and they occasionally adopt a harsh, dramatic quality that is quite beyond his other songs. Brahms refused to have them performed, suggesting that they were of great personal importance to him.

"Denn es gehet dem Menschen" (It is for a person [as it is for an animal]), from Ecclesiastes 3:19–22, focuses on the transience of life. The text notes that people, just like animals, must die. In D minor, Brahms' setting conveys this transience through changes in tempo, meter and texture. The song proceeds with a turning melody, never leaving D minor; a quiet shift to a 3/4 meter and Allegro tempo bring with it denser and more complex harmonies, climaxing with the appearance of a new texture and the question, "Who knows if the soul of a person rises upward?". "Ich wandte mich und sahe an alle" (I turned and looked upon everyone), sets Ecclesiastes 4:1–3. The opening notes, over a stumbling accompaniment, anticipate the beginning of the next song. This is the most recitative-like of the four songs.

The text for "O Tod, o Tod, wie bitter bist du" comes from Ecclesiastes 41:1–2; Brahms alters the opening text, "O Tod, wie bitter bist du" (O death, how bitter you are) to "O Tod, wie wohl tust du dem Dürftigen" (O death, how good you are to the poor) when it returns for the second time. A musical metamorphosis accompanies this textual one, reflecting a shift in attitude from the bleak to the reassuring. Death, although final, alleviates suffering. The fourth and final song, "Wenn ich mit Menschen- und mit Engelzungen redete" (If I speak with the tongues of humans of angels), is drawn from 1 Corinthians 13; it is both a paean to, and a eulogy for, love. *—John Palmer*

Recommended:

- ○ **Centenary Collection 1950: Dietrich Fischer-Dieskau** / Fischer-Dieskau, H. Klust / 1998 / DG 459012

○ **Alexander Kipnis sings Brahms & Wolf** / A. Kipnis, G. Moore / Preiser 89204

○ **Brahms: 8 Gypsy Songs** / DeGaetani, Kalish / 1993 / Arabesque 6141

Zigeunerlieder (1886)

Johannes Brahms' music often divulged a Gypsy influence, and it is thus hardly surprising that he also adapted Hungarian folk music at different times in his career—or what was thought to be genuine Hungarian folk music. His first major effort here was the *21 Hungarian Dances* (1852–69). *Zigeunerlieder* (Gypsy Songs) came from the other end of his career (1887) and consists of 11 untitled songs scored for vocal quartet and piano on texts by Hugo Conrat. Shortly after completing them, Brahms arranged eight for single voice and piano, selecting Nos. 1 through 7 and 11. It must be remembered that while these songs adapt certain folk elements, the music is largely Brahms' own, the melodies—not to mention the harmonies—having typical Brahmsian features. No. 1 is lively and fiery, but its music has little that is exotic and, like most items in the set, could pass for pure Brahms. Its single verse of text tells of an unfaithful maiden and her Gypsy ex-lover singing of his sorrows. The second song features much passion and drama, too, the text once more recounting love woes. While there may be Gypsy and Hungarian features to the theme, it has that dark, passionate Brahmsian drama, not unlike that in the opening of the composer's *Piano Concerto No. 2*'s Scherzo. No. 3 is a playful love song full of lightness and sunshine. The ensuing song features much the same light mood, with the text telling of a young woman's cherished memories of her lover's first kiss. No. 5 is hearty in its celebratory joy, jaunty and carefree in its rhythmic accents, its text telling of a young man taking his girl to a dance. The ensuing song, also about courtship, is delicate at the outset and effervescent in its rapid tempo, but turns muscular later on and thereafter deftly juxtaposes the two expressive manners. No. 7 is slow and Romantic in its lyrical theme and warm harmonies, sounding more like some of Brahms' lieder. It offers much-needed contrast to the generally lively manner of the preceding songs. The last number here is joyous and, once again, has little that is Gypsy-like in its sonorities. The text also deals with love. Most songs in this delightful collection last from a minute to a minute-and-a-half. *—Robert Cummings*

Recommended:

○ **Brahms: Lieder** / Groop, Lubimov / Ondine 896

○ **Brahms: Lieder** / von Otter, Forsberg / 1990 / DG 429727

○ **Brahms: Lieder** / J. Norman, Barenboim / 2000 / DG 459469

CHORAL

Alto Rhapsody, Op. 53 (1869)

Brahms composed the *Alto Rhapsody*, Op. 53 (1869) as a wedding gift for Julie Schumann, the daughter of Robert and Clara Schumann, who was for a time the object of the composer's affections. Forced to abandon his undeclared love upon her engagement to another man, Brahms sublimated his grief in this work for alto, male chorus, and orchestra. Shortly after completing the work, Brahms showed it to Clara Schumann, prompting her to write in her diary, "A few days ago Johannes showed me a wonderful work.... He called it *his* bridal song. It is long since I have received so profound an impression; it shook me by the deep-felt grief of its words and music." The *Alto Rhapsody* was first performed in Jena on March 3, 1870 of the same year.

The text consists of three stanzas from Johann Wolfgang von Goethe's *Harzreise im Winter* (Harz Mountain Journey in Winter); together they make for a self-contained poetic and dramatic unit in which desolation gives way to the possibility of consolation. Brahms set each of the stanzas differently. The first, which introduces the wanderer's plight, receives the freest, most rhapsodic musical treatment; the fragmented voice part never repeats an idea, and there is a sense of aimless resignation. Significantly, it seems that the first lines of the first stanza were the last measures Brahms composed; the text "Who is that in the distance? His path is obscured in the thicket...." may indeed have encapsulated the composer's own feelings.

The second section, marked by a faster tempo and more agitated rhythm, becomes an intense plea for pity on behalf of the lost wanderer: Is there to be no consolation for him? Brahms organized the second stanza along the lines of a da capo aria; the first lines of the stanza return at the end with the same melody and an only slightly modified accompaniment.

The chorus makes its first appearance in the third stanza, which takes the form of a simple, hymn-like song. The warm harmonies of the chorus and the straightforward phrases are indeed a balm for the first two stanzas; perhaps the wanderer will indeed find hope and consolation. Though they begin homophonically, the alto's solo and the four choir parts eventually gain some measure of independence; the overall effect is that of a duet for alto and choir. Aside from a few flirtations with flat keys, the music remains in C major throughout.

The *Alto Rhapsody* has remained one of Brahms' most popular and successful works; the sincerity of its sentiment and the universality of its plea for future contentment have given it a timeless quality that transcends its occasional inspiration. *—AMG*

Recommended:

○ **Brahms: Symphony 1; Tragic Overture; Alto Rhapsody** / Klemperer (cond.), C. Ludwig, Philharmonia Orch. / 1999 / EMI 67029

○ **Brahms: Symphony 2; Academic Festival Overture; Alto Rhapsody** / C. Abbado (cond.), Lipovsek, Berlin PO / 1998 / DG 459054

○ **Brahms: Symphony 1; Alto Rhapsody** / C. Krauss (cond.), Ferrier, London PO / 2000 / Dutton 1210

Choral music for mixed voices & piano (1858–1884)

Johannes Brahms (1833–1897) wrote for mixed vocal ensembles and piano throughout his compositional career. The first three sets of duets were composed in his native Hamburg. The *Vier Duette*, Op. 28, for alto and baritone with piano from 1860 and 1862 and the *Drei Quartette*, Op. 31, for soprano, alto, tenor, and bass from 1859 and 1863 were given their premiere in Vienna in 1862 as part of Brahms' introduction to Vienna. But his earliest set of duets, the *Drei Duette*, Op. 20, for soprano and alto with piano from 1858 and 1860 were deemed by the composer too passionate and too indiscrete to premiere until 1878. After settling in Vienna, Brahms wrote a series of works essentially extolling its musical charms. The wonderfully romantic and deeply ironic *Liebeslieder Walzes*, Op. 52, for vocal quartet and two pianos from 1869, was premiered in Vienna 1870 and was followed five years later by the even more romantic and ironic *Neue Liebeslieder Walzes*, Op. 65, for the same forces from 1875 and premiered in Vienna 1875. During the same period, Brahms wrote the sentimental *Vier Duette*, Op. 61, for soprano and alto in 1874 and premiered in Basle in 1890; the archaic *Vier Balladen und Romanzen*, Op. 75, for soprano, alto, and tenor with piano from 1878 premiered in Vienna in 1879; the romantic *Drei Quartette*, Op. 64, from 1863 and 1874 and premiered in Vienna in 1869 and 1875; the deeply nostalgic *Fünf Duette*, Op. 66, for soprano and alto with piano from 1875 and premiered in Vienna 1878; and the exquisite *Vier Quartette*, Op. 92, from 1877 and 1884 premiered in Basle and Leipzig in 1885 and 1893. Brahms final two sets of quartets, the *Drei Quartette aus Zigeunerlieder*, Op. 103, from 1887 and premiered in both Frankfurt and London the same year, are the essence of the gypsy spirit in Brahms' music, and the final set of *Sechs Quartette*, Op. 112, from 1891 and posthumously premiered, begin with two of the most sublime works in Brahms' repertoire for mixed chorus and end with the supremely nostalgic *Vier Zigeunerlieder*. *—James Leonard*

Recommended:

○ **Brahms: Quartets for Four Solo Voices & Piano** / Beegle (cond.), New York Vocal Arts Ens. / 2000 / Arabesque 6725

○ **Brahms: Choral Works** / Parkman (cond.), Danish National Radio Chamber Choir / 2000 / Chandos 9806

Ein deutsches Requiem (German Requiem), Op. 45 (1857–1868)

Johannes Brahms' *Ein deutsches Requiem* (1863–67) is not a setting of the German translation of the standard requiem text. Rather, Brahms set a selection of Bible verses in German, treating death and its repercussions, and emphasizing consolation over religious observance. He avoided explicitly Christian references, at one time even suggesting that the work be called the "Human Requiem." The *German Requiem* took shape gradually, undergoing a number of revisions and additions in the course of its creation. First performed in a six-movement version in 1868, the work had its emotional roots in the death of the composer's mother three years earlier. The maternal spirit of much of the text, with its words of consolation that speak more of memory of the dead than return of the dead is a direct allusion his mother's death in 1865, and a reflection of Brahms' disillusionment with dogmatic religion. As a counter to this, there is a more paternal element in the second, third, and sixth movements, which invoke the inevitability of death and its eventual defeat. In spite of its evolving over a period of 11 years, there is a unity of style, mood, and form that is surprising in a work not planned as a unit from the beginning. There are some disparities in balance and scoring, however, the breadth, power, and sheer beauty of the work surely rank it among the great masterpieces of choral-orchestral music.

The first person to see the "finished" score was the other important woman in Brahms' life, Clara Schuman, who wrote to him, "I am completely filled with your *Requiem*, it...takes hold of a person's whole being like very little else." In 1869, Brahms inserted a new movement as the fifth of the work's seven, and in this, its present form, the *Requiem* was presented at the inaugural concert at Leipzig's Gewandhaus concert hall. Over the next decade the work was performed more than one hundred times in German-speaking countries alone. The *Requiem*, which predated all of the composer's symphonies, was the first large-scale orchestral piece for which Brahms gained universal acclaim; its radiant warmth has made it a perennial audience favorite.

Recent intepretations of the *German Requiem* seem to be evolving from a tradition of automatic application of the formula "slow = reverent" into a newer approach that observes Brahms' often faster, more flowing tempos. Listeners with the desire to perform the work themselves but without the conjunction of choir, orchestra, and will in their immediate communities may wish to investigate Brahms' own arrangement of the work for piano, four hands. *—AMG*

Recommended:

- ○ **Brahms: Ein deutsches Requiem** / Klemperer (cond.), Schwarzkopf, Fischer-Dieskau, Philharmonia Orch. / 1998 / EMI 66955
- ○ **Brahms: Ein deutsches Requiem** / Blomstedt (cond.), Norberg-Schulz, Holzmair, San Francisco SO / 1995 / London 443771
- ○ **Brahms: Ein deutsches Requiem** / J. E. Gardiner (cond.), Gilfry, Margiono, Orch. Revolutionnaire et Romantique / 1991 / Philips 432140
- ○ **Brahms: Ein deutsches Requiem; 2 Live Performances** / Furtwängler (cond.), Lindberg-Torlind, Sönnerstedt, Schwarzkopf, Hotter, Stockholm PO, Lucerne Festival Orch. / Music & Arts 1085

Motets (1856–1889)

Brahms wrote a great deal of a cappella sacred choral music, but he published only three works under the title motet: the *Two Motets for Five-Part Chorus*, Op. 29; the *Two Motets for Four- and Six-part Chorus*, Op. 74; and the *Three Motets for Four- and Eight-part Chorus*, Op. 110. Although an agnostic, Brahms took his texts from the *Bible* and from Lutheran scriptures. And although a nineteenth century composer, Brahms took his contrapuntal forms from earlier music, particularly that of Schütz and Bach. Despite these apparent contradictions, the motets are completely sincere: Brahms was a musical conservative who always composed in traditional forms and he was also a true German who believed that the spirit of the nation was expressed in its spiritual literature. More importantly, Brahms himself found comfort in both traditional musical forms and traditional spiritual literature, and his motets are the expression of his own deepest emotions in some of his profoundest music.

The *Motets*, Op. 29, were written in about 1860. The first, "Es ist das Heil" (It is the Redeemer), sets a text by Paul Speratus as a chorale harmonization concluding with a cantus firmus fugue. The second, "Schaffe in mir, Gott" (Create in me, God), sets three verses of *Psalm 51*, alternating between two strictly canonic and two fugal sections. Although this sounds complicated, the motets sound wholly lyrical in their devotional fervor.

The *Motets*, Op. 74, were written at two different points in Brahms' career. Portions of the first were originally part of his unpublished *Canonic Mass* of the mid-1850s and much of the second is thought to have been composed in 1863–64. However, the motets were put in their published form in 1877. As with his *Ein deutsches Requiem*, Brahms chose his texts for the first motet, *Warum ist das Licht gegeben den Mühseligen?* (Why is light given to those who suffer), from various sources to express his own pessimistic *weltanschauung*: the despairing cry of Job, the harsh anguish of James, and the gloomy consolation of Luther. The music itself is grimly chromatic with its repeated choral shouts of "Warum" and its twisted chromatic fugue. The second motet, *O Heiland reisse die Himmel auf* (O Savior, rend the heavens) sets the text of an unknown author to music that is as ineffably consoling as it is brilliantly contrapuntal.

The *Motets*, Op. 110, were all composed in 1889 and continue the polyphonic pessimism of the Op. 74 set. The first, *Ich aber bin elend* (But I am in misery), sets verses from *Psalm 69* and *Exodus* for double choir; the second, *Ach, arme Welt* (O, wretched world), sets an anonymous poem as a strophic choral song; and the third, *Wenn wir in höchsten Nöten sein* (When we are in greatest need) sets a four-verse by Paul Eber to alternating contrapuntal and homophonic music. *—James Leonard*

Recommended:

- ○ **Brahms: Geistliche Chormusik** / M. Creed (cond.), RIAS-Kammerchor / HM 901122
- ○ **Brahms: Sämlichte Chorwerke a cappella** / Hauschild (cond.), Rundfunkchor Leipzig / 1997 / Orfeo 026974

Dennis Brain

b. May 17, 1921, London, England, **d.** Sep. 1, 1957, Hatfield, England
French Horn Player

Few instrumentalists of the twenieth century did more to establish a solo role for an instrument than Dennis Brain. By age 36, he had helped restore the four Mozart and two Strauss horn concertos to the repertory, inspired Hindemith, Britten, and others to write for his instrument, and generally set the standard for twentieth century horn soloists.

Born in 1921, Brain was raised in a London horn-playing family. Both his father, Aubrey Brain, and his uncle played professionally, as did their father, Alfred Brain Sr., himself the son of a horn player. (His other brother, Leonard, was a noted oboist.) In 1936, he began studies with his father at the Royal Academy of Music, and two years later made an acclaimed London debut as a soloist in Bach's *Brandenburg Concerto No. 1* with the Busch Chamber Players.

Brain soon became a frequent soloist with the Royal Air Force Central Band, with which he filled the position of principal horn during World War II. His growing reputation was cemented during a goodwill tour of America, during which he received an invitation from Leopold Stokowski to join the Philadelphia Orchestra after the war. This was just one of several invitations that Brain received, however, and he eventually took the job of principal horn with the Royal Philharmonic. Later he moved on to become principal horn of the Philharmonia Orchestra.

All the while, Brain was a sought-after horn soloist and chamber musician. During the postwar years, he made a series of now-classic recordings of concertos by Mozart, Strauss, and Hindemith, as well as of various chamber and recital works. Among the additions to the horn literature directly inspired by Brain were works by Britten, Hindemith, Malcom Arnold, and Gordon Jacob. His virtuosic command of the instrument stimulated two of Britten's greatest chamber works, the *Serenade for Tenor, Horn and Strings* (1943) and the *Canticle* (1953).

Brain took up conducting as well and founded a wind quintet that won him considerable fame. It was following a concert by this quintet at the Edinburgh Festival on September 1, 1957, that Brain was killed in a car accident on his way back to London. Benjamin Britten has written of that fateful night that "it has robbed us of an artist with the unique combination of superb technical command of his instrument, great musicianship, a lively and intelligent interest in music of all sorts, and a fine performing temperament, coupled with a charming personality." *—Brian Wise*

Recommended:

- ○ **Dennis Brain** / Susskind, Galliera (conds.), Brain, London PO, Halle Orchestra, Griller SQ / Pearl 0026
- ○ **Strauss & Hindemith Concertos** / Sawallisch, Hindemith (conds.), Brain, London PO / 2002 / EMI 67783
- ○ **Brain** / Brain, various artists / 2001 / BBC Legends 4066
- ○ **Mozart: Horn Concertos 1–4** / Karajan (cond.), Brain, James, Horsley, Waters, Dennis Brain Wind Ensemble, Philharmonia Orch, & Chorus / 1998 / EMI 66950

Julian Bream

b. Jul. 15, 1933, London, England
Guitarist

Originally taught by his father, Julian Bream (b. 1933) made his debut with the Cheltham Guitar Circle at the age of 14. By the age of 16, already a seasoned recitalist, he entered the Royal College of Music. He made his London debut in 1950, but it was his appearance in November of 1951 at Wigmore Hall that propelled his career to international success. This led him first to Switzerland in 1954, followed by a European tour, and in 1958, the United States.

In 1950, Bream took up the Renaissance lute, and began a life-long fascination with Elizabethan music. His work with the tenor Peter Pears, and especially his formation of the Julian Bream Consort began a revival of early consort music that has continued to the present day. In addition, his work with such contemporary composers Villa-Lobos, Britten, Bennet, Rawsthorne, Walton, Henze, Takemitsu, Tippett, and Arnold led to a revival of interest in guitar music.

Bream has recorded extensively, receiving numerous awards along the way including six from the National Academy of Recording Arts and Sciences, and a platinum disk from RCA. He has also produced a number of televised programs, including master classes, an eight-part retrospective on Spanish music, and a biography entitled *A Life in the Country*, first broadcast in 1976 by the BBC.

Among his many other awards are honorary doctorates from the Universities of Surrey and Leeds, an honorary membership in the Royal Academy of Music, an honorary fellowship in the Royal College of Music, and an honorary membership in the Royal Philharmonic Society. Julian Bream was the first musician of the post-war era to popularize classical guitar. His wide ranging interests in repertory, his impeccable technique and style, his instrumental role in the revival of Renaissance music, and his extensive recorded legacy place him as one of the giants of twentieth century guitar music. *—Steven Coburn*

Recommended:

- ○ **The Ultimate Guitar Collection** / Gardiner (cond.), Bream / 1996 / RCA 33705
- ○ **The Golden Age of English Lute Music** / Bream / 1993 / BMG 0902661584
- ○ **Music of Spain** / Bream / RCA 61608
- ○ **Spanish Guitar Recital** / Bream / 2001 / RCA 68016
- ○ **Julian Bream Plays Spanish Guitar Music** / Bream / 2001 / Westminster 471236

Alfred Brendel

b. Jan. 5, 1931, Wiesenberg, Moravia, Austria
Pianist

Alfred Brendel is the preeminent thinking pianist, a loner to whom fame came through the power of imaginative integrity, an artist who has achieved—at his best—a divinatory rapport with piano literature from Bach to Schoenberg. Yet by his account, "I did not come from a musical or intellectual family.... I have not been a child prodigy. I do not have a photographic memory; neither do I play faster than other people. I am not a good sight-reader." Born in Wiesenberg, Moravia—in the latter-day Czech Republic—in 1931, he received piano lessons from ages 6 to 16, as the family moved from Zagreb to Graz, and studied composition privately while supporting himself in a variety of odd jobs. Brendel was among the first generation to learn from recordings, the legacies of Cortot, Kempff, Schnabel, Furtwängler, and Toscanini proving especially valuable. Master classes with Eduard Steuermann—a pupil of Busoni and Schoenberg—and Edwin Fischer crowned his scarce tuition. A 1948 debut recital in Graz marked the beginning of his career, launched by taking a prize at the Busoni Competition in Bolzano in 1949. Busoni's example, his mysticism and Faustian striving, fascinated the young Brendel—he recorded Busoni's *Fantasia Contrappuntistica* in the early 1950s—but proved a detour while prompting an extraordinary insight into the music of Liszt. The ensnaring and gradual liberation from Busoni's influence may be traced in the several essays Brendel wrote about him in *Musical Thoughts & After-Thoughts.* Fischer came to mean more. "With Fischer," Brendel wrote in 1960, "one was in more immediate contact with the music: there was no curtain before the soul when he communicated with the audience. One other musician, Furtwängler, conveyed to the same degree this sensation of music not being played, but rather happening by itself." Armed with such ideals, Brendel embarked upon an international recital and recording career which, in the decade of the 1960s, saw his reputation grow throughout Europe and North America as he became a frequent guest with the world's greatest orchestras. He performed the entire cycle of Beethoven sonatas in London's Wigmore Hall in 1962, and recorded them for Vox. In the 1970s he became an exclusive Philips artist, touring and recording prolifically, not only the Classical masters—Haydn, Mozart, Beethoven, Schubert, and Schumann—but Liszt, Mussorgsky, Stravinsky, Bartók, and Schoenberg, and garnering numerous awards. He has published a volume of comedic poetry. In 2004 he appeared in concert with his son, cellist Adrian Brendel. *—Adrian Corleonis*

Recommended:

- ○ **Mozart: Piano Concertos, K271, 503** / Brendel / 2002 / Philips 470287
- ○ **Schubert: Impromptus** / Brendel / Philips 411040
- ○ **Art Of Alfred Brendel Vol. 1** / Brendel / 1996 / Philips 446921
- ○ **Schubert: Piano Sonatas, D575, 894, 959 & 960** / Brendel / 2001 / Philips 456573
- ○ **Beethoven: Piano Concertos 1 & 4** / Rattle (cond.), Brendel, Vienna PO / 2001 / Philips 462782
- ○ **Brendel plays Beethoven Sonatas, Vol. 1** / Brendel / 1991 / Vox 5028
- ○ **Haydn: 11 Piano Sonatas** / Brendel / Philips 416643
- ○ **Young Brendel** / Brendel / 2001 / Vox 3601

Havergal Brian

b. Jan. 29, 1876, Dresden, Staffordshire, England, **d.** Nov. 28, 1972, Dresden, Staffordshire, England

Composer: Choral

Lauded for his "courage and fortitude in the face of total neglect," over the course of a creative life of 80 years—one of the longest ever—Havergal Brian composed big and ambitious works, including 32 symphonies and several operas, most of which went unperformed in his lifetime. Since his death, he has moved from near total obscurity to recognition as one of twentieth century England's most significant composers.

Both of Brian's parents sang in a choir, and his earliest musical experiences were of singing and playing organ in the local church. He took some rudimentary music lessons, but was largely self-taught through studying scores and taking part in local amateur performances. After supporting himself for a time as a carpenter's assistant and working for a coal mine and a timber firm, Brian decided to devote himself to music.

His first successes as a composer were part-songs and choral works for various British music festivals. Through those experiences he befriended Sir Edward Elgar and Sir Henry Wood; the latter's performance of Brian's *English Suite No. 1* (1904) inspired an anonymous patron to help Brian get his music published. In 1912, Brian moved to London. He was very poor, his works weren't being performed, and at one time he contemplated suicide. He did brief service in World War I; after the war, he worked as a freelance music copyist and for many years did writing and editing work for publications like *Musical Opinion* and *Musical World.* All the while, he was composing huge pieces of music, such as the comic opera *The Tigers* (written 1916–18, orchestrated 1918–30) and the *Gothic Symphony* (1919–27).

After completing his four-hour long opera *Prometheus Unbound* (after Shelley, 1937–44), Brian stopped composing for a few years. But in 1948, as he put it once, "the muse returned with a rush." He then embarked on the most prolific period of his career: from 1948 to 1968 he completed 27 symphonies, four operas, and various other instrumental works. Twenty-two of those 27 symphonies were written after Brian had turned 80, and seven were written after his ninetieth birthday. With the completion of his *Symphony No. 32* in A flat in October 1968, Brian decided he no longer had any impulse to compose. He died at age 96.

Brian was 78 years old before he heard one of his symphonies performed, in a 1954 BBC concert. Performances of his works have remained fairly rare, though the pace picked up with the formation of the Havergal Brian Society. His most notorious work is still his *Symphony No. 1*, the *Gothic* which for years was listed in the Guinness Book of World Records as the "Largest Symphony." Close to two hours in length, the work calls for a vast orchestra (supplemented by four brass bands and organ), four soloists, two choirs, and children's choir. Completed back in 1927, the symphony only received its first commercial recording in 1990. *—Chris Morrison*

Overview of Works (1892–1967)

Only in the closing decades of the twentieth century did Havergal Brian begin to develop a public profile through sparse performances and recordings—vast tracts of his enormous oeuvre remain *terra incognita.* An inheritor of the great English choral tradition, between 1905 and 1925, Brian composed 80 part songs notable for their adventurous deployment of voices, frequent onomatopoeia, and orchestral ambitions hand-in-hand with considerable charm and occasional sentimentality. Though he left a large body of song and piano music, it is his 32 symphonies upon which Brian's notoriety rests. The *Gothic Symphony*, his first extant work in the medium, and largest—calling for soloists, quadruple chorus, children's chorus, four brass bands, and a vastly augmented orchestra—occupied him from 1919 to 1927. Playing just under two hours, it established his disconcertingly idiosyncratic style on an encyclopedic scale. Though his use of tonality is expanded and often ambiguous, he nevertheless employs it as an organizing principle. The *Gothic*, and the more compact *Second* and *Third* symphonies of the early 1930s, proceed by counter-intuitive disjunctions, sudden *coups de théâtre* unfolding with grand—or grandiose—extravagance, at once exhilarating and appalling. Obstreperous, truculent, garrulous, violent, bizarre, lurid, grotesque, these discontinuities—relieved by oases of lyricism, evocations of light—succeed each other with a relentless, stultifying, formal forward movement. The effect is similar to Gnostic literature, or Blake's prophetic books, in which terrifying presences hover and cosmic portents —baleful and beautiful—are visited upon the Earth, but without resolution, as movements or entire works may not so much end as simply stop or disintegrate. Between 1948—as he turned 70—and 1968, Brian composed 27 symphonies and four large operas. The later symphonies telescope the manner of the earlier, though each has a strikingly individual character: the magical *Sixth* (inspired by Synge's *Deirdre of the Sorrows*); sunny *Seventh*; knotty and motivically allusive *No. 16*; wryly serene *No. 31*, albeit laced with Brian's habitual vehemence (augmented brass, side drum). Only two of Brian's five operas remain unperformed, though their exposure (through BBC broadcasts) is so infrequent as to leave them in the limbo of the unknown. Orchestral excerpts from *The Tigers* (1916–18) suggest a talent for satire, albeit on a Brobdingnagian scale, and a transcendent orchestral conception making for visionary meta-opera. Mainstream listeners will find Brian excessive and disconcerting, while his admirers will cite Blake's proverb, "The road of excess leads to the palace of wisdom." *—Adrian Corleonis*

Recommended:

- ○ **Orchestral Works of Havergal Brian** / G. H. Smith (cond.), Hull Youth SO / 1994 / Campion 1331/2
- ○ **Brian: The Complete Piano Music** / Raymond Clarke, E. King, Spong / 1997 / Minerva Athene 12

CHORAL

Symphony No. 1 in D minor ("The Gothic") (1919–1927)

English composer Havergal Brian spent eight years working on his mammoth *Symphony No. 1 in D minor, "The Gothic,"* composing it during the evenings while spending his days making a pittance copying music. Begun in 1919 and completed in 1927, *The Gothic* is a by-product of World War I, which many Britons felt signified the end of all that was decent and incorruptible in the world. The forces required to perform *The Gothic* earned Brian recognition in the *Guinness Book of World Records* for being the largest ever asked for in the history of Western music: four vocal soloists, a children's chorus numbering 100 voices, and an adult chorus of four double choirs numbering no less than 500 voices. Add to this an on-stage orchestra of 32 winds, 24 brass, 4 tympani, and 18 percussionists, 4 keyboards and harps, and 82 strings. In addition to this already huge ensemble there are four off-stage groups consisting of 24 brass players and a tympanist in each. This works out to around 800 parts, and depending on how the conductor feels the need to balance out the chorus and orchestra mix to achieve clarity, a performance of *The Gothic* can easily involve more than 1,000 people.

The full score was brought out by Cranz & Co. in 1932 and for many years, like Charles Ives' own publication of the *Concord Sonata*, was trotted out by music professors in order to demonstrate to students an extreme example of impractical musical lunacy. Brian's timing for the introduction of *The Gothic* couldn't have been worse; between the wars, Western music was strongly oriented toward piquancy and neo-Classic concision of expression. In the 1930s anything referred to as "gothic" smacked of undesirable Romanticism that young composers of the day went out of their way to avoid; certainly a score as big and bloated as Brian's could be nothing more than a white elephant. Not everyone shared this view; composer Richard Strauss, himself facing stylistic eclipse, admired Brian's work, as did conductor Eugene Goossens, who tried unsuccessfully to mount a performance of *The Gothic* at one of the Cincinnati May Festivals of the 1930s.

It was finally heard for the first time in 1961 in London with an amateur group under conductor Bryan Fairfax; at this time the composer was 85 years old. Sir Adrian Boult gave the first professional performance at the *Royal Albert Hall* on October 30, 1966, and it was issued on a pirated LP. Although the sound of the LP was poor, it at least convinced musicians that there might be something to *The Gothic*. The work is so loud at times that it is difficult to record well; nonetheless, conductor Ondrej Lenard achieved this end for Naxos in 1989. Now that it can truly be heard, it is clear that the symphony is "gothic" in terms of architecture; musicologist Paul Rapoport has likened its six parts to the six points on the cruciform plan of a gothic cathedral. It embodies influences ranging from Elgar to Edgard Varèse to Renaissance part writing, and culminates in a massive setting of the Latin Te Deum, which Brian decided to set only after abandoning a text extracted from Goethe's *Faust*. Despite its unwieldy size and length, running to nearly two hours, *The Gothic* is never boring; indeed, new details emerge through repeated hearings no matter how many times it is enjoyed. It is no small miracle that a composer of working-class origins such as Brian could create a complex work so rich in multiple meanings that easily rivals and exceeds the size of the Beethoven *Ninth* or Mahler's *Eighth*, yet is addressed to the future and shaped in the materials of the past. *—Uncle Dave Lewis*

Recommended:

- ○ **Brian: Symphony 1, "The Gothic"** / Lenard (cond.), Jenisová, D. Pecková, Dolezal, Mikulas, Slovak Radio SO and PO / 2004 / Naxos 8557418-19

Frank Bridge

b. Feb. 26, 1879, Brighton, England, **d.** Jan. 10, 1941, Eastbourne, England

Composer: Orchestral

Frank Bridge studied violin and composition at the Royal College of Music, graduating in 1904. A scholarship enabled him to study with Charles Villiers Stanford for four years (1899–1903). Bridge quickly established a reputation as a gifted violist and conductor. In 1906, he played with the Joachim Quartet, and he was a member of the English String Quartet through 1915. He conducted some operas at the Savoy Theatre and Covent Garden, and when Sir Thomas Beecham organized his New Symphony Orchestra in 1906, he named Bridge as his assistant. Bridge also befriended Sir Henry Wood and occasionally substituted for him as conductor at Queen's Hall; Wood later became an important champion of Bridge's music. During this period, Bridge was writing mostly chamber music and songs. His few orchestral works of the time were much influenced by the French Impressionists; the first of them to become part of the standard repertoire was the suite *The Sea* (1911).

World War I was a traumatic time for Bridge, an ardent pacifist. One can hear more dissonance and darkness creeping into such works as the *Cello Sonata in D minor* (1913–17) and the *Quartet No. 2 in G minor* (1915). After several years of near-silence, Bridge's next big work signaled a large shift in style. The *Piano Sonata* (1921–24) was written in memory of composer Ernest Farrar, who was killed in action in France, in 1917. In it, one hears considerably more dissonance, abrupt changes of mood and tempo, and a more angular and aggressive sound. This stylistic evolution continued in works like the third (1926) and fourth (1937) string quartets, which flirt with Schoenberg-like atonality.

In his last two decades, Bridge composed, occasionally conducted, and did some travelling, including trips to the United States in 1923, 1934, and 1938. He also did some private teaching. Certainly his best-known pupil was Benjamin Britten, who was an 11-year-old prodigy when Bridge met him in 1924. Britten retained a great affection for his teacher, and paid tribute to him in the *Variations on a Theme of Frank Bridge* (1937), based on the second of the latter's *Three Idylls for String Quartet* (1906). Britten was also partly responsible for the subsequent interest in Bridge's music.

Among Bridge's later compositions were a lovely opera, *The Christmas Rose* (begun 1919, set aside for years and completed only in 1930), as well as several important chamber and orchestral works. His last completed composition was the *Rebus Overture* (1940); he also left a symphony for strings unfinished at his death. *—Chris Morrison*

Overview of Works (1901–1941)

Although it holds a less prominent position in the twentieth century repertoire than those of many of his contemporaries, the œuvre of Frank Bridge uniquely represents a pivotal moment in modern British music. It seems that English music has always maintained a tight grip on tradition. Bridge's work extends, on one end, almost seamlessly out of the late Romanticism of Brahms, and on the other, into the tonally conflicted terrain of his successors (including Britten, his only composition student).

Bridge's prolific early years produced a wealth of music known for its craftsmanship and accessibility. The art song was a favored genre, and the dozens he produced between 1900 and 1920 included settings of Shakespeare, Shelley, Tennyson, Keats, Coleridge, and numerous others. His chamber music of the period sometimes experimented with different approaches to standard forms, as in the "Phantasies" for piano trio and quartet (1905, 1907, and 1910), while his orchestral works tended toward the pictorial, as in *The Sea* (1911), a suite, and *Summer* (1914), a symphonic poem. Scholar Anthony Payne identifies the *Piano Sonata* from 1921 as a turning point in Bridge's career, perhaps emblematic of his reaction to World War I. The *Piano Sonata* and subsequent works, such as his later string quartets (1926, 1937), take far greater liberties with harmonic language, sometimes to the point of atonality, and articulated this new language within a more unsettled and restless rhythmic and structural context. During the 1920s and 1930s Bridge also devoted considerably more of his attention to orchestral music, incorporating his expanded musical language while at the same time remaining prone to the programmatic. Bridge's focus on instrumental music, and perhaps the aesthetic implications of his later compositional style, lead him away from vocal music; in fact, he wrote no songs or choral pieces after 1925. Subsequent to his death in 1941, Bridge's works fell out of circulation and remained forgotten for decades before enjoying a limited rediscovery near the century's end. *—Jeremy Grimshaw*

Recommended:

- ○ **Bridge: Works for String Quartet** / Maggini Quartet / 1995 / Naxos 553718
- ○ **Bridge: Complete Music for Piano Vol. 1** / Peter Jacobs / Continuum 1016
- ○ **The Songs of Frank Bridge** / J. Watson, L. Winter, MacDougall, Finley, Vignoles / Hyperion 67181
- ○ **Bridge: Music for Viola** / L. Williams, J. Rigby, D. Norris, / 1999 / ASV 1064

ORCHESTRAL

The Sea, suite (1910–1911)

Not only was this aural seascape one of Frank Bridge's most successful works, but it was the piece that "knocked sideways" the ten-year-old Benjamin Britten, who would go on to study with Bridge and champion his music. *The Sea*, however, is a plush late Romantic score not really characteristic of Bridge's fully mature, more austere music. To a degree, it can be confused with such Arnold Bax oceanic tone poems as *Garden of Fand*, *Tintagel*, and *On the Sea-Shore*.

Of the first movement, Bridge wrote, "'Seascape' paints the sea on a summer morning. From high drifts is seen a great expanse of waters lying in the sunlight. Warm breezes play over the surface." Fragments of a harmonically vague theme float through the orchestra, then come together into a broad melody that surges to an early climax. The music repeatedly swells and recedes through the course of this movement, relying on colorful woodwind solos in the quiet sections and full string and brass proclamations for the grander statements.

"Sea-foam," wrote Bridge, "froths among the low-lying rocks and pools on the shore, playfully not stormy." This is a brief, mercurial scherzo, with quicksilver little woodwind solos weaving their repeated notes through fuller orchestral material, most notably a broad horn passage.

Third comes the slow movement, "Moonlight," which Bridge described as "a calm sea at night. The first moonbeams are struggling to pierce through dark clouds, which eventually pass over, leaving the sea shimmering in full moonlight." This nocturne begins as a huge orchestral sigh, a tender, quiet, harp-accompanied inhalation followed by a long, firm, crescendoing exhalation of related material, a troubling little cough in the brass, and then a more extended section in which the material breathes more steadily and quietly.

"Storm," the finale, is almost self-explanatory. Wrote Bridge, "Wind, rain and tempestuous seas, with the lulling of the storm an [allusion] to the first number is heard and which may be regarded as the sea-lover's dedication to the sea." Despite much conventional churning in the strings and woodwinds, complete with cymbal crashes, chorale-like brass passages also ride over some of the effects. Again, the music ebbs and flows, and once the storm's last flurries seem to have receded into the low woodwinds, Bridge brings back the big, sweeping theme from the first movement as a brief but splendid coda for full orchestra. *—James Reel*

Recommended:

- ○ **Britten: Four Sea Interludes; Passacaglia; Bridge: The Sea; Bax: On The Sea-Shore** / Handley (cond.), Ulster Orch. / 1986 / Chandos 8473
- ○ **Britten the Perfomer: Britten, Bridge & Holst** / Britten (cond.), English CO / 1999 / BBC Legends 8007

Summer, tone poem (1914)

The middle period of Frank Bridge's compositional career consists of four works, the first of which is the tone poem for orchestra, *Summer* (1915). This work was the first to be completed after the success of another orchestral piece, *Dance Poem* (1913), in which the composer made considerable progress toward an individualized style. The next two compositions of Bridge's middle period were *Two Poems for Orchestra* (1915), a work based on a couple of poems by Richard Jefferies, and the *Second String Quartet*, also completed in 1915. The final composition of this period is the *Cello Sonata* (1917), which Bridge actually began sketching in 1913. In the next ten years, the composer would not finish another major work on a similar level of the *Cello Sonata*. Each subsequent work of the middle period, including *Summer*, showed some indications of the eventual path that the composer was to take.

Summer is a lushly written piece for orchestra in which the extremely lyrical melodic material in many respects resembles the themes found in Bridge's other compositions up to this point. Also similar to previous works is the way in which Bridge presents a countermelody to promote melodic development. Also characteristic of the composer is the technically perfect part-writing. Yet *Summer* has distinctive and attractive qualities. By mimicking the harmonic language of the previous English generation, Bridge achieved a sense of a pastoral setting in his piece. By using modal harmonies and incorporating diatonic dissonances, Bridge achieved something like the robust English pastoral sound of Frederick Delius, among others. Bridge had recently come into contact with the works of Delius, as well as John Ireland and Arnold Bax. Formally, *Summer* likewise owes something to the ideas of these composers; its form is largely dictated by alternating moods or sonorities, in which the orchestration used is widely varied from section to section.

Bridge's familiarity with the orchestra had greatly increased since he had begun to be invited to accept conducting engagements with such groups as the New Symphony Orchestra. He also was desired as a conductor of operas, appearing in this fashion at the Savoy Theatre and at Covent Garden. He was even asked to fill in at Promenade Concerts when the regular conductor, Henry Wood, was not able. Bridge was so skilled at score-reading and musical interpretation that he was available to accept conducting assignments on very short notice. Fittingly, Bridge himself conducted the first performance of *Summer* on March 13, 1916. *—Chris Boyes*

Recommended:

- ○ **Bridge: Suite for Strings; Summer; Butterworth & Bantock** / del Mar (cond.), Bournemouth Sinfonietta / 1993 / Chandos 6566

Keith Brion

b. 1933

Conductor

Keith Brion occupies a most unique niche in music: he is a reincarnation (of sorts) of John Philip Sousa. Brion has combined his already considerable musical prowess with his knowledge, devotion, and resemblance to (with the help of some accoutrements) the John Philip Sousa of the 1920s. In this persona, Brion leads his New Sousa Band in an uncanny re-creation of a typical Sousa band concert of the era, with meticulous attention to the programming, interpretation, and even Sousa's own mannerisms.

After studies in music education at West Chester State University and piccolo studies with John Krell, Brion taught in New Jersey schools while obtaining a master's degree at Rutgers University. During this time, he played piccolo in the New Jersey Symphony and found time to form the North Jersey Wind Symphony, as well as playing in park concerts and parades. As a symphony conductor, Brion has led the Philadelphia, Boston Pops, and European orchestras to name a few, but it is with the wind band that he is most at home. Among the most noted ensembles over which he has presided are the Goldman Band; the Allentown Band; and the United States Marine, Army, and Coast Guard bands. Brion, a former director of bands at Yale, took that institution's band to Amsterdam's Concertgebouw for a concert devoted to the works of Yale alumnus Charles Ives, solidifying his credentials as a fervent ambassador of American music.

In 1978, Brion first appeared in the persona of John Philip Sousa with the Yale Band. The following year, he organized and debuted his New Sousa Band. The ensemble continues to thrive, the conductor himself stepping into the persona of the March King. To complete the visual effect, Brion dons the black, gold-trimmed uniform, medals, pince-nez, white gloves (celebrated for Sousa having never worn a pair twice), and sports a well-cropped white moustache, Sousa having removed his famous beard for good after World War I. This is only the start, for the younger man has scrupulously studied footage and written accounts to produce the style and mannerisms of the legendary bandsman. Equally authentic is the programming, featuring the many arrangements of classical fare by Sousa, period pieces, potpourris, solos, and the encores in the form of the famous marches. To this day, the ensemble is a crowd-pleaser. Sousa, who felt that entertaining the audience is paramount, would approve. Brion prefers to refer to his performances as "portrayal" rather than impersonation. Indeed, the thorough research, as well as the high musical quality of the concerts, places them on a higher plane than mimicry. And as bands have for decades now inclined toward arrangements of more current popular fare, it is through musicians such as Brion, and a younger generation of band musicians, that the music of Sousa (and Goldman, Alford, Fillmore, etc.) will remain present and vital. Brion has also edited editions of the band music of Sousa, Ives, Percy Grainger, and nineteenth century bandsman D.W. Reeves. *—Wayne Reisig*

Recommended:

- ○ **Sousa: Music for Wind Band Vol. I** / Brion (cond.), Royal Artillery Band / 2000 / Naxos 559058
- ○ **Herbert: Beloved Songs & Classic Miniatures** / Brion (cond.), Slovak RSO / 1999 / Naxos 559026

Benjamin Britten

b. Nov. 22, 1913, Lowestoft, Suffolk, England, **d.** Dec. 4, 1976, Aldeburgh, England

Composer: Opera, Vocal, Choral, Chamber Music, Symphonic, Orchestral, Concerto

With the arrival of Benjamin Britten on the international music scene, many felt that English music gained its greatest genius since Purcell. A composer of wide-ranging talents, Britten found in the human voice an especial source of inspiration, an affinity that resulted in a remarkable body of work, ranging from operas like *Peter Grimes* (1944–45) and *Death in Venice* (1973) to song cycles like the *Serenade for tenor, horn, and strings* (1943) to the massive choral work *War Requiem* (1961). He also produced much music for orchestra and chamber ensembles, including symphonies, concerti, and chamber and solo works. Britten's father was a prosperous oral surgeon in the town of Lowestoft, Suffolk; his mother was a leader in the local choral society. When Benjamin's musical aptitude became evident, the family engaged composer Frank Bridge to supervise his musical education. Bridge's tutelage was one of the formative and lasting influences on Britten's compositional development; Britten eventually paid tribute to his teacher in his Op. 10, the *Variations on a Theme by Frank Bridge* (1937). Britten's formal training also included studies at the Royal College of Music (1930–33).

Upon graduation from the RCM, Britten obtained a position scoring documentaries (on prosaic themes like "Sorting Office") for the Royal Post Office film unit. Working on a tight budget, he learned how to extract the maximum variety of color and musical effectiveness from the smallest combinations of instruments, producing dozens of such scores from 1935 to 1938. He rapidly emerged as the most promising British composer of his generation and entered into collaborative relationships that exerted a profound influence upon his creative life. Among the most important of his professional associates were literary figures like W.H. Auden, and later, E.M. Forster. None, however, played as central a role in Britten's life as the tenor Peter Pears, who was Britten's closest intimate, both personally and professionally, from the late 1930s to the composer's death. Pears' voice inspired a number of Britten's vocal cycles and opera roles, and the two often joined forces in song recitals and, from 1948, in the organization and administration of the Aldeburgh Festival.

A steadfast pacifist, Britten left England in 1939 as war loomed over Europe. He spent four years in the United States and Canada, his compositional pace barely slackening, as evidenced by the production of works like the *Sinfonia da Requiem* (1940), the song cycle *Seven Sonnets of Michelangelo* (1940), and his first effort for the stage, *Paul Bunyan* (1940–41). Eventually, the poetry of George Crabbe drew Britten back to England. With a Koussevitzky Commission backing him, the composer wrote the enormously successful opera *Peter Grimes* (1944–45), which marked the greatest turning point in his career. His fame secure, Britten over the next several decades wrote a dozen more operas, several of which—*Albert Herring* (1947), *Billy Budd* (1951), *The Turn of the Screw* (1954), *A Midsummer Night's Dream* (1960), *Death in Venice* (1973)—became instant and permanent fixtures of the repertoire. He also continued to produce much vocal, orchestral, and chamber music, including *Songs and Proverbs of William Blake* (1965), the three *Cello Suites* (1961–64) and the *Cello Symphony* (1963), written for Mstislav Rostropovich, and the *Third String Quartet* (1975).

Britten suffered a stroke during heart surgery in 1971, which resulted in something of a slowdown in his creative activities. Nonetheless, he continued to compose until his death in 1976, by which time he was recognized as one of the principal musical figures of the twentieth century. *—Michael Rodman*

OPERA

Albert Herring, Op. 39 (1947)

In this charming adaptation of a story by Guy de Maupassant, Britten transplants the characters to his own neighborhood, a borough in East Anglia. As usual, absolutely everyone in the cast is brilliantly and economically characterized: you would swear you know someone just like them. It's 1900, and Lady Billows is concerned with declining morality among the young folk. She decides to revive the old tradition of honoring the most virtuous maiden of the village "Queen of the May." She sets her secretary, Florence, to figure out just who that would be but is crushed to learn that no girl qualifies. As Florence puts it, "Country virgins (if there be such) think too little and see too much."

Instead Lady Billows and her crowd (the town cop, the vicar, the schoolmistress, etc.) quite unilaterally decide to single out as "King of the May" the virginal mama's boy Albert, presumed to be a simpleton, who spends all his time running his shrew of a mother's greengrocer's shop. Albert is humiliated by the honor, but Mum forces him to accept because the May King crown carries with it a substantial purse from Lady Billows. The purse is the undoing of Her Ladyship's aims and Albert's liberation: emboldened by some rum that some others of his own age have used to spike the glass of lemonade he is served at his "coronation," Albert takes some of the money and goes off on a pub-crawl in the next village. He is presumed missing and dead, but comes back no longer a boy but a man, as they say. He delights in telling Mum, Her Ladyship, and the whole village about the "sordid, evil" degradation their paragon has done the previous night ("I didn't lay it on too thick, did I?" he later asks one of his confidants), sends Lady Billows politely but firmly on her way, and when his mother lights into him, shuts her up with a decisive "That'll do, Mum," to the delight of all the young people.

This is a chamber opera. Although it has a large cast, it is scored for only about a dozen instruments, which means that it is performed only in the special context of chamber operas and rarely on major operatic stages. Even so, it is something of a favorite among its kind: the music is unfailingly attractive and takes delightful advantage of every opportunity for comedy and satire. For instance, when Albert drinks the rum-laced lemonade, the orchestra plays the "Love Potion" theme from Wagner's *Tristan und Isolde*. A rumor of Albert's corpse having been discovered brings about a gong-accompanied dirge which is at once comical and touching: The feelings of Albert's mother and the others are genuinely grieving at this point. Britten's word-setting is delightful: in performance, a lot rides on clear projection of the words so that the humor is clearly conveyed. Comedy requires precise timing, and Britten has as much of a way with that as any other great composer of comic opera has ever had. Thus, one of the great modern gems of comic opera, Albert Herring was premiered at Glyndebourne on June 20, 1947, with Britten conducting and Peter Pears in the title role; it was the inaugural production for the Aldeburgh Festival in 1948. *—AMG*

Synopsis:

Act One. The opera opens in Lady Billows' house as she shouts various orders concerning the management of the village to Florence, who feels distinctly overworked ("One Lifetime, One Brain"). Miss Wordsworth, Mr. Gedge, Mr. Upfold, and Superintendent Budd arrive and chat until Lady Billows sweeps in and they discuss their task: they must select a May Queen. Lady Billows sings that the title rewards virtue ("May Queen! May Queen!"), something in distinctly short supply; each nominee is found to be less than a model of purity ("The First Suggestion on My List"). They lament the decline in morality ("Oh, Bitter, Bitter Is the Fruit"), and Lady Billows makes her indignation known ("Is This All You Can Bring? Each Single Name"). Finally, having decided the only virtuous person in the village is a young man, Albert Herring ("Is Albert Virtuous?"), they decide on a "May King! May King!" The next scene takes place in the village, where children play outside and steal apples from the store. Sid drives them out and rewards himself with some of their loot. Albert comes in and Sid teases him that his mother doesn't let him have any real fun ("Tickling a Trout"). Albert tries to ignore this, even when Nancy comes in and the two sweethearts agree to meet that night ("Meet Me at Quarter Past Eight"). The thought makes Albert uncomfortable, and when they have gone, he wonders whether he is missing something ("He's Much Too Busy"). Florence comes to tell him that Lady Billows and the others are on their way. The selection group arrives and tells Albert of the honor to be bestowed upon him, along with a prize of 25 pounds. Unlike his mother, he is not at all enthusiastic, and when the others have gone, he says he won't do it. She sends him up to his room as the children taunt him for letting his mother bully him.

Act Two. At the May festival, with Nancy and Florence setting up the tables, Florence is very upset because Sid is late with the extra meat. When he does show up, saying he had a puncture in his bicycle wheel, she scolds him ("For Three Precious Weeks") and then bustles off. Sid tells Nancy how silly Albert looks being all dressed in white with orange blossoms in his hair and being fussed over, and she asks him the real reason for his delay; she can tell he's been up to something. They go out, and Miss Wordsworth rehearses the children in a song to celebrate the crowning of the May King. They leave, and when Sid and Nancy return, he shows her the bottle of rum he stopped to buy, and pours it, over her half-hearted protests, into Albert's glass. The procession comes in and children give flowers and sing to an increasingly awkward Albert. Lady Billows makes a speech ("I'm Full of Happiness") exhorting all present to lead lives of virtue and sobriety, and there follow other speeches and gifts. Albert is called upon to make a speech but is so embarrassed that he can say only "Thank you very much," and he gladly sits down again. He drinks the lemonade and begins to hiccup, trying to stop it by drinking more, and they all settle down to eat. In the next scene, the rum has had its effect and Albert staggers into the shop, singing a version of the song in his own praise, "Albert the Good," and then wonders why Nancy was looking at him so oddly. He regrets that he is so shy with girls, and when he hears Sid whistling to Nancy and watches them meet and kiss, he decides to take the prize money and go have some fun with it ("Heaven Helps Those Who Help Themselves").

Act Three. Nancy is overwhelmed with guilt, for Albert has disappeared; even though the whole village is searching, he can't be found ("What Would Mrs. Herring Say?"). Sid comes in, muddy and disgruntled, and they fight; he thinks Albert has just gone off, while she is convinced that he's been killed in an accident. Superintendent Budd comes in and reports no progress. Mrs. Herring comes in, broken with grief, and when Budd asks her for a photograph of Albert, sends Nancy to get one. When Nancy returns, she laments, "It is all that I have to remember him by!" Nancy tries to comfort her. Lady Billows comes in, calling for Scotland Yard, and Albert's orange blossom wreath is brought in; it was found in the well. General lamentations begin ("In the Midst of Life Is Death"). Albert comes in and asks what is going on. They round on him for making them so worried, and he says that he's sorry about that, which doesn't appease them. He only nods yes or no to their questions, and finally comes out with the whole story ("I Can't Remember Everything"). He went out to get thoroughly drunk, and when they react in disgust, he turns on his mother, saying that it was her overprotectiveness that made him explode. He admits it wasn't much fun, but he did it. Sid and Nancy approve, but Lady Billows predicts a dire end for him and storms out; he politely holds the door for her and the others. When his mother turns on him, he tells her that it's enough, and she runs into the other room, crying. He remorsefully asks Sid and Nancy if he went too far; Nancy responds with a hearty kiss, to Sid's brief disgruntlement. Albert throws the wreath into the audience as all exclaim "Jolly good riddance." *—Ann Feeney*

Recommended:

- ○ **Britten: Albert Herring** / Britten (cond.), Pears, Cantelo, C. Wilson, Brannigan, English CO / 1989 / London 421849
- ○ **Britten: Albert Herring** / Hickox (cond.), Gilchrist, Stephen, Williams, Richardson, City of London Sinfonia / 2003 / Chandos 10036
- ○ **Britten: Albert Herring** / D. Gilbert (cond.), Pfund, Powell, Altman, Balach, Manhattan School of Music Orch. / 1997 / Vox 7900

Billy Budd, Op. 50 (1951)

After the sweepingly successful *Peter Grimes* of 1945, Benjamin Britten moved into the realm of chamber opera for several years, producing such well-loved works as *The Rape of Lucretia* and *Albert Herring* and concocting a new version of John Gay's perennial favorite, *The Beggar's Opera*. Only with a 1951 adaptation of Herman Melville's *Billy Budd* did the composer move back into the realm of massive, symphonically conceived opera. *Billy Budd*, written to a libretto by E.M. Forster and Eric Crozier, is a formidable, even menacing work in which nearly every bar testifies to the distance—in terms of musical sophistication and narrative/musical structure—traveled by Britten between 1945 and 1951. His decision in 1961 to condense the four-act work into a new two-act mold was, likewise, the sign of an ever-maturing pen, and had the very palpable effect of raising the opera from the relative obscurity surrounding its initial premiere to the more general appreciation among musicians and opera lovers it has enjoyed since the 1960 premiere of the revised version. It may never equal *Peter Grimes* in the public eye, but it is in almost every conceivable way that work's superior.

Billy Budd is a truly through-composed opera: here, Britten has gotten beyond the need for constant sectionalization that marks his first theatrical entries. Here also, even more than in *Peter Grimes* (in which there are intermittent episodes of distinctly light character), Britten uses weighty musical forces to hammer in an even weightier psychological substance; a very particular color (certainly one of isolation and constriction, and perhaps also of nearly panic-stricken obsession) is achieved and maintained throughout *Billy Budd* by both the restricted physical area (the action takes place entirely on board ship) and the use of male voices exclusively throughout. The narrative affords no room for gentleness beyond the singing of a few chanteys in the third scene of Act I, and Britten is wise enough to avoid inserting extramusical delicacies merely to increase the opera's popularity among casual operagoers.

Billy Budd takes place at sea on board the HMS *Indomitable* during the 1797 French wars. Budd is himself a new recruit to the ship, and falls prey to the treachery of Claggart, the Master-at-Arms. From the moment Billy sets foot on deck his fate is sealed, and yet, as Captain Vere himself tells us in the Epilogue (which takes place, as does the Prologue, many years after the actual action of the drama), Billy's death is not entirely without cause or devoid of positive repercussions. Britten takes it upon himself, however, to challenge through music the effort to justify the hanging of an innocent lad on the basis of nothing better then martial laws, and the large composite structures with which he works are built up of insinuating gestures that refuse to allow even a moment's peace; if justification is to be had, it will not be easily won. Even tonality itself, normally so comforting to twentieth century audiences, is used to such intentionally conflicted ends that it becomes a looming (if fractured) darkness that only the final B flat of the Captain's Epilogue can pierce. Throughout, the work paradoxically evokes the expanse of the wide-open ocean and the claustrophobia of dozens of men forced to live and work on the confines of a wooden sailing ship. *—Blair Johnston*

Synopsis:

Prologue. The elderly Captain Vere muses over the events aboard the HMS Indomitable that led to the tragic demise of Billy Budd. The rest of the opera, except for the Epilogue, proceeds as a flashback to 1797.

Act One. A guard boat pulls up to the HMS *Indomitable* with three new conscripts from the ship Rights O' Man for war service, one of whom is the cheery, handsome Billy Budd. Despite his tendency to stammer when he becomes excited, he immediately impresses Master-at-Arms John Claggart with his positive attitude and willingness to serve. Claggart is bitter about life, but Billy sympathizes with him and quickly makes friends, among whom is the old sailor Dansker, who warns him to keep his distance from Claggart.

At a meeting a week later in the Captain's quarters, Vere and his officers deride French culture and ideas, especially those that precipitated the Revolution. Budd, with his charm and having come from the Rights O' Man, is singled out as a potential threat in spreading such ideas. But Vere completely dismisses the suggestion.

On the berth-deck, Billy catches Squeak searching his belongings. A fight ensues, broken up by Claggart, who, unknown to Billy, had ordered the search. Claggart privately reveals his hatred of the young Billy Budd because of his handsome looks and inherent kindness. Claggart pressures the obsequious novice to partake of another plot and, fearful of a flogging on trumped-up charges, he agrees. That night he wakes Billy and attempts to draw him into a plan of mutiny, but fails. Dansker later warns Billy again about Claggart, but the youth remains disbelieving.

Act Two. On the main deck several days later, an uneventful encounter with a French ship interrupts the deceitful Claggart in his account to Captain Vere of mutiny aboard the ship. When the military engagement ends, Claggart finishes his story, accusing Billy of attempting to bribe the novice into joining the treasonous plot. Vere summons Billy to his cabin and when Claggart falsely accuses him, Billy begins stammering, failing miserably to defend himself. He strikes Claggart, who falls to the floor dead. The ship's officers are assembled and Billy, who is not present, is sentenced to death. The Captain agonizes over Billy's fate and comes to see himself as his executioner.

On the bay of the gun deck the following morning, Dansker offers Billy hope with news that a mutiny is indeed brewing, because the sailors want to save him from execution. Billy, however, asks him to put an end to it, declaring it is fate that decrees his death.

Later, on the main deck with all present, Billy is brought out and read his sentence of death. He wishes the Captain well and is taken off. A mutiny nearly does erupt as he is executed.

Epilogue. The elderly Vere still ponders the incident, knowing he could have saved Billy, but believing now that it was, ironically, Billy who was his savior. But has Vere found relief of his mental anguish in this rationale? *—Robert Cummings*

Recommended:

○ **Britten: Billy Budd** / Nagano (cond.), Hampson, Rolfe Johnson, Halfvarson, Halle Orch. / 1994 / Erato 21631

○ **Britten: Billy Budd** / Hickox (cond.), Keenlyside, Langridge, Tomlinson, London SO / 2000 / Chandos 9826

○ **Britten: Billy Budd** / Britten (cond.), Glossop, Pears, J. Langdon, Shirley-Quirk, London SO / 1989 / London 417428

Gloriana, Op. 53 (1953; revised 1966)

Britten's three-act opera *Gloriana* was composed as a coronation opera in honor of Her Royal Majesty Queen Elizabeth II. Britten wanted an opera with sumptuous pageantry and a powerful story about Queen Elizabeth I and her love, in her advanced years, for the young Earl of Essex, whom she called "Robin." Britten had as his librettist William Plomer, a talented writer and strong dramatist. The premiere took place in the Royal Opera House at Covent Garden on June 8, 1953, before an aristocratic audience. The young Queen Elizabeth II was said to be delighted and flattered by the event, but the response of the audience was polite and muted.

Like coronation and royal operas of the previous several hundred years, Britten includes many tableaux of dances, processions, and state ceremonies, bringing the audience into an intensely formal and regal setting. With this sumptuousness Britten sought to flatter the new Queen. Throughout, he celebrates English history in music and dance. His influences include the traditional English masques, which historically had been used to entertain royalty, the music of the Elizabethans, of Purcell, and even of English chant. The opera opens with a fanfare, a tournament, and royal processions, and before the first act is over, there is a masque to entertain the Queen and her company. The singers' parts in the masque are in a lively, contrapuntal, a cappella style, setting them apart from the surrounding dramatic dialogue.

The second act contains a tableaux of Elizabethan dances, scored with prominent parts for reed instruments and drums. Even though the tonalities of the dance pieces are modern, the orchestral colors and the old dance forms bring immediacy to the ancient Elizabethan setting. Within this gay party atmosphere, the plot begins to develop, and Elizabeth stages a "burlesque" meant to shame her rival, the wife of Essex.

The characters of the intense drama are well drawn by Plomer and Britten. Elizabeth evolves through her struggles as a defenseless and jealous lover into a defeated monarch who must order the execution of her beloved. She is seen courting the love of her people, praying in private for strength, and creating jealous scenes in public. Her duets with Essex are superb, as she hands him the political power that proves his downfall. Her right-hand man is a smooth politician, and the characters who surround Essex and incite him to treason are handled with liveliness and energy. The initial performance of *Gloriana* was panned by the critics, not on grounds of the opera's musical worth, but because the portrait Plomer's story paints of the aging Elizabeth I was perceived as unflattering. Although the opera was eventually a box-office hit, intially the English could not bear the idea that the myths of the Elizabethan age were not upheld in a coronation opera meant to honor their new sovereign.*—Rita Laurance*

Synopsis:

Act One. As the opera opens, a tournament is in progress, and a festival atmosphere prevails. Lord Mountjoy wins the tournament and is to be congratulated by the Queen, but the Earl of Essex, jealous of the attention given to a perceived rival, denigrates his prowess in the field and insults him. They fight, and Essex is hurt. The Queen and her retinue arrive on the scene, and she urges the two to make up. Sir Walter Raleigh is in attendance, and he helps them make peace.

The Queen and Cecil, her right-hand man and counselor, are conferring at the beginning of the second scene. Cecil counsels the Queen against becoming too emotionally involved with Essex, and although she soothes Cecil's worries, she admits openly that she loves Essex. However, she tells him, she is dedicated to serving her country and her people as a royal Prince, and she will not let any entanglements come between her and her duties of state. Essex arrives. When Cecil exits, the two are left alone to sing together and talk idly. The Queen is filled with tenderness for him, and he plays two beautiful lute songs for her, after which they have their first duet of the opera. He takes this opportunity to urge her to let him head the English army in Ireland, promising to defeat the rebel Tyrone and win back Ireland for the Crown. She doesn't answer his request, and he leaves, disheartened. Privately, she prays for strength. She does not want to fail as a Prince because of her frailty in love.

Act Two. The second act opens with the Queen's arrival at Norwich. The Recorder has a public speech, and then the Queen and her retinue are presented with an entertainment. It is a lively masque, featuring the characters Time and Concord. The Queen is delighted, but Essex, at her side, wishes to be free of public events.

Later, Lord Mountjoy and Lady Penelope Rich have a clandestine meeting in the garden. The two are secret lovers and wish to be alone together. Essex and his wife are walking in the same garden, complaining of the Queen's treatment of them. The four meet and come together in a lively quartet in which they express their frustrations and their treasonable sentiments toward Elizabeth. Lady Essex warns them all to be cautious, but the other three are at the limits of their patience and want to rule England themselves.

At the Palace of Whitehall, a great festivity of dancing has been arranged. Essex has made a point of having a beautiful and fashionable dress made for Lady Essex for the occasion. When they arrive, all eyes are on Lady Essex as she dances with her husband. Her gown is the most expensive and sumptuous one there, and the Queen is enraged. She arranges a recess, during which time all are expected to change clothes. She takes this opportunity to have her attendants steal Lady Essex's gown. Elizabeth appears after the pause in the new gown, which is much too small for her and makes her look freakish. The entire company is aghast, and Lady Essex bursts into tears. Elizabeth leaves triumphantly, having shamed her rival, and Mountjoy and Essex express their anger at her behavior. But then Queen Elizabeth returns. She has changed into her own garments, and she tells Essex that she has decided to send him to Ireland after all. Pacified, the Earl promises to vanquish the rebel Tyrone and bring honor to his country and their Queen.

Act Three. The Queen is at her dressing table preparing for the day. She is still in her nightdress, and her wig is at her side. Her wisps of gray hair fall about her wrinkled face, and her balding head makes her look old and frail. Essex makes his way into the room, even though the Queen's maids attempt to keep him from her. He has returned from Ireland defeated by the rebel forces, and he begs the Queen to listen to his pleas. He suspects that political enemies have turned her against him. She replies that he has failed his country and the Crown, and she tells him to leave—he has intruded on her when she was barely dressed, only to bring her the news that Ireland is still not in their possession.

Cecil warns her that Essex is at the head of a rebellious faction, and she agrees to have him watched. During the second scene, we see Essex and his rabble in action, trying to stir up revolt against the Queen. Eventually Essex is caught, brought to trial, and convicted of treason. However, Elizabeth hesitates at the signing of his death warrant, for he is still her favorite and she is loath to part with him. Lady Essex, Lord Mountjoy, and Lady Rich all plead for the Earl to the Queen, and Elizabeth is almost moved. However, Lady Rich, with her strident hysteria and bold desperation, gradually infuriates her, and the warrant is signed.

At the end of the opera, Elizabeth is alone. Cecil urges her to announce to her people whom she has selected as a successor, but she rebukes him. She is not ready to die, but she sees that he expects the event at any moment. He replies that perhaps she should just ready herself for bed and get some rest. When he leaves, her loneliness and isolation are complete. Her death is approaching, but she is not ready to stop ruling or to stop courting the love of her people. *—Rita Laurance*

Recommended:

○ **Britten: Gloriana** / Mackerras (cond.), Bairstow, Langridge, Opie, Y. Kenny, Welsh National Opera / 1993 / Argo 440213

A Midsummer Night's Dream, Op. 64 (1960)

For the 1960 Aldeburgh Festival, Britten realized that he did not have time to have a libretto written and then compose an opera for the event. He and Peter Pears hit on the idea of simply cutting and shaping Shakespeare's play into an opera text. It is one of opera's happiest adaptations of plays of the Bard and, needless to say, the most faithful. Of course, Britten had had the play in mind as a possible opera for some time. (There is only one-half of one sentence in the text that is not original Shakespeare.)

To condense the play, he begins it already in the enchanted woods, in the world of the fairies. The fairies are divided into two camps, supporting one or the other of the battling Fairy Queen and King, Tytania, and Oberon. The initial sound of the opera is a wonderful description of the darkening woods itself; beginning on the lowest register of the string basses a tremolando and then a glissando. The idea expands in scope throughout the entire string section, sighing chromatically. This idea recurs as a sort of ritornello between all sections of Act I, and blossoms into an accompaniment for the fairies' lullaby to Tytania at the end of the act. The fairies enter to glittering percussion. Britten's orchestration is unlike that of any other opera; the orchestra is rather small, but includes a sizeable group of metallic percussion and, in a remarkable touch, a harp and a harpsichord, and a bright Baroque trumpet and tuned snare drum to accompany Puck (a speaking and acrobatic role). Deployment of vocal forces is also unique. The humans all have "normal" voices, although, interestingly, the two sets of lovers are cross-matched, the tenor with the mezzo, while the baritone is paired with the soprano. The "Rustics" range from a squeaky comic tenor to a low bass. But the fairies all have special voices; except for the royalty and Puck they are all child singers; Tytania is a glittery coloratura soprano; Oberon is a countertenor.

Act II also has a remarkable ritornello: The whole act is based on a progression of four chords, scored respectively for strings, brass, woodwinds, and percussion. None of the chords shares a note with any of the other chords, and together they constitute all 12 chromatic notes.

But then the opera as a whole is filled with the most remarkable inventiveness. Britten shows remarkable sympathy with all the characters, giving them music with real passion and anger. He gives Oberon some musical lines of real menace as he hatches plans to put a spell on his Queen. *—Joseph Stevenson*

Synopsis:

Act One. The first act opens in the woods. Tytania's troupe of fairies come in ("Over hill, over dale"), occasionally alarmed by Puck's interruptions. Tytania and Oberon enter ("Ill-met by moonlight") and quarrel over a young boy whom Tytania insists on keeping in her entourage, though Oberon wants him for his. She storms out, and Oberon calls for Puck to bring him the magic herb that will make a person fall madly in love with the next being her or she sees. He leaves, and Lysander and Hermia enter, fleeing her forced marriage to Demetrius. They vow their love and leave. Oberon returns, plotting his scheme further, and he withdraws as Lysander and Helena enter. Lysander is looking for Hermia, but Helena tries to persuade him to forget Hermia and turn to her, instead, vowing that she faithfully adores him ("I am your spaniel"). When they leave, Oberon decides to take a role in these lovers' lives and calls for Puck, who returns with the magic plant ("I know a bank where the wild thyme grows"). They leave and the six rustics come in to rehearse *Pyramus and Thisbe*, the play they will perform for the wedding of Theseus and Hippolyta. Peter Quince assigns roles, a process made livelier by Bottom's various demands. When they leave, Lysander and Hermia enter, totally lost, and fall asleep. Puck, confused about their identities, squeezes the herb's juice onto Lysander's eyelids as he sleeps. When Demetrius and Helena come in and Lysander wakes up, Helena is the first one he sees, and he immediately vows his love for her. She runs off and Lysander goes to chase her, and when Hermia wakes up, she goes to chase Lysander. Tytania returns with her fairies, and they sing her to sleep ("You spotted snakes with double tongue"). Oberon comes in and squeezes the herb onto her eyes, casting a spell to make her awaken at the presence of some unworthy, lowly thing.

Act Two. Tytania is still asleep, and when the rustics come in to rehearse, she sleeps through even Bottom's incessant suggestions for improvements and Quince's concerns about the various stage effects. Puck comes in and watches, and when Bottom makes his exit, follows him. Bottom returns, Puck having transformed his head into a donkey's, and the rustics run out in fright. Bottom is confused, though he sings to keep his spirits up ("The woosel-cock"), the more so when Tytania awakens and immediately falls in love with him. She orders her fairies to attend to his every need ("Be kind and courteous"), though their dainty offerings are not exactly a match for his tastes. He falls asleep, as does Tytania. Puck and Oberon return, and while Oberon is delighted at the success of his plot for revenge against Tytania, he realizes that Puck hasn't done so well with the humans. Demetrius and Hermia enter. Puck goes off to bring Helena and Lysander in, and Oberon squeezes more of the herb on Demetrius' eyes ("Flower of this purple dye"). When Helena and Lysander enter, there is general quarreling. Helena and Hermia spit insults and leave, and the men go off to duel. Oberon and Puck return; Puck gets another scolding and is ordered to set things right. Demetrius and Lysander are made to get so lost in the woods that they're too exhausted to fight, and with applications of the (fortunately available) antidote, the fairies sing a lullaby, "On the ground sleep sound."

Act Three. The final act opens with the lovers, Tytania, and Bottom all asleep (again). Oberon, who has now taken the boy for his own, drops the antidote into Tytania's eyes, and as she wakes up, they are reconciled. They leave at the sound of Theseus' horns, and the lovers then wake up ("And I have found"). Bottom wakes up after they leave, confused by what he imagines to have been a dream. The rustics come in and they rush off to perform. In the palace, where Hippolyta and Theseus are impatient for the ceremonies and celebrations to be over, the lovers come to ask Theseus' blessing. The rustics perform the play, which they take quite seriously even though it is a parody of a tragedy, complete with parted lovers, a foiled elopement, a mad scene, and the deaths of the lovers. At the conclusion there is dancing, and at midnight, the six lovers are ready to obey Theseus ("Lovers, to bed"). After all have left, the fairies return, first to make fun of the play ("Now the hungry lion roars") and then to dance ("Now until the break of day"). *—Ann Feeney*

Recommended:

- ○ **Britten: A Midsummer Night's Dream** / Britten (cond.), Deller, Pears, Shirley-Quirk, Watts, London SO / 1990 / London 425663
- ○ **Britten: A Midsummer Night's Dream** / C. Davis (cond.), McNair, Asawa, A. Lloyd, London SO / 1996 / Philips 454122

Peter Grimes, Op. 33 (1945)

It would not be an exaggeration to say that Benjamin Britten's works for the stage (17 in all) single-handedly restored the vitality and relevance of English-language opera, which had been virtually dormant since the death of Henry Purcell, and integrated themselves into the performing repertory to an extent that has eluded every composer since Puccini and Strauss. *Peter Grimes* was Britten's first full-scale operatic composition and the decisive salvo in his quest to become a force in the genre. Its immediate success gained him international stature, and its score proved a seminal foundation upon which he would build and expand for the rest of his career.

The inspiration for *Peter Grimes* came to Britten and his collaborator/partner, Peter Pears, while they were living in the United States. A reading of George Crabbe's epic poem *The Borough* filled Britten with a longing for his home country—specifically the coastal town of Aldeburgh, which was central to Crabbe's writing—and ignited his imagination. The means to realize the project came from Serge Koussevitzky, who offered Britten a generous commission for the work. Britten and Pears set to work on a tentative outline immediately, and by the time of their return to England (March 1942) they had loosely adapted a story line from Crabbe's original, which the playwright and journalist Montagu Slater then used as the basis for his libretto.

In adapting Crabbe's story, Britten and Pears created the quintessential antihero—a man whose complete, and perhaps deserved, alienation from society is the very source of his sympathy. While the Grimes of Crabbe's poem is a relatively one-dimensional villain, sadistic and cruel, the central character of Britten's opera is conflicted and driven, no more villain than victim. Standing apart from society so completely, Grimes actually gives "character" to the Borough in which he lives; the unity of hostile sentiment among its citizens forges them into a larger dramatic presence. The town itself seems to be opposed to Grimes and to be the driving force behind his tragic downfall.

Elements of *Peter Grimes* are reminiscent of nineteenth century French grand opera and the tendency of the genre to put individuals against larger, often unstoppable forces. Grimes' inexorable march toward tragedy seems to nullify any faith in free will or in his power to swim against the tide of events. Public scorn, and the desire to succeed in spite of rejection—even the harsh storm that besets the town—all seem predestined to bring about his torment, and in fighting against these things his faults become all the more apparent. He is a man overwhelmed by circumstance and by his own inner conflicts. He is a failure.

Britten's score, on the other hand, is a resounding success. It is rich with modal inflections, rhythmic intricacies, and cleverly layered musical ideas, all of which are bound by a taut and economical structure. The four orchestral interludes are especially effective, both in their musical invention and their ability to advance the drama without the need for complementary stage action; Britten excerpted them into a concert suite in the years following the work's premiere.

Although the tonal language of *Peter Grimes* is conservative by Britten's later standards, he clearly drew upon his score as a template for other works. In *Grimes* can be heard glimmers of *The Rape of Lucretia*, *A Midsummer Night's Dream*, *Billy Budd*, the *Canticles*, and the choral cantata *Rejoice in the Lamb*, and at all times it exhibits his innate blending of the lyrical and the driven, the dissonant and the peaceful, the vital and the surreal—the very qualities that so well suited him to opera.*—Allen Schrott*

Synopsis:

Prologue. The setting is Moot Hall in a small town in England in the early part of the nineteenth century. One of the boys apprenticing under Peter Grimes, a local fisherman, has died, and an inquest into the event is being held. The hall is bustling with people. Mr. Swallow, the coroner, after conducting a thorough interrogation, pronounces a verdict of death by misadventure, but orders Grimes to take on no further boy apprentices. Grimes isn't satisfied that the townspeople won't continue to suspect his guilt in the affair. Ellen Orford, the school mistress, tries to reassure Grimes that his name will be cleared.

Act One. The act opens a few days later on a seaside street near the Moot Hall and the Boar, the local pub. Ned Keene tells Grimes, who is finding difficulty in managing the boat by himself, that a potential new apprentice has been found. Orford agrees to go fetch the boy, named John, despite vehement general disapproval. A fearful storm rises just after she has gone off in the carrier's cart to fetch the boy, so the townspeople dock their boats hastily, bring in all the nets, and board up the windows of the houses. Grimes discusses with Balstrode, a retired merchant shipper, the reputation he has earned since the accident, and his desire to marry Orford. Balstrode tries to make him see that Orford would marry him now, but Grimes is unshaken in his belief he must acquire wealth first.

The second scene takes place in the interior of the Boar that evening, past the normal closing time. The pub is bristling with people, while the storm howls on outside. News reaches them that a coast road has been flooded and a cliff near Grimes' hut has been washed out. Quarrels begin to brew. A weather-beaten Grimes arrives and is served up abuse from every side ("His exercise is not with men but with killing boys!"), and a man named Boles tries to assault him. When Orford returns with John at last, Grimes leaves with him.

Act Two. On a sunny Sunday morning sometime later, Orford is sunning herself by the ocean with the young John while the morning church service is going on nearby. Hymns are interjected throughout the scene. She discovers worrisome tears in John's jacket, and deep bruises on his neck. The consequent argument between her and Grimes, who arrives to take the boy out to work, ends with him striking her. A few neighbors overhear, and news that "Grimes is at his exercise" spreads rapidly. People arrive to investigate. They're divided regarding Grimes and heated comments pass back and forth. Grimes has meanwhile gone off with John to the fishing hut.

The second scene is set in Grimes' hut. John is sobbing miserably while Grimes is urging him to get ready to go to sea, growing increasingly frustrated. He hears the sounds of a party of men approaching, hurls insults at the boy for slowing him down, and finally he sends him scrambling down the cliff in order to make their getaway quick. Just as the men knock, a scream is heard as John falls to his death. Grimes runs down after him, and the men enter an empty hut.

Act Three. A few nights later many people are about, enjoying drinks at the Boar and a subscription dance in the Hall. It is assumed that the absent Grimes and John are out fishing. Orford is overheard talking of the sweater she embroidered for the boy: it washed up on the shore. When it is noticed that Grimes' boat has returned to harbor, Swallow orders the constable to round up a posse of men to arrest Grimes.

A few hours later at the harbor, raving, exhausted, and desperate, Grimes is sneaking back to his boat. Occasional cries of the manhunt pierce the fog, and a foghorn makes a melancholy sound. Orford and Balstrode find Grimes. She suggests that practically his only honorable option left is to take the boat out into the night and go down with it. He does so. The very end of the opera occurs a few hours later, just at dawn. As the town is waking up, a coast guard report comes in that a boat has sunk far out at sea. But the news is dismissed as fanciful rumor. *—Donato Mancini*

Recommended:

- ○ **Britten: Peter Grimes** / Britten (cond.), Pears, Brannigan, Lanigan, Kelly, Covent Garden Opera Orch. / 1985 / London 414577
- ○ **Britten: Peter Grimes** / C. Davis (cond.), Vickers, H. Harper, J. Summers, Covent Garden Royal Opera Orch. / 1999 / Philips 462847

Turn of the Screw, Op. 54 (1954)

Some have called it "the perfect opera libretto." Mrs. Myfanwy Piper provided Britten with an adaptation of the novella by Henry James; this wordy, ambiguous text is magically turned into a concise psychological thriller about a governess placed in charge of two orphaned children at the estate of their uncle. The uncle is unwilling to provide any parenting. He simply orders the governess not to bother him about anything having to do with the children. Isolated at the estate, the governess soon perceives that two malevolent ghosts (of the master's valet and of the former governess) are fighting her for the very souls of the children. In a final confrontation, the girl is taken away from harm by the old housekeeper, but the boy's final struggle to renounce the evil influence proves too much for him, and he dies. Were there really ghosts, or was the psychological struggle actually an outgrowth of the repressed sexuality of the governess? James' novella is ambiguous; Britten seems on the surface to cast the ghosts as real (his opera gives them voices and words to sing, which James did not do), but there is enough of a question that it can be staged either way. The dramatic and musical form is masterly. One theme, twisting its way around all notes of the scale, dominates the opera, whose 15 scenes and prologue each constitute a variation on the theme. Doubt creeps in slowly in Act One, as scenes of idyllic upper-class country life are subtly darkened by references to death until the ghosts finally appear and call to the children. Act Two presents a struggle between the ghosts and the governess, with the tension tightening each step of the way. Britten uses only 13 instruments and six voices in this opera, but he creates a breathtaking variety of sounds from these resources. Because of its small scale the work is not played in the larger opera houses very often, but it is accepted as a masterpiece of the growing genre of chamber opera. *—Joseph Stevenson*

Synopsis:

Prologue. A soloist ("It is a curious story") describes how the Governess met the children's handsome young uncle and guardian, hesitated about accepting his offer to care for them, especially since he insisted that she never correspond with him, but eventually agreed.

Act One. The act opens with a theme, "On the Journey," that will recur in varied form throughout the opera as the governess wonders what things will be like and tries to overcome her fears ("Nearly There"). In Variation One, "The Welcome," the children excitedly await her arrival. She enters and is immediately delighted ("How Charming They Are"), and Mrs. Grose talkatively assures her they are good children. Variation Two, "The Letter," opens with the Governess receiving a letter from Miles' school, saying that he has been expelled. She and Mrs. Grose refuse to believe that he is bad, especially when they look out the window and see him playing with Flora ("Lavender's Blue, Diddle, Diddle"). In Variation Three, "The Tower," the Governess strolls about in the grounds, contemplating how happy she is despite all her past fears and wishing only that she could see the children's guardian again. Peter Quint appears briefly on the tower, and for a moment she thinks that it is the guardian, but after he disappears, she wonders who he might have been. In Variation Four, "The Window," Flora and Miles are playing ("Tom, Tom, the Piper's Son"), and they leave as the Governess enters. She sees Quint in the window, staring at her, and she is terrified. She describes the mysterious intruder to Mrs. Grose, who tells the Governess that Quint had been the guardian's valet. She says that he was "too free" with Miles and also with Miss Jessel, the Governess' predecessor ("He Had His Will, Morning and Night"). Miss Jessel died, and Quint died shortly thereafter in a fall. The Governess is determined to protect the children. In Variation Five, "Lessons," Miles recites a Latin lesson ("Many Nouns in 'Is' We Find") as Flora plays. Miles then sings a strange song, "Malo." In Variation Six, "The Lake," Flora and the Governess come to the lake in the park, and Flora is astounded at how big it is even though the Governess tells her it is actually quite small. Flora sings a strangely ominous nonsense lullaby to her doll ("Dolly Must Sleep"). In Variation Seven, "At Night," Quint calls to Miles ("I Am All Things Strange and Bold"), and Miles eagerly listens. Miss Jessel similarly calls to Flora, and Quint's and Miss Jessel's voices blend ("On the Paths"). The children promise to come to them. The Governess and Mrs. Grose come out and ask what the children are doing out of bed. Miles comments: "I am bad, aren't I?"

Act Two. The act opens with Variation Eight, "Colloquy and Soliloquy." Miss Jessel and Quint sing of their past ("Why Did You Call Me"), and Quint says that he is intent on finding an obedient friend to feed his mounting power. In their duet, they declare that when they have bound others, "the ceremony of innocence is drowned." The Governess is desperate and confused ("Lost in My Labyrinth I See No Truth"). Variation Nine, "The Bells," is set in the churchyard, where Miles and Flora sing a psalm that gradually turns into nonsense ("O Sing Unto Them a New Song"). The Governess is terrified, but Mrs. Grose tries to reassure her. Miles hangs back from entering and obliquely questions the Governess, asking her whether his uncle thinks what she thinks. She is aghast ("It Was a Challenge"). Variation Ten, "Miss Jessel," takes place in the schoolroom, where Miss Jessel sits at the desk, lamenting that where she suffered, she must find peace. The Governess comes in and confronts her, but Miss Jessel seems not to see her. When Miss Jessel disappears, the Governess writes to the guardian. In Variation 11, "The Bedroom," Miles is getting undressed and singing his Malo song. The Governess comes and tries to get him to confide in her, but he restlessly turns away from her. Quint calls to him, and when the candle goes out, he sweetly tells the Governess that he blew it out. In Variation 12, "Quint," he persuades Miles to steal the letter ("So! She Has Written"). In Variation 13, Miles plays the piano. Mrs. Grose still calls him a good boy, but the Governess just calls him clever. Mrs. Grose helps Flora play cat's cradle ("Cradles for Cats"). Flora urges her, almost hypnotically, to go to sleep, and she slips away. The Governess turns around, and when she notices, wakes Mrs. Grose up. They go to find her. Miles continues playing. In Variation 14, "Flora," she waits by the lake. The Governess and Mrs. Grose find her, and Miss Jessel appears and calls to Flora. Mrs. Grose cannot see her, and Flora furiously turns on the Governess, saying she can't see anything either and shrieking that she hates her. The Governess is desolated, "Ah! My Friend, You Have Forsaken Me." In Variation 15, "Miles," Mrs. Grose has heard Flora talking in her sleep and, horrified by what the child said, is taking her to the guardian. Mrs. Grose says that the letter disappeared, and the Governess realizes that Miles took it. Flora and Mrs. Grose leave and Miles comes in. He is suavely attentive, and Quint appears. She questions Miles, and Quint urges him not to betray him. She becomes insistent ("Who? Who?") and screaming ("Peter Quint, You Devil"), Miles collapses. The Governess thinks she has won, but when she sees he is dead, she wonders what they have done between them and leaves, almost deliriously singing "Malo." *—Ann Feeney*

Recommended:

- ○ **Britten: The Turn of the Screw** / Britten (cond.), Pears, Vyvyan, Cross, D. Hemmings, English Opera Group / 1990 / London 425672
- ○ **Britten: The Turn of the Screw** / Harding (cond.), Bostridge, J. Rodgers, Henschel, Tierney, Mahler CO / 2002 / Virgin 45521

VOCAL

A Ceremony of Carols, Op. 28 (1942; revised 1943)

Benjamin Britten's decision to leave the United States in 1942 was not easily arrived at, but when he was finally on his way homeward-bound, his troubled conscience—it was wartime, after all—seems to have been more than just a little bit soothed. Over the course of the long journey he began a series of choral works (two were finished during the voyage) that have remained among the most thoroughly popular of all his non-operatic compositions. The second of the two works completed on the ship is the now-famous *Ceremony of Carols*, Op. 28, for treble voices (properly a choir of boys, but more often sung by women's chorus) and harp. (The first piece was the *Hymn to St. Cecilia*.)

The 12 pieces of the *Ceremony of Carols* have, over the last half century, become a perennial part of the English-speaking world's Christmastime celebrations. The *Ceremony* is not Britten's first compilation of holiday music—*A Boy is Born*, from almost a decade earlier, has that distinction. In *A Boy is Born*, Britten used the mixed choir in a very instrumental way. For the *Ceremony*, on the other hand, Britten adopts a mock-archaic manner that allows him to weave the modal and linear qualities of his sources into his own very different harmonic and structural language.

The *Ceremony* begins with an a cappella plainsong procession (the traditional *Hodie Christus natus est*, "Today, Christ is born") and ends with a recession on the same melody. Between these two pillars are nine carols and, between the sixth and seventh carols, a brilliantly evocative solo harp interlude.

The harp's ostinato introduction to the first carol, "Wolcum Yole!" (No. 2, as the procession is "officially" No. 1), sets up the unusual acoustic tone (unmistakably designed to make use of the amplifying powers of large English cathedrals) of the *Ceremony*. The delicate vocal homophony of No. 2 is maintained throughout the following "There is no Rose," while No. 4, "That younge child," affords the opportunity for one treble soloist to emerge from the semitone-inflected harp background. "Balulalow" (No. 5), which alternates soloist with ensemble, is more clearly tonal than No. 4, its F sharp minor context making frequent and, in the end, decisive digressions to the parallel major. "As dew in Aprille" (No. 6) develops the chromatic fluctuations provided in the previous number into an oscillation between E flat major and C major (with the dissonant E flat still riding along on top). The sixth carol, "This little Babe" (No. 7), is surely the most famous of the set. A hemiola-ridden accompaniment provides support for a curiously anxious interpretation of the melody that soon erupts into a driving, three-voice canon in which the voices seem to chase one another without ever actually making any progress in the pursuit. The harp positively shimmers with sonority and texture during its three-minute interlude, providing what is, to many listeners, the most appealing music of the entire *Ceremony*. "In Freezing Winter Night" (No. 9) sets up major second dissonances against shivering harp tremolos. Two treble soloists emerge, almost lifelessly, during the reprise of the opening. The last two carols, "Spring Carol" (No. 10) and "Adam lay i-bounden" (No. 11) are set up in thoroughly contrasting fashion, though, in fact, they form two parts of one larger musical blueprint. "Spring Carol" rides along a harp ostinato that hints at D major without ever giving us a real resolution, while "Adam lay i- bounden" takes off in motoric fashion after a pair of incisive "deo gratias" gestures. *—Blair Johnston*

Recommended:

- ○ **Britten: A Ceremony of Carols** / Cleobury (cond.), King's College Choir / 1991 / Argo 433215
- ○ **Britten: A Ceremony of Carols** / D. Hill (cond.), Westminster Cathedral Choir / 1986 / Hyperion 66220
- ○ **A Robert Shaw Christmas: Angels on High** / Shaw (cond.), Robert Shaw Chamber Singers / 1997 / Telarc 80461

The Holy Sonnets of John Donne, Op. 35 (1945)

This song cycle for piano and tenor voice is one of the largest and most profound of Benjamin Britten's many vocal publications, and one of the most distinguished of the twentieth century.

It is the third major song cycle he composed specifically for the voice of Peter Pears, his life partner. Although Britten and Pears had been reading Donne as early as two years earlier, serious work on the cycle was triggered by a specific occasion for performance, Pears and Britten planned a Purcell commemorative concert set for November 1945 at Wigmore Hall. Britten decided to write a cycle in the spirit of Purcell's *Divine Hymns* to include on the program.

But it is another experience, a particular recital, that impelled the emotional depth of this cycle. Almost as soon as the war ended in Europe, Yehudi Menuhin began touring Europe. Britten joined him for concerts in Germany, which included a performance on July 27 for survivors of the Belsen concentration camp.

The cycle begins with "O my blacke Soule," to a stark, hammering piano accompaniment and a vocal setting that emphasizes Donne's rhythmic patterns. "Batter my heart" is a demonic perpetual motion piece at high speed, calling for utmost flexibility, range, and power on the part of the tenor.

A stunned quietness rules the third song, "O might these sighes and teares." The traditional musical representation of a sigh, the interval of the falling second, dominates this song, and from this point the half-step relationship is the most important structural element of the cycle.

"Oh, to vex me" is another moto perpetuo in the piano part, although the line of the voice part is more broken. It ends with a literal shaking in the singer's voice to illustrate the words.

The fifth song, "What if this present" asks the unsettling question, what if this were the earth's last night? Would Christ's crucifixion be in vain as far as the poet's soul is concerned? The tormented answer is "No." This song, the central point in the cycle, is also its darkest moment.

More peaceful, calmly oscillating piano chords begin a path to redemption in "Since she whom I lov'd." Since she is now in heaven, the poet is thinking "wholly on heavenly things."

The seventh song, "At the round earths imagin'd corners," expresses certainty in resurrection and judgment and prays to be taught true repentance. The piano accompaniment has a remarkable ringing effect.

This prayer is continued in "Thou has made me"; the poet begs for grace more for God's sake (lest His work of creation be in vain) than the poet's own. The music is again rushing and agitated, but now this seems directed towards resolution rather than despair, which is found in the final song, the famous "Death be not proud," for "One short sleepe past. Wee wake eternally, And death shall be no more; Death, thou shalt die." The music has an assured, regular tread as the it becomes a lullaby welcoming this final rest. *—Joseph Stevenson*

Recommended:

- ○ **Britten: Billy Budd** / Pears, Britten / 1989 / London 417428
- ○ **20th Century English Art Songs: Britten & Quilter** / P. A. Kelly, Recchiuti / 1995 / GM Recordings 2022

Les Illuminations, song cycle for high voice & strings, Op. 18 (1939)

Les Illuminations (1939), is a song cycle written for high voice (soprano or tenor) and string orchestra. While on a weekend excursion, Britten read poems by the nineteenth century Frenchman Arthur Rimbaud, and stated, "I must put them to music." Whereas many composers—even the notoriously nationalistic French—had passed over Rimbaud's works, considering them too thorny for lyrical settings, Britten was deeply affected by them and felt a strong affinity with the author; especially familiar to Britten was Rimbaud's sense of cynicism, and a longing for the innocence of childhood. *Les Illuminations* was completed on October 25, 1939, and was dedicated to the Swiss soprano, Sophie Wyss, who gave the premiere in London, 1940 (she had previously given the first performance of Britten's *Our Hunting Fathers* in 1936).

Les Illuminations dates from Britten's "American" period (1939–42), a remarkably productive time during which he also completed his *First String Quartet* (1941), his *Sinfonia da Requiem* (1940), and the *Michelangelo Sonnets* (1940). In writing *Les Illuminations*, he not only embraced the French language, but also distinctly French elements of style; this marks the beginnings of his move away from certain identifiable "Britishisms," and toward a more cosmopolitan and personal style (The *Michelangelo Sonnets* embraced Italian characteristics with similarly open arms).

The piece opens with a Fanfare in which Britten imitates the sound of two trumpets with a violin and a viola. The second movement is titled "Villes," and is about the industrialization of cities; the constant eighth note pattern conveys the mechanical sounds of the city. The third movement of the song cycle is divided into two parts, "Phrase," a simple song, and "Antique," a dance-like piece. The next movement, "Royaute," is ceremonious in its portrayal of a couple wishing for and attaining royalty—at least in their own minds! "Marine," the sixth song, sets the vocal line against an ostinato accompaniment; this leads into an orchestral interlude. The seventh movement, "Being Beauteous," has an erotically-charged text, while the text of "Parade" describes the participants in the titular spectacle. The last movement is befittingly titled "Depart." *—AMG*

Recommended:

- ○ **Les Illuminations; Sinfonia da Requiem; 7 Sonnets** / Britten (cond.), Pears, CBS SO / 1995 / NMC 30

On this Island, song cycle, Op. 11 (1937)

In the mid-1930s, shortly after the deaths of both his mother and his father in the same short span of time, Benjamin Britten joined the circle of artists clustered around the brilliant poet W.H. Auden. Generally disillusioned with British life, aesthetic tastes, and conventional morality, this group adopted a cynical outlook and a fashionable affinity for left-wing politics. These personal matters are relevant to a discussion of this music because this song cycle (the first of many brilliant collections in Britten's oeuvre) is one of the first Britten works on which they had a direct impact. The five poems of the cycle were written by Auden and are typically complex, with obscure allusions and obvious delight in virtuosity in handling the words. Britten gave them unusually stark settings.

Among them is a song called "Nocturne," probably the first of Britten's evocations of dreaming in a slow-breathed sleep, an image that haunts his music thereafter. The opening "Let the florid music praise" contains figures suggesting trumpet calls, but a subversive and sensual little waltz-figure is also present, a hint at the side of their lives that Auden, Britten, and their friends had to keep hidden—homosexuality was then punishable as a crime in the U.K. The final song is a jazzy number making clear Britten and Auden's disdain for contemporary societal values. The work is highly regarded as Britten's first song cycle and is full of impressive compositional touches, but the disillusionment at its core has denied it the success of the later cycles. Soprano Sophie Wyss gave its first performance, with Britten himself at the piano, on November 19, 1937, a couple of days before the composer's twenty-fourth birthday. *—Joseph Stevenson*

Recommended:

○ **On This Island** / L. Dawson, Martineau / 2001 / Hyperion 67227

Serenade, for tenor, horn & strings, Op. 31 (1943)

On his way back from America in 1942, Britten began two choral works, *Hymn to Saint Cecilia* and *A Ceremony of Carols*, that were premiered the same year. But morale-boosting concerts with tenor Peter Pears (both were conscientious objectors and already lifelong partners) preoccupied them for the next 11 months. Not until he was hospitalized with measles early in 1943 did Britten began to compose again, working on what he described as "6 Nocturnes for Peter and a lovely young horn player, Dennis Brain, & Strings." He dedicated the finished *Serenade* to Edward Sackville-West, who later wrote: "The subject is Night... the lengthening shadow, the distant bugle at sunset, the Baroque panoply of the starry sky, the heavy angels of sleep; but also the cloak of evil—the worm in the heart of [William Blake's] rose, the secret sense of sin in the heart of man. The whole sequence forms an Elegy or Nocturnal, as Donne would have called it." It was premiered with Walter Goehr and his orchestra in London's Wigmore Hall on October 15, 1943.

The horn plays unaccompanied on natural (rather than tempered) harmonics at the beginning and the end, onstage in the Prologue. In the Pastoral, the first song, in D flat, Charles Cotton's seventeenth century words "could be a description of a Constable landscape... [while] the horn continues to play in imitative diatonic phrases." So wrote Humphrey Carpenter in his 1992 biography of Britten. In the succeeding Nocturne (words by Alfred Lord Tennyson, ABA form, E flat and C major), the horn echoes and later embellishes its partner's jaunty, triplet-filled melody. Next, in the Blake *Elegy*, subject matter darkens the music landscape. Its extended horn preface and postlude are dominated by descending half-step intervals, eerily so at the end—symbolizing "the sense of sin" that had its origin, for Britten, in boarding and public schools that he both dreaded and despised. The anonymous, fifteenth century *Lyke Wake Dirge* follows in grim G minor, and is keened by the tenor at the upper extreme of his voice, keeping the half-step intervals from the Elegy. Here, however, they ascend. Carpenter calls this "a relentless funeral march in the strings... the tenor's swoops up the octave suggest mortal terror of judgment." Its fugal character turns ghoulish at the horn's rude intrusion more than halfway through. The B flat setting of Ben Jonson's *Hymn to Diana*, goddess of the moon as well as the chase, is marked "presto e leggiero." Triplet-filled hunting calls and scales passages on the horn are imitated by the tenor in a cadenza near the end. The sixth and final song lets the horn rest while the tenor sings Keats' sonnet about the healing power of sleep, albeit uneasily, almost pleading on repeated high D's at the end ("seal the hushèd casket of my soul") over a sustained D by two solo violins and viola. From offstage, the horn repeats the Prologue note for note in an Epilogue. *—Roger Dettmer*

Recommended:

○ **Britten: Serenade; Les Illuminations; Nocturne** / Britten (cond.), Pears, Tuckwell, London SO / 1986 / London 417153

○ **Ian Bostridge: Britten** / Metzmacher (cond.), Bostridge, Neunecker, Bamberg Symphoniker / 1999 / EMI 56871

Songs and Proverbs of W. Blake, Op. 74 (1965)

English composer Benjamin Britten wrote more than 100 songs for voice and piano, many of them arranged in cycles. Britten typically composed his song cycles with a particular singer in mind: more often than not his friend, the tenor Peter Pears. The cycle *Songs and Proverbs of William Blake* was composed for a particular singer: not Pears this time, but the famous baritone Dietrich Fischer-Dieskau, who had sung in the premiere of Britten's *War Requiem* in 1962. Fischer-Dieskau premiered the William Blake songs at the 1965 Aldeburgh Festival. Peter Pears chose the texts for Britten to set, selecting poems from Blake's *Songs of Innocence and of Experience*, written between 1789 and 1793. Pears also chose some of Blake's "Proverbs of Hell" from *The Marriage of Heaven and Hell*, to be interspersed between the poems. Blake's poems explore humanity's woes and the tensions between innocence and experience, from the bleak misery of the child in "The Chimney Sweeper" to the cold, cruel victory of "A Poison Tree." Britten's musical settings closely follow the text, with both the vocal lines and piano parts setting the mood for each song. Britten's vigorous, agitated setting of "The Tyger," for example, neatly captures the poem's seething energy, while "Every Night and Every Morn" is set like a chorale, emphasizing the poem's spiritual concerns: "God Appears and God is Light/To those poor Souls who dwell in Night." The Proverbs, each only a few lines long, are transitional, leading from one song to the next. This song cycle requires a huge amount of stamina from its vocalist, with extremely long phrases and held notes in uncomfortable portions of the range of a baritone. *—Alexander Carpenter*

Recommended:

○ **Benjamin Britten: The Red Cuckatoo, Holy Sonnets Donne & others** / Bostridge, G. Johnson / 1995 / Hyperion 66823

Seven Sonnets of Michelangelo, Op. 22 (1940)

Benjamin Britten's three-year sojourn in the United States is considered by many scholars to be a turning point in his career, marking the beginning of his creative maturity. Among the finest works composed during this period are the *Seven Sonnets of Michelangelo* (1940), for tenor and piano, based on the romantic sonnets of the famed Renaissance artist Michelangelo Buonarroti. This song cycle was the first of many compositions Britten conceived for his life-long partner and collaborator Peter Pears, who accompanied Britten to America in 1939. As with other works written for Pears, these songs succeed on the combined merits of two things: the deeply personal expressiveness that arose from his relationship with Pears—to whom the *Sonnets* are dedicated—and the well-developed craftsmanship that infused them with universal human and artistic themes.

Seven Sonnets of Michelangelo was completed by November 30, 1940, but the cycle was not premiered until two years later, after the composer and singer had returned to London. This delay occurred because Pears did not feel ready to present the extremely taxing work; he took lessons in the U.S. in order to add strength to his voice and increase his range. Upon returning to England in the midst of World War II, the two artists gained exemptions from duty in the armed forces due to their artistic contributions. Pears and Britten agreed to tour the country performing recitals for the Council for the Encouragement of Music and the Arts. *Seven Sonnets of Michelangelo* was given its premiere on September 23, 1942, in London in Wigmore Hall. Critics cited the seven songs as the best English examples in the genre since the time of Purcell, and also recognized the growth of the composer's language during his time in America. The premiere, in fact, was so successful that just as the composer was leaving the stage, executives from the Decca record company approached him in order to produce a recording of the piece. According to Britten, the resulting recording "sold enormously."

By leaving the texts of the *Sonnets* in their original Italian, Britten retained their particular formal and phonetic character; it also allowed for a fusion of his own, very British, sensibilities with the more expansive lyricism that is characteristic of the Italian tradition. In this way, the *Sonnets* are similar to Britten's earlier composition, *Les Illuminations* (1939), which allowed for a similar English/French symbiosis. The last of the *Sonnets* (XXIV: "Spirto ben nato") is often singled out as the finest piece in the cycle. *—AMG*

Recommended:

○ **Benjamin Britten** / Pears, Britten / Pearl 9177

○ **Britten: Songs** / Rolfe Johnson, G. Johnson / 2001 / Helios 55067

○ **Britten: Winter Winds; On This Island; 7 Sonnets** / Tear, Ledger / 2000 / EMI 573995

CHORAL

Hymn to St. Cecilia, Op. 27 (1942; revised 1966)

The early 1940s were a difficult time for Benjamin Britten, whose pacifist ideals led to an uneasy relationship with a British public fired with passion and fighting spirit in the face of World War II. Partly to provide comfort for his fellow Britons and partly to salve his own troubled conscience, Britten produced a variety of striking religious choral works that take a place among his best-known and most beloved music. Surely no choral society or harpist is unfamiliar with the *Ceremony of Carols* (1942), and *Rejoice in the Lamb* (1943) is similarly a staple of the modern choral repertoire.

While perhaps less familiar than those works, the *Hymn to St. Cecilia*, Op. 27 (1942), is an imaginative, important example of Britten's singular gift for melding words and music. In relation to Britten's career, the work provides a distinctive bridge between the accomplishments of a young if immensely talented prentice and those of the more sophisticated composer who was to soon burst onto the international scene with the opera *Peter Grimes* (1944–45).

Britten had focused almost exclusively on instrumental music during the 1930s, and it comes as no surprise that his earliest choral works, such as *Te Deum (1936)* and *Ballad of Heroes* (1939), are filled with vocal imitation of instrumental effects. In *Hymn to St. Cecilia*, however, Britten begins to incorporate superficial gestures of this sort into a more truly choral style in which the vocal forces are frequently deployed in rich parallel triads.

The text of the *Hymn* consists of three poems of W.H. Auden, each followed by a four-line invocation to Cecilia, the patron saint of music. Britten's setting is not really a hymn in the traditional sense of the word, but rather a three-movement structure, like a cantata in miniature, that sets the sonorous triads of the first poem against the rapid-fire vocal scherzo of the second and the ground-bass design of the third. The somber cycling of the last poem is interrupted in the middle to make way for a soaring solo for boy soprano. The invocation is set in delicate unisons and octaves after the first poem, blossoming into a fuller texture at the end of the scherzo movement. Beyond this use of a text refrain, Britten achieves further formal unity by fitting to the final statement of the invocation to "Blessed Cecilia" the music that opened the Hymn.—*Blair Johnston*

Recommended:

- ○ **Britten: Saint Nicolas; Hymn to Saint Cecilia** / M. Best (cond.), Rolfe Johnson, Corydon Singers, English CO / 1989 / Hyperion 66333
- ○ **Britten: Sacred and Profane** / M. Creed (cond.), RIAS-Kammerchor / 2001 / HM 901734

Rejoice in the Lamb, cantata, Op. 30 (1943)

Benjamin Britten's festival cantata *Rejoice in the Lamb* (1943), written for chorus and organ, is regarded as one of his most interesting compositions. Although the cantata is technically one of Britten's "occasional" works, meaning that the piece was composed for some sort of event, it is an important step in his journey to compositional maturity. This piece is highly praised partly because of Britten's unusual choice of the text from the poem *Jubilate Agno*, by the mentally disturbed eighteenth century poet Christopher Smart. However, Britten's brilliant setting of the poetry is the real accomplishment in artistry. Immediately after *Rejoice in the Lamb*, Britten composed two works that affirmed his technical mastery, the *Serenade for Tenor, Horn, and Strings* (1943) and the opera *Peter Grimes* (1944–45).

Rejoice in the Lamb was commissioned by the vicar of St. Matthew's Church in Northampton, for the occasion of the church's 50th anniversary, and was first performed there on September 21, 1943. Its vicar, Walter Hussey, was well known for being a patron of the arts. Smart's *Jubilate Agno* is an antiphonal poem, of which only half still remains. Britten does not use all of the material, but it is noted by Smart scholars that he selected an excellent representation. Smart writes about the glory of God shining through religious icons, such as David, but he also sees this glory through other strange things, such as his cat and a bothersome mouse, the letters of the alphabet, and musical instruments. Smart also discusses his confinement to the mental asylum by comparing his suffering to that of his Savior. *Jubilate Agno* is thought by some to be the mad ranting of a mad poet, but Britten recognized in Smart a naive, childlike faith in his own beliefs. Apparently the message of Smart's poetry remained with Britten, as portions of *Rejoice in the Lamb* were read at the composer's funeral. The commissioner of the piece, Walter Hussey, gave the address at Britten's memorial service.

The cantata only lasts about 15 minutes and is one continuous movement, but ten separate sections can be discerned. The often changing musical texture is necessary due to Smart's constant shifts in subject. The second section sets the passage about biblical figures quite ceremoniously. The fourth section, which involves Smart's cat, named Jeoffrey, and a mouse, is well conceived with both animals being perfectly conveyed by the organ part. —*Chris Boyes*

Recommended:

- ○ **Bernstein & Britten** / Dale Warland Singers / 1999 / American Choral 123

Spring Symphony, Op. 44 (1949)

Britten's Op. 44 is a symphony only in the broadest understanding of that term; it's really a song cycle for three soloists, chorus, and orchestra on texts concerning the departure of winter and the renewal and rebirth brought by spring. The Koussevitzky Music Foundation commissioned it, but Sergey Koussevitzky and the Boston Symphony Orchestra—the work's dedicatees—gave the second performance; the premiere was conducted by Eduard van Beinum at the 1949 Holland Festival.

Britten had initially considered using Medieval Latin texts, but ultimately settled on English lyric verse mainly from the sixteenth and seventeenth centuries. He said that he found inspiration in "a particularly lovely spring day in East Suffolk"; no doubt he also found inspiration, or at least precedent, for the form of his work in Gustav Holst's *Choral Symphony*.

The first of the four movements begins deep in winter, a slow introduction featuring the icy tones of the vibraphone. It sets "Shine Out, Fair Sun," a prayer in winter for the coming of spring, which may be by George Chapman (Britten's attribution is the safe "Anon."). The orchestra alternates with unaccompanied chorus here, but the forces come together for three concise, quick treatments of lighthearted poems by Edmund Spenser ("The Merry Cuckoo"), Thomas Nashe ("Spring, the Sweet Spring," with soloists imitating birdcalls), and John Clare ("The Driving Boy"). Part One broadens out, but loses none of its humor (Molto moderato ma giocoso) in its concluding section, John Milton's "The Morning Star." The second song is for tenor; the fourth features a boys' choir and the soprano singing over choral whistling.

In the composer's words, Part Two, the symphony's slow movement, considers "the darker side of spring—the fading violets, rain and night." An alto is featured in Robert Herrick's "To Violets" (here renamed "Welcome Maids of Honour"). Next comes a more tranquil treatment for tenor of Henry Vaughan's "The Shower" (retitled "Waters Above"), and finally a setting for alto of portions of "Summer Night" by Britten's contemporary W.H. Auden.

The third movement, the scherzo, is a suite of dance-songs: Richard Barnefield's "When Will My May Come" (with tenor), George Peele's "Fair and Fair" (with tenor and soprano), and William Blake's "Sound the Flute." Part Four is a Mayday festival, based mostly on a sung version of a joyous speech from Beaumont and Fletcher's comic play *The Knight of the Burning Pestle*, raucously set. This provides waltzing counterpoint at the end with an almost shouted version of the anonymous thirteenth century round "Sumer Is Icumen In," ending the cycle from winter to summer. —*James Reel*

Recommended:

- ○ **Britten: Spring Symphony; Four Sea Interludes** / Previn (cond.), K. Walters, J. Baker, Tear, London SO / 1993 / EMI 64736

War Requiem, Op. 66 (1961)

Benjamin Britten spent most of the 1950s adding to a string of successful operas that had begun with *Peter Grimes* in the mid-1940s. Though he took a brief sojourn from opera to write the *War Requiem*, it is clear that the dramatic spirit that fueled his operatic efforts carried over into this work, his most monumental effort. While the *Requiem* is in its own way even more overtly theatrical than Verdi's well-known *Requiem* (described by Hans von Bülow as "an opera in ecclesiastical guise"), it cannot properly be thought of as an opera without staging. The musical procedures of Britten's operas were quite well established by 1961, and the *War Requiem* really has little to do with them. The work instead relies on simple, sectional musical means to convey a pattern of thought that even listeners unfamiliar with the often confusing realm of mid-twentieth century music can follow with little trouble.

Indeed, such an immediately accessible idiom was one of the composer's basic goals when he set himself to interpolating the anti-war poetry of Wilfred Owen (killed in action just one week before the Armistice of 1918) into the traditional requiem scheme. The *War Requiem* is by no means pure music, nor could its various sections conceivably stand alone. It is a work with a basic human message, simple and uncontrived and utterly reliant on the distribution of textual materials (separate instrumental and vocal forces are assigned to the two disparate bodies of text) to achieve its impact. The work attained an almost immediate rapport with English-speaking audiences around the world after its May 9, 1962, premiere at the new Coventry Cathedral, and to many it remains Britten's supreme achievement.

On a structural level, the *War Requiem* is massive, its six large movements, each comprising several smaller sections, of some 90 minutes' total duration. From the bells and chantlike chorus in the opening bars of the Requiem aeternam, Britten's use of the tritone as a basic unifying device is obvious. A boys' choir breaks in with the Te decet hymnus, only to be interrupted by Owen's poem "What passing-bells" set as a tenor solo. (The solo tenor and baritone sing all the poetic texts.) The restless tritone gives way to a moment of temporary repose at the end of this first movement, which resolves on an F major chord.

The Dies Irae, containing no fewer than ten separate subsections, is the longest of the six movements, while the following Offertorium and Sanctus together comprise only six sections of music. The Dies Irae closes with a quiet choral Pie Jesu, while the Sanctus is the only movement to end with one of Owen's poems, the grim baritone solo "After the blast of lightning." Chillingly, the closing Dona nobis pacem (Grant us peace) of the following Agnus Dei is sung not by the chorus, as might be expected, but rather by the anguished tenor soloist. At the end of the final Libera me, however, some peace, or at least rest, is reached at last as the unaccompanied chorus finds the strength, after a lengthy and tortured tumult, to resolve the burdensome tritone to the sonorous F major chord of the final "Amen." —*Blair Johnston*

Recommended:

- ○ **Britten: War Requiem** / Pears, Fischer-Dieskau, Vishnievskaya, London SO / London 414383

CHAMBER MUSIC

Six Metamorphoses after Ovid, for oboe, Op. 49 (1951)

Benjamin Britten's *Six Metamorphoses* for oboe solo, Op. 49, of 1951 are his only substantial instrumental pieces to appear in his otherwise almost exclusively-theatrical 1950s. The next real concert piece after the *Metamorphoses* would be the *Sonata for cello and piano* of 1961. Britten's only work for solo oboe takes Ovid's famous literary work by the same name as its starting point. The work focuses six episodes into musical sequences that give full expression to both Britten's melodic ingenuity and the oboe's expressive range, which is expanded to include far more than just traditional technical idioms and coloristic possibilities.

Certainly one might well wonder, upon first encountering the *Metamorphoses*, why Britten chose an instrument as seemingly limited as the oboe. However rich in tone, it is basically without extensive change in color throughout its two-and-a-half octave range and is generally monophonic. Yet, upon further acquaintance with the music, it becomes clear that it is these very restrictions that attracted Britten to the instrument and which allow his melodic and harmonic metamorphoses to take center stage, unfolding with great clarity. By restricting himself so thoroughly, the musical processes can remain pure throughout the six movements.

"Pan, who played upon the reed pipe" begins with a brief six-note gesture that will be reshaped to produce all the vital material of the movement. Obviously, the many fermatas and rests that pop up throughout this and the other five movements are not only for the purposes of isolating different musical fragments, but also designed to keep the performer from passing out. Abstract, non-linear use of pseudo-traditional harmonies such as triads, dominant seventh chords with irregular resolutions, etc., abound in the following movements, telling the stories of Phaeton and Niobe. After a musical portrayal of Bacchus, Britten moves on to the appropriately reflective tale of Narcissus and finally to the waterlogged cellular variations of Ovid's Arethusa. *—Blair Johnston*

Recommended:

○ **Britten: Music for Oboe; Music for Piano** / S. Francis / 1995 / Hyperion 66776

Suite No. 1 for cello, Op. 72 (1964)

Any composer who writes a suite for unaccompanied cello takes inspiration from Johann Sebastian Bach's glorious models in some measure. Benjamin Britten, however, was just as inspired by the great cellist Mstislav Rostropovich's rich, romantic playing of the Bach suites as by the suites themselves. Britten wrote three solo suites for Rostropovich; this first one dates from 1964.

The compositional tactics here are a blend of Baroque and modern. Britten features a rich, sunny Canto at the start of the work, which is replayed in two other movements and takes on a different character each time. The first two movements proper pay homage to Bach. A fugue comes first, using Bach's technique of suggesting contrapuntal movement that is impossible to play on the cello. Yet the fugue subject is not conventional; it is snaky, with little rhythmic disturbances that make it difficult to pin down. The working-out of the subject is fairly conventional, but the music fades away at the end, leading into a movement titled "Lamento." This movement distinctly recalls the Sarabande from Bach's Fifth Cello suite; both feature winding, slow, sad and beautiful melodies played with no double stops. After a more timid version of the Canto, Britten plays with modern styles. A "Serenata" suggests an introspective flamenco with its use of pizzicato. Next, a "Marcia" begins with an oddly tinkly melody and moves into bolder strokes from the cello. These lose energy and fade into eerie high notes, which in turn lead into the next Canto—a much sadder statement than the previous two. The next movement, titled "Bordone: Moderato quasi recitativo," plays with the Baroque idea of monodic recitative over a droning bass. Finally, a devilish "Moto perpetuo" movement, with a driven, almost angry theme, begins at full speed. Britten brings back the Canto theme to stop the moto perpetuo theme in its tracks, and from there the Canto theme strives to subdue the moto perpetuo theme. They come to an uneasy truce at the movement's end. *—Andrew Lindemann Malone*

Recommended:

○ **Britten: Cello Suites 1–3** / Mørk / 2000 / Virgin 45399

Suite No. 2 for cello, Op. 80 (1967)

Like its predecessor, Benjamin Britten's Cello Suite No. 2 (1967) was inspired both by Johann Sebastian Bach's suites for solo cello and the artistry of cellist Mstislav Rostropovich. Like the first suite, the second blends Baroque forms with Britten's modern sensibility. Thus, the first two movements, a "Declamato" and a fugue, are similar in basic structure to a Bach prelude and fugue. The "Declamato" has an improvised, rhapsodic feel, sounding like an impassioned speech; quiet, pleading passages yield unexpectedly to angry, bold gestures from the cello. A very slow fugue follows. Britten makes extensive use of the *style brisé* here, which allows the composer to suggest, with melodic lines shifting between pitch levels, counterpoint that cannot actually be played on the cello. Since the fugue is so slow, however, the melodic lines are somewhat difficult to follow, giving the movement a mysterious air. A short Scherzo follows, featuring breakneck melodic motion occasionally interrupted by a four-note upward motive that seems to break off mid-flight; the whole movement seems to abhor coming to rest. Britten makes use of an unusual technique in the following Andante lento, having the cellist play a sustained melody on one string while plucking out the accompaniment on another. The winding, sad melody goes through a few variations, including one played entirely pizzicato, before ending up about where it started. The final Ciaccona, a favorite form of both Bach and Britten, carries the most weight of the movements; it is by far the longest and the fastest. The Ciaccona sounds more like a Baroque movement than any other, as it adheres relatively closely to proper chaconne form. The music moves quickly between emotional extremes, at one moment robust and joyous, at another tender and slower, but retains an almost irrepressible forward momentum until the final resolute note. Much like Britten's first cello suite, this suite is a highly creative and vital artistic response both to Bach's writing and Rostropovich's playing. *—Andrew Lindemann Malone*

Recommended:

○ **Britten: Three Suites for Violoncello Solo** / Wispelwey / 2001 / Channel Classics 17198

Suite No. 3 for cello, Op. 87 (1971; revised 1974)

The long train of purely instrumental compositions that Benjamin Britten began in the 1930s had, by the early 1950s, come almost to a standstill, and for a time he seems to have felt that his real musical future lay exclusively in the theater. The abandonment of concert music had taken place, not so coincidentally, after the sweeping success of *Peter Grimes* and the early chamber operas. Just as the association with tenor Peter Pears was crucial in helping to focus Britten's dramatic sensibilities, Britten's developing friendship with Soviet cellist Mstislav Rostropovich played an intimate role in helping to draw the composer back into the realm of pure instrumental composition. In all, five works designed for Rostropovich's very deft music-making were produced, starting with the *Cello Sonata* of 1961 and ending with the *Third Suite for cello solo*, Op. 87 of 1971.

A composer setting out to create an extensive multi-movement work for a solo string instrument can hardly avoid the influence of J.S. Bach's six such works each for both violin and cello. Britten is no exception, and throughout all three Suites we can clearly hear Bach, obviously not in the immediate musical style, but rather in the general technical blueprints and syntactic measures employed. In particular, the underlying principle of harmony by implication—a way to get around the basic technical limitations of an instrument designed more or less for single-line melodic gestures—is drawn straight from Britten's awareness of both Bach's works and the same pre-Classical lute pieces that inspired Britten's *Nocturnal* for guitar.

The Suite consists of nine individual movements which are, however, so completely thematically interconnected that the work resembles a large set of variations on a group of themes as much as a true multi-movement composition. The four melodies that Britten draws upon throughout the work are all of Russian extraction, obviously in deference to the work's dedicatee. They include three folksongs known to Britten through Tchaikovsky's transcriptions and one fragment of plainsong from the Eastern Orthodox Church liturgy for the dead. They are deployed in a manner seemingly opposite to the Classical exposition/development progression. As the first eight movements unfold, we catch only fragmentary glimpses of the four melodies as they are fused together to create new melodies and gestures for each new movement. Only at the very end of the Suite does Britten allow for a direct and unadulterated presentation of the four themes.

First, the introductory Lento movement sets up a tonally-vague series of recitando gestures (the Orthodox plainchant is the informing theme here) against a steady open C string pedal. A March follows, giving its two buoyant themes a traditional exposition and mini-development, but deflecting away into the lyric third movement (Canto) before the expected recapitulation is allowed to peek through. Sonorous arpeggiations provide a sure foundation for the following Lento, while the plucked chords of the fifth movement serve to introduce the remarkable fugue (on a sweeping subject drawn from one of Tchaikovsky's melodies) that follows. Vague, almost ghostlike thematic outlines pop up in movement seven, followed in turn by a rambunctious perpetual motion. The final movement makes thorough use of passacaglia technique; the repeated ground is drawn quite simply from the basic intervallic substance of the Russian plainchant melody. At the very end the three underlying folksongs are sung out without any foreign accoutrements whatsoever. *—Blair Johnston*

Recommended:

○ **Tavener: The Protecting Veil; Britten: Cello Suite 3** / Isserlis / 2000 / Virgin 61849

Variations on a Theme by Frank Bridge, for strings, Op. 10 (1937)

Benjamin Britten began taking composition lessons from Frank Bridge in the year of 1927. Bridge was fairly well known as a composer and a viola player, but his greatest contribution was definitely in the role of a teacher. Britten also was a violist and greatly admired Bridge's playing. Over the next few years, Britten grew immensely as a musician and as an individual. His raw talent in composition was refined and his ideals were formed under the tutelage of Bridge. In 1932, Britten wished to compose a tribute piece for his teacher and began work on a set of variations on a theme from one of Bridge's works. The young composer soon was distracted from this project and was forced to temporarily abandon work on it.

Five years later, the opportunity arose for Britten to complete the dedication composition for Bridge, and to fulfill a rather important commission. Boyd Neel, an English conductor, founded the first chamber string orchestra consisting only of players of virtuosic ability in England. The reputation of this orchestra soon spread quickly across Europe, and Neel's ensemble was invited, in May 1937, to perform at the Salzburg Festival, which was occurring the upcoming August. The only condition was that the group was required to perform a new work by a British composer. Britten was not well known at the time, but Neel had conducted his film score for *Love from a Stranger* (1936). Neel remembered being astonished by the quickness in which Britten could compose quality music. With only three months until his scheduled performance, Neel asked Britten to accept the commission and to work fast. Neel could not have expected that Britten would have completed a composition sketch of *Variations on a Theme by Frank Bridge* (1937) only ten days after accepting the task. The work was fully scored for Neel's string orchestra within a month. The finished score is dated July 12, 1937, and is dedicated "to F.B. A tribute with affection and admiration." The theme is from the second of Bridge's *Three Idylls* for string quartet.

This set of ten variations were definitely a challenge for Neel's virtuoso orchestra. With Britten's experience of playing the viola, the parts were not impossible, but they did take the performers to the boundaries of their abilities. At the orchestra's first rehearsal of the piece, the principal violist was having difficulty with a passage involving harmonics. Britten and Bridge both happened to be present at the rehearsal, and both subsequently played the passage without error.

Variations on a Theme by Frank Bridge was premiered at the Salzburg Festival on August 27, 1937, and was immediately received by the Europeans as a fine composition. The London premiere took place on October 5, 1937. For the first time, Britten's name was known on an international level as the work was performed over 50 times within the first two years of its composition in Europe and the United States. *—Chris Boyes*

Recommended:

○ **Britten: Young Person's Guide; Simple Symphony; Bridge Variations** / Britten, English CO / 1986 / London 417509

SYMPHONIC

Simple Symphony, Op. 4 (1934)

At the age of 20, perhaps feeling nostalgic, Britten set about recasting a handful of old piano tunes and song melodies from his pre-teen years into a four-movement work for string orchestra. Entitled *A Simple Symphony* (1933–34), the work contains the irresistible charm of youth projected as an array of musical colors that, although combined in a relatively sophisticated manner, retain at least the impression of innocence. The symphony's widespread popularity can be attributed to several factors, among the most significant of which is its idiomatic string writing—scoring of such technical ease that amateur ensembles and student orchestras can feel confident in undertaking it. Perhaps the real reason for the work's appeal, however, is the way that Britten refuses to wholly subordinate the pleasantly cliché-ridden fruits of his youth to the more sophisticated musical syntax that, by the mid-1930s, was emerging as the driving force behind such works as the choral *Te Deum* (1934) and the orchestral *Variations on a Theme of Frank Bridge* (1937).

However near and dear these melodies may have been to Britten's heart, he clearly felt it necessary to apply a substantial amount of touch-up as he forged them into a symphonic form. For example, the colorful twists and turns of the first movement, "Boisterous Bourée," do not really represent Britten as a child composer as much as they do a maturing composer's desire to reawaken the spirit of an earlier time. However, the movement does retain a certain juvenile spirit, especially in its heavy emphasis on the melodic contours and rhythmic cadences of English folksong.

The Presto possibile "Playful Pizzicato," with its rounded, wittily arpeggiated theme, is just what its title would seem to indicate. The trio section makes effective use of an irregular phrase structure (i.e., empty bars shape the gestures into three-bar groups). Its material is derived from a 1924 Scherzo for piano and a song that apparently dates from later in that same year.

The "Sentimental Saraband" unfolds in a straightforward ternary (ABA) form, its somber main theme first announced by the violins over a stubborn G pedal in the cellos and basses. A second melody, originally part of a waltz, is, by comparison, quite translucent, as are the gently repeated chords of the coda.

After an introduction made up of naively dramatic open fifths, the "Frolicsome Finale" takes off with a subject that recalls the cello theme of the "Boisterous Bourée"; the chromatically descending inner lines are, however, unique to this final movement. After a contrasting second theme, the first idea undergoes development. Soon enough a recapitulation arrives, during which the second theme is cast in an almost heroic light. A grand pause ushers in the kinetic coda. *—Blair Johnston*

Recommended:

○ **Bitten: Young Person's Guide; Bridge Variations; Simple Symphony** / Britten (cond.), English CO / 1986 / London 417509

ORCHESTRAL

Four Sea Interludes from Peter Grimes, Op. 33a (1944)

It has been said that with the emergence of Benjamin Britten, England produced its first composer equal in stature to longtime favorite son Henry Purcell. There are indeed strong connections between the two—indeed, Britten's sympathy for the music of the Baroque master was such that he made a number of arrangements, transcriptions, and realizations of Purcell's works—though undoubtedly this assertion is based primarily on both composers' complete mastery of the operatic medium. Britten's *Peter Grimes* (1944–45), based upon a poem of George Crabbe, has taken a place among the most important contributions to opera by a composer in any century. The struggles of its characters—most prominently, those of the tortured Grimes himself—are refracted through the metaphor of the sea, which is the lifeblood of the Borough in which the drama is set. Britten's own affinity for the nautical intimately colors the musical and dramatic action throughout. Perhaps *Peter Grimes'* most elequent expression of these concerns emerges, ironically, in those segments of the opera whose traditional role is to provide "coverage" during scene changes between acts.

The *Four Sea Interludes* (1944) constitute a suite of entr'actes that, in addition to serving a practical function, infuse the opera with probing psychological cues and suggestions. Composer John Ireland remarked upon the shattering impact of these orchestral episodes: "He really has achieved something remarkable here.... It was not pleasant or uplifting—rather Satanic, I thought." The *Interludes'* deliberate function on Britten's part is underscored by the particular care and attention that attended their creation. Apropos of the "Storm" Interlude, which Britten was asked to lengthen for practical reasons, the composer remarked that it was "like someone who came to an architect when he had just finished building a cathedral, gave him a huge slab of stone, and said, 'Here, you must find room for this.'" The *Interludes* are presented thus: "Dawn," "Sunday Morning," "Moonlight," and "Storm." Each is invested with Britten's most picturesque instrumental sense, from the emergent warmth of the triads in the low brass which bloom beneath intermittent, burbling arpegii in "Dawn" to the boiling, tempestuous morass—punctuated by Grimes' soaring "What harbor shelters peace?" motive—of "Storm." Both "Sunday Morning," with the bustle of the Borough's citizens making their way to church for morning services, and the serene respite provided by "Moonlight" display Britten's keen dramatic sense in effectively foreshadowing the action which follows. *—Michael Rodman*

Recommended:

○ **Bernstein: The Final Concert** / Bernstein (cond.), Boston SO / Tanglewood 431768

○ **Britten: Young Person's Guide; Suite on English Folk Themes & others** / Hickox (cond.), Bournemouth Sinfonietta / 1993 / Chandos 9221

Young Person's Guide to the Orchestra (Variations and Fugue on a Theme of Purcell), Op. 34 (1946)

While many composers have tried their hand at creating music with special appeal for young audiences, few nations have produced as many artists deft at so particular a craft as Great Britain. Sir Edward Elgar is perhaps the godfather of this musical line, having produced such genuinely touching, non-condescending gems as *Starlight Express* (1915) and the two *Wand of Youth* suites (1907 and 1908), warmly nostalgic works about childhood that demonstrate the composer's success both in relating effortlessly to youngsters and understanding the concept of childhood from afar.

In this regard as well as others, Benjamin Britten was Elgar's worthy successor. Britten never really escaped the lure of subjective musical innocence, yet maintained a perspective that allowed him to produce an "educational" work with the sophistication and polish of *The Young Person's Guide to the Orchestra*, Op. 34.

Britten had always been fond of the music of Henry Purcell. When asked to compose a short instructional piece to be used in a film for schools, he plundered a hornpipe from Purcell's *Abdelazer, or The Moor's Revenge* (1695) as a theme for a set of variations that colorfully puts the entire orchestra through its paces. After a brash tutti statement of the melody, each of the orchestra's four main sections—woodwinds, strings, brass, percussion—is showcased in successive variations, after which the theme is restated in all its tutti grandeur.

Each instrument type is granted some time in the spotlight. In the first, woodwind variation, impish flutes set the stage for a languid oboe duet against a pulsating string background; the clarinets take off in a circus-style whirlwind, only gradually becoming more circumspect. As the string section sets up a pattern of incisive staccati, the pompous bassoons take over to finish the woodwind showcase. Mock-virtuoso violins, sultry violas, and syncopated cellos each have their say in the string variation, and even the plodding bass musters some fiery scales and noble melodies. Britten excelled at writing for the harp, and a dramatic solo for the instrument, introduced by a stoic gong stroke, is no exception. A fanfare of horns and martial trumpet calls riding atop a galloping snare drum rhythm give way to the lower brass in the brass variation. The percussion variation begins with the timpani accompanied by excited string figures; the xylophone solo in particular stands out, as do the castanets and colorful string harmonics.

If the preceding music has perhaps seemed a trifle common—indeed, the work has at times come under critical attack for its loosely wrought connections—the following fugue, whose quicksilver subject is introduced by a pair of flutes, certainly cannot be so regarded. The grandest moment in the entire work arrives with the return of Purcell's theme—which to this point in the fugue has served as a countersubject—in its original form at the climax. Half the orchestra carries on the wild figurations of the subject, and the two melodies are sung out by the entire orchestra in glorious double counterpoint.—*Blair Johnston*

Recommended:

○ **Britten: Young Person's Guide; Simple Symphony; Bridge Variations** / Britten (cond.), English CO, London SO / 1986 / London 417509

○ **David Bowie Narrates Prokofiev's "Peter and the Wolf"** / Ormandy (cond.), Philadelphia Orch. / 1992 / RCA Victor 60878

CONCERTO

Cello Symphony, Op. 68 (1963; revised 1964)

Benjamin Britten wrote his *Symphony for Cello and Orchestra*, Op. 68, in 1963 for Mstislav Rostropovich. Having already composed a sonata for this extraordinary cellist and musician, he would eventually also dedicate to him the three solo suites and the *Tema "Sacher."*

Britten's choice to call a work for solo cello and orchestra a symphony, while unusual, seems logical on reflection: though it is as demanding as that for any concerto, the solo part is woven into the texture of the orchestra, trading off melodic motives and subsidiary roles with other instruments. Also, the piece comprises four movements, more typical of the symphonic genre than that of the concerto. The cello begins the first movement, Allegro Maestoso, right away with no orchestral introduction, another characteristic that helps to break the idea of the piece as a concerto. The first passage is built on dissonant chords in the cello part, which is agitated from the start. The cello part gains in intensity, hits a period of relief, and then begins rebuilding. In the more intense moments it is as if the orchestra is prodding the cellist along. The cello part shifts in terms of melodic importance. Usually it appears as the solo melody, but sometimes it creates background texture while another instrument has the melody. There is a middle section that is expressive and lyrical, but then the intensity reappears and builds for some time before finally dying away at the end of the movement.

The second movement, marked Presto Inquieto, is restless in character, full of energetic undercurrents, even in the more lyrical sections. The cello and orchestra trade off the underlying energy as the melody swirls over the top of everything. Soft in overall dynamic range, this movement has an eerie feel to it.

The following Adagio begins with a timpani roll and a beautiful, rich solo cello melody. The strings accompany in a similar manner, but the agitated timpani sharply contrast the melodic feel. The timpani returns throughout, like a heartbeat pounding to interrupt the otherwise tranquil mood. The adagio leads into the cello cadenza, explosive, dissonant, and melodically intense. It leads directly into the fourth movement, a Passacaglia. The cello part continues the cadenza melody that becomes the ground bass part as the trumpets enter with a new melodic motif. These two tunes, intertwined, set the stage for six variations and a coda to follow. Some of the variations feature the cello more than others, but the orchestra plays a prominent role in most parts. The overall texture grows thick at times, but in the end the cello cuts through it all to create an exciting finale. —*Emily Stoops*

Recommended:

○ **Britten: Young Person's Guide; Cello Symphony; Sea Interludes; Pärt** / N. Järvi (cond.), Mørk, Bergen PO / 1988 / Bis 420

Violin Concerto in D minor, Op. 15 (1939; revised 1950)

Composed in 1939, this violin concerto was written at the close of a magical decade for violinists in which more great concertos for their instrument appeared than any other time (Stravinsky, Bartók, Bloch, Hindemith, Berg, Prokofiev, Khachaturian, Sessions, Walton). It has never really been absent from the repertoire, but violinists who are seeking to add a concerto of this era to their repertoires generally choose the Stravinsky, Berg, or Prokofiev in preference to it. It is one of the first works Britten wrote after resettling in the United States. Britten uses a novel procedure in his sonata allegro (here, actually marked "moderato con moto") first movement: the gentle and tender opening theme (which is initially announced over a soft timpani figure) vies in the development with the aggressive second subject and wins by absorbing all the elements of the second theme into itself; when the recapitulation comes, the second subject is entirely absent. The middle movement is a scherzo which has aspects of the first, including the opening drum pattern. For the finale, the largest movement of the score, Britten provided the first of his notable line of magnificent passacaglias. Britten devised a theme of a sort that would return in important works: a patterned set of notes that moves itself around the circle of 12 available tones. He uses it to reach a conclusion that, rarely for violin concertos (a genre that usually ends with a flourish), concludes in territory unsettled as to whether it is major or minor. —*Joseph Stevenson*

Recommended:

○ **Britten: Violin Concerto; Walton: Viola Concerto** / Rostropovich (cond.), Vengerov, London SO / 2003 / EMI 57510

Leo Brouwer

b. Mar. 1, 1939, Havana, Cuba
Composer: Chamber Music

Progressive Cuban composer and conductor Leo Brouwer was encouraged musically by his father, an amateur guitarist, and began playing the guitar when he was 13. He then became a descendant in an important guitar lineage: Isaac Nicola, his first real instructor, had studied under Emilio Pujol, who himself had been a student of Francisco Tárrega.

Brouwer gave his first performance at 17 and soon was composing music as well. His *Prelude* was written in 1956 followed by *Fugue* in 1959. He furthered his musical education in America, studying composition at the Juilliard School and at Hart College in Hartford.

He became director of the Music Department of the Cinema Institute of Cuba in 1961 as well as professor of composition in the Music Conservatory and musical advisor to the National Radio and Television Chair of Havana. He was also named director of the experimental department of the Cuban Institute of Cinema Arts and Industry, where he continued his own work as composer.

Brouwer was the first Cuban composer to use aleatory forms in his compositions. His varied output includes many works for guitar; percussion; prepared and non-prepared piano; a ballet; a chorus of 12 members, three children, and harp; and several orchestral pieces. He has also written music for more than 100 films.

Brouwer's early compositions reflect a Cuban influence and are strongly rhythmic while his later works veer towards a more minimalist style. His passion for the guitar has remained and he is perhaps best known for his *Etudes Simples*, a group of 20 studies for the classical guitar where technique and musicality function as one. Brouwer has also explored the possibilities of large-scale works for the guitar, particularly in a piece written for the 1979 Esztergom Guitar Competition in Hungary. For the event, Brouwer composed a piece utilizing an orchestra composed of 200 guitarists.

Beyond his compositional output, Brouwer has conducted some of the world's leading orchestras including the Philharmonic Orchestra of Berlin, BBC Concert Orchestra, Orchestra Nouvelle Philharmonic de Paris, and the Symphonic Orchestra of Madrid. In addition, Brouwer retains duties as principal conductor of the Cordoba Symphony in Spain, artistic director of the Havana Symphony and a member of the International Council of Music. Brouwer has also participated as a guitarist and composer in the festivals of Aldeburgh, Avignon, Edinburgh, Spoleto, Berlin, Toronto, Martinique, and Rome, among others. —*Tod Whitesel*

CHAMBER MUSIC

Works for Guitar (1955)

Cuban-born Leo (Juan Leovigildo) Brouwer has been called one of the most important composers for guitar in the later twentieth and early twenty-first centuries. His output includes numerous compositions for solo performance, such as preludes, studies (*20 Simple Studies*), dances, and various free-form pieces, as well as compositions involving orchestra, which include six concertos and a concerto for guitar, violin, and strings (*Omaggio a Paganini*; 1994–95).

Brouwer has exhibited various trends in his style over the years, including folk influences (particularly Afro-Cuban), serial methods, and minimalism. His guitar music has generally been quite tuneful and approachable throughout most of his stylistic phases. The concertos are probably the most important group of works in his guitar output. The third, *Concerto Elegiaco* (1985) and fourth, *Concerto de Toronto* (1990), are probably the most popular. The former, written for virtuoso guitarist Julian Bream, is cast in three movements—"Tranquillo," Interlude, and Finale (Toccata)—and is generally elegiac in character as its nickname suggests, but it is not without its share of tension and brilliant rhythmic music, as demonstrated by the colorful Toccata. The *Concerto de Toronto* also has three movements—Moderato, Theme and Variations, and Tempo Libero, Allegro—and features a charming melody in the middle panel on which Brouwer fashions a series of highly inventive variations. The fifth concerto, *Concerto de Helsinki* (1992), has also received attention and may well advance toward repertory status. Also cast in three movements, each with a subtitle—"Spaces," "Lightness and Heaviness," and "Luminosity"—the work divulges the composer's minimalist tendencies and is powerfully atmospheric both in its often hypnotic guitar writing and haunting orchestral scoring.

Brouwer's solo works can hardly be neglected; even among the first several pieces will one rarely hear immature or awkward writing. The earliest ones, such as *Preludio* (1956), *Danza Caracteristica* (1957), and the two-movement *Elogio de la Danza* (1964), reflect the Afro-Cuban folk influence mentioned earlier. Without doubt, the most popular collection of guitar pieces in Brouwer's output is the 1981 *Preludios Epigrammaticos for guitar*, probably his most heavily recorded major effort. Many will find their lyricism dry but subtle; their generally unhurried tempos somewhat lacking in variety, but essential in the creation of mood; and atmosphere.

There are many other important solo works, of course, such as a powerful 1990 sonata, the 1978 *Berceuse, Cancion de Cuna*, and the *Canticum 1968*, all of which are deserving of greater attention. There are charming chamber works involving guitar, too, including the 1958 effort *Homenaje a Falla for guitar, flute, oboe, and clarinet.* While evaluation of Brouwer's art will continue well into the twenty-first century, it is safe to declare that many of his guitar compositions will live on within and well beyond the borders of Cuba, having already been performed and recorded by some of the finest virtuoso guitarists of the day, including John Williams and Julian Bream. *—Robert Cummings*

Recommended:

○ **Leo Brouwer: La obra guitarrística** / A. Rodriguez / Egrem 8001

○ **Leo Brouwer: Guitar Music, Vol. 1** / Cobo / 1997 / Naxos 553630

○ **Brouwer: From Yesterday to Penny Lane; Concierto de Toronto** / Brouwer (cond.), Guerra, Orquesta Sinfónica Nacional / 1993 / Egrem 60

Cancion de Cuna, for guitar (ca. 1970)

Cuban composer Leo Brouwer has been strongly identified with the guitar throughout his career. While his style often divulged folk influences—especially early in his career—it was generally individual, even though Afro-Cuban elements still seeped into it. Probably inspired by *Canción de Cuna* (Cradle Song) by Federico Garcia Lorca (1898–1936), Spanish poet and dramatist, this *Berceuse* has a lullaby-like manner in its gentle, serene theme.

It opens with a pizzicato rhythmic idea, after which a simple but lovely theme is introduced, really a more developed version of the rhythmic motif. It is somewhat restricted in its range and has a rocking, soothing character in its unhurried gait. The opening material returns and, in fact, alternates with the main theme throughout. A brief second subject, which begins with a lively ascending run, appears twice to offer imaginative contrast while not actually breaking the dreamy mood. The piece ends quietly with the gentle rhythmic motif having the last say. Lasting nearly four minutes, this beautiful work must be counted as at least a minor masterpiece in the guitar literature. *—Robert Cummings*

Recommended:

○ **Cantos y Danzas** / Barrueco / 1998 / EMI 556578

○ **Seven Latin American Composers** / Guiscafre / 1999 / Jaime Guiscafre 000

Danza Característica, for guitar (1957)

This is among the earliest of Brouwer's compositions and thus divulges his penchant for mixing African and Cuban folk elements. Yet, despite whatever ethnic influences one hears in this music, it has an individual stamp of its own, a bold style. And Brouwer was only 18 when he wrote the piece, having begun study of the guitar just five years earlier. The work carries a subtitle that suggests humor—*Get off of the Sidewalk* (Quitate de la acera).

The piece opens with a busy running figure, after which several rhythmic motifs are heard in succession, each seemingly attempting to ignite a more permanent thematic flow. The final one is a blunt bouncy statement whose emphatic manner and sense of drama fails to bring a resolution to the roiling atmosphere. A brief middle-section theme of childlike character offers a moment of respite, but the tension soon begins building again and the main thematic material is reprised. Lasting about two minutes, this piece, replete with rich colors and sonic effects, is a delight most guitar fanciers should find to their liking. *—Robert Cummings*

Recommended:

○ **John Williams: Spirit of the Guitar** / J. Williams / 1989 / Sony 44898

El decamerón negro (Black Decameron), for guitar (1981)

Cuban composer Leo Brouwer's three-movement work *El Decamerón negro* ("Black Decameron") rapidly became recognized as one of the most important additions to the solo guitar repertory of the last quarter of the twentieth century.

Brouwer (b. 1939) studied in the United States during the last half of the 1950s at the University of Hartford and at the Juilliard School of Music and studied composition with Stefan Wolpe and Vincent Persichetti. He held a number of important posts in Cuban musical life and beginning around 1962 he became a leader of avant-garde music in Cuba and was frequently heard at the Warsaw Autumn festivals, one of the leading venues for new music. He used serial (12-tone) and aleatory (chance) devices in his music of this period. The guitarist has written a notable body of works for that instrument, though he has much music for other instruments as well.

Around 1980, just before this piece was composed, he began to edge away from the avant-garde vocabulary of his earlier works. He succinctly described the course of the music of his time, as it affected his stylistic development, as follows: "The avant-garde put an end to a monotonous dialogue which existed in music and replaced it with very aggressive language, which became too aggressive and which lacked equilibrium. Human beings, today, need a more cordial form of expression, more warm, more tangible."

Composition of this suite stems from his hearing the playing of the Canadian guitar virtuoso Sharon Isbin in 1975: "I was possessed by the clarity and poetry in her playing, as well as by her technical accuracy and perfection—her music-making was sheer pleasure." He added, "from the very first two notes I had found the interpreter: Sharon Isbin." Brouwer composed the music and dedicated to Isbin without telling her, "just imagining how it would sound in her hands." She premiered it in 1983.

The suite is neo-Romantic in style, Brouwer says, and is programmatic. It is based on love stories from Africa, collected from folk sources during the nineteenth century by the German anthropologist Leon Frobenius. It is in three movements, which may be played in any order. These notes follow the order recorded by Isbin.

"El arpa del guerrero" (The Warrior's Harp) contrasts dramatic and rhythmic passages with lyrical moments. A warrior is banished because he has taken up playing the harp. But he returns to lead his people in battle when invaded. After his victory, he is condemned to exile again, but escapes with his lover.

"La huida de los amantes por el valle de los ecos" (Flight of the Lovers through the Valley of Echoes) seems to follow their flight. Horseback rhythms alternate with love music, and there is a dazzling portrayal of the sound of the horse's hooves echoing off the valley walls.

"Balada de la doncella enamorada" (Ballad of the Young Girl in Love) is a passionate rondo using one of the love tunes of the prior movement. *—Joseph Stevenson*

Recommended:

○ **Road to the Sun: Latin Romances for Guitar** / Isbin / 1990 / Virgin 59591

Ojos Brujos, for guitar (ca. 1970)

Havana-born Leo Brouwer has as strong a connection to the guitar as almost any other twentieth- or twenty-first century composer. Yet, he also has written prolifically in other genres, such as film music, with more than 60 scores to his credit, ballet, choral and chamber music. His style can be eclectic, though early on it divulged an influence of African and Cuban folk music, a mix he has never completely gotten away from. This work, *Ojos Brujos* (Sorcerer's Eyes), features a memorable melody, which Brouwer borrowed from composer Gonzalo Roig.

The tune has a sentimental, somewhat sad sense in its nocturnal character, and Brouwer, a master arranger of music, even of popular music for guitar, milks it for all its touching beauty. The theme has a mostly descending contour and a serene, peaceful manner, as if whatever sadness that inspired it is quite bearable. In the middle section a lovely variant appears, after which the melody switches to the lower ranges and the music turns, if not brighter, a bit less melancholy. The work lasts about two minutes and enjoyed a good measure of popularity. *—Robert Cummings*

Recommended:

○ **Possession** / Afshar / 2002 / Archer 1919

Earle Brown

b. Dec. 26, 1926, Lunenburg, MA, **d.** Jul. 2, 2002, Rye, NY

Composer: Avant-Garde

Earle Brown was born in Lunenberg, a farm town in Worcester County in central Massachusetts. He picked up the trumpet at age ten and led a small dance band through high school. While at Northwestern University in Chicago, studying engineering and mathematics, Brown played weekends in a "territory" jazz band. He joined the Air Force to become a pilot, but wound up in an Army band unit. Therein Brown met a fellow player who sparked his interest in the Joseph Schillinger method of musical composition. After Brown was discharged, he embarked on four years of study at Schillinger House in Boston (now Berklee School of Music) under Brogue Henning. His earliest works, such as the *Music for Violin, Cello and Piano,* are 12-tone based and make use of methods derived from the Schillinger system.

In 1951, in Denver Earle Brown first met composer John Cage. Cage invited Brown to move to New York City the following year. Earle Brown worked with Cage and David Tudor in the *Project for Music for Magnetic Tape.* During that time, Brown created a key pioneering electronic work, the *Octet for Eight Loudspeakers,* the first piece of musique concrète to be executed in multi-track stereo. Later that year, Brown worked on a series of compositions entitled *Folio* that one by one began to reduce certain elements of notation. In *December, 1952* Brown dispensed with conventional notation altogether, utilizing instead a simple graph as the composition with instructions for performance. *December, 1952* is recognized as a landmark work of the 1950s, as it introduced graphic notation, which would soon be widely adopted into the mainstream of the avant-garde.

Brown is often lumped together with Cage, Tudor, Morton Feldman, and Christian Wolff as the "New York School." This is a convenient handle used to identify New York composers of the 1950s who were, in approach, seen as analogous in music to the Abstract Expressionist style of painting then current among New York-based artists. They were all friends, and it is true that Jackson Pollock and his drip canvases provided a major source of inspiration to Earle Brown, as did the spindly mobiles of Alexander Calder. But to lump Brown in with any specific era or style does not do him justice. In later compositions he moved into realms where he took greater amounts of the music back, and put the ordering of the material into the hands of the a conductor. In 1964, Brown and Leonard Bernstein both conducted the premiere of his *Available Forms I* with the New York Philharmonic, and Brown since composed several large-scale orchestral works. At the other end of the spectrum, some Brown pieces are completely notated and only a few seconds in length.

Earle Brown took a very active role in personally attending to performances and recordings of his own music. Brown enjoyed composer residencies at Cologne, Basle, the University of California at Los Angeles, the California Institute of the Arts, University of Southern California, the University of California at Berkeley, Peabody, University of Cincinnati, Indiana University in Bloomington, the American Academy at Rome, and at Yale. The Peabody Institute of Music awarded Brown an honorary Doctorate of Music in 1970; he also received a Guggenheim Fellowship and an award from the National Institute of Arts and Letters. Brown said "I have certainly never been embarrassed by writing a beautiful melody, a very lyrical passage, or what I consider a beautiful chord progression. But I'm also interested in activating the interaction between composers and performers, and making music a more collaborative world—not in all cases, but some." *—Uncle Dave Lewis*

AVANT-GARDE

Available Forms I for 18 instruments (1961)

Composed in 1961, Earle Brown's *Available Forms* is an open-form work in graphic notation for 18 performers. It deals with sound and form as flexible materials that can be molded, shaped, modified, and arranged in real time by cues from the conductor. Consequently, each performance may sound completely different from any other. The score consists of six loose pages (similar to John Cage's *Variations* and other works) with four or five numbered musical "events" on each page—in other words, "available forms." In performance, these numbered events may occur in any order, according to the discretion of the conductor. The conductor cues each new event by gesturing with the appropriate number of fingers. In devising the pliable structures of *Available Forms*, Brown was particularly influenced by the mobile sculptures of Alexander Calder.

There have been many wonderful performances of this work; especially notable are the ones by conductor/composer Bruno Maderna. A work along similar principles and aesthetics is Brown's *Available Forms II* written for 98 instrumentalists and two conductors premiered at the Venice Biennale in 1962. Brown is one of the few composers to truly understand the possibilities of "indeterminate" composition and how to make works using indeterminacy into a rich experience for both performances and listeners. In *Available Forms*, Brown calls for music-making rooted in the spontaneous moment, trusting in the spirit, musical intelligence, and awareness of performers. The piece is then not just a mirror of the composer, but the performers and conductor as well. *—"Blue Gene" Tyranny*

Octet I for 8 loudspeakers (1953)

Octet I for Eight Loudspeakers was created as the second work undertaken by The Project for Music for Magnetic Tape. This was an enterprise begun by composer John Cage in order to explore the possibilities of creating electronic music directly onto magnetic tape, a technological development that had only lately become available. The main participants in the project were composers Cage, Earle Brown, and David Tudor, with the husband and wife team Louis and Bebe Barron providing studio access and a library of sounds. The first piece produced by the team was Cage's *Williams Mix*, completed on January 16, 1953.

Earle Brown's *Octet I for Eight Loudspeakers* was constructed immediately afterward, and like *Williams Mix*, it was created in eight-channel Surround Sound. This was achieved by making eight separate half-track mono tapes to be played on eight tape machines—Brown's score contains a diagram recommending placement for the individual speakers. In the twenty-first century the technology to create a Surround Sound CD capable of playing back all eight channels in exactly the configuration Brown originally specified is a reality; this indicates how ahead of its time The Project for Music for Magnetic Tape really was.

In terms of content, *Octet I for eight Loudspeakers* utilizes the same basic cricket and frog sounds collected by the Barrons that appear in *Williams Mix*, but has an entirely different effect. Whereas the Cage work was derived from a 183-page score and a typically rigorous application of the *I Ching*, Brown based his composition on a simple graphic score of only a few pages. The pieces are roughly equal in length, but the Brown is as spatially distinct and understated as the Cage is dense. Brown created a sequel to this work entitled *Octet II*, of which the score is still extant, but it was never realized in Brown's lifetime. *—Uncle Dave Lewis*

Recommended:

- ○ **Earle Brown: Times Five; Octet I; Decmeber 1952 & others** / E. Brown / 2000 / CRI 851

Iona Brown

b. Jan. 7, 1941, Salisbury, England, **d.** Jun. 5, 2004, Salisbury, England
Violinist, Conductor

Iona Brown, violinist and conductor, was best known for her work with chamber orchestras. Her family was a highly musical one, and she was encouraged to explore her talents from a young age. She joined the National Youth Orchestra of Great Britain in 1955, remaining with it for five years. She was then sent to the Continent to study; her teachers were Hugh Maguire in London, Remy Principe in Rome, and Henryk Szeryng in Paris and Nice. She also studied music in Vienna and Brussels.

While also working in the Philharmonia Orchestra (1963–66), Brown joined the Academy of St Martin-in-the-Fields in 1964 as a violinist and quickly developed an interest in conducting. She made her debut as conductor of a *Proms* concert in 1965, appearing regularly with the Academy ever since. In 1974 Marriner decreased the time he spend with the Academy, and named Brown as artistic director. Since then she has often conducted the Academy in concert and on a large number of recordings, primarily on the Philips label. In 1981 she also became artistic and music director of the Norwegian Chamber Orchestra. She brought it into the front rank of international rank chamber ensembles; in 1967 she received an appointment as music director of the Los Angeles Chamber Orchestra. She conducted many of the world's major symphony orchestras, including the Saint Louis Symphony, the San Francisco Symphony, and the City of Birmingham Symphony Orchestra (of which she was guest director from 1985 to 1989). In 1996 she was appointed chief conductor of the Danish Philharmonic Orchestra.

As a violinist, she recorded Bartók's *Second Violin Concerto* and David Blake's violin concerto, which was written for her. She was awarded the Order of the British Empire in 1986 and the Knight of First Class Order of Merit of Norway in 1991. *—Joseph Stevenson*

Recommended:

- ○ **Vivaldi: La Cetra** / Marriner (cond.), Brown, Hogwood, Bennett, Latchem, Academy of St. Martin-in-the-Fields / 1996 / London 448110
- ○ **Grieg & Nielsen: Music for Strings** / Brown (cond.), Norwegian CO / 1996 / Virgin 45224
- ○ **Mozart: Violin Concertos 1, 3 & 5** / Brown (violin & cond.), Academy of St. Martin-in-the-Fields / 1992 / London 433170
- ○ **Vaughan Williams: The Lark Ascending, etc.** / Marriner (cond.), Brown, Bennett, Kanga, Shingles, Academy of St. Martin-in-the-Fields / 1985 / Argo 414595

John Browning

b. May 22, 1933, Denver, CO, **d.** Jan. 26, 2003, Sister Bay, WI
Pianist

John Browning ranks among the very few truly virtuoso pianists of the post-Vladimir Horowitz era. A large technique, the ability to draw a broad spectrum of colors and deep reserves of sound from his instrument, and total investment in his work have marked him as one of the most important artists of his time. Among his American contemporaries, he alone has sustained a career in which there has been only a steady enrichment of artistry without detours caused by injury or emotional crisis.

His parents were both musicians: his father a violinist, his mother a pianist. He grew up in Denver and began keyboard studies at five years of age. He recalls the aftermath of a civic concert in which composer/pianist Béla Bartók and violinist Joseph Szigeti visited his parents' home and he saw his mother sitting at her piano turning pages for Bartók. His first public appearance came as soloist with the Denver Symphony at the age of ten. Summer classes with Josef and Rosina Lhévinne later led to more extended study with Mrs. Lhévinne at Juilliard School of Music in New York. When the family moved to Los Angeles, further studies with Lee Pattison solidified an increasingly solid technique and introduced him to most of the works that now form his repertory.

Several major awards propelled Browning to a successful career. In 1954, he won the Steinway Centennial Award, in 1955 he placed first in the esteemed Leventritt Competition, and in 1956 he gained second prize in the Queen Elisabeth International Music Competition in Brussels.

In 1956, Browning made his debut with the New York Philharmonic and has since appeared in nearly every important music center in the world. His debut recording, taped when he was 25 and now available once more on CD, reveals a fully-fledged musician, already in complete possession of a polished technique and a probing musicality.

Browning's artistry attracted the attention of composer Samuel Barber, and in 1962 a new piano concerto was introduced to the public in New York with Browning performing under the direction of Erich Leinsdorf. The Barber *Piano Concerto* was applauded by the critics and audience alike and has, ever since, remained the centerpiece of Browning's repertory. Two recordings were made, the first with George Szell and the Cleveland Orchestra, the second with Leonard Slatkin directing the St. Louis Symphony. The latter was awarded the first of two Grammys won by Browning (his second was for a collection of Barber solo piano pieces).

A select repertory, all of it tailored to a pianist of Olympian power and authority, embraces Mozart, Beethoven, Chopin, Brahms, Tchaikovsky, Rachmaninov, Prokofiev, and Ravel. Among later twentieth century composers, Barber figures prominently, as does Richard Cumming, who has also written several solo piano works for Browning.

In addition to appearances with most of the major orchestras in the United States and Europe, Browning has toured Russia on four occasions and is a regular guest at America's most celebrated summer festivals. He has been featured at Ravinia, Tanglewood, the Blossom Music Festival, Wolf Trap, and at Lincoln Center's Mostly Mozart Festival. *—Erik Eriksson*

Recommended:

- ○ **Barber** / Slatkin (cond.), Browning, St. Louis SO / 1991 / RCA 60732
- ○ **Liszt** / Browning / 1985 / Delos 3022
- ○ **Barber** / Browning / 1988 / Phoenix USA 105

Max Bruch

b. Jan. 6, 1838, Cologne, Germany, **d.** Oct. 20, 1920, Friedenau, Germany
Composer: Concerto, Chamber Music

While the music of Max Bruch generally strikes listeners as beautiful, imaginative, and high-minded, critics have tended to relegate him to the status of a minor master. Bruch started composing as a child, displaying an extraordinary musical talent which was recognized as such by Ignaz Moscheles. In 1852, he wrote a symphony and a string quartet, the latter work bringing him a scholarship from the Frankfurt-based Mozart foundation, which enabled him to study with Ferdinand Breunung, Ferdinand Hiller, and Carl Reinecke. In 1858, having embarked on a teaching career in Cologne, he produced his first opera, *Scherz, List und Rache*. He visited several important German cultural centers between 1861 and 1862. From 1862 to 1864, Bruch lived in Mannheim, where he wrote his cantata, *Frithjof*, which audiences received with great enthusiasm. In addition, Bruch's opera *Loreley* was produced in 1863. After leaving his Mannheim post, Bruch visited Paris and Brussels, eventually accepting the position of music director in Koblenz in 1865. In 1867, Bruch became Court Kapellmeister in Sonderhausen, remaining at that post until 1870. That year, Bruch moved to Berlin, where his third opera, *Hermione*, was produced in 1872. Between 1873 and 1878, Bruch, enjoying his reputation as an eminent German composer, worked independently in Bonn. In 1881, however, he resumed his career as a conductor, succeeding Julius Benedict as conductor of the Liverpool Philharmonic Society in England, but he did not get along with the players, who had rather lax standards. In 1883 Bruch left Liverpool and became director of the Breslau (now Wroclaw, Poland) Orchesterverein, where he stayed through the end of the season in 1890.

That autumn, Bruch took up an appointment as professor of composition at the Berlin Hochschule für Musik, working there until his retirement in 1910 and retaining his rank as a professor there until his death in 1920.

During his lifetime he had a reputation as destined to become one of music's great composers. Bruch's best-known work is without doubt his passionately romantic *Violin Concerto No. 1 in G minor* (1868), a major item in the standard violin repertoire. His next most often played work is the single-movement work for cello and orchestra, *Kol Nidrei*. This lovely composition is representative of his interest in setting melodic material originating from other ethnic groups; he wrote works on Russian, Swedish, Scottish, and Celtic melodies as well. These other works, and his symphonies, have not worn well and are rarities, sometimes revived in the concert hall and on records and on those occasions usually favorably surprising the audience for their beauty and fine workmanship. *—Joseph Stevenson*

CONCERTO

Concerto for clarinet, viola & orchestra in E minor, Op. 88 (1911)

This work from late in Max Bruch's career, though written when atonality and dissonance were coming to the fore, is very much music of the Romantic age, or at least of the period's more classically reserved, Brahmsian element. Bruch avoids sharp contrasts and dramatic outbursts; he seems to be taking his cue from the similarities between the two solo instruments, whose ranges are practically identical.

It's the viola that gets the first word in the opening Andante con moto, in a short, rhapsodic passage punctuated by orchestral chords. The clarinet then voices the same material itself, and the two instruments begin to intertwine. But the clarinet utters the first statement of the movement's true principal theme, a long, slow, autumnal melody. Bruch then undertakes a pattern of phrase trading between the soloists, rounding off the movement's subsections with small duets. The composer basically employs sonata form, but the structure is obscured by the slow harmonic and metrical motion; the music seems more rhapsodic than it really is.

Although marked Allegro molto, the second movement sounds no faster than the first, thanks to Bruch's reliance on longer-held notes. The soloists here work in duet far more consistently than in the first movement. Again, the writing is highly lyrical, although it lacks truly memorable melodies. Pizzicato accompaniment brings a little more animation to the movement's second episode, although the solo lines remain long and maintain a nostalgic feeling. The first section returns in full, and what initially seems to be a reappearance of the second section turns out to be merely a coda.

The concluding Allegro molto promises more vigor with its opening brass fanfares and swirling string figures, the latter soon picked up by the soloists in turn. If the slow movement at times suggested late Richard Strauss, particularly the later composer's *Duet Concertino*, the more outgoing portions of this movement seem to have influenced the early symphonies of Franz Schmidt. These animated passages, spurred on by the orchestra, alternate with slightly more subdued sections showcasing the soloists, who work through busy material derived from the opening section. *—James Reel*

Recommended:

- ○ **The Clarinet in Concert** / A. Francis (cond.), T. King, N. Imai, London SO / 1997 / Hyperion 22017

Kol Nidrei, Op. 47

German composer Max Bruch subtitled his *Kol Nidrei* "An Adagio on Hebrew Themes for Cello and Orchestra." Composed in 1881, the work is based on two Jewish themes that Bruch described as "first-class." "The first is an age-old Hebrew song of atonement, the second (D major) is the middle section of a moving and truly magnificent song 'O Weep for Those That Wept on Babel's Stream' (setting words by the English poet Byron), equally very old. I got to know both melodies in Berlin, where I had much to do with the children of Israel in the Choral Society," wrote the composer. However, as has been pointed out by Jewish musicians and scholars since the work's premiere, Bruch's secular treatment of the themes hardly qualifies his *Kol Nidrei*, a piece of Jewish music. As Bruch himself recognized, his *Kol Nidrei* is no more a Jewish work than his *Scottish Fantasy* is a Scottish work. In both works, Bruch treated the themes as folk tunes that he took as themes for art music compositions. Bruch was, nevertheless, a master at transforming his "folk tunes" into art music, but still retaining their folk elements. The combination of Bruch's late Romantic expressive harmonies and his Jewish themes created a work of great power and beauty that has maintained its place in the repertoire. *—James Leonard*

Recommended:

- ○ **Romantic Adagios** / Vladimir Ashkenazy (cond.), Harrell, Philharmonia Orch. / 1999 / Decca 466710

Scottish Fantasy, Op. 46

Bruch composed this work in 1880 for violinist Pablo de Sarasate, who played the first performance at Hamburg in September of that year. The orchestra includes two each of winds, trumpets and percussion, four horns, three trombones, and timpani. The Nazis lumped Bruch among a host of "racially impure" composers (including Mendelssohn and Mahler) whose music they banned. Yet this son of a noted soprano and a civil servant was descended from German-Protestant stock. Although his canon included two string quartets and nearly 50 works for chorus and orchestra, he is chiefly remembered today for the first violin concerto, the *Scottish Fantasy*, and a variation setting for cello and orchestra of the Yom Kippur chant *Kol Nidrei*—most likely the reason for his blacklisting by the "Thousand-Year Reich."

Following Paganini's meteoric career after he left Italy, the most famous nineteenth century violinists were German-schooled Joseph Joachim (who played the definitive version of Bruch's first concerto in 1868), and the virtuosic Spanish showman, Pablo de Sarasate. For the latter, Bruch composed not only his second concerto (in 1877) and *Scottish Fantasy*, but a failed third concerto and a serenade. Bruch wrote more for Sarasate than did any other composer, and while Bruch was fonder of his *Second Concerto*, the *Fantasia Freely Using Scottish Folk Melodies* (the present work's formal title) proved to be far more popular.

Bruch freely admitted the influence exerted upon the work by Sir Walter Scott, whose writings had ensnared Bruch's attention during a conducting stint in England in 1880; Scott's *Lady of the Lake* inspired a subsequent cantata, *Das Feuerkreuz*. The *Fantasia* opens with a slow, solemnly bardic introduction for brass and harp, and then a recitative for the soloist on a soft cushion of strings. This leads directly to an Adagio cantabile in E flat major, based on the song *"Auld Robin Morris,"* with the harp nearly as prominent as the violin's decorations.

The G major second movement has various titles—"Scherzo: Allegro" and "Dance"—and is based on "Hey, the Dusty Miller." Drone basses imitate the sound of bagpipes, while the violin adds all manner of pyrotechnics after it introduces the tune on double-stopped strings (two strings played with one stroke of the bow). The merriment ends with a bridge passage recalling "Auld Robin Morris." This leads without pause to the third movement, a set of plushly sonorous variations in slower time, Andante sostenuto, on the song "I'm Down for Lack o' Johnnie." The violin rhapsodizes eloquently throughout, and concludes with a memorable sigh.

Bruch gave his finale the same warlike marking, Allegro guerriero, that Mendelssohn used in the last movement of his *Scottish Symphony*. "Scots wha hae" is the dominant folk melody, legendarily sung by Robert the Bruce at the Battle of Bannockburn. The violin adds excitement by playing on two, three, even four strings simultaneously until a tender reprise of the first movement. "Scots wha hae" returns, however, to conclude the four-movement work rousingly. *—Roger Dettmer*

Recommended:

- ○ **Bruch: The Complete Violin Concertos** / Masur (cond.), Accardo, Leipzig Gewandhaus Orch. / 1998 / Philips 462167
- ○ **David Oistrakh: Bruch, Berlioz** / Rozhdestvensky (cond.), D. Oistrakh, USSR SO / 1997 / Russian Revelation 10051
- ○ **Sibelius: Violin Concerto; Bruch: Scottish Fantasy** / Mehta (cond.), Midori, Isreal PO / 1994 / Sony 58967

Violin Concerto No. 1 in G minor, Op. 26 (1864–1867)

Bruch wrote six substantial multi-movement works for violin and orchestra, but only this—the first of his three official concertos—and his *Scottish Fantasy* remain familiar today. Compensating for such neglect is the fact that this is one of the most popular nineteenth century concertos in the repertory, which is all the more remarkable because it was the first big orchestral work Bruch ever published. It didn't come easily to him. Bruch first sketched out the concerto in 1857, but withdrew it after its 1866 premiere. After a thorough revision based on suggestions from a number of violinists and composers, most notably the violin virtuoso Joseph Joachim, Bruch released a final version in 1868. It was premiered by and dedicated to Joachim. Although he cast the work in the traditional fast-slow-fast sequence, Bruch generated each movement in sonata form, connecting them all without pause.

The first movement, Allegro moderato, carries the subtitle *Vorspiel* (Prelude), a holdover from when Bruch was intending to call this a fantasy rather than concerto. A quiet timpani roll and a few disconsolate woodwind phrases set the stage for the violin's meditative entrance, a melody that rises gradually. This is all repeated a bit more assertively, until the full orchestra takes forceful control of the woodwind motif, and the violin spins out a long, impassioned theme over quivering strings and ominous timpani thuds. The second principal subject is more songful and lies lower in the violin's range, until a series of trills take it into a more ardent high register where it hovers for quite some time. The first theme is presented again, double-stops doubling its intensity. This launches the development section, a stormy sequence for the orchestra during which the violin holds its peace. In the return to the movement's opening bars, the violin's solo phrases now serve as abbreviated cadenzas. A short orchestral recapitulation-coda combo leads to the second movement.

The Adagio is a nostalgic aria for the violin. The solo writing becomes increasingly intricate, drifting into a more ardent, but less clearly defined second subject that culminates in three heaving sighs for the orchestra and then the soloist. Bruch subjects all this to a heart-on-sleeve development, deeply emotional without quite becoming mawkish. The recapitulation eases off and inserts a very brief pause before the final movement.

That's the Allegro energetico, which after a careful orchestral buildup turns out to be a joyful dance in a faintly Hungarian style (a tribute both to Joachim, who was Hungarian, and to the Joachim-influenced finale of the Brahms *Violin Concerto*). The dance theme is succeeded by some scurrying virtuosic material for the soloist and then a grand romantic melody that creates a climax of its own near the end of the exposition section. Bruch's idea of development here is largely a matter of repeating everything transposed and played at a slightly higher emotional pitch. It's the Hungarian dance that carries the concerto to an exhilarating conclusion that one could hardly anticipate from the work's gloomy beginning. *—James Reel*

Recommended:

- ○ **The Complete Violin Concertos** / Masur (cond.), Accardo, Leipzig Gewandhaus Orch. / 1998 / Philips 462167
- ○ **Mozart: Violin Concerto 5; Bruch: Violin Concerto 1** / Karajan (cond.), Mutter, Berlin PO / 1998 / DG 459042

Violin Concerto No. 2 in D minor, Op. 44

While violinist Joseph Joachim had a hand in fine-tuning Max Bruch's first violin concerto, Pablo Sarasate was the direct inspiration for Bruch's second concerto. This is unfortunate, for Bruch provided the Spanish soloist a virtuoso vehicle lacking the balance and direct expression that made his first concerto so popular.

This concerto begins with a long Adagio non troppo, which Johannes Brahms found altogether troppo: "Normal people cannot endure it," he wrote. The movement is in sonata form, the violin singing out a first theme tailored specifically to what Bruch called Sarasate's "soulful" style. This is the concerto's strongest movement, with highly expressive writing for the soloist over unobtrusive, but effective, ominous support from the orchestra. Despite a few high-tension passages replete with double stops, this movement does not require fireworks from the soloist.

The brief second movement, described as a recitative, picks up the pace somewhat with a sequence of declamatory passages for the violin, cheered on by orchestral outbursts, that link the outer movements thematically. The movement also functions somewhat as a big, accompanied cadenza.

The finale, an Allegro molto in loose sonata form, brings on the pyrotechnics. The soloist uses the rather Lalo-like themes as little more than an excuse for virtuosic display, with the orchestra almost fully subservient to the violin's survey of bowing effects and showy double-stop writing. The music does ease off from time to time, but these more relaxed episodes still require ardent playing from the soloist, and the rip-roaring final measures are clearly designed to bring an audience to its feet. *—James Reel*

Recommended:

- ○ **Bruch: The Complete Violin Concertos** / Masur (cond.), Accardo, Leipzig Gewandhaus Orch. / 1998 / Philips 462167

Violin Concerto No. 3 in D minor, Op. 58

So far as most of the music-loving public is concerned, there is just one Max Bruch violin concerto, and the *Concerto No. 3 in D minor for violin and orchestra*, Op. 58, is not it. Many fine violinists, in fact, go their whole lives without knowing that this piece even exists. Bruch's *Concerto No. 1 in G minor*, Op. 26, has long been a standard of the violin repertory; the *Concerto No. 2 in D minor*, Op. 44, is its occasionally played cousin. The *Concerto No. 3* (1890–91), is, on the other hand, a musical unicorn: since it has almost never been played, its existence is for many the stuff only of musicological folklore.

However, Bruch and the *Concerto No. 3*'s dedicatee, violinist Joseph Joachim, were always fond of the piece, despite its lack of commercial and popular success. Bruch originally wrote just a single movement, an Allegro (now the first movement); but Joachim convinced him to compose two further movements and make a full three-movement piece of it.

The opening Allegro energico is firm and rigid—steel-rimmed, if you will—to a degree not often heard in Bruch's music. There is little in Bruch's earlier two violin concertos to compare with the climactic recapitulation of the *Concerto No. 3*'s first movement: here, the snare-drum-like main theme in triplets heard at the beginning of the movement is positively beaten into submission by a fortissimo tutti—the orchestra seems almost a percussion battery, and listeners are left stunned that Bruch, master melodist and a man generally thought to have been not "edgy" enough to leave a real mark on music history, could be so forceful.

This opening movement has three themes, the first two of which work together as the primary theme-group in D minor. The third is a sweet-toned thing in quiet A major, ingratiating with its quarter note neighbor note figures; in concert-sonata formal terms, it counts as not a "third," but a "second" theme. The solo violin enters after a moderate-sized opening tutti, spinning an obbligato web around the first two themes, which have already been offered by the orchestra, flying up and down the fingerboard in the electrifying way that Bruch loved so much.

The second movement, Adagio, is an instrumental song in B flat major. Its tempo may be slower and its tone gentler than the first movement's, but the violinist's fingers must move just as fast: much of the Adagio is played out in 30-second notes, again taking the form of a filigree in and around the thread of melody played by orchestra.

For a finale, Bruch composed a snappy Allegro molto with a staccatissimo main tune. A sumptuous melodic idea featuring the kind of rich parallel sixths in the finale of the Concerto No. 2 serves as a contrasting second theme. It is, of course, the fiery opening idea that gets the honor of closing the concerto. *—Blair Johnston*

Recommended:

- ○ **Bruch: The Complete Violin Concertos** / Masur (cond.), Accardo, Leipzig Gewandhaus Orch. / 1998 / Philips 462167

CHAMBER MUSIC

Eight Pieces for clarinet, viola or cello & piano, Op. 83

Bruch was over 70 when he wrote these pieces; their autumnal nature isn't surprising, given the composer's age and the fact that his form of Romanticism was being displaced by more innovative techniques. Each of these items is a character piece, although they carry no titles more descriptive than tempo indications. All but the seventh are in minor keys, and are designed to draw the mellowest sound possible from the instruments.

The set is framed by quiet pieces. No. 1 is an A minor Andante. Its tentative main theme is introduced by the piano, which then recedes to an accompanimental role while the Schumannesque melody is played in turn by the viola and clarinet. Although the piano retains a constant presence, the clarinet and viola rarely play together. More often they're like an old married couple, completing each other's thoughts.

No. 2 in B minor is a brief Allegro còn moto with a quietly roiling piano undercurrent; this dark, restless piece would have been at home in any of Brahms' chamber or piano works from the 1890s.

No. 3 in C minor, Andante con moto, is the suite's most extended movement. It's a study in contrast between the rhapsodic, recitative-like material for viola and the introverted lyricism of the clarinet. Each of those instruments enjoys a very long passage to itself with piano accompaniment (actually the viola gets two), but the full ensemble comes together in the last quarter of the piece, which is dominated by the clarinet's material.

No. 4, Allegro agitato, packs a bit of D minor humor into its mere three minutes; the instruments' occasional self-mocking trills imply that the music's agitation isn't to be taken entirely seriously.

No. 5 is an F minor Andante influenced by Rumanian folk music. The viola intones a bardic theme over the piano's rolled chords, after which the clarinet presents its own yearning melody with counterpoint from the viola and chordal accompaniment in the piano. All three instruments join forces for the gloomy remainder of the movement.

No. 6, Andante con moto, is a delicate nocturne, another piece in the late style of Brahms. Although it's the clarinet that introduces the melody, Bruch integrates all three instruments more thoroughly than in any prior movement.

No. 7 is the suite's sole major-mode piece, an Allegro vivace ma non troppo in B major. It's a charming rondo full of Mendelssohnian verve and the barest hint of an Italian folk dance in the section that binds the piece together.

The subdued mood returns in the beginning of No. 8, a Moderato in E flat minor. The music's ardor builds through the second quarter of the piece but subsides without reaching a full climax; it follows the same pattern toward the end, gradually receding into silence. —*James Reel*

Recommended:

○ **Bruch: Concerto for Clarinet & Viola; 8 Pieces for Clarinet, Viola & Piano; Romance** / P. Meyer, Caussé, Duchable / 2001 / Apex 89229

Anton Bruckner

b. Sep. 4, 1824, Ansfelden, Austria, **d.** Oct. 11, 1896, Vienna, Austria

Composer: Symphonic, Choral, Chamber Music

Although Bruckner wrote a great deal of sacred choral music (including not only his grandly conceived *Mass No. 3*, but also his more intimate *Mass No. 2* and his astringent motets, which fuse Renaissance and nineteenth century techniques), he is best known for his symphonies: two unnumbered apprentice works, eight completed mature symphonies, and the first three movements of a Ninth (The finale has been reconstructed by several hands, but most performances include just the movements Bruckner completed). The symphonies, influenced to some extent by Wagner and identified with his school by the Viennese public, are monumental: expansive in scale, rigorous (if sometimes gigantist) in formal design, and often elaborate in their contrapuntal writing. Their sonorities are stately and organ-like; the Viennese critic Graf wrote that Bruckner "pondered over chords and chord associations as a medieval architect contemplated the original forms of a Gothic cathedral." Despite occasional folk influences in the scherzos, his symphonies are uniformly high-minded, even religious, in spirit. Together, they form the weightiest body of symphonies between Schubert (whom he greatly admired) and Mahler.

Bruckner was born in the town of Ansfelden, Austria, on September 4, 1824, and he spent the first years of his career as a choirmaster for a group of monks and as a church organist in Linz. After several years of studying composition and counterpoint by mail, he passed exams at the Vienna Conservatory in 1861. In the early 1860s he created his first large works, including a Symphony in D minor that he later derisively named "die Nullte," the *Symphony No. 0*. He was present at the premiere of Wagner's *Tristan und Isolde* in 1865, and remained a near fanatical admirer of Wagner, but the extent to which his own vast musical structures were modeled on Wagner's is a matter of debate. He landed a teaching post at the Conservatory in 1868, but always retained something of his original rustic character. An often-repeated anecdote tells how he gave a tip to the aristocratic conductor Hans Richter after a successful rehearsal of his *Symphony No. 4*, telling Richter to go and buy himself a beer. Bruckner died in Vienna on October 11, 1896. —*AMG*

SYMPHONIC

Symphony No. 0 in D minor ("Die Nullte"), WAB 100 (ca. 1863)

The curious numeration of Anton Bruckner's Symphony No. 0 would imply that its composition preceded his First (1868). Yet its date is ambiguous. It is most generally agreed that its genesis was in 1863 and it was substantially revised into its definitive form in 1869, after Bruckner had made the significant acquaintance of Beethoven's Ninth. In its first rehearsal by the Vienna Philharmonic, conductor Otto Dessoff, upon examining the first movement, asked where the main theme was. This was all it took for the sensitive composer to shelve the work until the penultimate year of his life. Although reluctant to include the symphony in his official canon, he was hesistant to discard it altogether and thus appended the curious designation for which it is famous, along with the words "only an attempt."

It shows many anticipations of Bruckner's mature style and the composer used the work as a sort of thematic woodshed for the creation of subsequent works. The scurrying opening motive is so unusual that it is understandable that Dessoff could not identify it as a theme. The overall harmonic layout is strikingly similar to the opening of the *Third Symphony*, also in D minor. The second theme is similar in mood to that of the *Seventh Symphony*, its lyricism set against a softly tread march. What is unusual is the brief reappearance of the opening theme before the third theme is stated, a typical Brucknerian hymn-theme. Anticipation of the *Third Symphony* can be heard in the development, where a whirlwind transformation of the main theme vies with a chorale-like transformation of the other themes. The recapitulation already reveals Bruckner's tendency to telescope this section while avoiding verbatim restatement. The beginning of the coda uses a motive heard later in the *Sixth Symphony* and the *Te Deum*. The second movement is more in the mood of an andante than a typical Bruckner adagio, although it does unfold at a leisurely pace. In song form, a hymn-like theme alternates with lighter lyrical one. Most conspicuously absent is the working up to a steeple-like climax present in all of Bruckner's slow movements from the Third on. The following scherzo is neither heavy-footed nor Valkyrie-like, but shows the influence of Schubert's symphonic scherzi, while the trio is chromatic in a way somewhat different from Bruckner's later style. A brooding introduction over pulsating woodwinds opens the finale, with the first theme proper bursting forth forte in unison, quite similar to the opening of Beethoven's Ninth. The second theme is unusual for being mercurial, a mood rare in any Bruckner, but the typical "gesangperiod" follows in the third theme. The development shows many Brucknerian devices including insistent unisons and trailing woodwind figurations. Again the recapitulation is terse. A brief diminuendo precedes the short vigourous coda, not yet the deliberate inexorable buildup against a reverberating tonic typical of the composer. None the less, the "Zero" symphony is a worthy work in perspective, accepted as part of the canon with the other nine. — *Wayne Reisig*

Recommended:

○ **Bruckner: Symphony No. 0 In D Minor, "Die Nullte" Wab. 100** / Guschlbauer (cond.), Bruckner Orchester Linz / Camerata 257

○ **Bruckner: Symphony No. 0** / Marriner (cond.), Stuttgart Radio SO / Delta 14091

Symphony No. 00 in F minor ("Study Symphony"), WAB 99 (ca. 1864)

The *Study Symphony* (often catalogued as the *Symphony No. 00*) was composed, along with the *Overture in G minor* and the *112th Psalm*, at the conclusion of Bruckner's studies in form and orchestration with Otto Kitzler. Bruckner clearly considered the work a student exercise, going so far as to indicate that in the heading; however, the fact that Bruckner did not destroy or suppress the score suggests that he attached some merit to it. The *Symphony No. 00* is a work of its time, showing the clear influence of Schumann; yet at certain points the voice of the mature Bruckner makes itself heard. In the first movement, the addition of a fourth subject to the otherwise conventional sonata form is a distinct touch, showing the composer's already-evident inclination toward form expansion. The slow movement is an andante, lovely in itself although not yet inhabiting the spiritually introspective world of the later adagios. The following scherzo, however, already shows Bruckner's knack for producing happy, vital, and infectious movements in that genre. And while the finale has been described as "academic" or, at best, in step with its times, there are premonitory brass chorales and a passage in the coda which anticipates a corresponding passage in the *Eighth Symphony*. Throughout, the orchestration is effective and shows a sense of variety and color, even if it is not characteristic of Bruckner's later technique in that area. While Bruckner may have been correct in not wanting the F minor symphony to be part of his canon, it is a fascinating part of Bruckner-study, often giving tantalizing glimpses of things to come. — *Wayne Gerard Reisig*

Recommended:

○ **Anton Bruckner** / Vladimir Ashkenazy (cond.), Berlin SO / Ondine 920

Symphony No. 1 in C minor ("The Saucy Maid"), WAB 101 (ca. 1866; revised 1877)

The work today known universally as Anton Bruckner's *Symphony No. 1* in C minor was far from being his first attempt in the symphonic genre. Like most of its siblings, it underwent several revisions, for the composer was given to near-pathological self doubt, and lacked almost all confidence in his own abilities. The eminent Bruckner scholar Robert Haas described no less than four separate versions—those of 1866, 1877, 1891, and 1893. Only two versions of the symphony are generally known and performed; they are called the "Linz" and "Vienna" versions. The Linz version corresponds to the 1877 version, not the 1866 version as often claimed. The 1866 version heard at the premiere also differed from the 1877 score in a number of ways, especially in the Finale. The Vienna version, too, departed widely and often from earlier editions of the score. For some considerable time, the "Linz" version enjoyed limited success. Subsequently, Bruckner's 1891 Vienna version was adopted as the definitive version of the work, however today (largely thanks to the work of pioneering scholars like Robert Haas and Leopold Nowak) the original Linz score has been rehabilitated as the standard performing version of the *First Symphony*.

Although Bruckner's formative models were the symphonies of Beethoven, Schumann, and Mendelssohn, he was also profoundly affected by the music of Richard Wagner, which to a greater or lesser degree, permeates almost all of his music. Wagner's influence can be felt in each of the four movements of the *First Symphony*, from externals (such as the extended duration of the Adagio slow movement) to the remarkably progressive harmonic language employed. The opening movement (Allegro) is cast in conventional sonata form. But unusually, the exposition also includes an additional third theme, given out by the trombones, an architectural device which is more typically encountered in Bruckner's later works. The slow movement is placed second. Set predominantly in the key of F minor, the language is both confessional and at the same time deeply expressive and solemn. Then comes the rhythmically propulsive Scherzo, derived from a number of rustic-sounding thematic groups, dispersed around a central trio section in a more relaxed vein. Much later in his life, Bruckner observed "never was I so bold and daring" when writing about his first symphony. It seems probable that the reference applied chiefly to the Finale of this work, outwardly a positive and forthright expression of optimism and confidence in the grace of the God whom Bruckner faithfully honored throughout his life, but certainly both "bold" and "daring" in the masterfully diverse and effective use of counterpoint in the treatment of three highly contrasted thematic ideas. —*Michael Jameson*

Recommended:

- ○ **Bruckner: 9 Symphonies** / Jochum (cond.), Berlin PO / DG B000001302
- ○ **Bruckner: Symphony 1 (1866)** / Tintner (cond.), Scottish National Orch. / 2000 / Naxos 554430
- ○ **Bruckner: Symphony 1** / Solti, Chicago SO / 2000 / Angel 73905

Symphony No. 2 in C minor ("Symphony of Pauses"), WAB 102 (1871–1872; revised 1873)

Bruckner composed his *Second Symphony* during the years 1871–1872. It is set in the traditional four movements, and is no more gargantuan than Schubert's *"Great" C major Symphony*. However, this work is genuinely predictive of Bruckner's later style, both in its balanced synthesis of classical elements and in the Wagnerian chromaticism of its musical ethos. The second exists in no fewer than five different versions! In hindsight, it's easy to see why Bruckner's contemporaries advised him to overhaul the score, for during the autumn of 1872, the members of the Vienna Philharmonic dismissed it as unplayable, though it had already won the admiration of Franz Liszt. The symphony was introduced to Vienna audiences on October 26, 1873, after a wealthy patron, Johann Merbeck, had volunteered to underwrite costs. Now, the new symphony received enthusiastic approval from critics and public alike; Bruckner received an ovation, and even the feared critic Hanslick temporarily stayed his barbed pen, finding positive things to say about the piece. In 1877, aged 53, Bruckner produced a subsequent revision, but as Hans Christian Schmidt-Banse observes, "this music continues, even today, to disturb and puzzle its listeners and refuses to provide a quick fix...."

The opening movement (moderato) adopts conventional sonata form, although Bruckner takes a strangely fragmented approach in the management of his thematic material. The peremptory conclusion of the movement—a coda of just 17 bars—was more suggestive of a composer laboring against self-doubt than any lack of technical skill. That quality is much in evidence in the slow movement (Andante) which now follows: like many of Bruckner's slow movements, this one has a hymn-like, devotional character, although again the fragmentary nature of the musical language, and its hesitant quality, suggest a certain lack of confidence. The Scherzo is more forthright and declamatory. While only passing allusions to the original dance forms remains, the thundering rhythmic gestures are not effectively countered by more relaxed material: only the trio section affords any sense of calm. Very soon, the music returns to the rustic, rough-hewn abrasiveness of the surrounding scherzo material. That same rambling, discursive quality which prompted calls for Bruckner to revise the work is even more palpable in the Finale (moderato). The first real theme does not arrive for a considerable time, though when it does, its thematic associations with the pounding themes of the Scherzo do not pass unnoticed. The second subject group, too, begins after a series of fits and starts, and its pastoral nature is soon swamped by a church chorale. One interesting feature, however, is the series of fleeting cyclic reminiscences of the first movement. But almost all commentators have found this symphony unconvincing in its attempts to unify musical opposites: as Schmidt-Banse concludes "however much he struggles to reconcile them, Bruckner's antitheses always seem to resist all attempts at reconciliation." —*Michael Jameson*

Recommended:

- ○ **Bruckner: Symphony 2** / Eichhorn (cond.), Bruckner Orchester Linz / Camerata 442
- ○ **Bruckner: The Complete Symphonies** / Jochum (cond.), Staatskapelle Dresden / 2000 / Angel 73905
- ○ **Bruckner: Symphony 2** / Giulini (cond.), Vienna SO / 2001 / Testament 1210

Symphony No. 3 in D minor ("Wagner"), WAB 103 (1872–1873; revised 1874)

British musicologist Deryck Cooke described the third as "the least perfect, but not the least magnificent" of Anton Bruckner's nine symphonies. The work has undergone a convoluted evolution however; when Cooke described "its present intolerable state of complexity," just six versions existed, all completed between 1873 and 1889. Recent research has raised that total to nine editions of Bruckner's so-called "Wagner" symphony.

When Bruckner initially submitted the score to Otto Dessoff, the puzzled conductor retorted, "but where is the main tune?" So began the tortuous gestation of the *Third Symphony*, as Bruckner's well-intentioned students and supporters proposed their own "improvements." Incredibly, the original text of 1873 was finally published only in 1977, some 103 years after its composition. This was the version the composer inscribed to his hero Richard Wagner, with the words "to the unreachable world-famous noble master of poetry and music."

The symphony is sprinkled with suggestions of Wagner's operas, chiefly *Die Walküre*, *Tannhäuser*, and *Lohengrin*. But it adheres to Classical models and as usual for Bruckner is quite distinct from Wagner in its basically abstract, elevated outlook. In every incarnation it comprises four movements, a structure from which Bruckner never deviated. The first begins as the solo trumpet announces a striking motto theme, followed by the announcement of a noble horn melody. Not unusually for Bruckner, the first movement exposition has three thematic groups, ending with a quotation from his own *Mass in D minor*. The development section, too, has the typical Bruckner imprint of a second main theme stated in contrary motion, before the lead-up to the recapitulation. The coda offers the main motif as a canon for trumpets and trombones, and the movement ends majestically.

The Adagio, set in quiet reverential style at the outset, was the subject of major revision; the original 1876 movement was some 38 bars longer than that of the regularly heard 1877 revision. The third movement is an irrepressible, headlong scherzo of formidable power. It contrasts vehement outer sections with a beautiful trio section characterized by a lyrical theme for the violas.

The finale begins in a mood of similar determination, but the contrasting second thematic grouping presents an enigmatic juxtaposition of idioms. Bruckner contrasts a polka-like idea for the violins with a solemn brass chorale, answered by the woodwinds. The composer's biographer August Göllerich recalled strolling around a Vienna suburb with Bruckner and hearing popular dance music coming from a tavern, adjacent to a funeral home in which the body of a famous cathedral architect awaited interment. "Listen!" Bruckner exclaimed. "Here is dancing, while over there the master lies in his coffin. That's life—that's what I wanted to show in my *Third Symphony*. The Polka symbolises life's joys, and the Chorale its pain and sorrow." But this great work ends in a mood of triumphant affirmation, as the opening trumpet motto theme returns to crown a short but decisive coda, now majestically transfigured into the major key. —*Michael Jameson*

Recommended:

- ○ **Bruckner: Symphony 3** / Nagano (cond.), Deutsches SO Berlin / HM 801817
- ○ **Bruckner: 9 Symphonies** / Jochum (cond.), Symphonie Orch. des Bayerischen Rundfunks / DG 429079
- ○ **Bruckner: Symphony 3** / Sinopoli (cond.), Staatskapelle Dresden / 1990 / DG 62935
- ○ **Bruckner: Symphony 3** / Barenboim (cond.), Berlin PO / 1996 / Teldec 13160

Symphony No. 4 in E flat major ("Romantic"), WAB 104 (1874; revised 1878)

Bruckner's *Fourth Symphony* was the one which began a reversal of the composer's fortunes for the better. The Vienna premiere under Hans Richter in 1880 was a resounding success. So elated was the composer that after a very promising rehearsal he pressed a coin into the conductor's hand with the enjoinder to have a beer. At the performance, Bruckner was called out for a bow after each movement.

The original version of 1874 was reworked into an almost totally new work, the most conspicuous changes being the replacement of the mysterious-sounding original scherzo with the now familiar "Hunting" one; a new finale subtitled "Volkfest" replaced the original, only to be replaced again with a less programmatic one two years later. Along with extensive reworking of the first two movements, these changes were all incorporated into the version most commonly known and performed today, being designated as the version of 1878–80. A further 1887–88 revision by Bruckner's pupils Lowe and Schalk has largely disappeared.

The subtitle "Romantic" was derived from a program which Bruckner was persuaded by friends to append to the work, evoking images of medieval knights, castles, hunting, and other things. That Bruckner halfheartedly accepted the suggestion may be divined from his reply to a query regarding the finale: "I've quite forgotten what image I had in mind." And yet, the first movement's designation of "Dawn at a medieval citadel... knights sally forth from the gates on proud chargers... the wonder of nature surrounds them..." is admittedly a bit appropriate. Against a mysterious tremolo a horn call emerges to be followed by the weighty and heroic main theme; a more idyllic "song period" follows, evocative of nature and replete with bird calls, followed in turn by a more imposing third subject; the movement's climax is a broad and blazing brass chorale which caps the development; the recapitulation ends with the horns powerfully repeating the symphony's opening notes against reiterated forte chords. The slow movement, a softly-treading andante in lieu of the usual Bruckner adagio, is said to represent a tryst of two medieval lovers; this alternates with a more spiritual chorale-like episode and works up to a climax for full orchestra which seems to invoke heroism more than romance. The following scherzo is perhaps the only undisputed tone-painting in the symphony, a rollicking, thundering depiction of a medieval hunt which is a tour-de-force for the horns; the trio is one of Bruckner's most engaging Ländlers, saturated with the serenity of the countryside. The finale of the 1880 version is expansive and episodic, commencing with a prolonged crescendo of an introduction and erupting into a theme derived from the opening of the symphony; a relaxed, winsome second theme alternates with passages of Wagnerian intensity and occasional fleeting references to the preceding movements; the long coda is a typically Brucknerian workup to a sonorous tapestry of sound with the work's opening motive woven into the fabric, bringing to a close what is often deemed the first of Bruckner's mature symphonies. — *Wayne Gerard Reisig*

Recommended:

- ○ **Bruno Walter The Edition; Bruckner Symphony 4** / B. Walter (cond.), Columbia SO / 1996 / Sony 10233

○ **Bruckner: Symphonie 4; Sibelius: Nächtlicher Ritt und Sonnenaufgang** / Jochum (cond.), Berlin PO / 1996 / DG 449718

○ **Bruckner: Symphony 4** / Wand (cond.), Berlin PO / 1990 / RCA Victor 62935

Symphony No. 5 in B flat major ("Tragic" / "Church of Faith" / "Pizzicato"), WAB 105 (1875–1876; revised 1877)

Bruckner's Symphony No. 5 *in B flat* stands at the fulcrum of his symphonic output. Among his most intellectually daunting creations, the Fifth has never attained the popularity of the Fourth or Seventh symphonies, and its complexity proved a barrier to performance during the composer's lifetime. It was given only twice, and then never as Bruckner intended.

As is typical of the composer's works, Bruckner's Fifth was the product of a lengthy gestation. Work began on the great Adagio on February 14, 1875; then came the opening movement and Scherzo, with the monumental Finale reaching completion in May 1877. Even then, however, Bruckner was not satisfied, and he was not finished with his modifications until January 4, 1878. He dedicated the work to Carl von Stremeyr, Austria's enlightened and sympathetic minister for education and culture, who had been instrumental in helping Bruckner secure a professorship at Vienna University.

This is the only Bruckner symphony to begin with a slow introduction, and the opening motif is heard again at the start of the finale. The devotional atmosphere of the outset leads to an Allegro of raw power; its ostinato dotted- rhythm figure eventually gives way to a more subdued secondary idea, beginning with pizzicato strings. Dialogue between horn and flute heralds the development section, though again the relentlessness of the dotted motif becomes obsessive. It even continues to dominate the colossal coda.

The oboe begins the languid, deeply eloquent Adagio, against a triplet accompaniment from pizzicato lower strings. The rhythmic connection between this supporting device and the beginning of the first movement Allegro only becomes clear when the second theme arrives, cast in rich, deep harmonies for full strings. As the movement continues, the two thematic groups are reviewed in turn, as Bruckner explores their contrapuntal possibilities to the fullest. Most of the Scherzo's material has already been heard previously in the symphony, and the links with the pizzicato opening of the slow movement, now presented at a much faster tempo and now played arco (with the bow), soon become apparent. The trio section affords effective contrast, and brings a shift in key from D minor to the symphony's home key of B flat.

Many commentators discuss the influence of the finale of Beethoven's *"Choral" Symphony* upon the last movement of Bruckner's Fifth, though in fact the resemblances hardly extend beyond the opening of the movement. Whereas Beethoven reviews themes from earlier in his work, and then dismisses them, the germinal thematic idea of Bruckner's finale derives clearly enough from the major themes that have gone before. What follows is an extraordinarily masterful display of contrapuntal skill; this sonata movement also contains an astounding double fugue, though three distinct main ideas are present. The last of these, a nobly expansive chorale for full brass returns to crown the mighty resolution of the symphony, in its unforgettably powerful coda. *—Michael Jameson*

Recommended:

○ **Bruckner: Symphony 5** / Knappertsbusch (cond.), Vienna PO / 1995 / London 448581

○ **Bruckner: Symphony 5** / Eichhorn (cond.), Bruckner Orchester Linz / Camerata 335

○ **Bruckner: Symphonies 5 & 7** / Ormandy (cond.), Philadelphia Orch. / 2001 / Sony 45669

○ **Bruckner: The Complete Symphonies** / Jochum (cond.), Dresden Staatskapelle / 2000 / Angel 73905

○ **Furtwängler Recordings 1942–1944 Vol. 2** / Furtwängler (cond.), Berlin PO / 2001 / DG 471294

Symphony No. 6 in A major ("Philosophic"), WAB 106 (1879–1881)

Bruckner completed his *Symphony No. 6* in A major in September 1881. It was not performed complete during his lifetime, although in February 1883, the two middle movements were played by the Vienna Philharmonic. The first complete reading, under the young Gustav Mahler, was given on February 26, 1899, but with a number of substantial cuts and other amendments made to the score. Although a work with many fine passages, and a great deal of internal consistency, the sixth has always been regarded as somewhat imperfect; as Bruckner specialist Georg Tintner put it, it consists of "three perfect movements, and one that is somewhat problematic."

Considering the vast scale of its predecessor, the sixth is a work of comparatively modest proportions; yet it is distinguished by richly varied orchestration and hugely contrasted thematic ideas. The opening movement begins with an urgent rhythmic ostinato played by the violins; the unsettled first subject gradually gives way to a secondary theme that is altogether more lyrical in quality. The opening ostinato figure returns frequently and unaltered as the movement progresses, and becomes especially potent at the climax of the development section. During the coda, trumpets and horns challenge each other antiphonally, as if sounding across vast distances of time and space.

The Adagio which follows is Bruckner's only symphonic slow movement in conventional sonata form. The hymn-like F major opening theme suggests reverential awe in an elegiac string threnody, over which the oboe responds plaintively. A second theme lightens the texture, with a richly-hued episode for strings, but particularly impressive is the extended and yearning coda, after the manner of a funeral march. The scherzo is perhaps the most fantastical of any to be found among Bruckner's nine symphonies; whereas others are bucolic and rustic in mood, this is demonic and threatening, its fearsome tensions only assuaged during the more relaxed trio section.

The finale presents an austere, purposeful idea for the violins, on which the second clarinet comments; a contrasting lyrical melody follows. The music progresses in urgent style—a quality emphasised by frequent gestures of harmonic ambiguity, and in a brilliant and virtuosic passage for the violins. When the long-awaited resolution arrives, Bruckner brings back the ostinato rhythm heard at the start of the symphony, along with its main first subject idea, now played by three trombones. *—Michael Jameson*

Recommended:

○ **Bruckner: Symphony 6; Wagner: Wesendonck-Lieder** / Klemperer (cond.), New Philharmonia Orch. / 1999 / EMI 567037

○ **Anton Bruckner: Symphony 6** / Tintner (cond.), New Zealand SO / 1995 / Naxos 553453

○ **Bruckner: Symphony 6** / Eichhorn (cond.), Bruckner Orchester Linz / Camerata 345

○ **Bruckner: 9 Symphonies** / Jochum (cond.), Bavarian Radio Sinfonie-Orchester / DG B000001302

Symphony No. 7 in E major ("Lyric"), WAB 107 (1881–1883)

Having recently gained acceptance in Vienna with the premiere of the *Fourth Symphony*, Anton Bruckner received a visit from famed conductor Artur Nikisch who offered to premier the composer's *Seventh Symphony*. The concert took place in Leipzig with the Gewandhaus Orchestra on December 30, 1884; Hans Richter and the Vienna Philharmonic gave the symphony its local premiere in January 1885. Despite a cool reception from the critics, the work was an enormous success, and public enthusiasm helped to solidify Bruckner's growing reputation. Among the accolades was a telegram from Johann Strauss Jr. which read "Am deeply moved. It was the musical experience of my life." Unlike most of his other symphonies, Bruckner's *Seventh* underwent virtually no revision; the one point of concern was a cymbal crash at the Adagio's climax which Bruckner added at the suggestion of friends, but then subsequently removed.

The symphony commences with a string tremolo from which the searching main theme arises; this theme is said to have been whistled to Bruckner in a dream by his late friend Ignaz Dorn, and it reappears throughout the symphony in subtle transformations. This is followed by a plaintive, yet animated, theme for woodwinds, and followed in turn by an imposing dance-like third theme. The development is expansive, making effective use of theme inversion, and the recapitulation is varied; a long crescendo using fragments of the opening theme forms a glowing and dynamic coda.

The deeply felt second movement, an adagio in song form, is mournful and dignified. Said to have been inspired by a premonition of Richard Wagner's death, the opening threnody breaks into a sonorous hymn for strings. This alternates with a beautiful arching theme which offers consolation at each appearance. The climax occurs with the third appearance of the movement's opening theme which, against an ostinato of rising sextuplets, is propelled to a blazing C major climax. Finally, a dirge for Wagner tubas, said to have been composed upon Bruckner's learning of Wagner's passing, follows as coda with the strings intoning a poignant transformation of the symphony's main theme.

With a contrast as stunning as the corresponding moment in Beethoven's *Eroica*, the windswept Scherzo which follows is one of Bruckner's best. The main theme is said to have been derived from the crowing of a cock; the wistfully nostalgic trio is deeply affecting.

The finale opens with an athletic transformation of the symphony's opening theme. This is followed by beautifully modulating chorale for strings against a walking bass, and in turn following by a thundering unison transformation of the opening theme in minor. These three wonderfully contrasting ideas are interwoven deliberately, yet with great animation and vigor, until the heartily extroverted coda brings home the symphony's opening theme in the full orchestra. *—Wayne Gerard Reisig*

Recommended:

○ **Symphonie 7** / Szell (cond.), Vienna PO / 1994 / Sony 47646

○ **Bruckner: Symphony 7** / Tintner (cond.), Royal Scottish National Orch. / 1997 / Naxos 554269

○ **Bruckner: Symphony 7; Motets** / Jochum (cond.), Berlin PO / 1998 / DG 459026

○ **Symphony 7** / Furtwängler (cond.), Berlin PO / Music & Arts 698

Symphony No. 8 in C minor ("Apocalyptic" / "The German Michel"), WAB 108 (1884–1887; revised 1887)

In 1887, an elated Anton Bruckner sent the score of his eighth symphony to his newly found champion, conductor Hermann Levi. The accompanying letter read, "To my artistic father. Alleluia! May it find grace!" Nevertheless, this immense symphony, dwarfing anything in history before it, was greeted with trepidation by the conductor. After the recent breakthrough success of the *Symphony No. 7*, Levi was reluctant to hurt the composer's feelings, so he sent a friend to break the news to Bruckner. The result was a nervous collapse on the part 8 of the sensitive, self-doubting composer—and, upon recuperation, an extensive revision of the symphony. In its new form—somewhat pruned and with many dramatic new features (including a different ending to the first movement and a new trio)—the still imposing work was premiered in 1892 under Hans Richter with the Vienna Philharmonic. A more complete triumph could hardly have been hoped for. Bruckner's rival Brahms heartily joined in the long ovation, while the critic Hanslick, the bane of Bruckner's existence, fled the hall amidst jeers and hisses from the audience.

Even in its revised form the work was the longest symphony on record, with a performance time of roughly 80 minutes. The stern character of the work earned it the nickname "Apocalyptic" (a subtitle which has largely fallen by the wayside), and indeed there is the impression of an eruption as the highly chromatic opening theme thunders out in the full orchestra. A complex of solemn themes unfolds, and an almost cosmic battle occurs in the development section; the recapitulation reaches an awesome climax against an obstinate brass figure; the grim, fading coda, appended in the revision, was described by the composer as a "wake."

The immense scherzo, one of Bruckner's best, is constructed around an infectious carillon-like figure, and was said by the composer to represent the German national figure "Cousin Michael." The trio is expansive and dreamlike in quality.

The following adagio is perhaps the longest in the literature and it unfolds in visions of religious ecstasy, reaching a climax similar but structurally surpassing that of the *Symphony No. 7*. The serenity of its coda is jarringly contrasted with the opening of the finale in which the opening urgency of the first movement returns with even greater intensity. Militant fanfares hammer out the main theme against a jabbing ostinato; a meditative second theme and a rhythmic third are worked out on a vast scale; the sudden return of the opening theme in the recapitulation is one of the most terrifying moments in all of Bruckner's music. The coda to the entire symphony is perhaps Bruckner's greatest orchestral achievement. Over a slow, inexorable build-up the main theme of each movement is reworked in a major key and played in counterpoint with the others, bringing this titanic work to an awe-inspiring close. *—Wayne Gerard Reisig*

Recommended:

- ○ **Bruckner: Symphonie 8** / Karajan (cond.), Vienna PO / 1989 / DG 427611
- ○ **Bruckner: Symphonies 8; 0** / Tintner (cond.), National SO of Ireland / 2001 / Naxos 501101
- ○ **Bruckner: Complete Symphonies** / Jochum (cond.), Staatskapelle Dresden / 2000 / Angel 73905
- ○ **Bruckner: Symphony 8** / Furtwängler (cond.), Vienna PO / Music & Arts 764

Symphony No. 9 in D minor ("Unfinished"), WAB 109 (1887–1896)

As Bruckner progressed on his ninth and last symphony, he daily petitioned God for the strength to complete it, saying "If He takes the pen from my hand, it is His responsibility." From 1889 to 1896, the composer doggedly worked on the *Ninth*. But on October 11, 1896, after a morning walk, Bruckner went home and quietly passed away, leaving behind what is possibly the greatest unfinished symphony since Schubert's.

The *Ninth* is often cited as one of the most important musical links between the nineteenth and twentieth centuries, taking the innovations of Wagner's *Tristan* a step further. The pounding rhythms of the scherzo seem to look ahead to Stravinsky and Bartók while the wide interval leaps and grinding dissonance look ahead to the Second Viennese School. Although the three movement torso is the standard format for presenting Bruckner's last symphonic essay, the final sketches (which have been recorded along with a few "completed" versions of the finale) show that despite failing health and occasional mental detachment, Bruckner's musical mind remained virile and imaginative to the end. The immense fourth movement would have surpassed even the *Eighth*'s in scale, utilizing a fugue and quotes from the *Te Deum*. Yet, there is something satisfying and uplifting in closing with the adagio.

The solemn drone against which the symphony commences sets the stage for an otherworldly conflict, evolving into a whirlwind and erupting into the shattering main theme. This is followed by a characteristic hymn-like passage and a restless rocking-like third theme; in the development section a twisting 6/8 motive emerges and will later be used as a propelling device against which the apocalyptic coda plays out, ending on a menacing open fifth. No hint of a peasant dance or earthly image is left in the pounding, demonic scherzo, placed second in order; even the trio, while starting out with elfin lightness, soon evolves into a mysterious, half-lit dreamscape of vague and unsettling images. The following adagio is considered the composer's valedictory to life. The tortured leap of a ninth ushers in a slow-unfolding vision which explodes, *Tristan*-like, into a climax of spiritual ecstasy. This is followed by a beautiful, autumnal song-theme which seems to radiate from a nostalgic looking-back on life's joys; then appears an austere march-like theme derived from the symphony's opening. Against a stuttering sixteenth note figure, the autumnal theme makes a last appearance. It is gradually joined by a noble hymn-like theme which gradually sours with dissonance while becoming even more intense in its attempted fervor; this works up to the famous seven note dissonance, grinding and terrible, and is followed by an even more terrible silence, as though staring into a void. But then, stealthily a motive from the movement's opening drifts the music to a final serene plane. In the coda, Bruckner fondly quotes from his *Eighth* and *Seventh* symphonies, taking an eloquent and affecting leave of the world. *—Wayne Gerard Reisig*

Recommended:

- ○ **Bruckner: Symphony 9** / C. Davis (cond.), London SO / 2002 / LSO Live 23
- ○ **Bruckner: Symphony 9** / Tintner (cond.), Royal Scottish National Orch. / 1999 / Naxos 554268
- ○ **Bruckner: 9 Symphonien** / Jochum (cond.), Berlin PO / DG 474990
- ○ **Bruckner: Symphony 9** / von Hausegger (cond.), Munich PO / Preiser 90148
- ○ **Bruckner: Symphony 9; Wagner:Tristan Prelude & Liebestod** / Furtwängler (cond.), Berlin PO / Music & Arts 730

CHORAL

Ave Maria, motet, WAB 6 (ca. 1861)

This is Bruckner's second, and most popular, of three settings of the Latin *Ave Maria*, each in the key of F major. It was written for a May 12, 1861, celebration to commemorate the founding of a local choral group, the *Liedertafel Frohsinn*, of which Bruckner was then director. One of a number of works he composed just after finishing counterpoint studies with Simon Sechter, it is generally regarded as the piece in which Bruckner first realized his mature style of vocal composition. Scored for a seven-part, a cappella chorus, the women's voices sing the first lines, never moving far from the F major triad. The men's voices take up the next lines in similar fashion, modulating until all join in A major block chords at the name of Jesus, repeating the name three times in a crescendo. The choir then breaks into imitative counterpoint to return to the home key and finish the prayer. The composition ends with a plagal cadence, the traditional chords of the "Amen" usually found in Protestant hymns. The whole work has a homophonic, yet rich and warm sound that reflects the coming together of Bruckner's understanding of older compositional forms and styles, his Romantic sensibility of expression, and his personal beliefs. *—Patsy Morita*

Recommended:

- ○ **Bruckner: Ave Maria; Gostliche Chöre; Motets** / Flamig (cond.), Dresdener Kreuzchor / Capriccio 10081
- ○ **Anton Bruckner: Messe en mi Mineur; Motets** / Herreweghe (cond.), Collegium Vocale, Ens. Musique Oblique / HM 901322
- ○ **Bruckner: Te Deum; Motetten; 150 Psalm** / Jochum (cond.) Bavarian Radio Chorus / 1999 / DG 457743

Locus iste, gradual, WAB 23 (ca. 1869)

Bruckner's gradual *Locus Iste* for a cappella chorus is an expressively beautiful work dating from the end of his Linz years. The brief work was written for the dedication of the votive chapel of the Linz Cathedral, making it contemporary with the *Symphony No. 0* and the *F minor Mass*.

Locus Iste shows the 45-year-old composer finding his own voice even within the three-odd minutes of the work. The overall mood is one of warmth despite the astringent means of unaccompanied chorus, in contrast to some of Bruckner's modal works in the same medium. The overall shape of the opening melody and its harmony bears some resemblance to the Pilgrims' Chorus from Wagner's *Tannhäuser*, a not too surprising influence on the younger man during that period. However, a dramatic modulation at the word "inestimabile" leads to a passage premonitory of the mature Bruckner, recalling the words "Tu devicto aculeo" from the *Te Deum* and providing a dramatic contrast with the initial lyricism of the opening, the latter of which returns. A melisma-like elongation of the word "Deo" brings this gently spiritual work to a close. *—Wayne Gerard Reisig*

Recommended:

- ○ **Bruckner: Mass 1; Motets** / J. E.Gardiner (cond.), Monteverdi Choir, Vienna PO / DG 459674
- ○ **Bruckner: Mass in E minor; Motets** / Herreweghe (cond.), Le Chapelle Royale / HM 2981322

Mass No. 2, for chorus & winds in E minor, WAB 27 (ca. 1866)

While Bruckner is known chiefly as one of the most important symphonists in music history, he was equally adept in the field of sacred music. The later *Te Deum* and *Psalm 150* show the composer applying his mature symphonic language to the religious medium, yielding works of striking passion and originality. However, Bruckner's earlier sacred works, especially the masses, are fascinating in that they show the amount of expertise he had amassed as a church musician and organist, that skill in turn coming to terms with his newly discovered influences in secular music. The *E minor Mass* of 1866 was wrought as Bruckner was cutting a path through the revelatory world of Richard Wagner. Thus it is a work which straddles both worlds, yet is fully integrated. It elicits admiration from even those who are otherwise lukewarm to Bruckner's oeuvre. Many have cited this and the other two masses as among the most important sacred works of the Romantic era. Also, the number of themes from the *E minor Mass* which will reappear in Bruckner's later works provide another vein of fascination as a glimpse into the composer's creative processes.

The opening Kyrie is in E minor and reflects Bruckner's grounding in the Italian Renaissance masters; almost totally a cappella, the brass enters periodically to punctuate the climaxes. If the Kyrie looks back, the succeeding Gloria in C major is ablaze with flashes of the later Bruckner, featuring a melisma by the horns which would appear in the trio of the *Sixth Symphony*. Similarly, the Credo yields material which would emerge again in Bruckner's later years, specifically in the *Te Deum* and the scherzo of the *Eighth Symphony*; in three sections, the two outer ones in C major flank the repose of the second in F major. The following Sanctus in G major begins a cappella. The subsequent grinding entry of the brass as it joins the chorus produces a remarkable passage of great intensity which foreshadows much sacred music of the twentieth century. This resolves to the more reflective mood of the Benedictus, cast in sonata form, which moves with gentle animation; the blaze-up of the coda is almost frightening in its suddenness. The closing Agnus Dei in E minor is ethereal in character and alternates the Renaissance tradition with Wagner-Liszt chromaticism. Its final measures anticipate those of the *Seventh Symphony*'s slow movement, bringing the *Mass* to a correspondingly serene close. *—Wayne Gerard Reisig*

Recommended:

- ○ **Bruchner: Missa No. 2; Psalm 150; Te Deum** / Rilling (cond.), Bach-Collegium Stuttgart, Gachinger Kantorei Stuttgart / 1997 / Haenssler 98119
- ○ **Anton Bruckner: Messe en mi Mineur; Motets** / Herreweghe (cond.), Collegium Vocale, Ens. Musique Oblique, Chapelle Royale / HM 901322
- ○ **Bruckner: Die 3 Messen** / Jochum (cond.), Schmidhuber (cond.), Bavarian Radio SO, Bavarian Radio Chorus / DG 447409

Os justi, gradual, WAB 30 (ca. 1879)

Anton Bruckner's motet *Os justi* is an eight-part setting for mixed chorus of a text derived from Psalm 36, verses 30 and 31: "The mouth of the just shall meditate wisdom, and his tongue shall speak judgment. The law of his God is in his heart, and his steps shall not be supplanted. Alleluia." The work was composed in 1879, and subsequently published in 1886. Around the same time, Bruckner had just begun work on the opening movement of his *Symphony No. 6*. This particular motet, when first heard in Vienna on June 6, 1880, was the first completely new work by Bruckner to be performed there since the disastrous premiere (in 1877) of the Third Symphony. On this occasion, *Os justi* was inserted as an offertory within a performance of Bruckner's *Mass in D minor*, which itself had not been performed in Vienna for some 13 years.

This work was one of "Four Graduals" published in 1886, which together rank as some of the most revolutionary and original liturgical settings of Bruckner's Vienna years. With these settings (the others are *Locus iste*, *Virga Jesse*, and *Christus factus est*), the composer now consciously strove to distance himself from the reforming endeavors of the Cecilian group founded by Franz Xaver Witt. The principal objective of that group lay in its efforts to restore the archaic purist modality of Palestrina's works to modern ecclesiastical music, on the grounds that most music of the times sought to achieve "unduly profane seductiveness" through effect rather than piety.

In many respects Bruckner's setting would seem to have endorsed such aspirations. *Os justi* was in fact dedicated to another prominent Cecilianist, Ignaz Traumihler, the organist of St. Florian Abbey. Bruckner wrote to him in the following terms: "I should be very pleased if you found pleasure in the piece. It is written entirely without any sharps or flats, and without the chord of the 7th, and without any 6-4 chords, and also without any chordal combinations of four and five simultaneous notes." Even so, as Derek Watson has concluded, "despite the severity of these restrictions, this motet is profoundly emotional in its effect." Bruckner's infusion of Romantic feeling into a spare, archaizing choral language is unique. A central main section in counterpoint is introduced by a chordal passage, and the work ends with a chant-like Alleluia. *—Michael Jameson*

Recommended:

- ○ **Bruckner: Ave Maria; Geistliche Chöre; Motets** / Flamig (cond.), Dredener Kreuzchor / Capriccio 10081
- ○ **Anton Bruckner: Messe en mi Mineur; Motets** / Herreweghe (cond.), La Chapelle Royale, Collegium Vocale, Ens. Musique Oblique / HM 901322
- ○ **Bruckner: Te Deum; Motetten; 150 Psalm** / Jochum (cond.), Bavarian Radio Chorus / 1999 / DG 457743
- ○ **Lika As A Hart; Pslams & Spiritual Songs** / Flummerfelt (cond.), Parrella, Westminster Choir / Chesky 138

Te Deum, WAB 45 (1881–1884)

Although they speak much of the same language as the symphonies and masses, Anton Bruckner's other choral works tend towards a certain conciseness, being epic by implication. This can be said of his *Te Deum*, arguably the crown of his sacred music. Bruckner singled out this work as his own personal favorite, referring to it as "the pride of my life." It is certainly one of the most positive, joyous, and compelling ever to come from his pen and is believed to have been the last music of his which he attended in live performance. Composed from 1881 to 1884, it is contemporary with the *Seventh Symphony*, with which it shares some very significant thematic material. The *Te Deum* reflects the contemporary frame of mind of its composer, being one of elation and thankfulness for his long-delayed success and acceptance. The then-recent performance of the *Fourth Symphony* by the Vienna Philharmonic under Hans Richter had been the breakthrough for Bruckner.

As with the later *Psalm 150*, there are moments in the *Te Deum* where barbaric opulence coexists with intense spirituality, a quality harking back to the Baroque arts. The work opens in blazing C major, propelled by a powerful open-fifths motive in the strings. The chorus and the rest of the ensemble enter as the music moves through processes and modulations distinctly Brucknerian. The following F minor section, "Te Ergo," is serene yet imploring in nature, featuring an expressive tenor solo and a solo violin which can hardly fail to bring to mind the "Benedictus" from Beethoven's *Missa Solemnis*. The central section, "Aeterna Fac," is in Bruckner's favored key of D minor and is almost apocalyptic in its fury. Propelled by a rhythmic device similar to one used in the *Sixth Symphony* and *String Quintet*, it draws on the full resources of the chorus and orchestra before coming to and abrupt unresolved cadence. The "Salvum Fac Populum" section follows, being essentially a repeat of the "Te Ergo," this time with women's voices accompanying the tenor. This leads to the "Per Singulos" which recalls the fervor and energy of the opening. The overall symmetry of the work is now apparent, but the final section is an apotheosis built entirely on the words "In Te Domine Speravi. Non confundar in Aeternum" ("In Thee, Lord, I have trusted. Never let me be confounded"), words which form a motto for Bruckner's life work. The section culminates in a joyous fugue and is followed by an intensely haunting and impassioned chorale, the latter of which would later be used to great effect in the slow movement of the *Seventh Symphony*. The opening string figure returns as the full ensemble carries the *Te Deum* to a terse yet powerful conclusion. *—Wayne Gerard Reisig*

Recommended:

- ○ **Bruckner: Te Deum; Mass in D minor** / M. Best (cond.), J. Rodgers, Wyn-Rogers, K. Lewis, A. Miles, Corydon Singers & Orch. / 1993 / Hyperion 66650
- ○ **Bruckner: Te Deum; Os justi** / Jochum (cond.), Stader, Siegelinde Wagner, Häfliger, Berlin Philharmonic Chorus / 1999 / DG 457743
- ○ **Bruckner: Te Deum; Mozart: Requiem** / Walter (cond.), Yeend, Lipton, D. Lloyd, M. Harrell, New York PO / 1995 / Sony 64480

Virga Jesse, gradual, WAB 52 (ca. 1885)

The course of Anton Bruckner's musical development may have taken a new turn when he first made the acquaintance of Wagner's music in the 1860s, but to regard him as a simple musical offshoot of Wagner, a disciple who brought to the symphony something of what Wagner brought to music drama, is both inaccurate and unfair. Indeed, an understanding of Bruckner's own sacred music—both the large masses and such smaller works as the a cappella motet *Virga Jesse floruit* of 1885—provides many keys to understanding Bruckner's immense symphonic works. *Virga Jesse floruit*, which is one of comparatively few sacred works composed after Bruckner turned to symphonies, reminds us once again that even the idea of classifying Bruckner as a Romantic is not without problems. His musical mind-set was, as has often and rightly been observed, more of the Renaissance or even the pre-Renaissance than nineteenth century modern, and no amount of chromatic elaboration and structural expansion can hide the fact that, psychologically speaking, his symphonies have nothing whatever to do with the throbbing, searching new ways of Liszt, Wagner, and company. In *Virga Jesse floruit*, Bruckner very consciously draws on an ancient musical heritage, spinning out rich, pure lines in a style reminiscent of Palestrina and the *stile antico*. It is as if time itself has no meaning to Bruckner, and in his music-making—long or short, old or new—his identity remains the same.

Virga Jesse floruit is one of Bruckner's most famous pieces; it is sung at Christmastime by choirs, amateur and professional, around the globe. The brief gradual text translates something as follows: "The rod of Jesse flourished; a virgin produced both God and man: and God restored peace, reconciling both lowest and highest within Himself. Alleluia." Bruckner's 92 measures of music move from a group of isolated phrases at the beginning of the piece through some expansive imitative play on the text "pacem Deus reddidit," and finally to the staggered alleluias, at first ecstatic and then absolutely tender, that fill the final third of this most effective piece. *—Blair Johnston*

Recommended:

- ○ **Advent at St. Paul's** / J. Scott (cond.), St. Paul's Cathedral Choir / 1997 / Hyperion 66994
- ○ **Bruckner: Ave Maria; Geistliche Chöre; Motets** / Flämig (cond.), Dresdner Kreuzchor / Capriccio 10081

CHAMBER MUSIC

String Quintet in F major, WAB 112 (ca. 1879)

The idea of Anton Bruckner as a composer of chamber music may seem inconceivable to those given to quick misjudgment. His *String Quintet* of 1879, his sole mature chamber work, shows that Bruckner was completely at ease and eloquent in the medium. Created between the *Fifth* and *Sixth* symphonies, the music seems to be striving for orchestral utterance in only a few spots (if that can even be considered a flaw). Otherwise, the composer completely integrated his characteristic vernacular into the chamber idiom in this concise and well-crafted work.

The main theme of the first movement is more lyrical and searching than a typical Bruckner opening, making the work a cousin to the *Seventh Symphony* in that regard. The theme is passed from one instrument to the next until a typical Brucknerian octave unison evolves. The second subject is a characteristic "Gesangperiode," less Austrian in flavor than Bruckner's other music of this type. A leisurely expansive development follows, including Bruckner's favored device of theme inversion. The recapitulation is telescoped, as was the composer's wont in later works, and a characteristic reiterative coda closes the movement. The scherzo comes second, as in the last two symphonies, and is quite unlike any other by Bruckner. It combines an elfin spirit with the rhythm of the composer's beloved Ländler. The trio section is yet another curiosity for Bruckner—it is in the style of an old-fashioned minuet, even if the composer's modern modulations peer through the eighteenth century framework.

The third movement again seems to inhabit the world of the *Seventh Symphony*, with many of its turns of phrase and cadences recalling the later work's adagio; yet overall a solid peacefulness diverges from the mournfulness of the *Seventh*'s slow movement. The second theme continues this serene and reflective spirit, recalling the corresponding theme in the *Third Symphony*'s adagio. The two themes are woven into an elaborate tapestry of development. A gypsy-like descent of sixteenth notes leads to a more plaintive transformation of the second theme; the opening is recalled once more before the calm of the lulling coda. The finale gives ample proof that conciseness was not beyond Bruckner's capabilities when it suited what he needed to say. The first subject is highly animated and motive-derived rather than thematic. A striking transition which seems to flirt with atonality leads to the second theme, another typical "Gesangperiode." The rhythmic third subject features stark, angular counterpoint, anticipating that of the first movement of the *Sixth Symphony*. The development is leisurely, focusing on the more lyrical elements of the exposition. There is only the faintest suggestion of a recapitulation, with the earlier themes fleetingly referred to. In the coda is there a tendency to break through to an orchestral utterance; one can hear echoes of the symphony's final measures. This concluding gesture notwithstanding, the work inspires speculation as to what Bruckner might have accomplished further in the chamber-music vein. *— Wayne Gerard Reisig*

Recommended:

- ○ **Bruckner: String Quintet; Intermezzo; Strauss: Prelude to Capriccio** / Raphael Ens. / 1994 / Hyperion 66704
- ○ **Bruckner: Streichquintett F-dur** / Melos Quartette, E. Santiago / HM 1951421

Frans Brueggen

b. Oct. 30, 1934, Amsterdam, Netherlands
Conductor, Recorder Player

Frans Brueggen became one of the world's top recorder players and a leader in the revival of Baroque and other early music before switching his emphasis to conducting and gaining equal acclaim. He studied the recorder and the standard transverse flute, as well as musicology at the University of Amsterdam. Attending the Muzieklyceum, Amsterdam, he embarked upon recorder studies with Kees Otten, who was a student of Karl Dolmetsch, the great rediscoverer of the instrument in the twentieth century. Brueggen decided to specialize in the recorder and in historical versions of the transverse flute. He became the first student of the Muzieklyceum to graduate with a diploma in recorder.

Thanks to the confluence of his own talents and the tremendous reawakening of interest in early music in the 1960s and 1970s, Brueggen evolved into something of an international recorder star. He was known for a brilliant and rapidly fluent technique and total devotion to historical accuracy, often established by his own research. Yet he was musical and often deeply affecting in performance. Brueggen is credited with inspiring succeeding generations of players; he became a highly respected teacher not only of the instrument but also of interpretation and performance practice. He joined the faculty of the Royal Conservatory of The Hague as professor of flute and in 1972–73 was the visiting Erasmus Professor of late Baroque Music at Harvard University. Brueggen has written exercise compositions for recorder students and treatises on playing the instrument. He has also prepared editions of Baroque music.

Though recognized for his recorder performances in the early music field, Brueggen also commissioned several new works for the instrument, including *Gesti* (1966) by Luciano Berio. He began to conduct music of various eras, and formed an avant-garde music group called Sourcream. Gradually he began to emphasize conducting and in 1981 founded the Orchestra of the 18th Century, an international group of specialists in early instrument performance who gather twice yearly in Amsterdam for concerts and touring. They play music of the later Baroque era (Purcell, Rameau, Bach, Handel, Vivaldi, and their contemporaries), the Classical era including Beethoven, and occasionally works from the earliest days of musical Romanticism, such as that of Mendelssohn.

He also been guest conductor with some of the most famous standard-repertory orchestras: the Orchestre de Paris, the Royal Concertgebouw Orchestra of Amsterdam, the Chicago Symphony Orchestra, the City of Birmingham Symphony Orchestra, the Vienna Philharmonic, the Rotterdam Philharmonic, the Chamber Orchestra of Europe, the Berlin Radio Symphony Orchestra, and many others. As an opera conductor he has led Mozart's *Mitridate, King of Ponto* in Zurich and Gluck's *Orfeo* at the Lyons National Opera. In 1991, he was invited by Simon Rattle to participate in a series of recordings of music of Bach and Haydn with the Orchestra of the Age of Enlightenment, another leading Baroque-Classical specialty orchestra. He has made well over a hundred recordings, both as a recorder player and a conductor. *—Joseph Stevenson*

Recommended:

- ○ **Rameau: Suites from Naïs & Zoroastre** / Brueggen (cond.), Orchestra of the 18th Century / 2001 / Glossa 921106
- ○ **Telemann: Recorder Sonatas & Fantasias** / Brueggen, Bylsma, Leonhardt / 1995 / Teldec 93688
- ○ **Schubert: Symphonies 2, 3, & 5** / Brueggen (cond.), Orchestra of the 18th Century / 1996 / Philips 446100
- ○ **Haydn: Symphonies 88 & 89** / Brueggen (cond.), Orchestra of the 18th Century / 2000 / Philips 462602
- ○ **Haydn:The Paris Symphonies** / Brueggen (cond.), Orchestra of the 18th Century / 1999 / Philips 462111
- ○ **Italian Recorder Sonatas: Frans Brüggen, Vol. 2** / Bylsma, Brueggen, Leonhardt / 1995 / Teldec 93669

Nicolaus Bruhns

b. 1665, Schwabstedt, Germany, **d.** Mar. 29, 1697, Husum, Germany
Composer

Although he had a short life and wrote very little music that survives, Nicolaus Bruhns is considered important in the development of North German Baroque music for bringing a new virtuosity to his vocal writing.

The Bruhns family was among the musical dynasties that one encounters all over the history of German music in the 1600s. They lived in northern Germany and southern Denmark. Paul Bruhns (d. 1655) was a lutenist who had three musical sons, of whom the middle, also named Paul, was Nicolaus' father. Paul the Younger got a musical job in Schwabstedt by marrying the daughter of the town organist there and inherited it. (This was a common practice in the area at the time.)

When Nicolaus showed uncommon musical talent at an early age, Paul sent him to live with Paul's younger brother, Peter, in Lübeck, a town with a livelier musical life and, hence, better teachers. Primary among them was the great organist Dietrich Buxtehude, who considered Nicolaus his best pupil. Nicolaus also studied violin with his uncle Peter.

As a young musician, Nicolaus got work early in his career thanks to Buxtehude's glowing letter of recommendation. He worked for several years at Copenhagen as a virtuoso violinist and composer. This gave Bruhns a chance to get to know Italian musicians, popular with the citizens at the time, and their music, which included a virtuoso element not common in German music at the time.

He auditioned for the open post of organist of the Stadtkirche of Husum on March 29, 1689. The city council hired him right away, remarking that "since never before has the city heard his like in composition and performance on all manner of instruments." He was a hit from the start. The city fathers of the larger city of Kiel heard him play and tried to lure him away with more money. Husum, a nice and thriving town, knew what a treasure it had, and, as such, approved a special increase in the salary for his position (taking care to note that it was a special case, for Bruhns alone). Bruhns stayed there until his death in 1697.

None of his chamber music has survived, which is especially unfortunate since witnesses make reference to his use of innovative double stops to make it sound like there are more instruments playing than was actually the case. He was known for playing two or three solo lines simultaneously on the violin while playing the bass line on organ pedals. Bruhns' four preludes and fugues are obviously influenced by Buxtehude. After a brilliant opening prelude, the fugues are also inventive in their use of echo effects. His toccatas are technically brilliant and have especially inventive pedal passages. His sacred concertos for chorus have the virtuosity of Italian instrumental concertos. *—Joseph Stevenson*

Overview of Works (ca. 1685–1697)

Twelve or Thirteen (depending on how you count them) sacred vocal pieces and five works for organ: this is all that survives of Nicolaus Bruhns' music. And yet these few items have generated enough interest over the years, especially after the early music revivals of the twentieth century, to keep Bruhns' name from fading completely into obscurity. Bruhns was quite famous in his day—the eminent composer, theorist, and writer Johann Mattheson was among those who sang his praises, and we know that J.S. Bach was familiar with his music even a generation later—and, scant though the extant selection most certainly is, we can be glad for the pittance of Bruhns' music that history has seen fit to hand down to us.

Two of the vocal works have Latin texts; the rest are in German. Of the former, a *De profundis* for solo singer, two violins, and continuo is especially striking. Three of the German-language items are likewise for solo voice, while the others are written for vocal duet, trio, or quartet with various-sized instrumental ensembles as accompaniment. *Ich liege und schlaffe*, for vocal quartet, four strings, bassoon, and continuo, may well be the finest of all, though it, like the rest of Bruhns' music, is not at all well known. There are no true choral pieces, but some of the four-voice works are sometimes sung by small ensembles.

Four organ pieces of the prelude-and-fugue variety have survived; each follows quite clearly in the footsteps of Dietrich Buxtehude, with whom Bruhns studied as a youth; they are set in the keys of G major, G minor, E minor, and E minor again. There is also a setting of the chorale *Nun komm der Heiden Heiland*, likewise in the Buxtehude vein. *—Blair Johnston*

Recommended:

○ **Nikolaus Bruhns: Deutsche Kantaten** / Junghanel (cond.), Cantus Colln / HM 901752

○ **Nikolaus Bruhns: Organ Works** / Ghielmi / Winter & Winter 70

Gavin Bryars

b. Jan. 16, 1943, Goole, Yorkshire, England

Composer: Avant-garde

Gavin Bryars displays nearly all the trademarks of late twentieth/early twenty-first century classical music: versatility, integration of visual arts and multimedia, explorations of nontraditional approaches, and extensive collaborations with other composers and arts organizations. Like several of his contemporaries, he has attracted popular attention through the combined innovation and approachability of his compositions, and writes articulately on a wide variety of music and musicians. His first love in music was jazz, and he performed as a bassist with Derek Bailey and Tony Oxley. Some of this influence shows in his use of improvisation. In the late 1960s, he began to study and work with several other innovative composers, including John Cage and Cornelius Cardew. In 1969, he began teaching at the Portsmouth College of Art, where he helped found the Portsmouth Sinfonia, and also wrote his first major composition, *The Sinking of the Titanic*. This first foray into musical conceptual art was inspired by his considering what the sounds of the band that continued to play as the ship sank would have been like in the watery environment. Two years later, he composed *Jesus' Blood Never Failed Me Yet*, a work in which he combined a tape looping the voice of a man in a homeless shelter, singing the title phrase, and a musical background. In 1981, he followed on the success of the Portsmouth Sinfonia by creating the Gavin Bryars Ensemble. Rather than following traditional ensemble structures based on a group of instruments, Bryars chose instead to make it a group of musicians who would work well and creatively together. This resulted in constant changes in the ensemble's musical textures and capacities, though low strings have tended to predominate its sound. He wrote his most famous opera, *Medea*, in 1984 and it premiered at the Opera de Lyon. In 1988, he wrote his first work for the Hilliard Ensemble, *Glorious Hill*, beginning a long-standing collaboration, as well as material for the opening of the Tate Gallery in Liverpool. He wrote *The War in Heaven* for the BBC Symphony Orchestra in 1993. In 1998, the English National Opera premiered his second opera, *Doctor Ox's Experiment*, based on a story by science fiction writer Jules Verne, and he also began his *First Book of Madrigals* for the Hilliard Ensemble, completed in 2000. 1999 marked his first incursion into film music, with his score for *Unless the Eye Catch Fire*, a striking series of variations on a chorale theme. In 2002, he wrote his *Second Book of Madrigals* (Bryars plans five more books) for the Trio Mediaeval Sextet and also appeared as bassist in *By the Vaar* at *the Vancouver Jazz Festival*. He also collaborated with choreographer Carolyn Carlson on *Writing on Water*, which premiered in Venice, and wrote his third opera, *G*. In the early 1990s, after Point Music recorded *The Sinking of the Titanic* and *Jesus' Blood Never Failed Me Yet*, both recordings became classical best-sellers. *—Ann Feeney*

AVANT-GARDE

Jesus' Blood Never Failed Me Yet (1971)

Jesus' Blood Never Failed Me Yet is one of Gavin Bryars' most minimalistically constructed pieces, and at the same time one of his most emotionally intimate. Borrowing as it does a piece of tape-recorded "documentary" material of a religiously charged nature, the work finds itself in the company of a number of important minimalist and postminimalist works, including Steve Reich's seminal *It's Gonna' Rain*, John Adams' *Christian Zeal and Activity*, and Brian Eno and David Byrne's *Jezebel Spirit* (from *My Life in the Bush of Ghosts*). Bryars' piece, however, assumes a much larger scale than even the longest of these pieces, unfolding and reiterating itself over the course of some 75 minutes. Whereas minimalist music is sometimes offhandedly associated the emotional neutralization of repeated materials, Bryars' work has the opposite effect: rather than numbing the listener's sensibilities, it heightens them; rather then imposing a postmodern indifference toward the subject matter, it forces a confrontation with it.

The taped excerpt that serves as the "source material" of the work came from the cutting room floor of a documentary film made by the composer's friend, Alan Power, in 1971. Power had conducted interviews with a number of homeless or otherwise down-and-out residents of one of London's rougher quarters. Among the footage was a passage in which an transient old man sang a quiet spiritual tune: "Jesus' blood never failed me yet, never failed me yet... this one thing I know, for he loves me so." The man, Bryars was told, was of destitute circumstances but of a sound mind (he avoided alcohol altogether), and seemed quite unfazed by the apparent disparity between his difficult life and the sentiments of the song.

As it appears in Bryars' work, the old man's song emerges slowly from silence, making several repetitions before it can be heard in its entirety. Bryars then slowly introduces an accompanimental chord progression that is first played by a string quartet, then eventually enhanced by the addition of plucked bass and guitar. As the instruments subsequently fade out, the old man's song continues and is eventually underscored, cumulatively, by a much richer sounding ensemble of low strings (for which Bryars has a special taste), then woodwinds, brass, and delicate percussion, and finally full orchestra and choir. At the textural apex the old man is joined, in an odd multimedia duet, with celebrity hobo Tom Waits. (Apparently, an early version of the piece Bryars had completed in 1971 had been one of Waits' favorite recordings, and he jumped at Bryars' invitation to participate in the later, extended version). Their duet concluded, Waits continues singing, to the accompaniment of high strings, while the "real" hobo's voice fades away completely. Such extended exposure to the little tune, heightened by Bryars' slowly evolving orchestrational variations, has a sobering effect. "Although the old man died before he could hear what I had done with his singing," writes Bryars, "the piece remains as a restrained testament to his spirit and optimism." *—Jeremy Grimshaw*

Recommended:

○ **Bryars: Jesus' Blood Never Failed Me Yet** / Riesman (cond.), Hampton SQ, Waits / 1993 / Point Music 438823

The Sinking of the Titanic (1969)

Gavin Bryars' haunting multimedia work *The Sinking of the Titanic* is a mixture of musical narrative, documentary, and meditation, drawing heavily upon various historical accounts of the sinking of the famous ship and weaving numerous details of the story into a surreal and multi-layered web of music and sound. The project began in 1969 and over the subsequent 25 years underwent numerous additions and alterations. Many of these enhancements grew out of new information that emerged about the ship, including the discovery of the ship's hull and remaining contents in 1985.

In composing the work Bryars brought together a wide range of sonic elements, including strings, winds, a variety of percussion sounds, bass, and electric guitar, as well as a number of electronic effects—many of them evoking the sounds of large metal objects being bent, scraped, and twisted. These instrumental timbres and sound effects are joined by two distinct but equally poignant vocal elements: a children's choir, and recordings of interviews with survivors of the disaster.

The inspiration for the work came from the composer's discovery of a report by a survivor that, in the last moments before the ship tipped and sank into the water, a band on the deck of the ship continued to play. The observer, who was working frantically to send out a wireless communication for help, first heard the band playing ragtime music. Later, as he was swimming away from the sinking ship, he heard strains of the Episcopal hymn *Autumn*. The hymn continued, the observer recalled, even as the ship tipped upright on its nose and plummeted into the ocean.

This hymn serves as the central musical layer of the work, performed primarily by strings and joined at various points by other instruments and ethereal choir voices. The hymn music proper is subjected to a number of variations and tropes, and is interrupted by the occasional chime or woodblock. This musical layer is joined by a variety of sustained sounds, including tam-tams, bass drums, and highly evocative water gongs (a gong whose pitch is lowered by dipping it in a tub of water while it is being struck). Intermittently, barely decipherable excerpts from news reports and survivor interviews emerge from the mix as well. The various layers of sound are subjected to careful sound engineering, with heavy reverberation and other alterations applied. This element is crucial to the piece's narrative quality, so much so, in fact, that on the 1994 recording the sound designer is listed among the instrumentalists. The idea, the composer explains, is that the band continues to play even as they and their instruments are submerged in the water. At the end of the work the reverberation effects disappear as the musicians emerge once again from the depths as an apparition. *—Jeremy Grimshaw*

Jack Brymer

b. Jan. 27, 1915, South Shields, England, **d.** Sep. 15, 2003, Brighton, England
Clarinetist

Widely considered the dean of British clarinetists up to his death in 2003, Jack Brymer once said that "the ability to play the clarinet is the ability to overcome the imperfections of the instrument," adding that "there's no such thing as a perfect clarinet, never was and never will be." Brymer was working as a schoolteacher and had just given his debut recital on BBC Radio when his friend Dennis Brain, the prominent horn player, suggested that he audition for the empty first clarinet chair in Britain's new Royal Philharmonic Orchestra in 1947. He was picked by conductor Sir Thomas Beecham and remained with the Royal Philharmonic for 16 years, later joining the BBC Symphony (1963–1972) and the London Symphony (1972–1985, retiring on his 70th birthday). Brymer's three recordings of Mozart's Clarinet Concerto are considered classics, and one was heard in the film *Out of Africa.* He also recorded other clarinet and wind ensemble music of Mozart, as well as several Romantic-era concertos, but he knew and performed more music than he ever recorded. One other Jack Brymer performance that everyone knows, however, is that of the clarinet part in the long orchestral crescendo in the Beatles' "A Day in the Life." Atypically for players of his time, Brymer also investigated music by some of the lesser-known composers of the Classical era. Brymer wrote two books, hosted radio programs, and served as a professor at several top British music schools, including the Royal Military School of Music. From time to time he played jazz clarinet in British clubs, and he also recorded as part of the jazz group of his best-known student, saxophonist John Harle. *—James Manheim*

Recommended:

- ○ **Mozart: Complete Wind Music** / Brymer / London 455794
- ○ **Mozart: Clarinet Concerto; Oboe Concerto** / Marriner (cond.), Brymer, Black, Academy of St. Martin-in-the-Fields / Philips 416483

John Bull

b. ca. 1562, Old Radnor, Radnorshire, England, **d.** Mar. 12, 1628, Antwerp, Belgium
Composer

John Bull, an early example of the species of virtuoso performer/composer, lived in a time of cultural and political ferment in England. Unlike most of his contemporaries, however, he traveled extensively and became acquainted with the musical styles of other European countries, particularly the Netherlands.

At about age 11 Bull became a chorister and, nine years later, organist at Hereford Cathedral. In 1574, when only 22 years old, he was appointed Master of the Choristers at the Cathedral, and in the same year to a similar post at the Chapel Royal of King Charles I in London. His subsequent career might have easily been lived out in the cloistered calm of great churches was it not that Bull was a reckless, argumentative man who courted disaster in both his private and public life.

Bull graduated as Doctor of Music at both Cambridge and Oxford Universities (1589 and 1592). From 1597, when he was a Public Reader at Gresham College, London, he frequently fell foul of the College authorities and in 1607, the year he was married, was forced to resign. However, despite journeys abroad as an organ consultant, he continued as organist at the King's Chapel.

In 1613, Bull was charged with adultery and fled to the Netherlands, claiming religious persecution as the reason for his sudden departure. During his flight from England, many of Bull's manuscripts were lost, though 120 canons, a dozen or so anthems and a large quantity of keyboard music survived.

In 1614, diplomatic pressures from England brought dismissal from a post Bull held in Brussels with Archduke Albert, and in 1617 he moved to Antwerp Cathedral as organist, an appointment he held until his death.

One of the composers of the a golden age of English choral and keyboard music that includes Byrd and Tallis, Bull frequently used the "free-voiced" textures that mark the period of transition from Renaissance to early Baroque, yet his sacred music reflects the contrapuntal complexity of J.S. Bach. His intricate plainsong settings and hexachord fantasias for organ also show a continental influence; the virginal music is more English in character, and includes highly ornamented variations and fantasias. Under Bull's influence, the simple melodic style of popular songs and folk tunes became a starting-point for elaborate excursions into keyboard virtuosity; the anthems and multi-part canons are more direct in feeling, and preserve the formal structures of English masters such as Tallis. *—Roy Brewer*

Overview of Works (ca. 1590–1625)

The English composer, keyboard virtuoso, and organ builder John Bull (1562/3–1628) was one of a group of English composers who had a profound influence on the development of early seventeenth century keyboard music by composers such as Sweelinck. Following a career as a Gentleman of the Chapel Royal, and (from 1597) as the first Public Reader in music at Gresham College, London, Bull was forced to flee to mainland Europe after being accused of adultery. There, like his compatriot and fellow composer Peter Philips, he settled in Belgium, where he claimed to be a persecuted Catholic and was offered the post of organist of Antwerp Cathedral.

Bull's compositions fall into three groups, a body of church music consisting mainly of anthems, music for keyboard (virginals or organ), and some 50 works for viols. Much of the sacred music was lost after Bull fled to Europe, and today it is the keyboard works that are especially valued. Around 150 such works are extant, compositions that include all the major forms of the period: variations based on the popular tunes of the day, plainsong, or built over bass patterns; stylized dances such as the pavan and galliard (invariably coupled together to make a slow-fast pairing), alman, and coranto; and free contrapuntal compositions such as preludes and fantasias, or fancies (as they were often called in England). It is in the last-named genre that Bull, and composers like Philips and Giles Farnaby exerted the strongest influence, going well beyond the fantasias of Italian composers in expanding the form. Many of Bull's linked pavans and galliards are expansive works incorporating bold harmonies and brilliantly inventive writing. Among notable examples are the *Chromatic (Queen Elizabeth's) Pavan and Galliard,* possibly composed in the wake of the death of Elizabeth I, and the three sets known as *Quadran Pavans and Galliards.*

Many of these works make considerable technical demand on their performer, particularly those involving variations. *The King's Hunt,* one of Bull's most famous works, is a colorful programmatic piece based on two themes which are marvelously developed through a series of increasingly virtuosic variants. Many of Bull's keyboard works appeared in *Parthenia* (1613), the first published collection of keyboard works, while the famous *Fitzwilliam Virginal Book* also includes a substantial number. Of the few anthems that survive, four are unaccompanied "full" anthems (purely choral), and another three are "verse" anthems for soloists, choir, and instrumental ensemble. One of the latter, the six-part *Almighty God, who by the leading,* was one of the most popular cathedral works of the day. *—Brian Robins*

Recommended:

- ○ **Doctor Bull's Good Night** / Hantaï / 1999 / Astrée 128543
- ○ **Bull: Pavans And Galliards** / Payne / 1995 / Bis 729

Grace Bumbry

b. Jan. 4, 1937, St. Louis, MO
Mezzo-Soprano

As a youth Grace Melzia Ann Bumbry sang in church choirs. In 1955 she entered Northwestern University, where she studied voice with Lotte Lehman, and transferred with her to the Music Academy of the West in Santa Barbara, California. In 1958 she was joint winner of the Metropolitan Opera Auditions, sharing first place with Martina Arroyo. She won some other prizes, and made her professional debut in a recital in London in 1959. Her first operatic appearance was at the Paris Opéra, as Amneris in Verdi's *Aida.* It was one of the most spectacular operatic debuts in history; Bumbry became an instant star and was invited to join the roster of the Basle Opera. She made operatic history in 1961 when she was engaged by Wieland Wagner to sing at the Bayreuth Festival and became the first black singer to perform in that shrine of Wagnerian opera. Furthermore, musical historian Nicolas Slomimsky has pointed out that she was the first African American to make a professional operatic as a goddess, for her debut at Bayreuth was as Venus in *Tannhäuser,* July 23, 1961. Bumbry embarked on a concert tour of the United States and was invited by Jacqueline Kennedy to sing at the White House, on February 20, 1962. She also followed up her smash success at Bayreuth with appearances as Venus at the Chicago Lyric Opera and at Lyons, France.

Bumbry's 1963 London debut came in the role of Princess Eboli in Verdi's *Don Carlos,* and she gave her first Metropolitan Opera performance in the same role in 1965. Among the other roles she undertook were those of Lady Macbeth in Verdi's *Macbeth* and Carmen in Bizet's opera. During the 1960s Bumbry worked on extending her range. In 1970 at the Vienna Staatsoper, she sang the part of Santuzza, making her debut as a soprano. She sang Richard Strauss's *Salome* at Covent Garden the same year, and her first appearance in Puccini's *Tosca* at the Metropolitan Opera came in 1971. She maintained her mezzo voice while triumphing in soprano parts, such as *Jenufa* in Janáček's opera and as Ariane in Dukas' *Bluebeard.* Between operatic performances she established a fine recital career, stressing the core repertory of German lieder. Her attractions as a performer include a commanding stage presence with an effective and understated acting technique. She has a very warm voice with rich tone quality throughout the mezzo range, although it loses some of its distinctiveness in the very upper part of her soprano register. She is among the few sopranos who have sung both the roles of Aida and Amneris in *Aida* and both Venus and Elisabeth in Wagner's *Tannhäuser.* *—Joseph Stevenson*

Recommended:

- ○ **Lieder & Arias** / Mehta, Ceccato (conds.), Bumbry, Corelli, Hokanson, Giaiotti, Orchestra del Teatro Municipa / 2001 / EMI 567675

- **Bizet: Carmen** / Frühbeck de Burgos (cond.), Freni, Bumbry, Vickers, Paskalis, Paris National Opera Theater / 2003 / EMI 85505
- **Verdi: Aida** / Leinsdorf (cond.), Alldis, Price, Domingo, Milnes, Bumbry, London SO / 1999 / RCA 39498

Adolf Busch

b. Aug. 8, 1891, Siegen, Westphalia, Germany, **d.** Jun. 9, 1952, Guilford, Vermont
Violinist

Adolf Georg Wilhelm Busch was born into a musical family that included his older brother, conductor Fritz Busch. Trained on the violin from age three, Adolph Busch entered the Cologne Conservatory at age 11. He studied conducting and composition with the school's director, Fritz Steinbach, and pursued further composition training with Hugo Gruters. Busch began a long performing association with composer Max Reger in 1907 and received his first major orchestral appointment in 1912 as leader of the Viennese Konzertverein. Following an attempt at organizing a performing group in 1913—which fell apart amid the turmoil of World War I—he cofounded the Busch Quartet in 1918. During the early 1920s, with Gosta Andreasson, Karl Doktor, and Paul Grummer in the group, the ensemble achieved international renown for its performances and in 1930, Busch's younger brother Hermann Busch succeeded Grummer as their cellist. Throughout the late 1920s and the early 1930s, he achieved renown throughout Europe in a dual career, as a member of the Busch Quartet and as a soloist, celebrated for his performances of the Beethoven and Brahms violin concertos, while the quartet was particularly successful with the Beethoven quartets. He was also noted as a teacher and his students included figures such as Yehudi Menuhin. Busch composed as well, very much in the mold of Reger, but his recognition rests upon his work as a re-creative musician. During the mid-1930s, he founded the Busch Chamber Players, whose stripped-down interpretations of such Baroque works as Bach's *Brandenburg Concertos* achieved great popularity in their time and marked an important early step in removing the layers of Romantic-era bombast that had been applied to them. The group's subsequent recordings in England of these pieces and the suites for orchestra, and works such as the Handel Op. 6 concerti grossi, were unique in their time and remain highly prized. Busch also organized a piano trio with his brother Hermann and pianist Rudolf Serkin, who also served as his accompanist and subsequently married Busch's daughter. Busch moved to the United States in 1939 and the Busch Quartet was re-formed by 1941. He remained active as a soloist, as well as a member of the chamber group for the remainder of his life, and he also conducted orchestras. In 1950, two years before his death, Busch founded the Marlboro School of Music. —*Bruce Eder*

Recommended:

- **Bach: Orchestral Music** / Busch, etc. / 2001 / Andante 1986
- **Great Violinists Volume 5: Adolf Busch** / Busch, Seidler-Winkler, Busch SQ / 1992 / Symposium 1109
- **Adolf Busch Plays Brahms** / Busch, Steinberg (cond.), Kell, Busch SQ / Music & Arts 1107

Antoine Busnois

b. ca. 1436, Busnes, France, **d.** Nov. 6, 1492, Bruges, Belgium
Composer: Choral

"Worthy of the immortal gods" was the fifteenth century theorist Johannes Tinctoris' assessment of the music of Antoine Busnois (as well as that of Johannes Ockeghem). The twentieth century, as well, has identified in this composer a crucial link between Guillaume Dufay and Josquin Desprez. His chansons, masses, and secular vocal polyphony represent some of the finest (and most plentiful) examples of French music of the latter half of the fifteenth century; yet Antonius de Busne, *dit* Busnoys, often seems unjustly eclipsed by his esteemed contemporaries.

Busnois' family history and early life remain somewhat shrouded in the historical mists. His name (in the Artois dialect) most likely indicates the town of Busne (similarly, Gilles from Bins was styled "Binchois"). Since Busnois had advanced to the priesthood by 1460, the period 1436–39 is suggested for his birthdate. His name and the location of his early benefices suggest Flanders/Artois/Hainaut as the general area of his first training in music, though 1450s service to the Court of Brittany is also possible.

The earliest documentary evidence of his life, shockingly, is a Vatican petition (1461) for absolution from the sentence of excommunication. The young priest apparently beat another priest bloody within the cathedral close, organized five further gang assaults on him, and then continued to celebrate mass while under sentence! It seems the Pope pardoned these youthful indiscretions, however, as Busnois recevied promotion to Acolyte and then to Subdeacon around Easter of 1465.

Busnois by now was a choir clerk in the Abbey of St.-Martin in Tours, where Ockeghem himself served as Treasurer. Also by this time, his many accomplishments as courtly poet and musician were already being recorded in a series of central manuscript *Chansonniers* in the Loire Valley. Autobiographical evidence in one set of these songs hints strongly of an extravagant society love affair between the priest and a Parisian noblewoman.

After one further year in French lands, serving a Potiers church from September to July 1465 as Master of the Choirboys, Busnois was dismissed, perhaps for financial irregularities. Less than a year later, he is documented in service to the Court of Burgundy, the most important position of his career. His motet *In hydraulis* praises Ockeghem and calls himself an "unworthy singer of the Count of Charolais"; this Count was crowned Duke of Burgundy on June 15, 1467, and Busnois followed Charles the Bold onto the international stage. His service was at first unofficial, but tenured by November of 1470; he provided a variety of musical and courtly duties to the peripatetic court until well after Charles' death. He sang regular liturgical observances in the Duke's chapel, followed the Duke on military campaigns, and even undertook a diplomatic embassy of some secrecy at one point (this last could have entailed a "poaching" mission to secure singers from a rival prince's chapel). His few surviving sacred works, with a number of chansons, may date from this service.

After Charles' January 1477 death, Busnois entered the service of his daughter and heir, Marie of Burgundy. Upon her marriage to the Maximilian I later the same year, he transferred his service to the chapel of the Hapsburg Emperor. Busnois is documented at least sporadically in this well-remunerated position until April 1483. Two anomalous Italian-texted pieces attributed to him have suggested his presence sometime in Italy, but one of these certainly is an Italian contrafactum of a French piece, and the other is more likely the work of a Florentine. The final documentary reference to Busnois indicates his death: the Chapter of St.-Saveur in Bruges met on November 6, 1492, to consider replacements for their recently deceased musical director. —*Timothy Dickey*

Overview of Works (ca. 1450–1490)

Just as the consummate chanson composer, Gilles Binchois, was eclipsed by Guillaume Dufay, Antoine Busnois has often suffered in comparison with his contemporary, Johannes Ockeghem. But should Ockeghem's few masses outweigh Busnois' manifold chansons? Composer, singer, and poet, Busnois was acknowledged one of the most excellent musicians of the fifteenth century. He has justly regained stature through scholarly collection of his sacred works, and revaluation of the scintillating craft of his chansons. He was one of the first composers to bring the "modern" techniques of imitation into all genres of music, and was instrumental in shaping the "spatial integrity" of independent vocal lines. His melodic writing itself is marked by airy and wide-spanned melodies, energized by sequences and syncopation. A professional singer himself, perhaps he took as much delight in writing for the human voice—exploiting the entire modal octave in characteristic, syncopated ascents—as singers still derive from performing his music.

Busnois' output of chansons first formed the cornerstone of his reputation. More than 65 pieces survive, scattered widely throughout the lavish chansonniers commissioned as status symbols in both France and Italy. Most of his songs set Rondeaux and Bergerettes, the courtly formes fixes. They also somewhat favor topics of restrained, "courtly" love, though he set a number of decidedly more earthy, popular tunes.

His skill at writing imitation is frequently evident, often on a structural level (as in the regular points of imitation in *Centmille escus,* or *Ma vostre cuer*). Sometimes the voices inhabit spatially distinct ranges, though he freely experiments with scoring, as in the three overlapping baritones in *Bel acueil.* A group of singular pieces allude through acrostics and other puzzles to an apparent society affair between Busnois (possibly writing text himself) and a "Jacqueline de Haqueville."

Contemporary manuscripts also preserve at least two masses by him, with a number of highly individual motets. His *Missa O crux lignum* shows a strongly rational organization, which alternates reduced textures (often imitative) and fuller sonorities containing the cantus firmus. The *Missa L'homme armé* adds to this kind of structural planning a staggering level of complexity in mathematical proportions, corresponding perhaps both to the Pythagorean harmonic ratios, and the organization of the Burgundian chivalric Order of the Golden Fleece; it may have been the seminal work in a lengthy tradition of masses on this tune. (Busnois has also been advanced as a possible composer of a series of six anonymous *L'homme armé masses* presented to the King of Naples.)

Many of his other Latin-texted works display similar levels of intellectual artifice: *Anthoni usque limina* with its self-referential text and "bell" canon, *Regina coeli II* with its chant cantus firmus in strict canon, *In hydraulis* with its symbolically Pythagorean Tenor and erudite references to Ockeghem and his music. At the same time, he could find his way to such a charming and unassuming little piece as the welcome song *Noel noel.* —*Timothy Dickey*

Recommended:

- **Busnoys: In Hydraulis & Other Works** / Blachly (cond.), Pomerium / 1993 / Dorian 90184
- **Busnois: Magnificat; In Hydraulis; Missa O Crux Lingnum** / van der Kamp (cond.), Kapel der Lage Landen / Emergo 3954

CHORAL

Missa "L'homme armé" (ca. 1460)

In 1453, when Byzantium fell to the Turks, Pope Pius II called for a new Crusade. Crusading fervor resounded strongly in the neo-chivalric culture of the Duchy of Burgundy. One unexpected fruit of this climate may have been the elevation of a little chanson rustique, a popular ditty about the "armed man" ("L'Homme armé"), into an internationally popular song, and the inspiration for one of the most famed clusters of compositions in the Renaissance. Either Robert Morton or Antoine Busnois, both singers at the court of the Burgundian Duke Charles the Bold, included the *L'Homme armé* tune into a satirical quodlibet (a song that presents other well-known tunes in humorous or clever combinations), *Il sera pour vous*, and sometime in the late 1460s the first of a long line of masses took the tune as cantus firmus. All told, some 40 masses in the late fifteenth and sixteenth centuries would be composed on *L'Homme armé*. Although probably not the first to be composed, that by Antoine Busnois is apparently seminal to the ongoing tradition. The intricacies in his treatment of the *L'Homme armé* cantus firmus line, coupled with the excitement of his often richly imitative counterpoint in the outer voices, give a freshness and novelty to the piece. Guillaume Dufay may have quoted Busnois in his *Missa L'Homme armé*, and Jacob Obrecht models his own mass directly on that of Busnois. A splendid set of six such masses, preserved anonymously in a manuscript presented to the King of Naples by the Burgundian Court, betray a structural and symbolic debt to Busnois, and his name has been suggested as composer for them as well. Some facets of Busnois' cantus firmus treatment do seem quite unusual. Whereas the *L'Homme armé* tune divides neatly into three segments, he divides it instead into two parts in the Kyrie and Agnus Dei, and at seemingly random places in the inner three movements. His compositional artifice transposes the tenor melody down a fourth in the Credo, using a Latin canon (a written instruction in the music telling performers how to assemble the parts); in the Agnus Dei he gives the cantus firmus in augmented inversion. Though he adds no ornamentation to the cantus firmus, leaving its jaunty rhythms and horn call of falling fifths clearly audible, different mensuration signs (time signatures) produce different paces in the tenor voice relative to the other three. The Neapolitan theorist Johannes Tinctoris, in fact, though he praised Busnois as one of the most literate composers of the day, criticized his choices of mensuration in this piece. These idiosyncrasies, in fact, result in part from the composer's conscious adoption of a hyper-rational program within the Mass. Medieval music theory credits Pythagoras with the discovery of musical consonance, and the expression of intervals and chords by means of simple ratios. Busnois' selection of mensurations allows him to manipulate the length of the various movements of the Mass so that they not only relate in groups of threes (the perfect number of the Trinity), but also present ratios which symbolically correspond to the Pythagorean intervals. The lone exception is the Et incarnatus, which at the literal center of this Mass, lasts 31 tempora (units of time). Thirty-one happens to be the exact number of knights invested with membership in Charles the Bold's Order of the Golden Fleece, inaugurated in 1468. The importance of the same number to several of the anonymous Naples *L'Homme armé* masses suggests a strong connection between the entire group and the Burgundian Court, again centering on the remarkable person of Antoine Busnois. *—Timothy Dickey*

Recommended:

- ○ **Busnois: Missa L'homme armé; Domarto: Missa Spiritus almus** / Kirkman (cond.), Binchois Consort / 2002 / Hyperion 67319

Ferruccio Busoni

b. Apr. 1, 1866, Empoli, Italy, **d.** Jul. 27, 1924, Berlin, Germany
Composer: Keyboard, Concerto, Orchestral, Opera

Ferruccio Busoni was the son of an Italian clarinet virtuoso who was a harsh and demanding pedagogue. Under the thumb of his father, Busoni developed a virtuoso keyboard technique that is in itself the stuff of legend. He began composing early, adding opus numbers to his works from the beginning. Reaching Opus 40 at age 17, Busoni decided go backward to number 31 and start over, causing no end of grief to scholars who attempted to edit his works later.

From an early age, Busoni pursued a serious interest in the music of J.S. Bach, Mozart, Beethoven, and Liszt. Although Busoni's reputation as a piano virtuoso of the first rank was established in Europe by the end of the 1880s, he first made his mark as an editor of Bach's keyboard music. While today these editions are regarded as among the most intrusive and heavily marked Bach scores ever made, Busoni's marginal remarks about Bach's thought processes and the analytic value of these comments influenced Bach scholars and composers for generations.

In 1896, Busoni found his mature compositional voice in the *Violin Sonata No. 2*, Op. 36b, which takes a theme of Bach and submits it to a complex series of variations. In 1904, Busoni followed that with his huge piano concerto. Cast in five movements, it runs 90 minutes and contains parts for a chorus. In 1907, Busoni published a series of writings as *Sketch for a New Esthetic of Music*. This book proposes a wide variety of new compositional techniques then relatively uninvestigated in Western music, such as microtonal scales and electronics. By 1912, Busoni had composed his first entirely non-key centered composition, the *Sonatina seconda*. The basis for his definitive style is to be found here; it is neither wholly tonal nor completely atonal, but is placed in a sort of harmonic netherworld in between. In the years left to him, Busoni composed four operas, *Die Brautwahl* (1912), *Arlecchino* (1915), *Turandot* (1917) and *Doktor Faust* (1924). His major keyboard work is the *Fantasia Contrappuntistica* (1911–22), a piece that concludes with a massive fugue built out of the unfinished *Contrapunctus XXIV* of Bach's *Die Kunst der Fuge*.

Busoni conducted master classes in composition and taught piano. Among his composition students, Kurt Weill made perhaps the most masterly use of Busoni's Apollonian approach to opera and his quirky sense of harmony. Another Busoni pupil, Otto Luening, helped pioneer the use of electronics in music. As a piano teacher, Busoni also started off an international school of super-virtuosos. Claudio Arrau and Egon Petri are good examples of what Busoni wrought in terms of pianists. As to Busoni's own playing, there are some phonograph records of him made in 1919 and an enormous number of piano rolls. The records only hint at what his playing might've sounded like, but some of the better rolls offer a more generous sample of his artistry at the keyboard.

After his death, Busoni was regarded as a great piano virtuoso whose own music was seemingly incomprehensible. Busoni's thinking would have a more decisive impact on later composers, such as John Cage and Morton Feldman, and in the early 1980s, his music would experience a small-scale revival of interest. There is little reason to be afraid of Busoni, as his best music is tremendously exciting, accessible, and endlessly thought-provoking. *—Uncle Dave Lewis*

KEYBOARD

Bach Transcriptions (1914–1919)

In an epilogue to Ferruccio Busoni's complete edition of Bach's keyboard works, the pianist/composer wrote, "I have my father to thank for the good fortune that he kept me strictly to the study of Bach in my childhood, and that in a time and in a country in which the master was rated little higher than Carl Czerny. He educated me in this way to be a 'German' musician and showed me the path which I never entirely deserted, though at the same time I never cast off the Latin qualities given to me by nature." Over the years, Busoni's dedication to Bach led him to compose numerous works invoking Bach's style, assemble the above-mentioned complete edition of the Bach keyboard works, and arrange many of Bach's works for the modern piano. Busoni transcribed Bach throughout his life, both for concert use and his own edification. Most of the Bach transcriptions were published in a set called the *Bach-Busoni gesammelte Ausgabe* (Collected Edition of Bach-Busoni) of 1920, which also included an annotated version of the *Well-Tempered Clavier*, a few were published along with the Busoni Edition.

Especially before the advent of widespread recording technology, many listeners heard Bach's keyboard works first in Busoni's transcriptions. Many of these are fairly straightforward, simply recasting organ music for the piano without much alteration; the more ambitious transcriptions, however, have aroused controversy ever since they were published, especially among Bach purists. Busoni felt free to add chords, additional lines of counterpoint, and varied repeats to already-dense compositions. Defenders of Busoni have cited his desire to exploit the resources of the modern piano, but it is still hard to imagine why Busoni felt it necessary to arrange, for example, the *Goldberg Variations*, one of the summits of keyboard virtuosity.

Busoni's transcriptions seem rather to have been motivated by a desire first to serve the genius of J.S. Bach, and then to respond to the old master in his own rather cerebral musical language. Heard in this light, many of the transcriptions are quite fascinating. Some have a gentle simplicity and unforced eloquence, like many of the chorale preludes. Others take more drastic measures. One of the most dramatic transcriptions is the *Chaconne in D Minor*, originally part of the *Second Partita* for solo violin. Obviously, there would be no question of attempting to imitate the original instrument on the piano; however, the new instrument allows Busoni to include and elaborate on the chords which the violin can only suggest, making for an illuminating listening experience, halfway between Bach and Busoni and none the worse for it. All these pieces work spectacularly well for the piano, giving both players and listeners a fresh insight on Bach. *—Andrew Lindemann Malone*

Recommended:

- ○ **Busoni: Klavierbearbeitungen Bach'scher Werke** / Rösel / 1993 / Berlin Classics 0010882
- ○ **Songs Without Words** / Perahia / 1999 / Sony 66511

Elegies (1907–1908)

Ferruccio Busoni published six *Elegies* in 1907, shortly after publication of his groundbreaking book, *Toward a New Aesthetic of Music*, an avant-garde manifesto in which he outlined the directions he believed music should take in the twentieth century, including expanded tonalities, atonality, and electronic music. Far from exemplifying such futuristic ideas, the *Elegies* actually occupy a middle ground between the late-Romantic tendencies of Busoni's first decades as a composer and the modernistic sound-world of his mature compositions. Although each piece can stand on its own, the *Elegies* make a satisfying cycle, with a profoundly moving conclusion in the seventh elegy, *Berceuse*.

The first elegy, "Nach der Wendlung. Recuillement" (After the Turning Point. Self-Communion), is thematically entirely new. A thoughtful and harmonically ambiguous meditation, it effectively introduces the subsequent elegies, which treat their recycled themes in new and similarly ambiguous ways. The second elegy, "All'Italia," employs two themes from Busoni's hyper-Romantic piano concerto: a moody barcarolle from its central third movement and a Neapolitan tarantella from its wild fourth movement. The dark and thoughtful atmosphere is heightened in the third elegy, "Meine Seele bangt und hofft zu Dir" (My soul is afraid and hopes in Thee), which is a freely developed chorale prelude based on Bach's *Allein Gott in der Hoh' sei Ehr.* It builds to a fine climax of dissonant chordal intensity before subsiding to a brooding conclusion. Busoni later used this powerful music as the springboard for his massive *Fantasia Contrappuntistica* of 1910. The fourth and fifth elegies take their themes from Busoni's *Turandot Suite*, a concert hall work inspired by Gozzi's well-known play. The fourth, "Turandots Frauengemach" ("Turandot in the Women's Quarters"), is based on the Elizabethan song "Greensleeves," which had been mistakenly included in the book of Chinese melodies that Busoni used as the source for the suite. Busoni's first opera, *Die Brautwahl* (The Spectre-Bride), was the source for the sixth elegy, "Erscheinung. Notturno" ("Apparition. Nocturne"), an appropriately ghostly bit of mood-painting. In 1909, Busoni added a seventh elegy, *Berceuse*, which was a transcription for piano of his *Berceuse élégaique* for orchestra, written as a memorial to his mother, who had died in May of that year. Each of the elegies was dedicated to a pianist that Busoni admired. The first was dedicated to Austrian pianist Gottfried Galston, the second to Busoni's greatest pupil, Egon Petri, the third to Russian pianist Gregor Beklemischev, the fourth to Polish-American pianist Michael von Zadora (also a Busoni pupil). The fifth elegy was dedicated to Busoni's English pupil, O'Neill Phillips, who died young, the sixth to Hungarian pianist Leo Kestenberg (yet another Busoni protégé), and the seventh to Dutch pianist and composer Johan Wijsman. *—Mark Satola*

Recommended:

○ **John Ogdon; Rachmaninov: Etudes tableaux; Busoni Piano Works** / Ogdon / 2003 / Testament 1295

Fantasia contrappuntistica, transcription of Bach, for 2 pianos (1922)

On tour in the United States in January 1910, Busoni ran across a friend from his student days in Leipzig, Bernhard Ziehn, a richly cultivated musician and contrapuntal theorist. Busoni, at the time preoccupied with editing *The Art of Fugue* for an edition of Bach's keyboard works, was also at an aesthetic turning point. The pianist/composer was developing a new, "Faustian" musical language dominated by melody—not in the form of memorable tunes, but as "the ruler of all voices and all emotions... as the bearer of the idea and the begetter of harmony, in short, the most highly developed (not the most complicated) polyphony." Discussions between Busoni and Ziehn turned to the final, unfinished fugue from *The Art of Fugue*, which has three subjects and which breaks off as Bach works his name—in German musical nomenclature, equivalent to the notes B flat-A-C-B—into the texture. The manner in which Bach had intended to complete the work had long been the subject of speculation. Ziehn's theory of symmetrical inversion, in which themes retain their intervallic integrity without regard to the resulting harmony, stimulated Busoni's own imagination.

For the remainder of the tour, the composer continued labors on his oft-revised piano work, then titled *Grosse Fuge*. To its massive ten-part structure—four fugues, three variations, intermezzo, cadenza, and coda—Busoni added a chorale prelude, reworked from the third of his *Elegies* (1907) for piano, as well as a reminiscence of the chorale before the coda-stretta. In this final form, the so-called *edizione definitiva*, Busoni retitled the work *Fantasia contrappuntistica*. "The piece is a disproportionate task for ten fingers," he wrote with considerable understatement, "whereas divided between twenty it would be easy and transparent for player and listener alike." Busoni arranged the work for two pianos in June 1921.

Considerably expanded for the two-piano version, the alternately luminous and declamatory fantasy on Bach's chorale "Ehre sei Gott in der Höhe" that opens the *Fantasia* suggests not faith but anxiety, a spiritual crisis. Busoni transcribed Bach's tripartite unfinished fugue, freely and with some subtle chromatic additions, into Fugues I, II, and III of the *Fantasia*. Fugue III continues in an ascetically chromatic idiom from the point at which Bach's fragment breaks off, hovering between delirium and mounting hysteria until a climax, a tempestoso salvo of interlocked octaves. As scholar and conductor Antony Beaumont puts it, "with the aid of Ziehn's symmetrical inversion, Busoni assembles a panoply of tense, tersely argued counterpoint. The play of theme against theme unleashes a stream of harmonic surprises...."

A sotto voce Intermezzo, marked occultamente, and later, visionario, works over the B-A-C-H motive like an invocation. Three progressively more animated variations, the second of which contains a nod to the B-A-C-H motive, transform the fugal subjects. The third variation, marked by triplets poco a poco crescendo, achieves a fiery climax from which the Cadenza gradually retreats, dissolving into arpeggios in which the B-A-C-H motive seems to float. This surreally blithe moment is short-lived as Fugue IV, driven by dotted rhythms, combines in a stunning *tour de force* the three subjects of Bach's fugue, the B-A-C-H motive, and the central subject of *The Art of Fugue*. Over the B-A-C-H motive, now heard as an ostinato, a reminiscence of the chorale glows dolcissimo in the treble; this leads to the Stretta, which begins sotto voce and grows to end this work of intensely concentrated power with a cataclysmic pronouncement of the subject of Fugue I. *—Adrian Corleonis*

Recommended:

○ **Mozart, Reger, Busoni: Music for Two Pianos** / A. Schiff, P. Serkin / 1999 / ECM 465062

Sonatinas (1910–1920)

Ferruccio Busoni's *Sonatinas* provide a handy summary of his stylistic evolution and historical interests. These six works variously explore Lisztian virtuosity; the return to the musical virtues of past masters like Bach that Busoni expounded as "Young Classicism"; the melodic, harmonic, and rhythmic adventurousness of Busoni's contemporary, Arnold Schoenberg; and Busoni's increasing interest in the Faust legend.

Despite its frequent dissonance, the *Sonatina No. 1* (1910) is almost entirely tonal and even ends with a C major cadence. Structured as a series of connected episodes based on two main themes, this technically difficult work moves through major, minor, and whole tone scales and into harmonic realms suggestive of Schoenberg's experimentation with 12-tone music.

In a diary entry of June 25, 1912, Busoni wrote "Two to one = Boy to girl," contrasting the relative delicacy of the *Sonatina No. 1* with the more aggressive *Sonatina No. 2* (1912). The later work is freer in structure than its predecessor, as Busoni abandons bar lines in parts of the work and even refers to it as "senza tonalità." At this time, Busoni was beginning his examination of the stories associated with Faust and he thought of the *Sonatina No. 2* as a study for his opera *Doktor Faust*; one theme from the piano work turns up as the opera's "Student's theme."

After the relatively experimental nature of the first two *Sonatinas*, the *Third* (1915)—subtitled "Sonatina for the Use of the American Child, Madeline M., Composed for the Harpsichord"—reflects Busoni's "Young Classicism." The piece is actually a miniature suite in five connected sections, including a prelude and fughetta, a rather sardonic March suggestive of the neo-Classical music of Igor Stravinsky, a short chorale, and a "Polacca" that is also heard in Busoni's opera *Arlecchino*.

Composed in the last days of 1917, the *Sonatina No. 4* is dedicated to Busoni's son Benvenuto. It is a calm, if not unclouded, reflection on Christmas, with thematic links again with *Doktor Faust* and an effective evocation of tolling bells.

Busoni had a long-standing fascination with the music of Johann Sebastian Bach. His many transcriptions and arrangements of Bach's music were collected and published in a deluxe edition in 1918. To close out the final volume of that set, Busoni created the *Sonatina No. 5*, a recasting of Bach's *Little Fantasy and Fugue in D minor*, BWV 905, that is in equal parts Bach and Busoni.

Another of Busoni's lifelong interests was the music of Franz Liszt. In his forward to an edition of Liszt's *Fantasy on Themes From Don Giovanni*, Busoni speculated on the possibility of creating a similar work using themes from Bizet's famous opera *Carmen*. That plan came to fruition in 1920 with the *Sonatina No. 6*, which employs numerous themes from Bizet's work, including the familiar *Flower Song* and *Habanera*. This lighthearted work actually ends with a poignant, rather dark coda that provides an ironic commentary on what came before. *—Chris Morrison*

Recommended:

○ **The Legendary Busoni Recordings** / Paul Jacobs / 1979 / Arbiter 124

Sonatina for piano No. 6 ("Fantasia da camera super Carmen") (1920)

Composed between 1910 and 1918, the first five of Busoni's sonatinas are signal items in the esoteric endeavor of fashioning a new, Faustian musical language that parallels the similar path of Schoenberg. Capping the series with an old-fashioned Lisztian operatic fantasy in the *Sonatina super Carmen* has, therefore, struck critics and commentators as incongruous. But heard against the backdrop of its era, rife with virulent political jostling reflected in swift aesthetic crosscurrents, it looms as a musical manifesto, a validation of Nietzsche's anti-Wagnerian admiration for Bizet's *Carmen* and a realization of the philosopher's call to "Mediterraneanize music."

Born in Italy, Busoni was justly proud of his heritage, yet he lived in Berlin for 30 years and wrote his stage works and songs in German. In this fiercely chauvinistic milieu, he never ceased to be an outsider. Typically, while on tour in New York in 1915, with the exuberantly begun Great War turning grim, news that he had been seen chatting with Saint-Saëns during a performance of *Carmen* at the Metropolitan Opera provoked a scandal in Berlin. His cosmopolitanism could only be viewed as disloyalty. To his "disciple" Egon Petri, he wrote: "The German is the greatest sufferer from *Heimweh*: he loves to make poems about it. Art is at home everywhere. The German is bourgeois, art is aristocratic." A visit to Paris in March 1920 he described as "like a homecoming for me... to find life on the grand scale again...." And under this stimulus he composed the *Sonatina super Carmen* there in the same month.

The best of Liszt's operatic fantasies touch upon a few salient moments in a grand pianistic design with the effect of a dramatic distillation or summary. Seizing upon four high points from Bellini's opera and working them with ever greater magniloquence to a whelming conclusion, Liszt's *Norma Fantasy* (of which Busoni was a compelling interpreter) provides the archetype and richest example. Busoni follows this model; but where Liszt is expansive, flamboyant, and luxuriant, Busoni's utterance is rapid, concentrated, and allusive. Sparkling octaves and thirds evoke the opening of Act Four—the crowd, the vendors, the anticipation—to segue into Don José's "Flower Song," heard in the piano's middle register, garlanded in scintillant arpeggios ranging over the entire keyboard, and cunningly combined with the Fate motif as it sinks to a murmur before Carmen's teasing *Habanera*. Beginning dolce, vagamente, the dance intensifies to a spinning seduction before dissolving suddenly into the entrance of the toreadors, brilliantly conjured with astounding economy. This, too, dissolves—into an andante visionario in which the Fate motif looms, strangely muted. Petri's classic 1936 recording of the *Sonatina super Carmen* plays just under six-and-a-half minutes.

Busoni gave the work its premiere in London's Wigmore Hall on June 22, 1920. Critic and composer Kaikhosru Sorabji was in the audience and commented: "The vulgar commonplace Bizet tunes lose all their own identity, although not rhythmically distorted, and are for the time being 'controlled' by Busoni in a way that recalls the control of a psychic sensitive by some powerful discarnate entity.... It was amusing to feel the audience at the Wigmore a little horrified and frightened by something the likes of which they had certainly never known before." That, too, is Faustian. *—Adrian Corleonis*

Recommended:

- ○ **Marc-André Hamelin Live at Wigmore Hall** / Hamelin / 1994 / Hyperion 66765
- ○ **The Legendary Busoni Recordings** / Paul Jacobs / 1979 / Arbiter 124

CONCERTO

Piano Concerto in C major, Op. 39 (1903–1904)

Ferruccio Busoni's *Piano Concerto*—a 70-minute, five-movement work whose performing forces include a male chorus—is likely the most massive work for soloist and orchestra in the repertory; the composer himself once referred to it as "my Skyscraper Concerto." What is most remarkable about the Concerto is that the immense labor of the musicians yields a momument of absolute music, signifying nothing but itself. Stylistically, the work is a synthesis of turn-of-the-twentieth century past and present, as well as the twin legacies of the composer's German and Italian parentage.

Busoni eschews a "display" role for the soloist—though the piano part requires both considerable technique and stamina—instead calling for an equal partnership of piano and orchestra. The opening movement, Prologo e Introito, begins with a lengthy orchestral introduction, followed by the piano's entrance with an extended series of massive chords. This expansive movement progresses through a variety of moods, introducing motives that recur throughout the work. The second movement, Pezzo giocoso, is a lively rondo filled with dance rhythms, which finally drifts into silence. The central Pezzo serioso, about 20 minutes long, is itself divided into four parts: "Introdactio," darkly colored and suggestive of some primordial mist; "prima pars," which rises to a great and noble climax; "altera pars," stormy music marked by harmonies that anticipate the mature language of Prokofiev and Stravinsky; and "ultima pars," in which the music returns to its mysterious beginnings. The fourth movement, All' italina, is a spectacular, virtuosic tarantella which leads directly into the final Cantico. Here the chorus joins in with words from Oehlenschlaeger's *Aladdin*: "Now the dead world is fully enlivened/Praising godliness the poem grows silent." The piano underscores the chorus and orchestra before bursting free in a jubilant coda.*—Sol Louis Siegel*

Recommended:

- ○ **Busoni: Piano Concerto** / Elder (cond.), Hamelin, City of Birmingham SO / 1999 / Hyperion 67143
- ○ **Busoni: Piano Concerto** / C. von Dohnányi (cond.), Ohlsson, Cleveland Orch. / 1989 / Telarc 80207

ORCHESTRAL

Berceuse élégiaque, Op. 42 (1909)

Busoni wrote his *Berceuse élégiaque* for orchestra (1909) as a memorial to his mother, who died in May of that year. The work, subtitled "Des Mannes Wiegenlied am Sarge seiner Mutter" (The Man's Cradle Song at His Mother's Coffin), also carries the inscription "The child's cradle rocks, the hazard of his fate reels; life's path fades, fades away into the eternal distance."

In the *Berceuse*, Busoni makes one of his first ventures into the realm of atonality, exhibiting a highly original style that is all the more moving and impressive for its resolutely quiet nature. The orchestration is delicate, exploiting the possibilities of tone color in a manner similar to that in Schoenberg's *Five Pieces for Orchestra*, written in the same year, but not performed until 1912.

The *Berceuse élégiaque* was premiered in New York City on February 21, 1911 in a concert conducted by the ailing Gustav Mahler. The occasion was, as it turns out, the great composer/conductor's final public appearance. *—Mark Satola*

Recommended:

- ○ **Busoni: Orchestral Works** / N. Järvi (cond.), BBC PO / 2002 / Chandos 9920
- ○ **Michael Gielen conducts Skrjabin, Busoni, Ravel & Strawinsky** / Gielen (cond.), SWF SO Baden-Baden & Freiburg / 1998 / Haenssler 93059

Turandot, suite from the opera, Op. 41 (1905)

Busoni composed this suite in 1905 and introduced it with the Berlin Philharmonic on October 21 of that year. Its lavish scoring includes triple winds (which double two piccolos, English horn, bass clarinet, contrabassoon), four trumpets, and four percussionists. Busoni—born six years after Mahler, four after Debussy, two after Richard Strauss—died in his fifties, as the first two did. If heredity didn't endow him with quite their creative genius, he was surely the thinking man's Romantic, with a fascinating musical vocabulary. Although most famous as a keyboard titan, one of the legendary virtuosi in a golden age, he was also a composer, scholar, teacher, and sometime conductor.

Antony Beaumont conjectures that the pending centennial (in 1906) of playwright Carlo Gozzi's death prompted Busoni to compose music for *Turandot*, the best known of the aristocratic Venetian's ten *fiabe* (fairy tales), written between 1761 and 1765 to protest the new bourgeois realism in Carlo Goldoni's rehabilitation of *commedia dell'arte*. Carl Maria von Weber had written an overture and six pieces in 1809 for Schiller's German adaptation of the play (part of which Hindemith used in his 1943 *Symphonic Metamorphosis*). But Busoni knew the original, and created both this eight-movement suite and, in 1911, a full complement of incidental music for the play.

Busoni indicated that "most of the themes are taken, sometimes unaltered, sometimes adapted, from Arabian, Chinese and Indian music" (the oldest *Turandot* literature came from twelfth century Persia, where *Turan-doht* meant "Chinese daughter"). Even though the suite was completed well in advance of the fully functional music for the play, it is genuine incidental music, with lengthy specific references made to Gozzi's play in Busoni's notes. Of the Alla marcia (The Execution, the City Gate, and the Departure) movement, for example, he writes: "Over the city gate of Peking are several heads on pikes, of princes who sought the hand of proud, sagacious and cruel Princess Turandot, but failed to solve three riddles posed by her. Prince Calaf, against the warning of friends, is so smitten with her beauty that he insists on undertaking the dangerous quest. Strange music is heard, built on a monotonous timpani motif, heralding the judge who approaches with his retinue to collect a new head.... Even this does not deter Calaf; he tears himself away, determined to win the princess or die."

Of Turandot's March, Busoni wrote: "Entrance of Princess Turandot, interspersed with the Turandot theme [first played pianissimo by low strings, later by violins]... melancholy, voluptuous and sinister." For Beaumont this "most extended movement of the suite offers a complete tone-picture of icy beauty...'Cruelty—Passion—veiled Beauty—unveiled Beauty.' Her theme is the second of three authentic Chinese melodies [associated with Turandot, originally collected by Rousseau]: Weber used the first, Puccini the third." Written 15 years before Puccini began (but never finished) the more famous operatic *Turandot*, Busoni's work lies in Puccini's shadow. On its own merits, however, it forms an interesting chapter in the evolving story of Orientalism. *—Roger Dettmer*

Recommended:

- ○ **Busoni: Turandot Suite; Sarabande et Cortège; Berceuse élégiaque** / S. Wong (cond.), Hong Kong PO / 2002 / Naxos 555373
- ○ **Busoni: Turandot Suite; Casella: Paganiniana; Martucci: 3 Pieces** / Muti (cond.), PO La Scala / 1993 / Sony 53280

OPERA

Arlecchino or The Windows, Op. 50 (1914–1916)

This fast-paced, witty, and attractive comic opera comes as a surprise to those who accept Busoni's ill-deserved reputation for academic dullness, and it foreshadows the neo-Classical trend that would appear strongly in Western music after World War I. In 1912 Busoni saw a revival of commedia dell'arte—the traditional theatrical form featuring the stock characters of the trickster Harlequin—and was inspired to begin work on a libretto, finishing it in 1914. Work on the music was interrupted by the composer's departure from Germany during World War I, only to be completed in Switzerland in 1916. (In the interim he adapted some of the music for an orchestral piece called *Rondo Arleccinesco*.)

Busoni's stated goal was to write an "Italian national opera," but the opera is in German. The reasons for this are practical: it seemed to Busoni that the many

German city opera houses, which were more innovative than those in Italy, would be more likely to play the work. The Zurich Opera was immediately interested, but asked for a companion piece to make a full evening with the one-act *Arlecchino*; Busoni quickly wrote an operatic setting of Carlo Gozzi's *Turandot* (nearly a decade before Puccini's more famous version). The composer conducted the premiere of both in Zürich on May 11, 1917.

Arlecchino is firmly tonal, and its emotional content is highly stylized. These elements, along with the frequent quoting of earlier music (Mozart and Donizetti, and even the love motive from Wagner's *Tristan und Isolde*) makes the connection to neo-Classicism.

Busoni presents his story in four scenes. In "Arlecchino as Rogue," the anti-hero narrowly escapes detection in a tryst with Annunziata (wife of the tailor Ser Matteo) by convincing the cuckolded husband that the "barbarian army" is gathering for attack. In "Arlecchino as Warrior," the trickster shows up in military uniform with his "guard" and enlists Matteo to fight against the barbarians. In "Arlecchino as Husband, his wife, Columbina, appears to scold him for his infidelity." The finale, "Arlecchino as Conqueror," sees Leandro (slain in a duel) reviving from death; the way is now clear for him to elope with Annunziata. *—Joseph Stevenson*

Synopsis:

Ferruccio Busoni's libretto for his opera *Arlecchino* plays off of the stylized characters of the traditional Italian *commedia dell'arte*, staged in a distanced, winking style characteristic of the composer's operatic style. Thus, when the title character first appears on-stage, he delivers a Prologue directly to the audience: "The sense of what the characters may say/may well escape an all too literal mind... The little world in miniature is treated, and truth in masquerade is counterfeited."

Act One—"Arlecchino as Rogue". Friendly old tailor Matteo is seated on his front stoop, reading aloud from Dante as he works. Even as he ponders the hellish fate of the unfaithful as described in the *Divine Comedy*, his own wife Annunziata is upstairs with the promiscuous Arlecchino. Making his escape, Arlecchino leaps from the window and lands at Matteo's feet. Thinking quickly, Arlecchino tells the tailor that barbarians are laying siege of the town; as he ushers Matteo into the house, he swipes the tailors coat and keys. As Arlecchino escapes, Abbate Conspicuo and Dottore Bombasto stroll by and call to Matteo; informed of the (imaginary) barbarians, they run to warn the mayor, but are somehow diverted to the pub instead.

Act Two—"Arlecchino as Warrior". The protagonist appears disguised in phony military regalia and enlists Matteo into the service. Matteo answers the call, assembling a hodgepodge uniform, and reports for service. Dante in hand (Arlecchino assures him that culture must not be a casualty in this war!), Matteo heads off, leaving Annunziata unguarded.

Act Three—"Arlecchino as Husband". The full extent of Arlecchino's intrigues becomes clearer with the appearance of his own wife, Colombina. She gives her errant spouse a severe tongue lashing, but he remains defiant, even as her angry complaints soften into sorrowful pleas. Sneaking away, Arlecchino returns to Annunziata. In the meantime, Leandro the troubadour appears, learns of Colombina's plight, and melodramatically commits to her cause. When Arlecchino returns, he sends Colombina off to the pub and handily fells Leandro in a duel.

Act Four—"Arlecchino as Conqueror". Colombina leaves the cabin with the Abbot and the Doctor on her arms. Properly drunk, they decide to warn the Mayor of the barbarians after all. To Colombina's horror, however, they encounter Leandro's lifeless, crumpled form in the street. Detecting a breath of life, the Abbot prays for help; his prayer is answered by the clumsily miraculous appearance of the "Ass of Providence," which carries the awakened Leandro to the hospital. In the meantime, Arlecchino appears atop the house proclaiming his triumph and freedom, then flees with Annunziata, who has left a note telling Matteo that she has gone to church. Finding the note upon his return from the "battle," the befuddled tailor resumes his work and his reading—continuing, oblivious, even as Arlecchino steps to the footlights to show off his mistress to the audience. *—Jeremy Grimshaw*

Recommended:

○ **Busoni: Arlecchino** / Albrecht (cond.), S. Lorenz, Worle, Pape, Matic, Deutsches Radio SO Berlin / Capriccio 60038

Doktor Faust (1916–1925)

German-Italian composer Ferruccio Busoni's final, unfinished work was his opera *Doktor Faust*. Although he spoke of setting *Faust* as early as 1904, he was reluctant to attempt a setting of Goethe's *Faust* because of that play's enormous scale and scope. Finally, using an old German puppet play version of the Faust legend as his model, he wrote the libretto himself in a few days at the end of 1914. Composing the music would occupy the rest of his life. His pupil Philipp Jarnach completed it, and the work was premiered in Dresden in 1925.

An intentionally fragmentary work even in its finished portions, Busoni's *Doktor Faust* stands aside from both the Italian verismo of Puccini and the German post-Romanticism of Strauss. Busoni's own aesthetic, which might be called New Classicism, is clear, clean, and direct, emphasizing melody, but not the extravagantly emotional melodies of the Italian operatic tradition. Instead the work features coolly expressive, flexible melody. Although the harmonic language of *Doktor Faust* is based on counterpoint, it ultimately sounds more like Liszt's transcriptions of Bach than like Strauss or Wagner. The composer uses the contrast between diatonic and chromatic passages to expressive effect. Busoni's libretto divides the action of the plot into six unequal parts: two prologues, an interlude, and three long scenes for the principal action. Both prologues take place in Faust's study and are concerned with his pact with the devil. The brief interlude records his first crimes: desecration of a church and the murder of an adversary. The three long scenes follow Faust's career as a magician, a seducer, and a murderer, and, in the last scene, his end. However, Busoni avoids the transcendental Christian endings of either transfiguration or damnation and instead has Faust transform himself into "eternal will."

Busoni's *Doktor Faust* is infrequently staged or recorded. Its recondite musical language and lack of stage action has restricted its appreciation to a small number of cognoscenti. The music is rich in allusions to past styles. The long spoken Prologue and Epilogue are not set to music and usually not performed, so the work begins with "Symphonia: Easter Vesper and Nascent Spring"—a rich orchestral texture that leads into a depiction of the birth of nature (flowing melodies with open, modern harmonies). During the Second Prologue, Faust invokes Lucifer, whose voice is made up of a chorus of voices (!) accompanied by drums. A lively philosophical discussion opens the Second Scene in a tavern in Wittenberg. Faust quotes Luther as a thinly disguised musical quotation from "A Mighty Fortress is Our God" occurs in the orchestral part. A contrapuntal uproar (in German and Latin) later breaks out among the Protestants and the Catholics. *—AMG*

Synopsis:

Prologue One. The story's setting is sixteenth century Europe. The First Prologue takes place in the Wittenberg study of Faust, where his protégée, Wagner, enters to announce that three students possessing a magical book are anxious to meet him. Faust immediately suspects it will give him special powers and thus receives them excitedly. The students, all dressed in black, present him with the book and a key to open it.

Prologue Two. In this Prologue Faust carries out the ritual necessary to unleash the book's powers. After five evil spirits appear and fail to entice him, Mephistopheles materializes and promises to meet his every worldly desire, provided Faust will do his evil bidding for all eternity. At first he declines the proposal, but Mephistopheles reminds him of his many troubles, including the threat of death by the brother of a woman, Gretchen, he had seduced. Faust finally agrees and signs the unholy pact with Mephistopheles.

Interlude. As Gretchen's brother prays in the cathedral, Mephistopheles deceives several soldiers into believing he is a criminal. They kill him.

Scene One. This scene takes place at the palace of the Duke of Parma, where Faust is received now as a man of extraordinary powers. He causes the Duchess of Parma to fall in love with him and astonishes those in attendance with his trickery. The jealous Duke attempts to poison Faust, but Mephistopheles intercedes to save him.

Scene Two. This scene takes place at an inn in Wittenberg. Faust tells of his amorous adventures with the Duchess. Mephistopheles, disguised as a messenger, announces the Duchess' death, and presents Faust with a token of the pair's illicit affair, a newborn baby's corpse. Mephistopheles then turns it into straw and sets it afire, the smoke producing the image of Helen of Troy. The three students enter and request return of the book and key, items Faust now claims are destroyed. They warn him of imminent death.

Scene Three. The final scene begins with Faust traipsing along a snow-covered street in Wittenberg. He hears the ominous Dies Irae theme and fears eternal damnation. He decides to perform a good deed in hopes of redemption, and thus gives money to a woman beggar holding an infant. She turns out to be the Duchess. Faust attempts to enter the nearby church, but is hampered by Gretchen's murdered brother at the door. Faust finally enters the church and observes the image of Helen of Troy on a crucifix. He cries out. Faust makes a final attempt at redemption by covering the corpse of the infant with his cloak and creating a circle on the ground with his sash. He steps into the circle and says magic words. Suddenly he falls dead and a youthful figure carrying a green branch rises from his corpse and departs. *—Robert Cummings*

Recommended:

○ **Busoni: Doktor Faust** / Nagano (cond.), Henschel, Begley, Hollop, Fischer-Dieskau, Orch. du L'Opéra National Lyon / 1999 / Erato 25501

George Butterworth

b. Jul. 12, 1885, London, England, **d.** Aug. 5, 1916, Pozières, France

Composer: Orchestral, Vocal

George Butterworth was the best-known of a generation of prominent musicians whose careers or lives were cut short by the hostilities of World War I. His reputation as a composer rests on a handful of exquisitely fashioned small-scale works which were strongly influenced by his studies in English folk song.

Butterworth was the son of a talented singer (Julia Wigan) and a prominent railway executive (Sir Alexander Kaye Butterworth, head of the North Eastern

Railway). His mother gave him his first musical instruction as a child in Yorkshire, and so fertile was the ground in which the seed of music had been planted, that by the time Butterworth was a schoolboy at Eton, the school orchestra had given a performance of his *Barcarolle*, in 1903. Nevertheless, it was the gray and solemn life of a solicitor for which George was being groomed, and upon his matriculation at Trinity College, Oxford, he began the requisite study of Greats.

While at Trinity, however, Butterworth encountered two musical "greats," the seminal folk song collector and editor Cecil Sharp and the composer Ralph Vaughan Williams. They encouraged his very evident musical abilities, and soon Butterworth was accompanying Vaughan Williams on folk song–collecting excursions into the English countryside. As might be expected, law was quickly abandoned in favor of music.

Leaving Oxford for London, Butterworth threw himself into a welter of activity, studying for a short time at the Royal College of Music, teaching, writing music criticism for the *Times*, and composing. He was also active with the English Folk Song and Dance Society. His friendship with Vaughan Williams, meantime, had deepened both personally and professionally, and it was in the latter realm that Butterworth performed an invaluable service for the older composer when he helped reconstruct, from assembled orchestral parts, the full score of Vaughan Williams' *A London Symphony*, the autograph of which had been sent to conductor Fritz Busch in Dresden in 1914 and had been lost at the outbreak of war. Butterworth also wrote the program notes for the symphony's premiere later that year under Geoffrey Toye. Vaughan Williams afterward dedicated his symphonic masterpiece to Butterworth's memory.

Despite his successes, Butterworth was plagued throughout his short life by a sense of purposelessness. The eruption of war in 1914, however, seems to have catalyzed him. He enlisted immediately in the Duke of Cornwall's Durham Light Infantry, and his brazen valor in battle soon brought him a lieutenant's rank. Butterworth was posthumously awarded the Military Cross for his bold defense of a strategically important trench network, which was later named for him. He was killed at Pozieres leading a raid during the Battle of the Somme.

George Butterworth's most famous work is his orchestral rhapsody *A Shropshire Lad*, inspired by A.E. Housman's poetry and thematically related to his earlier Housman song cycle of the same name. Its premiere in 1913 at the Leeds Festival under Artur Nikisch was a gratifying success for the young composer. Other works include *Two English Idylls* and *The Banks of Green Willow* for small orchestra. The slender catalog of Butterworth's music, in which a refined and elegiac sensibility is informed with the poignancy of English folk song, was reduced further when the composer, just before leaving England for the trenches in 1915, destroyed those manuscripts which he deemed unworthy of survival. *—Mark Satola*

ORCHESTRAL

The Banks of Green Willow, idyll (1913)

Though George Butterworth referred to his *Banks of Green Willow* as an "idyll for small orchestra," the work is more like a miniature, and very English, tone poem. Though broadly based on a folk song, the music strays further and further from a simple, unassuming tone—first into quiet contemplation, then toward a dramatic climax far removed from the spirit of the source material. The work is structured as an arch characterized by a meditative beginning and ending. Butterworth was undoubtedly influenced by the English folksong revival of the 1900s, but his surviving compositions are generally more individual and, perhaps, more "European" in style than those of his contemporaneous countrymen. There is a melancholy undertone to this otherwise sunny work that, in hindsight, may seem like a premonition: a few years later, the 31-year old composer was killed in World War I. *—Roy Brewer*

Recommended:

- ○ **Greensleeves: English Classics** / Marriner (cond.), Academy of St. Martin-in-the-Fields / 1999 / Decca 460637
- ○ **Bridge, Butterworth & Bantock** / del Mar (cond.), Bournemouth Sinfonietta / 1993 / Chandos 6566

Two English Idylls (1911)

Because George Butterworth sometimes referred to his two most popular orchestral pieces, *The Banks of Green Willow* and *A Shropshire Lad*, as "idylls" (the latter more formally as "rhapsody"), some people mistakenly assume these to be the works gathered under the title *Two English Idylls*. Actually, the *Two English Idylls* are quite separate and independent items, although, like *The Banks of Green Willow*, they are based on English folk songs.

Both proceed at a measured pace, but the first opens with a jaunty oboe tune that eventually swells into an exuberant, lushly scored passage dominated by the strings. The oboe, with bassoon counterpoint, introduces a more lyrical and antique-sounding melody, with commentary from the flutes, other winds, and strings. The clarinet comes along with yet another good-natured tune, this one with a skip to its rhythm, and all of this material, including a passage resembling an Irish dance, passes through the orchestra in various combinations and guises before a quiet return to the opening melody. For this idyll, Butterworth has incorporated the folk songs "Dabbling in the Dew," "Just as the Tide Was Flowing," and "Henry Martin."

The second idyll, again introduced by the oboe, begins with a very lyrical melody soon taken up by the strings. Darker, more hesitant material arises in the low strings and woodwinds, and the violins soon come to the fore with an impassioned central climax. Again, Butterworth gently works through the melodic material, taking full advantage of the woodwind colors and, near the end, solo violin. The piece ends quietly and the overall tone of this idyll, which is based on "Phoebe and the Dark-Eyed Sailor," is pastoral and wistfully nostalgic. *—James Reel*

Recommended:

- ○ **Fantasia On Greensleeves** / Marriner (cond.), Academy of St. Martin-in-the-Fields / 1997 / London 452707
- ○ **Butterworth, Parry & Bridge** / Boughton (cond.), English CO / 1987 / Nimbus 5068

A Shropshire Lad, rhapsody (1912)

The *Rhapsody*, an orchestral epilogue to the composer's song cycle of the same name, is in the form of an elegy. Butterworth was the first of several English composers to set poems from A.E. Housman's A Shropshire Lad, and chose those that mourn the lives and deaths of "redcoats" (British soldiers). Though the poems were written well before 1914, the music is now inseparable from the bleak years of the World War I, when it was written. The main theme is a meditation on one of Butterworth's most haunting songs, "The Cherry Tree." Though scored for a large orchestra, it is mostly somber, quiet music, with a climax towards the end as the trumpets poignantly echo the song tune, after which the somber mood returns. The *Rhapsody* ends with funereal drum beats that sound eerily prophetic: Butterworth was killed in the last year of the war, at age 31. *—Roy Brewer*

Recommended:

- ○ **Fantasia On Greensleeves** / Marriner, Academy of St. Martin-in-the-Fields / 1997 / London 452707

VOCAL

Six Songs from "A Shropshire Lad" (1911)

Though Butterworth's settings of 23 poems in A.E. Housman's collection entitled *A Shropshire Lad* were written several years before World War II, they poignantly mirror the futility of the 1914–18 conflict: these "lads" represent the doomed youth of every war.

Butterworth wrote two Shropshire Lad cycles (in 1911 and 1912), but only six of the finest songs are usually performed today. The opening five notes of the first, "Loveliest of trees," a somber meditation on mortality, became the central melodic motif in Butterworth's powerful orchestral *Rhapsody* based on the cycle. The remaining five are "When I was one-and-twenty," "Look not in my eyes," "Think no more, lad," "The lads in their hundreds" and "Is my team ploughing."

Butterworth was strongly influenced by the English folk song revival, but there is little trace of such elements here beyond the composer's attraction to Housman's metrically simple, deceptively artless texts. A Schubertian quality of tender lyricism and deeply personal sadness characterizes all these songs. The final one, "Is my team ploughing," is a tour-de-force—a haunting dialogue between two men, one of whom has survived war and another, singing mezza voce, "who now lies under the land he used to plough."

Housman's words have been set to music by several English composers, though never more potently. The continuing popularity of Butterworth's set is due in some measure to the premonition it contains of the composer's own death in action on the Somme in 1916. An orchestral arrangement exists, but does not have the subtlety and delicacy of the original piano accompaniment. *—Roy Brewer*

Recommended:

- ○ **The Vagabond** / Terfel, Martineau / 1995 / DG 445946
- ○ **On the Idle Hill of Summer: Song Cycles** / T. Allen, G. Parsons / 2001 / EMI 67428

Dietrich Buxtehude

b. ca. 1637, Helsingborg [?], Denmark, **d.** May 9, 1707, Lübeck, Germany

Composer: Keyboard

Dietrich Buxtehude is probably most familiar to modern classical music audiences as the man who inspired the young Johann Sebastian Bach to make a lengthy pilgrimage to Lubeck, Buxtehude's place of employment and residence for most of his life, just to hear Buxtehude play the organ. But Buxtehude was a major figure among German Baroque composers in his own right. Though we do not have copies of much of the work that most impressed his contemporaries, Buxtehude nonetheless left behind a body of vocal and instrumental music which is distinguished by its contrapuntal skill, devotional atmosphere, and raw intensity. He helped develop the form of the church cantata, later perfected by Bach, and he was just as famous a virtuoso on the organ.

No documentation exists for Buxtehude's birth, though he said late in life that he was a native Dane. Since his father, Johannes, was organist and schoolmaster at

Oldesloe, Denmark, until 1638, it is a reasonable guess that Dietrich was born there. Johannes moved to Helsingborg in 1638 and to Helsingør in 1641 or 1642, where he stayed until 1671. After learning the organ at the feet of his father, Buxtehude became organist at his father's former church in Helsingør in 1657 or 1658; he then moved to a German-speaking congregation in Helsingborg in 1660. Buxtehude decided to stop following in his father's footsteps when the prestigious position of organist at the Marienkirche in Lubeck became available; after several others were rejected, Buxtehude got the job on April 11, 1868. He also married the outgoing organist's youngest daughter, Anna Margarethe Tunder, which may have been a condition of taking the post, and certainly was a condition when Buxtehude sought a replacement for himself. Buxtehude was organist at the Marienkirche for the rest of his life. His official duties were to provide congregational chorales and other musical interludes for every service, and to act as treasurer, secretary, and business manager of the church. He was most famous, however, for his *Abendmusik* concerts, held following the afternoon service on five Sundays a year and on special occasions. Although these concerts are universally described as extraordinary, and were the basis of most of Buxtehude's contemporary fame, very little music from them has survived. Two of the most famous *Abendmusik* concerts, held on December 2 and 3, 1705, and commemorating the death of Emperor Leopold I and the ascension of Joseph I, were probably attended by Bach on his pilgrimage. Buxtehude had an opportunity for early retirement in 1703, when Georg Friederic Handel and Johann Mattheson (famous organists both) visited him; Mattheson had been thinking of succeeding Buxtehude at his post, but balked at the requirement to marry Buxtehude's daughter Anna Margareta, and the visit came to nought. After Buxtehude died on May 9, 1707, the church found another organist willing to marry his daughter.

Historically, Buxtehude's organ music has been studied because of its direct influence on Bach; Buxtehude wrote the first truly idiomatic fugues for the organ and was one of the first to experiment with the structure that Bach later codified into the prelude and fugue. Buxtehude is generally considered the greatest organist between Scheidt and Bach and is regarded as the originator of the German organ toccata. However, in addition to the keyboard music that so impressed his contemporaries, he also wrote some extraordinary works for trios involving the viola da gamba. His vocal works shared the devotion and intellectual rigor of his instrumental work, and were also much admired. *—Andrew Lindemann Malone*

KEYBOARD

Chorale Preludes for organ (ca. 1670–1705)

As one might expect from a man who spent over 40 straight years as the organist of first the Marienkirche of Helsingør and then the Marienkirche of Lübeck—with duties centered around leading the congregation in the singing of Lutheran chorales, introducing the music, and then playing along with them—the list of organ chorale preludes fills quite a few pages in Dietrich Buxtehude's catalog of compositions. Including one fragmentary piece, there are 48 surviving individual Buxtehude organ chorales (including not only true chorale preludes but also chorale variations and lengthy chorale fantasias). Most (30) are brief settings in which the hymn melody is embedded in fresh polyphony, settings meant to remind the largely musically illiterate congregation of the tune. These are true chorale preludes (examples are *In dulci jubilio,* BuxWV 197 or *Gott der Vater wohn uns bei,* BuxWV 190), in which the tune is usually put in the uppermost voice and given some lively elaboration, and in which the pedal bass offers very free imitation on the chorale motives heard in the soprano voice.

Other Buxtehude organ chorales take much larger forms. An example is the enormous chorale fantasia on *Te deum laudamus,* BuxWV 218, which begins with a sizable and virtuosic Praeludium and then proceeds to build each phrase of the chorale tune into its own complete section of music; fiery organ showmanship, fugal display, and rich, multi-textured essays take root in long-note cantus-firmus presentations of the chorale phrases. The rarest kind of Buxtehude organ chorale is the set of chorale variations, in which the chorale melody repeated several times as a cantus firmus, each time in a different contrapuntal setting and possibly differently elaborated and ornamented; *Nun lob mein Seel' den Heeren,* BuxWV 213 contains three variations on the chorale tune, the first using just two manual voices, the second three manual voices, and the third allowing the pedals to join in and carry the melody.

Beyond forming a vital repertory unto themselves, Buxtehude's chorale preludes, variations, and fantasias can boast the lasting value of having influenced J.S. Bach's own chorale style to an enormous degree. In fact the influence of Buxtehude's music in general (not just the organ chorales) on J.S. Bach can hardly be overestimated. But the debt goes both ways, for it is to Bach that the survival of much of Buxtehude's music is owed—Bach carried dozens and dozens of Buxtehude pieces, including most of the organ chorales, back home with him after making his legendary trip, on foot, to hear the older master play. *—Blair Johnston*

Recommended:

○ **Buxtehude: Orgelwerke** / Koopman / 1989 / Novalis 150048

La Capricciosa, 32 variations for keyboard in G major, BuxWV 250 (ca. 1690)

It is interesting that Dietrich Buxtehude should today be known almost exclusively as a composer of organ music—the finest before J. S. Bach appeared on the scene a generation or two later—as Buxtehude actually spent much more of his time composing sacred vocal works and chamber music than he did writing for his own instrument. There was also a large and widely-admired body of harpsichord music, but none of it was published during Buxtehude's lifetime, and history with all its inscrutable whims has not seen fit to hand down very much of it. All of Buxtehude's extant harpsichord music was preserved in a single manuscript. There are just under 20 suites and several variations sets, one of which is BuxWV 250, a set of 32 variations on the well-known tune *La capricciosa.*

The aria, or theme, of BuxWV 250 is an eight-bar miniature binary (4+4) thing; each half is repeated. The work shouldn't really be called, as it sometimes is, a "theme and 32 variations"—for there are in fact 32 statements of the theme altogether, including the initial introductory one (rather, call it 32 variations or theme and 31 variations). Buxtehude proves inventive at making derivatives of the basic tune. He maintains the framework of the theme throughout his variations and uses various figures and rhythmic saturations to build interest. There are running 16th and eventually 32nd notes, snappy dotted rhythms and some rapid off beats; there is light imitation between voices, and there are a few variations that move into triple or compound meter (3/8, 6/8, and 12/8) and grow more dance-worthy. In the final variation, speedy, flaming scales in the bass get the spotlight as the right hand offers steady chords to move inexorably towards a bright close. *—Blair Johnston*

Recommended:

○ **Buxethude: Suites & Variations** / M. Meyerson / ASV 102

○ **Buxtehude: Harpsichord Music Vol. 3** / L. U. Mortensen / 1999 / Da Capo 224118

Passacaglia for organ in D minor, BuxWV 161 (ca. 1690)

The *Passacaglia for organ in D minor,* BuxWV 161, may well be Dietrich Buxtehude's most famous piece of music—but that does not mean, sadly, that it is by any stretch of the imagination well recognized. It is one of three ostinato-oriented, ground bass organ pieces (BuxWV 159–161; a related work is BuxWV 137, whose brief final section is a chaconne) in which Buxtehude refocused the lens of his quintessentially north German organ art to look at the Spanish-Italian chaconne and passacaglia forms—forms hitherto foreign to mainstream German organ music. Like nearly all of Buxtehude's music, BuxWV 161 has to this point remained undatable—the best we can do is say that it was probably composed during his 40-year tenure as organist at the Marienkirche at Lübeck, a post he held from 1668 to his death in 1707.

In the *Passacaglia,* Buxtehude assigns the repeating four-measure ground bass to the pedals, and allows the two hands to devise ever more elaborate filigree—here contrapuntally ordered, there made into more obviously virtuoso stuff—to go above it. Buxtehude builds a four-section plan from the modulations through which he puts the ground bass (D minor—F major—A minor—D minor); each section is exactly 30 measures in length, with a one-measure "fill" separating neighboring sections. It is easy to recognize, when encountering such an unwaveringly precise but flexible-sounding architecture, the extent to which such works as the *Passacaglia* influenced Buxtehude's spiritual descendent J.S. Bach, who is of course famed for his intricate and sometimes mathematical structural layouts, and who as a young man traveled some 200 miles on foot so that he might hear Buxtehude play. *—Blair Johnston*

Recommended:

○ **Buxtehude: Orgelwerke** / Koopman / 1989 / Novalis 150048

○ **Buxtehude: Organ Music Vol. 3** / Rubsam / 2003 / Naxos 555991

Praeludium for organ in C major, BuxWV 137 (ca. 1680)

Although its English title might lead one to believe otherwise, Dieterich Buxtehude's *Praeludium for organ in C major,* BuxWV 137—known as the *Prelude, Fugue and Chaconne*—is really not a very lengthy piece of music. It does indeed have three sections of music, the first of which is a free prelude, the second fugal, and the last built up from a ground bass. But each section is comparatively brief, and there are no breaks between the three (which is why Buxtehude called it simply *Praeludium,* a word that in his day could encompass works with many sections as well as those with few or one); the final Chaconne is differentiated from the other sections through a tempo change to Presto, as opposed to the undefined but probably moderato tempo of the opening. The Prelude portion of BuxWV 137—which is incidentally a work whose date of composition remains unknown and, given Buxtehude's long period of active composition can only be narrowed to the second half of the seventeenth century—is itself made up of several short, discrete musical sentences. The main idea from the first of them, an oscillating 16th note figure, is reforged first into the subject for the Fugue portion, and then, by way of more sweeping rhythmic changes, into the ground bass for the Chaconne section, which ends in an impressive quasi-cadenza blaze. *—Blair Johnston*

Recommended:

○ **Bach Encounters Buxtehude: A Journey to Lübeck, 1705** / Marshall / 2002 / Loft Recordings 1029

○ **Organ Music of Dietrich Buxtehude** / Kibbie / Arkay 6088

Semyon Bychkov

b. Nov. 30, 1952, Leningrad (St. Petersburg), USSR
Conductor

Semyon Bychkov's conducting is admired for its clarity, unexaggerated expression, and frankness in conveying the intent of the music, regardless of what he is conducting. He is equally comfortable conducting orchestral, choral, or operatic music. His first studies were of the piano, but he spent ten years (from the age of seven) at the Glinka Choir School in St. Petersburg singing in the choir and learning conducting. Bychkov then studied with Ilya Musin at the Leningrad Conservatory, earning such respect for his skills that he won the 1973 Rachmaninov Conducting Competition and was invited to conduct the Leningrad Philharmonic before his graduation. However, the concert and his graduation never happened. Bychkov had not been discreet about his views of Soviet policies and due to this, the concert was canceled. In 1974 the KGB handed him an exit visa. After a few months in Vienna and Italy, he found himself in New York, studying conducting at the Mannes College of Music. He then became conductor of the Grand Rapids [Michigan] Symphony, 1980–1984, and took American citizenship in 1983. At the same time, he was principal guest conductor of the Buffalo (NY) Philharmonic, eventually becoming its music director in 1985. However, it was a series of guest conducting jobs—including with the Berlin Philharmonic, and filling in for Bernard Haitink with the Concertgebouw and Rafael Kubelik with the New York Philharmonic—in 1984 that brought him international attention. Around the same time, his first recording, of Rossini's *Stabat Mater* on Philips, met with great success. Leaving the Buffalo position, Bychkov was named music director of the Orchestre de Paris in 1989, principal guest conductor of the St. Petersburg Philharmonic in 1990, principal guest conductor of Florence's Maggio Musicale in 1992, and chief conductor of the Dresden Semperoper in 1997. He stepped down from his Paris position in 1998 after being appointed conductor of the WDR Symphony Orchestra in Cologne. With that ensemble, he began a recording series of Shostakovich's symphonies, expanded its touring schedule, and premiered many new works by composers such as Magnus Lindberg and Nicholas Maw. In addition to the operas conducted in Dresden, Bychkov has also conducted *Elektra* at the Wiener Staatsoper, *Tristan und Isolde* at the Chicago Lyric Opera, and *Jenufa* in Florence. Bychkov's debut at New York's Metropolitan Opera occurred in June 2004, with Mussorgsky's *Boris Godunov.* Bychkov is married to pianist Marielle Labèque. —*Patsy Morita*

Recommended:

- ○ **Shostakovich: Symphony 8** / Bychkov (cond.), Orchester des WDR Koln / 2004 / Avie 43
- ○ **Mahler: Symphony 3** / Bychkov (cond.), Shikata, Lipovsek, Beck, Monkediek, Orchester des WDR Koln / 2003 / Avie 19
- ○ **Concertos for 2 Pianos by Mendelssohn & Bruch** / Bychkov (cond.), K&M Labeque, London PO / Philips 432095

Anner Bylsma

b. Feb. 17, 1934, The Hague, Netherlands
Cellist

Playing with impeccable technique and a beautiful, unadulterated tone, Anner Bylsma is acknowledged as a master cellist, comfortable in a wide range of music on both period and modern cellos. As they were for many gifted musicians, his first lessons were from a parent, in this case his father, also a multi-talented musician. At the age of 16, he enrolled at the Royal Conservatory, The Hague, to study with Carel van Leeuwen Boomkamp, principal cellist with the Concertgebouw Orchestra Amsterdam. It was Boomkamp who introduced Bylsma to the Baroque cello. Bylsma won the school's Prix d'excellence in 1957, and after becoming the Netherlands Opera Orchestra's principal cellist, he won first prize in the Casals Competition in Mexico in 1959. He himself then became principal cellist of the Concertgebouw in 1962. Six years later he left the orchestra to devote his performing career to solo and chamber ensemble touring. His chamber music collaborators often included period flutist Frans Brueggen, harpsichordist Gustav Leonhardt, and in the 1990s and 2000s keyboardists Malcolm Bilson and Jos van Immerseel. Bylsma was also a co-founder of the string chamber ensemble L'Archibudelli. As a solo performer he plays regularly with such orchestras as the Orpheus Chamber Orchestra, Tafelmusik, the Australian Chamber Orchestra, the Orchestra of the Age of Enlightenment, the Freiburger Barock, and the twentieth century music ensemble Rondom Kwartet.

Bylsma is also a noted scholar and teacher and author of *Bach—The Fencing Master,* about the first three of Bach's *Cello Suites.* His playing is always based on what he finds in the composers' manuscripts. However, he quickly admits that his interpretation of a work is not and should not be the only one, which he also impresses on his students. Although he doesn't like to use the term "authentic," it is in keeping with period performance that he avoids the use of steel strings, and this is a major element of his tone. Both his 1695 Gofriller cello and his 1865 Pressenda are strung with gut or silver-wrapped gut. He also has a five-string "violoncello piccolo" that he has used to record Bach's solo works.

His recordings can be found on a variety of labels, covering a variety of works, from Vivaldi to Hindemith. Many of his recordings on Sony, both as a soloist and with L'Archibudelli, have won the Edison prize, the Diapason d'or, the Liszt prize, and the Vivaldi prize. —*Patsy Morita*

Recommended:

- ○ **Vivaldi: Cello Sonatas** / Bylsma, Marcon (hpschd) / 2000 / Sony 51350
- ○ **Leo: 6 Cello Concerti** / Lamon (cond.), Bylsma, Tafelmusik Baroque Orch. / 1986 / Atma 2126
- ○ **Haydn: Last 4 Piano Trios** / Bylsma, Beths, Levin / 1993 / Sony 53120
- ○ **Bach: Cello Suites 1–3** / Bylsma / 2002 / Sony 89960
- ○ **Boccherini: String Quintets; Cello Sonatas** / Bylsma, S & W Kuijken, Van Dael, Smith, Stuurop / 1997 / Sony 63190

William Byrd

b. 1543, Lincoln [?], England, **d.** Jul. 4, 1623, Stondon Massey, Essex, England
Composer: Choral, Keyboard, Vocal, Chamber Music

Even in an era so richly stocked with great names, William Byrd demands particular attention as the most prodigiously talented, prolific, and versatile of his contemporaries. Byrd was born in about 1543, and it is assumed that he was a chorister in the Chapel Royal (his brothers were choristers at St. Paul's Cathedral) and a student of Thomas Tallis. He was named organist and master of choristers of Lincoln Cathedral at the age of 20, where he wrote most of his works in English and music for Anglican services. This music and his anthems provided the young English church with some of its finest music. In 1570 he was appointed a Gentleman of the Chapel Royal, where he shared the post of organist with Thomas Tallis. Queen Elizabeth I, despite Byrd's intense commitment to Catholicism, was one of his benefactors, and granted him and Tallis a patent to print music in 1575. Their first publication was a collection of five- to eight-part, Latin motets, but they published little else. Around the same time, Byrd began composing for the virginal. His contribution to the solo keyboard repertoire comprises some 125 pieces, mostly stylized dances or exceptionally inventive sets of variations which inaugurated a golden age of English keyboard composition.

During the 1580s and 1590s, Byrd's Catholicism was the driving motive for his music. As the persecutions of Catholics increased during this period, and occasionally touched on Byrd and his family, he wrote and openly published motets and three masses (one each in three, four, and five parts), which are his finest achievement in sacred music, almost certainly composed for small chapel gatherings of Catholics. Byrd had taken up the publishing business again, printing the first English songbook, *Psalmes, Sonets and Songs* in 1588. This and his other songbooks include Byrd's compositions in the leading secular genres of the day: the ayre or lute song, the madrigal, and the consort song for solo voice and viols. The consort song's finest hour came at the hands of Byrd, who preferred texts of a high moral (frequently religious) or metaphysical tone. They are notable for the way the viol parts lead an existence independent of the vocal line. He openly published two *Gradualia* in 1605 and 1607, with music for the Propers of all the major feast days. His last collection, *Psalmes, Songs and Sonnets* from 1611, consisted mostly of previously published works, but did include two of his viol consort works. Byrd is at his most distinguished in the free fantasias for consort, particularly the later pieces in five and six parts, works of exceptionally luxurious texture. Byrd's last songs were published in 1614, and he lived out his life comfortably at Stondon Massey, where he died in 1623. —*AMG*

CHORAL

Mass for Three Voices (ca. 1590)

The three unaccompanied masses Byrd composed during the 1590s are masterpieces of late Elizabethan polyphony. The *Mass for Three Voices* (1593–94), like its companions for four and five voices, is a setting of the sections of the Ordinary: Kyrie, Gloria, Credo, Sanctus, and Agnus Dei. Byrd wrote the work for use by Catholics during a period when celebration of the mass was strictly forbidden. Still, Catholics (or recusants, as they were then known in England), continued to perform their central act of worship under cover of strict secrecy. Byrd's masses were therefore composed for practical use and conceived expressly for small-scale, furtive performances. After moving from London to Essex in 1593, Byrd himself may have been involved in such acts of worship at the nearby home of Sir John Petre, a notable member of the Catholic community and a friend and patron of the composer.

The *Mass for Three Voices* is the briefest of Byrd's three masses, almost certainly because the opportunities for passing thematic material from one voice to another are restricted by such a small number of parts. There is no evidence that Byrd had a particular vocal disposition in mind, and the mass works as well for soprano, alto, and tenor as it does for alto, tenor, and bass, or even tenor, baritone, and bass. Such flexibility is obviously logical, given the conditions under which the work was originally intended to be sung. In each of his masses, Byrd was careful not to make the vocal writing too complex; the scoring in the present work is mainly syllabic, with little complex melismatic writing. Still, within such apparent austerity, Byrd produces many wonderfully expressive moments, with key passages in the text highlighted to great effect. —*Brian Robins*

Recommended:

- ○ **Byrd: 3 Masses** / P. Phillips (cond.), Tallis Scholars / 2001 / Gimell 345
- ○ **Byrd: The 3 Masses** / P. Hillier, Pro Arte Singers (i) / 2002 / HM 907223
- ○ **Byrd: Messes** / Deller, Deller Consort / HM 190211

Mass for Four Voices (1592–1593)

The *Mass for Four Voices* (1592–93) was likely the first of the three great unaccompanied polyphonic mass settings Byrd composed in the 1590s. All three masses are settings of the Ordinary: Kyrie, Gloria, Credo, Sanctus, and Agnus Dei. The scoring of the *Mass for Four Voices* is often thought to consist of the usual soprano, alto, tenor, and bass, but the closeness of the alto and tenor parts has led some authorities to believe that alto, tenor, baritone, and bass achieves a more satisfactory balance.

Like its fellows, this mass was composed for liturgical use by Byrd's fellow Catholics—a dangerous proposition, since celebration of the Catholic mass was forbidden in Elizabethan England under threat of severe penalties. The central act of the liturgy was therefore performed by Catholics, or recusants as they were termed, under conditions of strict secrecy. These conditions are reflected in Byrd's three settings, which entirely eschew the kind of exuberance and florid writing encountered in earlier Tudor settings of the mass. Instead, Byrd's contrapuntal writing is largely syllabic, with the lines treated to clean, clear imitative counterpoint. Byrd compensates for such implications of austerity with a superbly expressive setting that often points up key words or sections of the text in a manner rarely encountered in settings of the timeless and unchanging words of the Ordinary. Examples include the soaring lines at "et ascendit" (and ascended into Heaven), or the sublime beauty of the Agnus Dei, in which Byrd gradually builds the number of voices and complexity of the counterpoint to achieve a searing climax at the words "dona nobis pacem" (grant us Thy peace). Perhaps he was making a political plea on behalf of all persecuted Catholics, who could emerge into the light only with the brightness of the work's very last sonority. —*Brian Robins*

Recommended:

- ○ **Byrd: 3 Masses** / P. Phillips (cond.), Tallis Scholars, / 2001 / Gimell 345
- ○ **Byrd: The 3 Masses** / P. Hillier, Pro Arte Singers (i) / 2002 / HM 907223
- ○ **Byrd: Messes** / A. Deller, Deller Consort / HM 190211

Mass for Five Voices (ca. 1590)

No single piece could by itself hope to exemplify the scintillating and multi-faceted musical style of William Byrd. Codifying such elements as the keyboard virtuosity of Alfonso Ferrabosco, the imitative counterpoint of Continental musica reservata, and a varied heritage of English cathedral music from Taverner to Tallis, Byrd's music in the broadest reading has been cited as a prime factor in the forging of Elizabethan culture. The *Mass in Five Voices* does capture the predicament of its composer's personal faith, and the facility and grace of his musical skill.

Byrd, despite serving as a Gentleman of the Chapel Royal in London and composing well for the Anglican service, privately maintained a devout Catholic faith; his home was often cited in the 1580s as a seat of recusancy, and his family sustained persecution and yearly fines for their faith. In 1593, he moved to the provincial estate of Stondon Massey, apparently under the protection of Catholic patrons such as the Pastons, the Petres, and the Earl of Worcester. So strong, in fact, was his protection (and his obstinacy) in a climate when mere possession of a copy of his Catholic *Gradualia* was once grounds for arrest, that Byrd boldly published the three Masses with his name printed on the top right corner of every printed page. Many motets of the *Gradualia*, as well as the three Mass settings probably first served the illegal (and thus intimate) underground Masses celebrated at Sir John Petre's Ingatestone Hall.

None of the three Masses (printed by Thomas East for four voices in 1592–93, three voices 1593–94, and five voices 1594–95) uses the common Continental device of parodying a model composition; they do not rely on a preconceived unifying thematic web. Byrd does seem, however, to have revised and reworked some musical ideas from one mass to the next, and all three are unified by a conservative and beautifully sculpted tone of "classical" counterpoint. The *Mass in Five Voices*, published last, links several movements by means of freely composed, but repeated, themes. Though it partakes of the fuller textures and antiphonal effects made possible by the fifth voice, its tone is the most reserved and distant. Among its many aural felicities are the strong musical emphasis on the text (cherished by Byrd) "Et unam Sanctam Catholicam et Apostolicam Ecclesiam," (And [I believe in] the one Holy, Catholic, and Apostolic Church), and the assured and nearly mystical peace of the final "Dona nobis pacem" (Give us peace). —*Timothy Dickey*

Recommended:

- ○ **Byrd: 3 Masses** / P. Phillips (cond.), Tallis Scholars / 2001 / Gimell 345
- ○ **William Byrd: The 3 Masses** / P. Hillier, Pro Arte Singers (i) / 2002 / HM 907223
- ○ **William Byrd: Mass for Five Voices** / D. Hill, Winchester Cathedral Choir / 1996 / Hyperion 66837

KEYBOARD

Works for Keyboard (ca. 1570–1600)

Though Byrd's choral works have long been counted among the monuments of British music, his works for keyboard remained relatively less known until recent years. A host of recordings and writings, however, have made clear that Byrd's keyboard music shows his genius at its fullest and is perhaps even more historically influential than his vocal music, much of it written under the cloak of Catholic secrecy in Anglican Elizabethan England. English music for the virginal (a small early harpsichord with the keyboard to one side of its front panel) existed before Byrd, but he was the tradition's first great exponent. (Byrd's music is also playable on Italian harpsichords and was often so performed in his own day.) Keyboard music dates from all phases of Byrd's career, from organ music composed during Byrd's tenure at Lincoln Cathedral in the 1560s to the keyboard compendium *My Lady Nevells Booke* of 1591 and to music written during Byrd's old age under the influence of the many younger keyboard composers, including John Bull and Orlando Gibbons, whom Byrd inspired. His 127 keyboard works include 56 consisting of paired pavans and galliards, a slow, duple meter dance followed by a faster one in triple meter. Within this seemingly restricted format, and in his 11 ground bass pieces and 14 variation sets, Byrd displays limitless melodic invention and a strong contrapuntal sense rivaling that of his choral masterpieces. Some of the pavans and galliards, a genre that for other composers served as light music often suitable for flowery dedications to a patron, display complicated derivations from ground bass lines and other intellectual devices that inspired composer Thomas Tomkins to call one of Byrd's pieces "excellent for matter," while a similar piece by Byrd's successor Bull was merely "excellent for the hand." Byrd's complete keyboard music was issued on a set of seven CDs by the Hyperion label in 2001 by harpsichordist Davitt Moroney, who has compared Byrd's pavans and galliards to the preludes and fugues of Bach's *Well-Tempered Clavier* or the 32 piano sonatas of Beethoven. —*James Manheim*

Recommended:

- ○ **Byrd: The Complete Keyboard Music** / Moroney / 1999 / Hyperion 66551/7
- ○ **Byrd: Music for the Virginals** / Häkkinen / Alba 148

VOCAL

Sacred Vocal Music (ca. 1563–1623)

William Byrd (ca. 1540–1623) was the most important English composer of the latter half of the sixteenth century. An extraordinarily versatile musician, his output covers every major genre of the period: sacred works, keyboard music, secular song, and compositions for a consort of viols. His sacred music falls into two categories: music to Latin texts, much of it composed for the Catholic liturgy, and works written for the newly-established Anglican Protestant church.

As a Catholic himself, Byrd made a vital contribution to the clandestine repertoire that enabled England's Catholics to continue their worship—an illegal activity in Elizabethan England. Despite such religious persecution, much of Byrd's sacred music was published during his lifetime. In 1575 he and his senior colleague Thomas Tallis (also a Catholic) were granted the first publishing monopoly in England by Elizabeth I, who despite her efforts to control Catholicism held both composers in high esteem. The result was *Cantiones Sacrae* (1575), which includes 17 motets by each composer. Byrd's contribution not only shows him writing in the broad, richly sonorous style inherited from earlier Tudor composers, but also more modern works with a narrower, more concentrated vocal range and close imitative polyphony. This trend is still more marked in the three masses in three, four, and five parts composed and published during the 1590s. Here Byrd purges all suggestion of display to keep within the capabilities of small recusant communities celebrating mass in secrecy. Deeply expressive, with key sections of the text tellingly highlighted, the masses are one of the glories of late Renaissance polyphony.

The *Gradualia*, Byrd's greatest religious publication appeared in two volumes, published in 1605 and 1607. It is a substantial, varied collection in which Byrd includes music for the Propers of the liturgy throughout the church's year. Not the least interesting aspect of this magnificent anthology, drawn from various stages of the composer's career, are "political" works in which Byrd makes sometimes thinly disguised allusions to the plight of his fellow Catholics.

Byrd's contribution to the liturgy of the Anglican church is smaller, but of high quality. The demands made of composers for Anglican service music were very different to the polyphonic complexity of Latin church music—the principal requirement being a textural clarity that called for simpler textures, and largely syllabic settings. These qualities are apparent in Byrd's Anglican service music, which includes accompanied verse anthems, unaccompanied choral anthems, and the Great Service. The last named is so-called to distinguish it from Short Services, simpler settings of the canticles of Morning Service (Venite, Te Deum, and Benedicite) and Evening Service (Magnificat, and Nunc dimittis). Byrd's Great Service is one of the most elaborate of the period, making greater use of polyphony than was often the case. Finally, brief mention must be made of a group of sacred songs, mostly consort songs with an accompaniment of viols. *—Brian Robins*

Recommended:

- ○ **Byrd: Ave Verum Corpus, Motets & Anthems** / Rutter (cond.), Cambridge Singers / 1989 / Collegium 110
- ○ **Byrd Edition 4: Cantiones Sacrae 1575** / Carwood (cond.), The Cardinall's Musick / 1999 / ASV Gaudeamus 197
- ○ **Byrd Edition 2: Early Latin Church Music** / Carwood (cond.), The Cardinall's Musick / 1998 / ASV Gaudeamus 178

Secular Vocal Works (ca. 1563–1623)

The most versatile English composer of his day, William Byrd (1539 or 1540–1623) made substantial and important contributions to a wide range of genres that include Latin and English church music, keyboard music, works for an ensemble, or consort, of viols, and secular song. The principal forms of secular song during the Tudor and Elizabethan period were works of the madrigalian type—set for either three, four, or five unaccompanied voices—and the consort song with viol accompaniment, the latter usually set for a solo singer, but occasionally as a duet. Many of Byrd's part-songs were published during the composer's lifetime in three major collections: *Psalmes, Sonets, and Songs of Sadnes and Pitie* (1588), *Songs of Sundrie Nature* (1589), and *Psalmes, Songs and Sonnets* (1611). As the titles suggest, the range of topics is wide, ranging from devotional religious songs to the kind of lovelorn conceits beloved of Elizabethan poets, and rustic humorous songs. Byrd's settings cover an equally wide gamut of styles, ranging from dense polyphony to near-homophonic strophic songs.

Possibly even more important are Byrd's consort songs. Until supplanted by the lute song at the end of the sixteenth century, the consort song (accompanied by a group of viols) was the principal mode of solo vocal music in Tudor and Elizabethan England; it reaches a pinnacle in Byrd's songs, of which there are some 30 secular examples. Their greatness arises from Byrd's skillful synthesis between voice and instruments; the latter frequently complement the sentiment of the text in masterly fashion, as in one of the most famous, *Ye sacred muses*, an elegiac song composed on the death of Byrd's senior colleague and friend, Thomas Tallis. As with the part songs, the variety of topics covered is wide, and includes both lighter and serious settings—the latter, as in *Wretched Albinus* including sometimes daring political commentary on the persecution of Byrd's fellow Catholics. *—Brian Robins*

Recommended:

- ○ **The Early Byrd Vol. 1** / I Fagiolini, Fretwork, S. Yates / 1995 / Chandos 578
- ○ **Byrd: Consort Songs** / R. Blaze, Concordia / Hyperion 67397

CHAMBER MUSIC

Viol Music (ca. 1570–1600)

Music composed for a group, or consort, of viols (consisting of the treble, alto, and bass members of the viol family) was the principal form of instrumental chamber music during the Tudor, Elizabethan, and Jacobean periods. The establishment of the Protestant church in England was marked by a decline of interest in sacred music, mirrored by a commensurate rise of secular arts like poetry and song. Instrumental music, either for viol consort or the lute enjoyed a golden age during this period. Among those who contributed to the viol consort repertoire during this period, William Byrd, the greatest English composer of his age, enjoys a special place. While not large in volume (there are 23 complete works extant; a number of others exist in too fragmentary a state to be reconstructed) his viol consort works cover a substantial period of his composing career.

The earliest of Byrd's consort works follow models by composers such as Christopher Tye—usually a polyphonic composition based around a short piece of plainsong. Among these are the three-part *Sermone blando*, believed to be Byrd's earliest surviving consort work, and three settings of the hymn *Christe qui lux* in four parts. From composing such pieces Byrd learned the discipline of weaving a contrapuntal piece around a cantus firmus.

The five In nomine in five parts belong to the same genre, but are more mature works. Byrd's handling of this peculiarly English form, based on the setting of the words "in nomine Domine" from John Taverner's *Missa Gloria tibi trinitas*, displays a greater freedom from the constraints of the cantus firmus than the earlier pieces. Byrd's next consort work is *Browning*, a set of variations on the popular tune also known as "The leaves be green," composed around 1680. Here Byrd places the melody in the lowest part, forming a function akin to a ground bass; this was an unusual practice for the time.

Finally, there is a group of mature compositions, mostly believed to date from the 1680s. Prime among these are a group of fantasias, freely composed works in three, four, five, and six parts. Along with a six-part Pavan and Galliard that was probably Byrd's last consort work, the two six-part fantasias show the composer at the peak of his powers, relishing the freedom and richness of sonority obtainable from a sextet of instruments. The second of them is especially outstanding, a superbly crafted medley that manages to incorporate an exuberant version of *Greensleeves* before proceeding to a final coda of quiet beauty. The six-part *Pavan and Galliard* is equally fine, Byrd skillfully unifying the themes of these two stylized dances to a degree unique during this period. *—Brian Robins*

Recommended:

- ○ **Byrd: The Consort Music** / Fretwork / 1994 / Virgin 45031
- ○ **Byrd: Virginals & Consorts** / Sempé (cond.), Capriccio Stravagante / 1997 / Astreé 8611

C

Montserrat Caballé

b. Apr. 12, 1933, Barcelona, Spain
Soprano

Montserrat Caballé's career, which began with a legendary lucky break, would eventually make her one of Spain's greatest sopranos—equaled in status and reputation only by her fellow Barcelonian, Victoria de los Angeles.

Her full birth name is Maria de Montserrat Viviana Concepción Caballé i Folch. She is named after the famous Catalan monastery of Montserrat. It is said that her parents feared that they would lose her and vowed that if she were born alive and well they would christen her with the monastery's name.

She learned singing at her convent school; at the age of eight, she entered the Conservatorio del Liceo in Barcelona. Her most important teachers were Eugenia Kenny, Conchita Badea, and Napoleone Annovazzi. When she graduated in 1954, she won the Liceo's Gold Medal.

Caballé made her professional debut in Madrid in the oratorio *El pesebre* (The Manger) by the great Catalan cellist Pau (Pablo) Casals. She then went to Italy, where she received a few minor roles at various houses.

In 1956, she joined the Basle Opera; she was working her way through the smaller roles when one of the principal singers took ill and she took over the role of Mimì in Puccini's *La Bohéme*. Her unqualified success in that part led to promotion to starring roles, including Pamina (*The Magic Flute*), Puccini's *Tosca*, Verdi's *Aïda*, Marta in Eugén d'Albert's *Tiefland*, and the Richard Strauss roles of Arabella, Chrysothemis (*Elektra*), and Salome.

She steadily gained a European reputation, singing in Bremen, Milan, Vienna, Barcelona, and Lisbon, taking such diverse roles as Violetta (*La Traviata*), Tatiana (*Yevgeny Onegin*), Dvořák's *Armida* and *Rusalka*, and Marie in Berg's *Wozzeck*. She debuted at *La Scala* in 1960 as a Flower Maiden in *Parsifal*. She sang in Mexico City in 1964 as Massenet's Manon.

In April 20, 1965, on extremely short notice, she substituted for the indisposed Marilyn Horne in a concert performance in Donizetti's *Lucrezia Borgia*, achieving a thunderous success and "overnight" superstardom. She became one of the leading figures in the revival of interest in the bel canto operas of Bellini and Donizetti, many of which were staged especially for her. Caballé's performances as Elizabeth I (*Roberto Devereaux*) and that monarch's rival Mary Queen of Scots (*Maria Stuarda*) are legendary. In 1971, she sang a memorable concert performance of *Maria Stuarda* in which her fellow Barcelonian José Carreras made his London debut, and after that she helped advance his career. She made her Metropolitan Opera debut in 1965 as Marguerite in *Faust*.

Caballé's career has centered around Verdi's important dramatic roles, but has also embraced the Marschallin (*Rosenkavalier*), the Countess (*Marriage of Figaro*), and Queen Isabella (in the premiere of Leonardo Balada's *Cristobál Colón* in Barcelona in 1989).

Caballé has had unusual crossover success. In addition to singing on two tracks on an album by New Age composer Vangelis, she is famous for collaborating with the late Freddie Mercury of the rock group Queen, who wrote *Exercises in Free Love* for her. She appeared on his hit album *Barcelona*. That album and its primary single rose high on the pop charts.

In 1964, she married Spanish tenor Bernabé Marti. They have two children, Bernabé Marti Jr. and Montserrat Marti, who is herself a succesful soprano. In 1997, Caballé co-founded an important annual vocal competition in the Principality of Andorra, the Concurs Internacional de Cant Montserrat Caballé. She conducts master classes in conjunction with that competition. *—Joseph Stevenson*

Recommended:

○ **Montserrat Caballé: Ultimate Collection** / Caballé, various artists / 1999 / RCA 63464

○ **Verdi: Don Carlo** / Giulini (cond.), Domingo, Caballé, Verrett, Milnes, Royal Opera House Orch. & Chorus / 2000 / Angel 67397

○ **Bellini: Norma** / Bonynge (cond.), Pavarotti, Ramey, Sutherland, Caballé, Welsh National Opera Orch. & Chorus / 1988 / London 414476

○ **Leoncavallo: Pagliacci** / Santi (cond.), Domingo, Caballé, Milnes, Etheridge, London SO / 1998 / RCA 50168

Juan Bautista José Cabanilles

b. Sep. 6, 1644, Algemesi, near Valencia, Spain, **d.** Apr. 29, 1712, Valencia, Spain
Composer

Cabanilles was born in Algemesi, and his first name is shown variously as Juan and Joan; some works ascribed to "José Cabanillas" are now confirmed as belonging to his output and not that of another composer. Outside of his baptismal certificate, nothing is known of him until 1665, when the 21-year-old Cabanilles was appointed second organist at Valencia Cathedral, replacing the departing Jerónimo de la Torre. Somehow the issue that Cabanilles was not yet a priest was discreetly avoided, and thus he was not prevented from being promoted to first organist in April 1666. Cabanilles was finally ordained as a priest in September 1668. From then on, little is known of Cabanilles' activity, although he is said to have traveled north to France on occasion to play certain high holy feast days. In 1703, his health began to decline, and Cabanilles soon began to rotate a number of substitute organists in order to keep his position filled in Valencia. He died there, aged 67, in 1712.

Much of what is known, and the survival of many of Cabanilles works, is owed to the industriousness of his student Josep Elias. The manuscripts that Elias conserved and others of Cabanilles reside within the Library of Cataluña in Barcelona, which also publishes an edition of the works of this composer. Cabanilles' surviving output is rather extensive, numbering to nearly 200 pieces, all but eight written for the organ. Ninety are Tientos, monothematic in nature and based on the Renaissance form of the ricercar. Cabanilles' *Tientos de falsas* are noted for their liberal use of chromaticism and dark modal coloring. This approach has led some writers to cite Cabanilles as a harmonic revolutionary, but his approach is likely more reactionary. Cabanilles was one of the lone holdouts to Renaissance mannerism in an era where greater Europe was concerned with Baroque forms and major/minor key orientation. Nonetheless, Cabanilles' style was in keeping with trends in seventeenth century Spain. Cabanilles also composed polyphonic elaboration of chant and several works in variation form over a repeating bass figure, which he variably called passacalles, galiarda, paseos, and xacara. Cabanilles also experimented in six works with the Italian form of toccata. Of his *Battle Pieces* the famous *Battala Imperiale* has been discovered to be the work of Johann Kasper Kerll, not Cabanilles.

Valencia is a major port of call in Spain, and Cabanilles' music betrays some superficial elements derived from Italian practices, demonstrating that he knew contemporary Italian music. As the Kerll piece is found among Cabanilles' manuscripts, this seems to confirm his awareness of German music, and he may have known something about Franco-Flemish music as well. But overall, Cabanilles' music is overwhelmingly Spanish in character, and in his own time he was considered the last major figure in the line of "mystic" Spanish organists that begins with Antonio de Cabezón and continues through de Heredia, de Arauxo, and Coelho. Eight sacred vocal works survive in Cabanilles' catalog; a fragmentary mass, Magnificat, and six motets, of which the four-voice *"Mortales que amais a un Dios immortal"* utilizes a tune which would later coincidentally turn up in the *St. Matthew Passion* of Johann Sebastian Bach. His pupil, Josep Elias, who wrote, "the world will vanish before a second Cabanilles comes," gives an indication of the high regard in which Cabanilles was held in his day. *—Uncle Dave Lewis*

Overview of Works (ca. 1665–1710)

Juan Bautista Jose Cabanilles has been called the finest Spanish organist and organ music composer of the seventeenth century, and he may well have been—no mean feat, to be sure. His music is inventive and graceful, contrapuntally sturdy without seeming overly rhetorical or stodgy. It is not, however, the music of a man much interested in the musical developments of the middle Baroque: Cabanilles seems a composer who would have been quite content to have his country and his art remain in the cherished ways of the sixteenth and seventeenth centuries. Still, it wouldn't be proper to call his music outdated for its time; rather, consider him a musician whose taste for the rich and unique organ music traditions of pre-Baroque and early-Baroque Spain outweighed most other factors and allowed him to develop a style in which the best of the old shakes hands with a select few traits of the new. There are passages that sound almost as if J.S. Bach had written them, but more often than not Cabanilles moves straight from such episodes into passages built around a characteristically Spanish modal display that reaches back all the way into the Renaissance.

Cabanilles composed a great deal of music. There are some Latin sacred vocal works (including a mass, a Magnificat, and a Beatus vir, the last two for rich 12-voice ensembles) and a handful of Spanish-text vocal pieces. But the bread and butter of his catalog, of course, are the 400-plus essays, some small and some large, for organ. Cabanilles sometimes tackled forms whose counterparts in other languages we immediately recognize—passacalles, gallardas, tocatas and the like. Far more numerous, though, are his works of the tiento variety. The tiento was a uniquely Spanish (and Portuguese) keyboard composition that is best described as a cross between a toccata, a fantasia, a prelude, and a ricercar—it can take characteristics of any or all of them in any combination and any order. Juan Bautista Jose Cabanilles is considered the last great composer of tientos, just as his stylistic predecessor Antonio de Cabezón, a century and a half earlier, is commonly felt to have been the first great composer of them. Cabanilles also composed a large body (more than 150) of organ "verses" meant to be inserted into the liturgy. —*Blair Johnston*

Recommended:

○ **Cabanilles: Batalles, Tientos & Passacalles** / Savall (cond.), Hesperion XX / 1998 / Alia Vox 9801

Antonio de Cabezón

b. ca. 1510, Castrillo de Matajudios, Spain, **d.** Mar. 26, 1566, Madrid, Spain
Composer

One of the first composers to write prolifically for keyboard, Antonio Cabezón was innovative and influential. His works anticipated the potential of both the organ and clavichord—later explored to a greater degree by Jan Pieterszoon Sweelinck (1562–1621) and Manuel Rodrigues Coelho (1583–1635), both of whom were influenced by Cabezón—and his treatise on keyboard performance advocated the use of the thumb, which was unusual for the time. Fortunate to have led a privileged existence, Cabezón entered easily into the circles of Spanish nobility, and spent much of his life in the service of royalty.

Born into a noble family (landowners in Castillo de Matajudíos and Castrojeriz), Antonio Cabezón was either blind from birth or blinded in early childhood. His first musical training was probably from a local organist; it is certain that he continued his studies in Palencia with Garcia de Baeza, organist at the Burgos Cathedral. While in Palencia, Cabezón lived with his relative, Esteban Martinez de Cabezón, canon of Burgos Cathedral.

In 1525, excellent recommendations helped Cabezón move from Palencia to Toledo, where he took up a position in the new royal chapel of Queen Isabella; he became principal organist a year later. He later played in the chamber consort of Charles V. Cabezón married the wealthy Luisa Núñez (1538), and relocated to Avila, his new wife's native city. Their five children also secured positions with the royal family.

After Queen Isabella died in 1539, Cabezón remained in the service of her children, one of whom was Prince Philip, the future king; by the time of Philip's accession, Cabezón played only for Philip's chapel. As part of the Royal retinue, Cabezón traveled to Germany, Luxembourg, the Netherlands (October 1548–July 1551), and later to England (July 1554–January 1556). During these excursions, he was exposed to a great deal of music, some of which he transcribed. More importantly, Cabezón exerted an influence upon the keyboard composers whom he met.

The few of Cabezón's pieces that were printed during his lifetime appeared in Luis Venegas de Henestrosa's *Libro de cifra neuva* of 1557. Cabezón's son, Hernando (1541–1602), published most his father's known works after Cabezón's death.

Cabezón's music was influenced by that of the Franco-Flemish composers, particularly Josquin DesPrez, but his works are clearly in the Spanish instrumental tradition; his keyboard writing is masterfully idiomatic. Striking modulations mark his music, which is infused with modal chromaticism; an adventurous use of intervals (discouraged by contemporary theorists) enabled him to develop a colorful harmonic palette. His motivic approach to melodic writing produced intensely woven, unified works that relied primarily on augmentation and diminution of a primary idea for variation and development.

Cabezón composed in a wide variety of instrumental genres, including tientos, (ricercari), glosas, diferencias, falsobordone, versos, hymns, and canons. He treated *diferencias*, or variations on tunes, in an original manner by placing the cantus firmus in a different voice in each variation; this technique was later adopted by William Byrd (1543–1623).—*John Palmer*

Overview of Works (ca. 1530–1665)

The graceful, stylized works of Antonio de Cabezón were key contributors to the first true flowering of keyboard music in Spain during the early sixteenth century. Not be confused with his brother or his sons, some of whom were also prominent musicians of the day, Cabezón may be considered the first great champion in the noble line of Renaissance/Baroque Spanish organists—a lineage that culminated in (and, for some, ended with) Juan Bautista Jose Cabanilles at the turn of the eighteenth century.

Cabezón, who was blind from infancy, composed music for both organ and clavichord. His tientos (highly sectional pieces that sometimes paraphrase preexisting music) are among his most significant works. Building on the long-established practice of Spanish vihuela players, Cabezón also made many arrangements (also called glosses or glosas) of other composers' music—including motets by Josquin and other Flemish composers—for his own instruments. There are also many sets of diferencias (variations) that take up pre-existing cantus firmi. Cabezón's music must be considered modal rather than tonal, but, at the same time, he was fluent in a rich harmonic language whose connections with music of the future are, from our modern vantage point, sometimes startlingly evident. —*Blair Johnston*

Recommended:

○ **Cabezón: Obras de Musica para Tecla** / Baiano / Symphonia 98156

○ **Antonio de Cabezón: Works for Organ** / Gonzalez Uriol / Motette 12291

○ **Cabezón: Tientos y Glosados** / Wimmer (cond.), Ens. Accentus / 2001 / Naxos 554836

Giulio Caccini

b. Oct. 8, 1551, Tivoli [?], Italy, **d.** Dec. 10, 1618, Florence, Italy
Composer: Vocal

Giulio Caccini, one of music's true pioneers, was an important Italian composer of the early Baroque era, noted for his songs and lone opera *Euridice*. In the former genre he was most influential, leading the way in establishing the new monodic style that flourished in Italy after 1600. He may have been the first Florentine composer to write an opera; certainly *Euridice* was the first published (1600).

Caccini was born around 1545, probably in Rome, though there is some evidence to suggest Tivoli was his birthplace. After vocal and instrumental studies in Rome, he was taken to Florence by the influential arts patron, Cosimo I de Medici, who was captivated by the youth's singing. Caccini would be accepted into the Medici Court there, though he first took further vocal instruction from Scipione delle Palle at Cosimo's expense. It appears Caccini developed a considerable reputation as a singer in Florence either before beginning service in the Medici Court or concurrently with his early years there.

Around 1574, Caccini became associated with the Camerata, a Florentine musical association headed, in effect, by Count Giovanni de' Bardi. This group would wield great influence in the arts and produce the first operas. By the time the composer reached his early thirties he was a famous tenor, well-connected with the Medici family and with other artists and prominent Florentine citizens. Caccini regularly sang and performed on viol and other instruments in Court masques during this period. Still, he would not attain an important position in the Medici Court until 1600.

By the early 1580s Caccini was working on a new song style whose manner typically consisted of an elegant melodic line sensitive to the inflections in the text, supported by rather subdued diatonic chordal accompaniment, and colored by improvisatory embellishments. He may not have actually introduced many compositions before 1589, the year when Court records first make reference to his compositional activities, in this instance relating to the celebrations surrounding the marriage of Grand Duke Ferdinando I. Caccini had also become a respected teacher by this time, though his foremost pupil would be his daughter, Francesca (1587–1640), who became a well-known singer and composer in the first half of the seventeenth century. Caccini's two other children, Pompeo and Settimia, studied under him as well, the latter, like her sister, achieving fame as both a singer and composer.

On a trip to Rome in 1592, Caccini's new song style was reportedly well-received. In the next decade his reputation as a composer, as well as his standing at the Medici Court increased dramatically, in the latter venue culminating in his elevation to music director in 1600. He completed his opera, *Euridice*, by that year, too, probably to edge out his famous rival Peri, who was also doing a setting. Caccini's opera was first staged in Florence on December 5, 1602, with success.

1602 was also the year that Caccini's presented his most famous collection of vocal music, *Le nuove musiche* (The new music). It contains madrigals, arias, and some additional music to an earlier work, *Il rapimento di Cefalo* (1600), a so-called pastoral drama, something of a precursor to opera.

In 1604, Caccini and his family were invited to the French Court, where Henry IV tried to enlist the vocal services of his daughter, whom he called the greatest singer in France. After Caccini returned, he remained in the service of the Medici Court, but became far less active as a composer. Caccini died on or about December 7, 1618, and was buried three days later. —*Robert Cummings*

VOCAL

Le Nuove Musiche, arias and madrigals for voice & continuo (1601–1602)

Giulio Caccini wanted to secure his place in music history. In the preface to his 1602 publication *Le Nuove Musiche*, Caccini insists that he himself invented the new genre of monody, which would change the face of music across the entire century. Caccini was not actually monody's sole inventor, and *Le Nuove Musiche* was not technically even the first monodic collection published. It nevertheless enjoyed a spectacular influence, going through numerous reprintings and inspiring countless later composers. To this day, *Le Nuove Musiche* remains one of the best-known musical publications of all time; very few contemporary collections of solo songs fail to include an excerpt.

The monodic genre of *Le Nuove Musiche* first took root and grew in Renaissance Florence. Caccini, with Jacopo Peri, Ottavio Rinuccini, and Vincenzo Galilei, established the revolutionary experimental music studio known as the Florentine Camerata. Meeting in the home of Count Giovanni de' Bardi, the Camerata considered the very principles of music. They believed that ancient Greek stage music achieved its dramatic effect because it was performed by a single voice; the polyphonic madrigal of their own time had exhausted the possibilities of musical expression. They sought a new and newly affective musical form. They pioneered the new style of solo operatic singing and the solo monodic madrigal; Florentines first heard their new music in public during the city's 1600 *feste*. The ambitious Caccini (also jealous of Peri) named his published collection *The New Music*, and claimed in the preface to have himself invented the style decades before.

The musical style of *Le Nuove Musiche* is founded on vocal virtuosity (Caccini was an excellent bass). The book contains 22 songs, 12 madrigals, and ten arias, each for a solo singer accompanied by citarrone or other stringed continuo instrument. The madrigals do not showcase the kind of mimetic word-painting famous in the sixteenth century madrigal; Caccini's settings achieve their power by sensitive reflection of the poetic structure, and by carefully mapped displays of vocal ornamentation. Some of the ornaments are helpfully explained in the volume's preface; many others are written in to the printed score. Among the madrigals are some of his best-known compositions: *Amarilli mia bella* and *Perfidissimo volto*. The arias adopt a similar compositional profile, setting strophic Italian canzona texts. Caccini closes the collection with a set of monodic opera excerpts. In 1614 he was driven by the success of *Le Nuove Musiche* to release a second volume. —*Timothy Dickey*

Recommended:

○ **Caccini: Le Nuove Musiche** / Savall (con.), Schola Cantorum Basiliensis / DHM 77164

John Cage

b. Sep. 5, 1912, Los Angeles, CA, **d.** Aug. 12, 1992, New York, NY

Composer: Avant-garde, Keyboard, Chamber Music, Vocal, Concerto, Orchestral

Even after his death, John Cage remains a controversial figure. Famously challenging the very notion of what music is, Cage remained on the leading edge of both playful and profound experimentalism for the greater part of his career, collaborating with and influencing generations of composers, writers, dancers, and visual artists. One of his best-known and most sonically intriguing innovations, the prepared piano, had become an almost commonplace compositional resource by the end of the twentieth century. Years before the invention of the synthesizer, he was in the forefront in the exploration of electric and electronic sound sources, using oscillators, turntables, and amplification to musical ends. He pioneered the use of graphic notation and, in employing chance operations to determine musical parameters, was the leading light for one cadre of the avant-garde that included Morton Feldman, Christian Wolff, Earle Brown, and Pauline Oliveros. Cage produced works of "performance art" years before the term was coined, and his *4'33"* (1952)—in which the performers are instructed to remain silent for four minutes and thirty-three seconds—takes a place among the most notorious touchstones of twentieth century music.

Cage was born on September 5, 1912, in Los Angeles, California. After boyhood piano lessons, he pursued both formal and informal musical studies that ranged from classes at Pomona College to cultural excursions throughout Europe to lessons with American composer Adolph Weiss.

Cage's true mentors were Henry Cowell and Arnold Schoenberg, two very different musical personalities. Cage's music from the 1930s and 1940s demonstrates the direct influence of both Schoenberg and Cowell, and is marked especially by the use of percussion instruments and the prepared piano. While Cage's early music was based, like Schoenberg's, primarily on the organization of pitch, rhythmic structures became increasingly important, no doubt due in part to the composer's associations with the world of dance. He had worked as a dance accompanist at UCLA and then took a similar position at the Cornish School of the Arts in Seattle, Washington, in 1938. Here he met, and developed a working relationship, with choreographer/dancer Merce Cunningham.

The most important aesthetic development in Cage's career came as a result of his studies of Eastern philosophies, especially Zen Buddhism, in the late 1940s and throughout the 1950s. The result was music derived, at least in part, from quasi-random decisions determined by the *I Ching* (the Chinese Book of Changes). Instead of imposing an inviolable order upon the conventional elements of Western music, Cage endeavored "to make a musical composition[,] the continuity of which is free of individual taste and memory (psychology) and also of the literature and 'traditions' of the art." The embodiment of this philosophy is well illustrated by Cage's *Imaginary Landscape No. 4* (1951). The score calls for the prescribed manipulations of knobs on twelve radios; the aural result is dependent on what happens to be on the airwaves at the instant of performance. In "composing" works in such a fashion, Cage ensured that each realization of the score would provide a unique sonic experience.

Cage's ecumenically experimental spirit continued to thrive into the 1960s and beyond. The "environmental extravaganza" *Musicircus* (1967) incorporates everything from rock music to pantomime to film; *HPSCHD* (1967) mixes computer technology with the music of Mozart, Beethoven, and Chopin. *Child of Tree* (1975) calls for the amplification of a potted plant, *Inlets* (1977) for four conch shells and the sound of fire, and *Il Treno* (1978) for "prepared trains."

Though his career unfolded largely without the confines of the musical establishment in America, Cage became something of a beloved elder statesman of music in his later years, honored with formal distinctions and concerts marking his major birthdays. He died in New York City on August 12, 1992.—*Michael Rodman*

AVANT-GARDE

4'33" (1952)

4'33" and its alternative realization (*4'33" No. 2*) are perhaps the most elegantly simple and controversial of all of Cage's works. The score consists of the notations I. Tacet, II. Tacet, III. Tacet. Perhaps what is called for is an action that will give the sense of three moments in time and will also make the presence of an undisturbed, eternal silence felt—not a negative act, but an affirmation of silence, the element that is necessary for any meaningful sound gesture. The first realization made of this piece was by David Tudor, who quietly opened and closed the keyboard lid of a piano three times to create a performance of four minutes and 33 seconds' duration. It can, of course, be performed for any duration, and has been. The version *0'00"/Solo* (to be performed in any way by anyone,) written for Yoko Ono and Toshi Ichiyanagi in Tokyo, October 24, 1962, further elucidates this experience by indicating a kind of non-clock time or eternal presence, and indicating that the piece can also embody other extremes of infinite compression or loudness: "In a situation provided with maximum amplification (no feedback), perform a disciplined action. With any interruptions. Fulfilling in whole or part an obligation to others.... No attention to be given the situation (electronic, musical, theatrical)... the first performance was the writing of this manuscript... this is 4'33" (*No. 2*) and also Pt. 3 of a work of which *Atlas Eclipticalis* is Pt. 1."

There are probably as many reactions/meanings/interpretations of *4'33"* as there are possible realizations. And that will always be the undisturbed ("The Way that can be told of is not the unvarying way," *Tao Te Ching*), elusive, quite timeless beauty of this piece. Aside from all these considerations, it is charmingly warm and disarming to simply share this peaceful moment (unselfconsciously) with the rest of the audience. —*"Blue Gene" Tyranny*

Recommended:

○ **4'33": Cage, Cage-Harrison, Varése, Chávez** / Amadinda Percussion Group / Hungaroton 12991

○ **45'; 34'46.776; 31'57.9864; 27'10.554 & others** / E. Blum, M. Schroeder, Schulkowsky, Uitti, Vigeland / 1991 / Hat Hut 6070

Fontana Mix (1958)

John Cage's 1958 title *Fontana Mix* is attached to two related, but historically distinctly separate, entities, the score published by C.F. Peters (1960) and the four multi channel tapes Cage prepared from it at the Studio di Fonologia in Milan. The score Cage created for *Fontana Mix* consists of 20 sheets, ten transparencies inscribed with points (or dots), a single transparency bearing a straight line and ten plain white sheets with squiggly lines. By means of an included graph and a straight line, the performer uses the sheets in combination as a "tool" to assemble a realization of *Fontana Mix*. In executing the tape, Cage divided his sound sources into six classes; city sounds, country sounds, electronic sounds, manually produced (meaning "instrumental") sounds, wind-produced sounds (such as singing), and small sounds that require amplification, such as crickets chirping. Coordinate points drawn from the transparencies determine the class of each tape sound, inches of tape used, its volume, timbre, mixing, and other elements. Cage once described the score of *Fontana Mix* as "a camera from which anyone can take a photograph."

The creation of the four audio tapes comprising *Fontana Mix* were not created without some difficulty. The tapes were not coming out to the same coordinates as the score, and the problem wasn't solved until Cage realized that he was editing with both eyes open and that his Italian second engineer was cutting with one eye closed. The difference in tape inches proved sufficient to throw the whole work off the plan.

Both the score and tape of *Fontana Mix* provided Cage with a rich source of variables from which to garner new pieces. A cycle of Cage works emerged in the years 1958–60 that either draw information from the *Fontana Mix* score or make use of the tapes; *Aria* and *Music Walk* (both 1958), *Sounds of Venice* and *Walter Walk* (both 1959) and *Theater Piece* (1960). A 1960 *Time 2000* series recording of soprano Cathy Berberian combining *Aria* with *Fontana Mix* is a frequently cited example, chosen to exemplify Cage's compositional efforts in this period. Likewise celebrated is Cage's 1959 Folkways recording of *Indeterminacy*, where David Tudor once again pressed the *Fontana Mix* tapes into service behind Cage's droll narration of 90 short stories. Cage has also suggested that *Fontana Mix* may be used in conjunction with *Solo for Voice 2* (1960) and *Songbooks* (1970).

Long after their creation, the *Fontana Mix* tapes continue to inspire audio artists within the field of electronica. There is a group called Fontana Mix in honor of Cage's creation and the group the Tape-Beatles has recorded a "Euro pop dance mix" of the work. Other significant realizations of the score as published include the 1964 Max Neuhaus version for electronic percussion entitled *Feed*, a later (1967) Tudor-Cage version scored for piano and electronic circuits and an audio-architectonic environment (1998) created in Stuttgart, Germany by artist David Wendland. *—Uncle Dave Lewis*

Recommended:

○ **John Cage: Fontana Mix & Solo for Voice 2** / E. Blum / 1993 / Hat Hut 6125

HPSCHD, for up to 7 harpsichords & up to 51 tapes (1967–1969)

Pronounced harpsichord, *HPSCHD* (the computer handle for harpsichord) was commissioned by the Swiss harpsichord aficionado Antoinette Vischer, who had to pester John Cage for several years before he agreed to do it. The reason for the delay was that, as Cage put it "I've always hated the harpsichord, it reminds me of a sewing machine." Perhaps as an antidote, the massive *HPSCHD* can be performed with from one to 51 tracks of computer-generated sound along with live performances by one to seven harpsichordists performing compositions by Mozart, Beethoven, Chopin, Gottschalk, Busoni, and Schoenberg that have been abstracted by chance operations. Completed in 1968, the work is more accurately considered a collaboration between Cage and Lejaren Hiller, who worked on it together at the University of Illinois' Electronic Music Studio in Champaign.

The compositional procedure behind *HPSCHD* enabled a meeting ground where Cage's use of chance operations and Hiller's use of mathematical probability could meet. This was facilitated by Fortran programmer Ed Kobrin, who devised a random number generator based on hexagrams found in the I Ching. The work required over 18,000 such "coin tosses" and as Hiller has stated, "Every note was a mutual decision." Each of the 885,000 "decisions" included not only pitch, but duration, attack, decay, and timbre. Additional computer programs by programming pioneer Max Matthews and Hiller affected tuning, note sequence, silence, and repetition. These programs became essential to the work, and pushed their computers to the breaking point. The aural result was undeniably complex, a new kind of chamber music that had never been heard before. And as Cage pointed out "Disorganization can result from the accumulation of organizations having fine differences." Hiller also created a program called KNOBS which enabled a print-out of 10,000 different "solutions" or scores to be included with the recorded version of the work, enabling the listener to "participate" by accordingly altering tone, volume, and panning controls while listening at home.

HPSCHD was premiered on May 16, 1969 at Assembly Hall on the University of Illinois campus, to an audience of 6,000. The amassed equipment included seven amplifiers, 208 computer-generated tapes, 52 projectors, 64 slide projects, eight movie projectors, 6,400 slides, 40 movies, a 340 foot circular screen, and several rectangular screens. In a space capable of holding up to 16,000 people, the audience was free to circulate and view/hear the work from different angles. Just as previous Cage works had predated minimalism (*String Quartet in Four Parts*), (the three *Constructions in Metal*) and the turntabling of hip-hop *Cartridge Music*), the premiere of *HPSCHD* seems to have, in some ways, envisioned the rave. *—AMG*

Number Pieces (1987–1992)

The so-called "Number Pieces" date from the last five years of John Cage's life (he died in 1992), and represent the fullest distillation of his musical and aesthetic philosophies. They are at once an exercise in boundaries and in freedom; their seemingly sterile titles, consisting only of number names and numerals, indicate not only limitations, but the wide space of possibilities between them. The works, which number nearly 50, are organized rather efficiently: each piece is assigned a number, spelled out as a word, indicating the number of players required; a superscript numeral attached to the number name indicates the pieces chronological order in relation to other pieces for the same number of players. Thus, *Four*^{3} is the third work in the series requiring four performers, while *Two*^{6} is the sixth piece for a duo of players. Pieces with unique numbers of performers bear no superscript; for example, there is only one *Thirteen* in the series.

The titles of the works convey only the faintest and most abstract indications of their sound; that is, we obviously might expect a more varied sonic terrain from *Fifty-Eight*, for example. The specific instrumentations for the various pieces, however, represent a wide variety. The performers in *Four*^{3}, for example, play violin, piano, and a variety of rain sticks; the lone performer in *One*^{12} is a person delivering a lecture. And even if many of the pieces can be characterized by a general sense of space and focus, with individual sound events often surrounded by generous expanses of silence, the compelling aspect of the works is not the leisure in which they indulge while unfolding, but rather the microscopic attention that they compel the listener to devote. The parameters within which the events occur are somewhat flexible, although some specific actions are supplied. (For example, the violinist and pianist in *Two*^{6}, composed in the year of Cage's death, deliver sequences of tones derived from Satie's famous protominimalist marathon for piano, *Vexations*.) In applying temporal aspects to the events in a given number piece, Cage uses various systems of sound modules and time brackets, which allow the performer to make certain decisions as to the moment of attack and the duration of individual sounds or silences. This does not relieve the performer of any burden, however, but imposes one: each decision is utterly exposed; freed from any expectations of tonal, melodic, or gestural convention, each sound stands as "pure music," its existence and execution anything but arbitrary. *—Jeremy Grimshaw*

Recommended:

○ **Cage: Four^3; One^5; Two^6** / M. Joste, Flamer, Alchourroun, Michaut / 1995 / Mode 44

○ **John Cage: Ten; Ryoanji, Fourteen** / Ives Ens / 1994 / Hat Hut 6159

Roaratorio: An Irish Circus on Finnegan's Wake (1979)

In the late 1970s, Klaus Schoning of West German Radio, asked John Cage to compose some music especially for broadcast. Specifically, he asked Cage to write something to accompany Cage's own text piece, *Writing for the Second Time Through Finnegan's Wake*, *Finnegan's Wake* being the notoriously unread great novel by James Joyce.

The hour-long piece is built in three layers. First, there is the sound of Cage reading his text, which is 41 pages of mesostic poems he pulled out of *Finnegan's Wake*. Second is what Cage called a circus of Irish music. All the essentials are there: folk songs (which Joyce himself sang as he strolled in Dublin), fiddle, flute, uillean pipes, and bodhran drum. Instructed to listen only to themselves, the five performers who play the folk music do so completely independent of each other and of the rest of *Roaratorio*. When first contemplating *Roaratorio*, Cage made a huge list (more than 4,000 items) of the sounds he noticed mentioned in Joyce's novel. He thought that simply presenting these sounds back to back would "bring the novel to music." Using this as a starting point, the third layer of *Roaratorio* is made up of such sounds—machines, bells, voices, a fart, crowds, various birds and animals, sounds of nature, etc.—and of ambient noise recorded by Cage himself in 626 of the Irish locations mentioned in *Finnegan's Wake*, which has 626 pages. As you can imagine, the result is cacophonous. *Roaratorio* simply enacts in music the punning simultaneities of Joyce's hyper-complicated novel by piling-up loads of "Irish" audio material. Irish tradition, place, language, history, music, time, and all the Irishness of what sounds Irish are tossed in a heavy sonic salad. Cage admitted that as they made the piece (he had several assistants), he had no idea how the result would come off. By the time all the multi-tracking was done, his reading was barely audible. Luckily for listeners, the density constantly fluctuates so that *Roaratorio* feels purposeful rather than pointlessly busy. The folk melodies offer easy clarity amidst the digressive tangle and they also give *Roaratorio* an overall mood of cheerful nostalgia.

The fact that Cage won the Carl Sczuka prize for *Roaratorio* is probably more indicative of the belated desire to celebrate Cage's achievements than of *Roaratorio's* particular excellence as a work of art. Perhaps it also expresses the judges' delight that some avant-garde music left them feeling uplifted for a change. *Roaratorio* follows its arbitrary structural plans as rigorously as any of Cage's other music, but instead of being weirdly unrecognizable and spare, it's dreamy, warm, and Pink Floyd-like. *—Donato Mancini*

Recommended:

○ **John Cage: Roaratorio** / Heaney, Malloy, Glackin, Ennis, Mercier, Cage / 1994 / Wergo 6303

○ **John Cage: Roaratorio** / Heaney, Malloy, Glackin, Ennis, Mercier, Cage / 2002 / Mode 28

KEYBOARD

In a Landscape, for piano or harp (1948)

Fresh from achieving notoriety with his invention of the prepared piano (meaning one attached various dampers, mutes, and noisy things to the strings inside the piano to transform it from a harmonic instrument into a box of percussion sounds), Cage wrote *In a Landscape* for the dancer Louise Lippold in 1948.

It is a companion piece to *Dream*, written the same year for Merce Cunningham, and uses the same compositional technique. Namely, it is limited to only a certain number of tones and depends on the use of sustained notes to make its effect. In comparison with the earlier work, though, it uses more different notes and therefore has a more expansive feeling.

Cage wrote the piece to the rhythmic structure of the dance piece as conceived first by Lippold, who gave him the counts of the dance. He credits the lack of organization that was the usual state of these lists of counts with leading him to his ideas of "structural rhythm."

The tonal oddity of this piece is that all the notes are contained in two octaves. One of the two uses a mode based on B flat, while the other octave has only notes of a mode in the key of G. Shifts from one octave to another create a bitonal effect that creates a momentary impression of being out of tune, which gives *In a Landscape* a uniquely haunting quality. *—Joseph Stevenson*

Recommended:

○ **Cage: Daughters of the Lonesome Isle** / M. L. Tan / 1994 / New Albion 070

○ **Cage: In a Landscape** / S. Drury / 1994 / Catalyst 0902661980

Music of Changes (1951)

Composed in 1951, this work in four books created an entirely new sound in the literature for piano through new performing techniques and a radically novel compositional aesthetic. These instrument techniques include a sophisticated use of natural and artificial harmonics, a complex interplay of silently depressed keys to produce these harmonics, muting and striking the strings, the continuous use of all three pedals to create interpenetrations of sound layers, vastly differing octave displacements, striking of the piano body, playing on the strings with various objects, and the use of extreme dynamics within a moment/event, thus producing subtle inflections and nuances. The (secondary) emotional effect is that of a mysterious aura in some sections and of breathtaking and energetic virtuosity in others.

In composing the work, Cage used the *I-Ching* (the ancient Chinese "Book of Changes") to create charts of individual musical parameters such as superpositions (how many events happen at one time within a given space), tempi, durations (including silences), and dynamics. In other words, charts of individual musical parameters in linear sequences that were accessed (quasi-) randomly by coin tosses, similar to the method of accessing the hexagram-coded sequences of the *I-Ching* itself. Some charts were considered "mobile," where an event passes in time to be replaced by another. Other events are considered immobile when they recur or repeat, and this function changes with a coin toss related to the numbering systems. The interaction of these charts required Cage to enter an even subtler conceptual area calling for decisions on further conditions, such as apparent interferences, actual and potential audibility, etc. This conception is a sharp contrast to the more constructivist procedures of the serialists of that period, like Pierre Boulez and Karlheinz Stockhausen. "The sounds enter the time-space centered within themselves, unimpeded by service to any abstraction, their 360 degrees of circumference free for an infinite play of interpenetration...." (Cage) *—"Blue Gene" Tyranny*

Recommended:

○ **Cage: Music of Changes** / Henck / 1988 / Wergo 60099

○ **Cage: Complete Piano Music Vol. 3; Music of Changes** / Schleiermacher / 1998 / MDG 6130786

Sonatas and Interludes, for prepared piano (1948)

Lasting over 70 minutes and comprised of 16 sonatas and four interludes, John Cage's *Sonatas and Interludes* is his most substantial work for his invention, the prepared piano. Completed in March of 1948, the work is dedicated to Maro Ajemian, who premiered it in New York City at Carnegie Hall on January 11, 1949.

Students of music history have probably seen photographs of pianos fitted by Cage with all sorts of foreign objects—bits of rubber stuffed between strings, hammers fitted with tacks, perhaps even a wooden spoon poking out from the instrument's entrails at an odd angle. The so-called prepared piano, for which the *Sonatas and Interludes* are composed, provides the means by which a single instrument is able to evoke a wide variety of colors, timbres, and textures. The score, then, indicates not the sounds to be heard, but the action to be taken. Striking a particular key might produce a pitch, a hi-hat-like sizzle, or a wooden thump. Cage originally conceived the prepared piano for his 1938 work *Bachannale*, in response to a request from dancer Syvilla Forte to provide music for a six-minute dance that had no budget and space for no more than one pianist. He used it again in *A Book of Music* (1944) and *Three Dances* (1945) before employing it in *Sonatas and Interludes* in 1948. The sound is immediately engaging, and because of the differences between various pianos and the numerous varieties of weather stripping, thumb tacks, and wooden spoons available, each performance or recording is distinct. The work conjures a world of sound that is variously serene, haunting, percussive, and surreal.

Each movement examines a particular emotion, with a palette drawn from the Indian tradition that includes heroism, eroticism, wonder, mirth, sorrow, fear, anger, and tranquility. Another important principle at work in the *Sonatas and Interludes* is that of micro/macrocosmic structure. In short, this means that local elements of the structure reflect the overall form of the piece. We can look at the first Sonata in the series as an example. Explaining micro/macro structure requires what is perhaps a frightening amount of math, but reveals a very interesting principle at work. The base unit of this structure is a phrase consisting of seven beats. The first section of the bipartite sonata consists of two phrases, each with a length equivalent to seven measures in 2/2 time, or 28 quarter notes—making the entire first section, with the notated repeat, 112 quarter notes long. The second section also consists of two phrases, but each of these is only 21 quarter notes long, the equivalent of seven measures in 3/4 time—making the second section, with its repeat, 84 quarter notes long. This creates a structural four-to-three ratio, and makes the total length of the work, then, 196 quarter notes—the equivalent of seven times seven measures in 2/2. Thus the length of each phrase resonates with the length of the entire work, and the parsing of seven into four and three gives the work its principal formal division. By composing within this carefully controlled structure, Cage is free to make uncontrolled decisions of pitch, rhythm, and timbre in the moment-to-moment, while maintaining an overarching holistic continuity. *—Jeremy Grimshaw*

Recommended:

○ **Cage: Piano Works 2, Sonatas & Interludes** / Vandré / 1996 / Mode 50

○ **Cage: Sonatas and Interludes; Henck: Festeburger Fantasien** / Henck / 2003 / ECM B000021102

○ **Cage: Sonatas and Interludes** / Beth Berman / 1999 / Naxos 559042

Suite for Toy Piano (1948)

Aside from his *Music for Wind Instruments* written a decade earlier, John Cage (1912–92) was known in 1948 for his works for percussion, for piano, and for prepared piano, mostly written for dance companies. The prepared piano gained him wide notoriety as he attached washers, nuts, bolts, strips of paper, and rubber muting objects to the piano strings; each score contains drawings and precise instructions showing where to put these implements.

The purpose of all this fooling around with the innards of the piano was to change the piano, in effect, into a "percussion ensemble in a box" that could be played by a single player. The sounds Cage obtained tended to be unemotional and hard-edged, and he deliberately restricted his available palette to a few notes.

Cage enjoyed the chiming sound of the toy piano and clearly was predisposed to write for a keyboard that produced, again, hard-edged and unemotional sounds from a limited-note palette. Another factor that obviously predisposed him to write this suite was his major occupation of that year: he had gone to teach at Black Mountain College in North Carolina. (While teaching there in 1944 he had organized an event that is generally acknowledged as the first instance of what two decades later came to be called "a happening.") His 1948 project was a 25-concert series featuring the music of French composer Erik Satie.

The simplicity of Satie's music is evident in this suite. The work is in five brief movements, none more than two minutes in length. Cage announces the musical material of the first piece in the form of an incomplete scale. The toy piano is a very limited instrument; it has not much more than an octave of diatonic notes. Cage starts by restricting this instrument even more, using only five notes in the middle of the instrument. The next three notes expand the note palette until all keys on the toy instrument can be used, and then the final movement reverts back to five notes. The music has an intimate and charming, if somewhat deliberately bland quality.

In 1963, Cage's friend Lou Harrison made an orchestral arrangement of the *Suite for Toy Piano*. This version uses a large orchestra. With the full resources of the orchestra, Harrison adds remarkable amounts of character to the work. He does not harmonize or add additional notes, but he does double the notes at the octave. The sound of the orchestration is at times stately, at times exotic (sometimes even far-Eastern). Harrison's orchestration is far in result from the intentions or sound of Cage's original, but it is beguiling to the ear. And Cage, who loved the idea that his music was unpredictable, did not complain when Harrison created a sound for this music that the composer never dreamt of. *—Joseph Stevenson*

Recommended:

○ **Cage: Daughters of the Lonesome Isle** / M. L. Tan / 1994 / New Albion 070

CHAMBER MUSIC

First Construction (In Metal), for 6 percussionists (1939)

"Since Arnold Schoenberg had impressed upon me the structural function of tonality," wrote John Cage, "I felt the need of finding some structural means adequate to composing for percussion." The solution that Cage developed and utilized in the *First Construction in Metal* (1939) for percussion sextet, provided the structural foundation for much of the composer's output until the early 1950s.

The system Cage employed has been described as a "micro/macrocosmic" structure: in essence, local structures reflect the overall form of the piece. The First Construction is based on a 16 measure palindrome divided 4-3-2-3-4. The entire work is comprised of 16 of these 16-bar units grouped into structural divisions according to this same pattern, plus a nine bar coda. Thus, the piece begins with four groups of 4-3-2-3-4, followed by three groups of 4-3-2-3-4, then two, and so on. It should be noted that these ratios refer only to lengths of the sections. Within these strict parameters, Cage freely explores and combines various sounds and rhythms. The initial group of four may loosely be called an exposition due to the appearance of numerous motifs, contrasting rhythmic patterns, and instrumental combinations that Cage later develops.

His ear for the innovative use of percussion demonstrates the influence of Henry Cowell, Cage's onetime teacher, as well as that of Edgard Varèse. The massive instrumental complement includes five thundersheets, four automobile brake drums, a 12-gong gamelan, a piano (the sound of which is altered by pressing a metal cylinder against the strings), water gong, and an array of bells and cymbals. *—Jeremy Grimshaw*

Recommended:

- ○ **Cage: Three Constructions** / Donald Knaack Percussion Ens. / 2003 / Tomato 2020
- ○ **Cage: Works for Percussion** / Quatour Helios / 1991 / Wergo 6203

VOCAL

Aria, for solo voice (1958)

This innovative and entertaining vocalise, originally written for Cathy Berberian, has become a new music "classic"; it is a conceptual precursor to the composer's *Song Books* series, *Aria No. 2*, and the *Europeras I-V*. The score indicates ten different vocal styles to be employed, notated in wavy lines (somewhat similar in appearance to Tibetan vocal notation) in ten different colors, and containing 16 black squares that indicate "non-musical" sounds. A text of fragments and phrases in five different languages (Armenian, Russian, Italian, French, and English, all of which have unique vowel sounds) are associated with the various wavy lines ("Hampartzuom Dirouhi Di questa terra Naprasno Conscience et Arise!"). The choice of the specific styles and the extra-musical sounds are made by the performer. For example, in the late Cathy Berberian's realization released on a vinyl recording in the 1960s, she chose to assign the dark blue color to jazz inflections, red to deep contralto intonations ("idyot a.k.u. oakhoa far-removed"), black with parallel dotted lines was delivered in Arnold Schoenberg's sprechstimme vocal style (a kind of pitched speech) ("Poost ya the burning bush"), black tint alone was identified with "dramatic," purple suggested the famous actress/singer Marlene Dietrich's breathy and sultry style ("Will you give me to tell you?"), yellow tinted material was delivered in a bright coloratura opera style ("Odyodzke cinq not as a birth but as love"), green was folk music timbres of various sorts, orange was Oriental (Chinese opera, etc.), light blue suggested baby sounds to Berberian, and brown was reserved for nasal intonations. The various extra-musical sounds in Berberian's realization consisted of electronic bursts and processed natural, extra-musical, or environmental sounds in a *musique concrète* manner. This radical composition not only introduced the element of indeterminacy to vocal music but also changed the nature of emotional gestures in singing by moving away from linear narrative and imagery to the expression and appreciation of these gestures as a kind of database available in ordinary language, and to the utilization of language as sound per se. *—"Blue Gene" Tyranny*

Recommended:

- ○ **A Chance Operation: The John Cage Tribute** / M. Monk / 1993 / Koch 37238
- ○ **John Cage: Litany for the Whale** / P. Hillier, S. Owens / 2002 / HM 907279

CONCERTO

Concerto, for prepared piano & chamber orchestra (1951)

This work is a successful balance of current and new ideas for Cage as he was in the throes of shedding already explored, almost accepted ideas of avant-garde composing in favor of a completely radical and American outlook. Cage is perhaps the most critical creator of a musical aesthetic as it pertains specifically to the United States, and here, two vital elements of his legacy are being fleshed out for the listener: prepared piano and chance operations. The composer had already written for prepared piano, *Sonatas and Interludes* for prepared piano from 1942 went on to become a twentieth century classic, but this is the first time it had been highlighted among other instruments. The chance operations are still not in full swing, but they do play an important role in the overall work. Using charts and number sequences, he created a chance operation system that dictated where notes and chords in different sonorities and durations are placed in the score. This produces some randomness, while Cage also composes parts of the score in a more standard process. Though the method is a complex one to explain, the result sounds natural and compelling. The orchestra of 22 players involves all sections of the standard ensemble. The concerto is in three parts, each simply called "first part," "second part," etc., and is about 20 minutes long. Among the composer's daring and large catalog, this piece is a definite success; wonder and investigation carry the concerto to a particular aesthetic where great works by Cage allow the imagination to flourish. His psychology was as inventive as it was artistic and when his music works it generates the joy of discovery. The emotions generated are not the standard, cathartic events, but they are edifying. When a work by Cage flops, it is invariably the failure of a new idea, rather than one that is tried and true. The *Concerto for Prepared Piano and Chamber Orchestra* is an enduring investigation that merits repeated listens and a comparison among different performances. Even the brilliant and hypercritical philosopher/music critic Theodor Adorno approved of it. Those who remain skeptical can approach a performance of the concerto as one among many paths for music, a path that may enrich the palette of future composers. *—John Keillor*

Recommended:

- ○ **Cage: The Piano Concertos** / Peltz (cond.), S. Drury, Callithumpian Consort of NE Conservatory / 1997 / Mode 57
- ○ **John Cage: Concerto for Prepared Piano & Chamber Orchestra; Sixty-Eight** / Vis (cond.), Regos, Bavarian Radio SO / 2003 / Col Legno 20088
- ○ **John Cage: The Seasons** / Russell Davies (cond.), M. L.Tan, American Composers Orch. / 2000 / ECM 465140

ORCHESTRAL

Atlas Eclipticalis (1961)

Named after the circle of stars surrounding the sun, John Cage's magnificent *Atlas Eclipticalis* was completed in 1961, while the composer was working at Wesleyan University. In the Wesleyan Observatory, Cage discovered some Czechoslovakian star maps. Guided by chance procedures, Cage placed transparent sheets over the charts and converted the stars into notes, eventually producing eighty-six individual instrumental parts. The parts consist of four pages of five systems, each system lasting sixty seconds. Curiously, each part is dedicated to a friend, colleague, or family member, including several composers and Cage's own parents (the second trombone part). Aside from the used of untuned percussion and microtones, pitch is indicated with traditional staff notation. Duration and loudness are shown graphically, by extended lines and the size of the note heads, respectively. The general dynamic level is quiet; occasionally, though, notes explode with great force. The conductor, too, has a part—there is no "score" as such—which guides the timing and distribution of parts within a performance. Still, the decisions of the individual performers are primary. Any number of the parts may be played, and thus the size of the ensemble may vary from a solo performer to a full orchestra. "Cosmic" characteristics mysteriously become apparent in performance. Though no specific tone-painting was intended, those rare performances with a full orchestra suggest vast universal events, while performances by a single player depict exquisite "singularities" in space. Cage commented, "I thought in writing *Atlas Eclipticalis* of the first line of a haiku poem, and of the stars as nirvana."

The work was premiered in Montreal, with a simultaneous performance of *Winter Music*, in 1961. At the 1964 American premiere by the New York Philharmonic, the "conductor" was actually a clock sculpture designed and built by Paul Williams. This performance was also distinguished by the use of amplification: contact microphones were placed on each instrument, then fed into a console and mixed according to chance procedures. Subsequent orchestral performances have tended towards bafflement and even sabotage on the part of performers, not to mention a lack of comprehension by concert audiences. *—"Blue Gene" Tyranny*

Recommended:

- ○ **Cage, Carter, Babbitt, Schuller** / Levine (cond.), Chicago SO / 1994 / DG 431698
- ○ **Cage: Concert for Piano & Orchestra; Atlas Eclipticalis** / Kotík (cond.), Kubera, Orch. of the S.E.M. Ens. / 1993 / Wergo 6216
- ○ **Cage: Atlas Eclipticalis & Winter Music; 103** / Kotík (cond.), Tudor, Orch. of the S.E.M. Ens. / 2000 / Asphodel 2000

Antonio Caldara

b. 1670, Venice, Italy, **d.** Dec. 28, 1736, Vienna, Austria

Composer

Caldara was born in Venice around 1670, and died in Vienna in 1736. He was the son of Giuseppe Caldara, a local violinist of no great fame. In his childhood, Caldara was a choirboy at St. Mark's Cathedral and also studied the viol, the cello, and keyboard. He may well have been a pupil of the *maestro di cappella* of St. Mark's, Giovanni Legrenzi, but this is uncertain. It is likewise uncertain just how much composing Caldara did in his early years, and only a few works survive from this time in his life (these works, interestingly, include the only instrumental chamber music Caldara ever wrote). Caldara likely traveled to Rome towards the end of the seventeenth century, but returned to Venice around 1698.

One year later, Caldara left Venice for Mantua: he was appointed *maestro di cappella da chiesa e dal teatro* to Ferdinando Carlo, the Duke of Mantua. The Duke had a reputation for a dedication to grandiose opera productions, the cost of which threw the finances of Mantua into disarray. It is difficult to determine exactly what Caldara was doing during the period of his employment with the Duke, for virtually none of his music from this time survives. Caldara remained in the Duke's service until 1707; the Duke died mysteriously the following year.

In 1708, Caldara was in Rome; while there, he composed oratorios and became acquainted with such luminaries as Handel, Alessandro and Domenico Scarlatti, and Antonio Corelli. In this same year, Caldara also composed a number of operas, including *Sofonisba*. Caldara settled into the musical life of Rome, becoming *maestro di cappella* to Prince Ruspoli and composing some four operas, nine oratorios, a number of vocal duets and trios, and 150 solo cantatas.

After marrying contralto Caterina Petrolli, Caldara left Rome in 1711, traveling to Vienna and Milan, then returning to Rome to fulfill his duties to the Prince. Between 1711 and 1715, Caldara composed, among other things, a significant collection of two and three voice motets. At the end of 1715, Caldara secured an appointment in Vienna as Vice-Kapellmeister under Fux; he left Rome for good in 1716, after composing some cantatas for his former patron, Prince Ruspoli, and settled in Vienna. Once in Vienna, Caldara was faced with a demanding new position in which he was required to compose many large and small scale dramatic works each year, including many operas and oratorios. In addition to his busy schedule, Caldara also accepted outside commissions, composing operas for nobles in Salzburg and Monrovia. He was well-respected and well-paid in Vienna (though he had a reputation for lavish spending), and was able to be active as a composer until his death.

Caldara is chiefly known as a composer of vocal music, and is especially remembered for his operas, many of which are settings of librettos by Zeno and Metasasio. His stylistic development as a composer, however, has been described as a movement from works that are carefully crafted, with attention given to both musical and dramatic elements (his pre-1716 works) to music that becomes increasingly less detailed and texturally thinner (post-1716), reflecting Caldara's pressing schedule in Vienna. *—Alexander Carpenter*

Overview of Works (ca. 1688–1736)

One of the most prolific composers of the Baroque, Venetian-born Antonio Caldara (1670–1736) spent the earlier part of his life in Venice, where he was trained at St. Mark's under Giovanni Legrenzi, and in Mantua as *maestro di cappella* to the Duke Ferdinando Carlo. In 1708 he left Mantua for Rome, subsequently also visiting Barcelona and Vienna. In 1716 he was appointed Vice-Kapellmeister under Johann Joseph Fux at the imperial court in Vienna, a position he retained until his death.

Caldara's huge output is centered almost entirely around vocal works: oratorios, operas, chamber cantatas, and (in his Viennese years) masses, although his first publications also include a number of trio sonatas. The musical styles employed in Caldara's operas and oratorios reflect not only the diversity of location in which he worked, but also the developments taking place during his lifetime—collectively and retrospectively summarized as the shift from the middle to the late Baroque. In operatic terms these changes, broadly speaking, show the move from the freer forms of seventeenth century opera to the static formalism of opera seria. The audiences for whom Caldara composed his operas influenced these changes of style. In Italy, Caldara was composing for public or semi-public opera houses whose audiences demanded lively, entertaining works in which variety was a key element. The demands on him in Vienna were diametrically different. There, Caldara had only one man to please, the Emperor Charles VI, whose predilection for highly formal, serious court opera played a large part in the "reform operas" of such librettists as Zeno and Metastasio, both of whom collaborated with Caldara in Vienna.

The emperor's conservatism was also responsible for his love of contrapuntal music, exemplified above all in the works of his Kapellmeister, J.J. Fux. After settling in Vienna, Caldara's music underwent a noticeable change in this respect: the light, airy Italian style of his earlier period was replaced by a weightier approach to orchestration incorporating a greater degree of counterpoint. This change of style is also apparent in Caldara's oratorios, and can be heard clearly in two works for which recordings are available. *Maddalena al piedi di Cristo* (Mary Magdalene at the Feet of Christ), composed around 1700, is written in the lighter, more brilliant manner of the composer's earlier works, with a colorful diversity of pictorial effects. *La Passione di Gesù Cristo Signor Nostro* (The Passion of Jesus Christ Our Lord) is one of the Passiontide oratorios composed for the Viennese court. Dating from 1729, it marks the occasion of Caldara's first collaboration with Metastasio, who had just been engaged by the court. Here one immediately notices the more solid, richly orchestrated approach and the less flamboyant vocal writing as compared with the earlier work. The choral sections of the festive masses Caldara composed for Vienna also show the contrapuntal influence of Fux, but the solo writing frequently looks forward to the lighter *galant* style emerging during the 1730s and 1740s. It is this combination of the serious Austrian polyphonic style coupled with airier, Italianate elements that we find carried forward into the sacred music of Haydn and Mozart. *—Brian Robins*

Recommended:

- ○ **Caldara: Maddalena ai piedi di Cristo** / Jacobs, Banchini (cond.), Scholl, Turk, Fink, Kiehr, Dominguez, Basiliensis Schola Cantorum Orch. / HM 90522122
- ○ **Caldara: Passione di Gesù Cristo Signor Nostro & Sinfonias** / Nemeth (cond.), Zadori, Fotiadis, Bentch, I. Kovacs, Savaria Baroque Orch. / Hungaroton 31862
- ○ **Caldara: Missa Dolorosa; Stabat Mater** / Clemencic (cond.), Aura Musicale, Budapest / 2000 / Naxos 554715
- ○ **Caldara: Sonate a Violoncello solo col basso** / L'Aura Soave / Tactus 670302

Maria Callas

b. Dec. 2, 1923, New York, NY, **d.** Sep. 16, 1977, Paris, France

Soprano

The fame and legacy of Maria Callas are nearly unsurpassed in the modern history of opera. Her fame has transcended the usual boundaries of classical music, and she has been the inspiration for several movies, an opera, and a successful Broadway musical. Her extensive catalogue of recordings remains among the most coveted and controversial for both her fans and detractors.

Though American by birth, Callas (née Maria Anne Sofia Cecilia Kalogeropoulos) was born of Greek parents, and at age 13 her mother took her back to Greece because of financial difficulties caused by the Great Depression. She studied voice at the Royal Academy of Music in Athens with Spanish coloratura soprano Elvira de Hildago and made rapid progress; she soon sang Santuzza in a student production of *Cavalleria rusticana*. Her professional debut came at age 16 in a minor role in Suppe's *Bocaccio*.

While still in Athens during World War II, Callas sang her first *Tosca* in 1942. In 1945, she returned to the United States and sang several auditions, but nothing came of her visit. Her first appearance in 1947 at Verona as *La Gioconda* brought her to the attention of Tullio Serafin; Serafin became her musical advisor for many years, acting as her coach and conductor of many of her performances.

The entire world of opera was stunned when, in 1949—while singing Brünnhilde in *Die Walküre* at Venice—she agreed to sing Elvira in Bellini's *I Puritani*, alternating performances during the same week. That same year she traveled to Buenos Aires to sing *Turandot* and *Norma*. In 1950, she sang *Aida* at the Teatro alla Scala, but she did not become a regular member there until 1952. The summer of 1950 took her Mexico City where, in one month, she sang *Norma*, *Aida*, *Tosca* and *Il trovatore*. During these early years, Callas would sing nearly any role offered including Isolde, Leonore in *La forza del destino*, Constanza in Mozart's *Die Entführung aus dem Serail*, and Elena in *I vespri siciliani*.

As she matured, Callas began to concentrate on a smaller core repertory, including Cherubini's *Medea*, Bellini's *Norma*, Puccini's *Tosca*, Bellini's *La Sonnambula*, and Donizetti's *Anna Bolena*. Most of her other roles were heard only in one series of performances. After 1959, she rarely appeared on the opera stage, but she did sing concerts in America and Europe. Her last opera performances were in June 1965, at Paris as *Norma*. She came out of retirement in 1973 to tour the world with Giuseppe di Stefano in a series of recitals. Although financially rewarding, the tour did nothing to enhance her reputation. In 1971, she gave a series of masterclasses at the *Juilliard School of Music* in New York which were quite successful. In 1977, she died of a sudden heart attack in her Paris apartment.

Maria Callas was one of the most controversial singers of the twentieth century. She had a wide range from high E to the F below the staff, and an innate feel for the style of bel canto roles, but she was most notable for bringing a commitment and intensity to her dramatic portrayals that was nearly unprecedented at the time. By 1957, her voice developed a wobble which grew worse in the following years. Always a perfectionist, she was very difficult to deal with from a management point of view: she was fired from the Metropolitan Opera in 1958 and she was estranged from Teatro alla Scala for several years. Her vocal decline coincided with the dissolution of her first marriage to Giovanni Meneghini and her affair with Aristotle Onassis. *—Richard LeSueur*

Recommended:

- ○ **Puccini: Tosca** / de Sabata (cond.), Callas, Gobbi, di Stefano, La Scala / 2003 / EMI 85644
- ○ **Bellini: Norma** / Serafin (cond.), Callas, Filippeschi, Stignani, Rossi-Lemeni, Caroli, Cavallari / 2003 / EMI 62642
- ○ **La Divina** / Callas, various artists / 1992 / EMI 54702
- ○ **Live in Stuttgart 1959** / Callas, Rescigno (cond.), South German RSO / 2003 / EMI 62682
- ○ **The Passion of Callas** / Callas, various artists / 2003 / EMI 57613
- ○ **Callas the Divine** / Callas, various artists / 1996 / Gala 100526

Giuseppe Maria Cambini

b. Feb. 13, 1746, Livorno, Italy, **d.** Dec. 1825, Bicêtre, France

Composer

Italian-born composer and violinist Giuseppe Maria Cambini was certainly one of the most prolific composers of the late eighteenth century, with well over 700 compositions (representing all the major musical forms of the day) to his name. Cambini was probably born in February of 1746 in Livorno, Italy (as recorded by nineteenth century Belgian historian Francois Fétis). While the details of his early years remain unknown, a number of fanciful legends have arisen over the centuries to fill the void: according to one account Cambini was taken captive by Barbary pirates during a voyage in 1766 and subjected to any number of indecencies and hardships before finally gaining his freedom through the intervention of an affluent merchant. Cambini himself did little to suppress such rumors, and may have even contributed to them; certainly his claim that he was a quartet partner of Boccherini and Nardini during his youth has been deemed fanciful by scholars.

While Cambini may have studied with Padre Martini as a young man, it is only upon his arrival in Paris around 1770 that we begin to acquire solid facts about the man. A performance at the Concerts Spirituels during May of 1773 introduced Cambini to Parisian audiences, and the subsequent publishing of his string quartet collection Op. 1 thrust him into the front rank of up-and-coming composers. Cambini composed prolifically throughout the next 30 years, maintaining his stride even through the Revolutionary years of the late 1780s and early 1790s.

Indeed, Cambini earned the approval of Revolutionary authorities by composing a number of popular songs for the cause.

After the turn of the century, however, critics began to take a less favorable view of Cambini's work, and during the first decade of the new century fewer and fewer of Cambini's pieces found their way into print. After 1810, almost nothing is known of his activities or even his whereabouts, and even the generally accepted date of his death (1825) is guesswork—he may well have died several years earlier.

At heart a composer for the masses, Cambini played little part in the radical musical developments of the Classical period. His music epitomizes the French galant style, emphasizing a simple brilliance and charm that requires little depth of understanding to appreciate. While his success as a theatrical composer was rather limited (despite having held positions at both the Théâtre Beaujolais and the Théâtre du Louvois), Cambini's over-600 purely instrumental works (including 149 string quartets, 114 string quintets, 9 symphonies orchestras of various sizes, and well over 100 trios for various instruments) were quite successful during his day. Even Wolfgang Amadeus Mozart, despite having developed a strong personal dislike of Cambini (whom he wrongly blamed for the cancellation of a concert of his works in Paris during the 1770s), is known to have praised Cambini's instrumental music for its lyric charm.—*Blair Johnston*

Overview of Works (ca. 1770–1810)

Italian composer and sometimes violinist Giuseppe Maria Cambini (1746–1825 [?]) appears to have been born in Livorno. Many details about his early life remain speculative, but he certainly journeyed to Paris in the early 1770s. A probably apocryphal legend held that he and his fiancée were captured by pirates and sold into slavery, then purchased by a wealthy Venetian. Of all the musical figures he is purported to have studied with, Manfredi seems the most plausible.

Upon arrival in Paris, Cambini was introduced to Gossec, and in May of 1773 he heard one of his symphonies concertantes performed under the direction of the older composer. In December of that same year, Cambini's Op. 1, a set of string quartets, was published. The symphonies proved pleasing to Paris audiences, sunny in their lyricism however unassuming they may have been. The prodigious amount of music written over the next two decades marked Cambini as one of the most indefatigable composers ever. By 1800, his complete works included nearly 600 instrumental works alone, consisting of: 400 works for various instruments and instrumental combinations, 144 string quartets, 9 symphonies, 17 concertos, 82 symphonies concertantes (published by several different houses, some 20 by subscription), several ballets, and a number of organ pieces. In addition, there were 14 operas written from 1778 to 1798 (12 of them produced in Paris); an oratorio, *La sacrifice d'Abraham* (1774); a *Miserere* (1775), presented at another Concert Spirituel; 15 patriotic hymns (that enabled him to come through the Revolutionary era unscathed), and a miscellany of solfeggi and other methods.

Of Cambini's operas only two survive intact, together with fragments of three others; all of them suggest that his purpose was to serve his public's tastes rather than to establish a new direction for the lyric theatre. During the 1770s and 1780s, his music was well-received, but during the 1790s he fell out of favor somewhat and got a reputation as a lightweight which he never either quite deserved or managed to surmount. In the 1780s and 1790s Cambini worked as a theatrical orchestra leader. Beginning in 1794, he directed concerts and composed chamber music for the arms manufacturer Armand Sequin. Around 1795, Cambini devoted himself less to the composition of music and more to writing about it, becoming an anonymous co-editor of the *Tablettes de Polymnie* in 1810.

Some think that Cambini's best work is to be found in his string quartets. Although the field of quartet composers was crowded at the time, Mozart is said to have found his quartets "quite lovely." One possibly unreliable story tells us that his ability as a violinist was such that he was invited to perform with the three most accomplished quartet players of the late eighteenth century. In any event, the airy style of Mozart's French-inflected works such as the Concerto for flute and harp may well have been forged at least in part by Cambini. —*Erik Eriksson*

Recommended:

- ○ **Cambini: Sinfonie** / Mangiocavallo (cond.), Academia Montis Regalis / 1999 / Opus 111 30244
- ○ **Cambini: 6 Trii Concertanti Op45** / Mercelli, Vignali, Carlini / Bongiovanni 5070
- ○ **Cambini: 6 Trii Concertanti Op26** / Trio Tourte / Tactus 740302

Cambridge Singers

f. 1981, Cembridge, England
Ensemble

The Cambridge Singers are a general-repertoire mixed-voice choir, one of the best known in the compact disc era. They are particularly associated with the wildly popular choral compositions of their founder, John Rutter, who established the group in 1981 expressly as a professional chamber choir for recording sessions. The initial nucleus of the group comprised seven former members of the Clare College Choir. All additional members had also been choral scholars in British colleges. In 1984 Rutter took the next step in the construction of his empire by creating the Collegium Records label in order to record the Cambridge Singers. This was at the very beginning of the compact disc era, and the Cambridge Singers had one of the first major successes for a small independent label in their recording of the original orchestration of Gabriel Fauré's *Requiem*, and other music by Fauré. The choir's beauty of tone and the exemplary recording of the album established both the label and the choir as top representatives of their type. Soon Collegium released the Singers in a recording of Rutter's own *Requiem*, a work much in the vein of the Fauré work, consolidating the reputation of the choir and the label, and arousing worldwide interest in Rutter's choral compositions, many of which are now frequently performed by choirs around the world. The Cambridge Singers are still primarily a recording ensemble, but they do make concert and church appearances. —*Joseph Stevenson*

Recommended:

- ○ **There is Sweet Music: English Choral Song 1890–1950** / Rutter (cond.), Padmore, Sears, Sheffield, Cambridge Singers / 2002 / Collegium 505
- ○ **The Cambridge Singers Christmas Album** / Rutter (cond.), Cambridge Singers, City of London Sinfonia / 2003 / Collegium 512
- ○ **Cambridge Singers A Cappella** / Rutter (cond.), Cambridge Singers, City of London Sinfonia / 2002 / Collegium 509
- ○ **The Cambridge Singers Collection** / Rutter, Hickox (cond.), King's Singers, Cambridge Singers, City of London Sinfonia / 1993 / Collegium 501
- ○ **The John Rutter Collection** / Rutter (cond.), Cambridge Singers, City of London Sinfonia / 2002 / Decca 472622

Thomas Campion

b. Feb. 12, 1567, London, England, **d.** Mar. 1, 1620, London, England
Composer

With John Dowland Campion was one of the most prolific composers of English lute songs, or Ayres. A true "renaissance man," Campion also wrote masques for court performances, a critique of English poetry and, in 1613, a treatise on counterpoint. He was also a trained physician. His works were widely disseminated; the best of them demonstrate a capacity for elegant melodic lines that perfectly matches the rhythm of English verse. Unlike most composers of songs, he wrote all of the poems he set to music himself.

Campion's father, John, was a cursitor of the Chancery Court; his mother, Lucy, had a significant sum of money from her previous marriage. On February 12, 1567, Thomas Campion was baptized at the church of St. Andrew, Holborn. Campion left home in 1581, matriculating at Peterhouse, Cambridge, but never completing a degree. In 1586, he entered Gray's Inn, one of the Inns of Court at which young noblemen learned "the ropes" of court life. There he established contacts with potential patrons, in part through his participation in performances of masques attended by members of the nobility, including Queen Elizabeth.

By the early 1590s Campion had become known as a poet; in 1595 he published a book of Latin poems that was particularly well received. His first collection of songs came six years later (1601) as part of Philip Rosseter's *A Book of Ayres*, the second half of which featured songs by Rosseter. In 1602, Campion's *Observations on the Art of English Poesie* appeared, in which he discussed rhyme, the structure of poetry, and the proper meters to use when setting English; his skillful setting of English texts is, arguably, the most impressive aspect of his music. For the next decade, Campion concentrated on the contribution of music to masques, including two printed as *The Lords Maske*, written in 1613. Unfortunately, only the texts of these works survive.

Campion studied medicine at the University of Caen, earning his M.D. on February 10, 1605. This did not derail his compositional activities, however: he composed masques for performance at the court of James I, and his *Two Bookes of Ayres* was published ca. 1614. A year later he was accused of participating in the plot to murder Sir Thomas Overby by the Earl and Countess of Somerset; however, Campion's name was eventually cleared. The *Third and Fourth Booke of Ayres* appeared in either 1617 or 1618, and Campion's last published work, *Tho. Campiani epigrammatum libi II*, was printed in 1619.

All of Campion's Ayres were for solo voice with lute accompaniment; however, many of the songs were printed with the parts for alto, tenor, and bass extracted from the lute texture. His attention to proper text setting of each verse of a poem is remarkable. Although he generally avoided superficial word-painting, he was not above the occasional illustrative passage. For example, in "Mistris since you so much desire," Campion sets the line, "but a little higher," four times in succession, each statement a step higher than the previous. His strict adherence to the rules of four-part counterpoint laid out in his treatise lends a measure of predictability to some of his Ayres, but the best examples show a composer capable of exquisite melodic tailoring, skillful contrapuntal writing, and technical mastery of the lute. —*John Palmer*

Overview of Works (ca. 1600–1619)

The English composer Thomas Campion (1567–1620) is paradigmatic of the Renaissance man. Trained as a lawyer, Campion later became a poet, a composer of lute songs, and a physician. As a young lawyer at Grey's Inn, London, he became involved in the vital world of Elizabethan theater and made social contacts that subsequently gained him royal patronage. During the 1590s he gained a reputation as a poet; several publications appeared at this time and during the early years of the following century.

Campion's verse is generally held in higher esteem than his musical settings of it; most of these appeared in a *Book of Ayres* of 1601, and in four further publications with the same title issued in pairs around 1613 and 1617. Nonetheless, he is the most important composer of English lute songs after John Dowland. In his settings, Campion did not attempt the close integration between voice and instrument that makes Dowland a unique composer in this genre, preferring to keep the role of the lute to that of accompaniment. His songs have an easy melodic appeal. They encompass a wide range of topics, from the risqué (as in the word play of "I care not for these Ladies") to the bucolic ("Jacke and Jone they think no ill"), and sometimes they include serious religious sentiments such as those expressed in "Never weather-beaten saile." Many of the songs have a strong narrative element, as in the delightful "It fell on a sommers daie," a thinly veiled story of welcome seduction. Campion's attitude to his art is neatly summed up in the preface to his fourth *Booke of Ayres*, where he writes: "All these Songs are mine if you express them well, otherwise they are your owne." *—Brian Robins*

Recommended:

- ○ **Move Now with Measured Sound: Music by Campion** / R. Blaze, E. Kenny / 2001 / Hyperion 67268
- ○ **Campion: Elizabethan Songs** / Minter, O'Dette / 2001 / HM Classical Express 3957023
- ○ **Campion: English Ayres** / Chance, North, Concordia / 2000 / Linn 105

André Campra

b. Feb. 4, 1660, Aix, Provence, France, **d.** Jun. 29, 1744, Versailles, France
Composer: Choral, Opera

The most significant composer for the French stage between Lully and Rameau, Campra was born in Aix-en-Provence in 1660. His father, an amateur violinist, provided him with his first music lessons, and while he was a slow learner at first, he did begin to show talent, and joined the choir of St. Sauveur in 1674. At one point he nearly lost his place in the choir when he was caught giving unauthorized performances in secular theaters on the side. In August of 1681 he became the music master at the church of Ste. Trophime in Arles, and two years later moved on to the same position at the Cathedral of St. Étienne in Toulouse. In 1694 he took a leave of absence that became permanent when he became music master at Notre Dame. Until he arrived in Paris he had composed mostly sacred music, but even though he had reached a top position in the world of church music, the dramatic stage once again began to draw his creativity.

in 1697, he presented a new form of his own invention, the opéra-ballet. A loosely plotted song-and-dance spectacle, *L'Europe galante* was well received by its aristocratic audience. Its successors, the similar divertissements *Vénus* (1698) and *The Venetian Carnival* (1699), were likewise successful. He had published these in his younger brother's name because he was afraid of losing his church appointment, but after these successes, he was confident in his ability to support himself with secular music. In 1700, he left Notre Dame and wrote his first opera, *Hesione*. Of the eight operas (or *tragédies-lyriques*) that followed, only *Tancrède* (1702) and *Idomenée* (1712) have been performed with any regularity in the twentieth century. Campra assumed a dominant position in the world of dramatic music; he was granted a publishing monopoly and, in 1718, an annual no-strings-attached pension by King Louis XV. In 1708, he wrote his first book of secular cantatas in French, specifying that he wanted to combine the liveliness of Italian music with the delicacy of French music; this was followed by a second book in 1714 and a third in 1728. In 1720, Campra began to write sacred music again, and in 1722 he was made master of the royal chapel and official composer and music director for the Prince of Conti. He wrote a good deal of material for the royal chapel between then and his retirement in 1742.

Campra's prolific writing was more or less evenly divided among opéra-ballet, sacred music, and tragic opera. While the opéra-ballet was intended as light entertainment, Campra's works in the form are musically sophisticated and varied. They combine characteristics of Italian music, particularly an emphasis on melody, with various influences from Lully, providing new ideas after French music had become somewhat stale under Lully's near-complete domination. Similarly, his tragic operas also show innovations, such as the highly atmospheric musical special effects of *Idomenée* and *Hesione*; these paved the way for Rameau's musical language. Like that of his contemporary Bach, Campra's sacred music also wove Italian influences into an essentially conservative idiom. *—Ann Feeney*

CHORAL

Motets (ca. 1700–1741)

Campra published his first of his five books of motets in 1695. Despite having begun his successful career as a dramatic composer, Campra continued to compose motets. These were published in four collections in 1700, 1703, 1706, and the last book in 1720. These motets are built on the model of Lully's motets, that is, they are settings of the psalms that divide the text into solos, duets, and occasionally choruses usually accompanied by organ and continuo. After returning to the church, Campra published only one collection of motets: *Motets for the Royal Vault* (1741). These are all grand motets, large-scale works for soloists, chorus, and orchestra, and his masterpieces in the genre. They include the *De profundis, Pange lingua, Regina coeli, Miserere, Lauda Jerusalem, Te Deum, Ecce Panic grass.* All Campra's motets are austere works with few overt opportunities for compositional or vocal display. Unlike his ballets and operas, Campra's motets are severely devotional works that suited the early years of the *grand siècle*. *—James Leonard*

Recommended:

- ○ **Campra: Grands Motets** / W. Christie (cond.), Les Arts Florissants (Choir), Les Arts Florissants (Orch.) / 2003 / Virgin 45618
- ○ **Campra: Motets** / Caudle (cond.), P. Hyde, del Pozo, P. Harvey, Canzona / 1999 / Etcetera 1201

Requiem Mass

Although he spent the middle years of his career writing operas, French composer André Campra (1660–1744) spent his youth and his old age—the years 1694–1700 and 1722–44—as a composer of church music. His most famous work for the church, his *Requiem Mass*, could have come from either period. The only original manuscript comes from a volume found in a library in Campra's hometown of Aix-en-Provence, but it gives no date of composition. Some writers point out that the duet for tenor and recorder in the Agnus Dei is also found in Campra's opera *L'Europa galante*, but this could mean either that the mass quoted the opera or the opera quoted the mass. And while Campra's virtuoso use of the choir is similar to his use of the choir in his late motets, the theatricality of the work recalls Campra's *Tancredi*. But while the origins of the work are debatable, its emotional and musical effectiveness is beyond debate. Setting the Latin text to music of great variety, depth, dignity, and ultimately blissful serenity, Campra's *Requiem* is the greatest French setting of the *Requiem* before Berlioz's. *—James Leonard*

Recommended:

- ○ **Campra: Messe de Requiem** / Herreweghe (cond.), La Chapelle Royale / HM 901251
- ○ **Campra: Requiem; Miserere** / Malgoire (cond.), Visse, Ragon, P. Harvey, La Grande Ecurie et la Chambre du Roy / 1998 / Virgin 6152823

OPERA

Idomenée, Rè di Creta (1712)

The death of Lully in 1687 opened doors previously closed to other French composers of opera, termed in France *tragédie en musique* or *tragédie lyrique*. Lully's monopoly gave way to the works of a generation of composers previously thwarted from seeing their works reach the stage of the Paris Opéra. One of the most notable of the younger generation of composers to benefit was André Campra (1660–1744), the leading French opera composer to flourish in the period between the dominance of the two French Baroque giants, Lully and Rameau. Between 1700 and 1735, Campra had 11 full-length operas produced at the Paris Opéra, in addition to a number of opera-ballets (a lighter form that he was responsible for creating), shorter ballets, and divertissements. All 11 follow the format established for tragédie by Lully: a prologue involving allegorical characters or gods and generally including praise for the ruling French monarch, followed by five acts which include danced divertissements. *Idomenée*, first produced at the Opéra on January 12, 1712, to a libretto by Antoine Danchet, falls into this category. The plot, set in Crete in the aftermath of the Trojan War, bears a strong resemblance to the Biblical story of Jephtha. Returning from the wars, the fleet of the Cretan king Idomeneus is threatened by destruction, averted only by the king's promise to the sea god Neptune to sacrifice the first person he sees on gaining land safely. That person turns out to be his own son, Idamante, and the opera is a powerful examination of a conflict between duty and filicide. At the end Idomeneus, driven mad by his predicament, kills Idamante, and is restrained from taking his own life by his retinue. Campra's music is notable for his dramatic use of the chorus and orchestra, apparent particularly in a passage in Act Two in which the fateful storm occurs. Nearly 60 years later, Danchet's libretto was adapted (with the ending changed to a happy outcome) for Mozart's use; the result was a work that would become his greatest serious opera, *Idomeneo, re di Creta*. *—Brian Robins*

Recommended:

- ○ **Campra: Idomenée** / W. Christie (cond.), Deletre, Fouchecourt, Piau, Zanetti, Les Arts Florissants / 1999 / HM 2901396/98

Canadian Brass

f. 1970, Toronto, Ontario, Canada
Ensemble

The Canadian Brass quickly rose to become the world's most popular brass brass quintet, pioneering a unique and entertaining stage format that has influenced numerous other chamber groups. There were no full-time touring brass quintets when the group formed as an experiment in 1970. At that time, most brass quintet music was played by members of local orchestras or music conservatories.

The impetus for the group came from trombonist Eugene Watts, a native of Sedalia, Missouri, and a graduate of the University of Missouri. He grew up with a strong interest in jazz, and played traditional Dixieland to help pay for college. After playing in the North Carolina, San Antonio, and Milwaukee symphony orchestras, he came to Toronto at the invitation of the Toronto Symphony's music director, Seiji Ozawa. He is a major contributor to the unique programming for Canadian Brass concerts, which range from traditional classical repertoire to less formal, and often humorous interactions with the audience.

Tuba player Charles Daellenbach is also a founding member. If Watts is the impetus for the group, Daellenbach is the catalyst. He and Watts tend to spark each other's humor, and their in-concert banter is part of the group's distinction. A native of Wisconsin, Daellenbach is from a German family with a long musical tradition. He earned a Ph.D. from Eastman at the age of 25 and was teaching at the University of Toronto when he met Watts.

Trumpeters Bill Philips (1970–72) and Stuart Laughton (1970–71) were founding members who became exhausted by the constant touring and subsequently left the group. The two longest tenures, excluding the founders, were Ron Romm (1971–2000), who had been a professional trumpeter in his family's band (the Romm-Antics) from the age of twelve, and Fred Mills (1972–96). Mills intended to be an original member, but could not join for the first year due to contract commitments.

Jens Lindemann, born in Germany but raised in Alberta, Canada, replaced Mills in 1996. He started playing the trumpet in grade school and was inspired by the Canadian Brass, who signed his trumpet case when he was 12 years old. Emulating the Brass, he obtained a gold-plated trumpet. He became soloist in an Edmonton orchestra at 16, and was well established when he joined the Canadian Brass. He brought to the Brass a special facility on the high piccolo trumpet, and also played C trumpet, cornet, and flugelhorn. In 2000, Lindemann left the ensemble to pursue a solo career, and was replaced by Josef Burgsteller.

Ryan Anthony joined the Brass in June 2000 at the age of 31. He is a former member of the Cleveland Orchestra and the Indianapolis Symphony. The older Brass members remember him as the 15-year-old member of a quintet that wowed them at a master class performance.

Graeme Page was the original French horn player of the Brass (1970–83). Succeeding him were Marty Hackleman (1983–86) and David Ohanian (1986–98), a founding member of the Empire Brass in 1972. The current horn player is Jeff Nelsen.

The Canadian Brass has enriched the brass quintet repertoire with many commissioned works and a large number of arrangements of music from the early Baroque onward. The quintet has made over fifty LP and CD releases, and have toured around the world. *—Joseph Stevenson*

Recommended:

○ **Canadian Brass Super Hits** / Canadian Brass, Berlin PO Brass Ens / 2000 / Sony 89270

○ **Sacred Brass** / Canadian Brass / 2002 / RCA 63868

Guido Cantelli

b. Apr. 7, 1920, Novara, Italy, **d.** Nov. 24, 1956, Paris, France
Conductor

Cantelli was both the youngest and shortest-lived of the world-class conductors born between 1908 and 1920, a remarkable group that included Karajan, Solti, Leinsdorf, Giulini, and Bernstein. His musical youth was conventional: early evidence of a gift, keyboard instruction, his first piano recital at 14, etc. Slonimsky wrote that he played in his father's military band. Cantelli entered the nearby Milan Conservatory, where he majored in conducting and composition (under Giorgio Ghedini). He returned to his home city in 1943 as director of the Theatre Coccia, opened in 1888 by Toscanini, who became his champion in the last decade of both their lives. However, Cantelli was forced to join the Italian army despite his outspoken loathing of Nazism. For this he was interned in a German labor camp near Stettin until illness finally required hospitalization at Bolzano. He escaped with a forged passport and lived in Milan under an assumed name until Fascist troops took him hostage. Following the liberation, Cantelli was freed to pursue conducting engagements. The La Scala Orchestra became his first, with Claudio Abbado's father as violin soloist. Operatic and concert engagements followed, first in Italy, then elsewhere in Europe including Budapest and Vienna. Within three seasons he proved himself deserving of the mercurial career that Toscanini launched.

The "Old Man" began his ninth decade looking for a younger associate to keep the NBC Symphony Orchestra (created for him in 1938) on course during his absences. La Scala's intendant, Antonio Ghiringhelli, took him to an off-season concert by Cantelli. Before it was half-over, Toscanini whispered "that is me directing this concert!" He arranged for the young conductor's immediate NBC debut on January 15, 1949. Afterwards, *Time* magazine featured a profile likening him physically to Frank Sinatra, but musically to Toscanini. Until NBC disbanded the orchestra in 1954, Cantelli conducted annually, beginning with four but expanding to eight programs. In 1951 he made the first of five annual appearances as a regular guest-conductor of the NY Philharmonic along with Bruno Walter and Szell. He recorded Vivaldi's *Seasons* with them for Columbia, but RCA and EMI owned his services contractually. With NBC he recorded four performances, with Walter Legge's London Philharmonia considerably more, a few in stereo.

Toscanini's endorsement proved a double-edged sword, however. Some NYP players echoed the complaint by two daily newspaper critics that the regular guests conducted too much standard repertory, perhaps because Cantelli was being groomed to take over. (With Mitropoulos on his way out, Bernstein would serve as a stopgap until Cantelli was "ready." Bernstein had lost Boston in 1949 because he was Jewish; in NYC the stigma was his Broadway career.) Cantelli had been a taskmaster who rehearsed and conducted without score; sluggish players resented him—so openly that he asked without success to be released from a late November 1956 engagement. La Scala formally named him music director on November 16 (to succeed Giulini, who had succeeded Victor de Sabata in 1953 but detested administrative duties). One week later, a Lineo Aereo Italiano plane from Milan to NYC crashed following a stopover at Orly Airport near Paris. Guido Cantelli was not among the survivors.

Toscanini died two months later without being told of Cantelli's death. Legge wrote in a memorial tribute to Cantelli, "no other conductor in the history of the art has established, so early in life, so wide a fame." While studio recordings validate that encomium, none quite captured the incandescence of his live performances. One of a kind, unmatched since, Cantelli was a supernova. *—Roger Dettmer*

Recommended:

○ **Cantelli: The Debussy Recordings** / Cantelli (cond.), London Philharmonia Orchestra / 1992 / Testament 1011

○ **NBC Broadcast Concerts, December 1950** / Cantelli (cond.), Miller, Marlowe, Bauchmann, Cooke, Robert Shaw Chorale, NBCSO / 2003 / Testament 1317

○ **Cantelli Conducts Schumann, Schubert, Mendelssohn** / Cantelli (cond.), Heifetz, New York PO, NBCSO / 2002 / Archipel 52

○ **Tchaikovsky: Symphony 6; Romeo & Juliet** / Cantelli (cond.), London PO / 1989 / EMI 769785

Joseph Marie Canteloube

b. Oct. 21, 1879, Annonay, France, **d.** Nov. 4, 1957, Paris, France
Composer: Vocal

Most notable as an arranger of French folk songs, Canteloube is unfortunately overlooked as a composer of original music. He is primarily remembered for the *Chants d'Auvergne* (1930–32), four sets of folk songs for voice and piano or orchestra, widely enjoyed for their color, naturalistic beauty, and charm.

When Canteloube began his studies with d'Indy at the Schola Cantorum in Paris in 1901, he soon showed a preference and talent for composing nature music, especially music that described the landscape of his native region, the Auvergne. He decided to seek inspiration and stimulus in folk song (as had d'Indy before him). Thus began his lifelong task of travelling throughout France to collect and arrange folk songs. Well into the 1940s, Canteloube busied himself with collecting songs and arranging them for choral, quartet, or solo voices with pianoforte or orchestra. Meanwhile he continued to produce original compositions, but as an arranger of folk music he was generally more successful. His other regional song arrangements include songs from Catalonia, Alsace, Angoumais, Languedoc, Touraine, and the Basque region. He served as editor of the *Anthologie des chants populaires français* (1939–44).

Outside of his prolific work in folk song, Canteloube's most ambitious projects were two operas which were both produced by the Paris Opéra. The first, *Le mas* (1910–13) won him the lucrative Prix Heugel in 1925. Apparently the production was not received well, for the work was never revived. This did not discourage Canteloube, for he began work the following year on *Vercingétorix* (1930–32), a nationalist opera celebrating the birth of French national unity. Composed to a libretto by E. Clémental and J. Louwyck, it was produced by the Opéra on June 22, 1933 to little acclaim. Like his first opera, *Vercingétorix* is said to have lacked a theatrical sense. *Vercingétorix* was the first opera ever to use the ondes martenot (an electronic keyboard instrument developed in the 1920s by French musician Maurice Martenot) in the orchestra. Both operas show Canteloube's patriotism. One of Canteloube's last notable efforts was, interestingly, not a musical piece, but a biography of d'Indy (1951). He was active as a composer into the 1950s. *—Rachael Unite*

VOCAL

Songs of the Auvergne (1923–1930)

Canteloube's acquaintance with the folk songs of Auvergne began with his birth in Annonay, about 50 kilometers south of Lyon. During walks through the mountains he heard both dance and vocal music, which entranced him even as a child. Late in life he wrote, "I lived at that time deep in the country in a region where the country folk would still willingly sing." When he asked them to sing, they did so without hesitation. As an adult he returned to the Auvergne to make recordings of folk songs.

Not long after meeting Vincent d'Indy (1851–1931) in 1902, Canteloube moved to Paris to study at d'Indy's independent conservatory; later he began assembling folk songs of the Auvergne and composing harmonizations for them. From 1923, Canteloube pursued the collection of folk songs from numerous regions of France with increasing intensity. Most of these were harmonized and set for a variety of ensembles, including voice with either piano or orchestra accompaniment, and a cappella arrangements for choir. His *Chants d'Auvergne* have become a staple of the concert repertoire.

To the end of his life, Canteloube championed through articles and lectures the idea of "regionalism" and its use of folk song material. When asked how he justified dressing "ancient" tunes with modern orchestra accompaniment, Canteloube responded: "Just because the peasant sings without accompaniment, that is not sufficient reason to imitate him. When the peasant sings at his work... there is an accompaniment which surrounds his song which would not be felt by those whose interest is purely academic. Only poets and artists will feel it...." Canteloube rationalized his inconsistencies by the typical invocation of the separation between mind and heart. All the songs of *Chants d'Auvergne* are in that region's *langue d'Oc* and many feature passages of nonsense syllables.

Canteloube's mastery of the elements of composition is clear throughout the *Chants d'Auvergne*. In the "Pastrouletta" we find a slow, but regular, voice part over a swelling accompaniment that comes forward between verses. The fourth of the set, "Pastouro, sé tu m'aymo" (Shepherdess, if you love me), stands out in its bouncy rhythms and rapid declamation. Accompanimental figures in the orchestra swirl about as the shepherdess' suitor offers her a dress and flowers in exchange for her love. Not surprisingly, "Lou Coucut" (The Cuckoo) begins with imitations of the Cuckoo's call in the orchestra. The voice part is among the liveliest of the set. "Lo fiolaire" (The Spinner) begins with rumbling low strings before the piano enters with a "spinning" motive. Instruments heterophonically follow the vocal line as the shepherdess explains how, when her shepherd asked her for a kiss, she gave him two. Woodwind sighs open the last of the *Chants d'Auvergne*, "Brezairola" (Lullaby), in which the narrator complains, quietly, that the baby will not go to sleep. As the song proceeds in regularly shaped phrases, the orchestra accompanies the new voice part of the second verse with the voice line from the first and begins rocking in the third, as the baby falls asleep. *—John Palmer*

Recommended:

- ○ **Canteloube: Chants d'Auvergne** / Nagano (cond.), Upshaw, Orch. de l'Opera National de Lyon / 2002 / Erato 44656
- ○ **Canteloube: Chants d'Auvergne** / J. Tate (cond.), Te Kanawa, English CO / 1990 / Decca 8001

Giacomo Carissimi

b. Apr. 18, 1605, Marini, Italy, **d.** Jan. 12, 1674, Rome, Italy

Composer: Choral

Perhaps worthy of being designated the father of the oratorio, Giacomo Carissimi was among the most important Italian composers of the seventeenth century. He is best remembered for his oratorios and cantatas. Carissimi was born somewhere near Rome and baptized on April 18, 1605; an exact date of birth is not known. He was the son of an artisan, but he must have received a good deal of early musical training, for at the age of 18 he was recorded as a member of the Tivoli Cathedral choir. In 1625, he became the organist at the cathedral, and soon after that began composing.

Carissimi received his first and only important appointment in 1629: he became *maestro di cappella* of the Collegio Germanico in Rome. The Collegio Germanico was, at that time, a major center for Jesuit learning; Carissimi's position there commanded considerable influence and respect, and the composer would remain there until his death. As *maestro di cappella*, Carissimi was responsible for the musical training of students, the directorship of the choir, and the preparation of music for services at the church of St. Apollinare. In 1637, he was ordained as a priest. Carissimi became well-known and well-respected in Italy and across Europe, and was invited to accept employment at a number of important churches and courts. He turned down the opportunity to succeed Monteverdi at the famous St. Mark's in Venice, however, and likewise declined to serve in the court of the governor of the Netherlands.

While it is difficult to accurately catalog and date Carissimi's music, it is certain that he was one of the originators of the oratorio genre. His oratorios are notable for their clear text settings, the importance given to the chorus, and the use of expressive gestures to intensify and illustrate meanings in the text. The influence of early opera, and of Monteverdi in particular, is evident in the oratorios, and Carissimi's free alternation of aria- and recitative-style passages is considered an important contribution to the development and refinement of operatic recitative. All the operatic means, however, are turned to religious ends; Carissimi's oratorios are sacred pieces, not the middle-class entertainments that Handel would create a century later. Carissimi also met with fame as a composer of cantatas, and, as with the oratorio, he advanced that genre substantially.

Carissimi was an influential figure, and several composers of the next generation bear the marks of his innovations and style. These included Alessandro Scarlatti in Italy, Christoph Bernhard in Germany, and Marc-Antoine Charpentier in France. *—Alexander Carpenter*

CHORAL

Jephte, oratorio (before Jun. 1648)

Oratorio, as a genre and to some extent a form, was just coming into its own when Giacomo Carissimi took it by the reins in the mid-seventeenth century. Carissimi, more than any other single composer, can be credited with having elevated oratorio from a downtrodden, half-baked hybrid of motet and opera to the lofty musico-religious essay-type that reached its zenith with the works of G.F. Handel about a century later. Fifteen oratorios with his name on them have survived (a few also exist in motet versions, showing how closely related the two genres really were); and the most famous of these, the most celebrated, and the most influential in its day, is the oratorio *Jephte*, for chorus and continuo, that Carissimi likely composed during the late 1640s.

Carissimi's chief contribution to the development of the oratorio was the placing of the chorus on a level more nearly equal to that of the narrator (who, in most seventeenth century Italian oratorios, is placed on a pedestal significantly above the other participants). What is meant by this is both that the sections of music marked "chorus" are of greater interest and importance in the musical drama, and that the actual singers of the choir are given more meaningful music to sing throughout the oratorio. Indeed, in *Jephte*, the role of narrator is in fact shared by the members of the six-part chorus (SSSATB), so that here the narrator is an alto solo, here it is a bass solo, there it is the entire chorus, and so on.

The story of *Jephte* is taken from the Book of Judges in the Old Testament, and there are two character roles: Jephte himself (a tenor), and the daughter (a soprano) whom he has vowed to sacrifice to the Lord. Carissimi keeps well within the bounds of the standard mid-seventeenth century musical syntax throughout *Jephte*; and he has no orchestra from which to draw colors and paint bold sonorities as a later oratorio composer would do. *Jephte* is for chorus and basso continuo alone, though of course one can do a great deal with "just" basso continuo, and it is likely that the vocal lines were reinforced by instruments during Carissimi's lifetime. But, plain though it may sound to ears more accustomed to listening for shocking progressivism and Technicolor splendor, this is an eminently well-balanced, fine-tuned, and deeply affective 20-some minutes of music, perfectly expressive of the text in ways that sometimes touch on madrigalism—and, after all, such virtues were the highest goal for most Baroque composers. *—Blair Johnston*

Synopsis:

The king of the Ammonites declared war upon Israel, and Jephte promises that if he is victorious in the battle, he will sacrifice the first creature to come out of his house to greet him upon his return. The narrator describes the fight and defeat of the Ammonites, "Transivit ergo Jephte," and his daughter is the first to come from the house to greet him, celebrating his victory by singing and dancing with her companions, "Incipite in tympanis." He sadly tells her of the oath he has sworn, "Heu, heu mihi, filia mea." She accepts her fate, but asks that first she be allowed to go into the mountains with her friends and lament that she died while still a virgin and without children. She mourns her destiny, "Plorate colles, dolente montes," with an echo responding, and the chorus joins in exhorting the children of Israel and its virgins to mourn for Jephte's daughter. *—Ann Feeney*

Recommended:

- ○ **Carissimi: Jephte; Jonas; Judicium Extremum** / J. E.Gardiner (cond.), Monteverdi Choir, His Majesty's Sagbutts and Cornetts, English Baroque Soloists / Erato 45466
- ○ **Love & Lament** / Van Veldhoven (cond.), Netherlands Bach Society, Cappella Figuralis / 2001 / Channel Classics 17098

John Alden Carpenter

b. Feb. 28, 1876, Park Ridge, IL, **d.** Apr. 26, 1951, Chicago, IL

Composer: Orchestral, Ballet

Though his music is less well known today than that of his more adventurous contemporary, Charles Ives, John Alden Carpenter was a fine composer notable for his songs, orchestral music and ballets. He was a student of John Knowles Paine at Harvard University, and though his music was mostly rooted in European traditions of the nineteenth century, he did begin to assimilate the sounds of distinctly American forms, most notably jazz.. Like Ives, Carpenter never pursued the life of a professional musician, choosing instead to work as vice-president of the family business, George B. Carpenter & Co., in Chicago.

Carpenter was born in Park Ridge, Illinois, and was a direct descendant of John Alden, a passenger on the Mayflower. He graduated from Harvard in 1897, and then continued his composition studies with Edward Elgar and Bernhard Ziehn. He made his debut as a composer with his *Violin Sonata* in 1912; it was premiered by the famous Mischa Elman. Soon after, he began publishing songs, piano music, and his first orchestral piece, *Adventures in a Perambulator*, which recounted in music his childhood memories of being wheeled around in a carriage by his nanny. In 1921 he began to strike a more modern tone with his jazz-inflected ballet, *Krazy*

Kat, which was based on the classic comic strip. Its success led to the commission of *Skyscrapers*, originally meant for Serge Diaghilev and the ballets russes, but eventually premiered by the Metropolitan Opera. Other important works include the symphonic poem, *Sea Drift* (1933), and his *Second Symphony*, which Bruno Walter premiered with the New York Philharmonic in 1942. Carpenter's most enduring works have been his many songs, including those to texts of Langston Hughes, Walt Whitman, and the Indian poet Rabindranath Tagore. *—AMG*

ORCHESTRAL

Adventures in a Perambulator (1914; revised 1941)

Composed in 1914 and revised in 1941, this set of six pieces for orchestra depict, in a tuneful and richly colorful American impressionist style, experiences and states of mind in a child's day. The work, probably patterned on the 1903 *Sinfonia Domestica* of Richard Strauss, was championed by Chicago Symphony conductor Frederick Stock, who conducted its premiere.

Each movement in the suite is accompanied by charming and humorous program notes written by the composer from the point of view of a baby (perhaps the composer's daughter Ginny). "En Voiture!" (All Aboard!) describes being bundled up "after my second breakfast" by an old nurse (open fifths and wind solos), and strapped into the baby carriage. The music becomes gradually airy and light like a sunny day, with an "all aboard" rhythm interspersed. The title of this movement suggests Carpenter's awareness of Debussy's *Children's Corner*. The second adventure is with "The Policeman," in a slightly over-important march tempo that breaks for some wisecracks: "Some sounds seem like smells. Some sights have echoes"... for instance, The Policeman... round like a ball, taller than my father... I try to analyze his appeal... I suspect it is his eye, and the way he walks. He walks like Doom." Adventure No. 3 is "The Hurdy-Gurdy," which alternates between a hurdy-gurdy waltz in reduced orchestration evoking that instrument and a passage for full orchestra, with hints of traditional tunes and popular songs wafting through. "Suddenly, at the climax of our excitement, I feel the approach of a phenomenon that I remember. It is the Policeman. He has stopped the music. He has frightened away the dark man and lady with their music box... but far off again I hear the forbidden music. Delightful forbidden music!" Adventure No. 4 occurs at "The Lake"; it is the most French and harmonically lush of the six movements, "I feel the quiver of the little waves as they escape from the big ones and come rushing up over the sand," Carpenter's baby says. "Their fear is pretended... Waves and Sunbeams!... This is My Lake!" The fifth adventure concerns some "Dogs": "We pass on. Probably there is nothing more in the World. If there is, it is superfluous. There IS. It is Dogs! ... not one of them—all of them... they laugh, they fight, they flirt, they run ... It is tremendous!" The last adventure is interior and is called "Dreams." Sounds from the day gradually quiet down, although impressions of the day's adventures continue to enter the child's reverie: "I lie very still. I am quite content... most of the time, my Mother and my Nurse have but one identity in my mind, but at night or when I close my eyes, I can easily tell them apart, for my Mother has the greater charm... how very large the world is. How many things there are!" Between a lullaby and *Scheherazade*-like textures, the music quietly closes. *—"Blue Gene" Tyranny*

Recommended:

- ○ **Carpenter: Adventures in a Perambulator; Symphonies 1 & 2** / J. M. Williams (cond.), National SO of Ukraine / 2001 / Naxos 559065
- ○ **Moore: Pageant of P.T. Barnum; Carpenter: Adventures; B. Rogers & B. Phillips** / Hanson (cond.), Eastman-Rochester Orch. / 1992 / Mercury 434319

Sea Drift, tone poem (1933; revised 1944)

Sea Drift is a rich, late Romantic work about 15 minutes long. As a part-time composer (he worked in his father's business in Chicago from 1909 to 1936) John Alden Carpenter often took a long time to realize a project. The nearly 20 years it took to write this one might, however, have more to do with a determination to avoid copying the sound of the many works written about the sea around the time Carpenter first thought of writing a symphonic seascape in 1915. Carpenter's immediate inspiration was Walt Whitman's collection of poems *Leaves of Grass*, which contain a section of poems about the sea under the heading *Sea Drift*. Ralph Vaughan Williams' *A Sea Symphony* and Frederick Delius' *Sea Drift* are settings of some of these poems, and Carpenter had also to deal with the existence of Debussy's *La Mer* (The Sea).

What attracted Carpenter's attention in this tone poem is the fact that Whitman uses the vast emptiness of the sea and its mighty force as a metaphor of separation and the forces that keep people apart and lonely. It is this aspect that Delius caught poignantly in his arch-Romantic *Sea Drift*.

Carpenter's treatment of the same emotion is, however, very different. There are two main motives in the work. One is a typically murmuring string figure, the other a melody announced in the oboe near the start of the work. Carpenter follows Franz Liszt's principle of thematic transformation, constantly metamorphosing them, changing both their shapes and their emotional quality. The music itself becomes a metaphor of the poem, for this constant slow change in its basic material causes the music to drift. The music has no sea-storms, and moments where the music enters a climax are few and subside rapidly. Towards the end the motives coalesce into a lyrical statement, as if a goal were sighted across an impossible expanse. The overall sound of the music is post-Romantic, with some Impressionist harmonies, though never enough to bring Debussy's work into mind. The interior nature of the music is unusual for sea-music. The unusually gentle nature of the orchestral writing and the harmonies make the listening easy, disguising the fact that for the work to make its true effect the listener really needs to pay attention to the thematic metamorphoses that constantly take place. One who just sits back and lets the ears soak up the pretty sounds, expecting pretty melodies and dramatic contrasts, may well miss the point. *—Joseph Stevenson*

Recommended:

- ○ **American Dreams** / Leppard (cond.), Indianapolis SO / 1999 / Decca 458157

BALLET

Krazy Kat, jazz pantomime (1921; revised 1940)

Composer John Alden Carpenter's hometown of Chicago had been "jazz-crazy" for about five years by the time he composed *Krazy Kat* in early 1921. Described as a "jazz pantomime," this choreographic sketch for small orchestra is not so much jazz as a reflection of its sound; only the final section of the work is truly syncopated, and there is no improvisation. However, Carpenter made his entry into the genre of jazz-inspired classics well ahead of practically everyone else in the game, save Ernst Schulhoff in Europe.

The proto-surreal comic strip adventures of George Herrimann's *Krazy Kat* provided the point of departure for Carpenter's music. The scenario of the work is credited to Herrimann, and the artist also provided illustrations for the handsome first edition of *Krazy Kat*, published in piano reduction by Schirmer in 1922. In the story, Krazy is seen sleeping beneath a tree when Bill Postem comes by to paste up an announcement for the Grand Ball (the wall in Herrimann's illustration, naturally, reads "post no bills.") Krazy awakes, reads the poster, and tries a few tentative dance steps, but "finds his feet heavy and numerous." A clothesline swings into view revealing a ballet skirt, which Krazy tries on to the improvement of his dance. Old Joe Stork drops a bundle on his way through, and Krazy opens it to discover a complete makeup kit and a pair of white cotton gloves.

Ignatz Mouse appears for the first time at this point. Ignatz's attempts to retrieve "an inviting brick" are thwarted by Officer Pup. Krazy is now made up and indulges in a bit of a Spanish dance. Then a "mysterious stranger" appears, obviously Ignatz is disguise; the "stranger" is bearing a huge bowl of catnip. Krazy inhales deeply and dances; having what Herrimann termed a "Class A fit." This provides Ignatz with just enough opportunity to bash Krazy with a brick. Krazy staggers back to the tree where she started at the opening of this piece, and returns to sleep.

After a trial performance of the music alone was given in Chicago on December 23, 1921, the premiere of the ballet was given at Town Hall in New York on January 20, 1922. Adolph Bolm danced the role of Krazy in front of a novel rolling backdrop painted by Herrimann himself, and Georges Barrère led the orchestra. The production received excellent publicity and was widely discussed; and critic Gilbert Seldes included both Carpenter's program notes and Herrimann's illustrations in his book *The Seven Lively Arts* in 1924. But as a musical work, *Krazy Kat* has failed to stick; with full knowledge of its scenario the music makes perfect sense, but without it the work seems episodic and lacking in form. Nonetheless, *Krazy Kat* is a fascinating artifact of its day, an early attempt to combine the "highbrow" element of concert music with the "lowbrow" forms of jazz and daily newspaper comics. *—Uncle Dave Lewis*

Recommended:

- ○ **Carpenter: Krazy Kat; H. F. Gilbert; A. Weiss & J. Powell** / C. Simmons (cond.), Z. Carno, Los Angeles PO / 1977 / New World 80228

Skyscrapers (1923–1924)

If a composer's career can ever be embodied in a single work, then *Skyscrapers* (1923–24)—subtitled "A Ballet of Modern American Life"—must be considered Carpenter's *magnum opus*. The composer's third and final ballet, *Skyscrapers* represents Carpenter at the pinnacle of his creativity and popularity. Carpenter's biographer, Howard Pollack, hails *Skyscrapers* as the composer's "boldest and brashest work, his *Rite of Spring*, so to speak...." Indeed, the ballet is a magnificent sonic canvas on which the composer paints a picture that could only have come from Jazz Age America.

Skyscrapers owes its genesis in part to Carpenter's fascination with Diaghilev's ballets russes. On a trip to Europe in 1923, Gerald Murphy, a leading light in the American artistic community in Paris in the 1920s, introduced the Carpenters to Diaghilev's circle. It soon came about that the Russian impresario asked Carpenter to produce a ballet embodying "the alternating violence of American life." This request may have been partially inspired by the press coverage of the Boston police strike in 1919, with its attendant violence and social breakdown. In any case, Carpenter immediately went to work on a large-scale piece with the working title "The Policeman's Holiday" in the fall of 1923. By the end of that year, however, he had begun to incline toward the world of machine and metal as the theme of his ballet.

Chicago in the 1920s led the world in the development and construction of skyscrapers, inspiring humorous comment, literature, visual art, and universal attention, whether in the form of admiration, envy, or horror. Carpenter took this towering symbol of American metropolitan life as a point of departure, noting that his new ballet was "simply based on the idea that in this country we work hard and play hard." A litany of misdirected communication and misunderstandings, coupled with Diaghilev's increasing dislike of the extent to which jazz was then "infecting" European music, led Diaghilev to decline to stage the work. Carpenter sought an American premiere for the work, and *Skyscrapers* at last debuted (with choreography by Sonny Lee) at the Metropolitan Opera in February 1926. Aside from purely musical considerations, the early performances of *Skyscrapers* marked the first time that African-American singers performed onstage at the Met, where the ballet enjoyed great success.

The primary influence at work in *Skyscrapers* is, by common consent, Stravinsky's ballet *Les noces* (1914–17), which Carpenter had seen performed during his European travels. Much of the music's "primitivism" is indeed Stravinskian in tenor but is also redolent of the American Indian influences Carpenter incorporates into several of his works. Generally, *Skyscrapers* was enthusiastically received by critics and audiences alike. While some commentators felt the work was too dependent upon the music of Stravinsky, most praised its jazz-inflected energy; the *New York Times*, for example, found the work "auspicious for the development of a specifically American art form." Under the title *Wolkenkratzer*, *Skyscrapers* received its European premiere in Munich in 1928, with choreography by Heinrich Kröller. Arriving as it did on the heels of Ernst Krenek's jazzy opera *Jonny spielt auf* (1927), it was an unequivocal success in Europe—a success thrown into relief when the Nazis banned *Skyscrapers* (and, indeed, all of Carpenter's music) as "undesirable" in 1938.

Though infrequently performed today, *Skyscrapers* remains an icon of 1920s urban Americana and a classic example of the "machinist" compositional aesthetic that enjoyed currency in the early part of the twentieth century. *—Tim Mahon*

Recommended:

- ○ **Skyscrapers: Symphonic Jazz** / Shilkret (cond.), Victor SO / 2002 / Naxos Jazz 8120644

José Carreras

b. Dec. 5, 1946, Barcelona, Spain
Tenor

José Carreras, one of the legendary "Three Tenors," was born Josep Carreras (Josep is his Catalan name, the equivalent of the Castilian Spanish José) in Barcelona in 1946. He began singing at a very early age; family lore holds that he serenaded passengers on a voyage home from Argentina when he was only five. He was inspired by the film biography *The Great Caruso*, starring Mario Lanza, and is said to have learned each and every aria contained within.

After a mere two years of voice lessons, the young Carreras sang *"La donna è mobile"* from Verdi's *Rigoletto* on Spanish National Radio—a performance that has been preserved and is included in one of his video biographies. He made his professional operatic debut at the age of eleven in Manuel de Falla's *El retablo de Maese Pedro*. This unique opera, written originally for a puppet theater, has as one of its primary roles an exceptionally difficult part for boy soprano—a part so challenging that it is rarely sung by a child, usually taken instead by an adult mezzo-soprano.

After his voice changed, he took up studies with Francisco Puig, then with Juan Ruax, whom Carreras now regards as his "artistic father." At Ruax's encouragement, he auditioned at the Barcelona Liceo and landed the small role of Flavio in Bellini's *Norma*. This small break would have enormous consequences, since it brought him into contact with the already-famous Montserrat Caballé, who was very taken with the young tenor and recommended him to her management. The resulting engagement, opposite Caballé in Donizetti's *Lucrezia Borgia* as Gennaro, is now generally considered his real debut as a tenor, and helped to launch his career.

Carreras made his American debut in 1972 at the New York City Opera as Pinkerton in Puccini's *Madama Butterfly*. His Covent Garden debut (1974) was as Alfredo in *La Traviata*, and his first appearance at the Salzburg Festival was in Verdi's *Requiem* at the request of maestro Herbert von Karajan. He first appeared at the Vienna State Opera as the Duke in *Rigoletto* (1974), at the Met the same year as Cavaradossi in *Tosca*, and as Riccardo in *Un Ballo in Maschera* in 1975.

By the age of 28 he had already sung 24 different roles in the leading opera houses of Europe and the Americas. This busy schedule gave rise to some controversy: critics sometimes found his voice strained and complained that he might be overtaxing himself. It was not immediately recognized that this tiredness masked the onset and development of the blood disease leukemia, not diagnosed until 1987, when it had reached an acute phase.

It was during his treatment that the Three Tenors phenomenon was born. Having competed ruthlessly with both Domingo and Pavarotti for ascendancy in the world of opera, he now struck up genuine friendships with both men, who supported him during his illness. Their first concert together was conceived as a fundraiser for the newly-created Josep Carreras International Leukemia Foundation. It drew a live audience in the tens of thousands and an international viewership of tens of millions. The resulting records and videos were phenomenal sellers.

Carreras is widely represented in operatic and concert recordings, numerous cross over recordings of various styles, and a large number of videos. He has over fifty complete opera recordings. His video biography, *A Life Story*, which included his battle with leukemia, won an international Emmy award. *—AMG*

Recommended:

- ○ **Carreras: The Golden Years** / Carreras, various artists / 1999 / Philips 462892
- ○ **The Very Best of José Carreras** / Carreras, various artists / 2003 / EMI 75903
- ○ **Verdi: Stiffelio** / Gardelli (cond.), Carreras, Ganzarolli, Sass, Manuguerra / 1989 / Philips 422432
- ○ **Zarzuela Recital** / Carreras, English CO / 1997 / Ensayo 9717

Elliott Carter

b. Dec. 11, 1908, New York, NY
Composer: Chamber Music, Keyboard, Orchestral, Symphonic, Concerto, Ballet

One of the most significant post-World War II American composers, Elliott Carter remains a forceful and eloquent voice into his tenth decade. From an early, quasi-neo-classical style, Carter has forged his own complex, dramatically oriented adaptation of serial methods.

His initial education was at the Horace Mann School and at Harvard, where he obtained a B.A. in English, in 1930; two years later, he got his M.A. in Music, after studies with Walter Piston and Gustav Holst. He also received early encouragement from Charles Ives. From Harvard, he went to Paris, studying at the Ecole Normale de Musique and taking private lessons with Nadia Boulanger. Carter had an interest in modern music almost from the beginning (in fact, he once said that he took his degrees at Harvard so he could be near the Boston Symphony Orchestra, which under Serge Koussevitzky's direction was performing a broad range of contemporary compositions at the time). But he also sang in a madrigal group and conducted choral concerts in Paris, and has pursued interests in mathematics, literature, and languages.

After his return to the U.S., he served as the musical director of the Ballet Caravan from 1937 to 1939. From 1940 on, Carter has held an impressive variety of teaching posts at, among others, St. John's College, Annapolis (1940–42); the Peabody Conservatory (1946–48); Columbia University (1948–50); Queen's College, New York (1955–56); Yale University (1960–62); the American Academy in Rome (1963 and 1967); and the Juilliard School (1972). Carter has also been the recipient of many honors and awards, including honorary doctorates from almost a dozen universities, many foundation grants, a Prix de Rome, two Guggenheim fellowships, and Pulitzer Prizes for his second (1960) and third (1973) string quartets.

His ballet *Pocahontas*, written for the Ballet Caravan, and the *Holiday Overture* (1944) are representative of Carter's early style, a fusion of Igor Stravinsky's Neo-Classicism and the American populism of Aaron Copland. In the mid-1940s, however, Carter decided that the style he had employed to that point avoided some important modes of expression. Subsequent works, such as the 1946 *Piano Sonata* and the 1948 *Cello Sonata*, employ more dissonance and rhythmic complexity. Carter developed his notion of "metrical modulation," in which one tempo leads gradually to another through changing the note values in different voices of the ensemble. One starts to hear this process in the *String Quartet No. 1* (1951), and colorful works like the *Variations for Orchestra* (1954–55), the *Double Concerto* (1961) and the *Quartet No. 2* develop those ideas further. Carter also occasionally develops dramatic scenarios for his compositions. The *Quartet No. 3*, for example, pits two duos (violin/viola and violin/cello) against one another as they play in different tempos and rhythms; Claus Adam of the Juilliard Quartet, which premiered the work, called it the most difficult work the Quartet had ever played.

Carter has gone on to write a total of five quartets, along with a variety of symphonic works, concertos, chamber and solo pieces and, in the late 1970s and early 1980s, a handful of vocal works. He has continued to be productive: Carter's *Symphonia: sum fluxae pretium spei* (1993–96), which he completed at the age of 88, was received with great enthusiasm. Carter astounded the music world by creating his first opera, *What Next?* (1998), at the age of 90. *—Chris Morrison*

CHAMBER MUSIC

Eight Etudes and a Fantasy, for woodwind quartet (1949–1950)

The poet Richard Wilbur once compared the thought process to a bat that flies blindly about its cavern, knowing through the darkness exactly where the walls are; the difference in the brain is that in certain moments of concentrated thought, "a graceful error may correct the cave." So much of Carter's music seems exploratory—not in an unfinished, experimental way, but rather as a conscious effort to test the boundaries and limits of all aspects of the aural experience. Within a certain harmonic system, for example, he might exploit the varied ways in which registral contrasts render the same pitches or intervals. His rhythmic processes stretch time into an elastic substance. In his *Eight Etudes and a Fantasy* for woodwind quartet (1950), Carter explores the sonic possibilities afforded by the instruments of a wind ensemble, producing a rich palette of textures and colors.

"Etude" usually implies that a work's actual or at least vestigial purpose is to serve as a technical study for the performer. Here, however, the "study" is directed toward the composer—or, more accurately, his students. The work originated as a series of exercises for an orchestration class Carter taught at Columbia University in 1949. At the class's disposal was a quartet of woodwinds, for which the students were assigned to compose pieces. Apparently Carter, unsatisfied with the students' efforts, put chalk to blackboard to demonstrate a more imaginative set of possibilities. Each of Carter's sketches took as its basis a particular figure or concept and explored its coloristic and textural possibilities. Later, the composer developed these sketches into the now well-known *Eight Etudes and a Fantasy.*

The first etude in the group seems to provide some preliminary aural diagnostics. Within its 24 measures it bounces between the rafters and the basement of the instruments' ranges—the flute's first gesture, for example, is a descending leap of more than two octaves—while also devising various kinds of relationships between the voices: unison, imitation, etc. Some of the etudes are exercises in pure sonority. Etude III, marked Adagio possibile, consists of a long-sustained D major chord. Voices enter and exit seamlessly on different chord tones, demonstrating the various colors possible within very fixed parameters. This idea is taken a step further in Etude VII, which consists of articulations of a single note.

Some of the etudes are more figural in their focus. Etude II is comprised almost entirely of a single, dizzying, arching string of 32nd notes. The germinal figure, which fills the better part of two measures, is passed from instrument to instrument, appearing at a different but consistent transposition in each voice. Carter's description of this etude sounds like one that might come from Messiaen: "four birds ... sing as birds do, sporadically, the same song over and over." Strict rules govern Etude IV, a game in which every figure is a quick half-step motion followed by a rest. At times the instruments are lined up in a row so that a chromatic line runs though the ensemble, while at others the voices create intermittent parallelism or undulating crosscurrents. Etude VI is peppered with trills, flutter tonguing, and special fingering effects. The registral acrobatics and intricacy of coordination among the instruments in Etude VIII make it one of the most challenging pieces in the woodwind repertory. The concluding Fantasy takes shape as a fugue, the episodes of which recall various moments in the previous studies. *—Jeremy Grimshaw*

Recommended:

○ **Best Of The New York Woodwind Quintet Vol. 1** / NY Woodwind Quintet / 1996 / Boston Skyline 137

Sonata for Cello and Piano (1948)

Elliott Carter's *Cello Sonata*, composed in 1948, marked a breakthrough for the composer. In it, he moved decisively away from his former populist style, which had been influenced by Copland, towards a style that was both more academic and more personal. The *Cello Sonata* utilizes devices that would recur often in later Carter compositions: metric modulation, complex relationships of tempo deployed to achieve continuity, subtle thematic and harmonic transformations, and most notably the assignment of a certain character to each instrument. In the *Cello Sonata*, a passionate cello opposes a coldly logical piano; though the two instruments occasionally come together, they never really resolve their differences.

This opposition is most prominent in the first movement, which Carter actually composed after the other three. Here the piano begins with regular, barely changing chords that sound more like the tick of a metronome than anything else. These form contrasts with broad, out-of-time lyrical outbursts from the cello. As the cello moans and sighs, the piano obliviously counts off; the feeling of alienation is palpable. At times the two instruments come together, but their meetings feel purely accidental. The second movement on its surface is a jazzy scherzo, with the piano and cello working on more intimate terms. However, even with all the syncopation, the cello still can be heard straying from the piano's tempo. The less explicit tension in this movement is brought to a sort of climax with a weirdly casual statement of the Dies irae just before the cello's quiet pizzicato coda. A restless quintuplet figure from the second movement provides the deceptive opening for the slower third. Here, Carter moves his themes through different, related rhythms to aid in their development. Cello and piano come closest together in this movement; they trade phrases, and support each other harmonically, but they are still two different characters having a dialogue, not two instruments speaking with one voice. The finale begins with music from the third movement, much as the third reused music from the second. In the finale, however, Carter borrows the lyricism of the third movement and whips it up into a propulsive frenzy that ultimately still fails to bring the two instruments together. As the work ends, the cello plays a few sad notes, while the piano remains unable to help.

One need not understand this work's forbiddingly complex methods of composition to appreciate their result; this is both an academically rigorous and a keenly communicative work. *—Andrew Malone*

Recommended:

○ **In The Shadow Of World War II** / Krosnick, Kalish / 1996 / Arabesque 6682

String Quartet No. 2 (1959)

Carter's *Second String Quartet* (1959) is structured as a drama in which each of the four players assumes a distinct and largely independent role; the composer even recommends that the members of the ensemble separate themselves spatially, though few quartets choose to do this, as it increases the already imposing technical difficulties of the piece. In contrast to the traditional view of the string quartet, in which homogeneiety is often a primary goal, the *Second Quartet* demands four individuals who observe and comment on one another as the music progresses. Carter further explored this idea of musical discourse among multiple, often conflicting personalities in the two great concerti of the following decade, the *Double Concerto* (1961) for piano, harpsichord, and chamber orchestras, and the *Piano Concerto* (1967). In both of these works, the soloists and orchestras occupy the sort of distinct, even opposing musical realms that are integral to the *Second Quartet.*

Each of the players in the *Second Quartet* assumes a unique voice: The first violin is instructed to play in a largely bravura manner, the cello takes on a Romantic character, and so on. The work's four main movements are separated by cadenzas, each featuring one of the instruments in a prominent role while the remaining players provide commentary on the musings of the soloist. The viola is the first member of the quartet to present a cadenza, which unfolds in a broad expressive manner. Throughout this passage the other three players burst in with violent exclamations, as though in anger at the viola's self-centeredness or in ridicule of its pompous manner. The ensuing Presto scherzando is followed by a cadenza for the cello, which struggles to preserve an atmosphere of freedom and melodiousness against the metric rigor demanded by the rest of the ensemble. The first violin's cadenza, which follows the lyrical Andante espressivo, is full of virtuosic highlights yet meets with no response whatsoever from the other three players. Significantly, there is no cadenza for the second violin, perhaps because of the rigid character of its part throughout the work.

Carter endeavors in the *Second Quartet* to emphasize the relationships between the players in the ensemble rather than imposing a preconceived dramatic structure. Instead of merely presenting the composer's musical ideas to an audience, the individual players are asked to actively join in the creation of the musical drama, each in a specific role. Carter added new dimension to the idea of chamber music by fusing a centuries-old genre and traditional musical performance with elements of theater, an innovation which exerted much influence on generations of American composers.

Both the *Second Quartet* and its successor, the *Third* (1971), were awarded the Pulitzer Prize, in no small part due to the expertise and commitment of the Juilliard Quartet at the works' premieres and in numerous subsequent performances. *—Blair Johnston*

Recommended:

○ **Elliott Carter: Quartets 1 & 2** / Composers Quartet / 1975 / Nonesuch 71249

KEYBOARD

Night Fantasies (1980)

"*Night Fantasies*," explains Carter in the preface to what is arguably one of his most delightfully intractable works, "is a piano piece of continuously changing moods, suggesting the fleeting thoughts and feelings that pass through the mind during a period of wakefulness at night.... In this score, I wanted to capture the fanciful, changeable quality of our inner life at a time when it is not dominated by strong, directive intentions or desires."

Night Fantasies (1980) was the result of a quadruple commission extended by some of Carter's most notable advocates and performers. Carter had Paul Jacobs, pianist of the New York Philharmonic, in mind when he composed the piano parts for his *Concerto for Orchestra* (1968–69). Ursula Oppens had performed Carter's works in several venues, including performances with the ensemble Speculum Musicae, of which she was a founding member. Gilbert Kalish had participated in the premiere of the composer's *Duo for violin and piano.* Pianist-scholar Charles Rosen had long been a champion of Carter's music, and had made the *Piano Sonata* (1946), Carter's only previous composition for solo piano, part of his standard repertory. *Night Fantasies* thus glows with an unusual reciprocal energy between performer and composer, especially apparent in recordings by the dedicatees. Carter knows his resources well, and utilizes them to their fullest; the performers speak Carter's musical language, and transform his sometimes cryptically difficult musical demands into fluent and fluid gestures. Which is not to say that this is by any means a gentle piece—otherwise the insomniac would be peacefully snoozing. The uninitiated listener will strain to follow musical thoughts in the same way that, between moments of consciousness, one struggles to reclaim reality from the elastic logic of dreams. While for some the thorny figures that dot Carter's sonic landscapes sound random and improvisatory, they are in fact carefully calculated. The composer's notorious rhythmic specifications—*Night Fantasies* begins, for example, with sustained notes articulated exactly four-fifths of the way into the first beat—suggest that Carter knows the precise flavor of (dis)order he wants at any given moment, never leaving it to chance. In fact, his complex metric ratios create an unseen but pervasive rhythmic skeleton that determines the position of surface features within the piece. For this reason, tempi and meter must be strictly observed and consistently deployed so that the so-called metric modulations (really tempo modulations) Carter frequently employs can be faithfully executed. (In this technique, the rate of pulse of a given division is used to set the speed of a subsequent division. For example, quintuplet eighth note rhythms in one measure might emerge as identical-sounding septuplets in the next, remaining "constant" as the metric context changes .)

Meticulous, too, are Carter's articulation indications. Throughout *Night Fantasies*, Carter specifies in detail when and how the damper, sostenuto, and una corda pedals are to be used; he likewise carefully controls note durations and dynamic nuances. Thematic organicism is difficult to find here; the piece is divided with invisible seams into overlapping and intermingling textural zones that continually produce new but vaguely familiar figurations. The harmonic language utilizes intervallic combinations that can be rearranged and inverted to create striking spatial and registral contrasts, the sort of extremes that only appear in the caricaturized thoughts of the half-conscious. Scholar, composer, and former Carter student David Schiff observes that works such as *Night Fantasies*, though extremely difficult to learn and perform, are not "extroverted show pieces. Rather, they seem intense acts of self-communion." *—Jeremy Grimshaw*

Recommended:

- ○ **American Piano Music of Our Time** / Oppens / Music & Arts 604
- ○ **Elliott Carter: Complete Music for Piano** / C. Rosen / 1997 / Bridge 9090

ORCHESTRAL

Elegy, for string orchestra (1952)

Originally composed in 1939 for cello and piano, Elliott Carter's *Elegy* took many shapes before it finally found the one that best pleased its composer. A second version, for string quartet, appeared in 1946, and then a third, for string orchestra, in 1952, before finally, in 1961, the final incarnation of the *Elegy* as a work for viola and piano came into being. To those who know Carter only through the works of the 1950s on this work in any of its forms (particularly in the pre-viola versions) might hardly seem like Carter at all. (In the 1961 revision, Carter made some changes to the basic music that bring it somewhat "forward" in time.) The means of expression in the piece are wholly traditional: it is linear, lyrical in its mode of inspiration, and tonal. It should not really be called the composer's most intimate work, but it is easy to excuse the listener who, having not yet dug a way into the Carter of later decades, happens to think so. The version for string orchestra has a depth and warmness of tone that, lovely in a formal way, perhaps make the piece a bit too public. *—Blair Johnston*

Recommended:

- ○ **American Music for Strings** / G. Schwarz (cond.), Los Angeles CO / 1980 / Nonesuch 79002
- ○ **Metamorphosen Performs Chamber Orchestral Works.** / S. Yoo (cond.), Metamorphosen CO / 1995 / Albany 194

SYMPHONIC

A Symphony of Three Orchestras (1976)

Carter's *A Symphony of Three Orchestras* (1976) typifies the composer's sophisticated manner of coordinating instrumental groups. Carter refers to the work as a symphony *of* three orchestras, rather than *for* three orchestras, to emphasize the idea of distinct ensembles sounding simultaneously rather than antiphonally. Orchestra I contains brass, strings, and timpani; Orchestra II, clarinets, piano, vibraphone, chimes, marimba, solo violins and basses, and a group of cellos; Orchestra III, flutes, oboes, bassoons, horns, violins, violas, basses, and non-pitched percussion instruments. Each orchestra plays four "movements" of differing characters, as in a traditional symphony. Each movement, however, is partially superimposed upon one from another of the three ensembles, creating a 12-movement structure of continuously overlapping sonic entities. In his preface to the score, Carter wrote:

"The listener, of course, is not meant, on first hearing, to identify the details of this continually shifting web of sound any more than he is to identify the modulations in *Tristan und Isolde*, but rather to hear and grasp the character of this kaleidoscope of musical themes as they are presented in varying contexts."

More than simply a technical tour de force, this approach is an attempt to reflect a fluid and complex reality in music. Carter continues:

"I do not want to give the impression of a simultaneous motion in which everybody's part is coordinated like a goose step. I do not want to write the kind of music that just marches on and marches off. I want it to seem like a crowd of people, or like waves on the sea—all things that signify a much more fluid and, to me, more human way of living."

The Symphony fulfilled Carter's longstanding desire to write a work based on the poem "The Bridge" by American poet Hart Crane (1899–1932). (The same poem, in fact, is also source of the title of Aaron Copland's *Appalachian Spring*.) Carter first encountered Crane's poetry while a student at Harvard in the 1920s; the poet's work later provided inspiration for Carter's ballet *Pocahontas* (1936) and the song *Voyage* (1943). "The Bridge" begins by describing the Brooklyn Bridge and New York harbor and unfolds as an examination of the paradoxes of industrial America in the 1920s. Carter believed that Crane's America, "for all its fascinating modernism, would eventually prove a paralyzing wasteland, depriving him of his poetic gift, even destroying him completely." The poet eventually committed suicide by throwing himself over the side of a ship into the Gulf of Mexico.

Carter's *Symphony*, like Crane's poem, suggests a continual descent. The work begins with the players in the highest registers of their instruments. The sound of the solo trumpet initiates a falling motion:

"How many dawns, chill from his rippling rest
The seagull's wings shall dip and pivot him,
Shedding white rings of tumult, building high
Over the chained bay waters
Liberty —
Then, with inviolate curve, forsake our eyes
As apparitional as sails that cross
Some page of figures to be filed away;
Till elevators drop us from our day. . . ."

Immediately preceding the work's conclusion, the music is interrupted by a series of violent crashes ("The forked crash of split thunder parts . . ."), after which the opening of the *Symphony* is mirrored in the lowest registers of the tuba and double basses.

Carter was commissioned to write the *Symphony* by the New York Philharmonic in celebration of the American Bicentennial. The *Symphony* is dedicated to Pierre Boulez and the New York Philharmonic, who premiered the work at New York's *Avery Fisher Hall* on February 17, 1977. *—Robert Adelson*

Recommended:

- ○ **Carter: A Symphony of Three Orchestras; Varèse** / Boulez (cond.), New York PO / 1995 / Sony 68334

CONCERTO

Concerto for Orchestra (1969)

The 1960s were the time of concertos for Elliott Carter: indeed, save for the *Eight Pieces* for timpanist that took all of the 1950s and over half of the 1960s to write, he composed nothing but concertos during that decade. First, in 1961, the *Double Concerto for harpsichord and piano* appeared. In 1965 the *Piano Concerto* was finished, and finally, in the last year of the decade, the *Concerto for Orchestra* took shape. The *Concerto for Orchestra* still ranks in some circles today, the fame of the string quartets and the achievements of the 1970s, 1980s, and 1990s notwithstanding, as Carter's most striking effort. It was commissioned by the New York Philharmonic Symphony Society in celebration of its 125th anniversary, composed while Carter was in residence at the American Academy in Rome, and premiered in New York in early 1970.

In this work, the large orchestra is broken down by register into four groups of instruments (high, high-middle, low-middle, and low). These take turns stepping on each other's toes as the four connected movements unfold (Allegro, Presto volando, Maestoso, and Allegro agitato). To each of these freshly organized families of instruments is added an appropriate group of percussion instruments. Carter's musical conception was not an absolute one: he seems to have organized certain elements of the concerto around the poem *Vents* by St. John Perse. Still, the purely musical architecture of the work is complicated even by Carter's usual standards, and the interested listener would do well to locate a copy of Carter's own "chart" for the work (in which certain matters of structure, pacing, and harmony are broken down movement by movement) and then listen, listen, listen. *—Blair Johnston*

Recommended:

- ○ **Carter: Concerto for Orchestra, Violin Concerto, 3 Occasions** / Knussen (cond.), London Sinfonietta / 1992 / Virgin 59271

Double Concerto, for harpsichord, piano & 2 chamber orchestras (1959–1961)

The first work in a threesome of Elliott Carter concertos that appeared during the 1960s, the *Double Concerto for harpsichord and piano with two chamber orchestras*, of 1959–61 is, as one looking at its title might well guess, a work whose instrumentation turned many heads when it first appeared. There are several concertos for two or more pianos and several for two or more harpsichords in the general repertoire, but a work in which the massive, sound-sustaining modern piano is pitted against the much smaller-toned, plucked harpsichord was a sensational one in 1961. Commissioned by the Fromm Foundation and composed with harpsichordist Ralph Kirkpatrick in mind, Carter's *Double Concerto* was premiered in the fall of 1961 with Kirkpatrick and pianist Charles Rosen in the starring roles. Igor Stravinsky, in his famous evaluation of the piece, called it "a masterpiece, by an American composer" (Stravinsky and Craft, *Dialogues and a Diary*, New York, 1963).

The purely acoustical difficulties of balancing a harpsichord and a piano and an orchestra are dealt with in a simple and effective way by Carter: there are in fact two differently constituted chamber orchestras, one to support and challenge the harpsichordist and one to support and challenge the pianist (each of the chamber orchestras has a full and varied percussion contingent). And, to draw an even clearer line of distinction between soloist and soloist, the harpsichord and piano parts are built out of completely different sets of intervals and rhythms, so that, in a matter of speaking, they make words and sentences in different languages out of different alphabets. Without the four percussionists acting as go-betweens, the harpsichordist and the pianist might have nothing to do with one another.

There are seven portions of music in the *Double Concerto*: 1. Introduction, 2. Cadenza for Harpsichord, 3. Allegro scherzando, 4. Adagio, 5. Presto, 6. Cadenzas for Piano (and continuation of the Presto), and 7. Coda. The music represents in some ways a new direction for Carter: theme and development, in any traditional sense, are gone altogether, completely replaced by the kind of continually evolving, layered music, in which a multiplicity of instrumental "characters" coalesce into a musical whole and in which time and sound are not always friendly compatriots, that has since been Carter's claim to fame. *—Blair Johnston*

Recommended:

○ **Carter: Sonata for Flute, Oboe, Cello & Harpsichord; Cello Sonata; Double Concerto** / H. Kolbe, A. Weisberg (conds.), Paul Jacobs, Kalish, Contemporary Chamber Ens. / 1992 / Nonesuch 79183

Piano Concerto (1964–1965)

Carter conceived his *Piano Concerto* as an 85th birthday present for Igor Stravinsky, who had been a proponent of Carter's music for some time. Written during a stay in Berlin in the mid-1960s, the Concerto is a tragic, even violent, piece that fuses the composer's love of formal, rhythmic, and harmonic complexity with a deeply human sense of contemporary social and political concerns. From the opening bars it is apparent that the orchestra and soloist are in active contention with one another. The solo writing is no mere elaboration of material presented by the orchestra, as one might expect of a more traditionally cast concerto; indeed, the antagonism between the two forces is emphasized by the composer's instruction to spatially separate the piano and orchestra. There is also a third party involved, a small concertino of seven players situated directly around the piano, which functions as a hard-working, if ultimately unsuccessful, intermediary between the warring bodies. The *Piano Concerto* is constructed upon a principle, familiar to connoisseurs of Carter's music, which the composer borrowed from the works of his early mentor Charles Ives: several musical layers, representing different spatial, temporal, or even philosophical, planes, are presented simultaneously. Thus, the *Piano Concerto* is really two irreconcilably different pieces of music forced into the same temporal space; for attentive listeners, the resulting conflict is electric.

As one would expect from a modernist like Carter, the *Piano Concerto*'s two substantial movements bear little resemblance to traditional formal plans. The work's musical material undergoes continual development, and there is no suggestion of anything like a reprise or recapitulation. The soloist, isolated behind the wall created by the concertino, presents capricious music, light and sensitive, while the orchestra lumbers along in representation of something far more menacing. Carter worked on the piece near an American weapons range; indeed, it is possible to hear a terrifying militarism in the orchestra's mechanical onslaught. There are few points of reference to previous events for either listener or performer as the work progresses, and few internal resolutions of the ongoing struggle between the soloist and the orchestra. As the concerto nears its conclusion, however, the two violently opposed forces come to something of a truce as their respective musical worlds become more complementary. In the end, however, there is no resolution, and the work closes with a lingering sense of despair. *—Blair Johnston*

Recommended:

○ **Elliott Carter: Piano Concerto** / Gielen (cond.), Oppens, Cincinnati SO / 1986 / New World 80347

BALLET

The Minotaur (1947)

Impresario Lincoln Kirstein commissioned Carter to write a ballet for performance by the Ballet Society of New York in 1947. The resulting work was *The Minotaur*, based on the ancient Greek mythological tale of a man-bull, the Cretan labyrinth in which he was imprisoned, and the Greek warrior, Theseus, who killed the Minotaur. Kirstein had previously commissioned Carter's only other ballet, *Pocahontas* (1939), which was performed by the Ballet Caravan. The Ballet Society, for which *The Minotaur* was commissioned, was an elite organization whose presentations were held inconspicuously at a high school in New York. The company gave productions with music by such composers as Hindemith and Stravinsky, both choreographed by George Balanchine. Also, the Ballet Society presented the first collaboration between John Cage and Merce Cunningham.

Balanchine was supposed to be the choreographer for *The Minotaur* as well. Before beginning his composition, Carter met with Balanchine to discuss the ballet and its specific scenes. Not long after, Balanchine suddenly left New York for Paris, in an attempt to become the new director of the Paris Ballet. The position never actually opened up, and Balanchine soon returned to New York. In the meantime, Carter and the Ballet Society offered the opportunity to choreograph *The Minotaur* to Balanchine's young assistant, John Taras. *The Minotaur* was premiered on March 26, 1947, and was praised by some and criticized by others. The ballet was performed for only two seasons before it was dropped. An orchestral suite was later fashioned by Carter, who excised about one-third of the music from the ballet score. Howard Hanson and the Eastman-Rochester Symphony Orchestra recorded this orchestral suite in 1956. The suite itself was choreographed in the late 1960s by John Butler, and this adaptation was performed in Boston in 1970. Carter felt that the orchestral suite was best fitted for the concert hall, while the ballet should not be presented without the entire original score.

The years of 1936 to 1948 comprise what could be considered Carter's early period, before the first work in his mature style, the *Cello Sonata* (1948). In the works from this period, Carter's music can be described as embodying a conflict between neo-classical restraint and the complex harmonic and rhythmic innovations that would become prevalent in his mature style. *The Minotaur* is a strong example of this contradiction in style. Much of the music is similar to Stravinsky's neo-classical pieces, but instances of polyrhythm, or separate lines played at different tempos, are also present. *—Chris Boyes*

Recommended:

○ **Carter: The Minotaur; Piano Sonata; 2 Songs** / Schwarz (cond.), New York Chamber Symphony / 1990 / Nonesuch 79248

Ferdinando Carulli

b. Feb. 1770, Naples, Italy, **d.** Feb. 17, 1841, Paris, France
Composer

Classical guitarists owe a debt of gratitude to this Italian-turned-Parisian guitar master. Ferdinando Carulli, born to an affluent, upper-class family, began his musical training under the tutelage of a priest; who was little more than a musical dilettante himself. Carulli first learned music on the cello. It was not until he was about 20 years of age that he took up the guitar, which at that time, more resembled a lute and might have five or six pairs of strings. From that time forward, Carulli devoted his life to developing the guitar as a classical instrument and to popularizing guitar music. Guitarists were few in Naples in Carulli's time; he, therefore, had to study on his own and consequently, he developed his own unique style as a composer and a guitarist. A significant part of his legacy was born from that experience and published as *Method*, Op. 27. This collection of guitar pieces was composed for novice guitarists and, as such, became very popular. Today, these pieces are still used for guitar instruction.

Carulli's early career focused on performing. His popularity in his native Naples soon led to performances across Europe, where he gained equal prominence. His composing did not begin in earnest until the early nineteenth century. Some of his earliest published works were from Milan around 1807. After Milan, he apparently spent some time in Venice, as evidenced by published manuscripts from there in the 1807–08 time period. By April 1808, however, Carulli had taken up residence in Paris. He enjoyed considerable success composing, performing, and teaching guitar. Over his lifetime, Carulli composed at least 400 pieces for the guitar, making him one of the most prolific composers of the century. One of his more popular pieces was *Trio*, Op. 12, for guitar, violin, and flute. Other pieces that exemplify his artistry include several serenades for guitar and violin and for flute and guitar. He wrote for guitar and piano, guitar and voice, guitar solo, and with his *Concerto*, Op. 8, guitar and orchestra.

Being a pioneer in his field, Carulli often had difficulty in getting some of his work published. Publishers were interested in works that were more simplistic, not willing to risk publishing works believed to be too difficult to perform for the average performer. Consequently, it is believed that many of what would have been Carulli's masterpieces were lost. This, no doubt, also played a role in Carulli's decision to self-publish. In addition to publishing some of his own works, he published the works of other guitarists as well.

Carulli was one of the few guitarists in Paris and the first to popularize classical guitar. He was so successful many burgeoning guitarists came to Paris to study under him. In addition to this influx of foreign students, many of whom were from Italy like himself, Carulli counted nobility and upper class Parisians as his students. His popularity was only surpassed when Fernando Sor arrived in Paris in 1823.

Carulli's interest in the guitar extended beyond composing, teaching, and performing to include guitar design and construction. He worked closely with the French guitar maker René Lacote to help evolve the guitar into the instrument it is today.

Ferdinando Carulli married Marie-Josephine Boyer from France in 1801. They had a son, Gustavo, with whom Ferdinando composed several pieces for guitar and piano. *—Bruce Lundgren*

Overview of Works (ca. 1809–1837)

The oeuvre of Italian musician and composer Ferdinando Carulli reflects his position as the most gifted guitarist of the first half of the nineteenth century. Carulli spent his career opening up new terrain for the guitar as a virtuosic solo instrument, both through his notoriety as a performer, as well as his skill as a teacher and composer, and his works introduced a number of innovative techniques that have since become the classical guitarist's stock and trade.

Aide from a single work for solo piano, the *Premier Pot-pourri*, Op. 77 (1814), and a handful of pieces for violin duo, Carulli's entire output—comprising well over 350 opus numbers—consists of works for one or more guitars, guitar and voice, or guitar with other instruments or ensembles. These include dozens of solo sonatas and sonatinas, such as the *Sonata sentimentale* ("Napoleon the Great"), Op. 33 (1807), and *Two Grand Sonatas*, Opp. 16 and 83 (1810, 1815). He also composed numerous smaller works for solo guitar, as well as pieces for the decacorde, a ten-stringed instrument of his own invention. Carulli's ensemble pieces include three concertos for guitar and orchestra, a number of chamber ensemble pieces, and two works designated as *Petit quator* and scored for guitar, violin, viola, and cello. He also wrote literally hundreds of duos for two guitars or guitar with violin, viola, flute, piano, harp, or voice.

In his compositions for guitar, Carulli sought to follow the ascendant path that virtuosic performers on more traditionally concertized instruments like the violin and piano were just beginning to forge at the beginning of the nineteenth century. Thus, virtually all of his works exhibit a balance between an expert display of technical prowess and more purely lyrical, musical concerns. Indeed, so extensive were Carulli's contributions that it is difficult to draw a clear line between virtuosity and expressivity. Whatever one's assessment of his compositional skill may be, perhaps his most enduring contribution to guitar music remains his extensive series of method books and writings on performing on and composing for the guitar. His inaugural *Méthode complette*, Op. 27 (1810), as well as the numerous supplemental studies and teaching pieces, became standard resources for countless performers throughout the subsequent century. *—Jeremy Grimshaw*

Recommended:

- ○ **Opere per Chitarra e Fortepiano Vol. 1** / Saracino, Palumbo / Nuova Era 7169
- ○ **Carulli: Guitar Sonatas Op21 Nos. 1–3 & Op5** / R. Savino / 1995 / Naxos 553301
- ○ **Carulli: Duetti e Trii** / Giorgio Sasso, Cardi, Guido Sasso / 2003 / Stradivarius 33586
- ○ **Opere per Chitarra e Fortepiano Vol. 3** / Saracino, Palumbo / Nuova Era 7167

Enrico Caruso

b. Feb. 25, 1873, Naples, Italy, **d.** Aug. 2, 1921, Naples, Italy
Tenor

The most famous operatic tenor of all time, Enrico Caruso (né Errico Caruso) was born on February 25, 1873 (not on February 27, as given in many reference books). He was the third child of his relatively poor parents—not the 18th, as is often repeated in popular myth. He began serious vocal studies with Guglielmo Vergine in 1891 and later studied with Vincenzo Lombardi. In 1895, he made his debut in *L'amico Francesco* by Domenico Morelli. That fall in Cairo, he sang *Cavalleria rusticana*, *La Traviata*, *Lucia di Lammermoor*, *La Gioconda*, and *Manon Lescaut*, all in less than four weeks.

His international fame began when he sang Loris in the premiere of Giordano's *Fedora* in 1898. In the following seasons, he sang at St. Petersburg, Moscow, Buenos Aires, Milan, Monte Carlo, and London. Arturo Toscanini conducted his Teatro alla Scala debut when he sang Rodolfo in *La Bohème*. Nellie Melba was his partner at his London debut in *Rigoletto*.

After making his very successful debut at the Metropolitan Opera as the Duke in *Rigoletto*, Caruso made the United States his primary operatic home. He spent the major part of each year singing there and usually had the honor of singing opening nights. He also took part in the annual Metropolitan Opera tour of the U.S., and in 1906 was caught in the great San Francisco earthquake right after his performance in *Carmen*. It was at the Metropolitan Opera that he sang the premiere of Puccini's *La fanciulla del West*.

As he aged, Caruso began to take on heavier roles including Samson, Eleazar in *La Juive*, and Vasco in *L'africaine*. After the tour each season, Caruso would travel to South America and/or Europe to sing and vacation. He never sang in his native city of Naples after 1902 because of a particularly nasty reception to his performances of Massenet's *Manon*. In 1920, he underwent several operations for pleurisy, but his health continued to decline afterwards. He returned to his native Naples, where he died in 1921.

Caruso's voice had a warmth, and an almost baritonal quality, which was different from the bright, ringing sound favored by most of the colleagues. The voice was extremely beautiful and he had an excellent feeling for the shape of a phrase. His sound recorded very well which helped to make his recordings among the most popular of his time; many of these selections have been available in one format or another since they were first issued. He was for many years the best selling classical performer in America.

Known as a generous colleague as well a great practical joker on stage, Caruso was welcome everywhere. He was a firm believer in good food, good wine, and a good cigar. However, whenever a friend was in a difficult situation, he was the first to offer help. One evening in Philadelphia when a colleague playing Colline became hoarse during a performance of *La bohème*, Caruso sang the bass aria for him to save the performance. During World War I, he sang in many benefit concerts to raise money for the war effort. To this day Caruso is imprinted in the imagination as the archetypal operatic tenor. *—Richard LeSueur*

Recommended:

- ○ **Caruso: Complete Recordings Vol. 1** / Caruso, etc. / 2000 / Naxos 110703
- ○ **The Early Recordings** / Caruso, etc. / 1999 / Nimbus 7900
- ○ **Greatest Tenor in the World** / Caruso, etc. / 1999 / BMG 63469 2
- ○ **The Legendary Caruso** / Caruso, etc. / 1999 / EMI 67006

Lisa Della Casa

b. Feb. 2, 1919, Burgdorf, Switzerland
Soprano

During her career, Swiss-born soprano Lisa Della Casa was known for her engaging portrayals of Mozart and Strauss roles, particularly Strauss' Arabella. She began her studies at the age of 15 with Margarete Haeser, who remained her only teacher. Della Casa made her debut as Cio-Cio-san in 1941 in Solothurn-Biel and in 1943 became a member of the Zürich City Theater. In normal times she no doubt would soon have been singing in houses in Germany, Austria, and Italy as well, but she remained in neutral Switzerland until after World War II ended in 1945. One of her first major appearances outside Switzerland was at the Salzburg Festival in 1947. Engaged for that production on the recommendation of Maria Cebotari, she sang the part of Zdenka in Strauss' *Arabella*. She was engaged right away to return the following year for another Strauss role, that of the Countess in *Capriccio*.

Della Casa became a member of the Vienna Staatsoper (Vienna State Opera) in 1947, but continued singing with the Zürich City Theater until 1950. In Zürich she sang a wide variety of roles: Pamina in *The Magic Flute*, Gilda in *Rigoletto*, and, unusually, Serena in *Porgy and Bess* (the Gershwin estate's insistance on all-black casting for that opera has not been followed in Europe as carefully as in the United States). She also sang a noted world premiere in Burkhard's *Die schwarze Spinne* as "The Young Woman" (1949) and created the triple role of the female leads in Gottfried von Einem's *Der Prozess* (1953).

She made her British debut as the Countess in Mozart's *Nozze di Figaro* at Glyndebourne in 1951, and sang the title role of Strauss's *Arabella* for the first time at her Munich debut the same year. Arabella became her signature role. Her first appearance at Covent Garden was in that role on a tour with the Bavarian Staatsoper. Critics found in her voice the "spring and silver" that Strauss said he called for in such parts, and her attractive and elegant looks and unmannered acting style made her an audience favorite.

She sang regularly at the Metropolitan Opera from 1953 to 1968, again appearing as Mozart's Countess. Of Mozart's heroines, she excelled in Donna Elvira, Donna Anna, Pamina, and Fiordiligi. She sang Chryothemis in Strauss's *Elektra*, in *Ariadne auf Naxos*, and even tried *Salome* (an attempt she admitted was an experiment). Since she had a wide range, she became one of the few singers to excel, in turn, in all three of the major parts in *Der Rosenkavalier*: Sophie, Octavian, and Die Marschallin.

In 1952, she received the honorary title of *Kammersängerin* of Austria. She was invited to sing at the Bayreuth Festspielhaus in 1952, where she appeared as Eva in *Die Meistersinger*. She was, however, bothered by the lingering sense of the darker side of German nationalism she sensed at that shrine to Richard Wagner and turned down all further requests to sing there.

She had a reputation as a thoughtful, highly principled artist and person. She was known for her criticism of the dishonorable aspects of the "music business" and loathed the intrigues, jealousies, and cabals that often infested the operatic world. She also felt that star egos prevented major singers from working together as ensembles. She retired from singing unexpectedly in 1974.*—Joseph Stevenson*

Recommended:

- ○ **Strauss: Arabella** / Solti (cond.), Della Casa, London, Dermota, Guden, Vienna PO / 1998 / Decca 460230
- ○ **Strauss: 4 Last Songs and more** / Bohm, Moral, Hollreiser (conds.), Della Casa, Guden, Poell, Schoeffler, Bierbach, Vienna PO / 2000 / Decca 467118
- ○ **Gluck: Orfeo ed Eurdice** / Monteux (cond.), Della Casa, Stevens, Peters, Rome Opera House Orch. / 2000 / RCA 63534

Pablo Casals

b. Dec. 29, 1876, Vendrell, Catalonia, Spain, **d.** Oct. 22, 1973, San Juan, Puerto Rico
Cellist

As the first modern cello virtuoso, Pablo Casals created a new appreciation of the instrument and its repertory when the concert stage was still considered the exclusive playground of the piano and violin. Casals also devoted his formidable musical skills to composition and conducting, leaving many insightful readings of the standard orchestral repertory to posterity via recordings. He is remembered today as much for his pacifism and regard for human life as for his musicianship (he once stated that "the life of a single child is worth more to me than all my music").

Casals came to his true instrument relatively late in life, having first developed some degree of skill on the piano, violin, and organ. Discovery of the cello at the age of 11 led to studies (from 1887 on) with J. Garcia at the Barcelona Municipal Music School. After a period of supporting himself playing in local cafés, Casals was granted a royal scholarship to the Madrid Conservatory in 1893, where he worked with Tomás Bretón, and later in Brussels in 1895.

After a brief tenure as a cellist at the Folies-Marigny music hall in Paris, Casals returned to teach and perform in Barcelona, and joined the first of a series of notable chamber ensembles with which he would be associated: a piano trio with Belgian violinist Crickboom and well known pianist and composer Enrique Granados. In 1919 Casals founded the Orquestra Pau Casals in Barcelona. Although the project was quite successful, the outbreak of civil war in 1936 forced its dissolution. Casals, who spoke out vehemently against the Franco regime, was forced to seek refuge in the Catalan village of Prades. Following the Second World War, saddened by the lack of any definitive action against the Franco regime by major world powers, Casals elected to cease performing as an act of protest.

Inspired by the Bach bicentenary celebrations of 1950 at the first annual Prades Festival, Casals came out of retirement to begin a new series of recordings and concerts. In 1956 he made a new home in Puerto Rico, where he founded the Puerto Rico Festival. Though nearing 85, he began a campaign for peace in 1962, traveling around the world to conduct performances of his oratorio *El pessebre* (The Manger). Casals continued to make occasional concert appearances until virtually the end of his life in 1973.

Casals' impact on cello playing in the twentieth century cannot be overestimated. His radical approach to bow and finger technique produced a mechanical prowess far beyond any other cellist of the late nineteenth or early twentieth centuries. In addition, Casals was the first cellist to incorporate the kind of left-hand shifting techniques which had been employed for decades by violinists, thus allowing for far greater agility on the cello than had been previously thought possible. Always scornful of "flashy," superficial virtuosi, Casals strove tirelessly to develop and maintain the kind of intense musical concentration which he considered to be the true artist's responsibility.

Casals' virtues as a composer are less unimpeachable; very little of his music was published during his life. Works such as his *Hymn to the United Nations* (1971), on text by W.H. Auden, and, of course, *El pessebre* (composed 1943–60) did receive numerous performances, but his works received little more than cursory notice by the musical establishment. However, the steadfast devotion which so defined his performing persona is evident in such works as the *Revérie for cello and piano* (1896), or the much later *Sonata for violin and piano*, which he worked on sporadically from about 1945 to 1972. *—Blair Johnston*

Recommended:

- ○ **The Legendary Pablo Casals** / Casals, Schulhof (piano) / 1999 / EMI 567008
- ○ **Bach: Cello Suites** / Casals / 2003 / EMI 62617
- ○ **Beethoven: Cello Sonatas 3–5** / Casals, Serkin (piano) / 1989 / Sony 45680
- ○ **Casals: Early Recordings 1925–1928** / Casals, Mednikoff, Gendron / 1994 / RCA 61616
- ○ **Beethoven: Trio 1; Schubert: Trio 2** / Casals, Horszowski, Istomin, Schneider, Fuchs / 1993 / Sony 58988
- ○ **Dvořák & Boccherini Cello Concertos; Bruch: Kol Nidrei** / Szell, Ronald (conds.), Casals, London SO, Czech PO / Opus Kura 2043

Alfredo Casella

b. Jul. 25, 1883, Turin, Italy, **d.** Mar. 5, 1947, Rome, Italy
Composer: Keyboard, Concerto, Orchestral

Alfredo Casella was an outstanding if uneven composer who led several of his contemporaries—Respighi, Malipiero, Pizzetti, and others—in a struggle to modernize Italian music. His interests as a composer and as an author of articles on music were highly cosmopolitan, as may be gathered from his early enthusiasms for Debussy, the Russian nationalists, Strauss, Bartók, and Schoenberg. Yet Casella was also intensely inspired by Italian culture, both its folkways and its Futurism movement.

His formal studies began in 1896 at the Paris Conservatory, under Fauré; he won first prize in piano in 1899, and soon was touring Europe and Russia as a pianist. He also began accepting guest-conducting stints in the early years of the century, a pursuit that would greatly occupy his time after World War I. But before the war the piano was his primary pastime, especially while he served as a keyboard instructor at the Paris Conservatory from 1912 to 1915. He spent most of the war back in Rome, succeeding Sgambati as piano professor at the Santa Cecilia Academy. In 1917 he founded the short-lived Società Nazionale di Musica, which produced controversial concerts of modern Italian and foreign music. Meanwhile, Casella was also one of the figures—again, including Respighi—pushing for a revival of Renaissance and Baroque Italian music. Beyond this, he published valuable editions of the keyboard works of J.S. Bach, Mozart, Beethoven, and Chopin.

Casella spent a great deal of his time in the 1920s as a guest conductor in the United States, appearing with orchestras in Chicago, Detroit, Cincinnati, Cleveland, and Los Angeles; his American debut in 1921 with the Philadelphia Orchestra showcased his talents as conductor, composer, and pianist. Casella conducted the Boston Pops from 1927 to 1929, but his advocacy of modern music annoyed the public. Nevertheless, his efforts on behalf of contemporary music (including his own works) were recognized with a substantial prize from the Musical Fund Society in Philadelphia in 1928, and with the Coolidge Prize in 1934.

In 1938, Casella made the dubious decision to return to Fascist Italy, and he remained in his homeland until his death. He seems to have been one of those naive Fascists who welcomed many of the movement's reforms without understanding their full implications. His opera *Il Deserto tentato* praised Mussolini's Ethiopian campaign, yet Casella was married to a French Jew and promulgated the music of the "degenerate" Jewish modernist Schoenberg.

As for his own compositions, the early works, particularly his first two symphonies (1905 and 1909), were extremely modernistic for their time; that is, they were influenced by Richard Strauss and Gustav Mahler (Casella even transcribed the latter's *Seventh Symphony* for piano, four hands). But Casella eventually settled into an energetic, spiky neo-classicism owing much to Stravinsky and something to Ravel. This more personal style became evident with his 1924 ballet *La Giara*. Ironically, Casella is now remembered less for his original works than for a couple of brilliant pastiches of earlier composers' pieces: *Scarlattiana* for piano and orchestra, and the vibrant *Paganiniana* for orchestra. The true breadth of his range and interests is evident from three works, one from each phase of his career: *Italia*, a 1910 orchestral rhapsody based on Italian folk tunes; the neo-classical 1925 *Partita for Piano and Orchestra*; and the quasi-serialist 1944 *Missa solemnis pro pace*. *—James Reel*

Overview of Works (1900–1944)

Best-known for his work as the head of the Italian section of the International Society for Contemporary Music and his advocacy of new music, Italian composer Alfredo Casella is hardly remembered as a composer. And when he is remembered, it is for uncharacteristic pastiche works like *Scarlattiana* (1926) after the works of Scarlatti or *Paganiniana* (1942) after the works of Paganini. The real Casella was a modernist composer who was the Italian equivalent of Stravinsky or Hindemith. Casella's works are generally divided by critics into three manners. The earliest manner (1900–13), exemplified by his *First* (1905) and *Second* (1908–09) symphonies, is marked by the influence of Mahler, whose works Casella conducted during his student years in Paris. The second manner (1913–20) is aggressively modernist and reveals the influence of Bartók and Schoenberg in works like the *Piano Sonatina* (1916) and the Tagore songs for voice and piano *L'adieu à la vie* (1915). Most of Casella's music was written in his third manner (1920–44), a neo-classical style that retained some small touches of modernism in its dissonant melodies and chromatic harmonies, but that was predominantly linear and lyrical with the influence of Italian folk songs, and indeed nineteenth century Italian opera was thoroughly dominant. Casella's masterpiece, the grand opera *La donna serpente* (The Woman Serpent) (1928–31), is his great work in the third style. Although there are hints of a monumental fourth manner in the late *Missa solemnis*, with its quasi-serial chromaticism, Casella died before he could realize its potential. *—James Leonard*

Recommended:

- ○ **Alfredo Casella: Piano Music** / S. I. Bartoli, Guerrini / 1998 / ASV 1023
- ○ **Alfredo Casella: Liriche** / Duo Alterno / Nuova Era 7371

KEYBOARD

Pagine di guerra, for piano, 4 hands, Op. 25 (1915)

In 1915, although Europe could not know it at the time, World War I had only just begun. Also in its infancy at that time was the use of silent film reels as a means of recording the events of war; it was this that inspired Italian composer Alfredo Casella's musical work *Pagine di guerra* ("Pages of War") for piano, four hands, Op. 25 (1915). Each of the four pieces in *Pagine di guerra*, which Casella describes as "short impressions," was suggested by a specific cinematic image of wartime Europe, as noted by Casella in the titles and subtitles.

The first is "Nel Belgio: sfilata di artiglieria pesante tedesca"; it concerns itself with the Germans' heavy artillery use in Belgium. The second, "In Francia: davanti alle rovine della cattedrale di Reims," translates as "In France: in front of the ruins of the Cathedral of Reims." No. 3 provides an image of Cossack cavalrymen and is titled, "In Russia: carica di cavalleria cosacca"; and the last "impression" is simply called "In Alsazia: croci di legno ..."—"wooden crosses...."

Pagine di guerra is of the bitingly dissonant and rhythmically punctuated style that Casella began to explore about a dozen years into the new century. The two pianists combine their strengths to create (in No. 1) a sharply percussive juxtaposition of staccato and legato; the march of men and artillery is made plain through the music. Parallelisms of the sort found throughout Debussy's work—fifths in the secondo part and entire chords in the primo part—draw the ancient and now-ruined Cathedral of Reims to life, while a lively Allegro molto vivace, at first quiet and "staccatissimo" but growing ever louder and more furious as the army draws nearer, calls the Cossack cavalry into musical existence. For the "wooden crosses..." music, Casella keeps things texturally simple and transparent; a lightly swaying berceuse and an ethereal final sonority (E major in the lower voices, D sharp major in the upper) remember the victims of war.

Casella fashioned an orchestral version of *Pagine di guerra* in 1918. *—Blair Johnston*

Recommended:

○ **Casella: Piano Music** / S. I. Bartoli, Guerrini / 1998 / ASV 1023

Pupazzetti, for piano, 4 hands, Op. 27 (1915; revised 1920)

The year 1915 was a year of pianoforte duets for Italian composer Alfredo Casella—first came *Pagine di guerra*, Op. 25, and then the better-known *Pupazzetti*, Op. 27, both for piano four hands. Never again did Casella write for piano four hands, and, as he quickly made orchestral versions of both *Pagine di guerra* and *Pupazzetti*, one wonders whether an orchestral work might in each case have been his original plan. Perhaps the realities of wartime musical life convinced him to first make a more practical version of each work for just two players.

Aside from the similarity of instrumentation and the shared year of creation, *Pupazzetti*, Op. 27, has little in common with *Pagine di guerra*, Op. 25; for while Op. 25 boldly faces the grimmer facts of war ("Pages of War" is a translation of its title), *Pupazzetti*, described by Casella as a group of five pieces for marionettes, seeks to provide a few moments of humorous escapism. Casella had, during the 1910s, begun to explore deeply the music of such progressive composers as Stravinsky and Schoenberg; given the puppet-oriented subject matter of the present work and its frequent focus on snappy, firmly punctuated rhythms, it is probably safe to say that Stravinsky's ballet *Petrushka* is among its immediate predecessors. But Casella's music is sufficiently his own to warrant the fame that these five pieces had during the 1920s and 1930s, especially in the orchestral version of 1920.

The five pieces of *Pupazzetti* are: 1. Marcetta, 2. Berceuse, 3. Serenata, 4. Notturnino, and 5. Polka. (One might note how *Pagine di guerra* and *Pupazzetti* are musically connected by the appearance in each of a shadowy, quietly swaying berceuse.) In addition to the orchestral version, Casella in 1918 shaped *Pupazzetti* into a work for nine chamber players. *—Blair Johnston*

Recommended:

○ **Works by Auric, Busoni, Casella, Hindemith, Ravel & Schoenberg** / Muller & Steigerwalt / 1992 / Centaur 2127

CONCERTO

Concerto for piano, violin, cello & orchestra, Op. 56 (1933)

Casella was an occasional visitor to Busoni's soirées at the latter's famous Berlin apartment—a meeting place for a new generation of artists (e.g., Weill, Vogel, Krenek) as well as all of cultivated Europe—and both men felt the pull of native *Italianità*, though where it became but one aspect of Busoni's ironic, increasingly esoteric art, it loomed as Casella's spiritual and musical salvation.

A prime example is Casella's so-called *Triple Concerto for Piano, Violin, Cello and Orchestra*, composed in 1933. A work for such forces cannot but invite comparison with Beethoven's *Triple Concerto*, and Casella was quick to call attention to differences. "While Beethoven deliberately gave each of the three instruments... a specifically bravura and brilliant function, in my Concerto the three solo instruments form a little block of sound which is contrasted with the orchestral mass exactly as the *concertino* is contrasted with the *ripieno* in the old concerto grosso. The form of the first movement recalls for the last time in my work the bi-thematic structure of Beethoven, but it is completely changed by a third theme which appears at the beginning of the introduction and which is combined with the others in the symphonic development." The choice of performing forces owes less to any former work, however, than to the fact that, from 1930, Casella, with violinist Alberto Poltronieri and cellist Arturo Bonucci, performed worldwide as the Trio Italiano; while the resurrection of the concerto grosso neatly combined an Italian model with the neo-classical turn Modernism had been taking over the preceding decade or so and forecasts similar works by Vaughan Williams and Bloch. The concerto's often harsh dissonance indicates a calculated truculence lending a fillip to the work's already robust gait and has no functional significance in its straightforward diatonic design. Of the central Largo, Casella justly notes that it is "without precedent in my other works because of its relative serenity and its luminous, soft transparency, which is probably due to the Sienese landscape where it was written." The concluding Rondò is a gigue, or tarantella, *in modo populare*, though its themes are original. The concerto received its premiere on November 17, 1933, at the Berlin Staatsoper with the Trio Italiano under the baton of Erich Kleiber. *—Adrian Corleonis*

Recommended:

○ **Casella: Triple Concerto, Concerto for strings, piano & percussion; Cello Concerto** / Panni (cond.), M. Rizzi, A. & F. Pepicelli, Orch. i Pomeriggi Musicali Milano / 1996 / Dynamic 169

ORCHESTRAL

Serenata for small orchestra, Op. 46bis (1930)

Alfredo Casella's *Serenata for small orchestra*, Op. 46bis of 1930, is an orchestral arrangement of the *Serenata* that he composed three years earlier for clarinet, bassoon, trumpet, violin, and cello (Op. 46 proper, a work upon which the Musical Fund Society of Philadelphia bestowed its First Prize in 1928). The only significant difference is that the orchestral version is in five movements, while the original is in six; Casella omitted the second movement of the original when making the chamber orchestra version.

The *Serenata* hearkens back to the occasional serenades of the eighteenth century, with its concise dance movements and light, entertaining style; gracefulness, in true neo-classical fashion, is here more important than cutting-edge musical narrative. The pieces in the *Serenata* are: 1. March, (2. Minuet, omitted in Op. 46bis), 3. Notturno, 4. Gavotte, 5. Cavatina, and 6. Finale (tarantella). *—Blair Johnston*

Recommended:

○ **Casella: Chamber Music** / Ex Novo Ens. / 2000 / ASV 1085

○ **Casella: Paganiniana; Serenata; La Giara** / C. Benda, Orch. della Svizzera Italiana / 1998 / Naxos 553706

Mario Castelnuovo-Tedesco

b. Apr. 3, 1895, Florence, Italy, **d.** Mar. 17, 1968, Hollywood, CA

Composer: Chamber Music, Concerto

Little of Italian-born composer Mario Castelnuovo-Tedesco's music has ever been published or performed. As a result, he is better remembered as a teacher of other well-known musicians (counting future luminaries André Previn and Jerry Goldsmith among his pupils) than as a composer in his own right.

Born in Florence during the last years of the nineteenth century, Castelnuovo-Tedesco studied piano and composition at the Florence Conservatory, eventually taking diplomas in both subjects (piano 1914, composition 1918). While primarily studying with noted Italian composer Ildebrando Pizzetti, Castelnuovo-Tedesco also attracted the attention of Italian composer, pianist and conductor Alfredo Casella, who would become one of the young composers earliest champions.

After successfully supporting himself as a freelance composer and pianist during the 1920s and 1930s, Castelnuovo-Tedesco, a Jew, found it advisable to leave Europe in 1939 to avoid persecution under the Hitler and Mussolini regimes. Relocating to California, he spent the next decade and a half scoring films for major studios (including *The Day of the Fox*, 1957), while concurrently serving on the faculty of the *Los Angeles Conservatory* (1946 on). In his later years Castelnuovo-Tedesco worked on an autobiography (left unfinished upon his death in 1968).

While far less than half of Castelnuovo-Tedesco's vast output has ever been released, it is generally acknowledged that his finest work is to be found in the earlier music (such as the short piano piece *Questo fu il carro della morte* from 1913). Even by the 1920s his rapid method of production and corresponding overestimation of his own skills had led to a style of composition which, although occasionally of high merit, frequently borders on formless self-indulgence. During the American period such works as the *Sonatina zoologica* show a tendency to revert to the simpler, altogether more successful music of his early days, though the tendency to inflate ideas beyond the scope demanded by their intrinsic merit remains apparent in works like *Tobias and the Angel*, Op. 204 from 1965.

Aside from a brief flirtation with serialism during the American years, Castelnuovo-Tedesco's basic style of composition remained unchanged from the 1920s onward; only the quality and scope of execution varied. Perhaps his most important contribution is to the literature for the guitar, for which the composer shows great fondness in his two concertos and many chamber pieces for the instrument (the second concerto being for two guitars).*—Blair Johnston*

CHAMBER MUSIC

Capriccio diabolico, for guitar ("Omaggio a Paganini"), Op. 85 (1935)

A few years before leaving Italy in 1938 in the face of rising anti-Semitism, Mario Castelnuovo-Tedesco had written this charming ten-minute piece, ostensibly as a tribute to Paganini. Having composed it for the guitar virtuoso Andrés Segovia, he consciously attempted to draw a parallel between himself and Paganini. Will the latter ever be separated from that disparaging word, diabolical? Naturally, one will recognize thematic references to Paganini here, but the music is still Castelnuovo-Tedesco's own, even if the listener is often stylistically taken back to the early nineteenth century. The work opens with a dramatic introduction based on the main theme, then goes on to present that theme in a lively creation that, not surprisingly, divulges an Italianate character. The melodic material is deftly worked out as the music takes on a heroic manner in the central sections. In the latter part of the piece, it grows increasingly difficult, as rapid-fire notes heighten tension and bring on blazing colors, the music building toward a virtuosic climax. This brilliant piece will appeal to most fanciers of serious guitar music. *—Robert Cummings*

Recommended:

○ **The Art of Segovia** / Segovia / 2002 / DG 471697

Platero y yó, for narrator & guitar, Op. 190 (1960)

Platero y Yo (*Platero and I*) exemplifies a late phase of Castelnuovo-Tedesco's style, during which he became more interested in the relationship between music and other arts. It is inspired by a book written in 1914 by Juan Ramon Jiménez (1881–1958), the Spanish poet who was awarded the Nobel Prize in Literature in 1956. The poet and the composer had intriguingly parallel lives: They were both sons of bankers and overcame parental opposition to focus their lives on their creative endeavors; they were both exiled from their Fascist home countries in 1939; both found refuge in America.

"Platero y yo" is the story of a poet and his silvery gray donkey who was both traveling companion and confidant. In 1960 Castelnuovo-Tedesco conceived for Andrés Segovia a work of 28 pieces for guitar and narrator (the poem contains more than 100 chapters). A performance of the entire work would take around 50 minutes. A selection of ten numbers for guitar only, was also sanctioned by the composer as a more concise portrait of the charming animal and his master. Castelnuovo-Tedesco cautioned that in such cases the audience should know the story of Platero and his poet. Castelnuovo-Tedesco divided the series into four groups of seven pieces, each section ending with a reflection on Platero's death. The pieces, which do not follow any order of the original chapters, range from descriptions of events in the lives of the poet and the donkey to the poet's reflections on the people and places they visit around their Spanish village. In much of the suite the music primarily supports the spoken words; there are no recurring themes or motives to represent the characters. The guitar paints musical pictures of birds, village festivals and dancing, the colors of the sky at twilight, at times using such techniques as staccato to represent trotting, harmonics in an address to the moon, habanera rhythms, and a toccata to welcome Spring. The nature of the music is as gentle as Platero himself. *—AMG*

Recommended:

○ **Platero & I** / Koonce, Dan Doyle, narrator / 1995 / Summit 1002

Sonata "Omaggio a Boccherini," for guitar, Op. 77 (1934)

As Mario Castelnuovo-Tedesco began to assume a more conspicuous presence in the musical world, he made the significant acquaintance of premier guitarist Andrés Segovia. Their subsequent friendship led in 1932 to the creation of the composer's first guitar works. The following year, Segovia suggested that Castelnuovo-Tedesco write a work in honor of his countryman Luigi Boccherini, who was well known. The result was the Op. 77 *Sonata, "Omaggio a Boccherini"* (Homage to Boccherini). The work is dedicated to Segovia, who contributed his expertise to the fingerings.

Berlioz once observed that it is impossible to compose properly for the guitar unless one is a player (which he was—but ironically he wrote almost nothing for the instrument). There is some truth in his contention, but with a modicum of knowledge of the instrument's physical capabilities, a composer such as Castelnuovo-Tedesco (himself a pianist) was able to provide challenging and rewarding entries in the guitarist's repertoire; a truly competent guitarist knows where alternate notes lie on the fingerboard and is well-equipped to leap hurdles. In the present work, the connection between eighteenth and twentieth centuries is more in the vein of Stravinsky than Prokofiev; knotty forms of tonality are contained within the archaic rhythms. The current work opens with a highly chromatic and energetic first movement, somewhat in the tempo of a gavotte and based primarily around a rocking motif. Although in the guitar-friendly key of D major, the piece uses much barring for a sharper, less lyrical sound, further compounded by shifting meters. A long held dolce chord on the tonic leads to the Andantino movement in G minor, melancholy in nature though alleviated somewhat midway by an allegretto section. Another long-held D chord, this time acting as dominant, leads to the minuet, also in G minor. Here is a delightful nod to the age of elegance, the most securely tonal of the movements, with the trio in the parallel major of G. Also less tonally ambiguous than the opening sections is the vivacious perpetuum mobile of the finale, which requires great agility on the part of the player; this is brought into contrast with a more chromatic "alla marcia." An unusual progression of full chords finally nestles itself into a perfectly voiced final cadence. *—Wayne Reisig*

Recommended:

○ **The Segovia Collection Vol. 2** / Segovia / 2003 / DG B000066302

CONCERTO

Guitar Concerto No. 1 in D major, Op. 99 (1939)

In the early 1930s Mario Castelnuovo-Tedesco became concerned about the situation of Jews in his native Italy. When severe purges hit the country in 1938, Castelnuovo-Tedesco, himself Jewish and a well-known figure in Italy's musical community, was quickly targeted. "I happened to be the 'pioneer,'" he wrote later. "My music was suddenly banished from the Italian radio and some performances of my works were cancelled." Official anti-Semitism drove Castelnuovo-Tedesco to emigrate to the United States in the summer of 1939. Settling initially in New York, he eventually became an American citizen and lived in the country until his death in Hollywood in 1968. It was during the stressful year of 1939 that he wrote the *Guitar Concerto No. 1*; the work was dedicated to legendary guitarist Andrés Segovia, who gave its first performance in Montevideo.

Castelnuovo-Tedesco composed dozens of works for the guitar, both solo and with orchestra. He understood the instrument and knew how to balance the comparatively quiet guitar with the volume of an orchestra. The composer has indicated that the present concerto's orchestration was designed "to give more the appearance and the color of the orchestra than the weight." In later years Segovia used the *Concerto* as a counterexample to the proposition that a solo guitar cannot be heard over an orchestra.

The first movement, Allegretto, opens with a mock-stately melody in a neoclassical style, and proceeds at an easygoing gait; its orchestration is quite transparent, sometimes taking on an almost Impressionistic shimmer. A short cadenza and a final flourish close the movement. The gently melancholy second movement, Andantino alla romanza, is based on three Italian folk songs. Segovia described it as Castelnuovo-Tedesco's "tender farewell to the hills of Tuscany which he was about to leave." A rustic, somewhat tongue-in-cheek tune is the basis of the third movement, Ritmico e cavalleresco. Slower, more mysterious regions are explored in a contrasting central section. An extensive cadenza, a return of the movement's opening melody, and a final flourish closes out the work. *—Chris Morrison*

Recommended:

○ **The Great Guitar Concertos** / C. Groves (cond.), J. Williams, English CO / 1989 / CBS 44791

Alfredo Catalani

b. Jun. 19, 1854, Lucca, Italy, **d.** Aug. 7, 1893, Milan, Italy

Composer: Opera

Alfredo Catalani created richly romantic operas intended to create a synthesis of Wagnerian opera and Italian operatic tradition.

Lucca was home to two established musical families, the Puccinis and the Catalanis. Alfredo was born four years ahead of Giacomo Puccini. He and young Puccini both studied music, as boys, with Fortunato Magi, Puccini's uncle. Catalani's progress was rapid, and he was sent to Paris where he studied with Bazzini, though he did not enroll at the Paris Conservatory. He returned to Lucca in 1873 to report for military service, but was rejected due to tuberculosis. He went to Naples to study with Antonio Bazzini. Bazzini introduced him to the salon of Clara Maffei, which was frequented by young artists, musicians, and literary figures like Arrigo Boito and Franco Faccio. They introduced him to Wagner's music, which made a large impression on him. Ignoring the developing trend of verismo opera, Catalani emulated Wagner in choosing, often, tales of the fantastic, with dramatic action. He received a commission from publisher Giovannina Lucca. The result, *Elda*, was based on the *Lorelei* legend and published in 1876 and performed in Turin with lukewarm results. *Dejanice*, the next opera, premiered in 1883 and did poorly.

Catalani was already in declining health due to his tuberculosis, and suffering from guilt over having an affair with his best friend's wife. He roused himself from depression to write a symphonic poem, *Hero and Leander*. Its success in 1885 gave him new confidence, and he wrote a successful opera, *Edmea*, which premiered at La Scala in 1886. The same year he was appointed professor of composition, at the Milan Conservatory to succeed Ponchielli.

Giovannina Lucca's publishing firm had been promoting his career, but it merged with the more powerful Ricordi firm. Ricordi was promoting Giacomo Puccini's career, and neglected Catalani, seriously damaging his prospects. He hired the composer Zanardi to carry out his planned revisions to *Elda*. Catalani got no support from Ricordi, and had to arrange for a performance himself. Retitled *Loreley*, the opera was given on February 16, 1890, in Turin, and was a success.

During this time, Catalani had been devoting his dwindling strength to writing a new opera, *La Wally*, based on a German romance. The conductor Mascheroni realized that the success of *Loreley* might make Ricordi more receptive to this new opera. Though Catalani was embittered by his treatment by the firm, Mascheroni brought about a reconciliation. Ricordi accepted the work and promoted it, securing a La Scala premiere on January 20, 1892. It was a huge success, particularly after it was adopted by Arturo Toscanini, who conducted it widely and even named his daughter "Wally." Catalani is remembered today almost entirely for *La Wally*. He started another opera, based on a Tolstoy text, but soon after starting work suffered a hemorrhage, and died five days later. *—Joseph Stevenson*

OPERA

La Wally (1892)

La Wally was premiered at a time when Italian verismo was emerging, but this opera was not a part of that school. Rather, it reflected its composer's interest in the works of Wagner and other figures of the late Romantic period. Although it is seldom performed outside of Europe (especially in Italy), the work is known to many opera enthusiasts through its Act One aria for the heroine, *"Ebben?... No andrò lontano,"* a haunting reverie on the theme of traveling alone and far from home. The aria, aside from its popularity as a concert piece among prominent spinto and dramatic sopranos, was introduced to viewers of the cult film *Diva.*

Catalani lived a short life. He was dead at the age of 39, only a year and a half following *La Wally*'s premiere at Milan's La Scala on January 20, 1892. This opera was his final stage work. Earlier, Catalani had enjoyed some success with *Elda* (1880), more so in its revised form as *Loreley*, first performed in 1890. *La Wally* enjoyed the presence of such celebrated singers as Emmy Destinn and Pasquale Amato when the Metropolitan Opera presented it for the first time in 1909. On the podium for those four performances was Arturo Toscanini, whose advocacy was important to such success as was enjoyed by Catalani's works. The setting for *La Wally* poses some difficulties in staging. The Swiss mountain scenes must give a sense of both height and depth. The conclusions of both the third and fourth acts fail if the audience cannot believe that the ravine, in the former, and the mountain pass, in the latter, are real and dangerous. Still, for the company with modern stage facilities, which can pull together a rich-voiced star soprano, a dramatic tenor, a baritone who exudes villainy and a conductor who can build and maintain a high level of tension, *La Wally* can be a rewarding venture. *—Erik Eriksson*

Synopsis:

Act One. The opera begins in the Swiss Alps, in a large square in Hochstoff. It is the 70th birthday of the landowner Stromminger, whose house is seen nearby. In the midst of conversation with Vincenzo Gellner, bailiff of the neighboring village of Sölden, young Walter passes in search of Stromminger's daughter, Wally. Walter is a ballad singer who often goes into the mountains with Wally to sing, and his presence arouses joking comments from the crowd. Gellner is in love with Wally, but she doesn't love him. When he presses the issue, declaring that she must be his, she counters that she is "free as light, as the wind" and will never be his. Despite her father's protests, she declares that she'll take to the road with Walter and that together they'll spend their days singing.

Act Two. It is a year later. Stromminger has died; Wally has inherited his wealth and holdings and has come back to the village. On the morning of Corpus Christi, Giuseppe Hagenbach is seen with his friends at Afra's Inn in Sölden, talking about how elusive Wally seems. Gellner approaches Wally to insist that Hagenbach is about to marry Afra. On the dance floor, a kissing game is begun. Hagenbach takes up a challenge to win from Wally a kiss. In doing this, he turns around the feather in his hat, a sign that whatever promises he makes do not need to be honored. He dances with Wally and tells her, "I want you, mine, mine, for always!" After Wally abandons herself to him, the other dancers begin to laugh. When Wally realizes that she has been deceived, she asks Gellner, "Do you still want me?" When the answer is yes, Wally tells him she wants Hagenbach dead.

Act Three. In the evening of that same day, Wally and Walter are seen strolling back to Hochstoff. As the sky darkens, Gellner returns and, after bidding his friends goodnight, extinguishes the street lamp and lies in wait near the bridge. Hagenbach is seen approaching, on his way to offer an apology to Wally. Gellner emerges swiftly from the shadows, attacking and heaving Hagenbach into the ravine below. He then taps on Wally's windowpane to inform her that her wishes have been attended to, but she, having been agonizing over her demand, is mortified. She grabs Gellner by the throat and forces him toward the bridge. As she hears a moan below, she lets go, and Gellner runs off. At Wally's cries for help, the townsfolk arrive and are able to pull Hagenbach from the ravine, his body lashed to Wally's. To Afra, she says, "God is returning him to you." Kissing Hagenbach, Wally cries, "Farewell, farewell."

Act Four. Wally has ventured off to her mountain cabin. Walter arrives to urge her to return to the village for Christmas. She declines, and Walter leaves her once more to her reverie. The voice of Hagenbach is heard in the distance, although at first Wally is hallucinating and does not comprehend it. When Hagenbach comes into view, he is stricken by the worry and suffering shown on her face. After telling her of his search for her, he cries, "I love you, Wally!" She tells him he cannot love from pity, but he protests that the kiss he had taken from her was truly a "kiss of love." A storm builds, but the lovers are scarcely aware of it at first. Finally, its ominous roar engulfs them both as Hagenbach tries to move down the trail from which he had come. He disappears in the storm, calling for Wally. Suddenly, he is heard to shout "The path has vanished!"—and soon thereafter a cry is heard from below. Wally is now thrown to the ground by the crashing avalanche. Clinging to the precipice, she stretches her arms outward, and with a cry of "open your arms to me, blessed heart," she leaps into the snow-whipped valley below. *—Erik Eriksson*

Recommended:

○ **Catalani: La Wally** / Cleva (cond.), Tebaldi, Del Monaco, Cappuccilli, Monte Carlo National Opera Orch. / 1989 / London 425417

Emilio de' Cavalieri

b. ca. 1550, Rome, Italy, **d.** Mar. 11, 1602, Rome, Italy

Composer: Vocal

Cavalieri was a major figure in the early Baroque, producing several of the cantatas and pastorales that led the way to Baroque-style oratorio and opera, as well as intermedi, ancestors of the intermezzo and of opera in general. His *La rappresentazione di Anima e di Corpo* is claimed by some music scholars as the first oratorio, by others as the first opera. Most of his works are lost, but contemporary writings and commentaries suggest that he might also have written the first recitative.

Unlike many composers, he was born into the aristocracy, and held various positions for the Rome branch of the de' Medici family, as well as that of organist for the Oratorio del Santissimo Crocifisso. When Ferdinando de' Medici became Grand Duke of Tuscany in 1587, Cavalieri went with him to Florence where he superintended the court's artistic employees, including artists and musicians, and was a sort of stage manager and producer for plays and dances, as well as Inspector General of Arts and Artists. Florence was home to the Camerata Fiorentina, of which Peri, Corsi, Marco da Gagliano, Giulio and his daughter Francesca Caccini, and Vincenzo Galilei were members, and is arguably the city where opera and oratorio were born. The first major performances of his works were in 1589, when Ferdinando married Christine of Lorraine, and among the entertainments were the play *La Pellegrina*, for which Cavalieri wrote intermedi (musical interludes somewhere between incidental music and intermezzos), including the *Ballo del Gran Duca*, for which many later composers wrote variations and improvisations. During the succeeding year, for further court entertainments, he wrote various pastorales and solo cantatas, none of which survive. However, since much of the music of his Florentine contemporaries survives, we do have a sense of what they might have been like.

In 1600, his *La rappresentazione di Anima e di Corpo* was first performed at the Oratorio della Vallicella in Rome. While often described as an oratorio, it was drawn from the old morality plays, and Cavalieri left specific instructions for its dramatic presentation as well as recommendations for the orchestration, choreography, and for the vocal ornamentation. It was originally performed as a three-act work with two intermezzos between each act. While he returned to Florence to supervise and participate in the entertainments celebrating the wedding of Maria de' Medici and Henry IV of France, he soon returned to Rome. His health and eyesight were both failing, and he died there shortly afterwards. *—Ann Feeney*

VOCAL

La rappresentatione di anima e di corpo, musical morality play (1600)

Morality plays date back to early medieval times, but this is nonetheless a seminal work in music drama. It was the first printed score to have a figured bass and the first musical morality play to survive fully intact. While the composer took advantage of its being the first *printed* recitar cantando (sung recitative) score to claim that the style was his sole invention, and Jacopo Peri declared him an innovator who made the new style possible, most scholars also give Peri and their contemporary Giulio Caccini roughly equal credit for the development of the style. Aside from these firsts, it also has extended and detailed recommendations for the performers, giving much more of a sense of how it would have been presented in its own time and at least an insight into general performance practices.

It was premiered in Rome, at the Oratorio (literally "prayer house," the musical style took on the name of the house, much like "zarzuela") of the Chiesa Nova, where the founder, Filippo Neri had started a tradition of performances of spiritual music for the public. While entertainment was a vital part of these presentations, the goal was to educate and to inspire meditation, and so in the notes, the composer instructs the singers to be sure to deliver the words clearly and with full attention to their meaning, and to act not only with their hands, but with other movements.

He also provided specifics for the singers' ornamentation and for the orchestration, and for performances in theaters, he even recommended certain steps and sequences for the dances, as well as writing an alternative eight-part choral ending if it was not possible to perform the four-part chorus with dances. (Peri was not only a composer and musical administrator for the Medici family, but also a voice teacher, dancer, and organist.)

While it lasts only about an hour, there are 90 separate musical numbers, including solos, choruses, recitatives, dialogs, and sinfonias. There is also a remarkable five-part sinfonia after the first act whose structure suggests the development of the modern symphony, with its emphasis on the interrelation of the contrasting parts.

Most of the creativity in this work, however, is concentrated in the style and structure, rather than the music itself, and it is easy to point out various musical clichés (especially in the rhythm), as well as a lack of expressiveness compared to Monteverdi or even Peri. However, it is still one of the most important examples of early music drama and provides an invaluable insight into early Baroque performance. *—Ann Feeney*

Recommended:

- ○ **Cavalieri: Rappresentazione di Anima e di Corpo** / Maerzendorfer (cond.), Sarroca, Jahn, Bomches, Mozarteum-Orchester Salzburg / 1999 / Orfeo d'Or 517992
- ○ **Cavalieri: Rappresentatione di Anima e di Corpo** / Vartolo (cond.), Cappella Musicale di San Petronio di Bologna / Naxos 554096

Pietro Francesco Cavalli

b. Feb. 14, 1602, Cremona, Italy, **d.** Jan. 14, 1676, Venice, Italy
Composer: Opera

After Monteverdi's death, Pietro Cavalli became the leading opera composer in Venice. Tremendously popular during his lifetime, he was soon forgotten after his death, and his operas vanished from the stage until their resurrection toward the end of the twentieth century.

Cavalli's father, G.B. Caletti, was probably his first music teacher. Federico Cavalli, the Venetian governor of Crema whose name Cavalli eventually adopted, was taken with young Francesco's voice and brought him back to Venice with him at the end of his term. Cavalli entered the *cappella* of St. Mark's in Venice as a boy soprano in 1616. After his voice changed, he remained in the *cappella* as a tenor.

During Cavalli's first 25 years at St. Mark's, he sang under the direction of Claudio Monteverdi (1567–1643), with whom he cultivated a relationship, and with whom he may have studied formally. His earliest known publication is a motet printed in Leonard Simonetti's *Ghirlanda sacra*, an anthology of motets by 26 composers.

Cavalli supplemented his income from St. Mark's by taking other positions in Venice, including that of organist at the church of Sts. Giovanni e Paolo. He also sang and played at numerous church festivals. His marriage (January 7, 1630) to Maria Sozomeno brought the composer a substantial dowry and some measure of financial independence.

Cavalli was appointed second organist at St. Marks in 1639; at approximately the same time, he invested in the Teatro San Cassiano (the first public opera house in Venice [built in 1637]), and began writing operas for that theater. This proved to be a sound financial venture for Cavalli, since he earned far more money writing for the theater than he did from his position at St. Mark's. By 1670, he had composed 41 stage works, most for the San Cassiano. Cavalli's *Egisto* (1643), *Ormindo* (1644), and *Calisto* were all especially successful productions; these, as well as others, have been revived in the twentieth century (often by Raymond Leppard, who greatly altered Cavalli's scores).

Cavalli visited Paris twice, and a modified version of his *Serse* (1654) was given there in 1660 as part of Louis XIV's wedding celebration. This represented a compromise, because the opera Cavalli had been commissioned to compose, *Ercole amante* (Hercules in love), was not completed in time for the performance. Finished in 1662, *Ercole amante* is notable among Cavalli's works for the use of orchestral strings to accompany recitative; earlier works had made use of basso continuo alone.

The most popular of Cavalli's operas was *Giasone*, composed in 1649; it is a perfect example of Cavalli's stark division between recitative and aria. In the perhaps inevitable comparison between *Giasone* and Cavalli's other operas with the works of Monteverdi, the younger composer's recitatives are less passionate, less probing into the psyche of the character, and lacking in the variety of Monteverdi's. However, Cavalli's arias are more developed than Monteverdi's. Strophic in format, Cavalli's arias are generally in triple meter and the words are set syllabically, except for occasional decorative melismas. In each opera, there is usually at least one lament, often employing a repeated, descending bass line and resembling a passacaglia.

It is in his sacred works that Cavalli most resembles Monteverdi; his earliest known sacred piece, *Cantate Domino*, could be mistaken for a work by the older master. The conservative nature of Cavalli's sacred works no doubt stems from his desire to maintain the musical tradition of St. Mark's, developed in previous decades by Gabrieli and Monteverdi. *—John Palmer*

OPERA

Egisto (ca. 1643)

Egisto survives as the most representative and, in modest terms, most-often staged of Cavalli's 40-plus operas. In the style of the time, Cavalli classified *L'Egisto* as a "favola drammatica musicale," or musical dramatic fable. The libretto by Giovanni Faustini was drawn from Roman mythology, safely avoiding overt references to current events or personalities. Musically, Cavalli kept his lines clear. The work follows the standard format for Venetian opera of this period, including a prologue in which allegorical characters and gods prepare the audience for a drama played out in three acts. Here these are complemented by scenes at the end of the first two acts in which such allegorical characters return to comment on the central action. Although most scenes involve at least two characters, each character sings in turn rather than overlapping with others; the most significant exceptions are a sprightly duet between Venus and Amor at the end of the first act and music for Egisto and Clori in the opera's final pages. Singing alternates between extended recitative and a leisurely, florid, and sometimes doleful aria. Instrumentation was a matter of what was available, the assumption being there would at least be a modest body of string players and some sort of continuo group embellishing the spare bass line. Today's performers must decide whether to try to reproduce the forces available at a specific theater in the 1640s or to assemble some idealized orchestra that's both historically valid and rich enough to suit modern tastes.

After an instrumental sinfonia, in the prologue, the character La notte (Night) temporarily cedes rule of the earth to L'aurora (Dawn). The main story commences with Act One, in which Cavalli's sweet, gentle music evokes an Arcadian setting. Clori and Lidio, a young nobleman, declare their love for each other while Climene, formerly engaged to Lidio, wakes Egisto, formerly engaged to Clori, from a nightmare. Under the hostile watch of Venus, goddess of love, Egisto and Clori had been kidnapped and separated; the same fate has befallen Lidio and Climene, and now all four oddly find themselves together on the same island. The complications which follow include mischief made by Climene's brother Hipparco and the god Amor. Naturally, everything works out in the end, and under Amor's influence, the lovers return to their pre-opera pairings. *—James Reel*

Synopsis:

Prologue. Spring has come to the island of Zante in the Ionian Sea, and the kingdom of shadows yields to the rising sun and the reign of Phoebus. In other words, day breaks.

Act One. Lidio, a young nobleman, is exchanging words of tenderness with Clori, the former fiancée of Egisto, a descendant of the god Helios. Egisto is sleeping—only sleeping—in a grove with Climene, Lidio's former fiancée. Climene rouses Egisto from his nightmares; the young man explains that he and Clori had been kidnapped by pirates and separated, and that the hatred of the goddess Venus makes his life miserable. It turns out that Climene and Lidio have shared a similar fate, and were abducted from their wedding altar. Now Egisto discovers Clori in Lidio's arms; he and Climene realized they have been wronged, and implore the god Amor to avenge them.

Climene's brother, Hipparco, has also fallen in love with Clori, who scorns him, so Hipparco, too, has a reason to wish ill to befall Lidio. Clori defends herself by maintaining that she is merely a plaything of Amor, who extinguished her love for Egisto and sparked a new passion for Lidio. Meanwhile, back on Olympus, Venus is indignant that Egisto has escaped peril; her son, Amor, vows to drive Egisto insane.

Act Two. Amor's plan is taking effect; Egisto wallows in his confusion of sadness, doubt, love, and hate. He stumbles upon Clori, who decides the best course is to pretend not to recognize Egisto, proclaiming her former lover to be dead. Egisto longs for death.

Now Climene confronts Lidio, whom she finds singing Clori's praises. Lidio declares that his relationship with Climene is long over, and leaves the young woman to her sorrow. Hipparco learns from his sister of Lidio's disloyalty, and swears vengeance. Dema, Climene's confidante, ponders the situation; the arrogant Clori will fail in the end, she believes, because her beauty will fade over time, but if Hipparco doesn't overcome his Clori fixation, he will be doomed to lifelong bachelorhood.

Act Three. Lidio and Clori pause in a romantic grove, he musing on love and she praising the work of Amor. Nearby, Hipparco insists that Climene stab Lidio in revenge for his disloyalty, leaving the dirty work to his sister as he prepares to "console" Clori. Climene confronts Lidio, dagger in hand, but cannot kill him, and senses that he loves her again—Amor has changed Lidio's heart. So far so good, but Amor complains that his job is made too difficult by the fickle moods of women.

Egisto rails against fickle Clori; his insanity intensifies. Clori feels that she is responsible for Egisto's state, and is weeping at his side when he comes to his senses. Amor has taken mercy on all the lovers—except the ardent Hipparco—and restores the relationships as they were before landing on Zante. *—James Reel*

Giasone (1648)

In 1637, history's very first public opera house was opened in Venice. The early success of the San Cassiano theater inspired numerous imitators, which came and went on a regular basis during much of the remainder of the seventeenth century. Ultimately, San Cassiano became one of the less important houses, but it did witness the birth of many of the operas of the most important Venetian composer of the latter half of the century, Pietro Francesco Cavalli (1602–76). Cavalli arrived in Venice as a chorister at St. Mark's at the end of 1616, singing under the direction of Monteverdi, then *maestro di cappella* at the basilica. Later he became organist and finally, in 1668, took over Monteverdi's old post. Beginning in 1639, Cavalli composed over 30 operas for Venetian houses, nearly half of which received their first performance at San Cassiano. Among those that did so was *Giasone*, first performed on January 5, 1649. The work marked Cavalli's only collaboration with the librettist Giacinto Andrea Cicognino, who loosely based his tale on Apollonius' *Argonautica*. The work's structure follows the usual format of Venetian opera, with a prologue followed by three acts. As is customary, the prologue features gods who introduce the drama. Here, Apollo and Cupid debate the likely outcome of a drama which concerns the amorous intrigues of Jason and his quest for the Golden Fleece. To a greater degree than was common even in Venetian opera, mythological heroes and royalty rub shoulders with comic characters drawn from the lower orders to produce a kaleidoscopic mélange of noble sentiment and low humor. Musically, *Giasone* is of importance for achieving what Cavalli had been edging toward in his previous operas—a distinctive separation between recitative and aria. *Giasone* became the most frequently performed opera of the seventeenth century; it was performed all over Italy and is the only opera known to have inspired a play. Ironically, late in the century a reaction against the opera set in among literary critics for the very reasons that audiences had enjoyed it. One writer complained that "the hotchpotch of characters brought about a total destruction of the rules of poetry." The opera was also attacked for creating a distinction between aria and recitative, thus destroying the dramatic veracity and fluidity that had been the aim of the creators of opera at the start of the century. By the turn of the eighteenth century, such sentiments were to lead directly to the reform of opera, with the development of strict division between serious and comic elements. *—Brian Robins*

Synopsis:

Prologue. The mythical figures of Love and the Sun are found arguing. The Sun, protector of Medea, Queen of Colchis, delights in the pending marriage of Medea to Jason, leader of the Argonauts. Love, protector of Hypsipyle, Queen of Lemnos, curses any romance born without his blessing.

Act One. Hercules complains to his colleague Besso that Jason's long nights in the arms of his lover might leave him exhausted when the call to battle comes. Jason emerges, still groggy, to face Hercules' complaints himself. He has already fathered twin sons by Hypsipyle, whom he left on Hercules' advice; succumbing to another lover will only weaken him further; moreover, his current love has yet to reveal her face. Meanwhile, Medea is confronted by Aegeus, King of Athens and her former lover. He begs her to show him a final mercy by killing him; she appears to consent, but at the last moment throws down the dagger in derision. Elsewhere, Orestes arrives in Colchis, sent by Hypsipyle to spy on Jason, and meets Demo, the stuttering dwarf from Aegeus' court, who tells of Jason's new lover. Back at the palace, Medea reveals herself to Jason as the lover—and the mother of two more twin sons.

Act Two. Hypsipyle meets Orestes, whose news of Jason puts her in despair. Jason, meanwhile, has gone away to battle and, under the protection of a magic ring given him by Medea, returns with the spoil: the Golden Fleece. His ship is pursued by Aegeus and Demo, who have discovered the identity of the King's rival. The gods conspire to wreck Jason's ship, but it is Demo's boat that sinks, while Love slyly directs Aeolus' winds back toward Hypsipyle. She appears on the shore, begging Jason to return; he pretends she is insane and leaves with Medea. The only romance to emerge is that between Besso and Hypsipyle's maid Alinda.

Act Three. A twisted sequence of events: Hypsipyle discovers Jason and Medea asleep in the woods; upon awakening, Jason promises his old love that he will return to her if she will leave Medea undisturbed. Medea hears all, though, and compels Jason to promise to kill Hypsipyle. In his most elaborate deceit, Jason tells Hypsipyle to meet Besso later and ask him if Jason's orders have been carried out—which question will be Besso's cue to take her to Jason; Besso, however, has received different instructions: whoever poses the question is to be thrown into the sea. Hypsipyle stops to nurse her children before going to Besso, and is delayed; it is Medea who arrives, hoping to find out if Hypsipyle has been killed. She inadvertently asks the secret question, and is tossed into the sea. Aegeus, who has survived his shipwreck, arrives just in time to save her. She swears her fidelity to him and, upon encountering Jason, encourages him to return to Hypsipyle. As the opera closes, the gods celebrate Love's triumph. *—Jeremy Grimshaw*

Recommended:

○ **Cavalli: Giasone** / R. Jacobs (cond.), Chance, Banditelli, Dubosc, Concerto Vocale / HM 2901282/84

Sergiu Celibidache

b. Jun. 28, 1912, Roman, Romania, **d.** Aug. 14, 1996, Paris, France

Conductor

Romanian-born conductor Sergiu Celibidache spent his early life in Jasí, capital of Moldavia, and in 1936 commenced music studies at the Hochschule für Musik in Berlin. At age 33, after winning a conducting competition organized by Berlin Radio, he became conductor of the reconstituted post-war Berlin Philharmonic Orchestra, and toured with it to the British and American sectors of occupied Germany. In 1952 he shared the podium with the exiled Furtwängler, the Berlin Philharmonic's general music director, on a tour of the United States. Later that year when Furtwängler was cleared of allegations of being a Nazi sympathizer and he returned to Germany, Celibidache's appointment with the Berlin PO was terminated.

Thereafter, the larger part of his career was with the Radio Orchestras of Stockholm (1964–71), Stuttgart (1971–77), and Paris (1973–75). From 1979 until his death, he was music director of the Munich Philharmonic Orchestra and general music director of the City of Munich. Between 1983 and 1984, he conducted the student orchestra at the Curtis Institute in Philadelphia, U.S.

When a music student in Berlin, Celibidache also attended Berlin University where he studied philosophy and formed the Buddhist beliefs he retained throughout his life. He preferred the immediacy of a live performance rather than recordings and, according to his son, felt that recordings prevented the listener's spontaneous involvement with the music and gave a distorted representation of reality. Thus, though widely admired as an outstanding conductor, many of Celibidache's recordings were unauthorized, and some were of poor sound quality. It was not until after his death that, with the cooperation of his family, EMI Classics and Deutsche Grammophon released a substantial number of recordings, mainly of broadcast performances with the Stuttgart and Munich orchestras, but also with the Mannheim Philharmonic and London Philharmonic Orchestra. The repertoire is almost entirely Romantic and Post-Romantic, including Beethoven, Bruckner, Brahms, Richard Strauss, Debussy, Ravel, Tchaikowsky, Respighi, and Berlioz.

It is perhaps ironic that Celibidache should have received his widest exposure through a medium he did not approve. Yet his intense, finely-balanced and deeply-felt interpretations made him one of the greatest names in twentieth century orchestral conducting. Above all, he was a superb technician. Celibidache could not have asked for a better memorial than the current library of recordings, especially those in *The Celibidache Edition*, which includes lengthy rehearsal recordings (one lasts for 45 minutes, complete with English translations). Deutsche Grammophon's selection is mainly from earlier recordings made with the Stuttgart Radio Orchestra. Proceeds from both labels are given to the Celibidache Foundation for the encouragement of young musicians and a humanitarian organization he set up to assist needy people in Tibet, Romania, and other parts of the world. His own compositions include four symphonies, a piano concerto, and an orchestral suite which he recorded for UNICEF with the Stuttgart Radio Symphony Orchestra. *—Roy Brewer*

Recommended:

○ **Bruckner: Symphonies 7–9** / Celibidache (cond.), SWR Stuttgart RSO / DG 445471

○ **Bruckner: Symphony 4** / Celibidache (cond.), Swedish RSO / 2000 / DG 459665

○ **Celibidache: From the collection of Deutsches Rundfunkarchiv** / Celibidache (cond.), Berger, Machula, Berlin PO, Berlin RSO / Music & Arts 1079

○ **Sibelius: Symphonies 2 & 5** / Celibidache (cond.), Swedish RSO / 2000 / DG 469072

○ **Brahms: Symphonies 2 & 3** / Celibidache (cond.), SWR Stuttgart RSO / DG 495637

Pierre Certon

b. ca. 1510, France [?], **d.** Feb. 23, 1572, Paris, France

Composer

Very little is known of the early life of sixteenth century French composer Pierre Certon. He may have been a pupil of composer Josquin Desprez, though there is little concrete evidence to support such an assertion; certainly Certon could not have been much more than ten or eleven years old at the time of Josquin's death in 1521. Certon first figures into the factual historical record with an appointment as matins clerk at Notre Dame Cathedral, Paris in October of 1529. Certon's headstrong nature seems to have caused something of a strain between himself and his superiors, and when he was indicted in 1530 for initiating sporting activities within the Cathedral courtyard (and for missing the holy service) only the pity of the administration saved the young musician from being thrown in prison.

In 1532 Certon relocated to the Sainte Chapelle, where he remained until his death 40 years later. Although hired as a clerk, from November 15, 1536 on, Certon was officially in charge of the choirboys as well; as the years went by he assumed further musical duties within the diocese without ever abandoning his primary role as master of choristers. Towards the end of his life he was awarded a number of titles, mostly honorary, which indicate the esteem in which he was held by Church and court, and in 1570—just two years before his death—he became the third composer to earn the title "Composer of Music for the King's Chapel" (though the implications of this title are only partly understood).

In addition to his sacred duties, Certon participated in a number of secular musical activities throughout his life, and developed friendships and contacts with figures as diverse as composer Claudin de Sermisy (Certon's *Déploration* in memory of Sermisy, composed sometime after Sermisy's death in 1562, remains a powerful work) and the printer Hubert Jullet (of whose daughter Certon became the godfather).

From Certon's respectable output, eight masses, a magnificat, a wide array of motets, and almost 300 chansons survive. Six of the eight masses use the common sixteenth century technique of parody (the reworking of material from a pre-existing piece into a new musical structure), while the motets tend to combine canonic or ostinato use of cantus firmi with music paraphrased from various chansons. Certon's earliest chansons are composed in a rather melodically fragmented way, while towards the end of his life (and especially in the 1570 collection *Les meslanges*) a more homophonic texture involving as many as seven or eight voices begins to take shape. *—Blair Johnston*

Overview of Works (ca. 1540–1570)

The early life of French composer Pierre Certon (ca. 1510–72) is shrouded in some mystery although it is known that he was attached to the Sainte-Chapelle in Paris for several decades and remained so until the time of his death. He may have been born in Melun. He was appointed a clerk at Notre-Dame Cathedral in 1529 and it is recorded that in 1530 he found himself in trouble for refusing to attend services and instead playing games on the grounds of Notre-Dame. Identified as "Clerc sous la prébende de M. de Colligny" as of May 1532, he was made master of choristers in November 1536 and is so identified in Book II of his motets issued in 1542. He was made permanent chaplain in 1548 and held that title along with his music responsibilities throughout the remainder of his life.

While not a creator of innovative, or even particularly striking melodies in his spiritual and secular chansons, Certon was a figure of considerable industry, composing eight masses which have survived in their entirety (three additional movements were published in 1553 and may have belonged to others which did not). In six of these works, Certon follows form and style similar to those of his predecessors and contemporaries (referred to as parody), while the other two are based upon chanson and plainchant, respectively. In his *Missa pro defunctis*, he employed very simple opening and closing movements in contrast to middle sections of greater complexity. Certon's *Déploration*, written upon the death of his colleague and friend Claudin de Sermisy, bears notable resemblance to that written by Josquin Desprez to honor Ockeghem. Another signal work of Certon's was his "fricassée" based on a theme by Sermisy, *Vivre ne puis content sans ma maistresse*, and completed in 1538.

Several sets of motets were completed by Certon, the first collection of 24 issued in 1542 with at least 20 more finished by 1553. While owing something to Sermisy, they embrace more far-reaching influences, including those of the northern European masters. Ostinatos and canons conjoin with more complex textures to support melodic lines often taken all but directly from existing plainchant.

Certon wrote nearly 300 chansons which, taken together, chronicle his progress toward greater assurance in melodic invention. His final collection known as *Les meslanges* (1570) numbers 96 items, 84 of which are reworkings of earlier chansons. The three- and four-part voicings have been expanded to four- to eight-part largely homophonic realizations. Only 12 chansons in this collection are original works. The title page lists Certon as *"compositeur de musique de la chapelle du Roy"* (only the third composer to have received this title) just as in 1567 he was identified as *"chantre de la chapelle du Roy."* Both titles undoubtedly were honorary, but entirely in keeping with the numerous acknowledgements accorded the composer during his last three decades. *—Erik Eriksson*

Recommended:

○ **Cum Jubilo** / H. Chaney (cond.), Chior of St. Ignatius of Antioch / 1993 / Music & Arts 4798

Antonio Cesti

b. Aug. 5, 1623, Arezzo, Italy, **d.** Oct. 14, 1669, Florence, Italy

Composer: Opera

Antonio Cesti was an important composer of the seventeenth century Italian Baroque, particularly in the field of opera. Born Pietro Cesti, he adopted the name Antonio when he joined the Franciscan order. He had already been a choir boy in Arezzo. Although details of his musical training are uncertain, it seems likely he studied with Abbatini, and possibly with Carissimi and Luigi Rossi. He joined the Franciscans in Volterra in 1637, was elected organist of the Cathedral there in 1643, and in 1645 was confirmed as master of music of the Volterra seminary and of the Cathedral.

The powerful Medici family became his patrons. Through them, he became acquainted with a literary group called the Accademia dei Percossi, who wrote texts for his cantatas and, eventually, opera libretti. It has been assumed that his first successful opera was *Orontea*, produced in Venice in 1649. However, evidence suggests this opera may have been written in 1656 for Innsbruck. Whatever the case, Cesti built an increasingly successful career as a secular composer and singer. He was reappointed at the cathedral in July 1649, but there were clearly conflicts between his vocation and his increasing material success outside the Church, which led to a love affair with the married singer Anna Maria Sardelli. Salvator Rosa, one of the members of the Percossi, wrote of it, "it is ever thus with anyone who would behave as though he were neither friar nor layman." In October the Superior-General of the Franciscans rebuked his monastery for permitting Cesti's "dishonorable and irregular life." Undeterred, Cesti wrote two more popular operas for Venice, *Il Cesare amante*, and *Alessandro vincitor di se stesso*, in 1651 and 1652. Cesti left the monastery in 1652 to accept a position at the court of Archduke Ferdinand Karl in Innsbruck, Austria. Although he made some trips back to Italy (primarily to recruit singers) he remained in that position through 1657.

He then moved to Rome, evidently with the ulterior purpose of ingratiating himself with the Pope so he could be released from his vows. Cesti, a fine tenor who often took leading roles in his own and others' operas, sang for the Pontiff four times, was released from his vows in March 1659, in the understanding he would remain a secular priest, and that year joined the Papal Choir. In 1661 the Pope granted him leave for a temporary trip to Florence in connection with the wedding festivities of Duke Cosimo III of Medici and the French Princess Marguerite Louise d'Orléans. From there, he went straight back to Innsbruck and Ferdinand Karl, while the angered Pope threatened to excommunicate him.

Cesti went on with continued success in opera and was even rewarded by the Archduke with an abbotship. When a new Duke inherited in 1665, Cesti moved with him to Vienna, affording him even greater scope for his operas. He died in 1669, and some sources indicate that his death was rather sudden, suggesting he may have been poisoned. *—Joseph Stevenson*

OPERA

Orontea (1649)

Although little known today, Antonio Cesti (1623–69) was one of the most important Italian composers of the second half of the seventeenth century, the only figure to seriously challenge the dominance of Cavalli as an opera composer. Born in Arezzo, he began his peripatetic career in Venice, Cavalli's own territory. His earliest Venetian operas, of which *Orontea* has frequently but erroneously been cited as one, conformed to the type popular in that city during the middle of the century. Such operas consisted of a prologue followed by three acts of swiftly moving drama involving a mixture of dramatic recitative, arioso, and strophic arias. Arias were most frequently allotted to the comic characters, usually servants and other members of the lower orders. By 1652, Cesti had been appointed to the Innsbruck court of the Archduke Ferdinand Karl, and in 1666 he joined the imperial court of the music-loving Leopold I in Vienna. There, intense activity culminated in the production of his gargantuan *Il pomo d'oro* in 1668, one of the most famous events in early operatic history. Spread over the two evenings, and featuring lavish staging, ballets, and a named cast of over 40 in addition to a large chorus, *Il pomo d'oro* is said to have run for over nine hours.

Orontea, first performed at the court theater in Innsbruck on February 19, 1656, makes rather more modest demands. Indeed, its high repute today is based on a plot of unusual dramatic veracity and on Cesti's sympathetic treatment of human characters as opposed to gods. The libretto, revised for Innsbruck by Giovanni Filippo Apolloni from a previous Venetian setting of the opera, revolves around Orontea, Queen of Egypt, who has forsworn love. Rather inconveniently, she falls in love with Alidoro, a humble young painter, who is revealed as a prince (and therefore an eligible suitor) only at the denouement. Although the plot, which also involves a secondary romantic couple, is handled with a light touch by both librettist and composer, it does not exclude some highly affecting music for the perplexed *Orontea*. But there are also many moments of high humor, a genre at which Cesti excelled. These particularly involve Gelone, a drunken court servant and his sidekick, the young page Tibrino. In its fluidity and its brilliant intersections of musical style and character, *Orontea* must be accounted one of the most successful operas in the later seventeenth century Venetian style. Along with Cavalli's *Giasone*, it was also one of the most popular, finding revival on many occasions. *—Brian Robins*

Synopsis:

Performances and recordings of this romantic comedy may differ in details because surviving manuscripts contain varying material, including extra arias and even a different prologue, but the general outline of the story holds constant.

Prologue. Old lady Philosophy and young god Love are bickering and taunting each other. Love decides to demonstrate the superiority of his worldview by flying off to Egypt to vanquish the philosophical Creonte, who mocks love.

Act One. Creonte, adviser to queen Orontea, is not mocking love at all; he urges his ruler to surrender her prideful freedom (her aversion to romantic entanglements) for the good of the realm (which would be more secure if she produced an heir). Just then, coincidentally, young page Tibrino leads in the handsome Alidoro, a foreigner and a commoner, who has been assaulted; he is accompanied by Aristea, his mother. Orontea is instantly smitten with the newcomer, a painter. While this infatuation begins to percolate, the drunken servant Gelone stumbles through a love scene involving courtiers Corindo and Silandra, whose affair will soon be threatened by Silandra's attraction to Alidoro. The act ends with a comic scene between Gelone and Tibrino, whose exchange does nothing to advance the plot.

Act Two. Orontea is marveling at her love-struck condition when who should arrive but her former confidante, Giacinta, who had been abducted years before and carried off to Phoenicia. Now she has made her way back to Egypt dressed as a boy. It turns out that Giacinta was the person who had attacked Alidoro, under orders from the lovesick and vengeful Queen of Phoenicia, whose court Alidoro had abandoned. Creonte prevents Orontea from killing Giacinta on the spot in retaliation for her assault of Alidoro. Giacinta flees and, in her boyish disguise, inadvertently catches the eye of old Aristea. Elsewhere, Silandra brushes off Corindo and enjoys an assignation with Alidoro. This comes to the attention of the jealous and furious

Orontea. Eventually, though, Alidoro realizes he truly loves not Silandra, but the queen.

Act Three. Silandra is trying to win back Alidoro, while servants gossip about the queen, mad with love. Creonte makes a formal objection to Orontea's infatuation with a commoner, so for the good of the realm, Orontea breaks off her involvement with Alidoro. He licks his wounds in the arms of Silandra, who now, perversely, is inclined to reconcile with Corindo. The action moves briskly as Aristea continues to pursue the disguised Giacinta, and Alidoro challenges Corindo to a duel over Silandra. Before the fight can take place, though, uproar ensues when a royal medallion resembling one owned by Orontea is found on Alidoro. It turns out that Alidoro is actually the son of the King of Phoenicia and had been kidnapped by pirates as a child and raised by Aristea, a pirate's wife. His pedigree established, Alidoro may now marry Orontea. The queen orders a double wedding: the reconciled Silandra and Corindo will join them at the altar. *—James Reel*

Recommended:

○ **Cesti: Cantate; Orontea (excerpts)** / R. Jacobs, Concerto Vocale / HM 901100

Emmanuel Chabrier

b. Jan. 18, 1841, Ambert, Puy-de-Dôme, France, **d.** Sep. 13, 1894, Paris, France
Composer: Orchestral, Keyboard, Opera

Although music seems to have been his passion all along, it was not until nearly the age of 40 that Chabrier turned to composition as his full time career. When he finally did this, he crafted works characterized by brilliance, wit, and vivid harmonic, rhythmic, and orchestral coloring.

As early as age six, Chabrier began piano lessons under the tutelage of a Spanish refugee named Saporta. At ten, he attended the Lycée Impérial at Clermont-Ferrand, where he continued his keyboard studies and began to try his hand at composition. Upon the insistence of his father, however, he relegated music to be his pastime; after two years in Paris at the Lycée Louis le Grand (or the Lycée Saint Louis—biographers disagree on which is the case), he began to study law. He continued also to take piano lessons and studied counterpoint and fugue, but when he took his law degree in 1862, he went to work for the Ministry of the Interior, where he worked for 18 years. During this time, he associated with the painter Manet and the poet Verlaine and fellow musicians including Duparc, d'Indy, Fauré, and Messager. On December 27, 1872, he married Marie Alice Dejean.

In 1879, he made his first visit to Germany in the company of Duparc; a performance of Wagner's *Tristan und Isolde* in Munich so moved him that he determined to quit the law and devote his life to music. He returned to Paris, resigned from the Ministry on 12 November 1880—just two months before his 40th birthday—and began to spend his days composing.

Before this monumental step, Chabrier had produced only two significant works, these being the operettas *L'Étoile* (1877) and *Une Éducation manquée* (1879); however, now freed of his routine job, he produced in short order *Dix Pièces pittoresques* for piano (1881), *Habanera* (1885), and *Bourrée fantasque* in 1891. His finest short work, the brilliant *España Rhapsody*, came forth in 1883; this piece alone established Chabrier as a composer of serious merit.

In the years 1884 and 1885 he worked as chorus master at the Château d'Eau where, among other projects, he assisted with a production of Wagner's *Tristan*. This close association with Wagner's music both developed his skill in orchestration and instilled in him some elements of Germanic style; in later years, these elements would appear in his own works, much to his own consternation and that of his musical compatriots in France.

Arguably Chabrier's finest work, the comic opera *Le Roi malgré lui* (based upon a comedy by François Ancelot) was premiered at the Opéra Comique on May 18, 1887. Still a rather old-fashioned work, in which sung portions were interspersed with stretches of dialogue, it was rebuffed by modernists; it was nonetheless considered spirited and delightfully original.

Considering his very late start and lack of substantial formal training, Chabrier must be regarded as brilliant. His music is extremely colorful, and he was particularly adept at integrating forces and resources to create a unified sound world. Not so much a dramatist as a lyricist, Chabrier seemed most comfortable writing in the realm of comedy; evidently this is an accurate reflection of his personality in general. He was a fundamental influence on Les Six, the group of young French composers who typified the emerging French nationalism in the generation following him; they took him as a model, stopping short of his later Wagnerian turn. He also heavily influenced the work of Maurice Ravel. When viewed in the context of his relatively short career, Chabrier's output indeed labels him as an overachiever.*—Michael Morrison*

ORCHESTRAL

España, rhapsody (1883)

From July to September 1882, Emmanuel Chabrier and his wife traveled in Spain, starting out from San Sebastián and winding up in Barcelona. Chabrier was enthralled with everything he saw and heard in Spain, and his impressions are recorded in an abundance of letters sent from the Iberian Peninsula by the composer to friends. In one such letter addressed to conductor Charles Lamoureux, Chabrier boldly states that "my rhythms, my tunes will arouse the whole orchestra to a feverish pitch of excitement; and you too will feel obliged to hold [your assistant] in your arms, so voluptuous will be my melodies." These were strong sentiments indeed, for up to this time Chabriér had been known primarily as a ne'er-do-well amateur composer of unsuccessful operettas.

All of that would change when the finished work, *España*, was given at the Concerts Lamoureux in Paris on November 4, 1883. It was immediately encored, and afterward routinely requested (and played) at Lamoureux Concerts and elsewhere for weeks afterward. The tunes were whistled in the streets of Paris. *España* made Chabrier an overnight celebrity in Paris, and he would reap the benefits of its fame to the end of his days. The work's single movement is in the shape of a Spanish dance in three beats, with a rhythm suggesting the strumming of a guitar.

España was written as a piano piece, and in later years Chabrier made something of a specialty out of it, pounding it out on bad pianos in cafés to the astonishment of onlookers. Of the work Chabrier himself said that "it is in F major and consists of nothing else." In this laconic statement there is a grain of truth; the primary melodic ideas that drive *España* are neither terribly original nor substantive. It is the tremendous rhythmic energy of the piece, combined with Chabrier's colorful orchestration, that puts the piece over. And it did have impact on other musicians for long afterward; Stravinsky, perhaps half-consciously, echoes the central trombone part of *España* in the final tableau of his *Petrushka* (1911). The work's delightful melody became a hit song in the 1950s under the unlikely title "Hot-Diggity."

While most experts do not hold Chabrier's *España* in the same exalted regard that they do his other orchestral works, such as *Marche Joyeuse* or *Bourrée fantasque*, the piece is still Chabrier's best-known composition as far as the public is concerned. It is worth noting that *España* did not do as well in Germany, where Chabrier's operas had already proved successful in German translations. In Spain, where the Spanish-flavored music of French composers such as Ravel, Debussy, and Bizet have long been respected and played, the Chabrier is yet looked upon as a weak sister of the zarzuela overture. Chabrier's realization of the Spanish idiom was so close to the "real thing" that in Spain it seemed too familiar. Although this might be seen as something of a backward compliment to *España*, it also echoes the sentiments of French musicologist Louis Bourgault-Ducoudray, who wrote shortly after the 1883 premiere, "Emmanuel Chabriér belongs to that school of pioneer composers who copy Nature and are above all concerned to respect the truth." *—Uncle Dave Lewis*

Recommended:

○ **Fantastic Philadelphians** / Ormandy (cond.), Philadelphia Orch. / 1999 / RCA 63313

○ **Chabrier: Orchestral Music** / Paray (cond.), Detroit SO / 2004 / Mercury 000339536

Joyeuse marche (Marche française) (1888)

The short *Joyeuse marche* of nineteenth century French composer Emmanuel Chabrier is his second most popular orchestral work, with his *España* taking the lead. Both of these works were written in 1888, along with his *Prélude pastorale*. Chabrier also drew that year upon his previously published piano pieces as a source for new orchestrations. Four 1881 vintage pieces from the *Dix Pièces pittoresques* were refashioned into the *Suite pastorale*, and Chabrier also pressed into orchestral service a *Habanera* written in 1885. All of these works were first presented at a concert conducted by Chabrier in Angers, France, on November 4, 1888. This group of pieces forms the core of Chabrier's stand-alone orchestral music.

As for the *Joyeuse marche*, it is indeed joyous, even comical. In this work, Chabrier interrupts a high-stepping march with little tongue-in-cheek quotations and technical surprises that were designed to amuse the audiences of his day and to furrow the brows of his colleagues. Modern audiences generally do not "get" the jokes, but the spirited good fun of the *Joyeuse marche* is enough to put the work over in any situation, and that is what has kept it vital as a concert favorite.

There are a couple of unusual facts relating to the *Joyeuse marche*. First of all, the work did originate as a piano solo, despite that most sources cite Chabrier's piano version as an "arrangement." Secondly, there is a considerable amount of confusion regarding the correct title of the work. At its 1888 premiere, the *Joyeuse marche* was entitled "Marche française." By the time of its Paris premiere the following year, the title had been changed to "Marche Joyeuse," and in 1890 it first appeared on a *Concerts Lamoureux* program as *Joyeuse marche*. The last-named title is used as the standard in France, probably as it represents Chabrier's own final thoughts on the matter. However, outside of France the title "Marche Joyeuse" appears interchangeably with *Joyeuse marche*, and in English-speaking nations this alternate title tends to be favored. *—Uncle Dave Lewis*

Recommended:

○ **Chabrier: España, Suite Pastorale** / Paray (cond.), Detroit SO / 1991 / Mercury 434303

Suite pastorale (1888)

"Without hesitation," Poulenc wrote, "I declare that the *Pièces pittoresques* are as important for French music as Debussy's *Préludes*." Only seven of the ten were given by Marie Poitevin at their *Société Nationale* premiere, August 9, 1881—according to Cortot—though among them were the four numbers Chabrier would later orchestrate as his *Suite pastorale*, and for which he seems to have had an especial fondness. But to speak of them merely as piano music, or of the *Suite pastorale* as a pianist's music orchestrated, as is sometimes done, is to miss Chabrier's distinctive compact richness and his exquisite awareness of style.

Ostensibly polite drawing room fare evoking pleasant country scenes, the first number of the *Suite pastorale*, "Idylle," on the keyboard, demands, *sans pedal*, a Lisztian legato for its fetching melody, simultaneously accompanied by two motoric parts in Alkanesque staccato. Though the pianistic allusions are lost, the superb and constantly varied resourcefulness with which their effects are transferred to the orchestra demonstrates the implicitness of Chabrier's orchestral imagination in one of his most pianistic pieces. After the quietly percolating animation of the "Idylle", the "Danse villageoise" has all the rumbustious vigor of a rustic clog dance. Turning raucous in its orchestral guise, it is set off by a fleet trio whose additions of instrumental color shade its spirited frolic with winsome grace. As in the first two pieces, the undulating charm of the gently ecstatic "Sous-bois" provides a foil for high-kicking gaiety in the concluding scherzo-valse. In their alternations of boisterousness and *tendresse*, we have the essential Chabrier.

Too often, such distinguished composers as Berlioz, Fauré, and Chabrier—quintessential Parisians all—were forced to seek recognition in the provinces or abroad. Chabrier orchestrated the *Suite pastorale* for a Chabrier festival offered by the Association Artistique of Angers, which he conducted November 4, 1888, with his *Habanera*, the *Joyeuse marche*, *Prélude pastoral*, and *España*. During rehearsals under his direction, the orchestra caught on immediately to his rollicking style and were convulsed with laughter, while the critics, though generally approving, felt obliged to comment on Chabrier's "Wagnerism"—an astounding charge as nothing could be further from the heavy metal solemnities of Wagner's scores than these scintillant, often coruscating, dialogues between subtlety and *éclat*. *—Adrian Corleonis*

Recommended:

○ **Dukas: La Péri; Chabrier: Suite Pastorale** / Tortelier (cond.), Ulster Orch. / 1990 / Chandos 8852

○ **Chabrier: Orchestral Works** / Paray (cond.), Detroit SO / 2004 / Mercury 000339536

KEYBOARD

10 Pièces pittoresques (1881)

Chabrier is one of the great originals. Through the common musical language of his day—the salon song, the piano genre piece, comic opera—he transformed everything he touched with an irresistible combination of verve, drollery, and refinement. His piano writing is *sui generis* and utterly inimitable because it is pure invention. "Without hesitation I declare that the *Pièces pittoresques* are as important for French music as Debussy's *Préludes*," Francis Poulenc noted. But that is hindsight—until late in his broken-off career, Chabrier was dismissed as an amateur, a dilettante. Maintaining by day a civil service career in the Ministry of the Interior, Chabrier entered capaciously into the life of the grand boulevards, the cafés, the salons, a-swarm with poets, artists, and musicians—thus this son of the Auvergne became the quintessential Parisian.

One would have had to be very discerning to detect genius—though it is there—in such sporadic productions as the *Marche des Cipayes* (1863) and the *Impromptu* (1873) for piano. His exquisitely spirited operettas, *L'Étoile* (1877) and *Une Éducation manquée* (1879), lifted the inspired fooling of Offenbach into a transcendental dimension, but they had only limited exposure.

In the summer of 1880, Chabrier made a pilgrimage to Munich with Henri Duparc to hear Wagner's *Tristan und Isolde*—a decisive experience leading to his resignation from the Ministry in November. And in 1881 the ten *Pièces pittoresques* appeared. Following their première, given by Marie Poitevin at a concert of the Société Nationale de musique, August 9, 1881, César Franck remarked, "We have just heard something quite extraordinary. This music is a link between our epoch and that of Couperin and Rameau."

The "Paysage" of the first number could be by Watteau—with a raucous *commedia del arte* troupe disembarking. The 18 bars of "Mélancolie" open on a daydream of exquisite wistfulness. "Tourbillon"—"whirlwind"—dusts up hat-snatching, skirt-lifting coruscations to vanish as suddenly as it began. Over an undulating ostinato, "Sous-bois" insinuates a melody redolent of the most blithesome happiness. Through the intricate exoticism of the "Mauresque," frolicsome can-can girls languorously disport themselves. Sans pedal, a fetching legato melody—*avec fraîcheur et naiveté*—spins out over an obsessive two-part staccato accompaniment to evoke an hypnotic "Idylle." The "Danse villageoise" is foot-stomping rustication recollected in crisply elegant satire, to contrast superbly with an "Improvisation" of extended Schumannesque fantasy. Wickedly self-parodying, the "Menuet pompeux" appealed sufficiently to the fastidious Ravel that he orchestrated it. And the "Scherzo-valse" brings the revels to a close with scintillant suggestions of supernatural gaiety.

The sustained alchemy of the *Pièces pittoresques* owes largely to what has since come to be called "crossover"—the *sec* crackle of the *style sévère* played off against sensual Lisztian legato, old modal inflections and new harmonic "audacities" (usually ascribed to Debussy in his prime), commonplace expectations met by the most persuasive melody—the genre piece touched with Falstaffian, Pan-ic genius.

Chabrier himself orchestrated the "Idylle," "Danse villageoise," "Sous-bois," and the "Scherzo-valse" in 1888 as the *Suite pastorale*. *—Adrian Corleonis*

Recommended:

○ **Piano Works of Chabrier** / Stott / 1995 / Unicorn Kanchana 9158

OPERA

Le roi malgré lui (1884–1887)

"I would rather have written *Le Roi malgré lui* than the *Ring of the Nibelungen*." So wrote Maurice Ravel of Emmanuel Chabrier's comic opera *Le Roi malgré lui*, or *The Reluctant King*. Chabrier's previous opera, *Gwendoline* (1885), to that time his most ambitious score, had been premiered in Brussels, Belgium, on April 10, 1886. It was very successful, but after just two performances the theater went bankrupt. Disappointed but not disillusioned, Chabrier launched straight into the writing of a new comic opera. Writers Emile de Najac and Paul Burani were given the job of turning Ancelot's 50-year-old play *Le Roi malgré lui* into a libretto. The result, however, was a confusing mess, so Chabrier had his poet friend Jean Richepin rewrite it. Richepin got well into the job but eventually gave up, disgusted, and Chabrier himself had to complete the revision. The music, however, proceeded with much less strain, and Chabrier completed it in early 1887 after just nine months of work, producing a lively and melodic score as well as a diverse one—patter song, love music, a bit of heavy Wagnerian drama (reflecting Chabrier's love of the music of the German master), and energetic dances are all part of the mix.

The opera is based, loosely, on historical figures and events. After the death of King Sigismund of Poland in 1572, the country became an elective monarchy and chose as its new king the Frenchman Henri of Valois, Duke of Anjou. Henri didn't really want to leave France, however, and Chabrier's opera deals with Henri's machinations to avoid becoming Poland's king. The opera ends with Henri's decision to become King of Poland after all; the historical Henri reigns there until 1574, at which point he returns to France to become its King on the death of his brother, King Charles IX.

Le Roi malgré lui was premiered by the Opéra-Comique of Paris on May 18, 1887. Despite the complexities of the plot, Chabrier's music won the day and the performance was very well received, with several numbers encored (although the librettists were booed). But, shades of *Gwendoline*, the theatre burnt down after just three performances. Six months later the opera was taken up again at the Théâtre Lyrique, Place du Châtelet, and thanks to the support of the noted Wagnerian conductor Felix Mottl, the opera was also performed several times in Germany. But the work seemed to lose favor with the public, to a large extent due to the poor libretto (which was revised substantially for revivals in 1888 and 1929), and it has seldom been performed since that 1929 revival. Some excerpts from the opera, notably the Fête polonaise from the beginning of Act II, have taken on their own life in the concert hall, ensuring that the work Chabrier once referred to as a "comic opera with elaborate undies" has not disappeared completely from view. *—Chris Morrison*

Synopsis:

Act One. Henri de Valois and his court are in a castle outside Krakow not long after Henri's election as King of Poland. The Comte de Nangis arrives with soldiers for the King's Guard; they sing their loyalty to Henri, who will be crowned the following day. Poland is largely united behind Henri, but the country's aristocrats, led by Prince Palatine Albert Laski, would rather have Archduke Ernest of Austria as their new king and are conspiring to that end. The Duke of Fritelli, who has been appointed Chamberlain by the French, is planning Henri's coronation procession—but no one knows that Fritelli is married to Laski's niece Alexina and is himself one of the conspirators. For his part, Nangis is in love with the slave Minka, who works for Laski; the two sing a love duet and agree to meet later that evening. Henri enters, depressed by being forced to abandon France to become Poland's king. Fritelli overhears part of Henri's sad aria in which he longingly sings of France and of a beautiful Polish princess with whom he'd had an affair in Venice some time back. Fritelli realizes that this princess is none other than his own wife Alexina! Alexina herself appears and tells Fritelli of a conspirators' meeting set for that evening at a ball at the home of her uncle Laski's; in a duet, Fritelli sings of his love for Alexina and Alexina of her ambitions for Fritelli's future. Minka enters looking for Nangis, but encounters Henri. Thinking him simply one of Nangis' friends, Minka tells Henri of Laski's plot and Fritelli's role in it. Henri is delighted, seeing an opportunity to leave Poland behind and return to France. The craven Fritelli is confronted and confesses all. Henri will grant him mercy, however, if Fritelli will take him to the conspirators' meeting. Henri will be disguised as Nangis, whom he imprisons to get him out of the way. Henri, Fritelli, and Alexina sing a comical trio in which they discuss their past alliances and the present conspiracy. Minka and the soldiers join the ensemble as Nangis escapes, unbeknownst to everyone.

Act Two. The Introduction and famous Fête polonaise open the act, accompanying the dancers' cries of delight at Prince Laski's ball. Henri (disguised as Nangis), Fritelli, and Alexina enter; they and Laski sing an ensemble of hidden identities and disloyal friends. Minka enters with a group of her fellow slave maidens, who inquire about her love interest. She responds in the lively "Gypsy's Song." Minka offers to help Henri and Fritelli in order to prove her love for Nangis, who has also quietly turned up at Laski's palace. Alexina and Henri meet and recall their happy times in Venice. Fritelli returns with Laski and the other conspirators; in the "Ensemble of the Conspiracy" Henri (still disguised as Nangis) joins the conspiracy—they've decided to kidnap the king-to-be. Henri enlists the real Nangis' help; Nangis will now disguise himself as Henri, and they plan to quickly leave Poland. Laski believes, however, that to simply kidnap and banish Henri leaves open the possibility of reprisals, so Henri must, after all, die. In Act Two's lengthy finale, Henri finally reveals himself to be the King, but isn't believed. So, back in disguise as Nangis, Henri agrees to drive the king (Nangis in disguise) out of Poland, as everyone is put into a panic by the arrival of the French.

Act Three. At a country inn, Fritelli sings a brief number with the innkeeper Basile as they discuss the two possible kings, Henri and Ernest of Austria. Alexina arrives, however, with the startling news that the conspiracy has been made public and Archduke Ernest has returned to Austria. She believes that she and other conspirators might be able to save themselves by saying that they were spying on the conspirators for Henri's benefit and were not themselves part of the plot, thereby perhaps winning his favor. Fritelli, however, is mostly worried that Alexina and Henri might take up their affair again. Minka then arrives, looking for Nangis; she believes that Nangis (still playing the role of Henri) has been killed—but just as she is about to kill herself in despair, Nangis appears, very much alive, and they sing an ecstatic duet. In the opera's finale, all the plots and hidden identities are revealed, Henri decides to accept the Polish crown, the lovers are reunited, and all ends happily. *—Chris Morrison*

George Whitefield Chadwick

b. Nov. 13, 1854, Lowell, MA, **d.** Apr. 4, 1931, Boston, MA

Composer: Orchestral

As an instructor, and eventually director, at the New England Conservatory of Music, George Whitefield Chadwick played an important role in the development of a uniquely American musical style. He was also one of the most significant of the Boston, or New England, school of composers. His music, although conservative in approach, is brilliantly orchestrated and reflects a subtle charm and sense of humor.

Chadwick grew up in a musical home. Both his parents were amateur musicians, and Chadwick got his first musical instruction in piano and harmony from his brother. More formal studies continued at the New England Conservatory in 1872. However, he didn't have enough money to complete his degree, so he worked in his father's insurance business for about three years. At age 21 he decided to pursue a career as a music educator and composer; he taught at Olivet College in 1876 and 1877. Then in the fall of 1877, Chadwick traveled to Germany, entering the Leipzig Conservatory where he studied with Carl Reinecke. He also received some organ lessons from Josef Rheinberger in Munich. His graduation piece from the Leipzig Conservatory was the *Rip Van Winkle Overture* (1879), which was premiered at the Conservatory and later became his first composition performed in America.

Returning to the United States in 1880, Chadwick set up a private teaching studio in Boston. Two years later he took a post as instructor in harmony and composition at the New England Conservatory. He also became the organist at Boston's South Congregational Church, a post he held for 17 years. In his spare time he composed works like the *Symphony No. 3* (1886), which won him a prize from the National Conservatory in New York.

In his years at the New England Conservatory, Chadwick instructed many of the most important of the next generation of American composers, such as Horatio Parker, William Grant Still, Henry Hadley, E. B. Hill, Daniel Gregory Mason, and Frederick Converse. After becoming Director of the Conservatory in 1897—a post he held for the rest of his life—Chadwick instituted some noteworthy changes, reforming the curriculum and organizing an opera workshop and a student orchestra. He also wrote influential textbooks such as *Harmony, A Course of Study* (1897, rev. 1922).

Chadwick was much in demand as a conductor, appearing frequently with U.S. orchestras. He also directed music festivals in Springfield (1897-1901) and Worcester (1889-99). Even with all this activity, he still managed to compose; among his most popular works are the four *Symphonic Sketches* (1895-1904) and the *Tam O'Shanter Overture* (1915). He eventually produced five operas, three symphonies, five string quartets, and a variety of other orchestral and chamber works. The conservatism of his music, however, led to its falling out of favor as the musical world changed dramatically in the early twentieth century. The Metropolitan Opera even refused to produce his tragic opera *The Padrone* (1912).

Chadwick was much honored during his lifetime. As early as 1897 he received an honorary degree from Yale University; eight years later he received another from Tufts College. In 1928, he was presented a gold medal by the Academy of Arts and Letters. And in 1930 a pair of music festivals (at the New England Conservatory and the Eastman School) marked the fiftieth anniversary of his return to the United States from his European studies. He died the following year. *—Chris Morrison*

Overview of Works (1879–1923)

Despite his position as patriarch of American music, George Whitefield Chadwick's compositions gathered dust for decades after his death before being brushed off and reintroduced to audiences near the end of the twentieth century. Though associated with the classicist style of the "Second School" of New England composers, Chadwick's consummate craftsmanship, as well as his efforts to innovate "from within" musical genres and idioms, helped establish the aesthetic footing on which much subsequent American music was built.

Chadwick composed in virtually every genre, ranging from art songs (well over 100 of them) to his gargantuan commission for the 1892 Chicago World's Fair—a work scored for literally hundreds of instrumentalists and thousands of voices. His reputation was first established with his instrumental works, namely his first two string quartets (1877, 1878) and a number of successful early orchestral efforts, including the overtures *Rip Van Winkle* (1879) and *Thalia* (1882), and his *Symphony No. 2* (1883–85), which was especially favored by Boston audiences. He also contributed as a composer and conductor to Boston's active choral society movement in the late nineteenth century. By the 1890s, Chadwick had developed a more distinctly "American" sound (some scholars have noted that his style exemplified—slightly ahead of the fact—Dvořák's opinions about American music). Around the turn of the century Chadwick reduced his output in order to devote more effort to his duties as director of the New England Conservatory; around the same time, and perhaps in contradistinction to the contemporaneous European artistic angst, his style began to favor even more the lucid and light moods that audiences had long appreciated in his music. Much of his post-1900 orchestral output treated programmatic subjects, as in the *Symphonic Sketches* (1895–1904), *Cleopatra* (1904), and *Tam O'Shanter* (1914–15), a work once described as "an American *Till Eulenspiegel*."

Chadwick made several operatic efforts, none of which gained a foothold in the repertoire. In fact, his first stage work, the comic operetta *The Peer and the Pauper* (1884) remained unperformed, though parts of it were recycled for *Tabasco* (1894), a burlesque that met with moderate success. His most ambitious operatic efforts, however, fell into neglect: the lyric drama *Judith* (1901) received only an unstaged concert performance, and the verismo opera *The Padrone* (1912), a strikingly realistic depiction of Italian immigrants and mafia corruption, was not performed at all—until a revival in Boston some 85 years later gave it new life. *—Jeremy Grimshaw*

Recommended:

- ○ **Chadwick: Aphrodite, Suite Symphonique & Elegy,** / Serebrier (cond.), Czech State PO, Brno / 1996 / Reference 74
- ○ **Chadwick: Symphonies 2 & 3** / N. Järvi (cond.), Detroit SO / 1998 / Chandos 9685

ORCHESTRAL

Melpomene, overture (1887)

Though George Chadwick was one of the most distinguished members of the so-called "Second New England School," his recognition as a composer of some consequence was delayed largely because he liked lighthearted musical subjects in an era when "great" music had to be "serious"—and when many critics simply dismissed "lighthearted" music as "lightweight." Chadwick remedied this perception problem with his very serious *Melpomene Overture*, named after the Muse of Tragedy. The tragic aspect of the music is generalized rather than specific, atmospheric rather than programmatic. The harmonic language is clearly influenced by Wagner and by *Tristan und Isolde* in particular.

The overture earned more respect than its equally worthy predecessor, the *Thalia Overture* (1882), named after the Muse of Comedy: After *Melpomene*'s premiere, the *Boston Evening Transcript* described it as the "best thing Mr. Chadwick has done." *—Joseph Stevenson*

Recommended:

- ○ **Chadwick: Aphrodite; Suite Symphonique & others** / Serebrier (cond.), Czech State PO, Brno / 2002 / Reference 2104

Symphonic Sketches (1895–1904)

Chadwick was a typical representative of the "New England School" of late Romantic American composers. His *Symphonic Sketches* was one of the few pieces that hung on and wasn't neglected as other works and composers of the New England School were. Although he wrote three large and academically respectable symphonies up to the year 1893, thereafter he wrote works that can be classed as lighter works in symphonic form. In addition to this half-hour long set of pictorial movements, he also composed a *Sinfonietta* and a *Suite Symphonique.*

The opening movement, "Jubilee," is in a well-realized and concise sonata-allegro form, a very up-tempo piece in which the composer obviously feels liberated because he decided not to call the whole work a "symphony." So he composes very "loosely" and naturally.

The second movement, "Noël," has a double meaning. It is a lullaby to mother and baby. Obviously the direct association is with Christmas, the Madonna, and Jesus. But it is also a tender portrait of Chadwick's own son Noël, born the same year he wrote it.

While the other movements are from the years 1895 and 1896, Chadwick wrote the scherzo movement, "Hobgoblin," in 1905. Chadwick takes a motive from Mendelssohn's music to *A Midsummer Night's Dream* associated with Puck (the "hobgoblin") and turns him into an all-American brat. The final movement, "A Vagrom Ballad," is based on a hobo song Chadwick heard while undertaking a commute to Springfield, MA, for a festival there. *—Joseph Stevenson*

Recommended:

- ○ **Chadwick: Symphonic Sketches; MacDowell & Peter** / Hanson (cond.), Eastman-Rochester Orch. / 1994 / Mercury 434337

Riccardo Chailly

b. Feb. 20, 1953, Milan, Italy
Conductor

Riccardo Chailly is the dynamic, and sometimes controversial, conductor of Amsterdam's Royal Concertgebouw Orchestra, known for his devotion to contemporary music, and for his attempts to modernize the ensemble's approach to the traditional symphonic repertory. His many recordings for the Decca label include modern masterworks by Zemlinsky, Hindemith, and Schnittke, the symphonies of Gustav Mahler, and a number of operas.

The son of composer Luciano Chailly, and a sometime rhythm and blues drummer, Chailly began his conducting career as Claudio Abbado's assistant at La Scala, cutting his teeth on the standard operatic literature. He attained considerable success as an opera conductor in his own right, making guest appearances at London's Covent Garden, the Metropolitan Opera, and numerous Italian and German houses; he also made several notable recordings, including an Andre Chénier with Luciano Pavarotti. Nevertheless, he decided to focus his energies on symphonic conducting instead, feeling that it offered a wider avenue for artistic exploration. To that end, he became the principle conductor of Berlin's Radio Symphony Orchestra in 1982, eventually leading them on their first North American tour in 1985; he was also the principal guest conductor of the London Philharmonic from 1982–1985.

In 1988, the newly rechristened Royal Concertgebouw Orchestra named the 35-year-old Chailly as its chief conductor and artistic director. This would prove to be the defining post of his career, and he would cut back on his touring and operatic engagements to make it the center of his artistic activities. The relationship with both the orchestra and its audience was rocky at first, marked by resentment toward his "modernistic" approach to the works of Bruckner, Mahler, and Brahms. (Among other things, Chailly moved the group away from its signature sound, and toward a more flexible palette of orchestral color, adaptable to the needs of each composer.) But after that adjustment, Chailly assumed a position of confident leadership over the group, maintaining its position as one of Europe's finest ensembles, but also establishing it as a source of innovation and fresh perspective.

Chailly is a noted champion of Edgard Varèse and Alexander Zemlinsky, both of whom he feels have been underappreciated. He also maintains an interest in the performance practice of the Baroque era, and in his performances of Bach's *St. Matthew Passion* he attempts to balance the sound of the modern orchestra with the style of the period. Still selectively active as an operatic conductor, Chailly has made several notable Rossini recordings, including *La cenerentola*, starring Cecilia Bartoli. Chailly has also assumed the leadership of the Orchestra symphonica Guiseppe Verdi, which is a professional Italian orchestra composed entirely of players between 18 and 25 years of age. *—Allen Schrott*

Recommended:

- ○ **Shostakovich: The Film Album** / Chailly (cond.), Kerr, Concertgebouw / 1999 / London 460792
- ○ **Varèse: The Complete Works** / Chailly (cond.), Leonard, Delunsch, Zoon, Royal Concertgebouw Orch. / 1998 / London 460208
- ○ **Rossini: La Cenerentola** / Chailly (cond.), Bartoli, Corbelli, Matteuzzi, Pertusi, Bologna Community Theater Orch. / 1993 / London 436902
- ○ **Mahler: Symphony; Totenfeier** / Chailly (cond.), Lang, Diener, Royal Concertgebouw Orch. / 2001 / Decca 470283

Feodor Chaliapin

b. Feb. 13, 1873, Kazan, Russia, **d.** Apr. 12, 1938, Paris, France
Bass

Feodor Chaliapin is perhaps the most legendary operatic bass in history. Possessed of a large and beautiful voice, he devoted himself to all aspects of his art—most significantly his dramatic portrayals—at a time when such things were not at all typical of singers. Chaliapin was born the son of Russian peasants and was apprenticed to a cobbler at the age of ten. However, a brief engagement with a touring opera and a fortuitous meeting with his first voice teacher, Dimitri Usatov (both during his teen years), alerted the young singer to the true extent of his musical potential. Usatov was, in fact, so impressed with the young man that he agreed to teach him free of charge.

In 1894, Chaliapin sang in St. Petersburg and soon was accepted at the Imperial Opera. In 1896, he sang with a private opera company in Moscow, making his debut as Ivan Susanin in Glinka's *A Life for the Tsar*, for which he received excellent reviews. At the same time, he gave many successful solo concerts. His first appearance outside Russia was in Boito's *Mefistofele* at Teatro alla Scala in 1901. He sang nearly every season at Monte Carlo from 1905 to 1937. His first role there was King Philip in *Don Carlo*, and there he created the role of *Don Quixote* in Massenet's setting of that tale. In 1933 he starred in a film about the same idealistic knight (this project was ultimately left incomplete, but it resulted in the fine *Don Quichotte* songs of both Maurice Ravel and Jacques Ibert).

In 1907, the bass made his Metropolitan Opera debut in Boito's *Mefistofele*, and later that season sang both Gounod's *Faust* (Mefistophele) and Mozart's *Don Giovanni* (Leporello). His return to the United States was delayed until 1921 when he sang the title role in *Boris Godunov*. He sang with the Metropolitan Opera until 1929.

In 1908, Chaliapin began his close association with Diaghilev in Paris, where many famous productions of Russian operas were staged. He sang several Russian roles at Covent Garden, London in 1913. In 1914, he returned to Russia and stayed until after World War I and the Great Revolution. In 1922, he immigrated to France, which remained his home for the remainder of his life.

Chaliapin appeared in nearly all of the great opera houses of Europe, as well as those of England and the United States; in 1935–36 he made a world tour, including performances in China and Japan.

Chaliapin was a large man with great dramatic flair, and he could portray any type of character. He was a master of make-up, and he used this skill to help create his characters. His voice was wide ranging, allowing him to sing baritone roles like *Eugene Onegin* as well as bass roles like Oroveso. In his recitals, he never revealed what he would sing; the printed program would simply say "Selections to be announced."

When he immigrated to Paris, he fell out of favor with the Russian government, but his native country's official posture toward him warmed when it became apparent that he was bringing Russian opera to people all over the world. Besides the Russian operas already mentioned, Chaliapin also sang *Khovanchina*, *Prince Igor*, Dargomyzhsky's *Rusalka*, *Sadko*, *Mozart and Salieri* (which he premiered), Rubinstein's *The Demon*, Serov's *Judith* and Gretchaninov's *Dobrinya Nikititsch*. His art is preserved on his many recordings made between 1901 and 1935 which document his wide ranging repertoire. Without his performances of *Boris Godunov*, the opera would probably not have had the enduring popularity that it has subsequently enjoyed. *—Richard LeSueur*

Recommended:

- ○ **Chaliapin: A Vocal Portrait** / Chaliapin, etc. / 2002 / Naxos 8110748-49
- ○ **Feodor Chaliapin Song Book** / Chaliapin, etc. / Preiser 89207

Cécile Chaminade

b. Aug. 8, 1857, Paris, France, **d.** Apr. 13, 1944, Monte Carlo, Monaco
Composer: Keyboard, Chamber Music, Vocal, Concerto

One of the relatively few women composers of her time to achieve great popularity, Cécile Chaminade was a child prodigy; she began playing the piano very early, and her first compositions date from the age of eight. Her father wouldn't allow her to attend the Paris Conservatoire, but she did work privately with many instructors, including Benjamin Godard, with whom she studied composition. She gave her first public recital at age 18, and from then on appeared frequently as a pianist all over the world, often playing her own music. She was a regular on British concert stages from the early 1890s, and was a guest of Queen Victoria during one of her British tours. Chaminade made her American debut in 1908, playing her *Concertstück*, Op. 40 (written around 1896) with the Philadelphia Orchestra. She was a big hit in America, and within a few years many Chaminade clubs sprang up around the country. In 1913 she was the first woman to receive the Legion of Honor from the French government.

A large percentage of Chaminade's nearly 400 compositions were published during her lifetime. About half of those are short piano pieces, some of which, like the *Scarf Dance* and *The Flatterer*, were once quite popular. She also wrote about 125 songs, as well as a few larger, more ambitious pieces like the ballet *Callirhoë* (1888), the comic opera *La Sevillane*, and the dramatic symphony *Les amazones* for chorus and orchestra (1888). She also composed two orchestral suites and a handful of chamber works, including two trios. *—Chris Morrison*

KEYBOARD

Etudes de concert, Op. 35 (ca. 1885)

Though she composed music in a variety of genres, the reputation of the French composer Cécile Chaminade rests for the most part on a handful of brief salon-type piano pieces—and it was clearly in this musical realm that she was most gifted. Even more demanding works like the six *Études de concert* for piano, Op. 35, of around 1885, which were most certainly composed with the drawing room quite out of mind and Chaminade's own very successful concert tours quite in mind, never really get very far from the sweet, scented (and as detractors would have it, cloistered and aesthetically thin) salon style. Chaminade was in her late twenties when she composed these *Études*: already several years past her professional debut as a pianist and moving full speed ahead towards international fame.

The *Études de concert* are big, meaty works that take up a great deal of space in notation (some 55 pages altogether) and demand a great deal of control from their performer. They are not, however, bombastic or densely virtuosic in the manner of a great many other late nineteenth century étude collections. No. 1 is a C major Scherzo that might best be described as an Allegro study in the rapid contrast of staccato and legato. Next up is an étude that Chaminade calls "Automne"; it is a deeply sonorous D flat major Lento with a luscious melody in the middle voice and a Con fuoco middle section in which earth-shaking tritones are heard moving in the bass. No. 3, "Fileuse," is sewn from gossamer 16th notes that wind down from above and then, a little later, "doodle-doodles" in contrary motion between the hands. No. 4 is an explosive Appassionato, No. 5 a Chopinesque Impromptu featuring a very lovely F major melody. The set ends with a vigorous Tarantelle, Allegro vivace in D major, hustling along by way of the tarantella's traditional 6/8 time. *—Blair Johnston*

Recommended:

○ **Chaminade: Piano Music** / Katahn / 1994 / Gasparo 247

Sérénade espagnole, Op. 150 (1895)

Cécile Chaminade's *Serenade espagnole* dates from 1895, at which time Chaminade's star had risen to a point where she was considered the top woman composer in the world. Also known as *Chanson espagnole*, the work is, along with the *Scarf Dance* and *The Flatterer*, among her best-known pieces. Originally for piano solo, the serenade also had wide currency as an arrangement for violin and piano by Fritz Kreisler.

Chaminade was a friend and admirer of George Bizet in her youth, and it is not too difficult to discern the flavor of *Carmen* in this charming little work. Brief and evocative, as is typical of beloved salon pieces from the era of homemade music, the serenade commences with a languid guitar-like accompaniment against which a Latin-infected folklike melody sings. The middle section escalates to the livelier tempo of a fandango until a brief cadenza ushers in a return to the sunny, somnolent ease of the opening. The work trails off, as though blissfully yielding to the lure of a siesta. *— Wayne Reisig*

Recommended:

○ **Mots d'Amour** / von Otter, Forsberg / DG 471331

CHAMBER MUSIC

Salon Music (ca. 1880–1915)

Chaminade's work is destined to be forever discussed in the vexed context of salon music, if only because her nearly 200 piano pieces and more than 125 mélodies were patently designed for home entertainment ranging from middle-class parlors to the fashionable salons where the social and artistic elite mingled. But if the term "salon music" is a critical commonplace, its definition is slippery, while its pejorative connotations are not always appropriate. Duparc's *Sérénade* (to a poem by Gabriel Marc), though it failed to pass muster with its composer, alluringly hovers at the frontier where charm and sentiment vault into passionate truth, a frontier richly colonized by Chaminade. A piece such as the once-popular *La lisonjera*, with its Spanish coloring—a Chaminade staple—may even venture mild satire. Many are no more than effusive fluff, character pieces (with such indicative titles as *L'Ondine*, *Automne*, *Libellules*, *Arlequine*, *Pas des écharpes*, *Valse tendre*, and the like), and songs rife with easy sentiment. But buried amid this amazing cascade, enshrining the happier side of *la belle époque*, there are pieces and mélodies which, like Chabrier's, aggrandize salon sentiments with such aureate invention that they transcend the genre. Among the latter, one might single out such fetching things as *L'anneau argent*, *Bonne humeur*, *Malgré nous*, *Mots d'amour*, or *Chanson triste*, among many others, while the *Valse carnavalesque*, *Pas des cymbals*, and *Danse païenne* for two pianos rival Chabrier's like-scored, incandescent *Trois valses romantiques*. On the other hand, attempts to strike a deeper note, as in *Tristesse*, Op. 104, or *Au pays dévasté* for piano (a reaction to the Great War), are undone by Chaminade's habitual mellifluous melodiousness and unfailingly brilliant surfaces. If her mélodies require some vocal prowess, her piano writing sits easily beneath the fingers—quite unlike Chabrier's—allowing even players of modest technique to achieve an ingratiatingly sonorous *éclat*. Winged with an easily engaging melodic flair and a preference for deft charm and upbeat tempi, the simple ternary form of most of her pieces is handled with such exquisite tact that they seem more substantial than they are. The salon as a social institution sharply declined after the Great War, and the American middle-class parlor—where her music thrived—all but disappeared after World War II, throwing Chaminade's genteel wealth of invention into the discard. Only near the end of the twentieth century did her work begin to re-emerge, largely thanks to the interest of such leading artists as Peter Jacobs, Bengt Forsberg, and Anne Sofie von Otter. *—Adrian Corleonis*

Recommended:

○ **Mots d'Amour** / von Otter, Forsberg / DG 471331

○ **Piano Music of Cécile Chaminade** / Peter Jacobs / 1992 / Hyperion 66584

○ **Chaminade: The 2 Piano Trios** / Tzigane Piano Trio / 1996 / ASV 965

Piano Trio No. 1 in G minor, Op. 11 (ca. 1880)

Although best known as a composer of salon-genre piano music, and also as a woman who made her way as a creative musician in a male-dominated field, Cecile Chaminade composed in many mediums, including orchestral, ballet, and chamber music. In the last named category, the *Piano Trio No. 1 in G minor*, composed when Chaminade was in her early twenties, is one of her best in the genre. Despite the modest proportions of the four-movement work and a certain clarity in the writing which is usually (but all too glibly) termed Gallic, there are some unexpected pleasures to be found upon hearing.

The opening allegro, in sonata form, while somewhat French in its reserve, has something of Brahms, and even her exact contemporary Elgar, in its darker brown hues, curiously autumnal for so young a composer, yet not oppressively so. The following andante boasts a lyrical main theme (Chaminade was a good tunesmith; some of her themes cry out for words) and a slightly contrapuntal midsection. This is followed by the brief Presto scherzo, propelled by bustling 32nd notes, cross-rhythms, and punctuated by horn-fifths. Although the Finale, Allegro molto, shows a classical bent towards a rapid, streamlined conclusion and is solidly tonal, there is a remarkable traversal through distantly related keys, strangely premonitory of the progressive tonality which the younger composers of her generation would fully explore years later. *— Wayne Reisig*

Recommended:

○ **PIano Trios By Ravel, Chaminade, Saint-Saëns** / Rembrandt Trio / 1993 / Dorian 90187

VOCAL

Songs for voice & piano (ca. 1880–1915)

While best-known for her piano and ballet pieces, Chaminade was also a prolific song composer, writing almost 140 over her lifetime. Her works were very popular during her day, both in Europe and in the United States, and she was even invited to compose for the first World's Fair at the Columbian Exposition in Chicago. (In fact, it was the financial rewards of the popularity of her salon pieces, including these songs, that drew her away from the larger-scale choral and orchestral works that had drawn critical enthusiasm, but far less of the money she needed to support her family after her father's death.) Rather like Fauré, Debussy, and Hahn, she concentrated on atmosphere and emotional expression, rarely aspiring to drama or psychological penetration. Also like theirs, her songs are full of a distinctively French charm, combining lightness of touch, elegance, and lyricism. She also shows her late nineteenth century roots in the use of chromaticism to add a usually understated sensuality to a moment. Unlike them, however, she often displays a sense of humor, even silliness, that seems to lead the way to Satie and Poulenc, as in the accompaniment to *Bonne humeur*, in which a walker describes a stroll on a rainy day and the piano occasionally suggests children jumping in puddles or wind blowing a sudden spurt of rain onto the walker's head. The tone is almost invariably light; even when the lover expresses an unrequited love, the suggestion is that the love will soon be appeased. For example, in *Tu me dirais*, when the lover declares that if the beloved were to tell any number of lies, the lover would believe them fully, the quick tempo, major key, and frequent use of dolce markings in both voice and piano suggest that this is a part of courtship rather than the Germanic angst that Schubert or Schumann or the Italianate despair Tosti might have given the same text; the last rising fourth in the piano line and high major chord give the impression of a teasing question, rather than resignition. The vocal line dominates her songs and the piano is rarely more than accompaniment, generally either providing arpeggios or a chordal underpinning. Even when, as in *Si j'étais jardinier*, there is an extended piano interlude between verses, it typically reiterates the vocal melody or elaborates its earlier theme, providing continuition rather than commentary. While her songs, as well as her other compositions, fell out of popular attention beginning around World War I, the late twentieth/early twenty-first century resurgence of interest in women composers and the championship of Swedish mezzo-soprano Anne Sofie von Otter have brought her songs more prominence, though not to a place in the standard vocal repertoire as before. *—Ann Feeney*

Recommended:

○ **Mots d'Amour** / von Otter, Forsberg / DG 471331

CONCERTO

Concertino for flute & orchestra, Op. 107 (1902)

Chaminade wrote the *Concertino* in 1902 as an examination piece for flute students at the Paris Conservatoire, where it was used for many years thereafter. The work is dedicated to the famed French flutist and teacher Paul Taffanel, who, after a long playing career in the Paris Opéra Orchestra (1864–90) and as a conductor, retired from public performance and served as flute professor at the Conservatoire from 1893 until his death in 1908. Chaminade's composition, with its wide-ranging, highly decorative solo part, does in fact provide quite a workout for the flutist. A broad and graceful melody opens the work. After a more active central section, marked Più animato agitato in the score, a short oboe phrase leads into a cadenza for the soloist. A reprise of the opening melody and a rousing coda conclude this melodic and attractive work. *—Chris Morrison*

Recommended:

- ○ **Laurel Zucker, Virtuoso Flutist** / Zucker, R. Sutherland / 1993 / Cantilena 660012
- ○ **Galway 60 Years 60 Flute Masterpieces Vol. 6: The French Tradition** / Dutoit (cond.), Galway, Royal PO / 1999 / RCA 63438

Michael Chance

b. Mar. 7, 1955, Penn, Buckinghamshire, England
Countertenor

Michael Chance is a leading British countertenor, in worldwide demand for male alto parts in opera, and as a recital, concert, and recording artist. He was a choral scholar at King's College, Cambridge—an adult-voice singer at the famous Choir of King's College Cambridge, receiving a full scholarship for singing daily services in the College Chapel during the school term. His major subject at Cambridge was English, but he received thorough musical and vocal training as a matter of course as a choral scholar.

After graduation, he studied voice with Rupert Bruce Lockhart. His operatic debut was in the Buxton Festival, where he sang the part of Apollo in Ronald Eyre's production of Cavalli's *Giasone* in 1983. He was a member of Kent Opera for three seasons. In 1985, his European debut was in Lyon, as Andronico in Handel's *Tamerlano* (1985).

He rapidly established a strong reputation. He is one of the newer sort of countertenor, whose vocal production is well supported and natural-sounding. As the bulk of the countertenor repertory is in Baroque opera, he has sung Tolomeo in Handel's *Giulio Cesare*, Ottone in Handel's *Agrippina* and Monteverdi's *L'incoronazione di Poppea*, and as Orpheus in both the Gluck and Monteverdi operas.

However, he is equally admired for his performances in newer operas featuring countertenors, and his roles in twentieth century opera include Oberon in Britten's *A Midsummer Night's Dream*, the Voice of Apollo in the same composer's *Death in Venice*, the Military Governor in Judith Weir's *A Night at the Chinese Opera*, and in Harrison Birtwistle's *The Second Mrs. Kong*. The latter two parts were written for him, for he is active in promoting new works. Composers he has worked with include Alexander Goehr, Richard Rodney Bennett, John Tavener, Anthony Powers, Tan Dun, and Elvis Costello.

He has sung at major opera houses such as the Teatro Colón in Buenos Aires, La Scala of Milan, at Covent Garden in London, and in opera houses in New York, Paris, Amsterdam, Lisbon, and Sydney.

Chance has made over 50 recordings, including the Grammy Award-winning release of Handel's *Semele* with John Nelson conducting. Other recordings include Mozart's *Ascanio in Alba*, Göehr's *The Death of Moses*, and Rolf's *Carmina burana* as well as the major oratorios and choral works of Handel and Bach. He appears in major festivals, such as the Glyndebourne Summer Opera, the Edinburgh Festival, the Salzburg Festival, and the Aix-en-Provence Festival. His concert appearances have taken him to major cities of Europe, the United Kingdom, North America, Japan, and Australia.

As a chamber recitalist he often works with the Baroque viol ensemble Fretwork and with Trevor Pinnock and the English Concert. He teaches at the Royal College of Music as a Visiting Professor. *—Joseph Stevenson*

Recommended:

- ○ **Purcell: Music for a While** / Chance, Boothby, North, Cole / 1996 / Columns 555008
- ○ **Elizabethan & Jacobean Lute Songs** / Chance, Wilson (lute) / 1993 / Chandos 0538

Sarah Chang

b. Dec. 10, 1980, Philadelphia, PA
Violinist

An American violinist of Korean heritage, Sarah Chang was already a celebrity as a prepubescent soloist; unlike many child prodigies, she made the transition to adulthood painlessly, and remains a high-profile soloist on the international circuit.

She began performing in public at age five; within two years, she had won the Starling scholarship to the Juilliard School, where she studied with Dorothy DeLay and Hyo Kang. At age eight, after only two years of study at Juilliard during which she still regarded playing the violin as a hobby, she auditioned for conductors Zubin Mehta and Riccardo Muti and bowled them over. She made her professional debut in 1988 performing Paganini's *Violin Concerto No. 1* with Mehta and the New York Philharmonic. Soon she found herself playing Paganini, Tchaikovsky, and Sibelius concertos with the world's greatest orchestras, with an EMI recording contract tucked into her frock. Initial features and reviews focused on the incongruity of such technical virtuosity coming from a cute little girl, and coverage during her teen years was similarly half awed, half patronizing.

As she approached her twenties, Chang began to enjoy more serious critical appraisal. One critic summarized her attributes as "consummate technical ease, a gorgeous, vibrant, flawlessly beautiful tone, and a heartfelt but unsentimental expressiveness." Conversely, some of her performances of Romantic repertory were sometimes criticized for being slightly emotionally disengaged.

Chang quickly became associated with concertos of not only Paganini but also Mendelssohn, Tchaikovsky, and Sibelius. She also advocated not-quite-standard concertos by Goldmark, Strauss, and Dvořák. But not until she was nearly 20 did Chang begin exploring chamber music with any frequency, initially playing in small festivals but also recording with other high-profile soloists on the EMI roster.

Less apparent from her discography is her interest in contemporary music. She has worked on new pieces with jazzman Eddie Karam, as well as Jack Elliott and Korean-American composer Donald Sur.

One area in which Chang has been slow to develop self-confidence is teaching. Feeling she was too young to be a credible authority, she didn't give her first master class until she was 22, and that was hidden away in Singapore. After that, she embarked on a small-scale series of recitals and educational events for rural and underserved populations in the United States.

Chang plays a 1717 Guarneri del Gesù; reluctant to expose it to hot lights, she uses a cheap but attractive stand-in violin for publicity photos. *—James Reel*

Recommended:

- ○ **Mendelssohn & Sibelius: Violin Concertos** / Jansons (cond.), Chang, Berlin PO / 1998 / EMI 56418
- ○ **Simply Sarah** / Chang, Abramovic (piano) / 1997 / EMI 56161
- ○ **Debut** / Chang, Rivers (piano) / 1992 / EMI 54352

Chanticleer

f. 1978, San Francisco, CA
Ensemble

Chanticleer may be the only independent full-time classical vocal ensemble in the United States. Since its inception in 1978, the group has developed an excellent reputation for its interpretation of music from many genres, and its bell-like sound has set a new ensemble standard.

Originally founded to sing Renaissance vocal repertoire, Chanticleer has toured worldwide and released more than twenty recordings. While most of Chanticleer's work is done a cappella, the group has collaborated such unusual projects as a fully-staged opera, recordings of jazz standards with the Don Haas Trio, and performances with the unorthodox Japanese dancers Eiko and Koma. Its repertoire ranges from chant to twentieth century pop. In 1978, founder Louis Botto, a graduate student in musicology, was disturbed by the fact that sacred Renaissance vocal music was so rarely performed. So he formed a group to sing this neglected repertoire. Trying to hold to the male-only Renaissance tradition, Botto asked friends who sang with him in the San Francisco Symphony Chorus and Grace Cathedral's Choir of Men and Boys to join the group. Rehearsals began, and the ensemble arranged a debut performance in San Francisco's historic Mission Dolores.

The works chosen for the debut included compositions by Renaissance composers whose music would become staples of the group's repertoire: Byrd, Ockeghem, Morley, Dufay, and Josquin. The members settled on the name Chanticleer in honor of the "clear-singing" rooster in Geoffrey Chaucer's *Canterbury Tales*, which Charlie Erikson, one of the baritones, was reading at the time. While maintaining its basic repertoire of Renaissance music, Chanticleer also began experimenting with music of other genres. The number of singers varied and eventually settled at 12.

In 1980, the ensemble participated in the Festival of Masses in San Francisco. Robert Shaw was the festival's conductor that year, and after hearing Chanticleer's solo concert proclaimed it "one of the most beautiful musical experiences" of his life. A turning point in Chanticleer's history came when Joseph Jennings, a countertenor, joined the group in 1983. Other members soon recognized his exceptional vocal and interpretive abilities and asked him to become Chanticleer's first music director. Since he accepted that position, Jennings' startling vocal clarity and innovative arrangements have become hallmarks of the ensemble.

International early music audiences began to find out about Chanticleer after a 1984 performance at a large scholarly conference in Belgium. Chanticleer created its own label, Chanticleer Records, releasing a tenth-anniversary CD in 1988. Over the next six years, the ensemble released ten recordings on its private label. These CDs sold well at Chanticleer's concerts, and in 1994 Teldec Classics International signed Chanticleer to an exclusive recording contract. The group's recordings suddenly became available all over North America and abroad. By 1991, Chanticleer was financially able to make all 12 of its members full-time employees, allowing the group to tour more frequently and take on a wide variety of projects. Since then the ensemble has performed and recorded with the London Studio Orchestra, jazz legend George Shearing, and the New York Philharmonic. In 1994, the group presented a critically acclaimed, fully staged performance of Benjamin Britten's opera *Curlew River.* In 1997 Chanticleer recorded works by Mexican Baroque composers Manuel de Zumaya and Ignácio de Jerusalem with an orchestra of period instruments. It has commissioned works by many of the late twentieth century's foremost composers, including David Conte, Morton Gould, Bernard Rands, and Chen Yi (who served as Chanticleer's composer-in-residence from 1993 to 1996). In 1999, Chanticleer released a collection of these works on its CD *Colors of Love.* *—Corie Stanton Root*

Recommended:

- ○ **A Portrait** / Chanticleer, London Studio Orch., Chanticleer Sinfonia / 2003 / Teldec 49702
- ○ **Tavener: Lamentations & Praises** / Chanticleer, Jennings (cond.) / 2001 / Teldec 41342
- ○ **Evening Prayer** / Chanticleer, Capriccio Stravagante / 2003 / Warner 60290
- ○ **Our American Journey** / Chanticleer / 2002 / Teldec 48556

La Chapelle Royale

f. 1977, Paris, France
Ensemble

La Chapelle Royale is one of a number of ensembles, vocal and instrumental, founded by the Belgian conductor and keyboard player Philippe Herreweghe. The group specializes in French music of the seventeenth and eighteenth centuries.

While Herreweghe was still a university student, he founded the Collegium Vocale of Ghent, one of the first groups dedicated to authentic performances of Baroque vocal and choral music. The Collegium became known for its concerts and recordings of German Baroque music, particularly the Bach cantatas. It was suggested to Herreweghe by Philippe Beaussant and Vincent Berthier de Lioncourt that Herreweghe should found a Paris-based group to devote the same sort of attention to the very different music of the French Baroque. They were associated with an academic organization called *L'Association La Chapelle Royale,* a group registered since 1901. Its name reflected its interest in music and musicians of the French Royal Chapel, which, under Louis XIV, had grown to a grand size and manner.

Herreweghe founded the musical ensemble La Chapelle Royale in 1977 and began performing vocal and instrumental music of the great composers of the French Baroque, including Lully, Lalande, Rameau, Couperin, and their contemporaries. However, it was with a Bach performance that La Chapelle Royale made its first big impression when, in 1980, it presented the first period-instrument performance of Bach's large-scale music in Paris.

It has become the world's leading ensemble dealing with the French Baroque repertory and has made over 60 compact discs for the Virgin Classics and Harmonia Mundi labels. It has traveled to most of the world's major classical music venues, and appears regularly at the leading music festivals of the world.

La Chapelle Royale has extended its period of interest backward into the Renaissance era and forward into the Classical and even early Romantic ages of music. When performing in choral works, La Chapelle Royale's vocal members function as its choir. As such, they have added to their acclaimed performances of music of the French *grand siècle* that of other eras, such as Mozart's *Requiem,* Beethoven's *Missa Solemnis* and *Ninth Symphony,* Berlioz's *L'enfance du Christ,* Schumann's *Scenes from Faust,* and Brahms' *A German Requiem.* *—Joseph Stevenson*

Recommended:

- ○ **Charpentier: Miserere; Motets** / Herreweghe (cond.), Chapelle Royale / HM 1951185
- ○ **Brahms: Motets** / Herreweghe (cond.), Collegium Vocale, Chapelle Royale / HM 901122
- ○ **Bach: Motets** / Herreweghe, Kooy, Crook, Reyghere, Mellon, Darras, Collegium Vocale, Chapelle Royale / HM 901231
- ○ **Schütz: Musikalische Exequien** / Herreweghe (cond.), Kooy, Junghanel, Fouchecourt, Reyghere, Chapelle Royale / HM 901261
- ○ **Josquin Desprez: Motets** / Herreweghe (cond.), Chapelle Royale / HM 901243

Michel Chapuis

b. Jan. 15, 1930, Dôle, Jura, France
Organist

Michel Chapuis' career as organist and as specialist in performance upon historically important instruments began at Cathedral of Dôle when he was quite young. He proceeded to study music in Paris; his teachers included Eduoard Souberbielle for organ, René Malherbe for composition, and Emile Poillot. In 1951, while studying under Marcel Dupré at the Conservatoire de Paris, Chapuis took first prize in organ and improvisation (the Prix Périlhou et Guilmant). He served as organist for the Paris churches of St. Germain l'Auxerrois (1951–54) and St. Nicolas des Champs (1954–72), accompanied at Notre Dame from 1955 to 1964, and was titular organist of St. Séverin from 1964. At the same time, he has held organ teaching posts at the prestigious conservatories of Strasbourg (1956–79), Besançon (1979–86), and finally Paris (1986–95). In 1995, Chapuis was named organist to the Versailles Royal Chapel. Both Chapuis' life as a teacher and as a performer have been dedicated to historically informed performance; his greatest contribution has been in musical interpretations upon historic instruments. In addition to performances of every surviving piece of French organ music from the seventeenth and eighteenth centuries on the Cliquot organ of St. Nicolas des Champs, he has produced numerous recordings matching early repertory to historic instruments: Daquin Noëls on the 1710 Silbermann organ of Marmoutier, Couperin on the 1772 organ by Brother Isnard of Tarascon in Saint-Maximin, Marchand on the 1782 Cliquot organ at Souvigny. Chapuis has also personally supervised several instrument restorations across France. *—Timothy Dickey*

Recommended:

- ○ **Noël à l'Orgue** / Chapuis / Valois 4637
- ○ **Bach Trio Sonatas** / Chapuis / Valois 4411

Gustave Charpentier

b. Jun. 25, 1860, Dieuze, Lorraine, France, **d.** Feb. 18, 1956, Paris, France
Composer: Opera

Charpentier was born in Dieuze, on June 25, 1860. He did not come from a musical family—his father was a baker—but his family encouraged his interest in music and allowed him to study the violin at an early age. His formal studies, however, did not begin until he was a teenager. He began working in a spinning mill in 1875, and gave violin lessons to his employer, Albert Lorthiois. Charpentier's musical abilities must have been impressive, for Lorthiois subsequently sponsored Charpentier for entrance into the Lille Conservatoire. Finally, in 1881, Charpentier was formally accepted into the Paris Conservatoire, where he studied violin with Massart, harmony with Pessard, and composition with Massenet. Charpentier's composition studies with Massenet began in 1885; surprisingly, only two years later, the young composer won the prestigious *Prix de Rome* for his cantata, *Didon.*

While living and composing in Rome at the Villa Medici—a condition of winning the *Prix de Rome*—Charpentier completed an number of important works, including a symphony entitled *La vie du poete,* and an orchestral suite, *Impressions d'Italie.* He also began work on an opera, *Louise,* which was destined to become his most famous work.

Charpentier returned to Paris in 1890 with the libretto for *Louise,* which he had written himself. The text of the opera concerned a dressmaker's shop girl named *Louise* and her life in Paris. Many of Charpentier's friends and colleagues suggested that the libretto was too realistic, too crude; the composer made a number of revisions to the text before finally completing the music in 1896. The opera was premiered at the Opera Comique early in 1900 and was an astounding success. It has been called a "roman musical," an early example of "verismo," and a "realist" drama; most importantly, *Louise* secured Charpentier's fame as a composer and earned him many honors, including election to the Academie des Beaux Arts. In 1900, he was also named a Chevalier of the Legion of Honor.

In 1902, Charpentier founded a school of music, the Conservatoire Populaire Mimi Pinson, which offered free musical instruction to Paris' many "midinettes"—the shop girls who were popularized in his *Louise.* Charpentier also organized successful festivals throughout the country, many of which featured his own music, and thus enlarged his fame.

Charpentier's next success was the opera *Julien* of 1913, essentially a sequel to *Louise.* Probably the second work in an intended trilogy (never to be completed), *Julien* was not as successful as *Louise,* but shares many of the latter's charateristics: both are naturalistic music dramas that include the sights and sounds of life on the streets of Paris.

After *Julien,* Charpentier completed virtually no music, and instead busied himself with organizing concerts and writing music criticism. Interested in modern technological developments like the gramophone, radio, and film, Charpentier participated in a film version of *Louise* in 1936; however, Charpentier became a recluse after World War II, and produced no more music until his death (Paris, February 18, 1956). *—Alexander Carpenter*

OPERA

Louise (1887–1896)

In 1887, Gustave Charpentier (1860–1956) was awarded the coveted *Prix de Rome,* one part of which consisted of support for a year's study in Rome. It was there, while living at the Villa Medici, that Charpentier began work on *Louise.* The composer himself created the scenario, based on his own time in Montmartre; Charpentier maintained that he was the sole author of the final libretto, but research has shown that he paid the poet Saint-Pol-Roux to write at least some of the text.

Charpentier once explained that in *Louise* he attempted to capture the voice of his generation, which may explain his extensive efforts at realism. After returning to Paris in 1890, he read the libretto to friends who suggested cutting down on the realistic tone and increasing the lyricism. Charpentier heeded this advice; but this may have weakened the work, since the most effective sections of the opera revolve around its verismo elements—elements which appeared before any of the so-called *verismo* operas of Puccini or Mascagni had been staged.

Nearly four years elapsed between the composition of *Louise* and its first performance. The main cause of the delay was the director of the Opéra-Comique, Léon Carvalho, who disliked the realism of the work and wanted to move the setting back to the era of Louis XV; he also wanted a "happy" ending, with total reconciliation of all characters. Charpentier would have none of this, waiting instead until 1898, when Albert Carré decided to produce *Louise* as written; sets were by Lucien Jusseaume, and André Messager conducted. *Louise* received its premiere at the Opéra-Comique in Paris on February 2, 1900. The vocal score was published in 1900; the full score followed in 1905.

A great success, *Louise* was performed a hundred times during its first season; undoubtedly, this success was due in large part to its proto-feminist theme. This is best seen in moments such as the final scene of Act One, when Louise's father suggests that "experience" is the best way to choose a good husband. Furthermore, statements spiced with political overtones that point up the inequalities in contemporary society struck a chord with young leftists. Because of these themes, *Louise* caused a stir even before its premiere; people talked and wrote of the "revolutionary" score and "immoral" subject matter.

Musically, however, the work is hardly revolutionary; it bears similarities to earlier works by Gounod and Massenet (who both admired *Louise*). This does not, however, mean that the score is unoriginal; there are many brilliant moments, such as the harmonically intriguing end of the first section of Act Two, in which a street vendor tries to sell his artichokes amid the hustle and bustle of Montmartre street life. The unbridled chromaticism of the duet between *Louise* and her mother in the third scene of Act One is also forward-looking. Charpentier's use of unusual instruments, such as the viola d'amore and, especially, a sewing machine, both promoted the realist cause and have insured *Louise* a place in the standard repertory.

Paul Dukas once wrote of *Louise*: "The first and last acts are those of a master; the other two are those of an artist; the whole is the work of a man." —*John Palmer*

Synopsis:

Act One. The opera opens in the working-class rooms of Louise's parents. It is evening. Louise is leaning out of the window, deep in conversation with the poet Julien. He is madly in love with her and tries to convince her to leave her parents' house and go away with him. She begs him not to torment her but coyly asks him to recount the first moment that he found himself in love with her. They exchange words of tenderest love as Louise's mother appears in the background, eavesdropping on the pair. They are speaking of the first times they met when Louise sees her mother and is dragged indoors by the arm. Her mother confronts her, angrily berating Louise about her clandestine meetings with Julien. While Louise pleads with her, she calls Julien a vagabond, deadbeat, and drunkard. Louise's father comes home from work, carrying a letter in his hand. The mother stirs the soup while Louise sets the table and her father reads the paper. Then they all sit down to dinner. He takes up the letter. It is from Julien, asking yet again for Louise's hand in marriage. Her father cautions her to forget him, saying that he is not worthy of her. He tries to comfort her as she dissolves in tears of distress.

Act Two. A tableaux of the waking city at dawn is spread before the audience. The streets begin to fill with merchandise sellers, ragpickers, and a seeker after pleasure. Housekeepers are beginning their morning marketing. A policeman stops for a conversation with a milkwoman. Finally Julien and a group of Bohemians enter. They are encouraging Julien to capture Louise on her way to work and steal her from her parents if necessary. While he contemplates his love for Louise, other girls on their way to work pass him and give him their greetings. He sees Louise and her mother in the now-bustling streets, and he begins to follow. The mother turns and orders Louise back into the house, then continues on her way. Julien enters and grabs Louise, demanding that she come away with him. They go out into the Paris streets arguing, until finally she breaks away and goes back inside.

At the sewing factory, the other girls comment on Louise's manner. They speculate that she is in love. A singer begins to serenade them at the window, and all except Louise lean out to listen. Louise recognizes the voice as that of Julien, and realizes that he is pleading with her still. At first the girls comment on his good looks and fine voice, but when he won't shut up, they begin to yell at him to go away. Finally, to their astonishment, Louise leaves and joins her lover.

Act Three. The act opens at the home of Julien at the top of Montmartre. He and Louise are seated together in the garden, for she has finally run away with him. She sings to him of her happiness and of the beauty of Paris. After an ecstatic love scene, crowds of people begin to fill the streets. A group of Bohemians enter and proclaim that it is time to crown the Muse of Montmartre. They have elected Louise, and she graciously accepts. Celebrations erupt, and Grisettes and Bohemians all break into song and dance. As they reach the height of merrymaking, Louise's mother appears on the scene. Louise runs and hides inside Julien's house while her mother pleads with Julien to release Louise. Her father is ill, and if she would but return home, the mother is sure all would be well. She promises that Louise will be allowed to return.

Act Four. The final act takes place at Louise's parents' house. Her father has recovered, and today has been his first day back at work. He is tired but well. Louise is still staying with them. She hopes to go back to Julien, but her parents keep her with them still, arguing against her returning to Montmartre. Her mother scolds her for obstinate sulking, and her father grabs her to him, pleading with her violently. Louise argues passionately for her right to freedom. She becomes delirious with visions of Paris and becomes bolder in her talk of her love for Julien. Finally her father, in a rage, tells her to go. Confused, Louise ventures forth, then finally flees, while her father cries out that the city of Paris has stolen his child from him. —*Rita Laurance*

Recommended:

○ **Charpentier: Louise** / Prêtre (cond.), Cotrubas, Domingo, New Philharmonia Orch. / 1990 / Sony 46429

Marc-Antoine Charpentier

b. 1643, Paris, France, **d.** Feb. 24, 1704, Paris, France

Composer: Choral, Opera, Chamber Music

Long completely forgotten and then hailed, in the twentieth century, as a Baroque genius, Charpentier was born in Paris, in 1643. In the mid-1660s, he traveled to Rome, where he spent three years studying with Carissimi and mastering the Italian style. Upon his return to Paris, Charpentier accepted employment and patronage from the powerful and pious Marie de Lorraine, known as Mademoiselle de Guise, last scion of the illustrious Guise family. In 1627, already known for his religious music, Charpentier agreed to provide incidental music for Molière's comedies. With astounding facility, the church composer wrote witty, charming, and delightful music in perfect consonance with Molière's comedic genius, as exemplified by the extraordinary score for *Le Malade imaginaire*. Nevertheless, church music remained Charpentier's primary vocation, and he steadily wrote masses, motets, hymns, and various other liturgical pieces. After Mademoiselle de Guise died in 1688, Charpentier found employment at the college Louis le Grand, where his accomplishments included the Latin oratorio *David et Jonathas*, a dramatic masterpiece. His next post was at the Jesuit Church of St. Louis, where he composed music for various aspects of the Catholic liturgy. In 1693, Charpentier's *Medea*, a *tragédie en musique*, had its premiere at the Academie Royale. If the composer thought this extraordinary work would secure him a royal appointment, he was mistaken, for the audience seemed deaf to the music. In 1698, Charpentier became music master for children at the Sainte-Chapelle, remaining there until his death. Two and a half centuries after Charpentier's death, millions heard the opening bars of his stunningly brilliant *Te Deum* (H. 146), selected as Eurovision's official theme. A master of harmonic and melodic invention, Charpentier satisfies the three prerequisites for beauty formulated by St. Thomas Aquinas: consonantia (harmony), integritas (perfection), and claritas (brilliance). This quintessentially Catholic composer ingeniously resolved the perceived conflict between faith and pure beauty by creating music in which devotion and beauty cannot be separated. Indeed, musicologist Catherine Cessac captured the essence of Charpentier's music when she wrote that the "grandeur and originality of Charpentier's music is due to a combination of exceptional musical talent and deep faith, each complementing the other." —*Zoran Minderovic*

CHORAL

Epitaphium Carpentarii, cantata, H. 474

Written as an homage to a deceased person, often a fellow composer, a *tombeau* is usually a heartfelt, sincere musical tribute. Charpentier's cantata *Epitaphium Carpentarii* (H. 474) may strike the listener as a deeply reverent work, but the Latin text identifies this astonishing composition as the composer's monument to himself. There are six characters in the strange cantata: two friends, three angels, and the ghost of Charpentier. To a listener who does not understand Latin, the music, particularly the exquisite melismatic traceries sung by the three angels, evokes a sonic dream world of tranquil gentleness. Discerning a certain velar transparency in this music, the listener, hearing the singers' clear diction, intuitively grasps the composer's desire to remove any obstacle to his story. And this story is anything but gentle. Charpentier, a gentle, modest, profoundly pious artist, creates an absurd, paradoxical, almost blasphemous parody of liturgical music with the aim of pouring scorn on François Chaperon, a decidedly unimportant composer whom Charpentier perceived as a rival and whose death Charpentier had to wait for (which occurred in 1698) to finally obtain a coveted post at the Sainte Chapelle. Lapsing into macaronic Latin, Charpentier condemns Chaperon's music as *musica capronica*, making the ridiculously obvious connection between *Capronus* (Chaperon) and *caprinus* (goat). Since nothing is known about Charpentier's inner life, it is quite reasonable to accept the *Epitaphium* as a "psychological portrait," as Charpentier scholar Catherine Cessac has suggested. According to Cessac, Charpentier's rather humble references to his unglamorous public career, not to mention his spectral appearance in the narrative, reflected the idea of a possible reflection of Bossuet's famous "Sermon on Death," or human insignificance in the divine scheme of things. True enough, but this is only one dimension of Charpentier's complex personality. The narrative also reveals an artist fully aware of his genius: the ultra-Catholic Charpentier blatantly trivializes the ideas of Purgatory and Heaven by describing Chaperon's music as the penance that the faithful will have to endure in order to reach the heavenly delights of Charpentier's music. "I was a musician," Charpentier's ghost declares, "considered good by good musicians, and ignorant by the ignorant ones. And since those who scorned me were more numerous than those who praised me, music brought me small honor and great burdens." Coming from a composer whose genius was consigned to oblivion for more than two centuries, these words sound truly prophetic. *—Zoran Minderovic*

Recommended:

- ○ **Charpentier: Orphée descendant aux enfers** / Ledroit, Ricercar Consort / 1987 / Ricercar 206722

Les Neuf leçons de ténèbres, H. 96–110 (1680)

In 587 B.C., the Babylonians destroyed the Temple in Jerusalem. A contemporary poet—traditionally thought to have been the Prophet Jeremiah—spoke of the desolation in a lengthy series of Lamentations. Thirteen centuries later, the Roman Catholic church adapted the Latin translation of the Lamentations as part of their ritual mourning for the death of Christ during Holy Week. Three Lamentation passages were chanted on each of three Holy Days in the evening Office of Tenebrae. The plangent Lamentations texts inspired composers beginning in the high Renaissance to write expressive polyphonic settings, and the practice continued unabated into the seventeenth century. During the extravagant reign of the "Sun King" Louis XIV, the Lamentations were sung in many prominent French churches. The style of the French Tenebrae music, however, owed as much to the flourishing of French opera as to its roots in the church's solemn chants. The *Tenebrae Lessons* of Marc-Antoine Charpentier, for instance, cloak their plainchant melodies in all the ornate trappings of the operatic idiom.

All told, Charpentier composed at least 31 separate pieces from the Tenebrae Lamentations, each more brimming with pathos than the last. As characteristic of his voluminous sacred vocal writing, Charpentier's harmonic language in the *Tenebrae Lessons* tends to the extravagant. His vocal melodies are carefully modest in proportion, but heavily encrusted with ornamentation. Among his earliest Lamentations settings are a complete set of *Neuf Leçons de Ténèbres*, composed in 1680 for the nuns of the Solitude de Port-Royal. (Even the names of the nuns who sang the first performance survive: Mère Ste-Cécile, Mère Camille, and Mère Desnots on contratenor.) In each of this set of nine lessons, Charpentier works with the Gregorian chant melody associated with the Lamentations. All of the acrostic Hebrew letters (Aleph, Beth, Gimel) that begin each verse, and most of the verses as well, open with clear, melodic references to the Gregorian chant. Melismas, however, with heavy ornamentations and even polyphonic expansion, quickly take over the musical substance of each verse.

A later volume of Charpentier's collected manuscript works (now preserved in the Bibliothéque Nationale) contains another large group of Lamentations settings. They comprise nine lessons, though not a complete set. Once again, the Gregorian chant melody remains present, yet heavily masked in rich musical ornament. These settings, possibly composed for the Ste-Chapelle, add to the operatic solo voices a full complement of instrumental accompaniment, and open with instrumental sinfonias. *—Timothy Dickey*

Recommended:

- ○ **Leçons De Ténèbres Du Jeudy Sainct** / W. Christie (cond.), R. Jacobs, J. Nelson, Verkinderen, Concerto Vocale / HM 901006
- ○ **Leçons De Ténèbres** / Lesne (cond.), Pelon, Purves, Greuillet, Il Seminario Musicale / 1995 / Virgin 45107

Te Deum, motet for soloists, chorus & orchestra, H. 146 (Feb. ?, ? 16??)

Marc-Antoine Charpentier was a seventeenth century Parisian composer who studied with Carissimi in Rome, and helped to set in motion the gradual infiltration of French Baroque music with Italian traits. His four settings of the *Te Deum* text (a hymn of thanksgiving, probably dating from the early Middle Ages) establish this compositional vein; of these four, H. 146 is undoubtedly the most popular, made famous by the adoption of its regal orchestral Prelude as the theme music for Eurovision (a Europe-wide TV distribution network run by the European Broadcasting Union) in the 1950s. The work was probably written in the early 1690s, perhaps in 1692 to mark the French victory at Steinkerque. Cast in D major (a key that Charpentier characterized as "joyous and warlike"), it alternates between delicate sections in an Italian style for the solo singers (often combined with solo wind instruments) and exultant choruses with French-style dotted rhythms and generally simple harmonies. Within movements there are also dramatic changes of meter or texture, a typical practice for Charpentier—one reflecting his view that "diversity in itself makes perfection." The work as a whole, then, exemplifies the peculiarly lyrical grandeur, the warmly Italianate inflection of French formality, that makes Charpentier's music so attractive. *—David A. McCarthy*

Recommended:

- ○ **Charpentier: Te Deum; Magnificat** / Marriner (cond.), Upshaw, A. Murray, Aler, Moll, Academy of St. Martin-in-the-Fieldsields / 1991 / EMI 54284
- ○ **Charpentier: Te Deum** / W. Christie, Les Arts Florissants / HM 926007

OPERA

Médée, H. 491 (1693)

Though it is one of the resplendent monuments of French Baroque opera, *Médée* is an anomaly, both in its composer's career and in its time. The bulk of Charpentier's vast output was for the private devotional use of his noble employers. Even so, he was no stranger to dramatic music, having composed many "dramatic motets" treating Biblical scenes, while his succession to Jean-Baptiste Lully as the house composer for Molière's Comédie Française not only gave him practical theater experience but made him Lully's rival. Apart from the privately performed *David et Jonathas* (1688), *Médée* is Charpentier's only other *tragédie lyrique*, and the only one to have been performed at the Opéra de Paris, known then as the Académie Royale de Musique. The premiere, December 4, 1693, met with a mixed reception falling out along party lines, the Lullistes objecting to Charpentier's Italianate violations of "pure" French style, and the work achieved only ten performances. Though he accepted the dedication of *Médée*, Louis XIV is not on record as having attended. Louis' nonchalant acknowledgement of Charpentier as "a good man," and that he "knew that there were very fine things in his opera," may have been in deference to the memory of Lully, who had died in 1687, but it has been more plausibly suggested that Medea's sorcery and poisoning of her rival—the opera's dramatic high points—too much resembled the infamous Montespan affair in which the royal mistress Françoise Athénaïs, Marquise de Montespan, attempted to hold the king's affections by a combination of witchcraft, aphrodisiacs, and attempts to poison the new favorite. One of the very few Charpentier works to have been published (Paris, 1694), *Médée* was produced again in Lille, November 17, 1700, a revival cut short by a theater fire, and not heard again—incredibly—until a 1984 Opera de Lyon performance led by Michel Corboz. The libretto by Thomas Corneille, younger brother of Pierre Corneille, the creator of classical French tragedy, is cast in the Lullian mold of prologue and five acts, replete with theatrical extenuations and danced *divertissements* which allowed Charpentier to give the best of himself while, so to speak, beating Lully at his own game. Following the obligatory Prologue, a frigid allegorical encomium to the Sun King, Charpentier's music lifts into supple warmth and an overflowing wealth of elegant invention shaped with polished brilliance making *Médée* the crowning work of French Baroque opera before Rameau. *—Adrian Corleonis*

Synopsis:

Prologue. This scene takes place in mythical but then-contemporary France. In it, commoners and shepherds, as well as the Gods of Victory and Glory, praise and defend Louis XIV, then King of France and, not coincidentally, an admirer of this opera.

Act One. Medea, Princess of Colchis, and Jason, Prince of Thessaly, plot the murder of King Pelias of Thessaly. Jason is indebted to her because of her aid in obtaining the golden fleece for him, but he is in love with Creusa, daughter of Creon, King of Corinth. Creusa, however, is to wed the Prince of Argos, Oronte. Medea must have the military support of Creon and Oronte to fend off an impending attack by her enemies in Thessaly. Later, when Jason is alone with his confidante Arcas, he deliberates his situation: is his love for Creusa stronger than his feelings of gratitude and indebtedness to Medea? Oronte arrives amid much fanfare.

Act Two. In a small hallway Creon informs Medea he will defeat her foes, but only if she consents to exile. The Corinthian King intends to retain the services of Jason and Oronte to bolster his kingdom's defenses, aware their love of Creusa will prove favorable to his plans. Medea agrees to Creon's proposal and turns her children (by Jason) over to Creusa. Jason has a rendezvous with Creusa where they declare their mutual love. The unsuspecting Oronte later joins them.

Act Three. Oronte learns of Jason's love for Creusa from Medea, after he proposes asylum in Argos to her for both Jason and her. Medea and Oronte talk of revenge, and when the former learns that Creon has announced the marriage of Jason and Creusa, she mixes a poison to sprinkle on a robe she had earlier given Creusa, a poison whose deadly properties can be ingested by contact.

Act Four. In a palace garden, Medea and Oronte discuss their plans of revenge. Upon the arrival of Creon, Medea uses her powers of sorcery to make him delusional and mentally deranged.

Act Five. At Medea's palace, Creusa, wearing the poison-laced robe, pleas with Medea to remove her dark powers over Creon. But it is too late: news arrives that Creon has murdered Oronte and then taken his own life. Medea kindles the poison in Creusa's robe and she falls dead as Jason clutches her. Medea then reveals to Jason that she has also murdered their children. *—Robert Cummings*

Recommended:

- ○ **Charpentier: Médée** / Christie (cond.), Hunt, Padmore, Deletre, Zanetti, Les Arts Florissants / Erato 96558

CHAMBER MUSIC

Noëls sur les Instruments, H. 534 (ca. 1693)

Marc-Antoine Charpentier might be best known for the reams of weighty sacred vocal music bearing his name, but even this serious and devout composer (his resume includes a long stint as music-master to the Paris Jesuits) did not eschew the joys of lighter musical entertainment such as that to be had from his ten *Noëls sur les Instruments*, H. 534, of around 1695. True, these ten instrumental settings of then-famous Christmas carols were apparently intended to be played during Advent and especially Christmas Eve church services, but there was a time-honored French Baroque tradition of "letting the hair down," even in church, during these final joyous moments before Christmas. Music that dances as happily and, at times, raucously as do these instrumental *Noëls* should probably bear a label warning: "die-hard proponents of grim, austere sacred music beware."

Charpentier's manuscripts for these happy truffles are not entirely specific as to the instrumentation intended, but it is clear that flutes (meaning recorders), string instruments, and basso continuo should be included. The ten carols, in no particular order (since Charpentier provided no particular order), are: "Les bourgeois de Châtre"; "Or nous dites, Marie"; "Laissez paître vos bêtes"; "Joseph est bien marié"; "Vous qui désirez sans fin"; "O créateur"; "A la venue de Noël"; "Une jeune pucelle"; "Où s'en vont ces gais bergers?"; and a second setting of "Les bourgeois de Châtre."

Charpentier's settings, while by no means complex, are not necessarily plain. The first "Les bourgeois de Châtre," for example, begins with a run-of-the-mill, homophonic statement of the carol melody by the whole ensemble. But then there is a comely trio during which the players band together into smaller groups and play around with the various phrases of the melody, offering some counterpoint here, a little imitation there. Finally, the opening music is played again, da capo. The setting of "Vous qui désirez sans fin," on the other hand, is more like a miniature set of variations on the carol melody. The second setting of "les bourgeois de Châtre," which should probably be played as the final number if the *Noëls* are played as a whole, is both more intricate and less repetitive than the first setting. *—Blair Johnston*

Recommended:

○ **Simphonies des Noëls** / Labadie (cond.), Les Violons du Roy / 1993 / Dorian 90180

○ **Noëls pour les instruments** / Poitier (cond.), Les Musiciens de Mademoiselle de Guise / 1999 / Bayard Musique 9630886

Ernest Chausson

b. Jan. 20, 1855, Paris, France, **d.** Jun. 10, 1899, Limay, France
Composer: Vocal, Concerto, Symphonic, Chamber Music

If Marcel Proust had written music, it might have sounded something like Ernest Chausson's: intensely passionate, yet rarely given to grand gestures. The effectiveness of Chausson's ardent, even erotic, musical language derives largely from the slithery chromatic style the composer inherited from his most important teacher, César Franck. Not a prolific composer, Chausson died in 1899, at the age of 44, from injuries sustained in a bicycle accident. Chausson's death silenced the most distinctive voice in French music in the generation immediately preceding Debussy's; indeed, Chausson's music forms an elegant, if swaying, bridge between Franck's lush, Wagnerian Romanticism and the sensuous Impressionist language of Debussy. Chausson came from a well-to-do family; in fact, comfortable circumstances throughout his entire life made it unnecessary for him to pursue a living as a musician. Although interested in music from a young age, Chausson pursued law studies at his father's behest. In 1877, he was sworn in as a lawyer in Paris; in the same year, he wrote his first work, the unpublished song *Lilias*. The impulse to devote himself to composition was sparked in 1879, when he attended a performance of Wagner's *Tristan und Isolde* in Munich and met there the sometime Wagner disciple Vincent d'Indy. Chausson entered the Paris Conservatory in the following year and began studies with Jules Massenet; his formal musical education was rounded out by private study with Franck. Chausson's talent flowered in short order; a number of even his earliest published works—especially the song set *Seven Melodies*, Op. 2 (1879–82)—have long been regarded as small masterpieces. As secretary of the Société Nationale de Musique (an organization founded by Saint-Saëns and others to promote the performance of French instrumental music) from 1886, Chausson became a full-fledged member of the Parisian musical community. His salon became a regular meeting place for literary and musical notables including Mallarmé, Debussy, Albéniz, pianist Alfred Cortot, and violinist/composer Eugène Ysaÿe. A prolific composer of songs, Chausson also composed works for voice and orchestra, choral music, and several operas. He is best known, however, for his chamber music—especially the *Concerto for piano, violin, and string quartet*, Op. 21 (1889–91) and the *Piano Quartet*, Op. 30 (1897)—and for imaginative orchestral works like the *Symphony in B flat major*, Op. 20 (1889–90) and the *Poème for violin and orchestra*, Op. 25 (1896). *—AMG*

VOCAL

Songs (1878–1897)

Chausson oscillated in self-doubt between morbid melancholy and manic gaiety. After taking his doctorate in law in the spring of 1877, he composed his first song, *Lilias*, that year, though he would not enroll in Massenet's instrumentation class at the Conservatoire until 1879. Having decided, at last, on music as a career, his ambition flourished in a number of ballads for solo voice, chorus, and orchestra composed between 1879 and 1881, though his dissatisfaction with them prevented their publication. Among these apprentice works is *L'Albatros* for voice and piano, from October 1879. Baudelaire's comparison of the poet with "the prince of clouds/Haunting the storm and mocking the archer" whose "giant wings prevent him from walking" on the earth appealed strongly to Chausson as an image of his own condition. Though hardly a masterpiece, its grandiose striving signals a shift of allegiance from Massenet to Franck, whose organ—and unofficial composition—class he audited at the Conservatoire, soon becoming an avid member of Franck's intimate circle. His first published songs, the *Sept melodies* of 1882, show him attempting to balance his gifts against the shapely, elegant conceits of Gautier and a new generation of Parnassian poets—Silvestre, Leconte de Lisle. The latter's *Nanny* and *Le Colibri* touch, respectively, Chausson's melancholic and manic strains, though with an assurance which mutes them to fluent sadness and ecstatic contemplation, while the setting of Louise Ackermann's *Hébé* achieves a classicizing, almost static, perfection. With the two collections of four mélodies each—to poems by Verlaine, Villiers de l'Isle Adam, Jean Lahor, and Maurice Bouchor—and the magnificent setting of Gautier's *La Caravane* composed through the mid-1880s, Chausson's harmonic language becomes more chromatically expressive as his grasp of feeling deepens. Of the two *Chansons de Miarka*, composed in 1888 to poems by Jean Richepin, *"La Pluie"* looks back to the Parnassian melodies while the oracular *"Les Morts"* forecasts the works of the 1890s. The three *Chansons de Shakespeare*, spanning the early to mid-1890s, achieve a concentrated utterance with the simplest means. With the settings of Maeterlinck collected under the title *Serres chaudes* ("Hothouses"), Chausson took the plunge into the new aesthetic world of symbolism, teeming with images of a shadowy, interior fullness against which the executants of everyday life are mere stick figures. In these songs, a stifling, hallucinatory demesne is evoked with a somber, chromatically rich harmony owing equally to the Wagner of *Tristan und Isolde* and the Franck of *Psyché*. Only with the *Trois Lieder de Camille Mauclair* of 1896 does Chausson come into his own—albeit inspired now by Schubert and Schumann—with depth of feeling and evocative power handled with a new, quintessential serenity. And with serenity came a new directness heard in *Deux Mélodies*, Op. 36, and the two late Verlaine settings, both 1898. *—Adrian Corleonis*

Recommended:

○ **Chausson: The Songs of Chausson** / Lott, A. Murray, McGreevy, Trakas, G. Johnson, Chilingirian Quartet / Hyperion 67321

○ **Debussy & Chausson: Mélodies** / Schäfer, Gage / 2000 / DG 459682

Chanson perpétuelle, for soprano & orchestra, Op. 37 (1898)

This family man was well-acquainted with the works of Schubert, Schumann, Mendelssohn, Beethoven, and Bach before he acquired a felicitous spirit from Massenet and an understanding of harmonic richness and cyclical form from Franck, with both of whom he studied at the Paris Conservatory. Having first completed legal studies, Chausson's late start in formal musical training required many years of persistence in order to reach refinement. In fact, it was only shortly before his death that Chausson entered his third and most triumphant period of output (1894–99) during which he fully mastered his technique and embraced new ways of thinking about and writing music. The music of his first and second periods, with shapely melodic lines, elegant harmonies, and elaborate and dramatic styles, showed the influence of Wagner and Massenet, whereas that of his third period grows in sonority and harmonic subtlety.

Chanson Perpetuelle (1898) provides an example of the direction in which Chausson was taking his music. The piece has an air of disenchantment and conveys the oppressive degree of Chausson's post-romantic world. The verse is a declaration of love to an absent lover and is taken directly from Charles Cros' poem *Chanson Perpetuelle*. Written for voice, piano, and orchestra (or string quartet/quintet), Chausson implies the title's perpetual recurrence by developing the work's introductory bars, a phrase in the minor mode, which rises to a fifth and falls to the third and tonic, as a predominant accompanimental figure to the tenderly longing syllabic vocal line. The only formal repetition of the piece is found within verse seven, when the music of the first verse is repeated. Chausson is remembered as one of the most prominent and influential members of the Franck circle, and after a period of cleansing himself of his early musical influences, he and other friends attempted to renew interest in pure forms of classicalism. *Chanson Perpetuelle* is an example of the type of purified music that the Franck circle might have been interested in, as it is free from the at-times-incomprehensible Wagnerian language and the Massenet-like use of excessive trills and arpeggios, which were found in Chausson's early works. *Chanson Perpetuelle* is a moving representation of the clarity and conciseness, which appeared in Chausson's final works. *—Meredith Gailey*

Recommended:

○ **La Bonne Chanson: French Chamber Songs** / Von Otter, Forsberg & Chamber Ensemble / 1996 / DG 447752

Poème de l'amour et de la mer, for voice & orchestra, Op. 19 (1882–1890; revised 1893)

Except in the domain of the mélodie, of which he became a supreme master, Chausson seems to have been more hindered than helped by words. The composition of his grand opera *Le roi Arthus*, for which he wrote a superb libretto, occupied him from 1886 until 1895. Likewise, he agonized over the setting of his friend Maurice Boucher's verses for the *Poème de l'amour et de la mer* from 1882 until 1890, visiting revisions upon the work again in 1893. Boucher (1855–1929) was not a great, nor even a very distinguished, poet. And that's perhaps as well, as his cliché-filled sketch of a seaside summer romance allowed Chausson extended opportunities, unhampered by undue explicitness, for mood and scene painting. The Parnassian inheritance—banal images of a time of lilacs and roses giving way to the metallic rustle of dead leaves as love dies—becomes transfigured in Chausson's music into an exquisite, frantic, almost palpable evocation of both the period (what is now thought of as "the Nineties") and the psychology of Romantic love. Part I, "La fleur des eaux," is a gentle seascape reflecting radiant, sunlit happiness, levitated by sensuous arabesques and fretted with anxious anticipation—"O sky that will reflect the color of her eyes"—to rise in a soaring climax before melting into an entranced, hymn-like, beatific vision of the beloved—"a beautiful girl was there upon the shore ... smiling with a tender wildness." Almost at once it is fraught with a premonition of the end—"What wild lament will sound the hour of farewell?"—as exaltation becomes a startled keening, for "my very soul is taken away from me, and the dull booming of the waves muffles my sobs." A brief orchestral interlude rehearses the poignant melody associated with the lost happiness of "le temps des lilas." With the final, extended section—"La mort de l'amour"—the season has turned, the weather has changed, the seascape returns with the tempestuous shimmer of "sauvage" sorcery as black skies and howling winds presage the beloved's sudden coldness—"my blood turned to ice at my love's strange smile.... I could read this fatal word in her wide eyes: oblivion." A final spellbinding lament for the irrecoverable, irremediable "time of lilacs and roses" (arranged in 1886 as a *mélodie* with piano accompaniment) ends on a sustained hush of desolation. Scored with a scintillating sumptuousness according a psychically penetrating prominence to the woodwinds, the *Poème de l'amour et de la mer* has become something of a Liebestod for mezzos, while the score is marked unequivocally "pour une voix (élevée) et orchestre." Curiously, the first performance was given in Brussels in 1893 at one of the prestigious and distinguished subscription concerts organized by Octave Maus, with the composer accompanying a tenor, one Désiré Demest, in his own arrangement for piano. *—Adrian Corleonis*

Recommended:

- ○ **Vesselina Kasarova Sings Berlioz, Ravel, Chausson** / P. Steinberg (cond.), Kasarova, Vienna ORF SO / 1995 / RCA Victor 68008
- ○ **Chausson: Poème; Symphony** / Dutoit (cond.), Le Roux, Montreal SO / 2000 / Decca 458010
- ○ **Baker: Chausson, Berlioz & Schoenberg** / Svetlanov (cond.), J. Baker, London SO / 2001 / BBC Legends 4077

CONCERTO

Concert, for violin, piano & string quartet in D major, Op. 21 (1889–1891)

This rich, warm-sounding, melodic example of late French Romanticism practically defies categorization. Although Chausson called it a "concerto" (*concert* in French), this composition for six players is certainly not that. "Sextet" would be wrong, because that name implies some equality among the players, missing here. The best description would be "duet (or concerto) for violin and piano with string quartet accompaniment." Chausson called the two main instruments "projections against the quartet background." For long stretches of the piece, virtually all the musical interest is in these two instruments; the other strings only occasionally respond.

Stytlistically it is clear that Chausson seeks to avoid the spell that Richard Wagner (1813–83) cast over late nineteenth century French music. He still uses the rich chromatic harmonies and the passionate melodic style that had come into French music in the 1870s and 1880s. But his textures and use of chords suggest an effort to find a non-Wagnerian sound through a deliberate archaism. One device he uses is parallel octaves in the part writing, which suggests old church chant. Another is the consistent use of the plagal cadence (the "church" or "amen" ending) instead of the ordinary type. These almost subconscious religious associations give the music the desired antique quality. In addition, Chausson frequently uses special effects such as arpeggios, trills, and tremolos.

The first movement is based on a three-note motive introduced at the start by the piano. A main theme grows from it. A speedup in tempo leads to one of the several unaccompanied duets for violin and piano in the work. Instead of classical-style development, Chausson offers a further flow of rich melody.

The second movement is in the old Baroque Sicilienne dance rhythm, with a light, restrained, and graceful mood. The violin has two fine themes. The third movement is a somber piece in slow tempo, featuring another section for the two main instruments without the quartet. This one is brooding and distracted in mood. The finale is in the bouncing triple-time gigue rhythm, but has the driving character of a toccata. Despite the rhythmic emphasis, Chausson introduces yet another rich and expressive melody, this time given to piano, as a contrast to the predominantly forward-moving melody.

Chausson dedicated the work to the famous Belgian violin virtuoso Eugène Ysaÿe, evidently in hopes that this would prompt him to play it. In fact, Ysaÿe did play the first performance, in Brussels in 1892, as the soloist, with pianist Auguste Pierret and members of the Ysaÿe Quartet. Upon finishing his creation, Chausson remarked: "Another failure!" Posterity vigorously disagrees. *—Joseph Stevenson*

Recommended:

- ○ **Chausson: Concert; Ravel: Trio** / J. Bell, Thibaudet, Takacs SQ / 1990 / London 425860
- ○ **Chausson: Concert for Violin, Piano and String Quartet** / Perlman, Bolet. Julliard SQ / 1983 / CBS 37814
- ○ **Chausson: Concert pour violon, piano & quatour à cordes** / R. Pasquier, Pennetier, Daugareil, Simonot, B. Pasquier, Pidoux, / 2000 / HM 1951135

Poème, for violin & orchestra, Op. 25 (1896)

On being asked by his friend, the renowned Belgian violinist Eugène Ysaÿe, for a violin concerto, Chausson dithered. The demands implied by the form, coupled with his high seriousness, loomed oppressively just as he was entering a new phase of freedom, fluency, and aureate fancy. It has been suggested by Chausson's biographer, Jean Gallois, that the *Poème*—with which he eventually answered Ysaÿe's request—was prompted by a Turgenev tale of jealousy and death in which the novelist's thwarted passion for the French mezzo-soprano, Pauline Viardot (1821–1910), is transposed into a fabulous Renaissance setting fraught with a magic potion, a violin whose music ravishes the soul, and a lover returned from the legendary orient. Chausson knew and frequently entertained Mme. Viardot—she who had created the role of Fidès in Meyerbeer's *Le Prophète*, who was an accomplished composer, painter, and writer, and upon whom Berlioz in his last decade had a lingering crush—and her husband. Thus the elements of what might have been the strangest of grand operas were in place. It is a mark of Chausson's genius that he eschewed the commonplaces of narrative to transmute those elements into a seamlessly compelling work for violin and orchestra—for the *Poème* is not program music. Rather, its high fantasy—superbly sustained—relies upon deftly dovetailed but clearly distinguished episodes, thematically linked.

Lento e misterioso, a harmonically rich introduction, rippled with thematic premonitions, immediately casts forth an enveloping aura of the fantastic, exalted, and exquisite, before the solo violin enters with a slow, elegiacally beguiling, doubly arched melody, echoed by the orchestra in a sensuous chorale. The violin answers with a solo variation in which the melody is accompanied by rapid scale and arpeggio figures, punctuated by frequent double stops, to magical effect. The orchestra responds with an extended Animato shimmer which the effusively varied violin theme seems to mesmerize as it soars aloft in ever more ecstatic flights. In a Molto animato gasp, the orchestra lunges over the theme's contours to begin a hectically syncopated accompaniment to the violin's riveting sorcery in rapid thirds, fourths, and sixths. For a brief, hesitating moment, passion seems exhausted. With a triplet-coiled ascent of three octaves, the violin rouses the orchestra, which responds again with the theme's chorale-like enunciation as it is slowly enchanted into another spate of enraptured shimmer over which the violin, with a lacing, lashing, feverishly entrancing new melody, brings all to a sudden climax. The chorale returns, vehement but giving way to weary finality as the violin croons and surges aloft to sink in chains of trills, spent, to a sumptuous cadence.

Composed between mid-April and mid-June 1896, the *Poème* was given its première at the Nancy Conservatoire on December 27 of that year by Ysaÿe, to whom it is dedicated. In a sublime gesture, Chausson's friend, Isaac Albéniz, secretly arranged for Breitkopf to publish the score, paying for it from his own pocket, to buoy the composer through one of his periodic bouts of self-doubt. *—Adrian Corleonis*

Recommended:

- ○ **Poème** / Litton (cond.), J. Bell, Royal PO / 1991 / London 433519
- ○ **Chausson: Poème; Symphony** / Dutoit (cond.), Juillet, OS de Montreal / 2000 / Decca 458010

SYMPHONIC

Symphony in B flat major, Op. 20 (1889–1890)

The mid-1880s witnessed the creation of a mighty handful of great French symphonies—Saint-Saëns' *"Organ" Symphony*, Lalo's *Symphony in G minor*, d'Indy's *Symphony on a French Mountain Air*, and César Franck's *Symphony in D minor* (begun in 1886 and completed in 1888). Having hit his mature compositional stride during this period, Chausson inevitably wished to add a symphony of his own to the series—hopefully one that would help him overcome his reputation as an affluent dilettante. His *B flat Symphony* was begun in September 1889 and completed in December of the following year. Its three-movement layout has prompted comparisons with that of his mentor, Franck—for instance, both employ the "cyclical" recall of themes from previous movements in the last, and make prominent use of the cor anglais—though perhaps the most significant common quality between the works is their intense mood of idealism. Chausson's preoccupation with symphonic forms and expression would carry over into his contemporaneous work on his opera, *Le Roi Arthus*, begun in 1886; it suffers somewhat from its self-conscious striving for nobility of utterance in formally wrought (sometimes overwrought) sections of "pure" music.

The Symphony opens with a brooding Lent introduction, the basic melodic shape of which will reoccur throughout the work; having the character of a prolonged sigh, it rises in ever more anxious iterations to a thunderously impassioned statement before giving way to a light, shimmering, syncopated, heraldic first theme (Allegro vivo). The following development—fraught with sudden shifts from minor to major and constant modulations—is animated by real conviction, as aureately ecstatic moments vie with tempestuous alarums. A brief recapitulation and coda round off the movement with a rare moment of relative triumph.

The second movement (Très lent), also with two themes, is a long-breathed lamentation, rising to a passionate climax and ending in the optimistic glow of a prolonged D major chord. In good cyclic fashion, the third movement (Animé) opens stormily, with a fanfare-like reminiscence of the first movement introduction ushering in thematic transformations of material from the preceding movements; the first movement's Allegro vivo theme receives special emphasis. Development and recapitulation seem to have reached an impasse when the opening motto theme is heard as a chorale—a Franckian ritual also strategically employed in symphonies by d'Indy and Magnard—which succeeds by the audacity of being scored for brass choir alone. Conferring a moment of mournful benediction, it is taken up by the orchestra in a grandiose peroration.

Of Wagnerian amplitude, the orchestral writing is graced by a glowing, almost impressionist, richness which compensates for such weaker passages as the repetitive third movement. In its grandeur and gloom, the Symphony is abreath with the aspirations and anxieties of the Franckist *table ronde*. *—Adrian Corleonis*

Recommended:

○ **Chausson: Poème; Symphony** / Dutoit (cond.), Montreal SO / 2000 / Decca 458010

○ **Chausson: Symphony; Ibert: Escales** / Mata (cond.), Dallas SO / 1994 / Dorian 90181

CHAMBER MUSIC

Piano Quartet in A major, Op. 30 (1897)

Chausson's music, at all stages, could be called psychological in its vaulting gamut of expression—from blackest melancholy to mercurially manic high spirits—traversed with startling suddenness by an unexpected modulation, a subtle nuance, a brilliant *coup de théâtre*. Indeed, the latter occur more often in his orchestral and chamber works than in his grand opera, *Le roi Arthus*, lending them a constant effect of shimmer between articulate darkness and blithe radiance. In the first decade of his maturity, in such things as the *Poème de l'amour et de la mer* (1882–90) and the *Symphony* (1889–90), this bipolar oscillation is tinged with a certain morbidity checked only by the application of formal procedures inspired by Franck. But from the mid-1890s, as Chausson entered his forties, a new prehension—a hectically fraught serenity (or hyper-aesthetic twist on the "serene anxiety" of his mentor, César Franck)—comes into play. Form and content, too, dovetail more deftly. The handful of works from this period are no less intense, impassioned, or volatile, but suffused with a new assurance that calls to mind Yeats' lines in his 1939 poem "Lapis Lazuli," reminding all that great actors "Do not break up their lines to weep./They know that Hamlet and Lear are gay; /Gaiety transfiguring all that dread." In this sense, the works of Chausson's last broken-off period have about them a tragic gaiety. One thinks of the *Serres chaudes* cycle of *mélodies*, the great *Poème for violin and orchestra*, the *Quelques danses* for piano, and—preeminently—of the sublime *Piano Quartet*. In marked contrast to the slow, agonizing gestation of many of his other works, the *Piano Quartet* was composed in a mere five weeks between July and September 1897. The cascading pentatonic theme that opens the work provides most of the first movement's Animé melodic material, with its peremptory head phrase and nether phrases lyrically shaped for contrast. Although the movement is written in orthodox sonata-allegro form, listeners are reminded, in a fine turn on Franck's "cyclic" practice, that it all originates from one long-breathed melody. Rapidly and with constant modulations, this unity in multiplicity unfurls its transformative fabric in coruscating brilliance. Marked Très calme, the second movement offers an orison-like lied, passionately worked, yielding to an imploring, insistently contrasting middle section before the lied returns with an air of wan melancholy. The brief third movement, woven around a folklike tune, passes—Simple et sans hâte—with sad, balletic grace. A tempestuous Animé burst announces the final, long, balancing movement largely given to languishing, dreamlike evocations—albeit dramatically rippled—of themes from the preceding movements to conclude with a recall of the lied and an oracular reminiscence of the work's opening cascading melody. While the *Concert for piano, violin, and string quartet* (1892), among Chausson's chamber works, has achieved something like popularity, critics and connoisseurs rate the seldom-heard *Piano Quartet* a far finer work, and not merely because of its unintentionally valedictory *geste*. *—Adrian Corleonis*

Recommended:

○ **Chausson: Concert; Piano Quartet** / Devoyon, Graffin, Chilingirian SQ / 1997 / Hyperion 66907

Carlos Chávez

b. Jun. 13, 1899, Mexico City, Mexico, **d.** Aug. 2, 1978, Mexico City, Mexico
Composer: Symphonic, Chamber Music, Orchestral, Ballet

Carlos Chávez was probably the most important Mexican composer of the twentieth century. Known for his seven symphonies, the ballets *La hija de Colquide* (The Dark Meadow), and *Toxcatl*—which uses his popular 1947 *Toccata for percussion*—his concertos for piano and violin (one each) and the four *Soli* (the third for orchestra and soloists and the others for winds), he was a composer who generally did not follow trends and fared better in purely orchestral or instrumental music. While Chávez's style is sometimes not recognizable as Latin, as it can often sound Stravinskyan and neo-classical, folk elements of Aztec and Mexican music rarely stay dormant for long, with their colorful rhythms, exotic percussion and characterful themes. Chávez also wrote two books, one of which was the influential *Toward a New Music: Music and Electricity*, from 1932.

Chávez's father died when he was three, but he and his five other siblings were generally well cared for by their mother, who was a school teacher. He studied piano with Asuncion Parra, having already developed a measure of proficiency from lessons in his early childhood from an older brother. Young Carlos advanced rapidly and by the age of eleven began studies with Ponce. While he received instruction only on piano during his early years, Chávez began to study instrumentation on his own. Throughout his career, in fact, he continued this practice: his copies of Beethoven's and Brahms' symphonies, for instance, contained all sorts of notations in his hand.

At 15, Chávez became a pupil of Ogazon and a year later took some instruction from Fuentes in harmony. Among his first important works was the *Piano Sextet* (1919), whose piano part he performed at its 1921 premiere. That same year Chávez began work on his Aztec ballet *El fuego Nuevo*, on a government commission.

Chávez married Otilia Ortiz in September 1922, then traveled to Europe and the United States with his bride over the next several years, finding the culture of the latter much more to his liking. In fact, he made many subsequent trips there and even lived in New York City from 1926 to 1928, where he developed friendships with Copland, Varèse and other important figures of the day. His only opera, *The Visitors*, would be premiered in New York in May 1957.

In 1924, Chávez began writing music articles for *El universal*, a Mexico City newspaper, and he continued to do so for most of the rest of his life. He also had developed ties in politics by now and soon received important appointments: directorship of the National Conservatory came in 1928; and in 1933 he took up the reins at the Public Education's fine arts department. But he remained busy composing during these years, too, completing his ballet *Caballos de vapor* in 1932 and turning out his first (1933) and second (1935–36) symphonies, as well as many other works.

In 1947, Chávez helped establish Mexico's National Institute of Fine Arts. He made a return trip to Europe two years later, but still found its culture of no great appeal to his sensibilities. Over the next two decades he composed more symphonies (his seventh coming in 1960 and his sixth in 1961), many songs, and chamber works. In 1958–59, he served as Charles Eliot Norton Chair of Poetics at Harvard University. In the 1970s, Chávez's inspiration seemed to vanish, as he produced no significant new work. *—Robert Cummings*

SYMPHONIC

Symphony No. 1 ("Sinfonía de Antígona") (1932)

Mexican composer/conductor/educator Carlos Chávez trained first as a pianist and later came to the art of composing to a great extent through self-instruction.

The first symphonic work by Carlos Chávez offers an example of the composer's working out of the Spanish musical tradition in terms relevant to his own time. That tradition addressed variation as the principal developmental device rather than form as found within the Austro-German heritage, based primarily on the sonata whether applied to solo and chamber music or to works of symphonic dimension. For this reason, the symphony was not strongly represented in Spanish music, not, that is, until Chávez began his exploration of the symphony based on motifs rather than on form. Proof of his process lies both in his copies of symphonic scores by the European masters (scores marked with notations of variations arising from basic themes) and in his own symphonies, all of which exemplify his preoccupation.

Sinfonía de Antígona is a brief, but eventful work, lasting approximately 11 minutes. In one continuous movement, it is founded upon a reexamination of the Greek modal system, employing differing modes (specifically the Dorian and Hypodorian) to convey the struggle within the heroine, Antigone, and her embattled relationship to her society. The symphony begins with woodwinds voicing a slowly oscillating, slightly dissonant melody. The strings next sound the austere theme, percussion punctuates, then winds are heard in octaves. Trilling high winds lead eerily to a steady rhythmic figure sounded by plucked strings. Softer string figures meander curiously before clashing brass chords interject ever more insistently. Drums then presage a return of the relatively quiet winds. Strings and winds are heard next in combination with the sounding of a high gong adding a sense of distance and anticipation. Just before the halfway mark, a faster rhythmic figure appears briefly, then winds combine with strings in a steadily broadening and ever grander effect, the percussion more urgent, reinforced by punching brass chords. The lower winds are heard beneath a flute, then the lower strings appear voicing open Copland-esque chords. The strings articulate a dancing figure and, as the conclusion approaches, the piece becomes once more slower, broader, simpler. Harp chords bring the symphony to an end. *—Erik Eriksson*

Recommended:

- ○ **Chávez: 3 Symphonies** / Bátiz (cond.) / 1999 / ASV 1058

Symphony No. 2 ("Sinfonía india") (1935)

In his first symphonic work, composer Carlos Chávez was inspired by the ancient Greeks. When he returned to the symphonic form, he turned to the Indian culture of his own hemisphere.

Though Chávez only rarely used authentic Native melodies only rarely, the *Sinfonia India* features actual themes discovered in his research. From the Huichol Indians of the state of Nayarit, he drew the first theme of the exposition. The introduction which opens the brief work, in a pentatonic scale, suggests a recalling, a conjuring of the past world of the Mexican Indian. Mixed meters (5/8, 2/4, 5/8, 3/4) give way to indigenous-style drumming before the Huichol theme makes its appearance. That theme steals in via the first violins and oboes over a sustained rhythmic pattern in the seconds and violas, a pattern carried over from the introduction. The Yaqui Indians of Sonora provided the second and third themes, while a Seri melody forms the basis for the finale. The concluding section is a sustained crescendo of rhythmic excitement and orchestral color, representing both a people and the vitality of their cultural voice.

This 15-minute work in one movement ranges in mood from joyful and dancing, to lyrical, to that of a solemn ritual procession. The sound of the work is colorful yet ascetic, as if it were a painting in primary earth colors. Throughout, there is exceptional use of percussion instruments. In the score, the composer specifies native percussion instruments, such as deer-hoof rattles. But he is also careful to list alternative instruments that the average symphony orchestra outside Mexico is likely to be able to get and which are more apt sound through a symphony at its full power. However, recordings made in Mexico and elsewhere often do use the "authentic" Mexican instruments and balance the sound so that they can be heard. *—Erik Eriksson*

Recommended:

- ○ **Latin American Masters: Orbon; Villa-Lobos; Estevez; Chávez** / Mata (cond.), Simon Bolivar SO of Venezuela / 1994 / Dorian 90179
- ○ **Chávez: 3 Symphonies** / Bátiz (cond.), Orquesta Filarmonica De La Ciudad De Mexico / 1999 / ASV 1058

Symphony No. 4 ("Sinfonía Romántica") (1952)

Carlos Chávez was one of the leading Mexican composers of the twentieth century and his six symphonies are clearly among his most important works. The *Fourth* here is probably the most popular after the *Second*, the "Sinfonía índia," which has appeared on numerous recordings. This later symphony is somewhat less exotic, but just as skillfully scored, and having a more traditional formal design. The "Sinfonía Romántica" features thematic ties among its three movements, the main theme of the opening panel appearing in different guises or in partial form throughout. This symphony sounds like many American compositions from this period, in particular like the robust and sometimes epic symphonies of David Diamond. Stravinsky can be noticed here, too, and of course, so can some colorful Latin flavors, most notably in the rhythm and percussion scoring. The joyous and aloof main theme in the Allegro first movement is immediately presented by the English horn, then taken up by strings and oboes. A second, somewhat dreamy melody is presented by the bassoon, later played by the trumpet. Other motifs appear to form new material and the development section that follows is terse but totally satisfying. The whole movement is quite attractive and fairly light in expressive manner. The short second movement (Molto lento) is deeper in its darker character. The main theme, partially derived from the first movement's main theme, is songful but tense and sorrowful. The finale opens with a full statement of the seemingly ubiquitous main theme from the opening panel, then moves on to present several other ideas and some imaginative development of the materials, featuring much interesting contrapuntal writing. This movement makes the symphony somewhat lopsided and unusual in that it is, at about ten minutes, nearly half the length of this 20-minute-plus work. *—Robert Cummings*

Recommended:

- ○ **Música Mexicana Vol. 8: Chávez, Revueltas** / Batiz (cond.), Royal PO / 1995 / ASV 942

CHAMBER MUSIC

Toccata, for 6 percussionists (1942)

This is one of the first major pieces written for percussion ensemble alone, and perhaps the first in a Classical, multi-movement form. As such, it is a brilliantly inventive piece, and is a cornerstone of the percussion ensemble repertoire. Chávez avoids using percussion to make a bunch of noise, nor does he use it to maintain a driving beat or imitate any folklore or dance movement at all. Toccata movements traditionally are fast movements with many repeated notes, an opportunity for virtuosic display. Chávez recalls that the root meaning of toccata is "toccare," meaning "to touch," and is meant to display the performer's touch, rather than lyrical gifts. Since the essence of percussion playing is that the instrument's sound by being touched, Chávez shows the possibilities of percussion at moderate tempos and mostly without melodic material. The first movement is primarily for drums; the second one casts a mysterious spell with mainly metallic instruments. Both types are combined for the scherzo. A wonder of this piece is that with all the exotic sound-material available to him Chávez kept such a pure, Classical feeling about this percussion masterpiece. *—Joseph Stevenson*

Recommended:

- ○ **Chávez: Xochipilli; Suite for Double Quartet; Tambuco; Energia; Toccata** / Mata (cond.), La Camerata & Tambuco / 1994 / Dorian 90215
- ○ **4'33"** / : Double Music, Varèse: Ionisation, Cage: Third Construction, Cage: Amores, Chávez: Toccata, Cage: / Amadinda Percussion Group / Hungaroton 12991

Xochipilli, an Imagined Aztec Music (1940)

Xochipilli, a work for wind quartet and percussion sextet, represents the synthesis and synergy of meticulous research, cultural introspection, archaeological speculation, and musical imagination that characterize much of the music of Mexican composer Carlos Chávez. Written in 1940, the work uses a unique mixture of modern and ancient musical instruments to speculate on the sonority and expressivity of a musical culture long since lost. The piece is named after an important figure in indigenous Mexican culture, the Aztec "Prince of Flowers." In addition to being the god of poetry, dance, and music, Xochipilli was also the god of joy and love and is depicted in ancient pictograms adorned with flowers and holding a barbed stick with which he pricked the hearts of men. As the work's subtitle suggests, it seeks only to "imagine" the kind of music that might have been performed by the worshipers of Xochipilli. None of the music from the period in question actually survives, of course, but many instruments from that era do. Chávez, ever interested in establishing as authentic a foundation as possible for his own creative forays into his native culture, undertook considerable research into these instruments in order to inform his music to the fullest extent. In fact, this work is perhaps his most "historically informed" piece. It calls for a variety of Aztec percussion instruments, including various huehuetls (skin drums), a pair of teponaxtles (double-tongued log drums), two omichicahuaztli (a notched bamboo shaft), and various kinds of shakers; in addition, a trombone is used to simulate the sound of a blown conch shell. These instruments, along with the traditional instruments in the ensemble, play figures and patterns whose connection with the past is entirely speculative; still, this "Imagined Aztec music" surely provides a hint of the sonority, or at least zeitgeist, of the musical followers of Xochipilli. And perhaps more importantly for Chávez, the work represented the kind of convergence that he saw in his own ancestry and heritage and his efforts as a Mexican composer: a mixture of vibrant native culture ultimately overtaken by and speaking largely through the voice of, but nonetheless adding its own energy to the "European" tradition. *—Jeremy Grimshaw*

Recommended:

- ○ **Chávez: Xochipilli; Suite for Double Quartet; Tambuco; Energia; Toccata** / Mata (cond.), La Camerata & Tambuco / 1994 / Dorian 90215

ORCHESTRAL

Toccata (1947)

Carlos Chávez's *Toccata para orquesta* was originally composed as incidental music for one scene of Salvador Novo's dramatization of *The Adventures of Don Quixote*, and was commissioned for this purpose by Mexico's National Institute of Fine Arts. The passage of time has removed the music from its dramatic context, and it now lives in the repertory as an orchestral showpiece. The work opens with a long pastoral section, played by a lone oboe, which calmly elaborates on a short opening motive. The music here is long-breathed and almost hypnotic, and it seems as though the oboe's song will never cease. Finally, the bassoon enters with a short, similarly ruminative solo, after which the rest of the winds, the strings, and the brass bring a new, energetic motive and rush the tempo to develop it. This new motive has a Mexican flavor common in Chávez's melodies, but the development is mainly concerned with propulsion and exuberantly varied and piquant orchestration. Chávez holds most of the orchestra in reserve until the *Toccata*'s closing pages, when he finally lets the percussion make some timely comments. Everything slows to a crawl for some triumphant final chords. The *Toccata para orquesta* is as immediately attractive a work as anything else Chávez ever wrote. *—Andrew Lindemann Malone*

Recommended:

- **Musica Mexicana Vol. 7: Chávez** / Batiz (cond.), State of Mexico SO / 1995 / ASV 927

BALLET

La hija de Cólquide ("Dark Meadow") (1943; revised 1946)

The renowned dancer-choreographer Martha Graham inspired the creation of *La hija de Cólquide* (The Daughter of Colchis), the fourth of Chávez's five ballets. She both commissioned the music from Chávez and formulated the initial concept for the work. The ancient Greek story of Medea was the starting point for a scenario in which modern themes were combined with elements familiar from Greek mythology. Chávez composed the ballet's music in 1943, scoring it for a double quartet of winds and strings. At the same time that he was creating the ballet in eight sections, Chávez was also assembling a five-movement suite from the music for full orchestra. By the time of its premiere at the Plymouth Theatre in New York on January 23, 1946, the ballet's title had changed to *Dark Meadow.* Graham choreographed the work, and Isamu Noguchi created the sets (one of his numerous collaborations with Graham).

Chávez had long been interested in classical Greek theatre—consider his incidental music from 1932 for Jean Cocteau's adaptation of Sophocles' *Antigone,* or the later cantata *Prometheus Bound* (1956). In the case of *La hija de Cólquide,* Chávez created a rather restrained score, much of it in a moderate-to-slow tempo, with little of the explosiveness one finds in so many of his works. The emphasis is on pastoral lyricism, some of it in the vein of Chávez's good friend Aaron Copland. There are impassioned moments in the score, such as the more threatening parts of the "Encantamiento" and "Peán" that serve as the second and fourth movements of the orchestral suite. But much of the music is quiet, such as the oboe solo that begins and ends the work or the string chorales that are so often featured. *—Chris Morrison*

Recommended:

- **Musica Mexicana Vol. 7: Chávez** / Bátiz (cond.), State of Mexico SO / 1995 / ASV 927

Shura Cherkassky

b. Oct. 7, 1909, Odessa, Russia, **d.** Dec. 27, 1995, London, England

Pianist

At his death, Cherkassky was almost universally remembered as the last great Romantic pianist. Cherkassky combined Romantic sensitivity of touch with the power of a modern player, and he traveled easily between works by the Romantics and those by Ives, Hindemith, Boulez, and Ligeti. This blend of talents served him well, particularly in works such as Mussorgsky's *Pictures at an Exhibition.* His parents brought him to the United States in 1923, and within a few years he began studies with Josef Hofmann at the newly founded Curtis Institute. Among his early performances were one with Walter Damrosch and the New York Symphony Orchestra, a performance at the White House, and a tour in 1928 that included Australia and South Africa. Although he also made a few recordings during the 1920s and 1930s, his career did not really take off until after World War II and his move to London. By that time, the pianists, like Hofmann, who had learned from the nineteenth century greats Liszt, Moszkowski, and others, were no longer around. Cherkassky was acknowledged as the heir of that particular school of performance, and just as Liszt and the others had had their own idiosyncrasies, he had his own individual style that seemed to give fresh meaning to everything he played. He toured almost continually around the world during his career, making some time nearly every year to take a holiday in Thailand. He made a successful debut in Russia in 1976 and returned for subsequent tours in 1977 and 1987. In 1986, New York's 92nd Street Y began annually presenting the Shura Cherkassky Recital Award to young artists, in honor of the many recitals Cherkassky had given there. Most of his recordings were made later in his life and cover most of his Romantic repertoire. The best representations of his work can be found on the Decca and Nimbus labels. *—Patsy Morita*

Recommended:

- **Rachmaninov: Concerto 3; Prokofiev: Concerto 2** / Nagano, Schwarz (conds.), Cherkassky, London PO, BBCSO / 2002 / BBC Legends 4092
- **Piano Masters: Shura Cherkassky** / Stokowski (cond.), Cherkassky, Hollywood Bowl SO / 2001 / Pearl 0138
- **Shura Cherkassky** / Cherkassky / 1999 / Philips 456742
- **Art of the Encore** / Cherkassky / 1995 / Nimbus 7708

Luigi Cherubini

b. Sep. 14, 1760, Florence, Italy, **d.** Mar. 15, 1842, Paris, France

Composer: Opera, Choral, Symphonic

Much admired by musicians, Cherubini was Beethoven's favorite contemporary composer. What Beethoven and many others particularly admired was Cherubini's ability to weave his polyphonic virtuosity, Classical stylistic polish, and a truly Romantic sense of drama into music of extraordinary depth and dramatic power. The work that made Cherubini's famous as a dramatist of exceptional psychological acumen was the opera *Medée,* based on the harrowing tragedy by Euripides. Cherubini also excelled as a church composer. In his sacred music, particularly the later works, Cherubini combined his profound knowledge and skill as a contrapuntalist with an ability to express, tempering a passionate dramatic impulse with the discipline of religious contemplation, the tremendous experience of faith.

Born in Florence, on September 14, 1760, Cherubini started studying music with his father; his first work, a mass and Credo, was performed in 1773. Five years later, he went to study with Giuseppe Sarti, composing his first opera, *Il Quinto Fabio,* during this apprenticeship. Returning to Florence in 1782, Cherubini continued composing operas. In 1785, following a successful visit to London, Cherubini traveled to Paris, permanently establishing himself in the French capital. His first work for the French stage, the opera *Démophon,* was produced in 1788. The following year, which marked the beginning of the French Revolution, Cherubini was named director of a new opera company, an enterprise initiated under the auspices of King Louis XVI's brother, who later ruled France as Louis XVIII. In 1791, Cherubini produced his opera *Lodoïska,* which was received with tremendous enthusiasm. In 1792, however, the opera company, viewed by revolutionaries as a royalist relic, ceased to exist, and Cherubini found refuge at a friend's country house in Normandy. Nevertheless, he returned to the capital in 1793, hoping, despite the dangerous political situation, to resume his career. Having made the proper political connections, Cherubini won an appointment at the Institut National de Musique. When the Institute became the Conservatoire National in 1795, Cherubini became one of its inspectors. During this period, Cherubini composed ephemeral works glorifying the new government.

A turning point in Cherubini's career was the 1797 production of *Medée.* As Philip G. Downs has observed, *Medée* is a brilliant synthesis of the opéra comique (with spoken dialogue), the tragédie lyrique (with a story from mythology), Gluck's opera, and the allegorical opera during the French Revolution. Medea, the mythological sorceress who murders her children, is traditionally portrayed as a demonic figure. Significantly, Cherubini's work, while conveying the sheer horror of Medea's actions, focuses on the chilling, sinister, yet profoundly human, nature of his protagonist's rage.

In 1805, Cherubini traveled to Vienna, where he met Haydn, Beethoven, and Napoleon, who had come to Vienna as a conqueror. The French Emperor, who never fully appreciated Cherubini's music, urged the composer to return to Paris. After his return, Cherubini fell into a deep depression, lost all interest in music, retired to the chateau of the Prince of Chimay, and turned to painting and botany. Fortunately, he was asked to compose a mass for the church in Chimay, and this request prompted him to return to music. His inspiration as powerful as ever, Cherubini devoted himself to composing music for the Church. In 1822, Cherubini became director of the Paris Conservatory, gaining the reputation of an excellent administrator. Although extremely busy at the Conservatory, Cherubini continued composing, writing, among other works, his profound *Requiem in D minor.* First performed in 1836, Cherubini's Requiem was also played at his funeral—according to his wishes. *—Zoran Minderovic*

OPERA

Médée (ca. 1797)

According to music historian Philip G. Downs, to Cherubini "falls the honor of having written the only opera of the 1790s (apart from Mozart's) to survive on the modern stage." First performed in Paris, in 1797, *Médée* is a complex and demanding work, requiring in its title role a soprano with what would later be called an exceptional bel canto voice as well as extraordinary dramatic talent. A moderate success, the opera was quickly forgotten in France. *Médée* was sometimes performed throughout the nineteenth century and in the early twentieth century, but it truly became established in the twentieth century opera repertoire in 1952 when Maria Callas sang the title role, also starring in Pier Paolo Pasolini's 1969 film version of Euripides's tragedy.

Immortalized by Euripides, the story of Medea has inspired numerous literary and musical works. Medea, the mythological sorceress and priestess of Hecate, murders her children when her husband, Jason, whom she had assisted in his successful quest for the Golden Fleece, repudiates her because he wishes to marry another woman. Traditional renditions of the story have portrayed Medea as a demonic figure, but Cherubini and his librettist, François-Benoit Hoffmann, while conveying the sheer horror of Medea's actions, bring out the humanity of a woman who is driven to unspeakable crimes by unbearable pain. As Downs has remarked, in the France of 1797, the story of Medea could have easily been interpreted as an allegory of the Revolution who devours her own children. Cherubini's work is a brilliant synthesis of several types of opera: opéra comique, tragédie lyrique, Gluck's operatic style, and the allegorical opera of the French Revolution. In this opera, Cherubini's mastery of harmony, counterpoint, and orchestration—which often anticipates the orchestral sound of Beethoven—truly comes to the fore.

Cherubini may lack the astounding melodic facility of Mozart, but his peerless handling of musical form and drama rewards the listener with an extraordinary operatic experience. This remarkable balance of drama and form is exemplified by Medea's aria in the first act of the opera. Cherubini and Mozart, Downs affirmed in his discussion of *Médée*, "stand alone as the two opera composers of the time with sufficient technical *savoir faire* to be able to accomplish what they set to do." *—Zoran Minderovic*

Synopsis:

Act One. At the palace of Creon, King of Corinth, his daughter Dirce expresses doubts about her upcoming marriage to Jason, leader of the Argonauts, because of a possible return of his evil wife Medea. Jason and several attendants reassure her, the former suggesting Medea is likely dead. She finally consents and Creon blesses the marriage, but a mysterious woman enters and reveals herself to be Medea. She wants Jason back, but Creon orders her banished. Using both threats and charm, she attempts to persuade Jason to return to her, but despite a weakening spirit, he refuses.

Act Two. In a chamber in Creon's palace, Medea's attendant Neris warns her that an angry crowd is gathering outside, demanding her life. Medea, enraged that Jason will not allow her to see her children, is fearless and decides to remain in the palace. Creon enters and urges her to flee, declaring he will be unable to save her from the wrath of the growing mob. Medea first attempts to sway Creon against Jason, but seeing her cause is hopeless, pleads with him to allow her one more day's stay at the palace. He finally acquiesces. Medea decides that Dirce must die for her to achieve vengeance against Jason. Jason enters and agrees to let their children stay with her for her final day at the palace. After he departs for pre-nuptial activities, Medea commands Neris to fetch the children, as well as several jewels she will use as wedding presents for Dirce. Jason, Dirce, Creon, and the wedding party enter the temple, as Medea rails against the event.

Act Three. On a hill in front of the temple, amid the roar of thunder, Medea invokes the powers of the gods to come to her aid. Neris enters with the children, Medea realizing her maternal sense is an encumbrance in her plan to kill them. Neris describes the scene at the wedding reception when she presented the gifts to Dirce, and Medea gleefully ponders the bride's grim fate once the poisoned jewels touch her skin. Medea orders Neris to take the children into the temple. Cries emanate from the palace, as Dirce is consumed by fire from the lethal jewels. Neris tells Jason of Medea's plan to slay the children, and he rushes toward the temple. When he arrives at the entrance he sees three Eumenides flanking Medea, who holds the bloody knife she used to stab the children. She curses Jason and tells him they will meet in Hades. The temple bursts into flames as she floats skyward. *—Robert Cummings*

Recommended:

- ○ **Cherubini: Medea** / Gardelli (cond.), G. Jones, Lorengar, Prevedi, Cossotto, Orch. Accdemia de Saint Cecilia, Rome / 1997 / Decca 452611
- ○ **Cherubini: Medea** / L .Bernstein (cond.), Callas, Barbieri, Modesti, Vercelli, La Scala Theater Orch. / 2002 / EMI 67909

CHORAL

Mass No. 5 in D minor (1811)

Although it is an exceedingly long work, the *Mass in D minor* took Cherubini only six months to complete. It is rich in melody, harmony, and instrumentation, and at times takes on an operatic sense of drama; but, in keeping with Cherubini's aesthetic, it retains a tone of solemnity and is consistently tailored to the meaning of the mass text. The Gloria has five sections, the Kyrie three complete movements, and the Credo six distinct divisions. These divisions into sections reflect the fragmentation of the text of the Ordinary, a practice which is typical of the period. Lasting almost 30 minutes, the monumental Gloria is the longest movement. With all of the resources of counterpoint at his disposal, Cherubini created a truly memorable piece, with beauties on every page. Its opening is incredibly forceful, vigorous, and uplifting. However, the sections of the Gloria contrast in mood and scoring. The "Benedicamus te" is hymn-like and pious, while the "Pax in terra hominibus" is delicate and refined. The "Gratias agimus tibi," which immediately follows the Kyrie, features three solo voices and a richly lyrical style of writing. This is the breath of fresh air needed before the audience encounters the monumentally dramatic "Qui Tollis." Everything about this section is dramatic and vivid. Here, the meaning of the text comes through with truthfulness and energy. The tragedy of sin and the anguish of the hopeless are clearly depicted in the vocal forces and orchestral accompaniment. The music is filled with human pathos and operatic emotion. Toward its close, the music turns to a heavenly pianissimo, as hope for the hopeless seems to shine through. The Credo includes a section for solo voices which creates a poetic image of the incarnation, the voices singing purely and simply over a delicate orchestral accompaniment. In the Crucifixus, an atmosphere of mystery and magic is created when the choir gently sings while the orchestra holds on to a single sustained note. What follows is the "Resurrexit," which surprises the listener with its unbridled energy and vigorous vitality. The Sanctus, Benedictus, and Agnus Dei, are lesser movements, although the Benedictus is noteworthy for its operatic splendor and spaciousness. *—Rita Laurance*

Recommended:

- ○ **Cherubini: Messa solenne per il Principe Esterházy** / Muti (cond.), Streit, Suzuki, Tilling, Bavarian Radio SO / 2001 / EMI 57166

Requiem No. 1 in C minor (1816)

Commissioned by the Bourbon family to honor the memory of Louis XVI, this *Requiem Mass* was first performed in 1816. This is a grandiose work which scholars have compared to Mozart's *Requiem*. Indeed, Cherubini's composition was hailed as a great accomplishment by a number of major composers, including Beethoven, Schumann, Brahms, and even Cherubini's arch-enemy Berlioz. Premiered throughout Europe in the 1820s to considerable acclaim, this *Requiem* has been performed fairly frequently, particularly in Germany. While the comparison with Mozart's *Requiem* may not be far-fetched, there are fundamental differences between the two works. First of all, there are no soloists in Cherubini's work; secondly, Cherubini's orchestration, which reflects the development of orchestration technique since Mozart's death, features truly Romantic brass and percussion effects. The Introitus and Kyrie are slow and gloom-laden, with the orchestra balanced toward the cellos and bassoons. The brief Graduale, however, is almost tender compared to the opening section. This moment of peace is soon shattered by the brass fanfare and ominous tam-tam stroke that introduce the initially frantic Dies Irae. It should be noted that these characteristic effects consisting of new brass and percussion timbres greatly influenced the arch-Romantic Berlioz, who delighted in excoriating Cherubini for his "traditionalism." The Dies Irae music soon subsides, but remains constantly troubled through such devices as soft but frantic falling phrases in the strings underlying steadier choral passages. Alternately laconic and theatrical, this movement also anticipates moments in Verdi's *Requiem*. In contrast, the smoothly assertive Offertorium seems almost confident. Its centerpiece and conclusion are grand fugues on the words "Quam olim Abrahae" ("Which Thou didst promise to Abraham"). The tiny yet powerful Sanctus provides a brief moment of light to show the way to Cherubini's restrained setting of Pie Jesu. This leads to an Agnus Dei that begins in deep mourning, builds very slowly to a brief tumultuous climax, recedes into a long, steady, low-key plea for eternal peace, and gradually fades away. *—James Reel*

Recommended:

- ○ **Cherubini: Requiem in C minor; Marche funèbre** / Best (cond.), Corydon Singers & Orch. / 1996 / Hyperion 66805

SYMPHONIC

Symphony in D major (ca. 1815)

Cherubini wrote 36 operas but only a single symphony. It is a solid, appealing work, but stylistically it straddles a transition between Mozart and Mendelssohn—a typical effort of Cherubini, the "conservative revolutionary." Because it's not easy to categorize as fully Classical or early Romantic, the symphony has been largely ignored, at least by major conductors. (The main exception was Arturo Toscanini, who programmed it at least twice and made a still-classic recording with the NBC Symphony Orchestra in 1952.) The work was commissioned in 1815 by the newly-formed London Philharmonic Society. Cherubini also transcribed the symphony as his *String Quartet No. 2*. The symphony begins with a Largo introduction, fragments of its stately string phrases echoed by the woodwinds. The string utterances become more gruff, the wind echoes more plaintive, and suddenly the first movement's main Allegro section erupts with a sunny, extroverted tune carried mainly by the strings. The more flowing second subject shifts into the minor mode without darkening the mood, and makes fuller use of the winds. This episode leads to frantic passagework that segues into the development section, an energetic, playful working-over of fragments drawn mainly from the first subject, although the second theme does put in an agitated appearance. This whole section anticipates the lean, agile, yet dynamic developments of Mendelssohn. Cherubini's melodies seem even more lively and forceful in the recapitulation and culminate in an energetic coda. The Larghetto cantabile begins with light, anticipatory material, as if to smooth the way for an opera aria. What would pass for the aria, though, seeps into the orchestra through what sounds like a transitional passage and builds a little climax even before it's apparent that a full-fledged theme has emerged. An explosion of jagged figures leads to an even more expansive but better-defined theme. Cherubini subjects all these elements to a brief, subtle development, the alterations consisting mainly of more elaborate accompaniments to the themes, interrupted by a few rough climaxes. The Minuet, marked Allegro non tanto, features a theme that shoots up like the eighteenth century Mannheim Rocket, and proceeds with a muscular exuberance and wit worthy of Haydn. The Trio section, with its melodramatically throbbing woodwinds and urgent but broken minor-mode melody, which creates an atmosphere of light-hearted charm. The finale, Allegro assai, burbles up from the cellos and basses through the string section, picking up the woodwinds along the way and develops into high-spirited and occasionally stormy material. Midway through the movement a chattering fugato develops, but this is soon displaced by a little recapitulation and a final stretto energetic enough to finish off a comic opera. *—James Reel*

Recommended:

- ○ **Luigi Cherubini: Symphony in D major** / H. Griffiths (cond.), Zurich CO / CPO 999521
- ○ **Arturo Toscanini: Great Symphonies Vol. 6** / Toscanini (cond.), NBC SO / 1999 / RCA Victor 59481

Chicago Brass Quintet

f. 1963, Chicago, IL
Ensemble

Established in 1963, the Chicago Brass Quintet was created to promote the appreciation and enjoyment of brass chamber music through public performances, educational workshops, broadcasts, recordings, and commissioning of new works. Its members were students at the Northwestern University School of Music.

The quintet has since performed throughout the United States, Canada, Europe, and Asia. Highlights have included guest performances for the International Trumpet Guild Conference in New York and London, a two-and-a-half-week tour of Hawaii, performances at the Kennedy Center, West Point Academy, numerous tours throughout Illinois and the Midwest, the South, and East Coast, and two tours of Brazil and Taiwan. The quintet has enjoyed a close association with Chicago's fine arts radio station, WFMT, often performing live from their studios for broadcast over National Public Radio and the CBC in Canada.

Ross Beacraft performs as principal trumpet with the Chicago Opera Theater, Concertante di Chicago, and the Elgin Symphony. In addition he has performed often with the Chicago Symphony, Lyric Opera, the Chicago Chamber Orchestra, Chicago's ballet and theater orchestras, and in many radio and television commercials. Beacraft, an Eastman School graduate, is coordinator of admissions for the DePaul University School of Music.

Trumpeter Matthew Lee is principal trumpet with the Illinois Philharmonic Orchestra, Chicago Sinfonietta, Light Opera Works Orchestra, and the Millar Brass Ensemble. A finalist in the Maurice Andre Solo Trumpet Competition in Paris, Mr. Lee also performs regularly with the Lyric Opera and Chicago Symphony Orchestra. A graduate of Western Illinois University and Northwestern University, he serves on the faculties of DePaul University and Elmhurst College.

Greg Flint, horn, performs frequently with the Lyric Opera and the Grant Park and Milwaukee Symphony Orchestras. He has toured with both Frank Sinatra and Aretha Franklin and enjoys performing a wide variety of music. A graduate of Northwestern University, Mr. Flint teaches at the DePaul University School of Music.

Trombonist James Mattern, founder of The Chicago Brass Quintet, has enjoyed a distinguished career as a performer, composer and arranger, performing with the Lyric Opera, Grant Park Symphony, Chicago's Contemporary Chamber Players, and Chicago's ballet and theater orchestras. A graduate of Lawrence University and Northwestern University, he has taught at Northern Illinois University and the DePaul University School of Music. His brass compositions and arrangements have been performed worldwide.

Dan Anderson is principal tuba with the Lake Forest Symphony Orchestra and in many of Chicago's theater orchestras. A respected jazz bassist, he performs often with many of Chicago's finest jazz artists. A graduate of the University of Illinois and Northwestern University, Mr. Anderson teaches at Columbia College and the DePaul University School of Music.

The quintet's commissions have added to the brass quintet literature new works by such composers as Cliff Colnot, James Mattern, Lawrence Rapchak, Dan Anderson, and J. Mark Scearce. Since 1981, the ensemble has released several recordings for the Crystal, Centaur, Delos, and Covenant labels. In March 1988, The Chicago Brass Quintet recorded a CD for GIA publications featuring the brass and choral music of Richard Proulx, former music director and composer in residence at Holy Name Cathedral.

The CBQ's repertoire embraces a wide range, including original pieces and transcriptions of masterworks from America, Western and Central Europe, the British Isles, and Russia, drawn from a span of many centuries. Arrangements of Broadway and jazz standards have also won them an appreciative following. *—Erik Eriksson*

Recommended:

- ○ **Virtuoso Brass** / Chicago Brass Quintet / 1991 / Delos 1022

Chicago Symphony Chorus

f. 1957, Chicago, Ill.
Ensemble

The Chicago Symphony Chorus is among the best choruses attached to a world-class symphony orchestra.

It was established in 1957, when the music director of the Chicago Symphony Orchestra, Fritz Reiner, engaged Margaret Hillis to develop a permanent chorus of a quality fit to partner the Chicago Symphony Orchestra at its concerts. Hillis already had a record of achievement: she was a junior golf champion and a civilian flying instructor for the U.S. Navy during World War II. She studied music at Indiana University and the Juilliard School (she had been a tuba and string bass player in her high school band), became assistant to America's leading choral conductor, Robert Shaw, and was conductor of the chorus of the American Opera Society in New York. She quickly fulfilled the mission given her by Reiner, developing one of the world's greatest choral groups.

Recordings of the Chicago Symphony Orchestra with its chorus have won a number of Grammy Awards. It also appears with visiting symphony orchestras when they wish to perform a choral/orchestral work. The chorus also tours with the orchestra and has been critically acclaimed for its performances in Europe, which include Berlioz's *Damnation of Faust*, Schoenberg's *Moses und Aron*, and Brahms' *Requiem*.

In 1994 Duain Wolfe succeeded Hillis as the chorus' director. He originated the orchestra and chorus' popular *Welcome Yule!* Christmas concert programs. *—Joseph Stevenson*

Recommended:

- ○ **Bach: Mass in B minor** / Solti (cond.), Hillis, Otter, Lott, Blochwitz, Chicago SO & Chorus / 1991 / Decca 430353
- ○ **Bach: Matthäus-Passion (Arias & Choruses)** / Solti (cond.), Hillis, Rao, Te Kanawa, Otter, Chicago SO & Chorus / 1990 / London 425691
- ○ **Beethoven: Symphony No. 9 "Choral"** / Solti (cond.), Hillis, Lorengar, Minton, Burrows, Chicago SO & Chorus / 1999 / London 460622
- ○ **Verdi: Requiem** / Solti (cond.), Price, Baker, Van Dam, Lucchetti, Chicago SO & Chorus / 1993 / RCA 61403

Chicago Symphony Orchestra

f. 1890, Chicago, IL
Ensemble

Through the leadership of some of the twentieth century's greatest conductors, the Chicago Symphony Orchestra has emerged as one of a handful of orchestras that can be safely regarded as the finest in the world. As Chicago, a major financial, manufacturing, shipping, and packing center on Lake Michigan, developed, so too did its musical life. In the early part of the nineteenth century the city was a major destination for touring ensembles; from 1850 to 1858 the city boasted the first important orchestra of its own, the Chicago Philharmonic. In 1890, Ferdinand W. Peck and other music lovers incorporated the Chicago Orchestral Association and hired German-born Theodore Thomas to become its first conductor. The new ensemble gave its first concert at the Auditorium Theater on October 16, 1890.

The Chicago Orchestra, as it was then known, gained national and international attention when Chicago hosted the World's Columbian Exposition in 1893. During the months-long festivities, Antonín Dvořák conducted an all-Czech concert; Ignace Paderewski was a featured soloist with the orchestra; and Richard Strauss assumed the podium as one of the first of a string of distinguished guest conductors in the orchestra's history. The orchestra's permanent home, Orchestra Hall, was completed in 1904. After Theodore Thomas' death in the following year, the ensemble was renamed the Theodore Thomas Orchestra. In 1912 it assumed its present name, the Chicago Symphony Orchestra, and Frederick Stock, who had served in the orchestra's viola section, became music director. To date, his 35-year tenure with the orchestra is the longest in its history. Stock and the orchestra made further history with a recording of Mendelssohn's *Wedding March*, the first-ever recording made by a major orchestra under an American music director. In 1920 Stock founded the Civic Music Student Orchestra (now the Civic Orchestra of Chicago), the first American training ensemble affiliated with a permanent professional orchestra.

The year 1934, the hundredth anniversary of the incorporation of Chicago, saw another World's Fair in the city, the Century of Progress Exposition. In three months the orchestra played 125 concerts on the fairgrounds. In commemoration of the orchestra's own fiftieth anniversary in 1940, Stock commissioned a series of new works that included contributions from Darius Milhaud, John Alden Carpenter, Roy Harris, and Igor Stravinsky.

During the Depression, meanwhile, a long-standing outdoor summer music series at Ravinia Park had gone bankrupt. In 1936, the CSO played its first concert at Ravinia, reviving the series and creating one of America's great summer musical events. In 1941, Stock hired the CSO's first full-time female member, hornist Helen Kotas.

After Stock's death in 1943, the all-but-forgotten Desire Dufauw became music director until 1947, ushering in a decade of short, turbulent tenures. Artur Rodzinski led the orchestra from 1948 to 1950, Rafael Kubelik from 1950 to 1953. Kubelik initiated the orchestra's great series of Mercury "Living Presence" recordings. With the arrival of the uncompromising Fritz Reiner in 1953, the orchestra entered a period during which it achieved unprecedented excellence. Reiner's recordings with the CSO on the RCA Victor label were a triumph of early stereo technology, and those of Strauss and Bartók (including *Music for Strings, Percussion and Celesta*, the first CSO recording to win a Grammy) remain, in the estimation of many, unsurpassed. Under Reiner, the orchestra engaged the outstanding Indiana-born choral conductor Margaret Hillis to build a permanent Chicago Symphony Chorus, which quicky evolved into a world-class ensemble in its own right.

Reiner's decade at the helm was followed by another troubled and relatively brief directorship, that of conductor Jean Martinon (1963–68). His "French" sound and repertory displeased critics and traditionalists.

Georg Solti's arrival as music director in 1969 marked the beginning of another great era in the orchestra's history. Solti took the CSO on its first overseas tour in 1971; both he and the orchestra garnered lavish (and sometimes astonished) praise during their month-long visit to Europe. In a gesture rarely afforded even the greatest musicians, Chicago gave the members of the orchestra a ticker-tape parade upon their return. In 1989, Solti stepped down as music director and was replaced by Daniel Barenboim. Under Barenboim and highly regarded guest conductors like Pierre Boulez, the orchestra has enjoyed a continued worldwide reputation, evidenced by its multiple Grammy Awards and other honors in the 1990s. In total, the CSO has appeared on over 900 recordings and collected dozens of Grammy awards—more, in fact, than any other individual or ensemble. *—AMG*

Recommended:

- ○ **Mahler: Symphony 8** / Solti (cond.), Popp, Auger, Shirley-Quirk, Kollo, Chicago SO / 1999 / Decca 460972
- ○ **Bartok** / Reiner (cond.), Chicago SO / 1993 / RCA 61504
- ○ **Respighi: Pines of Rome; Fountains of Rome** / Reiner (cond.), Chicago SO / 2000 / JVC 8
- ○ **The Reiner Sound** / Reiner (cond.), Chicago SO / 2001 / JVC 215
- ○ **Smetana: Má Vlast** / Kubelik (cond.), Chicago SO / 1996 / Mercury 434379

Chilingirian Quartet

f. 1971, London, England

Ensemble

The Chilingirian Quartet is one of the best-known string quartets based in Britain, with numerous recordings over a three-decade career. Its founder is Levon Chilingirian, born in Cyprus of Armenian descent to a family with a long musical heritage. He started playing the violin when he was five years old and had lessons with the violin virtuoso Manoug Parikian.

The Quartet began attracting attention soon after its founding in 1971 and appeared on the BBC early on. These broadcasts were followed by invitations to appear at the Edinburgh, Bath, and Aldeburgh Festivals, then by invitations to perform at major musical centers. They have become one of the best-known quartets around the world, traveling to all six inhabited continents and having played in more than thirty countries. These have included several coast-to-coast tours of the U.S., Mexico, and Canada, as well as tours to Australia and New Zealand, Japan, Africa, and South America. The Chilingirian Quartet plays annual series of concerts at London's Queen Elizabeth Hall and Wigmore Hall. Other major venues where they have frequently appeared include the Herkulessaal in Munich, Zurich's Tonhalle, the Vienna Konzerthaus, and the Tivoli in Copenhagen.

They have appeared in concert on most European national television stations, on National Public Radio in the U.S., and on the CBC. The group has recorded extensively on the EMI, RCA, CRD, Nimbus, Chandos, Conifer, and Virgin Records labels. These recordings have included a broad representation of the basic works in the quartet repertory, as well as music of lesser-known and contemporary composers. Among the latter are the world premieres of Hugh Wood's Quartets Nos. 1–4, quartet works of Stravinsky, Schnittke, Roslavets, and Firsova, and music of Arvo Pärt, Andrzej Panufnik, John Tavener, and Michael Tippett. Three of the Chilingirian members participated in the Bournemouth Symphony Orchestra's recording of Tippett's *Triple Concerto*.

In 1986 the Chilingirian was named Ensemble-in-Residence at the Royal College of Music in London and gives master classes there regularly. It won the Royal Philharmonic Society's Chamber Ensemble Award for 1995.

Levon Chilingirian is also the conductor of Camerata Roman, a chamber orchestra. He is a professor of violin on the faculty of the Royal College, and performs as a violin soloist, having appeared with the BBC Symphony Orchestra and the Liverpool Philharmonic. He plays a 1729 Stradivarius violin.

The other members of the Quartet are violinist Charles Sewart, violist Asdis Valdimarsdottir, and cellist Philip De Groote. *—Joseph Stevenson*

Recommended:

- ○ **Komitas-Aslamazian** / Chilingirian Quartet / 1997 / MEG 6
- ○ **Elgar: String Quartet; Piano Quintet** / Chilingirian Quartet, B. Roberts (piano) / 1994 / EMI 65099
- ○ **Prokofiev: String Quartets 1 & 2** / Chilingirian Quartet / 1991 / Chandos 8929

Frederic Chiu

b. 1964, Ithaca, NY

Pianist

American pianist Frederic Chiu was born to a Chinese immigrant family. Critics count his diverse background as one of his strengths, permitting him a wider point of view in studying the music he plays. On the other hand, his concert repertory is as centered on the classical European piano literature as that of any comparable player. Another part of his background gives him unusual insight into collaboration: his brother is a violinist, and as the pair was growing up Frederic often accompanied him.

He attended Indiana University, where he pursued a double major in piano performance and computer science. His piano teacher at Indiana was Karen Shaw, a pianist known for her powerful virtuosic interpretations. While attending Indiana he frequently participated in the violin class of the late teacher Josef Gingold as a class accompanist. One of his acquaintances from those years was one of Gingold's greatest pupils, Joshua Bell. Chiu frequently accompanies Bell and also with Pierre Amoyal. (The fact that Bell and Chiu are contracted with different record companies impedes the possibility of these two leading American instrumentalists collaborating on disc.)

After Indiana, he studied at the Juilliard School with Abbey Simon, Shaw's teacher. At that point he decided to base his performing career in Paris. Having settled in France, he co-founded (with violinist Philippe Graffin) the "Consonance Festival" in Saint Nazaire in 1991 and participates regularly in it, often collaborating with Jeremy Menuhin, the St. Lawrence Quartet, Christian Ivaldi, Gary Hoffman, or Jean-Yves Thibaudet.

In 1993, already considered one of the quickest-rising young pianists, he entered the Van Cliburn competition. His elimination before the final round resulted in a storm of protest, reminiscent of the 1980 scandal involving Ivo Pogorelich in the Chopin Competition. He received more publicity as a result than did the winner; the *New York Times* began referring to him as a "maverick pianist." Since then, he has received more positive recognition as the recipient of the Petscheck Award, the American Pianists Association Fellowship, and the 1996 Avery Fisher Career Grant. He has toured extensively in the United States and Europe, appearing with the major orchestras and in solo recitals in the major venues.

He records for the French Harmonia Mundi label, where he has completed several volumes of a critically acclaimed project to record all the piano music of Sergei Prokofiev, including the unpublished juvenilia and Chiu's own transcription of the suite from the film *Lt. Kizhe*. He is drawn to little-performed Romantic repertory, including the Mendelssohn piano sonatas and the great virtuoso piano transcriptions of the era, especially those of Franz Liszt. He has given lecture-concerts on Liszt's piano version of the Schubert song cycle *Schwanengesang*, which he had recorded for Harmonia Mundi. He has also recorded transcriptions of music by Rossini and, more conventionally, Ravel's piano music and Chopin's Opus 10 etudes. *—Joseph Stevenson*

Recommended:

- ○ **Virtuoso Piano Transcriptions** / Chiu / 2001 / Classical Express 3957054
- ○ **Grieg: Violin Sonatas** / Chiu, Amoyal (violin) / 2000 / HM 907256
- ○ **Prokofiev: Piano Music** / Chiu / 2001 / Classical Express 3957150
- ○ **Schubert-Liszt Lieder Transcriptions** / Chiu / 1998 / HM 907239

Choir of King's College, Cambridge

f. 1441, Cambridge, England

Ensemble

The Choir of King's College, Cambridge, is Britain's leading university chorus, part of that nation's rich tradition of choral singing. It was founded in 1441 on the order of King Henry VI for the purpose of providing daily singing of services in the magnificent chapel he had built at King's College. To this day the singing of these services is the purpose of the choir, which also sings on other occasions, with orchestras, on tours, and on recordings. The choir comprises 30 singers. These are 16 choristers (boy singers) and 14 choral scholars. The boys all receive education at the King's College School, a major British boarding school. The choral scholars (and the two additional organ scholars) are undergraduate students in various courses of study at King's College, itself, and, therefore, members of Cambridge University.

The choir has worldwide fame from its annual worldwide radio and television broadcasts at Christmas of the *Festival of Nine Lessons and Carols*. It frequently travels to sing in London, often with the leading orchestras of that city. In the 1990s the choir made tours of South Africa, Australia, Japan, Europe, the U.S., and Canada. In 1996 it sang a Christmas concert with the Philharmonia Orchestra at Royal Albert Hall.

It has formed a recording partnership with the Brandenburg Consort, a period-instrument ensemble. This has resulted in CDs of Handel's *Messiah* and the two *Passions* of Johann Sebastian Bach. The choir also supports new music, and has recorded albums of music of Górecki, Pärt, Tavener, Penderecki, Stravinsky, Panufnik, and many others, and has commissioned works from Richard Rodney Bennett, Alexander Goehr, Nicholas Maw, John Rutter, Stephen Dodgson, and James Macmillan, and requested American composer Stephen Paulus to contribute a new carol for the 1996 *Festival of Nine Lessons and Carols* broadcasts. It appears regularly on BBC Radio. One of its projects on that channel was a presentation of Easter Matins according to the *1549 Prayer Book*.*—Joseph Stevenson*

Recommended:

- ○ **Allegri, Palestrina, Lassus** / Guest (cond.), King's College Choir / 2002 / EMI 575560

- ○ **Handel: Coronation Anthems** / Cleobury (cond.), George, Blaze, Gritton, Blackadder, King's College Choir, Academy of Ancient Music / 2001 / EMI 57140
- ○ **Christmas Music from King's** / Willcocks (cond.), Spencer, Davis, Kampen, Whittaker, King's College Choir / 1996 / EMI 66244
- ○ **Psalms of David, Vol 1** / Willcocks (cond.), King's College Choir / 1998 / Angel 66784

Choir of St. Paul's Cathedral, London

f. 1127, London, England
Ensemble

For nearly 900 years, there has been a choir of boys and adult men at London's St. Paul's Cathedral. In 1127, the Bishop of London, Richard de Belmeis, founded what was the first choir school and made provision for "almonry" boys to serve the cathedral. At the time, the choir performed in what was the fourth Christian cathedral built on the site, the first of which, dedicated to St. Paul, was completed by 604, during the reign of King Aethelberht I. The fourth structure, the so-called "Old St. Paul's," fell into disrepair and, in the seventeenth century, succumbed to the combined threats of lightning, Cromwell's troops, and the great fire of 1666. Architect Christopher Wren (1632–1723) was contracted to build a new cathedral, a project that required 30 years to complete.

For the opening of the new cathedral, on December 2, 1697, John Blow (1694–1708), then Minister of the Choristers, composed the anthem *I was glad when they said unto me.* Blow was assisted by his pupil Jeremiah Clarke (1670–1707) (known for the *Trumpet Voluntary* arranged from one of his harpsichord pieces), who was to become the first official organist of the new cathedral. Purcell's *Te Deum* and *Jubilate* were also performed, accompanied by Father Smith's new organ.

Change came again in 1860, when the screen on which the organ was housed was removed. This increased the space in which the choir sang, greatly altering the acoustic environment. Nothing was done until 1872, when John Stainer, previously a chorister at the cathedral, was appointed organist, a position better described as "director of music." Stainer enlarged the choir, proposing a group of 40 boys and 18 Vicars Choral to fill the immense space. He also increased the rehearsal time and performances standards, developing a more professional approach. It was under Stainer that the repertoire of the choir began to grow and the present musical tradition was established.

Today the choir consists of 30 choristers (boy sopranos), eight probationers (who will become choristers) and 18 adults, six of whom are counter-tenors, six tenors, and six basses. The primary function of the choir is singing services in the cathedral. Evensong is sung every day, and on Sundays, there are three Choral Services—Matins, Eucharist, and Evensong. In 1990 John Scott took up the post of organist and director of music, assisted by sub-organist Huw Williams and his assistant, Richard Moorhouse.

Under John Scott's direction, the St. Paul's Cathedral Choir toured throughout Europe, Japan, and North and South America, made a great variety of critically acclaimed recordings, worked with many great orchestras and gave world premieres of numerous works composed especially for them. In 1997, the tercentenary of the opening of the Quire of St. Paul's for worship was honored with a year-long musical program (planned by John Scott) that included recordings, recitals, galas, orchestral and choral concerts, and a celebratory service in the presence of Her Majesty the Queen. All of this took place in addition to the annual performances of one of J.S. Bach's *Passions* during Holy Week, Handel's *Messiah* in Advent, the July orchestral masses and the daily performance of liturgical music for which the St. Paul's Choir is famous.

The choir's recordings include all 150 psalms of David, recorded over a period of seven years and released on compact disc in 12 volumes. By late 2000, they had produced seven recordings of English anthems and numerous recordings of works by various composers. *—John Palmer*

Recommended:

- ○ **Psalms from St. Paul's Vol. 1** / Scott (cond.), St. Paul's Cathedral Choir / 1993 / Hyperion 11001
- ○ **Coronation Anthems & Hymns** / Rose (cond.), Dearnley, , St. Paul's Cathedral Choir / 1994 / Guild 7102
- ○ **The Psalms of David** / Scott (cond.), St. Paul's Cathedral Choir / 2002 / Hyperion 44101/12
- ○ **The English Anthem** / Scott (cond.), Lucas, St. Paul's Cathedral Choir / 1990 / Hyperion 66374

Choir of Trinity College, Cambridge

f. 1553, Cambridge, England
Ensemble

The Choir of Trinity College Cambridge has one of the most ancient histories of any musical organization, actually predating the founding of the College itself by 229 years.

King's Hall was established as a college at Cambridge by King Edward II in 1317 and incorporated as such by Edward III in 1337. Under Edward II, when boy singers (or "choristers") left the choir of the Chapel Royal after their voices broke, they were enrolled in the King's Hall to continue their academic studies as a reward. Music was one of the disciplines of the King's Hall, and history's first Doctorate of Music was conferred in 1461 on a member of King's Hall, Thomas. St Just. (King's Hall was distinct from King's College, another Cambridge institution, founded by Henry VI.)

In 1546 King Henry VIII decided to establish a new college, Trinity College, which he intended to be the largest at Cambridge, by amalgamating King's Hall with Michaelhouse, a very small college founded in 1324 by Edward II's Chief Justice, Hervey de Stanton. It took the property of King's Hall and an endowment provided by property taken from some Catholic monasteries. Henry's successor, Queen Mary Tudor, ordered the construction of a new chapel on the site of the medieval King's Hall Chapel. It was completed during the reign of Elizabeth II in 1567. It includes two very old "Father Smith" organs (1694 and 1708), in their restored original cases. Mary Tudor in 1553 established the chapel choir with ten choristers, six lay-clerks, four priests, an organist, and a schoolmaster.

Trinity College became known for producing poets and other literary figures and scientists. Over the years these have included Newton, James Clerk Maxwell, Rutherford, Dryden, A.A. Milne, A.E. Housman, Byron, and six of the translators of the King James Bible. It was not especially well known for musicians, with the notable exception of Ralph Vaughan Williams and Charles Villiers Stanford, who attended the place at the same time. In the late 1890s Trinity College closed its choir school and relied on boy trebles drawn from a local grammar school to join the undergraduate lay-clerks in chapel services, which continued under conductors Alan Grey and Hubert Middleton until the 1950s. At that time the traditional men-and-boys constitution of the Chapel Choir was replaced by a larger choir of undergraduate men by Director of Music Raymond Leppard.

In 1982, a few years after Trinity College started admitting women, the Choir was re-formed as a mixed chorus comprising 24 choral scholars (students who, after passing a competitive audition, receive tuition to the College in exchange for singing at chapel services during the school term). As such, it is ironically one of the least traditional of British college chapel or church choirs. *—Joseph Stevenson*

Recommended:

- ○ **Hymns & Descants** / Trinity College Choir, Marlow / 1999 / Gmn.com 107

Fryderyk Chopin

b. Mar. 1, 1810, Zelazowa Wola, Poland, **d.** Oct. 17, 1849, Paris, France
Composer: Keyboard, Concerto, Vocal

Although a few major pianists, notably Glenn Gould, have dismissed his music as excessively ornamental and trivial, Fryderyk Chopin has long been recognized as one of the most significant and individual composers of the Romantic age. The bulk of his reputation rests on small-scale works that in other hands would have been mere salon trifles: waltzes, nocturnes, preludes, mazurkas, and polonaises (the last-named two groups reflecting his fervent Polish nationalism). These works link poetically expressive melody and restless harmony to high technical demands. Even his etudes survive as highly appealing concert pieces by emphasizing musical as well as technical values.

His birth date is a matter of controversy; the town registration of his birth specifies February 22, but Chopin always gave the date as March 1. His father was French, his mother Polish; he was raised in Warsaw by a family that mingled with intellectuals and members of the middle and upper classes, and as a teenager he spent two summers in the country, where he was exposed to Polish folk music. By the age of eight he was recognized as a child prodigy, performing in elegant salons and beginning to write his own pieces. Early on he studied composition with Josef Elsner, then took classes in various other music subjects as well as art and literature at the Warsaw Lyceum. In 1826 he enrolled at the University of Warsaw. He gave his first recital in Vienna in 1829, and over the next few years he performed at home and through much of German and Austria as well as in Paris. Feeling limited by Warsaw's cultural provincialism and uncomfortable with the publicity surrounding his performances there, he settled in Paris in 1832 and established himself as an exorbitantly paid piano teacher. In Paris he composed extensively, but limited his performances mainly to private salons.

In 1838 he began an affair with French novelist George Sand. The couple, along with Sand's children, spent a harsh winter in Majorca, where Chopin's health plummeted and he was diagnosed with consumption (tuberculosis). Chopin settled in with Sand in France, composing steadily although his increasing perfectionism slowed his output. By the mid-1840s, though, his health and romantic situation both had deteriorated. The affair ended in 1847 after, among other things, Sand had portrayed their relationship unflatteringly in her 1846 novel *Lucrezia Floriani.* Chopin then made an extended visit to the British Isles, but returned to Paris to die in 1849. *—James Reel*

KEYBOARD

Ballade No. 1 in G minor, Op. 23 (1831)

Chopin is credited with originating the Ballade genre for the piano. The Ballade had previously been associated exclusively with the literary world; it is found in the works of Goethe, Schiller, and other poets. In this Op. 23 effort, Chopin was said to have been inspired by the poem *"Konrad Wallenrod"* by Adam Mickiewicz. Mickiewicz, like Chopin and many other Polish artists, lived as an exile in Paris in the 1830s. Regardless of any programmatic comments associated with the *Ballade No. 1*, it is almost certainly not a depiction of specific events associated with this or any other Mickiewicz poem, but rather an expression of emotions associated with them.

The piece opens with a ponderous, somewhat hesitant introduction, and then the composer presents a melancholy theme that maintains the uncertain air of the opening. Gradually the tempo quickens, the emotional pitch turning fiery and passionate. Chopin then offers one of his most memorable melodies, a lovely, Romantic outpouring of rather simple, yet ingenious, construction: the theme revolves mainly around a three-note pattern, which sings and soars in its arch-like contour. The main theme returns briefly, but mostly to serve as a bridge; it builds up to a powerful statement of the alternate theme in one of Chopin's most passionate climactic moments in any of his works. The melody returns once again, now serene and confident in its demeanor. But a stormy and dark return of the main theme leads to a tragic and anxious ending, full of color and ambivalence. Without question, this is one of the composer's greatest compositions from his early Paris years. There would be three more Ballades, with perhaps only the *Ballade No. 4*, composed in 1842, equaling this first effort. Like many of Chopin's works, this *First Ballade* contains many technical and interpretive challenges for the soloist. *—Robert Cummings*

Recommended:

- ○ **Chopin: Ballades & Etudes** / Zimerman / DG 463051
- ○ **Ivan Moravec, Chopin: 4 Ballades, Mazurkaa, Barcarolle** / Moravec / 2001 / Supraphon 3583
- ○ **Chopin: 4 Ballades; Fantaisie, Op49; Prelude, Op45** / Pollini / DG 459683
- ○ **Chopin: 4 Ballades; 4 Scherzi** / Vladimir Ashkenazy / 1999 / Decca 466499

Ballade No. 2 in F major, Op. 38 (1839)

The dedicatee of Chopin's second *Ballade*, Robert Schumann, was hardly impressed; he found the piece "less artistic" than its predecessor, with the more intense episodes seeming a mere afterthought. This is a curious pronouncement, since those episodes, though brief, are essential to the ballade's structure and emotional impact. Chopin's literary inspiration may have been Adam Mickiewicz's poem "Switez," in which maidens escaping a besieged city drown themselves and are transformed into deadly flowers at the water's edge; this legendary Lake of the Wilis also inspired Mickiewicz's ballet *Giselle*. Chopin's composition begins as a simple idyll, the opening, gently rocking scene-setting phrases of a balladeer. At length a violent episode arises, full of impulsive but sonorous chords in the bass, with the right hand rushing up and down the keyboard. This soon subsides and the opening theme returns, only to hesitate and then mount in tension (as if the balladeer were becoming caught up in his story). Violence again erupts and the music reaches the height of its passion, the opening theme struggling to maintain a presence amid the onslaught. All this collapses, after which comes a brief, quiet conclusion, the opening theme bathed in melancholy and pessimism. *—James Reel*

Recommended:

- ○ **Chopin: 4 Ballades; Fantaisie Op49; Prelude Op45** / Pollini / DG 459683
- ○ **Chopin: Ballades & Etudes** / Zimerman / DG 463051
- ○ **Ivan Moravec Plays Chopin Vol. 2** / Moravec / 1994 / VAI Audio 1092
- ○ **Chopin: The Complete Piano Works Vol. 3: Ballades** / Ohlsson / 1991 / Arabesque 6630

Ballade No. 3 in A flat major, Op. 47 (1841)

This ballade, like its two predecessors, is assumed to draw on the poetry of Chopin's friend Adam Mickiewicz (Chopin never confirmed the precise sources or programs connected with these works). Dedicated to Princess Pauline de Noailles, one of the composer's pupils, the piece is said to be inspired by Mickiewicz's "Undine." It's the tale of a water sprite who falls in love with a mortal; she cannot have him because her watery embrace would be fatal. (The sprite appears in another celebrated piano work, the first movement of Ravel's *Gaspard de la nuit*.)

Far less turbulent than the other ballades, this one begins almost coyly, with a rising yet hesitant phrase in moderate tempo that gives way to a slightly more emphatic theme, dominated by its gently rocking rhythm, suggesting the waves of Undine's natural habitat. This material rises in volume and intensity, but quickly recedes into splashes and gentle cascades of notes in the keyboard's upper reaches.

This aquatic idyll gives way to a new section, still dominated by the rocking rhythm but now arising from a simple, almost childlike tune. Within a few measures this melody grows more complex and the music heaves with passion without becoming truly turbulent. The music ebbs, making way for a return of the section's opening material. Now more gradually, the tempo and filigree increase and recede again. The ballade's opening theme returns without overtly marking a new section; it's incorporated into the tempo and texture the music has already established, and propels a long, restless passage that builds to the most intense climax of all—yet one that suggests frustrated, passionate love rather than the high tragedy of the other ballades. *—James Reel*

Recommended:

- ○ **Sviatoslav Richter** / S. Richter / DG 457668
- ○ **Chopin: 4 Ballades; Fantaisie Op49; Prelude Op45** / Pollini / DG 459683
- ○ **Chopin: Ballades & Etudes** / Zimerman / DG 463051
- ○ **Ivan Moravec Plays Chopin Vol. 2** / Moravec / 1994 / VAI Audio 1092

Ballade No. 4 in F minor, Op. 52 (1842–1843)

Unlike its predecessors, this ballade has no clear link to the poetry of Adam Mickiewicz. Some observers have suggested as inspiration Mickiewicz's *The Three Brothers Budrys*, about siblings who go off to capture sables, disappear for a while, and ultimately return sharing a wife. It would be very difficult, though, to trace this story through Chopin's music, and the ballade's sequence of moods could easily apply to many other stories, or no particular story at all.

The F minor ballade, dedicated to Baronne Nathalie de Rothschild, follows the general pattern of its predecessors in relying on episodes of contrasting mood and thematic transformation, alternating very simple phrases with passages of great elaboration. The gentle opening is harmonically ambiguous, but settles into a delicate, wistful, decidedly F minor Slavic theme. Chopin repeats the theme, but not exactly; he alters the phrasing and the elaboration of the melody in subtle, expressive ways. The theme's next appearance is more troubled and fragmented; it becomes more agitated with the addition of an ornamental countermelody. After a climax, a lilting chordal section arrives. This material grows increasingly elaborate, and soon begins to intertwine with the first theme. Chopin thins the musical texture, brings everything to a brief halt, then reintroduces the first theme in a particularly dark, desolate mode. From this point, he essentially repeats the patterns he established in the work's first half, except that now the music is always more restless, with more complex accompanying lines and a higher pitch of excitement. The final section is particularly turbulent, ending with four feverish chords. *—James Reel*

Recommended:

- ○ **Chopin: 4 Ballades; Fantaisie Op49; Prelude Op45** / Pollini / DG 459683
- ○ **Horowitz at the Met** / Horowitz / 1992 / RCA 63314
- ○ **Ivan Moravec, Chopin: 4 Ballades; Mazurkas; Barcarolle** / Moravec / 2001 / Supraphon 3583
- ○ **Sviatoslav Richter: In Memoriam** / S. Richter / DG 457668

Barcarolle in F sharp major, Op. 60 (1845–1845)

This *Barcarolle* came in the latter part of Chopin's career, when his health was deteriorating from tuberculosis and his relationship with George Sand, one of the most successful novelists of her day, was beginning to crumble. But he remained fairly productive during this period and produced, among other compositions, this quite upbeat *Barcarolle in F major*. While it exhibits the rocking lilt associated with this genre of works, it does not invoke images of gondolas on waterways or other aquatic scenes. This piece is lushly Romantic throughout, both in musical style and in emotional temperament. The main theme, heard over a gentle swaying rhythm, exudes a brightness, an almost ecstatic glow in its long-breathed character and angular shape, fluttering here and turning charmingly demure there, then welling up with sweet passion before descending so elegantly. A sense of passion grows in the middle section buildup, too, but the music seems constrained here from reaching the ecstatic outpourings it alludes to until the return of the main theme, which first appears in a somewhat varied form and is played at a livelier tempo. After a reprise of it in its original guise, it reappears as the variant and leads to a passionate climax of great beauty. A lovely, playful coda closes out this masterpiece. *—Robert Cummings*

Recommended:

- ○ **Chopin: The Nocturnes** / Arrau / 2001 / Philips 464694
- ○ **Chopin: 4 Scherzi; Berceuse; Barcarolle** / Pollini / DG 431623
- ○ **Sviatoslav Richter Conducts Chopin, Debussy, Beethoven** / Richter / 1998 / Orfeo d'Or 491981

Berceuse in D flat major, Op. 57 (1844)

This is a late work in Chopin's oeuvre, coming at a time when the composer's output was in decline along with state of his health. He had spent the summer of 1843, when most of this work was written, in Nohant, at the residence of his lover, novelist Aurore Dupin Dudevant, better known by her pseudonym, George Sand. Some have suggested that the inspiration for this *Berceuse* or lullaby was the young daughter of singer Pauline Viardot, who had left the child in the care of Sand during that summer. Ultimately this assertion must be considered conjecture, but the character of the music would hardly seem at odds with it.

Chopin's expressive language here is uncomplicated and the music quite straightforward. Moreover, there is something childlike in the simplicity and playful innocence of the main theme. Yet, the composer invests more in the work's mood and character than one might realize. The main theme sounds dreamy and innocent at the outset, but as it unfolds atop one of Chopin's ostinato basses it gradually takes on subtle changes, becomes more sophisticated—perhaps more adult—as it sprouts new ideas and gathers ornamentation. Still, it never loses its innocent demeanor, even if there is a feeling the piece is gradually fading or decaying. When the end is reached, the mood has turned wistful, even somewhat disconsolate. A typical performance of the *Berceuse* lasts from four to five minutes. *—Robert Cummings*

Recommended:

○ **Chopin: Complete Piano Music Vol 1** / Biret / 1999 / Naxos 554527

○ **Chopin: Ballades & Etudes** / G. Hermann / DG 463051

Etudes, Op. 10 (1830–1832)

Before Chopin, there was a tradition of writing studies for the development of keyboard technique, but the pieces were primarily didactic. This set of 12 *Etudes*, dedicated to Liszt, represents a new form: concert pieces that serve a secondary function as development of advanced piano skills. Each etude begins with a pattern of pianistic figuration, which creates the specific technical problem for the etude and persists for the duration of the piece. That Chopin was able to create poetry in spite of such controlled and limited means of expression is a testament to his creative genius.

No. 1, in C major is nothing more than a series of wide-spanning arpeggios, expanding and contracting the right-hand, set over a simple sustained bass. It is a work of majestic beauty in spite of the simplicity of means.

No. 2, in A minor is a somewhat dry work, which exercises the last three fingers of the right hand. Rapid chromatic scales run up and down the keyboard to the accompaniment of detached chords. It is extraordinarily difficult to play smoothly.

With a beautifully lyrical melody, set rather simply, *Etude No. 3, in E major*, is contrasted with a more agitated middle section. The ability to differentiate melody from accompaniment in a single hand is exercised here. One of the easier etudes, Chopin thought this his finest melody.

Strong and independent fingers are required for the toccata-like *Etude No. 4, in C sharp minor.* Rapid passages alternate between the hands, creating an exciting, whirlwind effect. It is less difficult than it sounds.

The popular nickname for *Etude No. 5, in G flat major*, "Black Key," refers to the right-hand playing exclusively on the black keys. The mood is light and brilliant, created by rapid figuration over a chordal accompaniment. A strong and flexible rotation technique is required.

Etude No. 6, in E flat minor, is the easiest of the set, similar in technical requirements to No. 3. The mood is somber and plaintive, and there is no contrasting middle section.

The *Etude No. 7, in C major*, is a study in double notes. The right hand alternates rapidly between thirds and sixths, while the left hand carries the melody and bass. Musically a little insubstantial, it is valuable for the development of proper wrist and arm technique.

Etude No. 8, in F major, is a study in right-hand arpeggios and passagework. The left hand plays a somewhat jaunty melody while the right hand sweeps up and down the keyboard. Technically, it is similar in requirements to No. 4, but the wider range of the arpeggiation makes a legato execution more difficult.

Widely spaced figurations in the left hand of the ninth etude in F minor present the principal technical problems here. A breathless and passionate melody in the right hand propels the etude to a quietly effective ending. This is one of the easier etudes of the set.

A variety of technical problems are addressed in *Etude No. 10, in A flat major.* broken-chord rotation technique in the right hand, large skips and arpeggiation in the left hand, and differentiation of attack for both hands. Chopin basically presents a single idea repeated in a wide variety of articulations and phrasings. This etude is as ingenious as it is difficult.

Really nothing more than a chorale, the 11th etude in E flat major is a study in broken or arpeggiated chords. The difficulty lies in the wide span of the chords and in the tonal differentiation of the melody.

There is an apocryphal story that has Chopin writing his *Etude No. 12, in C minor, "Revolutionary,"* as a reaction to the burning of Warsaw in 1831. True or not, it is an extraordinarily impassioned work, belying its technical utility. Here, the requirements of No. 8 are reversed—the left hand provides the sweeping arpeggios and passagework while the right hand plays the heroic melody in octaves and chords. *—Steven Coburn*

Recommended:

○ **Chopin: 12 Etudes; 4 Rondos** / Chiu / 1997 / HM 907201

○ **Chopin: Etudes** / Pollini / 1980 / DG 413794

Etude No. 5 in G flat major, Op. 10/5 (1830–1832)

The 24 *Etudes* of Fryderyk Chopin (divided into two separate opuses, 10 and 25, but actually composed almost simultaneously) remain the most significant entries in that particular musical genre. Chopin refers, in a letter dating from the fall of 1829, to having written a study "in [his] own manner"; indeed, a great chasm stands between his achievements in the genre and the far drier attempts of his predecessors (one thinks of Moscheles, Czerny, and Hummel in particular). It was not Chopin's intent, as it was with many nineteenth century pianist-composers, to create studies of mere technique and raw dexterity; here, instead, are works with an inexhaustible array of textures, moods, and colors to explore. These are works meant for the concert hall as well as for the practice room. The 12 *Etudes* published as Chopin's Opus 10 are an indispensable tool of the modern pianist's craft: they are a rite of passage that no serious player can ignore.

Op. 10, No. 5 is the famous "Black key study" in G flat major: the right hand plays only the pentatonic group of pitches found on the black keys of the piano. Chopin himself was not fond of this etude, remarking that it is "the least interesting [of all the etudes] for those who do not know that it is written for the black keys alone." It has become fashionable among virtuosi to perform the work at lightning-fast tempos; the *Etude*, however, is not a showpiece by nature, and would be better served if performers instead emphasized its rather coquettish humor. *—Blair Johnston*

Recommended:

○ **Chopin: Piano Favourites** / Biret / 1995 / Naxos 553170

○ **Debut: John Browning** / J. Browning / 1999 / EMI 67017

Etudes, Op. 25 (1835–1837)

The Op. 10 Etudes were composed in the period 1829–32 and dedicated to Franz Liszt. This Op. 25 collection bears a dedication to Liszt's mistress, Countess Marie d'Agoult, a writer who used the pseudonym Daniel Stern. One reason Chopin attempted to capture Liszt's sympathies with the dedications had to do with the performance design of the pieces in the two sets: each was written to highlight some facet of pianism. For example, in the Op. 25 collection, No. 2, in F minor, is a study in cross rhythms, while No. 10, in B minor, is a study in legato octaves.

The first item in the Op. 25 set is nicknamed the "Aeolian Harp," owing to its soft and graceful arpeggios. The piece is lively and full of color, but slightly wistful in its dark gentleness. The second etude, mentioned above, sounds gossamer and utterly enchanting as the pianist's fingers glide along the keyboard to produce a busy yet elegant cascade of running notes. The third piece, in F major, gallops along with a theme that strikes the ear as the perfect mixture of joy and confidence.

The next three etudes all offer virtuosic challenges of substantial proportion—not that the others do not. The first of this trio, in A minor, hustles along and presents contrasts between legato and staccato. It has been linked to the virtuosity of the legendary violinist Paganini. The next, in E minor, is playful and has been called Lisztian, not simply because of its pianistic challenges but also because of its impish, devilish character. The last of this threesome, in G sharp minor, presents difficulties in its right-hand thirds. Its delicate sonorities and effervescent sprays of notes simply beguile the ear.

No. 7, in C sharp minor, is lyrical, and is by far the longest etude in either set, lasting around six minutes. Its expressive range and focus are probably greater than those in any of its companion pieces; most of its music is deeper, and its mood is sorrowful. The eighth etude, in D flat major, is joyous in its study of sixths, while the ensuing G flat piece, of similar mood, is more buoyant; the soloist is challenged once more in rendering the piece's divided octaves. This feature of octaves has been mentioned above in relation to the furious No. 10, whose lovely middle section provides wonderful contrast to the insistent rage of the main theme.

The 11th entry here, in A minor, is the famous *"Winter Wind" Etude*. Its proud theme evokes a wintry scene, with the busy right hand providing swirls of notes that seem to incarnate an angry wind. The last item in the set, in C minor, is a study in arpeggios. The mood is somber and agitated, and there is resemblance throughout to the first etude of the Op. 10 set.

A typical performance of the Op. 25 Etudes lasts from 30 to 35 minutes. *—Robert Cummings*

Recommended:

○ **Chopin: Etudes** / Pollini / 1980 / DG 413794

○ **Chopin: Etudes** / B. Berezovsky / 1991 / Teldec 73129

Fantasy in F minor/A flat major, Op. 49 (1841)

This is one of Chopin's largest compositions for solo piano, typically lasting well over ten minutes in performance. It is unusual not only in its length but in form: some have called it the "fifth" Ballade, but its 4/4 time, as opposed to the usual 6/8 of the ballade, perhaps ruled out that genre name. Certainly the work qualifies as a Fantasy in that it is loosely structured and extended, profuse in its melodicism, and quasi-improvisatory in nature. The ideal of unfettered imagination was a strong one in much of Chopin's music, however, and in fact this Fantasy bears some affinity with other big Chopin pieces of the early 1840s, such as the *Scherzo*, Op. 54 and the second and third piano sonatas. The work shows this master of the miniature applying himself to the problem of large-scale form, and in this respect is very much a worthy counterpart of earlier composed Fantasies such as Mozart's K. 457.

The challenge composers faced was to avoid the seeming contradiction between the ideals of composition and fantasy.

The piece starts off with a slow march-like theme which appears only once in the piece. There follow three main groups of themes, each preceded by a sort of bridge passage that serves as a refrain. This bridge is made up of arpeggios that rise upward and gradually increase in tempo. The mood imparted by the first group of themes is one of intensity and passion, of drive and excitement. Its chief theme is stormy and somewhat melancholy, and is the most dominant melody in the work. The mood of the second theme group is subdued and has an air of religiosity about its solemnity, while that of the third is a mixture of triumph and happy defiance. The refrain closes the piece, leaving the listener in awe at the many moods and colorful writing he or she has encountered in this somewhat enigmatic work. *—Robert Cummings*

Recommended:

- ○ **Kissin: Chopin Recorded at Carnegie Hall** / Kissin / 1993 / BMG Classics 902660445
- ○ **Great Pianists of the 20th Century: Vladimir Horowitz II** / Horowitz / 1999 / Philips 456844
- ○ **Chopin: 4 Ballades; Fantaisie Op49; Prelude Op45** / Pollini / DG 459683

Fantasy-Impromptu in C sharp minor, Op. 66 (1834)

Chopin wrote four impromptus—a French word suggesting improvisation—but affixed the word "fantaisie" (fantasy) only to the last one, perhaps implying a clearer form for the first three and a more rhapsodic nature for the last. In fact, though, it's in a fairly straightforward ABA pattern, with an unexpected twist in the coda. Chopin asked that this work, along with several others, be destroyed after his death (obviously his executors ignored him); it's speculated that he felt the piece was too derivative of the Op. 89 impromptu of Ignaz Moscheles. Chopin's manuscript carries the French inscription "Composed for the Baroness d'Este," which some people, notably pianist Artur Rubinstein, have interpreted to mean that the baroness commissioned the work for her exclusive use.

Following a dour, imposing opening note, the piece begins with fast, rippling figures in both hands. A second section, moving to D flat over left-hand triplets, offers a broad, lyrical melody with just a few touches of filigree near the ends of phrases. It serves as the basis of a couple of short quasi-variations, never straying far from the original theme. This melody, incidentally, was used about a century after its composition as the tune of the pop song *"I'm Always Chasing Rainbows."* The perpetual-motion opening section returns for what seems will be a fleet finale, but just before the end the music devolves into a swirling figure from which emerges a firm bass restatement of the second section's romantic theme, and the *Fantaisie-Impromptu* ends with a gentle arpeggio and a quiet chord. *—James Reel*

Recommended:

- ○ **Great Pianists of the 20th Century: Artur Rubinstein** / Rubinstein / Philips 456955
- ○ **Chopin: Favorite Piano Works** / Vladimir Ashkenazy / 1999 / Delta 14536
- ○ **Chopin: Sonata 2; 4 Nocturnes: Scherzo 2; Barcarolle** / Pletnev / 2000 / Virgin 61836

Impromptu in A flat major, Op. 29 (1837)

The term Impromptu has little technical meaning. Usually a composition for piano (or, occasionally, another solo instrument) that suggests improvisation, it is often thought of as a work resulting from sudden inspiration. Schubert composed eight impromptus in 1827. Of these, only one sounds improvisational, the others are highly organized, and one is a set of variations. Schumann's impromptus, Op. 5 and Op. 124/9, are also in the form of variations, as is a later piece by Balakirev. Like Schubert's, Chopin's four famous *Impromptus* are in ternary form (ABA). Similarities between the four works have led some writers to suggest that Chopin thought of the four as a "set" in which each successive impromptu is derived, in an improvisatory fashion, from the previous one.

Chopin composed the *Impromptu in A flat major,* Op. 29, in 1837, not long after he first met Aurore Dudevant (George Sand). The piece was first printed the same year in Paris. Although Op. 29 was the first impromptu Chopin published, it was the second he composed, and it shows a clear ternary form without the lengthy codas heard in his later ones. However, Chopin does employ a great amount of variation within the sections of the work, especially in the B section.

A triplet rhythm pervades the entire first section of the *Impromptu A flat major.* The wildly leaping, four-measure melody sounds twice, the second time modified to move swiftly into a contrasting theme. Although the new, chromatically sliding melody is very different from the main theme, Chopin maintains the triplet accompaniment figuration and the two-line texture. After passing through several harmonies, the new theme gives way to a return of the main theme, which is almost immediately altered in a developmental fashion, becoming more aggressive, and finally closes with an insistently repeated figure that builds anticipation. A quiet passage with a bell-like tone provides a transition to the B section.

In section B, Chopin dispenses with the triplet rhythm and frenetic energy of the first part of the impromptu, preferring a lyric, rising melody that moves mostly stepwise and is in F minor, the relative minor of A flat. Chopin's repeat of the initial phrase is decorated with flashy pianistic flourishes. The second phrase of this section appears four times in succession, each time embellished to a greater degree and with altered accompaniment in the left hand. Chopin curbs the energy of the B section only slightly before the return of section A. The triplet rhythm of the nearly note-for-note reprise of the A section ceases only at the very end, when a coda featuring hesitant statements of block chords closes the piece. *—John Palmer*

Recommended:

- ○ **Great Pianists of the 20th Century: Artur Rubinstein** / Rubinstein / Philips 456955
- ○ **Chopin, Pletnev** / Pletnev / 1997 / DG 453456

Impromptu in F sharp major, Op. 36 (1839)

Chopin composed the *Impromptu in F sharp major,* Op. 36, in 1839, not long after beginning his relationship with Aurore Dudevant (George Sand). The piece was first printed in Leipzig in 1840.

Chopin begins the *Impromptu in F sharp major* with a device he uses in several other works: it starts with a motive that has melodic characteristics, but eventually proves to be accompanimental. In this case, six measures of an idea occur in the left hand before another voice enters in the right, inverting the direction of the left-hand voice. What is most interesting is that the reiterated D sharp—C sharp at the end of this right-hand phrase also appears in the first two measures of the left-hand phrase. The second half of the theme is a flamboyant, six-measure phrase with a prominent dotted figure. Chopin repeats this pair of ideas, transposing the second of the two and extending it with a chordal passage that acts as a transition to the central section.

In D major, the central section employs the dotted figure from the A section in the bass to underpin a melody that gradually becomes thicker and more forceful over leaping octaves in the left hand. This dissolves quickly, heralding the return of the first theme, which begins, oddly, on F major, eventually returning to F sharp. The coda, as lengthy as the music that precedes it, begins with one of Chopin's technically dazzling passages. The extremely fast scales and turns of the right-hand line are given a simple accompaniment, allowing the listener to completely focus on the awesome technique necessary to perform the right-hand passage. *—John Palmer*

Recommended:

- ○ **Chopin: Waltzes; Impromptus** / Cziffra / 1999 / EMI 74975
- ○ **Rubinstein Collection Vol. 47: Chopin 14 Waltzes; Impromptus; Bolero** / Artur Rubinstein / 1999 / RCA Victor 63047

Impromptu in G flat major, Op. 51 (1842)

Dedicated to the Countess Esterházy, the *Impromptu in G flat major,* Op. 51, was composed in 1842 and published in 1843 in Leipzig. Unlike Chopin's other impromptus, that in G flat major is in a compound meter (12/8). Opening with a single line, the piece's texture grows increasingly dense throughout the first section. The similarity between the opening and the first theme of the *Impromptu in A flat major,* Op. 29, is apparent from the outset. Without repeating the first theme, Chopin moves on to the second, which begins with a rising scale and closes after a long chromatic descent. The subsequent repeat of this phrase is so varied and passes through such distant harmonies that it sounds like new material. Chopin skips the first two measures of the opening theme at the return; the first hint that these measures are actually introductory and not part of the theme.

For the opening of the B section, Chopin juxtaposes two measures of constant eighth note rhythm with two measures of slower moving chords. This four-measure complex happens twice, with some variation, before giving way to a new idea featuring scales that climb to the stratosphere. The second part of the trio is in 4/4 meter, but this is not immediately apparent because Chopin continues to write triplets for the right hand. Once the duplet eighth notes in the left hand create a polyrhythmic texture, however, the new meter becomes audible. The leaping tune and polyrhythm, emphasizing the dominant (D flat), eventually dissolve into a return of the first theme, which again is missing the introductory measures. Both section A themes follow in their original forms, as does the first part of section B. *—John Palmer*

Recommended:

- ○ **Great Pianists of the 20th Century: Artur Rubinstein** / Rubinstein / Philips 456955
- ○ **Chopin: Nocturnes** / Hewitt / 2004 / Hyperion 67371/2
- ○ **Chopin: Fantasy on Polish Airs; Impromptus & others** / Nakamatsu / 1999 / HM 907244

Mazurkas, Op. 41 (1838–1839)

Of all the genres that Chopin wrote in, perhaps the most personal is the mazurka, which recalls the rhythms, modes, and characteristics of Polish music, allowing the listener to experience a sense of the composer's native land. Combining the influences of classical Polish music with the traditional dances—namely, the Mazur, the

Kujawiak, and the Oberek—the mazurka allowed for a variety of compositional approaches and combinations. The result is a collection of 57 distinct short pieces, each with its own personality and flavor. The collection as a whole stands as an important part of the modern piano repertoire.

Op. 41 marks the half way point in the compositional development of Chopin's mazurkas, and in it we can see more daring experiments in mode, form, and character. The opening piece of the collection is in the Phrygian mode, and the form is enlarged to a rondo. A recurring theme includes a subtle melody line that expands and soars by the end of each phrase. This mazurka's contrasting sections include a more lively and dance-like passage and a more dramatic and frenzied portion. Ending with a coda, the piece simply melts away. Hymn-like in its beginning, the second mazurka develops into an expression of pure joy. Chopin maintains a rich chordal texture throughout the piece. The third piece of the set is rather brief, with a contrast between the recurring opening rhythmic chordal figure and the energetic, arching melody. The final mazurka is very much a waltz, friendly and warm in character. *—Kristen Grimshaw*

Recommended:

- ○ **Chopin: Complete Piano Works Vol. 11: Mazurkas** / Ohlsson / 1999 / Arabesque 6730
- ○ **Chopin: Complete Piano Music Vol. 4: Marzurkas Vol 2** / Biret / 1999 / Naxos 554530
- ○ **Rubinstein Collection Vol. 27: Chopin 51 Mazurkas** / Artur Rubinstein / 1999 / RCA 63027

Mazurkas, Op. 50 (1842)

Of the piano works of Chopin, the mazurka, perhaps more than his works in other genres, allowed him to experiment with different harmonic and melodic colors, unusual rhythmic patterns, and individualized, personal expressive traits. The genre draws upon the music of the composer's native Poland, including the dance forms of the Mazur (strong, irregular accents, moderate tempo), the Kujawiak (slow, flowing tempo, singing in nature, more subtle accents), and the Oberek (strong, irregular accents, fast tempo, spontaneous in nature). Just as each dance form has its own character, it also has a specific rhythmic formula. Some of Chopin's mazurkas are references to a specific dance, but many are something of a collage, assembling elements which sound like fragments of waltzes and nocturnes. The result is a richly varied repertoire of 57 pieces, each with its own individual traits. The later mazurkas show the development of (Chopin's compositional ability, as more space for expansion and development is provided in the longer pieces. Op. 50 begins with a grand and noble mazurka, rich in melodic and harmonic invention. The Aeolian mode which Chopin uses adds to a feeling of mystery and impending danger. What follows is an introspective, tender waltz, with a rhythmically stable, lighthearted middle passage. The third mazurka employs the rhythmic and characteristic traits of the Mazur, the Oberek, and the Kujawiak. In weaving the three together, Chopin uses several contrasting contrapuntal and accompanimental figures, including fugal imitation, thicker chordal textures, and waltz pattern bass lines. The piece appears to fade away, but it ends with two surprising and accented cadence chords.*—Kristen Grimshaw*

Recommended:

- ○ **Chopin Complete Piano Music Vol. 4: Mazurkas Vol. 2** / Biret / 1999 / Naxos 554530
- ○ **Chopin: Mazurkas** / Kapell / 1999 / RCA Victor 68990
- ○ **Chopin Complete Piano Works Vol. 11: Mazurkas** / Ohlsson / 1999 / Arabesque 6730

Mazurkas, Op. 56 (1843–1844)

The nineteenth century composer's penchant for the new and different led to the implementation of many new genres and forms, including the short character piece. The rise of national and patriotic feelings also contributed to the appearance of several dance forms and compositional genres previously unknown in the western European art world. It was in this environment of change and acceptance that Chopin appropriated, developed, and elevated the mazurka, an artistic blend of three native Polish dance forms, traditional Polish classical music, and the western aesthetics of Chopin's formal training. This miniature piece serves as an exploration in rhythmic, modal, harmonic, textural, and emotional variety, each mazurka a unique emanation of deep sources of inspiration. The mazurkas of Op. 56 display the dramatic contrast possible within the same genre. The first is a joyous, tender reflection, with an intimate salon feel. The contrasting sections demonstrate Chopin's lyrical ability, and the subtle change of melody between hands attest to his developing style. The second mazurka has a true Polish flavor, with a rhythmic drone accompaniment, irregular accents, and rustic grace note figures. The chromaticism and sophisticated imitation among the voices are further evidence of Chopin's maturing style. The dance-like second piece is followed by a mysterious and unusual third mazurka. The rhythmic ambiguity, combined with the stronger emphasis on the second and third beats, creates a truly native feel. The contrasting section bursts into a patriotic, rhythmic, chordal texture, but quickly returns to the original, winding theme.*—Kristen Grimshaw*

Recommended:

- ○ **Chopin: Complete Mazurkas** / Chiu / 1999 / HM 90747-48
- ○ **Rubinstein Collection Vol. 27: 51 Mazurkas** / Artur Rubinstein / 1999 / RCA 63027
- ○ **Complete Chopin Piano Works Vol. 11: Mazurkas** / Ohlsson / 1999 / Arabesque 6730

Mazurkas, Op. 59 (1845)

Although Chopin spent most of his adult life Paris, his roots were Polish. In homage to his homeland, he developed two genres of music, the polonaise and the mazurka. The mazurka takes much of its form from the native folk songs and dances of Poland, specifically the Mazur, the Kujawiak, and the Oberek. The unusual rhythmic patterns and irregular accents provided the basis for 57 mazurkas in total, each unique in character and texture. Because of the different sources of inspiration for the mazurka, each piece is a different combination of several ingredients of rhythm, harmony, tempo, and mood. This particular genre, more than any other, encouraged Chopin to revise and experiment freely. Unlike many of his other mazurkas collections, the pieces of Op. 59 do not contrast greatly amongst themselves. They share similar characteristics and textures, perhaps meant to unify the collection. The first piece in the set is highly chromatic, warm and rich in melodic and contrapuntal nuances. It serves as a tender portrait, the ending as unassuming as the opening. Pleasant and good-natured in its character, the second mazurka features a rich exchange between hands, a hallmark of Chopin's mature style. This piece ends with an ascending, winding lyrical line, which seems to disappear into the clouds. Resembling a polonaise, the third composition is noble and waltz-like in character. Having experimented with different contrapuntal devices, Chopin includes chromaticism, as well as some interesting descending chromatic chords in the accompaniment. While much interesting harmonic material is found in the lower voices, this particular composition is defined by the unaffected, expressive singing melody appears to be unaffected, soaring above the texture below. *—Kristen Grimshaw*

Recommended:

- ○ **Chopin Complete Edition Vol. 3: Mazurkas** / Luisada / DG 4630542
- ○ **Complete Chopin Piano Works Vol. 11: Mazurkas** / Ohlsson / 1999 / Arabesque 6730
- ○ **Chopin Complete Piano Music Vol. 4: Mazurkas Vol. 2** / Biret / 1999 / Naxos 554530

Mazurkas, Op. 63 (1846)

Chopin's piano music can be descriptive, as in the ballades or nocturnes, or can just explore the range of a certain genre, as in the scherzos and waltzes. Some genres, such as the mazurka, both explore formal boundaries and reflect feelings associated with particular places. The mazurkas draw upon Chopin's early years in Poland and the different classical and native forms of music which influenced the young composer. Folk dances such as the Mazur, the Kujawiak, and the Oberek, served as models for the mazurka. A few of the pieces actually draw directly upon one specific dance form, but most are an amalgamation of many ingredients. Although some of the mazurkas have a distinctly Polish flavor, other examples of this genre merely suggest, through subtle accents and rhythmic references, the original source of inspiration. Furthermore, each composition is a unique and personal reflection of the composer's memories of Poland. The later mazurkas of Chopin demonstrate the maturity of the composer's style. In addition, the mazurkas Op. 63 may suggest a maturing of the composer's emotional approach to the music as well. The opening Vivace is rhythmic and full of rustic flourishes, contrasted by interruptions of a rather simple melodic idea. There is much repetition throughout, with accents on the second and third beats, and a feeling of animation and excitement contrasting with warmth and simplicity. The second piece of the collection, marked Lento, is melancholy and pensive in its character. The mastery of lyricism one would expect from Chopin is certainly present, along with subtle nuances within the inner voices. The final mazurka of the set is a true Kujawaik, with its slow, singing flavor. The innocent, bittersweet, expressive, melody line works along with innovative contrapuntal devices and textural experimentation to create a mournful, intimate miniature.*—Kristen Grimshaw*

Recommended:

- ○ **Chopin: Mazurkas (Complete); Poloniases** / Brailowsky / 1997 / Sony 63237
- ○ **Chopin Complete Piano Music Vol. 4: Mazurkas Vol. 2** / Biret / 1999 / Naxos 554530
- ○ **Rubinstein Collection Vol. 27: 51 Mazurkas** / Artur Rubinstein / 1999 / RCA 63027

Mazurkas, Op. 67 (ca. 1835–1849)

Chopin drew upon both the classical traditions of Poland and its folk songs and dances to create the 57 mazurkas for piano, which stand as some of his most personal and intimate compositions. In composing the dance form, Chopin actually drew upon three traditional dances: the Mazur, the Kujawiak, and the Oberek. Each is in triple meter and often has the third or second beats accented. Some of his mazurkas draw directly from one of these dances, but most are a combination of the three, along with more classical influences. Thus Chopin was able to create a genre both personal and unique, adding much to the piano repertoire. The mazurkas of Op. 67, published posthumously, seem to represent the compositional style of the earlier collections, with the four-piece format, the shorter pieces, and the more good-natured tone. The first mazurka is amusing and flamboyant, with many flourishes and a dance-like character. The cheerful dialogue between the melody's two ranges is innovative and playful. The second piece of the set, marked Cantabile, is a brief but pleasant reflection. The contentment is found in the rhythmic and melodic stability; there are no surprises, but there are no disappointments. The third piece in the collection, again very brief, seems to have shed the pathos of the Op. 63 mazurkas, with its agreeable melody and character. The final mazurka, the first in the minor key, adds some heart to the collection. It displays the flourishes and rhythm of the dances, but with effortless melodic subtlety and warmth of tone. *—Kristen Grimshaw*

Recommended:

- ○ **Complete Chopin Piano Works Vol. 11: Mazurkas** / Ohlsson / 1999 / Arabesque 6730
- ○ **Chopin: Mazurkas** / Vladimir Ashkenazy / 1999 / London 448086
- ○ **Rubinstein Collection Vol. 27: 51 Mazurkas** / Artur Rubinstein / 1999 / RCA 63027

Mazurkas, Op. 68 (ca. 1830–1846)

It is universally agreed that the piano pieces of Fryderyk Chopin changed the way the piano was played, not in the technical sense, as in the pieces of Liszt, but in the expressive quality required by the pianist. The shorter works allowed Chopin to experiment with and to expand his compositional abilities, creating a truly distinct musical style. Perhaps the most unusual and individual of the shorter piano pieces is the mazurka, which reflects the merging of Chopin's classical training in Paris and his patriotism for his native Poland. While retaining the flavor and rhythm of the traditional Polish dances, the mazurkas also reflect the sophisticated melodic nuances and the coloristic harmonies found in Chopin's other compositional genres. The brief, intimate postcards from his homeland are perhaps some of Chopin's greatest contributions to the piano repertoire.

The mazurka collection of Opus 68, published posthumously, evokes a very nationalistic flavor throughout. The first mazurka contrasts outbursts of bold, patriotic chordal passages with lyrical, winding, melodic passages. The rhythmic energy drives the piece ahead, and the contrasting middle section, waltz-like in character, demonstrates the expansion of range and melody of Chopin's later works. The second piece of the set, marked Lento, is warm and unhurried. Its introspective and reminiscent flavor is contrasted by a more homophonic, chordal section with a rhythmically stable pulse. The mazurka is highly ornamented and rhythmically interesting. The third piece in the collection evokes a nationalistic feel, with its chordal texture interrupted by a brief, winding, ascending melodic figure. The contrast between the two is that of a military fanfare and a rustic dance. The final mazurka is a lyrical and expressive reflection, harmonically rich and full of melancholy. *—Kristen Grimshaw*

Recommended:

- ○ **Chopin Complete Piano Music Vol. 4: Mazurkas Vol. 2** / Biret / 1999 / Naxos 554530
- ○ **Complete Chopin Piano Works Vol. 11: Mazurkas** / Ohlsson / 1999 / Arabesque 6730
- ○ **Rubinstein Collection Vol. 27: 51 Mazurkas** / Rubinstein / 1999 / RCA 63027

Nocturnes, Op. 9 (1830–1832)

The 21 nocturnes of Fryderyk Chopin (of which only 20 were designated as such by the composer, the well-known *Nocturne in C sharp minor* of 1830 being in fact a pastiche of pre-existing music that only received the title nocturne upon publication in 1875) span virtually his entire creative career. Chopin inherited the form from Irish composer John Field; Field's influence is indeed palpable throughout Chopin's earliest published entries in the genre, the *Three Nocturnes*, Op. 9 (dedicated to the famous pianist Mme. Camille Pleyel, with whom several noted musicians of the day, including Berlioz and Liszt, fell in love), although even at this early stage in his development Chopin's melancholy-tinged chromaticism and sinewy melodies stand in stark contrast to the Irish composer's far simpler pieces.

The *Nocturne in B flat minor*, Op. 9, No. 1, is actually not Chopin's earliest work in the form: the *E minor Nocturne* published posthumously as Op. 72, No. 1, was composed in 1827, some three full years earlier. Nevertheless, it is with this elegiac, somewhat neglected B flat minor piece that Europe got its first real glimpse into Chopin's wondrous, rapidly-maturing musical mind. Chopin adapts Field's ternary (ABA) design to suit his more strophic organization, and it is thus also possible to hear the *B flat minor Nocturne* as a musical utterance in four, rather than three, distinct groups. The restrained melancholy of the opening passes through to a longer, melodically sultry middle section, only to return once again, inevitably, to the point of departure. Chopin expands the coda, once merely a kind of musical appendage, into a full-fledged partner in the musical drama. The final repose on the tonic major implies a deep sadness far beyond the expressive power of a more glaring minor mode ending.

The *Nocturne in E flat major*, Op. 9, No. 2, is very possibly the most famous work ever penned by the composer. In spite of the many tasteless renditions to which it has been subjected over the years (a great many of them on disc, and by performers of some stature), it remains a work of great charm. Of the three pieces in Opus 9, this is the one most heavily indebted to John Field, both in terms of its direct phrase structure and its generally rather simple atmosphere. Cast in the kind of two-part song formula beloved of nineteenth century salon musicians, Op. 9, No. 2, is one of the briefest of the nocturnes. There is little space indeed for sloppy sentimentality, even within the striking little cadenza that concludes the work.

Although it has remained in the shadow of its more famous companions, many feel that the *Nocturne in B flat major*, Op. 9, No. 3, is the finest of the group. Of the three, it most clearly outlines the language and dramatic ABA pattern of the more mature nocturnes, though it, like its companions, remains markedly Fieldian. Nowhere in his music is Chopin's great affinity for the human voice more apparent—both the aria-like ornamentation and gentle melodic sweep of the opening passage present a great challenge to the performer's powers of subtlety. The middle section is more agitated, indeed, almost march-like. Chopin begins the important coda with an abrupt and somewhat startling shift of harmony, while the final cadenza is of even greater range than that of the preceding nocturne. *—Blair Johnston*

Recommended:

- ○ **Chopin: Complete Nocturnes & Impromptus** / Arrau / 1997 / Philips 456336
- ○ **Chopin: The Nocturnes** / Pires / DG 447096

Nocturnes, Op. 15 (1830–1833)

Although composed just a few years after the Op. 9 nocturnes, Fryderyk Chopin's *Three Nocturnes*, Op. 15 (dedicated to friend and fellow pianist/composer Ferdinand Hiller—still a relatively unknown musical figure in the early 1830s), show a distinct stylistic advance over the earlier group. The emphasis on consummate mastery of the "salon" style, so crucial an element of the composer's earlier music, is abandoned in favor of a far more personal approach: here we can speak of the melodic contours and depth of feeling as being typically "Chopinesque."

The *Nocturne in F major*, Op. 15, No. 1, is of the passionate type which the composer first explored in the third and final nocturne of the Op. 9 bunch. A tender, loving Andante melody opens this clear-cut ABA form; the more agitated middle section (marked con fuoco) uses a dramatic double-note texture to good effect. Unusually for the nocturnes, no coda follows the serene reprise of the opening gesture: instead, two delicately arpeggiated chords bring the work to a tranquil close. Many have remarked that there seems to be nothing of nighttime about this particular nocturne (indeed, one can almost imagine sunlight leaking from the piece's seams).

More famous is the second piece of the opus, cast in the superbly pianistic (but still musically exotic) key of F sharp major. Here is a flawless miniature, equal to the best efforts of the more mature output from the composer's later years. In the hands of a capable performer the flowing opening melody has the power to transport audiences to a degree seldom achieved by composers of even the highest echelon. The central, doppio movimento section grows from an initial sotto voce texture to a brief climax of fiery abandon, with a repetitive quintuplet figure (still a musical oddity in 1833) running throughout. The nineteenth century German pianist and teacher Theodor Kullak remarked that the return of the heavenly opening theme "touches one like a benediction."

The G minor nocturne that concludes the Op. 15 collection was apparently inspired, to some degree, by the composer's attendance at a performance of Shakespeare's *Hamlet* (on the original manuscript Chopin wrote, "After a performance of *Hamlet*" only to later cross out the indication and replace it with the exclamation, itself a source of great insight into the composer's aesthetic views, "No! Let them guess for themselves!"). In Chopin's nocturne we can easily see a kind of musical crystallization of the tragic atmosphere of Shakespeare's work. Virtuosity is laid firmly aside as the composer instead explores the feverish realms of psychological despair. The opening gesture, marked Languido e rubato, builds to a local climax, replete with musical sobs and sighs; a more hopeful passage, ushered in by a glorious enharmonic modulation and three bell-like tones, follows (marked religioso). There is no reprise of the opening: instead the piece ends, if not hopefully, then with an air of generous acceptance. While some think Op. 15, No. 3, to be the weakest of the group, others—including Robert Schumann, an early advocate of Chopin's music—see in it a powerful outpouring of Romantic sentiment, in the truest sense of the term. Chopin, true to form, does not tell stories or paint pictures, but rather presents "pure" music of the most expressive kind. *—Blair Johnston*

Recommended:

- ○ **Chopin Nocturnes** / Moravec / Nonesuch 79233
- ○ **Chopin: The Complete Nocturnes And Impromptus** / Arrau / 1997 / Philips 456336
- ○ **Chopin: The Nocturnes** / Pires / DG 447096

Nocturnes, Op. 27 (1835)

The *Nocturnes*, Op. 27, dedicated to Mme. la Comtesse d'Appony, are Chopin's third publication in the genre. Many feel these two works to be among the very best of his compositions; they are certainly two of the most powerful—and famous—nocturnes he ever penned. The composer's conception of nocturne form (and sentiment), as embodied here, is virtually unrecognizable as the same genre he inherited from its inventor, the Irish composer John Field.

The first of the pair is cast in the melancholy, brooding key of C sharp minor, and employs the typical ABA form with coda. There is a piquant alternation between the minor and major third scale degrees throughout the opening gesture; the arpeggiated left-hand figuration, common throughout the Nocturnes, adds perhaps more to the atmosphere, in this case morbid and intentionally grating, than does the accompaniment of any other Nocturne. The central section is of a far more overtly passionate nature; the resigned coda is of its composer's finest silk.

The Nocturne in D flat major, Op. 27, No. 2 is of a different sentiment altogether, exploring the many sides of just one basic mood rather than presenting the kind of dramatic conflicts contained within its immediate predecessor. Two strophes are repeated three times each, varied with ever greater ingenuity upon each reiteration (the piece is one of the composer's most graceful essays in fioritura ornamental practices). The opening melody will be familiar to many who nevertheless cannot identify it by name (a fragment of the gesture melody even found its way into one of the James Bond movies, cleverly used in conjunction with deep-sea imagery). The static atmosphere of the opening (a wandering melody floating upon an unchanging D flat major background) is broken up by the unexpected intrusion of the minor subdominant a few bars later. The powerful main cadence of the piece (near to its end, but not actually the final cadence) is surely one of the most glorious moments in Chopin's entire output: the elaboration of an otherwise elementary 4-3 suspension by means of arpeggiation in the right hand is magical—the actual acoustic effect is more like that of stacked fourths. *—Blair Johnston*

Recommended:

- ○ **Chopin: The Complete Nocturnes & Impromptus** / Arrau / 1997 / Philips 456336
- ○ **Chopin Nocturnes** / Simon / VoxBox 447096
- ○ **Complete Chopin Piano Works Vol. 6; Nocturnes** / Ohlsson / 1995 / Arabesque 6653
- ○ **Chopin: The Nocturnes** / Pires / DG 447096
- ○ **Dinu Lipatti In Concert at Zürich and Amsterdam** / Lipatti / Palexa 509

Nocturnes, Op. 32 (1837)

The pair of nocturnes contained in Fryderyk Chopin's fourth published entry in the genre, Op. 32 (published in 1837 and dedicated to Mme. la Baronne de Billing) are something of a letdown after the brilliance and grace of the Op. 27 pair. Though each of the Op. 32 pieces exemplifies one of the composer's various approaches to nocturne form, the steady stream of craftsmanship that marked the previous pair of nocturnes (and also the following, Op. 37 pair) seems not so reliable here: in each of the Op. 32 nocturnes, moments of originality and power stick out in a way that they couldn't have, had the entirety of the pieces been sewn of finer silk.

Chopin composed three nocturnes in the key of B major; the *Nocturne in B major*, Op. 32, No. 1, is chronologically in the middle, and has found its way onto concert programs far less frequently than either of the other two. Following on the heels of the highly decorated *Nocturne in D flat major*, Op. 27, No. 2, this first piece in the set sings a tune of great simplicity. Decoration is kept to a minimum (for Chopin)—the watery texture and unassuming accompaniment make this easily one of the most "Classical" works ever penned by the composer. Of interest is the way that the main theme, an exercise in modesty and sweetness, is broken off during each presentation by a sudden, unexpected silence (each time reasserting itself by means of the captivating cadence that immediately follows this unwanted intrusion). The finest detail of this small work, by far, is its unexpectedly dramatic coda. A change of both mode (from major to minor) and texture (from quiet and unassuming to stormy and recitativo) make the conclusion a complete contrast to the first two thirds of the piece. There is no last-minute reprise of the opening atmosphere: the work ends, sullenly, with a sustained B natural in the bass.

The *Nocturne in A flat major*, Op. 32, No. 2, would, some 70 years after its original composition, become one of the most important parts of the famous ballet *Les sylphides* (one of the most popular ballets in the repertoire, *Les sylphides* consists solely of orchestrations of Chopin's music. Indeed, the graceful triple-meter flow of the work makes it easy to see why the choreographers selected this mild work as a kind of centerpiece. The nocturne opens with a very brief (two-bar), almost rhythmless introduction (a chorale-like plagal cadence figure that also serves as the work's final gesture), after which the body of the nocturne begins. Like the previous nocturne, simplicity of gesture is of the utmost importance throughout the opening section of the A flat nocturne. A stormier, more chromatic middle section, however, marks this second nocturne as fundamentally different than the first. The ternary form (ABA) of the work demands a repetition of the earlier section; it seems, however, to have been infected by the agitated atmosphere of the nocturne's center, and it takes the reprise some time to recapture the gentleness that is its rightful tone. The opening two bars, now pianissimo, serve as a coda. *—Blair Johnston*

Recommended:

- ○ **Chopin: The Complete Nocturnes And Impromptus** / Arrau / 1997 / Philips 456336
- ○ **Chopin: Piano Works** / Vasary / DG 469350

Nocturnes, Op. 37 (1838–1839)

Once regarded as the high-water mark of his work in the form, the two *Nocturnes* of Fryderyk Chopin's Opus 37 gradually fell into disservice during the course of the twentieth century. They are, nevertheless, wonderful specimens, being something of a hybrid between the more dramatic Opus 27 and the far simpler textures and moods of Opus 32. It is perhaps important that Robert Schumann considered these two works to be examples of Chopin at his finest, declaring them to be "of that nobler kind under which poetic ideality gleams more transparently (than the earlier *Nocturnes*)."

The first of the pair, the *Nocturne in G minor*, Op. 37, No. 1, is cast in the characteristic three-part (ternary) form. The opening and closing sections are of great sadness; the initially restrained primary theme quickly gains in passion upon its repetition some 16 bars into the piece, and only the sudden intrusion of a subito piano dynamic during the second phrase of the repetition curtails the torment. Consolation is found in the chorale-like chords of the central section of the piece; the texture is absolutely plain: not a single eighth note interrupts the procession of steady, quarter note chords, and no dynamic above piano is allowed by the composer. Some biographers have felt that this music represented Chopin's faith in the consoling power of religion. The reprise of the opening section is literal (if truncated to some degree).

The *Nocturne in G major*, Op. 34, No. 2, is of an altogether different breed, with its barcarolle-like meter and sweet melody in parallel voices. It is quite possible that this particular Nocturne was composed during or shortly after Chopin's 1838 stay with writer George Sand on the Island of Majorca, and that something of the warmer Mediterranean climate crept into the composer's pen. The second theme of the Nocturne, a simple tune that varies very little from its initial pattern, has been judged by many to be the most beautiful melody Chopin ever composed (Chopin recorded that he himself felt the melody of the E major Etude from Opus 10 to be his finest such achievement); at any rate, the theme is certainly a musical embodiment of the "less is more" doctrine. This second theme returns after a truncated reprise of the opening, more active material, and it wins out once again at the end of the piece. *—Blair Johnston*

Recommended:

- ○ **Chopin: The Complete Nocturnes & Impromptus** / Arrau / 1997 / Philips 456336
- ○ **Chopin: The Nocturnes** / Pires / DG 447096

Nocturnes, Op. 48 (1841)

Fryderyk Chopin's Nocturne output spans virtually his entire creative career. Some, like the three works of Opus 9 (his earliest published entry in the genre), owe a great deal to Irish composer John Field, from whom Chopin inherited the form. Others, like the two works published as Opus 27 and, particularly, the pair of Opus 48 Nocturnes, are so unique in tone and powerfully dramatic in scope that one almost feels them to be more aptly described as ballades in miniature. The *Two Nocturnes*, Op. 48, dedicated to Mlle. L. Duperré, were composed during 1841 and published during January of the following year; Chopin sold the copyright, along with those for the *Allegro de Concert*, Op. 46, the *Fantasie* Op. 49, and the *F sharp minor Polonaise*, Op. 44, for 2,000 francs. The 1840s were, in many significant ways, the most musically fruitful years of Chopin's short life; in the Opus 48 Nocturnes both the immediacy of emotional/psychological drama and the mastery of subtlety that so mark music of the composer's mature period are strikingly evident.

The *Nocturne in C minor*, Op. 48, No. 1 is one of the grandest of all Chopin's character pieces, both in sheer size and sentiment. The principal subject of the piece is an expression of the deepest grief; it is of melodies such as this that opponents of the composer have often used the term "sickly," particularly when such melodies are played without insight and by self-indulgent pianists. The central section, marked Doppio movimento (twice as fast), has a devout, march-like character. The reprise of the opening theme brings with it a great agitation that is only dispelled by the arrival of the magnificent coda.

The *Nocturne in F sharp minor*, Op. 48, No. 2, by comparison with its companion piece, is a work of much greater textural transparency. The main theme, restrained on the surface but bursting with passion underneath, is presented, repeated in ornamented fashion, and then followed by the radically different central section. Here, a change of mode from minor to major, and a totally redesigned metric scheme reflect a dramatic change in musical attitude. Chopin once told a student (Adolf Gutmann) that this middle section must be played like a recitative: "a tyrant commands," he said, referring to the first two declamatory chords, "and the other asks for mercy." —*Blair Johnston*

Recommended:

- ○ **Chopin: The Complete Nocturnes & Impromptus** / Arrau / 1997 / Philips 456336
- ○ **Chopin: The Nocturnes** / Pires / DG 447096

Nocturnes, Op. 55 (1842–1844)

The two noctures of Op. 55 were Fryderyk Chopin's penultimate group of nocturnes (only the Op. 67 pair were composed at a later date; all the posthumously published nocturnes actually came from the composer's younger days). The two pieces have had a turbulent and often unhappy history. While most musicians of the late twentieth century regarded them as two of the finest entries in the genre, during much of the nineteenth and early twentieth centuries, the pair was ignored by the majority of concertizing pianists. Certainly it is easy to understand the professional neglect heaped on the *Nocturne in F minor,* Op. 55, No. 1, which, due to its relative technical ease, has become the property of amateurs and students around the globe. The *E flat Nocturne,* Op. 55, No. 2, however, is a work of extraordinary power and a testament to both the masterly command of Chopin's later years and the distance he had traveled since the Fieldian nocturnes of his Op. 9.

The primary melody of the *Nocturne in F minor,* Op. 55, No. 1, has a bittersweet tang. The piece as a whole is cast in the characteristic (ABA) ternary form, with a dramatic and anxious middle section. An exciting stretto passage leads directly into the reprise of the opening theme, which has itself assimilated something of the second subject's agitation. A welcome harmonic change (from the minor to the major mode) as the coda progresses, and a trio of arpeggiated chords make a firm conclusion. This nocturne, though clearly less inspired than some of its brothers and sisters, makes an effective entry-level piece for those players and listeners seeking a clear glimpse of the composer's basic style.

The *Nocturne in E flat major,* Op. 55, No. 2, however, is a different matter altogether. Few pieces are less suitable for such an instructive purpose as that described above, and yet few are so eminently rewarding as a musical experience. Here there is no discrete sectional form, but rather a continuously developing melodic strand. If this causes a certain monotony, then it is the same brand of monotony that one's own inner stream of consciousness can, at times, engender. It is as if the composer has abandoned all the external trappings of nocturne "form" in order to place a greater emphasis on the essence of the genre's sentiment. The interested student of Chopin would do well to make a careful comparison of this work with the more famous *E flat Nocturne,* Op. 9, No. 2: the contrast is striking, and the greater skill of the later work cannot be overstated. A worthy coda (containing, around 12 bars from the end, a modulation of the finest and most expressive kind) serves as a conclusion to this unique work. —*Blair Johnston*

Recommended:

- ○ **Chopin: The Complete Nocturnes & Impromptus** / Arrau / 1997 / Philips 456336
- ○ **Chopin: The Nocturnes** / Pires / DG 447096

Nocturnes, Op. 62 (1846)

Although the *Two Nocturnes,* Op. 62, were composed three full years after the pair of Opus 55 works by the same title, the freedom of phrase design and thematic content in these, Fryderyk Chopin's final two essays in the form (the posthumous *Nocturne in E minor,* Op. 72, actually being a much earlier composition), indicate a compositional mindset very much drawn from and building upon the work he did on the second of the Op. 55 pieces. The Opus 62 nocturnes are so unique in every detail that it took musical Europe several decades to begin to appreciate just how important they really are: even as late as the early twentieth century it was common to dismiss these works as the products of a disease-weakened spirit, sickly, defeated, and sadly lacking in inspiration. Nothing could be further from the truth, as two such intimately expressive works as these—one is almost willing to assert that such musical privacy has no place in the public concert hall—have rarely found their way onto paper.

Chopin composed three nocturnes in the key of B major; the present one (Op. 62, No. 1) is now the most generally popular. A singing main theme is profusely decorated with strings of trills and non-harmonic tones (especially upon its reprise during the latter portion of the piece). There is a deftly executed modulation from the principal key to A flat major as the second, slightly more serious (but not starkly contrasting, as would be more traditionally acceptable) theme arrives. The reluctant accents of this middle section convey a poise and elegance that become all the more attractive in the hands of a skilled executant. There is, perhaps, more fioritura (that peculiarly operatic ornamentation that Chopin inherited from seventeenth and eighteenth century masters) about the reprise of the initial theme than in any of the composer's works since the famous *D flat major Nocturne* of the Opus 27 pair.

The *Nocturne in E major,* Op. 62, No. 2, was the last nocturne published during Chopin's lifetime. A warm, sustained (and entirely unsentimental) melody fills the opening and concluding portions of the piece. The central section is, like so many earlier nocturnes, more agitated in tone, though the effect is less worldly than in those previous examples, and more purely rhetorical. There is a kind of dialogue, containing many subtle melodic and intervallic imitations, between the two outer voices of the part-writing. During the coda Chopin seems reluctant to let go, almost as if, though a full three years from death, he guessed this to be his last entry in one of his most beloved genres. —*Blair Johnston*

Recommended:

- ○ **Chopin: The Complete Nocturnes & Impromptus** / Arrau / 1997 / Philips 456336
- ○ **Chopin: The Nocturnes** / Pires / DG 447096

Piano Sonata No. 2 in B flat minor, Op. 35 (1837)

Chopin wrote the Funeral March that became the third of the four movements here in 1837 and composed the other three movements two years later. Almost since it was first heard, this work was looked on not as a sonata in form, but as a collection of four rather diverse pieces the composer assembled under one musical roof, Robert Schumann being the first to make the charge of a lack of cohesion between the various movements. However, several musicologists in the late twentieth century pointed out a number of previously overlooked—or at least ignored—qualities in this composition that bind the movements as inseparable musical siblings.

The sonata can be viewed as something of a life cycle. The first movement serves as the life force, struggling, loving, and suffering. The ensuing Scherzo enacts demonic forces in the main section and good forces in the lyrical alternate melody of the trio section. When this movement ends with a partial recalling of the second theme, it is not clear which set of forces has emerged victorious. The third movement Funeral March represents death or mourning for the hero of the first two movements. The ghostly finale, with its swirls of dark winds, has evoked many ominous images in the minds of listeners, and serves the life cycle here as a kind of final picture of the deceased, who lies in his quiet grave, with the rustles of the wind the only disturbance above.

There are many thematic and harmonic relationships between the movements, too. The harmonies in the Funeral March can be noticed in all three of the other panels. Also, there is a thematic kinship between the alternate melody in the first movement and the lovely theme in the trio to the Scherzo. Other ties between the first two movements exist: both are stormy and hard-driven at the outset, and each features a lyrical second theme. The structural likeness between the main themes in both these movements is also worth noting: each is built on repeating motifs, the first part of which is presented twice before moving upward on the keyboard to complete the thematic idea.

In the end, this sonata, while unorthodox in some respects, is a painstakingly worked out composition of great subtlety, hardly comprised of a loosely strung-together set of piano pieces. But for all its grand and profound design, it has always been Chopin's themes and keyboard writing that have made this work popular. The third movement Funeral March theme is as famous as any ever written, and the compelling nature of the fast themes in the first movements, and their alternate melodies as well, have made this sonata popular the world over. A typical performance of the work lasts from 22 to 26 minutes. —*Robert Cummings*

Recommended:

- ○ **Chopin: Klaviersonaten 2 & 3** / Pollini / 1985 / DG 415346
- ○ **Chopin: Sonata in B flat minor; Berceuse; Ballade 4 & others** / Moravec / 2003 / Vox 7908
- ○ **Great Chopin Performers** / Pogorelich / Laserlight 15961
- ○ **Rachmaninov Plays Chopin** / Rachmaninov / 1994 / RCA Victor 62533

Piano Sonata No. 3 in B minor, Op. 58 (1844)

Although Chopin was essentially a miniaturist, he handled the sonata form with remarkable assurance. To a degree, his fairly hefty ballades, scherzos, and impromptus provided good preparation for writing the four movements of his third and final piano sonata, but this work's first movement, in particular, displays compositional skills that Chopin had few other opportunities to practice.

The first movement, Allegro maestoso, falls into traditional sonata form, constructed from a decisive and sometimes impulsive first theme and a more extended second theme, highly lyrical with a detailed accompanimental filigree—music that would not be out of place in Chopin's nocturnes. The musical texture thickens considerably in the central development section; Chopin devotes long passages to variants on the second subject, but much of the development is highly contrapuntal. Following the recapitulation, which again emphasizes the second subject, the movement ends with a surprisingly peaceful coda.

The very brief Scherzo, molto vivace, uses light, fleet, but finger-challenging E flat outer sections to frame a gentle and pensive trio section in B major. The ensuing slow movement, a Largo, is the heart of the sonata, conceptually as well as rhythmically. Stern but harmonically ambiguous chords lead to a delicate, nostalgic aria supported by a gentle heartbeat figure in the bass. This is soon supplanted by a long, flowing, rhapsodic section of quiet rumination. The opening theme, now with a more murmuring accompaniment, returns in more ornamented garb to escort the movement to its conclusion. The final movement, Presto, non tanto, makes a short transition from the Largo with a few swelling introductory bars that lead to the urgent, driving first theme of what turns out to be a rondo; this B minor material alternates with a contrasting, chord-launched section in the major designed to showcase the performer's agile fingerwork. Elements of both sections overlap for a grand coda. *—James Reel*

Recommended:

- ○ **Great Pianists of the 20th Century: Martha Argerich II** / Argerich / 1999 / Philips 456703
- ○ **Dinu Lipatti: Chopin; Brahms; Ravel; Liszt; Enesco** / Lipatti / EMI 63038
- ○ **Rubinstein Collection Vol. 46: Chopin Piano Sonatas 2 & 3** / Artur Rubinstein / 1991 / RCA Victor 60822
- ○ **Great Pianists of the 20th Century: Emil Gilels III** / Gilels / 1999 / Philips 456799
- ○ **Kissin: Chopin Sonata 3 & Mazurkas Recorded at Carnegie Hall** / Kissin / 1994 / RCA Victor 902662542

Polonaises, Op. 26 (1835)

These were the first two polonaises published in Chopin's lifetime, although he had written nine others prior to them, all of which would appear in posthumous publications. The first of this Op. 26 pair is in the key of C sharp minor and the second in E flat minor, an exceedingly rare choice, though Scriabin would use it occasionally some years later. Musicologists have made much of the melancholy keys of these polonaises, but in fact this composer could impart a sad mood to almost any key when he wanted.

Both of these polonaises, at around nine to ten minutes each, are not only about the same length, but of similar mood and structure, making them bona fide musical twins. The first begins grimly with emphatic descending chords, after which the gentle, melancholy main theme follows, seeming to struggle in its quiet upward climb. After its second appearance a warmer alternate melody appears to offer effective contrast and brighten the mood, but only briefly as the main theme returns. The middle section features a beautiful melody related to the alternate theme. This quiet section, a mixture of passion and sadness, ends when the intrusive opening chords jolt the listener and bring back the main material for a reprise and abrupt, quiet close.

The second polonaise's opening is ominous, beginning quietly, then becoming agitated before the main theme, itself a restless creation, mixing anxiety and melancholy, is given. The alternate melody is brighter, even jaunty in manner, somewhat relieving the dark atmosphere. The middle section features a theme which, like the slow one in the C sharp minor polonaise, is a variant of the alternate melody. The main material returns and the piece, like its sibling, ends quietly, though without the abruptness.

Both these polonaises are masterful compositions and must be regarded among Chopin's better efforts in the genre. *—Robert Cummings*

Recommended:

- ○ **Complete Chopin Piano Works Vol. 5: Polonaises & Impromptus** / Ohlsson / 1994 / Arabesque 6642

Polonaises, Op. 40 (1839)

The first of these two polonaises, the A major, nicknamed the *"Military,"* dates to 1838, and the latter, in C minor, comes from the winter of 1838–39. Both are well known in the composer's output, but the Military is clearly the more popular, while its dark sibling is deeper and perhaps the better piece.

That said, the *"Military" Polonaise* is a finely-crafted composition, whose bright colors and martial demeanor may flirt with the bombastic in places, but never quite attain it. What is remarkable about the piece is its deliberate Military stiffness: both hands play in-step much of the time, as if in response to the demanding beat of a military drum. This work's outer sections feature a memorable Chopin theme comprised of big chords in which the proud, muscular melody ascends in each of its three phrases, until a resolute plateau is reached. The middle section features greater freedom in the writing for the two hands of the soloist but still remains militaristic in its march-like manner. The recapitulation is a rather straightforward restatement of the main thematic material, with no coda following.

The C minor polonaise begins with an ominous theme in the bass, whose tolling-bell accompaniment of insistent chords imparts an atmosphere of grim urgency. While the mood brightens a bit with a livelier second subject, the dark character of the piece is relieved only in the gentle but schizophrenic middle section, whose subdued music is interrupted by violent outbursts seemingly intent on disrupting the calm, which one senses is only temporary at best, anyway. The foreboding main theme returns to close this sinister piece.

Anton Rubinstein related these works to the composer's beloved Poland, calling the first "Poland's Glory" and the latter "Poland's Collapse." Both these descriptions may be too specific and imply programmatic content that Chopin may never have intended, but they still have validity here since this composer wore his nationality proudly, not simply allowing it to seep into his music to become one of many characteristics, but encouraging it to become an essential ingredient. The *"Military" Polonaise* lasts about six minutes in a typical performance, while the C minor runs about eight minutes. *—Robert Cummings*

Recommended:

- ○ **Rubinstein Collection Vol. 28: Polonaises** / Artur Rubinstein / 1999 / RCA 63028
- ○ **Chopin: Polonaises; Fantaisie Impromptu; Tarantella; Berceuse** / Brailowsky / 1991 / Sony 46546

Polonaise in F sharp minor, Op. 44 (1841)

Despite its title, this is a composite work, with a mazurka embedded in the middle of the polonaise. (A polonaise is usually a dance in triple meter and moderate tempo, with the accent seeming to fall on the first beat thanks to its typical rhythmic pattern: a quarter note followed by two eighth notes, then four more quarters. A triple-meter mazurka, in Chopin's hands, tends to sound less belligerent and more graceful, with the accents shifting to the second or third beats.) The piece is dedicated to Princess Ludmilla de Beauveau, a prominent member of the Polish émigré community in Paris.

A short, menacing opening passage announces one of Chopin's most disturbing creations, a bold theme, defiant and rather sinister, with hammering chords and growling trills. It's answered, between statements, by a series of less aggressive melodic bits, sometimes apparently trying to soothe the main matter's fury, sometimes rising passionately across the keyboard. A second section takes this same material and strips it down to a savage bass ostinato with melodic fragments fluttering above. Suddenly the mood changes as the mazurka section begins. This is delicate music of moonlight and romance, its initial tinkly nature calling the courtly eighteenth century to mind. But soon the music slips into more ominous harmonies, two isolated torrents of notes dismiss the tender mazurka section, and the violent polonaise material from the beginning rumbles back in. At length, this reprise loses its force and seems about to fade into oblivion, but Chopin dismisses the work with one final angry gesture, a fortissimo chord of octaves. *—James Reel*

Recommended:

- ○ **Chopin: Polonaises** / Pollini / 1976 / DG 457711
- ○ **Rubinstein Collection Vol. 4: Chopin Polonaises** / Rubinstein / 1991 / RCA Victor 60822
- ○ **Complete Chopin Piano Works Vol. 5: Polonaises & Impromptus** / Ohlsson / 1994 / Arabesque 6642

Polonaise in A flat major ("Héroïque"), Op. 53 (1842–1843)

This polonaise, nicknamed the "Heroic," is one of Chopin's most popular works. It was written during a happy period in his life: his love affair with writer George Sand (Aurore Dupin Dudevant) was in full bloom, and the unpredictable tuberculosis which nearly killed him in early 1839 was temporarily behaving less lethally.

After a dramatic introduction, where the music immediately heightens the listener's expectations, the main theme of this polonaise is given, a defiant and heroic creation whose first several notes repeat emphatically before resolving in triumphant chords, which are usually arpeggiated by pianists owing to their wide span. The melody varies the second time around, providing a resolution of descending chords whose downward trajectory gives no hint of defeat or acquiescence. Indeed, the music remains optimistic and imparts a feeling of triumph even in the brief and defiant second subject.

The middle section offers a buildup in which the right hand's racing rhythmic figure, related to the main theme's repeating notes, prods the militaristic right hand onto further glories. A subdued, lyrical section of mysterious character follows, after which the main theme returns. The piece ends with an ecstatic, colorful rendition of the theme. Performances of the *A flat major Polonaise* typically last around seven minutes. *—Robert Cummings*

Recommended:

- ○ **Chopin: Polonaises** / Pollini / 1976 / DG 457711
- ○ **Rubinstein Collection Vol. 4: Polonaises** / Artur Rubinstein / 1991 / RCA Victor 60822
- ○ **Martha Argerich, Chopin: The Legendary 1965 Recording** / Argerich / 1999 / EMI 56805

Polonaise-fantasie in A flat major, Op. 61 (1846)

The *Polonaise-Fantasie* has much in common with the *Ballades*, but still retains the basic ternary dance form and the characteristic rhythms of the polonaise. A long and improvisatory introduction leads to the initial presentation of the polonaise material. This section is not a typical dance section divided into structured phrase groups. Instead, Chopin presents a theme in polonaise style that is subjected to continuing and ongoing variation and development. The effect, especially with the complex harmonies and frequent key changes, is one of a self-generating improvisation. Unlike all the previous polonaises, there is no literal duplication of material. This long and passionate section eventually leads to slow, lyrical and introspective central Lento. This entire section represents the usual trio, but as there is no actual reprise, it cannot really be considered as such. The Lento begins with a sustained, chordal melody over a richly melodic bass part. This leads to a passage that is a return to the polonaise character, but new material. A cadenza using double trills leads in turn to a partial reprise of the Introduction and the final brilliant peroration on the Lento theme. The principal polonaise material is never fully reprised.

Although it retains something of a ternary dance structure, the effect of the *Polonaise-Fantasie* is of an organic improvisation that grows and develops to a climax rather than as a dance with its set sections and repetitions. This characteristic places it formally with the *Ballades*, even though the principal material and rhythmic drive are more clearly polonaise-like. This is an extraordinarily complex and forward-looking work. The kind of continuing variation that Chopin uses here as well as the highly chromatic and adventurous harmony anticipate the techniques of Wagner and Mahler. In spite of its somewhat loose structure, the *Polonaise-Fantasie* remains as one of Chopin's greatest and most effective pieces. *—Steven Coburn*

Recommended:

- **Ivan Moravec Plays Chopin & Debussy** / Moravec / 1993 / Vox 5103
- **Chopin: Etudes; Préludes; Polonaises** / Pollini / 1998 / DG 431221
- **Chopin: Piano Music** / Horowitz / 2001 / RCA Victor 68008

Polonaises, Op. 71 (1827–1829)

Despite their high opus number, these polonaises are early works, the first likely dating to 1825, the latter pair probably coming in 1828. Chopin's first polonaise was written in 1817, when he was seven years old. The first of the Op. 71 works—the D minor—was actually his fifth polonaise, and the other two here, the B flat major and the F minor, were the seventh and eighth, respectively. Both of them show the composer as a more seasoned creator, closer to his mature style.

The D minor polonaise, though it divulges the influence of Mozart on its 15-year-old creator, is not a weak composition. After a brief introduction, the main theme is given, a mysterious and ominous melody in its first half, but turning quite playful and brighter in its latter moments. "Playful" is also the word to describe the middle section, although, in a kind of reverse of the scheme used for the main theme, it becomes serious before its close. In the end, while this is certainly a strong effort for such a young composer, it is not a major achievement.

The grander B flat major polonaise is not entirely free of Mozart's voice either, but it is clearly and instantly recognizable as Chopin and better constructed. After a brief, rather stern introduction, the long-breathed main theme is presented, a graceful and, in its bird-like twittering in the upper register, sweetly playful and elegant melody. The middle section, based on the previous material, is darker and full of tension. If Chopin is more concerned with beauty and grace in the main theme, he gives the middle panel a depth of expression that already shows a fine sense of contrast for a composer of his (then) 18 years. He closes with a recapitulation that presents the opening material with few changes.

The F minor polonaise may be the best of the three here. It is pure Chopin, mired in the kind of gloom that inspired him to write some of his finest music. Here, the main theme is haunting in its loneliness and the obsessiveness of the refrain-like resolution that closes each appearance. An ebullient alternate theme appears briefly as if to cheer up the spirits, but fails to break the generally dark atmosphere. The middle section does offer a change of mood, though its Romantic warmth is tinged with wistfulness and a sense of longing. The main and alternate themes return in the latter half, with the former closing the piece out.

The Op. 71 set is interesting because it shows the composer's style evolving from the naïve D minor polonaise to the more sophisticated B flat major, and finally to the masterful F minor. The latter two last about ten minutes each and the earliest about six minutes. *—Robert Cummings*

Recommended:

- **Chopin Polonaises** / Vladimir Ashkenazy / 1996 / Decca 452167
- **Complete Chopin Piano Works Vol. 5: Polonaises & Impromptus** / Ohlsson / 1994 / Arabesque 6642

Preludes, Op. 28 (1838–1839)

Fryderyk Chopin's *24 Preludes* were published in mid-1839, immediately after the composer's wintertime stay with writer George Sand on the island of Majorca. Chopin had been paid 2,000 francs for the copyright by Parisian publisher Camille Pleyel, son of the more famous Ignaz Pleyel. Evidence, some of it in the composer's own correspondence, seems to indicate that the majority of these works were composed in 1837 and 1838. For many of these pieces, the title Prelude can be a misleading one. The practice of "preluding" was very much alive during this period, and Chopin's preluding abilities are well-documented. During a live performance, preluding was a way of preparing the atmosphere of the major work by means of a brief, usually improvised, introductory piece that often made a modulation from the key of the preceding work to the key of the next. And while it is on record that Chopin did in fact employ some of the Preludes in this way, it seems indisputable that the real intent was for the Preludes to stand on their own, preferably in a complete performance. The selection of title may also be a nod in the direction of J.S. Bach, whose own *Preludes and Fugues* in all the major and minor keys, better known as the two books of the *Well-Tempered Clavier*, exerted a heavy influence on Chopin.

The gamut of emotions contained within the collection of 24 preludes is impressive. None of them is particularly long, and some of them, like the very first, are of almost disconcerting brevity. The truncated formal structures and abbreviated phrase patterns that result from this general miniaturization, far from diminishing the works' expressive power, actually serve to focus each of the pieces in an extraordinarily effective way. On a large scale, the *24 Preludes* are organized by key group: C major, its relative minor A minor, G major, its relative minor E major, and so on, moving up the circle of fifths until the final Prelude in D minor. *—Blair Johnston*

Recommended:

- **Chopin: Preludes** / Pollini / 1980 / DG 413796
- **Ivan Moravec Plays Chopin** / Moravec / 1993 / VAI Audio 1039
- **Chopin: PIano Concerto 2; 24 Preludes** / Pires / DG 437817
- **Chopin: Préludes, Op28** / Pogorelich / DG 429227
- **Great Pianists of the 20th Century: Alfred Cortot II** / Cortot / Philips 456754

Prelude No. 4 in E minor, Op. 28/4 (1838–1839)

For many of Chopin's *24 Preludes*, the title prelude can be a misleading one—while keyboard improvisation of one piece as a prelude to another was very much alive during the 1830s, and while it is on record that Chopin did in fact employ some of the preludes in this way, it seems indisputable that the real intent was for the preludes to stand on their own, preferably in a complete performance. The selection of title may be as much a nod in the direction of J. S. Bach, whose own *Preludes and Fugues* in all the major and minor keys (the two books of the *Well-Tempered Clavier*) exerted a heavy influence on Chopin.

The gamut of emotions contained within the collection is impressive. None of the preludes is particularly long, and some of them, like the very first, are of almost disconcerting brevity. One of the few preludes that expresses true sadness (in the proper sense of the word), the Prelude No. 4 in E minor (Largo), was performed at the composer's own funeral service (also on the program were the sixth and twentieth preludes and the Mozart *Requiem*). The languid, chordal accompaniment provides effective support for the prelude's tormented melody. Rarely has so much grief been poured to such powerful effect into so tiny a mold.

If the emotional tenor of this *E minor Prelude* can be tied to events in the composer's life, those events must have been devastating to have created such a despondent mood. That said, this famous prelude is a beautiful expression of such an abject sadness. The piece was one of 24 in the Op. 28 set that Chopin began in the aftermath of his breakup with Countess Delphine Potocka. He would begin an affair with writer George Sand (Aurore Dupin Dudevant) in 1838, however. If this work is related to his love life, it must have been written during its lowest nadir.

This prelude begins with a melody which might strike the uninitiated ear as merely gloomy descending chords, so long-breathed and obsessive it is in its slow-paced downward tread. The music seems to be weeping and growing more listless as its end nears. The gloomy harmony, enacted by the left hand in a repetitive funereal gait, imparts a sense of doom, as if expressing fateful tolling bells. This two-minute piece ends quietly, somberly, and resigned to its message of sadness. For all its sorrows, this is one of the most popular preludes in the set. *—AMG*

Recommended:

- **Chopin: Favourite Piano Pieces** / Argerich / 2000 / DG 469127
- **From the Archives: Sviatoslav Richter, Chopin** / S. Richter / Preiser 95001

Scherzo No. 1 in B minor, Op. 20 (ca. 1835)

Chopin composed six Scherzos, four of which were published as individual works, the fifth as part of the *Sonata*, Op. 35, and the sixth as part of the *Sonata*, Op. 58. The best known scherzos before Chopin are those by Beethoven and Mendelssohn, and these undoubtedly served as models for Chopin. However, in Chopin's more mature scherzos, all that seems to be left of these models is the 3/4 meter. For Chopin, the scherzo form (ABA, or ternary) was indeed a skeleton, just as ternary form was for all of his dance music, and he embellished upon this skeleton as he saw fit.

In the Opp. 20, 31, and 54 Scherzos, Chopin achieves his dramatic effect through the ternary form we find in most scherzos. The third of the four independent scherzos, Op. 39, is in a modified sonata form. A great extension and harmonic foray into distant keys create tension that is resolved with the reprise of the opening material. By delaying the reprise and pushing toward the end of the piece, Chopin increases the dramatic power of its arrival. Furthermore, the reprise is not always given in full, but leads to a coda that features new material. This type of composition stood in the face of the prevailing Germanic works of the time, which were constructed with the principle of "thematic unity." In the scherzos, as in most of Chopin's single-movement works, the overriding principle is departure and return.

Chopin's first Scherzo, Op. 20, does follow the strict ternary form of its models. In his later examples we find him approaching the form more flexibly. Composed in 1831–32, the Scherzo, Op. 20, was published in Leipzig in February of 1835. Writers have used terms such as "somber," "ironic" and "reckless" to describe the piece; no doubt these are reactions to different sections.

After an eight-measure introduction of two sustained chords, an arabesque-like figure begins that resembles the main idea of Chopin's *Fantasie-Impromptu*, Op. 56. This idea, distributed between the hands, becomes both melody and an accompaniment for sighing chords in the left hand. The first part of the scherzo moves agitatedly to the dominant before the repeat, closing with a leap up to sustained notes that will later become part of the transition to the trio and the introduction to the coda. The second, contrasting idea of the scherzo employs the same figuration as the main theme, but on new keys and with a different overall melodic shape. It is both quasi-developmental and insistently repetitive, with unusual harmonic shifts.

The central molt più lento section, the trio, is a masterpiece of polyphony, with two ideas in the right hand alone. The brightness of the trio's new key, B major, fades only a moment before the reprise of the first scherzo theme. Hesitant descending figures and the leaping idea from the first theme dissolve into a transition leading to the impetuous coda. Throughout the coda, accents on the first beat of the measure in the right hand vie for supremacy with accents on the second beat in the left hand. After a wash of chromatic scales, a few strident chords close the work in B minor. The dynamic range requested by Chopin in the closing measures of the scherzo pushes the music into the Lisztean range of power. *—John Palmer*

Recommended:

- ○ **Chopin: 4 Scherzi; Berceuse; Barcarolle** / Pollini / DG 431623
- ○ **Ivan Moravec Plays Chopin** / Moravec / 1993 / VAI Audio 1039
- ○ **Favorite Chopin** / Horowitz / 1987 / Sony 42306
- ○ **4 Ballades; 4 Scherzi** / Vladimir Ashkenazy / Decca 466499

Scherzo No. 2 in B flat minor, Op. 31 (1837)

Chopin's *Scherzo in B flat minor/D flat major* was published in Leipzig in the same year it was composed. It is the most popular of Chopin's scherzos. Chopin wished his students to perform the opening phrase of this scherzo in a manner that evoked the image of a mortuary. In a way, Chopin has ultimately gotten his wish, because the piece has been played to death. The problem with this is that our familiarity with the work can lead us to miss its many great moments. Among these are the vast contrasts in the first theme, with its wide leaps and pregnant pauses in the first half and rising and falling scales in the second.

The lengthy trio, in A major, is lacking entirely the somber atmosphere that pervades much of Chopin's music. Its opening idea, which brings to a halt the frenetic energy of the preceding scherzo, is serious, but it is the seriousness of a love song. A single line over sustained chords closes with a Gypsy music-like, dotted-rhythm tune that evaporates into the upper register. The contrasting segment of the trio is a layered idea with the main theme in the highest voice and a counter melody in the alto range with a rapid, duplet/triplet figure. The segment's initial emphasis on C sharp minor shifts to the dominant in its contrasting material, a passage of swirling eighth notes that encompasses nearly the full range of the piano. The "love song" returns, but this does not signal the end of the trio; instead, Chopin brings back the contrasting segment, this time preparing for the return to B flat minor, while working with his material in a developmental fashion. Near the end of the trio, Chopin works in a reference to the secondary scherzo theme.

As if infected by the mood of the trío, the return of the scherzo is less detached than its predecessor, with a sustained note after the second of the triplets. The shift to D flat major (the relative major of B flat minor) begins immediately, albeit surreptitiously. The powerful coda is an admixture of snippets from the scherzo that gives a firm close on D flat. *—John Palmer*

Recommended:

- ○ **Favourite Chopin** / Ashkenazy / 1992 / London 436389
- ○ **Frédéric Chopin** / Argerich / 1975 / DG 415836
- ○ **Chopin: 4 Scherzi; Berceuse; Barcarolle** / Pollini / DG 431623

Scherzo No. 3 in C sharp minor, Op. 39 (1839)

This third of the four independent scherzos, is in a modified sonata form. A great extension and harmonic foray into distant keys create tension that is resolved with the reprise of the opening material. By delaying the reprise and pushing toward the end of the piece Chopin increases the dramatic power of its arrival. Furthermore, the reprise is not always given in full, but leads to a coda that features new material. This type of composition stood in the face of "Germanic" works of the time, which are constructed with the principle of "thematic unity" in mind. In the scherzos, as in most of Chopin's single-movement works, the overriding principle is that of departure and return.

Creating tonal ambiguity is Chopin's primary intention in the amorphous first measures of the *C sharp minor Scherzo*. Several repetitions of the opening motive move downward chromatically without committing to any particular key. The motive itself creates metric ambiguity as well, for Chopin has directed to play four quarter notes in the space of three. The scherzo proper begins fortissimo with a theme consisting of descending quarter notes in groups of three, finally confirming C sharp minor. In the second half of the scherzo, this quarter-note theme becomes the accompaniment to a new, broad idea in the uppermost voice, the polyphony of the section increasing to three voices before the return to the first theme. Elements of sonata form creep into the piece as the return of the main theme modulates to prepare for the D flat major (enharmonic with C sharp major) of the trio.

Marked, "sostenuto" and "leggiero," the trio material provides a foil to the aggressive scherzo. Quiet, falling figures alternate with sustained chords as Chopin explores the range of the keyboard. At first diatonic, the trio becomes harmonically adventurous after the return of the opening, finally moving to C sharp minor for the scherzo reprise. After the scherzo material has run its course, the trio themes appear again, "resolved" to E major (the relative major of C sharp minor). Chopin continues freely with this material, returning to C sharp. In a surprising twist, Chopin closes the piece in C sharp major. As in a number of Chopin's mazurkas, the most intense harmonic activity occurs near the end of the work. The first two-thirds of the piece remain in the same key, although there is a change of mode from major to minor. *—John Palmer*

Recommended:

- ○ **Chopin: 4 Scherzi; Berceuse; Barcarolle** / Pollini / DG 431623
- ○ **Live from the Concertgebouw 1978 & 1979** / Argerich / 2000 / EMI 56975B
- ○ **Chopin Recital** / Pogorelich / DG 415123

Scherzo No. 4 in E major, Op. 54 (1842–1843)

Published in Leipzig in 1843, the Scherzo in E major, Op. 54, was composed in 1842. Not often performed, the piece is of a very different character than Chopin's previous works in this form, exhibiting more capriciousness and elegance than profundity. It is best described as bright and direct. The opening four measures, with their bare octaves, usher in an air of optimism that continues throughout the main theme, a combination of held chords and quickly rising arpeggios. The restatement of the theme is more densely harmonized and moves to A major for the contrasting material of the scherzo section, a complex of a unison passage linked to swirling eighth note figures. A plethora of ideas appears in the scherzo section as a return of the first theme occurs on the surprising key of A flat major. Chopin extends and develops the theme while returning to E major and the swirling eighth notes.

The brief A flat passage turns out to be an anticipation of the trio key, E flat major. Built mainly of scales, the trio's first theme moves to E major for a rhythmically ambiguous melody. Into the trio Chopin inserts a cursory restatement of scherzo material, then moves into uncharted territory, mixing development of previous material with new ideas in an extended passage enveloped in several harmonies. The rising arpeggios of the first theme become accompanimental material as the piece heads for the return of the scherzo, which is now even thicker than before with a pulsating eighth note accompaniment. The playful "recapitulation" includes a brief reference to trio material in its original key and closes with a nearly six-octave scale punctuated by E major chords. *—John Palmer*

Recommended:

- ○ **Chopin: 4 Scherzi; Berceuse; Barcarolle** / Pollini / DG 431623
- ○ **Chopin: Complete Piano Works Vol. 4: Scherzi & Variations** / Ohlsson, Chriss (cond.) / 1993 / Arabesque 6633
- ○ **Richter: Debussy, Chopin** / S. Richter / 1999 / BBC Legends 40212

Waltz in E minor, CT. 222 (1830)

This waltz is contemporary with the *First Piano Concerto* and was among the last works Chopin wrote before departing his beloved Poland—never, as it would turn out, to return. It came also at a time when the composer had fallen in love with Konstancja Gladowska, a young soprano. Thus, it is easy to understand this waltz's perkiness and playful demeanor, as well as its dreamy, charmed middle section.

The main theme is graceful in its nervous jauntiness, but turns reflective in typical Chopin style in the latter part, as it descends bracingly. Its lively manner and playfulness do seem to have an anxious undercurrent, as if the composer had already begun to realize that his relationship with the young singer was doomed. Following the lovely middle section the main theme returns but only partially, Chopin dispensing with its more reflective half, ending the piece rather abruptly. This waltz lasts just under three minutes in a typical performance. *—Robert Cummings*

Recommended:

- ○ **Chopin: 14 Valses** / Lipatti / 1997 / EMI 66222
- ○ **Complete Chopin Piano Works Vol. 7: Waltzes** / Ohlsson / 1996 / Arabesque 6669
- ○ **Rubinstein Collection Vol. 29: 14 Waltzes** / Artur Rubinstein / 1999 / RCA Victor 63029
- ○ **Chopin Waltzes** / Vladimir Ashkenazy / 1999 / Decca 460991

Waltz No. 1 in E flat major, Op. 18 (1831–1832)

Fryderyk Chopin's published waltzes (actually valses—a subtle but significant stylistic distinction) fall into two distinct categories: sparkling, highly ornamented jewels suitable, to at least some degree, for actual ballroom use; and more introspective, often rather melancholy, miniatures that are far removed from the fashionable Viennese waltzes of Joseph Lanner or Johann Strauss I. The earliest of the published waltzes (actually fifth in order of composition), the *Grande Valse brillante in E flat major*, Op.18, is an example of the former.

This aristocratic work presents its young composer in a particularly extroverted mood; surely the main theme of the work, introduced after a lively four-bar fanfare, is one of Chopin's most famous. The composer toys with a secondary, repeated-note gesture (marked leggieramente) before making a happily-chosen move to D flat major; the chromatic figure in parallel thirds that runs throughout a good part of this central section provides a good taste of the composer's more mature style. An extended version of the opening fanfare ushers in the reprise of the initial tune, which, upon reiteration some forty bars later, is broken up by the unexpected intrusion of two bar-long grand pauses.

While some, including the famous musicologist Huneker, have felt the (perhaps overly) effervescent quality of the Opus 18 Waltz to be vulgar, others see a kind of sly humor in the work's irrepressibly joyous tone. Whatever the Waltz's true sentiment is, Chopin, having visited Vienna and found the Viennese waltz to be entirely foreign to his nature (declaring, upon his return to Paris, that "I am still unable to play valses), seems wholly determined to reinvent the form in his own image. *—Blair Johnston*

Recommended:

- ○ **Complete Chopin Piano Works Vol. 7: Waltzes** / Ohlsson / 1996 / Arabesque 6669
- ○ **Chopin: 4 Ballades** / Perahia / 1994 / Sony 64399
- ○ **Chopin: 14 Waltzes; Barcarolle** / Lipatti / 1998 / EMI 66956

Waltzes, Op. 34 (1835–1838)

Authentic Viennese waltz style was almost entirely foreign to Fryderyk Chopin: when the Polish-born, Parisian-based composer returned from a journey to the Austrian capital he declared to a friend, "I have acquired nothing of that which is specially Viennese by nature, and accordingly I am still unable to play valses." Therefore, it was left to Chopin to reinvent the form on his own terms. The resulting, highly individual, output of waltzes divides easily into two categories: sparkling, highly ornamental jewels suitable for actual ballroom use, and more abstract miniatures that are far removed indeed from the fashionable Viennese waltzes of his time. The *Trois Valses brillantes*, Op. 34 contains one example of the former category (the first of the group) and two of the latter (the second and third).

The *Valse brillante in A flat major*, Op. 34, No. 1, is a kindred spirit to Chopin's earliest published work in the form, the *Valse brillante in E flat major*, Op. 18. Marked Vivace, this is a work truly suitable for the ballroom. While the opening fanfare of the Opus 18 Waltz lasts just four bars, that of this buoyant A flat major piece is extended to sixteen by the insertion of chromatically rising chords above a bass pedal. The body of the dance sparkles with wit and energy; the coda, which is somewhat less danceable than the rest of the work, is strikingly similar to that of the Preamble to Schumann's *Carnival*.

Very different in tone is the *Valse brillante in A minor*, Op. 34, No. 2 that follows—indeed, the title "Valse Brillant" hardly seems appropriate for such a melancholy, subdued work. Of all his waltzes this was Chopin's favorite; he positively bathes himself in languor and longing throughout. A change of mode (to A major) at bar 53 ushers in a melody of striking loveliness, which, in a moment of bittersweet inspiration, is echoed in the minor mode some sixteen bars later. The opening 16-bar gesture is brought back to serve as a conclusion.

The third waltz of the group, the *Valse brillante in F major*, Op. 34, No. 3, is more rightfully deserving of the "brillante" description than its immediate predecessor. Although quick (marked Vivace) and energetic, this is hardly a work that would find favor among elite nineteenth century dancers (it is, among other things, far too short). The waltz is not characterized by any particularly distinct thematic material; rather, its perpetual motion is driven forward in a seemingly improvisatory way. The pungent appoggiaturas contained in the fourth section of the piece have earned the Waltz the nickname the "Cat Valse" (as the unsubstantiated legend goes, Chopin's cat hopped up on the keyboard, his little paws striking the first notes of this passage). A buzz of witty activity draws the work to a close. *—Blair Johnston*

Recommended:

- ○ **Chopin: Etude, Ballades & Waltzes** / Anievas / EMI 74291
- ○ **Complete Chopin Piano Works Vol. 7: Waltzes** / Ohlsson / 1996 / Arabesque 6669

Waltzes, Op. 64 (1846–1847)

The *Trois Valses*, Op. 64 (published in 1847) were the last set of such works to be published during Fryderyk Chopin's lifetime and were among the very last works sketched by his prodigious pen before his disease rendered further work impossible. Each of the three is among the shortest of his entries in the waltz form, making them entirely unsuitable for effective use in the ballroom, a use that at this stage in his life, would have been unthinkable to the composer. They are, rather than actual dances, dance-poems that reflect the weakened composer's attitudes from three very different points of view. It is as if Chopin's latter-day musical personality were put through a prism, with the light of the resulting, rather distinct persona cast upon three separate sheets of music-paper.

The *Valse in D flat major*, Op. 64, No. 1, popularly known as the "*Minute Waltz*," is the only of the three which could conceivably be followed by mortal feet (it provides less opportunity for soloistic rubato than either of its companions). It must certainly not be played at such speed that it would actually be completed within a minute's time! Because the work is the technically most conquerable of all Chopin's waltzes, this work has lost some of its freshness through uncounted performances by pianists of lesser skill. It is, nevertheless, a work of enduring charm. A spinning little melodic cell (the pitches A flat, B flat, C, and the raised fourth scale degree, G natural), at first a seemingly rambling, aimless fragment, works its way seamlessly into the primary melody of this tiny work (only four pages, and Molto vivace at that). The cantabile of the middle section is Chopin at his most graceful.

More subdued (and strikingly Slavic in tone, with undercurrents of mazurka-rhythm mingling with the characteristic waltz figure) is the *Valse in C sharp minor*, Op. 64, No. 2 that follows. Although the opening is marked Tempo giusto, one hardly ever hears this work played without a heavy dose of rubato. The "veiled melancholy," as Huneker called it, of the primary melody is unrivalled among Chopin's works. The sad protagonist is called to the dance floor by a spinning passage in running eighth notes (which returns two times throughout the piece, each time its tiny antecedent-consequent phrase pair being stated twice), while the piu lento, D flat major middle section offers some consolation.

Chopin's final waltz, the *Valse in A flat major*, Op. 64, No. 3, is a piece of delicately-poised, Moderato-tempo beauty. It offers neither the whirling glee of Op. 64, No. 1, nor the melancholy of Op. 64, No. 2, but rather a musical item in which the more pure expression of perfect structural and harmonic balance is paramount. The central section (in C major) is a dialogue between two melodic voices. *—Blair Johnston*

Recommended:

- ○ **Vladimir Ashkenazy Plays Chopin (Hybrid SACD)** / Ashkenazy / 2002 / Decca 470608
- ○ **Complete Chopin Piano Works Vol. 7: Waltzes** / Ohlsson / 1996 / Arabesque 6669

Waltz No. 6 in D flat major ("Minute"), Op. 64/1 (1846–1847)

The *Minute Waltz* is the most famous of Chopin's waltzes and ranks among the best-loved pieces in the entire classical repertoire. Its sprightly mood and kinetic energy belie the composer's personal situation at the time of composition: his health was in serious decline and his relationship with novelist Aurore Dupin Dudevant, who wrote under the pseudonym of George Sand, was falling apart.

The theme of this waltz is its best-known feature. It begins as though hurriedly winding itself up; then, with the left hand anxiously maintaining the waltz rhythm, the right hand slithers elegantly upward and downward, finally resolving in quivering swirls of notes that ascend as they peak, then descend at the final climactic moment. The whole is held together by a little melodic cell and seems to shimmer in the hearing and before the eyes. This effervescent theme is perhaps indescribable, but that has not deterred the nickname-makers who have attached programmatic significance to the works of this determinedly abstract composer; the work is also known as the "Dog Waltz" because for some it suggests the image of a dog chasing its tail. (Legend has it that the waltz was inspired by Chopin's own pet.) The stately, singing middle section is more conventional, which is not to suggest that it is stale or hackneyed. Its nonchalance and relaxed manner provides the perfect contrast to the bustling energy of the opening theme. The piece closes with a restatement of its joyous and memorable initial creation.

Some of the work's popularity is due to its comparative technical simplicity; unlike much of Chopin's output, it is within reach of ambitious amateurs. Despite its nickname, the *Minute Waltz* lasts closer to two minutes in performance. *—Robert Cummings*

Recommended:

- ○ **The Chopin I Love** / Thibaudet / 1999 / Decca 466357
- ○ **Piano Greatest Hits** / Artur Rubinstein / 1994 / RCA Victor 62662
- ○ **Chopin: 14 Waltzes; Barcarolle** / Lipatti / 1998 / EMI 66956

Waltzes, Op. 69 (1829–1835)

Fryderyk Chopin's *Deux Valses*, Op. 69, were not published during his lifetime, and in fact are products of his earlier days. A rather clear distinction can be made between those of the composer's waltzes that could potentially be used for actual dancing purposes and those which serve more purely musical functions. In the Opus 69 publication, only the latter category is represented.

The *Valse in A flat major*, Op. 69, No. 1 (deemed by some nineteenth century writers to be in the key of F minor) dates from the year 1835. It is sometimes referred to by the nickname "L'Adieu," as it was presented to Marie Wodzinska shortly before Chopin departed from Dresden, where the work was composed, for Paris. Chopin had fallen deeply in love with "Mlle. Marie," as her name appears in the work's dedication, and had even proposed marriage; his status as a poor musician, however, caused Marie's parents to reject Chopin as a suitor. It is an expressive, Lento-tempo work, with a middle section that has something of the mazurka about it. By comparison with many of the other waltzes composed during the mid-1830s (those of Opus 34, for instance), Op. 69, No. 1 is not particularly striking, and one can easily understand the composer's decision–probably made for reasons both professional and personal–not to publish it.

The *Valse in B minor*, Op. 69, No. 2 was composed in 1829, and is one of several works that the composer hoped would be burnt upon his death (his wishes, as composers' wishes about such matters so often are, were ignored). It is a melancholy work with three primary melodies and a somewhat more optimistic middle section. Although popular, this is not one of Chopin's most important compositions. *–Blair Johnston*

Recommended:

○ **Complete Chopin Piano Works Vol. 7: Waltzes** / Ohlsson / 1996 / Arabesque 6669

○ **Chopin: 14 Waltzes; Barcarolle** / Lipatti / 1998 / EMI 66956

Waltzes, Op. 70 (1829–1832)

Chopin's waltz collections are often assemblages of pieces not necessarily from the same period. For example, the Op. 34 trio came from 1831 (No. 2), 1835 (No. 1), and 1838. The three comprising the Op. 70 set were composed in 1829 (No. 3), 1833 (No. 1), and 1841. Surprisingly, though, they show less evolution of style and manner than one might expect.

The first waltz, in G flat major, is vigorous and buoyant, full of color and joy in the outer sections, while the central panel is reflective and nostalgic. The second, in F minor, features one of those Chopin themes that, while generally light in character, is tinged with beautiful melancholy. The brief middle section is brighter and offers effective contrast. The third waltz, the earliest effort here, is the most emotionally neutral of the trio. The main theme is attractive and graceful, demure and cool, while the middle section is livelier and somewhat playful. Each of the three waltzes in the Op. 70 set lasts under three minutes in typical performances. *–Robert Cummings*

Recommended:

○ **Great Pianists of the 20th Century: Samson François** / François / 1996 / Philips 456778

CONCERTO

Andante spianato and Grande Polonaise, for piano & orchestra, Op. 22 (1830–1835)

The headnote and dating of this work may seem a bit confusing until one understands the background of this piece. In the winter of 1830–31, while in Vienna, Chopin wrote the *Grand Polonaise* for piano and orchestra, affixing to it the opus number of 22. Later he composed the *Andante spianato* and grafted it onto the *Grand Polonaise* to serve as an introduction, thereby forging a new, expanded work, also designated Op. 22. In the process he fashioned versions of the work for both piano solo and for piano and orchestra. This effort, incidentally, marked the last time that Chopin composed anything for orchestra.

The solo version begins with a lovely theme in the upper register, clearly of a Romantic bent. Like many of the composer's creations, there is something sad in its beauty, which to some will always represent the exiled Chopin's homesickness for his country and family. A consoling, mellow theme is next heard and after recalling some of the main material, this section ends quietly. The unusual (for music) word "spianato" means "level" or "smoothed," and these concepts give an idea of the music's tone.

The *Grand Polonaise* begins with a fanfare and then launches into one of the composer's more attractive dance themes. It is light and delicate, joyful and aristocratic, and full of the color and subtlety one associates with so many of Chopin's polonaises. Upon restatement, the theme is given more ornamentation and glitter. In its middle section the mood turns playful at the outset, but then becomes more intimate and subdued while retaining its dance-like character. Some passages here resemble parts of the first movement of the composer's *Piano Concerto No. 1* (1830). The main theme returns and the piece concludes with a brilliant coda, parts of which, once again, look back to the First Concerto, this time to its magical last-movement coda.

In the piano-orchestral version the piece begins the same way; the introduction, in fact, remains strictly for piano solo. The differences are noticed when the polonaise section starts, for here the orchestra delivers the introductory music, after which the piano takes up the dance theme. There is minimal accompaniment from the orchestra here and throughout, but some may prefer this version precisely because of Chopin's sparing use of the various instrumental sections.

The ending in the orchestral version is more brilliant and dramatic, but many will favor the piano solo rendition for its greater fluidity and less extroverted nature. One might observe that in the orchestral version the pianist is freed up to impart a greater sense of keyboard color; and indeed, its mood is a bit more playful. Essentially, however, one hears much the same music, since the piano is so utterly dominant throughout the orchestral version.

Both renditions are the same in duration, about 15 minutes each in a typical performance, with the *Andante spianato* section comprising about one third of the overall length. *–Robert Cummings*

Recommended:

○ **Chopin: Complete Works for Piano & Orchestra** / Inbal (cond.), Arrau, London PO / Philips 438338

○ **Richter: Liszt Concertos 1 & 2; Hungarian Fantasia; Chopin** / Kondrashin (cond.), S. Richter, London SO / 2000 / BBC Legends 4031

○ **Rachmaninoff: Paganini Rhapsody; Falla, Chopin** / Wallenstein (cond.), Artur Rubinstein, Symphony of the Air / 1997 / BMG 68886

Piano Concerto No. 1 in E minor, Op. 11 (1830)

Chopin, the son of a French father and a Polish mother, was born the same year as Schumann (one later than Mendelssohn, one before Liszt). Before consumption killed him in his 40th year, he had developed both an elegantly sensual pianism and a keyboard oeuvre without expressive parallel. His twin gods were Bach and Mozart (as if Haydn, Beethoven, and Schubert never existed); in turn he influenced keyboard composers for nearly a century after–Schumann, Liszt, Brahms, Dvořák, Debussy, Scriabin, Rachmaninov, and Ravel.

Although we cannot ignore developments in piano manufacture, especially by Pleyel of Paris, it was Chopin's artistry that prompted Schumann to write in 1830, "Hats off, gentlemen! A genius!" Parisian critics, who were then Europe's most cosmopolitan, dubbed him "the Ariel of the piano," although in his lifetime he played in public only 50 times, just once a solo recital, and for audiences usually no larger than 100 listeners.

Before his emigration to Paris in 1831 he had composed six works for piano and orchestra (but nothing orchestral after those), including two concertos published in reverse order. The E minor was issued in 1833, the F minor "Second" in 1836 although Chopin composed it in 1829, when he was 19. Both reflect his infatuation with Vincenzo Bellini's operas, especially *Norma*, whose ornamentation he adapted and personalized, to the extent of basing his theme-and-variations slow movement in *Concerto No. 1* on embellishments.

In the classical style that Mozart bequeathed to Beethoven, principal themes of the Allegro maestoso are introduced by the orchestra, at uncommon length which adds admirably to the suspense. Once the piano enters, it dominates. Although the opening subject is marked maestoso, subsequent ones are glowingly lyrical and gorgeously ornamented, even before their development in E minor/major. There is a coda but no cadenza per se (although the entire solo part may be likened to a cadenza).

Chopin wrote, during the composition of the Larghetto (E major/C sharp minor) homage to Bellini, "I am using muted strings–I wonder how they will sound?" He described it as having "a romantic, calm, and rather melancholy character . . . a kind of moonlight reverie on a beautiful spring night." There is no pause before–

The main theme of the Rondo: Vivace in E major has been called both a polka and a Krakowiac; beginning in E major, Chopin modulates to A major for the episode. Before a dashing conclusion, he ventures into E flat, then B major in the episode's return.

The concerto is altogether a prize although its orchestration is neither artful nor brilliant; nonetheless this compares favorably with Schumann's or Hummel's in a well-conducted performance, and the piano writing is nonpareil. *–Roger Dettmer*

Recommended:

○ **Chopin: Piano Concertos 1 & 2** / Giulini (cond.), Zimerman, Los Angeles PO / DG 415970

○ **Chopin: Piano Concertos 1 & 2** / Dutoit (cond.), Argerich, OS de Montreal / 1999 / EMI 56798

○ **Chopin: Piano Concertos 1 & 2** / Ormandy (cond.), Gilels, Philadelphia Orch. / 2002 / Sony 89836

○ **Grieg & Chopin: Piano Concertos** / Ackermann (cond.), Lipatti, Zurich Tonhalle Orch. / 2001 / EMI 74802

○ **Chopin: The 2 Piano Concertos** / (Chamber Version) / Shiraga, Yggdrasil SQ, Haukas / 1997 / BIS 847

Piano Concerto No. 2 in F minor, Op. 21 (1830)

The *Piano Concerto No. 2 in F minor* of Polish composer Fryderyk Chopin was actually composed before his *Piano Concerto No. 1 in E minor*. The F minor was begun in autumn 1829 and premiered on March, 3, 1830, while the E minor was begun shortly after the premiere of the F minor. The F minor is a less popular and more derivative work than the E minor; there is the sense that Chopin, having heard the F minor, decided to move beyond his models. The opening Maestoso movement of the F minor is clearly modeled on the concertos of Mozart's pupil, Hummel. The central Larghetto is based almost literally on the *Piano Concerto in*

G minor composed in 1820 by Ignaz Moscheles and the closing Allegro vivace is the most original movement of the three, a stylized Polish folk song. Within the movements, all the standard concerto principles are obeyed: an orchestra exposition of the main themes before a piano exposition of the same material, the usual contrast between the tonic minor and the relative major for the principal and subordinate themes, a lyrical slow movement in the relative minor, and a rondo-form finale in the tonic major. While Chopin's piano writing is idiomatic and highly personal—the lyrical melodies and their ornamentations could have been composed by no one else—his orchestral writing is at best competent. This, however, is less a fault than a decision: Chopin, the greatest composer for the piano of his age, would never let anything obscure the brilliance of his piano writing. *—James Leonard*

Recommended:

- ○ **Chopin: Piano Concerto 2; 24 Preludes** / Previn (cond.), Pires, Royal PO / DG 437817
- ○ **Chopin: 24 Preludes; Piano Concerto 2** / Rostropovich (cond), Argerich, National SO / 1998 / DG 459037
- ○ **Chopin: Piano Concertos 1 & 2** / Giulini (cond.), Zimerman, Los Angeles PO / DG 415970
- ○ **Chopin: Complete Works for Piano & Orchestra** / Inbal (cond.), Arrau, London PO / 1995 / Philips 438338
- ○ **Chopin: The 2 Piano Concertos** / (Chamber Version) / Shiraga, Yggdrasil SQ, Haukas / 1997 / BIS 847

Variations on "La ci darem" from Mozart's "Don Giovanni," for piano & orchestra in B flat major, Op. 2 (1827)

This was Chopin's first work in the piano and orchestra genre, a realm he was uncomfortable with from the beginning and one he would abandon in 1834, when he appended his *Andante Spianato* to the *Grande Polonaise* (1831), which actually involved little additional orchestral writing. What can generally be said about the composer's works for piano and orchestra—this Op. 2 effort included—is that the piano captures attention with its beauties and colors and originality, while the orchestra is cast in a mostly humdrum accompanimental role.

In this composition, Chopin does not use his variations to look beyond the emotions in the duet between Zerlina and Don Giovanni, thus eschewing suggestions, for example, of the latter's descent into hell, and avoiding expression of other extreme elements in the opera, as well. He chooses to simply focus on the innocence and romance in the duet. The work begins with an introduction based on fragments of the famous "La ci darem la mano" theme. This first section is marked Largo—Poco piu mosso, and has a rather stately air about it. There follows a rather straightforward rendering of the theme by the piano, with minimal playing by the orchestra except near the end when it takes up the theme. The exuberant first variation, marked Brilliante, is given next. It lasts but a minute, like most that follow, but is not short on color or energy or high spirits. The second variation, marked Veloce, ma accuratamente, is even more energetic, starting like a shot out of a gun on the keyboard, with the orchestra eventually entering to offer another view of the theme and serving to slacken the breathless pace of the music. The next variation, marked Sempre sostenuto, is more relaxed, though still brimming with energy and high spirits. Variation No. 4, Con bravura, presses ahead once more, and also maintains the bright mood. The string of short variations here—Nos. 1 through 4—finally comes to an end with the last section, marked Adagio—alla polacca, which is nearly as long as the Introduction and first four variations combined. It begins in a somber mood, but does not quite jettison the playful remnants spilling over from the previous sections. The first part is lovely and elegant, Chopin not yet finding the romance and passion in his style that would later permeate so much of his music. The latter half of this section finds the mood buoyant once again, but with the piano also turning on the fireworks.

This is a fine early work by Chopin and is often recorded and played in concert. A typical performance lasts from 17 to 19 minutes. *—Robert Cummings*

Recommended:

- ○ **Chopin: Complete Works for Piano & Orchestra** / Inbal (cond.), Arrau, London PO / 1993 / Philips 438338
- ○ **Chopin: Complete Works for Piano & Orchestra** / Beissel (cond.), Simon, Hamburg SO / VoxBox 5002

VOCAL

Songs, Op. 74 (1829–1836)

Though neglected for years by singers unacquainted with the Polish language and by audiences demanding performances of his familiar piano masterpieces, Chopin's songs for voice and piano have enjoyed a modest resurgence. Some musicologists believe that one of the earliest of these songs, "Precz z moich oczu!" (Out of My Sight!), usually dated 1830, might actually have been written as early as 1827. In any event, two decades of creative activity on Chopin's part yielded just 18 songs. (He seems to have conceived about 30, but, curiously, left some unfinished.) Sixteen were published in 1856–57, and two others appeared in 1910. It seems that Chopin never intended to have his songs published, though he apparently left Liszt and others with the impression he did.

The 17 songs in the Op. 74 set, arranged without regard to chronology in their published edition, fall into two categories: the romantic and the historical, or, put more simply, the personal and the public. All his songs are settings of text by Polish poets, 10 by Stefan Witwicki (1801–47) alone; all of those texts are taken from Witwicki's 1830 collection, *Idylls*. Chopin's apparent doubts about the artistic worth of his songs probably had something to do with his conviction that his best piano music was patently superior. The songs are indeed less distinctive works, but they offer much that is of interest, including unusual insights into the epic side of Chopin's thinking and a wealth of beautiful piano writing. It is also interesting to ponder the shortcomings of the songs in view of the fact that Chopin's pianistic language was itself heavily influenced by vocal music, specificially that of Bellini. The composer himself never partook in any concert performance of his songs, which offers further evidence of his doubts about them.

Among the romantic songs, there are several quite appealing works in Op. 74 set. "The Maiden's Wish" (No. 1, 1829), on texts by Witwicki, is a two-minute creation whose piano writing is most attractive. But the vocal part, too, is lovely and well-conceived. "Moja pieszczotka" (My Darling, 1837), No. 12, a setting of a poem by Adam Mickiewicz (1798–1855), is another worthwhile effort in the personal vein.

In the historical realm, there are several notable songs as well: "Wojak" (The Warrior, No. 10, 1830), another Witwicki setting, and two *Dumkas*, Nos. 11 and 13 in the set respectively, "Dwojaki koniec" (The Two Corpses) and "Nie ma czego trzeba" (I Want What I Have Not), both from 1845 on texts by Zaleski.

Other worthwhile songs in the Op. 74 collection include "S'piew z mogi/ly" (Hymn from the Tomb, No. 17, 1836), the longest of the group. The piano writing in most of the songs is imaginative, but often distracting in the sense that similarities to other, better-known compositions in the keyboard realm make themselves noticed. The entire Op. 74 set can be performed in about 50 minutes. *—Robert Cummings*

Recommended:

- ○ **Complete Chopin Piano Works Vol. 12: Songs** / Podles, Ohlsson / 2000 / Arabesque 6746
- ○ **Complete Chopin Edition Vol. 9: Songs** / Szmytka, Martineau / 1999 / DG 463072

Daniel Chorzempa

b. Dec. 7, 1944, Minneapolis, MN

Organist

Organist Daniel Chorzempa studied at the University of Minnesota from 1955–65, then at the Staatliche Musikhochschule in Cologne before returning to Minnesota to complete his Ph.D. in 1971. He began his career as a pianist, first in Hamburg and Cologne in 1969, then in Oxford and London in 1970 and 1971; however, it was his debut as an organist in London in 1969 that gained him critical acclaim.

Chorzempa's fluent, pianistic technique has allowed him to tackle some of the more virtuosic organ works, particularly those of Liszt and Reubke. It is also his background as a pianist that has led him to make a point of playing from memory, which is rare among organists, and at one time caused something of a sensation at his recitals. His recordings, in addition to the great nineteenth century virtuoso works, also encompass many of the traditional works by Bach. Since 1970, Chorzempa has been a member of the Studio für Elektronische Musik, Cologne, where he remains active as a composer of electronic music. *—Steven Coburn*

Recommended:

- ○ **Händel: Organ Concertos, Vol. 1** / Schroder (cond.), Chorzempa, Concerto Amsterdam / 2002 / PentaTone 5186103
- ○ **Widor: Symphonies 5 & 10** / Chorzempa / Philips 410054
- ○ **Bach: Popular Organ Music** / Chorzempa / Philips 410038

William Christie

b. Dec. 19, 1944, Buffalo, NY

Conductor, Harpsichordist

Long a leading figure in the early music performance movement, William Christie has been especially influential in restoring opera and French music to their rightful places in the Baroque repertory. He is the harpsichordist and leader of the ensemble Les Arts Florissants. Christie was born in Buffalo, New York, in 1944, and studied piano and organ as a young man. He attended Harvard, graduating with an art history degree and switching to music only for graduate study at the Yale School of Music. His teacher there was the pioneering harpsichordist Ralph Kirkpatrick, best known for his rediscovery and thorough exploration of the sonatas of Domenico Scarlatti. Christie moved to France in 1971; eventually he not only became a French citizen, but also was named a member of the Legion of Honor. Many early music performers have done stints in the contemporary-music world (and vice versa); between 1971 and 1975, as a member of the Five Centuries Ensemble, Christie participated in premieres of work by such notables as Luciano Berio and Morton Feldman.

Between 1976 and 1980 he played keyboards for the early music group Concerto Vocale, led by René Jacobs. In 1979, Christie founded Les Arts Florissants, an ensemble devoted to French, English, and Italian music of the seventeenth and eighteenth centuries. The group has done much to revive the difficult genre of French Baroque opera, with its arcane declamatory style; working with leading stage designers and choreographers, Christie has had special success with the operas of Marc-Antoine Charpentier and Jean-Philippe Rameau, rightful mainstays of the operatic repertory in their own times but almost forgotten since then. Since 1994, Christie and Les Arts Florissants have recorded for the major French label Erato, and the contract was renewed in 1999. That year saw the release of the Les Arts Florissants recording of Monteverdi's magnificent *Vespro della Beata Vergine* (the Vespers of 1610), and recordings of Mozart, Caldara, Lully and other composers were in the works. *—AMG*

Recommended:

- ○ **Lully: Les divertissements de Versailles** / Christie (cond.), Les Arts Florissants / 2002 / Erato 44655
- ○ **Purcell: The Fairy Queen** / Christie (cond.), Rousset, Dawson, Daniels, Fouchecourt, Les Arts Florissants / HM 901308
- ○ **Handel: Theodora** / Christie (cond.), Berg, Daneman, Taylor, Croft, Les Arts Florissants / 2003 / Erato 43181
- ○ **Rameau: Hippolyte et Aricie** / Christie (cond.), Agnew, Hunt, Padmore, Berg, Les Arts Florissants / Erato 063015517
- ○ **Monteverdi: Vespro della Beata Vergine** / Christie (cond.), Les Arts Florissants / 1998 / Erato 23139
- ○ **Charpentier: 2 Oratorios** / Christie (cond.), Les Arts Florissants / HM 195066

Boris Christoff

b. May 18, 1914, Plovdiv, Bulgaria, **d.** May 28, 1993, Rome, Italy
Bass

Boris Kirilov Christoff was born in Plovdiv, Bulgaria, on May 18, 1914. Educated as a lawyer, he was heard by Bulgaria's King Boris while singing in the famous Gusla Choir. The King granted a scholarship to allow him to travel to Rome for voice studies. There, Christoff's teacher was Riccardo Stracciari. He then traveled to Salzburg for further studies. At the end of World War II, after spending time in a Nazi labor camp, he was a refugee. He traveled again to Rome, where he made a debut in a concert. His first operatic performance was in the role of Colline in Puccini's *La bohème*; this was in Reggio Calabria. His first appearance in the opera with which would become most associated, Mussorgsky's *Boris Godunov*, was in the year 1947, when he sang the part of Pimen in Rome and in La Scala. He made his first appearances in the title role in 1949 at Covent Garden. He sang the role in most of the major opera houses of the world; it was also his debut role in the United States, at the San Francisco Opera House on September 25, 1956. In the United States he was particularly associated with the Chicago Lyric Opera from 1957 to 1963. His brother-in-law, incidentally, was another great bass, Tito Gobbi.

As a Slavic singer with something of a specialty in *Boris*, he was inevitably compared with the Russian bass Feodor Chaliapin. He was also a formidable stage actor, thereby bringing his roles special dramatic depth. His voice was beautifully controlled, round, and full-sounding, although it was not a big voice. He was able to make great dramatic use of excellent projection and outstanding tonal qualities in soft singing, the quality most often praised following his legendary performance at Covent Garden as King Philip II of Spain in Verdi's *Don Carlos*. Unlike Chaliapin, he also built a major reputation as a Verdian bass in addition to specializing in the Russian composers. He also made his mark in the major Wagnerian bass roles such as Hagen (*Götterdämmerung*), Gurnemanz (*Parsifal*), and King Marke (*Tristan und Isolde*) but sang as far afield as Rocco in Beethoven's *Fidelio* and the title role of Handel's *Giulio Cesare*. He recorded many of his major roles. He also maintained a notable career as a recital singer, and recorded a wide range of the songs of the Russian Romantic-era composers. *—Joseph Stevenson*

Recommended:

- ○ **Mussorgsky: Song Cycles** / Tzipine (cond.), Christoff, Labinsky, Française / 2003 / EMI 67997
- ○ **Verdi: Don Carlo** / Santini (cond.), Christoff, Gobbi, Clabassi, Stella, Opera di Roma Chorus & Orch. / 2000 / Angel 67479
- ○ **Italian Opera Arias** / Christoff, etc. / 1995 / EMI 65500

Harry Christophers

b. Dec. 26, 1953, Goudhurst, Kent, England
Conductor

English conductor Harry Christophers was educated at the Canterbury Cathedral Choir School and Magdalen College, Oxford. He founded the choral ensemble The Sixteen in 1977, which performs with an emphasis on early English polyphony, but also in a varied repertoire from the Renaissance to contemporary composers. He has led The Sixteen on tours throughout Europe, America, and the Far East, and on over 70 recordings. To perform music for choir and orchestra, Christophers founded the Symphony of Harmony & Invention. His recordings have been awarded two Grand Prix du Disque honors, two Deutsche Schallplatten prizes, two Diapason d'Or awards, and the 1992 Gramophone Early Music Award (for the first of the five-volume series *Music From the Eton Choirbook*). Christophers also performs as guest conductor with orchestras such as the English Chamber Orchestra, BBC Philharmonic, Deutsche Kammerphilharmonie, and the St. Louis Symphony. His operatic repertoire includes Monteverdi's *Il ritorno d'Ulisse*, Gluck's *Orfeo*, Handel's *Ariodante*, and Mozart's *Die Zauberflöte*. He conducted Monteverdi's *Coronation of Poppea* in September 2000 in his debut with the English National Opera. *—Robert Adelson*

Recommended:

- ○ **A Choral Pilgrimage: The Glories of Tudor Church Music** / Christophers (cond.), The Sixteen / 2000 / Linn 118
- ○ **The Symphony of Harmony & Invention** / Christophers (cond.), The Sixteen / 2000 / Linn 148
- ○ **Victoria: Tenebrae Responsories** / Christophers (cond.), The Sixteen / 1995 / Virgin 61221
- ○ **Taverner: Mass & Motets** / Christophers (cond.), The Sixteen / 2000 / Hyperion 55054

Kyung-Wha Chung

b. Mar. 26, 1948, Seoul, Korea
Violinist

Korea's long, rich tradition in the performing arts has helped it produce a number of internationally acclaimed classical musicians, despite its relatively short acquaintance with Western music. Kyung-Wha Chung was the first of Korea's performers to achieve this status. She is best known as a concert soloist, but is also recognized for her appearances with her younger brother, the pianist and conductor Myung-Whun, and elder sister, the cellist Myung-Wha, in the Chung Trio.

Born in Seoul, in 1948, Chung at first took up the piano; however, a magnetic introduction to the violin at the age of six inspired her to switch. After studying with Shin Sang Chul, she made her debut at the age of nine with the Seoul Symphonic Orchestra, playing Mendelssohn's *E minor Concerto*. When she was 12 years old, Chung toured Japan, and the following year moved to New York to study at the Juilliard School of Music with Ivan Galamian, with whom she worked until 1971.

In the late 1960s she took first prize at the Leventritt Competition (along with Pinchas Zukerman) and also appeared as a soloist with the New York Philharmonic Orchestra and the Pittsburgh Symphony Orchestra. She made her London debut with its Symphonic Orchestra in 1970, playing the *Tchaikovsky Concerto*. Shortly thereafter, she began to expand her circle of teachers by working with Josef Gingold, Szymon Goldberg, Paul Makanowitzky, and Joseph Szigeti. Her sonata partners have included Peter Frankl, Itamar Golan, Radu Lupu, Stephen Kovacevich, and Krystian Zimerman, and she has performed with leading conductors, such as André Previn, Georg Solti, and Lorin Maazel. Her brother, Myung-Whun, has also been the acting conductor when she has performed as soloist.

At the turn of the twenty-first century she maintained a rigorous touring schedule, performing more than 100 times a year. She was named one of the most prominent violinists of the latter part of the twentieth century by the *Sunday Times* of England, and took eight curtain calls in the mid-1990s when she played Bartók's *Second Violin Concerto* at a concert at the Champs Elysées Theater in Paris, organized to commemorate the 70th birthday of Pierre Boulez. The performance, which was recorded by EMI, was critically acclaimed and awarded the Gramophon Prize. Her other recordings, totaling over 20, include the concertos of Beethoven, Berg, Bruch, Elgar, Mendelssohn, Saint-Saëns, Sibelius, Tchaikovsky, and Walton, and are primarily under the Decca label.

As members of the Chung Trio, she and her siblings became the United Nations' first good-will anti-drug ambassadors for their concert-giving support of anti-drug campaigns in Rome, New York, Chicago, and other cities of the world. Kyung-Wha Chung has been showered with recognition for her sparkling, energetic personality, and for her concentrated, inspiring, and nearly technically perfect performances; she is considered one of the top violinists in the world. *—Meredith Gailey*

Recommended:

- ○ **Violin Concertos of Mendelssohn & Bruch** / Dutoit, Kempe (conds.), Chung, Royal PO, Montreal SO / 1999 / Decca 460976
- ○ **Violin Concertos of Berg & Bartók** / Solti (cond.), Chung, Chicago SO / 1984 / Decca 411804
- ○ **Violin Concertos of Tchaikovsky & Sibelius** / Chung, Previn (cond.), London SO / 1995 / London 425080
- ○ **Souvenirs** / Chung, Golan (piano) / 1999 / Angel 56827B

Myung-Whun Chung

b. Jan. 22, 1953, Seoul, Korea
Conductor

Myung-Whun Chung is one of the leading conductors of his generation. Also a prize-winning pianist, he is particularly noted for his interpretations of the music of French composer Olivier Messiaen.

There has rarely been as talented a group of siblings as Myung-Whun and his two older sisters, cellist Myung-Wha Chung (b. 1944) and violinist Kyung-Wha Chung (b. 1948). Myung-Whun made his performing debut as a pianist in Seoul at the age of seven. At eight, he flew to Seattle, Washington, to begin his American musical studies. He attended the Mannes School, and later the Juilliard School in New York. His teachers there were Nadia Reisenberg (piano) and Carl Bramburger (conducting).

Chung won the *New York Times* piano competition in 1970. He made a conducting debut back in Seoul in 1971, conducting the Korean Symphony Orchestra. In 1974, he entered the International Tchaikovsky Competition in Moscow as a pianist, winning second prize. He continued conducting studies at Juilliard, conducting both the New York Youth Orchestra and the Pre-College Orchestra of the Juilliard School. Carlo Maria Giulini, music director of the Los Angeles Philharmonic Orchestra, engaged Chung as his assistant in 1978. Two years later on Giulini's recommendation, the Orchestra named Chung its associate conductor. In 1984, Chung became music director and principal conductor of the Saarbrücken Radio Symphony Orchestra in Germany. He made his triumphant New York debut in 1986 conducting the Metropolitan Opera's production of Verdi's *Simon Boccanegra.* Later in 1986, he also delivered a brilliant performance in Paris of Prokofiev's rarely-heard opera *The Fiery Angel.* In 1987, he was appointed principal guest conductor of the Teatro Communale of Florence, Italy (1987–92). He received two major Italian awards during this period, the Premio Abbiata and the 1989 Arturo Toscanini Prize. In 1989 Chung became music director of the Opéra-Paris-Bastille. His performances included Messiaen's *Saint-François d'Assise* and Shostakovich's *Lady Macbeth of Mtsensk District.* He became noted for his renditions of the complex music of Messiaen. The composer rewarded Chung by dedicating to him his last work, the *Concert à Quatre* and entrusting him with its world premiere (1994). In 1992, the French government awarded him the Legion of Honor for his contributions to the Paris Opera. This did not prevent an angry parting resulting from a change of administration at the French Ministry of Culture in 1994. He has frequently guest conducted in such venues as La Scala Milan, the Royal Opera House Covent Garden, and the leading international orchestras. After leaving the Bastille Opera post he has been principal conductor of the Accademia Nazionale di Santa Cecilia and the Asia Philharmonic Orchestra.

In the early 1980s he began work to present "environmental concerts" to allow the audience to accept environmental problems "with their hearts." He seeks a closer relationship between the two parts of his divided country, and has premiered the music of Isang Yun, a South Korean-born composer with similar views. Chung held concerts to raise money for rice to be shipped to famine-stricken North Korea. When he won the Ho-Am Prize from the Samsung Group (worth $111,000), he donated it all to the Korean Red Cross to alleviate the starvation in North Korea.

He also promotes an anti-drug message in his concerts, leading him in 1992 to be named Ambassador of the Drug Control Program at the United Nations. He was 1995's UNESCO "Man of the Year" and in 1996 won the highest cultural award of the Korean government. He returned to Korea to become music director of the Korean Broadcasting Symphony, and is the first Honorary Cultural Ambassador for Korea. *—Joseph Stevenson*

Recommended:

- ○ **Messiaen: Concert à Quatre** / Chung (cond.), Rostropovich, Loriod, Cantin, Bastille Opera Orch. / 1995 / DG 445947
- ○ **Messiaen: Turangalîla Symphony** / Chung (cond.), Loriod, Loriod, Bastille Opera Orch. / DG 431781
- ○ **Messiaen: Eclairs sur l'au-delà** / Chung (cond.), Bastille Opera Orch. / 1994 / DG 439929

Charlotte Church

b. Feb. 21, 1986, Llandaff, Cardiff, England
Soprano

Charlotte Church exploded onto the classical recording scene at the age of 12 and enchanted audiences around the world with a remarkably mature voice.

Her story seems to confirm the notion that Wales is a land of naturally great singers. At the age of 11, she appeared on the British television program "Talking Telephone Numbers"; she sang "Pie Jesu" from the Andrew Lloyd Webber *Requiem.* Paul Burger, chairman and chief executive of Sony Music UK, saw the performance and immediately signed her to a recording contract.

The result was an album called *Voice of an Angel.* Its theme was primarily religious, with music ranging from hymns like *Amazing Grace* and *Jerusalem* to classical pieces like "Pie Jesu". Cautioned that classical recordings often sell copies numbering only in the low four figures, she and the recording world in general were surprised when it quickly sold over 600,000 copies in Britain alone—double platinum in that country.

The feat made her the youngest artist ever to have a No. 1 album on the classical charts. The disc also made the top five among albums in general (in the U.K.); again, she is the youngest artist ever to have an album rise so high on that chart. The recording went gold in the United States, and Charlotte performed on American television's *Late Night with David Letterman, The Tonight Show with Jay Leno, Oprah, Rosie, Good Morning America,* and *The Today Show,* and was booked to act and sing in an episode of the series *Touched by an Angel.*

Church performed at the 50th birthday celebrations for the Prince of Wales and at Pope John Paul II's Christmas Concert at the Vatican. In November 1999, she released her second album, *Charlotte Church,* while the first album remained on the album charts and the top of the Billboard Classical Crossover chart after three months. More secular than the first disc, *Charlotte Church* benefited from heavy marketing in American discount retail chains such as Target—virtually unprecedented for a classical CD.

Charlotte Church seemed to have the personality of a typical teenager, counting her meetings with Elton John, Will Smith, Danny DeVito and the Spice Girls as equal to those with her classical heroes and heroines such as Placido Domingo, Kiri Te Kanawa, and Kathleen Battle. As she approached adulthood, Church seemed restless and became a fixture of British tabloid gossip pages. Her *Prelude, Enchantment,* and *Dream a Dream* albums were firmly located on the pop side of the crossover equation and saw Church collaborating with yet newer crossover sensations like Josh Groban. *—Joseph Stevenson*

Recommended:

- ○ **Prelude: The Best of Charlotte Church** / Church, etc. / 2002 / Columbia 86990

Aldo Ciccolini

b. Aug. 15, 1925, Naples, Italy
Pianist

Italian pianist Aldo Ciccolini has enjoyed a long and varied career, but to many music lovers his name is most readily associated with the music of Erik Satie. Ciccolini was raised in Naples, where he studied at the Conservatory under pianist Paolo Denza, himself a onetime student of Ferruccio Busoni; Ciccolini made his debut there in 1942. In 1949 Ciccolini traveled to Paris to complete in a Long-Thibault contest—after he won first prize, Ciccolini decided to stay in Paris and continue his studies with Marguerite Long. Ciccolini made his New York debut in 1950. It was probably through Long that Ciccolini got to know the music of Satie.

Ciccolini started playing a wide range of Satie works on his programs of the 1950s, including many pieces that had been forgotten since the composer's death. This attracted attention among the musical cognoscenti in Paris, including some of the most forward-thinking musicians of the time. They recognized in Ciccolini's interpretations of Satie's works elements in keeping with current-day avant-garde approaches that had been previously overlooked. Ultimately this led to a revival of Satie's music and to Ciccolini's recorded versions of it for EMI; while the earliest of these recordings have proven the best sellers over time, Ciccolini has recorded the entire keyboard output of Satie twice over.

It is not fair to Ciccolini's talent, however, to limit him only to Satie, even as this association is the best-known in his particular case. Ciccolini has also recorded the complete piano sonatas of Beethoven, and has also performed the sonatas of Mozart and is renowned for his work with the music of French composers other than Satie, such as Chabrier, Saint-Saëns, Ravel, Debussy, and Fauré. Ciccolini is also an expert interpreter of the music of Liszt, and is equally well situated in concerto literature in addition to solo piano repertoire. Ciccolini is highly regarded as a teacher, holding a chair at the Paris Conservatoire from 1971 to 1989. In 2000 Ciccolini was named honorary president of the Associazione Musicale Aldo Ciccolini, an organization devoted to promoting the cause of cultural and musical events in his native city of Naples. *—Uncle Dave Lewis*

Recommended:

- ○ **Mozart: Sonatas, Vol. 1** / Ciccolini / 2000 / Arcobaleno 94412
- ○ **Satie: L'Oeuvre pour piano** / Ciccolini / 2001 / EMI 74534
- ○ **Granados: Goyescas; Albeniz: Iberia** / Ciccolini / EMI 62889

Johannes Ciconia

b. ca. 1335, Liège, Belgium, **d.** Dec. 1411, Padua, Italy
Composer

Johannes Ciconia was one of the most important Franco-Flemish composers of the pre-Renaissance era. His output encompassed both the secular and sacred realms and included, in the former, madrigals, ballata, virelai, and a Latin canon; and in the latter, mass movements (only Glorias and Credos, however), motets, and Latin songs. His style mixed Italian, specifically Pavian, features with those of the French so-called ars subtilior. It is believed that a substantial portion of his output was lost. Some of the surviving compositions, like the ballata *Amor per ti sempre,* may have been misattributed to him.

Ciconia was born in Liège, but details about the early years of his life are confusing and fraught with conjecture, so much so that it is often difficult to sift out the speculation from the facts. One factor contributing to the muddle is that there were two or three prominent men having the name of Johannes Ciconia with roots in Liège and living around the turn of the fifteenth century. Moreover, there is some speculation that the composer's often-given date of birth, "ca. 1370," is wrong by a whole generation; Ciconia conceivably could have been born as early as 1335. The reason for the wide gap in the two dates is that he may be confused with his father in certain biographical sources. Just who his father was is also a matter of controversy, since, according to a 1391 letter by Pope Boniface IX, a certain priest sired one Johannes Ciconia, who is thus referred to as illegitimate and thus placing him in Rome in the 1390s, which fits a likely scenario, as will be seen. There is a document confirming that Ciconia served as a choir boy in 1385 at the Liège Church, St. Jean l'Évangéliste, where a certain Johan de Chywongne was canon. This canon, another document suggests, was most probably the composer's father and the year 1370 the more likely time of Ciconia's birth. This last conclusion is supported most convincingly by the fact that all of Ciconia's surviving output can be dated to around and after 1390.

Ciconia himself was a cleric, though it is unclear whether he actually was a priest. In any event, he seems to have served Cardinal d'Alençon in Rome in the 1390s as *clericus capelle*, an important post usually occupied by young musicians. It is almost certain that Ciconia went into the service of Giangaleazzo Visconti at his Court in Pavia in the late 1390s, which would explain the composer's use of stylistic traits generally associated with Pavian music of the time. In 1401, Ciconia accepted a chaplaincy at the cathedral in Padua and a benefice at St. Biagio di Roncalea Church, also in Padua. It appears that only a handful of Ciconia's works date to the 1390s, with the rest coming during his Paduan period. In the years following his appointment at the cathedral, Ciconia was granted further benefices at nearby churches. He wrote a good many of his works for wealthy patrons, like the politically powerful Carrara family and Francesco Zabarella, a good friend and mentor. It is thus quite probable that the composer lived in very comfortable circumstances in his last decade, perhaps even with a measure of wealth. Ciconia retained his post with the cathedral until his death in June or July 1412. *—Robert Cummings*

Overview of Works (ca. 1394–1410)

The works of Johannes Ciconia represent the coexistence and convergence of a number of styles, bridging the end of the Middle Ages with the early Renaissance and intermingling various regional styles. For many scholars Ciconia represents a connection between the mannerist *ars subtilior* movement in France with the *Trecento* traditions of Italy. Ciconia's surviving works include secular music in both French and Italian traditions; motets in French and Latin, composed to mark important civic and religious occasions; and several liturgical works.

Represented among Ciconia's secular works are two closely related but geographically separated genres, the French virelai and the Italian ballata. Ciconia's ballata *O rosa bella* shows affinities with the early Italian madrigal in its expressive approach to text declamation and hints at word painting; the virelai *Sus une fontayne* exhibits the notationally complex rhythmic tricks of the *ars subtilior* as well as a clever and progressive employment of borrowed musical fragments. Artifice and technique figure prominently in Ciconia's pair of canonic songs as well. *Quod jactatur* has yet to be deciphered: only one line is given, and the rubric for extrapolating three voices from it has stumped scholars. Of Ciconia's four madrigals, *Una panthera* is the most well-known. Referring to the city of Lucca's mythical founding by a panther, the piece uses symbolic imagery as civic and political allusion. The madrigals in particular exhibit specifically Italianate musical traits, such as the quick triplet figurations, syncopations, and other rhythmic profiles inherited from the Trecento (but tempered somewhat when rendered in French notation).

Ciconia's motet style, in the two dozen or so surviving examples, is grounded firmly in the practices of northern Italy at the turn of the century. Some works, such as *Ut te per omnes* and *O felix templum*, employ isorhythmic principles of the Ars Nova, but in a less architectonic way; the tenors, rather than being culled from plainchant or other sources, are freely composed to fit the upper voice structures (rather than vice-versa); their repetition schemes are less complicated than those found in the isorhythmic motets of Machaut. In addition, Ciconia left a number of motets that are not structured according to isorhythmic principles.

Ciconia's mass movements are best represented by the handful of surviving Gloria-Credo pairs (of the type in use prior to the Continental adoption of the fully cyclical four- or five-movement Mass Ordinary). These works, for three or four voices, are necessarily less extrovert, but still representative of Ciconia's stylistic flexibility and a keen sense of expression and declamation. *—Jeremy Grimshaw*

Recommended:

- ○ **Ciconia: Motets; Virelais; Ballate; Madrigals** / All Francesca & Alta / 1994 / Opus 111 30101
- ○ **Homage to Johannes Ciconia** / Ens. PAN / 1992 / New Albion 048
- ○ **Ciconia: Oeuvre intégrale** / Van Nevel, Huelgas Ens. / 1997 / Pavane 7345

Francesco Cilea

b. Jul. 26, 1866, Palmi, Italy, **d.** Nov. 20, 1950, Varazze, Italy

Composer: Opera

Cilea wrote relatively few works, and only one, *Adriana Lecouvreur*, is performed with any kind of regularity. Musically and dramatically, he hovered between the nineteenth and twentieth centuries, writing verismo operas with a lightness that is somewhat reminiscent of bel canto. If his writing did not show musical genius, it showed mastery of his chosen style and a gift for pathos and lyricism.

He did not come from a wealthy family, and was discouraged by his family from pursuing a musical career, but with the aid an aunt, he was eventually allowed to apply for admission to the San Pietro di Majella Conservatory in Naples. There he was befriended by Francesco Florimo, a librarian, archivist, and teacher who encouraged him and introduced him to the music of Bellini, who became a lifelong inspiration. At first, he showed more promise as an instrumental composer than an operatic one, and some of his piano works were published by Ricordi while he was still a student. Upon graduating in 1889, he had modest successes with his first two operas, *Gina* and *La Tilda*, but achieved somewhat wider fame with *L'arlesiana*, premiered in 1897 (revised in 1898 and yet again in 1937.) However, not achieving the level of success he had hoped for, he had to be persuaded by his publisher, Sonzago, to continue writing rather than concentrating on music education. Upon graduating, he had taken a position as auxiliary professor of harmony and piano at the Conservatory.

In 1900, he began work on *Adriana Lecouvreur*, and it premiered in 1902, with the young Enrico Caruso, who had also sung the tenor lead, Federico, in *L'arlesiana*. In 1904, Cilea was popular enough that the Theatre Sarah Bernhardt in Paris was able to mount a season consisting solely of his works.

In 1907, his opera *Gloria* had its premiere at La Scala, conducted by Toscanini. It is far different from his previous operas, with a wide dramatic scope, extensive choral writing, and considerably more sophisticated orchestral writing. However, it was not as successful as he hoped, either at its premiere or in the revised version staged in 1932, and except for one tribute to Verdi (Il canto della vita) and the above-mentioned revisions to his other works, Cilea essentially stopped composing, and instead returned his focus to music education, teaching at the Palermo and Naples conservatories, among others. *—Ann Feeney*

OPERA

Adriana Lecouvreur (1902)

The life of Francesco Cilea (1866–1950) spanned several important periods in Italian opera. Born before the advent of verismo, he lived well past the end of the great outpouring of lyric theatre heard from Puccini, Mascagni, Leoncavallo, Giordano, and others of their time. Although several of his works enjoyed success during his lifetime, Cilea is known best for two operas, *L'Arlesiana*, premiered in 1896, and *Adriana Lecouvreur*, first staged at Milan's Teatro Lirico on November 6, 1902. It was the latter work that spread the composer's fame beyond his native country and provided, in addition, a role irresistible to lyric/dramatic sopranos—irresistible for both its soaring melodic invention and the opportunities it affords for dramatic acting (and overacting). Staged earnestly and sumptuously, it constitutes an engaging evening of music theatre.

Among its prime attractions are two arias for Adriana, well known by many who have never heard the entire work. From the first act comes "Io son l'umile ancella," in which the the heroine, an actress, maintains that she is merely a handmaid of the arts. As her death nears in the final act, she bids adieu, in the aria "Poveri fiori," to a love she believes is as faded as the withered (and poisoned) violets that she inhales. These are not the only exceptional solo moments in the score, however. The role of the Princess of Bouillon calls for a stellar dramatic mezzo-soprano and rewards her with an opening scene in Act Two that can sweep an audience away ("Acerba voluttà"). The aria's concluding section ("O vagabonda stella d'Oriente") expands to an electrifying climax, musically and theatrically thrilling—an assured showstopper for any singer of quality. The tenor, Maurizio, has his moments as well, although they are less flavorful than those for the leading women. No less important than the big occasions are those scenes which bind the story together. Cilea demonstrates a facility for handling conversation skillfully enough to further the action and never impede it. The music uses conventional harmony but employs very colorful orchestration in the service of an aesthetic that is often melodramatic but continuously effective.

The real Adriana (Adrienne Lecouvreur) was an actress of great celebrity who lived from 1692 to 1730 and revolutionized French theatre by her naturalistic approach to appearance and speech. Eschewing the declaiming of her lines, she impressed her audiences with the power of her presentation. In Cilea's opera, the actress is in love with Maurizio, Count of Saxony, whom she knows only as a soldier. Her rival for his love, the Princess de Bouillon, is angered by Maurizio's rejection of her advances and plans revenge upon the actress. When she is insulted by Adriana during the latter's public reading of certain scornful lines from Racine's *Phèdre*, she redoubles her resolve to do away with the actress. She poisons a clutch of violets and sends them to Adriana, certain that she will believe that they are being returned by Maurizio. He arrives to ask Adriana's hand in marriage shortly before she succumbs and dies. *—Erik Eriksson*

Synopsis:

Act One. In the green room of the Comédie Française in 1730, Michonnet, stage manager/factotum, mutters that he tolerates his difficult job only because of his hope of someday becoming a *sociétaire*, a position that would keep him near

Adriana Lecouvreur, the leading actress of the period. The backstage chaos is interrupted by the arrival of Prince de Bouillon, a protector of Lecouvreur's rival, Mademoiselle Duclos. The Prince, an amateur chemist, is accompanied by his toady, the Abbé of Chazeuil, a worldly cleric. Condescendingly inquiring as to La Duclos' whereabouts, the Prince learns that she is still dressing. The evening's full house is scarcely surprising, given that both La Lecouvreur and La Duclos are appearing on the same bill. When Adriana appears, she admonishes her admirers who offer her too much flattery; she is merely a handmaiden of the arts. When she admits that she learned everything from Michonnet, he nearly breaks into tears.

Told by Michonnet that Duclos has been hastily writing a note in her dressing room, the Prince vows that he will see its contents. The soldier Maurizio, Adriana's lover, has made his way to the green room. Adriana questions him about his chances for promotion, but he evades her inquiries. At the play's conclusion, the Prince is handed Duclos' letter by the Abbé, who has obtained it for him. The letter, addressed to the occupant of the third box on the right-hand side, reveals an assignation for later that very night. The Prince concludes that Maurizio must be the intended recipient and invites Adriana to the villa of her rival later that night in order to interrupt the rendezvous and subject Adriana to humiliation. Unbeknownst to the Prince, however, the letter was written at the behest of his wife, the Princess de Bouillon, whose own intent was the seduction and conquest of Maurizio. The Prince has the letter delivered to Maurizio in his box and delights in contemplating the havoc it will unleash.

Maurizio, unhappy over the interruption of his planned evening with Adriana, comes backstage. He thinks that he will pass a letter to Adriana breaking their tryst by substituting it for a prop letter needed for the play's action. Adriana is shaken, but the audience takes this to be an example of superlative acting. After the performance, the Prince invites the ensemble to dinner at his villa to celebrate Adriana's "triumph."

Act Two. In a salon at the villa, the Princess impatiently awaits the arrival of Maurizio. When he arrives, she tells him that his exploits (he is in fact a lieutenant and not a mere soldier) have gained the attention of the Queen, but that he has enemies as well. When Maurizio resists her advances, his entreaties that they remain friends brings forth a volley of scornful invective. When the Prince and the Abbé arrive, the Prince accuses Maurizio of engaging in a dalliance, but when challenged to a duel the Prince admits his ruse. Adriana arrives and learns to her relief of Maurizio's true rank. She is asked by him to assist an innocent woman hiding in the villa, someone he vows is not her rival. In the dark, Adriana gives the Princess a key to the garden gate as each protests that she loves Maurizio. The Princess makes her escape in a monumental rage, and Maurizio, believing that Adriana has accompanied the Princess, leaves. Adriana, feeling abandoned, collapses.

Act Three. In the Great Ballroom at the Prince's residence, arrangements for a reception are underway. When the guests arrive and are presented to the Prince and his wife, the Princess hears in Adriana's words of appreciation the voice of the woman who led her from certain ruin. Exercising great control, the Princess asks Adriana to favor the company with a recitation, but, when the actress observes the Princess and Maurizio in conversation, she directs the scornful concluding lines of her verses from Racine's *Phèdre* directly at the Princess. The Princess, insulted, vows revenge.

Act Four. In a room at her home, Adriana disconsolately tells Michonnet of her intention to retire. A small casket arrives containing withered violets. Believing them to be those she gave Maurizio, she presses them to her lips, drawing from them a poison applied in fact by the vengeful Princess. Maurizio arrives to explain his absence. As he begs forgiveness and announces his intent to marry her, she turns pale and slowly expires in his arms. *—Erik Eriksson*

Recommended:

- ○ **Cilea: Adriana Lecouvreur** / Levine (cond.), Scotto, Domingo, Obraztsova, Milnes, Philharmonia Orch. / Sony 34588
- ○ **Cilea: Adriana Lecouvreur** / Capuana (cond.), Tebaldi, Del Monaco, Simionato, Orch. dell'Accademia di Santa Cecila, Roma / 1991 / Decca 430256

L'Arlesiana (1897; revised 1898)

When librettist Leopoldo Mareneo approached Francesco Cilea with his *L'Arlesiana* libretto, the composer had not worked on an opera for over five years. Instead, he had been pouring his efforts into his position as a professor of piano in Naples and teacher of counterpoint at the Reale Instituto Musicale in Florence. From that moment on, Cilea fell into a pattern of composing an opera every five years. Unlike his later *Adriana Lecouvreur*, *L'Arlesiana* has never been successful outside Italy. It is a verismo opera, especially in its musical identification of its pastoral setting, but it is not innovative within that style. It is not quite popular music, but also not very sophisticated. Although it features a few French folk melodies (appropriate for its location, Provence) it does not reach back in time in search of a style. The voice of *L'Arlesiana* is fluid and clear, born in the simple, expressive, Italian melodic tradition Cilea inherited.

Cilea recognized the weaknesses of *L'Arlesiana.* In 1898, he condensed the original four acts to three and in 1910 he added the excellent aria for Rosa Mamai, "Esser madre è un inferno," and made further changes. In 1937, he attached a new prelude. Today, most critics attribute its weak effect to the mediocre libretto, which tells the tale of a family of Provençal farmers, one of whom falls in love with an Arles woman, whom he discovers to have been another man's mistress. Despite the love of another woman, the man is driven insane by jealousy and commits suicide.

Cilea's *L'Arlesiana* is often described as plebian and "folk-like," the very opposite of his *Adriana Lecouvreur* of 1902, which is blatantly sophisticated and mannered and the only one of Cilea's works performed today. From *L'Arlesiana* we occasionally hear the aria "E la solita storia del pastore" adored by tenors wishing to display their dynamic range and dramatic capabilities. This aria is occasionally referred to as the "Lamento di Federico." The success of the opera on its opening night had more to do with Caruso's interpretation of this aria than with the Cilea's score and Mareneo's libretto. What is most memorable about Cilea's *L'Arlesiana* are several emotional, powerful arias. To the two already mentioned Baldassare's "Come due tizzi" in the first act must be added.

It was at the premiere of Cilea's *L'Arlesiana* that Enrico Caruso, in the part of Federico, had his first great success. Cilea himself had chosen the young tenor for the part and coached him before the first performance, on November 27, 1897, at the Teatro Lirico in Milan. The success of *L'Arlesiana* prompted the publisher Sonzogno to place high hopes on the 31-year-old Cilea. *—John Palmer*

Synopsis:

Act One. Rosa Mamai has two sons living on her farm, the younger of whom, L'Innocente, is mentally slow. When the curtain rises, Baldassare, an old shepherd, entertains L'Innocente with "The Story of Monsieur Seguin." Rosa enters to ask Baldassare about a beautiful Arles woman whom Rosa's oldest son, Federico, wants to marry. This upsets Rosa because she knows nothing of the woman. Baldassare, too, is completely ignorant of the woman's past and points out that no one knows her. Rosa tells Vivetta, a childhood friend of Federico, that her son plans to marry and describes how Federico first met the young lady ("Era un giorno di festa"). This upsets Vivetta because she is in love with Federico, and her distress becomes apparent. Swooning, Federico arrives with his uncle, Marco. Marco has done some research and has decided that the young woman's family is acceptable; he encourages Federico to seek her hand in marriage. As those assembled celebrate the upcoming wedding ceremony, a cattle herder named Metifio arrives to speak to Baldassare and Rosa. Metifio informs them that the woman from Arles is fickle; she used to be his mistress and has letters to prove it. Federico is sick with despair because he simply cannot conceive of marrying such a person. Metifio leaves his letters with Federico and Rosa.

Act Two. The action takes place at a sheep pen near the lagoon of Vaccarès. Federico has run off. Baldassare, Rosa, and Vivetta search for him. During the search, Vivetta confesses to Rosa that she is in love with Federico. Rosa suggests that she seduce Federico to win him and make him forget the Arlesian woman, but Vivetta refuses. Baldassare finds Federico, who has given himself over to a life of hard labor in order to forget the woman who has such a strong hold on him "È la solita storia del pastore"). L'Innocente tries to help Federico by telling a story, but he falls asleep, as does Federico. Vivetta, now on the offensive, slips in, wakes up Federico, and tells him of her feelings. Federico is shocked and, in utter disdain, forcefully pushes Vivetta away from him, rejects her, and again runs off. His mother catches up with him and tries to bring him to his senses. Eventually, he calms down and decides to ask for Vivetta's love, not because he loves her, but because he feels it is the only way of ridding himself of the spell cast by the woman from Arles.

Act Three. It is the night of St. Eligius at the farm, and the betrothal of Federico and Vivetta is being celebrated. Vivetta is unsure of Federico's intentions, for he has kept Metifio's letters concerning the Arlesian woman for quite some time. Federico assures Vivetta that he is completely cured of the woman's "spell." Metifio arrives, asking for his letters and, in very passionate tones, tells those at the celebration that he intends to take the Arlesian woman away with him on his horse, for he is more attracted to her than ever. Federico overhears Metifio's monologue and becomes furiously jealous, attacking the cattle herder. Rosa separates the fighting men before they kill one another and takes Federico to his room. Rosa retires to her own room and prays to be rid of this new torment, which simply adds to all the others she has incurred as a mother ("Esser madre è un inferno"). L'Innocente then joins his mother and tries to console her. As he does so, Rosa notices that the boy is beginning to show signs of increased intelligence. Instead of cheering her up, this observation frightens her, because an old Provençal tradition states that a fool in the family brings good luck. Bad luck strikes the next morning. Federico has not slept during the night but lay tormented by thoughts of Metifio abducting the Arlesian woman. Rosa and Vivetta try to reason with him, but to no avail. Tortured by his own mind, he leaps out of the window of the tower to end his misery. *—John Palmer*

Recommended:

- ○ **Cilea: L'Arlesiana** / Basile (cond.), Tassinari,Tagliavini, Galli, Silveri, OS di Torino della RAI / 2001 / Warner Fonit 87469
- ○ **Cilea: L'Arlesiana** / Rosekrans (cond.), Zilio, Kelen, Spacagna, B. Anderson, Hungarian State SO / 1998 / EMI 66762

Domenico Cimarosa

b. Dec. 17, 1749, Aversa, Italy, **d.** Jan. 11, 1801, Venice, Italy
Composer: Opera

A composer who was quite familiar to Mozart's operatic audiences, Domenico Cimarosa was the prolific creator of over 60 operas. He was the son of a poor bricklayer, coming from a working-class family. He studied music at the Conservatorio Santa Maria di Loreto from 1761 until 1772. Among his teachers was the famous Piccinni, the rival of Gluck in France. His first opera was *Le stravaganza del conte.* It premiered in Naples in 1772, and its success was such that it brought Cimarosa immediate recognition. Cimarosa spent the next several years in Rome and Naples, and composed over twenty operas for these two cities. His operas were performed internationally in Paris, Vienna, Dresden, and London. In 1787, Catherine II invited him to St. Petersburg. During his stay in Russia, Cimarosa continued to compose at a prodigious rate. *La Cleopatra* and *La vergine del sole* are two works that were staged in 1788. Subsequently, Leopold II of Austria engaged him as court Kapellmeister in Vienna, to fill the position vacated by Salieri. One of Cimarosa's greatest successes was staged in Vienna. *Il matrimonio segreto*, a delightful comic opera full of invention and wit, immensely pleased the Emperor. He gave the entire cast supper, and had them perform the entire opera again that same evening. Although lacking Mozart's depth, Cimarosa's music does possess some of Mozart's qualities—in particular, a gift for the comic, buffo style.

After the death of the Emperor, Salieri was reappointed Kapellmeister, and Cimarosa was released. He left Vienna and returned to Naples where he entered the service of the King. He was hailed in Naples as a great operatic hero, and his *Il matrimonio segreto* was performed 57 times running. However, Cimarosa's last years were marked by misfortune. When the French Republican army marched into Naples, Cimarosa enthusiastically declared his support of the revolution. He was immediately thrown into prison and condemned to death. The King eventually released him, but banished him from Naples. Broken in spirit, Cimarosa attempted to return to Russia, but died in Venice in 1801. Because of rumors that he was poisoned, the government was obliged to perform an autopsy. In addition to operas, Cimarosa left behind oratorios, masses, and cantatas, and some instrumental music.—*Rita Laurance*

Overview of Works (1762–1801)

Domenico Cimarosa (1749–1801) was one of the most successful composers of his era. Born in Aversa, he received his early training as a singer in Naples, where his first stage works were performed. His fame as an opera composer spread rapidly throughout Italy; during the 1780s he composed works for Milan, Florence, Livorno, Rome, and Venice. In 1787 he was appointed *maestro di cappella* to the St. Petersburg court of Catherine the Great, where he succeeded a distinguished line of Italian composers. On his return from Russia, Cimarosa served for two years as Kapellmeister to Joseph I in Vienna before settling again in Naples, from whence republican sympathies forced him to flee to Venice, his final resting place.

While Cimarosa also composed a number of sacred works (many of them in his younger days in Naples), some attractive keyboard sonatas, and a few other instrumental works, his fame rests overwhelmingly on his nearly 60 operas. The vast majority of these are comic operas, the genre at which he excelled, which in many instances were performed in houses all over Europe. Cimarosa composed with extraordinary facility, his comic operas bubbling over with a good humor and high spirits that, by contemporary accounts, reflect the character of the man himself. While stylistically similar to the great comic operas of Mozart, Cimarosa's operas rarely sought to emulate the greater composer's profound psychological insights into the human condition, relying rather on an elegant sophistication and an unfailing ability to entertain his audiences. If he was at times let down by poor librettos, Cimarosa shows that when given a good book he was capable of approaching the Mozartean ideal.

Il matrimonio segreto (The Secret Marriage), the one opera of Cimarosa's that still holds the stage regularly today, perhaps comes closer than any other to doing so. Composed for Vienna in 1792, *Il matrimonio segreto* was immensely successful, running for 57 consecutive performances at the Burgtheater. It is a work that demonstrates Cimarosa's strengths at their best, fast-paced, and with many witty ensembles involving real dramatic flexibility and interaction between the characters. The opera is also notable for its colorful orchestration and effective wind writing that often approaches comparison with Mozart.

Il pittore parigino (The Parisian Painter), originally produced in Rome in 1781, was another enormously successful comic opera, particularly after being revised by Cimarosa in 1792, while *Armida immaginaria* (1777) is a highly enjoyable earlier Neapolitan work that shows the composer successfully exploiting the popular eighteenth century theme of feigned madness. Finally, mention should also be made of *Il maestro di cappella*, an enchanting short comic work that amusingly recounts the difficulties of a conductor attempting to rehearse his orchestra in a new work. While Cimarosa was responsible for few innovations, his operas will continue to be valued for his unfailing melodic invention and a gift for Italianate spirit and verve unmatched by his native contemporaries. —*Brian Robins*

Recommended:

- ○ **Cimarosa: Armida Immaginaria** / Hull (cond.), Colaianni, Edwards, Donadini, Guarnera, Orch. del Teatro Massimo "Bellini" de Catania / 1998 / Dynamic 205/1-3
- ○ **Cimarosa: Complete Sonatas** / Crudelli / 1994 / Arcobaleno 9367

OPERA

Il matrimonio segreto (1792)

Among Domenico Cimarosa's comic operas, *Il matrimonio segreto* is the most famous and best loved. Cimarosa was popular throughout Italy because he wrote for the Italian people, in a language with which they were familiar. His dramas are quickly paced, his humor drew on Italian theater traditions, his melodies are beautiful, singable, and extremely pleasing. His vocal writing is constantly varied, combining voices in new ways and setting words in varied ways: patter, secco recitative, a cappella part writing, and concerted ensembles. Before Cimarosa's day, vocal ensembles were usually reserved for the grand finale of each act.

Il matrimonio segreto was composed for the Vienna court opera. Cimarosa had been hired by the Empress Catherine the Great of Russia as her court composer. But by the time he took the post, the Russian court had ceased to put money into its operatic productions. He stayed in Russia until his contract expired, but then left to return to Italy. He passed through Vienna and wrote *Il matrimonio segreto* for the Emperor Leopold I. It was premiered at the Burgtheater in Vienna on February 7, 1792, to rave reviews. The production was such a success that every number was encored. Leopold was so happy with the opera that he asked the exhausted company to perform it a second time that same evening. Cimarosa was asked to stay on at the court of Leopold I as music director. However, Leopold soon died and the composer Salieri was reinstated, leaving Cimarosa without an official position. Cimarosa returned to Italy. But there the opera was just as popular as it had been in Vienna, if not more so. It became an international success and was translated into ten different languages and performed in as many different countries. It is one of the few eighteenth century *opere buffe* to have been revived in the twentieth century, and it remains in the repertoire of opera houses in the twenty-first.

The libretto for the work was written by Giovanni Bertati. It is an exceptionally fine text, with neatness of construction and stylish comedy. The source for the libretto was a British satire called *The Clandestine Marriage*, which in turn has as its origins *Mariage à la mode* by Hogarth. It lacks some of the underlying "heart" of Mozart's music, but by any other measure it compares well. The plot is, of course, about an attempt to thwart the leading couple's true love. In fact, Carolina and Paolino have married secretly because of the opposition of her father, the greedy Geronimo, a Bolognese merchant. Paolino believes that he can win the old man's acceptance by engineering a marriage between Geronimo's other daughter, Elisetta, to a wealthy young English Count. This backfires when Elisetta falls in love with Paolino and the Count with Carolina. The secretly married lovers then flee in desperation and are captured. When they reveal they are marriedm Geronimo accepts the fait accompli, any bitterness over the fact being alleviated when Elisetta and the Count decide they love each other, after all, and decide to marry. —*Rita Laurance*

Synopsis:

Act One. After a brilliant overture, the curtain rises on Paolino and Carolina, a pair of lovers who were married in secret several months ago. Carolina's father Geronimo is sure to be against the union, but they need to tell him about it, and soon. Geronimo has ambitions that he hoped would be realized through the marriage of his daughters to persons of rank and power. The two think that, although he is sure to disapprove of their marriage, perhaps when the elder daughter Elisetta marries a Count his anger will abate. They hope that they will be forgiven because they were behind the favorable match of Elisetta to Count Robinson. They have a touching love duet in which they discuss their future together, and then Paolino leaves to deliver a letter from the Count, asking for Elisetta's hand in marriage. When Geronimo understands its contents, he is overjoyed that his eldest is fated to be a member of the nobility. He is swept away by currents of joy and announces to all that the feast is in preparation. Too late, he realizes that Elisetta is not as happy about the situation as he is.

Elisetta picks a fight with Carolina for not showing her enough respect, while Fidalma tries to make peace between them. But Fidalma is secretly in love with Paolino and intends to marry him. To make matters worse, when the Count enters, he mistakes Carolina for his prospective wife. He is disappointed with Elisetta's homeliness and lack of grace, and he wants to marry Carolina instead. No one is happy about the situation except Geronimo, who is deaf and therefore doesn't understand what all of the fuss is about. Elisetta accuses Carolina of seducing the Count, and chaos ensues.

Act Two. Count Robinson and Geronimo embark on a duet in which they argue over the Count's marriage plans. While Geronimo insists that he must marry Elisetta, the Count refuses, and they argue about it. He finally offers to marry Carolina for half of the dowry that he was offered to marry the elder girl, and Geronimo agrees. Fidalma, meanwhile, declares her love for Paolino and her wish to marry him. Carolina and Paolino decide that they must run off together as soon as possible. After all of the characters have gone to bed, Carolina and Paolino attempt to make their getaway. When they are caught by the rest of the cast, they must admit that they are married, and have been for several months. Geronimo forgives them, and when the Count understands the situation, he decides to marry Elisetta instead. All ends happily. *—Rita Laurance*

Recommended:

- ○ **Cimarosa: Il matrimonio segreto** / Lopez-Cobos (cond.), LeRoux, A. M. Owens, Szmytka, A. Romero, CO de Lausanne / Cascavelle 1022
- ○ **Cimarosa: Il matrimonio segreto** / G. Bellini (cond.), Patterson, Matteuzzi, Antoniozzi, J. Williams, Orch. of Eastern Netherlands / 1995 / Arts 47117

Cincinnati Pops Orchestra

f. 1977, Cincinnati, OH

Ensemble

The Cincinnati Pops Orchestra is the name assumed by the Cincinnati Symphony Orchestra for an annual series of 13 to 20 Pops concerts currently conducted by American Erich Kunzel. The Cincinnati Pops Orchestra was officially established in 1977, and has played an important role in popularizing the Orchestra with Cincinnati audiences, particularly through their summertime Concerts in the Park series. Pops has been a tradition of Cincinnati since the 1870s. The progenitor to the Cincinnati Symphony Orchestra, the Cincinnati Grand Orchestra, performed pops concerts as a part of their regular programs. Musicians from the Grand Orchestra would later form the nucleus of the Cincinnati Symphony Orchestra, who, at 45 members strong, gave their inaugural performance on January 17, 1895.

The first director of the Orchestra was Frank Van der Stucken, a Texan of European parentage. His programming focused on modern composers such as Strauss (who also appeared as a guest conductor), Wagner, Tchaikovsky, and American Edward MacDowell.

The Orchestra disbanded in 1907 due to increasing debt and a labor dispute. It was reconstituted in 1909 with 77 hand-picked members, and a 27-year old director named Leopold Stokowski. One of his most important achievements during his three-year tenure was the programming of regular pops concerts.

After Stokowski left the Orchestra in 1912, Austrian Ernst Kunwald assumed the position of Director. Under him, the Orchestra undertook its first tour and first recording, both in 1917. The following season saw another new director, this time a Belgian, Eugène Ysaÿe. Ysaÿe led the Orchestra through four very successful seasons, and expanded its season, touring schedule, and membership. Whereas Kunwald's programming emphasized the Germanic repertoire, Ysaÿe emphasized the French. Ysaÿe left the Orchestra in 1922, to be replaced by Hungarian Fritz Reiner.

Reiner was a strict disciplinarian and held the Orchestra to a high standard. He made significant changes to the Orchestra's personnel, including hiring the first woman. His goal upon taking the position was to make the Orchestra one of the premier Orchestras in the country. When he left after nine years, his mission was clearly a success.

Eugene Goossens succeeded Reiner in 1931. Like his predecessors, he emphasized modern music, including American music, but he also led the Orchestra in opera and ballet performances. After Goossens left in 1947, American Thor Johnson became the music director. He continued the focus on modern and American music. Johnson started an outreach program to the communities of Cincinnati and increased the number of concerts held for young people.

After Johnson left the Orchestra in 1958, Max Rudolf assumed the position of director. Under his leadership, the Orchestra grew in size and expanded its concert series with Concerts in the Park and Area Artists Concerts. He led the Orchestra on a State Department sponsored world tour in 1966 that brought them world recognition. In 1965, Rudolf's assistant conductor, Erich Kunzel, assumed leadership of the Eight O'Clock Pops concerts that would lead to the development of the Cincinnati Pops Orchestra in 1977. Rudolf resigned from the CSO in 1969, and was followed by Thomas Schippers, Walter Susskind in 1978, Michael Gielen in 1980, and Jesús López-Cobos in 1986, all continuing the commitment of the CSO to the people of Cincinnati, and the world. *—Bruce Lundgren*

Recommended:

- ○ **Ein Straussfest** / Kunzel (cond.), Keyes, Cincinnati Pops Orch. / 1985 / Telarc 80098
- ○ **The Fantastic Stokowski** / Kunzel (cond.), Cincinnati Pops Orch. / 1994 / Telarc 80338
- ○ **Copland: Lincoln Portrait; Old American Songs** / Kunzel (cond.), Milnes, K. Hepburn, Cincinnati Pops Orch. / 1987 / Telarc 80117
- ○ **Classics at the Pops** / Kunzel (cond.), Northcut, Cincinnati Pops Orch. / 2004 / Telarc 80595
- ○ **Puttin' on the Ritz: Great Hollywood Musicals** / Kunzel (cond.), Stoll, Von Stade, Hadley, Feinstein, Cincinnati Pops Orch. / 1995 / Telarc 80366

City of Birmingham Symphony Orchestra

f. 1920, Birmingham, England

Ensemble

The City of Birmingham Symphony Orchestra was founded in 1920, becoming the first British orchestra to be funded by a city council. Its opening concert was conducted by British composer Edward Elgar. Since then, the orchestra has thrived as a bastion of musical culture in the Midlands. It has also gained a reputation for adventurous programming, underlined in recent years by the long, fruitful appointment of Simon Rattle as music director.

Birmingham is located to the northwest of London. It is one of the nation's major cities, but as with other urban centers such as Liverpool and Manchester, it has often been eclipsed by the capital in cultural matters. The centralization of British culture and power in London has nonetheless provided impetus for a competitive spirit out in the "regions," and Birmingham is no exception. The City of Birmingham Orchestra was founded by, among others, Neville Chamberlain, a prominent citizen who later became prime minister of the U.K. The orchestra's first conductor was Adrian Boult, who was quickly snapped up by the newly formed BBC Symphony Orchestra in London. Boult was replaced by one of his pupils, Leslie Heward. In 1932, Harold Gray, was named associate conductor, a post he held for nearly 50 years. In 1944, the musicians were hired on a full-time basis, and George Weldon was appointed music director to replace Heward, who had succumbed to tuberculosis.

In 1948, the orchestra was renamed City of Birmingham Symphony Orchestra (CBSO), the name it retains to this day. It began to expand its dominion with tours and London performances, including a debut at the Royal Albert Hall in London in 1951. An interesting appointment came in 1957 when Polish ex-patriot composer, Andrzej Panufnik, was named principal conductor. He lasted until 1960, when he returned to composing, but the emphasis on new music took hold. In 1962, the CBSO gave the first performances of Benjamin Britten's *War Requiem* at nearby Coventry Cathedral. This piece, which includes vocal soloists and choirs, is considered one of the major musical achievements of the post-war era in Britain.

In 1969, the young Frenchman Louis Frémaux was named principal conductor, and he led the orchestra through a series of well-received recordings for EMI. In 1980, Simon Rattle, just 25 years old but already a major talent, was appointed as Frémaux's successor, and he remained with the CBSO for almost 20 years. In that period, Rattle established himself as one of the world's top conductors, and the orchestra solidified its international reputation through tours and an impressive series of recordings. Rattle oversaw a number of interesting innovations during his tenure. One was the establishment of the Birmingham Contemporary Music Group (BCMG), a subset of the orchestra dedicated to performing the music of its time. In 1990, the young British composer Mark-Anthony Turnage was appointed composer in association, and he created a series of successful scores (such as *Three Screaming Popes*). In 1995, he was succeeded by Judith Weir, who followed up the Rattle's knighthood (still in his thirties!) with her own Companionship of the British Empire. Along with new British music, the CBSO commissioned works by international composers such as Luciano Berio, Tristan Murail, and Toru Takemitsu.

As Sir Rattle moved on to the Berlin Philharmonic in 2002, the CBSO continued its reputation as a forward-looking, world-class orchestra, rooted in a community proud of its independence. From Finland, the new Music Director Sakari Oramo was young, bright, and energetic, and lead the orchestra into the new millennium with enthusiasm and dedication. *—Jim Harley*

Recommended:

- ○ **Ravel: Daphnis & Chloé; Boléro** / Rattle (cond.), Birmingham SO / 2001 / EMI 74750
- ○ **Schoenberg, Webern, Berg: Orchestral Works** / Rattle (cond.), Auger, Birmingham SO / 2003 / EMI 75880
- ○ **Prokofiev: Scythian Suite; Symphony 5** / Rattle (cond.), Birmingham SO / 1993 / EMI 54577
- ○ **Rattle Conducts Britten** / Rattle (cond.), Tear, Gomez, Donohoe, White, Birmingham SO / 2000 / EMI 73983
- ○ **Adams: Harmonielehre; The Chairman Dances; 2 Fanfares** / Rattle (cond.), Holland, Warren, BSO / 1994 / EMI 55051

Mikolajus Konstantinas Čiurlionis

b. Sep. 22, 1875, Varena, Lithuania, **d.** Apr. 10, 1911, Pustelnik, Poland

Composer

Mikolajus Konstantinas Čiurlionis, whose musical career ceased when he fell into an abyss of depression, is best remembered for establishing professional art in Lithuania and for exemplifying the interests of the Symbolist and Modernist movements, through his paintings and his chromatic, mysterious, and folkloric—yet cosmopolitan—compositions. He was most strongly influenced in these areas midway through his life by his travels, his own reflections on the culture and politics of his fatherland, and by the attitudes of his close friend Eugeniusz Morawski, who was following the two movements when the men met.

As the son of the church organist of Druskininkai, Čiurlionis was exposed to music early in life and by the age of 14 he entered the music school associated with Prince Oginski's orchestra. His placement in the institution proved to be a wise decision and he ultimately received magisterial support to study at the Warsaw Conservatory under Sygietynski and the composer and conductor Zygmunt Noskowski. From there he attended the Leipzig Conservatory, where he was a student of the pianist, composer, and conductor Carl Reinecke and the theorist and composer Salomon Jadassohn. After achieving the competence to teach, Čiurlionis earned his living in Warsaw by giving private lessons.

After his interest in Lithuanian culture and politics was stimulated during travels near Russia, Čiurlionis moved to Vilnius in 1907 and allowed his music and art to be shaped by the influences there. In a few short years he learned to speak Lithuanian from Sofija Kymantaite (who later became his wife), directed voices of Vilniaus Kankles (Lithuania's first proficient choir), showed his own paintings in the First Lithuanian Art Exhibition, organized a follow-up display, and founded the Lithuanian Art Association (with the help of two other artists). His artwork was praised for his efforts to represent music in groups of paintings, and composers like Stravinsky showed their support by purchasing works. In his compositions Čiurlionis allowed the tedious rhythms; smooth, unembroidered melodies; and the hints of melancholy found in the country's folk songs to permeate and characterize his most mature music, especially in bass lines. Just one year after having moved to Vilnius he journeyed to St. Petersburg, where his compositions were heard in the "Evenings of Contemporary Music," on a program with Medtner and Scriabin, and his art was shown by the Union of Russian Artists. Unfortunately upon his return to Russia after a visit in his hometown of Druskininkai, he became seriously depressed, then was treated in a sanatorium near Warsaw, where he caught a fatal bout of pneumonia.

This greatly admired musician preferred to express himself through variations, did a great deal of exploration into polyphonic lines in the late half of his career, created many pieces that were marked by atonal harmony, and broadened his career through writings. The works that helped to establish Čiurlionis as a prominent composer include his orchestral work *Polonez* (1900), the cantata *De Profundis* (1899–1900), and the symphonic poems *Miske* (In the Forest) (which took the first prize at the Zamojski competition in Warsaw) and *Jura* (The Sea) (which he had once planned to transform into an opera, with the help of his wife). He also composed works for solo piano, string quartets and several songs for organs. His works are still recorded, and the most popular are his instrumental selections, which can be heard almost exclusively under the EMI and Marco Polo labels, featuring the directors M. Rubackytė and Lithuania's future president V. Landsbergis. *—Meredith Gailey*

Overview of Works (1898–1910)

Although Mikolajus Konstantinas Čiurlionis spent only a fraction of his adult life in his native Lithuania, his sense of ethnic identity profoundly influenced his work. Even as he absorbed the styles and techniques favored in the places he studied and worked (principally Warsaw, Leipzig, and St. Petersburg), his chamber, orchestral, and, especially, choral and piano works continually looked back to Lithuania. As scholar Jonathan Powell has observed, the Lithuanian in Čiurlionis' music can be both explicit and implicit. That is, while some pieces deliberately borrow or allude to Lithuanian tunes or gestures, others reflect on a more deep-rooted level of the composer's immersion in Lithuanian sounds: one often encounters, even in "non-Lithuanian" works, the rustic rhythmic simplicity, limited melodic palette, and small scalar range that Čiurlionis observed in his indigenous musical tradition. These elements fused with a forward-looking harmonic language that falls somewhere between the elaborate chromaticism and gestural flourish of Chopin, the mystical richness of Scriabin, and the chthonic rootedness of Bartók.

It is in the choral genre that Čiurlionis drew most heavily on folk sources. With the exceptions of the early cantata *De Profundis* (1899–1900), three mass movements, and a handful of other works, Čiurlionis' choral output consisted of more than 60 folk song arrangements. The composer's relatively few orchestral works frequently evoke landscape, as in the symphonic poems *In the Forest* from 1900 and *The Sea* from 1907; sketches also survive for a *Lithuanian Pastoral Symphony*, which was left incomplete at the composer's death. Čiurlionis' limited chamber output avoids the outwardly pictorial and tends toward the learned, as in his *Fugues and Canons for string trios and quartets*. Himself a piano prodigy, Čiurlionis was most prolific in the arena of keyboard music. His years of study in Warsaw infused much of his keyboard music with a lingering shadow of Chopin, as evinced by the dozens of nocturnes, mazurkas, and preludes Čiurlionis composed in his roughly decade-long career. He also composed a number of nature pictorials (*Lakstingala [The Nightingale]*, Op. 19) and landscape pieces (*Marios [The Sea]*, Op. 28), several theme and variation pieces, and a collection of 16 pieces on Lithuanian folk songs. *—Jeremy Grimshaw*

Recommended:

○ **Ciurlionis: Complete Piano Music Vol. 1** / Lahusen / Celestial Harmonies 13184

Dom Jean Claire

b. 1920, Tarbes, France
Conductor

Dom Jean Claire served as choirmaster at the Abbey of Solesmes in France from 1971 to 1996, succeeding Dom Joseph Gajard. He studied in classics and composition, entering the abbey in 1944. During his tenure as choirmaster, he made over 25 recordings of Gregorian chant and published numerous scholarly articles on the origins of Western modality. He is known for his refinement of the Solesmes style in which the duration of individual notes is flexibly interpreted rather than given a fixed measure. The Abbey of Solesmes has been the center of the modern revival of Gregorian chant performance since the mid-nineteenth century, and the monks of the abbey have provided the official chant books of the Catholic church from the beginning of the twentieth century. *—Robert Adelson*

Recommended:

○ **Easter** / Claire (dir.), Monastic Choir of St. Peter's Abbey, Solemnes / 1985 / Solesmes 822

○ **Tenebrae Of Good Friday** / Claire (dir.), Monastic Choir of St. Peter's Abbey, Solemnes / 1993 / Solesmes 834

Jeremiah Clarke

b. ca. 1674, London, England, **d.** Dec. 1, 1707, London, England
Composer: Chamber Music

Jeremiah Clarke was a popular composer and organist around the dawn of the eighteenth century, but his best-known piece was known for years as "Purcell's Trumpet Voluntary"—and later as the "Masterpiece Theater Theme."

The man whose music has been played at more nuptials in the English-speaking world than anyone but Wagner or Mendelssohn has no clearly established early history. In 1940 a researcher named E.H. Fellowes tentatively linked him to a family of choir singers at St George's Chapel, Windsor.

The earliest thing we really know about Clarke is that he was a boy choir singer in the Chapel Royal at the time of the coronation of James II. His voice changed in 1692; in that year he became the organist of Winchester College. He left there in 1696, and reappears in the record on June 6, 1699, when he was appointed a vicar-choral of St Paul's Cathedral, London. He received some promotions and titles, and in 1704 took the position of organist of the Chapel Royal, jointly with William Croft.

He wrote attractive and popular theater pieces, many effective anthems, and other sacred music, and some harpsichord pieces including *The Prince of Denmark's March*, which is the proper name for the piece of worldwide fame known as the *Trumpet Voluntary*. (The work itself has an interesting history. Its familiar trumpet, organ, and drum arrangement is of contemporary origin, but was inspired by a nineteenth century organ version that ascribed the tune to Henry Purcell, at the time one of the few names known to posterity from the then-shadowy Baroque era.)

Accounts of Clarke's life suggest that he was subject to periods of deep depression. He shot himself and was buried in the crypt of St. Paul's Cathedral. *—Joseph Stevenson*

CHAMBER MUSIC

The Prince of Denmark's March, for brass, winds & percussion in D major ("Trumpet Voluntary") (1700)

The initial source for the popular *Prince of Denmark's March*, long thought to be the work of Henry Purcell, is a seven-part suite for brass, winds, and percussion in the British Library of London. The untitled manuscript is the hand of Jeremiah Clarke, a composer at the Drury Lane Theater of London in the late seventeenth century. In 1700, Clarke contributed a keyboard arrangement of this piece to a publication titled *A Choice Collection of Ayres*.

The march is nothing musically extraordinary, even within the context of Clarke's own music, the originality and inventiveness of which is best experienced in the composer's sacred music, odes, songs, and keyboard works. Still, the tune has a certain gravity and regal pomp which has made it a favorite at weddings, church services, affairs of state, and other such occasions.

How the work came to be known as a "trumpet voluntary"—which it is not—and attributed to Purcell is a curious matter. An 1837 collection reprinted the piece with the attribution "Purcell?" Subsequent nineteenth century editions removed the question mark. In the 1930s, Sir Henry Wood made an arrangement of the piece for small orchestra which became well known through radio broadcasts, further spurring the work's popularity. Wood believed it to be Purcell's work, and even though the Clarke manuscript was already known to some scholars, the arrangement was published under the English Baroque master's name. For several decades the erroneous attribution persisted in various published editions and recordings; by the end of the twentieth century, the rightful identity of the composer seemed to have taken hold in most quarters. *—Uncle Dave Lewis*

Recommended:

○ **Favourite Baroque Classics** / R. Goodman (cond.), Brandenburg Consort / 1999 / Helios 55020

- ○ **The Classic Wedding Album** / Marriner (cond.), Wilbraham, Academy of St. Martin-in-the-Fields / 1999 / DG 445478
- ○ **Greatest Hits: Trumpet** / Kapp (cond.), Biggs, Press, Firth, NE Brass Ens. / 1994 / Sony 66702

Clemencic Consort

f. 1969, Vienna, Austria
Ensemble
The Clemencic Consort was founded in 1969 by recorder player and early music specialist René Clemencic. Clemencic was one of the first musicians to explore in depth, and perform, the music of the Middle Ages and Renaissance using the instruments and performance practice of the time. He formed the Clemencic Consort after leaving his previous group, the Ensemble Musica Antiqua (with which he had been involved since 1958).

The Clemencic Consort's repertoire is wide, drawing on music from the medieval period (like the twelfth century anonymous *Play of Daniel* and *Le Roman de Fauvel*) through the Renaissance and Baroque eras. They have even made occasional forays into modern avant-garde music, including some compositions by Clemencic himself. One of the Consort's specialties is the revival of little known operas from the seventeenth century, such as Jacopo Peri's *Euridice.*

The Consort has recorded extensively and won many awards, including the Edison Prize, Grand Prix du Disque, Diapason d'Or, and Prix Cecilia. *—Chris Morrison*

Recommended:

- ○ **Dufay: Cathedral Sounds** / Clemencic (dir.), Clemencic Consort / 2002 / Arte Nova 92584
- ○ **Carmina Burana** / Clemencic (dir.), Clemencic Consort / HM 90335
- ○ **Dunstable: Cathedral sounds** / Clemencic (dir.), Clemencic Consort / 1996 / Arte Nova 34055
- ○ **Machaut: La Messe de Nostre Dame** / Clemencic (dir.), Clemencic Consort / 2001 / Arte Nova 85289
- ○ **Danses de la Renaissance** / Clemencic (dir.), Clemencic Consort / HM 90610

René Clemencic

b. Feb. 27, 1928, Vienna, Austria
Conductor
"Lively authenticity" is one commentator's description of René Clemencic's musical performance aesthetic. The Viennese-born recorder player, composer, teacher, and conductor has sought this authentic mode of musical expression in an extremely wide range of musical experiences. Trained as a recorder player and keyboardist, earning a Ph.D. from Vienna University in 1956, Clemencic performs on a variety of early flutes, recorders, and other woodwind instruments. As an expansion of his instrumental career, Clemencic has founded two ensembles for early music in Vienna (a city which, in the 1950s, was widely acknowledged as the world's capital for historical performance): Musica Antiqua in 1958 and the Clemencic Consort in 1968. Also a teacher, he is a member of the Accademia Filharmonica Romana, frequently appearing in Siena to teach at the Accademia Musicale Chigiana. He maintains a large personal collection of early musical instruments. Clemencic's own compositions reflect his performing tastes and include music for recorders and oratorios in ancient languages (Greek and Hebrew). Clemencic's catalog of performance projects is both broad and prolific. At one temporal pole is his own experimental compositions. At the other, his ensemble the Clemencic Consort has brought to life several major repertories of the high Middle Ages, from the *Play of Daniel* and *Cantigas de Santa Maria* to a fiery presentation of the *Roman de Fauvel.* Very frequently, the group explores the use of improvisation within these repertoires. This allows Clemencic a very rich, sonic, and performative effect, most notable in a Spanish-Moorish flavor to his interpretation of Troubador lyrics. He has also widely recorded in the early Netherlandish Renaissance of Dufay, Ockeghem, and Obrecht, and in a wide variety of courtly and popular early dance styles. Finally, Clemencic has championed a number of neglected early operatic works, even producing fully staged versions of works by Peri, Draghi, Fux, Jean-Jacques Rousseau, and the Emperor Leopold I. *—Timothy Dickey*

Recommended:

- ○ **Caldara: Missa Doloroso; Stabat Mater** / Clemencic (dir.), Chorus of Italian Swiss Radio, Aura Musicale / 2000 / Naxos 554715
- ○ **René Clemencic & His Flutes** / Clemencic / HM 190384
- ○ **Cathedral Sounds: Ockeghem** / Clemencic (dir.), Clemencic Consort / 1998 / Arte Nova 56351

Clemens non Papa (Jacob Clement)

b. ca. 1510, Ieper, Belgium, **d.** ca. 1556, Dixmuiden, Belgium
Composer
The nickname "non Papa" seems to have been given to the Dutch composer Jacob Clemens by his publisher as a joke, to distinguish him either from the poet Jacobus Papa, or from the recently deceased Pope Clement VII. In the generation following the death of Josquin Desprez, Clemens non Papa was one of the most prolific and well-published composers of both sacred and secular music, but rather little is known of his life. A small number of chansons were published early in his life in Paris; after this his musical activities centered in modern-day Belgium and Holland. His professional appointments included positions at St. Donatian's in Bruges (where he served as Succentor from 1544–45), 's-Hertogenbosch (making music for a Marian confraternity in 1540), Ypres, and Leiden. Evidence also points to work in the private chapel of Philippe de Croy, one of the principal generals of Emperor Charles V, and perhaps a professional relationship to Charles himself. His death date itself may only be inferred from an uncompleted publication of 1556, and a *Deploration* on his death written in 1558.

His enormous surviving musical output—apparently written in the span of just over 15 years—comprises 15 "parody" masses, a requiem mass, two complete cycles of Magnificats, over 230 motets, a setting of the 150 psalms in Dutch, and nearly 90 French chansons. His musical style in the masses and motets, like that of his contemporaries Gombert and Willaert, often lacks the structural clarity for which their immediate predecessor Josquin was famous; it rather applies the techniques of pervading imitation to achieve a more uniform, seamless, and fluid surface. Often Clemens would extend a musical passage beyond its opening exposition by long sequential repetitions of imitative motives. He also experimented with imitative technique by crafting motives which allow inversion, or "tonal" answers in addition to strict imitation of the original notes. His "parody" masses demonstrate an advance in the infusion of the sections of the mass by a number of different motives from the music of his model. Clemens has also been credited with experimentation in, and propagation of, a "secret chromatic art": a kind of countercultural cryptic notational practice which could only be understood by the initiated among professional musicians (though obviously this is difficult to prove).

One outstanding late achievement of this composer is a complete polyphonic setting of the Dutch Psalter. Martin Luther's German vernacular translation of the psalms was published in Antwerp in 1534, followed in 1540 by a Dutch translation of the entire Psalter printed by Simon Cock. This volume, the *Souterliedekens,* listed one popular tune (love songs, drinking songs, ballads, and sacred tunes) for each psalm. Clemens set the entire set in simple, but polished, three-voiced polyphony, usually with the popular tune in the middle voice. His collection, published by Tylman Susato in 1556–57, differs from the contemporary Geneva Psalter in context as well as musical polish: Calvin's Psalter was intended for public worship, Clemens' for private devotions and social gatherings. *—Timothy Dickey*

Overview of Works (ca. 1530–1555)

Over a remarkably short span of time, generally reckoned at roughly 15 years, Jacobus Clemens "non Papa" established himself as one of the most prolific composers of the musical Renaissance. His close relationship with Antwerp-based printer Tylman Susato assured the wide circulation of much of his music. The hallmark of his musical style in his Latin-texted works, which include 15 masses, a requiem, and well over 200 motets, is a continuous texture of dense imitation. His imitation extends to a much greater length than those of most of his contemporaries, primarily due to the overlapping repetitions of motifs beyond their opening exposition. He used canonic procedure only rarely, however. In settings of various vernacular texts, his style showed more variety. Across all genres, he showed a profound gift for shaping melodic lines and a deep fascination with modal and tonal ambiguities, even perhaps participating in the so-called "Secret Chromatic Art" of occult musical chromaticism.

Clemens' mass ordinary cycles eschew the archaic technique of cantus firmus organization (a single line of chant or some other preexisting melody) in favor of a richly allusive parody procedure, wherein all the parts of an existing multipart work are used as the basis for the new composition. Eight of the masses take contemporary motets as models, and six are based on chansons. The infusion of his mass textures with a variety of musical motifs is typified in the *Missa Pastores Quidnam Vidistis* (based on his own motet), or the *Missa Quam pulchra es* (based on a *Song of Songs* motet by Lupi). Of the 233 motets, only eight use a cantus firmus, the rest are freely composed. Nearly all set liturgical texts—psalms, canticles, Old Testament prophets, and Christ-based and Marian passages from the New Testament—in a similar style of pervasive imitation. Chordal passages, which betray the Italian influence on many of Clemens' generation, are quite rare; they are used for special effect such as to represent the dignity of the Magi's gifts in *Magi veniunt,* or to highlight the motto of the particular confraternity that commissioned the motet *Ego Flos Campi. Fremuit spiritu Jesu* has occasioned much comment for its unique hidden chromaticism: this motet can be performed "straight" or, by rigid application of certain rules pertaining to the application of sharps and flats, may be sung so that it includes an unheard-of chromatic modulation from F to G flat. A complete setting of the *Psalter* in Flemish, the 159 elegant three-voiced settings published as the *Souterliedekens,* forms the centerpiece of Clemens' work in the vernacular tongues. In addition to this masterpiece of Reformation piety, perhaps as many as 89 French chansons, eight Dutch secular songs, eight textless pieces, and two intabulations survive from his secular output. Love and drinking are his favorite subjects for the songs. Some of the chansons are chordal, after the

"Parisian" fashion of Claudin de Sermisy (such as *Misericorde au martir amoureulx*), though here, too, his penchant for imitative practice holds sway. *La belle Margaritte* exemplifies this, as well as being one of the few instances of canonic writing in his entire oeuvre. —*Timothy Dickey*

Recommended:

○ **Clemens non Papa: Missa Pastores quidnam vidistis** / P. Phillips, Tallis Scholars / 2001 / Gimell 13

Muzio Clementi

b. Jan. 23, 1752, Rome, Italy, **d.** Mar. 10, 1832, Evesham, Worcestershire, England
Composer: Keyboard

Born shortly after Handel wrote his oratorio *Jephtha* and dead shortly after Berlioz wrote his *Symphonie fantastique*, Muzio Clementi failed to write anything equal to the originality of those two composers—or, certainly, equal to the best of his closer contemporaries, Mozart and Haydn. Yet Clementi remains a significant figure for his pioneering work on behalf of the newfangled piano, that percussive, expressive instrument that quickly displaced the harpsichord at the end of the eighteenth century. His full-scale sonatas and small studies exploited the possibilities of the early piano and groomed the technique of early pianists, and led him to be known as "the father of the piano." His influence on Beethoven has likely been underestimated.

Clementi was a child prodigy, with an appointment as an organist at age nine and an oratorio to his credit by the time he was 12. In 1766 Clementi's father was persuaded to take the boy to study in England, the country that would remain Clementi's base for the rest of his life. In the English countryside the youth undertook a rigid course of studies, emerging in 1773 for a spectacular debut in London as a composer and pianist. Had Clementi matured anywhere else in Europe, he might have limited himself to the organ and harpsichord; but the piano was enormously popular in England, and Clementi furthered his career by capitalizing on the instrument's expanded capabilities. In 1780, he went on tour to the Continental capitals; in Vienna, Emperor Joseph II instigated a friendly musical duel between Clementi and Mozart.

Clementi settled down in London in 1782, dividing his time between teaching (his pupils included Cramer, Meyerbeer, and Field), composing, and performing. In 1799, he co-founded a company that both published music and manufactured pianos. Toward the end of his life he traveled through Europe again and spent more and more time composing; during this time, he wrote several symphonies, but most have been lost. He is mainly remembered for his dozens of piano sonatas, and for his collection of studies, *Gradus ad Parnassum* (Steps Toward Parnassus), which has been the bane of piano students for two centuries and was parodied by Debussy in the opening movement of his *Children's Corner*. Clementi was the complete piano man, popularizing the instrument through his own performances, writing exercises to develop young pianists, writing sonatas for mature pianists to play, and manufacturing instruments for their use. —*James Reel*

KEYBOARD

Gradus ad Parnassum, Op. 44 (1817–1826)

That Clementi's great *Gradus ad Parnassum* (Steps Toward Parnassus) is so poorly and unaffectionately remembered today is one of the more unfortunate results of the mid- and late nineteenth century obsession with pure instrumental virtuosity in the wake of figures like Niccolò Paganini and Franz Liszt. *Gradus* comprises 100 pieces for solo piano Clementi wrote over a span of nearly five decades and published in three volumes (1817, 1819, and 1826). Clementi intended the collection to serve as an instructional tool, but it hardly reflects the dry, colorless vein of such famous pedagogical aids as Charles-Louis Hanon's *The Virtuoso Pianist*. Though *Gradus* contains simple technical exercises, it also includes graceful miniature sonatas, fugues, and deeply expressive, operatic fantasias designed to tap all of a player's musical resources.

In the late 1850s, more than 40 years after the publication of Volume I, famed pianist and Liszt pupil Carl Tausig prepared and eventually published an new edition of *Gradus ad Parnassum*. However, he included only the purely technical exercises, believing that it was only as raw practice fodder that Clementi's work was of value to contemporary pianists consumed with attaining ever-greater digital velocity and power. In subsequent generations, unfortunately, many musicians came to know Clementi's great compendium only in this defleshed, skeletal form. It was only in the last few decades of the twentieth century that a revival of interest in Clementi's music spurred a widespread revisitation of the work in its original incarnation.

Gradus ad Parnassum is, quite simply, a stunning achievement. Clementi was one of Europe's most famous musicians during his lifetime; in a famous keyboard duel with the formidable Mozart, the judges declared the contest a draw. This level of manual skill, plus a further forty years' experience, is at the heart of Clementi's Opus 44. As *Gradus* was written in bits and pieces over most of the composer's long career, the range of styles represented is impressive, from the almost Haydnesque Classicism of the famous Allegro (No. 62 in Clementi's original ordering) to the chromatically adventuresome pieces composed during the 1820s. The best known of the finger-exercise-variety pieces is probably No. 16, parodied by Claude Debussy in *"Doctor Gradus ad Parnassum"* from the piano suite *Children's Corner* (1906–08). —*Blair Johnston*

Recommended:

○ **Clementi: 23 Studi Obbligatori dal "Gradus ad Parnassum"** / Campanella / Fonit Cetra 54

Piano Sonatas (1771–1821)

Roman-born Muzio Clementi produced over 100 keyboard sonatas. Their influence is widely recognized, although Clementi's posthumous reputation as a theorist, teacher, and piano manufacturer now greatly outstrips his renown as a composer. Indeed, during the late twentieth century, it was largely through the advocacy of Vladimir Horowitz that Clementi's sonatas retained a foothold in the recital room. Deep-rooted antipathy is hard to overcome; Mozart rated Clementi "a mere mechanicus without a farthing's worth of taste or feeling," while Hugo Wolf wrote that "just to hear Clementi's terrible name sends shivers down my spine ... I've always crossed myself at its merest mention."

Clementi's sonatas were widely admired, especially and significantly by Beethoven, whose own works Clementi published. The early sonatas display an external brilliance which owes much to Domenico Scarlatti and his school. Clementi's personal style began to emerge decisively with his works published as Op. 10 through Op. 14, which rejected Scarlatti's influence in favor of the three-movement Viennese Classical sonata model. Increasingly greater reliance upon thematic development and a more acerbic melodic style, as for example in Clementi's two sonatas of Op. 34, anticipated Beethoven's early sonatas. While Beethoven's defiant heroism is manifestly absent in Clementi's output, the latter's style advanced exponentially after the advent of the modern pianoforte (in whose innovation Clementi took a decisive hand) in the early nineteenth century, so much so, in fact, that in his later sonatas it is the early piano music of Field and Chopin that is prefigured.

At its best, Clementi's sonata legacy is still of crucial importance, even if it does not capture attention through uncompromising effects of the sort devised by Beethoven. Though in his sonatas Clementi is no lawbreaker or iconoclast, his achievements in forging the basic language of the piano and in bridging the absolutism of Beethoven and the romantic-virtuoso league of Chopin, Liszt, and Thalberg should not be underestimated. Those critics who opine that Clementi's suppposed superficiality points to lack of self-insight have missed the point. As Anselm Gerhard writes, "the listener with an ear for subtle shades of meaning, for undertones and hidden details, will easily detect the sovereign seriousness of Clementi's musical thinking." —*Michael Jameson*

Recommended:

○ **Muzio Clementi: Piano Sonatas** / Demidenko / 1995 / Hyperion 66808

○ **Horowitz Plays Clementi** / Horowitz / 1989 / RCA 7753

○ **Muzio Clementi: Sonate, Duetti & Capricci Vol. 10** / Spada / 1997 / Arts 47232

Six Sonatinas ("Progressive Sonatinas"), Op. 36 (1797; revised 1813)

Every student of classical piano has learned at least one of Muzio Clementi's *"Progressive" Sonatinas*, Op. 36. The pieces were originally published in 1797 and have all but replaced his *Gradus ad Parnassum* as his most famous work. Clementi intended them as teaching tools, meant for the youth among the burgeoning amateur pianist public. It is a credit to him that they are still used just as he intended. They are "progressive" in that the difficulty of the sonatinas increases with each subsequent one. The first contains little for the left hand to do, but in the sixth, there are more complex rhythms, phrasing, and accompaniment, with the left hand taking the melody in a couple of spots. The emphasis throughout all is on basic piano skills: dynamic control, even touch, and melodic phrasing. However, within each one there are more specific lessons on ornamentation, arm and wrist motion, arpeggios, and more. When the set was re-published in 1803 as a supplement to Clementi's *Introduction to the Art of Playing on the Piano Forte*, he included specific instructions on how to play certain ornaments and interpret markings. For example, when discussing the use of staccato, he stated it should be reserved "to give spirit occasionally to certain passages, and to set off the higher beauties of the legato." *Sonatina No. 1 in C major* is the most widely known, with No. 3, also in C major, and *No. 6 in D major* following it in popularity. The theme of the opening of the first sonatina shows a strong resemblance to the opening of Scarlatti's *Sonata* K. 460. (Clementi had studied Scarlatti's works in his own youth.) The second movement of the *Sonatina No. 2* introduces easy dotted rhythms to be played dolce, with the note "dolce means sweet, as in taste; now and then swelling some notes." No. 3 is a study of scalar runs, while sextuplet figures are extensively used in the final movement of *Sonatina No. 4*. No. 5 has an "Original Swiss Air" with six-bar phrases instead of the usual four-bar ones. No. 6 is just two movements, brief but lively. The sonatinas have distinct characters, formed by graceful, charming melodies without much drama and, surprisingly, without much of that bane of the Classical era: the Alberti bass. —*Patsy Morita*

Recommended:

- ○ **Clementi: Piano Music** / Szokolay / 1995 / Naxos 550452
- ○ **The Classical Sonatina** / D. Blumenthal / Etcetera 2018

Louis-Nicolas Clérambault

b. Dec. 19, 1676, Paris, France, **d.** Oct. 26, 1749, Paris, France
Composer

Clérambault came from and later added to a family known for its musical service to French royalty; his father, Dominique Clérambault, was a musician for the king's violin consort (an ensemble of 24 violinists!), and he himself served both at Versailles and at royal churches. Both his sons were musicians and organists for royal churches, and one of them, César François Nicolas, was also a minor composer. He was one of the most respected composers and performers of his time, and, like Campra, helped to lead French music out of the musical isolation that Lully had imposed, adding more melodiousness and energy to the delicacy and grace that had become almost the sole considerations for composition and performance. Also like Campra, he added a strong Italian influence, but with a French style; one contemporary quotation says that "If Campra writes modulations in the Italian style, [his music] speaks in the French style." He was also one of the first composers to give names to his sonatas.

His first music lessons were with his father, but his main musical influences were Jean-Baptiste Moreau and Andre Raison, his two organ and composition teachers. As his reputation spread, he was appointed to the organist position at Saint Louis and became part of the musical forces of Versailles, responsible (together with Madame de Maintenon, the king's mistress) for the music for the king's private concerts. In 1697, he published his *Book of Airs*, followed by his *Book for the Harpsichord* in 1702. In 1710, he produced the first of his five books of cantatas (his second was in 1713, his third in 1716, his fourth in 1720, and the last in 1726), as well as his *Book for the Organ*. When Madame de Maintenon retired to Saint Cyr, a school and royal church founded by the king for the daughters of impoverished military officers, and known for the quality of its musical education, he became organist and music master there. Many of his motets and cantatas were written for the Demoiselles de Saint-Cyr, the girls' chorus. In 1715, he was appointed main organist at Saint Sulpice, where he had served as a deputy for several years, and in 1720, to the same position at Saint Jacques. His one major stage work was an allegory, *Le Soleil, Vainqueur des Nuages* (The Sun, Conqueror of Clouds), celebrating Louis XIV's recovery from illness (Louis was known as The Sun King, and took particular pleasure in works that glorified this image) and first performed at the Opera. He had continued writing four more books of cantatas, the last of which was published in 1726. They were among his most popular works, and frequently performed at the court as well as in various salons, the Jesuit colleges, and at Saint Cyr. After the end of the 1720s, he was far less prolific, and relatively few of these are important, though many, such as *Le départ du Roi* (The King's departure) written in 1745, were given major productions. *—Ann Feeney*

Overview of Works (1697–1745)

The Frenchman Louis-Nicolas Clérambault spent most of his career working for the Catholic church as a composer and organist. Like many French composers at the turn of the seventeenth century, Clérambault's style was an amalgam of the native French style of grandly elevated lyricism and imported Italian style of brilliant virtuosity and expressive drama. More than most composers of his generation, Clérambault was more fully able to fuse these two schools into a single characteristic style. In his lifetime, Clérambault published two kinds of music: cantatas and sacred choral music and clavecin and organ music. His 25 cantatas, 20 of which were published in five volumes appearing from 1710–26, are predominantly for one or two voices with or without instrumental accompaniment (of course, a continuo is present in all of them). The subjects are usually mythological—*Orphée*, *L'amour et Bacchus*—and the music is elegantly expressive with supple melodies and rich harmonies. Like most French religious composers of *le gran siècle*, Clérambault also composed motets published in five volumes as well as other large-scale sacred works including the single oratorio *L'histoire de la femme adultére*. Clérambault first became known as a keyboard player and his *Livre de l'orgue* (1710) testifies to his great but subtle virtuosity. He also published *Livre de pièces de clavecin* (1704) for home use. Unpublished in his lifetime but widely distributed in manuscript copies were his solo and trio sonatas for one or two violins and continuo. While his keyboard works were in the French tradition, his violin sonatas show him confronting, mastering, and besting the new school of Italian violin playing. *—James Leonard*

Recommended:

- ○ **Clérambault: Motets pour Saint Sulpice** / Lesne, Collard, Padmore, Il Seminario Musicale / 2000 / Virgin 45415
- ○ **Clérambault: Livre d'orgue; Chants du Salut** / J. Boyer, Mandrin, Les Demoiselles de Saint Cyr / 2000 / Virgin 61777
- ○ **Clérambault: Songs and Motets** / Mandrin, Les Demoiselles de Saint Cyr / 1998 / Virgin 61529

Cleveland Orchestra

f. 1918, Cleveland, OH
Ensemble

Since its founding, the Cleveland Orchestra has become a source of tremendous pride for the city of Cleveland. It is one of America's artistic treasures, an orchestra capable of playing as well as any in the world. Chamber music flourished in Cleveland from the middle of the nineteenth century on, but the orchestra was not founded until 1918. Adella P. Hughes, with the support of the Musical Arts Association, spearheaded the formation of the orchestra and engaged Russian-American conductor Nikolai Sokoloff to direct it. Sokoloff remained music director until 1933, and led national tours, educational concerts, commercial recordings, and radio broadcasts. Perhaps the most important legacy of his tenure is Severance Hall, which opened in 1931 and received immediate renown for both its acoustics and its aesthetics. In 1939 the hall was renovated and improved, and then reopened in January 2000 to renewed acclaim. Artur Rodzinski directed the orchestra from 1933 to 1943 and was followed by Erich Leinsdorf from 1943 to 1946. Both of these men contributed to Cleveland's budding reputation, but the golden age of orchestral playing in Cleveland came with the arrival of the now-legendary George Szell in 1946. One of the last of the old-time conductors, Szell ruled the orchestra with an iron fist, lashed out at players who he felt were giving less than full effort, erupted at even the smallest technical mistakes, and built the best orchestra in America. The Cleveland Orchestra under Szell played with marvelously clear textures, impeccable precision, perfect ensemble and inspiring passion. It was also astonishingly adaptable to different genres and styles of music; Szell liked to say that the specialty of the Cleveland Orchestra was that it had no specialty. The orchestra recorded extensively for Columbia (now Sony), toured internationally and staked its claim as the biggest of the Big Five American orchestras. In 1968, the orchestra began a long and fruitful association with composer and conductor Pierre Boulez. During the same year Szell opened the Blossom Music Centre, a summer concert venue owned by the orchestra, which has been enormously successful financially and musically. Szell died in 1970, but could have been music director for as long as he wanted. Boulez served as musical advisor until 1972, when Lorin Maazel became music director. While Maazel was and is a great conductor, the orchestra felt they had not been properly consulted in the decision to hire him, and his tenure was marked by controversy. His interpretations were seen as overly extreme, and although he kept the orchestra playing at a high technical level, he was never much loved by the city of Cleveland. The appointment of Christoph von Dohnányi as music director in 1982 started the Cleveland Orchestra on another long run of greatness. Dohnányi successfully preserved the tonal clarity of the Szell years, while broadening the orchestra's repertoire to include more new music and modern classics. Franz Welser-Möst succeeded Dohnányi in the 2002–03 season. To the extent that orchestras can be ranked, the Cleveland Orchestra is widely considered America's best, and the city of Cleveland supports its orchestra in the manner it deserves. *—Andrew Lindemann Malone*

Recommended:

- ○ **Dvořák: Slavonic Dances** / Szell (cond.), Cleveland Orch. / 2002 / Legacy 89845
- ○ **Stravinsky: The Fairy's Kiss** / Knussen (cond.), Shelton, Smith, King, Geber, Cleveland Orch. / DG 449 205
- ○ **Berlioz: Roméo et Juliette; Les Nuits D'Été** / Boulez (cond.), Porco, Diener, Tarver, Sedov, Cleveland Orch. & Chorus / 2003 / DG 1301
- ○ **Mussorgsky: Pictures at an Exhibition; Rimsky-Korsakov: Capriccio Espagnol** / Szell (cond.), Cleveland Orch. / 2001 / Sony 93019
- ○ **Beethoven: Symphonies 5 & 7** / Dohnányi (cond.), Cleveland Orch. / 1988 / Telarc 80163

Van Cliburn

b. Jul. 12, 1934, Shreveport, LA
Pianist

Kairos is a word used by ancient Greek writers to signify "the right point of time ... the exact or critical time ..." of action, a favorable planetary conjunction, or otherwise. Cliburn's career is an illustration. In the tensest days of the Cold War—of Civil Defense, air raid sirens, bomb shelters, atomic angst, and the launch of the Soviet satellite Sputnik that put the Russians first into space—handsome, lanky 6'4," 23-year-old Van Cliburn, with his Southerner's air of innocent modesty and tremendous keyboard technique, in April 1958 carried off the Gold Medal at the International Tchaikovsky Competition in Moscow with a transcendent performance of Tchaikovsky's *Piano Concerto No. 1*. Timing—*kairos*—and talent combined to make his triumph symbolic, heroic, and permanently memorable; the recording he made of it soon after, with Kiril Kondrashin conducting the RCA Victor Symphony Orchestra, is warmly glowing with an incomparable magic that has kept his performance competitive with later interpreters decade after decade. But such moments do not happen without preparation. Cliburn's mother, who had studied with Liszt pupil Arthur Friedheim, was his first teacher. He gave his first recital at four, played with the Houston Symphony at 13, and at 14 was heard in Carnegie Hall. Appearances, prizes, and awards followed in a regular spate without amounting to public recognition or a genuine career. At 17 he had begun studies with Rosina Lhévinne at the Juilliard School—taken with his mother's Liszt/Friedheim connection, he became an unself-conscious inheritor of the grand Romantic tradition. And it was Rosina Lhévinne who prompted his entrance to the Tchaikovsky Competition. Following his win, of course, Cliburn enjoyed a major career, and the recordings he made in the succeeding decade possess a large-scale grandeur. He was at his best in Romantic repertoire—Liszt, Chopin, Schumann, Grieg, MacDowell, Rachmaninov—though his Mozart and Beethoven can seem academic. And with the years, the grand manner devolved into careless mannerism as the public clamored for a reprise of the Tchaikovsky *Concerto No. 1*. He founded the Van Cliburn International Piano Competition in Fort Worth, TX, in 1962, to which he has devoted more time than to his own career as a performing artist. His return to the concert scene after a ten-year sabbatical was hardly noticed. But the legend, the peculiar *kairos* that realized itself through him, is imperishable. *—Adrian Corleonis*

Recommended:

- ○ **MacDowell: Concerto 2; Brahms: Concerto 2** / Reiner (cond.), Cliburn, Chicago SO / RCA 68480
- ○ **My Favorite Chopin** / Cliburn / 1962 / BMG 68813
- ○ **Beethoven: Concerto 5; Rachmaninoff: Concerto 2** / Reiner (cond.), Cliburn, Chicago SO / RCA 61961
- ○ **Tchaikovsky: Concerto 1** / Kondrashin (cond.), Cliburn / 2003 / JVC 24004

Andre Cluytens

b. Mar. 26, 1905, Antwerp, Belgium, **d.** Jun. 3, 1967, Neuilly, France

Conductor

André Cluytens was among the leading French conductors of his time. His father, Alphonse Cluytens, was also a conductor, and recognized the boy's musical talents. André was enrolled in the Royal Flemish Conservatory at the age of nine. He studied in the piano class of Emile Bosquet, and received first prize for piano at the age of 16. The next year he won first prize in harmony, theory, counterpoint, and fugue.

His father was conductor at the Royal French Theater of Antwerp. André became his assistant and a choirmaster there. When an illness prevented Alphonse from conducting, André made his performance debut in 1927 in Bizet's *Les Pêcheurs de perles*. After that experience he devoted his efforts to orchestral and opera conducting rather than choral work, and he became a resident conductor in the house.

In 1932 he accepted a position as the musical director of orchestral concerts at the Capitole de Toulouse, and he became a French citizen. In 1935 was appointed the opera director in Lyons. He was an assistant of Josef Krips in a summer series in Vichy and, once again, was called on to substitute when that conductor could not perform. He became musical director of the Lyons Opera in 1942, conductor of the Conservatoire Concerts and the French National Radio Orchestra in Paris in 1943, and in 1944 conducted at the Opéra de Paris. From 1947 to 1953 he was music director of the Paris Opéra-Comique, and in 1949 was appointed as principal conductor of the Conservatory Concerts. He retained that position for the rest of his life. In 1955 he was invited to conduct *Lohengrin* at the Bayreuth Festival, the first French person to appear on the podium there. He debuted in the United States in 1956, and in Britain in 1958, when he substituted for Otto Klemperer. He formed a close relationship with the Vienna State Opera, which he first conducted in 1956, becoming a permanent guest conductor in 1959. In 1960 he became conductor of the Belgian National Orchestra in Belgium, also holding that post until his death. He also formed a close link with the Berlin Philharmonic, with which he made a notable recording of the Beethoven symphonies. However, he was primarily known for French repertoire, premiering works by Françaix, Jolivet, Messiaen, Milhaud, Tomasi, Büsser, and Bondeville. He was invited back to Bayreuth in 1965, but by then increasing illness made that appearance impossible. *—Joseph Stevenson*

Recommended:

- ○ **André Cluytens** / Cluytens (cond.), Christoff, Lanigan, Berlin PO, London PO / EMI 75106
- ○ **André Cluytens Conducts Franck & d'Indy** / Cluytens (cond.), Ciccolini / 2002 / Testament 1237

Eric Coates

b. Aug. 27, 1886, Hucknall, Nottingham, England, **d.** Dec. 21, 1957, Chichester, England

Composer: Film Music, Orchestral

Eric Coates was perhaps the most important composer of symphonic light music in the first half of the twentieth century outside the Viennese sphere. He took the music genre and made it into as bona fide and influential an art form as that created by any member of the Strauss family. He is often regarded as the Mozart of a music world whose generally light emotional expression is colored by splashy orchestration and perky rhythms. Yet, his music featured an elegance and aristocratic air and could capture moods and, in stage works, story lines with deftly vivid imagery. Among his important compositions are the 1930 ballet *Snow White and the Seven Dwarfs*, revised eight years later and re-titled *The Enchanted Garden*; and *Springtime Suite* from 1937. Even though Coates composed music in a less serious genre, he must be regarded nearly as highly as England's other important figures from his time, Vaughan Williams, Sir Arnold Bax, and Gustav Holst.

The youngest of five children, whose physician father was an amateur flutist and whose mother was an accomplished pianist, Eric began study on the violin at age six. Later on he took up the viola. He showed no serious interest in composing until age 20 when he entered the Royal Academy of Music, where he studied viola with Lionel Tertis and composition with Frederick Corder.

In the period between 1908 and 1909, he wrote his first vocal works: *Four Old English Songs* and *Stonecracker John*. In 1910 he began playing the viola in the Beecham Symphony Orchestra and shortly afterward got a similar post in the Queen's Hall Orchestra, under Sir Henry Wood. He turned out his first orchestral work, the *Miniature Suite*, in 1911. Two years later, Coates married 18-year-old Phyllis Black, who would write lyrics for him and be of immense help to him throughout his career. Because of a progressive neuritis in his left hand and arm, Coates was exempt from military service during the war years. By 1919, however, the condition forced him to give up his first-chair viola post in the Queen's Hall Orchestra.

In 1927, Coates composed his orchestral suite *Four Ways*, which achieved considerable popularity. Perhaps his greatest success, though, came with the 1933 *London Suite*, which contained a section called "Knightsbridge," a march that took on a life apart from the suite when it was used to introduce the BBC radio program *In Town Tonight*, which became familiar to virtually every British listener during its 27-year run.

When his wife began working for the Red Cross in 1940, Coates was moved to write *Calling All Workers*, whose theme was subsequently used by the BBC for another radio show, *Music While You Work*. The orchestral suites *Four Centuries* (1942) and *Three Elizabeths* (1944) merely solidified his position now as the composer of the most familiar British music of all time.

In the postwar years, Coates continued to turn out popular scores, like *Music Everywhere* (1949) and the 1955 film score, *The Dam Busters*. The composer continued to be active as a conductor in his last years, taking up the baton at one notable Promenade concert in August 1956, after Sir Malcolm Sargent had led the orchestra in a Tchaikovsky work. The 70-year-old Coates led the ensemble in his *Four Centuries* Suite and drew an enthusiastic response from the audience. Coates suffered a stroke and died on December 23, 1957. *—Robert Cummings*

FILM MUSIC

The Dam Busters (1954)

Eric Coates' score for the celebrated 1954 film *The Dam Busters* is without question his most popular music. The film itself tells the story of an audacious bombing raid in which the RAF's specially chosen Lancaster bomber crews of 617 Squadron, led by Wing Commander Guy Gibson, flew deep into the heartland of Germany to destroy the three great dams which provided hydro-electric power to Germany's military hardware production facilities of the Ruhr. At the heart of this top-secret mission was Dr. Barnes-Wallis' famous "Bouncing Bomb"—a new if somewhat fanciful invention, originally widely mistrusted by the RAF top brass, but which proved to be the key to the successful completion of the night bombing raids of 1943.

Eric Coates' score, on which he collaborated with the conductor Muir Mathieson, is a perfect example of his affinity for patriotic music, embodying power, grandeur, and also sensitivity. The main march, which provides music for opening and closing titles and for many key moments, is particularly memorable. The passage of the movie in which the Lancaster crews are awaiting dispersal to their planes is deftly scored, with more solemn, reflective music depicting various pre-flight emotions, before Gibson is heard to say, "My watch says it's time to go." As the crews make their way to their planes, the big march returns, now with an almost Elgarian sense of patriotism.

There are many other sections in which Coates writes with touching pathos. For example, the music heard after Gibson's dog "Nipper," the station mascot, is killed by a car, or that which accompanies Barnes-Wallis' struggles to perfect his invention, knowing that his country's future may well depend on its success. But without doubt, the stirring Dam Busters March is the most enduring symbol of the film. *—Michael Jameson*

ORCHESTRAL

Calling All Workers, march (1940)

Eric Coates is identified with British light music in the way John Philip Sousa is with American band composition. While 1940 was a time during which war was breaking out across Europe, a time that would engulf England in a grim five-year struggle, the mood of the music in *Calling All Workers* might have seemed more appropriate as a prelude to a game of cricket. Not that its music is weakly crafted or lacking in character in any way; rather, its cheerful mood suggests the composer is oblivious to all the world's woes, so chipper and charmingly nonchalant is the music here. The piece opens up with a brief fanfare, then presents a bouncy main theme whose manner is at once joyous and busy. It is then heard in a second, quite mellow guise, the robustness from the opening tempered by a suavity that soothes. The ending is brilliant and full of color, capping this piece with a sense of total joy. The instrumentation in the orchestral version is more colorful than that in band arrangements. Certainly, most listeners attracted to light music should find that presentation superior. Coates himself recorded the march and used the orchestral version for this, one of his most popular works. *—Robert Cummings*

Recommended:

- ○ **British Light Music Classics** / Corp (cond.), New London Orch. / Hyperion 66868

The Three Elizabeths (1944)

It was the receipt of an unexpected letter from a certain Reverend Arthur A. Hall one day in 1941 which prompted Eric Coates to consider the notion of creating an orchestral suite based on the generations of the British royal family. The "Three Elizabeths" of the title depict three figures. The first movement, "Halcyon Days," suggests Elizabeth I (Tudor). This opens with a fanfare played by the horns, and then continues with a lively, animated figure which characterizes the Elizabethan appetite for swashbuckling adventure upon the high seas, very much as personified by the exploits of Sir Francis Drake. The opening horn fanfare returns triumphantly at the end of the movement, and in more restful guise; it then also serves to introduce the next section of the work, though in a slower tempo. This is Coates' portrait of Elizabeth of Glamis, the Queen Mother, and carries the subtitle "Springtime in Angus," in recognition of her lifelong love of the countryside of northern Scotland, and the pastoral surroundings amid which she spent her childhood years. There is a prominent and plaintive melody for solo oboe, possibly a reminder of a traditional Scottish folk ballad. Later on, a solo violin quotes the melody to which the Robert Burns setting of the poem "My Love Is like a Red, Red Rose" is sung. The *"Three Elizabeths" Suite* concludes with a rousing march entirely typical of Coates. It is entitled "Youth of Britain," and portended the new confidence and style epitomized by Princess Elizabeth, who became Queen Elizabeth II after acceding to the British throne in 1951. An opening trumpet flourish and bold main theme are in the style of Coates' famous *Knightsbridge March.* The suite reaches a proudly assertive final climax, again reflecting Coates' confidence in the spirit of a new generation of the English monarchy, and also looked forward to happier times of post-war regeneration. For Eric Coates, Princess Elizabeth and the "Youth of Britain" gave hope of a new and positive future even as the darkest days of World War II approached. *—Michael Jameson*

Recommended:

- ○ **Eric Coates: London Calling; Music for Wind Band 1** / G. Kingston (cond.), Royal Artillery Band / 1999 / Naxos 554488

Martin Codax

fl. mid-1200s

Composer: Vocal

Martin (or Martim) Codax (or Codaz) is the name of the author and composer of a set of seven poems (six with music) written on a leaf of parchment that was found in 1914 inside the binding of an old book. The poems are written in the Portuguese-Galician language. They are the only Galician-Portuguese music, aside from the *Cantigas de Santa Maria,* to survive from the Middle Ages and represent the oldest surviving written Spanish music.

Each of the six songs with music comprises four or six stanzas, made of a couplet followed by an unchanging refrain. In form, the composition appears to be a song cycle, concerning the feelings of a woman awaiting her lover by the sea in the coastal city of Vigo, in the west of Spain.

Commentators have tried to discover or deduce details of the composer's life, but have achieved no more than speculation. Because the work is love poetry, some have found a connection with courtly music of the time and speculate Codax was a member of the court of Ferdinand III. Others have suggested that he was a troubadour. They are not even certain whether he was Portuguese or Galician Spanish. The music itself has more connections with Galician folk music than with either Spanish court or troubadour music of the time. *—Joseph Stevenson*

VOCAL

Cantigas de Amigo (mid-1200s)

Spanish secular music in the vernacular grew directly out of the tradition of French troubadours from Provence and other parts of southern France. They infiltrated Italy and the Iberian peninsula, bringing with them the culture of courtly love. The earliest examples of Spanish monophonic song can be found in the seven *Cantigas de Amigo* by Martin Codax. Codax hailed from the Spanish town of Vigo in Galicia, close to Portugal, and may have had connections with the court of Don Dinis of Portugal. Known only in two manuscripts containing only the texts, the music was discovered early in the twentieth century by a Madrid bookseller. All three settings present the songs in the same order, suggesting that although there is no narrative, they were intended as a cycle devoted to a single subject: love. All are sung by a girl waiting on the seashore near Vigo for the return of her lover. Although much simpler in structure than troubadour songs, these tiny gems are filled with a melancholic longing that make them, in the words of one of their interpreters, "among the most passionate and moving pieces we have ever performed" (Philip Pickett). *—Brian Robins*

Recommended:

- ○ **Bella Domna: The Medieval Woman** / Sinfonye, Wishart (cond.) / 1988 / Hyperion 66283
- ○ **Music for Alfonso the Wise** / Dufay Collective / 2005 / HM 907390

Joel Cohen

b. May 23, 1943, Providence, RI

Conductor

In the United States, Joel Cohen is best known as the long-tenured helmsman of the Boston Camerata, and understandably so; but travel east across the Atlantic and you'll find him equally highly regarded as a lutenist, a radio broadcaster, and a producer of music films.

Cohen was born in Providence, RI, in 1942 and attended Brown University and Harvard University. After leaving Harvard, he spent two years in Paris, honing his skills as a composer under the wing of Nadia Boulanger. In 1968, just one year after returning to the U.S. from France, Cohen took up the directorship of the then-14-year-old Boston Camerata, which he has since built into a truly first-class organization. Cohen has never maintained a lengthy permanent academic post, but he has lectured at many universities (especially those in or near the metro Boston area, like Harvard University and Brandeis University).

Cohen has not really followed up on his training as a composer save by making arrangements of already-existing music; he has instead focused on directing, organizing, and to a lesser extent, performing. With the Boston Camerata, Cohen has made several dozen recordings (mostly of early music), some of which have earned prestigious awards. His 1989 disc of *Tristan et Iseult* won the grand Prix du Disque of the Académie Charles Cros in Paris. In 1990, Cohen founded a new group, the Camerata Meditarranea, to perform early music from the Mediterranean area. Cohen is the author of *Reprise: the Extraordinary Revival of Early Music* (Boston, 1985). *—Blair Johnston*

Recommended:

- ○ **Musique Judeo-Baroque** / Cohen (cond.), Boston Camerata / HM 1951021
- ○ **de Ventadorn: Le Fou sur le Pont** / Cohen (cond.), Camerata Mediterranea / 1994 / Erato 94825
- ○ **Le Roman de Fauvel** / Cohen, Boston Camerata, Ens. Project Ars Nova / 1995 / Erato 96392
- ○ **Tristan Et Iseult** / Cohen (cond.), Boston Camerata / 1987 / Erato 98482
- ○ **Carmina Burana** / Cohen (cond.), Boston Camerata / 1996 / Erato 14987
- ○ **Cantigas** / Cohen, Briouel (conds.), Camerata Mediterranea / 1999 / Erato 25498
- ○ **A Medieval Christmas** / Cohen (cond.), Boston Camerata / 1975 / Nonesuch 71315

Collegium Musicum 90

f. 1990, London, England

Ensemble

Collegium Musicum 90 is one of Britain's best known and highly regarded period instrument ensembles. One of its unusual features is that it was founded by and directed by two leaders, one most associated with historical music performance and the other with his work with standard modern orchestras.

Born in 1941, violinist Simon Standage is one of the best-known instrumentalists on London's busy period instruments stage. He has played in modern music ensembles, having been a sub-leader (i.e., assistant concertmaster) of the English Chamber Orchestra (1974–78) and leader (concertmaster) of the City of London Sinfonia (1980–89).

However, he became best known as the leader of the English Concert (1973–91), the famous period-instrument group founded by harpsichordist Trevor Pinnock, and as the first violinist of the Salomon Quartet, the first major British quartet to use period string instruments—instruments set up with the same sorts of strings, bows, bridges, and so forth as in the period of the music to be played.

Richard Hickox, six-and-a-half years younger, was an organ scholar at Queen's College Cambridge who in 1971 founded the City of London Sinfonia and the Richard Hickox Singers and specialized in Baroque music, but on regular instruments. Despite his initial reputation for Baroque music, his skills as a choral conductor in particular eclipsed it, and in 1976 he became the conductor of the London Symphony Chorus. He also has had leadership positions with the Netherlands Radio Philharmonic, the Northern Sinfonia, the San Diego Symphony Orchestra, and the London Symphony Orchestra.

It was in the midst of this success (which also included Hickox's frequent conducting of opera) that Standage and Hickox in 1990 co-founded the Collegium Musicum 90 to be a standing Baroque period orchestra. (The name Collegium Musicum, or "musical guild," has been used in the names of so many groups that it is practically a generic term for Baroque-era ensembles.) It has become Hickox's primary means of performing the Baroque music that interested him so much in the early part of his career.

Collegium Musicum 90 established itself quickly. It gained an exclusive contract with the British record company Chandos and has made several records. It has toured Europe and most of the major British music festivals. It has performed at the BBC Promenade Concerts, the City of London Festival, and the Cheltenham Festival, and its recording of Purcell's *Dido and Aeneas* was chosen by the BBC to be the soundtrack of a filmed version of the opera made in connection with the Purcell tercentenary observances in 1995. *—Joseph Stevenson*

Recommended:

- ○ **Handel: Concerti Grossi, Op. 6** / Standage (cond.), Collegium Musicum 90 / 1997 / Chandos 0600
- ○ **Haydn: London Symphonies Vol. 1** / Hickox (cond.), Collegium Musicum 90 / 2000 / Chandos 655
- ○ **Vivaldi: String Concertos, Vol. 1** / Standage (cond.), Collegium Musicum 90 / 1999 / Chandos 647

Collegium Vocale

f. 1970, Ghent, Belgium
Ensemble

The Collegium Vocale is a vocal ensemble known for its authentic performances of Baroque and pre-Baroque music.

The name "Collegium Vocale" is a generic term for a vocal ensemble with connections to a center of learning or other scholarly background. This is the best-known of several groups using the term as their name, and so, when it is necessary to avoid confusion, it is identified as the one founded in Ghent, Belgium. In 1970 the Belgian musician Philippe Herreweghe founded this Collegium Vocale to apply the fruits of researches into actual performance practices of the Baroque to vocal music performance. It was the first choir founded with an "authentic performance" purpose. Some of the issues involved include the proper use (or non-use) of such coloristic devices as vocal vibrato, and the appropriate and fluent use of ornamentation of the written line.

The Collegium quickly achieved a reputation for its stylistically correct performances of older music and found itself in demand by the leading conductors and orchestras in the early music movement. These included Gustav Leonhardt, Ton Koopman, and Nikolaus Harnoncourt, who were eager to match their period instrument ensembles with a chorus founded on the same principles in recordings of the great Baroque repertoire. This tradition has continued with conductors such as Sigiswald Kuijken, Paul Van Nevel, and René Jacobs. Collegium Vocale has frequently appeared with original instrument groups such as the Vienna Concentus Musicus and La Petite Bande, as well as modern instrument ensembles like the Concertgebouw of Amsterdam and the Vienna Philharmonic.

The Collegium Vocale has not restricted its repertoire to the Baroque. It also frequently performs great polyphonic music of the Renaissance. It also has extended its repertory to the Classical and even the Romantic era and, on rarer occasions, music of its own time. However, it still remains best known for its performances of German Baroque music, especially that of Johann Sebastian Bach.

It has recorded widely on several labels, producing well over 60 recordings for such labels as French Harmonia Mundi, Virgin, Ricercare, Accent, and Telefunken (now Teldec). In 1993 it was appointed "Cultural Ambassador of Flanders" by the Flemish regional government, a recognition of its wide touring activities, which have taken it to Asia and both Americas in addition to frequent visits around Europe. *—Joseph Stevenson*

Recommended:

- ○ **Bach: Johannes-Passion** / Herreweghe (cond.), Padmore, Scholl, Rubens, Volle, Collegium Vocale / HM 901748
- ○ **Polish Early Music** / Szamotul, Leopolita, Collegium Vocale / Dux 248
- ○ **Mendelssohn: Psaumes** / Herreweghe (cond.), Kooy, Lamy, Van Doeselaar, Harrhy, Collegium Vocale, Chapelle Royale / HM 901272
- ○ **Lassus: Moduli Quinis Vocibus, 1571** / Herreweghe (cond.), Collegium Vocale, Hannover Boys Choir Soloists / 2001 / Astree 10887

Columbia Symphony Orchestra

f. New York, NY
Ensemble

The Columbia Symphony Orchestra was a name linked to numerous ensembles recording at different times for Columbia Records. The name itself was an artifact from a time in which record labels and radio networks assembled and named their own orchestras, or used the name as a "cover" for the use of an orchestra that was contracted elsewhere.

The Columbia Symphony Orchestra name was used by Columbia Masterworks in the 1950s on New York recording sessions with an orchestra comprised of members of the New York Philharmonic, the Metropolitan Opera Orchestra, and the NBC Symphony. The label could hire members of those orchestras as freelance players, assemble an orchestra every bit as good as (and perhaps better than) the New York Philharmonic, and pay them for their work without having to pay royalties against sales to the Philharmonic or any of the players other than the conductor or soloist. This orchestra—as it appeared on monaural recordings made by Bruno Walter in New York between 1954 and early 1956, and with other New York-based conductors into the early 1960s—was a good ensemble, a match for the Philharmonic in the studio. Indeed, one of the most highly acclaimed and best selling recordings by Leonard Bernstein on the Columbia label—of George Gershwin's *An American In Paris*—was a Columbia Symphony Orchestra recording.

However, the Columbia Orchestra which appeared on Bruno Walter's stereo recordings from 1957 onward was something different and very special. Walter (1876–1962) had retired at age 80 after a very successful career recording with the New York Philharmonic, where he served as Musical Advisor from 1947 to 1949, and as a frequent guest conductor over the following seven years. In 1957, while living in California, he was approached by Columbia's executives with a new proposal. Told of the advent of stereo recording and the threat that it constituted to the future sales of monaural records, Walter was asked to undertake a new series of recordings in stereo to preserve his interpretations in the most modern sound possible, and to allow them to reach new generations of listeners.

The result was a new Columbia Symphony Orchestra, chosen specifically by and for Walter. This group was an ensemble of 50 to 70 members, assembled from the best freelance musicians on the West Coast, many of whom typically never took on orchestral work, but made the exception to work with Walter. It was one of the best recording orchestras ever assembled in the United States, incorporating many of the best characteristics of the Vienna Philharmonic and the Leipzig Gewandhaus—which Walter had conducted in Austria and Germany during the 1920s and 1930s—as well as the New York Philharmonic. This orchestra recorded much of the core Classical and Romantic repertoire under Walter's baton, including the late Mozart symphonies, Mahler's symphonies Nos. 1 and 9, the four Brahms symphonies, Dvořák's Symphonies Nos. 8 and 9, Schubert's Ninth, the Wagner orchestral music, and the complete Beethoven symphonies. *—Bruce Eder*

Recommended:

- ○ **Bruckner: Symphony 4** / Walter (cond.), Columbia SO / 1996 / Sony 64481
- ○ **Stravinsky: The Firebird; Scherzo à la Russe; Fireworks** / Stravinsky (cond.), Columbia SO, CBC SO / CBS 42432
- ○ **Mozart: Symphonies 25, 28, 29 & 35** / Walter (cond.), Columbia SO, New York PO / 1995 / Sony 64473
- ○ **Mahler: Symphonies 1 & 2; Lieder eines fahrenden Gesellen** / Walter (cond.), Forrester, Miller, Cundari, Columbia SO, New York PO, Westminster Choir / 1994 / Sony 64447
- ○ **Bach: Keyboard Concertos, Vol. 2** / Golschmann (cond.), Gould, Libove, Columbia SO / 2001 / Sony 87761

Concentus Musicus Wien

f. 1953, Vienna, Austria
Ensemble

The Concentus Musicus Wien (Concentus Musicus of Vienna) has long been one of the premier musical ensembles specializing in period instruments and techniques, with an immense discography. Austrian conductor and cellist Nikolaus Harnoncourt founded Concentus Musicus in Vienna in 1953. The ensemble, led by Harnoncourt's wife, Alice, on first violin and staffed with many of their young colleagues from the Vienna Symphony Orchestra, then prepared themselves for four years before giving their first concert. Vienna, home of musicologist Joseph Merkin, keyboardist Gustav Leonhardt, the Clemencic Consort, the Capella Academica, and the Vienna Recorder Ensemble, was already claiming worldwide attention for its early music performance. Yet Concentus Musicus exploded onto the musical scene, displaying a level of technical virtuosity unknown in most period-instrument orchestras of the time.

The group's award-laden and often controversial recording career began with Teldec (then Telefunken) in 1963. The repertories explored by Concentus Musicus, interestingly, have mimicked the trajectory of Western music history. The group's early programs sometimes featured re-creations of medieval and Renaissance music. The first recording project, however, presented the *Viol Fantasias* (1680) of Henry Purcell, and the ensemble quickly became known for its performance of the high Baroque. Among its many acclaimed interpretations of the music of J.S. Bach are the *Brandenburg Concerti* (first recorded in 1964), the *Orchestral Suites* (1966), the *St. John Passion* (1965), *Mass in B minor* (1968), *St. Matthew Passion* (1970), and a massive project to record the complete cantatas (undertaken between 1971 and 1990 with Gustav Leonhardt). In the meantime, the group participated in Zürich productions of all three Monteverdi operas in the 1970s and gave performances of Rameau, Telemann, Handel, and many others. From this deep expertise, the Concentus Musicus moved forward into the eighteenth century, giving sharp and highly energetic performances of Mozart and Haydn symphonies, choral works, and operas. It has received a Grammy and multiple awards of the French Grand Prix du Disque, the Edison Prize, the German Schallplattenpreis, and Preis der Deutschen Schallplattenkritik; the Bach cantata series earned them the Gramophone Award for Special Achievement.

The performing philosophy of Concentus Musicus follows the vision of founders Nikolaus and Alice Harnoncourt. Nikolaus has called his 1954 essay "On the Interpretation of Historical Music" the group's creed. In the face of what he sees as two conflicting approaches to past music—either to transplant it into the present and thus transform it, or academically transplant oneself into the past and thus lose connection with the present—his ideal uses past techniques and instruments to re-create a vibrant contemporary music. He treats the Baroque orchestra as an instrument "whose sound and technique aid and inspire us" to live and make music in the twentieth century. The sonic hallmarks of his approach include a virtuosic level of competence on the early instruments, a characteristic sharpness of musical articulation and accent, a carefully historic tuning system, and creative use of spatial elements to render the "Musical Dialogue." *—Timothy Dickey*

Recommended:

- ○ **Zelenka: Hipocondrie; Trio Sonata; Overture** / Harnoncourt (cond.), Vienna Concentus Musicus / 1997 / Teldec 17386
- ○ **Instrumental Music of 1600** / Harnoncourt (cond.), Vienna Concentus Musicus / 2004 / Artemis Classics 1277
- ○ **Haydn: Symphonies 30, 45 & 73** / Harnoncourt (cond.), Vienna Concentus Musicus / 1995 / Teldec 10016
- ○ **Monteverdi: L'Incoronazione di Poppea** / Harnoncourt (cond.), Berberian, Esswood, Langridge, Soderstrom, Vienna Concentus Musicus / 1993 / Teldec 42547

Le Concert des Nations

f. 1989

Ensemble

Taking its name from a 1726 set of trio sonatas by François Couperin, Le Concert des Nations is a period-instrument orchestra of young musicians from mostly Latin countries, standing in contrast to the proliferation of period instrument ensembles in Northern Europe and England. The orchestra was founded in 1989 by gambist Jordi Savall, who is also the group's conductor. The orchestra has recorded a varied repertoire spanning the seventeenth to nineteenth centuries. Its first recordings featured Charpentier's *Canticum ad Beatam Virginem Mariam*, Bach's orchestral suites and *Brandenburg Concertos*, and Haydn's *Seven Last Words of Christ on the Cross*. Its operatic repertoire includes Martín y Soler's *Una cosa rara* and *Il burbero di buon cuore* and Monteverdi's *L'Orfeo*. Under the baton of Savall, Le Concert des Nations has explored late eighteenth and early nineteenth century music, such as Mozart's *Requiem* and *Beethoven*'s "Eroica" symphony. Its recording of Handel's *Water Music* and *Music for the Royal Fireworks* was awarded an RTL prize in 1994. The orchestra's concerts and recordings have brought to light several more obscure composers, including the Spaniard J.C. Arriaga. Le Concert des Nations is the orchestra of La Capella Reial de Catalunya and is sponsored by the government of Catalonia. *—Robert Adelson*

Recommended:

- ○ **Biber: Battalia; Requiem** / Biber: Battalia in D C61, Biber: Requiem à 15 C7 / Savall (cond.), Capella Reial de Catalunya, Le Concert des Nations / Alia Vox 9825
- ○ **Bach: Musikalisches Opfer** / Bach: Musical Offering BWV1079 / Savall (cond.), Le Concert des Nations / Alia Vox 9817
- ○ **Marais: Alcione Suites** / Marais: Alcione / Savall (cond.), Le Concert des Nations / 2000 / Astree 9945
- ○ **Lully: L'Orchestre du Roi Soleil** / Lully: Le bourgeois gentilhomme LWV43, Lully: Alceste LWV50, Lully: L' Amour médecin LWV29, Lully: / Savall (cond.), Kraemer, Le Concert des Nations / Alia Vox 9807

Concertgebouw Orchestra

f. 1888, Amsterdam, Netherlands

Ensemble

This world-class orchestra takes its name and its origins from its home venue: the Concertgebouw (Concert Hall) located in the heart of Amsterdam. As part of the cultural renaissance that swept through the Netherlands in the 1880s, a group of wealthy Amsterdam businessmen decided that orchestral music should have a more prominent place in the city's artistic life and set about constructing a suitable concert hall. Completed in 1888, the Concertgebouw management engaged Willem Kes as conductor and hired musicians to fill this acoustically superb venue.

Kes took it upon himself not only to entertain, but to instruct. Much of the repertoire he chose consisted of important symphonic works, he programmed very little frivolous or contemporary music. He also insisted that his audiences adhere to the standard rules of concert etiquette, which was quite different from the raucous behavior common in Amsterdam's concert halls at that time. Although his rigidity was not initially well-received, when Kes moved on to conduct the Scottish Orchestra in 1895, he left a competent ensemble and a well-behaved, knowledgeable audience.

Following Kes was Willem Mengelberg, who conducted the Concertgebouw Orchestra for nearly 50 years and honed the group into a polished ensemble. Mengelberg's affinity for the music of Richard Strauss and Gustav Mahler and his reputation for adherence to the composer's intentions brought a wonderful sensitivity to the orchestra's performances. His rehearsal technique was musically demanding and highly disciplined, which allowed him to draw exciting and highly interpretive performances from the ensemble, thrilling Concertgebouw audiences. His energetic conducting style was widely acclaimed, and his insistence that the orchestra make recordings helped bring the ensemble to the world's attention. Although his interpretive approach sometimes overshadowed the orchestra's repertoire, Mengelberg made the Concertgebouw a "musical as well as architectural landmark."

After the war, management of the orchestra was taken over by the Dutch government and placed under the direction of Eduard van Beinum. His personable character and cooperative rehearsal technique brought out the best in the orchestra's members. This was most evident in the fluidity and inter-sectional sensitivity that characterized the Concertgebouw's postwar sound. Van Beinum also broadened the ensemble's repertoire to include contemporary works, especially those of Dutch composers, which not only brought new depth to orchestra's musical abilities, but also buoyed pride in the war-torn nation's native sons.

After the shock of Van Beinum's sudden death during a rehearsal in 1959, Bernard Haitink and Eugen Jochum shared the Concertgebouw podium until Haitink shouldered the full responsibility as chief conductor in 1964. Under Haitink's direction, it recorded and toured extensively. He established the Concertgebouw Orchestra Chorus, directed by Arthur Oldham, in 1980. He shared the podium with many distinguished guest conductors, such as Colin Davis, Antál Dorati, and Kiril Kondrashin, who was the orchestra's co-conductor from 1979 until his death in 1981. Haitink also began a long-term collaboration with Baroque and Classical music specialist Niklaus Harnoncourt, which led to significant refinement in the Concertgebouw's performances of works from these periods. This was especially notable in the orchestra's annual performance of Bach's *St. Matthew Passion* each Easter Sunday; a tradition since 1899. In addition, Haitink presided over the ensemble's 100th anniversary celebration, which included six performances of Mahler's *Symphony No. 8* that delighted audiences. Haitink stepped down from his long tenure as chief conductor at the end of the 1988–89 season and was replaced by Riccardo Chailly, who was a frequent and well-loved Concertgebouw guest conductor during Haitink's reign.

Through a series of sensitive and creative conductors and with the consistent support of its appreciative audiences, the Concertgebouw Orchestra has earned its reputation as the Netherlands' most distinguished orchestra. *—Corie Stanton Root*

Recommended:

- ○ **Concertgebouw Orchestra** / Beinum (cond.), Menuhin, Lipatti, Francescatti, Kolassi, Solomon, Concertgebouw / 2003 / Andante 4060
- ○ **Shostakovich: Symphony 8** / Haitink (cond.), Concertgebouw / 1993 / Decca 425071
- ○ **Shostakovich: Symphonies 6 & 12** / Haitink (cond.), Concertgebouw / 1993 / Decca 425067
- ○ **Charles Ives: Symphony 3; Orchestral Set 2** / Tilson Thomas (cond.), Concertgebouw / 1985 / Sony 37823
- ○ **Willem Mengelberg** / Mengelberg (cond.), Concertgebouw / 2002 / Andante 2966

Aaron Copland

b. Nov. 14, 1900, Brooklyn, NY, **d.** Dec. 2, 1990, North Tarrytown, NY

Composer: Ballet, Orchestral, Keyboard, Vocal, Symphonic, Film Music, Concerto, Chamber Music, Band Music, Opera

Few figures in American music loom as large as Aaron Copland. As one of the first wave of literary and musical expatriates in Paris during the 1920s, Copland returned to the United States with the means to assume, for the next half century, a central role in American music as composer, promoter, and educator. Copland's sheer popularity and iconic status are such that his music has transcended the concert hall and entered the popular consciousness; it both accompanies solemn and joyous celebrations the world over (*Fanfare for the Common Man*) and punctuates the familiar words "Beef: It's What's for Dinner!" (*Rodeo*) for millions of television viewers.

Copland was the youngest of five children born to Harris and Sarah Copland, Lithuanian Jewish immigrants who owned a department store in Brooklyn. He did not take formal piano lessons until he was 13, by which time he had also begun writing small pieces. Instead of attending college, Copland studied theory and composition with Rubin Goldmark and piano with Victor Wittgenstein and Clarence Adler, and attended as many concerts, operas, and ballets as possible. In 1921, he went to Fontainebleau, France, taking conducting and composition classes at the American Conservatory. He went on to study in Paris with Ricardo Viñes and Nadia Boulanger and spent the next three years soaking up all the European culture, both new and old, that he could. He learned to admire not only composers like Stravinsky, Milhaud, Fauré, and Mahler, but others such as author André Gide. Boulanger's performance of Copland's 1924 *Organ Symphony* with Koussevitzky was the beginning of a friendship between the conductor and composer that led to Copland's teaching at the Berkshire Music Center (Tanglewood) from 1940 until 1965.

After his return to America, Copland drifted toward an incisive, austere style that captured something of the sobriety of Depression-torn America. The most representative work of this period—the *Piano Variations* (1930)—remains one of the composer's seminal efforts. He tried to avoid taking a university position, instead writing for journals and newspapers, organizing concerts, and taking on administrative duties for composers' organizations, trying to promote American music. By the mid-1930s, taking the direct engagement of and communication with audiences as one of his central tenets, Copland's compositions developed (in parallel with other composers like Virgil Thomson and Roy Harris) an "American" style marked by folk influences, a new melodic and harmonic simplicity, and an appealing directness free from intellectual pretension. This is nowhere more in evidence than in Copland's ballets of this period, and it finally earned him the respect of the general public. While Copland gradually became less prolific from the mid-1950s on, he continued to experiment and explore "fresh" means of musical expression, including a highly individual adoption of 12-tone principles in works like the *Piano Fantasy* and *Connotations for orchestra*. Still, the fundamentally lyrical nature of Copland's language remained intact and occasionally emerged—with an often surprising retrospective air—in works like the *Duo for flute and piano* (1971). He continued to teach and write and received numerous awards both in America and abroad. In 1958, he began conducting orchestras around the world, performing works by 80 other composers as well as his own over the next 20 years. By the mid-1970s, Copland had for all intents and purposes ceased composing. One of the last of his creative accomplishments was the completion of his two-volume autobiography (with musicologist Vivian Perlis), an essential document in understanding the growth of American music in the twentieth century. *—AMG*

BALLET

Billy the Kid (1938)

It was ballet impresario Lincoln Kirstein who had the inspiration to bring together composer Aaron Copland and choreographer Eugene Loring to create a work based on the legend of Billy the Kid. Kirstein was particularly drawn to Walter Noble Burns' 1925 best-seller *The Saga of Billy the Kid*, a mix of lore, fantasy, and historical research. As related by Burns, Billy, a gambler, cattle rustler, and vigilante frontiersman, made his claim to fame in having killed a man for each of his 21 years. Loring devised a scenario which calls for four principals, along with "pioneers, men, women, Mexicans, and Indians." Much of the ballet's action, form, and mood reflects Burns' *Saga*, particularly the grotesque celebration which follows a central shoot-out scene.

Copland, having already composed works evocative of the American west and Mexico like *El Salon Mexico* (1933–36) and *Saga of the Prairies* (1937), was well prepared for this "cowboy ballet." The composer provided period flavor by incorporating six cowboy tunes into the score: "Great Granddad," "Git Along Little Dogie," "The Old Chisholm Trail," "Goodbye, Old Paint," "The Dying Cowboy," and "Trouble for the Range Cook."

Copland's score provides a vivid sonic depiction of prairie life. An opening processional is distinguished by Copland's trademark widely spaced "open" harmonies in the woodwinds, followed by a bass figure centered on a syncopated two-note motive. This plodding bass moves dramatically from pianissimo to a triple-forte climax, suggesting the laborious trudging of the settlers. The music of the processional brings the ballet full circle with its reappearance as the coda. "Street in a Frontier Town" moves from pastoral innocence to mechanistic violence, incorporating several cowboy tunes along the way. The rest of Billy's story moves unfolds in short vignettes, including "Card Game at Night" (also known as "Prairie Night"), which draws upon the familiar image of the lone cowboy, including snatches of "The Dying Cowboy." "Gun Battle" is dominated by violent percussion, the sounds of gunfire represented by snare and bass drums. In "Celebration After Billy's Capture" Copland neatly transforms the trudging bass of the opening processional into a dissonant "oompah" figure that underpins a crude bitonal melody, while a waltz section transforms "Trouble for the Range Cook" into an ironic ditty with solos in the trombone and bassoon. "Billy's Death" is a solemn epilogue for strings, harp, and winds.

Billy the Kid was first performed by the Ballet Caravan in Chicago in a two-piano version on October 6, 1938. The familiar version for full orchestra was premiered in New York on May 24, 1939 to critical and popular raves. In 1940 Copland extracted a concert suite from the ballet, the form in which the music is today most frequently heard. *—AMG*

Synopsis:

The action begins (c. 1877) in a frontier town in New Mexico. Billy (William Bonney), aged 12, is accompanied by his mother as he watches some rowdy cowboys roughhousing outside a saloon. A fight breaks out among them and Billy's mother is shot and killed by a stray bullet. Billy immediately reaches for his knife and takes vengeance on his mother's killer.

By 1885 Billy has earned a reputation as one of the West's boldest robbers, a crook who steals not just from the rich, but from the common man and woman as well. He kills a Land Agent and leads a gang of thieves in and out of trouble, from one criminal escapade to another.

During a card game, Billy is caught cheating by one of his friends, Pat Garrett. The two have an argument and Garrett rides off to join the side of law and order, and to eventually become a sheriff in pursuit of Billy.

Billy's gang and Garrett's posse have a bloody shootout, with many men on both sides falling dead. In the end, Billy is captured by Garrett and taken off to jail. The surviving members of the posse celebrate their victory.

Their celebration turns out to be premature, as Billy kills a jail guard and manages to escape. He flees into the desert where he is aided by sympathetic Mexicans and a few admiring young women. Billy becomes weary and falls asleep, dreaming that he has met a girl with whom he will settle down. In the dream he is tender and compassionate, no longer a notorious criminal. He awakens at the sound of horses galloping toward him, then hears a voice. He lights a cigarette and begins a dialogue with the stranger. His visitor, he quickly learns, is Pat Garrett, who tells him that lighting the cigarette was a mistake, its red glow making him a easier target under the dark skies. Garrett shoots Billy dead.

A large crowd gathers to view Billy at his funeral. They place a pistol at one hand and a knife at the other. *—Robert Cummings*

Recommended:

○ **Aaron Copland: Appalachian Spring; Billy The Kid; Danzon Cubano; El Salon Mexico** / Dorati (cond.), London SO / 1991 / Mercury 434301

Rodeo (1942)

The essential spirit of Aaron Copland's music is embodied perhaps nowhere so well as in his ballet scores, which are among his best-known works. Copland wrote *Rodeo* (1942) for Agnes de Mille, and it proved to be the choreographer's most enduring success. The scenario tells the story of a young woman, accomplished in all the skills of a cowpoke, who hopes to attract the attentions of the head wrangler on a ranch. In a decidedly pre-feminist resolution, he is unimpressed by her skill but succumbs to her charms when she trades her cowboy duds for a dress and shows a more "womanly" side at the rodeo dance.

Both the ballet and the popular concert suite derived from it are divided into four musical scenes. The opening "Buckaroo Holiday" incorporates two cowboy tunes, "If He Be A Buckaroo By His Trade" and "Sis Joe"; this section is marked by the use of ever-changing rhythms and unpredictable turns of harmony. The "Corral Nocturne," in an asymmetrical 5/4 meter, is a plaintive portrait of a cowgirl's loneliness. "Saturday Night Waltz" makes use of another cowboy song, "Goodbye, Old Paint," to which Copland adds his own stamp by the employment of cross-rhythms. "Hoe-Down" is undoubtedly the ballet's best-known episode, largely through its use as the music to accompany the words "Beef: It's What's for Dinner" on television. Written in the midst of Copland's "populist" period, *Rodeo* is distinguished throughout by the composer's exuberance, evocative sense of orchestral color, distinctive harmonic language, and singular expressivity.

Rodeo was premiered at the Metropolitan Opera House on October 16, 1942. To make the suite called *Four Dance Episodes from Rodeo*, Copland shortened four of the main dance scenes of the ballet and dropped some connecting music, including a delightful ricky-ticky barroom piano solo reputed to have been written by the young Leonard Bernstein for insertion into the ballet as a gift to his mentor. *—AMG*

Synopsis:

In the opening scene cowboys gather to rope and brand cattle, as well as to test their skills at bronco riding and other buckaroo challenges. The young Cowgirl steps forward to show she can compete with the men. She has an eye out for the Head Wrangler and is determined to impress him with her skills. At first some of the cowboys offer her encouragement, but her awkwardness lowers their expectations and they lose interest. She mounts a wild horse, calculating this fearless action will surely catch the attention of the Head Wrangler and the others. But the horse throws her off and she is humiliated. One cowboy, however, offers her genuine sympathy, but she is taunted by the city girls, who have just arrived for the square dance and party to be held that night at the ranch house. Worst of all, she notices the Head Wrangler walking off with the Rancher's Daughter.

At the festivities in the ranch house that night The Cowgirl, dressed in her bronco riding clothes observes the city girls in their pretty dresses and graceful movements, and the cowboys dancing with them and enjoying their company. All, she sees, are having a good time, while she stands alone, unnoticed. She runs outside, but returns a short while later wearing a beautiful dress and necklace, and having a lovely ribbon in her hair. The dancing stops when she reenters and all take note of her beauty and elegance. The Head Wrangler makes his way toward her, but she refuses his offer to dance. She turns down all others as well, but finally accepts one, that of the cowboy who had shown sympathy toward her when she was thrown from the horse. The two dance happily as the festivities resume. *—Robert Cummings*

Recommended:

- ○ **Gershwin: An American in Paris; Copland: Rodeo & others** / Dorati (cond.), Minneapolis SO / 1993 / Mercury 434329
- ○ **Copland: Rodeo; Billy The Kid; El Salón México; Danzón Cubano/** / Zinman (cond.), Baltimore SO / 1994 / Argo 440639
- ○ **Copland: Billy The Kid; Rodeo** / L. Bernstein (cond.), New York PO / 1981 / Sony 36727

ORCHESTRAL

An Outdoor Overture, for orchestra or band (1937–1941)

The *Outdoor Overture* was written for the High School of Music and Art in New York City at the urging of the school's director of music, Alexander Richter. Richter told Copland that the piece would be an "opening gun" in a campaign by the school entitled "American Music for American Youth." Richter therefore suggested that the piece be "optimistic in tone, which would have a definite appeal to the adolescent youth of this country."

A bold opening for the entire orchestra is followed by a long, carefree trumpet solo. A march-like theme is developed, followed abruptly by a lyrical melody in the strings. Another march theme builds up into a return to the opening material, followed by a dramatic conclusion in which all of the previous themes are combined. The music is unpretentious and joyful throughout, succeeding both as a genial concert opener and as a work with special appeal for young performers. *—Robert Gold*

Recommended:

- ○ **American Dreams** / Corporon (cond.), Cincinnati Wind Symphony / 1993 / Klavier 11048

Appalachian Spring, concert suite from the ballet (1945)

Long after its composition, Aaron Copland's *Appalachian Spring* remains both the composer's quintessential masterpiece and one of the definitive ballets of the twentieth century. Written on commission from dancer/choreographer Martha Graham, *Appalachian Spring* depicts the lives of a newly married pioneer couple in nineteenth century Pennsylvania. The scenario that emerges in the course of the dance "narrative" includes a house-raising, a sermon, a festive party, and the couple alone in a moment of hopeful reflection. Throughout, *Appalachian Spring* unfolds with a spirit of unfailing optimism (though, as is clear from the Hart Crane poem from which the ballet's name was derived—after the music was written—the "Spring" of the title actually refers to a wellspring, not the season).

The music of *Appalachian Spring* is at once characteristic of Copland's "Americana" style of the late 1930s and the 1940s. The harmonic language, based largely on triadic and other, mildly dissonant sonorities, is marked by an overall spareness and simplicity; at appropriate moments, though, Copland employs fuller, more luxurious textures. The melodic material varies according to the ballet's episodic nature: the introduction, for example, is ethereal and almost nonmelodic, but is immediately followed by leaping, spiky lines in which melodic fourths play a prominent role. What is undoubtedly the most famous tune from the ballet is not Copland's own: The composer presents the traditional Shaker hymn *Simple Gifts*, masterfully spinning a set of variations that progress toward the climax of the entire work, a final tutti statement of the theme marked by a particular dignity and grandeur. In keeping with the nature and purpose of the score, the rhythmic language is particuraly lively, even breathtaking, making *Appalachian Spring* among the most kinetic of any of Copland's works. Irregular, changing meters are a particularly notable feature; even when the music remains in a single meter, shifts of accent ensure a distinctive sense of constant motion and rhythmic surprise.

Practical and economic constraints led Copland to score the original version of the work for an ensemble of 13 instruments. Within a short time of the ballet's premiere, however, Copland arranged the music into a concert suite for full orchestra, in which form it is most fequently performed today. Many purists prefer the original instrumentation, which has, it must be said, a striking austerity and rawness that is largely smoothed over in the version for full orchestra. The latter, at the same time, presents its own beauties not present in the smaller-scale original. In any event, *Appalachian Spring* continues to flourish as a perennial favorite and remains Copland's most beloved contribution to the pantheon of twentieth century classics. *—AMG*

Recommended:

- ○ **Copland: Appalachian Spring; Rodeo; Billy the Kid; Fanfare for the Common Man** / L. Bernstein (cond.), New York PO / 1997 / Sony 63082

Three Latin American Sketches (1959–1971)

Copland's final work for orchestra was the remarkably youthful *Three Latin American Sketches*. Its second and third movements, "Paisaje Mexicano" and "Danza de Jalisco" were composed in Acapulco in 1959 on a commission by Gian Carlo Menotti for the Spoleto Festival, but only the latter was performed for that occasion. At the request of Andre Kostelanetz, Copland composed an additional movement, "Estribillo," based on a melodic fragment he heard in Venezuela, in 1971. Kostelanetz led the New York Philharmonic in the completed work, newly titled *Three Latin American Sketches*, on June 7, 1972.

Copland calls for an orchestra of flute, oboe, clarinet, bassoon, trumpet, two pianos, percussion, and strings. An extended percussion battery adds a requisite Latin tinge with claves, wood block, xylophone, ratchet, slap-stick, triangle, suspended cymbal, and conga drum.

All three movements employ traditional Latin melodies. "Estribillo" features an ardently syncopated phrase that moves through the different sections of the orchestra, much like the refrain-like sections associated with salsa and calypso music. The vaguely melancholic "Paisaje Mexicano" ("Mexican Landscape") recalls the composer's rural American landscapes, while the vigorous finale, "Danza de Jalisco" ("Dance from Jalisco," a province in northern Mexico) features the alternating 3/4 and 6/8 meters characteristic of Mexican dance, along with some optional hand-clapping for the pianists. While the *Sketches* take a place among Copland's lighter works, the composer advised that they are "not so light as to be pop-concert material." Indeed, biting dissonances and complex polyrhythms abound throughout. *—Brian Wise*

Recommended:

- ○ **Copland Conducts Copland: Our Town & others** / Copland (cond.), New Philharmonia Orch. / 1988 / Sony 42429

A Lincoln Portrait, for speaker & orchestra (1942)

Performed even more often than the composer's repertoire mainstay *Appalachian Spring*, Copland's *A Lincoln Portrait* has achieved the status of a legitimate American classic. The restraint and nobility of Copland's score and the inclusion of Abraham Lincoln's own words (including extracts from the Gettysburg Address) lends *A Lincoln Portrait* a dignity and sincere, non-jingoistic spirit rare in other "patriotic" music of the World War II era.

In 1942, conductor André Kostelanetz commissioned Copland, along with a number of other well-known composers, to provide a musical portrait of a famous American. After considering and then rejecting Walt Whitman as a subject—one of the other commissioned composers (Jerome Kern) had already chosen a literary figure, Mark Twain)—Copland decided upon Abraham Lincoln. Copland's friend and fellow composer Virgil Thomson pointed out the problems of adequately representing the greatness of a man such as Lincoln solely in music. The solution he suggested was to bring Lincoln *into* the music by writing the work for speaker and orchestra, the speaker declaiming Lincoln's own words. Copland embraced such a plan, producing one of the more successful examples of a concert work that incorporates narration. The role of speaker in major performances and recordings of *A Lincoln Portrait* has in fact been filled by luminaries from many fields of endeavor, ranging from Marian Anderson to Henry Fonda to Eleanor Roosevelt to Norman Schwarzkopf to Copland himself.

Listeners may find much of the text unfamiliar, since Copland drew his source material largely from lesser-known passages in Lincoln's writings and speeches. Copland reserves the famous phrase from the Gettysburg Address—"government of the people, by the people, and for the people"—for the work's climactic ending, maximizing the impact of the words.

In his program notes, Copland explains that *A Lincoln Portrait* is divided into three main parts. The first part is a portrayal of Lincoln, "the mysterious sense of fatality that surrounds Lincoln's personality, and near the end of the first section, something of his gentleness and simplicity of spirit." Allusions to the folk song "Springfield Mountain" (including a trumpet solo at the end of this section) aptly echo this characterization. The central section is a sprightly Allegro that evokes the times in which Lincoln lived: sleigh bells recall horse-drawn, nineteenth century transportation, while fragments of Stephen Foster's "Camptown Races" weave in and out of the texture. In the final section, the speaker assumes the voice of Lincoln himself. The words are for the most part set against a quiet, unobtrusive orchestral backdrop, with occasional, more prominent punctuations and responses from the ensemble. The work climaxes with a quotation from the Gettysburg Address, accompanied by a return of the the solo trumpet melody from the opening section. A powerful C major chord brings the work to a sonorous close. *—AMG*

Recommended:

- ○ **Portraits Of Freedom** / G. Schwarz (cond.), Jones, Seattle SO / 1993 / Delos 3140

Music for the Theatre, suite for small orchestra (1925)

Copland began his *Music for the Theatre* in May 1925 in New York City, but the bulk of the composition was written at the MacDowell Colony in New Hampshire during the summer. Having been impressed with Copland's earlier *Symphony for*

Organ and Orchestra (1924), conductor Sergey Koussevitzky (1874–1951) urged the League of Composers to commission an orchestral piece from Copland, to be performed the following season. *Music for the Theatre* received its first performance on November 20, 1925, by the Boston Symphony Orchestra under Koussevitzky, who directed another performance for the League of Composers on November 28.

In five movements, Copland's *Music for the Theatre* (the composer preferred the British spelling) represents a deliberate attempt to compose "American" music. It thus stands in contrast to the strongly European *Organ Symphony.* To establish an American style for the piece, Copland looked particularly to jazz and blues, an influence evident from the very beginning. The piece has no programmatic associations. As the composer explained, "the title simply implies that at times this music has a quality which is suggestive of the theatre." Devoid of linear counterpoint, *Music for the Theatre* is filled with melodies and harmonic accompaniments in the manner of a popular song.

Music for the Theatre is scored for a small orchestra consisting of winds, two trumpets, trombone, percussion, piano, and a small string ensemble. Theatrical aspects indeed abound in *Music for the Theatre,* which begins with a solo trumpet that announces the jazzy first theme after an unmetered repeated-note passage for trumpet that opens the sonata-form Prologue movement. Strings enter and provide accompaniment for the oboe that intones the second theme. The development section is climactic and leads to a return of the opening material. Polyrhythmic writing constantly pushes the music forward.

The "Dance" second movement, marked Allegro molto, is brief and frenetic with infectious rhythms; it incorporates the popular song "East Side, West Side." The *Lento* Interlude features lyrical writing and solo woodwind passages, and presents the same elegant melody three times on different instruments. The English horn opens with an introduction before the clarinet plays the primary theme over a transparent accompaniment of strings, piano, and glockenspiel.

In two parts, the lively "Burlesque" (Allegro vivo) bounces along in 3/8 time. Its two sections alternate in an ABAB pattern and propel the music forward to a witty close. Nothing new appears in the Molto moderato Epilogue, in which the mood and themes of the Prologue and Interlude return to round off the entire piece and create a very quiet close. *—John Palmer*

Recommended:

○ **Copland: Music for the Theatre; Piano Concerto & others** / Bernstein (cond.), New York PO / 1998 / Sony 60177

The Red Pony, suite from the film score (1948)

Having won Academy Award nominations for each of his first three Hollywood film scores—*Of Mice and Men* (1939), *Our Town* (1940), and *The North Star* (1943)—Copland was much in demand for further film music. When he finally decided to return to films after completing his *Symphony No. 3* in 1947, it was once again in collaboration with producer-director Lewis Milestone, with whom Copland had worked on the first and third of the films mentioned above. Milestone, whom Copland called "a classy and intelligent director," had decided to make his first color film an adaptation of John Steinbeck's novella *The Red Pony.* Once he had read, and liked, the Steinbeck book, Copland decided to join the project, agreeing to write and record approximately an hour of music—one of his largest musical efforts—in ten weeks for a significant (for the time, at least) fee of $15,000. The film and score were completed in 1948, with the film released the following year.

Steinbeck's novella tells the story of Jody Tiflin (renamed Tom in the film), a young boy who lives on a ranch near Salinas, CA, with his parents and the cowhand Billy Buck. The novella and film deal with the death of Tom's beloved pony Gabilan and the subsequent birth of Gabilan's foal, along with the relationships between the various characters and scenes of everyday life on the ranch. Steinbeck himself wrote the film's screenplay, slightly condensing and rearranging the action of his book.

Even before the film was released, Copland had decided to extract a concert suite from the score (premiered in Houston, TX, on October 30, 1948, by the Houston Symphony conducted by Efrem Kurtz). The six-movement suite contains:

(1) "Morning on the Ranch," which uses music from the beginning (early stirrings on the ranch) and ending (the birth of the foal) of the film;

(2) "The Gift," depicting the moment when Gabilan is given to Tom and his excited presentation of Gabilan to his friends;

(3) "Dream March and Circus Music," which accompanies two of Tom's daydreams—one in which he and Billy Buck lead an army of knights in armor into battle, another in which Tom is a circus ringmaster;

(4) "Walk to the Bunkhouse," with melodies representing Billy Buck as well as Tom's admiration for Billy and his mare;

(5) "Grandfather's Story," in which Tom's visiting grandfather tells about how he led a wagon train across the country; and

(6) "Happy Ending," which, like "Morning on the Ranch," uses material from the beginning and ending of the film. *—Chris Morrison*

Recommended:

○ **Copland: Music for Films** / L. Slatkin (cond.), St. Louis SO / 1994 / RCA Victor 902661699

El Salón México (1933–1936)

Copland's period as a full-time populist didn't begin until 1936, when he completed *El Salón México.* On a trip to Mexico in 1932, Copland resolved to write a piece using popular Mexican themes, and when he finally began its slow assembly the following year, he borrowed tunes from collections recently published by Ruben Campos and Frances Toor. The result is a gaudy souvenir, as Copland intended; he felt unqualified, as a foreigner, to write something more serious drawing from Mexico's history or its revolutionary present. He connected the piece with a dancehall he'd visited, El Salón México, a "hot spot," Copland wrote, where "one felt, in a very natural and unaffected way, a close contact with the Mexican people. It wasn't the music I heard, but the spirit that I felt there, which attracted me."

For this work, Copland favored the Mexican huapango rhythm, essentially a measure in 6/8 answered exuberantly by a measure in 3/4. The piece begins with rhythmic brass chords and a rising string figure, but almost immediately the music, having toyed with fragments of "El Palo Verde" and "La Jesusita," loses its energy and collapses with a thud. The trumpet lazily introduces the folk tune "El Mosco" over a wheezing, inebriated-sounding accompaniment. The lower winds bring on a slow, quiet, sexy, rhythmic theme of their own, which the strings take up more grandly. Next, the higher woodwinds announce a faster, jaunty tune, which is picked up in turn by other sections of the orchestra, although the strings and percussion quickly reduce it to little more than rhythm. The brass and percussion take the lead in developing this into a dynamic, strongly accented motif. This soon plays itself out, whereupon a softer, broader, dreamier section arises. This grows organically into a faster, more vigorous section whose most arresting feature is a raucous little tune for clarinet. Now Copland builds the excitement more patiently and gradually than before, layering on and then stripping away various sections of the orchestra. A tiny bit of "El Mosco" comes to dominate the proceedings, building to an exuberant finale that Copland intentionally sabotages with a percussive whack on the offbeat. *—James Reel*

Recommended:

○ **A Copland Celebration Vol. 1** / Copland (cond.), New Philharmonia Orch. / 2000 / Sony 89323

KEYBOARD

Danzón Cubano, for 2 pianos (1942)

Having already written the spicy *El Salón México* (1933–36), Copland, fresh from a return visit to Mexico in 1941, produced this colorful, if slightly less successful composition for two pianos for the 20th anniversary of the U.S. League of Composers. It was premiered at New York's Town Hall on December 17, 1942, with Copland and Leonard Bernstein at the pianos. Three years later, he orchestrated it, creating the version of the piece most often heard today. The work opens with a short, lively rhythmic theme, which is especially colorful here and throughout in the orchestral version. It remains relatively subdued, however, in accordance with the features of the Mexican danzón, a two-part dance somewhat restrained in its first half, but quite wild and driving in its latter part. The music in the opening half is playful and bouncy, its melodies exhibiting that typical stop-and-start quality heard in so many Copland works. There is a leisurely, somewhat mischievous sense to this cheery music, too, as if in preparation for the fireworks to come. Midway through, episodes of greater momentum appear, the rhythms turning spicier, the decibels louder, the sonorities often alluding to American jazz styles. But the music does not really explode until near the close, as the rhythmic character turns obsessive, almost mechanical. Still, just before the close, Copland deftly harnesses the runaway music before it gets out of hand. This attractive gem has a duration of about six or seven minutes. *—Robert Cummings*

Recommended:

○ **Gould, Piston & Copland: Music for 2 Pianos** / Pierce & Jonas / 1990 / Koch 3-7002

Piano Sonata (1939–1941)

Aaron Copland's *Piano Sonata* comes chronologically from the very heart of his "vernacular" period, but bears little stylistic resemblance to the works around it. The opening sketches date from June 1939, just after Copland had completed the incidental music he would later fashion into the tone poem *Quiet City.* In December 1940, Copland was named by Nelson Rockefeller to an advisory panel within the State Department's Office of Inter-American affairs. Copland spent most of 1941 touring South America as part of the Roosevelt administration's Good Neighbor policy, getting to know South American music and composers, giving master classes, and concertizing. In Santiago, Chile, in September, Copland put the finishing touches on the *Piano Sonata,* premiering it himself in Buenos Aires on October 21, 1941.

Copland once noted that "a piano work, in my case, (is written) when I am stuck with ideas that have nowhere else to go." Copland studied sonata form extensively with Rubin Goldmark in Cleveland as a youth, and sticks to standard sonata-allegro form very definitely in this *Sonata,* varying the opening Molto moderato with appropriate contrast and periods of roughly equal length. The Scherzo vivace alternates abrupt, jazz-derived ideas with a slower, more relaxed trio section. The final *Andante sostenuto* departs from standard sonata form, in that it takes its basic working material from the second movement *Trio* and consists of static chords, giving an impression of immobility, like a clock winding down.

Copland had relatively little to say about the *Piano Sonata*, although he was in general somewhat tight-lipped about his work, preferring to let the music speak for itself. However the *Sonata* is rarely discussed in the context of Copland's music, and is as seldom heard in concert, in spite of its historical placement among the most popular of his works. Indeed, the *Piano Sonata* inhabits both of Copland's main spheres of activity to that time, taking the spindly, naked forms of his vernacular music and combining them with the tougher language of his early *Piano Variations* (1930). Nonetheless, the *Piano Sonata* is one of his finest creations in terms of its concentration of expression, variety of mood, and its finely tuned balance of both seriousness and dry wit. One important early advocate of the Copland *Piano Sonata* was Leonard Bernstein, who played it expertly early in his career and made a fine recording of it for RCA Victor in 1947. *—Uncle Dave Lewis*

Recommended:

- ○ **Frick Collection Recital** / Kapell / 1998 / RCA Victor 68997

Piano Variations (1930)

While the observation that each of Aaron Copland's three major piano works—the Variations (1930), the Sonata (1939–41), and the Fantasy (1955–57)—signals a turning point in the composer's style is not quite accurate, it can be said that each of these works bears the distinctive stamp of its place in *Copland*'s creative development. The first of these, the *Piano Variations*, is perhaps the most characteristic of Copland's "modernist" works; it aptly reflects the composer's particular attention to an austerity of means in a context of angular melodies, irregular rhythms and meters, and pungent harmonies. Though his later ballets and concert works—written in a more overtly accessible vein—overshadowed the Variations in popularity, this work remains one of Copland's most notable accomplishments, the first certifiable masterpiece from the man who would emerge as the "dean of American composers." The work was highly influential (the young Leonard Bernstein was one of its early proponents), and its astringency was only slightly less bracing decades later, when Copland dusted it off and used it as the basis for his *Orchestral Variations* (1957).

The germinal material of the Variations is a four-note motive (E—C—D sharp—C sharp) whose compact collection of intervals gives rise to the tangy harmonies that so strongly characterize the work. The theme and 20 variations flow into one other without interruption; as Copland relates in *What to Listen for in Music*, the traditional roles of the theme and first variation are reversed, the initial statement of the theme making a strident and dramatic entrance, the first variation presenting a simpler, more subdued version.

Variations one through 11 treat the theme in a generally straightforward, if "bangy" and dissonant manner. Variations 12 through 19 are more rhythmically active and of a somewhat lighter tone, at times taking on the character of a scherzo. Variations 19 and 20 provide the impetus for a buildup into a tremendous coda. *—AMG*

Recommended:

- ○ **Copland: The Young Pioneers** / Leo Smit / Sony 66345

VOCAL

Old American Songs, Book 1 (1950)

Copland's interests in American vernacular traditions were most fully realized in his song arrangements for voice and piano. Varied in inspiration, these take on themes—political and religious, folk and theatrical—presenting a diversified portrait of America itself, linked by the unity of Copland's style. The five songs in the first set feature predominantly major modes, diatonic harmonies, and a certain directness in character. Copland's personal stamp is apparent in the comic minstrel song "The Boatman's Dance," (wherein he rewrote portions of the black dialect to avoid offensive racial implications); the sentimental love song "Long Time Ago"; the Shaker tune "Simple Gifts"; the topical song "The Dodger"; and the children's song "I Bought Me a Cat" (complete with barnyard sounds in the accompaniment). As always, he refashioned these tunes as he saw fit, whether by altering a few notes to smooth out the melody in "Simple Gifts," or condensing the number of stanzas in "The Dodger" from seven to three. The latter satirizes a political candidate, preacher, and lover, while stanzas about the lawyer, doctor, merchant, and farmer were omitted. Nevertheless, Copland's evocation of banjo playing marvelously captures the folk sensibility of the original. The *Five American Songs* were premiered by Peter Pears and Benjamin Britten at the Aldeburgh Festival on June 17, 1950, while baritone William Warfield gave the American premiere with Copland at the piano on January 28, 1951. *—Brian Wise*

Recommended:

- ○ **Modern American Vocal Works** / Copland (cond.), Warfield, Columbia SO / 1999 / Sony 60899
- ○ **Brahms & Copland: Songs** / W. Parker, Huckaby / 1987 / Centaur 2022

Old American Songs, Book 2 (1952)

The warm reception of the *Old American Songs* in 1951 prompted Copland to write an immediate sequel, *Old American Songs Book 2*, comprising settings of "The Little Horses," "Zion's Walls," "The Gold Willow Tree," "At the River," and "Ching-a-Ring Chaaw." Although they elicited little critical comment at the time, these became extremely popular and remain so to this day. As with the first set, Copland preserves the tunes' rhetorical directness and simple diatonic harmonies in his arrangements, while adding numerous personal touches. In the camp-meeting spiritual "Zion's Walls," for example, he adds a novel contrasting section based on his own countermelody to the original tune, while he entirely rearranges the ballad "The Gold Willow Tree." In "Ching-a-Ring Chaw" he purged the text of its racial implications and revised the story about African-American immigration to Haiti as a more general utopian fantasy. The *Old American Songs Book 2* were premiered by baritone William Warfield with Copland at the piano on July 24, 1953. During Copland's lifetime, these were widely associated with Warfield, who, like many singers since, preferred singing them in their orchestral arrangements over the piano versions. *—Brian Wise*

Recommended:

- ○ **Modern American Vocal Works** / Copland (cond.), Warfield, Columbia SO / 1999 / Sony 60899
- ○ **My Native Land: A Collection of American Songs** / Larmore, Palloc / 1997 / Teldec 16069

12 Poems of Emily Dickinson, song cycle (1949–1950)

The composition of his *12 Poems of Emily Dickinson* (1949–50) marks the beginning of a brief period during which Copland composed vocal music almost exclusively. It was his first major vocal piece, and some consider it one of the great song cycles of the twentieth century.

Copland hoped that the audience would perceive the work as a song cycle, although only the seventh and 12th songs in the set are thematically related. Features below the surface lend uniformity to Copland's settings. The interval of a third dominates the songs in both voice part and accompaniment, as do chord progressions that feature falling fourths. In general the songs are transparent, the piano part often consisting of only one line per hand. In addition, word painting appears in many of the songs.

The first line of "Nature, the gentlest mother" consists almost entirely of leaps of a third, particularly between B flat and D natural, while the piano delivers embellishments resembling bird calls. Agitated and even violent, "There came a wind like a bugle" opens with piano scales in strident ninths. Piano trills suggest the "quivering grass," while the church bell is evoked in accented left-hand notes. The accompaniment is generally simple in "Why do they shut me out of heaven?" and the melodic central section is enclosed by recitative-like material. "The world feels dusty" is a rumination on inevitable death, given a quiet setting.

Resignation is also at the core of "Heart, we will forget him," a poem on lost love. Copland evokes the loss and tragedy conveyed by the poem through falling fourths in the voice part, especially at the words, "thought may dim," on E, B, and F. With a very active accompaniment, Copland sets "Dear March, come in" in music with a dual time signature—6/8 in the piano and 2/4 in the voice. The resultant cross rhythms create a lively atmosphere in this bucolic welcoming of spring. "Sleep is supposed to be" marks the middle of the cycle, and after this song Copland specifies a significant pause. Arpeggios dominate both the voice and piano parts in this brittle song.

Spring is again the subject in "When they come back." Simpler than "Dear March," "When they come back" is rhythmically uniform and predominantly diatonic. Unlike the other songs, each of its verses begins with the same music. Copland sets Dickinson's dark "I felt a funeral in my brain" with a lugubrious accompaniment depicting the slow, heavy pace of a funeral procession. Bells clang as the piano and voice move mostly in different keys, creating an atmosphere of unease. Despair is once again conveyed through falling fourths. In contrast, "I've heard an organ talk sometimes" is calm, while rising phrases dominate "Going to Heaven." "The Chariot," (Copland's title for *Because I would not stop for death*), begins with the opening of "Sleep is supposed to be." The calm setting reflects the narrator's fearlessness in the face of death.

Copland orchestrated eight of the 12 *Dickinson Poems* between 1958 and 1970.*—John Palmer*

Recommended:

- ○ **12 Poems of Emily Dickinson; Songs of Rorem** / Curtin, Copland / 2001 / VAI Audio 1194
- ○ **Sallie Chisum Remembers Billy The Kid** / B. Bonney, Previn / 1998 / London 455511
- ○ **Aaron Copland 81st Birthday Concert at the Library of Congress** / DeGaetani, Smit / 1993 / Bridge 9046

SYMPHONIC

Symphony for Organ & Orchestra (1924)

American composer Aaron Copland was the first American student of French pedagogue Nadia Boulanger and spent the years from 1921–24 studying with her at

Fontainebleau. While there, he met many of the most important artists of the day, including the Russian émigré conductor Sergey Koussevitzky. These facts are all central to the creation of Copland's first great piece of music, his *Symphony for Organ and Orchestra*. Koussevitzky commissioned the work from Copland in anticipation of Boulanger's first appearance in America in 1925. Copland wrote the symphony while working as a pianist at a resort in Pennsylvania. The work was premiered in Carnegie Hall by the New York Symphony Orchestra under Walter Damrosch. Although composed in what was then the height of the avant-garde musical style—that is, with complex and pugnacious rhythms, tonal but pungent harmonies, and with spiky and brilliant orchestration—Copland's symphony is clearly the music of a young man who had studied the most advanced music of Europe and who was determined to make a huge impact with his first widely publicized piece. But it is also the music of an American composer: The long lines of the melodies and the specific shapes and intervals of the themes could only have been written by a composer born in the United States. *—James Leonard*

Recommended:

○ **Copland: Symphony for Organ & Orchestra; Symphony 3** / L. Bernstein (cond.), Biggs, New York PO / 1997 / Sony 63155

Symphony No. 3 (1944–1946)

The symphonic form is one Copland approached with some caution—the Third Symphony (1944–46) would be his last such effort—and that, like his three major piano works, helped to codify particular compositional concerns that occupied him at the time. Though the three symphonies (not including the *Dance Symphony* of 1925, which is more properly a suite) are clearly of the same composer and all exploit what have come to be identified as Copland hallmarks (including changing, dance-influenced rhythms and expressive gradations of orchestral color), each in its own way exists quite apart from the others. While, for example, the bumptious, impudent character that characterizes much of the Second Symphony (1932–33) lurks unmistakably in the Allegro molto of the Third, its essence and context are subtly distinctive; the relationship is one between cousins rather than siblings. More markedly, the symphonies represent an evolution—not necessarily in a predictable linear fashion, but in the more circumspect and elusive sphere of the composer's imagination.

The lyricism which is an overarching characteristic of the the Third Symphony was, according to Copland himself, inspired in large part by the knowledge that the work was commissioned and to be premiered by conductor Serge Koussevitsky and dedicated to the memory of his wife, Natalie. The first movement, Molto moderato, is thus imbued with a songful melodic expansiveness (looking forward, at times, to the composer's opera *The Tender Land*) emerging from the subdued, ever-expanding opening theme. The movement proceeds to a more assertive, brass-laden climax, which eventually dissipates into the calm of the opening via a series of bassi ostinati that gently underpin the gradually stilling activity above.

The opening of the Allegro molto announces at once the movement's jovial intent, the percussion crashes and brass rocket figure foreshadowing the fanfare of the last movement. The movement continues in the cast of a scherzo with trio, in turns assuming a martial drive and a humorous bounce; one direction in the score the composer provides for this music is "perky."

The third movement, Andantino quasi allegretto, opens with a dialogue among the strings that in gradual, subtle degrees introduces the rest of the orchestra; the winds, for example, enter by quietly doubling the strings so that their presence is realized almost only after the fact. A vocally fluid, converging "wedge" figure introduces a more rhapsodic and expansive section, characterized by plangent harmony and frequent parallel motion in the instruments that provides a gentle suggestion of medievalism.

A quiet wind and string chorale leads directly into the fourth movement, Molto deliberato—Allegro risoluto. In a particularly pregnant and dramatic stroke, the theme which forms the centerpiece of the last movement (perhaps best known as the basis for Copland's *Fanfare for the Common Man*), is introduced—not with its full complement of brass and percussion, but as a somewhat reflective meditation for the flutes and clarinets. It is quickly taken up by the whole orchestra, serving as introduction for the movement proper, which presents and develops two additional themes. Material from the first movement is later incorporated into the texture, here assuming a different, strengthened guise appropriate to the nobilmente, heroic character of the finale. The theme that opens the work, now newly emboldened, brings the Third Symphony to an exhilarating conclusion. *—Michael Rodman*

Recommended:

○ **Copland: Symphony 3; Quiet City** / Bernstein (cond.), New York PO / DG 419170

FILM MUSIC

Our Town (1940)

By the close of the 1930s, Aaron Copland had begun to compose avidly for the cinema, following his earlier successes writing for the stage. Indeed, his first film project probably gave him a taste for success, after his score for Ralph Steiner's documentary *The City* earned him widespread acclaim when first shown at the New York World's Fair in 1939. A second documentary commission followed in 1945, with *The Cummington Story*, produced for the U.S. government. Copland's other film scores of the WWII period were written exclusively for Hollywood.

When the Hollywood director Sol Lesser approached Copland to write music for his production of *Our Town* in 1940, the commission also provided that Copland should orchestrate his own work. The result, a plaintive and traditional musical accompaniment ideally suited to the character of Steinbeck's depiction of small-town American life, was instantly successful with audiences and critics alike. Copland also reworked the full score as a short concert suite, lasting just over ten minutes. This was premiered on June 9, 1940, by the Columbia Symphony Orchestra under Howard Barlow. Later, during 1942, Copland returned to this score (and others), when he selected passages from *The City*, *Of Mice and Men*, and also *Our Town*, working material from all three into an orchestral suite entitled simply *Music for the Movies*. *—Michael Jameson*

Recommended:

○ **Copland Conducts Copland: Our Town** / Copland (cond.), London SO / 1987 / Sony 46559

CONCERTO

Clarinet Concerto (1947–1948)

Copland began work on his *Clarinet Concerto* while traveling in Latin America in 1947. After setting it aside when he was unable to come up with a suitable theme for the second movement, Copland completed the work during his annual sojourn at Tanglewood in the following year. The Concerto, commissioned by the prominent clarinetist Benny Goodman, was premiered by Goodman and the NBC Symphony Orchestra in a broadcast of November 6, 1950. Though the initial critical reception of the work was less favorable than that which had greeted a number of Copland's other works, the Concerto gradually attained popularity among performers and audiences alike. It received a substantial boost in the year following its premiere, when choreographer Jerome Robbins adopted it as the musical setting for his ballet *The Pied Piper*.

Copland drew inspiration for the *Clarinet Concerto* from a number of sources. The work took shape under the influence of the Brazilian folk music Copland heard during his travels, while the second movement in particular was tailored to fit Goodman's own playing style and skills. (Copland's manuscript drafts, in fact, indicate a number of alterations made expressly to accommodate Goodman's technique.) The work is divided into two movements, the first marked "Slowly and expressively," the second, "Rather fast"; the two are connected by an extended cadenza for the soloist. The first movement is meditative and rhapsodic, combining dramatic leaps in the solo clarinet line with an unhurried, waltz-like accompaniment in the strings and harp. A more restive and harmonically adventurous section interrupts the lilt of the the triple meter, and the movement is rounded out by a return to its original mood.

The cadenza between the movements acts as a transition, extending the mood of the first movement and introducing the lively melodic and rhythmic material of the second. The piano, which sits silent during the first movement, is freely employed in the second, assuming both soloistic and less obtrusive textural roles. After a mysterious introduction, the clarinet introduces the melodic material of the movement, which is altered and recombined in a variety of jazzy contexts as the movement unfolds in a rondo-like form. The clarinet often declaims its line over an ostinato accompaniment, and at one point Copland heightens the jazzy atmosphere by directing the basses to play in a "slap-string" style. A concluding virtuosic coda has the clarinetist wailing in the upper ranges of the instrument and bringing the work to a close with a long glissando (in jazz, a "smear"), accompanied by the ensemble. *—AMG*

Recommended:

○ **Benny Goodman Collector's Edition** / Copland (cond.), B. Goodman, Columbia SO / 1986 / Sony 42227

○ **Copland: El Salón México; Clarinet Concerto & others** / Bernstein (cond.), S. Drucker, New York PO / DG 431672

Quiet City, for English horn, trumpet & strings (1940)

Aaron Copland's breathtakingly evocative *Quiet City* was finished in 1940. It was actually based on thematic material Copland had previously incorporated within a suite of incidental music written for a play by Irwin Shaw. This intensely concentrated tableau was characterized by its director as "a realistic fantasy…something which concerned the night thoughts of many very different kinds of people within a great city." Although only lightly scored for string orchestra with solo parts for English horn (cor anglais) and trumpet, Copland's *Quiet City* is among his most popular and successful works, a highly skilled yet nonetheless affectionate tribute to the wakeful nights of inhabitants of a great metropolis that never sleeps.

Irwin Shaw's play focused on two main characters. The first was a young Jewish boy, awestruck by the steely modernity of his city environment, yet still profoundly in touch with his own feelings and heritage. The obverse figure is that of a poor, dispossessed, and lonely man, for whom the city provides no refuge. These two personalities were portrayed in Copland's original incidental music by a jazz trumpet solo played by the Jewish boy, and a disconsolate, idly limping string theme, which according to Copland signified "the slogging gait" of a vagrant.

Quiet City, one of Aaron Copland's most internationally performed concert works, takes the form of a short through-composed suite, encapsulating the essence of Shaw's play. The music begins and ends with a depiction of the still night air of the slumbering city, invoked by the improvisatory sounds of the trumpeter, with the English horn portraying the homeless man. The spaciousness of Copland's musical textures has often been compared to the vastness of the American landscape, and *Quiet City* was emblematic of an urban, internalized facet of Americana. As Virgil Thompson wrote, Copland's orchestration was "plainer, cleaner-colored, deeply imaginative... it was theatrically functional." In *Quiet City* as in Copland's *Music for the Theatre*, the genius of modernism is heard in the way each expressive idea becomes a unique emotional construct, and also part of the unfolding drama of the work. *—Michael Jameson*

Recommended:

○ **Barber: Adagio for Strings; Ives: Symphony 3; Copland: Quiet City** / Marriner (cond.), Nicklin, Laird, Academy of St. Martin-in-the-Fields / 1987 / Decca 417818

CHAMBER MUSIC

Nonet, for 3 violins, 3 violas & 3 cellos (1960)

Copland's *Nonet for strings* was commissioned by the Dumbarton Oaks Research Library in Washington, D.C., to honor the 50th wedding anniversary of the library's main patrons, Mr. and Mrs. Robert Woods Bliss. The work is dedicated "after 40 years of friendship" to the famed music teacher Nadia Boulanger, with whom Copland had studied in Paris as a young man. Boulanger, a friend of the Bliss family, was to have conducted the *Nonet*'s first performance; however, Copland did not complete it in time for the scheduled premiere, and he himself led the first performance, with members of the National Symphony Orchestra, at a private subscription concert at Dumbarton Oaks on March 2, 1961.

Copland had on occasion conducted performances of the dark-hued viol music of Henry Purcell and may have taken some inspiration from that music in composing the *Nonet*, scored for the unusual, "bottom-heavy" (the composer's own words) combination of three violins, three violas, and three cellos. Though Copland didn't like the idea of a conventional string ensemble performing the *Nonet*, he sanctioned performances by larger bodies of strings, suggesting configurations of 24 players (12 violins and six each of violas and cellos), 36 players (18 violins, nine violas, nine cellos), or 48 players (24 violins, 12 violas, 12 cellos).

The single-movement *Nonet*, about 18 minutes long, is cast in something like an ABA arch form. The work's three opening chords provided Copland's initial inspiration for the work's form and sonic language. These chords expand into a longer main theme of a brooding, melancholy nature, played by the cellos. The textures tend to be dense; some sonorities involve as many as six different pitches. After the appearance of more consonant and lyrical material, the tempo speeds up for a lively, jazz-influenced central section. The lyrical music returns on the heels of some ghostly transitional material, and the work concludes with slow, powerfully elegiac music related to the opening. The *Nonet* was composed at a time when Copland was increasingly influenced by serial techniques, which are clearly in evidence in his previous major work, the *Piano Fantasy* (1955–57). While Copland makes individual use of serial techniques throughout the *Nonet*, it is not a 12-tone work in the conventional sense. *—Chris Morrison*

Recommended:

○ **A Copland Celebration Vol. 1** / Copland (cond.), Columbia Chamber Ens. / 2000 / Sony 89323

BAND MUSIC

Fanfare for the Common Man (1942)

Aaron Copland's iconic *Fanfare for the Common Man* is without question his most internationally popular work, not least because it was once featured in an album by the rock group Emerson, Lake & Palmer, in which form it reached a global audience of huge numbers. The piece, which is scored for brass ensemble with timpani, bass drum, and tam-tam, originally came into existence as the result of a commission from the conductor Eugene Goossens, who in 1942 was serving as music director of the Cincinnati Symphony Orchestra. The work was one of a set of 18 fanfares written by various American composers during the dark days of World War II, all of which were expressly intended to promote feelings of patriotism and national unity. Copland's contribution to the project has been the only one of the set to find a place in the regular orchestral repertory; its original siblings have faded away.

Analyzing its success, Stuart Ledbetter points out that "part of the reason for this is surely its splendid title, but even more is the soaring, heroic character of its opening trumpet theme." Appropriately, too, for a ceremonial expression of national pride, the fanfare begins with an arresting call to attention, with solemn, regular strokes from the percussion instruments, whose measured salvo precedes the first statement of the trumpet theme itself. The entire work is built around this original statement, which grows in intensity through exchanges of the theme between trombones and tuba, and then horns and trumpets. The score concludes with a magnificently effective percussion crescendo supporting a thrilling final sustained chord for the brass.

While Copland was working on his *Symphony No. 3* in the years 1944–46, he commented that he was "certainly reaching for the grandest gesture." Indeed, the grandiloquence and colossal sense of optimism that underlies what is widely regarded as the greatest symphony by any U.S. composer is stunningly crowned by the reappearance of the *Fanfare for the Common Man* as a preface to the final movement. Actually, however, as Anthony Burton suggests, it "provides a focus for the work in a more subtle way: its intervals, especially the rising fourth and fifth of the first phrase, permeate the thematic material of the entire symphony." *—Michael Jameson*

Recommended:

○ **Copland Conducts Copland: Fanfare for the Common Man & others** / Copland (cond.), London SO / 2003 / Sony 90403

OPERA

The Tender Land (1952–1954; revised 1955)

Though he essayed any number of musical genres with remarkable results—chamber music, symphonies, ballets—Aaron Copland only rarely ventured into the realm of opera in the 50-plus years of his compositional career. Copland's first such foray, the rarely heard "school opera" *The Second Hurricane* (1936), is of relatively little musical interest. It wasn't until the 1950s, in fact, that Copland made his first and only important contribution to the repertory with his two-act opera (revised from three acts) *The Tender Land*, completed in 1954.

One of the last works Copland wrote wholly in his characteristically lyrical "American" style (epitomized by works from the previous decade like *Appalachian Spring* and the *Symphony No. 3*), *The Tender Land* dramatizes a story that is well complemented by the spaciousness and elegant simplicity of Copland's music. Inspired by photographs in James Agee and Walker Evans' timeless account of Depression-era America, *Let Us Now Praise Famous Men*, Copland and librettist Horace Everett fashioned a drama centered around a farm girl on the verge of womanhood. On the eve of her graduation from high school, Laurie Moss is faced with life-defining choices regarding love, family ties, and independence. The theme of outsiders—groundlessly accused of wrongdoing—invading the peaceful world of rural America mirrors certain contemporaneous social concerns, not the least of which was the witch hunt for Communists under the direction of Senator Joseph McCarthy. Copland himself had been called to testify at the notorious congressional hearings.

The Tender Land underwent much revision both before and after its initial production at the New York City Opera on April 1, 1954. Though the work has never attained the popularity of other American operas of the same period like Douglas Moore's *The Ballad of Baby Doe* (1956) or Carlisle Floyd's *Susannah* (1955), it enjoyed something of a renaissance in the 1990s with numerous productions and the first-ever recording of the entire work. *—AMG*

Synopsis:

Act One. (The story takes place in rural America in spring, 1930s.) As schoolgirl Beth plays with her doll outside the farmhouse where she lives, Mr. Splinters, the mailman, delivers a package for her old sister Laurie. It turns out that the parcel has arrived just in time, since it contains the dress Laurie will wear at her high school graduation on the following day. Inside the house, the girls' mother, Ma Moss, offers an invitation to Mr. Splinters to attend the graduation party. The wholesome nature of the chat ends when the mailman reveals that two strangers seen in the area have raped two neighborhood girls. Laurie enters the house and is exasperated that her mother and grandfather are so overprotective of her.

A pair of suspicious-looking young drifters appear and meet Laurie. Grandpa is wary of them, but still takes them on as farmhands to work in the coming harvest. The naïve Laurie invites them to the graduation party, planned for that night. Alone, the two contrives a scheme to get Grandpa drunk so that they can make inroads with the pretty Laurie.

Act Two. At the party, the Moss family members and their guests enjoy dancing, food, and much celebrating. The plan is working smoothly, too, Grandfather gradually becoming tipsy. Ma Moss grows increasingly suspicious of the strangers, however, and soon asks Mr. Splinters to fetch the Sheriff. After dancing with Martin, Laurie, charmed by his engaging personality, goes out on the porch to be alone with the young fellow. Grandpa and Ma Moss catch the two sharing a kiss, Ma turning furious and accusing Martin and Top of being the rapists. No sooner is the accusation made than Mr. Splinters returns with news that the Sheriff has just apprehended the guilty pair. Still, Grandfather orders that the two be off the premises by morning.

Act Three. Laurie believes she is in love with Martin and has a secret rendezvous with him outside the house later that night. They work out a plan to elope, but later Martin and Top discuss their life as drifters and conclude it would not be suited to Laurie. They depart without her, and when Laurie finds them gone she decides not to remain for her graduation and also leaves. The opera concludes with Ma Moss focusing on her youngest daughter, Beth, seeing her now as the family's center of attention. Ma goes inside the house and leaves Beth outside to play, the scene resembling that at the story's outset. *—Robert Cummings*

Recommended:

○ **Copland: The Tender Land** / Brunelle (cond.), Jette, Comeaux, Hardy, Bohn, Plymouth Music Series Orch. / 1990 / Virgin 592532

John (Giovanni) Coprario

b. ca. 1575, England [?], **d.** 1626, London, England

Composer

John Coprario was one of the leading composers of post-Elizabethan England. He was highly respected for his songs and his instrumental music, which was original and trend setting.

He was an Englishman, born and bred, who affected an Italianized name. (Sometimes he went so far as to style himself Giovanni Coprario.) Although he signed his surname "Coprario," it was sometimes rendered "Coperario" during his lifetime. The original name seems to have been either Cooper or Cowper. He does not seem to be the John Cowper who was a chorister at Chichester Cathedral in 1575 and its choir director in 1595 and 1596.

One contemporary account says that the composer adopted his pseudonym after he spent substantial time in Italy, where the local people started calling him "Coperario." This may well be the case, but there is no evidence that he spent any time in Italy. However, he was on the Continent, in the Netherlands, at least, in 1603.

In 1606 he issued his first publication (also his earliest surviving music), *Funeral Teares*, written on the death of Charles Blount, the Earl of Devonshire. As early as 1607 he was engaged to write music for entertainment of a party including the King given by the Merchant Taylors' Company. At about that time he provided music frequently for Sir Robert Cecil, who became Earl of Salisbury in 1605 and Lord Treasurer in 1608. Salisbury made payments to him to cover lodgings, maintenance costs of instruments, and so forth.

In 1613 he composed the music for Campion's *Songs of Mourning, Bewailing the Untimely Death of Prince Henry*, which contains elegies specifically for various members of the royal family. At a happier occasion a bit earlier the same year he had written music for Campion's *The Lords Masque*, for the marriage of Princess Elizabeth to Elector Frederick, and accompanied the newlywed royal pair on their progress to Heidelberg. At the end of the year, he again collaborated with Campion to write three songs included in *The Masque of Squires*, for the wedding of the Earl of Somerset.

Coprario's other major patron besides the Earl of Salisbury was Edward Seymour, Earl of Hertford, until that elderly noble died in 1621. By that time Coprario also had a major position in the household of the Prince of Wales.

In 1625 Charles I appointed Coprario his composer-in-ordinary. Charles went on record as regarding some of Coprario's instrumental fantasias as "incomparable" and learned to play the bass-viol parts. Coprario did not enjoy his official appointment for long, dying within the year.

Coprario also wrote a concise and clear manual on composition, called *Rules How to Compose*, probably intended as teaching material for his pupil, William Lawes. Coprario was one of the first to compose for the lyra-viol. *—Joseph Stevenson*

Overview of Works (ca. 1605–1625)

Probably born plain John Cooper sometime between 1570 and 1580, Coprario (Coperario) is believed to have Italianized his name following a visit to the Continent in the entourage of Sir Robert Cecil in 1603. Later he joined the service of the Earl of Hertford, under whose patronage he was instructed to teach music to the Prince of Wales (the future Charles I), and to William Lawes, whose own style owes much to Coprario. Coprario maintained close contact with the royal family, gaining the post of composer-in-ordinary to Charles I on the latter's accession.

Except for the fact that he wrote little sacred music, Coprario's works closely mirror the taste of the day. An outstanding viol player himself, he made his most important contributions in the field of consort music. Notable here are his works in traditional fantasia form for two to five viols, which by Coprario's time were accompanied by organ. These freely composed works in several sections frequently show him going beyond the rather conservative style of his contemporaries in matters such as contrast of sonority. But Coprario's most radical innovation was inspired by Italian influences, for it appears to have been he who was first responsible for introducing to chamber works the violin, an instrument previously almost entirely restricted to dance music. Coprario was also responsible for introducing a new form, the so-called consort- or fantasia-suite, which added an almain and galliard to the fantasia to make a three-movement work. He scored these works for either one or two violins, bass viol, and organ (there are 16 for one, and eight for two violins). The most extensive movement remained the opening fantasia, which with its richly wrought counterpoint and introspective character carried the expressive burden of the "suite." The dance movements are generally lighter in character, with the galliards less concerned with contrapuntal texture than the foregoing fantasia and almain.

Coprario's lute songs, particularly those composed in memory of the Earl of Devonshire and the heir apparent, Prince Henry, whose premature death in 1612 shocked the nation, are distinguished by an unusually expressive approach that owes something to the Italian monodists. The passionate gravity of these solos and duets owes little to the standard run of ayres with lute. Finally, there are a number of lighter theater songs and music composed for masques. The latter includes the music Coprario contributed to *The Lord's Masque*, mounted in honor of the wedding of Princess Elizabeth and the Elector Palatine in 1613. *—Brian Robins*

Recommended:

○ **John Coprario: Consort Musicke** / Savall, Coin, Casademunt / 1999 / Astree 9923

Arcangelo Corelli

b. Feb. 17, 1653, Fusignano, Italy, **d.** Jan. 8, 1713, Rome, Italy

Composer: Concerto, Chamber Music

One of the seminal figures of Baroque music, Arcangelo Corelli was the first master of the modern violin, and the predominance of that instrument in the music of the following three centuries is his technical and pedagogical legacy. He managed to extract from it a beauty of tone and singing lyricism that were previously unknown; these qualities brought him international fame, both for his own performances and for those of his many students who began to disseminate his techniques. It would not be an overstatement to say that the fundamentals of modern string playing—including issues of both bowing and fingering—descend directly from Corelli.

Though he did not create the concerto grosso form, Corelli wrote the first significant compositions in the genre, laying the foundations for the achievements of Vivaldi, Handel, and Bach a generation later. The same can be said of his trio sonatas and solo violin sonatas, all of which show a greater stability of form and developed sense of harmonic progression than those of his predecessors. These compositions were influential not only because of their innovative use of form, terraced dynamics, and major/minor tonality, but also because they coincided with the flourishing music publishing industry in Italy; Corelli's fame and wealth led to the printing of nearly all of his works during his lifetime, and their wide circulation internationally. Indeed, composers and musicians studied his scores for many years following his death.

Corelli was born in the town of Fusignano in 1653 to a wealthy family. The details of his early life are unknown, but he most likely began his musical studies with a local priest before moving to Bologna where he studied at the Accademia Filarmonica. No later than 1675 (but perhaps earlier), Corelli moved to Rome, where he began appearing as a violinist in ensembles formed for various religious and civic occasions.

He soon emerged as one of the city's preeminent musicians and entered the service of Queen Christina of Sweden (the first of several influential patrons), who had established herself in Rome after abdicating her throne. Some of the young composers earliest works are dedicated to her, and were performed at her "academies." Following her death, Corelli entered the service of Cardinal Pamphili, who gave him a generous salary and a place to live; he would remain in the Cardinal's service until 1690, when the Cardinal left the city. Corelli's patronage was then assumed by the young (extremely young!) Cardinal Ottoboni, who had received his office through the intervention of Pope Alexander VIII, his uncle. This would prove extremely beneficial for Corelli, since his young employer quickly befriended him, paid him well, and was a great admirer of his music. Few musicians have ever enjoyed a more secure or lucrative relationship with a patron. In this position, Corelli achieved wide fame and extreme wealth, and upon his death in 1713 he was interred in the Pantheon. *—AMG*

CONCERTO

Concerti Grossi, Op. 6

Of all history's elite composers (and certainly of elite Baroque composers), Arcangelo Corelli may well have the least music to his name. Six publications' worth of solo and trio sonatas and concerti grossi, plus a handful of unpublished and possibly spurious works, are all he bequeathed to posterity; but what a magnificent and vastly influential lot that music is. By the time Corelli's *12 Concerti grossi*, Op. 6 were published, posthumously, in Amsterdam in 1714 (by Estienne Roger—famous for his sometimes underhanded Handel publications), Corelli was no longer at the forefront of Italian musical development—Vivaldi and company by then had that honor. But the music nevertheless drove a great deal of Europe into a renewed frenzy for the recently deceased Corelli's music, and the extent to which composers from country to country tried to duplicate the clean, clear style of the

Op. 6 works ("pure," "rich," and "grateful" are words the eighteenth century music historian Dr. Charles Burney used to describe these concerti grossi) cannot really be measured.

Corelli didn't compose Op. 6 from scratch just before its publication—much or even all of the music in the volume goes back many years, some as far as the 1680s or possibly even further. Corelli revised all of this old music in the years leading up to 1714, however, to bring it up to his own current standards and to make it more compatible with current taste. The first eight Op. 6 concerti grossi are cast in four-movement sonata da chiesa form, sometimes modified from what is now considered to be the sonata da chiesa norm, and in the case of No. 8 expanded to five movements, while the last four are examples of the more dance-oriented sonata da camera. Corelli, perhaps significantly, never actually used the term da chiesa, though he did specifically describe the last four works of Op. 6 as per camera. In Op. 6, as in all concerti grossi of the day, a small concertante group is set against a larger tutti ensemble. Interestingly enough, Corelli indicated that the tutti ensemble of Op. 6 can be eliminated if need be and the three soli—two violins and a cello—can play the music as though a trio sonata; but perhaps one shouldn't heed Corelli's words too much—such a performance results in the loss of some important music, and one imagines that the need would have to have been great for Corelli himself to have allowed such a performance. *Op. 6, No. 8 in G minor* is the famous five-movement *Christmas Concerto. —Blair Johnston*

Recommended:

- ○ **Corelli: Concerti Grossi Op. 6** / Corelli: Concerti Grossi Op6 / Banchini (cond.), J. Christensen, Ens. 415 / HM 901406
- ○ **Corelli: The 12 Concerti Grossi Op. 6** / Corelli: Concerti Grossi Op6 / Shepherd (cond.), Cantilena / 1981 / Chandos 8336/7/8

Concerto Grosso in G minor ("Christmas Concerto"), Op. 6/8

Although one cannot be sure, Arcangelo Corelli's famous *Christmas Concerto*—the *Concerto grosso in G minor,* Op. 6, No. 8 ("Fatto per la notte di Natale," as the inscription actually reads)—may well have been composed a full quarter century before it first appeared in print, posthumously, in 1714; there is a record of Corelli having, in 1690, performed a *Christmas Concerto* for the enjoyment of his then-new patron, Cardinal Pietro Ottoboni. The *Christmas Concerto* is easily Corelli's best-known piece of music, though isolated movements from the sonatas have, through other composers' adaptations, achieved vast individual fame. It is at heart an example of the sonata da chiesa, expanded from the usual four movements to five and incorporating into the last movement a rolling, 12/8 meter Pastorale ad libitum. Like the rest of the Op. 6 concerti, it is scored for a concertante group consisting of two violins and a cello and a larger tutti ensemble.

The normal slow-fast-slow-fast organization of the sonata da chiesa underlies everything that happens in the *Christmas Concerto*; but Corelli at several key points makes a concerted effort to turn that textbook organization on its head. Six measures of fiery Vivace preface the opening Grave movement, and the third movement (Adagio) has a central Allegro episode in which the first solo violin and first tutti violins suddenly break out with a rapid, ruffled sixteenth note oscillation (complex first movement structures that incorporate many changes of tempo are not at all unusual throughout Op. 6, indeed, the opening movement of Op. 6, No. 1 has no fewer than seven tempo indications in it!).

The second movement is in the usual binary form, and is built around Corelli's favorite kind of staggered, imitative suspensions. The fourth movement, *Vivace*, which would normally be the finale, is very short, so as to make room for the sizeable fifth movement, the body of which is an Allegro, but the true heart of which is that most famous of all Corelli music: the lovely, serene *Pastorale* (Largo). *—Blair Johnston*

Recommended:

- ○ **Per la Notte di Natale: Concertos & Cantatas for Christmas** / Standage (cond.), Collegium Musicum 90 / 1998 / Chandos 634
- ○ **Christmas Concertos** / Il Giardino Armonico / 1991 / Teldec 46013
- ○ **Albinoni: Adagio; Pachelbel: Canon & Gigue** / I Musici / 1992 / Philips 434787
- ○ **Corelli: 12 Concerti Grossi Op 6** / Pinnock (cond.), English Concert / 1998 / Archiv 459451

CHAMBER MUSIC

Trio sonatas (ca. 1689–1694)

The emergence of the full-fledged trio sonata at the hands of Arcangelo Corelli represents a defining moment in the development of Baroque music. Since the establishment of an idiomatic style of writing for the violin earlier in the seventeenth century, composers had increasingly sought to unify the disparate sectional nature of their compositions for the instrument. Virtuoso solo works gave way to pieces for two violins and continuo, in which more extended movements and imitative interplay between the three parts provided a greater sense of cohesion. Outstanding in this context are the sonatas of the Venetian Giovanni Legrenzi (1626–90). But it was the enormously successful and influential four sets of trio sonatas by Corelli that eventually established the genre as the dominant chamber music form of the Baroque.

The first, published in 1681 as Op. 1, immediately established Corelli, already famous in Rome as the most notable violin virtuoso of his day, as one of the foremost living instrumental composers. It consists of 12 sonatas in four movements, termed by their composer sonate da chiesa or church sonatas. They were known as such to emphasize their serious nature and to distinguish them from the type of sonata that included dance movements, such as those of the composer's Op. 2 (1685); this latter type was thus designated sonata da camera (chamber sonatas). Nearly all, whether church or chamber sonata, have a slow-fast-slow-fast scheme; deviations such as Op. 1, No. 4 in A minor, which opens with an Allegro, were rare at this time. These two publications were succeeded by two further sets of 12 sonatas, the sonate da chiesa of Op. 3, published in 1689, and a further group of a dozen sonate da camera, which appeared in 1694. Corelli's sonatas are particularly notable for the new breadth he brought to slow movements, often created by the composer's beautiful use of suspensions to create sustained, slow-moving passages harmonically enlivened by gentle dissonance. Quicker movements feature cleverly crafted imitation between the two violins, and, at times, the bass line. The relatively undemanding nature of the writing ensured a ready market for Corelli's sonatas among the rapidly growing numbers of amateur players. Within Corelli's lifetime they achieved the staggering total of no less than 78 reprints, and they continued to be reprinted throughout the eighteenth century. More important, they laid the framework for many dozens of works composed in imitation of these, though later composers such as Handel tended to blur the distinction between church and chamber sonata. *—Brian Robins*

Recommended:

- ○ **Corelli: Sonate da Chiesa Op3** / Gatti (cond.), Ens. Aurora / 1998 / Arcana 902
- ○ **Corelli: Sonatas for Strings Vol. 3** / Purcell Quartet / 1992 / Chandos 0526
- ○ **Corelli: Sonatas for Strings Vol. 2** / Purcell Quartet / 1991 / Chandos 0515

Violin Sonatas, Op. 5 (before 1700)

These dozen sonatas fully constitute one-sixth of Corelli's published output and strongly influenced the form of the violin sonata in the early decades of the eighteenth century. The collection is in many ways a condensation of Corelli's four earlier volumes of trio sonatas; here are solo sonatas (front-and-center violin, accompanied by a continuo section of at least a keyboard and usually cello or gamba, sometimes with the addition of theorbo or some other member of the lute family), with the works divided between six church sonatas (sonate da chiesa, the format of Corelli's Opp. 1 and 3 trio sonatas) and five chamber sonatas (sonate da camera, in the manner of Opp. 2 and 4). The final work follows neither convention; it's a theme with variations in a single movement. Although Corelli knew this music would be purchased and played mainly by amateurs, he requires a great deal of skill; this set is something of a compendium of violin technique ca. 1700.

Each of the six church sonatas consists of five movements carrying tempo indications rather than the names of dances. The first movement is always imposing and slow (marked either Grave or Adagio), the spacious tempo allowing florid melodic lines. This is always followed by a fast movement, either Allegro or Vivace, often a fugue whose counterpoint requires double and triple stops. Next comes a pair of movements, one fast and the other slow, although the order varies; these are lighter than what has come before, and may suggest some dance form without fully committing to one. The finale is fast, sometimes another fugue, sometimes dance-like (Corelli actually calls one "Giga").

The five chamber sonatas accomplish much the same sort of work with a lighter touch. They are in either four or five movements, the first always called Preludio and usually slow (except for *Sonata No. 7,* which is Vivace). Next come three movements in fast-slow-fast pattern. The first of these may be a Corrente, Allemanda, or Giga; the second is usually called Sarabanda; the third is generally a Giga (when that wasn't the basis of an earlier movement) or Gavotta. The 10th and 11th sonatas end with an extra Allegro, a Giga in the first case, a Gavotta in the second. The final sonata is a set of 24 variations on the old "La Folia" chord progression, offering a variety of tempo, character, and harmony, and ultimately requiring great virtuosity. *—James Reel*

Recommended:

- ○ **Corelli: Violin Sonatas Op. 5** / Sonnerie, N. North / 2003 / Virgin 562236
- ○ **Corelli: 12 sonate a violino e violone o cimbalo Op. 5** / Trio Veracini / 1996 / Novalis 150128

Franco Corelli

b. Apr. 8, 1921, Ancona, Italy, **d.** Oct. 29, 2003, Milan, Italy

Tenor

"Thrilling" is the word that inevitably seems to come up in discussion of Franco Corelli, whether in reference to his powerful, immediately identifiable voice or his matinee idol good looks. (He was one of the few tenors whose appearance was actually enhanced by Renaissance-style tights and after one such appearance was nicknamed "The Golden Calves.") He sang everything "Corelli-style," altering rhythms to suit his voice, inserting or prolonging high notes whenever he felt like it, and almost never displaying a high level of finesse, nuance, or sensitivity to phrasing; for his admirers, he was the quintessence of operatic excitement.

Rather unusually, he did not come from a musical family, discovered his own talent relatively late in life, and was almost completely self-taught. He had studied for an engineering career, but friends encouraged him to think about music, and he briefly studied at the Pesaro Conservatory when he was in his early twenties. In 1951, he won the Maggio Musicale competition, but he decided to discontinue formal musical studies shortly afterwards. Instead, he spent his time listening to recordings of great tenors of the past, particularly Caruso, Gigli, and Lauri-Volpi, in the repertoire which he himself hoped to sing. He made his operatic debut as Don José in a production of *Carmen* in Spoleto, also during 1951.

Despite not having the network of teachers that many students have, he quickly grew in reputation, appeared in a television production of Leoncavallo's *Pagliacci*, and made his La Scala debut in Spontini's *La Vestale* as Licinio, in 1954. His Covent Garden debut in 1957 was as Cavaradossi in Puccini's *Tosca*, and his Metropolitan Opera debut as Manrico in 1961. While he had a definite "bleat" in his voice during his early years that led to some critics dubbing him "PeCorelli" (Italian for "goat"), he did learn to overcome that, and also to add a ravishing pianissimo to his singing, though his phrasing remained more or less crude. Over the coming years, La Scala and the Met were the houses where he appeared most frequently. He constantly suffered from stage fright, and many of his divo antics, offstage and on, might have stemmed from that, but on stage, he cut a dashing figure, though somewhat more inclined to pose than to act. In one memorable staging of *Don Carlo*, feeling that Boris Christoff, the bass singing King Philip, was getting too much audience attention, he provoked a genuine sword fight with the no less feisty Christoff during the auto-da-fé scene, until a brave supernumerary (spear carrier) physically separated the two. In yet another staging of the same scene and opera, he didn't come out onto the stage until long after his cue; he had been in the middle of a dispute backstage, and wanted to win that before he came out to sing.

He sang a wide variety of roles from the Italian and French repertoire, including several works that had been relative obscurities, such as Meyerbeer's *Les Hugenots* and Donizetti's *Poliuto*. Appropriately, considering how he learned to sing, he made several recordings, mostly for EMI/Angel. Among the recordings that capture him at his best are an *Andrea Chenier*, conducted by Santini (EMI CDS5 65287-2) and a selection of arias and songs (EMI *Double Forte* CZS 569530 2.) *—Ann Feeney*

Recommended:

- ○ **The Very Best of Franco Corelli** / Corelli, etc. / 2003 / EMI 85084
- ○ **The Unknown Recordings** / Corelli, etc. / EMI 62699
- ○ **Giordano: Andrea Chenier** / Santini (cond.), Corelli, Stasio, Malagu, Modesti, Rome Opera Orch. & Chorus / 1994 / EMI 65287

John Corigliano

b. Feb. 16, 1938, New York, NY

Composer: Symphonic, Film Music, Keyboard, Opera

American composer John Corigliano (b. 1938) has summed up his artistic aims thus: "It has been fashionable of late for the artist to be misunderstood. I think it is the job of the composer to reach out to his audience with every means at his disposal.... Communication of his most important ideas should be the primary goal." Throughout the development of his career, Corigliano's "primary goal" of communication with the audience has remained ever in his sight. In an atmosphere in which audience responses to new music so often range from indifferent to adversarial, Corigliano takes a place among the few "serious" contemporary composers whose appeal has ranged beyond the new-music crowd to reach listeners steeped in more traditional, time-tested fare.

The son of longtime New York Philharmonic concertmaster John Corigliano Sr., Corigliano received his formal training at Columbia University and the Manhattan School of Music; his teachers included Otto Luening, Vittorio Giannini, and Paul Creston. Corigliano's father, with his from-the-trenches perspective on the world of classical music, at first discouraged John Jr. from pursuing a career in composition, all too aware of the difficulties that faced contemporary composers. However, after a stint as a music programmer for radio, Corigliano attracted international attention for his *Sonata for Violin and Piano* (1963), awarded the top prize at the 1964 Festival of Two Worlds in Spoleto, Italy.

From that point, he continued to evolve a musical language in which architecture, color, and overt drama are paramount. While his works are steeped in a Romantic aesthetic that makes liberal, unembarrassed use of tonality, Corigliano's inclusive sensibility has led him to also employ extended instrumental techniques, microtones, and elements of minimalism and serialism (sometimes in a parodistic context); more recently he has incorporated live electronics into his music. The orchestra is clearly Corigliano's native medium and the ensemble for which he has written his most compelling works. He has demonstrated an especial interest in the concerto; in his concerti for piano (1968), oboe (1975), clarinet (1977), flute (1981), and guitar (1993), Corigliano both approaches the relationship between soloist and orchestra from a fresh perspective and makes notably creative use of the instrumental resources at hand. The *Symphony No. 1* (1990), written in response to the AIDS crisis, is remarkable for its effective alchemy of intensely personal associations and musical potency; in 1991, it was awarded the Grawemeyer Award, the most lucrative prize in the world of contemporary classical music.

On an occasional basis since the 1980s, Corigliano has lent his abilities to producing film music of exceptional interest. His score for Ken Russell's *Altered States* (1980) was nominated for an Academy Award; nearly two decades later, he took home the Oscar for his score to François Girard's *The Red Violin* (1998). Though Corigliano's catalogue of chamber music remains relatively slender, works such as the Grammy-winning *String Quartet* (1995) and *Chiaroscuro* (1997) for two pianos suggest an increasing interest in writing for smaller forces.

The composer's affinity for the voice is at once evident in numerous vocal and choral works like the "memory play in the form of an oratorio" *Dylan Thomas Trilogy* (1999) and the song cycle *Tambourine Man: Seven Poems of Bob Dylan* (2000). His most ambitious work to date, the opera *The Ghosts of Versailles* (1991), has earned worldwide plaudits and, in a rare instance among contemporary operas, has enjoyed repeated productions since its premiere. *—Michael Rodman*

Overview of Works

The works of John Corigliano cover a wide range of media and ensembles, reflecting the composer's desire to create music that will reach a variety of audiences and speak to them in a musical language that holds meaning for them. On the one hand, Corigliano's orchestral works have been commissioned by the New York Philharmonic and the Chicago Symphony; on the other, his music for film has garnered acclaim as well as considerable commercial success. Unashamed to embrace "traditional" musical grammar (early reviews bore headlines like "Unfashionably Romantic" and "Highbrow Music to Hum"), Corigliano's traversal of chamber, orchestra, and stage genres has made him one of the most prolific and accessible composers to straddle the twentieth and twenty-first centuries. Corigliano's stage works, though not the most prominent aspect of his output, place Corigliano's playful historicism squarely in the spotlight. They combine disparate and often anachronistic elements together in the manner of postmodern pastiche. His first stage venture, *The Naked Carmen*, was completed in 1970. Billed as an "electric rock opera," the piece recast Bizet's favorite by drawing on Corigliano's recent experience arranging for rock albums. Two decades later, Corigliano's style received a rare stamp of approval: he premiered a new work at the Metropolitan Opera. Completed in 1991 in collaboration with librettist William Hoffman, *The Ghost of Versailles* imagines a posthumous romance between Marie Antoinette and the writer Beaumarchais (the author behind *The Barber of Seville* and *Marriage of Figaro*); the stage becomes a postmodern playground of allusions and appropriations as Beaumarchais attempts to stage a sequel to *Figaro* in a convoluted attempt to save Antoinette's life. Apart from stage works, Corigliano's oeuvre includes a number of vocal works, including some settings in the early 1970s of poems and translations by Richard Wilbur (*L'invitation au voyage*, *A Black November Turkey*), as well as a trio of choral pieces on texts by Dylan Thomas completed in 1976 and later turned into an oratorio in 1999. The following year saw the premiere of *Mr. Tambourine Man: Seven Poems of Bob Dylan*. Instrumental chamber works form a small but significant portion of his output as well, including a bassoon quartet (*How Like Pellucid Statues, Daddy*, 1994), a piece for brass ensemble (*Antiphon*, 1994), a piece for two microtonally tuned pianos (*Chiaroscuro*, 1997), and, most notably, the Grammy-winning *String Quartet* (1996). Corigliano's film scores (*Altered States*, 1981; *The Red Violin*, 1997) have received numerous awards as well. Orchestral music figures most prominently in Corigliano's work, including a trio of concertos for woodwind and orchestra (oboe concerto, 1975; clarinet concerto, 1977; *Pied Piper Fantasy for flute and orchestra*, 1982), as well as a number of overtures and fanfares. The weightiest of his orchestral works, however, is his *Symphony No. 1* from 1989. The work's first three movements memorialize, in turn, three of the composer's friends who had succumbed to AIDS; the fourth movement recalls all three before falling silent. *—Jeremy Grimshaw*

Recommended:

- ○ **John Corigliano** / L. L. Smith (cond.), Harth (cond.), Tocco, Louisville Orch. / 2001 / First Edition 2
- ○ **Corigliano: Symphony 2 & The Mannheim Rocket** / Storgaards (cond.), Helsinki PO / Ondine 1039
- ○ **The Red Violin (Original Motion Picture Soundtrack)** / Salonen (cond.), J. Bell, London PO / 1999 / Sony 63010
- ○ **John Corigliano: Creations & others** / Werthen (cond.), I Fiamminghi / Telarc 80421

SYMPHONIC

Symphony No. 1 (1988–1989)

John Corigliano completed his *Symphony No. 1* during his tenure as composer-in-residence for the Chicago Symphony Orchestra (1987 to 1990). Written in response to the AIDS epidemic, the work is as deeply personal as it is socially urgent: each of the first three movements eulogizes a close friend of the composer that died of AIDS.

The first movement (Apologue: "Of Rage and Remembrance") mourns the passing of a concert pianist. It begins rather ruthlessly, with the strike of the anvil and a shriek from the strings. A passage of stark orchestrational contrasts—ethereal strings, blaring brass, fitful percussion—eventually settles down, and from offstage, faintly, is heard a piano. It plays a tango by Isaac Albéniz that, in this context, transmits an ineffable mixture of irony, nostalgia, and melancholy. The ghostly piano fades in and out of the kaleidoscopic texture, which remains continually undecided between consolation and fury.

The second movement also begins with a series of jarring, percussive outbursts. Labeled a Tarantella, it is dedicated to a music executive and amateur pianist (who, incidentally, had also been the dedicatee of the final Tarantella of Corigliano's *Gazebo Dances* from years before). According to the composer, the second movement attempts to portray musically the alternating moments of dementia and clarity that his dying friend suffered. Fittingly, moments of stasis and calm are juxtaposed and overlapped with frenzied dances and foreboding brass and percussion figures. In one particularly dark moment, a sort of canon begins between the bass drum, contrabassoon, and tuba before the upper choirs join in a chaotic and cathartic dance. The schizophrenic movement ends with a grotesque scene of frantic percussion, brass glissandi, and finally, a vocalized shout from the players.

The third movement, subtitled "Giulio's Song," is much more emotionally lucid: a soft and austere background of strings (perhaps recalling the "silent druids" of Ives' *Unanswered Question*) set in relief the lush melody of the solo cello. A memorial to a cellist friend, Corigliano took melodies from an old tape recording of himself and his friend improvising, and incorporated them into the extended cello solo. The solo line takes place above a dodecaphonic chaconne, and also incorporates melodies from Corigliano's earlier settings of eulogies written by poet William Hoffman. Even here, however, remembrance finally cedes to rage, as the movement ends with a relentless crescendo of brass and percussion.

The final movement recalls all three friends: the faint tango from the phantom piano of the first movement; the struggle for mental clarity found in the second; and the plaintive cello from the third. The piece ends as the texture gradually thins out, finally leaving the cello on a sustained A that fades imperceptibly into silence.

Perhaps due in part to the social significance of *Symphony No. 1*, it was performed by nearly 100 symphonies worldwide within a decade. It also received the coveted Grawemeyer Award, and the recording by the Chicago Symphony won two Grammys. Corigliano reused some material from the *Symphony No. 1* in creating his later *Of Rage and Remembrance*. *—Jeremy Grimshaw*

Recommended:

- ○ **Corigliano: Symphony 1** / Barenboim (cond.), Hough, Sharp, Chicago SO / Erato 45601
- ○ **Of Rage And Remembrance** / L. Slatkin (cond.), Orkis, Garlick, Hardy, National SO / 1996 / RCA 68450

FILM MUSIC

Altered States (1980)

John Corigliano obtained an Oscar nomination for this, his first film score, an apt aural mirror of the movie's hallucinogenic imagery. *Altered States* is Ken Russell's treatment of a Paddy Chayevsky novel about a scientist whose experiments with mind-altering drugs and sensory deprivation lead to physical evolutionary regression—part Carlos Castañeda, part King Kong in miniature.

Corigliano didn't "go Hollywood" for this score; with one exception, the music shares the style of the concert works he'd been writing in the 1970s: timbrally vibrant, dramatic in its surges and contrasts, with liberal use of savage percussion, microtones, and harmonics. The exception is the love theme, an honestly Romantic melody that Corigliano restricts to a very small scale. It's a wistful, uncertain theme usually played by only a very few instruments; woodwind solos introduce it and sustain it, and when Corigliano does employ masses of instruments, it's generally to give the music a darker, more tragic coloring. Most notable is a version of the love theme for piano, violin, and cello, where it becomes a quiet, nostalgic waltz that would be right at home in the Tchaikovsky *Piano Trio*.

More typical are the segments for the hallucination and transformation scenes, which employ buzzing, howling effects reminiscent of Penderecki, Ligeti, and Xenakis. All the sounds are produced orchestrally, although Corigliano did sometimes manipulate them electronically in the studio. *—James Reel*

Recommended:

- ○ **Corigliano: Altered States** / C. Keene, Orch. / RCA Victor 3983

KEYBOARD

Gazebo Dances for piano, 4 hands (1972)

John Corigliano first conceived *Gazebo Dances* for piano, four hands. It did not receive its title, however, until he had arranged the piece for both orchestra and concert band in 1973. Each movement has a separate dedication: I. Overture, to Rose Corigliano and Etta Feinberg (both pianists); II. Waltz, to John Ardoin (a music critic); III. Adagio, to Heida Hermanns; IV. Tarantella, to Jack Romann and Christian Steiner.

Corigliano's title, *Gazebo Dances*, is derived from the dance music played by bands in New England country towns. These groups usually play in pavilions, or gazebos, while the public listens and dances. Three of the four movements refer to traditional types of pieces both in title and in style.

The overture, called "Rossini-like" by the composer, exhibits the contrasting moods and rhythmic buildup we associate with the Italian opera composer. Jazz elements are clear from the beginning, as are dance rhythms, suggested by the title of the piece. Aggressive chords open the overture then give way to a more tuneful segment. Repeated notes begin dominating the movement in the middle section and continue through to the end, which includes a brief reference to the initial tuneful passage that rounds out the structure.

Corigliano described the waltz movement as "peg-legged," no doubt because of its irregular accents. Unlike a genuine waltz, the stress is not always on the first beat of the 3/4 measure. Highly sectionalized and often hesitant in mood, the movement ends very quietly.

The longest movement in performance, the Adagio opens with repeated chords that help create the illusion of sustained melody. Slow and haunting, the opening theme dissolves as a more linear, double-note idea injects the music with more life, punctuated by deep bass notes. Gradually, the piece thickens as both the dynamic and dissonance increase. The tension is released as the music suddenly halts, after which bright chords descend from the highest register. Slowly and hesitantly, the linear section begins again and brings the movement to a close.

The Tarantella begins with a trochaic figure that soon accompanies the bouncy and rising main theme of this ABABA-form movement, the shortest of the four. The contrasting B section features deep bass thunder as a repeated octave figure begins in the highest register. The first return of the A material is nearly literal, while the first return of section B begins with a new idea. Corigliano drastically thickens the last A section, which closes with wild trills. Segments of this Tarantella appear in the Tarantella movement of Corigliano's *Symphony No. 1*.

Corigliano's Tarantella movement became tragically portentous. The tarantella has been believed, incorrectly, to be the cure for the insanity resulting from a tarantula bite (it is actually a courtship dance), because both the spider and the dance derive their names from the town of Taranto, in Southern Italy. One of the dedicatees of this movement of *Gazebo Dances* became insane because of AIDS dementia. *—John Palmer*

Recommended:

- ○ **John Corigliano** / L. L. Smith (cond.), Louisville Orch. / 2001 / First Edition 2

OPERA

Ghosts of Versailles (1991)

John Corigliano's *The Ghosts of Versailles* was commissioned by the Metropolitan Opera to mark the company's centenary. With a libretto by William M. Hoffman, the work was billed as a grand opera buffa in two acts. The world premiere took place at the Met in New York City on December 19, 1991. Among the cast were a number of opera superstars, including Teresa Stratas as Marie Antoinette, Renée Fleming as Rosina, Håkan Hagegård as Beaumarchais, and Marilyn Horne as Samira. Set and costume designs were by James Conklin and the performance was conducted by James Levine.

Hoffman's book for *The Ghosts of Versailles* was suggested by *La mère coupable* (1792), the third play in Pierre Beaumarchais' Figaro trilogy. Ghosts from the time of Louis XVI gather in Marie Antoinette's theater in the palace at Versailles. The ghost of Beaumarchais is in love with the ghost of Marie Antoinette, who is still miserable because of her execution 200 years earlier and is not interested in the playwright. Beaumarchais intends to cheer her up with a performance of a new theater piece entitled *A Figaro for Antonia*, enabling him to change history by saving the Queen from death. Antoinette comes to appreciate Beaumarchais' love for her and, instead of escaping her previous fate, elects to let history take its course, preferring Beaumarchais' love in the present to an unknown past.

Hoffman and Corigliano create three planes of action in *The Ghosts of Versailles*. The first of these is what Hoffman refers to as the ghosts' "world of eternity." The second is the world of the stage, represented by the ghosts' performance of the play, and the third is the world of history, inhabited by actual, historical mortals. The creators call for contrasting costumes between the ghosts watching the play and those performing, thus drawing a clear line between those on the stage and those on the stage-within-a-stage encompassed by Beaumarchais' *A Figaro for Antonia*. The historical plane intersects with the other planes only at the end, when the historical Antoinette is executed while those in the play-within-a-play escape to London in a balloon and the ghosts of Antoinette and Beaumarchais walk off into eternity.

The musical interest of the work lies largely in how Corigliano creates the proper historical contrasts between the ghost world, which is situated in the present day, and the ghosts' play, which takes place in the eighteenth century. For the pit orchestra Corigliano assembles a large group, including three flutes with piccolo, three oboes with English horn, four clarinets with bass clarinet, three bassoons with contrabassoon, four horns, four trumpets, three trombones, tuba, percussion, harp, piano, synthesizer, and strings. The onstage ensemble, meant to accompany Beaumarchais' play, is much smaller and calls for instruments associated with the period, including a harpsichord, mandolin, guitar, harp, violin, viola, three cellos, and two double basses. In *The Ghosts of Versailles*, Corigliano found an operatic story perfectly suited to the retrospective, eclectic spirit of today's music, and he ended up with one of contemporary opera's great successes. *—John Palmer*

Synopsis:

Act One: In Marie Antoinette's private theater in Versailles; the present Ghosts of members of the court during the reign of Louis XVI appear in the theater. King Louis enters and tells those assembled that a commoner is courting his wife, Marie Antoinette. However, this does not bother him. The bored ghosts perk up when they learn a new play by Beaumarchais will be staged. Beaumarchais enters and tells Marie Antoinette he is in love with her. Still tormented by memories of her horrible execution, Antoinette cannot be bothered with Beaumarchais, who hopes to cheer her up with a performance of his new play, *A Figaro for Antonia.*

A Figaro for Antonia opens with creditors and angry men in pursuit of Figaro. After he eludes them he explains the situation ("They wish they could kill me") and describes his past ("Diplomat, acrobat, teacher of etiquette"). This turns out to be a Prologue, which is warmly applauded, after which Beaumarchais announces that, with the aid of the Queen's diamond necklace, he will be able to change the past, preventing the French revolution and allowing the Queen to avoid her grisly death. Beaumarchais then sets the scene. The first act begins in 1793. Count Almaviva, the ambassador from Spain, plans to attend a party that night at the Turkish embassy, where he will sell the Queen's necklace to the English ambassador. (At this point, Louis XVI tells Beaumarchais to stop, but the playwright ignores him.) We learn that Rosina, Almaviva's wife, and her husband are separated because she has had a baby by Cherubino. Figaro and his wife, Susanna, will also appear. Léon, the son of Rosina and Cherubino, and Florestine, an illegitimate daughter of the Count, are in love. Almaviva, however, has forbidden them to marry and has promised Florestine to Bégearss, who we learn is the villain.

As the action begins, Figaro tells Almaviva that Bégearss is a spy working for the revolutionaries. Almaviva does not believe Figaro and fires him on the spot. Bégearss and his servant, Wilhelm, enter and speak with Almaviva. Figaro listens secretly to them and learns that Almaviva plans to sell the Queen's necklace that night at the Turkish embassy. Rosina enters and pleads with Almaviva to be kinder to her son, but he ignores her. As Rosina reminisces about her affair with Cherubino, Beaumarchais and the Queen join her in singing about love. The King is angered by the way Beaumarchais and the Queen become close on the stage, and he stabs Beaumarchais with his sword. Because Beaumarchais is a ghost, he does not die. Once everyone assembled realizes this, they all begin stabbing each other gleefully.

The scene changes to the Turkish embassy. Rosina and Susanna beg Alamaviva not to sell the necklace as Bégearss and Wilhelm wait to arrest Almaviva. Samira, a Turkish singer, enters and interrupts the transaction. Figaro, disguised as one of Samira's dancing girls, snatches the necklace from Almaviva and manages to escape, although his identity is discovered.

Act Two. As the ghosts debate whether or not Beaumarchais can alter the past, the onstage action continues. Almaviva, Rosina, Susanna, and Florestine wait for Figaro. Once Figaro shows up, he deviates from Beaumarchais's script and refuses to return the necklace. His plan is to sell it instead and to use the money to help the Almavivas escape, for they are more valuable than the Queen. Beaumarchais now stops the action and decides to enter the play himself to set things right. Susanna and Rosina sing a duet, and Figaro returns once again, but this time he is followed by Beaumarchais, who forces him and Susanna to watch a reenactment of Marie Antoinette's trial. Figaro is annoyed at this unfair course of events but is compelled to follow along. Next, on a Paris street, Bégearss incites a gang of women to crash a ball Almaviva is giving that evening.

The next scene is set at Almaviva's ball. Florestine is in despair because her father will not allow Léon into the ball. Léon shows up anyway, and he and Rosina sing of their mutual love. Afterward, Rosina again pleads with her father to let her marry Léon, but they are interrupted by Bégearss and his revolutionary ladies, who demand the Queen's necklace from Almaviva. To save Almaviva, Figaro gives Bégearss the necklace, but Bégearss still has the Almavivas taken to prison because Almaviva now will not allow him to marry Florestine. They disappear before Beaumarchais can help them, leaving Beaumarchais and Figaro alone.

The scene changes to a prison. The Almavivas are in a cell next to Marie Antoinette's. Rosina and Almaviva reconcile. Beaumarchais and Figaro enter and attempt to rescue them, but they discover that Wilhelm has the only key to the cells. Rosina pretends to be sick, and when Wilhelm enters the cell the others jump on him and take his keys. Bégearss arrives before they can escape, has Wilhelm arrested, and again demands Florestine's hand in marriage. Figaro and Wilhelm expose Bégearss as a spy and reveal that he has kept the necklace for himself instead of selling it and giving the money to the poor, as he said he had done. As the revolutionaries drag off Bégearss, the Almavivas escape, planning to go to America. Beaumarchais is left with the necklace and the keys to Antoinette's cell, which he starts to open. Antoinette, however, tells him not to change the past, for it will alter the present, and she does not want to take the chance of losing the love he has for her now. The Queen, with Beaumarchais, watches her own execution, and then the two exit. *—John Palmer*

William Cornysh

b. ca. 1470, England [?], **d.** Sep. 10, 1523, Hylden Manor, Kent, England

Composer

The *Eton Choirbook*, compiled for liturgical use at Eton College around 1500, provides a unique view of English music at the turn of the sixteenth century; no other comparable repertoire source for this time has survived the depredations of the English Reformation. Among the 25 choice composers represented stands the name of William Cornysh, contributing eight pieces to this national anthology of devotional music. He also composed 13 of the secular part songs in a 1520 anthology of music known as *Henry VIII's Songbook*, after its collector and principal contributor. Clearly Cornysh held the respect of King and Church alike; very little straightforward information about his life, however, survives. In fact, recent scholarship suggests that these two repertoires may be the work of two separate individuals: William Cornysh the elder, composer of the mature *Eton Choirbook* church music, and William Cornysh the younger (possibly his son), actor, singer, and courtier.

A small number of early documents list payments to a William Cornysh for compositions, and for participation in courtly dramas and "disguysings," the earliest dating from 1494. He spent time in prison starting in 1502, producing a pamphlet of versified defenses while incarcerated. Apparently his term was brief, as his 1501 appointment as a Gentleman of the Chapel Royal was never revoked, and he was appointed Master of the Children for the Chapel establishment in 1509, a position he held until his death in 1523. Records of court dramatic presentations in 1511 and 1514 credit him with musical collaboration, and his presence leading the royal singers across the Channel in 1513 and again at 1520 during the celebrations on the field of the Cloth of Gold is well-documented. As late as June 1522, the court received a play of his, celebrating the diplomatic visit by the Holy Roman Emperor.

The surviving sacred music of "Cornysh" in the *Eton Choirbook* shares with much of that repertory a thick, melismatic texture, a noble breadth of vocal range, and a penchant for biting cross-relations and other dissonances. His splendid and popular setting of the Marian text *Salve regina* from this source exemplifies the style. Indeed, his contributions to this volume bespeak a surprising maturity of hand. In his time, however, William Cornysh Jr. (presuming that both repertoires are his) seems to have been far better known for his secular work, as a song composer, actor, playwright, and stage director, and one at the center of the Tudor court's secular culture. A song of his from *Henry VIII's Songbook*, *A Robyn, gentle Robyn*, may have been the song Shakespeare intended the clown to sing in the fourth act of *Twelfth Night*. *—Timothy Dickey*

Overview of Works

The musical contribution of William Cornysh is difficult to assess for several reasons. The most obvious complication is the suggestion that a father-and-son pair of Williams may have both composed music surviving under the name Cornysh. The surviving music, indeed, makes up two distinct groups of pieces: a small number of sacred works, almost all contained in a single manuscript (*The Eton Choirbook*), and a group of 15 secular songs from the court of Henry VIII, some decades later. Furthermore, a considerable variety of musical style is evident in both. The composer of late fifteenth century church music and the master of Henry VIII's court entertainments—singer, composer, actor, playwright, and stage director—both demonstrate a consummate facility in the musical art.

The Cornysh works in *The Eton Choirbook* present a mature style comparable to that of his contemporary Robert Fayrfax (though often more audacious). A rich, five-voiced texture, covering a vast span of musical space, alternates with contrasting thinner textures for groups of solo singers. Individual vocal lines contain dazzling rhythmic complexities, and often combine to produce biting dissonances. Cornysh's setting of the *Magnificat*, surviving in the *Caius Choirbook*, shares these characteristics with the Salve Regina and Stabat Mater in *Eton*. However, the *Ave Maria Mater Dei* and *Gaude Virgo Mater Christi*, also in *Eton*, show a more restrained side of Cornysh's style, both using only four voices with a simpler style that approaches homophony at times.

The same composer (or his son) contributed heavily to the secular entertainments at Henry VIII's court. Several songbooks (one owned by Henry himself, who also dabbled in song composition) preserve vernacular songs attributed to Cornysh. Once again, a versatility of procedure characterizes this repertory. Several pieces, such as *And I were a maiden*, *You and I and Amyas*, and the double-entendre-rich *Blow thy horn, hunter*, appear in a simple style, principally chordal. Other songs, several in French, the courtly language, present a more "refined" polyphonic idiom (such as his *Adew mes amours*). Two pieces—*A robyn, gentle robyn* and *My love sche morneth*—though sounding a more simple style, hide canonic derivation within their structure. Finally, some jaunty, dance-inspired works such as *Trolly lolly lolly lo* and *Hoyda, hoyda, jolly Rutterkin* even approach the most current Parisian styles of the 1520s. —*Timothy Dickey*

Recommended:

○ **Cornysh: Stabat Mater** / P. Phillips, Tallis Scholars / 2001 / Gimell 14

Alfred Cortot

b. Sep. 26, 1877, Nyon, Switzerland, **d.** Jun. 15, 1962, Lausanne, France
Pianist

Pianist Alfred Denis Cortot's father was French and his mother Swiss. He studied at the Paris Conservatory with Decambes and others, winning first prize in piano in 1896. He made his debut the same year in Beethoven's *Third Piano Concerto.* Soon he became widely acclaimed as a performer of Beethoven concertos, appearing as a soloist in two prominent Parisian concert series. In 1898 he went to Bayreuth to study Wagner's music and was hired as a choral coach and then as an assistant conductor. Cortot brought Wagner to Paris, leading the first Paris performance of *Götterdämmerung* (May 1902), and a remarkable performance of *Tristan und Isolde* the next month. Also in 1902 he established his own concert series, the Association des Concerts A. Cortot. Although it lasted only two years, it did a lot towards breaking down the conservative French resistance to Wagner, particularly with a concert performance of *Parsifal*, and even the first French performances of Beethoven's *Missa Solemnis* and Brahms' *Requiem.* He also served contemporary French music by premiering works of Roussel, Magnard, and others.

In 1904 he became the conductor of the Concerts Populaires at Lille, and the following year he joined with cellist Pablo Casals and violinist Jacques Thibaud to form one of the greatest of permanently established piano trios, one which became a model of its type, touring frequently. This drew him back to the piano, which he had never given up despite his fame as a conductor. In 1907 he joined the faculty of the Paris Conservatory, teaching piano, but remained very active as a piano soloist and chamber music player. He gave up that position in 1917, feeling that his busy concert schedule had made it impossible to devote sufficient uninterrupted periods to teaching. In 1919 he founded the Ecole Normale de Musique, assembling a faculty of famous musicians. As the director, he taught a summer course in interpretation, which became famous. He continued a career performing piano around the world, including lecture recitals, and also guest conducted many orchestras. He also continued to premiere new French piano music. Cortot was a skillful and scholarly editor of great piano music, famous for his editions of most of Chopin's piano music. Cortot's teacher was a student of Chopin, and the grace of his Chopin performances, especially, remains breathtaking and should be recommended to all students of the piano; he also had a remarkable way with the music of Robert Schumann.

In 1943 Cortot founded the Chamber Music Society of the Paris Conservatory Concerts. However, his admiration for German culture served him ill when Germany occupied France between from 1940 to 1944, and he appeared to cooperate with them willingly. This led to his being shunned after the war both in France and elsewhere. By the time he returned to the concert stage, some years later, it was clear that his memory was failing. His main legacy remains in the records he made in the 1920s and 1930s. In addition, he was an avid collector and amassed, among other items, a large quantity of autograph scores and printed music. After his death, this collection was divided among several important libraries and universities; it remains an interesting view into the mind of a musician who was both a living link to Romantic Paris and a key figure of the twentieth century. —*Joseph Stevenson*

Recommended:

○ **Victor Recordings of 1919–1926** / Cortot / Pearl 9386

○ **Chopin: Preludes & Impromptus** / Cortot / EMI 61050

○ **Great Pianists: Alfred Cortot** / Munch, Ronald (conds.), Cortot, London PO / 2000 / Naxos 110613

○ **Alfred Cortot Plays French Concertos** / Barbirolli, Munch (conds.), Cortot, / Pearl 9491

○ **Alfred Cortot** / Cortot / 1999 / Philips 456751

Fiorenza Cossotto

b. Apr. 22, 1935, Crescentino, Italy
Mezzo-Soprano

While best known for the fiery, scenery-chewing Verdi roles such as Azucena, Amneris, Lady Macbeth, and Eboli, Fiorenza Cossotto was also a prominent performer of bel canto parts such as Rosina in Rossini's *Barbiere*, Leonora in *La favorita*, and Adalgisa in *Norma.* Such large and powerful mezzo voices, particularly with a secure top, are rare compared to the lyric mezzo, and from the late 1960s through the early 1980s, she was *the* Verdi mezzo, the successor to Simionato and the predecessor to Zajick.

After studying at the Turin Conservatory, she graduated in 1956 and then joined the training school of La Scala in Milan. She made her operatic debut as Sister Matilde in the world premiere of Poulenc's *The Dialogues of the Carmelites* in 1957. Her international debut was at the 1958 Wexford Festival as Giovanna Seymour in Donizetti's *Anna Bolena.* Her Covent Garden debut was in 1959 as Neris in Cherubini's *Medée*, with Callas in the title role. A 1961 performance of the lead in *La favorita* at La Scala led to wider fame and she made her Chicago debut in the same role in 1964 and as Amneris at the Met in 1968. She is married to bass singer Ivo Vinco. Among her recordings, the Amneris on EMI under Muti (EMI CDS7 47271–8) captures the fire and vigor of her performances. —*Ann Feeney*

Recommended:

○ **Verdi: Aida** / Muti (cond.), Domingo, Caballe, Ghiaurov, Cossotto, New Philharmonia / 2001 / EMI 67617

○ **Verdi: Il Trovatore** / Mehta (cond.), McCarthy, Price, Domingo, Milnes, Cossotto, New Philharmonia / 1998 / RCA 7432139504

Ileana Cotrubas

b. Jun. 9, 1939, Galati, Romania
Soprano

Ileana Cotrubas was one of the most expressive singing actresses of her era. She specialized in operatic roles calling for a degree of pathos, such as Violetta, Ilia in *Idomeneo*, Mimì, Gilda, and Mélisande, but she also had a gift for comedy that was well expressed in roles such as Susanna in *Le nozze di Figaro*, Norina in *Don Pasquale*, or Adina in *L'elisir d'Amore.* She held strong beliefs about staging, and more than once caused controversy by walking out of a production which she believed was inappropriate for the opera in question. Her voice and vocal production, too, were somewhat controversial: while her admirers praised it for the undefinable quality of "morbidezza" and for an almost childlike tone of vulnerability, others found it saccharine. Some listeners, too, found her audible breathing to be distracting. While the majority of her career was in opera, she also sang sacred music, particularly Mozart, and gave the occasional lieder recital.

Her family was a musical one, and she began her own singing career when she joined the Children's Chorus of Radio Romania at the age of nine, and by the age of 11 she had graduated to solo parts. Her family moved to Bucharest in 1952, and she enrolled at the Scoala Speciala de Musica, a musical training academy for children. In 1958, she continued her studies at the Ciprian Porumbescu Conservatory. In 1964, she made her operatic debut at the Bucharest Opera as Yniold in *Pelléas et Mélisande*, a role sung either by a boy soprano or an adult lyric soprano, and continued there, singing lyric and coloratura roles such as Gilda in *Rigoletto*, Oscar in *Un ballo in maschera*, Blonde in *The Abduction from the Seraglio*, and even Siebel in *Faust.* In 1965, she won the first prize at the International Singing Competition in Hertogenbosch, Holland, followed by similar success at the 1966 Radio Competition in Munich. She made her debut in England at the Glyndebourne Festival in 1969, singing Mélisande, and her Covent Garden debut in 1970 as Tatyana in *Eugene Onegin.* Throughout her career, she maintained close ties with both the Festival and Covent Garden, and maintained a home in Kent, England. In 1970, she signed a non-exclusive three-year contract with the Vienna State Opera, singing there and also making her U.S. debut at the Lyric Opera of Chicago as Mimì. In 1975, she made her La Scala debut on extremely brief notice, replacing an ill Mirella Freni as Mimì (a role that has been a calling card for both sopranos), and in 1977, made her Met debut in the same role. In 1981, she was named a Kammersangerin by the Austrian government. In 1989, she announced her retirement, and focused her energies on teaching. Her best-known pupil is Angela Gheorghiu, her Romanian compatriot.

In comic opera, her Adina in *L'elisir d'Amore* is excellent (Sony M2K 79210), and she also made a lovely and touching Violetta in *La traviata* (Deutsche Grammophon 35417). She also made a fine recital CD on Sony (SMK 60783), which features her in both her core repertoire and some roles she never sang on stage. —*Ann Feeney*

Recommended:

○ **Donizetti: L'elisir d'Amore** / Pritchard (cond.), Domingo, Cotrubas, Wixell, Evans, Royal Opera House Orch. / 1977 / CBS 34585

○ **Verdr: La Traviata** / C. Kleiber (cond.), Domingo, Milnes, Cotrubas, Foiani, Bavarian State Orch. / 1977 / DG 415132

○ **Famous Opera Arias** / Cotrubas, etc. / 1998 / Sony 60783

François Couperin

b. Nov. 10, 1668, Paris, France, **d.** Sep. 11, 1733, Paris, France
Composer: Keyboard, Chamber Music, Vocal

François Couperin was the most important member of the illustrious Couperin family and was one of the leading composers of the French Baroque era. He is best known for his harpsichord works, all of which are found in the collection of more than 220 pieces entitled *Pièces de clavecin*, consisting of four books. His music showed the influence of Lully and incorporated elements from the Italian school. Indeed, both these sources would be acknowledged by Couperin himself in two chamber works, *Apothéose de Corelli* (1724) and *Apothéose de Lully* (1725). Moreover, he successfully integrated the French and Italian styles in his *Les goûts réunis ou nouveaux concerts* (1724), a collection of chamber compositions for unspecified instruments. Many of his works were lost to posterity, as none of his original manuscripts has survived.

Couperin was born in Paris on November 10, 1668. His father, Charles, was an organist, and young François' early musical training probably came from him. Only child François and his mother were reasonably well cared for following Charles' death (probably in 1679), in part because of the kindness of Jacques Thomelin, organist at Saint-Jacques de la Boucherie, who looked after the young boy and instructed him in music.

Couperin became the organist at Saint-Gervais at age 17. In 1689, four years later, he married Marie-Anne Ansault, daughter of a wine merchant who had many relatives in other business endeavors. The following year, he published his so-called "organ masses," known as *Pièces d'orgue*, comprising two masses (*Messe des Paroisses* and *Messe des Couvents*) and several smaller pieces.

It was around this time that the composer came under the sway of the Italian school. He would display this influence in several chamber works he wrote in 1692 that he called *sonades*, a name that is a Gallic version of "sonata."

On December 26, 1693, Couperin was appointed organist at the Royal Chapel by King Louis XIV, sharing the post with Buterne, Nivers, and Lebègue, and performing his duties only in the first quarter of each year. He maintained his position at Saint-Gervais for the other three-quarters of the year. He also taught the Duke of Burgundy on harpsichord and six other princes and princesses. The composer would later write an important treatise on playing the harpsichord entitled, *L'Art de toucher le clavecin*.

Couperin wrote a fair amount of sacred non-liturgical vocal music for the Royal Chapel. Beginning around 1697, he wrote a series of motets, completed in 1702. They include *Motet Saint-Barthélemy*, *Motet de Sainte-Anne*, and *Motet de Saint-Augustin*.

In the early part of the eighteenth century, Couperin began composing a large number of works for the harpsichord, which would appear in the *Premier Livre* from the *Pièces de clavecin* in 1713. The Second Book was published in 1717, and the final two came in 1722 and 1730.

There is evidence that Couperin also found time for concerts in the early part of the eighteenth century in Versailles and other nearby locales. Actually, relatively is known about Couperin's life from about 1700 onward. There is record of his renting a country home in 1710 at Saint-Germain-en-Laye, confirming the view he was financially secure. In 1719, Couperin became harpsichordist to King Louis XV, a position he most probably had held in all but title for a number of years. By this time, he was recognized as the leading composer in France and the greatest exponent of organ and harpsichord teaching as well. Couperin died on September 11, 1733. *—Robert Cummings*

KEYBOARD

Pièces de clavecin

François Couperin, known as "Le Grand," was one of the leading French composers, an influential teacher, and harpsichordist to King Louis XIV (1638–1715). His keyboard works are unlike those of the other celebrated musicians resident at the king's palace in Versailles, and reflect Couperin's determination to bring international influences to bear on the somewhat rigid artistic conventions of the French court.

The four books of *Pièces de Clavecin* comprise 220 fairly short single-movement works arranged in 27 groups (or "ordres"). They include dance forms, character pieces, portraits, and impressionistic sketches, including representations of natural sounds. Many have descriptive titles. Their variety and lively wit make them one of the most important collections of eighteenth century keyboard music and, together with Couperin's treatise on interpretation, *L'Art de toucher le clavecin* (the art of playing the harpsichord) are an invaluable source of information on the keyboard styles of the French Baroque. As with other of his works, Couperin approved the performance of some *Pièces* (e.g., those in Book II) on instruments other than the harpsichord. No autograph manuscripts of Couperin's harpsichord works survive. The printed versions that appeared from 1713 to 1730 were later corrected by the composer and are now treasured as fine examples of classical music engraving. Nevertheless, certain problems remain.

Couperin used six sets of clefs and numerous special signs. Indications of speed and nuance—"sans lenteur," "tendrement," etc.,—are plentiful. However, later editions tended to contain many errors, all of which makes playing from early printings difficult. The first edition in conventional keyboard notation, edited by Johannes Brahms and Friedrich Chrysander, was published in 1888. Despite Chrysander's disconcerting remark in his preface that Couperin "is the first great composer for the pianoforte known in the history of music," this edition is probably as "complete and faithful" as Chrysander says it is. Vols. 1 and 2 and parts of Vols. 3 and 4 were reprinted by Dover Publications, New York, in 1988.

Couperin's meticulously annotated tables of signed ornaments and instructions on their correct performance enhance the value of the *Pièces*, and provides a unique insight by the composer himself into the keyboard style of the French Baroque. Unfortunately Couperin's aims were not always realized. In a preface to the *Pièces de Clavecin* Couperin observes, "I am always astonished, after the pains I have taken to indicate the appropriate ornaments for my pieces…to hear persons who have learnt them without heeding my instructions."

Anyone expecting a set of academic studies is in for an agreeable surprise: the pieces are full of originality and good humor. Some have fanciful titles and it is difficult not to imagine Couperin deriving a certain satisfaction from such baffling ones as "La prude" (the prude), "La diligente" (the diligent one), "Le gazoüillement" (the warbling one), "Les baricades mistérieuses" (the mysterious barricades), and "La fringante" (the frisky one). *—Roy Brewer*

Recommended:

○ **François Couperin: Premier livre de Pièces de clavecin** / Rousset / HM 90145052

L'Art de toucher le Clavecin

François Couperin was perhaps one of the most important composers of keyboard music in the Baroque era. Along with four books of harpsichord pieces, Couperin published a theoretical treatise on harpsichord playing, *L'Art de toucher le clavecin*, in two editions in 1716 and 1717. In the treatise, Couperin also included some instructional pieces: one allemande and a series of eight preludes. The allemande is a two-part invention largely comprised of canonic imitation. The preludes, quasi-improvisatory pieces, represent some of Couperin's best efforts with the form and suggest, in their balance and complexity, the preludes of J.S. Bach. *Prelude No. 1 in C major* consists of sequences of chords in suspension, as does *Prelude No. 2 in D minor*. *Prelude No. 3* is a polyphonic courante in G minor; the fourth, in the key of F, is similar to *Preludes No. 1* and *No. 2* in its use of suspensions. *Prelude No. 5* is perhaps the most fluid and free of the eight, and is in the key of A major. *Prelude No. 6* is an invention in B minor in which the complexity of the counterpoint creates metric displacement and dissolves the bar line. *Prelude No. 7 in B flat major* is highly ornamented and chromatic, while the final *Prelude No. 8 in E minor* is comprised of sequential patterns and ornate figuration. Couperin intended his preludes as warm-up exercises for his own music: a performer could use one of the preludes as preparatory tool, selecting and playing the appropriate prelude in the appropriate key before performing other works by Couperin in the same key. *—Alexander Carpenter*

Recommended:

○ **Couperin: Deuxième livre de Pièces de clavecin** / Rousset / HM 901447

CHAMBER MUSIC

L'Apothéose de Lully

Throughout the seventeenth century, the musical world in France was dominated by the argument that raged over the conflicting merits of the French and Italian styles. Following the death of Lully in 1687, some French composers began to seek to reconcile the stylistic argument. The catalyst for this new, pragmatic approach was the publication of the trio sonatas of Arcangelo Corelli, in Rome between 1681 and 1695. Enormously influential, these seminal works swept through Europe like wildfire. Among those in France to succumb to the Corellian conquest was the young François Couperin, who was referred to by one French pedagogue as the "passionate servant of the Italian." In fact, while never denying the Italian style, Couperin's elegant, refined music constantly reminds the listener of his nationality. In his mature years, Couperin would consciously seek a synthesis of the two styles, or "Goûts" (tastes), a development which would be consummated in two late chamber works, the *Apothéoses* dedicated respectively to the two great champions of the opposing styles, Lully and Corelli. The *Lully* was published in 1725, a year after the *Corelli Apotheosis*. It is scored in trio sonata format for two violins and basso continuo (viol and harpsichord). There are 13 movements, all bearing descriptive titles that betray the programmatic nature of the work. Thus, in the opening movement one finds Lully in the Elysian fields, in grave discourse with the shades that inhabit it. Later, Couperin depicts gestures typical of those found in Lully's operas (flashing scales to depict the flight of Mercury). While never losing its elegance, the music is often full of humor, as in the movement in which Lully is elevated to Parnassus. Here, little Italianate gestures remind one that Lully, the great champion of French music, was himself Italian-born. On Parnassus, Lully and Corelli meet and are persuaded by Apollo that the reunion of French and Italian music will achieve a musical perfection hitherto unknown. After each plays an air in his own style (Lully, first violin, and Corelli, second violin) in the final movement, "The Peace of Parnassus," the Muses of Italian and French music come together to produce the desired union. *—Brian Robins*

Recommended:

○ **Couperin: Les Apothéoses** / Hesperion XX / 1997 / Auvidis Fontalis 7709

○ **Couperin: L'Apotheose de Lulli** / W. Christie, Rousset / HM 901269

Les Nations, sonatas & suites for 2 violins & continuo

Les Nations is a collection of chamber works published by François Couperin in 1726. Issued in four separate books, it was intended "for the use of music academies and concerts," according to its title heading. It contains four extended works that feature movements in the French or the Italian manner, resulting in hybrid pieces that encompass both of the then sharply opposed styles. Such reconciliation runs like an *idée fixe* throughout Couperin's life, reaching its fruition in the true fusion achieved in the *Apotheosis of Corelli* (1724) and the *Apotheosis of Lully* (1725). Early in his career Couperin fell under the spell of Corelli's enormously successful trio sonatas for two violins and continuo, which had become familiar all over Europe. During the 1690s, he composed six sonatas in the *da chiesa* (church) style, clearly influenced by those of Corelli. Three of these were taken to form the Italian part of the works that appeared as *Les Nations*. To the four Italian movements in the typical slow-fast-slow-fast pattern of the church sonata, Couperin added four sets of dances in the French style, adapting the names previously given them in three instances: *La Pucelle* became *La Françoise*, *La Visionnaire* was renamed *L'Espagnole*, and *L'Astrée* became *La Piémontoise*. To these was added another bipartite sonata, *L'Impériale*, the *da chiesa* section of which comes from a sonata possibly composed around 1715. Although these works were almost certainly intended for two violins and continuo (harpsichord and bass viol), Couperin left no precise instructions as to instrumentation. Like many chamber works of the period, they are therefore also suitable for oboes or flutes, or combinations featuring the violin, flute, and oboe. *—Brian Robins*

Recommended:

○ **François Couperin: Les Nations** / Savall (cond.), Hesperion XX / Astree 7700

Le Parnasse, ou L'Apothéose de Corelli, trio sonata ("Les Goûts réunis")

Late in his life François Couperin composed two chamber works that summed up his musical thinking on the reconciliation between French and Italian styles. It was an argument that had dominated the musical scene in France for much of the seventeenth century, and one that gained new focus with the extraordinary success of the trio sonatas of Arcangelo Corelli during the 1680s and 1690s. In his younger days Couperin had been among those unable to resist the all-pervasive triumph of Corelli's sonatas. Among the works he composed during his twenties, several sonatas for two violins and continuo show Corelli's influence to such a degree that Couperin was branded for his "Italianisms." Couperin was in fact far too individual a composer to slavishly adhere to any style, and his great achievement was to seek a reconciliation that, in the words appended to the final movement of his *Lully Apotheosis*, would "achieve a new perfection in music." This philosophy was above all articulated in that work, which appeared in 1725, and the *Apotheosis of Corelli*, published the previous year. In taking the two greatest protagonists of the opposing styles for his subject matter, Couperin was clearly laying out the philosophy which had guided his artistic career. Like its sister work, the *Corelli Apotheosis* is scored in standard trio sonata form for two violins and continuo. There are seven movements, which, as in the Lully piece, are given picturesque titles and are clearly programmatic. The first movement finds the great Italian composer at the foot of Parnassus, gravely asking the Muses to admit him. The music has a typical Corellian breadth and seriousness. He is accepted and expresses his joy in a fugal movement. In the third movement Corelli relaxes by a fountain to long, sustained notes and suspensions. After a rapid movement recalling Corelli's virtuosity, he falls asleep to a "Sommeil," a dreamlike movement typical of those found in many Italian "church sonatas" of the period. He is awakened by the Muses to another lively movement, before finally expressing his thanks in a florid and dynamic fugue. Couperin's supreme achievement in the *Corelli Apotheosis* is to pay tribute to Corelli while never for one moment allowing us to forget that he is a French composer achieving a true reunion between the two styles. *—Brian Robins*

Recommended:

○ **Musique pour les Fètes du Roy** / Savall, Hesperion XX / 1999 / Astree 8669

○ **Couperin: L'Apothéose de Lulli** / W. Christie, Rousset / HM 1951269

VOCAL

Leçons de Ténèbres, for treble voice (or 2 treble voices) & continuo (ca. 1712)

François Couperin, called "le grand" to distinguish him from other members of his illustrious musical family, was principally known as a keyboard composer. He published four large volumes of keyboard music and a learned treatise on keyboard ornamentation; J.S. Bach even knew some of Couperin's harpsichord music. Yet as one of the favored organists within the French Chapelle Royale, François Couperin also was required to compose and perform sacred music for some of the greater feasts of the liturgical year. Couperin's contemporary Delalande served the Sun King with grand motets that deployed vast choral and instrumental forces; Couperin preferred smaller forms. It is thus in the realm of the petit motet where Couperin the miniaturist shines. His three *Leçons de Ténèbres* encapsulate the extreme pathos of their *Lamentations* texts within an intimate musical space.

In Couperin's time, the Catholic Church had been singing texts from the Lamentations of Jeremiah as a solemn observance of Holy Week for many centuries. For each of three nights—Holy Wednesday, Maundy Thursday, and Good Friday—the evening service of "Tenebrae" contained three lessons from the Old Testament book of Lamentations, and concluded by plunging the church into darkness. However, advances in music and fashion had somewhat changed the nature of the service. Many of the smarter set in Paris went to the Abbey of Longchamp on the outskirts of town to hear splendid operatic singers perform the *Lessons*; the church even charged admission. Couperin apparently wrote his *Tenebrae Lessons* for this very Abbey. Unfortunately, only three of Couperin's nine lessons survive. He published these three in the mid-1710s, between his first and second keyboard volumes; his preface refers to the composition of further lessons. The three surviving lessons (two for soprano and basso continuo, the third for soprano duet) serve the liturgy of Holy Wednesday and set the first 14 chapters of Lamentations 1. Couperin preserves the Hebrew letters that begin each verse; the poetic letters point out the acrostic nature of the original poem. Each letter he then sets in a lush, melismatic style. The bulk of the text arrives in a rich mixture of restrained French recitative style and daringly chromatic Italian arioso; highly dissonant ornaments encrust the surface. The entire piece slowly builds in expressive power: Couperin extends and embellishes the "Jerusalem, convertere" that concludes each lesson; the entire third lesson blossoms into duet textures, brimming with dissonant suspensions. *—Timothy Dickey*

Recommended:

○ **Couperin: Leçons de Ténèbres** / R. Jacobs (cond.), Concerto Vocale / HM 2981133

Louis Couperin

b. ca. 1626, Chaumes, France, **d.** Aug. 29, 1661, Paris, France

Composer

The Couperin family resembles, in many ways, the Bach family, though on a smaller scale: several generations of Couperins were important figures in the history of French music. Louis Couperin was the uncle to perhaps the best-known member of the Couperin family, François, also known as François le Grand. Louis was the son of Charles Couperin, organist of Chaume, and brother to Charles, also a successful organist and father to François.

Very little is known about the early years of Louis' life, other than that he must have received excellent musical training (probably from Chambonnières), for he became an overnight success when he finally arrived in Paris around 1651. Once in Paris, he secured a job as an organist at St. Gervais and also played treble viol in the royal chapel. He was a well-known and well-respected musician in Paris, and was closely connected to many of the most important musicians in the city.

Aproximately 215 of Couperin's works survive today, although it is very likely that he composed many more. Most of his compositions are works for keyboard, and indeed Couperin is considered one of the greatest French keyboard composers of the seventeenth century. His œuvre includes a great deal of music for organ, including a number of fugues, as well as music for the harpsichord. Couperin's harpsichord music has generated the most interest over the centuries: comprised largely of short dance pieces—allemandes, courantes, gigues, sarabandes, etc.—the harpsichord music is remarkable for its intensity and sudden harmonic, rhythmic, and melodic gestures.

Some scholars have suggested that Couperin was one of the first French harpsichord composers to adopt the new basso continuo style; others have noted that his style changed from medium to medium, so that the violin music, the organ music, and the harpsichord music each reveal a different facet of the same fertile musical imagination. *—Alexander Carpenter*

Overview of Works (ca. 1650–1659)

Although the works of Louis Couperin (ca. 1626–61) have been overshadowed by those of nephew François, he was arguably the finest French keyboard composer of the seventeenth century, a man whose works fully merit comparison with those of his more famous relative. He held the post of organist at St. Gervais in Paris, a prestigious position which would subsequently remain within the Couperin family throughout the seventeenth and eighteenth centuries.

Louis Couperin's extant output consists almost entirely of keyboard music for the harpsichord or organ. The one hundred thirty-four individual pieces for harpsichord fall into three principal categories: préludes, keyboard dances, and passacailles and chaconnes. The préludes are to be played *sans mesure*, or not in strict time, thus giving them a free, improvisatory character. Dance movements include allemandes, courantes, sarabandes, and gigues, in addition to more exotic French dances such as the bransle, and older stylized dances like the pavan and galliard. The passacailles and chaconnes are more extended movements built over repeated bass patterns. All of these pieces were designed to be mixed and matched by key in order to form ad hoc performing suites; typically each of these would include a prélude followed by group of four or five dances, and finally a chaconne (or passacaille).

Most of Couperin's organ music was unknown until the middle of the twentieth century, but since then approximately 70 works for that instrument have come to light and been published, allowing for a new assessment of Couperin's contributions to that repertory. The organ works cover a wide variety of type and form, but a large number are either free fantasias or fugues which confirm their composer as a leading exponent of seventeenth century counterpoint. Additionally, there are a number of works with Latin titles; these refer to hymns and other plainsong melodies, indicating that they are realizations of these tunes to be performed alternatim with sung chant.

Couperin's music owes much to the style of his teacher Chambonnières, who in turn owes a debt to the *style brisé* of French lutenists—so called because it gains much of its rich texture from the characteristic broken chord arpeggiations. However, Couperin added to the rather self-conscious, heavily ornamented music of Chambonnières a toughness and contrapuntal rigor that gives it a new, vigorous quality. These features are particularly notable in two of Couperin's superbly structured passacailles, those in C (No. 27) and G major/minor (No. 98), where the composer builds over a large-scale architectural plan to create impressively solemn edifices. One famous work which falls outside any of the categories mentioned above is the *Tombeau de Monsieur de Blanrocher*, an expressive and moving tribute composed in memory of a lutenist.—*Brian Robins*

Recommended:

- ○ **L. Couperin: Tombeau de M. de Blancrocher** / G. Wilson / 2003 / Naxos 8555936
- ○ **L. Couperin: Les piéces de clavessin I** / Verlet / 2000 / Naive 8822
- ○ **L. Couperin: Oeuvres pour orgue** / J. W. Jansen / 2000 / Virgin 61775

Henry Cowell

b. Mar. 11, 1897, Menlo Park, CA, **d.** Dec. 10, 1965, Shady, NY

Composer: Keyboard, Chamber Music, Orchestral, Symphonic, Concerto

Of all the early twentieth century American musical revolutionaries, perhaps composer Henry Cowell wielded the most vivid and far-reaching influence. Born in 1897 to a rural California family, Cowell began to study the violin at age five, though his parents' hopes of creating a prodigy on the instrument remained unfulfilled when the lessons had to be stopped on account of the boy's poor health. After his parents' divorce in 1903, Cowell spent several years traveling around the country visiting relatives with his mother. It was during one such journey in 1908 that he began to write his own music, his first known effort at composition being an unfinished setting of Longfellow's *Golden Legend*.

Until he began musical studies with Charles Seeger at the University of California at Berkeley in 1914, Cowell remained a basically self-taught musician, as well as a young man who had never spent so much as a day in school in his life. Seeger was impressed by the young Cowell's output—over 100 compositions of varying quality by 1914—but was much more interested in the young composer's hypercreative, open-minded musical personality. Free of the often confining attitudes which govern formal musical education, Cowell had come to view any sound as musical substance with which he could work, and his early music owes more to the influence of birdsong, machine noises and folk music than it does to any knowledge of earlier masterworks. In his 1912 work *The Tides of Manaunaun*, Cowell asks the pianist to use his or her fist, palm, and forearm on the keys of the instrument's bass register to evoke massive tidal waves; thus was born the tone cluster. Cowell used this and similar techniques in many later works, which proved to be highly influential for many of the "sound mass" composers of later decades, including Penderecki, Ligeti, and numerous electronic composers.

However, Seeger felt that without structure and guidelines Cowell would remain an unskilled, if impressively inventive, musician, and he encouraged the young composer to make a rigorous study of traditional harmony and counterpoint. In 1919, at Seeger's suggestion, Cowell finished a systematic treatise on his own music entitled *New Musical Resources*, in which he discusses new musical techniques, aesthetic directions, and possible alterations to the accepted system of musical notation. Concert appearances throughout North America and Europe during the 1920s earned Cowell countless friends and enemies throughout the musical establishment. Although he had earned the respect of such luminaries as Bartók and Schoenberg, his concerts frequently caused audience riots and invoked the wrath of critics who wondered if Cowell's headstrong independence disguised a lack of true musical craftsmanship. In the *Aeolian Harp* (1923), for piano, Cowell instructs the pianist to play "inside" the piano by sweeping, scraping, strumming, and muting the strings. *The Banshee* (1925) applies indeterminacy and graphic notation with instructions for the pianist to play exclusively inside the piano while an assistant holds down the damper pedal. Playing techniques include scraping the strings with a fingernail, and pizzicato effects, all performed in the lowest registers of the instrument, yielding resonant and primarily non-pitched waves of sound.

Later music, such as the *Amerind Suite* for piano (1939) and the *26 Simultaneous Mosaics* (1964) incorporate generous helpings of indeterminacy, though from the 1930s onward, Cowell's compositional language grew increasingly tonal and rhythmically simplified. He died in 1965 after several years of serious illness. —*Blair Johnston*

KEYBOARD

Advertisement (Third Encore to Dynamic Motion), HC 213/4 (1917)

Henry Cowell's *Advertisement* (HC 213/4) for piano was written in November 1917 as the "third encore" to his *Dynamic Motion*; it was first published as sheet music in 1922. As in *Dynamic Motion*, *Advertisement* records an impression of New York City—in this case, its flashing billboards and neon signs. Cowell described it as a "satire on repetitious advertising of a raucous nature."

After a short introduction (derived from *What's This*, Cowell's first encore to *Dynamic Motion*), Cowell launches into a passage that resembles a music hall tune gone wrong. Gradually the quirky texture explodes into a flurry of rapid-fire tone clusters played with the fists. Although these clusters are thoroughly notated in the score, Cowell's own recorded performances of *Advertisement*—made for CRI in 1957 and Folkways in 1963—differ radically from his printed markings; Cowell may have felt that an element of improvisation was appropriate, or perhaps the piece simply evolved over time with repeated playings.

While *The Tides of Manaunaun* may serve as Cowell's "signature" as pianist and composer, *Advertisement* acts as a more specific calling card for the tone cluster technique itself. Cowell's recordings of the piece were once included in primary-level teaching materials relating to modern music appreciation, and conductor/pianist Michael Tilson Thomas (who knows *Advertisement* from memory) played a few measures of it to illustrate the use of tone clusters in a CBS Television Young People's Concert in the 1970s. The unusually wide exposure of the piece (at least by the standards of frankly modern piano music), as well as its pictorial relevance to everyday life (who hasn't experienced a noisy day in the big city?), have made *Advertisement* an important watershed in the acceptance, presentation, and use of modern musical vocabulary. —*Uncle Dave Lewis*

Recommended:

- ○ **Henry Cowell: Piano Music** / H. Cowell / 1993 / Smithsonian Folkways 40801

Antinomy (Fourth Encore to Dynamic Motion), HC 213/5 (Dec. 1917)

The early twentieth century saw the emergence of a number of brash young composers who infused their piano works with a sense of an organic connection to the instrument. Many of Charles Ives' piano works and songs fit this category, with their ham-fisted harmonies and thick textures, as do the relentless attacks on the keyboard launched by George Antheil. Arguably, however, it was Henry Cowell whose piano output exerted the most outward pressure upon the stylistic and technical boundaries of piano music. Many of his works in this vein are well-known: the mysterious sounds emanating from the stroked and plucked entrails of the piano in *The Banshee* (1925) or the rustic autoharp evocations of the strummed chords in *The Aeolian Harp* (1923). Still, these are only two of a huge body of experimental piano works that Cowell began composing as a teenager. Many of these lesser-known works are likewise remarkable for the ambitious musical ideas they explore and even more remarkable considering the tender age at which Cowell created them. Included among these pieces less-familiar but deserving attention is Cowell's *Antinomy*, a brief but striking piece from 1917, the year of the composer's 20th birthday. From the outset, *Antinomy* continues certain lines of thought established earlier in *The Tides of Manaunaun*. Well-known for its use of tone clusters (executed with palms, flat hands, and even forearms) to evoke the sound and mood of a seascape, the piece combined mimetic sounds in one hand with melodic sounds in the other. In *Antinomy*, the two become fully integrated. While there are certainly moments of near-lucid melodic contour contrasted with indecipherable clusters of pitches, much of the piece explores the middle ground between the two. To be sure, the piece clearly has a predominant "tune," which falls within a diatonic field and appears at times without much dissonant interference (in fact, the melody was resurrected from a setting of Longfellow's *Golden Legend*, which Cowell undertook during his pre-teen years but never completed). This tune is set in opposition to the washes of sound in the left hand created (in the manner of *Manaunaun*) by blocks of contiguous pitches—the pianistic equivalent of broadband noise. The tone clusters move up and down the keyboard, carving out gestures whose general contours are clear even if the lines articulating those contours are thick and fuzzy. Approaching from the other direction, the melodic materials of the piece are sometimes rendered as groups of multiple notes rather than single ones; each note has a "wider" sonority, making it difficult to perceive the melodic shape until the clusters are heard as composite entities, drawing out melodies in broad, bold strokes. —*Jeremy Grimshaw*

Recommended:

- ○ **Henry Cowell: Piano Music** / H. Cowell / 1993 / Smithsonian Folkways 40801

The Banshee, for piano strings, HC 405 (1925)

In the late 1910s and early-mid 1920s, Henry Cowell made a study of extended techniques and sounds available on the piano, and incorporated these in a series of short compositions. One of these, *The Banshee* (1925), has become one of the composer's best-known works; it also manifests Cowell's longstanding interest in Irish mythology. The banshee (or banshie) is a female spirit who alerts a family to the impending death of one of its members by making a wailing sound underneath the windows of the family home. Cowell evokes this wailing sound, called "keening," by having the a pianist directly manipulate the strings of the instrument with his/her hands, at times scraping a fingernail along the strings to create an unearthly cry. Some have said that the result of this inside-the-piano technique is reminiscent of electronically generated sound. As was so often the case with him, Cowell returned to *The Banshee* in 1928–29, rearranging it for piano and orchestra as the first movement of his *Irish Suite*.

Two players are required, one standing at the piano's crook and the other holding down the damper pedal throughout. The music, written an octave higher than it sounds, requires the player standing at the crook to stroke and pluck the interior strings in one of 12 specified ways using either the flat of the hand, the fingernails, or the flesh of the fingers. Although all the notes are indicated and the piece is in rough ABA form with specific tempo instructions, these are not easily perceived by the listener, who hears only an eerie, otherworldly shrieking and wailing. *—Chris Morrison*

Recommended:

○ **Sound Forms For Piano** / R. Miller / New World 80203

Dynamic Motion, HC 213/1 (Nov. 1916)

Among Henry Cowell's early "tone cluster" pieces, *Dynamic Motion* probably elicited the most comment and controversy in its day—reaping rich rewards for the young modernist in terms of publicity. Cowell composed *Dynamic Motion* in November 1916 during a brief term spent enrolled in study at the Institute of Musical Art in New York. Cowell enlisted in the Army in February 1918, and it does not appear that he began to employ *Dynamic Motion* in public performances until his discharge in May 1919. *Dynamic Motion* was usually chosen to end Cowell's early recitals of "futurist" music, and is alluded to frequently by name in press coverage of his concerts.

One 1919 reporter tells us that Cowell's *Dynamic Motion* is "a musical impression of the New York Subway; the clamor in the subterranean darkness."

It begins with a loud series of cluster chords that build from the nucleus of an open fifth. This is followed by a series of wedge formations, with the clusters growing louder and larger as the wedges "spread out." The opening section is interrupted at points by a dissonantly stated bugle call-like figure. Then the "subway train" rolls in; a low, ominous cluster grows out of the darkness simulating the sound of the train's rumbling and its approach. This section is more frequently interrupted by the bugle call figure. When the train arrives at the platform, the bugle call figure "takes over" and is stated in huge clusters, answered by a wild confusion of showy display. When this reaches a saturation point, the piece drops down to a mysterious close, momentarily disturbed by the static chords heard during the opening.

Listening to *Dynamic Motion* in the twenty-first century, one is moved to imagine the effect this piece had on 1919 audiences. Indeed, the early press reports record that when Cowell played *Dynamic Motion* on one occasion, "three women lay in a dead faint in the aisle, and no less than ten men had refreshed themselves from the left hip." Cowell later claimed that reactions such as this inspired his undertaking the five "Encores to *Dynamic Motion*": *What's This?, Amiable Conversation, Advertisement, Antinomy,* and *Time Table.* However, all of these works were written shortly before Cowell entered the Army, and thus prior to his concert career.

Throughout *Dynamic Motion* and its five "Encores," Cowell works with a formal practice of "organizing sounds by their sounds." Mid-twentieth century scholars tended to fault this aspect of Cowell's work as a shortcoming resulting from an inexact grasp of formal development. The twenty-first century, which Cowell in his time sought to evoke as a "futurist," has come to his rescue in this regard. Looking back over more than a half century of developments in electronic music, clearly the concept of "organizing sounds by their sounds" is as natural a means of formalizing music as are pitch, harmony, or melody. *—Uncle Dave Lewis*

Recommended:

○ **Henry Cowell: Piano Music** / H. Cowell / 1993 / Smithsonian Folkways 40801

Exultation, HC 328 (May 1921)

Exultation, written in 1925, was once described by Henry Cowell as an "Irish walking tune." The piece is one of many Cowell wrote in the late 1910s and early 1920s based on his interest in Irish mythology. It also employs some of the adventuresome playing techniques that Cowell developed during the same period. Specifically, in *Exultation* he calls for the use of "arm-sized" tone clusters, or large groups of adjacent notes on the piano keyboard played simultaneously, using the palm or side of the hand or the forearm. That distinctive sound is just one feature of what is otherwise a sprightly, Irish-inflected tune over a stomping chordal accompaniment. Cowell returned to the composition twice in later years. He arranged it for string orchestra in 1930, and ten years after that used it once again as the second movement of his *Four Irish Tales for piano and orchestra,* assembled from various examples of his solo piano work. *—Chris Morrison*

Recommended:

○ **Exultation** / B. Gowen / 1998 / New World 80304

The Snows of Fuji-Yama, HC 395 (Aug. 1924)

Henry Cowell's piano miniatures are well known, many of them bearing titles with reference to legends or mythical figures or places. These frequently utilize "extended techniques," such as stroking the strings on the inside of the piano, as in *The Aeolian Harp* and *The Banshee,* or striking clusters of notes with the hand or forearm, as in *The Tides of Manaunaun. Snows of Fuji-Yama* (1924), one of his lesser-known works, was composed in this same spirit. As the composer explains, the piece takes its title from an old legend regarding the famous mountain, in which the snows that cap the peaks are found to be not snow at all, but rather lotus blossoms. Each blossom, the story goes, represents the soul of a different maiden.

This is a short piece, with a unique sound. Its vaguely exotic melody is rather straightforward, with simple figures in the lower ranges answered by more lyrical lines in the upper register. What gives the piece its character, however, is the clever way in which Cowell inflects each note in the melody with a shimmering tone cluster. These complex chords are executed simultaneously with the melody, and roughly follow its contours, but are delivered at a lower dynamic level so as to sound as an added resonance rather than a harmony or chord per se. The resulting timbre resembles some kind of imagined oriental bell or gong, with a clear fundamental pitch colored by a wide array of additional overtones. *—Jeremy Grimshaw*

Recommended:

○ **Henry Cowell: Piano Music** / H. Cowell / 1993 / Smithsonian Folkways 40801

The Tides of Manaunaun, prelude (from "The Building of Bamba"), HC 219/1 (Jul. 1917)

Henry Cowell's short piano piece *The Tides of Manaunaun* is usually referred to as a "Prelude" or "Introduction." In prefacing his 1963 Folkways recording of this work, Cowell stated that it was "written as a prelude to an opera based on Irish mythology," and that it represents Manaunaun, legendary Irish god of motion whose forces caused waves in bodies of water to flow.

In Cowell's piece, Manaunaun's "waves" are represented by large, sweeping tone clusters which are played using the left forearm. The folk-like melody of the piece is stated mostly in octaves in the right hand. While the pianistic means utilized in realizing Cowell's program are simple, his results are undeniably effective, as *The Tides of Manaunaun* has an orchestral sweep and grandeur that has long impressed itself on hearers who are not necessarily fans of modern music. In his later years, Cowell played this avant-garde piece in the White House for American presidents Franklin Delano Roosevelt and John F. Kennedy.

Cowell frequently programmed *The Tides of Manaunaun* to open his own recitals and used it as a way "in" for listeners unaccustomed to his sound and style. He often identified it as his first venture into the realm of piano tone clusters and dated it variously 1911 or 1912. The original manuscript of the work no longer exists, and Cowell may have destroyed it to protect the secret of Manaunaun's true, and somewhat later, origins. As he stipulates, *The Tides of Manaunaun* was conceived as a prelude to an opera based on Irish myth. This was *The Building of Bamba* (HC 219), best described as a "pageant" or "Mystery Play" written by John O. Varian, and presented at the headquarters of a Theosophist cult called The Temple of the People near San Luis Obispo, CA, in August 1917. Some of Cowell's friends recalled Cowell playing this piece, or some variant of it, before 1917, but apparently the score did not take shape until the composition of *The Building of Bamba.*

The Tides of Manaunaun was Henry Cowell's first published piece of music, having been issued as sheet music in 1922; this is the primary source for the music as it is known. His logic for attempting to backdate it may have been motivated by a desire to substantiate his claim to the tone cluster as his invention. Cowell need not have worried, as his first use of tone clusters in a notated piano piece appears in *Adventures of Harmony* (1913; HC 59) and is only predated by such archetypal experimentalists as Charles Ives, Charles-Henri Alkan, and Franz Liszt. *The Tides of Manaunaun* virtually cries out for orchestration, and in 1940 Cowell created an orchestral version as part of the suite *Four Irish Tales* (also known as *Tales of Our Countryside,* HC 605) at the request of conductor Leopold Stokowski. *—Uncle Dave Lewis*

Recommended:

○ **The Bad Boys!** / Schleiermacher / 1994 / Hat Hut 6144

○ **Henry Cowell: Piano Music** / H. Cowell / 1993 / Smithsonian Folkways 40801

○ **New Music** / D. S. Hays / 1999 / New Albion 103

CHAMBER MUSIC

Mosaic Quartet ("String Quartet No. 3"), HC 518 (1935)

Henry Cowell composed his *String Quartet No. 3,* otherwise known as the *Mosaic Quartet,* in 1935, a year before the beginning of the unfortunate string of events that led to his eventual (and, as he was later granted a full pardon, unjust) incarceration at a California state penitentiary. The *Mosaic Quartet* is the second of three quartets composed during the mid-1930s; with its aleatory structure and fascinatingly semi-diatonic harmonies, it is an intriguing centerpiece to an experimentally-minded triptych.

The *Mosaic Quartet* has five short movements (two pages of score each) in five different tempos. The order of the movements, and also the number of times each is played, is left up to the performers. Cowell does, however, suggest an arrangement in which little three-movement ternary patterns emerge and then all five are played in order at the end: 1. 2. 1. 3. 4. 3. 5. 4. 5. 1. 2. 3. 4. 5.

Movement 1 is a Largo that begins and ends clearly in E major, but moves through freely dissonant regions (but ones whose counterpoint is still clear) in-between. Movement 2 is an Allegro throughout which the first violin plays trills in the highest register. The three upper strings sustain quiet tones as the cello impetuously shoots off on its own in the Andante movement 3. Two-note gestures are exchanged in 4 (Allegretto), and triplets are tossed about throughout the Allegro non troppo final movement. *—Blair Johnston*

Recommended:

○ **Cowell: Mosaic** / Colorado SQ / 1999 / Mode 72

Ostinato Pianissimo, for 8 percussionists, HC 505 (1934)

The powerful interest in folk music and national styles that occurred in 1930s American art, theater, and music inspired a number of works for percussion ensemble, including those by John Cage, Lou Harrison and Edgard Varèse. Henry Cowell, already known for his "ultramodern" compositions, also tried to reflect this expanded musical awareness, as evidenced by this energetic and delightful piece for eight performers. In its way, it is an early kind of "world music," suggesting at times Javanese and Balinese gamelan, African drumming, South American village, South Indian classical instrumental, and of course contemporary American concert musics; but the overall conception is decidedly modern: a self-contained, quietly excited surface of contrasting tone colors. It is dedicated to the innovative and adventurous conductor and champion of modern music, Nicolas Slonimsky.

The composer indicates that most of the parts, except for the difficult xylophone part, can be played by "non-professionals." The "percussion band" necessary to create this timbral panorama consists of instruments of fixed tuning and those of indefinite pitch. To execute the two tuned "string piano" parts, the performers use their right hands to play the indicated pitches on the regular keyboard while their left hands dampen the interior strings in various ways (over several strings, near the bridge, at 1/4 the length of the string, etc.) to produce different harmonic partials. The xylophone part is in standard tuning, but the swift, manic, and rather snaky chromatic part is played with soft mallets, yielding a muted wooden tone. Eight rice bowls (the "jala tarang") of indefinite pitch are arranged according to relative highness and lowness. The same indeterminate relation holds for the two woodblocks, the tambourine (without rattles), and guiro (tapped with stick) pair, the two bongos, the three drums, and the three gongs (struck with padded and wood sticks).

The "ostinato" of the title refers to the invariant, cyclical rhythms of different lengths assigned to each player. The beginning of a cycle is marked by a loudly accented special event: a tone cluster for the string pianos, a major third for the xylophone, the striking of two bowls by the rice bowls player, two woodblocks by their player, two bongos by that performer, and a wood stick grace note on tynhe gongs. Additionally, most of the instruments indicate the end of each cycle with a trill or a tremolo that briefly builds in excitement and anticipation.

The overall dynamic is very soft unless accents are notated; in those cases, the accented events are "brought out sharply." The ensemble sound thus created is like a mysteriously shifting, polyrhythmic mobile exuding a strange ceremonial atmosphere. The last eight measures of the composition gradually build toward an overwhelming climax. This crescendo occurs as an accumulation initiated by a loud cluster in the first string piano, which is then progressively answered by the other instruments. *—"Blue Gene" Tyranny*

Recommended:

○ **Percussion Music** / Des Roches (cond.), New Jersey Percussion Ens. / Nonesuch 79150

Quartet Euphometric, for string quartet, HC 283 (1916–Sep. 1919)

Henry Cowell's *Quartet Euphometric* is the second of Cowell's "rhythm harmony quartets." Begun in 1916, concurrently with its companion work, *Quartet Romantic*, this composition wasn't completed until September 1919. It is scored for standard string quartet, but, as theoretically oriented piece, is considered apart from Cowell's established cycle of five string quartets. *Quartet Euphometric* is a very short work that can be performed in a couple of minutes.

As in *Quartet Romantic*, Cowell organizes the rhythm of the piece based on the overtone series derived from what was probably a short sketch in the form of a canon. However, Cowell makes considerable improvements over the *Quartet Romantic* in terms of transmitting his concept. Cowell keeps a tighter grasp on the highly independent individual melodic voices in this quartet by devising new means of notation. Laid out on just 11 staves, the piece introduces interesting innovations, including subdivisions within bars, as well as a triangular "sixth" note which signifies triplet-based figures. This eliminates the need for the bracketed rhythms, which in the *Quartet Romantic* had served only to render long sections of the score unplayable. As the piece is based in theory, the resultant music is rather nondescript, but since the work is so short, this, paradoxically, becomes part of *Quartet Euphometric*'s charm.

The Galimir String Quartet gave the earliest documented performance of the *Quartet Euphometric* at Philharmonic Hall in New York on February 12, 1964. It was published in 1974, along with *Quartet Romantic*, and has since become something of a favored genre piece among string quartets which specialize in American avant-garde repertoire. *—Uncle Dave Lewis*

Recommended:

○ **The Emerson String Quartet Plays 50 Years of American Music 1919–1969** / Emerson SQ / 1977 / New World 80453

○ **Short Stories** / Kronos Quartet / 1993 / Nonesuch 79310

Quartet Romantic, for 2 flutes, violin & viola, HC 223 (Sep. 1917)

The *Quartet Romantic for two flutes, violin, and viola* is the first of Henry Cowell's two "rhythm harmony" quartets, based on theoretical principles outlined in his book *New Musical Resources* (1930). The basic principle employed is the use of overtones—the numerous harmonics that give a fundamental pitch its characteristic sound and tone color, and of which we are usually unaware—to create perceptible musical patterns and events. Cowell first encountered this possibility when he entered the University of California at Berkeley, in 1914. Working with a friend in the physics department, Cowell discovered the overtone effects created by sounding two sirens. In *Quartet Romantic*, Cowell sought to apply the organizing principle suggested by the use of overtone series as a structural basis for composition.

Cowell composed the first section of *Quartet Romantic* in strict adherence to his basic plan, without regard for whether the music was playable in a practical sense. "This piece is humanly impossible to play!" Cowell noted upon the top page of his manuscript. "But if at some time in the future a performance does become possible, this is how I want it to sound." The most active melodic lines are to be found in the flutes; the rhythms of the violin and viola are stated in slower note values, providing the illusion of support, although the four parts are melodically independent. During the opening of the first movement, rhythms are exceedingly complex. To take a randomly chosen example, bar 22 calls for a bracketed value of 71/2 in the first flute, 6 in the second, 41/2 in the violin, and 21/4 in the viola. Eventually the first flute has a solo; then the other instruments gradually reenter, playing in quicker note values and in a more broken-up texture. Finally the whole movement repeats, and then closes with a brief coda that is made up mostly of stuttering, repeated notes. The second movement is shorter and more rhythmically conventional. The texture is thinly applied, some of it stated in two voices only. There is a brief, contrasting section where the instruments break into rapid figurations. The whole second movement of the *Quartet Romantic* is playable under average conditions.

Despite its basis in experimental techniques, the *Quartet Romantic* is aptly named, as its sound is warm and richly Romantic in texture, even though the piece has no tonal orientation. However, the lack of accents and the extreme flexibility of the rhythm tend to obscure any sense of punctuation; at times this highly disorienting music nearly sounds like it is traveling in reverse. Despite its extreme level of rhythmic flexibility, the *Quartet Romantic* leaves the impression of being rhythmically static. *Quartet Romantic* remained unpublished until 1974, and it was first heard at Alice Tully Hall, in 1978. This premiere and the recorded performance that followed it were achieved utilizing click tracks, like those used in motion picture synchronization. *—Uncle Dave Lewis*

Recommended:

○ **Quartet Romantic** / Palma, Schulte, Dunkel, J. Graham / 1998 / New World 80285

ORCHESTRAL

Persian Set, for chamber ensemble, HC 838 (Nov. 18, 1956–Feb. 8, 1957)

After spending the winter of 1956 in Tehran, Cowell was inspired to write this four-movement suite for small orchestral ensemble adapting elements of Iranian and Persian techniques and modes to Western conventions. Cowell called it "a simple record of musical contagion." He adds to the Western instruments found at Radio Tehran, which commissioned the work, the three-stringed Persian *tar*, which is usually replaced by a mandolin in American performances.

The first and longest movement, Moderato, sets the pattern for the rest by having one instrument, in this case clarinet, introduce a wide-ranging, at times ornate, theme, with a second instrument (here a violin) following the first in canon over a sustained accompaniment by other instruments. The melodies have a deliberately improvisatory feeling, and Cowell aims to create a very loose sort of polyphony inspired by the free improvisation of Iran's three- to five-man ensembles. The second movement, Allegretto, is propelled more by the drums and employs the fuller orchestra in highly colored, Persian-style material. The Lento follows the pattern of the first movement, generally with spare textures, and a brief Presto concludes the set with a lively dance that sounds both Persian and Elizabethan and includes some joyful shouts from the musicians. *—James Reel*

Recommended:

- ○ **Cowell: Persian Set; Goeb: Symphony 3 & B. Weber** / Stokowski (cond.), Leopold Stokowski SO / Citadel 88123
- ○ **Henry Cowell: Persian Set** / R. A. Clark (cond.), Manhattan CO / 2000 / Koch 7220

SYMPHONIC

Symphonies (1918–1965)

During the last two decades of his life, Henry Cowell produced an impressive number of symphonies—impressive for even a composer whose output includes nearly 1,000 works. The symphonies drew upon some of Cowell's principal musical interests, including non-Western musics and American folk music, but cast them in a thoroughly modern light. Cowell himself stressed that the musical allusions and borrowings so prevalent in his music were not meant to evoke a sense of exoticism or otherness, but a sense of unity and affinity: "My admiration and enjoyment of foreign musical cultures have led me to welcome types of musical treatment which show the close relationship between our musical concepts and those of other peoples."

Cowell's first two symphonies, from 1918 and 1938, predate Cowell's fully integrated interest in musical internationalism, and reflect instead his early experimentalist tendencies. Cowell's career as a symphonist begins in earnest with his *Symphony No. 3* from 1942. Nicknamed the *"Gaelic" Symphony*, the work reflects Cowell's own Irish roots. (This influence would appear in later works as well, such as the jig-inspired scherzo of the *Symphony No. 7*.) The *Fourth Symphony* followed four years later and reflected one of Cowell's most prolific obsessions: the genre of the hymn and fuguing tune. This music takes its cue from William Billings and the early American shape-note singers, whose rustic devotional singing involved a moderately paced hymn followed by a livelier tune in simple counterpoint or round. While Cowell's oeuvre includes a large number of works for various instrumentations bearing the designation "Hymn and Fuguing Tune," a number of his symphonies bear traces of the style or appropriate it in full. The *Fourth Symphony* closes with a fuguing tune, as does *Symphony No. 10*, which also includes a hymn and fuguing tune comprising its opening two movements. In his *Fifth Symphony* (1948), Cowell made an explicit attempt to trace affinities of various Western and non-Western musical ideas by constructing the symphony upon musical ideas simple enough to be at home in either context.

The early 1950s were Cowell's busiest years, symphonically speaking, with no less than five symphonies within a two-year period. Most notable among these are the *Seventh* and *Eleventh* symphonies. No. 7, from 1952, is scored for a small orchestra and subtitled "Seven Rituals of Music." Each of the work's seven movements takes as its programmatic subject a different phase—such as childhood, love, or war—in man's journey from life to death. The work is highly interconnected and cyclical, with themes that migrate from movement to movement like memories, and a finale (representing Death) that turns motives from each of the previous movements into fugal subjects. Among the symphonies from Cowell's last decade, the India-inspired No. 13 ("Madras," 1959), as well as the *Symphony No. 16* ("Icelandic," 1963), composed for the dedication of an auditorium in Reykjavik and featuring a combination of Lydian-tinged Icelandic folk music combined with hymn and fuguing techniques and even allusions to medieval polyphony. *—Jeremy Grimshaw*

Recommended:

- ○ **Henry Cowell** / Mester (cond.), Whitney (cond.), Louisville Orch. / 2001 / First Edition 3
- ○ **Cowell: Symphonies 7 & 16; Variations** / W. Strickland (cond.), Vienna SO, Iceland SO, Katowice Polish Radio Orch. / 1997 / CRI 740

CONCERTO

Hymn and Fuguing Tune No. 10, for oboe & string orchestra, HC 813 (1955)

In his mature years as a composer, Henry Cowell struck upon an idea that produced some 20 works for various instrumentation, which he designated as *Hymn and Fuguing Tunes*. Simply stated—by Cowell himself, in fact, in the pithiest of terms—a hymn and fuguing tune simply as "something slow followed by something fast." More specifically, the genre was inspired by the music of early American composers William Billings and William Walker. Recalling the sounds of Protestant hymnody from his youth, Cowell created a style of music that emulated the sturdy, melodic tunes found in the shape-note books Walker published in the pre-Civil War era and in the boisterously spiritual song gatherings of the Sacred Harp style. While Cowell certainly diverges from his models to a considerable degree, certain gestures and sonorities stand out as direct borrowings: strong, simple diatonic melodies, lucid triadic motions with little dissonance and virtually no chromaticism, and emphasis on "open" harmonies, such as the unadorned perfect fifth.

All these qualities are found in abundance in the piece under consideration here, the *Hymn and Fuguing Tune No. 10 for Oboe and Strings*. This work stands as a fair representative of the genre, both chronologically and stylistically, Cowell having settled comfortably into rendering the style for larger forces and taking some licenses according to his own tastes, while still observing some of its most essential and unique features. The first section, the Hymn, begins with a robust, lyrical theme introduced by the oboe. Its modern identity is given away from the outset, as the oboe's entrance immediately outlines a plaintive major seventh interval. The melody unfolds in a moderately paced triple meter, with an underlying B minor tonality that hints strongly at its relative major, D. The hymn tune undergoes various transformations as it moves through the orchestra, including a rendering in exact inversion. A central section features various combinations of instrumental trios, this exchange finally leading to a return of the opening material.

The *Fuguing Tune* takes the form of a nimble duple meter dance in D Dorian (a modality closely associated with the practices of Sacred Harp singing). The principal eight-bar melody is split in two, its halves passed around the orchestra. Its transformations are easy to track, as it begins with a strident upward leap of a perfect fifth. A subsequent development section contains all sorts of contrapuntal tricks, including stretto (one instrument picking up the melody before another is done with it), augmentation (stretching the tune out into longer notes), and inversion (flipping it upside down). As the melody undergoes this extensive working out, it seems to have its rougher edges smoothed, and when it emerges in the final coda, it is not only more lyrical, but has actually been transformed into a vibrant major mode. *—Jeremy Grimshaw*

Recommended:

- ○ **Henry Cowell: Fiddler's Jig; Air & Scherzo & others** / R. A. Clark (cond.), Lucarelli, Manhattan CO / 1994 / Koch 7282

Robert Craft

b. Oct. 20, 1923, Kingston, NY

Conductor

Robert Lawson Craft is an American conductor, noted for his association with Igor Stravinsky and his championing of the music of Anton Webern and other composers of the Second Viennese School.

Craft had a middle-class upbringing in upstate New York. After service as an Army medic during World War II, he studied at Juilliard and Berkshire Music Center and privately with Pierre Monteux. From 1947 to 1950 he conducted the Chamber Arts Society of New York, attracting attention for his adventurous programming.

His conducting led to a meeting with the 65-year-old Igor Stravinsky, who hired him as musical assistant and secretary. Moving to Stravinsky's home in Los Angeles, Craft assisted him with the English text of the opera *The Rake's Progress*. Craft also conducted two concert series in Los Angeles, the Evenings-on-the-Roof and its successor, the Monday Evening Concerts. Again, he scheduled music of Schoenberg, Webern, Varèse, late Stravinsky, and older music such as that of Gesualdo.

After the premiere of *The Rake* in 1951, Stravinsky found himself creatively blocked, but also unexpectedly stimulated by hearing Craft's performance of Schoenberg's *Septet*. The Russian master (generally considered the greatest rival of Schoenberg and his school) now asked Craft to provide some Schoenberg and Webern scores for study. Craft also gave Stravinsky Ernst Krenek's invaluable teaching books on the 12-tone system. Over the next few years Stravinsky startled the musical world by embracing Schoenberg's system. Craft's position with Stravinsky altered from assistant to collaborator. The composer welcomed Craft's suggestions and advice even to the shaping of some of his late works. Craft also began rehearsing orchestras for Stravinsky to conduct in concert and for a great series of recordings for Columbia Records, making both endeavors possible.

In connection with the composer's 75th birthday, Craft suggested that he and Stravinsky prepare a written interview dealing with the most frequently asked questions and release it to the press rather than subject the old man to long, repetitive personal interviews. This format proved so successful that Craft and Stravinsky co-wrote several volumes of Stravinsky's memoirs and thoughts on music. After Stravinsky's death, Craft continued to edit Stravinsky documentation and write his own memories of life with Stravinsky.

Craft has pursued his own career as a lecturer, conductor, writer, and musicologist. While recording the Columbia Stravinsky cycle, he used odd moments available during recording sessions to produce the first integral recordings of the complete numbered works of Anton Webern. The turn of the century found him recording the works of Stravinsky and of Schoenberg for Koch International Classics.

He is a highly skilled and precise conductor, who could no doubt have established a career of higher profile if he were more interested in the standard repertory and if he had not devoted much of his time to Stravinsky, both during and after the master's life. But he has gone firmly on record as saying the opportunity to know and work with the great man was, without doubt on his part, fully worth the trade-off. *—Joseph Stevenson*

Recommended:

- ○ **Stravinsky: Symphony of Psalms; Les Noces; Lamentations** / Craft (cond.), London PO / 2002 / Koch 7514

○ **Stravinsky: The Rite of Spring; Apollo** / Craft (cond.), London SO / 1996 / Koch 7359

○ **Music of Arnold Schoenberg, Vol 3** / Craft (cond.), Wyn-Rogers, London PO / 1999 / Koch 7463

Ruth Crawford Seeger

b. Jul. 3, 1901, East Liverpool, OH, **d.** Nov. 18, 1953, Chevy Chase, MD
Composer: Keyboard, Chamber Music, Choral

Ruth Crawford was born to an itinerant Methodist minister and his wife. Upon graduating from high school, Crawford entered Foster's School of Musical Art in Jacksonville, Florida, studying piano. The Foster School relocated to Miami in 1921, and Crawford enrolled in the American Conservatory of Music in Chicago. She stayed until 1929, studying composition and theory with Adolf Weidig. Weidig encouraged her early efforts, and with her first *Piano Preludes* of 1924 Crawford had already developed her own unique modern voice.

In 1926, Crawford composed her *Sonata for Violin and Piano*; performed at modern music concerts in the late 1920s, it prompted a critic to remark that Crawford could "sling dissonances like a man." She was recognized early on as a woman composer who did not fit the sentimental stereotypes associated with the standard profile. In Chicago, Crawford joined the circle of Djana Lavoie Herz, pianist and ex-follower of Scriabin; through Herz she met Dane Rudyhar, Henry Cowell, and pianist Richard Bühlig. Cowell quickly became a supporter of Crawford's work, arranging for performances of her music in New York and publishing it in the periodical *New Music Quarterly*. Crawford worked as a piano teacher for the children of poet Carl Sandburg; it was he who first interested her in American folk songs. She contributed arrangements to his 1927 book *The American Songbag*, and later created significant original settings to eight of his poems.

By 1930, Ruth Crawford was a force to be reckoned with in American modernism. Stylistically, her work stood out in its uncompromising use of dissonance, contrapuntal ostinati, striking choice of texts and tidy formal construction. In March 1930, Crawford won a Guggenheim Fellowship to travel to Europe; the first woman so honored. In Berlin, Crawford composed *Three Chants* set to a wordless text for women's chorus; this eerie, experimental work has no obvious parallels to any music written before the 1960s. The following year witnessed her most famous work, *String Quartet 1931*, and with its publication Crawford provided the definitive foil to the old maxim that women "just can't write" classical music with the strength and seriousness of male composers.

In 1929, she began study with Charles Seeger, a key figure in American music as a composer, theorist and musicologist. They married in 1932. She likewise adopted several of Seeger's theoretical methods that mark the works of her most productive period, 1930–33; however, her composing came to a virtual standstill around 1934. Among her children with Seeger were daughter Peggy and son Mike, both to become renowned folk singers and teachers in adulthood. In 1936, the Seegers moved to Washington, D.C., to work in folk song collecting for the Library of Congress. Crawford acted as transcriber for the book *Our Singing Country* and, with Charles Seeger, for *Folk Song USA*, both authored by John and Alan Lomax. As Ruth Crawford Seeger she published her own pioneering collection, *American Folk Songs for Children*, in 1948, designed for use in elementary grades. This and the other "Crawford Seeger" books are regarded as key texts in primary music education, and were widely adopted and imitated in the field. Crawford only returned to serious composition with the *Suite for Wind Quintet* in 1952. By the time it was completed, she learned she had cancer. Ruth Crawford died at the age of 52. *—Uncle Dave Lewis*

Overview of Works (1924–1952)

As she came of age in the post-Great War era of unprecedented musical experiment the young Ruth Crawford's first extant works (dating from her Chicago period between 1921–29), the *Piano Preludes* of 1924–25, already breathe what the vocal obbligato of Schoenberg's *String Quartet No. 2* called "the air of another planet," though her model is Scriabin's hallucinatory last manner. While they are not atonal, the tonal sense of these pieces is blurred by the use of augmented and diminished triads and the tritone. Octaves are economically eschewed as redundant. Ranging from 12 to 46 bars, interest hovers between the anxious avoidance of post-Romantic clichés and the permutation of close chromatic cells or small, but widely leaping motifs. A preoccupation with dreamlike, or hypnotic, states set off by movements worked from busily independent lines are typical strategies in the *Violin Sonata* (1926), *Music for Small Orchestra* (1926), *Suite for Five Winds and Piano* (1927), and *Suite for Strings and Piano* (1929). A setting of Carl Sandburg's "Rat Riddles" (1930), whose "accompaniment" is a quirkily vehement exegesis, makes explicit the combination of subtlety and dynamism in the works of this period. Her study of dissonant counterpoint in New York in 1930 with musicologist and theorist Charles Seeger brought a rationale, discipline, and formal point to her work that is evident in the *Four Diaphonic Suites* of that year. This uncompromising linear independence and cogency directly led to her *String Quartet* (1931). Though it plays for only 12 minutes, the quartet's harmonic abrasiveness, disjunct rhythms ("rhythmic dissonance"), and the palindromic form of its final movement (totally organized in tempo and dynamics) evince a substance and power that firmly place it, if in a side niche, among Modernism's triumphs. The melismatic, glissando-rippled *Three Chants for Women's Voices* (1930) recapture the mystical afflatus of her Chicago period with a new compositional rigor. Her career is divided by the irony of having fashioned an elite, hermetic language only to be overtaken by the Great Depression and the radical left reaction to it, which called upon her to speak for and to popular sentiment. The *Two Ricercare* (1932)—protest lyrics couched in her "advanced" manner—are ludicrous failures. With her marriage to Seeger in 1931, her life as a composer virtually ended, while her creative energies were employed in the cultivation of American folk song. *Rissolty, Rossolty* (1939), a brief orchestral rhapsody on folk materials, is an acerbic amalgamation of compositional economy, humor, and ready accessibility. A *Suite for Wind Quintet* (1952) returns to the manner of the string quartet with deft lightness. *—Adrian Corleonis*

Recommended:

○ **Ruth Crawford Seeger: String Quartet & Chamber Works** / Pellegrini Quartet, Ens. Aventure / CPO 999670

○ **The World of Ruth Crawford Seeger** / J. Lin, T. Jones (narr.) / 2001 / BIS 1310

○ **Ruth Crawford Seeger: Portrait** / Knussen (cond.), de Leeuw, L. Shelton, Schoenberg Ens. / DG 449925

KEYBOARD

Piano Study in Mixed Accents (1930)

Ruth Crawford Seeger's tiny piano piece *Piano Study in Mixed Accents* occupies three pages of printed music as published in October 1932, as part of volume six in Henry Cowell's *New Music Quarterly*. Although Crawford Seeger's pre-compositional strategy for the piece was laid out in 1929, the work was written between November and December 1930. Its earliest known public performance was over the Yiddish-language radio station WEVD in New York, in January 1933, as played by Crawford Seeger's protégé, composer Vivian Fine.

Crawford Seeger's biographer, Judith Tick, has described *Piano Study in Mixed Accents* as a "modernistic *Minute Waltz*." A single line of music is played in both hands, consisting of rapidly played 16th notes accented in a rugged, uneven fashion. *Piano Study in Mixed Accents* is conceived and executed in a tightly rigorous experimental milieu, and is barely a minute and a half in length. It is so short that it might take even an attentive listener a couple of tries to get it. However, the piece has an urgency and rhythmic drive that immediately perks up one's attention. While *Piano Study in Mixed Accents* is not famous, it has long been a favorite of pianists who specialize in twentieth century American literature. It is an appealing, accessible virtuoso concert encore, despite its origins in the avant-garde.

Although Crawford Seeger never adopted Schoenberg's serial methods, this piece—a double palindrome, constructed of a single, highly chromatic line—shows how close she came at times to embracing the older composer's idiom. The texture of the piece is monophonic (one voice only), with the two hands doubling each other at the octave. It is a toccata built of very short staccato notes. The palindromic aspects of the work exist in both the rhythm and in the melodic line: either is the same when read forward or backward, yet the two have different center points (if the melodic line is considered without note values). *—Uncle Dave Lewis*

Recommended:

○ **The World of Ruth Crawford Seeger** / J. Lin / 2001 / BIS 1310

CHAMBER MUSIC

String Quartet 1931 (1931)

Ruth Crawford (who married her composition teacher Charles Seeger in November 1931, shortly after writing this quartet) was among the most daring and accomplished American avant-garde composers. She wrote music in which a lot happens all at once, on every possible level. She exercised strict control over all aspects of the music, rhythm, and tone color, as well as the individual notes of the melodic lines, creating music of extraordinary dramatic tension. This quartet is often considered her masterpiece.

The quartet, a 12-minute work is fully as concentrated and advanced as any work for a similarly-sized ensemble produced by Anton Webern, Schoenberg's most radical disciple. The texture throughout favors lines that are highly independent from each other. The first movement, Rubato assai, has the kind of wide, arching intervals that are a part of the Webern-Schoenberg style, perhaps not surprising since Crawford wrote the quartet in Berlin during her Guggenheim Fellowship year of 1930–31. The way the movement increases in energy by piling up on itself, so to speak, is typical of Crawford's music and sets the work apart from its European models.

The second movement, Leggiero (lightly), is canonic, with imitative entrances cast in distinct registers; the lines of the music are often linked from one instrument to the next like a chain. The third movement is a remarkable study in what Crawford called "dissonant dynamics." Each of the four instruments has its own independent rise and fall in loudness on different held notes. The assertion of one particular note transfers the listener's attention to it, so the melody emerges note by note from an ever-shifting cloud of dissonance. Later, Crawford would attempt to make this effect even clearer to the audience by arranging this movement as an *Andante for string orchestra*, trusting that the conductor would control these emerging melodies even better than individual string players could.

The Allegro finale features hard-edged playing at the frog of the bow by the first violin, juxtaposed with fast unison or doubled answers by the other strings, posing a tricky problem in dynamic balance for the performers. As the movement progresses, the three lower strings adopt the material and manner of the violin, and vice versa, by stages, then return via the same path to the texture of the beginning. It's a bold concept, brilliantly executed.

This quartet represented both the high point of Crawford's career as an avant-garde composer and a premature end to it. The Seegers became Communists, necessarily involved in the "proletarian music movement." Crawford Seeger's music veered sharply in that direction with the couple's subsequent pioneering work in American folk song taking all her career time. She did not return to the path indicated by this great quartet again until 1952, by which time she was already fatally stricken with cancer. *—Joseph Stevenson*

Recommended:

- **Ruth Crawford Seeger: String Quartet & Chamber Works** / Pellegrini Quartet / CPO 999670
- **Ruth Crawford Seeger: Portrait** / Knussen (cond.), Schoenberg Ens. / DG 449925

CHORAL

Three Chants, for female chorus (1930)

Ruth Crawford (1901–53) was described by fellow composer Henry Cowell as having broken the stereotype of a "woman composer," which was presumably one who wrote lightweight, conservative, sentimental music. This work is typical of Crawford's music in being nothing like that.

Crawford (who married folk song expert and teacher Charles Seeger in 1931) had been studying and working in Chicago before she wrote this music. She was determined to create music in a new dissonant style, but with little reference to the 12-tone technique of Schoenberg. In addition, she was drawn to visionary or transcendental ideas and attempted to express these in her music. In 1930, Crawford won a Guggenheim Grant to travel and study in Europe. She wrote this composition in Berlin. She was interested in the Indian religious text, the *Bhagavad Gita*. When she could find no English translation, she made up her own imaginary language to create the impression of a mystical Asian text. The sound she was aiming for, and achieved brilliantly, is not the recreation of any sort of music she heard first-hand, but the attainment of a description she read about certain music possessing a "complex dissonant veil of sound." Harmonic motion in these three *Chants* tends to be slow. The harmonies themselves are densely packed into the range of women's voices, and sometimes involve all 12 tones of the chromatic scale sounding at once. The individual vocal lines in the piece are both polyphonic and heterophonic. This suggests nuns chanting freely rather than in chorus. The idea of heterophony was very important to Charles Seeger and was a part of the lessons in dissonant counterpoint he had already given her before she went on her European trip. The mood of the three chants is highly mysterious, striking a strangely serene and solemn mood, although with the threatening aspects of mysteries of any sort. The final chant features a soaring line for a solo soprano drawn from the chorus, and ends in a hushed statement of a chord of all notes. The second and most serene of the three chants was the only part recorded in the composer's lifetime; the first recording of the first and third chants and of the *Three Chants* as a whole did not occur until 1996. *—Joseph Stevenson*

Recommended:

- **Ruth Crawford Seeger: Portrait** / Knussen (cond.), New London Chamber Choir / DG 449925

Thomas Crecquillon

b. ca. 1480, France [?], **d.** ca. 1557, Béthune, France

Composer

Thomas Crecquillon was one of the leading northern European composers in the generation after Josquin Desprez. He was highly popular for his chansons, but his religious music is considered his most significant work.

Very little is known with any certainty about his life. An official document of the court of Holy Roman Emperor Charles V dated 1540 lists him as "m-re de la chappelle," and his music's title pages also recite that he was "maître de chapelle." This basically means that he was responsible for selecting, performing, and composing music for religious services on behalf of the emperor.

However, another source, Nicolaus Mameranus, who in the years 1547 and 1548 wrote a *Catalogus familiae* of the Imperial establishment in Cologne, referred to him only as a singer and a composer and implied that Canis was maître de chapelle. Also in 1547 a petition from the court singers referred to Crecquillon as "chapelain de la haute messe."

Whether he was maître de la chapelle or if he perhaps resigned the title by the time of Mameranus, he was in sufficiently high favor to have received a series of benefices. In 1540 he received income from Termonde and Béthune. In 1550 he received the benefices of St. Pierre, Louvain, and was canon at St. Aubin, Namur, which he resigned in 1552 to become canon of Termonde. In 1555 he was also canon of Béthune. In 1557 his successor there was named, most likely meaning that he died before then. Since there was a plague in the area at the time, that is the most likely cause of his death.

The first known publications of his music—and the only one we know to have occurred during his lifetime—was by Susato in 1544. It was a single volume called *Le tiers livre de chansons*. He left over 200 chansons and more than 100 motets, as well as a dozen masses and two cycles of Lamentations. He was a master of polyphony. His contemporaries mention him as one of the great composers of the Netherlands or Flemish school between Josquin and Lassus.

He uses imitation as his most important musical technique and was one of the greatest masters of it. Even when he wrote parody masses, he chose polyphonic works as the basis. His music has admirable qualities of invention and grandeur. The motion of his parts is smooth, and Crecquillon was not nearly as given to use dissonance and chromaticism as some of his contemporaries.

Claudio Monteverdi, about a century later, described him as a composer of the "first style." This description stems from the debate that broke out in the Roman Catholic Church at mid-century over the primacy of music or words in the composition of Church music, and means that Crecquillon allows the words to be submerged in the musical texture. Some commentators conclude that, masterly as his music is, Crecquillon often chooses technique over individuality. *—Joseph Stevenson*

Overview of Works (ca. 1540–1555)

An entire generation of composers between Josquin Desprez—at the turn of the sixteenth century—and Orlando di Lasso—near its end—often pass unnoticed in surveys of music history. Thomas Crecquillon, with his Franco-Flemish contemporaries Nicolas Gombert, Jacob Clemens non Papa, and Adrian Willaert, generally receives but perfunctory mention as a member of the lost "post-Josquin" generation. Yet the mid-century publishers Tylman Susato and Pierre Phalèse each published more pieces of Crecquillon than any other composer, including the wildly prolific Lasso. Several of Thomas' compositions were among the best-known hits of the century. His works were the subject of emulation and "parody" by composers across Europe, and he was highly touted by music theorists into the beginning of the next century. His twelve masses, roughly 125 motets, and over two hundred chansons helped establish the techniques of pervading imitation within the "Central Musical Language" of the Renaissance.

Though his only documented musical service is to the Flemish-speaking (and highly Catholic) court of the Holy Roman Emperor Charles V, Crecquillon's French chansons are often viewed as the cornerstone of his musical output. The chansons (most for four or five voices) appear in a large number of published and manuscript sources throughout the century, and several individual works achieved vast popularity. *Ung gay bergier*, for instance, was arranged at least 28 times for instrumental ensemble. Though a number of his texts are the work of well-known contemporary poets such as Clément Marot, most are unidentified. Even known poems are often adapted—apparently by the composer—for a specific event or context, by changing words, quoting middle stanzas, and the like. Quite freqeuntly, a chanson appears with a second (and even a third) piece of music as companions: *Chanson* and *Réponse*.

Two general strains of compositional practice are evident in Crecquillon's chansons (often both are found in the same piece). In line with current Parisian fashions, many—such as the paired chansons *Amour, partez* and *Au Dieu d'Amours*—adopt a more chordal and text-driven declamatory style. Others, such as *Si mon travail*, present the different aesthetic of Northern contrapuntal practice, with lines of text corresponding to structural "points" of imitation, each built around a single imitative motive. This type of imitative practice is even more consistently characteristic in Crecquillon's motets, whose texts are classically segmented into phrases marked by an opening imitation and proceeding to a cadence. A large number of the motets set texts from the Bible or from the Catholic liturgy, though several topical and celebratory motets indicate a courtly context for their composition. All but one of the Mass Ordinary cycles assume polyphonic models, both motets and chansons, often his own. Though some early masses seem rigid in their attitude towards the borrowed musical material, the best are among the most mature examples of the "parody" techniques so dear to the sixteenth century. *—Timothy Dickey*

Recommended:

- **Thomas Crecquillon Vol. 1: Missa Domine; Motets** / E. Ho (cond.), The Choir of the Church of the Advent, Boston / Arsis Audio 136
- **Thomas Crecquillon Vol. 2: Missa D'ung petit mot; Motets** / E. Ho (cond.), The Choir of the Church of the Advent, Boston / 2002 / Arsis Audio 146

Régine Crespin

b. Feb. 23, 1927, Marseilles, France
Soprano

Notwithstanding her great success in the German repertory, Régine Crespin was quintessentially a French artist. With an unmistakable sensuality betraying her origins in Mediterranean France, she was guided by an unfailing sense of elegance. Whether as Kundry, the Marschallin, Carmen, Didon, Amelia in *Un ballo in maschera*, or Sieglinde, her large, lush voice was deployed with refined abandon. Her top register, powerful and soaring when it was working as the singer wished, sometimes emerged congested, as tones that began as clarion would cloud over and lose their cutting edge. As it became increasingly problematic, Crespin looked toward roles only equivocally soprano, where she could rely on the luxurious amplitude of her middle and lower registers. Her Carmen, presented at the Metropolitan Opera in 1975 after a period of vocal restudy and a loss of weight, was distinctive for its subtle danger and meticulous delivery of text and vocal line.

Following studies at the Paris Conservatoire with Georges Jouatte and celebrated bass Paul Cabanel, Crespin made her debut in 1950 singing Elsa at *Mulhouse*. In August of that same year, she appeared for the first time at the Paris Opéra, the role once again being Elsa. Despite the self-evident resplendence of her voice and art, little else happened in the French capital and it was left to provincial theaters to witness the advance of Crespin's career. There, she grew into mastery of both the expected lyric/dramatic roles in the French repertory and spinto weight characters in Italian and German operas. With a major success in Paris as Reiza in Weber's *Oberon*, as well as in Poulenc's *Dialogues des Carmélites* (as Madame Lidoine), Crespin's reputation began to expand to other countries. In 1958, she appeared at Bayreuth, fulfilling Wieland Wagner's wish for a Kundry as Mediterranean temptress. Audiences at England's Glyndebourne Festival responded warmly to Crespin's womanly Marschallin in 1959 and Vienna hailed her passionate Sieglinde that same year. A Covent Garden debut in 1960 brought renewed acquaintance with her Marschallin and gained her still more ardent followers.

Chicago claimed Crespin for her American debut in 1962 and the reviews for her Tosca were adulatory. Critic Claudia Cassidy described her as "a singing actress of the first rank. She has what Callas has—intelligence, a born stage presence, subtlety, class, and a big spinto voice of individual timbre." Also in 1962 were debuts in Buenos Aires (where she sang such French roles as Cassandre and Didon in Berlioz's *Les Troyens*, Fauré's *Pénélope*, and the title role in Gluck's *Iphigénie en Tauride*) and New York. On November 19, Crespin made her first appearance at the Metropolitan Opera as Marschallin in a production enlisting Lotte Lehmann, that incomparable Marschallin of yesteryear, as director. Crespin was received enthusiastically and Lehmann herself later recalled that her younger colleague had begun rehearsals as rather "French," but had become "a typical Viennese woman" by the first performance. Lehmann, in her book on the operas of Richard Strauss, deemed Crespin "a magnificent Marschallin."

Crespin's San Francisco debut in 1966 found her shrill as Elisabeth in *Tannhäuser*, but both vocally comfortable and dramatically on point in the dual roles of Cassandre and Didon. In 1967, Crespin sang Marschallin in San Francisco.

By the early 1970s, vocal problems had dictated a move to roles with a lower tessitura, such as Carmen, Charlotte, and Madame de Croissy. Crespin retired in 1989. *—Erik Eriksson*

Recommended:

- ○ **Strauss: Der Rosenkavalier** / Solti (cond.), Pavarotti, Auger, Crespin, Minton, Vienna PO / 1998 / Decca 417493
- ○ **Wagner: Die Walküre** / Solti (cond.), Nilsson, Hotter, Ludwig, Crespin, Vienna PO / London 455559
- ○ **Berlioz: Les Nuits d'été; Ravel: Shéhérazade** / Ansermet (cond.), Crespin, Wustman, Orch. de la Suisse Romande / 1999 / Decca 460973

Paul Creston

b. Oct. 10, 1906, New York, NY, **d.** Aug. 24, 1985, San Diego, CA
Composer

As a composer, Paul Creston was about as self-made as he could be. Born Giuseppe Guttoveggio in New York City in 1906, Creston chose his professional surname from a high school play he'd been in, adopting "Paul" simply because it appealed to him. The son of poor Italian immigrants—his father was a housepainter—Creston was forced to leave high school after two years to work at a variety of jobs. Still, he educated himself in his free hours, practicing on a ten-dollar piano and studying the scores of the masters: Beethoven, Mozart, Brahms, Chopin, Debussy, Ravel, Stravinsky, and, above all, Johann Sebastian Bach. To fuel his nocturnal marathons, Creston bypassed coffee drinking altogether and took to smoking ground coffee beans in his pipe.

Recognition came late to Creston, who devoted his energies to composition only from 1932; but when the accolades and honors did come, they were many and impressive. Early performances of his music by Henry Cowell, a similarly accomplished autodidact, led to a 1938 Guggenheim fellowship. In 1941, Creston's *Symphony No. 1* received the annual award from the New York Music Critics' Circle. To his accelerating musical activities Creston added teaching duties, first at Swarthmore, and later at the New York College of Music (1963–67) and Central Washington State College (1968–75). His music was championed by a number of important conductors, including Toscanini, Ormandy, and Stokowski, but few were as committed to Creston's music as Howard Mitchell, longtime conductor of the National Symphony Orchestra of Washington, D.C.

Creston composed in a variety of forms; his catalogue includes six symphonies, 15 concerti (including some for neglected instruments like marimba and saxophone), and miscellaneous orchestral, chamber, choral, and vocal works. Creston demonstrated a particular affinity for the poetry of Walt Whitman, which inspired five major scores between 1934 and 1972. Though Creston's bold use of counterpoint often results in striking dissonance, he considered serialism a terrible mistake that would eventually be corrected. Accordingly, Creston's music is always distinctly tonal in the modern American idiom and possessed of a strong rhythmic sense. Rhythm is so central to Creston's aesthetic, in fact, that in addition to authoring two texts on rhythmic matters—*Principles of Rhythm* (1964) and *Rational Metric Notation* (1979)—the composer wrote a ten-volume series of 123 instructional piano works collectively titled *Rhythmicon* (1977).

From his earliest years as a composer, Creston maintained a post as organist of St. Malachy's Church in New York City (1934–67). There is a distinct religious sensibility to much of his music that is clearly evident in such works as the *Symphony No. 3* ("Three Mysteries"; 1950) and the orchestral meditation *Corinthians: XIII*, Op. 82 (1963). After retiring from his academic career, Creston moved to San Diego, where he died on August 24, 1985.*—Mark Satola*

Overview of Works (1932–1981)

The hallmark of Paul Creston's style lies in his deft manipulation of rhythm and of related elements, such as ostinatos. But one cannot underestimate his keen melodic talent and his imaginative harmonies, which, with his inventive rhythms, yielded music whose essence, as the composer asserted, was really about song and dance. Paul Creston, born Giuseppe Guttoveggio, wrote six symphonies, which probably comprise his most substantial body of work. His *First* (1940) drew immediate attention, elevating him to nearly front-rank status on the American scene. His *Second*, however, enjoyed broad popularity throughout the United States and even in Europe following its 1945 premiere. This two-movement work divulges a quite American sound, much in the vein of Hanson and Harris. Creston derives all his thematic material from seeds he cleverly planted in the first few bars. In a sense, this work is perfectly representative of his musical persona, with the first movement largely related to song and the second to dance. The 1950 *Third* was also a success, not least because it served as a venue for Creston to express his religious side. Each of its three movements depict a crucial event in the life of Christ. While the 1951 *Fourth* is also a worthy piece, it is the *Fifth* (1955) that some consider the composer's strongest symphony. Again, all the thematic material emerges from the opening, here presented in mysterious tones by the cellos and basses, after which much conflict emerges in the ensuing rhythmically dominated themes, conflict that is not resolved in this three-movement work until the conclusion of its powerful and dramatic finale. The *Sixth* (1981), for organ and orchestra, is not among his more successful symphonic compositions, but earlier efforts, such as the 15-minute tone poem *Corinthians XIII* (1963), evidenced his masterful skills at a time when his reputation was fading. *Walt Whitman* (1952), another symphonic poem, and *Choreografic Suite* (1965) are also quite worthy efforts, the latter disclosing a light character in its scoring, less muscle than one might expect in a dance work from this rhythmic-minded composer. His *Toccata for Orchestra* is a colorful piece that makes considerable demands on the ensemble's wind players.

Creston had a penchant for writing music for offbeat instruments, producing a saxophone concerto (1941), accordion concerto (1958), and other major works for marimba and trombone. He also composed scores for radio and television. In the keyboard realm, Creston's 1936 piano sonata comes across as an interesting early work but not quite on the level of *Metamorphoses* (1964), a brilliant variations composition. The 1952 *Suite for Flute, Viola, and Piano* and the *Concertino for Piano and Wind Quintet* (1969) are among the composer's more compelling chamber works. Creston's choral output includes his 1938 *Requiem* and 1949 *Missa Solemnis*, both well-crafted, but not major works. *—Robert Cummings*

Recommended:

- ○ **Creston: Symphony 5; Toccata; Partita** / S. Schwarz (cond.), Talvi, Goff, Seattle SO / 2003 / Naxos 8559153
- ○ **Creston: Symphonies 1–3** / Kuchar (cond.) National SO of Ukraine / 2000 / Naxos 559034

Richard Crooks

b. Jun. 26, 1900, Trenton, NJ, **d.** Sep. 29, 1972, Stanford, CA
Tenor

Richard Crooks began singing as a boy soprano in his local church. The famed contralto Ernestine Schumann-Heink heard the young Crooks at a performance of

Mendelssohn's *Elijah* and foresaw his promise; soon local choirmaster Sydney H. Bourne began formal voice training with him. With World War I's outbreak in 1917, Crooks lied about his age and enlisted to become a pilot in the Army Air Force. Before embarking to France, Crooks made a test record of his singing at the Columbia Records studio in New York, perhaps as insurance against an unlucky fate. Both he and his test survived the armistice.

Upon returning, Crooks studied with baritone Leon Rothier and the vocal coach/pianist Frank La Forge. Crooks' voice caught the attention of Walter Damrosch, who engaged him to sing *Siegfried* at a concert of the New York Symphony Orchestra in November 1922. From his first appearance, the New York press was abuzz about Crooks, and he shortly thereafter accepted a management contract. Victor Records signed Crooks as an artist in mid-1923, and in addition to solo records issued on the blue Victor label, Crooks appeared in Victor's series of anonymously performed operetta and musical theater "gems" in the black label "popular" series. Crooks continued to make these after he was established as a "Red Seal" artist.

Damrosch was intent on getting Crooks to study in Europe, but Crooks and his wife decided against this course of action. This did not prevent him from touring overseas, and in Hamburg in 1927 he made his operatic debut in *Tosca*. Crooks followed that with his Metropolitan Opera debut in 1930.

During this period Crooks was continuing to make scores of recordings for Victor, and some even in Europe. Crooks' strong, clear voice, crisp enunciation, and command of languages made him an ideal match for recording, and his records were popular sellers worldwide. After returning to New York in 1933 from his third tour of Europe, Crooks decided to record Schubert's *Die schöne Müllerin* in its entirety. To his profound disappointment, Victor did not release the records until 1941, and then only in a drastically shortened version. The complete *Die schöne Müllerin* with Crooks and La Forge would wait until 1997 for release, but this attempt to record such a large, "uncommercial" vocal work in the depths of the depression economy is an achievement which speaks for itself.

In 1933, Crooks instituted a highly popular series of radio broadcasts on the long-running Voice of Firestone program. He also finally joined the Metropolitan Opera's official roster. In the late 1930s, Crooks made tours of Australia and New Zealand that were so well received he had to add dates to his itinerary, delaying his return to the U.S. for months. One such delay, in 1939, was nearly costly, as the outbreak of the Second World War found Crooks and his wife stranded in Cape Town, South Africa. After he sang several concerts there, the Crooks found passage back to the U.S. on a cattle boat.

Ill health intervened, and in 1942 Crooks retired from the Metropolitan on the advice of his doctor. Crooks cancelled his Victor recording contract in 1945, and in 1950 ceased all professional work. In 1966, Crooks was honored at the Farewell Gala to the Old Met, this proving to be his final public appearance. Richard Crooks died at the age of 72, leaving behind a massive and rewarding legacy of commercial and radio recordings, some among the finest made by any tenor.
—Uncle Dave Lewis

Recommended:

- **The Stanford Archive Series** / Crooks, etc. / 1997 / Delos 5501
- **A Richard Crooks Serenade** / Crooks, etc. / 1997 / ASV 5240

Paul Crossley

b. May 17, 1944, Dewsbury, England
Pianist

English pianist Paul Crossley is world-renowned for his expertise and artistry in the interpretation of twentieth century keyboard literature. Although he has made his reputation as a pianist, Crossley began his studies on the organ at Mansfield College in Oxford; he first undertook serious instruction on piano in Leeds with Fanny Waterman, later founder of the Leeds International Piano Competition. In 1967 Crossley was awarded a scholarship to France in order to study with Yvonne Loriod and Olivier Messiaen and in 1968 won first prize in the Messiaen Piano Competition.

Paul Crossley first came to prominence in the concert world at the 1973 Bath Festival, premiering the *Piano Sonata No. 3* of Michael Tippett; likewise, Tippett's *Piano Sonata No. 4* (1983–84) would be entrusted to Crossley for its first performance. On the concert circuit, Crossley is most readily associated with "new music." He has given the first performances of piano works by composers Magnus Lindberg, Nicholas Maw, Hans Werner Henze, George Benjamin, Toru Takemitsu, John Adams, and Henryk Górecki. He has also made something of a specialty of the significant piano part in Messiaen's *Turangalîla Symphony* and has recorded it with Esa-Pekka Salonen and the Los Angeles Philharmonic. As a recording artist, Crossley has appeared on more than 50 releases, and has recorded the complete keyboard output of composers such as Tippett, Ravel, Poulenc, and Debussy. Crossley became an Internet music marketing pioneer in 2001 when he offered his complete recording of the piano works of Takemitsu through an Internet download at www.gmn.com before he released it at the retail level.
—Uncle Dave Lewis

Recommended:

- **Takemitsu: Riverrun; Water-Ways, etc.** / Knussen (cond.), Crossley, London Sinfonietta / 1991 / Virgin 7590202
- **Messiaen: Des Canyons aux Etoiles; Oiseaux Exotiques; Couleurs de la Cité Celeste** / E-P Salonen (cond.), Crossley, Thompson, Holland, Johnson, London Sinfonietta / 1988 / CBS 44762
- **Debussy: Complete Works For Solo Piano, Vol 1** / Crossley / 1993 / Sony 52583

George Crumb

b. Oct. 24, 1929, Charleston, WV
Composer: Chamber Music, Keyboard, Vocal, Choral

George Crumb was one of the most distinctive compositional voices to emerge in the second half of the twentieth century. A charter member of the "New Virtuosity" movement, Crumb developed an expansive musical palette noted for its emphasis on extended instrumental and vocal techniques, its rich and sophisticated musical allusions, an evocative theatricality, and a poet's sense of sonorous detail.

Crumb was born in West Virginia in 1929 into a musical family, and studied at various schools in the Midwest as well as at the Berlin Hochschule as a Fulbright Scholar. He eventually joined the faculty at the University of Pennsylvania, where he composed and taught for three decades. His highly intuitive approach to composition, with its emphasis on texture, timbre, and line, bore substantial fruit during the 1960s, including the *Madrigals* (1966–1969), *Eleven Echoes of Autumn* (1965), and, inspired by the Apollo 11 lunar landing, *Night of the Four Moons* (1969). *Echoes of Time and the River*, one of Crumb's rare orchestral works, earned the composer the Pulitzer Prize.

Crumb's style remained remarkably consistent during the subsequent decades. *Black Angels* (1970) used a dizzying arsenal of extended techniques to evoke a surreal soundscape of the Vietnam War. *Star Child* (1977) applied Crumb's acute ear for nuance to an impressive vocal/orchestral ensemble. *Ancient Voices of Children* (1970), with its unimaginable timbral variety and taxingly dramatic vocal lines, became a near-instant classic of the postwar period. It also demonstrated the resonance between his compositional style and the writing style of Garcia Lorca, whose poems would repeatedly serve as the inspiration for and/or words to a number of Crumb's pieces.

Crumb's works became known also for their almost choreographic visual elegance in performance—and, in fact, numerous dance companies have composed dance pieces to be performed with his work. Crumb's poignant use of musical borrowing and stylistic allusion also add a sense of reflective history and introspection to his compositions. In some cases, this visual approach to design spills over into the very notation: some of the pieces in the two-volume keyboard collection *Makrokosmos* (1972–1973) appear engraved on staves that turn and twist into a variety of curious Zodiac symbols. Having eschewed process-oriented compositional techniques, his output slowed in later years as greater demands were placed on his creative faculties to find continually new sounds and inspirations—though by the turn of the century, his historical importance was already firmly established.
—Jeremy Grimshaw

CHAMBER MUSIC

Black Angels (Images I), for electric string quartet (1970)

"There were terrifying things in the air," said George Crumb of the Vietnam War years. Events of the time provided inspiration for *Black Angels*, subtitled "Thirteen Images from the Dark Land." The score of this eerie, sometimes downright scary work (completed, by no means coincidentally given Crumb's fascination with numbers, on a Friday the 13th, in March 1970) is inscribed "in tempore belli" (in time of war). The Stanley Quartet gave *Black Angels* its premiere on October 23, 1970, in Ann Arbor, Michigan.

The quartet of stringed instruments is amplified "to the threshold of pain," and the musicians are called upon to play their instruments in many unusual ways, including trilling on the strings with thimble-capped fingers. The four players also whisper, chant, shout, and employ percussion instruments—maracas, tam-tams, and water-tuned crystal goblets. Crumb wrote of the work: "*Black Angels* was conceived as a kind of parable on our troubled contemporary world. The work portrays a voyage of the soul. The three stages of this voyage are Departure (fall from grace), Absence (spiritual annihilation), and Return (redemption)."

The first movement, Departure, begins abruptly and frighteningly with "Threnody I: Night of the Electric Insects," and moves into "Sounds of Bones and Flutes" and the mysterious "Lost Bells." Crashes of the tam-tam punctuate the wild "Devil-music," and the last section is a submerged-sounding evocation of Camille Saint-Saëns' *Danse macabre*. The movement ends with whispered counting from the musicians.

The opening section of the second movement, Absence, is titled "Pavana Lachrymae"; Schubert's *Death and the Maiden quartet* is quoted here in an evocation of ancient viol music. Yelling and further insect sounds are heard in "Threnody II:

Black Angels!" Viols are again imitated in "Sarabanda da la Muerte Oscura," and the movement closes with "Lost Bells (Echo)."

The final movement, Return, opens with "God-music," in which an ethereal glass harmonica effect from the water-tuned goblets combines with a wandering, nearly static melodic line. "Ancient Voices" consists mainly of a series of little pizzicato (plucked string) sounds. An almost silent "Ancient Voices (Echo)" leads into more pizzicato sounds and a reprise of the insect music in "Threnody III: Night of the Electric Insects." *—Chris Morrison*

Recommended:

- ○ **Black Angels** / Kronos Quartet / 1990 / Nonesuch 79242
- ○ **American String Quartets 1950–1970** / Concord SQ / 1995 / VoxBox 5143

Music for a Summer Evening (Makrokosmos III), for 2 amplified pianos & 2 percussionists (1974)

George Crumb completed *Makrokosmos III, Music for a Summer Evening* in February 1974. It is scored for two amplified pianos and percussion, expanding on the solo piano work of *Makrokosmos I and II* from 1972 and 1973 respectively. Bartók's *Sonata for two pianos and percussion* from 1937 partially inspired this work, and the pieces work well together on the same concert program. Thematically, *Makrokosmos III* is, like his earlier works in the series, concerned with the Babylonian zodiac and other pieces of his personal world view, drawing together many disparate elements to achieve a grander design. About 40 minutes long and divided into five specific sections, it is a work of art that brings to mind Mahler's claim that "a symphony is like the world; it must contain everything." The same can easily be said for this work. There are so many intertwined elements that one cannot hear the work upon repeated listenings without being rewarded by the further unveiling of additional interconnections and outside musical associations. A cosmology of benevolent spirituality is in operation in tandem with world history, different cultures, and music from throughout the ages. It is a work so successful and openhearted that *Makrokosmos III* is among the most frequently performed avant-garde chamber works from the second half of the twentieth century. The dedicatees were the same illustrious musicians that premiered the work at Swarthmore College on March 30, 1974, Gilbert Kalish, James Freeman, Raymond DesRoches, and Richard Fitz.

Crumb described the work's syntax as "more or less atonal, or more or less tonal." Crumb's personal musical syntax does not sound systematic. In fact, it is difficult to envision him describing in technical detail how his personal language works. It is music of intuitive organicism and highly idiosyncratic. The titles of the movements, such as the opening "Nocturnal Sounds (The Awakening)" seem chosen with little concern for the more worldly approaches toward art, though the titles of the three larger movements are taken from Quasimoto, Rilke, and Pascal. His is intimate music, pastoral, personal, and celestial. Its international quality is only partially related to Western art. Crumb uses Tibetan prayer stones and an African thumb piano in this piece, evoking a sympathy for all cultures that has been frequently imitated to a lesser effect. The furthest reaching quote in *Makrokosmos III* is in the last movement, "Music of the Starry Night," wherein Bach's D sharp minor fugue is quoted from the second book of the *Well-Tempered Clavier.* Among Crumb's many successful works, this one has perhaps the most evocative cultural polyphony. Like Messiaen, Crumb has a vast, universal viewpoint that translates seamlessly into his music. As a work of either composer continues, there is always more coming into the work from the most unlikely of sources. *—John Keillor*

Recommended:

- ○ **Crumb: Ancient Voices Of Children** / Kalish & J. Freeman, DesRoches, Fitz / 1971 / Nonesuch 79149
- ○ **Crumb: Madrigals; Makrokosmos III** / I. Lindgren & Dahlman, Kuisma, Asikainen / 1985 / BIS 261

KEYBOARD

Makrokosmos I, for amplified piano (1972)

Crumb's *Makrokosmos, Vol. I* (12 Fantasy-Pieces after the Zodiac for Amplified Piano) (1972) were written for his friend David Burge, who later recorded them for Nonesuch Records. Crumb has said that the title and format of the pieces "reflect my admiration for two great twentieth century composers of piano music—Béla Bartók and Claude Debussy." While composing, Crumb "was aware of certain recurrent haunting images... vivid... subliminal...." These were "the 'magical properties' of music; the problem of the origin of evil; the 'timelessness' of time; a sense of the profound ironies of life (so beautifully expressed in the music of Mozart and Mahler); the haunting words of Pascal 'Le silence éternel des espaces infinis m'effraie' (the eternal silence of infinite space terrifies me); and these few lines of Rilke: '... And in the nights the heavy earth is falling from all the stars down in loneliness. We are all falling. And yet there is One who holds this falling endlessly gently in his hands.'"

The *Makrokosmos* use the same alternative techniques inside and on the keyboard of the piano as the *Five Piano Pieces.* Like in his later *Madrigals,* Crumb has a penchant for organizing sets of pieces in 3 x 4 or 4 x 3 subsets. Each subset of the *Makrokosmos, Vol. 1* ends with a piece notated in a graph notation that is symbolic. Part One contains (1) Primeval Sounds (Genesis I)/Cancer, (2) Proteus/Pisces, (3) Pastorale (from the kingdom of Atlantis, ca. 10,000 B.C.)/Taurus, and (4) Crucifixus/Capricorn (written in the form of a cross, on the horizontal with "darkly mysterious" low harmonics, and on the vertical with a shouted "Christe!" accompanied by very deep and very high pitches and gradually receding in a "serene, transcendental" series of tiny variations on a high figure.

Part Two contains (5) The Phantom Gondolier/Scorpio, (6) Night-Spell I/Sagittarius, (7) Music of Shadows (for Aeolian Harp), and (8) The Magic Circle of Infinity (Moto Perpetuo)/Leo, written in the form of a circle, played "joyously, like a cosmic clockwork" initiated by a non-repeated passage of high clusters.

Part Three concludes with (9) The Abyss of Time/Virgo, (10) Spring-Fire/Aires, (11) Dream Images (Love-Death Music)/Gemini, and (12) the Spiral Galaxy/Aquarius, written in a spiral graphic. *—"Blue Gene" Tyranny*

Recommended:

- ○ **George Crumb: Makrokosmos I & II** / Henz-Diemond / 1989 / Musikszene Schweiz 6091
- ○ **George Crumb: Makrokosmos I & II** / M. Leng Tan / 2004 / Mode 142

Makrokosmos II, for amplified piano (1973)

George Crumb's *Makrokosmos, Volume II* (1973)—subtitled *12 Fantasy Pieces after the Zodiac*—is a sequel to *Makrokosmos, Volume I,* and was composed in 1972. Like its predecessor, it is a work for solo piano in which the pianist is asked to play his or her instrument in a fashion that would likely have left Franz Liszt and Johannes Brahms completely speechless. The instrument must be amplified so that the incredibly wide dynamic range (*ffff* to *pppp*) can be better felt by audience members far back from the stage; then, taking up where John Cage left off, the piano must be "prepared" beforehand by the insertion of foreign objects—a strip of paper, glass tumblers, etc.—into the string area to produce carefully calculated sonic effects. When it comes time to actually play the piano, the pianist must, in addition to employing ordinary keyboard techniques, stick his or her hands into the guts of the piano and pluck strings, knock on the soundboard, and so on. He or she must also, in vintage Crumb fashion, use his or her voice—"singing" certain mystic words, making rhythmic breath sounds, and at one point whistling. Naturally, the range of sounds produced during a performance of *Makrokosmos II* is stunning; this, combined with the sheer spectacle of one performer doing so many different things in one piece, have made the work one of Crumb's most famous.

The 12 pieces in *Makrokosmos* all have both proper names and zodialogical subtitles; they are laid out in three groups, or parts, of four pieces each. Part One contains: 1. "Morning Music" (Genesis II), which corresponds to Cancer; 2. "The Mystic Chord" [Sagittarius]; 3. "Rain-Death Variations" [Pisces]; and 4. "Twin Suns" (Doppelgänger aus der Ewigkeit) [Gemini]. Part Two is: 5. "Ghost Nocturne: for the Druids of Stonehenge" (Night-Spell II) [Virgo]; 6. "Gargoyles" [Taurus]; 7. "Tora! Tora! Tora!" (Cadenza Apocalittica) [Scorpio]; and 8. "A Prophecy of Nostradamus" [Aries]. Part 3 contains: 9. "Cosmic Wind" [Libra]; 10. "Voices from 'Corona Borealis'" [Aquarius]; 11. "Litany of the Galactic Bells" [Leo]; and, finally, 12. "Agnus Dei" [Capricorn].

The player or listener familiar with Crumb's *Four Nocturnes* for violin and piano will find the visual layout of the score of *Makrokosmos II,* and its multi-textured, semi-percussive sounds, very familiar. Three of the pieces (Nos. 4, 8, and 12—the final piece in each part) do, however, look completely differently than the others; in them, the music is printed in circles and spirals—Crumb calls these movements "symbols." *Makrokosmos II* lasts a little over 30 minutes in performance and is dedicated to pianist Robert Miller, who premiered it on November 12, 1974. *—Blair Johnston*

Recommended:

- ○ **George Crumb: Makrokosmos I & II** / Hudicek / 2002 / Furious Artisans 6805
- ○ **George Crumb: Makrokosmos I & II** / M. Leng Tan / 2004 / Mode 142

VOCAL

Ancient Voices of Children (1970)

George Crumb's *Ancient Voices of Children,* a song cycle for soprano and chamber ensemble, is one of several compositions by Crumb based on the poetry of Federico Garcia Lorca. In fact, the work is the eighth installment in what the composer considers a kind of "meta-cycle," one that includes such earlier Lorca settings as *Night Music* (1963), *Madrigals, Books I–VI* (1965), *Songs, Drones, and Refrains of Death* (1968), and *Night of the Four Moons,* from (1969). *Ancient Voices of Children* is the best-known of the series, and stands as one of the few pieces of late twentieth century avant-garde music that manages to appeal to a broad audience while at the same time maintaining a challenging harmonic and stylistic language and a highly sophisticated musical surface.

It is perhaps the complexity of the piece that appeals to listeners; Crumb's angular lines and surprising timbres do not seem to emerge from a theoretic premise but rather from a highly intuitive and often visceral emotional sense. In setting Lorca's evocative poetry and addressing its themes of childhood, aging, and death, Crumb renders the poetry with an intriguing theatrical sensibility. Crumb frequently calls on the soprano and the boy soprano featured in the piece to use extended vocal techniques and sound effects, thus blurring the boundaries between conversation, soliloquy, and song. Likewise, the oboist frequently uses unusual articulations and pitch bends, and also doubles on harmonica. The mandolinist plays deliberately out of tune, and also performs on the musical saw. The harpist sometimes plays with papers woven between the strings, while the keyboardist moves between a toy piano and an amplified "real" one. A trio of percussionists perform on a wide variety of instruments from around the world. Crumb seeks not only to blur boundaries between music, poetry, and drama, but likewise keeps porous the boundaries separating the musical elements involved in the piece: the instrumentalists are called upon occasionally to hum, speak, and whisper, while the singers sometimes are instructed at certain points to sing directly at the amplified and undampened strings of the piano in order to create shimmering fields of resonance.

Consisting of five songs, the cycle is comprised of five songs interspersed with interludes. In "El niño busca su voz," vocal gestures and noises gradually coalesce into words. The ambiguously exotic "Dance of the Ancient Earth" leads into the haunting second song, "Me he perdido muchas veces por el mar," followed by the more angular and rhythmically charged "¿De dónde vienes, amor, mi niño?" and the "Dance of the Sacred Life Cycle." The mournfully tranquil "Todas las tardes en Grandada, todas las tardes se muere un niño," with its combination of meditative drones and nostalgic instruments (including the toy piano and the harmonica) is perhaps the most memorable song in the cycle. The brief and spartan "Ghost Dance" introduces the intensely focused "Se ha llenado de luces me corazón de seda," with which this engaging and dramatic cycle ends. *—Jeremy Grimshaw*

Recommended:

- ○ **Crumb: Ancient Voices Of Children** / Weisberg (cond.), DeGaetani, Contemporary Chamber Ens. / 1971 / Nonesuch 79149
- ○ **Crumb: Ancient Voices Of Children & others** / P. Freeman (cond.), B. A. Martin, Orch. 2001 / 1998 / CRI 803

CHORAL

Star-Child (1977)

Even decades after its composition, George Crumb's *Star-Child*, from 1977, remains one of his most ambitious works. It calls for huge instrumental and vocal forces, including a huge percussion battery, and no fewer than four conductors, whose respective ensembles follow independent paths to form a loose, undulating, but coherent composite. This vast collection of sound colors reflects the breadth of the work's quasi-narrative arc: a "progression from darkness (or despair) to light (or joy and spiritual realization . . .)."

The first movement, an instrumental introduction, paints a translucent backdrop of hums; drones; faint, low gongs; and slow, sustained chord progressions in the strings. These chords appear throughout the work, a constant undercurrent representing the "Music of the Spheres." The opening vocal strains in the second movement depict a soul tormented by apocalyptical thoughts ("Deliver me, Lord, from eternal death on that terrible day . . ."). The soprano's line, which simmers for stretches before rising in ardent leaps, forms an intermittent, angular counterpoint with a solo trombone's ominous growls and violent outbursts; this clearly recalls the texture of Ives' *The Unanswered Question*, in which woodwinds and a trumpet make similar exchanges above faint string harmonies. A brief and haunting interlude, featuring low whines in the brass and rattling chains and gongs in the percusssion, propels listeners with a drum crescendo into the fourth, "Musica apocalyptica." Here Crumb introduces a male choir, which intones a tersely shouted version of the famous *Dies irae* plainchant and sets the percussion off into driving, odd-metered rhythms (which, in more than one moment, recall the noisier moments in Stravinsky's *Rite of Spring*). The subsequent interlude, "Seven Trumpets of the Apocalypse," adds a spatial element to its eschatological evocations by distributing the trumpets around the perimeter of the performance space. With the penultimate movement, "Adventus Puerorum Luminis"(Advent of the Children of Light), the piece begins its ascent toward its ecstatic culmination, "Hymnus pro novo tempore" (Hymn for the New Age), in which the soprano is joined by two children's choirs, situated antiphonally on opposite sides of the stage. This final movement, the longest in the piece, finds its apex not in boisterous exclamations, however, but in a serene return to the cosmic harmonies with which the composition began. The final voices heard come from the men's choir uttering, in a whisper that rises like an apparition from the sustained chords, "Deliver me, O Lord, from eternal death." *—Jeremy Grimshaw*

Recommended:

- ○ **Crumb 70th Birthday Album: Star-Child** / Conlin (cond.), Narucki, Warsaw National PO / 1999 / Bridge 9095

Hugues Cuénod

b. Jun. 26, 1902, Conseaux-sur-Vervey, France
Tenor

Hugues Cuénod is sometimes referred to as "the tenor without a voice," which is quite untrue. He has never claimed to have a beautiful voice, but he has created his own important niche in our musical lives.

Cuénod began his vocal studies as a baritone, but with his teacher's help worked the voice to a highly cultivated tenor. At first he sang primarily light music and cabaret songs, but in 1928 he sang in the French premiere of Krenek's *Jonny spielt auf*. His career took a change in direction when he began to sing early music under the direction of Nadia Boulanger. Performances of Cavalieri's *Rappresentatione di Anima et di Corpo* and Monteverdi madrigals brought him a reputation as an early music specialist, but he was equally at home with the music of his contemporaries. He sang in the premieres of *Le Diable boiteux* by Francaix and Stravinsky's *The Rake's Progress*, *Cantata*, and *Threni*. Cuénod sang many character roles in operas by Richard Strauss, Giuseppe Verdi, Wolfgang Amadeus Mozart, Claudio Monteverdi, and Leoš Janáček among others. He was one of the few tenors to sing the Astrologer in Rimsky-Korsakov's *Le coq d'Or* with all its high phrases. He made his Metropolitan Opera debut at the age of 85 as the Emperor in Puccini's *Turandot* (becoming the oldest person ever to debut at the Met!). He relished making a complete character in just a short period of time on stage. He was a regular visitor to the Glyndebourne Festival between 1954 and 1977 singing in operas by Stravinsky, Mozart, Strauss, Verdi, Mozart, Monteverdi, Ravel, Cavalli, Tchaikovsky, Massenet and Janáček.

Besides continuing to sing well into his eighties, Hugues Cuénod gave master classes and coached singers around the world. He did not teach voice, but rather taught the performer how to find their way of interpreting the song or opera at hand.

The voice of Hugues Cuénod was certainly not your typical tenor. It was thin, reedy, and very pure. The lack of sensuous beauty required the listener to concentrate on the text and the meaning of music. He was an excellent musician, which was why he was the favorite of so many composers. He simply tried to lay the music out as the composer intended.

Cuénod made many recordings over the years. The earliest important recordings are of Monteverdi madrigals. In the early LP era, he recorded a series of discs of vocal music of the pre-Baroque era. Later there were recordings of songs by Schubert, Fauré, and Debussy which have been reissued (LYS 342/3). He has also taken part in recordings of *L'enfant et les sortileges*, *Ariadne auf Naxos*, *Oedipus Rex*, *Les contes d'Hoffmann*, *L' Ormindo*, *Le nozze di Figaro*, *Benvenuto Cellini*, and the *St. Matthew Passion*. With Hilde Rossl-Majden, he recorded the complete *Schemelli-Liederbuch* of Bach. His recordings of Stravinsky's music are required listening for any devotee of that composer. *—Richard LeSueur*

Recommended:

- ○ **Cuénod: Inédits, 1948–1965** / Boulanger (cond.), Desarzens (cond.), Cuenod, Jaccottet, Lipatti / 2002 / Cascavelle 6158
- ○ **Cuénod: Le Maître de la Mélodie** / Cuenod, Parsons (piano) / 1992 / Nimbus 5337
- ○ **Hugues Cuénod (ténor)** / Cuenod, Cohen (piano) / 1995 / INA Memoire Vive 016

César Cui

b. Jan. 18, 1835, Vilnius, Russia, **d.** Mar. 26, 1918, Petrograd, Russia
Composer: Chamber Music

An engineer, military officer, and self-taught composer, César Cui was also a perceptive critic. As a member of the Mighty Handful of composers, he did much to help shape Russian nationalism in the nineteenth century.

Born in Poland, he was the son of a Lithuanian woman and a French officer who had been trapped in Russia following Napoleon's rout in 1812. Cui displayed precocious musical talent and was taught the pianoforte at an early age. He also received instruction in musical theory, but upon his graduation from school in Wilno, he chose to enter the School of Military Engineering in Saint Petersburg. He became a sub-professor at the Artillery School and Staff College and was recognized as an authority on fortification, even instructing Emperor Nicholas II. He ascended to the rank of lieutenant general and, as a collateral activity, took the post of president of the Imperial Russian Musical Society.

In 1857, Cui encountered Mily Balakirev and not only was his musical enthusiasm fired, he became a disciple of Balakirev and an ardent devotee of his Russian nationalist beliefs. As he did with most everyone else he met, Balakirev bullied Cui and made continual, insistent demands with regard to his compositional efforts. Cui began to compose in earnest and in 1859 produced his first operetta, *The Mandarin's Son*. It was an early and lackluster effort, but Cui pressed on, winning the prize of the Imperial Russian Music Society in 1860 for a work which combined chorus and orchestra. He had also composed his first three orchestral works: a pair of scherzos and an early tarantella.

Ten years elapsed before Cui produced another opera; it was an ambitious work, a drama in three acts based upon Heine's romantic tragedy *William Ratcliff.* It was premiered in Saint Petersburg in 1869, was well received, and established Cui's reputation as a composer of Russian opera. He followed this in 1875 with another large-scale dramatic work based upon the play *Angelo* by Victor Hugo. Posterity has come to view this as possibly the finest work of Cui's maturity, but it did not receive the adulation nor the popular acceptance of the earlier work.

In the meantime, Cui began to write reviews and essays on musical subjects and became a frequent and respected critic and contributor to many leading Russian papers. As a critic, Cui was perceptive and witty. His articles also appeared in both French and Belgian publications and he used these to call attention outside Russia to the growing nationalism of Russian music.

Though he produced many songs and other larger-scale vocal works, another 13 years passed before Cui produced another opera. This was *Le Flibustier,* based upon a play by Jean Richepin. Finally presented five years later, in 1894, it was enthusiastically received but did not endure. Between 1899 and 1903, he wrote more operas, continued to produce a few orchestral works, larger numbers of vocal pieces, and solo works for pianoforte during these years. As he finished his career, he generated three more operatic works, the last of which, *Puss-in-Boots,* was unfinished and unperformed at his death. *—Michael Morrison*

CHAMBER MUSIC

Kaleidoscope, 24 pieces for violin & piano, Op. 50 (1893)

Like so much of César Cui's music, the 24 miniatures that together make up the *Kaleidoscope* for violin and piano are forgotten—all but one of the 24, that is. Op. 50, No. 9 is the famous "Orientale," and has been a staple on violinists' encore lists (and also, through various arrangements, cellists') for a full century now. The other 23—well, suffice it to say that a full recording of *Kaleidoscope* didn't appear until that same full century was nearly up, and that the number of complete performances given by violinists of stature can probably be counted on one hand without using the thumb.

"Orientale" is drawn from the same stock of faux-Eastern gestures that Tchaikovsky and countless other lesser late nineteenth century composers drew from in their efforts to satiate the Orient-crazed Russian and French musical publics. (The *Nutcracker* contains probably the most famous such music.) There is only the slightest breeze of anything authentically Eastern in the music, but we would be remiss to denounce Op. 50, No. 9 on the grounds of stylistic inauthenticity—Cui, like Tchaikovsky (though Cui would not like to hear anyone say that anything about him was "like Tchaikovsky"—Cui was one of Tchaikovsky's most vehement critics), was simply taking colors from a then-exotic source and sprinkling them onto his music at will. The 6/8 time Allegretto rides along on a tambourine rhythm set up by the violin in the opening bars. The tune offered by the piano a few bars in, and later taken up, "con morbidezza," by the violin is built from flavorful augmented seconds. There is a tiny middle episode, not a section unto itself by any means, just a little wedge between two presentations of the main idea. At the reprise of the opening, the previously simple piano harmonies sprout some chromaticism, and the opening tambourine riff brings the curtain down at the end.

Of the other *Kaleidoscope* pieces, there is a Mazurka that is pulled off the shelf from time to very rare time, and also a sweet-toned "Lettre d'Amour" that has found a few fans over the years. Of more significance is the composer's *Violin Sonata in D,* Op. 86. *—Blair Johnston*

Recommended:

○ **Cui: Kaleidoscope; Violin Sonata** / Sheppard, Shorr / 1995 / Olympia 456

José Cura

b. Dec. 5, 1962, Rosario, Argentina
Tenor

José Cura emerged in the mid-1990s as one of the most distinctive and promising new tenor voices. His first instrument was the guitar, which he studied under Juan de Maestro, and his first public performance was as a choral conductor at the age of fifteen. He studied composition with Carlos Castro and piano with Zulma Cabrera. He entered the School of Arts of the National University of Rosario in 1982.

At that time he was undecided between a career in music or as a professional rugby player. He accepted the suggestion of the university's choirmaster that he study vocal technique. Horacio Amauri, one of his first teachers, taught him the basic foundation of singing. He has continued to receive lessons and coaching in Italian operatic style from Vittorio Terranova.

His initial performances were in unusual repertoire: his first stage performance was as the father in Hans Werner Henze's opera *Pollicino* in Verona in 1992, and he first garnered attention in Trieste, where he sang Jan in *Fraulein Julie* by Antonio Bibalo (1993).

In 1994 he won the International Operalia Competition and made his American debut. His London debut was in Verdi's *Stiffelio* in 1995. The London press predicted that he was an "Otello-in-waiting," a prediction he fulfilled in 1997 when he sang the great Verdi role in Turin with Claudio Abbado conducting. *USA Today* contrasted him to the stereotypical "brilliant, heroic tenor voice encased in the dumpiest of bodies and deployed by the dimmest of intellects," calling him "tall, smart, and handsome." Cura insists that he is "an actor who sings, not a singer who pretends to act." He maintains his interest in athletics through a serious bodybuilding regime and Kung-Fu training (he is a Black Belt). Thus, he makes a credible stage appearance as a hero, even as Samson, in Saint-Saëns' opera *Samson et Dalila,* which he has recorded. He prefers "the roles that [he] can act and where the plot is believable or something close to reality." He says he sings parts like Calaf (Puccini's *Turandot*) and Radamès (Verdi's *Aïda*) for the sake of the music, but does not enjoy them because they are "so one-dimensional that it is very difficult to make a believable character out of them." He calls Giordano's *Fedora* "a bitter pill" and says that in Bellini's *Norma* "you feel like you're in the middle of nonsense." But he likes Cavaradossi (in Puccini's *Tosca*) because the character of the political prisoner has reality today. He was slow to accept invitations to record because audio-only performances eliminate much of the acting part of the role. His first release was an acclaimed set of Puccini arias, which he delivered free of the post-Caruso "tradition" of vocal sobs and other histrionic effects. The album was conducted by Plácido Domingo.

In 2001, he became principal guest conductor of Sinfonia Varsovia. His work in the early 2000s has included a wide range of operatic performances and recordings, and he is especially noted for concert performances in which he both sings and serves as conductor. *—Joseph Stevenson*

Recommended:

○ **Puccini Arias** / Domingo (cond.), Cura, London PO / 1997 / Erato 18838

○ **Verismo** / Cura, Brewer, Owens, London Philharmonia Orch. / 1999 / Erato 27317

○ **Anhelo** / Cura, Bitetti, Delgado / 1998 / Erato 23138

Clifford Curzon

b. May 18, 1907, London, England, **d.** Sep. 1, 1982, London, England
Pianist

Clifford Curzon was among the finest English pianists of the twentieth century, known for his clear, ego-less performances of the German Classical and Romantic masterpieces. A quiet intellectual who nevertheless possessed a formidable technique, Curzon played everything from Mozart to Liszt with equal authority. His fans often cite this ability to emphasize the personality of each composer, rather than his own, as his most distinctive quality. Curzon recorded for the Decca label for over 30 years, leaving behind a modestly sized, but musically impressive catalog. His recordings of Mozart and Schubert are considered his best.

Curzon achieved success early, with a scholarship to London's Royal Academy of Music in 1919. His impressive student career earned him every prize available to a pianist at the Academy, and he made his professional debut in 1923—playing Bach's *Triple Concerto* with conductor Henry Wood at a Promenade Concert in Queen's Hall. In 1926, when still just 19 years old, he was invited to join the RAM faculty; he remained on the faculty there until 1932, when he became a full-time performing pianist. During his time teaching at the RAM, Curzon spent several extended periods abroad studying with great pianists: first with Artur Schnabel in Berlin, and then with Wanda Landowska and Nadia Boulanger in Paris. In 1936, Curzon made a recital tour of Europe with violist Lionel Tertis, and in 1939, he made his U.S. debut at New York's Town Hall. By 1941, he was making records for Decca, beginning a relationship that would last almost to the end of his life.

Curzon was an exacting perfectionist, often refusing to allow the release of recordings he felt were imperfect. This included recordings of Mozart concertos with the likes of George Szell, István Kertész, and Benjamin Britten conducting. For this and other reasons, he earned a reputation for being difficult, and at times highly temperamental—an irony, considering his generally retiring nature, and the restrained elegance of his playing. Curzon was knighted in 1977. *—Allen Schrott*

Recommended:

○ **Brahms, Franck, Litolff** / Szell, Boult (cond.),Curzon, London SO, London PO / 1999 / Decca 466376

○ **Mozart: Concertos Nos. 20, 23, 24, 26 & 27** / Britten (cond.), Kertesz (cond.), Curzon, English CO, London PO / 2001 / Decca 468491

○ **Decca Recordings, 1948–1964, Vol. 1** / Curzon, etc. / 2003 / Decca 000017602

○ **Clifford Curzon** / Kertesz (cond.), Curzon, London SO / 1999 / Philips 456757

Czech Philharmonic Orchestra

f. 1896, Prague, Bohemia (Czech Rep.)
Ensemble

The Czech Philharmonic Orchestra has a particularly strong reputation in the music of its own country and in French and twentieth century works as well. In 1894, the members of the orchestra of the Czech-speaking National Theater re-formed into the Czech Philharmonic Orchestra. Their first performance was on January 4,

1896, under the baton of Antonín Dvořák. Conductor Vaclav Talich is credited with actually building the CPO into a first-rate ensemble after Czech independence in 1918. Debuting with the orchestra in October 1918, Talich's thrilling premier of Josef Suk's *Ripening* led to his appointment as principal conductor, a post he held until 1941. During the Second World War and the German occupation, he displayed tremendous perseverance by programming Smetana's symphonic cycle *Má Vlast* (My Country), and was unjustly persecuted for this even after the liberation. Rafael Kubelik first conducted the Philharmonic at the age of 19 and was engaged as conductor in 1936. From 1937–1939 he led it on its tours of England, Belgium, and Italy. Kubelik was then named principal conductor of the Czech Philharmonic in 1942, establishing himself as a unique musical interpreter. On October 22, 1945, the orchestra lost its independent status when the Soviet-backed government nationalized Czechoslovakia. In 1948 Kubelik fled the country, leading to the brief appointment of Vaclav Neumann as music director, who was then succeeded from 1950–68 by Karel Ančerl. During Ančerl's tenure the orchestra's repertoire was expanded to include significant works of the twentieth century. At this time the orchestra's numerous recordings gained considerable acclaim, a series of which won prestigious international awards. In 1968 the CPO lost Ančerl, who left for Canada as Russian troops crushed the liberty-minded "Prague Spring" government. Vaclav Neumann was then re-appointed CPO chief conductor, a position he retained until 1990. The backbone of Neumann's repertoire was Czech music, particularly the entire symphonic and oratorio legacy of Antonín Dvořák, and of course Smetana's *Má Vlast* and the works of Janáček and Martinů, which he approached with special admiration. Neumann's contribution to the interpretation of Mahler's symphonic legacy was also substantial. Fortunately, the majority of his output as conductor has been captured on recordings, which have also won international recognition. In 1989 Neumann spearheaded a protest against the government's continued repression of artists. The orchestra joined the protest, becoming part of a process that brought down the Communist regime. The orchestra played Dvořák's *Te Deum* on December 29, 1989 in celebration of the election of Vaclav Havel as the Czech Republic's president.

On May 12, 1990, Rafael Kubelik returned from 42 years of exile to lead the orchestra in a thrilling performance of *Má Vlast*. However, the 1990s were a difficult decade for the orchestra, with numerous disagreements amongst the musicians. In June 1996, Vladimir Valek was finally appointed permanent conductor, but not chief conductor, a post that remained vacant. In January 1997, Vladimir Ashkenazy conducted the orchestra and was soon appointed chief conductor, effective January 1, 1998. He has since devoted himself to a broad range of tours, recordings and special projects with the aim of focusing appropriate attention on this great orchestra with its rich musical tradition. During the 1999/2000 season and coincident with the 10th anniversary of the Velvet Revolution, they appeared together in Europe, Japan, the United States, and South America, performing repertoire at the very heart of the orchestra's history and cultural identity, from Mozart and Mahler to Krasa, Janáček and Martinů. *—Joseph Stevenson*

Recommended:

- ○ **Václav Talich** / Talich (cond.), Czech PO, Slovak PO / EMI 75483
- ○ **Smetana: Má Vlast** / Kubelik (cond.), Czech PO / 1990 / Supraphon 111208
- ○ **Karel Ančerl Conducts Celebrated Overtures** / Ančerl (cond.), Czech PO / 1999 / Supraphon 011
- ○ **Charles Mackerras Conducts Janáček** / Mackerras (cond.), Czech PO / 2004 / Supraphon 3739
- ○ **Belohlavek Conducts Martinů** / Belohlavek (cond.), Saroun, Ruzicka, Czech PO / 2003 / Supraphon 3743
- ○ **Dvořák: Symphonies 7–9** / Neumann (cond.), Czech PO / 2003 / Supraphon 3705
- ○ **Vaclav Talich & Clemens Krauss** / Krauss, Talich (conds.), Vienna PO, Czech PO / 2000 / History 204557

György Cziffra

b. Nov. 5, 1921, Budapest, Hungary, **d.** Jan. 15, 1994, Paris, France

Pianist

György Cziffra was one of the most celebrated and individual piano virtuosos of the postwar decades in Europe, especially noted for his powers of improvisation and as a Liszt pianist.

He was born in a shantytown called Angels Court on the outskirts of Budapest to a family of gypsy musicians. The family was desperately poor, and ultimately both his father and a sister died of starvation.

He learned piano by watching an older sister's lessons. By the age of five, he was improvising requests from the audience at a circus. At ten, he was sent to the conservatory in Budapest. He was able to stay there only briefly, taking lessons from György Ferenczi and composition with Ernst von Dohnányi, supporting himself playing in nightclubs. He began to establish a recital career in Hungary, Holland, and Sweden. He married Zuleika shortly before he was drafted into the Hungarian army in 1941. After the war, he was imprisoned for a year in 1946.

Returning to his wife and small son, and with his mother and surviving sisters dependent on him, he worked for hours each day to recover his piano technique, making a living on tips from playing jazz in bars and cabarets each night. After the Communists gained full power in Hungary, Cziffra was imprisoned again, for political reasons, which meant that his captors also took his wife and son, György Cziffra Jr. The boy nearly died from the inhumane conditions in which he was held. Cziffra's Communist captors tortured him; knowing he was a pianist, they beat his hands and made him carry heavy pieces of stone. When he was released, the ligaments were so loose that he could not transmit the power of his arms through his wrists. After six months of exhaustive work, he recovered his top form. His records on the Hungarian label Qualiton and the Czechoslovak Supraphon label began to circulate in Western Europe, propelling him to legendary status.

When Russian troops poured into Hungary, the refugees fleeing ahead of them included the Cziffra family. After ten days on foot, they reached Vienna. He debuted there at the *Brahmssaal* on November 17, 1956, with outstanding success. Debuts elsewhere in Europe followed. After one recital in London, *The Daily Telegraph* said the audience "witnessed feats of piano playing probably never to be equalled, certainly never surpassed in their lifetime." Cziffra gained international stardom not without critical disfavor, adhering to a nineteenth century approach to music that allowed for taking "liberties" with the texts.

Cziffra settled in France with his family and took citizenship there. He undertook three major projects. One was the establishment of a piano competition in his name. The second was the purchase of the Royal Chapel of St. Frambourg near Senlis, which he made a non-sectarian shrine to spirituality and the arts, now known as the Foundation Cziffra. He also restored the organ at the Abbey of La Chaise Dieu and started a summer festival there, at the suggestion of his son, who became a conductor. It is known as the Salle Cziffra.

György Jr. tragically died in an accident in 1981, shortly after making his first commercial recordings. Cziffra refused to perform with an orchestra thereafter. He retired from recording in 1986 and left the stage in 1988. In the same year, France named him a cultural ambassador to a newly liberalized Hungary. He was diagnosed with cancer in the early 1990s, but died of a heart attack. He is buried in the cemetery of Senlis near the remains of his son, and his wife continues to direct the Foundation Cziffra. *—Joseph Stevenson*

Recommended:

- ○ **Liszt: Concerto 1; Grieg: Concerto; Gershwin: Rhapsody in Blue** / Lehel, Rozsnyai (conds.), Cziffra, Budapest SO, Hungarian State SO / Hungaroton 32134
- ○ **Gyorgy Cziffra, Piano** / Cziffra / Hungaroton 32056
- ○ **Cziffra: 1955–56** / Cziffra / Hungaroton 31569
- ○ **Cannon & Flowers** / Cziffra, Hungarian State SO / 1996 / APR 5545

D

Francesco d'Avalos

b. Apr. 11, 1930, Naples, Italy
Conductor

Francesco d'Avalos is probably better known as a conductor than as a composer, though he has been active throughout his career both with a baton and in composition. His fame came later on and is largely due to his recordings of orchestral music by Wagner, Muzio Clementi, and the lesser-known Giuseppe Martucci, all on smaller labels.

He did not show unusual talent at an early age, though he divulged a strong interest in music, listening often to the family's recording of Mahler's *Symphony No. 2* by Ormandy and the Minneapolis Symphony. He credited Italian composer Antonio Favasta with convincing his parents to arrange for his musical instruction. At 12, d'Avalos began study on the piano with Vincenzo Vitale. Three years later, he enrolled at the Conservatory of San Pietro a Majella in Naples. There, however, he could satisfy his needs only in the study of composition, not in conducting, his second ambition. He has acknowledged that Renato Parodi, who instructed him in composition and orchestration, was the teacher having the greatest influence on him. After receiving a diploma in composition from the San Pietro Conservatory in 1955, d'Avalos began studying conducting at Siena's Chigiana Academy with Paul van Kempen. After dropping out for a few years owing to the death of van Kempen in the first year, he returned to the academy to work with Celibidache and Ferrara. His first important works appeared during his Siena years, including the *Symphony No. 1*, for (wordless) soprano and orchestra (1955), and *Hymme an die Nacht* for orchestra (1958). He made his conducting debut in 1964, leading the Rome RAI Orchestra, and thereafter made numerous guest-conducting appearances throughout Europe. In 1979, he was engaged to teach composition at the Conservatory of San Pietro a Majella. He continued conducting and his first recordings began to appear in the 1980s. His most active period in the recording studio, however, has been the last decade of the twentieth century, during which he compiled a dozen or so releases. He composed his *Symphony No. 2 for Soprano and Orchestra* (on texts by Lenau and Shelley) in 1995. In the late 1990s, d'Avalos announced plans to record all five symphonies of Mendelssohn, as well as Liszt's complete orchestral works. He is still an active composer. *—Robert Cummings*

Recommended:

- ○ **Clementi: 2 Symphonies; Piano Concerto** / d'Avalos (cond.), Spada, London PO / 1992 / ASV 802
- ○ **Clementi: Complete Orchestral Works** / d'Avalos (cond.), Spada, London PO / 1992 / ASV 322
- ○ **Martucci: Complete Orchestral Works** / d'Avalos (cond.), Yakar, Caramiello, Clark, Ives, London PO / 1990 / ASV 408
- ○ **Brahms: Symphony 2; Variations on a Theme By Haydn; Academic Festival Overture** / d'Avalos (cond.), London PO / 1990 / ASV 744

Sigismondo d'India

b. ca. 1582, Palermo, Italy, **d.** Apr. 19, 1629, Modena (?), Italy
Composer: Vocal

All that is known about Sigismondo d'India's early life comes from what he said himself on the title pages of his publications: He claimed that he was of a noble Sicilian family and that he had received his training from "learned men of music." He was probably in Florence around 1600, judging from the dedication of his 1621 "Le musichi e balli" to the Queen Mother of France, Maria de' Medici. He published a book of madrigals in 1606, and its introduction suggests he was in Mantua. If so, he could have met Claudio Monteverdi there.

He visited Florence in 1608, earning the admiration of Vittoria Archilei and Caccini. Cardinal Farnese praised his songs when he visited Rome somewhat later, and in 1610, he was in Parma and Piacenza, where he supplied some festival music.

He settled down in Turin in 1611 when he became director of chamber music at the court of Carlo Emanuele I, Duke of Savoy. Most of his music dates from the period of his employment there. This was a position requiring the production of secular music, both instrumental and vocal. But it is most likely that his predilection was not for religious music. He produced music in the new style that deemphasized polyphony, which found great favor with the Duke.

Malicious courtiers undercut him with vicious gossip, and he left the court in 1623. From October 1623 to April 1624, he was attached to the Este court in Modena on a temporary basis. Moving on to Rome, he took a position with Cardinal Maurizio, who was a son of the Duke of Savoy, and shared his father's tastes. He produced more religious music at this time, including a famous *Missa Domine, clamavi ad te*, written for Pope Urban VIII. He also composed an opera with a religious theme, *Sant' Eustachio*. In the same year, 1625, d'India took a permanent position in the court of the Este family and directed a funeral mass for Isabella d'Este (it is not known if this was one written by him or someone else).

The historical record grows thin at this point: in 1627, he was competing for a commission for a marriage between the Farnese and Medici houses, but lost to Monteverdi. He was also appointed to the court of Maximilian I of Bavaria. It is not known whether he ever made it there, or exactly when, where, or how he died. A document dated April 19, 1629, is addressed to the heirs of Sig. d'India, establishing that he died some time earlier.

Sigismondo d'India is regarded as the most important early Italian composer of secular vocal music in the new monodic style, with the exception of Claudio Monteverdi. He also wrote very good polyphonic motets and madrigals. His music is marked by strong, dramatic emotional content and bold, original, and personal harmonic progressions. Among the most typical of his subjects are laments by rejected or jilted lovers, their heartbreak expressed in a reliance on chromatic half-steps and strong dissonances that resolve in unusual ways. *—Joseph Stevenson*

VOCAL

Madrigals (ca. 1605–1624)

The period bridging the late Renaissance and early Baroque was a time of heady experimentation in all phases of musical composition. The emergence of "monody," in essence melody line with harmonic accompaniment, led to a splintering off in compositional process, being designated as "stile moderno," as opposed to "stile antico," the older contrapuntal, equal-voice style. The enigmatic Sigismondo d'India was among the most prominent exponents of the new school. Although initially bracketed with the radicals of his period, the position d'India holds in music history is one analogous to Beethoven's in that he brought the old forms to a summit while infusing them with melodic and harmonic innovation. Largely, vocal music was d'India's favored medium for his expression of musical thought, especially the madrigal. Through his many essays in this form, one finds a wide variety of expression and musical thought coupled with innovation.

Among the then-new generation of composers of "continuo monody" (i.e., single line melody with the accompaniment indicated by figured bass), d'India's most striking innovation is perhaps his expressive use of speech-rhythm. Where this device is most commonly found in recitative, d'India's uses of chromaticism and daring harmonic progressions (two features he shares with his more famous contemporary Gesualdo) help blur the distinctions between lyrical aria and arioso and the more prosaic recitative. In his hands the former two take on a dramatic declamatory nature owing to the speech inflection, while the latter is expressively enhanced by the musical innovations. A fine example of the expressive use of these elements may be found in *O dolcezz', amarissime d'Amore*. The unwinding of the speech-rhythm is like a baring of one's thoughts on the bitter-sweetness of lost love, while the clever rapid alternation of D minor and D major (a device so effectively used by Schubert two centuries later) delineates the confused emotion of the protagonist, better never to have loved or to have loved and lost. Note also the melisma in measure 15, no longer mere embellishment but a cry of the heart. Melisma, too, can be used as a motivic unifier, as witness the chains of 32nd notes which are even visibly (as well as aurally) cohesive in *E pur tu parti*.

While the initial impression of the above process may be an invitation to formlessness or at best a freer form, d'India achieves structural unity through sectional repetition. And yet, this repetition is often handled with originality. The repeat of the opening phrase in *Piange, madonna*, for example, is virtually a variation on the theme. Where the music is more indisputably through-composed, d'India uses reiteration of a motive, as in the earlier example or, to use an arch-type, in *Ancidetemi pur*, where the phrase is spun to even greater length, an almost symphonic process. It may be said, then, that in the field of madrigal, d'India was a vital and imaginative rethinker. *— Wayne Reisig*

Recommended:

○ **Italian Madrigals** / Christie (cond.), Orlando Gibbons Viola Ens., Les Arts Florissants / 1998 / Teldec 23418

Songs (ca. 1605–1624)

Although very little would change socially as Western civilization moved from the sixteenth to the seventeenth century, there were many undercurrents of change in the arts, especially music. Among the movers in the field of vocal music were the visionary Gesualdo, opera pioneer Monteverdi, and Sigismondo d'India. The last, until recently the least well-known of the three, and something of a biographical enigma to this day, has come to be regarded as a figure who brought traditions to a culmination while cutting new paths, specifically in the musical language of his favored medium, the song.

d'India's songs can be broken down according to the three then-prominent types—aria, recitative, and arioso—and his unique approach may be identified in each. In the arias (as with the word's operatic association, the most lyrical of the categories), a large number of d'India's output are strophic, of which most of them are canzonette. These are simple diatonic melodies, structured from short, symmetric phrases and matched with simple, one-on-one counterpoint. *"Se bel rio"* is archetypical among this genre, the rhythmic contours of the figured bass rigidly adhering to the melody. In the recitative style, d'India's innovation is most conspicuously present, infusing with lyricism and emotion what had been a drier, more prosaic style, and utilizing that format more than any of his contemporaries in the monodist school. Perhaps the best example to show these traits within the said format is *"Là tra 'l sangue"*. If recitative was the apparatus of d'India's most pronounced innovation, his most expressive achievements can be found in the category of arioso. In this, the declamatory drama of the recitative merges with the lyricism of the aria. Most of the composer's madrigals are in this form, a fine example being *"Cara mia cetra"*. Here, an unusual tendency toward syncopation in the melody and a greater rhythmic independence in the accompaniment is seen.

In addition to obscuring the boundaries between these three major song types, d'India's innovations lie in his use of then-unusual melodic intervals to serve the ends of greater drama and expression (as in *"Là tra 'l sangue"*). Another conspicuous melodic feature is his use of florid arioso; in this, embellishment is no mere decoration, but is used to carry forward the flow of the music, as in *"Piangono al pianger mio"*. An embellishing phrase can even act as a structural unifier, as in the late-period *"Ancidetemi pur"*. Here, alternating cascades derived from two 16th and 32nd note phrases act as a thread to the musical fabric.

Although long a footnote in music history, d'India's still-recent emergence from the musicologist's shelf reveals him to be a visionary who was preoccupied with merging text and note. In his doing so, he strove for greater emotional and dramatic effect and may be regarded as one of the great early musical Mannerists. *—Wayne Reisig*

Recommended:

○ **Italian Madrigals** / Christie (cond.), Orlando Gibbons Viola Ens., Les Arts Florissants / 1998 / Teldec 23418

Vincent d'Indy

b. Mar. 27, 1851, Paris, France, **d.** Dec. 2, 1931, Paris, France

Composer: Orchestral, Concerto

Vincent d'Indy, the son of a French nobleman, was one of the leading figures in Parisian musical society during the closing years of the nineteenth century. His compositions, though not achieving lasting popularity, were characterized by their complexity and religious content. He composed in a variety of genres, including orchestral, chamber, piano, vocal, and opera. His legacy, however, rests also on his activities as an author and a teacher. He wrote two biographies, a book on his experiences in the Franco-Prussian War, numerous essays, and criticisms. His influence as a teacher can be heard in the works of many of his students, particularly those composers of opera, such as Madetoja and Roussel. D'Indy was an uncompromising classicist until his death, a position that frequently brought conflict with contemporary composers of the period.

D'Indy's strong beliefs and tendency toward narrow-mindedness stem from his childhood under his paternal grandmother's care, his own mother having died in childbirth. He was frequently described "as stubborn to the point of fanaticism." His religious beliefs ran deep, as did his anti-Semitism.

He was considered a child prodigy, but did not begin formal music lessons until his early teenage years. He began piano lessons in 1864 from Diemer and, in 1865, began instruction in harmony, counterpoint, and orchestration from Levignac. In 1872, d'Indy began studying in private with his most influential teacher, César Franck. He later audited Franck's organ class at the Paris Conservatory and subsequently became a registered student there. Vincent d'Indy would go on to be one of Franck's most ardent followers, champion, and biographer. His musical education was further developed through playing percussion and keyboard and through conducting.

Franck was the composer with the greatest influence on d'Indy, but others, Wagner in particular, also influenced the young composer. D'Indy attended the premiere of Wagner's Bayreuth theater in the summer of 1876 and the second Bayreuth festival in 1882, for the premiere of Wagner's *Parsifal*. D'Indy also became acquainted with Liszt and Brahms. D'Indy was a great admirer of Beethoven; so much so that he wrote a biography of the composer that was published in 1911.

D'Indy began composing in the late 1860s and had his first work published in 1870. He began his first grand opera, *Les burgraves* in 1869, but never finished it. His orchestral trilogy, *Wallenstein* premiered in 1880 under his direction. He won the Prix de Paris in 1884 with the cantata *Le chant de la cloche*. *Symphonie sur un theme montagnard français* (1886) is his only work to survive obscurity. D'Indy composed six operas, of which *Fervaal* (1895), sometimes referred to as the French *Parsifal*, was the most successful. Most of the librettos for his operas were written by d'Indy himself.

Teaching occupied a great deal of d'Indy's time. In 1894, along with Bordes and Guilmant, he founded the Schola Cantorum. Its original function as a society promoting performance of sacred music evolved into a school for the study and preservation of church music and French folk music. He taught composition at the school beginning in 1897, which resulted in his writings on composition *Traite de composition* (Paris, 1903–33). From 1912 to 1929, d'Indy taught orchestration and conducting at the Paris Conservatory.

D'Indy ultimately became the victim of his conservatism and his inability to accept contemporary trends in music that were so prevalent in France during the latter nineteenth and early twentieth centuries. The modernists prevailed and his music was forced out of favor. D'Indy, however, remained true to his artistic ideals until his death. *—Bruce Lundgren*

ORCHESTRAL

Istar, symphonic variations, Op. 42 (1896)

Composed in 1896, *Istar* is d'Indy at his most masterly and his most immediately attractive; the work manages to be at once a ravishing tone poem and a set of superbly proportioned symphonic variations. In the late 1880s, a viewing of the Assyrian sculptures in the British Museum had sparked d'Indy's enthusiasm, and when he came across a translation from an Assyrian epic, detailing Istar's progressive divestment as she descends to the underworld, his imagination was fired. In the fragment as it has come down to us, Istar's denudation is but the beginning of her trials, but the musical conceit it suggested—variations first with the theme revealed only at the end—proved irresistible, and d'Indy deftly transforms this terrifying goddess of love into a vulnerable yet seductive parisienne.

Undertaken in search of her dead lover, Dumuzi (or Tammuz), her adventure begins with a drooping horn call which hints at her own theme and represents Istar summoning the gatekeeper of the netherworld, followed immediately by a knocking motif slipping closely around a central insistent tone. The first variation, in which she is required to part with her tiara, offers a blaze of orchestral effects playing over the harmonization absent the theme. A more anxious version of the knocking motif leads to the second variation in which arabesques merely hint at her theme as Istar turns coquettish, removing her earrings. Indeed, the knocking motif at the third gate seems flirtatious, though the variation pleads effusively at the removal of her necklace. Briefly, anxiously, she knocks at the fourth gate, yet the divestment of her charmed breastplate is accomplished in a burst of Corybantic scintillations leading directly in an aggressive march to an assault on the fifth gate. As she removes her belt, the variation suggests a rising anxiety with the first firm outline of her theme. Suddenly, the knocking motif becomes an impassioned outburst—radiant, ecstatic—before the sixth gate opens and she casts aside her ankle bracelets in a moving imploration. Abrupt and apprehensive, the knocking motif opens the seventh gate to a variation of eerie skittishness punctuated by an enormous orchestral tutti as Istar's veil falls; naked, her theme is revealed in a great, long-breathed string unison. This breathtaking moment yields to a coda with the knocking motif now a triumphal cortège heralded by (in Léon Vallas' phrase) "une fanfare carillonnante."

Despite the program's suggestion of a 'dance of the seven veils' or striptease, it should be said that *Istar* is not sensual but sensuous, graced with the brilliant, transparent, and uniquely luminous scoring of d'Indy's maturity. The *longueurs* almost inevitably besetting d'Indy's more ambitious designs are forestalled here by an admirable concision in which the variations, nevertheless, comprise both a compelling psychological portrait and an eminently satisfying musical design.

The work was heard first at Brussels on January 10, 1897, given by the Concerts Ysaÿe, to whom it is dedicated. D'Indy himself conducted the first Paris performance with the Colonne Orchestra on January 16, 1898. It was successfully given as a ballet, with the composer conducting, by Natasha Trukhanova on April 22, 1912, and has been revived in that form a number of times since. *—Adrian Corleonis*

Recommended:

○ **Franck: Symphony in Dm; 3 Pieces; d'Indy: Istar** / Monteux (cond.), San Francisco SO / 1994 / BMG 61967

Souvenirs, tone poem, Op. 62 (1906)

Through December 1905, d'Indy was on tour in the United States conducting programs of recent French music—Franck's *Psyché et Eros*, Fauré's *Pelléas et Mélisande*

Suite, two of the Debussy *Nocturnes*, Dukas' *L'Apprenti sorcier*, Magnard's *Chant funèbre*, Chausson's *Symphony*, and his own *Istar* and *Symphony No. 2*—in Boston, New York, Philadelphia, and Washington, to receptions and reviews ranging from reserved (for his *Symphony*) to enthusiastic. Upon his return to France at the end of the month he found his wife in agony, apparently the victim of a cerebral aneurysm—she died in his arms during the early morning of the 30th. Theirs had been a love match. Isabelle de Pampalonne, whom he married as a young church organist, choirmaster of the Colonne Orchestra, and fledgling composer—albeit, also wealthy and aristocratic—was his cousin, and he had been obliged to outwait the objections and death of his grandmother, Countess Rézia d'Indy, to be joined to her on August 11, 1875. In 1881, d'Indy was occupied with rapturous protestations of devotion in his piano suite, *Poème des montagnes*, in which Isabelle's theme, frankly labeled "la bien-aimée," figures prominently. Isabelle's grandson, Yves de Becdelièvre, recalled that "My grandmother adored her husband, but she detested music." Isabelle, however, was determined to help her husband achieve his goals and maintained a closely organized household. As could only be expected after 30 years of happiness and shared adventure, Isabelle's death devastated d'Indy, leaving him temporarily at loose ends, but work afforded respite from grief.

Repairing to the family estate at Faugs, in the Ardèche, in the summer of 1906, he quickly put aside attempted work on incidental music for an adaptation of *Phèdre* and embarked, almost secretively, on the composition of a large tone poem, *Souvenirs*, dedicated "à la memoire de la bien-aimée." Completed by year's end, the work was given a semi-private audition by the Société Nationale on April 20, 1907. Only at the insistence of friends, with whom he'd shared the score, was he persuaded to publish the work and allow it to be performed at a Colonne Concert on December 22. Once again, Isabelle's "bien-aimée" theme figures prominently in this poignant, almost frantic, intensely personal evocation of lost happiness, worked with the sum of d'Indy's art. *—Adrian Corleonis*

Recommended:

- ○ **Indy: Symphony 2; Souvenirs** / DePreist (cond.), Monte Carlo PO / 1995 / Koch 7280

CONCERTO

Symphony on a French Mountain Air, for piano & orchestra, Op. 25 (1886)

Though greatly gifted and an indefatigable learner, Vincent d'Indy was not a prodigy. Born with a decided intellectual bent, he felt compelled to make a systematic assessment of the Romantic heritage which meant for him mainly Beethoven, Berlioz, Wagner, and his own mentor, César Franck. It's little wonder that the matching of matter to manner should have been problematic for him at all stages of his career, or that he was well into his thirties by the time he developed a characteristic style. The *Symphony on a French Mountain Air* (1886) is the first large step in the composer's angular gait toward a distinctive musical language. From childhood, d'Indy had spent his summers at the family estate at Chabret in the Cevennes. In the mid-1880s, he took a villa in nearby Faugs, from which he could glimpse Mont Blanc. He began to notate the folk songs he encountered on his rambles to the country; the melody upon which he based the Symphony is a shepherd's tune which he heard "in the distance from the top of Tortous, between Saint-Péyrau and Toulaud...." Given d'Indy's intense involvement in Parisian musical life, it is well to recall Martin Cooper's observation that "In spite of his conscious professionalism, one side of him remained a patriarchal countryman with something of the air of a visitor to Paris and a background of health and earthiness...." Begun as a Fantaisie for piano and orchestra, the Symphony eventually assumed its present three-movement structure—anticipating the symphonies of Franck and Chausson—while retaining a prominent role for the piano. D'Indy may have been inspired by Franck's *Les djinns* (1884) and *Variations symphoniques* (1885), in which rich webs of piano figuration accompany the orchestra; similarly, it may have been more than coincidence that the Symphony was composed in the same year as the premiere of Saint-Saëns' *Symphony No. 3*, a work notable for the grand integration of organ and piano into its orchestral texture. The use of a "cyclic" theme—in which melodic contour is preserved, though rhythm and character may vary drastically—as a unifying device throughout has an obvious antecedent in Berlioz's *Symphonie fantastique* (1830). Over an atmospheric string tremolo, the shepherd's air sounds wistfully on the cor anglais, spreading with an infectious lift to the other woodwinds and the strings and then to the piano, which emblazons it with soaring brilliance. The lambently descending second theme proves a worthy foil to the shepherd's melody; their blithely engaging dialogue provides a substantial development before the coda, which is ushered in by the cor anglais. In the Andante, the lilting form of the air smooths out into expansive lyrical flight. The melodic fragments alternate fleetingly—now brilliantly, now adumbrated—teasing the ear for the animé revelations of the Finale. Here, the air's lilting gestures return, at times with the mien of a rowdy rigaudon, interleaved with reminiscences that gradually recall the source of the work's multihued transformations. The Symphony is the freshest and most spontaneous manifestation of its creator's musical personality, and its enduring popularity is wholly deserved. *—Adrian Corleonis*

Recommended:

- ○ **Cluytens Conducts Franck & d'Indy** / Cluytens (cond.), Ciccolini, Societe des Concerts du Conservatoire / 2002 / Testament 1237
- ○ **Franck & D'Indy: Symphonies** / Dutoit (cond.), Thibaudet, Montreal SO / 1991 / London 430278

D'Oyly Carte Chorus & Orchestra

f. 1878, London, England
Ensemble

The D'Oyly Carte Chorus and Orchestra was an offshoot of the D'Oyly Carte Opera Company, which first took shape in London in the 1870s. But there is more to the story of failed-composer but successful-impresario Richard D'Oyly Carte and his company than just a date and a place: the course of twentieth century British music and even the very physical landscape of the city of London were dramatically affected by the work of Carte. After abandoning his efforts to establish himself as a composer (he wrote three operettas in the late 1860s and early 1870s, none of which met with any real success), Carte decided to set himself up as an impresario, and shifted his energies towards connecting well-known international performers (Adelina Patti and Oscar Wilde, to name a couple) with prominent London concert halls and theaters. By 1875, he was serving as manager of the Royalty Theatre, and in 1877, building from the wild success of his Gilbert and Sullivan productions, he founded a new organization called the Comedy Opera Company; by 1879 the company was known simply as the D'Oyly Carte Opera Company. British light musical theater now had a solid base from which to reach an ever-wider and more-appreciative mid-Victorian audience. Gilbert and Sullivan works remained the mainstay of Carte's theater repertoire, and he built a new hall especially for their production: the now-famous Savoy Theatre, which happens to have been the first all-electric civic hall in Great Britain.

Richard D'Oyly Carte then spread his managerial wings and began tackling serious, dramatic English-libretto operas, which were generally avoided by British promoters in that day. But this focus on native musicians made Carte well-loved throughout London and was key to the success of his operations, both in the comic and serious realms. Again, drawing on his vast resources, he built a new theater especially for these dramatic operas: the Royal English Opera House (later renamed the Palace Theatre), whose first musical inhabitant was Sir Arthur Sullivan's grand opera *Ivanhoe* (1890). Although this new venture raked in significantly less money than the comic operettas, Carte had succeeded in bringing serious British opera to the Londoners, and twentieth century British musicians, especially that great champion of English opera Benjamin Britten, could be extremely grateful for that.

The Chorus and Orchestra offshoot of Carte's company, along with several touring companies, helped spread his name throughout the English-speaking world. Richard D'Oyly Carte died in 1901; his son Rupert took over the D'Oyly Carte Opera Company during World War I, and it remained in the family until 1982, when it disbanded. The company was re-formed in 1988, and is resident in South London. *—Blair Johnston*

Recommended:

- ○ **The Pirates Of Penzance** / Godfrey (cond.), Masterson, Adams, Allister, Brannigan, Royal PO, D'Oyly Carte Chorus & Orch. / 1993 / London 436292
- ○ **H.M.S. Pinafore** / Godfrey (cond.), Reed, Adams, Knight, Cook, New SO of London, D'Oyly Carte Chorus & Orch. / 1989 / London 414283
- ○ **Sullivan: The Mikado** / Nash (cond.), Masterson, Reed, Wales, Ayldon, Royal PO, D'Oyly Carte Chorus & Orch. / London 425190

Dale Warland Singers

f. 1971, St. Paul, MN
Ensemble

The Dale Warland Singers are an American choral group founded in 1971 by Dale Warland. It is a professional, 40-voice a cappella chorus recognized as one of the finest in the United States. Based in the Minneapolis/St. Paul, MN, area, they frequently tour both in the United States and abroad.

In 1990, the group represented North America in the Second World Symposium on Choral Music in Helsinki. They have appeared on the nationwide radio programs St. Paul Sunday and A Prairie Home Companion and primarily record on the American Choral Catalog label and have released over 20 compact discs. Their annual Echoes of Christmas and Cathedral Classics broadcasts are also heard on stations across the U.S. The group was the first-ever recipient of the Margaret Hillis Achievement Award for Choral Excellence in 1992.

The Warland Singers enjoy a reputation for promoting the composition of new and exciting choral repertoire. Among the composers they have commissioned for new music are Libby Larsen, Stephen Harrison Paulus, Carol Barnett, George Shearing, Peter Schickele, Dominick Argento, Augusta Read Thomas, and Bernard Rands.

Although the Dale Warland Singers are primarily an a cappella group, they do collaborate and have joined the St. Paul Chamber Orchestra and the Minnesota Orchestra for concerts and have sung with the James Sewell Ballet. The group also participates in a larger chorus, the Warland Symphonic Chorus. In that, Dale Warland Singers members join and form the experienced core of a larger chorus otherwise made up of volunteer singers from the Twin Cities area.

Since its founding, the group has had the same music director: Dale Warland, who has earned degrees at St. Olaf College, the University of Minnesota, and the University of Southern California. Prior to devoting himself to full-time work with the Singers, Warland had served for 19 years as director of choral music at Macalester College, St. Paul, MN. He has also been on the faculty of the All Japan Chorus League National Competition in Fukuoka, Japan. *—Joseph Stevenson*

Recommended:

- ○ **Argento: Walden Pond** / Warland (cond.), Dale Warland Singers, Lark Quartet / 2003 / Gothic 49217
- ○ **A Rose in Winter** / Warland (cond.), Dale Warland Singers / 1997 / d'Note 1022
- ○ **Christmas with the Dale Warland Singers** / Warland (cond.), Dale Warland Singers / 2002 / Gothic 49208
- ○ **Cathedral Classics** / Warland (cond.), Dale Warland Singers / 1994 / American Choral 120

Luigi Dallapiccola

b. Feb. 3, 1904, Pisino d'Istria, Italy, **d.** Feb. 19, 1975, Florence, Italy

Composer: Keyboard, Vocal, Choral, Opera

Luigi Dallapiccola, Italian pianist and composer, became an ardent admirer of the Second Viennese School early in his career. He was the first Italian composer to work within the 12-tone system, and his work in atonality led to his being considered one of Italy's most important composers in the twentieth century. The impact of both World Wars can be heard in his compositions, and he used atonality in the service of rich melodies that conveyed his very personal themes. Though he is widely known for his 12-tone instrumental compositions, he achieved an equal reputation for his operas, even though he only completed three. Dallapiccola also had a successful career as a pianist, during which he was in a long-standing partnership with violinist Sandro Materassi. His career spanned more than 50 years of performing, teaching, writing, and composing. He received membership in several national academies of arts, and was awarded the Albert Schweitzer Prize shortly after his death.

Dallapiccola began his studies in music at an early age; he was eight when he began studying piano, and two years later he began studies in composition. His formal studies were derailed with the coming of World War I. In 1917, his family, along with several others, was deported to Graz, Austria, where they were interned for almost two years. During this period, he was introduced to Austro-German opera, particularly that of Mozart and Wagner. His family returned to Istria in 1919 and he continued his formal education, traveling to Trieste to study piano and harmony. In 1922, he entered the Conservatorio Luigi Cherubini in Florence where he studied piano with Consolo and, later, composition under Vito Frazzi.

Dallapiccola joined the faculty of Cherubini Conservatory in 1934; a relationship that lasted until his retirement in 1967. His work, teaching piano to composition students, allowed him to travel widely where he was introduced to many different works and composers. It was through these travels that Dallapiccola met Alban Berg, one of the principals of the Second Viennese School. He met another principal, Anton Webern, in 1942 in Vienna. Their influence can be heard in Dallapiccola's first two operas *Volo di notte* (1937–39) and *Il prigionia* (1948), and in the works *Liriche greche* (1942–45), which was composed as a memorial to Webern, and *Cinque frammenti di Saffo* (1942). In addition to his operas, Dallapiccola composed several film scores, works for orchestra, chamber music, choral music, and songs.

The theme of several of Dallapiccola's works revolved around the concept of liberty. Three of his more renowned works, *Canti di prigionia* (Songs of Prison, 1941), *Il prigionia* (The Prisoner), and *Canti di liberazione* (Songs of Liberation, 1955) all incorporate this central theme. Undoubtedly this theme arose from his experiences in Graz during World War I and the time he and his Jewish wife, Laura, spent in hiding after Mussolini announced his anti-Semitic policies.

Luigi Dallapiccola was active until late in life. He traveled widely throughout Europe, England, the U.S., and Argentina. In addition to composing and performing, he was a consummate lecturer and teacher. He taught at several schools in the U.S., including Berkshire Music Center at Tanglewood, Queens College in New York, University of California at Berkeley, Dartmouth College, and at the Aspen Music School. He also lectured at the Instituto Torcuato di Tella in Buenos Aires. Dallapiccola also wrote widely. His writing began in the mid-1940s for the publication *Il mondo europeo* and continued throughout his career. *—Bruce Lundgren*

KEYBOARD

Quaderno musicale di Annalibera (1952)

The children of composers often have dedications bestowed upon them, and the pieces so dedicated are normally simple, appropriately childlike works. Luigi Dallapiccola's *Quaderno musicale di Annalibera* (Annalibera's musical notebook), however,—dedicated to his daughter Annalibera on her eighth birthday—is a dense 12-tone work whose name, form, and content all pay tribute to Johann Sebastian Bach. The work was written (during a 1952 journey across America) for the Pittsburgh International Contemporary Music Festival. Its sixth movement, "Ornaments," would go on to serve as the basis of Dallapiccola's *Songs of Liberation*, leading some to suspect that the *Quaderno* was a preparatory work for the later piece; the whole notebook was later transcribed as the *Variations for Orchestra*.

This is music of no mean interest—strictly constructed, and sharply characterized—but it may have left young Annalibera a little bewildered. A movement titled "Symbol" opens the work, and within its first five bars it openly states the B-A-C-H (in English notation B-A-C-B flat) over an exaggeratedly regular bass line. The ten short movements which follow alternate between freely expressive movements with names like "Accents," "Shadows," and "Colors," and various species of canon titled with a term Bach used in the *Art of Fugue*, "Contrapunctus."

Some of the free movements are lyrical, like "Lines," which spreads a serene melody over a bass line of broken chords. Others explore rhythm, like "Accents," in which the irregular meter is smashed out in chords. "Shadows" is particularly interesting, as it juxtaposes different pianistic colors simultaneously, so one can hear the ghost of something quiet while a rugged chord is played.

The contrapuntal pieces are complex; the second is in contrary motion and the third is a crab canon, in which the two parts are played together, one the reverse of the other. Yet Dallapiccola manipulates the textures in a way that maintains their nonacademic interest and expressivity. For example, the "Contrapunctus secundus," which is marked Poco allegretto; alla Serenata in the score, takes on an almost nocturnal aspect, with staccato notes that recall the strumming of mandolins.

Dallapiccola's *Quaderno* is an interesting and personal tribute to and assimilation of Bach and some of the most difficult music ever dedicated to an eight-year-old. *—Andrew Lindemann Malone*

Recommended:

- ○ **Dallapiccola: The Solo Piano Music & Castelnuovo-Tedesco** / Monetti / 1998 / ASV 1034

VOCAL

Parole di San Paolo, for high voice & 11 instruments (1964)

Patron of music Elizabeth Sprague Coolidge died in 1953, but the foundation she established in 1925, which had commissioned so many twentieth century masterpieces while she lived (e.g., Bartók's *String Quartet No. 5*, Schoenberg's *Third* and *Fourth* quartets, Stravinsky's *Apollon musagète*, Ravel's *Chansons madécasses*, Copland's *Appalachian Spring*) continued to underwrite new works after her death, and, in fact, continues to sponsor composers today. Dallapiccola had been the recipient of the foundation's generosity in 1956 with a commission for the *Cinque Canti*, songs on ancient Greek fragments (translated by Salvatore Quasimodo) for baritone and chamber ensemble, and would be again for *Sicut umbra* in 1970, three songs to Spanish poems by Juan Ramón Jiménez for mezzo-soprano and a chamber ensemble of flutes, clarinets, strings, vibraphone, celesta, and harp. The similarly scored *Parole di San Paolo* (1964) for mezzo-soprano or boy's voice was, likewise, a Coolidge Foundation commission, given its first performance at the Library of Congress under the auspices of the Elizabeth Sprague Coolidge Foundation, October 30, 1964, with Nancy Williams, soloist, and the composer conducting. The text is drawn from the brief 13th chapter of St. Paul's *First Letter to the Corinthians*, the often-quoted encomium to charity beginning "Though I speak with the tongues of men and of angels, and have not charity, I am become as sounding brass or a tinkling cymbal." "Charity" translates the Vulgate's "charitas" (or "caritas," Greek "agape") and differs in meaning both from the Classical usage of "dear," in the sense of costly, and the commonplace notion of its English derivation, namely, contributions to worthy causes: St. Paul's "charitas" is disinterested, unconditional, "divine" love. In Dallapiccola's hands this becomes an intense meditation, volatile in its response to every nuance. By this late stage in his career, the serialism first embraced in the early 1930s had become second nature, a personal language allowing Dallapiccola a rare eloquence and expressive power with very few strokes, though his distinctive Klangfarben—an exquisite pointillism: the aural equivalent of stars against a moonless night—requires the unusual ensemble of two flutes, two clarinets, piano, celesta, harp, vibraphone, xylorimba, viola, and cello. The vocal writing calls for utmost suppleness to expressively render the Italianate arioso line with its melismatic feints dovetailing with varieties of parlato, including Sprechstimme on certain words—"linguis ... prophetiam"—imparting an aura of profound thought deepening into incantation. Despite the rigors of its utterance, the *Parole di San Paolo* seems to follow a logic of pure expressiveness. *—Adrian Corleonis*

Recommended:

- ○ **Orchestra Of Our Time** / Thome (cond.), Valente, Orch. of Our Time / 1995 / VoxBox 5144

CHORAL

Canti di Prigionia, for chorus, 2 pianos, 2 harps & percussion (1938–1941)

By his own admission, Dallapiccola didn't know what he was doing when he wrote his early 12-tone works, including *Canti di Prigionia*. No systematic explanation of Schoenberg's system was available to him, so he unwittingly broke the "rules" being developed by the Second Viennese School and employed dodecaphony freely, not systematically, varying his timbral and tonal fabrics and often implying a traditional tonality. His first "wrong" move in *Canti di Prigionia* (Songs of Imprisonment) was in the very opening bars in having the timpani quote the Medieval *Dies Irae* theme and echo that in the pianos, thus setting up very traditional, tonal expectations. As the score progresses, it remains highly lyrical, often employing only fragments of tone rows in ways that accommodate traditional, emotive expression. This is not sensual music, though, in the manner of Berg; the instrumental timbres of keyboards and percussion are austere and generally non-melodic and the choral lines, while long and often intense, avoid voluptuous harmonies as they repeat elements of the brief texts again and again. Dallapiccola initially welcomed the rise of Benito Mussolini, but quickly became alarmed by fascism's racist course (especially since his fiancée was Jewish). Indignant and having just read Stefan Zweig's *Mary Stuart*, Dallapiccola intended, he later wrote, "to transform the prayer of the queen as an individual into a song for all mankind; I wanted to dwell at length upon the word 'libera' in the music, to have this divine word shouted by everyone." The text, which Dallapiccola set in Latin, was: "O Lord God! I have hoped in Thee. O dearest Jesus! Deliver me now. In harsh chains, in pitiable pain, I desire Thee. Languishing, moaning, and kneeling, I worship Thee, I implore that you free me." The composer finished this initial section, "Preghiera de Maria Stuarda" (Prayer of Mary Stuart) for mixed chorus, in 1939, and heard it first performed on Belgian Radio the following year. He then turned to four short verses by sixth century philosopher Boethius, who fell victim to Emperor Theodoric, setting them for female chorus and completing the movement in 1940. The text of this "Invocazione di Boezio" (Invocation of Boethius) from the *Consolations of Philosophy* was: "Happy is he who has been able to contemplate clearly the fount of good, happy he who has been able to unbind the chains of the burdensome earth." By late 1941, he had completed the triptych with "Congedo di Girolamo Savanarola" (Farewell of Girolamo Savanarola), for mixed chorus: "Let the world oppress, the enemy attack. I fear nothing for in Thee, O Lord, have I put my trust, for Thou art my hope, for Thou hast established the highest refuge of all." The full work was first performed on December 11, 1941, the day Mussolini declared war on the United States. The score was soon banned and Dallapiccola and his wife went into hiding in 1943. They and the score re-emerged in a safer postwar world. *—James Reel*

Recommended:

○ **Dallapiccola: Il Prigioniero; Canti di Prigionia** / Salonen (cond.), Swedish Radio Orch. & Choir / 1995 / Sony 68323

OPERA

Il Prigioniero (1944–1948)

Il Prigioniero is one of the enduring masterpieces of twentieth century opera. The similarly inspired choral *Canti di prigionia* (1938–41) accompanies *Il Prigioniero* as Dallapiccola's central and most successful large-scale works. Composed between 1944 and 1948, the composer's libretto is a curious amalgam of Romantic and *décadent, fin de siècle* oddments informed by the political realities of the Fascist era, to which it is a response. Dallapiccola's extensive account of the genesis of *Il Prigioniero* begins with his schoolboy discovery of Victor Hugo's poem *La rose de l'infante*, with its glimpse of the Hapsburg monarch Philip II—with his centralized authority and support for the Inquisition, he appears as the prototype of such twentieth century dictators as Hitler, Mussolini, and Stalin—holding the world in a bloody death grip. This claustrophobic prehension suffuses the opera. The action is taken from *La Torture par l'espérance*, to which Dallapiccola's wife introduced him in June 1939, though the hero of Villiers de l'Isle Adam's brief, Poe-like tale, Rabbi Aser Abarbanel, becomes the nameless prisoner of Dallapiccola's title, representing the political prisoners of all times. The addition of details from Charles de Coster's epic of Flemish resistance to Spanish domination, *La légende... d'Ulenspiegel et de Lamme Goedzak* (1867), conflates the story with events from the reign of Philip's father, Charles V, namely the warning of the approach of the Spanish fleet by Ghent's great bell, Roelandt, whose motif, representing revolution, is woven through the fabric of the score. Remarkably, the work possesses an integrity and theatrical power transcending its stylistic confluence. In Dallapiccola's distinctive musical idiom, too, several tributaries may be traced. A near-Debussyan sensuousness, for instance, is dodecaphonically articulated in a way owing more to Berg than to Schoenberg—the diatonic shaping of the tone row representing liberty tellingly contrasting with the predominantly dissonant harmony, to recall Berg's use of a chorale in his *Violin Concerto* to suggest transfiguration. The impress of Webern's work is also felt in Dallapiccola's exquisitely tense pointillism. The frequent alternation of declamation and angular arioso, for which one might find a precedent in verismo opera or the Verdi of *Falstaff*, lends the whole an Italianate cast. Finally, a certain mysticism suffuses *Il Prigioniero* with an eerie radiance. Shifting sensibilities may be measured by comparing Verdi's *Don Carlos* (1866), which views the same political events from the perspective of kings, princes, and nobles with bittersweet, often pungent, Romanticism, and Dallapiccola's modern parable of anonymous horror forecasting the "detainees" and "disappeared" of the world. *—Adrian Corleonis*

Synopsis:

The story is set in Flanders, during the uprising against King Philip II, and is inspired by the story of a rabbi tortured during the Inquisition. But because Dallapiccola makes the prisoner of the title less specifically rabbinical, and because he conceived the opera during World War II, stage directors often move the action to Nazi Germany or its overrun territories.

Prologue. The Prisoner's mother, dressed in mourning black, sings of her longing for her son, and recounts her recurring nightmare about the oppressive King Philip. Her monologue is swamped by an off-stage chorus singing in Latin, representing the power of the Inquisition.

In the first of the four main scenes, the mother visits the Prisoner, presumably for the last time, in his horrible cell. The Prisoner speaks of the darkness in his cell and the darkness in his heart, and his unimaginable suffering. But then one day, he recounts, his jailer broke his long silence with two words: "My brother." From that time, the jailer's implied friendship has given the Prisoner the strength to survive the ongoing whippings, burnings, and lacerations.

His mother leaves, and in the second scene the jailer appears. He tries to give the Prisoner hope by announcing a revolt in Flanders; the Flemish people are rising against Philip and the jailer predicts the downfall of both king and Inquisition. The jailer reports that even the beggars are fighting, on land, river, and sea. With the jailer's words, the Prisoner realizes he can now hope for freedom—particularly since when the jailer departs, he leaves the cell door unlocked.

In the third scene, the Prisoner, navigating the subterraneous passageways in the course of his escape, has found his way into a dungeon; torturers move about in the dark while he prays. He cowers in the darkness, yet is amazed when two passing priests glance in his direction but fail to notice him. The Prisoner presses on, and by the fourth scene finds himself in a nocturnal garden. Believing he has finally achieved liberty, he ecstatically embraces a great cedar tree, but two enormous arms reach out from the tree and trap him. Now comes the familiar voice of the jailer, saying with irony, "My brother." The jailer is actually the Grand Inquisitor, who has inflicted upon the Prisoner the ultimate torture, that of hope. As the chorus intones the Latin hymn of the Inquisition, the jailer/Inquisitor leads the Prisoner off to the pyre. *—James Reel*

Recommended:

○ **Dallapiccola: Il Prigioniero; Canti di Prigionia** / Salonen (cond.), Bryn-Julson, Hynninen, Swedish Radio Orch. / 1995 / Sony 68323

Dallas Symphony Orchestra

f. May 22, 1900, Dallas, TX

Ensemble

As was often the case in the U.S., German immigrants and their descendants in Dallas founded a choral society, in this case called the Frohsinn Singing Society. Its conductor, Hans Kreissig, assembled musicians to accompany them and in 1890 co-founded the Dallas Symphony Club. Its members played and rehearsed privately. By May 22, 1900, they determined they were ready for public performance. However, it was 1905 before the orchestra, now named the Beethoven Symphony Orchestra and conducted by Walter J. Fried, announced a regular series of scheduled concerts. Carl Venth, taking over in 1911, renamed it the Dallas Symphony Orchestra. Anti-German sentiment closed it in 1914.

Fried resumed leadership when the Orchestra reassembled in 1918 and remained its director until his unexpected death in 1925. His successor was Dr. Paul van Katwijk, dean of the School of Music at Southern Methodist University (SMU). His reorganization of the orchestra into a fully professional organization led to improved performances and crowds of as many as 4,000 a night at the Music Hall.

The 1930 discovery of oil somewhat insulated Dallas from the Great Depression, but the Texas Centennial celebrations almost eradicated the Orchestra, as many regular donors to the Symphony transferred their philanthropy to the Centennial Committee, and construction of the Centennial Park blocked access to the Music Hall. Miss Sudie Williams almost single-handedly kept the orchestra going until 1942, when conductor Jacques Singer (1938–42) and several musicians joined the armed forces.

In 1945 rising Hungarian conductor Antal Dorati, a great orchestra builder, took the podium and began to raise the Dallas Symphony to major artistic rank. It soon started to make radio broadcasts and recordings. Walter Hendl, succeeding him in 1949, was less flamboyant, but also practical and a good orchestra builder. During his tenure, the orchestra moved its venue to the acoustically preferable McFarlin Auditorium at SMU.

Hendl's departure in 1958 began a difficult period. The world-famous conductor Paul Kletzki left prematurely in 1962 due to health problems. Sir Georg Solti was the next director, but was frequently absent, often appearing as guest conductor elsewhere, and left after one year. His assistant, Donald Johanos, took over as music director. His artistic success and notable recordings for the Vox Group did not prevent the orchestra from sliding into regular deficits. He left in 1970. His successor, Anshel Brusilow, resigned in 1972 after almost continuous controversy. Highly respected maestro Max Rudolf was too late to save the situation. The Symphony was so deeply in debt that in 1974 banks suspended its credit, Rudolf resigned, and the season was cancelled.

A reorganized Dallas Symphony resumed concerts in spring 1975 under guest conductor Louis Lane. He developed the orchestra into a full-time group with a 52-week-per-year contract. The exciting Mexican conductor Eduardo Mata became music director in 1977. He built the orchestra into a first-rate ensemble and brought it to Carnegie Hall for a visit. The symphony made notable recordings for RCA during the early digital years. Mata also oversaw the building of the orchestra's new concert hall, the acoustically acclaimed Eugene McDermott Concert Hall in the Morton H. Meyerson Symphony Center, located in an area set aside as the Dallas Arts District.

Drawn by the excellent acoustics, Dorian Records began a series of acclaimed recordings there under Mata, which continued when Mata left the orchestra at the end of the 1992–93 season. His replacement was the energetic young American conductor Andrew Litton, who continued the Dorian recordings and led the orchestra in its first national television broadcast in 1995. By critical consensus, he maintained and even improved the group's high artistic standards. *—Joseph Stevenson*

Recommended:

- ○ **Ravel: Orchestral Music** / Mata (cond.), Dallas SO / 2001 / RCA 68015
- ○ **An American Tapestry** / Litton (cond.), Dallas SO / 1996 / Dorian 90224
- ○ **Shostakovich: Symphony 7** / Mata (cond.), Dallas SO / 1992 / Dorian 90161

David Daniels

b. Mar. 12, 1966, Spartanburg, SC

Countertenor

David Daniels emerged in the 1990s as one of the strongest members of a crop of new countertenors. His parents were both voice teachers, and he trained for a number of years as a tenor, but it was not until his decision to explore the countertenor repertory that his voice found its best aspect. He also fell in love with the Baroque repertory, which is the primary source of roles associated with the countertenor voice. He has said that Handel's music has more emotion than even the histrionic "verismo" school of Italian opera, and he has become particularly associated with the role of Nero in Monteverdi's *L'Incoronazione di Poppea.* He sang it with the Florida Grand Opera in one of his early appearances, and gained international fame in the part with the Glimmerglass Opera's production in 1994, reprising the role with that company at the Brooklyn Academy of Music in 1996.

Daniels' voice is strong and is representative of a newer style of more masculine countertenor singing, free of the typical hooty sound of earlier exponents of this voice range. Of his Nero performance, the *Wall Street Journal* said that he "brought down the house with ferocious coloratura." He debuted with the Glyndebourne Festival Opera in 1996 as Didymus in Handel's *Theodora*, with stage direction by Peter Sellars, in a performance that was called riveting. He often sings in the most prominent twentieth century countertenor role, Oberon in Britten's *A Midsummer Night's Dream*, which was his London debut role with the English National Opera. His other repertory includes Handel's *Tamerlano, Xerxes* and *Jephtha* (his Salzburg Festival debut role), Sesto in *Giulio Cesare* (his Metropolitan Opera debut role in 1999) and, in concert, an unusual selection of works ranging from Baroque to Britten and including such composers as Debussy, Gounod, and Massenet. In 1997 he became the first countertenor to win the coveted Richard Tucker Award. *—Joseph Stevenson*

Recommended:

- ○ **A Quiet Thing** / Daniels, Ogden / 2003 / Virgin 45601
- ○ **Handel: Rinaldo** / Hogwood (cond.), Bartoli, Daniels, Bott, Finley, Academy of Ancient Music / 2000 / Decca 467087
- ○ **Handel: Operatic Arias** / Norrington (cond.), Daniels, Montgomery, Orch. of the Age of Enlightenment / 1998 / Virgin 45326
- ○ **Serenade** / Daniels, Katz / 2000 / Virgin 45400

Franz Danzi

b. Jun. 15, 1763, Schwetzingen, Germany, **d.** Apr. 13, 1826, Karlsruhe, Germany

Composer

Italian composer Franz Danzi was an influence on Carl Maria von Weber and is sometimes classified as a "pre-Romantic" composer. He was the third musical child of Innozenz Danzi, an Italian cellist and member of the famous Mannheim Orchestra. Franz took cello, keyboard, and singing lessons from his father and won a job as cellist himself at Mannheim when he was only 15.

In March 1778 the Palatine electoral court and the orchestra moved to Munich, the elder Danzi went also, but Franz stayed behind to become a member of the newly organized National Theater orchestra; the Elector hoped to establish a German musical theater to counter the vogue for Italian works. Danzi also studied at the Abbé Vogler Mannheim School of Music. The effort to establish a German theater meant work for talented composers, and although Danzi was young, he was given assignments to write incidental music.

In 1783 Danzi's father retired as cellist in the orchestra in Munich, and Franz went there to take his place. Thanks to his theatrical experience, Danzi was asked to compose an opera in Munich, a comic opera called *Mitternachtsstunde* (In the Midnight Hour). It was a hit, published, and played in many theaters. In 1790 Danzi married; he and his wife toured widely in Europe for several years and landed in Venice, where he became Kapellmeister, and she became prima donna of the Guardasoni company.

Danzi returned to Munich and in 1798 took a job supervising German musical theater and church music at the court. Two years later his wife died, and he also faced opposition from rival composers and the new elector. In 1807 he took an appointment as Kapellmeister in the court of King Frederick II of Württemberg in Stuttgart. In some respects it was a difficult appointment, but Danzi had one great compensation for the trials he endured: the fledgling composer Carl Maria von Weber was the secretary to the King's brother.

Although they were of different generations, Danzi and Weber became close personal and professional friends. Danzi was a trusted mentor to whom Weber showed his opera in progress, *Silvana*, for comments and assistance in working out problems. Danzi also organized the premiere of Weber's *Abu Hassan.* In 1812, after Weber fled Stuttgart to evade his father's debts, Danzi was given the additional duty of the teaching of musical composition in the new Institute of Art. He ended his career as Kapellmeister at the Baden court in Karlsruhe until his death, continuing to promote and produce Weber's works.

Danzi's operas were well known in his time; *Iphigenie in Aulis* was an unusual example for the time of a German opera with continuous music and no dialogue. He also wrote a large quantity of orchestral and chamber music, and songs. While works fell into classical forms, he kept up with modern harmonic ideas, on view among other places in the unusual amount of chromaticism he tended to use in the inner voices of his pieces.*—Joseph Stevenson*

Overview of Works (ca. 1780–1823)

Franz Ignaz Danzi, Beethoven's contemporary, at first glance seems to represent the anchored musical tradition, while the master of Bonn blazed new paths. Yet if one looks (listens) a bit more intently, ruminations of the then-emerging Romantic movement in his music may be perceived. A cellist in the Mannheim Orchestra from the age of 15, Danzi prolifically composed in all mediums, particularly opera and chamber music. In his lifetime, he was celebrated for the accomplishments in the former, although today his name is most readily associated with the latter, particularly wind instruments. Like many of the early Romantics, Danzi's interests spilled over into the other arts, in his case literature and poetry. Some of the latter provided text for his *Deutsche Lieder*, Op. 15, as well as, it is believed, the libretto for his own *Turandot* over a century before Puccini. He also provided a libretto for the opera *Die OpernProbe* by fellow composer Poissl. Danzi's other operas fall into the category of the German singspiel, typified by Mozart's *Die Zauberflöte*, and includes a setting of *Iphigenie in Aulis, Silvana*, and the early *Cleopatra.* While these are works of their time, representing the Sturm und Drang school, his comic fare, including *Die Mitternachtstunde* and *Der Kuss*, seem to look ahead with imaginative orchestration and a more expanded chromatic palette. His other vocal and choral music is more in step with the conventions of his time, as is a small body of keyboard work. In his instrumental work, Danzi drew on his experience with the Mannheim Orchestra. His larger scale works are, for the most part, concerti and sinfonia concertante. It is, for the most part, his chamber work that is most admired, particularly his horn and clarinet works, wind quintets, and sextets. Like so many of the prototypical Romantics (mature Beethoven, Schubert, Weber), a more impassioned language is put through the rigors of traditional formal processes. That Danzi has never received the recognition of the said composers may be attributed to his excessively by-the-book processes, yet juxtaposed with this is a consistently daring incursion into chromatic and harmonic adventurousness that is bound to draw a listener in. *— Wayne Reisig*

Recommended:

- ○ **Danzi: Wind Quintets Vol. 3** / Berlin Philharmonic Wind Quintet, Derwinger / 1991 / Bis 592
- ○ **Danzi: Bassoon Concertos** / Pasquet (cond.), Holder, Neubrandenburger PO / 1999 / Naxos 554273
- ○ **Danzi: Flute Concertos** / Stadlmair (cond.), Adorjan, Munich CO / Classic Collection 99875

Michael Daugherty

b. Apr. 28, 1954, Cedar Rapids, IA

Composer: Symphonic, Chamber Music

Michael Daugherty was born in 1954 in Cedar Rapids, IA. Raised in a family of musicians (his father was a dance band drummer), Daugherty was subject to many different influences, and began playing keyboards in jazz, rock, and funk bands. It was these early influences and loves that later informed his formal music writing; his chamber music and symphonic works alike are based on references to American popular culture, including Elvis Presley, J. Edgar Hoover, *I Love Lucy*, UFOs, Rosa Parks, spaghetti Western movies, and Barbie dolls. With these pieces, Daugherty has risen to be one of the most performed and talked-about composers of his time.

Daugherty received his bachelor's degree from North Texas State University in 1976. It was there that he composed his first work for orchestra. He then received a master of music degree from the Manhattan School of Music. Daugherty left the states on a Fulbright fellowship to attend Boulez's IRCAM in Paris in 1979. In 1980, he began his final graduate studies at Yale University. After completing the course-work requirement of the degree, he moved to Hamburg, Germany, to study privately with György Ligeti.

In 1986, Daugherty received his Doctor of Musical Arts degree from Yale University and was hired to teach composition at the Oberlin Conservatory. The following year, he came to national attention after winning a Kennedy Center Friedheim award for *Snap, Blue like an Orange!* Over the next few years, Daugherty's music began to be performed all over the United States and appeared on many recordings. Some of the pieces he wrote at this time were the *Metropolis Symphony* for orchestra, *Sing Sing: J. Edgar Hoover* for 3 Elvis impersonators and string quartet, *Bizzaro* for symphonic winds, and *Dead Elvis* for chamber ensemble. Daugherty received critical acclaim and audience approval for his work including awards and fellowships from the American Academy of Arts and Letters, Lincoln Center, the Guggenheim Foundation, and the National Endowment for the Arts.

Daugherty began teaching at the University of Michigan in 1991. Commissions during this period included *Jackie-O* for the Houston Grand Opera, *UFO* for percussionist Evelyn Glennie and orchestra, *Spaghetti Western* for English horn and orchestra for the Philadelphia Orchestra, and *Hell's Angels*, a concerto for bassoon quartet and orchestra. The Detroit Symphony, as part of his four-year appointment as composer-in-residence, premiered *Motor City Triptych* in 2000. *—DJ Sparr*

SYMPHONIC

Metropolis Symphony (1988–1993)

Michael Daugherty is an American composer (b. 1954) who uses icons of pop culture in the way earlier composers used folk tales and classic legends. He composed this symphony between 1988 and 1993, receiving his initial inspiration from the ceremonies in Cleveland celebrating the first appearance of Superman in action comics. It is scored for a standard orchestra, plus synthesizer and an expanded percussion section. Taking another inspiration from American composer Charles Ives (1874–1954), it uses various styles, often applied in layers of music in different rhythms, drawing on symphonic, rock, jazz, funk, and avant-garde elements. It is a high-energy piece.

The first movement depicts Lex Luthor, the evil scientist and tycoon who is Superman's most persistent villain. The solo violin remakes one of its traditional roles—impersonating the devil—into a characterization of Lex. Its perpetual-motion figurations are chased by the orchestra, which includes four police whistles. The music is mysterious and brooding, with microtones and buildups that lead to the planet Krypton's apocalypse. The scherzo of the symphony is "Mxyzptlk," an imp from the Fifth Dimension who visits Metropolis regularly. He can only be banished back if he is tricked into saying his name backward. (Forward, by the way, it is pronounced "mixes-pit-lick.") The movement uses a lot of spatial effects. "Oh, Lois!" is also a fast movement (its tempo marking is "faster than a speeding bullet"). Although Lois is Superman's love interest, this is not a romantic movement; instead it keeps the Man of Steel busy throughout, rushing to her rescue time after time. The dance in "Red Cape Tango" is a dance of death, based on the Dies Irae chant. Legato and staccato portions alternate. A tango rhythm is ultimately lost in Superman's struggle to the death with Doomsday. This year-long story arch had just concluded its run in the comic books when Daugherty wrote the movement. The comic-book Superman was later revived, in a different form, but Daugherty has said that this is his last Superman piece. *—Joseph Stevenson*

Recommended:

○ **Daugherty: Metropolis Symphony** / Zinman (cond.), Controulis, Greenberg, Sparks, Baltimore SO / 1996 / Argo 452103

CHAMBER MUSIC

Dead Elvis (1993)

In Michael Daugherty's *Dead Elvis*, the King of rock & roll is personified by, of all things, a bassoon—played by an appropriately dressed and coifed Elvis impersonator—accompanied by clarinet, trumpet, trombone, one percussionist, violin, and double bass. The piece uses the same instrumentation as Stravinsky's *L'histoire du soldat*, and is analogous to the story of that famous work: Elvis sells his soul to record agents, Hollywood, and Las Vegas in somewhat the same way that Stravinsky's violinist sells his soul to the devil.

The main musical motive of the piece is the Dies Irae chant, which is programmatically used in reference to Elvis' death. This medieval chant for the Day of Judgment is the first motive we hear, and appears either as melody or accompaniment in every movement of the piece. Each of *Dead Elvis*' distinct sections starts sparsely and quietly and then builds progressively to be busy and loud; aside from this, however, the movements are musically dissimilar, ranging from the beautiful legato bassoon solos with lounge-style background music, to exciting trades of short motives from the other instruments in a rock style, to more complicated twentieth century counterpoint in other sections. Over the course of the piece, it is easy to imagine the journey of Elvis from a young man to a burned-out Vegas lounge act. *—DJ Sparr*

Recommended:

○ **Absolute Mix** / K. Jarvi (cond.), Absolute Ens. / 2000 / CCn'C 702

Mario Davidovsky

b. Mar. 4, 1934, Buenos Aires, Argentina
Composer: Chamber Music

Mario Davidovsky is a renowned composer who is best known for his work in electronic music. He received the Pulitzer Prize in 1971 for his *Synchronism No. 6* for piano and tape. Davidovsky began his musical training at the early age of seven while still residing in Argentina. He went on to study at the Collegium Musium before entering the Bartolome Mitre School at the University of Buenos Aires. He began composing at age 13 and studied under Guillermo Graetzer.

In 1958, Davidovsky traveled to the U.S. to study at the Berkshire Music Center with Aaron Copland, who was not a fan of electronic music, believing it to be limited by its reliance on electronic media. Milton Babbitt encouraged Davidovsky to permanently move to New York City in 1960. Since coming to the U.S., he has taught at the Manhattan School of Music, Yale University, City University, City University of New York, the University of Pennsylvania, and the University of Michigan. He also was a visiting professor at the Di Tella Institute in Argentina, and in January 1994, he joined the music department at Harvard University.

In addition to his teaching and composing, Davidovsky served as director of the Koussevitsky Foundation at the Library of Congress, director of the Fromm Foundation at Harvard University, and chairman of the Electronic Music Center at Columbia University. He founded and served as the vice president of the Robert Miller Fund for Music. Davidovsky has been the recipient of numerous awards and commissions. He has received two Guggenheim Fellowships, the Brandeis Creative University Creative Arts Award, a Koussevitsky Fellowship, the Williams Foundation Fellowship, and two Rockefeller Fellowships. He became a member of the American Academy of Arts and Letters in 1982. In 1997, he received the honored Christopher and Stephan Kaske Foundation Music prize for his contributions in developing contemporary music.

His many commissions have come from such prestigious institutions as Harvard's Fromm Foundation, the Julliard String Quartet, the Pan American Union, the Koussevitsky Foundation, Yale University, the Emerson String Quartet, the San Francisco Symphony Orchestra, and the Philadelphia Orchestra. In addition, he has received commissions from Speculum Musicae, the Naumburg Foundation, and the Orpheus Chamber Orchestra. Davidovsky is perhaps best known for combining live instrumental performances with pre-recorded electronic sound. He composed a series of eight *Synchronisms* for various instruments. Mario Davidovsky is currently the Fanny P. Mason Professor of Music at Harvard University. *—Bruce Lundgren*

CHAMBER MUSIC

Synchronisms, for various instruments (1963)

Mario Davidovsky's *Synchronisms*, composed over the course of several decades beginning in 1963, stands as one of the most significant pieces in the electro-acoustic repertoire. The engaging structures and surfaces found throughout *Synchronisms* reflect the new parameters of artistic creation afforded by advanced electronic and computer-aided sound production methods. Each of the works in the *Synchronisms* series features an acoustic instrument or ensemble performing in tandem with a recording of electronically generated sounds; in each case, the electronic sounds engage in a complex timbral counterpoint with the tones and articulations of the soloist or ensemble. "One of the central ideas of these pieces," the composer states, "is the search to find ways of embedding both the acoustic and the electronic into a single, coherent musical and aesthetic space." By engaging with each instrument on a purely acoustic, timbral level, Davidovsky opens up entirely new avenues of exploration; the sounds an instrument is able to produce, rather than just the motives or chords it is able to play, become subject to variation. Likewise, Davidovsky utilizes the "spatial" element of stereophonic sound afforded by the electronic medium to interact with the instrumental element, literally, from various angles. In *Synchronism No. 6* for piano and tape, which secured for the composer the Pulitzer Prize for music in 1970, the percussive articulation of the piano is echoed in caricature by a broad spectrum of snaps, pops, and blasts of broadband noise; elsewhere, a pedaled legato melody blends with sustained electronic tones. *Synchronism No. 10* (1992) takes advantage of the innumerable ways in which one can create sound on the guitar. The piece begins with an extended guitar solo (senza electronics) which, in many ways, assumes the texture of one of Davidovsky's electronic works. It utilizes a wide array of timbres and articulations ranging from aggressive strumming, to hovering harmonics, to percussive knocks on the instrument frame. In the meantime, at about the midway point, the electronic element enters rather seamlessly as distant harmonics or lingering resonances. As the electronic element becomes more involved, the guitar part becomes more streamlined and less erratic, thus giving the piece a kind of overall dovetail structure. In the two *Synchronisms* for string instruments, No. 3 for violoncello and No. 9 for violin, as well as No. 1 for solo flute, busy electronic clouds spin off of instrumental gestures and finish off particularly forceful passages with pointed punctuations and clever retorts. Fully half of the *Synchronisms* extend the palette of sounds even further by employing electronic sounds in tandem with instrumental ensembles. These include No. 2 (1963, for flute, clarinet, violin, cello), No. 4 (1967, for chorus), No. 5 (1969, for percussion quintet), No. 7 (1973, for orchestra), and No. 8 (1974, for wind quintet). *—Jeremy Grimshaw*

Recommended:

- ○ **Boston Musica Viva Plays Schwanter, Ives & others** / Boston Musica Viva / 1987 / Delos 1011
- ○ **Secret Geometry; Music for Piano & Electronic Tape** / Karis / 1996 / CRI 707
- ○ **Jennifer Frautschi: Solovision** / Frautschi / 2003 / Artek 16
- ○ **Davidovsky: Flashbacks** / D. Starobin / 2000 / Bridge 9097

Dennis Russell Davies

b. Apr. 16, 1944, Toledo, OH

Conductor

Though respected for his interpretations of works that range across the entire repertoire, American conductor Dennis Russell Davies is particularly well known for his skillful presentations of new music. Davies' formal training includes studies at the Juilliard School of Music, where his conducting teachers were Jean Morel and Jorge Mester. He made his conducting debut in 1968, leading the Juilliard Ensemble in performances at the Spoleto Festival. In 1969, Davies led the same group (under the name "The Ensemble") in the famed concert series "New and Newer Music" at Lincoln Center. In 1970, he led the premiere performance of Luciano Berio's opera *Opera* at the Santa Fe Festival.

The conductor's first appointment was as music director of the Norwalk Symphony (1968–73). From 1972 to 1980 he was music director of the St. Paul Chamber Orchestra and, from 1974, director of the Cabrillo Music Festival. Davies made his European operatic debut with a production of Debussy's *Pelléas et Mélisande* at the Netherlands Opera in 1973. In 1977, he became a founding member and music director of the American Composers Orchestra, a New York ensemble specializing in new music. His tenure with that ensemble, which continued to 2001, represents one of the longest such associations on the American orchestral scene. In 1978, Davies became the second American (after Thomas Schippers) to be asked to conduct at the Wagner Festival in Bayreuth, where he led performances of *The Flying Dutchman* through 1980. Davies held the post of music director of the Württemburg State Theater in Stuttgart from 1980 to 1987. There, in addition to premiering works like Henze's *The English Cat*, Glass' *Akhnaten*, and Bolcom's *Songs of Innocence and Experience*, he attracted attention for controversial productions of more familiar repertoire.

Davies has lived in Germany since 1980, although he spends much of his professional life in the United States. In 1991 he became director of the Brooklyn Academy of Music and principal conductor of the Brooklyn Philharmonic. He debuted at the Metropolitan Opera in 1996, conducting the premiere of Glass' *The Voyage*. In the 1990s he also premiered Berio's *Un re in Ascolto* at the Chicago Lyric Opera and Schwertsik's operetta *Der ewige Frieden* in Bonn and Vienna. Davies assumed the post of chief conductor of the Stuttgart Chamber Orchestra in 1996. In 2002, he took on chief conductor position of both the Linz Opera and the Bruckner Orchestra Linz.

Davies is amply represented on recordings, especially of new music. His label associations include projects with Nonesuch, ECM, Point, Argo, Tzadik, MusicMasters, and CRI. *—AMG*

Recommended:

- ○ **Mozart: Piano Concertos; Adagio & Fugue** / Davies (cond.), Jarrett, Stuttgart CO / 1999 / ECM 462651
- ○ **Davies Performs Philip Glass** / Davies (cond. & piano), Rascher Saxophone Quartet, Stuttgart CO / 2004 / Orange Mountain Music 11
- ○ **Lou Harrison: Drums Along the Pacific** / Davies (cond.), Gamelan Sekar Kembar, William Winant Percussion Group / 2003 / New Albion 122
- ○ **Glass: Symphony 3** / Davies (cond.), Stuttgart CO / 2000 / Nonesuch 79581
- ○ **Glanville-Hicks, Harrison, Riley** / Davies, Fairweather (cond.), Jarrett, Brooks, Riley, Brooklyn PO, Voices Saintpaulia / 1992 / MusicMasters 67089

Sir Peter Maxwell Davies

b. Sep. 8, 1934, Manchester, England

Composer: Musical Theater, Orchestral, Concerto, Symphonic, Opera

Known to his friends simply as Max, Sir Peter Maxwell Davies is one of the most prolific and frequently performed of British composers. His several hundred compositions draw from an eclectic array of influences, from Indian music to serialism to Renaissance polyphony. Davies has also worked tirelessly in the area of music education and as an environmental activist.

The precocious Davies made his musical debut in a BBC broadcast at age eight. His education continued at Leigh Grammar School and from 1952 at Manchester University, where he received an M.A. in 1957. He also attended the Royal Manchester College of Music from 1952 to 1956, where he and fellow musicians Sir Harrison Birtwistle, John Ogdon, Alexander Goehr, and Elgar Howarth formed New Music Manchester—a group devoted to the performance of twentieth century works. The Italian government provided Davies with a scholarship in 1957, allowing him to study in Italy for a year with Goffredo Petrassi.

From 1959 to 1962, Davies was director of music at the Cirencester Grammar School, where he developed a teaching method based on musical performance. Since then he has written often for children, and continues to devote significant time to education. He spent the next two years in the United States, studying at Princeton University's graduate school with Roger Sessions and Earl Kim on a Harkness Fellowship. He wrote *The Shepherd's Calendar* (1965) for young singers and instrumentalists for the 1965 UNESCO Conference on Music in Education in Sydney, Australia, and was a visiting composer at Adelaide University in 1966.

Back in England in 1967, Davies formed the Pierrot Players with Birtwistle. The Players specialized in performances of contemporary music, and Davies wrote many works for them, including his infamous *Eight Songs for a Mad King* (1969). He took over sole directorship of the Players in 1970, reforming them as the Fires of London (which he continued to lead and compose for until he disbanded the group in 1987). During the 1960s, Davies became interested in John Taverner, the sixteenth century English composer. In 1962, he wrote the award-winning *First Fantasia on an In Nomine of John Taverner*, and started work on his first opera, *Taverner*, which was premiered in 1972.

In 1970, Davies relocated to the Orkney Islands; Orcadian subject matter, in particular, the writings of George Mackay Brown and the Orcadian St. Magnus became a significant part of his music. Brown's writings have inspired works like *Black Pentecost* (1979) and the massive *Orkney Saga* project (the first two of its proposed fourteen parts appeared in 1997). In 1977, Davies organized the St. Magnus Festival, which he directed until 1986. *The Yellow Cake Revue* for singers and piano (1980) features a text by Davies criticizing proposed uranium mining in the Orkneys and is just one of his compositions reflecting his environmental concerns.

Davies received his knighthood in 1987. Two years earlier, he became the Associate Composer-Conductor of the Scottish Chamber Orchestra, an association which led to the *Strathclyde Concerto Project*, a set of ten concertos for various instruments written over the years 1987 to 1996. His interest in children's music continued with the frequently performed *The Turn of the Tide* (1992), in which Davies' music is combined with compositions by school children. Among his numerous commissioned works are *An Orkney Wedding, with Sunrise* (1984), written for the centennial of the Boston Pops; *The Doctor of Myddfai* (1995), his second full-scale opera, written for the fiftieth anniversary of the Welsh National Opera; and the *Symphony No. 8, "Antarctic"* (2000), commissioned by the Philharmonia Orchestra. *—Chris Morrison*

MUSICAL THEATER

Eight Songs for a Mad King, J. 80 (1969)

"This Organ was George the third for Birds to sing," reads a note accompanying a small mechanical organ willed to Sir Peter Maxwell Davies in 2000. Its previous owner had once shown it to Randolph Stow, who was so intrigued by its music and its history that he composed a series of eight poems, which Peter Maxwell Davies then set to music and devised as a semi-theatrical work for male vocalist, piano, violin, cello, flute, clarinet, and percussion. The resulting work, *Eight Songs for a Mad King*, was completed in 1969 and stands as one of the most distinctive, and arguably one of the most disturbing, musical works from the twentieth century. Inspired by the little mechanical organ's repertoire of eight tunes, the eight songs depict several documented and imagined events from King George III's famous and well-documented descent into insanity. The work draws on various extremes of compositional and performance technique to explore the emotional and expressive extremes of a disturbed mind, and remains the best-known example of Davies' eclectic musical style.

Perhaps the most distinctive characteristic of this work is the timbral array utilized by the vocalist. The part spans a range of over four octaves, and employs all manner of noises: Sprechgesang (something between highly inflected speech and song), falsetto, glissandi, portamenti, grunts, burbles, howls, and screeches. In the course of the work, the King attempts to teach his bullfinches to sing; the birds are "played" by the winds and strings, who perform within cages. This creates surreal dialogues between voice and instruments, demanding incredible virtuosity from both. The effect has a powerful stage impact; at one point in the seventh song, the King grows so frustrated with this enterprise that he grabs the violinist's instrument and smashes it to pieces.

Other dramatic associations are created as well; the "Lady-in-Waiting" whom George tries to engage in conversation in Scene Three is represented by the flute; his rant in Scene Six is largely directed at the clarinet; the cellist takes the role of the River Thames in Scene Four, carrying the King momentarily away from his troubles; and in the first and last scenes the percussionist stands as the King's sentry, always keeping him under close guard and finally escorting His howling Highness off stage at the end with solemn, whip-like drum beats. The piano throughout assumes no particular roles but alternately provides commentary on the proceedings and takes the part of harpsichord continuo for the numerous musical quotations and allusions.

Representation even extends beyond instrumentation; in one scene, the notes on the page of the score are arranged so as to resemble a cage visually—the one in which the bullfinches are kept, as well as the one in which the King feels himself trapped. The music itself throughout the work is a strange hodgepodge of various materials, from fox-trot to Handel's *Messiah*, the highly anachronistic juxtapositions creating the kind of disorientation for the listener that George himself might have experienced during his less-than-lucid moments. *—Jeremy Grimshaw*

Synopsis:

As an exploration of (and at some points an exercise in) insanity, Peter Maxwell Davies' music theater work for ensemble and male soloist, *Eight Songs for a Mad King*, follows a circuitous and calculatedly confused plot line, one that seeks to embody an intermittently lucid mind caught in a chronic struggle with a fractured frame of reality. The songs are settings of poems by Randolph Stow inspired by actual accounts of the life of King George III, whose reign at the end of the eighteenth century and the beginning of the nineteenth was marred by bouts with porphyria, a disorder that frequently led him to dementia and hallucinations. The events outlined in the eight scenes are cobbled together from a combination of new text by Stow and quotations from firsthand transcriptions of King George's words, uttered during a number of his "spells." Throughout the piece the King musically converses with the violin, flute, clarinet, and cello, which represent both the bullfinches that the King attempted to teach to sing, as well as various other characters or ideas; the percussionist represents the King's keeper.

In the first scene, titled "The Sentry," the King fancies himself setting out on a walk in the countryside. Approaching the gate of the royal grounds, he extends a friendly greeting to the guard. As he looks for his key, he makes small talk with the lad and promises to give him a cabbage from the garden next month. He commands that the door be opened but cannot find his key, and suddenly lapses into hallucination ("Ach! My kingdom is snakes and dancing, my Kingdom is locks and slithering!"). He realizes that the guard is not there to keep intruders out, but rather to keep His Mad Majesty in. He begs for the sentry's pity.

Unable to leave the grounds (and is it known for certain whether the previous scene has been a real or imagined encounter?), the King nonetheless imagines himself on a walk in Scene Two ("A Country Walk"). The beauty of nature, however, is transformed into grotesquerie as trees take on hideous forms and ivy turns into snakes. In Scene Three, "The Lady-in-Waiting," the King finds himself in an imaginary conversation with a young woman, represented by the flute. His self-consciousness about his mental instability is apparent as he repeatedly begs the imagined woman not to leave and assures her that he means no harm. The fourth scene finds the King on a boat floating down the River Thames, which is represented in the music by the cello. He imagines the current carrying him far away from his present troubles—to Eden, Hannover, Bermuda, or perhaps America. "I am weary of this feint," he mourns. "I am alone."

The King yearns again for companionship in Scene Five, "The Phantom Queen." According to historical accounts, George occasionally would imagine that he and his real-life wife Queen Charlotte had divorced and that he had married Lady Esther Pembroke, whose beauty had been known far and wide in earlier decades. He voices the suspicion that his captors, the doctors, have chained her up just like him and disputes their suggestion that someone besides Esther is the real Queen. Scene Six, "The Counterfeit," is difficult to decipher, as its text is excerpted verbatim from a transcription of one of King George's impromptu delusional speeches. He insists that he is not "ill," just "nervous," and he begs his caretakers to tell him the truth. Doctor Heberden, he states, has been honest with him, but Sir George (?) has told him a white lie. "But I hate a white lie!" he cries. "If you tell me a lie, let it be a black lie!"

In Scene Seven, "Country Dance," George imagines himself in the middle of a country festival, reveling with the locals. "The landlord, at the Three Tuns," he divulges, "makes the best purl in Windsor." The gaiety is punctuated by incongruous references to Handel's *Messiah*, with which the King urges the partygoers to "Comfort ye, my people, with singing and dancing." Suddenly, however, he is overcome by revulsion toward the decadent state of the populace. "Sin! Sin! Sin!" he charges, then threatens, in an outburst from an actual interview with the King, that "I shall rule with a rod of iron!" It is during this scene that, in live performances, the enraged King commandeers the violinist's instrument and smashes it. According to the composer, "This is not just the killing of a bullfinch—it is a giving-in to insanity and a ritual murder by the King of a part of himself." In the final scene the King mourns his own passing and delivers his own eulogy. "A good-hearted gentleman," he recalls. "A humble servant of God." He then recounts his own madness, including several documented events—his mistaking of a tree for King Frederick of Prussia, a physical attack against his son, his covering of the mirrors in his quarters to avoid the sight of his sunken, crazed eyes. He also chronicles his mistreatment at the hands of his keepers. As his eulogy ends he is escorted from the stage by the percussionist, whose slow and stark beats on a drum elicit howls of anguish from the Mad King. *—Jeremy Grimshaw*

Recommended:

○ **Maxwell Davies: Miss Donnithorne's Maggot; 8 Songs for a Mad King** / Maxwell Davies (cond.), J. Eastman, The Fires of London / 1987 / Unicorn 9052

Vesalii Icones, J. 85 (1969)

Composer Peter Maxwell Davies has an elegant analogy to explain the complex convergence of elements that comprises *Vesalii icones* (1969)—his part-ballet, part-chamber music, part-performance art piece for solo dancer, cello, and instrumental ensemble. He sees the work's various constituent parts as figures painted on panes of glass which are layered with intervening space, so that the eye can shift focus from one pane to another; at the same time, no matter which layer demands attention at any given time, each layer effects the perception of all the others. In the music of *Vesalii icones*, these layers can be identified as plainchant, "popular" or jazz music, and that of Davies himself, whose style amalgamates the previous ones.

This kind of synergistic combination finds a counterpart in the work's crucial visual elements. In fact, the work's genesis can be traced to the composer's purchase of a facsimile edition of *De Humani corporis fabrica*, the groundbreaking illustrated guide to human anatomy by the sixteenth century Belgian physiologist Andreas Vesalius. Vesalius' detailed drawings, based on studies originally performed on the stolen bodies of criminals left hanging at the gallows, depict the human figure in everyday scenes—walking down a country road, hailing a friend, leaning against a wall. Disconcertingly, however, the posing figures are depicted in several degrees of dissection or disembowelment, with varying layers of muscle and tendon cut away to reveal the workings of the body. In composing a piece based on these drawings, Davies associated these figures with the so-called "stations of the cross," the various events leading up to and including Christ's crucifixion. The work comprises 14 scenes; in each, the dancer navigates between exploring the movements and gestures suggested by one of Vesalius' diagrams, and the emotions suggested by one of the stations of the cross.

As in his famous theatrical cycle, *Eight Songs for a Mad King*, Davies' musical realization of his dramatic scheme is at times extremely jarring. The score calls for a hodgepodge of odd timbres. Flute, clarinet, and viola are joined by a cello soloist, who at various times seems to execute the role of Pilate, the flagellator, and—with the sawing motion of the bow, Vesalius himself. A percussionist augments a large battery of standard instruments with such things as chains, a biscuit tin full of broken glass, a typewriter, and a "short length of scaffolding"; a pianist doubles on, among other things, an out-of-tune autoharp, four lengths of bamboo, and a music box "chosen for the unsuitability of its tune." In addition, in the scene depicting Christ being mocked by his guards, the dancer is instructed to play a sharply irreverent fox-trot on a "honky tonk" (out-of-tune) piano. The most shocking event, however, occurs in the last scene, in which the resurrected figure emerging from the tomb turns out to be the Antichrist. According to Davies, this apparent blasphemy actually bears a moral message: "that one should not be taken in by appearances." *—Jeremy Grimshaw*

Synopsis:

Though Peter Maxwell Davies does classify his *Vesalli Icones* as a "music-theatre work for solo dancer, cello and instrumental ensemble," a synopsis of the action that takes place over the course of the work is less than straightforward and requires some introductory explanation. The music and dance follow a series of episodes, but do so along two concurrent and rather complexly convergent strands. Each of the 14 episodes explore in tandem one of the Stations of the Cross from Christian tradition and one of the drawings from Vesalius' *De humani corporis fabrica*. Each scene begins with the dancer assuming a position from one of Vesalius' illustrations, then shifting to depict a loosely "corresponding" station. As the composer describes it, each anatomical drawing inspires certain technical explorations on the part of the dancer, which are executed "in the light of the ritual and emotional experience suggested by the station."

The first episode compares Vesalius' *Prima musculorum tabula* with Christ's suffering in the garden. One sees a certain immediate correspondence in the anatomee's sorrowful and pleading heavenward glance. At this point, only the top layer of skin is removed, revealing the outermost muscular systems intact. The second scene, beginning with the left-side view shown in Vesalius' *Tabula II*, takes as its countersubject Judas Iscariot's betrayal of Jesus. The body in *Tabula III* remains intact for the encounter between Christ and Pilate, but for Jesus' ensuing flagellation in scene four, Vesalius' *Tabula IV* is shown with some initial layers of muscle and tendon peeled away. In scene five, in which Christ is condemned to death, the figure assumes a pose similar to that of the opening scene, save that in Vesalius' fifth tabula layers of muscle and bone are now pulled away and hang from his limbs and torso. The first half of the work ends with the mocking of Christ; here the figure seems to take on the role of an observer, with head tilted back and mouth open as if in laughter. Interestingly, this effect is exaggerated in Vesalius' drawing by the peeling away of the skin and muscles surrounding the mouth.

The convergence in the seventh scene is rather gruesome. Bearing the title "Christ receives the cross," it utilizes the seventh tabula of the *De humani corporis fabrica*, which depicts a partially dissected and disembowelled body hanging from a noose. In *Tabula VIII*: "Saint Veronica wipes His face," the figure leans against a wall, nearly shorn of all its musculature. For the subsequent scene, "Christ prepared for death," the nearly intact body in Vesalius' *Tabula IX* turns its back to the viewer, suggesting departure. *Tabula XI*, associated by the composer with Christ's death, depicts a similar stance, though the figure is partially dissected and the skull is opened to reveal the brain. A finger extended upwards into the air suggests heavenly ascension. *Tabula XII*, associated with the descent from the cross, shows the same figure, hands extended downward, another layer of flesh removed, while the figure in *Tabula XIII*, corresponding with the entombment, is nearly skeletal. For the final scene, Davies drastically alters the biblical element in his story. The armless, nearly fleshless figure of Vesalius' *Tabula XIV* leans against a stone bench; the Resurrection associated with this scene is not that of Christ, but of the Antichrist, who places an everlasting curse on Christendom. This final gesture, the composer insists, is not sacrilegious, but moral: "it is a matter of distinguishing the false from the real, that one should not be taken by appearances." *—Jeremy Grimshaw*

Recommended:

○ **Maxwell Davies: Vesalii Icones; Bairns of Brugh; Runes from a Holy Island** / Maxwell Davies (cond.), Ward-Clarke, The Fires of London / 1994 / Unicorn 2068

ORCHESTRAL

Mavis in Las Vegas, theme and variations, J. 287 (1997)

Heading north from the Las Vegas airport one encounters an enormous billboard that encapsulates the wildly postmodern spirit of this boldly overblown city: next to a picture of a Prince look-alike appear the words "Accept no *other* imitation." Such was the immediate impression felt by composer Peter Maxwell Davies upon arriving there during a tour of the United States with the BBC Philharmonic in 1995. "The most unreal synthetic city in the middle of the desert," recalled Davies, whose home on the tranquil shores of Hoy Island in the Orkneys could find no more exact opposite than the glitz of Vegas. "Gambling, quick weddings, and the cult of kitsch so tacky as to be a source of wonder and inspiration." The sharp irony that Davies had proven himself so capable of evoking was thus tempered with a sense of campy fondness in the composition of *Mavis in Las Vegas: Theme and Variations for Orchestra*.

The composer arrived at the title and concept of this ode to oddity when, while still in Vegas, he came across an article in a London newspaper documenting recent events in his U.S. tour. The reporter recounted his difficulty in contacting the composer for a prearranged interview because of a clerical error on the part of an employee at the Flamingo Hilton: apparently the name "Maxwell Davies" had been mistakenly conflated to "Mavis." This delightful mistake inspired the composer to create an entire musical persona around this imagined woman, a kind of desert-dwelling Dame Edna, whose adventures in the city of sin Davies lavishly and lovingly depicts over the course of this 13-minute-long work.

Mavis herself is represented by a lush theme on the violin, rendered dolce, con vibrato sentimental ("sweetly, with a sentimental vibrato"). Davies then transports us to the casino, where the din of the slot machines, roulette wheels, and cocktail glasses is depicted by layer upon layer of motoric, polyrhythmic ostinatos. Aside from a few obnoxious stray tones (the result of one too many cocktails, no doubt) these putter along noisily in C major. Mavis finally appears on the scene. "I imagine her," describes the composer affectionately, "all outrageous flounces and hip-jerks, her generous ball-gown streaming, descending a magnificent (pink!) curved staircase into the gambling arena."

Mavis visits several other Vegas landmarks during her excursion, as well: a wedding chapel, a shrine to Elvis Presley, the fountains at Caesar's Palace. The visit to the Liberace museum offers a particularly rich font of sickly-sweet musical ephemera, with relentlessly melodramatic piano runs up and down the keyboard and a wonderfully inordinate amount of orchestral aplomb. The work concludes in front of the MGM hotel, as a crowd gathers to watch in wonder as the great plastic volcano erupts, right on schedule, with a magnesium flash and a digitized roar. A final rendering of the opening material indicates Mavis' gleeful approval, as every conclusory cliché is employed in drawing the work to a close. *—Jeremy Grimshaw*

Recommended:

○ **Maxwell Davies: Mavis in Las Vegas** / Maxwell Davies (cond.), BBC PO / 1998 / Collins 15242

An Orkney Wedding, with Sunrise, J. 205 (1985)

While textbook references to Peter Maxwell Davies usually focus on his studies of dark psychological dysfunction (most prominently the *Eight Songs for a Mad King*), one of his most popular works among symphony orchestra audiences is a much more lighthearted exercise. *An Orkney Wedding with Sunrise*, commissioned by John Williams and the Boston Pops Orchestra in 1985, is a delightfully vivid musical pictorial of a jubilant and rather boozy wedding party on the Orkneyan isle of Hoy, off the northern coast of the Scottish mainland.

In fact, the musical account is rendered first-hand. Though Davies traces his ancestral roots to Scotland, his musical roots took soil there when, beginning in 1970, he began traveling to Orkney for creative retreats. *An Orkney Wedding with Sunrise* was inspired by the composer's attendance at an actual wedding party on Hoy. The work is as extroverted as any of Davies', but joyously so—the exaggerated gestures reflect those of the scene's revelry, as well as the guest's increasing intoxication. The composer's characteristic hall-of-mirrors approach to musical allusion is employed with highly comic effect as lyrical and nostalgic (though generally not borrowed) tunes spin themselves into happy confusion, rhythms intermittently trip forward or hiccup, and harmonies sway and swoon with the rustic and boisterous crowd.

The work is highly pictorial, its episodic sections corresponding closely with the succession of events witnessed by the composer. As the piece opens the guests are just arriving, the sour weather outside contrasting the festivities inside the hall. To a processional tune passed around the woodwind section, the guests ceremoniously greet the bride and groom. The brass enter noisily as the first round of drinks are passed, the bouncy rhythms of the Scottish snap setting the melodic scene. The musicians then noisily tune their instruments in preparation for the evening's dances. With each new tune the group becomes audibly more intoxicated, the brass smearing their way through some passages and the melody occasionally stepping out of line. The insistent oom-pahs continue, however, increasing in tempo and rhythmic drive (while all the while slipping and sliding with increasing frequency). The lead fiddle seems particularly well stocked; a lilting solo waxes comically rhapsodic, with intermittent dizzy spells and moments of harmonic confusion. The dancing builds further until the whiskey takes its full effect and the partygoers drift from the dance floor. The party has apparently lasted all night, for as the guests leave they look across the water to see the first rays of dawn. At this point Davies works an ingenious bit of programmatic magic: a Highland bagpiper suddenly appears in the back of the concert hall. He passes majestically through the audience in full Scots regalia, playing a grand march as he approaches the orchestra. The stirring music carries a clever metaphor. The Highland pipes, not native to Orkney, represent the dawn as viewed by the Orkney party, the sun rising across the bay over Caithness. *—Jeremy Grimshaw*

Recommended:

○ **Maxwell Davies: A Celebration of Scotland** / Maxwell Davies (cond.), MacIlwham, Scottish CO / Unicorn-Kanchana 9070

Worldes Blis, J. 79 (1969)

The premiere of Peter Maxwell Davies' orchestral piece *Worldes Blis* (1969) caused a large portion of the audience to leave their seats, and the performance hall, rather noisily. Davies reported that the audience members who decided to stay booed at the conclusion of the composition. The concert took place in London at the Royal Albert Hall on August 28, 1969. Davies himself conducted the BBC Symphony Orchestra on this occasion. The extremely negative reaction of the audience is all the more surprising in view of the usual calmness of English concertgoers, but nothing happened on the scale of the riotous *Rite of Spring* premiere in 1913, when objects were thrown and audience members shouted at each other. Since the premiere of *Worldes Blis*, the composition has come to be accepted by many listeners and is widely regarded as a masterpiece of symphonic writing.

In *Worldes Blis*, Davies attempted to represent evil and terrible aspects of the world around him, such as violence, poverty, and injustice. Sections of the work meant to portray these conditions are marked by the aggressive and striking sounds that offended audiences at the premiere. On the day after the premiere, most reporters made no mention of the audience's reaction to Davies' work. Stanley Sadie, a musical critic and later editor of the New Grove Dictionary of Music and Musicians, wrote perhaps the only accurate account of the event. He acknowledged that the audience indeed had a right to leave if they so wished, but he criticized them for their "closed ears," and went on to suggest comically that the BBC should advertise such music as "suitable for adult listeners only."

Davies made the first sketches of this composition in 1963 and 1964 while he was at Princeton University on a Harkness Fellowship. A couple of years later, Davies continued his work on the piece while he temporarily served as Professor of Composition at the University of Adelaide in Australia. Davies greatly enjoyed this position due to the fact that he taught an exceptional group of young composers there. *Worldes Blis* is a monumental work for full orchestra, lasting an average of 40 minutes in performance. The piece starts calmly and continually builds throughout its duration, and for this reason has been compared to Ravel's *Bolero* (1928). Aspects of the world that Davies abhors are represented through this growing tension. Perhaps in reference to the work's extramusical associations, the composer termed it a "motet for orchestra." The tension is not released until just before the conclusion of the work, in a large climax. A short coda follows in which a calmness falls over the orchestra. —*Chris Boyes*

Recommended:

○ **Davies: Worldes Blis & others** / Maxwell Davies (cond.), Royal PO / 1993 / Collins 13902

CONCERTO

Strathclyde Concertos (1987–1996)

In late 1983, Peter Maxwell Davies was invited to conduct a few of his own works in front of the Scottish Chamber Orchestra. Since Davies had little conducting experience, he was hesitant to accept, but soon agreed. A year later, a new Managing Director of the SCO was appointed, Ian Ritchie. Ritchie created the position of Associate Composer/Conductor, the first of its kind. Davies was offered the post, which he gladly accepted. Later, Davies asked Ritchie, "What would you say if I suggested that I write a series of, say, ten concertos for you—one for each of the principals of the orchestra?" Ritchie agreed to the idea, but the question of funding was still unanswered. The Scottish Arts Council offered half of the funds needed and the other half was provided by the Strathclyde Regional Council. Thus was born the series of ten *Strathclyde Concertos*.

Together with Ritchie and Davies, the Council set up a plan to enrich the children of the region by using each concerto as a teaching tool. As each concerto was finished, a young composer chosen by the Council would visit the schools in a particular region of Strathclyde and would address the students concerning the concerto and the process of its composition. Then, the students would be asked to create compositions of their own. Also, the soloist for each concerto would visit the schools in the region and discuss the concerto from the performer's point of view. This plan was put into action with the ultimate goal of reconstructing the bond between composers, performers, and common people which had been severed by the avant-garde movement of the first part of the twentieth century. Throughout his career, Davies worked to reestablish music as something that all people could understand and enjoy. The composition of the concertos themselves was an ongoing project that proceeded over the course of the following decade.

These works include references to various aspects of the long concerto tradition, incorporating them into Davies' own unique tonal (but never Neo-Classical or Neo-Romantic) language. Each concerto is written for a different soloist or group of soloists. Davies tailored the accompanying orchestra in each concerto so as to not overshadow the solo instrument or instruments. In the *First Strathclyde Concerto for Oboe* (1986), the orchestra does not include any oboes or bassoons. Likewise, in the *Third Strathclyde Concerto for Horn and Trumpet* (1989), Davies excludes all of the brass instruments from the orchestra. For the *Sixth Strathclyde Concerto for Flute* (1991), Davies went even farther by removing all of the flutes, oboes, and violins from the orchestra, and by severely limiting the trumpet parts. The most demanding of the solo parts most likely lies in the *Second Strathclyde Concerto for Cello* (1987). In the last two of the *Strathclyde Concertos*, Davies increased the number of soloists. The *Ninth* (1994) is scored for six woodwind soloists, while the *Tenth* (1996) is a concerto for orchestra whose finale is a sort of recapitulation of ideas heard in the earlier concertos. —*Chris Boyes*

SYMPHONIC

Symphony No. 3, J. 203 (1984)

Peter Maxwell Davies' *Symphony No. 3* grew out of an aesthetic question that composers have pondered at least since the carefully calibrated proportions of the medieval isorhythmic motet: how to create a piece of music that resists the temporal plane on which it necessarily unfolds, and assumes instead a spatial quality. "When I wrote this symphony," the composer explains, "I thought of it in terms of purely abstract music, and involved myself with problems of large-scale articulation—that is, with musical architecture."

In fact, just as the motet Dufay wrote for the dedication of the Florence Dome in 1436 actually took musical cues from architectural features, Maxwell Davies likewise found inspiration in Brunelleschi's designs. This plays out indirectly, on the surface, in the composer's frequent use of plainchant. On a more structural level, though, the symphony's four movements are said to "articulate the same architectural outline in four different ways." The second movement, for example, depicts in tones the contours, lines, symmetries, and perspectives the eye would capture walking in a straight line from Brunelleschi's nave toward the altar; the third movement evokes the same scene, but with the proportions distorted, as if from a different point of view. The allegro first movement's gradual acceleration corresponds with the way visual lines of perspective draw nearer to each other as they approach vanishing points. The final movement stretches the material from the first into an elongated and slow finale.

Composed in 1984, the *Symphony No. 3* differs from his previous symphonic efforts in one particularly striking regard: while the earlier symphonies, like so many of his compositions, employed huge and varied percussion batteries, the *Symphony No. 3*'s sole drummer is a tympanist. His/her role is crucial, however: the drum beats help punctuate some of the most crucial features of the work's carefully wrought form. This less percussive, more fluid orchestral sound also brings the work into closer sonic proximity to another model: Mahler's *Symphony No. 9*. Not only does Maxwell Davies borrow from Mahler the idea of a slow finale, he also alludes to certain harmonic ideas and melodic figuration. Likewise, the *Symphony No. 3*'s overall form and its complex tonal and textural trajectories depict the kind of architectonic friction and collision found in the Mahlerian model, with huge, carefully paced climaxes counterpoised with, in the end, a lingering sense of uncertainty. "The music floats away," the composer described, "as if time has stood still." —*Jeremy Grimshaw*

Recommended:

○ **Maxwell Davies: Symphony 3** / Maxwell Davies, BBC PO / 1994 / Collins 14162

Symphony No. 5, J. 266 (1994)

Peter Maxwell Davies' oeuvre demonstrates a remarkably broad range of expression, from the unabashedly sentimental to the intellectually daunting. Certainly, one senses in his symphonies a distillation of the composer's masterful sense of drama (as demonstrated in his numerous theatrical/operatic works, and in his famous quasi-theatrical *Eight Songs for a Mad King*), his intimate knowledge of instrumental color (as made systematically clear in his series of *Strathclyde Concertos*), and his rigorous sense of musical structure. Davies' *Symphony No. 5*, composed in 1994 on a commission from the Philharmonia Orchestra, exemplifies Davies' particular brand of musical synergy, combining a complex and engaging harmonic language, a dizzying array of orchestrational moods and effects, and a seemingly spontaneous (though carefully constructed) overall form.

As in many of Davies' works, the harmonic language derives largely from a system of what the composer calls "magic squares." These precompositional devices correlate roughly with the matrixes generated from the 12-tone rows of Schoenberg and the second Viennese school, but differ in their pitch content. In fact, in this work Davies generates his pitch materials by extrapolating his "magic squares" from a preexisting plainchant source. The chant appears in the liturgical repertoire as *"Haec dies,"* taken from an Easter-related liturgical piece, and *"Domini audivi,"* taken from Habakkuk 3:3. The chant, which Davies had appropriated previously in *Chat Moss* from 1993, is not used in an explicit-enough fashion to draw particular attention to itself as a musical or religious allusion, and the complex transformations to which it is subjected are likely beyond the conscious comprehension of most listeners. Nonetheless, Davies' rather painstaking method (which reportedly produced considerable wastebasket filler as the piece was under development) results in a pervasive sense of conceptual unity, one that creates a strong-enough sense of compositional cohesion to grant Davies added room to experiment quite freely with formal parameters and orchestrational ideas.

Symphony No. 5 assumes a unique shape, one that seems to emerge from the musical materials themselves; scholars have found an affinity between the work's form and that of Sibelius' *Seventh Symphony*, which Davies conducted just before beginning his own *Fifth Symphony*. The work is cast in a single continuous movement, one whose overall construction is ambiguous and rather unpredictable. The score is divided clearly into 34 distinct sections, ranging anywhere from several minutes to only a few bars. These spill into each other in waves, giving the work an overall sense of uneasy but continuous momentum. Musical kernels gradually expand into walls of sound, reach a violent breaking point, then dissipate into moments of relative and fleeting repose, only to be stirred again into action by new melodic or orchestrational ideas. Nonetheless, a general arc can be derived from this fluid succession of musical passages: the first half of the work presents a variety of musical ideas in a rather free admixture, while the materials in the second half seem to polarize and tessellate into more starkly contrasting blocks of activity and stasis. —*Jeremy Grimshaw*

Recommended:

○ **Maxwell Davies: Symphony 5; Chat Moss & others** / Maxwell Davies (cond.), Philharmonia Orch. / 1995 / Collins 1460

Symphony No. 6, J. 280 (1996)

This is a large-scale three-movement symphony. It lasts about 50 minutes and comprises a pair of 20-minute end movements and an inner movement that is a bit less than half that length. Its style is strongly modern and uses the full chromatic scale nearly throughout, though mostly it retains a sense of being a tonal work. Its moods range from highly disturbed to raucous, with a finale that is mostly slow and meditative. Mostly it is highly dramatic and affecting throughout, though some of the most dissonant, loud, and rhythmic passages will upset a fair percentage of listeners.

As Sir Peter Maxwell Davies (born 1934) has often done, he based this work on a prior work. The earlier piece is an overture called *Time and the Raven*, written in 1995 for the Royal Philharmonic Orchestra to play on a tour honoring the United Nations on its 50th anniversary. From that work Davies took a slow theme of pentatonic character and used it as the basis of the new symphony. He states it on strings, with occasional glides between the notes that sound slightly Eastern.

The whole symphony is based on continuous transformation of the slow theme, which returns in its original form only at the end of the work. Davies says that the forms of the first two movements are paradoxical: "The first movement proper is a scherzo masquerading as a sonata-allegro, and the second a sonata-allegro masquerading as a scherzo."

This is possible because each of the two formal terms used in that description also implies a general mood. Scherzos typically begin with one musical idea (possibly with a contrasting one), and then in a central section offer an entirely different theme, which then yields back to the main scherzo music (usually in its original form). A sonata-allegro typically states two contrasting themes, subjects them to transformations in a middle section called the development, then repeats the original themes, more or less in their original forms. What Davies does is to use scherzo form as his first movement, basing the central section on a development of the main idea.

The first movement is serious and rather angry, the middle movement becomes violent, and the final movement (which echoes events of the first movement at formally important points in a kind of musical "rhyming scheme") is mostly slow and contemplative.

On the day Davies wrote its final bars, the poet George Mackay Brown died. Davies accordingly dedicated the symphony to Brown's memory. Davies has also said that the variety of light and shade and the intense colors and energy of the symphony constitute his reaction to the landscape of the Orkney Islands, where he lives. The work was premiered at Davies' own St. Magnus Festival held in the Islands, on June 22, 1996; it was played by the Royal Philharmonic Orchestra under the composer's direction. *—Joseph Stevenson*

Recommended:

○ **Maxwell Davies: Symphony 6; Time and the Raven** / Maxwell Davies, Royal PO / 1996 / Collins 1482

OPERA

The Lighthouse, chamber opera, J. 162 (1979)

One of the most mysterious stories from seafaring history dates from 1900, when a supply ship arrived at the lighthouse on the Flannan Isles to find its lamp dark and the station abandoned. The post, located on a remote shore in the Western Hebrides, had been manned by three keepers; no sign of their whereabouts remained, though their last meal reportedly sat half eaten on the table and the work log's last entry from a few days before left no clues as to the cause of the disappearance. This mystery was eventually chronicled in detail in a book by Craig Mair (*A Star for Seamen—The Stevenson Family of Engineers*, 1978), which in turn inspired composer Peter Maxwell Davies to elaborate the story into one of his most musically and dramatically engaging operas.

The work was commissioned for the Edinburgh International Festival, where it was premiered in 1980. The libretto, which Davies himself devised, utilizes the historical facts of the incident as a general framework but takes considerable license with the details and draws clever and fantastical speculations about the nature of the keepers' disappearance, effectively turning the work into a deeply psychological (and psychologically disturbed) drama of the kind for which Davies is so famous. An extended prologue lays out the general story in the form of a Court of Inquiry, at which the crew of the supply ship reports their findings. In doing so, they continually lapse into vivid reenactment, crisscrossing chronotopes in a way that allows for Davies' characteristic manipulations of stylistic juxtapositions. The prologue sets the scene for the work's single act, which introduces us to the trio of lighthouse keepers. In Davies' innovative rendering, their interpersonal tensions become aggravated by an apparent case of cabin fever, and they become haunted by ghosts from their dark and secret pasts. Their paranoia escalates into tragedy, culminating in a truly unexpected ending.

That Davies created both the libretto and the score can be observed in the inextricable connection in *The Lighthouse* between music and drama. One of Davies' strangest and most effective devices appears in the prologue, where the questions from the Court to the supply ship officials are posed by a French horn, located in the audience; likewise, certain points in the drama are highlighted or interconnected by purely musical means, thus melding the unfolding plot to the musical structure. The overall form of the work draws upon numerological principles drawn from the Tower of the Tarot, which finds surface resonance in an onstage card game. Such integration is enhanced by the vocal roster, which calls for three singers to switch between all of the roles: the officials who report the incident transform into the missing lighthouse keepers, and even step outside of the dramaturgical frame to comment in third-person-omniscient voice upon the proceedings of the opera. Such techniques allow Davies to construct elaborate symbolisms that transcend both music and text, the various musical and dramatic elements eventually combining with volatile force at the conclusion of the opera. *—Jeremy Grimshaw*

Synopsis:

Prologue. Edinburgh: an investigation is underway to determine the cause of three lighthouse keepers' disappearance. Three men (the only singers in the production) play the roles of the officers of the lighthouse supply ship that first arrived on the scene of the abandoned beacon. They field questions posed by a French horn positioned in the audience, framing their answers in such a way as to make the line of interrogation understood. As they describe their experience, the recollections become vivid and they intermittently break into pantomime and reenactment. The first officer describes a violent storm encountered on their trip, which disoriented them to such an extent that they thought they heard foghorns sounding from all directions. The waters suddenly became eerily still, he reports, and one of the men saw a triangle of lights fading into the mist. The fog parted to reveal the darkened lighthouse, which they carefully approached. Each man reports encountering different creatures near the shore: a trio of black selkies (seals), three black scarfs (bats), and three black gibbies (cats); these cryptic symbols clearly foreshadow the supernatural speculations to be elaborated in the second act. The officers describe the state of the lighthouse—all normal, save an overturned chair, an uneaten meal, and a broken glass. The men then step out of the scene, as it were, to report the court's findings and results: the disappearance is declared "death by misadventure"; because no one is found willing to replace the missing men, the lighthouse is rigged to be fully automated without human supervision, "its ghosts... shut in, sealed in, tight."

Act One. Arthur, Blazes, and Sandy, the three missing lighthouse keepers, sit down to their meal. Immediately the tension caused by their cramped quarters is established: Blazes mocks the sanctimoniousness with which Arthur, an overtly religious man, asks a blessing over the food. "Even your fine graces can't bless a meal when it's the same old nosh," Blazes insists. In an attempt to defuse tensions Sandy challenges Blazes to a game of cards while Arthur ascends the stairs to light the beacon lamp. Another argument ensues, however, sparked by accusations of cheating and aggravated by Arthur's return. Sandy again tries to lighten the mood by encouraging Blazes to treat his companions to a song. He obliges, crooning to the accompaniment of the violin and banjo a dark tale about a youthful thug who commits a violent murder while conducting a robbery, then lets his own father hang for the crime and his mother die in lunacy. "The moral of my tale," Blazes sings, "cannot fail to tease: if you're both clever and lucky, you can do just what you please." It is then Sandy's turn to sing. He chooses a love song that seems innocent at first, but its phallic symbols and sexual euphemisms become glaringly explicit when its phrases are juxtaposed into a polyphonic exchange with his companions. "I don't know what your song means," says the self-righteous Arthur, "but I disapprove." He then presents a number of his own— a fervent and energetic song about the God of Israel and his revenge against the Golden Calf and all who worship it. Arthur's fire and brimstone prompts Sandy to utter a quiet prayer to himself: "Preserve us from both the Golden Calf of his imagination and his jealous God."

While the men have been singing, the night has been settling in and the mist growing thick. Arthur ascends the stairs to sound the foghorn, enunciated by the French horn in the audience. As a storm outside swells, Blazes' past, as recounted in his apparently autobiographical ditty, comes back to haunt him with hallucinations. The pile of oilskins by the door rises up and takes the form of the old woman murdered during the robbery, while he sees his dead parents approaching the door calling him down to their ghoulish boat by the jetty. Sandy's closeted skeletons return, as well; his crimes are not made explicit, but his haunted visions suggest a past riddled with incest, pedophilia, and perhaps even murder. As his companions grow increasingly frantic, Arthur intones a dramatic recitative warning of the approach of the Beast, the Antichrist, come to claim them as his own. The lights of the Beast's three eyes appear in the distance, drawing closer, until they blind the audience. Behind the glare, the lighthouse keepers transform into the three officers, the three lights turning out to have been the lanterns of the supply boat. The officers carry the clothes of the lighthouse keepers over their arms. Attacked by the crazed keepers, they have disposed of them in some way. They conspire to report a mysteriously empty lighthouse; with the meal on the table, the lamps trimmed and filled. Then, in an unexpected twist, they reenter as the "relief lighthouse keepers," replaying in a ghostly and robotic fashion the first few lines from the beginning of the act. It is with these mysterious ellipses that the opera ends. *—Jeremy Grimshaw*

Taverner, J. 92 (1970)

British composer Peter Maxwell Davies demonstrated early in his career his masterful manipulation of jarring musical and dramatic juxtapositions—perhaps most notably in the decidedly uncomfortable rendition of "Comfort Ye My People" that appears in his *Eight Songs for a Mad King*. Likewise, a desire to problematize concepts of religiosity and morality has threaded its way throughout his musical career. Both these characteristics play prominently in Maxwell Davies's surreal and biographical two-act operatic effort from 1970, *Taverner*.

Maxwell Davies first drafted the outline and scenario of an opera based on the life of composer John Taverner (ca. 1490–1545) around 1956, and the project remained very much in his mind until he completed it in 1968. Evidently, he first had the idea as early as 1950. Between 1962 and 1964 Maxwell Davies composed two *Fantasias* on John Taverner's *In Nomine*, both of which share music with the opera. In these two works, Maxwell Davies experimented with processes he would employ in the opera, which makes use of actual music by Taverner. By 1968, *Taverner* was complete.

After a gestation period of nearly a decade, *Taverner* received its world premiere at the Royal Opera House in Covent Garden, London, in 1972. The work follows the life of John Taverner (not to be confused with post-minimalist composer John Tavener), insofar as that life is documented. In fact Maxwell Davies, who penned his own libretto for the opera, scoured the available primary sources dealing with Taverner's life and career, and actually appropriated much of the material verbatim. This combines to create a dark and, in the hands of Maxwell Davies, structurally imposing plot, one that folds over onto itself with haunting symmetries and dramatic inversions. The work begins in a courtroom, where the composer stands accused of heresy against the Catholic church. His musical talents mitigate the guilty verdict, placing him in an artistic and moral quandary; he must either continue to compose beautiful music for a church he finds increasingly corrupt, or, as part of his spiritual reorientation, renounce his musical as well as his religious past. Demonic forces eventually lead him to an unseemly resolution, one that turns the narrative on its head: as a zealous proponent of the English Reformation, he abandons his career as a composer, devoting all his energies instead to persecuting Catholicism and running monks out of their monasteries.

This plot line affords Maxwell Davies the opportunity to design dramatic polarities on numerous levels. Whereas Taverner appears first as defendant, he returns later as prosecutor. Visual aspects of the drama make full use of stark black and white color schemes. And of course, in the music itself, Maxwell Davies's characteristic and calculated anachronisms suggest that he intends his free biographical treatment to be viewed through a contemporary rather than a merely historical lens. This becomes most apparent in those scenes where music is provided by an onstage ensemble performing on Renaissance instruments, as well the various places where Maxwell Davies inserts snippets of Taverner's own music. These moments stretch taut the stylistic strands holding the opera together: elsewhere, the listener is confronted with Maxwell Davies's dissonant barrages of sound, which emanate from an unwieldy pit orchestra comprised of standard strings and winds, expanded brass, and a battalion of percussion instruments (including, among numerous more familiar objects, a knife with grinding wheel, a large cracked cymbal, and a disembowelled piano). The composer uses the essentially Medieval and Renaissance structural principal of the cantus firmus, that is, a theme which is used as the foundation for a piece of music. In the composer's hands, the plainsong *Gloria Tibi Trinitas* serves that function. Maxwell Davies pursues free musical invention over it, although he often fragments by such devices as octave displacement, rhythmic changes, and shifts of orchestral color. The opera is in eight scenes, and the events of one act frequently are mirrored by actions in the other act. Following the example of Alban Berg's opera *Wozzeck*, each scene is in a specific musical form, such as a verse anthem or a motet or a Renaissance dance. *—Jeremy Grimshaw*

Synopsis:

Act One. The opera begins in a courtroom, where Taverner himself faces charges of heresy against the Catholic Church. Acting as judge, the White Abbot warns Taverner of the deadly consequences of such actions. The composer nonetheless expresses his doubts in the church. The prosecution presents four witness, three of which present evidence against the accused: the composer's father recalls his son's volatile temperament; Taverner's Priest-Confessor, having accepted a bribe, provides damning testimony; even a choirboy from Oxford speaks out against his mentor. Only the composer's mistress, Rose, pleads on Taverner's behalf. Just when the sentence of death is about to be imposed, the Cardinal arrives and insists that the composer's music should mitigate his apostate tendencies. His life is thus spared.

The following scene finds Taverner back at the chapel, agonizing over his situation: whether to ride out the storm of his growing discontent and disbelief or to act upon his reformational desires. He finally decides to place his trust in God and await answers to his questions. Meanwhile, a chorus of monks sings reverently in Latin. Their words do not intone the liturgy, however, but rather an account of the opera's events up to this point. Appropriately, their texts are set to music derived from Taverner's own.

Scene Three finds the Cardinal in the throne room of the King (understood to be Henry VIII). They are accompanied by an on-stage ensemble of Renaissance musicians. The King devises a pretext of righteous doctrinal dissent in order to amass wealth and dispose of his wife (since to divorce the queen would be unacceptable to the Roman church). The Cardinal overcomes his misgivings and agrees to participate. Death himself, disguised as the court jester, watches over the proceedings.

Death appears in the following scene as well, working his charms to compel Taverner to voice his doubts. Two visions confront the composer: a pair of monks, one dressed in white, the other in black, hold aloft a white dove, then, engaging in a doctrinal dispute, crush it and set it aflame; the pope appears — in the form of an ape—declaring in screeching tones a death decree against the reformers. Taverner finally determines to devote his efforts to his hatred of the Roman church's unwieldy power. Death prompts him to abandon his family and his music, as well, but Rose, in the role of his muse, urges him to not deny his artistic essence. He is almost convinced by her when Death calls upon a troupe of demons, which perform an outrageously blasphemous passion play. Overwhelmed, Taverner finally forswears his music and makes an oath to further the cause of Protestantism by any means possible.

Act Two. The second act returns to the courtroom. This time, though, the formerly persecuted is now the persecutor: Taverner stands to hear evidence against the White Abbot. Witnesses appear to lodge accusations of idolatry and lust; the Priest-Confessor, no respector of persons, accepts a bribe from this prosecution as well in exchange for damning testimony. The Cardinal again appears and tries to intercede, but this time his face and voice are gone and his efforts are useless. Death, the Jester, spins a giant wheel of fortune as Taverner condemns the Abbot to death by fire.

The next scene is in the interior of the throne room, where once again an on-stage early music ensemble takes over from the pit orchestra, mimicking musical styles and postures from the early Renaissance and early Baroque eras. The Cardinal arrives, announcing the Pope's condemnation of the King's proposed divorce. Incensed, the King determines to cut off all financial ties to Rome and boldly assumes ecclesiastical authority over his kingdom. An Archbishop even arrives to bestow his blessing upon the king's self-appointment. It is clear, however, that it is not an Archbishop at all, but the Death/Jester in disguise.

Scene Three moves to the chapel, where the White Abbot and a group of monks are intoning the liturgy—specifically, an excerpt dealing with Jesus' betrayal at the hands of one of his apostles. As the mass proceeds toward the communion, Taverner suddenly cries out in shame and rage for having composed music for the church that he now finds corrupted and unwieldy. Just as the emblems are being raised, authorities enter and throw the wine to the floor. The monks intone Taverner's own Benedictus from the *Gloria tibi trinitas* as they exit the monastery.

The final scene moves from the chapel to a marketplace in Boston, Lincolnshire. An audience has assembled to witness the White Abbot face his death sentence. Taverner supervises, documenting the event to report to authorities. The accused is given the chance to speak his final words; he does so in a dramatic, extended solo passage that brings to culmination the somber moral of the opera: that man surrenders himself to evil when the parameters of his dogma—whatever it may be—supersede those of morality. Despite the chorus' pleas for clemency, Taverner commands the fire be lit. Rose mourns the monstrosity that her lover has become, and as the flames engulf the accused, Taverner utters a final fervent prayer. His cries are answered by fading vestiges of his own music, which draw the work to a close. *—Jeremy Grimshaw*

MISCELLANEOUS

Works for Young Performers

Although outside of the United Kingdom Peter Maxwell Davies is best known for dark, grotesque, polystylistic dramatic works (most famously, the *Eight Songs for a Mad King*), his oeuvre also includes a very large corpus of pieces and arrangements designed for performance by children and youth ensembles. Davies' pedagogical and artistic skill with children's music can be traced to his early career teaching at a preparatory school, and although his works for students are technically within the reach of reasonably skilled performers, they demonstrate considerable dramatic and musical sophistication. Many of them address narrative topics and myths that, like the best children's literature, appeal to older audiences as well.

Davies' output includes two early operas and a number of later music-theater works for children and teens. *Cinderella*, composed in 1978 for elementary-aged children, was followed in 1979 by *Two Fiddlers*, a rendering of an Orkney folk tale performed by preadolescents. Numerous theatrical works followed in the 1980s and 1990s. These range in length from short 15-minute scenarios to half-hour mini-musicals and touch upon a variety of subjects. *The Great Bank Robbery* (1989) is a cartoonish romp in three fast-paced scenes, while *Jupiter Landing* (1989) is a kind of *Where the Wild Things Are* set in outer space. *A Selkie Tale* from 1992 draws on folklore from the composer's adopted home on the Orkney Islands, off of Scotland's northern coast. Davies' stage works for children require various levels of skill and various numbers of instrumental performers, ranging from a few children on drums, rattles, and simple diatonic xylophones and glockenspiels, to small chamber orchestras involving strings, woodwinds, and brass. The composer serves as his own librettist, penning lighthearted and self-consciously corny texts.

A number of orchestral works also count among Davies' repertoire for young players, including the clever and concisely poignant *Five Klee Pictures* from 1959 (inspired by such whimsical paintings as the famous *Twittering Machine*); a series of arrangements, competed in 1959–60, of music by Byrd, Attaignant, Couperin, and others; and the original composition *Chat Mass* from 1993, which takes as its musical kernel the memorable Easter plainchant *Haec dies*, and which appears in brief snatches later within Davies' daunting *Symphony No. 5*. Davies' catalog also includes several works for various smaller student ensembles, including his *Three Studies for Percussion Ensemble* (1977), arrangements for brass quintet of works by Tallis and Gesualdo, and solo works for trumpet and guitar. Among his solo piano works for children, *Farewell to Stromness* and *Yesnaby Ground*, both from 1980, are especially endearing. Davies' works for student vocal ensembles are particularly thoughtful, including the wistfully nostalgic *Seven Songs Home* (1981), the serene sacred work *O Magnum Mysterium* (1960), and the lively *Shepherd's Calendar* (1985), a setting of four thirteenth century goliard songs. *—Jeremy Grimshaw*

Recommended:

- ○ **Maxwell Davies: Symphony 1** / Rattle (cond.), Philharmonia Orch. / 2003 / Universal 000109102
- ○ **Maxwell Davies: Chamber Works 1952–1987** / Pace, Cowley, Kreutzer Quartet / 2003 / Metier 92055
- ○ **Maxwell Davies: Mass; Missa parvula** / M. Baker (cond.), Quinney, Westminster Cathedral Choir / Hyperion 67454
- ○ **Maxwell Davies: Le Jongleur De Notre Dame; String Quartet** / Peltz (cond.), E. Albert, Arditti SQ, Opera Sacra Buffalo / 1997 / Mode 59

Andrew Davis

b. Feb. 2, 1944, Ashridge, Hertfordshire, England

Conductor

Sir Andrew Davis is one of the leading English conductors from the latter twentieth and early twenty-first centuries. He has conducted symphonic and operatic repertory with equal distinction and been praised for his performance of the music of British composers, in particular that of Vaughan Williams, Elgar, and especially of Michael Tippett.

Davis' musical talents gravitated toward the keyboard early on, and his first serious studies came with his enrollment at the Royal College of Music in London, followed by further instruction at King's College, Cambridge, where he excelled in organ performance and scholarship. The young Davis was gradually drawn toward conducting, however, studying with Franco Ferrara at Rome's Academy of St. Cecilia. His first major podium assignment came in 1970, when he was appointed associate conductor of the BBC Scottish Symphony Orchestra, a post he held for two years. Davis' ascent toward international recognition came quickly in the years that followed: he became the principal guest conductor of the Royal Liverpool Philharmonic in 1974 and the following year was appointed music director of the Toronto Symphony Orchestra. During his 13-year tenure in Toronto, Davis led many successful tours abroad and made a spate of celebrated recordings, including those of Handel's *Messiah* with soloists Florence Quivar, Kathleen Battle, and Samuel Ramey, and of Janáček's *Taras Bulba* and *The Cunning Little Vixen Suite*. When he left the TSO in 1988, it is generally agreed that he had noticeably improved the ensemble and greatly enhanced its international reputation. Davis did not sever ties with the TSO when he stepped down, since he became its conductor laureate—a very active one—and then served as the artistic advisor for the orchestra's 2002–03 season. In 1988, Davis accepted the directorship of the Glyndebourne Festival Opera and the following year was appointed chief conductor of the BBC Symphony Orchestra. With the BBC Symphony Orchestra, he led a number of successful tours abroad, including to Hong Kong (1990), the United States (1995), Austria (1997 Salzburg Festival), and three excursions to Japan (1990, 1993, 1997). Davis' recordings with the BBC Symphony Orchestra have included a variety of works from various periods, but among contemporary composers he has tended to favor the British, as attested by CD issues of compositions by Birtwistle (*The Mask of Orpheus*), David Sawer (*Byrnan Wood*), and others. In the 1990s, Davis also conducted concerts and made recordings with the Bavarian Radio Symphony Orchestra, the London Symphony Orchestra, the Stockholm Philharmonic Orchestra, and several others. He also conducted operatic performances at the Metropolitan Opera, San Francisco Opera, Covent Garden, La Scala, and the Bavarian State Opera, where his rendition of Benjamin Britten's *Peter Grimes* was critically acclaimed. In 1999, he was knighted and the following year he departed his BBC Symphony Orchestra and Glyndebourne posts. He then accepted the appointment of music director and principal conductor of the Chicago Lyric Opera, succeeding Bruno Bartoletti. For the 2002–03 season in Chicago, Davis chose to lead performances of Wagner's *Die Walküre*, Massenet's *Thaïs* (with Renée Fleming), and Verdi's *La traviata*. He also continues to remain active as a guest conductor in the concert halls and on the operatic stages in his native England and throughout the world. *—Robert Cummings*

Recommended:

- ○ **Delius: Orchestral Works** / Davis (cond.), BBCSO / 2001 / Teldec 89084
- ○ **Holst: The Planets; Egdon Heath** / Davis (cond.), BBCSO / 2001 / Teldec 89087
- ○ **Vaughan Williams: Sinfonia Antartica; A Pastoral Symphony** / Davis (cond.), Davis, Rozario, Bimson, BBCSO / 1997 / Teldec 13139

Sir Colin Davis

b. Sep. 25, 1927, Weybridge, England

Conductor

Sir Colin Davis became one of the world's best-known conductors during the last four decades of the twentieth century. He is particularly well known for his recordings of Berlioz and Sibelius. While playing the clarinet as a student at the Royal College of Music in London, he participated in a performance of Berlioz's oratorio *L'enfance du Christ*. He was deeply affected by the work, and decided then to become a conductor. A great obstacle in achieving his goal was his lack of skill at the piano. For that reason, he was barred from the conducting classes at the Royal College of Music and had to learn conducting on his own. He still admits that he plays piano "very badly, not worth talking about."

He was called to military service and was posted to the Band of the Household Cavalry. At that point he formed, with some fellow Royal College instrumentalists, an ensemble called the Kalmar Orchestra, which he often conducted. It soon evolved into the Chelsea Opera Group, a semi-professional organization. Davis became recognized for his professional and stylish performances of Mozart operas. In 1952 he became head of ballet music at Royal Festival Hall. He was an assistant conductor of the BBC Scottish Orchestra (1957–59). In 1958 he debuted at Covent Garden in *Die Entführung aus dem Serail*. In 1959, when Otto Klemperer became ill, he took over a performance of Mozart's *Don Giovanni* at the Royal Festival Hall, a performance that won him wide acclaim. In 1960 lightning struck twice when Thomas Beecham, scheduled to conduct Mozart's *Zauberflöte* at Glyndebourne, fell ill and Davis again made a brilliant substitution.

In 1961 he was appointed musical director of the Sadler's Wells Opera. He resigned from Sadler's Wells in 1964 to do more symphonic conducting, especially with the London Symphony Orchestra. In 1965 he was named a Commander of the Order of the British Empire. During this period he began to record widely, including a classic series of releases of the music of Hector Berlioz, including the first recording of the complete *Les Troyens*.

From 1967 to 1971 he was Principal Conductor of the BBC Symphony Orchestra, with the autonomy to pursue an adventurous policy of repertory. He conducted the Royal Opera Company on several occasions, again mainly in newer music, and emerged as a principal champion of Sir Michael Tippett's operas

He was chosen to succeed Sir Georg Solti as musical director of the Royal Opera House, Covent Garden, in 1971. While continuing to be praised for his Mozart and for unusual repertory, he received some criticism for his more standard selections, including a Wagner *Ring* cycle of 1974–76. Even so, he was asked to appear at Bayreuth, where his *Tannhäuser* in 1977 was the first appearance of a British conductor in the Wagnerian shrine. Over the years, he has become more at home in the core operatic and orchestral repertory.

In 1980 he received a knighthood from Queen Elizabeth II. In 1984 he accepted a position as chief conductor of the Bavarian Radio Symphony Orchestra in Munich. He took it on a tour of North America in 1986. In the same year, he resigned his position with the Royal Opera to have more time for guest conducting. He remained with the Munich Orchestra into 1994. He also was principal guest conductor with the Boston Symphony Orchestra. In 1995 he was appointed Principal Conductor of the London Symphony Orchestra. *—Joseph Stevenson*

Recommended:

- ○ **Berlioz: Symphonie Fantastique; Beatrice & Benedict Overture** / Davis (cond.), London SO / LSO Live 0007
- ○ **Berlioz: Requiem; Te Deum** / Davis (cond.), Kynaston, Dowd, Tagliavini, London SO & Chorus / 2001 / Philips 464689
- ○ **Handel: Messiah** / Davis (cond.), Harper, Watts, Shirley-Quirk, Pearson, London SO & Chorus / 1993 / Philips 438356
- ○ **Sibelius: The 7 Symphonies; Finlandia; Kullervo; etc.** / Davis (cond.), Martinpelto, Fredriksson, London SO & Chorus / 2003 / RCA 55706
- ○ **Britten: Peter Grimes** / Davis (cond.), Allen, Vickers, Harper, Allan, Royal Opera House Orch. / 1999 / Philips 462847

Gervase de Peyer

b. Apr. 11, 1926, London, England

Clarinetist

Gervase de Peyer had no trouble launching himself into cyberspace when the Internet era began, despite the fact that by then he had already been performing almost half a century. No slouch at self-promotion, he set up a lavish website where it is claimed that he is "the world's most recorded clarinetist." He certainly has created a vast discography, as diverse as it is extensive, and receiving praise way beyond his own cyber-hype. It is hard to conceive of a classical music collection that lacks his recordings and a case could be made that his work with the Melos Ensemble for EMI between 1960 and 1973 could constitute a reasonable start to a classical collection in itself.

He was born into a musical family of Swiss descent. The only real break in his dedication to the clarinet came during 1944 and 1945, when he performed British national service. In the late 1940s he began to work professionally with the Royal Philharmonic Orchestra under Sir Thomas Beecham and the Philharmonia Orchestra under such conductors as Herbert von Karajan, Guido Cantelli, and Otto Klemperer. He was engaged as principal clarinetist with the English Chamber Orchestra, the London Chamber Orchestra and the London Mozart Players, his repertoire including Finzi, Busoni, Nielsen, Seiber, Weber, and Mozart. In 1949 he was supported by The Arts Council of Great Britain on national solo tours, improving the climate for establishing The Melos Ensemble. This group comprised some dozen players including pianist Viola Tunnard, and was dedicated to performing the often neglected repertoire for extended chamber groups. Melos became closely involved with the contemporary composers of the day, especially Benjamin Britten, but this was just one aspect of the group's extensive activity.

In 1956, the music director of the London Symphony Orchestra selected Gervase de Peyer as his principal clarinetist, an appointment that lasted for 17 years and helped de Peyer acquire a formidable reputation throughout Britain and Europe. In 1964 de Peyer gave the London premiere of Francis Poulenc's *Clarinet Sonata*. Both Paul Hindemith and Aaron Copland, conducting their own clarinet concertos, chose him as soloist for their tours. De Peyer also toured extensively, performing many other standard concertos, and, with the Philharmonia Orchestra under the direction of Pierre Boulez, recorded Debussy's *Rhapsody for Clarinet and Orchestra*. This project was released on Columbia Records. He was a founding member of the Chamber Music Society of Lincoln Center in New York City. He toured the United States and appeared several times on the *Live from Lincoln Center* national television series with this group.

De Peyer has premiered many compositions as a soloist, usually working in close collaboration with the composers. This includes concertos by Arnold Cooke, Berthold Goldschmidt, Joseph Horovitz, Alun Hoddinott, William Mathias, Edwin Roxburgh, and Thea Musgrave's so-called *Peripatetic Concerto*, in which the soloist is required to move around among various sections of the orchestra during performances. In 1992 he founded the Melos Sinfonia of Washington which follows in the tradition of the Melos Ensemble. *—Eugene Chadbourne*

Recommended:

- ○ **Mozart and Brahms: Clarinet Quintets** / de Peyer, Melos Ens. / 2001 / Angel 74520
- ○ **English Music for Clarinet & Piano** / de Peyer, Pryor / 1987 / Chandos 8549
- ○ **French Music for Clarinet and Piano** / de Peyer, Pryor / 1987 / Chandos 8526

Victor de Sabata

b. Apr. 10, 1892, Trieste, Italy, **d.** Dec. 11, 1967, Santa Margherita Ligure, Italy
Conductor

Although he was a composer and a violinist and pianist of virtuoso caliber, Victor de Sabata (born Vittorio) was best known as one of the world's leading conductors, particularly of Italian opera.

His father was a chorus master who gave his son well-rounded musical training, including cello, oboe, clarinet, and bassoon. He went on to study at the Milan Conservatory, with counterpoint lessons from Michele Saladino and composition from Giacomo Orefice. He earned his diploma with a *Suite for Orchestra*. During the first few years of his career his concentrated on composition. His opera *Il macigno* (The Rock) was premiered at La Scala in 1917 and was frequently played during the next few years.

Arturo Toscanini (who frequently performed de Sabata's tone poem *Juventus* of 1919) encouraged de Sabata to consider a conducting career. He began to conduct in 1918, but continued composing as his conducting career gathered steam. He wrote several other orchestral works, mainly with an intriguing mixture of Romantic-era Italian lyricism and dramatic episodes. He soon became the conductor of the Monte Carlo Opera. With that company he gave the world premiere of Ravel's *L'enfant et les Sortilèges* in 1925. His first performance in the United States was with the Cincinnati Symphony in 1927. He conducted that orchestra through much of 1929, but left to assume a post at La Scala in Milan, debuting there in 1930 with Puccini's *La fanciulla del West*. He remained affiliated with La Scala to the end of his life. He concentrated on a broad spectrum of the traditional repertory, plus modern composers like Stravinsky, Debussy, Ravel, Puccini, Sibelius, Strauss, and his Italian contemporaries. He was active as a guest conductor, appearing at the Vienna State Opera in 1936 and the Berlin Philharmonic in 1939. He became closely associated with Wagner's *Tristan und Isolde*, leading him to be invited to conduct in Bayreuth in 1939. After World War II he resumed his international touring. He led a special series of all the Beethoven symphonies in 1947 with the London Philharmonic, brought the La Scala company to Britain in 1950, conducted 14 concerts in March, 1950 with the New York Philharmonic in Carnegie Hall, and conducted in several other American cities.

He was known for a precise ear and original interpretations. He had the elasticity of tempo characteristic of the Romantic era. This rhythmic freedom and his unusual interpretations caused him to be criticized in later years as eccentric, which bothered him. Ill health caused him to give up regular conducting in 1953, but not before he led one of the all-time classic opera recordings, Puccini's *Tosca*, with Callas, Di Stefano, and Gobbi. His conducting at the funeral of Toscanini on February 18, 1957, was his last performance. He remained associated with La Scala as artistic superintendent from 1953 until his death. *—Joseph Stevenson*

Recommended:

- ○ **Puccini: Tosca** / De Sabata (cond.), Callas, di Stefano, Gobbi, Calabrese, La Scala Theater Orch. & Chorus / 1997 / EMI 56304
- ○ **Verdi: Falstaff** / De Sabata (cond.), Tebaldi, Valletti, Nessi, Silveri, La Scala Theater Orch. & Chorus / 2001 / Urania 176
- ○ **Victor De Sabata** / De Sabata (cond.), Stignani, Baracchi, Zanelli, Cobelli, Righetti, Berlin PO, La Scala Theater Orch. / Pearl 0054

Claude Debussy

b. Aug. 22, 1862, St.-Germain-en-Laye, France, **d.** Mar. 25, 1918, Paris, France
Composer: Orchestral, Keyboard, Opera, Ballet, Chamber Music, Vocal, Concerto, Choral

Claude Debussy (born Achille-Claude Debussy) was among the most influential composers of the late nineteenth and early twentieth centuries. His mature compositions, distinctive and appealing, combined modernism and sensuality so successfully that their sheer beauty often obscures their technical innovation. Debussy is considered the founder and leading exponent of musical Impressionism (although he resisted the label), and his adoption of non-traditional scales and tonal structures was paradigmatic for many composers who followed.

The son of a shopkeeper and a seamstress, Debussy began piano studies at the Paris Conservatory at the age of 11. While a student there, he encountered the wealthy Nadezhda von Meck (most famous as Tchaikovsky's patroness), who employed him as a music teacher to her children; through travel, concerts and acquaintances, she provided him with a wealth of musical experience. Most importantly, she exposed the young Debussy to the works of Russian composers, such as Borodin and Mussorgsky, who would remain important influences on his music.

Debussy began composition studies in 1880, and in 1884 he won the prestigious Prix de Rome with his cantata *L'enfant prodigue*. This prize financed two years of further study in Rome—years that proved to be creatively frustrating. However, the period immediately following was fertile for the young composer; trips to Bayreuth and the Paris World Exhibition (1889) established, respectively, his determination to move away from the influence of Richard Wagner, and his interest in the music of Eastern cultures.

After a relatively bohemian period, during which Debussy formed friendships with many leading Parisian writers and musicians (not least of which were Mallarmé, Satie, and Chausson), the year 1894 saw the enormously successful premiere of his *Prélude à l'après-midi d'un faune* (Prelude to the Afternoon of a Faun)—a truly revolutionary work that brought his mature compositional voice into focus. His seminal opera *Pelléas et Mélisande*, completed the next year, would become a sensation at its first performance in 1902. The impact of those two works earned Debussy widespread recognition (as well as frequent attacks from critics, who failed to appreciate his forward-looking style), and over the first decade of the twentieth century he established himself as the leading figure in French music—so much so that the term "Debussysme" ("Debussyism"), used both positively and pejoratively, became fashionable in Paris. Debussy spent his remaining healthy years immersed in French musical society, writing as a critic, composing, and performing his own works internationally. He succumbed to colon cancer in 1918, having also suffered a deep depression brought on by the onset of World War I.

Debussy's personal life was punctuated by unfortunate incidents, most famously the attempted suicide of his first wife, Lilly Texier, whom he abandoned for the singer Emma Bardac. However, his subsequent marriage to Bardac, and their daughter Claude-Emma, whom they called "Chouchou" and who became the dedicatee of the composer's *Children's Corner* piano suite, provided the middle-aged Debussy with great personal joys.

Debussy wrote successfully in most every genre, adapting his distinctive compositional language to the demands of each. His orchestral works, of which *Prélude à l'après-midi d'un faune* and *La mer* (The Sea, 1905) are most familiar, established him as a master of instrumental color and texture. It is this attention to tone color—his layering of sound upon sound so that they blend to form a greater, evocative whole—that linked Debussy in the public mind to the Impressionist painters.

His works for solo piano, particularly his collections of Préludes and Etudes, which have remained staples of the repertoire since their composition, bring into relief his assimilation of elements from both Eastern cultures and antiquity—especially pentatonicism (the use of five-note scales), modality (the use of scales from ancient Greece and the medieval church), parallelism (the parallel movement of chords and lines), and the whole-tone scale (formed by dividing the octave into six equal intervals).

Pelléas et Mélisande and his collections of songs for solo voice establish the strength of his connection to French literature and poetry, especially the symbolist writers, and stand as some of the most understatedly expressive works in the repertory. The writings of Mallarmé, Maeterlinck, Baudelaire, and his childhood friend Paul Verlaine appear prominently among his chosen texts and joined symbiotically with the composer's own unique moods and forms of expression. *—Allen Schrott*

ORCHESTRAL

Images, for orchestra, L. 122 (1905–1912)

The three works which collectively form Claude Debussy's *Images* for orchestra, not to be confused with the two sets of piano works that go by the same title, are among the more immediately accessible and directly expressive of his later pieces. Although intended to be performed in succession, the *Images* are frequently heard independently of one another, especially the second, "Iberia," which remains among the composer's most frequently played orchestral works. The three works, which continue to be published as separate titles, were initially released at different times, with the first being composed and published several years after the second and third.

"Gigues" was written from 1909–12, and has a decidedly English flavor. Debussy quotes the English folk tune "The Keel Row" throughout as the tune ebbs and swirls in the colored orchestral texture, surfacing in one instrument, fading back into the texture, and then resurfacing on another instrument. Debussy makes striking use of the oboe d'amore in the opening "Gigues"—indeed, it can be said that this unique instrument constitutes more of a musical "theme" than does any actual melody. A plaintive tone predominates; the few hints of joyfulness are clearly the product of wistful fantasy.

The central "Iberia" (1905–08), itself divided into three movements, is more outgoing in nature (as French representations of Spanish music and culture almost invariably seem to be). The celebratory yet undeniably aristocratic atmosphere of "Iberia" owes a great deal to the earlier "Fêtes" from the *Nocturnes*, which rides the same fine line between the vernacular and the high-minded. Debussy's score even calls for guitars and castanets, a remarkable request at that time. There is a decadent flavor to "Parfums de la nuit," whose nocturnal activities form the center of the piece—dawn arrives with the feeling that nothing has actually happened. The last movement of "Iberia" is kaleidoscopic in feel: Debussy presents a series of disconnected, seemingly random (but actually not so in any sense) musical ideas in a manner that foreshadows his *Jeux* (1912) and the processes used by many later composers, including so-called aleatoric music. The raw exuberance of a Spanish celebration drives the music to heights of a strained passion, and at times seems to be an attempt to conceal a great melancholy.

The last of the *Images*, "Rondes de printemps," was composed between 1905 and 1909. It is a product of the same turn-of-the-century French obsession with spring that encouraged Diaghilev to commission Stravinsky's *Le Sacre du printemps*. Debussy had himself composed an orchestral work entitled Printemps as a young man, and countless musical and literary works from the period go by similar titles. In *Images* however, spring has nothing in common with Stravinsky's famous work. "Rondes de printemps" is an unassuming work based on one of Debussy's favorite nursery tunes, "Nous n'irons plus au bois," a melody he incorporated into a number of compositions. Like "Gigues," "Rondes de printemps" is introspective and nostalgic, short on activity and long on tone-color. "Debussy spreads color throughout the ensemble in a masterly, and deceptively simple display of orchestration, rather than focusing on a single instrument as he did in "Gigues."—*Blair Johnston*

Recommended:

- ○ **Debussy: Images; Prélude a l'après-midi d'un faune; Printemps** / Boulez (cond.), Cleveland Orch. / DG 435766
- ○ **Debussy: La Mer; Prélude a l'après-midi d'un faune; Nocturnes** / Munch (cond.), Boston SO / 2004 / RCA Victor 59416
- ○ **Debussy: La Mer; Images; Nocturnes & others** / Dutoit (cond.), Montreal SO / 1999 / Decca 460217
- ○ **Celibidache, Debussy** / Celibidache (cond.), Munich PO / 1997 / EMI 56520

La Mer, 3 symphonic sketches, L. 109 (1903–1905)

Debussy's *La Mer* (The Sea; 1903–05) is one of the most famous non-symphonic orchestral pieces ever written. During the 1890s, oceanic imagery had proven a recurrent source of inspiration for the composer. "Sirènes," the third of the *Nocturnes* (1897–99), and passages from the opera *Pelléas et Mélisande* (1893–1905) at once bear testament to a certain nautical bent. *La Mer*, however, goes a great deal farther than any previous work—by Debussy or any other composer—in capturing the raw essence of this most evocative of nature's faces. *La Mer* is no mere exercise in musical scene-painting, but rather a sonic representation of the myriad thoughts, moods, and basic instinctual reactions the sea draws from an individual human soul.

La Mer comprises three distinct movements: "De l'aube à midi sur la mer" (From Dawn to Noon on the Sea), "Jeux de vagues" (The Play of the Waves), and "Dialogue du vent et de la mer" (Dialogue of the Wind and the Sea). "De l'aube à midi sur la mer" unfolds in 6/8 following a Trés lent (very slow) introduction. As in so much of the composer's mature music, it is not always possible to draw a clear distinction between thematic material and accompaniment and texture. Indeed, texture itself is often paramount in Debussy's music; what few glimpses of discreet melodies the movement affords (such as the glassy violin solo that arrives some sixty bars into the piece, or the brief horn gesture soon after the metric change to 6/8) are soon subsumed into the complex orchestral fabric. There are passages during which the rhythmic and metric scheme is obscured, perhaps intentionally so, by as many as six or seven different layers of simultaneous activity. The movement ends with one of the most striking of the composer's musical affirmations: In an enigmatic gesture, the final forte-fortissimo brass attack dies away to piano as the movement draws to a close.

The scoring of "Jeux de vagues" is, on the whole, more austere than that of the first movement. Frequent trills and bursts of rhythmic vitality vividly bring to life the movement's frolicsome, unpredictable subject matter, while the extremely quiet ending purposely fails to resolve any of the musical expectations set out in the preceding, more active sections. The scoring of this passage (solo flute and harp harmonics) recalls the identical orchestration as used by the composer at the end of *Prélude à l'après-midi d'un faune* (Prelude to the Afternoon of a Faun; 1894), Indeed, these parallel passages are quite similiar in dramatic purpose.

The final "Dialogue" is a tumultuous juxtaposition of an urgent, articulated rhythmic gesture—first introduced pianissimo by the cellos and basses and ingeniously manipulated throughout the movement—with a grandiose legato idea that many have likened to the melodies of César Franck (an important influence upon the young Debussy). A sustained forte-fortissimo brings this violent, elemental work to a powerful close. —*Blair Johnston*

Recommended:

- ○ **Respighi: Pines of Rome; Fountains of Rome; Debussy: La Mer** / Reiner (cond.), Chicago SO / 1995 / RCA Victor 68079
- ○ **Debussy: La Mer; Images; Nocturnes & others** / Dutoit (cond.), Montreal SO / 1999 / Decca 460217
- ○ **Claude Debussy: La Mer; Nocturnes** / Boulez (cond.), Cleveland Orch. / 1995 / DG 439896
- ○ **Arturo Toscanini Vol. IX: French Orchestral Music** / Toscanini (cond.), NBC SO / 1997 / RCA Victor 66924
- ○ **Ravel, Debussy & Saint-Saëns** / Karajan (cond.), Berlin PO / 2003 / DG B000020302
- ○ **Debussy: La Mer; Prélude à l'après midi d'un faune; Nocturnes** / Vladimir Ashkenazy (cond.), Cleveland Orch. / Decca 467428

Nocturnes, for female chorus & orchestra, L. 91 (1897–1899)

Claude Debussy's *Three Nocturnes for Orchestra* went through several incarnations before eventually assuming their final form. They were sketched under the title "Trois scènes au crépuscule" as early as 1892, and prior to their completion in 1899, Debussy toyed with the idea of casting them as vehicles for solo violin and orchestra. Debussy's developing skill as an orchestral colorist, first hinted at in 1892 with the *Prelude to the Afternoon of a Faun*, comes to the fore in the *Nocturnes*, particularly the second, "Fêtes," which is regarded by many as one of the composers supreme creations.

A special role is allotted to the English horn in "Nuages" (Clouds), the first piece of the group. Thin, two-voice counterpoint in steady quarter notes provides a background for the English horn's rather plaintive gesture. The same melodic fragment is repeated several times with very little alteration or extension, interrupted occasionally by comments from the French horn section. A stark contrast is provided by a pentatonic interlude, scored for flute and harp against a sustained chordal background and marked "Un peu animé." The English horn raises its quiet voice again, only to dissolve against the pianissimo tremolo background as the flute takes up its melody one more time. The quietly pulsating pizzicati of "Nuages" conclusion provide a sense of "grey agony," as Debussy put it.

"Fêtes" (Festivals) will be friendly ground to any listener familiar with the final movement of Respighi's 1929 work along the same lines, *Feste Romane*. The juxtaposition of a forceful, even percussive, rhythmic ostinato in 12/8 time with the earthy tune of the brass band (representing the Garde Républicaine) provides for the same kind of multi-textural feel that Respighi would exploit even further three decades later. Through sheer repetition the music builds to several swaggering climaxes, only to be deflated each time and have to begin the process all over again. The music trails away into nothingness as the brass band finally completes its journey through the heart of the celebration. Remarkable about "Fêtes" is Debussy's ability to hint at raunchiness and vulgarity within the context of his own extremely refined sound world.

A vocalizing (i.e. textless) women's chorus is added to the ensemble for "Sirènes," the last, and in many ways the most evocative of the *Nocturnes*. One must not be misled by "Sirènes" repetitiveness and apparent simplicity—a simplicity meant to parallel the deceptively innocent charm of the mythological sea sirens—for here is a work of great subtlety indeed. The dense intricacy of the orchestral effects contained throughout the piece, set almost exclusively at a piano or pianissimo dynamic indication, has reminded more than one listener of the techniques of that most accomplished of orchestrators, Maurice Ravel. Debussy's methods, however, are entirely his own. Not surprisingly, the music drifts away into the sea, floating upon the few sparse harmonics of the two harpists. —*Blair Johnston*

Recommended:

- ○ **Claude Debussy: La Mer; Nocturnes** / Boulez (cond.), Cleveland Orch. / 1995 / DG 439896
- ○ **Debussy: Orchestral Music** / Haitink (cond.), Concertgebouw / 1993 / Philips 438742
- ○ **Debussy: La Mer; Images; Nocturnes** / Dutoit (cond.), Montreal SO & Chorus / 1999 / Decca 460217
- ○ **Claude Debussy** / C. Abbado (cond.), Boston SO / 2000 / DG 469130

Prélude à l'après-midi d'un faune (Prelude to the Afternoon of a Faun), L. 86 (1894)

The first of Debussy's trailblazing works—the 10-minute *Prélude à l'après-midi d'une faune*, written between 1892 and 1894—was received with delight by a Société Nationale audience that demanded its encore at its premiere in Paris on December 22, 1894, with Gustave Doret conducting. Almost everything else he wrote later provoked controversy, especially *Pelléas et Mélisande*, the opera he composed simultaneously (but did not complete until just before the first performance in 1902) with the *Prélude*. Both texts that inspired the 31-year-old composer were avant-garde: *"The Faun,"* "an eclogue" published in 1876 by Stephane Mallarmé (1842–98), self-proclaimed father of "symbolisme" in French verse, and *Pelléas*, an allegorical play by Maurice Maeterlinck.

Because of Mallarmé's deliberate obscurities, excerpts from a paraphrase by Edmund Gosse seem more useful for concert reading than the poem itself: "A faun—a simple, sensuous, passionate being—wakens in the forest at daybreak and tries to recall his experience of the previous afternoon. Was he the fortunate recipient of an actual visit from nymphs, white and golden goddesses… or is the memory but a shadow of a vision, no more substantial than the 'arid rain' of notes from his own flute?… Ah! the effort is too great for his poor brain…. So, when he has glutted upon a bunch of grapes… the delicious hour grows vaguer; experience or dream, he will never know which it was. The sun is warm, the grasses yielding; and he curls himself up again, after worshipping the efficacious star of wine, that he may pursue the dubious ecstasy with the more hopeful boskages of sleep…."

Form-fetishists have tried, without success, to diagram Debussy's *Prélude* (he never did write announced "interludes et paraphrase finale"). Hypotheses have ranged from three-part "song with midsection" to "theme and variations," but Felix Borowski may have said it best: "… a pastoral rhapsody without fixed form [whose] principal theme is given out in the solo flute, which colors the entire prelude… a dreamy melody, heard repeatedly." The key signature is E major and the rhythm 9/8 (triple meter in other words), yet Debussy was more absorbed by a C sharp to G natural tritone—until the more conventional, common-time middle section in D flat. His orchestra has no trumpets, trombones, tuba, or timpani, but it features three flutes, English horn, and four horns, plus two antique cymbals that share a total of just 10 notes near the end.

After Debussy played the music for Mallarmé on the piano, the poet said, "I wasn't expecting anything like that! This music prolongs the emotion of my poem and conjures up the scenery more vividly than any color." Following the premiere, he stated publicly that the work "presents no dissonance with my text: rather, it goes further into nostalgia and light with subtlety, malaise, and richness." In June 1897, he sent round a copy of the poem, inscribed:

"If you would know with what harmonious notes
"Your flute resounds, O sylvan deity,
"Then hearken to the light that shall be breathed
"Thereinto by Debussy's art." —*Roger Dettmer*

Recommended:

- ○ **Debussy: La Mer, Prélude à l'après-midi d'un faune, Nocturnes** / Ashkenazy (cond.), Cleveland Orch. / Decca 467428
- ○ **Debussy: La Mer, Images; Nocturnes & others** / Dutoit (cond.), Montreal SO / 1999 / Decca 460217
- ○ **Debussy: La Mer, Prélude à l'après-midi d'un faune & others** / Munch (cond.), Boston SO / 2004 / RCA Victor 61556
- ○ **Debussy: Images; Prélude a l'après-midi d'un faune** / Boulez (cond.), Cleveland Orch. / DG 435766

KEYBOARD

Deux Arabesques, L. 66 (1888–1891)

Although in his later years his piano compositions ranked among his best-known works, Claude Debussy was initially rather uncomfortable with the medium. Despite having been trained at the Paris Conservatoire as a professional pianist from age ten, it wasn't until he was nearly 30 that he produced his first substantial works for the instrument. Begun just a few years before the landmark Suite bergamasque, Debussy's *Two Arabesques* (1888–91) are among the earliest of his pieces to have maintained a place in the recital repertory.

Many of the hallmarks of Debussy's mature pianistic style are evident in the Arabesques, particularly in the first. Debussy's love of parallel chords—in this case, triads in first inversion—is apparent in the arpeggiation which opens the first Arabesque, and even more so when the same figuration recurs at much greater length toward the end of the piece. The music unfolds in an ABA form whose tonal scheme hinges on dominant harmonies with the addition of ninths and the occasional thirteenth. The first and third sections, more atmospheric than thematic, are characterized by the sort of rolling left-hand accompaniment that figures so prominently in the composer's later piano music. The A major middle section, foreshadowed by the work's opening triad, is both shorter and more thematically organized than its neighbors, though its primary melody is actually the inversion of a subsidiary motive from the A section.

The second Arabesque, marked allegretto scherzando, is altogether more energetic and sprightly than the first. Less harmonically innovative than its companion piece, it relies on tried-and-true harmonic formulae to define its G major tonality. Like the first Arabesque, the piece is shaped into an overall ABA form, again with a shorter middle section in the subdominant. Significantly, the triplet-sixteenth-plus-eighth rhythmic cell which dominates most of the second Arabesque is completely absent in the middle section, which instead features an ascending sequence of broken parallel thirds. Unlike the first Arabesque, the B-section material returns near the end of the piece, again making reference to C major, only to be rejected in favor of the primary rhythmic cell. A rather startling forte digression to B major seven bars before the end is quickly deflected back to the home key, and the music disintegrates into a series of increasingly quiet, quintessentially Debussyan punctuations. —*Blair Johnston*

Recommended:

- ○ **Debussy: Piano Works** / Rogé / 1994 / London 443021
- ○ **Debussy, Geoffrey Simon, The Philharmonia** / Simon (cond.), Philharmonia Orch. / 1991 / Cala 1001

Children's Corner, suite, L. 113 (1906–1908)

Children's Corner was written for Debussy's three-year-old daughter, Claude-Emma (nicknamed "Chou-Chou"), and bears the following dedication: "to my dear Chou-Chou, with the tender apologies of her father for what is to follow." The composer's sentiments were presumably an acknowledgement of the inevitable loss of innocence that comes with growing up, but his words take on a darker, more prophetic, hue in hindsight—Claude-Emma died from diphtheria only a year after Debussy's own death from cancer in 1918.

Though ostensibly children's pieces, the miniatures that make up Children's Corner are not meant for children to play; rather they are meant to evoke the mood and essence of childhood, and the fantasies of youth. The titles, all of them in English, reflect not only the rampant anglophilia in Paris at the time of composition (and Debussy's own affection for England), but also Chou-Chou's relationship with her English nanny, who helped to choose them. The set, as a whole, captures the particular charm of Debussy's piano music, in spirit if not in style. It possesses great humor and lightness, real beauty, and deceptive technical difficulties.

The first movement, "Doctor Gradus ad Parnassum," is a light-hearted reference to Muzio Clementi's well-known piano exercises, *Gradus ad Parnassum*, published in 1817. It parodies a child performing these exercises, initially tearing through the bright, fast passages and eventually becoming distracted, bored, and finally slamming down the final cadence with relief. This movement looks forward to Debussy's later *Etudes*, in which he lampoons the five-finger exercises of Carl Czerny. The second movement is about a toy elephant, and is called "Jimbo's Lullaby"; the ponderous gait of the elephant and the lightness of its stuffing are illustrated in whole-tone harmony. The third movement "Serenade for the Doll" is a quick, dance-like song for a little girl's favorite toy, while "Snow is Dancing" gives us a picture of falling ice crystals.

"The Little Shepherd" tells a story of a young shepherd, playing his pipe, dancing around the meadow, resting by a tree, and finally falling asleep. The last movement, "Golliwogg's Cake Walk," was inspired by American ragtime music, which, considered plebeian in its native country, had taken Europe by storm. Debussy also managed a tweak at Wagner, by quoting the famous *Tristan & Isolde* theme, and following it with a pianistic chuckle. It's title comes from Golliwogg, a doll that was popular in Chou-Chou's day, and a popular children's game associated with the doll. The game involved walking to the music (the steps required are specific, and seeing kids perform them is adorable) and whoever looked most enthused about getting cake received a slice.

The *Children's Corner* suite is certainly not characteristic of Debussy's ephemeral style—which by now had fully developed impressionistic qualities—however, it is a delightful work, and it showcases Debussy's ability to create unique tonal colors.—*AMG*

Recommended:

- ○ **Debussy: Estampes** / Tabe / 2001 / Chandos 9912
- ○ **Debussy: Images I & II; Children's Corner** / Michelangeli / DG 415372
- ○ **Debussy: The Complete Works For Piano** / Gieseking / EMI 65855

En blanc et noir, for 2 pianos, L. 134 (1915)

Debussy composed his piano duo *En blanc et noir* (In black and white; 1915) during a late creative outburst that also included the *Etudes* for piano (1915) and the completion of his edition of Chopin's works for the publisher Durand. The three sections of this suite are brilliant and colorful and seem more inspired (if no more original) than the *Etudes*. The work's originality was, apparently, recognized from the beginning: It was the premiere of *En blanc et noir* that prompted Saint-Saëns to exclaim, "One must at all costs bar the doors of the Institute to a gentleman capable of such atrocities!"

All three sections are highly effective and convey a depth of feeling occasionally lacking in the *Etudes*, but which resurfaces in the composer's final works, the *Sonata No. 1 in D minor* for cello and piano (1915) and the *Sonata No. 3 in G major* for violin and piano (1916–17). The first section, "Avec emportement" (With passion) is an energetic waltz that foreshadows the spirit of Ravel's *La valse* (1919–20) though lacks that work's sardonic nostalgia. "Lent sombre" (Slow and somber) was composed in memory of Debussy's friend Jacques Charlot, killed in World War I. This section, marked by a particular complexity, begins and ends with elegiac passages that flank a central Allegro, which itself spans the emotional gamut from despair to elation. (At one point Debussy quotes from the hymn "A Mighty Fortress is Our God.") The concluding section, Scherzando, is dedicated to Stravinsky; however, it has more in common with the impish humor of "Scarbo" from Ravel's *Gaspard de la nuit* (1908) than with anything Stravinsky ever wrote. The shortest and least serious section of the suite, the Scherzando brings the work to a spirited close. *—Steven Coburn*

Recommended:

- ○ **Great Pianists of the 20th Century: Robert Casadesus** / R. Casadesus & G. Casadesus / 1999 / Philips 456739
- ○ **Debussy: Etudes for Piano; En Blanc et Noir** / Paul Jacobs & Kalish / 1987 / Nonesuch 79161

Six épigraphes antiques, for piano, 4 hands, L. 131 (1914)

The *Six épigraphes antiques* (1914) are actually a reworking of incidental music Debussy wrote for a single performance of 12 of Louÿs' *Chansons de Bilitis*—staged as a recitation with "living tableaux"—on February 7, 1901. In reworking the incidental score (for two flutes, two harps, and celesta) into the *Épigraphes*, Debussy retained only about half of the original music. As might be expected with music originally intended to accompany a theatrical presentation, all of the *Épigraphes* are highly atmospheric.

"Pour invoquer Pan, dieu du vent d'été" (For Invoking Pan, God of the Summer Wind) depicts a languid summer day. The movement opens with a melody that evokes Pan playing his pipes and unfolds in a perfectly symmetrical arch (ABCBA) form. "Pour un tombeau sans nom" (For a Tomb Without Name) is a highly chromatic though subtle elegy. "Pour que la nuit soit propice" (So That the Night May be Propitious) is an expressive nocturne in a condensed sonata form. "Pour la danseuse aux crotales" (For the Dancer with Castanets) evokes its original instrumention with harp-like keyboard figuration; Debussy depicts the castanets with brief ornamental figures. "Pour l'Egyptienne" (For the Egyptian) is marked by a particularly improvisatory character; its ornate, dissonant quality anticipates the Night Music from Bartók's *Out of Doors Suite* (1926). The etude-like "Pour remercier la pluie au matin" (For Thanking the Morning Rain) is dominated by rapid chromatic figuration accompanied by a wide variety of melodic material. *—Steven Coburn*

Recommended:

- ○ **The Debussy Album** / K. & M. Labèque / Philips 454471

Estampes, L. 100 (1903)

"When you don't have any money to go on holiday, you must make do by using your imagination," Debussy wrote, and the first two pieces in his triptych *Estampes* constitute an exotic travelog; the third piece is stay-at-home music, watching the rain. "Estampes" means print or engraving, and these three pieces are musical depictions of particular moments at particular locales. They also represent an interior journey of sorts, a newly personal idiom for Debussy, who is now seemingly unconcerned with the conventions and expectations of the salon and the concert hall.

"Pagodes" (Pagodas) manages to seem still and flowing at the same time. The stillness comes from the score's long pedal point, as well as from the harmonic restriction of the pentatonic scale, which is highly characteristic of Asian music. Despite this stasis, the music ultimately conveys smooth motion, thanks to Debussy's imitation of Javanese gamelan music; it may also be an imitation of the "Laideronette, Empress of the Pagodas" movement from Ravel's *Ma mère l'oye*. The music hovers mostly at low and medium dynamic levels, rising for only a couple of sonorous climaxes that soon recede into the softly tinkling texture.

"Soirée dans Grenade" takes listeners to Spain, but again the tour guide is Ravel, whose *Habanera* covers much the same musical territory. Debussy uses the same rhythm—which, technically, is Cuban rather than Spanish, although the French strongly associated it with the Iberian peninsula. Debussy's dreamy treatment includes rather Moorish material and, except for two brief outbursts four-fifths of the way through, avoids the fast, fiery, flamenco-inspired effects that foreigners associate with Spanish music. Manuel de Falla thought highly enough of this piece to quote from it in his *Homage to Debussy*.

The final movement, in the great French keyboard tradition, is a toccata, although Debussy gives it a more fanciful title, "Jardins sous la pluie" (Gardens in the Rain). Judging from the movement's rapidity, this is quite a downpour, although there's little evidence of thunder or lightning; the challenge to the player is to maintain a light touch through most of the movement. The piece incorporates fragments of the French nursery songs *"Do, do l'enfant do"* and *"Nous n'irons plus au bois,"* suggesting a child unable to go out and play but taking great interest in the rain, watching snug behind some window. *—James Reel*

Recommended:

- ○ **Debussy: Piano Works** / Rogé / 1994 / London 443021
- ○ **Piano Music by Claude Debussy** / Rév / 1995 / Hyperion 44061
- ○ **Debussy: The Complete Works For Piano** / Gieseking / 195 / EMI 65855

Etudes, L. 136 (1915)

Early in 1915, disheartened by the menace of World War I and gravely ill with cancer, Claude Debussy (1862–1918) nevertheless managed to compose. The fruits of his labors, 12 *Etudes* (study pieces or exercises), would be his last important works for solo piano, and would represent a distillation of the composer's musical legacy. It was appropriate for Debussy—the most original composer for the piano since Franz Liszt—to join the ranks of étude composers. Equally fitting was his dedication of his two volumes to Fryderyk Chopin, noting that the serious nature of the exercises was offset by a charm reminiscent of the earlier master.

The *Etudes* are divided into two books, each different in conception. Book I is devoted to exploring the technical problems and musical possibilities inherent in different intervals (thirds, sixths, etc.), while Book II engages in the exploration of musical syntax and style. In all, the *Etudes* are witty, challenging, and inspired. Though academic in nature—and perhaps less easily digested than other of Debussy's works—they fall closely on the heels of his popular *Préludes* and *Images*, and reflect the same aesthetic concerns: complex harmonies, fragmented melodic lines, and colorful textures.

The first étude of Book I, "Pour les 'cinq doigts'—d'apres Monsieur Czerny" (For Five Fingers—after Mr. Czerny), is inspired by the five-finger exercises of Carl Czerny. Debussy pantomimes the pedantic works by placing figurations in grotesque juxtaposition and introducing bizarre modulations. "Pour les Tierces" (For Thirds) presents an extraordinary variety of patterns in parallel thirds, excepting those already encountered in "Tièrces alternées" from the second book of *Préludes*. "Pour les Quartes" (For Fourths) exercises the pianists ability in parallel fourths. Almost needless to say, quartal harmony abounds, making this étude more tonally adventurous than many of the others. "Pour les Sixtes" (For Sixths) is a slow and meditative work with two fast interludes, and one forte interruption. "Pour les Octaves" (For Octaves) combines chromaticism, whole-tone harmonies, and complex syncopation. Probably the most brilliant étude of both books, it is equally difficult to play. "Pour les huit doigts" (For Eight Fingers) is meant to be performed (the composer's suggestion) without the use of the thumbs, due to the division of the figuration into four-note scale patterns. It finds humor in its rigid insistence on four-note groupings and sudden ending.

Book II begins with "Pour les degrés chromatiques" (For Chromatic Intervals), an essay in the use of the chromatic scale, both compositionally and technically. "Pour les agréments" (For Ornaments) is one of the most fiendishly difficult works in the repertoire. The entire fabric of the music is created by juxtaposing musical embellishments, arpeggiations, and miniature cadenza-like passages. "Pour les notes répétées" (For Repeated Notes) requires a performer able to execute repeated tones with great rapidity while still maintaining the piece's humorous, scherzando atmosphere. One wry melodic fragment balances the otherwise relentlessly staccato texture. "Pour les sonorités opposées" (For Opposing Sonorities) emphasizes the kind of multiple-layered textures found earlier in the second set of *Images* and many of the préludes. "Pour les arpéges composés" (For Composed, or Written-out, Arpeggios), easily the best-known of all the études, redefines the arpeggio to include a variety of non-harmonic tones (such as the added second or the added ninth). "Pour les accords" (For Chords), is probably the nearest thing to a Romantic virtuoso piece that Debussy ever produced. Mammoth in conception and brutally difficult, this étude juxtaposes relentless perpetual motion with an almost uncomfortably still middle section. A truncated reprise precedes a driving conclusion that puts even the most skilled performer to a grueling test, both technically and interpretively. *—AMG*

Recommended:

- ○ **Debussy: 12 Etudes** / Uchida / Philips 422412
- ○ **Debussy: 12 Etudes; Boulez: Second Sonata** / Pollini / 2001 / DG 471359
- ○ **Debussy: L'Oeuvre Pour Piano** / Haas / Erato 94827

Images, Sets I & II, L. 110 & L. 111 (1905–1907)

Claude Debussy's two sets of *Images* for solo piano—not to be confused with the orchestral work by the same title—are often considered the first examples of the composer's wholly mature language and style. For nearly 20 years Debussy had struggled to come to grips with his own revolutionary musical viewpoint, and throughout the *Images* (six pieces in all) we find, in equal parts, an intense glorification of sensation and a new harmonic richness.

"Reflets dans l'eau" (Reflections on the Water), which opens Set I of *Images*, is frequently cited as one of Debussy's finest works, despite the composer's own dislike of the piece. Brief melodic fragments are set against an undulating background that covers the entire range of the instrument—the bass register employed with great stillness, the upper register shimmering and subtly distorted. The motion subsides towards the end, and the music disappears into a final, spacious D flat major sonority.

"Hommage à Rameau" (marked *dans le style d'une Sarabande*) probably owes its existence to Debussy's participation in the editing of Rameau's opera-ballets. While some have found the "Hommage" to be less successful than its companion pieces, others hear this affectionate tribute as a work of great power (it has been likened by one writer to the late piano sonatas of Beethoven).

The last piece in Set I of *Images* has no specific extra-musical connection and is titled, simply, "Mouvement." Fleet of foot (or hand) and rather enigmatic in expression, the piece opens with a rhythmically active but harmonically static passage. A few passionate outbursts precede the more thematically substantial (and much, much louder) middle section. Following a literal reprise of the opening material, "Mouvement" dissolves into a long diminuendo employing the absolute extremes of the instrument's range, with only a single, fragmentary melodic line filling the gap.

Set II of *Images* is one of the most striking things Debussy ever composed; he found it necessary to notate the entirety of the work on three staves to ensure clear articulation of his very complex pianistic textures. "Cloches à travers les feuilles" (Bells through the Leaves), which opens the set, simultaneously presents several layers of musical detail: a series of sustained chords supports a more rapid pentatonic figuration in the right hand, while the bell tones are themselves represented by a series of accented dyads (two notes, in this case usually major seconds) in the left.

Traditionally "oriental" sonorities take center stage for "Et la lune descend sur le temple qui fut" (literally, the Moon Descends on the Temple Which Was). Often these sonorities are intervals of fourths and fifths, set in a gamelan-like texture; Debussy had been enthralled with the gamelan ensemble ever since hearing it at the 1889 Paris Exposition. The result is a series of melodic fragments thrown together what seems to be an entirely free manner.

"Poissons d'or" (Goldfish) is perhaps the most famous piece in all of *Images*. The choreography of the hands at the keyboard is gracefulness itself, following the music as it shifts directions in the quick, almost random manner of fish. The line between theme and accompaniment is blurred in "Poissons," with the two frequently exchanging roles. The gradual accretion of musical material builds to a radiant climax, after which follows the famous black key against white key cadenza. A graceful coda brings the piece to a quiet close. *—Blair Johnston*

Recommended:

- ○ **Debussy: Piano Works** / Rogé / 1998 / EMI 66753
- ○ **Debussy: Images 1 & 2; Children's Corner** / Michelangeli / 1971 / DG 415372
- ○ **Great Pianists of the 20th Century: Ivan Moravec** / Moravec / 1998 / Philips 456910
- ○ **Debussy: Complete Piano Music Vol. 1** / W. Haas / 1993 / Philips 438718

L'isle joyeuse, L. 106 (1904)

Debussy's *L'isle joyeuse* (1903–04) was inspired by Watteau's painting *Embarkation for Cythere*. Debussy's work is a single movement in a highly modified sonata form. Using a technique similar to Chopin's alteration of sonata form in his ballades, the lyrical second subject returns at the brilliant conclusion as a fortissimo paean. *L'isle joyeuse* has an almost orchestral quality, as well as an unrelenting choreographic rhythmic drive. The cumulative effect is perfectly calculated and overwhelmingly successful. A number of hallmarks of Debussy's mature style—parallel sonorities, whole-tone structures, multiple layers of sound, atmospheric effects, melodic fragmentation—are in full evidence. *—Steven Coburn*

Recommended:

- ○ **Debussy: Estampes** / Tabe / 2001 / Chandos 9912
- ○ **Debussy: Preludes I; L'isle joyeuse** / Pollini / DG 445187
- ○ **Debussy: Clair de Lune** / Weissenberg / DG 445547
- ○ **Richter: Debussy & Chopin** / Richter / 1999 / BBC Legends 40212

Nocturne, L. 82 (1892)

This is a relatively early work by Debussy and thus does not divulge the Impressionist style that would permeate his keyboard compositions a few years hence. Still, it contains a sufficient quantity of his stylistic fingerprints, notably in its rich harmonies, to leave no doubts about authorship. That said, it also displays hints of Liszt in the opening, and of Massenet and perhaps even Fauré, in its thematic lushness.

The piece opens with a short, mysterious theme, rising from the bass region to the upper register, imparting a sweetness and gentleness that immediately summon middle-period Liszt. The ensuing theme, too, more than vaguely suggests Liszt at the outset, but then suddenly turns playful and somewhat capricious, then passionate and romantic, allowing in more sunlight than the work's title might suggest. The material from the opening returns, as does the main theme and secondary themes, all now more forceful, more passionate. The whole piece has a brightness in its romantic outpourings and a hesitant, almost Scriabin-esque sense of lyrical flow. A typical performance of the *Nocturne* lasts about seven minutes. *—Robert Cummings*

Recommended:

- ○ **Claude Debussy: Complete Piano Music Vol. II** / W. Haas / 1993 / Philips 438721
- ○ **Debussy Dreams** / Ciccolini / 1998 / EMI 66753
- ○ **Nightmoods** / C. Rosenberger / 1994 / Delos 3030

Petite suite, for piano, 4 hands, L. 65 (1888–1889)

On February 2, 1889, Claude Debussy himself collaborated with the pianist and publisher Jacques Durand in the first performance of the *Petite Suite*, for piano, four hands. Debussy's *Petite Suite* is a work of immediate lyric charm. But as a number of Debussy scholars have opined, it hardly seems to fit into the prevailing climate of deeply-felt Romantic utterance which characterizes many of Debussy's finest song settings, which are closely contemporaneous. As Frank Dawes, for example, writes of the work, "composed shortly after the *Ariettes oubliées* to poems by Verlaine, the *Suite* is in such sharp contrast to those remarkable songs that it could almost have come from another hand. Yet the suite, helped by an orchestration by Henri Büsser, has become even more popular than the Arabesques." Debussy clearly intended this music to be judged on its own merits, and on the basis of what it strove to achieve. Its purpose is to entertain, rather than to educate or intellectually challenge, and in this, Debussy's *Petite Suite* succeeds admirably.

The *Suite* comprises four individual movements, each one constructed in such a way as to give more or less equal opportunities to both pianists, not that the work is especially demanding to play, a further indication, perhaps, that Debussy intended these pieces for the amateur market. As in several of his early piano works, the prevailing style owes much to the lighter idioms of Delibes and Massenet, though in a sense, this genre was one which suited Debussy's highly personal language quite naturally. The first movement, "En bateau," also shows the clear influence of the equivalent movement of Fauré's *Dolly Suite*, composed some years earlier, in the sensitive and alluring disposition of the parts, as a sublime melody is floated above a broken chordal accompaniment. A passage towards the close is doubly prophetic, firstly because it employs a whole-tone scale, and also (writes Dawes) "in the little pattern of semi-quavers contributed by the secondo player, very like things in the later music used to symbolise ripples, eddies and whirlpools in water."

The next movement, "Cortège," is a brilliantly evocative processional, suggesting a marching band on a festival day (as does "Fêtes" in Debussy's *Images* for orchestra), while the penultimate movement, "Menuet," is generally regarded as the high point of the work. With its particularly subtle interplay, especially between the middle voices, it (writes Frank Dawes) "begins with suggestions of elfin pipes and horns... and the magical vanishing trick at the end has fairy horn-calls echoing faintly around the main melody in a way that suggests that Debussy's piano music was by now beginning to find a place in his unique dream-world." The final movement of Debussy's *Petite Suite*, entitled "Ballet," is an energetic dance, with a contrasting central section rooted in the world of French popular theatre music of the day. *—Michael Jameson*

Recommended:

- ○ **En Blanc et Noir: The Debussy Album** / Labeque Sisters / Philips 454471
- ○ **Debussy: Works for Two pianos** / Nagai, Achatz / 1991 / Bis 526

La plus que lente, waltz, L. 121 (1910)

The history of Debussy's celebrated waltz "La plus que lente" is an engaging one. The composer kept on his mantelpiece a small sculpture by Claudel entitled "La valse," and so skilled was its creator "in transforming rhythmic movement into mass," writes Paul Roberts (in his book *Images: The Piano Music of Claude Debussy*), "that one has the impression of being able to *touch* a waltz, of experiencing its essence in another medium." Like Ravel, who saw the waltz as the touchstone of decadence, and in *La valse* used it to suggest the inevitable collapse of imperial Vienna, Debussy was fascinated by the waltz form as much for its human and social implications as for its purely musical ones. Whereas in Debussy's virtuoso piano piece *Pour les octaves* the music expresses the inner meaning of the form—in Roberts' words, "its energy, movement, and line, and its power to excite and take the dancers out of themselves"—the intentions, and indeed the effect of "La plus que lente" are quite different.

The title might be translated into English as "The Even Slower Waltz"; at the time it carried subtle connotations beyond the evocation of a popular style. *La plus que lente* appeared soon after the publication of Book I of Debussy's *Preludes*, in 1910. It represented Debussy's laconic reaction to the pervasive influence of the slow waltz in France's coffee-houses, dance-halls, and salons. But, writes Frank

Howes, "'La plus que lente' is, in Debussy's wryly humorous way, the *valse lente* to outdo all others." Apparently Debussy handed the manuscript of this piece to the gypsy fiddler Leoni, whose Romany band played to great popular acclaim in the ballroom of the New Carlton Hotel in Paris. It was almost certainly here that Debussy got the idea for the work in the first place. Perhaps the composer was deliberately aiming "La plus que lente" at a less sophisticated audience than he normally wanted to address through his music, but it contained a vaguely condescending Stravinskyan irony that a hotel audience might or might not have detected. *—Michael Jameson*

Recommended:

○ **Debussy for Daydreaming** / Arrau / 1995 / Philips 446484

○ **Claude Debussy: The Composer as Pianist** / Debussy (piano roll) / 2000 / Pierian 1

Pour le piano, suite, L. 95 (1894–1901)

Claude Debussy began his three movement piano suite, *Pour le piano*, L. 95, around 1896 and completed it in 1903. There was a great deal of evolution in the composer's style during these years; his songs and orchestral writing had become wholly unique. It was not until this late date in his career (he was in his late thirties when he began this suite) that Debussy chose to incorporate the idiomatic challenges of the piano into his personal vocabulary. Looking at the whole of his output, with such piano masterpieces as *Estampes* and his Etudes to his credit, it is difficult to imagine why it took so long for the composer to begin writing great piano music.

The suite's opening Prélude has a fast, savvy infectiousness, using the whole-tone scale and closing with a harp-like cadenza flourish that is unmistakably Debussyan. There is a broad palette of tone colors at work in the opening movement, featuring wide contrasts in register and breadth of chords. The opening builds from an initial, fast and steady line into a grand, overture-like section within the first minute. From there the opening material is then transformed into a totally different texture that heads to the same declamatory, ritornello-style moment. The differing colors and the general tone of this prelude suggest orchestral writing, which is what Debussy's hero, Chopin, abhorred in Beethoven's solo piano music. On the whole, the effect is both familiar and exotic, with shades of near-ancient music (such as Rameau's), and Javanese gamelan. Chopin comes to mind as well, though it is easy to imagine him taking exception to this comparison. It is undeniable, though, that the real power of French piano music is most readily identified with Debussy and Chopin's mature keyboard compositions. Both have a unique reverence for the pianist's position as a master of an exceptional instrument and a language that is specific to it.

In the second movement, Sarabande, is actually a revision of the "Sarabande" found in his *Images (oubliées)* of 1894. In it, the composer is having a very personal conversation through the piano. Like Debussy's *D'un cahier d'esquisses*, the keyboard is a vehicle for an extra-musical level of communication; the listener seems almost beside the point as the composer maintains a loving dialogue with music; there are no fireworks whatsoever. Alert listeners may regard this work as among the most intimate music for the keyboard. There is also a certain affinity for the piano music of the composer's friend, Erik Satie, whose 1887 *Sarabande* may well have inspired the tone of Debussy's own movement. Debussy may have been the superior craftsman, but Satie's pianistic ability to deliver the straight goods, the meaningful understatement, has always been under appreciated for its influence on his good friend Claude.

The suite's finale is a Toccata that is poised and energetic, extroverted and graceful. Performers will find it daunting and enlightening. Demanding unflappable technique and poise, it concludes the suite admirably with the message that Debussy has mastered the piano's unique language on his own terms. *—John Keillor*

Recommended:

○ **Piano Music by Claude Debussy** / Rev / 1995 / Hyperion 44061

○ **Debussy: Piano Music** / Entremont / 2003 / Sony 54451

○ **Great Pianists of the 20th Century: Ivan Moravec** / Moravec / 1998 / Philips 456910

○ **Debussy: Piano Works** / Rogé / 1994 / London 443021

Préludes, Book I, L. 117 (1907–1910)

Each of Debussy's *Préludes, Book I* (1907–10) is a short but substantial work that conveys a particular mood or impression suggested by its title. Still, as musicologist Rollo Myers notes, "the pictorial element [is not] unduly stressed if stressed at all; these *Préludes* are pure music." In accordance with the composer's practice of assigning a title only after the completion of a work, the titles of the *Préludes* are placed at the foot of each, rather than at the head. The *Préludes* represent the pinnacle of Debussy's keyboard art; each may be rightly regarded as a miniature masterpiece.

1. *Danseuses de Delphes* (Delphic Dancers): This is a slow, hypnotic, stately sarabande that utilizes multiple layers of parallel chords in unusual five-bar groupings.

2. *Voiles* (Sails): Whole-tone scales and pentatonic harmonies provide the musical substance of this mysterious and evocative tone poem. The spirit and character of this work recall *Jeux de vagues* (Play of waves), the second movement of *La mer* (1903–05).

3. *Le vent dans la plaine* (Wind on the Plain): Rapid figuration depicts the whirling winds, twice interrupted by sudden chordal outbursts. Much of the work's impact derives from the extreme, effective economy of its material.

4. *Les sons et les parfums tournent dans l'air du soir* (Sounds and Scents Mix in the Evening Air): The title of this *Prélude* was taken from Baudelaire's *Fleurs du mal*, the inspiration for this slow, waltz-like nocturne. The work makes active use of three themes, all in the same key, demanding the utmost sensitivity and imagination from the pianist.

5. *Les collines d'Anacapri* (The Hills of Anacapri): This is a lively scherzo in tarantella rhythm, with a slower central section in imitation of Italian folk song. The piano writing is particularly colorful and brilliantly effective.

6. *Des pas sur la neige* (Footprints in the Snow): Debussy depicts a barren winter snowscape with a plaintive, harmonically static dirge. The slow, sustained legato underpins the powerfully hypnotic atmosphere.

7. *Ce qu'a vu le vent d'ouest* (What the West Wind Saw): Rapid, sweeping arpeggios, fast alternating chord passages, and thundering tremolos characterize this brilliant, virtuosic showpiece. It is virtually an étude, fiercely aggressive and calling upon the full resources of the pianist.

8. *La fille aux cheveux de lin* (The Girl with Flaxen Hair): The title of this, one of the most familiar of the *Préludes*, comes from Leconte de Lisle's *Scottish Song*. Debussy's use of modality lends an archaic air to this charming, delicate work.

9. *La sérénade interrompue* (The Interrupted Serenade): A Spaniard wooing his sweetheart with the sounds of his voice and his guitar is thwarted by several noisy interruptions. Debussy effectively recreates a Spanish-inflected guitar sound on the keyboard, treating the interruptions with wry humor.

10. *La cathédral engloutie* (The Sunken Cathedral): Debussy effects a striking musical depiction of the mythical submerged cathedral of Ys with "archaicisms" like modality and parallel harmonies. The work's rhythmic stasis, combined with its massive sonorities, creates an overwhelming sense of awe and grandeur.

11. *La danse de Puck* (The Dance of Puck): Shakespeare's Puck is depicted here as a witty and capricious elf. Light, rapid figurations and sudden shifts of register and dynamics require an exceptional degree of pianistic control.

12. *Minstrels* (Minstrels): The last of the *Préludes* from Book I is a sardonic parody of the music heard in turn-of-the-century music halls. Crisp rhythms and "popular" harmonies punctuated by sharp dissonance anticipate elements in the music of Stravinsky and Poulenc. *—Steven Coburn*

Recommended:

○ **Debussy: Preludes I; L'isle joyeuse** / Pollini / DG 445187

○ **Claude Debussy** / Michelangeli / 2000 / DG 469130

○ **Debussy: Préludes I & II** / Gieseking / 2000 / Angel 67262

○ **Debussy & Chopin** / Richter / 1999 / BBC Legends 40212

Préludes, Book II, L. 123 (1910–1912)

The works in Debussy's second book of *Préludes* (1910–13) are similar in intent to those of *Book* (1907–10). Several of them look ahead to Debussy's later style, in which the composer's earlier impressionistic, almost Romantic poetry was supplanted by a greater concentration upon technique and neoclassical objectivity. In addition, perhaps because Debussy's style is so prone to mannerism, several of the *Préludes* in *Book II* bear strong similarities to those from the earlier set.

1. *Brouillards* (Mists): Quietly teeming, delicate, and atmospheric, the texture is dominated by sweeping arpeggios that require a high degree of control on the part of the pianist. Harmonically, the work is quite advanced, with a strong suggestion of polytonality.

2. *Feuilles mortes* (Dead Leaves): The main theme of this *Prélude* is so similar to that of *Les sons et les parfums tournement dans l'air du soir* (Sounds and Scents Mix in the Evening Air) from *Book I*, it seems an intentional parody. The overall mood likewise recalls that of the earlier work.

3. *La Puerta del Vino* (The Gateway of the Alhambra Palace): One of the most effective *Préludes* of the set, this Spanish-inflected work has the rhythm of a habanera throughout.

4. *Les fées sont d'exquises danseuses* (The Fairies are Exquisite Dancers): The wispy, delicate figuration of this work calls for extraordinary facility and lightness on the part of the pianist.

5. *Bruyères* (Heaths): Similar in mood and style to *La fille aux cheveux de lin* from *Book I*, *Bruyères*, a depiction of an idyllic English landscape, is also one of the least demanding Préludes from a technical standpoint.

6. *Général Lavine—eccentric*: In this *Prélude*, Debussy portrays the famous American juggler with enormous wit, making ingenious use of incisive rhythms and sudden contrasts. Perhaps reflecting common "showbiz" origins, it is similar in mood and style to *Minstrels* from *Book I*.

7. *La terrasse des audiences du clair de lune* (The Terrace of the Audiences of Moonlight): This subtle *Prélude* is based on a phrase from the French children's

song "*Au clair de la lune*." The many artfully constructed mood changes are difficult to convey and require great sensitivity on the part of the pianist.

8. *Ondine*: Debussy depicts the legendary water sprite with a subtly changing atmosphere, as in the previous *Prélude*. Typical "water-like" arpeggiated figuration alternates with scherzando outbursts.

9. *Hommage à S. Pickwick Esq., P.P.M.P.C.* (after Dickens' *Posthumous Papers of the Pickwick Club*): The protagonist of Dickens' novel is musically personified by imitations of whistling, echoes of an English music hall, and a quote from *God Save the Queen*.

10. *Canope*: This *Prélude*, similar in style and content to *Et la lune descend sur le temple qui fût* (And the Moon Descends on the Ruined Temple) from the second set of *Images* (1907), is a mournful depiction of an Egyptian burial urn.

11. *Tierces alternées* (Alternating Thirds): This is a brilliant study in thirds that anticipates the style of the *Etudes* (1915). Debussy achieves great effect through a subtle rise and fall of dynamics, using a minimum of musical material.

12. *Feux d'artifice* (Fireworks): The last of Debussy's *Préludes* is a musical portrait of a fireworks display over Paris. Brilliant arpeggios, trills, and rapid chord passages characterize this, the most technically challenging of the *Préludes*. The work comes to an effective close with a distant quote of *La Marseillaise* sounded over a hushed tremolo. *—Steven Coburn*

Recommended:

- ○ **Debussy: Préludes for Piano Books 1 & 2** / P. Jacobs / 1997 / Nonesuch 79474
- ○ **Debussy: Préludes Vol. 2** / Michelangeli / DG B000001602
- ○ **Richter: Debussy & Chopin** / S. Richter / 1999 / BBC Legends 40212

Rêverie, L. 68 (1890)

The year 1890 witnessed the first flowering of French composer Claude Debussy's piano music in print, as the *Deux Arabesques*, the four-hand *Petite Suite* and, most significantly, the *Suite bergamasque* all found their way into published editions. Debussy was considerably less satisfied when Paris-based publisher Eugène Fromont issued his piano piece *Rêverie* from an old manuscript that had been lying about for some time. "I very much regret your decision to publish *Rêverie*," Debussy testily wrote to Fromont. "I wrote it in a hurry years ago and purely for commercial purposes. It is a work of no significance and, frankly, I consider it absolutely no good."

Debussy's low opinion of *Rêverie* has not prevented it from taking pride of place among the very best known of his piano works. Debussy's original manuscript is no longer extant, and in terms of dating, that of the first published edition, as reflected above, is generally accepted. But in actuality, *Rêverie* was composed sometime between 1880 and 1884. As such, it is a milestone, as it represents the earliest known instance of Debussy working in the "impressionistic" musical vocabulary that eventually became his trademark.

The piece starts with a modal accompaniment figure that is started on the weakest beat of the bar. As Debussy's plaintive, simple melody gets underway on the beat, there is a rhythmic instability at first between the two parts. This is further obscured due to the wandering modal orientation of the harmony. The piece does not get firmly on the ground until the sixth bar. Debussy applies his melody lightly, and provides a bare, largely arpeggiated accompaniment that is rich in suspensions such as sevenths, ninths, and seconds. *Rêverie* is wholly satisfying as a mood or relaxation piece, and unlike the vast wealth of similarly intentioned salon music that also appeared in the 1880s, it does not in the least seem dated.

The first American edition of *Rêverie* appeared in 1895, and since then the piece has become a popular concert favorite in the United States. The American pianist Harold Bauer helped to popularize *Rêverie* early in the twentieth century through a rather simplified arrangement of his own, thus establishing a trend toward adaptation of *Rêverie* that yet continues. *Rêverie* has been arranged countless times for a wide array of instrumental forces; the version for harp in particular is considered a staple in the literature for the instrument. Jazz musicians have long known the piece, and its influence may have helped to shape the harmonic approach of jazz in general. In 1938, bandleader Larry Clinton recomposed *Rêverie* into a hit song entitled *"My Reverie."* In 1974 an electronic version from Isao Tomita's album *Snowflakes are Dancing* helped to popularize the work even further. Of Debussy's works, *Rêverie* has exceeded all expectations in terms of its performance within the commercial milieu, the very aspect of the piece that caused its composer to practically disown it. *—Uncle Dave Lewis*

Recommended:

- ○ **My Favorite Debussy** / Cliburn / 1999 / BMG 0902663567
- ○ **Debussy: Piano Works** / Rogé / 1994 / London 443021

Suite bergamasque, L. 75 (1890; revised 1905)

It is difficult to establish an appropriate chronological place for Claude Debussy's *Suite bergamasque* within his output. He originally composed the piece in 1890, but it was not published until 1905, and the extent to which he revised it during the interval is unclear. Certainly the published work is a great stylistic advance over the few short piano works which preceded it during the late 1880s and early 1890s, but whether that advance is due to an early maturity or to much later alteration will perhaps always elude historians.

The Suite, Debussy's tribute to the French Baroque *clavecinistes* (harpsichordists), comprises four individual movements: Prélude, Menuet, *Clair de lune*, and Passepied. It is interesting to note that Debussy originally titled the third and fourth pieces "Promenade sentimentale" and "Pavane," respectively, and changed their titles only shortly before publishing the Suite in 1905. This has caused many to question the purported connection between the much-celebrated *Clair de lune* and Paul Verlaine's poem of the same name. However, Debussy's connection with Verlaine's poetry is far reaching enough for the association to be meaningful. He had already set the poem *"Clair de lune,"* as well as several others, for voice and piano on two separate occasions by 1891, and the word bergamasque is itself contained within that particular text.

The Prelude, an F major piece cast in ternary (ABA) form, unfolds in an aristocratic, unhurried way. The opening declamation, spanning some four octaves, is nobleness itself, while the B section, in A minor, is devoted to more thoughtful ideas. Perhaps the best music in the Prelude is contained within the lengthy passage that connects the middle section to the reprise of the opening. The Menuet presents the best glimpse of Debussy's emerging compositional voice. Save for its 3/4 meter there is little trace of the traditional minuet form to be found. Especially notable is the absence of a trio section. *Clair de lune* is perhaps the most famous work Debussy ever penned. Although Debussy's reliance on left-hand arpeggios throughout the piece can lead to a somewhat mechanical effect in the hands of less skilled performers, *Clair de lune* has a way of drawing the listener into its magical atmosphere. Particularly striking are the opening gestures, still and quiet, and a passage in parallel octaves that connects the opening to the more active middle-section. The Passepied that ends the Suite is cast in 4/4 time, betraying its origins as a pavane, since the traditional Passepied is invariably found in 3/4 time. As is the case with the Menuet, Debussy is making reference to an antiquated dance form without actually making use of it. *—Blair Johnston*

Recommended:

- ○ **Debussy: Piano Work** / Rogé / 1994 / London 443021
- ○ **Debussy & Ravel: Piano Music** / Stott / 1991 / Conifer 51755
- ○ **Debussy: Children's Corner; Suite Bergamasque, etc.** / Pludermacher / HM 7901504

OPERA

Pelléas et Mélisande, L. 88 (1893–1902)

Claude Debussy's sole completed opera, *Pelléas et Mélisande* (he worked, to little avail, on several during his younger days), is based on the Maurice Maeterlinck play that also inspired works by both Schoenberg and Jean Sibelius. Debussy began the first sketches of the opera as early as 1889, though the work did not take its final form until shortly before its Paris premiere in 1902. It was the composer's intention to produce a kind of opera in which the music served the subtleties of text far better (he felt) than the dominant opera style of his day (i.e. the work of Wagner and his immediate successors) did. Thus, while the techniques of *Pelléas* are frequently Wagnerian in origin, they serve so radically different a purpose as to render the resemblance barely recognizable.

Debussy exploits the utter simplicity of Maeterlinck's allegorical plot and allows the music to assume a texture of thoroughgoing delicacy. It is this fragility, sustained with consummate skill throughout the five-act opera, that, more than any other single feature, draws the most powerful response from both audiences and musicians involved in productions of the work. Subtle musical suggestion is the key to Debussy's magic in *Pelléas*. Wagner's celebrated leitmotif techniques are modified to make them less of a "visiting card technique," as Debussy himself once described the German composer's method, and more of a way to draw vague musical shapes that represent characters' psychological conditions. Maeterlinck's pessimistic denial of free will finds expression in the uncertain, intentionally non-directional nature of much of Debussy's music (many of the musical motifs themselves seem to have trouble deciding which direction to turn next, so to speak, and undergo a certain amount of internal repetition before finally shooting off in a new direction). Debussy's setting of French texts was never less than superb, and in *Pelléas* he achieves wonders—the instrumental/vocal balance is such that few listeners will ever be aware of just how dense the orchestration is, while the psychological nature of the play (and its lack of stage action) allows the relationship between music and text to unfold in a spacious way that affords each character plenty of time to explore the depths of his or her individual experience. Although it is safe to say that few twentieth century operas could feasibly exist in their present forms had Debussy not found time to complete *Pelléas et Mélisande*, the work has never achieved the public adulation bestowed upon many of its "dependents." Perhaps it is the very qualities that make the work so uniquely powerful—its emotional vagueness, the way its apparently simple plot and undramatic (in a Wagnerian sense) music disguise a wealth of textual and musical complexities—that are to blame for its general neglect. In many ways, however, *Pelléas* is a profoundly intimate work, and one wonders whether it is not better kept so. *—Blair Johnston*

Synopsis:

Act One. In a forest in the fictional kingdom of Allemonde, Golaud enters, lost, and notices Mélisande, huddled and crying. He asks her why, and she tries to run, telling him not to touch her. He tells her he won't hurt her, then exclaims at her beauty. He asks who hurt her, and she answers, "Everyone," and says that she fled to this place from very far away. He asks what is glimmering in the water, and she answers that it's "the crown he gave me," but won't let him retrieve it. He leads her out.

In the castle of the kingdom, Genevieve (the mother of Pelléas and Golaud) reads a letter that Golaud sent to Pelléas, saying he has married Mélisande but still knows nothing about her. He asks Pelléas to show a light if Mélisande will be welcome; if not, he will leave and not return. King Arkel had planned another marriage for Golaud, but accepts the situation. Pelléas enters, weeping because of the approaching death of a friend, but Arkel says he must stay with his father, who is gravely ill. Outside, Genevieve and Mélisande talk. Pelléas enters, and they watch a ship leaving. When Genevieve goes, Pelléas tells Mélisande he is leaving, but doesn't answer when she asks why.

Act Two. Pelléas and Mélisande are near a well, at noon. To his alarm, she leans over it, murmruring that her hair can touch the water. He questions her about her first meeting with Golaud. She tells him that Golaud wanted to kiss her, but she didn't want him to. She begins to play with her wedding ring, tossing it over the water, and it falls in. She asks what they will tell Golaud, and Pelléas answers, "the truth."

Inside, Golaud is in bed, bandaged. He tells Mélisande he was thrown from his horse, just at the stroke of noon. She is sad, and he wonders whether it is because of Pelléas, who is silent around her, but she insists that it's because it is so dark and gloomy. He laughingly tries to comfort her, but when he notices her ring is gone, he becomes so upset that she tells him she lost it in a cave, gathering shells for Golaud's son Yniold. He orders her to go find it immediately, and when she protests that she is afraid, he tells her to take Pelléas. Outside the cave, Pelléas tells Mélisande she must enter, so she can describe the ring. She is frightened when the moonlight reveals three sleeping beggars, and they leave.

Act Three. Mélisande is singing childishly to herself, combing her hair. Pelléas enters, and she leans out. He tells her how beautiful she is and that he is leaving tomorrow. She refuses to reach out her hand to him if he leaves, and he agrees to wait. He exclaims blissfully as her hair cascades about him. It becomes entangled on branches, whereupon Golaud discovers them and chides them for playing in the dark like children. Golaud takes Pelléas into the castle vaults, and, while holding him, tells him to lean over to smell the scent of death in the chasms. Pelléas gasps, and they leave. On the terrace, Pelléas joyously breathes the fresh air. Golaud tells him not to upset Mélisande, who is pregnant. Outside Mélisande's bedroom, Golaud cajoles and threatens Yniold to persuade him to tell him what Pelléas and Mélisande do when they are alone together, and he lifts him up to watch them. Yniold says they are sitting silently looking at the lamp, and, frightened, cries and asks to be let down.

Act Four. Pelléas tells Mélisande he is leaving and asks her to meet him. He also tells her that his father expressed the opinion that he had the grave, friendly look of someone who is about to die, and has told him to leave the castle soon. Arkel comes in and tells them that since Pelléas' father is recovering, the castle will be more cheerful for Mélisande. Golaud comes in and roughly pushes Mélisande away, demanding that she bring his sword. He mutters about her eyes, and Arkel says he sees only great innocence in them. Golaud exclaims sardonically and roughly orders her to shut them, then seizes her by her hair and yanks her back and forth, laughing. Arkel intervenes, and Golaud leaves. Arkel says that if he were God, he would take pity on the human heart.

In the park, Yniold is trying to move a rock; his ball has fallen behind it. He hears sheep bleating and asks the shepherd why they do that. The shepherd answers that it's because he is not taking them to the sheepfold, and Yniold asks why, but gets no answer. Pelléas is waiting for Mélisande, confused but intent on telling her what is in his heart. She joins him, and they quietly admit they love one another. They hear the castle doors being locked and exclaim that everything is lost, everything is won. Golaud finds them and kills Pelléas, as Mélisande flees.

Act Five. Mélisande has given birth prematurely, but a doctor tells Golaud that she is only slightly wounded. Golaud is tortured by the thought that he killed Pelléas for no reason; he and Mélisande were kissing like children. When she awakens, she talks mysteriously, and Golaud asks to be left alone with her. He begs her to tell him whether she loved Pelléas, and she answers yes, but when he asks if they were guilty, she says no, despite his shouted insistence. The doctor and Arkel return; Golaud groans that he has killed Mélisande, and they give her her baby, who she says will weep as well. The servants come in, and, sensing the moment of her death, kneel. Arkel says that Mélisande was a tiny, mysterious creature, like everyone else in the world, and that now it is the baby's turn to live. *—Ann Feeney*

Recommended:

- ○ **Debussy: Pelléas et Mélisande** / C. Abbado (cond.), Ewing, F. LeRoux, Van Dam, Courtis, Vienna PO / DG 435344
- ○ **Debussy: Pelléas et Mélisande** / Karajan (cond.), Stilwell, Von Stade, Van Dam, Raimondi, Berlin PO / 1999 / EMI 67168
- ○ **Debussy: Pelléas et Mélisande** / Boulez (cond.), Söderström, Shirley, D. McIntyre, D. Ward, Royal Opera House Orch. Covent Garden / 1991 / Sony 47265
- ○ **Debussy: Pelléas Et Mélisande: A Collector's Pelléas** / P. Coppola & Truc (conds.), Croiza, Panzera, Brothier, Dufranne / 1995 / VAI Audio 1093

BALLET

Jeux, L. 126 (1912–1913)

Jeux is a ballet. The story for the work was suggested by the Russian dancer and choreographer Vladimir Nijinsky, famous for his association with Igor Stravinsky, Sergei Diaghilev, and the ballets russes. Nijinsky had danced in Debussy's *L'après midi d'une faune* in 1912, and apparently felt some affinity with Debussy and his music. Debussy rejected Nijinsky's original scenario, which included a game of tennis and a crashing airplane; instead, Debussy proposed a scenario in which two women and a man become involved in a love triangle while searching for a lost tennis ball one evening. Premiered in 1913 by the Ballets russes, the ballet is set at a tennis court, where a man happens upon two women. The man turns on the charm, and flirts with one until he gets a kiss, making the other jealous. The second girl then dances with the man, while the first leaves. They join together at the end, and the ballet ends with a tennis ball rolling across the stage, edging the trio offstage.

The ballet has been criticized for its inaccessibility, and indeed it is an intimidating, complicated work. Absent from the work are repeating themes, clear tonal centers, and simple functional harmonies, making the work somewhat reminiscent of Arnold Schoenberg's atonal modernist opera of 1909, *Erwartung*, in which "themes" are heard only once, and motivic material is abandoned almost immediately after it is heard. *Jeux* contains a number of techniques carried over from Debussy's earlier opera *Pelléas et Mélisande*—most notably what Arthur Denk calls "diatonic saturation," a technique which exhausts all of the diatonic pitches in embellishing a single chord. The ballet also contains moments of bitonality, in the form of superimposed contrasting diatonic sonorities, and moments of near-atonality. However, there is ultimately a subtle overarching tonal framework (using modal, pentatonic, major, and minor tonalities) connecting the various episodes of the work.

Jeux was premiered just two weeks before Stravinsky's then scandalous *Le sacre du printemps*, and Debussy was deeply impressed by *Le sacre*. There are a number of similarities between the two ballets, most notably the adventurous harmonies that stretch the limits of tonality. Debussy's ballet marks a turning point in his career, perhaps even a moment of crisis, and ultimately it would be Stravinsky whose influence would push Debussy in a new musical direction. *—Alexander Carpenter*

Recommended:

- ○ **Debussy: La Mer; Images; Nocturnes & others** / Dutoit (cond.), Montreal SO / 1999 / Decca 460217
- ○ **Debussy: La Mer; Images; Nocturnes** / Boulez (cond.), Cleveland Orch. / 1995 / DG 439896
- ○ **Debussy: Orchestral Works 1** / Martinon (cond.), O.R.T.F. / 1998 / EMI 72667

CHAMBER MUSIC

Cello Sonata, L. 135 (1915)

Although they represent only half of a projected series of works, Debussy's three chamber sonatas bear testimony to the composer's developing identification with a more abstract—that is, less visually, textually, or otherwise extramusically oriented—musical process. The first of these works, the *Sonata No. 1 for cello and piano* (1915), is cast in three movements, the last two of which are played without break. The Prologue opens with a noble keyboard statement in D minor, well-defined harmonically (an unusual feature in Debussy's music) and tinged with modal color, to which the cello provides a highly ornamental response. The entire movement is but 51 measures in length, yet encompasses a wealth of expression. Throughout, musical phrases are allowed to develop and collapse with no clear boundaries; as with much of the composer's later music, the distinction between melody and ornamentation is deliberately obscured. The absolute saturation of the ensuing Sérénade (marked Modérément animé) with the percussive tones of the cellist's pizzicati came as a great shock to Parisian audiences of Debussy's own time. The few arco passages that invade the texture quickly dissolve away, save for an outburst of triplet rhythms midway through the movement. The bass staccati in the piano serve to make the occasional melodic, legato inserts all the more powerful. The finale, marked Animé, follows without pause. At 123 bars, it is of greater length than the two previous movements together. Although in performance its quicker tempo compensates for its proportions to some degree, a great deal of the Sonata's musical weight is invested in this energetic movement. Debussy calls for the cello to play with a "light and nervous" character, while he includes no fewer than 17 tempo indications that emphasize the psychological tension. The music builds to several climaxes, only to have the bottom drop out each time in one of Debussy's favorite musical strategies. The cello makes a final passionate, unaccompanied melodic plea, as at the beginning of the entire work, before the Sonata concludes in a flurry of great percussive strength. *—Blair Johnston*

Recommended:

○ **Maisky & Argerich Live in Japan** / Argerich, Maisky / 2001 / DG 471346

○ **Schubert: Arpeggione Sonata & Schumann, Debussy** / Rostropovich, Britten / 1999 / Decca 460974

○ **Janos Starker: Chopin, Bartók, Mendelssohn & others** / Starker, Sebok / 1995 / Philips 434358

Violin Sonata, L. 140 (1916–1917)

Debussy's *Sonata for violin and piano,* third in a projected series of six chamber sonatas, was the last work the composer completed before his death in 1918. Progress on the sonata caused Debussy a great deal of frustration; in the end, he felt that it never really came together the way he had originally intended. Nevertheless, the work remains a powerful, forward-looking effort that manages to fuse elements of mainstream concert tradition with a wholehearted affinity for gypsy violin playing.

The sonata unfolds in three movements: Allegro vivo, Intermède (Fantasque et léger), and Finale (Très animé). A broadly melodic flavor informs the first movement, enough so that Debussy clearly felt no need to include the separate slow movement typical of traditional sonatas. Indeed, the extremely legato gestures, frequent hemiolas, and generally long note values belie the movement's Allegro vivo indication, which, rather than reflecting the surface detail of the music, seems calculated to prompt the performers to provide a constant undercurrent of urgency. More active are the piano's arpeggio figurations as the music moves through several keys in preparation for the reprise of the opening material; even these, however, are marked pianissimo.

Of the three movements the Intermède is the most "fantastic," moving with ease between music marked scherzando and that of a more improvisatory nature. A wonderful chromatic melody, marked "expressif *et sans* rigueur," enters midway through the movement and is repeated just before the return of the opening material (now recast in a fuller, less rhapsodic fashion). A burst of energy from the violin is quickly extinguished as the movement dies away into nothingness.

Debussy had the most difficulty with the sonata's final movement. The opening theme of the first movement returns in the violin, accompanied by the piano in figuration that recalls the composer's *Les estampes* (1903). After this introductory gesture, the finale proper begins with an explosion of unaccompanied activity in the violin. This almost incessant stream of sixteenth notes is suspended on only a few occasions, each marking vital structural points; in one particularly striking instance, the movement's main motive sounds pianissimo against a static, B flat major background. Unusually for Debussy, the work ends with a staunch fortissimo affirmation of the home key of G major.

In his last few compositions Debussy began to move away from the kind of pictorial, sensual music that had driven his work for the previous 15 or 20 years. Indeed, the Sonata for violin and piano provides a glimpse of what purely abstract musical wonders the composer might have wrought had he not succumbed to cancer at the age of 55. *—Blair Johnston*

Recommended:

○ **French Violin Sonatas** / Midori, R. McDonald / 2002 / Sony 89699

○ **Anne-Sophie Mutter: The Berlin Recital** / Mutter, Orkis / 1995 / DG 445826

Sonate en trio for flute, viola, & harp, L. 137 (1915)

Claude Debussy's *Sonata for flute, viola, and harp* (1915) is the second entry in a projected series of six chamber sonatas (of which the composer completed three). The Sonata is at once evocative and emotionally ambiguous, though a great deal less harmonically adventuresome than its two companions; Debussy once remarked that he didn't know whether it "should move us to laughter or to tears. Perhaps both?" The Sonata opens with a freely constructed movement marked Pastorale: Lento, dolce rubato. Debussy subjects six essential musical cells to a free variation treatment as the music unfolds. When he reprises these melodic strands, he does so without regard for their initial ordering, and yet with a clear dramatic impact. The atmosphere, seemingly relaxed, is nonetheless charged with a sense of repressed passion; the pause in the second measure, for instance, is positively bursting with psychological tension. The second movement, Interlude: Tempo di minuetto, recalls the Menuet of Debussy's *Suite bergamasque* (1890) in its vague implication—rather than explicit modeling—of a dance form; here, though, the rhythmic structure is more sharply defined. In the finale, marked Allegro moderato ma risoluto, the reason for Debussy's decision to abandon the Sonata's original scoring—flute, oboe, and harp—becomes clear. Without the viola's passionate pizzicati, the finale would lose much of its essential character; indeed, its opening would be unrecognizable. Listening to such an abstract, non-representational movement, it is easy to understand why Debussy was moved on one occasion to refer to anyone who described such music as "impressionistic" as an "imbecile." *—Blair Johnston*

Recommended:

○ **Franck & Debussy: Sonatas; Ravel: Introduction & Allegro** / Melos Ens. of London / 1988 / London 421154

○ **Flute & Harp** / Rampal, Laskine, Pasquier / Erato 45837

String Quartet, L. 85 (Op. 10) (1893)

Debussy began work on the composition of his only string quartet in 1892. Little documentary evidence, save for one or two passing oblique references in letters to friends remains to indicate his rate of progress. The final movement, however, caused him no little trouble, and only in August 1893 did Debussy feel able to write to his colleague André Poniatowski that "I think I can finally show you the last movement of the quartet, which has made me really miserable!"

Cast in the traditional four movements, Debussy's *Quartet* in G minor, Op. 10 has as its most distinctive feature its overarching preoccupation with timbre and sonority. The work as a whole offers a compendium of string-playing techniques, yet it also displays a concision of thought rare, perhaps, in a composition often regarded (along with the quarte by Ravel) as one of the seminal impressionist works in the string quartet genre.

Its fascinating and readily palpable thematic concentration seems all the more remarkable when one realizes that the very first theme of the opening movement (Animé et très décidé) comes to furnish almost all of the diverse thematic components for the entire work. Another ingenious feature (possibly less immediately apparent to the listener at first hearing), is that the quartet is less dominated by melodic or harmonic considerations than by a rhythmic flexibility which carries the potential for seemingly endless variety. In this respect, Debussy's string quartet seems to strongly prefigure those by Bartók. Yet it remains unmistakably a work dominated by the sensuality and *longueurs* of French late nineteenth century Romanticism, a strong feature of the slow third movement (Andantino doucement expressif).

The work is also strongly predictive of the disjunctive and highly polarized new musical language that would assert itself in the two decades following its completion. The Scherzo (Assez vif et bien rythmé), for example, makes use of the disruptive sonic confrontations that can occur when rapidly alternating pizzicato and bowed passages produce what one commentator has described as "a confusion that forces the listener to concentrate on the textures, rather than the linear form of the music." These apparently disparate elements are then welded together in a finale of striking economy of means, and only at the close does it become really clear that the opening gestures of the work have actually altered themselves and coalesced to produce an organic unity of some 25 minutes' duration.

The work was to be dedicated to Ernest Chausson, whose personal reservations eventually diverted the composer's original intentions. Debussy sold his score for a mere 250 francs to the publishers Durand & Cie., who, as he later recalled, "were cynical enough about it to freely admit that what they were paying me didn't cover all the labor this 'work' has entailed." Not surprisingly, the quartet was widely misunderstood at its premiere, given by the Ysayë Quartet on December 29, 1893. At the time, the composer Guy Ropartz was the lone voice in a wilderness of critical lack of interest; he described the quartet as a work "dominated by the influence of young Russia (interestingly, Debussy's patroness in the early 1880s had been Nadezhda von Meck, better known for her support of Tchaikovsky); there are poetic themes, rare sonorities, the first two movements being particularly remarkable." *—Michael Jameson*

Recommended:

○ **Debussy & Ravel: String Quartets** / Emerson SQ / DG 445509

○ **Debussy & Ravel: String Quartets** / Quartetto Italiano / 2001 / Philips 464699

○ **Debussy, Ravel, Stravinsky: String Quartets** / Alban Berg Quartet / 2001 / EMI 67551

○ **Claude Debussy** / Melos-Quartett Stuttgart / 2000 / DG 469130

○ **Quartets: Debussy, Ravel & Dutilleux** / Julliard SQ / 1993 / Sony 52554

Syrinx, for solo flute, L. 129 (1913)

Asked by his frequent correspondent, the poet and dramatist Gabriel Mourey, to provide a score for his adaptation of the Psyche myth, Debussy expressed his reluctance thus: "What kind of genius is required to revive this ancient myth from which all the feathers of the wings of love have been plucked?" In the end, however, the composer sufficiently mustered his creative powers to produce a short incidental work for Mourey's play. Although *Syrinx* (1913) may seem relatively uncomplicated on the surface, especially since it calls only for a lone flute, its modest appearance belies its substance. In its simplicity of utterance and highly emotive language, *Syrinx* immediately recalls Debussy's *Prelude à l'après midi d'un faune* (1892–94), and, likewise, evokes that work's sensual Symbolist resonances, inspired by the poetry of Mallarmé.

In both works, the composer's musical language is immensely cultured and, at the same time, in the forefront of contemporaneous musical modernism. This is most powerfully evident in the use of whole-tone scales and other devices that lend the music a strange ambiguity. In *Syrinx*, Debussy de-emphasizes, even dispenses with, conventional tonal centers; much of the work's potency instead derives from its delicate, fragmentary melodies and highly seductive timbral effects. Scholar Edward Lockspeiser points out that, significantly, given its implied association with the first of Debussy's *Chansons de Bilitis* (1900–01), *Syrinx* was originally titled "Flûte de Pan." He further opines that "it is as exquisitely and lovingly designed as the flute solo for Mallarmé's mythological faun. It was the one project that was not allowed nebulously to float about in Debussy's mind during his long friendship with Mourey." *—Michael Jameson*

Recommended:

- ○ **Incantation** / Zukerman / 1996 / Delos 3184
- ○ **Music, My Love** / Rampal / 1989 / CBS 45548

VOCAL

Songs (1879–1915)

"The strongest influence on Debussy is that of writers, not of musicians," wrote composer Paul Dukas. "Verlaine, Mallarmé, and Laforgue gave us new tones, new qualities of sound. They projected onto words a luminosity that had never been seen before.... Like musicians they brought together images and their correspondences in sound." Claude Debussy's songs are, to a significant degree, extensions of his instrumental music, which is guided more by timbre, effect, and subtly shifting emotions than by traditional notions of musical form. The songs are not especially tuneful, as are those of Fauré and Poulenc, but they are lyrical; they float the voice gracefully and naturally over the varied textures of pastel piano accompaniment. And while the color and direction of the vocal line are closely attuned to the meanings of every word and phrase, a Debussy song conveys a precise atmosphere even to listeners who don't understand French.

Of course, this is true more of Debussy's mature work than his early songs, and it must be noted that he wrote nearly half his 80 songs by 1885, when he was only 23. These first pieces are more conventional, very pleasant but not highly distinctive examples of French *mélodie.* Debussy's favorite poets to dress in music during this period were such well-known Romantic figures as Alfred de Musset and Leconte de Lisle, as well as the less familiar Vincent Hyspa and André Girod. The outstanding song from this period is *Beau Soir,* a haunting appreciation of an evening scene.

The turning point in Debussy's song production came around 1882 with *Mandoline,* his first setting of a poem by Paul Verlaine. This is a delicate scherzo, the vocal line undulating over flurries from the keyboard. Debussy would set 18 more Verlaine poems, most of them published in the collections *Ariettes oubliées* (1887) and *Fêtes galantes* (1891, 1904). Particularly in the two sets of *Fêtes galantes,* the vocal lines become more sinuous, the harmonies more unstable and sensual; the piano parts, while always providing sensitive support for the voice, are now more elaborate, and could almost hold their own in the piano suites Debussy was writing at the time. Paul Baudelaire, poet of perfumed corruption, was another important source of texts during this period.

But in the early 1890s, Debussy needed greater freedom than that allowed by verse, and began setting prose to music, starting with his own texts for *Proses lyriques* (1892–93). The pinnacle of Debussy's prose treatments came in 1897 with the *Chansons de Bilitis,* three languorous, hypnotic settings of erotic nymph-and-satyr texts by Pierre Louys. Here, the piano accompaniment is becoming simpler and colder.

By the early years of the twentieth century Debussy grew interested in French Baroque music and even older French poetry. These years are dominated by treatments of the rondels and ballads of Charles d'Orléans, Tristan L'Hermite, and François Villon in such cycles as *Trois Chansons de France, Le Promenoir des deux amants,* and *Trois Ballades de François Villon*—somber settings all. *—James Reel*

Recommended:

- ○ **Debussy: Mélodies** / Baldwin, Ameling, Von Stade, Souzay, Command, Mesple / EMI 64095
- ○ **Debussy: Mélodies** / Piau, Immerseel / 2003 / Naive 4932
- ○ **Debussy: Songs** / Maltman, Martineau / 2003 / Hyperion 67357

Ariettes oubliées, L. 60 (1885–1887; revised 1903)

These settings of some of the best-known poems of Paul Verlaine mark Debussy's transition from a traditional composer in the style of Gounod to a more individual artist, although here the operative word is "individual" rather than "original": the young Debussy, in sauntering away from his French idols, is hooking his arm into that of Richard Wagner. The music is highly chromatic and tonally ambiguous, traits that Debussy would make his own in the next few years. Also, Debussy begins to make heavy use of the dominant ninth chord, one of his later trademarks; indeed, the very beginning of the first song is a series of falling ninths.

Debussy set Verlaine's poetry 19 times through his career; the texts are rich in long, lazy vowels and seductively repetitive consonants. The first item in *Ariettes oubliées* is typical of Verlaine's work and a highly adept musical setting by Debussy: the gauzy, floating melodic line perfectly reflects the text of *C'est l'extase langoureuse,* in all its languorous ecstasy. Next is *Il pleure dans mon coeur,* with the piano accompanying the long vocal lines with what would become Debussy's typical "raindrop" music; the singer notes that it rains in her heart as it rains in the town, but can't understand the source of her sadness. "It's pain's darkest state/not to know why/without love, without hate/my heart feels such weight."

The third song is *L'ombre des arbes* (The Shadows of the Trees), another doleful piece in which the singer's state of mind reflects (rather than is reflected by) a sad, solemn landscape. Everything brightens significantly with *Chevaux de bois,* initially celebrating the energy of merry-go-round horses turning in their circular route, although midway through the mood changes to sadness and wistfulness, reflecting the knowledge that these are not living creatures.

The last two songs are "Green" and "Spleen"—the titles are in English, because Verlaine liked their sound. Debussy, following Verlaine, referred to this pair of songs as aquarelles, and the music does have a light, wispy, watercolor character. "Green" is a love song that begins with offerings from nature (fruits, flowers, leaves in the trees) and ends with a falling into slumber. "Spleen" is a song of despair—the sky is too blue, the sea too green, all because the loved one has done something "atrocious." The vocal line becomes intentionally monotonous, and the music fades away, listlessly. *—James Reel*

Recommended:

- ○ **Songs of Debussy and Mozart** / Banse, A. Schiff / 2003 / ECM 000019202
- ○ **Forgotten Songs: Dawn Upshaw sings Debussy** / Upshaw, J. Levine / 1997 / Sony 67190
- ○ **Voyage à Paris** / Von Stade, Katz / 1995 / RCA 902662711

Chansons de Bilitis, song cycle, L. 90 (1897–1898)

Debussy's *Trois Chansons de Bilitis* were published in their original form for voice and piano in 1897, with a dedication to the writer André Gide. The texts were those of the well-known prose poems by Pierre Louÿs. As Edward Lockspeiser writes, these songs "provide the most moving revelations of the hedonistic, pagan art of Debussy, a reminder that the antique grace and splendour of the earlier *Après-midi d'un faune* was not only still alive in the composer's imagination, but that it was capable of a more remote, and therefore still more poignant spiritualization. Indeed, one may go further and conjecture that Bilitis and the Mallarméan faun are in a sense the illegitimate progenitors of the ultimate glory of Debussyan paganism, *Le Martyre de saint Sebastien.*"

The second song of the group, as it was eventually published, was in fact the first to be written. It was printed and issued independently in the October 1897 issue of the journal *L'Image,* while the surrounding panels of this triptych, "La Flûte de Pan" and "Le Tombeau des Naïades," were both finished in September 1898. Notable for their sensuality and beguiling mild eroticism, the three chansons were first performed in public at a Société Nationale de Musique concert on March 17, 1900, when Debussy himself accompanied Blanche Marot at the piano. Later in 1900, Fernand Samuel, director of the Théâtre des Variétés, approached Louÿs suggesting the cycle could perhaps also be recited and mimed, whereupon Debussy was asked to remodel and enlarge the score appropriately. He provided a reworking for pairs of harps and flutes with celesta, which was finally presented at the Salle des Fêtes of Le Journal on June 7, 1901.

The first of the *Trois Chansons,* "La flûte de Pan," suggests something of the pastoral simplicity evoked to such palpably sensuous effect in Debussy's *Syrinx* for solo flute. "La Chevelure" is at once more declamatory and confident in style; but once again, amid the calmly undulating expressive lines of the vocal part, it is possible to clearly recognize the powerfully erotic language Debussy used so graphically in the Tower Scene of his opera *Pelléas et Mélisande.* A number of critics, among them Romain Rolland, have identified the spirit of Jules Massenet in this song. Massenet "whose spirit (says Rolland) will continue to slumber in the heart of every Frenchman" was noted for lyrical elegance, but also for his forthright exuberance, a passionate quality which emerges also powerfully enough in this dream of ecstatic lovemaking between Pan and Bilitis.

In the final song, "Le Tombeau des Naïades," explains Lockspeiser, "Bilitis is following the lonely trail of a faun to the distant tomb of the naiads," in this glacial setting in which Debussy's crystalline-textured accompaniment etches mysterious footprints in the fresh snow. Finally Bilitis reaches the vast blocks of ice that Pan has hewn from the naiads' mausoleum and, says Lockspeiser, the reflection of a wintry sky "is marvellously transformed in this music into a remote, icy and colourless disillusionment." *—Michael Jameson*

Recommended:

- ○ **Berlioz: Les Nuits d'été; Ravel: Shéhérazade** / Crespin, Wustman / 1999 / Decca 460973
- ○ **Night Songs** / Fleming, Thibaudet / 2001 / Decca 467697
- ○ **Debussy: Mélodies** / Command, Baldwin / EMI 64095

Fêtes galantes, Set I, L. 80 (1891)

Debussy composed his first set of *Fêtes Galantes* in 1882, at the age of 20. The three texts come from a similarly-titled collection of verse by Paul Verlaine, who, in turn, took his inspiration from eighteenth century French paintings, most notably those of Watteau. Full of mystery and subtle wit, these poems—featuring elegantly costumed characters engaged in the pursuit of love—were also set by Gabriel Fauré.

Although these are youthful songs, they reveal the composer's already subtle sense of eroticism, as well as the seeds of his thoroughly French mature aesthetic. In this sense, Verlaine was the ideal source for poetic inspiration: like Debussy, Verlaine was a hedonist of legendary proportions, and along with his fellow Symbolist writers he was already deconstructing the overbearing seriousness of Wagnerian drama to produce something far more suited to the Parisian temperament—seriousness about pleasure (as Debussy would often say, "Happiness is no laughing matter"). The result is successful in every regard. While capturing the spirit of fun embedded in these poems, Debussy manages to infuse them with a gentle sentimentality that makes the characters within deserving of a deeper sympathy. The first and third songs, "En Sourdine" (Muted) and "Clair de Lune" (Moonlight), form thoughtful and sensuous bookends to the middle song, "Fantoches" (Marionettes), which features the playful antics of characters from the Italian Commedia Dell'arte. Debussy's graceful melodies and accompaniments are typically colorful, and attentive to turns of phrase and meaning; as much as any of his mature songs, these showcase the composer's talent for imprinting his compositions with a unique sound world that proves an extremely flexible framework for declamation, while at the same time never losing sight of its distinctive qualities. *—AMG*

Recommended:

○ **Debussy: Mélodies** / Ameling, Baldwin / EMI 64095

○ **Songs of Debussy and Mozart** / Schiff, Banse / 2003 / ECM 000019202

Fêtes galantes, Set II, L. 104 (1904)

Written more than 12 years after *Fêtes Galantes I*, this sequel is likewise taken from the poetic works of Paul Verlaine. The differences between the two sets of *Fêtes Galantes* illuminate the stylistic growth that occurred between the beginnings of Debussy's career and the apex of his productivity: dealing with the most ephemeral of topics and moods, these three songs are among the most subtle and mysterious that Debussy ever wrote—arguably his finest. His use of color and texture, especially in the piano, help to illuminate the characters as they experience the complexities of the sensual world about them.

Fêtes Galantes II occupies an expressive netherworld that straddles the real and unreal, the waking and the dream state. This tone is immediately established in the first song, "Les Ingénus" ("The Innocents"), as the singer recalls the images and impressions from the first awakening of his interest in the opposite sex. The accompanimental ostinato—ticking with clock-like regularity—restrains the voice rhythmically and expressively; the effect is of a memory so vivid, so strong, that the one relating is entranced. The climax of the song speaks of how the sight of female skin was almost unbearable to the singer's once young and foolish senses; he seems to momentarily forget himself as the music escalates beyond its hushed sensibilities and allows for an outburst. This fades, however, and, as is typical of Verlaine's symbolist aesthetic, we are left to decipher the specific consequences of this first encounter without benefit of an explanation.

"Le faune" ("The Faun"), which follows, also makes use of an ostinato. But, whereas that of the first song is somewhat dry and ephemeral, this repeated pattern of open fifths and octaves in the bass register immediately establishes a new affect: innocence has given way to full-fledged sensual experience. The narrator speaks, as if still in the time, to his partner in a presumably erotic encounter; neither participant is sure of his/her exact motive, but both have surrendered to the beat of the drums, as embodied by the piano ostinato. Unrelenting in rhythm and rich sonic texture, this song is as hypnotic as one imagines the moment to have been.

The third song of the group, "Colloque Sentimental," is especially interesting; it brings to life the ghostly dialogue of two lovers, long since dead, as they relive their moments together. The singer assumes both roles, one rhapsodic and nostalgic, and the other terse—perhaps even bitter. Unlike the first two songs, there is no ostinato, and the song takes on a much more sprawling, appropriately conversational quality. The "rhapsodic" voice, impassioned in memory, sings phrases drawn from Debussy's most sensuous pen; that of the terse partner inhabits less optimistic, dry music—he (she) is not anxious to remember. The song, like the event it embodies, is incredibly fragile, easily broken by a careless vocal phrase or pianistic accent.

The fidelity implied by these two ghostly lovers, presumed to be faithful even beyond the grave, has been linked by some biographers to Debussy's newly formed union with the singer Emma Bardac, mother-to-be of his beloved daughter, Claude-Emma (Chou-chou). A notorious philanderer in his past (the suicide attempt of his recently abandoned wife caused an international scandal in the music community), he perhaps wanted to express his intentions of "turning a new leaf." Whatever the inspiration, Verlaine's delicate and evocative poems drew from Debussy some of his most satisfying (yet appropriately fleeting) settings. *—AMG*

Recommended:

○ **Debussy: Mélodies** / Souzay, Baldwin / EMI 64095

Trois poèmes de Mallarmé, L. 127 (1913)

These pieces, Debussy's last set of songs, were composed at a time when his health was in serious decline, the world was on the brink of war and revolution, and music itself was in the beginnings of great upheaval. The composer himself was starting to move into new directions and while the music here is not quite revolutionary, it is bold and innovative: melody does not flow, and the daring harmonies match the quirkiness of the text. Some have suggested that Debussy felt a duty to set texts by Stéphane Mallarmé, since it was that poet's work which inspired the composer's great breakthrough orchestral composition, *Prélude à l'après-midi d'un faune* (1892–94). True, Debussy had already written the song *Apparition* (1884) using a Mallarmé text, but that was an early and not particularly strong effort.

The first song in this set, "Soupir" (Sigh), features a typical Debussy vocal line, but the accompaniment is appropriately cold in its sometimes mechanistic sounds. The mood is one of detachment and desolation, perfect for conveying the autumnal elements of Mallarmé's text. The second song, "Placet futile" (Futile Petition), has an intellectual air about it, and a dry sort of humor that effectively conveys the spirit of the text, which tells of the declaration of love to the figure of a shepherdess on a teacup. The last song, "Éventail" (Fan), has an almost off-the-wall manner in places, again appropriate for the text, which is said to lack a clear meaning. In sum, these songs are important works in Debussy's vocal output and represent some of his more inventive creations in any genre. *—Robert Cummings*

Recommended:

○ **Debussy: Mélodies** / Piau, Immerseel / 2003 / Naive 4932

○ **Debussy: Mélodies** / Ameling, Baldwin / EMI 64095

CONCERTO

Rhapsody for alto saxophone & orchestra, L. 98 (1901–1911)

Many great composers have accepted commissions for new works, and then never managed to bring them to fruition; Debussy was certainly no exception. A composer who found it exceptionally difficult to write anything to order, Debussy found the composition of his *Rhapsodie for alto saxophone and orchestra*—which had been requested in 1903 by Elisa Hall, President of the Boston Orchestral Club—a particularly disagreeable task.

Hall had taken up the saxophone—as yet still rather unfashionable prior to the jazz era, when the instrument came into its own—in the hope that it would improve a respiratory weakness from which she suffered. With little regard for the cost, she set about commissioning a substantial array of new works for the instrument, which then had a very small repertory, and approached several prominent French composers, including Debussy. Debussy, who cared little for the instrument and knew almost nothing of its technical capabilities, would not fulfill the commission for the *Rhapsodie* for several years; indeed, when he did submit his score, it was incomplete and unorchestrated.

Not easily deterred, Hall traveled to Paris, pressing for a completion date. Debussy wrote to André Messager of her visit in somewhat ungracious terms: "The Americans are proverbially tenacious... the saxophone lady has arrived, and is inquiring about her piece. Of course, I have assured her that it is the only subject that occupies my thoughts... so here I am, searching desperately for novel combinations calculated to show off this aquatic instrument." And to Albert Louÿs, he confided "Considering this piece was ordered, and paid for... and (its proceeds) eaten more than a year ago, I realise that I am behindhand with it. The saxophone is a reed instrument with whose habits I am not very well acquainted. Does it indulge in romantic tenderness like the clarinet?"

In 1905, Hall performed one of her other commissions in Paris, and Debussy, who was present, later wrote that he thought it ridiculous to see a woman in a pink frock playing on such an ungainly instrument, adding that it was not his desire to perpetuate the spectacle. However, in 1911 Debussy again resumed work on the piece, and finally sent Hall a rough draft of just three or four staves, with much of the score still missing. Jean Roger-Ducasse undertook the task of completing the work after the composer's death, in a manner which showed how well he understood Debussy's musical language.

Originally, the work was to be called "Rhapsodie Orientale"; subsequently, it became the "Rhapsodie at a Société Nationale de Musique event Mauresque," possibly a more appropriate title, since this straightforward work owes much to Spanish idioms. The *Rhapsodie* was premiered in its completed form on May 11, 1919, conducted by André Caplet and featuring saxophonist Yves Mayeur as soloist. *—Michael Jameson*

Recommended:

○ **Saxophone Concertos** / Marriner (cond.), Harle, Academy of St. Martin-in-the-Fields / 1997 / EMI 72109

○ **Music for Saxophone & Orchestra** / Brabbins (cond.), Kerkezos, Philharmonia Orch. / 2002 / Naxos 8557063

CHORAL

Trois chansons de Charles d'Orléans, L. 92 (1898–1908)

The *Trois Chansons de Charles d'Orléans* (Three Songs of Charles d'Orléans}) falls into a sparsely populated category of Debussy's output—that of unaccompanied choral music. In fact, discounting unpublished and unfinished works, it is the only such piece he composed. For that reason alone, these songs are valuable in the study and understanding of the composer's works; apart from such academic and personal considerations, this music has broad appeal as well.

The three songs are settings of poems by Charles Duc d'Orléans (1394–1465). The first is entitled "Dieu! qu'il la fait bon regarder!" (God! but she is fair!). The music is ethereal and subdued, and features at times a religiosity of mood, the whole offering a mixture of Renaissance and modern sounds and putting an interesting and rare retrospective spin on the composer's harmonic thinking. The next song, "Quand j'ai ouy le tambourin" (When I heard the tambourine), is also somewhat ethereal, but the music is livelier and a bit more colorful, too. The contrapuntal writing here—and in fact throughout the set—is quite effective. The last song, "Yver, vous n'estes qu'un villain" (Winter, You're Naught but a Rogue), is also colorful and quite spirited. In the end, the three pieces in this collection are all worthwhile and must be ranked as important efforts in Debussy's output. The first and last songs date from 1898, and the middle from 1908, the year the collection was published. *—Robert Cummings*

Recommended:

- ○ **Appear & Inspire** / Shaw (cond.), Robert Shaw Festival Singers / 1996 / Telarc 80408
- ○ **Debussy: Mélodies** / Command, Baldwin / EMI 64095

La Demoiselle élue, L. 62 (1887–1888)

This was another early cantata from Debussy and easily among his strongest efforts in the choral genre. Of course, in the twentieth century, he completely abandoned that realm, unless one counts some unpublished efforts and the unaccompanied choral works, *Trois Chansons de Charles d'Orléans* (1908) and *Ode à la France* (1916–17), which he sketched out but did not complete.

Debussy reorchestrated *La damoiselle élue* (The Blessed Damozel) in 1902, but left the music and text intact otherwise. The text he used was from the English poet Dante Gabriel Rossetti (1828–82), in a translation provided by G. Sarrazin. The Blessed Damozel is portrayed by the soprano in this work, while narrative portions of the text are divided between the women's chorus and contralto soloist, who serves as the Narrator. The music is beautiful and well-crafted, with little in it that could be called naïve. The choral and orchestral writing both are assured, even masterful. In the Prelude, Debussy introduces three themes that reappear in the harmonies throughout the score. There are certainly signs of the mature composer here, even if there is nothing revolutionary in the music, nothing quite like his watershed work, *Prélude à l'après-midi d'un faune* (1892–94). Yet, there are more than a few moments that augur its coming, and there are fewer noticeable influences in the score. In sum, this is one of the composer's better early large works, and clearly one of his finest choral compositions. *—Robert Cummings*

Recommended:

- ○ **Bidú Sayão: La Demoiselle èlue; Opera Arias** / Ormandy (cond.), Sayão, Philadelphia Orch. / 1997 / Sony 63221
- ○ **Inghelbrecht: Debussy Prélude à l'après; Nocturnes & others** / Inghelbrecht (cond.), Gorge, J. Joly, Orch. Nationale de RF / 2001 / Testament 1212
- ○ **Debussy: Nocturnes; La Damoiselle élue; Le Martyre** / Salonen (cond.), Upshaw, Rasmussen, Los Angeles PO / 1994 / Sony 58952

L' Enfant prodigue, scène lyrique, L. 57 (1884; revised 1907)

This piece for voices and orchestra, often referred to as a cantata, is one of Debussy's earliest large works. It dates from the composer's student years, during which he came under the spell of several influences that resulted in music often unlike the Debussy most listeners know. That is not to say this work is without merit, because it has its fair share. A 1906–08 revision was undertaken by the mature composer who now looked with scorn, if not outright ridicule, upon some sections of the work. In any event, the music and vocal writing here are reasonably attractive, even if it belongs to the period of time before the composer found his own style.

Debussy scored *L'Enfant prodigue* for soprano, tenor, baritone, and orchestra, and used a text by Edouard Guinand. The music was heavily influenced by Massenet, though there are moments when the mature composer emerges (the opening, for example, bears a vague resemblance to some of the music in the composer's *Le Martyre de Saint-Sébastien*, from 1911). Debussy employs leitmotives that he associates with the three characters—Lia, the mother, Simeon, the father, and Azael, the son. There are exotic elements in the score that some have linked to the composer's then-recent exposure to Russian music. The cantata is divided into eight scenes, with the procession and dance music from the third sounding perhaps the most Debussyan, not least because this was, along with the ensuing section—*Ces airs joyeux* (These joyous airs)—the most heavily revised music in the score.

Debussy was only 22 when he wrote the original version, which was good enough to win first prize in the Prix de Rome contest in 1884. *—Robert Cummings*

Recommended:

- ○ **Debussy: L'Enfant Prodigue; La Damoiselle Elue** / Bertini (cond.), Norman, Carreras, Fischer-Dieskau / Orfeo 12821

Jan DeGaetani

b. Jul. 10, 1933, Massillon, OH, **d.** Sep. 15, 1989, Rochester, NY

Mezzo-Soprano

The remarkably versatile mezzo-soprano Jan DeGaetani studied voice at the Juilliard School of Music in New York with Sergius Kagen. She made her debut in New York in 1958. Her international reputation was established when she sang the premiere of George Crumb's *Ancient Voices of Children* in 1970 at the Library of Congress in Washington, D.C. She has also sung the premieres of works by Peter Maxwell Davies (*A stone litany*; *Black Pentecost*), Richard Wernick (*Visions of wonder and terror*), William Schuman (*In sweet music*), and Elliott Carter (*Syringa*). Although best known for her singing of contemporary music, Jan DeGaetani sang a wide variety of music ranging from the medieval *Play of Herod* to songs of John Dowland, German lieder, French mélodies, and songs of Stephen Foster and Charles Ives.

During her career, DeGaetani appeared with most of the major English and American orchestras, usually in works by contemporary composers. Her regular appearances with the Contemporary Chamber Ensemble evoked many fine performances, including Schoenberg's *Pierrot Lunaire*. She also appeared with the Chamber Music Society of Lincoln Center and with Speculum Musicae.

Always an intelligent performer, DeGaetani had a voice with great expressive range; she was one of the rare singers of contemporary music to garner not only critical praise, but also popularity with the general public. In 1973, she was appointed a professor of voice at the Eastman School of Music in Rochester, NY, where she remained on the faculty until her death. Among her students, the most outstanding is the soprano Dawn Upshaw. During the summers, she also taught at the Aspen Music Festival. She often gave master classes in conjunction with her recital tours in order to pass her love of contemporary music on to the next generation. *—Richard LeSueur*

Recommended:

- ○ **Charles Ives Songs** / DeGaetani, Kalish (piano) / 1976 / Nonesuch 71325
- ○ **Crumb: Ancient Voices Of Children** / Weisberg (cond.), Kalish, Jolles, Desroches, Fitz, Contemporary Chamber Ens. / 1971 / Nonesuch 79149
- ○ **Schoenberg: Pierrot lunaire; Book of the Hanging Gardens** / Weisberg (cond.), DeGaetani, Kalish, Rudiakov, Nyfenger, Benjamin, Bloom, Contemporary Chamber Ensemble / 1990 / Nonesuch 79237
- ○ **Schubert & Wolf Songs** / DeGaetani, Kalish (piano) / 1992 / Nonesuch 79263
- ○ **Copland: 81st Birthday Concert** / DeGaetani, Smit (piano) / 1993 / Bridge 9046
- ○ **Ives & Crumb** / DeGaetani, Kalish (piano) / 1987 / Bridge 9006

David Del Tredici

b. Mar. 16, 1937, Cloverdale, CA

Composer

A composer known more than anything else for his large series of works based upon Lewis Carroll's *Alice's Adventures in Wonderland* and *Through the Looking Glass*, Del Tredici has achieved popularity as a composer caught between the extremes of the serialism of his education and a strong drift toward tonality. As a result, his music is often suffused with tonally driven melodies with serialist undertones.

Del Tredici earned his bachelor's degree at the University of California at Berkeley and his master's at Princeton University, studying with such names as Roger Sessions, Earl Kim, Robert Helps, Bernhard Abramowitsh, Arnold Elston, and Seymour Shifrin. As a pianist he earned the Kimber Award in 1955, and as a composer has been given numerous awards, including the Pulitzer in 1980 (for *In Memory of a Summer Day*) and the National Academy of Arts and Letters award in 1968. He has been on the faculties of Harvard University, SUNY Buffalo, Boston University, City College, and Graduate School, and City College of New York. He has also been composer in residence for several organizations, including Tanglewood and the New York Philharmonic Orchestra, among others.

Final Alice is considered by many to be one of Del Tredici's finest works, if not his finest. The work is harmonically somewhat simple, implying the type of tonality many modern composers have driven away from. However, Del Tredici uses this static harmonic language to draw the listener's (as well as the performer's) attention to the other aspects of the works, such as resolutions that seem continuously deceptive, rarely seen time signatures, and the counting, in Italian, to 13. This last is especially important to note, since "tredici" means "13" in Italian. Indeed, this number plays an important role in his work, especially in this piece, and is used as a type of signature, much as Bach did several centuries before.

This is not to imply that Del Tredici's works are harmonically unimportant, boring, or stagnant. Quite the opposite is true. Indeed, strong comparisons could be made to the music of Wagner, with harmonic alterations taking place over extended durations, and themes based upon fairy tales or stories. His harmonies can also be heard as extensions of ideas presented in the late nineteenth century, giving his music a neo-Romantic feel, a category fitting much of his music in the *Alice* series.

Because of his use of extended harmonic changes, combination of serial and tonal ideas, and late Romantic style of harmonic writing and orchestration, Del Tredici has earned a place in the world of serious music as an innovator of new harmonic and theatrical writing; it is for this reason and the impression of his music on generations to follow that he has earned his place in musical history. *—Michael Blostein*

Alice Cycle, for various ensembles (1963–1996)

At least 20 pieces altogether of David Del Tredici are either settings of or programmatic musings on stories by Lewis Carroll. Though not arranged as a "cycle," per se, Del Tredici's various musical responses to Carroll's "Wonderland" tales (*Alice in Wonderland* and *Through the Looking Glass*) constitute as comprehensive a musical treatment of a literary topic as can be found in music of the twentieth century. In fact, all of Del Tredici's works completed between 1968 and 1996 are based on scenes or ideas from Carroll's "Wonderland" tales, beginning with *Pop-Pourri*, a "Cantata of the Sacred and Profane" that set Carroll's "Turtle Soup" and "Jabberwocky" together with a Bach chorale and a *Litany of the Blessed Virgin*; and continuing through to *Heavy Metal Alice*, a work for brass quintet. Along the way, Del Tredici's "Alice cycle" grew to include everything from an opera (*Dum Dee Twiddle*, 1995), to smaller-scale pieces for solo piano (*Virtuoso Alice*, 1984) or chorus (*Acrostic Song*, 1982), to multi-movement orchestral works (*An Alice Symphony*, 1969; *Final Alice*, 1976). The first works in the series take specific portions from Carroll's books and either render them in song or follow them as musical narratives. Several of these works draw not only on Carroll's tales, but also the "critical commentary" and parallel sources elucidated by Martin Gardiner's *Annotated Alice*. The musical style of these earlier works reflects Del Tredici's development of a personal compositional voice, from his training and early interest in atonality to his eventual return to tonality, albeit tonality of a sometimes distinctive flavor. In addition, virtually all of the pieces from this period (not counting later arrangements of isolated movements, etc.) use a kind of concertante textural structure. Del Tredici approaches this traditional setup in rather non-traditional ways, however: against the orchestral tutti in *Pop-Pourri*, for example, the concertante ensemble includes an amplified soprano solo and a four-piece rock band; the five movements of *An Alice Symphony* (selections from which are sometimes performed or recorded under the titles "Illustrated Alice" or "In Wonderland") features in its concertante group, among other things, mandolin, banjo, and accordion. Other works from the period include two medium-length works, *Adventures Underground* (1971) and *Vintage Alice* (1972), both using ensembles similar to that of the *Alice Symphony*, and the hour-long orchestral song cycle *Final Alice* (1976).

Between 1977 and 1981, Del Tredici composed the longest of the Alice pieces, *Child Alice*, an evening-long work reflecting on the events that lead Carroll to publish *Alice in Wonderland* and *Through the Looking Glass*. The Alice here is Alice Pleasance Liddell, who, along with her sisters, encouraged Carroll to publish the stories he had improvised for them as he rowed with them in a boat on the River Thames. Del Tredici imagines these scenes in four movements: "In Memory of a Summer Day," "Quaint Events," "Happy Voices," and "All in the Golden Afternoon." *—Jeremy Grimshaw*

Recommended:

- ○ **Vintage Alice** / Knussen (cond.), Shelton, Harshagen, Wiersma, Rijke, ASKO Ens. / 2003 / DG 000141502
- ○ **Perle, Del Tredici, Thorne** / Boriskin / 1989 / New World 80380
- ○ **Del Tredici: An Alice Symphony** / Knussen (cond.), Bryn-Julson, Tanglewood Music Center Orch. / 1995 / CRI 688

Léo Delibes

b. Feb. 21, 1836, St.-Germain-du-Val, Sarthe, Franc, **d.** Jan. 16, 1891, Paris, France
Composer: Opera, Ballet

Léo Delibes was the first notable composer of ballet to emerge after the death of Rameau, the art of ballet composition having suffered a period of neglect in the interim. Delibes was the first to craft a full-length ballet score with the care and distinction already common among the best opera composers; not only could he produce buoyant, memorable tunes, but he delivered them in sparkling orchestrations. He also wrote several operas, of which *Lakmé*—which generated one popular aria (the "Bell Song") and a now-ubiquitous duet—is the best known.

Delibes studied at the Paris Conservatory under Adolphe Adam. In 1853, he became accompanist at the Théâtre-Lyrique, moving to the same position at the prestigious Paris Opéra ten years later. His great success as a composer of music for the theater in the 1870s and early 1880s gained him a professorship in composition at the conservatory in 1881, and membership in the French Institute in 1884.

The French did not place much value on instrumental music during Delibes' youth, so the emerging composer concentrated on light-hearted operettas and farces in the manner of Offenbach. His first opportunity to work on a large ballet score came in 1866, when he collaborated with Ludwig Minkus on *La Source*. The success of this ballet led eventually to commissions for the two works that would again raise ballet music to its highest level: *Coppélia* (1870), based on a story of E.T.A. Hoffmann, and *Sylvia* (1876), based on a mythological theme. The former is still produced regularly; both light, graceful works generated concert suites that, although not as common in the concert hall as they might be, have been frequently recorded.

Meanwhile, Delibes honed his skill as an opera composer. Most notable are his opéra comique *Le Roi l'a dit* (1873) and his more serious, exotic *Lakmé* (1883). Delibes's church music (he once worked as an organist) has fallen by the wayside, as have most of his colorful songs, with the exception of *Les Filles de Cadiz*, which exudes the same Franco-Spanish air as Bizet's *Carmen*.

His most important work, clearly, was for the stage, particularly those two 90-minute ballet scores. Their significance, beyond their own merits, is the direct influence they had on Tchaikovsky, whose mastery of the symphonic ballet owes everything to *Coppélia* and *Sylvia*. *—James Reel*

OPERA

Lakmé (1883)

Lakmé is a three-act opera with a libretto by Edmond Gondinet and Philippe Gille. Gondinet thought the subject particularly suited to the soprano voice of Marie van Zandt, a rising young vocal star whom he admired. The subject comes from a novel by Pierre Loti. Delibes composed the music between 1881 and 1882, but the premiere took place the following April 1883 at the Opéra-Comique of Paris. Typical of its age, the story makes use of an exotic location, Hindu religious rituals, tension and conflict between the natives and the British settlers, and conflicts surrounding the two main lovers, who both have obligations and loyalties that war with their passion for one another. The music is rich and sensuous, with an oriental flavor during the crowd scenes and scenes of religious rites. This oriental flavor defines the ambiance of the story, giving an aural background even where there is no narrative. Meyerbeer's *L'Africaine* makes similar use of the contrasts between Europeans and "pagans," and also has a love triangle which crosses ethnic boundaries in much the same way. And the subtle colors and harmonies that create this "exotic" world blending European culture with foreign elements were also inspired by Meyerbeer and Bizet. The opera was very well-received by the public and was produced many times at the Opéra-Comique. It achieved international popularity as well, and all in all is as great a work as Delibes' ballets *Sylvia* and *Coppélia*.

Lakmé was based on a novel by Pierre Loti, with strong autobiographical elements inspired by a romance the author experienced while living in Tahiti. Rarahu, the woman involved, eventually died from alcoholism. The basic outline of the story was retained, but Delibes transferred the story to India so that the cultural conflict could be one between the British and the Brahmin Hindus. And instead of alcohol being the cause of his heroine's downfall, Delibes chose as the means of her demise the poetic device of a poisonous flower, the datura (which outside of the operatic stage is not deadly).

The hinge-piece of the opera is the famous "Bell Song" (De la fille du paria). It is sung by Lakmé at the behest of her father, the Brahmin priest Nilakantha. Unbeknownst to her, he intends to use her beauty and beautiful singing to ensnare a trespasser. A British officer named Gérald is one of a group of Englishmen who has trespassed on holy ground despite a warning that this was forbidden on pain of death. He saw Lakmé and fell in love with her instantly, and she with him. Nilakantha observed the last part of their meeting, but fled without being clearly seen.

Delibes' topic suggested musical contrasts between the British and the Eastern characters and locales; it is modal melodies that give the opera its distinctiveness and particular charm. Besides the wonderful "Bell Song, " there are various "Oriental" dances and passages intended to depict Hindu ceremonial music. Even though the growth of world-spanning media and field recordings has shown us just how inauthentic this music is, the opera continues to seem exotic in mood. Even though the opera is a fairly rare visitor to the stage outside France, the "Bell Song" has always been popular. *—AMG*

Synopsis:

Act One. The opera takes place in British-ruled India. The scene is the idyllic landscape around a Hindu temple. Lakmé is the daughter of a Hindu priest and leader named Nilakantha, a radical visionary who wants revenge against the British for their tyrannical rule. The British have forbidden the practice of the Hindu religion, but Nilakantha continues to raise his daughter in Indian religious traditions. As the opera opens, a group of Hindus are led in an invocation to the gods. Lakmé's voice soars above the others in exuberant coloratura. Nilakantha leaves, and Lakmé remains behind. She and her slave Mallika decide to bathe in the river. She leaves behind her jewels on a rock, and they go off together in a boat. The scene is empty when two British officers, a pair of young girls, and their governess appear. They have never been to the Hindu temple, and they find everything exotic and strange. One of the officers, Frédéric, tells the rest of the group about a strange Brahmin priest with a beautiful daughter. The two live in hiding, he says, and the priest has planted poisonous flowers all around their hut to protect his daughter, whom he prizes above all else. The group finds Lakmé's jewelry, and Gérald, the other officer, decides to make a sketch of it. Of an artistic temperament, he has brought his pastels along on their excursion. The others leave, and Gérald indulges in romantic fantasies about the owner of the jewels. Lakmé and Mallika return, and Gérald hides. Lakmé sings a beautiful song and then spies Gérald. She sends Mallika and Hadji to look for her father and then tells Gérald that he is risking death by trespassing on their grounds. Gérald has fallen instantly in love with the beautiful girl, however, and sings her a passionate love song. She responds, joining him in a love duet. But the sound of her father's return interrupts them, and she hastily sends Gérald away. When Nilakantha appears he rages against the profanation of his temple grounds.

Act Two. At a market, a mixed crowd of Indians and foreigners loiters. Mistress Bentson, the governess of the two girls in Act One, is having her pockets picked. She is soon rescued by Frédéric, however, in a light, comical scene. Frédéric and Gérald are due to be stationed in another province of India. The market closes, and a public festival featuring dancers and music begins. Nilakantha has brought Lakmé to the market, hoping that she will attract the attention of the soldiers who trespassed on his temple grounds. He introduces her to the crowd as a traditional Hindu singer. Lakmé sings the famous bell song, about a Hindu maiden who rescues a stranger by using her bells and charms against the wild beasts of the forests. The stranger turns out to be the god Vishnu. The two fall in love, and he takes her with him to the heavens. No British soldier comes forward at the sound of Lakmé's voice, much to Nilakantha's frustration, so he commands his daughter to continue with her singing. She tries to convince her father that Brahma would forgive a stranger for trespassing, but to no avail. As she resumes her singing she finally sees Gérald in the crowd. She stops, but it is too late. As she faints, he rushes up to her and catches her in his arms. Nilakantha now thinks that he knows the identity of the soldier who profaned his temple grounds, and plots his death. There will be a procession later that evening, and plenty of opportunities to kill Gérald. Gérald and Lakmé sing of their love for one another, and they plan to run away and live in hiding so that they can be together always.

The procession of the goddess Dourga begins, and as it is winding through the streets, Brahmin priests chant religious hymns. Frédéric reflects on Gérald's infatuation with an Indian girl. He thinks that when they are both called away to another province, Gérald will forget her, and all will be well. But as the British soldiers are standing about watching the procession pass by, Nilakantha sees his opportunity. He stabs Gérald and quickly flees. Lakmé rushes to her lover's aid. Finding that he is only wounded, she has Hadji take him to a secret hiding place in the forest. There the two, she hopes, can live happily ever after.

Act Three. In the forest, Gérald lies wounded with Lakmé in attendance. She sings him a lullaby, and they have a happy love scene. She tells him of some waters not far off which guarantee that those who drink of it will love one another forever. She leaves to fetch some water for them, and Frédéric arrives. A path made up of drops of blood led him to his friend. He reminds Gérald of his duties as a soldier, and for the first time since his arrival in the woods, Gérald's infatuation with Lakmé lessens. He hears the marching of troops in the distance and realizes that he must go. When Lakmé returns, she knows immediately that Gérald is planning to leave her. So she gives him some of the sacred water, but she also eats a leaf of the poisonous datura tree. They pledge their eternal love for one another, and she tells him that she is dying. They have a final love scene which is interrupted by the arrival of Nilakantha. Gérald despairs, but Nilakantha is content that Lakmé will live on in heaven. *—Rita Laurance*

Recommended:

- ○ **Delibes: Lakmé** / Lombard (cond.), Mesplé, Benoit, Linval, Soyer, Theatre National de L'opera-Comique / 2002 / EMI 67745
- ○ **Delibes: Lakmé** / Bonynge (cond.), Sutherland, Bacquier, Berbie, Sinclair, Monte Carlo National Opera Orch. / 1989 / London 425485
- ○ **Delibes: Lakmé** / Plasson (cond.), Dessay, Van Dam, Leguerinel, Petibon, Toulouse Orch. / 1998 / EMI 56569

BALLET

Coppélia, ou La fille aux yeux d'émail (1870)

The premiere of the ballet *Coppélia*, on May 25, 1870, at the Paris Opera, was an overwhelming success, and paved the way for the future developments of the classical ballet of the nineteenth century. *Coppélia* had been in rehearsal since 1868, and had seen many setbacks. It took Delibes some time to compose the music, and in the meantime, the choreographer was obliged to look for a new prima donna, due to the illness of his lead dancer. Swanilda at the premiere was performed by a prodigy by the name of Giuseppina Bozzacchi. Franz was performed "en travestie" by another female star, Eugenie Fiocre, and Coppélia was played by a real, mechanical doll. Because the male lead was played by a woman dancer, there wasn't a classical pas de deux written for the lovers. Instead, the ballet closes with a divertissement called "Fete del la Cloche," which features the ringing of the village bell. It is filled with dances and festivities meant to close the Opera on a high note.

The music for *Coppélia* ranks with that of the ballets by Tchaikovsky. It is colorful, sensitive, full of nuance and spirit. Its lyricism inspires motion, and it advanced the technique of the leitmotif in theatrical music. Each of the characters is identified by its own leitmotif, and leitmotifs also set the mood and atmosphere of each number. Color and timbre are Delibes' *forte*. He uses both to exquisite effect, communicating emotional content with his diverse palette. He was well acquainted with Slavic music and eastern European dance forms. For the first time, the czardas, a Hungarian dance, is included among the dance numbers. There are also mazurkas and Slavic themes throughout the ballet. The ethnic and national color adds character to the work, and follows Romantic ballet traditions. Romanticism was on the wane when Delibes composed the score for *Coppélia*, and his evocative and impressionistic score prefigures future developments of the nineteenth century.

The librettist for *Coppélia* was Charles Nuttier. He took his story from E.T.A. Hoffmann's *Der Sandmann*, but he was also influenced by the comedy *La Fille mal Gardée*, which has characters derived from the commedia dell'arte. The story of *Coppélia*, though taken from Hoffmann's gothic tale, is a light-hearted love story, which features a mechanical doll as the heroine's arch rival and a comical villain. Although Dr. Coppélius is still a somewhat sinister figure, he is also the springboard for comic events. *Coppélia* was the first ballet to feature a mechanical doll coming to life as part of the plot, and it formed a precedent for future ballet plots of the century. *—Rita Laurance*

Synopsis:

Act One. The curtain opens on the Village Square. Coppélius emerges from his house at the right of the stage. His business is unknown to his fellow citizens, and he is rumored to be an alchemist. On the balcony of his house, Coppélia, the girl believed by townsfolk as Coppélius' daughter, sits reading a book. He re-enters the house. From another home emerges Swanilda, a young girl in love with a local peasant, Franz. Seeing Coppélia from the street, Swanilda attempts to draw her attention with fancy footwork and broad gestures. Coppélia seemingly ignores her. Swanilda is angered by the snub, but hears Franz approaching from the distance and hides herself.

Franz enters with a bold swagger. As he strides in, he blows a kiss to Coppélia, who waves back, much to the shock of the hidden Swanilda. She emerges to redress Franz for his lack of faithfulness. A group of merry villagers arrive, dancing a Mazurka. The Burgomaster announces that the Lord of the Manor is making the gift of a bell to the Town Square, and all couples who marry during the ensuing celebration will be awarded a dowry. Attention turns to Swanilda and Franz, but Swanilda is still petulant. Picking up a plant, variously described as an ear of corn or staff of wheat, Swanilda holds it to her head. If the plant talks to her, then Franz loves her. To Franz' dismay, she soon casts the plant to the ground and declares that their engagement is ended. Franz storms away angrily, and Swanilda joins in a lively Czardas with the band of villagers.

After nightfall, Coppélius slowly exits his house, wrapping his key in a large handkerchief. Some villagers surprise Coppélius and set upon him, spinning him about and mocking him. In the ensuing confusion, the key is lost. Making his escape, Coppélius heads off in a huff. Swanilda then enters in the company of other village girls, discovers Coppélius' key, and slips inside the house to confront her rival. The others join her, showing signs of apprehension. Franz arrives with a ladder, convinced that Swanilda is no longer interested in him and determined to win the heart of Coppélia. Before he can advance, an angry Coppélius returns and chases him off. He has now noticed the key is missing, and is stunned to find the door to his home standing wide open. Coppélius rushes inside.

Act Two. Scene One. (Note: In the original version, the two following scenes are presented as "Act II" and "Act III". Standard practice dictates that the scenes are combined within a single act.) Inside Coppélius' workshop, Swanilda and her coterie discover that it is filled with a variety of life-size dolls that are amazingly realistic. Swanilda discovers that Coppélia, too, is a mechanical doll. Delighted at uncovering Coppélius' secret, Swanilda and her friends wind up all the dolls and set them loose. This is the scene that, to his horror, Coppélius happens upon. He chases Swanilda's friends away, although Swanilda remains behind, hidden.

The ladder appears at the window and Franz climbs through. Coppélius is about to eject the young man, until he learns of the latter's love interest in Coppélia. Coppélius offers to introduce Franz to Coppélia, then plies him with drink until Franz passes out. Coppélius produces a large book, from which he intends to cast a magic spell to bring life to Coppélia. Calling her forth, he is unaware that Swanilda has assumed Coppélia's clothing. Swanilda plays along with Coppélius' 'experiment;' refining her mechanical steps into more assured ones. Clothing Swanilda in a mantilla, Coppélius watches as she dances a Bolero. Coppélius then adds a kilt to Swanilda's wardrobe, and she breaks out into a jig. Swanilda soon tires of this game, and begins to wreak havoc. Franz, awakened by the commotion, rushes back down the ladder, followed by Swanilda.

Coppélius pulls back the curtain to discover his beloved Coppélia, minus her garment and shattered beyond repair.

Act Two. Scene Two. At the ceremony for the bell, the now wizened up Franz and his bride Swanilda are awaiting their wedding. Coppélius storms in, demanding to be compensated for his destroyed property. He is awarded a handsome sum by the Lord of the Manor, and departs, satisfied, if not happy. Then a series of dances relating to the wedding ceremony are given. To close the ballet, the whole company engages in a lively Galop. *—Uncle Dave Lewis*

Recommended:

- ○ **Delibes: Coppélia, Delibes: Sylvia** / Dorati (cond.), Minneapolis SO / 1992 / Mercury 434313
- ○ **Delibes: 3 Ballets** / Bonynge (cond.), National PO / Decca 460418

Sylvia, ou La nymphe de Diane (1876)

French composer Léo Delibes' three-act mythological ballet *Sylvia* is something of the poor unknown cousin of his far more famous *Coppélia* of six years earlier, and yet it too is music of great grace, charm and beauty. As a musical genre, ballet spent most of the nineteenth century in a pitiable condition, and conventional musicology tells us that it was only the great works of Tchaikovsky that raised the genre to the style and symphonic quality that today we take for granted; in all fairness, however, Delibes, whose ballets just barely predate those of the great Russian, came very close to achieving the same kind of pinnacle, and it is worth noting that Tchaikovsky himself remarked that he felt his *Swan Lake* to be "poor stuff compared to *Sylvia*." *Sylvia*'s rise to repertoire position really began not at its 1876 Paris Opera premiere, but rather with a 1900 revival in St. Petersburg. In the century or so since, *Sylvia* has popped up in major ballet theaters on a semi-regular basis; it is far better known, however, outside the theater, via one or another of the orchestral suites that various people have drawn from the full score.

Torquato Tasso's *Aminta* was the source from which Delibes' librettists, Jules Barbier and the Baron de Reinach, drew the story of Sylvia, the Nymphe de Diane (the Nymph of Diana).

Delibes' masterful score betrays a heavy debt to the heavy Wagnerian dramatic style then all the rage throughout Europe—particularly in the Prelude, with its bombastic and richly-scored opening and then its shimmering, luxurious pianissimo gestures—but at the same time manages to retain something of the textural clarity and sectionalization more typical of French music. There is gorgeous melody throughout the three acts, aptly reflecting Sylvia's sensual plot while only rarely dipping too far into the sentimental bucket.

"Faunes et Dryades," a scherzo from the beginning of Act I, mixes a lovely cello tune together with more witty woodwind gestures and some pert pizzicati. In the "Valse lente" from the same act, Delibes manages to impart that most aristocratic of dance-forms with a high-minded humor, while in the "Cortège rustique," a happy flute melody plays around with the mock-exotic tones of open fifths, tambourine and triangle.

Highlights of Act II include the "Pas des Éthiopiens," with its striking tritones between the strings and horns and drum-accompanied piccolo flute solo, and the eminently graceful "Chant bacchique."

The "Pizzicato Polka" of Act III has achieved some fame outside the ballet, and for good reason. The use of an alto saxophone in the "Barcarolle" from that same act was certainly unusual for the day, but the instrument is fittingly smooth against the rolling waves of the string and harp background. The first of the final two numbers, "Le Temple de Diane," is dramatic tension all the way through, from the tremolo build-up and blatantly Wagnerian descending string scales right up to the seamless transition to the beginning "Apparition d'Endymion," an epilogue that brings the ballet to a triumphant E major close. *—Blair Johnston*

Synopsis:

Act One. The scene is a mysterious wood, where dwells the goddess Diana and her sylvan nymphs. A stream flows through the trees, and the wood is softly lit by moonlight. All kinds of woodland creatures people the clearing; they relax in the moonlit stream and chase one another about playfully. Sylvans wrap dryads in garlands of flowers and pretend to hold them captive. All is idyllically happy, until the company of sylvans hears the approach of human footsteps. It is a shepherd invading their sacred territory in the middle of the night. Aminta, for so he is called, puts down his staff and makes as if to rest. He is reflecting on memories of this magic wood. At one time, he thought he saw a beautiful nymph of Diana, and she captured his heart forever with her beauty. He longs to relive this moment and looks about him for any sign of her. Seeing a statue of the god of love in the clearing, he begins to pray to it. The hunting call of a horn is heard in the distance. Aminta is overwhelmed with joy, for he is sure that Eros has granted him his wish and that Sylvia approaches. He hides and waits for the arrival of the beautiful nymph.

Sylvia enters with her company of huntresses. They all decide to take a break from their hunting and bathe and relax in the stream. Sylvia swings fearlessly from a tree branch, skidding over the water with her toes, while the others go for a swim. Aminta is ecstatic with love at the sight of her, but he is not alone. The evil Orion, hiding in a thicket, also watches the beautiful nymphs. Suddenly, one of the nymphs finds Aminta's staff, and they are all furious at the thought that a mortal may have seen them bathing. They gather their weapons and go searching for the vile intruder. When they find Aminta, they force him to kneel before Sylvia. He is so in love with her that all he can do is gaze fearlessly at her angry countenance. She demands an explanation, and he offers her his heart full of love and his life. She decides to wreak vengeance against Eros, for the presumption that he has shown in letting a mortal fall in love with her. She shoots an arrow at the statue, but Aminta takes the arrow instead. As a response, the statue lets loose an arrow that pierces the heart of Sylvia, who falls to the ground stricken as if dead. Orion has been watching and, seeing her weak, waylays her as she departs. He abducts the nymph and carries her off to his grotto. The statue of Eros comes to life and revives Aminta, and Aminta leaves to rescue his beloved Sylvia.

Act Two. In the grotto of Orion, Sylvia is held captive at his pleasure. He is surrounded by his female slaves, all of whom try to entice Sylvia to remain. They shower her with gifts and jewels, and she pretends to revel with the dark huntsman. He has never before tried fermented drinks, so she takes some grapes from the slaves and concocts a type of wine. At first, he refuses the proffered drink, but after she has drunk a glass, he also has some. Liking the wine, he drinks glass after glass until he is completely inebriated. The slaves also crush the grapes and drink. She leads them in a dance in honor of the god Bacchus, and their celebrations get wilder and wilder. Finally, the drunken Orion tries to take her in his arms and clasp her to him. She makes him chase her about until he passes out from drink and exhaustion. Then she prays to the god Eros for assistance, and he appears. In a flash, he makes Orion's grotto disappear, and the freed Sylvia sees Aminta sitting forlornly among the rocks.

Act Three. The scene is a seashore near a temple of Diana. Celebrating villagers have put together a festival in honor of Bacchus. Thalia and Terpsichore are both in attendance, the latter with her lyre. Priests, young girls, and bacchantes all begin the celebrations. Bacchus' chariot appears in the heavens, for he, too, is attending the festivities. Aminta enters, filled with despair, for he cannot find his beloved Sylvia. The bacchantes attempt to cheer him up with reveling. One of the dancing girls is Sylvia in disguise, and he is irresistibly drawn to her. He follows her about until Eros intervenes and reveals her identity to him. The two lovers have a joyful reunion.

Orion arrives at the festival. He is angry with the lovers and threatens them with death. The frightened Sylvia takes refuge in the temple of Diana, as Aminta prepares to defend himself against the evil hunter. However, Orion ignores Aminta and tries to follow Sylvia into the temple. He swings his axe against the closed doors, which finally give way at the third blow. As the doors fly open, Sylvia can be seen kneeling before the goddess Diana, who has her bow drawn to defend the hapless nymph. When Orion tries to capture Sylvia, Diana lets loose the arrow in her bow and strikes him dead. But then Diana angrily turns against Sylvia. Aminta and Sylvia plead for forgiveness, but must tell Diana that they have been slain by the arrows of Eros. At first, she refuses to forgive them, for Sylvia has broken her vows, but Eros reminds her of her own love for Endymion. The vision of the gods smiles down on the lovers as the curtain falls. *—Rita Laurance*

Recommended:

- ○ **Delibes: Coppélia; Sylvia** / Fistoulari (cond.), London SO / 1992 / Mercury 434313
- ○ **Delibes: Sylvia; Saint-Saëns: Henry VIII** / Mogrelia (cond.), Razumovsky Sinfonia / 1995 / Naxos 553338

Frederick Delius

b. Jan. 29, 1862, Bradford, England, **d.** Jun. 10, 1934, Grez-sur-Loing, France

Composer: Orchestral, Choral

Frederick Delius was an English composer who forged a unique version of the Impressionist musical language of the early twentieth century. He was born in Bradford, England, in 1862, and died in Grez-sur-Loing, France, in 1934. He did not come from a musical family; rather, his father owned a wool company and hoped that his son would follow a career in business. Delius, however, wanted to study music, and though his father did not approve of music as a profession, he did not discourage music-making as a pastime; thus, Delius was allowed to study the violin and the piano. To his father's dismay, he also spent much of his youth sneaking away from school to attend concerts and opera performances. When he completed school, he went to work for his father in the family business. In 1884, he left England for Florida, where he worked on a plantation as an orange grower. While in Florida, he began studying music with Thomas Ward, a musician and teacher from Jacksonville. Delius proved to be a failure as an orange grower, and began supporting himself as a musician. In 1886, his father arranged for him to spend a year and a half studying music in Germany at the Leipzig Conservatory. Though Delius would later insist that he learned very little of importance during his stay in Leipzig, it was there that he met Grieg, with whom he forged a lifelong friendship. Grieg convinced Delius' father to allow the young man to become a composer, and

Delius, with the support of his formerly reluctant father, soon moved to Paris and began living the life of an artist.

Once in Paris, Delius began composing in earnest, and towards the end of the nineteenth century had already completed two operas, *Irmelin* and *The Magic Fountain*. In the first decade of the twentieth century, Delius married the painter Jelka Rosen and produced a number of important works, including the opera *A Village Romeo and Juliet*, the large-scale choral works *Appalachia* and *A Mass of Life* (based on the writings of Nietzsche), a *piano concerto*, and a number of songs and chamber pieces. His music was well-received throughout Europe, and Delius was quite successful up until World War I, when he was forced to leave France for England. Despite his renown in continental Europe, Delius was virtually unknown in his native England, and his stay there was marred by financial difficulties. After the war, Delius returned to France, where the syphilis he had contracted in Florida gradually caused him to become paralyzed and blind. Ironically, as Delius became increasingly infirm, his fame began to spread. This was due in large part to the efforts of English composer Sir Thomas Beecham, who championed Delius' music and organized a Delius Festival in 1929. Though terribly ill, Delius nonetheless still wanted to compose, and in 1928 enlisted the services of English musician Eric Fenby, to whom he dictated music (Fenby would later write a book about Delius). Towards the end of his life, Delius was made Companion of Honor by King George V of England, and was awarded an honorary degree in music by Oxford University. Before his death, Delius was able to hear his music over the radio and on record, but these accomplishments paled before the terrible deterioration of his health, and he died in seclusion. *—Alexander Carpenter*

ORCHESTRAL

Appalachia (American Rhapsody) (1896)

Frederick Delius first composed *Appalachia*, subtitled "Variations on an Old Slave Song with final chorus," in 1896. He returned to the work six years later and recomposed, enlarged, and expanded it. The second version was premiered by Hans Haym at the *1904* Elberfeld Festival, and the work was published in this version. In his twenties, Delius had been sent to Florida by his father to manage an orange plantation. Although he failed as a farmer, Delius loved the folk songs of the blacks working with him. He later used these songs as the basis of some of the themes of his *Florida Suite* and elaborated them most fully and evocatively in *Appalachia*. With its long Molto moderato Tranquillo introduction, its languorous Misterioso and Lento variations, and its climatic closing Lento chorus, the work's tempos are slow and its mood is dreamy. *Appalachia's* colors are soft and warm and its textures are humid and turgid and the addition of the chorus only deepens the voluptuous sensuality of the work. As always in Delius' music, faster tempos are often clumsy and never sustained for very long. But also as always in Delius' music, when *Appalachia* is at its warmest and most humid, it is unequaled for creating a mood of overwhelming sexual nostalgia. *—James Leonard*

Recommended:

- ○ **Delius: Orchestral Works** / Barbirolli (cond.), Halle Orch. / 1994 / EMI 65119

Two Aquarelles, for strings (1936)

Nietzsche underlined his attack on Wagner's "incapacity for . . . organic form" by calling him "our greatest miniaturist in music who crowds into the smallest space an infinity of sense and sweetness. His wealth of colors, of half shadows, of the secrecies of dying light spoils one to such an extent that afterward all other musicians seem too robust." The remark could refer as well—or better—to the mature works of Delius, who, as man and artist, drew most deeply from, respectively, Nietzsche and Wagner. With World War I raging, Delius had been busy throughout the winter and spring of 1917 at his home in the French village of Grez-sur-Loing, completing the tone poem *Eventyr*, revising his *String Quartet*, and composing two brief, mixed a cappella part songs for *To be sung of a summer night on the water*. To his young friend Philip Heseltine—known to all lovers of English song as Peter Warlock—he wrote on the May 27 that "It is a great thing to be able to isolate ones [sic] self completely: altho' not very practical." The part songs received their first performance only on June 28, 1921, at a London concert by Kennedy Scott and his Oriana Madrigal Society. Vocalizing on wordless vocables, both songs evince an immediate lyrical lift, transporting the listener to other realms, in down-distilled, immensely filled, meltingly sensuous evocations. The first song takes one to a realm of fairy, of beauty heartbreakingly beyond human passion; the second (with its tenor solo set against diaphanously shifting harmonies) is magically redolent of a bliss surpassing all mortal cares. Words, here, would have been inadequate—and too limiting—for the sudden seductive nostalgia felt for a world never known or even dimly suspected.

In the fall of 1932, with the composer now blind and paralyzed, the part songs were arranged for string orchestra as *Two Aquarelles* by Eric Fenby, a young, intrepid Yorkshire musician to whom Delius dictated a surprising number of fine, late works. What is haunting in the choral version becomes caressing and consoling in the string arrangement. It is a mere musicological nicety that bars them from the list of the composer's original works—the *Two Aquarelles* are as nearly pure Delius as it was possible for another hand to come, and were done, moreover, under the composer's supervision. Here, then, is "an infinity of sense and sweetness crowded into the smallest space," for Fenby's own classic, lovingly lingering recording of the *Two Aquarelles* with the strings of the Royal Philharmonic Orchestra lasts just under five minutes. *—Adrian Corleonis*

Recommended:

- ○ **Barbirolli Conducts Delius** / Barbirolli (cond.), Halle Orch. / 1996 / Cedar 1005
- ○ **English String Miniatures, Vol. 4** / Lloyd-Jones (cond.), Northern Sinfonia Chorus / 2002 / Naxos 555070
- ○ **The Delius Collection, Vol. 7** / Lloyd Webber, Holmes / Unicorn Kanchana 2077

Brigg Fair (An English Rhapsody) (1907)

Delius hit his stride as a composer around the turn of the twentieth century in such works as *Mitternachtslied* (1898) (a setting of the "Night Song" from Nietzsche's *Also sprach Zarathustra* which he later incorporated into *A Mass of Life*); the tone poem *Paris-The Song of a Great City* (1899), and the opera *A Village Romeo and Juliet* (1900–1). Those works and others, moreover, had been performed in Germany with marked success and established Delius' reputation on the continent, though little of his music had been heard in England.

In the spring of 1907, he was in London arranging for performances of his *Piano Concerto* and *Appalachia*. It may have been at the home of the painter John Singer Sargent that he met Percy Grainger, a kindred spirit in his inveterate roaming of Scandinavia, friendship with Grieg, and intense dislike of the conventional attitude which identified genuine music only with the German classical tradition. Grainger, meanwhile, had been assiduously collecting Scandinavian and English folk song, which he used as the basis of many of his compositions.

One of the pieces he showed Delius was a setting of "Brigg Fair" for tenor and a cappella chorus, the words and music of which Grainger had gleaned two years before from one Joseph Taylor, a Lincolnshire man in his early seventies. Not only was Delius much taken with the tune, but he recognized that he and Grainger also shared an affinity for a similar sort of post-Wagnerian, meltingly chromatic harmony. Sealing their friendship, which was to remain lifelong, Grainger gladly gave permission for Delius to use "Brigg Fair" as the basis of a large orchestral work.

Brigg Fair: An English Rhapsody was composed over the summer of 1907 and dedicated to Grainger; it received its first performance at Liverpool under Granville Bantock on January 18, 1908 (though the premiere has been widely and incorrectly ascribed to Hermann Suter at Basle the preceding year). Further performances followed quickly by Landon Ronald and the Hallé Orchestra in Birmingham on February 19 and Beecham with the New Symphony Orchestra in Queen's Hall, London, on March 31. For the latter occasion, Grainger brought Joseph Taylor to town to sit with him and Delius for the performance.

After the brief, atmospheric introduction, as the oboe introduces the theme, Taylor is said to have stood and sung the opening verse of "his" tune—"It was on the fifth of August, the weather fine and fair, /unto Brigg Fair I did repair, for love I was inclined. . . ." In his little book on Delius, Philip Heseltine—known to all lovers of English song as Peter Warlock—notes that "he has, quite unconsciously, harked back to the very form in which the old English composers of the time of Queen Elizabeth were in the habit of adumbrating the popular melodies of the day—that is to say the cumulative variation form which afterwards grew formal in the *passacaglia*, in which the theme is repeated, intact or with very slight rhythmical modifications, in each variation, always surrounded with a new harmonic, contrapuntal, or rhythmic embroidery. In Delius' work there is a brief and lovely interlude—a kind of happy love-song, which is not derived from the main theme: otherwise the form is identical with that employed by John Bull, William Byrd, Giles Farnaby, and many another more than three hundred years ago." *—Adrian Corleonis*

Recommended:

- ○ **Delius: Orchestral Works** / Temirkanov, Mackerras, Seaman (conds.), Royal PO / Tring 036
- ○ **Delius: Orchestral Works** / Beecham (cond.), Royal PO / 2001 / EMI 67553
- ○ **Delius: Orchestral Works** / Barbirolli (cond.), Halle Orch. / 1994 / EMI 65119

Florida, suite (1887; revised 1889)

The *Florida Suite* is the stuff of legend. After a desultory school career and a rather wavering application to the family wool business, young Delius persuaded his father to stake him as master of a hundred-acre orange plantation along the St. Johns River, south of Jacksonville, Florida. Taking a Cunard liner from Liverpool, he arrived in late March 1884 and remained until September 1885. The impact of those months can hardly be overestimated, for it was here, in this lushly tropical setting, with its glowing spectrum of lurid natural splendors and preternatural quiet, that he recognized his vocation and took his first real steps toward it. When Delius took possession of Solano Grove, he had just turned 22. The critic, Cecil Gray, who knew the composer well in his later years, ascribed to this period "... that which is known to mystics as 'the state of illumination,' a kind of ecstatic revelation which may only last for a split second of time, but which he who has known it spends the rest of his life trying to recapture...I knew, too, the exact moment at which that experience must have occurred...and when I asked him if it were so and if I were right, he was surprised and admitted that I was. The occasion was one summer night, when he was sitting out on the verandah of his house in his orange grove...and the sound came to him from the near distance of the voices of the negroes in the plantation, singing in chorus. It is the rapture of this moment that Delius is perpetually seeking to communicate in all his most characteristic work."

It is highly unlikely that Delius ever turned a dime (or a shilling) cultivating oranges, and his father eventually capitulated to *force majeure* by allowing him a period of study at the Leipzig Conservatory (beginning in the fall of 1886). While his actual studies at the conservatory proved relatively uninspiring, they did bring him into contact with Edvard Grieg, whose music and friendship would serve to cement his desire to become a composer. Grieg's lyrical suites also offered a convenient, if temporary, model that allowed the young Delius to give expression to the richness of his Florida experience. The resulting *Florida Suite*, was composed over 1886–87.

The work is in four broadly expansive movements. The first, "Daybreak-Dance," opens with a lyrically rippling, ever more animated, evocation which gives way to a dance, "La Calinda"; this dance is one of the most ravishing moments in Delius' *oeuvre*, and he would make use of it again in his opera, *Koanga*. The second, "By the River," is a melodically effusive, fluently ingratiating elegy with two strains, laid out in a simple ABA design. In "Sunset-Near the Plantation," another spate of rhapsodic tone-painting again gives way to a spirited dance. The fourth movement, "At Night," opens with a horn quartet suggesting at once muted fanfares and plantation slaves singing a spiritual from across the water; this eventually yields to an alternately blithe and impassioned love song.

Delius must at some time have been assiduous in his studies, for he has the orchestra well in hand in this, his first large work. For the price of a barrel of beer, he heard the *Florida Suite* once in early 1888, in the company of Grieg and Christian Sinding, given by a restaurant orchestra in Leipzig; after this performance, he revised two movements and laid the work aside. It remained for Sir Thomas Beecham to discover and give it a proper premiere in 1937, three years after Delius' death. *—Adrian Corleonis*

Recommended:

- ○ **Delius: Orchestral Music** / Handley (cond.), Ulster Orch. / 2000 / Chandos 6628
- ○ **Delius: Florida Suite; Songs of Sunset; Over the Hills and Far Away** / Beecham (cond.), Royal PO / 2002 / EMI 575788

Hassan, incidental music (1920–1923)

When *Hassan* reached the stage of His Majesty's Theatre, London, on September 20, 1923, it arrived out of a web of destinies almost as quixotic as the spectacle itself. The play's author, James Elroy Flecker (1884–1915), had been dead eight years. Its champion, producer Basil Dean, had seen the work through a series of revisions and postponements from before the Great War and had considered a number of composers—including Ravel—for the copious amount of incidental music it would require. A chance hearing of *A Village Romeo and Juliet* in the spring of 1920 persuaded him that Delius was his man. Delius, in failing health, was ever more dependent on royalties from the sale of his scores. Once his enthusiasm had been sparked, work proceeded rapidly, with Philip Heseltine writing the composer's pencilled drafts into full score, and the original version of the music was completed before year's end. Despite Flecker's modest success while he lived, *Hassan* had generated a large posthumous interest, and further delays handed the premiere, in German translation and employing Delius' original score, to Darmstadt, at the Hessische Landes-Theater on June 1, 1923. Meanwhile, for the London production, more music was required, and Delius, now firmly in the grip of the syphilitic infection, working against time and unable to hold a pencil, dictated the new pieces to his wife. When Percy Grainger dropped by on a chance visit, he was pressed into service to compose, anonymously, a brief section of the Act II ballet. The London production of *Hassan* proved a considerable success, opening before a distinguished audience and running for a respectable 281 performances to glowing critical notices. Delius was able to attend the last rehearsals and the virtuosic first night, with Eugene Goossens conducting.

Hassan is a curiously distinguished item in that seemingly inexhaustible vogue for orientalia which includes, among hundreds of ephemeral oddments, Gilbert and Sullivan's surefire *Mikado* (1885), Edward Knoblock's wildly successful play, *Kismet* (1911), the phenomenally long-running Asche/Norton musical, *Chu Chin Chow* (1916), and Puccini's enduring *Turandot* (1926). Though minor, Flecker's vein of poetry was genuine. Said to have been inspired by a volume of farcical plays which he read in Turkish, Flecker's verse nevertheless owes everything to Edwardian notions of "elevated" language, while its "orientalism" harks back to Edward Fitzgerald's translation of *The Rubaiyat*. Thus, a banal tale of intrigue, betrayal, romance, and sudden shifts of fortune is given dignity by a languorous beauty and mild satire highlighting an inevitable disillusionment. And it was, no doubt, this eloquence born of deep disenchantment which led Delius to compose some of his most straightforwardly enchanting music.

The numbers range from fanfares, melodramas, choruses, interludes—some of them snippets but a few bars long—and brief atmospheric preludes to the celebrated, wordlessly vocalized, Serenade (heard thrice) and an elaborate ballet sequence (choreographed for the lavish London production by no less than Michel Fokine). Despite his discomfiture by the limitations of a 26-instrument theater orchestra, nearly everything he composed for *Hassan* is rife with Delian touches—meltingly evocative choral apostrophes, some preludes so imbued with Delian nostalgia as to be abbreviated tone poems, and the final superbly moving chorus, "We take the golden road to Samarkand." The upshot was an aureate, slightly bittersweet, post-Romantic confection wholly out of touch with the Jazz Age antics which surrounded it. *—Adrian Corleonis*

Recommended:

- ○ **Delius: Orchestral Works** / Barbirolli (cond.), Tear, Halle Orch. / 1994 / EMI 65119
- ○ **Delius: Arabesk; Hassan; Sea Drift** / Norby, etc. / Sony 47680

In a Summer Garden, rhapsody (1909; revised 1912)

Many of Delius' works are visual in character, so much so that they can be discussed in terms more closely associated with painting: hues, highlights, shadow, perspective. In the composer's *In a Summer Garden* (1908–1909), the scene in question is Delius' own garden in Grez-sur-Loing, France. Despite the full-sized orchestral forces called for, Delius deploys the instruments in a manner that produces the effect of a chamber work.

In a Summer Garden opens with a chant-like tune for wind quintet, echoed by strings; the oboe part includes a flitting phrase that proves important to the rhythmic development of the entire work. The orchestra introduces a more spacious melody in the violas. As a nearby river comes into view, horns and trumpets herald a brief, rapturous climax that slowly winds down to shadowed harmonies as the aestival vision fades away.*—Roy Brewer*

Recommended:

- ○ **Delius: Orchestral Works** / Barbirolli (cond.), Halle Orch. / 1994 / EMI 65119
- ○ **Vaughan Williams & Delius** / Ormandy (cond.), Philadelphia Orch. / 1996 / Sony 62645

Irmelin, prelude (1931)

Based on themes from Delius' 1892 opera, *Irmelin*, this prelude is actually a free-standing orchestral piece, not an introduction to the stage work. Delius dictated it in 1931 to his amanuensis, Eric Fenby, and it was first performed when Sir Thomas Beecham used it as an interlude in a 1935 production of another early Delius opera, *Koanga*.

The prelude begins with a small, rising motif with a little fall at the end, whispered by individual woodwinds and passed to the strings. (The woodwinds, indeed, play a central role through this piece.) The themes are wispy and fragmentary; the second and third main sections contain pastoral melodies that seem more extended, but they merely rely on gently repeated small gestures. The opening theme returns in a string duet, seeming especially nostalgic and nocturnal, and the prelude ends with the clarinet crooning the melody on a soft bed of strings. *—James Reel*

Recommended:

- ○ **Delius: Orchestral Works** / Barbirolli (cond.), London SO / 1994 / EMI 65119
- ○ **George Szell** / Szell (cond.), Cleveland Orch. / EMI 75962

On Hearing the First Cuckoo in Spring / Summer Night on the River (1911–1912)

The *Two Pieces for small orchestra* are exquisite tone poems depicting two adjacent seasons. They were written after Delius completed his last opera, *Fennimore and Gerda*, which demonstrated the shift to his later style of composition. These two works, however, also look back to his earlier, very personal style. Both are scored for a reduced orchestra of flute, oboe, two clarinets, two bassoons, two horns, and strings.

"On Hearing the First Cuckoo in Spring" (1912) opens on a beautiful sustained major seventh chord followed by the oboe introducing a pastoral bird-like pattern. Then "with easy flowing movement," a song in triple meter is introduced in the strings with drones in the cellos and basses. The simple, sweet, pastoral, modal melody is harmonized by Delius with chromatic passing tones that at times give the impression of bitonality when set against the lower harmonic roots. The melody is built in cumulative phrases, until the oboe has learned the whole tune and now steps forward as a solo underscored by lovely strings. The clarinet then comes forward with an authentic "cuckoo" call. The middle section of the tune is developed as the "cuckoo" clarinet enters at several points. The strings create a small looping pattern just before the ending, and manifest some simple yet rich new harmonies. A major chord dies away to silence. The piece is based on the Norwegian folk song "In Ola Valley, in Ola Dale," and is, to some extent, a transcription of Edvard Grieg's own treatment of the piece in his *Norwegian Folksongs* for piano, Op. 66.

"Summer-night on the river" (1911), one of the few thoroughly impressionist pieces by this composer, opens with gently sighing winds, over a droning pedal point in the muted double basses, and sustained horn notes. The string section enters, their muted sound creating a rich yet somber timbre. There is the beginning of a sea-faring melody but it quickly transforms into undulating figures and trills that perfectly describe a flowing river. A solo cello sings out with a lyrical theme, which is taken over by a solo violin, soon joined by a solo viola, all surrounded by the flowing patterns. The solo violin melody becomes "softer and softer as if dying away in the distance." There is a mystical and atmospheric coda with trilling chromatics in the solo violin, supported by sustained and pizzicato strings. The river in question is the Loing, upon which the wildly blossoming garden of Delius' villa, in the French village of Grez, near Fontainebleau, faced; this distilled tone poem—playing between six and seven minutes—is the upshot of many meditative hours spent there. *—"Blue Gene" Tyranny*

Recommended:

- ○ **Delius: Orchestral Works** / Barbirolli (cond.), London SO / 1994 / EMI 65119
- ○ **Delius: Orchestral Works** / Mackerras (cond.), Welsh National Opera Orch. / 1999 / Decca 460290

A Song Before Sunrise, for small orchestra (1918)

In the summer of 1918, with the Great War grinding slowly to its end and the troubling symptoms of syphilitic paralysis—which over the next seven years would turn the vigorous Delius into a helpless invalid—on the rise, the composer sought a cure in the baths at Biarritz, where he composed *A Song Before Sunrise.* In its brevity (playing about six minutes), keenness of orchestral detail, and evocative power, it might easily make a third to the *Two Pieces for Small Orchestra*—"On Hearing the First Cuckoo in Spring" and "Summer Night on the River"—from before the war. Indeed, it has the character of "'Cuckoo' revisited," though where the latter and its companion exude an elegiac, almost mystical, rapture, *A Song Before Sunrise* is redolent with tongue-in-cheek blitheness. Delius is even said to have likened the clarinet figure in the last bars to a rooster's sunrise greeting. Dedicated to Philip Heseltine—known as Peter Warlock to all lovers of English song—the piece was first given by Sir Henry Wood at a Promenade Concert in September, 1923. *—Adrian Corleonis*

Recommended:

- ○ **Delius: Orchestral Works** / Barbirolli (cond.), Halle Orch. / 1994 / EMI 65119
- ○ **Delius: Orchestral Works** / Beecham (cond.), Royal PO / 2001 / EMI 67553

CHORAL

A Mass of Life (Eine Messe des Lebens) (1905)

Delius was an ardent Nietzschean; the text of this large work for chorus, soloists, and orchestra comes from that philosopher's *Also sprach Zarathustra.* Zarathustra embodies the concept of the superior man of the future, possessing the Will to say "Yes" to Life at its highest. This work is in no sense a Christian mass, for it uses none of the liturgical words of the mass. Rather, it uses Nietzsche's words to celebrate Life, and in its selection of words from various parts of the poem, gives an overview of the entire life of Zarathustra beginning with his address to the Will. It is powerful and sensual music, depicting many of the same images found in Richard Strauss' famous tone poem inspired by the same source. Dances, inner meditations, and pastorale scenes coexist with scenes of great mystery and of grandeur in this 100-minute piece. There is one textual issue concerning the words. Delius originally set the English translation of John Bernhoff. Even before the first full performance of the work conductor Thomas Beecham recognized that this translation was hopeless, and commissioned a new translation which he fit to Delius' music (presumably with the latter's consent). Since then it has become more fashionable to use Nietzsche's original German. *—Joseph Stevenson*

Recommended:

- ○ **Delius: Requiem; Mass Of Life** / Hickox (cond.), Rodgers, Rigby, Robson, Coleman-Wright, Bournemouth Sinfonietta / 1997 / Chandos 9515

Alfred Deller

b. May 31, 1912, Margate, England, **d.** Jul. 16, 1979, Bologna, Italy

Countertenor

Alfred Deller was the first renowned countertenor. As a child, Deller studied voice first with his father as a boy soprano, and when his voice changed he continued his singing as a countertenor. He joined the Canterbury Cathedral choir in 1940, where Michael Tippett heard him and invited him to London to make his debut. He came to the attention of the English public after a 1946 radio broadcast of Purcell's *Come, ye sons of art, away.* During the early years of his career, he concentrated on performing English Baroque and pre-Baroque composers such as Purcell and Dowland. In 1950 he formed the Deller Consort, a group which dedicated itself to performing early music using authentic performance practice. For many years, the group toured Europe and the Americas, bringing the music of this period to a new public. In 1964, Deller's son, Mark, joined the Deller Consort, also as a countertenor. Deller founded the Stour Music Festival in 1963 in order to have another venue for his Consort and to team with other early music specialists such as Frans Brueggen and Gustav Leonhardt. In 1960, he sang the role of Oberon in the premiere of Benjamin Britten's *A Midsummer Night's Dream.* This was the first important countertenor role in opera of the twentieth century. He repeated the role at Covent Garden Opera House, London, the following year. Other composers who wrote works specifically for Deller include Fricker, Mellers, Ridout, and Rubbra. In 1970, he was named a Commander of the Order of the British Empire. He died while on vacation in Italy.

Alfred Deller set the standard for countertenors for many years. His voice was very light with a wonderful lyric quality. He was most effective in the more contemplative pieces, but when necessary he was able to sing very florid pieces extremely well. Although he could sing the dramatic arias of Handel, he never allowed his voice to be pushed beyond its basically light sound. Deller's recordings cover the entire range of his repertoire from the lute songs of Dowland to Benjamin Britten's *A Midsummer Night's Dream* with many stops along the way. Without Alfred Deller, the international recognition of countertenor voice might not have come as quickly as it did. *—Richard LeSueur*

Recommended:

- ○ **HMV Recordings, 1949–54** / Deller, etc. / 1995 / EMI 65501
- ○ **The English Madrigal School** / Deller, Deller Consort / 1994 / Vanguard 2533
- ○ **Dowland: Lute Songs** / Deller, Spencer, North, Consort of Six / HM 290244/45
- ○ **Deller's Choice** / Deller, Leonhardt / 2003 / Vanguard 1250
- ○ **O Ravishing Delight: Airs Anglais** / Deller / HM 190215
- ○ **Shakespeare Songs** / Deller, Dupre, Deller Consort / HM 195202

Norman Dello Joio

b. Jan. 24, 1913, New York, NY

Composer

First active as a professional musician in 1927, composer Norman Dello Joio remained a prominent figure on the American landscape at the turn of the next century. A delicate understanding of musical craft as well as an honest, accessible musical language have earned him many critical successes and the gratitude of countless audiences, though at times he has been rejected by the musical establishment (thinking him to be too accessible to be taken as a serious composer).

Dello Joio's father and godfather were both skilled organists who took it in hand to train the boy on the instrument. At fourteen, Dello Joio's skill had developed enough to earn him a position at the Star of the Sea Church in New York, where constant exposure to traditional Catholic liturgical music made a lasting impression on the young musician. After attending All Hallow's Institute from 1926 to 1930 and the College of the City of New York from 1932 to 1934 Dello Joio sought more serious musical training at the Institute of Musical Art (1936) and at the Juilliard School (1939–41). Brief studies with Hindemith in 1941 (at Tanglewood and Yale University) were vital in shaping Dello Joio's compositional outlook.

Throughout his long career Dello Joio held numerous faculty appointments (including positions at Sarah Lawrence College, the Mannes College of Music, and Boston University) and was the recipient of many scholarly honors (including a Pulitzer Prize in 1957 for his string orchestra work *Meditations on Ecclesiastes* and two Guggenheim fellowships).

Encouraged by Hindemith to shape his compositional identity to suit those influences which compelled him in the most natural way, Dello Joio developed a musical language which effectively synthesizes the worlds of Italian opera, liturgical music, and jazz. While he is sometimes charged with being overly theatrical in his musical gestures, Dello Joio's music never resorts to garishness or overindulgence (as does the music of a great many other "accessible" composers), and it seems likely that a good number of his pieces (such as the *Meditations* or the second version of the opera *The Triumph of St. Joan,* 1959) will continue to occupy a place in the repertoire.*—Blair Johnston*

Overview of Works

Although Norman Dello Joio trained as an organist, he realized as a graduate student at Juilliard that his true calling was that of a composer. He studied under Wagenaar at Juilliard and Hindemith at Tanglewood, the latter advising him that "Your music is lyrical by nature, don't ever forget that." It was a lesson that Dello Joio took to mean he didn't have to sacrifice to a system. In the late 1940s and 1950s, Dello Joio was recognized as one of the foremost composers in America. His music was harmonically tonal, melodically lyrical, syncopatedly rhythmic, and extravagantly colorful. He has written an enormous amount of music, including three operas, eight ballets, 45 choral works, more than 30 orchestral works, 25 songs, 20 chamber works, ten works for band, nine television scores, and many works for solo piano. Among his best-known works are those associated with his opera *The Triumph of St. Joan* (1959), including *The Triumph of St. Joan Symphony* (1952); his many works on New York subjects, including *New York Profiles* (1949); and his sacred oratorio *The Lamentation of Saul* for baritone and full orchestra (1970).

His most popular music was written for the television series *Air Power* (1957). —*James Leonard*

Recommended:

- ○ **Music for Martha Graham Vol. 3** / Chivzhel (cond.) / 1994 / Koch International Classics 7167
- ○ **Dello Joio: Complete Works for Piano Vol. 1** / Torok / 1999 / Albany 344
- ○ **Dello Joio** / Slatkin, Whitney (conds.), Louisville Orch. / 2003 / First Edition 19

Nikolai Demidenko

b. Jul. 1, 1955, Anisimovo, Russia

Pianist

Nikolai Demidenko is a celebrated piano virtuoso, considered a leading exponent of the Russian school of playing. His blend of technical brilliance and musical vision have earned him consistent raves since he first emerged on the international scene in the mid-1980s, and he has become a musical fixture in his adopted home of Great Britain, where he gained citizenship in 1995.

Demidenko began playing before the age of five, learning on his grandfather's old, beaten-up piano. By the age of six, he was a student of Anna Kantor (Evgeny Kissin's teacher) at the Gnessin School of Music. An obstinate student who disliked scales and technique, Demidenko still made swift progress, and he eventually entered the Moscow Conservatory. There, he studied with Dmitri Bashkirov, whom Demidenko credits with fostering his more individual qualities as a player, as well as ironing out the remaining wrinkles in his technique. Reaching the finals of both the 1976 Montreal competition and the 1978 Tchaikovsky competition in Moscow (where he played through an acute case of the flu) served as a final springboard to professional recognition.

A 1985 tour with the Moscow Radio Symphony Orchestra introduced Demidenko to the West, and in particular Great Britain, where he would become a resident in 1990. While teaching piano at the University of Surrey, Demidenko has steadily built an international career of the highest caliber, playing concertos with many of Europe's greatest orchestras and conductors, and playing a landmark series of recitals in London's Wigmore Hall. His recordings of Medtner, Mussorgsky, and Busoni have been particularly well-received, and he has established himself as a leading interpreter of Liszt and Chopin. Demidenko has also ventured into earlier composers, such as Bach, Mozart, and Scarlatti, playing with a degree of rhythmic freedom (rubato) that cuts against the grain of studied performance practice; Demidenko feels that it is an essential ingredient of their music. —*Allen Schrott*

Recommended:

- ○ **Live at Wigmore Hall** / Demidenko / 1998 / Hyperion 22024
- ○ **Bach-Busoni: Transcriptions Vol. 2** / Demidenko / 2002 / Hyperion 67324
- ○ **Prokofiev: Concertos 2 & 3** / Lazarev (cond.), Demidenko, London PO / 1996 / Hyperion 66858
- ○ **Medtner: Concerto 2; Concerto 3** / Maksymiuk (cond.), Demidenko, BBC Scottish SO / 1992 / Hyperion 66580

Jörg Demus

b. Dec. 2, 1928, St. Pölten, Austria

Pianist, Fortepianist

Jörg Demus is a highly regarded pianist and one of the finest of accompanists. He is noted for combining a basically Romantic sound and line with an interest in historic keyboard interpretation and early model pianos.

He entered the Vienna Academy of Music at the age of 11, where he studied piano and conducting, graduating in 1945. He continued to study conducting with Josef Krips and Hans Swarowsky, while also taking composition classes. He made his debut as a pianist at the age of 14, while still a student at the Conservatory.

From 1951–53, he was a pupil of Yves Nat in Paris. In 1953, he attended master classes with Gieseking in Saarbrücken, and studied interpretation further with Wilhelm Kempff, Arturo Benedetti Michelangeli, and Edwin Fischer.

He made his debut as a mature artist in Vienna in 1953. In 1956, he won the Busoni Prize of the International Competition for Pianists. He maintained a notable solo career, especially noted for personal interpretations of Bach and flexible, colorful renditions of Debussy. He also was well regarded for the main line of German piano music from Mozart to Schumann, and for his performances of the piano music of César Franck. He was a recipient of the Beethoven Ring and the Mozart Medal of Vienna.

He was a sensitive accompanist, and worked with singers of the highest caliber, including Elisabeth Schwarzkopf and Dietrich Fischer-Diskau. His version of Schubert's *Winterreise*, with Fischer-Dieskau, is perhaps the most critically acclaimed of all recordings of this great song cycle.

He also accompanied violinists (Josef Suk, for instance) and cellists (Antonio Janigro). He sometimes appears in piano duet and two-piano concerts with Paul Badura-Skoda, who shares Demus' interest in older keyboard instruments. Demus acquired several notable examples of early instruments, including harpsichords and pianos by Broadwood, Clements, and Conrad Graf, and has recorded appropriate music on them.

He has also authored several essays, a book on interpretation, and, as co-author with Badura-Skoda, an analysis of the Beethoven piano sonatas. —*Joseph Stevenson*

Recommended:

- ○ **Fraz Schubert: Winterreise** / Fischer-Dieskau, Demus / DG 447421
- ○ **Mozart: Concertos 8, 23 & 26** / Demus, Aureum Collegium / 1995 / RCA 77417
- ○ **Beethoven: Sonatas for Cello & Piano** / Janigro, Demus / 2003 / Vanguard 1218
- ○ **Demus Plays Debussy, Chopin & Schubert** / Demus / Astoria 21005/6

Edison Vassilievich Denisov

b. Apr. 6, 1929, Tomsk, Siberia, Russia, **d.** Nov. 24, 1996, Paris, France

Composer

Edison Vasilyevich Denisov was one of the leading composers who emerged in the Soviet Union after the death of Stalin and used avant-garde techniques in their music despite the disapproval of the Communist Party. His father was an electrical engineer in Tomsk, and named his son Edison in honor of the American inventor and because the name is an anagram of Denisov (omitting the final "v"). Edison was interested in mathematics, music, and painting. He taught himself to play a number of folk instruments, and from 1946 to 1950 studied piano at Tomsk Music College. At the same time he was a student of mathematics and mechanics at Tomsk University (1946–51).

Then he decided to pursue musical studies, traveling to Moscow to enter the Conservatory there and remaining until 1956. His piano teacher was Vladimir Belov and his composition instructor was Vissarion Shebalin. He also studied orchestration with Nikolai Rakov and musical analysis with Viktor Zuckerman. He became a faculty member of the Conservatory in 1960 and over the years taught orchestration, analysis of musical forms, and composition. His early music shows the beginning of his lifelong interest in using Russian folk materials.

During the early 1960s he made a thorough study of the major composers of the twentieth century, including the officially disfavored Stravinsky, Schoenberg, Webern, Berg, Nono, and Stockhausen, plus Lutosławski and Bartók. Denisov's major work that consolidated this study and demonstrated that there was an interest in avant-garde music in the U.S.S.R. was *The Sun of the Incas*, premiered in Leningrad in 1964 and soon played in Western Europe by Bruno Maderna and Pierre Boulez.

In the 1960s Denisov often used rigorous serial procedures, and often tightly restricted formal ideas, such as the one reflected in the title of his *Crescendo e diminuendo* for harpsichord and 12 strings (1965). During the following year he had a tendency to write music in larger forms, often in the form of concertos. Many of these works were composed for Western performers, such as saxophonist Jean-Marie Londeix, oboist Heinz Holliger, clarinetist Eduard Brunner, and flutist Aurèle Nicolet. One Soviet performer who did champion Denisov's work was the Latvian violinist Gidon Kremer, and he even premiered Denisov's *Violin Concerto* in Milan, rather than in the Soviet Union.

During this decade Denisov started using techniques other than the 12-tone system, including aleatory (chance) techniques, electronic music, new playing techniques, and microtones. His music became less rigidly systematic. In his mature music (generally that written from 1980 onward) he usually employed various techniques freely. Russian folk music made a reappearance in this music, but often used in heterophonic textures.

The late Soviet policy of perestroika allowed Denisov to cultivate close ties with the West and employ avant-garde techniques with more freedom. In 1990 he became head of the Moscow Association of Contemporary Music. In 1991, at the invitation of Pierre Boulez, he went to work at IRCAM, the French experimental music institute. —*Joseph Stevenson*

Overview of Works (1951–1995)

Russian composer Edison Denisov was one of the more prominent composers of the post-Shostakovich generation. Trained first as a mathematician, Denisov's music is a unique combination of the most advanced international compositional procedures of his time fused with Russian folk and liturgical melodies. While utilizing serial, aleatoric, and tape methods of composition, Denisov's music is essentially lyrical. As he wrote, "Beauty is a principal factor in my work. This means not only beautiful sound, which, naturally, has nothing to do with outward prettiness, but beauty here means beautiful ideas as understood by mathematicians, or by Bach and Webern." Denisov's earliest published music was in the populist Soviet style in the opera *Ivan-soldat* (1959) and the oratorio *Siberian Soil* (1961). But with the delicately scored and intensely lyrical *Le soleil des Incas* (The Sun of the Incas) (1964) and the song cycle *Italian Songs* (1964) on texts by Blok, Denisov found his own style as a composer. And while his music continued to incorporate other influences (he was the director of the Experimental Studio of Electronic Music in Moscow from 1968–72), melody remained of paramount importance to him. Even in his later large-scale orchestral works, such as *Peinture* (Painting) (1970), *Violin Concerto for Gidon Kremer* (1977), and his symphony (1988), with their manifold contrapuntal complexities are quintessentially lyrical in conception and execution. *—James Leonard*

Recommended:

○ **Denisov: Painting; Sonata for saxophone; etc.** / Otaka (cond.), DeLangle, Kelangle, Buckland, Delangle, BBC National Orch. Wales / 1994 / Bis 665

○ **Denisov: Concerto for 2 Violas & Harpsichord; Chamber Music; etc.** / Markiz (cond.), Imai, DeMan, Vahle, Nieuw Sinfonietta Amsterdam / 1991 / Bis 518

○ **Denisov: Colin et Chloe; Cello Concerto; etc.** / Monighetti, etc. / Melodiya 1000107

○ **Denisov: Ode; Clarinet Quintet; Clarinet Concerto** / Kakhidze (cond.), Levin, Brunner, Sadlo, Bavarian RSO / 1994 / Col Legno 31864

○ **Denisov: Choral Works** / Aastvorova (dir.), New Moscow Choir / HM 35272

○ **Denisov: Symphonie** / Barenboim (cond.), Paris Orch. / Erato 45600

○ **Denisov: Complete Piano Works** / Armengaud / Mandala 4888

○ **Denisov: Piano Concerto; Peinture** / Hauschild (cond.), Philipp, Berlin RSO, Leipzig RSO / 1996 / Berlin Classics 0092602

Natalie Dessay

b. Apr. 19, 1965, Lyon, France

Soprano

French coloratura soprano Natalie Dessay emerged on the international scene in the 1990s. A graduate of the Bordeaux Conservatoire, she took first prize in the Premier Prix de Concourse (First Prize of the Competition) in the France-Telecom Les Voix Nouvelles Competition, and then entered the Paris Opéra's training program for talented young singers, the Ecole d'Art Lyric (School of Lyric Art). There she sang Elisa in a production of Mozart's *Il Rè Pastore*.

After winning the International Mozart Competition of the Vienna State Opera in 1991, she received invitations for concert and recital appearances, most notably an all-Mozart recital on the stage of La Scala in Milan. She also made a recital recording with EMI Classics of Mozart arias that was an extraordinary success.

Quickly engaged by major opera houses around the world, she sang Blondchen in *Die Entführung aus dem Serail*, Madame Herz in *Der Schauspieldirektor*, *Zaïde* (the title role at the Opéra de Lyon and the Paris Opéra-Bastille), Adele (*Die Fledermaus* in Geneva), and Zerbinetta (*Ariadne auf Naxos* in Lyon and at the Bastille).

In 1992, Dessay debuted as Olympia in Offenbach's *Tales of Hoffmann*, and in 1993, she sang at the opening of the New Lyon Opéra. In the same year she joined the roster of the Vienna Staatsoper, with a triumphant performance as Blondchen. She sang there in acclaimed production of *Tales of Hoffmann* (again as Olympia) with Plácido Domingo, and as Sophie in Strauss' *Der Rosenkavalier* opposite Anne Sofie von Otter.

Another Strauss opera was the vehicle for her debut at the Metropolitan Opera in New York in 1994, where she sang Fiakermilli in *Arabella*. In that year, she also added to her credits the Queen of the Night (Mozart's *Magic Flute*) in the Aix-en-Provence Festival, and the title role of Delibes' *Lakmé* at the Opéra-Comique in Paris.

Dessay enlarged the scope of her repertory in 1996, singing Strauss' rarely heard *Die Schweigsame Frau* (The Silent Woman) on her home stage in Vienna, Stravinsky's *Nightingale* at the Châtelet under Boulez, and Ophelia in Thomas' *Hamlet* at the Geneva Opera. Since then she has added Berg's *Lulu*, Offenbach's *Orphée aux Enfers*, *La Sonnambula*, *Lucia di Lammermoor*, Massenet's *Manon*, and Susanna in *Le nozze di Figaro* to her repertory.

Her recital album, *Vocalises*, with Michael Schonwandt conducting the Berlin Symphony Orchestra, won a Diapason d'Or award and a Classique d'Or RTL in 1998. EMI's recording of *Lakmé* with Michel Plasson conducting and Dessay in the title role won the award for French Recording of the Year at the Victoires dé la Musique Classique. Other releases include Offenbach's *Orphée* and a Mozart aria disc on Virgin.*—Joseph Stevenson*

Recommended:

○ **Mozart Heroines** / Langree (cond.), Dessay, Age of Enlightenment / 2000 / Virgin 45447

○ **French Opera Arias** / Lanceron, Fournillier (conds.), Dessay, Burles, Monte Carlo PO / 1996 / EMI 56159

○ **Donizetti: Lucie de Lammermoor** / Pido (cond.), Dessay, Alagna, Cavallier, Tezier, Lyon National Opera Orch. & Chorus / 2002 / Virgin 45528

○ **Airs d'opéras français** / Plasson (cond.), Reiss, Dessay, Gotkovski, Kotlarski, Orchestre National du Capitol / 2003 / Virgin 45610

Emmy Destinn

b. Feb. 26, 1878, Prague, Bohemia (Czech Rep.), **d.** Jan. 28, 1930, Ceské Budejovice, Czechoslovakia

Soprano

Czech soprano Emmy Destinn's family name was Kittl, but she chose her stage name by adapting that of her voice teacher Marie Lowe-Destinn. In her later career, she used only the Czech form of that name, Destinnova. Her first musical studies were on the violin which she first played in a public concert at age eight. At 14, she started to study voice and at the age of 20 she made her debut at Berlin as Santuzza in *Cavalleria Rusticana*. She was immediately given a five-year contract with the Berlin Imperial Opera. In 1901, she sang Senta in Wagner's *Fliegende Holländer* to great acclaim, which led to her London debut as Donna Anna in Mozart's *Don Giovanni*. In London, she also sang *Aida* and *Madama Butterfly*. In 1904 at Berlin, she sang in the world premiere of Leoncavallo's *Der Roland von Berlin*. During this period, she also sang in Vienna, Prague, Hamburg, Leipzig, Dresden, and Paris. At London in 1908, she created the title role in *Tess* by Erlanger. That same year, she came to the Metropolitan Opera House in New York, making her debut as Aida. It was there that she created Minnie in Puccini's *La Fanciulla del West* with Caruso and Toscanini. She returned to her homeland during World War I and worked for national independence, and at one point she was interned at her home for her activities. In 1919, she returned to the Metropolitan Opera for two seasons. It is said that Destinn could sing over 80 operas on a moment's notice and at one Metropolitan Opera performance when a colleague was ailing, she sang the off-stage Priestess as well as Aida in the same performance. In 1926, she gave her final stage performances. She lived out her life in Straz, Bohemia, and occasionally gave concerts, primarily benefit performances.

Destinn had a beautiful, rich soprano voice with an extensive range. It was a very expressive voice with complete command of the dynamic range. The voice recorded very well and she recorded over 200 items. Her complete recordings have been issued on CD (Ultraphon 11 2136-2 600) with many titles being recorded several times during her long recorded career. Her 1908 recording of *Carmen* with Karl Jorn (Marston CDA 52022) was one of the earliest complete opera recordings and is sung in German. It gives a wonderful example of her vocalism and her ability to create a character. Among the best recorded of her discs are the Victors which include arias from *Madama Butterfly*, *Aida*, *La Gioconda*, and *Trovatore* (Romophone 81002-2). Of her earliest recordings, the Act 4 duet from *Les Huguenots* with Karl Jorn is especially impressive. Besides *Carmen*, in 1908, Destinn also recorded a complete *Faust* by Gounod. This recording was also sung in German with Karl Jorn as Faust. Emmy Destinn was one of the greatest sopranos of the first quarter of the twentieth century, and we are fortunate that her voice recorded so well. *—Richard LeSueur*

Recommended:

○ **Emmy Destinn** / Seidler-Winkler (cond.), Destinn, Jorn, Duchene / 2003 / Nimbus 7910

○ **Emmy Destin** / Destinn, etc. / Pearl 9172

Detroit Symphony Orchestra

f. 1914, Detroit, MI

Ensemble

Like the city of Detroit itself, the Detroit Symphony Orchestra has had to deal with many difficulties, from disintegrating venues to financial crises. But through all its trials and tribulations, the DSO has maintained a consistently high level of musicianship and technical skill, directly representative of the many distinguished conductors who have directed the group. The DSO was founded in 1914 by ten young society women who each contributed $100 to the enterprise and secured $10 commitments from 100 other people. The ladies hired Weston Gales to conduct, and the DSO played its first concert on February 26, 1914. Gales' name is not much remembered in Detroit; the orchestra blossomed with the appointment of the Russian pianist Ossip Gabrilowitsch as the music director in 1918. Gabrilowitsch encouraged the construction of Orchestra Hall, which was immediately hailed for its fine acoustics. He also raised the DSO's profile nationally and internationally through concertizing and (especially) radio broadcasts. With Gabrilowitsch conducting and the famed pianist Artur Schnabel playing, the DSO took part in the world's first radio broadcast of a symphonic concert in 1922; later, the DSO was featured on the nationally broadcast Ford Symphony Hour. Unfortunately, two years after Gabrilowitsch died in 1937, Orchestra Hall was closed due to lack of funds to maintain it. The orchestra went through a difficult stretch, during which it was disbanded twice, until the 1951 hiring of French conductor Paul Paray. Paray's mastery of French repertoire brought international attention to the DSO; during his tenure, some claimed the world's best French orchestra was actually in Detroit. He was succeeded by the distinguished musician Sixten Ehrling, but then the orchestra went through another down period in the 1970s. Antal Dorati, the fine Czech conductor, was brought in to lead in 1977, but financial problems crippled the orchestra. These problems continued through 1987, when the orchestra's cumulative deficits reached $8 million; its endowment was only $14 million. The musicians stopped work for 12 weeks, claiming that both management and current music director Gunther Herbig were inept. Finally, both sides made concessions; Herbig was dismissed, and replaced with the esteemed Estonian conductor Neeme Järvi, while the orchestra's musicians accepted a substantial pay cut. Meanwhile, a group called Save Orchestra Hall had staved off numerous attempts by the city to demolish the now-decrepit structure, and managed to raise enough funds to restore it to its former glory. In 1989, the DSO moved back in. With Järvi's creative, stimulating direction drawing in the ticket buyers, and the glorious old-new hall proving an eminently suitable recording venue, the DSO took steps towards financial rejuvenation. Thankfully, the DSO never lost its artistic distinction; those who expect Detroit to be incapable of producing a distinguished orchestra are always surprised by the DSO's precise playing, tonal beauty, and ability to convey emotion. The DSO recorded for Chandos with Järvi and is currently heard nationally on General Motors' nationally broadcast Mark of Excellence radio series.

In 2003, the DSO successfully opened the Max M. Fischer Music Center, which includes the modernized Orchestra Hall, a second performance hall, and an education center, even as Järvi announced his departure at the end of the 2004–2005 season. —*Andrew Lindemann Malone*

Recommended:

- ○ **Paul Paray Conducts Dances of Death** / Paray (cond.), DSO / 1994 / Mercury 434336
- ○ **Stravinsky: The Firebird** / Dorati (cond.), DSO / 1984 / London 410109
- ○ **Ives: Symphonies 1 & 2** / Järvi (cond.), DSO / 2002 / Chandos 10031
- ○ **Copland: Symphony 3; Harris: Symphony 3** / Jarvi (cond.), DSO / 1996 / Chandos 9474
- ○ **Paray Conducts Chabrier** / Paray (cond.), DSO / 1991 / Mercury 434303
- ○ **Paray Conducts Ibert & Ravel** / Paray (cond.), DSO / 1990 / Mercury 432003
- ○ **Paray Conducts Saint-Saëns & Paray** / Paray (cond.), DSO / 1991 / Mercury 432719

Giuseppe di Stefano

b. Jul. 24, 1921, Motta Sant'Anastasia, Italy
Tenor

Giuseppe di Stefano began to study voice as he trained for the priesthood in a Jesuit seminary in Milan; his teachers included Luigi Montesanto and Mariano Stabile. Mobilized into the Fascist army at the age of 19, di Stefano helped make ends meet by singing popular music under the pseudonym of "Nino Florio." Deciding he'd had enough of service under Mussolini, di Stefano deserted to neutral Switzerland in 1943. Though di Stefano was interned as a refugee, he made his way singing on Swiss radio broadcasts, succeeding in building a small following. At war's end di Stefano returned to Italy and began his singing career in earnest, debuting as Chevalier des Grieux in Massenet's *Manon* at a performance held in Reggio Emilia on April 20, 1946.

Word spread like wildfire throughout Italy about di Stefano's talent, and he made his La Scala debut less than a year later, repeating his role as des Grieux. Di Stefano's reputation was further assisted with a series of recordings undertaken at this time in which he sang Neapolitan and other kinds of light Italian songs. Some of these early di Stefano recordings are yet regarded as the finest in this genre. The Metropolitan Opera of New York soon became interested, and di Stefano made his bow at the Met in *Rigoletto* on February 25, 1948.

For many opera lovers, the name of Giuseppe di Stefano is inextricably linked with that of legendary soprano Maria Callas. Di Stefano first appeared with Callas in a production of *La traviata* given at São Paulo on September 9, 1951. Afterward he appeared frequently alongside Callas on stage and in recordings, the most celebrated of the latter being a 1953 EMI of *Tosca*, regarded by many in the operatic fold as the finest recorded *Tosca* in existence. Clearly there was some compatibility between Callas and di Stefano; both emphasizing emotional, powerful singing colored with sensual warmth. With Callas, di Stefano recorded a total of ten complete operas. Di Stefano also partnered Leontyne Price in a celebrated *Tosca* led by Herbert von Karajan for London/Decca in 1961.

As in the case of Callas, problems with di Stefano's voice began to surface early on. In the late 1950s, di Stefano began to take on heavy roles, such as Calaf in *Turandot*, wreaking havoc on his clear and light tenor voice. By the early 1960s, di Stefano was unable to sing a true pianissimo, resorting instead to shouting, aspirating, and breaking registers. Nonetheless, di Stefano maintained a full schedule of engagements throughout the 1960s and into the 1970s. In 1973–74, di Stefano and Callas embarked on an ill-advised world concert tour. The end result, unfortunately, was that the public got to hear what pitiable wrecks these two great singers had made of their voices. This disastrous tour spelled a sad end to both their professional careers.

However, di Stefano has since returned to the stage to sing minor roles on occasion, the last recorded instance being in Rome in 1992. While the efforts of his later singing has injured the reputation of di Stefano in some quarters, there's no denying that he was one of the finest tenor voices to emerge in the wake of World War II. —*Uncle Dave Lewis*

Recommended:

- ○ **Early Treasures** / di Stefano, Moser / Preiser 93432
- ○ **The Very Best of Giuseppe di Stefano** / di Stefano, etc. / 2003 / EMI 85087
- ○ **Puccini: Tosca** / De Sabata (cond.), Callas, di Stefano, Gobbi, Calabrese, La Scala Theater Orchestra & Chorus / 1997 / EMI 56304

David Diamond

b. Jul. 9, 1915, Rochester, NY, **d.** Jun. 13, 2005, Rochester, NY
Composer: Orchestral, Symphonic

One of the twentieth century's most venerated musicians, American composer David Diamond was born in Rochester, New York in 1915. He showed exceptional musical promise as a young boy, and at age 12 began studies at the newly formed Cleveland Institute of Music, returning to Rochester in 1930 to take lessons from Bernard Rogers at the Eastman School. A year of work with Roger Sessions (partly through the Dalcroze Institute in New York) in 1935 was followed by a two-year stay in Paris, during which time, in addition to formal studies with Nadia Boulanger, Diamond made the acquaintance of Stravinsky and Ravel (the latter having a particularly strong impact on the 21-year-old composer's musical outlook).

Recognition came early for Diamond, and by 1938 he had already been awarded the Juilliard Publication Award for his 1936 orchestral work *Psalm* and the first of three Guggenheim Fellowships. Major conductors took note of Diamond's colorful orchestral style and in 1941 his *First Symphony* was premiered by Dimitri Mitropoulos and the New York Philharmonic, launching Diamond's 60-year reign as one the country's pre-eminent symphonists. A study of Diamond's 11 symphonies is, in effect, the study of a constantly evolving compositional ethic.

Appointed Fulbright Professor at the University of Rome in 1951, Diamond remained in Italy (especially Florence, a city he came to love) until 1965, when he returned to the U.S. to take over as head of the composition department at the Manhattan School of Music. In addition to serving as vice-president of the National Institute of the Arts, Diamond was an active member of ASCAP. Diamond became professor of composition at The Juilliard School in 1973, where he taught well into the 1990s. In 1986, Diamond received the William Schuman Lifetime Achievement Award. In 1991 he was awarded the Gold Medal of the American Academy of Arts and Letters and the Edward MacDowell Gold Medal for Lifetime Achievement. Then, in 1995, he was a recipient of the National Medal of Arts in a ceremony at the White House.

Best known as a symphonist, Diamond emerged in the late 1930s as a basically diatonic composer with strong Romantic roots and a natural flair for effective structural drama. By the 1950s, however, an ever-increasing interest in chromaticism led to his adoption of some serial techniques, which he synthesized into a highly personalized musical language. Diamond's orchestral and chamber music, the backbone of his contribution to the repertory, displays a keen interest in counterpoint and a craftsmanlike command of melody that owes something to his abiding love of Ravel. During the last years of the twentieth century, the popular Adagio from the *Symphony No.11* fueled something of a renewed public interest in Diamond and his music. —*Blair Johnston*

Overview of Works

A good case can be made that the musically conservative David Diamond is the greatest symphonist among twentieth century American composers. Even his upbeat *Symphony No. 1* (1940–41) already discloses his brilliant craftsmanship, although it is the *Second* (1942–43) which garnered attention and prompted many of his admirers to tout it as his greatest symphony. The work has been called Brucknerian, but it is quite the eclectic Diamond's own, written in an epic, dark style with large first and third movements (Adagio funebre and Andante espressivo, quasi adagio, respectively); it is powerful and profoundly gripping. The somewhat Stravinskyian *Symphony No. 3* (1945) bustles with that typical Diamond energy and contrapuntal activity in the first and third movements and turns gentler and lyrical in the two alternating panels. The 15-minute *Fourth* (1945), though not programmatic, deals with issues of life and death, opening in a serene manner and closing triumphantly. The next three symphonies were not as successful, but are well-crafted works nonetheless. The *Symphony No. 8* (1960) may well be the composer's most difficult for the listener, but a rewarding one still. That said, Diamond remained a tonal composer throughout his career and this two-movement symphony is one of the composer's deeper and more unsettling creations. The *Symphony No. 11* (1989–92) demonstrated that the elderly Diamond was still capable of writing masterful, touching symphonic music. Diamond wrote many other large orchestral compositions, including a piano concerto (1949–50), cello concerto (1938), flute concerto (1984–85), and three violin concertos (1936; 1947; 1967–68). Of these last-named works, the *Violin Concerto No. 2* has probably garnered the most attention, largely because of the lovely lyrical writing in the first two movements and spirited rhythmic manner of the finale. With the 1936 ballet suite *Tom*, Diamond appears to have written music in a cowboy idiom before Copland, and though his score is uneven, it must be counted among unjustly overlooked works by American composers. His *Music for Romeo and Juliet* (1947) may not attain the dramatic levels achieved by Prokofiev and Tchaikovsky, but it is nevertheless a colorful, evocative score. Diamond also produced a large body of work for smaller orchestral ensembles, including his most popular, *Rounds* (1944), an effervescent piece in three short movements for string orchestra. *Elegy in Memory of Maurice Ravel* (1938–39) for strings and percussion, is a touching work of melancholy character. Diamond's songs, unfortunately, have largely been ignored. They include the brilliant cycles *We Two* (1964; Shakespeare), *Hebrew Melodies* (1967–68; Byron), and *The Fall* (1970; Agee). Individual songs of note include *i shall imagine life* and *If you can't* (both e.e. cummings) and *My Little Mother* (Mansfield). Diamond's ten string quartets and two piano quintets (the last from 1996) are significant works in his considerable body of chamber music. One of his most popular compositions here is the lovely *Concert Piece for Flute and Harp* (1989). *—Robert Cummings*

Recommended:

- ○ **Diamond: Chamber Music** / Notre Dame String Trio, Votapek / 1999 / Centaur 2437
- ○ **Diamond: String Quartets 2, 9 & 10** / Potomac SQ / 2002 / Albany 540
- ○ **Diamond: Symphony 3; Psalm; Kaddish** / Schwarz (cond.), Starker, Seattle SO / 2003 / Naxos 8559155
- ○ **Diamond: Symphony 1; Violin Concerto 2** / Schwarz (cond.), Talvi, Seattle SO / 2003 / Naxos 8559157
- ○ **Diamond: Chamber Music** / The Chicago Chamber Musicians / 1995 / Cedille 23

ORCHESTRAL

Elegy in Memory of Maurice Ravel (1938–1939)

Like Copland and so many other American composers of his time, Diamond traveled to Paris to study and absorb the latest artistic trends. There, in 1928, he met Maurice Ravel, a composer then at the height of his reputation. Diamond struck up a friendship with the French master that lasted until the latter's death on December 27, 1937. The *Elegy* (1937) was the young Diamond's expression of grief at this great loss.

About seven minutes in duration, the *Elegy* was originally scored for brass, harps, and percussion; Diamond also made made a version for strings and percussion. In both cases the work is permeated with darkness and tragedy, with pain and an overwhelming sense of grief. The brass version is starker, more biting, while the string adaptation is gentler in its anguished outpourings. Nonetheless, both are emotionally disconsolate in equal measure, the glacial pacing only adding to the sense of morbidity. The dark-hued ending, with its barren textures, lends a particular sense of desolation. Many, including Elliott Carter, have praised the *Elegy* as one of the finest works of its kind from the period. *—Robert Cummings*

Recommended:

- ○ **John Adams conducts American Elegies** / Adams (cond.), Orch. of St. Luke's / 1991 / Nonesuch 79249

Romeo and Juliet, incidental music (1947)

The *New Grove Dictionary* and other reference works have listed this score as dating to 1944. That, however, was the year Diamond wrote the concert piece, *Music for Shakespeare's Romeo and Juliet*, a different score upon which the later incidental music is based. The reason the composer wrote the second *Romeo and Juliet* is that actress Olivia de Havilland, and producers Dwight Wiman and Peter Glenville wanted to use Diamond's concert music for their 1951 staging of Shakespeare's tragedy, but with certain excisions not approved of by him. Diamond, however, offered to write incidental music tailored to the play, and the producers agreed.

There are many famous *Romeo and Juliet* scores, of course, particularly those by Tchaikovsky, Prokofiev, Berlioz, and Gounod. It would thus be hard to pretend that this Diamond effort, solid though it is, ranks with these. Yet its love music is attractive in its tender lyricism and light scoring, and is uncommonly warm for Diamond. If the music for Juliet and her nurse lacks the tuneful playfulness heard in the Prokofiev ballet, at least it is catchy and atmospheric here, and fully convincing. For the deaths of Romeo and Juliet, Diamond produced some of his best music, full of intensity and heartfelt tragedy.

What is remarkable about both versions of Diamond's *Romeo and Juliet* is their unabashed American flavor. This is pure Diamond, giving Shakespeare's doomed teenage lovers a New-World spirit that features less darkness and more vibrancy. *—Robert Cummings*

Recommended:

- ○ **Great American Composers Collection** / Schwarz (cond.), NY Chamber Symphony / 2002 / Delos 3708

Rounds, for string orchestra (1944)

America's multi-faceted and prolific composer Diamond composed *Rounds* in 1944, and it continues to be his most "popular" piece in much the way that Samuel Barber's early *Adagio* (likewise for strings) remains his most "popular." Diamond was born five years later than Barber, who followed Howard Hanson, Walter Piston, Virgil Thomson, and Aaron Copland by a decade or more. As they say in film circles, that generation "wrapped" in 1918 with Leonard Bernstein's birth.

For a 1983 Nonesuch recording of *Rounds* by Gerard Schwarz, the latest and most comprehensive champion of David Diamond's music, the composer wrote the following: "*Rounds for String Orchestra* was commissioned by Dimitri Mitropoulos and composed in June and July 1944, in New York City; [full scoring] was completed at Rhinebeck, New York. Almost all of the new music Mitropoulos had been performing at the time was of the 12-note school, and he was undergoing depression and doubts as to the quality of melancholia in this music.... Write me a happy work. These are distressing times, most of the difficult music I play is distressing. Make me happy." The result was this work, which *The New York Times* critic, Olin Downes, in his review of a Koussevitzky's performance with the Boston Symphony called "admirably fashioned, joyous and vernal...there is laughter in the music. And no waste notes!" The two outer Allegro movements enclose a slow movement of lyric intensity. Canonic and fugal devices of imitation control the three movements, which are played without pause. The work was first performed by Mitropoulos on November 24, 1944, with the Minneapolis [today Minnesota] Symphony, then repeated by other orchestras. Critical and public success when Koussevitzky performed it on tour encouraged further performances by major orchestras under Artur Rodzinski, George Szell, Bernstein, Fritz Reiner, Max Rudolf, Aaron Copland, and abroad as well. It remained one of his most frequently performed works. *Rounds* received a special citation by the New York Music Critics' Circle in 1945. *—Roger Dettmer*

Recommended:

- ○ **American Music for Strings** / Schwarz (cond.), Los Angeles CO / 1980 / Nonesuch 79002
- ○ **Entre Amis** / Bernardi (cond.), CBC Vancouver Orch. / 1986 / CBC 5050

SYMPHONIC

Symphony No. 4 (1945)

Diamond completed this work on November 3, 1945. Leonard Bernstein conducted the first performance with the Boston Symphony Orchestra on January 28, 1948. It is scored for quadruple winds, trumpets, and percussion, six horns, three trombones, tuba, timpani, two harps, piano, and string choir.

Diamond enjoyed a creative heyday in the 1940s, composing four symphonies and starting a fifth (not completed, however, till 1964). For Philadelphia performances of the *Fourth Symphony* in 1977, Diamond provided a lengthy analysis without reference, however, to a 1945 "program" that stated its three movements (dedicated to the memory of Mme. Natalie Koussevitzky, "Magni Nominis Umbra") symbolized "a state of uninterrupted sleep... the transition from sleep to wakefulness... and the eternal wakening to death."

In 1977 he wrote (in part), "I consider the [the Fourth] my smallest large symphony. Small in the sense that not only is it short... but form is never allowed to exceed the needs of the material. Yet materials, although of a modest nature, are expansive, [and] somewhat transcendental in the way they go beyond themselves...."

The first movement is marked Allegretto. "A sonata-form movement in alla breve [2/2] tempo. Exposition: first theme (A minor) of a tender and pastoral lyricism in two large phrases; the first half of it played by muted violins and cellos at the beginning, the second half by violins and violas without mutes, ushered in by a cortege-like accompaniment. The second theme (D minor, solo oboe) has a simple, jovial, carefree quality. Subsequent development is the largest and most extensive section, [followed by] a short recapitulation of only the first theme, and a short coda...."

Next is the Andante. "Its Adagio introduction has a chorale-like brass theme of a religious and supplicating nature. Restatement by the strings [leads to] the Exposition—a long cantilena theme in the violas, followed by a second theme whose first half is played by three clarinets, its second half by violins. [The latter part] is elaborated, bringing about a climax [after which] the second theme continues to sing itself out."

The final movement is an Allegro. "The symphony's one brioso movement combines scherzo and rondo-finale. After brass stridently proclaim the main theme, a rhythmic percussion figure intrudes itself repeatedly as the movement gains momentum—Mercurial, sometimes elfin. I chose materials of a strongly contrasting character to produce dramatic flourishes of almost theatrical evocativeness, so that what may have seemed earthbound at the start is released at the end." *—Roger Dettmer*

Recommended:

- ○ **American Masters: Harris, Thompson, Diamond** / Bernstein (cond.), New York PO / 1998 / Sony 60594
- ○ **Diamond: Symphonies 2 & 4; Concerto for Orchestra** / Schwarz (cond.), Seattle SO / 1990 / Delos 3093

Hugo Distler

b. Jun. 24, 1908, Nuremberg, Germany, **d.** Nov. 1, 1942, Berlin, Germany
Composer: Choral, Concerto

Persecuted because of his beliefs and his innovative music, Hugo Distler's life is a study in perseverance and faith. Born the illegitimate child of seamstress Helene Distler and a Stuttgart manufacturer, Distler was taken in by his grandparents after his mother married and left for America. Distler was allowed to study piano and music theory while attending the local Gymnasium, and in 1927, he entered the Leipzig Conservatory, where he studied theory and piano. Later, at the Institute for Church Music, he studied organ with Günther Ramin, organist of the famous Thomaskirche. In 1931, he took the position of organist and cantor at Jakobkirche (Church of St. James) in Lübeck. This was the beginning of 11 years of inspired composition. He was married in Lübeck in 1933 and participated in the Lübeck Singing and Playing Circle. His collection of 52 two- and three-part choral pieces for each Sunday of the year, entitled *Der Jahrkreis*, Op. 5, was published in 1933. Distler demonstrates a refreshing originality in the settings of these traditional religious and folk tunes from the Reformation and the seventeenth century. In 1934, Distler premiered his unusual composition *Totentanz* (Dance of Death) for a cappella chorus and speakers, which was inspired by the Totentanz fresco at the St. Mary's Church. In 1935, he wrote his popular *Die Weihnachtsgeschichte*, Op. 10 (The Christmas Story), an inspired and tender piece for four-part a cappella chorus and four soloists. Its rich and complex modal harmonies evoke ancient, archaic images. There are seven variations on the traditional song *Es ist ein Ros' entsprungen* (A Rose Did Spring Up From a Tender Root) that separate sections of the work. The chorus aids the narration at several points, notably on the multiply repeated (for emphasis) line "Zu Bethlehem im jüdischen Lande" (To Bethlehem in the Jewish countries). Distler was sticking his neck out simply to remind his audience that Jesus was a Jew. Criticism from the Nazis was gradually mounting for Distler's exclusive composition of religious music and his membership in the Lutheran Confessional Church, which publicly opposed the state's anti-Christian and anti-Semitic policies and actions that were supported by the fanatical, so-called German Christians' Faith Movement. In 1937, Distler was appointed a lecturer at the Württemburg Musikhochschule in Stuttgart and became leader of the Esslinger Singakademie. Distler lived his most successful years at Vaihingen in Stuttgart between 1937 and 1940. His *Mörike Chorliederbuch* was premiered in Graz by the Stuttgart Hochschule Choir. In autumn 1940, Distler was hired as a professor at the Berliner Hochschule für Musik, and in 1942 he took over the direction of the Berlin state and church choirs. Meanwhile, his music had been declared "entartete Kunst" (degenerate art) by the Nazi state. On account of air raids, his family was evacuated to Ahlbeck on the Ostsee and he remained alone in Berlin. Because of physical and psychological exhaustion, Distler ended his life by inhaling gas. Today, Distler is recognized as the foremost representative of contemporary church music. *—"Blue Gene" Tyranny*

Overview of Works (1927–1942)

Hugo Distler was a consummate German church musician: he was an organist, a restorer of organs, a director of choral ensembles, a church music director, a teacher, and not least, a composer of both vocal and organ music for the church. Although his death by suicide in 1942 prohibited him from completing what would have been his two greatest works, a *St. John Passion* and an enormous oratorio entitled *Die Welt alter*, his many motets and choruses are wonderful examples of his style. Rooted in the music of Bach and especially Schütz, Distler's music is essentially polyphonic in conception and execution, tonal but with intense chromaticism, and relentlessly rhythmic. In both his sacred and secular vocal music, he is a master at wordpainting and at getting the many meanings of his texts expressed in his music. Of his sacred choral music, Distler's best-known work is his *Totentanz* from the *Geistliche Chormusik* for chorus (1934–41). His great secular choral work, the *Mörike Chorliederbuch*, was published in three parts—one for female voices, one for male voices, and one for mixed choir (1938–39). Like Bach, Distler was known as a virtuoso organist and his works for organ, particularly the two *Partitas—Nun komm, der Heiden Heiland* (1932) and *Wachet Auf, Ruhft Uns die Stimme* (1934–35)—as well as his two *Trio Sonatas* (both 1938–39), reveal a mastery of the instrument unmatched by any German composer since Reger. *—James Leonard*

Recommended:

- ○ **Distler: Das Orgelwerk Vol. 1** / Schoof / 1995 / Thorofon 2293
- ○ **Distler: Motets** / Stegmann (cond.), Berlin Vocal Ensemble / 1994 / Cantate 58007

CHORAL

Mörike-Chorliederbuch, Op. 19 (1938–1939)

Hugo Distler's *Mörike-Chorliederbuch* (Mörike Choral Song Book) was published in three volumes in 1939 by Bärenreiter. The first book is set for mixed choir, the second for female chorus and third for male chorus. As in the previous settings of Hugo Wolf and Josef Rheinberger before him, Distler drew inspiration from the small but significant catalog of poems written by Eduard Mörike (1804–75). But Distler's music in no way resembles that of the earlier masters. Distler's mature choral composition recalls seventeenth century Baroque practice, both in its basic sound and in its manner of text painting. But the *Mörike-Chorliederbuch* is liberally spiced with mild dissonances that place it firmly in the middle twentieth century. Distler's clear, homophonic texture is practically free of chromaticism and complex counterpoint. For English-speaking listeners, once the language barrier has been breached, there is not one aspect of this work which is unenjoyable or difficult to grasp from a purely musical angle. The premiere of a selected number of pieces from the *Mörike-Chorliederbuch* was given in National Socialist Germany on June 26, 1939, and this was a rare triumph for a composer whose career was severely compromised by his status as a "degenerate artist" under the Nazis. *—Uncle Dave Lewis*

Recommended:

- ○ **Distler: Mörike-Chorliederbuch** / Stegmann (dir.), Berlin Vocal Ens. / Musicaphon 56820
- ○ **Distler: Mörike-Chorliederbuch** / Grube (dir), Berlin Arts Academy Chamber Choir / 1994 / Thorofon 2231

CONCERTO

Harpsichord Concerto, Op. 14 (1935–1936)

Hugo Distler's *Harpsichord Concerto*, Op. 14, was composed between the years 1935 and 1936. It is the second such work in his catalog, preceded in 1932 by his *Chamber Concerto for harpsichord and 11 instruments*. Add to that Distler's later piano concerto (1937) and his incidental music for the play *Barbe Bleue* (1940) and you have his entire output in terms of orchestral music. At this point in Distler's life, the Nazi hierarchy was beginning to take note of his fervent dedication to the Protestant church and the advanced nature of his harmonic style, neither of which placed him in good stead with the Nazi party. The premiere of the *Harpsichord Concerto* was given in Hamburg in 1936 with Distler as soloist and Hans Hofmann conducting. After the performance, cultural authorities within the Third Reich would not allow Bärenreiter to publish the score until the third movement was removed, as they disapproved of its sound and style. This would be one of the first steps along the path that took Distler from a promising career as a major voice among young German composers of sacred music to that of a "degenerate artist." Needless to say, the third movement was ultimately restored to the work, and as a whole, Distler's *Harpsichord Concerto*, Op. 14, is an astounding piece, rich with ideas that still sound fresh and structurally as tight as a drum. Although his so-called neo-Baroque approach may have worked most idiomatically in Distler's choral works and organ compositions, there's no denying the unique harmonic profile of Distler's music and his deft handling of the ripieno-styled accompaniment. One wonders what Distler might have achieved in orchestral music had he been spared from the scrutiny of authorities, and ultimately, his tragic fate. *—Uncle Dave Lewis*

Recommended:

- ○ **Distler: Cembalo-Konzerte** / Haselbock (cond. & hpschd.), Vienna Academy Orch. / 1999 / Thorofon 2403

Karl Ditters von Dittersdorf

b. Nov. 2, 1739, Vienna, Austria, **d.** Oct. 24, 1799, Neuhof, Bohemia
Composer: Concerto

Karl Ditters von Dittersdorf, born simply Karl Ditters, was an Austrian contemporary of Haydn and one of the most popular composers in Europe in his day. As a virtuoso violinist and prolific composer he was a favorite of various court ensembles. His popularity was said to rival that of Haydn, Gluck, and Mozart. During his sixty years of life, he composed over 120 symphonies, 45 operas, a myriad of sacred and chamber works, and completed his autobiography two days before his death. Although his music had circulated all over Europe, he never found a source of stable patronage as Haydn did, and he reportedly died in dire financial straits.

Ditters began his career as a violin virtuoso. Employed in a church orchestra at age 10 or 11, he moved on to the court orchestra of the Prince of Sachsen-Hildburghausen. There he studied composition under Giuseppe Bonno, the court composer and Kapellmeister. He also met Gluck, a fellow violinist, and Haydn. In 1761, at age 21, Ditters was appointed court violinist. Two years later, in 1763, he made his first trip abroad, traveling to Italy with Gluck and performing.

Ditters left the imperial court in 1764 after a dispute. He became Kapellmeister for the court of the Bishop of Grosswardein, in what is now Romania, and produced mostly sacred music for five years. After a dispute with Empress Maria Theresia, the Bishop disbanded his chapel, leaving Ditters unemployed. The following year, Ditters became acquainted with the Prince-Bishop of Breslau, Schaffgotsch, who appointed Ditters court composer in 1770. The court was located in the small hamlet of Johannisberg, and to persuade Ditters to remain in such an out-of-the-way locale, the prince bestowed upon him many honors and titles, including the Order of the Golden Spur and the position of Overseer of Forests and Chief Magistrate. In 1772 Ditters gained noble status and appended "von Dittersdorf" to his surname.

During his years in Johannisberg, Ditters composed numerous symphonies, chamber works, and operas. This period is considered his most creative, and for a time he was in the running to succeed Gassmann as Kapellmeister at the court of Emperor Joseph II. In the middle 1780s, several of his compositions were performed in prestigious circumstances. The imperial palace was the venue for performances of six of his twelve "Ovid" symphonies. As a symphonist Ditters gained a reputation for humor and formal inventiveness, and even today those adventurous musicians who unearth his works are likely to be delighted by those same qualities.

The year 1786 proved to be a defining one for Ditters: his comic opera, *Der Apotheker und der Doktor* (The Pharmacist and the Doctor) premiered in Vienna with overwhelming success. It soon became the most popular opera in Europe, rapidly spreading to opera houses across the continent. Riding on a wave of popularity, Ditters composed eight more comic operas over the next five years, and these *singspiele*, works with spoken dialogue and folkish elements, proved extremely influential over the next half century. Among their direct successors was Mozart's Die Zauberflöte.

In the middle 1790s, Ditters' employment with the Prince-Bishop Schaffgotsch came to an end. History is obscure about why, but the separation was caused either by the Prince's death or by court intrigues that led to Ditters' expulsion. Ditters' popularity began fading as well. Facing an impoverished future, Ditters found another patron in Baron Ignaz von Stillfried, who in 1795 installed the composer in his castle in southern Bohemia. His final years were spent editing his works and writing his autobiographical *Lebenbeschreibung* (Leipzig, 1801). *—Bruce Lundgren*

Overview of Works (ca. 1765–1797)

Born in Vienna as Carl Ditters in 1739, Dittersdorf gained the name by which he is now known through his ennoblement by the Empress Maria Theresa (1733). His working life was peripatetic, including spells in various parts of the Habsburg empire in the service of princes and archbishops. Frequent return visits to Vienna punctuate these travels, and in 1784 he participated in the famous quartet party, which included Haydn, Mozart, and the distinguished Bohemian composer Vanhal as its remaining members.

Today Dittersdorf's achievements as a composer, like those of his contemporaries, have been nearly totally overshadowed by those of Haydn and Mozart; yet at the height of his fame he was noted as one of the leading composers of German opera. Although his earliest works in the field were in the pervasive Italian opera buffa style, it was in the emerging German style (actively promoted by the Emperor Joseph II) that Dittersdorf saw his greatest success—*Der Apotheker und der Doktor* (1786). This immensely successful comic opera established a vogue for German opera in Vienna dominated by Dittersdorf until the more overtly populist style of Mozart's *Die Zauberflöte* (1791). *Doktor und Apotheker* (the name by which the opera is generally known today) was followed by 20 German operas composed between 1786 and 1798. One of Dittersdorf's major achievements was to introduce to German opera the fast-paced, multi-sectional finales of opera buffa, driven by situation rather than character, as in the instance of Mozart's operas. Arias tend to be tuneful and simpler than those in Italian opera, with less opportunity for bravura display. Topics tend to be typical of those of later eighteenth century comic opera, with trials, tribulations, and intrigue happily resolved in a denouement.

Dittersdorf also composed in most of the other popular forms of the day. His oratorios on Old Testament themes, in particular *Ester* (1773), *Isacco* (1776), and *Giobbe* (1786), were much valued in the day, particularly by Joseph II, who is reputed to have wished to offer Dittersdorf the position of court Kapellmeister after attending a performance of *Ester*. Like Haydn, whose style is often evoked, Dittersdorf composed over 100 symphonies. They are notable for the composer's use of folk-like melodies (one clear analogy with Haydn) and his propensity for descriptive titles. Notable among such works are six symphonies devoted to topics from Ovid's *Metamorphosis* (ca. 1785). In general, Dittersdorf preferred the four-movement form of the symphony established in Vienna during the early years of the genre, although he was not averse to switching the order of movements. In addition, Dittersdorf also composed a substantial body of concertos and chamber music, including a published set of six string quartets whose wit and good nature again owes something to Haydn. Dittersdorf was the author of a delightful autobiography which was republished by the Da Capo Press in 1970. *—Brian Robins*

Recommended:

- ○ **Dittersdorf: 6 Symphonies after Ovid's Metamorphoses** / Shepherd (cond.), Cantilena / 1987 / Chandos 8564/5
- ○ **Dittersdorf: String Quartets 1–3; String Quintet 1** / Kubin Qt., Hosek / 1999 / Multisonic 310477
- ○ **Dittersdorf: Viola & Double Bass Concertos** / Vajnar (cond.), Thuri, Maly, Posta / Supraphon 0951
- ○ **Dittersdorf: Oboe Concertos** / Rolla (cond.), Lencses, Franz Liszt CO / Hungaroton 32062

CONCERTO

Harp Concerto in A major

Although Karl Ditters von Dittersdorf's *Concerto for harp and orchestra in A major* is a favorite of concerto-starved harpists the world over, the fact remains that Dittersdorf never composed an original harp concerto: this most attractive work is a transcription—by Dittersdorf himself—of one of his five harpsichord concertos. If, however, one considers the tonal characteristics of the harp and the harpsichord (and at the same time ponders the origin of the word "harpsichord"), one will quickly recognize that such a transcription makes pretty good sense. In this three-movement concerto we are reminded of just why it was that Dittersdorf was considered, during his lifetime, to be one of the top-ranked composers of the day (Haydn and Mozart included): grace, charm, sophisticated wit—they all find their way into the streamlined melodic contours of the piece.

Because the orchestra used in the concerto features a pair of oboes and a pair of horns, the work is sometimes called a concerto for harp, 2 oboes, 2 horns, and string orchestra. One mustn't, however, get the idea that either the oboes or the horns are part of some solo group—the spotlight is most assuredly on the harp and the harp alone, and sometimes the wind instruments are left out of the performance altogether. The three movements are: 1. Allegro, 2. Larghetto, 3. Allegretto (Rondo). *—Blair Johnston*

Recommended:

- ○ **Great Works For Harp** / Kuentz (cond.), Zabaleta, Paul Kuentz CO / 1993 / DG 439693

Christoph von Dohnányi

b. Sep. 8, 1929, Berlin, Germany

Conductor

Christoph von Dohnányi gained renown as one of the world's most versatile conductors in the last decades of the twentieth century and beyond, earning particular distinction for his interpretations of Romantic music and that of the Second Viennese School. The grandson of the well-known Hungarian composer Ernst von Dohnányi (1877–1960), Dohnányi studied the piano in his youth. Both his personal life and his musical education were disrupted by World War II; his father and his uncle, Dietrich Bonhoeffer, were executed by the Nazis for their complicity in a plot to assassinate Adolf Hitler.

After the war, Dohnányi studied law at the University of Munich and entered the Munich Musikhochschule in 1948, taking the institution's top prize in composition and conducting within a few years. He traveled to the United States to study music with his grandfather, who had emigrated to Florida in 1949 and was the composer-in-residence at Florida State University in Tallahassee. In a rite of passage for conductors of his generation, Dohnányi also made the pilgrimage to the Tanglewood Music Center to study conducting with Leonard Bernstein.

He returned to Germany and in 1952 assumed posts at the Frankfurt Opera, then under the leadership of Georg Solti. His career continued apace with posts as Generalmusikdirektor in Lübeck (1957–63) and Kassel (1963–69), chief conductor of the Cologne Radio Symphony Orchestra (1964–69), director of the Frankfurt Opera (1968–77), and Intendent and Principal Conductor of the Hamburg State Opera (1978–84). Highlights of his career to that point include conducting the world premieres of two of Henze's operas, *Der Junge Lord* in 1965 and *Die Bassariden* in 1966. A full schedule of guest engagements included concerts with the great orchestras of Europe and operas at Covent Garden, La Scala, the Metropolitan in New York, and elsewhere.

In 1984 he assumed his most influential post, as music director of the Cleveland Orchestra. With that ensemble, Dohnányi produced a diverse, well-received body of recordings ranging from the music of Mozart and Schubert to that of Ives, Varése, and Lutosławski. He further honed and maintained the orchestra's razor-sharp sense of ensemble and infused its overall sound with a distinctive warmth. He was succeeded as music director by Franz Welser-Möst in 2002.

In 1997 Dohnányi became principal conductor of the Philharmonia Orchestra in London. He has received numerous honors, including the commander's Cross of the Republic of Austria, Germany's Commander's Cross of the Order of Merit, and the Bartók Prize of Hungary. In 2004 Dohnányi became chief conductor of the NDR Symphony in Hamburg, Germany. *—Joseph Stevenson*

Recommended:

- ○ **Mahler: Symphony 9** / Dohnányi (cond.), Cleveland Orch. / 1999 / Decca 458902
- ○ **Henze: Die Bassariden** / Dohnányi (cond.), Meyer, Paskalis, Lagger, Melchert, Vienna PO / 2003 / Orfeo 605032
- ○ **Ives & Ruggles** / Dohnányi (cond.), Morrell, Cleveland Orch. & Chorus / 1995 / London 443776
- ○ **Webern** / Dohnányi (cond.), Cleveland Orch. / 1995 / London 444593
- ○ **Dvořák: 3 Great Symphonies** / Dohnányi (cond.), Cleveland Orch. / 1996 / London 452182

Ernst von Dohnányi

b. Jul. 27, 1877, Bratislava, Slovakia, **d.** Feb. 9, 1960, New York, NY
Composer: Chamber Music, Orchestral, Concerto

Among the dominant figures in Hungarian music during the first half of the twentieth century, pianist, composer, and conductor Ernst von Dohnányi is still regarded as the most versatile musician to emerge from that country since Franz Liszt. Dohnányi was born in present-day Bratislava in 1877, where he received his earliest musical instruction (piano and the rudiments of theory) from a local church organist and friend of the family. Entering the Budapest Academy in 1894, Dohnányi studied piano with Thóman and composition with Koessler for three years before making his 1898 debut as a pianist in London (under the baton of Hans Richter). Dohnányi's astounding skills at the keyboard earned him quick recognition throughout the musical establishment, even as his early compositions began to win approval. Brahms himself organized the Vienna premiere of Dohnányi's 1895 *Piano Quintet in C minor*, Op. 1 (despite its opus, the work is not the composer's first, following some 70 earlier efforts), and in 1899 his *Piano Concerto*, Op. 5, won the Bösendorfer Prize for piano composition.

At Joachim's invitation Dohnányi served on the faculty of the Berlin Hochschule from 1905 to 1915, after which he returned to Budapest to take a more active part in his homeland's musical development. Traditionally, the majority of Hungarian musical talent left the homeland for training and careers in the more financially and culturally rewarding European careers. Hoping to curb this trend, Dohnányi committed himself to the cause of then-lesser-known Hungarian composers such as Bartók and Kodály, and, in doing so, changed the landscape of Hungarian music forever. These years were busy indeed: in addition to his own activities as a composer and as a professor of piano at the Budapest Academy, Dohnányi maintained a hectic performance schedule including over 100 annual appearances in Budapest alone!

Ousted from the Academy in 1919 by the new fascist regime, Dohnányi took to the podium, first as chief conductor for the Budapest Philharmonic Society (1919–44) and later with the New York State Symphony Orchestra as well (1925 on). His concert career slowed somewhat during the 1930s (owing to persistent illness), and he returned to the Academy as director in 1934, but when the Second World War erupted, Dohnányi chose to resign from the Academy rather than conform to its anti-Semitic demands. Dohnányi refused to dismiss members of his Budapest orchestra on racial or religious grounds, and eventually disbanded the Philharmonic to avoid such action. Frustrated by the state of affairs in his homeland during the early 1940s, he relocated to Austria in 1944 (a highly criticized move which would later make reappearance on the international music scene difficult) and, in 1949, accepted a position at Florida State College in Tallahassee. Dohnányi continued to perform and conduct on a limited basis until his death in 1960.

Although his reputation as one of the century's greatest pianists is secure, Dohnányi's fame as a composer has suffered from the whims and fancies of the twentieth century. Heavily influenced by Brahms during his youth (most noticeably in the first *Piano Quintet*), Dohnányi soon developed a style which owes more to the noble structures of German Classicism than to late Romantic or early twentieth century aesthetics (and unlike Bartók or Kodály, owes very little to eastern European folk music). While his output includes entries in virtually every genre (including three operas and two symphonies, the first very early and the second relatively late, from 1901 and 1943 respectively), it is his masterful chamber music, particularly the three string quartets and two piano quintets, which remains vital to the repertoire. *—Blair Johnston*

CHAMBER MUSIC

Serenade for violin, viola & cello in C major, Op. 10 (1902)

The *Serenade in C for violin, viola, and cello*, which took shape during the first year of the twentieth century, is widely considered to be Dohnányi's finest early chamber work. It seems unusual that it was with an essay in this underrepresented genre that Dohnányi first made his mark as a composer of chamber music, since historically examples of truly "great" string trios are few and far between. In this work, Dohnányi devised a novel reinterpretation of Classical serenade form in a work of five movements. Unlike Beethoven's *Serenade*, Op. 8, Dohnányi does not end the work with a reprise of its opening march section. Instead, this is a brilliant curtain-raiser, providing the players ample opportunity to capture the listener's attention for what is to come. There follows a contrasting Romance, in which the lyrical subject matter is equally shared amongst the ensemble. The subtlety of the scoring also permits each instrument to exploit its most sonorous register. The central movement is a Scherzo, imposing strenuous demands on the players and affording little respite from fast-moving passagework, despite the equality of instrumental dialogue. As both Mozart (in his *Divertimento in E flat (K. 563)*) and Beethoven demonstrated, no work in this form is complete without a variation movement, and although this is much the longest in Dohnányi's example, the many harmonic and thematic twists attest to the composer's imagination and craftsmanship. In a final concession to the world of Classicism, the *Serenade* ends with a movement in Rondo form. There, however, any real similarity between Dohnányi's Op. 10 and its Viennese forbears must end. With its highly charged thematic language and distinctly modernistic harmonies, the Rondo brings to a close one of the few examples of string trio to have become popular during the twentieth century. *—Michael Jameson*

Recommended:

- ○ **Chamber Music** / Domus / 2001 / Angel 61904
- ○ **Dohnányi: Serenade; ; Kodály: Serenade; etc.** / Silverstein, Hoffman, Neubauer, Lincoln Center Chamber Music Society / 1993 / Delos 3151

ORCHESTRAL

Variations on a Nursery Song, for piano & orchestra, Op. 25 (1914)

Dohnányi was one of a trilogy of fine Hungarian composers (the others are Bartók and Kodály) who emerged at about the same time. Unlike the other two, he never took a deep interest in the authentic national folk music or embraced a modernistic twentieth century idiom. He remained in a late-Romantic, post-Brahmsian mode, but composed a considerable amount of fine music in that style. Much of it has been overlooked because the dominant attitude of the twentieth century demanding unceasing "progress" in compositional techniques prompted snap judgments that such music as Dohnányi's was "reactionary." Even so, this piece retained a toehold in the repertoire because of its fine workmanship, high entertainment value, and attractive sound. Scored for piano and orchestra, it is nearly a full-fledged piano concerto in single-movement variation form. It is also a musical joke of the highest order. It begins with a lengthy and solemnly important-sounding introduction that could be from a Wagnerian drama. This mighty promise of weighty things to come halts with a drum stroke, at which point the piano enters playing, in the simplest way, the little tune known as *"Twinkle, Twinkle, Little Star."* The rest of the work is a set of variations on that tune, each one in a parody of a well-known musical style, including a delicious send-up of *The Sorcerer's Apprentice*. It ends with a joyous romp. It is similar in style to Rachmaninov's *Paganini Rhapsody*, but concerned with humor rather than romance. *—Joseph Stevenson*

Recommended:

- ○ **Tchaikovsky: Piano Concerto 1, etc.** / Dohnányi (cond.), Wild, New Philharmonia / 1988 / Chesky 13
- ○ **Dohnányi: Viel of Pierrette; Suite; Variations on a Nursery Theme** / Bamert (cond.), Shelley, BBCPO / 1999 / Chandos 9733
- ○ **Rachmaninov: Piano Concerto 2; Rhapsody on a Theme of Paganini; etc.** / Boult (cond.), Katchen, London PO / 1996 / London 448604

CONCERTO

Piano Concerto No. 1 in E minor, Op. 5 (1897–1898)

Written in 1897–98, the *Piano Concerto No. 1 in E minor*, Op. 5, of Ernst von Dohnányi is clearly the work of an extremely skilled musical epigone. Harmonically, thematically, and structurally, there is nothing in the work that the most reactionary musical conservative would have found innovative, much less radical or modern. Cast in the standard three-movement concerto form of a highly dramatic Allegro followed by a contemplative and then passionate Andante and concluded with a exciting climactic Vivace, Dohnányi does add certain small, individual touches: an Adagio maestoso introduction that contains the motive seed out of which the work's themes grow and a Cadenza con orchestra in the heart of the closing Vivace. This is not to say that the concerto is without its charms: Dohnányi's fundamentally conservative Brahmsian manner is spiced with touches of Hungarian turns of phrase and harmonic pungencies. But in an era when Strauss and Mahler were approaching atonality and Schoenberg, Berg, and Webern were about to cross over into atonality, Dohnányi's *First* sounds distinctly old-fashioned. *—James Leonard*

Recommended:

- ○ **Dohnányi: Piano Concerto 1; Ruralia Hungarica** / Bamert (cond.), Shelley, BBCPO / 2002 / Chandos 9649
- ○ **Dohnányi: Piano Concertos 1 & 2** / Glushchenko (cond.), Roscoe, BBC Scottish SO / 1993 / Hyperion 66684

Plácido Domingo

b. Jan. 21, 1941, Madrid, Spain
Tenor

Plácido Domingo's parents were both singers of zarzuela, Spain's distinctive national form of musical theater. They founded their own zarzuela troupe in Mexico, where Plácido appeared with them in child roles. He studied voice with Carlo Morelli at Mexico's National Conservatory (1955–57), and took the small role of Borsa in Verdi's *Rigoletto* with the National Opera in Mexico City in 1959. His first appearance in a leading tenor role was as Alfredo in Verdi's *La Traviata* in Monterrey, Mexico, in 1961, and he made his U.S. debut the same year as Arturo in *Lucia di Lammermoor* with the Dallas Civic Opera.

Domingo's New York debut was as Pinkerton in Puccini's *Madama Butterfly* at the New York City Opera, October 17, 1965. After a 1966 stadium performance, his debut on the Metropolitan Opera stage occurred on September 28, 1968, as Maurice de Saxe in *Adriana Lecouvreur.* His first appearances at major houses such as Milan's La Scala (1968), the Vienna State Opera (1967), and London's Covent Garden (1971) established him as one of the greatest lyric tenors of his time, and, remarkably, as a formidable dramatic tenor besides. He has a bright, forceful voice, excellent stage presence, and superb musicianship, studying his parts from full orchestral score when possible. Commanding one of the largest active repertories among his contemporaries, he is often called upon as an emergency substitute. In one memorable case he flew from Europe to San Francisco, studying his part while in the air. He was met by a limousine and changed into his costume while traveling to the opera house by police escort.

Domingo is noted for his musical interests beyond singing. He began conducting, making his debut with *La Traviata* at the New York City Opera in 1973. He conducted *La Bohème* at the Met, and commissioned the opera *Goya*, on the life of the great Spanish painter, from Gian-Carlo Menotti, appearing as the painter in the work's premiere in Washington, D.C. If he had taken up conducting as a hedge against vocal decline, the measure proved unnecessary. Little diminishment is evident in his singing; he has used the darkening of his voice to his advantage, moving further into the dramatic tenor repertoire and even taking on Wagnerian roles such as Lohengrin, Parsifal, and Tristan. He has been especially identified with Verdi's *Otello*, and appeared in the work's official 100th anniversary performance at La Scala in 1987.

For much of his career he was put forward as a rival with his near-contemporaries, the Italian tenor Luciano Pavarotti and fellow Spaniard José Carreras. When Carreras was hospitalized for leukemia in the 1980s, Pavarotti and Domingo both visited him, and the three brought to an end whatever rivalry might actually have existed. After Carreras' recovery, the three operatic stars formed an unprecedented partnership founded on their common love of soccer. They united every four years at the World Cup tournament for a monster gala concert called "The Three Tenors." The compact discs and video releases of these events then went on to become immense best sellers.

In later years Domingo appeared in concerts for Mexican earthquake relief and AIDS benefits, and has sung and conducted increasingly in zarzuela presentations, on stage and in recordings. In 1993, he founded the "Operalia" competition for young singers. He also turned to administration, becoming artistic director for the Washington Opera (1996) and the Los Angeles Opera (2000). *—Joseph Stevenson*

Recommended:

- ○ **The Essential Plácido Domingo** / Domingo, etc. / 2004 / Sony 92845
- ○ **Verdi: Otello** / Levine (cond.), Domingo, Scotto, Milnes / 1998 / RCA 7432139501
- ○ **Verdi: Don Carlo** / Giulini (cond.), Domingo, Caballé, Verrett, Milnes, Estes / 2000 / Angel 67397
- ○ **The Young Domingo** / Domingo, etc. / 1999 / RCA 63527
- ○ **Be My Love** / Domingo, etc. / DG 469631

Gaetano Donizetti

b. Nov. 29, 1797, Bergamo, Italy, **d.** Apr. 8, 1848, Bergamo, Italy

Composer: Opera

Gaetano Donizetti was among the most important composers of bel canto opera in both Italian and French in the first half of the nineteenth Century. Many of Donizetti's more than 60 operas are still part of the modern repertoire and continue to challenge singers for their musical and technical demands. Donizetti stands stylistically between Rossini and Verdi; his scenes are usually more expanded in structure than those of Rossini, but he never blurred the lines between set pieces and recitative as Verdi did in his middle-period and late works. Often compared to his contemporary, Bellini, Donizetti produced a wider variety of operas and showed a greater stylistic flexibility, even if he never quite achieved the sheer beauty of Bellini's greatest works.

Donizetti was educated in Bergamo, the town of his birth, studying with the opera composer Simon Mayr from 1806 to 1814. His youthful works include chamber operas, religious works, and some chamber music. Donizetti's first opera of note was *La Zingara*, which was premiered in Naples in 1822. He continued to work in Naples throughout the 1820's and 1830's, where he was active as both a conductor and composer.

In 1830, Donizetti finally achieved international fame with his opera *Anna Bolena*; notable for its expressive music and more extended scenes, it established Donizetti as one of the leading contemporary opera composers. The comic opera *L'elisir d'amore* (1832) and the tragic *Lucrezia Borgia* (1833) came shortly after. Donizetti's next work was *Maria Stuarda*, followed the same year by *Lucia di Lammermoor* (1835), which became an internationally recognized masterpiece. The Elizabethan tragedy *Roberto Devereux* (1837) completed his trilogy of operas that chronicle the English court from Henry VIII to Elizabeth I.

Donizetti's operas from the late 1830s were unable to match the success of *Lucia*, and when Donizetti was passed over for the directorship of the Naples Conservatory in 1840, he moved to Paris. There he composed the opera comique *La fille du Régiment* (1840), which was celebrated immediately for its charm and virtuosity. Later that year he completed *La favorite* (1840), another major contribution to the French repertoire. In 1842 Donizetti was appointed Kapellmeister of the Austrian court in Vienna, but retained his association with Paris.

Among Donizetti's last operas are *Maria di Rohan* (1843), an important historic opera, and his French tragedy *Dom Sébastian* (1843). *Caterina Cornaro* (1843) is also one of his finest works for its strong dramatic content. These late operas, although rarely performed, are serious works that set the standard for Verdi. *—Steven Coburn*

OPERA

Anna Bolena (1830)

Anna Bolena marked a turning point in the career of Gaetano Donizetti. He was already known throughout the operatic world as a successful composer of opere buffe, but his serious operas had not been accepted by the critics or the public. With *Anna Bolena*, an opera seria in two acts, Donizetti became one of Italy's foremost operatic composers, respected and loved internationally as well as at home.

The opera was composed with Donizetti's typical haste. Contracted to compose an opera for the Teatro Carcano on August 1, 1830, Donizetti didn't receive his text from Felice Romani until November 10, but the opera went into rehearsal exactly one month later and premiered on December 26 of the same year. *Anna Bolena* is the first of what are known as Donizetti's "queen" operas, all set during England's Tudor period. It was both the first opera to be written and also the first chronologically in its setting. The subsequent operas show Elizabeth I, Anne's daughter, both as a foil to Mary Queen of Scots (*Maria Stuarda*), and as an aging, jealous lover (in *Roberto Devereux*). These operas are as well known for their dramatic as for their musical demands, especially for the soprano. In each, the soprano has a fiery scene that closes the opera, after some extremely demanding music preceding the last act. Part of the success of the *Anna Bolena* premiere was due to the stellar cast, which included the soprano Giuditta Pasta as Anna and the tenor G.B. Rubini in the role of Percy.

The subject for the opera is taken from English history and concerns the fate of one of Henry VIII's many wives. Romani turned Anne Boleyn's life into a powerful drama of innocence and injustice, heroism, and love. The libretto is superior, and the text contains many dramatic and musical opportunities for the composer. Both acts are carefully structured, and each twist in the plot and each detail in the score moves the drama forward. Arias are carefully prepared; love scenes and conflict scenes are juxtaposed with scenes for chorus or for larger groups of players. And brilliant ensembles bring the main portions of the drama to closure.

The characters are thoroughly developed, particularly those of Giovanna (Jane) Seymour and Anna Bolena—rivals in love and in music. Giovanna's music is afflicted, impassioned, and sung in the lower, richer voice of the mezzo-soprano. Her character provides much of the tension and drama of the opera as she torments herself over the fate of her rival. Her love scenes with Enrico are scenes of conflict as she pleads for Anna's life and pits her will against that of the monarch's. However, Anna has the heroine's part. Contrary to the portrait of her often painted by historians, Felice Romani paints her as a noble martyr who faces her downfall with heroic fortitude and even forgiveness. Her music exudes radiant innocence and heroism.

Prison scenes were standard fare in traditional serious opera, and Romani's drama contains not one but two of them; one for Percy and Rochefort that takes place in the Tower of London, and one for the solitary Anna. They allow for a change of scene and mood, for introspection and reflection, and for a solitary character to reveal herself or himself before the audience. In between the two prison scenes is a scene devoted entirely to a somber chorus, which makes the section into a tripartite structure. Anna's subsequent music is finely spun, with light accompaniments, delicate use of timbres, declamation, and arioso vocal writing. It is a dramatic and musical showcase for the soprano, who must traverse a full range of emotions and technical demands in the course of a short text. Anna is also given a preghiera, or prayer, to sing as she faces her end heroically, forgiving the iniquity and injustice of Henry and Giovanna. *—Rita Laurance*

Synopsis:

Act One. The opera opens at Windsor Castle, in the apartments of the Queen. It is during the reign of King Enrico VIII, and Anna Bolena is his queen. Giovanna Seymour is concerned lest anyone discover that she and the King are in love, for she is aware that Anna Bolena's fate would then be in her hands. When the two lovers meet, Enrico makes veiled threats against Anna. Both lovers are tired of clandestine meetings and long to be together, but Giovanna pleads with him to have mercy on Anna. Rochefort, Anna's brother, meets Percy in the parks of Windsor Castle and is surprised that he has returned from exile. Rochefort and the entire court know that King Enrico has changed in his attitude towards Anna. Only the Queen is unaware that Henry has a new love. Percy was madly in love with Anna when they were younger and confesses that he has feelings for her still. A huge hunting party has been arranged to amuse the court. All arrive in the park where Percy and Rochefort are conversing, Anna included. When Percy begins to betray himself in front of the King, Rochefort is sure that all is lost. Percy cannot keep from becoming agitated in the Queen's presence, and thus displaying his affection for her. King Enrico, for his part, is perfectly pleased about Percy's discomfiture, for all he wants is an excuse to be rid of his cumbersome wife.

In a room of Anna's, Smeton, a servant, has entered the chamber in order to return a small portrait of the Queen which he has borrowed. He, too, is in love with Anna and reverently kisses the picture before going to replace it. He hears someone approaching and hides. It is Anna and Rochefort. Rochefort begs her to give Percy an audience, for he is dying of love for her. She finally agrees, and Percy confesses his love for Anna. She admits that the King now abhors her. But although she is deeply moved by his protestations, she urges him to flee the country and go back into exile. She is a married woman, she insists, and cannot return his love. Percy takes out his sword and is about to commit suicide when Smeton steps out of his hiding place to stop him. The melee is interrupted by the arrival of the King, who thinks that he has caught the lovers at last. Smeton protests that Anna is innocent, but the miniature of the queen falls from his coat, and he is arrested as well. As the act closes, the Queen stands accused of infidelity.

Act Two. Anna is under arrest, held in some rooms of the palace. Giovanna enters and pleads with her to save herself. She believes that the king will spare Anna if she will only confess her guilt. When Anna demands to know how she knows this, Giovanna is forced to admit that she is the lover of the king. Anna is outraged and refuses to confess. Giovanna prostrates herself before the queen and begs her forgiveness.

Anna's trial is scheduled to take place, and the council convenes to hear testimony. But her accuser is the King, and her fate is sealed. Smeton confesses to being the Queen's lover, thinking that the King will now spare her, but she is condemned. Enrico is further enraged when Percy openly declares his love for Anna. King Enrico and Giovanna again argue over the fate of Anna. He insists that justice is the province of a King, and that justice demands that Anna must die. When he tells her that she should be Queen, she rejects his offer of a kingdom and tells him that her prayers no longer bring her comfort.

The King has offered to let Percy and Rochefort go free, but they have decided to die with the Queen, out of loyalty. Anna contemplates her unhappiness and sad fate as well as her youthful love for the gallant Percy. Percy and Rochefort are brought to her, and she becomes delirious when she learns that they, too, are to die. Smeton begs her for forgiveness, and she begins to say her final prayers. Cannon shots announce the wedding of Giovanna Seymour to King Enrico. She is outraged that wedding festivities are to accompany her execution. But she prays to God to forgive the lovers' iniquity, and the curtain falls. *—Rita Laurance*

Recommended:

○ **Donizetti: Anna Bolena** / Rudel (cond.), Sills, Verrett, Plishka, Lloyd, London SO / 2000 / DG 465957

○ **Donizetti: Anna Bolena** / Gavazzeni (cond.), Callas, Simionato, Clabassi, Raimondi, La Scala Theater Orch. / 1997 / EMI 66471

○ **Donizetti: Anna Bolena** / Varviso (cond.), Souliotis, Horne, Alexander, Ghiarov, Vienna State Opera Orch. / 1997 / London 455069

Don Pasquale (1843)

Don Pasquale is one of the great masterpieces of Italian comic opera, ranking with Rossini's *Il barbiere di Siviglia* and Verdi's *Falstaff.* The premiere took place at the Théâtre Italien in Paris, on January 3, 1843. Later that spring it appeared first at the Teatro alla Scala of Milan, then at the Kärntnertortheater in Vienna, and finally at Her Majesty's Theater in London. Although Donizetti was reputed to have finished this, his 64th opera, in a mere two weeks, it was hugely successful at each of these venues and gained rapid recognition throughout Europe. It was first heard in New York City in 1846 and has enjoyed unflagging popularity worldwide ever since.

The charming libretto, which revolves around the elderly Don Pasquale's ill-fated foray into marriage with a young girl, is by Giovanni Ruffini, but is more properly considered a collaborative effort between him and the composer. Ruffini (who narrowly avoided death by escaping from an Italian prison, where he was to be put to death for "revolutionary" activities), wrote the original libretto for Donizetti in Paris, basing his story on Angelo Anelli's earlier libretto for Stefano Pavesi's opera, *Ser Mercantonio.* However, Donizetti (who often wrote his own comic libretti) made such substantial changes to the text during composition that Ruffini refused to sign his name to the finished product. As a result, the authorship of the libretto was for some years in question.

The score to *Don Pasquale* is often described as Mozartean, and while its affect is clearly of the nineteenth, rather than eighteenth, century, it does recall the earlier master's ability to create vivid characterizations within a taut musical framework. Donizetti also succeeds in humanizing his subjects without ever sacrificing a light-hearted spirit of comedy. Norina is an especially gratifying character, both a strong-willed comic heroine and a sympathetic lover. She is full of intelligent wit, humor, tender sensibilities, and charm. The character of Don Pasquale, the rich bachelor determined to sire his own heirs at the age of 70, offers rich food for comedy without ever sacrificing his overriding sympathy. In each case, characters' emotions are skillfully delineated by musical style and texture: dramatic declamation, patter music, expressive roulades, and tender lyricism blend seamlessly.

The second act is rightfully considered one of Donizetti's finest achievements. Still following the traditional divisions of number opera, it proceeds with such natural pacing and dramatic progression that it seems to form one through-composed gesture. It begins as a trio, as Norina and Doctor Malatesta arrive at Don Pasquale's house. Patter dialogue between the two men contrasts with the nervous melodic outpourings of Norina, who sings first in staccato notes, then in dotted rhythms, and finally in irrepressible roulades. When Ernesto enters, he is given heroic declamatory vocal lines. The conclusion of the resulting quartet is delightfully various and complex, with each character maintaining his or her particular musical identity while contributing to overall effect.

Other memorable moments from *Don Pasquale* include the scheming Dr. Malatesta's aria, "Bella siccome un angelo," which has become a lyrical centerpiece of the baritone repertory, Don Pasquale's delightful "Un foco insolito," and Norina's cavatina, "Quel guardo, il cavaliere... So anch'io la virtù magica." Throughout the score, Donizetti succeeds in matching the wit and humor of the score with musical invention. *—AMG*

Synopsis:

Act One. The opera opens in the home of Don Pasquale, a wealthy aged bachelor looking to be married. He is anxiously awaiting the arrival of his friend Dr. Malatesta, who he hopes has found him a suitable bride. He glances repeatedly at the time while muttering to himself about his irresponsible nephew. Dr. Malatesta arrives and tells Don Pasquale that he has indeed found a bride for him. She is ravishingly beautiful, innocent, and pure. When Dr. Malatesta tells him that the lady in question is his own sister, Don Pasquale resolves to be married at once. He has the doctor send for her immediately and sings a vigorous aria in which he boasts that he will soon be the father of six children. He makes plans to disinherit his disobedient nephew.

Ernesto, Don Pasquale's nephew, enters, and Don Pasquale begins to upbraid him. He is angry that Ernesto refused to marry someone whom he had picked out for him. Don Pasquale announces that he, himself, is about to be married, and that unless Ernesto does as he asks he will be turned out of the house. Ernesto is shocked at his uncle and insists that he loves only Norina, an attractive widow. Don Pasquale repeats his threats, glad that his nephew has finally gotten his due.

Scene Two opens in the rooms of Norina, who is deeply absorbed in a romantic novel. She is musing of love when she receives a letter from Ernesto, saying that he is leaving Rome. Dr. Malatesta arrives, and she hands him the letter angrily. The two had been forming a plan to fool Don Pasquale, but evidently it backfired. Dr. Malatesta calms her fears, saying that he can convince Ernesto to remain. He has a plan. He has convinced Don Pasquale to marry his sister Sofronia, but Norina will take her place, and when the two have been married by a false notary, it will be up to Norina to make Don Pasquale miserable. No harm will come to Ernesto, and in fact he will probably be allowed to marry whomever he wishes.

Act Two. Ernesto is lamenting his fate and grieving that he must part from his beloved Norina. He plans on going to foreign lands and ending his days there, never to see her again. He exits, and in comes Don Pasquale, attired in rich array. He takes a turn about the room admiring himself, thinking that he cuts quite a figure for a man of 70! Malatesta arrives with Norina, veiled demurely. Norina acts the part of an incredibly shy and frightened young girl, clinging to her "brother" Malatesta during the entire interview. She is finally persuaded to remove her veil, and Don Pasquale is struck by her beauty. He tells Malatesta that if she is willing, the two can be married at once. A notary is brought in and the terms settled. Norina, thought to be Sofronia Malatesta, is to be complete mistress of the house and owner of everything. She and Don Pasquale both sign the contract, and the notary looks around for another witness. Just then Ernesto enters, and Dr. Malatesta and Norina are horrified. They are sure that Ernesto will give away their plot, for he is still unaware of their scheming. As Ernesto looks at Norina in rage, Malatesta hastily tries to convince him in an aside that all will be well. He finally agrees to sign the wedding contract as the second witness, and the fun begins.

Norina tells Don Pasquale that he is too old to accompany her on walks, so she will retain his nephew as her companion. She orders more servants, carriages, and furniture, and she issues commands to the chef to prepare a dinner for 50 for that very evening. The fuming Don Pasquale is silenced repeatedly as his new "wife" makes demand upon demand. As the curtain closes, Malatesta is warning Norina and Ernesto not to let Don Pasquale see their love for one another.

Act Three. Don Pasquale is seated in front of a pile of bills, and the servants bustle about taking new orders from Norina. The room is buried in new dresses, hats, and garments of all kinds, and they hasten to put the room in order. Norina sweeps into the room grandly, dressed in her finest clothing, and heads for the door without even glancing at her husband. When he demands to know her plans, she replies that she is going to the theater. He begins to rage and tells her that if she returns too late, she will find the door locked. She replies very sweetly that at his age he should get his rest, but her youthfulness requires some activity. As she leaves, she drops a mysterious letter from a lover. This is the final straw for Don Pasquale, and he decides that he wants a divorce. He sends for Dr. Malatesta. While Ernesto hides, he tells all of his complaints to Malatesta, rounding off his long list of accusations against Norina with the latest: she plans to meet a lover on his own grounds. The two plan to catch Norina with her lover that evening. If she is guilty, Dr. Malatesta will be responsible for her punishment.

The final scene opens with a serenade for Ernesto and a beautiful duet for the two lovers. The two are in the garden summer house speaking of their love for one another when Dr. Malatesta and Don Pasquale enter the garden. Ernesto quietly slips into the house, and Norina/Sofronia stages a scene. While Pasquale insists that he wants a divorce, Malatesta makes him believe that it will be possible to get rid of his sister Sofronia if Ernesto is allowed to marry the widow Norina. Sofronia will not want to remain in a house with two mistresses. Don Pasquale agrees, and the ruse is revealed. At first he fumes at the three of them, but finally he relents and gives them his blessing. *—Rita Laurance*

Recommended:

○ **Donizetti: Don Pasquale** / Muti (cond.), Freni, Bruscantini, Winbergh, Fabbris, Nucci, London PO / 1984 / EMI 47068

○ **Donizetti: Don Pasquale** / Ferro (cond.), Hendricks, Bacquier, Quilico, Schirrer, Canonici, Lyon Opera Orch. / Erato 45487

L'elisir d'amore (1832)

The commission for Donizetti's *L'Elisir d'amore* came shortly after the dismal failure of Donizetti's *Ugo, Conte di Parigi* at Milan's La Scala Theatre. Eager to redeem himself with the Italian public, he delivered the completed work to the Teatro Canobbiano (also a Milanese theatre) in a mere six weeks' time. The premiere, on May 12, 1832, was a brilliant success with both critics and the public, and the first run alone lasted for 33 performances. *L'elisir* remains an important work in the repertory of major opera houses in the twenty-first century.

The work is a comedy, a melodramma giocosa in two acts, composed to a libretto by Felice Romani. Romani based his book on the libretto for Daniel Francois Auber's *Le Philtre*, which was penned by Eugène Scribe. The two productions occured less than a year apart and in fact shared some of the same performers. In reworking the story, Romani made some important additions, including Nemorino's aria, "Una furtiva lagrima," which is the most famous excerpt from the opera (aside from its inherent qualities, this aria is notable for having launched Enrico Caruso's rise to fame when he sang it to repeated ovations at La Scala in 1900). From the first discussions of the opera with Romani, through the adaptation of the original text by Scribe, to completion, work on the opera took only three weeks. With this 1832 score Donizetti achieved his first enduring success.

L'elisir is a good-natured story in which the peasant Nemorino attempts to win the heart of his love, Adina, through the injestion of a farcical magic elixir (in fact merely Bordeaux wine). The phony "medicine man," Dr. Dulcamara, and the superlatively stuffy army sergeant, Belcore (who is Nemorino's rival for Adina's love), fill out the roster. An important aspect of the opera is its fine group of characterizations, especially that of Dr. Dulcamara. This slippery salesman contrasts nicely with the tender sincerity of the two lovers. He is given typical buffo music, such as a patter song, which makes him a lively and dynamic force in the unfolding of the story.

The opening music for *L'elisir d'amore* is multi-sectional, with an Allegro introduction and a Larghetto theme and variations. It is almost like an opening Baroque sinfonia, with no relation to the content of the story to follow. Much has been written about the skill with which both librettist and composer balance the humor and rustic, bumptious nature of the story with tender sentiments and pathos. Nemorino has always been an important role for tenors. While the plot is being set up through the interactions between the other characters, Nemorino intervenes with pleas of love to his beloved Adina. His pathos filled "Adina, credemi" leads right into one of the most important ensembles of the opera, a divergent trio in which Adina and Belcore seem to side against the woeful and lovelorn Nemorino. But it is his loving heart which triumphs in the end over all the obstacles that he himself helps to put in his way. *—Rita Laurance*

Synopsis:

Act One. The opera opens in the countryside on a beautiful summer's day. Adina and her friends are sitting in front of her farmhouse, reading and conversing. The peasants are taking a break from their labors, and one of them, Nemorino, stands off to the side and gazes with desperate longing at Adina. She reads aloud from her book the story of *Tristan and Isolde*, and she tells how Isolde's indifference to Tristan was changed to passion by a magic love potion. All comment that they would like to obtain such a potion.

Sergeant Belcore arrives with his soldiers and pompously marches right up to Adina. He tells her of his love for her in a bold and self-assured manner, and he insists that she should return his love. Then he decides that he has made a good impression. Adina and her friends laugh at his confidence, but Adina offers his men some wine and hospitality. Nemorino, looking on, envies the Sergeant and his swagger. But Adina knows that Nemorino is lovelorn, and she quickly tells him to find someone else to fancy. For her heart is free, and she prefers it that way.

In the village square, trumpet sounds herald the arrival of an important personage. A magnificent carriage enters, and all marvel at its opulence. Some member of royalty must be approaching! It is Doctor Dulcamara, a rich and famous quack renowned for his miraculous potion known as a cure-all. In reality it is Bordeaux wine. He offers to sell bottles of his miracle medicine for only one scudo each, and villagers crowd about his carriage enthusiastically. Nemorino, lagging in the back of the crowd, gradually works his way up to Doctor Dulcamara and asks him whether he knows of the love potion of Queen Isolde. Dulcamara offers him a bottle of his cure-all for only one gold piece, saying that it is the same magic potion that cured the hard-hearted Isolde herself. In a comic duet, Doctor Dulcamara laughs at the foolish gullibility of Nemorino while advising him of the best way to drink his potion. He is confident that by the time the potion is supposed to have worked its magic, he will be far out of town. Nemorino on his part is sure that he has found the solution to all of his ills. He confides his love for Adina and rejoices that soon it will be requited.

Nemorino drinks the entire bottle of wine and begins singing and dancing about. He sees Adina approaching but ignores her, for he is sure that by the morrow she will be hopelessly in love with him. As he continues his capers, Adina decides that he has gone a little mad and is irritated that he now ignores her. Sergeant Belcore strides in, and Adina decides to try to make Nemorino jealous. She tells the sergeant loudly enough for Nemorino to hear that she loves him, and that they can be married. But Nemorino continues dancing and thinking of the powers of the elixir. By the next morning, Adina will be sorry. But Belcore announces that they can wed immediately. The desperate Nemorino begs Adina to wait just one more day. But Adina is now thoroughly miffed at him, and she tells Belcore to send for the notary at once. The act closes on the laments of the drunken Nemorino.

Act Two. At Adina's farmhouse a wedding feast has been prepared. All are celebrating, and Adina and Doctor Dulcamara sing a duet about a beautiful lady gondolier and her loves. Adina looks around desperately for Nemorino, who is absent. She proceeded with this ruse of a wedding only to get even with him for ignoring her, and now he is nowhere to be found. The notary arrives, and Sergeant Belcore expects to be married that instant. Adina goes off with the notary and tells the sergeant that she would like to postpone the wedding.

Meanwhile Nemorino arrives, filled with despair. Doctor Dulcamara offers him another bottle of elixir but of course wants payment. In order to obtain money to buy some more elixir, Nemorino decides to enlist in the army. He is encouraged by Sergeant Belcore, who tells him that he will be given 20 scudi immediately upon signing the contract.

After getting his money, Nemorino drinks over a quart of Doctor Dulcamara's Bordeaux wine and staggers about the village square in drunken glory. There are rumors flying that now Nemorino has become rich, through a wealthy uncle's demise, and all the girls of the village pay him respect. He is considerably more confident than he was a few hours ago and swaggers around pompously. When Adina and Dulcamara enter the square, they find Nemorino surrounded by admiring, flirting girls. Adina is enraged at his behavior, and the good doctor is quite confused at the success of his elixir. Nemorino boldly tells Adina that now she is suffering from unrequited love, just as he has had to suffer. And he leaves with the village girls to go dancing!

Doctor Dulcamara tells Adina that he sold Nemorino a bottle of the same elixir that cured Queen Isolde, and offers to sell Adina a few pints. Adina has her own plan, however, and decides to win Nemorino back with true affection. Nemorino returns to the village square, unhappy over the sorrow he has caused his beloved Adina. And Adina enters and returns his enlistment papers, telling him that he should stay at home with his friends and with those who care for him. They pour out their love for one another in a passionate duet and decide to be married. Doctor Dulcamara brings the news that Nemorino's uncle has indeed died and left him a huge fortune, and announces to all who will listen that his elixir brings wealth as well as happiness in love. As the curtain falls, Doctor Dulcamara is selling off all of his bottles of Bordeaux wine to the villagers present, and all are celebrating. *—Rita Laurance*

Recommended:

○ **Donizetti: L'Elisir D'Amore** / Viotti (cond.), Alagna, Devia, Spagnoli, Pratico / Erato 98483

○ **Donizetti: L'Elisir D'Amore** / Bonynge (cond.), Pavarotti, Sutherland, Casula, Malas / 1985 / London 414461

○ **Donizetti: L'Elisir D'Amore** / Levine (cond.), Pavarotti, Battle, Dara, Nucci, Upshaw / DG 429744

La favorita (1840)

La favorita started life in French as a work for the Parisian Théâtre de la Renaissance, titled *L'ange de Nisida*. Due to the ill-timed bankruptcy of that theater, it was never produced, but Donizetti managed to parlay the failed effort into a new work for the Paris Opéra in 1840. For this new production, the esteemed French librettist Eugène Scribe adapted Alphonse Royer and Gustave Vaëz's original libretto, shifting its focus to the touching story of Léonor de Guzman, favored mistress of

King Alphonse XI of Castille. These skillful alterations allowed Donizetti to preserve the lion's share of his original score, which contains some of the finest music of his career. The entire fourth act and most of the first three survived the transition intact; the primary changes were the composition of new arias, more suitable for the new drama as well as for the first cast at the Opéra. The premiere took place on December 2, 1840, and was an incredible triumph for both singers and composer. The work is a big grand opera in the classic French mold, with ballets, pageantry, ceremony, and large choral scenes, combining a historical and religious setting with a passionate love story. The many moods and colors of the opera are enhanced by the sheer beauty of Donizetti's melodies. The drama is powerful and moving, with full-blooded, complex characters.

The work is a tragedy built around the ill-fated love affair between the king's mistress, Léonor, and a young novice monk, Fernand, who, not knowing her true identity, betrays his vows to pursue her. Frustrated by circumstance, obligation and misunderstanding, their love is realized only at her death. Highlights from the score include the two lovers' impassioned duets from the first and last acts ("Mon idole" and "Viens, viens, je cède éperdu"), as well as Fernand's famous fourth-act aria, "Ange si pur" (better-known in its Italian version, "Spirto gentil"). On the whole, the score shows Donizetti at his most consistently inventive and resourceful.

The score was a hit at the Paris Opéra and was performed consistently until the early twentieth century. Since that time it has receded in its native France and become more widely known in its Italian translation. The use of different translations and performing editions has led to considerable corruption of Donizetti's original score and has somewhat eroded critical opinion of the work, but it has always held a place in the repertory. *—AMG*

Synopsis:

Act One. The opera takes place in fourteenth century Spain, opening at the monastery of St. James in Compostella. After a dramatic overture, the curtain rises on a group of monks proceeding through the monastery and chanting. Fernand, a novice monk, hesitates when the others enter the chapel. Balthazar, head of the order, questions him as to the cause of his unease. Fernand replies that he is madly in love and cannot go through with his monastic vows. Although she is totally unknown to him, he fell in love with a noblewoman and cannot get his mind off of her. The prior replies that perhaps all he needs is some directed prayer. He reasons with the younger monk, warning him of the evils of the outside world, but Fernand is positive that the situation is completely hopeless.

On the island of St. Leon, a group of women sing the praises of their lady, Léonor de Gussmann. It is the noblewoman Léonor whom Fernand loves. Although she is the mistress of King Alphonse of Spain, she requites his love. She and her ladies expect his arrival at any moment. When his ship docks at the port, they teasingly blindfold him and tell him to wait. Léonor arrives, and they declare their passion for one another. But when he offers to marry her, she refuses. She is still the mistress of the king, and she knows that Fernand could find a more suitable wife. She has used her influence to procure him a position in the king's army, and he will now be able to make a name for himself. She gives him a note saying that he is to open it later, for it will explain everything. Alone, Fernand reads the letter, but its contents bring him no closer to the truth. He still is unaware that she is the king's mistress. Instead, he thinks that she has refused him temporarily. It is obvious that she loves him. When he has become a great warrior she will marry him.

Act Two. The act opens on King Alphonse at the palace at Alcazar. He is happily contemplating the army's recent set of victories against the Moors, which were brought about by a young hero named Fernand. A message arrives from the Pope, and it casts a pall on his happy mood. The pope disapproves of his infatuation with Léonor de Gussmann; word has reached him that the King has set aside his lawful wife in favor of Léonor. Léonor enters and complains that all are turned against her because of her position as his mistress. While the King sings of his undying love for her, she begs him to let her go free.

Festivities begin in celebration of the recent set of Spanish victories. Don Gaspar brings the king a letter that was meant for Léonor, but that he has intercepted. It is from some unknown lover and was sent to Léonor's servant Inès. As Alphonse prepares to question her about it, Balthazar enters and breaks up the celebrations. He has brought the news that the Pope has called for King Alphonse's immediate excommunication! The Church demands that the king reject his lover and go back to his wife. Unless Alphonse complies immediately, he and all of his followers will be barred from receiving Holy Sacraments. The entire court is horrified as King Alphonse angrily refuses to renounce Léonor.

Act Three. At the palace of Alcazar, more celebrations are about to take place. They are in honor of the young hero Fernand. When Fernand enters, Alphonse tells him that he will be granted any boon that he asks, out of gratitude for his service to the throne of Spain. Fernand confesses to the king that he is deeply in love with a noblewoman and wants nothing more than to be allowed to marry her. As Léonor arrives, Fernand tells the court that it is Léonor whom he loves. The amused king grants his request, telling Léonor to be faithful to her new husband.

Léonor now feels obliged to tell Alphonse everything. She is sure that he will refuse to marry her when he finds out the truth. She gives a note to her servant, confessing to Fernand that she is the king's mistress. But Inès is again intercepted by Don Gasparo, and the note goes undelivered. All assemble for the ceremony elevating Fernand to the rank of a noble. He is made the Count of Badajou and Marquis of Montreal. He has not received Léonor's letter, so his attitude towards her is completely unchanged. He still loves her, and they go off to get married. But at the chapel, several of the king's courtiers scorn Fernand and insult him horribly. When Balthazar enters the chapel and learns that the two are married, he is scandalized. He quickly reveals to Fernand Léonor's status as the king's mistress. Fernand angrily rejects the recent honors done to him by the king and returns to the monastery. The heartbroken Léonor learns too late that Inès was arrested before she was able to deliver the letter. Fernand no longer loves her, and she is ruined.

Act Four. Monks once again chant their prayers; Fernand has entered the monastery once again. A visitor arrives to see him. Balthazar tells Fernand that it is another novice who is near death, but it is Léonor in disguise. She has come to explain herself to Fernand, although she no longer has any hopes that he will forgive her or love her again. She hears the chanting of the monks, and as she passes out, Fernand arrives at the scene. When he recognizes her, he is at first angry but is soon moved to pity by her weakness. She confesses everything, and he loves her again. But it is too late. Léonor dies in his arms, and the monks pray for her soul. Fernand contemplates the morrow, expecting to join her in heaven. *—Rita Laurance*

Recommended:

- ○ **Donizetti: La favorita** / Viotti (cond.), Vargas, Kasarova, Michaels-Moore, Piccoli, Munich Radio Orch. / 2000 / RCA 7432166229
- ○ **Donizetti: La favorita** / Ruhlmann (cond.), Lapeyrette, Opera-Comique Chorus & Orch. / 1998 / Marston 52010

La fille du régiment (1840)

La fille du régiment is a French comic opera in three acts, with a libretto by Jules de Saint-Georges and Jean Francois Bayard. It is one of the more important operas by Donizetti composed for the French stage. The work premiered at the Paris Opéra-Comique on February 11, 1840. Among the most popular of Donizetti's works, it nearly failed at its premiere due to organized hostility from other composers. Berlioz reviewed the opening night and offered damning criticisms of the score. He called the opera a pastiche of earlier works, insinuated that the music had been borrowed from another opera by another composer, Adam, and offered the blanket opinion that the entire opera lacked any new ideas whatsoever. Donizetti, he averred, was preparing a total of seven different operas for various theaters around Paris, and all in one year, so he probably had not given much thought to the music of *La fille du régiment.* He was treating the French public "cavalierly." Donizetti was quick to respond to his colleague's criticisms, and the opera eventually had a successful first run. It was performed a total of 44 times at the Opéra-Comique in 1840 and was then revived often over the rest of the century. An Italian version was prepared by Donizetti and the librettist Calisto Bassi, and was premiered at the Teatro alla Scala of Milan later that same year. Although the plot is dreadfully simple, the music sparkles and shines, and the characters of the story are sympathetic.

In *La fille du régiment,* Donizetti combined military band music and actual songs of the 21st French regiment with sentimental arias and ensembles full of elegant, graceful melody. The opera takes place around the year 1815, when the French occupied the Tyrol area; the heroine of the title, Marie, is the manager of a military canteen for the regiment., in love with a local peasant named Tonio who is suspected of being a spy. The soldiers gallantly treat her as a "daughter of the regiment." Newly established in Paris, Donizetti cannily presented the French with an opera calculated to appeal to his hosts, involving kindly French soldiers, plenty of patriotic moments, and flag-waving scenes, and, of course,*l'amour.* The soldier's chorus "Rataplan, Rataplan," in praise of the glory of victory, and the final aria, "Salut à la France," gave Parisians their chance to relive some of France's better military moments. In Marie and Sulpice's opening number, the vocal lines imitate military bugle calls and drum rolls, and the orchestration is brilliant and lively. Marie's stature as the "daughter" of the regiment is reinforced through the robustness of her music and youthful vivacity of her character. Choruses of soldiers combine with love scenes and songs based on dance rhythms to produce a lively tableaux throughout.

The work has much in common with one of Donizetti's other great comedies, *L'elisir d'amore.* Each features comic military music, a continuous flow of melody, and most of all, a sparingly but beautifully used element of pathos (consider Marie's "Il faut partir" in Act I and Tonio's "Pour me rapprocher de Marie" in Act II). Aside from an opportunity for touchingly heartfelt music, this dimension of human emotion highlights the comedy as well as making the ending seem that much happier. Donizetti also added parody to the comedy; in Marie's singing lesson, he pokes fun at overly affected vocal display and excessive sentimentality, and his combination of the ribald (for those days) regimental song with wild coloratura more associated with romantic outbursts also pokes fun at bel canto convention.

The work remains an operatic standard. During times of war, various patriotic tunes (and the uniforms of various armies) have been interpolated into the music. *—AMG*

Synopsis:

Act One. The opera takes place in the mountains of Austria. Napoleon is occupying the territory known as Tyrol, and the peasants watch from the mountains as their forces battle the French. The Countess of Berkenfeld and her retinue kneel in prayer, asking for aid for the Tyrolese. They find themselves trapped by the battle, unable to progress to the Countess' castle at Berkenfeld. When all is clear, scouts announce that the battle has ceased and that they can breathe more easily for now. There is a cottage in the clearing, and they all take refuge, undecided as to how to proceed.

Sergeant Sulpizio of Napoleon's 21st regiment enters, boasting that the French have completely routed their enemy. Maria, called the daughter of the regiment because she was found and raised by its men, also enters. The two embrace affectionately and then sing a vigorous duet about the joys of living in the army, of winning in battle, and of the credit they do their country. After they have paraded around for a bit, Sulpizio tells Maria that the time has come when she must seek a suitable husband. She replies that she already has fallen in love, with a Tyrolean man who recently saved her life. Just then, French soldiers drag in a young Tyrolean man on suspicions of spying. It is Tonio, the object of Maria's affection. Maria begins to argue with the French soldiers on his behalf, insisting that they must not mistreat him for her sake. When he breaks free from his captors, the two have a short love scene in which he promises to be hers forever. Sulpizio catches the two embracing and threatens Tonio, insisting that Maria should marry one of the French soldiers, someone more worthy of her. Tonio scoffs at Sulpizio and runs off, and Maria also flees the scene.

Sulpizio is prevented from pursuing Maria or Tonio by the arrival of the Countess of Berkenfeld. She and her servant Ortensio request safe passage back to their castle. But Sulpizio stops, for he knows of the Berkenfeld castle through the last will and testament of Maria's father. Her father was a Captain in Napoleon's army and died on the battlefield. His last request was that Maria be given to her relatives living in Berkenfeld castle, for she is half Tyrolean and the daughter of the Countess' sister. The Sergeant produces papers which prove her parentage. Maria enters, with her customary bravado, shocking the Countess with her manly behavior. The two are introduced, and Maria is informed that she has been discharged from the service. Grief-stricken at having to part with her company of comrades, she is carried off in the carriage with her aunt and servant.

Tonio now has entered the service of the French in order to be near his beloved Maria. He and the French soldiers sing the famous "Rataplan" chorus in honor of bravery in battle and embrace as comrades in arms. But when he asks their permission to marry the "daughter of the regiment," they aren't so sure that they approve. He insists that two are terribly in love, and they finally give their consent. But poor Tonio is just in time to see Maria leave. She sings a tender goodbye to him as she goes off with the Countess of Berkenfeld.

Act Two. At Berkenfeld castle, Maria is being trained in the social arts in order to become the wife of a Baron or Count. She is quite unhappy. Sulpizio, having been wounded in battle, arrives and hopes to get some rest. Maria confides that she longs only for her beloved Tonio and the rest of her friends in the army, but is told that he and all of the regiment are missing. The Countess enters the drawing room. She wishes to rehearse Maria in a song, to be sung that very evening at a social gathering, at which she will be presented with a suitor. Maria starts to sing, but the song is sickeningly pompous, and she obviously hates it. Sulpizio, in an effort to cheer her up, leads her in the boisterous military chorus of "Rataplan." The Countess tries to quell their rising spirits but eventually flees the room in distress when they begin dancing and marching about.

Maria laments that she will have nothing but dullness for the rest of her life and expresses her sadness that she will never see Tonio again. But just then, a group of soldiers arrives. It is the 21st regiment, and Tonio is among them! All crowd into the salon of the Countess of Berkenfeld and have a joyful reunion.

But the Countess returns, and announces that Maria is to marry the Duke of Crackenthorp that very day. She sends Maria to her room in tears and banishes the protesting Tonio from the house. Then she confides in Sulpizio that Maria is really her own daughter, and that it is her wish the she marry the duke. Will Sulpizio help convince Maria that it is for the best? The pre-signed nuptial contract arrives with the ducal court, headed by his mother the Duchess. And then they all await the decision of Maria. But just as she is about to agree to go through with the wedding, the regiment returns. They announce that they will not let their darling "vivandière" marry against her will. Tonio, they say, is her true love, and the two must marry at once and be true to their love for one another. The Countess is taken aback, but when Maria sides with the men, she blesses the marriage of the two lovers. Could she do otherwise? All ends in rejoicing. *—Rita Laurance*

Recommended:

- ○ **Donizetti: La Fille du régiment** / Bonynge (cond.), Pavarotti, Sutherland, Sinclair, Garrett, Covent Garden Royal Opera House Orch. / 1986 / London 414520
- ○ **Donizetti: La Fille du régiment** / Panni (cond.), Gruberova, Van der Walt, Hansen, Bunz, Munich Radio Orch. / 1995 / Nightingale 70566
- ○ **Donizetti: La Fille du régiment** / Campanella (cond.), Anderson, Kraus, Trempont, T'hezan, Paris National Opera Theater Orch. / 2002 / EMI 575260

Linda di Chamounix (1842)

Even for an opera, this libretto is unusually sappy, complete with a sweet, naive heroine, her poor but honest and proud parents, a nobleman in disguise who falls in love with aforesaid heroine, his family insisting that he marry another, a kindly village prefect, a villain who all but twirls his moustache, a sad song about a fallen woman, and of course, given all this, a mad scene for the heroine.

But the villain in *Linda de Chamounix* is unusual, despite all the trouble he causes, and despite the obligatory dramatic ensemble when Linda's parents realize his intentions are not good: he is sung by a basso buffo and is a comic figure rather than a menacing one. The contrast is drawn most strongly in the second-act duet when he makes buffo-style advances towards Linda, and she rejects them in a style right out of opera seria. It's this lightness that keeps the story from becoming completely laughable for modern listeners. For example, the heroine reacts to a request for an embrace from her beloved with a horror that would be more credible if he had asked her to embrace a venomous snake!

The opera is best known for Linda's sparkling "Ah, tardai troppo…O luce di quest'anima" from the first act, a delightful showpiece for coloratura agility and one of opera's most demanding entrance scenes. But the rest of the work has appealing melodies as well, and even despite the plot, the music for Linda's father, with its tenderness, anger, and pride, seems to be pointing the way towards the fathers that Verdi depicted so powerfully in *Luisa Miller, Rigoletto,* and *Giovanna d'Arco.*

The role of Linda di Chamounix was originally created by one of the great coloratura stars of the time, Eugenia Tadolini. Donizetti so loved her performance that he said she had turned Linda's mad scene into a dramatic vehicle superior to even that of Lucia Di Lammermoor. The premiere, on May 19, 1842, was such a success that Donizetti was called out for bows at the end of the performance a total of 17 times; the theater was packed every night of its first run, and the work received great critical praise. The success of *Linda* would eventually lead to Donizetti's appointment as Kapellmeister at the Austrian court.

For its Paris premiere (1842), *Linda di Chamounix* again benefited from a singer's star power. For his Parisian Linda, Fanny Taccinardi-Persiani, Donizetti composed an additional set piece, entitled "O luce di quest'anima," which has remained an extremely important work in the coloratura repertoire. The dual successes of its Vienna and Paris premieres guaranteed the work's popularity through the end of the nineteenth century, but its revivals declined sharply in the twentieth century. The opera now occupies a marginal place in the repertory—not quite obscure, but not on a level with the composer's more frequently performed works. *—AMG*

Synopsis:

Act One. The opera takes place in the French-Italian Alps in the eighteenth century. The villagers of Chamounix journey to Paris to work in the factories, in order to supplement the income they earn from their small farms. Linda is one of the village maidens of Chamounix. Her family is very poor, and they stand to lose their entire farm unless they can get some kind of monetary help from the Marquis di Boisfleury. But he has designs on the unsuspecting Linda. He sees her family's vulnerability and hopes to persuade her to become his mistress, in exchange for the security of her family lands. She, meanwhile, is in love with Carlo, who she thinks is a penniless painter. But he is really the Viscount de Sirval. Linda's parents decide to send her off to Paris to work in the factories, along with Pierotto, a hurdy-gurdy player, and the other silk workers of the region, to keep her from the wicked attentions of the opportunistic Marquis.

Act Two. The second act opens in Paris. Carlo has installed Linda in a luxurious apartment, and she is never in want of anything. She knows that he is really the Viscount de Sirval, but they have an entirely innocent relationship, and he acts honorably towards her always. She sends her parents money from time to time and appears in society along with the Viscount. Pierotto sees her at her apartments and decides that she must be the mistress of a very wealthy man. She reassures him that the Viscount has been truly correct in his behavior and gives him a purse of gold. The Marquis also pays Linda a visit at her new lodgings, hoping to convince her to become his mistress. But she is insulted by his brash offers and quickly sends him on his way. Carlo reveals in a soliloquy that his mother has discovered that he has been keeping Linda in a lavish apartment in town, and that she is threatening to cut off his inheritance. He must marry someone of her choosing, or she will have Linda thrown into prison as a prostitute. He is afraid to tell Linda of his plight, for the wedding preparations are already underway.

Linda's father Antonio comes to Paris. He mistakes Linda for a noblewoman and pleads with her for help in saving his farm. She is moved that he doesn't recognize her. But when she tells him who she is, and gives him the money that he needs, he assumes the worst. He curses her, and leaves her. Then Pierotto brings the news that Carlo has married someone of his mother's choosing. Linda goes completely mad, and it seems that all is lost. The faithful Pierotto takes her with him back to her home town of Chamounix. Carlo is there waiting for her there. He did not get married, and her sanity is immediately restored when he tells her that he loves her and wants to marry her. *—Rita Laurance*

Recommended:

- ○ **Donizetti: Linda di Chamounix** / Haider (cond.), Sporrong, Groop, Gruberova, Kim, Swedish RSO / 1993 / Nightingale 70561
- ○ **Donizetti: Linda di Chamounix** / Gavazzeni (cond.), Kraus, Bruson, Dara, Rinaldi / 2000 / Opera d'Oro 1269
- ○ **Donizetti: Linda di Chamounix** / Bellini (cond.), Salomaa, Devia, Canonici, Antoniozzi, Eastern Netherlands Orch. / 1995 / Arts 47151

Lucia di Lammermoor (1835; revised 1839)

From Sir Walter Scott's melodramatic novel *The Bride of Lammermoor*, librettist Salvatore Cammarano cobbled together one of the most contrived and ridiculous plots in all of opera. The opera is saved and made great by Donizetti's flood of fabulous music, which includes one of the greatest of all coloratura parts in the title role. It's got blood and thunder, great choruses, the sextet "Chi mi frena," and above all, the celebrated Mad Scene. Scott's novel had already inspired three operatic treatments by the time of this one. Cammarano had not had much work as a librettist previous to his writing of *Lucia*, but afterwards he and Donizetti became close partners. *Lucia di Lammermoor* remains one of Donizetti's most popular works.

In the latter part of 1834, Donizetti signed a contract with the Royal Theaters of Naples to compose three operas, the first of which he was to have ready by July of 1835. After a lengthy process, the premiere of *Lucia* took place on September 26 at the Teatro San Carlo of Naples. The audience gave the opera an almost ecstatic reception. They cheered each of the individual arias during the opera, and Donizetti and all of the cast were called out for repeated ovations.

The music of the opera was composed with the talents and abilities of the original cast in mind. As the lead soprano in the role of Lucia, Donizetti had chosen Fanny Tacchinardi-Persiani, who was known for her technical abilities. She created the role of Lucia during its initial run, and it was for her that Donizetti composed the incredibly difficult mad scene, which is filled with vocal pyrotechnics and fioritura. From the nineteenth to the twenty-first century, this mad scene has been a showcase for sopranos with technical agility. But it is also an eerily dramatic scene, filled with psychological overtones. Many of the tunes are taken from earlier songs in the opera and twisted in order to show Lucia's demented state of mind. The choruses and narrative flow directly into Lucia's recitative and double aria, showing us her vulnerability right before her death. And the Tomb scene for Edgardo follows, with beautiful, dramatic music. With his suicide, the lovers are joined in death.

The other famous piece from *Lucia di Lammermoor* is the sextet at the end of Act Two. This is the climax to the other two acts, and is one of the most powerful and dramatic moments of the opera. It begins with the entrance of Edgardo, as he enters the castle of the Lammermoor to find the entire Lammermoor clan gathered in honor of Lucia's wedding. The emotional conflict between the various characters ignites into an energetic ensemble piece. *—Rita Laurance*

Synopsis:

Act One. The opera takes place in Scotland, in the early eighteenth century. The backdrop of the action is a horrible feud between the Lammermoors and the Ravenswoods, who are sworn and bitter enemies. By the time the opera opens, all but the last of the Ravenswoods have been slain. The sole survivor is the heroic and gallant Sir Edgardo of Ravenswood. When his father was slain, all of his lands were confiscated by the Lammermoors, and he now lives in the ruins of a castle at Wolfscrag. As the opera opens, Lord Enrico Ashton of Lammermoor also has fallen on hard times. He reveals to his friend Raimondo that he has lost his fortune and that Sir Edgardo still haunts his steps, waiting for revenge. He has asked his sister Lucia to marry a man of his choosing, but she refuses. Raimondo tells him that she is still suffering from the loss of her mother, but Sir Enrico scoffs at the suggestion. He scornfully tells the latter that his sister has been meeting a lover in secret, and he has reason to believe that her lover is none other than his cursed enemy Edgardo. And his men have seen a stranger prowling about the grounds lately; all are convinced that it is he. Bitterly, Enrico rages that he wants nothing but to be avenged against his sister and her lover.

That evening, Lucia goes forth with her servant Elisa to meet Edgardo on the grounds of the castle. She tells Elisa a legend of a ghost that haunts the grounds. A Ravenswood man murdered his lover here, and her soul still walks the park. And one evening, her spirit came to warn Lucia of an unhappy ending to her affair with Edgardo. But Lucia sings only of her undying love for him, and she goes to meet him with a full heart. He wishes to make peace with her brother and to formally request her hand in marriage. But Lucia warns Edgardo that he is in danger and that he must not seek out Enrico. Edgardo is angered, but she persuades him to let love prevail. He tells Lucia that he must leave for France that very night on business, and that he will be gone for several months. They exchange rings and vows of fidelity, then sing a passionate love aria as the act closes.

Act Two. Several months later at the Ravenswood castle, Enrico is still plotting against his foe in an effort to ruin his sister's love affair and hurt both of them. He has arranged a marriage between Lucia and Lord Arturo Bucklaw in the hopes that the union will bring wealth into the family. In order to get Lucia to agree to such a proposal, Enrico and his Captain of the Guard Raimondo have confiscated all of the love letters Lucia and Edgardo have written to one another. They decide to make Lucia to believe that Edgardo has been unfaithful, and that he plans on marrying someone else. Enrico hands her a forged letter from Edgardo in which he breaks his engagement vows to her. But instead of being persuaded to forget her lover, Lucia faints and begins to plead for death. Then Enrico confesses his circumstances to her. He needs her to go through with the wedding, he says, for he has committed treason against the state and will surely be executed if he doesn't gain some powerful and politically influential friends. This match, he asserts, is the only thing that will save him from certain death and ruin. But Lucia hears none of his pleas for aid. Her heart is broken, and she knows no reason. While trumpets announce the arrival of the court of Lord Bucklaw, Lucia insists that death is now the only thing she wishes for. But when all assemble for the wedding feast and Lord Bucklaw signs the marriage contract, Lucia is persuaded to do likewise. Just as she does so, a stranger bursts into the room.

It is Edgardo. He confronts the assembled guests, his sword drawn, threatening a fight. He has come to claim Lucia at last, and he insists that she is his. But Enrico presents him with the marriage contract, which Lucia cannot deny she has just signed. Bitter and angry, he gives her ring to her and demands his own in return. As the curtain falls, he rushes dramatically from the room.

Act Three. The curtain opens on a Lucia who has gone completely mad. She believes herself to be with her lover Edgardo, so she walks in a world of rarefied happiness. There are guests assembled in the hall. A distraught Raimondo rushes in to inform them that Lucia has murdered Lord Arturo Bucklaw. He saw her standing over his body with a knife, completely unaware of what she had done. She is thoroughly mad, he breathes in a horrified whisper. Lucia wanders into the room, completely disheveled. She talks to Edgardo in her ravings, confessing her love and fidelity to him as she longs for death to come and claim her.

Meanwhile, Edgardo is brooding back at his castle at Wolfscrag. He thinks that Lucia has found happiness in a new love, and he too longs only for death. Villagers enter with the gossip of Lucia's madness and crime. They tell him that Lucia is dying and calling for him constantly. Overcome with love for her, he is about to go to her when a death knell announces that she too has passed away. Edgardo breaks down in mourning and finally kills himself in his misery. The opera closes in mourning and in prayer. *—Rita Laurance*

Recommended:

- ○ **Donizetti: Lucia de Lammermoor** / Serafin (cond.), Callas, Cappuccilli, Tagliavini, Elkins, London PO / 1997 / EMI 56284
- ○ **Donizetti: Lucia de Lammermoor** / French version / Pido (cond.), Dessay, Alagna, Cavallier, Tezier, Lyon National Opera Orch. / 2002 / Virgin 45528
- ○ **Donizetti: Lucia de Lammermoor** / Bonynge (cond.), Gruberova, Miles, Montague, Agache, London SO / 1992 / Teldec 72306
- ○ **Donizetti: Lucia de Lammermoor** / Pretre (cond.), Moffo, Bergonzi, Flagello, Sereni, RCA Italiana Opera Orch. / 1966 / RCA 6504
- ○ **Donizetti: Lucia de Lammermoor** / Schippers (cond.), Sills, Bennett, Cappuccilli, Bergonzi, London SO / DG 471250

Lucrezia Borgia (1833; revised 1840)

Lucrezia Borgia was the most popular of all of Donizetti's operas during the nineteenth century, for its dark subject matter and somber tone appealed powerfully to Romantic sensibilities. The premiere took place on December 26, 1833, to mixed reviews, due to a variety of problems. But the work quickly gained in popularity, and its first run lasted for 33 performances.

The composer Mercadante had been hired by the Teatro La Scala of Milan to compose the opening opera of their *Carnivale* season; he and Felice Romani worked on an opera based on the life of Sappho. But the management of the theater was in disarray, and the project failed. So Donizetti was contracted to compose a new work based on the life of Lucrezia Borgia instead. Romani remained the librettist, basing his story on the play *Lucrèce Borgia* by the French author Victor Hugo. Historians will debate the exact extent of Lucrezia's involvement in her brother's and father's crimes, but this opera is not concerned with historical fact. Lucrezia is a vengeful, cunning, ambitious multiple murderess, with only one spot of human feeling, her love for her son Gennaro, whom she had given away at birth for his own safety.

Henrriette Meric-Lalande was to be the lead soprano in the premiere. Well past her vocal prime, she nevertheless still demanded prima donna treatment and added to Donizetti's difficulties by demanding a closing bravura aria. The problem for Donizetti was dramatic: Lucrezia dies at the end, surrounded by the bodies of her victims, who include her own son. Finally Donizetti gave in to Meric-Lalande and wrote her a showcase aria; when the opera was revived in 1840, however, he took out the aria and gave Lucrezia an *arioso* solo instead, creating an ending filled with pathos and horror.

Lucrezia Borgia is truly an ensemble opera; there are 12 significant roles, and while he retained the traditional four principals, he elevated the other eight characters to nearly equal status. The grim subject is reflected in the generally dark color of the vocal writing; there are few female voices in the chorus, and among the leads, only Lucrezia is a soprano. Orsini is a contralto, and the remaining voices are tenors and basses. This emphasis on the lower vocal timbres leaves the soprano voice of Lucrezia in relief, giving her aural prominence throughout the opera and evoking the psychological dominance she wields over the other characters.

Hugo's complex drama could not be turned into a typical nineteenth century operatic structure: the individual acts do not build up to large ensemble endings, and there is no love interest save for the bond that exists between Lucrezia and Gennaro. Hugo wrote of Lucrezia that her character is one of "moral deformity purified by motherhood." She is a monster, but she wins our sympathy in the end. To portray this monster, Donizetti wrote that he wanted new effects which would make his audience shudder. Every detail in scoring serves this end: when Lucrezia appears among her victims to announce that they all have been poisoned, we are truly horrified. The somber chorus, the death throes of Gennaro and his friends, and the offstage chorus singing the service for the dead all contribute to the effect. Historians will debate the exact extent of Lucrezia's involvement in her brother's and father's crimes, but this opera is not concerned with historical fact. Lucrezia is a vengeful, cunning, ambitious multiple murderess, with only one spot of human feeling, her love for her son, whom she had given away at birth, for his own safety. *—Rita Laurance*

Synopsis:

Prologue. In sixteenth century Venice, Gennaro, Orsini, and their friends, along with Gubetta, enjoy the beautiful night. Gubetta mentions Lucrezia Borgia, and the others immediately express their hatred for her. Gennaro is bored, and he falls asleep as Orsini tells a story: after Gennaro saved his life after a battle and they swore eternal friendship, a specter appeared, telling them that they would die together and to beware Lucrezia Borgia ("Nella fatal di Rimini"). Orsini cannot shake off his forebodings ("Fede a fallaci") and they leave. Lucrezia enters, masked, and looks at Gennaro lovingly ("Tranquillo ei posa"). Gubetta returns and warns her she may be subject to insult in Venice. She sends him away and contemplates Gennaro ("Com'e bello"), praying that he will never know who she is. Alfonso and Rustighello recognize her when she takes off her mask to dry her tears, and Alfonso orders Gennaro brought to him. Lucrezia bends to kiss Gennaro ("Si voli il primo"), and he awakens. She hastily remasks, but he immediately pays court to her. He feels a strong empathy and tells her of his past ("Di pescatore ignobile"); raised by a fisherman, he was led away one day by a man who gave him weapons, a horse, and a letter from his real mother, who had to hide him and herself from her persecutors. Lucrezia weeps and urges him always to love his mother, which he assures her he does ("Ama tua madre"). The others return, and, recognizing her, denounce her for her many crimes ("Maffio Orsini, signora, son io") despite Gennaro's attempts to defend her. Finally, they tell him she is the infamous Lucrezia Borgia, and he recoils.

Act One. In Ferrara, outside Gennaro's house, Alfonso oversees Rustighello's plans to kidnap Gennaro ("Vieni, la mia vendetta"); he has no fears of repercussions ("Qualunque sia l'evento"). They leave, and the young men enter, teasing Gennaro about Lucrezia. He denies any attraction, and to prove his contempt he tears down the letter B in the name Borgia on crest of her home, leaving it as "orgia" (orgy). Rustighello enters with a group of brigands, and Astolfo comes on separately. He has been told to bring Gennaro to Lucrezia, but seeing himself outnumbered by Rustighello's forces retreats as they break down Gennaro's door. In Alfonso's place, he readies poison for Gennaro. Lucrezia enters, incensed at the insult to her name and demanding that he kill the culprit, and he sardonically agrees. Gennaro is brought in, to Lucrezia's horror, and admits his guilt. Lucrezia asks to speak to Alfonso alone, and now begs mercy, but he refuses ("Vi chiedo, o signore"), telling her he knows she is trying to protect her lover. She begs for pity and then threatens him ("Oh! A te bada"), reminding him he is her fourth husband. He warns her that in Ferrara she is in his power. Gennaro is brought back in, and Alfonso pretends to have forgiven him. Alfonso, despite Lucrezia's whispered pleas, offers him the poisoned wine, which he drinks ("Guai se ti sfugge"), and then leaves him with Lucrezia. She tells him he has been poisoned and gives him the antidote, which, despite his initial suspicion, he drinks. He leaves by a hidden exit.

Act Two. Outside Gennaro's house, Rustighello and the bandits declare that the Duke will still be avenged ("Rischiarata e la finestra"). They leave, and Orsini comes and knocks. Gennaro comes out, and Orsini asks him to stay in Ferrara and come to the party at Princess Negroni's. Gennaro says he fears for his life, but Orsini persuades him to stay ("Non sai tu di donna"). They vow to remain together until death. Rustighello and the brigands comment that he is headed into a deadly trap.

In the Negroni palace, the young men are attending a lavish banquet, most of them getting drunk. Gubetta deliberately picks a fight with Orsini ("Io ti daro, balordo"), and the women leave. Gubetta and Orsini calm down, and a servant brings another bottle of wine. Gennaro notices uneasily that Gubetta doesn't drink from this new bottle, but Orsini is unimpressed, and sings a drinking song, "Il segreto per esser felice," declaring the secret of happiness is not giving a thought to tomorrow. They hear voices chanting a lament, but they assume the women are just playing a prank, and Orsini goes on with the second verse. The lights go out and the doors are locked, and Lucrezia enters, heavily guarded. She informs them that she is avenging the insult they paid her in Venice; she has poisoned them all, and five graves are ready for them. Gennaro informs her that six are needed, and she immediately orders the guards to take the others away. He shows her the bottle of the antidote, which he kept, but she tells him there is enough only for him, and he refuses to drink it. He takes a knife from the table to kill her, and she begs him not to shed his own blood; he is a Borgia. She renews her pleas for him to drink the antidote ("M'odi, ah! m'odi"). He refuses again, and she begs him to drink for the sake of his mother. He accuses her of being his mother's persecutor, and she finally reveals she is his mother. He dies, and she cries out in grief. Alfonso, Rustighello, and some ladies enter, and Lucrezia tells them that Gennaro was not her lover, but her son, whose virtue she hoped would have been her own redemption ("Era desso il figlio mio"). She falls into the arms of one of the ladies as the opera ends. Throughout the libretto, there are very veiled hints that Gennaro is Lucrezia's son by her brother, Cesare, which is the reason for her silence throughout. *—Ann Feeney*

Recommended:

○ **Donizetti: Lucrezia Borgia** / Perlea (cond.), Antonellini, Caballe, Verrett, Flagello, RCA Italiana Opera Orch. / 1989 / RCA 6642

Maria Stuarda (1834)

Maria Stuarda, one of the so-called "Tudor operas," takes almost as many liberties with geography as it does with history. However, Donizetti knew what would and wouldn't make good theater, and fiction triumphed over history.

Both female protagonists are sharply drawn in all of their different emotional aspects, and the climax of the conflict between Elizabeth and Mary comes in a personal confrontation between the two queens. Mary loses all of her reserve in the face of Elizabeth's insults, and calls her "the bastard daughter of a harlot." This highly effective scene in the opera contributed to Donizetti's difficulties. The two prima donnas playing Mary and Elizabeth at the initial production hated one another so much that when the moment came for Del Serre, playing Mary, to insult Elizabeth, she is said to have been so convincing in her delivery that the other singer, Giuseppina Ronzi, attacked her, bit and scratched her, pulled her hair, and so physically overpowered her that she had to be carried out of the theater. Even so, the dress rehearsal was very well received, and Donizetti's music was judged superb. The climactic screamfest would have resonances down through the subsequent history of Italian opera, but soon Donizetti found his opera ensnared in political difficulties.

The history of *Maria Stuarda* is long and complicated. Although it is in the repertory today, it was performed in its original version only once during Donizetti's lifetime, and modern performances are based on scores of varying authenticity. The source of *Maria Stuarda* is the play *Maria Stuart*, by Friedrich von Schiller, translated into Italian by Andrea Maffei and subsequently put into libretto form by Giuseppe Bardari. The subject matter would turn out to be the biggest problem for Donizetti, who saw his new tragedia lyrica banned for the depiction of royalty on stage. Only by transplanting much of the music into a new libretto was Donizetti able to have the work performed. This version, under the title of *Buondelmonte* was first offered at the *Teatro San Carlo* in Naples, October 18, 1834.

The first real performance of the original *Maria Stuarda* was given at La Scala, in Milan, on December 30, 1835. It featured the famous Maria Malibran in the title role and was a political scandal because she refused to incorporate changes deemed necessary by government censors. The work was again banned, and Donizetti would never again attempt a true revival (although watered-down versions continued to be produced during his lifetime). *—AMG*

Synopsis:

Act One. Setting: England, 1567, palace of Westminster and Fotheringay Castle.

The Queen (Elizabeth I) is under pressure to marry the Dauphin of France, but she secretly harbors feelings for the Earl of Leicester. She is also unsure of how to deal with Mary, Queen of Scots, whom she has imprisoned at Fotheringay Castle, and whom many consider a threat to the throne. Meanwhile, the Earl of Leicester has received a letter from Mary, whom he once loved, asking his help in obtaining a meeting with the Queen. Confronted by Elizabeth, Leicester admits to the letter and, after enduring her jealousy, convinces her to meet with Mary.

Act Two. Leicester arrives at Fotheringay and prepares Mary for her imminent meeting with Elizabeth. He assures her of his allegiance and asks for her hand in marriage. When Elizabeth arrives, she finds Mary unpalatably proud, and accuses her of treachery (both in politics and love) and murder. Unable to bear such accusations, Mary openly insults the Queen's bloodlines ("Figlia impura di Bolena") and proclaims her innocence. Elizabeth summons her guards and threatens to have Mary put to death.

Act Three. At Westminster, Elizabeth weighs the decision to sign Mary's death warrant; Cecil urges her to sign, and Leicester pleads for clemency. Elizabeth, who until this point has been unsure of her actions, is angered by Leicester's apparent feelings for her rival and decides to sign. To make her point especially clear, she orders him to witness the execution himself. Cecil, happy at this turn of events, personally delivers the sentence to Mary. Talbot, who has always wished for reconciliation between Mary and Elizabeth, pities her and takes her confession (a Catholic rite, which, if discovered, would have been an act of treason against the Protestant sovereign). During the confession, Mary confronts—perhaps really, perhaps figuratively—the ghost of her dead husband, of whose murder she is accused. She resolves her conscience and lays the blame instead on Elizabeth. When the time of execution comes, Mary makes a final protestation, but finally resigns to her fate. Leicester watches ruefully as she is taken to die. *—Allen Schrott*

Recommended:

- ○ **Donizetti: Maria Stuarda** / Bonynge (cond.), Sutherland, Tourangeau, Pavarotti / 1990 / London 425410
- ○ **Donizetti: Maria Stuarda** / Ceccato (cond.), Sills, Farrell, Quilico, Burrows / 2001 / DG 465961

Poliuto (1838)

Verdi may be the composer with the best-known troubles with the censors of Italian theater, but this Donizetti work was actually banned by the king of Naples, even after the censors had passed it. (The depiction of the martyrdom of early Christian saints was considered inappropriate material for entertainment.) The angry composer left for Paris, where by 1840 he had produced a revision, written for the French taste, with different recitatives, a new finale for the first act, new arias and trios, and the inevitable ballet. Eugène Scribe wrote a French libretto that was closer to Corneille's original play, placing at the center of the drama the characters of the two lovers, Pauline and Poliuto. Donizetti took great pains to suit his music to the new French text; the opera was expanded from three acts into four; and the drama became both more static and more powerful. Opera houses have presented both versions since then, but the original Italian one has appeared slightly more frequently.

The first scene is one of Donizetti's most strongly atmospheric. The Christians meet secretly in a cave. As a hint of the fate that awaits them, a Roman-style march lurks under their meditative hymn, suggesting the march to the arena where they will be killed by wild animals. The subsequent meditative, sonorous prayer during which Poliuto is baptized, and which Paolina overhears, is followed by a particularly limpid melody for the deeply affected Paolina. The ensemble that ends the first act is noteworthy, beginning with a slow, suspenseful melody sung first by Severo, then by Paolina. Poliuto's sweeping melody leads the rest of the voices into the various lines of the ensemble; dramatic recitative passages conclude when Poliuto overturns the altar, and his stretta leads into the fiery final tutti section. The hushed, menacing aria and chorus of Callistene and the Roman priests in the second act is quite effective, as is the final duet of Paolina and Poliuto, in which she expresses her newfound faith in sparkling trills while he sings of the joys of Heaven in an expansive melody. The concluding ensemble, if not one of Donizetti's most original, makes a well-crafted and satisfying finale. *—Ann Feeney*

Synopsis:

Act One. Act One, "The Baptism," takes place outside a cave. A chorus of Christian worshippers comes to meet in secret ("O Dio tutelare"). As they descend into the cavern, they look forward to their inevitable deaths as martyrs. Poliuto and Nearco enter, preparing for his baptism as a Christian, and he speaks of his troubled feelings. He loves his wife dearly, but her frequent tears and words of love in her sleep make him suspect she loves another. He adds that he has confided in Callistene, who agrees with him. Nearco warns him against trusting Callistene and assures him that Paolina is a virtuous wife. Poliuto prays for peace ("D'un alma troppo fervida"), and they enter. Paolina has followed them and enters. She is afraid that Poliuto has joined the Christians, and when Nearco emerges from the cave, she questions him. He tells her it is the truth but reminds her that Poliuto's life depends upon her silence. He goes back, and she listens to the rites. She finds herself deeply moved by the prayers, particularly when they pray for their enemies ("Di quai suavi lagrime"). Poliuto and the rest return, and Nearco tells them that the proconsul Severo is not dead in battle, as had been reported, but has come to the region to kill any Christians there. Paolina is at first overjoyed that the man she loves is alive, but then despairs, as she is married to another ("Ah! Egli vive?"). In the public square the crowd sings Severo's praises, but he thinks only of Paolina ("Di tua beltade immagine"). He is distraught to learn that thinking him dead, she has married Poliuto ("Altrui porgesti").

Act Two. Act Two, "The Neophyte," opens in Felice's house. Callistene hints to Severo that Paolina was ordered to marry Poliuto. Callistene leaves, secretly intent on destroying Paolina, who had rejected him. When Severo and Paolina meet, they are both desperate with grief ("Il più lieto"), but she insists on remaining faithful to her husband. Callistene brings Poliuto into the house, and they see but do not overhear her pleas to Severo to leave, and his vows that he will never forget her ("Quest'alma è troppo debole"). All leave except Poliuto, who is furious at the apparent betrayal ("Fu macchiato l'onor mio") and swears revenge. A Christian comes in and tells him that Nearco has been arrested and taken to the Temple of Jupiter. Poliuto is overwhelmed with religious zeal and rejects his anger and wish for revenge ("Sfolgoro divino raggio"). In the temple, priests are chanting to Jupiter ("Celeste un'aura") as the people pray and Callistene vows to destroy all enemies of their religion. Nearco is brought in and ordered, under threat of torture, to reveal the name of the neophyte he inducted. He refuses, but Poliuto comes forward and declares his new faith. The priests, Severo, Callistene, and Felice call for his torture and death. Paolina prays for his safety, vowing that if the Nazzarene (Jesus) saves her husband, she herself will worship him. Poliuto is still disturbed by his feelings for Paolina, and Nearco rejoices in the future rewards that martyrdom will bring, in the ensemble "La sacrilega parola." Paolina begs for Poliuto's life, but the priests refuse, and he, thinking her a hypocrite, overturns the altar at which they were married ("Lasciami in pace morire omai"), to her despair. Severo realizes she will regard him as Poliuto's murderer, Felice tries to comfort her, and the priests call for Poliuto's punishment.

Act Three. The final act opens in a sacred grove where the crowd looks forward to the impending executions in the circus. When they leave, some priests and Callistene enter, and he tells them that other Christians have come forward to join Nearco and Poliuto in death. He urges them to keep the mob inflamed for blood ("Alimento alla fiamma"). In the prison, Poliuto is asleep, and when he awakens he sings of a dream in which he saw Paolina proven innocent. She herself enters and, weeping, pleads with him to flee ("Ah! fuggi da morte orribil contanto"), but he reassures her that he will be reborn in Heaven. She is so moved by his constancy that she declares only a true deity could inspire such courage, and she resolves to die with him. When he tries to dissuade her, she repeats his own words of confidence in their faith, and they anticipate eternal life together ("Il suon dell'arpe angeliche"), blissfully calling one another husband and wife and embracing. In the amphitheater, Severo gives Poliuto a chance to renounce Christianity and save his life, but he refuses. He orders Poliuto dragged into the circus to be killed by animals, and Paolina demands to join him. Severo and Felice are horrified, but Callistene is delighted. Severo pleads with her, begging her to relent for her father's sake, not for his own ("No, d'amor non favello gli accenti"), but she remains firm, saying she will pray for her father and for him as well. Other Christians are heard praying, declaring themselves happy to die for their faith, and Callistene and the priests pronounce curses on them. Severo is horrified to find that he worships Paolina more than his own gods, and as Paolina, Poliuto, and the Christians are led into the arena, he draws his sword to kill himself, but is stopped by the guards as the curtain falls. *—Ann Feeney*

Recommended:

- ○ **Donizetti: Poliuto** / Votto (cond.), Corelli, Bastianini, Morresi, Palma, La Scala Theater Orch. / 1997 / EMI 65448
- ○ **Donizetti: Poliuto** / Caetani (cond.), Grossmann, Carreras, Ricciarelli, Pons, Vienna SO / 1989 / CBS 44821

Roberto Devereux (Il Conte di Essex) (1837)

Robert Devereaux is one of several Donizetti operas based on stories from English history. It is also one of many settings of the story of Queen Elizabeth I and her love for Robert Dudley, Earl of Essex. Salvatore Cammarano's libretto is said to have been largely taken from Felice Romani's *Il Comte d'Essex*, which was set by the composer Saviero Mercadante in 1833; however, he also used a number of French dramatic treatments of the same story, notably those of Pierre Corneille and Francois Ancelot as source material. The plot gave Donizetti an opportunity to create another magnificently tragic heroine—a woman conflicted over her love for a man, and the knowledge that he has betrayed her both politically and by loving another woman. The course of the opera witnesses the assault of these cruel truths upon her spirit, until she finally becomes emotionally unhinged at the end.

Donizetti's project faced numerous challenges: a cholera epidemic was raging in Naples at the time, and people were afraid to go out of doors, let alone go to the theater; and in the two-year period leading up to the work's composition Donizetti had lost two children, his mother, father, and his wife, Virginia. Still, the composer honored his contract with the Teatro San Carlo, delivering the completed opera as promised—only one month after Virginia's death. The 1837 premiere was only a moderate success, and the work lay largely dormant from about 1850 until renewed interest in music of the bel canto emerged in the later twentieth century.

Even though it was not one of Donizetti's more popular operas, the score to *Robert Devereaux* contains many beautiful passages. The vocal writing for Queen Elizabeth is dramatically effective; her tortured emotions and confused rage are aptly portrayed in her brilliant coloratura roulades. Her characterization is one of the strongest elements of the opera; it even overshadows the tender love interest in the plot of *Robert Devereaux* and Sarah, Duchess of Nottingham—although Robert's execution and Sarah's bereavement are cruel sufferings, the real tragedy is the torn psyche of the lovelorn queen. Her frustrated rage is finally vented on the two Nottinghams after Robert's execution in her final aria "Qual sangue versato" (That spilled blood), as she promises to be revenged on them for having been tricked into executing her own lover. The orchestral highlights to the opera include the opening overture, which contrasts a theme based on the melody to *God Save the Queen* with the lyrical theme from Robert's cabaletta, sung while he is alone in the tower, contemplating his death. *—Rita Laurance*

Synopsis:

Act One. As the opera opens, Sarah, Duchess of Nottingham, is weeping while reading about Rosamund Clifford, the rival of Eleanor of Aquitaine in love, and the victim of her jealous wrath. She can only think of her own predicament, and tries to hide her disordered feelings from the rest of the ladies of the court. Queen Elizabeth enters with the news that she expects to receive Robert, Earl of Essex, soon. He has returned from Ireland having been accused of treason, but Elizabeth still loves him and hopes through an interview to be persuaded that he still loves her, too. Cecil, her advisor, enters with Robert's death warrant, and urges the Queen to sign it quickly. But she dismisses him.

Robert enters, and Elizabeth orders everyone else to leave. She reminds him that she once gave him a ring as a token of her love, and that all he will ever need to do to gain her pardon is to send the ring back to her as a token of his. She begins to question him closely, and he assumes that she knows that he is in love with Sarah. As he dissembles to her, she becomes enraged and decides that she will indeed sign his death warrant. But she wants to know the name of her hated rival. She exits grandly.

The Earl of Nottingham assures Robert that he will plead his cause to the Council. Cecil summons him away to decide Robert's fate. Robert goes to see Sarah. He is angry that she married while he was absent. Couldn't she have waited for his return? Didn't their love mean enough to her? But she tells him that the Queen insisted on her marriage to Nottingham. She begs him to flee for his own safety, and he realizes that she still loves him. He throws the Queen's ring on the table between them, and vows to be true to her forever. Sarah gives him a blue scarf that she has been embroidering as a farewell keepsake.

Act Two. In the Great Hall of Westminster, all are awaiting news from the council about Robert's fate. Word is brought that he has been condemned to death. Sir Walter Raleigh, who arrested him, reports that Robert was found with a blue scarf concealed next to his heart. He presents it to Elizabeth, who now has proof of Robert's infidelity. She demands that he be brought before her immediately. Nottingham enters with the death warrant, still pleading with the Queen to spare Robert's life. When Robert is led in, Elizabeth brandishes the blue scarf in front of his face. She demands to know who gave it to him. When Nottingham sees it, he recognizes it as his wife's and also becomes enraged. He moves as if to attack Robert, but is restrained by the Queen. Robert refuses to name the person who gave him the scarf and is led away to be executed the following dawn.

Act Three. The distraught Sarah is anxiously waiting for news of her lover. A servant enters with a last letter from Robert, instructing her to take the Queen her ring and to beg for mercy. But Nottingham enters and grabs the latter. He decides to have Sarah confined to her quarters. He accuses her of infidelity, but she repeatedly protests her innocence. Through the window, she sees Robert being led to the tower, but she is powerless to do anything to save him.

Robert is locked in his prison cell and his only hope for clemency from the Queen is if Sarah can get the ring to her in time. He longs to defend Sarah to her husband, and to fight him on the field of honor for his unjust accusations of her. Elizabeth anxiously awaits the hour of Robert's execution. She longs for her old love to send her the ring that she gave him, for even now she would pardon him everything. As Robert is led to the block, Sarah finally enters with the ring. She was able to break free and now tearfully confesses everything, and she begs for mercy from the angry Elizabeth. But it is too late. A cannon shot announces Robert's death. Nottingham proudly tells Elizabeth that he wanted revenge, and he is happy that he got it. Elizabeth orders the Nottinghams led away and collapses in grief. She longs only for death, and the curtain falls. *—Rita Laurance*

Recommended:

- ○ **Donizetti: Roberto Devereux** / Mackerras (cond.), Sills, Taweel, Howell, Allan, Royal PO / 2000 / DG 465964
- ○ **Donizetti: Roberto Devereux** / Domingo, etc. / Melodram 270107

Antal Dorati

b. Apr. 9, 1906, Budapest, Hungary, **d.** Nov. 13, 1988, Gerzensee, near Bern, Switzerland

Conductor

Conductor Antal Dorati was known for his crisp, rhythmically alert performances and as a highly respected ensemble builder. Both of Dorati's parents were professional musicians, and he learned to play the cello as a child. He also began composition lessons with Leó Weiner when he was just 12, completing three youthful operas before entering the National Hungarian Royal Academy of Music at 14. There, he continued to take composition with Weiner, but also from Zoltán Kodály, and piano with Béla Bartók. The works of the two latter men would become specialties in his conducting career. His first professional position, just after graduating in 1924, was as *répétiteur* at the Budapest Royal Opera House, where he soon conducted, as well. In 1928, he went to the Dresden Opera to be assistant to Fritz Busch for a year, then was appointed music director in Münster, where he stayed until 1933. Dorati then joined the conducting staff of the ballets russes de Monte Carlo. During the 1930s, in addition to his ballet russes position, Dorati began guest-conducting in Europe and America. Named music director of the American Ballet Theater in 1941, he made the most of his first opportunity to demonstrate his ability to build an orchestra, quickly establishing a professional ensemble. He did the same to revitalize the Dallas Symphony Orchestra during his 1945–1949 tenure. In 1947 Dorati became an American citizen. Each of his appointments was marked by special achievements for the conductor and orchestra together. With the Minneapolis Symphony Orchestra (1949–60), he made a number of well-regarded Mercury Living Presence recordings. When he left the BBC Symphony Orchestra in 1963 after four years, he was honored with a concert of his compositions. He then took over the Stockholm Philharmonic (1966–70). With the National Symphony Orchestra (1970–77) and the Detroit Symphony Orchestra he helped inaugurate new and renovated concert spaces, respectively. In addition, he continued to guest conduct and form close relationships with other orchestras, taking a particular interest in the refugee orchestra, the Philharmonia Hungarica. He eventually recorded all of Haydn's symphonies with that ensemble, and also recorded eight of Haydn's operas with the Lausanne Chamber Orchestra. Dorati's nearly 600 recordings and his skills brought him many prizes and honors over the years. When he retired, he was able to turn to other creative outlets, such as writing, drawing, and painting. *—Patsy Morita*

Recommended:

- ○ **Tchaikovsky: 1812 Overture, Romeo & Juliet, etc.** / Dorati (cond.), Detroit SO, National SO / 1987 / London 417742
- ○ **Delibes: Coppelia; Sylvia** / Dorati, Fistoulari (conds.), London SO, Minneapolis SO / 1992 / Mercury 434313
- ○ **American Classics** / Dorati, Zinman (conds.), Detroit SO, Baltimore SO / 1999 / London 460656
- ○ **Respighi: Ancient Dances & Airs** / Dorati (cond.), Hungarica Philharmonia / Mercury 434304
- ○ **Tchaikovsky: Complete Suites For Orchestra** / Dorati (cond.), New Philharmonia Orch. / 1996 / Philips 454253
- ○ **Bartók: Miraculous Mandarin; Divertimento; Sonata for 2 Pianos & Percussion** / Dorati (cond.), Ponse, Frid, London SO, BBCSO / 1995 / Mercury 434362
- ○ **Rachmaninoff: Concertos 2 & 3; 2 Preludes** / Dorati (cond.), Janis, London SO, Minnesota Orch. / 1991 / Mercury 432759

John Dowland

b. 1563, London [?], England, **d.** Feb. 20, 1626, London, England

Composer: Chamber Music, Vocal

Melancholy was all the rage in Elizabethan England, and John Dowland was the most stylish composer of his time. "Semper Dowland, semper dolens" was his motto, and much of his music is indeed exquisitely dolorous. Although he was a talented singer, Dowland mainly followed a dual career as a composer and lutenist. He was the period's most renowned and significant composer of lute solos, and especially ayres (also called lute songs), and a gifted writer of consort music.

Nothing is known of Dowland's youth; even his date and place of birth are uncertain. It is clear, though, that in 1580 he went to Paris in the service of the ambassador to the French court. Dowland converted to Catholicism during this time, and later claimed that this excluded him from employment at the Protestant court of Elizabeth I in 1594 (actually, the court was cutting costs and left the position unfilled for five years). In 1598, Dowland became lutenist to Christian IV of Denmark, but he was dismissed for unsatisfactory conduct in 1606. Between 1609 and 1612 he entered the service of Theophilus, Lord Howard de Walden, and finally in 1612, he was appointed one of the "musicians for the lutes" to James I of England.

Dowland managed to respect tradition while absorbing the trends he encountered on the Continent. Dominating Dowland's output is a form called the lute song or ayre. It was peculiar to English music, and was systematized somewhat by the 1597 publication of Dowland's *First Booke of Songes or Ayres.* These early songs are simple strophic settings, often in dance forms, with an almost complete absence of chromaticism. Continental influences come to the fore in such later songs as *In darkness let me dwell* (1610) and *Lasso vita mia* (1612), full of declamation, chromaticism, and dissonance.

Dowland also wrote a significant amount of instrumental music, much of it for solo lute and some for consort. There are some ninety works for solo lute; many are dances, often with highly embellished variations. Even here the Continental influence shows; such chromatic fantasies as *Forlorne Hope fancye and Farewell* are far more intense than the lute music of any other English (or, for that matter, Continental) composer of the time. Among the consort works, Dowland's *Lachrimae*, or *Seaven Teares Figured in Seaven Passionate Pavans* (1604), became one of the most celebrated compositions of the late Renaissance. *—James Reel*

CHAMBER MUSIC

Works for Lute (ca. 1590–1610)

During the course of the sixteenth century the lute became established as the "prince of instruments." It was admired for its expressive qualities, and its most renowned performers gained a prestige allowed few other musicians. Among such may be numbered the English composer and lutenist John Dowland (1563–1626), who was especially famed for his improvisations. Dowland's conversion to Catholicism almost certainly hampered his sought-after progress at the court of Elizabeth I, where he was unsuccessful in gaining a post in the 1590s. Travels in Europe followed, and in 1598 Dowland accepted an invitation to join the Danish court of Christian IV, of which he remained a highly respected member until 1606. After returning to London, he finally gained a post as lutenist at the court of James I in 1612.

With few exceptions, and in marked contrast to his songs and viol consort works, the music Dowland composed for the lute remained unpublished, although it had been his avowed intention to issue a collection of his best pieces. Notwithstanding, nearly 100 pieces are extant, their sources ranging widely throughout Europe. They form a body of works of great diversity, ranging from tiny, lighthearted trifles sometimes lasting under a minute, to large-scale—often profound—pieces that reflect Dowland's propensity for melancholy. The classic example of the latter is *Semper Dowland, Semper Dolens* (P. 9; numbers referring to Diana Poulton's catalog of Dowland's works), a superb piece whose punning title tells its own story.

One marked feature of all Dowland's lute music is the high quality of its melodic invention, an asset that allowed its composer to convert a number of pieces into lute songs. The most famous example is *Lachrimae* (P. 15), published in the *Second Book of Songes* (1600) as *Flow my teares.* Even when writing in standard dance forms of the period such as the slow, serious pavan and the lighter, swifter galliard, Dowland produced works of considerable contrast. As a great improviser, the lute also showed Dowland was a master of one of the most important technical devices in the lutenist's arsenal—the art of playing divisions. This decorative feature includes filling in scalar figures, and arpeggiations to flesh out the bare bones of a melody, and is particularly effective in slower moving pieces like pavans. Such writing can also be heard in pieces in more overtly free form, of which the most notable are four chromatic fantasias, or "fancys" as Dowland sometimes called them. All touch depths of profound sadness, none more so than *Forlorn Hope Fancy* (P. 2), where the music's despair is reflected in extraordinary harmonies. *—Brian Robins*

Recommended:

- ○ **Dowland: Selected Lute Music** / Lindberg / Bis 824
- ○ **Dowland: Complete Solo Lute Music** / Lindberg / 1994 / Bis 722/744
- ○ **Dowland: Complete Lute Works Vol. 1** / O'Dette / 1995 / HM 907160

Lachrimae, or Seaven Teares, for 5 viols/violins & lute (before 1604)

It seems likely that one of the reasons John Dowland returned briefly to England in the late summer of 1603 after nearly ten years abroad was to oversee the publication of one of his most famous works, the *Lachrimae, or Seaven Teares,* which, in a none-too-subtle effort to ingratiate himself with the English court, he dedicated to Queen Anne. In the event it availed Dowland nothing, for he failed to gain a long-sought post at the English court, almost certainly because Anne did not wish to be seen poaching one of her brother's, King Christian IV of Denmark, most highly valued court musicians. *Lachrimae* is scored for a "broken" (or mixed) consort of five viols and lute. In essence, the work is a collection of dance music, a series of seven slow moving pavans succeeded by "diuers [diverse] other Pavans, Galliards, and Almands." The unique form of the work lies in the separation of the two genres into two quite distinct groups. The motive for such an innovative approach is soon established, since the series of pavans with which it opens are linked by a single idea, the so-called "falling tear" motif heard at the outset of the opening pavan, "Lachrimae Antiquae," an idea familiar from Dowland's famous song *Flow my tear* (from the *Second Book of Songs* published in 1600). Each of the six pavans that follows is a variant of the opening piece, each having its own distinctive character. The result is one of the greatest works in the canon of English chamber music, a work whose cumulative power over the course of its seven successive slow movements cannot fail to move the listener. Dowland obviously recognized how unusual the succession of the seven pavans was. In the prefatory dedication to Queen Anne he writes: "And though the title doth promise teares, unfit guests in these joyous times, yet no doubt pleasant are the teares which Musicke weeps, neither are teares always shed in sorrowe, but sometimes in joy and gladnesse," words that also provide a key to the understanding of a work that, while melancholy in general character, is by no means universally sad. For example the fifth piece, "Lachrimae coactea" is often regarded as a parody of the preceding "Lachrimae tristes," the intensely profound pavan that lies at the heart of the work. Many of the remaining pieces in the collection were arranged from pre-existent lute works, which Dowland arranged for his "broken" consort. Among them are a number of well known pieces such as the "King of Denmark's Galiard," "Captaine Piper his Galiard," and "Semper Dowland semper dolens," the play on words which the composer employed to describe his melancholy nature. *—Brian Robins*

Recommended:

- ○ **Lachrimae** / Parley of Instruments, Renaissance Violin Band / 1993 / Hyperion 66637
- ○ **Dowland: Lachrimae or Seven Teares** / Savall (cond.), Hesperion XX / 2000 / Astree 9949

VOCAL

Songs with Lute (ca. 1590–1612)

John Dowland is credited with developing the solo song with lute accompaniment, which enjoyed an incredible vogue in England around the turn of the seventeenth century. His first collection, or *Book,* of songs was published in 1597, though he had begun writing and singing them in about 1589, when this new song form began replacing the madrigal as the popular choice in England. He produced his *Second Book of Songs or Ayres* in 1600, by which time he, a Catholic from Protestant England, was serving in the Court of King Christian IV of Denmark. His *Third Book* appeared in 1603 and the *Fourth* and final book, entitled *A Pilgrim's Solace,* in 1612. There are 84 songs in the four books, and another three that appeared in his son Robert's 1614 publication called *Musical Banquet.*

Dowland's secular songs (he did write a small amount of sacred music, lute music, and other instrumental and vocal works) were for one voice and lute, or for four voices; this flexibility of performing medium was undoubtedly an element of his success. He also allowed for substitution in the accompaniment in some of the songs, specifying use of the orpharion and viols.

The composer's *First Book* is generally regarded as his least impressive collection. The songs are strophic and while items like *Away with these self loving lads* are attractive, the scope of invention is, on the whole, only modest; the composer hardly strayed from convention in his harmonies and often used popular dance melodies of the day. Still, the collection became immensely popular and must be counted as an artistic success.

At least one song from the set, *Come heavy sleep,* is recognized as a masterpiece that augurs his later, more innovative efforts. It is a dark and melancholy creation that shows the composer was already developing a profound sense of the potential unity between music and text. Among his later works that showed this tendency at its full gestation is *"In this trembling shadow"* (*Book Four*), really a sacred song whose contrapuntal writing and haunting character are masterfully fashioned. *"When sin sore wounding"* (*Book Four*) is similar in its mood and just as brilliantly imagined.

The composer's 1610 song *In darkness let me dwell* has often been cited as his greatest effort. Certainly its melodic originality, as well as its unusual lute harmonies, set it worlds apart from anything else from its time. But Dowland was also effective when he set text of less grim subject matter to music. *When Phoebus first did Daphne love* (*Book Three*) is a brief but delightful song, as is the chipper and colorful *Fine knack for Ladies* from *Book Two.*

Dowland's music is important not just for its innate mastery but for its influence on succeeding English and European composers. His writing for the lute, as popular in the sixteenth and seventeenth centuries as the piano in the nineteenth and twentieth, was also innovative, often supplying the musical fabric with vivid color and haunting atmosphere. *—Robert Cummings*

Recommended:

- ○ **Dowland: The First Booke of Songes** / Covey-Crump, Lindberg / 1988 / Bis 430
- ○ **Dowland: Lute Songs** / Oberlin, Iadone / 1994 / Lyrichord 8011

Drottningholm Court Baroque Ensemble

f. 1971, Stockholmn, Sweden
Ensemble

The Drottningholm Court Baroque Ensemble was founded in 1971 by Lars Brolin using players from within the Stockholm Royal Opera Orchestra. The band takes its name from the Drottningholm Slottstheater, built on the island of Mälaren located directly opposite the city of Stockholm by King Gustaf III in 1766. The theater, built primarily for opera performances, was later incorporated into the Royal Palace complex, also built by Gustaf III and not completed until 1782. In 1792 Gustaf III was assassinated in the Drottningholm Slottstheater during a masquerade ball, an event that was later incorporated into an opera, Giuseppe Verdi's *Un ballo in maschera.* Gustaf's successor threatened to tear the Slottstheater down, but ultimately the building was simply locked up, encapsulating its original theatrical machinery, curtains, and interiors in an unchanged form for the next century and a half. Theatrical stagings were revived at the Slottstheater staring in the early 1920s, and the theater's unique eighteenth century ambiance has been utilized as a setting for Ingmar Bergman's 1976 film of Mozart's *The Magic Flute.*

Needless to say, once you uncover an eighteenth century theater neatly locked away, as in a time capsule, you would want an appropriate period instrument musical ensemble to go with it. Yet it took five decades for musical scholarship to catch up with such an exigency. Once it was founded, another 15 years passed before the Drottningholm Court Baroque Ensemble was up to the business of recording. Its maiden effort, a 1986 rendering of Vivaldi's *The Four Seasons* led by Nils-Erik Sparf on the Swedish Bis label, was received with accolades of acclaim by reviewers and listeners everywhere. In the past two decades, the talents of the Drottningholm Court Baroque Ensemble have sustained them through roughly two dozen recordings for labels such as Bis, Naxos, Musica Sveciae, and Proprius. In the opening years of the twentieth century, subsidies from the Swedish government began to dry up in the face of hard economic times, and the Drottningholm Slottstheater was forced to shorten its season. Nonetheless, in recent years the theater has found the means to commission new operas from contemporary composers in addition to staging the Baroque- and Classical-period opera revivals that constitute its main fare. The Drottningholm Court Baroque Ensemble is kin to its sister organization, the Drottningholm Court Theatre Orchestra. *—Uncle Dave Lewis*

Recommended:

- ○ **Anne Sofie von Otter with the Drottningholm Baroque Ensemble** / Otter, Drottningholm Court Baroque Ens. / 1990 / Proprius 9008

Jacob Druckman

b. Jun. 26, 1928, Philadelphia, PA, **d.** May 24, 1996, Milford, CT
Composer

Jacob Druckman was an American composer and teacher known for his advanced sense of timbre and color. His music covers many genres and ensemble types, from chamber works such as *Interlude* (1953), the Pulitzer Prize-winning *Windows* (1972) for orchestra, and *Animus III* (1969) for clarinet, tape and live electroincs.

Druckman began his career at age ten, studying composition and violin for several years under Louis Gessenway. His formal studies began during the summer of 1949 at the Berkshire Music Center in Tanglewood, Massachusetts, where he studied with Aaron Copland. He followed this with studies at the Juilliard School with Vincent Persichetti, Peter Mennin, and Bernard Wagenaar. As a Fulbright Scholar, he worked with Tony Aubin at the Ecole Normale de Musique in Paris from 1954–56. Some of his other honors and positions included studies as a Guggenheim Fellow in 1968 at Office de Radiodiffusion—Television Francaise in Paris; professorships at Juilliard, Bard College, and Yale (where he was the chair of the music department); as well as composer-in-residence for the Aspen Festival, Tanglewood, and the New York Philharmonic.

As with many composers of his generation, Druckman began his creative endeavors with a personalized approach to serialism, and an exploration into the newly emerging field of electronics. One of Druckman's most distinctive attributes was his remarkable affinity for instrumental color and timbre. His electronic works are excellent examples, such as *Animus I*, for trombone and tape. *Windows* provides a remarkable journey into a kaleidoscope of orchestral sound, achieved by combining shifting instrumental timbres with striking harmonic colors. Druckman also believed that music should convey emotion, which was reflected by the theatrical elements he built into much of his work. For example, in *Animus III*, for clarinet and tape, the tape part symbolizes another, more virtuostic player whose intent is to gradually overwhelm and even demoralize the clarinetist. The gradual shift is further eludicated by interruptions in the solo part where the performer speaks to the audience, beginning with an air of confidence that later grows into uncertainty. Druckman's music also frequently refered to pre-existing works and styles. He was particularly known for literal quotation, often drawing from a wide range of European and American music history. In the orchestral *Prism* (1980), he draws on material from the operas of Charpentier, Cherubini, and particularly Cavalli, which caused a revival in the latter's works, in order to retell the myth of Jason and Medea from different angles. Druckman abstracts the borrowings into a skein of atonal lines and dense, textural webs. *—Michael Blostein*

Overview of Works (1948–1996)

Jacob Druckman was one of the more important American composers from the latter half of the twentieth century. He was often associated with the movement called New Romanticism, but his music cannot be called Romantic or even warmly lyrical. It could take on such features at times, but for the most part it was eclectic and reflected an abstract expressionism using atonal and electronic techniques. Often, too, Druckman quoted from the music of other composers in his works.

In his earliest compositions, Druckman divulged a neo-Classical style, as displayed in his 1949 *Duo for Violin and Piano*, a work divulging the influence of Bartók and Debussy, the latter a composer Druckman much admired. The 1950 chamber piece *Divertimento* is another example of neo-Classicism in his work. Gradually, Druckman's expressive language grew more modernist and transition works like *Dark Upon the Harp* (1961–62) for mezzo-soprano, brass quintet, and percussion (using psalms for texts), already exhibited a more progressive manner while hinting at popular, almost Broadway-style music (as in the setting of *Psalm 30*). With the appearance of his 1966 *String Quartet No. 2*, where Druckman turns somewhat experimental in his use of serial techniques, his expressive manner deepens, but also becomes more austere. In 1966, Druckman also began his *Animus* series, consisting of works for instrumentalists and tape. There would be four in all, the first three coming in the years 1966–69 and the last in 1977. *Animus II, for soprano, percussion, and tape* projects a wild character, with electronic sounds that powerfully punctuate the sense of eroticism conveyed by the singer. Perhaps Druckman's most famous effort was his 1972 *Windows*, his first essay for large orchestra that was awarded a Pulitzer Prize. An homage to Debussy, the work surprisingly does not quote from his works, but its style and atmosphere evokes that composer's orchestral scores in its colorful, sostenuto tutti chords that are periodically broken up by brief passages of a different character, thus representing the *Windows* in the title. Some of the more successful examples of Druckman quoting from other composers' works are his *Delizie contente che l'aime beate* (1973), scored for wind quintet and tape, in which he uses a theme from an aria in Cavalli's *Il Giasone*. In Druckman's three-movement work *Prism* (1980), he quotes from Cavalli again, as well as from Cherubini and Charpentier, the three having written operas about Medea, which serve as Druckman's unifying source for his quotations. In his orchestral composition *Aureole* (1979), he does not so much quote from Bernstein as build thematic material from his Kaddish melody from the *Symphony No. 3, "Kaddish."* In Druckman's later works—those from about 1980 on—his music grew a bit more approachable and perhaps more substantial in expressive depth. Late orchestral compositions like *Brangle* (1989), *Counterpoise* (1994, for soprano and orchestra), and the piano concerto (1996), his last major work, are all highly rewarding efforts. *—Robert Cummings*

Recommended:

- ○ **Druckman: Brangle; Counterpoise; Viola Concerto** / Zinman, Sawallisch (conds.), Upshaw, Diaz, Philadelphia Orch. / 2001 / New World 80560
- ○ **Druckman: String Quartets 2 & 3; Reflections on the Nature of Water; Dark Wind** / Group for Contemporary Music / 1998 / Koch 7409
- ○ **Music of Jacob Druckman** / New York Philomusica / 1997 / NY Philomusica Records 30005

Jacqueline Du Pré

b. Jan. 26, 1945, Oxford, England, **d.** Oct. 19, 1987, London, England
Cellist

Her story is one of the most legendary of all twentieth century musicians' stories, and also, sadly, one of the most tragic. Cellist Jacqueline Du Pré, born on January 26, 1945, in Oxford, England, to Derek and Iris Du Pré. (Despite the family name, Derek Du Pré was not French, but rather of British Channel Island ancestry; he could trace his lineage back to the Norman Conquest). She blossomed young and achieved international fame in a few short years during the mid-1960s, during which same time she joined Daniel Barenboim in one of history's most celebrated musical marriages. But her career was shattered in the early 1970s—not even a decade into its maturity—by multiple sclerosis.

It was through her mother Iris, a pianist and teacher, that young Jacqueline was first introduced to music. She was given a cello at age four, began lessons with Alison Dalrymple at the London Violoncello School some months later, and by age ten was studying with William Pleeth, eventually enrolling as his student at London's Guildhall School of Music. While at Guildhall she was the recipient of virtually all the school's internal awards and recognitions, meanwhile taking lessons with Pablo Casals in Switzerland and Paul Tortelier in Paris. Graduating from Guildhall in 1960, she began to make her first true professional appearances, appearing with the BBC Orchestra in 1961 and performing the Elgar concerto at Wigmore Hall in London that same year, playing on a 1672 Antonio Stradivarius cello presented to her by an anonymous patron. Further concert appearances and, in particular, a series of recordings quickly established her as the premiere young cellist of her generation, and, in many minds, the premiere British-born performer to have appeared in many generations.

In 1964, she was given the Davidoff Stradivarius (now in the possession of Yo-Yo Ma), and it was with this instrument that she made her Carnegie Hall debut on May 14, 1965. She engaged in further studies with Mstislav Rostropovich around that same time, even taking the final examination at the Moscow Conservatory in 1966—the same year she met Daniel Barenboim, whom she married the following June. Du Pré's personal and professional relationship with Barenboim opened up whole new opportunities for chamber music experience, and her collaborations with such up-and-coming luminaries as Pinchas Zukerman and Itzhak Perlman sold thousands of both recordings and tickets (and, eventually, videos).

In 1971, Du Pré began to feel that all was not well with her body and, thus, her playing, and she took the entirety of the following year off. In 1973 she was diagnosed with multiple sclerosis, and, except for a pair of performances that year and some sonata recordings (Chopin and Franck), her career as a performer was over. She remained active as a teacher, however, for many years afterwards. In 1976, she was awarded the O.B.E., and in 1982 she was named Musician of the Year by the Incorporated Society of Musicians. She passed away on October 19, 1987, at the age of 42.

Jacqueline Du Pré's physical gift for her instrument was prodigious; but it was her sheer joy in music making that endeared her to the world's audiences. Although some found her physical involvement during performance distasteful, few could find reason to complain about the sonic result. The scintillating, rapturous tone she produced was positively intoxicating, and remains so today through recordings.

Her renditions of the Elgar and Dvořák concertos, and of the Schumann concerto, are especially beloved. *—Blair Johnston*

Recommended:

- ○ **Impressions** / Barbirolli, Barenboim (conds.), Du Pre, Zukerman, London SO, English CO / 1988 / EMI 69707
- ○ **Concertos by Dvořák & Schumann** / Barenboim (cond.), Du Pre, Chicago SO, New Philharmonia Orch. / 2004 / EMI 62805
- ○ **Concertos by Haydn & Boccherini** / Barbirolli, Barenboim (conds.), Du Pre, Zukerman, London SO, English CO / 1998 / EMI 66948
- ○ **Brahms: Sonatas 1 & 2; Bruch: Kol Nidrei** / Du Pre, Barenboim, Israel PO / 2002 / EMI 57293
- ○ **Beethoven: Sonatas & Variations** / Du Pre, Barenboim (piano) / 1999 / Angel 73332

François-René Duchable

b. Apr. 22, 1952, Paris, France

Pianist

Pianist François-René Duchable was born in Paris in 1952. He studied at the Paris Conservatory, and at the age of 13 won the institution's first prize in piano. Three years later he placed 11th at the Queen Elisabeth of Belgium competition in Brussels, and in 1973 he won the Prix de la Fondation Sacha Schneider; at that time Duchable caught the attention of the legendary Artur Rubinstein, who encouraged him to pursue a solo career and helped him secure his first important engagements. Since then, Duchable has enjoyed an uninterupted and highly succesful concert career in Europe, the United States, Canada, and Japan.

Duchable has been recognized for his performances of a wide swath of the standard repertory, including the concertos of Beethoven, Brahms, Schumann, Bartók and Ravel, and solo piano works of Lizst, Chopin, and Poulenc. He has appeared at many prestigious music festivals, including those of Salzburg, Lucerne, Berlin, the London Proms, Lockenhaus, and the Flanders Festival, and has presented concerts at London's Royal Festival Hall, the Philharmonie in Berlin, and the Musikverein in Vienna. As an orchestral soloist, Duchable has performed with the London Philharmonic, the Berlin Philharmonic, the Rotterdam Philharmonic, the Orchestre de Paris, the Orchestre de la Suisse Romande, and the Montreal Symphony. *—Robert Adelson*

Recommended:

- ○ **Duchable Plays Chopin, Schumann, Liszt** / Duchable / 2003 / Virgin 545574
- ○ **Liszt: Sonata in B minor; 2 Légendes** / Duchable / 1985 / Erato 88091
- ○ **Duchable Plays Bach, Beethoven, Scarlatti, Mozart** / Duchable / 2003 / Virgin 545575
- ○ **Duchable Plays Chopin** / Duchable / 2003 / Virgin 545572

Guillaume Dufay

b. ca. 1397, Cambrai [?], France, **d.** Nov. 27, 1474, Cambrai, France

Composer: Vocal, Choral

Guillaume Dufay commenced a meteoric musical career as a simple choirboy at Cambrai Cathedral in 1409. Before his death, Dufay would lead the papal chapel, consort with popes and dukes, collaborate with Donatello and Brunelleschi, and be reckoned the first composer of the Renaissance. His birthdate is unknown—the suggestion 1397 stems from the date of his priestly ordination—but his lengthy contact with Cambrai Cathedral and the Vatican, combined with evidence internal to his music, means that his life is quite well documented. His choirboy service apparently lasted until his voice broke in 1413 or 1414, when he was given a small chaplaincy. His early musical training came from choirmasters Nicholas Malin and the composer Richard Loqueville. The unusual gift of a book (the *Doctrinale*) in 1411 or 1412 testifies to the boy's intellectual abilities.

Cambrai's famous bishop Pierre d'Ailly took an active part in the Council of Constance (1414–18), and Dufay's presence in his retinue could explain several points: his absence from Cambrai from November 1414, his early exposure to English music, and his contacts with the Malatesta family. After a brief tenure as subdeacon in Cambrai's St.-Géry, Dufay took up service with the Malatesta in Pesaro/Rimini. Two lavish wedding pieces, another motet, and a number of chansons date from this service, probably from 1420–24. The health of his mother caused Dufay to return North, likely settling briefly in Laon, but the composer left for Italy again in 1426, bidding farewell to the fine wines of his homeland in the autobiographical *Adieu ces bons vins*.

Dufay stayed for some months in Bologna in the retinue of Cardinal Louis Aleman, possibly beginning his law degree there, but by December 1428 he had assumed a lucrative post in the Papal Chapel. Under Pope Martin V, the Chapel singers enjoyed a strong salary as well as the opportunity to hold several absentee benefice incomes; the musicians' fortunes improved further under the patronage of his successor, Eugenius IV (for whom Dufay wrote three more motets). However, Roman political turmoil helped push Dufay into the waiting arms of the Ducal Court of Savoy in 1433. As choirmaster there, his compositional life flourished, yielding a large cycle of hymn settings and many mature songs. A 1435 promotion to first singer (and choirmaster) lured him back to the Papal Chapel, now resident in Medicean Florence; among other pieces, Dufay gave the City of the Lily *Nuper rosarum flores* for the completion of Ghiberti's dome and the consecration of her Cathedral.

Dufay returned to a canonicate at Cambrai Cathedral by December 1439, where he would remain for most of the remainder of his life. Only a trip to Italy in 1450, possibly to contribute the *St. Anthony Mass* for the dedication of Donatello's altar in Padua, and a final period of Savoyard service from 1452 to 1458, broke this semi-retirement. He took on a number of administrative tasks, such as ambassador to the Court of Burgundy (with which he apparently maintained a lifelong relationship), and musically led the *petit vicaires* as well as supervising the recopying of the Cathedral's chantbooks. He also composed several late cantus firmus masses, a lost requiem, and a plainchant Marian Office. At his death in 1474, Dufay left a sizable fortune (including cash, jewelry, furniture, and books), as well as musical provisions for his own memorial services. He also left an outstanding musical reputation and an exceptionally long shadow upon generations of composers to come. *—Timothy Dickey*

Overview of Works (ca. 1420–1470)

In the 1440s, Martin le Franc credited Guillaume Dufay with a revolutionary and fresh musical sensibility; this judgment laid the foundation for the enduring view of Dufay as a musical "father of the Renaissance." The four masses he wrote late in life seem music's first compositionally virtuoso masterpieces, unified, large-scale works that offer multiple brilliancies. More skeptical historians view Dufay's achievement more in terms of invention than of innovation, but his utter command of musical techniques over a varied and prolific career is inarguable. He assimilated various then-current musical forms, both sacred and secular, and an array of international stylistic features drawn from Loqueville, Dunstable, Ciconia, and others, and he left some two hundred compositions and a long shadow of influence over his contemporaries. His facile style of composing for four voices and his late cyclic masses set the stage for the generation of Josquin and Obrecht.

The Northerner Dufay composed chansons–multipart French secular songs–throughout his life, though at least two-thirds of them apparently were written before about 1440. His favorite form was the Rondeau, though occasions such as a 1423 Savoyard wedding often warranted the weightier Ballade. The earlier songs are based on an essential duet of the cantus and tenor parts, with the contratenor filling in and supporting the harmonic framework. Though each piece is individual, many analysts note their consistently graceful melodic lines. Brief untexted introductions and phrase interludes are common. A large group of songs, probably dating from Dufay's tenure at the court of Savoy in the 1450s, generally display greater economy of melodic means.

The grander occasions of state also provided the context for Dufay's isorhythmic motets, a form dating back more than a century that featured a cantus firmus, often a piece of chant, repeated in a complex proportional fashion (for instance, the melody and the rhythm might be repeated at different rates, so that the initial melody and rhythm would no longer coincide). Dufay's motets surpass in scope and technical proficiency those of his predecessors. *Supremum est mortalibus*, for instance, though in only three voices, presents an elegant variety of textures, including fauxbourdon. *Eccelsie militantis*, in five voices, contains three cantus firmus voices, two of which paraphrase different chant melodies for the Angel Gabriel (both pieces were written for Pope Eugenius IV, Gabriele Condulmer). The famed motet for the dedication of Florence Cathedral, *Nuper rosarum flores*, places two isomelic (melodically unified) upper voices over a pair of tenors whose proportional scheme may derive from the architecture of the Cathedral itself.

Dufay's varied ecclesiastical posts called forth a wide spectrum of liturgical compositions. Among these common liturgical items are three-voiced chant-based settings of Antiphons, Magnificats, Sequences, and an influential cycle of Hymn settings covering the entire liturgical year. Many of these pieces are linked to English discant and Continental improvisatory practice; the chant is slightly ornamented in the uppermost voice (again his elegant melodies are foregrounded). A vast group of Mass Proper settings preserved in Trento have been attributed to Dufay; an entire Marian Office in new plainchant, comissioned from him by Cambrai, was discovered in 1985. His compositional career reached its summit in the four late masses, with the new English technique of unifying the movements around a single preexistent cantus firmus. Each of these four-voiced masses was apparently conceived as a self-sufficient "masterwork." The prodigious *L'homme armé Mass* contains a crab canon at its climax; the *Missa Ecce ancilla Domini* juxtaposes two similar chants throughout. The *Missa Ave regina coelorum*, on his own Marian antiphon, may have solemnified the 1472 dedication of Cambrai Cathedral. Dufay's will stipulated that it be sung at his deathbed. *—Timothy Dickey*

Recommended:

- ○ **Dufay: Chansons** / Posch (cond.), Unicorn Ens. / 1996 / Naxos 553458
- ○ **Dufay: O gemma, lux** / Nevel (cond.), Huelgas Ens. / HM 901700

VOCAL

Songs (ca. 1420–1460)

While the four cantus firmus Masses of his late years are considered the zenith of his music, Dufay's songs are by far his most popular works. This is partly because they contain all the essential beauties of his music in a highly accessible short-form. But it is not only that, for the songs have an intimate lyricism and poetic charm that isn't found in the more ambitious works. More than 70 chansons survive by Dufay, with an unknowable number lost. One of the essential things to grasp in Dufay's music is the unusual continuity of his approach across the many forms he worked in. Whether listening to an isorhythmic motet, a mass, or a quaint rondeau, we recognize that one mind is at work. The chansons, to a student of Dufay, read rather like a great artist's sketchbooks, containing clear indications of the mainstays of his style at each point in his development.

Most of these very tonal-sounding songs are for three voices, in the form of the rondeau, but there are also bergerettes, virelai, and ballades, while a few are through-composed or in unusual motet-like forms. They can be divided into two main stylistic periods, but considerable variety is found within those. Despite the basic continuity of style, each song stands on its own, often indicating a focused effort to solve a specific technical riddle. The years up to 1440, during which most of the chansons were composed, show a brilliant young composer restless to distinguish himself as the outstanding musical technician of his day. They are happy pieces, full of experimental touches, and glittering with Dufay's brilliant melody. For the most part they follow clear dance-related metrical schemes. The tune-bearing discantus essentially acts in duet with the tenor, while the contratenor fills in the harmonies and provides touches of color essential to the total effect.

Dufay's secular music drops off after 1440, but the comparatively few songs from that point on reveal an ever-deepening maturity of style that culminates after 1450, especially from 1460 onwards. Dufay tended more and more in these to equalize the voices stylistically, so that all would unfold at the same rate, none more florid than the other, while maintaining the stated contrapuntal hierarchy. Dufay turned an about face on his experimental, exhibitionistic tendencies in order to refine, with an astonishing success, the highest courtly modes of art song current at the time. He was mainly seeking in the late years to perfect his control of dissonance and achieve greater harmonic clarity, but the sense of rhythm also changes profoundly for the better. Rhythms and phrase lengths become more and more numerically irregular, until modern transcriptions into 3/4 or 6/8, although correct for the early works and still convenient, no longer bear any real relation to the rhythmic structure. The results, somberly gorgeous, for the overall mood becomes quite dark, have an economy of melody, and a kind of balanced, quiet perfection rarely found in any music. *—Donato Mancini*

Recommended:

○ **Dufay: Complete Secular Music** / London Medieval Ens. / 1997 / L'Oiseau-Lyre 452557

Resvelliés vous et faites chiere lye, ballade (1423)

The Malatestas were a large, extraordinarily powerful family in the Italian Renaissance; their dual branches controlled the towns of Pesaro and Rimini. Although they eventually succumbed to bitter rivalry, during the time when Dufay was among their artistic beneficiaries they were still in a powerful alliance, and had their main base in Rimini.

The three surviving works Dufay is known to have composed for the family are the magnificent isorhythmic motet *Vasilissa ergo gaude* (the first datable composition in Dufay's oeuvre), and two ballades: *Mon chier ami* and *Resvelliés vous. Resvelliés vous* was composed for the marriage of Carlo Malatesta da Pesaro to Vittoria di Lorenzo Colonna, celebrated at Rimini on July 18, 1423. Ballades were one of the customary forms used for such occasions, probably because the recurring refrain line could contain a reference to the patron, underscoring again and again the name of the one being honored: "Charle gentil, qu'on dit de Malateste." To emphasize further, Dufay sets "Charle gentil" in block-chord homorhythm. Though musically incongruous, these blatant musical references to patrons appear in a number of Dufay's works—the fifteenth century equivalent of today's hilarious "product placements" in films.

In spite of this, the chanson is quite beautiful—certainly not burdened by Charles' presence. Dufay was clearly satisfied with the work since he made *Resvelliés vous* the musical basis for his first surviving mass cycle, the inaccurately named *Missa Sine nomine.* The mass may in fact have been sung at the wedding also.

The two main sections of Resvelliés vous have different meters; the contrast between them brings their principle melodies into sharp relief. The rich counterpoint generally follows the movement of the topmost discantus voice, with the two lower parts shadowing it in gesture and manner. Rhythmic contrast is the key to Dufay's thinking here; it is also used within each section to maintain interest within the discantus voice. The wealth of material here indeed suggests a greater structural capacity than a mere ballade, and so it's no surprise that *Resvelliés vous* became the foundation of a much more ambitious, important work. *—Donato Mancini*

Recommended:

○ **Dufay: Chansons** / Posch (cond.), Unicorn Ens. / 1996 / Naxos 553458

CHORAL

Ave Regina caelorum, antiphon

The motet *Ave regina caelorum* is among the most beloved works in Dufay's oeuvre, and historically a favorite among the rich body of fifteenth century polyphony. Its popularity perhaps derives from its position near the juncture between the architectonic approach to form inherited from the isorhythmic motet of de Vitry and Machaut in the fourteenth century and the more flowing and expressive contours that would characterize vocal music of the mature Renaissance. To be sure, its use of the tenor cantus firmus holds the entire polyphonic structure together and lends the motet its overall shape. Still, as Dufay and his contemporaries became more adept at the new genre of the four-voice, cyclical cantus firmus mass, their attention was occupied less by the sheer constructional demands of cantus firmus integration and focused more on the genre's expressive possibilities. As exemplified in the work under consideration, this trend toward greater expressivity became more pronounced in the so-called "tenor motet," which was not obligated to meet the same liturgical demands as the mass.

The *Ave regina caelorum,* which is usually given the Roman numeral designation "III" to distinguish it from two earlier motets on the same antiphon, was composed sometime before 1464, the year in which it was copied into a manuscript at Cambrai. Stylistically it distinguishes itself from earlier motet styles in its use of the cantus firmus. Whereas in Dufay's famous *Nuper rosarum flores* from 1436, for example, the tenor is rendered in long notes that serve as a kind of undergirding, the tenor in *Ave regina* is given a more clearly defined rhythmic profile, one that embeds it more seamlessly within the overall polyphonic fabric. In fact, at the beginning of the motet, before the tenor even enters with the cantus firmus, the three other voices take turns "foreshadowing" the antiphon melody; thus, when the tenor finally appears, the cantus firmus does not seem like a sturdy structural pillar so much as the natural outgrowth of a series of imitative entries. Dufay's use of texture likewise presages the style of the Josquin generation in his use of different paired voice combinations.

Perhaps the most distinctive aspects of the piece, however, are the personalized interpolations with which Dufay tropes the antiphon text. In both interpolations, which are punctuated by unexpected shifts to C minor, Dufay makes the devotional tone of the motet a deeply personal one: the first, "Miserere tui labentis Dufay" (Have mercy on your dying Dufay), corresponds with the composer's request that the motet be sung at his death bed; the second, "Miserere, miserere supplicanti Dufay" (Have mercy, have mercy on your supplicant Dufay), is accompanied by particularly haunting music—so distinctive, in fact, that it reappears without its text (but unmistakable nonetheless) in Dufay's final cyclic cantus firmus mass, the *Missa Ave regina caelorum* (1472). *—Jeremy Grimshaw*

Recommended:

○ **Dufay: Missa Puisque je vis; Loyset Compère: Omnium bonorum plena** / Kirkman (cond.), Binchois Consort / 2003 / Hyperion 67368

Mass for St. Anthony of Padua (ca. 1450)

Two of the immediately noticeable features of this work are its rhythmic vigor and plurality of content. The usual devices to unify a mass—normally a common melody of the tenor of all the movements—are absent here: from the first, one is plunged into a musically dense world where every moment is ultimately as important as the next in the unfolding of the musical narrative. In this it echoes certain modern developmental forms, like in R. Strauss' *Death and Transfiguration,* which start with a musical idea and develop it continuously, without turning back, right until the end of the piece, by which time the material has been changed beyond recognition, although the listener has been there every step of the way. The experience of Dufay's virtuosically composed mass is similarly impressive in character, constantly pushing itself forward, as it does, through an incredible wealth of musical ideas. It feels like Dufay wishes both to give us his ideal versions and to found a new school of composition with each setting.

The Introit and Kyrie settle slowly into a richness of polyphony that's merely a prelude to the almost explosive Gloria. The Gloria is perhaps the fullest climax of the mass, using rhythms of a complexity that no one else in Dufay's day could have written, along with its most adventurous harmonies. The gradual begins on the same plateau, eventually settling down in its middle section, into a duet between tenor and countertenor. Here we get to appreciate Dufay's quick witted counterpoint without mediation before the return of the full choir and a steep rise, stretching through the Alleluia, towards the Credo where the next musical climax is. The Offertory is perhaps the most patient and lyrical movement of the mass. It shows, beside all the elaborate cleverness, what a hushed loveliness Dufay was capable of. *—Donato Mancini*

Recommended:

○ **Dufay: Music for St. Anthony of Padua** / Kirkman (cond.), Binchois Consort / 1996 / Hyperion 66854

○ **Dufay: Mass for St. Anthony of Padua** / Blachly (cond.), Pomerium / 1996 / Archiv 447772

Missa Ecce ancilla Domini (1463)

A prominent historian and profound admirer of Guillaume Dufay's music once called the composer's four late cantus firmus masses a "summary of Dufay's work." Each of the four last masses uses an advanced four-voiced texture, and each apparently was planned as a unique aesthetic whole. One of these masses daringly uses a secular song as the rigidly structural cantus firmus; a second offers Dufay's scintillating contribution to the growing tradition of *L'homme armé* masses. Dufay's final and most complex mass, on *Missa Ave regina coelorum*, probably graced the consecration ceremonies for Cambrai Cathedral in 1472, and was also sung at his deathbed. The *Missa Ecce ancilla Domini*, Dufay's penultimate mass, stands somewhat aloof from these three companions. Some of its compositional techniques—such as its overt, two-voiced "motto" opening for each movement and its unembellished plainchant tenor—stand unabashedly in the well-worn footsteps of older musical traditions. Its aural profile and its double plainchant cantus firmus, on the other hand, present a more intimate and personal side of the composer's worship music instead of the more extroverted and heavily structural of the other late masses. Some of the *Missa Ecce ancilla*'s intimate character derives from the comparatively light vocal scoring: nearly half of the mass proceeds only in duo textures. These duos most commonly alternate with full, four-voiced textures when the tenor is singing one of the canti firmi. The duple alternation of duo and full textures may have had symbolic connotations for Dufay, related to the canti firmi. Both *Ecce ancilla Domini* and *Beata es Maria*, the tenor's invariable second melody, properly serve two liturgical functions. One is the Feast of the Annunication (March 25), when Gabriel spoke the words to Mary of her coming divine pregnancy. The second is the so-called "Golden Mass" sung on Advent Wednesdays, when many late-medieval churches featured dramatic recitations of the same angelic dialogue with Mary. In every movement of Dufay's mass (save one), two roughly equal sections include the tenor singing the chant melody, without much melodic elaboration, to Mary's "Behold, I am the Lord's handmaid," followed by its cousin's dramatic response later in *Luke 2*, "Blessed are you, Mary." The manuscript choirbook that preserves Dufay's mass even has both chant texts written into the tenor voice rather than the mass ordinary, so there is no mistaking the dialogue. Regis and Ockeghem both apparently knew Dufay's *Missa Ecce ancilla Domini*, borrowing its concepts and melodies when writing their own Annunciation Masses. *—Timothy Dickey*

Recommended:

○ **Dufay: Missa Ecce ancilla Domini** / Vellard (dir.), Gilles Binchois Ens. / 1994 / Virgin 45050

○ **Dufay: Missa Ecce ancilla Domini; Missa Se la face ay pale; Magnificat quinti toni** / Choir of the Church of Advent, Boston / Arsis Audio 118

Missa L'homme armé (ca. 1460)

"Beware the armed man!" was a cry familiar to the ears of the late feudal culture of the "Autumn of the Middle Ages." Pope Pius II died in Ancona while trying to garner support for a new Crusade to wrest Constantinople from the hand of the Turks, who had conquered the city in 1453. This crusading project and the stylized chivalric ethos of the Burgundian court of Charles the Bold provide historical context for the immediately popular monophonic hit song *L'homme armé*. Robert Morton and Antoine Busnois, singers and composers to the Burgundian dukes, have been variously credited with the first polyphonic setting of the tune. In fact, the song engendered a vast family of compositions—some 40 masses over the late fifteenth and early sixteenth centuries. While Johannes Ockeghem may have been the first to complete a cycle of five Mass ordinary movements based upon the *L'homme armé* chanson, Busnois' *Missa L'homme armé* proved seminal to the tradition. The coeval *Missa L'homme armé* of Guillaume Dufay appears to quote music from Busnois, and thus likely dates from the last decade of Dufay's life. As in all four of Dufay's late cantus firmus masses, the central organizational device is a pre-existent melody in the tenor voice, stated at least once in each of the five Mass movements. Unlike the *Missa Se la face ay pale*, however (and unlike the more overt cantus firmus statements in Busnois and Ockeghem's *L'homme armé* masses), Dufay twists and disguises the chanson melody, altering it, ornamenting it, and subjecting it to a dazzling array of compositional permutations. Dufay apportions the tripartite structure of the *L'homme armé* melody across the three sections of the Kyrie, with tenor cantus firmus entries sneaking in from adjacent bass notes, hiding among melodic similarities permeating other voices, and elaborated with a "tag" in Kyrie I and a diminution of the melody appended to Kyrie II. The entire melody appears twice in the Gloria, once with melodic ornamentation and shuffled rhythmic values, and a second time with further rhythmic alteration. The opening duo of this movement (and that of the following Credo) uses the motto opening first heard in the Kyrie, lending some audible support to the cyclic structure. The Credo movement follows a similar pattern to the Gloria: opening with a tremendously long duo, continuing with a structure containing an identical cantus firmus statement, and climaxing in a rhythmically intense third statement in diminution and a long free-composed "tag." Sanctus presents fragments of the tenor melody only at first, but then a complete statement without any alteration in the second Osanna. The most celebrated compositional fancy in this setting occurs in the third Agnus Dei movement, Dufay's famous "crab canon." The tenor voice is given the familiar *L'homme armé* tune, with a Latin inscription "Cancer eat plenus sed redeat medius," translated "The Crab goes out full but comes back half." Part of the solution to this witty instruction involves rhythmic diminution: the "coming back," or second statement of the melody, should halve all rhythmic values. But the crustacean invocation indicates a further complexity: retrograde motion the first time, as the crab "goes out" walking backwards. Dufay's clever gambit certainly sparked a tradition of competition and compositional challenge in the nascent family of *L'homme armé* mass settings. *—Timothy Dickey*

Recommended:

○ **Dufay: Missa L'homme armé; Supremum est mortalibus bonum** / Summerly (cond.), Oxford Camerata / 1995 / Naxos 553087

○ **Offertorium** / Savall (dir.), Capella Reial de Catalunya / 1997 / Fontalis 9906

Missa Se la face ay pale (ca. 1450)

Guillaume Dufay composed the ballade *Se la face ay pale* in the 1430s, perhaps for a Savoy wedding in 1434. Its courtly text speaks in clever, punning rhymes of the pale-faced, dejected lover. Another Savoyard event—such as the 1451 wedding of the Dauphin Louis of Savoy—may have provided the context later for him to construct an entire cantus firmus mass setting upon the tenor line of his chanson. English composers early in the century had begun to experiment with devices for the musical unification of all five movements of the Mass Ordinary. Leonel Power's *Missa Alma redemptoris* and John Dunstable's *Missa Rex seculorum*, as well as anonymous settings of the *Missa veterem hominem* and the *Missa Caput*, all present a single cantus firmus melody in the tenor voice in each mass movement, after the fashion of the isorhythmic motet; other English masses essay tunes borrowed from secular song. Dufay's *Missa se la face ay pale* most likely is the earliest surviving mass setting to do both. The chanson tenor melody, divided into three phrases and sung in the tenor voice of the Mass throughout, provides the framework for each movement of the Mass. In the Kyrie, Sanctus, and Agnus Dei, this cantus firmus is given once over the course of each movement, with duo sections punctuating the structure; the "wordier" movements Gloria and Credo give the tenor melody three times each. This lends to the Mass a complex and "advanced" sense of structural unity by linking groups of movements as subsets within the structure. The outer pair of movements—Kyrie and Agnus—apportion the three cantus firmus sections to their tripartite structures as follows: AB/none (duo texture)/C. The inner pair—Gloria and Credo—present the entire melody three time, with proportional reductions in the ratio 3:2:1. By the end of each, the tenor's long notes give way to a rhythmic intensity similar to that of the other voices, building a fine climax. These two movements, thus, become a pair of isorhythmic motets of equal length, with identical trajectories. Dufay creates further audible connections across the mass by means of a motto opening: four movements begin with the same melody in the upper voice, while the Kyrie opening clearly alludes to the same melody. This very motto acknowledges the composer's debt to English concepts, as its melodic contour closely parodies the motto opening to the famous English Caput Mass. Furthermore, near the end of each of Dufay's movements, a sunny fanfare section shines through in all four voices: a series of interlocking and overlapping C major triadic motifs, borrowed from the characteristic sound of the chanson model. This jolly concluding passage, as well as the modal clarity of major-key cadences throughout the cycle, make Dufay's *Se la face ay pale Mass* the most joyful sounding of his group of four late cantus firmus settings. Its sonic world belies the stereotypical distress of the chanson's bereft lover, aptly describing the presumed nuptial bliss celebrated in the Mass. *—Timothy Dickey*

Recommended:

○ **Dufay: Se la Face ay Pale** / Binkley (dir.), Pro Arte Singers / Focus 934

○ **Dufay: Se la Face ay Pale** / Munrow (dir.), Early Music Consort of London / 1996 / Virgin 61283

Nuper rosarum flores, isorhythmic motet (1463)

On March 25, 1436, a great procession wound through the streets of Florence. Church prelates, led by Pope Eugenius IV himself, and the *Signoria* of the Italian city-state, led by Cosimo de' Medici, marched with ranks of musicians along a ceremonial wooden bridge from the steps of Santa Maria Novella to the newly completed Cathedral, Santa Maria del Fiore. There the Cardinal of Venice would offer Mass and the Heir of St. Peter would officiate in the liturgy of Dedication. For the Cathedral of Florence, the "cradle of the Renaissance," Ghiberti crafted her Baptistry's bronze "Doors of Paradise," Luca della Robbia and Donatello carved her *cantoria*. Filippo Brunelleschi had now crowned her with a momumental dome. And for the event, the director of the Papal choir, Guillaume Dufay, presented new compositions, including the celebratory isorhythmic motet *Nuper rosarum flores*. The text, probably written by Dufay himself, consists of four Latin stanzas, seven lines of seven syllables each. It addresses St. Mary of Flowers, as she was known in Florence, offering the church to her and asking for her perpetual intercession for her Florentine people. The upper two voice parts (often dividing for further harmonic richness) sing this text in four sections, each beginning with a duet of 28 breves' duration and concluding with 28 breves of music for all four voices. The upper melodies are free-flowing and rhythmically active, though melodic fragments are recycled later in the piece (a technique known as isomelism). One exceptional moment in the counterpoint occurs when the text mentions the name "Eugenius": the texture suddenly clarifies, so that the Pope may be gratified to hear his own name sung. The fourfold structure of the motet derives from the isorhythmic plan of the lower voices, which sing a long-note cantus firmus in canon with one another. Their melody and text is a plainchant: "Terribilis est locus iste," from the liturgy for the Dedication of a Church. Specifically, Dufay uses the first 14 notes of this famous chant. Then the lower voices sing their melody in four different rhythmic configurations, by the application of different mensurations to each section. This results in a durational ratio of 6:4:2:3. While the compositional device of isorhythm was common in the fifteenth century, especially for large occasional pieces, Dufay's choice of ratios here is unique for its complexity. In a famous article, published in 1973, Charles Warren argued that this unique set of ratios corresponded to the large-scale architectural dimensions of the Cathedral—nave, crossing, apse, and dome. This theory was later challenged by musicologist Craig Wright, who, nevertheless, further elucidated the presence of carefully crafted numerology in Dufay's composition. The unique isorhythmic ratio chosen to honor the Florentine Cathedral may symbolize instead the Old Testament Temple of Solomon, whose overall length, length of nave and sanctuary, and height were 60:40:20:30 cubits. The number seven—crucial to the sectional divisions and to the structure of the poem—relates to the seven pillars of the Temple, the sevenfold gifts of the Holy Spirit (which filled the Temple at its dedication), and the seven censings of the altar in the Dedication service. The Temple symbolism is then overlaid with Marian meaning, as seven signified the Virgin Mary's perfection: seven joys, seven sorrows, seven feasts. The Virgin, whose womb was the temple which nurtured the incarnate Christ, is richly honored in the symbolic language of her Florentine temple's dedication. *—Timothy Dickey*

Recommended:

- ○ **1000 Years of Sacred Music** / Hillier (dir.), Hilliard Ens. / 2002 / Virgin 562126
- ○ **Dufay: O gemma, lux** / Nevel (dir.), Huelgas Ens. / HM 901700

Paul Dukas

b. Oct. 1, 1865, Paris, France, **d.** May 17, 1935, Paris, France

Composer: Orchestral, Symphonic, Chamber Music, Ballet, Opera

Paul Dukas' music, like his life, straddled the Romantic and modern periods (and encompassed a still wider range of influences), and he remained true to classial structures well into the twentieth century. Born in 1865 to the family of a cultured Parisian banker, he was the second of three children; his mother was the musician in the family and she died when he was five. He studied the piano without displaying special aptitude in music until he was 14. While convalescing from an illness, he started composing, and from that point on, he gravitated toward music, enrolling at the Paris Conservatoire when he was 16. He studied harmony, piano, conducting, and orchestration and at 17, he wrote his first two adult compositions, overtures to Goethe's *Götz von Berlichingen* and Shakespeare's *King Lear.* He formally studied composition with Ernest Guiraud but left the conservatory in 1888, frustrated over his inability to win any prizes for his early work and he was being confronted by the military draft. Following his service in the army, he returned to civilian life as a critic and composer, enjoying his first success in the latter capacity in 1892 with the premiere of his overture *Polyeucte.* The same year, he began the first of several attempts to compose an opera, but he was to see no success in that genre for years to come; rather, he wrote his two most well-known instrumental works: the *Symphony in C* (1896) and *The Sorcerer's Apprentice* (1897). The latter, based on Goethe's "Der Zauberlehrling," became one of the most popular orchestral works of the late Romantic era with its rich coloration, and it was quickly taken into the repertory of conductors around the world. For the next decade, he devoted himself to an opera, *Ariane et Barbe-bleue,* based on the work of Maurice Maeterlinck, while continuing to write criticism and completing his *Sonata for piano in E flat minor* (1900). Dukas completed his ballet *La Péri* in 1912, but his later output was blighted by an increasingly self-critical outlook, which caused him to abandon and destroy many works. Only four pieces from the last 23 years of his life ever saw the light of day. In his final decades, Dukas achieved renown as a teacher and his students included Messiaen and Duruflé. In 1940, five years after his death, Dukas and *The Sorcerer's Apprentice* became enshrined in American popular culture through the use of the work in the movie *Fantasia.* *—Bruce Eder*

ORCHESTRAL

The Sorcerer's Apprentice (L'apprenti sorcier), symphonic scherzo (1897)

On January 3, 1897, the premiere of Dukas' great *Symphony in C* met with a cool reception. An impressive Beethovenian overture, *Polyeucte* (inspired by Corneille's play), had been heard in 1892, the year in which Dukas began his career as a critic, covering productions of Wagner operas in London. Behind him lay an undistinguished apprenticeship at the Paris Conservatoire and a year's military service. Older colleagues, d'Indy and Saint-Saëns foremost, recognized his talent. The latter tapped him to orchestrate Guiraud's uncompleted *Frédégonde,* and edit several operas for a new Rameau edition, despite the fact that he lacked a public profile. That literally changed overnight on May 18, 1897, with the premiere of *The Sorcerer's Apprentice;* it became one of the most popular orchestral works ever penned, long before Disney's animated version for the 1940 film *Fantasia.*

The public has always responded avidly to pictorial and literary associations in music. In matching Goethe's laconic ballad *Das Zauberlehrling* with an orchestral showpiece, Dukas found unmistakable musical equivalents for the events of the poem, and did so with formal concision. Teasingly called a scherzo by its composer, this resourceful, brilliantly orchestrated work is cast as a compact sonata movement with four themes that are tenuously alluded to in a brief introduction depicting an aura of mystery as the old sorcerer leaves his atelier. Quietly descending thirds in the strings suggest magic—and later the water that magic summons—yielding to the softly enunciated broomstick theme on clarinets. The apprentice makes a sudden appearance in a skittering, vacillating rush before quiet descends again, and the commanding theme of the master's spell is heard as if from a distance, on muted brass. With startling abruptness, the spell motif rings out on trumpets combined with the broomstick motif pizzicato. The magic has been worked and the introduction ends with a single tympani stroke. The exposition proper begins now as the lurching broomstick theme gradually shudders to strident, marchlike life, drawing in the descending minor thirds signifying water and sorcery. Development proceeds relentlessly with the enchanted broomstick filling the apprentice's bath, which overflows, becoming an inundation. Despite his frantic cries and the partial enunciation of the spell motif—or the apprentice has forgotten the words—the broomstick heedlessly continues. To a mighty climax, he seizes an axe and cuts the broom in two. For a moment this seems to have worked. But slowly, shudderingly, "two" brooms—the theme in canon—begin to draw water, initiating the recapitulation. Tension escalates even more alarmingly, but this time the climax is capped by the authoritative pronouncement of the spell motif, signaling the master's return, at which a crashing orchestral tutti brings all to a halt. The mysterious quiet of the beginning returns as the waters dissipate and the apprentice's theme, now supplicating, is heard twice before a triplet rush to the final "once upon a time" chord.

The indebtedness of the stormier parts of *The Sorcerer's Apprentice* to the *Ride of the Valkyries* has been noted a number of times, while the adroit use of Wagner-like motifs is self-evident. Nietzsche referred to Wagner as "the old Sorcerer"—it is not too much to see in *The Sorcerer's Apprentice,* a masterpiece demonstrating that Dukas had not only learned "the lessons of the Master," but cunningly combined them with the French penchant for formal clarity. *—Adrian Corleonis*

Recommended:

- ○ **Fête à la Française** / Dutoit (cond.), Montreal SO / 1989 / London 421527
- ○ **Cantelli Conducts Dukas, Ravel, Falla, Rossini, Casella** / Cantelli, etc. / Testament 1017

SYMPHONIC

Symphony in C major (1895–1896)

During *la belle époque,* very few French composers wrote symphonies and, aside from Saint-Saëns, fewer still wrote more than one. There was Lalo's *Symphony in G minor* (1886), Franck's *Symphony in D minor* (1888), Chausson's *Symphony in B flat major* (1889), and Dukas' *Symphony in C major* (1896). All except the Franck symphony are hardly known outside of France, but the Dukas symphony is probably the least known of them all. Only his fourth published work, Dukas completed his symphony the year after he finished his tone poem *The Sorcerer's Apprentice,* that is, after he considered that he had reached maturity as a composer. Like Franck and Chausson's symphonies, Dukas' symphony is in three movements. Unlike them, it does not use a single motif, an *idée fixe,* to unify the work, but, like them, it does use Wagnerian chromatic harmonies as the basis of its musical language. Nevertheless, Dukas' symphony is a powerful and distinctive work whose tone of exuberant optimism is a welcome tonic after the heavy late-Romanticism of Franck and Chausson. The opening Allegro non troppo vivace, ma con fuoco has three themes: an agitated first theme in C major, a lyrical theme in A minor, and a fanfare theme in F major. After a quiet return of the first theme, the development deliberately moves toward the recapitulation of the three themes, the first two in C major, the third in F major. The coda begins calmly, but rises to a magnificent climax. The central Andante espressivo e sostenuto also has three themes: an expansive first theme in E minor, a tender second theme in E major, and a lyrical third theme that winds its way through many modulations back to the first two themes' recapitulation. The closing Allegro spiritoso is a rondo with two episodes: a vigorous rondo theme followed by a chromatic episode and a gentler, more lyrical episode. After the third statement of the rondo theme, Dukas combines all three themes in a Presto coda that takes the movement and the symphony to its exultant close. *—James Leonard*

Recommended:

○ **Slatkin Conducts Dukas** / Slatkin (cond.), National Orch. of France / 1999 / BMG 68802

CHAMBER MUSIC

Villanelle, for horn & piano (1906)

It may seem odd that the composer who created the stunningly brilliant *Sorcerer's Apprentice* produced practically no other enduring music. In his *Villanelle*, Dukas reveals a gift for molding simple materials into an evocative vignette. Dukas interprets "villanelle," which translates from the Italian equivalent as "country girl," in a musical context that suggests something more like "scenes in a rural setting." The composer produced *Villanelle* as an entry in a competition for which only the solo part and sketches for the orchestration were required. Dukas himself never got around to fleshing out the instrumental texture; so, while it is often played with piano accompaniment, full concert versions of the work are not, strictly speaking, Dukas' own. The writing for the solo horn, in any event, is fetching and effective. Dukas' indications in the score specify that certain passages must be played as though on a natural (valveless) horn; as a result, the piece is not chromatically rich, relying instead on the charm of its melodic material and its taut organization. At about six minutes in length, the *Villanelle* is a miniature and—because of the scarcity of works by the composer—a rare gem. *—Michael Morrison*

Recommended:

○ **French Music for Horn & Piano** / Tuckwell, Blumenthal / 1992 / Etcetera 1135

○ **Brian, Kell, Goossens play Schumann & Beethoven** / Brain, Moore / 1993 / Testament 1022

BALLET

La Péri (1911–1912)

Dukas' final significant work, the 20-minute ballet *La Péri* (subtitled "Poème dansé") was written for dancer N. Truhanova and was premiered by her on a program that also included dances to Schmitt's *La tragédie de Salomé*, d'Indy's *Istar*, and Ravel's *Valses nobles et sentimentales* (here retitled *Adélaide*). *La Péri* fit perfectly in this company, with its dreamy manipulation of two exotic themes in an orchestration Dukas intended to resemble "a kind of translucent, dazzling enamel." This is Dukas' most Impressionistic score, with the primary themes used as vehicles for explorations of mood and timbre. The orchestra can make a powerful noise in the work's many passionate sections, but at least half the score is given over to quiet washes of strings and delicate swirls of woodwinds, with Middle Eastern flavor provided by a few extra percussion instruments, notably the tambourine. In the story, which is based on an ancient Persian legend, Iskender (Alexander the Great) at last finds the Flower of Immortality in the hand of a sleeping Péri, or fairy. Iskender snatches the flower, which distresses the now wide-awake Péri; without it, she cannot serve Ormuzd, the god of light. Iskender becomes aroused by the Péri, who performs a seductive dance while the Flower of Immortality causes Iskender's face to glow red with desire. Realizing himself unworthy, he willingly hands back the flower; with it, the Péri rises into the light while Iskender recedes into the shadows and, presumably, death. The score begins with a regal, questing brass fanfare in ternary form, a piece written, and often played, separately. The dance music itself falls into three parts. The first opens with shimmering strings and mysterious horn calls, leading to variations on Iskender's sinuous, ever surging-and-receding theme. A mysterious transition leads to the second part, the Péri's dance, which is really a set of variations on her own more ecstatic theme. Dukas then developed the two themes together, eventually bringing them to a shattering climax. The final part is a brief epilog in which the Péri's theme, now dreamy and increasingly distant, mingles for the last time with Iskender's, which is now much calmer and broader than it initially was. The music dies away into the muted horn calls of the beginning. *—James Reel*

Recommended:

○ **Dukas: La Péri; Symphony in C; The Sorcerer's Apprentice; etc.** / Lopez-Cobos (cond.), Cincinnati SO / 1999 / Telarc 80515

○ **Ravel, Debussy, Dukas** / Jordan (cond.), Suisse Romande Orch. / 1999 / Cascavelle 5004

OPERA

Ariane et Barbe-Bleue (1899–1907)

Even among Dukas' relatively small, self-circumscribed output, *Ariane et Barbe-Bleu* is considered a masterwork. It is also considered one of the two supremely outstanding French operas of the twentieth century—the other one being Debussy's *Pelléas et Mélisande*. Both operas take their librettos practically wholesale from plays by the contemporary master Symbolist, Maurice Maeterlinck, and musically follow that author's penchant for understatement and suggestion. Both operas, though "anti-Wagnerian" in concept, are undeniably indebted to Wagnerian techniques, and bear hallmarks of musical Impressionism.

Dukas' opera, however, is not an emulation of Debussy's, even though it often seems to be about to veer into Debussy-ism. At one point this is absolutely intentional: when Ariane calls to Mélisande in Act II, the theme from Act I, scene 3 of *Pelléas et Mélisande*. The rich harmony and orchestration also keep tending towards sounding like Mussorgsky, Richard Strauss, and Wagner himself. The centrality and self-possession of Ariane in Maeterlinck's 1901 play carry over to the opera, and differ significantly from the more short-phrased dialogues of *Pelléas et Mélisande*. Indeed, Barbe-Bleu gets decidedly short shrift. After Ariane, the only other important part is that of La Nourrice (the nurse), and she mainly functions as a medium for the self-expression of the title character.

The influence of Debussy's *Pelléas et Mélisande* is quite well noted. Much less is said about Dukas' *Ariane et Barbe-Bleu*. Its harmony and orchestration were widely respected, and its influence particularly on musical Expressionism was great, particularly with Schreker, Schoenberg, and Berg. Bartók's 1911 opera *A Kékszakállú Herceg Vára* (*Bluebeard's Castle*) uses a libretto based on the Maeterlinck play, though significantly altered and simplified. Many have detected the spirit of Richard Strauss and Dukas in the sumptuous orchestral music accompanying the openings of the seven locked doors in Bartók's opera.

Although the performance at the premiere of *Ariane et Barbe-Bleu* at the Opéra-Comique on May 10, 1907, was less than ideal, it certainly didn't have all the difficulties that had beset *Pelléas et Mélisande* five years earlier. For one thing, Maeterlinck's wife, Georgette Leblanc, did get to sing the title female role in Dukas' opera—a fact that couldn't have hurt it from that author's point of view. Subsequent performances improved, and the opera went on to enjoy more than modest success, both in France and other countries. In 1935, months after Dukas' death, it entered the repertory of the Paris Opéra at the famed Palais Garnier. *—Neil Cardew-Fanning*

Synopsis:

Act One. A crowd of vociferous peasants is gathered outside Barbe-Bleu's castle, discussing him and his newest wife. They ask if Barbe-Bleu killed his five previous wives, will Ariane be next, does she know of this history, and, are the five still living but confined to a dungeon? Ariane and her nurse enter the large hall of the castle. Barbe-Bleu has given Ariane seven keys: six silver, the seventh gold. He has forbidden Ariane to use the latter one. Ariane feels that this key must be the one to unlock his secret, and it is therefore the only one she wants to use. The nurse takes the silver keys and one-by-one unlocks the six doors, revealing various gems and jewels. Only the diamonds tantalize Ariane, as she has a passion for light. She unlocks the seventh door with the forbidden key and hears the voices of the previous wives down below. She is about to enter and descend a stairway when Barbe-Bleu returns to the castle, and discovering what she has done, chides her for her disobedience. He attempts to take her away, and as she contends with him, the nurse lets the peasants in to rescue her. Ariane assures them that she is neither hurt nor in danger, and asks them to leave, shutting the door after them. Barbe-Bleu flees.

Act Two. Ariane and her nurse (bearing a lamp) enter the nearly dark underground vault. They find Barbe-Bleu's five former wives scared and confused, their clothing in tatters. Ariane calls them individually and says she has come to free them. After a drop of water extinguishes the lamp, the wives lead her through the gloom to a corner where there is some light. She finds an obstructed portal, which she forcibly opens to reveal a large window emitting some light. Ariane shatters the glass with a stone. An incredibly bright light penetrates the dungeon, so great that even Ariane is bedazzled by it. She bids the five wives to gaze out on the world they've been shut away from, and leads them joyfully out of their prison.

Act Three. The seven women have been unable to leave the castle as the drawbridges have been raised and water has suddenly filled the moat. Ariane encourages the wives, newly clothed, to prepare for freedom and deck themselves with flowers and jewels (that were behind the six doors). As Barbe-Bleu returns with his bodyguard, he is attacked by the peasants, wounded and bound. They bring him into the hall to allow the wives to avenge themselves. Ariane dismisses the peasants, cuts Barbe-Bleu's bonds, and the former wives attend to his wounds. As Ariane and the nurse are about to leave, Ariane enjoins the women to come with her to freedom. They decline, and two of them shut the gate behind her. *—Neil Cardew-Fanning*

Recommended:

○ **Dukas: Ariane et Barbe-Bleue** / Jordan (cond.) ,Ciesinski, Bacquier, French Radio Orch. / Erato 45663

John Dunstable

b. ca. 1390, England [?], **d.** Dec. 24, 1453, London, England

Composer: Choral

Dunstable's name suggests he may have been born in the town of Dunstable in Bedfordshire, England. Sources from his time, including a possible signature of his own, spell his name "Dunstaple." The birthdate of 1390 is surmised from the appearance of his earliest known datable works, the motets *Veni sancte spiritus* and *Preco preheminencie*, heard during the celebrations that followed in the wake of English King Henry V's victories in the Battle of Agincourt. These pieces were repeated at Canterbury Cathedral for the King and the Holy Roman Emperor Sigismund in 1416; this is the only connection that can be drawn between Dunstable and Canterbury. This could suggest Canterbury composer Leonel Power, author of the *Old Hall Manuscript*, knew Dunstable, and Power may have been Dunstable's teacher. The work of Dunstable and Power is so similar that in several instances contemporary manuscript copies bear attributions to both composers for the same pieces.

Dunstable disappears from the historical record until 1427, when it is established that he was then in France in the service of Henry V's younger brother John of Lancaster, Duke of Bedford. Dunstable is also shown to be in the retinue of the notorious dowager Queen, Joan of Navarre, from 1428. The historical record relating to Dunstable's service to the Plantagenets is unclear, but this may mean that Dunstable traveled quite frequently between England and France, in service of both courts. During his travels abroad Dunstable may have become acquainted with his greatest admirers, the Franco-Flemish composers Guilliaume Dufay and Gilles Binchois. Fifteenth century treatises acknowledge the impact made by English music on French musicians during this period. This reflects the concurrent political situation as well, as much of the territory of France, including Paris itself, lay in English hands from 1420 to 1450, the final phase of the Hundred Years War. Dunstable benefited directly from this situation when the Duke of Bedford died in 1435, as Bedford awarded to Dunstable generous land grants in Normandy. Queen Joan remembered him a handsome annuity at her death in 1437. Dunstable was also an astronomer of considerable acclaim in his day, and astronomical charts believed to be in his own hand yet survive. However, all of his music is only known in copies made by other scribes. Most of Dunstable's music is preserved in sources located in Italy and Germany, rather than England, where just a scant remainder of contemporary examples remains.

Only a tiny fraction of Dunstable's work is of the secular variety, and of these the most widely circulated piece, *O Rosa bella*, is now known to be the work of Dunstable's younger contemporary John Bedyngham. Although Dunstable's musical output is primarily sacred, there is no evidence to suggest that he held any post as a cleric. When Dunstable died in 1453, he was both wealthy and famous, and his reputation as a composer survived well into the first part of the sixteenth century. Another presumed associate of Dunstable's, John Wheathampstead, abbot of Saint Albans, composed two epitaphs to Dunstable's memory, one of which reads "with (Dunstable) as judge, Urania learned how to unfold the secrets of Heaven. This man was your glory, O Music; who had dispersed your sweet art through the world. The 'star' transmigrates to the stars; may the citizens of Heaven receive him as one of their own." *—Uncle Dave Lewis*

CHORAL

Overview of Works (ca. 1410–1453)

A famous poem of Martin le Franc credits Dunstable with primacy in creating a sonic revolution early in the fifteenth century. According to the *Champion des Dames*, the first composers of the "Renaissance" on the Continent, Dufay and Binchois, adopted the sound of the "English countenance," the *Contenance Angloise*, led by Dunstable. John Dunstaple (in the more contemporary English spelling), also a renowned mathematician and astronomer, sang for the Duke of Bedford, Regent of occupied France; the wide dissemination of his music in Continental sources demonstrates his musical influence. Among his stylistic traits, those most likely to pertain to the "sweetness" praised by Le Franc and others are the high level of consonance and full triadic harmonies (though his cadence formulations are often archaic); this practice is likewise evident among the works of many English contemporaries such as Leonel Power. Dunstable is also known for the last great flowering of isorhythm, for careful patterning of textural changes, and (again with Power) for an epochal development: cyclic linking of the various movements of the Mass Ordinary.

Almost half of Dunstable's surviving musical compositions are Mass Ordinary settings. Though several movements stand alone, at least one Gloria setting was clearly composed in conjunction with the following Credo (both, unusually, in four voices); as many as three other such pairs, Gloria and Credo or Sanctus and Agnus Dei, may be adduced from voicing, tonal, and motivic relations. In addition, as many as four mass cycles, unified by means of a single tenor melody, survive with attributions to Dunstable. These include the Gloria/Credo pair set above isorhythmic elaborations of "Jesu Christe Fili Dei," a Kyrie-through-Sanctus cycle on single statements of "Da gaudiorum praemia," a complete mass setting upon different rhythmic outworkings of the chant "Rex seculorum," and a Missa "Sine nomine" upon an unidentified chant melody; these last two, unfortunately, have conflicting attributions to Leonel Power and John Benet.

While other English composers of the time cultivated the genre of the cyclic mass, Dunstable's enthusiasm for the archaic isorhythmic motet seems unsurpassed. He contributed at least 12 compositions in this genre, mostly in a thick four-voiced texture, with two or three competing simultaneous texts. The structural tenor, as in the tradition Dunstable inherited, is formed around rhythmically proportional transformations of a single preexistent liturgical chant; in his motets, however, all four voices are generally necessary to the counterpoint. In several pieces, the "free" voices are to some extent bound by isorhythmic proportions, and even may recycle entire melodic phrases. Dunstable's best-known work, the motet *Veni Sancte Spiritus*, adds to the highly cerebral mix a different plainchant paraphrased in the uppermost voice, and certain levels of number symbolism; the untarnished beauty of the work despite these constraints testifies to his compositional skill.

Most of the remaining works surviving from his pen are three-voiced settings of other Latin liturgical works; texts of Marian devotion are especially favored. The well-known setting of the Song of Solomon text *Quam pulchra es* provides perhaps the most exaggerated example of Dunstable's "sweetness" of pan-consonance. A number of these pieces, such as the Marian antiphons *Ave regina* and *Regina coeli*, give the liturgical chant in often lavish paraphrase in the upper voice; only the hymn *Crux fidelis* presents a middle-voice chant. A complete setting of the Magnificat, alternating two-voiced and three-voiced verses, is marked by a rich, sonorous character, and often shows signs of the English improvisatory practice of "Faburden." Only two secular compositions are thought to be his (one, *O rosa bella*, is certainly not), though he certainly must have contributed to the burgeoning tradition of the English carol. *—Timothy Dickey*

Recommended:

- ○ **Dunstable: Cathedral Sounds** / Clemencic, Mason, Chum, Clemencic Consort / 1996 / Arte Nova 34055
- ○ **Dunstaple: Musician to the Plantagenets** / Orlando Consort / 1995 / Metronome 1009

Preco preheminencie, isorhythmic motet (ca. 1410–1453)

News of a great victory came to King Henry V of England on August 21, 1416. His brother, John, the Duke of Bedford, followed up the recent English victory at Agincourt by breaking the siege of Harfleur and advancing the English cause in the Hundred Years' War. An immediate service of thanksgiving was called in Canterbury Cathedral, in which both King Henry and the Holy Roman Emperor Sigismund took part. A contemporary verse chronicling the solemn event lists each piece of music sung; a motet for Saint John the Baptist (Bedford's patron saint) with *Inter natos mulierum* and the unique text *Preco preheminencie* featuring prominently. This yields one of the only surviving clues to a performance of music by Bedford's famous musician, John Dunstable. Both Italian and English sources preserve copies of his isorhythmic motet for St. John, *Preco preheminencie*.

Three of Dunstable's four voices sing different texts (following the vibrant tradition of multi-texted motets in fourteenth century France). The voice upon which the piece's structure is founded, the tenor, sings a fragment of a plainchant antiphon for the Nativity of John the Baptist in the Sarum (English) Rite, *Inter natos mulierum* (*Matt 11:11*; *Luke 7:28*). The more florid upper pair of voices sings texts apparently unique to this setting: "Preco preheminencie" and "Precursor premittitur." Both are highly rhythmic, with clear poetic couplets; both present a nearly overwhelming use of alliteration within their texts and between one another ("The preacher preceded the Prince of preeminence," and "The precursor is pre-sent to prepare the people" in Howlett's translation). These two texts, one presenting the moment of Christ's baptism by John and the other John's imprisonment, might preserve pieces of the same poem.

Musically, *Preco preheminencie* follows a classical pattern of isorhythmic structure in the lower pair of voices. Two iterations of a rhythmic pattern (or talea) are allotted to the 24 notes of the tenor melody (the isorhythmic color). The tenor voice sings this entire isorhythmic complex three times, with note values decreasing in the proportion of 3:2:1. Each new (faster) statement in the tenor and the textless contratenor bassus is preceded by rests, filled by duet passages in the upper voice pair whose lines show Dunstable's characteristic use of triadic openings, fluid rhythms, and melodic grace. The "harmony-bearing" lower pair provides a platform for the more song-like upper pair, gradually building the rhythmic crescendo. *—Timothy Dickey*

Recommended:

- ○ **The Medieval Experience** / Turner (cond.), Pro Cantione Antiqua / 1995 / Archiv 449082
- ○ **Dunstaple: Musician to the Plantagenets** / Orlando Gibbons Viola Ens. / 1995 / Metronome 1009

Puisque m'amor, rondeau (ca. 1410–1453)

When Martin le Franc, in his famous early 1400s poem "Le champion des dames," praised the "English face" of contemporary music, he was probably thinking of John Dunstable. But as the bitterly ironic winds of history would have it, people now know and quote (at least in history classes) le Franc's line by heart, but know almost nothing of the celebrity he cites. Dunstable's biography is an illegible palimpsest upon the more readable pages of the time in which he lived. And while Dunstable's music is now quite well known and oft played (thanks to scholars like Margaret Bent), his place in history still cedes to early Renaissance composers like Guillaume Dufay and Gilles Binchois—both of whom poet le Franc referred to as influenced by Dunstable's new musical face. There are, however, some concretized traces of Dunstable, the big-man-on-the-Renaissance-campus. One materializes in countless versions of his modest little chanson *Puisque m'amour.* There is perhaps no musical culture closer to popular-song tradition than that of the medieval and early Renaissance song. Here, like there, a good tune goes a long way, and its celebrity becomes synonymous with how many covers it receives, how much it's reworked and arranged. Think of the Beatles' "Come Together"—Dunstable's *Puisque m'amour* is a distant foil at the top of a more aristocratic hit parade. It exists in four versions that shave off its third voice, the contratenor; it also shows up with newly written contratenors, one of the musical middle ages' favorite ways to complement the original composer: imagination is thanked by being pitted against a new imagination. On top of this selection of vocal reworkings, *Puisque m'amour* also survives in a number of instrumental arrangements, for organ or possibly for simpler keyboard mechanisms that predate the harpsichord. These revisions tend to take advantage of the instrument's main privilege: since it could not expect to compete with the voice in its flexibility, continuity, and nuance of expressive inflection, it convolutes vocal lines into virtuosic folds of rapid ornament. So why the popularity? Is the song that good? Well, it's hard to listen with back-then ears, against which the hearing of present age is comparable to sight in a completely darkened room. Outlines are barely perceptible, and even then only able to be discerned after a long period of acclimation. Likewise with Dunstable's chanson: it may sound to contemporary ears much like most other three-voice ditties of the early 1400s. But on closer listen, the ears will gradually glean the prized "English face" le Franc so lauded. It can be heard in the sweetness of the thirds and sixths; in the cool, lucid roundness of the harmonic scheme that expands and contracts from bare octaves to concentrated unisons via its iconic passageway of dulcet affections. In addition to this Anglo-earmark, the chanson treats its text in a strikingly idiosyncratic manner; the rondeau form (AbaAabAB) is not structured into individual sections by the music, but treated like prose, around which the music freely courses in its creativity. *—Seth Brodsky*

Recommended:

○ **Das Buxheimer Orgelbuch, Vol. 1** / Payne / 1995 / Naxos 553466

Quam pulcra es, antiphon (ca. 1410–1453)

A famous passage by Martin le Franc in his *Champion des dames* (c. 1441) speaks of the *contenance angloise,* the new sweetness of English music as the apparently more barbaric Continental musicians recently encountered it. Martin credits Guillaume Dufay and Gilles Binchois with imitating the "English countenance" and bringing a rebirth of musical beauty to French-speaking lands; his judgment has provided the beginning of most historical concepts of the "Renaissance" in music. Although other prominent courtly musicians of the English fifteenth century certainly contributed to the style and assisted in transmitting this style to a France which Henry V had recently conquered, the composer whom Martin le Franc specifically names as leader among the English is John Dunstable. Dunstable was a mathematician, astrologer, and musician in the service of the Duke of Bedford, Regent of occupied France from 1422 till 1435. This period of Dunstable's service across the Channel might explain the survival in numerous Continental music manuscripts of his motet *Quam pulchra es.* The text of *Quam pulchra es* serves as a processional before the mass in the Sarum Rite (English plainchant according to the traditions of Salisbury Cathedral). The English chant for Sundays in summer and autumn and for Saturdays throughout the year, provided often elaborate processionals for the entry of clergy and other celebrants. Many of these chants in the fifteenth century were devotedly Marian in cast; several, including *Quam pulchra es,* use the sensual texts of the Song of Solomon. In the original Hebrew of the Old Testament, the Song may have preserved Israelite wedding poetry or an allegory of God's relationship to His people. In Medieval Catholic exegesis, the most common sublimation of its erotic content applied the Song allegorically to devotion of the Virgin Mary; the explicit nature of the imagery remained. A literal translation of *Quam pulchra es* (from Song of Songs 7:6–7, 11–12) for instance, ends with the lover's promise to go into the fields and enjoy the ripeness of her breasts. Musically, Dunstable reacts to the lush imagery of his text with an exquisite sweetness of sound. The three (male) voices relate most often to one another in pure triadic fashion; his "pan-consonant" harmony is so well controlled that no structurally important beat anywhere in the piece receives a dissonance. Imperfect consonances—thirds and sixths—predominate over the "perfect," but more austere fifths and octaves. The rhythms of the text drive those of the musical motives, lending a clarity of declamation to the piece. The composer also reveals some sensitivity to nuances of textual meaning, as in the graceful melismas on the luscious adjectives *deliciis* and *eburnea,* the contrasting steadfastness of the imitative motive on *caput,* and the dramatic invitation of fermata-marked chords when the text asks the beloved to come (*veni*). Many of these aspects, in fact, are not at all characteristic of the general style of Dunstable's motets. But *Quam pulchra es* was one of his most popular pieces in the fifteenth century and remains in the foundation of his fame. *—Timothy Dickey*

Recommended:

○ **Dunstable: Motets** / Hilliard Ens. / 1997 / Virgin 61342

Duo Crommelynck

f. 1974, Vienna, Austria, **db.** Jul. 14, 1994
Ensemble

Belgian pianist Patrick Crommelynck (born 1947) co-founded Duo Crommelynck with his Tokyo-born wife Taeko Kuwata (born 1945) in the 1970s. They had a splendid turn as a piano duo, carving out a solid reputation during a time when competition among piano duos was tough in Europe, given the popularity of such high-profile acts as the Pekinels and the Labèques. The Duo Crommelynck recorded many CDs, all for the Swiss Claves label, and their three-disc set of the four-hand works of Schubert won a Grand Prix du Disque from the Academie du Charles Cros. The senseless double suicide that claimed the pair in July 1994 was a tragedy that has few, if any, parallels in the history of classical music. *—Uncle Dave Lewis*

Recommended:

○ **Schubert: Works for Piano 4 Hands, Vol. 3** / Crommelynck Duo / 1994 / Claves 509413

○ **Dvořák: Complete Works for Piano 4 Hands, Vol. 2** / Crommelynck Duo / 1991 / Claves 509107

Henri Duparc

b. Jan. 21, 1848, Paris, France, **d.** Feb. 12, 1933, Mont-de-Marsan, France
Composer: Vocal

Examination of the life of Henri Duparc often leads one not to explore what he accomplished but to speculate on what he might have accomplished. While Sibelius and Copland wrote virtually nothing over their last 30 years of life, presumably because their inspiration had been tapped out after producing sizable outputs, Duparc simply stopped composing in 1885, at age 36, in the midst of a burgeoning career. His oeuvre comprised 13 songs, some incomplete works like his opera *Roussalka,* and other compositions, which he later would not acknowledge or only grudgingly acknowledge, such as his symphonic poem, *Lenore.* His greatest contribution was in his songs, which demonstrated a sophistication in uniting the text with the music, in using fairly elaborate contrapuntal elements in the accompaniment, and in eschewing overly sentimental moods often heard in the songs of other French composers of the time. While Duparc was obviously not a major composer, he was a minor figure who clearly demonstrated talents that might have elevated him to the front rank.

As a child and teen Henri Duparc showed an interest in many fields and possessed an extraordinary intellectual capacity. Yet, he also divulged a sensitive, sometimes hesitant nature. He initially began studying for a career in law, but concurrently took piano lessons from César Franck. Later he studied composition with him and soon began writing music. He typically destroyed his early works, not satisfied with aspects of his style, or with the entirety of the piece itself.

In 1868, his *Five Mélodies,* for voice and piano, were published, marking his first major surviving song collection. Shortly afterward he expressed doubts about three of them (*Serenade, Romance de Mignon,* and *Le galop*), though he ultimately allowed their survival. From this early period there exists a *Sonata for piano and cello* (1867), not published but in manuscript form, held by his daughter's estate.

In 1869, Duparc received his first substantial exposure to Wagner's music when he traveled to Munich for several performances. There he met Liszt, who introduced him to Wagner at that year's Bayreuth Festival. Wagner became a hero to Duparc, and at times a noticeable influence in his music. The composer would make numerous trips to Bayreuth over the next several decades, often with friends like Chabrier.

By the early 1870s Duparc was turning toward the orchestra. In 1874 he wrote *Poéme nocturne,* which was premiered in April that year at a Société National concert. Only the first of the three parts, however, has survived. Also, Duparc composed the aforementioned symphonic poem, *Lénore,* in 1875. Four years later, still in the thrall of Wagner, though not stylistically now, he began work on his opera *Roussalka.*

In 1885, Duparc abruptly abandoned composition, at least in part owing to a neurasthenia, which may have had psychological manifestations. The composer had an acute sense of pain and other physical discomforts, but managed a reasonably normal life with his wife and family. Though he composed no new music after 1885, in the early 1900s he did revise some earlier works, like the 1868 *Five Mélodies* and the *Poéme nocturne* of 1874.

In the early 1900s Duparc became blind. Always a religious man and growing more so in his later years, he traveled to the shrine known for miracles in Lourdes, France, in 1906. He seemed to accept his blindness, and toward the end of his life he suffered from paralysis. *—Robert Cummings*

VOCAL

Songs (1868–1886)

The matter of Wagnerism in France—or of "the French Wagnerians"—has been almost wholly misunderstood in terms of baleful *à rebours* influence and slavish imitation. Of the composers usually cited—Chabrier, Fauré, Chausson, d'Indy, Duparc—only the systematic d'Indy would lavish a half-dozen years of his youth on such a

Wagnerian white elephant—*Fervaal* (1889–95). Duparc, on the other hand, who made excursions to Munich to hear Wagner operas with d'Indy, his fellow Franck pupil, around the time of the Franco-Prussian War, instinctively realized what Nietzsche would later make explicit in *The Case of Wagner*. "... Wagner is admirable and gracious only in the invention of what is smallest, in spinning out the details. Here one is entirely justified in proclaiming him a master of the first rank, as our greatest *miniaturist* in music who crowds into the smallest space an infinity of sense and sweetness. His wealth of colors, of half shadows, of the secrets of dying light spoils one to such an extent that afterward almost all other musicians seem too robust."

That could serve admirably to describe Duparc's *mélodies*. But he, too, was haunted by the desire to compose an opera, and considered *King Lear and Cymbeline*, *Francesca da Rimini*, and Molière's *Amphitryon* as possible subjects before settling upon Pushkin's *Roussalka*, which occupied him for years, and the score of which he destroyed, rewrote, and destroyed again. Nonetheless, by 1868 he had already composed *Sérénade*, *Romance de Mignon*, *Le galope*, *Soupir*, and *Chanson triste*. The *Romance de Mignon* was a disappointingly wan rendering of Goethe's poem ("Kennst du das Land?"), while *Le galope* is merely effective. *Sérénade* is salon fare—but *superior* salon fare. *Soupir* and *Chanson triste*, on the other hand, were admitted to the exclusive canon of 13 *mélodies* by which Duparc ultimately wished to be known, and moreover, must have revealed to him how "an infinity of sense and sweetness" could be "crowded into the smallest space" while dispensing with the dramaturgical detritus of libretto, plot, *mise en scène*, and so on. *Au pays où se fait la guerre* (1869–70, orchestrated 1876) is, in fact, a concentrated operatic scene salvaged from *Roussalka*. The hallucinatory *La vague et la cloche* (ca. 1871, orchestrated 1913) presents a gripping interior drama, while the incisive but subtle *Le manoir de Rosemonde* (1879, orchestrated 1912)—"Like a dog, love has bitten me"—is shadowed in Symbolist nightmare. The exquisite *Tristanesque Extase* (1874) demonstrated how Wagner's sensual languor could be appropriated and down-distilled in the *mélodie*. And *Phidylé* (1882, orchestrated 1891–92) illumines Leconte de Lisle's prim conceits in an effulgent answer to the "Liebestod." *Lamento* (1883), set earlier by Berlioz and Fauré. *Elégie* (1874), *Sérénade florentine* (1880–81), and *Testament* (1883, orchestrated 1900–01), also discover multidimensional intensity in poems that seem fairly flat. Yet Duparc rose superbly to Baudelaire's verse in the glowing, nostalgia-rife *La vie antérieure* (1884, orchestrated 1911–13) and—his best-known *mélodie*—*L'invitation au voyage* (1870, orchestrated 1892?), shimmering with "half shadows and the secrets of dying light." *—Adrian Corleonis*

Recommended:

○ **Songs of Henri Duparc** / Allen, Walker, Vignoles / 1989 / Hyperion 66323

Desmond Dupré

b. Dec. 19, 1916, London, England, **d.** Aug. 16, 1974, Tonbridge, England

Lutenist

Desmond Dupré was a pioneer in the performance of lute and viola da gamba during the twentieth century early music revival. After studying chemistry at Oxford, he began his musical training at the Royal College of Music in 1946, where he studied cello with Ivor James and harmony with Herbert Howells. The following year, he taught himself the viol and started to perform professionally as a guitarist and also as a cellist with the Boyd Neel Orchestra. In 1950, he made his first of many recordings with Alfred Deller, accompanying him on the guitar. After teaching himself the lute, he used that instrument for further collaborations with Deller, including a 1951 Wigmore Hall debut recital, and became the first president of the Lute Society (1956–73). Dupré performed regularly with other leading early music groups, including the Julian Bream Consort, the Jacobean Consort of Viols, and Musica Reservata. He recorded Bach's sonatas for viola da gamba and harpsichord with Thurston Dart, and Dart reconstructed a Handel concerto for lute and harp, which Dupré premiered. *—Robert Adelson*

Recommended:

○ **Love Songs in Shakespeare's Time** / Iadone, Dupre & Oberlin (lutes) / 1999 / Fine Tune 4420

○ **Shakespeare Songs** / Deller (cond.), Dupre, Deller Consort / HM 195202

○ **The Three Ravens** / Deller, Dupre / 2003 / Vanguard 1252

Marcel Dupré

b. May 3, 1886, Rouen, France, **d.** May 30, 1971, Meudon, France

Composer: Keyboard

Marcel Dupré was the foremost French organ virtuoso of his time, an heir to the great tradition of Romantic French organ playing and composing. Dupré was famed for his ability to improvise; he also composed substantial works and was a widely traveled recitalist and an influential teacher.

His pedigree as a French organist was impeccable. His father and two grandfathers were organists and choirmasters, and he was tutored privately by Guilmant in 1898. Dupré studied at the Paris Conservatory (1902–14) with Vierne, Diémer, and Widor. He had already given his first organ recital at age ten, had been appointed organist at St. Vivien at 12, and had had his oratorio *Le Songe de Jacob* performed (in his home) at 15. As a youth he also took long walks with the organ builder Cavaillé-Coll; the two discussed organ construction. In 1914, after already having won conservatory prizes for organ and fugue, he received the Grand Prix de Rome for his cantata *Psyché*.

In 1920 Dupré gave a series of ten recitals in which he played from memory the complete organ works of J.S. Bach; he had learned the music during World War I, for which he had been found unfit for duty. He toured extensively as a virtuoso, giving as many as 110 recitals in a single trip and making ten tours of the U.S. alone between 1921 and 1948. Dupré celebrated his 1,900th concert in 1953. He frequently improvised fugues and organ symphonies from themes suggested by musicians in the audience; his *Symphonie-Passion* and *Le Chemin de la croix* (The Way of the Cross) were first improvised in performance (in Philadelphia and Brussels, respectively) and later notated. His written compositions include a series of 76 chorales, a concerto for organ and orchestra, and two symphonies for solo organ. Dupré also wrote several texts on organ technique and improvisation. All his music has a tonal basis overlaid with high chromaticism. His habit of using chords in rapid bunches was soon picked up by his pupils Alain and Messiaen.

Dupré's academic appointments included a professorship at the Paris Conservatory from 1926 (an institution he directed from 1954 to 1956) and oversight of the American Conservatory at Fontainebleau (1947–54). From 1934 until his death at age 85, he also served as organist (succeeding Widor) at St. Sulpice. *—James Reel*

KEYBOARD

79 Chorales, Op. 28 (1931)

These 79 chorales for organ, based on the melodies of 79 chorales used by J.S. Bach in his chorale preludes, were composed in 1931. Dupré wrote them (mostly on the beach during a family vacation) for a friend who owned a small household organ and wanted to learn to play Bach chorales but wasn't yet up to the challenge. They range from simple harmonizations to works with more active (and more chromatic) accompanying voices that approach the complexities of their models, and for an aspiring organist they are one-of-a-kind teaching pieces. Most are in four parts, with the chorale in the soprano or tenor voice; in a few, it is in the bass and is played by the pedals. Several have simple canonic or fugal treatments. Each chorale fills one page of printed music, and some are burnished with chromatic touches that mark them as characteristic works of their composer. Dupré seemed ambivalent about the value of these works. Several times he stated he hadn't intended them for public performance, but he occasionally included them in concerts and even recorded three of them on a small organ of his own in 1934. They are attractive on their own and are of immense interest for the way they make manifest the suffusing presence of J.S. Bach in musical pedagogy. Anyone trying to become a self-taught organist, of course, would do well to lay hands on a copy of these. A complete performance of all 79 chorales will fit on a single CD. *—James Manheim*

Recommended:

○ **Dupré: Complete Organ Works, Vol. 12** / Filsell / 2000 / Guild 7203

○ **Dupré: Works for Organ, Vol. 9** / Neswick / 1999 / Naxos 554378

Symphonie-Passion, Op. 23 (1924)

According to both the composer and those who were in the audience, French composer Marcel Dupré, one of the greatest of French organ players, apparently improvised a four-movement symphony for organ while giving a recital in Wanamaker Auditorium in Philadelphia on December 8, 1921. Some sources claim that Dupré returned to France and immediately began to write down and further elaborate the improvisation while others assert that he only began work on it three years later. But whatever the truth of the matter is, the work that was published as the *Symphonie-Passion* for organ, Op. 23, has proven to be the most popular of all Dupré's organ works. Part of the reason for this popularity is the fact that the work is based on four pre-existing liturgical themes that thereby ensure instant recognition in the audience. But the largest part of the work's success is simply because it contains some of Dupré's most appealing and dramatic music.

The *Symphonie-Passion* is laid out in four movements: "Le monde dans l'attente du Sauveur" (The World Awaiting Its Savior), "Nativité," "Crucifixion," and "Résurrection." In the opening movement, an agitated original first subject is contrasted with the serene plainsong *Jesu, Redemptor omniu*. The second movement describes the scene at the stable in Bethlehem, the arrival of the three Magi, and concludes with the Christmas hymn *Adeste fideles*. The third movement describes the scene on Golgotha with a series of jagged, so-called "nail" chords over a merciless ostinato rhythm, concluding with a gentle statement of *Stabat Mater dolorosa* theme. The closing movement is a huge, written out crescendo based on the plainsong *Adoro te devote*. *—James Leonard*

Recommended:

○ **Romantic French & German Organ Music** / Long / 1990 / Koch 7008

○ **Dupré: Works for organ** / Engels / 1999 / Naxos 553920

Variations on an Old Noël, Op. 20 (1922)

In the early 1920s, Marcel Dupré was making his name primarily as a performer, offering the complete works of Bach from memory in ten Paris recitals and then embarking on a tour to conquer the United States. He nevertheless found time to compose, and one of his most popular works from that period is this set of variations on an old French Christmas tune. Dupré somberly sets out the simple melody, then proceeds with ten brief variations. On paper, the approach looks academic, with a variation in canonic form, one in thirds, and so on. Aurally, though, the set is quite rich and Romantic. The theme itself rarely strays far from its original form, but is pictured in a series of increasingly fantastic harmonic and accompanimental landscapes. Some are whimsical, begging for reedy registrations; others are gnarled and mildly dissonant; one imitates the procedures and sonorities of medieval organ music, while another calls to mind a circus calliope. The ninth variation, a muscular little fugue, leads to the finale, a grand, loud restatement of the theme under a frantic babble of notes. Dupré was a gifted improviser and it was surely music such as this, performed off the cuff, that particularly impressed Americans during the tour that immediately preceded the notation of this work. *—James Reel*

Recommended:

- ○ **Daniel Roth Plays Marcel Dupré** / Roth / 1999 / Motette 12581
- ○ **Organ Music by Marcel Dupré** / Scott / 1986 / Hyperion 66205

Maurice Duruflé

b. Jan. 11, 1902, Louviers, Eure, France, **d.** Jun. 16, 1986, Paris, France
Composer: Choral, Keyboard

French organist and composer Maurice Duruflé is known for a small number of extraordinary compositions, among which the *Requiem* is perhaps the finest and most often performed. His works, which, due to his crippling self-criticism, number only 14, are based on Gregorian chant. Characteristically, these melodies, which retain their original suppleness, are surrounded by complex modal harmonies that are generated by an intricate web of polyphony.

Duruflé was born in Louviers, in the Normandy, France. At the age of ten, he entered the choir school at the Rouen cathedral, where he studied piano, organ and theory with Jules Haelling. It is during this time that Duruflé developed his affinity for Gregorian chant. Duruflé moved to Paris in 1919, where he studied with Charles Tournemire, organist at St. Clotilde, where Duruflé later became his assistant. He later became the assistant of Louis Vierne at Notre Dame.

In 1920, Duruflé entered the Paris Conservatoire, where studied organ with Eugène Gigout, harmony with Jean Gallon, accompaniment with Estyle, counterpoint and fugue with Georges Caussade, and composition with Paul Dukas. At the Conservatoire, Duruflé took first prizes in the areas of organ, harmony, accompaniment, counterpoint and fugue, and composition. In 1929, he won a prize from the Amis de l'Orgue for interpretation and improvisation.

In 1930, he was appointed to the position of organist at St. Etienne-du-Mont, a position he held for the remainder of his life, sharing the appointment with his wife after 1953. That same year, he was again honored by the Amis de l'Orgue, this time for his *Prelude, adagio et choral varié sur le 'Veni Creator,'* Op. 4. In 1936, Duruflé received the Blumenthal Foundation Prize. In 1943, he became Dupré's assistant for the organ class at the Paris Conservatoire. He was also appointed professor of harmony, a position that he held until 1969. The Duruflé *Requiem* was premiered in 1947, by Desormière.

Duruflé was also a highly esteemed organist. He toured extensively throughout Europe and North America. His performing career was ended by an automobile accident in May of 1975 that left him virtually bed ridden until his death in 1986. *—Stephen Kingsbury*

CHORAL

Missa "Cum Jubilo," Op. 11 (1966)

In 1928, Maurice Duruflé entered Paul Dukas' composition class at the *Paris Conservatoire.* He seems to have learned there the proud, ingrown habit of self-criticism, and that one's music must be *very* good indeed to be made public. Dukas was notorious for destroying ambitious works—almost consigned to the flames, the superbly glowing *La Péri* survives to give a measure of the music that perished; this limited his catalog to a scant 12 published works, albeit they included an opera, a symphony, a piano sonata, and variation set, and the phenomenally popular *L'Apprenti sorcier* which are among the towering works of French music.

Duruflé, on the other hand, was primarily an organist and church musician, and his sphere of activity was far more limited. But within that sphere he achieved a unique utterance in a handful of suavely radiant works which loom as more enduring than bronze. Because both men composed urbane requiems rife with tidings of comfort and repose, Duruflé has been taken as a sort of poor cousin of Fauré. But where the latter employed modal coloring and a suggestion of chant, Duruflé absorbed Gregorian melody as a second nature, and its long-breathed, supple phrasing informs an otherwise smartly up-to-date idiom with an enchanting aura of timelessness.

This is nowhere truer than in the *Messe "Cum jubilo,"* especially in light of the blithely serene Kyrie. But in the Gloria—playing a bit over five minutes, the longest of the mass' five succinct sections—the chant-inspired central baritone solo ("Qui tollis") is flanked by jubilant affirmations which could almost be by the Poulenc of *Les Mamelles de Tiresias*, and quite disarming in their juxtaposition. The Sanctus opens on a glowing mystical note, rises to a solemn paean of praise ("Hosanna in excelsis"), and retreats as if in awe. A baritone solo intones the very brief Benedictus with comforting assurance, to questioning interjections from the organ. And in the Agnus Dei, the music seems to hover, abashed before the central mystery, yet lingering.

As he did for his requiem, Duruflé left three scorings for the *"Cum jubilo" Mass.* There are versions for large orchestra, small orchestra, and organ—all of which retain the original's unusual vocal forces: a chorus of baritones in unison, with baritone solo. Dedicated to Marie-Madeleine Duruflé, the work received its premiere at the Salle Pleyel, Paris on December 18, 1966, with Camille Maurane taking the solo, the Stéphane Caillat Choir, and the Lamoureux Orchestra led by Jean-Baptiste Marie. *—Adrian Corleonis*

Recommended:

- ○ **Duruflé: Requiem; Messe "cum jubilo"; Motets** / Plasson (cond.), Toulouse Orch., Orfeon Donostiarra / 1999 / EMI 56878

Four Motets on Gregorian Themes, Op. 10 (1960)

Duruflé's choral setting of "Ubi caritas" is one of the most popular sacred a cappella works of the twentieth century; it is, however, only one of a group of four works of equally high caliber. The *Four Motets*, written just before the final version of the composer's *Requiem*, are dedicated to Auguste Le Guennant, the director of the Gregorian Institute in Paris at the time. Each is based on a different Gregorian chant tune which remains prominent throughout; this process is similar to that employed in the *Requiem*, lending the pieces a flexible, speech-like rhythm. The incipit (the first few notes) of the original melody is given in neumatic chant notation at the beginning of each motet.

Each of the motets is quite short—a trait that is typical of Duruflé (even the *Requiem*, his largest work, is composed of nine much smaller units). Also typical is his use of Renaissance contrapuntal techniques in the service of a rich harmony derived from that of Fauré and Ravel. Performed as a set, the *Four Motets* have a classic arch shape, reaching a climax in the third motet ("Tu es Petrus"), then, in "Tantum ergo," returning to the mood of serene contemplation first established in "Ubi caritas."

The text of "Ubi caritas" ("Where charity and love are, there is God") is an antiphon usually sung on Maundy Thursday during the washing of the feet. This is the most famous of the motets, and an example of Duruflé's style at its best: rhythmic flexibility, strong part-writing, and rich harmony provide a serene background for the chant melody. The opening phrase returns briefly at the end (Duruflé, like Chopin and other composers who tended toward shorter compositions, usually composed in ternary form), and leads to an appended "amen."

"Tota pulchra es" ("You are all-beautiful") is a setting of antiphons from the feast of the immaculate conception of the Virgin Mary, and is sung only by the sopranos and altos. The opening melody serves as a kind of refrain, coming back twice. The pace is rather faster than in the "Ubi caritas," and leads into the climactic third motet.

"Tu es Petrus" ("You are Peter") is the shortest of the motets, and is a setting of the Jesus's renaming of his disciple Simon by the Greek for "rock," and then saying that "upon this rock will I build my church" (Matthew 16:18). The latter phrase is stated three times in Duruflé's setting, perhaps reflecting Peter's later three denials of Jesus. "Tu es Petrus" is much more rhythmic than the other motets, and builds to a loud climax.

In "Tantum ergo" (the last two verses of the "Pange lingua" eucharistic hymn traditionally attributed to Thomas Aquinas), the chant is sung in long notes by the sopranos. The melody is imitated and varied by the tenors, while the other voices are freely composed, with an effect similar to cantus firmus settings of chants from the Renaissance period. There are no accidentals (notes outside the key in which it is written), and very little harmonic tension. The motet, like the "Ubi caritas," ends peacefully on a low chord with the word "amen." *—David A. McCarthy*

Recommended:

- ○ **Duruflé: Requiem; Mass 'Cum Jubilo'; motets** / O'Donnell (cond.), Westminster Cathedral Choir / 1995 / Hyperion 66757
- ○ **Duruflé: Requiem; 4 Motets** / Best (cond.), Corydon Singers / 1986 / Hyperion 66191
- ○ **Lux Aeterna** / Hill (cond.), Winchester Cathedral Choir / 2002 / Virgin 562086

Requiem, Op. 9 (1947)

In 1947, Maurice Duruflé was already working on a suite of pieces for organ based on the Gregorian chants for the requiem mass (the service for the dead), when he was commissioned by his publisher Durand to write a large-scale work based on those texts. The resulting *Requiem*, originally for orchestra and chorus, is the culmination of Duruflé's style, mixing chant, quasi-Renaissance counterpoint, and sumptuous harmony derived from Fauré, Debussy, and Ravel.

Duruflé made three versions of this work; the final one, completed in 1961, is for choir, string orchestra, trumpets, and organ; it is the most practical and the most commonly used. He used the same text as Fauré had done in his *Requiem* of 1889, omitting the Dies Irae (Day of Wrath) section which, although it provided some of the most spectacular music in the Mozart, Berlioz, and Verdi settings, was not compatible with the gentler, more reassuring tone of the work. This peaceful quality is in many ways simply a reflection of the *Requiem*'s indebtedness to Gregorian chant, the flowing, easy quality of which serves as a musical template for many of the movements (chant formed a large part of Duruflé's musical upbringing: from 1912 to 1918 he was a boy chorister at the cathedral in Rouen, where the services were almost entirely chanted, and his professional education was at the Paris Conservatoire, where harmonizing chant melodies was a large part of the training for organists). Duruflé presents the chants quite clearly, much as in the *Four Motets on Gregorian themes*. The serene mood is enhanced by pervasive imitative counterpoint in a quasi-Renaissance melodic style. There is often a similarity of sound between Duruflé's music and that of Vaughan Williams, who briefly studied in France and also used modal melodies and counterpoint, though for him these archaic-sounding techniques were inspired by English folk music and the composers of the Tudor era. With Duruflé, the modal counterpoint is supported by rich, and very French, added-note harmonies.

Duruflé's grounding in the past is evident throughout the *Requiem*. The opening movement, one of the most beautiful in twentieth century music, sets a mood for the rest of the piece: running sixteenths (a favorite device of Duruflé's) create a wash of sound, preparing the entrance of the tenors and basses intoning the requiem chant, soon accompanied by a wordless vocalise from the women's voices. The original chant melodies are present in many of the movements; a striking instance is the Kyrie, where the trumpets sound the chant melody in long notes over a busy contrapuntal texture in the choir (which in turn is based on a rhythmicized version of the chant). The effect is similar to that of Bach's famous cantus firmus cantata opening movements—*Wachet Auf* and *Ein' feste Burg* are good examples. Another striking section is the Pie Jesu, which Duruflé sets in a style very similar to Fauré, with a mezzo-soprano solo accompanied only by organ and cello. In the final movement, In Paradisum, the sopranos, supported by full chords in the strings, sing the incantatory chant promising the deceased a peaceful welcome into heaven. At the words "chorus angelorum te suscipiat" (May the choir of angels receive you), the other singers enter with a beautiful, slowly descending passage to end the work. Duruflé's wife has said that while composing his *Requiem*, which is dedicated to the memory of his father, Duruflé "cried several times"; it is indeed one of the most moving religious works of the twentieth century. *—David A. McCarthy*

Recommended:

- ○ **Requiems of Duruflé & Faure** / Best (cond.), Trotter, English CO, Corydon Singers / 1998 / Hyperion 67070
- ○ **Duruflé: Requiem; Messe "Cum jubilo"; Motets** / Plasson (cond.), Alain, Hampson, Otter, Toulouse Orch., Orfeon Donostiarra / 1999 / EMI 56878
- ○ **Duruflé: Requiem; Mass "Cum jubilo"** / O'Connell (dir.), Simcock, Keenlyside, Webber, Clein, Westminster Cathedral Choir / 1995 / Hyperion 66757

KEYBOARD

Prelude and Fugue on the name Alain, Op. 7 (1942)

Born to a family of musicians in 1911—his sister is the renowned organist Marie-Claire Alain—the precocious Jehan Alain was forging a pungently distinctive personal style from the musical upheavals of the young century while still a student at the Paris Conservatoire, with Dupré for organ and the skeptical Dukas for composition. Among his contemporaries—Messiaen, Daniel-Lesur, Poulenc, Duruflé—he was recognized as a peer. While still taking classes, his skirling, jazzy *Litanies* (1937) achieved fame with organists around the world. Mobilized in August 1939, he fought in Flanders, participated in the evacuation of Dunkirk, and was killed in action near Saumur in 1940, aged 29, leaving behind some 127 works.

Duruflé's *Prélude et fugue sur le nom d'Alain*, Op. 7 is an homage to his fallen friend, composed in 1942. By manipulating the alphabet around those letters with musical significance, Duruflé finds an equivalent for Alain in the notes ADAAF, which yield a syncopated theme picked out against the *Prélude*'s flickering scherzo, thrice interrupted by a plangently descending quoted from *Litanies*. Its slowing last announcement ends the *Prélude* and leads directly to the attractive fugal subject, which undergoes a regular exposition. The development suggests a radiant smile before the scherzo returns, contrapuntally worked to a brilliant climax of great power. *—Adrian Corleonis*

Recommended:

- ○ **Organ Fireworks, Vol. 8** / Herrick / 1997 / Hyperion 66978
- ○ **Maurice & Marie-Madeleine Chevalier** / Durufle-Chevalier / 1999 / Gothic 49107

Suite, Op. 5 (1933)

Duruflé's *Suite*, Op. 5 represents one of the high points in the composer's substantial output for the organ. As with his other works for the instrument, it makes considerable demands on the player. The first movement, a Prelude in E flat minor, is constructed as a large arch. It opens with a funereal theme that exploits the organ's darkest, most brooding colors. As the movement progresses, the brighter organ stops slowly overcome the darkness of the opening until the grand sound of the full instrument bursts forth. From this great expanse of sound, Duruflé gradually returns to the contemplative mood of the opening.

The second movement is a graceful Sicilienne. The plaintive theme is isolated in various solo stops, accompanied by an eighth note figuration; these episodes alternate with a chordal texture played on string stops. The final Toccata, one of the most difficult pieces in the organ literature, is a sonic whirlwind that eschews the sort of consistent pattern of fast notes that characterizes many French organ toccatas; rather, it unfolds in a more improvisatory spirit. *—Darren Wong*

Recommended:

- ○ **French Symphonic Masterpieces** / Davidsson / 2002 / Loft Recordings 1054
- ○ **Organ Music by Maurice Duruflé** / Scott / 1990 / Hyperion 66368

Jan Ladislav Dussek

b. Feb. 12, 1760, Tschaslau, Bohemia (Czech Rep.), **d.** Mar. 20, 1812, St.-Germain-en-Laye, France

Composer

Jan Ladislav Dussek (Czech family name Dusík) was the first truly important touring piano virtuoso and a highly popular composer, although his music rapidly fell into obscurity. It was somewhat revived in the late nineteenth century, and 100 years after that was recognized for its originality. Primarily for piano, it is brilliant in effect, with fast, exciting figurations and other elements intended to dazzle. He was one of the first to write specific pedaling instructions into his scores. His music anticipates many aspects of later Romantic piano composers, to a surprising degree.

He was the son of Jan Dussek (1738–1818), a well-known local musician in Bohemia. He studied piano from the age of five, and began playing the organ at nine. He also had a fine voice, joining the boy choir of the Minorite church in Iglau (Jihlava). In 1778 he attended the University of Prague for one term.

He almost always had a job as organist and made public appearances as pianist. An artillery officer, Count Männer, took him on a concert tour in Germany. In 1780, he was piano teacher to the stadtholder's children in The Hague. He met C.P.E. Bach in Hamburg, in 1782, who may have taught him for a while. Dussek pressed on east, playing before Empress Catherine II in 1783. He left Russia quickly, with rumors that he was implicated in a plot against the Empress, and found refuge in Lithuania as Prince Karl Radziwill's Kapellmeister for the next two years.

He then toured Germany and France, playing glass harmonica as well as piano, and again making a huge impression with his virtuoso playing. In addition to having remarkable finger fluency and power, Dussek was able to make a singing, legato tone out of what is essentially a percussion instrument. The secret was the detailed study of the sustaining pedals of the piano, unprecedented at the time. He was the first pianist to turn the piano so that instead of facing the audience across the long axis of the instrument, he sat with his right profile presented to the audience, allowing the piano lid to be opened to reflect and project the sound outward.

He appeared before the French court, playing for Marie Antoinette. With the Revolution, Dussek fled to London, anticipating that his aristocratic ties would be unpopular with the new regime. He spent 11 years in London, where he was praised by Haydn. He encouraged the English piano-maker Broadwood to adopt a longer keyboard, six octaves wide. He married Sophia Corri, whose father was a conductor originally from Naples. She was an accomplished singer, pianist, and harp player, and often appeared with her husband. They had one child, Olivia. Dussek and his father-in-law went into business as music publishers and failed spectacularly by 1799. Corri was thrown into prison, and Dussek fled the country, leaving wife and daughter behind.

He resumed his European concert career and in October 1804, was appointmented Kapellmeister by Prince Louis Ferdinand of Prussia, who loved music so much, he took his musicians with him to the battlefields. Wild stories of these visits were told by Ludwig Spohr, the violinist and composer, who was also along. Dussek wrote his popular piano sonata, *Elégie harmonique*, Op. 61, after the Prince was killed in battle.

In September, 1807, Dussek accepted a position with the French minister Talleyrand and remained in that job until death. Contemporary accounts suggest that his powers were in no way diminished until the final months of his life, when he was bedridden, suffering from gout and other ailments, including excessive drinking and extreme obesity. *—Joseph Stevenson*

Overview of Works (1779–1813)

The nearly complete abandonment of Jan Ladislav Dussek's music shortly after his death in 1812 can pretty much be blamed on Beethoven. No, the brilliant Bonn-born musician bore Dussek no animus; but by the 1820s Beethoven's new, volatile brand of music making had so captivated European audiences that for the next half century, many seemed willing to forget that there ever had been a composer filling the gap between the age of Mozart and Haydn and their new hero. Dussek was himself one of the greatest pianists of his era, and his music, the vast majority of which features the piano, shows it. The performer must travel a difficult course, one not just virtuosic and physically tiresome but also emotionally dense and psychologically complex. Dussek has been labeled a mere showman, but he was not a one-sided figure at all. No touring pianist who adds a bit of glass harmonica playing to his programs, as Dussek did, could ever be called one-sided.

The list of Dussek's works is long. First and foremost are 41 sonatas for piano or piano four-hands. These pieces were the first to receive posthumous attention, when Breitkopf and Härtel reprinted them in the 1860s and 1870s, and among them are a few works that rightly belong with the masterworks of the genre. The two-movement *Sonata in F sharp minor,* Op. 61, an "Élégie harmonique sur la mort du Prince Louis Ferdinand," of 1806 is one, as is the *Piano Sonata in C minor,* Op. 35, No. 3, of 1797, whose imprint some hear in the sonatas that Beethoven composed around the same time. At the end of the Dussek timeline is *L'invocation,* a sonata in F minor, Op. 77, composed in 1812; it is a long four-movement thing, weighty and noble—a brilliant valedictory work.

Dussek composed about 18 piano concertos (some alternately for harp), a few of which are no longer extant. They occupy a unique realm of the Classical concerto: not the prim and proper concertos of Haydn and Mozart but also not the square, vigorous ones of Beethoven. They are today less well known than the sonatas, though one cannot help but be surprised that more harpists have not taken this body of work into their repertoires. Dussek also composed chamber music, including 87 sonatas or sonatinas for piano and violin (sometimes with cello accompaniment) and more than a dozen quintets, duos, etc. for other instruments. There is one 1797 item for violin, cello, piano, and percussion that goes by the unlikely name *The Naval Battle and Complete Defeat of the Dutch.*

Schooled by Jesuits and having pursued a course of university study in theology, Dussek inevitably put his talents, at least once, towards a sacred end—one of his last works is a *Missa Solemnis* without opus number for chorus, vocal soloists, and orchestra. While living in England in the 1790s he also tried writing music for stage, but without much success. Works like *The Captive of Spilberg* (1798) are best assigned to footnotes in the Dussek biography. *—Blair Johnston*

Recommended:

- ○ **Dussek & the Harp** / Perrett, Verney, Ellis, Cole / 2001 / Meridian 84451
- ○ **Piano Works of Dussek, Vol. 1** / Marvin / 1976 / Dorian 80110
- ○ **Dussek: Piano Concertos** / Staier (cond. & piano), Cologne Concerto / Capriccio 10444
- ○ **Dussek: Chamber Music with piano** / Conway, Blume, Croshaw, Shillito, Lynn / 2000 / Meridian 84383

Henri Dutilleux

b. Jan. 22, 1916, Angers, France

Composer: Chamber Music, Orchestral, Concerto

Henri Dutilleux is a hard-working French contemporary composer who emphasizes quality over quantity, shuns systems of formal organization, and writes rock-solid music tailored to the needs of specific ensembles. Dutilleux, independence of spirit sets him apart from many of his colleagues in France. His concern for instrumental color, spatial relationships among instrumental groups, and heterodox sense of spirituality maintains the French lineage of modernism that stems from the music of Debussy through the work of Messiaen. Dutilleux is deeply inspired by visual art, his orchestral work *Timbres, espace, mouvement* (1978) being directly inspired by Vincent van Gogh's painting *The Starry Night.*

Dutilleux was born the grandson of organist and composer Julien Koszul, who was onetime director of the Roubaix Conservatoire, a close friend of Gabriel Fauré, and helped foster the career of Albert Roussel. Dutilleux studied at the Douai Conservatoire until 1933 when he enrolled in the Paris Conservatoire. His third Prix de Rome cantata, *L'anneau de Roi,* won the Premier Prix in 1938, but the outbreak of war curtailed his award. Dutilleux served as a stretcher-bearer, and later as a singing coach at the French opera. It was during the war that Dutilleux began to stake out his reputation as a composer in works such as the *Sonatina for flute & piano* (1943) and the song *Chanson de la deportée* (1945). Ever conscious of the quality of his small work list, Dutilleux has renounced all of the pieces that predate the *Piano Sonata* (1946–1948), written for his new bride, pianist Genevieve Joy. At war's end Dutilleux took a job as a producer for the ORTF (French public radio) that he kept until 1963. In this capacity his unit sponsored "radiophonic" pieces by Pierre Schaeffer, Antonín Artaud, and others. As a composer, Dutilleux elected to stay in the background, working hard and patiently waiting his turn.

That recognition came with his *Symphony No. 1* (1951), which led to interest in Dutilleux, particularly among performers who have kept a stream of commissions coming his way since then. Among the artists who have had works written for them by Dutilleux are cellist Mstislav Rostropovich, the Juilliard String Quartet, violinist Anne-Sophie Mutter, the Boston Symphony Orchestra, and Swiss conductor Paul Sacher. Many of these works, such as the string quartet *Ainsi le nuit* (1977), the orchestral pieces *The Shadows of Time* (1997), and *Métaboles* (1964), are already regarded as masterworks of Western literature. *—Uncle Dave Lewis*

CHAMBER MUSIC

Ainsi la nuit, for string quartet (1973–1976)

Ainsi la nuit (1976) was commissioned by the Koussevitzky Foundation and was intended for performance by the Juilliard Quartet. Before starting on the actual composition, Dutilleux spent some time studying the intricacies of string-playing techniques of the time. He had not attempted to write a work for string quartet since his days as a student at the Paris Conservatoire. The composer has stated that Webern's *Six Bagatelles* (1913) were most beneficial in helping him get up to date. Dutilleux also looked over Berg's *Lyric Suite* (1926), as well as compositions for string quartet by Beethoven and Bartók. After making a series of sketches in which he practiced writing for string quartet, the composer sent three completed pieces to the Juilliard Quartet. These pieces, entitled *Nuits* (1974), have musical material which was later used in the final version of *Ainsi la nuit.* Dutilleux completed *Ainsi la nuit* in 1976 and the work was premiered on January 6, 1977, in Paris, but not by the Juilliard Quartet. Actually, the premiere was given by the Quatuor Parrenin. The Juilliard Quartet would first perform the composition in the Library of Congress at Washington D.C. on April 13, 1978.

The final version of the piece has seven movements with four "parentheses" lying in between the first five movements. Dutilleux did not like to leave the individual movements of his works untitled. The seven movements of *Ainsi la nuit* are "Nocturne I," "Miroir d'espace," "Litanies I," "Litanies II," "Constellations," "Nocturne II," and "Temps suspendu." The "parentheses" are mostly used to recall or foreshadow musical material in the rest of the work. For this reason, *Ainsi la nuit* is often associated with the idea of memory.

Many of the characteristics of Dutilleux's later works are displayed in *Ainsi la nuit,* including "fan-shaped" writing, the outlining of a tonal triad in a seemingly atonal work, and a similarity of some melodies to the modality of Gregorian chant. Dutilleux's "fan-shaped" writing can best be described through a piano composition in which the placement of the pianist's fingers create a mirror image between the hands. In *Ainsi la nuit,* this is accomplished through the voices of the four string instruments. Many of Dutilleux's pieces from the same period as *Ainsi la nuit* also make use of "fan-shaped" writing. It has also been discovered that in some of Dutilleux's later works, a tonal triad is outlined over the course of the piece by an emphasis on individual pitches. This is also true in *Ainsi la nuit,* as a D major triad is outlined with each successive pitch being centered upon in a separate movement. The pitch D is emphasized in the untitled introduction, while F sharp is the most important pitch in the fourth movement, "Litanies II." Finally, in "Constellations," the climax of the piece, the pitch A is the central pitch. The Gregorian influences in "Nocturne I," as well as the opening of "Litanies II," were acknowledged in Dutilleux's own program note. *—Chris Boyes*

Recommended:

- ○ **Dutilleux & Dusapin** / Arditti SQ / 1994 / Disques Montaigne 782016
- ○ **Debussy, Ravel & Dutilleux** / Juilliard Qt. / 1993 / Sony 52554

Flute Sonatina (1943)

Predating his official Opus 1 (the *Piano Sonata*) by five years, Henri Dutilleux's *Flute Sonatina* hardly reflects the composer's distinctive mature style; it's in a more generic, sometimes saucy French manner. The Paris Conservatory commissioned it as a test piece for the graduating flutists of 1942.

Lasting barely ten minutes, the sonatina falls into three sections played without pause. It begins with a mysterious, tonally ambiguous flute theme played over an angular, rising and falling piano motif that strongly recalls the style of Dmitry Kabalevsky. The flute offers some brighter material as a bridge to a restatement of the opening piano melody, now appropriated fully by the flute and sounding gradually more playful. A fast, tense, and questioning flute cadenza leads to an expressive, lyrical andante reminiscent of Poulenc in his most serious instrumental mode. Excitement eventually builds until the piano takes over with a jubilant, if initially frantic, melody. This burbling material soon becomes the flute's property, and the remainder of the section tests the flutist's articulation, breath control, and agility in music that grows increasingly lighthearted. Near the end, a challenging cadenza alludes to motifs from all three sections of the sonatina, with the piano joining for an accelerando through the final, bright measures. *—James Reel*

Recommended:

- ○ **Sonatines for flute & piano** / Bernold, Tharaud / 2000 / HM 901710

ORCHESTRAL

Métaboles (1959–1964)

After Henri Dutilleux completed this work, which was commissioned by the Cleveland Orchestra under George Szell, he looked up all the words beginning with the prefix "meta-" in the dictionary to find a title for it. He eventually settled on *Métaboles* because, in physiology, the word refers to the continuous, incremental chemical transformation of one compound into another. In Dutilleux's piece, the word describes the structure of the work, as each of the five brief orchestral movements is a transformation of the movement that succeeds it, and the final movement combines all that has come before. "Incantatoire," the first movement, begins with sustained E naturals in the winds, punctuated by sharp chords from the orchestra. The E natural becomes a pivotal point for the entire work. The remainder of the movement opposes freer melodies on the clarinet, flute, and trumpet to the E naturals. The strings only have the melody for a brief period in "Incantatoire," and that brief melody becomes the basis for the second movement, "Lineaire," written solely for the strings. Throughout the movement, there is only one prominent melodic line at a time, which gives it a "linear" feel. The music itself is slow and nocturnal, with Dutilleux's marvelous ear for timbres providing some gorgeous sounds. "Obsessionnel," is the skittish third movement that takes an idea from "Lineaire," makes it faster and more rhythmic, and entrusts it mainly to the brass, although pizzicato strings play a large role, as well. "Torpide," the fourth movement, features percussion accents on a series of sustained chords in the winds and brass, which are slowed-down remnants of the third movement. Dutilleux's use of percussion is highly inventive in using motion to suggest a lack of motion. The last movement is marked "Flamboyant," and it brings all the instruments together. After all the instruments have entered playing characteristic music from the first four movements, the winds play the E natural chords from the first movement. The whole orchestra then rushes headlong into a rousing coda. Dutilleux's highly individual orchestration always pleases the ear, and the formal methods he uses in *Métaboles* unify the work. *—Andrew Lindemann Malone*

Recommended:

○ **Honegger: Symphony 4; Dutilleux: Metaboles** / Munch (cond.), ORTF / Erato 45689

○ **Dutilleux: Symphony 2; Métaboles; etc.** / Saraste (cond.), Toronto SO / Finlandia 25324

Timbres, espace, mouvement, ou La Nuit étoilée (1976–1978; revised 1990)

Henri Dutilleux's *Timbres, espace, mouvement ou La nuit etoilée* (Timbres, space, movement or The starry night) depends on its spatial organization of instruments as much as its musical organization to convey meaning. Inspired in an oblique fashion by van Gogh's famous painting *La nuit etoilée*, Dutilleux decided to create a work where the movement of music through physical space, as well as through time, represents astrological phenomena. Twelve cellos are placed in a row in front of the conductor. Immediately behind them are the woodwinds: two flutes, three oboes, oboe d'amore, E flat clarinet, two clarinets in A, bass clarinet, three bassoons, and a contrabassoon. Next comes a brass row, containing four horns, three trumpets, three trombones, and a tuba. Percussion, tympani, and double basses form the last row, and a celesta and a harp are placed in between the cellos and percussion to the left. The instrumentation produces a sound that is highly polarized between the woodwinds and the low strings, and the spatial organization lets Dutilleux move themes fluidly through space within the orchestra. This large orchestra also allows Dutilleux to indulge what he has described as his "delight in sound as such." The outer movements of this work are both named for astrological phenomena; the first is called "Nebuleuse" and the third is called "Constellations." These emphasize a continuous metamorphosis of themes and timbres moving across the orchestra. The "compositional space" between high and low establishes itself with the entry of high, quiet woodwinds followed by the low strings, and the tension between these two sections remains a key idea throughout. Originally, "Nebuleuse" and "Constellations" were the entire work, but in 1998, as a recording was being made, Dutilleux decided to add an Interlude for the cellos alone. Again, Dutilleux organizes the space of the sound; the four lines at first assigned to three cellos apiece soon collapse and mutate, and the organization of the cellos keeps changing according to numeric patterns until the end of the movement, when the cellos slowly fade out from left to right. Throughout this work, Dutilleux produces gorgeous sounds from his orchestra, and the final chorale-like chords in "Constellations" seem to both realize the possibilities of the work and point in new directions. *Timbres, espace, mouvement* works equally well in conception and realization. *—Andrew Lindemann Malone*

Recommended:

○ **Dutilleux: Timbres; Métaboles; Mystère de l'instant** / Rostropovich (cond.), National Orch. of France / Erato 45626

○ **Dutilleux: Complete Orchestral Works** / Tortelier (cond.), BBCPO / 2000 / Chandos 9853

CONCERTO

Tout un monde lointain . . . , cello concerto (1967–1970)

Although it is one of the most significant concertante works for cello and orchestra to have appeared during the second part of the twentieth century, the words "cello concerto" do not appear anywhere on the score of *Tout un Monde Lointain* (A Whole Remote World). Dutilleux took this title from Baudelaire's poem "La chevelure," from which the individual titles of the five movements are also taken. These ("Enigma," "Gaze," "Surges," "Mirrors," and "Hymn") suggest something of the atmosphere of the whole, but are not to be interpreted too literally. Structurally, the work is extremely complex. The opening movement sets out a basic dialogue between solo cello and orchestra, wide-ranging in tempo and registral effects, but with no sense of resolution between the protagonists. The music is cast as a set of variations on the 12-note theme heard at the outset and cross-referenced in each of the successive movements. The second and fourth sections are slow moving, while the third has the function of a scherzo, with solo writing of enormous technical difficulty. The final movement ("Hymn") is in the form of a vibrant Allegro, though the enigmatic overall feel of the work is still evident here. Dutilleux was commissioned to write the work by Igor Markevitch, who wanted a new concerto for Mstislav Rostropovich to perform with his Lamoureux Orchestra in the mid-1960s. Ironically, by the time Dutilleux began to write it, Markevitch had been replaced and the work was premiered by Rostropovich and the Paris Orchestra in Aix-en-Provence in 1970. *—Michael Jameson*

Recommended:

○ **Dutilleux & Lutosławski: Cello Concertos** / Baudo (cond.), Rostropovich, Paris Orch. / Angel 67868

Charles Dutoit

b. Oct. 7, 1936, Lausanne, France

Conductor

One of the world's foremost conductors, Charles Dutoit is especially noted for his performances of French, Russian, and twentieth century music. Dutoit began his studies at the Lausanne Conservatory (violin, piano, and orchestral conducting), and later continued in Geneva. In 1958 he received his diploma in conducting and went to Alceo Galliera at the Accademia Musicale Chigiana in Siena. In 1959 he took additional training in orchestral conducting in Tanglewood. From 1957 to 1959 Dutoit worked as a violist in Europe and South America before returning to Switzerland to conduct. In 1959 he was appointed as a guest conductor of the Orchestre de la Suisse Romande and the Lausanne Chamber Orchestra. From 1964 to 1966 he worked as a conductor for Radio Zurich, and from 1965–67 he conducted ballet at the Vienna Opera. He succeeded Paul Kletzki as the head of the Bern Symphony Orchestra (1968–78). In addition to his work in Bern, he directed the National Symphony Orchestra of Mexico from 1973 to 1975, and the Symphony Orchestra of Göteborg from 1975 to 1978. In 1977 Dutoit obtained the major appointment of his career: music director of the Montreal Symphony Orchestra. He quickly elevated the Montreal to international acclaim. He notably improved the orchestra's scheduling of Classical-era works, particularly the symphonies of Haydn. He is also noted for the championing of new Canadian music. Dutoit has been the artistic director and principal conductor of the Philadelphia Orchestra's concert series at the Saratoga Performing Arts Center in Saratoga Springs, New York, and has also directed the orchestra's summer series at the Mann Music Center in Philadelphia. In 1990, Dutoit became music director of the Orchestre National de France. Since September 1996, he has been the principal conductor of the NHK Symphony Orchestra in Tokyo and as of September 1998, also their music director. In April 2002, Dutoit resigned his position with the Montreal Symphony.

While in Montreal, Dutoit established an impressive legacy of recordings that won over forty national and international awards including the Grand Prix du Président de la République (France), the High Fidelity International Record Critics' Award, the Amsterdam Edison Award, the Japan Record Academy Award, the German Music Critics' Award, as well as numerous Juno awards. Dutoit and the Montreal received their first Grammy Award in 1996 for Best Opera Recording of Berlioz's *Les Troyens* and more recently, a second Grammy for their 1999 recording of Prokofiev's *Piano Concertos* Nos. 1 and 3, and Bartók's *Piano Concerto No. 3* with pianist Martha Argerich (Dutoit's former wife). The Montreal and Dutoit also recently won a Juno Award for their recording of Respighi's *La Boutique Fantasque* and *Impressioni brasiliane*.

Between 1981 and 2001, Dutoit and the Montreal undertook significant tours of Europe, the Far East, South America and the United States. Dutoit has conducted all the major orchestras of the world including those in Cleveland, Chicago, Los Angeles, the Israel Philharmonic Orchestra, the Berlin and Munich Philharmonics, and the Royal Concertgebouw Orchestra. Since his operatic debut at Covent Garden in 1983, he has conducted the Metropolitan Opera and at the Deutsche Oper in Berlin.

Dutoit has received numerous awards and distinctions including honorary doctorates from McGill University, the Université de Montréal, and the Université Laval. In 1982 Dutoit was named Musician of the Year by the Canadian Music Council, and in 1988 he received the Canadian Music Council Medal in recognition of his contribution to music in Canada. Also in 1988, the French government made Dutoit an *Officier de l'Ordre des Arts et des Lettres*, and in 1996, he was promoted to *Commandeur de l'Ordre des Arts et des Lettres*. *—AMG*

Recommended:

○ **Debussy Orchestral Music** / Dutoit (cond.), MSO / 1999 / Decca 460217

○ **Respighi Orchestral Music** / Dutoit (cond.), MSO / 1999 / Decca 455983

○ **Holst: The Planets** / Dutoit (cond.), MSO / 1998 / London 460606

○ **Gubaidulina: Offertorium; Hommage à T.S. Eliot** / Dutoit (cond.), Kremer, Geringas, Zimmermann, Brunner, BSO / DG 427336

○ **Ravel: Boléro** / Dutoit (cond.), MSO / 1999 / Decca 460214

○ **Ravel: Daphnis et Chloé** / Dutoit (cond.), Hutchins, Zirbel, MSO / 1999 / Decca 458605

○ **Chopin: Concertos 1 & 2** / Dutoit (cond.), Argerich, MSO / 1999 / EMI 56798

Antonín Dvořák

b. Sep. 8, 1841, Mühlhausen, Germany, **d.** May 1, 1904, Prague, Bohemia (Czech Republic)

Composer: Symphonic, Orchestral, Concerto, Chamber Music, Keyboard, Opera, Vocal, Choral

Widely regarded as the most distinguished of Czech composers, Antonín Dvořák (1841–1904) produced attractive and vigorous music possessed of clear formal outlines, melodies that are both memorable and spontaneous-sounding, and a colorful, effective instrumental sense. Dvořák is considered one of the major figures of nationalism, both proselytizing for and making actual use of folk influences, which he expertly combined with Classical forms in works of all genres. His symphonies are among his most widely appreciated works; the *Symphony No. 9* ("From the New World," 1893) takes a place among the finest and most popular examples of the symphonic literature. Similarly, his *Cello Concerto* (1894–95) is one of the cornerstones of the repertory, providing the soloist an opportunity for virtuosic flair and soaring expressivity. Dvořák displayed special skill in writing for chamber ensembles, producing dozens of such works; among these, his 14 string quartets (1862–95), the *"American" Quintet* (1893) and the *"Dumky" Trio* (1890–91) are outstanding examples of their respective genres, overflowing with attractive folklike melodies set like jewels into the solid fixtures of Brahmsian absolute forms.

Dvořák's "American" and "New World" works arose during the composer's sojourn in the United States in the early 1890s; he was uneasy with American high society and retreated to a small, predominantly Czech town in Iowa for summer vacations during his stay. However, he did make the acquaintance of the pioneering African-American baritone H.T. Burleigh, who may have influenced the seemingly spiritual-like melodies in the "New World" symphony and other works; some claim that the similarity resulted instead from a natural affinity between African-American and Eastern European melodic structures.

By that time, Dvořák was among the most celebrated of European composers, seen by many as the heir to Brahms, who had championed Dvořák during the younger composer's long climb to the top. The son of a butcher and occasional zither player, Dvořák studied the organ in Prague as a young man and worked variously as a café violist and church organist during the 1860s and 1870s while creating a growing body of symphonies, chamber music, and Czech-language opera. For three years in the 1870s he won a government grant (the Viennese critic Hanslick was among the judges) designed to help the careers of struggling young creative artists. Brahms gained for Dvořák a contract with his own publisher, Simrock, in 1877; the association proved a profitable one despite an initial controversy that flared when Dvořák insisted on including Czech-language work titles on the printed covers, a novelty in those musically German-dominated times. In the 1880s and 1890s Dvořák's reputation became international in scope thanks to a series of major masterpieces that included the Seventh, Eighth, and "New World" symphonies. At the end of his life he turned to opera once again; *Rusalka*, from 1901, incorporates Wagnerian influences into the musical telling of its legend-based story, and remains the most frequently performed of the composer's vocal works. Dvořák, a professor at Prague University from 1891 on, exerted a deep influence on Czech music of the twentieth century; among his students was Josef Suk, who also became his son-in-law. *—AMG*

SYMPHONIC

Symphonies Nos. 1–4 (1865–1874)

While the themes of Dvořák's *Symphony No. 9 "From the New World"* are among the most familiar in the mainstream classical repertoire, and many of his orchestral works count among favorites among modern audiences, his first forays into the symphonic realm fell into decades of obscurity shortly after their completion.

Dvořák composed his *Symphony No. 1 in C minor* over a five-week period in 1865. Although bearing the title *The Bells of Zlonice*, the work reportedly bears no program or implicit narrative, the title having been added after the fact before entering the work in a contest—which he lost. In fact, after the competition the score was never returned to him, but by sheer luck it reemerged in 1923. Aspiring to a Beethovenesque flavor in terms of thematic approach, it has since enjoyed a few performances and a number of recordings, and of its four movements the coy scherzo has won particular favor. Dvořák's *Second Symphony in B flat major*, also cast in the traditional four-movement mold, dates from 1865 as well. Conveying an orchestrational atmosphere influenced by Wagner, it nonetheless occasionally admits the kind of folksy melodic tone that makes some of Dvořák's later themes so memorable; though initially unsure of the work's quality, the composer revised it two decades later and gave it an opus number (Op. 4).

Dvořák's *Third Symphony*, composed in 1873, exhibits even more pronounced Wagnerian tendencies. It adopts a three-movement structure, with an Allegro Moderato leading to a pensive Adagio molto, and a fast-paced Finale. Smetana and the Prague Philharmonic gave the work its premiere in 1874. Although the *Fourth Symphony* followed at a close interval, it seems to demonstrate a level of symphonic development that the composer had not yet reached in his previous attempts. His taste for distinctive rhythms coalesced with his melodic skill. With the *Fourth Symphony*, one observer put it, Dvořák demonstrates that "he understands the art of deep breathing: his music does not pant." There is a stark contrast of themes in the first movement, with the turbulent tension between triplets and sixteenth notes at the beginning foiled by the subsequent lyricism of the developmental material. The second movement, an Andante theme and variations, is emotive in its contours but restrained in its development, particularly in its timid approached to cadences. The Scherzo spins out of three perfunctory opening chords into a rhythmically diverse series of episodes, while the Finale takes a more measured but still energetic pace.

Although recordings undertaken during the latter part of the twentieth century have, at the very least, testified to the existence of these works (previous generations called his sixth symphonic effort "No. 1"!) they have yet to garner the attention given to Dvořák's later works. After all, while Brahms waited with famous caution before attempting his first symphony at 44, Dvořák jumped in without apprehension in his mid-twenties. Still, while the artistic value of these works may be subject to debate, their historical importance warrants fair consideration. *—Jeremy Grimshaw*

Recommended:

○ **Dvořák: Symphonies 1–3** / Neumann (cond.), Czech PO / 2003 / Supraphon 3703

Symphony No. 5 in F major, Op. 76 (Jun. 15, 1875–Jul. 23, 1875; revised 1887)

Dvořák's *Symphony No. 5* owes its genesis to a fortuitous series of events in the composer's life. At age 32, his lady friend informed him that she was pregnant, and the two were hastily married; having poor financial prospects, Dvořák did what any penniless composer of today would do: he applied for a grant. He submitted a couple of early symphonies and some chamber music to be considered for the Austrian State Prize; the judges for this contest were none other than the eminent critic Eduard Hanslick, the conductor Johann Herbeck, and the composer Johannes Brahms. Much to his surprise, Dvořák impressed the committee and he received the grant. The immediate imperatives were easily met: his son was born into good financial circumstances. An unexpected, and very fortunate, side effect was the resultant arrangement with Brahms' publisher, Fritz Simrock.

It was Simrock who began the arbitrary use of opus numbers and numbering of Dvořák's symphonies—a practice that caused much confusion in later years. Being an astute business man, he knew perfectly well that works with higher opus number would sell better than lower numbers, and what Dvořák wanted to call his Fourth Symphony, Op. 24 (he had discarded his First Symphony altogether), was actually published as Symphony No. 3, Op. 76. It was not until the mid-twentieth century that all the confusion was cleared up, and the nine symphonies were numbered in their proper chronological sequence.

The *Fifth Symphony* is a finely crafted work, and an advancement beyond the best of the composer's early symphonies. It opens in a leisurely manner with an arpeggiated theme for two clarinets; this opening idea returns to dominate the development section, and the movement closes with a peaceful coda.

The Andante con moto is dominated by a plaintive, melancholy cello theme that is reminiscent of the opening of Tchaikovsky's *First Piano Concerto*. Dvořák continuously varies this tune, toying with the opening figure and deriving new accompaniment figures from it. Without pause, the music moves into a transition to the Scherzo, a vivacious, colorfully scored movement full of delightfully unexpected contrasts.

The Finale begins in the "wrong" key of A minor; when the music finally moves to the tonic key of F major, the effect is striking and dramatic. Reminiscences of the opening theme of the first movement conclude the Finale, which is not only the finest movement of the work, but one of Dvořák's most outstanding symphonic movements.

The *Symphony No. 5* received its debut in Prague on March 25, 1879, with Adolf Cech conducting. It was subsequently dedicated to Hans von Bülow, who was a tireless advocate of the composer's symphonic works. *—Brian Wise*

Recommended:

○ **Dvořák: Symphonies 4–6** / Neumann (cond.), Czech PO / 2003 / Supraphon 3704

○ **Dvořák: Nine Symphonies** / Kubelik (cond.), Berlin PO / DG 463158

○ **Dvořák: The Symphonies** / Kertesz (cond.), London SO / 1991 / London 430046

Symphony No. 6 in D major, Op. 60 (Aug. 27, 1880–Oct. 15, 1880)

This was published as Dvořák's *Symphony No. 1*, but it was not renumbered as the *Sixth* until the mid-twentieth century, when earlier symphonies were recognized as a legitimate part of his canon. Composed in 1880, it came exactly halfway between the 1875 Fifth and 1885 Seventh, and thus is a pivotal work in the composer's oeuvre, standing as the last major work from his Slavic period and appearing as a transition of sorts to the more mature symphonic masterpieces to come, namely the last three symphonies, No. 7, No. 8, and No. 9 (*New World Symphony*). Dvořák acknowledged Brahms as a model in the earlier part of his career and in the *Sixth*, he was still under his spell. This symphony also reveals lingering folk influences from Dvořák's then-recent first volume of the *Slavonic Dances* (1878). The first movement is both effervescent and epic, forging a mixture of joyous abandon and Bohemian nationalist pride. Marked Allegro non tanto, this sunny movement has a Brahmsian character in sound, but lacks the weight and expressive depth of the Brahms symphonies, though it is still a rewarding listening experience, especially in its ecstatic close. The second movement Adagio is lovely, imparting a sense of Romantic warmth in its main theme and lush scoring. The middle section is intense and stormy. Perhaps the most effective movement in the symphony is the shortest (about seven minutes), the ensuing Scherzo. Marked Presto and subtitled "Furiant," a once-popular Bohemian dance in 3/4 timing, it opens at a furious pace with a colorful theme that sounds less dance-like and more good-naturedly rowdy. The trio is calm and playful, offering deft contrast to the fury of the outer sections. The finale (Allegro con spirito) is both joyous and heroic in its colorful main theme. The alternate theme is playful and nonchalant, and Dvořák's development of his material has a Brahmsian intensity in the central section. *—Robert Cummings*

Recommended:

- ○ **Dvořák: Symphonies 4–6** / Neumann (cond.), Czech PO / 2003 / Supraphon 3704
- ○ **Dvořák: Symphony 6; Suk: Serenade** / Talich (cond.), Czech PO / 1991 / Koch 7060
- ○ **Dvořák: Nine Symphonies** / Kubelik (cond.), Berlin PO / DG 463158
- ○ **Dvořák: The Symphonies** / Kertesz (cond.), London SO / 1991 / London 430046

Symphony No. 7 in D minor, Op. 70 (Dec. 13, 1884–Mar. 17, 1885; revised Jun. 1885)

Many consider Antonín Dvořák's *Symphony No. 7 in D minor*, Op. 70, the pinnacle of his achievement as a composer. Indeed, never before had he risen to such a height, and one can make a formidable case that he never again did, the immense and just popularity of the *"New World" Symphony* notwithstanding. Dvořák had spent a full five years away from the symphonic domain when, in December 1884, he began plotting his course through the *Symphony No. 7*. The interval had been an important if not especially prolific one; the works of this period had been significant (for example the *Piano Trio in F minor*, Op. 65, the *String Quartet No. 11 in C*, Op. 61), and when the time came to compose the *Symphony No. 7* Dvořák was prepared. The commission came from the London Philharmonic Society, to whose membership Dvořák had been elected in 1884.

The four-movement Classical plan was Dvořák's bread and butter as a composer. Here the movements are: Allegro maestoso, Poco Adagio, Vivace (the Scherzo), and Allegro.

A less likely main theme for a symphony than the wistful, lyric pianissimo idea offered by the violas and cellos at the opening of the first movement would be hard to come by. But it is not long before the drooping pendant at the end of the melody is converted, by means of some characteristic Dvořák hemiolas, into something far more electrifying, and from that point the movement is off and running. The second theme, in B flat major and introduced by a rich rising chromatic passage in the violins and woodwinds, has the aspect of a carefree summer day to it. The slow movement begins simply, contentedly—the clarinet providing an airy tune that hovers between the keys of B flat and F major. There is, as the movement gradually reveals itself, passion enough. The hemiola-ridden main tune of the Scherzo, which is probably the most famous movement in the symphony, draws us into an extraordinary and compelling realm in which vivacious rhythm and undeniable melancholy are made to walk hand-in-hand.

Prominent augmented seconds and an abundant use of the raised fourth scale degree provide the finale's principal theme and the music around it with a peculiar and subtly exotic pungency. A major becomes the launching pad for a fluffy second theme in the cellos. The assertive quarter note thrusts of the symphony's final bars manage to break through the wall of D minor into the adjacent field of D major, and the matter ends in a blaze of glory. *—Blair Johnston*

Recommended:

- ○ **Dvořák: Symphonies 7 & 8** / Neumann (cond.), Czech PO / Supraphon 111960
- ○ **Dvořák: Nine Symphonies** / Kubelik (cond.), Berlin PO / DG 463158
- ○ **Dvořák: Symphony 7** / Davis (cond.), London SO / 2003 / LSO Live 14
- ○ **George Szell** / Szell (cond.), Cleveland Orch. / 1998 / Heritage 63151
- ○ **Dvořák: The Symphonies** / Kertesz (cond.), London SO / 1991 / London 430046

Symphony No. 8 in G major, Op. 88 (Aug. 26, 1889–Nov. 8, 1889)

Dvořák had been embarrassed when mature works were issued as early ones, while his nationalism had been offended by the persistent Germanizing of his first name as "Anton." In 1889, no longer a *naïf provincial*, Dvořák chose to interpret the offer of 1,000 deutschmarks—5,000 less than he had paid for the instantly popular Seventh—as publisher Fritz Simrock's first right of refusal, and sold his new Eighth to the British firm of Novello, who published it as No. 4. Novello considered it a privilege to buy the work; Simrock never repeated his mistake.

When Cambridge University honored Dvořák as a Doctor of Music in 1892, he submitted the *Eighth Symphony* as his obligatory "exercise." Thus it came to be called the "English" Symphony for many years, despite its obvious Czech grammar and diction— Dvořák's declaration of independence, in fact, from Germanic influences in the first seven symphonies.

Dvořák united all four sections of the Eighth with a rising three-note figure, first heard in the opening measure of the opening movement; from this come the main themes there and in the finale. The work abounds in structural symmetries and subtleties, which reveal themselves once one becomes familiar with its charming Czech-rooted melodies and rhythms. Organization of this caliber is the handiwork of a master composer in complete control of what he wants to say and how to say it.

A melody in G minor, which returns later on before the development section and again (albeit altered in mood) before the recapitulation, is introduced in the Allegron con brio before G major arrives with the main theme, bird-like in character as played on the flute. Dvořák moves to E major for a gently contrasting second theme, then to B minor for a march-like third subject; but G major prevails at the end.

In the Adagio, duple meter replaces common time, while the key of C replaces G (C being the dominant of G). An ABAB structure begins quietly in C minor, but metamorphoses in the repeated sections suggest a variation-pattern with a wistful character.

Dvořák shocked purists by writing an Allegretto grazioso waltz movement, as Tchaikovsky had done in his *Fifth Symphony* a year earlier. It is, however, unmistakably a Slavonic waltz in G minor, whose G major trio lends itself even less to ballroom dancing, yet is a dance. After a repeat of the song section, a fast coda in 2/4 time sets up both the meter and the key of the finale.

Beethoven might have applauded Dvořák's theme-and-variations-structure within-a-song-and-trio frame of the final Allegro ma non troppo. Following a trumpet fanfare, a two-part theme emerges whose halves are repeated, then four variations, all in G major. The trio is a three-part march in C minor, after which the fanfare returns with four more variations in tow. *—Roger Dettmer*

Recommended:

- ○ **Dvořák: Symphonies 7 & 8** / Neumann (cond.), Czech PO / Supraphon 111960
- ○ **Dvořák: Symphony 8; Concert Overtures** / Talich (cond.), Czech PO / Supraphon 1898
- ○ **Dvořák: Symphonies 8 & 9** / Szell (cond.), Cleveland Orch. / 2001 / Sony 89413
- ○ **Dvořák: The Symphonies** / Kertesz (cond.), London SO / 1991 / London 430046
- ○ **Dvořák: Symphonies 8 & 9** / Kubelik (cond.), Berlin PO / 1973 / DG 447412

Symphony No. 9 in E minor ("From the New World"), Op. 95 (Jan. 10, 1893–May 24, 1893)

Dvořák composed this work in 1893; Anton Seidl conducted the premiere with the New York Philharmonic Society on December 16, 1893.

His most popular work from his time spent in America was the swan-song symphony he subtitled *From the New World*. Chauvinists among us still claim that its themes are either Amerindian or African-American, which Dvořák refuted in 1900: "Omit the nonsense about my having made use of 'American' motifs.... I tried only to write in the spirit of those national melodies." This dust-up managed to ignore influences both stronger and more subtle. Dvořák already knew Tchaikovsky's *Fifth Symphony*, completed in 1888, and he likewise used a motto-theme to link the four movements in his symphony in E minor. The introduction can be made to sound a lot more Tchaikovskian, indeed, than a subsequent theme can be made to sound like "Swing Low, Sweet Chariot," as alleged. Beyond the Slavic gravitas of both symphonies, however, Dvořák's musical signature was intrinsically Czech, even in the Largo movement that represented, he once said, Hiawatha at the grave site of Minnehaha (a quasi-Spiritual, "Goin' Home" text was created post facto by a white American pupil). By the time he heard any Amerind music, during the summer of 1893 near a Czech settlement at Spillville, Iowa, Dvořák had finished the *Ninth Symphony*. From the structural standpoint, two sonata-form movements (with an exposition repeat in the first) bracket two movements in song form (ABA), all of them with brief introductions and codas.

The 2/4 Allegro molto has an Adagio preface in 4/8 time. Horns introduce the motto theme, answered by clarinets and bassoons, then strings. Flutes and oboes play a melody in G minor before the "Swing Low" closing subject shifts from minor to G major. Sectional development omits the G minor tune; reprise and coda are distillations.

The Largo begins in D flat major, far from single sharped E minor. A plaintive English horn melody dominates both here and later on. In between—in a C sharp minor section marked Un poco più mosso—winds introduce two themes, more palpitant than the D flat section's big tune, before the motto makes a sinister appearance.

Song sections marked Scherzo: Molto vivace, in E minor, pay homage less to Indian pow-wows than to the scherzo movement of Beethoven's *Ninth Symphony.* A briefer subject in E major recalls the G major closing theme of the first movement, followed by the motto. The Poco sostenuto Trio is pure Czech, beginning in C major, with a G major second theme related to the Beethoven rhythm in sections A and A.

Allegro con fuoco is the marking of the final movement with a martial main theme in E minor for horns and trumpets. The clarinet counters with a nostalgic subtheme, after which flutes and fiddles play a closing subject in G major. The development combines music from previous movements with the main theme of movement four. Following the recap, a Grand Coda ends with a fortissimo restatement of the motto, then a diminuendo to pianissimo on the final chord. *—Roger Dettmer*

Recommended:

- ○ **Dvořák; Symphony 9; 3 Overtures** / Czech PO, Ashkenazy (cond.) / Ondine 962
- ○ **Dvořák: Nine Symphonies** / Kubelik (cond.), Berlin PO / DG 463158
- ○ **Dvořák; Symphony 9; Slavonic Dances; Smetana: Moldau** / Szell (cond.), Cleveland Orch. / 1987 / CBS 42417
- ○ **Dvořák; Symphony 9; Symphonic Variations** / Davis (cond.), Concertgebouw / Philips 429349
- ○ **Dvořák; Symphony 9;** / Kertesz (cond.), London SO / 1998 / London 460604

ORCHESTRAL

Carnival, concert overture, Op. 92 (Jul. 28, 1891–Sep. 12, 1891)

In many ways, the 1890s represented for Dvořák a time of creative and personal renaissance. It was during this decade that he made his first forays into the New World, the direct result of which included the production of a wealth of American-inflected chamber music as well as the composer's best-known work, the *Symphony No. 9* (1893). The latter proved to be Dvořák's final essay in that form, signaling, perhaps, his increasing interest in other genres. In addition to the operatic stops and starts that occupied much of the composer's attention in the 1890s, Dvořák produced a substantial body of self-contained orchestral works in the guise of overtures and tone poems.

The *Carnival Overture,* Op. 92 (1891), was the second of a group of three works by the composer collectively titled "Nature, Life, and Love." An operatic spirit—one is struck by certain *Carmen*-esque flashes, for example—informs the overture throughout, as does a prevailing ebullience and stomping, folk dance-like energy. A brief central Andantino con moto episode of sedate, almost nocturnal character is distinguished by more expansive melodies and the use of the English horn, one of Dvořák's favorite instruments, in an unusual role: sounding an ostinato accompaniment rather than the melody proper. The overture ends in a spirit similar to that in which it begins, aptly embodying the festal atmosphere suggested by its title. *—Michael Rodman*

Recommended:

- ○ **Dvořák: New World Symphony; Smetana: Bartered Bride; Weinberger: Polka & Fugue** / Reiner (cond.), Chicago SO / 1995 / RCA 62587
- ○ **Dvořák: The Nine Symphonies** / Kubelik (cond.), Bavarian RSO / DG 463158
- ○ **Dvořák: Symphony 8; Concert Overtures** / Talich (cond.), Czech PO / Supraphon 1898
- ○ **George Szell** / Szell (cond.), Cleveland Orch. / 1998 / Heritage 63151

Czech Suite, Op. 39 (1879)

Antonín Dvořák composed this music in 1879 (during April, it is believed); Adolf Cech conducted the premiere on May 16 of that year, in Prague.

When Johannes Brahms recommended Dvořák's work to his own Berlin publisher, Simrock concurred, thereby initiating a selective association in 1879 that included only some of the pieces Brahms had mentioned. First, though, Simrock commissioned and published the initial set of *Slavonic Dances,* Op. 46, for piano four hands and for orchestra, too. While these made Dvořák quickly famous, he became unhappy with several Simrock business practices: He protested the Germanizing of his first name as "Anton," in vain. He was embarrassed by high opus numbers given to early works, implying they were new. The biggest bone of contention, however, was Simrock's stinginess, coupled with a first right of refusal for all future works. This accounts for the *Czech Suite's* low opus number, although it was composed after the first set of *Slavonic Dances* (Op. 46) and the three *Slavonic Rhapsodies* (Op. 45). John Warrack has written that "[Dvořák] was evading an agreement for future works by pretending that this was an old one." Ironically, Simrock published it, but not until 1881. Even more ironically, it was destined to become a Cinderella among Dvořák's orchestral works.

All of the movements are dance-based, even the opening Praeludium in D, additionally marked Pastorale; Allegro moderato, which evokes indigenous bagpipes (*dudy* in Czech; *Dudelsack* in German) that Svanda played incomparably in Jaromír Weinberger's subsequent opera of that name. While Warrack found a "suggestion of a polka under the oboe melody," a full-scale polka follows ebulliently in F major (Allegretto grazioso; 2/4). The central movement in the piece has a double designation: both Sousedská (a Bohemian version of the waltz, here in B flat major) and Minuetto, with a tempo marking of Allegro giusto, although Warrack remarked that "it is not really either so much as a Mazurka, the strong accent falling on the second beat in each bar." A slow movement follows in G major, a 9/8 Romanza to be played Andante con moto, with a colloquy for flute and English horn. A melody from this returns during the course of a superb concluding Furiant in F major, marked Presto (in 3/4 time, characterized by cross-rhythms). There's even a genuine folk song quoted, although Dvořák preferred to compose delectable counterfeits—a movement in any event that begs to be encored. *—Roger Dettmer*

Recommended:

- ○ **Dvořák: Czech Suite; Janáček: Suite for Strings** / Prague CO / Supraphon 110055
- ○ **Dvořák: Czeska Suita Op. 39; String Quintet Op. 77** / Ensemble Acht / 2004 / MDG Scene 6031259

The Golden Spinning Wheel (Zlatý kolovrat), symphonic poem, Op. 109 (Jan. 15, 1896–Apr. 25, 1896)

The *The Golden Spinning Wheel,* or *Zlatý kolovrat,* Op. 109, is the third of Antonín Dvořák's four 1896 orchestral tone poems on subjects taken from the poetry of Karel Jaromír Erben. Its plot, put simply, is quite ludicrous; that Dvořák should succeed in making a fine piece of music from it is a testament to the notion, oft-stated and oftener-demonstrated by composers throughout the nineteenth century, that a sensible plot line is by no means necessarily the best choice for a program-music subject. Dvořák sketched *The Golden Spinning Wheel* during January and February of 1896 and orchestrated it some weeks later. At its premiere in October 1896, Dvořák's critics and colleagues alike found the work too long; as a result, a number of cuts concocted by Dvořák's friend and son-in-law Josef Suk are generally made, not necessarily to the work's betterment.

Erben's *Zlatý kolovrat* tells the tale of a king who falls in love with a simple peasant girl. After he has invited her to his castle, her evil stepmother kills her, cuts off her feet and hands and removes her eyes, and substitutes her own daughter—who is apparently the stepdaughter's spitting image—in her place. Unwittingly, the king weds the evil daughter, but, fortunately, an old man stumbles across the body of the king's beloved. He sends his young lad up to the castle three times—to exchange three items, including a golden spinning wheel, for the hands, feet, and eyes of the dead daughter—and then proceeds to resurrect the king's beloved. The golden spinning wheel turns out to be the stepmother's and daughter's undoing: when the king's new bride begins to spin, the magic spinning wheel spins out the awful truth. The king seeks out his true beloved in the forest and the two live happily ever after, while the evil stepmother and daughter are eaten by wolves.

Dvořák's treatment of this material is very free indeed. Much of the music of *The Golden Spinning Wheel* really does spin, starting with the rolling cello triplets of the very opening (which are presumably intended to reproduce the gallop of the king's horse). There is a pleasing economy to the way that the horn fanfare idea that announces the king at the opening takes on new shapes as the work unfolds; the most colorful of these is the harshly dissonant version in parallel seventh chords (over an uncooperative pedal-point) that depicts part of the king's encounter with the evil stepmother and her daughter. Dvořák pulls out all the stops at the end, when the violins soar up to the heights of the reunited lovers' passion; in the final bars, as the king's fanfare is given a robust Allegro ma non troppo treatment, one can almost hear them riding off into the sunset. *—Blair Johnston*

Recommended:

- ○ **Dvořák: Slavonic Dances; Overtures; Symphonic Poems** / Kubelik (cond.), Bavarian RSO / DG 469366
- ○ **Dvořák: Symphonic Poems After Erben** / Talich (cond.), Czech PO / 1993 / Supraphon 119002001
- ○ **Dvořák: Symphonic Poems** / Neumann (cond.), Czech PO / Supraphon 0199

In Nature's Realm (V přírode), concert overture, Op. 91 (Mar. 31, 1891–Jul. 8, 1891)

The philosophical overtones of Dvořák's overture *In Nature's Realm* were perhaps best summarized by his biographer Otakar Sourek: "Deeply religious in feeling, above all he saw in Nature the unfathomable work of a Divine Will, but in a certain pantheistic sense he also saw it as the giver of Life, which is both beautiful and ugly." Thus, in addition to picturesque tone painting, Dvořák aimed to create spiritual overtones. The work was composed between March 31 and July 8, 1891, and dedicated to Cambridge University, which honored him with a doctorate on June 16 of that year.

The overture is in a standard sonata form, framed by a few introductory measures and a simple epilogue. After a lively dance theme, the lyrical second subject occurs in the mediant major, a key rarely used in this way by Dvořák. Until the closing epilogue—which features a pentatonic, chorale-like motif based on a Czech hymn—the overture revels of bird songs and other natural sounds, revealing the composer's love for his home in the spruce forest of Vysoká where the work was written. The overture has many features that place it in the long tradition begun by Beethoven's "Pastoral" symphony, but the hymn motif is quite an individual feature.

In Nature's Realm forms the first portion of a programmatic trilogy that Dvořák had undertaken at the contemplative age of 50. The second and third overtures were the *Carnival*, Op. 92 and *Othello*, Op. 93. —*Brian Wise*

Recommended:

- ○ **Dvořák: Symphony 8; Concert Overtures** / Talich (cond.), Czech PO / Supraphon 1898
- ○ **Dvořák: Slavonic Dances; Overtures; Symphonic Poems** / Kubelik (cond.), Bavarian RSO / DG 469366
- ○ **Dvořák; Symphony 9; 3 Overtures** / Ashkenazy (cond.), Czech PO / Ondine 962

Legends, Op. 59 (Nov. 13, 1881–Dec. 9, 1881)

Like the two sets of *Slavonic Dances* by Czech composer Antonín Dvořák, the *Legends* for orchestra were originally conceived and executed as piano duets. Unlike the *Slavonic Dances*, however, the *Legends* are more lyrical and song-like with fewer dance-like rhythms, darker harmonies, and slightly more complex structures. Composed in summer 1881 as a relaxation from the recently completed *Symphony No. 6*, Dvořák orchestrated the *Legends* in the autumn of that year. Although not nearly as popular as the *Slavonic Dances*, the *Legends* were lauded by no less a composer than Brahms. As he wrote their mutual publisher: "Please give Dvořák my greetings and tell him how much his *Legends* have given me lasting pleasure. They are a fascinating work, and the man's fresh, exuberant, rich powers of invention are enviable."

1. Allegretto: This is fiercely set in archaically inflected D minor and the *Legend No. 1* sounds faux-frightening.

2. Molto moderato: Smoothly lyrical music in G major alternates with yearning music in G minor in the *Legend No. 2*.

3. Allegro giusto: Shifting between passionate G minor and yearning G major, the *Legend No. 3* is a harmonic and emotional mirror image of the *Second*.

4. Allegro maestoso: The archaic tone of the opening Legend returns in the bardic solo horn call that starts the *Legend No. 4* in C major. The most balladic and longest of the *Legends*, the Fourth moves from bardic call to heroic march to excited climax.

5. Allegro giusto: With its gently plucked harp and gently flowing melody, the *Legend No. 5* in A flat major is said to have been inspired by the devotional painting Dvořák favored.

6. Allegro con moto: Set in Romantic C sharp minor, the *Legend No. 6* is a lilting nocturne with a warmly ardent woodwind trio.

7. Allegretto grazioso: Like its title, the *Legend No. 7* in A major starts gracefully in the violins, but builds to a dramatic ending for horns and winds.

8. Un poco allegretto e grazioso: The *Legend No. 8* is a pastoral picture in the pastoral key signature of F major and the pastoral time signature of 6/8. Like the preceding Legend, it is predominantly graceful in tone.

9. Andante con moto: The shortest piece in the set, the *Legend No. 9* starts and ends in D major with a D minor central section. Although its themes are folk-song like, Dvořák uses canonic entrances, invertible counterpoint, and pedal points to enliven the music.

10. Andante: The *Legend No. 10* slides between dramatic B flat minor and lyrical B flat major and brings the *Legends* to a warm and tender conclusion. —*James Leonard*

Recommended:

- ○ **Dvořák: Stabat Mater; Legends** / Kubelik (cond.), English CO / DG 453025
- ○ **Dvořák: Symphonic Variations; Scherzo capriccioso; Legends** / Mackerras (cond.), Czech PO / 2002 / Supraphon 3533

My Home (Domov muj), concert overture, Op. 62 (1882)

Dvořák's concert overture *My Home* (1882) is a prized rarity in the classical repertoire: a patriotic work of generally high quality. Originally intended to serve as incidental music for F.F. Samberk's play *Josef Kajetán Tyl*, *My Home* was rarely performed in this context, and it soon took on a new life as an independent concert work.

My Home makes use of two melodies: the bucolic folk song "Na tom naem dvore" and Skroup's "Kde domov muv?," most familiar as the Czech national anthem. After a brief introduction, the folk song provides the basis for the first subject, though at a tempo more in the manner of a Slavonic dance. Skroup's theme provides the lyrical second subject.

The work proceeds effectively in a traditional sonata form, though some commentators have suggested that the coda provides a somewhat pompous, hollow, and unsatisfying conclusion. Regardless, the work is attractively orchestrated and is a successful exemplar of music from one of the composer's most productive periods. —*Brian Wise*

Recommended:

- ○ **Dvořák: Slavonic Dances; Overtures; Symphonic Poems** / Kubelik (cond.), Bavarian RSO / DG 469366
- ○ **Dvořák: Symphony 6; Overtures** / Ancerl (cond.), Czech PO / Supraphon 111926

Nocturne for strings in B major, Op. 40 (revised 1883)

It took Antonín Dvořák many years to get his feet firmly planted as a composer, and during his journeyman years we very often find him not quite sure what to do with pieces that seemed to be failures but which he was loath to simply destroy (in the end, he did destroy most of his early music). Sometimes, as with both the famous *Romance for violin*, Op. 11 and the *Nocturne in B major for string orchestra*, Op. 40, Dvořák managed to salvage something of real value from a piece that he had previously counted as a total failure. In the case of the *Nocturne*, the cast-away piece upon which Dvořák drew was the *String Quartet in E minor* of late 1870, B. 19; the quartet, which is in one extended movement, did not meet Dvořák's expectations, but the Andante religioso middle section was too good to bury. It was so dear to the composer, in fact, that he resurrected it three times: once for the *Nocturne for strings*, another time for a separate version of the same piece, for solo violin with piano or strings (published with the string version as Op. 40), and a third time (actually the earliest of the three, chronologically speaking) for the original slow movement, eventually replaced, of the *G major String Quintet*, Op. 77 of 1875. The Op. 40 string-orchestra Nocturne was given a final touch-up by Dvořák just before its publication in 1883. The following year he conducted the work in London, at a Crystal Palace concert that did much to broaden his international reputation. It remains a lovely concert interlude for an orchestra's string section.

The *Nocturne* is a slow movement, Molto adagio, in 12/8 time. The wonderful arch-shaped melody, begun by the cellos and basses in unaccompanied, pianissimo octaves has a peculiar cross-rhythm in its second bar. When the first violins take this theme over four bars later, the second violins and violas jump in with sumptuous parallel thirds. The entire first half of the piece is played over a dominant pedal; when finally resolution is made to B, Dvořák provides music that is rich and flows elegantly to its serene final cadence. Here, as in nearly every one of his chamber works, Dvořák proves that he has few peers as a master of the slow movement. —*Blair Johnston*

Recommended:

- ○ **Smetana: Má Vlast; etc.** / Dorati (cond.), Detroit SO / 1994 / Decca 443015
- ○ **Dvořák: Serenade; Waldesruhe; Notturno** / Schwarz (cond.), Los Angeles CO / 1982 / Delos 3011

The Noon Witch (Polednice), symphonic poem, Op. 108 (Jan. 11, 1896–Feb. 27, 1896)

Like each of his other four tone poems—save only the last—Antonín Dvořák's second orchestral tone poem, *Polednice*, or *The Noon Witch*, Op. 108, is modeled after a poem by Czech poet Karol Jaromír Erben. Dvořák's sudden urge to try his hand at true program music was so strong that he hadn't yet even finished sketching out *The Water Goblin*, Op. 107—his first symphonic poem—when he started plotting his musical course through Erben's *Polednice* in mid-January 1896. *The Noon Witch* is, it must be said, a very attractive and justly famous piece of music; to some, it is the finest of Dvořák's tone poems. Dvořák's achievement is made all the more impressive by the realization that he took just three days to sketch the work out, and then, in February, two weeks to orchestrate it.

Erben's poem tells of the legendary Noon Witch, summoned by a mother to call her reckless and restless child to order. Unfortunately, the Noon Witch effects the fainting of the mother and the suffocation of the child; when the father returns home and wakens his wife the two discover and lament their loss. Dvořák treats the poem in a kind of continuous miniature symphonic form. The four ordinary movements of a symphony are all in place, but are played without breaks between them.

At the beginning of the opening Allegretto is introduced the happy, frolicking little motive that will be reshaped into a large portion of *The Noon Witch*'s material; there is shortly a brief foreshadowing of the Andante sostenuto music that will form the second movement, easily dispatched by the child as he continues to horse around. Things grow very heated, and only the arrival of the actual Andante sostenuto can tame matters; but it is not a comfortable tameness, for ever within this music—with its gripping semitone oscillations and its bizarre tune for bassoon and bass clarinet—is the mother's threat of summoning the Noon Witch. As the child becomes unmanageable once again, the mother makes good her threat, and the Witch arrives and dances a wild dance (Allegro—the scherzo movement) in which the happy clarinet motive of the opening is tossed about upside down. The final movement of this pseudo-symphony, Andante, is full of sharp articulations and pained rhythms: the father has returned and the tragedy is revealed—and all the passionate pleading of the strings (maestoso, triple-forte) cannot return his child to him. *—Blair Johnston*

Recommended:

- ○ **Dvořák: Slavonic Dances; Overtures; Symphonic Poems** / Kubelik (cond.), Bavarian RSO / DG 469366
- ○ **Dvořák: Symphonic Poems** / Talich, Czech PO / 1993 / Supraphon 119002001
- ○ **Dvořák: Symphonic Poems** / Neumann (cond.), Czech PO / Supraphon 0199

Othello, concert overture, Op. 93 (1891–1892)

Antonín Dvořák didn't compose an actual tone poem until less than half a decade before the turn of the twentieth century; he did, however, dabble on the fringes of program music with the three overtures for orchestra that he called, collectively, *Nature, Life and Love.* The third of these—*Love*—took its dramatic basis from what might seem an unlikely source (at least if one is seeking an optimistic appraisal of romance): Shakespeare's *Othello.* Dvořák seems himself to have been somewhat uncomfortable with calling the Op. 93 overture *Othello*, and he toyed with the idea of providing a less specific title. In the end he opted to stick with *Othello*, but always emphasized that the connection between the music of Op. 93 and Shakespeare's work was as much in his mind as on the music-paper. The *Othello* overture was composed during late 1891 and early 1892, and first performed, along with Op. 91 and Op. 92 (*Nature* and *Life*, respectively), during April 1892 in Prague.

The *Othello* overture is a fine piece, from the rich pseudo-archaisms of the very opening (the impression of the Renaissance is palpable in Dvořák's archaic harmonization of the opening phrase), to the violent jealousy of the Allegro con brio that follows shortly thereafter, to the vicious murder of Desdemona (the specific moment of the murder is actually indicated by Dvořák on the score), to the fevered final bars when Othello, pushed to the edge of his sanity, forgives Desdemona and kills himself. The work is very possibly the most grim of all Dvořák's compositions—the biting dissonance of the last bars, and in particular one moment at which we are treated to the shock of F sharp, G natural, D natural, and D sharp all at the same time—and as a result it has never matched its immediate predecessor, the *Carnival Overture*, Op. 92, in popularity. However, in terms of the composer's craft and inspiration it is easily superior to that work, and the fact that its treasures are enjoyed by fewer does not mean that they are less. *—Blair Johnston*

Recommended:

- ○ **Dvořák: Symphony 8; Concert Overtures** / Talich (cond.), Czech PO / Supraphon 1898
- ○ **Dvořák: Slavonic Dances; Overtures; Symphonic Poems** / Kubelik (cond.), Bavarian RSO / DG 469366
- ○ **Dvořák: Othello Overture; Symphony 9** / Abbado (cond.), Berlin PO / 1999 / DG 457651

Scherzo capriccioso, Op. 66 (Apr. 4, 1883–May 2, 1883)

Antonín Dvořák's 1883 *Scherzo capriccioso* for orchestra, Op. 66, is one of the most thoroughly enjoyable musical sweetmeats—in the best sense of that word—to have graced the world's concert halls over the last century-and-a-quarter. These were the years of Dvořák's first real international fame, and the joy of once and for all escaping poverty can be heard throughout this happy-go-lucky orchestral showpiece. Dvořák wrote the *Scherzo capriccioso* during April and early May 1883, and it was given its Prague premiere already during the latter month; a much more noteworthy performance came about the following year when Dvořák himself conducted the *Scherzo capriccioso* during his first visit to London.

There really is a great deal of capriciousness to Op. 66. At the very start of the piece the solo horn playfully begins the main tune in the "wrong" key—B flat—and it is up to the rest of the orchestra to find the way over to the real home base: D flat major. The main tune is an almost circus-like affair; a second melody arrives in the guise of a waltz. During the middle of the Scherzo the cor anglais manages, on the strength of simple melodic beauty, to temporarily substitute a little calm D major for the energetic playfulness that has thus far been the work's focus. A horn duet begins the Scherzo's coda, which then proceeds to afford the harpist a chance to make a *Nutcracker*-like arpeggio solo; a rousing climax is drawn after the solo horn once again chides the orchestra to action. *—Blair Johnston*

Recommended:

- ○ **Dvořák: The Nine Symphonies** / Kubelik (cond.), Bavarian RSO / DG 463158
- ○ **Dvořák: Symphonic Variations; Scherzo capriccioso; Legends** / Mackerras (cond.), Czech PO / 2002 / Supraphon 3533
- ○ **Rudolf Kempe Conducts Smetana, Dvořák, Humperdinck** / Kempe (cond.), Royal PO / 2002 / Testament 1279

Serenade for strings in E major, Op. 22 (May 3, 1875–May 14, 1875)

Much of Antonín Dvořák's most famous work, such as the *Slavonic Dances*, is music of a most unpretentious variety; yet this impression of musical innocence, perfectly charming and unsoiled by the occasionally overwrought struggles of Romanticism, inevitably stirs something remarkable in listeners. This is certainly true of the *Serenade in E major for string orchestra*, Op. 22 (1875), which is greatly cherished by those who know it well. In a sometimes disappointing genre explored most often by journeyman composers still finding their creative way, it stands out as a near-faultlessly crafted five-movement gem.

The *Serenade*, Op. 22, usually lasts just under 30 minutes in performance. Unlike the normal symphony of the day, the first movement (Moderato) is the briefest of the lot. Its primary theme is a guileless inverted-arch melody that is made the subject of playful imitation; delicately-pointed dotted rhythms fill the central, G major section. More than once, the C sharp minor Tempo di Valse second movement shows a better-than-passing resemblance to Chopin's *C sharp minor Waltz*, Op. 64, No. 2, though Dvořák never veers far from his own Bohemian space; certainly a five-measure waltz-phrase like Dvořák's main idea is something Chopin would have reconsidered. The third movement, Scherzo, is a Vivace zinger; the Larghetto's main tune is a beautifully resigned. The rhythm and shape of the introductory measures of the finale to Beethoven's *Ninth Symphony* sneak into the start of the *Serenade*'s finale (Allegro vivace). The themes of first the Larghetto and then the Moderato first movement make encore appearances as the finale unfolds. *—Blair Johnston*

Recommended:

- ○ **Dvořák: Serenades** / Chung (cond.), Vienna PO / 2003 / DG 000019602
- ○ **Dvořák: Serenades** / Marriner (cond.), Academy of St. Martin-in-the-Fields / Philips 400020

Serenade for winds & strings in D minor, Op. 44 (Jan. 4, 1878–Jan. 18, 1878)

In 1875 Brahms replaced Johann Herbeck on the Austrian governmental panel that awarded financial aid to "young, poor, and talented artists." The chairman, Eduard Hanslick, showed Brahms music that Dvořák had sent with his application in 1874 (resulting in annual stipends of 400 gulden through 1878).

Hanslick suggested that Dvořák write Brahms, who asked permission to send the *Moravian Duets* of 1876 to his own publisher, Berlin-based Fritz Simrock. Not only did Simrock issue them, but he also commissioned the first set of *Slavonic Dances* (Op. 46) that made Dvořák suddenly and widely famous at the age of 37. A long-term contract enabled Dvořák to quit his job as cathedral organist in Prague and concentrate on composing. His subsequent productivity was prodigious: one has to go back to Schubert to find another major composer who wrote so much so quickly of such quality since Schubert.

His plans included three serenades. The first, for strings, had already been written in 1875. The D minor followed in 1878, for pairs of oboes, clarinets, and bassoons, contrabassoon, three horns, cello, and string bass. Begun on January 4, it was finished two weeks later and first performed on November 17 in Prague with Dvořák himself conducting. In April 1879, Simrock published it with a dedication to the Berlin critic Louis Ehlert, an early champion. After studying the score, Brahms wrote to Joseph Joachim that "a more lovely, refreshing impression of real, rich, and charming creative talent you can't easily have.... I think it must be pleasure for the wind players." There never was a third serenade; materials earmarked for it were used in the 1879 *Czech Suite*.

The first movement of the D minor serenade is a march-like Moderato that begins in the style of Mozart's Salzburg serenades. But Dvořák's melodies, rhythms, and harmonic vocabulary remain emphatically Czech. A tripartite structure includes a beguiling middle section in F major, introduced by clarinets. The F major Minuetto is really a sousedská, a slow Bohemian dance in triple time used several times elsewhere by Dvořák. The trio in B flat is a syncopated furiant, marked Presto, based on a motif from the Minuetto, which returns before the end. The slow third movement, Andante con moto in A major, is altogether more serious—passionately romantic, too, in a middle section with outstandingly beautiful music for solo clarinet and oboe. Dvořák's Allegro molto finale takes lovable liberties with conventional rondo form. March material from Movement One begins it, but now swaggeringly. Episodes include a sweetly sophisticated polka before the march theme reappears for the last time, followed by a coda both saucy and sonorous in D major. *—Roger Dettmer*

Recommended:

- ○ **Greatest Hits** / de Waart (cond.), Netherlands Wind Ens. / 2003 / Philips 472678
- ○ **Dvořák: Serenade; String Quintet** / Lincoln Center Chamber Music Society / 1995 / Delos 3152

Slavonic Rhapsodies, Op. 45 (Feb. 13, 1878–Dec. 3, 1878)

1878 was an important year for Antonín Dvořák: Dvořák's friend Johannes Brahms helped lift him from the pit of obscurity by arranging for the German publication of his *Moravian Duets*; consequently, he received the commission for the first volume of his *Slavonic Dances* that, to this day, remain, alongside the *"New World" Symphony*, Dvořák's best-known music. These events mark the beginning of

Dvořák's so-called "Slavonic" period (late 1870s–early 1880s), during which he responded directly to public demand and his publisher's wishes by composing music explicitly Bohemian/Czech/Moravian in tone, style, and to some extent, design. The three *Slavonic Rhapsodies* for orchestra, Op. 45, of 1878, are the largest manifestations of that financially lucrative musical vein.

The first of the three *Slavonic Rhapsodies*, Op. 45, No. 1 in D major, was composed during February and March 1878 and thus actually predates the *Slavonic Dances*; No. 2 in G minor and No. 3 in A flat major followed in autumn and early winter, respectively. The orchestra employed is reasonably large; the usual contingent of winds and strings is augmented by harp and a sizeable percussion brigade. The three pieces coalesce to form a cycle of sorts, though one hardly ever hears them played together as a set.

The most memorable feature of No. 1 is the central march-like episode, while No. 2 is distinguished by its many shifts between 3/4 and 4/4 time. The third *Slavonic Rhapsody* opens with a harp solo whose substance is immediately taken up by the woodwinds, and proceeds to explore a series of good-natured tunes; the grand climax seems to dissolve away elusively without a final resolution, but in the end two bright chords draw the piece to the cadence we crave. *—Blair Johnston*

Recommended:

- ○ **Dvořák: Symphony 5; Slavonic Rhapsodies** / Sejna (cond.), Czech PO / Supraphon 1917
- ○ **Dvořák: Slavonic Rhapsodies; My Home; Hero's Song** / Gregor (cond.), Czech PO / 2002 / Supraphon 3607

Symphonic Variations, Op. 78 (Aug. 6, 1877–Sep. 28, 1877)

During four days in the middle of January 1877, Antonín Dvořák composed the three part-songs for male voices (now known as B. 66), the first two of which are settings of Moravian folk poems. While the third song of B. 66, "Huslaf" (The Fiddler), cannot boast a folk origin, it can claim a much greater distinction than either of its two sister-pieces: seven months after its composition, Dvořák used its music as the theme for his *Symphonic Variations* for orchestra, Op. 78. The *Symphonic Variations*, composed in August and September of 1877, were premiered in Prague within three months of Dvořák putting his signature to the manuscript. The work was almost immediately thrown into the pit of neglect, however—Dvořák's publishers were uninterested in buying it, and, until the famous conductor Hans Richter took the work under his wing in the late 1880s, it remained a stranger to the concert hall. The now-famous success of Richter's 1887 London and Vienna performances of the *Symphonic Variations* more than made up for this neglect, and the work, while perhaps nowhere near Dvořák's best-known symphonies and string quartets in popularity, has since joined Brahms' *Variations on a Theme by Joseph Haydn*, Op. 56 as the most frequently played of all orchestral variations-sets.

Following the initial presentation of the 20-measure, C major theme, there are 27 variations and an extended Allegro maestoso finale. The theme itself is wonderfully suited for the purpose of variation-making: the irregular lengths of its three phrases (the first and third of which are basically identical, making a miniature ABA design)—7, 6, and 7 bars, respectively—help to avoid metric monotony and provide all kinds of possibilities for expansion and condensation, and the chromatic descents and rises of the melody provide useful stepping-stones that are immediately recognizable no matter how far from the original theme Dvorˇák's development might take us. At first, Dvorˇák tinkers with the theme very little—countermelodies are added, textures take new shapes. But as the variations progress, the theme becomes a fountain of material for extended inventions, some of which reach several dozen measures in length. The finale, as per tradition, exposes the theme as a fugue-subject before bursting forth into a vigorous and ever-faster orchestral workout. *—Blair Johnston*

Recommended:

- ○ **Dvořák: Requiem; Symphonic Variations; Kodály: Psalmus Hungaricus** / Kertesz (cond.), London SO / 2001 / Decca 468487
- ○ **Dvořák: Slavonic Dances; Overtures; Symphonic Poems** / Kubelik (cond.), Bavarian RSO / DG 469366
- ○ **Dvořák: Legends; Symphonic Variations** / Sejna (cond.), Czech PO / Supraphon 1919

The Water Goblin (Vodník), symphonic poem, Op. 107 (Jan. 6, 1896–Feb. 11, 1896)

The first three of Antonín Dvořák's five orchestral tone poems were put to paper in rapid succession during early 1896. Each of these three, and for that matter the fourth (which followed after an interval of several months), takes a poem by Karel Jaromír Erben as its dramatic basis; in the case of Dvořák's virgin effort in the territory, that poem is *Vodník*, or, the *Water Goblin*. The tone poem *The Water Goblin*, Op. 106, composed between the first week of January and the second week of February, was not the first of this initial threesome of tone poems to be performed—*The Golden Spinning Wheel*, Op. 109, has that honor—but it certainly didn't have to wait very long for its own premiere: on November 21, 1896 it was played by a London orchestra led by Henry Wood (not yet Sir).

Dvořák treats Erben's poem in what amounts to a rondo form, somewhat modified from the standard layout. The cruel Water Goblin is introduced in the opening Allegro vivo. We learn of a maiden and her mother in a rich Andante sostenuto. The Allegro vivo music bursts forth again as the Water Goblin snatches the poor maiden up and transports her down to his lair underneath the lake. As the unfortunate captive suffers we are provided a painfully chromatic Andante mesto come prima; she sings a lullaby (Un poco più lento e molto tranquillo), and finally convinces the Water Goblin—now in fact her husband—to let her go and visit her mother one last time. Her homecoming is a sad one indeed: the daughter's own child (sired by the Water Goblin) has remained down under the lake to ensure her return, and she has but one day to spend with her mother above. Still, there is real warmth to the B major Lento assai of their reunion; hardly any time has passed, however, before the Allegro vivo announces the arrival of the Water Goblin to take back his captive bride. The mother turns him away, and, true to his cruel word, he sends them the decapitated body of the daughter's child. Here the poem ends, but not the music: a grim timpani roll ushers in an Andante sostenuto coda—music absolutely frozen with horror. *—Blair Johnston*

Recommended:

- ○ **Dvořák: Wild Dove; Noon Witch; Water Goblin** / Talich (cond.), Czech PO / Panton 811100
- ○ **Dvořák: Slavonic Dances; Overtures; Symphonic Poems** / Kubelik (cond.), Bavarian RSO / DG 469366
- ○ **Dvořák: Symphonic Poems** / Neumann (cond.), Czech PO / Supraphon 0199

The Wild Dove (Holoubek), symphonic poem, Op. 110 (Oct. 22, 1896–Nov. 18, 1896)

After composing his first three orchestral tone poems in a frenzy of activity at the opening of 1896, Antonín Dvořák took several months off to do other things before starting work on his fourth, *The Wild Dove*, Op. 110, in late October. The premiere of the work, which took place the following March, was conducted by a then up-and-coming Leoš Janáček—but, of course, by the late 1890s Dvořák was one of Europe's most established musicians, and Janáček's name is by no means the most prominent among those who conducted the premieres of Dvořák's five tone poems; Hans Richter, Henry Wood, and Gustav Mahler make fine podium peers!

The Wild Dove (or, The Wood Dove), like Dvořák's first three tone poems, takes a poem by Karol Jaromír Erben as its dramatic starting point. Four musical "scenes" relate the story of a woman who poisons her husband (there is a grim funeral march) to wed another man (everything grows bright and a happy dance commences), and when she hears a gentle dove-call above her dead husband's grave, her suppressed guilt is brought to the surface and she takes her own life (an Andante in which the dove is heard in the winds and harp). Dvořák adds a musical epilogue after the sordid tale has run its course. *—Blair Johnston*

Recommended:

- ○ **Dvořák: Wild Dove; Noon Witch; Water Goblin** / Talich (cond.), Czech PO / Panton 811100
- ○ **Dvořák: Slavonic Dances; Overtures; Symphonic Poems** / Kubelik (cond.), Bavarian RSO / DG 469366
- ○ **Dvořák: Symphony 6; Wood Dove** / Belohlavek (cond.), Czech PO / 1993 / Chandos 9170

CONCERTO

Cello Concerto in B minor, Op. 104 (Nov. 8, 1894–Feb. 9, 1895; revised Jun. 11, 1895)

Opus 104 was Dvořák's second and final attempt at writing a cello concerto. The first, a 50-minute work in A major, was written very early in his career (1865), when his style was still markedly derived from those of his models—of which Mozart, Haydn, Beethoven, and Schubert are most notable. He had also recently encountered the music of Richard Wagner, which perhaps helps to explain the grand scale of the work. The resulting effort was not very satisfactory to the composer, and Dvořák never bothered to orchestrate it; he would not attempt to write another (the work at hand) until thirty years later, after he had written all nine of his symphonies (not to mention numerous operatic, choral, orchestral, chamber, piano, and vocal works). Upon reading through the finished product, completed in February 1895, Dvořák's colleague and friend, Brahms, is said to have remarked, "Why on earth didn't I know that one could write a cello concerto like this? Had I known, I would have written one long ago."

The first performance was given in 1896 in London under Dvořák's own direction, with Leo Stern as the soloist. The cellist was to have been Hanus Wihan (a close friend of the composer, to whom the work was dedicated), but there were misunderstandings surrounding Wihan's suggested revisions (including the addition of a last-movement cadenza) to the publisher without the composer's consent. Wihan did eventually perform the work, as did many other artists; the concerto has retained a solid place in the modern repertory.

Although the concerto's solo part is demanding, the work is by no means a bravura showpiece. Instead, the orchestra and soloist form an integral whole; Dvořák's refusal to accept Wihan's somewhat flashy revisions to the solo part show that he was determined to make the piece much more than a vehicle for virtuosity. Throughout the work there is a freshness of invention and sense of inevitable direction that betrays nothing of the thorough and painstaking revisions Dvořák himself undertook; it seems instead to have flowed effortlessly from the composer's pen.

The first movement (Allegro) is constructed around two main themes, the first of which (in B minor) is surprisingly brief, and the second of which (largely pentatonic, stated by solo horn), was one of the composer's personal favorites. The passing of these ideas back and forth between the soloist and orchestra allows for substantial thematic development; the first, brief theme is given substantially more weight in the eventual recapitulation.

In contrast to the dynamic first movement, the second (Adagio ma non troppo) opens with a more peaceful theme in G major. A middle section in G minor incorporates the melody from Dvořák's own song, "Leave me alone"—a favorite tune of his sister-in-law, Josefina Kaunitzova, who had taken ill during the concerto's composition. Dvořák was very devoted to her, and her death not long after his return home would cause him to revise the end of the work to include the same song in a lengthy epilogue. The finale (Allegro moderato) is an energetic rondo, followed by an epilogue which recalls the opening of the first movement, as well as the song mentioned above. *—Allen Schrott*

Recommended:

- ○ **Dvořák: Cello Concerto; Symphony 9** / Szell (cond.), Casals, Czech PO / 1995 / Dutton 5002
- ○ **Dvořák: Cello Concerto; Tchaikovsky: Rococo Variations** / Karajan (cond.), Rostropovich, Berlin PO / DG 447413
- ○ **Dvořák: Cello Concerto** / Celibidache (cond.), Du Pre, Swedish RSO / 2000 / DG 469070
- ○ **Dvořák: Cello Concerto** / Munch (cond.), Piatigorsky, Boston SO / 2001 / JVC 14

Piano Concerto in G minor, Op. 33 (1876)

Antonín Dvořák composed his only virtuoso vehicle for pianoforte and orchestra during the late summer months of 1876, at the prompting of a notable Czech pianist. The *Piano Concerto in G minor*, Op. 33, is often described as Dvořák's first effort at concerto composition, but in fact this is not so: he had, a dozen or so years earlier, made what might be called a first draft of a concerto for cello and orchestra—an apprentice piece that quite naturally pales when placed next to his mature cello concerto of 1894–95. It is usually, but certainly not always accurately, assumed that a pianoforte concerto is a vehicle for better and loftier musical thoughts than is a concerto for string instruments (the assumption goes back to Mozart and Beethoven, for whom it does indeed hold true), and Dvořák—himself far more a string player than a pianist—seems to have approached his *Piano Concerto* with that assumption in mind. The work is epic in style, grand in architecture, and sewn from an immediately and urgently dramatic fabric very different in kind from that used for the *Violin Concerto*, Op. 53 of just a few years later.

Even Dvořák devotees, however, are forced to admit that the *Piano Concerto* is not a completely successful piece of music. Some of the problems come from the piano writing, which is at times imbalanced and unwieldy. Many pianists have edited and rewritten the pianoforte part of the concerto over the years, but, in the end, something is lost in these rewrites. It takes a superb pianist to pull off Dvořák's original, but it can be done: Sviatoslav Richter is perhaps the finest exponent the work has yet known.

There is a full orchestral exposition at the start of the Allegro agitato first movement (again unlike the *Violin Concerto*, in which the soloist intrudes after just a few bars). The principal theme is symphonic in tone; the second theme veers towards something very chorale-like. A bombastic cadenza is the only sure sign that the work is not really a symphony accidentally scored for piano and orchestra.

The Andante sostenuto in D major is serene, and follows a harmonic path full of quiet surprises. The Allegro con brio finale is started by the soloist, a vintage Beethoven move, and proceeds to romp around in vintage Dvor˘ák style; there is an undisguised Bohemianism to the energetic principal ideas of this rondo. *—Blair Johnston*

Recommended:

- ○ **Dvořák: Piano Concerto; Schubert: Fantasy** / C. Kleiber (cond.), Richter, Bavarian State Orch. / 1998 / EMI 66947
- ○ **Dvořák: Piano Concerto** / Belohlavek (cond.), Moravec, Czech PO / Supraphon 3067
- ○ **Dvořák: Piano Concerto** / Somogyi (cond.), Firkušný, Vienna State Opera Orch. / 2002 / Westminster 471266

Romance for violin & orchestra in F minor, Op. 11 (1873; revised 1877)

As is the case with the *Nocturne for strings*, Op. 40, Antonín Dvořák's *Romance in F minor for violin and piano* (alternately orchestra, both versions being authentic to the composer), Op. 11 is in fact salvaged from an aborted string quartet. Dvořák seems to have been born to write slow movements; it was the crafting of workable outer movements that took painstaking work. It comes as no surprise, then, that when he decided to disown the *String Quartet in F minor*, Op. 9 (1873),it was only the slow movement that he saved and revised. The result of this revision, carried out over the course of the following few years, is the *Romance in F minor*.

Much of the music in the *Romance* is original and had no place in the abandoned string quartet movement—it is only the principal theme, a thoroughly lovely cantabile, that is shared by both. Dvořák mines a rich vein of expression even in the piano introduction—the ephemeral modulation to G flat major and the bell-like countermelody are especially memorable. There is a second theme that rises up as if it is lighter than the musical air around it. Throughout the piece there is plenty of fingerwork for the violinist, but even at its most bravura there is always a lyricism to it that makes one think twice before calling it virtuosic. *—Blair Johnston*

Recommended:

- ○ **Dvořák: Violin Concerto; Romance; Suk: Fantasia** / Ancerl (cond.), Suk, Czech PO / 2002 / Supraphon 3668
- ○ **Dvořák: Violin Concerto; Romance** / Mehta (cond.), Midori, New York PO / 1992 / Sony 44923

Rondo for cello & orchestra in G minor, Op. 94 (Oct. 16, 1893–Oct. 22, 1893)

It is said that Dvořák spent an entire Christmas Day working on his *Rondo in G minor for cello and piano*, Op. 94 (1891). The work is dedicated to Hanus Wihan, the cellist of the Bohemian String Quartet and, later, the dedicatee of the composer's *Cello Concerto* (1894–95). Dvořák had been touring Bohemia with the cellist and another musician; noting that there was no solo piece to show off Wihan's abilities, the composer produced the Rondo to fill the gap.

The Rondo's main theme has a slightly morose feel, largely because of its key of G minor. Despite its melancholic tinge, the melody is spirited and dance-like in the manner so characteristic of the composer's chamber music. The first section is followed by a more lyrical, optimistic passage in which the cello sings out until the accompaniment takes over the melody. This lyrical atmosphere is short-lived, however, as the mood grows uneasy before moving on to the next section. The following section shows off the cello's virtuosic capabilities as the instrument joyfully soars into its high registers. The return of the lyrical section brings more development; with a final statement of the cello's melody, less wistful and a little gloomier this time, the Rondo draws to a quiet close. Although the Rondo is effective with its piano accompaniment, Dvořák also made an orchestral version that lends the work an extra measure of color and drama; both incarnations of this imaginative work remain active in the repertoire. *—Emily Stoops*

Recommended:

- ○ **Gaspar Cassado Cello Masterpieces** / Perlea (cond.), Cassado, Vienna Pro Musica Orch. / 1992 / Vox 5502
- ○ **Dvořák: Cello Concerto; Silent Woods; Rondo** / Neumann (cond.), May, Czech PO / Supraphon 1544

Silent Woods (Klid), for cello & orchestra, Op. 68/5 (Oct. 28, 1893)

Besides the famous *Concerto in B minor*, Op. 104, Dvořák wrote precious little music for solo cello; Dvořák was never especially fond of the instrument (legend has it that his decision to compose a cello concerto was a shock even to him). In fact, there is really just a single original composition for cello beyond the *Concerto*: the *Rondo in G minor*, Op. 94 (there was an early sonata, but it has survived only in fragments). The rest of Dvořák's cello pieces, including *Silent Woods*, B. 182, are arrangements of music originally intended for other instruments. This non-originality has, however, been no hindrance to the fame of a work such as *Silent Woods*, and it is safe to say that it is today better known in its cello-and-orchestra (or cello-and-piano) clothing than it is in its original piano duet garb.

Dvořák composed the piano duets *From the Bohemian Forest*, B. 133 in 1883–1884; he selected the fifth of that group for arrangement as a solo cello vehicle about ten years later. *Silent Woods* (whose original Czech title, *Klid*, might be better translated as "Rest" or "Quiet") is a lovely work, endowed with long and sumptuous melody, tenacious syncopations, and a gently plodding bass line in which we can almost hear Dvořák quietly tramping though the Czech woods. A little flute solo (in the orchestral version, of course) ushers in a more active middle section. The close of the piece is perfectly drawn-out—how can we blame Dvořák for not wanting to end so charming a piece as this? *—Blair Johnston*

Recommended:

- ○ **Dvořák: Cello Concerto; Silent Woods; Rondo** / Neumann (cond.), May, Czech PO / Supraphon 1544
- ○ **Jacqueline du Pré Concerto Collection** / Barenboim (cond.), Du Pre, Chicago SO / 2000 / EMI 67341

Violin Concerto in A minor, Op. 53 (1879)

Dvořák composed this music in 1879 and revised it twice, in 1880 and 1882. František Ondricek played the premiere on October 14, 1883, with the composer conducting. Herr Doktor Professor Joseph Joachim never hesitated to "correct" concertos that younger composers submitted for his approval. From Max Bruch's in *G minor* in 1865, he graduated to Brahms' *D major* in 1878, then to Dvořák's *A minor* toward the end of 1879. But Joachim didn't just revise solo parts; he suggested changes in musical structure and orchestration that Bruch obsequiously obeyed, with the upshot that his—and Brahms'—were introduced to the world by Joachim. Not Dvořák's, though, despite a dedication to Herr Doktor Professor as well as revisions that the violinist deemed essential. (Joachim, in passing, was a proficient composer without being in any way distinctive, vide a violin concerto "in the Hungarian manner.") He waited two years before acknowledging Dvořák's changes, then wanted more ("some passages... were too difficult to perform"), chiding Dvořák, who was both a violinist and a violist, for "not having played in some time." Joachim allowed that he "was pleased by the many true beauties of your work, which it will be a pleasure for me to perform," doubting in the next breath that "in its present shape [it is] ripe for the public, especially because of its orchestral accompaniment, which is still rather heavy." Herr Doktor Professor invited Dvořák to Berlin for a play-through by the student orchestra at his Hochschule für Musik. A representative of the composer's Berlin-based publisher, Fritz Simrock, also attended, and had his own criticisms to add. Exasperated by now and not a little offended, Dvořák insisted the piece be published instanter. When this was done, he sought someone else to play the premiere. Although for the rest of the nineteenth century, the concerto was as popular as Beethoven's (even more so than Brahms'), Joachim never did play it. Just as certain structural innovations in the Bruch G minor had put him off, Dvořák's even freer, more imaginative approach to form was disturbing.

Rather than a heaven-storming first movement, an ameliorative Adagio and an insouciant finale, Dvořák dispensed with any long orchestral introduction (as Mendelssohn's had done 35 years earlier, and Bruch, too). He also abbreviated the first-movement reprise (Allegro ma non troppo in common time), and wrote a 13-bar transition (quasi moderato) that connected it to the second movement (Adagio ma non troppo in triple meter). Although F major is the root key of his sweetly reflective Romanza, Dvořák takes us on expressive side trips into D (major and minor), E, and A flat major.

Most probably, the sticking point for Joachim (not above being a fogy) was Dvořák's elaborate, intricate, uniquely Czech finale—a hybrid sonatina-rondo that starts with a recurring main-theme furiant in A major (Allegro giocoso, ma non troppo, 3/8 time). Four subsections celebrate the composer's national heritage, reminding us that he composed the first book of *Slavonic Dances*, Op. 46/1–8, a year before he undertook he violin concerto. The first of these is in F sharp major, but more striking is a D minor dumka in 2/4 time halfway through, in which a sun-dappled sky until this moment suddenly clouds over. But the key is A major, and the mood subsequently ebullient when this material repeats. More furiant follows before a high-spirited coda. *—Roger Dettmer*

Recommended:

- ○ **Dvořák: Violin Concerto; Suk: Fantasia** / Ancerl (cond.), Suk, Czech PO / 2002 / Supraphon 3668
- ○ **Dvořák: Violin Concerto; Piano Quintet** / Davis (cond.), Chang, London SO / 2003 / EMI 57521
- ○ **Schumann & Dvořák: Violin Concertos** / Enescu (cond.), Menuhin, Orch. of thr Paris Conservtory / 2002 / Naxos 8110966

CHAMBER MUSIC

Bagatelles for 2 violins, cello & harmonium, Op. 47 (May 1, 1878–May 12, 1878)

Antonín Dvořák's *Five Bagatelles*, Op. 47, in addition to two violins and cello, make use of the harmonium, a reed-type organ that was perfected around 1842. Although the harmonium is not commonly heard today, it was popular in the middle to later part of the nineteenth century. Dvořák wrote the *Bagatelles* in 1878. Around the time, he was playing a lot of chamber music with close friends. One of these, Josef Srb-Debrnov, owned a harmonium, and speculation is that Dvořák omitted the viola part (his own instrument) and played the harmonium instead.

Bagatelles are short pieces usually heard in sets, and Dvořák wrote his as a group of five. The first bagatelle is an Allegretto Scherzando in a minor key. It is spirited and full of contrasts of mood as it slips back and forth from minor into major. The harmonium functions in this movement as a bass part while the cello part, typically the "bass" of most quartets, functions as a middle part by playing moving pizzicato lines. The violins have the melody and harmony, which is rich and melancholy, although the cello does occasionally mirror the melodic lines of the upper instruments. The harmonium is the least "present," simply serving to create an overall texture, as it does through much of the five pieces. It is not until the very end that the harmonium has a brief solo, closing out the movement.

The second bagatelle is lyrical and flowing, less dance-like than the first bagatelle. It is marked in the tempo of a minuet (Grazioso), but sounds more rich and lush, less delicate, than a usual minuet.

The third bagatelle hearkens back to the first bagatelle with the same main theme, but there are darker-sounding twists and turns, making it dramatically different from its predecessor. It is rhythmically livelier and contains stormier contrasts to the main theme.

The fourth is a canon with an Andante con moto marking. The pastoral-type melody, which gets passed from instrument to instrument, is similar in many ways to so many of Dvořák's other andante melodies, particularly the *American Quartet* and the *Symphony No. 9 from the New World*. This melody has an open and uncomplicated feel that is expanded and elaborated upon, growing in emotion to a high point, then easing back into tranquility.

The final bagatelle is an allegretto that once again uses the theme from the first. This time it is more lighthearted and playful with a feeling that it is quickly moving forward. In addition, it has a contrasting section, making this movement twice as long as the others. Once again, the moods change quickly, not only between the sections, but within them as well. The original theme returns at the end, creating a sense that the bagatelles as a whole have come full-circle. *—Emily Stoops*

Recommended:

- ○ **Dvořák: String Quartets Opp. 96 & 105; Bagatelles** / Takacs SQ / 1991 / London 430077
- ○ **Domus** / / 1992 / Virgin 59245

Cypresses (Ohlas písní [Echoes of Songs]), for string quartet (Apr. 21, 1887–May 21, 1887)

In his youth, Dvořák wrote a set of 18 songs based on the poems of the Moravian writer Gustav Pfleger-Moravský´, and called them *Cypresses*. He dedicated them to the composer Karel Bendl, though they were, in fact, addressed to the young actress Josefina Cermáková, who later became his wife. In later life, he rearranged 12 of them for string quartet, and it is usually in this form they are now played. The music is gently romantic, rarely sentimental, and full of Dvořák's gift for fluid melody. To hear all 12 in succession is, perhaps, rather like eating a whole box of chocolates at one go; but *Cypresses* is a good example of the lyricism found in Dvořák's more fully developed chamber works. The pervasive gentle melancholy of these pieces is lightened by dance rhythms. In any performance of *Cypresses* it is useful to know the title of the song on which the movement is based, so as to have a clue to its mood and inspiration, for these are truly "emotions recollected in tranquillity." *—Roy Brewer*

Recommended:

- ○ **Dvořák: The String Quartets; Cypresses** / Prague SQ / DG 429193
- ○ **Dvořák: String Quartet 10; Cypresses** / Panocha Qt. / 2000 / Supraphon 111457

Piano Quartet No. 2 in E flat major, Op. 87 (Jul. 10, 1889–Aug. 19, 1889)

Dvořák's *Piano Quartet in E flat major*, Op. 87 had its premiere in November of 1890, just before the creative beginnings of the great *"Dumky" trio*, Op. 90. The quartet, however, while not devoid of folk influences, falls on the pan-European side of the duality that pervaded and animated Dvořák's work. Its outer movements are expansive, quite Brahmsian essays in sonata form, with characteristic touches in the instrumental writing such as the rapid exchange of tremolos between violin and viola at the end of the first movement. The second movement, marked Lento, is one of Dvořák's most purely lyrical, with a sequence of five themes, shifting in mood. The third movement, the most folkloristic of the four, consists of two contrasting dances; its central section deploys the piano in such a way that it sounds, perhaps, like a hammer dulcimer or other Eastern European folk instrument. The work is an unjustly neglected masterpiece of the chamber music repertoire, an unfailing crowd-pleaser but possessed of an originality that makes it worthy to stand beside the more complex corners of Brahms' chamber output. *—AMG*

Recommended:

- ○ **Dvořák: 2 Piano Quartets; Piano Quintet; Bagatelles** / Firkušný, Juilliard SQ / 1989 / CBS 45672
- ○ **Rubinstein Collection, Vol. 66** / Rubinstein, Guarneri Quartet / 1999 / RCA 63066
- ○ **Dvořák: Piano Quartets 1 & 2** / Hala, Suk, Kodousek, Chuchro / Supraphon 111464

Piano Quintet in A major, Op. 81 (Aug. 18, 1887–Oct. 3, 1887)

In the early 1870s Antonín Dvořák wrote a *Piano Quintet in A major* that was published as Op. 5. Always dissatisfied with it, he attempted in 1887 to revise it for republication. Instead, he cast it aside and immediately set about composing a brand new piano quintet in the same key. This product, the *Piano Quintet in A major*, Op. 81 (now called No. 2, though Dvořák surely would not have liked to hear it called so), is a complete success and a central masterwork of Romantic-era chamber music. Written between August and early October of 1887, it is a work that now stands alongside the Brahms *F minor Piano Quintet* as one of the twin peaks of the repertoire written for piano and string quartet. The three legs of the Dvořák stylistic triad—Brahmsian depth and warmth, Eastern European folk flavor, and sheer melodicism—are held in perfect balance here.

The *Piano Quintet, Op. 81* is in the traditional four movements (though the use of a schizophrenic dumka as the slow movement is more than a bit nontraditional): Allegro ma non tanto, Andante con moto (the dumka), Molto vivace (a scherzo), and Allegro. The cello introduces a famous melody atop a warm bed of the piano's arpeggiations at the start of the first movement; but barely a dozen bars go by before the music takes a jolting turn to the minor mode and shoots forth towards a rousing, fortissimo C major phrase (if only four bars are remembered by a listener while driving home from the concert, it will be these). A second theme area in C sharp minor provides the basis for a movement that falls essentially into the long tradition of sonata form.

The dumka was a Ukrainian lament or ballad that often contained several sections with contrasting moods; Dvořák incorporated dumky into several compositions. The dumka movement in this quintet is in F sharp minor. Its beautiful and introverted main theme is turned on its head first by a lighthearted D major interlude (Un pochettino più mosso) and then, after a reprise during which the viola plays the main tune in canon with the piano, by a fabulous Vivace during which a sprightly version of the main tune's first notes is tossed about between the players. The scherzo is called a "Furiant" in the score; at first it shows none of the metric alternations inherent in that particular Bohemian dance, but as the trio section unfolds Dvořák provides some nice three-against-four and two-against-threes rhythmic passages. The rondo finale starts with a burst of *secco* string eighth notes against rapid syncopation in the piano. The refrain theme thoroughly enjoys its time on center stage, hustling and bustling forward on folkish sixteenth notes. *—Blair Johnston*

Recommended:

- ○ **Dvořák: String Quartet 12; Piano Quintet** / Firkušný, Juilliard SQ / 1992 / Sony 48170
- ○ **Dvořák: Piano Quintet; Piano Quartet** / Pressler, Emerson SQ / 1994 / DG 439868

Piano Trio No. 3 in F minor, Op. 65 (Feb. 1, 1883–Mar. 31, 1883)

One of the most fascinating topics for study in the arts is the phenomenon of the striking, seemingly sudden increase in a composer's artistry made evident by comparing two works of the same type. Only seven years intervene between this work and Dvořák's second trio for piano, violin, and cello. Yet in this work there is much more maturity, control over musical material, and depth of feeling than in the prior work. More than just the seven more years of experience accounts for these. During this period the composer experienced professional disappointment after writing operas that did not find acceptance, formed a friendship with Johannes Brahms that provided a chance to share ideas about music, and suffered the death of his mother.

This music is darker in tone than the two earlier trios, and has an immediately evident seriousness of purpose. In the realm of development of his craft, Dvořák here shows a much greater understanding of writing for the piano in a chamber-music context.

At nearly 40 minutes, this is Dvořák's largest work for piano trio. The first movement is full of passion. It begins without introduction, yet the character of the opening theme is brooding and ominous. The second subject is tender. The first gets most of the attention in a passionate development section, and the recapitulation is dramatically convincing.

Dvořák originally placed the slow movement next, but in revising the work before its first performance placed the relatively brief (six-minute) scherzo movement as relief between two movements that are both over ten minutes long. Instead of being a scherzo per se, this movement is actually in the rhythm of a polka. The slow movement is surely bears the marks of the composer's friendship with Brahms. The finale, allegro con brio, starts off with the lightness of a dance movement, but it soon turns heroic, with a very dramatic development. At the very end the dance-like idea begins anew and the trio whirls to its conclusion. *—Joseph Stevenson*

Recommended:

- ○ **Dvořák: Complete Piano Trios** / Suk Trio / 2001 / Supraphon 3545
- ○ **Dvořák: Piano Trios** / Oistrakh, Oborin, Knushevitzky / Monitor 72070
- ○ **Dvořák: Complete Piano Trios** / Beaux Arts Trio / 1996 / Philips 454259

Piano Trio No. 4 in E minor ("Dumky"), Op. 90 (Nov. 1890–Feb. 12, 1891)

The manic-depressive nature of this, Dvořák's most celebrated chamber score after the *"American" Quartet*, derives not from the psychology of a suffering artist, but from the folk music form on which the entire work is based. Dumky is the plural of dumka, a Ukrainian lament; dumka is a diminutive of duma, a Ukrainian epic or ballad. Dvořák, like some others before him, combined the various elements of the dumka or duma, ending up with a format that alternates slow, melancholy, melismatic sections with fast Slavic dances.

For this trio, Dvořák assembled six dumky, each in a different key; the result seems more like a suite of songs and dances than a traditional piano trio, avoiding as it does standard development or even true variation of themes. Except for the lively fifth dumka, each begins with slow material that recurs later in the movement, following the lively sections. The first begins in E minor with a cello lamentation, which is soon picked up by the violin; this breaks in later in the movement, after it has been displaced by a cheerful dance. The second movement again finds the cello taking the lead in a C sharp minor meditation, which gives way to an increasingly lively dance. For the third movement, the key shifts to A major for a lyrical interlude, which unexpectedly lurches into the minor for the faster material. A bridge in D minor crosses over to a scherzo in F and D major, after which the D minor bridge leads out of the movement again. The fifth movement dispenses with slow material; it's a strongly rhythmic Allegro in E flat major. The final movement begins Lento maestoso in C minor; this section alternates with one of the most vigorous dances in the trio, which ends the work on an exuberant note. *—James Reel*

Recommended:

- ○ **Ahn Trio** / / 1998 / EMI 56674
- ○ **Dvořák: Complete Piano Trios** / Suk Trio / 2001 / Supraphon 3545
- ○ **Dvořák: Piano Trios** / Oistrakh, Oborin, Knushevitzky / Monitor 72070
- ○ **Dvořák: Piano Trios** / Golub Kaplan Carr Trio / 1999 / Arabesque 6726

Romantic Pieces, for violin & piano, Op. 75 (1887)

Antonín Dvořák's *Romantic Pieces*, Op. 75 (1887), comprise four charming miniatures for violin and piano. Perhaps surprisingly, they owe their existence to the modest musical skills of a young man who rented a room in Dvořák house. This subtenant was a chemistry student by day and an amateur violinist by night, and Dvořák took it upon himself to compose a string trio that Dvořák, the student, and the student's violin teacher could play together for fun. The resulting work, the *Terzetto*, Op. 74, proved too difficult for the young amateur, and so Dvořák composed a much simpler trio, the *Bagatelles* for two violins and viola, Op. 75a. This latter work was well within the student's grasp, but as an item of music Dvořák found it rather unsatisfying; so he took its four numbers and rewrote them for violin and piano as the *Romantic Pieces*, Op. 75.

Each of the *Romantic Pieces* originally had a title, but they were removed by the time of publication. Op. 75, No. 1 (originally Cavatina) is a comely B flat major Allegro moderato with a simple sequential melody and a constant long-short-short rhythm in the accompaniment. No. 2 (Capriccio) is more boisterous and features the pungent raised fourth so common in Bohemian music. No. 3 (Romance), is a flowing Allegro appassionato in the same key as the first piece. The G minor melody of the final number, Larghetto (Elegy), is broken up into many passionate, breathless bits; here more than in any of the other *Romantic Pieces* the addition of the piano's deep bass is welcome (in the original versions of the pieces the bass range was limited to the compass of the viola). *—Blair Johnston*

Recommended:

- ○ **Best of Dvořák** / Suk, Hala / 2001 / Supraphon 3572
- ○ **Dvořák: Piano Quintet; Romantic Pieces** / Accardo, Canino, Batjer / 1994 / Dynamic 51
- ○ **Itzhak Perlman** / Perlman, Sanders / EMI 47399

Sonatina for violin & piano in G major ("Indian Lament"), Op. 100 (Nov. 19, 1893–Dec. 3, 1893)

If the *"New World" Symphony*, Op. 95 and the *"American" String Quartet*, Op. 95 are the best-known products of Antonín Dvořák's years in the United States, the little *Sonatina in G major for violin and piano*, Op. 100—sometimes called the *"Indian Lament" Sonatina*—may well be the most obscure; yet it is a charming work that deserves better than its relegation to the learning books of young violinists. To hear it played by highly skilled musicians is, for many, to hear the piece for the first time.

The *Sonatina*, which Dvořák probably composed during the same year as those two more famous works (1893), is in four movements: Allegro risoluto, Larghetto, Scherzo (molto vivace), and Allegro. The first movement's principal tune has a firm rhythmic spine, its second tune a gentle plaintiveness; there is just a hint of American folk music in the movement—a light syncopation here (perhaps Dvořák's favorite "Americanism"), a modal inflection there, a pentatonic scale there.

The following Larghetto earned the *Sonatina* the nickname "Indian Lament." The succession of its three melodies—one in G minor, one in B flat major, and one in G major—has to it the same wistfulness, and the same sudden brightening and then softening of mood, that we hear in the famous slow movement of the *"New World" Symphony*.

The Scherzo takes the very first gesture of the Allegro risoluto as its starting-point. The Allegro finale is a substantial sonata-allegro movement, with three wonderful themes to claim as its own: the opening, syncopated idea in G major, a subsidiary thought in E minor, very dancelike and built around a repeating marcato cell, and finally a rich tranquillo melody (very much out of the "New World" trough) that closes the exposition. *—Blair Johnston*

Recommended:

- ○ **Dvořák** / Suk, Hala / Supraphon 111466
- ○ **Favorite Violin Encores** / Grumiaux, Hajdii / 1995 / Philips 446560

String Quartet No. 10 in E flat major, Op. 51 (Dec. 25, 1878–Mar. 28, 1879)

The immense popularity of Antonín Dvořák's colorful Slavonic works of the 1870s—the *Slavonic Dances* and *Slavonic Rhapsodies*, the *Moravian Duets*, and so on—was not without its price (a price familiar to many composers, authors, and actors): European fame was attained, yes, but for quite some time afterwards Dvořák's more substantial compositions were of almost no interest to his publishers, who were content to reap the near-endless harvest of the Slavonic-style works; furthermore, to the public and even many fellow musicians, Dvořák was suddenly typecast as an author of Bohemian novelties. However, Dvořák felt this to be a small price for escaping absolute poverty, and he continued to satisfy the demand for Slavonic works (for a time, anyway). So when the first violinist of the then-famous Florentine Quartet asked Dvořák to write a "Slavonic work" for the group, Dvořák was only too happy to comply. Composed between Christmas Day, 1878, and spring of 1879, the *String Quartet No. 10 in E flat*, Op. 51—the *"Slavonic" Quartet*, as it is sometimes called—is the result of that commission.

This quartet is the first of a pair of works that would temporarily wrap up Dvořák's work in that medium (the other is No. 11 in C major—an interval of 12 years would pass before Dvořák would again compose an original work for string quartet). Like so many of Dvořák's mature string quartets, the charms of this piece go far beyond the superficial attractions of its folk-music colorations. The opening of the Allegro non troppo first movement is perfectly relaxed; the main tune and its bouncing, dance-like counterpart vie for attention. The dance tune earns a major victory when it is selected to begin the recapitulation; but when all is said and done it is the calm first tune that draws a close.

The most obviously Slavonic movement of the quartet is the second, an Andante con moto dumka with bursts furiant sections in the middle (the dumka and the furiant are both dance forms native to Dvořák's homeland). The third movement is a Romanza in B flat major, one of Dvořák's loveliest thoughts.

Dance is again the germ from which the Allegro assai finale grows; a lively two-step colors the movement's sonata-form landmarks. *—Blair Johnston*

Recommended:

- ○ **Dvořák: Piano Quartet; String Quartet Op. 51** / Takacs SQ / 1999 / Decca 466197
- ○ **Dvořák: The String Quartets** / Prague SQ / DG 429193
- ○ **Dvořák: String Quartet 10; Cypresses** / Panocha Qt. / 2000 / Supraphon 111457

String Quartet No. 12 in F major ("American"), Op. 96 (1893)

Antonín Dvořák hadn't composed a string quartet in 12 years when, in the summer of 1893, he sat down to compose the *String Quartet No. 12 in F major*, Op. 96; the resulting *"American" String Quartet* is, along with the *"New World" Symphony* and perhaps a handful of the *Slavonic Dances*, the only Dvořák music that many music-lovers have ever learned to recognize.

Dvořák spent three years in the United States (1892–95) as the director of the newly-founded National Conservatory of Music in New York; it was during a vacation in rural Iowa that this beloved string quartet was written. Dvořák's progress on the work was so quick and satisfying that he scrawled out a sentence of gratitude to God at the end of his first draft! On the following New Year's Day the quartet received its Boston premiere, and it lost little time sewing itself into the fabric of the world's quartet repertoire.

There is more of America to the Opus 96 quartet than just its name and place of composition—Dvořák was fascinated by Native American and African American music, and throughout the *"American" Quartet* we can hear these new colors mixing in with his own usual quartet method. Many of the themes are pentatonically derived (the pentatonic scale being composed of five notes and containing no semitones); syncopation and snappy rhythm are found in abundance.

The viola gets things moving in the Allegro ma non troppo first movement with a happy, workaday tune that exploits the warm growl of its lowest register. The inviting A major melody that rounds off the exposition has just the slightest touch of America to it, and we are made to love it all the more for its reticence on that matter. A peculiar fugato in F minor, begun with enthusiasm by the second violinist, intrudes upon the development just before the lovely recapitulation.

It may have been 12 years since he had last produced a slow movement for quartet, but Dvořák's legendary slow-movement touch is as golden as ever in the Lento second movement of Op. 96 (no mean feat, as the previous quartet slow movement—that of Op. 61 in C major—is a masterpiece of its kind). The scherzo is Dvořák's usual rhythmically playful thing; according to Dvořák, birdsong is quoted by the first violin in the main music.

The finale hustles and bustles along on a very energetic, syncopated rhythm in the second violin and viola that shortly transforms itself into a patchwork of shifting accents. The first violin sings, first capriciously and then voluptuously, atop this motoric accompaniment. A completely different tone is drawn during the somber central portion. *—Blair Johnston*

Recommended:

- ○ **Dvořák, Tchaikovsky & Borodin Quartets** / Emerson SQ / 1994 / DG 445551
- ○ **Dvořák: The String Quartets** / Prague SQ / DG 429193
- ○ **Dvořák: String Quartets Opp 105 & 96** / Takacs SQ / 1991 / London 430077
- ○ **Dvořák & Smetana: String Quartets** / Alban Berg Quartet / 1991 / EMI 54215

String Quartet No. 13 in G major, Op. 106 (Dec. 9, 1895)

Dvořák was in such good spirits when he finally left the United States to return to Europe in the spring of 1895 that he spent many weeks just savoring the joy of being home; when he eventually started to work again in November, that joy found very palpable expression in the *String Quartet No. 13 in G major*, Op. 106. It would be tough to come up with a more unabashedly happy beginning to a piece of music than the opening bars of the first movement; there is extraordinary life to the scherzo movement; and the slow movement is one of the glories of Dvořák's whole catalog. In October 1896, this gem was introduced to the world by the famous Bohemian String Quartet.

The ordinary four movements are in operation here: Allegro moderato, Adagio ma non troppo, Molto vivace, and Andante sostenuto—Allegro con fuoco. Dvořák is too fine a composer to allow his personal sentiments to affect the balance of a piece for the worse, and after the first movement's carefree opening he allows the viola and cello to ponder some sober thoughts in bare octaves. But the violins will have none of this, and reroute the music back into G major with some ecstatic flourishes, so infectious that the lower strings have no choice but to take them up as well. A second theme arrives in the unlikely key of B flat major; it, too, is unconcerned and unaffected.

The Adagio is as deep and honest an expression of contentment as Dvořák ever wrote. The many shifts from E flat major to the parallel minor serve only to reinforce that sentiment by way of absence.

The scherzo is punctuated and vibrant. As often as not the instruments are waging war against one another, which makes the gentle trio section a real pleasure. In the slow introduction to the finale Dvořák finds his way into (and immediately out of) a realm that Jean Sibelius called home. The body of the movement can hardly control its own ebullience, though from time to time one wonders if perhaps it should. *—Blair Johnston*

Recommended:

- ○ **Dvořák: The String Quartets** / Prague SQ / DG 429193
- ○ **Dvořák: String Quartets 13 & 14** / Panocha Quartet / Supraphon 111459
- ○ **Dvořák: String Quartets, Opp 105 & 106** / Melos Quartet / HM 901709

String Quartet No. 14 in A flat major, Op. 105 (Mar. 26, 1895–Dec. 30, 1895)

Antonín Dvořák's final piece of chamber music, the *String Quartet No. 14* in A flat major, Op. 105, was begun before Dvořák had yet even thought of composing the *String Quartet No. 13* in G major, Op. 106, but it was put aside for many months and not finished until just after Christmas, 1895; by that time Dvořák had already put the final touches on the G major work, which explains the order of their opus numbers.

It is not hard to understand why Dvořák abandoned the *String Quartet No. 14* for a time: the first sketches of the piece date from his final, homesick weeks in the United States, and to expect him to immediately resume work on the piece upon his return to Prague, giving himself no time to regain his bearings, would be expecting too much. These two final quartets are a dual crown upon the head of a glorious string quartet output that spans better than 30 years (more than half of them years of mature work); there are some who would say that none since, including the twentieth century Russians and Soviets, have managed to master the medium so well.

The somber, apparently directionless opening bars (Adagio ma non troppo) of the first movement are as stark a contrast to the joyous outbursts in the exposition of the G major quartet as one could imagine; but by the time Dvořák has wheeled his way around to the Allegro appassionato body of the movement, the cello's uncertain idea has been transformed into something sparkling and cheery in the violin. "Appassionato" is certainly an appropriate indication for this many-faced movement, which expands in all directions to dramatic realms that would normally be far beyond the bounds of a movement less than ten minutes in duration.

The constant hemiolas of the Molto vivace second movement (the scherzo movement) transport us straight into the world of the traditional Bohemian furiant dance. The F major Lento molto e cantabile is at first a simple, attractive song; when Dvořák decides to adorn his tune with melting countermelodies and chromatic adornments, it becomes something else altogether. The way that Dvořák effortlessly floats from the bizarre cello figuration and ominous tremolos that begin the Allegro non troppo finale straight into the effusive, dancing body of the movement is simply wonderful. *—Blair Johnston*

Recommended:

- ○ **Dvořák: String Quartets 13 & 14** / Panocha Quartet / Supraphon 111459
- ○ **Dvořák: The String Quartets** / Prague SQ / 1977 / DG 463165
- ○ **Dvořák: String Quartets Opp 96 & 105** / Takacs SQ / 1991 / London 430077

String Quintet in G major, Op. 77 (1875; rev. 1883, 1888)

Dvořák's *String Quintet in G major* was originally planned as a five-movement work for string quartet plus bass, with the order of movements being Allegro con fuoco, Intermezzo, Scherzo, Poco Andante, and Finale. All the movements except the Intermezzo were composed in 1875; the Intermezzo was a recomposed and rescored version of the slow movement of his unpublished *String Quartet in E minor* from 1870. In 1883, however, Dvořák removed the Intermezzo from the quintet, recomposed and rescored it again, and published it separately as his

Nocturne for string orchestra. The four-movement version of the quintet was published in 1888 as Dvořák's Op. 77, although a more accurate chronological listing would be Op. 18. The quintet itself is a wonderful example of Dvořák's first maturity as a composer, that is, the period after he had taught himself how to compose and after he had rejected his youthful enthusiasm for Wagner, the period in which Dvořák became Dvořák. The work is cast in classical Viennese forms like Dvořák's models Mozart and Schubert, with the opening movement set in sonata form, the slow movements in ternary form, the Scherzo having a central trio, and the closing movement in rondo form. But Dvořák was also at the height of his first enthusiasm for Bohemian music, and each of the movements is indelibly marked with Bohemian melting melodies, poignant harmonies, and vigorous rhythms. Although like most of Dvořák's chamber music except his *Piano Quintet* and his *"American" String Quartet*, the *String Quintet in G major* is generally ignored in the concert hall and on disc, it is as worthy of attention as the string quintets of Brahms. *—James Leonard*

Recommended:

- ○ **Dvořák: String Quintet 2; String Sextet; Intermezzo** / Panocha Quartet, Nejtek / Supraphon 111461
- ○ **Dvořák: String Quintet 2; Intermezzo; String Quartet In E** / Buckoke, Coull SQ / 1994 / Hyperion 66679

String Quintet in E flat major ("American"), Op. 97 (Jun. 26, 1893–Aug. 1, 1893)

Dvořák's *E flat String Quintet ("American")* was written around the same time as the *Symphony No. 9* ("New World"); like that famous work, it is based partly on Native and Black American themes. Unlike the salon atmosphere that characterized string quartets of the era, the *American Quintet* is full of wonderful, populist tunes, even though their pentatonic origins may be more Slavonic than American. The String Quartet No. 2 received its premiere on January 12, 1894 at New York's Carnegie Hall.

The direct impetus for this Quintet came on Dvořák's first long vacation in the United States, at the Czech settlement of Spillville in northeast Iowa. During his stay, a band of American Indians arrived to sell medicinal herbs to the locals and stage a celebration. Dvořák came into contact with the Indians on a daily basis, and on two or three occasions he attended small gatherings at a local inn, where they performed their traditional songs and dances for him.

The Czech-American violinist Josef J. Kovarik recalled that one of the melodies he heard the Indians sing at the time bore a resemblance to the second subject of the Quintet's first movement. Indeed, at bars 63–64, Dvořák incorporates the transformed fragment of an Indian song—a so called "Indian drum rhythm." Other "Indian" elements that appear in the movement, as well as the finale, include pentatonic themes and short, oft-repeated phrases.

No less striking is the Larghetto movement—a set of variations that follows Haydn's example by having a double theme, half in major and half in minor. Dvořák had originally drafted it as a setting of S. F. Smith's "American National Anthem" (*My country, 'tis of thee*); he even hinted at the time in a letter to his publisher, Simrock, that he was considering expanding it into an independent work for baritone, chorus and orchestra. The *Finale*, has distant precursors in the cimbalom theme in the finale of Schubert's *Trio in E flat*, Op. 100, as well as the presto of Smetana's *Trio in G minor*. *—Brian Wise*

Recommended:

- ○ **Dvořák: String Quintets** / Panocha Quartet, Kluson / 2000 / Supraphon 111460-2131
- ○ **Dvořák: American Quartet; Quintette** / Talich Quartet, Bukac / 2002 / Calliope 9331

String Sextet in A major, Op. 48 (May 14, 1878–May 27, 1878)

Dvořák approached this sextet with confidence, fresh from the success of his *Slavonic Dances*. It's a particularly Czech-sounding work, less beholden to German models than some of his earlier scores, although there is a Schubertian abundance of endearing melodies.

The first movement, Allegro moderato, is based on three contrasting but generally sunny themes spun out at length but awarded a comparatively short development before being recapitulated in F sharp instead of the expected tonic key. The second movement is marked Dumka (Elegie): Poco allegretto, and has an improvisatory feeling thanks to its asymmetrical phrases. It begins with a sighing melody that might serve as a lullaby if it weren't played over a pizzicato, march-like accompaniment. At length this gives way to a slower, gypsy-like section without fully abandoning the gently marching pizzicato. The opening material returns for the final third of the movement. Next comes an even more thoroughly Czech movement, a Presto designated as a Furiant. Although it lacks the cross rhythms associated with that dance form, it is indeed a vigorous, highly physical piece, more playful than imposing. The central trio section eases off a bit, and includes a reference to, though not an exact quotation from, Dvořák's *Slavonic Dance No. 1*. The final movement is a B minor theme with five variations. The theme, marked Allegretto grazioso, quasi andantino, evokes an eighteenth century minuet. The first variation gives the theme a more flowing character, with the accompaniment lines providing a gentle ebb and flow. The second variation is a little Mendelssohnian scherzo; the third is contemplative and even mysterious, again alluding to an earlier *Slavonic Dance*. The fourth continues in this vein, but now with an agitated undercurrent, and the fifth, making good use of pizzicato, transfers this material to a more bucolic realm. A final section seems to be another full variation, more energetic now, but it turns out to be a long, boisterous stretta, which Dvořák seems reluctant to bring to a full close. *—James Reel*

Recommended:

- ○ **Dvořák: String Quintet 2; String Sextet; Intermezzo** / Panocha Quartet, Kanka, Kluson / Supraphon 111461
- ○ **Dvořák & Tchaikovsky: String Sextets** / Chang, Christ, Hartog, Faust, etc. / 2002 / EMI 57243

Terzetto for 2 violins & viola in C major, Op. 74 (Jan. 7, 1887–Jan. 14, 1887)

Antonín Dvořák's *Terzetto* (trio) in C major, Op. 74 was composed in the second week of 1887 (Jan. 7–14) for the express purpose of amateur music making. A young chemistry student with a love of the violin was at the time renting rooms in the Dvořák house, and Dvořák thought it would be fun to take up the viola once again (Dvořák had made a living playing the instrument in early adulthood) and play some music with the young student and his violin teacher. Unfortunately, both of the *Terzetto*'s violin parts proved excessively difficult for the enthusiastic, but more-or-less unskilled, amateur and Dvořák was forced to write a new piece for them to play (Op. 75a, finished the following week but, until well into the twentieth century, published only in an arrangement for violin and piano). Happily enough, however, we still have the *Terzetto*. The piece is a truffle, but a thoroughly enjoyable one; if it happens that it is a richer experience to play the *Terzetto* than to hear it, we can only smile and note that such was Dvořák's intent at the time.

The *Terzetto* is in four movements: Allegro ma non troppo, Larghetto, Vivace (scherzo), and Tema con variazioni. The first movement has a rather innocent main theme, the gestures of which are thrown about by the two other voices as a children's toy. In the Larghetto Dvořák manages to create the impression of a countermelody when the melody is given a second statement simply by taking the middle voice and moving it up top. The scherzo is a wonderful movement (it would be better if the viola had another octave to it to provide a richer bass!) built along the same vigorously rhythmic thematic lines that we find in the scherzos for larger ensembles. The theme and variations finale takes up a tune that is poised somewhat indecisively between C major and C minor. *—Blair Johnston*

Recommended:

- ○ **Dvořák: String Quartet 1; Terzetto; Drobnosti** / Panocha Quartet Supraphon 111451
- ○ **Dvořák: String Quartet; Terzetto** / Vlach Quartet 1996 / Naxos 553373

KEYBOARD

Humoresques, Op. 101 (Aug. 7, 1894–Aug. 27, 1894)

The eight humoresques of Antonín Dvořák's Op. 101 are largely forgotten today—all but one of them, that is. The *Humoresque in G flat major, No. 7*, Op. 101 is surely one of the world's most famous short pieces, and has been since it was first published. Arrangements of this slight work have been made for every imaginable instrument and ensemble, most of them by the original publisher (N. Simrock) with Dvořák's knowledge; the arrangement made for violin and piano by Fritz Kreisler was so famous in its day that many forgot altogether that the work was originally for piano.

The *Humoresques* are among Dvořák's last works for keyboard. Composed in 1894, they are followed only by the *Two Pieces*, B. 188 ("Berceuse" and "Capriccio"), written later the same year. As such, they represent the composer's mature synthesis of the character piece genre with his innate, spontaneous sense of melody and the ever-present influence of his native Czech folk music. All eight of the *Humoresques* are, at times, reminiscent of Johannes Brahms in their combination of relatively conservative musical language, robust textures, and warm tunefulness.

It took Dvořák a few years to put the pieces of Op. 101 into their finished shapes. He jotted down most of the melodies and themes during his stay in the United States (1892–95), but he didn't set about fleshing them out until the summer of 1894 (during a brief and welcome return to Bohemia for the summer). At first he thought of calling the set *New Scottish Dances* (a follow-up to the *Scottish Dances*, Op. 41 of the late 1870s), since they all follow the basic duple-meter and simple rondo-type plan of an Ecossaise dance. But he decided instead to give them the less specific title, *Humoresques*. *—AMG*

Recommended:

- ○ **Rudolf Firkušný Plays** / Firkušný / 1992 / Vox 5058
- ○ **Dvořák: Music for Violin & Piano Vol. 2** / Jacobson, Stanzeleit / 1995 / Meridian 84281
- ○ **Romantic Piano Favourites Vol. 1** / Szokolay / 1995 / Naxos 8.550052

Slavonic Dances, for piano, 4 hands (Apr. 1878–Jan. 5, 1887)

Brahms' publisher Simrock asked Dvořák to write a set of *Slavonic Dances* for piano, four hands, in hopes that they might achieve the same financial success of

Brahms' first set of *Hungarian Dances*. Dvořák agreed and produced the first of his two sets of *Slavonic Dances*, Op. 46, between March 18 and May 7, 1878. He orchestrated all eight of them in August, that same year. The composer produced the second set of eight (Op. 72), again for Simrock, in 1886, once more making versions for piano, four hands, and for orchestra. Dvořák used folk forms but no folk themes in either of his two books of *Slavonic Dances*. The first book's No. 1, in C major, is furiant, like the set's G minor closing piece. As the form's name suggests, the music is quite lively in both these efforts, though each has moments of respite. No. 2 is a dumka in E minor, a charming slow dance here of great color and melodic appeal. No. 10 and No. 12 in the Op. 72 set are also attractive dumkas, both showing perhaps a little more subtlety in expressive manner and orchestration. No. 3 is a lively and infectious polka in A flat major, while the ensuing F major dance is a sousedská, a 3/4 time number which here is charming in its catchy, folk-ish melody and mostly relaxed but festive character. There two more sousedskas in the *Slavonic Dances*, the D major No. 6 (a colorful, graceful piece of sunny character) and No. 16 in A flat major, Op. 72 (a better work in its dream-like character and subtly understated manner). No. 5 in A major, No. 7 in C minor, and No. 11 in F major all use the form called skocná, known as a jumping dance. Not surprisingly, they are lively and effervescent pieces of great charm and playfulness. Op. 72's No. 9 in B major is an odzemek, an energetic, light dance occasionally boisterous here in its festive character. No. 13 is a spacírka, a colorful Czech dance which, in this B flat minor effort, mixes slow and fast music with a fine sense for contrast. The ensuing polonaise, in B flat major, exhibits a bucolic manner in its tuneful charm, while No. 15 in C major is a kolo, an energetic Serbian dance, which here effervesces with an almost ecstatic sense of festivity. *—Robert Cummings*

Recommended:

- ○ **Dvořák: Complete Works for Piano 4 Hands, Vol. 2** / Crommelynck Duo / 1991 / Claves 509107
- ○ **Dvořák: Slavonic Dances** / Szell (cond.), Cleveland Orch. / 2002 / Legacy 89845

OPERA

Rusalka, Op. 114 (Apr. 21, 1900–Nov. 27, 1900)

After Antonín Dvořák had conquered the musical world—he was considered the greatest Czech composer in Bohemia, the greatest composer after Brahms in Austria and Germany, the successor of Mendelssohn in England, and the greatest composer in the world in the United States—he returned to Bohemia to write the national operas of his people. He started with *Kate and The Devil* (1899) and ended with *Armida* (1904), but between them composed the great Czech national opera, *Rusalka*. Written in a single burst of inspiration between April 21 and November 27, 1901, to a text by Jaroslav Kvapil based on Hans Christian Andersen, *Rusalka* is a Bohemian "Little Mermaid." Telling the sad story of a water sprite who longs for human love, *Rusalka* is a three-act opera set in its first and last acts in the lakes of Bohemia, with a central act depicting an interrupted wedding feast. Although it hews basically to the composer's distinctive mix of nationalism, lyricism, and Brahmsian classical thinking, the influence of Wagner is readily apparent in the use of leitmotif musical character identifiers, and more generally in the derivation of the story from ancient and fantastic legend. Its melodies are based on the cadences of the Czech language; its harmonies are lushly late Romantic, sometimes almost Impressionistic but always sweetly and sensuously Czech; its cavatinas, arias, and set pieces are derived from the folk ballads of Czech poetry; and its lyricism is deep, passionate, and all-suffusing. Dvořák's *Rusalka* rivals the operas of Smetana and Janáček as the supreme expression of what it means to be Czech in music. *—James Leonard*

Synopsis:

Act One. The action in this fairy tale opera begins in a meadow in a heavily wooded area near a lake. The water gnome Vodnik is teased by water nymphs. Rusalka, his daughter, has more serious matters on her mind. She tells Vodnik she is in love with a man, the Prince, who frequently swims in the lake. Vodnik discerns that she desires to become a human and is repulsed at the thought. He advises that she must seek the aid of the witch Jezibaba, whom Rusalka immediately seeks out. The sorceress changes her into a beautiful but mute woman, cautioning her that if her human lover betrays her, both will suffer eternal damnation. The Prince sees the transformed Rusalka and is immediately enamored of her beauty.

Act Two. The scene opens on the grounds within the castle of the Prince. The Gamekeeper and Kitchen Boy talk of the Prince's odd behavior ever since he met Rusalka. The Prince plans to marry her, but is alarmed at her strange ways and especially at her speechless manner. Guests begin arriving for dancing and festivities, and during the celebrations Vodnik, from near the lake, sings sadly about Rusalka and her inevitable failure in love. Rusalka, who is growing progressively disenchanted with her new life, flees into the nearby forest and over to the lake. Her voice restored, she beseeches Vodnik to forgive her for her foolish venture. A foreign Princess at the festivities catches the Prince's eye, and he declares his love for her. Rusalka returns and, finding the two together, is rejected by the Prince. But he in turn is rejected by the Princess.

Act Three. The scene is near the lake, where Rusalka bemoans her awful fate. Jezibaba agrees to return her to her water nymph form, but she must agree to kill the Prince. She refuses the awful proposal. The Gamekeeper and Kitchen Boy bring news that the Prince is seriously ill and ask Jezibaba to come to his aid. Vodnik rises from the lake and drives them off, angered by their deceit in claiming that Rusalka had been unfaithful to the Prince. The Prince staggers along, sick and delusional, and begs Rusalka to come back to him. She informs him that kissing him would bring both death and damnation. The Prince entreats her to kiss him anyway, and she obliges. He dies, and she asks God's forgiveness for him. Then she dives into the lake, descending to its deepest, demon-inhabited regions. *—Robert Cummings*

Recommended:

- ○ **Dvořák: Rusalka** / Neumann (cond.), Beňačková, Novák, Ochman, Soukupova, Czech PO / Supraphon 3641
- ○ **Dvořák: Rusalka** / Mackerras (cond.), Fleming, Heppner, Kusnjer, Hawlata, Czech PO / 1998 / London 460568

VOCAL

Biblical Songs (Biblické písně), Op. 99 (Mar. 5, 1894–Mar. 26, 1894)

The *Biblical Songs* were all composed in March 1894, while Dvořák was in the United States. It is thought that the composer's turn to religious subjects was a reflection of his homesickness—he had been in America for a year already—and also an expression of sorrow over the recent deaths of a number of fellow composers, including his friend Tchaikovsky. Dvořák composed relatively little religious music, and was not entirely comfortable writing it, but the texts of the *Biblical Songs* were perfectly suited to his expressive needs, and he completed them quickly and with relative ease.

Dvořák chose the texts himself from the Book of Psalms, selecting verses from 13 different psalms. Musically, the songs reflect a number of different influences, including the Negro spirituals to which Dvořák had been exposed while in America. The songs contain a blend of pentatonic and conventional diatonic progressions, with some complex modulations which serve to dramatize the text; almost all of the 10 songs are slow and contemplative in nature. The composer orchestrated the first five songs of the set in 1895, and the remaining songs were orchestrated by V. Zemánek for their publication in 1929. Interestingly, these songs have been both lauded as Dvořák's best, and criticized as his worst: those who praise them songs claim that they are works of great religious sincerity, while others see them as overly conventional, too simplistic, and lacking in variety when performed as a set. *—Alexander Carpenter*

Recommended:

- ○ **Dvořák: Songs** / Pecková, Gage / 2001 / Supraphon 3437
- ○ **Dvořák: Biblical Songs; Gypsy Songs** / Moravec, Soukupova / Supraphon 0206
- ○ **Dvořák: Biblical Songs** / Lapsansky, Kusnjer / Supraphon 3247

Cypresses (Cyprise), song cycle (Jul. 10, 1865–Jul. 27, 1865)

When Dvořák, then just under 24 years of age, took up a book of Gustav Pfleger-Moravsky´'s Moravian love poems and set them to music in July of 1865, he was entranced by an actress named Josefina Cermáková. The resulting song cycle, *Cypresses* (B. 11), representing Dvořák's first attempt at song writing, is full of deep feeling, sentiment, and clearly betrays the composer's youthful exuberance in love; however, it is also unfortunately poor—or at best uneven—music. Pfleger-Moravsky´'s verse is not to blame for *Cypresses*' deficiencies: Dvořák, who had thus far spent all his time working at instrumental composition, simply hadn't yet any real notion how to capture poetry in song and, furthermore, how to supply an apt piano accompaniment for the voice. Dvořák was one of history's more honest and objective composers, and it didn't take him long to realize that, although the 28 songs contained some lovely vocal melodies, his cycle was a failure; the music would remain near and dear to his heart however (Josefina's rejection of him had ensured that much; later on, she would become Dvořák's sister-in-law, and we can only wonder at his internal response to that turn of events), and he revised and adapted its music many times throughout the years, most notably in the string quartet work *Cypresses* of 1887 and in the *Love Songs*, Op. 83 of 1888. *—Blair Johnston*

Recommended:

- ○ **Popp** / , Gage / 1999 / BBC 4025
- ○ **Dvořák: Biblical Songs; Cypresses** / Langridge, Kvapil / Unicorn Kanchana 9115

Gypsy Melodies (Zigeunermelodien), Op. 55 (Jan. 18, 1880–Feb. 23, 1880)

Dvořák's *Gypsy Melodies* is a cycle of 10 songs composed for the tenor Gustav Walter, who sang with the Vienna Court Opera and was a great admirer of Dvořák. The composer used Walter's own German translations of the original Czech texts as the basis of his settings. While exact dates for these songs are unknown, it is thought that they were written in just a few day at the end of February 1880. The songs display Dvořák's ever-increasing skill at vocal composition; their vocal melodies are supple and natural, and the piano accompaniment is often interesting—vivacious and dance-like. Despite the cycle's title, the songs are not written in an authentic gypsy idiom, but they do reflect in general the character of gypsy music, filtered through Dvořák's own compositional style. *—Alexander Carpenter*

Recommended:

○ **Dvořák: Songs** / Pecková, Gage / 2001 / Supraphon 3437

○ **Dvořák: Biblical Songs** / Lapsansky, Kusnjer / Supraphon 3247

CHORAL

Mass in D major, Op. 86 (Mar. 24, 1892–Jun. 15, 1892)

It was for the private consecration of the Czech philanthropist Josef Hlávka's personal chapel that Antonín Dvořák composed, in 1887, his *Mass in D major*, Op. 86, for chorus, soloists, and organ. As his sole surviving setting of the Mass Ordinary (another setting was among the early works that Dvořák destroyed), the *Mass* has been overshadowed by the justly well-known *Requiem* of a few years later; Dvořák, however, remained interested in the work even after composing the *Requiem*: in 1892 he took the trouble to re-score the organ part for orchestra.

The *Mass in D*, whose solo parts, as the composer indicates, can be sung by "small chorus" instead, is in the usual six sections: Kyrie, Gloria, Credo, Sanctus, Benedictus, and Agnus Dei. The soloists (or small chorus singers) get their first chance to shine during the central Christe eleison portion of the serene Kyrie. The Gloria is, as per tradition, exuberant, the Credo multi-sectioned. The latter's warm B flat major Allegro moderato gives way to G minor during the central Et incarnatus est and Et resurrexit tertua strains, but is put back in place when the opening music is reprised for Credo in Spiritum Sanctum; a kind of da capo form is thus created. The Sanctus is a boisterous alla breve, the Benedictus a Lento whose choral writing is imitative in absolutely unstrict ways. The final Agnus Dei is more properly fugal, though the subject is so wonderfully melodious that one would hardly suspect it of harboring such strict imitative designs.*—Blair Johnston*

Recommended:

○ **Dvořák: Mass in D major; Te Deum** / Smetacek (cond.), Machotkova, Jedlicka, Lindauer, Tvrzský, Prague SO / Supraphon 111821

○ **Dvořák: Mass in D major; Te Deum** / Polyansky (cond.), Russian State SO / 1996 / Chandos 9505

Stabat Mater, Op. 58 (Feb. 19, 1876–Nov. 13, 1877)

Antonín Dvořák's *Stabat Mater* for four vocal soloists (SATB), chorus, and orchestra, Op. 58 is a work born of deep sorrow. The death of his infant daughter in late 1875 (tragically, she never passed her second day of life) moved Dvořák, a devout Catholic, to begin the *Stabat Mater* in February 1876; the deaths of his other daughter and only son in August and September of the following year moved him to finish the work. The *Stabat Mater dolorosa* sequence is, of course, well-suited for expressing a parent's agony, for the text itself tells of a parent's anguish, Mary bereaved. For all the depth of feeling that Dvořák poured into the *Stabat Mater*, Op. 58, he seems not to have considered it an especially private piece of music; indeed, it was one of the composer's biggest triumphs to date at its Prague premiere in on December 23, 1880.

Dvořák sets the *Stabat Mater dolorosa* sequence in ten sections of music that, for the most part (and with some exceptions), alternate between chorus and soloists. The opening Andante con moto begins with a substantial orchestral introduction—as pained a specimen of B minor as the late nineteenth century ever produced, filled with little chromatic descents that just weep. The soloists enter with music that sounds like heartbeats, pianissimo and very hollow; the chorus follows shortly. This lengthy first number is a major achievement the likes of which any composer would covet.

Quartet and chorus make their respective cases separately in Nos. 2 and 3; in No. 4, which presents the Fac ut urdeat cor meum text in a B flat minor Largo, the bass soloist explores the depths of "His Passion." In No. 6, the tenor soloist brightens things up a bit (B major) as he lies at Jesus' feet "in adoration." Some of the opening number's quiet agony is recalled at the start of the final number, "Quando corpus morietur," but the "glory of Paradise" dissolves the Holy Mother's pain, and Dvořák is able to end his *Stabat Mater* in a blissful expanse of D major, triumphant at first, utterly tranquil at the last. *—Blair Johnston*

Recommended:

○ **Dvořák: Stabat Mater** / Sawallisch (cond.), Beňačková, Dvorsky, Rootering, Wenkel, Czech PO / Supraphon 103561

○ **Dvořák: Stabat Mater** / Kubelik (cond.), Jurinac, Hoppe, Merriman, Crass, Bavarian Radio Orch. / Living Stage 1006

○ **Dvořák: Stabat Mater; Suk: Asrael** / Talich (cond.), Blachut, Kalas, Tikalova, Krasova, Czech PO / Supraphon 111902

Te Deum, Op. 103 (Jun. 25, 1892–Jul. 28, 1892)

Antonín Dvořák's arrival in the United States in the autumn of 1892 was nearly coincident with the fourth centennial of Columbus' landing in the New World, and Dvořák's sponsor asked him to compose a new choral work to be performed at the celebrations. A poem by Joseph Rodman Drake was to be the text for this new work, but Dvořák did not receive the completed text in time (although he eventually did set it as *The American Flag*, Op. 102). So, during the summer of 1892, he instead composed the *Te Deum* for soprano and bass vocal soloists, chorus, and orchestra, Op. 103. The work represents something of Dvořák's musical thinking immediately prior to the important American phase of his career.

Dvořák shapes the *Te Deum* text into four sections of music that more or less correspond with four-movement symphonic form. Midway through the opening Allegro moderato maestoso movement, the soprano soloist comes out of the woodwork to help out with the "Sanctus Dominus Deus" text; the tranquil lyricism of her melody forms a perfect contrast to the stately choral music and vigorous orchestral sixteenth notes of the rest of the movement.

The slow movement, Lento maestoso, begins in E flat major with an enthusiastic bass solo. By the end of the Lento Dvořák has moved to G flat major, in preparation for the B minor key of the following scherzo-like "movement" (with the text "Aeterna fac cum Sanctis tuis").

The finale is an expansive and flexible thing—tempo and key develop freely, beginning Lento and B major and finishing in G major with exactly the same tempo as the opening section of the *Te Deum*. The outline of the solo soprano melody that opens this section is something that, by all rights, should not work, but which, through Dvořák's magical pen, does, and how! At the end of the work, as both key and tempo recall the *Te Deum*'s opening, the jubilant sixteenth note motive from that opening is called out of retirement as well, so that a happy conclusion may be drawn from a cyclical detail. *—Blair Johnston*

Recommended:

○ **Dvořák** / Smetacek (cond.), Maffeo, Czech PO / Supraphon 111821

○ **Dvořák: Symphony 9; Te Deum** / Neumann (cond.), Beňačková, Soucek, Czech PO / Supraphon 1961

E

Eastman Wind Ensemble

f. 1951, Rochester, NY

Ensemble

In 1951, under the direction of Frederick Fennell, a group of wind, brass, and percussion students at the Eastman School of Music in Rochester, New York, performed a groundbreaking concert. On the program were several names quite familiar to the Western musical canon, including (Willaert, Lasso, Mozart, Beethoven, Stravinsky), as well as a few less-familiar faces, such as seventeenth century composers Samuel Scheidt and Johann Pezel, and twentieth century American Carl Ruggles. The pieces themselves, however, were in an even more obscure vein: a motet for double brass choir by Lasso, a trombone quartet by Beethoven, and Stravinsky's *Symphonies for Wind Instruments*. In an effort to create an ensemble that could fulfill the traditional social and musical functions of a band, while at the same time endeavoring to create its own sonorities and foster its own compositions, Fennell and his students established the Eastman Wind Ensemble. In the ensuing years, Fennell and his group would play a crucial and prominent role in shaping the character of this new, historically grounded but uniquely American genre.

In addition to performing works involving only portions of its constituency (works for brass or winds only, for example), the Wind Ensemble as it came to be defined—largely through its development at Eastman—shed the usual doubled parts of the traditional band, so that the composer could carefully shape, weigh, and balance sonorities with one player on a part. Over the course of the ensuing decades, this concept became widely institutionalized, attracting a large number of composers, performers, and audiences to the genre.

Central to the Eastman Wind Ensemble's pioneering role in the realm of "serious" wind music was its prolific recorded output during the Fennell years. Raoul Camus, writing in the *New Grove Dictionary of American Music*, observed that "Fennell's pioneering series of 24 recordings for Mercury brought about a reconsideration of the wind medium and established performance and literature models for the more than 20,000 wind ensembles that were subsequently established in American schools." These recordings included important works by such notable twentieth century composers as Paul Hindemith, Arnold Schoenberg, Vincent Persichetti, and Krysztof Penderecki; the Ensemble's recorded output also reflected the desire, reflected in that first concert, to rescue neglected works of the past. One album for example, was dedicated entirely to works by Giovanni Gabrieli. The ensemble's notoriety also increased through numerous radio broadcasts heard throughout the country, and through several national and international tours.

In 1962, Fennell passed the baton of the Eastman Wind Symphony to Clyde Roller, an Eastman graduate who had previously conducted the Amarillo Symphony. Two years later, the conductorship was assumed by another Eastman grad, Donald Hunsberger. Hunsberger had been an apprentice to Fennell, and under his new direction, the Eastman Wind Ensemble continued to greatly influence the character of the symphonic winds genre. From 1967–70, the Ensemble helped define and stimulate the wind repertory canon by collaborating on a project with MCA Music and Decca Records, in which performances of new works by the Ensemble were coordinated with the publication of scores and part sets by MCA, as well as the release of recordings on Decca.

In the last decades of the twentieth century, the Eastman Wind Ensemble continued to serve as a model for collegiate wind organizations worldwide, touring extensively in Europe and Asia, and continuing to perform and record important works by noted composers including Christopher Rouse, Joseph Schwantner, and Wynton Marsalis. *—Jeremy Grimshaw*

Recommended:

- ○ **Screamers** / Fennell (cond.), Eastman Wind Ens. / 1991 / Philips 432019
- ○ **Sullivan; Rossini-Respighi; etc.** / Fennell (cond.), Eastman Wind Ens. / 1992 / Mercury 434322
- ○ **Grainger; Persichetti; etc.** / Fennell (cond.), Eastman Wind Ens. / 1991 / Philips 432754
- ○ **Holst & Vaughan Williams** / Fennell (cond.), Eastman Wind Ens. / 1999 / Mercury 462960
- ○ **Sousa Marches** / Fennell (cond.), Eastman Wind Ens. / 1992 / Philips 434300

Max van Egmond

b. Feb. 1, 1936, Semarang, Dutch East Indies (Indonesia)

Baritone

With a voice essentially bass-baritone in range but with a lighter, more baritonal coloring, Max van Egmond achieved considerable fame through his series of Bach oratorio recordings made for Teldec under the direction of Nikolaus Harnoncourt and Gustav Leonhardt. His smooth, soft-edged timbre fit the lyric approach Harnoncourt favored, if missing something of the fire and intensity brought to Bach's bass arias by certain other singers such as Dietrich Fischer-Dieskau and John Shirley-Quirk. In collaboration with these celebrated conductors, however, he found his way to an understanding of period music performance that has maintained its authority through several decades of evolving practice; his singing invariably met the highest standards for musical integrity. Born in the former Dutch East Indies, Max van Egmond continued his schooling in Holland following World War II. At Hilversum, he studied with Tine van Willigen de Lorme, also taking lessons from Dr. Anton van der Horst. At the age of 18, he joined the Nerderlandse Bach Vereniging (Netherlander Bach Society). In 1959, he was a prizewinner in the 's-Hertogenbosch Voice Competition following his friend and soprano colleague Elly Ameling, who had similarly distinguished herself three years earlier. The young bass baritone won awards at Brussels that same year and at Munich in 1964. While Egmond had made his professional debut in a performance of Bach's *St. Matthew Passion* at Naarden in 1954, it was only in the aftermath of his competition awards that he devoted himself full-time to the music profession. He quickly gained an international following in oratorio, especially after being engaged for Teldec's massive project to record the complete passions, cantatas, and masses of Bach. Although he appeared with success in recital and in opera, his reputation as a singer of oratorio outranked his standing in other areas, especially with the record-buying public. With Harnoncourt, Leonhardt, and Frans Brueggen, he became the leading choice in other venues and under other conductors for the performance of these works. His performances and recordings with the Ricercar Consort helped revive interest in seventeenth century German oratorio. Recognition came from his own country in the form of numerous honors and citations. Queen Beatrix bestowed a special decoration celebrating his decades of service to Holland's musical life. While his expertise inclined him toward the performance of period opera, Egmond occasionally ventured into more contemporary fields, performing at the Netherlands Opera in world premieres of Jurriaan Andriessen's *Het Zwarte Blondje* in 1962 and of Anthony Hopkins' *Three's Company* in 1963. The singer even sang Quinault in a 1966 production of Cilea's *Adriana Lecouvreur* in 1966, a venture available in a live recording. Egmond has pursued a productive career as a teacher as well. As early as 1972, he was engaged as a teacher of singing and interpretation at Amsterdam's Muzieklyceum and from 1980 to 1995 (the year of his public retirement), he was a professor at the Sweelinck Conservatory at Amsterdam. In the United States, he forged a long-term relationship with the Baroque Performance Institute at Oberlin; since 1978, he has taught classes in interpretation, technique, and vocal diction (his own diction was of remarkable clarity). In addition to numerous master classes around the world, Egmond offers instruction each year at Mateus, Portugal, and has guided many promising singers into fruitful careers. One of his star pupils has been Dutch bass Harry van der Kamp, who, like his teacher, has made a name for himself in Baroque music performance. *—Erik Eriksson*

Recommended:

- ○ **Das Kantatenwerk, Vol.1** / Harnoncourt (cond.), Egmond, Equiluz, Concentus Musicus Wien / Teldec 35027
- ○ **Baroque Cantatas** / Egmond, Farr (hpschd) / Etcetera 1056

Sir Edward Elgar

b. Jun. 2, 1857, Broadheath, England, **d.** Feb. 23, 1934, Worcester, England

Composer: Orchestral, Symphonic, Chamber Music, Concerto, Choral, Keyboard

One of the preeminent musical figures of his time, Sir Edward William Elgar (1857–1934) bridged the nineteenth and twentieth centuries as the finest English composer since the days of Handel and Purcell. Elgar's father owned a music shop and was a church organist who taught his son piano, organ, and violin; apart from this instruction, Elgar was basically self-taught as a musician. At the age of 16, the composer became a freelance musician and for the remainder of his life never took a permanent job. He conducted locally, performed, taught, and composed, scraping by until his marriage to Caroline Alice Roberts, a published novelist of some wealth, in 1889.

Elgar had by this time achieved only limited recognition. He and his wife moved to London, where he scarcely fared better in advancing his career. They couple eventually retreated to Worcester, Elgar suffering from bitter self-doubt and depression. Alice stood by him the entire time, her unfailing confidence restoring his spirits. He was further buoyed by the success of his *Imperial March*, Op. 32, which earned him a publisher and a vital friendship with August Jaeger, his editor and confidant. In 1899, Elgar composed one of his best-known works, the *"Enigma" Variations*, Op. 36, which catapulted him to fame. The work is a cryptic tribute to Alice and to the many friends who stood behind the composer in the shaky early days of his career. German conductor Hans Richter proclaimed it a masterpiece, and his performances of the work in Britain and Germany established the composer's lasting success.

Elgar's most fruitful period was the first decade of the twentieth century, during which he wrote some of his noblest, most expressive music, including the *Symphony No. 1 in A flat major*, Op. 55 (1907–08) and the *Violin Concerto in B minor*, Op. 61 (1909–10). His best-known works from this period, however, are the first four of his *Pomp and Circumstance Marches* (1901–07); the first of these, subtitled "Land of Hope and Glory," became an unofficial second national anthem for the British Empire.

Elgar suffered a blow when Jaeger (the "Nimrod" of the "Enigma" Variations) died in 1909. The composer's productivity dropped, and the horrors of World War I deepened his melancholy outlook. His music became more intimate, even anguished; still, he wrote some of his best chamber music during this period, as well as the masterly *Cello Concerto in E minor*, Op. 85 (1919), whose deep feeling of sadness and impending loss surely relates to the final illness of his faithful Alice, who died in 1920.

For some time after that, he wrote little of significance but made a historic foray into the recording studios when new electrical recording processes were developed; the fortunate result was a number of masterly interpretations of his own orchestral music that have survived for posterity. In the early 1930s, Elgar set to work on a Third Symphony, left unfinished at his death in 1934. The work was brought to a generally well-received realization by Anthony Payne in the late 1990s and was subsequently recorded. *–AMG*

ORCHESTRAL

Cockaigne Overture, concert overture ("In London Town"), Op. 40 (1900–1901)

Edward Elgar's second extant orchestral overture, the *Cockaigne Overture*, Op. 40, originated in 1901, just a year or two after the completion of the famous *Enigma Variations*. Cockaigne was a medieval notion, a fictitious land of flowing wine and easy living that Elgar used as a backdrop for a light-hearted musical description of vivacious, turn-of-the-century London, as seen and heard through the eyes and ears of a young couple. Elgar seems to have planned a follow-up to Cockaigne in which he would explore the city's darker aspects ("City of Dreadful Night" was to be the subtitle), but nothing ever came of the idea.

The *Cockaigne Overture*, subtitled "In London Town," is a relatively brief piece of music—about 350 bars all told—cast in a traditional sonata-allegro form. A scherzando opening offers bits and pieces of themes that will presently take on more definite shapes and roles; the main "London" theme in C major, broad and sure, is given by the violins after a compelling introductory passage. A typically broad-spanned melody in E flat reflects on the couple's love for each other: the tender but passionate striving of the melody's initial octave leap could not be more typically "Elgarian." The "London" theme is given a treatment in diminution (a saucy rendition supposedly meant to represent the impudent disdain of the London youths for their stodgy elders), roving about harmonically, before the coda reviews our main themes and dissolves into the development section.

After a timid beginning in B flat major, the development soon bursts forth into a full-scale brass-band parade that, through sheer force, compels the entire orchestra to join in. Elgar's musical portrayal of the band as it grows distant again is striking: not wishing to resort to such bluntly obvious tactics as placing instruments offstage or in the balconies, the composer instead uses harmonic discrepancy (initially a sustained F pedal in the nearby orchestra against the band theme in G flat major in the increasingly distant clarinets) to create the illusion of separation and even distance.

In the wake of all this tumult our young couple wanders into a church. Here Elgar's theme is of the most moving and eloquent kind, and yet the brash youngsters outside can still find it in themselves to ridicule its incessant, dogmatic nature (cheekily and effectively represented by an overuse of melodic sequence). A complex contrapuntal structure is built up from all these various melodic fragments until, by sheer accretion, a recapitulation is forced upon the scene. Although this final portion of the overture remains thoroughly in the C major tonality that underlies the entire work, Elgar does make an effective harmonic digression to E flat major for the reprise of the pompous, "nobilmente" London theme. *–Blair Johnston*

Recommended:

- ○ **Elgar: Symphony 2; Cockaigne Overture; Dream Children 1** / Barbirolli (cond.), Halle Orch. / 1997 / EMI 66399
- ○ **Elgar: Cockaigne Overture; Symphony 2** / Boult (cond.), London PO / 1991 / EMI 764014
- ○ **Elgar** / Barbirolli (cond.), Philharmonia / 1997 / EMI 66323

Dream Children, for small orchestra, Op. 43 (1902)

The breadth of Elgar's literary knowledge is apparent by the extensive allusions which occur in title and content of his music. His best-known composition, after all, draws its title from an obscure line in *Othello* ("Pride, pomp and circumstance of glorious war!"). In the present work, *Dream Children*, the composer was moved by one of Charles Lamb's "Essays of Elia" for *London Magazine*, by the same title. In this cryptic yet haunting essay, Lamb recounts the vanishing before his eyes of two children to whom he has related a tale, this upon his awakening from a dream. The sad valedictory of the phantom children, suggested by the expression on their features runs "... We are nothing; less than nothing, and dreams. We are only what might have been. . . . " Deeply moved, Elgar quoted the entire paragraph from which the quote is drawn at the head of the score. The work received its premiere just three days after the composer's mother's death.

The restraint of this small but affecting work adds to its poignancy. The woodwind dominated first of the two movements is delicately scored; both the opening and the harp-driven middle section share a surreal melancholy. The second movement, attempting to alleviate the gloom, is in gently swinging 3/4 time and would seem to be of a carefree disposition, were it not for its context. Quite possibly the composer meant to depict the children as they might have existed. This gentle and less morbid movement fades into a reminiscence of the work's opening, closing with a major-key transformation of the same. *– Wayne Reisig*

Recommended:

- ○ **Sir Adrian Boult Conducts Elgar** / Boult (cond.), PO / 1997 / Testament 1106
- ○ **Elgar's Nursery Suite** / Boughton (cond.), English SO / 1995 / Nimbus 7029
- ○ **Elgar: Symphony 2; Cockaigne Overture; Dream Children 1** / Barbirolli (cond.), Hallé Orch. / 1997 / EMI 66399

Elegy, for strings, Op. 58 (1909)

Although written on commission to honor the memory of the Rev. Robert Hadden, ward of the Worshipful Company of Musicians, one can hear in Elgar's *Elegy for strings* deeply felt echoes of "Nimrod." The composer's closest friend and advisor, Augustus Jaeger, had passed away only one month before, so it is hardly surprising that that most eloquent of the *Enigma Variations* peers through the bars of this short work.

It is tempting to compare this brief but eloquent work to one from a few years previous, the adagietto from Mahler's *Fifth Symphony*. The two are structurally arch-shaped, speak closely related emotional languages, and are similarly scored. The Elgar work retains a stoic yet deeply felt dignity that sidesteps the angst of the Mahler symphony movement. Yet from the outset, the *Elegy* speaks a more intense language than usual for the composer, containing very dense string writing and more dissonance than the norm. Some consolation is to be found in the middle section, which is also highly reminiscent of the composer's earlier string music—perhaps a deliberate touch of poignancy, for those works were wrought during a much happier time in the composer's life. With the reprise of the opening section the arch of the music touches down to a somber yet calmly accepting close. *– Wayne Reisig*

Recommended:

- ○ **Elgar: Symphony 2; Elegy; Sospiro** / Barbirolli (cond.), New Philharmonia / 1993 / EMI 64724
- ○ **Elgar: Enigma Variations** / Boughton (cond.), English SO / 1994 / Nimbus 7015

Enigma Variations, Op. 36 (1898–1899)

At the end of an overlong day laden with teaching and other duties, Edward Elgar lit a cigar, sat at his piano and began idling over the keys. To amuse his wife, the composer began to improvise a tune and played it several times, turning each reprise into a caricature of the way one of their friends might have played it or of their personal characteristics. "I believe that you are doing something which has never been done before," exclaimed Mrs. Elgar. Thus was born one of music's great works of original conception, and Elgar's greatest large-scale "hit": the *Enigma Variations*. The enigma is twofold: each of the 14 variations refers to a friend of Elgar's, who is depicted by the nature of the music, or by sonic imitation of laughs, vocal inflections, or quirks, or by more abstract allusions. The other enigma is the presence of a larger "unheard" theme which is never stated but which according to the composer is very well known. The identity of the phantom tune left the world with the composer, and guesses have ranged from "God Save the King" to a simple major scale.

This apparatus aside, the variations contain some of the most charming and deeply felt music Elgar ever penned, more than redeeming the work from the status of mere gimmickry. The main theme is hesitating, lean and haunting, and is reprised with the passionate first variation that represents Caroline, the composer's wife, a constant source of encouragement and inspiration. The remaining variations are as follows:

II. H.D.S.-P.—Hew Stuart-Powell, a pianist with whom Elgar played chamber music.

III. R.B.T.—Richard Townsend, whose vocal pitch would rise when excited.

IV. W.M.B.—William Baker, who after barking out plans for the day would leave the room with a vigorous door-slam

V. R.P.A.—Richard Arnold, son of the writer Matthew Arnold, who would punctuate serious discourse with a nervous laugh.

VI. Isobel Fitton, a violist.

VII. Troyte—Arthur Griffith, an architect and raucous pianist.

VIII. W.N.—Winifred Norbury, a gracious and gentle friend.

IX. Nimrod—Augustus Jaeger, Elgar's close friend. The most beautiful and famous of the variations, this music describes a nighttime walk when Jaeger gave verbal encouragement to composer, recalling Beethoven's determination in adversity. "Jaeger" means "hunter in German, and Nimrod was a biblical hunter.

X. Dorabella—Dora Penny, whose infectious laugh is depicted in the woodwinds.

XI. G.R.S.—George Sinclair, an organist depicted frolicking with his bulldog, Dan.

XII. B.G.N.—Basil Nevinson, a cellist.

XIII. ***—The identity of this person is not known, but she is thought to have been on an ocean voyage at the time—this divined from a quote from Mendelssohn's "Calm Sea and Prosperous Voyage."

XIV. E.D.U.—Elgar himself. "Edu" was Caroline's nickname for her husband. This heartily extroverted, even boisterous, finale ties together the first variation and the Nimrod themes, as though to suggest that the composer has taken advice to heart and is determined to succeed. The entry of an organ in the final measures brings the work to a confident, happy close. *—Wayne Reisig*

Recommended:

- ○ **Elgar: Violin Concerto; Enigma Variations** / Elgar (cond.), Royal Albert Hall Orch. / 1999 / EMI 66994
- ○ **Barbirolli Elgar Album** / Barbirolli (cond.), Hallé Orch. / 2000 / Dutton 1017
- ○ **Holst: The Planets; Elgar: Enigma Variations** / Boult (cond.), London SO / 2002 / EMI 67749
- ○ **Elgar: Cockaigne; Introduction; Serenade; Enigma Variations** / Davis (cond.), BBCSO / 1991 / Teldec 73279
- ○ **Elgar: Enigma Variations; Sibelius: Violin Concerto; Weber: Konzertstück** / Monteux (cond.), Concertgebouw / Audiophile Classics 560

Falstaff, symphonic study in C minor, Op. 68 (1913)

This work confidently embraces the European traditions of symphonic writing, and does not suffer in comparison with the symphonic poems of Richard Strauss; yet it is among Elgar's most distinctly English inspirations. *Falstaff* works both as a portrait of a larger-than-life character ("not only witty in [him]self, but the cause that wit is in others") and as an evocation of the colorful and confident England of Shakespeare's *Henry IV* parts one and two, and *Henry V*. Here, Falstaff the man is the "knight, gentleman and soldier"—a high-living, hard-drinking giant of a man, full of braggadocio and ready humor—rather than the pathetic buffoon of *The Merry Wives of Windsor*.

The characters of Sir John and Prince Hal are deftly drawn in music; contrasting themes underline their uneasy relationship. There is also room for placid "interludes" such as "Gloucestershire, Shallow's Orchard," which serve as reminders of Elgar's unerring skill at orchestral landscape-painting.

Falstaff is indeed very pictorial music; in scene after scene, characters and places come to life through evocations of color, rhythm and melodic contour.

The sequence depicting Falstaff's death inevitably recalls the closing section of Richard Strauss' *Don Quixote*, but it is without Strauss' more extroverted dramatics. Snatches of old songs run through the old knight's head until, to the sound of muffled drums, he breathes his last—a gentleman to the last.

Falstaff is an extremely effective piece of musical storytelling; it is vivid, engaging, and full of gentle humor. However, its purely musical construction would give complete satisfaction without knowing anything about *Shakespeare's* plays, or the times in which he lived. *—Roy Brewer*

Recommended:

- ○ **Elgar: Enigma Variations; Falstaff** / Barbirolli (cond.), Philharmonia / EMI 66322
- ○ **Elgar: The Symphonies; Falstaff** / Elgar (cond.), London SO / 1992 / EMI 54560
- ○ **Sir Adrian Boult Conducts Elgar** / Boult (cond.), London PO / 1997 / Testament 1106
- ○ **Elgar: Falstaff; Elegy; Sanguine Fan** / Lloyd-Jones (cond.), English Northern Philharmonia / 1999 / Naxos 553879

Imperial March, Op. 32 (1897)

Although he had not yet broken through to an international audience with the *Enigma Variations* and the *Pomp and Circumstance* marches, Elgar was already making a name for himself in England when he asked for a musical contribution to the upcoming Diamond Jubilee of Queen Victoria. In 1897, he responded with this *Imperial March* for orchestra.

Although the work is generally conventional in utterance, Elgar here put something of his own fingerprint on the traditional British ceremonial march. After a restrained, deliberately paced first theme, the striking second theme offers a radical departure. Highly percussive and rhythmic, it borders on what Victorian standards would have deemed excessive and even barbaric. Perhaps the composer intended to evoke the Janissary music of the previous century. The exoticism was appropriate to the work's imperial theme, for the British Empire now extended to even more exotic lands than had the Austrian of Mozart's day. This unusual music, however, is abutted by a more restrained trio in Elgar's engaging childlike mode. With the reprise of the opening, the bold second theme is worked into the coda. Elgar introduced just the right amount of daring in the march, still staying within the bounds of dignity; the work met with acclaim and paved the way to future knighthood for its composer. *—Wayne Reisig*

Recommended:

- ○ **Sir Adrian Boult conducts English Music** / Boult (cond.), BBCSO / 1994 / VAI 1067
- ○ **Elgar** / Menuhin (cond.), Royal PO / 1998 / Virgin 61430

In the South, concert overture ("Alassio"), Op. 50 (1904)

The British custom of retreating to Italy's sunnier climes formed the basis of Elgar's concert overture *In the South*. By 1904, the public was eagerly awaiting the composer's first symphony, but Elgar's self-criticism led him to put a partially completed symphony on hold. He then offered up the present work, the longest single symphonic movement he had written up to that point. *In the South* had grown out of a merry excursion to the Italian town of Alassio and the neighboring village Moglio. Elgar spent most of the 1904 winter working on the overture. After its premiere comparisons with Richard Strauss' *Aus Italien* were inevitable, but these irritated Elgar even when favorable.

In the South paints a sunny Mediterranean postcard picture, yet is not quite as finely wrought as the *Cockaigne Overture*. It is fun nonetheless and shows Elgar to be a knowing hand at orchestral color. Typically, some of the musical material was of curious genesis, as will be seen. The opening theme came from an 1899 depiction of Dan the bulldog (immortalized in Enigma Variation XI) triumphant after a fight; the composer described the reoworked theme as "Joy of living (wine and macaroni)." This theme is juxtaposed with a nobilmente continuation. The second theme proper is a plaintive depiction of a shepherd grazing his flock among the ruins of an old church, the piping of his reed fulute sketched by the woodwinds. There follows a vivacious theme drawn from Elgar's delight in silly wordplay; when it was suggested that one could "roll" to and from the hillside village of Moglio, the composer toyed with the phrase "Moglio, Moglio, roglio, roglio" and applied the resulting speech rhythm to the theme. A fragment of this music yields another lively tune, which Elgar named "Fanny Moglio." The shepherd and "Fanny" themes are worked out in the development, which, in its increasing dissonances and frenetic rhythms, does suggest Strauss. The introduction of a sterner section in minor was said by Elgar to represent the conflicts and wars which peppered the Italian landscape through the ages (this puzzled Elgar's friend and reviewer Jaeger, who wondered why Italy in particular). The passage resolves back to the pastoral tune of the shepherd. Against a pedal the recapitulation commences. The sun-drenched coda features interplay of the two fragments of the opening theme and the "Fanny Moglio" theme, and, against a tympani roll, brings this agreeable travelogue to an end. *—Wayne Reisig*

Recommended:

- ○ **Elgar: In the South; Walton: Partita; Britten: Sinfonia da Requiem** / Barbirolli (cond.), Halle Orch. / 1999 / BBC 4013
- ○ **Elgar: Overtures** / Gibson (cond.), Scottish National Orch. / 2002 / Chandos 6652

Nursery Suite (1930)

Elgar's *Nursery Suite* (1930) represents the composer's last trip to the tune quarry of his youth in search of musical inspiration. As was always the case in such instances, Elgar makes clever use of such "borrowings," here forging his musical materials into a delightful set of children's pieces. Elgar, who after a fallow decade had resumed his previous level of activity, asked (and received) permission to dedicate the suite to the Duchess of York (the future Queen Mother), Princess Elizabeth (the future Queen), and Princess Margaret. The premiere of the work was actually a May 1931 recording session at which the Duke and Duchess of York were present.

In approaching the world of the young, some artists, like *Peter Pan* scribe J.M. Barrie, tend to look back longingly from an adult vantage point. Others, like *Winnie the Pooh* creator A.A. Milne, are able to plunge right into the child's world and assimilate with delight. Elgar straddles both of these approaches, always possessed of a sense of what is whimsical, even cheeky; at the same time, a sense of tender, wistful nostalgia is never far away.

The *Nursery Suite* is the music of a grandparent, aunt, or uncle among children, on the floor or at the playground. The first of the seven movements, "Aubade," recalls memories of serene awakening in the composer's most characteristic pastoral idiom. The following "Serious Doll," surely one for looking at but not playing with, is dominated by an active yet fragile flute solo. The frenetic "Busy-ness" (an example of Elgar's beloved wordplay) will strike a chord with anyone who has had charge of a two-year-old. A glum waltz entrusted to solo violin characterizes "The Sad Doll," but the merriment of the outdoors returns with "The Wagon Passes," in which the approach, passing, and vanishing of a horse-drawn cart is depicted through the movement's dynamic curve. The happy mood continues with "The Merry Doll," in which the instruments' higher registers evoke unbridled young laughter. The final movement, "Dreams-envoy," begins with a resigned winding-down, followed by a transitional violin cadenza, which in turns leads to flashes of previous themes, much as the day's thoughts swirl about in the twilight area before slumber and in dreaming. The last music heard is the "Aubade," signaling the start of a new day. *—Wayne Reisig*

Recommended:

- ○ **Sir Adrian Boult Conducts Elgar** / Boult (cond.), London PO / 1997 / Testament 1106
- ○ **Elgar: Wand of Youth Suites; Nursery Suite** / Thomson (cond.), Ulster Orch. / 1983 / Chandos 8318

Pomp and Circumstance, marches, Op. 39 (1901–1930)

Like so many of his countrymen during the late nineteenth and early twentieth centuries, British composer Edward Elgar was ardently patriotic. Combined with his natural militaristic turn (he had, after all, married the daughter of an army general) and love of ceremony, this patriotism made Elgar perfectly suited to author a long and distinguished line of Marches; ultimately, these would take a place not only in the traditional occasional music of his own country, but also in that of Britain's sister-nations across the Atlantic. The five *Pomp and Circumstance* marches, published collectively as Opus 39 but actually composed over a period of almost thirty years, are without a doubt the best known of his pieces in this peculiarly British genre. Though their collective title, drawn from a line in Shakespeare's *Othello* describing "the pomp and circumstance of glorious war," clearly allies them with the British military tradition, the musicality and variety (and even charm) of these five pieces render them enjoyable *sans* any nationalist association.

The first in the set, in D major (1901), earned Elgar his knighthood; it was later adapted into the *Coronation Ode* and given the well-known lyrics "Land of Hope and Glory." The famous trio section is as recognizable as the *Union Jack*, now virtually ubiquitous at high school and university graduation ceremonies. If one can put aside its over-familiarity, this is a very beautiful theme; as the composer himself described it in very unceremonious language, "I've got a tune in my head that's going to knock 'em dead!"

The A minor march that follows was composed almost simultaneously with the preceding one; it has never achieved anything like the fame of its sister-piece, and yet it is in many ways a better work. The trio in particular could hardly be a more striking contrast to the G major melody of the first march.

Elgar must have been in a particularly dramatic mood when he penned the *Pomp and Circumstance March No. 3 in C minor* (completed in 1904). This is no militaristic exercise, but rather a dramatic orchestral poem. Three bassoons offer vague hints of a melody during the subdued opening, but the quietude is not sustained for long, as a massive brass-laden crescendo paves the way for a broad main tune. The light theme and staccato accompaniment of the A flat major trio offer a well-earned reprieve from the physicality of the march-proper.

March No. 4 in G major, composed in 1907 recalls something of the general enthusiasm of the famous first March. The main march idea is built on a single rhythmic cell, while the C major trio is marked "nobilmente."

Almost 25 years would pass before the composer completed the fifth *Pomp and Circumstance March*, but upon hearing the result it quickly becomes apparent that Elgar saved the best for last. The main melodic idea is all youth and exuberance (especially considering that its composer was well over seventy at the time), and Elgar provides the trio section with a broad melody that is at least the equal of the G major tune in the first March. *—AMG*

Recommended:

- ○ **Elgar: Pomp & Circumstance Marches** / Barbirolli (cond.), Philharmonia / 1997 / EMI 66323
- ○ **Elgar: Enigma Variations; Pomp & Circumstance Marches** / Boult (cond.), London PO / 1991 / EMI 64015
- ○ **Edward Elgar** / Gibson (cond.), Scottish National Orch. / 1999 / Chandos 2404

Serenade, for strings in E minor, Op. 20 (1892)

Nothing disturbs the graceful amiability of this early work, begun a year before Elgar's marriage in 1889. These "little tunes," as the composer called them, are about as far as one can get from the patriotic fervor of the *Pomp and Circumstance* marches and the emotional intensity of the larger orchestral works.

All three movements, Allegro piacevole, Larghetto and Allegretto, are enchanting: the first liltingly rhythmic, the second a meditation of serene beauty on a melody similar to that of the Lento movement in the *Symphony No. 1*, the third a genial reworking of first-movement themes.

The opening movement, in 6/8 time, is based around an opening theme which is suffused with the feel of English ballad; perhaps some snatch of West-Country melody caught the young composer's ear and worked its way into his creative process. It weaves in and out of minor and major before yielding to the no less serene second theme, bearing Elgar's trademark interval of a seventh leap. This same thumbprint figure can be found in the sensitive following movement, in which there is a constant unfolding of melody rather than contrasting themes. A *Tristan*-like turn, as well as a phrase which seems to be a quotation from that opera (Elgar was an unashamed admirer of Wagner's music), are worked up to a crest which subsides; overall, though, the music is purged of excessive chromaticism, and any Wagnerisms used in a very different and sensitive context. The closing movement uses a sunny and winsome theme also in 6/8 and returns to the seventh leap of the opening movement, the theme in its final resolution bearing a curious resemblance to the trio of the last *Pomp and Circumstance* nearly 40 years later. Coincidental? Perhaps, but also indicative that nothing is incongruous within one's own frame of reference.

Elgar, himself a violinist, was sensitive to the coloration of the string orchestra, and his touch does not falter throughout a work which he described as being "real stringy." There is no straining after effect and no obvious personal or pictorial associations—all is pure music as well as pure poetry. Yet anyone who knows the English countryside around Hereford where Elgar lived can hardly fail, especially in the second movement, to be reminded of that peaceful, solitary landscape.

The composer made an arrangement of the *Serenade* for piano duet, though it is now difficult to think of it other than in its original form. *—AMG*

Recommended:

- ○ **English Orchestral Works** / Groves (cond.), Royal PO / Carlton 670068
- ○ **Elgar: Symphony 1; etc.** / Boult (cond.), London PO / 1991 / EMI 64013
- ○ **Elgar: Cello Concerto; etc.** / Sinopoli (cond.), Philharmonia / 1999 / Decca 460624

Sospiri, adagio for strings, harp & organ, Op. 70 (1913–1914)

Elgar's *Sospiri* was premiered on August 11, 1914, and in less than two weeks the world would be forever changed. Much of the composer's music from this period is read as an elegy to a disappearing golden age: the long-fading close of the *Second Symphony*, Falstaff being dismissed by the new young king. Granted, these readings have the benefit of hindsight. Yet in the case of *Sospiri* the interpretation seems reasonable, for world events were rapidly drawing to a head, and a sense of world-weariness, albeit restrained, is deeply felt in this brief, unusual work. The composer's wife, in fact, said that the work was "like a breath of peace on a perturbed world." The title is Italian for "sighs" or "sighing."

Although Elgar said that as a whole he did not care for French music, there is something quite Gallic in the Fauré-like delicacy and clarity of the writing here. This impression is due in part to the ethereal scoring for strings, harp, and organ (the organ part, unusually, is ad lib). The main melody enters dissonantly over the harmony, and the resolution, as well as the wide intervals, seem evocative of the title. After the reprise of the opening, the different voices, each from a different entry point, glide to a long-held final cadence that brings to rest this sensitive essay in resigned serenity. *—Wayne Reisig*

Recommended:

- ○ **Elgar: Symphony 2; Sospiri** / Barbirolli (cond.), New Philharmonia / 1993 / EMI 64724
- ○ **Elgar: Symphony 2; Sospiri** / Tate (cond.), London SO / 1991 / EMI 54192

SYMPHONIC

Symphony No. 1 in A flat major, Op. 55 (1907–1908)

In 1908, its first year of existence, this symphony received more than 100 public performances and was widely hailed as the first great British symphony. Expansive in style and large in scale, it is nevertheless a deeply personal and in some ways enigmatic work. Elgar insisted that it had "no program beyond a wide experience of human life ... and a massive hope in the future," and should be played "elastically and mystically." The music does, however, provide a glimpse of Elgar's private world of memories, feelings and places, for every note is characteristic of its creator.

The opening Andante, marked with Elgar's favorite direction of "nobilmente" (with the cautionary addition "e semplice"), is a solemn marching tune in the unusual key of A flat, with something of the ceremonial nature of Elgar's imperial style. This leads to a series of thematic motifs, including a brief "motto" theme that returns at various times and in various ways throughout all four movements. Some of the ideas are little more than fragments which, as the symphony develops, will go through a series of transformations, variations, and passing allusions. A peaceful episode introduced by violins is repeated by woodwinds, after which the movement becomes increasingly agitated. The march tune of the first section returns in what appears a conventional recapitulation, but here is extended into a magical meditation on earlier themes, with brilliant writing for violins, violas, and harps gradually spreading over the whole orchestra until the motto theme returns in triumph on horns and trumpets.

The second movement starts with typical Elgarian swagger, followed by a quieter section scored with wonderful airiness and freedom. When conducting the work the composer asked the orchestra to play it "like something you hear down by the river." Wisps of melody create an atmosphere of enchantment; but mysterious changes start to occur. These herald the tranquil third movement, Lento, which the conductor Hans Richter (to whom the symphony is dedicated) called "an Adagio such as Beethoven might have written." Marked Espressivo e dolce, this is perhaps, the finest of all Elgar's slow movements—a sustained pastoral reverie evoking the Herefordshire countryside that the composer knew and loved.

The fourth movement sees a return of the restless spirits, this time with haunting undertones. The ghostly atmosphere is dispelled by the marching theme of the first movement, propelled with gathering momentum towards the final bars in which violins and brass leap exultantly about in giddy cross rhythms before the orchestra unites to assert the "massive hope" that lies at the heart of the work. *—Roy Brewer*

Recommended:

- ○ **Elgar: Symphony 1; etc.** / Boult (cond.), London PO / 1991 / EMI 64013
- ○ **Elgar: Cockaigne Overture; Symphony 1** / Barbirolli (cond.), Philharmonia / 1993 / EMI 64511
- ○ **Elgar: The Symphonies; Falstaff** / Elgar (cond.), LSP / 1992 / EMI 54560
- ○ **Elgar: Symphony 1; Pomp & Circumstance Marches** / Zinman (cond.), Baltimore SO / 1992 / Telarc 80310

Symphony No. 2 in E flat major, Op. 63 (1909–1911)

Having achieved unprecedented success with his *Symphony No. 1*, Elgar was now fully confident of his symphonic prowess and threw himself into work on its successor. The composer, usually flippant about even his most ambitious works, spoke from his heart regarding his latest opus, proclaiming, "I have written out of my soul." And indeed the public anxiously awaited a repeat of the grandiloquent, "feel-good" sentiment of the A flat symphony, only to be stymied by the very different *Symphony No. 2* at its 1911 premiere. The tepid applause that greeted the work disappointed Elgar, who exclaimed, "They sat there like stuffed pigs!" The slow movement may have struck a chord with a populace still grieving the death of a popular monarch, but the long sunset of the entire work's close was unsettling to an audience that would have preferred an ending of assertion and optimism. Time has been kinder to the work, which is now viewed as a poignant epilogue to an age of innocence.

The well-read Elgar selected a line from Shelley, "Rarely, rarely comest thou, Spirit of Delight," putting the essence of that thought into a theme that as a cyclic unifier throughout the symphony. Without any fanfare, this theme sweeps the work into the energetic swing of the first movement, a complex of lively and varied themes that unfold kaleidoscopically. Midway through the first movement a new theme emerges, also with a significance to be revealed later; this theme is as mysterious and unsettling as a lost soul. The buoyant mood reappears for the recapitulation, and the recurring "spirit of delight" theme is joyously hammered out as the terse coda.

No greater contrast could be imagined than the following adagio, which follows the great tradition of Beethoven's *Eroica* and Bruckner's *Seventh*. It is a study in dignified mourning. Opening with a plaintive lament, the movement assumes a funereal mantle and seeks solace in contrasting themes, including a soaring *Tristan*-like theme which seems a desperate grasping for illusive joy. An intense climax is reached and subsides into a ghostly transformation of the "spirit of delight" theme before the return of the wistful opening brings the movement full circle. Relief is attempted in the scherzo, by turns mercurial, gypsy-like, and playful. Where one would expect a trio comes instead the mysterious theme from the first movement, worked up to a frightening, pounding climax described by Elgar as the pounding in one's head during a fever. The finale, unlike any other in the literature, commences with a subtle, leisurely theme which gives way to a typically Elgarian nobilmente theme and a closing martial one. The central section is fugal and warlike, with the climax occurring over a long-held high trumpet note, followed by an exotic Celtic theme with muted cymbal. The recapitulation reviews the opening themes in succession. Then comes for one last time the "spirit of delight" theme, in augmentation and glowingly orchestrated into a most beautifully serene and poignant close to the symphony. *—Wayne Reisig*

Recommended:

- ○ **Elgar: Cockaigne Overture; Symphony 2** / Boult (cond.), London PO / 1991 / EMI 764014
- ○ **Elgar: Symphony 2** / Barbirolli (cond.), Halle Orch. / 1993 / EMI 64724
- ○ **Elgar: The Symphonies; Falstaff** / Elgar (cond.), London SO / 1992 / EMI 54560
- ○ **Complete Symphonies** / Previn (cond.), London SO / 1996 / Philips 454250

CHAMBER MUSIC

String Quartet in E minor, Op. 83 (1918)

The *String Quartet in E minor* was the second of Elgar's three chamber works to come from the autumnal idyll at the cottage in Sussex in 1918. In it he seemed to come nearest to the ideal of Brahms, whom he greatly admired. Although highly expressive, the mood is comparatively restrained, and thus design becomes paramount. This is in contrast with the subsequent *Piano Quintet* in which novelty of structure and intensity of emotion are conspicuous features. Also, Elgar seems quite content within the restrictions of the chamber idiom, whereas in the *Quintet* one senses a frequent desire to bust loose into an orchestral one.

In 12/8, the first movement (Allegro moderato) possesses a searching nature, not so much in a questing, Romantic sense, but more on the nature of a puzzle to be solved. The opening chordal sonorities sound much like Renaissance music, but this quickly expands into a typical Elgarian melody; notable is a sequence of falling fourths rather than Elgar's fingerprint interval of a seventh. The second subject is serene yet devoid of excessive sentiment. The development very energetically works these two ideas with an amazing range of color for this comparatively limited medium; this reaches a climax and there is a sudden brief shift into duple meter, then a diminuendo which leads back to the recapitulation. A false close suddenly wells up into the high register of the instruments, and the work closes with an allusion to the opening figure.

The second movement, a lovely poco andante in 3/8, was a favorite of the composer's wife. It possesses warmth yet avoids pathos. The main theme combines a characteristic Elgarian melody with English folk song and is somewhat reminiscent of the "Angel's Farewell" from *Gerontius*. Rather than a second subject, a fragment of the opening theme is taken and worked over; plucked strings and a chromatic fortissimo herald a return of the main theme. There follows a second episode which is worked over in much the same way. The opening theme returns and the movement ends on a note of serenity.

"Vivacity" would seem more appropriate than "energy" to describe the allegro molto Finale in 4/4. The first subject immediately "plunges in" with a joie de vivre. The melodic, rhythmic, and harmonic texture of the music constantly changes, as though being spun out; the term "kaleidoscopic," once used to describe the processes in Elgar's symphonies before they were better understood, is more apt an adjective here. There is a less deliberate slowing to the second dolce subject which, despite the indication, is likewise too varied to allow any sentimental mulling-over; a few curiously Brucknerian sequence modulations appear. This subsides and the development commences. Elgar seems to return to the Classical concept of the finale as a "wrapping up" rather than a summit to be scaled. Thus the recapitulation is along conventional lines until a wild flurry of sixteenth notes brings the work to an almost abrupt stop, and then a terse yet vigorous and positive fortissimo conclusion. *—Wayne Gerard Reisig*

Recommended:

- ○ **Elgar: String Quartet; Piano Quintet** / Chilingirian Quartet, Roberts / 1994 / EMI 65099
- ○ **Elgar: String Quartet; Piano Quintet** / Medici Quartet, Bingham / 1985 / Meridian 84082
- ○ **Elgar: String Quartet; Piano Quintet** / Sorrel Quartet, Ian Brown / 2001 / Chandos 9894
- ○ **Elgar: String Quartet; Piano Quintet** / Donohoe, Maggini SQ / 1997 / Naxos 553737

CONCERTO

Cello Concerto in E minor, Op. 85 (1919)

Edward Elgar's *Concerto for cello and orchestra in E minor*, from the year 1919, is the last major work the composer penned (a *Third Symphony* remained in draft form at his death in 1934). While the instrumental forces remain basically equivalent to those used in the *Violin Concerto*, Elgar has amplified the tender, searching intimacy of that earlier work to such a degree that one might call the *Cello Concerto* not just introspective but searing and almost ascetic. It is an exceedingly complex but immediately touching work that makes a fitting epilogue to Elgar's lifetime in music.

The concerto is poured into a four-movement mold, yet still takes only about half an hour to perform—far less than any of Elgar's other large instrumental works. This restraint is mirrored by remarkably transparent orchestration. The work begins with four bars of solo cello recitative that firmly outline the home key of E minor. The subsequent Moderato entrance of the orchestra offers little immediate support for that key, really winding down to the tonic only after six bars of restless 9/8 melody built on a single rhythmic cell. During the 12/8 middle section Elgar makes good use of the contrast between E minor and E major. A recapitulation of the opening is made, but soon enough the movement has dissolved into a handful of uncertain pizzicati.

Elgar brings back the opening recitative, much altered (and buoyantly beginning where the first movement's pizzicati left off), to begin the following Scherzo. After twice pleading with the orchestra to join its cause, the cello finally rouses the group into an eighth note driven perpetual motion (Allegro molto). Elgar paints a miniature portrait of his own very characteristic lyric style in the relatively brief E flat major second theme.

A wonderful melody in B flat major is sung by the soloist throughout the Adagio third movement. Here Elgar's indebtedness to Schumann, the slow movement of whose own cello concerto also employs this song without words approach, is clearly evident. The life span of this one melodic strand is a bare 60 bars, yet it conveys deeper passion than do five times that many bars of the composer's earlier music. The movement ends on the dominant, paving the way for an attacca opening of the Finale.

After initially falling in with the B flat major of the Adagio, the Finale makes an eight-bar move back to its rightful E minor tonal center. The main idea of the movement (marked, like so many of the composer's favorite thoughts, "nobilmente") is given out first by the soloist in half-recitative and then, after a rude tutti interruption and a brief pause, by the entire ensemble, Allegro non troppo. A second theme recalls both the G major tonality and the impish sentiment of the Scherzo movement. As the Finale draws near its finish, Elgar undertakes an extended and very moving reminiscence: first on the melody of the Adagio movement and then reaching back to the recitative that began the entire half-hour journey. Two terse chords re-energize the movement's fast-twitch muscle fiber, and 16 bars later the curtain comes down. *—Blair Johnston*

Recommended:

- ○ **Elgar: Cello Concerto; Enigma Variations; Marches** / Barenboim (cond.), Du Pre, Philadelphia Orch. / 1999 / Sony 60789
- ○ **Elgar: Cello Concerto; Respighi: Adagio con variazioni; etc.** / Rozhdestvensky (cond.), Rostropovich, Moscow PO / Russian Disc 11104
- ○ **Elgar: Cello Concerto; Sea Pictures** / Barbirolli (cond.), Du Pre, London SO / 1997 / EMI 56219
- ○ **Elgar & Walton: Cello Concertos** / Previn (cond.), Ma, London SO / 1985 / CBS 39541
- ○ **Elgar: Cello Concerto; Bruch: Kol Nidrei; Brahms: Cello Sonata 2** / Boult (cond.), Casals, BBCSO / 2001 / Classica d'Oro 4007

Introduction and Allegro, for string quartet & string orchestra in G major, Op. 47 (1905)

From its first notes, Elgar's *Introduction and Allegro,* Op. 47 (1905) identifies itself as "open air" music. The orchestra, complemented by the gentler timbre of the string quartet, clearly lends itself to the composer's adoption of the Baroque concerto grosso form, though the composer makes no attempt to imitate earlier styles. The work's vitality and effect instead lie entirely in its overall freedom and imaginative sweep.

Elgar proved himself particularly adept in writing for strings in such works as the *Serenade,* Op. 20 (1892), the *"Enigma" Variations,* Op. 36 (1898–99), and his symphonies. In the Introduction and Allegro, he replaces intimacy and intricacy with bold, song-like melodies that evolve into a clearly defined structure. The string writing falls so felicitously under the players' fingers and bows that the work is just as popular with performers as it is with audiences.

The bold, formal introduction is followed by a striking contrast of mood in a wistful tune with more than a hint of Celtic twilight. The composer found innocent pleasure in puzzles of all kinds, and wrote of hearing the melody as "distant singing" while on holiday in Wales; however, there is no further evidence of its origin. The tune is variously expanded throughout—at one point it becomes part of a decidedly unacademic fugue—in a manner that might have seemed prosaic in less capable hands. The work is crowned by final, thrilling, seemingly inevitable tutti return of the "Welsh" tune. *—Roy Brewer*

Recommended:

- ○ **Elgar: Cello Concerto; etc.** / Barbirolli (cond.), Halle Orch. / 1991 / EMI 63955
- ○ **Elgar & Vaughan Williams** / Barbirolli (cond.), Allegri SQ, City of London Sinfonia / 2000 / Angel 67264

Violin Concerto in B minor, Op. 61 (1909–1910)

As a youth, Sir Edward Elgar was a devoted student of the violin; later on in life, as his orchestral skills began to unfold, the violin concerto became a form of great interest to him, and, though he completed only one such work, it is indeed a spectacular entry in the genre. The *Concerto for violin and orchestra in B minor,* Op. 61, appeared in 1910 and was given its first performance on November 10 of that year. It was slow to gain acceptance into the regular performing repertory, and it remains, for many reasons (not the least of which are a complex, demanding structure and extensive technical hurdles), a rather neglected work. In the hands of an intelligent and capable soloist/conductor pair, however, the work's unique juxtaposition of electric virtuosity and moving intimacy cannot fail to please.

Elgar places one of his famous enigmas at the head of the score, whose Spanish inscription translates as "In here is enshrined the soul of.....," with the five dots indicating the name of some individual with whom Elgar felt the work to be intimately associated. The work is cast in the standard three movements, but Elgar's characteristically rhapsodic approach to tempo and highly episodic musical architecture tend to obscure the usual landmarks of concerto form. And yet we must not think of the work as overly sectional, for, as anyone who has heard Elgar's own recording of the work (made with a teenage Yehudi Menuhin as soloist) will attest, all of these smaller episodes are meant to flow together into larger, seamless bodies of music.

The opening movement begins with one of the longest orchestral expositions in the concerto repertory, containing no fewer than three themes. The solo violin enters, darkly, on the G-string, with a closing version of the searching first theme. Various meditations—both lyric and virtuosic, and frequently quite chromatic—are made on each of the themes during the soloist's exposition and subsequent development. The exact moment of recapitulation is intentionally blurred, and the incessant tension between soloist and ensemble is such that no room can be found for a traditional cadenza.

The Andante second movement is one of the simplest-sounding pieces of music one can find, and yet it is of the cleverest and most intricate construction. Upon its entrance, the solo violin assumes a countermelodic role while the orchestral fiddlers continue on with the lovely B flat major melody that opened the movement. A second thematic idea is less settled than the first. During the central section the orchestra interjects and then develops a moving "nobilmente" phrase. This same idea ushers in the reprise of the movement's main theme, now even more intimate-sounding than before.

The Finale treads on some innovative musical ground, not so much in the way its richly varied theme groups are continuously developed (against fiendishly difficult violin arabesques, arpeggios, scales and chords) throughout the movement, but rather during the colorful accompanied cadenza that precedes the final grandiose conclusion (Schumann's *Cello Concerto,* a work Elgar knew, employs the same unusual device). Indeed, the cadenza is the very heart and soul of the movement, and all the musical fireworks that precede it are just a drawn-out introduction. During the cadenza (which features a background of tremolo pizzicati, a string effect that Elgar seems to have invented), melodies from the previous movements are revisited. Most striking of all is a powerful, wonderfully subdued rendition of the Andante's main theme. *—Blair Johnston*

Recommended:

- ○ **Elgar & Bruch: Violin Concertos** / Elgar (cond.), Menuhin, London SO / 1999 / Naxos 110902
- ○ **Elgar: Violin Concerto** / Handley (cond.), Kennedy, London PO / EMI 63795
- ○ **Elgar: Violin Concerto; Enigma Variations** / Elgar (cond.), Menuhin, London SO / 1999 / EMI 66994
- ○ **Elgar & Delius: Violin Concertos** / Boult (cond.), Menuhin, New Philharmonia / 1993 / EMI 64725

CHORAL

The Dream of Gerontius, oratorio, Op. 38 (1900)

"This, if anything of mine, is worth your memory," wrote Edward Elgar (quoting Ruskin) regarding his oratorio *The Dream of Gerontius.* The composer, often self-deprecating about even his most ambitious works, fetlt that this effort, inspired by a poem of Cardinal Newman, represented his finest music. Elgar received a copy of Newman's poem as a wedding present from his priest, and it struck a particular chord with him; in fact, the poem—which explained Roman Catholic theological views on the immortal soul in an accessible manner—had a tremendous vogue in the late Victorian era. Elgar edited the text down to about half its orginal size for the sake of musical economy, but he managed to do so without altering the essence of the poem. The 1900 premiere under Richter at the Birmingham Festival was marred by insufficient rehearsal, but at its German premiere a year later it was hailed as a masterpiece. Subsequent British performances quickly established the work in the repertory.

The central character of Gerontius is an imperfect, yet decent, man who is riddled with doubts on his deathbed. An angel comes to him during his last moments to give him a glimpse of the afterlife, culminating in an overwhelming vision of God. Gently the angel returns his ward to a death which will now be a peaceful transition. The prelude to the oratorio commences with a fade-in, as a candle's light would gradually illuminate a dark room. Here the hesitating, vague rhythm would seem to represent the labored breathing of the dying man. A typically Elgarian martial theme emerges, in major but quickly souring into anguished minor, evoking a crisis of faith. Part One of the oratorio proper commences; it consists of a dialogue between Gerontius, alternately offering supplication and despairing, and the clerical assistants, praying for his soul. Hope is found in the buoyant and noble "Proficisere" of the priest ("Go upon thy journey, Christian soul!"), in Elgar's nobilmente mode, answered by the chorus of assistants and subsiding to a serene close. Part Two commences, again nebulous but purged of torment, as Gerontius' soul speculates on this strange new existence and is joined by his angel who will lead him to the Almighty. They travel past the underworld, depicted in the "Demon's Chorus" by a restless, shadowy fugue punctuated by grotesque laughter. The angel assures the soul that they are past their harm, and presently they come before the choir of angels, depicted in the work's most glorious music, "Praise to the Holiest." This ethereal and childlike section is usually performed by a children's chorus. The soul is brought before God, inspiring uncomprehending awe; at this point comes Gerontius' moving aria, "Take me away." The angel soothes Gerontius and returns him to a gentler leave-taking, as the oratorio comes to a serene, transfigured close with "The Angel's Farewell," perhaps Elgar's most sensitive music. *—Wayne Reisig*

Recommended:

- ○ **Elgar: The Dream of Gerontius; Merry Makers** / Boult (cond.), Gedda, Watts, Lloyd, John Alldis Choir, New Philharmonia / 1998 / EMI 66540
- ○ **Elgar: The Dream of Gerontius** / Barbirolli (cond.), Baker, Lewis, Borg, Ambrosian Singers, Halle Orch. / 1999 / EMI 73579
- ○ **Elgar: The Dream of Gerontius; Parry: Blest Pair of Sirens; I was glad** / Hickox (cond.), Howell, Elms, Davies, Palmer, London SO / 1988 / Chandos 8641
- ○ **Elgar Conducts "The Dream Of Gerontius"** / Elgar (cond.), Balfour, Wilson, Heyner, Royal Albert Hall Orch. / Opal 9810

KEYBOARD

Organ Sonata in G major, Op. 28 (1895)

It seems curious that Elgar's output of works for the organ is so small considering that much of his formative musical experience was from the loft, first by deputizing for his father at St. George's Church and later succeeding him as organist. The few examples that exist do show Elgar to have a firm understanding of the instrument's potential, along with his own individuality and imagination stamped upon them. The *Sonata in G* could be termed an early work, although the composer was almost 40 at the time. Typical Elgarian melody is not as obvious as in other works, but it is well-crafted, concise, and imaginative; it leads one to wish that Elgar had produced more in that genre, especially after he had totally developed his musical character and idiom.

In the first movement a bold, confident first subject initially bears a striking resemblance to Handel's "and He shall reign forever and ever more" from the *Messiah*, but swiftly branches out. The second subject, although nobilmente, does not possess the typical Elgar character denoted by that word, but seems to bear some of the influence of early Wagner. A fragment from the first theme emerges near the end and leads to a development section that is brief and subtle. The recapitulation is conventional enough. A powerful statement of the opening bars leads to the coda. The lighter second movement is more of an intermezzo than a scherzo. In ABA form, the first theme has a relaxed, strolling air; the second has a somewhat Celtic feel with its Scottish snap. The noble and expressive third movement's main melody hints at mature Elgar and *Lohengrin*-period Wagner. An enharmonic modulation (key of B flat to F sharp) leads to the middle section. After the repeat of the first theme, the coda features the two themes played in polyphony. The restless opening of the fourth movement recalls early Romanticism when it vies between G minor and major; proceeding in perpetual animation that leads to a transformation of the lyrical theme of the preceding movement, now at a less solemn canter. The third subject is extroverted and terse, with all stops pulled out. As in the first movement, the development is concise. In the recapitulation, the first theme emerges in the higher register and noble second theme is transformed into a march. A powerful coda over sustained pedals brings the work to a close. *—Wayne Gerard Reisig*

Recommended:

- ○ **Elgar: Complete Works for Organ** / Butt / 2002 / HM 907281

Osian Ellis

b. Feb. 8, 1928, Ffynnongroew, Wales, England

Harpist

Osian Ellis is a former principal harpist for the London Symphony Orchestra, and he is probably happy about that. The Welshman once described his own personal outlook as "philosophical" and indicated that a symphony harpist had to be that way, since a good deal of his or her time is spent sitting in the wings. When a solo feature is actually offered, it is most often in one of the same half-dozen repertoire pieces, such as the *Mephisto Waltz No. 1* by Franz Liszt, which comes complete with a demonic rave-up of a harp cadenza at the finale. Yes, this piece is a specialty of Ellis', but this performer's varied interests and deep respect for his instrument's legacy have led to a career that has consisted of much more than just waiting for a chance to play. He was associated closely with Benjamin Britten, but has established a repertoire that stretches back to medieval British and Spanish music as well as the traditional harp music of Wales.

His stay with the London Symphony began in 1961, shortly after he first began his involvement with Britten. He was a creative player during his LSO days, and was even known to toss in his own solos while performing with the orchestra. Britten's *Suite for Harp* was composed in 1969 after Ellis asked the composer for a solo piece, and was premiered during that year's Aldeburgh Festival. Ellis toured extensively in America and Europe with tenor Sir Peter Pears from 1973 to 1980, prompting eager composers to submit songs to the duo. That included Britten, who came up with *Canticle V* and *The Birthday Hansel* during this period, the latter piece a special request from the queen. After this Ellis began to be referred to as "the queen's harpist." Ellis and Britten also collaborated closely on the 1976 *Eight Folk Song Arrangements*, with Ellis creating virtuoso harp accompaniment as well as English lyrics for Welsh text.

Ellis has been a constant champion of his instrument, conducting multi-harp workshops and leading the Osian Ellis Harp Ensemble. In 1999 he conducted a 12-harp ensemble at a special concert for the Florida International Festival, where he was photographed practicing harp on the beach. He has also had compositions written for him by Menotti, William Schuman, William Mathias, and Alun Hoddinott. He frequently performs excerpts from the harp compositions by Danish composer Jorgan Jersild, many of which are dedicated to Ellis.

When the Melos Ensemble was formed in London in the late 1960s, Ellis was a natural choice to become harpist. The ensemble consisted of about a dozen musicians and was dedicated to performing the often neglected repertoire for extended chamber ensemble, in the case of the harp leading to the impressionist masterpieces of Ravel and Debussy.

Ellis has also had a superb academic career. He is a former professor of harp at the Royal Academy of Music and in 2000 was made an Honorary Fellow by the University of Wales. His short book *The History of the Harp in Wales* was published by the University of Wales Press. He has been the subject of several full length documentaries produced by British and Welsh television, the latter filmed when he was just beginning his career. *—Eugene Chadbourne*

Recommended:

- ○ **Ravel: Introduction & Allegro; etc.** / Ellis, Melos Ensemble / 1997 / London 452891
- ○ **Mozart: Clarinet Concerto; Concerto for Flute & Harp** / Leppard (cond.), Bennett, Ellis, Johnson, English CO / 1996 / ASV 532

Mischa Elman

b. Jan. 20, 1891, Talnoy, Russia, **d.** Apr. 5, 1967, New York, NY

Violinist

Elman was the second prodigy pupil of Leopold Auer (after Efrem Zimbalist) to become internationally famous before adolescence. Their Hungarian-born teacher—a student of Joachim and subsequent mentor of Toscha Seidel, Jascha Heifetz and Nathan Milstein—was appointed professor of violin at the St. Petersburg Imperial Conservatory in 1868. He remained until the Revolution, then moved to the U.S. In 1878, Tchaikovsky dedicated his violin concerto to Auer, but withdrew the honor when the latter declared it "unplayable." Later on, Auer recanted, performed the work repeatedly, and made a point of teaching it to all his students including Elman, who came to cherish it as his own.

Mischa was 11 when his father brought him to Auer, vacationing in Odessa, where the family had moved to further the boy's natural talent. When he played Paganini's *24th Caprice* and the Wieniawski *Second Concerto*, Auer insisted the Imperial Conservatory accept him immediately. In St. Petersburg, Mischa gave private concerts for arts patrons, one of whom, the Grand Duke of Mecklenburg-Strelitz, gave him an Amati violin. Progress was so rapid that Auer decided Mischa should play a concert in Berlin (where a 10-year-old protégé of Joachim had created a sensation in 1903).

On October 13, 1904, the day before his debut, Elman played privately for Joachim, who could only manage to say, "I am speechless." Not so the audience, which cheered the 13-year-old phenomenon. In 1905 he took England by storm, and joined Nellie Melba and Enrico Caruso in a concert at Buckingham Palace for Edward VII and Alfonso of Spain. Called "the greatest violinist in the world" by London critics, Elman made his American debut in Carnegie Hall on December 10, 1908—one month shy of his 17th birthday—playing the Tchaikovsky concerto with the Russian Symphony Society of New York. Victor Records promptly signed him to a contract (salon music mainly, played with impeccable intonation and rich tone, but with nineteenth century mannerisms forever retained). Elman also made a series of recordings with Caruso and Frances Alda, and excerpts from works by Dittersdorf, Haydn, Mozart, and Schubert with an "Elman String Quartet." By 1912, he had appeared with every major U.S. orchestra, including 31 performances with the

Boston Symphony! By 1913, his annual record royalties were $35,000, and in 1916 Carl Sandburg wrote a paean to his playing entitled *Bath*.

Then Heifetz, who was Auer's masterpiece, made his American debut in Carnegie Hall on October 27, 1917. He was 16, a decade younger than Elman, who asked his box-partner at intermission, "Isn't it getting hot in here?" "Not for pianists," Leopold Godowsky famously replied. Elman continued touring far and wide, but a supernova had usurped his celebrity—a technician nonpareil, a musician in the "modern" tradition, although Elman continued to be celebrated as "the violinist with the golden tone." In 1926, Vitaphone made a six-minute "full-sound" film of him playing Dvořák and Gossec. Then came concerto recordings: his first Tchaikovsky in 1929, others later, although he didn't make a complete sonata recording until after World War II. In 1951, Elman switched to London Decca, recording concertos conducted by Boult, the young Solti, and Krips (Mozart with treacle). The last decade found him recording in Vienna for Vanguard, but never the Martinů *Second Concerto* he commissioned in 1943—only Khachaturian's populist artifact. In 1962, *A Golden Hour from the Royal Opera House* on BBC-TV sandwiched Elman, playing two salon trifles, between flamenco by José Greco and a Royal Ballet pas de deux. Then Callas and di Stefano came on, and got the lion's share of attention and applause. *—Roger Dettmer*

Recommended:

- ○ **Elman Plays Sonatas & Encores** / Elman, Seiger (piano) / 2004 / Testament 1344
- ○ **Hebraic & Russian Melodies** / Elman, Seiger (piano) / Vanguard 8030
- ○ **Elman Collection, Vol. 1** / Elman, etc. / 2000 / Doremi 7736
- ○ **Elman: Victor Recordings, 1910–1911** / Elman, Kahn (piano) / 1990 / Biddulph 035

Emerson String Quartet

f. 1976

Ensemble

The Emerson String Quartet is one of the world's great chamber ensembles, especially known for its exhilarating performances of twentieth century classics. Founded in 1976, the Quartet was named in honor of the New England poet and philosopher Ralph Waldo Emerson. The two remaining founding members, violinists Eugene Drucker and Philip Setzer, each won a Bronze Medal at the 1976 Queen Elisabeth of Belgium International Violin Competition. The two of them alternate between first and second violin in the Quartet.

Previously, Eugene Drucker had won a prize at the International Violin Competition in Montreal. He was born in New York and has a B.A. in English and Comparative Literature from Columbia University, and an Artist Diploma from the Juilliard School of Music, where he studied with Oscar Shumsky. He has recorded the complete solo violin works of Bach, and Bartók's sonatas and violin duos. He plays a 1686 Stradivari violin.

Philip Setzer is a native of Cleveland, Ohio, and also a pupil of Oscar Shumsky at Juilliard. His parents were both members of the Cleveland Orchestra and in Cleveland his violin teachers were Joseph Gingold and Rafael Drurian, both concertmasters of the orchestra. Setzer is a Visiting Professor of Violin at the Hartt School of Music at the University of Hartford, and in 1997 participated as a member of the faculty in the Isaac Stern Chamber Music Workshop at Carnegie Hall, and in 1998 at Stern's Chamber Music Encounter in Jerusalem. He premiered Paul Epstein's *Matinée Concerto* in 1989. His violin is a 1793 Nicolus Lupot made in Orleans.

Violist Lawrence Dutton is also is on the faculty at Hartt and participates in the Chamber Music Encounters in Israel. He earned Bachelors and Masters Degrees at Juilliard, where his viola teacher was Lilian Fuchs. Earlier, he studied at Eastman School with Francis Tursi. He is also a member of the Masters Piano Quartet. His instrument is a Pietro Giovanni Mantegazza dated Milan, 1796.

Cellist David Finckel also tours extensively as a cello soloist with his wife, the pianist Wu Han. He debuted in New York in 1998 and made his first European and Japanese recital tours during the same season. He is a director of ArtistLed, the first Interned-based recording company to be owned and directed by musicians, and in 1998 became artistic director of the La Jolla SummerFest chamber music festival.

The Emerson Quartet gives over a hundred concerts annually. They have won six Grammy Awards, one for Best Classical Album, and Gramophone Magazine's "Record of the Year Award." Their set of the complete Bartók Quartets (1987) is widely acclaimed as the recorded version of choice. They have also recorded the Ives and Barber Quartets, works by Meyers and Rorem, and in a three-year project, the complete Shostakovich Quartets in live recordings made at the Aspen Music Festival. *—Joseph Stevenson*

Recommended:

- ○ **Bartók: Six Quartets** / Emerson SQ / DG 423657
- ○ **American Originals** / Emerson SQ / 1992 / DG 435864
- ○ **Beethoven: Quartets, Opp 59/3; 132** / Emerson SQ / 1998 / DG 459063
- ○ **Mozart: Quartets KV387 & 421** / Emerson SQ / DG 439861
- ○ **Prokofiev: Quartets 1 & 2; Sonata for 2 Violins** / Emerson SQ / 1991 / DG 431772

Empire Brass

f. 1971

Ensemble

Since its inception in 1971, the Empire Brass has remained virtually unrivaled among brass quintets for sheer virtuosity and diversity of repertoire. Each of the ensemble's five members—trumpeter and founding member Rolf Smedvig, trumpeter Marc Brian Reese, French hornist Greg Miller, trombonist Mark Hetzler, and tubist Kenneth Amis—have held leading positions with American orchestras, and the members perform some 100 concerts together annually.

While many brass quintets focus on either mainstream, crowd-pleasing repertoire or a more "serious," scholarly approach, the Empire has found a steady middle-ground in its various activities. The ensemble is equally at home in the antiphonal works that Gabrieli composed for St. Mark's Cathedral in Venice, or the exuberant show-stopping Broadway tunes of Richard Rodgers and Andrew Lloyd Webber.

As proponents of the quintet medium, the Empire has recorded a series of best-selling CDs that include *Romantic Brass*, an anthology of Spanish and French music; *Class Brass—On the Edge*, featuring transcriptions of Khachaturian, Prokofiev, Bernstein, and Copland; *Passage*, a concept album juxtaposing medieval chant arrangements with electronic percussion; and the latest, *King's Court and Celtic Fair*, a collection of English Renaissance music.

The Empire Brass has been featured on network television, on ABC's *Good Morning America*, NBC's *Today Show* and *Sunday Today*, and PBS's *Mr. Roger's Neighborhood*. They are regular guests on commercial radio networks as well, including NPR's *Performance Today*.

A persuasive advocate for the art form, the Empire was the first brass ensemble to win the prestigious Naumberg chamber music award. It has served as Faculty Quartet-in-Residence at Boston University for 13 years, and has led the Empire Brass Seminar at the Tanglewood Institute for over 20 years, where students from around the world come to study with the quintet. Since 1991, the quintet has also been acting as visiting brass consultants at London's Royal Academy of Music.

In both pops and traditional settings, the Empire is regularly featured with such major orchestras as the Chicago Symphony, Boston Symphony, Philadelphia Orchestra, New York Philharmonic, Toronto Symphony, Detroit Symphony, Cincinnati Symphony, and Zurich's Tonhalle Orchester. It regularly makes appearances at leader summer festivals, including Ravinia, Tanglewood, Caramoor, Saratoga and Chautauqua. It has toured the Far East thirteen times, and regularly performs in Europe. *—Brian Wise*

Recommended:

- ○ **The Glory of Gabrieli** / Empire Brass / 2002 / Telarc 80553
- ○ **Passage 138 B.C.–A.D. 1611** / Empire Brass / 1994 / Telarc 80355
- ○ **Empire Brass: Greatest Hits** / Empire Brass / 1997 / Telarc 80438

George Enescu

b. Aug. 19, 1881, Liveni-Virnav, Romania, **d.** May 3, 1955, Paris, France

Composer: Symphonic, Orchestral, Chamber Music, Opera

George Enescu is still considered the greatest of all Romanian composers. While he is widely known for just one famous opus, he was in reality a very imaginative, highly skilled composer of music possessing great depth and subtlety, as well as being one of the great concert violinists of his time. For appearances in the West he adapted his name to a form that would prompt the French to pronounce it correctly: Georges Enesco.

He was given a violin and lessons at the age of four, progressing very rapidly and beginning to compose a year later. Legend has it his first teacher was a Romany fiddler. He entered the conservatory of the Gesellschaft der Musikfreunde in Vienna in 1888. His primary violin teacher was Joseph Hellmesberger. He took piano from Ernst Ludwig and harmony, theory, and composition from Robert Fuchs. He made his violin debut in 1889 in Slanic, Moravia. He remained in the Conservatory until 1894, regarded as a fully formed virtuoso at the age of 13. Nevertheless, he went on to the Paris Conservatory for more violin studies, and took harmony, theory, and composition from Dubois, Gédalge, Massenet, and Fauré. This mixture of late Romantic German and French training helped give his music its distinctive quality.

In 1897 the Concerts Colonne gave a concert of his works. The work he decided to designate as his first mature piece, the *Poème Roumaine*, Op. 1, premiered in 1898. That same year he started conducting the Romanian Philharmonic Society in Bucharest.

Enescu quickly established one of the most important solo and chamber music careers of the time. His recital partner was the great French pianist Alfred Cortot, and he formed a piano trio with Louis Fournier and Alfredo Casella in 1902, and in 1904 the Enescu Quartet. He joined the faculties of the École Normal and the American Conservatory in Paris.

In the meantime, he took an active part in building a classical concert life in his native Romania. He formed a Philharmonic Orchestra in the town of Iasi, and a

Composers' Society. He wrote his most famous works, the two *Romanian Rhapsodies*, Op. 11, for the Philharmonic. He also worked closely with the Conservatories in Bucharest and Iasi. In 1912 he funded a "George Enescu Prize" in composition, and played the world premieres of the winning works.

He made his first appearances in the United States in 1923, as violinist and guest conductor with the Philadelphia Orchestra. The brilliant young American prodigy, Yehudi Menuhin, became his most famous pupil. Others were Gitlis, Grumiaux, and Ferras. Through the 1930s he continued work as a violinist, conductor, teacher, musicologist, and organizer, while as a composer he toiled on his powerful opera *Oedipus*.

When World War II broke out, he happened to be at his country estate in Romania and was more or less stuck there for the duration. After the war ended, he went to New York, where he watched a Soviet-backed government take over his country. He remained in New York, increasingly incapacitated by arthritis. He gave a farewell concert with Menuhin in 1950, then returned to Paris. He suffered a stroke in 1954. As a result of it, he spent ten months almost entirely paralyzed. *—Joseph Stevenson*

SYMPHONIC

Symphony No. 1 in E flat major, Op. 13 (1905)

Scored for orchestra, wordless chorus, organ, and piano, this is a long way removed from any of Enescu's four so-called "School" symphonies written in the 1890s. Dedicated to Alfred Casella, this is an optimistic and idealistic Romantic work, owing much to Brahms and Wagner (especially *Tristan*) but also Berlioz, Franck, and Dukas. It was an immediate critical and popular success on its premiere in 1906. This probably results largely from the fact that, though it is a musically complex and densely structured work, most of its complexity is hidden from the listener, leaving only the sweeping grandeur of its Romantic thematic material to form a lasting impression. *—Tim Mahon*

Recommended:

- ○ **Enescu: Symphonies 1 & 3** / Rozhdestvensky (cond.), BBCPO / 1996 / Chandos 9507
- ○ **Enescu: Orchestral Works** / Mandeal (cond.), "George Enescu" Bucharest PO / 1997 / Arte Nova 49145

Symphony No. 2 in A major, Op. 17 (Sep. 4, 1912–Nov. 18, 1914)

This symphony was written during years when George Enescu was very busy as a leading concert violinist of his times. He was always a careful and slow worker, so like many of his major compositions this symphony took several years to complete. It was first performed in Bucharest on March 28, 1915, an event that could not make a large impression in Western Europe, which was then consumed in World War I. The A major tonality and the bustling, optimistic quality of the opening of the symphony are reminiscent of Mendelssohn's *"Italian" Symphony*, although the harmonies soon prove to be more enriched, in a style somewhere between the late Romantic and the Impressionistic. The first theme is broad and arching. Before the introduction of a second theme there is an unusual group of short motives, lyrical in nature, all extensions of elements of the first subject. Therefore, in this unusual structure Enescu manages to start the process of symphonic development before he has finished the exposition section of the form. The second theme itself is both lyrical and energetic, and again comprises a group of melodic ideas, which allows itself to slip away from the expected new key of E but into E flat, a distant key which gives an impression of a large, all-embracing structure. After a very rich and imaginative development and recapitulation, the movement ends in A minor.

The slow movement occupies a strange tonal position: It features the clash of the keys of B flat and G sharp. These two notes surround the symphony's home key of A, and their conflict tends to pull both tonalities towards that note, reaffirming the central tonality of the symphony without really using it much. The orchestration is breathtakingly beautiful, the music is passionate, and the musical effect (due to the unusual use of tonality and other factors) is remarkably original. The final movement begins in E flat, which is as remote from A major as possible. This again evokes a sense of mysterious spaces, of distances. The slow, ominously martial introduction uses a descending phrase which reappears later in Enescu's great opera *Oedipus* as a motive of Fate. The orchestra bursts out into a unison phrase, launching the Allegro body of the movement proper, and banishing the Fate motive. The vigorous and heroically martial rhythms propel the symphony toward a conclusion. Suddenly the Fate motive reappears, but the opening themes of the symphony recur in a thrilling coda. Worthy as it is, this symphony is not frequently played. Its 55-minute length makes it a risky choice for the major spot on a symphony concert. *—Joseph Stevenson*

Recommended:

- ○ **Enescu: Symphony 2; Romanian Rhapsody 2** / Rozhdestvensky (cond.), BBCPO / 1997 / Chandos 9537
- ○ **Enescu: Symphony 2; Vox Maris** / Andreescu (cond.), "George Enescu" State PO / 1988 / Marco Polo 223142

Symphony No. 3 in C major, Op. 21 (May 18, 1916–Aug. 20, 1918)

A monumental and distinctly Brahmsian work, Enescu's *Third Symphony* is an emotionally intense war symphony of grandiose dimension. Scored for orchestra and chorus, it calls for large forces to be deployed in execution of the composer's vision—12 double basses, for example, including two soli. It anticipates *Oedipe* in its philosophical approach and indeed in some of its thematic material which finds its way into Enescu's magnum opus. Its lavish orchestration and its entry into a completely new world of harmonic thinking for the composer make it a much more advanced work than the *Second Symphony*, for example. But it is a much less difficult symphony to grasp, since its melodic lines and majestic expressiveness lead the listener unerringly through the sweeping scope of the first two movements to the sparsely orchestrated and carillon-like conclusion. *—Tim Mahon*

Recommended:

- ○ **Enescu: Symphony 3; Romanian Rhapsody 1** / Rozhdestvensky (cond.), BBCPO / 1998 / Chandos 9633
- ○ **Enescu: Orchestral Works** / Mandeal (cond.), "George Enescu" Bucharest PO / 1997 / Arte Nova 49145

ORCHESTRAL

Two Romanian Rhapsodies, Op. 11 (Aug. 14, 1901–Oct. 26, 1901)

Enescu came to regard his *Romanian Rhapsodies* as sins of his youth, folkloric pop pieces that hardly reflected the more serious works of his maturity. But in truth, these pieces, particularly the first, are all that most people know of Romania's most famous composer. They follow in the traditions of such nineteenth century pieces as Liszt's *Hungarian Rhapsodies* and Dvořák's *Slavonic Rhapsodies*, adapting indigenous melodies, dance rhythms, and to some degree forms to the needs and expectations of the Romantic orchestra and its audience.

The first rhapsody takes its general inspiration from Liszt, employing the slow-fast pattern of his *Hungarian Rhapsodies* (and for that matter of the Czech dumka, as employed by Dvořák). Enescu initially conveys the intimate, gypsy folk-band nature of this music by assigning the melodies to solo and duo instruments before pulling together the entire orchestra for the later, forcefully swirling dances.

If the first rhapsody is mostly about dance, the second is a collection of songs. It's mostly leisurely music based on folk tunes, often employing the characteristic drone of Eastern European music and spending a great deal of time in the minor mode. Although it swells to a pair of climaxes, the music is generally tender and ends quietly. Not a noisy crowd-pleaser, it lies in the shadow of its predecessor. *—James Reel*

Recommended:

- ○ **Ravel, Lalo, Enescu** / Silvestri (cond.), Czech PO / 2000 / Supraphon 3514
- ○ **Liszt & Enesco Rhapsodies** / Dorati (cond.), London SO / 1991 / Mercury 432015

CHAMBER MUSIC

Violin Sonata No. 3 in A minor (dans le caractere populaire roumain), Op. 25 (Aug. 21, 1926–Nov. 18, 1926)

Enescu deliberately called this sonata "in Roumanian character" (dans la caractère populaire roumaine), not "in Roumanian style" because to him the two phrases meant entirely different things. To him, "in the style of" meant creating something new in imitation of another thing, whereas "in the character of" meant borrowing the traits of something that already existed. For his *Violin Sonata No. 3*, Enescu borrowed Gypsy violin techniques to create his themes. He did not want to use existing folk melodies because he felt he could do nothing more than state and restate them, there was no way for him musically to develop them further as you would normally develop the subject of a sonata-allegro form. He used quarter tones and chromatic modes to break down the tonality of the piece, repeated and superimposed rhythmic and harmonic devices, and detailed throughout the score specific bowing actions and ornaments as were used by Gypsy musicians. Not only does the violinist end up sounding like a true Gypsy violinist, but for much of the sonata the pianist ends up sounding like a cimbalomist, with careful use of the pedal; quick, short, repeated notes; and glissandos to re-create the sound of the hammered instrument. For all of its improvisational sound, the sonata is actually carefully constructed in three movements. The first, Moderato malinconio, is a sonata-allegro based on two contrasting subjects: the first a lament, the second much more animated. The opening of the second movement, Andante sostenuto e misterioso, features quietly repeated notes in the piano, on top of which the violin plays a long passage in harmonics. From there it becomes a darkly atmospheric, and at times dramatic, musical painting. The final Allegro con brio ma non troppo mosso is a rondo with a march-like subject, which breaks down into something more of a dance or improvisation in its episodes. It ends with a series of stern chords and a final, conclusive fillip from the violin. *—Patsy Morita*

Recommended:

- ○ **Ida Haendel & Vladimir Ashkenazy** / Haendel, Ashkenazy / 2000 / Decca 455488

OPERA

Oedipe (1921–Apr. 27, 1931)

Georges Enescu's only opera constitutes a fascinating sidebar in the history of opera. A work of enormous scale, *Oedipe* has not attracted many opera producers who have the means to mount a convincing production, nor has it caught the attention of a broad audience through the creditable recordings it has been accorded. Still, it has drawn a small but fiercely enthusiastic body of admirers and remains a superior work whose day may yet come.

Enescu, who excelled as pianist, violinist, conductor, pedagogue and composer, approached his the task of composition with measured deliberation. *Oedipe* was one of only 33 works completed in his lifetime. Inspired by a performance of Sophocles' *Oedipus the King* at the Comédie-Française in 1909, he found himself unable to begin composition until 1921. Although portions were performed in concert during the 1920s, orchestration of the entire work was not finished until 1931, and still more tinkering was done by the composer up to the moment of its 1936 premiere. For that first production, bass-baritone André Pernet, one of France's most respected singing actors, appeared in the title role.

More philosophical, less starkly tragic than Stravinsky's *Oedipus Rex*, Enescu's opera unfolds over four acts and three hours' running time. While Sophocles' *Oedipus the King* provided the basis for the third act, and *Oedipus at Colonnus* the essential story for the final act, other Greek epic tales informed the rest of the work. Using a range of contemporary effects, including quarter tones, Enescu infused his opera with vast musical interest.

Set in antiquity, *Oedipe* begins in Thebes with a dark, portentous prelude that establishes the psychological complexity of the score. Edmund Fleg's libretto follows the tragedy familiar to most secondary students: people celebrate the child born to King Laius and Queen Jocasta; there are warnings that the child will kill his father and marry his mother; and Laius orders the Shepherd to take the child to the mountains and abandon him. In the second act's second scene, Oedipus kills Laius at a crossroads and, after answering the riddles of the Sphinx, returns to Thebes in triumph. In the third act, Oedipus learns the truth about his parentage and accepts his own sentence of banishment. In Act Four, however, Fleg affords Oedipus the redemption missing in Stravinsky's opera: justified and with sight restored, Oedipus can contemplate his final hours in peace. *—Erik Eriksson*

Synopsis:

Act One. The action takes place in ancient Greece, at the palace of Laius, King of Thebes. A son has been born to Laius and Queen Jocasta, and a lavish celebration of the event is taking place. But the festivities come to a sudden end when the prophet Tiresias foretells that the child, defiant of the gods in birth, will one day slay his father and marry his mother. Laius and Jocasta decide to circumvent the prediction by ordering the child's death.

Act Two. A shepherd, under orders to kill the baby, gives him instead to Phorbas, who substitutes him for the dead infant left in his charge, the son of King Polybus and Queen Merope of Corinth. The spared child, named Oedipus, grows up believing that Polybus and Merope are his birth parents. When he is 20 years old an oracle tells him of his grim destiny, but Oedipus assumes that it pertains to Polybus and Merope. He ponders fleeing Corinth as his only hope to avoid fulfilling the prophecy that he will murder Polybus and marry Merope. Merope notices his troubled state and assures him that rumors she is not his real mother are untrue. But Oedipus reveals the oracle's prophecy to her and soon leaves Corinth.

Oedipus walks along a road near Thebes, while the Shepherd who saved him watches from nearby. As a storm swirls in the skies, Laius and attendants approach in the distance on a chariot. Oedipus curses Fate and raises his staff in defiance. Laius sees the gesture as threatening, and a violent brawl ensues; Oedipus kills Laius and his two attendants.

As he approaches Thebes, Oedipus is warned that the Sphinx has been posing riddles to passers-by who, when they fail to solve them, die. The citizenry is hoping that someone can solve her riddle, thereby destroying the Sphinx. Oedipus decides he will become the liberator of the city. He approaches the Sphinx and is asked to name "something or someone greater than Fate." He responds, "Man," and the Sphinx dies. Oedipus is greeted as the new King of Thebes and will soon marry the widowed Queen, Jocasta.

Act Three. Twenty years have passed. Oedipus has fathered seven children with Jocasta and has governed Thebes skillfully. But the city is ravaged by a plague which, according to an oracle, will not relent until Laius' murderer, who resides in Thebes, is brought to justice. Creon, Jocasta's brother, enlists the aid of Tiresias to find the culprit, and the seer accuses Oedipus. Oedipus considers the charge a ploy to overthrow him and place Creon in power. But when the old shepherd and Phorbas enter and tell their stories, he sees the truth. Jocasta commits suicide, and Oedipus inflicts blindness upon himself. He flees with his daughter Antigone, thus ridding the city of the plague.

Act Four (Epilogue). Years later, the elderly Oedipus, still accompanied by Antigone, prepares to meet with Theseus, King of Athens, in a grove inhabited by the Furies. Creon enters and informs him of new hardships in Thebes, and asks Oedipus to return. He declines, and when Creon attempts the abduction of Antigone to force his return, Theseus enters with attendants. He charges Oedipus with incest and patricide, but Oedipus asserts that he never committed his will to those acts and is therefore both innocent and victorious over Fate. His sight is restored. Oedipus walks off into a bright light, then disappears, the Furies declaring him pure. *—Robert Cummings*

Recommended:

○ **Enesco: Oedipe** / Foster (cond.), Van Dam, Gedda, Hendricks, Bacquier, Monte Carlo PO / 1990 / EMI 754011

English Baroque Soloists

f. 1978

Ensemble

Although the English Baroque Soloists was officially established as a chamber ensemble of period instruments in 1978, the group actually gave its first concert at the 1977 Innsbruck Festival of Early Music in a performance of Handel's *Acis and Galatea.* Founded by John Eliot Gardiner, the group regularly performs throughout England and Europe. It has given a number of concerts in two London halls, the Barbican and St. John's Smith Square. The English Baroque Soloists drew many of their original members from another group Gardiner had founded (in 1968), the Monteverdi Orchestra.

Shortly after their founding, it was Bach and Handel who were largely the focus of the EBS. However, the EBS became closely associated with Mozart's music, mainly because of its numerous, generally highly acclaimed recordings of his works. In 1984, Gardiner and the EBS launched a series for the label Archiv Produktion devoted to Mozart's concertos for piano and orchestra with soloist Malcolm Bilson (using a fortepiano) and the first such cycle using period instruments. Two years later, with the concerto series ongoing, they launched another Mozart project, this one to cover the mature symphonies for Philips. In summer 1990, the EBS debuted at the Salzburg Festival, giving three concerts, all to critical acclaim. The group has since returned numerous times and has also subsequently toured Vienna and Innsbruck. With the release in 1990 of *Piano Concerto No. 24* (K. 491) and *No. 27* (K. 595), the piano concerto series was completed, but the EBS and Gardiner immediately set to work recording the seven mature operas of Mozart for Archiv Produktion. The first release in this cycle, *Idomeneo,* won Gramophone's Best Opera Award in 1991. In that same year. Gardiner, the EBS, and the Monteverdi Choir appeared in a live BBC television broadcast of Mozart's *Requiem* performed at the Palau de la Música Catalana. The last issue in the Gardiner/EBS Mozart operas series, *Die Zauberflöte,* was released in 1996, after which they turned to the music of Bach.

In the late 1990s, a new series of recordings began with the release in 2000 of Bach's *Cantatas No. 6 "Bleib bei uns, denn es will Abend"* (BWV 6) and *No. 66, "Erfreut euch, ihr Herzen"* (BWV 66). Along with the Monteverdi Choir, Gardiner and the EBS performed the entire cycle of 198 Bach cantatas throughout various European churches in 2000. But the EBS was hardly focusing on only Mozart or Bach in 1990s: its performance at Covent Garden in 1995 of Haydn's *Die Schöpfung* (The Creation) was enthusiastically received and led to a successful 1997 recording on Archiv Produktion. Also in 1995, the EBS and the Monteverdi Choir performed the music for the film *England, My England,* a highly acclaimed movie directed by Tony Palmer, about English composer Henry Purcell. That same year, Gardiner, the EBS, and Monteverdi Choir issued a multi-disc set on the label Erato devoted to Purcell's music.

The touring schedule of the EBS has been one of the busiest of any orchestra's. In 2002, for example, it included performances of Weber's *Oberon* in Paris and London; of sixteenth and seventeenth century church music in numerous cities throughout the U.K.; Bach cantatas in Utrecht, Köthen, and Wiesbaden; and numerous other performances in Brussels, Zurich, Baden-Baden, Vienna, Turin, and Athens. As of 2002, the EBS appeared on about 70 recordings, making it one of the most heavily recorded orchestras over the years since its founding. *—Robert Cummings*

Recommended:

○ **Monteverdi: L'Orfeo** / Gardiner (cond.), Otter, Chance, Dawson, English Baroque Soloists / Archiv 419250

○ **Mozart: The Piano Concertos** / Gardiner (cond.), Bilson, Tan, Levin, English Baroque Soloists / Archiv 463111

○ **Händel: Messiah** / Gardiner (cond.), Brett, Ross, Robbin, Johnson, English Baroque Soloists / 1992 / Philips 434297

○ **Mozart: Mass in C minor** / Gardiner (cond.), McNair, Beznosiuk, Johnson, Montague, English Baroque Soloists / Philips 420210

○ **Haydn: 6 Great Masses** / Gardiner (cond.), Brown, Finley, Ziesak, Pregardien, English Baroque Soloists / 2003 / Philips 000132502

○ **Bach: Mass In B Minor** / Gardiner (cond.), English Baroque Soloists / Archiv 415514

English Chamber Orchestra

f. 1948

Ensemble

Considered one of the most distinguished chamber orchestras in the world, the English Chamber Orchestra was formed in 1948 by Arnold Goldsborough for the purpose of performing Baroque music. Similar in musical philosophy and organization to the Academy of St. Martin-in-the-Fields, the ensemble is financially self-supporting and has no permanent home venue. The orchestra presents an annual concert series in London and also tours internationally. Over its history, the ensemble has expanded its repertoire to include a wide range of chamber music from various musical periods and is flexible in size, ranging from 24 to 38 musicians.

Originally named the Goldsborough Orchestra, the ensemble changed its name to the English Chamber Orchestra (ECO) in 1960 in accordance with the needs of the group's growing reputation. At the same time, The English Chamber Orchestra and Music Society was formed as the promotion arm of the organization.

Like many other chamber orchestras, the ECO employs no full-time musicians but hires its players on a contract basis. This allows the orchestra to be flexible in size and structure according to the needs of its repertoire and concert venues and also gives the musicians the opportunity to work in a variety of other situations. The freedom this provides is key to the fresh approach this orchestra takes in its performances through its use of a system of co-principal groupings of players. Under this system, two principal players share each chair and are contracted to play a set number of performances in a given season.

The ECO has performed for numerous important occasions including a command performance before Queen Elizabeth II at the Queen Elizabeth Hall inaugural concert in 1967. Other performances of note are the first color television recording of music for the BBC and the wedding of Prince Charles and Diana, Princess of Wales in 1981. The ensemble has been associated with the music of Benjamin Britten since it became resident orchestra at the Aldeburgh Festival in 1961.

Until 1985, the orchestra chose to work without a principal conductor, instead inviting a series of talented guest artists to lead the ensemble. The ECO has a reputation for giving young conductors important opportunities. Among those who have benefited from this policy are Sir Colin Davis, Daniel Barenboim, and Pinchas Zukerman. During the orchestra's Silver Anniversary celebration in 1985, it was announced that Jeffrey Tate had been chosen to fill the newly created position of principal conductor, and in 2000 he was succeeded by Ralf Gothóni.

Tremendously versatile and musically polished, the English Chamber Orchestra is fully deserving of its reputation as one of the finest chamber orchestras in the world. *—Corie Stanton Root*

Recommended:

- ○ **Gavin Byars: Farewell to Philosophy** / Judd (cond.), Lloyd Webber, Haden, English CO, Nexus / 1996 / Point 454126
- ○ **Wynton Marsalis: The London Concert** / Leppard (cond.), Newman (cond.), Marsalis, Bennett, Lin, English CO / 2004 / Sony 93084
- ○ **Elgar: Chamber Works** / Goodwin (cond.), Bennett, Ellis, Gonley, Price, English CO / 2001 / HM 907258

English Concert

f. 1973

Ensemble

The English Concert is an "authentic performance" ensemble, founded by harpsichordist and conductor Trevor Pinnock in 1973. The group quickly established itself as one of Britain's leading orchestras in the then-young field of performing Baroque works on Baroque instruments. The English Concert and the energetic Pinnock helped put historical performance on the charts. The orchestra has a reputation for stylish, lively, and high-quality music-making. Its sound is light, bright, and clear. Its strings usually employ no vibrato, and its winds have a woody, attractive tone that blends well with strings and with the fortepiano. Generally the orchestra applies only a light swelling on sustained string notes. In explaining the orchestra's choice to specialize in original instruments (or painstakingly authentic re-creations of them), Pinnock explains, "The answer is simple—we wanted to use the most suitable tools for the job. These instruments were good enough for Bach—surely they're good enough for us." In 1983, the English Concert Choir was established, to perform and record choral works with the instrumental ensemble. After 30 years leading the group, Pinnock stepped down and turned the music directorship over to Andrew Manze.

Recording for Deutsche Grammophon's Archiv imprint, Harmonia Mundi, and its own label, Avie, the English Concert has released over 70 albums, many of which have won top recording awards such as the Grand Prix du Disque and Grammophon Awards. With Pinnock leading, it has recorded complete symphonies of Mozart, Bach's *Brandenburg Concerti* and *Orchestral Suites*, and many Haydn symphonies and Vivaldi concertos. In addition it has participated in recordings of Haydn masses and Handel oratorios and operas. It has toured extensively in Europe and Asia, including a 1998 25th-anniversary tour. *—Joseph Stevenson*

Recommended:

- ○ **Haydn: The "Sturm und Drang" Symphonies** / Pinnock (cond.), English Concert / Archiv 463731
- ○ **Handel: Orchestral Works** / Pinnock (cond.), Standage, Comberti, Pleeth, Wilcock, English Concert / Archiv 463094
- ○ **Vivaldi: Concertos** / Pinnock (cond.), Standage, Goodman, Pickett, English Concert / Archiv 471317
- ○ **Bach: 6 Brandenburg Concertos; 4 Orchestral Suites** / Pinnock (cond.), Halstead, Standage, Medlam, English Concert / 1982 / Archiv 423492
- ○ **Handel: Complete Organ Concertos** / Pinnock (cond.), Preston, Standage, Pleeth, Holliger, English Concert / 2002 / Archiv 469358

Brian Eno

b. May 15, 1948, Woodbridge, Suffolk, England

Composer: Avant-garde

Born Brian Peter George St. John le Baptiste de la Salle Eno in Woodbridge, England, Brian Eno took his early music training at art school in Ipswich and Winchester, where he studied with composers Christian Wolff and George Brecht. His classical training of the 1960s also included work with the Scratch Orchestra and the Portsmouth Sinfonia. In 1964 Eno turned his focus to rock music, first with the band the Black Aces and then with Maxwell Demon. Eno's better-known third effort was the 1971 formation of Roxy Music with Bryan Ferry. After two albums, including the self-titled 1972 project and 1973's *For Your Pleasure*, Eno left the group to pursue a solo career.

In 1973, Eno collaborated with King Crimson guitarist Robert Fripp for an experimental album of tape delay manipulations called *No Pussyfooting*. *Here Come the Warm Jets* (1974) is a collection of experimental pop songs on which Eno revisits his Roxy Music role as "sound manipulator." After touring extensively and performing with The Winkies, Eno's suffered from a collapsed lung in 1974. He returned later that year with *Taking Tiger Mountain (By Strategy)*, a project which utilized a set of "Oblique Strategies," which served as an aid for chance composition. In 1975, Eno began further experiments with ambient music and minimalism, including the highly regarded *Another Green World*. That same year Eno formed Obscure, a record company which specialized in experimental music, including his second ambient project, *Discreet Music* (1975) and Harold Budd's *Pavilion of Dreams*.

Eno continued in his collaborative efforts, working with David Bowie on *Low* (1977), *Heroes* (1977), *Lodger* (1979), and the German group Cluster. He produced a compilation album called *No New York*, which included the music of groups such as DNA, The Contortions, Mars, and Teenage Jesus and the Jerks, as well as Devo's 1978 debut album *Q. Are we Not Men? A. We Are Devo!*. Eno's work with ambient music continued, including *Music for Airports* (1979), the first in a series intended as background music. Perhaps the most fruitful collaboration of the time was with the Talking Heads, including 1978's *More Songs about Buildings and Food*, 1979's *Fear of Music*, and 1980's *Remain in Light*. In 1981, Eno and the Talking Heads' lead singer David Byrne produced *My Life in the Bush of Ghosts*, which combined electronic music, stylized African drumming, and "found" spoken material from around the world. This album was a continuation of the "fourth world" concept of trumpeter Jon Hassell, which began on the 1980 Hassell/Eno collaboration *Fourth World Vol. 1: Possible Musics* album.

Work with producer Daniel Lanois launched a successful series of albums with the band U2, including *The Joshua Tree* and *Achtung Baby*. He continued to work on his solo material, including 1982's *On Land* and 1983's *Apollo Atmospheres and Soundtracks*, as well as a collaboration with artist Christine Alicino in 1985's soundtrack *Thursday Afternoon*.

The 1990s found Eno involved in various solo projects such as *Nerve Net* and *The Shutov Assembly* in 1992, and *Glitterbug*, the soundtrack to a 1994 Derek Jarman film. His output in subsequent years spanned several genres and media: a diary published as *A Year with Swollen Appendices*, a multimedia project with Laurie Anderson, and even an "aural screen saver" for personal computers entitled *Generative Music* I (1996). In 1995, Eno also reunited with David Bowie for the industrial-rock project *Outside*. In 2000, Eno's art installation *Kites* was shown in art galleries around the world, including the *Kiasma* in Helsinki, Finland. *—Kristen Grimshaw*

AVANT-GARDE

Ambient 1: Music for Airports (1978)

Before there was a style of music called "ambient"—with offshoots reaching into classical, world, and "new age" musics, as well as electronica and a variety of dance-based sub-genres—the phrase "ambient music" was largely connected to Brian Eno. Eno, known in part for his work with groups like Roxy Music, Talking Heads and U2, has also produced a significant catalog of his own music. Some of his albums are relatively conventional collections of songs, but others are more experimental in approach and sound, including several which might be termed "ambient."

Generically speaking, "ambient music" is music that evolves very slowly through subtle textural changes, and tends not to have a pronounced beat or prominent melodic content. As early as 1975 Eno theorized on the possibilities for such music: "we might simply use it to 'tint' the environment, we might use it 'diagrammatically,' we might use it to modify our moods in almost subliminal ways." That year he was forced to spend several months in bed after an automobile accident. At one point an album of harp music was playing, very quietly, in his room. Since he was unable to get out of bed to turn it up, the music mixed with the sounds of a rainstorm outside and simply became part of the room's environment. Expanding on this revelatory moment and taking further inspiration from Erik Satie's notion of "musique d'ameublement" or "furniture music"—which exists in the environment like furniture but doesn't dominate one's attention—Eno explored something like an ambient approach in albums like *Discreet Music* (1975), and embraced the idea entirely in *Ambient 1: Music for Airports*, recorded in 1978 and released the following year.

In an essay that accompanied the album, Eno talked about the more common form of background music, "familiar tunes arranged and orchestrated in a lightweight and derivative manner." He imagined a different sort of background music that would enhance an environment and "induce calm and a space to think," and that would maintain some musical interest but "be as ignorable as it is interesting." Although he went on to create many albums which might be generally described as ambient, the "Ambient" series proper featured only four recordings: *Music for Airports*; *Ambient 2: The Plateaux of Mirror by Harold Budd and Eno* (1980); *Ambient 3: Day of Radiance by Laraaji* (1981); and Eno's own *Ambient 4: On Land* (1982).

Music for Airports is made up of four pieces. *1/1*, co-written by Eno, Robert Wyatt and Rhett Davies, takes a gentle, Satie-like piano tune and repeats it many times, accompanied by Eno's characteristically murky, studio-generated textures. "1/2" overlaps long notes from electronically distorted female voices, and "2/1" combines voices with a spare piano line. The album's last piece, "2/2," is for synthesizers.

The music took on new life in 1998 when the New York-based new music group Bang on a Can created its own arrangements for live musicians and performed *Music for Airports* frequently in concert. *—Chris Morrison*

Recommended:

○ **Eno: Ambient 1: Music for Airports** / Fast, Gomez, Wyatt, Zelninger / EG 17

Discreet Music, for electronics (1975)

Discreet Music is, strictly speaking, the very first piece of ambient music ever composed as such. It came out in the same week as Lou Reed's notorious soundscape experiment *Metal Machine Music*, an interesting fact, considering that ambient has now partly evolved in the direction of greater harshness. The word ambience means atmosphere or mood, and that's what this music essentially is: a mood, a feeling, a texture. Eno realized at a certain moment (as did Glenn Gould) that Muzak is only a bad idea when the music being used is bad. His ambient pieces are therefore partly an attempt to forge a style of background music that won't have the subliminally detrimental effects Muzak is widely thought (by music-lovers) to have. He instructs in the liner notes to play *Discreet Music* at a barely audible volume, but the rich timbres make it tempting to want to hear it more clearly. Yet even when turned right up, *Discreet Music* remains completely unobtrusive. It can be expected that once there exists an easy to use ambient music-generating program for non-musicians, shopping malls won't be haunted with songs from *The Lion King* arranged for wind quintet and synthesizer, but instead will be haunted with tasteful, weightless process music, not unlike *Discreet Music*, which sounds as if it could have been composed tomorrow. Ambient was only brutalized in the press for ten years before its importance became widely acknowledged. Now its influence can be heard in some of the most aggressive forms of rock music, as well as in productions for the concert hall by young composers. The compositional technique of *Discreet Music* involves a fixed, limited set of melodic lines in evolving, changing relation to each other. It's a structure that recalls the mobile constructions of Alexander Calder. With a flexible mind, it can be seen that it somewhat resembles the method of medieval isorhythmic motets and relates to serial and chance composition of the 1950s. Not that Eno was thinking of these (he knows, but hates, classical music), but his concepts aren't merely rock & roll folly either; they have first cousins in serious practice. His role in *Discreet Music*, however, was perhaps more radically passive than in any music before it. There are two brief lines played on clarinet-like synthesizer settings. Loosely compatible and of different proportions, with some rests in between, Eno set them both looping so they endlessly recur, usually together, but never in exactly the same vertical relationship. Behind this is an echoey, synthetic wash and the timbres undergo slight, subtle alterations throughout. The mood can be described as a diffuse, utopic cheerfulness. As a composer, Eno did almost zilch. If such a "de-personalized" music makes purists object, Eno's own words certainly make it sound warmly humane: "If you leave your own personality out of the frame, you are inviting the listener to enter it instead." Listening to a piece as sweet and comforting as *Discreet Music*, it's certainly easy to believe. *—Donato Mancini*

Recommended:

○ **Discreet Music** / / Editions EG EEGCD23

Thursday Afternoon, for electronics (1985)

The story of "ambient" music begins with a legend. While in hospital, due to a car accident, hopped-up on painkillers, Brian Eno asked his nurse to play a record of harp music he had brought with him. She did so, and left the room, but didn't turn the volume up high enough. He found himself captive, unable to hear anything of it except the loudest notes that pierced the soft background noise of rain. As he got over his frustration and began to enjoy himself, the revelation struck him: ambient music was born. What's extraordinary is how lovingly ambient music was embraced in the popular sphere. By the 1990s the ambient principle had deeply infiltrated pop music, giving rise to innumerable imitations and hybrid genres. Eno had become a musical saint.

Possibly the first piece of music ever composed specifically for compact disc, *Thursday Afternoon* was created about ten years after Eno's first ambient piece, *Discreet Music*. His fetching term for the compositional style of *Thursday Afternoon* is "holographic." Like a holograph, any small part of the piece shows the whole in lower resolution. From start to finish *Thursday Afternoon* barely changes at all; the minute changes that do occur are completely inconsequential in the total effect. Against a constant, watery synth wash we hear random droplets of echoing piano, the drooping moans of a bass frequency, bells, faint bird calls, and an occasional shudder of processed electric organ. It's a lazy morning dream of a perfect English summer afternoon.

Since the work was composed as part of a gallery installation of seven video paintings by Christine Alicino, Eno ties the aesthetic of Thursday Afternoon to the condition of video and film. Because they are normally single-viewing media, both are propelled by plot and surprise, the result being that they are speeding up as more and more dazzle and pizzazz are packed in to delay the inevitable decline in interest. Against this current that will only bring "increasing hysteria and exoticism," Eno has created a radically simple, static work which remains still while we are invited to (mentally) walk around in it.

Rather than telling us something, this inherently healing music opens a dreamlike architectural dimension within whatever environment it may offer itself. Rather than telling us something, it creates a huge, high-ceilinged room within a room within the imagination. Nothing intrudes on the suspended-animation calm; we're left to dream our way in, to populate its yawning spaces with anything we fancy. It makes no argument for our attention, nor for its importance or even for its presence. The elements of melody, harmony and rhythm all remain, but in a seriously diminished, vestigial form, less forceful than a infant's pinkie toe. Comparisons have been made of this music to colored tapestries, but it is far less obtrusive than even that image suggests. It mingles so seamlessly with the environment that halfway through you might turn to put on another CD, having graciously forgotten that there's already music on. *—Donato Mancini*

Recommended:

○ **Thursday Afternoon** / / Editions EG EGCD64

Ensemble 415

f. 1981

Ensemble

Chiara Banchini founded Ensemble 415 in 1981. The ensemble is noted for its performances of Italian Baroque string music on period instruments. Banchini was among the better Baroque violinists performing at the end of the twentieth century, and the ensemble is at its best performing concerti featuring their director as solost. Their performances of music such as Vivaldi, Corelli, Boccherini, Muffat, and Tartini offer an opportunity to hear less well-known Baroque repertoire by composers who were very well known during the eighteenth century. *—Andrus Madsen*

Recommended:

○ **Corelli: Concerti grossi Op. 6** / Banchini, Christensen, Ensemble 415 / HM 2901406/07

○ **Muffat: Armonico tributo** / Banchini, Christensen, Ensemble 415 / HM 1951581

Ensemble Clément Janequin

f. 1978, Paris, France

Ensemble

In the late 1970s and early 1980s, as the music world was being reshaped by the emergence of the great English a cappella ensembles (Gothic Voices, the Tallis Scholars, the Hilliard Ensemble), a virtuoso countertenor from France launched a sonic revolution of his own. The singer, Dominique Visse, founded the Ensemble Clément Janequin in 1978, and over the twenty years of the group's career it has virtually come to own the performance of Renaissance French music. The ensemble's characteristic panache and vigor has produced authoritative interpretations, especially for the sixteenth century chanson repertory. Among the ensemble's many recordings, more than ten collections of French vernacular music have taken center stage. These have included music of the group's namesake, Clément Janequin and his contemporary Claudin de Sermisy, as well as Anthoine de Bertrand, Costeley, Roland de Lassus, and Claude le Jeune.

Much that is unique to the sound of Ensemble Clément Janequin derives from the peculiar artistry of its founder. Dominique Visse is a celebrated countertenor with a long list of operatic triumphs, from Baroque performances under William Christie and René Jacobs to a premiere of Luciano Berio's *Outis.* His bright, facile, and often irreverent virtuosity may be heard in the upper reaches of nearly every piece recorded by the Ensemble, and has helped mold the other players musically. The ensemble performs primarily with one or two voices to a part, bringing to the foreground the individuality of musical lines. The bright and often nasal vocal quality of Vissé's other singers, with some subtle ornamentation, heightens this vertical differentiation. Instrumental accompaniment (from lutes and gambas to organs, cornetts and sackbuts in a Janequin mass recording), though frequent, remains generally unobtrusive.

Utter sympathy with the individuality of texts, however, trumps every other feature of the group's performances. Its first recording, a 1982 collection of Janequin and Sermisy chansons entitled "Les cris de Paris" (The Cries of Paris) palpably demonstrates such text-based stylistic differentiation. The simple bourgeois dignity of the mainstream "Parisian" chanson starkly contrasts with the farcical drama of the title track and with the onomatopoeic "La bataille" (The Battle). The ensemble cultivates for both types of music a forthright, almost rustic sound, but when texts call for evocative dramatic sounds (or bawdy humor, another specialty), its performance is sparked by whispers, shouts, and a generally Carnivalesque soundscape. For sacred repertory (recordings of masses by Le Jeune, La Rue, and a fine rendition of the Josquin *Missa Pange lingua*), the group adopts a sound which is more spacious but no less vibrant. The ensemble's projects have also included a series of recordings of French settings of the poetry of Pierre de Ronsard and of Rabelais, and, in 1998, a venture into the Spanish Golden Age. —*Timothy Dickey*

Recommended:

○ **Les Cris de Paris: Chansons de Janequin & Sermisy** / Visse (dir.), Clement Janequin Ensemble / HM 7901072

○ **Lassus: Chansons** / Visse (dir.), Clement Janequin Ensemble / HM 1951391

○ **Sermisy: Leçons de Ténèbres** / Visse (dir.), Clement Janequin Ensemble / HM 2901131

○ **Janequin: Le Chant des Oyseaulx** / Visse (dir.), Clement Janequin Ensemble / HM 901099

○ **Josquin: Chansons** / Visse (dir.), Clement Janequin Ensemble / HM 1951279

Ensemble InterContemporain

f. 1976, Paris, France

Ensemble

Based in Paris, the Ensemble Intercontemporain is one of the leading performance organizations devoted to new music, and is closely associated with composer/conductor Pierre Boulez, a leader of the European musical avant-garde establishment. Boulez developed the idea of the Ensemble during the planning stages for IRCAM (The Institut de Recherche et de Coordination Acoustique/Musique). IRCAM was established by the French government as an international center for experimental music, to further pursue the explorations that Boulez, Iannis Xenakis, Bruno Maderna, and Luciano Berio had been carrying out with either government, broadcasting organization, or university assistance.

IRCAM was planned to have the latest in computer and electronic music technology, and to be located underneath the new Georges Pompidou Center in Paris. Boulez, whose public pronouncements concerning the present and future of music tend to be absolutist, concluded that the advances of the twentieth century called into question the nineteenth century institution of the symphony orchestra. He proposed to establish a more flexible structure designed to play new works, which are often quite variable in instrumentation. His suggestion, patterned on the recent success of the London Sinfonietta (founded in 1968 to play twentieth century music), was for an in-house ensemble. He decided on its size and instrumentation by referring to the works of Austrian composer Anton Webern. Accordingly, Boulez proposed a 31-member group containing all the instruments needed to perform the chamber works of Boulez, as well as important works by Igor Stravinsky, Webern and Arnold Schoenberg.

In 1976, Michel Guy, the French Minister of Culture, approved the plan for the Ensemble Intercontemporain, and the organization was quickly formed. Boulez, who has been in charge of the Ensemble since its inception, invited 31 players to make up the Ensemble. The Ensemble uses an innovative staffing plan where members sign to long-term contracts, but they are required only two-thirds of the normal working time. The rest of the time remains at the musicians' discretion, affording them the opportunity to refresh themselves with different musical activities that the busy members of standard full-time orchestras often don't have time for. Furthermore, Ensemble members often function as a soloists within the group. Smaller sub-groups of the Ensemble are often billed as "Soloists of Ensemble Intercontemporain."

Organizationally, Ensemble Intercontemporain is not a part of IRCAM, although it usually performs there and is widely regarded as an IRCAM's group. In the first twenty years of its existence, the Ensemble performed over 1400 different works, including 200 world premieres, of which 115 were specifically commissioned for the group.

The Ensemble's emphasis is certainly on new works, but it saves a place in its schedule for works considered "classics" of the twentieth century. The Ensemble has recorded frequently, including works by iconoclastic American composer Frank Zappa (1940–93), in an album called *The Perfect Stranger*, although Zappa complained that it was under-rehearsed and inaccurate. —*Joseph Stevenson*

Recommended:

○ **Stockhausen: Donnerstag** / Stockhausen (cond.), Sperry, Arrignon, Gambill, Holle, InterContemporain Ens. / 1992 / Stockhausen-Verlag 030

○ **Boulez: Pli selon Pli** / Schafer (cond.), InterContemporain Ens. / DG 471344

○ **Boulez Conducts Webern** / Boulez (cond.), Aimard, Oelze, Pollet, InterContemporain Ens., BBC Singers / DG 437786

○ **Ligeti Concertos** / Boulez (cond.), Queyras, Aimard, Gawriloff, InterContemporain Ens. / DG 439808

Kurt Equiluz

b. Jun. 13, 1929, Vienna, Austria

Tenor

One of the most distinguished Bach tenors of the twentieth century, Kurt Equiluz began his singing career as soloist with the Vienna Boys Choir. After studies in music theory, harp, and singing at the Austrian State Academy for Music and Art in Vienna, he won several major competitions, including the International Singing Competition in England (1947–48) and the Vienna Mozart Competition (1949). He joined the Vienna State Opera Chorus in 1950 and went on to distinguish himself in 69 different roles, including Pedrillo in Mozart's *Die Entführung aus dem Serail*, Don Curzio in Mozart's *Le nozze di Figaro*, Scaramuccio in Strauss' *Ariadne auf Naxos*, Balthasar Zorn in the Wagner's *Die Meistersinger*, Spoletta in Puccini's *Tosca*, Kaiser Altoum in Puccini's *Turandot*, Monostatos in Mozart's *Die Zauberflöte*, and Rossillon in Léhar's *Lustigen Witwe*. In 1987, he gave his final performance on the opera stage in Gluck's *Iphigénie en Aulide*. With a vocal style best suited to oratorio and lieder, his reputation largely rests on his performances in the complete cycle of Bach cantatas and Passions directed by Harnoncourt and Leonhardt. In 1971, Equiluz was was appointed as professor in Musikhochschule of Graz, and in 1982 as professor at the Wiener Musikakademie. —*Robert Adelson*

Recommended:

○ **Mozart: Requiem** / Harnoncourt (cond.), Equiluz, Holl, Yakar, Wenkel, Concentus Musicus Vienna / 1983 / Teldec 842756

○ **Das Kantatenwerk, Vol.1** / Harnoncourt (cond.), Egmond, Equiluz, Concentus Musicus Vienna / Teldec 35027

Eroica Trio

f. 1986, New York, NY

Ensemble

The Eroica Trio became one of the best-known and most exciting new piano trios in the 1990s, and is among the most successful all-women chamber ensembles in the world. The three members are New Yorkers, born with close connections to the classical music world, and long-time friends.

Pianist Erika Nickrenz is the daughter of former concert pianist and Grammy Award winning classical record producer Joanna Nickrenz and Scott Nickrenz, a leading violinist and founding member of the Orpheus Trio and the Lenox, Claremont, and Vermeer String Quartets. Erika started piano at six, studied with German Diaz at the Claudio Arrau School, then debuted at New York's Town Hall playing a concerto at eleven. She met Adela Peña at the Greenwich House Music School when they were both nine and they played sonatas together.

Adela Peña was raised by parents who were fans of the great violinist Jascha Heifetz and noticed that as a baby Adela would cry if they turned off his recording of the Beethoven concerto before it was over. She asked for a violin at age four. She studied with Rochelle Walton for eight years and at Greenwich House studying chamber music. She then attended the pre-college program of the Juilliard School of Music, where her primary teacher was Margaret Pardee.

Meanwhile, Erika went to the Red Fox Music Camp to study with Isabelle Sant'Ambrogio, grandmother of Sara Sant'Ambrogio. Sara's father was a cellist in the Boston Symphony Orchestra, then moved to St. Louis where he is the principal cellist for the St. Louis Symphony.

All three were admitted to the Juilliard School, where they studied chamber music with Felix Galimir and founded the Eroica, taking its name, meaning "heroic," from the title of Beethoven's *Third Symphony.* In 1991, the Trio won the Naumberg Award, which gave them a Lincoln Center Debut performance. They quickly gained a reputation for passion and excitement in their performances, and for innovative programs that span over three hundred years of music history.

The Trio played at Carnegie Hall for the first time in 1997, and gained an exclusive five-CD recording contract with EMI Classics. The debut album reflected the diversity of their repertory by including music of Maurice Ravel, Benjamin Godard, Gershwin, and Paul Schoenfield's *Café Music.* The disc was NPR Performance Today's Debut Recording of the Year and a Top Ten Recording of 1997 according to *Time Out New York.* The second disc was more traditional, comprising trios of Rachmaninov, Shostakovich, and Dvořák. The Eroica's third disc was a Baroque recital, and the fourth disc featured music of Piazzolla, Villa-Lobos, and Turina.

The Eroica is one of the most active of piano trios in the field of orchestral performance. It plays more concerts of Beethoven's *Triple Concerto* (the leading work for trio and orchestra) than any other group, and has commissioned two full-scale works for trio and orchestra, which they were scheduled to premiere with the Milwaukee and St. Louis Symphonies in the 2001–2002 seasons. They also premiered *Tango for Seven* by Raimundo Penaforte for an innovative combination: string trio plus string quartet, which they played with the St. Lawrence String Quartet.

The Trio has appeared on many television programs and in articles in music, entertainment and fashion magazines, perhaps reflecting their stage appearance: since 1999, their concert-wear has been specially designed by Carmen Marc Valvo. They have appeared around the world, and often teach at schools, ranging from general music education appearances in elementary schools to master classes for accomplished music students. *—Joseph Stevenson*

Recommended:

- ○ **Eroica Trio** / / 1997 / EMI 56482
- ○ **Pasión** / Eroica Trio / 2000 / Angel 57033B
- ○ **Brahms: Trios 1 & 2** / Eroica Trio / 2002 / EMI 57199

Christoph Eschenbach

b. Feb. 20, 1940, Breslau (Wroclaw), Poland
Conductor, Pianist

Christoph Eschenbach overcame the most difficult of circumstances to become one of the finest pianists and conductors of the late twentieth century. He was orphaned at a young age: his mother died in childbirth and his father, the musicologist Heribert Ringmann, was killed in battle during World War II. His adoptive grandmother was then killed while trying to extract him and herself from the path of the Allied armies. Fortunately for the young boy, his mother's cousin, Wallydore Eschenbach, tracked him down after the war and adopted him from the refugee camp that would likely have claimed his life. It is from her side of the family that he eventually took his better-known surname.

Eschenbach began studying piano at the age of eight, taught by his adoptive mother. She quickly realized his talents and enrolled him in the Hamburg Hochschule für Musik, where he studied both piano and conducting. As a boy he won First Prize in the 1952 Steinway Piano Competition, and in 1962 he took second prize in the Munich International competition; however, it was with his first prize at the Clara Haskil Competition in Montreux, France, in 1965, that he finally made his mark. This new notoriety led to a London concert debut in 1966, and a prestigious debut with the Cleveland Orchestra and George Szell in 1969. Szell was impressed with his musicianship and gave him lessons in conducting, starting a close relationship that lasted until Szell's death in 1970.

Eschenbach was soon essaying a wide repertory in concert tours throughout Europe and America. Notable in his programs were a large number of works from twentieth century composers, such as Bartók, Henze, Rihm, Reimann, Blacher, and Ruzicka; however, his performances of Mozart, Beethoven, and Schubert were considered revelatory.

Eschenbach made his conducting debut in 1972 with a performance of Bruckner's *Symphony No. 3,* soon followed by Verdi's *La Traviata* at Darmstadt in 1978. In 1979 he was named general music director of the Rheinland-Pfalz State Philharmonic (through 1981). He was permanent guest conductor, then chief conductor of the Zürich Tonhalle Orchestra (1971–85).

In 1988 he began his most significant and productive association to date as music director of the Houston Symphony Orchestra, where he remained until 1999. Although the orchestra was already established as one of America's finer major symphonies, Eschenbach improved its standards, heightened its international reputation, and broadened its repertory. He also formed the Houston Symphony Chamber Players from its ranks. Eschenbach conducted the Houston Symphony in recordings on the Koch International, Virgin, RCA Red Seal, Telarc, and Carlton labels. These included standard fare such as some highly regarded Brahms and Tchaikovsky recordings and all of the major Mozart wind concertos (with the orchestra's own soloists). He and the Houston Symphony also recorded Kurt Weill's *The Rise and Fall of the City Mahagonny* suite, Tobias Picker's *Les Encantadoras,* and the violin concertos of John Adams and Philip Glass.

From 1991 to 1998 he was co-artistic director of the Pacific Music Festival, along with Michael Tilson Thomas. In 1994 Eschenbach was appointed music director of the *Ravinia Festival,* the summer outdoor season of the Chicago Symphony Orchestra. In the 1998–99 season he became music director of the North German Radio Symphony Orchestra of Hamburg, and, concurrently, artistic director of its Schleswig-Holstein Festival. In 2003, he became music director of the Philadelphia Orchestra. *—AMG*

Recommended:

- ○ **Christoph Eschenbach** / Karajan (cond.), Eschenbach, Berlin PO / 1999 / Philips 456763
- ○ **Strauss: 4 Last Songs; Songs with Orchestra; Rosenkavalier Suite** / Eschenbach (cond.), Fleming, Houston SO / 2004 / RCA 59408
- ○ **Mozart: The Piano Sonatas** / Eschenbach / 1971 / DG 463137
- ○ **Violin Concertos of Adams & Glass** / Eschenbach (cond.), McDuffie, Houston SO / 1999 / Telarc 80494
- ○ **Schnittke: Complete Violin Concertos** / Eschenbach (cond.), Kremer, Senft, Philharmonia Orch. / 2000 / Teldec 26866
- ○ **Schoenberg: Pelleas und Melisnade; Webern: Passacaglia** / Eschenbach, Houston SO / 1995 / Koch 37316

Paul Esswood

b. Jun. 6, 1942, West Bridgeford
Countertenor

Before the emergence of David Daniels as a countertenor superstar, Paul Esswood alone offered a rounded, settled, womanly sound spun around a firm, even vibrato. He quickly made his way among conductors who appreciated both his conscientious musicianship and beautiful sound. His now-legendary series of Bach recordings made with Nikolaus Harnoncourt in the 1970s still gives much pleasure even though Baroque-period performing styles have evolved since then. Esswood trained at the Royal Academy of Music from 1961, studying under baritone Gordon Clinton. Beginning in 1964, he was a lay vicar at Westminster Abbey, remaining in that position until 1971. During that same period, several significant debuts took place; his first professional performance took place in a 1965 broadcast of the *Messiah* with conductor Charles Mackerras (with whom he later recorded the work) and in 1968, he made his stage debut in Cavalli's *Erismena* in Berkeley, CA. The following year, he made his European opera debut singing the title role in Scarlatti's *Il Tigrane* at Basle. His fluency and command in Baroque operas quickly led to other performances in stage works by Monteverdi, Scarlatti, and Handel. During 1971 alone, he appeared in all three of Monteverdi's best-known operas, essaying *Il ritorno d'Ulisse in patria* in Vienna, *Orfeo* at the *Salzburg Festival,* and *L'Incoronazione di Poppea* in Amsterdam. During the 1976–77 season at Zurich, Esswood repeated the Monteverdi works in a cycle of productions directed by Jean Ponnelle with Harnoncourt conducting, which was subsequently recorded and filmed for worldwide broadcast. Polish composer Krzysztof Penderecki's *Paradise Lost* featured Esswood in the role of Death at both its 1978 premiere in Chicago and at La Scala the following season. In 1984, Esswood created the title role in Philip Glass' *Akhnaten* at Stuttgart (another role of his subsequently released on recording) and in 1988, he sang Oberon in Britten's *A Midsummer Night's Dream* in Cologne. At Karlsruhe's *1990 Handel Festival,* he performed the title role in *Admeto* and sang *Riccardo Primo* during the *1991 English Bach Festival* at Covent Garden. A later premiere found Esswood creating the role of Seff in Herbert Willi's *Schlafes Bruder* in Zürich and repeating the role in a second production at Innsbruck. In addition to opera, Esswood has been active as a recitalist and concert singer. On both the concert stage and at many of the world's leading festivals, he has performed works spanning several centuries, including the period of Romanticism, and works from modern times. In addition to Penderecki's *Paradise Lost,* Esswood also sang the premiere of his *Magnificat.* Two premieres of works by Alfred Schnittke featured performances by Esswood: the *Faust Cantata* and the *Symphony No. 2 "St. Florian,"* the latter yet another example of his work now available on disc. During a long career, Esswood has participated in more than 150 recordings, including no fewer than four of Handel's *Messiah.* His Bach series for Teldec includes the complete cantatas, while his solo recordings engage the music of Purcell, Schumann, and Britten with many others in between. Since 1985, Esswood has been a professor of Baroque vocal studies at the Royal Academy of Music. In 1967, he co-founded the *Pro Cantione Antiqua.* *—Erik Eriksson*

Recommended:

- ○ **Songs to My Lady: English Songs & Lute Pieces** / Esswood / HM 1903012
- ○ **Glass: Akhnaten** / Davies (cond.), Esswood, Hauptmann, Vargas, Liebermann, Stuttgart State Opera Orch. & Chorus / 2003 / Sony 91141
- ○ **Monteverdi: L'Incoronazione di Poppea** / Harnoncourt (cond.), Berberian, Esswood, Langridge, Soderstrom, Vienna Concentus Musicus / 1993 / Teldec 42547
- ○ **Bach: Sacred Cantatas** / Harnoncourt, Leonhardt (conds.), Hampson, Egmond, Esswood, Jacobs, Vienna Concentus Musicus / 1994 / Teldec 91765

○ **Bach: Matthäus-Passion** / Harnoncourt (cond.), Esswood, Egmond, Equiluz, Rogers, Vienna Concentus Musicus / 1994 / Teldec 42509

Simon Estes

b. Feb. 2, 1938, Centerville, IA

Bass

One of just a few African-American male singers who has had a top-rank international operatic career, bass-baritone Simon Estes grew up in Iowa in a house without heat or indoor plumbing. He sang in church as a youth, but when he enrolled at the University of Iowa in the late 1950s he had never heard an opera and had no idea he wanted to become a professional singer. He joined an a cappella quartet called the Old Gold Singers, where a professor of voice heard him and invited him to listen to some recordings of opera. Estes took to the music immediately and moved on to study at the Julliard School in New York and later in Europe. Office workers at New York's NAACP office passed the hat to pay for his trip.

Estes attracted attention when he won a silver medal at the Tchaikovsky Competition in Moscow in 1966, and soon he was winning major roles in European houses. He became identified with Wagner roles, and in 1978 he became the first African-American male to sing a lead role at the Wagnerian shrine of Bayreuth (in *Der fliegende Holländer*). His Metropolitan Opera debut in New York came in 1982, in *Tannhäuser*, and he made a return appearance three years later, as Porgy in Gershwin's *Porgy and Bess*. That production was one of the hits of the 1980s at the Met, and for a time Estes was a familiar face in newspapers and magazines, and even on television.

Outspoken about the lack of opportunities for black male singers in opera, even compared with black women, Estes suffered the effects of racism on many occasions. At one Italian production of *Aida* he was forced to wear white makeup, and he was once accused of jewelry theft while staying at a hotel in the American South in the 1970s. Estes pointed to the virtually all-white world of opera administration as a factor in holding back African-American singers; audiences, he believed, were interested in the voice above all else.

With a repertory that topped 100 roles, Estes has remained a familiar figure on operatic stages for several decades. His 1999 autobiography, *In His Own Voice*, was notable in that it was accompanied by a CD illustrating the development of his voice over time. —*James Manheim*

Recommended:

○ **Bizet: Carmen** / Ozawa (cond.), Freni, Norman, Estes, Rivenq, National Orch. of France / 2002 / Decca 470417

○ **Wagner: Der fliegende Holländer** / Nelsson (cond.), Salminen, Estes, Clark, Schunk, Bayreuth Festival Orch. / 1992 / Philips 434599

○ **Stravinsky: Oedipus Rex** / Salonen (cond.), Otter, Gedda, Cole, Estes, Swedish Radio Orch. / 1992 / Sony 48057

Estonian Philharmonic Chamber Choir

f. 1981

Ensemble

The Estonian Philharmonic Chamber Choir was founded in 1981 by Tõnu Kaljuste. It succeeded the amateur chamber choir Ellerhein (founded by Kaljuste's father, Heino Kaljuste, in 1966), which in turn had succeeded the children's choir Ellerhein founded in 1951. Tõnu Kaljuste served as the choir's principal conductor and artistic director until Paul Hillier assumed leadership of the choir in 2001. The choir performs repertoire ranging from Gregorian chant to contemporary composers and is particularly noted for its performances of the music of Arvo Pärt and other Estonian composers. The choir has also performed with numerous guest conductors, including David Willcocks, Helmuth Rilling, Claudio Abbado, Anders Öhrwall, Jon Washburn, Eric Ericson, Ward Swingle, and Ivan Fisher. In 1991, the choir won three gold medals and was awarded the Grand Prix at the Takarazuka Chamber Choir Competition in Japan. It has toured the United States, Canada, Japan, Australia, and Europe. —*Robert Adelson*

Recommended:

○ **Pärt: Beatus** / Kaljuste (cond.), Bowers-Broadbent, Urb, Kogermann, Salumae, Saul, Estonian Phil. Choir / 2003 / Virgin 562205

○ **The Powers of Heaven** / Hillier (cond.), Estonian Phil. Choir / 2003 / HM 907318

○ **Tormis: Casting a spell...** / Kaljuste (cond.), Estonian Phil. Choir / 1996 / Virgin 45185

○ **Pärt: Kanon Pokajanen** / Kaljuste (cond.), Estonian Phil. Choir / 1998 / ECM 457834

Jacob van Eyck

b. ca. 1590, Netherlands, **d.** Mar. 26, 1657, Utrecht, Netherlands

Composer: Chamber Music

Jacob van Eyck was a blind Dutch carillonist, recorder player, and composer. Though he is known today largely for his collection of recorder solos, *Der Fluyten Lust-hof*, his contributions to the art of carillon-making and playing were substantial.

Van Eyck spent his early years at Heusden in southern Holland before being appointed carillonist in Utrecht in 1625, and had several pupils. He was the first to discover the link between the overtone structure and the shape of the bell. In partnership with the famous bellfounders, the Hemony brothers, he worked out the dimensions for the "pure" bell, which spread throughout Europe and became the standard carillon bells. His theory is still used by bellfounders today. Van Eyck's bells have a minor overtone series causing the characteristic melancholy sound of a well-tuned carillon.

In addition to his carillon duties, the cathedral paid Van Eyck an additional salary to wander the grounds of Utrecht cathedral and entertain the passers-by with songs on his recorder. He (presumably consequently) became a skilled improviser on a theme and three collections of his variations for descant recorder were published: Euterpe and the two parts of Der Fluyten Lust-hof (or "The Flute's Pleasure-Garden"). Der Fluyten Lust-hof contains 144 sets of variations on a variety of melodies popular in Renaissance Holland. One of the best known is the variation on Dowland's *Pavane Lacrymae*. Although Van Eyck wrote them for amateur musicians, the different sets commonly increase in technical difficulty towards the end. Some of them are very difficult indeed. This is one of the largest Renaissance collections of solo recorder music. It is particularly unusual as the instrument used is the less popular descant recorder rather than the more common alto. —*David Cashman*

CHAMBER MUSIC

Der Fluyten Lust-hof (ca. 1646)

Little is known of van Eyck, other than that he held the post of carillonneur at Utrecht Cathedral in the Netherlands in 1624, and in 1648, two years after the publication of *Der Fluyten Lust-hof* (The Flute's Pleasure Garden), was given a raise of 50 guilders by the town council because "he delighted the strollers in the [cathedral] cemetery with the sound of his little flute."

The original edition of 150 pieces was published in two parts; its title page of which gives the contents as comprising "psalms, pavanes, Allemands, courantes, ballets, airs, etc., ... artistically presented with figurations and variations." Written for a solo instrument, the work contains, in addition to the aforementioned types, free variations of a more virtuoso character, such as an "Echo Fantasia" and six modal variations on "Enels Nachtegaltje" (The Nightingale). There are no indications of speed, phrasing, or ornamentation, but the simplicity and liveliness of these predominantly short pieces have survived the years to charm both professional and amateur players, and many selections have been edited and published in modern editions. Van Eyck's "little flute" was almost certainly a soprano recorder, and this is still the most appropriate instrument on which to play the pieces.

These innocent inventions contrast strikingly with the complex and serious works associated with the seventeenth century Netherlands school of composers, and the thought of this humble, talented functionary moving around the quiet churchyard "delighting the strollers," his music blending with bells of the carillon, is touching and evocative. —*Roy Brewer*

Recommended:

○ **Eyck: Der Fluyten Lust-Hof** / M. Verbruggen / 1993 / HM 907072

Hans Fagius

b. Apr. 10, 1951, Norköpping, Sweden

Organist

As the artist who has recorded longest with the BIS label, Hans Fagius has an impressive repertoire that includes organ music of several eras. Fagius' early organ lessons were with Nils Eriksson and Bengt Berg. His 1974 soloist's diploma from the Stockholm's Royal College of Music was earned under Alf Linder. That same year, he made his public debut in Stockholm. He spent the following year in Paris, doing private study with Maurice Duruflé. Fagius then began giving concerts, traveling to America and Australia, as well as throughout Europe. Although he has focused more and more on the Baroque, doing his own research into the era, he has performed and recorded organ works of the Renaissance, Baroque, and Romantic eras, and works by Swedish composers of all eras. In the early 1980s in Stockholm, and again in 1996 in Copenhagen, Fagius performed a series of recitals to present the entirety of J.S. Bach's organ works, which he has also recorded. In addition, he has recorded the organ symphonies of Widor; the complete organ music of Kodály; and several duet albums with artists such as David Sanger, organ; Mats Jansson, piano; Rolf Leanderson, baritone; and Gunilla von Bahr, flute. Fagius has taught at the Royal Danish Conservatory since 1989 and the Swedish Royal Academy of Music since 1998. *—Patsy Morita*

Recommended:

○ **Hans Fagius Plays Organ Favorites** / Fagius / 1987 / Bis 365

○ **Hans Fagius** / Fagius / 1980 / Bis 156

○ **Bach: Orgelbüchlein** / Fagius / 1986 / Bis 329

Manuel de Falla

b. Nov. 23, 1876, Cádiz, Spain, **d.** Nov. 14, 1946, Alta Gracia, Córdoba, Argentina

Composer: Ballet, Chamber Music, Keyboard, Concerto, Opera, Vocal

Part Spanish nationalist, part Impressionist, and part Neo-Classicist, Manuel de Falla is difficult to peg, but is widely regarded as the most distinguished Spanish composer of the early twentieth century. His output is small but choice, and revolves largely around music for the stage. Falla's reputation is based primarily on two lavishly Iberian ballet scores: *El amor brujo* (Love, the Magician), from which is drawn the *Ritual Fire Dance* (a pops favorite, often heard in piano or guitar transcriptions), and the splashy *El Sombrero de tres picos* (The Three-Cornered Hat). He also gained a permanent place in the concert repertory with his evocative piano concerto, *Nights in the Gardens of Spain.*

Born in 1876, Falla first took piano lessons from his mother in Cádiz, and later moved to Madrid to continue the piano and to study composition with Felipe Pedrell, the musical scholar who had earlier pointed Isaac Albéniz toward Spanish folk music as a source for his compositions. Pedrell interested Falla in Renaissance Spanish church music, folk music, and native opera. The latter two influences are strongly felt in *La Vida breve* (Life Is Short), an opera (a sort of Spanish *Cavalleria rusticana*) for which Falla won a prize in 1905, although the work was not premiered until 1913.

A second significant aesthetic influence resulted from Falla's 1907 move to Paris, where he met and fell under the Impressionist spell of Claude Debussy, Paul Dukas, and Maurice Ravel. It was in Paris that he published his first piano pieces and songs. In 1914 Falla was back in Madrid, working on the application of a quasi-Impressionistic idiom to intensely Spanish subjects; *El amor brujo* drew on Andalusian folk music. Falla wrote another ballet in 1917, *El Corregidor y la molinera* (The Magistrate and the Miller Girl). Diaghilev persuaded him to expand the score for a ballet by Léonide Massine to be called *El sombrero de tres picos*, and excerpts from the full score have become a staple of the concert repertory. In between the two ballets came *Nights in the Gardens of Spain*, a suite of three richly scored impressions for piano and orchestra, again evoking Andalusia.

In the 1920s, Falla altered his stylistic direction, coming under the influence of Stravinsky's Neo-Classicism. Works from this period include the puppet opera *El retablo de Maese Pedro* (The Altarpiece of Maese Pedro), based on an episode from *Don Quixtote*, and a harpsichord concerto, with the folk inspiration now Castilian rather than Andalusian. After 1926 he essentially retired, living first in Mallorca and, from 1939, in Argentina. He was essentially apolitical, but the rise of fascism in Spain contributed to his decision to remain in Latin America after traveling there for a conducting engagement. He spent his final years in the Argentine desert, at work on a giant cantata, *Atlántida*, which remained unfinished at his death in 1946. *—James Reel*

BALLET

El Amor brujo (1915–1917)

There has been an enormous amount of confusion about the various versions of Manuel de Falla's ballet *El amor brujo*, even down to the translation of the title, which properly is "Love the Magician." Falla composed the work in 1914–15, using a story by María and Gregorio Martinez-Sierra about a young Gypsy woman, Candelas, who wins back her indifferent lover's affections, not with magic (which she tries), but with the magic of love. Hence, "Love the Magician." In 1916, Falla arranged a rendition of the work for sextet and small orchestra. The following year, he made a concert version of the work, also for small orchestra. Later, he fashioned a piano suite from it and finally, a second ballet version (1925) that features expanded orchestration, elimination of the narration, small cuts and plot changes, and a different order to the numbers. It is this second version of *El amor brujo* that is the most popular today, both in concert halls and recording studios. Each rendition has two scenes and features a mezzo-soprano soloist. The most immediately obvious difference to the listener between the two ballet versions lies in the scoring: the original was written for 14 instruments only, while the latter is scored for a more standard-sized ensemble. Their lengths vary considerably, too, with the original lasting 10 to 15 minutes longer. The discarding of the narration accounts in part for the reduction in length, but not all since much of it is spoken during instrumental sections. Perhaps the most noticeable difference in the re-arrangement of the numbers comes with the appearance of the work's most-famous theme, that of the *Ritual Fire Dance.* It is first heard fourth in the original, "Dance at the End of the Day," whereas the fourth number in the later version is the very brief "The Apparition." This is followed by the "Dance of Terror," neither of which contains that theme, though the eighth does. Another example of Falla's re-arrangement of the music is the shifting of "Song of Love's Sorrow" from the second in the original, to the third number in the second ballet version. There are, of course, further differences in the order of the numbers, as well as slightly different titles to some of them, but on the whole the work remains in spirit quite the same in both versions. Some listeners will be distracted by the narration, because it often intrudes on the music: the aforementioned No. 4 in the original ballet version, for instance, features narration at the beginning of the number, though it is only very brief. Others will want it to enhance the dramatic elements in the story and will also favor the more delicate scoring of the original. *—Robert Cummings*

Synopsis:

Scene One. The setting is a seaside either in Cádiz or Malaga. It is night. Candelas, a young Gypsy woman, sits with an old Gypsy woman on a room. A small brazier sits on the floor, and the two sit by it, reading their cards. The sea pounds loudly outside. Candelas fears the sea speaks ill, but the old woman cautions here that the sea says nothing. Occasionally, the voice of another young Gypsy girl, waiting outside for her lover, is heard.

Everything seems an ill omen to Candelas—the wind blowing out the lamp, the way the cards fall, a dog barking in the street. She reads the cards by the light of her cigarette, then angrily throws them down, saying that they tell her "that he has never loved me." She gets up and sings "Canción del amor dolido" (The song of sorrowful love).

Midnight strikes and the brief music of a "Sortilegio" (Magic Spell) sounds. Candelas laments that she has lived through another day without seeing him. Hoping to follow a good path the next day, she relights the brazier, throws on incense, and dances "Danza del fin de dia" (Dance of the End of the Day), which contains the music that later would be retitled "Danza Rituel del Fuego" (Ritual Fire Dance).

When the dance is over, she can hear through the window that the younger Gypsy girl is rejoicing because her lover has arrived. Sadly, Candelas watches the girl go to meet him, then sings the sad "Romance del pescador" (Romance of the fisherman) a song of lost love. Its words give her an answer: she must go to the cave of the witch. "If she does not give me an answer, then I wish to die!" she proclaims.

Scene Two. The introduction to Scene Two, which is set in the witch's cave, is the number "El Fuego fatuo" (Will-o'-the-Wisp). The curtain comes up to reveal the cave in a fantastic moonlit landscape. Will-o'-the-Wisp dances madly about the scene and the cave.

To music called "El terror," Candelas walks the path approaching the cave. She calls three times and receives no answer, meanwhile Will-o'-the-Wisp hides itself and its dim light in the corner where the witch's magical paraphernalia is kept. Hearing no answer, Candelas timidly enters the cave to discover it empty. Perhaps the witch is out visiting the Devil, or riding on her broomstick, she thinks. The flickering light of the Will-o'-the-Wisp seems to draw her toward the charms, potions, and herbs in the corner, but she jerks her hand back at the last minute everytime she is close to touching one. "If I were brave enough I would work the spell," she muses. She steels herself, shuts her eyes, reaches out—and touches the magic objects. A dull sound like thunder peals out and Will-o'-the-Wisp comes out from hiding to attack Candelas for defiling the magic.

Will-o'-the-Wisp attacks her and she dances frantically to get away from it, but in resisting it she also gains strength and confidence, and soon it yields before her, finally fleeing out the cave entrance ("Danza de la fuego fatuo"). Following a musical interlude called "Alucinaciones" (Hallucinations), she sings "Canción del Fuego fatuo" (Song of the Will-o'-the-Wisp).

Having gained control of the cave, she uses the magic items to work a spell. ("Conjuro para reconquistar al amor perdido"—Conjuration to recapture lost love) The stage grows dark as the almost full moon sets a little before dawn. When it turns pitch black, the sound of chains being dragged echoes through the cave.

Suddenly sweet music is heard ("El amor popular"—Popular love, a title that means that the strange music takes on the sound of a popular love song). A red dot appears on the path. It is the cigar being smoked by Candelas' lover, approaching on the path. Candelas' notices it and recognizes him before he is aware of her presence. She decides to play a trick on him to pay him back for the heartache she has suffered. At that point his cigar goes out.

The Gypsy man asks if there is someone in the cave who can light his cigar. Candelas disguises her voice to invite him in, and in an aside says she will light a flame to burn his heart. He enters the cave and lights his cigar with the fire that burns therein, and makes to leave. Candelas, still hidden in the darkness, remarks that he is in a hurry. The Gypsy replies that two dark eyes are waiting to shine with love when he returns. Candelas says she will have to wait a long time, emerges from the shadows (a veil concealing her identity), and dances and sings a seductive dance that weaves its spell around him ("Danza y canción de la bruja fingida"—Dance and song of the pretend witch). She chastises him for loving a Gypsy girl and throwing her over for another woman, and orders him away. Instead he approaches. She pretends to be the witch, and says if he touches her his hand will burn. But he can't resist trying to approach her as she continues to dance sensuously. He tries to grab her but succeeds only in removing the veil.

Stunned, he recognizes her as Candelas, who now says she will leave him in darkness forever. As the sun rises and "Las campanas del amanecer" (The bells of daybreak) are heard, he begs Candelas' forgiveness. She continues to walk away, as he follows, calling her name. "The day is dawning; let my glory ring out!" she cries in triumph. *—Joseph Stevenson*

Recommended:

- ○ **Falla: Three Cornered Hat; El Amor Brujo** / Dutoit (cond.), Tourangeau, Montreal SO / 1983 / London 410008
- ○ **Falla: La vida breve; El amor brujo; El sombrero de tres picos** / Giulini (cond.), Los Angeles, London PO / 2001 / EMI 67590

El Sombrero de tres picos (1917–1919)

When Serge Diaghilev took his ballets russes on tour in Spain, he approached Manuel de Falla for a work for his troupe. Diaghilev was introduced to Falla's pantomime *El Corregidor y la molinera*, which Falla had written between 1915 and 1917. (Pedro de Alarcón's popular story had also been used by Hugo Wolf for an opera in 1895.) Diaghilev asked Falla to expand the work into a one-act ballet, *El sombrero de tres picos*, which was premiered in London on July 22, 1919, with Ernest Ansermet conducting, choreography by Leonide Massine, and sets designed by Pablo Picasso. Both the pantomime and the ballet were a return to Falla's roots in many respects. He had spent time in Paris, learning to love and use the techniques of Debussy, Ravel, and Stravinsky, among others, and been criticized for it. This story was based on Spanish folk-ways and Falla's music used Spanish folk idioms and dances. The debut of the ballet by a foreign company, with "modern" choreography, was also criticized, but the work was highly successful overall. Two suites of excerpts have become some of Falla's most well-known works heard in concert halls. A fanfare-like introduction, complete with castanets, clapping, shouts of "Olé," and a mezzo-soprano's warning that the Devil is about, precedes the two-part ballet. The first part opens with an afternoon scene of the miller and his wife at work, a blackbird (the piccolo) singing along. When the tricorne-wearing magistrate comes to romance the miller's wife, it is marked by the bassoon. She dances a fandango and flirts with him, but ultimately she refuses him. That evening, the neighbors dance seguidillas and the miller gives his own driven farruca. Referencing Fate's knock from Beethoven's *Symphony No. 5*, the miller is arrested and the mezzo-soprano warns the abandoned wife. The bassoon again marks the return of the Corregidor dancing his refined, old-fashioned minuet. This is interrupted by a wild splash of the strings, harp, and woodwinds as he falls into the millrace. The miller, who has escaped, comes back to thwart the magistrate. The neighbors dance a jota, to celebrate the magistrate's humiliation. Although employing many Spanish-flavored rhythms and turns of musical phrase, Falla's music still shows traits of what he learned in Paris: the translucency of harmony and colorful use of orchestral timbres. It is so vivid and eloquent that the action is obvious and delightful even without seeing the ballet dancers. *—Patsy Morita*

Synopsis:

(The story is set in a small Spanish village, presumably around the turn of the twentieth century.) The miller and his wife live an idyllic life in their pleasant village. Things change quickly for them, however, when the womanizing Corregidor, or provincial governor, arrives. He is an elderly man who wears a three-cornered hat, which signifies his rank in the local government. He boldly makes advances to the miller's wife and is not only rebuffed but ridiculed.

The governor will not stand for such treatment by simple folk and orders the miller arrested. When he is taken away, the Corregidor carries on with his pursuit of the miller's wife. She pushes him into a nearby river, however, and, outraged and drenched, he hurries away to dry his clothes. He soon reappears wearing a nightshirt he finds in the miller's home, and the wardrobe change results in some cleverly humorous mix-ups. The miller has made a successful jailbreak and sees the governor attired so, thus concluding he has made inroads in his quest to seduce his wife. He swears vengeance on the old scoundrel. Soldiers arrive and arrest the governor, mistaking him for the miller. The confusion ends when villagers appear and expel the Corregidor and the soldiers, after which the miller and his wife are reunited and all rejoice in the happy ending. *—Robert Cummings*

Recommended:

- ○ **Falla: La vida breve; El amor brujo; El sombrero de tres picos** / Frühbeck de Burgos (cond.), Philharmonia / 2001 / EMI 67590
- ○ **Falla: Three Cornered Hat; El Amor Brujo** / Dutoit (cond.), Montreal SO / 1983 / London 410008

CHAMBER MUSIC

Homenaje pour "Le tombeau de Claude Debussy," for guitar (1920)

At only three minutes in length, this piece had an influence on guitar writing that is disproportionate to its dimensions. It was composed as a contribution to a special edition of the Paris *Revue musicale* which would be a "tombeau" for Claude Debussy, who had died in 1918. Falla readily agreed, for Debussy had been important in giving him confidence as a composer and promoting interest in his music in France.

Meanwhile, the Spanish guitar virtuoso Miguel Llobet Soles had requested a solo guitar piece. Falla fulfilled both requests with this three-minute work in the rhythm of a slow habanera, dignified but not funereal in tread, restrained on the surface but with an impression of intense emotion beneath. At the end, Falla briefly quotes Debussy's piano work *Soirée dans Grenade*, honoring Debussy directly and also paying homage to the city of Grenada, which is where Falla composed the piece. He prepared a piano transcription of the work immediately, and the guitar version was published in the December 1922 *Revue musicale*. Falla's original autograph of the work, however, has been lost. In 1936, Llobet published his own edition of the music, but it diverges significantly from the 1922 publication. In the absence of any authority for the changes in the Llobet version, commentators assume that the 1922 text is authentic. In 1938–39 Falla orchestrated this composition, along with similar musical tributes he had written for composers Arbós, Dukas, and Pedrell, to make his last completed composition, *Homenajes* (Homages) for orchestra. *—Joseph Stevenson*

Recommended:

- ○ **Spanish Guitar Music** / Williams / 2002 / Legacy 89837

Suite Populaire Espagnole, for violin & piano (1926)

Just before Manuel de Falla left Paris to return to Spain in 1914, he completed his harmonizations of *Siete canciones populares españoles* for voice and piano using natural overtones to accompany the melody notes rather than traditional modal scales. Violinist Paul Kochanski (1887–1934) worked with Falla to transcribe six of the songs for violin and piano, leaving out the *Seguidilla murciana*. Since then, the songs have become the most famous of any of Kochanski's transcriptions, and many transcriptions for other instruments also have been made of the songs (including the *Seguidilla*). Kochanski's work was entitled *Suite populaire espagnole*, and that same title has been used for most of the other arrangements as well. The ordering of the songs in Kochanski's arrangement did not follow Falla's original score, but many performers prefer to restore Falla's numbering. Kochanski's suite begins with *El paño moruno* (The Moorish Cloth), to which Kochanski added pizzicato figures. The next songs, *Nana* (a lullaby) and *Canción*, are both based on popular published tunes. *Jota* is Falla's own work in the style of folk dance music from Aragon; for this song Kochanski uses pizzicato chords as if to imitate castanets. The most famous of the songs by far is *Asturiana*, a lament from northern Spain, played on muted strings. The final *Polo* is again an original Falla piece in the style of a folk dance, sometimes described as gypsy- or flamenco-like. *—Patsy Morita*

Recommended:

○ **Daniel Shafran, cello** / Shafran / 1952 / Omega 1026

○ **Jacqueline du Pré: Early BBC Recordings 1961–1965** / du Pré, Lush / 1999 / EMI 73377

KEYBOARD

Four Spanish pieces (Cuatro Piezas españolas) (1906–1909)

The piano did not figure as importantly in Falla's career as may be expected of the man who succeeded Albéniz and Granados as Spain's most prominent composer. Yet his *Obras Españolas* mark the first tentative flowering of Falla's own voice and were significantly dedicated to Albéniz. Strictly speaking, only three of these pieces are Spanish; the second item, "Cubana," is a colonial import. The first movement, "Aragonesa," is strongly indebted to Albéniz, although Falla's textures are generally less dense. This is nevertheless a glittering showpiece based on dance rhythms of Spain's Aragon region. Like each of its companions, it ends pianissimo. "Cubana" is quieter and smokier, but not substantially slower. "Montanesa" provides the suite's slow movement, a dreamy Spanish barcarolle with a brief, extroverted middle section. "Andaluza" takes listeners to the home office of flamenco music, incorporating buleria and zapateado rhythms for a heel-stomping finale until, that is, the final pianissimo. These pieces lack the nervous shimmer of Falla's *Nights in the Gardens of Spain* and *Fantasía Baetica*, but they are well-wrought examples of Spanish nationalism that could almost pass as a fifth book of Albéniz' *Ibéria*. *—James Reel*

Recommended:

○ **Essential Falla** / Larrocha / 1999 / Decca 466128

○ **Spanish Album** / Rodriguez / 1997 / Elan 2206

CONCERTO

Concerto for Harpsichord & 5 instruments (1923–1926)

This spiky neo-Classical *Concerto for Harpsichord* defies everyone's expectations. Most listeners anticipate the Impressionism of Falla's *Nights in the Gardens of Spain* or the Romantic Spanish color of *The Three-Cornered Hat*. Harpsichordist Wanda Landowska, who commissioned the piece, expected a full-blown concerto with the harpsichord having the dominant role. What Falla gave her was, in effect, a sextet in which the harpsichord was only one of six equal partners. Landowska duly gave the first performance in 1926, but bothered to play it only a couple of more times before entirely abandoning it. Knowing that new music for harpsichord would enjoy few hearings in the 1920s, Falla authorized performance of this work on the piano, but only if the pianist tried hard to emulate the harpsichord's sound. Inspired by the harpsichord's antique nature, Falla incorporated old popular, religious, and courtly Spanish melodies into the concerto and took as his stylistic inspiration the busy, clattering little sonatas of eighteenth century Spanish-based composers Domenico Scarlatti and Antonio Soler. But to position this as music of the twentieth century, Falla employed piquant, wrong-note harmonies in the manner of Stravinsky. Indeed, Stravinsky's *L'histoire du soldat* echoes through the snotty first-movement violin part. The harpsichord races into that compact opening Allegro, ignoring the dissonant, cautionary chordal cries of the other instruments. Soon, the flute and oboe try to wrest control of the music away from the hyperactive harpsichord, playing a fifteenth century Castilian folk song in octaves. The various instruments toss this tune around, sometimes spitting it out in staccato bursts and sometimes stretching it out as if to mock the harpsichord's difficulty playing legato melodies. The Lento (giubiloso ed energico) begins with rolled chords from the harpsichord—a lush sound by this instrument's standards—over which the winds, again playing in octaves, offer an austere melody that initially seems to be little more than a cautious scale. It soon evolves into a motif subjected to a canonic imitation so close that the instruments always seem at harmonic odds. Falla apparently intended to evoke Medieval religious ecstasy with this music; inscribed in the score is a reference to the feast of Corpus Christi. Finally comes the Vivace (flessibile, scherzando), a toybox of Baroque effects—trills and swoops—piled into a witty, high-spirited, and largely bitonal dance. *—James Reel*

Recommended:

○ **Falla: Master Peter's Puppet Show; Psyché; Harpsichord Concerto** / Mata (cond.), Puyana, Soloists of Mexico / Dorian 90214

○ **The Essential Falla** / Rattle (cond.), Constable, London Sinfonietta / 1999 / Decca 466128

Noches en los jardines de España (Nights in the Gardens of Spain), for piano & orchestra (1909–1916)

For Falla to gain the freedom of harmonic thinking to become the twentieth century's best-known and most effective author of Spanish music, he paradoxically had to leave Spain and study in Paris, principally with Paul Dukas. By absorbing the free harmonic approach and rich orchestral effects of the likes of Debussy and Ravel, Falla found the vocabulary he need for his own expressions of his native land. *Nights in the Gardens of Spain*, the most shimmeringly Impressionistic of Falla's major works, is a wistful, sultry triptych for piano and orchestra. It begins with a depiction of the gardens of the Generalife near the Alhambra, evoking Granada's Moorish history. Falla's use of the orchestra is colorful but delicate, including distant horn calls and *sul ponticello* effects in the strings to embellish a quivering piano line.

The second movement, "Danza lejana" (Distant Dance), moves to some unspecified, perhaps imaginary garden. Although the dance fragments do indeed begin as if from a distance, they soon come to the forefront, the piano sometimes accompanied by aggressive strumming effects in the strings, and sometimes quietly playing agitated passages over delicate, dark little woodwind solos. Without a pause, this leads into the fast final movement, "In the Gardens of the Sierra de Córdoba." Here the strumming effects become even more prominent, with both orchestra and piano engaging in heavily rhythmic passages inspired by gypsy and flamenco music. But a slower, mysterious Andalusian tune also insinuates itself into the movement, and has the last say as the strings take control of the quiet, soaring melody. *—James Reel*

Recommended:

○ **Chopin, Falla & Rachmaninoff** / Jorda (cond.), Rubinstein, San Francisco SO / 1997 / BMG 68886

○ **The Essential Falla** / Frühbeck de Burgos (cond.), Larrocha, Philharmonia / 1999 / Decca 466128

OPERA

La Vida breve (1905–1913)

The Spanish master Manuel de Falla was a slow-working and fastidious composer who produced a small number of perfectly crafted masterpieces. But he served a kind of apprenticeship writing zarzuelas, six of them in three years' time. This Spanish genre of semi-popular musical drama got him no respect as a serious composer, so he was tempted to try writing a real opera, albeit one full of Spanish and Gypsy folk elements, when the San Fernando Academy of Fine Arts announced a competition for a new opera, with a prompt premiere performance offered as part of the prize.

Falla composed this opera on a text by Carlos Fernández Shaw. The "short life" of the title belongs to a young, love-struck Gypsy girl named Salud, who is hopelessly in love with Paco, a cad who strings her along although he is betrothed to a rich girl of his own station in life. Salud establishes the truth only on the night of their wedding, when she looks into her rival's family courtyard. She then confronts her faithless lover, bitterly accusing him. When he further betrays her by insisting that she is lying, she falls dead at his feet as her family curses him.

The opera is full of colorful Spanish music, including two well-known and often-excerpted Spanish Dances. In addition, the scene around Salud's house involves work songs for a group of offstage blacksmiths, and the wedding party scene is full of flamenco music.

The promised premiere fell through. In disappointment, Falla moved to Paris to study and work there, hoping for more respect that he received at home. The French, particularly Debussy and Dukas, did appreciate the way Falla used his Spanish heritage in music, and Falla's works began to receive performances. Eventually he secured a production of *La vida breve* at the Municipal Casino Theater in Nice, on April 1, 1913. The opera was given there in a French translation by Paul Milliet, with some adjustment of the vocal line by Falla to fit the new text. It was in that form that the work gained its initial international fame. The Spanish premiere soon followed, in November 1914 in Madrid.

The opera shows Falla's deep understanding of the music of Andalusia, particularly the Gypsy music, flamenco, also known as cante jondo. Although an early opera by de Falla, *La Vida Breve* already shows his deep commitment to indigenous Andalusian music, Moorish folk elements, and themes of a cosmic and transcendental nature. Falla left what conductor Eduardo Mata considered to be an interpretational problem in his handling of cante jondo: all such passages in the opera are written for an unembellished line with uniform strummed guitar chords in 3/8 time. This, Mata thought, was an insurance policy that would let the opera be performed even where there was no authentic flamenco guitarist or cantaor available. Most performances and recordings of the opera render it as written. Mata believed that Falla intended, where possible, a real flamenco performance, with improvisation based on his written parts, even when these players and singers might use a more modern flamenco style than Falla knew decades earlier. *—Joseph Stevenson*

Synopsis:

Act One. The opera opens at the home of Salud, a gypsy girl who lives with her extended family in the gypsy quarter of Granada. Salud's grandmother attends to her cage of birds, fussing over one that is ill. It makes her think of her granddaughter, who is sick to death with love. Vendors in the street below sing of their wares, and groups of Spanish girls stroll by, giggling and talking. Salud enters, and sounds from the forge of blacksmiths next door are heard. As they work they sing of those born to misfortune, and Salud rages against her faithless lover, who is ever absent. She begs her grandmother to go and watch for him, for he is late and was expected some time ago. The chorus of blacksmiths continues to sing, and Salud sings the aria "Vivan los que rien!" (Long live those that laugh).

The grandmother finally returns with the news that Paco, the lover, has arrived. He and Salud have a touching love scene in which he promises fidelity. While the two lovers talk, Salud's Uncle Sarvaor comes in and tells the grandmother that Paco is lying to Salud. He is to be married the very next day to a wealthy girl and will abandon her. The grandmother convinces him to say nothing, and they both steal from the room.

A symphonic interlude paints a beautiful picture of Granada at dusk. The city is seen from the heights of Sacro Monte. Birds sing from the branches of the orange and pomegranate trees. Scenes of the waterways and sounds of Spanish dance music merge in an exotic urban portrait. As dark comes, the voices of the people singing and chatting die away into silence.

Act Two. We are in the midst of the wedding celebrations of Paco and Carmela. The setting is the home of Carmela and her brother Manuel. Friends and family of bride and groom fill the garden walks and join in the celebrations. Flamenco guitar rhythms and dance music entertain the guests.

Salud, followed by her grandmother and uncle, sneaks into the grounds behinds the celebrations. Bitter and dejected, she longs to see her faithless Paco one last time. Spying him through a window crevice, she sings to him of how she has died of unhappiness and is no more.

Paco stiffens and turns pale at the sound of Salud's voice. Salud and her uncle enter the courtyard and confront him, in front of all of the wedding guests. At first Paco calls out her name, but when she denounces him, telling those gathered that her very room still echoes with his recent words of love, he tells them that she is lying. He yells to the servants to throw her out of the celebrations. She cannot believe her ears. She takes one step forward, murmurs his name with tender love, then veers unsteadily on her feet and collapses in death. The grandmother and uncle curse Paco as the curtain falls. *—Rita Laurance*

Recommended:

○ **Falla: La vida breve; El amor brujo; El sombrero de tres picos** / Frühbeck de Burgos (cond.), Los Angeles, Cossutta, Narke, Moreno, National Orch. of Spain / 2001 / EMI 67590

○ **Falla: La Vida Breve** / Lopez-Cobos (cond.), Porco, Cid, Nafe, Wadsworth, Cincinnati SO / 1992 / Telarc 80317

VOCAL

Seven Popular Spanish Songs (Siete canciones populares españolas) (1914)

Manuel de Falla had made some studies into the natural overtone series produced by musical vibrations, particularly a treatise by Louis Lucas called *L'Acoustique Nouvelle* (New Acoustics). Lucas had argued that the notes suitable for polyphonic support of a melody are those reflected in the natural overtone series of the sounding note or the note taken as the fundamental tonic. Falla had found that the typical seven-note major or minor scales and the standard harmonies and progressions based on them somehow seemed false when used to set much folk music, particularly those using other kinds of scales or modes. He developed his own ideas of harmony based on Lucas and applied them to a Greek folk song. He liked the results so much he decided to try the same approach to Spanish folk songs or settings of Spanish folk poetry. The settings in *Siete Canciones Españolas* use folk and original melodies, and sometimes even adaptations of the previously published accompaniments to these melodies.

The first song is a famous one from Andalusia called "The Moorish Cloth" (El Paño Moruno), and has the florid vocal line and strumming, guitar-like accompaniment that has become a feature of Spanish music. Falla used this theme also in his ballet *The Three-Cornered Hat.* The accompaniment of the next one ("Seguidilla Murciana" or "Seguidilla," a dance from Murcia) suggests guitar and drum. Third is a lament called "Asturiana," named after the region of northern Spain where it was discovered and published by José Hurtado and B. Fernández. Falla's harmonic innovations include using the fourth degree of the scale as pedal point, teasing the ear into wondering whether that note might be the true center of the song. The ensuing "Jota" is another dance-song, this time from Aragon, followed by "Nana," a lullaby from Andalusia that appears to have been brought to Spain by gypsies from India. Falla told a friend he could remember his mother singing it to him "before he was old enough to think." Number six, simply titled "Canción" (Popular song) is just what its title says, a folk song virtually unchanged by Falla. The finale, called "Polo," is a brilliant Gypsy song, again with guitar-like accompaniment.

The soprano Luisa Vela sang the first public performance of the songs on January 14, 1915, with the composer accompanying. They repeated the cycle to great acclaim during an intermission of the successful first production of *La Vida Breve.* It was immediately chosen by the National Music Society of Madrid for the inaugural concert in its new series, February 8, 1915. Subsequently, Falla's friend and pupil the composer Ernesto Halffter made a highly effective orchestral arrangement of the accompaniment and it has been widely transcribed as an instrumental work for various combinations under the title *Suite populaire espagnole.* *—Joseph Stevenson*

Recommended:

○ **Falla: La vida breve; El amor brujo; El sombrero de tres picos** / Los Angeles, Soriano / 2001 / EMI 67590

○ **Conchita Supervia: In Opera And Song** / Supervia, Marshall / 1992 / Nimbus 7836

Giles Farnaby

b. ca. 1563, England, **d.** Nov. 25, 1640, London, England

Composer

A talented and original, if somewhat uneven, composer of the English Elizabethan and Jacobean age, Giles Farnaby was noted especially for his music for the virginal, a domestic keyboard instrument.

His parents were Thomas and Jane Farnaby. Some accounts conclude that he was of Huguenot descent on his mother's side, since she gave a bequest to the Dutch Reformed and French Protestant churches. Thomas was a joiner (cabinet maker), and trained Giles (sometimes spelled Gyles) in that craft. Farnaby gave "joiner" as his occupation for most of his life.

Farnaby's Uncle Nicholas was also a woodworker, and specialized in making virginals. Farnaby sought a degree in music, studying at Christ Church, Oxford from 1580 to 1592. It is likely that he was also working at the family trade during this period. In 1587 he married Katherine Roane at St. Helen's Church, Bishopsgate. They settled in that parish and had five children, including two daughters named Philadelphia (the first Philadelphia died in infancy). Richard Farnaby and Joyous Farnaby, two of the sons, also became composers.

In 1592 Farnaby wrote nine settings published in Thomas East's *Whole Book of Psalms.* In 1598 he published 20 *Canzonets to Four Voices.* Around 1600 the Farnabys moved to Aisthorpe in Lincolnshire, where they received the lease of an estate in return for Farnaby's instructing Sir Nicholas Saunderson's children in music. By 1611 they were back in London, where they lived in the parish of St. Giles, Cripplegate, until Farnaby's death.

Farnaby had one other publication, *The Psalmes of David,* for voices and viols. He wrote a considerable number of works that were never published, but of his keyboard works appear in the *Fitzwilliam Virginal Book,* the widely distributed English keyboard collection of the day. The best of these pieces are highly spontaneous and original, and in general his style was advanced for the time. The best of his virginal works are perhaps his 11 keyboard fantasias in variation form. His polyphonic works are less praiseworthy, for his large-scale formal thinking was not at the level of his imaginative variation and fantasia treatments.

Farnaby's secular vocal works, the canzonets, are engagingly tuneful, with novel harmonic ideas. *—AMG*

Overview of Works (ca. 1625–1639)

English composer Giles Farnaby was born into a family of joiners and apparently practiced that profession as his main source of income. However, he was also trained as a composer, graduating from Oxford with a bachelor's degree in 1592, and he was listed as a "virginal-maker" in a census done in 1596. The multifarious nature of Farnaby's many careers seems to have diminished his achievement as a composer. While his contemporaries Byrd, Gibbons, Morley, and Bull were more accomplished and polished composers, Farnaby remained something of an amateur. Nevertheless, Farnaby's music has a freshness and spontaneity that their more thought-through music lacks. Best-known for his keyboard works, 51 of which appear in the famous *Fitzwilliam Virginal Book,* Farnaby's music at its best is lyrical, improvisatory, and often deeply felt. While many of his work's have evocative titles, such as *A Toy* and *Giles Farnaby's Dream,* these titles give little clue as to what the music is like. Farnaby also wrote secular vocal works, songs, and madrigal-like harmonizations of popular songs of the day, which while charming, reveal less of the man than his keyboard music. *—James Leonard*

Recommended:

○ **Farnaby's Dream** / Hantai / Adda 581172

○ **Farnaby: Virginal Music** / Tracey, Dery, Skowroneck, Merzdorf, Nobili, Dobernecker / 1993 / FSM Adagio 91614

Geraldine Farrar

b. Feb. 28, 1882, Melrose, MA, **d.** Mar. 11, 1967, Ridgefield, CT

Soprano

Farrar was one of the early stars of the Metropolitan Opera, with a glamorous voice richly matched by her physical presence, and her insistence that she was not a singer but a singing actress. Her recordings were widely popular, and she also made several silent films, including the famous 1915 *Carmen* with Cecil B. DeMille. Her singing ranged from the technically brilliant to the severely flawed, but the essential charm of her voice and her magnetic personality (together with a near-genius for publicity), were enough to ensure her fame. And of course, the debate still lingers over the Butterfly duet. Caruso allegedly came to a recording session after several drinks, and according to many, she substituted "He had a highball" for one of Butterfly's lines. She denied it afterwards, and many listeners swear that the consonants are just distorted, others swear that her substitution is there as clear as day.

She made her public singing debut at age 12, portraying legendary soprano Jenny Lind at a springtime carnival, and began serious voice lessons after that. After studying in Boston, she went to New York, where she studied with Emma Thursby, and was introduced to Lillian Nordica and Nellie Melba. She was also given a successful audition for the Met, but her mother encouraged her to turn their offer down until she was more fully prepared. Her operatic debut was as Marguerite at the Court Opera in Berlin, and even though she sang the role in Italian, while the rest of the cast performed in German, her youthful charm and fresh voice made her a sensation. (And she first entered the gossip columns when rumor had it that she and the Crown Prince were having an affair.) One of her dreams was realized when Lilli Lehmann extended an invitation to study with her. In 1905, she sang at the Munich Opera with Richard Strauss conducting; he suggested that she sing Salome, and he would be glad to make any changes to the vocal line she required, since he was convinced her "Dance of the Seven Veils" would be such a triumph. Her Metropolitan Opera debut was in 1906 as Juliette in Gounod's *Romeo et Juliette*, opening that year's opera season. She soon became the Met's reigning soprano, provoking (probably quite deliberately) near scandals by such realistic touches as singing the scene in Juliette's bedroom while lying down, wearing a nightgown. She was immensely popular with younger opera lovers, who became known as her "Gerry flappers." In 1910, she created the role of the Goose Girl in Humperdinck's *Königskinder* (where she made a sensation by appearing with real geese, which she had trained herself, on stage). Her first Carmen was in 1914, and that following summer, she made the DeMille film, followed by several others, *Maria Rosa*, *Temptation*, *Joan the Woman* (about Joan of Arc), *The Woman God Forgot*, and *The World and Its Woman*. Many film critics still single her work out for praise (a comparatively rare tribute for opera singers who have made movies, let alone silent ones!) In 1918 she created the title role in Puccini's *Suor Angelica*. Her Met farewell was in 1922 in Leoncavallo's Zaza, and was one of the most emotional nights at the Met; her fans even pulled her limousine back to her hotel. Her last concert was in 1931. *—Ann Feeney*

Recommended:

○ **Farrar In Italian Opera** / Farrar, etc. / 1994 / Nimbus 7857

○ **Farrar in French Opera** / Farrar, etc. / 1995 / Nimbus 7872

Eileen Farrell

b. Feb. 13, 1920, Willimantic, CT, **d.** Mar. 23, 2002, Park Ridge, NJ

Soprano

While opera singers who dabble in popular music are common, those who do so successfully are rare, and those with large dramatic voices who do so are rarer still. Eileen Farrell was as authentic and natural a blues and jazz singer as she was an operatic soprano. She was in fact much more comfortable on the concert stage, on radio, and in the recording studio than in the opera house. She sang relatively few fully-staged performances and was ambivalent about opera and particularly opera house management throughout her entire career (when she taught at Indiana University, she hung a sign outside her office that read, "Help stamp out opera.") Her voice was huge, but capable of great nuances in volume and expressiveness as well as rapid and accurate coloratura, letting her sing bel canto roles such as Cherubini's Medea, the spinto-coloratura Leonora in Verdi's *Il trovatore*, the verismo Santuzza in *Cavalleria Rusticana*, and the great Wagner parts of Isolde and Brünnhilde (in concert).

Her parents were both singers, *The Singing O'Farrells*, and recognizing her potential, sent her to study voice in New York. She auditioned for various radio shows and was hired by CBS for chorus and ensemble work. In 1941, she got her own program, Eileen Farrell Sings, where she performed songs and lighter classical music. She remained with them until 1947, when she began to explore other venues, including the Bach Aria Group. She also began studying with Eleanor McLellan, who helped her hone her vocal technique, particularly helping her develop a pianissimo. In 1955, she sang for the film dramatization of singer Marjorie Lawrence's life, *Interrupted Melody* (Eleanor Parker acted the role), and the music, ranging from folk to Brünnhilde's immolation scene, showed off her power, rich voice, and versatility. In 1957, she appeared for the first time on the opera stage, as Santuzza in Mascagni's *Cavalleria Rusticana* in Tampa, FL, and two years later, sang for the first time in London, in a recital. She made her Metropolitan Opera debut in 1960 in the title role of Gluck's *Alceste*, and in 1962, won a Grammy with her album, *Songs*. Her relationship with Met management was an uncomfortable one, partly due to differences of personalities and her finding the repertoire they offered unchallenging, and her contract was allowed to drop in 1965. Towards the end of the decade, her voice was beginning to show signs of wear at the very top, and Farrell moved back into jazz and blues recordings, and taught music at Indiana University. She made her last record in 1993, at the age of 72. Farrell died on March 23, 2002. *—Ann Feeney*

Recommended:

○ **Farrell Sings Johnny Mercer** / Farrell, Pugh, McGlohon / 1991 / Reference 44

○ **Farrell Sings Verdi** / Farrell, etc. / Sony 62358

○ **Donizetti: Maria Stuarda** / Ceccato (cond.), Farrell, Sills, Quilico, Burrows, London PO / 2001 / DG 465961

Brigitte Fassbaender

b. Jul. 3, 1939, Berlin, Germany

Mezzo-Soprano

Brigitte Fassbaender is a prominent mezzo-soprano known for her acclaimed performances of the standard opera repertoire. Born in Berlin, in 1939, she had a childhood dream of becoming an actress, just her like mother, the film star Sabine Peters. As she realized how good her singing voice was, Fassbaender auditioned for the Nuremberg Conservatory, where her father, the famous baritone Willi Domgraf-Fassbaender taught. She studied with her father from 1957 until 1961, and in 1961 made her debut at the Bavarian State Opera as a Page in *Lohengrin*. However, she considers Nicklaus in *Les contes d'Hoffmann* her debut role; it was her first truly solo part. A 1962 telecast of *Eugene Onegin* with Fritz Wunderlich, in which she sang Olga, has been preserved. She sang minor roles for several years, and in 1965 got her big break when she was assigned the role of Clarice in Rossini's *La pietra del paragone*. She also sang at the Deutsche Oper am Rhein, Düsseldorf-Duisburg, Stuttgart, and Frankfurt am Main. In 1971, she sang Octavian in *Der Rosenkavalier* for her debut at London's Covent Garden. This role also served for her debut at the Metropolitan Opera, in 1974. Because of her admirable figure she was always in demand for trouser roles such as Octavian, Cherubino in *The Marriage of Figaro*, Sextus in *La Clemenza di Tito*, and Prince Orlovsky in *Die Fledermaus*. At the Salzburg Festival she sang Dorabella in *Così fan tutte* from 1972 until 1978; in 1989, she returned as Klytemnestra in *Elektra*. She also appeared there as Eboli in *Don Carlos* and Amneris in *Aida*, under the direction of Karajan. In 1983 and 1984, she sang Waltraute in *Götterdämmerung*, at Bayreuth. At Vienna, in 1976, Fassbaender sang in the world premiere of Einem's *Kabale und Liebe*. Her career took her to the major opera houses, including Milan, Tokyo, Paris, San Francisco, and Geneva. She made each of her characters a living entity, embellishing them with touches which made them unique. She was a favored singer of many conductors, including Herbert von Karajan and Carlos Kleiber. Fassbaender was also a highly esteemed recitalist and concert performer. She was most successful with narrative songs, particularly when she had the opportunity to tell a complete story and create one or more characters. In her performances, Fassbaender respected the dramatic and musical needs of a composition, without allowing either to overpower her interpretation. She was especially admired for her interpretation of Mahler's *Das Lied von der Erde* and Brahms' *Alto Rhapsody*. Her lieder recitals were always eagerly anticipated, particularly her performances of Schubert and Schumann. In 1987, Fassbaender's Deutsche Grammophon recording of songs by Liszt and Strauss brought her a Grammophone Award. Fassbaender's other critically acclaimed recordings include Schubert's *Winterreise*, Karl Loewe's *Frauenliebe*, and *Die Schöne Magelone* by Brahms. She appeared less often in oratorios, because of her busy opera schedule, however, remained in demand for works of Bach, Rossini, and Mendelssohn. As she cut back singing in opera houses, she began a second career as a stage director, beginning at Coburg with Rossini's *La Cenerentola*. Since that time, she has staged many operas, including *Der Rosenkavalier* and Franz Schreker's *Der ferne Klang*. Having retired as an opera singer, she teaches vocal music at the Musikhochscule in Munich. *—Richard LeSueur*

Recommended:

○ **Schubert: The Complete Songs Vol. 11** / Fassbaender, Johnson (piano) / 1991 / Hyperion 33011

○ **Strauss: Die Fledermaus** / Previn (cond.), Te Kanawa, Krause, Fassbaender, Leech, Vienna PO / 1991 / Philips 432157

○ **Brahms: Die schöne Magelone** / Fassbaender, Leonskaja (piano) / 1994 / Teldec 90854

○ **Verdi: Il Trovatore** / Giulini (cond.), Domingo, Fassbaender, Giacomotti, Stasio, St. Cecilia Academy Orch. / DG 423858

Gabriel Fauré

b. May 12, 1845, Pamiers, Ariège, France, **d.** Nov. 4, 1924, Paris, France

Composer: Chamber Music, Vocal, Choral, Keyboard, Concerto, Orchestral, Opera

When Gabriel Fauré was a boy, Berlioz had just written *La damnation de Faust* and Henry David Thoreau was writing *Walden*. By the time of his death, Stravinsky had written *The Rite of Spring* and World War I had ended in the devastation of Europe. In this dramatic period in history, Fauré strove to bring together the best of traditional and progressive music and, in the process, created some of the most exquisite works in the French repertoire. He was one of the most advanced figures in French musical circles and influenced a generation of composers world-wide.

Fauré was the youngest child of a school headmaster and spent many hours playing the harmonium in the chapel next to his father's school. Fauré's father enrolled the nine-year-old as a boarder at the *École Niedermeyer* in Paris, where he remained for 11 years, learning church music, organ, piano, harmony, counterpoint, and literature. In 1861, Saint-Saëns joined the school and introduced Fauré and other students to the works of more contemporary composers such as Schumann, Liszt, and Wagner. Fauré's earliest songs and piano pieces date from this period, just before his graduation in 1865, which he achieved with awards in almost every subject. For the next several years, he took on various organist positions, served for a time in the Imperial Guard, and taught. In 1871 he and his friends—d'Indy, Lalo, Duparc, and Chabrier—formed the *Société Nationale de Musique*, and soon after, Saint-Saëns introduced him to the salon of Pauline Viardot and Parisian musical high society. Fauré wrote his first important chamber works (the *Violin Sonata No. 1* and *Piano Quartet No. 1*), then set out on a series of musical expeditions to meet Liszt and Wagner. Throughout the 1880s, he held various positions and continued to write songs and piano pieces, but felt unsure enough of his compositional talents to attempt anything much larger than incidental music. Fauré's pieces began to show a complexity of musical line and harmony which were to become the hallmarks of his music. He began to develop a highly original approach to tonality, in which modal harmony and altered scales figured largely. The next decade, however, is when Fauré came into his own. He was named composition professor at the Paris Conservatoire in 1896. His music, although considered too advanced by most, gained recognition amongst his musical friends. This was his first truly productive phase, seeing the completion of his *Requiem*, the *Cinq Mélodies*, and the *Dolly Suite*, among other works. Using an economy of expression and boldness of harmony, he built the musical bridge over which his students—such as Maurice Ravel and Nadia Boulanger—would cross on their journey into the twentieth century. In 1905, he was named director of the conservatory and made several significant reforms. Ironically, this position gave his works more exposure, but it reduced his time for composition and came when he was increasingly bothered by hearing problems. Fauré's works of this period show the last, most sophisticated stages of his writing, streamlined and elegant in form. During World War I, Fauré essentially remained in Paris and had another extremely productive phase, producing, among other things, *Le Jardin clos* and the *Fantaisie for piano and orchestra,* Op. 111, which show a force and violence that make them among the most powerful pieces in French music. In 1920 he retired from the school, and the following year gave up his music critic position with *Le Figaro*, which he had held since 1903. Between then and his death in 1924, he would produce his great, last works: several chamber works and the song cycle *L'horizon chimérique*. *—AMG*

CHAMBER MUSIC

Cello Sonata No. 1 in D minor, Op. 109 (1917)

No sooner had Fauré completed the *Second Violin Sonata*—which inaugurates the chamber works of his final, old master, phase—than he began the *Sonata No. 1 for Cello and Piano* in the spring of 1917, completing the final movement August 18. Dramatic and impassioned, it has a direct and soaring disposition that sets it apart from its equivocal, uncertain predecessor. For instance, both begin with a sharply accented syncopation on the piano, but where the violin's entrance seemed skittish, the cello erupts in a peremptory, angry, commanding reworking of a theme from the discarded *Symphony in D minor* of 1884; the upward skips of this theme are something of a Fauréenne archetype, heard also in *Pénélope*. This is immediately succeeded by a lyrical second theme—a mere phrase, really—which poses a buoyant contrast to the first theme's agitation, and whose interplay is carried through with a narrative sureness. In its vehemence and power, this movement belies the image of Fauré as an urbane "master of charms," as Debussy called him, and points to his underrated strengths as a dramatic composer, evident in the operas *Prométhée* and *Pénélope*.

The great Andante again introduces two contrasting themes without prologue—a dotted figure and a berceuse-like sigh—from whose slender suggestions Fauré weaves a spellbinding cantando dialogue. The concluding Allegro commodo, again direct and simple, offers an effusive, accented melody followed by a leaping melodic fragment; the composer works these together canonically into an effervescent, yet serene statement.

In tandem with the *Second Violin Sonata*, the *Cello Sonata No. 1* had its premiere at a concert of the Société Nationale de Musique, November 10, 1917, by André Hekking, cello, and Alfred Cortot taking the piano part. *—Adrian Corleonis*

Recommended:

- **Fauré: Chamber Music Vol. 1** / Collard, Lodeon / 1988 / EMI 569261
- **Fauré: Élégie; Debussy: Sonata; Fauré: Sonatas** / Tortelier, Hubeau / Erato 45660

Cello Sonata No. 2 in G minor, Op. 117 (1921)

The Cello Sonata No. 2 occupied Fauré from February to November 1921, as the composer passed his seventy-fifth birthday plagued by deafness, illness, and the infirmities of age. The work's restlessly percolating first movement opens with a long, agitated melody, which the second theme, elegiac but hustled by relentless élan, cannot placate. The brisk canonic interplay between the two suggests passionate regret whose upshot, in the final bars, is a wan smile, more a memory than acceptance. The central Andante, curiously, is a literal transcription of the *Chant funéraire* (1921) for military band, which Fauré had earlier written on commission from the state to commemorate the hundredth anniversary of Napoleon's death. (Fauré originally wrote the music on three staves; the work was arranged for band by the leader of the Garde républicaine, Guillaume Belay.) In both settings, it is a somber, nobly imposing statement, a mourning processional that temporarily halts for a moment of tender elegy, rising to an animated crescendo before the slow, inexorable, tread begins once more. The surprise of the B flat major Allegro vivo is that the agitation of the first movement is here transformed in fantastic, continually modulating scintillations into a wry but genuine grin. Following its premiere by cellist André Hekking and pianist Alfred Cortot at a concert of the Société Nationale de Musique on May 13, 1922, Vincent d'Indy was moved to write to Fauré: "I want to tell you that I'm still under the spell of your beautiful Cello Sonata.... The Andante is a masterpiece of sensitivity and expression, and I love the finale, so perky and delightful.... How lucky you are to stay young like that!" *—Adrian Corleonis*

Recommended:

- **Fauré: Chamber Music Vol. 1** / Collard, Lodeon / 1988 / EMI 569261
- **Fauré: Élégie; Debussy: Sonata; Fauré: Sonatas** / Tortelier, Hubeau / Erato 45660
- **Schumann: Phantasiestücke; Shostakovich: Moderato; Fauré: Romance; Sonata** / Duo Postiglione Stuttgart / FSM Adagio 97721

Élégie, for cello & piano in C minor, Op. 24 (1880)

To his publisher Julien Hamelle on June 24, 1880, Fauré wrote, "I was very sorry you could not be at Saint-Saëns' on Monday. My cello piece was excellently received, which greatly encourages me to go on and do the whole sonata." As he entered the decade, Fauré's music became more subtle, allusive, and inward, leaving the style of broadly conceived melodic eloquence—in which this single movement is couched—more or less behind. Indeed, the exquisite *Ballade*, which may be said to have inaugurated this new phase, dates from the year before. This single movement for cello and piano was given its official premiere at the Société Nationale concert of December 15, 1883, by cellist Jules Loëb, to whom it is dedicated. Titled *Élégie*, it was published by Hamelle the same year. Fauré made an orchestral version of the piece in about 1897, which Hamelle eventually published in 1901. Curiously, as if the *Élégie* represented unfinished business, the great Andante of the *Cello Sonata No. 2* of 1921 is cut from the same cloth.

The simple grandeur of its ABA layout, in which the most telling melody is allowed to sing without complication, no doubt accounts for the *Élégie*'s phenomenal appeal. Over steady, dirge-like chords, the cello dramatically embarks upon an expansive lament that quietens as it unfolds in tones of somber oration. Then, accompanied by the cello, the piano essays an effusive song—as of joy recalled in grief—taken up by the cello to culminate in a sudden vehement (and rather unconvincing) cadenza before the funereal opening returns, shadowed by the central section's plaint, to sing itself into nothingness.

The *Élégie*'s immediate popularity prompted Hamelle to press Fauré for similar surefire pieces, to which is owed such things as *Papillon for cello and piano* (1884), the *Romance for cello and piano* (1894), the *Fantaisie for flute and piano* (1898), and so on. If Fauré's reputation with a larger public largely rests upon these often heard small numbers, to the detriment of his richer, elusive later works, it is worth noting that he never lost the common touch—the ability to speak directly and with compelling charm to the least sophisticated. *—Adrian Corleonis*

Recommended:

- **Pierre Fournier: Dvořák Cello Concerto** / Fournier, Lush / 1993 / Testament 1016
- **The Musical Circle of John Singer Sargent** / Navarra, D'Arco / 1998 / HM 986003
- **Maurice Maréchal Book 3** / Maréchal, Fauré / 1998 / Fono Enterprise 99356

Fantaisie, for flute & piano in E minor, Op. 79 (Jul. 28, 1898)

French musicians had been making pilgrimages to Germany to hear the Wagner operas since the 1860s with the fervor of Grail seekers; thus, it is hardly surprising to find Parisian salons devoted almost wholly to the cult of *der Meister* later in the century. Of these, the most remarkable must surely have been the "Petit Bayreuth" organized by Judge Antoine Lascoux, at which scenes from the operas were performed by whatever talent was on hand. A contemporary sketch of one of these evenings, published in *Le Journal* for November 23, 1899, reported that "The orchestra (a chamber one) included several unusual performers: besides d'Indy,

Fauré, Messager, Raoul Pugno, and Taffanel, Lascoux played first violin." Paul Taffanel (1844–1908), often called the father of the modern French school of the flute, was a busy man, active at the Opéra de Paris, in the Conservatoire concerts, as the leader of the L'Orchestre de la Société des Instruments à Vent (which commissioned, among many other works, d'Indy's *Chansons et danses*), and, from 1893, as a professor at the Conservatoire. Fauré was appointed professor of composition there in October 1896, and it was almost inevitable that Taffanel should ask him, in the spring of 1898, to write a sight-reading piece and a *concours* composition for the July examinations. No doubt owing to Wagnerian camaraderie, Fauré passed the orchestration of his incidental music for Maeterlinck's *Pelléas et Mélisande*, on which he had been feverishly working, to his pupil Charles Koechlin, so he could get to grips with the *concours* piece. The *Fantaisie for flute and piano* occupied him from the beginning of June until at least mid-July, though its fluent brilliance belies the effort that went into it. Opening with a brief sicilienne of great charm, the *Fantaisie* soon gets down to its raison d'être with a winsomely chirping tune riffled by mercurial pyrotechnics. Writing to Koechlin on his way to London on June 10, 1898, for the June 21 premiere of *Pelléas*, Fauré complained, "I am drowned in the Taffanel and plunged up to my neck in scales, arpeggios, and staccati! I have already perpetrated 104 bars of this irksome torture...." But for the adept musician who can, as intended, take its virtuoso demands in stride, the *Fantaisie* affords an airily effusive, scintillantly rapturous, and wholly un-Wagnerian spate of liquid silver. Its first performance was given by the *concours* winner, one Gaston Blanquart, on July 28, 1898. Despite the grumbling Fauré lavished on the piece, he seems to have prepared an orchestral version, which is now lost. In 1957, Louis Aubert made an orchestral arrangement published by the firm of Hamelle the year after. *—Adrian Corleonis*

Recommended:

- ○ **Celebration for Flute & Orchestra** / Bedford (cond.), Bennett, English CO / 1989 / ASV 652
- ○ **Serenade** / Galway, etc. / 1989 / BMG 60033
- ○ **Romantic Flute Concertos** / Vandernoot (cond.), Grauwels, Belgian Radio & Television Orch. / 2002 / Naxos 8555977

Impromptu for harp in D flat major, Op. 86 (Jul. 1904)

Though no one but Fauré could have written it, not the least curious thing about the *Impromptu for harp* is how atypical of Fauré it seems, despite the expansive length at which its slender materials are worked. Another curious matter is that Fauré transcribed it for piano as an *Impromptu for piano No. 6,* Op. 86bis. The boldly strummed chords of the opening (a positively carillon-like effect on the piano) are a kind of bardic call to order harking back to the world of Chopin's *Ballades*—though without sounding like Chopin, either—to a legendary demesne luminous with the stuff of dreams. For the initial heraldic motif is met immediately by a dreamingly distracted meno mosso melody in plucked gossamer as part of an ever-expanding dialogue moving from the instrument's throaty lower register to its aerial highest, dissolving in glistening runs and glittering arpeggios to return with greater vehemence answered by more lambent fantasy. Cumulative tension dissipates suddenly in a conventional coda.

Composed in July 1904 for a harp *concours* at the Conservatoire, it was heard there for the first time on the 25th of that month in a performance by Mlle Charlotte Landrin—soon to marry Jacques Lerolle, Chausson's brother-in-law. *—Adrian Corleonis*

Recommended:

- ○ **Magic Of The Harp** / Laskine / Erato 92131
- ○ **Sky Music** / Kondonassis / 1996 / Telarc 80418
- ○ **Romantic Evening Music for Harp** / Vigh / Laserlight 14090

Morceau de Concours (Morceau de lecture), for flute & piano in F major (1898)

Often called the father of the modern French school of flute playing, Paul Taffanel (1844–1908) taught at the Paris Conservatoire from 1893. When his friend, Fauré, was appointed professor of composition there in October 1896 it was natural that Taffanel should turn to him for a *concours* composition—a brilliant virtuoso number which Fauré worked over with slavish care and titled *Fantaisie*, Op. 79—and a brief sight-reading piece, properly titled *Morceau de lecture*. The latter, composed in July 1898, is a mere arabesque dutifully spun out in the requisite scales, arpeggios, grace notes, and mordents, the apt execution of which demonstrates proficiency. Over a spare piano accompaniment, this functional exercise plays out slowly for a minute-and-a-half with only the faintest redolence of the *fauréenne*. *—Adrian Corleonis*

Recommended:

- ○ **Paula Robison: Carmen Fantasy** / Robison, Sanders / 1992 / Vanguard 4058

Papillon, for cello & piano, Op. 77 (1884)

"Butterfly or dungfly, call it what you like," Fauré wrote to his publisher, Hamelle, acceding at last to that worthy request to title a small piece for cello and piano, composed in 1884, *Papillon*. Impressed by the popularity—and sales—of Fauré's *Élégie* (1880), Hamelle had prodded the composer to produce a frankly virtuoso piece for cello. The upshot was slight, in terms both of duration and inspiration. In under three minutes, four rapid sections and a codetta flash by—animated arpeggios for the cello leading into an expansive melody before the cello's brilliant opening returns, rippled by recollections of the central section, ascending suddenly to the tonic at the end. Startling, airy, and not without charm, *Papillon* is over before one grasps that the engaging shimmer is a mirage of no substance. The composer's recalcitrance regarding the title delayed publication until 1898. It immediately became, and has remained, one of Fauré's most often played pieces. *—Adrian Corleonis*

Recommended:

- ○ **Andre Navarra** / Navarra, Kisselhoff, D'Arco / 1988 / Calliope 9854
- ○ **Fauré: Complete Works for Cello** / Isserlis, Devoyon / 1995 / RCA 68049

Piano Quartet No. 1 in C minor, Op. 15 (1876–1879; revised 1883)

Looking back in 1922, Fauré noted that "The fact of the matter is that before 1870 I would not have dreamt of composing a sonata or a quartet. At that time a young musician had no chance of getting such works performed. It was only after Saint-Saëns had founded the National Music Society in 1871, the chief function of which was to perform the works of young composers, that I set to work." The encouragement given to French composers by the Société Nationale de Musique can hardly be overestimated; with his mentor, Saint-Saëns, Fauré joined Franck, d'Indy, Duparc, Lalo, and Massenet, among others, in the establishment of this concert organization which helped break the stranglehold of opera upon French musical life. But Fauré's sanguine remark about "setting to work" overlooks the "indolence" with which he reproached himself frequently in his youth—his *First Violin Sonata* was not begun until 1875, and the *First Piano Quartet* not until the year after, to be completed in 1879. Meanwhile—apart from a discarded *Symphony in F*—he had been finding his way stylistically in the intimate purlieu of the mélodie. It is also misleading to say (as is often done) that there was no chamber music in France before the Société Nationale—Alkan, Franchomme, Louise Farrenc, Lalo, Castillon, and Saint-Saëns himself all made notable contributions to the genre well before the founding of the SNM. Nevertheless, that venerable organization brought focus to French soul-searching, helping to embed chamber and symphonic music in the cultural mainstream.

There are a number of remarkable things about Fauré's *First Piano Quartet* which mark it as a prominent turning point. One notes first the complete assurance in his shapely handling of sonata form, fastidious craft in a coruscating dialogue of parts, the richness and indelible personality of its deftly worked melodic material, and unfailingly adept writing for piano. Worth noting, too, is the combination of a highly refined personal style with compelling high spirits. Above all, his *First Piano Quartet* strikes persuasively not merely the *urbane* (the epithet which clings to Fauré), but the *urban* tone which George Bernard Shaw made explicit when he noted that "From Mozart I learned the art of saying important things conversationally."

Romanticism and its doleful heroics are left behind in this work, as are the frivolous, the formulaic, and the balletic. The first movement holds one through its fluent melding of energy and lyricism. The Scherzo surprises with blithe, pizzicato pricked, *perpetuum mobile* fantasy. The great Adagio demonstrates that profound passion is not incompatible with balance and classical purity of line. And a soaring Allegro molto caps all with a gracefully poised major/minor shimmer of gaiety.

Fauré was at the piano for the first performance of the *First Piano Quartet* with the Société Nationale on February 11, 1880. Responding to criticism from colleagues, he revised the finale. Thus, the work attained its final form only in 1883. *—Adrian Corleonis*

Recommended:

- ○ **Fauré: Piano Quartets 1 & 2** / Domus / Hyperion 66166
- ○ **Fauré: La Musique de Chambre** / Navarra, Hubeau, Gallois-Montbrun, Lequien / Erato 39137

Piano Quartet No. 2 in G minor, Op. 45 (1885–1886)

"This may be tempestuous music," wrote Max Harrison in the liner notes to the 1992 Philips recording of Gabriel Fauré's *Piano Quartet in G minor No. 2*, "but it is also closely argued." Such a description suggests a conception of "music as rhetoric" that is usually much more closely identified with the eighteenth century German tradition than the musical circles of *fin de siècle* France. Still, the observation holds true. Though known for his capacity for stretching melodies beyond the strictures of foursquare phrases and coloring his harmonic schemes with vibrant modal inflections and innovative progressions, Fauré's mature, mid-career works, as exemplified by the G minor quartet (Op. 45, 1886), sustain their lyricism and validate their progressive harmonic languages through tightly woven structures. This tendency is not unique to the Op. 45 quartet; a strong sense of thematic cohesion and sensitivity toward structural pacing is also evident, for example, in the *Piano Quartet No. 1*, Op. 15 (1879). As in the earlier work, Fauré draws close connections between his forceful and lyrical themes, sometimes casting different veils on the same material. At the same time, however, Fauré's lines are crafted in such a way as to suggest continuity rather than segmentation; a strong sense of form is present, but the seams are well hidden. The quartet's four movements offer striking contrasts of character. The first movement, Allegro molto moderato, presents a bold minor-mode theme (the characteristic chromatic inflections of which actually suggest Phrygian), the contours of which closely relate to subsequent, more lyrical, themes. The movement as a whole conveys an urgency that takes a sly turn in the scherzo second movement, Allegro molto, which is propelled by a continual figurational motion and rhythmic intensity, and which echoes motifs from the first movement. The third movement, Adagio non troppo, is at once serene and unassuming, with long, lyrical lines in the viola alternating with tiptoeing chords in the piano. The piano executes nimble acrobatics in the final movement, Allegro molto, while the string melodies swirl around each other, then coalesce in forceful unisons. These moments of clarity are not articulated as musical consequences, however, but rather emerge naturally from the piece's dramatic contours. If the work, then, is "closely argued," it conveys its expression through persuasion rather than force of logic. Perhaps not rhetorical oration, then, but certainly a convincing soliloquy. *—Jeremy Grimshaw*

Recommended:

○ **Fauré: Piano Quartets 1 & 2** / Domus / 1985 / Hyperion 20166

○ **Fauré: Piano Quartets** / Schubert Ens. of London / 1999 / Quicksilva 6237

Piano Quintet No. 1 in D minor, Op. 89 (1890–1905)

Perhaps nothing else in Fauré's oeuvre cost him so much trouble for seeming so effortlessly spontaneous than the *Piano Quintet No. 1*. As early as 1887, he was jotting the melody of the work's Finale. And by the end of 1890, the work was sketched almost completely, though only the exposition of the first movement had been fully composed. Fauré's son Emanuel recalled hearing this fragment tried out at home by the Quatuor Ysaÿe. "But I only heard it that once," he told leading Fauré scholar Jean-Michel Nectoux. "One day I plucked up my courage and timidly sang to my father the first bars of this 'vanished' tune. I'll never forget how he threw his arms around me and embraced me, then sat down at the piano and played me the whole of the opening paragraph." It is indeed a memorable passage, with its quietly rippling arpeggios over which a serenely beguiling melody floats, like a messenger from a bourne quite as fantastic as that of Yeats' "sleepy country, where swans fly round/Coupled with golden chains, and sing as they fly." The development of this *donnée* seems to have been the sticking point. In the upshot, the *Quintet* was set aside for the Verlaine cycles, the *Cinq Mélodies "de Venise"* (1891) and *La Bonne chanson* (1892–94), which open on yet other strange enchantments. Though the work was briefly taken up again in 1896, it required intense labor through the summer holidays from 1903 to 1905 before Fauré had shaped the elements of this over-rich opus to his satisfaction.

The first-movement Molto moderato laces the ethereality of the opening with the involvements of a second and, eventually, a third theme that do not so much contrast with as complement the first theme to elaborate a spellbinding demesne. The dream deepens in the great central Adagio as a berceuse-like melody makes modulatory explorations, simultaneously raising the temperature of the first movement to a note of quiet passion that becomes more rapt as a more animated counter-melody enters into dialogue. After so much penumbral introspection, the gaiety of the concluding D major Allegretto moderato falls like a sudden shaft of sunlight. A rondo, its refrain, possesses the engaging ingenuousness of a *chanson populaire*. Moments of drama, with divagations into the minor, lend substance to insouciance and a contrasting radiance to the springing giddiness of the coda. Part of the *Piano Quintet No. 1*'s fascination owes to the inspiration of Fauré at the most opulent period of his career—the Verlaine years—worked with a cunning, old-masterly hand as the composer embarked upon his final manner. The casual hearer, for instance, will be delighted by an unbroken arch of glorious melody, while the close listener will be drawn into a transparently fluent web wrought of the subtlest contrapuntal art.

Dedicated to Eugène Ysaÿe, the *Piano Quintet No. 1* was given its premiere in Brussels by the Quatuor Ysaÿe, with Blanche Selva at the piano, on March 23, 1906. *—Adrian Corleonis*

Recommended:

○ **Fauré: Piano Quintets** / Domus / 1995 / Hyperion 66766

○ **Fauré: Piano Quintets 1 & 2** / Orth, Auryn Quartet / CPO 999357

Piano Trio in D minor, Op. 120 (1922–1923)

After an award of the Légion d'honneur and some gentle prodding, Fauré—now completely deaf—gave up his directorship of the Paris Conservatoire on October 1, 1920. On the second day of 1922, with the triumph of his *Piano Quintet No. 2* the previous spring fading into memory, he wrote to his friend Fernand Bourgeat, "I feel dreadfully the onset of old age and I regret not finding my freedom sooner… I've done good work even so. I've finished a 13th nocturne." In March, from Nice, he wrote to his wife, "I'm doing absolutely nothing and haven't thought of two notes worth writing down since I've been here. Have I come to the end of my resources?" Jacques Durand, his publisher, had suggested in January that he compose a trio for piano, violin, and cello, but Fauré would not take up the challenge until April in Paris. Staying at Argèles through July to revisit childhood haunts, he asked that sketches for the *Trio* be sent after him—only to contract bronchial pneumonia near the end of the month. By mid-August he was back in Annecy-le-Vieux, in Savoy, where the *Piano Quintet No. 2* had taken shape over the summers of 1919 and 1920. "I've started a trio for clarinet (or violin), cello, and piano," he wrote to his wife on September 26, 1922. "The trouble is that I can't work for long at a time. My worst tribulation is perpetual fatigue." Returning to Paris for the winter, he completed the *Trio* in mid-February 1923. Durand published it the same year as a *Trio for piano, violin, and violoncello*, probably with the composer's assent—the violin part contains passages of double-stopping—while the idea of using a clarinet seems to have quietly fallen by the wayside.

Despite its small scale and general restraint, much happens in the succinct opening Allegro ma non troppo. Two long-breathed melodies—the first wavering between elegy and lament, the second trailing a childhood memory of distant bells—receive a replete exposition and contrapuntal development, with a new exposition (rather than a recapitulation) and development rounded with a coda of defiant despair. The Andantino, the most extensive of the *Trio*'s three movements and the one with which Fauré had begun the composition, opens with a fiat of the most lambent lyricism shared by violin and cello, answered by a piquantly harmonized, heart-stopping melody on the piano from whose interplay he spins a delicate, exquisitely modulated, but puissant pathos. Much has been made of the resemblance of the Finale's opening *rappel à l'ordre* and the cry "Ridi, Pagliaccio" from Leoncavallo's *Pagliacci* (e.g., "La commedia è finita"). Tempting as that may be, an allusion was unintended. More remarkable is that the phrase, several times repeated, introduces an elegantly rumbustious, thumpingly accented, *plein air* rustic dance—a last surprise from the old magician. The premiere was given at a concert of the Société Nationale de Musique on May 12, 1923, by Robert Krettly, violin; Jacques Patté, cello; and Tatiana Sanzévitch, piano. *—Adrian Corleonis*

Recommended:

○ **Debussy, Fauré, Ravel: Piano Trios** / Florestan Trio / 1999 / Hyperion 67114

○ **Fauré: Quintettes; Quatuors; Trio** / Quatuor Via Nova / 1994 / Erato 96953

○ **French Piano Trios** / Golub Kaplan Carr Trio / 1994 / Arabesque 6643

Sicilienne, for cello & piano, Op. 78 (Apr. 16, 1898)

The *Sicilienne* is among Fauré's most familiar pieces; it began life as an orchestral sketch in March 1893, intended as incidental music for a revival of Molière's *Le Bourgeois gentilhomme* at Paul Porel's *Eden-Théâtre*. Left incomplete as that establishment went bankrupt, Fauré rounded it off and arranged it for cello and piano only in 1898, even as he passed the score along to his pupil Charles Koechlin to orchestrate as an item in the incidental music for a London production of Maeterlinck's *Pelléas et Mélisande*, where it introduces the scene at the beginning of Act Two, in which Mélisande's wedding ring slips from her finger and disappears into a well as she plays gently with Pelléas—a use for which it seems predestined. In this form it was first heard with the play's opening at the Prince of Wales' Theatre on June 21, 1898, with Fauré conducting. Given its effectiveness, it was inevitable that Fauré should have included it among the four numbers of his *Pelléas et Mélisande Suite*, heard for the first time on December 1, 1912, conducted by André Messager. The common practice of publishers in issuing multiple arrangements of works likely to catch on—for piano, or piano and solo instrument—ensured that the *Sicilienne*'s lilting wistfulness would become known around the world in the version for cello and piano, published in London by Metzler and Hamelle in Paris in 1898. Like a zephyr, the *Sicilienne*, with its hypnotically fluid melody carried, as it were, on waves of soothing arpeggiation, evokes a mood of mildly delirious nostalgia. If all music, as Vladimir Jankélévitch has remarked, is nostalgic in a certain manner, the *Sicilienne* is nostalgic music par excellence, for it embodies a truly existential, or perhaps mysterious, yearning for some undefined, imagined place, a Sicily in the luxuriant realm of dreams. *—Adrian Corleonis*

Recommended:

○ **Fauré: Chamber Music Vol. 1** / Collard, Lodeon / 1988 / EMI 569261

○ **The Swan** / Chang, Collard / 2000 / EMI 57052

String Quartet in E minor, Op. 121 (1923–1924)

"Every day I'm writing a little music, a very little it's true. And as so often has been the case, I don't yet know what these first fumblings will turn into," Fauré writes to his wife from Annecy-le-Vieux, Savoy, where he spent the summer of 1923. As sketches made in July began to take shape in the fall, the composer admitted to his wife, in a letter from September 9, that "I've started a quartet for strings, without *piano*. It's a medium in which Beethoven was particularly active, which is enough to give all those people who are not Beethoven the jitters!" Superstitiously wary, Fauré kept his work on the quartet a secret. By September 12, the great central Andante had been completed. Composition of the first movement was taken up in Paris in the fall, alternating with episodes of physical decline—he passed his 79th birthday on May 12, 1924. And it was only in late June, on holiday in Divonne, above Lake Geneva, that his creative energy returned. His son, Philippe Fauré-Fremiet, recalled that "On the fourth day he placed his manuscript paper on the table and quietly started on the finale of his *String Quartet*. He was no longer strong enough to walk." Moving on to Annecy at the end of July, he continued to compose, completing the *Finale* on September 11. Exhausted, by September 19 he had come down with double pneumonia. Instructions were given that the quartet was not to be published or performed before it had been heard by a select group of friends—including Dukas, Pierre Lalo, and Camille Bellaigue—who would decide whether the work was worthy. By mid-October he had shaken the pneumonia off, but at the beginning of November he was in pain and disoriented, and on the early morning of November 4, 1924, he died.

When an extensive *Allegro for violin and orchestra* from 1878–79—all that remains of an abandoned violin concerto—was exhumed and recorded in 1989, one could not fail to be astounded and moved to hear the two principal themes familiar from the Allegro of the old master's *String Quartet*, very little altered, in the context of youthful romanticism. The essential Fauré persists through all vicissitudes. In the microcosmic intimacy of the quartet, the first theme suggests a muted *de profundis clamavi*, the second an aspiring prayer. Their development is concise and contrapuntally constructed, with a special eloquence entrusted to the viola. Likewise, the three themes of the Andante—the most extensive movement—are polyphonically wrought to a quietly intense, incandescent contemplation radiating an aura of light parsed, with infinite sweetness and tenderness, in ever more ethereal gradations. And with its percolating pizzicati, the rondo Finale looms as a serenade and dance, which not without compassion, casts a wry eye on life and love.

The first performance was given at a concert of the Société Nationale de Musique on June 12, 1925, with Jacques Thibaud and Robert Krettly (violins), Maurice Vieux (viola), and André Hekking (cello). —*Adrian Corleonis*

Recommended:

- ○ **Fauré: Chamber Music Vol. 2** / Parrenin SQ / 1988 / EMI 569264
- ○ **Ravel & Fauré: String Quartets** / Ad Libitum SQ / 2000 / Naxos 554722

Violin Sonata No. 1 in A major, Op. 13 (1876)

Beginning in the middle of the last half of the nineteenth century there appeared a number of exquisite French violin sonatas which share the elements of lovely melodies, elegant expression, tasteful and sincere emotionalism, and well-balanced forms, as well as occupying a special place in the repertoire and affections of violinists the world around. Franck, Saint-Saëns, Fauré, Debussy, and Ravel are all contributors to this line of great sonatas.

Fauré, in fact, contributed two such sonatas, separated by 40 years, of which this one is by far the best known, and may be said to have initiated the line. Florent Schmitt correctly wrote that its appearance "marks a red-letter day in the history of chamber music."

Each movement has at least one achingly lovely lyrical theme. The passionate first theme is shared by both instruments (piano and violin are treated as partners throughout the work, rather than as soloist and accompaniment). The second movement, Andante, is reticent, almost shy, in character, with a fine melody for violin. The Scherzo is light-hearted in its outer sections, but lyricism returns in its central section, or "trio." Finally, the last movement is dramatic and emotional, yet even here there is an interlude with a lovely romantic theme. —*Joseph Stevenson*

Recommended:

- ○ **Thibaud & Cortot** / Thibaud, Cortot / EMI 763032
- ○ **Fauré: Chamber Music Vol. 1** / Collard, Dumay / 1988 / EMI 569261
- ○ **Fauré: Violin Sonatas** / Osostowicz, Tomes / 1999 / Hyperion 55030
- ○ **Fauré: Violin Sonata 1; Debussy: Violin Sonata; Saint-Saëns: Violin Sonata 1** / Chee-Yun, Eguchi / 1993 / Denon 75625

Violin Sonata No. 2 in E minor, Op. 108 (1916)

To hear the *First* and *Second Violin Sonatas* together is to comprehend how astoundingly far Fauré traveled, as man and artist, in the 40 years between them. Where the popular *First* is all lyric charm, the neglected *Second* is an extenuation—subtle, elliptical, elusive—as formally and emotionally complex as a late tale by Henry James. Tellingly, it was begun in the turbulent summer of 1916 and completed by year's end.

The first movement (Allegro non troppo) opens with a peremptorily syncopated motif, followed by an anxiously wavering melodic tendril above the staff; this settles into the anxious, contrapuntally involved second subject. The liberties taken with sonata form—an exposition repeated four times with expanding enrichments—is offset by a dramatic tautness in whose toils E minor is transmuted into a brilliantly agitated E major. In its restless compulsiveness, this movement may be seen as a statement on the nerve-wracking envelopement of France in the horrific grip of the Great War—with Fauré's own younger son, Philippe, away at the front.

The great central Andante salvages a long-breathed, hesitant theme from the discarded *Symphony in D minor* of 1884, met by a consoling espressivo melody that mutes the anxiety of the modulations in the previous movement without wholly eliminating their feeling. Likewise, the Allegro non troppo rondo finale broaches an engagingly winsome refrain which comes all too soon to modulatory grief in its interleaving play; this is all deftly managed, but—even with its brilliant major resolution—like happiness mimicked, or a welcoming smile flickering into a disturbing grimace.

If the *First Violin Sonata* is entrancing, the *Second* is arresting, and in it Fauré's art is at its simplest and most masterful, recalling lines from the beginning of Rilke's *Duino Elegies*—"Beauty's nothing / but beginning of Terror we're still just able to bear...."

The *Sonata* was first heard at a concert of the Société Nationale de Musique, November 10, 1917, with Lucien Capet on violin, accompanied by Alfred Cortot. It is dedicated to "Her Majesty Elisabeth, Queen of the Belgians," herself a fine violinist. —*Adrian Corleonis*

Recommended:

- ○ **Fauré: Chamber Music Vol. 1** / Collard, Dumay / 1988 / EMI 569261
- ○ **Fauré: Violin Sonatas** / Osostowicz, Tomes / 1999 / Hyperion 55030
- ○ **Fauré: Sonates pour violon et piano** / Faust, Boffard / HM 901741

VOCAL

Songs (1861–1921)

Fauré's Opus 1 was a giddy salon romance, *Le Papillon et la fleur*, to a lyric trifle by Victor Hugo, which he composed in 1861 as a student of 16 at the École Niedermeyer. It stands as the droll herald of the most distinguished body of song in the French language. Fauré's career links the world of popularly inspired Romantic song—the world of Berlioz's *Irlande* and Lalo's robustly picturesque romances—and an austere, hieratic Modernism which comes to the fore as the twentieth century dawns. The earliest songs are generally strophic or in simple ABA form, but also immediately rife with atmosphere and Fauré's highly personal melos—the still-performed *Dans les ruines d'un abbaye*, for instance, dates from 1866 and the exquisite *Lydia* from 1870. From 1871 on, Fauré seeks an ever closer integration of word and form, with successive stanzas taking on a different color and aura, underwritten by more ingeniously elaborate piano accompaniments, as in *L'Absent* and *Chant d'automne*, in which the facile romance gives way to the more subtly descriptive mélodie. The influence of Pauline Viardot and her circle becomes apparent about 1872 in such things as *La Chanson du pêcheur*—a muted aria in all but name—*Ici-bas*, *Tristesse*, *Après un rêve*, *Nell*, and the *Sérénade toscane*, in an Italianately shaped lyricism which, though often passionate, is never floridly operatic. The apogee of this manner is reached in the *Poème d'un jour* of 1878, three melodies which mirror the emotional fallout of Marianne Viardot's breaking of her engagement to Fauré. The succeeding era, from 1879 until the turn of the century, encompasses Fauré's ripest, most richly sensuous, and harmonically shimmering melodies as all facets of his art achieve a suavely scintillant integration, embracing the Parnassian and Symbolist poems with an expressive aura which exceeds music as Verlaine's melodious verse exceeds poetry. Such things as *Notre amour* (to a poem by Armand Silvestre), *Le Secret* (Silvestre), *Les Roses d'Ispahan* (Leconte de Lisle), *Nocturne* (Villiers de l'Isle-Adam), and, above all, the Verlaine settings—*Clair de lune* (1887, contemporary with the *Requiem*) and *Spleen*—are characteristic. Verlaine, in fact, is the poet through whom Fauré attains the ultimate throw of his lyric art in the expressive divination of the *Cinq Mélodies de Venise* (1891) and the incandescence of the cycle, *La Bonne chanson* (1892), whose seeming melodic superabundance is subtly, sinuously interwoven from a number of small motifs kindling in chromatic, radiant polyphony. With the new century came a new concision, a striving for absolute simplicity in which an ever-sparer, old-masterly clairvoyance crystallizes, so to speak, the poems' symbolism, in the cycles *La Chanson d'Ève* (1906), *Le Jardin clos* (1914)—both by Charles van Leberghe, *Mirages* (1919; Renée de Brimont), and *L'Horizon chimérique* (1921; Jean de la Ville de Mirmont) in which the hermetic, visionary manner attains its final, attenuated form. —*Adrian Corleonis*

Recommended:

- ○ **Fauré: Intégrale des Mélodies** / Ameling, Souzay, Baldwin / EMI 64079
- ○ **Fauré: Mélodies** / Hendricks, Dalberto / EMI 49841

Après un rêve ("Levati sol que luna è levata"), song, Op. 7/1 (1877)

Gabriel Fauré's *"Après un rêve,"* Op. 7/1, a setting of an anonymous poem translated by Romain Bussine, is one of the composer's best-known works for voice. The text describes a dream in which the narrator and her beloved come together in an almost otherworldly meeting, followed by a longing to return to this dream state after awakening: "In a sleep which your image charmed, I dreamt of happiness, ardent mirage.... You called me, and I left the earth, to flee with you towards the light.... Return, return, radiant, mysterious night!"

Though light, the piano accompaniment provides an underlying pulse, lending the song a sense of propulsion; at the same time, the vocal line is appropriately dreamy and languid. While the vocal range is not especially demanding, the accompaniment provides little pitch support for the voice's sometimes unusual intervals. When well performed, this richly expressive song is one of the most impressive and moving in the entire repertoire. —*Ann Feeney*

Recommended:

- ○ **Nuit d'Etoiles** / Gens, Vignoles / 2000 / EMI 45360
- ○ **Fauré: Mélodies** / Schmiege, Sulzen / 1994 / Orfeo 347941

○ **Dinu Lipatti: Les Inédits** / Lipatti, Janigro / Archiphon 112

○ **Night Songs** / Fleming, Thibaudet / 2001 / Decca 467697

La Bonne chanson, song cycle, Op. 61 (1892–1894)

Having completed the *Five Venetian Songs*, Gabriel Fauré wrote a friend feeling that he had just about exhausted for himself the musical potential of the poetry of Paul Verlaine. Luckily for the history of the song cycle, Fauré was to return once more to the French poet, composing the nine-song cycle *La bonne chanson*. Later in his life Fauré was to claim that he had never written anything as spontaneously as *La bonne chanson*.

Fauré carefully selected certain poems and even stanzas from Verlaine, reordering them to tell the story of a young couple in love. The cycle begins with "Une Sainte en son aureole" (A saint in her halo). Fauré's overall tonal plan in the cycle is highly idiosyncratic, and even within songs the harmonic sequences are often surprising. Fauré unifies the cycle instead with five musical motifs, the first of which, a lyrically descending melody, is heard at the beginning of "Une Sainte"; it returns both at the end of the song and of the whole cycle. The setting is light-hearted, establishing the uncharacteristically (for Fauré) happy mood of the composition. "Puisque l'aube grandit" (Since daybreak grows) follows, also in triple meter. The accompaniment plays dramatically broad arpeggios against a legato melodic line. The more serene "La lune blanche" (The pale moon) is third, with even more pronounced chromaticism, in the rare key of F sharp major. The fourth song, "J'allais par des chemins perfides" (I went down some treacherous paths) shifts to F sharp minor; it contains the most harmonic contortions as well as a further realization of an ascending bass-voice motif appearing at the end of the previous setting. "J'ai Presque peur, en verite" (I almost fear, in truth) is the first song of the cycle in duple meter. Fauré sets the text, a confession of love, in wonderfully anxious phrases. "Avant que tu ne t'en ailles" (Before you leave) uncharacteristically wavers in its tempo between a lyrical adagio and impetuous allegro. The arpeggios return in "Donc, ce sera par un clair jour d'ete" (So, it will be on a clear day of summer); a less-complicated mood follows in "N'est-ce pas?" (Is it not so?) with long vocal phrases. The ninth and final song, "L'Hiver a cesse" (Winter has ended), combines all the motifs of the work in an exuberant and colorful finish.

At the time considered revolutionary for its harmonic procedures, *La bonne chanson* has since been enshrined in art song repertoire. Fauré later arranged the piano accompaniment for piano and string quintet, but confessed to a friend that he preferred the original. Lyric baritone Maurice Bages premiered the cycle in April 1894, accompanied by the composer. Inspired by love, Fauré cast his usual caution to the wind in creating a vibrantly original work; the result, in the words of scholar Jean-Michel Nectoux, "reaches the proportions almost of a vocal symphony." *–Thomas Oram*

Recommended:

○ **La Bonne Chanson** / Otter, Forsberg / 1996 / DG 447752

○ **Fauré: Intégrale des Mélodies** / Souzay, Baldwin / EMI 64079

○ **Fauré: Mélodies** / Hendricks, Dalberto / EMI 49841

○ **Fauré, Debussy: Mélodies** / Danco, Agosti / 2003 / Testament 1289

La chanson d'Eve, song cycle, Op. 95 (1906–1910)

La chanson d'Eve inaugurates Fauré's last, "old master," manner—inward, stripped, and tellingly direct. By the time the initial setting, *Crépuscule*, arrived, composed June 4, 1906, and freshly engraved from the publisher in late August, Fauré had decided that it was to be part of a cycle and had already begun what was to become the first number, *Paradis*. *Prima verba* followed in late September, though the composition of the remaining seven songs was spread over 1908–10, delayed by his duties as director of the Conservatoire and work on the grand opera *Pénélope* (1907–12).

In *La chanson d'Eve*, by Belgian poet Charles Van Lerberghe (1861–1907), Fauré found an extensive art nouveau meditation on the feminine ideal—wraithlike, mysterious, and (as Eve) primordial. *Crépuscule* had been adapted from the *Chanson de Mélisande*, composed originally to English words for the London production of Maeterlinck's play, and *Paradis* opens with Mélisande's theme—a recurring motif. For in the symbolist aesthetic, Eve and Mélisande are interchangeable—fleeting, elusive faces of the eternal feminine. But where Mélisande is passive, Eve is an instrument of creation who, in *Prima verba*, awakens to sensuous prehension all that she names—"How the soul of the fountains and woods... sings in my voice.... Words dormant for aeons finally come to life on my lips in sounds, in flowers." Through the luminous, prismatically refracted pantheism of the central songs, Eve is revealed as at once an innocent, both daughter and lover of God, and the *magna mater*, mother of all. But *Crépuscule* shudders with a premonition of the inevitable reversal—"What is it that comes and flutters in my heart like a wounded bird?" And the final song—*O Mort, poussière d'étoiles*—brings numbness and extinction—"Come, dark breath in which I flicker like a flame intoxicated by the wind!"

In *La chanson d'Eve*, the lyricism of *La bonne chanson* has been sublimated in a sort of chant, lifting into arioso at moments of maximal expressiveness, to project the words, the poems' profuse images. Throughout, occasional subtle deployments of the whole tone scale evoke Paradise pristine on "the first morning of the world." The piano's part, too, seems ancient and modern at once in its alternation of severe imitation and radiant shimmer, piquant with modally inflected modulations couching the vocal line in anxious rapture. In his *Adagia*, Wallace Stevens noted that "Poetry must resist the intelligence almost successfully." In *La chanson d'Eve*, Fauré's recondite idiom—sensuously engaging and hieratically distanced—meets that criterion in a way that must remain hidden from all but connoisseurs and the most devoted of the composer's admirers. Following the first performance on April 20, 1910, at the initial concert of the newly formed Société Musicale Indépendante by Jeanne Raunay, with Fauré at the piano, Ravel wrote, "My dear Maestro, How I should have liked to express my delight to you... after La chanson d'Eve... I was too moved...." *–Adrian Corleonis*

Recommended:

○ **Fauré: Intégrale des Mélodies** / Ameling, Baldwin / EMI 64079

○ **Fauré: Mélodies Vol. 4** / Walker, Krause, Martineau / 2000 / CRD 3479

○ **Jan DeGaetani in Concert Vol. 1** / de Gaetani, Luvisi / 1991 / Bridge 9023

Clair de lune, song, Op. 46/2 (1887)

In Fauré's setting of *Les Présents*—the first of his Two Songs, Op. 46 (1887)—Villiers de l'Isle Adam's elusive poetry seems to hover between joy and sadness, twilight and myth. The Watteau *paysage* of its companion, *Clair de lune*—Fauré's first Verlaine setting—is enveloped in the moonlight of pure fantasy as archetypal stick-figure masqueraders "Play the lute and dance, / And are almost sad under their fantastic disguises!" An impassive vocal line croons in merely occasional agreement with the piano's quasi-plucked accompaniment, which is caught up and engulfed in an archaic minuet which eventually gives way to arpeggiated rapport with the vocal line before the suddenly enchanted exclamation "Au calme clair de lune, triste et beau...." Soon, though, the minuet returns to reach its cadence.

Clair de lune represents Fauré's first excursion into the ideal landscape to which he would return several times as a supreme master of the mélodie—notably, in the *Mélodies de Venise*, Op. 58 (1891), *La Bonne Chanson*, Op. 61 (1892–94), and the fantastic divertissement *Masques et bergamasques*, Op. (1919), in which *Clair de lune* would find its predestined place. By contrast, Debussy's second, more successful setting of *Clair de lune*, from his first collection of *Fêtes galantes* (1891), perhaps protests too much in sensuous striving to evoke a realm which Fauré calls up persuasively in a subtle, deceptively simple *fait accompli*. *–Adrian Corleonis*

Recommended:

○ **A Program of Song** / Price, Garvey / 1993 / RCA 61499

○ **Fauré: Intégrale des Mélodies** / Ameling, Souzay, Baldwin / EMI 64079

○ **Nuit d'Etoiles** / Gens, Vignoles / 2000 / EMI 45360

L'horizon chimérique, song cycle, Op. 118 (1921)

The song cycle *L'horizon chimérique* (1921) is Fauré's last vocal work, and indeed, one of the final works in the composer's catalogue. For the composer's audiences, these four poems by Jean de la Ville de Mirmont, with their images of the sea and of departures, would have had a level of poignant irony: the young Mirmont had been killed only a few years earlier in World War I.

Each of the songs depicts a different aspect of the sea and, even more important, the emotions it evokes. The first, "La mer est infinie et mes rêves sont fous," is quick and restless but free of turmoil. The second, "Je me suis embarqué sur un vasseau qui danse," unfolds with a repeated but slightly uneven rhythmic pattern that suggests the rolling of a ship. The third, "Diane, Séléné lune de beau métal," depicts the light of the moon on the still sea. The last, "Vaisseux, nous vous aurons aimés en pure perte," is the grandest of the four, with majestic lines in both voice and accompaniment. While it returns to the key of the first song, the text speaks of leaving the sea, belonging to the land, and yet still feeling an intense longing for the vast expanse of water.

These songs are often thought of as taking a place among Fauré's most virile efforts for the voice, and certainly the last song in particular has a sturdier tone than many of the composer's earlier works. The pensive delicacy that marked so many of those earlier songs, however, is still present here. All of the songs begin with a light touch, and there are some characteristically delicate moments, as in the last stanza of "Je me suis embarqué sur un vasseau qui danse," with its familiar slow crescendo and relatively rapid decrescendo.*–Ann Feeney*

Recommended:

○ **Fauré: Intégrale des Mélodies** / Ameling, Souzay, Baldwin / EMI 64079

○ **The Sea** / Allen, Vignoles / 1987 / Hyperion 66165

○ **L'Horizon Chimérique** / Sylvan, Breitman / 1996 / Nonesuch 79371

Mirages, song cycle, Op. 113 (1919)

In the summer of 1919, Fauré's utterance became more withdrawn and contemplative, more simple and luminous. Having worked his old-masterly style to vigorous valedictions with the fiery *First Cello Sonata* and the great *Fantaisie* for piano and orchestra, and having gently closed the door on his career as "master of charms" with his largely retrospective *Masques et bergamasques*, he produced his song cycle, *Mirages*. While their vocal technique looks back to *La Chanson d'Eve* (1906–10) in a *chant*-like projection of words and images, their form is tighter, their sparely expressive accompaniments more richly integrated, and their harmonic language developed with the utmost economy.

When his friend, Gabriel Hanotaux, showed him the newly published volume of *Mirages* by the Baronne Antoine de Brimont—a society dilettante—Fauré at once recognized a verbal suggestiveness admirably suited to his music. In "Cygne sur l'eau," the first of these songs, "The black swan swims towards the fleeing unknown." In "Reflets dans l'eau," the quietly anxious, wave-like, rocking accompaniment of "Cygne sur l'eau" becomes serene, though harmonized with subtle piquancy as the swan confronts "the azure depths of time gone by"—simply, tellingly, the ripples are reflected by the piano. This rare pictorial effect may be heard as a metaphor for the composer's dying words to his sons—"When I am no longer here you will hear it said of my works: 'After all, that was nothing much to write home about!' You must not let that hurt or depress you. It is the way of the world.... There is always a moment of oblivion."

In the tranquil stillness of the "Jardin nocturne," earthly delights—"Your scents of iris, jasmine and roses, your somber charms of desire and boredom"—are met for the last time. The final mélodie, "Danseuse," calls up as from a great distance the lure of the erotic—the dance evoked powerfully with a laconic ostinato snap—to end as "wetness shines, a vain kiss, along your smooth thighs, vain dancer!"

Introduced to Fauré by her professor at the Conservatoire early in 1919, Madeleine Grey learned the difficult *La Chanson d'Eve* rapidly and with sufficient acuity to earn the composer's admiration when she performed it at a Fauré Gala on May 30, the composer at the piano. Fauré composed the *Mirages* specifically for her, and Mlle Grey gave their première at a Société Nationale concert on December 27, 1919, accompanied by Fauré—his last performance in that venue. *—Adrian Corleonis*

Recommended:

○ **Fauré: Intégrale des Mélodies** / Souzay, Baldwin / EMI 64079

○ **Fauré: Mélodies Vol. 4** / Walker, Krause, Martineau / 2000 / CRD 3479

○ **Fauré: Mélodies** / Felix, Guiomar / 1994 / Arcana 28

Poème d'un jour, song cycle, Op. 21 (1878)

There is something exaggerated in the combination of the cycle's title, "Poem of a day," and the depiction of an entire cycle of a disappointed love—delirious idealization, romantic despair as the ideal is shattered, and finally cool indifference—events that typically require more than 24 hours' evolution. Fauré's setting captures this exaggerated sensibility, but without the sentimentality that, for example, his compatriot Massenet lavished on his opera of obsessive sensibility, *Werther*.

The first song, "Rencontre," begins in a kind of rapt wonder, with arpeggios swooping upwards in the accompaniment and the vocal line marked dolce. The two verses are close to identical, climaxing in an ecstatic mezzo forte high note expanding to forte before the concluding phrase. The quick tempo and fast motion in the accompaniment give the song the same rushing sense that the poem conveys, the instant infatuation before even knowing the beloved one.

The second, the only song in the cycle in a minor key, is much faster, allegro con fuoco, and even violent in the passionate phrasing. Typically Fauré's songs are sung piano, with occasional mezzo fortes or fortes, but here he wrote the opposite, with most of the vocal lines in a raging forte, complete, of course, with lavish high notes and octave leaps. There are relatively few rests in the relatively long vocal lines, further enhancing the impression of a near-breathless outburst. Again, the two verses are more or less similar.

The last song returns to the major key. This is almost a précis of the emotional journey of the cycle. The tone of this song is more or less dispassionate, with both voice and accompaniment moving in more or less scalar steps until the word "fumee," with the upward fourth and the following piano arpeggio suggesting smoke blowing away, followed by the key change. But even in the brief section before the repeat of the first theme, while there are wider intervals and even a mezzo forte on "fleurs," and a slightly more restless accompaniment, after the change back to the original key and vocal theme, the accompaniment even takes on a lightly accented syncopation, adding to the effect of near-carelessness. *—Ann Feeney*

Recommended:

○ **Fauré: Intégrale des Mélodies** / Souzay, Baldwin / EMI 64079

○ **Fauré: Mélodies** / Hendricks, Dalberto / EMI 49841

○ **Fabulous Victoria de los Angeles** / Los Angeles, Soriano / 1993 / EMI 650612

CHORAL

Cantique de Jean Racine, for chorus & organ, Op. 11 (1865; revised 1866)

At all stages of his career, Fauré was visited by suavely persuasive flights of fantasy transcending (or consolidating) the perennial refinement of his style. In the 20-year-old student's *Cantique de Jean Racine*, Op. 11 (1865), the serene ardor of his four-part setting maintains its interest through the three brief stanzas of Racine's prayer—"Word of God, one with the Most-High.... Pour on us the fire of thy mighty grace"—with a poise into which his years of apprenticeship at the École Niedermeyer are graciously subsumed. Fauré had been a boarder at the prestigious Parisian music school from his ninth year, absorbing the lore of modal music and Renaissance polyphony which would not enjoy a public revival until the concerts of the Schola Cantorum in the early 1890s.

From Niedermeyer's death in 1861, Fauré was taught by the young Saint-Saëns, who was but a decade older, thus beginning a lifelong friendship which no doubt gave a fillip to the younger man's instinct for lucidity, classical proportion, and the sublimation of passion to supreme, subtly wrought eloquence. The *Cantique de Jean Racine* took the École Niedermeyer's first prize for composition in 1865, capping Fauré's student years with a prophetic triumph. Looking back in 1905, the mature composer saw fit to orchestrate the work's organ part for small orchestra. *—Adrian Corleonis*

Recommended:

○ **Fauré: Requiem** / Best (cond.), Corydon Singers / Hyperion 66292

○ **Fauré: Cantique de Jean Racine; Oeuvres chorales** / Alldis (cond.), Houbart, Vocal Group of France / 1984 / EMI Classics 65562

Messe basse (1906–1907)

While on vacation in Normandy in the summer of 1881, Fauré and his pupil André Messager wrote the *Messe des pêcheurs de Villerville* for the small church in the town where they were staying. The church's musicans were both fewer in number and less thoroughly trained than those found in the churches of Paris; accordingly, the composers wrote in a style well suited to amateur performers, but still musically appealing. This approach must have held some personal resonance for Fauré, whose musical career had begun in similarly informal, ad hoc circumstances.

Fauré wrote the *Messe*'s Sanctus, Gloria, and Agnus Dei, while Messager wrote the Kyrie and the O salutaris; no Credo was included. In 1882, the pair collaborated on a version of the work with orchestra. In 1906, Fauré reworked and partially recomposed the *Messe*, leaving out those sections that had been composed by Messager. This version of the work, commonly known by the title *Messe basse*, is that most frequently performed today. The *Messe basse* calls for a somewhat different instrumentation than its predecessor, including soprano solo, women's choir, and organ.

In all versions of the *Messe*, the writing has much of the ethereal clarity and lyric lightness that imbue nearly all of Fauré's sacred music, an effect particularly enhanced by the use of massed female voices. Fauré made little attempt to pictorialize the various texts, instead employing a relatively similar texture throughout. He later used a similar technique in the famous *Requiem* (1887–99), in which he evokes an overall mood rather than creating a theatrical flow à la similar works by Mozart and Verdi. *—Ann Feeney*

Recommended:

○ **Fauré: Requiem, etc.** / Best (cond.), George, Scott, Poulenard, Seers, Corydon Singers, English CO / Hyperion 66292

○ **Fauré: Requiem, etc.** / Corboz (cond.), Alain, Steyer, Paris Audite Nova Choir / Teldec 17897

Pavane, for orchestra & chorus ad lib, Op. 50 (1887)

The years 1886 and 1887 were among the most productive of Fauré's career. In addition to the *Piano Quartet No. 2*, Fauré produced two of his best-known works during these years, the *Requiem* and the *Pavane*. The first version of the *Pavane*, for orchestra alone, was written for the Vicomtesse Elisabeth Greffuhle, one of Fauré's many patronesses. Fauré later made a version of the work that included a choral setting of a text by Comte Robert de Montesquiou, a cousin of the Vicomtesse. The text, written in imitation of Verlaine, evokes images of eighteenth century courtship with its old-fashioned references and pastoral names. In addition to these two versions, Fauré made a transcription for flute and woodwinds, and another for solo piano; the latter version was one of the few works of which Fauré himself made a recording.

Like the *Requiem*, the *Pavane* employs a muted palette, a language more of elegance than of emphasis. The pavane's origins as a stately Renaissance dance are evident in Fauré's reconception: A steady pizzicato undercurrent provides a grounding for the swaying, languid rhythm of the melodic line and Fauré's characteristic seductive harmonies. In the choral version, the musical discourse is set up as a dialogue between the male and female voices; both groups occasionally unite in passages about the power of love. *—Ann Feeney*

Recommended:

○ **Vaughan Williams: Tallis Fantasia; Barber: Adagio; etc.** / Slatkin (cond.), St. Louis SO / 1981 / Telarc 80059

○ **Gabriel Fauré** / Ozawa (cond.), Boston SO / 2001 / DG 469268

Requiem, Op. 48 (1887–1900)

Given the enormous and enduring popularity of Fauré's *Requiem*, it is curious to contemplate the sheer haphazardness by which this familiar masterpiece took shape. The initial version of 1887–88 included but five movements, lacking the Offertorium and the Libera me, and was scored moreover for mixed choir and organ, harp, tympani, violas, and cellos divided, and double basses, with a boy soprano (for the Pie Jesu), and a solo violin for the Sanctus. This version was first heard at the Madeleine, where Fauré was choirmaster, on January 16, 1888, with children taking the soprano choral parts and the young Louis Aubert singing the Pie Jesu. These gentle prayers were found to be dangerous "novelties" by the Madeleine's vicar, and the composer was reprimanded for them immediately following the ceremony. By May, two trumpets and two horns had been added. And in June 1889, the Offertorium was composed and added with a Libera me dating from 1877. Parts for trombones, bassoons, and violins were sketched and may have been included in a performance at the Madeleine on January 21, 1893—the manuscripts are ambiguous. Likewise, it is not known whether the elision of several bars from the Kyrie was made before or after that performance. Attempts to reconstruct the intimate, "authentic" 1893 chamber ensemble version of the *Requiem* have yielded two editions: one by composer and choral director John Rutter, the other by Fauré scholar Jean-Michel Nectoux. Although similar, these editions differ in details of both scoring and text. Meanwhile, a third and final version of the *Requiem* with full orchestra was prepared in 1899, though it has been impossible to establish whether the instrumentation is Fauré's or that of his pupil, Jean Roger-Ducasse. This "symphonic" *Requiem*—the version most often performed and recorded—had its premiere at the Trocadéro, July 12, 1900, with a chorus of 250, a Torrès taking the Pie Jesu (a number that had to be encored), Eugène Gigout at the organ, and the orchestra and chorus of the Conservatoire under the direction of Paul Taffanel.

Throughout, the suggestion of Gregorian chant informed by modern measure and melos lends Fauré's idiom immediate appeal and an aura of timelessness at once. The *Requiem*'s seven movements form an arch whose keystone and crown is the central Pie Jesu—the lone voice petitioning its savior for eternal rest in long-breathed, classically balanced, tender, and infinitely moving phrases—flanked by the serene lift of the Sanctus (over which an exquisite violin cantilena wafts) and the gently consoling Agnus Dei. Coming before and after, respectively, the somber Offertorium and Libera me are reminders of judgment, the more effective for being understated, with their baritone solos standing forth from the choral body to plead for deliverance and rest. At the extreme points, the opening darkly hued Introit and Kyrie are balanced by the sublime radiance of the final In Paradisum—"There may the choir of angels receive thee, and, with Lazarus, once a beggar, mayst thou have eternal rest." *—Adrian Corleonis*

Recommended:

○ **Fauré: Requiem** / Giulini (cond.), Battle, Schmidt, Farrell, Philharmonia / DG 419243

○ **Fauré: Requiem** / Cluytens (cond.), Los Angeles, Fischer-Dieskau, Puig-Roget, Conservatory Concert Society Orch. / 1998 / EMI 66946

KEYBOARD

Dolly, suite for piano, 4 hands, Op. 56 (1893–1896)

The *Dolly Suite* is a set of six short character pieces for piano duet which Fauré composed over the years 1893 to 1896. The set is dedicated to Hélène Bardac ("Dolly"), daughter of the singer, Emma Bardac, with whom Fauré enjoyed a brief relationship in the 1890s. Mme. Bardac would go on to become the second wife of Claude Debussy in 1905; Debussy composed his own homage to domesticity, the *Children's Corner Suite*, for their daughter together, Claude-Emma.

Hélène and her family are at the center of the *Dolly Suite*, which begins with "Berceuse," a peaceful nursery song. "Mi-a-ou"—sometimes taken to be a playful evocation of a cat—was originally intended as a portrait of Hélène's brother Raoul (the title comes from Hélène's attempt to pronounce her brother's name). Fauré wrote the third movement, "Le jardin de Dolly," as a New Year's present for Hélène in 1895. The sly "Kitty Valse" was likewise a present for her, this time for her birthday in 1896. The "Kitty" of the title is brother Raoul's pet dog. The Suite concludes with the romantic "Tendresse" and a spirited bit of Spanish music, "Le pas espagnol."

The *Dolly Suite* displays the refinement, charm, and harmonic transparency that characterizes much of Fauré's piano music, while also maintaining a somewhat childlike naïveté. Unlike some music for piano, four hands, the suite is very light in texture, rarely exploring the depths of sonority that are available with two players at the keyboard. The *Dolly Suite* is also frequently heard in an orchestral arrangement made in 1906 by Henri Rabaud. *—Chris Morrison*

Recommended:

○ **French Masterpieces for Piano 4 Hands** / Crommelynck Duo / 1992 / Claves 509214

○ **Fauré: Complete Music for Piano** / Stott, Roscoe / 1995 / Hyperion 66911

○ **Dolly Suite & Narnia Suite** / Marriner (cond.), Academy of St. Martin-in-the-Fields / 1996 / ASV 6182

Impromptus (1881–1904)

Though Fauré seldom composed at the piano, it was his preferred instrument. Not only did it give him mastery of something complete, but it represented a neutral medium for conveying music qua music, that is, music as an essentially abstract art—decidedly *not* without feeling, but—unencumbered by irrelevant associations suggested by the genre piece titles publishers felt it necessary to attach (e.g., "Paysage," "Mélancolie," "Sous-bois," etc., from Chabrier's *Pièces pittoresques*). In the upshot, the "impromptu" designation for five piano works and a harp piece may not be Fauré's, though it is not inappropriate in suggesting a fugitive, spontaneous outpouring. Toward the end of his life, Fauré proposed to his publishers a collection of his works in which the first three impromptus, composed between 1881 and 1883, should be bound with the four *Valse-caprices* from the same period, thus lending an insight into his own self-assessment—these are all pieces of scintillant éclat and surface charm, though each of the successive impromptus strikes more deeply and with greater mastery than the last. In dramatic contrast, the *Fourth Impromptu*, composed in 1905, catches Fauré at a stylistic crossroads. Opening with peremptory incisiveness, it seems to revisit the brilliantly soaring world of the earlier impromptus, but with agitated dissatisfaction turning to diffident near-truculence in its middle section. And though tonal, the vacillations of key prove provocative and unsettling. The very brief *Fifth Impromptu* of 1909 extends this manner in barbed gossamer (the oxymoron suggests the enigmatic feel of the stylistic compound) to a veritable whole tone ride to the abyss of atonality—a remarkable statement from the composer of the lyric *Pénélope*, the opera upon whose composition he had just embarked! The so-called *Sixth Impromptu*, Op. 86bis, is a transcription of the *Impromptu for Harp* composed in 1904, in which the world of the early impromptus and valse-caprices is touched with grandiosity, a ballade-like aura of the legendary, a note of the heraldic. Taken together, the impromptus provide a peculiarly telling aural glimpse of the chasm which opened between Fauré the seductive lyricist, darling of the opulent salons, the master of the exquisite, and the restless—if still disarmingly suave—Modernist who looms ever more nakedly and insistently after the turn of the century. *—Adrian Corleonis*

Recommended:

○ **Fauré: The Complete Music for Piano** / Stott / 1995 / Hyperion 66911

Nocturnes (1875–1921)

Inaugurated by John Field and wrought with a combination of sensuousness, fantasy, and drama by Chopin, the nocturne is not a form but a genre. In Fauré's hands, the genre gives rise to an emotional expansiveness that becomes more complex and revealing as one follows the 30-year-old post-romantic master of the first nocturnes into the heart of the early modern era as the old master of the last *13 Nocturnes)* in 1921.

Though published by Hamelle in 1883 as Op. 33, the first three nocturnes date from 1875, 1881, and 1883, respectively. From the beginning, one notices the open, airy textures and profusion of melody, along with the "accompaniments," which are seldom without melodic implication. Though Fauré never sounds academic, his thinking is naturally contrapuntal, requiring an exceptional pianist to realize his cantando richness. Late in his career, he noted in a letter to his wife that "There's no place for padding in piano music, one has to pay in cash and make it consistently interesting. It is perhaps the most difficult genre of all, if one aims to be as good as possible—and I certainly do." One could say that the early nocturnes follow an ABA plan, beginning with a lyrical idea giving way to a passionately animated central section before returning to the opening, amplified and garlanded with thematic recalls. The central section of the great *Nocturne No. 4* (1884), on the other hand, is a tranquillamente web of arpeggios in both hands, pierced by a slow, distant tolling of bells building to a rapturously incandescent crescendo—one of the most evocative moments in all of Fauré's works. The *Fourth* and *Fifth* nocturnes are contemporary with the composer's Parnassian phase, and such things as the *Madrigal* (Armand Silvestre), *Aurore* (Silvestre), and *Les roses d'Ispahan* (Leconte de Lisle), whose lyric exquisiteness they share.

The *Sixth* and *Seventh* nocturnes (1894 and 1898, respectively) look forward in the angularity of their lyricism, and backward in their arpeggio-gusted mood of sheer ecstasy. They are also more formally involved, with recalls breaking up the sectional pattern, as if in dialogue. Fauré's harmonic palette—never less than subtly refined—here becomes adventurous, adding an acute note of modulatory suspense, while the *Seventh*'s obsessive syncopated lurch and grinding dissonances strike a peremptory, gnomic note. This Sphinx-like utterance is at its sparest, briefest, and most powerful in the *Ninth* and *Tenth* nocturnes (both 1908), whose idiom is given a revelatory twist in the elegiac *Eleventh* (1913), "In remembrance of Noëmi Lalo," and the nostalgia-haunted *Twelfth*. The airy, wistful tissue of the so-called *Eighth* (1902) is an interloper, having been saddled with the title when Hamelle published it as the last of the *Huit Pièces brèves*. The final, *Thirteenth*, completed on the last day of 1921, reverts to the pattern of the *First*, opening with a despairing, dissonant chorale, yielding to a flight of passionate regret and defiant fantasy before the chorale returns in utter resignation. *—Adrian Corleonis*

Recommended:

○ **Fauré: Nocturnes** / Collard / 1987 / EMI 691492

○ **Fauré: Nocturnes, Impromptus, Romances, Barcarolles** / Stott / 1986 / Conifer 51138

Préludes, Op. 103 (1909–1910)

Composed in 1910, the *Préludes* are Fauré at his most old-masterly. They are also exactly contemporary with Debussy's first book of *Préludes*; where the latter, for all their exquisiteness, are extroverted public statements, Fauré's are a concentrated, inward utterance. The first three *Préludes* date from January and were performed for the first time by Marguerite Long at a Société Nationale concert on May 17, 1910, before being published by Heugel that year. But over July and into the autumn six more *Préludes* followed, and it seems that Fauré then intended to work his way through the cycle of major and minor keys—a plan which fell by the wayside with the resumption of work on his lyric drama, *Pénélope*. The remaining six were issued separately by Heugel the following year and eventually published together with the initial *Préludes* in a single collection in 1923. If their piecemeal appearance and small number helped drop them into obscurity, they are comparable, nevertheless, to Chopin's and Debussy's contributions to the genre in point of pith and emotional power.

In D flat, the first prélude looks back to the Verlaine settings of the 1890s wistfully and with *tendresse*, interrupted by a plangent B section which seems to toll the passing hour, rising to a tense climax soothed by the return of the initial strain and rounded with a coda-like a benediction. Likewise, the restless C sharp triplets of the second prélude are met by a carillon-like admonition. The third prélude seems to recall the dreaming, hesitant interludes of the joyous *Third Impromptu* for piano, of 1883, in a somber G minor rife with nostalgia. In F, the fourth prélude looks forward and backward; it includes a phrase which turns up again in the Menuet of Masques et bergamasques in 1918, and also harks back to the blithe world of the Verlaine settings. The following D minor outburst takes one by surprise—anger yielding almost conversationally to resignation. In E flat, the sixth prélude takes the form of a canon at the octave in a severe, obsessive meditation. The anxious flight of the seventh prélude, in A—composed in early September—is associated with the final illness of Fauré's father-in-law, the sculptor, Emanuel Fremiet. The tiny C minor study in repeated notes suggests a wryly *sec* serenade; the final prélude in E minor—a mere 33 bars—calls to mind the meditative compactness of Bach, albeit with an harmonic motility lending its straightforward statement tortuous piquancy. Taken together, the *Préludes* afford several direct, hence rare, glimpses of Fauré's inner being—in Wallace Stevens' phrase, "a self returning mostly memory." *—Adrian Corleonis*

Recommended:

- ○ **Fauré: Nocturnes** / Collard / 1987 / EMI 691492
- ○ **Fauré: Complete Music for Piano** / Stott / 1995 / Hyperion 66911
- ○ **Robert Casadesus** / Casadesus / 1999 / Philips 456739

CONCERTO

Ballade for piano & orchestra in F sharp major, Op. 19 (Apr. 1881)

The two versions of Fauré's *Ballade*—the first for solo piano, the second for piano and orchestra—have very few bar-to-bar discrepancies, but their effects are quite different. The solo version, using Chopin's *Ballades* as its obvious model, is thick, large-scaled, and passionate; the concerto version, by redistributing the thematic and harmonic strands, seems leaner and more elegant. Fauré showed an early version of the solo *Ballade* to Franz Liszt in 1877; the older composer played part of it, then asked Fauré to finish, saying, "I have no more fingers." The writing is elaborate and formidably difficult in the solo version. The more accessible version with orchestra, which the composer premiered with Edouard Colonne's orchestra in 1881, is no longer a display of virtuosity; this version seems more relaxed, even prettier. Debussy caustically dismissed it as overly charming and effeminate. The *Ballade* enjoys a very free form—"somewhat outside what is usually done," in the composer's admission—but essentially falls into three initial sections, each developing its own theme, followed by a fourth section that combines the second and third themes. In the version with orchestra, Fauré added a bar just before the flute solo that hints at the third theme, thus now incorporating some form of all the thematic material into the work's first 40 bars. The opening Andante cantabile, in F sharp major, introduces the A theme, a lyrical melody over a gently palpitating left-hand accompaniment, with the orchestra delicately supporting and answering the piano's phrases. The piano part soon becomes more declamatory and intense, but then relaxes into the sorts of arpeggios and runs that the score's detractors deemed too frivolously decorative. Some unsettling modulations lead to the E flat minor Allegretto section, dominated by the B theme. This decadent, falling motif is more impetuous (by Fauré's gentle standards) and sends the pianist into long passages of runs and trills. The harmony brightens to B major for the Allegro section (framed by two short Andante interludes), which centers on the rocking and trilling C theme. The final section, Allegro molto moderato, returns to the opening tonality of F sharp major and gracefully intertwines the second and third themes with busy, sparkling piano writing. Fauré eschews a bravura ending, wrapping up the *Ballade* with a few quiet, arpeggiated flourishes. *—James Reel*

Recommended:

- ○ **Marguerite Long** / Cluytens (cond.), Long, Conservatory Concert Society Orch. / 1997 / EMI 7224529
- ○ **Fauré: Complete Music for Piano** / Stott / 1995 / Hyperion 66911
- ○ **Fauré: Orchestra Works** / Tortelier (cond.), Stott, BBCPO / 1995 / Chandos 9416

Berceuse for violin & orchestra in D major, Op. 16 (1879; revised 1898)

In addition to his two fine sonatas for violin and piano, which stand among the most important French examples of the genre, Gabriel Fauré also composed a number of smaller scale works for this instrumental combination. Fauré's first violin sonata, in A major, Op. 13, which was written in 1875, seems to reflect the composer's skill and natural sensitivity as a creator of vocal music; and it is this same facility at "vocalizing" an instrumental line which distinguishes Fauré's best-known single movement work for the piano and violin combination, the *Berceuse in D major*, Op. 16.

The work dates from 1879, four years after the completion of the *First Violin Sonata*. It takes the form of a single movement, often highly concentrated in mood, but nevertheless somewhat limited in emotional range and of little more than three and a half minutes overall duration. The work was first performed in Paris, at one of the concerts promoted by the influential Société Nationale de la Musique, on February 14, 1880. The composer himself played the piano accompaniment for the violinist Ovide Musin, one of Fauré's most enthusiastic and committed champions.

Ovide Musin also premiered the alternative version of the work, in its arrangement for violin and orchestra, at a further concert held in Paris two months later. As Keith Anderson has written, "The Berceuse proved widely popular, something that was not entirely to Fauré's advantage, since its appearance in salon and even cafe repertoire might have been seen to detract from rather than add to his reputation." *—Michael Jameson*

Recommended:

- ○ **Ysaÿe: Violinist & Conductor** / DeCreus (cond.), Ysaÿe, Cincinatti SO / 1996 / Sony 62337
- ○ **Romance** / Levine (cond.), Mutter, Vienna PO / 1995 / DG 447070

ORCHESTRAL

Masques et bergamasques, suite, Op. 112 (1919)

Fauré's last, inwardly turning manner—spare, abrupt, arching toward ever finer gradations of luminosity—had been embarked upon for more than a decade when Prince Albert I of Monaco asked him in 1918 (at Saint-Saëns' prompting) for a brief *divertissement* to be performed at the Monte Carlo theater, which would become known as *Masques et bergamasques*. In collaboration with theater director Raoul Gunsbourg and René Fauchois, librettist of *Pénélope*, Fauré was to provide music for a *fête galant* in the spirit of Verlaine, drawing largely upon his earlier works. In the upshot, only the orchestrated version of the *mélodie Clair de lune*, from 1888, contained verse by "the Faun" (as Verlaine was known to his café cronies), though the *Pavane for chorus and orchestra* of 1887 featured lines by Count Robert de Montesquiou deliberately imitative of Verlaine's style. *Madrigal for chorus and orchestra* (1884) and the *mélodie Le plus doux chemin* (1904) to poems by Armand Silvestre dovetailed well with the spirit of the thing. The slender conceit of the scenario, in which the commedia del arte characters who flit through Verlaine's early verse appear in person to observe and mock the eighteenth century lords and ladies accustomed to being entertained by *them*, owes as much to Watteau—who inspired the décor—as to the poet.

For the Overture and two orchestral numbers, Fauré revised movements of an abandoned symphony dating from 1869—his 24th year—to which he added a Pastorale, the only newly composed music for *Masques et bergamasques*. The latter revives his *galant* style with a loving, old-masterly touch. While the Overture is not pastiche, the young Fauré was obviously moved by classical models—Reynaldo Hahn disarmingly suggested "Mozart imitating Fauré." Likewise, the Gavotte and Menuet were inspired by an even more remote era. Following the horrors of the Great War, and taken together, the oddments of this elegant trifle loomed larger than their sum. They still evoke a grand nostalgia, not merely for the *belle époque*, but for the eternally enchanted *paysages* that haunt Verlaine's early verse. And the freshly felicitous first orchestral essays, indeed, seem predestined for just this use. The Pastorale was Fauré's last orchestral work—in its brief magic there is something of Prospero's "Our revels now are ended." The Monte Carlo production opened April 10, 1919, scoring an immediate success, which led to it being restaged at the Paris Opéra-Comique on March 4, 1920. As a theater piece, *Masques et bergamasques* has frequently been revived in France, while the suite of orchestral numbers drawn from it—Overture, Gavotte, Menuet, and Pastorale—has achieved an enduring popularity the world over. *—Adrian Corleonis*

Recommended:

- ○ **Fauré: Orchestral Works; Incidental Music** / Plasson (cond.), Orch. of the Capitol of Toulouse / 2001 / EMI 74840
- ○ **Pavane: Ravel - Satie - Fauré** / Orpheus CO / DG 449186

Pelléas et Mélisande, incidental music and suite, Op. 80 (1898)

Fauré composed this music between May 16 and June 5, 1898, and conducted it in the Prince of Wales Theatre at London on June 21. He extracted a three-movement suite, published in 1901, and added the Sicilienne in 1909. Fauré courted a gentle muse during a long career that brought him recognition, acclaim, and great honors only after his 50th birthday, despite the fact that his talent had revealed itself at an early age. He was a full-time student in Paris before his tenth birthday, at a school devoted to religious music of the fifteenth, sixteenth, and seventeenth centuries, where he boarded free for a decade. When the founder died in 1861, Camille Saint-Saëns replaced him. Not only did he instruct Fauré in composition, piano and organ, but introduced him to the music of Schumann, Liszt, and Wagner.

After graduation, Fauré made his livelihood in Paris as an assistant or deputy organist until, in 1896, he was appointed both principal at the prestigious Madeleine and professor of composition at the Conservatoire. In 1905, he was appointed director of the latter institution, and served until deafness and poor health obliged him to retire, in 1920.

Never altogether comfortable as an orchestral composer, he specialized in piano, vocal, and chamber music. In later years, especially when his deteriorating hearing played acoustic tricks on him, he solicited help from his students, including Ravel, Charles Koechlin, Florent Schmitt, George Enescu, Nadia Boulanger, and Jules Roger-Ducasse, his favorite.

In 1898, the celebrated actress Mrs. Patrick Campell commissioned incidental music for a London production, in English, of *Pelléas et Mélisande*. He asked Koechlin to orchestrate seventeen cues (including a borrowed Sicilienne from 1893), composed in a three-week hurry. After London, Fauré himself rescored three of them as a concert suite, adding Sicilienne a decade later. It is his masterpiece for orchestra—tasteful, sweetly charming, expressively "proper" and basically chaste, as befits a play that depends on mood for its effect rather than on events.

The "Prélude" depicts the forest in which Golaud discovers fragile, amnesiac Mélisande. Beginning in G major, Quasi adagio, until Golaud's hunting horn approaches, it returns to G for a quiet close. "La fileuse" is the music before Act III, depicting Mélisande at her spinning wheel with Pelléas in rapt attendance—same key and 3/4 time as the "Prélude." The tempo is Andantino quasi allegretto for its oboe and horn solos amid gently whirring strings. Sicilienne, from Act II of the play, is Fauré's portrait of Mélisande, no matter that he borrowed and rescored it for solo flute, harp, and strings. The tempo is slightly quicker (Allegretto molto moderato), the key B flat major, the rhythm 6/8. "La mort de Mélisande" accompanied her cortège in Act V—muted, poignant music marked Molto adagio that was played at Fauré's funeral in 1924. *—Roger Dettmer*

Recommended:

- ○ **Fauré: Orchestral Works; Incidental Music** / Plasson (cond.), Von Stade, Och. of the Capitol of Toulouse / 2001 / EMI 74840
- ○ **Fauré: Requiem; Pelléas et Mélisande, Suite; Pavane** / Dutoit (cond.), Te Kanawa, Milnes, Montreal SO / 1988 / London 421440
- ○ **Fauré: Requiem; Pelléas et Mélisande, Suite; Pavane** / Zinman (cond.), Gomez, Rotterdam PO / 2001 / Philips 464701

Shylock, incidental music and suite, Op. 57 (1889)

"For the first three performances I'll have a reasonable little theatre orchestra. But from the fourth night onwards the *Odéon*'s economic cutbacks begin to take effect: several of the good players are being dropped and instead they're hiring all the useless, feeble and superannuated hacks they can scrape together from the Luxembourg quarter. I can see there's a bumpy ride ahead." Thus said Fauré to his friend and patroness, Countess Elisabeth Greffulhe, before conducting *Shylock*'s premiere on December 17, 1889. As things turned out, Edmond Haraucourt's facile adaptation of Shakespeare's *Merchant of Venice* ran for a respectable 56 performances, drawing critical praise for the sets, but only occasional perfunctory notice for one of Fauré's most exquisite scores. No doubt, the stage business rendered this urbane music—much of it employed to accompany dialogue—truly incidental. For the suite, Fauré dropped several numbers, composed a brief introduction to the "Chanson," expanded the "Epithalame," and augmented the orchestration. In this recension—the form in which the music was published and is invariably performed—*Shylock* was heard to better advantage at a concert of the Société Nationale de Musique on May 17, 1890, conducted by Gabriel Marie, with one M. Lepestre taking the tenor numbers.

Shylock is contemporary with Fauré's discovery of Verlaine—he had already set *Spleen* in 1888, while the *Cinq Mélodies "de Venise"* were to follow in 1891—and anticipates his gallant "Venetian" style, particularly in the two tenor *mélodies*. Indeed, as he was composing, he wrote to Countess Greffulhe in October 1889 that "I had to find for *Shylock* a musical phrase with a certain penetration, like Venetian moonlight, and now I've got it!" This is the ethereal violin melody that floats aloft through the *Nocturne*, suggesting Shakespeare's "How sweet the moonlight sleeps upon this bank. . . ." Opening the suite, on the other hand, the *Chanson* lavishes a disarmingly sanguine charm upon Haraucourt's interpolated verse fluff—"Oh! The girls! Come you sweet-voiced girls/'Tis time to forget your pride and virtue. . . ." The tenor's so-called *Madrigal* is, by comparison, primly and archaically suggestive, matching Haraucourt's invocations of Flora, Pomona, and Astarte, to convey the beauty of "she whom I love." Coming between them, the misleadingly titled *Entr'acte*—with fanfares heralding the entrance of Portia's suitors—is a velvety, gracious bit of pomp and circumstance. The few evocative phrases accompanying Bassanio in the play, as he chooses the casket containing Portia's portrait, have been worked into a substantial, moving "Epithalame" for the suite. The Nocturne follows, with its lunar magic. And a surprisingly breezy Finale, adorned with pizzicato scintillations, offers suave assurance that matters of great pith, moment, and romance have ended well. Fauré has rendered the poetry of the piece splendidly and perhaps too ideally—in Paris, even Shakespeare becomes Parisian, or, more precisely, Fauréen. Or, perhaps it is better said that in Fauré's *Shylock* music, the spirits of Shakespeare and Verlaine mingle in urbane incandescence. *—Adrian Corleonis*

Recommended:

- ○ **Fauré: Orchestral Works** / Plasson (cond.), Orch. of the Capitol of Toulouse / 2001 / EMI 74840
- ○ **Desire-Emile Inghelbrecht** / Inghelbrecht (cond.), National Orch. de la Radiodiffusion Francaise / 2002 / Testament 1266

OPERA

Pénélope (1913)

Following the success of his large-scale music for an outdoors production of *Promethée*, Gabriel Fauré let it be known that he was definitely shopping for a suitable libretto.

Meanwhile a virtual palace coup in the administration of the Paris Conservatoire over the stuffiness and hidebound traditionalism of its curriculum and methods resulted in the appointment of Fauré, the choice of the radical faction, as director of the Conservatoire in 1905. He took this post seriously, taking personal interest in the students and working to reform the curriculum.

Soon thereafter he became interested in a libretto by René Fauchois based on the concluding portion of Homer's *Odyssey*, dealing with the return of Odysseus to Ithaka, where his faithful wife, Penelope, has been cunningly putting off the advances of suitors for her hand (and her husband's throne). The subject is a venerable one as an operatic text: Monteverdi wrote one of the earliest of all operas on the subject of *Il ritorno d'Ulisse in patria* in 1641. Fauré composed the opera primarily during summer breaks from the Conservatoire, so it took five years to write.

Fauré's music epitomized French refinement and reserve. He feared that this quality of restraint might work against the popularity of the opera; he wrote to his wife in 1909 a letter distancing himself from the three opera composers most popular in France at the time, worrying that the French public accepted only "the excessive if always justifiable polyphony of Wagner, the chiaroscuro of Debussy, or Massenet's contemptibly passionate squirmings." He felt himself most like Saint-Saëns and noted that the public was indifferent to the operas of his old friend. "All that gives me shivers down the spine!" he added.

The first performance of the opera was on March 4, 1913, at the Opéra de Monte-Carlo, with Lucienne Bréval conducting. Fauré considered that production more or less a trial run for the Paris premiere two months later at the Théâtre des Champs-Elysées. Fauré's fears proved justified. While the opera has always been highly regarded, its deliberately unspectacular, restrained tone has not made it an audience favorite. It is unoperatic in tone; its main vocal numbers are more like Fauré's exquisite art songs (mélodies) than arias and recitatives, and they should be interpreted that way rather than with overt dramaticism. It was overshadowed by other major musical events of the same time, most notably the premiere of Stravinsky's *Rite of Spring* at the same theater a few weeks later. *Pénélope* was revived in 1919 with much the same results. It has been not infrequently revived, but it has not entered the French or international repertory. *—Joseph Stevenson*

Synopsis:

Act One. In a vestibule outside Penelope's bedroom, some maidservants sit spinning at looms. Voices and laughter are heard off-stage: they come from Penelope's many frustrated suitors. While waiting for her to choose one of them, they've been feasting every night. The giddy maidservants extol the virtues of the various suitors and are puzzled as to why Penelope doesn't choose one. Eurymachus, a suitor, enters. He asks one of the maidservants to bring Penelope a message that she should come join the feasting. But the Queen is absorbed in her grief. Eurycleé, one of the elder maidservants, scornfully orders the suitors to leave. There is a scuffle, which ends when Antinoös makes the threat that they will fetch the Queen themselves.

Penelope appears at the top of the stairs, leaning for support on Eurynome, the old housekeeper. She scolds the suitors for their indiscretion, and Antinoös counters with a plea that she has had enough time—ten years—to make up her mind. Penelope remains convinced that Ulysses will return. They try to hold her to a promise that once she had finished weaving a shroud for Ulysses' father, she would choose among the suitors. She gives in but reveals that she has only woven a tiny part of the shroud. They feel tricked.

Finally Ulysses returns, disguised as a beggar. Eurymachus tries to shoo him away, but Penelope makes him welcome. Antinoös, as the suitors have every night for many years, asks Penelope to take her place at the feasting table, and again she declines. In turn, Antinoös invites the maidservants to join them. The women happily accept. Penelope has Euryclée, the maidservant to Ulysses himself, wash the beggar's feet and serve him food. Euryclée seems to recognize the master, an intuition confirmed by certain scars, but he threatens to strangle her if she makes his identity known.

Penelope, thinking she is alone, sets to her work at the loom. As she has every night, she undoes the weaving work of the day. But the impatient suitors catch her in the act. They swear that the very next day, she'll marry one of them. Her hateful curses fall on deaf ears. Penelope makes ready to leave with Euryclée and the beggar, planning to climb to the top of a hill overlooking the sea. She hopes to catch sight of Ulysses' ship. Left alone momentarily, Ulysses looks around his wife's chamber with great satisfaction. Penelope returns to give the beggar a heavy cloak against the cold.

Act Two. Atop the hill, Eumée praises the beauty of the sea and the night. There is a white marble column there, decorated with rose garlands, with a bench encircling it. A shepherd greets him. Penelope arrives with her party and reveals that she frequently returns here to remember her husband. Eumée vows his loyalty and states his desire to take revenge on the suitors. Penelope turns to the beggar, asking questions about his origins and about how he knows of her husband. When she expresses fears that Ulysses has betrayed her with other women, he reassures her. As Euryclée urges them return to the palace, Penelope tearfully reveals the unwanted marriage that is set to occur on the morrow. The cunning beggar suggests a contest, which she agrees to: she will choose the suitor who is able to bend Ulysses' famous bow. Ulysses, left alone on the hilltop, reveals his identity to Eumée. They rejoice and Ulysses recruits the shepherds to help punish the suitors.

Act Three. In the great hall of the palace, Ulysses hides his avenging weapon—a sword once used by Hercules—beneath Penelope's throne. Euryclée enters; Ulysses entreats her to make sure that Penelope follows the plan and confirms the plans with Eumée. The suitors come in and set the maidservants to decorating the palace. Eurymachus complains of ill omens he has seen that day.

Finally Penelope arrives. At Antinoös' request to hear her choice, she reveals the terms of the contest. She has visions of the wrath of the gods crushing the shameless suitors. They all fail to bend the bow, but the beggar steps forth and easily wins. Now Ulysses reveals himself and brandishes Hercules' sword. The shepherds come in as arranged, and the unarmed suitors are slaughtered to the last man. King Ulysses and Queen Penelope are reunited at last and rejoice in each other's loyalty. The people of Ithaca raise thankful prayers to Zeus. *—Donato Mancini*

Recommended:

- ○ **Fauré: Pénélope** / Lloyd-Jones (cond.), Walker, English, Allan, Oliver / 2002 / Gala 705
- ○ **Fauré: Pénélope** / Dutoit (cond.), Norman, Van Dam, Huttenlocher, LeRoux / Erato 45405

Robert Fayrfax

b. Apr. 23, 1464, Deeping Gate, Lincolnshire, England, **d.** Oct. 24, 1521, St. Albans, England (?)

Composer

A contemporary of William Cornysh and John Taverner, Robert Fayrfax was the most successful English Tudor composer, receiving high honors from King Henry VIII. In 1511, he earned the very first doctor of music degree granted by Oxford University. Although he wrote in many genres, both vocal and instrumental, he is best remembered for his mass settings.

The first 30 years of his life yield no biographical information. Historical records first identify him in 1497 as a Gentleman of the Chapel Royal, a position he held until his death. He received two doctorates in music, the first at Cambridge University (1504), for which he wrote the mass *O quam glorifica*, and the second from Oxford University (1511). A favorite of Henry VIII, he accompanied the king as lead musician to the highest courtly functions, such as the funeral of Henry VII, the coronation of Henry VIII (both in 1509), and Henry VIII's famous meeting with Francis I of France (1520). In addition to numerous monetary and honorary rewards, in 1514 he was made Knight of the King's Alms, a position which guaranteed a lifetime annuity.

Twenty-nine works survive, including six cyclic masses, votive antiphons, Magnificat settings, as well as secular part-songs and instrumental dances. Only a few can be dated; comparing the early and late works shows that, while his contrapuntal technique is remarkably consistent, the mature compositions achieve greater independence of the voices and more controlled dissonant effects.

Most of his religious music is scored for the typical English five-voice ensemble (soprano, alto, high tenor, tenor, and bass). Stylistic features which distinguish his works include a greater propensity for textural and metrical contrasts, along with a restrained melodic style which eschews acrobatic vocal displays in favor of a more balanced line. Fayrfax's compositions show a rather advanced sense of harmonic movement, particularly at cadences. Imitation is used more for decorative effect than as a contrapuntal process.

The mass *O bone Jesu* provides an early example of English parody technique, borrowing material from his antiphon of the same name. The other five are written in the time-honored cantus firmus genre, meaning that free-composed voices are set in counterpoint to a phrase of plainchant, sung by the tenor in long sustained notes. His handling of the cantus firmus varies greatly: the highly technical doctoral composition, *Missa O quam glorifica*, uses a very long cantus heard only once per movement. At the opposite extreme, the *Missa Albanus* has a nine-note cantus, repeated frequently in many clever variations, at times forwards, backwards, or upside-down. All the masses alternate full sections with passages scored for fewer voices, more vocally demanding, but never overtly brilliant. *—Natalie Boisvert*

Overview of Works (ca. 1505–1520)

Gentleman of the Chapel Royal, Doctor of Music at Cambridge (later "incorporated" into the doctorate at Oxford), courtier to Henry VII, and apparent favorite of Henry VIII, Robert Fayrfax shone over the early Tudor age. His music survives in many of the prominent English manuscript sources surviving from the turn of the sixteenth century—the *Eton Choirbook*, the *Lambeth Choirbook*, and the "Fayrfax MS]" of part-songs—and presents the image of an assured and versatile, if somewhat conservative, composer. A comparatively vast repertoire of 29 pieces of his music survives; this includes six complete mass cycles, two magnificat settings, ten antiphons, eight secular songs, and three instrumental pieces. It seems certain that most of his music was performed in the highest circles: the Chapel Royal (with a mass and magnificat "Regali" perhaps even celebrating the coronation of Henry VIII), the renowned Eton College Choir, and the musicians attending the Tudor Court itself.

The bulk of Fayrfax's sacred music employs the five voice parts standard for English music of his time. Structual constrasts are achieved through changes in meter, as well as alternations between full five-voiced textures and reduced trio sections (a stylistic precursor to the "full" and "verse" textures of the later English anthem). His harmonic progressions are fairly advanced and often rife with pungent dissonances. The vocal rhythms abound in four-against-three syncopations and other complexities. He generally treats imitation as a decorative feature, rather than a structural one. The early Marian antiphon Salve regina, surviving complete in the *Eton Choirbook*, exemplifies this style. Another five-voiced Marian work, *Eterne laudis lilium*, cleverly hides an acrostic of the name of Queen Elizabeth of York within its dense Latin text. Both settings of the magnificat—one using material from "O bone Jesu," the other subtexted "Regali"—give polyphony for the even-numbered verses, and contrast different vocal scorings in the interior verses.

All but one of Fayrfax's six masses are based upon a plainsong cantus firmus, following a lengthy English tradition. (Also in typical insular fashion, none of the cycles contains a Kyrie set in polyphony.) The composer treats these chant models in different fashion in each mass, however. The chant "Regali ex progenie" is quoted twice in the tenor voice in each movement of the *Missa Regali ex progenie*, while the lengthier chant "O quam glorifica" only appears once per movement in the Missa O quam (written as Fayrfax's graduation "exercise" for the Cambridge Doctorate in 1504). The *Missa Albanus* takes as its cantus firmus the first nine notes of an antiphon for the patron saint of St. Alban's Abbey, where Fayrfax worked; this tune is quoted some 40 times, including passages in inversion, retrograde, and retrograde inversion, culminating in a climactic passage through all voices during the final *Dona nobis pacem*. The *Missa O bone Jesu*, while not employing a chant melody, borrows from Fayrfax's own antiphon *O bone Jesu*, and may be the first surviving example of English "parody" style.

The "Fayrfax Manuscript" derives its name from an eighteenth century family possession, but also from this composer's strong representation therein. Seven of his vernacular partsongs are preserved there. All but one of his secular songs are for three voices; all deal with themes of courtly love popular in the early Tudor court. These settings most frequently set the lines of text in partially imitative fashion, climaxing in rhythmically challenging florid melismas. Two of his surviving pieces for instrumental consort require the performers to derive the tenor by means of an intellectual puzzle canon. *—Timothy Dickey*

Recommended:

- ○ **Fayrfax: The Masses** / Carwood (cond.), Cardinall's Musick / 2001 / ASV 353
- ○ **Fayrfax: Missa Albanus; Aeternae laudis lilium** / Christophers (cond.), Sixteen / 1988 / Hyperion 66073
- ○ **Fayrfax: Missa O quam glorifica; Ave Dei Patris filia** / Carwood (cond.), Cardinall's Musick, / 1995 / ASV 142

Jill Feldman

b. May 21, 1952, Los Angeles, CA

Soprano

Among early and Baroque music specialists, soprano Jill Feldman has built a major reputation since the end of the 1970s, both for her prodigious technical skills and for her ability to communicate the meaning behind a text. She studied in San Francisco and the University of California at Santa Barbara, where she was a musicology major. Her studies in European and Elizabethan literature drew her to the music of Shakespeare's period, and she later became an expert in vocal styles of the sixteenth and seventeenth centuries. Feldman studied with Lillian Loran and made her operatic debut in 1980 in the role of Music in a Berkeley, CA, production of Claudio Monteverdi's *Orfeo*. She was also the recipient of an Alfred Hertz Scholarship that enabled her to pursue the perfection of her command of period vocal technique under Andrea von Ramm in Basel. Feldman later portrayed Clerio in Francesco Cavalli's *Erismena* in Spoleto, Italy, at the Festival dei due Mondi, and toured with the medieval music group Sequentia, where she performed the *Ordo Virtutum* of Hildegard von Bingen. Her career took a great leap forward in 1981 when Feldman joined the Parisian period music ensemble Les Arts Florissants, through which she essayed the title role in Marc-Antoine Charpentier's *Médée* at *the Salle Pleyel* in Paris in 1984; the work earned all concerned a Gramophone Record Award in England and the Grand Prix du Disque de Montreux when it was recorded and released in 1985 on the Harmonia Mundi label. She subsequently toured America with the Philharmonia Baroque Orchestra, performing repertory by George Frideric Handel, including the oratorio *Susanna* and the cantata *Clori, Tirsi, e Fileno*, of which she also made award-winning recordings. Feldman has been widely praised not only for her technical perfection but also for her ability to communicate the meaning of texts that are usually up to half a millennium old (and may well not have been heard in ensuing centuries)—she has also been responsible for reviving such unheard-in-modern times roles as Vita in Marco Marazolli's sixteenth century *La vita humana*. The latter work was done in association with the Scottish Early Music Consort of Glasgow, with which Feldman has been associated since the mid-1980s. She has also recorded with such celebrated conductors as Frans Brueggen on Haydn's *The Creation*, and Andrew Parrot on Handel's *Carmelite Vespers*. Her frequent collaborators include harpsichordist Kenneth Weiss and viola da gamba virtuoso Paolo Pandolfo. Feldman has also been a noted teacher, conducting master classes in America and Europe, and has trained such notable younger performers as Anabela Marcos and the male soprano Yves la Pech. *—Bruce Eder*

Recommended:

- ○ **Purcell: from Orpheus Britannicus** / Holman, Cunningham, Feldman, North / 1992 / Arcana 2
- ○ **Der Fluyten Lust Hof** / Feldman, Lislevand, Marq / 1997 / Astrée 8588
- ○ **Udite Amanti: 17th Century Italian Love Songs** / Feldman, North / 1991 / Linn 005
- ○ **Purcell: Dido & Aeneas** / Christie (cond.), Laurens, Sicot, Feldman, Cantor, Les Arts Florissants Orchestra & Chorus / HM 905173

Morton Feldman

b. Jan. 12, 1926, New York, NY, **d.** Sep. 3, 1987, Buffalo, NY

Composer: Chamber Music, Keyboard, Choral

Morton Feldman was a unique and influential American composer. His experimentation with non-traditional notation, improvisation, and timbre led to a characteristic style that emphasized isolated and usually quiet points or moments of sound. His work with John Cage and his association with the avant-garde of American painters, including Pollock, Rauschenberg, and Rothko helped him to discard traditional music aesthetics for a less ordered and more intuitive, "moment form" approach to structure. His earlier work of the 1950s utilized graphic notation in which only approximate indications were given to the performers. This eventually proved unsatisfactory to Feldman because it allowed for non-idiomatic, uncontrolled improvisation. Throughout the decade, he experimented with different versions of notation that gave varying amounts of freedom to the performers. The first experiment was to abolish rhythmic notation altogether. The pitches were specified exactly with open note heads, but all other elements were left entirely up to the performers. The second experiment involved giving an identical written part to several players with the intention of producing "a series of reverberations from an identical sound source." A work that is indicative of this reverberation technique is the *Piece for 4 Pianos* (1957). Feldman's third innovation of this period was a variation on the first one. Once again, note durations were left up to the performers, but in this case, all other elements were notated precisely. In his *Prince of Denmark* (1964), for solo percussion, the graphic notation is a key that assists the performer in making their own version of the piece.

By 1970, using conventional notation, his distinctive doctrine of quietness, stillness and lack of dramatic rhetoric was fully in place. Feldman's best-known chamber works of this period include *The Viola in My Life* (1970–71), *Rothko Chapel* (1971), and *Why Patterns* (1978). In his last compositions, Feldman became interested in the use of time and proportion. The resulting pieces became greatly expanded in scale, at least nine lasting more than ninety minutes. His composition *For Philip Guston* lasts four hours, and his *String Quartet II* can take up to six hours to perform. Yet even in his last works, Feldman's method is apparently intuitive, as he never admitted to, nor has any theorist been able to uncover, any systematic means of pitch selection.

Feldman's first teachers were Wallingford Riegger and Stefan Wolpe, but it was his meeting with John Cage in 1950 that set his entire future direction and musical aesthetic. Cage's circle of composers, which also included Christian Wolff and Earle Brown, combined with the influence of the visual artists that Feldman befriended, allowed him to develop his personal and instinctual method of composing. Feldman lived and worked in New York throughout most of his earlier creative career. In 1973, he was offered the Edgar Varèse Chair in composition at the University of New York at Buffalo, which he held until his death in 1987. *—Steven Coburn*

CHAMBER MUSIC

For Frank O'Hara, for flute, clarinet, percussion, piano, violin & cello (1973)

Feldman had two purposes in writing *For Frank O'Hara*: to fulfill a commission to celebrate the 10th anniversary of the Center of the Creative and Performing Arts at the State University of New York at Buffalo, and to mourn the 1966 death of poet Frank O'Hara, run over at age 40 by a beach taxi on Fire Island. Regarding this 18-minute piece, Feldman wrote, "My primary concern (as in all my music) is to sustain a 'flat surface' with a minimum of contrast." The music is exceptionally quiet; separately and in combination, the string and wind instruments play long, static notes, sometimes colored by brief, soft clusters from the piano and vague timbral splashes from the percussion—perhaps a distant tympani roll, perhaps a gentle ping from a pitched instrument. Brief moments of silence also become part of the musical expression. The score patiently proceeds in this manner from beginning to end, avoiding any sense of variation, development, climax, or finality. The music's partisans appreciate its pure, steady, meditative quality; its detractors may be reminded of Ravel's denigration of his own *Bolero* as "15 minutes of orchestration without music." *—James Reel*

Recommended:

- ○ **Feldman: Viola in My Life 2; For Frank O'Hara; Routine Investigations; etc.** / Recherche Ens. / 2000 / Disques Montaigne 782126
- ○ **Feldman: For Frank O'Hara; Bass Clarinet & Percussion; De Kooning** / Lubman (cond.), New Millennium Ens. / 2000 / Koch 7466

For Philip Guston, for flute, piano & percussion (1984)

It was during the late 1970s that American experimentalist composer Morton Feldman began to produce scores whose immense dimensions—the durations of some of these works boggled the minds of even some of the most radical and free-thinking American artists of the day—define the music as much as the selection of pitches and rhythms and tone colors. The 1984 chamber work *For Philip Guston* certainly qualifies as a mammoth piece of music: it takes over four hours to play. Performances of it have not surprisingly been few and far between—but a number of good recordings have appeared over the years! The experience of listening to Feldman's mature music might be likened to submersion into a sea of inactive, unmoving sound—perspectives change, colors shift, but the musical "object" does not (Feldman was more influenced by painters than by musicians during his formative years, and it shows). One might even venture to say that during the four-plus hours of *For Philip Guston* nothing ever happens, but, then again, it was never Feldman's intent to produce anything even vaguely resembling traditional musical rhetoric.

For Philip Guston, which is written for flute, percussion, and piano (the pianist doubles on celesta and the flutist is asked to also play alto flute), is in one long, continuous, spaciously scored movement. Rhythms shift and overlap with changes of pitch and register in a kind of kaleidoscopic manner, sometimes repeating again and again and only gradually taking on new shapes, other times spinning around with relatively great haste. Melody as we know it is absolutely absent: the music is usually given to us just one note at a time. The piano part is notated on just one staff. *—Blair Johnston*

Recommended:

- ○ **Feldman: For Philip Guston** / California EAR Unit / 1997 / Bridge 9078
- ○ **Feldman: For Philip Guston** / Blum, Williams, Vigeland / 1992 / Hat Hut 46104

The King of Denmark, for percussion (1964)

The King of Denmark counts among a group of "graphic notation" pieces composed by Morton Feldman in the late 1950s and early 1960s. The work, scored for one player on unspecified percussion instruments, exemplifies the common characterization of Feldman as a "musical pointillist"—perhaps to as great a degree as any composition in his oeuvre—and demonstrates both Feldman's intense focus on individual musical moments and his careful use of silence as a musical element. The unique notation employed in the piece de-emphasizes the importance of specific pitches or particular timbres, controlling only the overall density and rate of the musical materials while leaving most other decisions in the hands of the performer.

A classic in the modern percussion repertoire, the work indicates at only a few places the particular percussion instruments to be used. In fact, the notes themselves are rather flexible in terms of their pitch and rhythmic placement as well. Feldman uses a musical staff divided into three stacked rows, each row representing a general or relative low, middle, or high range. In order to indicate divisions of time, the rows are divided by evenly spaced vertical lines, each of which indicates the passing of one second of time. Feldman does not use regular note heads or rhythmic figures to indicate musical events, however; rather, he uses a simple set of Arabic and Roman numerals to indicate approximate sound event-densities within a given period of time and within a certain general pitch range. For example, an Arabic numeral "3" appearing in the top row during the same time column as a "1" appearing within the bottom row indicates that within that second of time, the performer is to execute three high-pitched sounds and one low-pitch sound of his/her choice. Roman numerals indicate sounds to be executed simultaneously; thus a Roman numeral "II" spanning all three pitch rows and filling three time divisions indicates that during that period of three seconds, two sounds in any range should be struck at the same time. Throughout the score one also finds several passages in which there are no sounds, or very few, for several seconds at the time. The spartan intensity of this texture is enhanced even further by the curious instruction that none of the percussion instruments should be played with sticks or mallets, but rather struck as quietly as possible with fingertips. These barely audible sounds and long silences have the effect of minutely focusing the listeners ears, as if each individual sound event or event group were examined under the scrutiny of a high-powered sonic microscope. *—Jeremy Grimshaw*

Recommended:

- ○ **Markussion: Heavy Loaded Percussion Recital** / H. Schiff, Leoson, Swedish RSO / Nosag 71
- ○ **The New York School 2** / Schleiermacher, Blum, Williams / 1994 / Hat Hut 6146
- ○ **Perkin At Merkin** / Pugliese / 1991 / Mode 25

Madame Press Died Last Week at 90, for 12 instruments (1970)

Morton Feldman became famous for his very quiet pieces, devoted to exploring diminutive musical ideas in great detail. Some of them are exceptionally long, but this four-minute piece is a brief elegy for the composer's childhood piano teacher, Madame Maurina Press. She was a teacher from Russia, said to have taught the Tsar's children. Feldman recalled that she had a Russian way of just putting the finger down, producing a simple note, "...and you wanted to faint." She gave her 12-year-old pupil the music of Scriabin and Busoni transcriptions of Bach piano music.

When she died in 1970 at, as the title says, the age of 90, Feldman wrote a piece in memory of her. But this was also one of his first exercises in the kind of quiet texture for which he would eventually become famous. Slowly moving notes played by individual instruments perhaps suggest those "simple notes" that Madame Press illustrated. A repeated major third figure in the flute and trumpet suggests a cuckoo clock sounding from somewhere in the distance, and never stops. A chime further suggests a clock. The coaxing, gentle harmonies have something old-world about them and help maintain the quiet ensemble sound. *—Joseph Stevenson*

Recommended:

- ○ **John Adams conducts American Elegies** / Adams (cond.), Orch. of St. Luke's / 1991 / Nonesuch 79249

The Viola in My Life 1–4, for viola & ensembles (1970–1971)

Parts 1 to 3 of this touching series, written in 1970, are for solo viola and small chamber ensemble (violin, cello, piano, flute, clarinet, and percussion) and Part IV (usually written with a roman numeral to distinguish it from the earlier parts), commissioned by the Venice Biennale and written in 1971, is scored for viola and a slightly expanded standard orchestra. These are straightforward, elegant, and thoroughly engaging compositions.

This series belongs to that unusual group among Feldman's work which include autobiographical elements in the form of melodies or simple patterns relating to events in his life—pieces such as *Rothko Chapel*, *For Philip Guston*, and *Madame Press Died Last Week at Ninety*. These melodies and patterns "stand out" in contrast to Feldman's usual and ideal "flat surface" texture.

Feldman structures the viola pieces by cycling particular gestures, effects, and chord forms by employing sophisticated, and ultimately expressive, formal procedures.

A gradually unfolded plaintive melody for the viola begins Part 1, accompanied by non-vibrato, dry harmonics on the strings combined with single flute tones and isolated vibraphone chords; sometimes only the snare drum, tympani, castanets, and viola play together.

Part 2 is characterized by long held tones in the viola part, and varying ways of moving away from that tone by the other instruments—this procedure results in many exquisite harmonies. Towards the end there are slightly varied patterns onto which the instruments lock. The last two notes of the viola, a major third melodic interval, seem to sum up the idea that motivated this part.

At the beginning and end of Part 3 is a tone row stated quickly by the viola. From the first tone row, a steady unfolding by the viola follows, together with isolated piano chords, creating the hypnotic effect of highlighting the harmonic and emotional flavor of these single tones in changing settings (the piano chords).

Part IV is played "very quiet, all attacks at a minimum with no feeling of a beat." To further enable his performers in creating this texture, all of the brass and the strings (except contrabasses) are played with mutes throughout the composition. The viola soloist plays both with and without the mute. Many string notes, especially the pizzicati, are in extreme registers, and airy harmonics are frequently employed (also in the harp part). Most often the strings play rich, sustained harmonies in the middle ranges. Some unusual sounds are created by using fingers to play the various drums, turning the motors off on vibraphones (for a thin, non-vibrato tone), employing fluttertongue in the woodwinds and brass in muted mid-range clusters, and pizzicati shakes on string clusters. The viola, using ascending runs and sudden stresses, becomes more expressive toward the end. Suddenly the orchestra steps forward in fortississimo and highlights quietude by returning immediately to pianississimo. This inevitable resonant decay of a loud action is again demonstrated in the last three measures by the piano, viola, and bass. *—"Blue Gene" Tyranny*

Recommended:

- ○ **Feldman: The Viola in my Life; False Relationships & the Extended Ending; Why Patterns?** / Robison, Barab, Desroches, Ajemian, Bloom, Phillips, Tudor / 1992 / CRI 620

Why Patterns?, for flute, percussion & piano (1978)

The answer to the disarming question posed by the title of *Why Patterns?* was several times given by Feldman himself. He said that while looking at Anatolian-patterned rugs he noticed subtle variations of hue within the each area of color because the hand-dyed yarn used was dyed in small quantities making complete uniformity impossible. Feldman always made it clear that visual art exerted a stronger influence on his subtle approach to composition than any music did. The microchromatic effect produced by the differently dyed yarns woven together, therefore, were inherently attractive to him, and his mind turned to seek possible analogies in music. He asked what in music could "best accommodate, by equally simple musical means, musical color?" The answer of course was patterns. As with many revelations, conversions, and other intellectual epiphanies, Feldman was struck so hard not because the idea was completely new but because it crystallized in words the things he'd been thinking, through his music, for a long time already. And so thanks partly to the habits of Anatolian rug makers, *Why Patterns?* and the music of that period began Feldman's major (and final) creative phase when he arguably composed all of his works of lasting importance. In *Why Patterns?* he put together timbrally distinct instruments that all have a dry sound—flute/bass, piano/celesta, glockenspiel/vibraphone (the three performers double on their respective instruments). Each instrument goes very much its own way throughout the work, playing rhythmically subtle, patterned motifs with a sharp visuality to them. They are idiomatic little statements often framed by hair-breadth rests, and the time signatures, already unusual enough, change with virtually every measure so that the sounds are really always hovering, like brightly colored clouds floating across a dark pond of silence. Toward the end of the piece, which lasts only a half an hour, the patterns of the three instruments finally fall into some alignment by way of a conclusion, but none is ever situated for the ear as musically more important than the others, nor thrust into a musical foreground, so the music flattens out gorgeously into a shimmering, patterned surface in which listeners can lose themselves. *—Donato Mancini*

Recommended:

- ○ **Feldman: Rothko Chapel; Why Patterns?** / California EAR Unit / 1991 / New Albion 039
- ○ **Feldman: The Viola in my Life; False Relationships & the Extended Ending; Why Patterns?** / Blum, Williams, Feldman / 1992 / CRI 620
- ○ **Feldman: Crippled Symmetry; Why Patterns?** / Blum, Williams, Vigeland / 1991 / Hat Hut 6080

KEYBOARD

Extensions 4, for 3 pianos (1953)

Extensions 4 for three pianos, of approximately six and a half minutes duration, was written in 1952–54. The term "extension" in this piece refers to the distance that sounds played "as loud as possible" stand out against the generally quiet dynamic surface level. This work gives an enjoyable rhythmic character to the abstractionism aesthetics of the 1950s (without any compromise of compositional technique on Feldman's part). The overall structure of this piece forms a remarkable and continually intriguing balance of the periods of on-rushing rhythmically bouncing gestures consisting of quickly interweaving material from the three pianos and the periods of gradually increasing silence that separate the larger gestures. Within the delightful rhythmic combinations, momentary loops are formed, but they arise and disappear quickly compared to the other "Extensions"—in *Extensions 4* there is typically only one repetition of an event within a single part, rather than the longer looping phrases that form a noticeable character in the other pieces. The exception to this are some brief moments of imitation between the pianos and, at one point, a very brief relatively loud and fast gesture with all three pianos that sounds like a mechanical piano—quick and even pulses in the middle voices and a single note repeated several times in the high treble range. Toward the conclusion, the events become more spaced apart and generally quieter, but the pointillistic texture is still maintained, and, without any coda, the piece simply ends at one point, still in character. *— "Blue Gene" Tyranny*

Recommended:

- ○ **For Stefan Wolpe; Extensions 4; etc.** / Recherche Ens. / 1995 / Disques Montaigne 782048
- ○ **Morton Feldman: First Recordings, 1950s** / Vandre (cond.), Turfan Ens. / 1999 / Mode 66

CHORAL

Rothko Chapel (1971)

After inventing graph notation with his *Projection I* for solo cello in 1950, Feldman began in the 1960s to write works that used long tones and wordless singing. They were played very quietly, bringing out sounds, harmonic content, and other elements that could not be otherwise heard. This created a sustained, changing but unbroken "flat surface with a minimum of contrast." Written in 1971, *Rothko Chapel* was designed as a consciously meditative work for this architectural space in Houston, Texas, itself constructed as a place for contemplation for persons of all faiths or none. This work, designed to be heard by a listener surrounded with the sounds of the chapel itself, contains slightly more contrasting material that is usual for Feldman, beginning with a long melodic viola solo defined at both ends by quiet tympani rolls. A second section introduces a wordless chorus (on a vocable between "oh" and a closed "ah" sound) intoning beautiful chords ("certain intervals throughout the work have the ring of the synagogue," Feldman says), paced gently by chimes and some rattling percussion; eventually the viola enters again with its long, plaintive melody, and a slow continuous pulse on two tympani notes underlines the music; the chorus begins to sustain a very long unbroken chord (the singers stagger their breaths), paced by chimes. In the third section, an interlude is created for an angelic solo soprano voice (the melody was written "on the day of Stravinsky's funeral service in New York"), viola alternately bowed and pizzicato, and gentle tympani rolls. This moves, seamlessly, into an ending section, a "collage effect" with chorus, a "quasi-Hebraic" melody on the viola (written when Feldman was fifteen), and an unchanging simple reiterated rhythmic pattern on vibraphone. A deeply felt work presented in a simple, beautiful and unaffected realization, evocative of natural religious feeling. *—"Blue Gene" Tyranny*

Recommended:

- ○ **Feldman: Rothko Chapel; Why Patterns?** / Brett, Winant, Abel, Rosenak, Dietrich, California-Berkeley / 1991 / New Albion 039

Frederick Fennell

b. Jul. 2, 1914, Cleveland, OH, **d.** Dec. 7, 2004

Conductor

The growing number of serious compositions for wind ensemble, and the large number of institutionalized ensembles to play them, are in large part due to the efforts of Frederick Fennell. Though his career took him to the orchestral podiums of Cleveland, Boston, Miami, and elsewhere, it is his notoriety as a conductor of music for winds, his prolific recorded output, and his role as the founder of the Eastman Wind Ensemble that perhaps most strongly denote his career.

Fennell was born in Cleveland in 1914. After high school, he entered the Eastman School of Music, pursuing a degree in percussion performance from the only institution in the country to offer one at that time. Fennell became a fixture at Eastman, going on to receive a master's degree in 1939, and being hired in that same year to conduct several instrumental ensembles; he remained at Eastman until 1965. During his years there he transformed concert band into a multifaceted musical wind ensemble that could tap into the large body of long overlooked wind and brass concert music, and establishing a unique tradition and sonority for which new works could be created.

His ideas first took shape in 1951, when under his baton a group of woodwind, brass, and percussion players staged a concert featuring several works from composers as wide-ranging as Adrian Willaert, Orlando Di Lasso, Giovanni Gabrieli, Mozart, and Beethoven. Fennell not only resurrected "lost" works, but gave due attention to new ones: Stravinsky was represented, as was the American composer Carl Ruggles. "This program," wrote Fennell, "argues strongly against the old complaint leveled against wind instruments that there is no music written for them which is of sufficient interest to make anyone care to hear it performed." And thus the Eastman Wind Ensemble was born.

The growth of wind ensembles and wind music was also aided by Fennell's and the Eastman Wind Ensemble's impressive output of recordings. Raoul Camus, documenting Fennell's career for the *New Grove Dictionary of American Music*, observed that "Fennell's pioneering series of 24 recordings for Mercury brought about a reconsideration of the wind medium and established performance and literature models for the more than 20,000 wind ensembles that were subsequently established in American schools."

Fennell's innovations appear in retrospect to be part of a larger effort in the mid-twentieth century to establish a distinctive American musical sound and identity. It was during Fennell's years at Eastman that his colleague Howard Hanson established an annual symposium to foster new American music for orchestra—a project that inspired a similar effort on Fennell's part, to elicit works for winds from American composers. Fennell definitely saw his wind ensemble project as a patriotic contribution to Western culture. "Granting the rich inheritance with which the American music heritage began [that is, the inheritance of the European musical tradition], it is not surprising that we finally have emerged as a people worthy of that legacy." In creating an ensemble that could variously serve an educational function, execute original and transcribed works from the Western canon, and foster the creation of new works (and, as evidenced by the widely-ranging styles within subsequent wind repertories, entirely new sonorities), Fennell helped define the character of American music, and the role of music in American society. *—Jeremy Grimshaw*

Recommended:

- ○ **Marches I've Missed** / Fennell (cond.), Dallas Wind Symphony / 1998 / Reference 85
- ○ **Hands Across The Sea** / Fennell (cond.), Eastman Wind Ens. / 1994 / Mercury 434334
- ○ **Country Gardens** / Fennell (cond.), Eastman-Rochester Pops Orch. London Pops Orch. / 1993 / Mercury 434330
- ○ **Screamers** / Fennell (cond.), Eastman Wind Ens. / 1991 / Philips 432019

Brian Ferneyhough

b. Jan. 16, 1943, Coventry, England

Composer

Within a generation of highly influential, progressively modernist English composers, Brian Ferneyhough (b. 1941 in Coventry) maintains perhaps the highest profile and most distinctive voice. Most of Ferneyhough's early training in music came from playing in, and conducting a brass band. He began formal training at the Birmingham School of Music, although the school provided no courses in composition. He went on to study composition with Lennox Berkeley at the Royal Academy of Music. After traveling to the Netherlands for the 1968 Gaudeamus Week, he decided to move to Europe, where he worked with Ton de Leeuw in Amsterdam and with Klaus Huber in Switzerland.

In addition to his influence as a composer, Ferneyhough has established an important legacy as a teacher. From 1973 to 1986 he taught at the Musikhochschule Freiburg, and from 1976 has been a frequent instructor at the Darmstadt Summer courses. From 1987 to 2000 he was Professor of Music at the University of California, San Diego, and in 2000 he became affiliated with Stanford University. Renowned former pupils include the Finns Kaija Saariaho and Magnus Lindberg. Ferneyhough's interest in the classical music of the twentieth century was piqued when he heard a recording of Varèse's *Octandre* while in his mid-teens. Further exposure to the music of Webern, Schoenberg, Boulez and other "modernists" came through scores found at the libraries of Coventry and the Birmingham school. Ferneyhough followed these leads to writings about the Second Viennese School by René Leibowitz and articles on current music in such publications as *Die Reihe*, which provided him with information on the background and techniques of serialism. Ferneyhough's first acknowledged composition is the *Four miniatures for flute and piano* (1965). Other important early works include the mixed ensemble piece *Prometheus* and the *Sonatas for String Quartet*, both pieces of substantial length and complexity completed in 1967.

By the 1980s, Ferneyhough's dense, highly structured, post-serial compositional approach came to be known as the "New Complexity." This term, to some degree a reaction to "New Romanticism," also describes the music of fellow countrymen Michael Finnissy and James Dillon, and is considered a musical analog to literary and architectural Deconstructivism. Ferneyhough's major 1970s work includes the three *Time and Motion Studies*: I for bass clarinet, II for solo cello with electronics, and III for 16 solo voices with electronics and percussion. Other works include *Transit* for six solo voices and chamber orchestra and the orchestral *La Terre est un homme* (1976–79). Part of the composer's philosophy involved the dynamics of notation versus interpretation, leading him to write works whose performance, as notated, was unattainable by the instrumentalist. This is particularly true of the solo works of the period, especially *Unity Capsule* for solo flute, in which the notation of this evidently monophonic work required up to four staves at once.

In the early 1980s Ferneyhough worked at IRCAM, researching the possibilities of instrument-computer interactivity, with few concrete compositional results. His concern for confronting the history of notational and performance praxis continued in the 1980s in scores such as *Lemma-Icon-Epigram* for solo piano (1981), the *Carceri d'invenzione* series (through 1987), *La chute d'Icare*, and String Quartets 2–4. Important pieces in the 1990s include *On Stellar Magnitudes* for mezzo-soprano and five instruments (1994), *Allgebrah* for oboe and nine solo strings (1990–96), *Masons noires* (1992–98), and a Carnegie Hall commission for pianist Maurizio Pollini, The Doctrine of Similarity, premiered in March 2000. *—Robert Kirzinger*

Overview of Works (1963)

British composer Brian Ferneyhough is an important figure in the history of late twentieth century music. Considered part of the vanguard of the so-called school of New Complexity, Ferneyhough is renowned—or notorious—for composing music that is fiendishly difficult, for both performers and audiences alike. His music is philosophical or metaphysical in orientation; that is, the surface complexity of the music is a natural outgrowth of the underlying complex philosophical ideas that inspire and structure his works. Many of his compositions make use of some kind of serial procedure, and often feature microtones. Structure and sense in his music also rely heavily on a dialectic of figure and gesture; that is, timbre, density, stasis, action, and comprehensibility constitute the identities of discrete musical lines, which enter into a kind of elaborate dialogue as a work progresses.

While Ferneyhough did study at the Royal Academy of Music and at the Amsterdam Conservatory, he a largely self-taught composer. His music reflects the influence of several important, formative sources, namely the music of Anton Webern, Pierre Boulez, and Karlheinz Stockhausen. Ferneyhough's early works, dating from the early to mid-1960s, include a *Sonata for two pianos*, an assortment of pieces for solo piano, and *Coloratura for oboe and piano*, among others. These works particularly display the influence of the serial compositions of Boulez and Stockhausen. Ferneyhough's *Miniatures* for flute and piano (1964) suggest a Webernian interest in intensity, concision, and compression.

In the 1970s, Ferneyhough's music took a turn towards indeterminacy, employing random elements in both form and musical content. Works from this period include the well-known piece *Cassandra's Dream Song*, as well as *Sieben Sterne* (Seven Stars). As of the mid-1970s, Ferneyhough largely abandoned indeterminacy as a compositional technique, and began composing music that placed exacting demands on performers. This is particularly evident in pieces like the *Time and Motion Studies I and II*, composed between 1971 and 1977, which also include electro-acoustic elements.

As Ferneyhough matured as a composer in the 1980s, his music began to reflect an engagement with the past, in particular with pre-Modern and early Modern German and Austrian composers, most notably Arnold Schoenberg. This engagement resulted in a number of remarkable works for string quartet, including the *String Quartets Nos. 2–5*, *Adagissimo*, and a *String Trio*. These pieces are complex musical essays that explore relationships between instruments and employ contrast and transformation as compositional principles. Form, in these later works, is often subject to subversion by insurgent musical elements, reflecting Ferneyhough's ongoing musico-philosophical concerns with the problem of form and the question of meaning.

Ferneyhough's music stands in sharp contrast to another trend in later twentieth century music: New Romanticism or New Simplicity. Ferneyhough's compositions, in the face of this trend, continue to be unapologetically complex and cerebral. *—Alexander Carpenter*

Recommended:

- ○ **Ferneyhough 1** / Arditti SQ, Arcadian Academy / 1994 / Disques Montaigne 789002
- ○ **Ferneyhough 2** / Arditti SQ, Arcadian Academy, ASKO Ens. / 1996 / Disques Montaigne 782029
- ○ **Ferneyhough: String Quartet 4; Kurze Schatten II; etc.** / Arditti SQ, ASKO Ens. / Naive 782169
- ○ **Ferneyhough: Prometheus; La chute d'Icare; On Stellar Magnitudes; etc.** / Nagy (cond.), Bernasconi, Pomarico, Castellani, Molinari, Renggli, Contrechamps Ens. / Accord 205772

Kathleen Ferrier

b. Apr. 22, 1912, Higher Walton, England, **d.** Oct. 8, 1953, London, England
Contralto

Although her career was tragically short, Kathleen Ferrier was among the most famous English singers of the twentieth century. Her contralto voice—a rarity in itself—was characterized by a firm, warm tone that found its expressive niche in the great works of oratorio and art song, as well as in her two operatic roles (only two!): Lucretia in Britten's *The Rape of Lucretia* and Orfeo in Gluck's *Orfeo ed Euridice*.

Born in Lancashire on April 22, 1912, Ferrier studied the piano with great success as a child and intended a concert career; her concurrent vocal studies were considered more recreational in nature. In her mid-20s, however, after taking two first prizes at the 1937 Carlisle Festival—one for piano and one for singing—she made the decision to pursue singing as her vocation. She studied with J.E. Hutchinson in Newcastle upon Tyne, then with Roy Henderson in London.

During the years of World War II Ferrier toured widely in England, gaining a reputation as an especially fine concert artist. She joined the Bach Choir in London, and was alto soloist for a 1943 performance of Handel's *Messiah* at Westminster Abbey. Benjamin Britten first put her on the operatic stage at Glyndebourne on July 12, 1946, in the premiere of his chamber opera *The Rape of Lucretia*. She then toured with the work throughout England and appeared on an historic recording of major extracts from the work conducted by the composer. Britten would later compose the alto part in his *Canticle No. 2* for her.

She appeared in the United States for the first time in Mahler's *Das Lied von der Erde* with the New York Philharmonic and Bruno Walter; her subsequent recording of the work—also under Walter's direction—remains a classic. Walter also appeared as her accompanist in lieder recitals in Edinburgh and London. Another of Ferrier's notable successes was the part of the Angel in Elgar's *The Dream of Gerontius*.

In February 1953, Covent Garden staged Gluck's *Orfeo ed Euridice* specifically for Ferrier, who was deemed ideal for the part of Orpheus. However, she was able to appear in only two of the scheduled four performances because of weakness caused by her already advanced cancer. These were her last appearances; she died in London on October 8, 1953. Before she died she was made a Commander of the Order of the British Empire. *—AMG*

Recommended:

- ○ **Mahler: Das Lied von der Erde; 3 Rückert Lieder** / Walter (cond.), Ferrier, Patzak, Vienna PO / 2000 / Decca 466576
- ○ **Songs My Father Taught Me** / Goodall, Goldsborough (conds.), Ferrier, Brannigan, Stone / 1993 / Gala 318
- ○ **Gluck: Orfeo ed Euridice** / Stiedry (cond.), Ferrier, Ayars, Vlachopoulos, Francis, Southern Philharmonia Orch. / 2002 / Dutton 9730

Emanuel Feuermann

b. Nov. 22, 1902, Kolomed, Ukraine, **d.** May 25, 1942, New York, NY
Cellist

Emanuel Feuermann's father was a self-taught violinist and cellist. Emanuel's elder brother, Zigmund, was a prodigy on the violin. Their father presented Emanuel with a violin, but the boy insisted on holding it upright, like a cello, so his father bought him a small cello. The family moved to Vienna so Zigmund could continue his violin studies and launch a concert career. Emanuel took lessons from Fridrich Buxbaum, the principal cellist of the Vienna Philharmonic and a member of the Rosé String Quartet. Later, Feuermann became a pupil of Anton Walter at the Vienna Music Academy.

When Feuermann was ten years old, he heard the debut of Pablo Casals in Vienna in 1912. Feuermann realized that the great Catalan cellist was "truly re-creating the instrument." He demanded to study more substantial works. Feuermann's concert debut was in Vienna in February 1914, playing the Haydn *D Major Concerto* with Felix Weingartner conducting the Vienna Philharmonic Orchestra. The debut was a success, but not spectacular. He joined his brother on a concert tour with his father.

In 1917 Emanuel went to study with Julius Klengel. Now Feuermann began to soak up training, music, and general knowledge. He systematically divided his day into practice sessions, work in music theory, piano practice, and building a repertoire. He interspersed this with avid reading. In 1918 the cello professor at the Gürzenich Conservatoire in Cologne, Friedrich Grützmacher, died. Klengel proposed Feuermann replace him. Sixteen-year-old Feuermann was hired, with full responsibilities of a professorship, but not the august title.

During the 1920s Feuermann added frequent and arduous concert tours and appearances to his schedule and began making recordings. He joined the faculty of the Berlin Hochschule für Musik in 1929, now ready for the title of professor. He formed a string trio with Joseph Wolfstahl (later replaced by Szymon Goldberg) on violin and Paul Hindemith on viola. This famous trio made several recordings, including a one of Hindemith's *String Trio No. 2*.

The ascension to power of the Nazi Party in 1933 left him looking for a place to settle. He took a world tour in 1934 and 1935, with a pair of memorable New York concerts in January 1935. He and his wife settled in Zurich, where he gave master classes and based his touring career. He traveled to Austria, where he was trapped when Hitler's forces poured in to take the country. Violinist Bronisław Huberman managed to get Feuermann out and into Palestine. A month later Feuermann, his wife, and his daughter arrived in New York and applied for citizenship. He taught at the Curtis Institute in Philadelphia and in summers settled in Los Angeles, where he gave master classes. There, he could be close to Jascha Heifetz and Artur Rubinstein, making up one of the greatest of trio ensembles.

Following the example of his early idol Casals, Feuermann advanced the instrument's playing technique. He worked hard to eliminate the remainder of a nasal tone that had been thought part of the natural sound of the instrument. He stressed the role of the entire body in playing the instrument. He is credited, along with Casals, as having established the cello as a solo instrument. On May 19, 1942, he was admitted for routine, minor surgery. As a result of carelessness, peritonitis set in and he died six days later at the age of 39. *—Joseph Stevenson*

Recommended:

- ○ **Piano Trios of Schubert & Beethoven** / Rubinstein, Heifetz, Feuermann / RCA 60926
- ○ **Cello Concertos of Haydn & Dvořák** / Sargent, Taube (conds.), Feuermann, Berlin State Opera Orch. / 2000 / Naxos 110908
- ○ **The Young Feuerman** / Feuermann, etc. / Pearl 9077

Zdeněk Fibich

b. Dec. 21, 1850, Všebořice, Bohemia, **d.** Oct. 15, 1900, Prague, Bohemia
Composer: Keyboard

Fibich was the third of the leading Czech composers of the last half of the nineteenth century, after Smetana and Dvořák. His music is strongly Romantic and often intensely personal. Less nationalistic than was fashionable for much of his later life and early posterity, his works have only recently begun to meet a revival of interest.

Fibich's mother was a from a cultured Viennese family, while his father was a Czech forestry official. He was born in a remote rural town and later moved to another, Liban. All his life he retained a love of nature. Fibich was home-schooled by his mother until he was nine; she also taught him piano, and then referred him to a local priest, Frantisek Cerny, for studies in music theory. He later attended a private music school in Prague; by the end of his schooling, Fibich had written over 50 compositions. Most were piano pieces and songs, but some were more ambitious, including an attempt at music for the final part of *Romeo and Juliet* and a symphony sketched out on four open staves. In 1865 he entered the Leipzig Conservatory, studying with Ignaz Moscheles and others. He returned to Bohemia in 1870, lived with his parents a year until he had turned 21, and then moved to Prague.

He began composing full-time, writing an opera, *Bukovin*, to a libretto by the same writer responsible for Smetana's *The Bartered Bride*. In 1873 he married Ruzena Hanusova and took a position directing a choir in Vilnius, Lithuania. His tone poem of that year, *Zaboj, Slavoj, and Ludek*, deeply influenced Smetana's nascent *Má Vlast*. Soon the newlyweds were expecting twins, but Fibich suffered the loss of his wife, her sister, and both babies over the next two years.

Fibich took a job at the Provisional Theater in Prague, and married a third Hanusova sister, Betty, in 1875. They had a son, Richard, in 1876. This baby survived, but the marriage did not. Finding that his theatrical duties took him away from composition, Fibich gave them up in favor of a position at the Russian Orthodox Church in Prague in 1878. He wrote a fairly successful opera, *Blanik*, and became interested in the unusual musical form of the melodrama. He came to be one of the most successful composers in that genre.

In 1881 Fibich resigned from his church position and devoted himself full-time to composing and teaching. Soon he fell in love with a pupil, a singer named Anezka Schulzová, and eventually abandoned his wife and son for her. Miss Schulzová was a well-read young woman who directed Fibich toward texts with a feminist orientation. Indeed, of his last four operas, she wrote the texts for three of them. *Sarka* (1897), about a Czech female military leader, was his most successful work, in part due to its patriotic theme.

Fibich also began writing an immense series of short piano works called *Moods, Impressions, and Reminiscences*, composed between 1891 and 1899. They form virtually a musical diary of his affair with Schulzová, and often they are exceptionally intimate and passionate. In 1899 he returned to a position as producer at the Provisional Theater, now called the National Theater. He died unexpectedly of a kidney infection in 1900. *—Joseph Stevenson*

Overview of Works (1865–1900)

Czech composer Zdeněk Fibich was the best trained and most internationally oriented of the Czech Romantic composers after Dvořák and Smetana. Unfortunately, these qualities seem to have lowered his standing both at home and in the Czech Republic. While Dvořák and Smetana and their successors Janáček, Novák, and Suk all sound clearly Czech in their folk song-based melodies, piquant and supple harmonies, and especially their sparkling orchestrations with prominent woodwind writing. Fibich sounds more like a highly skilled and fluent international composer of the second half of the nineteenth century. After he graduated from the Leipzig Conservatory, where he was trained under students of Mendelssohn, Fibich spent his early years learning the musical language and styles of Paris and Germany. When he returned to his homeland in his early twenties—then a part of the Austro-Hungarian empire called Bohemia—he continued to speak German both literally and musically. His early symphonies—the *First* (1877–83) and the *Second* (1892–93)—have little that could specifically be called Czech in them. Their structures are conventionally Mendelssohnian and their dramatic themes do not sound especially individualistic. Even his early overtures and tone poems based on Czech subjects—*Toman and the Wood Nymph* (1874–75) and *A Night in Karlsteine* (1886)—could have been written by an Austrian or German composer. But despite the seeming lack of surface characteristics that could be called Czech in Fibich's early work, there is something deeply Czech in Fibich's later music: a sweetness-tinged melancholy, a flexible sense of harmony, and, above all, a sensuous and even erotic lyricism. These qualities are most easily heard in his piano miniatures *Moods, Impressions & Reminisces* (1868–1900). These 376 pieces are an erotic musical diary of Fibich's affair with Anezka Schulzová in which he records everything from walks they took together to descriptions of nearly every part of her body. The themes and harmonies of the *Moods, Impressions & Reminisces* show Fibich at his most intimate and least studied and are arguably his most personal and characteristic works. Despite the obvious inwardness and essential privacy of these pieces, Fibich began to appropriate their themes and harmonies for his operas and stage works. Thus, his operas *The Bride of Messina* (1882–83), based on Schiller, and *Hedy* (1894–95), based on Byron, have some of the same sensuously lyrical melodies and warmly erotic harmonies as the *Moods, Impressions & Reminisces*. Arguably Fibich's greatest achievement as a composer was his monumental trilogy of melodramas *Hippodamia* (1888–91) based on Sophocles and Euripides. With speaking parts declaimed above a web of dramatic leitmotifs whose passionate lyricism is clothed in opulent orchestral colors, Fibich created an immense and moving fusion of play and opera. If he had lived past his 50th year, there is no telling how Fibich would have developed this mood of composition. *—James Leonard*

Recommended:

- ○ **Zdeněk Fibich** / Albrecht (cond.), Czech PO / 1995 / Orfeo 350951
- ○ **Fibich: Sarka** / Cambreling (cond.), Beňačková, Kirilova, Urbanova, Lotric / 2000 / Orfeo 541002
- ○ **Fibich: Overtures & Symphonic Poems** / Valek (cond.), Prague SO / 1994 / Supraphon 1823
- ○ **Fibich: Complete Symphonies** / Järvi (cond.), Detroit SO / 1998 / Chandos 9682
- ○ **Fibich: Works for Violin & Piano** / Suk, Hala / 2000 / Supraphon 3473

KEYBOARD

Malírské studies (Studies of Paintings), Op. 56 (1898–1899)

Czech composer Zdeněk Fibich successfully wrote in many forms—opera, symphony, symphonic poem, chamber music—but he composed more music for piano than any other instrument. Most of these pieces are collected in his *Moods, Impressions & Reminiscences*. His only other large work for solo piano is his *Malírské Studies* (Studies of Paintings), Op. 56, five pieces based on paintings that Fibich admired or for which he felt a particular affinity. Composed in the late 1890s toward the end of what would prove to be a short life—Fibich died unexpectedly of a kidney infection at the age of 50—the *Malírské Studies* combine Fibich's richly Romantic melodies with lush chromatic harmonies to create what are arguably his best works for the piano. Two of the five are particularly impressive: "The Dance of the Blessed" based on Fra Angelico's *The Last Judgment*; a Lisztian tone poem for piano of rapturous serenity; and "Io and Jupiter," based on Correggio's sensuous painting of the same name, which in its passionate eroticism is said to depict or evoke an episode from Fibich's ongoing love affair with one of his students. *—James Leonard*

Recommended:

- ○ **Anthology Of Czech Piano Music Vol. 5** / Kvapil / 1994 / Unicorn Kanchana 9149

Moods, Impressions & Reminiscences, Opp. 41, 44, 47 & 57 (1892–1899)

The piano cycle *Moods, Impressions, and Reminiscences*, by Zdeněk Fibich (1850–1900) originally comprised several hundred mostly short pieces, of which some 376 in total survive. The set owes its origin to the almost pathologically obsessive infatuation to which Fibich succumbed on meeting a much younger woman—after which he quickly left his second wife, a devoted but unprepossessing woman named Betty Hanušová. Fibich had married Betty's sister Rùzena in 1873. Upon her death she entrusted her husband to Betty, whom he married more out of duty than any emotional attachment. It was an awkward if domestically secure arrangement, and for a number of years, Fibich immersed himself fully in life as a freelance composer. Then he met and fell in love with one of his piano pupils, Anezka Schulzová (1868–1905), in 1886.

Anezka was an attractive, intelligent, and emancipated young woman who became Fibich's composition student. Their steamy romance scandalized Prague society and also set back the composer's professional aspirations. Nonetheless, their love affair resulted in this huge collection of intimate sound pictures that forms a very personal diary of the relationship. The pieces encapsulate the young woman's capricious moods, depict Fibich's own impressions of her at different times of day, and even offer fairly explicit musical representations of various parts of her body. The pieces also recall many events they shared together, and a considerable number carried Fibich's own detailed annotations, which, for obvious reasons of propriety and decency, did not find their way into any of the published editions. A total of 352 of Fibich's *Moods, Impressions, and Reminiscences* were published, 127 as his Op. 41 in 1894, 35 more as Op. 44 a year later, and a further 24 posthumously in 1902 as Op. 57. *—Michael Jameson*

Recommended:

- ○ **Moods, Impressions & Souvenirs** / Howard / 1995 / Chandos 9381

Arthur Fiedler

b. Dec. 17, 1894, Boston, MA, **d.** Jul. 10, 1979, Boston, MA
Conductor

A populist programmer, avuncular podium presence, and constant visitor to small-town concert halls and living room televisions, Arthur Fiedler personified orchestral music in America. He was less glamorous, less intellectual, and in many ways less respected than Leonard Bernstein, but those deficiencies worked to Fiedler's advantage in the minds of ordinary Americans. He also enjoyed greater longevity on his home turf—nearly 50 years in the national limelight, as opposed to Bernstein's one decade of unmatched glory in New York before running off to Europe to become another gray eminence. Fiedler's success, though, was also the source of some frustration; he was forever pigeonholed as a pops conductor.

He had studied violin with his father, Emanuel Fiedler, a member of the Boston Symphony Orchestra (as was Arthur's uncle Benny). In 1909 his father took him to Berlin to study violin with Willy Hess; young Arthur also took a class in chamber music with Ernst von Dohnányi and studied conducting. In 1913 he and two Fiedlers unrelated to him formed the Fiedler Trio. But he fled World War I in 1915, settling into the second-violin section of the BSO under Karl Muck. Fiedler later moved to the viola section, and doubled on celesta and other keyboard and percussion instruments. In 1924 he organized the 25 member Boston Sinfonietta (later known as the Arthur Fiedler Sinfonietta), drawn from members of the BSO, taking it on tour through New England.

In 1929 Fiedler started a series of free outdoor summer concerts at the Esplanade on the banks of Boston's Charles River, playing popular American music and light classical pieces. Soon the concerts attracted audiences in the thousands. The BSO noticed, and in 1930 engaged Fiedler to conduct the Boston Pops, succeeding Alfredo Casella. He remained with the Pops until his death, gaining the distinction of holding the longest music directorship of an American orchestra. For nearly half a century he maintained the Esplanade formula of popular music mixed with classics, some of them new but rather light works such as (Walton's *Façade*, Shchedrin's *Carmen Ballet*). Concert conditions were poor—the audience was seated at tables, clinking beer glasses and pushing chairs around—but Fiedler seemed to revel in the festive atmosphere.

He was a social animal, and he loved to ride on fire engines. Fiedler's antics were harmless and, indeed, contributed to his Everyman appeal, but his willingness to make commercial endorsements for everything from whisky to orange juice hurt his prestige in conservative Boston; he was never allowed to conduct in the BSO's regular subscription series (although he did record *Dvořák's "New World" Symphony* with the orchestra). Still, he was tremendously popular nationwide; he led pops concerts by the San Francisco Symphony from 1951 to 1978, and also began to make international appearances as a guest conductor in 1957. He received the Presidential Medal of Freedom in 1977, and a footbridge near the Esplanade bears his name.

Fiedler and the Boston Pops recorded from the 1950s through the 1970s with RCA records (with brief excursions to other labels toward the end), issuing disc after disc of classical overtures and ballet pieces, as well as arrangements of movie themes, Beatles hits, and other pop tunes. Pops concerts were packaged as fast-moving one-hour shows on the PBS television network. Critics usually ignored or snickered at Fiedler's handling of pop music, but they almost always approved of the verve he brought to light and not-so-light classics; indeed, his 1930s recording of a particular Beethoven overture was held in higher esteem than Toscanini's. Whether Fiedler's Beethoven *Seventh* could have stood up to Toscanini's will never be known. *—James Reel*

Recommended:

- ○ **Fiedler Greatest Hits** / Fiedler (cond.), Boston Pops Orch. / 1991 / BMG 60835
- ○ **Arthur Fiedler and Boston Pops at the Movies** / Fiedler (cond.), Boston Pops Orch. / 2003 / BMG 47947
- ○ **Carmen Ballet** / Fiedler (cond.), Boston Pops Orch. / 1999 / BMG 63308

John Field

b. Jul. 26, 1782, Dublin, Ireland, **d.** Jan. 23, 1837, Moscow, Russia

Composer: Keyboard, Concerto

John Field, the greatest Irish musical figure of the Romantic era, developed a highly influential keyboard style that provided a direct path to the music of Chopin. In contrast to his immediate predecessors, Field wrote music that calls for characteristically expressive and sensitive performance rather than virtuosic bravura. According to renowned and respected musicians like Spohr, Glinka, and Hummel, Field's playing was marked by a particular sweetness and delicacy and an emphasis on color and tasteful expressivity. Such qualities are reflected in Field's best-known and most influential compositions, primarily his nocturnes. At a time when piano music was typified by forms and genres like the sonata, theme and variations, fantasia, rondo, and fugue, the development of an independent composition emphasizing mood rather than thematic development or embellishment was both original and important. The development of the keyboard character piece paved the way for generations of Romantic composers, including Mendelssohn, Schumann, and Chopin, all of whom were indebted to Field.

In addition to numerous nocturnes, Field also produced a significant amount of other music for piano solo or piano in combination with other instruments. Field's first published works, the *Three Sonatas*, Op. 1, are interesting mainly for the fact that, having been written under the influence of Clementi, they present the only structurally conventional works in Field's output. Otherwise, they are uninteresting and derivative. While more original in style, the remainder of Field's works are episodic in form and rely upon melodic charm and invention for effect. The composer's many dances, rondos, and various other short works are mostly insignificant, tossed off for Field's own use on specific occasions. The seven piano concerti, on the other hand, are wholly representative of the typical virtuoso concerti of the period, and while they lack originality, Field makes effective, idiomatic use of the instrument.

Field began his piano studies with his father, and later studied with Tommaso Giordani. He made his debut at the age of nine; in the following year, Field and his family moved to London, where the young musician was apprenticed to composer/piano manufacturer Muzio Clementi. On February 7, 1799, Field premiered his *Piano Concerto No. 1*; shortly afterward, his apprenticeship with Clementi expired. For the next two years, Field was in demand as a soloist in London but continued to work for Clementi. Their relationship continued through 1803, when Field chose to remain in St. Petersburg after his appearance there during a tour. Spohr's autobiography suggests that Field was poorly treated by his former master, and St. Petersburg may have provided Field's first real opportunity to establish an independent career. Field, at any rate, lived in Russia for the rest of his life, achieving rather remarkable success as both pianist and composer. Shortly after his death, his works faded into obscurity; today, however, his legacy as a seminal figure in Romantic piano composition is secure. *—Steven Coburn*

KEYBOARD

Nocturnes (1812–1835)

At the time of their first publication, John Field's nocturnes were unique. Single-movement piano pieces were either variations on a theme, fugues, rondos, or multi-mood fantasies. Field's nocturnes are not constructed after any of these formal patterns or processes and, in opposition to the contemporary trend, do not follow an extra-musical program. They each expound a single mood (usually melancholy), are simple in form, and present virtuosic embellishments of melodies. In general, the accompaniment is in the left hand and requires significant use of the sustain pedal, while the right hand is responsible for the expressive melodic material. All of them evince what Liszt referred to as Field's "pearly" piano sound. Field's nocturnes influenced not only Chopin's works of the same name, but other works as well. For instance, Chopin's *Etude in E flat minor*, Op. 10, No. 6, conspicuously resembles Field's *Nocturne No. 3 in A flat major*.

In E flat major, *Nocturne No. 1* is simple and tranquil, with little harmonic variation. *No. 2* in C minor is filled with nervous agitation and intense expression amplified by outbursts of ornamentation with a single-note line soaring above an arpeggio-dominated accompaniment. The third nocturne verges on the degree of chromaticism in Chopin's works. All three of these date from 1812.

Field's second set of nocturnes appeared in 1817. *No. 4*, in its harmonic adventurousness, shows the growth of Field's compositional powers . In contrast is the popular fifth nocturne, in B flat major, with its almost stark musical material. *No. 6*, in F major, has been given the nickname "Cradle Song," and its restless, nervous mood belies this sobriquet.

No. 7, in C major (1821), is marked "Dreamily" and produces its effect through some of Field's richest harmonies and most flamboyant ornaments, all supporting the evocation of a distant, ringing bell. Field achieves contrast in the central section mainly through increased intensity rather than new material. *No. 8*, in A major was first published in 1811 as a "pastorale," in which version it was 35 measures longer. When it was printed in its present form, in 1815, it still was not titled "Nocturne" but rather as one of three *Romances for Piano*. Its central section is an excellent example of Field's ability to embellish a simple line. *Nos. 8* and *9* were not entitled "Nocturne" until 1835.

Despondent and unsettled, *No. 10*, in E minor (1822), features two recitative-like sections that break the forward motion. Like *No. 8*, *No. 11* (1833) explores repeated notes, while the diminutive *No. 12* (1834) is more decorative. *No. 13* (1834) has a song-like melody and formal structure, while the excellent and long *No. 14* (1835), with its busy main theme, is tonally ambiguous. *No. 16* (1836) is fueled by the contrast between its song-like cantando and agitated scherzo sections. In *No. 17* (1832), Field experiments with harmonies and greatly extends his melodies. Contrast is at its greatest in *No. 18* (1832), and its characteristics have led some critics to not include it among the "true" nocturnes. *—John Palmer*

Recommended:

- ○ **Field: 15 Nocturnes** / O'Conor / 1990 / Telarc 80199
- ○ **Field: 15 Nocturnes** / Spada / 1995 / Arts 47181

CONCERTO

Piano Concerto No. 1 in E flat major, H. 27 (1799)

John Field was a musician of the top order. He was also, however, undisciplined when it came to both life and music, something that hurt his career and musical stature in two ways: he whiled away long periods drinking himself into debt and sickness and ultimately cutting years off of his life, and he never mastered the fine art of musical form well enough to tackle large forms with the suavity and assuredness that might have kept his name on the tongues of future generations. Field nevertheless composed seven piano concertos, and all have their virtues; some, indeed, are extremely attractive pieces, however much deficiencies of architecture might count against them.

Field's *Concerto No. 1 in E flat major* was composed in 1798 or 1799, when Field was still a teenager apprenticed to Muzio Clementi. The occasion of its premiere—February 7, 1799, at King's Theatre in London (the concert was described as one to help support old and "decayed" English musicians!)—was a most happy one for Field, and he was immediately launched into the professional English music circuit. Not until 1815 or 1816, however, was the concerto published by Breitkopf and Härtel of Germany.

Field's piano concertos, like the rest of his music, were largely abandoned after the first half of the nineteenth century, and today there are special difficulties in putting together authoritative editions of them. The original editions consisted of piano parts and separate orchestral parts; no full scores were printed, which means that the scholar must piece the works back together by collecting whatever parts can be found and consulting whatever manuscripts might happen to have survived. Add to this the fact that Field and his publishers often arranged the concertos for performance by a solo pianist without orchestra (resulting in multiple versions of the same music), and you can have a real headache. What listeners can be relatively certain of, however, is that the orchestration of the concertos is Field's own, or at least mostly Field's own. His father, Robert Field, was a violinist of some accomplishment, and he seems to have given his son sound advice on the matter of instrumental deployment.

The *Concerto No. 1 in E flat major* is in three movements: Allegro, "Air Eccosais," and Rondo. The first movement begins with an energetic idea from the orchestra, complete with a recurrent, snappy accented second beat; the soloist enters with florid, keyboard-spanning music that seems quite a tangent from the solid, concise theme set up by the violins at the start of the piece. The second theme is a nifty idea in broken octaves that is cleverly thrown backwards off the beat by one eighth note—a very novel thing for 1799. The "Air Eccosais" is an ornamented instrumental rendition of the Scottish song *"Within a Mile of Edinboro Town,"* while the Rondo is a nimble dash in 2/4 meter. *—Blair Johnston*

Recommended:

- ○ **Field: Piano Concertos 1 & 2** / Bamert (cond.), O'Rourke, London Mozart Players / 1995 / Chandos 9368
- ○ **Field: Piano Concertos 1 & 3** / Haslam (cond.), Frith, Northern Sinfonia of England / 1997 / Naxos 556770

Piano Concerto No. 2 in A flat major, H. 31 (1811)

John Field's second foray into the realm of the piano concerto, the *Piano Concerto No. 2 in A flat major* has always been his most famous and for a large part of the nineteenth century was a staple of the concert artist's and teacher's repertoire. It's not really certain when he wrote the piece—sometime between 1805 and 1811, most likely—and it may in fact be that the *Concerto No. 2* was actually the third of his concertos to be composed and that it and the *Concerto No. 3* got flip-flopped somewhere along the way (Field's first four concertos were published more or less simultaneously in 1815–16, and Field was hardly the type of composer to keep notes on his music and its chronology).

The *Concerto No. 2* is really quite better than the youthful *Concerto No. 1* (composed back in 1798 or 1799). *No. 1* opens bright and brash and, while undeniably impressive for a teenage work, continues in a more or less generic fashion. At the start of *No. 2*, on the other hand, all is velvet and subdued. The audience is given to understand, in these first bars, that tunefulness and ingratiating sound will be more important in the concerto than flash and dazzle or iron-backed tutti drama; but when the soloist enters in a bravura torrent of sound, it is learned that all is not to be lyric and gentle. And when martial dotted rhythms invade the movement and drive it forward through its wild, loud center, one cannot but think of the powerhouse virtuosi yet to come in the century—indeed, such virtuosi loved this piece. Soloist and orchestra are in perfect conflict with one another—background and foreground are made palpable not just by dynamics and the employment of colorless accompaniment, but by a juxtaposition of basic musical characters: smooth, refined on the one hand, electrifying on the other. Herein lies the genius of Field's *Concerto No. 2*. It is, one must say, a remarkably modern approach to concerto writing.

The concerto, like most of Field's, has three movements: Allegro moderato, Poco Adagio, and Rondo. There is a justly famous B major episode in the middle of the first movement—it shines and shines, and the pianist conjures up a brand new melody to play for it. The E flat major second movement is marked molto espressivo and was published separately in 1811 under the title *Serenade*. The finale is, like the finale of the *Concerto No. 1*, a rondo romp in 2/4 meter. *—Blair Johnston*

Recommended:

- ○ **Field: Piano Concertos 1 & 2** / Bamert (cond.), O'Rourke, London Mozart Players / 1995 / Chandos 9368
- ○ **Field: Piano Concertos 2 & 3** / Stern (cond.), Staier, Cologne Concerto / 1999 / Teldec 21475

Piano Concerto No. 3 in E flat major, H. 32 (1811)

There is room for some debate about whether Field's *Concerto No. 3 in E flat major for piano and orchestra* was originally a multi-movement concerto at all. In two rather than Field's customary three movements, it may have been put together by German publishers Breitkopf and Härtel, with Field's participation, when they were publishing the first batch of Field piano concertos in 1815 and 1816. The second movement, a rondo in polonaise style, is known to have been written before 1809, when it was published in Russia as an individual piece under the name "Polonaise favorite en forme de Rondeau." It is known that sometimes Field wrote only two movements for his concertos and then inserted an arrangement of one or another of his nocturnes as a slow middle movement. Could it be that in the case of the *Concerto No. 3* this process of ad-hoc assembly was carried one step further? The first movement of the *Concerto No. 3* may have been composed and then abandoned; and when it came time to publish, it would have been a simple and practical thing to "borrow" the aforementioned polonaise movement for use as a finale. While no slow movement was ever permanently attached to the concerto, there are records of Field performing it with one of his nocturnes at the center. Of course, it may well be that any or all of Field's seven piano concertos were in fact put together in such a way, and that the seams were just hidden better than they were for *No. 3*. The issue is clouded a bit by the fact that the polonaise movement exists in multiple versions. The solo piano version is without an extended middle section heard in the concerto finale version. Was this now-you-hear-it-now-you-don't middle section added for the concerto, or was it taken out for the solo version? The chronology may never be clarified.

Many people believe that at least the first movement of the *Concerto No. 3* predates Field's *Concerto No. 2*. In the usual two-theme Allegro sonata-concerto form, it has little of the sophistication that makes the *Concerto No. 2* so attractive a piece of music. It was, as a result, forgotten even before the rest of Field's music was forgotten during the latter half of the nineteenth century.

The polonaise second movement, on the other hand, lasted far longer. Bright and bouncy and in 3/4 meter, it is dedicated to Clementi, Field's teacher, and seems to foreshadow some of the polonaises of Chopin, who knew and admired many of Field's pieces (most famously, the nocturnes, a genre in which Chopin borrowed quite liberally from Field). The episode heard in the concerto version but not heard in the solo piano version is a series of wide arpeggios in C major, a nice digression from the snappy E flat major of the rest of the movement. *—Blair Johnston*

Recommended:

- ○ **Field: Piano Concertos 3 & 5** / Bamert (cond.), O'Rourke, London Mozart Players / 1996 / Chandos 9495
- ○ **Field: Piano Concertos 2 & 3** / Mackerras (cond.), O'Conor, Scottish CO / 1994 / Telarc 80370
- ○ **Field: Piano Concertos 2 & 3** / Stern (cond.), Staier, Cologne Concerto / 1999 / Teldec 21475

Piano Concerto No. 4 in E flat major, H. 28 (1819)

When German publishers Breitkopf and Härtel set out to issue the very first editions of John Field's first four piano concertos in 1815 and 1816, they perhaps didn't realize that one had already slipped by them—the *Concerto No. 4 in E flat major* had been published in St. Petersburg, Russia, in 1814. This fourth concerto marks a return to the three-movement form heard in Field's first two concertos, after a brief digression to two-movement form for the *Concerto No. 3*. (It is also further evidence of Field's deep love for E flat major—three of the first four concertos are cast in that key!) While never as famous as the *Concerto No. 2 in A flat major*, this work is widely regarded as Field's best piano concerto. Field himself must have liked it, for he took the trouble to make a complete arrangement for solo piano as late as 1824.

The concerto's first movement is the usual sectionalized compound of lyricism and virtuosity. Smooth strings and woodwinds at the opening, piano comes in more forcefully. Field called the second movement a Siciliano; do not wait, however, for the characteristic dotted sicilienne rhythm, for it never comes. In G minor, it is to be played at Poco adagio tempo, and exists in early and late versions that give us a glimpse at Field's compositional process—that process seems often to have been quick draft and gradual revision. The Allegretto rondo that finishes the concerto is wonderfully spirited; Field seems to be enjoying himself thoroughly, and from time to time the piano and orchestra come very close (perilously close, to some tastes) to seeming like a couple dancing a do-si-do. *—Blair Johnston*

Recommended:

- ○ **Field: Piano Concertos 4 & 6** / Bamert (cond.), O'Rourke, London Mozart Players / 1996 / Chandos 9442
- ○ **Field: Piano Concertos 2 & 4** / Haslam (cond.), Frith, Northern Sinfonia of England / 1997 / Naxos 553771

Piano Concerto No. 5 in C major, H. 39 (1817)
John Field himself named this concerto "L'incendie par l'orage," roughly translated as "Fire by Lightning." The work is believed to have two inspirations: Daniel Steibelt's 1798 piano concerto "L'incendie de Moscou" and Beethoven's *Pastoral Symphony*. Steibelt was, like Field, a resident of St. Petersburg; his concerto referred to the fires of Moscow that met Napoleon's army in 1812. Field's opening movement bears resemblance to the Beethoven in its depiction of a storm and the calm aftermath. It is not known if Field's title bears any relation to an actual event. The first movement, Allegro moderato, begins in C major with a mild, lyrical first theme and more stirring second theme. The piano exposition essentially ornaments these themes in the same florid style found in his *Nocturnes*. The development section of the movement, in C minor, is the storm itself, filled with unresolved diminished seventh chords helping to depict the violence of the storm. A tam-tam signals the end of the storm and the recapitulation of the themes, with an extremely brief cadenza rounding out the movement. The following Adagio is not so much a full movement, than it is a slow introduction to the Allegro finale, an animated, carefree rondo with a brilliant coda. *—Patsy Morita*

Recommended:

○ **Field: Piano Concertos 3 & 5** / Bamert (cond.), O'Rourke, London Mozart Players / 1996 / Chandos 9495

○ **Field: Piano Concertos 5 & 6** / Haslam (cond.), Frith, Northern Sinfonia Chorus / 2002 / Naxos 554221

Piano Concerto No. 6 in C major, H. 49 (1819; revised 1820)
After having lived in St. Petersburg for close to a decade, Field, along with his wife Adelaide and their newborn son, moved to Smolensk in 1819. By that time, the marriage was close to ending, however, and soon after the move, Adelaide left Field and carried on an independent career as a piano teacher. It was in these stressful circumstances that Field composed the sixth of his seven piano concertos. The *Concerto No. 6* was given its premiere in 1819 and after a revision the following year, was eventually published in both Moscow and Leipzig in 1823. Field had made quite an impression with the *Piano Concerto No. 5*, with its vivid portrait of a firestorm. The *Concerto No. 6*, despite its length and complexity, did not go over quite so well. But it still contains a number of delightful ideas and provides the kind of opportunities for display on the part of the soloist that Field's enthusiasts had come to expect. The lengthy first movement, which accounts for nearly two-thirds of the concerto's half-hour duration, begins with a lighthearted march theme that recurs throughout the movement, as does the more flowing second idea. Field actually provides a number of themes that are worked over in a rhapsodic fashion. A noteworthy episode in the key of B flat—featuring a theme in the pianist's left hand over triplets in the right hand and quiet chords from the orchestra—bears a resemblance to Schubert's *Der Wanderer*, although Field likely didn't know of this contemporaneous piece. The second movement is an arrangement of Field's gentle *Nocturne No. 6* transposed from its original key of F into E major. This song without words is light and graceful, with transparent orchestral backing. A rather exotic, quasi-Oriental theme acts as the refrain of the Rondo final movement, in which the soloist gets an opportunity to shine in Field's exciting, extravagant piano writing. *—Chris Morrison*

Recommended:

○ **Field: Piano Concertos 4 & 6** / Bamert (cond.), O'Rourke, London Mozart Players / 1996 / Chandos 9442

Piano Concerto No. 7 in C minor, H. 58 (1822; revised 1822)
The first movement of what would be John Field's final piano concerto, No. 7 in C minor, was first performed by the composer in March 1822. Field was traveling between St. Petersburg and Moscow at the time, making his living primarily by teaching and concertizing. It was the beginning of a period of ill-health, depression, and very little composition that lasted eight years. He did not complete the concerto until 1831, around the time he made his last visit to England. Field premiered the work in Paris on Christmas Day 1832. Not having written such a large work in some time, he was worried about his and its reception, and with some justification, because the audience was much the same as had heard Chopin's Paris debut the year before. The critics did not think the concerto was his best work, but the audience enjoyed Field's playing enough to ask him to repeat a portion of the concerto. In this concerto, as in his others, Field borrows from his other works. The first movement, Allegro moderato, begins with the tympani and woodwinds quietly introducing a theme that came from a previously written albumleaf, followed by a vigorous secondary theme on the violin. Neither theme is really developed, as two somewhat unrelated interludes are used instead of a development section before the recapitulation and coda. The first interlude, a slow one in G major, is what was eventually published as his *Nocturne No. 12*, but it is unclear which came first, the nocturne or the concerto. The second interlude, in A major, returns to the movement's original tempo, but has a syncopated piano supported by strings, woodwinds, and horn. The second movement is a rondo, with which Field always ended his concertos. However, there is more of a partnership between the soloist and orchestra in this one than in the others. In this instance, the rondo theme feels almost like a Viennese waltz and was particularly admired by Schumann. In contrast to the facileness of the theme, the intervening passages show how imaginative Field could be. There are a couple of interesting episodes in this movement as well: a passage for strings featuring pregnant pauses and a brief adagio passage right before the coda featuring a small trumpet fanfare. Also, in contrast to the C minor opening movement, this one is in the happier C major. *—Patsy Morita*

Recommended:

○ **Field: Piano Concerto 7; Divertissment 1 & 2; etc.** / Bamert (cond.), O'Rourke, London Mozart Players / 1997 / Chandos 9534

Montserrat Figueras

b. Barcelona, Spain
Soprano
Soprano Montserrat Figueras is an early music singer best known for her work with the group Hespèrion XX (now known as Hespèrion XXI). A member of a musical family, she studied singing as a young girl with Jordi Albareda, originally as part of her studies to be an actress. She joined a local chorus called Aleluya, and then, having developed an interest in early music, she joined Enris Gispert's Catalan early music ensemble Ars Musicae.

In 1968, Figueras married Jordi Savall, who was then a viol player for Ars Musicae. Together they traveled to Basel, Switzerland, to study there in the Schola Cantorum Basiliensis and the Basle Music Academy. She, Savall, and keyboard player Ton Koopman recorded a successful LP called *El barroco español*. She and Savall, together with Lorenzo Alpert and Hopkinson Smith, then founded Hespèrion XX, specializing in early music of the Italian and Iberian peninsulas.

Figueras also frequently performs with La Capella Reial de la Catalunya. Her solo programs center around repertory from the Renaissance and Baroque periods, but also include some modern works, as well as some Mozart. *—Joseph Stevenson*

Recommended:

○ **Luys Milan: El Maestro, 1536** / Figueras, Smith / 2002 / Astrée 9976

○ **El Cant de la Sibil-la I: Catalunya** / Savall (cond.), Figueras, Bernardini, Capella Reial de Catalunya / 2002 / Astree 9971

○ **Isabel I: Reina de Castilla** / Figueras, etc. / 2004 / Alia Vox 9838

○ **Dufay** / Figueras, Savall, Lawrence-King / Travelling 1006

Irving Fine

b. Dec. 3, 1914, Boston, MA, **d.** Aug. 23, 1962, Boston, MA
Composer: Chamber Music, Orchestral
Aaron Copland described his friend and colleague Irving Fine as belonging to what he called the American "Stravinsky school," and indeed much of Fine's early work shows the influence of Stravinsky as well as Hindemith. A tonal language that is basically dissonant characterizes these early works. In later works, such as the *String Quartet* (1952) and the *Fantasia for string trio* (1956), Fine worked to integrate elements of serialism into his earlier tonal approach. Although he continued to experiment with serial technique, Fine's late works show more of an interest in contrapuntal and rhythmic organization. In addition to his work as a composer, Fine was a well-known teacher and conductor. He also wrote articles and reviews, which were published in such journals as *Modern Music*, *Notes*, and *Musical America* as well as in the *New York Times*.

Fine lived most of his life in and around the city of his birth. After attending the public schools in Boston and Winthrop, MA, he studied composition with Hill and Piston at Harvard University, earning a B.A. in 1937 and an M.A. in 1938. He went on to study in Cambridge, MA, and in Paris with Nadia Boulanger, as well as studying orchestral conducting with Serge Koussevitzky at the Berkshire Music Center at Tanglewood in Lenox, MA. Fine taught in the music department at Harvard from 1939 to 1950, where, in addition to his teaching duties, he conducted the Harvard Glee Club. In 1950, he became a professor at Brandeis University in Waltham, MA. Also, during the summers from 1946 to 1957, he was on the composition staff at the Berkshire Music Center. Over the course of his career, Fine received two Guggenheim Fellowships, the National Institute of Arts and Letters Award, a Fulbright Research Fellowship, as well as many other awards and grants. At the time of his death, in addition to serving as professor of music at Brandeis, he was the chairman of the Brandeis School of Creative Arts. *—Stephen Kingsbury*

CHAMBER MUSIC

Partita for wind quintet (1948)
Irving Fine's *Partita for woodwind quintet* certainly shows the influence of Igor Stravinsky's neo-classicism, from its antique title to its piquant harmonies and strong rhythms. But Fine had a lyricism all his own to offer, and the *Partita*, using an unusual structure, creates space for it to blossom. An Introduction and Theme first movement establishes the mood early, with high-spirited bursts of melody from all the instruments; one of these, toward the end of the movement, serves as material for the following extended Variation movement, which is as long as the entire preceding movement. Here the textures become even busier, with numerous

quick, running lines and carefree trills ornamenting the theme. Fanfare-like music from the horn introduces music which is a little more nervous. An interlude, with a slow, yearning melody and limpid harmonies, leads into a playful gigue. Here, the music starts and stops seemingly on a whim, veering off in new directions or returning to old ones; the impressive thing is how Fine keeps a basic melodic line present through most of the whirling. The final moments of the gigue, which stop, go into another direction, and end with a sweet final chord, would seem to provide a fine conclusion, but the work is not over. Fine titles an entire movement Coda, closing out the *Partita* with an unexpected seriousness. The beginning and end of the movement slowly unspool melodies and ornament them with sprays of repeated notes; the middle feels almost like a funeral march, at one point conjuring strident major-mode chords and immediately settling back into the minor. Fine's wit and pathos both shine in the *Partita*, making it one of his more appealing works. *—Andrew Lindemann Malone*

Recommended:

○ **Fine: Notturno; Partita; String Quartet; Hour-Glass** / Schwarz, Hoose (conds.), Jolles, Dane, Los Angeles CO, New York Chamber Symphony of The 92nd Street Y / 1988 / Elektra Nonesuch 79175

ORCHESTRAL

Serious Song: A Lament, for strings (1955)

Through most of his abbreviated life (he died in his forties), Irving Fine was essentially a neo-Classicist who at the end moved toward a dissonant style influenced by 12-tone techniques. Yet his *Serious Song*, written near the height of his career, is a deeply lyrical, almost Romantic work. The composer called it "an extended aria for string orchestra," and it is as direct in its form as in its expression.

Fine composed *Serious Song* on commission from the Louisville Orchestra. Carefully avoiding any overripe harmonic effects that would draw comparisons with Samuel Barber's *Adagio for Strings*, the piece begins with a searching yet severe unison statement by the violins of its first principal theme. The key is a constantly fluctuating E major and minor, so modal that Fine settled on calling it "E Phrygian." This theme receives a flowing, contrapuntal development, but soon gives way to the piece's extended, more animated central section essentially in C minor and calling to mind certain passages of Stravinsky's *Apollo*. This second section itself falls into three parts: first, a new, more active theme, then its development with what Fine called "considerable tonal digression," and finally a restatement of the theme as it originally appeared, but with a climax leading to the third section of the overall work, which returns to the material from the very beginning. Here the tonality is mostly E major and the textures thin out, but constant tremolando and pizzicato effects preclude any sense of peace. The work fades out into a couple of glum, triple-pianissimo plucked notes. *—James Reel*

Recommended:

○ **Metamorphosen Performs Chamber Orchestra Works** / Metamorphosen CO / 1995 / Albany 194

Gerald Finzi

b. Jul. 14, 1901, London, England, **d.** Sep. 27, 1956, Oxford, England

Composer: Vocal, Concerto, Chamber Music

A pacifist who believed that creative artists were the prime representatives of a civilization, Gerald Finzi is perhaps best known as a composer of songs. He believed that all texts of artistic merit can be set by composers who wish to work with their artistic substance; none are either too fine or too familiar. Many of his songs are set in an aria-like style. His accompaniments, designed to complement and support the material of the singer, are often reminiscent of the treatment given his short orchestral works. Finzi was influenced in his melodic and harmonic vocabulary by the music of Elgar and Vaughan Williams. His works also show a strong influence by the music of J.S. Bach.

The son of an English ship broker, Gerald Finzi began to study music with Ernest Farrar in 1914. When Farrar joined the army in 1916, Finzi began to study with Edward Bairstow at York. In 1922, drawn to the English countryside, Finzi moved to Painswick in Gloucestershire to work in isolation. Then, in 1925, on advice from Boult, Finzi began to study counterpoint with R.O. Morris in London. From 1930 to 1933, he taught composition at the Royal Academy of Music.

In 1933, Finzi married artist Joyce Black. In 1935, the couple moved to Aldbourne in Wiltshire. Then, in 1937 they built a house, designed for them to work in, on a 16-acre site on the Hampshire hills at Ashmansworth. From this base of operations, Finzi composed, assembled a music library, and tended an orchard of rare apple trees. He also traveled, taking whatever adjudication, examination, or committee work was offered him.

In the winter of 1939, Finzi founded the Newbury String Players, a group consisting mostly of amateur musicians. Since Finzi was neither a pianist nor a singer, the orchestra became the composer's primary performance vehicle. Through this ensemble, he became an advocate of many young performers and composers, as well as a champion of English works from the eighteenth century. He kept the group together from 1941 to 1945, during which he worked at the Ministry of War Transport in London.

In 1951, Finzi learned that he suffered from a form of leukemia. He was told that he had, at the most, ten more years to live. He kept this news within his family, simply continuing to work between his treatments. In 1955, he gave the Crees lectures at the Royal College of Music; providing a somewhat provocative survey of the history and aesthetics of English song during which he presented his principles of text setting.

However, the leukemia eventually weakened the composer's resistance to infection. He died of shingles in 1956, after a chance encounter with chicken pox at the 1956 Gloucester Festival. After his death, his library of music from 1740 to 1780, at the time considered the finest collection of materials from that period in all of England, was donated to St. Andrews University, in Fife. His library of English literature, from which he had drawn so much of his inspiration, is located in the Finzi Book Room at the Reading University Library. *—Stephen Kingsbury*

VOCAL

Dies Natalis, cantata for soprano or tenor & strings, Op. 8 (1925–1939)

Gerald Finzi began this five-movement song cycle for high voice and strings in the 1920s, but did not complete it until 1939. Finzi was a particularly voracious reader (his library numbered well over 3000 books), with a wide interest in literature. The texts of these poems are by Thomas Traherne (ca. 1637–74), an Anglican clergyman whose writing has a strong metaphysical side. The four poems chosen by Finzi are the immediate first thoughts of a newborn baby, if one can accept as a convention of the work that such an infant can form deep thoughts in striking philosophical language. There is an implication that these are Jesus' thoughts, also implying this is a Christmas cantata. The work is tonal and melodic; the harmonic language is not far from that of Finzi's mentor Ralph Vaughan Williams. The string writing is highly effective, and all the vocal lines flow naturally and seem to lie beautifully in the voice.

The opening movement, "Intrada," sets the meditative tone of the work, and introduces motives that are important in the following initial vocal section, called "Rhapsody (Recitativo stromentato)." Finzi was a master at creating extended recitative, which in his hands always has strong melodic appeal and a sense of drama. The text here is from Traherne's *Centuries of Meditation*. The baby at the instant of birth perceives the world as an apparent paradise: "All appear'd new, and strange at first, inexpressibly rare and delightful and beautiful."

The third movement, "Rapture" is subtitled "Danza." The sheer joy of being alive is expressed in exultant words and a strong dancing melody. Finzi was inspired to seek this mood by two examples of religious art: the famous Botticelli painting "Nativity," which he saw in the British National Gallery, and some carved angels in the March Church in the Fenlands of England.

"Wonder (Arioso)" expresses amazement as the new innocent perceives the Divinity that lies beyond all things, even itself. Bright, mysterious, and lovely dissonances sparkle in the string accompaniment. The final section, "The Salutation (Aria)," is a flowing song with the style of a Bach chorale, introducing a sense of mystery and meditation as the baby begins its first contemplation of its purpose.

The cycle was premiered in 1940 with Elsie Suddaby as the singer. Its first recording, later in the 1940s, was by the great English soprano Joan Cross. Since then tenors have been its most frequent performers (almost invariably when it comes to recordings). *—Joseph Stevenson*

Recommended:

○ **Finzi: Intimations of Immortality; Dies Natalis** / Best (cond.), Ainsley, Corydon Orch. / 1996 / Hyperion 66876

○ **Finzi: Dies natalis** / Handley (cond.), Evans, Bournemouth Sinfonietta / 1997 / Conifer 51285

Let Us Garlands Bring, song cycle, Op. 18 (1929–1942)

This is a highly attractive cycle of Shakespeare texts, dealing with love and the passage of time by Gerald Finzi, who is regarded as one of the finer British vocal composers of his time. The long gestation period of these poems—which take only about 15 minutes to sing through—is typical of the composer, who worked on many compositions over the same period. He would typically work out a piece, then put it aside to return to it over time for serious editing, or perhaps waiting for an idea for a needed additional touch, until the music became highly polished, direct, sincere, and high-minded.

The five poems are:

1. *Come away, come away, death.* The tempo and initial feeling of the song are dirge-like, but when the narrator proclaims "I am slain by a fair cruel maid," the mood of the song lightens—still sad in tone, but the listener realizes from the music as well as the words that this is the kind of being slain that future love will likely cure.

2. *Who is Silvia?* This song is the opposite in mood, an admiring portrait of a beloved beautiful woman. The final line of the song provides the title for the song cycle, "To her let us garlands bring." The song is faster, with a lightly dancing lilt.

3. *Fear No More the Heat o' the Sun.* This is a gentle song in a compound meter that states the attractions that the grave holds, that promises an end to the fears

and worries of life. The gentle sarabande-like motion of the song continues until a striking change takes place in the final verse: Its first four lines are a kind of recitative in even note values over a static, pulseless chord. In the end, on the lines "Quiet consummation have; and renowned be thy grave," the voice gently takes up the rocking rhythm of the first parts, but the accompaniment remain nearly still, and without rhythmic life.

4. *O Mistress Mine.* This song is a call for a kiss, now, rather than waiting and losing the opportunity to life's uncertainties. The mood of the song is light and carefree.

5. *It was a lover and his lass.* One of Shakespeare's best known and lightest verses inspires a joyful dancing verse, exultant in the very idea of love.

The cycle, for baritone and piano (or string orchestra), had its premiere on October 12, 1942, at the famous series of National Gallery Lunchtime Concerts in London (a program devised to use the building for morale purposes after all the pictures had been taken out during the German bombing of London). The date was the 70th birthday of Ralph Vaughan Williams. Finzi dedicated the cycle to that composer, who called "Fear no more the heat o' the sun" one of the loveliest songs he had ever heard. The cycle has become one of Finzi's best-known works. *—Joseph Stevenson*

Recommended:

○ **The Vagabond** / Terfel, Martineau / 1995 / DG 445946

Till Earth Outwears, song cycle, Op. 19 (1927–1956)

By his mid-20s, Finzi's manner of composition—which he likened to a "coral insect, building his reef out of the transitory world around him and making a solid structure to last long after his fragile and uncertain life"—was established, with little in the way of development to follow. The songs, which often grew from phrases and sketches jotted over a period of years, possess at once an improvisational spontaneity animating sustained meditation in which the unlikeliest verse is opened and illumined in music, as Howard Ferguson remarked, "that seems not only appropriate but utterly inevitable." Ferguson, a younger composition pupil of Finzi's teacher R.O. Morris, was a kindred spirit—a keen if minor talent cultivating a small but vibrant range—who became not only a lifelong friend but, as a pianist, one of Finzi's most divinatory interpreters. After Finzi's death, in collaboration with the composer's widow and son, Ferguson in 1957 prepared four posthumous collections of songs, *Oh Fair to See* and *To a Poet* to words by various poets, and two to poems by Thomas Hardy, whose fatalistic observation of country life was the song of the earth Finzi most often and most knowingly sang. For convenience' sake, the six Hardy songs for low voice were collected as *I Said to Love* and the seven for high voice—tenor or soprano—as *Till Earth Outwears.* The final song, "Life laughs onward," which Finzi had noted as suitable for either baritone or tenor, has been transposed up, from F to G, by the editors "in order to fit it into the high voice Hardy set where its contrasting mood is specially useful." Though the ordering is not his, the spirit is. As was his wont, Finzi no doubt wished to bring the number of songs in these collections to ten each—those in *Till Earth Outwears* ranging in date of composition from 1927 to 1956, the year of his death. His conservatively tonal idiom, with an occasional "wrong note" dissonance registering some wry asperity, lends a peculiarly fitting aura of understatement—the more moving for eschewing insistence, indignation, or protest—to Hardy's prevailing mood of alienated acknowledgement ("And some day hence, towards Paradise/And all its blest-if such should be/I will lift glad, afar-off eyes/Though it contains no place for me"). And if there are no memorable tunes, precisely enunciated declamation is softened by melody occasionally blossoming into extended arioso to compound a visionary eloquence, uniquely moving. *—Adrian Corleonis*

Recommended:

○ **Earth & Air & Rain** / Hill, Benson / 1989 / Hyperion 66161

○ **Oh Fair to See** / Kaasch, Lockwood / 2000 / Globe 5202

A Young Man's Exhortation, 10 songs, Op. 14 (1926–1929)

Finzi's working life, 1920 to 1956, encompassed the jazz age, *Gebrauchsmusik,* neo-Classicism, *Neue Sachlichkeit,* the rise and hegemony of serialism, the beginnings of electronic music, and many another fad and fashion making the motley fabric of Modernism, all heard, if heard at all, from the great distance of the English countryside where seasonal procession enacts the fragile beauty and transience of human life reflected in his conservatively tonal music. He was the type of diligent scholar, the artist *savant,* whose intense cultivation of English pastorale produced a minor but evergreen body of work in which the lives of country folk, their fleeting joys, the drama of aging, the vicissitudes of memory, and missed opportunity are caught in a timeless utterance. Vocal music comprises roughly two thirds of Finzi's output, and of some 60 songs for solo voice and piano, over half are settings of poems by Thomas Hardy.

The ten songs of *A Young Man's Exhortation* are divided into two equal parts, each headed by an inscription in the Latin of the Vulgate—*Mane floreat, et transeat, Psalm 89* (*Psalm 90* of the *King James Bible,* "In the morning it flourisheth and groweth up"); and *Vespere decidat, induret, et arescat* (ibid., "In the evening it is cut down, and withereth"). Composed between 1926 and 1929, the songs were published in 1933—the year of his marriage to artist Joyce Black—the only one of Finzi's vocal collections intended as a cycle. If Hardy's poignantly wry, grotesquely moving observations make his verse the authentic voice of rural England, his often knotted syntax militates against musical setting. But Finzi takes him in a musical prose employing the simplest means—a vocal line hovering between arioso and declamation supported by an open, seemingly improvised accompaniment, often no more than two voices in imitative arabesques dimpled with nuance or dilating with deft suggestion, to point the poem's movement and project its punch in melancholy meditations. Rarely, but tunefully, as in *"Budmouth Dears"* ("When we lay where Budmouth Beach is, O, the girls were fresh as peaches…"—the performing indication is "Storming march"), Finzi yields up something like a conventional song. And in *"The Comet at Yell'ham",* he touches, in the fewest of notes, the sidereal mystery in which lives are rapt. Far from the madding crowd, as Hardy has it, Finzi's sturdily exquisite art sings a song of the earth which, if bittersweet in its grasp of the eternal verities, is also reassuring. *—Adrian Corleonis*

Recommended:

○ **Earth & Air & Rain** / Hill, Benson / 1989 / Hyperion 66161

○ **Finzi: Song Cycles** / Brunner, Lisovich / 1998 / Gasparo 335

CONCERTO

Clarinet Concerto in C minor, Op. 31 (1948–1949)

Finzi was to some degree an intractable character, but this was only sporadically evident in his music, which tended to be extremely lyrical and audience-friendly. Perhaps the true balance of his personality is reflected in his *Clarinet Concerto,* which gives the soloist generous melodies with which to seduce a sometimes obdurate orchestral accompaniment. Finzi wrote the work for the 1949 Three Choirs Festival, and conducted its first performance (with soloist Frederick Thurston).

The first movement, Allegro vigoroso, launches with a stern orchestral opening answered with surprising softness by the clarinet. The soloist plays the same meandering theme, but now it seems more searching than declamatory. All the movement's thematic material springs from this line; during the soloist's few rests the string orchestra is inclined to vigorous outbursts, but it provides restrained support as the clarinet explores the music's more gently expressive possibilities. The soloists adopts the orchestra's dry vehemence only during and immediately after a brief cadenza near the movement's end.

The Adagio (marked "ma senza rigore," hinting at a much freer style than before), is introduced by the strings, high and grave, soon echoed by the clarinet in a high register. The strings establish an atmosphere of both tenderness and nobility, rather in the style of a slow movement by Fauré, while the clarinet rhapsodizes freely. The movement proceeds as an increasingly ornamented meditation for the clarinet, the music's character hardly changing save for a small climax just past the halfway point.

Breaking the mood is the concluding Rondo (Allegro giocoso), which revolves around a quick, good-natured and innocent tune. The intervening episodes are initially more pensive, with one downward-gliding theme again recalling Fauré; later they become more playful, and except for a late reference to the first movement, this is happy music that never quite approaches the elusive extreme of pure joy until the final few measures. *—James Reel*

Recommended:

○ **Finzi: Clarinet Concerto** / Griffiths (cond.), Plane, Northern Sinfonia / 1998 / Naxos 553566

○ **Stanford & Finzi: Clarinet Concertos** / Francis (cond.), King, Philharmonia / 2001 / Hyperion 55101

Eclogue, for piano & strings in F major, Op. 10 (ca. 1925–1929; revised ca. 1940)

Finzi began work on this piece sometime in the late 1920s, around the same time he was writing his *Grand Fantasia and Toccata for piano & orchestra*; he originally intended to incorporate both pieces into a concerto—not necessarily the same concerto—but nothing came of that plan. Finzi reworked the *Eclogue* twice so that it could stand alone, but it wasn't published or performed until 1957, one year after his death.

An eclogue is a poem in which shepherds converse; the genre originated with poets of classical antiquity, notably Virgil, and became popular again in the sixteenth century, often expanded into full-length plays or operas. Finzi's *Eclogue* is a comparatively modest quarter-hour movement for piano and strings. It begins with a gentle melody for piano, written for two imitative voices and featuring the occasional ornament that ties the music to its sixteenth century inspiration. The string orchestra enters with its own brief statement of the theme, but almost immediately withdraws to the subsidiary role it will play through most of the work. The piece progresses through a series of elaborations on the theme, building to a midpoint climax that manages to be both stately and passionate, but soon falling back to simpler, almost singsong material inspired by the skeleton of the principal melody. The strings take over for what seems to be the traditional buildup to a cadenza, but in this case the solo piano passage that follows is merely a low-key, bittersweet treatment of the material. The shepherd-lovers apparently part company at this point, as they so often do in eclogues, for the closing pages of the score are dark and resigned. *—James Reel*

Recommended:

- ○ **Finzi: Cello Concerto; Grand Fantasia & Toccata; Eclogue** / Griffiths (cond.), Donohoe, Northern Sinfonia / 2001 / Naxos 555766
- ○ **An English Suite: Music by Finzi, Parry & Bridge** / Boughton (cond.), Jones, English String Orch. / 1993 / Nimbus 5366

CHAMBER MUSIC

5 Bagatelles for clarinet & piano, Op. 23 (1941–1943)

"A mere bagatelle" usually indicates some light, throwaway piece, but Finzi labored over his *Five Bagatelles* for nearly two decades, and the results have become favorites among Anglo-American clarinetists. Finzi began the set sometime in the 1920s, early in his career, but didn't complete it until during World War II. There also exists a later arrangement for clarinet and string orchestra by Lawrence Ashmore.

The set consists of three slow movements, quite distinct from one another, framed by fast opening and closing movements. First comes a Prelude with an exuberant initial section, repeated at the end, interrupted by a more restrained middle section that builds to a dark climax. The Romance, the first of the slow movements, is lyrical and sweet. The miniscule Carol that follows begins with a light but foursquare rhythm that soon proves to be more flexible, bringing interest to the very simple melody (the tune was written for the children of fellow composer Herbert Howells). The "Forlana," still in a slow tempo and featuring a rather antique, pastoral melody, seems to have a slightly quicker pulse thanks to its rocking rhythm. Had the tempo been a bit slower, Finzi might have held to his original title for this piece, Berceuse. The final movement, Fughetta, is vigorous and witty, if not a textbook model of counterpoint. It's a fitting conclusion to a suite of pieces that are light and charming, but not at all trivial. *—James Reel*

Recommended:

- ○ **English Music for Clarinet & Piano** / de Peyer, Pryor / 1987 / Chandos 8549
- ○ **English Music for Clarinet** / King, Benson / 1997 / Hyperion 22027

Rudolf Firkušný

b. Feb. 11, 1912, Napajedla, Moravia (Czech Rep.), **d.** Jul. 19, 1994, Staatsburg, NY

Pianist

Firkušný studied both piano and composition with Janáček; from 1920 to 1927, at the Brno Conservatory with Ruzena Kurzová; and at the Prague Conservatory with Vilém Kurz and Rudolf Karel. From 1929–30, he also studied composition with Suk. Firkušný made his debut in Prague in 1922 and pursued an active career in Eastern Europe until 1933, when he first played in England, and 1938, when he made his United States debut. His compositions include a piano concerto, premiered in 1930, a string quartet, and various piano pieces and songs.

After his American debut, Firkušný established an international career as a pianist, later teaching at Juilliard and the Aspen School of Music. Although best known for the standard nineteenth century repertory, Firkušný was also known for his chamber performances and his championing of both contemporary and lesser known works. He gave premieres of works by Menotti, Barber, Ginastera, Hanson, and Martinů, among others, and championed the works of Dvořák and Janáček in particular. Firkušný was noted more for his refinement of style rather than for his virtuosity. *—Steven Coburn*

Recommended:

- ○ **Leoš Janáček: Piano Works** / Kubelik (cond.), Firkušný, Bavarian RSO / 1997 / DG 449764
- ○ **Rudolf Firkušný Plays...** / Firkušný / 1992 / Vox 5058
- ○ **Martinü: Concertos 2, 3 & 4** / Pesek, Rybar (conds.), Firkušný, Czech PO / 1994 / RCA 61934

Adam Fischer

b. Sep. 9, 1949, Budapest, Hungary

Conductor

Adam Fischer was born into a family of conductors. His father Sandor Fischer conducted the Budapest Radio Orchestra. His brother Iván, and a cousin, György, are also conductors. The Fischers lived across the street from the Budapest Opera House, and he attended his first concert at the age of five. When Haydn's *"Surprise" Symphony* was played, he decided to be a conductor so *he* could make the audience jump. He made his conducting debut at the age of seven, leading an ensemble of children playing toy instruments and singing.

He studied at the Budapest School of Music, sang in the children's choir of the Hungarian State Opera, and took the role of the Third Boy in Mozartıs *Magic Flute*. He took higher musical studies at the Vienna State Academy, including studies with Hans Swarowsky. In 1973 he was a co-winner of the first prize in the Guido Cantelli Conducting Competition in Milan.

Fischer began his conducting career in a traditional manner, with a job as repetiteur at the Vienna State Opera. He had a major break when he took over a scheduled performance of *Fidelio* in Munich when Karl Böhm became ill, leading to a regular engagement to conduct the new production of Dvořákıs *Rusalka* with Hildegard Behrens. He was principal conductor in Karlsruhe for five years, general music director of Freiburg (1981–83), and music director of the Kassel Opera (1987–92). While in Kassel (the site of one of Gustav Mahlerıs early jobs) he founded an international Gustav Mahler Festival.

He is the founder and music director of the Austro-Hungarian Haydn Orchestra, which plays in the original Esterházy Estate in the very room where Haydn premiered most of his symphonies, and has recorded Haydnıs symphonies with them. He has worked in most of the major opera houses and led most of the worldıs great orchestras.

He now lives in Hamburg, Germany, with his wife, Doris; a daughter, Golda; and a son, Aron. In the 1990s he was surprised to meet for the first time relatives living in the United States. In 1999 he became chief conductor of the Danish Radio Sinfonietta and in the following year was named general music director of the National Theater Mannheim. He also made a successful debut conducting the *Ring* cycle at the Bayreuth Festival in 2001, being asked to return annually for the following three years. *—Joseph Stevenson*

Recommended:

- ○ **Bartók: The 3 Piano Concertos** / Fischer (cond.), Sandor, Hungarian State SO / 1990 / CBS 45835
- ○ **Haydn: Complete Symphonies** / Fischer (cond.), Austro-Hungarian Haydn Orch. / Brilliant 99925
- ○ **The Salieri Album** / Fischer (cond.), Bartoli, Osele, Orchestra of the Age of Enlightenment / 2003 / Decca 000109702

Annie Fischer

b. Jul. 5, 1914, Budapest, Hungary, **d.** Apr. 10, 1995, Budapest, Hungary

Pianist

Hungarian pianist Annie Fischer made her debut at the age of 10 and studied with Ernst von Dohnányi at the Franz Liszt Academy of Music. Her performance of the Liszt *Sonata in B minor* won Fischer first prize at the 1933 Liszt International Piano Competition, but her concert career was barely underway when war broke out; Fischer fled to Sweden. Afterwards Fischer returned to Hungary, and although she made her New York debut in 1961, she was only seldom seen in the United States and based her career in continental Europe. In her native Hungary, Fischer was particularly well vaulted and was awarded the Kossuth Prize three times. Mozart and Beethoven were Fischer's bread and butter composers, but she also excelled in later Romantic repertoire and in a few modern works, most notably the *Piano Concerto No. 3* of Béla Bartók.

Although regarded as one of the world's greatest pianists late in life, Fischer only seldom recorded, and disliked doing so. Shortly after Fischer's death in 1995, the Hungaroton label issued a complete recording of Fischer in the 32 Beethoven *Piano Sonatas*. Fischer had been working on this set for the better part of two decades, but prior to that time she had not seen fit to release these recordings. Fischer was an intense and powerful pianist who responded most strongly to her own inner sense of inspiration and drive. In works where this approach was an advantage, such as the *"Hammerklavier" Sonata* of Beethoven, Fischer was second to none. *—Uncle Dave Lewis*

Recommended:

- ○ **Mozart: Concertos, K466 & 467** / Lukacs (cond.), Fischer, Budapest SO / Hungaroton 31492
- ○ **Beethoven: Complete Piano Sonatas** / Fischer / 2001 / Hungaroton 41003

Edwin Fischer

b. Oct. 6, 1886, Basel, Switzerland, **d.** Jan. 24, 1960, Zurich, Switzerland

Pianist

Edwin Fischer was one of the great pianists of the twentieth century, and among the finest piano pedagogues of all time. At the Basle Conservatory his teacher was Hans Huber. He then studied in Berlin with Martin Krause.

He was taught at Berlin's Stern Conservatory, where he remained from 1905 until World War I, when he returned to Switzerland. He established himself as one of the finest pianists of his generation after the war. He became particularly associated with the major works of the great German masters, including Bach, Beethoven, and Brahms.

In 1926 he also became conductor of the Lübeck Musikverein and continued his conducting career in Munich from 1928 to 1932, as director of the Bachverein there. He transferred the base of his career to Berlin in 1932, when he became a member of the faculty of the Berlin Hochschule für Musik, succeeding Arthur Schnabel.

He also founded a chamber orchestra. His increasing interest in Classical and Baroque music led him to reinstate the authentic method of leading the ensemble from the keyboard while realizing the basso continuo.

While his concept of the music of that era remained essentially Romantic in concept, he sought to recover the classical purity of his favored composers, deemphasizing excessive emotionalism and shifts in the basic pulse. As a result, he was typed as an intellectual pianist.

In 1942 he withdrew to Switzerland. After the war, he resumed appearing in chamber music and solo performance throughout Europe. His master classes in Lucerne were in high demand. He founded a foundation, the Edwin-Fischer-Stiftung, to support the beginning of promising young musicians' careers and to aid other needy musicians. As an academic and pedagogue, he published valuable books on musical interpretation and teaching. *—Joseph Stevenson*

Recommended:

- ○ **Bach: Well-Tempered Clavier, Book 1** / Fischer / 2000 / Naxos 110651–52
- ○ **Edwin Fischer Plays Beethoven** / Fischer / Pearl 9218
- ○ **Edwin Fischer** / Fischer / Pearl 9481

Iván Fischer

b. Jan. 20, 1951, Budapest, Hungary
Conductor

A member of a distinguished Hungarian musical family, Iván Fischer was one of top young conductors to emerge from Eastern Europe toward the end of the twentieth century. From 1965 to 1970, Fischer studied at the Béla Bartók Conservatory in Budapest and, in 1974 in Vienna, as a conducting student with Swarowsky. Between 1975 and 1976, he conducted in Milan, Florence, Vienna, and Budapest, and also won a BBC competition for conductors which led to many engagements in Britain and an appointment as co-principal conductor of the Northern Sinfonia Orchestra, based at Newcastle-upon-Tyne. In 1983, he toured the Far East with the London Symphony Orchestra and in the same year was appointed musical director of Kent Opera, one of Britain's leading provincial opera companies.

Fischer has made a number of fine recordings, mainly of the Classical and Romantic orchestral repertory, and of Donizetti's opera *Don Pasquale* and Paisiello's *Barber of Seville*.

Iván should not be confused with his younger brother Ádám, who also studied at the Béla Bartók Conservatory and has also followed a successful conducting career. *—Roy Brewer*

Recommended:

- ○ **Dvořák: Symphonies 8 & 9** / Fischer (cond.), Budapest Festival Orch. / 2001 / Philips 464640
- ○ **Kodály: Háry János, etc.** / Fischer (cond.), Budapest Festival Orch. / 1999 / Philips 462824

Dietrich Fischer-Dieskau

b. May 28, 1925, Berlin, Germany
Baritone

During a career that spanned nearly five decades, Dietrich Fischer-Dieskau established himself as one of the most accomplished performing artists of the twentieth century. He is widely considered to have been the finest modern interpreter of German lieder, and his extensive operatic career was noted for fine musicianship and powerful characterization. He has also made important contributions as an author, conductor, and teacher.

Born in Berlin on May 28, 1925, Fischer-Dieskau began his vocal studies at the age of sixteen, only shortly before being drafted into the Nazi Wehrmacht. After two years as a prisoner of war, the young baritone returned to Germany and soon made his oratorio debut in Brahms' *Ein deutsches Requiem*, and his stage debut in Verdi's *Don Carlos* (Posa). Engaged as the 'house' lyric baritone (kammersänger) at the Berlin Städtische Oper, he also began making guest appearances at the Vienna Staatsoper, and the Salzburg Festival. In the early 1950's he began a series of engagements at the Bayreuth festival, establishing a lasting relationship with the music of Wagner, especially the role of Wolfram in *Tannhäuser*. In the following decades, Fischer-Dieskau would traverse an impressive range of operatic roles, including *Don Giovanni* in Mozart's eponymous work, Mittenhofer in Hans Werner Henze's *Elegy for Young Lovers*, and John the Baptist in Strauss' *Salome*; his most critically admired performances were as Don Alfonso in *Così fan tutte*, Germont père in *La Traviata*, and Count Almaviva in *Le nozze di Figaro*.

Fischer-Dieskau's recital career began equally early and impressively—with a 1948 Radio Berlin broadcast of Schubert's *Winterreise*; however, it was with his first concerts and recordings with the English collaborative pianist Gerald Moore that his international fame began to spread. Together, the two of them recorded every song of Schubert, Schumann and Wolf (excluding those few that are generally reserved for the female voice) and considerable portions of those by Brahms, Strauss, Loewe, and Beethoven. This catalogue of repertoire is impressive for its sheer size, and even more so for its consistent excellence; while opinions have sometimes diverged on the subjective merits of Fischer-Dieskau's voice, there is no question that his performances of lieder represented the perfect wedding of poetry and lyricism—the very essence of the lied. While his collaboration with Gerald Moore was singular in its productivity, Fischer-Dieskau was by no means a "one-pianist" man. His work with accompanist Jörg Demus represents an impressive catalogue of its own, and he made memorable appearances and recordings with many other leading musicians, such as Alfred Brendel, Vladimir Horowitz, Daniel Barenboim, and Sviatoslav Richter. Also, his repertoire was by no means limited to works of the Romantic masters; he has championed the works of lesser-known composers, such as Othmar Schoeck. His cumulative body of recorded performances is stunning, perhaps best illustrated by the number of pieces of which his discography contains multiple (sometimes as many as four!) performances. A number of composers wrote works for him, the most notable of which is Benjamin Britten (*Songs and Proverbs of William Blake*), whose *War Requiem* the baritone also premiered in 1962.

Certainly Fischer-Dieskau is best characterized by his performances of works for voice and piano, in which his imagination, musicianship, and vocal timbre were showcased to the fullest. However, he made equal strides in the realm of orchestral lieder; his performances of Mahler's *Lieder eines fahrenden Gesellen*, *Rückert Lieder*, and *Kindertotenlieder* are some of the finest on record. Other works he performed with orchestra included the *Michelangelo Sonnets* of Dmitri Shostakovich, Brahms' *German Requiem*, and numerous cantatas of Bach and Telemann.*—Allen Schrott*

Recommended:

- ○ **Schubert: Winterreise** / Fischer-Dieskau, Demus (piano) / DG 447421
- ○ **Mahler: Songs** / Fischer-Dieskau, etc. / 2001 / EMI 67557
- ○ **Wolf: Italienisches Liederbuch** / Fischer-Dieskau, Schwarzkopf, Moore / 2003 / EMI 62651
- ○ **Brahms: Songs** / Fischer-Dieskau, Moore / 1985 / Orfeo 140201
- ○ **Wagner: Tannhäuser** / Gerdes (cond.), Nilsson, Fischer-Dieskau, Adam, Windgassen, German Opera Orch. / 2002 / DG 471708
- ○ **The Very Best of Dietrich Fischer-Dieskau** / Fischer-Dieskau, etc. / 2003 / EMI 75922
- ○ **Schubert: Goethe-Lieder** / Fischer-Dieskau, Moore & Demus / DG 457747

Eliot Fisk

b. Aug. 10, 1954, Philadelphia, PA
Guitarist

In article after article, the one thing that is always mentioned in addition to Eliot Fisk's skills as a guitarist and transcriber is his commitment to music as a changing force in peoples' lives. He firmly and enthusiastically advocates more teaching of music in schools and more active community involvement by musicians. He himself gives recitals at schools, prisons, retirement homes, and other community institutions whenever his concert and teaching schedules allow it. This dedication is credited to his upbringing in a Quaker home. His father bought both a banjo and a guitar for seven-year-old Fisk, hoping that Fisk would like one of the instruments. Fisk settled on the guitar and virtually taught himself to play, spending hours practicing each day as a teenager. He took a bachelor's and master's degree in music from Yale, where he studied with harpsichordists Ralph Kirkpatrick and Albert Fuller. His guitar teachers included Oscar Ghiglia and Alirio Diaz, but his mentor was Andrés Segovia. Fisk's talent was so admired by Segovia that the latter's widow gave Fisk the exclusive first rights to perform and record some of Segovia's compositions that were found in the mid-1990s. That album, *Segovia—Canciones Populares*, became one of Billboard's Classical Chart best-sellers. What makes Fisk stand out as a performer are his passionate, intense playing, whether it be Bach or Scarlatti, Berio or Rochberg, and his transcriptions that remain true to the original works' musical intentions, but are idiomatic of the guitar. His recording of the Paganini's *Caprices (24)* was called "daring" and also became a best-seller. Many of his transcriptions are of Baroque works, but he has also performed the music of Mozart and Haydn. In addition to the works dedicated to him by Berio and Rochberg, Fisk has also premiered new works for guitar by Ernesto Halffter, Robert Beaser, and Leonardo Balada. Fisk performs as much chamber music as he does concerto or solo music, most frequently with flutist Paula Robison, but also with string quartets, flamenco guitarist Paco Peña, vocalist Ute Lemper, and Turkish music specialist Burhan Öçal. Shortly after graduating from Yale, Fisk was asked to help establish that school's guitar program. He has taught at the Cologne Hochschule für Musik, and in 1989 started teaching at the Salzburg Mozarteum and at the New England Conservatory since 1996. *—Patsy Morita*

Recommended:

- ○ **Best of Eliot Fisk** / Fisk, etc. / 1995 / MusicMasters 67151
- ○ **Eliot Fisk: Für Eliot** / Fisk / 1995 / GSP 1008
- ○ **Eliot Fisk Plays Guitar Fantasies** / Fisk / 1989 / MusicMasters 60169

Kirsten Flagstad

b. Jul. 12, 1895, Hamar, Norway, **d.** Dec. 7, 1962, Oslo, Norway
Soprano

Born into a musical family (her father was a conductor, her mother a pianist and vocal coach), Kirsten Flagstad studied music from an early age and made her debut while still a student as Nuri in d'Albert's *Tiefland* in 1913. For the following 18 years, she sang only in the Scandinavian countries in such works as *Der Freischütz* and *Die Fledermaus* (the role she performed most often in her career). In 1932, she sang her first Isolde in a guest performance in Berlin. This lead to an audition at Bayreuth where she sang Sieglinde and Gutrune in 1934. She attained overnight worldwide recognition after her February 2, 1935, Metropolitan Opera debut as Sieglinde and her Isolde four days later. By April 17 of that year, she had also sung Brunnhilde in both *Die Walküre* and *Götterdämmerung*, Elsa in *Lohengrin*, Elisabeth in *Tannhäuser* and Kundry in *Parisfal*. From that time, she was regarded by many to be the best Wagnerian soprano in the world, although her rivals included Fieda Leider, Marjorie Lawrence, and Helen Traubel. In 1936 and 1937, she sang Isolde, Brunnhilde, and Senta in London to great acclaim. During this period she also sang at San Francisco, Chicago, and Buenos Aires.

In 1941, Flagstad returned to Norway to be with her husband, which led to rumors that she was a Nazi sympathizer. However, the only appearances she made outside of Norway were in Switzerland. She never sang for Nazi officials at any time. Her husband, who had business dealings with the occupation forces as well as the resistance, was arrested after the war, and she was forced to overcome hard feelings held by many. Her first major appearances were in London singing Isolde and Brunhilde. She sang four seasons at the Royal Opera, Covent Garden, and then appeared in a fabled production of Purcell's *Dido and Aeneas* at the Mermaid Theater. She returned to the Metropolitan Opera in 1950 and during her final seasons there sang Brunhilde, Isolde, *Fidelio*, and the title role in Gluck's *Alceste*, the role of her farewell. In 1949 and 1950, she appeared in *Fidelio* at the Salzburg Festival, her only appearances there.

In 1950, she sang the world premiere of the *Four Last Songs* by Richard Strauss in London under the direction of Wilhelm Furtwängler, who led many of her greatest performances and recordings. Throughout her career, she gave recital tours bringing to the public many fine songs by Scandinavian composers, especially Sibelius and Grieg. Her concert repertoire ranged from the Beethoven *Missa Solemnis* and Rossini's *Stabat Mater* to songs of Schubert, Brahms, and Mahler. After her retirement from the opera stage, she continued to appear in recital and concert until 1957. Her last appearance in the United States came in an benefit concert for the Symphony of the Air. After her retirement, she continued to make recordings, including a highly acclaimed performance of Fricka in the first complete recording of Wagner's *Das Rheingold*, and in 1958 was named general manager of the new Norwegian National Opera.

The voice of Kirsten Flagstad was a full dramatic soprano with great warmth. Unlike the voice of Birgit Nilsson, which was like a laser beam, Flagstad's voice enveloped the listener in a cushion of sound. She brought her characters to life primarily through vocal means; the overt theatricality of the later twentieth century was not part of her dramatic arsenal nor was it seen in any of her colleagues. Her many appearances with Lauritz Melchior at the *Metropolitan Opera* and at other houses in the 1930s made the music dramas of Wagner the core of the repertoire at these houses. *—Richard LeSueur*

Recommended:

- ○ **Wagner: Das Rheingold** / Solti (cond.), Flagstad, London, Kmentt, Wachter, Vienna PO / 1997 / London 455556
- ○ **Flagstad** / Flagstad, etc. / 1993 / Nimbus 7847
- ○ **Flagstad in Song** / Flagstad, McArthur / 1995 / Nimbus 7871

Leon Fleisher

b. Jul. 23, 1928, San Francisco, CA
Pianist

Leon Fleisher became one of the most distinguished pianists of the twentieth century, maintaining that status even after injuring his right hand. He is known for deeply studied yet equally deeply felt performances of major repertoire and is the world's leading master of left-hand literature.

His father was a tailor and his mother a singing teacher, who gave him his first music lessons. He studied piano with Lev Schorr, debuted at age eight, and at an early age was sent to Europe to study with Artur Schnabel. He played the Liszt *A major concerto* in San Francisco at the age of 14 and at the New York Philharmonic at the age of 16 he played Brahms' *D minor concerto* (November 4, 1944). In 1952, he became the first American musician to win a prize at the Queen Elizabeth of Belgium International Competition.

He began the typical concert life of one of the world's great artists, recording for Columbia Masterworks. He was hailed as one of America's ten-best musicians and proclaimed the "true heir of Schnabel." He made recordings of the five Beethoven concertos with George Szell and the Cleveland Orchestra that are among the greatest piano concerto recordings. In 1959, he joined the faculty of the Peabody Conservatory in Baltimore. He was known for his exhaustive practice schedule. In 1964, he made a widely praised recording of Brahms' *B flat Concerto*, but in preparing for it stressed his right hand, which eventually clenched. Focal dystonia was the eventual diagnosis. Fleisher turned to the left-hand repertoire and commissioned new works to be added to that literature.

He founded the Theater Chamber Players of the Kennedy Center in 1967, became music director of the Annapolis, MD, symphony orchestra, and associate conductor of the Baltimore Symphony in 1973. Meanwhile, he became one of the great teachers of piano, numbering André Watts and Lorin Hollander among his pupils. Students at Peabody call him the "Obi-Wan Kenobi of the keyboard."

Meanwhile, he pursued various treatments for his hand, including acupuncture, biofeedback, and, in 1981, surgery. Although he played Franck's *Symphonic Variations* with the Baltimore Symphony, he was dissatisfied with the results. In the late 1990s, using a therapy system called Rolfing, he succeeded in recovering, and in 1995 quietly resumed performing with both hands. He was acclaimed for his performance of Brahms' *D minor* in September 1999 in San Francisco and remained active. *—Joseph Stevenson*

Recommended:

- ○ **Brahms: Concertos, Waltzes, Variations** / Szell (cond.), Fleisher, Eskin, Cleveland Orch. / 1997 / Sony 63225
- ○ **Britten, Ravel & Prokofiev** / Ozawa (cond.), Fleisher, BSO / 1992 / Sony 47188
- ○ **Leon Fleisher Recital** / Fleisher / 1993 / Sony 48081
- ○ **Beethoven: 5 Piano Concertos; Triple Concerto** / Szell, Ormandy (conds.), Fleisher, Istomin, Stern, Rose, Cleveland Orch., Philadelphia Orch. / 1992 / Sony 48397

Renée Fleming

b. Feb. 14, 1959, Indiana, PA
Soprano

Renee Fleming is among the most widely admired American singers of the late twentieth and early twenty-first centuries. She has a wide variety of roles in her repertoire, and works to maintain a balance between Mozart roles, such as the Countess in *The Marriage of Figaro*, with heavier ones such as Desdemona in Verdi's *Otello*, in order to preserve both nuance and power in her voice. She is an especially noted Ellen Orford, Rusalka, Amelia in *Simon Boccanegra*, and Marschallin in *Der Rosenkavalier*. She created the role of the Countess in Corigliano's *The Ghosts of Versailles* in 1991, that of Madame Tourvel in Conrad Susa's *Dangerous Liaisons* in 1994, and Blanche in Andre Previn's *A Streetcar Named Desire* in 1998, and won both the George London and the Richard Tucker Prizes.

Fleming's parents were both high school vocal music teachers, and she describes her mother's influence as that of the "classic stage mother"; she was made to sing in any musical function that came up. While she dislikes the fact that singing became a chore, she later found the discipline that it instilled to be useful to her as a professional. In 1981, she graduated from State University of New York at Potsdam with a degree in music education, and continued her musical studies at the Eastman School of Music, which she credits with giving her a strong academic and theoretical background as well as continued vocal training.

From 1983 to 1987, she was enrolled in the American Opera Center at Juilliard, where she met Beverley Johnson, the voice teacher with whom she would continue to study throughout her career. Fleming also recalls with admiration the year she spent studying lieder with Arleen Auger, on a Fulbright Scholarship.

In 1986 she made her professional opera debut in *Die Entführung aus dem Serail* in Salzburg. Singing Constanze, one of the most difficult roles in the soprano repertoire, made her recognize that her vocal technique still needed work, as did her self-confidence to perform in public. She worked on both with renewed determination, and two years later, in 1988, she won the Met National Council Auditions and the George London Prize (in the same week) and the Eleanor McCollum Competition in Houston.

She sang the Countess in Mozart's *Le Nozze di Figaro* at the Houston Grand Opera (starting a long time association with that house), made her New York City Opera debut in 1989 as Mimi in *La Bohème*, and made her Covent Garden debut as Glauce in Cherubini's Medea later that same year. In 1991, she made her Met debut, stepping in for an indisposed Felicity Lott as the Countess in *The Marriage of Figaro*. The Countess became her calling card, and she made her San Francisco debut later that year in the same role, as well as her 1993 Vienna State Opera and 1994 Glyndebourne debuts. Her 1993 La Scala debut was as Donna Elvira (*Don Giovanni*).

Since that time, Fleming has been in constant demand in opera houses worldwide. After avoiding certain major roles for many years, she made a triumphant appearance as Violetta in *La traviata* at the Metropolitan Opera in 2003. Her combination of vocal beauty, stylistic versatility, and uncommon commitment to dramatic portrayal has worked to make her an instant draw anywhere she appears. A Fleming appearance in Verdi's *Otello* or in Handel's *Alcina* is likely to be equally satisfying—and the same cannot be said for many singers. *—Ann Feeney*

Recommended:

- ○ **Bel Canto** / Summers (cond.), Fleming, Feld, Jepson, Orch. of St. Luke's, Maggio Musicale Fiorentino / 2002 / Decca 467101

- ○ **Handel: Alcina** / Christie (cond.), Carsen, Fleming, Graham, Dessay, Les Arts Florissants Orch. & Chorus / Teldec 80233
- ○ **Dvořák: Rusalka** / Mackerras (cond.), Fleming, Heppner, Kusnjer, Hawlata, Czech PO / 1998 / London 460568
- ○ **Signatures-Great Opera Scenes** / Solti (cond.), Fleming, Summers, Diadkova, London SO / 1997 / London 455760
- ○ **The Beautiful Voice** / Mackerras, Tate (conds.), Fleming, Ellis, Watson, Greensmith, English CO, London Voices / 1998 / London 458858

Juan Diego Flórez

b. Jan. 13, 1973, Lima, Peru
Tenor

Sometimes promoted as the successor to Luciano Pavarotti, Peru's Juan Diego Flórez is actually a very different kind of tenor, and one of a sort that has not been seen much in recent years: his voice is light, extremely athletic, and suited above all to the bel canto tenor roles of the early nineteenth century. Among the accomplishments of his young career was the restoration of a difficult passage, long considered unsingable, in the role of Almaviva in Rossini's *Il barbiere di Siviglia* (The Barber of Seville). His primary vocal model is not Pavarotti but the Spanish tenor Alfredo Kraus—a performer less well known to the general public but equally well admired among opera cognoscenti.

Born in 1973 in Lima to a folk guitarist father, Flórez sang when he was young in a rock band that specialized in Beatles and Led Zeppelin covers. What set him on the road to an operatic career was a free voice course he took in conjunction with membership in his high school choir. He enrolled at the Lima Conservatory when he was 17, moving on from there to Philadelphia's Curtis Institute on a full scholarship. One mentor was Peruvian tenor Ernesto Palacio, who became Flórez's manager.

At the 1996 Pesaro Festival in Italy, Flórez was booked to sing a minor role in Rossini's *Ricciardo e Zoraide* but took over the lead role in a newly unearthed Rossini opera called *Matilde di Shabran* after the scheduled tenor had to cancel. Rhapsodic praise from hard-to-please Italian opera fans led to a debut at La Scala in Gluck's *Armide* and then to the rest of the world's major opera houses over the next several years. His Metropolitan Opera debut in New York came in 2002 as Almaviva in *Il barbiere*—a role that is emerging as one of his specialties.

Possessed of good looks and trademark curly hair that have elicited nearly universal comment among music writers, Flórez faced pressure to assume the mantle of opera megastardom. He has won praise from close observers of the operatic scene, however, for taking account of the unusual nature of his voice and sticking to the repertory to which he is best suited, avoiding for the most part the heavier roles of Verdi and reintroducing audiences to something of the full fire that might have been heard on an Italian stage of the early nineteenth century. "I think I know my limitations," Flórez told the *Economist* in 2002. "I have been offered Mozart's Mitridate. I looked at the part, but it's all just a little low, and he's just a bit too angry all the time. It's not for me."

Booked at this writing through the year 2009, Flórez has released three solo albums on the Decca label: one of Rossini arias, one (*Una furtiva lagrima*) including arias by Bellini and Donizetti, and 2004's *Great Tenor Arias*, which in the words of London's *Observer* newspaper "confirms his growing reputation as one of the most exciting vocal talents around." He has expressed an interest in exploring the repertory of Peruvian song. *—James Manheim*

Recommended:

- ○ **Great Tenor Arias** / Flórez, Rizzi (cond.) / 2004 / Decca 313602
- ○ **Rossini Arias** / Flórez, Chailly (cond.) / 2002 / Decca 470024
- ○ **Rossini: Le Comte Ory** / López-Cobos (cond.), Flórez, Bonfadelli, Miles, Todorovitch / 2004 / DG 292302

Friedrich von Flotow

b. Apr. 27, 1813, Teutendorf, Germany, **d.** Jan. 24, 1883, Darmstadt, Germany
Composer: Opera

Friedrich Adolf Ferdinand Flotow, Freiherr von Teutendorf, became one of the best-known figures in popular German opera. His opera *Martha* was a staple of the nineteenth century repertory.

As his lengthy name and title indicate, Flotow came from an aristocratic family. His father was an estate owner who wanted his son to become a government official, but did not oppose his growing interest in music. Flotow attended the Paris Conservatory from 1828 to 1830, studying composition with Antonin Reicha and taking in the city's lively operatic scene with its productions of works by Auber, Meyerbeer, Rossini, and Donizetti.

Revolution broke out in Paris in 1830, and Flotow quickly left for Teutendorf, taking with him what he had written of his first opera, *Pierre et Cathérine*, finishing it there. The work concerned Tsar Peter the Great's incognito stint as a shipbuilder in Holland. In a German translation by Flotow's uncle, it was performed several times in small German towns.

Flotow returned to Paris, trying to break into the operatic big time. After some private performances of small works, he gained recognition when he collaborated with the better-established Albert Grisar, writing numbers for a pair of new operas, *Lady Melvil* (1838) and *L'eau merveilleuse* (1839). He agreed to write another joint opera, *Le naufrage de la Méduse*, with Grisar and Auguste Pilati. Flotow wrote both acts two and three of the successful opera. A Hamburg company then contracted to perform it, but a fire at the theater destroyed the manuscript. Flotow entirely rewrote it with a new German libretto by Friedrich Wilhelm Reise, under the name *Die Matrosen*. The two worked together congenially and produced two other operas, *Alessandro Stradella* (which actually preceded *Die Matrosen*), and *Martha*. Those two operas, Flotow's greatest successes, are the only ones still staged; *Martha* was given all over Europe and America. Interestingly, its most famous music is the familiar Thomas Moore Irish ballad, *"The Last Rose of Summer,"* which plays a role in the plot. Flotow once again fled Paris during the Revolution of 1848.

In 1849 Flotow married Elise von Zadow, who died shortly after the birth of their only son. In his grief, Flotow lived for a while with a friend, Putlitz, at the latter's estate at Retzien. Putlitz wrote the text for some of Flotow's operas after this, but none had more than moderate success. In 1853 Flotow married Anna Theen, a 20-year-old dancer; the couple had two sons, who both survived into maturity, and in 1855 Flotow took a position as intendant of the grand ducal court theater in Schwerin, retaining that position until 1863. He wrote an opera there, as well as some occasional works. After moving back to Vienna, he divorced his wife in 1867 and married her much younger sister, Rose Theen, a singer. They bought a villa in Lower Austria, lived there until 1873 when Flotow moved back to Teutendorf, and in 1880 moved to Darmstadt, Flotow's last residence.

Flotow's many operas failed to enter the repertoire partly because he tended to choose serious topics, while his talent ran toward rather sentimental, undemanding music. Only in *Martha* did he chose a text that matched his music exactly. He wrote a large number of songs that are often very nice, but have that cloying Victorian quality. His relatively small quantity of instrumental music shows a true dramatic flair, and his operas have many defenders among those who have studied them closely.*—Joseph Stevenson*

OPERA

Martha (1847)

The libretto to *Martha* is by W. Friedrich, the pen name of Friedrich Wilhelm Riese (?1805–79), a prolific German playwright. Friedrich had written a libretto on the same theme in 1845–46 for Eduard Stiegmann's *Lady Harriet*. The *Martha* project was set in motion by a commission from the Vienna Court Opera, which prompted Flotow to expand his ballet, *Lady Harriette, ou La Servante de Greenwich* (1844), into an opera. *Martha, oder Der Markt zu Richmond* premiered in Vienna, at the Kärntnertortheater, on November 25, 1847. It is Flotow's most popular opera and remains so to this day, staged regularly in opera houses throughout the world.

The ingredients of *Martha*'s popular success are not difficult to identify. One important element is certainly that Flotow's *Martha* was the first German comic opera to abandon spoken dialogue and employ continuous music. This serves to heighten the effect of the excellent libretto with its clever couplets and tightly organized tale. There are, of course, clearly defined musical numbers, which allow for audience applause after particularly stirring arias and ensembles.

The plot of Flotow's *Martha* is conventional and accessible. Two young men seek two young women, find them, lose them, and are reunited with them at the end. Along the way there are disguises and mistaken identities, bucolic settings, crowd scenes, royal splendor, and sincere, deep emotions from the principal characters. In its plot, *Martha* is reminiscent of Mozart's *Così fan tutte*; in its light-hearted score, dramatic pace and situations, as well as its happy ending, it looks ahead to operetta. Lyonel's lyric tenor solos soar relentlessly while Sir Tristan's buffo bass part forms a *Falstaff*-like foil to the serious situations. As one might expect, the couples come together according to both social standing and voice part. The noble Lady Harriet, who poses as Martha, is the archetypal French coloratura soprano and ends up with Lyonel, who in the final act learns of his nobility, which explains his high, lyric tenor material. Plumkett, a farmer and bass, hitches up with Nancy, Lady Harriet's waiting maid and a mezzo-soprano.

There are numerous highlights in *Martha*, including Lady Harriet's "Letzte Rose," in the second act, which is the Irish folk song, *The Last Rose of Summer*, as published by Thomas Moore in his *Irish Melodies* of 1813. Motives from the song make up the material of the powerful quintet, "Mag der Himmel euch vergeben" (May heaven forgive you), which closes the third act. This detail is only one of many examples of Flotow's desire to unify his score melodically, including the several, referential repetitions of the "Letzte Rose" theme in the opera. Plumkett's drinking song early in Act III, "Könnt ihr ergründen" (Can you explain), is surpassed only by Lyonel's "Ach, so fromm" (Ah, so gentle), a show-stopper and favorite recital piece. *—John Palmer*

Synopsis:

Act One. Lady Harriet Durham, the maid of honor to Queen Anne of England, is bored of her courtly life and wishes she were in love. When her maid, Nancy, tries to cheer her up it only makes her feel worse. Lady Harriet is being pursued by her cousin, Lord Tristan, whom she finds to be a boorish dandy and who is, at the moment, trying to woo her. Singing peasant girls pass by Harriet's home on their way to the Richmond fair and give Harriet an idea: She, Nancy, and Lord Tristan will dress as peasants and will go with the commoners to the fair, where farmers bid for the year-long services of young ladies. Lord Tristan will use the name "Bob," Nancy will go by "Julia" and Lady Harriet will be known as "Martha."

Act Two. The farmers Lionel and Plunkett enter the square discussing their hopes at finding servant-girls. Lionel's father, on the run from the law, brought Lionel with him to Plunkett's family home. The two stayed with the Plunketts until the father died, never having revealed his identity or origins. Lionel was left with only a ring, which his father said he should show to the Queen if ever he found himself in serious trouble. The Sheriff then opens the festivities and explains that any young lady who accepts payment for her services must remain with that farmer for an entire year. The assembled farmers set about finding maids, but Lionel and Plunkett cannot decide which ones to choose. As "Martha" and "Julia" enter, dragging the reluctant "Bob" behind them, they attract attention because of Bob's loud insistence that they all go home immediately. Martha then exclaims that Bob is trying to force her to serve on his farm, whereupon the commoners shout that there are plenty of available girls, many of whom then swarm around him. Martha and Julia, now alone with Plunkett and Lionel, offer their services and accept the farmers' meager payment. The women's afternoon diversion backfires, however, for when they try to return home with Bob, the Sheriff reminds them of their one-year commitment and forces them to leave with their new masters. Bob tries to help, but his held back by other farmers.

Act Three. When the farmers tell their new servants to begin working, the women announce they are unfamiliar with housework. The men begin to show the women how to spin thread, at which moment "Julia" escapes. Plunkett chases after her, leaving Lionel with "Martha." Lionel tells Martha he has amorous feelings for her and asks her to marry him, saying that he can overlook her lowly station in life. Martha finds this very amusing and continues the charade. She refuses his offer of marriage but does agree to sing a folksong ("Letzte Rose"). At midnight, Julia is back in the farmhouse and locked in a room with Martha. Lord Tristan shows up outside and taps on the women's window. Before the farmers can stop them, the women escape and return to their aristocratic lives.

Act Four. Plunkett is drinking with friends at a tavern when the Queen Anne's hunting party arrives. Among them is Nancy. When Plunkett recognizes her he tries to force her to return to the farmhouse with him. Nancy denies knowing him and the armed servants chase him away. Lionel enters and tells of his pain at the loss of his maid, Martha ("Ach so fromm"). In his troubled state he does not notice as Lady Harriet and Lord Tristan appear. Once again, Tristan is trying to woo Harriet, but she asks him to leave and, in an aside, admits she misses Lionel. Lionel hears her voice and kneels before her, proclaiming his love. Lady Harriet knows that she must keep her earlier escapade a secret and denies having ever met Lionel. When Lionel becomes furious, Lady Harriet calls on Lord Tristan and the others, who do not believe Lionel's explanation that Lady Harriet disguised herself, posing as a servant girl, and came to his house. Lady Harriet accuses Lionel of being crazy, and he is arrested. Before Lionel is led off to prison, a quintet begins ("Mag der Himmel euch vergeben") and Lionel gives Plunkett the ring from his father, telling Plunkett to take it to the Queen.

Act Five. Before the curtain rises, the Queen identified Lionel's ring as that belonging to the Earl of Derby, unjustly banished years before, and she has released Lionel. Lady Harriet now comes to Lionel to reveal to him his true identity and to ask him to forgive her and to marry her. Of course, Lionel rejects her offer. Plunkett and Nancy, however, are on good terms and in love, and Harriet asks for their help in winning Lionel.

Outside of the farmhouse peasants erect a mock Richmond fair and dress one of the farmers as the Sheriff. The play within a play begins as "Martha" and "Julia" enter in peasant clothes to meet Plunkett and the depressed Lionel at the "fair." As before, the women offer their services to Plunkett and Lionel, who give in and embrace their new lovers. The crowd celebrates. *—John Palmer*

Recommended:

○ **Flotow: Martha** / Schuler (cond.), Berger, Anders, Greindl, Fuchs, Staatskapelle Berlin / 1994 / Berlin Classics 0021632

Carlisle Floyd

b. Jun. 11, 1926, Latta, SC

Composer: Opera

The accessible operas of this American composer include the international success *Susannah*, a repertory mainstay ever since its compostion. Floyd employed a distinctive harmonic language based on fourths and fifths to create melodies and harmonies inspired by American folk tunes, and he was an effective dramatist in the vein opened up by Puccini and mined by Hindemith.

Carlisle Sessions Floyd was born in South Carolina to a Methodist pastor whose wife was a pianist. Lessons with his mother started at age ten, and at 16 Floyd went to Converse College in Spartanburg to study piano with Ernst Bacon. When Bacon was named to the faculty at Syracuse University in 1945, Floyd relocated in order to continue his course of study. Floyd earned his bachelor's in music at Syracuse in 1946, and took up a position teaching piano at Florida State University in Tallahassee, where he remained until 1976, eventually adding composition and opera workshops to his curriculum.

From the beginning of his career, Carlisle Floyd was interested primarily in opera, and furnished all of his own libretti. His first effort in the genre was *Slow Dusk* (1949) given at Syracuse. Floyd's next opera, *Fugitives* (1951), was withdrawn after a single performance at Florida State. *Susannah* (1955) was based on the apocryphal biblical story of Susannah and the elders, but transferred to rural Tennessee, and was an immediate smash when heard at the New York City Opera in 1956. The 29-year-old Floyd won, in quick succession, the New York Music Critics' Circle Award, a Guggenheim Foundation grant, and the envy of many of his colleagues. *Susannah* has gone on to become Floyd's best-known and most frequently produced work; it requires only modest economic means to produce.

Floyd's next undertaking, *Wuthering Heights* (1958–59), proved troublesome, after it was first performed in Santa Fe in July, 1958. Floyd found it necessary to rewrite the entire third act. His next project, *The Passion of Jonathan Wade* (1962) remains Floyd' s largest-scale opera, requiring seven principals and an orchestra roughly the dimension of that required by Puccini. In the midst of *Jonathan Wade*, Floyd managed to work up *The Sojourner and Mollie Sinclair* for the tercentenary celebration of North Carolina in 1963. *Markheim* followed in New Orleans in 1966, and in Seattle in 1970 Floyd finally scored his second unchallenged hit, *Of Mice and Men*, based on John Steinbeck's novel. Like *Susannah*, this work has enjoyed numerous revivals both with regional professional opera companies and in university productions.

In 1972 aspiring opera producer David Gockley attended a Cincinnati Opera performance of *Of Mice and Men*, and it opened his eyes to the potential of contemporary American works. Soon after, Gockley assumed control of the Houston Grand Opera, and in 1976 convinced Floyd to leave his long-time post at Florida State to assume the position as HGO's co-director. Floyd's first work for Houston was *Bilby's Doll* (1976) based on the witch hunts in Colonial Massachusetts. Floyd's next Houston Production was *Willie Stark* (1981), a fictionalized account of Louisiana governor Huey Long based on Robert Penn Warren's novel *All the King's Men*. In the 1980s Floyd turned his attention to a major overhaul of *The Passion of Jonathan Wade*, essentially composing an entirely new opera out of the old. The tremendous success accorded to the new *Jonathan Wade* upon its launch in Houston in 1991 helped to re-establish critical interest in Floyd as a composer. What may be Floyd's valedictory opera, *Cold Sassy Tree* (2000) was a joint commission from five opera companies including Houston, and was both critically and financially a success.

His non-operatic works are mostly vocal cycles, including *The Mystery* (1960, written for Phyllis Curtin), *Citizen of Paradise* (1983, for Suzanne Mentzer) and the cantata *A Time to Dance* (1994). Floyd has also written a *Piano Sonata* and several short orchestral pieces. *—Uncle Dave Lewis*

OPERA

Cold Sassy Tree (2000)

Floyd is arguably the most "American" of United States composers. His stage works are almost exclusively drawn from works by American authors and set in the United States, and even when drawn from other sources, such as the Biblical story of Susannah, are direct looks at the flaws and virtues of America and American society. Musically, and again typical of Floyd, this opera draws from American music, most notably folk and hymns, but also with elements of jazz. *Cold Sassy Tree*, based on the best seller by Olive Ann Burns, which Floyd himself adapted for the libretto, shows the changes that unexpected love and behaviors can cause in a small town and explores small-town small-mindedness, though with far less tragic consequences than those in *Susannah*. The townspeople here are more foolish than venomous and the music is less biting in its depiction of them. In fact, Floyd himself argued that the piece is essentially a comedy, despite the serious and even tragic elements. For many critics, this work represented Floyd's final triumph as a composer (many even compared it to Verdi's final opera, *Falstaff*, also a comedy from a composer far more associated with tragedy), particularly in its blending of social comedy and drama and musical accessibility without banality or mere tunesmithing. For example, in the arioso when Rucker Lattermore rebukes the townsfolk for their refusal to accept his marriage, the interaction of his vocal line and the orchestra are masterful; the orchestra seems to reflect upon rather than illustrate his allusions, not falling into the trap of overt illustration of the birds or children he describes, and protects the moment from bombast and sentimentality by not backing his voice until the conclusion, which ends soberly rather than with a simplistic flourish. The opera was commissioned jointly by the Austin Lyric Opera, Baltimore Opera, Houston Grand Opera, Opera Carolina, and San Diego Opera, and premiered at the Houston Grand Opera on April 14, 2000. (This work was Floyd's fourth commission from the HGO) *—Ann Feeney*

Synopsis:

Act One. The opera is set in spring of the year 1900, in Cold Sassy Tree, GA, a small town. Tongues wag over the impeding marriage of local merchant Rucker

Lattimore to a young Northern widow named Love Simpson. The Lattimore family's problems are compounded when Rucker's grandson, Will Tweedy (who narrates the action), begins spending time with a young woman from "the wrong side of the tracks" named Lightfoot McClendon and saying that he wants to become a writer. Love Simpson tries to explain her relationship to Rucker Lattimore's daughters, Mary and Loma, saying that in return for keeping house for him she will inherit the house in the end. As an orphan, she says, she never knew anything more than a room in a boardinghouse.

The good people of Cold Sassy Tree will have none of it, and at church the following Sunday they turn a cold shoulder to Love Simpson. Will Tweedy and Love stalk out of the service, and Rucker Lattimore installs himself in his own living room as preacher of his own church. The act ends with a trio as Will, Love, and Rucker sing a pointed Doxology.

Act Two. It is the following summer, and Love has moved into Rucker's house. Rucker's daughters bewail all the changes that have taken place—Love has redone the house, and Rucker has even shaved off his beloved beard. A rancher named Camp shows up, and it turns out that he was once engaged to Love. But she sends him packing back to Texas. Lightfoot, meanwhile, has been forced to drop out of school for financial reasons. She talks to Will about her hope that she can further her education, and Will says that he can get her a job in Rucker's general store. The two embrace but are caught by Loma, who rebukes them. Will, in retaliation, begins spreading rumors about Loma, but Rucker asks him to apologize.

Rucker, to surprise Love, has electricity and plumbing installed in the house. She begins to realize that although theirs was a marriage of convenience, she is beginning to have real feelings for him. She reveals to him that she was abused as a child. Although she is afraid that he will consider her damaged goods, Rucker instead proposes that she become his wife in a physical sense.

Act Three. Several months later in fall, Love encounters a group of town gossips at a store. Now, however, she has learned to deal with them by flattery. Rucker tries to convince Will to take over the general store instead of pursuing his dream of becoming a writer. The issue becomes critical sooner than anyone expected when Rucker is shot during a robbery while he is closing the store and is seriously wounded. During a family vigil at his bedside, Rucker tells Will that he should follow his dream after all. He says to Love that she was the one he had always searched for. Love tries to tell him that she is pregnant with his child, getting the words in just before Rucker dies.

Lamenting Rucker's death as he talks to Lightfoot, Will reveals that Rucker's will has specified a town-wide party to be held in his memory. Will persuades Love to reveal her pregnancy, and she does so. The townspeople react with shock, but most are now reconciled to the marriage and its new offspring. Love is finally accepted into the bosom of Rucker's family, and members of the crowd congratulate her and join in a celebration of Rucker's memory. *—James Manheim*

Recommended:

○ **Floyd: Cold Sassy Tree** / Summers (cond.), Holloway, Christin, Marcinko, Jones, Houston Grand Opera Orch. / 2005 / Albany Troy 758/59

Of Mice and Men (1969)

American composer Carlisle Floyd is known for his verismo operas with modest production requirements and lean dramas, which are imbued with American musical folk idioms. *Of Mice and Men*, composed in 1970, marked a turning point in Floyd's musical style. Greater chromaticism and harmonic experimentation, as well as stage innovations, made this work Floyd's biggest success with both critics and public. It was premiered on January 22, 1970, by the Seattle Opera Association in Washington. The text was written by Floyd and adapted from the John Steinbeck novel. Floyd usually composes for a small orchestra with little unusual combinations. Here he has included an extensive percussion section that includes a gong, whip, and glockenspiel, xylophone, and vibraphone. He uses celesta and harp as the continuo instruments. The orchestral texture is extremely flexible, making use of constant meter changes to adapt to the rhythms of the sung text and orchestral interludes and passages that introduce and depict the character of the various scenes. The opera is through-composed and the voices of the orchestral instruments are always present. *—Rita Laurance*

Synopsis:

Act One. This is the story of two migrant farmhands, the level-headed George and his mentally disadvantaged companion Lennie. The first act opens in the middle of a cycle that it seems has been repeated several times: Lennie, whose physical strength is constantly foiled by his hapless clumsiness, has gotten into trouble, forcing them to flee one job and go looking for another one elsewhere. Camping out on the run, sirens whining in the distance, Lennie urges George to describe once again their common dream: to earn enough money to buy a farm of their own. Lennie takes particular delight in imagining taking care of the animals, as he is deeply fond of pets. Sadly, his affection caused him to inadvertently kill his last one, a mouse, by stroking it too hard; only at George's stern insistence does he discard its body. Come morning, the men arrive at their new place of employment, a ranch owned by the disagreeable Curley and his wife, a neglected woman whose domestic despair leads her to flirt with the ranch hands. On their first day at work George and Lennie witness both birth and death: their co-worker Slim's dog has just had puppies, one of which Lennie begs to call his own; the old hound owned by Candy, a fellow ranch hand, is so decrepit and smelly that another worker, Carlson, insists on putting it out of its (and their) misery.

Act Two. George and Lennie have found an advertisement for a farm that they think they can earn enough money to buy, and Candy offers to join with them and split the cost. Their pipe dream is disrupted by Curley's wife, who enters the bunkhouse against her husband's orders and the men's protests. Curley soon finds her there and, suspecting mischief, starts pummeling Lennie. Confused and defensive, Lennie grips Curley's hand so tight he crushes it. Humiliated, it is only at the insistence of the other men that Curley agrees not to fire Lennie.

Act Three. Lennie, again confusing affection with aggression, has cuddled his puppy too forcefully and killed it. He is hiding it in the hay loft when Curley's wife appears, suitcase in hand, ready to leave for good. Thinking him harmless and childlike, she allows Lennie to stroke her hair. She becomes uneasy, however, and Lennie tries to muffle her protests; in a panic, he accidentally snaps her neck. When the other men find her body, Slim gives George some grim advice: to find Lennie and shoot him before the inevitable lynch mob gets him. In the final scene, George finds the terrified Lennie, and consoles him by reciting once again their dream. As Lennie becomes lost in the reverie of his imagination, George, brokenhearted and desperate, draws his gun and fires. *—Jeremy Grimshaw*

Recommended:

○ **Floyd: Of Mice and Men** / Summers (cond.), Futral, Maddalena, Patrick, Evans, Houston Grand Opera Orch. / 2003 / Albany 621/22

Susannah (1953–1954)

Carlisle Floyd's *Susannah* achieved success beyond that of almost any other American opera. By the end of the twentieth century, it had been mounted not only by regional companies, but by major houses such as Chicago's Lyric Opera and the Metropolitan Opera in New York City. It has found favor overseas as well, with its simple dramatic and lyric balance, straightforward telling of a compelling tale, and an immediately accessible score. Countless aspiring sopranos have utilized *Susannah*'s Act I aria "Ain't it a Pretty Night" as an audition piece.

Floyd's choice of subject was strongly influenced by political events of the McCarthy era. The composer has said that McCarthyism "took all kinds of forms: suspicion, and the idea that accusation was all that was needed as proof of guilt. It terrified and enraged me." The South that he used for a setting (Tennessee) was well known to him, Floyd having been raised in small-town South Carolina. To describe *Susannah* merely as folk opera, however, is to ignore the assurance and sophistication with which he handles his orchestration. Bigotry, lust, seduction, and revenge may be elementary subjects, but Floyd manages to allow them their full impact while not oversimplifying. While he employed folk tunes, hymns, and dances, they are woven into the opera's fabric quite seamlessly.

Susannah herself is the kind of figure close to Floyd's affections and concerns, a figure who lives on the periphery of organized society. Seen by church elders bathing in a stream, she is a subject to raise fears among those who see and lust inwardly. The elders' embarrassment over their feelings is transmuted into cries that Susannah is wicked and must repent. She is shunned by her fellow church members. The itinerant preacher, Blitch, seeking first to save her, then only to comfort her, seduces her and, in the act, is horrified to realize that she is innocent. But by now, even his protests are of no avail against the aroused community. In the end, Susannah is left alone, isolated, hardened by her victimization. *—Erik Eriksson*

Synopsis:

Act One.

In the churchyard during a square dance, the wives of the church elders are waiting for the arrival of a traveling preacher. Most of the men try to partner with Susannah, and Mrs. McLean, noticing her own husband eye her, convinces the wives that a girl that pretty, raised by a brother who drinks, must be wicked. Blitch comes in and introduces himself ("I am the Reverend Olin Blitch"), announcing his intentions to cast out devils and make sinners repent. He notices Susannah and heads over to dance with her as Mrs. McLean declares that Susannah will come to no good. Later that evening, at the old Polk farm house, Little Bat walks Susannah home. She is unaware that he has a crush on her. She is still excited from the dance but laughs when he says that the men, including the preacher, were courting her. She sings about the night and her dreams of leaving the valley one day, to see what life in the big city is like ("Ain't it a pretty night"). Sam comes in, and Little Bat runs off. He teases her that soon she'll keeping house for a husband, and she, laughing it off, asks him to sing the "Jaybird Song." They dance around the yard and then sink back, both sighing "Ain't it a pretty night." The next morning, Susannah goes to bathe in the creek, and the elders, looking for a place for baptisms, see her and rapidly become lustful and then outraged. They leave, vowing to tell the whole village about her evil nature and to make her repent. That evening, at a church picnic, everyone is gossiping about Susannah, adding rumor to rumor. When she comes, everyone treats her coldly, and finally Mrs. McLean venomously tells her she isn't welcome there. Nobody speaks up for her, and she rushes away, fighting tears. Back at the house, Little Bat creeps up to tell Susannah that the elders saw her bathing and want to run her out of the church and the valley. She protests that she's done nothing wrong, but he continues by saying that everyone believes no man is safe from her. He even admits that his parents bullied him into saying that she seduced him. She orders him away, and Sam comes out, awakened by the noise. He tries to explain the malicious part of human nature ("It's about the way people is made, I reckon"), and that ("It must make the good Lord sad"). When he reiterates that there's nothing they can do but wait, she bursts into tears and begs him to sing "Jaybird" again.

Act Two. Susannah and Sam are talking about how badly she is treated now. He tells her he has to go fetch meat from his traps and urges her to go to the prayer meeting to show she doesn't believe she's done anything wrong. She is reluctant, but he persuades her. In the church, Blitch preaches thunder-and-brimstone sermons ("I'm fixin' to tell y' 'bout a feller I knowed"). Susannah is sitting alone in the back. As the congregation sings, "Come, sinner, tonight's the night," he begins to address her directly, urging her to come forward and confess her sins. Almost in a trance, she starts towards the altar, but seeing him burst into a triumphant smile, she cries out in protest and runs out. Alone outside her house, she sings a desolate song, "The trees on the mountain." Blitch has followed her and is friendly at first, but then insists again that she confess and repent. She repeats that she's done nothing wrong, and he turns to leave. After a moment, he turns back, and tells her that sometimes he longs for a woman's love ("I'm a lonely man, Susannah"). She offers no resistance when he leads her indoors.

In the church the next morning, he is praying, aghast at what he has done ("Hear me, O Lord"), having realized too late that she was a virgin. He prays for her and for forgiveness. In response to his message, the elders and their wives come in, followed by Susannah. He orders them to ask Susannah's forgiveness for spreading false rumors, but when asked how he can declare that she was innocent, he can only feebly answer that God told him. They leave in disbelief, and when, alone with Susannah, he asks for her forgiveness, she coldly tells him she's forgotten what the word "forgive" means. Back at their home, Sam returns, drunk. She tells him what happened, saying she was just too tired to put up any resistance while he was out getting drunk, not there to help her. He swears that he will kill Blitch, to which she tersely responds, "That'd do a lot of good." As she goes inside, he takes a shotgun and runs off. She calls him for supper, and when she comes out looking for him and sees the missing gun, then hears a shot, she falls to her knees, crying desperately and praying to be forgiven for whatever wrong she has done. Little Bat rushes in, telling her that Sam shot Blitch while he was leading the baptisms, and Blitch died, praying out loud for her. He tells her a mob is coming to hang Sam if they catch him, and to run her out of the valley. He hides as the mob enters ("Get out, get out, Susannah"). She stands firm, laughing defiantly, and when they advance, she threatens them with another gun. They back off, though still menacing her, and Little Bat emerges from hiding. She pretends to want to make love, and when he approaches eagerly, she slaps him and laughs again as he runs away. —*Ann Feeney*

Recommended:

- ○ **Floyd: Susannah** / Nagano (cond.), Brossmann, Erlo, Ramey, Hadley, Lyon National Opera Orch. / 1994 / Virgin 45039
- ○ **Floyd: Susannah** / Andersson (cond.), Curtin, Treigle, Cassilly, Long, Brim, New Orleans Opera Orch. / 1995 / VAI Audio 1115

Joseph Flummerfelt

b. Feb. 24, 1937, Vincennes, IN

Conductor

Joseph Flummerfelt's choral conducting career has traced a steady yet meteoric trajectory: for over 25 years, his performances have been well known across the world's most prestigious concert halls and in over 35 recordings on 12 different labels. Flummerfelt attended DePauw University for his first studies in organ and church music, graduating in 1958. He followed this with a master's degree in choral conducting from the Philadelphia Conservatory of Music (1962) and a doctorate from the University of Illinois (1971); he also studied under Nadia Boulanger, Julius Herford, and Elaine Brown. In addition to serving for 23 years as *maestro di coro* for the Festival of Two Worlds in Spoleto, Italy, Flummerfelt has been director of choral activities for the American spin-off *Spoleto USA* in Charleston, SC, since 1977. He made his conducting debut with the New York Philharmonic in 1988 and serves as chorusmaster for that ensemble. He has also founded and continues to direct the New York Choral Artists. He taught at the University of Illinois (1963–64), DePauw University (1964–68), and Florida State University (1968–71), before joining the faculty at Westminster Choir College (beginning in 1971). Among his many awards are the French Prix du Président de la République, two Grammy nominations, and four honorary doctorates. —*Timothy Dickey*

Recommended:

- ○ **O Magnum Mysterium** / Flummerfelt (cond.), Westminster Choir / 1992 / Chesky 83

Folger Consort

f. 1976, Washington, DC

Ensemble

The Folger Consort is an early music ensemble associated with the Folger Shakespeare Library in Washington, DC. The group was founded in 1976 by lutenist/guitarist/harpist Christopher Kendall, and to this day he and fellow founding member and viol and recorder player Robert Eisenstein form the core of the ensemble. Having met as students at Ohio's Antioch College, Kendall and Eisenstein shortly thereafter formed a group that became the resident music ensemble for the Folger Library. Within a short time, it took on a life of its own, the Folger Consort becoming an American exponent of early Celtic-Anglo-European music, which, after all, has a tradition going back to the time of the Roanoke Colony and Sir Walter Raleigh. Although the ensemble specializes in music of the Renaissance, its repertoire extends well past the sixteenth century in both directions, covering repertoire from the high Middle Ages all the way through to the eighteenth century. In addition to extensive live concerts and National Public Radio broadcasts, the Folger Consort produces one recording per year. So far, their body of recorded work gives an example of the ensemble's broad range, from twelfth century Christmas carols to Swiss-Austrian Alpine airs. In addition to guest performers, past members have included Tina Chancey and Scott Reiss. The latter has expanded the borders of the consort, by association at least, through the crossover ensemble Hesperus by playing blues and jazz on the recorder, citing providing a link with the improvisational tradition in much early music. Similarly, the Folger Consort remains an active and important New World link to the Old World tradition. It is based, with the rest of the Folger organization, in Washington, DC. —*Wayne Reisig*

Recommended:

- ○ **A Distant Mirror** / Folger Consort / 1994 / Delos 1003
- ○ **A Medieval Tapestry** / Folger Consort / 1990 / Bard 9003
- ○ **Of Kindly Lust And Love's Inspiring** / Minter (cond.), Folger Consort, Ensemble V/I / 1993 / Bard 9308

Arthur Foote

b. Mar. 5, 1853, Salem, MA, **d.** Apr. 8, 1937, Boston, MA

Composer: Orchestral, Concerto

Arthur Foote's music fits the mood of his time and place: turn-of-the-century New England. It was lyrical, conservative, Germanic, not arrestingly original, but expressive and formally clear. He was a major figure in his day; many of his orchestral works were premiered by the Boston Symphony. Foote tended to favor abstract forms; he wrote suites and a serenade for string orchestra, a cello concerto, a violin sonata, three string quartets, and the like. But he did occasionally venture into program music, notably with his "symphonic prologue" *Francesca da Rimini* and his *Four Character Pieces after Omar Khayyám* for orchestra. His cantatas, now long-forgotten, drew inspiration from Romantic poetry and art, as exemplified by *The Farewell of Hiawatha* and *The Wreck of the Hesperus.*

After childhood piano studies, Foote entered Harvard in 1870, originally intending to study law, but also enrolled in the music curriculum. There, he studied with John Knowles Paine, and, in 1875 he received the first M.A. degree in music awarded in America. The next year, Foote attended the first Bayreuth festival, but the music of Wagner had less impact on his style than that of Schumann and Brahms—which was the case for most of Foote's New England circle of German-born or—trained musicians. In 1878 he became organist in Boston's First Unitarian Church, a post he held until 1910, but one that inspired him to write surprisingly little organ music. Instead, he concentrated on songs (more than 100), as well as chamber and symphonic music. He organized a chamber-music concert series in Boston that ran from 1881 until the turn of the century, and frequently played piano with the Kneisel Quartet between 1890 and 1910; with them, he performed many of his own works. A longtime music teacher (his 50-year career began as a private instructor and culminated in a 1921 appointment to the New England Conservatory), Foote was an early member of the Music Teachers National Association, and a founding member of the American Guild of Organists, of which he was president from 1909 to 1912. He also worked as an arranger and editor for the Boston publisher Arthur P. Schmidt, taking the pseudonyms Ferdinand Meyer and Carl Erich.

Foote also produced several manuals; his *Modern Harmony in Its Theory and Practice,* written with W.R. Spalding and first published in 1905, was still in print in the late 1970s under the title *Harmony.*—*James Reel*

ORCHESTRAL

Suite for strings in E major, Op. 63 (1907; revised 1908)

American composer Arthur Foote's most famous piece of orchestral concert music, the *Suite for string orchestra in E major,* Op. 63, of 1907–09 (not to be confused with either the *Suite for string orchestra in E major,* Op. 12, of 1886 or the *Serenade for strings in E major,* Op. 25) is a piece of which he himself was quite fond, as he specifically mentions in his autobiography, and of which the American—and especially New England—musical public was quite fond for a full two or three decades after it was first composed. The suite, Op. 63, was premiered on April 16, 1909, by the Boston Symphony Orchestra, August Max Fiedler conducting.

The suite originally had four movements, but Foote eventually cut one of them and left only: 1. Praeludium, 2. Pizzicato and Adagietto, 3. Fugue. (The discarded movement was a Theme and Variations.) The Praeludium begins with a tune in the first violins and some syncopated accompaniment in the seconds and violas, and never veers more than a few degrees from this basic layout or that particular melody. Still, the tune is carefully planned for maximum effect, and there is great breadth and variety of expression drawn from it, including a not-too-strong climax moment. The Pizzicato and Adagietto is, as its name implies, a movement containing two quite contrasting types of music (it is not, however, the two-section movement its name would also seem to imply, but rather a three-section one—the opening Pizzicato music comes back after the Adagietto). Plucked music, Capriccioso, Allegretto, in a galloping 6/8 time A minor fills the opening portion, and then the strings throw mutes on their instruments for the introspective (and arco) central Adagietto. The Fugue is built from an Allegro giusto E minor subject first offered by the second violins and then given a go by the first violins, cellos/basses, and finally the violas. *—Blair Johnston*

Recommended:

○ **Kenneth Klein, Conductor** / Klein (cond.), London SO / 1997 / Albany 235

○ **American Dreams** / Leppard (cond.), Indianapolis SO / 1999 / Decca 458157

CONCERTO

A Night Piece, for flute & strings (1922; revised 1934)

Arthur Foote was an American often associated with a group of composers known as the Boston Six, the others being Edward MacDowell, John Knowles Paine, Horatio Parker, George Chadwick, and Amy Cheney Beach. This enclave is important in the development of American music because its members were among the first to write first-rate serious music that at least partially broke from European styles. Known for his songs and chamber music, Foote was one of the more important of the group, and this work, *A Night Piece*, is one of his most popular and most representative compositions. That said, its music may be better-known in its original guise, as the Nocturne section of Foote's 1918 *Nocturne and Scherzo*, for flute and string quartet. The larger scoring here was done at the behest of conductor Pierre Monteux. *A Night Piece* may be slightly more atmospheric than the original in capturing the somewhat wistful exoticism of the main theme. When the strings take up the melody after the flute's rendition of it, they impart a greater sense of warmth. The livelier alternate theme is playful and sweet, perfectly matched by Foote to the perky sonorities of the flute. Lasting about eight minutes, the work is subdued throughout, its Romanticism slightly cool and Delian-sounding, and its writing, especially for the flute, quite deftly imagined. *—Robert Cummings*

Recommended:

○ **Alexa Still, Flute** / Braithwaite (cond.), Still, New Zealand CO / 1991 / Koch 7063

Antoine Forqueray

b. ca. 1672, Paris, France, **d.** Jun. 28, 1745, Mantes, France

Composer: Chamber Music

Antoine Forqueray was the first major virtuoso of the bass viol, a favorite instrument of King Louis XIV. His surviving compositions are, likewise, the earliest important music for that instrument, technically demanding and possessing a piquant harmonic style.

Forqueray appeared before the king at the age of ten, playing the already-obsolescent "basse de violin." The king was delighted, and ordered the lad taught the bass viol. On December 31, 1689, he was appointed *Musician ordinaire de la chambre du roy*. Forqueray had a technique that astonished even violinists with its fluency. He entertained the king with Italian-style preludes. Forqueray also became a noted teacher of the high-born, including the Elector of Bavaria and the Duke of Orléans.

In 1697 he married Henriette-Angelique Houssou, a keyboard player and daughter of a church organist. The pair gave concerts, but the marriage was not a success. This might have been because of Forqueray's lavish way of life (he was well-paid by the king) and exaggerated, self-important and downright unpleasant personality. They separated permanently after 13 years, following a series of quarrels and shorter separations.

Around 1730 he retired to a country estate in Mantes, making infrequent appearances at court. He was listed as "veteran" member of the household, in effect retired at full pay, but with no duty to appear.

He treated his son, Jean-Baptiste Forqueray (1669–82), horribly. He had him thrown into debtors' prison in 1719, and exiled in 1725. This son, also a great bassist, succeeded to his father's court position in 1742. Upon his father's death, Jean-Baptiste published a book of viol pieces: three of his own and 29 of his father's. Antoine Forqueray is primarily remembered for the music in that publication, and for a few other of his pieces that were published elsewhere and are less adventurous works. *—Joseph Stevenson*

CHAMBER MUSIC

Pieces de viole & continuo, Book 1

By all reports, French composer Antoine Forqueray (1671–1745) was one of the greatest virtuosos of his time. According to his contemporaries, his virtuosity on the bass viol was legendary; even the great Marin Marais applauded his genius. For all that, apparently no one praised the man who is universally described as proud to the point of hubris about his musical talents, a bad husband, and a worse father—he had his son thrown into debtor's prison and later exiled. Despite this excessively harsh treatment, Forqueray's son, Jean-Baptiste, published the only edition of his father's music, the 34 pieces arranged in five suites of the *Book One* of his father's *Pièces de viole* were published posthumously. Forqueray was said to have composed more than 300 pieces for this instrument, but, unfortunately, most of them appear to be permanently lost. Of those pieces that survive in *Book One*, each demonstrates Forqueray's superlative abilities as a composer and performer. With strong, singing lines and highly ornate embellishments; fantastic modulations that are nevertheless grounded in his thorough knowledge of harmony; and a noble and even elevated tone and a kind of impious emotionality, Forqueray's *Book One* is one of the highest examples of music for the bass viol in existence. *—James Leonard*

Recommended:

○ **Forqueray: Pieces de Viole** / Koopman, Savall, Coin / 1988 / Astrée 7762

○ **Forqueray: Works for Harpsichord** / Rousset / 2001 / Decca 466976

Maureen Forrester

b. Jul. 25, 1930, Montreal, Quebec, Canada

Contralto

Canada's most famous contralto, Maureen Forrester, began her vocal studies with Sally Martin in Montreal and later studied with Frank Rowe and Bernard Diamant. Her first professional appearance came in a recital at Montreal in 1953, and she began a musical collaboration with pianist John Newmark which lasted until his death in 1991. In 1955 she went to Paris for a recital, and her New York debut recital was one year later. That recital brought her to the attention of Bruno Walter who asked her to sing the contralto solos in the *Second Symphony* of Mahler with the New York Philharmonic the following season. This appearance was the beginning of her international fame, as Walter considered her an outstanding interpreter of Mahler's music. During the early years of her career, she concentrated on concert and recital programs. Her first important operatic appearance came in 1962 at Toronto in Gluck's *Orfeo ed Euridice*. In 1966 she debuted at the New York City Opera as Cornelia in Handel's *Giulio Cesare* with Beverly Sills and Norman Treigle. She made her Metropolitan Opera debut as Erda in *Das Rheingold* in 1975. Her excellent comic timing brought critical acclaim for her appearances as the Step-Mother in Massenet's *Cendrillon*, the Witch in *Hansel and Gretel* and as the Fairy Queen in Sullivan's *Iolanthe* at Stratford. In her later years, she was in great demand as the Countess in Tchaikovsky's *Queen of Spades* and in Poulenc's *Dialogues des Carmelites*.

From 1965 to 1974, she was a member of the Bach Aria Group and made many tours of the United States and Canada with that group. Her solo recital tours took her around the world and, ever a staunch supporter of Canadian composers, she regularly included their songs on her programs. The most important of the works she championed was Fleming's *The Confession Stone*. Although her orchestral repertoire ranged from Bach and Pergolesi to Elgar and Casals, it was as an interpreter of Mahler that Forrester is best remembered, most especially for the *Second Symphony* and *Das Lied von der Erde*. Maureen Forrester's voice was a dark, rich contralto, but with an ease in the upper register which allowed her to sing some mezzo-soprano parts including the Verdi *Requiem* and Brangäne in Wagner's *Tristan and Isolde*. Although a large voice, it was very flexible which created a demand for her in the oratorios of Bach and Handel, as well as other Baroque composers, which she sang all over the world. In the 1960s and 1970s, she averaged around 120 performances a year, while raising five children.

Forrester enjoyed teaching, and from 1966 until 1971, she headed the voice department at the Philadelphia Academy of Music. After leaving the Academy of Music, she continued to teach privately in Toronto and to give master classes in conjunction with her recitals. In 1983, she began a five-year term as chairman of the Canada Council for the Arts. She published her autobiography, *Out of Character*, in 1986, the same year she was named a Companion of the Order of Canada. Maureen Forrester remained one of the great contraltos of the twentieth century throughout her long performing career. *—Richard LeSueur*

Recommended:

○ **Grande Dame of Song** / Forrester, etc. / CBC 2017

○ **Handel Arias** / Forrester, etc. / 1992 / CBC 2002

Lukas Foss

b. Aug. 15, 1922, Berlin, Germany

Composer: Concerto, Vocal, Chamber Music

American composer, conductor, and educator Lukas Foss has contributed profoundly to the circulation and appreciation of music of the twentieth century. He began his musical studies in Berlin, where he studied piano and theory with Julius Goldstein. Goldstein introduced Foss to the music of Bach, Mozart, and Beethoven, which had a profound effect on Foss musical development. In 1933, Foss went to Paris where he studied piano with Lazare Lévy as well as composition with Noël Gallon, orchestration with Felix Wolfes, and flute with Louis Moyse. Foss remained in Paris until 1937, when he moved with his family to the United States, continuing his musical instruction at the Curtis Institute of Music in Philadelphia. In addition, Foss studied conducting with Koussevitzky during the summers from 1939 to 1943 at the Berkshire Music Center. He also studied composition with Paul Hindemith as a special student at Yale from 1939 to 1940.

Foss began to compose at the age of seven and was first published at 15. At the age of 22, he won the New York Music Critic's Award for his cantata *Prairie*, which was premiered by the Collegiate Chorale, under the direction of Robert Shaw. From 1944–50, Foss served as the pianist of the Boston Symphony Orchestra. In 1945, he was the youngest composer ever to receive a Guggenheim fellowship. From 1950–51, he was a fellow at the American Academy in Rome, and received a Fulbright grant for 1950–52.

In February of 1953, Foss received an appointment as professor of music at the University of California at Los Angeles—succeeding Arnold Schoenberg—where he taught composition and conducting. While at UCLA, Foss founded the groundbreaking Improvisation Chamber Ensemble. He served from 1963–70 as music director and conductor of the Buffalo Philharmonic Orchestra. In 1963, at the State University of New York at Buffalo, Foss founded, and became the director of, the Center for Creative and Performing Arts. In 1971, Foss became the conductor of the Brooklyn Philharmonic, a position which he held until 1990 when he was named Conductor-Laureate. In 1972, he was appointed conductor of the Kol Israel Orchestra of Jerusalem. From 1972–73, Foss served as composer-in-residence at the Manhattan School of Music in New York, and from 1981–86, was conductor of the Milwaukee Symphony.

Foss is a member of the American Academy of Arts and Letters, and from 1989–90, served as composer in residence at the Tanglewood Music Center. Foss became professor of music at the School for the Arts at Boston University in 1991. He has also traveled widely, appearing as a guest conductor with many American and European Orchestras, and lecturing at many North American colleges and universities, including Harvard and Carnegie Mellon.

The compositions of Lukas Foss illustrate two main periods in his artistic development, separated by a middle, avant-garde phase. The works of his first period are predominantly neo-classic in style, and reflect his love of Bach and Stravinsky. In the transitional period he fused elements of controlled improvisation and chance operations with 12-tone, and serialist techniques. Notable works of this period include the *Baroque Variations* for orchestra, and the chamber works *Time Cycle* (1960), *Thirteen Ways of Looking at a Blackbird* (1978), and *Echoi* (1963). His later period works, including the *Renaissance Concerto* (1990) for flute, embrace a wide variety of musical references, displaying a keen awareness of idioms and styles that span the history of western art music. —*Stephen Kingsbury*

CONCERTO

Renaissance Concerto, for flute & orchestra (1985)

Twentieth century composers from Igor Stravinsky to Alfred Schnittke and everywhere in between explored material from the Renaissance and Baroque periods in their own compositions. When Lukas Foss was asked by flutist Carol Wincenc to compose a concerto for flute, he settled on the sound of Renaissance music as both a target and a point of departure. The resulting concerto uses transcriptions, evocations, and extensions to create, as Foss describes it, "an homage to something I love, a handshake across the centuries." The precariousness of this concerto's balance between ancient pipings and the thoroughly modern sound of Foss make it both a little unsettling and quite riveting. While a normal Renaissance suite might have opened with a sarabande, Foss' "Intrada" is, as he describes it, "part flute cadenza, part chorale, and part circus music." The flute-cadenza passages seem to be composed entirely of period-appropriate ornamental trills and runs, without an intervening melody; these mix with a jaunty processional melody in the winds, then a sonorous brass chorale delivered by trumpets from high perches on opposite corners of the stage to evoke music played from atop town walls. A "Baroque Interlude (after Rameau)" follows, which transcribes that master's harpsichord piece "L'enharmonique," from *Nouvelles suites de pièces de clavecin*, for flute, harpsichord, and full orchestra. The scoring is thin and open, as high notes in flute and harpsichord and pizzicato plucking mingle with precise timpani taps. The somewhat distorted melody becomes chirpy in Foss' flute transcription, leading to a coda featuring a couple of jokey delays. The third movement is titled "Recitative (after Monteverdi)," and the flute part is freely adapted from a recitative from *Orfeo*. In a move away from *Orfeo*, the flute is supported by soft dissonant washes in the strings, echoed in canon by an offstage ensemble. Occasionally, the orchestral flute imitates the soloist as well. The textures are dreamlike, and the slowly shifting harmonies become almost hypnotic. This mood is dispersed quickly by the spirited canon which begins "Jouissance," derived from a madrigal by Melville. Soon, however, this yields to a flutter-tongued flute cadenza, which in turn yields to strange evocations of Galilei, Gesualdo, and Peri. After these have left the stage, the flutist reenters over eerie glissandos in the strings and leaves the stage as well, its music dropping from forte to pianissimo and then to mere key-clicks as the soloists walks off. Foss' response to Renaissance music is individual and inventive. —*Andrew Lindemann Malone*

Recommended:

○ **Lukas Foss** / Foss (cond.), Wincenc, Brooklyn PO / 1989 / New World 80375

VOCAL

Song of Songs, for soprano & orchestra (1946)

Conceived in 1946 when the composer was in his mid-twenties, Lukas Foss' orchestral song cycle on the biblical *Song of Songs* is chronologically and stylistically situated among his early neo-Classical works, along with such pieces as the *Symphony in G* (1944) and the *Symphony of Chorales* (1956). In approaching the evocative and often erotic *Song of Songs*, texts from which have been set by countless composers, Foss chose rather subdued verses in which divine and romantic love are conflated through subtle metaphors rather than explicit descriptions. The expressive depth of the chosen texts remain, but leave room for emotional elaboration and nuance through Foss' orchestral rendering. In fact, the four movements of the piece actually draw on several different portions of the text, arranged in such a way as to lend each movement and the work as a whole a compelling dramatic contour that is further articulated through music. Much of the first movement, which primarily draws on the regenerative images of the wind and the dawn from the fourth biblical song, is obsessive over an initial gesture of a rising fifth followed by a lower neighbor tone. Beginning in the winds as an ostinato, it multiplies to permeate the orchestral texture in dense imitation. The entrance of the voice highlights a new gesture, which likewise infiltrates the accompaniment. A change of mood brings a change of pace and whereas before, the soloist elaborated the words in a fluid, reiterative manner, the words are now declaimed with sturdy, unadorned purpose while the orchestra lurches forward with new urgency. The second movement, marked Aria, is in a lilting, syncopated 6/8 meter and a folkish minor mode that corresponds with the playful insistence of the text: "Come my beloved, let us go forth into the fields... Let us see if the vine flourish...." The metaphor of springtime and its emerging flora assumes a more seductive tone in the recitative-like middle section, followed by a da capo that resumes the coy play of the opening. The third movement is the most dramatic, perhaps partly for what is not contained therein. Foss omits the rather explicit sexual metaphors found in the text surrounding his excerpted lines, retaining only the description of the speaker's intense longing for her love and her vain search for him. The score fills in the gaps in the text, however, with a highly chromatic, harmonic language and an almost expressionistically fluid texture that surges and ebbs in waves of ascending lines. The vocal line takes on a conflicted, angular quality, reaching its dramatic peak with an exposed high A that suddenly leaps downwards a full octave and a half. The brief but emotionally concentrated fourth movement, with a harmonic lucidity and measured pace that starkly contrasts the anxiety of the third, elegantly sets the most tender and devotional of the texts, a line taken from the eighth song: "Set me as a seal upon thine heart... as a seal upon thine arm: for love is stronger than death." —*Jeremy Grimshaw*

Recommended:

○ **Time Cycle** / Bernstein (cond.), Tourel, New York PO / 1997 / Sony 63164

Time Cycle, for soprano & orchestra (1959–1960)

Some see clocks and other timekeepers as friendly reminders, while others see them as necessary evils or mere appliances, but few find them particularly threatening. However, the four texts that make up Lukas Foss' *Time Cycle* are dark and fatalistic in their view of the clock—indeed time itself.

At the time of its composition, Foss was parting ways with his traditional, tonal language in the late 1950s and early 1960s, trying his hand first at a very individualized kind of serial music, and then experimenting with new and progressive techniques in keeping with the innovatory nature of 1960s art music. Standing as it does near the beginning of this new phase, *Time Cycle* occupies relatively tame musical ground as compared to some of Foss' later 1960s work (with its graphic scores, semi-aleatory features, etc.).

The music is full of complex counterpoint, and the disjunct melody leaps within the atonal framework; rhythm and meter are shifting and unpredictable. The four songs are connected by the common motive of time, in a nonmusical sense, and a shared chord made of C sharp, A, B, and D sharp. In performance, they may be alternated with three optional, improvised interludes.

The first song, "We're Late," with words by W. H. Auden, is a riddle of time, purpose, life, and death, written as a precise, enigmatic canon. The second song, "When the Bells Justle," from a poem by A. E. Housman, is a reflection on the error of one's own actions, provoked by the tolling of bells. Written as a little scherzo, the horns and trumpets simulate the sound of the bells before they are actually heard. The voice resembles this focal timbre as well. "Sechzehnter Januar" (January 16th), based on an entry from Franz Kafka's diaries, contains the sentence that inspired Foss' use of contrasting tempos, one of the cycle's principal musical techniques. It reads, "The clocks do not synchronize: the inner one chases in an inhuman manner, the outer one goes haltingly at its usual pace." The rest of the poet's words describe the chaotic relationship that so many individuals of the modern world have with time. The final song, "O Mensch, gib Acht" (O Human, Take Heed!) with text from Nietzsche's *Thus Spake Zarathustra*, reveals the poet's deep dreamlike desire for eternity. Each of the 11 lines of the tonal and diatonic vocal part are interrupted by strokes of the midnight clock, as played by the piano, celesta, harp, and percussion. In the background, a chromatic, atonal canon at the fourth moves gracefully through the piece. This song contains the most complicated method of musical organization in the entire cycle: after the men in the orchestra whisper the hour, the clock chimes the passing of time and the meter changes; the number of quarter notes in each measure momentarily corresponds to the number of strikes, which always enter on the last beat of the measure; overall the song is held together with an undetectable 3/2 time signature that reemerges when the clock is silent.

Time Cycle was composed for soprano Adele Addison under a commission from the Ford Foundation's Humanities and Arts Program. In addition to receiving the New York Critics Circle Award in 1961, the cycle was honored by the New York Philharmonic as the first composition the group ever repeated at its premiere. This rare event took place under the direction of Leonard Bernstein at Carnegie Hall Philharmonic on October 20, 1960. *—AMG*

Recommended:

○ **Time Cycle** / Bernstein (cond.), Columbia SO / 1997 / Sony 63164

CHAMBER MUSIC

Capriccio for cello & piano (1948)

Lukas Foss' *Capriccio* is a short piece, lasting only about six minutes total. It is easy to hear the influence of other American composers, particularly that of Aaron Copland. The opening theme sounds like it is straight out of a Western film or ballet, such as *Billy the Kid*. The cello plays the energetic theme as if to set the stage for events to come. When the piano takes the melody, the cello uses rhythmic and playful double stops across the four strings, soon adding special bow effects and pizzicato to enhance the liveliness. Cello and piano continue to exchange melodies, and then the first melody comes back to interrupt the flow of the double stops. The piece then makes a transition to an expressive cello theme. This makes use of the lower range of the instrument, in addition to the upper register.

From here, Foss develops the theme, clipping along in his rhythmic and playful manner, adding a little bit more storminess and gaining in rhythmic and melodic complexity as he goes along. Throughout all of this, the first melody periodically comes back, explosively interrupting the various musical textures. Foss always makes use of the various ranges and dynamic capabilities of the two instruments, creating excitement and drama. Harmonics are used to create a special texture in the cello part at several points. The piece hits a major high point as the cello screams out in the upper register while the piano has crashing chords, and then everything drops immediately to almost nothing, ready to start over again.

Next comes a brief but expressive cello line, followed by the same type of double stop passage that occured earlier in the piece. Once again, the playfulness returns to form a brief coda of sorts. The first melody returns with a final flourish, then fades quickly to an ending that is a good deal calmer than the rest of the piece.

Foss' *Capriccio* is a very popular work among cellists performing twentieth century works. Its energetic drive and virtuosity makes the piece a lot of fun for performers and audiences alike.

It was written for cellist Gregor Piatigorsky, but dedicated to the late Natalie Koussevitsky, the first wife of Serge Koussevitsky. At the time of its composition, Foss was the pianist for the Boston Symphony under Koussevitsky. The piece was premiered at Tanglewood in 1946 by Piatigorsky and Foss and was well received. Twelve years later, the two recorded the *Capriccio*. *—Emily Stoops*

Recommended:

○ **Cello Charms** / Rudiakov, Levy / 1994 / Centaur 2192

Stephen Collins Foster

b. Jul. 4, 1826, Lawrenceville, PA, **d.** Jan. 13, 1864, New York, NY

Composer: Vocal

Stephen Foster stands as the first great American composer of popular songs. It is often difficult to classify his style, as it contains folk, popular, and classical elements, yet remains a product of none of these entirely. *My Old Kentucky Home, Oh! Susanna, Old Folks at Home*, and many of his other songs have become so popular and familiar they are often viewed as folk music. Foster's instrumental music, which included *Santa Anna's Retreat from Buena Vista* (1848) and *The Social Orchestra* (1854), was far less successful. He also wrote hymns and Sunday school songs for children. Foster was probably the first American composer who attempted to support himself by writing songs. In this endeavor he failed, earning 15,000 dollars over his 11 year career and turning increasingly to alcohol. One cannot help but notice the similarities between his tragically short life and that of his near contemporary in American literature, Edgar Allan Poe.

Foster was born on July 4, 1826, a fateful independence day—the 50th—that some will say cursed him, since this was the very same day on which Thomas Jefferson and John Adams died. Foster was the youngest of nine surviving children—ten, actually, since a son fathered by Foster's father also lived with the family. Young Stephen's education was varied, coming from both tutors and private schools. It is generally believed that he received instruction in music from Henry Kleber, a German-born musician who was a merchant, impresario, composer, and performer, and also a prominent figure on the Pittsburgh cultural scene.

While in his teens, Foster formed a club with his brother Morrison and a friend, whose activities included singing. It is thought that *Oh! Susanna* may have been composed for this group. Foster published his first song, *Open Thy Lattice Love*, when he was just 18.

Two years later, he took a bookkeeping position with his brother Dunning's Cincinnati-based steamship business. Shortly afterward, he sold *Oh! Susanna* to a Cincinnati publisher for a mere 100 dollars. After its appearance, over twenty other editions were issued by other publishers, yielding not a dime to Foster owing to the lack of strong copyright laws. In about 1849 he signed a contract with the Firth, Pond, & Co. publishing house of New York, preparing a career in songwriting.

In 1850 Foster left his brother's employ and married Jane Denny MacDowell. Ironically, his only exposure to the deep South would come in 1852 with a belated honeymoon excursion by steamship to New Orleans.

In 1854, Foster, his wife, and daughter Marion (b. 1852) settled in Pittsburgh, where the composer struggled to support them on his scant royalties. He may have developed ties to the growing abolitionist movement now, owing to his relationship with boyhood friend, Charles Shiras, an abolitionist with whom he collaborated to write a song around this time. When his parents died in 1855, Foster sank into a deep depression from which he never fully recovered.

Foster and his family lived in boarding houses for a time, since their finances were continually scarce. The composer's addiction to alcohol and their mediocre living conditions contributed to the deterioration of the marriage. Foster and his family traveled to New York in 1860, but his wife returned to Pittsburgh with Marion a year later. The composer stayed on in New York and continued to drink heavily. Sick with a fever in January 1864, he fell and struck his head on a wash basin, and died three days later. *—Robert Cummings*

VOCAL

Songs (1844–1864)

Stephen Foster was the first composer of songs to consistently strike the rich vein of American vernacular melody based on folk, rather than European, material. In reference to his "plantation" songs, Foster used the term "Ethiopian" to describe the African-American-derived melodies that were his specialty, his other works identified as belonging to the "parlor" genre. Foster once stated "I find I cannot write at all unless I write for public approbation," and he demonstrated unprecedented skill at finding the right combination of words and music to capture nineteenth century America's fancies. Foster's songs find their expression in nostalgia, nonsense, sorrow, and in particular the concept of "home" and what it meant to Americans. Foster's melodies are simply constructed, often making use of a repeated phrase or exclamation to aid easy retention. 203 works are known from Foster; only two are non-vocal, but include *The Social Orchestra*, a collection of orchestral arrangements made of popular tunes. Within the body of his work, 132 songs are by Foster alone and 62 were written in collaboration with others, or set with texts drawn from other literary sources.

Foster's career began shortly after he settled into a bookkeeping job in Cincinnati in 1844, largely thorough his contact with E.P. Christy and his troupe of minstrels. In 1848, writing for Christy, Foster enjoyed his first two successes, *Uncle Ned* and *Oh! Susanna*. In 1850, Foster resettled in Pittsburgh and began his association with publishers Firth & Pond Co. of New York. Between 1850–51 Foster enjoyed a string of successes, including *Nelly Bly, Gwine to Rune All Night (De Camptown Races), Ah! May the Red Rose Live Alway!, Wilt Thou Be Gone, Love?, Ring, Ring de Banjo!*, and *Old Folks at Home*. The Ethiopian songs were issued crediting Christy as composer, Foster electing to conceal his own identity. Personal pride over *Old Folks At Home* forced Foster to rethink this decision. Under his own name in 1852–55 Foster published *Massa's in de Cold Ground, My Old Kentucky Home, Old Dog Tray, Jeanie With the Light Brown Hair*, and *Come Where My Love Lies Dreaming*.

After the great effort taken, and little remuneration received, resulting from Foster's instrumental collection *The Social Orchestra*, he ran into a long dry spell. Advances received from Firth & Pond did not result in new works, and by 1860 the company had dropped Foster from their rolls. Foster resettled in New York City that year, working as a freelancer. In these years Foster produced little of lasting value, however,

Old Black Joe dates from 1860. This song is of particular importance, despite its notoriety, as it was readily absorbed into the tradition of African-American spirituals, lasting there well into the twentieth century. Following Foster's premature death in an accident in 1864, an older song, *Beautiful Dreamer,* was marketed as Foster's "last" and gained tremendous popularity. Another, *The Voices That Are Gone* appeared the year after his death, and is recognized as one of Foster's best. *—Uncle Dave Lewis*

Recommended:

○ **Songs By Stephen Foster** / de Gaetani, Guinn, Kalish / 1987 / Nonesuch 79158

○ **American Dreamer** / Hampson, etc. / 1992 / EMI 54621

Pierre Fournier

b. Jun. 24, 1906, Paris, France, **d.** Jan. 8, 1986, Geneva, Switzerland
Cellist

Pierre Léon Marie Fournier was born into a military family. His father was a general; his mother was musical and taught him piano lessons. At the age of nine, he suffered a mild attack of polio. Weakness of his legs made pedaling the piano difficult. So he turned to the cello, and after making rapid progress, he was admitted to the Paris Conservatoire. His teachers there were Paul Bazelaire and Anton Hekking; he graduated in 1924 at the age of 17. Fournier made his debut the year after his graduation. This was a solo appearance with the Concerts Colonne Orchestra, which received favorable notices. The almost invariable comment in reviews was the perfection of his bowing technique. He began a successful career as a touring concert artist and as a performer in chamber music concerts, gaining a great reputation in Europe.

In 1937 to 1939, he was the director of cello studies at the Ecole Normal. It was often said that he became a friendly rival with his contemporary, cellist Paul Tortelier, and after attending a Tortelier concert remarked to him, "Paul, I wish I had your left hand." Tortelier responded, "Pierre, I wish I had your right." To Fournier, the secret of his great right hand (i.e., bowing technique) was keeping the elbow high, holding the bow firmly, but allowing the hand and arm to move fluidly. He prescribed the Sevcik violin bowing studies for his cello students.

In 1941, he became a member of the faculty at the Paris Conservatoire, but during the war years, his concert touring career was impossible. Once the war was over, though, was able to resume and he rapidly increased in fame and international stature. His old audience found that he had grown in artistic depth. Hungarian violinist Joseph Szigeti, meeting Fournier in rehearsals for a 1947 Edinburgh Festival appearance, had not heard him for over ten years and wrote that he was "tremendously impressed by the Apollonian beauty and poise that his playing had acquired in the intervening years. Szigeti, Fournier, violist William Primrose, and pianist Artur Schnabel formed a piano quartet in those years and gave some fabled concerts at which they played virtually all of Schubert's and Brahms' piano chamber music. Sadly, the BBC acetate air checks of this cycle were allowed to deteriorate and have been lost.

Fournier made his first U.S. tour in 1948. His chamber music partner Artur Schnabel spread the word among cellists, other musicians, and critics that they were to be visited by a great new cellist. The New York and Boston critics were ecstatic. He had to give up his Conservatoire post because of his expanding concert career; he appeared in Moscow for the first time in 1959. Commentator Lev Grinberg wrote that he was notable for a romantic interpretation; clarity of form; vivid phrasing; and clean, broad bowing all "aimed at revealing the content."

He had a broad repertoire, including Bach, Boccherini, the Romantics, Debussy, Hindemith, and Prokofiev. Composers Martinů, Martinon, Martin, Roussel, and Poulenc all wrote works for him. He had a standing Friday night date to privately play chamber music with Alfred Cortot, the eminent French pianist, at which they might be visited by musicians like Jacques Thibaud. In 1953, he became a Chevalier of the Legion of Honor and was promoted to officer in 1963.

In 1972, he retired to Switzerland and gave master classes. He still gave concerts, even as late as 1984 when he was 78, and a London critic praised the fluency of his playing and his strong and solid left-hand technique. *—Joseph Stevenson*

Recommended:

○ **Pierre Fornier, Violoncello** / Martinon, Wallenstein (conds.), Fournier, Berlin POa, Lamoureux Concert Assoc. / 1999 / DG 457761

○ **Bach: 6 Suiten für Violoncello solo** / Fournier / 1996 / Archiv 449711

○ **Dvořák, Schubert & Tchaikovsky** / Celibidache, Bigot (cond.), Fournier, Hubeau, Lamoureux Concert Assoc. / Pearl 9198

○ **Beethoven: Complete Sonatas for Cello & Piano** / Fournier, Schnabel / 2002 / Classica d'Oro 4020

Virgil Fox

b. May 3, 1912, Princeton, IL **d.** Oct. 25, 1980, Palm Beach, FL
Organist

Virgil Fox was one of the most popular and accomplished classical organists of his time. He often generated controversy because of his flamboyant performance style, which involved the use of lights during live performances and often liberal changes to the scores he was playing. Yet Fox, a brilliant technician and insightful interpreter, maintained broad appeal and never used ostentation or eccentricity to camouflage diminishing technique or failing skills.

By age ten, Virgil Keel Fox had developed sufficient skills to serve as organist at local church services, and after four more years he displayed virtuoso skills in his first public concert, in Cincinnati. At age 16, he began studying with Wilhelm Middelschulte, then organist of the Chicago Orchestra (now the Chicago Symphony Orchestra). In 1929, Fox won first prize in the National Federation of Music Clubs' Biennial Contest, held in Boston. Fox gave two particularly prestigious recitals at age 19, the first in London's Kingway Hall and the latter in Carnegie Hall, audiences on both sides of the Atlantic greeting his performances with enthusiasm. He enrolled at the Peabody School of Music in Baltimore in 1931, where he studied organ with Louis Robert. He graduated one year later with an artist's diploma, then traveled to France where he studied from 1931–33 with Marcel Dupré. In 1938, Fox returned to Peabody as head of the organ department, a post he retained until 1942, when he enlisted in the military service. As a member of the Army Air Force, Fox gave numerous recitals during the war to draw financial support for the Allied effort. He was discharged in 1946 and that year accepted the position as organist of New York's Riverside Church, where he remained until 1965. There he cultivated much of his trademark flamboyance. Over the years, Fox performed three times at the White House, ironically enough it was on the piano. In 1952, he was selected to represent the U.S. State Department in Bern, Switzerland, at the First International Conference of Sacred Music. Fox participated in one of the most memorable organ concerts in New York's history when he joined E. Power Biggs and Catharine Crozier in 1962 to play in the inaugural concert for the New York Philharmonic's new organ at Philharmonic Hall (Lincoln Center). By this time, Fox was already active in the recording studio, turning out numerous LPs of music, from Bach and Handel to Fibich and Jongen. He made around 60 recordings in his lifetime, many of which are still available in various reissues on a number of labels. Fox's accomplishments were recognized in the academic world when he received an honorary doctorate degree from Bucknell University, in Lewisburg, PA, in 1963, and a Distinguished Alumni Award from the Peabody Conservatory in 1964. He helped design the new Rodgers organ for Carnegie Hall and gave the instrument's inaugural recital in 1974. Three years later, he gave a memorable sold-out Bach concert at the Kennedy Center. Typically, Fox would tour the country during these years playing a large Rodgers electronic organ and provide lighting effects to accompany his performances. In 1976, Fox was diagnosed with cancer and succumbed four years later in Palm Beach, FL. Amazingly, despite his deteriorating health, Fox, known to be strong-willed and deeply religious, performed his last concert only a month before, on September 26, at the opening concert of the 1980–81 season of the Dallas Symphony Orchestra. *—Robert Cummings*

Recommended:

○ **Heavy Organ At Carnegie Hall 1973** / Fox / 1997 / RCA 902668816

○ **Saint-Saëns: Organ Symphony** / Ormandy (cond.), Fox, Philadelphia Orch. / 1985 / RCA Victor 66134

Jean Françaix

b. May 23, 1912, Le Mans, France, **d.** Sep. 25, 1997, Paris, France
Composer: Chamber Music

Composer Jean Françaix wrote in an accessible, attractive style that often led listeners and commentators to ignore the depth and originality present in much of his music. His father was the director of the Le Mans Conservatory. His mother was a teacher and choir director on its staff. He began to study piano when he was four. Before he was ten he had music lessons from Isidor Philipp (piano) and Nadia Boulanger (harmony, counterpoint, composition). He published a composition at the age of ten, *Pour Jacqueline,* a piano suite dedicated to his baby cousin.

In 1930 he won first prize in piano at the Paris Conservatory. Pierre Monteux premiered his *Symphony* in 1932. In the same year he wrote his *Concertino for Piano & Orchestra.* The premiere of the work in 1934 made Françaix's reputation. He quickly came into demand. Ballets russes de Monte Carlo commissioned a ballet, *Scuola di ballo* (Dance School), choreographed by Léonide Massine, based on themes of Boccherini. Another ballet, *Le Roi nu* (The Naked King or The Emperor's New Clothes), was premiered by the Paris Opera in 1935. He wrote a piano concerto in 1936 and played it on his first American trip, in 1938. He toured often with cellist Maurice Gendron, the Trio Pasquier, and later, with his daughter Claude as a piano duo partner.

Françaix was also known for his orchestrations of works by Chopin, Schubert, Chabrier, and Mozart. Poulenc requested that Françaix orchestrate *L'histoire de Babar* for him. Françaix transcribed many of his own works for the Mainz Wind Ensemble.

The light, witty character of Françaix's music has caused some to dismiss it as frivolous. Others have decried the fact that his style remained static throughout his life. In reality, he had found all he needed and achieved his mature voice immediately. His orchestrations are always clear and sparkling, his forms precise and neo-Classical, his emotions reserved. Françaix had little use for the Romantic esthetic of the composer pouring his inner soul into the music. In this, he was primarily influenced by Ravel. However, he sometimes wrote works of great depth. His masterwork among this sort of composition is *L'Apocalypse de St Jean*, written in 1939, the year World War II began. The work is mystical, even ecstatic, with plain flowing melodies reminiscent of old chant. It was premiered in 1942 at the Conservatory, conducted by Charles Munch. It was played at a memorial concert for Françaix in Le Mans in 1999, its first French performance since 1951. *—Joseph Stevenson*

Overview of Works (1932–1994)

French composer Jean Françaix exemplifies all that is truly French in twentieth century French music. Although fundamentally a conservative composer, Françaix's supple and expressive melodies, his highly refined harmonic sensibility, his brilliant surfaces, and tremendous depths make him far more than merely a lesser Poulenc or Milhaud. Françaix successfully wrote in every medium, from his passionately grand operas, especially *La Princesse de Cleves* (The Princess of Cleves) (1965), to his lightly droll ballet *Les demoiselles de la nuit* (The Girls of the Night) (1948); from his cataclysmic oratorio *L'apocalypse de St. Jean* (The Apocalypse of Saint John) (1939) to his affectionate yet playful *Cinq portraits de jeunes filles for piano* (Five Portraits of Young Girls) (1936). Françaix's style and music did not develop over his long career: He was already wholly himself at the premiere of his piano concerto (1936) when he 17 and his personality deepened, but did not change over time. *—James Leonard*

Recommended:

- ○ **Françaix spielt Françaix** / Françaix, etc. / Wergo 6087
- ○ **Françaix: Concerto for guitar; Concerto for harpsichord; Trio** / Gawriloff, Goritzki, Segre, Françaix / Wergo 6198
- ○ **Françaix: La Bergère Enchantée** / A & E Frohlich, Swete / 1996 / Orfeo 388961
- ○ **Françaix: Organ Works** / Essl / 1995 / Fermate 20018
- ○ **Françaix: Scuolo de Ballo; Symphonie** / Fischer (cond.), Ulster Orch., / 2002 / Hyperion 67323
- ○ **Françaix: Concertino; Les bosquets de Cythère; Les malheurs de Sophie** / Fischer (cond.), Cassard, Ulster Orch. / 2004 / Hyperion 67384

CHAMBER MUSIC

L'heure du berger, for 8 woodwinds & piano (1947)

L'heure de berger is actually three brief character sketches of Parisian café life. Francaix wrote the piece in 1947, the story goes, for a Paris restaurant to use in the background as its customers dined. Francaix wrote what he called *la musique sérieuse sans gravité* (serious music without weight), providing witty, accurate descriptions in sound of three types of people seen while at the café. The first movement is "Les vieux beaux" (The Old Dandies). The piano plays a jaunty accompaniment for the woodwinds' ironic, gliding sighs, as if the dandies are remembering the good old days. A quicker central section breaks into gossipy sixteenth notes between the flute and bassoon, with the occasional butting in of the horn, but the sighs return, those days are gone. In the second movement, the clarinet describes the teasing "Pin-Up Girls" in delightful arpeggios while the flute, oboe, horn, and bassoon parade around and the piano is silent. The set ends with "Les petits nerveux" (Nervous Children). All the instruments skitter around, their melody lines moving against each other. The trio section finds them better organized, with the flute and oboe playing offbeat, against the others. The opening section is repeated, followed by a coda wherein the nervous excitement builds to an inevitable collapse. *—Patsy Morita*

Recommended:

- ○ **Jean Françaix** / Gaudier Ens. / 1998 / Hyperion 67036
- ○ **Hexagon Plays Poulenc, Saint-Saëns, Roussel, Françaix** / Hexagon / 1997 / Bridge 9079

Petit quatuor, for saxophone quartet (1935)

Lean and deceptively simple, Jean Françaix's 1935 *Petit quatuor* (Little Quartet) for four saxophones is, along with the *Piano Concertino* of 1932, evidence that Françaix, though technically still a student during the first half of the 1930s, was already at 20–25 years old a composer of rare technical accomplishment. It is no simple thing to compose a piece of music that sounds utterly unruffled and plain, that is built from the most elementary rhythmic and melodic building blocks, and yet holds the audience's attention by virtue of its elegant poise and balance. If the *Petit quatuor* has never been as well-known or admired as the *Piano Concertino*, it is probably due to the fact that saxophone music in general has hardly been elevated to the status of traditional concert hall genres; this is, however, a state of affairs that a large number of twenty-first century saxophone ensembles are passionately trying to change, and many of them have taken up the *Petit quatuor* as part of their quest—with the happy result that a new, cleaned-up edition of the piece was issued by Schott publishers during the mid-1990s.

The *Petit quatuor* is, as expected from the name, not a long piece. Ten minutes is enough to play its three movements, which are scored for the usual saxophone quartet combination of soprano, alto, tenor and baritone instruments. Movement 1 is an Allegro titled Gaguenardise. An ABA form, the movement's outer sections are made from spry, staccato-filled music, while the central portion is by way of contrast almost wholly legato—long lines that overlap from one instrument to another, quite unlike the simultaneous attacks heard in the outer sections. The dynamic range is extreme indeed: ppp to fff are demanded, allowing the players to indulge in the especially fine dynamic control that their instruments allow (a legendary feature of the saxophone, this dynamic control was a big selling point when the instrument was introduced during the eighteenth century).

The second movement is slower, and calls for only three players—the soprano saxophone is tacet. Lento ma non troppo, it bears the songful title Cantilène and is shaped into one large arch that rises up from ppp only to fall back down at the end. As with the central portion of the Gaguenardise movement, the Cantilène is legato in the extreme.

The playful third movement is described by Françaix as a Sérénade comique; the four performers engage in a bouncing, teasing 3/8 meter skirmish, led by the soprano saxophonist who, having rested his or her chops during the second movement, has a few more bleeps and bloops and trills and runs than his or her comrades. *—Blair Johnston*

Recommended:

- ○ **Rollin' Phones: Saxophone Quartet** / Rollin' Phones / 1989 / Bis 466

Tema con variazioni, for clarinet & piano (1974)

Jean Françaix composed his *Tema con variazioni for clarinet and piano* in 1974 on a commission from the Paris Conservatoire. Although used as that year's "Pièce de Concours" in the Conservatoire's clarinet department, Françaix dedicated the *Tema con variazioni* to his grandson, Olivier. The theme is soberly stated in a tempo marked Largo, and this is followed by a florid and impressive set of six variations. The piece is generally cheerful, jazzy in feeling and its appeal is immediate, rather unlike what you would expect from a contemporary composer in that day and age. Luckily for Françaix, his decision to hold out against current trends paid off in the long run, as this is one of only a few chamber works of the 1970s to enter the standard repertoire. The *Tema con variazioni* has been recorded many times and may be found listed as a required work in many collegiate level clarinet courses. Inasmuch as it may be compared to other works within the long-running cycle of Pièces de Concours for clarinet, the Françaix *Tema con variazioni* runs a close third in popularity to similar works by André Messager (1899) and Henri Rabaud (1901). In 1978, Françaix dusted off the *Tema con variazioni* and recast it for clarinet and string orchestra, and while the result was as good as can be expected, this version has enjoyed nowhere near the popularity of the original for clarinet and piano. *—Uncle Dave Lewis*

Recommended:

- ○ **Moonflowers, Baby!** / Cohler, Gordon / Crystal 733

Woodwind Quintet No. 1 (1948)

Nearly 40 years separate Jean Françaix's two *Quintets* for wind instruments. The earlier of the two dates from 1948, when Louis Courtinat, French horn player with the Orchestre National de la Radiodiffusion Française, asked Françaix for a quintet for his colleagues. As the composer later related, the work was to be "very demanding, permitting the five players to display their virtuosity to the fullest!" Françaix continued, "Even though I am, by nature, a peaceable sort of person, I did my best to be nasty. And I seem to have succeeded, for these gentlemen had to closet themselves for six months in order to get through it." The *Quintet* proved to be a hit, "achieving a success beyond my wildest dreams."

The first movement opens with a laid-back, not-quite-serious slow introduction. When the music speeds to Allegro assai, it is with a light-hearted tune suggestive of the music hall, surrounded by decorative arpeggios. The genial Presto second movement acts as a scherzo, and the slow third movement is a set of variations on a lyrical melody. The final movement is marked Tempo di Marcia Francese; the jolly march melody leads into a contrapuntal central section. Françaix concludes the work with a quiet and humorous coda. *—Chris Morrison*

Recommended:

- ○ **Printemps** / BPO Wind Quintet / Bis 536

Zino Francescatti

b. Aug. 9, 1902, Marseilles, France, **d.** Sep. 17, 1991, La Ciotat, France
Violinist

Though indeed of Italian background, violinist Zino Francescatti was a Frenchman, born in Marseilles in 1902. His real name was René-Charles Francescatti. Both his parents played the violin, and his father René had been a student of Paganini. The younger Francescatti performed the Paganini *Violin Concerto No. 1* at his official Paris debut in 1925.

By that time Francescatti was already an experienced performer. He gave his first concert at age five and played the Beethoven violin concerto at ten. From his late teens he concertized regularly, and after arriving in Paris in 1924 he formed a duo with none less than Maurice Ravel and embarked on an international tour. In the 1920s and 1930s Francescatti toured the globe, although his U.S. debut didn't come until 1939, once again with the Paganini *Concerto No. 1*, in a New York Philharmonic concert.

Despite his fondness for Paganini, Francescatti was more identified with elegant, natural-seeming playing than with sheer virtuoso fireworks. Later in life he toured and recorded with the similarly fluid French pianist Robert Casadesus in duo repertory; they recorded a complete set of Beethoven's violin and piano sonatas, lyrical works ideally suited to their combined styles. Living in New York but often returning to France to perform and teach, Francescatti made durable recordings of several major repertory works, including the Beethoven concerto with conductor Bruno Walter and the Columbia Symphony Orchestra. Francescatti retired in 1976, moved back to France, and sold his prized Stradivarius instrument to Salvatore Accardo. In 1987 he used part of the proceeds to establish an educational foundation and a violin competition in the city of Aix-en-Provence.

Despite the deep-rooted European traditions exemplified in his playing, Francescatti's memory has not been particularly well served by reissue houses. An exception, however, is the Bridge release *An Evening of Paganini* (Great Performances from The Library of Congress, Vol. 17), which won a Best Recording of the Year award from *Fanfare* magazine. The disc presents a 1954 Paganini recital Francescatti gave with pianist Artur Balsam. The *Zino Francescatti in Performance* two-disc set released by the Music & Arts label offers Francescatti concerto performances from the 1940s and 1950s with various orchestras. Some of his original concerto recordings on the Columbia label have been reissued as part of the Sony Masterworks Heritage series. *—James Manheim*

Recommended:

- ○ **Concertos Vol. 1** / Watts, Oistrakh, Francescatti, Serkin / Sony 52516
- ○ **Zino Francescatti Vol. 1** / Wallenstein (cond.), Francescatti, Los Angeles PO / 2002 / Doremi 7780
- ○ **An Evening of Paganini** / Francescatti, Balsam / 2002 / Bridge 9125
- ○ **Beethoven: Violin Sonatas 5, 9, & 10** / Francescatti, Casadesus / 1990 / Sony 46342

César Franck

b. Dec. 10, 1822, Liège, Belgium, **d.** Nov. 8, 1890, Paris, France

Composer: Keyboard, Symphonic, Orchestral, Chamber Music, Concerto, Vocal, Choral

César Franck is an important composer from the latter half of the nineteenth century, particularly in the realms of symphonic, chamber, organ and piano music. His stage works were uniformly unsuccessful, though his choral compositions fared somewhat better. Born in Liège (in the French region which in 1830 became part of a new state, Belgium), on December 10, 1822, he led a group of young composers, among them d'Indy, Duparc, and Dukas, who found much to admire in his highly individual post-Romantic style, with its rich, innovative harmonies, sometimes terse melodies, and skilled contrapuntal writing. This group, sometimes known as "la bande à Franck," steered French composition toward symphonic and chamber music, finally breaking the stranglehold of the more conservative opera over French music.

Franck was a keyboard player of extraordinary ability who had a short stint as a touring piano virtuoso before moving to Paris and throwing himself into musical studies. In addition, he was an organist at several major churches during his career, and his skills on the organ accounted in great part for his compositional interest in that instrument; his organ compositions stand at the apex of the Romantic organ repertoire. Franck was a man of strong religious convictions throughout his life, which often motivated him to compose works based on biblical texts or on other church sources. For much of his life he was organist at the Paris churches of Saint-Jean-Saint-François and then Saint-Clothilde, and in 1872 he became a professor at the Paris Conservatoire.

Individual and instantly recognizable though his music was, it owes a debt to Liszt and Wagner, especially to the latter's *Tristan und Isolde* and several other late works. He tended to use rather quick modulations, another inheritance from Wagner, and shifting harmonies. There is a Germanic ponderousness in some of his compositions; consider, for example, the opening of the *Symphony in D minor* of 1888, probably Franck's most famous composition. In this work, one hears a mixture of paradoxical elements so typical of the composer: for example, moments of peace and serenity barely conceal an undercurrent of disquiet. In this symphony, Franck, adapts the Lisztian-Wagnerian predilection toward cyclical structure and melodic motto to an abstract symphonic form. Another characteristic of Franck's music is extended homophonic writing, as exemplified in his choral symphonic poem *Psyché*.

Franck died in Paris on November 8, 1890. By the turn of the century he had become the leading figure associated with the "Old School" in France, while Debussy came to represent the "progressive" forces. *—AMG*

KEYBOARD

Trois Chorals, for organ (1890)

In the park facing the suburban Paris basilica of Sainte-Clotilde, where Franck was organist for 32 years, there is a memorial sculpture by Alfred Lenoir, which places the composer before the manuals, head bowed, rapt in meditation as an angel, shielding him with outspread wings, whispers. Indeed, Franck's best music often evokes the voices of angels, a sense of being suspended (as he was in the organ loft) between earth and heaven, the worldly and the divine. Hence, the "serene anxiety" which the critic, Georges-Jean Aubry, attributed to him. In the *Trois Chorals*, his final work, this mystical hovering attains its most richly compelling form.

At the suggestion of the publisher, Auguste Durand, Franck began the *Chorals* while on summer holiday at Nemours and completed them on his return to Paris—the third and last choral is dated September 30, 1890. On October 2, he played them on a piano for his organ class at the Conservatoire—which included Vierne and Tournemire—with his last student, Guillaume Lekeu, taking the pedal part. An accident the preceding May, in which Franck had been struck in the chest by an omnibus, had left him weakened. A chill taken at the beginning of October soon turned to pleurisy, but he insisted on returning to the loft of Sainte-Clotilde on October 20 to determine the registration of the *Chorals*. He came home to take to his bed, his condition wavering, his mind deliriously occupied with a fugue, and died on the morning of November 8.

The formal plan of the first, *E major Choral* has been the subject of debate; the difficulty lies in attempting to equate what Franck has actually done with pre-existing models. Franck himself tried to explain to his students that "You will see, the *Choral* is not the thing itself—the *true* choral *becomes* in the course of the work." It opens with a flood of melody which Vincent d'Indy analyzed into seven thematic cells, of which, only the last—a six bar phrase—resembles what J. S. Bach would have understood as "choral." The work proceeds through an ever more fantastic, chromatically saturated series of contrapuntal variations, in which one or another of the cells informs every voice, imparting a polyphonic incandescence, transcending mere *punctus contra punctus* cleverness, until the Bach-like fragment stands forth tutta forza and exultant.

The *B minor Choral* is a free passacaglia, through which the travails of faith take on virtuoso swagger to end with hard-won tranquillity. Opening with toccata-like brilliance, the third, *A Minor Choral* introduces a proper four-voice choral which eventually subdues the coruscations before rising in great arpeggiated chords to a central dolce espressivo cantilena. This incantatory stream of liquid silver pours forth like ardent prayer, with growing modulatory and contrapuntal involvement until it attains a great, pedal-underlined slargando climax. The flickering scintillations of the opening return, surmounted by the choral and subdued again to a docile accompaniment. Wrought to a suspenseful coda, it ends on a triumphant A major tierce de Picardie. *—Adrian Corleonis*

Recommended:

- ○ **Marcel Dupré Recital** / Dupré / 1992 / Mercury 434311

Final, for organ in B flat major, Op. 21 (ca. 1862)

Franck was appointed organist and choirmaster of the suburban Paris basilica of Sainte-Clotilde in 1858, as construction was being completed. Neither was the superb Cavaillé-Coll organ ready—in fact, Franck did not inaugurate the instrument until a public concert of December 19, 1859. Yet there is no doubt that it reawakened his interest in composition, which had flagged after a youthful spate of undistinguished virtuoso fantasies, songs, sacred pieces, an unproduced opera and opéra comique, four remarkable *Trios* (1843) that impressed Liszt, and a startling symphonic poem, *Ce qu'on entend sur la montagne* (1845–47), which anticipates the vast opening of *Das Rheingold*, but remained unpublished and unheard. Their precise dating is disputed, but the *Six Pièces for organ* seem to have taken shape between 1858 and 1864, though they were only published in 1868. Not without charm, the *Fantaisie, Pastorale, and Prière* breathe the air of religious sentiment. The *Prélude, fugue et variation* looks ahead to the great piano triptychs—the *Prélude, choral et fugue* (1884) and the *Prélude, aria et final* (1886–87)—while the groundbreaking *Grande pièce symphonique* embodies the lessons of the master in its grandeur and the sure shaping of its material. Beethoven's example also informs the *Final*, which may be described as an exuberant, substantial *sortie*, though its robust, fanfare-like opening theme, given to the pedals, soon complemented by a serene melody over a running accompaniment, spaciously developed, suggests a sonata first movement. Its bravura winding up, on the other hand, is not innocent of an opéra comique vulgarity effervescently similar to some manic moments in the great (and misleadingly titled) *Impromptu*, Op. 69, of his friend Charles-Valentin Alkan, dedicatee of the *Grande Pièce symphonique*. The *Final* was dedicated to the once famous organist Louis James Alfred Lefébure-Wély, and was heard for the first time with Franck's premiere of the *Six Pièces* at Sainte-Clotilde on November 17, 1864. *—Adrian Corleonis*

Recommended:

- ○ **Franck: Great Organ Works Vol. 1** / Lebrun / 2001 / Naxos 554697
- ○ **Franck: Great Organ Works** / Alain / 1996 / Erato 12706
- ○ **Franck: Complete Masterworks for Organ** / Murray / 1990 / Telarc 80234

Grande pièce symphonique, for organ in F sharp minor, Op. 17 (1860–1862)

It cannot be doubted that Franck was one of the most gifted musicians of the nineteenth century. After a brief, frustrating career as a reluctant child prodigy and virtuoso, Franck escaped from his tyrannical father into marriage and the modest life of a church organist, though his ambitions were anything but small. By 1847, when he took his first post as organist, at Notre Dame de Lorette, the greatest challenge facing a serious composer was the attainment of a comprehensive certainty of style. If Saint-Saëns, Gounod, and Bizet looked back to Classical models for their symphonies, Franck—with his preternatural aptitude for counterpoint—espoused the works of Bach and the later Beethoven as his models, though his assimilation of these two (at that time) rather recondite tributaries proved both haphazard and creatively transforming.

When Franck moved into a new post as organist of the just-constructed, soon-to-be fashionable Parisian basilica of Sainte-Clotilde, with its superb Cavaillé-Coll organ, he was spurred to his first attempt to cut through the Gordian knot of style with his *Six Pieces for Organ.* Though their precise dating is disputed, they seem to have taken shape between 1858 and 1864. As one might expect, they are a rather mixed bag, with the *Prière* essaying facile religious sentiments, yet with that touch of chromatic yearning which marked Franck as a mystic to his contemporaries; the *Prélude, Fugue et Variation* looking ahead to the great piano triptychs of the 1880s; a *Final* touched with the spirit of Offenbach; and the imposing *Grande Pièce symphonique* which demonstrated that the great Romantic organ could rival an orchestra in works of symphonic scope.

Revealingly, it is dedicated to Charles-Valentin Alkan, a composer and virtuoso given to facetious stylistic toying. More to the point, in 1857 Alkan had published his monumental *Douze Études dans tous les tons mineurs,* Op. 39, which included—for solo piano—a symphonie in four movements, and the stupendous concerto in three. Though played without a break, the *Grande Pièce symphonique* is usually analyzed as being in three movements—the development of the central Andante leads to a scherzo-like Allegro, as in the great *Symphony in D Minor* (1888). The opening Andante serioso makes large gestures soon halted by a second, anxiously questioning theme, and the two are developed in something very much like sonata first movement form. The central Andante is notable mainly for its cloying, chromatically pleading melody. After reminiscences of the foregoing, in the manner of the last movement of Beethoven's *Ninth Symphony,* the initial theme is fugally worked to a brilliantly resounding peroration. It was heard for the first time with Franck's premiere of the *Six Pièces* at Sainte-Clotilde on November 17, 1864. *—Adrian Corleonis*

Recommended:

○ **Michael Murray Plays Dupré, Franck, Widor** / Murray / 2002 / Telarc 60516
○ **Organ Works of César Franck** / Guillou / 1990 / Dorian 90135
○ **Franck: Great Organ Works** / Alain / 1996 / Erato 12706

Pastorale, for organ in E major, Op. 19 (1863)

In the Baroque period, the term "pastoral" tied in to nativity music, as with the "Pastoral Symphony" from Handel's *Messiah* and a number of Italian concertos. One might expect that association to carry over to a later pastorale for organ, an instrument with religious connotations, but in his Op. 19 *Pastorale* Franck seems to have envisioned a secular nature scene more typical of the Romantic era, along the lines of Beethoven's "Pastoral" symphony. This composition was published as part of Franck's *Six Pieces for Large Organ,* but these works do not constitute a formal cycle; each item carries its own opus number and stands alone musically from the others. The *Pastorale* is dedicated to the great organ builder Aristide Cavaillé-Coll and is a modest display of the symphonic sonorities of the organ Cavaillé-Coll installed at Franck's church, Ste. Clotilde. It takes the sturdy song form ABA, with the outer sections based on two themes. One is rippling yet peaceful, played at a moderate tempo, and the second is based on a series of warm, not at all imposing chords. The central section, introduced by a trumpet-like fanfare, slips into the minor mode and is dominated by quick, staccato chords that produce a sense of speed and mild tension, soothed by a more legato melody. The A section returns after a little fugato passage, now combining its two themes, which are tainted with a bit of the B section's sixteenth note agitation. *—James Reel*

Recommended:

○ **Franck: Great Organ Works Vol. 2** / Lebrun / 2001 / Naxos 554698
○ **Franck: Great Organ Works** / Alain / 1996 / Erato 12706

Trois Pieces, for organ (1878)

Franck was titular organist at the newly constructed and soon to be fashionable Parisian basilica Ste. Clotilde from 1858 until his death in 1890. Considering that the organ was Franck's preferred instrument, he composed—discounting a number of small, if characteristic harmonium pieces—surprisingly little for it, though each of his dozen organ works is a milestone in his oeuvre. With the *Six Pièces* of the early 1860s, for instance, he turned his back on the popular vein of *grandes fantaisies* and *variations brillantes* that had occupied his years as a reluctant piano virtuoso for embarkation on a mature style prompted by Beethoven, Liszt, and a blossoming of latent Romantic sensibility evident as early as the unpublished orchestral poem *Ce qu'on entend sur la montagne* of 1845–47 (after Victor Hugo's poem, which had also inspired Liszt). The *Three Chorals* were Franck's last works, which he was revising on his deathbed, the grand culmination of a lifetime informed by the richest harmonic palette in Western music. Between them, the *Trois Pièces,* composed in 1878, are contemporary with the startlingly sensual *Quintet for piano and strings,* and loom as part of that spate of compositions in which the mature style of his last dozen or so years was confidently achieved: the symphonic poems *Les Éolides* (1875–76) and *Le Chasseur maudit* (1882); the piano triptychs *Prélude, choral et fugue* (1884) and *Prélude, aria et final* (1888); a violin sonata (1886); and many more. Franck's "disciple" Vincent d'Indy noted that the *Trois Pièces* were "written expressly for the inauguration of the colossal organ"—another Cavaillé-Coll instrument—"at the Trocadéro during the exhibition of 1878. . . . " And he singled out for praise the Cantabile, "with its suave and devotional theme" and its "wonderful canon which, moving with unbroken ease, forms the adornment of the melody, written by the master on purpose to display the warm, expressive quality of the new clarinet stop, recently discovered by Cavaillé-Coll." The pieces flanking the yearningly intimate Cantabile have an appropriately public character, the *Fantaisie in A* beginning with a stentorian theme in unison octaves—magnificently woven against a falling/rising wisp of lyricism into a sonic tapestry of light in darkness—while the *Pièce heroïque* opens with dramatic swagger to essay a moment of anxious prayer before being moved by a rocking figure on the pedals to a trenchantly *triomphale* conclusion. *—Adrian Corleonis*

Recommended:

○ **Popular Organ Music** / Walsh / Priory 477
○ **Franck: Great Organ Works** / Alain / 1996 / Erato 12706

Prélude, aria, et final, for piano (1886–1887)

Franck's miserable teenage years as a reluctant virtuoso, prodded by his tyrannical father to work his way through countless *grandes fantaisies* for piano on operatic airs, evidently left him with a distaste for the piano as an object of composition. In any case, Franck's appointment in 1858 as organist at the new basilica of Sainte-Clotilde made him master of its splendid Cavaillé-Coll organ, to which he began to confide his choicest thoughts. It was not until the end of his life that he composed again for the piano, creating the *Prélude, Choral et Fugue* in 1884 for Marie Poitevin, and its companion, the *Prélude, Aria et Final,* in 1886 and 1887 for the remarkable young pianist Léontine-Marie Bordes-Pène. The latter work is dedicated to Bordes-Pène, and she gave its first performance at a concert of the Société Nationale de Musique on May 12, 1888.

To Alfred Cortot (who made a classic recording of the *Prélude, Aria et Final* in 1932), the Prélude's opening theme evoked a choir of angels by Piero della Francesca, hymning the nativity. Other commentators describe it fairly as a march, though the deportment of its serene gait conveys radiant aspiration—we hear a maestoso soft thunder. Franck had enormous hands, and he asks, without comment, for the pianist to span a series of elevenths, and even a thirteenth, without evident discomfort—a feat beyond the grasp of many. A second theme brings the inevitable note of anxiety and a development in which the first theme takes on a risoluto swagger. After a climax, a third theme, sostenuto e serioso, is introduced in bare octaves and immediately beset by masterful, rich contrapuntal involvements that weave an aura of sighing suspense and high drama before the first theme returns to end the Prélude with virile assertiveness. In all but name, this is a sonata first movement molded after the manner of Beethoven's last sonatas. After a 15-bar introduction, the Aria—molto espressivo ma semplice—makes its appearance, its melodic magic soon magnified in octaves, extrapolated in fluent legatissimo textures, and wrought to a rapt climax. Marked Allegro molto ed agitato, the Final begins with a harried chase in echoing octaves and octave volleys that scare up a chromatically wailing figure suggestive of demoniac possession. Heralded by an animato flourish of detached octaves in counterpoint, a carillon-like theme resounds in the instrument's central register, soon garlanded in triplets, to announce salvation. In good cyclic fashion, these themes blossom from germs and phrases in the preceding movements, and proceed to a great developmental struggle of light in darkness which is, at sublime length, resolved as the Prélude's opening theme and the Aria are woven together in silvery rapture. *—Adrian Corleonis*

Recommended:

○ **Alfred Cortot 2** / Cortot / 1999 / Philips 456754
○ **Franck: Piano Music** / Hough / 1997 / Hyperion 66918
○ **Franck: Prélude, Aria et Final; Prélude, Fugue et Variation; Violin Sonata** / Nagai / 2000 / Bis 1056

Prélude, choral, et fugue, for piano (1884)

In 1874 a new pianistic star, the 19-year-old Marie Poitevin, blazed into the pianistic firmament, taking first prize at the Paris Conservatoire. A pupil of Elie Miriam Delaborde, she was praised not only for her transcendental *mécanisme* and her powerful, richly colored sonority, but for "an all too rare artistic conscience, which makes it a duty to sacrifice nothing to effect and lends her playing a remarkable purity of style" (Victor Dolmetsch, *Le Ménestral,* March 12, 1882). Franck, who taught an organ class at the Conservatoire, could hardly fail to be captivated, and for her debut at the Société National de Musique, Marie was entrusted with the second performance of his *Quintet for Piano and Strings.* On April 8, 1880, Marie gave the premiere of six of the *Dix pièces pittoresques* by his friend, Chabrier. Franck's comment on the occasion—"We have just heard something quite extraordinary—music which links our era with that of Couperin and Rameau"—no doubt owes nearly as much to Mlle Poitevin's *style sévère* "purity" as it does to the scintillant crispness of Chabrier's muse, which lends a clue to the clarity and dry brilliance (difficult to obtain on a latter-day grand piano) which Franck's age took for granted. And she played Bach—at that time a fairly recondite taste—superbly. Franck, himself a great organist and a Bach devotee, was not only enchanted but creatively stirred, confiding to his pupils his wish to "enrich" the French pianistic repertoire with substantial works.

Not until the spring of 1884 did Franck come to grips, in an era contentiously preoccupied with Wagner and just beginning to appreciate Beethoven's later works, with the task of reviving the forms which had moved Bach. Accordingly, a searchingly ruminative prélude and the swiftly running fugue—beginning with angst-laden drama to conclude in triumphantly incandescent peals—were composed together. Only then did the lack of something expressively and architecturally linking become apparent, prompting the composition of the great harped chorale, resounding across the keyboard and requiring the left hand to reach over into the treble to chime the theme. The upshot is an elaborately figured, chromatically inflected, and texturally rich essay in which doubt and faith, darkness and light, oscillate until a final ecstatic resolution. Mlle Poitevin, to whom the *Prélude, Choral et Fugue* is dedicated, gave the work its premiere at the *Salle Pleyel*, under the auspices of the Société National de Musique on January 24, 1885. It was published in the same year by Enoch. *—Adrian Corleonis*

Recommended:

○ **Alfred Cortot 2** / Cortot / 1999 / Philips 456754

○ **Franck: Piano Music** / Hough / 1997 / Hyperion 66918

○ **Artur Rubinstein 3** / Rubinstein / 1999 / Philips 456967

Prélude, fugue, et variations, for piano & harmonium, Op. 18 (ca. 1873)

César Franck's *Prélude, fugue et variations* has become a popular work among organists and is familiar to music lovers even though they may not know its title or composer. Written in 1862, it is a part of the larger *Six Pièces pour le Grand Orgue.* After having worked as organist at the parish of Saint-Jean-Saint-François for seven years, Franck obtained the same appointment at Sainte-Clotilde, where he had been choirmaster for some time. It was at the latter church that he received his inspiration for *Prélude.* At his new post, he met with a monumental artistic challenge when the inventor-builder Aristide Cavaillé-Coll finished construction on a three-manual grand organ for the church in 1859. For the dedication of this instrument on December 19 of the same year, Franck played his *Final in B Flat Major,* Op. 21. His attachment to this particular organ was so great that it inspired him to immediately compose *Six Pièces pour le Grand Orgue* (1860–62), which he followed with *Trois Pièces pour le Grand Orgue* (1878) and *Trois Chorals* (1890). These works were written at the height of the Romantic organ's popularity, which stretched between 1830 and 1930. This period's most popular organists were Charles-Marie Widor, Alexandre Pierre François Boëly, Louis Lefébure-Wély and of course, Franck, who in time became known as the only true "equal" of Johann Sebastian Bach as a composer for the organ. The *Prélude* was dedicated to Camille Saint-Saëns. The two men had similar posts and influences, and had both studied with François Benoist at the Paris Conservatoire.

A pastoral *Prélude* opens the work with a seductive oboe cantilena in the upper voice. Tournemire commented on the feel of this movement when he asked, "Can you not imagine a shepherd piping the beauties of nature…?" A brief bridge of nine bars of chordal harmony leads to the freely moving austere "fugue" that is parallel to Bach's *A major Fugue.* A satisfying link is made between this section and "variations" over a dominant pedal. The final portion returns to the work's opening oboe cantilena; here it soars through "Mendelssohnian" counterpoint that is both flowing and refreshing, bringing the work to a quiet end. When Franck composed *Prélude, fugue et variations,* along with the other five works in *Six Pièces pour le Grand Orgue,* he not only gracefully honored the new instrument at Sainte-Clotilde, but he also added greater majesty to the repertoire of the organ. *—Meredith Gailey*

Recommended:

○ **Awadagin Pratt Plays Franck, Bach, etc.** / Pratt / 1997 / EMI 55293

Prière, for organ in C sharp minor, Op. 20 (ca. 1860)

César Franck was a deeply spiritual man; his compositions such as *Prière* (Prayer) in C sharp minor reflect his true nature. Composed in 1860, during his 25-year characteristically religious period, this work was written for organ as a personal meditation on grief, hope, and faith. It stirs up the historical purpose of this devotional instrument. The work represents the divine thoughts of an organist questioning the unfathomable mystery of the hereafter, overwhelmed by anguish. This masterpiece of lyricism makes it easy to imagine sound pouring from pipes which are positioned between heaven and earth, played by a solitary organist, acting as a mediator between God and man. This was the role that Franck allowed himself to occupy when he composed *Prière* and other religious works.

Just one of the *Six Pièces pour le Grand Orgue* (1860–62), *Prière* was dedicated to the remarkable François Benoist, who taught for years as a professor of organ at the Paris Conservatoire. In the composition, Franck uses his much-adored registration of Foundation stops on the Pédale, Grand Orgue, Positif, and Récit together with the Hautbois. With its subtle use of the swell-box, the work reached the pinnacle of expressive organ writing. The first theme is an indeterminately long melodic phrase that feels as though it is springing from itself. It is in strict five-part harmony, cast in the manner of a chorale tune. This subject creates the foundation of the entire work and reappears either in cells, which form different episodes in the development, or is blended into one of the second theme's singing phrases. The composition grows to ecstatic heights of expression when a Gregorian chant-like solo recitative for the Trompette of the Récit merges with a restatement of the opening to close the work on a somber note. Using the fugal and canonical devices that Franck loved so much, the composition is rich and lyrical, straightforward, but profound. The astonishing musical and spiritual revolution which this piece achieves distinguishes it from other works of this period.

Alive during a time when the secular music of Mozart, Gluck, Beethoven, Schubert, and Schumann was celebrated, Franck had an interest in composition that was an antithesis of the majority of his fellow Frenchmen; he sought to return the organ to paths of spirituality and liturgical use. For the mastery of his instrument and the depth of his works, Franck has been considered the only true "equal" of Johann Sebastian Bach as a composer for the organ. His other religious compositions include *Les béatitudes* (1869–79), *Ave Maria* (1863), *Rédemption* (1871–72), and *Les Sermon sur la Montagne* (circa 1846). In short, Franck was a simple, warm-hearted man was devoted to his work, to teaching, to composition, and to his instrument. He came closer to achieving his goal of restoring the taste for "pure music" in France, when he composed the spiritually touching *Prière* in 1860. *—Meredith Gailey*

Recommended:

○ **Franck: Complete Organ Music** / Sanger / 1987 / Bis 214

○ **Franck: Great Organ Works** / Alain / 1996 / Erato 12706

SYMPHONIC

Symphony in D minor, Op. 48 (1886–1888)

The most brilliant of Belgian composer César Franck's compositions were written during the final decade of his life; the *Symphonic Variations* for piano and orchestra, the famous *Violin Sonata,* the *D major String Quartet,* and, perhaps most important, the *Symphony in D minor* are all the products of a single, remarkable five-year period. The Symphony, by no means an immediate success with critics or audiences, has nevertheless become so fused with the popular image of César Franck that it is nearly impossible to think of him without also thinking of this 40-minute orchestral juggernaut. And yet the work is by no means an empty audience-pleaser: as with all of his final compositions, the Symphony shows a superb synthesis of Franck's own uniquely rich harmonic language and cyclic themes with the traditions of Viennese Classicism that he had come to revere later in life (principally through the music of Beethoven).

Franck casts his Symphony in the still-rather unusual three-movement mold. A richly chromatic Lento introduction (almost agonizingly slow) presents the fundamental motivic unit of the first movement: a three-note dotted figure that moves down by semitone and then moves back up again by any either minor third or perfect fourth. The Allegro non troppo body of the movement takes off with a strident, fortissimo utterance of that same basic three note idea and its answer. An angry descending figure imitated at the half-bar, and a more searching, melodic idea round off the material, but Franck, refusing to be bound by tradition, cuts off the motion after just 20 bars to make another go at the introduction, this time a minor third higher (in F minor). Once again, the Allegro non troppo is achieved, and this time the body of the movement is allowed to work itself out. Over the course of the action, a new and triumphant melody (initially in F major) is introduced: this idea, sometimes known as the "faith" motif, will return in the Finale to powerful effect. The B flat minor second movement (Allegretto) displays characteristics of both slow movement and scherzo. The gentle, triple meter dance tune of the English horn (an instrument whose inclusion in a symphonic work was strongly objected to by the Parisian critics of the day) has something of the feel of a Medieval French ballad or dance. The gentle strumming of the harp and pizzicato strings gives way to a more searchingly chromatic consequent melodic strain, attired in attractive sixteenth notes. The middle (scherzo) section of the movement offers a delightful, contrasting dotted melody in E flat major. Throughout this movement, pauses in the rhythmic flow (indicated by fermatas) are used in a graceful manner. The Finale (Allegro non troppo) is altogether more exuberant in tone, beginning with bright wind attacks against a solid background of octave Ds in the strings. A sudden shift to pianissimo is made for the highly syncopated but still flowing main theme (cellos and bassoons, dolce cantabile). As this melody is taken through the characteristically Franckian chromatic depths, both the main theme of the Allegretto and the "faith" motif from the first movement (now offered a more tender treatment) return to fulfill the Symphony's cyclic element. On its second appearance in this movement, the Allegretto theme takes on a power and volume that one wouldn't think possible given its gentle contours during the middle movement. The happy opening melody returns to make a joyous end. *—Blair Johnston*

Recommended:

- ○ **Franck: Symphony** / Munch (cond.), Boston SO / 2002 / JVC 18
- ○ **Franck & Rachmaninoff: Symphonies** / Paray (cond.), Detroit SO / 1996 / Mercury 434368

ORCHESTRAL

Le Chasseur maudit, symphonic poem (1882)

Despite his reputation as an idealistic cultivator of "pure" music, Franck was as desirous of success as any other composer. And success in Paris meant either opera or an exciting orchestral work capable of firing the popular imagination, that is, the symphonic poem. During Franck's last and richest creative period, an inordinate amount of time was given to the composition of two operas, *Hulda* (1882–85) and *Ghiselle* (1889–90), which, though undone by incredibly mediocre books, contain some of his finest music and which remain almost wholly unknown. The symphonic poem began to take hold among French composers with Saint-Saëns' *Le Rouet d'Omphale* in 1871, followed by *Phaëton* (1873) and the enduringly popular *Danse macabre* (1874). Among Franck's pupils, d'Indy's imposing *Wallenstein* trilogy was completed the same year, and Franck's *Les Éolides* followed in 1876. The next three years were given to the completion of his oratorio, *Les Béatitudes*, with which he was largely preoccupied through the decade 1869–79, and which he considered his masterpiece. That behind him, he dashed off *Rebecca*, a small oratorio intended to capitalize on the continuing vogue for things Oriental first sparked by Felicien David's *Le Désert* in 1844.

It was almost certainly Duparc who then turned Franck's attention to Gottfried August Bürger's ballad, *Der wilde Jäger*, for the subject of his own 1875 tone poem, *Lénore*, had been taken from another Bürger ballad. Laurence Davies, the eminent critic and author *César Franck and His Circle*, dismisses Bürger's narrative as "a Lisztian tale of adventure about a Count who defies the Sabbath to go hunting," thus trivializing both its import and its musical suggestiveness which Franck rang into ringing bronze in *Le Chasseur maudit*. The errant nobleman pursues the hunt with preternatural savagery while committing the same trespasses for which Satan was banished from heaven—pride, sacrilege, and defiance. From the distant bells to the fury of the hunt and the count's seizure by demons who condemn him to ride the skies throughout eternity, Franck unfolds the tale with the relish of a savvy raconteur who knows how to call to his aid spellbinding melody, viscerally gripping detail, and richly evocative orchestral color. The work was given its premiere at the 132nd concert of the Société National de Musique, *Salle Érard* on March 31, 1883, conducted by Édouard Colonne, where it shared a program with the tone poem, *Viviane* (1882), by his pupil, Chausson. *—Adrian Corleonis*

Recommended:

- ○ **Franck** / Cluytens (cond.), National Orch. of Belgium / 1995 / EMI 65153
- ○ **Franck: Psyché; Le Chasseur maudit** / Otaka (cond.), BBC National Orch. Wales / 1995 / Chandos 9342

CHAMBER MUSIC

Piano Quintet in F minor (1878–1879)

The *Piano Quintet*, one of the earliest masterpieces of Franck, marked his return to chamber music after more than 35 years. The work was dedicated to Saint-Saëns who, although he played the piano part in the premiere, so strongly disapproved of the musical language of the composer that he rejected the dedication.

The first movement opens with a dramatic introduction, Molto moderato quasi lento, by the bowed strings. The piano replies in a gentle manner. The strings restate their opening. The piano turns even more gentle. The dialogue continues along similar lines until the piano suddenly launches into the Allegro. The second subject is characterized by a wistful inflection to minor. The development reaches a stormy climax. A passage mirrors the introduction. The reprise is very intense, but it concludes fading away. The second movement, Lento, con molto sentimento, is also in sonata form. It opens with a motive with a falling figure on the first violin, with a background of repeated chords of the piano. The atmosphere gradually turns more tragic. Then, a gentle melody in the lower strings is accompanied by piano in the high register. In the central section, the piano brings back the second subject of the opening Allegro. The reprise is again highly dramatic. The finale, Allegro non troppo ma con fuoco, is characterized by a relentless rhythmic drive. It opens with a repeated soft motive in the strings from which the first subject emerges. The second subject begins with a piano theme accompanied by the strings. The agitation continues throughout. Near the ending, the second subject of the Allegro reappears. But the rhythmic urgency resumes and brings the work to an intense conclusion. *—Hector Bellman*

Recommended:

- ○ **The Hollywood String Quartet** / Hollywood SQ, Aller / 1995 / Testament 1077
- ○ **Edition Lockenhaus Vol. 1/2** / Kremer, Zimmermann, Feeney, Rabinovitch, Hagen / 1985 / ECM 827024

Violin Sonata in A major (1886)

Aside from the *Symphony in D minor*, which has become a staple of the concert hall, the *Violin Sonata* (1886) is Franck's best-known work, and rightly so: It is a superb synthesis of Franck's own uniquely rich harmonic language and thematic cyclicism and the Viennese Classical tradition that he came to hold so dear in the later stages of his career.

The Sonata was composed as a wedding present for the famous Belgian violinist Eugene Ysaÿe, who performed it at his matrimonial celebrations on September 26, 1886. The work's popularity is suggested by the number and variety of arrangements that were eventually made, including versions for flute, cello, viola, and even tuba; of these, however, only the arrangement for cello received the composer's stamp of approval.

The Sonata begins not with a fiery quick movement, but rather with a poetic Allegretto moderato in 9/8 time. After a tentative opening gesture, the music builds to a compelling fortissimo climax. As the violin rejoins the discourse, the drama ebbs to a dolcissimo reprise of the opening. Another climax, this time moving toward the tonic A major, follows, and the movement ends with a brief codetta.

The tender relief of the first movement's conclusion is extremely short-lived, however, as a low sixteenth note rumbling in the piano soon overflows into a full-blooded Allegro. The syncopated main tune is taken over by the violin, and things settle down just long enough for a quasi lento interlude and some fragmented episodic reconstructions of the movement's three main motivic strands. A recapitulation, with suitable harmonic reorganization of the material, follows, and the coda, initially misterioso but increasingly tumultuous, provides an electrifying finish.

The third movement, Recitativo-Fantasia, is in many ways the most immediately striking in the Sonata. The piano makes an introductory gesture that draws on the same rising-third gesture that provided the first movement's main theme, to which the violin responds unaccompanied. The tranquil, almost other-worldly middle section introduces the two striving themes, with characteristic triplet-rhythm accompaniment, that will return in glorious attire in the Finale.

The total defeat that seems to mark the conclusion of the third movement is immediately dispelled by the happy opening of the Finale. Although the initial melody, treated in exact canonic imitation between the instruments, is original to the last movement, the first of the two melodies from the central section of the third movement also makes a return. After an appropriate mingling of these ideas—and a colorful interlude built on a subsidiary motive from the opening movement—a tremendous buildup climaxes in the passionate fortissimo return of the second of the two third-movement themes and is immediately repeated a whole step higher. As the dam bursts the opening canonic theme returns once more to bring the work to a cheerful close. *—Blair Johnston*

Recommended:

- ○ **Alfred Cortot Plays Cesar Franck** / Cortot, Thibaud / 1996 / Biddulph 027
- ○ **Argerich - Perlman** / Argerich, Perlman / 1999 / Angel 56815B
- ○ **David Oistrakh Edition** / Oistrakh, Richter / 1997 / Melodiya 40710
- ○ **Midori - Robert McDonald** / Midori, McDonald / 1997 / Sony 63331
- ○ **Rubinstein Collection Vol. 7** / Rubinstein, Heifetz / 1999 / RCA 63007

CONCERTO

Symphonic Variations, for piano & orchestra (1885)

One of the glitterati of the French music scene, Louis Diémer (1843–1919) had taken the piano part in Franck's Victor Hugo-inspired *Les Djinns, for piano and orchestra*, on March 15, 1885; he earned for the composer a rare plaudit from the press: "interesting work... for the direct originality of its thought and the admirable polish of its style." The *Ménestrel's* critic continued: "As I listened to the fine logic of these developments and the arresting effects of the blending of the piano with the orchestra, I was struck by the thought of how sad it is that the name of this eminent musician is so rarely seen on programs, too little honored at a time when he is one of the masters of our epoch, and will indubitably remain one."

This proved prophetic. Franck was delighted and credited his success to Diémer's brilliant playing—*sec, léger*, and articulated with lightning precision—which he promised to reward with "a little something." Good to his word, Franck dedicated his orchestration of the *Variations symphoniques* to Diémer. He began work in the summer of 1885, and completed it on December 12. In his ultimate, old master phase, Franck transformed everything he touched. The orchestral highlighting of pianistic virtuosity—heard in such works of his youth as the *Variations brillantes sur l'air du Pré aux clercs* (1834) or the *Variations brillantes sur le ronde favorite de Gustave III* (1834–35)—or the Lisztian heroics of the soloist locked in combat with the orchestra are left behind in the *Variations symphoniques* in favor of the deft dovetailing of piano and orchestra. This use of the piano as a concertante instrument would be taken up by Vincent d'Indy in his *Symphonie sur un chant montagnard française* (1886) and in turn, be adopted as far afield as Ferruccio Busoni's massive five-movement *Piano Concerto* (1904).

The strings open with a menacing dotted figure in unison, answered by the piano with a plaintively drooping phrase whose dialogue gives way to a second theme introduced by pizzicato woodwinds and strings. An appasionato development leads shortly to six seamless variations on the second theme through which the piano decorates, comments, alludes, and accompanies, as the mood shifts from triumphant assertion to mystical absorption and languishing, muted sighs. A sudden trill in both hands, two octaves apart, prompts the orchestra to begin the extensive, rhapsodic finale in which the thematic material of the preceding is wrought to an incandescent apotheosis. Without doubt, the irresistible, surefire breeziness of this finish has insured the *Variations symphoniques* first place in popularity among Franck's works.

Curiously, the première, at the annual orchestral concert of the Société Nationale de Musique, May 1,1886, with Diémer at the piano, passed almost without mention. At the second performance, an all-Franck concert on January 30 of the following year—again featuring Diémer—the surefire misfired as the aging conductor, Jules Pasdeloup, miscued the orchestra's entrance. *—Adrian Corleonis*

Recommended:

- ○ **Moravec Plays Schumann & Franck** / Neumann (cond.), Moravec, Czech PO / 2000 / Supraphon 3508
- ○ **Gershwin: Rhapsody in Blue; Falla: Nights in the Gardens of Spain; Franck: Symphonic Variations** / Dutoit (cond.), Entremont, Philadelphia Orch. / 1997 / Sony 62643
- ○ **Alfred Cortot** / Ronald (cond.), Cortot, London PO / 2000 / Naxos 110613

VOCAL

Panis angelicus, for tenor, organ, harp, cello & bass (1872)

Franck's music is shot through from beginning to end with a vein of sensual, sometimes cloying, sweetness heard, for instance, in such early piano works as the *Églogue* (1842) or the ambitious *Ballade* (1844). It is chromatically distilled with an old-masterly touch, in many pieces of the vast, posthumously published collections for harmonium, the two volumes of *L'Organiste*. Conflict, in Franck, is almost always psychological—an inner torment—rather than dramatic, and when, in his operas or the great oratorio *Les Béatitudes*, dramatic situations are to the fore, he falls back on operatic formulas—not necessarily unconvincing or ineffective (as often said), but not his most telling or original music, either. On the other hand, his habit of rapture lends his devotional works an ecstatic sweetness that is peculiar to himself. His setting of *Panis angelicus*—a hymn for the elevation proclaiming that the bread of angels shall be the bread of men, the humble, and the poor—is the classic instance in its brevity, its contemplative melodiousness, and its suggestive scoring for organ, harp, and cello. But it is also characteristic that, after a brief central section, the return of the opening phrases should place the voice in canon with the cello. Composed in 1872, *Panis angelicus* is the last in a mixed bag of liturgical works, crowned by the first version of the oratorio *Rédemption*, following in the wake of the Franco-Prussian War as the *bande à* Franck, his inner circle of disciples—Alexis de Castillon, Augusta Holmès, Henri Duparc, Vincent d'Indy, Ernest Chausson, Albert Cahen, and Arthur Coquard—began to cluster around him. He was, moreover, on the threshold of his last and greatest creative period. In the same year *Panis angelicus* was substituted for an *O Salutaris* in the *Messe à trios voix* of 1860, as the latter went to press. At the insistence of S. Bornemann, the publisher, the original *Messe à trois voix*, scored for and often performed with orchestra, was transcribed for organ, harp, cello, and double-bass to render the work more readily saleable. *Panis angelicus* lacks a double-bass part, which is just as well—the utter simplicity, suavely ardent sentiment, and sure execution, which have made it one of Franck's most enduringly popular works, could only have been compromised by elaboration. *—Adrian Corleonis*

Recommended:

- ○ **Jessye Norman** / Gibson (cond.), Norman, Ambrosian Singers, Royal PO / Philips 400019
- ○ **The #1 Christmas Album** / Adler (cond.), Pavarotti, National PO / 2001 / Decca 470022
- ○ **Allegri - Miserere** / Marlow, Trinity College Choir / 1993 / Conifer 16851

CHORAL

Psyché, symphonic poem for chorus & orchestra (1887–1888)

Vincent d'Indy's portrait of Franck as the *pater seraphicus* of music—selfless, saintly, and wise—shepherding his small but influential band of disciples in the green pastures of noble idealism is surprisingly accurate as far as it goes, though it carefully bowdlerizes a recurrent undertow of barely suppressed sensuality. Marooned in an unhappy marriage and a career as church organist, Franck's intense inner life became apparent only at chance moments, and most fully in his music.

Thus, it is telling that one of his most ambitious works, *Psyché*—a vast "symphonic poem" for chorus and orchestra in seven movements—was composed in secret in his vacation retreat at Combs-la-Ville-Quincy over the summer of 1886. To his friend and pupil, the composer Arthur Coquard, he confided that *Psyché* had been contemplated over "many years," though the progress of the composition is noted on the manuscript with a compulsive punctilio—e.g., "'Les jardins d'Éros,' 18 August, (4 o'clock)." Orchestration was accomplished the following summer. The story is drawn from the second century *Metamorphoses* (often translated as *The Golden Ass*) of Lucius Apuleius which tells of Eros' nocturnally veiled love for the mortal Psyche, Psyche's wish to behold her lover face to face, and the lovers' parting and reconciliation. In Franck's retelling, Psyché first dreams of Éros, then is carried by zephyrs to Éros' secret garden, where the orchestra enacts a rapturous love duet as the chorus (sopranos I and II, tenors) warns her that she must never seek to see the face of her mysterious lover. In its undulating melodic richness and sensuous scoring Franck captures more nearly than anything in music what Blake called "the lineaments of gratified desire." The aftermath of her transgression—narrated by the chorus—is as profoundly moving as the final luminous apotheosis is compellingly ecstatic. *Psyché's* premiere, at a concert of the Société National de Musique on March 10, 1888, disconcerted listeners and provoked controversy, with the dedicatee, d'Indy, insisting that the music was an allegory of the love of God, and others—not least, the composer's family—hearing in it an execrable carnality. As Nietzsche noted, "The degree and kind of a man's sexuality reach up into the ultimate pinnacle of his spirit." Largely neglected, *Psyché* looms as Franck's most revealing testament. *—Adrian Corleonis*

Recommended:

- ○ **Franck: Psyché; Le Chasseur maudit** / Otaka (cond.), BBC National Orch. Wales / 1995 / Chandos 9342
- ○ **Franck: Symphony; Psyché** / Latham-Koenig (cond.), Strasbourg PO / 2002 / Avie 0003

Samson François

b. May 18, 1924, Frankfurt, Germany, **d.** Oct. 22, 1970, Paris, France

Pianist

A pupil of Alfred Cortot, but standing apart from others who also studied with the French master, Samson François was a pianist of exceptional persuasiveness in live performance, but only intermittently as arresting in the recording studio. Nonetheless, he left on disc several samples of work approaching his best concert form, albeit with some evidence of the eccentricities critics complained about. His interests were wider than his recorded legacy might suggest; even at his most idiosyncratic, he offered moments of wry humor and rare magic. His life was recalled in some detail in Jérôme Spycket's biography *Scarbo*, published in 1985. In addition to studies in Paris with Yvonne Lefébure and the esteemed Marguerite Long, François was a student of Alfred Cortot at L'École Normale de Musique, the school Cortot cofounded with Auguste Mangeot. Before François had reached the age of 20, he won the Long-Thibaud Competition and thereafter embarked on a career, one of international scale once World War II had ended. Even during the war, Jacques Thibaud brought François to the attention of Walter Legge, the English recording producer turned wartime concert organizer; François was soon flown to England for an extended tour of factories and camps. Concentrating on the Romantic piano literature, and especially the French repertory, he was acclaimed for his performances of Liszt, Schumann, and Chopin, as well as Fauré, Debussy, and Ravel. His Prokofiev, too, was impressive. French critics and audiences were especially receptive to his virtuosic approach. François found an appreciative audience in London as well, and enjoyed a largely positive reputation there during his mature years. François' early death denied the world a chance to hear how the pianist might have developed had he lived longer, but his recordings, some reissued in the new millennium, preserve sufficient work of high interest to assure him a place as a major artist. Among his remastered and re-released recordings are discs of the Chopin and Ravel piano concertos on EMI's *Great Recordings of the Century* series. The former, recorded with the Orchestre National de L'Opera de Monte Carlo and its then-director Louis Frémaux, reveals much of what made François special. Containing what *Gramophone Magazine* deemed "personal and immediate" playing, the artist's quicksilver intensity was awarded with a Diapason d'Or upon its original release. The Ravel recording holds both the concertos, accompanied by André Cluytens and the Orchestre de la Société des Concerts du Conservatoire, and a mercurial account of the composer's *Gaspard de la nuit*, all of it a fitting remembrance of an artist who pursued his own singular vision. This disc was originally a recipient of the Prix de L'Académie du Disque français. Among François' other pursuits was that of composition. Among his recordings is one of his own piano concerto. In addition, he once composed music for the legendary jazz singer and cabaret artist Peggy Lee. *—Erik Eriksson*

Recommended:

- ○ **Chopin: Piano Concertos** / Fremaux (cond.), François, Monte Carlo National Opera Orch. / 2000 / Angel 67261
- ○ **Ravel: Piano Concertos, Gaspard de la Nuit** / Cluytens (cond.), François, Conservatory Concert Society Orch. / 1998 / EMI 66957
- ○ **Chopin: Piano Works Vol. 1** / Fremaux (cond.), François, Monte Carlo National Opera Orch. / 2001 / EMI 74457

Franz Liszt Chamber Orchestra

f. 1963, Budapest, Hungary
Ensemble

The Franz Liszt Chamber Orchestra was founded in 1963 by former students at the Franz Liszt Music Academy in Budapest. Its repertoire ranges from Monteverdi to music by contemporary composers. János Rolla, one of Hungary's leading violinists, has been concertmaster of the orchestra since its inception. The orchestra has made more than 200 recordings for the Hungaroton label and has released other discs for CBS, Teldec, EMI, Erato, Denon, and Sony Classical. The orchestra has received three Grand Prix awards of the French Academie du Disque in Paris, including one for a recording of Handel cantatas and one for Vivaldi motets, and has received numerous Hungarian "Record of the Year" awards. Together with presenting 30–35 concerts each year at home, the orchestra has toured in Europe, the United States, and Japan, and has been featured at festivals such as Besançon, Edinburgh, Bath, Flanders, Helsinki, Lucerne, Montreaux, and Salzburg. The orchestra has collaborated with many noted instrumentalists, including Jean-Pierre Rampal, Maurice André, Martha Argerich, Mstislav Rostropovich, Henryk Szeryng, Sir Yehudi Menuhin, and Isaac Stern. *—Robert Adelson*

Recommended:

- ○ **Bartók: Music for Srtings, Percussion & Celeste; Divertimento for Strings** / Rolla (cond.), Franz Liszt CO / Hungaroton 12531
- ○ **Haydn: Piano Concertos** / Ax, Franz Liszt CO / 2001 / Legacy 89853

Mirella Freni

b. Feb. 27, 1935, Modena, Italy
Soprano

Mirella Freni is the textbook example of a lyric soprano who expanded wisely to the spinto roles, conserving her voice so that even in her sixties she still possessed enough vocal freshness and bloom that she made a credible Mimi in theaters all over the world. (In Italy, one of her nicknames is "La Prudentissima," or "the most prudent one.") She is also a highly sympathetic actor in both comedies and more serious roles.

In an amusing coincidence, she and Pavarotti shared the same wet nurse as a child (both of their mothers worked in a tobacco factory, making their own milk unsuitable) and she later joked that he obviously got the bigger share of the milk. The granddaughter of Valentina Bartomesi, Freni was a child prodigy, singing *"Sempre libera"* in her first public performance at the age of ten. At 12, she made her broadcast debut singing *"Un bel di"* in a radio competition. Beniamino Gigli, a competition judge, warned her that she could damage her voice if she continued to sing opera with her voice still so undeveloped. She waited until she was 17 to begin studying again. Her new teacher was Ettore Campogalliani, whose most-celebrated student had been Renata Tebaldi.

Two years later, in 1955, she made her stage debut as Micaela in *Carmen*, one of her favorite and most effective roles. At this point, she briefly postponed further career development when she married conductor Leone Magiera and had a child (whom she named Micaela, after her debut role), but resumed singing again in 1958, when she won the Viotti competition in Vercelli, Italy. The prize was the role of Mimi in *La bohème* in Turin, a role in which she later made her Met, La Scala, Chicago, and San Francisco debuts. In 1960, she made her Glyndebourne debut as Zerlina, in 1961 her Covent Garden debut as Nanetta in *Falstaff*, and in 1963 her La Scala debut as Mimi in *La bohème* in the now-famous Zeffirelli production. Herbert von Karajan was the conductor for the La Scala Bohème, and he became one of her prominent supporters; as he did with many singers, he encouraged her to move toward heavier repertoire, such as Desdemona in *Otello*, which she first sang with him in 1970 and also filmed with Jon Vickers and Peter Glossop in a movie directed and conducted by Karajan. At that time, he declared that he had waited 40 years to hear such a Desdemona. She started to add more of these lyrico-spinto roles to her stage repertoire and also filmed the role of Madama Butterfly with Karajan. However, she absolutely refused to sing the title role of Turandot when he asked her to in 1980, and he subsequently refused to work with her again.

In 1981, she married Bulgarian bass Nicolai Ghiaurov, who encouraged her to examine the Russian repertoire. At first, she began to add Russian songs to her recitals, with his musical and language coaching, and then in the late 1980s, she was ready to sing the role of Tatiana in *Eugene Onegin*. In 1990, she took on Lisa (*The Queen of Spades*). In the mid-1990s, she started singing Giordano roles for the first time, not only Fedora, a role typically beloved by divas toward the end of their careers, but the title role of Madame Sans-Gene, a comedic, even occasionally farcical role. In 1990, she received the order *Cavaliere della Gran Croce della Republica Italiana* and the *Légion d'Honneur* in 1993. *—Ann Feeney*

Recommended:

- ○ **Puccini: La Bohème** / Karajan (cond.), Freni, Pavarotti, Ghiaurov, Panerai, Berlin PO / 1987 / London 421049
- ○ **The Very Best of Mirella Freni** / Freni, etc. / 2003 / EMI 75909
- ○ **Gounod: Faust** / Prétre (cond.), Domingo, Freni, Allen, Ghiaurov, Paris National Opera Theater Orch. / EMI 47493
- ○ **Mirella Freni Vol. 1** / Freni, etc. / 2000 / Opera d'Oro 2032

Girolamo Frescobaldi

b. Sep. 1583, Ferrara, Italy, **d.** Mar. 1, 1643, Rome, Italy
Composer

Girolamo Frescobaldi was a major composer from the late Renaissance and early Baroque periods whose keyboard works rank among the most important of his time. His sacred and secular vocal music is generally assessed to be less important but still significant. Frescobaldi appears to have learned much of his deft contrapuntal skill and harmonic boldness from his teacher Luzzaschi. The 12 *Fantasie* (1608) are notable for their brilliantly wrought counterpoint, but also for their somewhat arid intellectual character. The two books of *Toccate*, from 1615 and 1627, are both innovative, with the latter set showing greater structural complexity.

Frescobaldi was born in Ferrara probably in mid-September, 1583. His first teacher was likely his father, believed to be an organist. Girolamo became something of a child prodigy on the organ and was taken on as a pupil by Court organist Luzzasco Luzzaschi, who was also a respected composer.

At 14 Frescobaldi became organist at the Academia della Morte in Ferrara. With a prodigious talent and an apparently strong desire to further his career, he decided to travel to Rome in about 1599. Not much is known about his early years there. From January till June, 1607, he served as organist at Santa Maria in Trastevere. He might have continued in the position but for an offer from his friend and arts patron, Guido Bentivoglio, Archbishop of Rhodes. Bentivoglio departed Rome for Flanders on June 11, 1607, with Frescobaldi accompanying him as part of his entourage, intending to enter his service as a musician with duties not entirely clear. In 1608 the young composer's first works were published, a collection of madrigals and three canzonas, which appeared in Alessandro Raverji's publication, *Canzoni*.

Frescobaldi stayed in Brussels for less than a year, returning to Rome to assume the post of organist (October 31, 1608) at the Cappella Giulia at St. Peter's in Rome, thanks to the efforts of the influential Bentivoglio family. The organist's position was not a high-paying one, but finances were hardly a problem now: with his appointment to St. Peter's came service for Enzo Bentivoglio, ambassador to Rome from Ferrara. That position involved teaching the musicians in the ambassador's musical group or concertino.

In about 1612, Frescobaldi began employment for the wealthy Cardinal Aldobrandini, who paid him nearly twice the salary he earned from his organist post at St. Peter's. On February 18, 1613, Frescobaldi married Orsola del Pino, who had already given birth to his son and was pregnant with a second child. With publication in 1615 of ten Ricercari and five Canzoni, both for keyboard, Frescobaldi's growing prominence clearly placed him in the forefront of Italian musicians.

For the next 13 years, the composer would experience his most productive period, turning out collections of ricecars, canzonas and other works. In 1624, his 12 Capriccios for keyboard appeared, and three years later, volume two of his Toccatas. On November 28, 1628, the composer departed to become Court organist in Florence, having been granted a leave from St. Peter's. Not much is known about his six-year stint in Florence, though he produced the two volumes of arias and other vocal works there, *Arie musicali*. The composer returned to his St. Peter's post in April, 1634.

Frescobaldi's keyboard collection, *Canzoni da sonare*, was published in late that same year. Other important publications would come now as well, including the 12 Toccate, (two volumes) of 1637, which were reissues of the earlier ones. That same year he also began teaching Vienna Court organist Johann Jacob Froberger, who would study with him until 1641. Frescobaldi died on March 1, 1643. *—Robert Cummings*

Overview of Works (ca. 1608–1637)

One of the leading composers from the late Renaissance and early Baroque periods, Girolamo Frescobaldi (1583–1643) is known mostly for his keyboard works, which are among the most important of his time. His vocal music, while occasionally masterful, is on the whole less significant. Frescobaldi's keyboard compositions divulge the influence of the Neapolitan School, and probably owe something to Gesualdo, who with a group of performers and composers, visited Ferrara in 1594, where the young composer lived. Frescobaldi's keyboard music also owes a debt to that of his teacher, Luzzasco Luzzaschi, particularly in its contrapuntal and harmonic elements.

The *12 Fantasie* (1608), though a bit dry and cerebral, show Frescobaldi's deftly innovative counterpoint and solidly-conceived structures. His two volumes of

Toccate, the first containing 12 (1615) and the second 11 (1627), show remarkable development over earlier efforts, especially in their bold use of color and form. An examination of these two volumes reveals the evolution of Frescobaldi's harmonic content; whereas the first shows him still employing the very linear, modal approach that was typical of the late Renaissance, the second confirms his shift to the major/minor sonorities that would give rise to what we now call the "common practice era."

Other significant keyboard works included *Ten Ricercari* and *Five Canzoni*, both of 1615, *12 Capriccios* (1624), and the *12 Toccate* (1637). All of these works give evidence to Frescobaldi's own mastery at the keyboard, and surely have their roots in improvisation.

As mentioned above, Frescobaldi's vocal music is not generally regarded as highly as his keyboard works. He wrote no operas or oratorios but did have a significant output in both the sacred and secular genres. Among his most important efforts here is the two-volume *Arie Musicali* (1630), which contains many arias and solo songs.

Frescobaldi also composed a large number of madrigals, which appeared in a 1608 Antwerp publication. The composer was said to have written them in Brussels in 1607 or 1608. These vocal works once more divulge the influence of Luzzaschi, who is credited with founding the Ferrarese madrigal style. Frescobaldi's madrigals clearly fall under the umbrella of that style, not least because they show a preference for polyphony over homophony.

In the end, Frescobaldi is viewed as an innovator within a conservative framework. He did not tear down tradition, but rather built upon it, using novel ideas in large-scale instrumental works. His influence was vast, spreading throughout Europe in the decades that followed his death, holding sway to one degree or other with most important Baroque composers in the instrumental realm, including J. S. Bach. Ironically, it was Frescobaldi's bias for keyboard composition—and eschewing of opera—that caused his reputation to fade over the next couple of centuries. —*Robert Cummings*

Recommended:

- ○ **Frescobaldi: Keyboard Music** / Vartolo / 2002 / Naxos 553547-48
- ○ **Frescobaldi: Arie, toccate e canzoni** / Caserta / 2000 / BIS 1166
- ○ **Frescobaldi: Il Primo Libro di Capricci** / Butt / 1998 / HM 09332
- ○ **Frescobaldi: Works for Harpsichord** / Asperen / 1987 / Teldec 843774
- ○ **Frescobaldi: Motets** / Cantalupi / Tactus 580602
- ○ **Frescobaldi: Fiori Musicali** / Novenko / Supraphon 111862

Fretwork

f. 1985, London, England
Ensemble

One might doubt, upon first hearing the name Fretwork, that the group in question is a serious-minded viol sextet specializing in pre-Classical music from their native Britain; Fretwork might, after all, sound more like the name of a 1980s Euro-rock band. But it is precisely that unpretentious design, that appeal to the not-esoterically-minded masses of listeners who easily tire of textbook approaches to early music performance, that has enabled the men and women of Fretwork to lift themselves into the top rank of the world's performing ensembles—no small feat for a viol consort.

Fretwork was founded in Britain in 1985 and made its debut at Wigmore Hall the following year. It maintains, as mentioned, a reputation as exponents first and foremost of English music (William Byrd, Thomas Tallis, Henry Purcell, William Lawes, et al); but it has also been the catalyst for the composition of several new pieces of music (Tan Dun and George Benjamin being key among the composers represented in this category), thus allowing audiences to hear a kind of hybrid music-making—old meets new in the most obvious of ways—that has not very often been tried. The group also edits and publishes music under the label Fretwork Editions. —*Blair Johnston*

Recommended:

- ○ **Byrd: Complete Consort Music** / Fretwork / 1994 / Virgin 45031
- ○ **Purcell: The Fantazias & In Nomines** / Fretwork / 1995 / Virgin 45062
- ○ **Tavener: The Hidden Face** / Chance, Daniel, Wilcock, Fretwork / 2001 / HM 907285
- ○ **Goe Nightly Cares** / Wilson, Chance, Fretwork / 1990 / Virgin 59586
- ○ **Dowland: Lachrimae** / Fretwork / 1993 / Virgin 45005
- ○ **With a Merrie Noyse** / Ives, Harvey, Connolly, Covey-Crump, Harrold, Fretwork / 2003 / HM 907337

Ferenc Fricsay

b. Aug. 9, 1914, Budapest, Hungary, **d.** Feb. 20, 1963, Basle, Switzerland
Conductor

Ferenc Fricsay's career lasted barely 20 years, but during that time, he became one of the most acclaimed conductors of his generation and left behind a body of recordings that are still admired. Fricsay studied at the Budapest Academy of Music under both Zoltán Kodály and Béla Bartók, whose music he later championed. His first conducting appointment came in 1936, in Szeged, where he remained until 1944. His debut conducting the Budapest Opera was in 1939 and in 1945 he was appointed the company's music director, taking the parallel appointment with the Budapest Philharmonic. At the 1947 Salzburg Festival, when conductor Otto Klemperer was forced to withdraw from conducting the premiere of Gottfried Von Einem's opera *Dantons Tod*, Fricsay stepped in, receiving international accolades for a sterling performance. The next year he conducted the world premiere of Frank Martin's *Zaubertrank*, and the year after that Carl Orff's *Antigone*. In 1948, Fricsay made his Berlin debut with Verdi's *Don Carlos* in a production that also featured the debut of baritone Dietrich Fischer-Dieskau. Thereafter he served as a guest conductor throughout Europe, based in Berlin, where he served as music director of the Stadtische Oper and the American Sector Symphony Orchestra (RIAS), later renamed the Berlin Radio Symphony Orchestra. Fricsay was best known in Europe as an operatic conductor, acclaimed for his Mozart and Verdi, among other composers, but in America he made his debut with the Boston Symphony Orchestra in 1953. He was conductor of the Houston Symphony Orchestra in 1954, but resigned after one season due to policy disagreements with the board of directors. In 1956, Fricsay became music director of the Bavarian State Opera and after two seasons, returned to Berlin to resume the music directorship of the Berlin Radio Symphony Orchestra. In 1961, Fricsay conducted a performance of Mozart's *Don Giovanni* to commemorate the re-opening of the Deutsche Oper.

Fricsay's approach to conducting was influenced heavily by Toscanini, whose relationship with the NBC Symphony he used as a model for his own work with the Berlin Radio Symphony. He emphasized strict tempos and precise playing, with a close adherence to the score. As an operatic conductor, however, he was not afraid to challenge customs and conventions, both in his conception of a work and his way of realizing performances of striking vitality.

Fricsay began developing serious health problems in the 1950s. The vivaciousness of his earlier performances was replaced by a more measured, reflective approach to music as his physical condition deteriorated, and by the end of the 1950s, when he would normally have been expected to be in his prime as a conductor and recording artist, his strength was beginning to fail him. When he died, Fricsay left behind a small, precious body of recordings.

Fricsay had signed an exclusive contract with Deutsche Grammophon in 1948 and during the next decade or so, delivered a body of work heavy with award-winning recordings. Fricsay's remarkable textural clarity was captured on record with the help of his close understanding of recording techniques. Perhaps his most-acclaimed record was Mozart's *The Magic Flute*, made in 1955 with Rita Streich, Maria Stader, Ernst Haefliger, and Dietrich Fischer-Dieskau (who, though completely unsuited for the role physically, sings up a storm as Pageno), which remains a highly recommended performance. His recording of *Don Giovanni* from 1958 is also considered a definitive performance. He was also one of the most-acclaimed interpreters of Bartók, his reputation (and those of his recordings) rivalling that of Fritz Reiner, whose work with the composer is often cited as definitive. —*Bruce Eder*

Recommended:

- ○ **Ferenc Fricsay: A Life in Music** / Fricsay (cond.) / 2003 / DG 000085402
- ○ **Von Einem: Dantons Tod** / Fricsay (cond.), Hann, Alsen, Wernigk, Schoffler, Vienna PO / 2001 / Opera d'Oro 1316
- ○ **Bartok: Concertos 1–3** / Fricsay (cond.), Anda, Berlin RSO / DG 447399
- ○ **Ferenc Fricsay** / Fricsay (cond.), Vienna PO, Berlin RSO, Berlin RIAS-SO / EMI 75109

Ignaz Friedman

b. Feb. 14, 1882, Podgórze, Poland, **d.** Jan. 26, 1948, Sydney, Australia
Pianist

Ignaz (or Ignacy) Friedman was one of the most important pianists from the early decades of the twentieth century, ranking in stature with such keyboard stalwarts as Josef Hofmann, Sergey Rachmaninov, Josef Lhevinne, and Leopold Godowsky. His contemporaries were among his greatest admirers: Horowitz, a friend but generally taciturn in offering praise to rivals, was said to have assessed Friedman's technique as stronger than his own. Friedman was also a composer with a fairly substantial output, mainly of piano works or of chamber music involving the piano. He also transcribed many compositions for his instrument and edited Chopin's complete piano works, as well as selected ones by Beethoven, Liszt, and others.

Friedman was from the same place of birth as Josef Hofmann. Young Ignaz was drawn to music early on, no doubt because of his musician father, who was a member of a local orchestra. Friedman's first significant instruction on piano came from Flora Grzywinska in Kraków. He enrolled at the Leipzig Conservatory in 1900, where he studied composition with Hugo Riemann. The following year, he left for Vienna to study with composer and piano pedagogue Theodore Leschetizky. After three years of instruction from him, Friedman decided to launch his career in Vienna in November 1904, with performances of the Brahms, Liszt, and Tchaikovsky first piano concertos. His playing was enthusiastically received, as were the several encores he performed in between the concertos and at the close. The following year, he went on tour, thereafter rarely dropping out of the public eye, appearing with orchestras and giving recitals mainly in Europe until the 1920s, when he expanded his schedule to include concert dates in the United States, Australia, New Zealand, Asia (including Japan), and parts of the Middle East. More than a few of his contemporaries would wonder at the energy he displayed to remain on tour almost constantly until 1943. He established residence in Berlin around 1905, but fled Germany in 1914 at the onset of World War I to settle in Copenhagen. While Friedman is hardly remembered as a composer, he did produce several interesting works, perhaps the most compelling of which came during the war years, a piano quintet, published in Leipzig in 1918. In 1920, Friedman gave his first concert tour of the United States, which paved the way for 11 return trips in the next two decades. On one of them, in 1923, he made his first recording (Schubert/Liszt—*Hark, Hark! The Lark!*) for Columbia Records. In 1925–26, he recorded more music for the same label, including Chopin's *Etude No. 7 in C,* Op. 10, and *Etude No. 12 in C minor "Revolutionary,"* as well as works by Mozart and Scarlatti. He would go on to record such staples as the Grieg piano concerto, the Beethoven *Sonata No. 14 "Moonlight,"* and Liszt's *La campanella* (arr. Busoni). By 2002, these works—and the entire recorded legacy of Friedman—were available on reissues on various labels. Friedman remained as active in the 1930s as in the previous decades, but as political tensions grew in Europe, he decided to resettle once more, this time in Australia. There, and in New Zealand, he gave many successful concerts, some of which were broadcast. In 1943, Friedman retired from concert activity, owing to a partially debilitating paralysis in his left hand. *—Robert Cummings*

Recommended:

- ○ **Complete Recordings Vol. 1** / Friedman / 2002 / Naxos 8110684
- ○ **Liszt & Chopin** / Friedman / 1996 / Nimbus 8805
- ○ **Ignacy Friedman** / Friedman / 1999 / Philips 456784

Johann Jacob Froberger

b. May 19, 1616, Stuttgart, Germany, **d.** May 7, 1667, Héricourt, Haute-Saône, France

Composer

The cosmopolitan composer and harpsichordist Johann Jacob Froberger (1616–67) was born in Stuttgart. He spent much of his professional life at the court of Vienna but traveled widely to Italy, France, England, and the Netherlands. In his keyboard compositions, he acknowledged the divergent styles of his European contemporaries while forging a highly personal and musically powerful synthesis. Serving the Viennese *Hofkapelle* from 1634 until 1645, he was granted a stipend from the Italophile Emperor Ferdinand III to travel to Italy and supplement his musical training by studying with Girolamo Frescobaldi. He studied in Rome from late 1637 until 1641 and made a second trip to Rome, Florence, and Mantua before 1649. An extensive period of travel from 1649 to 1653 probably included trips to Paris (where he met Chambonnières and Louis Couperin), the Spanish Netherlands, and England. After a second period in Vienna as principal organist to the Imperial court from 1653 to 1658, he retired to the estate of Princess Sybilla of Württemburg-Montbeliard, where he died suddenly at a Vespers service in 1667.

Most of his (almost exclusively keyboard) music was published posthumously beginning in the last decade of the seventeenth century, at a ripe moment in the forging of High Baroque German national artistic consciousness. Thus his style, blending Italian and French genres and techniques with quintessentially "German" contrapuntal thinking, was immediately perceived as a foundation of this national style. In many of Froberger's autographed copies of his music, the different genres are separated and anthologized, with attention to the distinctive notational practices. The ricercars, fantasias and other polyphonic pieces are notated in open score, to highlight the independence of the voices. Conversely, the Italianate toccatas, are notated in the Italian style of one six-line staff above a seven-line staff, clearly delineating the two hands. These pieces show the influence of his teacher Frescobaldi as well as of Merulo; Froberger's organization of the pieces into contrasting rhapsodic and fugal sections, however, follows more the practice of Michelangelo Rossi. The other Italian genre in which Froberger composed is the canzona, or capriccio. Froberger's harpsichord suites published in the 1690s gave the impression that he "invented" the generic structure which would dominate eighteenth century keyboard music: a suite of bipartite dance movements in the same key, in the order Allemande—Courante—Sarabande—Gigue. This misconception, disproved by the presence of regular, but differing, orders in his own manuscripts, has long been the cornerstone of the composer's historical position. Nevertheless, Froberger did assimilate the French dance genres, grouping them in suites by key, and (especially in the Allemandes), incorporating some of the Italian improvisatory character into the dance structure. This yielded fuller-voiced pieces in a lute-derived style the French called style brisé. His other personal innovation in the dance suites was the substitution of the first dance by an affective miniature character piece with a descriptive title; these were often laments on the death of prominent court figures. *—Timothy Dickey*

Overview of Works (ca. 1640–1656)

While Johann Jacob Froberger (1616–67) is an unfamiliar name to many, he was the most prominent and respected composer of keyboard music in his day. Bach arrived on the musical scene several decades after Froberger's death and found he could hardly escape the late master's unique voice. All but two of Froberger's works are for keyboard, but his output embraced a variety of forms, including ricercares, toccatas, capriccios, canzonas, fantasias, and many French dance forms (sarabandes, allemandes, courantes, etc.) used to comprise a suite, a genre he is credited with developing for the harpsichord (or clavichord). The ricercares, toccatas, and other Italian-derived forms were written for organ or harpsichord. The dates of many of his compositions are uncertain, since many were first published several decades after his death.

Froberger's style featured much use of counterpoint, but less imaginatively and boldly than Bach. Other characteristics include the use of fugal subjects and variation techniques. His structures tended to be less complex than Bach's or those of other later Baroque composers.

It is generally accepted that Froberger's greatest works are the *Suites.* Typically they consist of a handful of dance pieces of short duration. For example, the *Suite No. 7,* in E minor, consists of the usual four: an allemande, gigue, courante, and sarabande. *No. 8,* in A major, follows the same pattern. *No. 30,* in A minor—one of his more often-performed efforts—leads off with a piece entitled *Plainte faite à Londres pour passer la melancholie,* which is, in effect, an allemande. The rest of the suite follows the same gigue-courante-sarabande pattern as in the other suites.

Among his more popular suites are *Nos. 12,* in C major, (whose opening allemande carries the lengthy subtitle *Lamento sopra la dolorosa perdita della Real Mstà de Ferdinando IV*); *18,* in G minor; and *29,* in E flat major. A lone allemande by Froberger has become probably his most popular composition, the character piece entitled *Tombeau de Monsieur Blancrocher* (1652). It was inspired, the story goes, by the death of the Parisian lutenist Blancrocher, who fell from a ladder and later died in the comforting arms of Froberger. Lasting around six minutes, this is one of the composer's longer and more heartfelt allemandes.

While the suite genre is generally thought to contain Froberger's best music, his other keyboard works rival them in popularity. Of the 17 capriccios, *No. 6,* in C major, may be the most popular. As a genre, it appears his 25 toccatas have attracted the most attention among the Italian-form pieces. *Nos. 1* (A minor), *2* (D minor), *3* (G major), *6* (G minor), *13* (E minor), and *16* (C major) are some of the more commonly heard toccatas. Among the 15 ricercares, *Nos. 1* (D minor) and *6* (F sharp minor) have achieved some currency over the years, too. There are also 17 capriccios, eight fantasias, and six canzonas in Froberger's output, most of high quality. *—Robert Cummings*

Recommended:

- ○ **Froberger: Ou l'intranquillité** / Verlet / 2000 / Astree 8805
- ○ **Froberger: Suites de clavecin & Toccatas** / Rousset / HM 1951372
- ○ **Froberger: Fantasia** / Rampe / 1998 / Veritas 5453082

Rafael Frühbeck de Burgos

b. Sep. 15, 1933, Burgos, Spain

Conductor

Rafael Frühbeck de Burgos, eminent Spanish conductor, was born to a Spanish mother and a German father. He was educated at the Music Academy of Bilbao and the Munich Conservatory, and completed his studies at the University of Madrid. His first post as conductor was with the Municipal Orchestra of Bilbao. In 1962, Frühbeck de Burgos began a lifelong association with the National Orchestra of Spain, and was its chief conductor from that time until 1978. His international reputation began with the success of his first appearance with the Philadelphia Orchestra. He has served as music director for the Montreal Symphony (1974–76), the Dusseldorf Symphoniker (1966–71), and the Deutsche Oper in Berlin (1992–97). Frühbeck de Burgos has also been named chief conductor of the Vienna Symphony and has held guest conductorships with the National Symphony Orchestra of Washington, D.C. and the Yomiuri Nippon Symphony in Japan.

Frühbeck de Burgos has recorded extensively with English Decca, EMI/Angel, IMP Classics, Chandos and Collins Classics. First and foremost, he is regarded for his interpretations of Spanish music, and has recorded the major works of Falla in addition to Rodrigo, Montsalvatge, Ravel, and Granados. His recording of Falla's *Nights In the Gardens of Spain* with pianist Alicia de Larrocha is judged the best on disc by many critics. Frühbeck de Burgos made several recordings backing vocalist Victoria de Los Angeles in Spanish songs and zarzuela arias for EMI. He has made his own arrangement for orchestra of Albeniz's *Suite española,* and it has become a concert staple. Outside of Spanish music, Frühbeck de Burgos has also contributed fine recordings of Bizet's *Carmen* with Grace Bumbry and Jon Vickers in the cast, and justly celebrated discs of Orff's *Carmina Burana,* Mozart's *Requiem* and Stravinsky's *Rite of Spring.* He is regarded as a sensitive and sympathetic accompanist in concerto literature, and has partnered with such luminaries as violinists Yehudi Menhuin and Nathan Milstein, pianists Arturo Benedetti Michelangeli, Louis Lortie, and clarinetist Karl Leister. Frühbeck de Burgos is also a renowned interpreter of the music of Mendelssohn and has made recordings of *Elijah* and the complete incidental music to *A Midsummer Night's Dream*, which have been critically praised.

Frühbeck de Burgos has never been recorded in the work of Mahler, but his broadcasts of Mahler's symphonies have been highly respected, and in 1996 he was awarded the Gold Medal of the International Gustav Mahler Society in Vienna. Since the late 1990s, he has been touring the world with the National Orchestra of Spain as its conductor emeritus. *—Uncle Dave Lewis*

Recommended:

○ **Albeniz, Turina & Falla** / Frühbeck de Burgos (cond.), Larrocha, London PO / 1984 / London 4102892

○ **Spanish Spectacular** / Frühbeck de Burgos (cond.), London SO / IMP 924

○ **Falla: La vida breve; El amor brujo; El sombrero de tres picos** / Giulini, Frühbeck de Burgos (conds.), Los Angeles, Gerard, Soriano, Challan, London PO, National Orch. of Spain / 2001 / EMI 67590

Wilhelm Furtwängler

b. Jan. 25, 1886, Berlin, Germany, **d.** Nov. 30, 1954, Baden-Baden, Germany

Conductor

Although born in Berlin, conductor Wilhelm Furtwängler spent his childhood in Munich, where his father was a professor. After his talents were recognized at an early age, he was removed from school and educated privately. Furtwängler's teachers included the composer Joseph Rheinberger and the conductor Felix Mottl. By the age of 17 the young musician had written numerous works and had his conducting debut three years later with the Kaim Orchestra, where he directed the opening Largo from his own first symphony, Beethoven's overture *Die Weihe des Hauses*, and Bruckner's *Ninth Symphony*. The ambivalent response to his music and the financial instability that composition offered caused him to focus his energies on conducting.

Furtwängler's first position was at the Breslau Stadttheater in 1906 and 1907. He went to Zurich the next season, followed by an apprenticeship at the Munich Court Opera under the auspices of his teacher Mottl. From 1911 to 1921, Furtwängler served as music director of various ensembles in Lübeck, Mannheim, Frankfurt, and Vienna. From 1920 to 1922, he served as conductor of the Berlin Staatskapelle. At the age of 35, the conductor took the baton at the celebrated Berlin Philharmonic and concurrently held the same position at the Leipzig Gewandhaus Orchestra, where he remained until 1928. Furtwängler led the New York Philharmonic from 1927 to 1929, but eventually declined an offer to remain there. It was during those years that Furtwängler was appointed music director of the Vienna Philharmonic. As the 1920s drew to a close, he held positions throughout Europe, including those at the Bayreuth and Salzburg festivals (1931–32) and the Berlin State Opera (1933). In 1932, he was awarded the Goethe Gold Medal.

When the Nazis came into power in 1933, Furtwängler strongly and publicly opposed the Nazi agenda, despite pride in his German heritage, and refused to give the Nazi salute, even in Hitler's presence. In 1934, when Hindemith's *Mathis de Maler* was banned by the Nazi party, Furtwängler unilaterally resigned from all of his posts, aided numerous Jewish musicians under Nazi persecution, and refused to conduct in Nazi-occupied areas. Furtwängler eventually fled to Switzerland at the suggestion of Albert Speer. When, in 1936, the New York Philharmonic offered him the position of music director, he was dissuaded from accepting the position by anti-Nazi sentiment. After the war's conclusion, the Allied command cleared Furtwängler of charges of being a Nazi sympathizer, although the American government did not "denazify" Furtwängler until 1946. In 1949, the Chicago Symphony Orchestra courted the German conductor, but its board of directors quickly withdrew its offer under the heavy and largely unjustified criticism from the orchestra's musicians.

Always welcomed in Europe, Furtwängler enjoyed continued success throughout the region. While uninterested in recording live performances, citing the impossibility for technology to capture a mood or aesthetic, he was responsible for countless recordings, most of which were made after the war. His dedication to the works of Beethoven was unsurpassed, and his enthusiasm towards the contemporary compositions of the time impressive, evidenced by his aggressive programming. Furtwängler's idiosyncratic approach to the repertoire and spontaneous interpretations were unique to say the least. Furtwängler remained a popular artist and kept a busy schedule conducting throughout Europe until his death in Baden-Baden in 1954. According to his second wife Elisabeth Ackermann, he died a darkened and melancholy man, troubled by the atrocious history his beloved Germany had written. *—David Brensilver*

Recommended:

○ **Wagner: Tristan und Isolde** / Furtwängler (cond.), Flagstad, Fischer-Dieskau, Schock, Suthaus, London PO / 2001 / EMI 85873

○ **Beethoven: Symphonie 9** / Furtwängler (cond.), Seefried, Dermota, Anday, Schoffler, Vienna PO / DG 435325

○ **Schubert: Symphony 9; Haydn: Symphony 88** / Furtwängler (cond.), Berlin PO / DG 447439

○ **Wagner: Der Ring des Nibelungen** / Furtwängler (cond.), Flagstad, Konetzni, Herrmann, Lorenz / Virtuoso 99082

○ **Beethoven: The 9 Symphonies** / Furtwängler (cond.), Schwarzkopf, Hongen, Hopf, Edelmann, Vienna PO, Bayreuth Festival Orch., Stockholm PO / 2000 / EMI 67496

○ **Mozart: Don Giovanni** / Furtwängler (cond.), Schwarzkopf, Siepi, Dermota, Berger, Salzburg Festival Orch. / Music & Arts 1129

○ **Brahms: The 4 Symphonies; Haydn Variations** / Furtwängler (cond.), Berlin PO / 1989 / Virtuoso 2699072

Johann Joseph Fux

b. 1660, Hirtenfeld, Styria, Austria, **d.** Feb. 13, 1741, Vienna, Austria

Composer

Born into a peasant family, Austrian composer and music theorist Johann Joseph Fux (1660–1741) showed a strong interest in music from childhood. In 1680, he entered the Jesuit University in Graz. In 1681, his skill in the musical arts earned him entrance to the imperial Ferdinandeum, a residential school run by the Jesuits, which was designed to give special priority to musically gifted students. By the end of 1683, Fux was listed as a student of at the Jesuit University at Ingolstadt. Until the end of 1688, he also served as the organist at St. Moritz, in Inglostadt. His movements after 1688 are uncertain, but the influence of Corelli and Bolognese composers suggests a study trip to Italy, perhaps under princely patronage.

After this time, Fux was in the service of a Hungarian bishop, presumably Leopold, Count von Kollonitsch, who, despite becoming Archbishop of Esztergom and Primate of Hungary, often made his residence in Vienna. On two visits to the Archbishop, Emperor Leopold I, heard some masses by Fux, which he praised highly. From this point on, Fux enjoyed imperial favour to an ever increasing degree. In 1696 Fux married C.J. Schnitzenbaum, the daughter of a secretary in the Lower Austrian government. In 1698 the emperor appointed Fux court composer, going over the heads of both his Kapellmeister and Chief Steward. Fux also served as organist at the Schottenkirche in Vienna until 1702.

Around the year 1700, at the emperor's expense, he traveled to Rome to study under Pasquini. After Leopold's death, Fux retained the office of court composer under Joseph I, who ruled from 1705 to 1711. On 1 October 1705, Fux took on the added responsibility of vice-Kapellmeister at St. Stephen's Cathedral in Vienna. He concentrated his efforts at St. Stephen's on the music which was performed before the statue of Our Lady of Patsch, which had been brought to Vienna and placed on the high alter of the cathedral in 1697 by Emperor Leopold I. In 1712, Fux succeeded J.M. Zacher as Kapellmeister at St. Steven's, a position he was to hold for the next three years. Meanwhile, in 1713, after the ascension of Charles VI to the imperial throne, Fux became vice-Kapellmeister to the court and Kapellmeister to Wilhelmine Amalia, the widow of Joseph I. With the death of M.A. Ziani, Charles VI appointed Fux to the position of principal court Kapellmeister. Fux occupied this important post until his death in 1741.

Today, Fux is perhaps best known for his counterpoint treatise *Gradus Ad Parnassum*, written in 1725. In this text, written in dialogue form after the works of Plato, Fux outlines the rules of counterpoint according to the usage of Palestrina. In the text, it is Palestrina who plays the role of the teacher Aloisius, while Fux himself is the student. As a composer, Fux wrote many secular works, including both operas and secular oratorios, but he was first and foremost a composer of music for the church. Here, Fux composed in two distinct styles; the stylus a cappella, in which he took the music of Palestrina as his model, and the stylus mixtus. It is this musical conservatism, as both a theorist and composer, that made the music of Fux the culmination of Baroque music in Austria. At the same time, his reliance on contrapuntal technique helped to lay the foundations of Viennese Classicism. *—Stephen Kingsbury*

Overview of Works (ca. 1685–1730)

Johann Joseph Fux (1660–1741) was one of the most distinguished composers at the Viennese imperial court during its most opulent era. He first joined the court around 1683 during the reign of the highly musical Leopold I, later serving both the short-lived Joseph I and Charles VI; the latter appointed him Kapellmeister in 1718, a position he held until his death. His musical style is based on a mixture of the solid background of the old-fashioned contrapuntal style favored at the Viennese court, and more progressive styles assimilated during a visit to Rome in 1700 to study with the influential composer and teacher Bernardo Pasquini.

Although Fux composed some instrumental music, including seven partitas (suites) for wind and strings published in 1701 as *Concentus musico-instrumentalis*, he was particularly renowned for his sacred vocal works. Among these are over 80 masses, some composed in strict polyphonic a cappella style, but the majority of which combine contrapuntal choral elements with Italianate solos and an orchestral accompaniment.

Of equal importance are a large number of dramatic oratorios and sepolcri. The latter are a form of oratorio for Holy Week that appears to have been peculiar to the Viennese court. They were much cultivated by the devout Leopold I, who contributed a number of examples of his own to the genre. Staged works, sepolcri take their name from the opening scene in which a black drape covering of a sepulcher symbolizing Christ's tomb is slowly removed. In earlier examples the characters were all allegorical, but later real personages from the Passion story were introduced, gradually replacing the allegorical characters until the sepolcro became indistinguishable from oratorio. Fux composed at least 15 sepolcri, of which a fine late example of the "pure" type, *Il Fonte della Salute* (1716), has been recorded. In addition to masses, oratorios, and sepolcri, he also composed three requiems and a large-scale festive Te Deum.

Fux's contribution to opera is only marginally less important. All 18 Italian operas conform to the festive and lavishly produced form in favor at court: extravagantly staged works with massive architectural sets, and subject matter that involved some glorification of Emperor and court. The Viennese court operas of Fux and others indeed played an important role in the emergence of opera seria as a dominant form, and it is no surprise to discover that two of the leading "reformers," the librettists Apostolo Zeno and Pietro Metastasio were both employed at the Viennese court during Fux's period as Kapellmeister.

In addition to his musical compositions, Fux was an important theorist whose *Gradus ad Parnassum* (1725) is famous as a bible of the contrapuntal style. Yet for all his conservatism, Fux left a lasting influence on Viennese sacred music, elements of his style being clearly apparent in the more archaic passages of the religious works of Haydn and Mozart. *—Brian Robins*

Recommended:

- ○ **Fux: Il Fonte della Salute** / Haselbock (cond.), Monoyios, Perillo, Chum, Vienna Academy Orch. / CPO 999680-2.2
- ○ **Fux: Requiem** / Clemencic (cond.), Clemencic Consort / 1995 / Arte Nova 27777
- ○ **Fux: Dafne in Lauro** / Clemencic (cond.), Piccollo, Sluis, Akerlund, Klietmann / 1990 / Nuova Era 7345

G

Andrea Gabrieli

b. ca. 1532, Venice, Italy, **d.** Aug. 30, 1585, Venice, Italy
Composer

The Basilica of San Marco in Venice boasted one of the most prestigious musical establishments of the sixteenth century. Adrian Willaert founded a veritable "Venetian School" of composition; it later flowered in the works of Giovanni Gabrieli and Claudio Monteverdi, and maintained its prominence well into the eighteenth century. In addition to the choirmaster/composer, San Marco employed two organists. Beginning with Annibale Padovano, these musicians also established their own internationally recognized school of playing and improvisation. Andrea Gabrieli, though often overshadowed by his nephew Giovanni, contributed mightily to both the composition and organ playing at San Marco early in its musical Renaissance.

Though very little information about his early life survives, it seems evident that Andrea Gabrieli quickly entered the musical profession. His death certificate lists his age as "about 52," leading to a birth date of 1532 or 1533; he was probably born in the Cannaregio quarter of Venice. In the early 1550s, he may have been studying music with Vincenzo Ruffo in Verona; Gabrieli returned to Venice, however, to serve as organist in his old parish church. At the age of 25, he lost a stiff competition to replace one of the San Marco organists (Claudio Merulo won). The next few years of Gabrieli's life remain a mystery. He next surfaces in Germany in 1562, where he was accompanying the Ducal Chapel of Munich—and its director Orlande de Lassus—on a state visit to Frankfurt; Gabrieli's connection to Lassus resulted in both great musical inspiration and splendid political contacts. By 1564, Gabrieli was employed in some capacity at San Marco, finally obtaining a post as organist in 1566, which he retained until his death in 1585.

There are several indices for measuring Gabrieli's vast musical influence. Though he frequently shied away from publishing his music, posthumous editions demonstrate his wide output in every genre of Venetian sacred, secular, and dramatic music. One posthumous print, the *Concerti* (1587), was still influentially selling copies in 1650. In addition to composing music for some of the greatest Venetian ceremonial occasions, Gabrieli's music often was dedicated to highly important figures such as Pope Gregory XIII and bankers such as the Saracini and the Fuggers. Finally, he cemented a musical legacy through his numerous (and in turn influential) students: Lodovico Zacconi and his nephew Giovanni Gabrieli in Italy, and Gregor Aichinger and Hans Leo Hassler, who both traveled from Germany to learn the Venetian style from Gabrieli. *—Timothy Dickey*

Overview of Works (1565–1585)

Along with his more famous nephew, Giovanni, Andrea Gabrieli was a seminal figure in the transition from the polyphonic style of the Renaissance to the more harmonically based style that acted as a bridge to the Baroque. Most authorities agree that the catalyst in the development of his style was his encounter with Orlando di Lassus in Munich. Although younger than Gabrieli, Lassus was already one of the most renowned composers in Europe, a master of every secular and sacred style of the day, and a musical polymath as capable of writing nonsense songs (in German, Latin, French, and Italian) as he was sublime religious masterpieces. His musical language was built on a love of color and sonority coupled with melodic gifts often expressed with relatively simple harmonic support. It seems to have been precisely these qualities that had such a profound influence on Gabrieli, for the works composed after his return to Venice exploit such characteristics to a considerable degree. He also adopted Lassus' diversity, composing an extensive body of secular music that includes both contrapuntal madrigals, and lighter forms such as the villanelle, which he specifically adapted to the taste of Venetian lowlife humor.

But it is for the ceremonial music composed for St. Mark's that Andrea Gabrieli is best known. With its many galleries, St. Mark's was ideally suited to the development of the polychoral style, which involved the spatial separation of groups of both singers and instrumentalists to form multiple choirs. Such writing, although originally introduced by Willaert and others, is inextricably associated with the two Gabrielis, whose antiphonal motets, brilliant instrumental canzonas, and even works exploiting spatially separated organs echoed around St. Mark's in the years preceding Monteverdi's arrival there as maestro. Such works were dependent on vivid contrasts of sonority, but, more crucially, blocks of harmony that fatally undermined the contrapuntal complexities of polyphony. In many of the grandest works of this kind, such as the motet *Omnes Gentes*, set for 16 voices divided into four choirs, Gabrieli achieves a monumental effect of overwhelming grandeur. His organ and harpsichord works are also important for the manner in which they developed a virtuoso keyboard style based on great technical brilliance. *—Brian Robins*

Recommended:

- ○ **A. Gabrieli: Missa Pater Peccavi, Motets, and Instumental Music** / Roberts (cond.), His Majesty's Sagbutts and Cornetts / Hyperion 67167
- ○ **A. Gabrieli: Madrigali e Canzoni** / Cordes (dir.), Weser Renaissance / CPO 999642
- ○ **A. Gabrieli: Psalmi Davidici** / Picotti (cond.), Capella Dvcale Venetia / 2002 / CPO 999863
- ○ **A. Gabrieli: The Madrigal in Venice** / Hollingworth, Blaze, Quinteiro, Devine, Mulroy, Pierron, I Fagiolini, English Cornett & Sackbut Ens. / 2003 / Chandos 697
- ○ **A. Gabrieli: Missa Apostolorum** / Conti (cond.), Cera, More Antiquo / 2001 / Dynamic 361

Giovanni Gabrieli

b. ca. 1555, Venice, Italy, **d.** Aug. 12, 1612, Venice, Italy
Composer

Giovanni Gabrieli is an important transitional figure between the Renaissance and Baroque eras and their associated musical styles. The distinctive sound of his music derived in part from his association with St. Mark's Cathedral in Venice, long one of the most important churches in Europe, and for which he wrote both vocal and instrumental works. Through his compositions and his work with several significant pupils, Gabrieli substantially influenced the development of music in the seventeenth century.

Very little is known about his early years; he probably studied with his famous uncle Andrea Gabrieli, who was also a composer, and organist at St. Mark's. Like his uncle, Gabrieli lived in Germany for several years, and was employed at the court of Duke Albrecht V in Munich from around 1575 until the Duke's death in 1579. Soon after that Gabrieli returned to Italy, and in 1585 became the organist for the Scuola Grande di San Rocco, a religious confraternity; he would hold that post for the rest of his life. That same year (1585), Gabrieli became organist at St. Mark's and, on his uncle's death in 1586, assumed his position as its principal composer (Gabrieli also edited a number of his uncle's compositions for posthumous publication).

At that time, Venice was a very cosmopolitan city and something of a musical crossroads. Much of the city's musical activity centered around St. Mark's Cathedral, which had long attracted many great musicians. The Cathedral's unusual layout, with its two choir lofts facing each other (each with its own organ), led to the development of what has been called the Venetian style of composition—a colorful and dramatic style often involving multiple choirs and instrumental ensembles; many of Gabrieli's motets and other religious choral works are written for two or four choirs, divided into a dozen or more separate parts. Gabrieli also became one of the first composers to write choral works including parts for instrumental ensembles; the motet *In ecclesiis*, as an example, calls for two choirs, soloists, organ, brass, and strings. Gabrieli wrote a number of secular vocal works (most or all of them before 1600), and a number of pieces for organ in a quasi-improvisational style.

Gabrieli composed many purely instrumental works in forms such as the canzoni and ricercari, which had become increasingly popular in the sixteenth century. Several of these were published with some of his choral music in the collection *Sacrae symphoniae* (1597). This publication was very popular all over Europe and attracted for Gabrieli a number of prominent pupils, the best known of which were Heinrich Schütz (who studied with him between 1609 and 1612) and Michael Praetorius. More of Gabrieli's instrumental pieces were published posthumously in *Canzoni e sonate* (1615). Some of these works were particularly innovative: the *Sonata pian e forte* was one of the first documented compositions to employ dynamic markings, and the *Sonata per tre violini* was one of the first to use a basso continuo, anticipating the later trio sonata. His instrumental works are now seen as the culmination of the development of instrumental music in the sixteenth century.

From around 1606, Gabrieli suffered from a kidney stone that reduced his activities, and eventually led to his death. *—Chris Morrison*

Overview of Works (ca. 1585–1612)

Succeeding his uncle and mentor, Andrea Gabrieli, as organist at St. Mark's Cathedral in Venice, Giovannni Gabrieli became one of the most influential composers of the late sixteenth and early seventeenth centuries. His body of sacred works, both choral and instrumental, stand as a reflection of the grandeur of St. Mark's itself, as well as of late Renaissance Venice in general.

Andrea Gabrieli's earliest published works were in a secular vein, composed during his study under Orlando de Lassus at the Court of Duke Albrecht V. One of these, a five-voice madrigal titled *Quand'io ero giovinetto*, appeared in published anthologies of works written under Albrecht's employ. Five madrigals are were also included in a 1587 collection of works by Giovanni's famous uncle, Andrea Gabrieli. Giovanni composed a handful of other secular works throughout his career, for various special occasions. Several of these are wedding commissions: *Sacro tempio d'honor*, for example, was commissioned for the wedding festivities of Francesco di Medici, Duke of Tuscany, while Gabrieli composed *Scherza Amarilli e Clori* on the occasion of a wedding of Nuremburgian nobility.

The lion's share of his compositional output, however, was for church use. His earliest sacred works reflect the influence of his uncle Andrea in the emphasis on chordal, syllabic settings, as well as the use of cori spezzati (divided choirs). *O magnum mysterium*, a work for eight voices from his concerti from 1587, characterizes this period in Gabrieli's career with its elegant but uncomplicated use of split choirs, its straightforward homophonic textures, and its structural symmetries. His subsequent development is exemplified in his two large bodies of choral works, the *Sacrae Symphonie, Liber I* (1597) and *Liber II* (1615). *Liber I* contains over 40 liturgical or otherwise sacred works for choirs of between six and 16 voices, some with instrumental support. Here, one finds Gabrieli engaging more frequently in imitative rather than homophonic writing, and often utilizing vocal texture, rather than harmonies and cadences, to articulate structural points. His use of multiple choirs also becomes more elaborate and involved, often in conjunction with creative integration of multiple instrumental ensembles. The second volume of *Sacrae Symphonie*, published posthumously, shows Gabrieli stretching the boundaries of Renaissance vocal writing, employing more complex imitative textures and introducing more adventurous melodic and harmonic practices. The six-voice motet *Timor et Tremor*, for example, demonstrates a wider variety of rhythmic figures, as well as a forward-looking approach to dissonance and chromaticism.

Gabrieli's instrumental works deserve consideration as well. As organist at San Marco, Gabrieli composed toccatas, ricercars, fantasias, and several organ motets for keyboard and vocal ensemble. His best-known instrumental works, however, are his canzons for ensembles for various sizes. These, like much of his sacred music, emphasized alternating, contrasting musical sections (and utilized the architecture of San Marco) by dividing the ensembles into two or more antiphonal choirs that would have been situated in various positions throughout the performance venue. Among them is the famous *Sonata pian e forte*, the first extant work in musical history to specify dynamics and, in its deliberate exploitation of extreme contrasts of both sonority and dynamics, a work which points forward to the essential elements of the emergent Baroque style. *—Jeremy Grimshaw*

Recommended:

- ○ **G. Gabrieli: Music for Brass Vol. 1** / Crees (cond.), London SO / 1997 / Naxos 553609
- ○ **G. Gabrieli: Canzoni et sonate** / Clemencic (cond.), Fontegara Consort / Tactus 550701
- ○ **G. Gabrieli: Canzonas & Sonatas from Sacrae Symphoniae 1597** / Roberts (cond.), His Majesty's Sagbutts and Cornetts / 1997 / Hyperion 66908
- ○ **Gabrieli in San Marco** / Negri (cond.), Biggs, Gregg Smith Singers, Edward Tarr Brass Ens., Texas Boys Choir, Gabrieli Consort "La Fenice" / 1996 / Sony 62426

Niels Wilhelm Gade

b. Feb. 22, 1817, Copenhagen, Denmark, **d.** Dec. 21, 1890, Copenhagen, Denmark

Composer: Orchestral, Symphonic

A multifaceted musician, Niels Wilhelm Gade was probably the most important figure in nineteenth century Danish music, making his mark as a composer, conductor, organist, violinist, teacher, and administrator. He furthered the careers of many important musicians, among them Edvard Grieg and Carl Nielsen, and played a major role in bringing Scandinavian music to the world's notice.

Both of Gade's parents were musical; his father was a cabinetmaker who turned to making musical instruments. As his family was poor, Gade received no formal music schooling until he was 15. He studied violin with F.T. Wexschall, a violinist in the Royal Orchestra, and theory and composition with Andreas Peter Berggreen. Berggreen was also a noted folklorist and passed along to Gade an interest in Danish folk music and literature. Gade made his debut as a violinist in 1833, and the following year became a junior player in the Royal Orchestra.

His earliest compositions date from his teens. His official Op. 1, the overture *Efterklange af Ossian* (Echoes of Ossian, 1840), was much praised and won Gade a Copenhagen Musical Society prize. When his *Symphony No. 1 in C minor*, Op. 5 (1841–42) was not accepted for performance in Denmark, Gade sent it to Felix Mendelssohn in Leipzig, who loved the work and programmed it in 1843. That same year, Gade was given a government grant that allowed him to travel to Leipzig. He met Mendelssohn, who engaged him as assistant conductor of the Gewandhaus Orchestra and as a teacher at the Leipzig Conservatory. Not surprisingly, many of Gade's compositions of the time, such as the *Symphony No. 3 in A minor*, Op. 15 (1847), strongly reflect Mendelssohn's influence. After Mendelssohn's death in 1847, Gade became principal conductor of the Gewandhaus, but when war broke out between Prussia and Denmark in 1848, Gade returned to Denmark.

Gade was always very much engaged in Copenhagen's musical life: he conducted concerts, played the organ in churches, and provided music for ceremonial occasions. He also founded an orchestra and choir that in later years gave many significant performances, including the premieres of many of Gade's own compositions. In 1852 he married Emma Sophie Hartmann, the daughter of composer J.P.E. Hartmann, and composed two works for her: the *Spring Fantasy*, Op. 23 for voices, piano and orchestra; and as a wedding present, the *Symphony No. 5 in D minor*, Op. 25. She died just a few years later, however, and Gade remarried in 1857. In 1866, he became the director of the new Copenhagen Academy of Music, where for many years he taught composition and music history; among his students was Carl Nielsen. His teaching and administrative schedules allowed him to compose only during the summer months.

Gade specialized in cantatas (or as he sometimes called them, "Koncertstykke") for soloists, chorus and orchestra, many taking their themes from Danish folklore. Perhaps the most popular of these is *Elverskud*, Op. 30 (The Elf-King's Daughter, 1853). His cantata *Psyche*, Op. 60 (1881–82) was written for a Birmingham music festival; by that time Gade was known all over Europe. He ultimately produced eight symphonies, many chamber works and cantatas, and a variety of shorter character pieces and songs. *—Chris Morrison*

Overview of Works (1836–1889)

Niels Wilhelm Gade (1817–90) was the greatest figure in Danish music in the nineteenth century, and his is the only Danish music composed between Buxtehude and Nielsen that is still performed internationally. His earliest successful works were his *Echoes of Ossian Overture* (1840) and his *Symphony No. 1 in C minor* (1842), characterful works of early Romanticism with a sweetness to their themes and a fantasy to their structure that sounds specifically Danish. But when the Danish musical establishment did not accept the innovations of his symphony, Gade sent it to Mendelssohn in Leipzig, where it was premiered in 1843. His *Symphony No. 2 in E major* of the same year was a less individual work as Gade sought to incorporate the language of German Romanticism into his own style. The six subsequent symphonies composed from 1847 through 1871 are progressively stronger works, but Gade's music slowly lost its earlier exuberance. After this, Gade turned for the most part to more overtly expressive and more grandiose choral orchestral works culminating in the enormous *Psyche* from 1882 and *Der Storm* from 1889. *—James Leonard*

Recommended:

- ○ **Gade: Symphonies Vol. 1** / Hogwood (cond.), Danish Radio SO / 2000 / Chandos 9862
- ○ **Gade: Works for String Orchestra** / Frowein (cond.); Cologne Sinfonietta / 1996 / Antes 319088
- ○ **Gade: Octet; Sextet** / BPO String Octet / 2001 / MDG 3081102

ORCHESTRAL

Efterklange af Ossian (Echoes of Ossian), overture, Op. 1 (1840)

Niels Wilhelm Gade enjoyed a musical reputation well known outside of his homeland. Felix Mendelssohn, an early champion of his work, became a close associate. Shades of all the significant composers of the German Romantic style (Schubert, Schumann, Liszt, and especially Mendelssohn) can be heard in Gade's music.

Echoes of Ossian, Op. 1, is a concert overture inspired by a Danish poem about a magical bird. It was Gade's first important work, winning a prize from the Copenhagen Musical Society. The piece is typical of the concert overture sonata form of that time: a slow, soft introduction that presents the principal theme in the minor (the melody is based on an actual Danish folksong); this theme becomes the unifying "glue" throughout as its character is manipulated and transformed in terms of key, rhythm, tempo, instrumentation, etc.; appearance of a contrasting theme in major leads to an exciting development section. Gade's lyrical gift and sense of drama are already in evidence in this compelling composition. *—Mona DeQuis*

Recommended:

- ○ **Gade: Symphony 1; Hamlet Overture; Echoes of Ossian Overture** / Kitajenko (cond.), Danish Radio SO / 1996 / Chandos 9422

○ **King Frederik IX conducts The Danish National RSO** / King Frederik IX (cond.), Danish RSO / 2000 / Dacapo 224158-59

SYMPHONIC

Symphony No.1 in C minor ("On Sjoland's Fair Plains"), Op. 5 (1841–1842)

Niels Wilhelm Gade, a Danish composer, conductor, and teacher of the mid-nineteenth century, enjoyed a lengthy and successful musical career. Gade's theory teacher was Andreas Peter Berggreen, a composer who believed in establishing and preserving a "musical identity" for Denmark by arranging and publishing authentic Danish folk songs. While Gade acknowledged the importance of a clearly defined national style, his own work is deeply entrenched in the German Romantic tradition: echoes of late Schubert, Schumann, and especially, Felix Mendelssohn, one of Gade's greatest champions. So close was the relationship of the two composers that Gade became principal conductor of the Leipzig Gewandhaus Orchestra following Mendelssohn's death in 1847.

Initially rejected by the Copenhagen Music Society, *Symphony No. 1* (the first of eight symphonies) found an ardent supporter in Mendelssohn who conducted its first performance in Leipzig. Several Danish folk songs are utilized as thematic material throughout the four movements. Moderato con moto—Allegro energico starts solemnly, then breaks into a dramatic, confident dotted rhythm, much like Schumann. With the Scherzo: Allegro risoluto quasi presto, one cannot help but be reminded of Mendelssohn's *A Midsummer Night's Dream* and *Symphony No. 4 "Italian."* The Andantino grazioso is extremely Mendelssohnian with its beautifully sustained melody. The Finale: Molto allegro ma con fuoco is infectious in its exuberance and admirable for its skillful thematic development. Related melodic material is used in each movement, giving the work a strong sense of unity, an important feature of the Romantic style. *—Mona DeQuis*

Recommended:

○ **Gade: Symphony 1; Hamlet Overture; Echoes of Ossian Overture** / Kitajenko (cond.), Danish RSO / 1996 / Chandos 9422

○ **Gade: Symphonies 1 & 2** / Schoenwandt (cond.), Copenhagen Collegium Musicum / Marco Polo 9201

Irwin Gage

b. Sep. 4, 1939, Cleveland, OH

Pianist

Based in Germany, the American pianist Irwin Gage has become one of the best-known piano accompanists for German and other lieder singers.

His father was Hungarian and his mother Russian. At the University of Michigan and Yale University, he studied piano, musicology, and literature. He found himself developing a particular interest in art song, which led him to continue his studies in Vienna, where he attended the Akademie für Musik. There his teachers were Hilde Lang-Rulh and Erik Werba. He also had private consultations with Otto Erich Deutsch and Helene Berg. To strengthen his knowledge of French vocal literature he studied in Paris with Pierre Bernac, the great singer and associate of composer Francis Poulenc.

He made a debut in Vienna in 1973 as soloist with the Vienna Philharmonic conducted by Claudio Abbado and occasionally does play solo performances. However, he has found the highest demand for his skills as an accompanist. Among the internationally famous vocal artists who have requested him for their recitals are Arleen Auger, Francisco Araiza, Peter Schreier, René Kollo, Lucia Popp, François Le Roux, Jessye Norman, Gundula Janowitz, Dietrich Fischer-Dieskau, Cheryl Studer, Cornelia Kallisch, Tom Krause, and Julie Kaufmann.

Gage also has a strong interest in continuing the great tradition of lieder recitals, and, therefore, pays close attention to emerging younger singers. It is considered a sign of promise when Gage consents to appear with them in full recitals. Among these younger singers have been Roman Trekel, Matthias Goerne, Dietrich Henschel, Christine Schäfer, Christiane Oelze, Monika Bacelli, Michael Schade, Dagmar Peckova, and Kurt Streit. He is a co-founder and regular participant in the "Freunde des Liedes" series, which, five times a year, presents several young singers. In addition to the German-language lieder repertory (from Beethoven to Hindemith and beyond), he has presented extensive concert series devoted to French and English songs by such composers as Chausson, Poulenc, Vaughan Williams, and recordings of songs by Purcell, Ravel, Dvořák, Debussy, Milhaud, and Sibelius.

He has won several major recording prizes, including the Grand Prix du Disque, the Deutschen Schallplattenpreis, the Edison Prize, and the Gramophone Prize. In 1979 he began teaching classes in lieder interpretation at the University of Zürich. He also conducts master classes in Europe, Japan, and the U.S.

In the recording studio, he has made noted recordings with Elly Ameling, Lucia Popp, Chistine Schäfer, Elisabeth Speiser, Cheryl Studer, Jessye Norman, Christa Ludwig, Tom Krause, René Kollo, Julie Kaufmann, Brigitte Fassbaender, and Gundula Janowitz. On the Arcanta label he has produced two albums of *Songs without Voice* (Lieder ohne Stimme), featuring Brahms and Schubert songs played as piano solos.*—Joseph Stevenson*

Recommended:

○ **Debussy & Chausson: Mélodies** / Schafer, Gage / 2000 / DG 459682

○ **Wolf: Songs to the Poetry of Goethe & Mörike** / Augér, Gage / 1992 / Hyperion 66590

○ **Brahms Lieder** / Fassbaender, Riebl, Gage / 2000 / Arts 47614

Amelita Galli-Curci

b. Nov. 18, 1882, Milan, Italy, **d.** Nov. 26, 1963, La Jolla, CA

Soprano

Amelita Galli-Curci was one of the first female operatic stars of the phonograph. Among the many tributes paid her was one from Compton Mackenzie, the founder of *Gramophone* magazine, who said he could accept old age if he had as many records of Galli-Curci as of Caruso.

Her background was Italian and Spanish. Born Amelita Galli, she was a piano student in a well-to-do musical household. The well-known opera composer Mascagni visited her parents and on hearing her play and sing recommended that she become a singer. After that, Amelita diligently taught herself. She made her debut in 1906 as Gilda in *Rigoletto*, which remained a favorite role, and she took about ten years—a fairly typical amount of time—to become a star. She married the Marchese di Sineri and added his family name of Curci to her own. On her birthday in 1916 she scored a major triumph in Chicago, in *Rigoletto*, that made her an international star.

She had a fluid, clear, very beautiful voice and a great gift for sustaining lyric lines. She was at her best in roles calling for grace, pathos, and happiness and had neither the stage temperament nor the dramatic style needed for fiery, tempestuous parts. She is said to have lacked stage presence. Her voice recorded very well, particularly in the acoustic process, where it was taken down with such clarity and resonance that listeners supposed it was a large-sounding voice, which it was not, in person. The adjective that live listeners used frequently for her voice was "celestial." Her range at her peak was to the E above high C.

During the last days of the acoustic recording era (around 1924) musicians began to notice a curious lack of precision in intonation above the note F. At the same time, the top notes of her range began to lose their penetration. This was at the same time the shift to electrical recording took place. In 1935 it was discovered that she had a goiter, a form of throat tumor that had progressively been closing off the flow of her breath. It was surgically removed, but she never recovered her vocal powers. *—Joseph Stevenson*

Recommended:

○ **Amelita Galli-Curci Recital** / Pasternack, Bourdon (conds.), Galli-Curci, Barone, Lapitino, Berenguer / Opera 54566

○ **Lo! Here the Gentle Lark** / Pasternack, Bourdon (conds.), Galli-Curci, Schipa, Samuels, Victor Orch. / 1996 / ASV 5201

○ **Galli-Curci** / Pasternack, Bourdon (conds.), Luca, Schipa, Lapitino, Berenguer / 1990 / Nimbus 7806

Baldassare Galuppi

b. Oct. 18, 1706, Burano Island, Italy, **d.** Jan. 3, 1785, Venice, Italy

Composer

Baldassare Galuppi, a key figure in the history of Italian comic opera, was for some time known only through his mention in Robert Browning's poem "A Toccata of Galuppi's." Galuppi's father was a barber and violinist who gave his son elementary music lessons. By the age of 16 he had composed an opera, *La fede nell'incostanza ossia Gli amici rivali.* It was a spectacular failure; the curtain had to be brought down before the audience rioted. The puzzled young man went to the composer Benedetto Marcello to try to find out why. The mentor took him to task for daring to write an opera before he was ready, and made him promise not to compose anything for three years, but to undertake study with Antonio Lotti, who called Galuppi his best pupil.

Galuppi went to Florence to work as a harpsichord player in the orchestra of Teatro della Pergola in 1726. He returned to Venice and formed a partnership with a writer friend of his from school, G.B. Peschetti. His second attempt at opera, *Dorinda,*(1729), was a major success. For the rest of his life he averaged about two operas per year, and they were played of Italy's major theaters. In 1740 the Ospedale dei Mendicanti (which included a conservatory) hired him as music director; he established a superb orchestra and church music for the institution. Meanwhile, Galuppi accepted an offer in 1741 from the Earl of Middlesex to write opera seria for his theater in the Haymarket, London. His first effort was moderately well received, and each successive opera was more popular than the last.

On returning to Italy in 1743 he took note of the cutting-edge Neapolitan innovation, opera buffa, and tried his hand at it. After some initial failures these comic operas, too, started to catch on. In 1748 he was appointed maestro of the cappella ducale at St. Mark's cathedral (and in 1762 was promoted to the head position, maestro di cappella, considered the top musical job in Venice). In 1751 the pressure of these positions led him to give up the position at the Mendicanti. His first comic success was *L'Arcadia in Brenta*, to a libretto by Carlo Goldoni, with whom Galuppi forged a partnership. Galuppi's best operas were played widely in Europe, and he was hired to go to Russia as music director of Catherine the Great's chapel. There he inaugurated an Italian dominance of Russian operatic life that lasted until Glinka's time; in addition, he introduced Western counterpoint into the music of the Russian Orthodox Church. Galuppi returned to Venice in 1768, resumed his duties at St. Mark's, and became chorus master at the Ospedale degli Incurabili. He phased out theatrical work, writing more keyboard music, sacred works, and oratorios.

Small in stature, he was described by the touring musical scholar Burney as an "agile little cricket" of a man. Burney also considered Galuppi one of the best operatic composers of the age, and the twentieth century's revival of interest in that era tended to confirm that opinion. His comic operas in particular are built of short, varied vocal phrases, with a strong melodic line and lively rhythms. He was adept at musical characterization and situational thinking. His orchestration was notable; winds mark important moments, and in finales he allowed the flow of string writing to carry the main melodic material while the voices exchange dialogue realistically. Galuppi's keyboard music, including over 130 sonatas, shows a bright, idiomatic, and lively style of writing, and establishes him as a major Italian composer for harpsichord and piano after Domenico Scarlatti. *—Joseph Stevenson*

Overview of Works (1722–1782)

Born on the island of Burano in the Venetian lagoon, Baldassare Galuppi (1706–85) was one of the most important Italian opera composers of the mid-eighteenth century. He initially established a reputation as a keyboard player, playing in opera houses in Venice and contributing occasional arias. From such modest beginnings, Galuppi progressed to a collaborative opera and eventually began to receive commissions of his own from both Venice and, eventually, further afield. By the time of his death he was a renowned figure of not inconsiderable wealth and merited a lavish requiem mass at St. Mark's.

About 100 operas by Galuppi are known, if rarely performed. He was unusual in achieving almost equal success in both the major forms of the day, opera seria and opera buffa. Although it is his innovations in the field of comic opera that are most frequently commented on, he composed more serious than comic operas, setting a number of librettos by such famous librettists in the field as Apostolo Zeno and Pietro Metastasio. Although his earlier opera serie maintain the rigid structure of the long da capo aria with its modulatory repeat of the opening section, after about 1750 Galuppi increasingly sought to simplify it, thus taking the first steps toward the reform operas of Jommelli, Traetta, and Gluck.

His influence on comic opera was even greater. He possessed the traditional Italian qualities of melodic grace and ease, coupled with an ability to express himself lucidly and with charm. His most fruitful collaboration in this area was with the Venetian playwright and librettist Carlo Goldoni, whose ingenious plots are an appealing mix of local situations, intrigue, and sentimental romance. Around 15 of Galuppi's comic operas, which he generally styled dramma giocosa, are set to plots by Goldoni and many of them, such as *Il filosofo di campagna* (1754), achieved fame throughout Europe. One of Galuppi's most important innovations was the introduction of swiftly moving ensemble act finales, a feature taken up and developed by Haydn and Mozart in their operas.

His orchestration is also notable, with clarity of line that largely eschews contrapuntal complexity, and thematic material frequently shared between singer and orchestra. In addition to his operas, Galuppi also composed a number of oratorios and keyboard sonatas, the latter in an easygoing, facile style that underlines his place as a composer whose music belongs more to the pre-classical style than the baroque. *—Brian Robins*

Recommended:

- ○ **Galuppi: Il mondo alla roversa** / Fasolis (cond.), Zanasi, Pennicchi, Dominguez, Serafini, Barocchisti / 2001 / Chandos 676
- ○ **Galuppi: Complete Harpsichord Concertos** / Peiretti (cond.), Accademia Dei Solinghi / 1999 / Dynamic 215/1-2
- ○ **Galuppi: Concerti a Quattro** / L'Offerta Musicale / Tactus 700701
- ○ **Galuppi: Musica Sacra** / Pirona (cond.), Nemeth, Gonzalez, Savaria Baroque Orch. / 2000 / Hungaroton 31828
- ○ **Galuppi: L'amante di tutte** / Fracassi, Campanella, Antonucci, Peirone, Castiglioni, Piacenza SO / 2003 / Bongiovanni 2318

James Galway

b. Dec. 8, 1939, Belfast, Northern Ireland
Flutist

Rivaled in fame among contemporary flutists only by Jean-Pierre Rampal, James Galway has earned both runaway popularity and critical respect. He has embraced the flute repertoire of all eras, including contemporary music. Part of his popularity is due to his sparkling, lively stage personality, which occasionally leads observers to compare him to a leprechaun.

In one interview, piqued by this recurrent comment on his Irishness, he pointed out that he came not from idyllic emerald green surroundings, but from the sooty industrial region of Belfast, within sight of the shipyard where the Titanic was built. He began to play the penny whistle when he was two years old, and he often uses the instrument in his encores. At least one of the concertos written for him also calls for him to substitute whistle for flute in several passages. When he started regular flute lessons, he developed quickly and won three top prizes in a local flute contest just two years later.

At that point Galway decided to make flute playing a career. He studied at London's Royal College of Music and Guildhall School. His first professional job was with the wind band at the Royal Shakespeare Theatre in Stratford-upon-Avon. He then spent 15 years as an orchestral player, most notably as first-chair flutist in the Berlin Philharmonic under Karajan (1969–75). Finally he decided to give up the security of an orchestral job to become a touring soloist and chamber player. In his first season he made 120 appearances. Soon his charm and the rich yet light tone of his gold-plated A.K. Cooper flute were familiar to concert audiences around the world. He also held a teaching position at the Eastman School of Music in the United States.

Galway's success has been due partly to the wide range of his repertoire. He has performed traditional flute repertoire in both orchestral and chamber settings. He is committed to renewing that repertoire through the introduction of new music and has commissioned works from composers including Henri Lazarof, Thea Musgrave, John Corigliano, and Lowell Liebermann. And, though he once stated that he intended to avoid pops or crossover repertoire, he has often released top-selling recordings of this kind. His personality transmits well over television, and part of his unusually wide popularity for a classical musician has come through broadcasts on the BBC and elsewhere. He has participated in Irish music recordings, often with the famous Irish band *The Chieftains* (as on 2002's *Celtic Spectacular*, and in the 1980s he collaborated with the U.S. country singer Sylvia on *The Wayward Wind*. The late 1990s saw the release of such Galway albums as *Un-Break My Heart*, consisting of flute-and-orchestra settings of top cinematic hits, and *Tango del Fuego*, Galway's contribution to the growing tango craze.

In 2001, Galway was knighted by Queen Elizabeth II. He was recently heard on the soundtrack of the film *The Lord of the Rings: The Return of the King*. His wife Jeanne Galway is also an accomplished flutist who has performed together with her husband and on her own. *—AMG*

Recommended:

- ○ **The Lark in the Clear Air** / Galway, Bairn, Fujikake, Boersma / 1994 / RCA 61379
- ○ **Pachelbel Canon and Other Baroque Favorites** / Galway / RCA 61928
- ○ **Annie's Song and Other Galway Favorites** / Galway / RCA 60747
- ○ **60 Years, 60 Flute Masterpieces Vol. 3: Mozart** / Galway, etc. / 1999 / RCA 63435
- ○ **60 Years, 60 Flute Masterpieces Vol. 6: The French Tradition** / Galway, etc. / 1999 / RCA 63438
- ○ **Very Best of James Galway** / Galway, etc. / 2002 / RCA 63950

Lamberto Gardelli

b. Nov. 6, 1914, Venice, Italy, **d.** Jul. 17, 1998, Munich, Germany
Conductor

Although born and trained in Italy, Lamberto Gardelli underwent his most crucial development during the ten years he spent as resident conductor of the Swedish Royal Opera in Stockholm. His work there from 1946 to 1955 coincided with the emergence of several singers who went on to international careers and focused on the Italian repertory for which he achieved his greatest celebrity. Although he failed to achieve the superstar level, he was a conscientious and often galvanizing master of the podium. While his American appearances were far fewer in number than those in Europe, his reputation was secured by his many recordings, all of which reflected his stylish and thorough approach to opera. He was also a notable symphonic conductor, albeit one whose concert appearances took second place to his work in the opera house.

After studying at Pesaro's Liceo Musicale Rossini and further training in Rome, Gardelli was chosen by Tullio Serafin to be his assistant in the Eternal City. Gardelli's 1944 conducting debut was made in Rome at the Teatro Reale dell'Opera in Verdi's *La traviata*. Following other successes in his native country, Gardelli was appointed resident in Stockholm, remaining there until 1955. From 1955 to 1961, he was engaged by the Danish State Radio Symphony where he polished his acquaintance with the symphonic repertory. Gardelli's next appointment was with the Budapest Opera where he continued to conduct for more than three decades. Through this relationship, he came to make a number of recordings, many of them of works in the Italian repertory utilizing casts mixing Hungarian and Italian artists. Under his guidance, a number of Hungarian singers grew into stylistically informed Verdi performers.

Gardelli made his American debut conducting a concert performance of *I Capuleti e i Montecchi* at Carnegie Hall. As a result of the positive impression he made there, he was engaged by the Metropolitan Opera for the 1965–66 season, making his first appearance on January 30, 1966, leading *Andrea Chénier*. A *Madama Butterfly* the following year, though well enough conducted, was all that the Metropolitan had to offer that fitted Gardelli's schedule; he thereafter concentrated on work in Europe.

England also heard Gardelli for the first time in 1964 when he led Verdi's *Macbeth* in a Glyndebourne production. Gardelli's first opera at Covent Garden in 1969 was another Verdi title, *Otello*, shaped with both fire and attention to detail. The conductor became a favored presence in England and his reliability led to his being called upon often to lead recordings. Eventually, his discography grew to encompass such Verdi works as *Nabucco*, *I Lombardi*, *Macbeth*, and *La forza del destino*. His recording of Rossini's *Guillaume Tell* (in French) drew together a strong cast and balanced dramatic force with elegance of expression, both vocally and orchestrally. Gardelli's association with the Hungarian company Hungaroton resulted in important recordings of operas by Respighi, including *Belfagor* (from 1922), *Egiziaca* (1931), and *La fiamma* (1934).

In addition to his podium work, Gardelli was a composer whose oeuvre included symphonic works, lyric pieces, and five operas, the final three of which are portions of a trilogy. Two operas, *Alba novella* and *L'Etrusco*, were written in the 1930s. Of the trilogy—*Il sogno* (1942), *L'impresario delle Americhe* (1959), and *Il demono* (1971)—only the second named was performed during Gardelli's lifetime. It was given a broadcast production for Budapest Television in 1982. —*Erik Eriksson*

Recommended:

- ○ **Rossini: Guillaume Tell** / Gardelli (cond.), Gedda, Caballe, Bacquier, Howel, Royal PO / 1995 / EMI 69951
- ○ **Verdi: Stiffelio** / Gardelli (cond.), Carreras, Ganzarolli, Venuti, Moser / 1989 / Philips 422432

Mary Garden

b. Feb. 20, 1874, Aberdeen, Scotland, **d.** Jan. 3, 1967, Inverurie, Scotland
Soprano

Despite Mary Garden's Scottish birth and return to roots in 1939, Paris and Chicago were the centers of her career as a diva with a difference. In Ronald L. Davis' words, she was "gracious and charming, but above all things, brainy," as much an actress as a singer, "the Sarah Bernhardt of the operatic stage." Her range was formidable. She informed one interviewer that "I have 34 roles in three languages which I have learned completely. Sixteen were written for me." Those 16 did not include Debussy's *Mélisande*, but the composer chose and coached her for the first (and at that time only) performance of *Pelléas* on 20 April 1902, at Paris' Opéra-Comique. Debussy wrote in her score, "You alone will remain the woman and artist I had hardly dared hope for." He also coached and cherished Maggie Teyte later on, but Garden was the original. She introduced *Mélisande* to New York in 1908 (at Oscar Hammerstein's Met competitor, the Manhattan Opera House), and to Chicago at a matinee on 3 November 1910, two days after their new Grand Opera Company debuted in Adler and Sullivan's Auditorium Theater. Garden, noted for her "stillness" as Mélisande, continued to sing the role until 1931, her last year in Chicago, where she reigned for 21 seasons, one of them as "directa" (her coinage) of the notoriously costly season of 1921–22: a $1.1 million deficit.

In 1934, Garden sang her final opera, Alfano's *Resurrection*, fittingly, at the Opéra-Comique. She had debuted there as Charpentier's Louise on April 13, 1900, two months after the premiere, replacing Marthe Rotion, who fell ill after the second act. This, too, became a Garden specialty for the next 30 years. Instantly famous, she created Pierné's *La fille de Tabarin* even before Mélisande. In 1905 Massenet wrote *Cendrillon* for her; Erlanger added *Aphrodite* in 1906. She also performed Gounod's *Marguerite and Juliet*, Verdi's *La traviata*, Puccini's *Tosca*, Montemezzi's *Fiora*, and Honegger's *Judith* (in 1927).

It was Strauss' *Salome*, however, that made her a sensation stateside when she sang it on January 27, 1909, for Hammerstein, in Oscar Wilde's original French. She spent two years learning the role, tried it out in Paris, but didn't become notorious until New York, then Chicago, in November 1910 (where her audience was so scandalized that a third performance was canceled, but played without incident on tour in Milwaukee). She revived *Salome* in 1921, during her "directa" season, but again a third Chicago performance was canceled, although Milwaukee and 12 other cities welcomed it without incident. By then 47, Garden retired the role, although it remained one she "enjoyed the most" along with Mélisande, Louise, Carmen, Février's *Monna Vanna*, and two by Massenet—*Thaïs* and *Le Jongleur de Notre Dame*.

Massenet was in fact the composer she performed most, also singing Manon, Cléopâtre, *Werther*'s Charlotte, *Don Quichotte*'s Dulcinée, *La Navarraise*, and finally Sappho. *Jongleur* was her final Chicago performance, although she returned in 1935 to give master classes, and a lecture tour in 1947. Before retiring to Scotland, she worked in Hollywood as a "technical advisor" on operatic sequences.

Garden was brought to the U.S. as a child—Bridgeport, Connecticut, first, then Chicago where she studied singing until, in 1896, a patron sponsored two years in Paris. When Garden ran out of money, Sybil Sanderson (Massenet's original *Thaïs*) befriended her. But from 1900 on, Mary Garden became the Maria Callas of her era: none less than James Gibbons Huneker (1860–1921) devoted four chapters of *Bedouins* to her in 1920, despite his detestation of Debussy's *Pelléas*! —*Roger Dettmer*

Recommended:

- ○ **Mary Garden Recordings** / Garden / Pearl 9067
- ○ **Mary Garden: The Complete Victor Recordings (1926–1929)** / Bourdon, Shilkret (conds.), Garden, Dansereau, Russell / 1994 / Romophone 81008

John Eliot Gardiner

b. Apr. 20, 1943, Springhead, Dorset, England
Conductor

John Eliot Gardiner is one of the leading conductors in the active "authentic performances" movement in England, performing Baroque music but also extending his range into later repertoire. He first conducted at the age of 15, and after finishing school he studied at King's College, Cambridge. While still an undergraduate, he conducted the combined Oxford and Cambridge Singers on a 1964 tour of the Middle East and founded the Monteverdi Choir, which has consistently performed on his recordings since.

After graduation, he went to Paris to study with Nadia Boulanger and then studied as a postgraduate at King's College, London, with early music leader Thurston Dart. His first notable engagement as a conductor was at a Promenade Concert in London in 1969 and he first conducted an opera in London (Gluck's *Iphigénie en Tauride*) at Covent Garden in 1973.

He had continued conducting the Monteverdi Choir, then founded the English Baroque Soloists, specializing in Baroque music played on original-style instruments. The EBS first appeared at the 1977 Innsbruck Festival of Early Music and has appeared with the Monteverdi Choir on many recordings.

He made his American debut in 1979 leading the Dallas Symphony Orchestra, part of an active and often overlooked aspect of his career: conducting standard repertoire on modern instruments. This included a period as principal conductor (1980–83) of the CBC Vancouver Symphony Orchestra; music director of the Opera de Lyon (1983–88), which included founding an entirely new orchestra; and principal conductor of the North German Radio Symphony Orchestra in Hamburg (1991–94).

He expanded his activities in the original-style instruments movement by recognizing that from the Classical era and well into the Romantic age there were distinctly different instrument designs than those that are standard today. As a result, he founded another new orchestra, the Orchéstre Révolutionnaire et Romantique, to specialize in that period with authentic instruments.

He has also been an active guest conductor, leading major orchestras of the world, including the Cleveland, Berlin Philharmonic, Royal Concertgebouw, Vienna Philharmonic, and Philharmonia orchestras, and has conducted the Puccini opera *Manon Lescaut* at Glyndebourne. He led a cycle of all seven mature Mozart operas and has conducted over 250 recordings on Deutsche Grammophon and Erato labels. He and Herbert von Karajan share the record for the most Gramophone Awards in a single year (three), while Gardiner has won more of them over the years than any other artist. —*Joseph Stevenson*

Recommended:

- ○ **Le nozze di Figaro** / Gardiner (cond.), Terfel, Martinpelto, Mason, Clarkson, Monteverdi Choir, EBS / Archiv 439871
- ○ **Monteverdi: L'Orfeo** / Gardiner (cond.), Otter, Chance, Dawson, His Majesty's Sagbutts and Co., EBS / Archiv 419250
- ○ **Bach: Advent Cantatas** / Gardiner (cond.), Argenta, Johnson, Bär, Lang, Monteverdi Choir, EBS / 1992 / Archiv 463588
- ○ **Mozart: Requiem, KV.626/Kyrie In D** / Gardiner (cond.), Otter, Bonney, Addison, Blochwitz, Monteverdi Choir, EBS / Philips 420197
- ○ **Händel: Messiah** / Gardiner (cond.), Brett, Ross, Robbin, Johnson, Monteverdi Choir, EBS / 1992 / Philips 434297
- ○ **Haydn: 6 Great Masses** / Gardiner (cond.), Brown, Finley, Ziesak, Pregardien, Monteverdi Choir, EBS / 2003 / Philips 000132502
- ○ **Mozart: The Piano Concertos** / Gardiner (cond.), Bilson, Tan, Levin, EBS / Archiv 463111

Denis Gaultier

b. 1603, Marseilles (?), France, **d.** Jan. 1672, Paris, France
Composer: Chamber Music

Denis Gaultier was a leading lute player in Paris in the early Baroque era, and also a notable composer for the instrument.

There were many lutenists with the name Gaultier, or close variants of it. Denis was cousin to Ennemond Gaultier, but related to none of the other prominent Gaultiers. Ennemond was born at Nèves, near Villette in 1575, and died near there in 1651. Ennemond is often referred to as le vieux Gaultier or Gaultier de Lyons, while Denis is called Gaultier le jeune or Gaultier de Paris, so that the two can be distinguished. Even so, during the time that their lives overlapped there is considerable confusion. Ennemond obtained a high appointment around 1600 and became a famous court lutenist and teacher. As the younger Denis quickly became famous, writers of the time did not usually make the effort to identify which they are talking about, so misattributions of their music and events in their lives persist up until the time that Ennemond left Paris to retire in 1631. Things are not made easier for the historian by the fact that both men were in the habit of signing the works with just their surname.

Denis was a pupil of Charles Racquet. He came to Paris as a young man and quickly became well known. He did not seek a court appointment and appears to have made a living as a freelance player and composer and as a teacher. Between Denis and Ennemond, the Gaultiers and a number of the important lute players of the time, including Dufaut, Dubuts, and Charles Mouton, shared mutual admiration.

Denis published two important volumes which, according to their title pages contained only his own music. (These are *La rhétorique des dieux* and *Pièces de luth sur trois differens modes nouveaux*.) However, other publications contain some of the compositions in these books, but attribute them to Ennemond. Denis began *Livre de tablature*, but did not live to complete it. In it, an approximately equal number of pieces are attributed singly either to Denis or Ennemond, but these might be the work of Denis's pupil Montarcis, who completed and edited the book for publication.

Pièces de luth and *Livre de tablature* both begin with a brief instruction manual for playing the lute, of some value in determining playing styles of the period. *La rhétorique* is the most substantial of Gaultier's publications, with compositions grouped into the 12 classical Greek modes.

Ennemond and Denis participated in the elevation of the lute from an instrument used mainly to accompany songs to a solo instrument. Denis was one of the developers of the style brisé of playing, which created the illusion that it was polyphonic. He and Ennemond evidently invented the particularly French form called the tombeau, a slowish piece in allemande rhythm written as a memorial to a deceased person. *—Joseph Stevenson*

CHAMBER MUSIC

Works for Lute (ca. 1669–1672)

It was not always easy for seventeenth century music publishers, patrons, and musicians to tell the lute music of Denis Gaultier from that of his older cousin Ennemond Gaultier—a piece might be attributed to Denis in one seventeenth century volume, but the identical piece to Ennemond in another—and it is not always an easy task today. What is certain beyond any doubt, however, is that these two French lutenist-composers did more to champion the cause of their instrument during that century than any other musician of the day (save perhaps John Dowland across the English Channel, and he didn't make it much more than a quarter of the way through the century).

Two large volumes of lute music attributed to Denis Gaultier were published during his lifetime (both actually contain items that are now thought to be works of Ennemond). The first, *La rhétorique des dieux* (Rhetoric of the Gods), appeared in about 1655; the second, *Pièces de luth sur trois différens modes nouveaux* (Lute Pieces in three different new modes), appeared in ca. 1669. A third volume, *Livre de tablature des pièces de Mr. Gaultier Sr. de Nève et de Mr. Gaultier son cousin* (Tablature Book of Pieces by Mr. Gaultier Sr. of Nève and Mr. Gaultier his cousin), appeared in 1672 (the year of Denis Gaultier's death) and, as its title indicates, contains music by both Gaultiers.

These volumes are filled with suites made up of the courtly dances of the day—pavanes, allemandes, gigues, courantes, sarabandes, for some of which Gaultier supplied descriptive little names (e.g. "Minerve," "Orphée," and "Echo"; Minerva and Orpheus are just two of the mythological characters drawn in the aptly-named *Rhetoric of the Gods*). As composers of the Baroque were wont to do, Gaultier flavors these suites with a variety of non-dance pieces—preludes, chaconnes, and, apparently for the very first time in lute music, funeral tombeaux (one of which, unhappily enough, is a "Tombeau de Mademoiselle Gaultier").

Both Gaultier cousins notated their music in lute tablature, which meant that few non-lutenists could read it. But the influence of the Gaultier lute music can nevertheless be felt throughout the later Baroque years—even after the lute was taken to the brink of extinction. After all, harpsichord composers of the seventeenth century (like Froberger and Böhm) modeled their dance suites explicitly after earlier lute suites, as, by extension, did those of the early eighteenth century (like J.S. Bach), and the Gaultiers were certainly at the top of the lutenist-composer class. *—Blair Johnston*

Recommended:

- ○ **Gaultier: La Rhétorique des Dieux** / Pernot / 1989 / Accord 200702
- ○ **Gaultier: La Rhétorique des Dieux** / Smith / 1976 / Astree 7778

Andrei Gavrilov

b. Sep. 21, 1955, Moscow, Russia
Pianist

A protégé of the great Russian pianist Sviatoslav Richter, Andrei Gavrilov won the 1974 Tchaikovsky Competition, revealing himself as, in the words of Harold Schonberg, "a virtuoso, sometimes an explosive one, who has Horowitz instincts that are not yet under control." Schonberg, reflecting much of the general feeling about Gavrilov, also expressed gratitude for the artist's temperament, an element notably missing from most of his supremely well-schooled, but more cautious contemporaries. In the years since he emerged as such a vivid personality, much remains the same: Gavrilov is still a brilliant artist who does not always command his unquestioned resources, however high the level of excitement. Gavrilov began his musical training with his mother, who stressed the need to search for emotional content in performance. By contrast, his second teacher, Tatiana Kestner, was a product of the German school and emphasized form and musical ideas rather than emotion. His official studies concluded with Lev Naumov, an esteemed pedagogue who imposed some order on his young student's unruly temperament. Winning the 1974 Tchaikovsky Competition thrust Gavrilov into the international spotlight and he soon traveled abroad, first to Europe and, by 1976, to England and America. In spite of certain reservations harbored by critics, the public was ecstatic and responded with standing ovations in venue after venue. Gavrilov appeared with the leading orchestras and undertook a tour of Japan in 1979. While Soviet officials were delighted to show off their newest piano virtuoso, their pleasure was replaced by censure after reports of Gavrilov's critical remarks about the state of music in the Soviet Union reached their attention. Upon Gavrilov's return to Russia after his Japanese junket, he found his career at full stop. Only after a half-decade of intense difficulties and his eventual accommodation to the regime was he be able to resume his overseas appearances. Coincident with his new tours, both the critics and the public were quicker to comment on his eccentricities and exaggerations. Still, those who longed for the strong stamp of personality allied with an often-staggering technique continued to rate Gavrilov highly. Those not fortunate enough to see Gavrilov in person have had available a number of impressive recordings, among them a disc of Chopin's Op. 10 and Op. 25 etudes. His pacing is frequently hair-raisingly brisk, but a sense of poetry is never lacking. While Gavrilov's recording of Rachmaninov's *Piano Concerto No. 3* released shortly after his Tchaikovsky Competition victory was rapturously acclaimed and won numerous awards, a remake with Riccardo Muti was much less successful, sounding like a compendium of the excesses and peculiarities noted in many of the pianist's live appearances. On the plus side again is Gavrilov's recording of Balakirev's tortuous *Islamey*, which is full of sweep, passion, and astonishing articulation. Gavrilov, rather surprisingly, has given some notable performances of Bach: the *French Suites*, concertos, and the *Goldberg Variations* were all committed to disc. After earlier recordings for a major label, Gavrilov was heard on disc in the 1990s as a part of the Edition Monastery Maulbronn. In the new millennium, Gavrilov's live appearances are still dramatic events. Favoring tunics for concert dress, long hair sometimes tied in a ponytail, he remains a highly physical artist, twisting and bobbing at the keyboard, gazing heavenward or staring at the audience. Still intensely Romantic in his playing, he remains a brilliant technician and, frequently, an illuminating artist. *—Erik Eriksson*

Recommended:

- ○ **Andrei Gavrilov** / Gavrilov / 1999 / Philips 456787
- ○ **Gavrilov Plays Scriabin** / Gavrilov / 1984 / EMI 473462
- ○ **Bach: French Suites; English Suite 3; Italian Concerto** / Gavrilov / 1996 / EMI 69479

John Gay

b. Sep. 1685, Barnstaple, Devon, England, **d.** Dec. 4, 1732, London, England
Composer: Opera

John Gay would probably be remembered today as a minor English poet were it not for *The Beggar's Opera*. Scathingly satiric, groundbreakingly original, and inordinately popular, it instantly made Gay one of the most famous composers of his day. Even today, Gay is best remembered for *The Beggar's Opera*, and that masterwork still retains all its power.

Gay attended grammar school as soon as he was old enough, but his parents had both died by 1695, and an uncle took him in until 1702. His poetic gift did not manifest itself immediately, as he apprenticed to a silk merchant in London, returned home briefly and returned to London to work as a secretary. In 1708, however, Gay met Alexander Pope, the greatest poet of his day, and began publishing. Soon he was a member of a famous clique of satirists, the "Martinus Scriblerus Club," comprising not only Gay and Pope, but Jonathan Swift and Dr. John Arbuthnot as well. While most of Gay's output was in the form of satiric poems and essays, he wrote stage works and ballads as well. He found himself involved with London's operatic community when no less a composer than Georg Friederic Handel wrote *Acis and Galatea* using Gay's libretto; it was Handel's first score for an English libretto.

Yet *The Beggar's Opera* still seemed to have come out of nowhere. Gay had invented the "ballad opera" form, in which spoken dialogue is combined with popular melodies, and at the same time produced an outrageous satire in which criminality and vice are celebrated, perhaps not wholly ironically. Even Gay's friends were not sure of its merit, and Gay had difficulty in getting it staged. Finally, John Rich at Lincoln's Inns Fields (one of the two major theaters) reluctantly decided to risk production. *The Beggar's Opera* was first performed on January 29, 1728, and Gay was soon a very famous and rich man. Audiences flocked to hear tales of real inhabitants of the underworld, rather than the two-dimensional figures which populated most operas. These audiences also appreciated the arias, which set words they could understand to tunes they knew. The opera contained attacks on opera itself (Handel's opera *Rinaldo* was raided for a heroic march which the thieves sing just before setting out for an evening of robbery), English jurisprudence, and conventional ideas of morality; Gay's not-very-subtle attacks on Horace Walpole and his government, however, were what caused Walpole to ban Gay's sequel to *The Beggar's Opera*, *Polly*. *Polly* was unperformed until 1779, when audiences were bewildered by the then-topical references in the text. It never achieved the renown of *The Beggar's Opera*. Gay composed one more ballad opera, *Achilles*, but it too was unsuccessful commercially and artistically.

Still, Gay had become a major figure in English literature on the basis of his one stunning success, and when he died, he was buried in the Poet's Corner at Westminster Abbey. Even after Gay's death, however, the ballad opera form he invented lived on, influencing the development of the singspiel of Wolfgang Amadeus Mozart and the much later genre of the American musical. The playright Bertolt Brecht and the composer Kurt Weill paid Gay the ultimate compliment by using his plot and most of his characters in their update of Gay's work, *Die Dreigroschenoper* (*The Threepenny Opera*). *—Andrew Lindemann Malone*

OPERA

The Beggar's Opera (1728)

The Beggar's Opera was the biggest hit of the eighteenth century, surpassing all other operatic and entertainment productions in popularity and in box office receipts. It brought wealth to the producer and author and was responsible for the birth of the first musical comedy stars. These included Lavinia Fenton, who later married a duke, and the famous Kitty Clive, grand dame of comedy of the London stage. *The Beggar's Opera* started a rage for ballad operas of all kinds, and even contributed to the emergence of singspiel in Germany. When revived in the twentieth century, *The Beggar's Opera* also drew an extensive audience and inspired such works as Kurt Weill's *Threepenny Opera*.

It was revolutionary in its conception. Although other plays had included ballad songs, this one made use of 69 tunes, most of them preexisting and known to the audience by other titles and with other words. Most of these were originally contained in Thomas D'Urfey's collection called *Wit and Mirth: or Pills to Purge Melancholy*. This included tunes originating in England, France, and Italy; some were composed by Purcell, others by Eccles, and they were sung with words about events with which everyone in England was familiar. Of the tunes that don't come from D'Urfey's *Pills*, there are melodies by Handel, Bononcini, Frescobaldi, Geminiani, and more. The sprightly overture and bass line accompaniments for the songs were written by Dr. Pepusch, but it is said that Gay himself picked out the song tunes and interpolated them into his riotously funny satire on British life.

The main characters in his play come from Newgate; they are all thieves, whores, highwaymen, and vagabonds, many inspired by famous criminals of the time. In addition to showing the extent of crime and poverty in London at the time, Gay uses his characters to satirize the upper echelons of British society, especially the licentious and thieving prime minister Sir Robert Walpole. A poor beggar, the supposed author of the work, introduces the play.

Gay's wit is sharp, and there are few stones left unturned. He heavily satirizes the ever popular Italian opera seria conventions and helped bring about the decline of Italian opera in London as a result. Gay invents a reprieve for Macheath, in imitation of the contrived happy endings of the Italian genre. He makes sure to include a series of simile arias of the Italian type which compare the singer to a flower, bee, ship, etc. As *The Beggar's Opera* opens, Gay's Beggar assures the audience that Polly and Lucy, his two leading ladies, have exactly the same amount of music and the same number of lines, a reference to the feud between Faustian and Cozen, two prima donnas at the Royal Academy of Music at the time. Lawyers are given their fair share of barbs, and injustice is sung of by the major criminals in the play. Murder is discussed as a business expediency, and the plight of women is also taken up. *—Rita Laurance*

Synopsis:

Prologue. The Beggar introduces himself to one of the players as a sometime poet. He tells the audience that the work was originally meant to honor the wedding of two ballad singers, and that just for them, he has included simile arias, just like the ones composed for Italian operas. He has also included a Prison Scene, also standard Italian opera fare, and plenty of pathetic music for the ladies. In fact, all the details of the Italian opera have been observed except for the Recitative, which he has left out for the sake of the drama. He then calls for the beginning of the overture, and exits.

Act One. Scene one introduces Peachum, head of a vast gang of thieves. He is studying his book of accounts when Filch enters with the latest news of all the rogues. As Mrs. Peachum enters, he begins to discuss the fate of one Bob Booty. Mrs. Peachum argues on behalf of the men for, she says, there has not been a murder in seven months. Mrs. Peachum mentions that their young Polly looks to be in love with Macheath. Mrs. Peachum takes Filch to her own room, there to ply him with cordials and learn the gossip about Polly and Macheath. When Polly enters, Peachum tells her that he doesn't mind her trifling with customers, but that he will slit her throat if he finds that she has married. Mrs. Peachum enters in a rage and announces that the wench has gone and gotten married. Peachum counsels Polly to murder her husband and thus gain whatever fortune he possesses. While Polly insists that she loves Macheath, her parents tell her that she is a shame to all womankind. Polly exits, but overhears the two Peachums decide to have Macheath "peach'd" the very next session.

At the end of the act, Polly tells Macheath that he must flee. After words of tender love, they part.

Act Two. In a tavern near Newgate, members of Peachum's gang are sitting around having drinks and talking. Macheath enters, and Matt of the Mint invites him to go speak with some passengers on the Western Road, but Macheath says he must keep out of Peachum's way. Matt suggests that they give out that Macheath has quit.

Macheath, alone, contemplates the foolishness of women. He sends for all of his lady friends. Musicians strike up a dance, and a song follows. He entertains all of his lady friends. They put their arms about Macheath's neck to give him a kiss, but make signs to Peachum and the constables, who are waiting outside. Macheath is taken into custody.

At Newgate, Turnkey and Lockit make Captain Macheath welcome in the jail. As Macheath sings of his plight, Lucy Lockit enters. She is both Macheath's mistress and the daughter of the jailer, and she already knows of his affair with Polly Peachum. He insists that he is still unmarried.

Meanwhile, Peachum is negotiating a fee for having betrayed Macheath. The government, it seems, is broke, and Peachum complains that he cannot afford to turn in his own men for nothing. He and Lockit enter into a bitter argument and threaten to have each other hung. Lucy enters whimpering, and pleads for Macheath. Macheath asks Lucy to offer her father some money, for he is sure that a bribe will free him. She promises to help him when Polly Peachum enters. Polly throws her arms about Macheath and wails that all is lost. Lucy Lockit steps forward, and both women begin to argue over him. Macheath tells Polly to quit pretending that they are married. Finally, Peachum arrives and drags Polly away with him. Macheath assures Lucy that he is faithful, and that Polly is merely fantasizing. He convinces her to help him escape by stealing the keys from her father while he is asleep.

Act Three. When he discovers that Macheath is gone, Lockit becomes suspicious of Lucy. She finally confesses that she helped him out of love, even though she is convinced that he is truly married to Polly Peachum. Filch and Black Moll, two of Peachum's gang, are in the next room. Lockit discovers from them Peachum's whereabouts and vows to learn all he can so that he can recapture Macheath. Meanwhile, Macheath is off with other gang members arranging times and places to gather and pick pockets.

Peachum is back at the warehouse for all of his stolen goods. With Lockit, he is looking over his accounts. Lockit counsels Peachum to watch Polly carefully. For between Lucy and Polly, they should be able to capture Macheath again. Mrs. Diana Trapes, a good customer of Peachum's, brings news of Macheath's whereabouts, and they promise her good deals on any stolen goods.

Back at Newgate, Lucy is torn apart by jealousy. Filch and Polly enter. Polly and Lucy seem to make up and reconcile. Each thinks that the other is better loved by Macheath. Lucy offers her a drink (with poison in it), but Polly drops it to the floor when the news arrives of Macheath's recapture. Polly and Lucy both set upon Macheath in distress and then plead to their fathers for Macheath, but Peachum and Lockit assure them that he is to die that very day.

Macheath has a moving prison scene in which he sings of his plight, and then Polly and Lucy again set upon him. Four more women enter, each with a child in tow, and Macheath desperately decides that he is more than ready to die. Just then, one of the players enters and objects to the ending. Why, if Macheath were to be hung, that would make this opera a downright tragedy! So a reprieve is invented, and all ends with a merry dance and song. *—Rita Laurance*

Recommended:

- ○ **Gay: Beggar's Opera** / Barlow (cond.), Daniels, Thompson, Walker, Honeyman, Broadside Band / 1991 / Hyperion 66591
- ○ **Gay: Beggar's Opera** / Sargent (cond.), Sinclair, Brannigan, Morison, Wallace, Pro Arte Orch. / 1995 / EMI 68926

○ **Gay: Beggar's Opera** / Barlow (cond.), Elliott, Kwella, Broadside Band / HM 901071

Severino Gazzelloni

b. Jan. 5, 1919, Roccasecca, Italy, **d.** Nov. 21, 1992, Camino, Italy
Flutist

This remarkable flutist and teacher was just as much at home with contemporary music as with the classics. He began his studies as a pupil at the Conservatorio di Santa Cecilia in Rome. He was the flute soloist of the Symphony Orchestra of RAI (Italian Radio) in Rome and became internationally known as an exponent of avant-garde music who premiered a vast repertoire of new works. He was the first to record flute music by Evangelisti, Luciano Berio, Matsudaira, Castiglioni, Messiaen, and Bruno Maderna. Many musicians consider him one of the greatest flutists, and many composers have dedicated compositions to him. He performed with many contemporary ensembles, including Pierre Boulez's groups, and with avant-garde pianist Aloys Kontarsky. Likewise, Gazzelloni was well ahead of his time in featuring a range of Baroque music, including Vivaldi's flute concertos, in his performances. *—"Blue Gene" Tyranny*

Recommended:

○ **Vivaldi: Complete Flute Concertos** / Gazzelloni, Steinberg, I Musici / 1996 / Philips 454256

○ **Severino Gazzelloni Plays Nino Rota** / Gazzelloni / CAM 006

Nicolai Gedda

b. Jul. 11, 1925, Stockholm, Sweden
Tenor

Nicolai Gedda—possessor of one of the widest-ranging repertoires ever, phenomenal technique, and a bright, resonant voice with clarion high notes and a seductive mezza voice—had one of the finest singing careers of the twentieth century. He excelled in music of English, French, German, Italian, Russian, American, and Swedish composers, and was equally adept in traversing styles from the Baroque to the contemporary; he was as noted a performer of oratorio and songs as of opera. His performances were masterpieces of authentic style, from language and diction to phrasing. While performing Samuel Barber's *Vanessa*, in which he created the role of Anatol, critics consistently acclaimed his diction as the finest in the cast, even though he shared the stage with Rosalind Elias and Eleanor Steber—both native speakers of English.

Gedda's father was Russian, his mother Swedish, and in 1929 his parents moved to Leipzig, where his father became cantor and choirmaster of a Russian Orthodox Church. As a child he sang in the church and performed Russian songs at weddings and parties. Having no wish to remain in Germany as the Nazi party rose to power, the family returned to Sweden in 1934.

As a teenager, he developed a strong ambition to become an opera singer, but unable to come up with the money to fund his studies, he became a bank teller, though he continued to participate in singing competitions. A wealthy bank client who was also an instrumentalist with the Stockholm Opera happened to hear Gedda mention his aspirations, and asked Karl-Martin Oehmann, a music teacher who had himself been an operatic tenor, to take him on as a pupil. Gedda later credited the development of his spectacular technique to Oehmann's teaching. Shortly thereafter, he won the Christine Nielsson Scholarship, which enabled him to begin music studies at the Stockholm Conservatory as a full time pupil in 1950.

In 1952, Gedda's recording and performing careers began simultaneously. Walter Legge, the famous producer for EMI, was in Sweden, and agreed to audition some of the students. He was immediately bowled over by Gedda's voice, musicianship, and technique; given that Gedda spoke fluent Russian, he signed him on the spot to take on the role of Dmitri in his upcoming recording of *Boris Godunov*, starring Boris Christoff—all despite the fact that Gedda had yet to make his stage debut (which came only a short time later, in a production of Adolphe Adam's *Le Postillon de Lonjumeau*)! This began a lifelong association with EMI.

He made his La Scala debut in the 1952–53 season as Don Ottavio (Mozart's *Don Giovanni*), and Carl Orff asked him to create the role of the Bridegroom in *Il Trionfo dell'Afrodite*; his Paris Opera debut in 1954 was as Huon in Weber's *Oberon*, and his Covent Garden debut in 1954 was as the Duke of Mantua. These were soon followed by debuts at Salzburg (Don Ottavio, 1957) and the Metropolitan Opera (*Faust*).

His life-long association with EMI has made him one of the most widely-recorded tenors, though in the compact disc era, EMI has been rather dilatory in re-releasing many of his recordings.*—Ann Feeney*

Recommended:

○ **The Very Best of Nicolai Gedda** / Gedda, etc. / 2003 / EMI 85090

○ **Lehar: Das Land des Lächelns; Die lustige Witwe** / Ackermann (cond.), Schwarzkopf, Gedda, Kunz, Loose, London PO / Angel 67529

○ **Massenet: Werther** / Prêtre (cond.), Los Angeles, Gedda, Benoit, Mesplé / 2003 / EMI 62630

Francesco Geminiani

b. Dec. 5, 1687, Lucca, Italy, **d.** Sep. 17, 1762, Dublin, Ireland
Composer: Concerto

Geminiani was an important and influential Italian violinist, composer, and theorist. During his life, he was overshadowed by Corelli, Handel, and Vivaldi, and he is still relatively obscure today in spite of the great originality and beauty of his compositions and his considerable place in music history's march. Geminiani, a student of Corelli, expanded the art of violin playing to a level previously thought unattainable. Many of the techniques he introduced or developed are now part of the standard technique of the violinist. Likewise, his practical treatises on music inspired numerous successors. The most important one, *The Art of Playing on the Violin* (1751), was the first instruction manual addressed to advanced players from a professional viewpoint, as opposed to a primer for beginners. His *The Art of Accompaniment on the Harpsichord* is likewise unique for its point of view, being framed from the soloist's perspective rather than the accompanist's. Geminiani published a number of other treatises on harmony, guitar playing, and further aspects of violin playing. As a composer, Geminiani accomplished little in the way of structural innovation. Mostly, he followed Corelli's models in his numerous sonatas and concertos, but his music is generally richer, harmonically somewhat more complex, and substantially more difficult to play than that of his former teacher, with a certain free and creative flair. The underestimation of his influence was not just a result of the Romantic eclipse of all things Baroque, but began even in his own day: Geminiani somehow incurred the critical wrath of the most influential British music writer of the day, Charles Burney.

Geminiani was born in 1687 and began his studies in Milan, but he encountered his most important teachers, Corelli and Alessandro Scarlatti, when he moved to Rome. Before 1714, he held several posts in Italy, including those in Lucca and Naples, but met with little success. In 1714, his career took a sharp turn upward when he moved to London. He quickly met with acclaim as a virtuoso performer and soon earned ongoing support from several influential patrons. Between 1716, when his Op. 1 violin sonatas were published and 1726, when his arrangements of Corelli's sonatas were published as Op. 5, little is known of Geminiani's whereabouts or activities. From 1727 through the middle or late 1740s, Geminiani continued to live in London, making several trips to Ireland and publishing more sonatas and concertos. He was also most active during this time as a soloist and conductor. Although he continued to perform occasionally, his later years were spent primarily in teaching and writing and publishing his various treatises. In 1759, he moved to Dublin, and he returned to England only once more before his death in 1762.*—Steven Coburn*

Overview of Works (ca. 1716–1754)

Born in Lucca, Italy, Francesco Geminiani (1687–1762) was a pupil of Archangello Corelli, one of the most important and influential violinists of his day. In 1714, Geminiani arrived in London, at that time a mecca for many Continental musicians attracted by lavish private patronage and a thriving public concert life; he remained there for the rest of his life, while making several visits to Dublin, where he died.

Like his master Corelli (and highly unusual for this time period) Geminiani's output is wholly devoted to instrumental music. His first publication was a set of *Violin Sonatas*, Op. 1 (1716), works that he reissued in revised form in 1739; this process of consistent revision was to be a hallmark of Geminiani's work as a composer. His first major published collections are two sets of six concerti grossi, Op. 2 (1732) and Op. 3 (1733), which established him as a major composer.

Although Geminiani had received the tutelage of Corelli and his music superficially shares many of the characteristics of the great Roman master, he was no slavish imitator of his teacher; he was a highly individual and at times even eccentric composer, fond of piquant harmonies and unusual textures. He departed from Corelli's model for the concerto grosso by scoring his own for a solo or concertino group consisting of a quartet (two violins, viola, and cello), rather than the trio (two violins and cello) favored by the older composer and many of his followers, Handel included. At the same time, Geminiani's orchestra (ripieno) has only two violin parts and bass to support the concertino. This rather odd disposition leaves the solo viola with no orchestral support, but results in a richness of texture that is one of the defining features of his style. He also favored contrapuntal writing to a greater degree than Corelli, as, for example, in the opening Allegro of *Concerto grosso No. 3 in E minor, Op. 3*, earning the praise of the historian Charles Burney, who although somewhat ambivalent toward Geminiani, praised his "skill in diversifying the parts."

A third set of original concertos (Geminiani had also issued a set arranged from Corelli's *Violin Sonatas*, Op. 5) followed in 1746, the scoring now expanded to include violas in the ripieno. In 1756, a larger-scale orchestral work, music for a staged pantomime, *The Inchanted Forrest*, was given at the Tuileries in Paris and published shortly afterwards. In addition to concertos, Geminiani published a number of chamber sonatas, of which the fine set of *Six Cello Sonatas*, Op. 5 deserves particular attention. In addition to his musical works, he also published a number of theoretical treatises that provide valuable primary source material for modern scholars. Of these, the most important is *The Art of Playing the Violin* (1751), which was addressed to advanced players and became extremely influential. —*Brian Robins*

Recommended:

○ **Geminiani: Concerti Grossi, Op7** / Brown (cond.), Academy of St. Martin-in-the-Fields / 1990 / ASV 724

○ **Geminiani: Concerti Grossi, Vol. 1** / Krcek (cond.), Istropolitana Capella / 1997 / Naxos 553019

○ **Geminiani: 6 Sonatas for cello, Op5** / Simpson, Spieth / Solstice SO 034

○ **Geminiani: Pièces de Clavecin** / Bonizzoni / 2001 / Glossa 921504

CONCERTO

Six Concerti Grossi, Op. 3 (1732; revised 1755)

Geminiani's first set of concertos had merely been arrangements of violin sonatas by his teacher Corelli. By the time of his Op. 3 collection, though, Geminiani is clearly his own master, although still steeped in the practices of Corelli. Geminiani follows the usual concerto grosso format, with a small solo group, the concertino, playing off the main body of strings with keyboard continuo, the ripieno players. But his figurations, harmonies, and textures are rather eccentric compared to Corelli's smoother models. Furthermore, he takes the unusual step of adding a viola to the concertino ensemble, filling out its texture, but neglects to provide for a viola section in the ripieno group. A 1755 revision corrects this "oversight," but musicians today tend to prefer Geminiani's original version.

In all but the fourth concerto, Geminiani adheres to the standard slow-fast-slow-fast pattern of movements. His part-writing is full and complex for the period, leading some contemporaries, notably Charles Burney, to complain of "confusion" resulting from the busy, dissimilar lines for each instrumental section. Also striking is Geminiani's habit of moving through an unlikely sequence of harmonies along the way to establishing or reestablishing the tonic key. Meanwhile, especially in the fast movements, Geminiani tends to rely on jagged, emphatically repeated little motifs in the manner of Domenico Scarlatti. The music sounded remarkably wild in its time.

Highlights among the six concertos include the virtuosic writing for the solo group, particularly the violin, in the first concerto; the relatively (and unusually) independent viola writing in the last movement of the second concerto; the imaginative contrapuntal material in the fast movements of the third concerto (including a four-part fugue on a chromatic subject); and the dramatic harmonic swings of the second movement of the fifth concerto, ranging through B flat major, C minor, D minor, and even F major along the way to the home key of G minor. —*James Reel*

Recommended:

○ **Geminiani: Concerti grossi, Op3** / Biondi (cond.), Europa Galante / 1997 / Opus 111 30172

Valery Gergiev

b. Sep. 21, 1953, Moscow, Russia

Conductor

Valery Gergiev emerged in the 1980s as one of the most exciting new conductors, particularly of opera and ballet, and has maintained and enhanced his reputation ever since. He is also known for the rather gruff, unshaven appearance he cultivates. Born in Moscow to Ossetian parents, he showed tremendous musical talent in early childhood. Deciding while still in his teens that he wanted to become a conductor, Gergiev entered the conducting class of Ilya Musin at the Leningrad (now St. Petersburg) Conservatory. In 1975 and still a student, he won the All Union Conductors' Competition in Moscow in 1975. The following year, Gergiev won the Herbert von Karajan Conductors' Competition in Berlin. In 1977, the 24-year-old Gergiev was appointed assistant conductor at the Kirov Opera under Yuri Temirkanov. He made his debut the next year, conducting Prokofiev's immense opera *War and Peace*. This and other exciting opera performances marked the arrival of an extraordinary conductor. In 1981, Gergiev became director of the Armenian State Orchestra, conducting widely throughout the Soviet Union. He was appointed music director of the Kirov in 1988, when Temirkanov left to take over the Leningrad Philharmonic. Starting his tenure at the Kirov with immense energy and enthusiasm, Gergiev developed the company's orchestra to the point that it rivaled the famed Philharmonic. As director of the Mariinsky Theater (the historic home of the Kirov Opera and Ballet companies), he organized a successful annual Stars of the White Nights festival in St. Petersburg.

Gergiev has traveled widely, taking the Kirov companies all over the world. During the 1997–98 season, for example, Gergiev conducted several Kirov productions, including Mussorgsky's *Boris Godunov* at the Théatre des Champs-Elysées in Paris and Borodin's *Prince Igor* at the Metropolitan Opera in New York. His subsequent engagements included a production of *Boris Godunov* at the Met. Following his North American debut in 1991, when he conducted a San Francisco Opera production of *War and Peace*, Gergiev has led major opera companies and symphony orchestras around the world. Known for fiery performances of Russian repertoire, he is also an acclaimed interpreter of more standard fare. Appointed principal guest conductor of the Metropolitan Opera in 1997, Gergiev is also principal conductor of the Rotterdam Philharmonic Orchestra. In addition, he is in charge of numerous festivals, including the Rotterdam Philharmonic/Gergiev Festival, the Mikkeli International Festival in Finland, the Peace to the Caucasus Festival, and the Red Sea International Music Festival in Eilat, Israel. Gergiev's many CD and video recordings include the classical Russian opera repertoire; symphonic works by Rachmaninov, Shostakovich, and Borodin; as well as the complete Prokofiev piano concertos. —*Joseph Stevenson*

Recommended:

○ **Prokofiev: Love for Three Oranges** / Gergiev (cond.), Diadkova, Pluzhnikov, Kit, Akimov, Kirov Chorus & Orch. / 2001 / Philips 462913

○ **Stravinsky: Rite of Spring; Scriabin: Poem of Ecstasy** / Gergiev (cond.), Kirov Chorus & Orch. / 2001 / Philips 468035

○ **Tchaikovsky: Nutcracker** / Gergiev (cond.), Kirov Chorus & Orch. / 1998 / Philips 462114

○ **Tchaikovsky: Sleeping Beauty** / Gergiev (cond.), Kirov Orch. / 1993 / Philips 434922

○ **Shostakovich: Symphonies 5 & 9** / Gergiev (cond.), Mariinsky (Kirov) Theater Orch. / 2004 / Philips 000248702

Roberto Gerhard

b. Sep. 25, 1896, Valls, Spain, **d.** Jan. 5, 1970, Cambridge, England

Composer

The first major Spanish musician to ally himself with Arnold Schoenberg and the Second Viennese School, Catalan composer Roberto Gerhard nevertheless developed a wholly individual musical language that drew equally from serial techniques, traditional tonal syntax, and the powerful Spanish tradition into which he was born. Born in 1896 to a family of Swiss origin, Gerhard showed evidence of musical skill at an early age. Although his parents were not supportive of his wish to make a serious study of music (and even sent him away to Switzerland to discourage him from this course), by age nineteen Gerhard was studying privately with two of the most prominent Spanish musicians of the early twentieth century: pianist Enrique Granados and composer Felipe Pedrell. Gerhard's work with Granados was cut short by the latter's tragic death aboard the H.M.S. Sussex (which was torpedoed by a German U-boat in 1916), but he continued to study with Pedrell until 1922, when, in an effort to broaden his musical horizons, he relocated to Vienna.

In Vienna, Gerhard found his way into Schoenberg's circle, of which he remained an active part (even moving to Berlin when Schoenberg was made a professor in that city) until his return to Barcelona in 1929. Gerhard was offered a position on the faculty of the Ecola Normal de la Generalitat in 1931, and from 1932 on was a member of the Advisory Council to the Catalan Minister of Fine Arts. Although performances of his music at International Society for Contemporary Music festivals throughout the 1930s had begun to earn Gerhard a more international reputation as a composer, the outbreak of civil war in 1938 and subsequent defeat of the Republican forces (of which Gerhard was a supporter, having even served on the Central Music Council of the Spanish Republican Government in 1937) forced Gerhard to flee the country. He eventually found his way to Great Britain.

Gerhard remained virtually unknown to the musical public of his adopted country for the next 15 years, and even the majority of British composers were unaware of his presence at Cambridge (where Gerhard had been offered a research scholarship by Cambridge historian and musicologist Edward Dent). By the mid-1950s, however, further ISCM performances and the premiere of his *Symphony No. 1* in Baden-Baden (1955) resulted in an increased awareness of Gerhard's merits as a composer; from 1960 until his death in 1970 he served as visiting professor and composer-in-residence at universities and festivals around the globe (including the Tanglewood Music Center and the University of Michigan). He was made a Commander of the Order of the British Empire (C.B.E.) in 1967 and a Fellow of University College, Cambridge the following year.

Gerhard's earliest music, such as the *Seven Haiku for voice and chamber group* (on the strength of which he earned a place in Schoenberg's class) show a wide range of influences. By the end of Gerhard's time with Schoenberg he had begun to assimilate certain serial ideas; pieces like the *Wind Quintet* of 1928, however, show Gerhard's reluctance to use strict 12-tone techniques. It would not be until the 1950s that Gerhard fully synthesized his own very textural and atmospheric style with a more rigorous 12-tone underpinning. After his emigration to Great Britain in 1939, Gerhard made most of his income composing scores for various television, film, theater and radio productions; the composer's lighter side can be seen in a group of arrangements he made (under a pseudonym) of Spanish popular tunes in 1943. —*Blair Johnston*

Overview of Works (1914–1969)

Catalan composer Roberto Gerhard started his compositional life as a student of Granados and his earliest works, the song cycle *L'infantament meravellós de Schahrazada* (1919) and a piano trio (1919), were written in the Spanish popular style with florid melodies, piquant but tonal harmonies, bright colors, and a rhythmic pulse that underlays—and to a large extent controls—all of the other compositional elements. Rather than continue in this vein or gravitating to Paris as many Spanish composers of his generation had, Gerhard decided to continue his musical education by studying composition with Arnold Schoenberg, first in Vienna and later in Berlin. During the five years (1923–28) he spent with Schoenberg, Gerhard not only learned how to compose with 12 tones related only to each other—Schoenberg's serial method of composition—but more importantly, Gerhard heard all manner of modern music. Although the music he composed after he returned to Barcelona in 1929 was not always harmonically organized along serial lines, Gerhard's fundamentally Spanish style was infused with modernist elements. His ballets of the 1930s, *Ariel* (1934) and *Soirées de Barcelone* (1936–1938), were Spanish in their rhythmic drive, but their more angular melodies and more dissonant harmonies placed them in the larger context of modernism. Gerhard's sympathies with the Republican Government forced him to leave Spain after Franco's victory in 1939 and he eventually settled in Cambridge, England, where he spent the rest of his life. During his first decade in his adopted country, he continued to compose music on Spanish subjects in a Spanish style, but this style was becoming more and more amalgamated with Gerhard's international modernism. The two key works from this period, the ballet *Don Quixote* (1940–41) and the opera *The Duenna* (1945–47), retained Spanish rhythms and melodies, but Gerhard's harmonies and structures transformed them into surface aspects of the scores and not their deep musical essence. In the works of his maturity, Gerhard's style became an combination of highly stylized Spanish rhythms, serial harmonies and structures, an almost anathematic concept of melody, and an expansively colorful percussion-based orchestration. The principal works of Gerhard's maturity and the works upon which his posthumous reputation rest are the five symphonies—the *First* (1952–53), the *Second* (1957–59), the *Third ("Collages")* (1961), the *Fourth ("New York")* (1967), and the *Fifth* (1969)—plus the *Concerto for orchestra* (1965), the *Epithalamion* (1966), and the oratorio *The Plague* (1963–64) based on Camus. In these works, Gerhard perfected a wholly modernist symphonic style that is at once intellectually rigorous in its form and yet still rhythmically exciting and brilliantly colorful. *—James Leonard*

Recommended:

- ○ **Gerhard: Symphony 1; Violin Concerto** / Bamert (cond.), Charlier, BBC SO / 1998 / Chandos 9599
- ○ **Gerhard: Symphony 3** / Bamert (cond.), Tozer / 1997 / Chandos 9556
- ○ **Gerhard: Symphony 4; Pandora Suite** / Bamert (cond.), BBCSO / 1999 / Chandos 9651
- ○ **Gerhard: Symphony 2; Concerto for Orchestra** / Bamert (cond.), BBCSO / 1999 / Chandos 9694
- ○ **Gerhard: Piano Trio; Cello Sonata; Chaconne; Gemini** / Balding, Cole, Lissimore, cantamen / 1996 / Metier 92012
- ○ **Gerhard: Cancionero de Pedrell; Pandora Suite; Alegrías Suite; Haiku** / Benet / HM 901500

German Bach Soloists

f. 1960

Ensemble

The German Bach Soloists are a world-renowned instrumental, and sometimes vocal, ensemble that specializes in performing the works of Johann Sebastian Bach. The group has also recorded works by composers such as Georg Philipp Telemann, Joseph Fiala, Domenico Scarlatti, in addition to violin concertos of Mozart. Although the ensemble does not limit itself only to Bach, it programs music mostly from within the confines of the Baroque period. The German Bach Soloists consists of professional players mostly from Germany.

German conductor and oboist Helmut Winschermann founded the chamber orchestra Deutsche Bachsolisten (German Bach Soloists) in 1960. A longtime professor at the Staatlichen Hochschule für Musik and Detmold College of Music, Winschermann was named an honorary member of the Royal Academy of Music in London in 1995. Winschermann has led the German Bach Soloists since its beginning. With Winschermann conducting, the ensemble has toured regularly to several continents throughout the world. Occasionally guest conductors have stood in Winschermann's place, such as conductor Wolfgang Gönnenwein, who has led several choirs and ensembles in Stuttgart. Also, conductor Klaus Martin Ziegler has made some recordings with the chamber ensemble.

Many of the German Bach Soloists' recordings are on the Laserlight budget label, although certain selections may be found on Philips Classics. The German Bach Soloists are quite excellent in their realm of specialization, appealing to most audiences who love the Baroque and similar music. *—AMG*

Recommended:

- ○ **Bach: Brandenburg Concertos 1–4 & 6** / Winschermann (cond.), Deutsche Bachsolisten / 1993 / Laserlight 14131
- ○ **Mozart: Violin Concertos 3–5** / Winschermann (cond.), Altenburger, Deutsche Bachsolisten / 1988 / Laserlight 15525

George Gershwin

b. Sep. 26, 1898, Brooklyn, NY, **d.** Jul. 11, 1937, Hollywood, CA

Composer: Concerto, Orchestral, Opera, Vocal, Film Music, Keyboard, Chamber Music
Pianist

The great musical border crosser of the twentieth century, George Gershwin excelled in the fields of concert music and popular song alike. The son of Jewish immigrants from Russia, he was born Jacob Gershvin in Brooklyn on September 26, 1898. His father ran a great variety of small businesses, and George, in the words of the New Grove Dictionary of Music, "excelled at street sports." He also studied the piano and was introduced to the European classics by his teacher, Charles Hambitzer.

Gershwin immersed himself in popular music after dropping out of school in 1914 and getting a job as a salesman for the music publisher Remick. He was influenced by ragtime and stride piano music, and as a songwriter enjoyed his first hit in 1920 with "Swanee," recorded by the leading vocalist of the time, Al Jolson. Gershwin and his brother Ira became one of the great creative teams in the history of music, each attuned to the considerable subtleties of which the other was capable. Their 1924 musical *Lady, Be Good* gained wide familiarity thanks to its hit song, "Fascinating Rhythm." Gershwin also wrote works for the concert hall: *Rhapsody in Blue* (1924), best known in an orchestration by Ferde Grofé; the *Piano Concerto in F* of 1925; and 1928's *An American in Paris* have been audience favorites since their respective premieres. Probably Gershwin's most famous work was the uncategorizable *Porgy and Bess*; "folk opera" was an early attempt at description. Set among African-American residents of Charleston, South Carolina, *Porgy and Bess* includes the song "Summertime," heavily recorded by both popular and classical artists.

Gershwin continued to write popular songs and musicals; 1930 brought the successful show *Girl Crazy* and its catchy yet strikingly complex hit number "I Got Rhythm." The 1932 show *Of Thee I Sing* was especially notable for its crackling political satire. Gershwin went to Hollywood in 1936 to write for the RKO film studio. In mid-1937 he began to complain of headaches, but doctors chalked his symptoms up to stress. In reality he was suffering from a brain tumor; he died on July 11, 1937.

The question of Gershwin's status as a classical composer is a live and productive one. Some observers have pointed out the strong resemblances between his popular and concert idioms, and it is certainly true that for all his studies of the classics over the years, Gershwin rarely wrestled with the problem of large-scale form, which one might regard as classical music's most definitive quest. His concert pieces consist of sequences of great melodies—perhaps expected in a piece called a "rhapsody" but less impressive for music aspiring to the status of "concerto" or even "tone poem," as *An American in Paris* was classified. Yet it was not only the American public that loved Gershwin's concert works. They were widely performed in Europe, where they shaped the jazz inflections that began to creep into the music of such composers as Maurice Ravel. Even the proponents of the difficult 12-tone system admired Gershwin's music: Gershwin hobnobbed with Alban Berg in Paris and played tennis with Arnold Schoenberg in Hollywood. "It seems to me beyond doubt that Gershwin was an innovator," Schoenberg wrote, and perhaps history will judge Gershwin as the first harbinger of a new music neither classical nor popular, drawing techniques from many sources and forms of musical knowledge. Who could ask for anything more? *—AMG*

Recommended:

- ○ **Gershwin plays Gershwin** / Whiteman (cond.), Gershwin, Paul Whiteman Orch., Van Eps Quartet / 2000 / Naxos 8120510
- ○ **Kickin' the Clouds Away** / Gershwin, Pollock / 2000 / Klavier 77031
- ○ **Rhapsody in Blue** / Tilson Thomas (cond.), Gershwin (piano roll), Jones, Vaughan, Gaffney, Simpkins, New York PO, Los Angeles PO, Buffalo PO, Columbia Jazz Band / 2004 / Sony 93018

CONCERTO

Concerto in F, for piano & orchestra (1925)

Gershwin successfully combined the sweep and mood of the typical Russian concerto with the blues, jazz, and rag elements he brought from his successful pop music career. And why not? His family had recently immigrated from Russia when he was born in 1898. He had, of course, been immensely successful as a pop tune composer and as a Broadway show composer before he wrote this 1925 concerto. It was, specifically, the success of his *Rhapsody in Blue* which led Walter Damrosch and the New York Symphony Society to commission this concerto. Gershwin resolved to orchestrate it himself (Grofé had done both the jazz band and the symphonic arrangements of the rhapsody.) Even if he had to delve into textbooks to learn orchestration and even to discover what the form of a concerto might be, he created an entirely successful work. Although some critics thought the concerto was derivative of Debussy and other composers, it is in fact a remarkably original and personally characteristic work for being any composer's first unassisted piece.

Gershwin was not ready for formal innovation; the three-movement form of the concerto is in fact textbook. The introduction is fresh, breezy, and contemporary, based on the rhythm of the very popular dance *Charleston* by James P. Johnson. A bassoon introduces the sprightly first theme, while the piano itself has the warm-hearted contrasting theme. Throughout the movement—and the concerto as a whole—the themes have jazz-like syncopations and make liberal use of the "blues scale."

The second movement is remarkable for its muted trumpet theme, a nocturnal, wistful tune with the potential to haunt the memory. It is contrasted with an upbeat, strolling theme on piano. The form of the movement is reminiscent of the slow movement of Dvořák's *New World Symphony*, and possesses the same kind of passionate outburst shortly before its conclusion.

A virtual fanfare for timpani, cymbals, and bass drum launches the highly energetic finale in rondo form. Like many of the fast themes of the whole concerto, its main subject makes good use of aggressively repeated notes. There is a lyrical theme which manages not to slow things down, initially. Gershwin recollects the second theme of the first movement and yet another melodic idea for muted trumpet with strings. Gershwin ends this high-energy romp with a brief coda. *—Joseph Stevenson*

Recommended:

- ○ **Music for Moderns, Vol. 1** / Whiteman (cond.), Bargy, Paul Whiteman Orch. / 2000 / Naxos 120505
- ○ **Levant Plays Gershwin** / Kostelanetz (cond.), Levant, New York PO / 1987 / CBS 42514
- ○ **Gershwin: Orchestral Works** / Fiedler (cond.), Wild, Boston Pops Orch. / 2001 / RCA 68019

Rhapsody in Blue, for piano & orchestra (1924)

George Gershwin's *Rhapsody in Blue*, arguably the most popular work for piano and orchestra written by an American, came about almost by accident. Toward the end of 1923, popular bandleader Paul Whiteman asked Gershwin if he'd consider writing a jazz concerto for his orchestra. Gershwin informally agreed to do so and returned to his regular beat of writing songs for Broadway shows. Imagine Gershwin's surprise on January 4, 1924, when his brother Ira brought along that day's edition of the *New York Evening Herald*, wherein Whiteman announced that George's jazz concerto was to be premiered at a program at New York's Aeolian Hall entitled "An Experiment in Modern Music" on February 12. This was barely more than a month away. The four-stave manuscript of *Rhapsody in Blue*, now in the Library of Congress, records that George began work on the piece on January 7, 1924. It was done by February 4, 1924, when arranger Ferde Grofé ordered the orchestral parts be made up in time for rehearsals. Then as now, it was standard procedure for a Broadway composer to use an orchestrator, and Grofé was then producing most of the Whiteman band's original arrangements and leading the rehearsals. George had other help, too: Ira suggested he use the slow second theme based on a melody already composed, and Victor Herbert advised George on some of the transitional material used to hold the movement together. Whiteman clarinetist Ross Gorman improvised the famous clarinet glissando that opens the work as a gag during rehearsals and George asked him to keep playing it that way. The title, *Rhapsody in Blue*, is not so much related to the final form of the piece as it was inspired by a painting of James McNeil Whistler entitled *Nocturne in Black and Gold*. The premiere of *Rhapsody in Blue* was a huge success and it was clear at the outset that the work had enormous commercial potential. Grofé created three more orchestrations of it—the first being a 21-part version for theater orchestra that became the standard text of the work for the next two decades. Grofé didn't create a version for full orchestra until 1942, and this is now the version that is most familiar and most frequently recorded. About this time, Grofé created yet another incarnation of *Rhapsody in Blue* for symphonic band in which the piano part is optional. *—Uncle Dave Lewis*

Recommended:

- ○ **Levant Plays Gershwin** / Ormandy (cond.), Levant, Philadelphia Orch. / 1987 / CBS 42514
- ○ **Gershwin: Rhapsody In Blue** / Fiedler (cond.), Wild, Boston Pops Orch. / 1997 / BMG 68792
- ○ **Gershwin: Rhapsody in Blue** / Tilson Thomas (cond.), Gershwin (piano roll), Columbia Jazz Band / 2004 / Sony Classical 93018

Variations on "I Got Rhythm," for piano & orchestra (1934)

Gershwin's famous tune "I Got Rhythm" (from the 1930 musical "Girl Crazy") was not only among the most popular of his hits with the public, but seems also to have become one of the composer's own favorites as well. It is well known that whenever he was attending a party, Gershwin would gravitate toward a piano and improvise on his own tunes. "I Got Rhythm" quickly became one of the tunes he used most often, but we have *Porgy and Bess* to thank for this published work for piano and orchestra. Gershwin took on extra work—a radio program and an extended tour—to earn money and clear the decks so that he could devote his time to that opera. In 1932 he prepared formal piano versions of some of his songs (collected as *George Gershwin's Song-Book*), and two years later he made an orchestral version that drew on his experiments-in-performance with "I Got Rhythm." Each variation decks the theme out in a new mood and new sound, even one that seems to spoof stereotypes of "Chinese" music. In one variation the song is transformed into a wholly new, broad melody. Gershwin at the time was in the midst of one of his periodic stretches of study of classical composition, and there are many nicely finished touches that make these variations into something beyond a notated improvisation. Fifteen minutes long, the work is often used as a companion to the *Rhapsody in Blue* and is an attractive addition in its own right to the canon of Gershwin's concert works. *—Joseph Stevenson*

Recommended:

- ○ **Gershwin: Orchestral Works** / Fiedler (cond.), Wild, Boston Pops Orch. / 2001 / RCA 68019
- ○ **Gershwin: Levant Plays Gershwin** / Levant, etc. / Sony 47681

ORCHESTRAL

An American in Paris, tone poem (1928)

After the stunning successes of Gershwin's *Rhapsody in Blue* (1924) and the *Piano Concerto in F* (1925), Walter Damrosch, then conductor of the New York Philharmonic, was anxious to capitalize on the young composer's growing fame. He requested a work from Gershwin for a first performance in Carnegie Hall in mid-December of 1928. Gershwin had journeyed to Paris and was thoroughly immersed in the mood of the French capital. He brought back authentic Parisian taxi horns, which were used as an integral part of the work. The piece is a true tone poem, inspired by extra-musical considerations—the sights, sounds, and moods of Paris. Deems Taylor, the 1920s composer and critic, furnished a blow-by-blow program for the piece from which I quote a brief excerpt: "You are to imagine an American visiting Paris, swinging down the Champs-Elysées on a mild sunny morning in May or June.... Our American's ears being open as well as his eyes, he notes with pleasure the sounds of the city. French taxicabs seem to amuse him particularly." Although he claimed not to have a program in mind when he wrote the work, Gershwin did sketch his own general scenario: "[A]n opening section, in which an American visitor strolls about Paris and 'absorbs the French atmosphere,' is followed by a rich blues with a strong rhythmic undercurrent," representing an episode of homesickness on the visitor's part. But the American overcomes his spell of depression and once again revels in the sights and sounds of Paris. "At the conclusion," according to the composer, "the street noises and French atmosphere are triumphant."

A three-part form is discernible in the composition. The slow middle section includes the famous "homesickness blues" solo by the trumpet, later interrupted by a Charleston-like, highly rhythmic figure also played by the trumpet. The harmonies in this work are spiced with stacked-third sonorities: ninth, eleventh, and thirteenth chords. Gershwin admitted that some influence of Debussy bore on the work, and indeed impressionistic passages can be heard in the section before the unforgettable bluesy trumpet solo. Readers interested in an in-depth analysis should consult Steven E. Gilbert's *The Music of Gershwin* (Yale University Press, 1995). While there are innumerable recordings of the work available, the most authentic one (although it lacks good sound) is the first one, made on February 4, 1929, with Nathaniel Shilkret conducting the Victor Symphony Orchestra (Victor 39563 and 39564; RCA AVM1-1740); this recording was available (as of 1999) in the Smithsonian Institution's 4-CD album titled *I Got Rhythm: The Music of George Gershwin*. Gershwin played the celeste part on this recording and obviously was present for the session, presumably indicating that Shilkret's interpretation was acceptable to the composer. *—Norbert Carnovale*

Recommended:

- ○ **Gershwin: Rhapsody in Blue; Concerto in F; American in Paris** / Previn, London SO / 1998 / EMI 66943
- ○ **Classic Gershwin** / Bernstein (cond.), New York PO / 1987 / CBS 42516

Catfish Row, symphonic suite (from "Porgy and Bess") (1935–1936)

The *Catfish Row Suite* is Gershwin's own purely instrumental adaptation of selected scenes from his opera *Porgy and Bess*. There are several named sections. The first, "Catfish Row," opens with the opera's overture and includes the "Jasbo Brown Blues" for solo piano. The movement continues with "Summertime," whose melody is assigned to various solo instruments in the orchestra. "Porgy Sings" commences with "I Got Plenty of Nuttin'" in the banjo and continues with "Bess, You is my Woman Now." The "Fugue" is the one used as background music during the fight between Porgy and Crown and to accompany the ultimate death of Crown. "Hurricane" is extracted from the opening of Act Two, Scene Three; a lyrical English horn-and-string melody is followed by a terrifying depiction of the storm. "Good Morning, Brother," also called "Occupational Humoresque," includes "Good Morning,

Brother," "Sure to Go to Heaven" (Children's Song), and the opera's finale, "Lord, I'm on my Way."

According to Edward Jablonski, "Though a scissors-and-paste job, Gershwin's suite is a carefully thought out musical précis of the score. He extracted five sections and bridged them successfully in an impressive compendium including many instrumental passages that had been jettisoned in Boston...." The work also confirms that Gershwin, who was sensitive to criticism of his compositional skills and had set out to prove his abilities in *Porgy and Bess*, was both capable and imaginative as an orchestrator.

Composer Robert Russell Bennett also prepared a suite from the opera (*Porgy and Bess: A Symphonic Picture*) which has enjoyed far more frequent performances than Gershwin's own suite.

The *Catfish Row Suite* was first heard on January 21, 1936, in a performance by the Philadelphia Orchestra at the Academy of Music. *—Norbert Carnovale*

Recommended:

○ **Gershwin: Works for Piano & Orchestra** / Slatkin (cond.), St. Louis SO / 1990 / Vox 5007

○ **Gershwin 100th Birthday Celebration** / Tilson Thomas (cond.), San Francisco SO / 1998 / RCA 902668931

Cuban Overture (1932)

George Gershwin was inspired to produce the colorful *Cuban Overture* by a vacation in Havana. A nonstop whirl of dancing and revelry drew the composer's attention to the particular rhythmic and instrumental characteristics of the rhumba. In addition to the Overture's more traditional orchestral forces, Gershwin calls for maracas, bongos, claves, and a guiro, directing in the score that they "be placed right in front of the conductor's desk." The Overture is a brilliant orchestral showpiece. Gershwin himself provided commentary for the work:

"In my composition I have endeavored to combine the Cuban rhythms with my own thematic material. The result is a symphonic overture which embodies the essence of the Cuban dance. It has three parts: the first part (Moderato e Molto Ritmato) is preceded by a (forte) introduction featuring some of the thematic material. Then comes a three-part contrapuntal episode leading to a second theme. The first part finishes with a recurrence of the first theme combined with fragments of the second. A solo clarinet cadenza leads to a middle part, which is in a plaintive mood. It is a gradually developing canon in a polytonal manner. This part concludes with a climax based on an ostinato of the theme in the canon, after which a sudden change in tempo brings us back to the rumba dance rhythms. The finale is a development of the preceding material in a stretto-like manner. This leads us back once again to the main theme. The work concludes with a coda that features the Cuban percussion instruments."

The Overture received its first performance as part of an all-Gershwin concert by the New York Philharmonic, conducted by Albert Coates at Lewisohn Stadium, on August 16, 1932. Editions of the Overture for both piano duet and piano duo have also been published and recorded. *—Norbert Carnovale*

Recommended:

○ **Gershwin: Complete Orchestra Collection** / Kunzel (cond.), Cincinnati Pops Orch. / 1998 / Telarc 80445

○ **Gershwin: Rhapsody in Blue; American In Paris; Porgy & Bess** / Maazel (cond.), Cleveland Orch. / 2003 / DG 473844

OPERA

Porgy and Bess (1935)

As the most embracing form of musical expression, opera could not fail to lure a composer of Gershwin's large ambitions. After a furiously paced apprenticeship mastering Broadway song-and-dance musical comedy formulas, from the mid-1920s—from *Rhapsody in Blue* (1924) on—Gershwin, working closely with his lyricist brother, Ira, composed to books which allowed greater scope for music. The sheer, Dionysian éclat of the dance music and generous, captivating melody lavished upon *Lady Be Good* (1924), *Oh, Kay* (1926), *Funny Face* (1927), and *Girl Crazy* (1930) enlarged the stick figures of their farcical plots into genuine characters. *Strike Up the Band* (1927, revised 1930), *Of Thee I Sing* (1931), and *Let 'em Eat Cake* (1933) already have operatic scope, and human dimension which only their coruscating satire holds in check. As early as 1922, in the one-act opera *Blue Monday*, Gershwin had shown a flair for drama with a confident mingling of pop, blues, and jazz, though it was unmatched by literary discrimination; and his scintillant score is undone by a ridiculous book. Through the late 1920s, he toyed with the notion of an opera on American Indian themes and even sketched one on a Jewish folk tale, *The Dybbuk*.

A reading of Southern poet DuBose Heyward's novel *Porgy*, in 1926, and a Theatre Guild production of Heyward's stage adaptation the following year, tantalized Gershwin, though the play's success and the composer's numerous other commitments delayed work on an operatic version until February 1934. In the course of an intense correspondence, Heyward and Gershwin, with Ira contributing lyrics, shaped the stage version into a musical conception. In June, Gershwin visited Charleston, staying for several weeks in a cottage on Ferry Island to absorb the African-American ambience from which Heyward had drawn his locale and characters. Back in New York by July 21, he continued hasty composition as he fielded new commitments and began thinking ahead to production and cast. Todd Duncan and Anne Brown were signed for the title roles, with the erratic but brilliant John W. Bubbles tapped for the central part of Sportin' Life. Composition was completed on August 23, 1935, and orchestration by September 2. The Boston tryout on September 30, 1935, garnered enthusiastic notices and a 15-minute ovation, but also frightened its producers by playing over three hours. In the upshot, some of the work's most original and dramatically revealing numbers were cut. By the time it opened on October 10 at New York's Alvin Theatre, *Porgy and Bess* hovered between the grand opera Gershwin had conceived and an over-elaborate musical, provoking mixed critical responses. Worse, audiences thinned drastically after the opening, and the show, though it played for 124 performances, lost money. Only in the last quarter of the twentieth century were Gershwin's intentions honored and his dramatic genius vindicated, prompting the conductor Lorin Maazel to note that "Gershwin's compassion for individuals is Verdian, his comprehension of them, Mozartean. His grasp of the folk-spirit is as firm and subtle as Mussorgsky's, his melodic inventiveness rivals Bellini's...."

Porgy and Bess revolves around the residents of Catfish Row, where drugs, violence, and hard times form a backdrop for a story of love between the title characters: Porgy—a poor cripple—and Bess, who finds herself alone after her lover, Crown, kills a man while gambling and then flees. The most famous moments from the score include "Summertime," which is sung by Clara to her baby at the opening of the opera; "Bess, you is my woman now," a duet between the two lovers; "My man's gone now," sung by the widow of the murdered gambler; and "I got plenty o' nuttin," Porgy's joyful anthem to simplicity. The choral numbers are unfailingly appealing. *—Adrian Corleonis*

Synopsis:

Act One. The opera opens on Catfish Row in Charleston. Some of the inhabitants are dancing, some of the men are playing craps, and Serena sings the lullaby, "Summertime" to her baby. Jake laughingly warns the baby that "A woman is a sometime thing." Some of the men sneer at Bess, Crown's latest lover, and when he defends her, tease the lame Porgy that he's in love with Bess. But he denies it, saying God meant him to be alone. Crown and Robbins fight over the game, and Crown kills Robbins, escaping in the subsequent tumult. Sportin' Life, the local drug dealer, takes the opportunity to try to persuade Bess to leave with him, but she rejects him. She tries to seek shelter with the other women, but they shut their doors. However, Porgy opens his door to her.

In Serena's room, she is holding a wake for Robbins. Neighbors are gathering to pray and collect money for a funeral. Porgy enters with Bess and leads a prayer, and Serena laments her husband's death ("My man's gone now"). A pair of white detectives come in and tell Serena to bury the body the next day, and, without any grounds, drag Peter off. After they leave, the undertaker agrees to bury Robbins although there isn't enough money to pay in advance. Bess leads a spiritual, "Oh, the train is in the station."

Act Two. The second act also opens on Catfish Row. Porgy and Bess are now lovers. As the men work, Porgy describes his happy life ("I got plenty o' nuttin"), pitying rich folks who are terrified of losing their wealth—all the things that he prizes are free. Maria chases Sportin' Life away from her shop ("I hates yo' struttin' style"). The cheerful mood is disrupted by a buzzard flying overhead, and the residents perceive it as a sign of coming misfortune ("Boss, dat bird means trouble"). Sportin' Life again tries to persuade Bess to leave with him, but Porgy frightens him off. Porgy and Bess sing of their love ("Bess, you is my woman now"). Rather than go to the big picnic on a nearby island, she wants to stay with him, but he tells her to go have fun, for her and himself. On Kittiwah Island, Sportin' Life sings ("It ain't necessarily so"), putting his cynical spin on biblical stories and expressing his own skepticism. Crown is in hiding on the island, and, catching Bess alone, half-forces, half-persuades her stay with him.

A week later, Jake ignores the signs of an impending storm and gets ready to go fishing. Bess has been ill, but the community is looking after her, and she is recovering. Bess admits to Porgy that she promised Crown she would return, and Porgy promises to help her ("I loves you, Porgy"). In Serena's room, after the storm has broken out, everyone is praying. Crown bursts into the room. He scandalizes everyone by mocking their prayers with the irreverent ("A red-headed woman"). Clara sees Jake's boat overturn, and only Crown will go to help. Clara rushes out, asking Bess to take care of her child.

Act Three. On Catfish Row once again, the women are mourning Clara's, Jake's, and Crown's deaths, but Sportin' Life tells them that Crown is still alive. They all leave, and from Porgy's room the voice of Bess is heard. Crown, seriously injured, comes onstage and goes to find Bess, but Porgy strangles him. Later, the police have no evidence but demand that Porgy view the body. He refuses, believing that a corpse will bleed in the presence of its murderer, and he is taken to jail. Bess is desolate and laments that "My man's gone now." Sportin' Life again tries to persuade her to leave with him, painting a glamorous picture of the life they would lead together in Harlem ("There's a boat that's leaving soon for New York"). Again she turns him down, but he leaves a package of "happy dust," drugs, on the doorstep. She waits for him to leave, then emerges and takes the package. A week later, Porgy returns, released for lack of evidence, which he credits to his closing his eyes when they made him look at Crown. Increasingly agitated at her absence, he asks where Bess is ("Oh, Bess, oh where's my Bess"), and they finally tell him she has left for New York with Sportin' Life. Even though they tell him New York is a thousand miles away, he gets into his goat-drawn cart and heads out to find her ("Oh, Lawd, I'm on my way"). *—Ann Feeney*

Recommended:

- ○ **Gershwin: Porgy & Bess** / Rattle (cond.), Marshall, White, Clarey, Simpson, London PO / 1980 / EMI 56220
- ○ **Gershwin: Porgy & Bess** / Engel (cond.), Fisher, Matthews, Williams, Carroll / 1998 / Sony 63322
- ○ **Gershwin: Porgy & Bess** / DeMain (cond.), Houston Grand Opera / 1977 / RCA 2109

VOCAL

Songs (1916–1937)

George Gershwin's songs make up the major part of his overall output, measure for measure matching and probably exceeding the amount of music he composed for "serious" purposes. Gershwin's songs are a mixed bag; some are mini-masterworks known to nearly everyone, yet some others are badly dated relics, revived only by specialists. The best of them, particularly the ones written with his brother Ira Gershwin, are every bit as significant as Gershwin's works for the concert hall.

Very early Gershwin songs, such as "When You Want 'em, You Can't Get 'em; When You've Got 'em, You Don't Want 'em" (1916) demonstrate that his basic approach to songwriting was in place from the beginning. He favored building his main theme out of a short, repeated melodic patterns varied with a subtly changing harmonic underpinning. Then Gershwin would wed this to a release phrase that sort of "sums up" what went before. Gershwin scored his first hit in 1920 when his song "Swanee" (1919; written with Irving Caesar) proved a big number for Al Jolson in the show *Sinbad*.

Apart from an isolated instance in 1918, George Gershwin did not collaborate with his older brother, lyricist Ira Gershwin, until the show "*Lady Be Good*" (1924). Once the brothers Gershwin started working together the team proved inseparable. Ira's lyrics utilized sophisticated, urbane and witty turns of phrase, often making use of a rhyme within a line ("maybe Tuesday will be my good news day"), a technique that proved a perfect complement to George's short, repetitive musical ideas. In "Lady Be Good" the brothers Gershwin also first worked with dancer Fred Astaire, a suave and genteel personality with only a limited vocal ability, but whose relaxed sense of phrasing and delivery seemed a perfect fit for the Gershwins' words and music. During the latter half of the 1920s the Gershwins experienced a run of hit Broadway shows including *Tip Toes* (1925), *Oh Kay!* (1926), *Funny Face* (1927), *Strike Up the Band* (1927; 1930) and *Girl Crazy* (1930). Most of the evergreens associated with the Gershwins originate in this period, such as "Fascinating Rhythm," "'S Wonderful," "Embraceable You," "Someone to Watch Over Me," "But Not for Me," and "I Got Rhythm." The classic Gershwin torch song, "The Man I Love" (1926) was not attached to a specific show, being inserted into several less than successful productions, but became a hit on its own terms.

Of Thee I Sing (1931), a biting contemporary political satire, was awarded the Pulitzer Prize for drama in 1932, the first musical so honored. It also proved a turning point for the Gershwin's partnership and its relation to Broadway, as their subsequent efforts were mostly failures. The Gershwins collaborated with author DuBose Heyward on the opera *Porgy and Bess*, opening to a mixed response in 1935; but in terms of songs the work resulted in "Summertime." Though technically an opera aria, "Summertime" remains the most popular and frequently recorded of all the songs written by the Gershwins.

In 1936 the Gershwins moved to Hollywood in hopes of improving their fortunes. Ira loved Hollywood, and George hated it; nonetheless the last songs that the team wrote together, mostly for Fred Astaire, were among the finest they produced: "They Can't Take That Away from Me," "Let's Call the Whole Thing Off," "Nice Work If You Can Get It," and "A Foggy Day." George's sudden death at age 38 didn't entirely end the collaboration with Ira; some later films utilized unused George Gershwin melodies with new Ira Gershwin lyrics added, and in other cases Ira added new lyrics to unsuccessful Gershwin melodies already used for other purposes. These posthumous efforts, though well-intentioned, added little of value to the Gershwins' reputation, but in George's lifetime they had already created a body of songs that are among the most naturally expressed, sparklingly witty and beloved body of song produced in America. *—Uncle Dave Lewis*

Recommended:

- ○ **He Loves & She Loves: Songs & Duets of George Gershwin** / Kaye, Sharp, Blier / Koch 7028
- ○ **It's Wonderful: Tribute to George Gershwin** / Hendricks, Bateman (cond.) / 2001 / EMI 57049
- ○ **Gershwin: Songs & Piano Music** / Morris, Bolcom / Nonesuch 79151
- ○ **The Song is Gershwin** / Jolson, Astaire, Tibbett, etc. / 1992 / ASV 5048

FILM MUSIC

Film music (1923–1937)

George Gershwin's contribution to film music is relatively small, just a handful of songs. These songs, however, have since become immortal Gershwin classics, among the most important works in his oeuvre. Gershwin began writing film music in earnest in 1936, shortly after the premiere of his opera *Porgy and Bess*. The opera was initially unsuccessful, and both George and Ira Gershwin had to face the reality of a declining Broadway. George had not really had a Broadway hit since 1931, and the public was becoming increasingly uninterested in his concert music. Ticket sales were down due to the Depression, and many of the best writers and composers had moved West to Hollywood. The overwhelming popularity of "talkies" could not be ignored, and so the Gershwins eventually decided to seek work in California.

George and Ira had worked on a film before, 1931's *Delicious*. While George wrote a few memorable tunes for this movie, most of the songs were comprised of pieces of older, unused material that George and Ira had stitched together. Hollywood was not impressed. Moreover, after *Porgy and Bess*, they began to regard Gershwin as a composer with "serious" pretensions, a "highbrow" composer rather than one who could write hits. Ira and George worked hard to disabuse the studios of this notion, and in 1936 managed to strike a deal with RKO to write songs for *Shall We Dance*, starring Fred Astaire and Ginger Rogers. The film, with its ridiculously simple plot, is by no means a cinematic heavyweight; its worth lies in the dancing and the songs. Gershwin composed a number of memorable songs for this film, including "They All Laughed," "They Can't Take That Away from Me," and "Let's Call the Whole Thing Off." In these songs, Gershwin's mature style is in full bloom: harmonic changes are more fluid, melodies are simplified but clever, and pentatonic scales are employed.

After the success of *Shall We Dance*, the Gershwins were hired by RKO to produce songs for two more films, *A Damsel in Distress* and *Goldwyn Follies*. For the former, George composed the songs "Nice Work if You Can Get It" and "Foggy Day (In London Town)." Because this film was set in England, Gershwin was also able to compose a few polyphonic pieces in the style of Renaissance madrigals. *Goldwyn Follies*, which Gershwin began work on in 1937, contained two memorable songs, "Love Walked In" and "Our Love Is Here to Stay." The latter was the last song Gershwin ever wrote. Failing health and disillusionment with Hollywood put an end to Gershwin's career as a film music composer. After working for the tyrannical Sam Goldwyn on *Goldwyn Follies*, Gershwin became resentful of the industry. He died of a brain tumor in July 1937, just months after completing the music for *Goldwyn Follies*. *—Alexander Carpenter*

Recommended:

- ○ **Gershwins In Hollywood** / Mauceri (cond.), Marshall, Hollywood Bowl Orch. / 1991 / Philips 434274

KEYBOARD

Gershwin Song-Book, 18 song transcriptions (1932)

"Playing my songs as frequently as I do at private parties," Gershwin noted, "I have naturally been led to compose numerous variations upon them, and to indulge the desire for complication and variety that every composer feels when he manipulates the same material over and over again." By 1932, when his publisher suggested a collection in his distinctive keyboard style, Gershwin could look back over a meteoric career and an impressive body of work. Indeed, only *Porgy and Bess*, a handful of musicals (including the superb *Let 'em Eat Cake*), and the *"I Got Rhythm" Variations* remained for him to compose before a brain tumor cut his life short on July 11, 1937. The album of 18 transcriptions with which he fulfilled his commission, however, are quite different in style from the few recordings he left of his improvisations. The *Song Book* versions are fresh compositions, most very brief—a mere two pages—but scintillant, suggestive, and witty. Double that length, "I Got Rhythm" looks forward to the *"I Got Rhythm" Variations for piano and orchestra* (1934), while "Liza" (to be played "Languidly") is spaciously developed. All are deft, polished, and rife with Gershwin's peculiar exuberance and inexhaustible invention. They are, moreover, of considerable historical interest. Gershwin, who rejected a "ghosted" introduction to write his own, notes that "The evolution of our popular pianistic style really began with the introduction of ragtime, just before the Spanish-American war, and came to its culmination point in the jazz era that followed upon the Great War. A number of names come crowding into my memory; Mike Bernard, Les Copeland, Melville Ellis, Lucky Roberts, Zez Confrey, Arden and Ohman, and others. Each of these was responsible for the popularization of a new technique.... To all of these predecessors I am indebted; some of the effects I use in my transcriptions derive from their style of playing the piano."

Gershwin is explicit, too, about touch. "Our study of the great romantic composers has trained us in the method of the legato, whereas our popular music asks for staccato effects, for almost a stencilled style. The rhythms of American popular music are more or less brittle; they should be made to snap, and at times to crackle." The songs he chose, however, show at least as much winsome croon—for instance, the ben cantando left-hand melody in "Do It Again" (to be played "Plaintively")—as crackle. The numbers also include his first hit, "Swanee," "Somebody Love Me," "The Man I Love," "Nobody but You," "I'll Build a Stairway to Paradise," "Lady Be Good," "Somebody Loves Me," "Sweet and Low Down," "Clap Yo' Hands," "Do Do," "My One and Only," "S'Wonderful," "That Certain Feeling," "Who Cares?," and "Strike Up the Band!"

Issued by Simon and Schuster in September 1932, the original edition featured the sheet music vocals followed by their transcriptions. And a special edition limited to 300 signed copies included a party song of broad ethnic humor, "Mischa, Yascha, Toscha, Sascha." *—Adrian Corleonis*

Recommended:

- ○ **Gershwin: Complete Piano Works** / Damerini / Musik Strasse 2106
- ○ **Gershwin: Piano Music** / Bolcom / 1987 / Nonesuch 79151

Impromptu in Two Keys (1929)

As he experimented with classical forms and procedures in the 1920s, George Gershwin left a number of sketches and fragments that were later unearthed as the reputation of his pop-classical fusions grew. The *Impromptu in Two Keys*, a 1924 sketch in which Gershwin inflects a pleasant song melody through unrelated keys, was first published through the efforts of Ira Gershwin in 1973. Amazing as it may seem, Gershwin had a keen if perhaps unfocused interest in contemporary musical developments in the 1920s. On the 1928 European trip that resulted in the tone poem *An American in Paris*, Gershwin met Alban Berg, repeatedly requested performances of the latter's *Lyric Suite*, and unsuccessfully sought composition lessons with the famed French pedagogue Nadia Boulanger. *—AMG*

Recommended:

- ○ **Gershwin: Original Works & Transcriptions for Solo Piano** / Buechner / 1993 / Connoisseur Society 4191
- ○ **Gershwin: Piano Music** / Bolcom / 1987 / Nonesuch 79151

Three Preludes (1926)

For some observers these three short piano pieces represent the apex of Gershwin's "classical" output. The two fast outer pieces, both marked Allegro ben rimato e deciso (fast, rhythmically, and decisively), are each hardly over one minute long, while the middle Prelude is a slow, three-minute blues piece. The Preludes combine the immediate appeal of Gershwin's longer concert pieces with the tight melodic logic and seeming musical inevitability of his songs. Gershwin here uses harmonies and intervals derived from popular music, treating them with a miniaturistic rigor that may even remind the hearer of Bartók. The Preludes evolved mostly between 1923 and 1926, although the theme of the third was based on that of the piano rag *Rialto Ripples*, one of Gershwin's earliest published compositions. They were originally envisioned as part of a large Bach-like cycle, to be entitled "The Melting Pot"; Gershwin presented five Preludes—the present three plus two earlier pieces that he had earlier called *Novelettes*—at a 1926 recital, but then wisely dropped the two Novelettes when the Preludes were published the following year. *—AMG*

Recommended:

- ○ **Gershwin Plays Gershwin** / Gershwin / Pearl 9483
- ○ **Tilson Thomas Performs & Conducts Gershwin** / Tilson Thomas / 1985 / CBS 39699

Rialto Ripples, rag (1916)

The Gershwin/Donaldson collaboration *Rialto Ripples* is generally recognized as Gershwin's first instrumental work. This brief, peppy piano solo combines elements of the ragtime idiom with the melodic and rhythmic hooks characteristic of the "novelty" music of the teens and twenties. *Ripples* follows a typical rag model, alternating the main melody with contrasting strains; the pervasive syncopated rhythms further point to the work's ragtime roots. While this work from the teenaged Gershwin shows little of the ingenuity and inventiveness of his more mature music, the sheer brashness and energetic swagger prefigure the composer's confidence in such later works as *Rhapsody in Blue*. *—Norbert Carnovale*

Recommended:

- ○ **Great American Piano II, Vol. 8** / Pennario / 1992 / Angel 64668
- ○ **Gershwin: Piano Music** / Bolcom / 1987 / Nonesuch 79151

CHAMBER MUSIC

Lullaby, for string quartet (ca. 1919)

The extent of Gershwin's early musical studies cannot now be known, though it was more encompassing than the myth of untutored genius will allow. And at all stages of his career he had what nothing can teach—a Schubertian gift for fluent, characteristic, and immediately compelling melody. Indeed, from his earliest days he carried with him what he called his tune book in which he jotted down the abundant ideas which came to him spontaneously. Even as his career began to open out, he continued to study with, among others, Edward Kilenyi, a well-respected private teacher who imparted the rudiments of harmony and orchestration. About this time, one of the "tunes" was worked into a piano piece, and it was as an exercise for Kilenyi, around 1919, that Gershwin scored it for string quartet as his *Lullaby*. Private copies soon circulated among friends and it was often performed at musical gatherings, to the young Gershwin's great satisfaction.

After a "tuning up" gesture, the slowly swinging blues melody is strutted in a skillfully varied exposition leading to a plaintively muted, hesitant moment which gives way to a rush of the warmest, most caressing lyricism before the initial blues returns to fade exquisitely.

In 1920 Gershwin was signed by George White to provide music for his annual *Scandals*. The first evening of *George White's Scandals* of 1922 featured *Blue Monday*, a one-act opera by Gershwin, which was largely undone by a melodramatically ludicrous book, though the score prefigures *Porgy and Bess* in its sureness of touch merging opera with the jazzy, popular *lingua franca* of the day to yield drama and character animated by demotic tang. The easy, gently swaying blues of the *Lullaby*'s opening became an aria for Vi, the generic jealous woman—"Has one of you seen my Joe"—in which she rhapsodizes her possessive affection for her smalltime gambler boyfriend. For a moment, its potent melodic appeal renders her credible.

Lullaby was published only in 1968, while its premiere recording by the Juilliard String Quartet in 1974 began its path to enduring popularity. *—Adrian Corleonis*

Recommended:

- ○ **Gershwin: Works for Piano & Orchestra** / Slatkin (cond.), St. Louis SO / 1990 / Vox 5007
- ○ **Essential Gershwin** / Chailly (cond.), Cleveland Orch. / 2003 / Decca 472780

Carlo Gesualdo

b. ca. 1561, Naples (?), Italy, **d.** Sep. 8, 1613, Naples, Italy

Composer: Vocal, Keyboard

Gesualdo's strength was his ability to combine a variety of unconventional strategies into the service of a deeply felt and psychologically effective whole. Gesualdo's style, once regarded as unique, has helped to open up an entire field of study relating to the avant-garde of the late sixteenth century, sometimes referred to by scholars as the "Mannerist Revolution." This movement vanished once Baroque style came to the forefront of music in Italy.

Gesualdo was born the second son of the Second Prince of Venosa, probably in the town that bears his family's name. After he received musical training from Stefano Felis and Giovanni de Macque, Gesualdo's earliest known work appears in 1585, when he was 19. That same year, his elder brother died at 20, making marriage an imperative for the younger Gesualdo. The bride was his first cousin, Maria d'Avalos, at age 25 already twice-widowed. They wed in Naples in 1586, and the following year an heir was born. Gesualdo discovered d'Avalos in an affair with the Duke of Andria. On October 17, 1590, Gesualdo, assisted by three servants, killed them both. The incident attracted public outrage, but there would be no trial, as authorities from both Church and State convened to dispose of the matter. Gesualdo's father died in 1591, and another marriage was arranged to Donna Leonora d'Este, taking place in Ferrara in February, 1594. In Ferrara, Gesualdo came into contact with court composer Luzzasco Luzzaschi and his "secret music," and became a close friend of the poet Torquato Tasso. Upon returning to his estate late in 1596, Gesualdo resolved to travel no more. In 1597, d'Este bore Gesualdo a second son who died in 1600, an event that plunged the Prince into a deep despair. The couple separated in 1608, and in 1610 d'Este began divorce proceedings against Gesualdo, but changed her mind and returned. In 1613, Gesualdo's elder son died, and Gesualdo himself followed on September 8 at age 47. He was known to be violently asthmatic his whole life. In later years, he would pursue masochistic practices which chronically served to weaken him physically, his spirit already broken by a decade of insanity.

Gesualdo's six books of Madrigals constitute the main body of his work. Books I and II (1594) are rooted in standard practice, but when compared to contemporary settings of the same poetry, they reveal a stubbornly individual mind at work. Book III (1595) shows a decreased reliance on pre-existing settings, and by Book IV (1596), all the texts used are original. Here, Gesualdo's mature style begins to emerge. Books V and VI did not appear until 1611, but in these editions, Gesualdo states the madrigals were written "15 years" prior to the date of publication, and were printed only to protect the works from plagiarists. While essentially diatonic in character, madrigals such as *Beltà, poi che t'assenti* and *Moro lasso* contain music which modulates so frequently it results in a disoriented sense of key. Dissonance is used liberally; passing tones cross relate, and there are passages of stepwise chromatic motion resulting in a suspended tonality. Gesualdo published three books of sacred music. The first two, entitled *Sacre Cantiones*, appeared in 1603, and in the second book Gesualdo expanded his usual five-part texture into six and seven parts, though two of the partbooks are lost. The third book, *Responsoria* (1611), represents Gesualdo's final musical statement. It is entirely in his late style, and the responses composed for the Good Friday service contains some of the most assured and eloquent music that Gesualdo composed. *—Uncle Dave Lewis*

VOCAL

Madrigals (ca. 1590–1610)

Although Carlo Gesualdo also composed church music, of which the darkly profound *Tenebrae Responsories* is the best-known example, his reputation rests largely on his madrigals. Six books were published for five voices (in 1594 [*Book I* and *Book II*], 1595, 1596, and 1611 [*Book V* and *Book VI*]), and one for six voices appeared posthumously, in 1626. Just as Gesualdo's lurid personal life has colored perceptions of the man, so his supposed unique originality as an example of extreme mannerist tendencies has distorted his image as a composer. In fact, the extreme dissonance and harmonic experimentation that drew Stravinsky and others to interest themselves in Gesualdo are by no means unique to him and have been recognized as being part of a broader picture that also includes the influence of Luzzasco Luzzaschi of Ferrara (acknowledged in *Book III* and *Book IV*) and such composers as Sigismondo d'India. It is not until the famous *Book V* and *Book VI* of the five-part madrigals that the boundaries of harmonic dissonance and wildly passionate expressionist utterances really come into their own. Here, too, one finds the violent contrasts of tempo and mood, and the strange melodic lines that have led observers to find reflections of the composer's personal neuroses in his music.

The less sensational *Book I* and *Book II* are of corrective value in proving that Gesualdo was thoroughly trained in contrapuntal techniques, thus undermining the theory advanced in some quarters that the more unruly elements in the later madrigals are the result of dilettantism and an imperfect compositional technique. A madrigal such as *Tirsi morir volea* (*Book I*, No. 12 & No. 13) clearly demonstrates the composer's confidence in handling imitative counterpoint. *Book III* and *Book IV*, the latter in particular, find Gesualdo developing a more personal idiom, one that not only shows the marked influence of his sojourn in Ferrara, but also develops a close relationship between text and music. In a madrigal such as *Or, che in gioia credea viver contento* (*Book IV*, No. 7) one also finds the kind of tortured melodic chromaticism that becomes so prevalent in the last books. Even in those books, where pieces like *Tu m'uccidi, o crudele* (*Book V*, No. 15) display the archetypal gamut of affects that have come to be viewed as a paradigm of Gesualdan style, madrigals free of extremes are to be found. *—Brian Robins*

Recommended:

○ **Gesualdo: Madrigals** / Christie (cond.), Les Arts Florissants / HM 901268

KEYBOARD

Canzon francese

Although the authorship of this short but extraordinary work had never been firmly attributed to Carlo Gesualdo, Prince of Venosa, it is generally programmed as one of his works. If it is, it is the only keyboard work of a composer principally known for his highly expressive Mannerist madrigals and darkly hued sacred works. The canzon has one of the most rigorous forms of late Renaissance keyboard works, a piece in strict contrapuntal style and structured in several sections. The *Canzon del Principe* conforms to such a description, but is especially remarkable for its extreme dissonance, chromaticism, and unexpected harmonic progressions, effects that it has been suggested could only have been associated in Gesualdo's mind with the archicembalo, a keyboard instrument with six manuals and 31 keys to each octave, and capable of playing all the diatonic, chromatic, and enharmonic notes known to ancient Greek theory. *—Brian Robins*

Recommended:

○ **Romanesca: Italian Music for Harpsichord** / Yates / 1997 / Chandos 0601

○ **Gesualdo: Madrigals** / Christie (cond.), Les Arts Florissants / HM 901268

Gagliarda del Principe di Venosa

There are exactly five known instrumental works of Don Carlo Gesualdo; certainly the most famous of these is the *Gagliarda del Principe di Venosa*. This comes from a manuscript collection of late Neapolitan Renaissance dances cataloged as No. 4.6.3. in the Naples Conservatory di San Pietro a Majella. Among the other composers who appear in this same source are Giovanni de Macque and Giovanni Trabaci, both of whom were known to Gesualdo on a personal basis, so that there is little doubt of the work's authenticity. The date of the work is unknown; theoretically it could've been written anywhere from 1585 up to Gesualdo's death in 1613. The collection in which it appears seems to have been put together in the years after Gesualdo died, probably in 1614–20.

This little Galliard, barely two minutes in length, is also in keeping stylistically with Gesualdo's harmonic approach, as it is largely made up of wandering chord progressions that fit alongside the five-step pattern of the galliard. Two or three short phrases even "sigh" in the fashion of Gesualdo's late madrigals. Scored in four voices and ostensibly for organ, it has been played in a variety of arrangements by groups in up to consort-sized ensembles. The *Gagliarda del Principe di Venosa* has captured the imagination of contemporary composers, for example Italian post-modernist Salvatore Sciarrino, who orchestrated and partly recomposed the piece as part of his work for voice and ensemble, *Le voci sottovetro* (1998). *—Uncle Dave Lewis*

Recommended:

○ **Italian Renaissance Dances, Vol. 1** / Douglass, King's Noyse / 2001 / Classical Express 3957159

Angela Gheorghiu

b. Sep. 7, 1965, Adjud, Romania

Soprano

Angela Gheorghiu is a Romanian soprano in demand the world over for leading roles in French and Italian operas, mostly of the nineteenth century. Her singing and career are spectacular in their own right, but Gheorghiu has gained an added measure of fame and publicity from her partnership with her husband, the tenor Roberto Alagna, which whom she performs frequently; they are the world of opera's best-known power couple.

Gheorghiu had success very quickly after her graduation from the Bucharest Academy in 1990, but her international career shifted into gear at England's Covent Garden, which engaged her as Zerlina in Mozart's *Don Giovanni* in 1992, and then as Mimi in Puccini's *La bohème* the same year. She received enormous critical praise for her singing there, and that house has continued to be a cornerstone of her career. In particular, her 1994 Violetta in *La traviata* was considered one of the finest performances of that role in many years. Gheorgiu quickly obtained a contract with Decca, for whom she has recorded Donizetti's *L'elisir d'Amore*, Puccini's *La bohème*, and an album called *My World*; her many recordings with Alagna are mostly on EMI, and include Bizet's *Carmen*, Verdi's *Il trovatore* and Puccini's *La rondine*. Since 1998 she has recorded exclusively for EMI, and has added Puccini's *Gianni Schicchi*, Gounod's *Roméo et Juliette*, Massenet's *Werther*, and an album of Verdi duets, *Verdi per due*, with Alagna and the Berlin Philharmonic Orchestra. At the turn of the new century, Gheorghiu was continuing to add new operas to her repertory, including *Luisa Miller*, *Pagliacci*, *Faust*, *Lucia di Lammermoor*, *La sonnambula*, *Tosca*, *Lucrezia Borgia*, and *Simon Boccanegra*.*—AMG*

Recommended:

○ **Massenet: Werther** / Pappano (cond.), Crayford, Toyne, Hampson, Gheorghiu, London SO / 1999 / EMI 56820

○ **The Essential Angela Gheorghiu** / Gheorghiu, etc. / 2004 / Decca 000228402

○ **Angela Gheorghiu—Diva** / Gheorghiu, etc. / 2004 / EMI 57706

Nicolai Ghiaurov

b. Sep. 13, 1929, Velingrad, Russia, **d.** Jun. 2, 2004, Modena, Italy

Bass

Ghiaurov excelled in both the Slavic and the Italian and French operatic repertoire, and he also moved with ease from serious to comic roles, though the serious roles played a greater part in his career. At times, he even took on some of the lower baritone roles, Mozart's *Don Giovanni* and Escamillo in Bizet's *Carmen*. He was also noted for his acting and compelling stage presence. During his prime, his voice was among the richest and most sonorous basses of the twentieth century, and even as much of its freshness and bloom was gone toward the end of his career, it retained its expressiveness and technical excellence.

Though his family was quite poor, they encouraged him to explore his interest in singing, and when he entered adolescence, he borrowed instruments so he could learn clarinet, violin, and trombone. He also began to take acting lessons, briefly considering a career as an actor rather than a musician. When he entered the army, where he was a clarinetist and conducted the chorus, his singing talents came to the attention of the authorities, who enabled him to study with Christo Brambarov, and later at the Moscow Conservatory. His studies were conservative—for the first year, he did nothing but vocal exercises over one octave—a fact to which he attributed his spectacular vocal longevity. Brambarov introduced him to Italian style, a rarity for Russian singers during that time. He made his stage debut as Don Basilio in Rossini's *The Barber of Seville* at the Sofia Opera in 1955 and made his Bolshoi debut as Pimen in *Boris Godunov* in 1957. His Italian debut was as Méphistophélès in Gounod's *Faust* at the Teatro Communale in Rome the next year. His Covent Garden debut came in 1962 as the Padre Guardiano in Verdi's *La forza del destino*. At the 1965 Salzburg Festival, he first sang the title role of Boris Godunov, a role generally considered the greatest challenge in the Russian bass repertoire. Aside from opera, he frequently performed and recorded Russian songs. Ghiaurov has established a place in musical history through his recorded legacy. His Boris was recorded commercially twice, once each in the "original" and Rimsky-Korsakov versions. He recorded *Don Carlos* in the studio three times, twice as Filippo and once (in the original French version) as the Grand Inquisitor. His early London/Decca aria recitals accurately document the size and beauty of his voice. He is also heard in Giulini's recording of Verdi's *Requiem*.

He was married to the Italian soprano Mirella Freni and participated in guiding her into her forays into the Russian repertoire, notably Tatiana in *Eugene Onegin* and Lisa in *Pique Dame*. *—Ann Feeney*

Recommended:

- ○ **Nicolai Ghiaurov** / Downes (cond.), Ghiaurov, London SO & Chorus / 2001 / Decca 467902
- ○ **Verdi: Messa da Requiem; 4 Pezzi Sacri** / Giulini (cond.), Schwarzkopf, Baker, Ludwig, Gedda, Ghiaurov, London Philharmonia Orch. & Chorus / 2001 / EMI 67563
- ○ **Mussorgsky: Boris Godunov** / Karajan (cond.), Ghiaurov, Talvela, Cvejic, Spiess, Vienna PO / 1988 / Decca 411862
- ○ **Gounod: Faust** / Pretre (cond.), Domingo, Freni, Allen, Ghiaurov, Paris National Opera Theater Orch. / EMI 47493

Il Giardino Armonico

f. 1985, Milan, Italy
Ensemble

Il Giardino Armonico is an Italian period instrument chamber ensemble specializing in vigorous and earthy performances of music from the Italian Baroque. Founded in 1985 in Milan, the group has a flexible membership with as few as three and as many as 30 players. Since 1989, the ensemble has been conducted by flutist Giovanni Antonini. The group has toured worldwide and developed an extensive discography, mostly on Teldec Classics. The group's recordings of concerti by Vivaldi have garnered awards such as the Diapason d'Or, Choc de la Musique, the Grand Prix des Discophiles, and the Gramophone Award. The Grammy award-winning *Vivaldi Album* (1999) on Decca featured Cecilia Bartoli singing previously unrecorded and mostly unperformed opera arias by Vivaldi. The group has performed in both concert and staged productions of many operas and oratorios from the seventeenth and eighteenth centuries, including Pergolesi's *La serva padrona*; Handel's *Agrippina*, *La resurrezione*, and *Il trionfo del tempo del disinganno*; and Hasse's *I pellegrini al sepolcro di nostro signore*. In 1993, the group performed Claudio Monteverdi's *L'Orfeo* in Milan to mark the 350th anniversary of the composer's birth. It regularly performs and records with a wide variety of soloists, including Cecilia Bartoli, Katia and Marielle Labèque, Eva Mei, Sumi Jo, Sara Mingardo, Lynne Dawson, Christoph Prégardien, Véronique Gens, Viktoria Mullova, and Giuliano Carmignola. Il Giardino Armonico's concerts and discography are notable for their inclusion of rarely performed works by composers such as Rossi, Riccio, Spadi, and Conti, alongside works such as Vivaldi's *The Four Seasons*. Even in the most familiar repertoire, the ensemble distinguishes itself by its lusty and energetic readings, replete with glissandos and imaginative ornamentation. *—Robert Adelson*

Recommended:

- ○ **Vivaldi: The Four Seasons** / Antonini (cond.), Il Giardino Armonico / Teldec 97671
- ○ **The Vivaldi Album** / Antonini (cond.), Bartoli, Arnold Schoenberg Choir, Il Giardino Armonico / 1999 / Decca 466569

Orlando Gibbons

b. Dec. 1583, Oxford, England, **d.** Jun. 5, 1625, Canterbury, England
Composer: Vocal, Keyboard

Orlando Gibbons was one of the most important English composers from the early seventeenth century, with only William Byrd eclipsing him in rank. His church music, exclusively written for the English Church, is among the most popular and enduring in his œuvre. Notable in this realm are his polyphonic anthems, *O clap your hands*, *Hosanna*, and *Lift up your head*. His two Services are also of great significance: the *Short Service* is polyphonic and the *Second Service* is a verse work with organ accompaniment. In the keyboard realm, several of his compositions have been widely declared of such masterful quality as to be unsurpassed by anything until the era of Bach. The *Fantasia of Four Parts*, from the *Parthenia* collection, is one such example. His fairly substantial output for keyboard includes many corantos, galliards, pavans, and fantasies. His *First Set of Madrigals and Mottets* demonstrate his considerable talents in the realm of secular music.

Orlando Gibbons was born in Oxford, probably no more than a week before Christmas, as his baptism took place on December 24, in St. Martin's Church, Oxford. With older siblings who were accomplished musicians, the young Orlando was raised in a musical environment strongly conducive to his burgeoning talents. It is likely that his first music training came from them, perhaps mostly from his brother Edward.

On February 14, 1596, Orlando became a member of the King's College Choir at Cambridge. His brother, Edward, was then master of the choristers there. Orlando served in the choir until the fall of 1598, afterward making periodic appearances there until May, 1599. By this time he was known to be composing music.

Earlier that same year he began studies at Cambridge University. In about 1603, Gibbons became a member of the Chapel Royal, and on March 21, 1605, he was appointed its organist. He was already regarded as one of the finest organists in England, and had become a respected composer, though he would not see his first works published for seven more years.

Gibbons graduated from Cambridge in 1606 and that summer married Elizabeth Patten, possibly only about 16 years old. There would be six surviving children from the marriage. The composer wrote a fair amount of music in the 1610s, but much of it would not appear until well after his death. The *First Set of Madrigals and Mottets, apt for Viols and Voyces* was published in 1612. A year later came the publication of six keyboard works in *Parthenia*, which was a collective effort in that it also included compositions by Bryd (eight) and Bull (seven). A collection of the composer's anthems appeared in Leighton's *Teares or Lamentacions of a Sorrowfull Soule* of 1614. They include *O Lord, I lift my heart to thee* and *O Lord, in thee is all my trust*, both for five voices. On July 19, 1615, the now widely known Gibbons was granted 150 pounds by King James I for his "faythfull service." In 1619, Gibbons was appointed to the royal post of Musician for the Virginals, while retaining his prestigious Chapel Royal post.

A collection of nine three-part works by him, titled *Fantasias*, was published in 1620. Three years later, Gibbons contributed 16 tunes to George Withers' collection, *Hymnes and Songs of the Church*. A 17th was added in a later manuscript. Gibbons accepted another post, in 1623, that of organist at Westminster Abbey. Two years later, he died suddenly in Canterbury, apparently of a stroke or related condition. *—Robert Cummings*

Overview of Works (ca. 1610–1625)

Orlando Gibbons, born into a highly musical family, served the English Crown as Gentleman of the Chapel Royal from shortly after the breaking of his voice until his untimely death; his music for the Anglican rite has been in near-constant use since the seventeenth century. As one of the most accomplished of the English "Virginals School," and one of two Royal Chapel organists, Gibbons also left an impressive corpus of keyboard music. Already in c. 1612, his music was included alongside that of William Byrd and John Bull in *Parthenia*. With varying performance contexts upon the virginal, the organ, or an imported Italian harpsichord, Gibbons' generally progressive and bravura-rich keyboard music was the foundation of his fame during his lifetime. He follows the example of Byrd in the forms and genres: Preludes, Variation sets upon popular "Grounds" (such as the florid composition upon *The Woods so Wild*), fugal *Fantasias* (ten, including a vast motivic expansion for "double organ," with two manuals, and the chromatically affective *Fantasia in G minor*), and dance forms. Unlike Byrd, he only set one pavan/galiard pair, the *Lord Salisbury*, which contains affective references to Dowland's pavan *Lachrymae*. Gibbons also apparently was one of the earliest to write music for the Jacobean theatre, with five keyboard "Masks," with evocative titles such as *Fairest Nymph* and *Welcome Home*.

Gibbons' vocal music, somewhat more conservative in outlook, comprises two complete Anglican Services (settings of the daily threefold set of liturgical canticles), nearly 30 anthems, and a small number of English madrigals. Madrigals such as the well-known *Silver Swanne* follow Byrd in contrapuntal simplicity and polish; the *Cries of London*, however, imaginatively mingles the ethos of Jannequin with the English "In Nomine" consort tradition. Simple chordal writing, suitable for the daily rite, suffices for several of the four-voiced "Full" anthems, and the First Service, though exceptions such as the Italianate polychoral richness of *O Clap Your Hands* often eclipse them. The *Second Service* and Gibbons' numerous verse anthems present more subtle and complex scoring between soloists, five-voiced choir, and accompanimental ensemble. Some of his finest, most vital, writing for voices appears in the likes of *This Is the Record of John*, and *We praise Thee, O Father*.

In addition, Gibbons contributed widely to the courtly and intimate genres of composition for instrumental ensemble, including richly imitative fantasias for up to six parts (and as few as an unusual two), In Nomines, and variations. Certain of his settings for ensemble upon the "great double basse"—possibly played by the new string band of Charles I—could preserve the earliest writing for the quintessentially Baroque trio-sonata texture. *—Timothy Dickey*

Recommended:

- ○ **Go from My Window** / Elliott, Concordia / 2001 / Metronome 1039
- ○ **Gibbons: Choral & Organ Music** / Summerly (dir.), Cummings, Oxford Camerata / 1995 / Naxos 553130
- ○ **Gibbons: Tudor Church Music** / Ledger (cond.), King's College Choir, London Early Music Group / 1990 / ASV 123
- ○ **Anthems by Orlando Gibbons** / Hill (cond.), Varcoe, Farr, Blaze, Winchester Cathedral Choir / 2000 / Hyperion 67116
- ○ **Gibbons: Fantasias, In Nomines & The Cries of London** / Nicholson (cond.), Fretwork, Red Byrd / 1996 / Virgin 45144
- ○ **Gibbons: Fantaisies Royales** / Savall, Coin, Casademunt, Sonnleitner / 2000 / Astree 9950

VOCAL

The silver swanne, madrigal for 5 voices (before 1612)

The madrigal arrived in England from Italy late in its history and enjoyed only a brief period of ascendancy. In general terms it is lighter in form than its Italian parent. It reached its apogee in the works of Thomas Morley, Thomas Weelkes, and John Wilbye, and one of the most famous of all examples was composed by Orlando Gibbons.

The silver Swanne is a madrigal for five voices which first appeared in Gibbons' First Set of Madrigals or Motetts of 5 Parts in 1612. The text is on the familiar topic of the song of the swan (it had featured in a number of Italian madrigals), which gives voice only in its death throes. To this Gibbons adds a topical sting in the final lines: "More Geese than Swannes now live, more fooles than wise." Musically this madrigal is atypical of the form in some ways, being less complex contrapuntally and relying more on its memorable melodic shape for its touching effect on the listener. This direct appeal was doubtless responsible for its enduring popularity, a popularity that was revived in the eighteenth century when it was frequently performed as an exemplar of the past glories of English music, and frequently republished in books of part-songs and glees. *—Brian Robins*

Recommended:

○ **Madrigal History Tour** / Rooley (cond.), King's Singers, Consort of Musicke / 1989 / EMI 69837

○ **English & Italian Renaissance Madrigals** / Hilliard Ens. / 1999 / Virgin 61671

○ **Gibbons: Consort & Keyboard Music; Songs & Anthems** / Rose Consort of Viols, Red Byrd / 1994 / Naxos 550603

KEYBOARD

Works for Keyboard

It is remarkable how small English composer Orlando Gibbons' keyboard oeuvre is, given that he was a virtuoso keyboardist. Gibbons, like Bach, was a busy church musician and a gifted improviser; unlike Bach, Gibbons apparently could not find the time to write much of his music down. Most of the pieces that survive—and there are less than 50—are short and likely date from Gibbons' years working in the Royal Chapel, though it is difficult to date some of the pieces with certainty. Scholars seem to accept, with some reluctance, that most of the keyboard music was probably composed between 1609–1619. It is also difficult to determine what instrument Gibbons was writing for, as his pieces do not always specify organ or virginals: some are only playable on one or the other, but some could be played on either. Gibbons' keyboard music consists of pavans, galliards, preludes, variations, and fantasies. His pavans and galliards—dance pieces—show the influence of two earlier English composers, William Byrd and John Bull, who both made significant contributions to the genre. It is interesting to note, however, that Gibbons' pavans and galliards deviate from the regular phrasing of Byrd's, becoming less danceable but more musically interesting. They typically feature the use of long sequences, rapid harmonic change, and elaborate figuration. The preludes and fantasies in Gibbons' keyboard oeuvre are not always easy to identify, as early sources do not always clearly differentiate between these genres. Preludes and fantasies are traditionally derived from improvisation and generally display a certain whimsy or melodic freedom. Gibbons' preludes tend toward virtuosic runs of quick notes over the top of simple harmonies. The fantasies are all in duple or common time, are less conservative than the preludes, and possess a greater formal flexibility and variety of melodic figures. They are also remarkable for their seemingly spontaneous generation of melodic ideas, which weave a complex polyphonic texture. Gibbons' variations for keyboard paint the clearest picture of the composer as a keyboard virtuoso. They also reflect the influence of Bull, who tended to compose complex variations. Gibbons' variations tend to be formally flexible, eschewing structure for astoundingly demanding virtuosic passages. This is in sharp contrast to Gibbons' predecessor Byrd, whose keyboard variations are more carefully structured. Many of Gibbons' variations also feature a repeating ground bass. *—Alexander Carpenter*

Recommended:

○ **Gibbons: Music for Harpsichord & Virginals** / Johnstone / 1999 / ASV 191

○ **The Woods So Wild** / Toll / 2001 / Linn 125

Walter Gieseking

b. Nov. 5, 1895, Lyon, France, **d.** Oct. 26, 1956, London, England

Pianist

It was with the repertoire of French masters that the German pianist Walter Gieseking became most famous. The impressionistic piano writing of Claude Debussy and Maurice Ravel required the most sensitive touch and attention to color and nuance, and Gieseking's finger acuity, imaginative pedaling, and, above all preternaturally alert ear made him an ideal interpreter of this music. Nevertheless, his own repertoire ranged widely across eras and national boundaries.

Largely self-taught as a pianist, Gieseking was born in Lyon, France, on November 5, 1895; with his family (his father was a distinguished doctor and entomologist), he traveled in France and Italy until he enrolled at the Hannover Conservatory, where he came under the tutelage of Karl Leimer, making his debut in 1915.

Gieseking was drafted into the German army a year after his first public performance but escaped combat by performing in his regimental band. After the war, he undertook the the life of a working musician, accompanying singers and instrumentalists, playing in chamber music ensembles, and working as an opera coach. He could hardly avoid the heady artistic atmosphere of postwar Germany, and he became an advocate of new music, playing works by Schoenberg, Busoni, Hindemith, Szymanowski, and Pfitzner, whose *Piano Concerto* he premiered under Fritz Busch in 1923. Subsequent debuts in London (1923), the United States (1926, Aeolian Hall, New York), and Paris (1928) were highly acclaimed, with audiences and critics responding enthusiastically to Gieseking's subtle shadings and contrapuntal clarity.

The Second World War brought controversy to Gieseking: like many other artists who remained in Germany during hostilities, he was accused of collaborating with the Nazis. His 1949 Carnegie Hall engagements caused such an uproar that they had to be cancelled; but he was eventually cleared of all charges by an Allied court in Germany. His concert career resumed with the success it had formerly enjoyed. To this activity he added a heavy schedule of recording, committing to disc the complete solo piano music of Mozart and the Beethoven concertos, as well as complete sets of Debussy's and Ravel's piano works. At the time of his death in London (October 26, 1956), Gieseking was engaged on a project to record all the Beethoven piano sonatas. His recordings of Debussy and Ravel are regarded as benchmarks for every subsequent performer.

Gieseking's autobiography, *So wurde ich Pianist*, was published posthumously in 1963; it seems never to have been translated into English. *—Mark Satola*

Recommended:

○ **Ravel: Complete Works for Solo Piano** / Gieseking / 2001 / EMI 74793

○ **Gieseking Performs Debussy** / Gieseking / 2004 / EMI 62800

○ **Gieseking—A Retrospective, Vol. 1** / Gieseking / Pearl 9930

○ **Beethoven: Sonatas 21, 23, 30 & 31** / Gieseking / 2001 / Angel 67586

○ **The London Years 1948–1960** / Karajan (cond.), Gieseking, Philharmonia Orch. / 1998 / EMI 66604

Beniamino Gigli

b. Mar. 20, 1890, Recanati, Italy, **d.** Nov. 30, 1957, Rome, Italy

Tenor

Beniamino Gigli was the foremost Italian tenor of the 1920s through the 1940s, possessed of a smooth, lush voice with a lyric sweetness often described as "honeyed." He became a Metropolitan Opera star, singing 28 roles there, and was a legitimate heir to the tenor Enrico Caruso, who had died at the beginning of the 1920s. No one person could fill Caruso's shoes, but it was widely conceded that Gigli inherited his lyrical and romantic parts, while Giovanni Martinelli took over the more heroic roles. Gigli was also one of the most-beloved performers of Italian song, with a special gift for the traditional Neapolitan repertoire. His singing was heavily mannered by modern standards, characterized by sobs, catches, and portamenti, but it had an inherent beauty and sincerity that are still easy to appreciate. Although an even more stylized actor than singer, Gigli had a successful film career, appearing in almost 20 films.

Gigli began his singing career as a child, performing for treats and coins at a local café. At age seven, he entered the choir of Recanati Cathedral, where his father was Sacristan. When he was 15 and still a boy soprano, he was recruited to sing the heroine in an operetta in the nearby city of Macerata; he did the production in drag! When he was 17, he moved to Rome to live with his brother, a student of sculpture; the two led a bohemian existence, frequently cold and hungry, until Gigli was offered a position as a servant in a wealthy household. There he was provided with room and board and given afternoons off to practice or to take lessons with a local teacher, Agnese Bonucci, who offered to teach him at no cost.

During World War I, a music-loving colonel saw to it that he was posted to a noncombat position in Rome and also encouraged him to audition at the famous Accademia di Santa Cecilia, where his evident musical talent led them to waive the normally required piano examination. He studied there for two years, and upon graduation won the famous Parma vocal competition. On the strength of that, he was offered roles at various small opera houses and made his official opera debut as Enzo in *La Gioconda* at Rovigo in the fall of 1914. By December 1916, he made his Rome Opera debut as Faust in Boito's *Mefistofele*. When the war was over, the recording company HMV set up a studio in Milan, and it was there that Gigli began his extensive recording career. In 1918, he made his La Scala debut also as Boito's Faust in a performance conducted by Toscanini. The next year, he made his first appearance in the Americas as Cavaradossi in *Tosca* at the Teatro Colon. His Met debut followed in November 1920, also as Faust, and he sang there every season until 1932.

His Covent Garden debut was not until 1930, as Andrea Chénier. After World War II, which he mostly spent in Italy, he largely restricted his singing to concert performances; his last public appearance was in May 1955, at a concert in Washington, D.C., ending a professional career of 41 years.

Gigli was one of the first singers to make complete opera recordings, including a particularly fine *Andrea Chénier* (EMI) and *Cavalleria rusticana* and *Pagliacci* released as a set on Nimbus. Among his solo CDs, a two-disc set on Pearl (Gemm) captures him in his youthful prime. *—Ann Feeney*

Recommended:

- ○ **Beniamino Gigli - In Opera And Song** / Gigli, etc. / 1997 / Nimbus 1763
- ○ **The Very Best of Beniamino Gigli** / Gigli, etc. / 2003 / EMI 85093
- ○ **Gigli Edition, Vol. 1: The Milan Recordings 1918–19** / Gigli, etc. / 2003 / Naxos 8110262
- ○ **Gigli Edition, Vol. 2: The Milan, Camden and New York Recordings 1919–22** / Gigli, etc. / 2003 / Naxos 8110263

Kenneth Gilbert

b. Dec. 16, 1931, Montreal, Quebec, Canada
Harpsichordist

Kenneth Gilbert has entwined scholarship and performance more closely than almost any other figure in the field of early music, making scholarship an art and performance a means of investigation. He has made well over 50 recordings, written numerous articles and reviews, and edited new publications of music by François Couperin, Domenico Scarlatti, Bach, Frescobaldi, and Rameau, among many others.

Gilbert was born and raised in Montreal, Quebec, Canada; his last name is pronounced as in French (zheel-BAIR). He has always retained strong ties to that city, but his career has been international. After studies at the Quebec Conservatory in Montreal he went to Europe, where his teachers included Nadia Boulanger and Maurice Duruflé. Gilbert's harpsichord teacher in France was Italian-born Landowska protégé Ruggero Gerlin. In 1953 Gilbert won a major European organ prize, and for much of the first part of his career he was primarily occupied with that instrument. He served as organist and music director at the Queen Mary Road United Church (now Rosedale Queen Mary United Church) in Montreal for 15 years, designing and supervising the installation of a new organ there. From 1957 to 1974 he taught at the Quebec Conservatory.

In the early 1960s, Gilbert won financial support from the Quebec government and later from the Canada Council to return to Europe for research purposes, and he began to become familiar with the original engraved printings of some of the monuments of Baroque keyboard music. A four-volume Gilbert edition of François Couperin's keyboard works published between 1968 and 1972 was the first of a series of harpsichord publications, and from about 1965 onward, Gilbert's interests as a performer shifted to the harpsichord.

Although he lived mostly in France in the 1970s and 1980s, Gilbert was active all over Europe, in Canada (where he was richly garlanded with national honors), and in the U.S. He taught at several European conservatories and universities, and in 1988 he became the first Canadian, and one of few foreigners of any nationality, to hold the post of professor at the Paris Conservatoire. Gilbert's recordings have been released on the Harmonia Mundi and Archiv labels, as well as a host of more specialized lines. He has focused on French music, and his recordings of works such as the *Premier livre de clavecin* by Chambonnières are considered standards. But he has also made major Bach recordings, including, for example, a 1989 Archiv release on which he performed the *Art of the Fugue*. *—James Manheim*

Recommended:

- ○ **Bach: Goldberg Variations** / Gilbert / HM 1951240
- ○ **Couperin: Pièces de clavecin I** / Gilbert / HM 190351
- ○ **D'Angelbert: Suites de clavecin; Tombeau de M. de Chambonnières** / Gilbert / HM 190941
- ○ **The Golden Age of English Organ Music** / Gilbert / Adda 581178
- ○ **Bach: The Well-Tempered Clavier, Book 1** / Gilbert / Archiv 474221

Emil Gilels

b. Oct. 19, 1916, Odessa, Russia, **d.** Oct. 14, 1985, Moscow, Russia
Pianist

Emil Gilels was one of the great pianists of history. He was a master of a wide repertory from the time of Bach to his own era, and one of the first pianists to adopt a modern, more objective style of playing and interpreting music.

His family was musical; his sister Elizaveta had a national reputation as a solo and chamber violinist, and married fellow violinist Leonid Kogan. Emil entered the Odessa Institute of Music and Drama in 1922 to study with Yakov Tkatch and Berthe Ringold. Following a successful debut as a child prodigy in 1929, he transferred to study with Reingbald at Odessa Conservatory. (Some biographies confuse Ringold and Reingbald.)

In 1933 he won the first All Union Musicians' Contests, initiating its rapid rise to become the leading musical performance competition in the U.S.S.R. Even with this success, he carefully continued his education, remaining at Odessa Conservatory until he graduated in 1935. After that he continued his studies as a graduate student at the Moscow Conservatory with Heinrich Neuhaus.

In 1938 he took another prestigious first prize at the Ysaÿe International Festival in Brussels. In the same year he was engaged as a teacher at Moscow Conservatory. He planned to launch his international career in 1939, beginning with a visit to the New York World's Fair, but the outbreak of World War II in Europe prevented his travel.

During the war he was evacuated to the East in 1941 when the German armies reached the outskirts of Moscow. He resumed his career in 1946, and soon won the Stalin Prize. He finally made his first appearance outside the Soviet Union in 1947, when he visited several European cities, but frigid diplomatic relations between Washington and Moscow prevented his appearance in the United States until 1955, when he became the first prominent Soviet performing artist to play a concert there on October 3, with the Tchaikovsky *First Piano Concerto* in Philadelphia, Eugene Ormandy conducting. The resulting storm of acclaim led to his returning to the U.S. 13 more times.

He debuted in England in 1959 to similar success. He became known for his refined yet powerful performances of great concentration and attention to the inner logic of the music. He was noted for his performances of Bach, Beethoven, Schubert, Schumann, Chopin, Liszt, Tchaikovsky, Brahms, and Shostakovich. He made numerous recordings, both for the Soviet state recording agencies (many of which are reappearing in improved sound on compact disc) and on Western labels. He was a two-time recipient the Order of Lenin. *—Joseph Stevenson*

Recommended:

- ○ **Emil Gilels** / Böhm, Ludwig (conds.), Gilels, Philharmonia Orch., Vienna PO / 1998 / Philips 456793
- ○ **Gilels Plays Liszt & Schubert** / Gilels / Orfeo 332931
- ○ **Beethoven: 4 Sonatas** / Gilels / 1996 / Russian Revelation 10029
- ○ **Grieg: Lyric Pieces** / Gilels / DG 449721
- ○ **Emil Gilels Legacy, Vol. 1** / Kondrashin (cond.), Gilels, Tchaikovsky SO, USSR SO / 1999 / Doremi 7747
- ○ **Gilels** / / 1999 / BBC 4015

Alberto Ginastera

b. Apr. 11, 1916, Buenos Aires, Argentina, **d.** Jun. 25, 1983, Geneva, Switzerland
Composer: Keyboard, Orchestral, Chamber Music, Vocal, Concerto, Ballet

Argentine modernist composer Alberto Ginastera began studying piano at the age of seven. Five years later, he entered Argentina's Williams Conservatory, graduating with a gold medal in conducting. From 1936 to 1938, he studied at the National Conservatory in Buenos Aires. Ginastera started composing around 1930, but he destroyed much of his early work. Known for his ability to effectively combine advanced and traditional musical styles, he gained recognition for the ballet *Panambí* (1936), which was popular later on when it was performed as an orchestral suite. For more than a decade, Ginastera enjoyed a prominent position in Argentine music, and his reputation was enhanced by successful performances of orchestral and stage pieces such as the ballet *Estancia* (1941). During this period, Ginastera's success was due in part to his incorporation of local and national themes. In 1941, he was appointed to a post at the National Conservatory. Disliked by Juan Peron's new government, however, Ginastera left Argentina in 1945, and traveled to the United States, where he stayed until 1947. Ginastera's American experience was remarkably eventful and enriching: he spent the time interacting with American composers, studying (he worked with Copland at Tanglewood), and attending concerts and musical festivals. Following his return to Argentina, Ginastera formed a League of Argentine Composers in 1948. He was named director of the Province Conservatory in La Plata but lost the position, again due to the government's animosity. Ginastera was appointed Dean of Musical Arts Sciences at the Argentine Catholic University in 1958. Through part of the 1950s, Ginastera still used a traditional, national idiom. In works composed in the 1960s and later, however, he broke new ground, successfully experimenting with a variety of contemporary styles and compositional techniques. His *Concerto for piano and orchestra No. 1* (1961) and *Cantata para América mágica* (1960) received high praise at the Interamerican Music Festival in 1961. A failure in Buenos Aires, Ginastera's opera *Don Rodrigo* (1964) had an excellent New York premiere in 1966, establishing him as one of the world's best large-scale opera composers. In Argentina, however, he kept encountering difficulties. For example, his dramatic cantata *Bomarzo* (1967) was banned because of its sexually explicit content. In 1971, Ginastera married the Argentine cellist Aurora Natola, and the couple settled in Geneva. Ginastera's reputation as a composer of structurally elaborate but also powerfully visceral music was solidified when his third opera, *Beatrix Cenci* (1971), which emphasized topics of rape and incest, was produced for the inauguration of the Kennedy Center in Washington. *—Graham Olson*

KEYBOARD

12 American Preludes, Op. 12 (1944)

Alberto Ginastera composed his *12 American Preludes* near the end of his early, most explicitly nationalistic period. As exemplified in works such as the *Danzas*

Argentinas, Op. 2, from 1937, and the *Creole Faust Overture* from 1944, Ginastera's first important pieces drew directly on regional folk styles and themes, especially those of his native Argentina. A similar approach can be found in the *American Preludes*, composed in 1944. The term "American" here is taken in a broader sense than Yankee listeners sometimes assume: the dozen short pieces in the series include musical evocations of, and tributes to, composers hailing from both North and South America. As Argentinean pianist Alberto Portugheis (arguably the foremost interpreter of Ginastera's piano music) described, "Ginastera tried in this work to translate musically the kaleidoscope of melodic and rhythmic turns similar to those of the American continent, from primitive pentatonic melodies to contemporary music." The works in the series are all miniatures ranging in length from 30 seconds to two minutes—hardly constituting individual forms or developments at all, while instead conveying concise but vivid emotional evocations. Some of these are suggested only vaguely by the individual pieces' titles.

The opening piece, "Accents," consists of an unbroken chain of chords spanning the entire keyboard, their metric delivery made clear by an emphasis on triple divisions. The subsequent movement, bearing the simple title "Sadness," is an exercise in economy; a plain and plaintive melody in the right hand accompanied by sparse, single notes in the left, and a Spartan counterpoint that finds repose only in the subtle shift to the major mode near the piece's end. The rest of the series unfolds similarly, in a series of textural and temporal contrasts that includes a pair of studies in pentatonic modes that are anachronistic in their mixture of simple melodic materials and modern gestures. The lively "Creole Dance" is an angular, etude-like study; "Octaves" presages some of the more technically demanding moments in Ginastera's *Piano Sonata No. 1* (1952); and the tranquil but mysterious "Pastorale" is constructed upon an unwavering two-note ostinato. Interspersed among the 12 pieces are tributes to specific American figures, including a furiously virtuosic ode to Roberto García Morillo; a melancholy melody dedicated to Juan José Castro; a playful, chromatically quirky tribute to Aaron Copland; and a dense, dark movement for Heitor Villa-Lobos. *—Jeremy Grimshaw*

Recommended:

○ **Ginastera: Complete Music for Piano & Piano Chamber Ensembles** / Nissman / 2001 / Pierian 0005/0006

Danzas argentinas, Op. 2 (1937)

The *Three Argentine Dances* constitute perhaps the most popular work in the piano literature of Argentina. They were written during the 20-year-old composer's early, nationalistic period. However, unlike many of his colleagues, Ginastera used folkloristic rhythms and melodic cells in a dissonant and virtuosic context, akin to Bartók's compositional world with its imaginary folklore. The first dance, "Danza del viejo boyero" (Dance of the Old Oxen-Keeper), is based on the rhythm of the *malambo,* a gaucho dance for a solo male that allows him to show off his tap-dancing talents. The second, "Danza de la moza donosa" (Dance of the Graceful Maiden), begins as a languid piece, turns rousing and intense, and then returns to its languor. The third piece, "Danza del gaucho matrero" (Dance of the Bandit Gaucho), is similar to the first but faster and makes use of recognizable melodic bits from Argentine folk music. *—Hector Bellman*

Recommended:

○ **Live from the Concertgebouw, 1978 & 1979** / Argerich / 2000 / Angel 56975B

Malambo, Op. 7 (1940)

Typical of Alberto Ginastera's appropriation of native Argentinean folk elements, the piano work *Malambo* (1940) spices a traditional dance form with nontraditional harmonies. The composer emphasizes the machismo of a gaucho's gestures by weighing down a folksy chord progression with chromaticism and polytonality. The nature of dance is initially clear, but gradually its gestures become more and more exaggerated and unwieldy, the harmonies more obscured, the texture saturated. This reaches an extreme when, near the end of the piece, the simple melody and repetitive accompanimental figures are completely overtaken by a series of upward-surging runs and polychordal outbursts. After taking a moment to reorient itself, *Malambo* returns to the unadorned dance material of the beginning, now repeated with increasing inertia as the work hurtles toward a forceful close. *—Jeremy Grimshaw*

Recommended:

○ **Ginastera: Piano Music, Vol. 1** / Delgado / M.A. Recordings 038

○ **Latin American Classics, Vol. 1** / Bátiz (cond.), Mexico Festival Orch. / 1994 / Naxos 550838

Piano Sonata No. 1, Op. 22 (1952)

Alberto Ginastera's *Piano Sonata No. 1*, Op. 22, exemplifies the stylistic traits associated with what scholars have described as Ginastera's "subjective nationalist" period. In earlier works, such as the *Danzas Argentinas*, Op. 2, from 1937, and the *Creole Faust Overture* from 1943, Ginastera borrowed from, modeled on, and/or made explicit references to dance and song styles from the folk traditions of his native Argentina. Beginning in the late 1940s and early 1950s, however, with such works as *Pampeana No. 1* (1947) and the orchestral piece *Ollantay* (1950), Ginastera tempered his earlier, explicitly nationalist style with a more cosmopolitan approach and a more sophisticated technical treatment of musical materials. Composed in 1952, the Op. 22 piano sonata reflects this more complex integration of national identity and compositional method through its fusion of lively, dance-derived rhythmic figurations, evocative textures, and modern musical forms and idioms. The dramatic first movement of the sonata, marked Allegro marcato, begins with aggressive chordal gestures emphasizing the extremes of the piano's range. The opening material and the subsequent, more lyrical theme, undergo a series of virtuosic figurational transformations organized in carefully paced arcs of intensity and repose. When the opening material returns at the end of the movement, it is intensified by a subtle shift upwards in its tonal orientation. The second movement, "Presto misterioso," conveys a palpably nervous energy, not only through its striking melodic material—a slithering line constituting a 12-tone row—but also through its unique texture: both hands play the same line in octaves at opposite ends of the keyboard, occasionally diverging for chromatic runs in contrary motion. The busy angst and relentless rhythmic drive of the second movement is sharply contrasted by the dreamy languor of the third, marked Adagio molto appassionato. The movement begins with sparse, ringing tones in arid, ascending arcs alternating with lyrical, introspective passages. The sinuous melodies of the latter section slowly gather momentum and eventually break into sensual, rhapsodic exclamations and florid figurations before subsiding again into a kind of narcotic haze. The Argentine element is perhaps most apparent in the driving syncopations and stylized bravado of the final movement. The right hand articulates angular ostinato figures while the bold octaves in the bass project a metrical emphasis that constantly shifts between 6/8 and 3/4, conveying in a modern musical language an indelible "gaucho" flavor. *—Jeremy Grimshaw*

Recommended:

○ **Ginastera: Complete Piano Music, Vol. 1** / Portugheis, Natola-Ginastera / 1993 / ASV 865

ORCHESTRAL

Creole Faust Overture (Obertura para el "Fausto" criollo), Op. 9 (1943)

In 1866, Argentinian politician and writer Ernesto del Campo had a chance to see a performance of Charles Gounod's opera *Faust* in Buenos Aires. The experience inspired him to write a tale called *El Fausto criollo* ("The Creole Faust"), which featured a gaucho telling a friend about watching a performance of *Faust* in Buenos Aires. The gaucho in del Campo's tale is plainly both captivated and confused by the theater, the production and the music itself, and he describes the performance in humorous terms. Del Campo's work was immensely popular in Argentina, and became a classic of Argentinian gaucho literature. In 1943, Alberto Ginastera was in the middle of his nationalist period, having already written works like the *Argentinian Dances* and the *Songs of Tucaman* which celebrated the melodies and rhythms of Argentinian folk music. *El Fausto criollo* seemed a natural subject for Ginastera, and so he wrote *Overture for "The Creole Faust"* in which ponderous European music (based partially on a few themes from Gounod's opera) competes with boisterous Argentinian music, with delightful results. Imposing chords open the overture, followed by a low, foreboding string melody. This melody moves gradually into a higher register, and becomes faster and faster, until without warning the orchestra breaks out into a high-spirited Argentinian dance. For the rest of the overture, Ginastera contrasts the two styles of music. The European music is generally written for massed strings and heavy brass, while the Argentinian music emphasizes woodwinds and exotic percussion. Thus, when Ginastera brings the woodwinds into a fugato that had formerly been for strings alone, we can sense that the music will move into the Argentinian mode soon. The two musics continue to yield unexpectedly to each other until the work's end, when the big opening chords come back and give way one last time to a spirited dance that closes the work. Ginastera's *Overture for "The Creole Faust"* is a skillful work that stays close to the exuberant spirit of its original text. *—Andrew Lindemann Malone*

Recommended:

○ **Fiesta in Hi-Fi** / Hanson (cond.), Eastman-Rochester Orch. / 1992 / Mercury 434324

○ **Caramelos Latinos** / Valdes (cond.), Simon Bolivar SO of Venezuela / 1995 / Dorian 90227

Variaciones concertantes, for chamber orchestra, Op. 23 (1953)

Alberto Ginastera composed this work, commissioned by the Argentine Friends of Music, in 1953. Igor Markevitch conducted the first performance on June 2 of that year, in Buenos Aires. It is scored for two flutes, piccolo, oboe, two clarinets, bassoon; two horns, trumpet, trombone; timpani; harp; and string choir. *Variaciones concertantes* germinated for five years before Ginastera formally composed it during the second of four creative periods in his life. *Variaciones concertantes* and *Pampeana No. 3* (for small and large orchestras, respectively) typify the second period (1948–61), which also hatched the *First Piano Sonata* and the *First String Quartet*, culminating in *Cantata para América mágica*.

Ginastera said that *Variaciones* has "a subjective character. Instead of employing folkloric materials, an Argentine atmosphere is obtained by the use of original melodies and rhythms... whose expressive tension has a pronounced Argentine accent." He called it "concerto-like," with some variations being decorative or ornamental, others "written in the modern form of metamorphosis, which consists in taking motives from the principal theme and constructing a new theme from them." The work is in 12 parts, played without interruption.

1. Theme for Cello and Harp (Adagio molto espressivo). While the harp plays variants of the so-called "guitar chord" (E-A-D-G-B-E), the solo cello sings a contemplative theme verging on sadness. The key of E, major and minor, is established immediately.

2. Interlude for Strings (same tempo). Like planes in an air-show, the music "peels away" from formation, chromatically.

3. Jocose Variation for Flute (Tempo giusto) has a bustling accompaniment, leading into—

4. Variation in the Style of a Scherzo for Clarinet (Vivace). The key switches to G; the rhythmic underpinning is a malambo, or gauchos' dance.

5. Dramatic Variation for Viola (Largo). Modal in character, this may remind some of Respighi's Gregorian-flavored music.

6. Canonic Variation for Oboe and Bassoon (Adagio tranquillo), in two parts, recalls the opening theme harmonically.

7. Rhythmic Variation for Trumpet and Trombone (Allegro) is another malambo, this one very brief.

8. Perpetual Motion Variation for Violin (same tempo). With an ABA ministructure, this too is brief and rhythmically impelled.

9. Pastoral Variation for Horn (Largamente) with a sostenuto string cushion—gently bitonal, although E major dominates.

10. Interlude for Winds (Moderato) is more assertively bitonal, otherwise archaic in style.

11. Reprise of the Theme for Double Bass (Adagio molto espressivo), harp-accompanied as before, but now markedly melancholic.

12. Variation-Finale in Rondo Style for Full Orchestra (Allegro molto) is a final evocation of the malambo. Whooping flutes and brass, pounding drums, and a string ostinato whip the piece to a rousing conclusion. *—Roger Dettmer*

Recommended:

○ **Ginastera: Variaciones concertantes; Glosses on Themes of Casals** / Ben-Dor (cond.), Israel CO / 1995 / Koch 7149

CHAMBER MUSIC

Guitar Sonata, Op. 47 (1976; revised 1981)

For many years, the Argentine composer Alberto Ginastera shied away from writing any music for guitar. As a non-player, writing for the instrument was difficult and this fact, he said, "checked my creativity, although the guitar is the national instrument of my homeland." It was only in the 1970s, when the Brazilian guitarist Carlos Barbosa-Lima asked for a composition, that he finally wrote for the guitar. At that time, he said, he realized that the "guitar repertoire in fact consisted solely of little pieces, with virtually no large, uniform works." Therefore he decided to write a sonata in the standard four, albeit concise, movements, each lasting between two and four minutes. The sonata was quickly recognized as one of the major pieces in the guitar repertory.

Ginastera added a few musical "special effects" to the usual sounds of the guitar. The opening "Esordio" is built on two themes: One has the quality of an exhortation, with accompaniment of punctuating chords. The other theme is more lyrical, with percussion effects. The second-movement Scherzo is perhaps the most extreme in its use of unusual sound effects: glissandi of both single notes and chords, strumming on the strings in the area where they are attached to their tuning pegs, and causing the strings to snap against the fingerboard punctuate a rhythmic movement. At times, the rhythm stops for some serious-sounding out-of-tempo statements, which are then interrupted by the scherzo. However, the third movement, the "Canto" is entirely unmeasured, like a flowing, improvised serenade, with frequent changes of tempo and spirit. The final movement is a vigorous rondo, with rhythms that can be traced back to pre-Columbian cultures of the Pampas. *—Joseph Stevenson*

Recommended:

○ **Piano & Guitar** / D & F Halasz / 1994 / Bis 671

Pampeana No. 2, rhapsody for cello & piano, Op. 21 (1950)

Ginastera gave the name "Pampeana"—relating to the Argentine pampas—to three rhapsodic works evoking his country's low-lying plains without quoting specific folk songs or dances. Although the third is a large-scale orchestral work, the first two are more compact pieces for violin (*No. 1*) or cello (*No. 2*) and piano. Written for cellist Aurora Natola, Ginastera's future second wife, the second *Pampeana* begins with a cello proclamation related to the declamations in gaucho singing competitions. The piano, initially restricted to sharp, intermittent chords, launches a vigorous folk rhythm and engages the cello in a brief dance, but soon the cello spins off into its own cadenza, full of double stops and pizzicato. The piano spends a couple of bars trying to lure the cello back to the dance floor, but the cello answers with low growls. Soon, the two instruments unite in a slow, nocturnal meditation; this continues at length, but eventually the instruments fall into a final, frenzied dance with hints of the malambo. *—James Reel*

Recommended:

○ **Le Grand Tango** / O'Riley, Brey / 1997 / Helicon 1025

String Quartet No. 1, Op. 20 (1948)

Ginastera waited until he was in his thirties and well established as a composer before writing his first string quartet. He was near the end of his initial stylistic period, which was strongly based on the music of his native Argentina, and would soon move to a more "international" style. The opening movement begins with an introduction, violent and declamatory in effect; the allegro begins with a vehement, almost savage melody played over hammered chords. The second subject is dance-like, but it is a rough, stamping dance; its development remains agitated, and the recapitulation is in reverse order, leading to a coda restating the opening declamatory statement. Movement two is a spectral scherzo, with rapid repeated-note figures, unusual bowing effects, and nervous rhythms. The third movement, a nocturne, finally breaks the aggressive mood with a lyrical melody for violin; this entire movement is based on the composer's characteristic "guitar" chord—the tones of the six open strings of the instrument played simultaniously. The finale is a rondo in the flavor of Argentine rural dances, featuring contrasting episodes in 5/8 time. *—Joseph Stevenson*

Recommended:

○ **Ginastera: The 3 String Quartets** / Lyric Quartet / 1996 / ASV 944

VOCAL

Two Songs, Op. 3 (1938)

Composed fairly early in Ginastera's career, the *Two Songs*, Op. 3 are characteristic of the composer's nationalistic period; both draw heavily upon traditional rhythms and accompanimental figures. The first, "Canción al Arbol del Olvido" (Song to the Tree of Forgetting), takes as its framework the rhythms of the milonga, an ancestor of the tango. It tells of a man who attempts to free his mind of his lover by sleeping under the tree of forgetfulness. His attempt is in vain, however: he "forgets to forget," and when he wakes, his beloved still haunts his mind. In the second song, "Canción a la Luna Lunanca" (Song for the Moon), the speaker compares the nightly return of the moon to his inevitable return to his lover. The texts of both songs are by Fernán Silva Valdés. *—Jeremy Grimshaw*

Recommended:

○ **Cancíones amatorías** / Fink, Vignoles / 2002 / Hyperion 67186

CONCERTO

Concerto for Strings, Op. 33 (1965)

To fulfill a commission from the National Institute of Culture and Fine Arts of Venezuela for a work to be premiered by Eugene Ormandy and the Philadelphia Orchestra at a 1966 festival in Caracas, Ginastera simply expanded much of his 1958 *String Quartet No. 2*. He jettisoned the first of the quartet's five movements, shuffled the others, beefed up the instrumentation, and, in places, composed additional passages. The quartet had been Ginastera's first entirely serial work, but its powerful rhythms and melodic contours tied it closely to Argentine folk dance and song. This is more apparent in the raw, direct four-instrument version; the string-orchestra expansion seems a bit more distant and abstract.

The concerto's first movement, Variazioni per i solisti, is derived from the quartet's second slow movement, Libero e rapsodico. Here it is a rhapsodic set of variations for the principals in each section, including double bass, with occasional support from the rest of the string body. In the manner of Ginastera's earlier *Variaciones concertantes*, each solo is really a challenging mini-cadenza. The theme itself is meditative and nocturnal, and very few of the variations change its character at all.

The Scherzo fantastico (the quartet's Presto magico), fast and feverish, makes free use of advanced techniques and sounds, with scratching col legno, splashing sul ponticello, and buzzing harmonics added to the more conventional pricks of pizzicato. The result, which also briefly employs aleatorics that look forward to Ginastera's *Glosses on Themes of Pablo Casals*, is more a study in timbre and effect than a development of themes.

The Adagio angoscioso is, as the title suggests, an anguished threnody, more densely scored than anything so far in the piece. The long, harmonically lost theme wanders through a sequence of transformations that create a gradual climax that falls off suddenly midway through the movement, making way for a slow, desolate fade-out.

The frenzied Finale furioso is Bartókian in its snap and intensity. It's as if the spirit of the conclusion of the Hungarian's *Music for Strings, Percussion and Celesta* had transmigrated into an Argentine gaucho dancing a malambo. *—James Reel*

Recommended:

○ **Ginastera: Concerto for Strings; Villa-Lobos: Suite for Strings; etc.** / Turovsky (cond.), I Musici de Montreal / 1996 / Chandos 9434

○ **Death of an Angel** / Hasaj, Spiller, Bariloche Camerata / 1998 / Dorian 90249

Harp Concerto, Op. 25 (1956)

Ginastera's choice of concerto instruments was mainly conventional; he wrote one concerto for violin and two each for piano and cello. Yet the fact that he also produced a concerto for harp shouldn't seem uncharacteristic; it can convincingly be considered a close relative of the guitar, and the guitar was essential to the Argentine folk music that so fascinated Ginastera. He wrote his *Harp Concerto* during a period when he was consolidating folk influences into a more rugged contemporary language; earlier, he had used folklore more directly, and later he would give it all up in favor of serialism and other advanced techniques.

The *Harp Concerto*'s first movement opens percussively and along with the third movement, are both inspired by the Argentine malambo, a 6/8 dance contest for gauchos that involves much stamping of heels. Argentina's tango embraces the eroticism of both sexes, but the rural malambo is purely virile; this is rather ironic in the context of this concerto, given that the harp is played by more women than men. The opening "Allegro giusto" is strongly rhythmic and viscerally exciting, although it does include as its second subject, material that is more mysterious and slightly antique-sounding, but still with a throbbing undercurrent. The slow second movement, "Molto moderato," keeps the harp in the foreground and employs the orchestra mainly for discrete support. The numinous, nocturnal ambience evokes Bartók, particularly with its use of celesta and a brief canonic passage for strings. A long solo cadenza (Liberamente capriccioso) opens the final movement. It surges and hesitates, incorporating special effects with pedals, fingernails, and harmonics without ever falling in line with the avant-garde (unlike Ginastera's *Violin Concerto* of the following decade). The inevitable harp glissandi are interrupted by a slap from the orchestra, which brings on another malambo (Vivace). The rhythmic pressure never lets up, not even when the orchestra is reduced to the strings' thumping under the wood of their bows. It all builds to a dissonant, exceptionally dramatic conclusion. *—James Reel*

Recommended:

○ **Ginastera: Harp Concerto; Estancia; Piano Concerto** / Batiz (cond.), Allen, Mexico City PO / 1989 / ASV 654

BALLET

Estancia, Op. 8 (1941)

In 1941, the American ballet director Lincoln Kirstein commissioned Ginastera for a "Ballet in One Act and Five Scenes, based on Argentine country life." The resulting work, *Estancia*, was to be performed by the American Ballet Caravan, a platform for young American choreographers whose aim was to move ballet away from Russian traditions (one of the company's biggest hits had been the 1938 ballet, *Billy the Kid*, with music by Copland). For *Estancia*, Kirstein planned to commission choreography from George Balanchine, and present the ballet in New York. It was not until 1952, at Argentina's Teatro Colón, however, that the complete *Estancia* would be performed, with choreography by Michel Borowski and sets by Dante Ortolani. The prior commission was abandoned after the Caravan suddenly disbanded after the troupe's Latin American tour in 1941.

In keeping with Kirstein's original request, the ballet takes place on the vast, grassy Argentine Pampas, on a farm or cattle ranch. Ginastera closely based his score on the great epic poem *Martín Fierro* by José Hernández (1873), which tells the story of the Argentinian cowboy, or gaucho. These downtrodden, nomadic, yet heroic individuals are the subject of much of the country's folklore.

Estancia represents the passage of a single day: dawn, morning, afternoon, night, and dawn. The ballet's action takes on an essentially symmetrical, arch-like structure, and simultaneously tells the story of simple love and symbolic resolution of the ways in which city life was encroaching on the old agrarian ways. Specifically, it tells of a city boy who watches, and falls in love with, a country maiden. After some initial contempt for him, her feelings turn to admiration after he proves his skill in taming wild horses. Romance, starlight and then the inevitable new day follow.

Employing a normal-size orchestra (though with extended percussion section), Ginastera evokes the earthy, evocative manner of Hernández's poetry with malambo rhythms, guitar-like sonorities and extracts (both sung and spoken) from the verse. Ginastera's music corresponds to the symmetry of the plot, with the horse-taming rodeo ("La doma") and the evening romance ("Idilio crepuscular") set as the central events. The two dawn scenes use versions of the same vivacious malambo-based material, while the central sequence of music is a vividly colored mosaic of dances evoking details of the activities of rural folk and visitors from the town.

In *Estancia*, Ginastera not only captures the rhythms of life on an Argentine ranch, but also provides a testament to the gaucho's now-vanished way of life; it also honors the spirit of Martín Fierro, "the unlucky gaucho, who has no one to call to, with no place of his own in all that space, and in all that darkness." *—Brian Wise*

Recommended:

○ **Música Iberoamericana** / Asensio (cond.), Spanish National Radio Orch. / 1993 / RTVE 65029

○ **Ginastera: Estancia; Panambí** / Ben-Dor (cond.) / 1998 / Conifer 51336

Umberto Giordano

b. Aug. 28, 1867, Foggia, Italy, **d.** Nov. 12, 1948, Milan, Italy

Composer: Opera

Umberto Giordano was born the son of a pharmacist who was against his son pursuing a career in music; the budding composer therefore learned the beginnings of his craft surreptitiously from Gaetano Briganti, a local maker of mechanical instruments. In 1880, Giordano's father finally lifted his objections, and Giordano entered the Naples Conservatory, where he studied somewhat irregularly until 1890. When Giordano was unable to attend at the Conservatory, he worked as a stagehand at the Teatro Dauno in Foggia.

In 1889 Giordano entered the Sonzogno Competition with his first one-act opera, *Marina*, which he had composed on a libretto purchased for only 25 lire. *Marina* placed sixth in the competition, and it earned the composer an invitation to play the score for the publisher Sonzogno personally—a compositional audition. When Giordano had finished playing the work, Sonzogno told him "I will not publish this opera, as I do not like the libretto. But I will engage you in a contract for a new work."

The agreement resulted in *Mala vita*, perhaps the grimmest verismo opera attempted to that point on the Italian stage. It was well received, especially in German-speaking countries, but a riot broke out at the work's premiere in Naples. In 1902, Giordano softened the dramatic edges of *Mala vita* and restaged it successfully in Naples as *Il Voto*.

Giordano's second opera, *Regina di Diaz*, was a certifiable flop, and Sonzogno threatened Giordano with a severance of contract. However, having unwittingly rescued the composer Pietro Mascagni from a tram accident in early 1896, Giordano was heartily repaid when Mascagni went to Sonzogno to argue on his behalf. This second chance resulted in what has become the composer's most famous work, *Andrea Chénier* (premiered March 28, 1896). Its libretto, drawn from events of the French Revolution, gave the initial producers pause, since political unrest was then high in Italy, and the work's effect on audiences was uncertain. But the work was greeted with huge enthusiasm, thanks in no small part to tenor Giuseppe Borgatti, who created the role of Andrea. The "Improvisation" and the aria, "La mamma morta," have remained popular excerpts.

The emergence of Giordano's next principal opera, *Fedora*, coincided with the appearance of yet another unknown tenor, Enrico Caruso; their mutual success gave rise to the saying, "*Fedora* made Caruso, and Caruso made *Fedora*." Giordano later claimed he had coached Caruso for the work using a cylinder phonograph to point out flaws in the voice; as Giordano once said, "I made a new Caruso out of him." While Caruso went on to the most brilliant career of any Italian tenor, the opera that "made" him is given to only infrequent revival.

Giordano went on to write more operas, but these did not enter the repertory. Notable among these efforts are: *Siberia* (1904), a huge, but not lasting success; *Madame Sans-Gene* (1915), which opened at New York's Metropolitan Opera with Geraldine Farrar in the lead role; *Le cena della befe* (1924), which marked Giordano's later turn away from the verismo style; and *Il re* (1929), in which Giordano broke completely with verismo, creating instead a light comedy that remained popular on European stages through the 1930s.

Aside from his operas, Giordano composed a considerable number of orchestral and chamber works, as well as one ballet, *L'astro magico* (1928). Giordano took a great deal of interest in recording technology, and helped found the *Discoteca di Stato* in Rome—the main Italian archive for historical recordings. Umberto Giordano died in Milan at the age of 81. *—Uncle Dave Lewis*

OPERA

Andrea Chénier (1896)

Giordano's *Andrea Chénier* (1896) is a fiery verisimo work very loosely based on the life and writings of a French poet who was guillotined during the French Revolution. The opera excitingly depicts the excesses of the French aristocracy, the idealism of the revolutionaries in their dreams of freedom, equality, and brotherhood, and the excesses of blood lust that ended the Revolution. The musical language is strongly post-Romantic, with gorgeous lyricism, fervent declamatory arias, and crashingly ominous passages depicting the crowds and tribunals that sent so many to their deaths. All of the characters are strongly drawn, from Chénier, the fervent supporter of the ideals of the Revolution, Maddalena, the formerly frivolous aristocrat, and Gérard, the lackey who became a Revolutionary leader, to the bit parts of the vindictive tribunal judges and members of the crowd.

The tale set against this backdrop is a love story between Chénier and Maddalena. Gérard is in love with Maddalena; in order to get her for himself, he has Chénier arrested. The aria in which he makes this fateful decision is one of the most dramatic in the baritone repertoire: He cynically writes the accusations he knows to be false, then remembers how Chénier himself inspired his now-tarnished revolutionary zeal. Upon learning of Chénier's arrest, Maddalena comes to Gérard for help, telling him of the death of her mother, the loss of her home, and how Chénier's love transformed her life. Though Gérard tries to save Chénier, the hero is condemned at the the corrupt trial, and Maddalena joins him in the prison so that they can die together. *—Ann Feeney*

Synopsis:

Act One. The first act takes place in a ballroom, where Gérard and the other servants are preparing for a party. Gérard is embittered by his and his father's life of inherited servitude, and he predicts the fall of the aristocracy ("Son sessant'anni"). Maddalena enters, and Gérard reflects on her beauty. The Countess bustles in, fussing over the arrangements, and Maddalena, tired of the silly dictates of fashion ("L'orribile gonnella"), declares she will wear a simple dress and one flower as ornament. The guests arrive and exchange elaborate compliments and gossip about the court and the prevalent mood of social unrest. They watch a pastoral entertainment ("O pastorelle, addio"), and the Countess is piqued when Chénier, a new visitor, does not recite to entertain her guests. Maddalena bets her friends that she can get Chénier to speak of love, and when she asks to hear his poetry, he compares its caprices to love. She laughs and he, stung, describes to her the contrast between the beauties of the country and the misery of its poverty ("Un di, all'azzurro spazio"), concluding that love is the soul of the world and declaring she does not know it. She is perturbed, and Gérard leads in a group of beggars, whom he announces as "His Highness, Misery." His father pleads for clemency, but Gérard instead leads him out as the Countess exclaims indignantly that they should treat such a charitable mistress so shabbily.

Act Two. Later, during the Terror, Bersi is flirting in a café with L'incredibile, declaring herself a lover of the Revolution ("Temer? Perché?"), but he is still suspicious that she has a connection with Chénier, once a Revolutionary leader but now under suspicion as a moderate. Roucher comes in and offers Chénier a passport, telling him he is in danger, but Chénier refuses to take it ("Credi al destino?"), saying he believes his destiny lies with a mysterious woman who writes him unsigned letters. Roucher examines the latest letter and is sure it is the effusion of some prostitute. They watch as members of the new government emerge, among them Gérard, who asks L'incredibile to find Maddalena for him. Bersi manages to whisper to Chénier to meet his letter-writer in a few minutes. He agrees, and as the crowd leaves, Maddalena enters, heavily veiled. On Chénier's return, she repeats his words about love, and he recognizes her—as does L'incredibile, who is watching. She tells him of how she has often thought of him ("Eravate possente"), and pleads for his help. They are soon singing a blissful love duet, "Ora soave," but are interrupted by Gérard, who claims Maddalena as his. Roucher, who has lingered, takes Maddalena to safety, and Chénier and Gérard fight. Gérard is wounded but recognizes Chénier. He urges him to flee, and when L'incredibile returns with a mob, he says he did not recognize his assailant.

Act Three. In the public room in the court, Mathieu harangues the crowd for money to help support the Revolution. Gérard, recovering, comes in and addresses them in heartfelt words ("Lacrime e sangue"), to which the crowd does respond. Madelon, a blind old woman brings her grandson, her sole surviving relative ("Son la vecchia Madelon"), whom she offers as a soldier. The crowd moves out, exuberantly dancing the Carmagnole, leaving Gérard and L'incredibile. He tells Gérard that now, with Chénier arrested, Maddalena will come to plead for him ("Donnina innamorata"), giving Gérard access to her. He urges Gérard to write an indictment of Chénier. Gérard begins to do so ("Nemico della patria"), but is overwhelmed by thoughts of how such abuse of his power betrays all his idealistic dreams. However, overwhelmed by his longing for Maddalena, he signs it. She comes in a moment later, and he reveals his passion for her ("Perché ti volli qui?"). She offers him her body in exchange for Chénier's life, and describes how Chénier's love changed her misery at the loss of her mother and her own constant fears and dangers into exaltation ("La mamma morta"). Gérard is overwhelmed by the power of her love and vows to save Chénier without demanding his price. People rush in to watch the trial, where various former aristocrats and officials are immediately condemned to death. Chénier is allowed to defend himself and does so, declaring himself a poet and soldier who fought with both pen and sword for his country ("Si, fui soldato"). Gérard denounces his own accusation as a lie, rushing to embrace Chénier, who is deeply moved, but Fouqier-Tinville renews the accusation on his own behalf, and Chénier is condemned to death as Maddalena cries out in agony.

Act Four. The finale takes place in the prison courtyard. Chénier reads his last poem, describing his death as the ending of a beautiful day in May ("Come un bel dì di maggio") and dedicating his last breath to the goddess of poetry. Gérard brings in Maddalena, who bribes Schmidt, the jailer, to let her take the place of another young woman who was condemned to die. Gérard goes to plead with Robespierre again for their lives, leaving Maddalena and Chénier alone. They welcome the idea of being united in death, declaring their love ("Vicino a te"), and as the cart to take them to the guillilotine arrives, they cry, "Long live death! Together!" *—Ann Feeney*

Recommended:

○ **Giordano: Andrea Chénier** / Santini (cond.), Corelli, Stasio, Malagu, Modesti, Rome Opera Orch. / 1994 / EMI 65287

○ **Giordano: Andrea Chénier** / Molajoli (cond.), Marini, Galeffi, Rasa, Bassi, La Scala Theater Orch. / 2000 / Naxos 110066-67

Fedora (1898)

Umberto Giordano's *Fedora*, based upon the play by Victorien Sardou, premiered just two and a half years after the composer's immensely successful *Andrea Chénier.* At Milan's Teatro Lirico, the protagonist was Gemma Bellinconi and her Loris was a young tenor named Enrico Caruso. Although hostile at the beginning, the audience slowly gained enthusiasm, and by the middle of the second act Caruso was obliged to repeat his aria. At the end, success was complete and within the next few years the opera was presented throughout Italy, Europe, and other parts of the world. While it failed to sustain its initial success, it has remained popular in its native country and enjoys continuing favor among sopranos who can both muster personal and vocal glamour and command the stage. Indeed, since the work's technical demands are fairly modest, it has become a harbor of refuge to aging prima donnas whose voices are still distinctive, even if less agile than they may have been. The solitary high C (optional) makes Fedora a viable role for dramatic mezzos, and many of its most riveting interpreters have been from the lower voice range. Tenors, too, despite second billing, relish the score's most memorable moment, a short, long-lined aria ("Amor to vieta") which unfolds with a fresh-minted lyricism few audiences can resist.

For a librettist, Giordano chose Arturo Colautti, a novelist and poet who later provided Francesco Cilea the text for his *Adriana Lecouvreur* (a work bearing certain similarities to *Fedora*). The Sardou play upon which Colautti based his libretto had long been of interest to Giordano, who felt it to be perfectly consonant with the verismo style.

Fedora, a Russian Princess, finds her fiancé Count Vladimir assassinated and swears chastity so long as his murderer is at large and unpunished. From Vladimir's St. Petersburg apartments to Fedora's Parisian home and thence to her Bernese Oberland villa, the settings are exotic, the characters aristocratic, the situations wrapped in intrigue. Count Loris Ipanoff, whom Fedora is certain killed her intended, admits that it was indeed he, not as a political activist, but a husband pursuing his wife's lover. Fedora, who has both ensnared Loris in a romantic involvement and has found herself attracted to him, learns the complete truth only after she dispatches a letter to the Russian embassy detailing Loris' confession and adding a paragraph about the arrest of Loris' brother, Valerian, that seems to implicate both in the Nihilist movement. Following a blissful interlude, Loris and Fedora are visited by the consequences of her letter. Loris learns that his brother has drowned in a subterranean cell and that their mother has died, grief-stricken. When Fedora pleads for forgiveness, Loris realizes that it was she who had sent the vengeful letter and curses her. Fedora takes poison. An antidote fails, Loris learns the entire story and Fedora dies, finally forgiven. *—Erik Eriksson*

Synopsis:

Act One. In Count Vladimir's St. Petersburg house, the servants gossip that Vladimir won't be back until dawn; he is celebrating his last night of freedom before marrying the rich Fedora, just in time to pay his debts. Fedora herself enters, saying she has been waiting for him. They send a servant to his club to look for him, and she examines a portrait, contemplating his eyes "glowing with fidelity" ("O grand'occhi lucenti di fede"). De Seriex, Grech, and servants help Vladimir in, gravely wounded. They take him into his bedroom, and Grech questions the servants. Cirillo describes hearing shots and seeing a man run past, dripping blood; then he found Vladimir wounded. Dmitri, a very young servant, remembers a man coming in and leaving without seeing Vladimir. Fedora grandly declares that he must be the culprit, and, on the cross she wears, she vows to avenge him. Dmitri finally remembers the man's name, Loris Ipanov, and Grech sends the police to his house, just across the street. Fedora watches intently, screaming for them to catch him, and a servant emerges to tell them that Vladimir is dead. Grech returns, reporting that Loris had already left. Fedora collapses.

Act Two. In her luxurious Parisian house, Fedora is giving a party. Olga flirts, declaring that politics are her passion, and de Seriex is surprised to see Loris there. Fedora tells him that she has caught the attention of Loris and intends to entice a confession out of him, though she admits that "perhaps" she has fallen in love herself. Boroff warns Loris against Fedora, but he declares that he is madly in love. Fedora says that she has substituted a cure for every ill in the reliquary case of her cross. Olga presents a pianist, Lazinski, as the next Chopin. When Olga snubs him, de Seriex calls her a Cossack, and she declares herself offended. He defends himself with a laughing tribute to Russian women ("La donna russa e femmina due volte"), angel and serpent, self-sacrificing and treacherous, and he greets Olga as the ideal. Fedora flirts with Loris ("Ma, dunque, è amore"), who responds that Love itself forbids her not to love him ("Amor ti vieta"). She says she is returning to Russia tomorrow, and he is stricken, since as an exile, he cannot return. She says she will ask the Czar for a pardon for him. As Lazinski plays, she asks for details of his crime, telling him to prove his innocence for her sake. He admits that he did kill Vladimir and says that he will return that night with proof of his moral innocence. De Seriex receives a dispatch saying that the Nihilists attempted to assassinate the Czar, and the party breaks up, with Grech and the police remaining. Fedora sends a letter to Yariskin, Vladimir's father and the Chief of Police, saying that Loris has confessed, and adds that his brother was an accomplice. They plan to abduct him to take him back to Russia when he leaves her house that night: a whistle will signal they are ready outside. They leave, and Loris returns. He tells her that he killed Vladimir over his wife ("Mia madre, la mia vecchia madre"). His mother had hired a companion, Wanda, who seduced him into a secret marriage. He was blissfully oblivious that she was betraying him with his own best man, Vladimir, until he found a letter arranging for a rendezvous. Fedora refuses to believe it until he gives her the note, in which Vladimir referred to his marriage as being made for money. She exclaims in anger, and Loris adds that he burst in upon them, that Vladimir fired at him but just wounded him, and that he killed him. Now he laments that he is an exile and will never see his family again ("Vedi, io piango"). She now declares that she loves him and will make up for his losses, and when she hears the signal, she asks him to stay the night.

Act Three. Offstage, at Fedora's Switzerland villa, peasants sing of the arriving spring ("Dice la capinera"). Fedora and Loris declare their love and kiss. Olga enters and informs them that the whole world bores her. Loris goes to fetch his mail, and de Seriex enters. He teases Olga about Lazinski, and then tells her Lazinski was a spy. She quickly recovers from the shock, and he suggests a bicycle ride. She happily goes off to change, and he turns to Fedora, telling her he really came for her sake. He explains ("Cade per l'empia sua crudeltà") that when her letter reached Yariskin, Loris' brother was being held in an underground fortress, which flooded, drowning him. At the shock of hearing the news, their mother died as well. Olga returns, and de Seriex leads her away. Alone, Fedora prays for Loris ("Dio di giustizia"). He returns, first reading a letter from Boroff saying that he has been pardoned. He bursts out with joy at the thought of being able to return to his family and to marry Fedora, but she is silent. The next letter brings him the news of the disaster ("Jariskin reco all'Imperatore"), also telling him of the letter from an unknown Russian woman in Paris that declared him and his brother proven guilty. He breaks down in grief but then declares they will go to Paris to find his hidden enemy. Fedora begs him instead to forgive that woman ("Forse con te li piange"), who perhaps is overwhelmed with grief and guilt. He angrily refuses, and at her continued pleading, he realizes she is the informer. He throws himself on her in rage, and she breaks away and drinks the poison from her cross. Fedora pleads again for Loris' forgiveness, which he finally grants. Whispering that she loves him, she dies. *—Ann Feeney*

Recommended:

○ **Giordano: Fedora** / Patane (cond.), Carreras, Marton, Kincses, Kovats, Hungarian Radio & Television SO / 1986 / CBS 42181

Mauro Giuliani

b. Jul. 27, 1781, Bisceglie, Italy, **d.** May 8, 1829, Naples, Italy
Composer: Chamber Music, Concerto

An acclaimed Italian guitar virtuoso and composer, Mauro Giuliani, along with Fernando Sor, was one of the last great classical proponents of his instrument until its revival in the early twentieth century. He studied counterpoint and the cello, but on the six-string guitar he was entirely self-taught, and that became his principal instrument early on. Italy abounded with fine guitarists at the beginning of the nineteenth century (Carulli remains the most familiar today), but few of them could make a living because of the public's preoccupation with opera. So Giuliani embarked on a successful tour of Europe when he was 19, and in 1806 he settled in Vienna, where he entered the musical circle of Diabelli, Moscheles, and Hummel. He solidified his reputation with the 1808 premiere of his *Guitar Concerto in A major*, Op. 30, and was soon heralded as the greatest living guitar virtuoso. Even Beethoven noticed Giuliani, and wrote a few guitar pieces especially for him. Perhaps to return the favor, Giuliani played cello in the 1813 premiere of Beethoven's *Symphony No. 7*.

Around 1814, Giuliani was named *virtuoso onorario di camera* to Napoleon's second wife, Empress Marie-Louise. But, deeply in debt, he returned to Italy in 1819. An 1823 trip to London brought him acclaim in the English-speaking world, and resulted in a short-lived fan publication called *The Giulianiad*. After this visit, the guitarist settled in Naples, enjoying the patronage of the court of the Kingdom of Two Sicilies. He became adept on an obscure instrument called the lyre-guitar (which was marketed mainly to female amateurs), and perfected the design of the "ghitarra di terza," an instrument with a shorter fingerboard than that of the regular "Spanish" guitar.

Giuliani published more than 200 works; his most durable pieces include three lyrical concertos in a late Classical/early Romantic style, and, for solo guitar, the *Grand Overture*, Op. 61, and a series of six sometimes long-winded suites, *Le Rossiniane*, based on tunes by Gioacchino Rossini. As a special help to other players, Giuliani notated his works on the treble clef in an innovative manner, with the rests and note-stem directions distinguishing the melody from the bass line and inner voices. *—James Reel*

Overview of Works (ca. 1806–1829)

Although Italian composer Mauro Giuliani also studied the cello, it was the guitar he focused on in his career as both a performer and composer. His three guitar concertos are the most important and influential of his roughly 220 compositions for the instrument. All three guitar concertos are cast in three movements, and surprisingly, the finales to both the *First* and *Third* are brilliant polonaises. The *Concerto No. 1* features an Allegro maestoso opening movement that offers a graceful, light main theme and livelier, even lighter alternate theme. The Andantino middle panel carries the parenthetical description Siciliano and does convey an Italianate songfulness in its passionate, dark melody while the closing Polonaise (Allegretto) is utterly charming in its rhythmic merriment. The *Concerto No. 2* (1812) frames a lovely Andantino, which has strains of the second-movement theme of Mozart's *Piano Concerto No. 20* and Mozart's style in general, with a noble and joyous Maestoso and a sprightly, colorful Rondo finale (Allegretto). The *Concerto No. 3* (ca. 1815) features an attractive march-like main theme in the first movement and a middle panel marked Andantino alla Siciliana that has bouncy, bright manner in its lyrical main theme. The Polonaise finale (Allegretto), once again, crowns the concerto with lively, colorful music. In all of the works, the guitar writing is masterful and quite challenging for the performer.

Among Giuliani's most popular solo guitar music are his *Rossiniana* works, six sets of pieces composed in the period 1820–28 and assigned the opus numbers 119 through 124. Among the more popular items here are *No. 1*, Op. 119; *No. 2*, Op. 120; and *No. 5*, Op. 123, all charming efforts based on themes from Rossini's operas. But these sets were hardly his only efforts that draw on works by other composers. He wrote a whole series of variation pieces for guitar that include the fairly substantial *Variations on a Theme by Paisiello* (ca. 1810), Op. 4, which opens with a lovely melody and goes on to present several highly imaginative variations. His *Variations on a Theme by Handel*, Op. 107, and *Variations on a March by Cherubini*, Op. 110, both dating to about 1828, divulge Giuliani's ability to adapt to the less fiery Germanic world of Handel in the former work, as well as to the more familiar lyricism inherent in Cherubini's music. Giuliani's *Grand Overture for Guitar* (1814) is also notable for its sense of drama and color.

His *Grand Potpourri*, Op. 53; the pair of four-movement works; the *Grand Serenade*, Op. 82; and *Grand Duo Concertant*, Op. 85, are three works scored for flute or violin and guitar. All are examples of his brilliant instrumental writing in the chamber music genre. Giuliani also produced a fairly sizable lieder output, which is generally neglected today owing to its somewhat less-inspired yield. *—Robert Cummings*

Recommended:

○ **Music of Giuliani** / Russell / Telarc 80525

○ **Giuliani: Variations** / Gallen / 2002 / Naxos 555284

○ **Giuliani: Duets for Flute & Guitar** / Kraft, Shulman / 2001 / Naxos 554560

CHAMBER MUSIC

Grand Duo Concertante, sonata for flute & guitar in A major, Op. 85 (ca. 1810)

Although the guitar is more closely associated with Spain than with any other country, it was Italy which brought it into the concert hall. Paganini, the famous violin virtuoso, was an avid and very able guitarist who frequently wrote for the instrument. Mauro Giuliani was the most celebrated concert guitarist of the time. He became famous during the late days of the Classical era, and even Beethoven wrote guitar music for him. His rise to fame paralleled that of Rossini. His instrumental style occupies similar ground in the continuum between the Classical and the Romantic eras.

This sonata was first written as work for flute and guitar. In keeping with the business practices of music of the day, Giuliani also had published a violin version. The music is very tuneful, using the kind of operatic Italian melody which Rossini was making popular. The sonata is nearly 20 minutes long and is a very pleasing, though hardly deep, work. *—Joseph Stevenson*

Recommended:

○ **Giuliani: Complete Works for flute & guitar, Vol. 1** / Savijoki, Helasvuo / 1988 / Bis 411

Grande Overture for guitar in A major, Op. 61 (ca. 1810)

Although he was a younger contemporary and colleague of Beethoven, Giuliani followed the more strictly classical principles of Mozart and Haydn. This is illustrated perfectly in his *Grand Overture*, which consists of a brief, slow, minor-mode introduction followed by a fully developed major-mode sonata-allegro structure. Giuliani himself was a guitar virtuoso, so this piece requires great facility and invites imaginative coloring from the player.

The introduction is quite simple; a gently throbbing ostinato bass note underlies brief passages that initially cascade downward and then rise expectantly. The movement's main matter is built upon good-natured, even bumptious, music that relies heavily on fast passagework and burbling tunes, with some sly partial scales and a couple of crescendos tossed in for humorous effect. Indeed, if this were orchestrated it would be indistinguishable from an opera overture by Giuliani's idol, Rossini. *—James Reel*

Recommended:

○ **Music of Giuliani** / Russell / Telarc 80525

CONCERTO

Guitar Concerto No. 1 in A major, Op. 30 (1808)

The guitar, and its relative the lute, enjoyed some popularity in the Renaissance and Baroque eras. But by the nineteenth century the lute was more or less obsolete and the guitar, which by then had taken its familiar six-string form, had fallen out of favor. Perhaps the best-known guitarist of that century was Mauro Giuliani, who, after moving to Vienna in his middle twenties, almost single-handedly brought the instrument back to public notice through his playing, composing, and teaching. He also wrote what might be the first true guitar concerto, his *Concerto No. 1 in A major*, which he premiered in Vienna in April 1808 to considerable acclaim.

The concerto is in the usual three movements. The first, Allegro maestoso, is a sonata-allegro based on two genial themes, both of which have a playful, Rossini-like cast. Once the orchestra presents the tunes, the guitar takes them up and develops them with a variety of embellishments and much technical display. The second movement, an Andantino, is marked Siciliano. It begins with a melancholy theme in the minor for strings, later taken by the guitar. Interestingly, the charming second tune is in the major, and the movement continues in the major to the end. A sprightly refrain opens the third movement Allegretto, a polonaise. Here, and throughout the concerto, the guitarist is kept quite busy; Giuliani illustrates why he had such a reputation as a virtuoso. *—Chris Morrison*

Recommended:

- ○ **Giuliani: Complete Guitar Concertos** / Marriner (cond.), P. Romero, Academy of St. Martin-in-the-Fields / 1996 / Philips 454262

Carlo Maria Giulini

b. May 9, 1914, Barletta, Italy, **d.** Jun. 14, 2005, Brescia, Italy
Conductor

An acclaimed and versatile conductor, Carlo Maria Giulini started his musical studies as a violinist, attending the Santa Cecilia Conservatory in Rome. He studied conducting with Bernardino Molinari at Santa Cecilia and Alfredo Casella at Accademia Chigiana in Siena. After graduation, he joined the Augusteo Orchestra in Rome as a violist. As an orchestral musician, he came in contact with the great conductors of the time, including Strauss, Mengelberg, Walter, Klemperer, and Furtwängler. After receiving his conscription notice for military service during World War II, Giulini, an ardent anti-Fascist, decided to go into hiding. When the Allies liberated Rome in 1944 he emerged and conducted the orchestra he used to play in (now known as the Orchestra of the Accademia di Santa Cecilia) in a Brahms symphony to celebrate the liberation. This was his debut as a conductor.

He was subsequently hired as an assistant conductor for the Italian Radio Orchestra, becoming chief conductor in 1946. During his tenure as conductor of the Italian Radio (RAI) Orchestra of Rome, he attracted notice for his innovative programming which included revivals of forgotten operas by Italian Baroque composers, such as Domenico Scarlatti. His theatrical debut was at Bergamo, in Verdi's *La Traviata*.

In 1950, he was sent to help organize a new RAI orchestra in Milan. His broadcast reviving the nearly forgotten Haydn opera *Il mondo della luna* was noticed by many, including legendary conductor Arturo Toscanini and La Scala's principal conductor, Victor de Sabata. He began conducting at Milan's La Scala opera house in 1952, debuting with Manuel de Falla's *La vida breve*. He was engaged as an assistant conductor, succeeding De Sabata as principal conductor in 1953. Among his most notable performances was a classic *Traviata* with Maria Callas. Giulini added new works to the La Scala repertory, including Bartók's *Bluebeard's Castle* and Monteverdi's *L'incoronazione di Poppea*, and worked with stage directors such as Franco Zeffirelli and Luchino Visconti. Although Giulini premiered in England at Glyndebourne in *Falstaff*, it was his direction of Visconti's production of *Don Carlos* at Covent Garden that made him well-known in Britain. In 1955, he debuted in the United States with the Chicago Symphony Orchestra.

Giulini developed a symphonic repertoire slowly, devoting much attention to each new score; thus, he did not conduct Mozart or Beethoven symphonies until he was in his fifties. He was appointed principal guest conductor of the Chicago Symphony in 1969, and was the director of the Vienna Symphony Orchestra from 1973 to 1976. He succeeded Zubin Mehta as musical director of the Los Angeles Philharmonic in 1978, remaining at that post until 1984.

Giulini's conducting incorporates elements of Furtwängler's and Toscanini's styles. His dynamism and purity of sound are reminiscent of Toscanini, but the spacious, Romantic approach reminds one of Furtwängler. His particular attentiveness to inner voices results in a rich sound. Giulini eschews podium theatrics or autocratic attitudes. Instead, he approaches the musicians as co-workers serving the music. After his retirement from Los Angeles, Giulini continued working as a guest conductor, mostly in Paris, Chicago, Milan, Berlin, and Vienna, and eventually limiting his activities to appearances with the major orchestras of these cities. *—Joseph Stevenson*

Recommended:

- ○ **Beethoven: Symphony 9** / Giulini (cond.), Tear, Shirley-Quirk, Armstrong, Reynolds, London SO & Chorus / 1998 / EMI 19695
- ○ **Verdi: Messa da Requiem; 4 Pezzi Sacri** / Giulini (cond.), Schwarzkopf, Baker, Ludwig, Gedda, Ghiaurov, Philharmonia Orch. & Chorus / 2001 / EMI 67563
- ○ **Rossini: Overtures** / Giulini (cond.), Philharmonia Orch. / 2004 / EMI 62804
- ○ **Beethoven: Violin Concerto** / Perlman, Giulini (cond.), Philharmonia Orch. / 1998 / EMI 66952

Philip Glass

b. Jan. 31, 1937, Baltimore, MD
Composer: Film Music, Opera, Chamber Music, Symphonic, Vocal

Philip Glass is generally regarded as one of the most prominent composers associated with the minimalist school, the other major figures being Steve Reich, Terry Riley, and John Adams. His style is quite recognizable, owing to its seeming simplicity of repeated sounds, comprised of evolving patterns of rhythms, which are often quite complex, and rhythmic themes. In some of his early works, like *Two Pages* (1967), the whole of the piece evolves from a single unit or idea that expands as notes are added. In later works, expansion comes via the lengthening of note values or through other inventive processes. Many describe his music in the minimalist vein as mesmerizing; others hear it as numbingly repetitive and devoid of variety in its simplicity. The latter view of his style is itself simplistic and fails to take into account the many subtleties and complexities found in his methods. Glass' mature style embraces more than just minimalism and thus must be viewed being more eclectic and far less dogmatic. There is greater emphasis on melody, less on controlling rhythmic patterns. His opera *Einstein on the Beach* (1975) was the first of an important triology of stage works, the other two being *Satygraha* (1980) and *Akhnaten* (1983). He is one of the most popular serious composers of the latter twentieth and early twenty-first centuries.

Glass showed musical talent early on, both on violin and flute. He graduated from the University of Chicago (he moved to Chicago in his teens) at the age of 19. He next enrolled at Juilliard, and had by then rejected serial techniques in composition in favor of more conventional styles, favoring the music of Ives, Copland, and Virgil Thomson. Over the next four years he studied with Reich, Persichetti, Milhaud, and Bergsma.

He later studied with Nadia Boulanger in Paris, and it was during this two-year period that he met and worked with sitar player Ravi Shankar, who introduced him to Indian music. He was intrigued by its sound and possibilities and attracted to Asian and Middle Eastern cultures. Eventually, he even converted to Buddhism. Glass later spoke of how greatly his 1966 visit to Tibet influenced his thinking, both musically and spiritually.

After returning to New York in 1967, Glass struggled financially and had to work as a cab driver and plumber for a time. Eventually, he established the Glass Ensemble in the early 1970s. This group consisted of seven players and used keyboards, woodwind instruments, and amplification of vocals. Though it also struggled at the outset, it eventually became immensely popular.

Glass' *Einstein on the Beach* was staged in 1976 and was his first large-scale triumph. By this time, too, his Ensemble was in greater demand, as were a good many of his other works. Since the 1980s, Glass' popularity has grown with the successes of his 1982 *Company*, for string quartet or string orchestra, the 1987 violin concerto, and the 1997 score, *Kundun*, written for the Martin Scorsese film. There have been other operas from Glass' pen, including *The Fall of the House of Usher* and *Orphée*. Among other works is the remarkable *Monsters of Grace*, for voices and instrumental ensemble, a mystical composition that uses light and other effects in performance.

Glass has received many awards, among which have been the Chevalier de l'Ordre des Arts et des Lettres in 1995, from the French government. Glass continues to write music and must be regarded as among the most important composers of his time. *—Robert Cummings*

FILM MUSIC

Koyaanisquatsi (1981–1983)

Koyaanisquatsi is an experimental film by Godfrey Reggio. It is a series of images, almost always with an altered time-base. Clouds race across the sky. Traffic moves at a frenetic pace. The contrails of aircraft move like meteors. When many of these everyday occurrences are viewed at such an abnormal speed, repetitive, predictable patterns emerge, particularly in the flow of pedestrian and vehicular traffic, making it look machine-like, predictable, and ultimately, futile. The title of the film is a Hopi word meaning "life out of balance." Oddly, and perhaps contrary to the intention of the film-maker, it is the scenes of human activity which present the most exhilarating, majestic images.

Philip Glass's minimalist score for the film turned into his first popular success. Typical of his style, it is static and repetitive, unfolding in rapid arpeggiated figures which tend to shift in blocks. This lends the work the impression of surface rapidity;

but underneath it all, the chords articulated by the arpeggios are static, consonant chords, with a very slow harmonic rhythm. A static majesty emerges, a sense of larger order imposed on the rippling surface that wonderfully enhances the content and theme of the film. As a marriage of music and images, the film and the score are truly meant for each other. Separated from the film, the music's capacity to give pleasure, or conversely to irritate the listener due to its stark simplicity and lack of progress, depends on the audience's sympathy with Philip Glass' music in general. *—Joseph Stevenson*

Recommended:

○ **Glass: Koyaanisqatsi** / Riesman (cond.), Philip Glass Ens. / 1998 / Nonesuch 79506

OPERA

La Belle et la Bête (1994)

Having sojourned in Paris in 1954 to study French, and having returned a decade later to study composition for three years (with Nadia Boulanger), Philip Glass' obsession with French culture comes as no surprise. The Bohemian lifestyle portrayed in his 1992 chamber opera adaptation of Jean Cocteau's film *Orphée* is a direct reflection of the life he lived and the artists with which he associated during his first stay in Paris. Another Cocteau film, *Les Enfants Terribles*, provided Glass with the inspiration for a ballet, and still another became part of what amounts to a multimedia theater piece, *La Belle et la Bête*. The music of this last work is highly integrated; Glass assigns particular themes to characters, objects, and situations, and as these elements recur in the film, they are duly reflected in the score. Glass' variety of timbral color is also very engaging. While one often hears rather "stock" electronic sounds used in his scores, the palette of electronica in *La Belle* is broadened and carefully woven into the orchestral fabric. Furthermore, the piece is a feat of technology. Glass envisioned an entirely new soundtrack to the 1946 film, requiring perfect timing and synchronization. The composer transcribed and timed all of the dialogue of the film and set it to music. Computers were employed to further align audio with video, which necessitated further rescoring. The final performance involved the singers standing in front of the screen onto which the film was projected, watching the characters they were portraying. The result is both an homage to the Cocteau film and a deconstruction of it. The story, which Glass interprets as an allegory of the artist, is presented visually, while the singers simultaneously portray and comment upon their characters. The audience is an outside witness to this double-faceted presentation. *—Jeremy Grimshaw*

Synopsis:

Haughty sisters Adelaide and Felicie are busily preparing for a night out, despite the torments of their brother, Ludovic, who delights in mocking their vanity. The attention of his friend, Avenant, is with the other sister, Beauty, who, like always, must stay home to clean the house. Left alone with her, Avenant professes his love and proposes marriage. Beauty declines, however; she must stay home and care for her father. Meanwhile, the Father appears with good news: his cargo ship, thought lost, has returned to port, saving the family from looming bankruptcy. Arriving at the port the next morning, however, the Father finds trouble: the ship has returned empty, leaving him with overwhelming debts. He doesn't even have money to rent a room, and must make the long journey home through the woods in the dark.

Losing his way, the Father happens upon a mysterious castle. Seeing no one around, he picks a single rose from the courtyard to take to Beauty. The Beast appears and accuses him of stealing; the penalty is death, unless one of his daughters is willing to come to the castle and take his place. The Beast sends him away on a magic horse that delivers him straight to his home. Upon hearing the story, Beauty eagerly offers to go to the castle and, despite her father's protests, mounts the magic horse and departs. Arriving at the castle, Beauty is frightened by her host's appearance but somewhat reassured by his hospitality, and, after a time, resigns herself to life in the castle. Still, even as she befriends the Beast, she grows homesick, and eventually begs a week's leave to visit her family. He warily succumbs to her pleas, but only after she solemnly vows to return; if she does not, he will die of grief. He gives her five items: the self-guided steed, the golden key to the pavilion in which a statue of Diana stands guard over his magical secrets, a glove that instantly transports its wearer anywhere, a mirror, and a rose.

The Father is overjoyed at Beauty's return; her siblings take interest primarily in the castle's purported riches. With the still lovesick Avenant, they plot to kill the Beast and take his treasures. The men steal the golden key and take off on the horse. At the same time, Beauty, peering into the mirror, sees the Beast crumpled in agony; donning the magic glove, she is transported to his side and tries to revive him. Arriving at the castle, the men peer down through the glass into Diana's pavilion; just as Avenant is about to break in, however, the statue of Diana comes to life and shoots an arrow through his heart. By the time his body hits the ground, he has become the Beast; the Beast, meanwhile, has been transformed into the handsome King Ardent (who, strangely, bears a striking resemblance to Avenant). Taking Beauty by the hand, Ardent carries her through the air toward his magical kingdom. *—Jeremy Grimshaw*

Recommended:

○ **Glass: La Belle et la Bête** / Riesman, Alekan (conds.), Goldray, Sterman, Gibson, Peck, Philip Glass Ens. / 1995 / Nonesuch 79347

the CIVIL warS: a tree is best measured when it is down, opera, Act V: the Rome section (1984)

The CIVIL warS: a tree is best measured when it is down was an ambitious theatrical project conceived by designer Robert Wilson to coincide with the 1984 Olympic Games in Los Angeles. Though arguably not an opera in the usual sense of the word, it was perhaps closest to that genre than to any other, since it combined elements of literature, music, movement, and the visual arts on a scale that perhaps only Wagner had ever attempted before. The work embraced the music, history, and culture of many different countries, and it was to be assembled from numerous parts, each representing the efforts of a different group of creative collaborators. However, due to financial and logistical difficulties the work was never performed as a whole, and only some of its component fragments have been performed or recorded.

Philip Glass's contribution to *the CIVIL warS* was the composition of its final act, commissioned by the Opera di Roma, and isolated scenes for Act I (the Cologne section). The text was a collaborative effort between Robert Wilson and Maita di Niscemi, and was based on the American Civil War, Native American folklore, and the writings of the Roman playwright Seneca. Glass completed the score, arguably his most earnestly operatic to date, in 1983. Unlike most of his compositions, which tend to revolve around chamber ensembles and synthesized sounds, it incorporates the full resources of the orchestra, and, therefore, represents a slight departure from his hallmark style. The characteristic minimalism is present, but it is tempered by a more lyrical impulse that allows for extended melodic ideas and some moments of real vocal elegance. *—AMG*

Synopsis:

Prologue. Earth Mother sings of a peaceful dawn. She is joined by Snow Owl in repeating the single word "death." Snow Owl then wonders where in the world he is, where he hears the nightbird calling. Abraham Lincoln begins his exhortation for evil in the world to cease. The idea is taken up by Snow Owl and Earth Mother, and all three, alternately as solos, in duet, and as a trio, repeat a prayer for peace as the music builds in agitation.

Scene A. The scene begins with the chorus optimistically repeating Lincoln's words from the Prologue. Then Giuseppe Garibaldi sings of the earth and nature's creations, the fluid music reflecting the lyrics. The music turns sharp as Garibaldi thinks of his struggles for peace in his country. Both the chorus' and Garibaldi's words are sung again.

Scene B. Robert E. Lee recites a gallimaufry of battle details in a variety of languages. Mary Todd Lincoln sings of the lone horseman at the end of a battle. It is actually a description of Lee as he surrendered at Appomattox, but the words and her music implies that it could also be describing Lincoln. An octet of persons from Greek and Roman myths encourages her remembrance of feelings on seeing the horseman. Robert E. Lee finishes the scene by relating the details of the surrender himself, as if he were the observer rather than the participant. Throughout the scene, the hymn tune *Jacob's Ladder* is woven into the music.

Scene C. The scene opens with a grand chorus imploring the hero to save the world. The mood becomes more uncertain as a younger Mrs. Lincoln rambles on in a long, somewhat incoherent soliloquy. Lincoln briefly repeats some of his text from the Prologue, asking that "If earth must still produce any evil…let it be mine"; almost as if to say that Mary Todd Lincoln's madness is another battle he will undertake. The octet, once again, offers its encouragement. Mrs. Lincoln begins her stream of consciousness once more, ending with her remembrance of feelings from the previous scene. Next, Hercules and his mother, Alcmene, offer each other moral support, as he struggles in the afterlife and she struggles in her grief. The opera ends with Hercules by himself, singing of his triumph over death. *—Patsy Morita*

Recommended:

○ **Glass: The Civil Wars** / Davies (cond.), Graves, Sabbatini, Zhou, Radvanovsky, American Composers Orch. / 1999 / Nonesuch 79487

Einstein on the Beach (1976)

"For me," Philip Glass once claimed, "minimalism was over in 1974." It was in the spring of that year that Glass began meeting with stage director Robert Wilson with the purpose of collaborating on a new work for musical theater. The result, *Einstein on the Beach*, changed the course of Glass's career while also blurring the boundaries between art music and pop music and dismantling the barriers that separated their respective audiences. Considering the grand theatrical scale of *Einstein*, the economy of means implied by minimalism was no longer appropriate for the task. The repetitive gestures and driving rhythms found in Glass's earlier works are still present, but piled upon each other in greater measure, and combined with image and word to create a synergistic effect of "maximalist" proportion.

Far from a "The Life and Times of…" approach, *Einstein on the Beach* is more an abstract, five-hour musing on Einstein's personality and ideas than a biographical sketch—an approach that Glass has described as a "portrait opera." All of the performers on stage sport the scientist's trademark short-sleeved white shirt, suspenders, and pipe, while a violinist wanders between proscenium and pit in full Einsteinian garb (complete with wig and moustache), representing the physicist's noted musical hobby. The actual texts are rather vague in their references to Einstein. In fact, his name is mentioned in just two places and in contexts that are completely unclear in their meaning.

The work is a kaleidoscopic look at technology and modern life, using the figure of Einstein as a sort of mantra, than it is a picture of Einstein the man. Three primary visual images recur within the work: trains (recalling the metaphors Einstein used to illustrate the theory of relativity and with which he played as a child); a trial/bed setting (modern life and modern science examined); and a spaceship/field (a metaphor for transcendence and/or an escape from nuclear disaster).

As Robert Wilson put it, "You don't have to listen to the words, because they don't mean anything. I'm not giving you puzzles to solve, only pictures to hear." Many of the most profound and moving elements of the work are, in fact, art by accident. Since the score calls for a chorus of untrained singers (who must also dance and act), Glass aided the performers learning his constantly shifting rhythms and melodies by having them sing numbers and solfège syllables (do-re-mi, etc.). The overall effect was so striking that it was used in performance. The fragmentary nature of the text owes to its various and unique origins. During their initial meetings, Glass and Wilson were sometimes joined by Christopher Knowles, a 14-year-old autistic boy. Knowles' contributions, which constitute about two thirds of the entire spoken text, are intriguingly sporadic in their subject matter.

While Glass's music for *Einstein on the Beach* bears strong familial resemblance to his earlier works, it served a new, unique dramatic function—one that would reappear in his next opera, *Satyagraha*, as well as his numerous film scores, including *The Thin Blue Line* and *Kundun*. *—Jeremy Grimshaw*

Synopsis:

Act One. (Each act is preceded and followed by a Knee Play, a vocal/orchestral interlude- or prelude-like piece.) The opera has no plot or conventional characters, but features a soprano, tenor, dancers, actors, and a violinist. The central theme of the work is an examination of the value or detriment of Einstein's Theory of Relativity. The flow of events is often nonlinear. The opening scene, subtitled "Train," takes place on a train, to reflect the example Einstein chose to explain the idea of time relativity. The second scene presents a "Trial," wherein the implications of Einstein's work are examined. Did he ever consider the significance of his discoveries? Did he know they might lead to the atomic age and nuclear horrors? Is Science on trial here? (The title of the opera suggests a link between Einstein and the 1959 nuclear doomsday novel and film *On the Beach*.) There follows a text about Paris, delivered by a speaker.

Act Two. This act is subtitled "Field with Spaceship." Two notes are repeated throughout, first played rapidly, then slowly, to depict time slowing and apparently to conjure the atmosphere of a ride on a spaceship. The next scene, "Night Train," reprises some elements of the opening scene.

Act Three. This act, subtitled "Trial/Prison," reprises parts of the text from the first trial and also repeatedly touches on the subject of grocery shopping. The subjects of court trials and jail sentences are also examined. The following dance scene reprises elements from the "Field with Spaceship" sequence.

Act Four. This act is subtitled "Building"; the term refers to the sense of building something up rather than to an edifice. The music calls to mind a rhythmic ride on a train. The next scene, "Bed," features Bach-like writing and a long, wordless soprano solo. The final scene, "Spaceship," may for some call to mind the movements of a spaceship. *—Robert Cummings*

Recommended:

○ **Glass: Einstein on the Beach** / Wilson (cond.), Riesman, Gibson, Peck, Hiskey, Landry, Glaser, Philip Glass Ens. / 1979 / CBS Masterworks 38875

○ **Glass: Einstein on the Beach** / Wilson (cond.), Riesman, Goldray, Sterman, Gibson, etc. / 1993 / Nonesuch 79323

Satyagraha (1980)

Following *Einstein on the Beach* by an interval of five years, Philip Glass' second operatic venture, *Satyagraha*, was more lucid in its structure and scope than its delightfully fragmentary and often unintelligible predecessor; it refined and tempered the musico-dramatic experiments from the first opera to create a vivid and moving theatrical experience. Although *Einstein on the Beach* created an international buzz and made Glass a celebrity virtually overnight, its monumental scale made it financially problematic and left Glass with little money. While working as a plumber and cab driver, Glass looked in vain for a new commission from an American opera company; finally it was the Netherlands Opera that provided him the opportunity to produce a new work, on the condition that it would be a "real opera"—that is, one that would have more coherent plot than *Einstein* and that would be scored for the traditional operatic voices and orchestra.

For his subject matter, Glass returned to an idea that had been rejected by *Einstein on the Beach* collaborator Robert Wilson: Gandhi. As in *Einstein*, Glass chose not to attempt an all-encompassing narrative, but rather offered what he called a "portrait opera" of the famous political figure. The opera focuses on an early period in Gandhi's life, when a year-long stint in South Africa as a legal aide led him into his life's work as an activist and political reformer. The philosophy of passive resistance that Gandhi developed during those years was given the name "Satyagraha," which translates (with some difficulty) as "truth-force" or "love-force." Recalling the kaleidoscopic quality of *Einstein*, *Satyagraha* moves easily through time and space, overseeing Gandhi's struggle for Indian freedom in South Africa from three outside perspectives. The first comes from Russian novelist and Nobel Prize winner Leo Tolstoy, who, according to Glass, had "the same combination of the political and the spiritual" as Gandhi. The overseer of the second act is Rabindranath Tagore, the Indian mystic and Nobel Prize-winning poet. Act Three is witnessed by Martin Luther King Jr., who fought a battle for African-Americans in the U.S. similar to the one Gandhi had fought for Indians in South Africa.

Despite the more conventional instrumental forces employed, *Satyagraha* maintains the streamlined sound Glass had developed with his ensemble of keyboards and winds. The orchestra for *Satyagraha* contains a full complement of strings (whereas *Einstein* had employed only a single violin), but the absence of brass and percussion and the inclusion of keyboards gives the orchestra Glass' unmistakable stamp. Likewise, the use of traditional operatic voices is overshadowed by the fact that they sing the text in the original Sanskrit, which reaches the untrained Western ear much as the numbers, solfège syllables, and ambiguous texts of *Einstein on the Beach* did: as a mesmerizing phonetic collage, underlaid by a pulsating, energetic score. *—Jeremy Grimshaw*

Synopsis:

The story takes place from 1896 to 1913, but events are not necessarily presented chronologically. In each act a historical figure—with a silent role in the opera—watches the action from above. The three, respectively, represent the past, present, and future.

Act One. The opening scene, The Kuru Field of Justice, draws on the Hindu epic Bhagavad-Ghita, with two mythical armies standing in opposition to each other, awaiting to do battle. The young leader of one of the armies, Arjuna, seeks advice from the gods to learn if it is moral to fight for a just cause in combat. Mohandas (Mahatma) Gandhi is enmeshed in the proceedings, which here and elsewhere deal with racial discrimination against Indians and South Africans. Gandhi develops the word Satyagraha, which unites two words from Sanskrit, truth and firmness (often translated as passive resistance), and forges ahead with his ideas of peaceful protest.

The ensuing scene, The Tolstoy Farm, depicts the commune established in 1910 to promote the Satyagraha principles among its residents. The third scene, The Vow, focuses on a 1906 public gathering in Johannesburg, South Africa, and the vow taken by those present to defy a racist government decree.

Act Two. In the first scene, Confrontation and Rescue, Gandhi is chased by a mob of white Europeans and protected from harm by the police superintendent's wife, who had gone outside for a stroll and encountered by chance the besieged Gandhi and the mob following him. The next scene, Indian Opinion, deals with the 1906 founding of Indian Opinion, a weekly human-rights journal. The concluding scene of the second act, subtitled Protest, depicts events from 1908, when a crowd of 2,300 Indians burned their alien registration cards in Johannesburg Park.

Act Three. The act's only scene, Newcastle March, deals with the historic protest in 1913 against racist laws by striking miners, who, along with women and children, marched 36 miles to their voluntary arrests. Subsequent peaceful acts of defiance against the laws and many arrests followed before the laws were finally repealed. *—Robert Cummings*

Recommended:

○ **Glass: Satyagraha** / Keene, Perry, Cummings, Reeve, McFarland, Liss, Woods, NYC Opera Orch. / 1985 / CBS 39672

CHAMBER MUSIC

Glassworks (1981)

By the time Philip Glass had finished two of his three quasi-biographical operas—*Einstein on the Beach* (1976), and *Satyagraha* (1980)—he had become one of the most prominent fixtures in the musical world. His success was such that by the early 1980s he had achieved a rare feat for a composer of "serious" music: signing an exclusive contract with the CBS Masterworks label. Still, his operas had been large and economically unwieldy, and Glass anticipated resistance towards the funding of his more expensive projects; so he devised a strategy wherein he would preemptively offset the financial obstacles of operatic recordings by intermittently releasing less expensive, more accessible, and marketable recordings. The first such project of this nature was the instrumental collection entitled *Glassworks*, which appeared on shelves in 1982. Featuring the Philip Glass Ensemble (which on this album includes piano, keyboards, organ, a handful of woodwinds, horns, and a few violas and cellos), *Glassworks* comprised six tracks ("Opening," Floe," "Islands,"

Rubric," Facades," and "Closing") with an amiably soft-edged minimalist sound, in an almost new-agey vein.

Critics often point to the success of *Glassworks*—within five years nearly 200,000 copies had been sold—as representative of Glass' "selling out"; others see it as simple business savvy (as scholar Keith Potter points out, Glass' *North Star* project from 1977 had similar commercial aspirations, but hadn't sold as well). Though *Glassworks* is rather lightweight, its gestures are familiar and Glass' characteristic rhythmic/melodic tricks do offer a certain amount of substance. It also exhibits a consistency and casual sophistication that seems quite strained in his next overtly commercial venture, *Songs from Liquid Days*. While *Glassworks* doesn't offer the challenges and poignancy of Glass' more serious works, at the very least it is easy on the ear. *—Jeremy Grimshaw*

Recommended:

○ **Glass: Glassworks** / Riesman, Gibson, Moe, Martin, etc. / 1982 / Sony 37265

SYMPHONIC

Low Symphony (1992)

Philip Glass has insisted that if his music involves a "crossover," it is on the part of the audience, not the composer. It might be more appropriate to say that Glass, particularly with the *Low Symphony* of 1992, is a composer that spans categories (and audiences) rather than occupying a niche between them. The *Low Symphony* is a curious treatment of themes from three songs, "Subterraneans," "Some Are," and "Warszawa," from *Low*, an album released by David Bowie and Brian Eno in 1977. It seems only appropriate that Glass would make the transition into mainstream pop culture via two other genre-defying artists.

Seminal figures in the progressive rock scene, Bowie and Eno created a sort of pop-experimental, proto-minimalist style that shared certain resonances with "art" music composers of the time. The similarities were not coincidental. In the late 1960s, Eno had been deeply impressed by a performance of Steve Reich's music. Later, when Philip Glass toured England in 1971, Eno and Bowie both attended a concert of his music at the Royal College of Art in London. It is possible, then, that Glass's *Low Symphony* contains ideas that Bowie/Eno borrowed from his music in the first place.

The opening of the first movement, "Subterraneans," is surprisingly lyrical. Gone are Glass' staple arpeggios and driving additive rhythms, in favor of sustained harmonies, feathery woodwind trills, and earnest, tuneful melodies. It suddenly changes moods, utilizing a battery of percussion instruments to set out on a rhythmic trajectory; the now-familiar themes are laid atop the pulsing texture with trademark ambiguity.

The second movement, "Some Are," begins with a repetitive texture in the strings reminiscent of Glass' string quartets. As the percussion and brass take over the rhythmic role, the strings pick up the theme, which betrays Bowie's pensive song style.

The final movement, "Warszawa," begins with gloomy deliberateness, a slow dirge of winds and percussion giving way to a unison, mostly unaccompanied lament in the low strings. The cellos and basses then undertake an accompanimental role, as the upper strings take melody. They too then become part of the texture as the winds enter with melodic material. The boundaries between foreground, middleground, and background are again blurred, as melodies step slip in and out the limelight and the overall textural composite.

The *Low Symphony* might remind the reader of Glass' previous foray into pop music, *Songs from Liquid Days* of 1986. It exhibits a thoughtfulness and integrity sometimes missing in the earlier pop collaboration—a collaboration that was initially conceived by record company executives who wanted to recoup some of the losses incurred from the recording of Glass' opera *Satyagraha*. The *Low Symphony* is a much more integrated and convincing juncture of styles and genres. *—Jeremy Grimshaw*

Recommended:

○ **Glass: Heroes Symphony; Low Symphony** / Davies (cond.), Brooklyn PO / 2003 / Philips 000084002

VOCAL

Songs from Liquid Days, for voice & chamber ensemble (1986)

In navigating the brackish waters of high art and low art that characterize his slick brand of post-minimalism, Philip Glass developed a clever business strategy for getting his more artistically ambitious (and more expensive) projects funded: according to his longtime producer, Kurt Munkacsi, Glass decided early on that by giving record company executives an occasional commercial success, he would find more flexibility when proposing less lucrative ventures. It was in this spirit that Glass composed and collaborated on *Songs from Liquid Days*, a collection of six songs for which Glass provided the music and a number of popular artists wrote lyrics. Released in 1986, partially as an entrepreneurial foil to the considerable expenses incurred by the recording of his opera *Satyagraha*, the recording turned out to be one of Glass' best-selling projects and further established Glass' position as an arbiter of pop and minimalist musical vocabularies.

Of course, one shouldn't get the idea that Glass' more commercial ventures are unsophisticated. His collaborators on *Liquid Days* generally appeal to the artsier end of the pop spectrum. (CBS tried to include Billy Joel, but Glass resisted.) Still, one senses a disjunction of genres that even the most postmodern ear might find hard to reconcile. Paul Simon provides the philosophically meandering lyrics for the opening track, "Changing Opinion." Glass' setting, however, lends it a kind of unnatural weight, as the pensive piano arpeggios and imposing orchestrational touches seem incongruous companions to passive lines like "We became aware of a hum in the room... it went mmmmmm." Likewise, the frenetic, syncopations and acutely dated synthesizer sounds of "Lightning," featuring lyrics by Suzanne Vega, strains perceptibly to have a techno edge, but comes off clumsily; Janice Pendarvis' satiny voice, while appealing, seems out of place on the 1986 recording. "Freezing," also with lyrics by Vega, is a much more convincing effort, partly because the ethereal texture of the pulsing strings blend nicely with Linda Ronstadt's voice. David Byrne's texts, featured in "Liquid Days" and "Open the Kingdom," are taken entirely too seriously; with lines like "Love needs a bath / Love could use a shave," one wishes to hear Glass' pensive settings ironically, but suspects they aren't meant that way. Laurie Anderson pens the words to the remaining song, "Forgetting," which Glass sets in alternating textures—ethereal, then ephemeral.

While this song cycle does lead a separate existence as a performable work separate from the recording, and though it remains one of Glass' most lucrative recordings, it rarely finds its way onto the recital stage. The character of the songs is shaped too distinctly by the singers who perform them, and the odd hybrid of styles perhaps seems sloppy to conservatory singers, on the one hand, and clunky and unhip to more progressive performers, on the other. When compared to Glass' groundbreaking and engaging stage works—and even some of his more carefully wrought orchestral scores—*Songs from Liquid Days*, though not entirely unredeemable, is rather unremarkable. *—Jeremy Grimshaw*

Recommended:

○ **Glass: Songs from Liquid Days** / Riesman, Gibson, Perry, Dunkel, Peck, Kripl, Fowler, Ronstadt, Kronos Quartet, Philip Glass Ens. / 1986 / CBS 39564

○ **Glass: Songs from Liquid Days; Vessels; 3 Songs** / Temple (dir.), Akhtar, Morgan, Crouch End Festival Chorus, National Sinfonia / 2000 / Silva Screen 6023

Alexander Konstantinovich Glazunov

b. Aug. 10, 1865, St. Petersburg, Russia, **d.** Mar. 21, 1936, Neuilly-sur-Seine, France

Composer: Orchestral, Symphonic, Concerto, Ballet

Born in 1865 in St. Petersburg, Glazunov was a leading Russian composer of the generation after Tchaikovsky. Doubtless owing to his exceptional mastery of and attentiveness to form, exemplified by his exceptional grasp of counterpoint, he has been described as a Romantic Classicist and therefore compared to Brahms. Furthermore, since he remained faithful to a traditional nineteenth century musical idiom, while some of his contemporaries pursued varieties of Modernism, critics have described Glazunov's music as academic and formal. But Glazunov's oeuvre, which includes a wide range of genres, cannot be easily reduced to mere critical formulas. At heart, Glazunov was a Romantic composer, and the spirit of his music comes to the fore in his *Violin Concerto in A Minor*, a richly melodic work, in which the expressive potential of the violin is fully realized.

Displaying an immense musical talent as a child, Glazunov started studying with Rimsky-Korsakov at the age of 15. Glazunov's progress was indeed astonishing, for he completed his *Symphony No. 1* at 16. In fact, his symphony, premiered by Balakirev in 1882, established, practically overnight, Glazunov's reputation as a great Russian composer. In 1884, the rich merchant and publisher Belyayev took Glazunov to Weimar, where the young composer met Liszt. Although absorbing many musical influences, particularly those of Liszt and Wagner, Glazunov eventually crafted an individual style, composing symphonies, ballets, and concertos for various instruments. Owing to his growing international fame as a symphonist, Glazunov was invited to conduct his works in Paris in 1889; an invitation from London came in 1896. During the 1890s, Glazunov composed some of his most successful works, including the fourth, fifth, and sixth symphonies, and the ballet *Raymonda*.

In 1899, Glazunov became an instructor in composition and orchestration at the St. Petersburg Conservatory. He resigned his post in the politically turbulent year of 1905, incensed by the government's politically motivated dismissal of Rimsky-Korsakov from his teaching position. However, when things returned to a semblance of normalcy, Glazunov was named head of the Conservatory. While his output may have diminished in terms of sheer quantity after 1905, Glazunov continued composing until the end of his life. After the Revolution of 1917, Glazunov, as director of a major national music school, worked hard, and with varying success, to protect his students from interference by a government which viewed music as an instrument of political propaganda. In addition, he felt isolated in a culture which rejected established musical traditions, and a general feeling of alienation finally prompted him to leave the Soviet Union in 1928.

Glazunov's life in exile, which included an unsuccessful tour of the United States, was difficult but did not suppress his creative energy. He traveled around the world for several years, eventually settling in Paris. Music composed during this period includes the *Concerto-Ballata for Cello and Orchestra* and the *Concerto for Alto Saxophone and Strings*, a standard work of the saxophone repertoire. Passionately interested in the distinctive characteristics of the instruments he composed for, Glazunov learned to play a variety of instruments, including, in addition to the obligatory piano, violin, cello, trumpet, trombone, French horn, clarinet, as well as several percussion instruments. Consequently, each of his concertos reflects a deep understanding of the instrument's nature and technical capabilities. Critics have reproached Glazunov for being too Western and insufficiently Russian. True, there are few traces in his music of Russian folk influences. However, while Glazunov's music certainly fits into the cosmopolitan culture of his time, it also embodies the unmistakable emotional and spiritual qualities which the attentive listener will recognize as Russian. *—Zoran Minderovic*

ORCHESTRAL

From the Middle Ages, suite in E major, Op. 79 (1902)

For Alexander Glazunov, the years immediately following his appointment in 1899 to the faculty of the St. Petersburg Conservatory marked the high point of his creative life—his greatest music all dates from the period from 1900–06. Among these works, the *Violin Concerto*, Op. 82 of 1904 and the *Symphony No. 8*, Op. 83 of 1906 are certainly the most admired, but there is a great deal of other, lesser-known but amply endowed music from this time. The orchestral suite *From the Middle Ages*, Op. 79 of 1902, a work in which Glazunov musically evokes enduring images of medieval Europe, is an example.

From the Middle Ages (Glazunov's title, in Russian, is *Iz srednikh vekov*) is in E major and has four midsize movements which serve almost as the four movements of a conventional symphony. In No. 1, Prelude, the composer moves from deep, bass-driven portent to amorous warmth of a most attractive kind—Glazunov's greatest strength was always his capacity for drawing broad lyric strokes from his instruments. He has not traditionally been a widely admired musician, but efforts like this Prelude give reason to reevaluate a century's worth of harsh judgments. No. 2, Scherzo, is a kind of *Danse macabre*, initiated by vehement strings, in which the traditional plainchant *Dies irae* can be heard. No. 3, "The Troubadour's Serenade," is a long-spun melody with a harp accompaniment at first, and then richer full orchestral support. The finale, No. 4, "The Crusaders," adopts the traditional European view of the medieval Crusaders as lofty Christian heroes and builds it up into a rousing, if perhaps vainglorious, musical epic that culminates in a brass-driven chorale. *—Blair Johnston*

Recommended:

- ○ **Glazunov: Orchestral Works, Vol. 2** / Krimets (cond.), Moscow SO / 1996 / Naxos 553537

Stenka Razin, symphonic poem in B minor, Op. 13 (1885)

Alexander Glazunov's brilliant *Stenka Razin* was one of the 20-year old composer's first successes. The work is a 16-minute tone poem in a style reminiscent of Tchaikovsky and Borodin; it was written, in fact, as a memorial to the latter. Stenka (the diminutive of Stepan) Razin was the leader of the Don Cossacks who rebelled against the ruling landowner during the reign of a weak czar. He was ultimately captured and executed, and quickly passed into legend, inspiring a body of enduring folk and epic literature. Glazunov's musical depiction is based on one such account, in which the hero has captured a Persian princess, along with other plunder, and sailed back to Russia. His servants and fellow fighters chide him for "going soft"; the young woman, they say, has dulled the fight in him. To prove them wrong, he offers Mother Volga "neither gold nor silver, but the most precious of all my possessions," throws the princess into the wide river, and leads his men into battle anew. The music is largely based on the well-known folk song "Song of the Volga Boatmen"; a contrasting "Persian" theme for clarinet represents the princess. *—Joseph Stevenson*

Recommended:

- ○ **Glazunov: Stenka Razin; Une fête slave; Cortège solonnel; Fantaisie; Mazurka; March** / Krimets (cond.), Moscow SO / 1996 / Naxos 553538
- ○ **Glazunov: Stenka Razin; The Sea; Spring; Suite** / Jarvi (cond.), Scottish National Orch. / 1997 / Chandos 7049

SYMPHONIC

Symphony No. 4 in E flat major, Op. 48 (1893)

Glazunov's *Symphony No. 4* (1893), dedicated to Anton Rubinstein, is representative of the composer's lifelong attempt to achieve some measure of reconciliation between the nationalist and traditional schools of music that found themselves at odds in Russia in the late nineteenth century. Rimsky-Korsakov found the work, particularly its orchestration, somewhat cumbersome; other critics, however, hailed it as a masterpiece and a sign of the rebirth of Glazunov's creativity.

The pastoral nature of the symphony's first movement takes as its point of departure a hauntingly beautiful and fundamentally Russian theme for the oboe. The Scherzo is dominated by a rustic, rhythmic dance-like motive. Glazunov's mastery at marshalling the orchestra's components into a cogent whole is clearly evident in the final Andante—Allegro. Here, the music builds inexorably to a stunning, majestic conclusion, echoing the natural splendor of the Caucasus Mountains which inspired the work.*—Tim Mahon*

Recommended:

- ○ **Glazunov: Symphonies 4 & 5** / Polyansky (cond.), Russian State SO / 1999 / Chandos 9739
- ○ **Glazunov: Orchestral Works, Vol. 7** / Anissimov (cond.), Moscow State SO / 1998 / Naxos 553561
- ○ **Mravinsky Edition: Vol. 11–20** / Mravinsky (cond.), Leningrad PO / 1995 / Melodiya 29459

Symphony No. 5 in B flat major, Op. 55 (1895)

The *Symphony No. 5* of Russian composer Alexander Glazunov is a fine example of the post-Tchaikovsky symphony of the Russian Silver Age. Composed in 1895—that is, one year after Tchaikovsky's premature death—Glazunov's *Fifth* is composed with memorable themes set in powerful forms and scored with craftsmanship. A masterfully optimistic work, Glazunov's *Fifth* takes the best elements from the Russian nationalist school of Balakirev and Borodin—the strong themes and muscular rhythms—and the best elements of cosmopolitan Russians like Rubinstein and Rimsky-Korsakov—tremendous formal control and harmonic cogency—and creates a symphony that rivals the best of contemporary works by European composers. The *Fifth* opens with a Maestoso introduction of great strength and confidence followed by a splendid sonata-form Allegro. The second movement is a light and elegant Scherzo, the third movement is a tenderly affectionate Andante, and the finale movement is a festive Allegro in modified sonata-rondo form. But while the movements are in the standard symphonic forms of the late and post-Romantic period, Glazunov's keen intelligence and open-hearted emotionalism fills these forms with glorious themes and harmonies. While Glazunov's earlier *Third* is as positive in tone and his later *Eighth* is as brilliantly composed, his *Fifth* is his most characteristic work. *—James Leonard*

Recommended:

- ○ **Glazunov: Symphonies 4 & 5** / Polyansky (cond.), Russian State SO / 1999 / Chandos 9739
- ○ **Glazunov: Symphonies 5 & 8** / Anissimov (cond.), Moscow State SO / 2000 / Naxos 553660
- ○ **Evgeny Mravinsky** / Mravinsky (cond.), Leningrad PO / EMI 75953

Symphony No. 6 in C minor, Op. 58 (1896)

While the *Symphony No. 6 in C minor*, Op. 58, of 1896 by Alexander Glazunov is not the most personally characteristic of his eight completed symphonies—the optimistic *Third* or the Olympian *Fifth* are more typical of his confident symphonic aesthetic—it is arguably the most typically Russian of his symphonies. Part of the reason for this is the scoring—violins in octaves above massed brass at its climaxes à la Tchaikovsky and gorgeously colorful woodwind writing in its central movements—part of it is the themes—ardent and powerful with a yearning quality characteristic of *fin de siècle* Russian symphonies—but most of it is the furious tone of the opening movement. With the darkly unfolding Adagio leading into a Allegro appassionato that balances a passionately despairing first theme with a fervently supplicating second theme, Glazunov's *Sixth* sounds like a Russian symphony composed after the death of Tchaikovsky. But the *Sixth* is more than the work of a symphonic epigone. While the tone of the opening movement sounds typically Russian, its chromatic melodic and cogent harmonic structure makes it sound much more modern than contemporary symphonies by Kalinnikov or even Rachmaninov. Even more modern are the *Sixth*'s second and fourth movements. The second movement is a theme and seven variations that slowly transmutes the tone of the symphony from the fury of the opening movement to one of calm acceptance. The brief third-movement Intermezzo that precedes the Finale is lighter in tone than anything else in the symphony. The Finale itself is one of Glazunov's most successful closing movements. With its magisterial Andante maestoso introduction announcing the chorale theme that will ultimately cap the movement, its highly contrasted themes—the first confidently striding in the winds Moderato maestoso, the second a lilting Scherzando theme for the flutes, horns, and strings—the Finale seems at first too episodic to cohere. Glazunov's superb technical skills, however, form all the Finale's material into an organic whole and the tone of the Finale—powerfully positive—is altogether Glazunov's own. *—James Leonard*

Recommended:

- ○ **Glazunov: Symphony 6; The Forest** / Anissimov (cond.), Moscow State SO / 2000 / Naxos 554293

○ **Glazunov: Symphonies 1 & 6** / Otaka (cond.), BBC National Orch. Wales / 2003 / Bis 1368

Symphony No. 7 in F major ("Pastoral"), Op. 77 (1902)

The *Symphony No. 7 in F major,* Op. 77, from 1902 by Alexander Glazunov is his most purposefully Germanic symphony. Called the "Pastoral'naya" (Pastoral), the *Seventh* from the start evokes the bucolic images of Beethoven's own F major pastoral symphony and indeed all of the F major pastoral works in the German canon. But beyond those deliberate references, the *Seventh* is wholly Glazunov's own: even in the austerely archaic Andante, the tone of the work is overwhelmingly positive and its goals almost always confidently attained. Like Glazunov's earlier symphonies, the *Seventh* combines Western forms with Russian content—even the piping shepherds of the opening movement have a Russian accent—but the *Seventh* more than any of its predecessors shows evidence of Glazunov's burgeoning interest in counterpoint. The development section of the opening movement and the string writing in the Andante are clearly linear in inspiration. For all its compositional mastery, however, the *Seventh* shows signs of decline in its concluding two movements. After the brilliant Scherzos of the *Fourth* and *Fifth* symphonies, the Allegro giocoso Scherzo of the *Seventh* seems pro forma in its jollity. And after the triumphal conclusions of the *Fifth* and *Sixth* symphonies, the rejoicing of the *Seventh's* Allegro maestoso Finale seems less convinced of its own success: the fierce central development seems more like an episode than an integrated part of the whole and the cymbals and triangle at the close seem predictably celebratory. *—James Leonard*

Recommended:

○ **Art Of Nikolai Golovanov, Vol. 8** / Golovanov (cond.), Moscow Large SO / Arlecchino 60

○ **Glazunov: Symphonies 2 & 7** / Annissov (cond.), Moscow SO / 1997 / Naxos 553769

CONCERTO

Piano Concerto No. 1 in F minor, Op. 92 (1910–1911)

Known as a conservative, Glazunov rarely, if ever, strayed in his vast output from the mold that tag denotes. His keyboard and orchestral works are especially Romantic in temperament, nineteenth century in outlook. His *Piano Concerto No. 1,* dating to 1910–11, came about near the beginning of an artistic crisis, a time when his artistry started to decline owing to his taxing work as director of the St. Petersburg Conservatory. Yet the *Piano Concerto No. 1* is generally considered one of his strongest compositions from this period, a superior effort to the later *Piano Concerto No. 2* (1917). The *Piano Concerto No. 1* is cast in two movements, the first an Allegro Moderato and the concluding panel a lengthy theme and variations that is really the center of gravity here. The work's form is borrowed from that of Beethoven's last piano sonata, Op. 111, whose two-movement (Allegro and Theme and Variations) structure would also inspire Prokofiev in his *Symphony No. 2* (1924–25). But Glazunov takes a different approach in this lush, richly Romantic work, neither scaling the transcendental heights of Beethoven nor attempting the "iron-and-steel" extravagance of Prokofiev. The concerto's first movement is colorful and tuneful, the theme and variations lush and brilliantly crafted, but neither attempts to etch out an especially individual character. It should not seem surprising that Glazunov, who had spent much time in England in 1907, divulges a somewhat Elgarian manner in his orchestration, especially of the second movement. Still, the work is not imitative and if it is not a major accomplishment, it is quite a worthwhile effort. *—Robert Cummings*

Recommended:

○ **Glazunov: Piano Concertos** / Yablonsky (cond.), Yablonskaya, Moscow State SO / 2000 / Naxos 553928

○ **Richter** / Kondrashin (cond.), , Moscow Youth SO / 1995 / Melodiya 29460

Piano Concerto No. 2 in B major, Op. 100 (1917)

Cast in a more traditional form—that is, in three movements—than the composer's *Piano Concerto No. 1* (1911), Alexander Glazunov's *Piano Concerto No. 2* is an altogether more reserved and mature work than its predecessor. The opening theme of the first movement (Andante sostenuto), which sets the mood for the entire work, forms a foundation upon which the composer liberally sprinkles dance-like rhythms and carefully crafted decorative motifs. The brief but powerful Andante draws much of its inspiration from the thematic material of the lyrical finale of the composer's *Piano Sonata No. 1* (1900). The Allegro finale is crowned by an anthem-like recapitulation of the main theme in the finest neoclassical tradition. *—Tim Mahon*

Recommended:

○ **Glazunov: Piano Concertos** / Yablonsky (cond.), Yablonskaya, Moscow State SO / 2000 / Naxos 553928

Saxophone Concerto in E flat major, Op. 109 (1934)

During his stay in Paris late in life, Glazunov heard the saxophone-rich band of the *Garde Républicaine* and was inspired to write two saxophone works: a chamber piece for four saxophones and this concerto for alto sax and string orchestra. Glazunov seems immune to the saxophone jazz that had invaded Paris; the concerto is entirely classical, although it does include some of the mildly folk-like themes akin to what Glazunov had employed in his earlier Russian scores. The one-movement work is a free rhapsody, essentially lyrical and sometimes melancholy, with a few extroverted scherzo interjections. For the most part, the strings keep to an unobtrusive supporting role. The tempo frequently changes and the concerto requires the soloist to demonstrate every musical skill: smooth, cantabile playing in the many slow sections; tonal control across a wide dynamic range as the melody winds up and down the scale; and, in the most intricate, animated passages, nimble fingering and effective glissandos. At almost the exact midpoint, the saxophone takes a long, increasingly agitated cadenza that dies away into a pathetic, sighing gesture; this is the basis of a sardonic transition to what initially seems to be a tarantella finale. Glazunov doesn't maintain the dancing rhythm all the way to the end, though; the soloist reminisces about the earlier, more lyrical themes while remaining animated, and the concerto concludes with trills and conventional bravura gestures. *—James Reel*

Recommended:

○ **Saxophone Concertos** / Marriner (cond.), Harle, Academy of St. Martin-in-the-Fields / 1997 / EMI 72109

○ **Extravaganza for Saxophone & Orchestra** / Trevor (cond.), Richtmeyer, Slovak RSO / 2003 / Albany 593

Violin Concerto in A minor, Op. 82 (1904)

This attractive concerto, small but offering plenty of special effects for the soloist, is probably the most widely played of Glazunov's works. It elegantly wraps up various Romantic takes on the concerto idea into an easily grasped package. The three movements of the traditional concerto are contained within the fast-slow-fast structure of this work's single movement, and the entire work, moreover, unfolds from the melodic material stated at the beginning, giving the concerto the character of a single sonata form movement. The moody slow section serves as a "development" of the opening material and builds to a spectacular cadenza. The final section, serving the function of a recapitulation, unleashes more soloistic fire. This concerto was a concert-hall favorite in the first half of the twentieth century and has continued to hold the stage even as most of Glazunov's other work has declined in popularity outside Russia. *—AMG*

Recommended:

○ **Dvořák: Violin Concerto; Glazunov: Violin Concerto; Schubert: Symphony 2** / Steinberg (cond.), Milstein, Pittsburgh SO / 1999 / Angel 67250

○ **Glazunov: Violin Concerto; Kabalevsky: Violin Concerto; Glière: Romance** / Kondrashin (cond.), Oistrakh, State SO of Russia / 1952 / Omega 1025

○ **Tchaikovsky & Glazunov: Violin Concertos** / Abbado (cond.), Vengerov, Berlin PO / 1995 / Teldec 90881

○ **The Concerto Collection** / Hendl (cond.), Heifetz, RCA Victor SO / 1994 / RCA Victor 61779

BALLET

Raymonda, Op. 57 (1896–1897)

Glazunov's score for the ballet *Raymonda,* Op. 57, props up a weak and fanciful narrative by novelist-journalist Lydia Pashkova, who submitted her ideas for a new scenario to Ivan Vsevolozhsky, director of the *Russian Imperial Theatres,* in 1895. *Raymonda* was originally produced in January 1898 at the Mariinsky (now Kirov) Theatre in St. Petersburg, with choreography by the great Marius Petipa. Prima ballerina Pierina Legnani (then in her benefit year) took the title role, with Sergei Legat as her suitor, the chivalrous knight Jean de Brienne.

The action takes place in medieval Hungary. Raymonda is to marry the crusader Jean de Brienne, but when he is summoned to take up arms abroad, Raymonda becomes the object of desire of the wicked Saracen infidel Abderakhman, who plots her abduction. The beneficent White Lady (a spirit committed to the guardianship of Raymonda's noble family line in perpetuity) suddenly appears at the critical moment. The planned kidnapping is thus foiled, and Jean de Brienne slays Abderakhman in battle with the sword.

The forgoing events, though entirely predictable, are spun out to occupy most of the ballet's first two acts. The third act focuses entirely on the betrothal and jubilant marriage celebrations for Raymonda and Jean de Brienne. Musically, this final act is composed of a series of divertissements and separate variations, one of which is the "pas classique hongroise," the most famous individual episode in the entire ballet. Though the somewhat ramshackle plot, with its banal and unsurprising outcome, is hardly an inspired literary creation, *Raymonda* survives in the repertory chiefly as the result of Glazunov's exquisite and imaginative score. Though Act III is occasionally presented on programs as a freestanding item, the complete ballet is seldom revived, overshadowed by the composer's more popular *The Seasons* (1898). *—Michael Jameson*

Recommended:

- ○ **Glazunov: Raymonda** / Annissov (cond.), Moscow SO / 1996 / Naxos 553503
- ○ **Glazunov: Raymonda** / Jarvi (cond.), Scottish National Orch. / 1986 / Chandos 8447

The Seasons, Op. 67 (1899)

Alexander Glazunov's ballet *The Seasons*, Op. 67, was composed for the Russian Imperial Ballet troupe, and first staged in February 1900 at the Mariinsky Theatre under the choreographic direction of Marius Petipa. The work is not, however, a ballet in the conventional sense, lacking as it does any clearly defined scenario. Instead, Glazunov's *The Seasons* is cast in the form of a series of (appropriately) four tableaux, each of which is further subdivided; this model is similar to that of Tchaikovsky's piano work of the same name, written a quarter-century earlier.

The ballet opens with a brief introduction, leading to the depiction of winter; its individual dances portray frost, ice, hail, and snow, respectively. Frost takes the form of a vigorous Polonaise, after which the violas and clarinets present a short dance suggesting ice. Hail takes the form of a scherzo, followed in turn by the waltz of the snow. Two gnomes then manage to dispel winter's grip by lighting a fire, in readiness for the arrival of spring, on the harp, to the gentle accompaniment of the zephyr, wild birds, and flowers. Following dances for each, the roses, the birds, and indeed the spring itself pass by, as the heat of high summer now approaches.

Summer's tableau is set amid the ripening corn, which dances along with wild poppies and cornflowers; all collapse exhausted in the heat, and as they rest, a group of water-bearing naiads arrive, dancing a graceful barcarole. A further dance follows, invoking the spirit of the corn, with an important clarinet solo. During the coda, fauns and satyrs try to carry off the spirit of the corn, but their attempts to do so are curtailed by the zephyr. Autumn is the season of new wine, and the fruits of the harvest. It is presented now by a wild dance to Bacchus, the god of the vintage. We hear fleeting references to themes from the earlier seasons, before the bacchanal of autumn returns, only to be eventually subdued as the leaves begin to fall from the trees. Finally, as the stage darkens, the stars of the heavens encircle the earth, a token of changeless, timeless eternity as the work draws to a close. *—Michael Jameson*

Recommended:

- ○ **Glazunov: Seasons; Scène dansante in A Op81, Glazunov: Scènes de ballet** / Anissimov (cond.), Moscow State SO / 1998 / Naxos 553915
- ○ **Glazunov: Seasons; Prokofiev: Cinderella** / Ashkenazy, Royal PO / 1999 / Decca 455349

Evelyn Glennie

b. Jul. 19, 1965, Aberdeen, Scotland

Percussionist

Evelyn Glennie, born in Aberdeen, Scotland, in 1965, is the world's foremost, and first full-time, solo percussionist. The recipient of enormous media attention due to her deafness, Glennie is likewise noteworthy for the variety of her repertoire and recording projects. She lost her hearing at the age of 12 and began to study timpani at that time, working extensively with her teacher to learn to sense percussion vibrations. Glennie made her professional debut in 1985, and it did not take long for her musical adventurousness to show itself. In addition to performing with classical ensembles, she commissioned new works (over 80 to date), single-handedly expanding the repertoire of works for solo percussion. An energetic concertizer, she is typically on the road for over 100 evenings a year, and has made 13 solo recordings.

Glennie crosses musical boundaries with unusual ease. In addition to performances with most of the major European and American classical orchestras, she has worked with the Kodo Japanese drummers, the experimental Icelandic pop vocalist Björk, Javanese gamelan ensembles, Brazilian samba bands, and other musicians on five continents. Her album *Shadow Behind the Iron Sun*, released in 2000, fulfilled Glennie's long-held desire to join forces with a pop producer, in this case the veteran American studio wizard Michael Brauer. The disc showcased the large collection of percussion instruments Glennie has mastered, including homemade instruments, most notably a set of cut and tuned car exhaust pipes, as well as sounds from around the world.

A composer herself, Glennie has written music for film and television in collaboration with the composer and web designer Greg Malcangi. She also plays the Great Highland bagpipes. Her numerous awards include "Scotswoman of the Decade," a Grammy award for her 1989 recording of Bartók's *Sonata for Two Pianos and Percussion*, and her designation as Officer of the British Empire at the age of 27, an honor very rarely given to anyone under 50.

Glennie does not mention her deafness in press materials, and she has been known to react with exasperation when asked about it to the exclusion of musical matters. She is profoundly deaf, meaning that while she cannot understand speech, she can hear some sound. What she hears is augmented, as it is for everyone else, by her sense of touch. The sensation of feeling vibrations is experienced by Glennie at various frequencies and in various parts of her body. She tends to feel low sounds in her legs and feet, and high ones on her face, neck, and chest. Glennie contends that hearing is a form of touch, and that everyone, whether "deaf" or not, processes sound in an individual way. Glennie's autobiography, *Good Vibrations*, appeared in 1990. *—AMG*

Recommended:

- ○ **Rhythm Song** / Glennie / RCA 60242
- ○ **Heath: African Sunrise; Manhattan Rave** / Glennie, Smith, Harle, London PO / 2000 / Black Box 1051
- ○ **Shadow Behind the Iron Sun** / Glennie, Smith / 1999 / RCA 63406
- ○ **Philip Glass: The Concerto Project, Vol. 1** / Schwarz (cond.), Glennie, Lloyd Webber, Haas, Royal Liverpool PO / 2004 / Orange Mountain Music 14

Reinhold Glière

b. Jan. 11, 1875, Kiev, Russia, **d.** Jun. 23, 1956, Moscow, Russia

Composer: Ballet, Vocal, Symphonic, Concerto

Although all of his important compositions came during the first half of the twentieth century, the body and style of his work place Glière solidly at the end of the nineteenth century in spirit. Having studied at both the Kiev and Moscow conservatories, he was infused with Russian Romanticism, and—even though he studied briefly in Berlin—it is safe to say that nothing he ever wrote sounded either modern or un-Russian. He studied theory under a student of Rimsky-Korsakov and, upon entering the Moscow Conservatory in 1894, studied composition and harmony with the likes of Arensky, Taneyev, and Ippolitov-Ivanov. In 1900 he was awarded the school's highest prize in composition, the gold medal. His monumental third symphony, subtitled "Ilya Murometz," which premiered in Moscow in 1912, propelled his career forward; in 1913 he was named director of the Kiev Conservatory, a position he held all through the Russian Revolution.

In 1920 he became professor of music at the Moscow Conservatory; his service there was interrupted only by the Second World War. While in Moscow, he taught Serge Prokofiev, Aram Khachaturian, and Alexander Mossolov, the spearhead of "Soviet realism."

Glière also became a political figure in Russia during the Stalin years, serving as chairman of the organizing committee of the Soviet Composers' Union from 1938 to 1948. His conventional, utterly Russian music found favor with Stalin and his cultural ministers; the extent to which Glière's reputation as a musician may have suffered because of this will forever remain speculative. Glière received many honors during this era, including the title of People's Artist of the Soviet Union.

Glière's body of work—which straddles the upheaval of the Russian Revolution, with fine pieces produced on both sides—is prodigious in quantity: besides his three symphonies, four string quartets, two complete operas, two ballets, and two concertos, he produced hundreds of songs, piano works, and chamber pieces. He is considered, along with his more famous predecessor, Tchaikovsky, to have been seminal in the development of Russian ballet; however, little of his music is heard outside Russia today. Glière's music is comfortably Romantic, invariably nationalistic, and skillfully crafted, often managing to combine beautiful melodies, inventive orchestration, and eye-popping bombast to great effect. *—Michael Morrison*

BALLET

The Red Poppy, Op. 70 (1926–1927; revised 1949)

Glière was a composer of the same generation of Rachmaninov, with whom the comparison is appropriate. Both composers wrote three symphonies, of which the Second Symphonies were composed in the same year. Their musical languages were similar in many respects, to the point of occasional resemblance. Both were happy to work in the Russian romantic tradition. But unlike Rachmaninov, who ran afoul of the October Revolution and went into permanent exile, Glière remained in Russia and adapted without great strain to the conservative artistic rules imposed by Stalinism. The 1926 ballet *The Red Poppy* was perhaps the most enduring success in a career that enjoyed the recognition of the regime, which named him People's Artist.

It is a full-length ballet, lasting two hours and comprising three acts and 36 numbers. The story takes place in a Chinese port. The main characters are Tao-Hoa, a Chinese girl, her manager, and the Russian captain. The action involves the revolt of the exploited coolies working in the docks, and several scenes in a cosmopolitan restaurant. This posed several problems to the composer, obliged to combine musical elements of diverse origin, from pentatonic melodies representing the Chinese setting, to a Charleston to suggest American influence, to the Internationale to portray the Russians. In view of these difficulties, Glière had a remarkable success in handling the materials. The most outstanding numbers were later collected in a suite—most of them belonging to the first act—that has become much better known than the complete ballet. The ballet opens with a pentatonic Introduction describing the docks. The Dance of the Coolies describe the oppression of the dock workers. Tao-Hoa enters in the following Scene, a beautiful lyrical moment. Several European dances follow, including the Boston Waltz. The Russian captain and sailors arrive, and there is a scene between Tao-Hoa and the captain where Glière masterly and inextricably combines the theme of the girl with the first phrase of the Internationale. This wonderful number is followed by the Variation with the Golden Fingers. The Coolies' Victory Dance that comes next is the one that opens the suite. The first act concludes with the famous Dance of the Russian Sailors that closes the suite. The second act takes place in an opium den, in an atmosphere of dream. The Dance of the Chinese Women precedes two dreamy adagios, an intense Prelude and a Procession and Sword Dance that sound like soundtrack music as well as "Phoenix." The lyrical Adagio is the emotional climax of the act. The third act opens with a Charleston. After several dances in the restaurant and the Chinese Theatre comes the rebellion and the interesting Scene of Confusion. The captain has a scene before the departure of his ship. The work concludes with an optimistic Apotheosis. *—Hector Bellman*

Recommended:

- ○ **Glière: Red Poppy** / Anichanov (cond.), St. Petersburg State SO / 1995 / Naxos 553496

VOCAL

Concerto for coloratura soprano & orchestra, Op. 82 (1943)

Reyngol'd Moritsevich Glier, or Reinhold Glière, as his name more commonly reads, is one of those fascinating Russian composers who witnessed the transition from the late Romantic period to the Soviet era. While Glière was born into the nationalist-driven (but ultimately French-oriented) musical world of mid-to-late nineteenth century Russia, he lived all the way up to 1956, gathering up armfuls of official Soviet artistic commendations and teaching, until 1941, at the Moscow Conservatory. During none of the U.S.S.R.'s various political or artistic upheavals, however, did he feel compelled to abandon his gently melodic musical style. The *Concerto for coloratura soprano and orchestra*, Op. 82 of 1942–43, shows that style off as well as any piece he wrote; it also demonstrates how little interested Glière was in the sharper, grittier music of Dmitry Shostakovich and his many followers.

The most striking thing about the *Concerto for coloratura soprano and orchestra*, Op. 82, is, of course, its instrumentation. The idea of writing music without text for a singer was not new (Glière's contemporary Sergey Rachmaninov wrote perhaps the most famous such piece, the treasured *Vocalise*, Op. 34, No. 14), but the idea of making a full-scale concerto for such an "instrument" certainly was. The concerto has two movements—Andante and Allegro—and lasts between ten and twelve minutes. A melancholy, unharmonized tune in the strings ushers in the first movement; the winds join in to fill out the texture, and the soprano promptly enters. Great spans of melody, thrown against washes of deep, rich orchestral texture, drive the movement from climax to climax. The warm Allegro has a great deal of lighthearted humor to it, and one can hear in it strands reminiscent of Tchaikovsky's ballets and even, somewhat more surprisingly, Wagner's music-dramas. *—Blair Johnston*

Recommended:

- ○ **Vocalises** / Schoenwandt (cond.), Dessay / 1998 / Angel 56565
- ○ **Glière: Harp Concerto; Concerto for Coloratura Soprano; Ginastera: Harp Concerto** / Hickox (cond.), Masters, Hulse, City of London Sinfonia / 1992 / Chandos 9094

SYMPHONIC

Symphony No. 2 in C minor, Op. 25 (1907–1908)

Although Glière's *Symphony No. 2* has never attained the popularity of his *Third* (subtitled "Ilya Murometz"), it is nevertheless one of the composer's more important works. Cast in four large movements, it exudes Glière's characteristic Russian style and conservative expressive language.

The first movement is marked Allegro pesante and opens dramatically with an epic theme of absolute Russian character, played at a more deliberate tempo than the marking would normally suggest. A passionate, almost Rachmaninovian alternate theme provides ample contrast amid the surrounding muscular, heroic, and more animated music. The development section builds to a dramatic climax, and the return of the main theme near the close adds to the epic sweep of the movement, despite the quiet ending.

The ensuing Scherzo, marked Allegro giocoso, is playful and lively in its outer sections, Romantic and mostly relaxed in its central Trio. As in the other movements, Glière's masterful scoring here enhances the colorful Russian character of the music. The Andante third movement is a theme and variations, the main theme richly Romantic, sounding like a mixture of Borodin and Rachmaninov. The variations that fill out the movement contrast moods—the lively and colorful with the soaring and passionate, the playful and fleet with the serenely beautiful.

The finale, marked Allegro vivace, may contain the most Russian-sounding music of all: the chipper folkish main theme, driving rhythms, and active tambourine, along with the composer's deft orchestration, impart a strong sense of both Russian fantasy (not unlike some of Rimsky-Korsakov's more colorful scores) and peasant festivity. The brief middle section features an exotic melody related to the main theme; it is followed by music even more celebratory than that heard at the outset. Soon, however, the mood develops a more epic character and the alternate theme appears in a stately, heroic guise to triumphantly crown the work. *—Robert Cummings*

Recommended:

- ○ **Glière: Symphony 2; Zaporozhy Cossacks** / Downes (cond.), BBCPO / 1992 / Chandos 9071
- ○ **Macal Conducts Glière** / Macal (cond.), New Jersey SO / 1996 / Delos 3178

Symphony No. 3 in B minor ("Ilya Murometz"), Op. 42 (1909–1911)

Glière, a Russian composer of French ancestry, was one of the more conservative figures of the twentieth century. His most famous large-scale work is this program symphony telling the tale of the legendary twelfth century figure Ilya Murometz. He is selected by a mighty "bogatyr," a Russian type of knight, to be his successor. Il'ya captures an outlaw named Solovei (which ironically means "nightingale"), and takes him to the castle of Vladimir, the Sun. Using Solovei's mighty voice as a weapon (before decapitating him) Murometz overcomes the defenses of the castle, and is welcomed inside by Vladimir. Finally, he is conquered when he and his forces are turned to stone. The idiom of the symphony is the rich romanticism of Rimsky-Korsakov and Tchaikovsky, with richer, more Wagnerian harmonies. It is also distinguished as one of the longest symphonies in the entire repertoire. Buyers of recordings of it should be aware of whether the version they are considering is complete or cut. *—Joseph Stevenson*

Recommended:

- ○ **Glière: Symphony 3** / Downes (cond.), BBCPO / 1991 / Chandos 9041
- ○ **Glière: Symphony 3** / Botstein (cond.), London SO / 2003 / Telarc 80609
- ○ **Glière: Symphony 3** / Johanos (cond.), Czecho-Slovak RSO / 1993 / Naxos 550858

CONCERTO

Harp Concerto in E flat major, Op. 74 (1938)

Glière was an exact contemporary of Ravel and only two years younger than Rachmaninov. He followed the latter's musical path, remaining firmly rooted in the styles of techniques he had learned in his youth and never strayed from the colorful Russian cosmopolitan style. But unlike Rachmaninov, he never left the broad territories of the Russian Empire or its successor, the Soviet Union. His avoidance of any modernist or radical sounds also kept him on the right side of the Soviet demand for accessible "Socialist Realist" art.

This concerto was written in 1938. It uses the instrument's idiomatic texture of arpeggiated chords very frequently; at other times rich chords are used and, in the second movement, a simple melodic texture introduces the main theme for a group of six variations and coda. For the most part the music is amiable and untroubled. When Glière wrote it he sought the advice of harpist Ksenia Erdeli as to the practicality of his music. Her suggestions were so helpful that he offered to give her credit in the publication as co-composer but she refused, insisting that her function was that of an editor. This, then, was the credit she received when the work appeared in print in Russia. However, at least one Western source confuses her with her niece Olga Erdeli, also an important harp soloist, and gives the latter undue credit as editor. *—Joseph Stevenson*

Recommended:

- ○ **Glière: Harp Concerto; Concerto for Coloratura Soprano; Ginastera: Harp Concerto** / Hickox (cond.), Masters, Hulse, City of London Sinfonia / 1992 / Chandos 9094
- ○ **Harp Concertos** / Bonynge (cond.), Ellis, London SO / 1997 / London 452585

Horn Concerto in B flat major, Op. 91 (1950)

With the addition of valves in the early part of the nineteenth century, the French horn suddenly evolved from the cumbersome, bugle-like accompanist it had been to a fully capable, full range solo instrument. And while many composers were taken with its range and unique tone, Reinhold Glière captured its full power and virtuosity in the concerto format. Written for Valeri Polekh, the solo horn player at the Bolshoi, his *Concerto in B flat* is unprecedented in both length and difficulty. Long at nearly 24 minutes and constructed without regard for the natural conveniences of the horn itself, it was inspired by and modeled after the barbarically difficult Tchaikovsky violin concerto. The result is a stirring piece in three movements, full of the sort of epic sweep and orchestral grandeur which Glière at his best could bring off as well as any Russian. Nearly as long as the other two movements combined, the first movement allegro begins with an orchestral tutti which brings on the soloist, who launches into a bright, singing theme. Although not complex, the movement provides for a cadenza which bridges to a more complicated second theme. The movement ends with an orchestral reprise of the tutti opening and without the horn itself. The second-movement andante sounds deceptively simple, but in it may be heard the chromatic complexity of the valved horn and the demands on the player are considerable. The movement ends on a sustained, muted high E flat. The finale is thoroughly Glière, with driving romantic energy, high drama, and satisfying cadences. The chromatic and dynamic demands on the player become greater and greater and at last a great, headlong, triple-tongued rush sweeps to the conclusion. *—Michael Morrison*

Recommended:

○ **Glière: Bronze Horseman Suite; Horn Concerto** / Downes (cond.), Watkins, BBCPO / 1995 / Chandos 9379

Mikhail Glinka

b. Jun. 1, 1804, Novospasskoye, Russia, **d.** Feb. 15, 1857, Berlin, Germany
Composer: Orchestral, Chamber Music, Opera

A well-educated child of privilege, Glinka became a fervent Russian nationalist. He is considered the father of Russian music, and exerted a significant influence on such great later composers as Tchaikovsky, Rimsky-Korsakov, and Stravinsky.

Glinka took piano, violin, and voice lessons, but he did not study music or composition seriously as a youth. His first job was as a government official, but, realizing how strongly he was drawn to music, he left to pursue both a general and a musical education. He studied for a time in Italy and spent the year 1833 studying composition in Berlin. He had composed some works during and prior to this time, but these were still derivative of prevailing Western European styles, and the year in Berlin only reinforced the non-Russian influences he felt.

Returning to Russia, he discovered the works of writers such as Pushkin and Gogol, who uncovered for him the wealth and depth of his Russian cultural heritage. Moved, he wrote his seminal, truly Russian work, *A Life for the Tsar*. It recounts how villainous Poles, in 1613, attempted to capture the Tsar and how a young hero, Ivan Sussanin, led the pursuing Poles on a wild goose chase at the ultimate cost of his life. The work premiered in 1836 and was an immediate success. It intermingled Russian and Polish folk tunes with Italian-style operatic passages and even anticipated Wagner's use of the leitmotif by employing recurring themes identified with specific characters. It also marked a new approach to orchestration in which the orchestra was essentially a member of the cast, not merely background accompaniment for the singers.

The year 1842 saw the premiere of Glinka's second great Russian opera, *Russlan and Lyudmila*. It was not as immediately successful as *A Life for the Tsar*, but ultimately was more influential. It contained Persian influences and made use of a seven-step whole-tone scale for the first time in European music.

His influence upon the Russian composers who followed him was immense; specifically he inspired Mily Balakirev, who gathered four other young Russian composers around him to form the so-called "Mighty Handful," and extended Glinka's effort to foster Russian nationalism in music and the arts in general. *—Michael Morrison*

ORCHESTRAL

Kamarinskaya (Russian scherzo), fantasy (1848)

An early example of Russian nationalism in orchestral music, this free variation-fantasy draws on two dissimilar Russian folk tunes, a wedding dance (*Kamarinskaya*) and a wedding song (*Over the Hills, the High Hills*). The opening bars are surprisingly menacing for a wedding-inspired piece, but soon they give way to the graceful *Over the Hills*, which almost immediately begins playing off an original countersubject, then disintegrates into material based merely on its first three notes. Soon the strings come to the rescue with the frisky if repetitive *Kamarinskaya* dance. The basic tune is only a couple of bars long; Glinka sustains interest by constantly varying its orchestration and harmonic and rhythmic settings. Glinka goes back to the beginning (minus the introduction) for a virtual repeat of all this, but varies the details, especially the instrumentation, and wraps it up with a lively hopak treatment of the dance tune. *—James Reel*

Recommended:

○ **Glinka: Orchestral Works** / Sinaisky (cond.), BBCPO / 2000 / Chandos 9861

○ **Favourite Encores** / Järvi (cond.), Detroit SO / 2001 / Chandos 6648

CHAMBER MUSIC

Trio pathétique, for clarinet, bassoon & piano in D minor (1832)

The *Trio Pathétique* by Mikhail Glinka is one of comparatively few piano trios by Russian composers to have found a place (albeit a fairly marginalized one) within the repertory. Even so, it is far less well known than similar works in the genre by Tchaikovsky, Rachmaninov, and Arensky. That's probably because, as Denby Richards has suggested, "Glinka's trio is not so it easily recognisable as a work by the 'Father of Russian music'... nor does it really fit the title which became attached to it in a published format, in its original scoring for piano, clarinet and bassoon."

The work (which may be played as a conventional piano trio or with clarinet replacing the violin) was composed in 1832. At the time, the 28-year-old Glinka was studying composition at the Milan Conservatory, having traveled to Italy in hopes that the warmer weather would ease his chronic chest condition. He came under the influence of Italian opera composers such as Donizetti and Bellini, which in part explains the character of this peculiarly un-Russian sounding work. As to the title, it is difficult to know whether it might refer to Glinka's daily endurance of the camphorated chest plasters prescribed by his doctors: more plausible, perhaps, is the suggestion that the term "Pathétique" refers to an unrequited romantic attachment. A note on the autograph score reads "I have known love only through the pain it brings," yet the prevailing mood of the work is genial rather than tragic.

The trio is laid out in the conventional four-movement form of the post-Beethoven/Schubert piano trio, and yet it retains the character of a through-composed single-movement piece. The first three movements are intended to be played straight through without a break, and the finale is little more than a brief epilogue which brings a return of material heard previously. The principal thematic idea is presented at the very outset; it is an enervated, unsettled motif which becomes ever more passionate and excitable with each succeeding appearance. Its restless quality counterpoises a luxuriant second idea, and another memorably beautiful melody given out by the cello in the central trio section of the Scherzo. Another wistful and elegiac motif comes later, in the penultimate episode of the work, following which all the various thematic blocks are reviewed during the finale and the work reaches a dramatic, even triumphant conclusion. *—Michael Jameson*

Recommended:

○ **Arensky & Glinka: Piano Trios** / Borodin Trio / 1987 / Chandos 8477

Viola Sonata (1825–1828)

An early work that Glinka never finished, the *Sonata in D minor for viola and piano* (1825–28) in later years has grown comely in the eyes of the world's violists, who are ever searching for additions to their unfortunately scanty nineteenth century repertory. It is—or, more properly, was to have been—a three-movement composition by which Glinka intended to move himself past the academic exercise pieces that had up to that point been occupying him and begin writing "real" music.

Glinka composed the first movement, Allegro moderato, in 1825, while living in St. Petersburg. He was, at this point in his life, only moderately trained in the arts of music, though passionately devoted to them. As far as instrumental music goes, he had composed a *Septet in E flat for winds and strings*, a *String Quartet in D major*, and some moderate-sized orchestral works, but as a lot they are only marginally successful music. The Allegro moderato movement of the *Viola Sonata*, built along traditional formal lines, but featuring a rich, singable melodicity all Glinka's own, has to be counted a great improvement upon those earlier works. Glinka the accomplished opera composer would be years yet in the making, and it would be utterly unfair to place the *Viola Sonata* next to, say, a Beethoven sonata from the early 1820s for comparison. But one can still imagine Glinka's joy when he played it through with friends in 1825, once playing piano and once playing viola, and found that he had indeed begun the musical breakthrough for which he had so longed.

The second and slower movement, Larghetto ma non troppo, was written a few years later while visiting Moscow in late April and early May 1828. Contrary to some reports, Glinka did in fact finish the Larghetto—it was the third movement, a rondo, that he began and abandoned (Glinka later wrote that he didn't even try to finish the rondo), not the second. He ended up quite happy with this songful B flat major slow movement—"rather clever" was Glinka's happy assessment.

Glinka planned and started work on a rondo finale built from a Russian folk theme. While the movement was never finished, his time was not completely wasted: he later used portions of the rondo music in a children's polka. Glinka revised the two finished movements of the *Viola Sonata* as late as the 1850s (further proof that he did finish the second movement), but the sonata was not published until well into the twentieth century. Borisovsky is sometimes credited with completing the work, but the matter is a confusing one, as the two movements that are performable (the fragmentary rondo is never played) were in fact finished by Glinka. Rather than completing the work, Borisovsky seems to have fleshed out the accompaniment part. *—Blair Johnston*

Recommended:

○ **Sonatas: Rubinstein, Glinka, Grechaninov** / Barshai, Nikolayeva / 1994 / Multisonic 310236

○ **The Russian Viola** / Imai, Pontinen / 1986 / Bis 358

OPERA

A Life for the Tsar (Zhizn' za tsarya) ("Ivan Susanin") (1834–1836)

Though overshadowed in the repertory by more frequently performed works like Mussorgsky's *Boris Godunov* and Tchaikovsky's *Eugene Onegin*, Glinka's *A Life for the Tsar* (1836) is a singularly important work in the history of opera. It was the first Russian opera to receive a foreign production (Prague, 1866), the first to establish itself permanently in the repertory, and the work which, in the view of many, marked the beginning of Russian nationalism in music.

A Life for the Tsar tells the story of the 1633 founding of the Romanov dynasty, which ruled Russia for nearly 300 years. It is the tale of Ivan Susanin, a peasant who sacrificed his life in order to thwart a Polish army force sent to kill the new boy Tsar (Michael Feodorvich) and install a Polish puppet ruler. (The focus on Susanin was virtually dictated by a Russian court rule that no member of the Romanov dynasty could be depicted on stage.) Glinka originally intended to call the opera *Ivan*

Susanin, but when Czar Nicholas I expressed his enthusiasm for the work during rehearsals, he adopted the present title.

The opera was highly popular in Russia until the end of the Romanov reign, and its reception abroad was similarly enthusiastic. However, the Bolshevik regime forced the opera, with its glorification of the Tsar, off the stage for 20 years. In 1939, a nascent nationalist spirit in the face of the Fascist threat prompted the opera's return to the Russian stage, this time under the earlier title that places its peasant hero front and center.

The opera's most effective parts are those that turn to the melodic style of Russian folk and liturgical music; there are also some memorable numbers based on Polish music. For all his unabashed nationalism, Glinka at times could hardly escape conventional Italian operatic formulas. Nevertheless, with its pageantry and gripping action, as well as Glinka's effective orchestration, *A Life for the Tsar* makes for exciting listening, and it still holds the stage well as a vital part of the Russian repertoire. *—Joseph Stevenson*

Synopsis:

Act One. The story is set in Russia and Poland in 1613. The opera opens in the Russian village of Domnino, where Ivan Susanin lives. The peasants sing happily, and Susanin's daughter Antonida eagerly looks forward to her marriage to Bogdan Sobinin. Susanin, however, sours her cheerful spirit when he declares that her wedding plans must be delayed as long as there is political uncertainty in the country; an incursion by a Polish army threatens Russian stability, and Tsarist succession remains in doubt owing to the Polish Prince Wladyslaw's claim to the throne. But Sobinin brings news of resistance to the Polish advance and announces that Mikhail Romanov has been elected Tsar by the assembly. The news is greeted joyfully and it is decided Antonida and Sobinin need not delay their marriage after all.

Act Two. At a ball given by the commander of the invading Polish army, there is much festivity among the guests, who are confident of triumph in the campaign. A messenger dampens their upbeat mood with news of Mikhail's election as Tsar. It is quickly decided that his installation must be prevented. A detachment is thus immediately assembled and heads for Kostroma, the Tsar-elect's temporary hideout.

Act Three. In his hut, Susanin discusses the election of Mikhail with Vanya, an orphan in his charge. The latter fears the Poles will capture Mikhail and thwart his ascension to the throne. But Susanin assures him that the new Tsar cannot be found, since knowledge of his whereabouts could, he believes, be revealed only by a traitor. Sobinin enters, followed by Antonida, and all four express joyous sentiments about the forthcoming marriage. Sobinin departs to complete preparations for the wedding. The sound of horses approaching the hut precedes the abrupt entry of Polish soldiers. They inquire after the whereabouts of the Tsar, and Susanin pretends to agree to take them to his hideout. Aside, he instructs Vanya to warn the Tsar and his retinue of the impending danger at the monastery where they are staying, while he misleads the Poles in their attempt to get there. Antonida fears her father will not return and begs him to stay, but he is forcibly taken away by the Poles. Friends soon enter, expecting to partake of a bridal party, but they learn from Antonida of her father's grim situation. Sobinin returns, and he and his peasant companions decide to pursue the Poles and rescue Susanin.

Act Four. In the forest that night, the searchers are lost and weary, but Sobinin encourages his posse to press onward. In the ensuing scene, Vanya arrives at the monastery and delivers the warning, urging all to flee with him.

In a snow-covered forest, the Poles begin to develop suspicions that they are being led astray by Susanin. They set camp for the night as Susanin realizes his demise is unavoidable. Later the Poles press him for the truth about his intentions, and he finally admits his deception, realizing that he has stalled them long enough for the Tsar to have made a successful getaway. The Poles kill Susanin.

Epilogue. A large crowd rejoices at the coronation of Tsar Mikhail in Red Square. In attendance are Antonida, Sobinin, and Vanya, who are told that the Tsar will always remember Susanin and his selfless act of bravery. *—Robert Cummings*

Recommended:

- ○ **Glinka: Ivan Susanin** / Marinov (cond.), Ghiuselev, Petkov, Stoyanova, Stanchev, Sofia National Opera Orch. / Capriccio 10783/85
- ○ **Glinka: Ivan Susanin** / Melik-Pashaev (cond.), Mikhailov, Nelepp, Spiller, Antonova, Bolshoi Theater Orch. / Preiser 90365
- ○ **Glinka: Ivan Susanin** / Tchakarov (cond.), Merritt, Pendachanska, Georgiev, Martinovich, Sofia Festival Orch. / 1991 / Sony 46487

Ruslan and Lyudmila (1837–1842)

Glinka's opera *Ruslan and Lyudmila* is not the first great Russian national opera—that honor goes to his *A Life for the Tsar*—but it is the definitive Russian opera. Shortly after the successful premiere of *A Life for the Tsar* in 1836, the director of the Imperial Theater suggested to Glinka Pushkin's mock-epic *Ruslan and Lyudmila.* But before the composer and poet could collaborate, the poet died in a duel, and although Glinka pushed ahead with the project, he did so without a librettist. As one of his friends noted, "The opera is almost finished and yet there is no text. A strange way of writing." The libretto was eventually written by Valerian Shirkov, but Glinka's dissatisfaction with it led him to bring in other writers and to even write some of it himself. Although *Ruslan and Lyudmila* was heavily cut and its final libretto roundly criticized, the premiere on November 27, 1842, was successful—one critic called it splendid, grandiose, and fascinating—and the work was given 31 times in its first season. But that number quickly diminished until the opera was withdrawn from the repertoire in 1848. Its first complete and uncut performance was given by Balakirev in Prague in 1867.

Glinka's opera is at once an epic and heroic quest opera and an intimate and lyrical opera, with both naturalistic and supernatural elements. Over the course of five acts, Ruslan's quest for the abducted Lyudmila takes him through music from all over: Russian music, Finnish music, Tartar music, Persian music, and, of course, Russian folk themes. All of these musics are wonderfully characterized, vividly rhythmic, and brilliantly orchestrated. To differentiate between the real world of Ruslan's Russia and the magical world of the villain Chernomor, Glinka uses earthy, tonal folk songs for the former and unearthly whole-tone harmonies for the latter. All of these disparate elements, however, are unified by Glinka's tremendous imagination and masterful compositional skills. *Ruslan and Lyudmila* influenced every subsequent Russian opera and Russian composer straight through to Shostakovich's *The Nose* 80 years later. *—James Leonard*

Synopsis:

Act One. This "magical" story is set in legendary times in Kiev. In the opening scene, the Knight Ruslan is about to marry Lyudmila, daughter of the Svietosar, Grand Prince of Kiev, as wedding festivities fill the Prince's assembly hall. In attendance are Ratmir and Farlaf, failed suitors of Lyudmila. Bayan begins singing, and his ominous song forecasts great tribulation for the couple—tribulation that will end happily, however. A thunderous noise is heard, followed by total darkness. During the brief blackout, Lyudmila is abducted by Tchernomor, the sorcerer dwarf. After light returns, Svietosar declares that whoever rescues his daughter will have her hand in marriage, in addition to half his kingdom. Ruslan, Ratmir, and Farlaf all depart in pursuit of Lyudmila and her captor.

Act Two. In his cave the benevolent sorcerer Finn reveals to Ruslan the name of Lyudmila's captor and advises him to travel north. In a wooded area in the following scene, Farlaf meets the sorceress Naina, once courted by Finn and now his enemy. She promises to help Farlaf in his quest, and he returns home to await further word from her.

On a misty battlefield, Ruslan seizes a lance and shield to replace weapons he has lost in battle. The fog lifts and he encounters the head of a giant, who attempts to blow him down. The knight, however, is unfazed and slashes the giant's head with his lance. The head acquiesces and gives Ruslan a magical sword. The knight inquires about the provenance of the weapon, and the head reveals that it belonged to Chernomor, his brother, and that only this sword can defeat him.

Act Three. At her castle, Naina sabotages Ratmir in his efforts to find Lyudmila by enchanting him with the singing of magical maidens. He becomes completely mesmerized by them, oblivious to all else around him. Gorislava, a maiden in love with Ratmir but forsaken by him for Lyudmila, observes his seeming trance. Ruslan, drawn to the castle by the powers of Naina, enters and observes Gorislava; the sight of her now enchants him, and his mission of rescue is suddenly forgotten. Finn appears, however, to save the day, driving off the maidens, waking both Ruslan and Ratmir from their spells, and turning the castle into a forest. Ratmir falls back in love with Gorislava, and Ruslan resumes his search for Lyudmila.

Act Four. Lyudmila is shown in Chernomor's magical gardens, where, depressed by her yearnings for Ruslan and for freedom, she ponders suicide. Ruslan arrives outside the gardens, and Chernomor, preparing to confront him in battle, casts a spell over Lyudmila. In the ensuing skirmish, the knight, with Ratmir and Gorislava in his company, dispatches the Sorcerer by cutting off his beard with the magical sword. But when Ruslan finds Lyudmila, he fails to revive her from her sleep.

Act Five. On their return trip to Kiev, the becharmed Lyudmila is abducted again, this time by Farlaf, who heads back to Svetozar to claim her as his bride, with Ruslan in pursuit. Finn appears and gives Ratmir a magical ring (to pass on to Ruslan) that will awaken her from her trance. In the final scene, Lyudmila lies on a bed in her father's assembly hall, with Farlaf attempting in vain to waken her, while Svietosar, courtiers, and others anxiously watch. Ruslan enters, accompanied by Ratmir and Gorislava, and the cowardly Farlaf immediately leaves. The knight rouses Lyudmila with the magical ring, and all rejoice as wedding festivities recommence. *—Robert Cummings*

Recommended:

- ○ **Glinka: Ruslan & Lyudmila** / Gergiev (cond.), Gorchakova, Diadkova, Pluzhnikov, Kit, Kirov Orch. / 1996 / Philips 456248
- ○ **Glinka: Ruslan & Lyudmila** / Simonov (cond.), Nesterenko, Maslennikov, Fomina, Morozov, Bolshoi Theater Orch. / 1996 / Melodiya 29348

Alma Gluck

b. May 11, 1884, Bucharest, Romania, **d.** Oct. 27, 1938, New York, NY
Soprano

Alma Gluck was one of the most popular sopranos of all time. Born Reba Fiersohn in Romania, she came to the United States as an infant. Her Metropolitan Opera debut as Sophie in Massenet's *Werther* launched her into a high-flying seven-year opera career, but later in life she devoted herself to concerts and recordings. She recorded for Victor, and her vintage 1915 recordings of songs such as *Listen to the Mocking Bird* and (*Carry Me Back to Old Virginny* sold millions of copies. So plentiful in supply, even in year 2001, are copies of Gluck's records that many 78 collectors regard them as "junk." However this is not a reflection on her artistry; Gluck's clarity of pronunciation, beauty of tone and accuracy in high ranges are still astounding. She was married to violinist Efrem Zimbalist, and like him taught at the Curtis Institute of Music in Philadelphia. Alma Gluck was the mother of popular television actor and part-time composer Efrem Zimbalist Jr., and her daughter is the writer Marcia Davenport. *—Uncle Dave Lewis*

Recommended:

- ○ **Alma Gluck** / Gluck, etc. / Marston 52001
- ○ **Alma Gluck** / Gluck, etc. / Pearl 9268

Christoph Willibald Gluck

b. Jul. 2, 1714, Erasbach, Germany, **d.** Nov. 15, 1787, Vienna, Austria
Composer: Opera

One of the great masters of eighteenth century opera, Gluck is known for his elegant synthesis of the French and Italian operatic traditions, exemplified by such remarkable works as *Orfeo ed Euridice* and *Alceste*. A native of the Upper Palatinate, Gluck first studied with the Czech cellist and composer (and Franciscan friar) Bohuslav Cernohorsky, later continuing his studies with Sammartini in Italy. Already known as an opera composer in the 1740s, Gluck visited Paris and London, where he met Handel. He married in 1750, settling in Vienna as an opera conductor.

In 1762, Gluck wrote his *Orfeo ed Euridice*, heralding a new era in the history of opera. Combining the Classical ideals of beauty and simplicity with an innate sense of dramatic impetus, it broke down many of the overwrought formal conventions of the Baroque and set the standard for a whole generation of operatic composers. In many ways, opera in the nineteenth century had its conception in the works of Gluck.

While Gluck achieved wide fame in his own time, his works are rare in opera houses today; he is primarily remembered as a reformer and revolutionary. In his dedication to *Alceste*, Gluck wrote that he "sought to confine music to its true function of serving poetry by expressing feelings and the situations of the story without interrupting and cooling off the action through useless and superfluous ornaments." This statement has often been interpreted as a desire to subordinate music to poetry; however, what inspired Gluck's reform was his belief that music gains in expressiveness when it is properly balanced with poetry. Thus, for example, by abolishing the traditional strict separation of recitative and aria, Gluck used music as a means of maintaining an uninterrupted flow of the dramatic action. Gluck's librettist for *Orfeo ed Euridice*, *Alceste*, and *Paride ed Elena*—the three works best representing his reformist ideas—was Ranieri de' Calzabigi, a poet and critic who anticipated some of the composer's fundamental ideas concerning poetry and music. For example, Calzabigi opposed the traditional poetic approach to mythology, exemplified by Pietro Metastasio, the greatest librettist of the opera seria tradition. While Metastasio's mythological figures appear as thinly disguised eighteenth century characters, Calzabigi's poetry strives to create an atmosphere of timelessness, which perfectly suited Gluck's artistic intentions.

After bringing his reforms to fruition, Gluck had several new works produced in Paris. The most remarkable of these works is *Armide* (1777), based on an old libretto by Philippe Quinault, which Lully used for his eponymous work in 1686. Viewed by conservatives as an attack on the French musical and literary traditions, Gluck's operas were targeted by a literary cabal, which decided to embrace Niccolò Piccinni, a respected composer of comic operas, as a standard-bearer. In a literary squabble reminiscent of the "quarrel of the buffoons" in 1752, the traditionalists proclaimed the superiority of traditional (that is: Italian, or, more precisely, Metastasian) opera over French opera, represented by the iconoclastic Gluck. It should be noted that the two composers, who respected each other, refused to participate in the war of words, leaving the polemics to Parisian pseudo-intellectuals.

In essence, Gluck's victory over his adversaries was the triumph of music. His works are regarded as seminal contributions to musical drama, and his ideas were gradually accepted, first by Piccinni himself, and later by Cherubini, who flourished as an opera composer in the 1790s and early 1800s. In the nineteenth century, Gluck's approach to opera was adopted by Spontini, who in turn influenced Berlioz as an opera composer. *—Zoran Minderovic*

OPERA

Alceste (1767)

Alceste, first performed in Vienna in December of 1767, was the second salvo in Christoph Willibald Gluck's famous campaign to reform Italian opera seria. Believing that operatic music should serve drama rather than asserting its own presence through virtuosity and ornament, Gluck set out to revive the dramatic ideals of Greek tragedy, and reclaim opera—that "most beautiful of spectacles"—from the performance traditions that had made it "ridiculous and wearisome" (as the composer wrote in his own preface to the score).

The original libretto for *Alceste* was adapted from Euripides by Calzabigi, a Livornese reform poet who sought to bring French influences into Italian opera. Changes from the play include the omission of the character of Hercules, who helps bring Alceste back from the underworld, focusing the drama instead around Alceste's self-sacrifice, and using a *deus ex machina* in the finale to bring about a happy ending. He also added two children and two servants to the drama, imitating Pietro Metastasio's habit of casting characters in matched pairs.

In Vienna, Gluck's Italian *Alceste* was extremely well received, but subsequent productions in Italy fared poorly. In 1776, Gluck and the librettist Marie François du Roullet rewrote the entire work for the Paris Opéra, creating the French version that would eventually supplant the original Italian in the repertory (the Italian version is rarely performed today, although there was a recording made in 1956 with Kirsten Flagstad in the title role). In the process of revision, du Roullet and Gluck turned back to the original Euripides play, reinstating the character of Hercules and thereby lightening the predominantly gloomy mood of the opera. They also completely revised the third act, adding a descent into Hades, a battle with the infernal spirits, and an extended celebratory divertissement at the end, when Alceste and Admetus are reunited. Gluck himself added a good bit of dramatic irony to the libretto.

Though the Italian and French versions differ in substantial ways, they both retain the same essential plot outline: Alceste, the Queen, sacrifices her own life to the gods of the underworld so that her husband's can be spared, but she is eventually spared as well. Most of the differences between the two scores come in the selective elaboration of certain scenes, and in the resolution of the plot. In the Italian version, the god Apollo spared Alceste from her fate, while in the French, Hercules battles the minions of the underworld on her behalf.

Gluck used various musical effects in his drama, such as the monotone chanting of the high priest, agitated or muted string textures, antiphonal effects in the chorus, and sweeping, spacious, arpeggiated figures. In "Non vi turbate, no," when Alceste pleads with the infernal deities, Gluck used the timbre of muted strings and English horns to create pathos. When the infernal powers come to claim Alceste, their music is filled with chromaticism, tremolandos, and a dramatic death knell. The high point of the French version is Alceste's air "Ah! divinités implacables!," in which she defies the inhabitants of the underworld. The air was adapted from an aria in the second act of the Italian version. *—AMG*

Synopsis:

Act One. *Alceste* is set in ancient Greece, in the era after the Trojan War. The first act opens outside the palace of Pherae in Thessaly, where the people pray to the gods to cure their ailing King Admète. A herald brings news of his impending death. Queen Alceste joins the crowd with her two children, Eumelo and Aspasia, and beseeches the gods to save the King. Inside a filled temple, in Scene Two, an oracle tells the crowd that Admète will surely die unless someone offers to take his place in death. Alceste agonizes over her love for her children, but decides to sacrifice herself. The High Priest informs her that the gods have accepted her offer.

Act Two. The scene opens in a dark forest as Ismene, attendant to Alceste, asks the Queen why she has come to this place, known to be sacred to the underworld gods. Alceste asks her to leave, and, after she is alone, offers herself as sacrifice to the gods for her husband. In the following scene, inside the palace, Evandre, confidante to the king, and others in attendance rejoice that Admète has recovered. But the King, unaware of Alceste's covenant with the gods, is distraught that a stranger will die in his place. He notices worry in his wife's face, and upon questioning her learns that she is the one to be sacrificed. Admète declares he will join his faithful wife in death. Alceste, urged by the people to forswear her pact, insists she will carry through with it.

Act Three. Admète, in a large hallway in his palace, tells Evandre of the tragic situation. Alceste enters with her children and bids them farewell. An infernal god appears to take Alceste away, but Admète pleads with him to take him as well. The god receives only Alceste, and she dies. In the ensuing scene of mourning, attended by Evandre and other courtiers, Admète enters, distraught over Alceste's death and lamenting that attendants had taken his weapons from him to frustrate his plans for suicide. The god Apollo appears suddenly and brings Alceste back to life. She is then reunited with her ecstatic husband, and the opera ends happily. This Italian version of Alceste was the first; a second one in French, with many changes in the score and libretto (introducing Hercules as a character), came in 1774 in a translation by du Roullet. *—Robert Cummings*

Recommended:

- ○ **Gluck: Alceste** / Ostman (cond.), Lavender, Degerfeldt, Drottningholm Court Theater / 1999 / Naxos 660066
- ○ **Gluck: Alceste** / Baudo (cond.), Gedda, Norman, Krause, Nimsgern, Bavarian RSO / Orfeo 27823

***Iphigénie en Aulide* (1774)**

In this work Gluck brought to opera a sense of drama that united the action of an opera in a single emotional arc, rather than allowing the form to serve as a mere excuse for florid singing. As such, it inspired Mozart and later composers, all the way up to Richard Wagner. Productions of it are fairly frequent. *Orfeo ed Euridice* had been Gluck's first attempt at producing an operatic work in Paris. But *Iphigénie en Aulide* was his first entirely French opera, written with a French text and composed with a Parisian audience in mind. He had declared in an open letter to the Parisians that his intention was to bridge gaps that had existed between French opera and the rest of the European continent. He had been reared as an Italian composer, had worked at the Viennese court, had composed French comic operas, had been influenced by the German singspiel, was an admirer of Handel, had composed ballets, and knew the Parisians' taste for opulence. With the help of the Dauphine Marie Antoinette, he was able to get his new dramatic work produced at the Paris Opéra, and *Iphigénie en Aulide* became a huge success.

Rameau was 81 at the time *Iphigénie* was premiered, and was involved in the rehearsals of his own last opera. Although his operatic language was subtle and varied, Rameau still worked in the tradition of Jean-Baptiste Lully, often using huge, splendid divertissements which, although spectacular, virtually stopped the dramatic action. With Gluck, everything served the poetics of the tragedy, and with *Iphigénie*'s success, the tradition of Lully was vanquished from the French stage.

Gluck's ideal was classical tragedy, which expressed the nobility of the human soul. His character delineation is thorough, and the full scope of human passions and emotions is expressed. The work is noble, grand, and humanistic. His new operatic style included constant orchestral involvement throughout the drama. Melodious and poignant, the music brings du Roullet's text to life, and the drama lives and breathes.

The music for the title role is exceptional. Iphigénie does not appear in the opera until all of the horrible building blocks of the plot have been set in p[lace. Dramatic choruses and solos for Agamemnon precede the heroine's arrival. Her entrance is hailed by a chorus of Greeks in a shimmering texture of soprano-dominated homophony in Scene Four of Act One. They are singing her praises as she and her mother Clytemnestra enter in a chariot. But she has no solo music until several more choruses and a solo for Clytemnestra have passed. When she finally does sing, her music is set apart by the complete innocence of its mood. Her lyrical aria is built around a light texture and filled with delicate ornaments. The many facets of her personality come through in the many shapes of the music she is given. *—Rita Laurance*

Synopsis:

Like many other serious operas of the Classical period, this one has a story taken from the ancient Greeks. The opera begins with an orchestral mood-piece rather than a formal overture; this flows into the opening scene in which Agamemnon addresses a pitiless command of the goddess Diana. She demands that he sacrifice his daughter, Iphigenia, as the price for allowing him to continue on to Troy. Torn between his civic duty and love for his daughter, Agamemnon attempts to convince her to leave Aulis by telling her that her love, Achilles, is unfaithful. This ruse fails.

At the planned wedding ceremony, Arcus proclaims the sacrifice, revealing that Agamemnon will perform it. Achilles is determined to save Iphigenia's life, and Agamemnon finally decides in her favor, ordering his wife to take her to Mycenae. But the people demand the sacrifice. Achilles swears to kill Agamemnon rather than permit it.

Iphigenia proudly consents to obey the will of the goddess and sings the aria "Adieu, conservez dans votre âme," often cited as the epitome of an emotionally and formally perfect Classical aria; in it she says goodbye to her people. She is led away, and the people pray to Diana to accept the sacrifice, but Achilles and his troops storm in and begin a battle to rescue her. Then the priest announces that the gods have been appeased, and no sacrifice is necessary. Iphigenia rejoins Achilles, and the people rejoice. In this work Gluck brings to opera a primacy of drama, which unites the opera in a single emotional arc, rather than allowing the form to serve as a mere excuse for florid singing. As such, it inspired Mozart and later composers, especially Richard Wagner. Productions of it are fairly frequent. *—Joseph Stevenson*

Recommended:

○ **Gluck: Iphigénie en Aulide** / Gardiner (cond.), Van Dam, Otter, Dawson, Laurens, English Baroque Soloists / Erato 45003

***Iphigénie en Tauride* (1779)**

Iphigénie en Tauride was one of Gluck's last operas, and the climax of his efforts to reform the French tragédies lyrique. It premiered in 1779 and was his biggest success on the Parisian stage, despite the efforts of Piccinnists to prevent the premiere. The Piccinni advocates preferred a traditional operatic style based on court idioms; Gluck's proponents favored innovation. Debate raged in the salons of Paris over the relative merits of each, and articles and letters were written in support and disparagement of both sides. But Gluck prevailed and the premiere went forward. His opera *Echo et Narcisse* was performed the same year but failed. The amount of work and the emotional involvement with the two operas cost Gluck his health, and he left for Vienna afterwards in a state of virtual collapse.

The story of *Iphigénie en Tauride* is taken from classical antiquity, and the setting is Tauris, after the Greek conquest of Troy. The libretto is by Nicolas-François Guillard and Roullet, who put together one of the finest librettos in the history of opera. The struggle is between the humanism and compassion of Iphigénie and the barbaric inhumanity of the court of King Thoas. There is no love intrigue in the plot, although the drama is filled with the conflicts of human passions. In the same time period, Goethe was writing his prose version of the story in which King Thoas is turned into a moral character, but in Gluck's libretto Thoas is so inhuman that justice is accomplished through his execution.

The opening prelude or "symphony" is sonorous and sumptuous, leading without pause into the following music The first section is full of graceful melody, but is soon replaced by an active con fuoco texture, heavy strings, and adventurous harmonies. This section leads straight into the first aria and chorus for Iphigenia, and makes for a dramatic opening to the opera. At once, a feeling of high tragedy is established. Scene three begins with a chorus of Scythians which uses tambourines, piccolos, and drums in an exotic texture. After a recitative for King Thoas, this same chorus returns as a refrain. A similar chorus for the Scythians for the same scoring acts as a frame in scene four of Act One, encompassing a ballet of four movements for the Scythians, and dramatic recitative passages for Thoas and Orestes.

The solo passages in this opera make use of a great variety of textures. Never sticking to a simple secco recitative, Gluck writes arioso passages, orchestral interjections, choral interjections, and a variety of accompaniment textures, tempi, and moods. In Act Two, scene five, Orestes and Iphigenia and a chorus of priestesses sing of the appearance of the shade of Clytemnestra in a texture which constantly varies. The emotions covered within the piece are confusion, anguish, distress, horror, vulnerability, even terror. In the scene that follows, Iphigenia and the chorus of priestesses sing to very light, flowing, orchestral accompaniment. The predominance of female voices, the flowing texture, the scoring for violins and harps, make this contrasting scene one of exquisite beauty. *—Rita Laurance*

Synopsis:

Act One. The story is set in ancient Tauris in the post-Trojan War era. The opening scene takes place amid a powerful storm at the sacred wood of Diana, where the high priestess Iphigénie and her priestesses pray to the goddess Diana. Iphigénie recalls a dream from the night before, in which she saw her mother Clytemnestra in pursuit of her father Agamemnon—whom she would murder. Worse, she saw her brother Oreste, King of Argos, and Mycenae, whom she then killed at the behest of some strange power. Iphigénie wants to die to join him.

Thoas, King of Tauris, enters, and, leery of the foreboding storm and on advice from oracles, commands Iphigénia to sacrifice a foreigner to satisfy the gods. Scythians, anxious to have a sacrifice carried out, enter and announce that two Greeks were tossed ashore during the storm. Thoas, over the objections of Iphigénie, orders that they be captured and sacrificed. The two turn out to be her brother Oreste and Pylade, King of Phocis, who, captured quickly, are told of their fate by Thoas.

Act Two. The scene opens in a room in the temple where victims of sacrifice await their slaughter. Oreste and Pylade are held in chains there, with an altar seen in the background. The latter is taken away, and Oreste, believing his friend is going to his execution, cries out to the gods, then collapses. He dreams of the Eumenides, who pursue him to avenge his killing of his mother, Clytemnestra. He awakens, and seeing Iphigénie mistakes her for his mother at first. Because the two have had no contact in many years, they do not recognize each other. Iphigénie inquires about events in Mycenae, and Oreste, without revealing his identity, relates news about the murder of Agamemnon by Clytemnestra, and her subsequent death at the hands of Oreste. Iphigénie becomes upset at the revelations, still not realizing the speaker is her brother.

Act Three. In her quarters, Iphigénie informs her priestesses that one of the two Greeks will be sent to her sister Electra to apprise her of their suffering in Tauris. For a moment she reflects on the likeness of one of the two captives to her brother. It is finally decided that Oreste will go to Greece to deliver the message to Electra. When they are alone, Oreste and Pylade argue over who should die, each wanting the other to survive. When Iphigénie returns, Oreste, threatening to take his life, convinces his sister to change her mind. Thus, Pylade is released and sent on the mission to Greece.

Act Four. Inside the temple of Diana, Iphigénie calls on Diana to give her the courage to perform the bloody sacrifice. Oreste is brought in by the priestesses and taken to the altar. Iphigénie raises the knife, but suddenly the two recognize each other, and there follows a moment of great joy for all present. But a Greek woman rushes in to reveal that Thoas, angered that one of the Greeks was released, is on his way to the temple. When he arrives he decides to carry out the sacrifice himself, even after learning the identity of Oreste. But Thoas is killed when Pylade returns with a large Greek army. Fighting breaks out between the Greeks and a band of Scythian warriors, but ends suddenly when the goddess Diana appears and commands an end to hostilities. She tells Oreste to return to Greece as King of Mycenae and to take Iphigénie with him. *—Robert Cummings*

Recommended:

- ○ **Gluck: Iphigénie en Tauride** / Gardiner (cond.), Brossmann, Erlo, Allen, Aler, Argenta, Lyon Opera Orch. / Philips 416148
- ○ **Gluck: Iphigénie en Tauride** / Pearlman (cond.), Cole, Goerke, West, Gilfry, Boston Baroque / 2000 / Telarc 80546
- ○ **Gluck: Iphigénie en Tauride** / Minkowski (cond.), Keenlyside, Delunsch, Naouri, Beuron, Les Musiciens du Louvre / Archiv 471133

Orfeo ed Euridice (1774)

Orfeo ed Euridice was one of three operas composed by Gluck in an attempt to reform the Italian opera seria. The opera seria had many dramatic drawbacks, among them a stiff libretto full of contrivances and formal musical patterns that were given precedence over dramatic flow.

Gluck had an admirable dramatic imagination that balked at all this regimentation. After he had come into contact with the librettist and poet Ranieri de' Calzabigi, he began to imagine a new form of dramatic opera. Calzabigi wanted to bring French influences to the Italian opera, and his libretti are monumental poetic works in an Italian rhetorical style. The libretto for *Orfeo ed Euridice* is noble and grand, and the ending employs a typical deus ex machina to bring about a happy ending for the lovers.

The grandeur of the libretto must have inspired Gluck, for his approach to the score is also monumental, as well as essentially orchestral in nature. The opera opens after the death of Euridice to a funereal choral tableau which is pierced by the cries of the anguished Orfeo. Huge dramatic choruses of shades and furies contrast starkly with the solo recitatives and arias of Orfeo as he searches for Euridice. Music of the Elysian Fields offers another contrast. Orfeo's aria here features a myriad of solo instruments. The entire scene is radiant and heavenly. The third act is particularly beautiful, as Gluck and Calzabigi turn the shade of Euridice into a complex lover and wife, unwilling to follow her husband blindly out of Hades, even though she has been called back to life. Her arguments and pleadings, her passion and confusion, create the torment in Orfeo that results in her being sent back to hell.

The premiere of 1762 was a great success, and when Gluck later decided to try to reform the French tragedies lyriques, he rewrote *Orfeo* and took it to the Parisian stage. The original Orfeo had been an alto castrato. In Paris the role had to be rewritten for a countertenor voice, as the French never used castrati, finding them ridiculous. The French version was also grander and more elaborate to suit the taste of the Parisians. The final happy ending was turned into a huge divertissement with ballet.

Orfeo ed Euridice achieved international renown and is still widely performed. In 1859 Berlioz made a third version of *Orfeo* which combined the French and Italian scores. He rewrote the part of *Orfeo* for Pauline Viardot, a female interpreter. In the nineteenth century the part was sung by a contralto as often as by a tenor, and in the twentieth century *Orfeo* was even been sung by a baritone. The most celebrated excerpt from it is not an aria, but the orchestral *Dance of the Blessed Spirits*. *—Rita Laurance*

Synopsis:

This opera is occasionally performed in a French version with different vocal casting, but the plot is unchanged.

Act One. The opera opens in the grove where Euridice is buried. Shepherds, shepherdesses, and nymphs lament her death and ask her to witness Orfeo's suffering ("Ah! se intorno a quest'urna") as they place flowers on her grave. Orfeo, meanwhile, sits to one side, occasionally calling her name, and then asks them to leave. He exclaims that he calls to her and to the gods ("Chiamo il mio ben così"), but to no avail. He finally resolves to seek her in Hades, the underworld, and hopes that its rulers will have pity on him. Amor descends and says that the gods will allow him to do so, and tells him to use the power of his music to plead his cause ("Dalla detra tua dolci toni"). However, he warns, he may not look at her until they are both back on the face of the earth; if he looks even once, she will return to the underworld forever. He urges Orfeo to have courage ("Gli sguardi tratieni") and leaves. Orfeo is briefly daunted by the task, particularly the ordeal of being unable to look at her, but finally declares that his sighing is over and that he will win his wife back ("Addio, o miei sospiri").

Act Two. Just outside Hades, the Furies stand guard. As they hear Orfeo approach, they demand to know who is defying their power ("Chi mai dell'Erebo forrale"). As he enters, they dance about wildly and sing of all the horrors inside. He begs them to be appeased and to listen to him ("Deh, placatevi con me"), and at first they merely shout "No!" But as he continues, they grow quieter. They ask him why he, a young man, is thinking of coming to this place of torment ("Misero, giovane"), and he answers that he is already tormented. He begs them to have pity for the sake of any grief they have ever felt, and they open the doors ("Le porte stridano"). As he departs, they dance again.

Act Three. The third act (often combined with Act Two) takes place in the Elysian Fields, the Greek paradise. Spirits dance the tranquil *Dance of the Blessed Spirits*, and one of the spirits (sometimes Euridice) sings of this beautiful refuge ("E quest'asilio ameno e grato"). Orfeo enters and sings in wonder of the pure sky and bright sunlight ("Che puro ciel! che chiaro sol"), but adds that even this perfect beauty cannot make him forget his loss. The spirits sing from the distance that Euridice is coming to him, and she appears, veiled. They tell her to be happy with her husband.

Act Four. In the fourth act, Orfeo and Euridice are still climbing back to the earth, and he urges her to hurry ("Ah! vieni"). She cannot understand why he will not look at her, and, increasingly unhappy, asks whether he no longer loves her. She finally turns back, saying that she does not want to return to life without his love. He repeats his pleas for her to come with him ("Su, e con me vieni, o cara"), but she refuses, tormented by her doubts, ("Che fiero momento"). Finally, he defies the gods' command and turns to her, but just as he looks at her and embraces her, she dies. He bursts out in the famous lament "Che faro senza Euridice," saying that life is meaningless without her and begging her to answer him. Declaring that he has no more hope, he draws his sword to kill himself. Amor suddenly appears and says that the gods have been moved by his sorrow and will restore her to life. He leads Euridice to him, and they leave together. In the temple dedicated to Amor, they all celebrate his triumph and declare that the entire world is subject to him ("Trionfi Amore"). As the shepherds, shepherdesses, and nymphs dance, Orfeo and Euridice are enthroned, and they and Amor sing that even love's pains bring joy ("Gaudio son al cuore queste pene"). *—Ann Feeney*

Recommended:

- ○ **Gluck: Orfeo ed Euridice** / Gardiner (cond.), McNair, Ragin, Sieden, English Baroque Soloists / 1993 / Philips 434093
- ○ **Gluck: Orfeo ed Euridice** / Solti (cond.), Horne, Donath, Lorengar, Royal Opera House Orch. Covent Garden / 1989 / London 417410
- ○ **Gluck: Orfeo ed Euridice** / Stiedry (cond.), Ferrier, Ayars, Vlachopoulos, Southern PO / 1998 / Dutton 5015
- ○ **Gluck: Orfeo ed Euridice** / Kuijken (cond.), Jacobs, Kweksilber, Falewicz, La Petite Bande / Accent 48223/24

Tito Gobbi

b. Oct. 24, 1915, Bassano del Grappa, Italy, **d.** Mar. 5, 1984, Rome, Italy

Baritone

Tito Gobbi was an admired operatic baritone. He originally studied at Padua University for a career in law, but he eventually gave that up in favor of pursuing voice lessons in Rome with Giulio Crimi. He made his operatic debut in the town of Gubbio in 1935, as Count Rodolfo in Bellini's *La sonnambula*. He was hired at Milan's La Scala for the 1935–36 season as an understudy; his first appearance there was as the Herald in Ildebrando Pizzetti's *Oreseolo*.

He won the international singing competition in Vienna in 1936. As a result he began getting improved billing; he sang the role of Germont in *La traviata* at the Teatro Reale in Rome in 1937. In the same year he sang Lelio in Ermanno Wolf-Ferrari's *Le donne curiose*, and continued singing secondary roles through 1939 there. He was promoted to primary roles and in 1941 sang Ford in Verdi's *Falstaff* during a visit by the company to Berlin in 1941. Meanwhile, in a guest appearance at Rieti he first sang the role of Scarpia in Puccini's *Tosca* in 1940. This was to become his best-known part.

Gobbi made his La Scala debut in a major role in 1942 as Belcore in *L'Elisir d'Amore*. However, the performance that made him famous was as Wozzeck in the first Italian performance of Alban Berg's opera in Rome in November, 1942. Fighting raged throughout Italy following the Allied invasions there in 1943, interrupting his career. After the war he began to include international appearances. He first appeared in Stockholm in 1947 as Rigoletto; in 1948 he went to Covent Garden in concerts and to San Francisco to debut as Figaro in Rossini's *Barber of Seville*. His London operatic debut was at Covent Garden as Belcore when the La Scala Company toured there. He appeared in Chicago in 1954 as Rossini's Figaro, and debuted at the Metropolitan Opera Company as Scarpia, January 13, 1956. He sang Don Giovanni in Salzburg in 1952 under von Karajan's direction.

He took up producing as well, often at Chicago, where he made regular appearances, and producing opera became an ever more important part of his career after 1965, which is when he produced a performance starring himself in the title role of Verdi's *Simon Boccanegra* in London.

Although he was particularly well known for his portrayal of Verdi's baritone roles (including Posa in *Don Carlos*), and of Puccini's (Scarpia, Jack Rance, Gianni Schicchi), he had a very large repertory of well over 100 roles, including such rare operas as Malipiero's *Ecuba* (as Ulysses), Teprulov in Rocca's *Monte Ivnor*, the Count of Albaforita in Persico's *La locandiera*, and operas by Lualdi, Napoli, and Ghedini. He was an excellent actor, had a high degree of musicianship and intelligence, had a flexible, rich, but not large baritone voice, and was at home in a wide variety of parts. He also appeared in 26 movies. He was the brother-in-law of another eminent singer, Boris Christoff. Gobbi retired from the operatic stage in 1979. He published an autobiography (*Tito Gobbi: My Life*, 1979) and *Tito Gobbi and His World of Italian Opera* (1984). He left a significant legacy of recorded performances, mainly made in the 1950s and 1960s. *—Joseph Stevenson*

Recommended:

- ○ **Puccini: Tosca** / Gobbi, etc. / 2003 / EMI 62675
- ○ **The Very Best of Tito Gobbi** / Gobbi, etc. / 2003 / EMI 85096

Benjamin Godard

b. Aug. 18, 1849, Paris, France, **d.** Jan. 10, 1895, Cannes, France

Composer: Chamber Music

The music of French composer Benjamin Godard, whose meteoric rise to fame during the late 1870s earned him a general popularity that eluded most of his Parisian contemporaries, has fallen out of the general repertory since his death in 1895. Godard was born in Paris on August 18, 1849, and was trained on the violin as a young boy (he was fortunate enough receive lessons from famed virtuoso Henri Vieuxtemps). After entering the Paris Conservatoire in 1863 (composition with Henri Reber) and making two unsuccessful bids in for the Prix de Rome (1866 and 1867), Godard earned a living as a violist until his music began to attract the attention of publishers during the final years of the 1860s. Godard's reputation as a skilled and prolific composer grew steadily during the 1870s, and when his *Le Tasse* (dramatic symphony for chorus, soloists, and orchestra) was awarded the Prix de la Ville de Paris in 1878 Godard entered the front rank of Parisian musicians.

Godard gained further attention when his music was made a focus of conductor Jules Étienne Pasdeloup's Concerts Populaires; Godard himself took over direction of the concerts during the mid-1880s, renaming them the Concerts Modernes, but the series never regained the success it had achieved under Pasdeloup. An interest in opera during the 1880s and 1890s led to the production of five dramatic operas, all popular failures (though the "Berceuse" from the 1888 opera *Jocelyn* is Godard's only well-known work). A comic opera, *La vivandière*, was left unfinished at the composer's death in 1895; the orchestration of the work was finished by another musician and the work was premiered in Paris later in the year.

Given Godard's instrumental background, it is not surprising that his chamber and symphonic works have the most to offer performers and listeners. The five symphonies (some with fanciful titles, e.g. *Symphonie gothique* or *Symphonie orientale*), while perhaps less rewarding than the music for violin (five sonatas for piano and violin, two concertos, of which the *Concerto romantique* is considered the superior, and an important solo violin sonata), are nevertheless superior to the operas, which fall rather short of their dramatic ambitions due to a lack of potent musical substance. Godard seems to have had little innate sympathy for the piano, and, although works for this instrument actually constitute a substantial portion of his total output, his piano music is generally rather trite. Perhaps Godard's widespread fame as a salon composer compelled him to compose such trifles, but he was not a miniaturist at heart, and his efforts in this vein are generally unsuccessful.

From 1887 on Godard was a member of the faculty at the Paris Conservatoire, and in 1889 he was named a *Chevalier* of the *Légion d'honneur*. *—Blair Johnston*

Overview of Works (ca. 1865–1894)

Benjamin Godard was at one time in the vanguard of the French school of the late nineteenth century. A child prodigy with a gift for the violin, he was enrolled at age ten in the Paris Conservatory and went on to become a prolific composer, much admired and renowned by his mid-twenties. Composing in all genres, he firmly embraced a tonality that was more in step with the first part of the century. He eschewed Wagner (around whom there was actually a strong cult in nineteenth century France) largely for his political and racial theories, as well as his compositions. Resistant to the chromaticism of his time, Godard's music found itself dated shortly after his death from tuberculosis at age 46. But by dint of its sheer beauty, coupled with Gallic restraint, Godard's music deserves more than a few non-audible print citations. It is, for the most part, his piano works and songs that wear Victorian purple, rendered mauve by their delicacy. These nonetheless range through the entire spectrum of technique and style, making them a fine and unusual resource for the imaginative piano teacher. In fact, some of his works in larger genres are innovative in concept, if not in fabric. His *Symphonie legendaire* is actually a song cycle with orchestral accompaniment, which could have been the structural model for Mahler's *Das Lied von der Erde*. The exoticism of his *Symphonie orientale* taps into authentic Far Eastern music rather than the conventional pentatonic stereotype. Some of this haunting sensitivity can be found in, curiously enough, what is probably his most well-known music, the "Berceuse," from his opera *Jocelyn*, with its plaintive, medieval-sounding, white-key harmonies. Sadly, nothing else from this opera, at one time widely known, has survived and this fate seems to have extended to his other operas, internationally at least. His last, *La vivandière*, a tale of father and son reconciliation during the French Revolution, was unfinished at his death and completed by Paul Vidal; à la Puccini's *Turandot*, it went on to great success in its time. At his best, the composer was an exponent of restrained and tasteful beauty, itself a timeless aesthetic. *—Wayne Reisig*

Recommended:

○ **Godard: Etudes, Op149** / Martin / 1995 / Marco Polo 223802

○ **Godard: Cello Sonata; 2 Pieces; Boëllmann: Cello Sanata; 2 Pieces** / Lidstrom, Forsberg / 1996 / Hyperion 66888

CHAMBER MUSIC

Suite de trois morceaux, for flute & piano in B flat major, Op. 116 (1889)

Although he achieved fame early in his career and maintained a certain level of popularity during his lifetime, the majority of music by French composer Benjamin Godard (1849–1895) has not retained its place in the repertoire. Indeed, with the exception of one piece of chamber music, all that is still performed and recorded of Godard's vast output are slivers of his slighter piano music. But that one piece of chamber music, the *Suite de trois morceaux*, is still immensely popular and will probably always be popular as long as there are virtuoso flutists and a competent pianist to accompany them. A short work in three movements—"Allegretto," "Idyll," and "Valse."—the suite is *musique de salon de la Belle Époque, par excellence*. Composed in 1890 for the great French flutist Paul Taffanel, the suite is elegantly tuneful, deeply nostalgic, and, in its final "Valse," incredibly virtuosic. While *salon music* is not nearly as popular as it once was, the lost world of salon music is brilliantly evoked by Godard's suite. The *Suite de trois morceaux* also exists in a version for flute and chamber orchestra. *—James Leonard*

Recommended:

○ **Fantaisie, Romantic French Flute Music** / Pople (cond.), Beckett, London Festival Orch. / 2000 / Black Box Class 1049

Leopold Godowsky

b. Feb. 13, 1870, Soshly, Lithuania, **d.** Nov. 21, 1938, New York, NY

Composer: Keyboard

Pianist

Leopold Godowsky was one of the most astonishing piano virtuosos of all time and a composer of remarkably difficult polyphonic music. His father was a physician who contracted cholera tending patients during an epidemic, dying when his son was only 18 months old. Godowsky and his mother were taken in by friends, who soon realized the toddler was exceptionally musical. He played violin and piano longer from an age earlier than he could remember, but he was told he played before he was two. He said he had no teacher that he could remember, certainly none past the age of four. He composed a minuet when he was five, with the middle section being a strict canon, "This is noteworthy," he said, "because up to that time I had never heard a canon." It was good enough that he was able to use it in a fully mature composition 23 years later.

Leopold's adoptive father, Louis Passinock, promoted his fame as a Wunderkind. To forestall his exploitation, a banker named Feinberg offered to finance his study at the Hochschule für Musik in Berlin. Leopold studied under Ernst Rudorff, but could only take three months of regimentation. He, his mother, and his "uncle" Passinock went to New York where he began to concertize at the age of thirteen. They booked him onto a tour of the West that eventually went bust, stranding the boy, who worked his way back to New York.

Again, a wealthy arts patron sought to "rescue" him. Leon Saxe arranged for him to go to Europe to study with the virtuoso Franz Liszt. By the time Leopold's ship reached Europe, Liszt was dead. But Camille Saint-Saëns, who had lost his children, became a mentor, mostly discussing interpretation and other esthetic manners. Godowsky had some success in Europe, but not enough to satisfy him, and returned to America.

There he had a career as a respected piano teacher in New York, Philadelphia, and Chicago. He developed the modern approach to piano playing, emphasizing economy of motion and release of weight (rather than direct muscle power) as the basis for playing. He began to arrange other composers' music, including a set of 53 exceptional etudes on Chopin's etudes, as well as other music. While teaching in Chicago, he gained a strong local reputation by giving recitals. An eight-recital set in 1897 and 1898 surveyed the history of nineteenth century piano literature.

Soon his fame spread, and he had triumphal performances in the U.S. and Europe. His December 6, 1900, concert at Beethoven Hall in Berlin was a triumph where he was acclaimed one of the greatest living pianists. Soon, he was the highest-paid solo instrumentalist in the world. He continued to write original piano music and his free adaptations of other music. In 1909, he became director of the Piano School of the Imperial Academy of Music in Vienna, the first Jew to take this post.

He was visiting Belgium for vacation in 1914 when the Germans invaded. He escaped to England and returned to the United States, where he made his home for the rest of his life. He moved his residence frequently and traveled widely, giving concerts in Mexico, South America, Yokohama, and Asia. His trip to Java inspired him to try to capture the sound of the gamelan orchestra in his suite *Phonoramas*. He lost much of his fortune in the 1929 stock market crash, then the next year had a severe stroke that ended his public career. He declined into depression and further illness before his death. *—Joseph Stevenson*

Recommended:

○ **Godowsky: Complete UK Columbia Recordings** / Godowsky / 1988 / APR 7010

○ **Leopold Godowsky** / Godowsky / 1999 / Philips 456805

Overview of Works (1888–1931)

In *The Great Pianists* (1963), Harold Schonberg rated Godowsky's music "of such complexity, burdened with such elaboration of detail, crossed with so many inner voices, that none but he could play it.... In his day it was said that he was composing for a future generation of pianists. If so, that generation has not yet arrived." In the early 1980s, it began to appear and, by the millennium, even Godowsky's most formidable works were heard. Apart from transcriptions of piano miniatures, arranged with Fritz Kreisler's assistance, Godowsky's compositions are for piano—though a piano rendered articulate as never before. Even as his work slipped into obscurity in the 1930s, every American parlor piano was graced by *Alt-Wien*, a nostalgia-rife, nuance-dimpled waltz from *Triakontameron* (1920), one of several collections of character pieces whose crossed hands effects and insinuating inner voices distilled the memory of a legendary prewar Europe. Pianistic prestidigitators might occasionally program Godowsky's Strauss transcriptions—*Künstlerleben, Fledermaus*, or *Wein, Weib, und Gesang* (1912)—in which the Waltz King's melodic flair and 3/4 lilt are wrought to an apotheosis of polyphonic fantastication. His masterwork, the *53 Studies on Chopin Etudes for piano* (1870–1914), Godowsky offered as a course "to develop the mechanical, technical, and musical possibilities of piano playing, to expand the peculiarly adapted nature of the instrument to polyphonic, polyrhythmic, and polydynamic work..." though often they are radical recompositions in which the themes and technical challenges of Chopin's *Études* are expanded in independent realizations. A number of them transcribed for the left hand alone, others combined, while Chopin's Op. 25/4 becomes a *Polonaise, No. 3*, of the Méthode a Menuetto, and so on. Playing an hour, the ruminative *Piano Sonata* (1911) deserves a place beside those of Dukas, d'Indy, and Rachmaninov, while the *Passacaglia* (1928)—44 variations, cadenza, and fugue on the first eight measures of Schubert's *"Unfinished" Symphony*—takes pride of place among similar works by Dukas, Reger, and Szymanowski. A dozen Schubert lieder (1922) become compelling piano works in Godowsky's loving transcriptions, while the dozen pieces of the *Java Suite* (1925)—souvenir of a voyage to the island—combine the rhythmic impetus and sonorous rapture of gamelan with Godowsky's own scintillant eloquence. Transcriptions from composers as diverse as Rameau, Weber, or Albéniz re-create their work with elaborate fullness, while pieces composed from the unaccompanied violin sonatas and cello suites of Bach (1924) seem to realize possibilities suggested by the originals, albeit beguilingly cast in a late Romantic harmonic vocabulary. *—Adrian Corleonis*

Recommended:

- ○ **Piano Music by Leopold Godowsky** / Waal / 1991 / Hyperion 66496
- ○ **Godowsky: Sonata; Passacaglia** / Hamelin / 2002 / Hyperion 67300
- ○ **Godowsky: Schubert Transcriptions** / Scherbakov / 2003 / Naxos 8225187

KEYBOARD

Java Suite, Book 1 (1924–1925)

Godowsky was one of the greatest piano virtuosos of his time, and his keyboard compositions typically required a technique at his level. The *Java Suite* here was one such work, but it also contains fine music in colorful writing whose exotic sonorities conjure Javanese images the composer observed on his visit to the Indonesian island in the 1920s. The *Java Suite* consists of four parts or books, each containing three pieces. Book I's leadoff work, "Gamelan," is a portrayal of the sonorities created by the gamelan, an orchestra dominated by percussion instruments. The music shimmers here in bright colors, the opening recalling Ravel from his *La vallée des cloches*. The mood then turns more robust and exotic in its bristling energy. "Wayang—Purwa" (Puppet Shadow Plays) is mostly serene and playful, while the third, "Hari Besaar" (The Great Day), one of the longest pieces in the set (lasting about five minutes), is colorful and lively, sounding at times like Rachmaninov draped in leis and equatorial sun. The music in these three pieces, and in indeed in the remaining books of the set as well, will appeal to those whose tastes favor the virtuosic writing of composers like Rachmaninov and Medtner and the exotic sounds of Asian and oriental music. *—Robert Cummings*

Recommended:

- ○ **Godowsky: Anthology of his American Recordings** / Godowsky / APR 7011
- ○ **Godowsky: Original Works & Transcriptions** / Hamelin / 1988 / Musica Viva 1026

53 Studies on Chopin Etudes (1870–1914)

Leopold Godowsky, the Polish-born piano virtuoso who made his career in America, was an outstanding technician of the piano, and restudied many aspects of playing, especially improving left-hand technique. Also famous for numerous piano transcriptions, he amplified and extended many of Chopin's etudes to create this set of 53 almost surreal transformations of them between 1900 and 1914, when he was touring Europe and teaching in Berlin. As if Chopin's originals weren't difficult enough, Godowsky adds additional parts, compounds the rhythms, sharpens the harmonies, superimposes one Chopin etude on top of another. Godowsky considered his purpose to expand the range of the piano to more complex textures, particularly as regards tone color, in addition to developing the mechanics and art of piano playing for the student of the set. He was careful to note that the original 26 Chopin etudes still existed, untouched and unspoiled by his alterations. Twenty-two of the Godowsky studies are for the left hand alone, and these, in particular, are revolutionary in their fingering. This music is so difficult that it has defeated many pianists' efforts to learn and present them as recital pieces. Taken simply as music, listening to them is a strange, almost Ivesian experience, as Chopin's familiar music floats as if wrapped in a sea foam of unexpected additional notes, sometimes altering the musical feeling to something like Impressionism, sometimes bizarrely contrasting one or two etudes with each other or with other rhythmic and musical ideas. All the while, the aware listener is bowled over as much by the sheer audacity of the concept as by the transcendent difficulty of the music. *—Joseph Stevenson*

Recommended:

- ○ **Godowsky: Complete Studies on Chopin's Etudes** / Hamelin / 2000 / Hyperion 67411/2
- ○ **Godowsky's Studies on the Chopin Etudes** / Grante / 2001 / Music & Arts 1093

Reinhard Goebel

b. Jul. 31, 1952, Siegen, Westphalia, Germany

Conductor

Reinhard Goebel has established himself, as both a violinist and conductor, as one of the leading exponents of Baroque historical performance practice. After studying violin at the Cologne Conservatory with Franzjosef Maier, then at the Folkwangschule in Essen with Saschko Gawriloff, he trained under Eduard Melkus and Marie Leonhardt. In 1973, after pursuing musicology studies for several years at Cologne University, he founded the instrumental ensemble Musica Antiqua Köln, initially made up of fellow students from the Cologne Conservatory. Since that time, he has performed with the ensemble as both soloist and director. In 1979, the ensemble gained an international reputation with its debut at London's Queen Elizabeth Hall during the annual English Bach Festival. After unexplained paralysis struck his right hand, Goebel abandoned his career as a solo violinist, although he continued to play with his group, bowing the violin with his left hand. Goebel has an extensive discography for Archiv Produktion and has helped revive interest in the music of several previously under-performed German composers of the seventeenth and eighteenth centuries, such as Heinichen, Schmelzer, Biber, and members of the Bach family. His recordings have won numerous awards: the Deutscher Schallplattenpreis in 1981 and 1982 (for chamber concertos by Telemann and *German Chamber Music Before Bach*, respectively); the Grand Prix International du Disque in 1987 (for *The Bach Family Before Johann Sebastian*); the Grand Prix National du Disque in 1984 (for Couperin's *Les Nations*); the Gramophone Award in 1984 (for chamber music by J.S. Bach); and the CD Compact Award in 1990 (for Telemann's *Tafelmusik*). Goebel's recording of Heinichen's *Dresden Concerti* won five important awards: the Jahrespreis der Deutschen Schallplattenkritik in 1993, the Gramophone Award in 1993, the *Prix Caecilia* in 1993, the Schallplattenpreis Echo-Klassik in 1994, and the CD Compact Award in 1994. *—Robert Adelson*

Recommended:

- ○ **Biber: Harmonia artificiosa** / Goebel (cond.), Cologne Musica Antiqua / Archiv 000218802
- ○ **Heinichen: Dresden Concerti** / Goebel (cond.), Cologne Musica Antiqua / Archiv 437549
- ○ **Bach: Brandenburg Concertos; Orchestral Suites; Chamber Music** / Goebel (cond.), Bauer, Staier, Linden, Schneider, Cologne Musica Antiqua / Archiv 471656
- ○ **Bachiana: Double Concertos** / Goebel (cond.), Hill, Fiedler, Schardt, Fischer, Cologne Musica Antiqua / Archiv 471579

Matthias Goerne

b. Mar. 31, 1967, Karl-Marx-Stadt, East Germany

Baritone

Matthias Goerne established a successful career as a baritone in Germany in the early 1990s and has expanded it to major appearances in other European countries and on recordings. His operatic experience began early, as a member of the City Opera in Weimar. He began professional-level voice training in 1985 with Hans Beyer in Leipzig, then continuing his studies with both Dietrich Fischer-Dieskau and Elisabeth Schwarzkopf. His taking second prize in the Robert Schumann Competition of 1989, and First Prizes in the Lindberg Salomon and Hugo Wolf competitions led to his being invited to sing in the Bach *St. Matthew Passion* in Leipzig in 1990 with conductor Kurt Masur. Other early appearances were with the NDR Radio Symphony Orchestra Hamburg, and the Bamberg Symphony Orchestra. Fischer-Dieskau recommended him for the Hindemith *Requiem for Those we Love* under Wolfgang Sawallisch.

He has become a notable Mahler interpreter, singing *Des Knaben Wunderhorn* with the Berlin RSO under Vladimir Ashkenazy and as a last-minute replacement for Fischer-Dieskau in *Kindertotenlieder*. Another notable part of his concert repertory is the Brahms *German Requiem*, in which he debuted, also on short notice, with Claus Peter Flor conducting in Zurich.

One of his earliest operatic successes came in 1992, when he sang the title role in Hans Werner Henze's *The Prince of Homburg* in a new production at Cologne. His Berlin Deutsche Oper debut was in a more traditional role for a young baritone, Marcello in Puccini's *La Bohéme*. Since the 1993–94 season he has been a member of the Dresden State Opera. In 2002, he debuted at Covent Garden as Wozzeck.

His first London appearance was at Wigmore Hall in 1994. He was invited back to that venue for the opening concert of the 1995–96 season, and five days later sang another solo recital there, accompanied by Graham Johnson, which received rave reviews. Since then, he has increased his activities as a singer of the German lieder repertory throughout Europe, usually accompanied by pianist Eric Schneider. He frequently broadcasts on German radio, and has recorded for the Hänssler, Berlin Classics, and Decca (London) labels, appearing on the latter in the important "Entartete Musik" series. He has participated in three volumes of the Hyperion series of the complete Schubert songs, including the disc devoted to *Der Winterreise*. His talent in lieder repertoire led to his appointment as professor of lied interpretation at the Robert-Schumann-Hochschule in Düsseldorf in 1991. *—Joseph Stevenson*

Recommended:

- ○ **Schubert: Die schöne Müllerin** / Goerne, Schneider (piano) / 2002 / Decca 470025
- ○ **Eisler: The Hollywood Songbook** / Goerne, Schneider (piano) / 1998 / London 460582
- ○ **Schumann: Liederkreis; 12 Gedichte** / Goerne, Schneider (piano) / 1999 / Decca 460797
- ○ **Matthias Goerne—Arias** / Goerne, Roschmann, Swedish Brass Quintet, Swedish RSO / 2000 / Decca 467263

Karl Goldmark

b. May 18, 1830, Keszthely, Hungary, **d.** Jan. 2, 1915, Vienna, Austria

Composer: Opera, Orchestral, Concerto

Composer Karl Goldmark, famous in Vienna throughout the second half of the nineteenth century, was born into an enormous Jewish family (Goldmark had over 20 siblings) in Hungary in 1830. The family moved to the outskirts of Ödenburg (now Sopron) in 1834, and seven years later Goldmark began to study the violin (in a most rudimentary way, his first teacher being a singer with little instrumental experience). After two years at the Ödenburg music school (1842–43) the talented but untrained 14-year-old was sent to Vienna for serious violin studies (1844). Forced for monetary reasons to abandon the lessons after a little over a year, but nevertheless determined to pursue music as a vocation, Goldmark managed to gain admittance first to the Vienna technical school and, in 1847, to the city's conservatory, where he studied violin with the respected performer Joseph Böhm and harmony (for a very brief time) with Gottfried Preyer.

Political troubles in the city in 1848—which shut down many Viennese institutions of learning, including the conservatory—forced Goldmark to abandon school after just a year of formal study. Working as a theater violinist and music teacher (first in Ödenburg and later in back in Vienna) for the next several years, Goldmark began trying to hone his skills as a composer, and in 1858 he organized a concert of his own music in Vienna. The concert was not a success, and Goldmark, disillusioned by the reception of his music in the city and uncomfortable with his lack of thorough compositional grounding, opted to relocate to Budapest, where he immersed himself in the music of Bach, Mozart, Haydn, and Beethoven and studied contemporary texts on musical form and language.

Upon his return to Vienna in 1860 Goldmark met with considerable and immediate success, and by the 1870s a string of successful works (such as the *String Quartet, Op. 8* of 1860, the *Sakuntala overture* of 1865, and, most significantly, the 1875 opera *Die Königin von Saba* [The Queen of Saba]) and the 1877 symphonic poem *Rustic Wedding* had placed Goldmark in the front tier of contemporary Austro-German composers. Despite the objections of many leading musicians (among them the outspoken critic Eduard Hanslick) who considered him to be just another second-rate Wagnerian, Goldmark remained an honored and very visible part of Viennese musical life until his death in 1915 at the age of 84.

Goldmark's musical influences were many and varied, beginning with his exposure to local folk dances while a child in Hungary, and later moving through Wagner towards a unique blend of German classicism and impressionism (a style he was just beginning to explore at the time of his death). Some of Goldmark's mature pieces, particularly the operas *Die Königin von Saba* and *Ein Wintermärchen* (A Winter Tale, 1908) and the Op.28 violin concerto, successfully employ a unique and beautiful language, rich in melody and warmly chromatic; at other times (as in most of the music for piano, an instrument for which Goldmark had little native sympathy) his work falls rather short of its hyper-expressive goal. *—Blair Johnston*

OPERA

Die Königin von Saba, Op. 27 (1869–1871)

Goldmark's first opera, *Die Königin von Saba* (The Queen of Sheba), proved to be his most famous and enduring work. Although most successful on German stages, *Die Königin von Saba* has played often outside that country and has been translated into numerous languages.

Goldmark first thought of composing an opera on the biblical character of the Queen of Sheba in 1863, and he charged Salomon Hermann Mosenthal with the task of drawing up a libretto. Based on the First Book of Kings, Chapter Ten, Mosenthal's first libretto was found unacceptable by Goldmark, and two years passed before Mosenthal was able to revise the text to his satisfaction. Goldmark began composing the opera in 1865 and eventually altered Mosenthal's original happy ending. Composition proved arduous, and Goldmark was able to finish only after he received a grant from the Hungarian government. *Die Königin von Saba* premiered on March 10, 1875, at the Vienna Court Opera.

In the Bible, the Queen of Sheba visits Jerusalem to see Solomon's court, speak with Solomon and "test him with subtle questions." He passes her tests, and she is very impressed with the palace and Solomon's prosperity. To this basic scenario Mosenthal added a love triangle. The Queen entrances one of Solomon's diplomats, Assad, who is betrothed to Sulamith, the daughter of Solomon's high priest. Although, in private, the Queen reveals her attraction to Assad, in public she denies even knowing him. This drives Assad to commit blasphemy. For this he is banished to the desert, where he dies in Sulamith's arms. The content of *Die Königin von Saba* is similar to that of Saint-Saëns' *Samson et Dalila*, which premiered two years after Goldmark's biblical tale.

Goldmark's debt to Wagner is clear not only from his actions—he helped form the Vienna Wagner Society—but in his music. *Die Königin von Saba* is filled with Wagnerian chromatic harmony and an occasional use of the leitmotif technqiue. What distinguishes Goldmark's work, however, is that this chromatic harmony supports songlike, closed forms that often contain Italianate, bel canto melodies. Declamation styles run the gamut from recitative to fluid arias to large choruses. Elements of French grand operas, particularly those of Meyerbeer, appear in the crowd scenes, the ballet in Act Three, and the historical subject matter. It is in the evocation of local color that Goldmark is at his best. Eastern modes and harmonic minor scales flavor the music surrounding the Queen of Sheba, while traditional Jewish melodies inform the music Goldmark uses for the religious ceremonies in the opera and the music associated with the Ark of the Covenant. All these aspects are conveyed with lush, masterfully manipulated orchestral tone colors that, again, bear the stamp of Wagner. *—John Palmer*

Synopsis:

Act One. The action takes place in Jerusalem during the reign of King Solomon. The High Priest and his daughter, Sulamith, wait in Solomon's temple for the arrival of Sulamith's fiancé, Assad. Assad has been away preparing for the arrival of the Queen of Sheba (a principality of Yemen), who wishes to visit Jerusalem and the court of Solomon, to witness the wonders of his palace, and to experience his wisdom at first hand. When Assad finally enters, he tells Sulamith that he no longer has the same feelings for her. He explains to Solomon and the others that he met an enchanting woman in a forest in Lebanon, and that she has filled his heart and changed his mind about his marriage plans. The Queen of Sheba then enters with her retinue. She begins speaking with Solomon and lifts her veil, revealing to Assad the face he saw in the forest in Lebanon. When Assad speaks to the Queen, she ignores him. This stuns the young Assad, whom Solomon advises to marry Sulamith as he had planned.

Act Two. In the palace garden, festivities celebrate the presence of the Queen of Sheba. The Queen, however, is distracted and leaves the crowd to be alone. Finding a quiet place, she contemplates, with some jealousy, Assad's coming marriage to Sulamith. The Queen's slave, Astaroth, enters and informs the Queen that Assad is nearby. The Queen has Astaroth lure Assad to the scene by singing a vocalise with an Eastern melody. This works, and Assad appears. He and the Queen enter into a lengthy dialogue and eventually a powerful duet, after which the two embrace. As in *Tristan und Isolde*, the two are interrupted by both dawn and temple guards, who enter and summon the "Sons of Israel" to early morning prayer.

Frustrated and afraid she will be recognized, the Queen leaves. The guards discover Assad and bring him to the temple. Amid praying Levites and priests, Assad and Sulamith are about to be married. When the Queen enters, claiming she has come to present to the couple a wedding gift, Assad becomes more ambivalent, but when he addresses the Queen, she again pretends not to know him. In anger, Assad shouts that the Queen is his god, an act of serious blasphemy, for he is standing beside the Ark of the Covenant when he does this. Amid outrage and confusion, guards take away Assad to prepare him for his punishment.

Act Three. A ballet, "Bienentanz der Almeen," and a bacchanale take place as part of the festivities for the Queen. It has been decided that Assad will be sentenced to death for his blasphemy, and the Queen tries to persuade Solomon to change his mind and spare the young man. Solomon, however, stands firmly by his decision, and the enraged Queen leaves, swearing vengeance. Sulamith and friends enter, praying and singing a song of mourning for Assad. Sulamith begins an impassioned soliloquy that is taken up by the entire ensemble, then leaves to suffer alone in the desert. As she exits, Solomon proclaims his vision of her dark future.

Act Four. As punishment for his actions, Assad has been banished from Jerusalem and forced to roam in the desert. The Queen comes after him, finds him, and tries to convince him to come with her. Despite his attraction to her, Assad rejects the Queen. After wandering through the desert for some time, Assad wishes for death, in part to free his mind from the weight of his blasphemy. As he says a prayer for Sulamith, the winds cover Assad completely with sand. Sulamith and her friends find Assad, barely alive, and during the ensuing duet they are reconciled. Assad dies in Sulamith's arms. *—John Palmer*

Recommended:

○ **Goldmark: Die Königin von Saba** / Fischer (cond.), Jerusalem, Kincses, Miller, Gregor, Takacs, Hungarian State Opera Orch. / 1997 / Hungaroton 12179/81

ORCHESTRAL

Rustic Wedding, symphonic poem in E flat major, Op. 26 (1888)

Karl Goldmark's *Rustic Wedding Symphony*, as it's usually called (even though it's cast in five movements rather than four, none of them even hinting at sonata form), hovers just at the edge of the standard repertory. It has been performed by the likes of Arturo Toscanini and Leonard Bernstein and is full of sensitively orchestrated, audience-pleasing tunes. Perhaps it could find a secure place in the concert hall if it were considered a Viennese counterpart to Smetana's *Má Vlast*—except that instead of roaring through epic, nationalist tales, Goldmark focuses on a simple country wedding to illustrate the cheerful and warm aspects of the complex Austrian character. The first movement, "Wedding March," is a series of variations on a bumptious, folk-like (but original) tune first heard in the low strings and soon embroidered with perky woodwind birdcalls. Each variation emphasizes a different group of instruments and brings a different but almost always festive character to the theme, except for a long, heartfelt, ultimately surging, and passionate section featuring the strings and minor key variations that foreshadow the more serious episodes in Elgar's *Enigma Variations*. The variations triumphantly end and the movement's overall effect and atmosphere are similar to Brahms' *Variations on a Theme by Haydn*; not coincidentally, Brahms admired this symphony. Next comes an intermezzo titled "Bridal Song." It begins with a gently playful, hesitant yet graceful melody; a short, brassy outburst ushers in a sweet, understated second subject. After the opening material repeats, a third, more serious theme arrives with the initial melody returning for a shy conclusion. The third movement, though marked Scherzo, is not the beefy sort of scherzo common since Beethoven, and although its alternate title is "Serenade," it's not very song-like. Again, the mood is playful and perky, and the trio section is happily bucolic. Goldmark sometimes puts a drone under the woodwind writing to emphasize the music's "rustic" character. "In the Garden" is a delicate andante, suggesting a loving, private al fresco conversation—and perhaps more—between the bride and groom. The long, ardent principal melody quietly begins, but very slowly builds to an ardent climax and recedes. The rest of the movement develops from fragments of this melody, handed gently from one group of instruments to another, with some episodes turning especially passionate. The finale is simply called "Dance." Fast and sometimes percussive, the movement vacillates between fugue and polka; the latter takes over, but not without a remembrance of "In the Garden" halfway through. *—James Reel*

Recommended:

○ **Dvořák: Slavonic Dances, etc.** / Bernstein (cond.), New York PO / 1999 / Sony 61836

○ **Goldmark: Rustic Wedding; Enescu: Roumanian Rhapsody in A Op11/1, Enescu: Roumanian Rhapsodies** / Abravanel (cond.), Utah SO / 1992 / Vanguard 5002

CONCERTO

Violin Concerto No. 1 in A minor, Op. 28 (1877)

The *Violin Concerto No. 1 in A minor*, Op. 28, by Karl Goldmark is his most frequently performed and recorded work. It is certain, however, that only the gripping virtuoso interest afforded by its rich and rewarding solo part has accorded the concerto a public status which now outstrips that of other formerly popular Goldmark's works, like his *Rustic Wedding Symphony*, and his operatic masterpiece *The Queen of Sheba*. The concerto was written in 1877 and received its first performance in Nuremberg (or Bremen, according to some sources) one year later.

A violinist by training, Goldmark knew well how to exploit the instrument's full potential, and in this work he created one of the nineteenth century masterworks of the violin repertory, deserving (on paper at least) to take its rightful place beside Romantic concertos by Mendelssohn, Tchaikovsky, Dvořák, Bruch, and others. As Benjamin Folkman writes, "the violin is very much a conciliator" in the opening movement (Allegro moderato) which begins with an abrupt-sounding march figure for the orchestra in angular, urgent dotted rhythms. This returns in more lyrical and reflective style with the first appearance of the soloist, to whom the luxuriant and expansive second subject group is also predominately entrusted. The development section is an ingenious fugato transformation of the first theme, now dispersed throughout the orchestra. The Andante in G major has a touching hymn-like quality, especially at the outset where the wind instruments provide an organ-like chordal accompaniment to the eloquent solo line. The devotional atmosphere is interrupted toward its close by a horn-call, and the violin immediately takes up the lively Allegretto theme of the finale. Stated a fourth lower, it re-establishes harmonic links with the idea given out at the very start of the concerto, but it has a completely different, more outgoing character, and its technical complexities (harmonics, double-stopping, and brilliant bow-work) are of true virtuoso difficulty. A more songful second subject idea follows, but the cadenza (usually heard in the first movement) only appears after another fugato-like orchestral development. The concerto ends with a further affirmative reprise for orchestra of the powerful opening figure of the concerto, thus giving the whole convincing structural unity. *—Michael Jameson*

Recommended:

○ **Milstein—Concert Performances & Broadcasts, 1942–1969** / Walter (cond.), Milstein, New York PO / Music & Arts 972

○ **Bell Plays Sibelius & Goldmark** / Bell, Salonen (cond.), Los Angeles PO New Music Group / 2000 / Sony 65949

Nicolas Gombert

b. ca. 1495, La Gorgue, Flanders (France) ?, **d.** ca. 1560

Composer

The German music theorist Hermann Finck wrote in 1556 that Nicolas Gombert had shown all musicians "the exact way to refinement." Finck claimed that Gombert had personally studied with the great Josquin Desprez, presumably in Josquin's final years at Condé-sur-l'Escaut; unfortunately, no independent confirmation of this master-pupil relationship exists, but Gombert's musical style of rich, pervasive imitation certainly builds upon the style of Josquin. His long service to the court chapel of the Holy Roman Emperor Charles V allowed Gombert to travel widely and transmit this musical style across the bounds of Europe. With his contemporaries, Adrian Willaert and Jacob Clemens non Papa, Gombert brought the style of the musical Renaissance to fruition; even as late as 1610, no less a musician as Claudio Monteverdi selected a motet of Gombert upon which to base a mass setting in his bid to become *Maestro di capella* at Venice's San Marco.

Gombert was born somewhere in Southern Flanders; the village of La Gorgue has been suggested based upon the presence of other families named Gombert there. From roughly 1526 until around 1540, Nicolas served the court chapel of Emperor Charles V, travelling throughout Charles' vast realms in Flanders, Italy, Austria, Germany, and, of course, Spain. As of 1529, he fulfilled the position of *maître des enfants* in the Chapel. Charles, a fervent Catholic (and later one of the initiators of the Council of Trent), apparently encouraged the composition of masses and motets among his personal musicians, though Gombert also produced a large number of courtly French chansons. Gombert also honored his imperial patron with several commemorative motets celebrating events in Charles' life: the birth of a son, the coronation of his brother as King of Hungary, and an important international treaty. Gombert's service was partially remunerated by a series of ecclesiastical benefice incomes from churches at Courtrai, Béthune, Lens, and Metz.

Gombert's name abruptly vanishes from the imperial paylists in 1540; the mathematician Jerome Cardan records the reason as Gombert's sexual violation of one of the boys in his charge; he was sentenced to penal servitude in the galley of a warship. Apparently, he continued to compose, however, and is said to have written certain "swan songs" which helped avert the Emperor's ire, and earned his pardon. By 1547—when he sent a letter and a motet to one of Charles' officers—he was residing in Tounai, where he eventually received a canonicate. He lived out his last years in peace at Tournai, dying some time between 1556 and 1561. *—Timothy Dickey*

Overview of Works (ca. 1527–1555)

Nicolas Gombert (ca. 1495–ca. 1560) was a Renaissance-era composer of high rank, considered in the sixteenth century to be a worthy rival of Adrian Willaert. While his reputation and frequency of performance may not now warrant such a lofty comparison, his output evinces several significant innovations.

Gombert's oeuvre includes 160 motets, eight Magnificat settings, and over 70 chansons. His masses might have turned out to be his most important body of work, but of the many he composed, only ten complete ones have survived. His *Missa Tempore paschali* still maintains some currency in the concert hall and on recording. It is notable in at least one respect: Gombert typically wrote two settings of the Agnus Dei for his masses, increasing the number of voices for the second; but for the one here he doubled the number from six to twelve to achieve a grander effect. Perhaps his greatest mass, however, was the *Missa Fors seulement*, for five voices. In this effort Gombert masterfully employed themes from chansons by Pipelare and Josquin Desprez, exploring to the fullest the possibilities of the Renaissance parody technique.

Gombert's motets have probably fared better down through the years than his masses, not least because vocal groups singing them can select particular favorites, whereas masses are usually performed whole. His two most popular motets—and probably his most widely performed works in any genre—are *Musae Jovis* and the four-part *Salve Regina*. In the former effort Gombert deftly fashioned material from Josquin Desprez for a cantus firmus, and in the latter he imaginatively drew on Marian and plainsong antiphons.

In his eight Magnificats the composer produced, by general consensus, some of his most masterful creations in the sacred genre. Set in each of the eight church modes, they feature assured writing for the required four voices—which swell to five or six at the end—that is often quite complex in its use of plainsong material.

A good handful of Gombert's chansons appear on recordings at least as often as anything else in his output. They are generally livelier and more lyrical than his sacred music, but still recognizably from his distinctive pen. Among his more popular efforts here are *Mille regretz*, which reworks a gorgeous chanson by Josquin Desprez, and *Puis qu'ainsi est* and *Je prens congié*. Gombert had a tendency to imitate sounds of nature or to depict scenes of activity within; his *Resveillez vous* evokes the sounds of birdcalls, and *Or escoutez* paints the breathless pursuit of a rabbit.

In sum, Gombert was an imaginative and quite consistent composer who occasionally could reach levels of profundity in his sacred music. He was one of the first who tended to treat voices equally, a stylistic facet demonstrated by one of his many imaginative devices: a motif is presented by one voice, then echoed by a succession of voices, creating a marvelous effect and drawing attention to all vocal parts. *—Robert Cummings*

Recommended:

○ **Gombert: Music from the Court of Charles V** / Nevel (cond.), Huelgas Ens. / 1992 / Sony 48249

○ **Gombert: Missa Tempore paschali; Magnificat octavi toni** / Henry's Eight / 1997 / Hyperion 66943

○ **Gombert: Credo; Magnificat Primi Toni; Manificat Octavi Toni, etc.** / Bo Holten (dir.), Vocal Group Ars Nova / Kontrapunkt 32038

○ **Gombert: 8-Part Credo; Motets** / Henry's Eight / 1996 / Hyperion 66828

○ **Gombert: Magnificats 1–4** / Phillips (dir.), Tallis Scholars / 2001 / Gimell 37

Richard Goode

b. Jun. 1, 1943, New York, NY

Pianist

One of the most respected recitalists of the day, Richard Goode turned to solo and concerto performances late in life. He had made a reputation for himself more as a chamber musician, with frequent participation at the Spoleto Festival and as a founding member of the Chamber Music Society of Lincoln Center.

Goode's musical genealogy is exceptional. Born on June 1, 1943, he grew up in the East Bronx, in a family that could be described as "semi-musical": his father was a piano tuner and an amateur violinist who hoped his son would take up the same instrument. He sent his son to a neighborhood piano teacher, believing that the keyboard instrument would give the boy the solid musical grounding he would need. When it became evident that the piano was where Richard's talents lay, his father sent him to study with Elvira Szigeti, aunt of the great Hungarian violinist Joseph Szigeti.

Through his association with Mrs. Szigeti, Goode came to the attention of arts patron Rosalie Leventritt, who arranged an audition for the ten-year-old with Rudolf Serkin. Serkin was impressed, and recommended him to Claude Frank. Subsequently Goode went on to study with Nadia Reisenberg, Karl Ulrich Schnabel, and Serkin himself, who reigned at the Curtis Institute in Philadelphia.

Goode's repertoire is anchored in the middle-European classics, and like Artur Schnabel, with whom he has often been favorably compared (by Karl Ulrich Schnabel, among others), he has made a specialty of the long-neglected piano sonatas of Franz Schubert. His early 1980s recordings of the complete piano sonatas of Beethoven, for Book-of-the-Month Records and Elektra/Nonesuch, brought his insightful artistry to a wider public. He has not eschewed modern music, though his tastes run toward a more conservative style of modernism; the works of George Perle are prominent in his repertoire.

A concern for the inner essence of music and its architectural balance has made him into an introspective artist; the self-effacement that so often goes with this introspection (plus a dollop of chronic stage fright) kept Goode from seeking out the solo concert spotlight for many years. It was only after the encouragement of respected friends and colleagues (Leonard Bernstein among them) that he left the relative security of playing chamber music and took the decisive step toward a solo career. Goode was 47 years old when he made his acclaimed Carnegie Hall debut with a program that included, characteristically, Schumann's *Davidsbündlertänze*.

Goode is possessed of a restless intellect and has developed passions for literature (*Moby Dick* and *Finnegan's Wake* rank high on his list). He has explored visual art extensively as well, noting that these seemingly extracurricular pursuits enhance his musical ones. With his wife Marcia, who is a violinist, he lives in New York City. *—Mark Satola*

Recommended:

○ **Schubert: Sonata in A; Klavierstück in E Flat** / Goode / 1985 / Nonesuch 78028

○ **Brahms: Clarinet Sonatas** / Goode, Stoltzman (clarinet) / 1982 / RCA 60036

○ **Beethoven: The Complete Sonatas** / Goode / 1993 / Nonesuch 79328

Benny Goodman

b. May 30, 1909, Chicago, IL, **d.** Jun. 13, 1996, New York, NY

Clarinetist

Clarinetist Benny Goodman, "the King of Swing," was one of the greatest artists and bandleaders in the history of jazz. However in 1938, at the height of his popularity, Goodman began to pursue classical music as a sideline, for the mere reason that he was bored—"how many choruses can you play on 'Oh Lady Be Good'?" he once mused. The one-time student of legendary Chicago clarinet teacher Fritz Schoepp became an expert interpreter of the Mozart *Clarinet Concerto*, K. 622 and mastered much of the standard literature for his instrument. Well before he ran through the major clarinet classics, Goodman began to commission works from contemporary composers such as Stravinsky and Copland. His first venture in this regard resulted in *Contrasts for clarinet, violin and piano* by Belà Bartók, and the 1940 Columbia record Goodman, Bartók and violinist Joseph Szigeti made of this work may well be the most astonishing historical recording of "modernist" music ever made. The reputation of Benny Goodman as a jazz player and bandleader is of such significance that it will never be superseded by his work as a classical musician, yet Goodman's devotion to classical music was so deep that when he died of a stroke while rehearsing in 1986, the music stand was open to the Brahms *Clarinet Quintet*, Op. 115. *—Uncle Dave Lewis*

Recommended:

○ **Benny Goodman: Mozart at Tanglewood** / Munch (cond.), Goodman, BSO, Boston Symphony SQ / 1997 / BMG 68804

○ **Bartók** / Goodman, Szigeti / 1991 / Sony 47676

Henryk Górecki

b. Dec. 6, 1933, Czernica, Poland

Composer: Symphonic, Chamber Music, Orchestral

Henryk Górecki is that rarity among contemporary composers: the originator of a full-fledged hit. A recording of his *Symphony No. 3* by the London Sinfonietta with soprano Dawn Upshaw climbed to the top of the British pop charts in the early 1990s. Górecki was among the Eastern European composers for whom contemporary stylistic trends (first serialism and then the various reactions against it) took on antiauthoritarian overtones, and who thus emerged in the forefront of late twentieth century music; in his works, stylistic originality seems a personal and political necessity.

Górecki was born in 1933 in the small town of Czernica in the Silesia region of Poland. He was trained as a primary-school teacher, and did not formally become a composer until the age of 22, when he enrolled at the State Higher School of Music in Katowice. He studied in Paris for a time and became acquainted with the leading edge of the Western avant-garde. The works of Webern, Stockhausen, and Messiaen were unavailable in Poland, suppressed by socialist-realist doctrines; but all of them, especially Messiaen, influenced Górecki's early music. Górecki became a professor at Katowice and went on to gain some official acceptance, ascending to the post of provost.

Górecki's music was always deeply rooted in Polish ideals, however, and it carries a sense of the emotional impact of the atrocities of the Second World War. He ran afoul of the authorities in the late 1970s, resigning his post as provost to protest the government's refusal to permit Pope John Paul II to visit Katowice. He later composed music to honor an injured Solidarity labor union activist. What gave his protests additional weight was that he had rejected Western hyper-modernism and created a new musical language that more directly served his ideals. Górecki had first gained recognition with *Scontri* (1959), a work very much of the avant-garde in its treatment of sonority and texture as primary structural elements. In the 1960s, however, Górecki's music offered harbingers of the eclecticism that would dominate contemporary music by the century's end. *Genesis* shows minimalist qualities, while *Three Pieces in the Old Style* manipulates modal and whole tone ideas, and *Lerchenmusik* quotes Beethoven, to name a few examples.

Górecki became interested in the folk music of his native region and investigated Polish music of the Medieval and Renaissance eras. In 1976 he synthesized the new trends in his music with the *Symphony No. 3*, subtitled "Symphony of Sorrowful Songs." Scored for soprano and orchestra, this hour-long piece contains three movements, quoting old religious and folk texts and incorporating folk tunes. It opens with a canon in the strings that builds gradually over a 12-minute span, with an effect comparable to that of Western minimalist composition but proceeding from different spiritual bases. (One of the animating principles of Górecki's work has been a fervent Roman Catholicism.) The work was recorded several times, but it was the 1993 release that caught fire—partly because it fit perfectly with the new and well-marketed trend toward "holy minimalism."

Despite his growing success, Górecki has continued to compose largely in response to inner creative dictates rather than according to any plan to increase his reputation. Much of his work in the 1980s and 1990s has been in the choral and chamber genres; the String Quartet No. 1, Op. 62 ("Already It Is Dusk"), was written for the Kronos Quartet, a successful U.S. ensemble devoted to new music, and further enhanced his reputation. The work used a Renaissance part-song as raw material, transforming it first into a dissonant but peaceful chorale and then into a folk-inflected dance. *—AMG*

Overview of Works

Polish composer Henryk Górecki is one of the most popular composers of the last half of the twentieth century. His vocal and chamber works of the 1970s and 1980s have been recorded many times and have sold millions of copies. Górecki's oeuvre, however, is more diverse than these works suggest, dating back to the late 1950s and reflecting an engagement with a number trends in contemporary composition.

Górecki's first work with opus number dates from 1955, a set of four preludes for piano. Other important works from the late 1950s include the *Sonata for Two Violins*, the *First Symphony*, the choral work *Epitafium*, and a number of songs and chamber works. In the late 1950s, Poland was slowly opening up to the West; consequently, young composers were being exposed to an array of new compositional techniques. Górecki quickly adopted the serial techniques exemplified by Pierre Boulez and the late Viennese miniaturist Anton Webern. Górecki's works from this time reflect the esthetic austerity of these latter two composers: *Epitafium* exemplifies Webernian compression, while other works, like the *First Symphony*, combine expressive gestures with sparse textures and splashes of instrumental color.

Serial procedures in Górecki's work were later undermined by his own intuitive, personal approach to composition. In the mid-1960s, Górecki composed two pivotal orchestral works: *Three Pieces in Old Style* and *Refren*. In the former, Górecki uses borrowed material—Renaissance-era Polish folk music—and adopts the modal style which will characterize his works of the 1970s; in the latter, serial technique is eschewed in favor of simplified formal structures and whole-tone harmonies. Together, these two works neatly foreshadow Górecki's esthetic orientation of subsequent decades.

In the 1970s and early 1980s, Górecki composed mostly vocal music. His *Second* and *Third* symphonies are perhaps the most important works of this era and utilize combinations of orchestra, choir, and solo voice. The *Second Symphony*, an enormous work composed to celebrate the 500th anniversary of the birth of Copernicus, follows the evolutionary path set out by the works of the 1960s: it is pervasively modal and consonant, and features the inclusion of Renaissance choral music. The *Third Symphony* of 1976 is unquestionably Górecki's most famous work, but it did not receive much attention until 1992, when it was recorded by soprano Dawn Upshaw and the London Sinfonietta. This work was so popular in part because of its moving text (a combination of a Polish folk song and hymn with a prayer found on the wall of a Gestapo prison cell), but also because of its slow, dramatic thickening of textures, simple, repeated melodic cells, and modal harmonies.

Górecki's subsequent compositions have largely been faithful to the esthetic developments of the 1970s and feature slow tempos, modal or diatonic musical language, the incorporation of old music, and an emphasis on minimal musical elements used to maximal effect. *—Alexander Carpenter*

Recommended:

- ○ **The Essential Górecki** / Krenz, Markowski (conds.), Warsaw National PO, Polish National SO / 1993 / Olympia 385
- ○ **Górecki: Miserere** / Nelson, Ding (cond.), / 1994 / Nonesuch 79348
- ○ **Górecki: Beatus Vir; Symphony 2** / Wit (cond.), Kilanowicz, Polish National RSO / 2001 / Naxos 555375

SYMPHONIC

Symphony No. 3 ("Symphony of Sorrowful Songs"), Op. 36 (1976)

Henryk Górecki has established himself as one of the most well-known composers of the late twentieth century, with a musical style whose poignancy and accessibility found a broad and diverse audience. His worldwide recognition was rather slow in coming, however, and although his orchestral and chamber works from the 1960s and 1970s found favor with audiences in Poland and some critics abroad, it was the *Third* that eventually catapulted Górecki into the classical music spotlight. The *Symphony No. 3*, subtitled "Symphony of Sorrowful Songs," is scored for orchestra with soprano soloist and is cast in three somber movements. The first and longest movement, marked Lento, sonstenuto tranquillo ma cantabile, begins with a slow, deliberative canon, the theme of which is adapted from an old Polish folk song. At its apex, the canon is interrupted by a soprano soloist singing a fervent lament for Jesus in the voice of Mary: "My chosen and lovely son, share with your mother all your wounds...." Her text is taken from the Songs of the Lysagóra, a sacred collection dating from the fifteenth century. In the shorter but equally powerful second movement, a spare harmonic background casts a shadowy pall over the heartwrenching maternal words that were found scrawled on the wall of a Gestapo prison by an 18-year-old female inmate. The tone here turns religious, as well: "Little mother, do not weep, Purest Queen of Heaven, pray, do not abandon me, Hail Mary." The third movement, constructed as a set of variations, once again visits the theme of a mother mourning for her son; its text and theme were derived from Polish folk song. Despite the *Third*'s intense expressivity and uncluttered musical language, its fame cannot be attributed to its style alone—and in fact, Górecki remained a relatively obscure figure to American audiences for some time after its composition, while three separate recordings of the piece enjoyed only average sales. However, in a happy convergence of musical style, shrewd marketing, and shifting public tastes, the 1992 recording of the work, featuring Dawn Upshaw and the London Sinfonietta, became an overnight hit and climbed up the classical as well as popular charts and sold over a million copies. Górecki's *"Sorrowful" Symphony* touched a more universal nerve and spoke to a broader audience than virtually any other classical work of its time. *—Jeremy Grimshaw*

Recommended:

- ○ **Górecki: Symphony 3** / Kord (cond.), Kozlowska, Warsaw PO / 1994 / Philips 442411
- ○ **Górecki: Symphony 3** / Zinman (cond.), Upshaw, London Sinfonietta / 1992 / Nonesuch 79282
- ○ **Górecki: Symphony 3** / Wit (cond.), Kilanowicz, Katowice RSO / 2001 / Naxos 550822

CHAMBER MUSIC

Recitatives & Ariosos: Lerchenmusik, for clarinet, cello & piano, Op. 53 (1984–1986)

In 1984, the reclusive Henryk Górecki was invited to attend a festival in Denmark, and to contribute a new piece. He had completed no scores between 1981 and 1984. As it turns out, *Lerchenmusik* wasn't quite to his satisfaction, and he withdrew it, presenting a revised version at the 1985 Warsaw Autumn Festival, then revising it again for a definitive premiere in April 1986. He hadn't touched the chamber music genre since 1970. This was the most ambitious instrumental work he had ever written.

Lerchenmusik falls into three movements, each being built from clear contrasting sections, underscoring the "recitatives" and "ariosos" of the full title. As a whole, the piece lasts some 45 minutes, an impressive musical architecture. The opening passage presents a slowly-unfolding melody in the low range of the cello over tolling octaves in the piano. This single idea lasts for some seven minutes, creating a solemn mood that is shattered by the outburst that follows. This middle section is relentlessly aggressive, juxtaposing short motives in repetitive structures that proceed in asymmetrical fashion. The bi-tonal chords of the piano add a biting resonance to the rising lydian motive that the clarinet plays as a clarion call over low, grinding patterns in the cello. This section, which hits the listener with shocking force, is over almost before you can catch your breath, returning to the solemn refrain of the opening. Different aspects of both types of material will be re-visited later.

The middle movement is a poignantly lyrical arioso for the clarinet, built upon the modal motive introduced earlier. The piano plays repeated bi-tonal chords that shift but rarely. The cello joins the clarinet in sweetly harmonious thirds, but as the dynamics build, the texture is intensified by shifting to gritty ninths. Górecki, with characteristic drama, notes that the climax should sound "ma delirioso-aggressivo-marcatissimo-ben tenuto e ancora—con molto passione con grande tensione"! To underscore his intent, the straining musicians are asked to play *ffff* and then crescendo. The urgency of this movement points to the composer's need to impart a maximum of expressive intensity.

The final movement is the most elaborate of the three. The gentle, plainsong-derived melody, sung by the widely-spaced clarinet and cello, accompanied by repeated chords in the piano, leads, magically, to a citation of the opening of Beethoven's *Piano Concerto No. 4*. The music also refers to Messiaen (his *Quatuor pour la fin du temps*, after all, uses these same three instruments, adding a violin), and to a "bird" motive that derives from the name of the commissioner, Louise Lerche-Lerchenborg ("Lerche" means "lark"). Eventually, one becomes aware that the bi-tonal chords of the piano have given way to pure triads, settling on a repeated A flat major chord. The piece ends with a drawn-out echo of the three-note lydian motive that has wound its way through the whole piece. *—Jim Harley*

Recommended:

- ○ **Lutoslawski: Dance Preludes; Górecki: Lerchenmusik; Prokofiev: Overture on Hebrew Themes** / Vistula Camerata / 1990 / Olympia 343

ORCHESTRAL

Three Pieces in Old Style, for strings (1963)

By 1963, Henryk Górecki had been abroad, twice, to Paris, Cologne, and Darmstadt, all pinnacles of modern music in Europe. Back home in Katowice, he was determined to develop his own style, one that would reject any artifice in its striving for simplicity and expressive force. Works such as his *Genesis* cycle epitomize that search. But there was another side of his development that was more nascent, and that was the desire to root his music in his native Polish soil, but in a way that wouldn't be exploitative or cliché. *Three Pieces in Old Style* was the first

"Polish" work to see the light, and it has gone on to become one of his most performed compositions.

Scored for strings, *Three Pieces* is far removed in style from his other works of that period. There are simple modal melodies, clear classical rhythms, triadic or diatonic harmonies, and direct dance-like forms. The outer two pieces contain no accidentals whatsoever, the first being in the major mode, the second in the minor, and the third in the Dorian mode. There are a couple of features, however, that point to Górecki's more individual style as it developed a few years later. One is that he subdivides the strings so as to sustain the individual notes of the melody. This creates an "aura" around the line, a form of resonance that marks the music as being contemporary rather than from an earlier era. The harmonic progressions, too, are not strongly directional. The first piece, for example, rocks back and forth between two chords, providing a sense of motion on the immediate scale, but a sense of stasis on the larger scale. The last piece contains a melody (taken from a sixteenth century Polish part song) that is played in parallel, each layer being a step lower than the original. The diatonic sonority remains throughout, but the harmonization of the melody becomes thick and vibrant. Górecki would make use of this technique in a number of works, notably his *Symphony No. 2*, from 1972.

Thus, while the *Three Pieces in Old Style* seems something of an anomaly when looking at Górecki's work in chronological order, it actually served as a catalyst for the coalescence of the composer's mature style, combining modernist techniques with traditional materials. —*Jim Harley*

Recommended:

- ○ **Górecki: Symphony 3; 3 Olden Style Pieces** / Wit (cond.), Polish National RSO / 2001 / Naxos 550822
- ○ **Szymanowski: Violin Concertos; Górecki: 3 Pieces in the Old Style; Baird: Colas Breugnon** / Maksymiuk (cond.), Polish CO / 2002 / EMI 575670

François-Joseph Gossec

b. Jan. 17, 1734, Vergnies, Netherlands, **d.** Feb. 16, 1829, Passy, France
Composer: Symphonic, Concerto, Choral

One of the leading figures of eighteenth century French music, Gossec was a versatile and prolific composer—particularly of instrumental music, as exemplified by his symphonies and string quartets. He enlarged the expressive capabilities of the orchestra, relying on his harmonic imagination and sense of sound texture; in many ways his experiments presage the works of Haydn and Beethoven. His choral music is also significant; his *Te Deum*, for example (written for 300 instrumentalists and a choir of more than 1,000 singers), foreshadows the later works of Berlioz.

Born in the historic Hainaut region (an incubator of great composers all the way back to the Renaissance), Gossec started his musical studies on the violin and the harpsichord. In 1741, he joined the choir of the Notre Dame Cathedral in Antwerp, continuing his music studies.

In 1751, Gossec went to Paris, armed with a letter of introduction to Rameau. The composer was so impressed by Gossec that he found him a position as violinist and bass player in the famous orchestra of La Pouplinière, conducted by Johann Stamitz (of Mannheim fame—thus his affinity for the emerging symphonic form). During this period, he produced large quantities of symphonic and chamber music; Gossec's symphonies composed in the 1750s and 1760s (mostly the three-movement Italianate variety) displayed an extraordinary range of form and orchestration.

In 1762 Louis-Joseph de Bourbon, Prince of Conde, appointed Gossec director of his private theater; however, despite some success, Gossec's operas did not show the same promise as his instrumental works. Gossec founded a new orchestra, the Concert des Amateurs, in 1769. This extraordinary ensemble attracted the best musicians of the time and performed many of Gossec's own symphonies, including his immensely popular *La chasse*. During his final season as director Gossec conducted the first performance of a symphony by Haydn in France.

In 1773, Gossec left the Concert des Amateurs, assuming the leadership of the Concert Spirituel. In addition, he worked for the Opéra, supervising the production of contemporary works. In 1774, Gossec's oratorio *La nativité* was performed at the Concert Spirituel. Among the innovations introduced in this work was a choir of angels, which Gossec put offstage, a device which Berlioz used in his oratorio *L'Enfance de Christ* (1854).

In 1780, Gossec obtained the post of sous-directeur of the Opéra, assuming the directorship, four years later, of the newly-founded Ecole Royale de Chant, which was under the Opéra's administrative control. During this period, Gossec continued composing symphonies, also writing works for the stage, including ballets, which were not very successful.

Unlike Cherubini, Gossec quickly adapted to the new cultural climate in the wake of the French Revolution. In 1789, he severed all his ties with the Opéra, which the revolutionary government regarded as a royalist institution. In addition, he placed his talent as a composer in the service of the new regime, composing popular pieces and organizing musical events to celebrate the Revolution. Prominent among Gossec's politically motivated composition is his massive *Te Deum* (1790), written to commemorate the storming of the Bastille.

While Gossec's output drastically diminished after 1800, works written during his final creative period include important works such as *Symphonie a 17 parties* (1809) and *Derniere messe des vivants* (1813).

Because of his enthusiastic support for the Revolution, Gossec was not treated well by the restored French monarchy. In 1816, King Louis XVIII dissolved the Conservatoire, which he doubtless perceived as an institution created by the Revolution, and Gossec was left without employment. He eventually moved to Passy, then a suburb of Paris, where he spent his remaining years. —*Zoran Minderovic*

Overview of Works (ca. 1753–1813)

Gossec, a Flemish composer active in Paris, is a somewhat marginal figure in general histories of music. He made, however, some significant contributions to the development of instrumental music in France in the late eighteenth and early nineteenth centuries, and was one of the most important composers of the Revolutionary period. Indeed he is remembered more for his general influence than for any particular work. In his *Messe des Morts*, the "Tuba mirum" employed two orchestras, one a wind ensemble positioned outside the church. The effect reportedly made an immense impression upon audiences of the day, and it seems to resound in the gargantuan parallel passage in Berlioz's *Requiem*.

Gossec's earliest works show the influence first of the Italian symphonists, then of Stamitz and the Mannheim School. These early works (circa 1750–60) include a collection of 24 symphonies and a number of sonatas: they are relatively unremarkable, essentially immature works, lacking technical adroitness and melodic inventiveness. Gossec later composed a significant number of string quartets and much chamber music: these small-scale works are counted among his best pieces because of their formal flexibility and occasionally audacious modulations to remote keys. His later symphonies, moreover, are also well regarded for their rich orchestral colors. Gossec also composed a number of operas and ballets; he was noted for comic opera, but most of his attempts at serious opera met with failure. Gossec had little facility with large forms, and many of his large-scale works suffered from repetitiveness and a lack of melodic interest. His smaller instrumental works shaped the Parisian musical world that Mozart notably failed to crack, but as a conductor he helped to spread Haydn's reputation in France. Gossec eventually became known for his use of sound effects, not only in his symphonies, but also in his religious and dramatic works, where orchestral effects were used to emphasize text and mood. His music also shows the increasing importance of wind instruments in Paris in the latter half of the eighteenth century, after German wind players began coming to France around 1770.

After 1798, Gossec emerged as an important figure in musical life in Revolutionary France. He composed a great deal of music celebrating the Revolution, including a *Te Deum*, a *Marche lugubre*, many patriotic songs, and dramatic works glorifying the new order in France. The massive opera *L'offrande à la liberté* endured as part of French musical life for decades. After the ascension of Napoleon in 1799, Gossec essentially ceased composing, producing only a few pedagogical works in his final years. —*Alexander Carpenter*

Recommended:

- ○ **Gossec: Grande Messe des Morts; Symphonie à 17 parties** / Fasolis (cond.), Crook, Invernizzi, Arruabarrena, Lugano Radio Orch. / 2001 / Naxos 554750-51
- ○ **Gossec: 4 Symphonies** / Sanderling (cond.), Bretagne Orch. / 2001 / ASV 1123
- ○ **Gossec: Quartets, Op14** / Nicolet, Trio Nouveau Pasquie / Talent 291050
- ○ **Gossec: Gavotte; Suite de Dances; Symphonies** / Sanderling (cond.), Bretagne Orch. / 2002 / ASV 1124

SYMPHONIC

Symphony in D major ("La caccia") (ca. 1773)

In 1773, French composer François-Joseph Gossec assumed the directorship of the Concert Spirituel. Although the organization had recently fallen on hard times and its orchestra was no longer the best in France, Gossec rebuilt both so thoroughly that the orchestra became the finest in Europe and the envy of Mozart and Haydn when they came to Paris. Part of Gossec's rehabilitation of the Concert Spirituel's orchestra took the form of the symphonies he wrote for them, starting with the *Symphony in D major No. 62* in the Brook catalog, also called *La caccia* or "The Hunt" because of its use of imitative hunting horns in its minuet. But the symphony is distinguished more by its wonderful fusion of Italianate melody, French elegance, and Mannheim school symphonic excitement. Written in four movements in the standard mid-eighteenth century order of fast-slow-dance-fast for the standard mid-eighteenth century ensemble of flutes, oboes, bassoons, strings, and in this case four horns, Gossec's *Symphony in D major* rivals those of Haydn and Mozart from the same period in style and grace. —*James Leonard*

Recommended:

- ○ **Gossec: 4 Symphonies** / Sanderling (cond.), Bretagne Orch. / 2001 / ASV 1123

CONCERTO

Tambourin, for flute & orchestra (1793)

Even the best-known composer in his/her lifetime may fall into obscurity after death. French composer François-Joseph Gossec was acknowledged to be the greatest instrumental composer at the close of the *ancien régime* in France (Marie Antoinette loved his music) and, in an amazing *volte face*, he was acknowledged to be the greatest composer of the Revolutionary and Napoleonic periods (Robespierre loved his music). While his operas and ballets for the *ancien régime* could not compare with Gluck from the same period, his orchestral symphonies were immensely successful. He was also, beyond all doubt, the composer of Revolutionary France, composing not only gargantuan works for public celebrations and ceremonies but even composing the *Hymn to the Supreme Being* which was, for a time, the hymn of the Revolution.

But all that has faded from memory and Gossec is instead remembered—if he is remembered at all—for having composed the *Tambourin for Flute and Orchestra*. Taken from his "divertissement-lyrique" *Le triomphe de la République*, it is nearly mandatory among flutists: James Galway and, of course, Jean-Pierre Rampal, have performed and recorded it numerous times. It also exists in a seemingly infinite number of arrangements for flute and every possible combination of instruments plus arrangements for nearly every possible solo instrument except, perhaps, sousaphone. But while the *Tambourin* is a charming little piece with an unforgettably delightful melody and sprightly rhythm, it is hardly representative of Gossec's greater achievement, and one can only imagine the old man whirling in his grave with the knowledge that it is his *Tambourin* that has gained a measure of immortality for him. *—James Leonard*

Recommended:

○ **Dances for flute** / Gerhardt (cond.), Galway, National PO / 1993 / RCA 60917

CHORAL

Te Deum, for 3 male voices & band (1790)

French composer François-Joseph Gossec had composed Te Deums and other celebratory church music for the *ancien régime*, most notably his *Te Deum* of 1779 in honor of the announcement of the pregnancy of Marie Antoinette. But, with the Revolution of 1789, Gossec's republican sympathies led him to rebel against the Bourbon monarchy, and he quickly sided with the people against the government of Louis XVI. Gossec was a musician and composer to the core, and his allegiance to revolutionary principles took the form of directing and writing music for the Revolution. After a series of military symphonies of 1789–90, Gossec composed a *Te Deum for Male Chorus and Wind Band* for the first Festival of Federation ceremony on the Champ-de-Mars for the one-year anniversary of the taking of the Bastille on July 14, 1790. The festival was celebrated by Talleyrand, a bishop who later renounced religion to become Napoleon's chief diplomat and, like Talleyrand, Gossec's *Te Deum* is both sacred and secular. Setting the liturgical Latin text to music scored for wind instruments and drums, rather than organ so that it might be better-heard at the outdoor festival, Gossec's *Te Deum* was only the first in a series of massive choral works he wrote during the Revolutionary and Napoleonic periods. The influence of these works on the massive choral works of Berlioz is incalculable. *—James Leonard*

Louis Moreau Gottschalk

b. May 8, 1829, New Orleans, LA, **d.** Dec. 18, 1869, Tijuca, Brazil

Composer: Keyboard, Symphonic

Gottschalk was the eldest son of a Jewish-English New Orleans real estate speculator and his French-descended bride. Gottschalk may have heard the drums at Place Congo in New Orleans, but his exposure to Creole melody likely came through his own household; his mother had grown up in Haiti and fled to Louisiana after that island's slave uprising. Piano study was undertaken with Narcisse Lettellier, and at age 11, Gottschalk was sent to Paris. Denied entrance to the Conservatoire, he continued with Charles Hallé and Camille Stamaty, adding composition with Pierre Maleden. His Paris debut at the Salle Pleyel in 1845 earned praise from Chopin. By the end of the 1840s, Gottschalk's first works, such as *Bamboula*, appeared. These syncopated pieces based on popular Creole melodies rapidly gained popularity worldwide. Gottschalk left Paris in 1852 to join his father in New York, only to encounter stiff competition from touring foreign artists. With his father's death in late 1853, Gottschalk inherited support of his mother and six siblings. In 1855, he signed a contract with publisher William Hall to issue several pieces, including *The Banjo* and *The Last Hope*. *The Last Hope* is a sad and sweetly melancholy piece, and it proved hugely popular. Gottschalk found himself obliged to repeat it at every concert, and wrote "even my paternal love for *The Last Hope* has succumbed under the terrible necessity of meeting it at every step." With an appearance at Dodsworth Hall in December 1855, Gottschalk finally found his audience. For the first time he was solvent, and at his mother's death in 1857 Gottschalk was released from his familial obligations. He embarked on a tour of the Caribbean and didn't return for five years. When this ended, America was in the midst of Civil War. Gottschalk supported the north, touring Union states until 1864. Gottschalk wearied of the horrors surrounding him, becoming an avid proponent of education, playing benefit concerts for public schools and libraries. During a tour to California in 1865, Gottschalk entered into an involvement with a young woman attending a seminary school in Oakland, and the press excoriated him. He escaped on a steamer bound for Panama City. Instead of returning to New York, he pressed on to Peru, Chile, Uruguay, and Argentina, staying one step ahead of revolutions, rioting, and cholera epidemics, but he began to break down under the strain. Gottschalk contracted malaria in Brazil in August 1869; still recovering, he was hit in the abdomen by a sandbag thrown by a student in São Paolo. In a concert at Rio de Janeiro on November 25, Gottschalk collapsed at the keyboard. He had appendicitis, which led to peritonitis. On December 18, 1869, Gottschalk died at the age of 40.

The impact of Gottschalk's music on the later development of ragtime might seem obvious, yet there is no proven link from him to the syncopated popular music he anticipated in works like *Bamboula*. The music of Scott Joplin and Jelly Roll Morton show traces of Gottschalk's melodic shape and rhythmic pulse, and the New Orleans-born Morton likewise studied under Lettellier. Nickelodeon pianists disserviced Gottschalk by loving him too well; pieces like *The Dying Poet* and *Morte!!* turned many a dramatic corner in silent movie houses, and the public began to identify these themes as cliché. By the 1940s, Gottschalk was condemned as hopelessly old-fashioned, and it would take decades of work by scholars to improve his critical fortunes. In his best music, Gottschalk was an American original; masterpieces like *Souvenir de Porto Rico, Union* and *O ma charmant, épargnez-moi!* transcend time through their emotional power, technical mastery, audacity, wit, and charm. *—Uncle Dave Lewis*

KEYBOARD

Bamboula, danse des nègres, Op. 2 (1844–1845)

Louis Moreau Gottschalk's first masterwork, *Bamboula*, Op. 2/RO 20, was written in the French town of Clermont-sur-l'Oise in 1848. Gottschalk was then only 19 years of age and an aspiring pianist who'd been sent overseas to study with European virtuosi. Already by this time Gottschalk had achieved some notoriety through his remarkable flair for the keyboard and his "savage" American origins. However, the bloody Paris Revolution of 1848 forced Gottschalk to flee, and a kindly psychiatrist, Dr. Eugene Woillez who was head of a large sanatorium located in Clermont-sur-l'Oise, offered safe haven. Woillez was a utopian idealist, and his mental institution was like a country club compared to the harsh conditions found in psychiatric facilities elsewhere. Here, Gottschalk was able to wait out the Revolution, practice, and compose in peace, and he produced a large number of works, including the first two pieces in his so-called "Louisiana Quartet," *Bamboula* and *La savane*.

Gottschalk's sister, Clara Gottschalk Peterson, left a firsthand account of the composition of *Bamboula* in her memoirs. Moreau, taken ill with the typhus then raging in Paris "was seen to wave his hands, which those around him supposed to be symptoms of the delirium. But during his convalescence he one day got up and wrote out *Bamboula*, which he said had been running in his brain during his illness." With Gottschalk's return to Parisian concert circles, *Bamboula* was unleashed upon a Paris that was fixated on all things American, and the piece was an immediate sensation throughout Europe. *Bamboula* is based on a Creole melody *"Quan' patate la cuite,"* basically meaning "barbecued potatoes," set in a highly syncopated fashion with a heavy emphasis on the downbeat. The minor melody used for contrast in the third strain is one of Gottschalk's most inspired and memorable creations.

The first performance of *Bamboula* took place at Gottschalk's debut at the Salle Pleyel in Paris on April 17, 1849. *Bamboula*'s first print appearance followed in the April 22, 1849, issue of *La France Musicale*. *Bamboula*'s African-Caribbean orientation is unmistakable, and practically unprecedented in the annals of concert music; the very name "Bamboula" is taken from a drum of African-Caribbean origin. This has led some commentators to speculate that *Bamboula* represents Gottschalk's alleged first-hand memories of the African slave dances held in Congo Square, New Orleans, in the 1830s. There is no evidence that Gottschalk ever witnessed these dances in person, and it is more likely that he picked up the tune within his own family (his mother was Creole). However, with *Bamboula*, Gottschalk helped set in motion the forces that led to the evolution of the African-American strain in nineteenth century music, resulting in ragtime beginning in the 1890s. *—Uncle Dave Lewis*

Recommended:

○ **Gottschalk: Piano Music** / Licad / 2003 / Naxos 559145

○ **Gottschalk: American Piano Music** / Rigai / 1992 / Smithsonian Folkways 40803

Le bananier, chanson nègre, Op. 5 (1846)

Le bananier, Op. 5/RO 21, was likely begun in 1848, during Louis Moreau Gottschalk's recovery from typhoid fever at a sanatorium in Clermont-sur-l'Oise run by his friend Dr. Eugene Woillez. If so, this little work wasn't yet complete when

Gottschalk returned to Paris at the start of 1849, for Gottschalk didn't begin to program it into his recitals until early December. At a Paris recital given in tandem with the violinist Max Mayer on January 11, 1850, the audience demanded an encore of *Le bananier*, and with its publication shortly thereafter, "*Bananier*-mania" broke out in Paris to the extent that it even eclipsed the popularity of *Bamboula*, Gottschalk's prior success.

Le bananier constitutes the third entry into Gottschalk's so-called "Louisiana Quartet" which began with *Bamboula* and *La savane*. It is a much simpler and shorter composition than *Bamboula*, consisting of variations on a single strain that is contrasted by a short release that is repeated twice, the second time with additional flourishes. Eventually a spray of 32nd note figures invades the texture, and this figuration develops into long runs that are both tricky to play and impressive to hear. Gottschalk's basic melody is built around minor thirds and harmonized with a drumbeat of open fifths. To American ears this immediately sounds like something based on Native American tribal music, but that may not have been Gottschalk's intention, as the work is designated "Chanson de nègre," and thus is probably based on an African-Caribbean model. Suffice it is that *Le bananier* proved exotic enough to capture the imagination of a Parisian public already preoccupied with a romantic notion of America, as fueled by the fictional novels of Chateaubriand and Gautier. *—Uncle Dave Lewis*

Recommended:

○ **Gottschalk: Piano Music** / Licad / 2003 / Naxos 8559145

○ **Gottschalk: Piano Music** / P. Martin / 1991 / Hyperion 66459

Le Banjo, esquisse américaine, Op. 15 (1854–1855)

Louis Moreau Gottschalk embarked upon a chaotic tour of the eastern United States in the spring and early summer of 1853. Exhausted, with no ground gained, Gottschalk retreated to Saratoga Springs in upstate New York. During the summer Gottschalk relaxed and undertook numerous compositions, among them the first version of *The Banjo*. After taking the piece through a major overhaul. Gottschalk submitted it for publication in 1854 as his Opus 15. First reaction to *The Banjo* was split, with the public taking to the piece immediately while Gottschalk's colleagues in the concert field felt at pains to make excuses for what they thought surely must be a momentary lapse of taste and reason on the composer's part.

Gottschalk was intimately familiar with banjo technique. In his native New Orleans, banjo playing by street musicians was a familiar sight. On one occasion, under his pseudonym "Seven Octaves," Gottschalk published a review of a concert performance by banjoist George Swaine Buckley in the *New York Morning Times*. Banjoists quickly recognized that Gottschalk's piano piece lay within the technical resources of their instrument with only minor adaptation, and incorporated it into their repertoires. Banjo instruction books of the nineteenth century sometimes credit Gottschalk for helping to establish the banjo as a "real" musical instrument.

Beginning with a variant of the main melody stated in octaves, the first strain of *The Banjo* takes the form of a long introduction made up of several periods, played in the middle range of the piano. The main melody is stated in the treble, and hardly gets off the ground before it is answered by a fiendishly tough passage in 16ths with the emphasis always on the downbeat, sometimes held there by a discreetly inserted tie. Thundering octaves take us back to the beginning of the introduction, and the whole thing is heard again. Gottschalk closes with a brilliant pair of variations on a melody strongly resembling that of Stephen Foster's *Camptown Races*. (The piece also contains echoes of the spiritual "Roll, Jordan, Roll.") In these last passages Gottschalk successfully suggests the "frailing" style of banjo playing on the keyboard.

After Gottschalk's death in 1869, the composer's original version of *The Banjo* was published as his Op. 82 under the erroneous title of *The Banjo No. 2*. In its own time, the Op. 15 version was greatly popular, but no match for Gottschalk's omnipresent masterpiece of Victorian sentiment, *The Last Hope*. One and a half centuries later, *The Last Hope* is but a faded memory from a past era, and *The Banjo* stands as Louis Moreau Gottschalk's most famous and enduring composition, in addition to a favorite encore of piano virtuosi the world around. *—Uncle Dave Lewis*

Recommended:

○ **Gottschalk: Piano Music** / Licad / 2003 / Naxos 8559145

○ **Grand Piano: Arthur Friedheim** / Friedheim (piano roll) / 1998 / Nimbus 8815

The Last Hope, meditation, Op. 16 (1854)

Gottschalk, who was quick to divine and appropriate every nativist strain—whether in France, Spain, Cuba, or the South American nations—returned to the United States early in 1854 from a triumphal Cuban tour with a clutch of new pieces, "one of them, " he notes, "of a melancholy character with which was associated a touching episode of my journey to Santiago… that seemed to me to unite the conditions requisite for popularity." *The Last Hope* came at a moment when the vein of the popular imagination was assiduously being worked by ballads depicting languishing, doomed, expiring maidens, thus fulfilling Edgar Allan Poe's requirement for the most poetic of all subjects. Surprisingly, given the stunning popularity that soon overtook the piece, its first publishers, Firth Pond & Co. in New York, moved but a few copies and *The Last Hope* did not embark upon its half century of phenomenal popularity until 1855, when the rights were transferred to William Hall & Son, who issued a revised version. In 1856, Gottschalk wrote to his friend Gustave Chouquet in Paris of the origin of *The Last Hope*, which Chouquet shared with the readers of *La France musicale* and which soon came to be appended to copies of the sheet music. "During his stay at Cuba, Gottschalk found himself at S-, where a woman of mind and heart… conceived for him at once the most active sympathy.… Struck down by an incurable malady, Madame S-… could alone find forgetfulness… while listening to her dear pianist.… One evening, while suffering more than usual-'In pity,' said she… 'in pity, my dear Moreau, one little melody, the last hope!' And Gottschalk commenced to improvise an air at once plaintive and pleasing.… " *The Last Hope* was the first of many similar effusions—including *The Dying Poet, O Loving Heart, Trust On, Morte!!* —described by Gottschalk's cataloguer, critic Robert Offergeld, with deadly accuracy as "le style pianola," "sad titles, *vox angelica* melodies, pathetic barbershop harmony, and lots of runs on cue." After an elaborately cloying introduction, *The Last Hope*'s lilting 3/4 melody spins out amid garlands of arabesque and filigree in a tune whose celestial aspirations, wedded several times to Victorian pieties (*Softly Now the Light of Day, Holy Spirit, Truth Divine, Father of Eternal Grace*) earned it a place in countless Protestant hymnals. *The Last Hope* became an obligatory staple of Gottschalk's recitals and its demand dogged his steps throughout the remainder of his career. *—Adrian Corleonis*

Recommended:

○ **Gottschalk: Piano Music—3** / P. Martin / 1997 / Hyperion 66915

○ **Great American Piano I: Gottschalk** / Pennario / 1992 / Angel 64667

O Ma Charmante, épargnez-moi!, caprice, Op. 44 (1861)

O Ma Charmante, Epargnez-Moi! (Oh, my charmer, spare me) in many ways captures the essence of the musical personality of its creator, Louis Moreau Gottschalk, the first American to make an international reputation as a virtuoso concert pianist and composer of piano music. His works soaked up the often exotic manner of the Creole music from his native Louisiana. By the time he had written this piece Gottschalk had already drawn considerable attention with the popular-styled, enormously successful pair, *Last Hope* and *Tournament Galop*, both from 1854.

O Ma Charmante opens with a lovely serene melody whose character is both forlorn and serene. The theme soon turns somewhat exotic, taking on an almost salon-like character in its mixture of the sweetly nocturnal and the sonically glossy. There later appears a dreamy childlike variant, charming in its seeming innocence, cute in its deftly conceived upper-register sonorities. Lasting about three minutes, this richly tuneful piece will appeal to those with an interest both in American keyboard and folk music. *—Robert Cummings*

Recommended:

○ **Cuba Piano** / Moura Castro / 1997 / Ensayo 9722

○ **Gottschalk: 40 Works for Piano** / Mandel / 1995 / Vox 3033

Pasquinade, caprice, Op. 59 (1869)

Gottschalk wrote his *Pasquinade* (literally "lampoon"), one of his final works, in Rio de Janeiro in 1869. Published initially in that city, the work was first circulated in the United States shortly after Gottschalk's death. Written when such "salon pieces" enjoyed especial currency, *Pasquinade* was enormously popular, especially in the composer's hometown of New Orleans.

Pasquinade is a short, alluring, highly syncopated dance. An introduction consisting of a repeated tattoo, answered by thundering octaves in the bass, is followed by a statement of the main theme. The second strain boldly anticipates ragtime, with its repeated use of a sixteenth-eighth-sixteenth rhythm over a high-stepping, march-like accompaniment. At the end of the second recapitulation of the theme, a twittering figure appears in the top octave of the piano and continues as the main theme is repeated, posing a particular challenge to the pianist. After a brief, colorful minor-key episode, florid passagework brings the work to its close.

Pasquinade was still quite popular at the turn of the century, and was particularly beloved of Sousa's band, which recorded it for Victor in 1901. (In this arrangement, the "twittering" role is assumed by the piccolo.) *—Uncle Dave Lewis*

Recommended:

○ **Gottschalk: Piano Music** / Licad / 2003 / Naxos 8559145

○ **A Gottschalk Festival** / List / 1990 / Vox Box 5009

Souvenir de Porto Rico, marche des gibaros, Op. 31 (1857)

Souvenir de Porto Rico, marche des gibaros, Op. 31, was written at a sugar plantation located outside the village of Barceloneta, Puerto Rico, in the fall of 1857. Pianist Louis Moreau Gottschalk, singer Adelina Patti, and Patti's father were taking a vacation from their concert schedule. While the Pattis would return to their touring life after about a month, Gottschalk remianed in the Caribbean for nearly five years, absorbing the music around him and composing practically nonstop.

The "Gibaros" in the title were farmers who tilled the land in the interior of Puerto Rico. In this work, strolling musicians are heard marching as if from the distance; as they approach, the main tune is sounded in the middle register of the piano. It is a traditional Puerto Rican song, *"Si me dan pasteles, dénmelos calientes"* (If You Give Me Cakes, Give Me Hot Ones"), that is heard in the streets around Christmastime. This is juxtaposed with a simple progression that gets more elaborate as the two strains are put through a series of eight variations. Midway through the sixth variation, Gottschalk breaks into a modulation to a new key, syncopating this section in a manner that strongly suggests the swinging rhythm of ragtime or tango music. At the time Gottschalk lived in Puerto Rico, 37 percent of the island's population was made up of Afro-Caribbean slaves. Though many of his works incorporate African American rhythms, *Souvenir de Porto Rico* is as close as Gottschalk came to something that sounds like jazz. After the climax is reached, Gottschalk lowers the music back down to where it started, and the Gibaros march away into the distance.

Gottschalk left behind his impressions of the surroundings that produced *Souvenir de Porto Rico* in his own words: "[I was] perched upon the edge of a crater, [and] my cabin overlooked the whole country. Every evening I moved my piano out upon the terrace, and played for myself alone, everything that the scene opened up before me inspired. It was there that I composed '*Marche des Gibaros*.'" *—Uncle Dave Lewis*

Recommended:

- ○ **Gottschalk: Piano Music** / Licad / 2003 / Naxos 8559145
- ○ **Masters of the Keyboard** / Ivan Davis / 1993 / DG B000193202

SYMPHONIC

Symphony No. 1 ("La nuit des tropiques") (1858–1859)

Gottschalk wrote his first symphony—less a symphony, actually, than two linked tone poems—during a multi-year tour of the Caribbean. The circumstances of its composition are unclear, but it seems that Gottschalk did the bulk of the work in Cuba, Martinique, and Guadalupe. The first movement was probably composed in 1858, with the title *Nuit dans les tropiques*, and was premiered in Havana in 1860 during one of Gottschalk's "monster concerts." The second movement was apparently written in 1859, first appearing under the title *Une Fête sous les tropiques*. The whole thing is scored for 150 players, including a huge primary orchestra, a full band, and extra percussion that includes bamboulas and other tropical drums. Not surprisingly, after Gottschalk's death there were no subsequent performances of the impractically scored *Night in the Tropics* for decades. The manuscript or an excellent copy of the score remained in Havana, but was stolen in 1932; somehow, the manuscript did find its way to the New York Public Library by the 1950s. The symphony was first heard in the United States in 1948 in a two-piano arrangement by John Kirkpatrick, based on work by Nicolás Ruiz y Espadero. The first complete American performance of the orchestral version was in 1955, using Howard Shanet's arrangement for reduced forces. Eventually, Igor Buketoff prepared an edition employing Gottschalk's original orchestration. All three versions have been recorded and some other variants also exist. The first movement is a broad, lyrical Andante free of any American touches. It takes its general inspiration from the *Symphonie fantastique* of Berlioz, Gottschalk's mentor, as well as the works of Wagner. Strings dominate the first several minutes of the movement, building a very gradual crescendo and then drawing the woodwinds and brass into a supporting role in a more agitated section. After a sustained, dramatic episode, the movement winds down into the opening string material. The thematic model, and to some degree a structural one as well, is clearly Wagner's *Tannhäuser* overture. Gottschalk cuts loose in the second movement Allegro moderato. Deploying the full percussion section and now making more prominent use of the winds and brass, the movement sways and bumps to the Cuban rumba rhythm, which was unknown in the U.S. during Gottschalk's lifetime; this may be that dance's first orchestral setting. Gottschalk insinuates a little fugue near the climax to provide his symphony some academic solidity, but the splashy music never skips a Latin beat. *—James Reel*

Recommended:

- ○ **Gottschalk: A Night in the Tropics** / R. Rosenberg (cond.), Hot Springs Music Festival / 2000 / Naxos 559036
- ○ **A Gottschalk Festival** / S. Adler (cond.), Berlin SO / 1990 / Vox 5009

Glenn Gould

b. Sep. 25, 1932, Toronto, Ontario, **d.** Oct. 4, 1982, Toronto, Ontario
Pianist

The defining moment of Glenn Gould's career came in 1964 when, at the age of 31, he withdrew from all public performance. The move was viewed by audiences and critics as willful and bewildering, and was seen as evidence that despite his demonstrably supreme artistry he was, in the argot of the common man, a nut.

But, as George Szell once said of him, "That nut [was] a genius." In his short international career, which spanned only 24 years, Glenn Gould changed the way the music world thought about performance practice, recording, and the music of Johann Sebastian Bach.

Glenn Gould was born to comfortable middle-class parents in Toronto in 1932. A pampered only child, Gould demonstrated his remarkable talents quite early and in 1943 entered the Toronto Conservatory of Music, where he quickly came to the attention of its director, Sir Ernest MacMillan. On MacMillan's recommendation, Gould was taken on as a student by the Chilean-born pedagogue Alberto Guerrero, whose own style was partly the basis for Gould's own sensitive touch. Gould once described Guerrero's keyboard technique as not so much striking the keys as "pulling them down." The other influence on Gould's technique was his experience playing the organ, wherein the tracker action is particularly responsive to variations in finger pressure.

Gould made his debut at the age of 16, playing Beethoven's fourth piano concerto in Toronto. He followed this triumph with tours across Canada and frequent broadcast performances over the CBC, introducing him to the studio enviroment which would remain a focus of his life thereafter. Gould leaped into international acclaim, in fact, through a studio production: his now-legendary 1955 Columbia Masterworks recording of Bach's *Goldberg Variations*. This recording, which has never been out of print in the 50 years since its first release, established Gould as a performer who combined penetrating insight (his *Goldberg Variations* was nothing short of a complete rethinking of the piece) and artistic daring with daunting technical prowess.

Gould's immediate fame brought international demand, and he responded with worldwide concert appearances; he met these with considerable reluctance, however, and quickly gained a reputation for last-minute cancellations. His dislike of performing in public, of being "looked at" by audiences, allowed a natural tendency of hypochondria to blossom (it was a convenient cancellation excuse), and he soon became the habitue of specialists ranging from chiropractors to psychiatrists. Long before quitting the stage forever, Gould had made frequent threats to do so, so that his 1964 decision was no surprise to those who knew him.

Following his withdrawal, Gould threw himself into a frenzy of recording, writing, and radio documentary production. His method of splicing together single performances from dozens of takes was initially viewed as something of an artistic fraud, though the technique was eventually adopted, in less exhaustive form, by the recording industry in subsequent years. His radio documentaries were less successful: a trilogy about life in Canada's northern territories combined multiple interviews in contrapuntal ways, an interesting idea that nevertheless rendered the sense of what was being said more or less unintelligible.

Though plagued by many imaginary maladies, Gould suffered from a very real hypertension that eventually led to a massive stroke, which he suffered in 1982, and from which he never recovered. He died in Toronto General Hospital, one week after being stricken, on October 4, 1982, at age 50. *—Mark Satola*

Recommended:

- ○ **Liszt: Piano Transcription of Beethoven's Symphony 6** / Gould / 1992 / Sony 52637
- ○ **Bach: Italian Concerto; Partitas 1 & 2** / Gould / 1999 / Sony 6141
- ○ **Glenn Gould: Solitude Trilogy** / Gould, etc. / 1992 / CBC 2003-3
- ○ **Images** / Stokowski (cond.), Gould, American SO / 1995 / Sony 62588
- ○ **Gould Conducts & Plays Wagner** / Gould (cond.), Members of the Toronto SO / 1994 / Sony 52650
- ○ **Bach: The Goldberg Variations** / Gould / 2003 / Sony 90387
- ○ **Schoenberg: Piano Works** / Craft (cond.), Gould, Armin, Shulmann, Bloemendal, Juilliard SQ, CBCSO / 1994 / Sony 52664

Morton Gould

b. Dec. 10, 1913, Richmond Hill, NY, **d.** Feb. 21, 1996, Orlando, FL
Composer: Orchestral, Ballet

Morton Gould was an important American composer, generally overshadowed by Copland, Barber, and Bernstein. Like Bernstein, he wrote in both popular and classical styles and often mixed the two. Many record collectors around the middle of the twentieth century knew him primarily as a conductor of popular music, as well as of newer works in the realm of serious music. His "classical" style in composition generally offered few challenges to listeners and often featured well-known themes of a patriotic or folk origin, or were based on melodies from American composers out of the past. *Foster Gallery* (1939) and *American Ballads* (1976) fall into this realm.

Gould was born in Richmond Hill, Long Island, New York. He was a musical prodigy of a rare order, playing the piano and composing by age four. His parents were strongly supportive of their young son and helped to get his first work, a waltz entitled *Just Six*, both performed and published when he was still only six years old.

By age eight, he was performing regularly on radio broadcasts. Later, he studied at the Institute of Musical Arts in New York and in New York University, where he was instructed in composition by Vincent Jones. He also studied piano with Abby Whiteside. In his late teens, Gould played piano in vaudeville and radio in various freelancing assignments, but also held positions with Radio City Music Hall and NBC. At age 21, (1934) he landed a conducting post with WOR Radio, regularly leading an orchestra in popular music fare. He recorded for RCA beginning in the 1930s and made piano rolls for Ampico.

One of Gould's first successes in composition was his *Chorale and Fugue in Jazz* (1935), which received a prestigious premiere on January 2, 1936, with Leopold Stokowski leading the Philadelphia Orchestra. Gould was beginning to turn out many significant compositions now: his *Piano Concerto* came in 1937 and his *Violin Concerto* in 1938. The following year, he wrote the aforementioned work based on popular Stephen Foster themes, *Foster Gallery*, which was subsequently recorded by Arthur Fiedler and The Boston Pops Orchestra.

Gould became music director of the popular radio programs "The Chrysler Hour" and "Cresta Blanca Carnival" in the 1940s. He composed three symphonies (of four) in that decade, as well as a spate of other works, including his *Viola Concerto* (1943) and *Fall River Legend* (1947).

Gould also wrote for Broadway, turning out *Billion Dollar Baby* in 1945 and *Arms and the Girl* in 1950. In 1944, he appeared in the film *Delightfully Dangerous*, for which he wrote the score. His career scoring films continued with other efforts including *Cinerama Holiday* (1955) and *Windjammer* (1958). He also composed numerous scores for television shows in the 1960s and 1970s. His last important effort here was for the mini-series *Holocaust* (1978), which starred Meryl Streep. In 1966, Gould received a Grammy award for his recording with the Chicago Symphony Orchestra of the Ives' *First Symphony*.

Gould continued to write concert music, as well, though one might assert that the film world may ultimately have sabotaged his chances somewhat to attain a higher level of art. Still, his *Symphony of Spirituals* and *American Ballads*, both premiered in 1976, demonstrated his undiminished talent. From 1986 until 1994 he served as president of the American Society of Composers, Authors and Publishers (ASCAP). In 1995, Gould received a Pulitzer Prize for his composition *Stringmusic*. *—Robert Cummings*

Overview of Works (1933–1996)

American composer Morton Gould was one of the most prolific, most accomplished, and above all, most American composers in the history of American music. In his long career, Gould effectively wrote in every genre from musicals, *Billion Dollar Baby* (1945); to ballet, *Fall River Legend* (1947); to the television mini-series, *Holocaust* (1976); to symphonic music, *Stringmusic* (1995); and his music incorporated elements of nearly every American musical style from high classical to country & western and even rap. A brilliant orchestrator, Gould's music is also distinguished by its sparkling rhythms and its highly polished surface. A serious classical composer with numerous commissions and prizes to his credit, Gould was also actively involved in popular culture, serving as the staff pianist at the newly opened Radio City Music Hall and a musical advisor for both the NBC and CBS television networks. Among his best-known works are the ballet *Fall River Legend* based on the story of Lizzie Borden, *American Salute* for orchestra, the *West Point Symphony* for band, and *Symphony of Spirituals* for orchestra, composed for the American bicentennial. *—James Leonard*

Recommended:

- ○ **Gould: American Ballads; Foster Gallery; American Salute** / Kuchar (cond.), National SO of Ukraine / 2000 / Naxos 559005
- ○ **Gould: Show Piece; Piano Concerto; String Music** / Miller (cond.), Hodgkinson, Albany SO / 1998 / Albany 300
- ○ **Billion Dollar Baby** / Lavine, Bassi, Green, McCormick, Scott, Chenoweth, Gravitte, Aibel, Cast Ens., Darrah, Kudisch, Nicholaw, Pistone, Rhiann, Roberts, Shaich, Shull / 2000 / Original Cast 4304

ORCHESTRAL

American Salute (1942)

Musical artillery written literally overnight for a patriotic World War II radio broadcast, Morton Gould's *American Salute* is a short set of variations on the Civil War song "When Johnny Comes Marching Home." A sputtering, machine-gun fanfare subsides into a quiet woodwind statement of the theme over a staccato accompaniment that evokes Morse code. The theme is restated with different timbres more than varied, always with that quick, ostinato rhythm, until the brass section breaks out with its own bombastic, syncopated treatment halfway through. The frenzy subsides into a *Taps*-like approach, with the woodwinds and strings then interjecting a bit of humor before the full orchestra revs up with an energetic statement leading to a rapid-fire finale. The work was premiered in 1943 on the radio show, "Cresta Blanca Carnival," with Gould conducting. Gould himself did not consider this piece to be anything special. Late in his life, the composer stated that "it was just a setting. I was doing a million of those things." The composition has endeared itself to many, though, due to Gould's creativity in producing an inspiring orchestral work from a folk melody. *—James Reel*

Recommended:

- ○ **American Masterpieces** / Ormandy (cond.), Philadelphia Orch. / 1997 / Sony 63034

Pavane (1935)

One of Morton Gould's greatest hits, the *Pavane*, is often played and recorded on its own. But it's actually the middle movement of his *American Symphonette No. 2*, a populist, jazzy suite written for radio performance. As conceived in sixteenth century Italy, a pavane is a slow, processional dance, usually in 4/2 or 4/4. Gould's treatment of the form is more of a saucy saunter with a swing of the hips. From the beginning, Gould hoped this would catch on as a pops piece, and initially spelled the title with a double N, discouraging musically inexperienced, monolingual Americans from rhyming the word with "vein."

An allegretto lasting no more than three and a half minutes, this *Pavane* manages to pack in an abundance of tunes over a subtle boogie-woogie ostinato. The arch-like thematic structure, ABACDCABA, opens with a soft, jaunty, syncopated melody for muted trumpet, followed by a somewhat questioning second subject and a repeat of the first tune. The C section includes a fragmentary flute melody that could be an homage to Fauré's even more famous *Pavane*. The strings take over with a rhythmic figure derived from the initial tune, while the woodwinds and then brass intone a short melody of long-held notes that bleeds into the flute motif. The piece then proceeds to its conclusion, mirroring the material that has come before.

Fragments of the Pavane were later worked into such straight-ahead jazz pieces as John Coltrane's "Impressions," Dizzy Gillespie's "Bebop" and "April B," and David Baker's "Wes Montgomery in Memoriam." *—James Reel*

Recommended:

- ○ **Charmaine** / Mantovani (cond.), Mantovani & His Orch. / 2004 / Living Era 5500

BALLET

Fall River Legend (1947)

Lizzie Borden took an ax, according to the children's rhyme, and whacked her father and mother in August 1892. The sensational trial of the sedate "Miss Lizzie," age 33, drew attention far beyond the town limits of Fall River, MA. Despite heavy evidence against her, Borden was acquitted. In 1948, choreographer Agnes de Mille and composer Morton Gould collaborated on a balletic treatment of the tale, assuming Borden's guilt, probing her psychological motivations, and ending with her conviction and hanging.

The full ballet includes about 45 to 50 minutes of music and includes a few spoken lines; it consists of a prologue, seven scenes, and an epilogue. Gould took his inspiration from New England hymns and dance tunes, but each of his themes is original. The music is strongly if irregularly rhythmic and just dissonant enough to convey village exuberance and a troubled psyche. The opening orchestral shriek of anguish is as discordant as the score ever gets, though.

In 1952, Gould drew a suite of six pieces from the ballet, which strips out the pantomime and other purely dramatic sequences and presents only the pieces that can comfortably stand alone. It fuses the full ballet's two initial sections, Prologue and Waltzes, excising the short "Indictment" passage read by an actor. After the grim, forceful Prologue, the Waltzes seem almost frantic; here Borden, known as The Accused, is remembering not entirely happy scenes from her childhood. Both the ballet and suite continue with Elegy, gentle music led primarily by woodwinds, with the strings taking over for a wistful waltz passage. The next 15 minutes of music with little independent interest—Interlude, Dirge, Lullaby, Serenade, and "Axe"—are omitted from the suite, which picks up with "Church Social," where a syncopated brass tune evolves into a gruff, repetitive treatment of a melodic fragment that could come from some old hymn. Most of this music is loud, outgoing, and roughly festive. "Hymnal Variations" are gentle elaborations on a brief, meandering chorale tune of Gould's own invention. "Cotillion" is a boisterous piece exploiting the full orchestra, with whooping horns and jittering, repetitive thematic kernels reminiscent of barn-dance music. The suite omits another chunk of pantomime-supporting sequences—"Cotillion Coda," "Death Dance," "Mob Scene"—and goes directly to the Epilogue, a funereal dirge with the strings playing a jagged figure over a lurching rhythm, with the Prologue's woodwind shrieks and brass snarls returning to bring the score full circle. *—James Reel*

Recommended:

- ○ **Composers Conduct** / Morton Gould & His Orchestra / RCA 61505

Charles Gounod

b. Jun. 18, 1818, Paris, France, **d.** Oct. 18, 1893, St. Cloud, France

Composer: Opera, Vocal, Choral, Keyboard

Composer Charles Gounod, responsible for some of classical music's true evergreens, began his musical studies early in life under his mother, a fine pianist. He entered the Paris Conservatoire, where he studied with Halévy in the hopes of becoming a composer. In 1837 he met with his first successes in that field, winning the second place Prix de Rome for his composition *Marie Stuart et Rizzio*. In 1839 he won the Prix de Rome with his cantata *Fernand*, and went to study in Italy. His early years were influenced by the music of Palestrina and the old masters as well as the music of Schumann and Berlioz. When he returned to Paris after this sojourn he acquired a position as an organist at the Mission Etrangères. He studied theology and developed an interest in literature and reading. It was expected that eventually he would take orders and become a cleric. He continued to compose, but during this time his compositions were primarily liturgical.

Gounod's first opera was premiered in 1851. It was not a success due to its lack of dramatic qualities. He took a conducting position and began to teach, and continued to compose choral works and masses. Two more operas were failures before Gounod finally composed one that was popular with the public. Perhaps the subject matter inspired the latent dramatist in him, for it was a setting of the story of *Faust,* the story of an intellectual seduced by the devil, but redeemed by love. Produced at the Théâtre Lyrique in 1859, it was an instant success with the French public and has remained in the repertory of opera houses all over the globe. None of Gounod's other operas was as successful, although portions have remained popular and are given in concert form. His *Romeo et Juliette* of 1867 contains much fine music, particularly the song of Queen Mab, the duets, the page's song, and the duel scene of Act Three. By the end of his life, Gounod had again become very religious, turning into something of a mystic. He composed primarily religious music, music that reflected the influence of Jules Massenet and Georges Bizet. *—Rita Laurance*

OPERA

Faust (1856–1859; revised 1868)

The first French translations of Goethe's *Faust*—a literary staple for Romantics everywhere—appeared in 1823, but, as even Goethe noted, they were surpassed in quality by Gérard de Nerval's 1827 translation. After these early translations, French art saw a profusion of popular plays, musical works, and paintings based on the story. Gounod's operatic treatment, *Faust,* which premièred on March 19, 1859, at Paris' Théâtre-Lyrique to great acclaim, is one of a number of musical treatments of the theme by French musicians; these include Louise Bertin's opera *Fausto* (1831) and Hector Berlioz's "dramatic legend" *La Damnation de Faust* (1846).

Jules Barbier constructed the libretto for Gounod's *Faust* from excerpts which he lifted, with the author's permission, from Michel Carré's play *Faust et Marguerite* (1850). Carré gave Barbier carte blanche to borrow from his play; he himself was busy writing the libretto for Meyerbeer's *Le Padron de Ploërmel* (Dinorah), and had no interest in adapting the play for operatic treatment.

The rehearsal process leading up to the premiere was difficult; Gounod made substantial cuts to his score and replaced the leading tenor, who was found to be inadequate, during the dress rehearsal. This original version contained spoken dialogue rather than recitative; in 1860 Gounod supplied music for these sections, thereby making the opera viable for performance in opera houses outside of France. The work indeed enjoyed considerable popularity internationally. It benefited especially from the circumstances of its London premiere, for which Gounod composed the now-famous aria "Avant de quitter ces lieux." The role of Marguerite's brother, Valentin, originally contained no aria, but the composer was persuaded to add it on the merits of the talented baritone, Charles Santley; this aria is now among the most popular excerpts from the score. For *Faust's* premiere at the Paris Opéra in 1869, Gounod composed a complete ballet to be placed near the beginning of Act Five; it was arguably this production, the work's most lavish yet, that propelled *Faust* to its position of unchallenged popularity in France—a position it maintained for the better part of a century.

The music of Gounod's *Faust* shows at every turn its membership in the lineage of French grand opera; numbers of strongly defined form, bel canto lyricism, and expressive orchestration all mark the score. Many major scenes are beautifully set by distinctive orchestral textures. The apparition of Marguerite at her spinning wheel in Act One, Scene Two is introduced by hushed strings and woodwinds and sparkling notes in the harp; the first violins illustrate the perpetual motion of Maguerite's spinning wheel with a magical filigree of 32nd notes, foreshadowing her spinning song ("Il ne revient pas") in Act Four. A chorale of trumpet and trombones announces the entrance of the pious Valentin in Act Two, Scene Two; his first aria ("Avant de quitter ces lieux") follows, in orthodox ternary (ABA) form. Rondo form is implied in the structure of Act Two, Scene Five, in which the recurring waltz music of a ball alternates with contrasting episodes of individual expression. *Faust's* Act Three cavatina ("Salut! demeure chaste et pure") is a classic example of a traditional grand opera ternary-form cavatina. Perhaps the best-known number of the opera is Marguerite's brooding Act Four, Scene Six chanson ("Il était un roi de Thulé"), a modified take on the strophic couplet common in grand opera. Also of note is Méfistoféle's crass and saccharine serenade, "Vous qui fete l'endormie," which he sings to the sleeping Marguerite; his complete disregard for her human worth makes for a dramatic foil to her piety and eventual redemption. The addition of the solo organ in Act Four, Scene Three, is another striking orchestral feature.

As shown with moderate accuracy in the film *The Age of Innocence,* Faust long seemed the inevitable opening-night presentation of the Metropolitan Opera House in New York. *—Jennifer Hambrick*

Synopsis:

Act One. In Faust's study, in sixteenth century Germany, he gloomily reflects that his lifetime of study has brought him no wisdom ("Rien! En vain j'interroge"). He prepares to poison himself, but when he hears songs in praise of God he is angry that God has done nothing for him. He invokes the devil, who promptly appears, offers to grant him his wishes, and suggests riches, glory, or power. Faust instead wants youth ("A moi les plaisirs"). Mephistopheles agrees, saying he will serve Faust on earth if Faust will serve him in Hell afterwards. Faust hesitates, but at a vision of Marguerite, Faust agrees. Mephistopheles turns the poison into an elixir of youth, and they leave, reprising Faust's paean to youth.

Act Two. In the square, villagers are drinking and celebrating ("Vin ou bière"). Valentin contemplates the sacred medal Marguerite has given him for protection in war, and he entrusts her to Siebel and prays for her safety ("Avant de quitter ces lieux"). Wagner, another solider, starts to sing a raucous song, but Mephistopheles interrupts with a cynical song about the Golden Calf, which humanity still worships ("Le veau d'or est toujours début"). He then tells fortunes, predicting for Wagner he will die in war, for Siebel that any flower he picks for Marguerite will wither, and for Valentin that he will soon be killed. He then commands the inn's statue of Bacchus to produce a better drink and toasts Marguerite. The men are suspicious, and Mephistopheles draws a protective circle around himself; it shatters Valentin's sword when he attacks. However, they drive the devil back by holding their hilts in the form of a cross ("De l'enfer qui vient"). They leave, and Faust, entering, demands Marguerite. Mephistopheles reassures him. The chorus returns, dancing ("Ainsi que la brise"), and Marguerite appears. Mephistopheles obstructs Siebel, and Faust asks to escort her. She refuses and leaves, but Faust ecstatically declares his love as the dancing resumes.

Act Three. In her garden, Siebel tries to pick a bouquet for Marguerite ("Faites-lui mes aveux"), but until he dips his hand in holy water, the flowers wither. Faust and Mephistopheles enter, and Mephistopheles leaves to fetch jewels to entice Marguerite. Faust rhapsodizes on the purity of her home ("Quel trouble... Salut, demeure chaste et pure"). When Mephistopheles returns, Faust is briefly troubled by scruples, which Mephistopheles quickly overcomes. Marguerite enters, remembering the handsome stranger she has seen before, and as she spins, she sings a ballad about a king who was faithful to his queen's memory ("Il était un roi en Thule"). She finds and tries on the jewels, exclaiming in delight at seeing herself in a mirror ("Ah! Je ris de me voir si belle"). Marthe enters, and Mephistopheles and Faust follow a moment later. Mephistopheles flirtatiously leads Marthe off. Faust and Marguerite begin to talk; Marguerite tells him of her simple life and the loss of her baby sister. Mephistopheles returns to watch and to hide from Marthe. Marguerite is half-afraid of Faust and her new-growing love ("Il se fait tard"), but he courts her still more ardently before leaving. Mephistopheles tells him to wait and listen, and when Marguerite, thinking herself alone, murmurs of her love, he rushes into her arms.

Act Four. Months later, in her room, Marguerite laments her deserted state and hears others mocking her from outside ("Elles se cachaient... Il ne revient pas"). Siebel comes to assure her of his absolute devotion ("Si le bonheur"), and she goes to church to pray for her child and her lover. There she kneels, but Mephistopheles ("Non, tu ne prieras pas") tells her she is damned. As she hears the chorus singing of the Day of Judgment, she frantically prays for mercy and collapses. In the square, the soldiers return, singing of glory ("Gloire immortelle de nos aieux"). Valentin affectionately greets Siebel, asking about Marguerite. Siebel can only stammer, and Valentin rushes inside. Faust and Mephistopheles return, Faust troubled by his conscience, but Mephistopheles sings a taunting serenade ("Vous qui faites l'endormie"). Valentin emerges, demanding satisfaction for his dishonor ("Que voulez-vous"). Faust is stricken at the thought of killing but is driven to fight, and Mephistopheles protects him once Valentin angrily throws away the sacred medal. Valentin is mortally wounded, and when the villagers, Marguerite, and Siebel rush in, he curses Marguerite despite Siebel's pleas ("Ecoute-moi bien, Marguerite").

Act Five. The fifth act is often cut. On Walpurgis Night, will-o-the-wisps sing ("Dans les bruyeres") and Mephistopheles leads Faust in. He transforms the scene into a glittering palace adorned with the great beauties and courtesans of history ("Jusq'aux premiers feux du matin"), and Faust, tiring of remorse, welcomes drunkenness and pleasure ("Doux nectar dans ton ivresse"). But he is sobered by a vision of Marguerite with a bloody ring around her neck, and the palace disappears. Faust demands to be taken to her.

Act Six. The last act takes place inside the prison where Marguerite, now insane, is awaiting execution for the murder of her child. Mephistopheles gives Faust the keys to her cell and leaves to ready the horses for their escape. Faust is overwhelmed at the consequences ("Mon coeur est pénétré d'épouvante"). She recognizes him ("Oui, c'est toi, je t'aime"), but her mind wanders back to their first meeting and to the garden where they met. Mephistopheles bursts in, telling them to hurry or they will be lost ("Alerte, alerte, ou vous êtes perdus"), but in the final trio, "Anges purs, anges radieux," she prays to the angels to protect her as Faust urges her to come and Mephistopheles warns him against wasting any more time. She exclaims that Faust's hand is bloody and cries out that he horrifies her. As she falls dead, Mephistopheles declares she is judged, but an angel chorus exclaims that she is saved and lifts her soul to heaven, singing of Christ's resurrection ("Christ est ressuscité"). In some stagings, Mephistopheles drags Faust to hell; in others, Faust kneels in prayer. *—Ann Feeney*

Recommended:

- **Gounod: Faust** / Pretre (cond.), Freni, Domingo, Ghiaurov, Allen / 1986 / EMI 47493
- **Gounod: Faust** / Bonynge (cond.), Sutherland, Corelli, Ghiaurov / 2002 / Decca 470563

Roméo et Juliette (1865–1871; revised 1888)

Charles Gounod had composed eight operas before completing *Roméo et Juliette* in 1867. Eight years had passed since Gounod's *Faust* propelled him to fame as an opera composer, and in between that work and *Roméo et Juliette* stood four dramatic works whose merits had not been consistently acclaimed. *Roméo et Juliette* premièred at Paris' Théâtre-Lyrique in 1867, and was first performed at the Opéra in 1888. Although it stands in second place to *Faust*, *Roméo et Juliette* remains one of Gounod's best-loved creations.

Jules Barbier and Michel Carré followed Shakespeare's tragedy closely, but with some alterations, in crafting their libretto for Gounod's *Roméo et Juliette*. Earlier in the century, Paris had experienced "Shakespearomanie" as French Romantics were overwhelmed by the transcendent drama of the playwright's works. Gounod's *Roméo et Juliette* comes relatively late in a line of operatic treatments of the subject, about many of which Hector Berlioz wrote less than flatteringly in his 1859 essay on Vincenzo Bellini's *I Capuleti e i Montecchi* (1830).

Indeed, some of Gounod's music recalls that of Berlioz's *Roméo et Juliette* symphony. Gounod begins his opera's overture with a theme stated three times by the trombones, followed by a fugato passage in the strings, essentially reversing the string fugato passage and low brass oration of the Introduction of the Berlioz work. The crystalline orchestration of Mercutio's *Ballade de la Reine Mab* in Gounod's *Roméo et Juliette* owes a debt to Berlioz's purely instrumental *Queen Mab Scherzo*, in which high woodwinds and buoyant violins musically characterize the mischievous dream fairy, and in which orchestration, as Beth Shamgar noted in 1988, plays a central role in articulating the narrative of Shakespeare's Queen Mab speech. Gounod's treatment of the tomb scene recalls Berlioz's purely instrumental version of it in his symphony. Sputtering fortissimo chords in the trombones—later scored for trombones, horns, woodwinds, and strings—convey Romeo's convulsions as the poison he drinks, believing Juliet to be dead, takes effect. Berlioz had conceived a similar, although more rhythmically charged, musical treatment of this aspect of the tomb scene. Quite apart from Berlioz's influence, Gounod's *Roméo et Juliette* opera contains the standard features of French opera, including arias in traditional formal arrangements, virtuosic solo vocal writing, large choral finales derived from smaller ensemble pieces, and instances of diagetic music. Juliette's Act One ariette (*Ah! Je veux vivre dans ce rêve qui m'enivre*) is a tuneful rondo-form waltz (a generic to the music of the Capulets' party that constitutes the basis of this scene) showcasing coloratura moments in a lyrical context. At the end of Act Three, a chorus of townspeople unites with the principal soloists in a grand finale. The solo organ music in Act Four functions simultaneously as diagetic music for the choir's procession to the wedding planned for Juliette and Paris and as an introduction to Capulet's aria *Ma fille cede aux vœux du fiancé*, which it continues to accompany. *—Jennifer Hambrick*

Synopsis:

Act One. After a prelude recounting the tragic consequences of the enmity between the Montagues and Capulets ("Verone vit jadis"), the opera opens at the Capulets' splendid masked ball. Capulet leads Juliette in and presents her to the crowd. She sings of her excitement ("Ecoutez! Ecoutez!"), and he heartily urges all to enjoy themselves ("Allons! jeunes gens"). Mercutio and Romeo enter with their friends, but Romeo is anxious and wants to leave without causing any trouble. When he says he had a dream, Mercutio teases him with the Ballad of Queen Mab ("Mab, la reine des mensonges"), who brings dreams. However, when Romeo catches a glimpse of Juliette, he is instantly smitten, and his friends laugh that he has obviously forgotten Rosaline, the woman with whom he had been infatuated. Juliette and her nurse enter, and Juliette, in a waltz song ("Je veux vivre"), says she doesn't want to marry yet, but rather to enjoy her youth while she can. When the nurse leaves, summoned by Gregorio, Romeo immediately courts a pleased but coy Juliette ("Ange adorable") in their two-voice madrigal. However, when Tybalt enters, Juliette says she is the daughter of Capulet, much to Romeo's dismay. Though Romeo has immediately remasked, Tybalt recognizes his voice as he leaves. He is all for pursuing and killing Romeo, even as Juliet exclaims in horror that she loves her enemy. Capulet, however, insists that the party continue without incident and restrains him.

Act Two. In Juliette's garden, mocked by his friends, Romeo climbs the wall to enter. Alone, he sings the rhapsodic "L'amour... ah, lève-toi soleil" and then overhears her speaking to herself of her love for him. They join in an ardent duet but are briefly interrupted by Gregorio and servants, who stop to tease Gertrude that he has doubtless come to court her. In their subsequent duet, "O nuit divine," Juliette asks whether he means to marry her; if his feelings are only trifling, then she wishes he would leave her to her sorrow. He kneels at her feet, declaring that she rules him completely. Gertrude calls from offstage, and Romeo and Juliet tenderly bid one another farewell.

Act Three. In Friar Laurent's cell, Romeo asks the monk to officiate at his marriage to Juliet. Juliet and Gertrude appear, and as she keeps watch outside, they exchange their vows and pray in the trio "Dieu qui fis." Gertrude enters once more, and all join in thanking God for their happiness. The second scene takes place outside the Capulet palace, where Stephano sings an insulting ballad, "Que fais-tu." Gregorio and servants come out and they fight, though not too seriously. Mercutio enters and says that a grown man fighting a boy is worthy of the Capulets. Tybalt appears, and he and Mercutio exchange insults and fight. Romeo enters and tries to stop them, but when he refuses to fight in response to Tybalt's insults, Mercutio does so, and as the others sing threats, Romeo laments the hatred between the families. Mercutio is mortally wounded, and Romeo forgets his resolve and fights Tybalt, who falls, dying. Capulet enters and promises to fulfill Tybalt's last wish, that Juliette marry Paris immediately. All sing of the misery the day has brought ("O jour de deuil"). The Duke enters and banishes Romeo, commanding him to leave before dawn on pain of death. Despite the Duke's orders, both sides sing of their desire for revenge. Romeo vows to see Juliette once more, even if it costs him his life.

Act Four. The scene is set in Juliette's room, where she pardons him for the death ("Va! Je t'ai pardone"), and they sing of their blissful wedding night ("Nuit d'hyménée"). They hear a bird singing and alternatingly declare it the nightingale, confidant of love, or the lark, announcing the dawn. He leaves when it is clear that it is dawn, and she prays for his safety. Gertrude enters, agitated and followed by Laurent and Capulet, who announce she is to marry Paris at once. Laurent gives her a potion that will make her appear to be dead ("Buvez donc"). She will be taken to the vaults, where Romeo and Laurent will wait for her to revive. Alone, she is frightened, but resolved ("Amour, ranime mon courage"). When the wedding procession enters, before Paris can put the ring on her finger, she declares that hate is the cradle of this fatal love and that the coffin will be her wedding bed. She falls, apparently lifeless, into Capulet's arms.

Act Five. In the first scene, Laurent learns that the letter he sent to Romeo describing the plan did not arrive. Stephano, who was carrying it, was attacked by the Capulets and was unable to deliver it. He rushes out to warn Romeo. In the burial vault, Juliet lies on a bier. Romeo breaks in ("Salut, tombeau") and speaks of the place as a shining, radiant palace, due to Juliette's presence. He lovingly contemplates her beauty, and drinks poison. She awakens a moment later, and for a moment they are ecstatically reunited ("Viens! fuyons"), but he staggers and wildly denounces the family cruelty that has brought him to the gates of heaven only to die. She is aghast as he tells her that thinking her dead, he has taken poison, and he tries to comfort her ("Console-toi"). As he falls, she takes a dagger and drives it into her heart. In a last embrace, they beg God to forgive them. *—Ann Feeney*

Recommended:

- **Gounod: Romeo & Juliette** / Plasson (cond.), Van Dam, Alagna, Gheorghiu, Henry, Toulouse Orch. / 1998 / EMI 56123
- **Gounod: Romeo & Juliette** / Lombard (cond.), Corelli, Freni, Depraz, Thau, Paris National Opera Theater Orch. / 1994 / EMI 65290
- **Gounod: Romeo & Juliette** / Ruhlmann (cond.), Journet, Affre, Dupre, Boyer, Theatre National de L'Opéra-Comique / 1994 / VAI Audio 1064

VOCAL

Ave Maria (ca. 1852)

Ah, the famous Bach/Gounod *Ave Maria*. So familiar and lyrical, a wedding music standard, it seems to be a naturally pious work. And yet it has a little-known history that reveals a different kind of devotional intent. The melody that Gounod wrote to go with the first prelude from Book One of Bach's *Well-Tempered Clavier* began as an improvisation made one evening after dinner with friends. The arpeggiated chords of the prelude work as the accompaniment to the cantilena melody, not unlike a song by Mendelssohn or a Bellini aria. Gounod's father-in-law wrote it down and not only had a violinist and choir perform it for Gounod, but also sold it to a publisher (he did give the money to Gounod). The *Méditation*, as the first published version for violin and piano was named, was an instant success, with publishers rushing out various arrangements for different instruments. How the Latin text of "Ave Maria" ended up attached to the melody is the real story. The composer, with his penchants for romance and drama, would frequently become infatuated by young, married women. According to the family story, Gounod was at one time enchanted by a young woman by the name of Rosalie. He found a poem by Alphonse de Lamartine, *Vers sur un album*, which he set to the *Méditation*'s melody, thinking it would be an appropriate gift for Rosalie. Although the text is innocent enough, Rosalie's mother deemed the gift inappropriate. She politely suggested the "Ave Maria" text as an alternative. Taking the hint, Gounod made minor changes to adjust the melody to the text, and a classical music hit was born. *—Patsy Morita*

Recommended:

○ **Songs By Charles Gounod** / Johnson, Murray / 1993 / Hyperion 66801/2

○ **Ave Maria: Myth of Mary** / Wolff, Froschauer (condd.), Hampson, Domingo, Saint Paul CO, VSO / 1999 / Teldec 21480

CHORAL

Messe solennelle de Sainte Cécile, in G major

Although Charles Gounod is today better known for his operas, his contemporary Camille Saint-Saëns contended that "In the faint distant future when inexorable time has completed its work and the operas of Gounod are forever in repose in the dusty sanctuary of libraries, the *Messe de Sainte Cécile*, the *Rédemption* and the oratorio *Mors et Vita* will still retain life. They will show coming generations what a splendid musician lent luster and renown to France in the nineteenth century."

While Saint-Saëns' analysis fell short of the mark, it was understandable that he should have written what he did. Gounod's works for the church far outnumber his 13 operas and continued to occupy his attention long after his last stage work had been premiered. Indeed, given his earliest predilections (he undertook a course in theology at Saint-Sulpice and referred to himself for a time as Abbé Gounod), he might easily have confined himself to the composition of sacred works.

Gounod approached the writing of his *Messe Sainte Cécile* with the same reverence that had informed his creative life from the beginning. Even other composers recognized that this was no mere posturing; after winning the Grand Prix de Rome in 1839, Gounod spent much time at the Sistine Chapel studying the works of the sixteenth century masters. During the summer of 1855, while at work on the *Sainte Cécile Mass*, he wrote to his mother, "During the afternoons I usually go to the woods and read selections from my beloved Sainte Augustin. I have translated them; that is my time of reflection. Following that, I contemplate my mass."

Gounod took some liberties with the liturgical text of the mass. In the Agnus Dei he changed the words slightly and added the "Domine Salvum," which is heard three times at the conclusion. Following the composer's lifetime, the reference to the Emperor Napoleon III was changed to "Domine salva fac Republicam" (Lord, deliver thy people). Throughout, one hears the composer's quintessentially French discernment added to his great respect for the major sacred composers of the past.

The premiere took place at the church of Saint-Eustache on November 22, 1855, and led Saint-Saëns to comment that "The appearance of the *Messe Saint-Cécile* caused a kind of shock. This simplicity, this grandeur, this serene light which rose before the musical world like a breaking dawn, troubled people enormously." He concluded by saying, "at first one was dazzled, then charmed, then conquered." *—Erik Eriksson*

Recommended:

○ **Gounod: Messe Solennelle; Petite Symphonie** / Hartemann (cond.), Lorengar, Hoppe, Crass, Puig-Roget, Societe des Concerts du Conservatoire / 2001 / EMI 74730

KEYBOARD

Funeral March of a Marionette, in D minor

This small piano piece is a light-hearted piece of musical grotesquerie, a mock funeral procession with a jaunty beat and a carefree tune over a humorously not-slow-enough funeral march rhythm. Gounod himself, recognizing its popularity, set it for orchestra in 1879. Other composers have arranged it for various combinations, and the piece gained international fame beginning in the 1950s when it was selected as the sardonic theme music introducing appearances by film director Alfred Hitchcock at the beginnings and ends of his television anthology series on suspense and the grotesque, *Alfred Hitchcock Presents*. Gounod's dead marionette is now as unseverably linked in most people's minds with the portly British filmmaker as Rossini's *William Tell Overture* has been with the Lone Ranger.

The piece has a little program: the marionette has died in a duel, and the funeral procession enters. A contrasting central section depicts the "mourners" stopping off for refreshments at an inn on the funeral route. At the end, though, Gounod lets a little more solemnity show. *—Joseph Stevenson*

Recommended:

○ **Tortelier's French Bonbons** / Tortelier (cond.), BBCPO / 1999 / Chandos 9765

○ **Great Marches** / Ormandy (cond.), Philadelphia Orch. / 1997 / Sony 63052

Susan Graham

b. Jul. 23, 1960, Roswell, NM

Mezzo-Soprano

Born in Roswell, New Mexico in 1960, mezzo-soprano Susan Graham began her professional operatic and concert career shortly after completing a master's degree in music at the Manhattan School of Music. A participant in the San Francisco Opera's Merola young artists' program and a winner of the Metropolitan Opera Auditions, she quickly gained a foothold in the major performing venues in the United States, including the Santa Fe Opera (Dorabella in *Cosí fan tutte*), St. Louis Opera (Erika in Samuel Barber's *Vanessa*), Chicago Lyric Opera (Annius in Mozart's *La Clemenza di Tito*), and Seattle Opera (Charlotte in Massenet's *Werther* and Stephano in Gounod's *Roméo et Juliet*). In 1989 she made her Carnegie Hall debut in Mahler's *Des Knaben Wunderhorn*, and sang the title role in the first American and British stagings of Massenet's *Chérubin*. Her Metropolitan Opera debut was in the 1991–92 season, during which she sang Second Lady in *The Magic Flute*, Cherubino in *The Marriage of Figaro* and Tebaldo in Verdi's *Don Carlos*.

During the 1990s, Graham established herself as an artist of international caliber, and added the opera houses of San Francisco, Lyon, Salzburg, Covent Garden, and Vienna to her performing schedule. During this period she also issued a number of recordings, including a highly regarded performance of Berlioz' *Nuits d'été*, and a collaborative effort with sopranos Renée Fleming and Barbara Bonney entitled *Strauss Heriones*. A 1998 release, entitled *La Belle Époque: Songs of Reynaldo Hahn* was a successful follow-up to her earlier Berlioz effort, and confirmed her achievements as an interpreter of French music.

In the year 2000, Graham sang the starring role of Sister Helen Prejean in Jake Heggie's *Dead Man Walking*, a work commissioned by and first performed at the San Francisco Opera. The production was a critical and popular success, and—particularly because of its association with Sister Prejean's well-known book and the equally popular movie rendering—brought Graham a measure of media exposure unusual for an operatic singer. *—Allen Schrott*

Recommended:

○ **La Belle Époque** / Graham, Vignoles (piano) / 1998 / Sony 60168

○ **Heggie: Dead Man Walking** / Summers (cond.), Solomon, Robertson, Von Stade, Graham, San Francisco Opera Orch. / 2001 / Erato 86238

○ **Susan Graham at Carnegie Hall** / Graham, Martineau (piano) / 2003 / Erato 60293

Percy Grainger

b. Jul. 8, 1882, Brighton, Melbourne, Australia, **d.** Feb. 20, 1961, White Plains, NY

Composer: Keyboard, Band Music, Orchestral

Percy Grainger was known during his lifetime as a virtuoso pianist and arranger of popular English folk song. His primary contribution to music, however, lies in his prolific and largely unexamined output as a composer of expert and highly original works. Because so much of his work remains unknown, there have been no composers of note that can be linked to his influence. Nevertheless, once Grainger's unique and unusual output becomes more widely disseminated, this is apt to change.

Early in his life, Grainger rejected the central European tradition of Western classical music, seeking instead a "democratic" music that was more closely related to natural sounds, speech, and world music. In his quest to assimilate as much unique musical culture as possible, Grainger became one of the first ethnomusicologists to use the wax cylinder phonograph in the collection and transcription of indigenous music. His arrangements of many of these are among the best ever done, capturing not only the melodies and harmonies, but also the timbres, inflections, and performance styles of each individual piece. In his own compositions, Grainger experimented with nontraditional rhythms, forms, and instrumental combinations in an attempt to create what he called "free music." He also created a large body of more traditional works and arrangements intended for more popular consumption, motivated, no doubt, by his experience with the Edwardian music hall and later with the U.S. Army Band (where he earned his American citizenship in 1918).

Grainger's early years were spent in Melbourne where he studied first with his mother, and later with Louis Pabst. From 1895–99 he attended the Hoch Conservatory in Frankfurt, Germany, and then settled in London in 1901. The next ten years or so were devoted to a combination of concert touring and folk song collection. Grainger's early reputation was as a brilliant and eccentric pianist, and it was this talent that not only provided his income for the rest of his life, but also brought him into contact with other composers. Grieg and Delius, in particular, had great influence on Grainger's development of a sympathy and sensitivity toward unique national and folk styles. In 1914, Grainger moved to New York, beginning a long career as a composer, arranger, collector of folk music, and educator. In 1925 and 1927 he collected and published over 200 Danish folk songs, and returned to Australia in 1924, 1926, and from 1934–35 in order to establish a Grainger Museum at the University of Melbourne devoted to ethnomusicological research. His final years were spent completing and arranging his earlier works and trying to develop a workable form of his "free music" using primarily theremins, one of the earliest electronic instruments. The project remained incomplete, and Grainger died embittered and in relative obscurity, known only for a handful of light works that he referred to derogatorily as his "fripperies." *—Steven Coburn*

KEYBOARD

Children's March "Over the Hills and Far Away" (1916–1918; revised 1920)

After making a stir in London as a pianist and composer from the opening years of the twentieth century, and doing valuable work collecting English folk song, Grainger hastily embarked for New York in the summer of 1914 as the Great War began. In America, he made a similar splash performing and having his own works widely performed. With the United States' entry into the war on April 5, 1917, popular support for the Allied effort rendered his conscientious objector stance untenable and threatened to break the large strides his career had taken. On a sudden whim on June 9, 1917, he bought a soprano saxophone and enlisted at Fort Totten as a bandsman, from which he was promptly assigned to the 15th Band of the Coast Artillery Corps, Fort Hamilton, South Brooklyn. Bandleader Rocco Resta was a friend from civilian life and Grainger spent a quietly productive time practicing wind instruments, conducting on occasion for Resta, and composing.

Among the works begun or completed during this period, the *Children's March "Over the Hills and Far Away,"* scored for winds, percussion, and piano, is one of his happiest inspirations, encapsulating both a newly found fondness for wind sonorities and his essentially childlike nature. The piece bears no relation to the like-named, richly evocative variations of his friend Delius, composed in 1897, though both explore realms of archetypal innocence. Begun in 1916 and completed in 1918, Grainger's work is dedicated—tantalizingly and for posterity, mysteriously—to "my playmate beyond the hills." A brief excerpt "dished up for piano" (as Grainger described his arrangements) was also made in 1918 and the transcription for piano, four hands, of the entire piece followed in 1920.

A few preludizing bars bring an infectiously skipping melody quietly in to be richly varied in alternations from entrancingly confiding to riotously gay as the music modulates downward through a cycle of fifths —F, B flat, E flat, A flat—and back, though halting at the return to B flat as the music dies away, suggesting some merrily unfinished business just out of earshot. The four-hands version compensates for the audacious band scoring (e.g., tambourine, castanets, snare drum, and a xylophone mallet striking a piano bass string at the peroration) with the virtuosity of splashily skirling passage work, sweeping glissandi, and sheer pulsating gusto. Grainger performed the four hands version with his friend Ernest Hutcheson as part of a benefit concert for Moritz Moszkowski at Carnegie Hall on December 21, 1921, sharing the stage with such luminaries as Ossip Gabrilowitsch (Mark Twain's son-in-law, by the way), Alfredo Casella, Ignaz Friedman, Josef Lhevinne, Wilhelm Backhaus, and Leo Ornstein. *—Adrian Corleonis*

Recommended:

○ **Grainger: To the Fore!** / Brion (cond.), Michigan State U. Symphonic Band / 1990 / Delos 3101

○ **Grainger: Complete Piano Music** / Jones / 1997 / Nimbus 1767

Country Gardens, folk song arrangement (1908–1936)

This short tune, in the style of an English morris dance, is the most popular individual small piece written by the folk-oriented Australian composer Percy Grainger. As is typical of Grainger's music, he arranged it (or "dished it up, " as he would have said) in several different forms. There are delightful versions for piano four-hands as well as solo piano, for band, and for orchestra. In 1949, conductor Leopold Stokowski proposed to record an album of Grainger's music and asked the composer for new versions of these pieces "in which all the colorful instruments of the modern orchestra could be employed."

Grainger was at first irritated at the implicit criticism that his existing version was not good enough for Stokowski, but the request made him reconsider the original arrangements. In the process he found fresh possibilities in them. The "arrangement for Leopold Stokowski" emphasized the woodwinds and added so many new harmonic twists and additional ideas that it diverged substantially from the more familiar versions, and is regarded by most commentators as the most interesting version of the piece. *—Joseph Stevenson*

Recommended:

○ **The Parlour Grand, Vol. 2** / Silverman / 1997 / Marquis Classics 81201

Handel in the Strand (1911–1952)

It has been Grainger's fate to be remembered more for what he called his "fripperies" than for his more serious works. *Handel in the Strand* is a perennial favorite, and well illustrates the wit and invention that brought him wide popularity after he settled in London in 1901. Australian-born, but a true cosmopolitan due to his travels in Europe and the U.S., Grainger was an exception to the high-minded seriousness of many of the early twentieth century English school of composers, with which he is often associated.

An unconventional personality and a formidable concert pianist, Grainger was influenced by the English folk song movement and arranged a number of traditional songs, including (another "frippery") *Molly on the Shore.* His compositions are highly original for their time and contain a variety of experimental techniques, such as jazz cross rhythms and improvisation.

The syncopated, perky tunes that form the basis of this work are clearly Handelian in character, though with a touch of Cockney arrogance—an amiable caricature of the Baroque liking for dance movements, complete with elaborate counterpoint, a canon, and a fugue. The technical detail is remarkable, yet never obfuscates the tuneful, lighthearted nature of the piece. Such virtuosity occurs in Grainger's more extended works but rarely sounds as engaging as in it does in this lively frolic.

Grainger's habit of writing several versions of the same work makes the dating of this and other works difficult. One- and two-piano (and other) arrangements exist, but the orchestral version is undoubtedly the most attractive. *—Roy Brewer*

Recommended:

○ **Fennell Conducts Grainger & Coates** / Fennell (cond.), Eastman-Rochester Pops Orch. / 1993 / Mercury 434330

Irish Tune from County Derry, folk song arrangement (1902–1913)

Despite the clinical title, this is one of the most sentimental of all Irish folk melodies, given a particularly rich arrangement. Grainger made several arrangements, in fact, and in terms of musical substance those for instrumental ensembles are all quite similar (string orchestra with one or two horns in 1913, winds in 1918, full orchestra in 1949, and chamber orchestra in 1952). Grainger found the melody in a collection of Irish folk tunes and professed to know no exact title for it; actually, it's well known as both "Londonderry Air" and "Danny Boy."

The timbral details vary from one arrangement to the next, but in general Grainger introduces the theme low in the ensemble, the first few phrases played simply but then with the counterpoint above becoming increasingly complex and chromatic. The melody receives a second treatment in a higher register, and then recedes into the middle of the instrumental texture for a third, grander statement. All the while the counterpoint becomes freer and more harmonically independent, particularly in the final version, with its almost Ivesian waywardness. *—James Reel*

Recommended:

○ **Vaughan Williams: Tallis Fantasia; Barber: Adagio; etc.** / Slatkin (cond.), St. Louis SO / 1981 / Telarc 80059

Molly on the Shore, folk song arrangement (1907–1947)

Grainger's source for this lively piece was the *Complete Petrie Collection of the Ancient Music of Ireland,* edited by composer Charles Villiers Stanford. Grainger cribbed two tunes, actually, both of them reels from County Cork: "Temple Hill" and "Molly on the Shore." Grainger's treatment keeps the pianist's fingers flying, although he employs such a wide variety of dynamics and coloristic effects that it never seems like a cheap knuckle-buster. He introduces the two tunes almost unharmonized, then slaps them through a short series of lively variations, jolting from one dynamic extreme to the other and enveloping it all in extremely detailed pedaling directions. *—James Reel*

Recommended:

○ **Grainger: Piano Music** / Hamelin / 1996 / Hyperion 66884

BAND MUSIC

Lincolnshire Posy, suite (1905–1937)

In the same years (1905–06) that Bartók and Kodály began roaming the Hungarian and Transylvanian countryside in search of a genuine Magyar heritage of folk song, Percy Grainger was similarly engaged in the English and Scandinavian hinterlands. He met Grieg—much of whose work may be said to valorize Norwegian folk songs—in 1906, while the previous year he had begun to rummage through Lincolnshire, seeking out folk singers and painstakingly transcribing their art. In this, he was at odds with other collectors, such as Cecil Sharp and the young Ralph Vaughan Williams, whose transcriptions of folk songs aimed at offering the urban public definitive versions that could be repeated strophically—folk songs in the abstract—where Grainger sought to capture the endless, peculiar variations his singers brought to a given melody. In a preface to *Lincolnshire Posy,* Grainger noted, "No concert singer I have ever heard approached these rural warblers in variety of tone-quality, range of dynamics, rhythmic resourcefulness and individuality of style... our folksingers were lords of their own domain—were at once performers and creators. For they bent all the songs to suit their personal artistic tastes and personal vocal resources...." When Grainger was commissioned in 1937 by the American Bandmasters' Association to compose a piece for that year's convention in Milwaukee, it is hardly surprising to find him, by then long an American citizen ensconced in White Plains, NY, looking back and rendering a loving tribute to the era in which he was in closest touch with the song of the earth. Of the six parts making his "bunch of musical wildflowers," Grainger wrote, "Each number is intended to be a kind of musical portrait of the singer who sang its underlying melody... a musical portrait of the singer's personality no less than of his habits of song...." The upshot is not folk song "arrangements," but small tone poems, evocations at once modally archaic and briskly modern, ranging from the laconic fanfare of *Lisbon (Dublin Bay)* through the noble poignance of *Horkstow Grange,* the eerie drama of *Rufford*

Park Poachers, to the blithe insouciance of *The Brisk Young Sailor*, the volatile narrative grandeur of *Lord Melbourne*, and the dancing tumult of *The Lost Lady Found*. The Grainger-led premiere of *Lincolnshire Posy* was given by the American Bandmasters' Association on March 7, 1937, and has come to be regarded as his finest work. *—Adrian Corleonis*

Recommended:

○ **Grainger; Persichetti, etc.** / Fennell (cond.), Eastman Wind Ens. / 1991 / Philips 432754

○ **Music of Percy Grainger, Vol. 1** / Green (cond.), University of Houston Wind Ens. / Mark Custom 1086

ORCHESTRAL

The Warriors ("Music to an Imaginary Ballet") (1913–1916)

The average concertgoer knows Grainger as the arranger of nice folk songs like *Irish Tune from County Derry* and *Lincolnshire Posey*. In reality he was one of the most individualistic figures in music. One of the oddest pieces he composed was this 19-minute ballet score from the years just before World War I.

Now, the warriors in this ballet do no fighting. Grainger himself described the story of the ballet best: "Ghosts of male and female warrior types of all times and places" have gathered "for an orgy of war-like dances, processions, and merry-makings broken, or accompanied, by amorous interludes."

The Warriors is a mad, almost stream-of-consciousness composition that sounds as though it were an improvisation begun with no idea where it was destined to go. Its textures range from popular song to intense, complex independent streams of music that no one (except, of course, Charles Ives) had dreams of. It takes three conductors, at times, to lead the offstage ensembles, which oftentimes proceed at independent meters and harmonies. In addition, the percussion section, which seems constantly to be standing aside from the music and commenting on it, is virtually a separate orchestra.

There's nothing much like it; it definitely does not "make sense" in any formal way. At any given moment it is impossible to know how the music got there. But its unceasing good spirits and sheer flamboyance, finally, carry the day. *—Joseph Stevenson*

Recommended:

○ **Holst: Planets; Grainger: Warriors** / Gardiner (cond.), Philharmonia / 2003 / DG 000033736

Enrique Granados

b. Jul. 27, 1867, Lérida, Spain, **d.** Mar. 24, 1916, At sea (in the English Channel)

Composer: Keyboard, Vocal, Opera

One of the most colorful turn-of-the-century Spanish musicians, composer and pianist Enrique Granados is best remembered for his evocative solo piano works; his output also includes a great deal of orchestral music and six operas (only the last of which has gained any fame). Born in 1867 to an officer in the Spanish army, Granados received his first musical instruction from an army bandmaster. Further studies in Barcelona with Jurnet (piano) and Pedrell (composition) prepared the young musician for a brief but highly influential stay in Paris (1887–89), during which Granados worked under well-known Parisian pianist and teacher Charles de Bériot (son of the famous violinist of the same name). Granados' earliest mature work, the *Valses poéticos* of 1887, was completed around this time.

After returning to Barcelona in 1890 Granados spent the next decade building a dual career as pianist and composer, forming a successful piano trio with the Belgian violinist Crickboom and the young Pablo Casals. His first opera, *Maria del Carmen*, was well received at its premiere in 1898, after which the Order of Carlos III (a Spanish knighthood) was bestowed upon Granados by a supportive government. Granados was quick to follow up on this success, and two more operas were produced in the next five years.

For the 1900 season Granados founded the Society of Classical Concerts (Sociedad de Conciertos Clásicos) in Barcelona, which, although short-lived, gave him the confidence to create his own piano school the following year (known as the Granados School, or *Academia Granados*). The school was a success, and Granados maintained his involvement with it until his death.

Granados was one of the great pianists of the late nineteenth and early twentieth centuries. Virtually all his music relies heavily on the Catalan and Spanish folk idiom (e.g. *Twelve Spanish Pieces*, or *Six Pieces on Spanish Popular Songs*), which, along with fellow Spaniard Isaac Albéniz, Granados was instrumental in bringing to the attention of the contemporary European musical establishment. *Goyescas*, begun in 1902 but not finished until 1911, is perhaps his mightiest achievement. (Granados also produced an opera by the same name—both the pianistic and operatic incarnations of the work take the striking visuals of Goya as their inspiration.)

In 1916, while returning from the U.S.A. (where the opera *Goyescas* had received a New York premiere on January 26, 1916, and where Granados had performed in the White House for President Wilson), the liner Sussex was torpedoed by a German U-boat. Among the casualties were Granados and his wife of 24 years. *—Blair Johnston*

KEYBOARD

Allegro de concierto, in C major, Op. 46 (1903–1904)

There are numerous works in the piano repertory, representing composers from virtually every era and nation, which are famous (or even infamous) by name but which, for whatever reason, are rarely played. Enrique Granados' *Allegro de concierto for piano in C sharp major*, Op. 46, H. 6, is such a work. The *Allegro de concierto*'s fame is not especially difficult to understand, nor is its paradoxical obscurity: fiendishly difficult works nearly always attain a kind of legendary status, and such works are also, on account of that very difficulty, forbidden fruit for most players. Moreover, Granados is not generally held in the same esteem as other composers of precipitously difficult piano music—like Liszt, or even Granados' colleague Isaac Albéniz—and so there have traditionally been few pianists willing to put in the time required to add his music to their portfolio. However, the glorious *Allegro* is beginning at last to find a better home in the repertoire.

Just as with the Liszt models that Granados clearly had in mind when composing (probably sometime during the 1890s), the heart and soul of the *Allegro de concierto* grows from the epic struggle of the performer to conquer the music and the instrument. The element of virtuosity is not something applied as garnish, but rather the very foundation of the work's aesthetic. The pianist who can plunge through its 15-or-so pages really does provide for his audience a transcendental experience (to borrow Liszt's own term for such super-virtuoso spiritual elevation). Granados' harmonies are rich, his figurations sparkling; and the few bona fide melodies that rise to the top of the constant broth of arpeggiations have a lyricism so deeply wrought that the work is never in danger of coming across as an etude. *—Blair Johnston*

Recommended:

○ **Granados** / Larrocha / 1985 / London 410288

○ **Liselotte Weiss** / Weiss / 1975 / Bis 23

Goyescas, Books 1–2 (1909–1911)

The piano suite *Goyescas*, considered by many the pinnacle of this Spanish composer's output, was composed between 1909 and 1911. In four sections and lasting about 55 minutes in performance, the work takes its inspiration from the art of the eighteenth century Spaniard Francisco Goya (1746–1828), specifically from a set of sketches of Spanish life that Granados had seen in the Prado museum in Madrid. The *Goyescas* use passages reminiscent of the eighteenth century Spanish-resident keyboard composer Domenico Scarlatti to evoke Goya's time, fusing that aspect effectively with the Spanish nationalism for which the composer was best known (and that was certainly relevant as well to Goya's turbulent life amidst Napoleonic occupation). The suite is fearsomely difficult in places; its first interpreter was the composer himself, who was best known in his own day as a touring virtuoso. For modern listeners, Granados' transfer of the propulsive rhythms of flamenco guitar music to the keyboard is one of the piece's most attractive features. A runaway success in France as well as in Spain, the *Goyescas* brought the composer invitations to convert the work into an opera, and Granados complied. With the outbreak of World War I in Europe, plans for the opera's premiere were shelved, but it was staged, with the composer present, at New York's Metropolitan Opera in January of 1916. Granados hobnobbed with President Woodrow Wilson and missed his boat back to Spain. The boat that he and his wife finally did take was hit by a torpedo launched from a German submarine; in a scene reminiscent of the finale of *Titanic*, Granados abandoned a life raft in an attempt to save his wife. Both of them drowned. *—AMG*

Recommended:

○ **Albéniz: Iberia; Granados: Goyescas** / Larrocha / 1996 / London 448191

○ **Granados: Goyescas** / Riva / 1999 / Naxos 8554403

Spanish Dances, Op. 37 (1888–1890)

These 12 perennial crowd pleasers were composed by Granados in support of his own pianistic career at various times during the late 1880s and early 1890s and later collected into four published books. Compared by critics at the time with the Norwegian nationalist works of Grieg, they are short works that draw on Spanish dance rhythms and forms. Grieg in turn is said to have admired them, as did Saint-Saëns and Massenet, contemporary masters of the French scene that shaped Granados' own style. They are colorful and infectious rather than really pathbreaking; piano pedagogue Maurice Hinson once wrote that '[t]hey vibrate like living organisms, pulsating with sun-drenched energies." Granados, however, had immersed himself in Spanish folk music as a result of studies with the pioneering Spanish musicologist Enrique Pedrell, and some of these works delve into unusual dance rhythms and pursue their musical implications. Through their considerable popularity and their wide reach into folk culture, these dances helped pave the way for the nationalistic path Spanish music would take for much of the twentieth century. Three of them were made into orchestra pieces in 1892 and are still known in those versions. The twelve dances are titled Galante, Orientale, Fandango, Villanesca, Andaluza, Rondalla aragonesa, Valenciana, Sardana, Romántica, Melancólica, Arabesca, and Bolero. —*AMG*

Recommended:

- ○ **Granados: Spanish Dances** / Larrocha / London 414557
- ○ **Granados: Danzas españolas** / Hewitt / 1994 / Musica Viva 1074

Valses poéticos (ca. 1887)

Like so many of Enrique Granados' compositions, the *Valses poéticos* for solo piano, H 147, are impossible to date with any real certainty; however, they have been tentatively assigned to the years 1886 and 1887—around the same time that Granados moved from Barcelona to Paris in order to take piano lessons from the Paris Conservatoire's Charles de Beriot (son of the legendary violinist by the same name and teacher also of Maurice Ravel). There are seven wonderfully fragrant waltzes in the *Valses poéticos*, to which are applied a not insignificant (and utterly un-waltz-like) Vivace molto introduction and, after the seventh waltz, a colorful and clever coda.

Valse No. 1 is marked Melódico and unfolds using the kind of almost ordinary, but actually jarred-just-a little-out-of-alignment harmonies for which Granados is famous and, for some, much beloved; it is written for the most part in just two melodic lines (though the lower one is arpeggiated and thus acts the part of more than one voice), and in the second half of its two-verse design, the bass line takes over the lightly strolling tune for a time. *Valse No. 2* is a noble thing in F major, *Valse No. 3* a slow (lento) and melancholy counterpart. Things brighten with the arrival of *No. 4*, a B flat major wisp that Granados marks Allegro humoristico, and that same key carries over into the following number. The high point of the set arrives in the form of a deeply felt F sharp minor Quasi ad libitum (sentimental) *No. 6*, while its follow-up, *No. 7* Vivo, pits hand against hand in a battle of dextrous wits. The coda begins as a spry and, as it begins to roll, rather chromatic 6/8 time Presto/Vivace, but eventually winds down—much to our surprise—into a literal and complete reprise of the elegant *Valse No. 1*. —*Blair Johnston*

Recommended:

- ○ **Granados: Piano Music Vol. 4** / Riva / 2001 / Naxos 554629
- ○ **Granados: Spanish Dances** / Larrocha / 1995 / BMG 68184

VOCAL

Canciónes amatorias (1915)

Not so famous in the world of art song as the *Tonadillas al estilo antiguo* but in some ways more truly representative of their composer's craft, the seven songs of Enrique Granados' *Canciones amatorias* for voice and piano, H. 24—settings of a series of Spanish folk love poems—cannot (like many other works by Granados) be dated reliably. They were probably composed sometime during the first decade of the twentieth century. Whereas the *Tonadillas* are by definition compact songs (the word tonadilla means basically "little song") in a traditional style, the seven *Canciones amatorias* are longer and more flexibly built songs, spun from imaginative, wandering melodies and silk-textured piano lines that dip from time to time into the trove of Spanish/Latin American folk idioms that inform, at a basic level, every aspect of Granados' highly personal language.

The songs are: 1. "Descúbrase el pensamiento de mi secreto cuidado," 2. "Mañanica era," 3. "Llorad, corazón, que tenéis razón," 4. "Mira que soy niña, ¡amor, déjame!" 5. "No lloréis ojuelos," 6. "Iban al pinar," and 7. "Gracia mía." —*Blair Johnston*

Recommended:

- ○ **Songs of Spain** / Los Angeles, Larrocha / EMI 66937
- ○ **Art of Pilar Lorengar** / Lorengar, Larrocha / 2003 / Decca 473317
- ○ **Canciones Españolas** / Bayo, Alvarez-Parejo / Claves 509205

Tonadillas al estilo antiguo

Though Enrique Granados himself remains a largely underappreciated and in some ways even murky figure, his *Tonadillas al estilo antiguo*, H136, settings of a group of poems by Fernando Periquet for voice and piano, have long and widely been considered a precious peak in the Spanish song repertoire. In this collection, which was first published in 1912, Granados' love of radiant but subtle harmonies, shimmering piano textures, and of archaic-sounding and often folklike melodies finds full expression.

Tonadillas al estilo antiguo is not, properly speaking, a song cycle; its songs are not all written for the same voice type, and the last one is a duet. But there is no doubting that the songs are all from the same batch, so to speak, and they do fit together as a single performance quite nicely. Although the number of songs is usually listed as ten, there are for all intents and purposes 12; the ninth song, "La maja dolorosa," is really three songs in one.

The texts tell of majos and majas (men and women of Madrid) and their sundry romantic interactions. (The word tonadilla means simply little *tonada*, or little song, and all the songs in the set are quite brief.) The first, "Amor y odio" (Love and Hate), is an Allegretto, half in G minor and half in G major; even at its darkest, however, there is no room for despair or self-pity, the piano skips lightly along, gently prodding the singer. The Spanish idiom is fully invoked for the second, "Callejeo," a tale of a woman scorned wandering the streets of Spain in search of the man who betrayed her. A series of three songs tell of three majos, one discreet, one forgotten, and one timid, and then in the sixth song, "El mirar de la maja," a maja tells, to a persistent staccato accompaniment figure, of the effect her fiery, passionate gaze has on her beloved. In the seventh, the adorable "El tra la la y el punteado," a maja informs her man that she intends to keep on singing no matter what he does or says to her. A maja devoted to Goya takes the stage in number eight, and then a bereaved maja sings of her loss in the three-part "La maja dolorosa." The final duet is titled "Las currutacas modestas" (The Modest Lovers). —*Blair Johnston*

Recommended:

- ○ **Songs of Spain** / Los Angeles, Moore, Soriano / EMI 66937
- ○ **España** / Johnson, Murray / 1993 / Hyperion 66176
- ○ **Art of Pilar Lorengar** / Lorengar, Larrocha / 2003 / Decca 473317
- ○ **Catalan Piano Tradition** / Larrocha, Supervia, Marshall, Badia / VAI Audio 1001

OPERA

Goyescas (1913–1915)

During 1909 and 1911, Granados was inspired by Spanish painter Francisco Goya's cartoons and tapestry sketches—with their vividly flavored and atmospheric depictions of life in Madrid—to write two piano suites that captured the vitality and colors of Goya's paintings. Pianist Ernest Schelling suggested the work would lend itself to an opera, and Granados began to sketch out a possible dramatic structure, beginning to work with Fernando Periquet (Zuaznabar). When they had a basic plot outlined, Granados began composing the music. While about half of the material is drawn from the piano pieces, Granados wrote a good deal of original music for it as well. This includes the now-famous intermezzo, which he wrote overnight upon realizing that the first version was too short to allow for the scene change. Even for the sections that were reworked, Granados took full advantage of the possibilities of the additional colors that orchestration and voices could add. It was originally scheduled to premiere at the Paris Opera, but the circumstances of World War I forced the Opera to cancel its plans. Granados then brought the piece to the Metropolitan Opera, where it premiered with an almost entirely Italian cast, including Giuseppe de Luca and Giovanni Martinelli. (Lucrezia Bori, who was of Spanish descent, was originally cast for Rosario, but was unavailable), and paired with Leoncavallo's *Pagliacci*. Despite this initial casting, the opera's structure, brevity (approximately an hour in performance), and consistent use of Spanish (including Andalusian, Madrileno, and Catalan) folk themes from popular songs strongly link this piece to the zarzuela tradition, and it has been performed with equal success by zarzuela troupes and opera houses, though despite critical acclaim it has not entered the standard opera house repertoire outside of Spain. Excerpts, however, such as the above-mentioned intermezzo and the breathtaking vocal arrangement of *La maja y el ruiseñor* (The Maja and the Nightingale), have remained in the concert hall repertoire since the work's premiere. —*Ann Feeney*

Synopsis:

Scene One. The action takes place in Madrid, ca. 1800, and centers on four characters: the dashing bullfighter Paquiro, his attractive fiancée Pepa, the beautiful noblewoman Rosario, and her lover Fernando, who serves as a Captain in the Royal Guard. At the Campo de la Florida hotel, a group of young fans gather around Paquiro, who is receptive to their praise and admiration for him. Pepa soon arrives and shortly afterward, Rosario, who catches Paquiro's eye. He offers to take her to a dance that evening, and Pepa becomes jealous and enraged, swearing to take vengeance on Rosario. Fernando arrives, and it will be he, not Paquiro, who escorts Rosario to the dance.

Scene Two. This scene takes place in a small tavern. Paquiro and Fernando have a violent encounter, Rosario being at the center of the quarrel. The two decide to settle their dispute by arranging a duel.

Scene Three. Rosario is alone in her garden, but is soon joined by Fernando and the two renew their pledge of love for each other. The mood is passionate and tense, as the moment of the duel nears. Soon a bell tolls to announce the event. A shadowy figure (that of Paquiro) is seen in the background passing by. Fernando departs, followed by Rosario. The duel is not seen on-stage. A scream is heard and Rosario drags the mortally wounded Fernando back into her garden, where he dies. —*Robert Cummings*

Recommended:

- ○ **Granados: Goyescas** / Ros-Marba (cond.), Bayo, Vargas, Baquerizo, Casariego, Madrid SO / 1996 / Valois 4791
- ○ **De Falla: La Vida Breve; Granados: Goyescas** / Frühbeck de Burgos (cond.), Damiani, Chung, Angeletti, Orch. del Teatro Lirico di Cagliari / 2002 / Dynamic 380/1

Marcel Grandjany

b. Sep. 3, 1891, Paris, France, **d.** Feb. 24, 1975, New York, NY

Renowned harpist, composer, and teacher Grandjany began his harp studies at the age of eight with Henriette Renié. At 11 he was admitted to the Paris Conservatoire, studying with Hasselmans, and he won the Premier Prix at age 13. When he was 17 he offered his first public recital at the Salle Erard, and debuted with the Concerts Lamoreux Orchestra. These concerts were very successful and launched the young man on an international solo career, including a recital with Maurice Ravel in Paris in 1913, his London debut in 1922, and his New York debut less than two years later. Grandjany was also a professional organist, playing during the years of World War I at the Sacre-Coeur Basilica.

Grandjany headed the harp department of the Fontainebleau Summer School from 1921 to 1926, after which he moved to America, concertizing and teaching, eventually accepting an appointment as chairman of the harp department at the Juilliard School of Music in 1938, and was made a U.S. citizen in 1945. He remained on the faculty until his death in 1975. In addition to a few private students, Grandjany was also on the staff of the Montreal Conservatory from 1943 to 1963, and the Manhattan School of Music, where he taught from 1956 until 1967. His final recital was in 1967.

As a teacher his influence is hard to overstate. His method is taught all over the world, a distinction he shares with the method of his colleague Salzedo, resulting in something of an "us versus them" rivalry in the arena of harp pedagogy.

Grandjany was known as a sensuous harpist, his technique enhanced by his large, spatula-shaped fingertips. His many pieces for harp solo and for harp in ensemble are acclaimed for their obvious archetypal idiomatic beauty for the instrument. Highlights from his catalog include the *Poème for harp, horn, and orchestra*; the *Aria in Classic Style for harp and strings*; and the solo pieces *Children's Hour Suite, Colorado Trail, Divertissement, Rhapsody, Fantasia on a Theme of Haydn*, and *The Erie Canal*. *—Gerald Brennan*

Carl Heinrich Graun

b. May 7, 1704, Wahrenbrück, Germany, **d.** Aug. 8, 1759, Berlin, Germany

Composer

Composer Carl Heinrich Graun, one of the leading lights of German opera in the eighteenth century, was one of three musical brothers. After singing and composing opera in Brunswick, he entered the service of Crown Prince Frederick who, after becoming King, appointed Graun Director of the Berlin Royal Opera. Along with Johann Adoph Hasse (1699–1783), Graun was the primary composer of Italian opera in Germany in the mid-eighteenth century.

Graun's uncle may have given him his first lessons in music; in 1714 he entered the Dresden Kreuzschule, where he sang in the choir under the direction of J.Z. Grundig and composed a significant amount of church music. In 1718 he became a student at the University of Leipzig; there he studied singing with Grundig, organ with Emanuel Benisch, keyboard with Christian Pezold, and composition with J.C. Schmidt—then Kapellmeister of the Dresden Opera. However, it was the Dresden Opera itself that exerted the most profound influence on Graun; there he witnessed the growth in Dresden of contemporary opera seria.

In 1725, Graun was engaged as a tenor in the Brunswick Opera; two years later he was made vice-Kapellmeister and produced the first of six operas for that stage. In 1733, Crown Prince Frederick (the Great)—who already employed Graun's older brother, Johann Gottlieb—attempted to acquire Graun; the composer accepted after obtaining release from Brunswick in March, 1735. Until Frederick became king in 1740 Graun taught his new employer music theory, directed the chamber orchestra, and composed and performed Italian cantatas at the Prince's residence in Rheinsberg. Once Frederick acceded to the throne Graun was made Royal Kapellmeister, given an excellent salary, and immediately sent to Italy to engage singers for Frederick's new opera. On December 7, 1742, the new Royal Berlin Opera House opened with Graun's *Cesare e Cleopatra*.

Graun's work dominated the stage at the Berlin Opera; he composed 26 operas for the house. There were problems, however: Frederick occasionally required Graun to rewrite an aria he did not like and, in *Demofoonte* (1746), the king substituted an aria by Hasse for one of Graun's. Around 1745, the King demanded Graun switch from the French overture to the Italian sinfonia and he usually edited—sometimes even wrote—the librettos for Graun's dramas. These restrictions and interferences made the operas somewhat formulaic, but Graun still managed to weave a German sense of counterpoint into the Italianate coloratura texture, and his works are peppered with brilliant moments.

Der Tod Jesu (The Death of Jesus) of 1755 remained popular in Germany until the end of the nineteenth century, due primarily to its excellent da capo arias. Because of their expressive chromatic inflections and nervous rhythms, the recitatives are often described as deriving from the *Empfindsamer Stil* ("Feeling style") of the mid-eighteenth century.

Graun was at the leading edge of developments in the da capo aria, many of which incorporate aspects of instrumental composition, particularly rudimentary sonata form. For example, instead of maintaining the same key through the principle section of the aria, Graun often sets the latter part of the section in a secondary key. During the return of this music, however, the material initially in the secondary key is transposed to the tonic. Occasionally Graun eliminated the return to the first section of the aria, instead writing a shorter aria type called a cavatina. One example is his "Godi l'amabile," from *Montezuma*. In this case, the modification was made at the request of Frederick the Great, who had written the libretto. *—John Palmer*

Overview of Works (ca. 1726–1753)

In company with Johann Hasse, Carl Heinrich Graun (ca. 1703–59) was the preeminent native-born composer of Italian opera in Germany. Also a tenor, his first important post was in that capacity at the Brunswick court, where he eventually rose to become vice-Kapellmeister, and for which he composed six operas. In 1734, he entered the service of Crown Prince Frederick of Prussia (later Frederick the Great), where he remained for the rest of his life, becoming Kapellmeister (1740) and chief composer to the Berlin Opera.

Frederick, an able composer himself, created a glittering musical establishment at his court at Potsdam, gathering around him musicians such as Quantz and C.P.E. Bach. He took a positive, not to say dictatorial, approach to all musical matters at Potsdam; virtually all the music composed for him had to bear the stamp of his personal approval to be successful (the reason C.P.E. Bach achieved less success in Berlin than he merited). Graun carefully maintained his relationship with the monarch by ensuring that the operas he composed for him conformed to Frederick's taste.

In all, Graun composed over 20 operas for the Berlin Opera, mostly opere serie with long, fully developed da capo arias and based on the mythological and legendary topics that were the staple of the genre. A number are set to librettos by the two major librettists of the day, Pietro Metastasio and Apostolo Zeno, but Graun also set books by resident court poets and, in four instances, Frederick himself.

Remarkably, for a composer who never set foot in Italy (although he did encounter the great Venetian master Lotti during his student days in Dresden), Graun's style is totally Italianized in its understanding of how to write for the voice. But along with strong signs of Neapolitan influence, his operas also display more German traits—especially their attention to counterpoint. His writing is often at its best in tenderly expressed adagios, precisely the kind of music Frederick liked the best.

Any valid assessment of Graun's operas must await their revival. Only one, *Cesare e Cleopatra*, the work which opened the new Berlin Opera House in December 1742, has received a recording; it confirms the composer's gift for mellifluous vocal writing. Critical opinion, both contemporary and modern, has tended to focus on the dominating king's interference in Graun's operas, which according to one eighteenth century writer were written entirely to the king's taste, with whatever was not liked being "struck out, even if it was the best piece in the opera."

Graun was also the composer of a number of instrumental works (although his brother Johann Gottlieb was the more talented in this area), secular cantatas, and sacred works. Among the latter is his oratorio *Der Tod Jesu* (a libretto also set by Graun's friend Telemann), universally considered to be his masterpiece and, in keeping with his cantatas, a more personal utterance since it was not subjected to the close scrutiny of Graun's royal master. *—Brian Robins*

Recommended:

- ○ **Graun: Cleopatra & Cesare** / Jacobs (cond.), Dawson, Vermillion, Williams, Popken, Cologne Concerto / HM 2901561/63
- ○ **Graun: Der Tod Jesu** / Kuijken (cond.), Genz, Schwabe, Genz, Kerkhove, La Petite Bande / 2004 / Hyperion 67446

Denyce Graves

b. Mar. 7, 1964, Washington, DC

Mezzo-Soprano

Denyce Graves rose from modest origins to become one of the finest mezzo-sopranos in the world. She was born in a rough area of southwest Washington, DC. Her father left her family when Graves was one year old, and her mother struggled to support the family through most of her childhood. Graves' early musical education was limited to singing gospel in her church's choir. When a few of Graves' junior high school teachers encouraged her to attend the Duke Ellington School for the Arts, one of Washington's most prestigious public schools, she decided to go even though she had no particular interest in music. The interest, needless to say, developed; at the Ellington School, she studied French melodies, German lieder, and jazz in addition to the operatic arias which would eventually make her famous. The Ellington School's program was a strong one, and by graduation Graves had developed her gift enough that Oberlin College in Ohio granted her a scholarship.

Graves got her first major exposure at the Houston Grand Opera, for which she performed from 1988 to 1990. Her reputation grew quickly, particularly on the strength of her exciting interpretations of the title roles in Georges Bizet's *Carmen* and Camille Saint-Saëns' *Samson et Dalila.* Graves made her Metropolitan Opera debut in the 1995–96 season, singing *Carmen.* Her star has only risen since then. She has worked with conductors including Riccardo Chailly, Charles Dutoit, Zubin Mehta, Placido Domingo, and Mstislav Rostropovich; shared a stage with singers such as Domingo, José Cura, and the popular crossover sensation Andrea Bocelli; and sung at opera houses including the Royal Opera at Covent Garden, La Scala Milan, Vienna Staatsoper, and Opera Nationale de Paris.

Graves' fame does not stem only from her concerts and operatic roles; she has made efforts to branch out and draw nontraditional audiences into classical music. The PBS special *Denyce Graves: A Cathedral Christmas* was taped at Washington's National Cathedral and airs every year on PBS during the Christmas season. She also frequently appears on the children's program *Sesame Street.* Crossover repertoire and spirituals make frequent appearances in her recitals, and the year 2003 saw a major crossover release from Graves featuring Latin American matterial, *The Lost Days.* Whether she is performing a Scarlatti cantata, a popular song, or something in between, Graves' voice is marvelously expressive and vibrant. Intelligent musicianship and a mesmerizing stage presence complete the package and guarantee a strong turnout at any Graves concert. Graves is married to lutenist David Perry and resides in Leesburg, Virginia. *—Andrew Lindemann Malone*

Recommended:

- ○ **French Opera Arias** / Graves, Soustrot (cond.), Monte Carlo PO / 2004 / Virgin 62277
- ○ **Voce di Donna** / Graves, Barbacini (cond.), Munich Radio Orch. / 1999 / RCA 902663509
- ○ **Heroines of French Romantic Opera** / Graves, Soustrot (cond.), Monte Carlo PO / 1994 / FNAC 592056

Gregg Smith Singers

f. 1955, Los Angeles, CA
Ensemble

The Gregg Smith Singers are one of the world's primary small choral ensembles, particularly among those with a reputation for twentieth century music. When Gregg Smith founded a vocal ensemble, he was an assistant in the UCLA (University of California at Los Angeles) Department of Music. In 1958 the group made its first appearance on the international musical scene, and later appeared at the Brussels World's Fair. Shortly, the Singers came to the attention of Igor Stravinsky, who chose it as his favored vocal ensemble, particularly in his historic series of recordings for the Columbia label. This association continued for twelve years until the great composer's death in 1971. Smith himself was chosen to conduct the chorus and orchestra for Stravinsky's funeral services in Venice.

The Singers undertook their second European tour in 1971; since then they continued touring frequently, totaling 34 tours by the end of the century. Since 1973 the Singers have been based in New York City, and makes annual appearances at the Adirondack Musical Festival at Lake Saranac, New York, and conducts the North Country Choral Workshop at Saranac Lake, open to high school students. More than a thousand students have completed this course. In the 1980s it became associated with New York City's "Art Connection" concerts.

The GSS's recording activities (which began even earlier than the Stravinsky collaboration with a recording on the Verve jazz label) has included for Vox, Everest, CRI, Lovely Music, and many others. Over the years it has participated in concerts and recordings with such conductors as Bernstein, Stokowski, Ormandy, and many others.

Seventy percent of the repertory of the Singers is American music, extending from Stephen Foster, Victor Herbert, Ives, Copland, and William Schuman, to late twentieth century composers such as Roger Reynolds, Jacob Druckman, Elliott Carter, Ned Rorem, and Louise Talma. In 1978 it received the Ditson Conductor's prize for service to American music, and in 1988 the Berliasky Prize of the American Academy in Rome. It won three Grammy awards, one each for *The Glory of Gabrieli, New Music of Charles Ives,* and another Ives disk, *General Booth Enters into Heaven. —Joseph Stevenson*

Recommended:

- ○ **La Noche: Modern Mexican Choral Masterpieces** / Smith (cond.), Rees, Gregg Smith Singers / 2001 / Newport 85639
- ○ **I Hear America Singing** / Smith (cond.), Rees, Clark, Reuter, Dorsey, Gregg Smith Singers, Adirondack CO / 1996 / Vox 3037
- ○ **William Billings—The Continental Harmonist** / Smith (cond.), Gregg Smith Singers, Adirondack CO / 1991 / Premier 1008

Gregorian Chant

Gregorian Chant, or plainchant, is the great body of monophonic song developed by the early Christian church for use in worship. Most chant texts are drawn from the Latin Vulgate, which is the Holy Bible as translated and edited by the Roman Catholic Church. Since the Middle Ages, chants have been collected and published in various groupings. In the standard 1903 *Editio Vaticana,* chants are divided by liturgical type. masses are compiled in a volume known as the *Gradual.* The second volume is known as the *Breviary* and contains the Offices or "Hours," psalm settings, chants for Saints' or Feast Days, hymns, sequences, and other occasional pieces. Strict regulations dictate when these works are to be performed.

Prior to about 800 A.D., music and liturgy varied widely across the Holy Roman Empire. Nowhere was this more problematic than in Gaul, where churches and monasteries displayed a chaotic variety of practices nearly unique to each house of worship. Reforms instituted in Gaul under King Pippin III in 754, with encouragement from Rome and the support of Pippin's successor, Charlemagne, led to the creation of a standard body of chant. Regional churches were forced to conform to this standard, although Milan was spared. The notion identifying Gregory the Great (d. 604) as the divinely inspired composer of the chant (hence the term "Gregorian chant") is unsupportable historically. Nevertheless, the standardization process to which the story indirectly points was a crucially important development. For standardization called forth notation, a process that changed the course of European music.

Early chant notation utilized a wide variety of "neumes," which we might informally call squiggles that indicate the rise and fall of the voice. Over several centuries, simple clefs were devised and a single staff line employed. When eleventh century French theorist Guido of Arezzo introduced a staff of four lines, the result was a chant notation still comprehensible today—at least in the realm of melody.

Chants were and are classified according to various other parameters besides liturgical function. Eighth and ninth century monastic theorists of chant adopted a system of eight standard modes adapted from ancient Greek writings; each mode was associated with a reciting tone used for large stretches of text. Chants are also referred to as syllabic (having one note per syllable), neumatic (mostly with several notes for each syllable), or melismatic (having many notes for each syllable). The towering melismatic chants of the Mass Proper (the parts of the mass that change over the liturgical year) are perhaps the most satisfying for modern listeners; some think that these very florid chants are among the oldest preserved in the repertory.

The chant repertory was not static; monks continued to create new chants even after the rise of polyphony. In the fourteenth and fifteenth centuries there was an unprecedented increase in the number of sequences, hymns, tropes, and other incidental pieces added to the liturgy. These were not necessarily limited to the Vulgate; many are based on sacred poems and reflect the influence of popular taste. The Council of Trent in 1508 barred the tropes from sacred practice, limiting the number of acceptable sequences to three and allowing only a few hymns to remain in use.

In the nineteenth century, Benedictine monks at the Abbey of Solesmes undertook an exhaustive review of old plainchant sources; the *Editio Vaticana* that resulted remains a standard source of the liturgical chant used in Roman Catholic Churches throughout the world until the 1960s. The *Liber Usualis,* a standard-use chant book, is a compilation of frequently sung chants selected from among the many that exist for every part of the liturgy. *—Uncle Dave Lewis*

Recommended:

- ○ **Chant** / Santo Domingo de Silos Abbey Monks' Choir / 1994 / Angel 55138
- ○ **Gregorian Chant** / Ruhland (cond.), Niederaltaicher Scholaren Choralschola / 1994 / Sony 53899
- ○ **Gregorian Chant** / Joppich (cond.) / 2000 / DG 469241
- ○ **Hymnen** / Ruhland (cond.), Capella Antiqua München / Seon 62939
- ○ **Mysteria: Gregorian Chants** / Chanticleer / 1995 / Teldec 99203
- ○ **La Messe Concélebré du Jeudi-Saint** / Monastic Choir of the Abbey of St. Peter / 1990 / Solesmes 831
- ○ **Mysteria: Gregorian Chants** / Chanticleer / 1995 / Teldec 99203
- ○ **Ego sum Resurrectio: Gregorian Chant for the Dead** / Randon (cond.), Aurora Surgit / 1995 / Naxos 553192
- ○ **Chant** / The Benedictine Monks of Santo Domingo de Silos / 1994 / Angel 55138
- ○ **Eastertide** / Monastic Choir of the Abbey of St. Peter / 1985 / Solesmes 825
- ○ **Vespers And Compline** / Monastic Choir of the Abbey of St. Peter / 1985 / Solesmes 15
- ○ **Tenebrae Of Good Friday** / Claire, Monastic Choir of the Abbey of St. Peter / 1993 / Solesmes 5
- ○ **Paschale Mysterium** / Ruhland (cond.), Munich Choral School Capella Antiqua / 1998 / Seon 60360
- ○ **In Passione et Morte Domini: Gregorian Chant for Good Friday** / Turco, Nova Schola Gregoriana / Naxos 550952

André Grétry

b. Feb. 8, 1741, Liège, Belgium, **d.** Sep. 24, 1813, Montmorency, France
Composer

André Ernest Modeste Grétry was born in Liège (now in Belgium) on February 8, 1741. He learned music from his father, a violinist, and became a choirboy. After the young Grétry was brutally beaten for tardiness, he developed the habit of arriving so early for each of the three daily services that he spent long periods shivering on the church steps during winters. This may have accounted for his susceptibility to respiratory infections that eventually led to tuberculosis. In 1761 Grétry traveled to Rome, where he spent some years as a student of Casali; despite the city's burgeoning operatic scene, he produced mostly sacred music during these years (1761–65). As a music teacher in Geneva in 1766, Grétry met Voltaire; at the writer's suggestion, he went to Paris, where he soon established himself as an operatic composer of some consequence. He met a Mlle. Grandon and apparently took a liking to her, judging from the appearance of the first of their three children prior to their marriage in 1771.

Grétry's central position in French opera (especially opéra comique) was undisputed during his lifetime, though the ascendancy of younger rivals such as Cherubini and Méhul eventually stole some of his thunder. Despite bouts of ill health, he maintained a more or less regular composition schedule of two new operas a year. He was decorated and received a pension from the King which, of course, was cancelled by the Revolution; finding favor with the new regime, however, he received a doubled pension by order of Napoleon, who also accorded him the Legion of Honor. Grétry eventually purchased Rousseau's "Ermitage" near Montmorency and eased into retirement there as his musical style became outdated. He died at the estate in 1813.

Though never repertoire mainstays after the composer's lifetime, Gretry's operas enjoyed renewed interest as opera companies and audiences began to rediscover such unjustly overlooked composers of the Classical era. *Richard Coeur-de-lion* (1784) remains a seminal masterpiece of the opéra comique style; *Zemire et Azor* (1771), based on the story of *Beauty and the Beast*, received well-regarded productions in the 1980s and 1990s. Grétry's operas, despite a sometimes offhanded approach to the more academic rules of composition, are notable for a distinctive declamatory style, inventive use of ensembles, and graceful charm. *—AMG*

Overview of Works (ca. 1760–1810)

French composer of Belgian extraction André-Ernest-Modeste Grétry (1741–1813) was the greatest composer of French opéra-comique during the *gran siècle*. Although he also wrote sacred music, chamber music, and symphonies (now lost), his highest achievement is contained in his 66 works for the stage. From his return to France in 1767 after his education in Rome and his exposure there to Pergolesi's comic operas, Grétry quickly achieved a success that transcended the disputes of all the Parisian cliques. Over his two decades of fame, Grétry's brilliantly supple and expressive melodies—his ability to articulate character in a handful of notes and then to develop that character throughout the length of the opera—was demonstrated in work after work and won him the friendship of the French royal family. Among the best of his works are *Zemire et Azor* (1771), *La caravane du Caire* (The Caravan to Cairo) (1783), and *Panurge dans l'isle des lanterns* (Panurge and the Island of Lanterns) (1785). His greatest work is commonly held to be *Richard coeur de lion* (Richard the Lion-Hearted) (1784). However, a series of unfortunate events in the late 1780s—the deaths of all three of his daughters from tuberculosis and the destruction of French society because of the Revolution—quickly reversed his fortunes. The deaths deeply depressed him, and the Revolution lost him his patrons and his audience. In addition, the Revolutionary government was hardly about to condone works in which the royalist Grétry extolled the virtues of the nobility, nor were they all that impressed by his attempts to curry their favor with insincere works praising the Revolution. He turned to writing and turned out many books, including eight volumes of memoirs. His funeral was spectacular in the grandest Empire style, but his music was almost completely forgotten after his death. *—James Leonard*

Recommended:

- ○ **Grétry: Suites & Overtures** / Sanderling (cond.), Bretagne Orch. / 2001 / ASV 1095
- ○ **Grétry: Zémire et Azor** / Doneux (cond.), Mesple, Orliac, Bufkens, Gorp, Belgian Radio & Television CO / 2002 / EMI 575290

Edvard Grieg

b. Jun. 15, 1843, Bergen, Norway, **d.** Sep. 4, 1907, Bergen, Norway

Composer: Concerto, Keyboard, Orchestral, Chamber Music, Vocal

Composer Edvard Grieg, the icon of Norwegian music, left his home in Bergen, Norway to study at the conservatory in Leipzig. There he began his formal musical education under the auspices of Ignaz Moscheles (piano) and Carl Reinecke (composition). While in school, the young composer saw the premiere of his first work, his *String Quartet in D minor*, performed in Karlshamn, Sweden. Despite being diagnosed with a form of tuberculosis, which left him with only one functioning lung, Grieg graduated from the conservatory in 1862. The composer had an intense desire to develop a national style of composition, but recognized the importance of becoming well versed in the work of the European masters, and consequently relocated to Copenhagen, studying with Niels Gade. He was thus able to remain in Scandanavia, while working in a thriving cultural center. In 1867 against his family's better judgment, Grieg married his cousin Nina Hagerup, a talented pianist, but whose vocal abilities enchanted the composer even more. Shortly after their wedding, the couple moved to Oslo, where Grieg supported them by teaching piano and conducting. He and his wife traveled extensively throughout Europe and it was during a period of time spent in Denmark, the composer wrote his landmark opus, the *Piano Concerto in A minor*. The premiere was given in 1869, with Edmund Neupert as the soloist. The piece was received with an enthusiasm that would attach itself to the composer's reputation for the remainder of his career.

Grieg admired his literary contemporaries and forged a productive partnership with Bjørnstjerne Bjørnson, playwright and poet, with whom he staged performances of such works as *Before a Southern Convert*, and *Bergliot*. While Bjornson struggled with his output, Grieg met and befriended Henrik Ibsen. The forthcoming collaboration would prove significant for both, as Grieg would supply incidental music to Ibsen's *Peer Gynt*. The premiere was performed to critical acclaim and eventually led to Grieg's scoring of *Peer Gynt* into Suites 1 and 2 (1888 and 1893 respectively).

As a result of the success of *Peer Gynt*, Grieg enjoyed tremendous celebrity and continued to travel extensively, often meeting internationally renowned composers such as Tchaikovsky, Brahms, and Liszt, among others. In addition to a grant he was awarded in 1874, Grieg was able to earn the majority of his money by adhering to a vigorous schedule of recital tours. He served briefly as the music director of the Bergen Symphony Orchestra, and from 1880–82, held the same position at the Bergen Harmonien. In 1885, Grieg and his wife relocated once again, this time to his native Bergen, Norway, where he built their celebrated home, Troldhaugen. The property, a popular tourist destination to this day, features a secondary building overlooking the water, which the composer used as his work area, as he could only work in solitude. He and his wife summered in Norway and departed each fall for European tours that would last the remainder of the year. Grieg also conducted extensively throughout his country.

Grieg was adored wherever he traveled and lived at a pace that would eventually catch up with him. Edvard Grieg died of chronic fatigue, with much credit given to his lifelong health problems, in his hometown of Bergen.

Norway's most famous composer, dedicated his career to the pursuit of a national sound. The respect he had for his predecessors illustrates the sincerity with which he worked towards this goal. He wrote in the Romantic tradition with, in his own words, the determination to "create a national form of music, which could give the Norwegian people an identity." *—David Brensilver*

CONCERTO

Piano Concerto in A minor, Op. 16 (1868; revised 1907)

Grieg was born on Norway's fjord-coast in the same year that Leipzig's storied Konservatorium opened under the direction of Felix Mendelssohn. By the time Ole Bull, the Norse Paganini, persuaded Grieg's parents to send their gifted 15-year old there for instruction, Mendelssohn was already dead 11 years. His successors were solid, German-schooled academicians whom Edvard hated, and against whom he rebelled. Ever after, he made five years in Leipzig sound like a prison sentence. That he learned so much from allegedly hidebound and uncaring teachers validates the soundness of their instruction. Most notably, Grieg absorbed the salient stylistic traits of Mendelssohn and Schumann (who taught there briefly before moving to Dresden). Indeed, his *Piano Concerto* could be called Schumannesque (likewise in A minor) without invalidating its Scandinavian character or Lisztian flourishes. Despite posthumous scorn for Grieg's large solo oeuvre during much of the twentieth century, his natural habitat was the keyboard. Grieg composed this music in 1868 for himself to play; however, Edmund Neupert played the first public performance in Copenhagen on April 3, 1869.

A government grant enabled Grieg to visit Italy in 1869, where he showed the work to Liszt at his residence near Rome. The kindly Abbé played it at sight with unconcealed pleasure (brilliantly, too, although for Grieg "rather too quickly" during the opening part). Liszt encouraged him to "go on, and don't let anything scare you," but tastelessly suggested that the second subject of the first movement be played by a trumpet instead of cellos. Grieg didn't restore it to the strings until his revision of 1905–06.

The concerto opens with a drum-roll and solo flourish, after which the winds play a simple, unsophisticated main theme that the piano preempts, and embroiders at length, Allegro, molto moderato. The cello subject (più lento—a little slower) is contrastingly "soulful." Trumpets usher in the development, and later on the reprise. A solo cadenza comes just before the end. In the second movement, the key shifts from A minor to D flat major. This structurally uncomplicated Adagio in 3/8 time begins introspectively with muted strings. The piano rhapsodizes until a dramatically angular version of the main theme shatters the mood.

Eventually, calm is restored, and a quiet ending leads without pause to the third movement another quick-but-not-too-quick movement in A minor, additionally marked marcato, whose structure combines sonata and rondo. The piano introduces a main theme based on the 2/4 rhythm of a Norwegian folk dance, the halling. The second subject is quirkier and more elaborate but no less folk-like. The solo flute initiates a tranquil episode, after which the main theme returns for extended development. A short solo cadenza precedes Grieg's long-delayed transition from minor to major for yet another dance, this one in 3/4 time at an accelerated tempo. During a final cadenza, Lisztian bravura blows away any lingering traces of Schumann. *—Roger Dettmer*

Recommended:

- ○ **Michelangeli Plays Grieg & Debussy** / Frühbeck de Burgos (cond.), Michelangeli, New Philharmonia / 2000 / BBC 4043
- ○ **Grieg & Schumann: Piano Concertos** / Matacic (cond.), Richter, Monte Carlo National Opera Orch. / 2003 / EMI 67987
- ○ **Rubinstein Collection, Vol. 13** / Ormandy (cond.), Rubinstein, Philadelphia Orch. / 1999 / RCA 63013
- ○ **Grieg & Schumann: Piano Concertos** / Davis (cond.), Kovacevich, BBCSO / 2001 / Philips 464702

KEYBOARD

Ballade in G minor ("In the Form of Variations on a Norwegian Melody"), Op. 24 (1875–1876)

From Edvard Grieg's extensive body of works for piano, history has, of course, singled out the *Concerto in A minor* for special treatment, but there are a number of other musical gems hidden among the ranks. Many of the *Lyric Pieces* (ten books, in all) are quite becoming, and the four *Album Leaves* have earned a special place in the hearts of a handful of pianists; but it is the striking *Ballade in G minor*, Op. 24, in which the brightest and best of his pianistic sentiments find expression.

The *Ballade*, composed during 1875 and early 1876, takes the melody of an ancient Norwegian folk ballad, "Den nordlansk hondestand" ("The Northland Peasantry"), as the source material for a handful of ingenious variations. Grieg sets the initial presentation of the somber, repetitive theme (Andante espressivo) against a chromatically sliding bass and two colorful middle voices. The delicate opening phrase is all contained within a single lengthy slur and marked piano e molto legato; a middle melodic strain offers a more lighthearted thought.

The first nine variations are simple elaborations of the theme that retain its basic length and melodic outline. In the first variation, the steady three-four quarter notes of the theme dissolve into gentle offbeat triplets; the process of acceleration (built in to the note-values, not played out by the performer) continues in the following allegro agitato, which fills every beat of its expanded nine-eight meter with 16th notes. Although marked Adagio, the third variation retains something of the flowing 16th note character that has been developing in the previous variation.

The fourth variation is impish and chromatic, while the fifth (Piu lento) balances fiery single-voice recitando gestures with calmer but fuller cadential figures. Variations five and six are both canons at the octave that fall under an Allegro scherzando indication.

Deeply contrasting is the following Lento—a kind of funeral march. The main theme is given, darkly, over a slow offbeat in the very low bass register; the recurring pedal tone is usually interpreted to be a musical representation of a bell tolling. The ninth variation is not so much a real section unto itself, but rather more of a transition to the remainder of the *Ballade*: four variations that are cast as continuous sections of one large Finale.

The tenth variation, or first section of the Finale (marked poco allegro e alla burla) is a witty and technically challenging dance. Variation 11 is marked piú animato, and moves to harmonically distant areas. After a characteristic modulation has been made back to the key of G, the mighty, Meno allegro e maestoso (variation 12) begins. This is a Lisztian outburst of sheer pianistic forcefulness: powerful downbeat chords are offset by strong octaves in the extreme registers of the instrument. Both the three-four meter and the original minor mode of the theme are back for Allegro furioso—and Grieg really does mean furious. Fiery arpeggiated chords moving in opposite directions struggle against one another; the tension of contrary motion is heightened by sharp harmonic conflict. Resolution occurs at the beginning of the last variation (prestissimo), a breathtaking plunge back into the theme as we first heard it—now even more subdued and melancholy than it was before. *—Blair Johnston*

Recommended:

- ○ **Grieg & His Circle Play Grieg** / Godowsky / Pearl 9933
- ○ **Rubinstein Collection, Vol. 13** / Rubinstein / 1999 / RCA 63013
- ○ **Grieg: Piano Music, Vol. 3** / Steen-Noekleberg / 1995 / Naxos 550883

Lyric Pieces (1864–1901)

Edvard Grieg's *Lyric Pieces for solo piano* consist of ten separate suites, each containing a number of relatively short character pieces. These ten suites were composed over the span of Grieg's compositional career and are representative of the composer's extraordinary gift for writing for the piano. Each of the 66 *Lyric Pieces* is an attempt to convey to the listener a certain scene or mood through lyrical means. Because of the relative lack of technical difficulty of many of the pieces, it is often believed that Grieg composed them for students of the piano.

The *Lyric Pieces I*, Op. 12 (1867) brought Grieg his first taste of success in the musical world. The first piece is titled "Arietta," in which the music is presented flowingly in a three-voice texture throughout. The second movement is the first waltz of many in the *Lyric Pieces*. Grieg did not compose the next installment in his series, *Lyric Pieces II*, Op. 38, until 1883. Grieg had advanced considerably in compositional maturity by this point. The new work was highly anticipated after the great success of *Lyric Pieces I*.

Three years later, Grieg composed *Lyric Pieces III*, Op. 43. In the six pieces of this suite, the composer perfected the art of the short character piece for solo piano. The second piece, "The Solitary Traveler," tells the story of a lonesome person with no permanent home. The last movement of *Lyric Pieces III* is "To Spring," in which Grieg effectively conveys the beauty of the Norwegian springtime. The *Lyric Pieces IV*, Op. 47 (1888) are not as straightforward as the previous three suites. Many of the movements have a nervous quality. Also, it is difficult for the performer to keep a steady tempo throughout the pieces.

In *Lyric Pieces V*, Op. 54 (1891), the level of virtuosity required has risen dramatically from that of the first *Lyric Pieces*. The third piece, "March of the Dwarfs," is the best example of the pianistic brilliance required to perform this suite. Extremely fast passages, played loudly and softly throughout, are sure to challenge any potential performer and dazzle any audience. A darker mood emerges in *Lyric Pieces VI*, Op. 57 (1893). Menacing bass accompaniments and denser harmonies help to give this impression. This slight stylistic detour is rethought, as a lighter mood returns in *Lyric Pieces VII*, Op. 62 (1895).

The next suite, *Lyric Pieces VIII*, Op. 65 (1896), is the most expressive and weighty of the series. This new solemnity is most evident in the fifth piece, "Ballad." *Lyric Pieces IX*, Op. 68 (1898) starts with the most exciting first movement of the entire suite. This first piece, "Sailor's Song," is meant to be played quickly and aggressively. The final suite of the series is *Lyric Pieces X*, Op. 71 (1901). The last piece of the series, "Remembrances," recalls the melody of the very first piece of the series, "Arietta." *—Chris Boyes*

Recommended:

- ○ **Grieg: Lyric Pieces** / Steen-Noekleberg / 1997 / Naxos 554051

Piano Sonata in E minor, Op. 7 (1865; revised 1887)

Early on in his career, before discovering his talents for miniatures, songs, and incidental music, Edvard Grieg tried his hand at more traditional concert music in its then rigidly codified styles and forms. Indeed, the list of Grieg's almost entirely unplayed early compositions reads like a text of essential concert music varieties: a symphony, some chamber sonatas, an abandoned string quartet, a piano concerto. The first of all these standard concert works to be completed was the *Sonata for piano in E minor*, Op. 7 (1865, revised 1887), a work so obscure that one can dig through book after book without catching a single reference to it and plunder shelf after shelf without finding either a copy or a recording.

And yet, for all that obscurity—and despite Grieg's admitted discomfort with such works—the *Piano Sonata in E minor* is, in its own way, quite an appealing work, like a colorful and clever, but admittedly underdeveloped child. The first of its four movements, Allegro moderato, rides forth on a vital theme that seems to want to plumb the very depths of the earth; if the figurations that surround it and the manner in which it is built up over the course of the movement seem somewhat juvenile, the same might be said of many a more-famous sonata composer's earliest efforts. The Andante molto second movement has just a touch of the same time-stands-still magic that graces the slow movement of the composer's *Piano Concerto* (written some three years later). The third movement—Alla minuetto, ma poco più lento—may be uncomfortably heavy-handed, but its peculiar Nordic flavor and odd dissonances at least add novelty. The finale gallops forth in 6/8 meter and has a chorale-like second subject which, during the recapitulation, achieves the happy E major in which the sonata closes. *—Blair Johnston*

Recommended:

- ○ **Andsnes Plays Greig** / Andsnes / 1993 / Virgin 59300
- ○ **Grieg: Lyric Pieces; Sonata; 7 Fugues** / Pletnev / 2000 / DG 459671

Slåtter (Norwegian Peasant Dances), Op. 72 (1902–1903)

In April 1888, Edvard Grieg was contacted by Knut Dale, who requested that the composer aid him in an effort to notate some of the slåtter, or folk-dance tunes, that he was known for performing on the hardanger-fiddle. The hardanger-fiddle was regarded as the national instrument of Norway at the time. These folk-dance tunes, most of which had been passed along for many generations, were passed to Dale from another fiddler, Torgier Augundsson, who was also known as Myllarguten, or The Miller's Boy. Augundsson often performed at Bull's National Theater in the town of Bergen in 1850. Grieg was not initially eager about the project due to the certain difficulty of transcribing this traditional style of folk-music. Yet he decided to arrange for the preservation of these folk-dance tunes because he feared that they would be forever lost in later times. The composer contacted the Norwegian violinist Johan Halvorsen in October of 1901 requesting that he spend time with Dale, in order to notate a number of the slatter. Grieg would then transcribe the folk-dance tunes for solo piano. By the end of the year, Halvorsen had completed the transcription of 17 of Dale's best folk-dance tunes. Grieg spent almost an entire year working on arranging Halvorsen's work for piano, to produce his *Norwegian Dances* (1902).

Norwegian Dances was published in its two versions, Halvorsen's for violin and his own for piano, in one volume at Grieg's insistence. The composer also insisted that it be made clear that his transcription for piano was based on Halvorsen's work. Both versions also include information on the extensive background of the folk-dance tunes. Although the material for this work was conceived of originally by Grieg, it is nevertheless an important step in his musical development, as well as in the course of the early twentieth century. In fact, in 1906, the work made quite an impression on the young Impressionist musicians of Paris, who referred to it as "the new Grieg."

The first of these folk-dance tunes for piano is "Havard Gibeon's Bridal March," which is rhythmically strict throughout. The next of the tunes, "Jon Vestafe's Sprindans," can be described rhythmically as being bouncy. Jon Vestafe, according to legend, was suspected of murder and at his trial he asked for just one wish, to play one slatt. He played so amazingly that he was immediately set free. The sixth slatter, "Myllarguten's Gangar," is very complex rhythmically with confusing patterns of accenting and slurring. The eighth folk-dance tune is "Myllarguten's Wedding March," a somber song which was written by Augundsson for a former love interest who left him to marry someone else. Arguably the finest piece of the cycle is the 11th slatter, "Knut Lurasen's Halling II." It is the most stylistically varied of the entire set of folk-dance tunes. The 13th folk-dance tune contains the most dissonant passages of the composition, but also has very tender sections. The final slatter transcription ends the work fittingly in a stately, nationalistic manner. *—Chris Boyes*

Recommended:

- ○ **Grieg: Complete Piano Music, Vol. 9** / Knardahl / 1979 / Bis 112
- ○ **Grieg: Piano Music, Vol. 4** / Steen-Noekleberg / 1995 / Naxos 550884

Stimmungen (Moods), Op. 73 (1898–1905)

Feeble and ailing, Grieg produced little in his final years aside from these seven mood pieces for piano. For the set, he dipped into sketches going back as far as 1867, but he did all the real work on the pieces in the early years of the twentieth century. Grieg intended to produce a suite of items larger in scale than his popular *Lyric Pieces*, but although his tone here is more serious, in truth these constitute only a minor enlargement of scope. Grieg was an expert miniaturist and folklorist and he put both strengths to use in this suite, nearly his swan song. The nostalgic first movement, "Resignation," expresses longing for his Danish friend and fellow composer Julius Röntgen. It's a very brief piece, with a slightly agitated section in the middle. "Scherzo-Impromptu" is a playful piece hinting at Grieg's Norwegian style; it's basically monothematic, but contrasting treatments of the theme (including a thoughtful passage near the end) give it an episodic quality. "A Ride at Night" is the most substantial item in the set, a nearly five-minute tone poem for piano lacking a specific program, but initially evoking such terrifying nocturnal equestrian excursions as Liszt's *Mazeppa* and Sibelius' *Night Ride & Sunrise*. At least that's true of the fast outer sections, with their sinister harmonic touches; the middle is an incongruously innocent respite, as if the horse had paused for a snack in a moonlit meadow. The flowing, pastoral "Folk Melody" borrows a ram's horn tune from the Valdres district, which Grieg found in L.M. Lindeman's collection of folk songs. The fifth movement, "Study (Homage to Chopin)," is a virtuosic interlude that had its origins in Grieg's 1867 sketches for his first set of *Lyric Pieces*. "Students' Serenade" employs singsong melodies tucked amid dark introductory and bridge material that sounds strangely ominous. The concluding "Mountaineer's Song" is a nationalist piece, modal and haunting, evoking Norway's rugged landscape with wandering melodies and unsettled harmonies. *—James Reel*

Recommended:

- ○ **Grieg: Complete Piano Music, Vol. 9** / Knardahl / 1979 / Bis 112
- ○ **Grieg: Piano Music, Vol. 1** / Steen-Noekleberg / 1995 / Naxos 550881

ORCHESTRAL

Two Elegiac Melodies, Op. 34 (1880)

The *Two Elegiac Melodies*, Op. 34, (1880) of Norwegian composer Edvard Grieg are string orchestral transcriptions of two songs from his Op. 33 set on texts by Norwegian poet Aasmund Olavsson Vinje. While Grieg has neither expanded nor recomposed the songs for string orchestra, his scoring is so magnificent—so full of poignant touches and tender nuances—that the works sound almost as beautiful in this guise as they did in their original form. The first *Elegiac Melody*, "The Wounded Heart," begins with two heartbreaking phrases in the minor and closes with two heart-consoling phrases in the major. In three verses, the melody of "The Wounded Heart" is first quietly stated in the violins, then more emphatically in the cellos, then passionately in the violins with an ardent countermelody in the cellos. The second *Elegiac Melody*, "Last Spring," has one of the most moving tunes Grieg ever composed, a tune that loves the goodness of life and the beauty of the world even as it fades away into infinity. In two verses, "Last Spring" is quintessential Grieg and replete with felicities: the moment when four solo violins take the tune up to the top of the world in the second verse may be the single most affecting passage in all Grieg. *—James Leonard*

Recommended:

- ○ **Complete Music for String Orchestra** / Norwegian CO / Bis 147
- ○ **Grieg, Sibelius: Romantic Music for Strings** / Leaper (cond.), Istropolitana Capella / 1989 / Naxos 550330
- ○ **NightMoods: Winter Dreams** / various / 1997 / DG 453908

Fra Holberg tid (From Holberg's Time), for strings ("Holberg Suite"), Op. 40 (1885)

While most every work, large or small, produced by composer Edvard Grieg bears the stamp of rightness and focused simplicity, writing music did not always come easily to him. During many of his earlier years, other duties were necessary for making ends meet—directing the Harmonien Orchestra of Bergen, for example. Even over his final two decades, Grieg was obliged to undertake grueling tours as a piano soloist. In 1885, a new home, Troldhaugen, began to provide a place of solitude and comfort. Despite the fact that Ludvig Holberg (1684–1754) lived most of his life in Denmark and was considered the father of Danish literature, his birthplace was Bergen, Norway, and on the bicentenary of his birth, Norwegians heartily celebrated. Even as a resident of Denmark, Holberg recalled his childhood in his works and celebrated the time he spent there. Educated at the universities of Copenhagen and Oxford, Holberg is regarded as having established Danish as a literary language. Prior to his time, Danish was employed only in ballads and hymns; plays were presented in French or German. Besides more than a dozen successful plays (several of them comedies), he wrote a history of his adopted country and published a collection of philosophical treatises. Notwithstanding his stronger relationship to Denmark, Norwegians were pleased to acknowledge Holberg, and Grieg, also a Bergen native, was one of those who directed the planning for the event. As early as 1878, he contributed a fee from his publisher toward the construction of a Holberg statue in Bergen. Further, he wrote two works, the first for male voices, a *Cantata for the Unveiling of the Holberg Memorial*, and a second (of more lasting consequence) entitled *From Holberg's Time: Suite in Olden Style*. Grieg himself premiered the piano suite just days after the dedication of the memorial. Its great success led Grieg to score it for string orchestra the following year, and both versions enjoy enduring popularity. The suite in five sections was intended by Grieg to recall the dance suites that might have been heard during Holberg's lifetime, which roughly corresponded to the period of the late Baroque. The first section, marked "Praeludium," is of such simple radiance that it unforgettably imprints itself on the listener's consciousness. Its predominant cadence, a gently skipping motif, is heard in clusters of three, the second and third each descending a whole tone. The contrasting Sarabande moves soberly, reflectively, and with unfailing elegance. The Gavotte that forms the third section beguilingly trips over the course of its three minutes, yielding to the Andante religioso tempo of the Aria. The final section, a Rigaudon, returns the listener to the buoyant mood of the beginning prelude. Through each of the five sections, the level of invention is matched by a refinement and purity of feeling that marks this as among the most cherishable short works of the late nineteenth century. *—AMG*

Recommended:

- ○ **Grieg: Complete Music with Orchestra** / Järvi (cond.), Gothenburg SO / DG 471300

Lyric Suite (1904)

Edvard Grieg composed and published about 60 so-called "Lyric Pieces" for piano over a period of almost 40 years, from the time of his first real creative outpouring to just a few years before his death in 1907. The six *Lyric Pieces* contained in Opus 54 are considered to be some of his finest products, and it is not surprising that he selected four of them for the charming orchestral *Lyric Suite*.

As it turns out, the idea to orchestrate some of the *Lyric Pieces* was not Grieg's at all. In 1903 it came to Grieg's attention that four pieces from the Opus 54 bunch had been orchestrated by the well-known conductor Anton Seidl; though enthusiastic about the idea, Grieg was not altogether satisfied by Seidl's rather Wagnerian approach. After securing the legal rights from Seidl's widow in 1904, Grieg proceeded to adapt the arrangements of three of them to better suit the translucent textures of the original piano ideas; the orchestration of the first piece in the suite is entirely Grieg's own. (It is touching to note that Grieg handed over the 1,000 marks he received from the sale of the *Lyric Suite* to Seidl's widow.)

Both the Opus 54 piano group and the *Lyric Suite* open with a dramatic piece called *Shepherd Boy*. It moves from a delicate but breathless opening melody to a tumultuous crescendo to fortissimo, only to eventually return to the fragile realm from which it came. The shimmering final chord is reminiscent of the one that begins the famous *Anitra's Dance* from the first *Peer Gynt Suite*.

Gangar, the title of the second piece, means "walking tune"; the music is steady and sure in a way that the first piece was not. A syncopated motivic idea is set against an unwavering background of dotted eighth- notes; the middle section makes a charming use of dynamic contrast—one can almost imagine that this is a heated conversation during the walk, one speaker tumultuous and agitated, the other far more subdued. The rising harmonies of the coda, set to two contrasting rhythms, evaporate in a striking way.

March of the Dwarves is not only the finest piece in the *Lyric Suite*, it is probably also the best of any of the *Lyric Pieces* and a contender for one of the top three or four slots in all of Grieg's music. Cast in a well-defined ABA form, it contrasts the firm, rhythmic (Dwarves are marching, after all!) material of the outer sections with one of the composer's most sublime lyrical melodies. Grieg writes some very long crescendos and diminuendos, as if the marchers draw near and then pass.

The last piece in the *Suite* is the well-known *Notturno* (Nocturne), an ethereal glimpse into a musical world in which traditional rhythm—even the basic concepts of downbeat and upbeat—are suspended. There is a rich, well-deserved two measure Adagio at the end. *—Blair Johnston*

Recommended:

- **Grieg: Norwegian Dances; Symphonic Dances; Lyric Suite (Hybrid SACD)** / Ruud (cond.), Bergen PO / 2003 / BIS 1291
- **Grieg: Peer Gynt Suites; Lyric Suite; Sigurd Jorasalfar** / Jarvi (cond.), Gothenburg SO / DG 427807

Peer Gynt, incidental music, Op. 23 (1874–1875; revised 1885)

The incidental music Edvard Grieg composed for Henrik Ibsen's play *Peer Gynt* (1867) stands, along with his *Holberg Suite* and *Piano Concerto*, among his most universally popular orchestral works. By common consent, the music itself achieved far more for Ibsen's vast and bewildering dramatic poem than any mere stage performance alone could have done, and therein lies a problem. For as Ibsen's English biographer Michael Meyer writes, Grieg's music "turns the play into a jolly Hans Andersen fairy tale," one thing its author would certainly never have wished for. And the critic and playwright George Bernard Shaw, a fervent advocate of Ibsen's works, similarly concluded that in his music Grieg "could only catch a few superficial points in the play instead of getting to the very heart and brain of it." That may well be the case, but Grieg's *Peer Gynt* incidental music has nevertheless become a universal favorite, and it is not difficult to understand why.

Ibsen decided to adapt his verse drama for performance at the Christiana (Oslo) Theatre in 1874, recognizing that his sprawling five-act play would benefit greatly from the addition of a musical score. Grieg's music was first heard there in February 1876, but the initial production run was radically curtailed after fire destroyed the sets and costumes. The score, however, was enthusiastically received by the critics, and Grieg subsequently saw an opportunity to establish a separate identity for the music itself and drew from the more than two dozen numbers of the complete work two concert suites, Opp. 46 and 54. Conductors sometimes assemble ad hoc suites of their own as well.

The most popular numbers are "In the Hall of the Mountain King" (a textbook example of the dramatic potency of cumulative crescendo and accelerando, illustrating Grieg's fondness for Germanic orchestral effects), in which Peer Gynt bargains for his life after the assembled Trolls call for his blood, and the highly evocative "Morning Mood" with its lovely flute solo and expansive orchestral language—the music depicts, incidentally, not a fresh Nordic sunrise, but rather a Saharan dawn in Act IV of Ibsen's drama! Other memorable moments include the fragile lyric utterances of "Solveig's Song," the beguiling "Anitra's Dance," the poignant "Death of Åse," "Peer Gynt's Homecoming: Stormy Evening at Sea," and his eventual "Shipwreck." As Anthony Burton writes, "the curtain falls as Peer's long and eventful journey finally comes to its end." *—Michael Jameson*

Recommended:

- **Grieg: Orchestral Music** / Beecham (cond.), Royal PO / 1998 / EMI 66966
- **Schumann: Piano Concerto; Grieg: Lyric Suite; Franck: Symphonic Variations; etc.** / Barbirolli (cond.), Halle Orch. / 1995 / Seraphim 568522

Sigurd Jorsalfar, suite, Op. 56 (1872; revised 1892)

Norwegian composer Edvard Grieg wrote eight pieces of incidental music plus opening fanfares for Bjørnstjerne Bjørnson's historical play *Sigurd Jorsalfar* (Sigurd the Crusader) at three different points in his compositional career. The original five pieces of incidental music—the intermezzo "Borghild's Dream," "The Matching Game," "The Northland Folk," "The Homage March," and "The King's Song"—were composed in Oslo in spring 1872 for the premiere performance of the play on April 10 of that year. Thirty-one years later, Grieg added a further three pieces—the Prelude to Act I, two Interludes, and an opening fanfare—for the 1903 production of the play in Stuttgart. In between, Grieg prepared a concert suite in 1892 from the original music, which became the basis for his 1903 version. The music for the concert suite for *Sigurd Jorsalfar* consists of three pieces from the 1872 incidental music, but re-ordered and, in one case, greatly expanded. The suite starts with "The Matching Game"—a confident march that begins quietly for the winds, but builds to an impressive climax for full orchestra with a folksong-like trio—"Borghild's Dream"—an appropriately mysterious work with hushed two-part counterpoint for the strings giving way to frightening music for full orchestra—and the closing "Homage March." The latter was vastly enlarged for concert suite in 1892. The original 1872 version had consisted of a noble tune first stated by the solo cello and heroic tune given to the solo trumpet. In the 1892 version, Grieg added an opening fanfare and, more significantly, a spacious central trio with strummed chords in the harp beneath a yearning lyrical theme for the strings. *—James Leonard*

Recommended:

- **Grieg: Peer Gynt Suites; Lyric Suite; Sigurd Jorasalfar** / Jarvi (cond.), Gothenburg SO / DG 427807

Symphonic Dances, Op. 64 (1896–1898)

The tunes upon which these four dances are founded are of folk origin, most of them taken from a collection assembled by Norwegian composer Ludvig M. Lindemann (1812–87). In fact, Grieg appended to the title of this work the phrase "after Norwegian themes." His use and development of these folk melodies fits a fantasia-like treatment here more than a symphonic one. The opening dance (Allegro moderato e marcato) is derivative of a so-called "halling," a Norwegian country dance possibly having Scottish origins. The music has a lively, celebratory air about it in the outer sections, while in the central part it is initially subdued and somewhat exotic, but intensifies before yielding back to the main material. The second dance (Allegretto grazioso) is also taken from a halling, but revels in a serene and relaxed atmosphere, confident and utterly joyful in its nonchalance. The middle section is lively and playful. The third dance number, marked Allegro giocoso, draws on a melody used for a spring dance from the Aamot region, in Hedmark County, Norway. It begins in a playful, subdued manner but turns festive and vigorous, then yields to a mostly relaxed middle section. The last dance opens with an Andante introduction, after which a march (Allegro molto e risoluto) is introduced that bears similarity to the main theme in Sibelius' 1893 tone poem *En Saga*. Yet, the likeness is purely coincidental since Grieg's thematic source was a country ballad. The lovely trio section here features the melody from a folk wedding song from the Valders region. At around ten minutes, the last dance is the longest of the four by far, and probably the most substantive as well. Together, the four dances have a duration of nearly half an hour. Grieg also made an arrangement of them for piano, four hands, and while it is a well-crafted effort, it cannot supplant the more colorful and musically appropriate orchestral rendition. *—Robert Cummings*

Recommended:

- **Grieg: Peer Gynt—Suites 1 & 2; Symphonic Dances** / Berglund (cond.), Bournemouth Sinfonietta / 2001 / EMI 74731

CHAMBER MUSIC

Cello Sonata in A minor, Op. 36 (1882–1883)

For some, it comes as a great surprise that Edvard Grieg's catalog contains five sonatas: one for piano solo, three for violin and piano, and one for cello and piano. All of these but two—the third and last violin sonata (Op. 45) and the *Cello Sonata*—are very early works, composed by Grieg in the mid-1860s. The *Sonata for cello and piano in A minor*, Op. 36 (1883), on the other hand, is the work of a composer almost 20 years older; while Grieg's frustrations and difficulties with traditional genres (sonata, string quartet, symphony, and the like) are well-documented in his personal letters, the *Cello Sonata*'s urgent and energetic dramatic thrust, as well as voluptuous, satiny songfulness, have ensured its position as one of the three or four best-loved late nineteenth century cello sonatas.

The *Cello Sonata* is in three movements: Allegro agitato, Andante molto tranquillo, and Allegro—allegro molto. The first movement's opening theme is as full of sturm und drang as they come; its second gushes with a most extraordinary warmth. There is, quite unexpectedly, a little cadenza for the cellist midway through the movement, just before the recapitulation; one cannot help but notice that when the pianist enters again the music takes a rumbling, ominous tone quite like one heard in the cadenza of the famous *Piano Concerto*'s first movement. The slow movement is in a warm F major; as the opening musical paragraph gives way to the second and third paragraphs, it becomes clear that all is not as innocent and sweetly lyrical as the lovely opening melody would suggest. Indeed, there is real desperation in the middle of the movement. After a quiet introduction, the lengthy finale assumes the shape of a dark-hued goblin-dance that ends in robust A major. *—Blair Johnston*

Recommended:

- **Grieg: Cello Sonata; String Quartet, Op27** / Mork / 2002 / Virgin 45505
- **Grieg: Cello Sonata; Brahms: Cello Sonata 1** / Rostropovich / AS Disc 11035
- **Delius & Grieg: Complete Music for Cello & Piano** / Lloyd Webber, Forsberg / 1998 / Philips 454458

String Quartet No. 1 in G minor, Op. 27 (1877–1878)

Grieg was, at root, a miniaturist. He did not often work in the large scale of the sonata form; his entire completed literature in this form consists of a symphony that he suppressed, one concerto, one cello sonata, three violin sonatas, and this quartet. (Later, he wrote two movements toward another one.) It was composed in 1877–78. It is an exceedingly attractive and untroubled work, with a melodic spirit that recalls his best songs or piano works. One song-like figure in particular is used throughout. Grieg does treat his material in sonata fashion, but not rigorously. There is a feeling of Norwegian peasant dances in the scherzo, while the finale trots merrily with a saltarello rhythm. It is, in short, a lovable work, heart-warming in the way that Grieg's music so often is. *—Joseph Stevenson*

Recommended:

○ **Mendelssohn: Quartet 2; Grieg: Quartet In G Minor** / Shanghai Quartet / 1994 / Delos 3153

○ **Grieg & Johansen: String Quartets** / Oslo SQ / 1994 / Naxos 550879

Violin Sonata No. 3 in C minor, Op. 45 (1886–1887)

In January 1900, Grieg performed his three violin sonatas with Wilma Neruda-Hallé in Copenhagen. Afterward, he wrote to his friend the Norwegian poet Bjørnstjerne Bjørnson that his violin sonata trilogy was closely related to his own life's experiences. "They characterize the three periods of my own evolution," he explained. "The first, ingenious and full of new ideas; the second, nationalistic, and the third, turned toward vaster horizons." Indeed, in the series of violin sonatas we do sense a logical, natural progression that may well seem autobiographical.

The set of three culminates with the massive C minor sonata, Op. 45, written in 1887. Whereas each of the previous sonatas had been set down in a matter of just a few weeks, Op. 45 was begun in the autumn of 1886 and was finished, according to the composer's journal, on January 21 of the following year. The work was dedicated to the painter Franz von Lehnbach, and had its premiere at the *Neues Gewandhaus* in Leipzig on December 10, 1887, in a performance by the Russian violinist Adolf Brodsky with Grieg himself at the piano. The work was enthusiastically hailed by critics and public alike. Within a very short time, it had entered the repertories of other leading violinists of the day, among them Wieniawski, Ysaÿe, and Kreisler.

Although Grieg characterized the piece as the product of newfound inspiration found during a time of personal happiness, such origins are hardly reflected by the terse urgency of the thematic material—nor by the choice of key, a defiantly Beethovenian C minor. The dimensions are expansive, and the work takes about 25 minutes to perform. The opening movement (Allegretto molto ed appassionato) offers a tense first-subject motif, with the second group altogether more relaxed and consoling in mood. The darkly somber development section is based entirely upon the first theme, which also makes a further appearance after the recapitulation just prior to the very dramatic coda. There follows a slow movement (Allegretto espressivo alla Romanza) in the serene tonality of E major. Interestingly, piano and violin assume quite independent roles here; though each is heard in the noble main theme (some 44 measures in length), there is little sense of dialogue or equitable exchange between the two. The individuality of the two instruments is heightened to a surprising extent here, and even in the final section the two are never fully reconciled. The finale (Allegro animato) has a sonata structure (ABAB–Coda) without a development section, the lack of which is compensated for in a series of daring modulations that involve digressions into A flat major and F major. In the words of Rune J. Andersen, the piece contains "universal and national elements fused into something deeply personal and specifically Griegian." *—Michael Jameson*

Recommended:

○ **Rachmaninov: Complete Recordings** / Rachmaninov, Kreisler / 1992 / RCA 61265

○ **Grieg: Violin Sonatas** / Chiu, Amoyal / 2000 / HM 907256

VOCAL

Songs (1859–1905)

Edvard Grieg composed at least 180 songs for solo voice and piano, the vast majority of which were written between 1864 and 1900. The reason for Grieg's sudden interest in the genre of the song was his engagement to Nina Hagerup, a talented singer; most of his songs were composed with her in mind. Their personal and musical relationship carried on as they moved to the capital city of Norway together in 1866, where they were to stay until 1874. Nina retired from public performance around the end of the century, and Grieg composed his last songs in 1900.

The generally high quality of Grieg's songs owes a lot to the composer's fortunate exposure to what was then a golden age of Norwegian lyric poetry. Also, he was familiar works in Danish, and had set German texts during his student years at the Leipzig Conservatory. All of Grieg's songs are in one of these three languages, and they are the elements that most readily divide his song output into meaningful groups.

Grieg's German lieder (mostly student compositions) were his earliest attempts in the genre. His *Four Songs for Alto*, Op. 2 (1861), are based on poems by Chamisso and Heine. His next set of songs, *Six Songs* (1864), was completed in the year of his engagement to Nina. These settings of texts by Chamisso, Heine, and Uhland are dedicated to "Fräulein Nina Hagerup."

The composer moved on to Danish texts with his *Four Romances*, Op. 10 (1864), based on texts by Christian Winter. There is a noticeable maturation of Grieg's style in his *Melodies of the Heart*, Op. 5 (1865). These four songs marked the beginning of Grieg's affinity for the poetry of Hans Christian Andersen. Two later opuses would also feature lyrics of Andersen.

Grieg's first songs with Norwegian text were his *Romances and Ballads*, Op. 9 (1866), set to poetry by Andreas Munch. Much of this work is reminiscent of a type of lyric song popular in Scandinavia at the time, known as the romance. From this point on, Grieg composed nearly all of his songs to only Norwegian texts. Some of his later songs, beginning with the *Twelve Melodies of Vinje*, Op. 33 (1880), are settings of the *landsmal* dialect of the Norwegian language, which grew in popularity during Grieg's lifetime. *—Chris Boyes*

Recommended:

○ **Grieg: Lieder** / Otter, Forsberg / 1992 / DG 437521

○ **Songs, Vols. 1 & 2** / Hagegård, Jones / 1993 / BMG 61630

○ **Grieg: Songs, Vol. 1** / Groop, Derwinger / 1993 / Bis 637

○ **Grieg: Songs, Vol. 2** / Groop, Ranta / 1996 / Bis 787

12 Melodies after Poems by Vinje, Op. 33 (1873–1880)

In April 1880, Grieg began composing again after a long period of travel and performing. He was inspired by the poetry of Aasmund Olafsson Vinje. Vinje (1818–70) was truly a poet of the nineteenth century, his Romanticism following in the footsteps of Heine, Byron, and Goethe, and with a nationalistic feeling not only for subject matter, but also for language, using a "country" version of Norwegian. This suited Grieg's desire to use Norwegian folk idioms in his music, and these songs are considered his first genuinely Norwegian songs. Grieg initially set 15 poems, but published only ten of these in Op. 33, adding two others that he had composed earlier. The songs were published in two books, in multiple languages. Grieg worked closely with the translators, hoping to accurately capture the feel of the original texts, but not always succeeding, even with that close relative of Norwegian, Danish. This helps explain why the songs are much better known in Norway than anywhere else. From the simplicity of a description of nature in *Langs ei Å* to the breathless dance of the fleeting vision in *Eit Syn*, and the dissonance of bitterness in *Eit vennestykke* (A Broken Friendship), the music is determined by the text in each song; the mood and words of the poem determine the mood and harmonies of the music. Most of the songs are strophic, all are representative of Grieg's gift for melody, and even if the folk music idioms are not obvious, the songs are unmistakably Grieg's. The set begins with *Guten* (The Youth), a warning to a restless youth. This is followed by what is probably Grieg's best-known song (other than *Solveig's Song*), *Våren* (Spring), later orchestrated along with the third song, *Den sårede* (The Wounded Heart). *Langs ei Å* (Beside the Stream), the fifth song, was written in 1877, while the seventh, *Gamle Mor* (The Old Mother), was written in 1873, but neither is out of place with the later songs. No. 6, *Eit Syn* (A Vision), is one of the more popular of the 12, as are No. 9, *Ved Rundarne* (At Rondane), and the final song, *Fyremål* (The Goal). In that final song, the bitterness inherent in much of the others is resolved through Vinje's hopeful text and Grieg's strong-minded, melodious opening and lyrical middle section of his setting. *—Patsy Morita*

Recommended:

○ **Grieg: Lieder** / Otter, Forsberg / 1992 / DG 437521

○ **Grieg: The Complete Songs, Vol. 4** / Groop, Vignoles / 2002 / Bis 1257

Charles Tomlinson Griffes

b. Sep. 17, 1884, Elmira, NY, **d.** Apr. 8, 1920, New York, NY

Composer: Keyboard, Orchestral, Concerto, Ballet

Charles Tomlinson Griffes was among the most distinctive and poetic of American composers. In the 15 years of his artistic maturity, his style evolved from German-derived post-Romanticism to a particularly personal adaptation of French Impressionism, and finally to a strong and individual style of his own. Most commentators regard his as the greatest talent of his generation.

His older sister, Katharine, started giving him piano lessons when he was young, passing on what she learned from her own teacher, Mary Selina Broughton. When the boy was 15, he started studying directly with Ms. Broughton, who was on the faculty of Elmira Free Academy. She also taught him "taste" and "gentility," and persuaded his parents that he had such talent that he should be encouraged to become a musician. She even subsidized his travel to Berlin, where he studied piano with Ernst Jedliczka and Gottfried Galston at the Stern'sche Conservatory; his counterpoint instructors were Max Lowengard and Wilhelm Klatte, and his composition professors were Philippe Rüfer and Engelbert Humperdinck. Griffes appeared at a Conservatory concert as a piano soloist in 1904, to high acclaim; but by then his interests had turned toward composition, somewhat to Ms. Broughton's disappointment. He left the Conservatory to study privately and intensively with Humperdinck, and continued in piano with Galston. He made some money by taking in pupils in piano and harmony, and by giving some concerts.

During his German period, he wrote German-language songs and a *Symphonische Phantasie*. He returned to the United States in September, 1907, accepting a job at the Hackley School of Tarrytown, New York, where he remained until his death in 1920 (of pneumonia, perhaps due to the 1919–20 influenza epidemic).

Since he died young, and because the position was a relatively minor one within the world of music, biographical information has been romanticized over the years, suggesting that Griffes was trapped in a menial job, living in poverty. In fact, he found the job interesting and was much liked by fellow faculty members and students—he was certainly not starving. Furthermore, the job included a lengthy summer period during which he could devote himself entirely to composition and promote his works in nearby New York.

During his own lifetime, piano works such as the *Roman Sketches* appeared and were appreciated for their poetic and descriptive beauty. The tone poem *The Pleasure Dome of Kublai Khan*, the Japanese ballet *Sho-jo*, *Five Poems of Ancient China and Japan*, and a major chamber ballet, *The Kairn of Koridwen*, all received major premieres, drawing attention to Griffes as a composer possessed of a unique voice, exceptional craftsmanship, and melodic inventiveness. His later pieces, such as the *Notturno for Orchestra* (1918) and the *Piano Sonata* are most illustrative of his mature voice; in these works, the influences of his German and French models are completely assimilated into his own harmonically adventurous palate. *—Joseph Stevenson*

KEYBOARD

Piano Sonata (1917–1918)

Although *The White Peacock*, *The Lake at Evening*, and *The Pleasure Dome of Kubla Khan* remain the best known works of American composer Charles T. Griffes, his *Sonata for Piano* represents his highest musical achievement. The *Sonata for Piano* has its roots in an unfinished work that Griffes undertook in the fall of 1917, not long after completing his incidental music for the Celtic play *The Kairn of Koridwen*. The unfinished piece was the torso of a *Sonata for Piano* that Griffes was ultimately to abandon in December of that year. At that point, Griffes decided to start over from scratch, and happily completed the 15-minute sonata in just one month. Griffes himself gave the premiere of the *Sonata for Piano* at a concert of his works held at the MacDowell Club in New York on February 26, 1918. At this juncture the sonata was cast in a single movement only; however, during preparation of the work for publication, Griffes changed his mind and divided the piece in three movements to be played without pause.

The *Sonata for Piano* is unique among Griffes' output. Whereas his earlier music tended to rely on a variety of approaches ranging from German-styled post-Romanticism to pseudo-oriental exotica, Griffes demonstrates a tough and single-minded attitude in the *Sonata for Piano*. The sonata shares little if anything with stylistic traits exhibited in Griffes' earlier works, and is cut from whole cloth that is free from exterior influences. Griffes' *Sonata for Piano* is dramatic, even tempestuous, dynamic (much of it is played forte) and makes quite liberal use of dissonance, although that is not to say the sonata is in any way disorienting to listen to. Griffes adheres strongly to a predetermined strategy of key relationships, and exercises a masterly control over the overall structure. Griffes does not digress, and his *Sonata for Piano* is a taut, highly disciplined, and compelling realization of his ideas.

Griffes' *Sonata for Piano* came along at a time when an important younger generation of American composers was coming of age, and few, if any, escaped the example it provided. Virgil Thomson once said that the sonata was "shockingly original." Critical reception to the sonata was immediate and overwhelmingly positive, with pianist/composer Rudolf Ganz proclaiming it as "the finest abstract work in American piano literature." The quality of the Griffes *Sonata for Piano* is attested to by the fact that since its introduction in 1918 there have been relatively few serious challenges to its status in this regard. The Griffes sonata has such "long legs," in fact, that in 1941, upon receipt of a manuscript copy of this sonata, Griffes' publisher G. Schirmer thought it a newly discovered work, and promptly signed a contract with the Griffes family to publish it. Only then did Schirmer realize that they'd already had it in their catalog for 20 years. *—Uncle Dave Lewis*

Recommended:

○ **Griffes: Works for Piano** / Wehr / 1996 / Connoisseur Society 4205

○ **4 American Piano Sonatas** / Doppmann / 1999 / Equilibrium 27

Roman Sketches, suite, Op. 7 (1915–1916)

The reputation of Charles Tomlinson Griffes as the "American Impressionist" mainly rests on his three best-known piano suites: the *Three Tone-Pictures*, Op. 5 (1910–11); the *Fantasy Pieces*, Op. 6 (1915); and the instant suite. They are all the result of Griffes' encounter with French Impressionist music in the shape of Ravel's *Jeux d'eaux*. In the *Roman Sketches*, Griffes retains French Impressionist harmony, but reasserts his penchant for clear-cut melodies and employs the harmonies to create a flow that carries the music rather than mainly coloring it in Debussy's fashion.

The *Roman Sketches* is a substantial suite of four pieces between three and a half and seven minutes in length. They are inspired by the poetry of William Sharp, published in a collection called *Sospiri di Roma* (Sighs of Rome). While Sharp's poems are not highly regarded now, they elicited some of Griffes' most personal and characteristic music. Each of the four movements flows naturally from the imagery of the poems, yet stands on its own as a fully satisfying musical composition that, if anything, conveys the pictures Sharp intended to portray better than the poet did. Considered purely in terms of their compositional technique and their utilization of the piano, the *Sketches* are nothing short of masterly in addition to being exceptionally beautiful and atmospheric pieces of music.

"The White Peacock" is the most famous, not only of this set, but of all Griffes' music. Griffes was fond of peacocks and saw his first white one in the Berlin zoo. He came to collect pictures of them, and it is quite likely that Sharp's poem about one first drew his attention to *Sospiri di Roma*. The piece has an unusually sensuous melody, with arpeggiated "fans" in the piano that obviously represent the male bird spreading his tail in the species' trademark display.

"Nightfall" creatively uses the minor second. This dissonance, normally considered one of the harshest, becomes an atmospheric blur when Griffes places it consistently in the low bass. It seems to cast a growing shadow as the sky darkens, and a sad though calm theme is heard higher on the keyboard.

"The Fountain of the Acqua Paola" is Griffes' answer to Ravel's *Jeux d'eaux*, though it is more tender than Ravel's or Franz Liszt's *Jeux d'eaux à la Villa d'Este*, its two most immediate predecessors.

The remarkable "Clouds" depicts cumulus clouds sailing tranquilly late in the day as they take on the colors of sunset. Since Griffes associated particular colors with particularly keys, he boldly mixes chords and tonalities as the clouds take on different colors, making a more brilliant effect than the deliberately gray sounds of Debussy's *Nuages*. The composer provided an outstanding orchestration of this movement as well as of "The White Peacock." *—Joseph Stevenson*

Recommended:

○ **Griffes: Complete Piano Works, Vol. 1** / Lewin / 1999 / Naxos 559023

○ **MacDowell: Griffes, Vol. I** / Tocco / 1984 / Gasparo 231

Tone-Pictures, Op. 5 (1910–1915)

Charles Tomlinson Griffes was part of the early generation of American composers who received their musical higher education in Germany. But the course of his musical development was reoriented to a new direction after he heard a performance of Ravel's *Jeux d'eau* (Fountains). This work with its brilliance, its mysterious and new harmonic language, and its unsettled harmonic ambiguity suited Griffes well. The French Impressionists' tendency to write brief descriptive movements rather than music of German formal structures also was closer to Griffes' natural inclinations. (It would not be until the end of his sadly shortened life—he died of complications from the disastrous influenza epidemic of 1918–20—that he turned back to academic forms with stunning originality in his *Piano Sonata*.)

If one must seek, for description's sake, a comparison to the *Three Tone Pictures* in the works of the French Impressionist masters, Ravel's *Gaspard de la nuit* and Debussy's *Images* for piano (particularly *Reflets dans l'eau*, *Cloches à travers les feuilles*, and *Et la lune descend sur le temple qui fût*) seem to come closest. In common with many of these six movements by the French masters, Griffes uses a hypnotic ostinato rhythm, obsessively tied to one note, as a leading harmonic and structure device. In common with Debussy, Griffes was drawn to the poetry of Edgar Allen Poe and uses epigrams from Poe as headings for two of the *Three Tone Poems*. The important thing is that Griffes' music, despite their being strongly influenced by Debussy and Ravel at this point, is fully capable of withstanding any sort of comparison with the works it is modeled after.

The first movement, "The Lake at Evening," was inspired by a line from Yeats, "lake water lapping with low sounds by the shore." It is the prettiest and most purely melodic of the *Tone Pictures*, with a tender melodic line that still retains the feeling of German Romanticism, creating a charming effect against the French harmonies and the disturbing repeated note.

"The Vale of Dreams" is more thoroughly tied to French Impressionism in its style, though there is a streak of Scriabin's harmonies involved here, also. The music seems to descend sadly to the place of dreams, depicted in the harmonic stillness that prevails in the last measures.

"The Night Wind," the final movement, is not a strong storm, but is a portrait of a gusty wind that seems to come from some mystic source. When its chromatic scurrying abates and the music rests on a shimmering dissonant chord, it is as though the wind has brought with it the breath of a mystic realm.

Griffes revised "The Night Wind" in 1915, when the suite became the first of his piano music to be published. He also arranged it for woodwinds and harp in the same year, and in 1919 made an orchestration for piano, wind quintet, and string quintet or string ensemble. *—Joseph Stevenson*

Recommended:

○ **Griffes: Collected Works for Piano** / Oldham / 1997 / New World 80310

○ **MacDowell & Griffes, Vol. 4** / Tocco / 1984 / Gasparo 234

ORCHESTRAL

The Pleasure-Dome of Kubla Khan, tone poem, Op. 8 (1917)

This work began as a piano piece written in 1912, but its definitive form is its orchestral version, completed in 1917 and introduced by the Boston Symphony under Pierre Monteux in 1919. The work was rapturously received by the audience and received glowing notices from the critics. It is one of a very few short orchestral pieces by the composer, who died the following year at the age of 36, and is unmistakably the work of an artist who could have achieved exceptionally important status in American musical history. In style the work is similar to those of contemporary French composers such as Debussy, Ravel, Roussel, and Ibert: it is rich, sweeping, brilliantly orchestrated.

The literary source, of course, is Coleridge's famous unfinished poem, and it faithfully mirrors the poem's startling juxtapositions of imagery of sunniness and "caves of ice." In the music, we perceive both glitter and darkness, stateliness and reverie, languorousness and frenzy. That's a lot for ten minutes of music!

In short, it is a seductively lovely piece. It sets interpretational problems for the conductor because of the sheer variety and number of its musical episodes. Occupying the position of something of a dead end in history (rather than being the introduction of a major new talent who would go on and develop even greater music), it has not become a major item in the repertoire. But it gains friends whenever it is played.

Griffes completed the first incarnation of the piano *Pleasure Dome of Kubla Khan* by July 1912, when he played it along with *The Vale of Dreams* for composer Arthur Farwell. At the beginning of 1913, Griffes submitted it, along with other new works such as *The Lake at Evening*, to the publisher G. Schirmer in New York, who rejected the entire group. Griffes was advised that he was "writing too dreamily and subjectively, and needed to get out into the outer world more." However, Griffes was also recommended to composer Ferruccio Busoni, who happened to be coming to New York to concertize in the weeks ahead. Busoni wrote a strong letter of recommendation for Griffes after reviewing several of his pieces, which helped to pave the way for Griffes at Schirmer. Busoni was most impressed with *Kubla Khan* in particular, but he suggested that Griffes either trim the piece or orchestrate it.

In 1915, Griffes dutifully prepared a streamlined *Pleasure Dome of Kubla Khan* for piano. But he soon got caught up in creating the orchestral piece, which was completed in 1917. After that, both piano versions went back into the drawer, not to be heard again for nearly 70 years. *The Pleasure Dome of Kubla Khan* in its original piano incarnation, startlingly different from the orchestral version, is profitably approached on its own terms. It contains some of Griffes' most florid and colorful writing for the instrument. The work is written at a level of difficulty so high that there is ample music for four hands, but some exceptional pianists are able to manage it with two. *—Joseph Stevenson*

Recommended:

○ **All American Favorites** / Schwarz (cond.), Seattle SO / 1994 / Delos 3180

CONCERTO

Poem, for flute & orchestra (1918)

This is one of the best of all single-movement concerted works for flute and orchestra, a masterpiece of less than ten minutes' length that displays all the potential of the flute as a solo instrument. Its composer was an American who had a tragically short life, living from 1884 to 1920. Moreover, Griffes was a painstaking composer who wrote his works slowly. His income from teaching was so meager that he had to copy out parts for his orchestral scores himself to get performances, which was sheer drudge work. The strain of repeatedly staying up through the night to do this is said to have broken his health.

He wrote this *Poem* for the famous French flutist Georges Barrère, who played it with the New York Symphony Society, Walter Damrosch conducting, on November 16, 1919. In keeping abreast of European musical developments, Griffes had adopted some harmonic practices from Debussy, and this music has the cool sensuality and sense of antiquity associated with the French master. It is not quite right to say that the music is some sort of "American Impressionism," for the harmonies still tend to be functional (i.e. are used in their accustomed role as the energizer of forward progress in the music) rather than coloristic.

Above all, the piece is extraordinarily beautiful. It is scored for a small orchestra of strings with the addition of two horns that add an extraordinary magical touch to the sonorities. There is effective use of percussion, lightly applied. The form of the work is that of a Liszt rhapsody: a languorous slow flute solo in a nocturnal atmosphere is succeeded by a lithe, fast dance. The first part lets the flute show off its sheer beauty of tone, while the second displays exceptional virtuosity in its rapid figurations. *—Joseph Stevenson*

Recommended:

○ **Hanson Conducts Barber, Piston, Griffes, McCauley, Kennan, Bergsma** / Hanson (cond.), Mariano, Eastman-Rochester Orch. / 1992 / Mercury 434307

BALLET

The Kairn of Koridwen (1916)

The Kairn of Koridwen: A Druid Legend, or, "The Sanctuary of the Goddess of the Moon," was originally composed in piano score form—not as a piano part—then arranged by composer Charles Griffes. The original, complete manuscript for the dance drama in two scenes, written for eight solo instruments, was scattered. In the 1960s, a score was reconstructed by the Free Library of Philadelphia.

The Kairn of Koridwen consists of an unusual group of instruments. Griffes was exploring Oriental music, and thus, the arrangement does not utilize any strings. The scoring for the pantomime is: flute, two B flat clarinets, two horns in F, celesta, harp, and piano. The *Kairn* utilizes a synthetic scale that causes the harmonies to consist of a large quantity of augmented seconds, fourths, and fifths. Because of the synthetic scale, and also the manner in which Griffes wrote the manuscript, it is difficult to tell exactly what key each of the scenes is in. Although the piece sounds somewhat Impressionistic, Griffes' use of atonality is heightened.

Kairn is adapted from a text by Edouard Schure (1841–1929), *Les Grandes Legendes de France*. The tale is about druidesses who worship Koridwen, the goddess of the moon. One druidess, Carmelis, has to choose between her love, the Gallic warrior, Mordred, and her religion. According to her religion, Carmelis is supposed to kill Mordred for seeking a prophecy, but cannot. She reveals to Mordred the secret of his future, then sends him away. Carmelis wants to believe that she will find a happier life after death. The druidesses then find Carmelis dead.

The music is intended for dance, and the characters are meant to convey a story without using customary dance steps. The piece consists of "Scene One: Introduction," beginning with a lone clarinet; "Bringing out the Cauldron," an ominous view of what is to come, portrayed by dissonant, heavy chords; "Fury of the Priestesses" a flurry of flute, horn, and harp; "Scene Two: Introduction," a free-floating intertwining of instruments; "She Begins to Rise," serene colors portrayed along with disturbances; and "Dirge," a slow passage that paints a dismal picture. *—Sylvia Typaldos*

Recommended:

○ **Griffes: Goddess Of The Moon** / Perspectives Ens. / 1998 / Newport 85634

Hélène Grimaud

b. Nov. 7, 1969, Aix-en-Provence, France

Pianist

Although small-framed and attractive, Hélène Grimaud is a pianist who defies feminine stereotypes. Her favored repertory has been Brahms, Beethoven, Rachmaninov, Schumann, and Liszt, not the less muscular music of Mozart (which she didn't perform until she was 21), Poulenc, or Chopin. From her early twenties on, Grimaud's lush sound and sweeping interpretations drew comparisons to such pianists as Martha Argerich and Jorge Bolet.

Although born in France, Grimaud has not identified herself with French culture and music. She is of North African, Corsican, and Italian Jewish heritage (her family changed its name from Grimaldi before she was born), and from her early adulthood she has been based in the United States.

An "agitated and agitating" child by her own admission, Grimaud started studying the piano at nine with Jacqueline Courtin of the Aix Conservatoire, simply as a channel for her surplus energy. After only three years, she was able to play Schumann's *Papillons*, the first movement of Beethoven's *Waldstein Sonata*, and Fauré's *Barcarolle No. 5* impressively, and after further lessons with Pierre Barbizet in Marseilles, she entered the Paris Conservatory at 13. In Paris, as an impatient and rebellious student of Jacques Rouvier, Genevieve Joy, and Christian Ivaldi, she insisted on learning repertory at a faster pace than the conservatory system allowed; on her own, she arranged to play the Chopin *Concerto in F minor* with the conservatory orchestra back in Aix when she was 14. Rouvier, impressed, gave a tape of that concert to a producer for Denon and that company, initially not realizing that Grimaud was in her early teens, recorded her in Rachmaninov's *Sonata No. 2* and *Etudes-Tableaux*, Op. 33. That CD garnered a Grand Prix du Disque; Grimaud was only 16. On the strength of that and a French radio broadcast, in 1987 she began playing concerts outside the conservatory, including an engagement at age 18 with Daniel Barenboim and the Orchestre de Paris (only her fourth public concert).

She maintains friendships with Barenboim, Martha Argerich, and Gidon Kremer and greatly admires the work of Vladimir Horowitz and Glenn Gould, yet she is never as prone to waywardness as those musicians. Grimaud does share Gould's fascination with clear counterpoint and Argerich's and Kremer's general intensity. Yet her treatment of Brahms, for example, avoids attention-getting extremes of tempo and instead follows what she has called a "pulsation that's very close to the ideal heartbeat," while also clarifying the textures. She is willing to take risks in performance, but only those that illuminate the music rather than spotlight the soloist. In Rachmaninov, she emphasizes what she calls the music's "nobility of heart" and lyricism rather than its virtuosity. She has said that she tired of flashy pieces like Liszt's *Hungarian Rhapsodies* as a teenager and in her twenties, started to focus especially on such monolithic Austro-Germanic composers as Bach, Beethoven, Brahms, and Berg.

Grimaud is extremely private, but her known eccentricities are no more extreme than a habit of learning music mostly by running it through her head rather than drilling it into her fingers. Perhaps it is this technique that has led to her concentration on overall musical line and color rather than moment-to-moment virtuosity. Grimaud took a university degree in animal behavior by correspondence, intending to be a biologist if music didn't work out. Since 1991, when she settled in the United States, her primary non-musical interest has been wolf conservation involving the preservation of wolves in their natural habitat as a critical element of biodiversity. To this end, she established the educational non-profit Wolf Conservation Center in upstate New York, where she has lived since 1997. *—James Reel*

Recommended:

- ○ **Credo** / Salonen (cond.), Larsen, Grimaud, Swedish Radio Choir, Swedish RSO / 2003 / DG 000173202
- ○ **Grimaud Plays Rachmaninoff** / Grimaud / 1993 / Denon 1054
- ○ **Piano Concertos of Gershwin & Ravel** / Zinman (cond.), Grimaud, Baltimore SO / 1997 / Erato 19571
- ○ **Beethoven: Concerto 4; Sonatas Opp109 & 110** / Masur (cond.), Grimaud, New York PO / 1999 / Teldec 398426869

Ferde Grofé

b. Mar. 27, 1892, New York, NY, **d.** Apr. 3, 1972, Santa Monica, CA

Composer: Orchestral

Ferdinand Rudolph von Grofé was born into a musical family. His maternal grandfather, Bernard Bierlich, was first-desk cellist with the Metropolitan Opera Orchestra. His mother was also a cellist, his father a singing actor, and when grandfather Bierlich moved to Los Angeles, he became first cellist of the Los Angeles Philharmonic, where Grofé's uncle Julius was already concertmaster.

Young Ferdinand was taken to Los Angeles shortly after he was born. He made quick progress in learning to read music and play piano. After his father died in 1899, his mother took him with her when she went to study music in Leipzig for three years. She returned to Los Angeles, opened a studio, and soon afterwards remarried.

Grofé was an indifferent student, always spending time learning new band instruments. He ran away from home after his stepfather refused to let him quit school and worked at unskilled jobs, writing popular songs at night. These brought him to the attention of The Elks (an American benevolent association), who commissioned him to write a special song for their 1909 convention; the song gained some popularity. Soon Grofé joined his grandfather and uncle in the Philharmonic, as a violist. In his spare time he played in dance halls, sometimes billing himself as "Professor Grofé." He founded his own jazz band in San Francisco and wrote arrangements for it.

In 1919 bandleader Paul Whiteman heard one of these arrangements. Grofé accepted a job as pianist and arranger, and immediately started taking orchestration lessons from Pietro Floridia. His very first arrangement for Whiteman was a success: "Whispering" became a million-selling hit. When the Whiteman band relocated to New York, Grofé went with them. His orchestral ideas laid the foundation for what became the big-band sound. More important, he conceived the basic format that makes jazz playing in large ensembles possible: the contrasting of fully written-out orchestra passages with improvised "breaks."

In 1923 Whiteman conceived a concert to be given at Aeolian Hall in New York. "An Experiment in Modern Music" presented a number of jazz-style classically composed pieces played by the Whiteman Band, many scored by Grofé. Among them was George Gershwin's *Rhapsody in Blue*, in Grofé's orchestration. The event made Grofé nearly as famous as Gershwin, and Grofé's symphonic version of the work has become the one best known to audiences.

Grofé began to widen his ambitions as a composer. He wrote the *Mississippi Suite* and, a few years later, the *Grand Canyon Suite* for the Whiteman orchestra, later enlarging them for symphony. In 1931 he resigned from the Whiteman organization and became conductor of the Capitol Theater orchestra in New York, hosted a network radio program, and was appointed to teach orchestration at the Juilliard School in 1939. During World War II he tirelessly conducted service bands and USO shows.

After the war he continued to write generally light music with a jazzy American flavor. A piano concerto was his most ambitious composition in a pure classical idiom. He also tried to follow up on the Mississippi and Grand Canyon suites with innumerable musical portraits of the American scene, including suites named for the Hudson River, Death Valley, Hollywood, San Francisco, New England, Virginia City, the World's Fair, and Mark Twain, as well as an *Aviators' Suite*, an *Atlantic Crossing Suite*, and a *Niagara Falls Suite*. These were generally played a few times and set aside. However, at the very end of the twentieth century there were some revivals of this forgotten music. Grofé died in Los Angeles shortly after his 80th birthday. *—Joseph Stevenson*

ORCHESTRAL

Grand Canyon Suite (1931)

This is by far the most popular of many suites by this master orchestrator depicting scenic wonders of America (others include the *Mississippi* and *Death Valley*). It is effective and entirely direct, with the clear melodism of American popular song. Originally written for Paul Whiteman's concert jazz band, Grofé, scored it expertly for symphony orchestra, and filled it with outstanding musical effects. The suite begins with a dynamic "Sunrise," even prefacing it with the faint rumbling of the expanding air that can just barely be perceived when sunrise is experienced in a place of utter quiet. The second movement, with eerie, static harmonies, pictures the nearby Painted Desert. The center movement, "On the Trail" is the most famous: a humorous depiction of the ride that may be undertaken on the backs of patient mules (not "burros"!), descending to the tumbling waters of the Colorado River at the bottom of the Canyon, and including a stop for a snack in a cabin with a music box. The spectacular sunset is depicted in a movement possessing a theme of Puccinian ardor and loveliness, sweetly scored for the high strings including harmonics and touched by the glitter of celesta. Finally, a pounding desert thunderstorm at night illuminates and shakes the canyon with thunder and lightning, before the clouds disperse showing the canyon in glorious moonlight. *—Joseph Stevenson*

Recommended:

- ○ **Grofé: Grand Canyon Suite; Gershwin: Catfish Row** / Kunzel (cond.), Ruder, Cincinnati Pops Orch. / 1987 / Telarc 80086

Mississippi: A Journey in Tones ("Mississippi Suite") (1925)

Five years before he created his trademark *Grand Canyon Suite*, Ferde Grofé—a composer with an obvious penchant for large subjects—wrote a four-movement suite depicting scenes along the Mississippi River. In the first section, "Father of Waters," a series of dark opening chords gives way to a serene, flowing theme, suggesting the movement of the river itself. "Huckleberry Finn" is a nod to author Mark Twain's close association with the Mississippi; Grofé musically recalls the shenanigans of Twain's fictional hero in a sort of stomping march in two parts that surround a quiet, brief, interlude. The "Old Creole Days" of the third section are languid in the extreme. "Mardi Gras" opens with syncopated, jaunty riffs; although the music rises in volume and intensity, it unfolds in a manner rather serene for an evocation of the raucous, Dionysian celebration. *—Michael Morrison*

Recommended:

- ○ **Modern American Music of Ferde Grofé** / Stulen (cond.), Beau Hunks / 1998 / Basta 9083
- ○ **Grofé: Grand Canyon Suite; Mississippe Suite** / Kostelanetz (cond.), New York PO / 1982 / CBS 37759
- ○ **Great American Grofé** / Slatkin (cond.), Hollywood Bowl SO / 1997 / Angel 66387

Niagara Falls Suite (1961)

One of Grofé's last orchestral works, this piece lies somewhere between a Romantic tone poem and a documentary soundtrack. The New York State Power Authority commissioned it to commemorate the opening of the Robert Moses Power Plant at Niagara Falls. The premiere was with Grofé leading the Buffalo Philharmonic at that facility on February 10, 1961.

The first movement is entitled "The Thunder of the Waters," an image perfectly captured by Grofé. A low roaring tremolo on the bass drums and tympani introduces the cascading falls, described by a constant cycle of descending scales from the woodwinds. The brass choir plays a theme of a general Native American character. Cymbal crashes and imitations of the "Indian" theme are added, then the theme is underscored with mysterious tremolo strings on chromatic walking patterns, followed by heavily accented afterbeats. The movement concludes with a massive reiteration of the previous elements.

The second movement is the "Devil's Hole Massacre" which is a musical narrative about the Native American ambush on September 14, 1763, of 25 British wagons. The first half begins with a plaintive English horn solo over a snaking chromatic line. Imagine the wagon train making its way through the mysterious territory while being watched by their enemies. Suddenly a single pedal glissando is sounded by a tympanum. A pause, then the fighting breaks out with gunshots imitated on the snare drums, and aggressive cries of the attackers imitated by attacked grace-note beats in the winds. The whole orchestra gradually rises in pitch and becomes like a turbulent maelstrom. The movements concludes with a slowly pulsed morendo.

The third movement, "The Honeymooners," depicts the modern cultural icon of the Falls as a retreat for newlyweds. The theme and orchestration suggest a typical nineteenth century sentimental tune that might be played on Sunday at the local park by a small band under the pavilion.

The final movement is "Power of Niagara—1961." Grofé pulls out all the stops and reveals himself as a master of orchestration. The drums roar, the cymbals crash, the strings trill, the brass join in cyclic counterpoint as the giant powerhouse is depicted. This becomes a wildly rhythmic dance. Suddenly, a noble brass choir theme seems to celebrate the dedication ceremony. Again the machine starts up with anvil and cymbal, sirens, a Mack truck horn(!), a syncopated brass theme, whirling woodwinds, snare drum rolls. "The Honeymooners" theme is recontextualized as a stupendous Hollywood ending. *—"Blue Gene" Tyranny*

Recommended:

○ **Grofé: Grand Canyon Suite** / Stromberg (cond.), Bournemouth Sinfonietta / 2001 / Naxos 5110002

Three Shades of Blue (1927)

Ferde Grofé was one of the triad, with George Gershwin and bandleader Paul Whiteman, that created the so-called symphonic jazz of the 1920s. That movement went well beyond its most famous manifestation, Gershwin's *Rhapsody in Blue*, orchestrated several times by Grofé; this fusion of classical music and jazz, most revealingly described by Whiteman as having the goal of "making an honest woman out of jazz," fell into obscurity after the Depression but mightily influenced the music of Duke Ellington and the whole pantheon of jazz composers who followed him. Grofé continued to turn out jazz-flavored orchestral works through the 1920s and 1930s, with even the familiar *Grand Canyon Suite* originating as a commission for Whiteman's 1931 wedding. One sparkling example, no less brilliantly orchestrated than Grofé's large symphonic pieces, is the set of pieces for small orchestra entitled *Three Shades of Blue* (1927). Recently unearthed by the Beau Hunks, a Dutch ensemble specializing in the music of the Whiteman orbit, the *Three Shades of Blue* are short orchestral essays ("Indigo," "Alice Blue," and "Heliotrope"), each three or four minutes long, that loosely evoke jazz rhythms and blues tonality. Those looking for Gershwin-like music will be disappointed, for neither Grofé nor any other white composer of the mid-1920s had Gershwin's understanding of African-American rhythm. Grofé, however, effectively evokes jazz rather than trying to write it, constructing his little pieces around shifting accents that suggest syncopation. Especially effective is "Alice Blue," which begins as a deceptively simple waltz, but develops into a sequence of hemiolas that leave the listener delightfully unsure of what to expect next. The final "Heliotrope" offers a similar treatment of march music, with some quite dissonant material blaring out from the brasses. The moderate-tempo "Indigo" shows Grofé's orchestration at its best, with new colors emerging to complement each rhythmic twist and a piano poking its head out to accomplish graceful transitions and to evoke the nightclub ambiance. These shades of blue would add color to any orchestral concert in either jazz or classical spheres. *—James Manheim*

Recommended:

○ **Modern American Music of Ferde Grofé** / Stulen (cond.), Beau Hunks / 1998 / Basta 9083

Monica Groop

b. Apr. 14, 1958, Helsinki, Finland

Mezzo-Soprano

One of several international singing stars in her time from the musically rich nation of Finland, mezzo-soprano Monica Groop emerged as a leading operatic figure in the 1990s. With an orientation towards Germanic repertory rather than Italian, she is also highly active on the recital and concert stages.

Groop's musical education culminated at the Sibelius Academy in Helsinki. In the 1986 summer season she participated in the Savonlinna Opera, then joined the Finnish National Opera. Her professional operatic debut was with that company in 1987 as Charlotte, the leading female character in Massenet's *Werther*. During her time on the Finnish National Opera's roster she sang the parts of Olga in Tchaikovsky's *Evgeny Onegin*, Dorabella in Mozart's *Così fan tutte*, Sesto in his *La clemenza di Tito*, and Octavian in Richard Strauss' *Der Rosenkavalier*.

In 1989, Groop entered the famous Cardiff Singer of the World Competition in Wales, and attracted attention as a finalist. She began her emergence in the international scene at about that time, especially with performances as Cherubino in Mozart's *Le nozze di Figaro* in the Aix-en-Provence Festival in 1991 and in the same year debuted at Covent Garden in the Royal Opera's production of Wagner's *Der Ring des Nibelungen*, as Wellgunde and Waltraute.

Her stardom is not the result of one dramatic star-making appearance, but she considers 1994 her breakout year. It was on the recital stage that she gained major international recognition with her debuts at Carnegie Hall in New York and Wigmore Hall in London, the most important recital venues of their respective countries. The *New York Times* wrote "A new mezzo has joined the star parade." In the same year she was invited back to Covent Garden in the role of Varvara in Janáček's *Kát'a Kabanová*.

The *Times* review was taking cognizance of the presence of an unusual number of important mezzo-sopranos currently active. Following the success of Cecilia Bartoli, there has been a reawakening of interest in the lower female voice range, manifested in such things as the tendency to return to the original mezzo-soprano parts for many leading Rossini heroines, and resumption of the use of female mezzos in heroic roles in many Baroque operas.

Groop's statements suggest that she sees the presence of other mezzos of similar international stature in a positive way, giving her an opportunity to specialize in the repertory most congenial to her. "The bel canto tradition is not close to me," she has said (referring to the style of operatic singing most associated with Rossini, Bellini, and Donizetti), "and Bartoli and [Jennifer] Larmore are brilliant practitioners of that side of things. I have sung a great deal of Mozart, and now I am ready for Strauss."

Accordingly, in 1995 she added the Straussian role of The Composer (*Ariadne auf Naxos*) to her repertory in performances in Frankfurt. In the same year she made worldwide news by her portrayal of Debussy's *Mélisande* in a controversial production staged by Peter Sellars in Los Angeles.

Since then she has been in such demand that she spends nearly 300 days a year away from her home. She has made over 40 recordings with major labels such as Decca, Sony Classics, Harmonia Mundi, CPO, Accent, Chandos, BIS, and Finlandia. Her recorded repertory includes music of composers as diverse as Bach, Mozart, Mendelssohn, Haydn, Grieg, Sibelius, Vivaldi, Sarasate, Kálmán, Madetoja, and Pettersson. They include the first recordings of Vivaldi's *Ottone* and Donizetti's *Linda di Chamounix*. She has appeared in the world's major opera houses, and in concert with the greatest conductors and orchestras, including both standard ensembles and original instruments groups. *—Joseph Stevenson*

Recommended:

○ **Grieg: Songs, Vol. 1** / Groop, Derwinger (piano) / 1993 / Bis 637

○ **Art of the Romantic Song** / Groop, Jansen, Lubimov, Angervo, Jubilate Choir / 2001 / Ondine 986

○ **Pettersson: Complete Songs** / Groop, Garben (piano) / 1998 / CPO 999499

Charles Groves

b. Mar. 10, 1915, London, England, **d.** Jun. 20, 1992, London, England

Conductor

Charles Groves was a major British conductor of the twentieth century, one of a relative few content to hold posts with only U.K.-based orchestras, though he led many performances by various European and American ensembles. He was well-known as an interpreter of large scores, including operas, often obscure operas. He was first among English conductors to lead performances of the entire canon of Mahler symphonies.

Groves studied music as a chorister at St. Paul's Cathedral Choir School and later enrolled at the Royal College of Music, where he focused on piano and organ studies. He also took an interest in choral and orchestral music, leading many ensembles in both venues during his student years. He worked with Toscanini in performances of Beethoven's *Missa Solemnis* and the Brahms and Verdi requiems. In 1938, the BBC Theatre Chorus engaged Groves to serve as a chorus master. Six years later, he was appointed conductor of the Manchester-based BBC Northern Orchestra (later named the BBC Philharmonic), his first such permanent assignment. He established a reputation for high performance standards in this post and for inclusion of unusual repertory. He left the BBC NO in 1951 and assumed duties as conductor of the Bournemouth Municipal Orchestra the following year. He immediately made numerous changes in the ensemble, which had been plagued by many troubles in the postwar years. The group's repertory was extended to include opera, performed in conjunction with the Welsh National Opera, and the orchestra's name was changed in 1954 to the Bournemouth Symphony Orchestra. His fine work with the Welsh National Opera and with operatic repertory in general did not go unnoticed: in 1961, he was appointed director of the Welsh National Opera, becoming the first conductor to hold the post in a full-time capacity. Once more, Groves expanded the repertory of his new ensemble, adding Wagner's *Lohengrin* and other major works previously ignored. Not only did Groves divulge an adventurous streak in his inclusion of new works, but he quite consistently brought them off with much acclaim. In 1963, Groves became the permanent music director of what would become the most-respected British ensemble not based in London, the Royal Liverpool Philharmonic. He took the group on a highly acclaimed tour of Germany and Switzerland in 1966. The following year, Groves took on a concurrent assignment as associate conductor of the London-based Royal Philharmonic Orchestra. Further tours for both his groups ensued in the next few years. With the Royal Liverpool Philharmonic Orchestra, he returned to Germany and Switzerland in 1968 to critical acclaim, and in 1970 toured Poland, where he scored a notable triumph at the Festival of Modern Music (Warsaw); with the RPO, he toured the United States to generally enthusiastic receptions. In 1973, Groves was knighted; five years later, he was appointed music director of the English National Opera, without doubt attaining one of the most coveted positions in British opera. But he quickly found the post incompatible with his manner of leadership and resigned the following year. For the last decade or so of his career, Groves guest-conducted ensembles throughout the world.

Of his numerous recordings, many are still available on a variety of labels. Not surprisingly, he displayed a fondness in both concert and recording venues for the music of Delius, Vaughan Williams, Arnold, Maxwell Davies, and of other British composers. *—Robert Cummings*

Recommended:

- ○ **Delius: Koanga; The Song of the High Hills** / Groves (cond.), Estes, Herincx, Allister, Temperley, London SO / 2003 / EMI 585142
- ○ **Sullivan: Cello Concerto; Irish Symphony; Overture di Ballo** / Mackerras, Groves (conds.), Lloyd Webber, London SO, Royal Liverpool Phil. / 1993 / EMI 64726
- ○ **English Orchestral Works** / Groves (cond.), Royal PO / Carlton 670068

Edita Gruberová

b. Dec. 23, 1946, Bratislava, Czechoslovakia
Soprano

Edita Gruberová is a coloratura soprano, best known for her performances of Mozart and Strauss operas, but also strongly identified with the bel canto revival. She studied in her hometown of Bratislava, and then in Vienna and Prague, finally making her professional debut as Rosina in Rossini's *Barber of Seville* at the Slovak National Theater in 1968. An engagement to sing Mozart's Queen of the Night with the Vienna State Opera in 1970 was pivotal in establishing her career. She joined the company as a regular member in 1972, and before long she had made successful debuts at Glyndebourne (1973), the Salzburg Festival (1974, as Thibault in Verdi's *Don Carlo* with Karajan), and the Metropolitan Opera (1977, again as Mozart's Queen). During the late 1970s and early 1980s she debuted at many of the world's other major houses, including Covent Garden, La Scala, and the Chicago Lyric, but her schedule remained focused around the houses of central Europe—a trend that has continued throughout her career. As of 2004, Gruberová was still pursuing a full schedule of operatic and concert appearances.

Other Mozart roles that Gruberová is strongly associated with include Constanze in *Die Entführung aus dem Serail* and, somewhat surprisingly, Donna Anna in *Don Giovanni*—a more lyrical role that lacks the high-flying coloratura that is usually her calling card. Her performances of Zerbinetta in Strauss' *Ariadne auf Naxos* are considered among the best ever heard. Among the bel canto operas, Donizetti's *Lucia* and *Anna Bolena*, Rossini's *Semiramide*, and Bellini's *I Capuleti e I Montecchi* have figured prominently in her success. *—Allen Schrott*

Recommended:

- ○ **Edita Gruberová: Famous Opera Arias** / Gardelli (cond.), Gruberova, Munich Radio Orch. / 1985 / Orfeo 101841
- ○ **Queen of Coloratura** / Gruberova, etc. / 1994 / Teldec 93691

Arthur Grumiaux

b. Mar. 21, 1921, Villers-Perwin, Belgium, **d.** Oct. 16, 1986, Brussels, Belgium
Violinist

Of the Franco-Belgian school, Arthur Grumiaux is considered to have been one of the few truly great violin virtuosi of the twentieth century. In his relatively short life his achievements were superb. He brought to performances guaranteed technical command, faithfulness to the composer's intent, and sensitivity toward the intricate delineations of musical structure. His fame was built upon extraordinary violin concerto performances and chamber-music appearances with his own Grumiaux Trio.

Grumiaux was born in Villers-Perwin, Belgium, in 1921, to a working-class family, and it was his grandfather who urged him to begin music studies at the age of four. He trained on violin and piano with the Fernand Quintet at the Charleroi Conservatory, where he took first prize at the age of 11. The following year he advanced his studies by working with Alfred Dubois at the Royal Conservatory in Brussels, and also worked on counterpoint and fugue with Jean Absil. He received his first few major awards prior to reaching the age of 20; he took the Henry Vieuxtemps and François Prume prizes in 1939, and received the Prix de Virtuosité from the Belgian government in 1940. During this time he also studied composition privately in Paris with the famous Romanian violinist Georges Enesco, Menuhin's teacher. His debuts were made in Belgium with the Brussels Philharmonic Orchestra playing Mendelssohn's concerto, and in Britain with the BBC Symphonic Orchestra in 1945. Due to the German invasion of his homeland, there existed a short time gap between these two important events. During that time he played privately with several small ensembles, while refraining from public performance of any kind. Regardless of this slight delay in the initiation of his international career, once started, it quickly developed. Following his British debut, he advanced into Belgium academia when he was appointed professor of violin at the Royal Conservatory, where he had once studied. There, he emphasized the importance of phrasing, the quality of sound, and the high technical standards of artistry.

Grumiaux's playing has been included on over 30 recordings, nearly all under Philips, although his name is also seen on the labels of EMI, Belart and Music & Arts. The titles on these releases tend to be the compositions of Bach, Beethoven, Brahms, Mozart, and Schubert, and on occasion include works by Ravel and Debussy. One of his greatest joys in life was his partnership with the pianist Clara Haskil. On occasion, the two would switch instruments for a different perspective and relationship. Grumiaux was left with a professional and personal absence when she died from a fall at a train station, en route to a concert with him. In addition to his solo work, he has recorded Mozart quintets with the Grumiaux Ensemble, and various selections with the Grumiaux Trio, comprised of the Hungarian husband-wife duo Georges Janzer (violin) and Eva Czako (cello). His successful performance career led up to royal recognition, as in 1973, he was knighted baron by King Baudouin, for his services to music, thus, sharing the title with Paganini. Despite a struggle with diabetes, he continued a rigorous schedule of recording and concert performances, primarily in Western Europe, until a sudden stroke in Brussels took his life in 1986. At the age of 65, Grumiaux left behind the memory of his elegant and solid musicianship. *—Meredith Gailey*

Recommended:

- ○ **Mozart: Violin Concertos** / Leppard, Davis (conds.), Grumiaux, London SO, New Philharmonia Orch. / 1993 / Philips 438323
- ○ **Violin Concertos of Brahms & Bruch** / Davis, Wallberg (conds.), Grumiaux, New Philharmonia Orch. / 2004 / Universal Classics 000217602
- ○ **Bach: Complete Music for Solo Violin** / Grumiaux / 1993 / Philips 438736
- ○ **Historic Philips Recordings, 1953–1962** / Grumiaux, etc. / 2003 / Philips 000017902
- ○ **Favourite Violin Concertos** / Grumiaux, etc. / 1994 / Philips 442287

Guarneri Quartet

f. 1964, Marlboro, VT
Ensemble

Until the year 2000, the New York City-based Guarneri Quartet consisted of the same four players who comprised the group at its 1964 founding: Arnold Steinhardt (violin), a former assistant concertmaster under Szell in the Cleveland Orchestra; John Dalley (violin), a one-time member of the Oberlin Quartet; Michael Tree (viola), formerly a highly respected concert violinist who converted to the viola; and David Soyer (cello), previously a member of several chamber ensembles, including the Bach Aria Group. Few chamber groups have maintained both the same personnel and such a consistent level of renown for so enduring a period. In 2000, Peter Wiley replaced David Soyer as the group's cellist. He is a former member of the Beaux Arts Trio.

The Guarneri Quartet's roots date to the 1964 Marlboro Festival, where as individual musicians they appeared with various ensembles and with pianist Rudolf Serkin. At the urging of violinist Alexander Schneider, the group collectively agreed to form a string quartet, taking their name from the famous Italian family of violin makers. It quickly achieved critical acclaim with 1965 appearances at the Spoleto Festival and Metropolitan Museum of Art. The group has since regularly appeared at the latter venue and have established other such recurring events, such as the Lincoln Center-based series entitled Guarneri and Friends, which began in 1973. The Guarneri Quartet also made immediate headway in the recording venue, with its traversal of the 16 Beethoven quartets (and *Grosse Fugue*) for RCA, issued from 1966–69, which received several prestigious awards. The group gave highly acclaimed performances of all the Beethoven quartets in a historic 1970 series of concerts in London. For the first decade or so of its existence, the Guarneri players had developed a reputation largely associated with eighteenth and nineteenth century repertory staples, but in the mid-1970s, the group shifted its focus to include important works from the twentieth century, like the six quartets of Béla Bartók, which the quartet also recorded to critical acclaim. Its repertory would later broaden to include not only works by Stravinsky, but Henze (piano quintet) and Rorem (*String Quartet No. 3*). Most of the group's early recordings appeared on RCA, but they moved to Philips in 1986, their first issue coming late that year with the Smetana *String Quartet No. 1, "From My Life."* They rerecorded much of their repertory for Philips including the Beethoven quartets. In the late 1990s, the group also started issuing recordings on the Arabesque label and in 2001, they made their first compact disc for a new label, Surrounded by Entertainment.

The Guarneri Quartet has also garnered numerous awards apart from those associated with its many recordings. In 1982, New York's Mayor Edward Koch gave the group the New York Seal of Recognition and the State University of New York (S.U.N.Y.) issued members honorary doctorate degrees in 1983, their second such citation, the first coming in 1976 from the University of South Florida.

The Guarneri Quartet has also reached its audiences via numerous broadcasts over radio and several appearances on television, including a particularly notable one from 1990 on the CBS Network's *Sunday Morning* program, hosted by Charles Kuralt, which featured an interview with the players. The group was also the subject of a 1989 film entitled *High Fidelity—The Guarneri String Quartet.* Several books have focused on their artistry, as well, including the 1986 Alfred A. Knopf publication *The Art of Quartet Playing: The Guarneri in Conversation with David Blum.* In 1998, Farrar, Straus, and Giroux published Arnold Steinhardt's own book *Indivisible By Four: A String Quartet in Pursuit of Harmony.* *—Robert Cummings*

Recommended:

- ○ **Beethoven: Late String Quartets** / Guarneri Quartet / 1990 / RCA 60458
- ○ **Schubert: String Quartets 13 & 14** / Guarneri Quartet / 1997 / Arabesque 6687

Sofiya Gubaydulina

b. Oct. 24, 1931, Chistopol', Tatar Republic, USSR

Composer: Chamber Music, Keyboard

"I am a religious person... and by 'religion' I mean re-ligio, the re-tying of a bond ... restoring the legato of life. Life divides man into many pieces... There is no weightier occupation than the recomposition of spiritual integrity through the composition of music."—Sofiya Gubaydulina

In Russian composer Sofiya Gubaydulina's 1986 symphony *Slïshu... umolko* ("I hear... silence"), the composer writes a cadenza for conductor. The orchestra is largely silent save for a few rumblings from bass drums, during which the conductor melds this quasi-silence into strong but delicate contours; with agonizingly slow precision, the conductor eventually brings her hands upwards, tracing a Christmas-tree shape, until they are fully stretched towards the heavens. She flips her hands upwards, and the organ, nestled deep in the orchestra, catches the gesture and begins the symphony's apocalyptic final movement. The gesture is wonderfully symbolic of Gubaydulina's work in general, obsessed as it is with the "other sides" of music—with "re-tying the bonds" between gesture and sound, sound and silence, silence and noise, this sensate world and the super-sensate next. From early works like *Night in Memphis* (1968) through the now classic *Offertorium and Seven Last Words* of the early 1980s, and up to the *Double Viola Concerto "Two Paths"* from 1999, Gubaydulina's music traces an impassioned commitment "to restore a sense of integrity" to both art and life. In this sense her music is unabashedly re-ligious: it finds and binds the fissures which mark human solitude, with a brazen honesty rare in music even today.

Sofia Asgatovna Gubaydulina was born on October 24, 1931, in Chistopol', in the Tatar Republic; growing up there, Gubaydulina would bind peculiar fusion of Eastern and Western into dramatic polarities in her later work. She graduated from the Kazan' Conservatory in 1954 having studied composition and piano; she then left for Moscow, where she studied at the Conservatory with Nikolay Peyko until 1959, and then with Shebalin until 1963. Already by this time, Gubaydulina was marked as an "irresponsible" composer on "a mistaken path"; Shostakovich, among others, supported her however, advising her to "continue along [her] mistaken path." By the mid-1970s Gubaydulina founded a folk-instrument improvisation group with fellow composers Victor Suslin and Vyacheslav Artyomov called Astreja, still active in the late 1990s. Today Gubaydulina is a successful freelance composer, having won a number of prestigious composition prizes and grants.

In many ways, the cross is the most potent symbol in Gubaydulina's work—it is the consummate node of intersection, the site of re-tying both as a mark of salvation and greatest suffering. So many of her works contain cross imagery, often through elaborate, predestined meeting-and-diverging points for distinct sounding bodies or musical concepts. Hence the great "crossings" of 1979's *In Croce* (between cello and organ), 1981's *Rejoice* (cello and violin), 1982's *Seven Last Words* (cello, bayan, and strings), and 1980's *Offertorium* (violin and orchestra). And in the 12-movement symphony, the crux occurs between sound (the orchestra) and silence itself (the pantomiming conductor), each on its own desperately etched trajectory. But what perhaps most astonishing about Gubaydulina's music is how, amidst such formally rigorous edifices (the cross, the mass-sequence, the Fibonacci series), a voice of such supple, passionate directness arises. Gubaydulina's work, even while unfolding an apocalyptic itinerary, often sounds breathed out in the moment, in- and ex-pired, systolic and organic; filaments or melody float, buffet, and fall, even as a musical cataclysm ferments. This tight religious knot of opposites may well account for Gubaydulina's success in the West in the late twentieth century; she is now certainly considered one of the most important composers alive today. *—Seth Brodsky*

CHAMBER MUSIC

In croce, for cello & organ or bayan (1979)

One of the many works in which Sofiya Gubaydulina makes reference to Christian themes and imagery, *In croce* was composed in 1979 for cellist Vladimir Tonkha, who, along with organist Oleg Yanchenko gave the work its first performance in the concert hall of the Moscow Conservatory. Later on, Gubaydulina began to incorporate the bayan, the Russian push-button accordion, into her works, and she and bayan player Elsbeth Moser rearranged *In croce* for cello and bayan in 1992.

The work's title can mean either "On the Cross" or "Cross-Wise," and it carres a musical meaning, along with the obvious Christian one. Roughly speaking, the organ (or bayan) begins the work playing comparatively diatonic music in the upper part of its register, while the cello plays spare tones in its lower register. Both instruments center their activities on the note E. As the work progresses the two instruments begin to approach each other, eventually crossing in the most aggressive passage. After some wild playing from both instruments, the mood grows hushed again; dissonant chords in the organ accompany the barest of textures from the cello as they both converge again on E. The work's ending is quiet and somber. *—Chris Morrison*

Recommended:

○ **Sofia Gubaidulina** / Ivashkin, Hicks / 2001 / Chandos 9958

○ **Gubaidulina: In Croce; Silenzio; Sieben Worte** / Kliegel, Moser / 1995 / Naxos 553557

Ten Preludes for cello (1974)

Another composer might have called Sofiya Gubaydulina's *Ten Preludes for solo cello* etudes instead of preludes. After all, each explores a different technique for producing sound on the cello, ranging from the mundane to the exotic. These preludes might also be called variations, for a motive introduced in the first of the ten preludes shapes the content of each of its successors, whether melodically or harmonically. Yet both of these titles might have implied a sort of academic exploration of the cello's potential, and while Gubaydulina is certainly interested in exploring that potential, the exploration is always in the service of music. The motive is introduced right away in the first variation, in alternating whole tones and semitones that make jagged feints in staccato notes. This texture is juxtaposed with legato playing, which closes the prelude by first making the motive quick and slithery, then finally slow and songful. Legato playing begins the second prelude, but the contrast here is with staccato once again, as the cello's broad, rich legato melodies are interrupted by staccato notes, trailing off into silence. The third prelude contrasts passages played with and without a mute, in a movement that could remind one of the *Sarabande in C major* from Johann Sebastian Bach's *Suite No. 5 for solo cello*: it features dark chromaticism, a winding melody, and deep feeling, and there are no double stops. Spiccato bowing, in which the cellist allows the bow to bounce on the string, imparts a suitably nervous feel to the fourth prelude, while the fifth exploits the eerie sounds which a cellist can make playing sul ponticello (on the bridge) and sul tasto (on the fingerboard). The sixth prelude is entirely written in harmonics—unnerving to hear for a long period, particularly when Gubaydulina throws in strange staccato playing, nervous slides, and even double-stopped harmonics. The cellist must play at the heel (al tacco) and the point (al punto) of the bow in the seventh prelude, which emphasizes guttural sounds with near-constant motion. After the eighth and ninth preludes contrast pizzicato and bowed playing, the tenth and final prelude is written for no bow at all, instead favoring Bartókian pizzicati, pizzicati glissandi, and even a weird tremolo effect which, the composer has written, should be "reminiscent of a snare drum." The quiet, cryptic music of this prelude provides an enigmatic conclusion to an interesting work. *—Andrew Lindemann Malone*

Recommended:

○ **Sofia Gubaidulina** / Ivashkin / 2001 / Chandos 9958

The Seven Last Words, for cello, bayan & strings (1982)

Drawing upon her own faith and upon musical examples provided in past centuries by Heinrich Schütz and Franz Josef Haydn, Gubaydulina composed her *Sem' slov na kreste* (*The Seven Words on the Cross*) in 1982. Unlike the two earlier works, Gubaydulina's is entirely instrumental (although she does borrow one thematic idea from Schütz's work). The first performance of the work came in that same year of 1982, with cellist Vladimir Tonkha and bayan soloist Friedrich Lips (to whom the work is dedicated), along with the Ricercar Chamber Orchestra conducted by Y. Nikolayevsky.

In order to classify and characterize the various musical devices used in her works, Gubaydulina has created what has been dubbed a "parameter of expression." In the present work, some of the string orchestra's parts are marked "consonant expression" (i.e., played legato, with consistent sound), whereas the cello and bayan are marked "dissonant expression" (with pizzicati in the cello and tone clusters and wide leaps in the bayan). These qualities are not consistent throughout the 40-plus minutes of this work, but they do give a general idea of the musical content.

To convey the idea of the Cross, Gubaydulina relied on musical metaphors. She has written of how the cello moves "through glissandi of the neighboring strings," of how the bayan (a Russian accordion) crosses through the orchestra, and of the string orchestra's "glissando crossings from unison to multi-octave textures and again back to unison (the figure of the Cross)." The cello and bayan enter tentatively, and their isolated notes resound into space in the first movement, "Father, forgive them, for they know not what they do." Here and in the second movement, "Woman, behold thy son—Son, behold thy mother," the two soloists' spare utterances are followed by a ghostly chorale from the string orchestra. Throughout, the reedy sound of the bayan reminds the listener of the instrument's folk origins.

An expressionistic cello line is juxtaposed with those ethereal strings in movement three, "Verily, I say unto thee: today thou shalt be with me in paradise." In the fourth movement, "My God, my God, why hast thou forsaken me?," the very earthbound sounds of the cello and bayan offer strong contrasts with the almost disembodied sounds of the string orchestra. The music becomes strident and intense at this point. By contrast, "I thirst," the fifth movement, is very spare and desolate. Aggressive tone clusters from the bayan mark "It is accomplished," with gently rocking strings in the background. The final movement, "Father, into thy hands I commend my spirit," begins with quiet gestures from the cello and bayan. The strings join in, and the texture grows dense and anxious. But the tension recedes and the music ends quietly. *—Chris Morrison*

Recommended:

- ○ **Gubaydulina: Seven Last Words, In croce** / Rosensteiner (cond.), CO Diagonal / Wergo 6263
- ○ **Gubaidulina: In croce; Silenzio; Sieben Worte** / Selmeczi (cond.), Kliegel, Moser, Rabus, Transylvanica Camerata / 1995 / Naxos 553557

KEYBOARD

Chaconne (1963)

Written on a commission from pianist Marina Mdivani in 1962, Sofiya Gubaydulina's *Ciacona* has been deemed a "student work" by its author, not worthy of the same recognition as pieces written only a few years later (1965 saw the composition of what she considered her "opus one"). It is true that Gubaydulina's mature style is present here only in occasional glimmers and foretastes, but the *Ciacona* is nevertheless quite a satisfying work to listen to, the product of both a good student of music at work and a ferocious creative temperament which would eventually find its full expression. At first, the *Ciacona* seems to be a perfectly typical modern example of the old Baroque form. It begins with a properly sonorous, arresting eight-bar idea, potent with harmonic possibility, and the initial moves Gubaydulina makes with it—quickening the tempo of the accompaniment, moving the idea from top to bottom to middle, overlaying a melody in another rhythm—would have been familiar to Bach, even if the quite modern harmonies would not have been. Yet Gubaydulina shows imagination in the way she develops the material, working the textures to a point where quick, rippling melodies are opposed to huge smashes of chords. Finally a fugato, nervous and thrilling, takes off from the wreckage of one particularly emphatic series of chords, signaling Gubaydulina's complete abandonment of the eight-bar form. After a crashing climax, the tempo becomes slower and the music quieter, and the textures rebuild themselves from the basic harmonic relations suggested by the theme. Soon this music too has begun racing, and one last blistering run up the keyboard sets the stage for the unaltered return of the initial ciacona theme. Motoric chords in the bass guide the piece to a quiet conclusion. Gubaydulina may have been indebted to an ancient form when composing this piece, but it is clear that she had mastered it and begun to think of original ways of modifying it. Anyone who does not expect mature Gubaydulina will enjoy this work. *—Andrew Lindemann Malone*

Recommended:

- ○ **Solo Piano Works** / Haefliger / Sony 53960
- ○ **Live at Wigmore Hall** / Demidenko / 1998 / Hyperion 22024

Jean Guillou

b. May 18, 1930, Angers, France

Organist

Jean Guillou was one of the most prominent and respected organists in Europe, but it took the CD boom of the late 1980s to turn him into something of a recording star. Guillou entered the Paris Conservatory in 1945, studying keyboard and composition with teachers including Marcel Dupré, Olivier Messiaen, and Maurice Duruflé. In 1953, at age 23, he joined the faculty of the Intituto de Alta Cultura in Lisbon. In 1958, Guillou moved to West Berlin, where he established himself as a recitalist and also published his first original compositions for solo organ and chamber ensemble. In 1963, Guillou was appointed organist at the Church of St. Eustache in Paris, a position he has had ever since. He subsequently toured Eastern Europe, Japan, and the United States. His recitals became renowned for their inventiveness and wit, Guillou freely intermingling his interpretations of works by Johann Sebastian Bach and César Franck, and arrangements of non-keyboard works by composers such as Franz Josef Haydn, as well as his own original compositions. Guillou's performances are noted for their dramatic flair and showmanship, which has made him something of a flamboyant star on his instrument.

As a composer, he has written numerous pieces that explore the sonorities of the organ in combination with other instruments, such as the cello in his *Fantasie Concertante* and with soprano in his *Andromeda*, based on the work of Gerard Manley Hopkins. He has also written concerti for the piano, an instrument on which he is thoroughly proficient though less celebrated, and authored an oratorio, *The Last Judgment* (1965); one symphonic work, his *Judith-Symphonie* (1971) for mezzo soprano and orchestra; and *Hypérion* (1987) for organ and orchestra. He has also revived the major keyboard works of Julius Reubke, a student of Franz Liszt who died tragically young. Guillou has written books on organ performance and the history and design of the instrument and is well-known within the music community as a leading scholar, conducting international master classes in Zurich since 1970.

He has made numerous acclaimed recordings that have earned him recognition around the world. For Philips, he recorded such works as *Alice au pays de l'orgue*, a musical journey inspired by Lewis Carroll's *Alice in Wonderland*, and the *Fantasie Concertante*. He has also done extensive recording for the audiophile Dorian label—the latter include his performances of Bach's *Goldberg Variations* and own organ transcriptions of Igor Stravinsky's *Petrushka* and Modest Mussorgsky's *Pictures at an Exhibition*—the latter disc found an especially large audience during the CD boom of the late 1980s, both as a result of the work's inherent popularity and as a serious follow-up to rock organist Keith Emerson's Moog synthesizer-based approach to the work from two decades earlier. This activity overlapped with Guillou's performances of the complete solo organ works of Bach in conjunction with the composer's tercentenary. *—Bruce Eder*

Recommended:

- ○ **The Great Organ of Saint-Eustache** / Guillou / 1989 / Dorian 90134
- ○ **The Art of Improvisation** / Guillou / 1991 / Dorian 90101
- ○ **Stravinsky: Petrushka; Mussorgsky: Pictures at an Exhibition** / Guillou / 1989 / Dorian 90117
- ○ **The Organ Works of Bach, Vol. 1** / Guillou / 1990 / Dorian 90111

Friedrich Gulda

b. May 16, 1930, Vienna, Austria, **d.** Jan. 27, 2000, Vienna, Austria

Pianist

Born in Vienna in 1930, Friedrich Gulda started piano lessons at the age of seven. At 12 he enrolled in the Vienna Music Academy, and four years later he received first prize in the Geneva International Music Festival. In 1949 Gulda toured Europe and South America, earning international acclaim for his treatments of Bach, Mozart, and Beethoven, and the following year he made a successful debut at Carnegie Hall. He also began recording for Decca around this time. Gulda was often grouped with Jörg Demus and Paul Badura-Skoda; all were young Viennese pianists oriented toward the heart of the city's musical tradition.

Gulda's involvement with jazz began after a 1951 encounter with trumpeter Dizzy Gillespie following a performance with the Chicago Symphony. Five years later, Gulda played his first American jazz concert at New York's Birdland club, followed by a performance at the Newport Jazz Festival. After this, Gulda formed the Eurojazz Orchestra, a jazz combo and big band that drew from both jazz and classical compositions. In 1966, ten years after his Birdland appearance, Gulda organized a modern jazz competition in his native city. He was awarded the Vienna Academy's Beethoven Ring in 1970, but later returned it to protest what he regarded as a constricting educational system. A lone wolf to the end, Gulda developed a core of admirers but didn't have much interaction with adherents of the then-flourishing third stream trend of fusing classical and jazz.

Over time, as he began to pursue parallel careers and even combine classical and jazz elements within a single concert, there developed a perception of Gulda as an eccentric. He gained the dubious moniker of "terrorist pianist." This reputation intensified when the pianist abruptly called off major performances more than once. One such incident occurred in 1988, as organizers of a Salzburg music festival objected to Gulda's inclusion of jazz musician Joe Zawinul on the program; Gulda and Zawinul would collaborate often in the late 1980s and early 1990s. After faking his own death in 1999 and staging a party in honor of his own resurrection, Gulda experienced the real thing on January 27, 2000, after a heart attack in Vienna. Although he continued to perform classical music for his entire life, the bulk of Gulda's classical recordings date from the 1950s through the 1970s. He has been honored with inclusion in EMI's *Great Pianists of the Twentieth Century* series. *—AMG*

Recommended:

- ○ **Mozart: Concertos 25 & 26; Beethoven: Sonata 22** / Collins (cond.), Gulda, New SO of London / 2003 / Testament 1301
- ○ **Mozart: Piano Concertos 9, 17, 20 & 24** / Gulda, etc. / 2003 / Artemis 1185
- ○ **Beethoven: Sonata 32; Gulda: Wintermeditation** / Gulda / Philips 412114
- ○ **Friedrich Gulda** / Gulda / 1999 / Philips 456817
- ○ **Bach: The Well-Tempered Clavier, Book 1** / Gulda / 1995 / Philips 446545

Ludwig Güttler

b. Jun. 13, 1943, Sosa, Saxony, East Germany

Trumpeter

Ludwig Güttler has been called "the Pavarotti of wind instruments" and the "King of Trumpets," but he is almost as well known for his research, teaching, and dedication to the culture of Saxony as for his playing of the trumpet and horn. Güttler first took music lessons at the age of five; when he was 14, he began playing the trumpet. At the Hochschule für Musik in Leipzig, he studied with Armin Mennel between 1961 and 1965. He then became solo trumpeter for Halle's Handel Festival Orchestra and then the Dresden Philharmonic, where he remained until 1980. At the same time, he became instrumental in the founding of three ensembles to further expand the performance of seventeenth and eighteenth century wind literature on period instruments: the Leipziger Bach-Collegium (1976), the Ludwig Güttler Wind Ensemble (1978), and the Virtuosi Saxoniae (1985). He performs and records both as soloist and conductor with all of these groups. He also regularly performs and records with his duo partner, organist Friedrich Kircheis. Throughout his career, he has looked for works for the trumpet and other wind instruments that have been left undiscovered in libraries, archives, and castles all over Germany, further enhancing the available eighteenth century wind repertoire. Güttler was a professor at the Dresden Hochschule für Musik from 1972 to 1990, taught annually at the Weimar International Music Seminar, and frequently gives master classes and serves on competition juries. Güttler also founded the annual Musikwoche Hitzacker festival in 1986, a multifaceted presentation of concerts, recitals, workshops, and exhibits, and conducts local opera productions. Numerous awards have been bestowed on him for his playing, his recordings, his research, and his civic activities. Güttler, who has a degree in architecture, has been a key figure in the restoration of Dresden's Frauenkirche and is a member of Saxony's Cultural Senate and Academy of Arts. This seemingly indefatigable artist has a catalog of more than 50 recordings, primarily on the Berlin Classics and Capriccio labels. *—Patsy Morita*

Recommended:

○ **Virtuoso Concertos** / Guttler, Saxoniae Virtuosi, Leipzig Bach Collegium / Capriccio 10394

○ **Bach: Cantatas with Corno Da Caccia** / Pommer, Rotzsch (conds.), Buchner, Guttler, Palm, Sandau, New Bach Collegium Musicum / Capriccio 10027

○ **Italian Trumpet Concertos** / Pommer (cond.), Guttler, New Bach Collegium Musicum Le, Berlin Chamber Orchestra / Capriccio 10020

○ **Telemann: Trumpet Concerto; Trumpet Suite; Overture** / Winschermann, Pommer (conds.), Guttler, Basch, Koster, Schroeder, Deutsche Bachsolisten, New Bach Collegium Musicum / Laserlight 15659

Jerry Hadley

b. Jun. 16, 1952, Princeton, IL

Tenor

Hadley is one of the most thoughtful singers of the late twentieth and early twenty-first centuries, and one who has explored a wide range of repertoire, with a special interest in contemporary works. While he began his career with a voice ideal for Mozart and bel canto, possessing a warmly lyrical timbre that was one of the most beautiful since Wunderlich, like all too many lyric tenors, Hadley ranged too early into heavier roles without a voice or technique that was fully prepared for their demands. While he lost much of that vocal freshness and bloom too early, the musicianship and scrupulous approaches to the roles he takes on (for example, he will not record a role unless he has sung it on stage, and wrote the English-language translation for his recording of Lehár's *The Land of Smiles*) still make him one of the most interesting tenors of his generation.

He was interested in singing from an early age and performed in *Up with People.* He went to the University of Illinois to study music, where a friend persuaded him to audition for a performance of *The Magic Flute.* He landed the role of Tamino, and was persuaded to take up an operatic career. His opera debut was at the Sarasota Opera as Lionel in von Flotow's *Martha* in 1978. He began a long association with the New York City Opera in 1979, debuting as Arturo in *Lucia di Lammermoor.* (His stage debut was not an auspicious one dramatically. Arturo appears on stage for only about fifteen minutes, but being unfamiliar with the staging, Hadley found himself catching a chair on his sword and dragging it across the stage before he could disentangle it, setting his plumed hat on fire, and being whacked by a chorus member's sword in an area that could have led to some unexpected high notes. These were only the most notable mishaps.)

Thereafter, he sang roles such as Pinkerton, Des Grieux (Massenet), Tom Rakewell, and Faust (Gounod) at the NYCO. His European debut was in 1982 as Nemorino at the Vienna State Opera, the same year that he won the Richard Tucker Competition. In 1983, he made his Glyndebourne debut as Idamante in Mozart's *Idomeneo,* and his Covent Garden debut the next year as Fenton in *Falstaff.* His Met debut was in 1987 as Des Grieux. However, such roles as Offenbach's Hoffmann and a technique that often "drew on capital" (forced itself) began to take their toll on his vocal flexibility and stamina in the 1980s, and his pitch was not as secure as it had been, and there was a certain rawness in his voice that had not been there before.

He has been a champion of twentieth century music, both operatic and popular; in 1997, he created the title role on Myron Fink's *The Conquistador,* and in 1999, that of John Harbison's *The Great Gatsby,* and he also created the tenor lead in Paul McCartney's *Liverpool Oratorio.* He recorded an exemplary Sam in Floyd's *Susannah* (Virgin Classics 72435 45039 2 4), and *Standing Room Only* (BMG 09026 61370 2), a vividly characterized collection of songs from musicals. *—Ann Feeney*

Recommended:

- ○ **The World Is Beautiful: Viennese Operetta Arias** / Bonynge (cond.), Hadley, Munich Radio Orch. / 2003 / RCA 68542
- ○ **Stravinsky: The Rake's Progress** / Nagano (cond.), Upshaw, Ramey, Lloyd, Hadley, Lyon Opera Orch. / 1996 / Erato 12715

Ida Haendel

b. Dec. 15, 1928, Chelm, Poland

Violinist

The respect held by other musicians for the talents of violinist Ida Haendel is almost as total as her obscurity in the mind of the general public. What commands this respect is her large tone, assured and dedicated technique, and refreshing musicality. Haendel took up the violin at the age of three. She won her first competition, the Huberman Prize, when she was five, playing Beethoven's *Violin Concerto,* and was a finalist at the age of seven in the Wieniawski Competition. She and her parents traveled around Western Europe for a few years, during which time she did some studies with Enescu. Eventually, the family settled in London, where she was a student of Carl Flesch. In 1937, she made her first appearance at the *Promenade* concerts, where she continues to perform. It was around the time of her 1939 debut with Sir Henry Wood that the debate over her age developed. At the time, London would not allow children under the age of 14 to perform on Sundays, so 11-year-old Ida and her manager lied about her age in order for her to play. During World War II, Haendel played for English troops and participated in Myra Hess' National Gallery concerts. She also made many recordings during the early 1940s, but it wasn't until she toured America in 1946 and began annual tours of Europe, as well as appearing in South America and Asia, that her name began to be known outside of England. She was the soloist invited to tour China with John Pritchard and the London Philharmonic in 1973. She and her family moved to Canada in 1952, but she now splits her time between Miami and London. Her signature pieces are the concertos of Sibelius, Elgar, Walton, Brahms, and Britten. Both Sibelius and Walton personally praised her performances of their works. She premiered Dallapiccola's *Tartiniana seconda* in 1957 and Allan Pettersson's *Violin Concerto No. 2,* which was dedicated to her, in 1980. Haendel was given the Sibelius prize in 1982 and created a Commander of the British Empire in 1991. While not as well recognized as she should be, she continues to be a much-sought-after soloist by conductors such as Vladimir Ashkenazy, Simon Rattle, Zubin Mehta, and Seiji Ozawa, and is admired by younger violinists such as Anne-Sophie Mutter and Maxim Vengerov. *—Patsy Morita*

Recommended:

- ○ **Popular Encores** / Haendel, Parsons / 2002 / Testament 1259
- ○ **Sibelius: Violin Concerto; Serenades** / Berglund (cond.), Haendel, Bournemouth Sinfonietta / 2002 / EMI 75236
- ○ **Ida Haendel Vol. 1** / Haendel, etc. / 1998 / Doremi 7726

Håkan Hagegård

b. Nov. 25, 1945, Karlstad, Sweden

Baritone

Hagegård is a singer at home in a variety of styles, from lieder to Swedish song to opera, from a variety of time periods, though he is probably best known for his performances of Romantic-era music. His voice is particularly suited to these nineteenth century composers, having a rich, warm timbre capable of a wide range of colorations. However, he has also championed twentieth century music, creating the part of Beaumarchais in John Corigliano's *The Ghosts of Versailles,* singing Nick Shadow in a film of *The Rake's Progress,* and recording the part of Captain von Trapp in Rogers and Hammerstein's *The Sound of Music.* He studied with Tito Gobbi, also known for using his voice to color and focus upon the meaning of the text as well as illuminating the music, and studied lieder with Gerald Moore, perhaps the most influential lieder teacher (and accompanist) of the last half of the twentieth century.

While his family enjoyed music, and nearly every member sang or played an instrument, the focus was on enjoying it as a family rather than on performing, or even having any aspirations to public performance. However, his interest ran deeper (as did that of his cousin, Erland Hagegård, who also became an operatic baritone), and he first studied music locally, and then went on to the Royal Academy of Music in Stockholm in 1967. He made his opera debut only a year later, as Papageno, perhaps his most famous role, at the Stockholm Opera. Upon graduating, he continued his studies with masters; Erik Werba and Gerald Moore in Salzburg and London and Tito Gobbi in Italy, as well as becoming a member of the Stockholm Opera from 1970, where he remained until 1979. He made his international debut at Glyndebourne as the Count in Strauss' *Capriccio,* and in 1975, he came to the attention of the opera world as Papageno in the famous Ingmar Bergman film of Mozart's *The Magic Flute.* His Metropolitan Opera debut was in 1978 as Malatesta in Donizetti's *Don Pasquale,* and his La Scala debut in 1985 as Papageno.

He founded the HageGarden Music Center, a retreat in a rustic area, but one with modern equipment for communications and recording, where he conducts master classes. He and soprano Barbara Bonney were married for a time. Caprice released two of his LP recordings, one of Swedish songs, another of operatic arias, as one CD. His *Die Schöne Müllerin* on RCA, with Emanuel Ax, is exemplary. *—Ann Feeney*

Recommended:

- ○ **Schubert: Winterreise** / Hagegård, Schuback / 1983 / RCA 14861

○ **Schumann: Liederkreis; 8 Songs** / Hagegård, Schuback / 1986 / RCA 5664

○ **Songs Of Brahms, Sibelius & Stenhammar** / Hagegård, Jones / 1997 / RCA 68097

Hilary Hahn

b. Nov. 27, 1979, Lexington, VA

Violinist

Hilary Hahn emerged in 1997 as a remarkably complete violinist at the age of 17. She recalls that she started violin because at the age of three, while she and her father were out for a walk, she noticed a sign outside a prep school that said "Music Lessons, Four Years Old and Up." She wandered inside. "I remember watching a little boy play 'Twinkle, Twinkle' on a little violin. I knew when I saw him that it was something I really wanted to try." After beginning lessons, she was soon referred to teacher Klara Berkovich. Berkovich was revered in her Russian homeland for her 25-year career as a teacher at the Leningrad School for the Musically Gifted. Berkovich used to tell Hahn "You only have to practice on days you eat." Hahn came to love the regimen of practicing, spending five and a half hours a day at the violin. As for the rest of her education, much of it came through home-schooling courses so that she would have sufficient time for music. At the age of nine she debuted with the Baltimore Symphony Orchestra. She credits Baltimore's conductor David Zinman, as one of her primary mentors.

At ten she enrolled in Philadelphia's Curtis School of Music, spending weekdays staying with her father in that city. Her violin teacher there was Jascha Brodsky. She won the prestigious Avery Fisher Career Development Grant at the age of 15 and she graduated from Curtis with a Bachelor of Music degree at the age of 19. Her usual schedule was to practice and study most days, with an average of a week or two a month spent in travelling and performing.

Hahn has appeared with the symphony orchestras of St. Louis, Cologne, Cleveland, and many others; at the end of the year 2000 she moved straight from a recital tour into an international concerto tour that included appearances in England, Germany, Japan, and Singapore. Hahn's first CD release, on Sony, was a best-selling set of Bach solo sonatas and partitas. In 1999 her recording of the Beethoven violin concerto, with Zinman conducting the Baltimore Symphony, was nominated for a Grammy award, and something of a publicity juggernaut began to build around the slender, technically flawless prodigy. Hahn's third release fell squarely amidst the effort by Sony to broaden the classical music public by focusing on accessible works. Bluegrass-classical fusionist Edgar Meyer composed a concerto especially for Hahn, and it was paired with the perennially crowd-pleasing concerto of Samuel Barber. Her 2002 recording of the Mendelssohn and Shostakovich (No. 1) concertos was also a Grammy winner. *—Joseph Stevenson*

Recommended:

○ **Hahn Plays Bach** / Hahn / 1997 / Sony 62793

○ **Violin Concertos of Brahms & Stravinsky** / Marriner (cond.), Hahn, Academy of St. Martin-in-the-Fields / 2001 / Sony 89649

○ **Violin Concertos of Barber & Meyer** / Wolff (cond.), Hahn, St. Paul CO / 2000 / Sony 89029

Reynaldo Hahn

b. Aug. 9, 1875, Caracas, Venezuela, **d.** Jan. 28, 1947, Paris, France

Composer

Reynaldo Hahn is often considered an archetypal French composer—a product of effective French music education coupled with the cosmopolitan atmosphere of Paris. The fact that Hahn was not actually French (he was born in Caracas, Venezuela) has never deterred this notion—even among the nationalistic French—since he made Paris his home for nearly his entire life. Today, as he was during his life, he is best known for his vocal works, ranging from serious opera and operetta to solo songs. His affinity for both the stage and the human voice eventually led to his appointment in 1945 as director of the Paris Opéra.

Hahn's parents were of German and Venezuelan extraction; when he was three years old the family relocated to Paris, where Hahn entered the Paris Conservatoire in 1886. He studied harmony with Théodore Dubois, piano with Decombes and composition with Jules Massenet. Massenet's influence is clear in one of Hahn's earliest, and most famous, songs, *Si mes vers avaient des ailes* (If my verses had wings); written when the composer was only 13, it is a charming setting of verses by Victor Hugo. The combined forces of Massenet's advocacy on his behalf (enough to have his cycle of songs on the poetry of Paul Verlaine, Chansons grises, published in 1893) and Hahn's own fine singing voice (enabling him to accompany himself in salons and concert halls) helped to establish his reputation in the city.

Early in his career, Hahn made the acquaintance of Sarah Bernhardt and Marcel Proust; Proust, especially, would instill in Hahn a deep appreciation and understanding of poetry, which had a profound effect on Hahn's approach to vocal composition. Hahn once wrote, "The genuine beauty of singing consists in a perfect unison, an amalgam, a mysterious alloy of the singing and the speaking voice, or to put it better, the melody and the spoken word." Hahn found himself seduced by the poetry of Victor Hugo, Théophile Gautier, and Paul Verlaine; he put his efforts toward creating musical phrasing and rhythmic gestures that would allow the words to speak for themselves. Hahn believed that "[o]nly form can give a piece a chance of lasting. . . . " This perhaps explains his predilection for the older, repetitive formal structures evident in some of his songs, such as *"L'automne"* (Autumn), *"Le printemps"* (Spring) and *"Quand je fus pris au pavillion"* (When I was Lured to her Pavilion).

Hahn's first stage composition was incidental music for Daudet's *L'obstacle* in 1890; his first opera to reach the stage was the three-act *L'île du rêve*, performed in Paris at the Opéra-Comique in 1898; a more successful serious opera appeared in 1935 (*Le marchand de Venise*, in three acts, with a libretto by Zamacoïs, after Shakespeare). Notably, with *Le marchand de Venise*, Hahn deliberately returned to the "old-fashioned" division between musical numbers and recitatives and returned the orchestra to a purely accompanimental role. Hahn's most important ballet, *Le dieu bleu*, was composed in 1912 for Diaghilev's company (to a scenario by Cocteau and Madrazo). By far, Hahn's most successful theater piece is his operetta, *Ciboulette*; it premiered to instant acclaim in Paris in 1923, and has received innumerable performances since.

As a conductor and impresario at the Paris Opéra, Hahn favored the operas of Mozart; he found the earlier composer so fascinating, in fact, that he composed a musical comedy on his life (*Mozart*, 1925), in which he included pastiches of Mozart's own music. *—John Palmer*

Overview of Works (1887–1947)

Venezuelan-born French composer Reynaldo Hahn (1874–1947) was the foremost composer of French operetta of his day. He revealed his talents early, composing ingratiatingly enjoyable songs at the age of 13 that he sang with a pleasant voice (there are several recordings of the mature Hahn singing). All of the elements of his style were immediately apparent, even in his earliest works: free and unaffected melodies of elegant lightness and charm set above conventional but effective harmonies and unobtrusive accompaniments. Hahn's first "hit" was *L'ile du reve* (The Island of Dreams) (1898), which was staged at the Opera-comique when Hahn was 24, followed by 24 more operettas, operas, and ballets. Among the most popular of these stage works were the musical comedy *Mozart* (1925), the ballet *Le dieu bleu* (The Blue God) (1912) written for Diaghilev, and his still popular three-act operetta *Ciboulette* (1923). He also continued to write songs and song cycles, as well as a violin concerto (1927), a piano concerto (1931), two string quartets, plus other chamber music and a great deal of light piano music. Friends with Sarah Bernhardt and Marcel Proust, Hahn was also a conductor who spent most of his re-creative dividing his time between being the music director of the opera at the Cannes Casino and of the summer festival at Salzburg before becoming the director of the Paris Opera in 1945. *—James Leonard*

Recommended:

○ **La Belle Époque** / Graham, Vignoles / 1998 / Sony 60168

○ **Hahn: Le Rossignol Éperdu** / Wild / 2001 / Ivory 72006

○ **Songs by Reynaldo Hahn** / Layton, Johnson, Varcoe, Bostridge, Lott, Bickley, Gould, London Schubert Chorale / 1996 / Hyperion 67141/2

○ **Chansons Grises & other songs by Hahn** / Hill, Johnson / 2000 / Hyperion 55040

○ **Hahn: Piano Quartet; Violin Sonata & Other Chamber Music** / Coombs, Groote, Sewart, Inoue, Room-Music / 2004 / Hyperion 67391

Emmanuelle Haïm

Conductor, Harpsichordist

A sensational new figure on the Baroque music scene in the early 2000s, conductor Emmanuelle Haïm electrified audiences with her passionate interpretations of operatic and choral works. She has never studied conducting formally, and, like many other performers involved with older repertoire, she first came to early music only in adulthood. Haïm has never divulged her birthdate, but music suffused her family background. In her deep ancestry was a family of Breton organmakers, and her Hungarian stepfather passed time as friends with both Andras Schiff and Zoltan Kocsis. Emmanuelle and her siblings performed chamber music at these high-level gatherings, and she soon decided on a musical career.

At first Haïm studied piano, but in her mid-twenties she switched to harpsichord because she wanted to participate in a performance of Bach's *St. Matthew Passion* and couldn't think of another way to become involved. Among her teachers at the Paris Conservatoire were Kenneth Gilbert and Christophe Rousset, and she was soon pulling down top prizes. Her harpsichord skills were spotted by conductor William Christie, and for a decade Haïm performed with his ensemble, Les Arts Florissants. Though neither Haïm nor Christie realized it at the time, she was also studying conducting. "Bill is a showman; he has a sense of the life and rhythm of a show," Haïm later explained to the *Independent*. She also performed Baroque and Classical repertory with big-name conductors such as Simon Rattle, who would later encourage her in her own conducting efforts. And she was a noted accompanist who worked with Cecilia Bartoli, among others.

Haïm's conducting debut was as unplanned as her turn toward the harpsichord; a group of instrumentalist friends wanted practice working with singers, and Haïm agreed to helm an impromptu ensemble. She began to find opportunities as a Baroque opera conductor, and in 2000 she formed an ensemble of her own, Le Concert d'Astrée. That put Haïm and her enthusiasm squarely in the spotlight ("like a ballerina on speed" was the *Independent*'s description of Haïm in rehearsal), and engagements and support began to flow her way. (Le Concert d'Astrée is backed by France Télécom, but not by the French government.) In 2003 Haïm conducted Monteverdi's *Orfeo* at the Barbican in London in a series of six sold-out performances featuring star tenor Ian Bostridge. She made numerous guest-conducting appearances, but declined chances to move into mainstream repertory. Haïm was slated to conduct *Orfeo* in 20 performances across France in the 2005–2006 season. *—James Manheim*

Recommended:

- **Handel: Aci, Galatea e Polifemo** / Haïm (cond.), Piau, Mingardo, Naouri, Le Concert D'Astree / 2003 / Virgin 45557
- **Monteverdi: L'Orfeo** / Haïm (cond.), Dessay, Bostridge, Agnew, Gens, Le Concert D'Astree, European Voices / 2004 / Virgin 45642
- **Purcell: Dido & Aeneas** / Haïm (cond.), Halsey, Lowe, Graham, Bostridge, Daniels, Le Concert D'Astree, European Voices / 2003 / Virgin 45605

Bernard Haitink

b. Mar. 4, 1929, Amsterdam, Netherlands
Conductor

Born in 1929, Bernard Haitink is regarded as one of the finest conductors of the twentieth century: with a wide repertory, and meticulous, yet exciting, performances. He studied violin at Amsterdam Conservatory, and began his musical career as a violinist in the Netherlands Radio Philharmonic. At the Conservatory, he studied conducting with Felix Hupka, later taking conducting courses with Ferdinand Leitner. He was eventually named second conductor with the Radio Union, leading four different orchestras or ensembles. He was promoted to principal conductor of the Netherlands Radio Philharmonic at the age of 27.

After a strong showing in a last-minute replacement at the Amsterdam Concertgebouw in Cherubini's *Requiem* in 1956, the Concertgebouw Orchestra frequently engaged him as a guest conductor. After Eduard van Beinum died, two conductors were named co-principal conductors of the Concertgebouw: Haitink (at 32 the youngest principal conductor ever), and the veteran Eugen Jochum. Two years later, Jochum left, leaving Haitink in charge. He became the principal conductor and then artistic director of the London Philharmonic Orchestra, retaining that position until 1979.

He also frequently conducted opera productions in England as music director of the Glyndebourne Festival (1977–88). He became music director of the Royal Opera in Covent Garden (London) in 1987, and has seen the company through the difficult period when its house was closed for radical renovations through the end of the 1990s.

In 1988 his association with the Concertgebouw Orchestra ended when he resigned in protest over governmental economic measures that in his view, affected the quality of the orchestra. He has increased his guest appearances in the years since, appearing with the Berlin Philharmonic, Vienna Philharmonic, London Philharmonic, London Symphony Orchestra, and the Boston Symphony Orchestra, of which he is the Principal Guest Conductor. Reconciliation with the Concertgebouw occurred several years after his departure when the orchestra named him its Conductor Laureate, the first time the Concertgebouw has bestowed the title, in recognition of his great contribution to their history over a 30-year period. In 1999 they invited him to lead them in a set of Concertgebouw concerts called the "Carte Blanche" Series. In it he led the Royal Opera House Orchestra, the Vienna Philharmonic, the Dresden Staatskapelle, Berlin Philharmonic, European Union Youth Orchestra, and Netherlands Radio Orchestra, as well as the Concertgebouw Orchestra.

He has made a large quantity of records under a wide ranging repertory. These have included complete symphonies of Vaughan Williams, Mahler, Bruckner, Beethoven, Shostakovich, and Brahms, and many other works. He has won numerous awards, an honorary British knighthood, and the House Order of Orange-Nassau, given to him by the Queen of the Netherlands.*—Joseph Stevenson*

Recommended:

- **Shostakovich: Symphony 7** / Haitink (cond.), London PO / 1993 / Decca 425068
- **Mahler: Symphonies 4 & 5** / Haitink (cond.), McNair, Berlin PO / 2004 / Philips 475445
- **Stravinsky: The Great Ballets** / Haitink, Markevitch (conds.), Grunberg, London PO, London SO / 1993 / Philips 438350
- **Shostakovich: Symphonies 5 & 9** / Haitink (cond.), Concertgebouw, London PO / 1993 / Decca 425066
- **Ravel: Bolero, etc.** / Haitink (cond.), Royal Concertgebouw Orch. / 2003 / Philips 000044102

Fromental Halévy

b. May 27, 1799, Paris, France, **d.** Mar. 17, 1862, Nice, France
Composer: Opera

Jacques Fromental Halévy was an accomplished composer, teacher and essayist on music. A pupil of Cherubini, Halévy also studied in Italy. His best known opera, *La juive*, is a primary example of French grand opera. He composed over 30 operas, as well as cantatas, ballets, and songs.

In 1807, Elias Levy and his wife, Julie Meyer, changed the family name from Levy to Halévy. The next year, their precocious son, Jacques-François-Fromental, entered the Paris Conservatoire. By 1811, the young Halévy had become a composition student of Luigi Cherubini (1760–1842), who would champion his young pupil's work. Halévy also studied with H.M. Berton (1767–1844) and Étienne Méhul (1763–1817), but it was his contact with Cherubini that would have the most profound effect on his life and music.

Halévy won the Prix de Rome in 1819, allowing him to study in Rome for a year. While in Italy, Halévy experimented with Italian genres, including opera; in 1822 he traveled to Vienna, where he conversed with Beethoven on a number of occasions. After his return to Paris, Halévy was primarily concerned with achieving success in the theater. He did, however, channel his energy into other activities, such as teaching: in 1827 he was appointed professor of harmony at the Conservatoire, and later of counterpoint and composition. Among his students were Gounod, Massé, Bizet, and Saint-Saëns. Halévy became *chef du chant* at the Théâtre-Italien in 1826 and held the same position at the Opéra in 1829–45.

By 1825, Halévy had completed four operas, plus the finale of a fifth—none of which would ever be performed. *L'artisan* was his first work to reach the stage, receiving its premiere on January 30, 1827, at the Opéra-Comique; reviews were mixed, but it was not a total failure. In 1829 Halévy achieved significant success at the Opéra-Comique with *Le dilettante d'Avignon*, which remained in the house's repertory for several years. After becoming *chef du chant* at the *Opéra*, Halévy composed two ballets for that venue; in the meantime, he continued writing comic operas and garnering moderate praise.

Halévy's first attempt at grand opera, the five-act *La juive* (The Jewish Woman) of 1835, was a huge popular success. Eugène Scribe (1791–1861), who—along with Giacomo Meyerbeer (1791–1864)—invented the spectacular genre, supplied the libretto. *La juive* provided exactly the kind of grandeur sought by Louis Véron, director of the Paris Opéra, and became as much a central part of the French opera repertory as the works of Meyerbeer. In the same year, Halévy achieved another success, this time at the Opéra-Comique with *L'éclair*. Throughout the rest of his career, Halévy alternated between comic and grand opera composition.

Although not as popular as *La juive*, Halévy's *Le reine di Chypre* (1841) and *Charles VI* (1843) are equally great musical achievements, if not greater. Halévy's versatility comes to the fore in *Le reine di Chypre*, for which Saint-Georges' libretto required music befitting numerous exotic locales and strange characters; Wagner praised the work, writing of Halévy's work in general, "I have never heard dramatic music that has transported me so completely to a particular historical epoch." *—John Palmer*

OPERA

La Juive (1835)

The premiere of *La Juive*, on February 23, 1835, was the most opulent and grand of any production of the Paris Opéra up to that time. Critics and public marveled at the accuracy with which the scenes and costumes re-created fifteenth century courts and churches. The knights, it was reported, had on real armor, and the Emperor was covered in glittering ingots of gold. Every historical detail of costume and setting was closely followed.

The libretto, by Eugène Scribe, sets a story of love between two central characters (Rachel and Léopold) against a backdrop of religious, political, and personal conflict. This libretto, along with the one Scribe provided for Meyerbeer's *Les Huguenots*, would help to change the course of French grand opera. Crowd scenes and themes of political conflict focused attention on issues of social unrest, bigotry, persecution, and class status. In these dramas, individuals were diminished and their surrounding social forces brought to life, embodied by the crowd. Obvious machinations of plot are employed to bring music to the forefront; realism is sacrificed in the interest of spectacle and drama on the grandest of scales. The result was a grand opera just as resplendent as those of the past, but one filled with modern social awareness.

Halévy's expansive score matches the splendor of the story with grand music, impassioned and passionate. The opera was greatly admired by Mahler, Berlioz, and Richard Wagner, who overcame his anti-Semitism temporarily in order to be inspired by Halévy's music and sense of drama. The story of the opera gave Halévy plenty of opportunity to write large dramatic tableaux. There is an angry, intolerant crowd in the first act, and a Passover seder in the second. Act Three contains celebrations in honor of the Emperor Léopold that make use of chorus, pantomime, and ballet. The spectacular festivities are interrupted by the dramatic high point of the story, in which Rachel denounces the Emperor in front of his entire court for having courted her, a Jew, for marriage. In the final act, a chorus of bloodthirsty townspeople, who are anticipating the execution of Rachel and her father because of the denouncement, contains some of the finest and most dramatic music of the opera.

Act Four closes with the most famous number in the opera, a solo for the hero Eléazar (Rachel's father): he contemplates sacrificing Rachel for the sake of his own revenge against the Cardinal, a powerful persecutor of the Jews. English horns and bass pizzicati give a Semitic flavor to the orchestration, as does the melodic use of augmented seconds. Here, Eléazar stands as a quintessential hero of French grand opera—both savior and demon, loyal father and fanatic—as his torn psyche is brought to life in this aria. *—Rita Laurance*

Synopsis:

Before the beginning of the opera's action, Cardinal de Brogni had been chief magistrate of fifteenth century Rome. During a war, his house was burned, his wife died, and his infant daughter vanished. He entered the priesthood, rising to the rank of cardinal.

Act One. The opera opens in a public square. Inside, the choir sings a Te Deum, and outside, the townspeople mutter about Eléazar, who is working while the Christians are in church. He emerges to glare defiantly, but Rachel asks him to return inside to avoid a confrontation. Léopold enters in disguise, and though Albert recognizes him, he agrees not to tell. Albert tells him that the emperor is arriving to open a council to reunite all sects of the Christian faith, something that Léopold himself has helped make possible through his defeat of the Hussites, a heretic group. Ruggiero announces a public holiday in celebration of Prince Léopold's victory and then questions Eléazar. Eléazar defiantly reminds him that his own sons were burnt at the stake for defying Christian laws, and Ruggiero threatens him, but Brogni, who remembers him from their earlier days in Rome, stops him, praying that God will enlighten the Jews ("Si la rigueur"), and that tolerance and forgiveness will prevail. He adds that he hopes he and Eléazar can be friends. Léopold, whom Rachel knows as Samuel, a Jewish artisan, serenades her ("Loin de son amie"). She invites him to join them for Passover. The townspeople enter, drinking and celebrating the holiday ("Hâtons-nous, car l'heure s'avance"), and are about to attack Eléazar and Rachel for the crime of standing on the church stairs to better see the festivities ("Au lac, oui"). Léopold, backed by Albert, saves them, to Rachel's bewilderment. Eléazar sings of his hatred for the Christians.

Act Two. During the Passover celebration, Eléazar prays ("O Dieu, Dieu de nos pères") and then curses anyone who might betray their feast ("Si trahison ou perfidie"). Léopold covertly drops his Passover bread, further increasing Rachel's worries. Eléazar prays again ("Dieu, que ma voix") but is interrupted by a knock on the door. The other Jews leave, but Eléazar tells "Samuel" to stay. Eudoxie enters and orders a gold chain as a returning gift for her husband ("Tu possèdes, dit-on"). Léopold is perturbed at the thought that he is betraying both her and Rachel. When she has left, Rachel asks Samuel for an explanation, and he insists that he will tell her later, in private. She waits for him ("Il va venir"), frightened but still deeply in love. He arrives and admits that he is a Christian, and she is bitterly angry, but he pleads that he loves her ("Lorsqu'a toi je me suis"). Eléazar catches them together and furiously declares that it is only the fact that Samuel is a fellow Jew that keeps him from killing him ("Je vois son front coupable"). Léopold says that in fact he is a Christian, and Eléazar strikes at him, but Rachel intervenes. Eléazar agrees to allow them to marry, but when Léopold says it is impossible, he again becomes furious.

Act Three. In the castle, Eudoxie happily anticipates her husband's return ("Assez longtemps la crainte"). Rachel asks to be allowed to serve her for just one day; she has followed Léopold there and wants to find his true identity. Eudoxie agrees and lovingly greets Léopold when he enters, but he is still morose ("Mon doux seigneur et maître"). At a banquet celebrating Léopold's victory, the Emperor has performers dance to entertain his guests, who include Brogni and Eudoxie. They sing of Léopold's triumph ("Sonnez, clairons"). Eléazar and Rachel enter with the necklace Eudoxie ordered, and when she is about to give it to Léopold, Rachel snatches it back and accuses him of consorting with a Jewish woman, herself, to general horror ("Je frissonne et succombe"). Léopold does not deny it, and Eléazar sarcastically asks if Léopold is above the law against miscegenation. He, Rachel, and Léopold are all condemned to die by Brogni, who pronounces a curse on them ("Vous, qui du Dieu vivant").

Act Four. Eudoxie pleads with Rachel to retract the charges, as she still loves Léopold and wants to save him. She at first refuses, and then, to demonstrate that a despised Jew can be more merciful than a Christian, and herself still in love, agrees ("Dieu tutelaire"). Brogni then comes and begs her to save herself by becoming a Christian. She refuses, to his dismay ("Mourir, mourir si jeune"), and he sends for Eléazar, whom he begs to save Rachel by himself converting. Eléazar refuses and tells Brogni that his daughter was saved from the fire by a Jewish man. She is still alive and he knows where she is, but he will avenge himself for their hatred by dying with the secret. Brogni pleads with him uselessly ("Ah! j'implore en tremblant"). Alone, Eléazar is torn between his hatred for the Christians and his love for Rachel, who is the daughter in question. He has devoted his life to her happiness, and now, by his silence, he is giving her to the executioner. He hesitates, but hearing the vicious chorus outside calling for death to the Jews ("Au bucher, les Juifs"), he chooses revenge and martyrdom instead.

Act Five. Léopold is banished rather than killed after Rachel recants her accusation. Eléazar and Rachel are brought in, where they are to be killed by being thrown in boiling oil (in many productions, this is changed to burning at the stake or hanging). Eléazar asks her whether, seeing the scaffold, she wishes to save herself by converting, but she refuses, preferring martyrdom ("C'est le ciel"). She is killed, and Eléazar tells Brogni that it was his daughter who just died. *—Ann Feeney*

Recommended:

- ○ **Halévy: La Juive** / Guadagno (cond.), Tucker, Etheridge, Fyson, Noble, New Philharmonia / Myto 3222
- ○ **Halévy: La Juive** / Young (cond.), Miles, Shicoff, Isokoski, Gati, Vienna State Opera / 2002 / RCA 79596

Hallé Orchestra

f. 1857, Manchester, England

Ensemble

The oldest of all of Britain's venerable orchestral ensembles, the Hallé Orchestra of Manchester was formed in 1857 by Charles Hallé, a German conductor and pianist. Hallé was hired to conduct a large orchestra in daily concerts for five months during an art exposition. Hallé found he could not bear to break up the fine orchestra thus created and, at his own financial risk, established the "Hallé Concerts" on January 30, 1858.

The orchestra played 30 concerts a year, becoming known for high standards and a wide repertory, but eventually it became enmeshed in the great clash between pro-German and anti-German sentiments that marked the British musical scene at the end of the nineteenth century. After Hallé's death in 1895 three Manchester businessmen put up a financial guarantee to sustain the orchestra. They engaged Hans Richter as conductor, but also hired Frederic Cowen as interim conductor. When Richter finally arrived in October, 1899, this aroused the anger of Cowen's supporters, who opposed Richter and his heavily Germanic programming. They remained unhappy when another German, Michael Balling, took over on Richter's departure in 1911.

World War I left he orchestra without a permanent conductor until 1920, when British conductor Hamilton Harty was appointed. He is credited with revitalizing the orchestra's spirits, standards, and repertory, but resigned in 1933 in a dispute over his outside engagements.

Malcolm Sargent was appointed conductor in 1939, but the outbreak of World War II prevented him from actually taking over. Meanwhile, in 1934 a deal had been struck to supply musicians for a new BBC Northern Orchestra, a studio ensemble. Soon the Hallé found it could not control its own schedule because the BBC had first call on these 35 players, who were used extensively in wartime morale concerts. Matters got even worse when the Hallé's home, the Free Trade Hall, was destroyed by bombs.

The orchestra's board severed the BBC contract and announced a 200-concert-per-year schedule. Only four of the players formerly shared with the BBC stayed with the Hallé. The British conductor John Barbirolli, finding New York uncongenial, returned home as conductor. Somehow, despite wartime scarcity and his own long absence, Barbirolli found 30 fresh players, and drilled the orchestra to its highest level yet. He remained at the helm for 25 years, semi-retiring as conductor laureate for life in 1968.

His successor, James Loughran, maintained the ensemble's standards, but did not have the international star appeal of Barbirolli. Loughran was succeeded by Stanislaw Skrowaczewski and, in 1991, by American conductor Kent Nagano.

At the end of the twentieth century, the Hallé has once again had competition from its old rival. In 1973 the BBCNO started playing public concerts, and in 1980 it was renamed the BBC Philharmonic and enlarged to full orchestra size. Both orchestras share quarters in Manchester's new Bridgewater Hall. In 1998, the accounting firm KPMG reported to the Hallé board that chaotic management, huge debts, and an operating loss of 600,000 pounds in the prior financial year threatened the immediate demise of the orchestra. But its four biggest sponsors and another 11 corporations called the "Hallé Family" came to the Hallé's financial rescue.

Nagano improved the quality and international recognition of the orchestra, which received a Grammy award for its recording of John Adams' *El Dorado.* However, Nagano's contract was not renewed after its expiration in the summer of 2000; Mark Elder was selected as the next music director. *—Joseph Stevenson*

Recommended:

- ○ **Elgar: Symphony 2** / Barbirolli (cond.), NPO, Hallé Orch. / 1993 / EMI 64724
- ○ **Sibelius: Finlandia, etc.** / Barbirolli (cond.), Hallé Orch. / 1988 / EMI 769205
- ○ **Adams: El Dorado** / Nagano, Adams (conds.), Hallé Orch., London Sinfonietta / 1996 / Nonesuch 79359

Marc-André Hamelin

b. Sep. 5, 1961, Montréal, Quebec, Canada
Pianist
Canadian Marc-André Hamelin is one of the world's most highly regarded piano virtuosos. He has a wide-ranging and large repertory with an uncommonly large proportion of little-known keyboard works of several eras in music. Critic Carol Bergeron of the Montréal newspaper *Le Devoir* called him "Glenn Gould's only worthy successor," and the *New York Times*' Harold Schonberg described him as a "super-virtuoso."

He studied at the Vincent d'Indy School of Music (part of the University of Sherbrooke in Montréal) and continued his musical education in the United States at Temple University in Philadelphia, earning his bachelor's and master's degrees there. His teachers were Russell Sherman, Harvey Weeden, and Yvonne Hubert. He still makes his home in Philadelphia.

In 1985, he launched his career with a first prize victory in the Carnegie Hall International American Music Competition. Since then, he has appeared in recital in a large list of international venues. A partial list includes New York, Philadelphia, Toronto, Montréal, Washington, Tokyo, Amsterdam, Berlin, Frankfurt, Istanbul, Luxembourg, Milan, Munich, Paris, Vienna, London, and Belfast. He tends increasingly to present series of thematically linked recitals. For instance, he appeared in the Manchester, England, Glories of the Piano Festival, a 1994 Wigmore Hall (London) series called Virtuoso Romantics, and in 1999, he began a six-recital three-year series of Tokyo appearances collectively called "150 years of Pianism with Marc-André Hamelin."

He has appeared in orchestral concerts in Toronto, Vancouver, Montréal, Chicago, Houston, Indianapolis, Minneapolis, Philadelphia, Birmingham, London, Ulster, Lahti, Amsterdam, Manchester, Edinburgh, and Belfast. Festival performances include the Blackheath Halls Pianoworks Festival, the Diszniki Chopin Festival, La Grange de Meslay en Touraine, the Lanaudière Festival, the Ruhr Piano Festival, the Ravinia Festival, La Roque d'Antheron, the Singapore International Piano Festival, the Snape Maltings Proms, the Schloss vor Hussum Rarities of Piano Music, the Valldemossa Chopin Festival, the Festival of Consonances, the St. Nazaire Festival, the Espoo Festival (near Helsinki, Finland), and the Tallinn Festival in Estonia.

He has performed in concert or recital with such organizations and artists as the Chicago Symphony Orchestra, the Houston Symphony Orchestra, the Indianapolis Symphony Orchestra, the Minnesota Orchestra, the Philadelphia Orchestra, the City of Birmingham Symphony Orchestra, the Montréal Symphony, the Polish National Radio Orchestra, the Orchestre de la Suisse Romande, the Ulster Orchestra, the CBC Vancouver Symphony Orchestra, the Royal Concertgebouw Orchestra, the BBC Philharmonic, the Lahti Symphony Orchestra, the Netherlands Radio Orchestra, the BBC Scottish Symphony Orchestra, and the Australian Chamber Orchestra, and conductors Andrew Davis, Stanislaw Skrowaczewski, David Zinman, Dmitri Sitkovetsky, Osmo Vänskä, Dennis Russell Davies, Jukka-Pekka Saraste, Christoph Eschenbach, and Günther Herbig.

His activities in the recording studio have reflected his interest in unusual music. He has recorded works of Alkan, Bolcom, Busoni, Catoire (a virtually unknown Russian composer), Godowsky, Eckhardt-Gramatté, Grainger, Henselt, Korngold, Ives, Medtner, Reger, Rzewski, Sorabji, and Wolpe. Larger-scale projects have included a multi-disc set of the piano music of Heitor Villa-Lobos, the complete Godowski elaborations on Chopin etudes, and the complete piano sonatas of Medtner and Scriabin. The Alkan album won the Canadian Juno Award, the Grainger recording received the Soundscapes Award 1997, and a set called "Composer-Pianists from Alkan to Hamelin" was the Preis der Deutschen Schallplatten Kritik in 1997 and 1998.

In 1994, Hamelin joined with a group of other well-known Canadian pianists (Janina Fialkowska, Jon Kimura Parker, Angela Hewitt, Angela Cheng, and André Laplante) to form Piano Six. This unique musical partnership brings their playing to small and far-flung communities in the vastness of Canada as its members provide their service for minimal fees that permit ordinary people to afford to attend. *—Joseph Stevenson*

Recommended:

- ○ **Alkan: Symphony for Solo Piano** / Hamelin / 2001 / Hyperion 67218
- ○ **The Composer Pianists** / Hamelin / 1998 / Hyperion 67050
- ○ **Godowsky: Complete Studies on Chopin's Etudes** / Hamelin / 2000 / Hyperion 67411/2
- ○ **Liszt: Paganini Studies; Schubert March Transcriptions** / Hamelin / 2002 / Hyperion 67370
- ○ **Busoni: Concerto** / Elder (cond.), Hamelin, City of Birmingham SO / 1999 / Hyperion 67143

Thomas Hampson

b. Jun. 28, 1955, Elkhart, IN
Baritone
Thomas Hampson possesses one of the most rich and mellow baritone voices of the postwar generations, complete with ringing top notes. His quick musical intelligence enables him not only to sing a vast and varied repertoire in song, lieder, oratorio, musical theater, operetta, and opera, but to write most of his own (very scholarly) program notes, and in addition to all that, was listed by *People* magazine in 1993 as one of the 50 most beautiful people in the world. Like his friend and frequent musical associate, Jerry Hadley, he is an avid student of history and in preparing lieder or opera roles, he often draws from history, literature, and cultural studies of the period. He is also an active teacher of both technique and interpretation. When he was in high school, president of the student body and active in the Model U.N., he was first exposed to symphonic music and then sang in the school choir and later the Spokane Chorale. After he sang a solo in an arts festival, Dr. Sister Marietta Coyle, who had herself studied with Lotte Lehmann, another singer who focused deeply on meaning and interpretation, told him that if he wanted to explore his talent, he should call her. At that point, Hampson was more interested in a career in law and politics. Nonetheless, he began serious voice lessons with her, making his opera debut as the Father in *Hansel and Gretel* in a small local production in 1974.

In 1978, he began summer classes at the Music Academy of the West, studying with Horst Gunther and Martial Singher, the famous baritone. In college, he balanced both potential careers by getting a B.A. in government from Eastern Washington University and a B.F.A. in voice performance from Fort Wright College. However, by 1980, when he won second place in the Met's Western Region competition and in the San Francisco Merola Program auditions, his plans focused more and more on music. In the Merola program, he studied with Elisabeth Schwarzkopf, another of the great lieder teachers. In September of that year, he went to Europe and was hired at the Dusseldorf Opera. His career began to expand, particularly when at the Dusseldorf Opera he graduated to more important roles, and in 1984, he was engaged by the Zurich Opera. During the same year, Schwarzkopf and the Walter Legge Foundation sponsored his debut recital in Wigmore Hall in London. In 1986, he made his Met debut as the Count in *Le nozze di Figaro* and his Vienna State Opera debut as Gugliemo in *Così.* Two years later, he made his Salzburg Festival debut as the Count. In 1994, he created the role of the Vicomte de Valmont in the world premiere of Conrad Susa's *Dangerous Liaisons.* During the 1990s, he began teaching master classes and in 1997, he received the Citation of Merit for Lifetime Contribution to Music and Education from the National Arts Club of America.

He has recorded widely with special concentrations in German and American song, both familiar and more obscure. In musical theater, his recording of Cole Porter songs (EMI) has just the right tongue-in-cheek sophistication for the comic songs and the heart-on-the-sleeve lyric emotional expression for the romantic ones. In lieder, his recital, including *Dichterliebe* and *An die Ferne Geliebte* (EMI), shows off his voice and excellent German diction and in opera, his recording of the French version of *Don Carlos* also on EMI is outstanding. *—Ann Feeney*

Recommended:

- ○ **Beethoven, Berlioz, Franz, Grieg, Liszt, Loewe, Schumann, Wagner: Songs** / Hampson, Parsons / 2002 / EMI 575187
- ○ **A Portrait** / Hampson, etc. / 1997 / EMI 572037
- ○ **Ives, Griffes, MacDowell: Lieder** / Hampson, Guzelimian / 1991 / Teldec 72168
- ○ **An Old Song Re-Sung** / Hampson, Guzelimian / 1990 / EMI 54051

George Frideric Handel

b. Feb. 23, 1685, Halle, Germany, **d.** Apr. 14, 1759, London, England
Composer: Opera, Choral, Orchestral, Concerto, Keyboard, Chamber Music
Most music lovers have encountered George Frederick Handel through holiday-time renditions of the *Messiah*'s "Hallelujah" chorus. And many of them know and love that oratorio of Christ's life and death, as well as a few other greatest hits like the orchestral *Water Music* and *Royal Fireworks Music*, and perhaps *Judas Maccabeus* or one of the other English oratorios. Yet his operas, for which he was widely known in his own time, are the province mainly of specialists in Baroque music, and the events of his life, even though they reflected some of the most important musical issues of the day, have never become as familiar as the careers of Bach or Mozart. Perhaps the single word that best describes his life and music is "cosmopolitan": he was a German composer, trained in Italy, who spent most of his life in England.

Handel was born in the German city of Halle on February 23, 1685. His father noted but did not nurture his musical talent, and he had to sneak a small keyboard instrument into his attic to practice. As a child he studied music with Friedrich Wilhelm Zachow, organist at the Liebfrauenkirche, and for a time he seemed destined for a career as a church organist himself. After studying law briefly at the University of Halle, Handel began serving as organist on March 13, 1702, at the Domkirche there. Dissatisfied, he took a post as violinist in the Hamburg opera orchestra in 1703, and his frustration with musically provincial northern Germany was perhaps shown when he fought a duel the following year with the composer Matheson over the accompaniment to one of Matheson's operas. In 1706 Handel took off for Italy, then the font of operatic innovation, and mastered contemporary trends in Italian serious opera. He returned to Germany to become court composer in Hannover, whose rulers were linked by family ties with the British throne; his patron there, the Elector of Hannover, became King George I of England. English audiences took to his 1711 opera *Rinaldo*, and several years later Handel jumped at the chance to move to England permanently. He impressed King George early on with the *Water Music* of 1716, written as entertainment for a royal boat outing.

Through the 1720s Handel composed Italian operatic masterpieces for London stages: *Ottone*, *Serse* (Xerxes), and other works often based on classical stories. His popularity was dented, though, by new English-language works of a less formal character, and in the 1730s and 1740s Handel turned to the oratorio, a grand form that attracted England's new middle-class audiences. Not only *Messiah* but also *Israel in Egypt*, *Samson*, *Saul*, and many other works established him as a venerated elder of English music. The oratorios displayed to maximum effect Handel's melodic gift and the sense of timing he brought to big choral numbers. Among the most popular of all the oratorios was *Judas Maccabeus*, composed in 32 days in 1746. Handel presented the oratorio six times during its first season and about 40 times before his death 12 years later, conducting it 30 times himself. In 1737, Handel suffered a stroke, which caused both temporary paralysis in his right arm and some loss of his mental faculties, but he recovered sufficiently to carry on most normal activity. He was urged to write an autobiography, but never did. Blind in old age, he continued to compose. He died in London on April 14, 1759. Beethoven thought Handel the greatest of all his predecessors; he once said, "I would bare my head and kneel at his grave." *—AMG*

OPERA

Agrippina, HWV 6 (1709)

The 21-year-old Handel arrived in Italy in the fall of 1706. Although documentation on the early part of his tour is scarce, it is safe to assume that his first port of call was Florence, where he had been invited by Prince Ferdinando de'Medici. It was there that his first Italian opera, *Rodrigo*, was produced in November. Following its successful production, Handel appears to have spent the following winter in Venice, where he made the acquaintance of Domenico Scarlatti and probably met Cardinal Vincenzo Grimani. It was Grimani, a learned churchman and diplomat, who, two years later, would write the libretto of Handel's Venetian opera *Agrippina*. This was one of the finest libretti Handel would set. Unlike the sources of many operas of the period, which favored mythological stories, *Agrippina* is based on history.

The story is set in the Rome of the young Nero, and the plot is centered around the machinations of his mother Agrippina to get him on the imperial throne. Other principal characters are the Emperor Claudius, Agrippina's husband Otho, the emperor's lieutenant, and his beloved, the flirtatious Poppea, who is also desired by both Claudius and Nero. From this story, Grimani fashioned a typically Venetian libretto in which intrigue, witty observations, and a certain black humor prevail. However, avoiding the amoral conclusion of Monteverdi's *L'incoronazione di Poppea*, composed in Venice some 70 years earlier, Grimani's libretto does not allow all the evil schemes to triumph. In keeping with the tenets of earlier Venetian opera, which had not yet been confined to the straitjacket of opera seria form, there is a flexibility in *Agrippina* rarely encountered in Handel's later London operas. In addition to the expected da capo arias, there are a number of ariettas, ariosos, and cavatinas, as well as a quartet, a trio, and a couple of choruses, the last rarely found in opera seria. This work is typical of the fresh, exuberantly inventive music Handel composed during his Italian years, a period during which he first became feted as a celebrity. The exact date of the first performance of *Agrippina* at the Teatro San Giovanni Gristostomo, which was owned by the librettist Grimani, is not known, but a likely time is early January 1710, just after the start of the Carnival season. The production was a tremendous success for Handel, who, according to his earliest biographer Mainwaring, was greeted with continual cries of "Vivo il caro Sassone" (Long live the dear Saxon). Subsequently, the opera was repeated on 26 successive nights, an astonishing feat at this time, and one made all the more remarkable by the fact that operas by two of the leading Venetian composers of the day, Gasparini and Lotti, were concurrently playing in other opera houses in the city. *—Brian Robins*

Synopsis:

Act One. The story takes place in Rome around 50 A.D. Agrippina, wife of Emperor Claudio, receives news of his death while he is staying in Britain. She decides that her son Nero can ascend to the throne with the proper, if unseemly, political moves, and she finds him a quite willing party to her plans. Agrippina also enlists the aid of two unsavory characters, Pallante and Narciso, both of them her lovers. But announcement of the Emperor's return by Lesbo, his servant, at least temporarily defeats her plan. It is revealed that Claudius' life was saved by Ottone, and that his reward for the deed is succession to the throne.

But an obvious obstacle to his future reign is his love for Poppea, who is also the object of the affections of both Claudius and Nero. Agrippina learns from Poppea of her relationship with Ottone and concocts a scheme. She convinces Poppea that Ottone is willing to give her up for the throne and further asks her to reveal his treachery to Claudius, in order to turn him against Ottone. The ploy works, and both Claudius and Poppea come to view Ottone as untrustworthy.

Act Two. Together, Narciso and Pallante decide that Agrippina cannot be trusted, either. Meanwhile, Agrippina flatters Claudius upon his arrival and fully convinces him that Ottone is a traitor. Nero and Poppea second the opinion and make the condemnation of Ottone unanimous. Ottone denounces the charge and hands Poppea a sword with which to stab him. She cannot, and she returns the weapon in the knowledge she still loves him, and because she finds his claims of innocence credible. Agrippina deepens her intrigues by making separate promises of greater rank to both Pallante and Narciso in return for killing Ottone, as well as each other. She also convinces Claudius to declare Nero his successor in order to head off any possible acts of treachery from a potential usurper.

Act Three. Poppea arranges to have her three suitors arrive in her quarters at different times, hiding the first two (Ottone and Nero) behind a curtain. Claudius denounces Nero, and the latter is exposed for his part in plotting to gain succession. Ottone tells Poppea that his love for her supersedes his desire to become Emperor. Pallante and Narciso betray Agrippina's intrigues to Claudius, but the Emperor is dubious of their claims. In a brilliant stroke of deceit, Agrippina admits to her scheming but maintains her actions were always taken with Claudius' welfare in mind. Both Pallante and Narciso have little choice but to confirm her claims; otherwise they will be implicated further.

Claudius summons Ottone, Poppea, and Nero, and declares Ottone his successor while giving Poppea's hand in marriage to Nero. But Ottone renounces succession to the throne in favor of Poppea. Claudius then announces Nero as successor and accepts Ottone's choice for marriage. The goddess Juno then appears and confers her blessing on their union. *—Robert Cummings*

Recommended:

- ○ **Handel: Agrippina** / Gardiner (cond.), Otter, Chance, Robson, Ross, English Baroque Soloists / 1997 / Philips 438009
- ○ **Handel: Agrippina** / McGegan (cond.), Savaria Capella / 1991 / HM 907063

Alcina, HWV 34 (1735)

Handel premiered the opera *Alcina* on April 26, 1735. Like *Orlando*, this magic opera is based on cantos from Ariosto's *Orlando Furioso* and has a fairy-tale aspect about it. Handel turned the character of Alcina, a siren who disposes of her ex-lovers by turning them into all kinds of objects, into a powerful but evil sorceress, a vulnerable woman, and finally a defeated, despairing queen. Her six arias cast her in many moods as the plot progresses and she faces her own downfall. In "Ah! mio Cor" and "Ombre pallide," she is the rejected woman, desolate and despairing, then angry and vengeful. "Ma quando tornerai" is a resolution aria in which she gathers her strength together and vows revenge against the lover who deserted her. Not only does Ruggiero desert her, but at the end of Act Two her magic powers also fail her. In a dramatically accompanied recitative, she invokes the evil spirits to aid her but ends up calling to the empty skies in angular intervals that are answered by silence.

The other characters are well developed and complex as well. The hero Ruggiero begins the opera under Alcina's spell, completely unmanly and petty. However, as the drama progresses, he grows into his heroic stature and breaks the spells that bind Alcina's victims. In Act III, Ruggiero has a resolution aria as well, in which he compares himself to a tigress. The brilliant vocal writing is accompanied by horns and shows him finally in a truly heroic light.

Alcina was heavily influenced by French trends at the time. It shows Handel's knowledge of Rameau, his ability to write a ballet spectacle and make use of the chorus in the French manner, to hold large scenes together and integrate it into the drama. The second scene of the first act sets the stage for the drama with typically French glitter, as the pleasure's of Alcina's enchanted court are displayed in a spectacle of dance and chorus. The finale is also a ballet, as Alcina's spells are broken and her former lovers regain their human forms.

All of the contrasting elements of *Alcina* are interwoven to create the drama. Any omission would damage the whole. And although the ending is a happy one for the lovers Bradamante and Ruggiero, and for the victims of Alcina, hers is the central figure. Her powerful character draws us into the tragedy that is revealed through her loss of power. *—Rita Laurance*

Synopsis:

Act One. Act One opens during the time of the Crusades in a wilderness, where Bradamante, dressed as a man, and Melisso enter. Morgana comes out, and they tell her they have been shipwrecked. She immediately falls in love with Bradamante ("O s'apre al riso"). In Alcina's magnificent palace, they notice Ruggiero holding a mirror for Alcina as she adorns herself. Alcina welcomes them and tells Ruggiero to show them around, reminding him of all the places associated with their love ("Di', cor mio, quanto t'amai"). Oberto comes in, asking whether anyone has news of his father Astolfo, who took refuge with Alcina and then disappeared ("Chi m'insegna il caro padre?"). Bradamante tells Ruggiero that she is Ricciardo, Bradamante's brother, and accuses him of desertion. He scornfully ignores the accusation ("Di te mi rido"), thinking only of Alcina. When he leaves,

Oronte accuses Bradamante of stealing Morgana, but Morgana comes in and prevents a fight. Bradamante reflects on jealousy ("E gelosia"). Oronte pleads in vain with Morgana. Ruggiero comes looking for Alcina, and Oronte tells him of how Alcina turned all her former lovers into animals, plants, and stones, warning him that she will tire of him as well ("Semplicetto! a donna credi?"). Ruggiero accuses Alcina of now loving Bradamante, which she denies; she assures him of her love ("Si, son quella"). Bradamante tells Ruggiero she is Bradamante, but Melisso persuades Ruggiero that she is raving. Ruggiero dares her to steal Alcina ("La bocca vaga"). Morgana tries to persuade Bradamante to flee, saying that Alcina, to appease Ruggiero's jealousy, has agreed to turn him into an animal. Bradamante asks her to persuade Alcina that he wants Morgana, not Alcina, and a delighted Morgana agrees ("Torna mi a vagheggiar").

Act Two. Melisso, disguised as Atlante, Ruggiero's former tutor, reproaches him for abandoning his duty for Alcina's sake. He gives him a ring that dispels the illusion of the beautiful castle, and Ruggiero is overwhelmed with remorse. He tells Melisso to inform Alcina that he no longer loves her and promises to return to Bradamante. Melisso urges him to hide his feelings when around Alcina and to ask to go hunting so that he can escape. He urges him to think of Bradamante ("Pensa a chi geme"). When Bradamante enters, Ruggiero sadly addresses him as Ricciardo, asking his forgiveness, and she reveals that she is really Bradamante. He is confused, thinks that this is a trick of Alcina's and leaves, to Bradamante's anger ("Vorrei vendicarmi"). Ruggiero himself cannot sort out his emotions or what he is seeing ("Mi lusinga il dolce aggetto"). In her garden, Alcina prays before a statue of Circe, preparing to turn Bradamante into an animal, but Morgana comes in and dissuades her, assuring her that Bradamante presents no threat to Ruggiero—he loves her, not Alcina ("Ama, sospira, ma non ti offende"). Alcina asks Ruggiero why he looks so troubled, and he says that he is restless for action and asks her to allow him to go hunting. She is hurt that he wants to be away from her for even a short while, but agrees, and he declares that he is faithful to the one he loves ("Mio bel tesoro"), adding in an aside that it's not to her. Oberto tells her that his search for his father is still unsuccessful, and she puts her treasures at his disposal, assuring him of her motherly affection and promising that he will see his father very soon. He is still uncertain, but encouraged ("Tra speme e timore"). Oronte comes in and tells Alcina that Ruggiero is using the hunt as a cover for escape, and she varies between fury and grief at the thought that her love has been rejected ("Ah! mio cor! schernito sei!"). Oronte tells Morgana that Bradamante is leaving her, and she refuses to believe it. Oronte is disappointed that he still loves her ("E un folle, e un vile affetto"). Ruggiero again begs Bradamante's forgiveness, but she tells him to stop apologizing and start fleeing. Morgana, who has overheard, is furious. Ruggiero is still slightly ambivalent about leaving such beautiful surroundings, though he knows they are deceptive ("Verdi prati, selve amene"). In her chamber, Alcina casts a spell to summon spirits to help her recapture Ruggiero's affections, but when it is unsuccessful she fears that she has lost her powers ("Ombre pallide, lo so, mi udite").

Act Three. Oronte rejects Morgana, who has returned to him, using her own words, but he softens at her coaxing ("Credete al mio dolore"), and he admits to himself that he still loves her ("Un momento di contento"). Alcina confronts Ruggiero as he makes his escape and tries to persuade him to stay with her by reminding him of all her love and then threatening that when he falls into her power, this is the last time she will be compassionate ("Ma quando tornerai"). Ruggiero warns Bradamante and Melisso of Alcina's wrath ("Sta nell'Ircana pietrosa tana"). Bradamante vows to break all of Alcina's spells and rejoices that Ruggiero again loves her ("All'alma fedel"). Oronte tells Alcina that Ruggiero has defeated her soldiers and now threatens the island. She is heartbroken ("Mi restano le lagrime"). Outside, near a cage of wild beasts, Alcina commands Oberto to kill one of the lions, but he recognizes his father and threatens her with the spear she gave him ("Barbara! io ben lo so"). Alcina again pleads with Ruggiero, and she and Bradamante exchange threats. Ruggiero moves to break the urn that contains the source of her power, and when her pleas are ineffective, she and Morgana flee. The enchanted animals and rocks are restored to human form ("Dall'orror di notte cieca"), and the opera ends with their rejoicing ("Dopo tante amare pene"). *—Ann Feeney*

Recommended:

○ **Handel: Alcina** / Christie (cond.), Carsen, Fleming, Graham, Dessay, Arts Florissants Orch. & Chorus / Teldec 80233

Alessandro, HWV 21 (1726)

Alessandro was Handel's ninth opera for the Royal Academy of Music, which had been formed "for carrying on Operas" in London in 1719. Under the joint directorship of Handel and the poet Paolo Antonio Rolli, the company was initially so successful that by the 1722–23 season it had attracted some of the greatest singers of the day. They included the soprano Francesca Cuzzoni (later the wife of the composer Hasse) and the castrato Francesco Bernardi, known as Senesino. By the fall of 1725, however, the novelty of the Academy's productions was over, and in an effort to boost flagging fortunes Handel engaged (at the huge fee of £2,500) another of the great prima donnas of the day, Faustina Bordoni. The vehicle chosen for the Academy's three fabulous stars to make their first joint appearance was *Alessandro,* the libretto of which was provided by Rolli.

The plot is set in the time of the victorious Asian campaigns of Alexander the Great. At his camp there are two intensely jealous rivals (thus reflecting the real life rivalry between Bordoni and Cuzzoni, which culminated in a famous onstage fight) for his affections: the Scythian princess Lisaura, and Roxana, a Persian princess who is a captive of Alexander's. It is the great conqueror's inability to make up his mind between the two that provokes the ensuing tale of intrigue and plotting. Cast in the usual three acts, *Alessandro* follows the familiar pattern of recitative and da capo aria, but there are also a number of ariosos, accompanied recitatives, and ensemble numbers. The care taken by Handel and his librettist to preserve absolute parity between his stars is nowhere better reflected than at the end of the opera, where in a continuous sequence leading up to the final chorus each soprano is given a duet with Alexander, after which the three join in a trio. Much of the story is treated in lighthearted fashion, with understandably dazzling coloratura arias to keep the three stars content. If *Alessandro* hardly counts among the greatest of Handel's London operas, it remains a superb vehicle for virtuoso singing and a highly enjoyable experience for its audience. Handel completed the score on April 11, 1726, and the first performance took place at the King's Theatre, London just over three weeks later on May 5. Given the enormous public interest in the first joint appearance of Cuzzoni and Bordoni, *Alessandro* was predictably a great success. The opera enjoyed a run of 11 consecutive performances that would probably have continued had not Senesino, perhaps feeling overshadowed, decided to make a sudden return to Italy for "health" reasons. *—Brian Robins*

Synopsis:

Act One. The story is set in and around the city of Oxidraca, in the fourth century B.C., at the time of Alexander the Great's Asian campaigns. Alexander is waging an attack against Oxidraca. He is wellserved and encouraged by his faithful captain, Leonnatus, and soon breaks through, entering the city. News of his victory is announced by Indian King Taxiles to the two women who vie for Alexander's love, Roxana, a princess living in captivity, and Lisaura, whom Taxiles loves, but without knowledge of her affections for Alexander. Alexander has already declared himself a god (the son of Jupiter) and he is received by all his subordinates, Leonnatus, and fellow captains Cleon and Clitusas, as well as by Taxiles, as a great conqueror. Cleon is in love with Roxana, but serves Alexander faithfully, even offering a sacrifice to him in the temple. Clitus is far less sycophantic: he denies Alexander's divinity, thus sending Alexander into a rage. He forces Clitus to the ground and Roxana and Lisaura work to calm him.

Act Two. In a garden, Roxana pretends to be sleeping and listens as Alexander declares his love for her. But then he expresses equally romantic sentiments for Lisaura, who is also present. Each of the women then reveals to him that they are aware of his feelings for the other, but both still strongly desire him despite his apparent duplicity. Lisaura turns down Taxiles' offer for courtship in hopes she may win over Alexander. Roxana pleads to be freed, and Alexander consents to her release, but she then declares she would rather remain his captive. Alexander decides that he will have to choose between the two and appears to favor Roxana when he implies to Lisaura that he must forsake further pursuit of her.

Alexander also decides it is time to reward those in his military service in recent campaigns. When he proposes to give Clitus the Indies, he rejects the offer, again expressing rejection of Alexander's divinity, this time by berating him for not recognizing Philip as his true father and asserting that Jupiter is. Once more Alexander is enraged, and Taxiles intercedes to prevent him from killing Clitus.

In the dramatic moment that follows, Alexander orders Clitus imprisoned on charges of treachery and conspiracy when the canopy above his throne collapses, nearly hitting him with what might have been deadly force. When Roxana is apprised of these events, she faints, prompting Alexander to conclude her concern for him proves her love. On the way to put down a minor insurrection among the people, Alexander tells her they will enjoy each other's love upon his return.

Act Three. In his prison cell, Clitus is visited by Cleon. Leonnatus soon appears with a contingent of soldiers and orders Cleon held and Clitus released. He tells the latter that Macedonian insurgents will support him in his efforts to topple Alexander. They depart, but Cleon is soon set free by his men and hurries off to alert Alexander. Roxana and Lisaura agree to share Alexander in love, but he convinces the latter to accept Taxiles as a husband. He then learns of the Macedonian scheme to overthrow him from Roxana, and decides to confront the conspirators and dare them to contest his authority. When the challenge is made, they shrink in the face of his charismatic manner and bravery. Clitus pleas to be pardoned and Alexander forgives him. A celebration in the temple follows, with Alexander declaring his love for Roxana. *—Robert Cummings*

Recommended:

○ **Handel: Alessandro** / Nowakowski (cond.), Anderson, Atkinson, Price, Terzian, Sinfonia Varsovia / Koch 100303

Ariodante, HWV 33 (1734)

Ariodante was composed in a turbulent time in Handel's career. Called by subsequent writers the Opera of the Nobility, the Prince of Wales and the nobility had created their own opera company in 1733, formed out of many of the musicians and performers of Handel's company. He was forced to find new singers and to come up with the funds to do productions himself. At the end of his lease of the King's Theatre in Haymarket, Handel was also forced to find a new stage. He applied to John Rich, the manager of the theater at Covent Garden, who produced comedies and pantomimes and agreed to let Handel fill out his season with operas. In addition, Handel was required to use the ballet company of Marie Salle, the famous French dancer. Handel's new opera company included a young, rising castrato named Carestini. Gifted with a large vocal range and incredible technique, the title role of Ariodante was written for him. His arias are not only technically virtuosic, they are dramatically demanding as well. One can not believe when one hears them that moments of such intense drama have been created within such a brilliant bravura vocal context. Some of the highpoints of the opera are his "Con l'ali di costanza" and "Dopo notte," which display thrilling vocal acrobatics. "Scherza infida" is a study is passion and jealousy, rage and confusion. In this opera Handel expands his da capo aria form to ever greater proportions, creating monumental works full of powerful emotion. The female lead, Cecilia Young, was also a youthful star, and a tenor was a recent recruit from the Chapel Royal. Handel put off the premiere of his new work, while he rewrote some of it, and adapted into the drama spectacles which used Marie Salle's dance troupe. At the ends of the first and third acts are sumptuous ballets that add to the dramatic mood of the opera, but the most effective ballet is integrated into the action in the second act when Ginevra goes mad. She begins seeing frightening visions, and the ballet dancers represent these mental horrors. The act concludes powerfully, with a dramatic, accompanied recitative for the distraught Ginevra. The libretto of *Ariodante* was adapted from a libretto by Antonio Salvi, one of the finest opera seria librettists of the age. The text was shortened, and the drama made more intense, while the arias were expanded into emotional powerhouses. The main theme is infidelity, as Ginevra is falsely accused and goes mad. Because the punishment for a wife's infidelity was death in Scotland, the action takes place there, heightening the dramatic meaning of the libretto. *—Rita Laurance*

Synopsis:

Act One. The story is set in Edinburgh, Scotland, in the Middle Ages. In her quarters, the daughter of the King of Scotland, Ginevra, confides to her attendant Dalinda that she is in love with Prince Ariodante and that her father is fully supportive of her choice. Polinesso, the Duke of Albany, enters and announces he is in love with Ginevra, but she tells him he is repulsive, without the least appeal for her. After she leaves, Dalinda reveals to the Duke that Ginevra's suitor is Ariodante, and divulges her own interest in Polinesso. The Duke then decides to plot against Ariodante, using Dalinda as a puppet in his plans.

In a rendezvous in the palace gardens, Ariodante and Ginevra declare their love for each other and the King orders his attendant, Odoardo, to arrange their wedding for the following day. Polinesso pretends to be in love with Dalinda to inveigle her into his plot against Ariodante. Believing his plan is directed at Ginevra, and naïvely in love with him, she agrees to take part. Lurcanio, Ariodante's brother, reveals to Dalinda his love for her, but she declares she is not interested in him.

Act Two. Under a moonlit sky outside the royal chambers, Polinesso pretends to know nothing of Ariodante's forthcoming marriage to Ginevra and tells him he is her lover. Dalinda, dressed in Ginevra's clothes, opens the door to the private quarters and lets Polinesso in. Ariodante is devastated by the sight and decides to commit suicide. Lurcanio, who overheard Polinesso's claims, stops him and suggests that his brother take revenge on the unfaithful woman.

A short while later in a palace gallery, Odoardo informs the King that Ariodante has jumped from a cliff into the sea, presumably to his death. When Ginevra is told she falls to the floor unconscious. Lurcanio goes to the King and charges Ginevra with driving his brother to his death, owing to her clandestine affair with Polinesso. He swears to the veracity of documents he presents making his claims. The King pronounces his charges true, and the bewildered Ginevra seems to go mad for a time.

Act Three. Ashore, the despairing Ariodante has survived the plunge into the sea. But he soon encounters Dalinda, who is fleeing assassins hired by Polinesso to silence the only person who can betray his intrigues. The knight saves her from them, and Dalinda, now mindful of Polinesso's duplicity, reveals his scheme to Ariodante.

The King asks that a champion be appointed in the cause of his daughter against Lurcanio, and Polinesso volunteers. Ginevra, sentenced to die for her illicit behavior, is brought in and told that he will serve as her champion. She protests, but to no avail.

On a sporting field, Lurcanio and Polinesso meet in a duel, the latter sustaining a mortal blow. Lurcanio then announces he will challenge anyone else who cares to take up Ginevra's cause. A knight steps forward whose identity is at first concealed by a lowered visor. He is soon revealed to be Ariodante, who asks the King to pardon Dalinda for her unwitting role in the dastardly plot. Word comes now that Polinesso confessed his treachery, then died. Dalinda is pardoned and consents to become the wife of Lurcanio. The King and Ariodante go to Ginevra's quarters with news of the happy turn of events. The lovers reunited, the opera ends joyfully. *—Robert Cummings*

Recommended:

- ○ **Handel: Ariodante** / Minkowski (cond.), Otter, Dawson, Podles, Croft, Cangemi, Les Musiciens du Louvre / Archiv 457271
- ○ **Handel: Ariodante** / McGegan (cond.), Muller, Hunt, Lane, Saffer, Gondek, Freiburg Baroque Orch. / 1996 / Hyperion 907146

Berenice, Regina d'Egitto, HWV 38 (1737)

Berenice was the third new opera produced by Handel for the 1736–37 opera season at Covent Garden Theatre. All three had the castrato Conti as the lead man. And all three were failures. Although the Opera of the Nobility had collapsed by the end of the season, and were further in debt even than Handel, Handel's season was not a success either, and he became physically ill from exhaustion. He suffered from his first "paralytic stroke" as the newspapers called it in April, before the premiere of *Berenice.* He was forced to watch his opera from the seats, rather than conduct it from the harpsichord. The libretto for *Berenice* was again taken from one by Salvi, and concerns Berenice, the Queen of Egypt, and her husband-to-be Alessandro. The love intrigues that surround the cast of characters is complicated, confusing, and elaborate, but all is worked into the required happy ending by the close of the opera. Although Berenice's music is good, and so is much of the rest of the cast's, the opera was only performed three or four times. The score is given a variety of treatments by the inclusion of duets and accompagnato recitativo, as well as three entrance cavatinas. The opera seria convention places the grand da capo aria at the end of the scene, culminating the emotions and actions which transpire during the recitative which precedes it. This climax at the end of the scene allows the singer to exit in glory; however, it is dramatically stunting, for the action does not develop past it. Handel preferred writing the entrance cavatina, as he did in this opera, so that the action could be introduced by a substantial musical number, the tension built through the recitative, and then discharged in an aria or duet. This appreciation for more flexible scenic constructions dates all the way back to his operatic days in Hamburg, in his youth. It is more characteristic of German opera writing than Italian. *—Rita Laurance*

Synopsis:

Act One. The story takes place in Egypt, ca. 80 B.C. Egyptian Queen Berenice has consented to marry a Roman for the political well being of her people. It is a difficult sacrifice for her to make since she is in love with the Macedonian Demetrio, who is an ally to the Egyptian enemy, King Mitridate of Pontus. The Roman envoy Fabio presents Berenice with his country's choice of a husband for her, Prince Alessandro. Alessandro immediately falls in love with her, but Berenice is less receptive to him and resents having her husband chosen for her. Fabio advises Alessandro that if the Egyptian Queen rejects him, he must marry her sister Selene.

Demetrio secretly meets with Selene in her private chambers. The two are lovers, unbeknownst to Berenice, who Demetrio suggests can be toppled with the aid of Mitridate, leaving Selene to claim the throne. After his departure, Selene is informed that Berenice must marry Alessandro and that Demetrio must be put to death, all to satisfy Rome. Berenice announces she will marry Arsace, who is also in love with Selene, but not mutually. Selene's odd reaction to the news causes Berenice to conclude her sister is in love with Arsace. Alessandro thwarts an attempt on Demetrio's life in the palace, and Berenice then decides to vigorously defend Demetrio against his enemies.

Act Two. Fabio brings news that Rome now demands that Alessandro marry Selene. Berenice, believing Selene and Arsace betrothed, refuses compliance with the request and is thus threatened by war. Demetrio is depressed in the knowledge Selene will marry Arsace and begins plotting against Egypt, intending to call on Mitridate and even the Furies for help. Alessandro yearns for Berenice's love amid Aristobolo's pleas to Arsace to abandon Selene so that she can marry Alessandro. Arsace finally yields.

Demetrio accuses Selene of betraying him for Arsace and threatens to kill him. He further confesses he never loved Berenice, and his admission is overheard by her. Berenice angrily demands that Selene marry Arsace. Arsace, however, is intent on stepping aside for Alessandro, but the latter rejects the offer because of his steadfast love for Berenice. Berenice is enraged at Demetrio and orders him imprisoned. In the tower jail he declares his love for Selene.

Act Three. Aware that Demetrio is madly in love with Selene, Berenice decides to allow Fabio to select the man she will marry. She gives the Roman envoy her signet ring with the understanding that the chosen one will return it to her.

Arsace renews his interest in Selene and she agrees to marry him if he can gain Demetrio's release. Having been given Berenice's ring by Fabio instead of the Queen herself, Alessandro passes it on to Arsace, unwilling to be the "chosen" one. Arsace takes it, intending to explain Alessandro's position to Berenice. The Queen orders Demetrio executed and his head presented to her in the temple.

Selene pleads with Berenice to spare Demetrio, and Arsace presents her with the ring and offers to trade places with Demetrio. Alessandro then tells Berenice he could not accept the ring because he wanted her to personally choose him for her husband, instead of Fabio, the Roman representative. Berenice is won over by his noble manner and charm and realizes she is in love with Alessandro after all. She decides to place Demetrio's fate in the hands of Alessandro, who orders him released. Demetrio is then reunited with Selene, and the opera ends happily. *—Robert Cummings*

Recommended:

○ **Handel: Berenice** / Palmer (cond.), Baird, Fortunato, Minter, Lane, Brewer Baroque CO / 1995 / Newport Classic 85620

Giulio Cesare in Egitto, HWV 17 (1724; revised 1725)

One of Handel's greatest and most successful operas, *Giulio Cesare* was first performed at the King's Theatre in London on February 20, 1724, when it ran for 13 performances. Handel subsequently revived the work on three occasions, the last in 1732. It was composed for the Italian opera season of the Royal Academy, the organization formed by a group of noblemen under Handel's musical direction in 1719. From its inception, the Academy had sought to present some of the greatest singers of the day to London audiences; the original cast of *Giulio Cesare* was no exception: the great castrato Senesino (Caesar), and Francesca Cuzzoni (Cleopatra), one of the leading prima donnas of the day, took the stage to premiere Handel's work.

By the conventions of the day, *Giulio Cesare* is unusual in a number of respects, not least of which is its subject matter. Based as it is on the famous historical love affair between Julius Caesar and Cleopatra, it departs from the more traditional realm (at least for opera seria of the time) of mythology. Around this central argument an excellent libretto, cast in the usual three acts by Nicola Haym, weaves a story of political intrigue and treachery involving Cleopatra's brother and co-ruler of Egypt, Tolomeo (Ptolemy).

Giulio Cesare was the only opera Handel composed for the Royal Academy during 1724, and he lavished extra time and care on a score that frequently breaches the conventions of its genre. To a greater degree than in any other of Handel's operas, there is a flexibility of design that departs from the rigid alternation of recitative and da capo aria. Handel's orchestration is also richer than in any other of his operas. Nowhere is this richness and flexibility better demonstrated than in the extraordinary scene in Act Two in which Cleopatra attempts to seduce Caesar by revealing to him a pageant set on the slopes of Mount Parnassus. Here Handel employs a double orchestra, one on stage including harp, theorbo, and viola da gamba, combined with the main body in a ravishing symphony of sensuality.

Above all, perhaps, the greatness of *Giulio Cesare* resides in the person of Cleopatra, for whom the composer created one of the most acute and vividly drawn characterizations in operatic history. In the course of her eight arias, Cleopatra's progress from a self-confident ruler and vivacious flirt to mature young woman is charted with unparalleled sympathy and insight. Nowhere is she more affecting than in adversity, particularly after her imprisonment by Tolomeo, when she is given three magnificent arias, culminating in her famous "Piangerò." While it is Cleopatra who dominates the opera, the other major characters are also unusually well drawn—Caesar truly heroic yet vulnerably susceptible, and Tolomeo a more rounded and convincing villain than is frequently the case. While Handel may have later equaled the achievement of *Giulio Cesare* in *Orlando and Alcina*, it attains an overall level he never surpassed. *—Brian Robins*

Synopsis:

Act One. Egypt; 48–47 B.C. Caesar has defeated his rival Pompey in battle and now pursues him in Egypt. Greeted there as a great conqueror, Caesar is petitioned by Pompey's wife, Cornelia, and son, Sextus, to make peace. Caesar acquiesces and decides to reconcile with Pompey, but the Egyptian General Achilla carries a gift from Ptolemy, King of Egypt—Pompey's head. Horrified, Caesar declares that Ptolemy must pay for his brutality. Cornelia attempts suicide; Curius, once her lover, proposes marriage to her, an offer she rejects. Sextus resolves to take revenge against Ptolemy.

In her palace, Cleopatra learns of Ptolemy's role in Pompey's demise from her confidant Nirenus. She quickly calculates that she can assume sole rule of the country by seducing and winning over Caesar. Meanwhile, Achilla informs Ptolemy his attempt to curry favor with Caesar by presenting him with Pompey's head backfired. Achilla then offers to assassinate Caesar, if Ptolemy will give Cornelia to him.

Cleopatra, accompanied by Nirenus, appears in Caesar's camp, presenting herself as Lydia, a noble woman cheated of her wealth by Ptolemy. She enchants both Caesar and Curius. The dispirited Cornelia once again fails at suicide, her son intervening. Cleopatra, posing as a Queen's attendant, enlists the aid of Cornelia and Sextus in her plot against Ptolemy. While Caesar is shown the royal quarters at Ptolemy's palace, Cornelia and Sextus arrive and their harsh words draw the wrath of Ptolemy, who imprisons the latter and consigns the former to menial work in the gardens. Achilla attempts to woo Cornelia, but is rejected.

Act Two. Nirenus takes Caesar into the garden of cedars, from where he views Cleopatra, still believing she is Lydia, seated on the throne of Virtue in the Palace of Pleasure. He approaches her but she suddenly disappears from his view. Nirenus informs him they will meet later on. Meanwhile, Ptolemy urges Achilla to carry out his plan against Caesar, but privately declares Achilla cannot have Cornelia. Ptolemy makes advances to Cornelia but is also rejected. Sextus, freed from prison by Nirenus, is encouraged by her to strike down Ptolemy during a planned encounter between him and Cornelia.

Curius arrives at Cleopatra's quarters to warn Caesar of a plot against him. Cleopatra, who had pretended to be asleep, now divulges her identity. She urges Caesar to escape, but he decides to confront the conspirators. Meanwhile, Ptolemy declares he will have Cornelia; moments later he is saved by Achillas from the vengeance-minded Sextus. Achilla later tells Ptolemy that Caesar is reportedly drowned, and when Ptolemy asks for Cornelia, he is refused. Sextus, disappointed at his failed attempt on Ptolemy, resolves, with his mother's encouragement, to make a second effort.

Act Three. Achilla switches allegiances to Cleopatra, but her forces are defeated by Ptolemy's; she is taken captive and Achilla is wounded. Caesar has escaped drowning and washes ashore. Soon he witnesses Achilla's confession of Pompey's murder to Nirenus and Sextus, and his giving the latter a seal authorizing command over a large army. But Caesar confiscates the seal, vowing to free Cleopatra and Cornelia. Caesar and his army defeat Ptolemy's palace forces. Meanwhile, Cornelia desperately fends off Ptolemy's advances, but Sextus soon enters and kills the King. Cornelia and Sextus announce news of Ptolemy's death to Caesar and Cleopatra at the harbor. The former cannot accept Ptolemy's crown from Cleopatra, but he declares his love for her, as she does for him. The two agree that she will rule Egypt under the guidance of Rome. *—Robert Cummings*

Recommended:

○ **Handel: Julius Caesar** / Jacobs (cond.), Zanasi, Ragin, Schlick, Larmore, Concerto Köln / HM 901385

○ **Handel: Julius Caesar** / Rudel (cond.), Sills, Forrester, Treigle, Malas, NYC Opera Orch. / 1967 / RCA 6182

○ **Handel: Julius Caesar** / Minkowski (cond.), Otter, Kozena, Ewing, Bertin, Les Musiciens du Louvre / 2003 / Archiv 000031402

○ **Handel: Julius Caesar** / Mackerras (cond.), Baker, James, Walker, Jones, Bowman, English National Opera Orch. / 1999 / Chandos 3019

Ottone, re di Germania, HWV 15 (1722; revised 1726)

George Frideric Handel had the biggest hit of the London Italian opera season of 1723 with his *Ottone, re di Germania* (Otto, King of Germany). A two-and-a-half hour, three-act opera, *Ottone* had a libretto by Nicola Haym, based on the first century story of Otto, the barbarian king of Germany, who travels to decadent Rome to marry Theophanes, the Princess of the Eastern Empire. As in any great opera, there is a powerful story about love thwarted and regained and, as in any Italian opera of the period, there is convoluted palace intrigue. But, also as in any Italian opera of the period, every problem was solved by the end of the opera and every character lived happily ever after. Among the best-known arias from *Ottone* are "La speranza e giunta" (Hope is with us); "Vieni, o figlio" (Come, my son); and "Tanti affani" (Such troubles). However, the real reason for *Ottone*'s success was the presence of three of the greatest singers of the time taking the three principal roles: Senesino, Cussoni, and Berenstadt. The second most popular of Handel's Italian operas, *Ottone* was given 34 performances in Handel's life. *—James Leonard*

Synopsis:

Act One. The story takes place in Rome and the surrounding area in 972 A.D. Ottone, King of Germany, is on his way to Rome to marry Teofane, daughter of Romano, Emperor of the East. He is delayed, however, by a clash at sea with the notorious pirate Emireno. In a Roman courtyard, Gismonda, widow of the tyrant Berengario, schemes to have her son Adalberto marry Teofane by impersonating Ottone. He agrees to carry out the plan and when he meets Teofane in the guise of Ottone, she is disappointed that his appearance is markedly different from his face in a portrait she possesses. His talk of marriage is distressing and she calls the portrait a "false image."

Ottone arrives in Rome with the captured Emireno (really, Basilio, brother of Teofane), whom he sends off to jail. Matilda, Adalberto's fiancée, has learned of his plans to marry Teofane and informs Ottone, who agrees to aid her in her plot for revenge.

In Teofane's palace, Gismonda impersonates Ottone's mother, Adelaide, but soon learns of the arrival of Ottone in Rome. She urges her son to challenge his forces immediately. Adalberto does so and is soundly defeated.

Act Two. As Adalberto is being taken to prison, he is disparaged by Matilda for his faithlessness and by his mother for ineptitude. Matilda still loves him, however, and decides to plead with Ottone for his life, despite the objections of Gismonda, who will not deign to make such a request even though she still cares for Adalberto.

Matilda meets with Ottone while Teofane listens unseen. Ottone refuses to pardon Adalberto, but embraces Matilda to show compassion, an action misinterpreted by Teofane as an expression of love. Matilda is angered by Ottone's lack of mercy for Adalberto and turns against him. When Ottone and Teofane finally meet, she reproaches him for betraying her in favor of Matilda. He then charges her with infidelity for agreeing to wed Adalberto. Alone in a garden, Teofane ponders her unhappiness.

Meanwhile, Matilda aids in the escape of Adalberto and Emireno from prison. She also meets with Ottone again, once more their conversation misunderstood by the eavesdropping Teofane. Emireno, intent on returning to his pirate life, invites Adalberto to join him. He does so, but drags along the unwilling Teofane.

Act Three. As Ottone worries over the disappearance of Teofane, Gismonda defiantly warns him of the dangers he must face, since Adalberto is now at large. During a storm, Emireno and the others have sought refuge in a wooded area on shore. Adalberto wanders off temporarily to seek shelter, leaving Emireno and Teofane alone. When the latter speaks of family members searching for her, Emireno suddenly realizes Teofane is his sister. Adalberto returns just as Emireno attempts to embrace her, and a scuffle breaks out. Emireno wins out and vows to do his sister's bidding.

In a palace courtyard, Gismonda informs Ottone of Matilda's role in the escape. But Matilda turns contrite and declares she will kill the unfaithful Adalberto. Emireno soon returns with Adalberto, and Ottone orders the latter's execution. Matilda prepares to carry out the sentence, but feels pity for Adalberto after he confesses his infidelity and dark intrigues. Ottone and Teofane are reconciled, the latter revealing the identity of Emireno to all. Matilda convinces Ottone to free Adalberto and she declares her love for him. The principal characters appeal for peace and love and the opera ends happily. *—Robert Cummings*

Recommended:

- ○ **Handel: Ottone** / McGegan (cond.), Minter, Popken, Saffer, Spence, Freiburg Baroque Orch. / HM 907073
- ○ **Handel: Ottone** / King (cond.), George, Smith, Visse, Bowman, King's Consort / 1993 / Hyperion 66751

Rinaldo, HWV 7 (1711; revised 1717)

After composing two Italian operas for Hamburg, two Italian oratorios for Rome, and a third Italian opera for Venice, George Frideric Handel moved to England in 1710 to compose his first Italian opera for London. Produced in the Queen's Theater in the Haymarket on February 24, 1711, *Rinaldo* would certainly have been an enormous success if the librettist and impresario Aaron Hill had not neglected to pay the tradesmen, thereby causing the Lord Chamberlain to revoke Hill's theater license nine days after the premiere. But *Rinaldo* paved the way for the quick success of Handel and Italian opera in London and the work was revived in 1712, then again in 1717, and again in 1731.

Hill's libretto is based on Tasso's epic poem on the First Crusade *Gerusalamme liberata*, but with a new plot and a new female lead to give the story appeal to a then-contemporary London audience. Handel's music is in part a pastiche drawn from many of his earlier dramatic works, and in part a newly composed work with deeply expressive arias and recitative adorned with extravagant trumpet and woodwind writing. Together, Hill's libretto and Handel's music create a powerful and plangent opera with strong and sympathetic leads in Rinaldo and Almirenda and a superbly coherent and convincing score. *—James Leonard*

Synopsis:

Act One. The action takes place near Jerusalem during the first of the eight Crusades, in the period 1095–1101. Goffredo leads his Christian armies toward Jerusalem, intent on capturing the city. He recalls his promising the hand of his daughter Almirena in marriage to the knight Rinaldo once Jerusalem is taken. The Saracen King Argante of Jerusalem appears and negotiates a three-day truce with Goffredo. The King then enlists the aid of the Sorceress-Queen of Damascus, Armida, who soon arrives in a dragon-drawn chariot. She assesses the King's desperate situation and decides to focus her plans on Rinaldo and Almirena as a means of halting the Christian advance, deciding to draw the former away from his military duties by abducting the latter and using her as bait. After Rinaldo learns of the kidnapping of Almirena, he swears revenge against her abductors. He also seeks advice from a hermit magician at the urging of Eustazio, Goffredo's brother.

Act Two. While searching for Almirena at a seashore, Rinaldo, Goffredo, and Eustazio see mermaids at play. Soon a spirit, appearing as a beautiful woman, induces Rinaldo to board a boat despite the attempts of his companions to restrain him. He sails off into the distance, headed toward the palace of Armida.

Almirena is being held captive there, fending off the advances of the persistent King Argante. When Rinaldo arrives, Armida is overjoyed and makes overtures to him. He rejects her. In her resourcefulness, however, she transforms her appearance to that of Almirena, but the trick ultimately does not fool him. (In the 1731 revised version, Armida merely imitates Almirena's voice.) Argante soon appears and believes Armida is Almirena, and thus resumes making advances to her, offering to set her free if she acquiesces to them. But his promises and scheming only precipitate a clash with Armida, who makes her identity known to him. (In the revised version a quarrel breaks out when Armida observes Argante admiring Almirena's portrait.)

Act Three. Goffredo and Eustazio consult with the hermit magician who had advised Rinaldo at the end of the first act. He directs them to Armida's palace, warning them of the monstrous creatures guarding it, but giving them magic wands to overcome them. Meanwhile, Armida is about to kill Almirena, but Rinaldo intervenes and raises his sword to strike down Armida, but is prevented by the Furies.

Goffredo and Eustazio ascend the mountain upon which the palace rests and, arriving at the enchanted building, tap their wands against its gate. The mountain vanishes and eventually the palace, as well, leaving the scene in the desert outside Jerusalem. Rinaldo and Goffredo prepare to do battle, and Armida and Argante reconcile and make provision for attack. Both the pagan forces and the Christian forces march in review before their respective leaders, then do battle with each other. The Christian army wins out and Argante and Armida are captured. Both embrace Christianity, are pardoned, and make plans to marry. (In the revised version, they flee on a chariot, remaining loyal to their pagan beliefs.) *—Robert Cummings*

Recommended:

- ○ **Handel: Rinaldo** / Jacobs (cond.), Visse, Genaux, Zazzo, Persson, Freiburg Baroque Orch. / 2003 / HM 901796/98
- ○ **Handel: Rinaldo** / Hogwood (cond.), Bartoli, Daniels, Bott, Finley, Academy of Ancient Music / 2000 / Decca 467087
- ○ **Handel: Rinaldo** / Malgoire (cond.), Brett, Esswood, Cotrubas, Watkinson, Grande Ecurie et la Chambre du Roy / 1997 / Sony 34592

Rodelinda, regina de' Langobardi, HWV 19 (1725)

Rodelinda came at the highest point of Handel's career, when he was exceptionally financially successful, incredibly popular, and beloved by his public and by the court and nobility of England. His productions at the King's Theatre in London were well subsidized by the crown. He was able to hire the finest singers in Europe, to have the best stage scenery built, and to have the finest costumes and machinery. He even had a good librettist. Three masterworks were composed by Handel at this time. Roughly between the years 1723 and 1725, Handel composed *Giulio Cesare*, *Tamerlano*, and *Rodelinda*. *Giulio Cesare* and *Tamerlano* are particularly virile works with heroic, strong, male characters. *Rodelinda's* hero is a woman, and the plot almost develops into a rescue opera in the manner of *Fidelio*. The story shows the heroine torn between her emotions as a wife and woman, and her duties as Queen. Handel's female audience was especially appreciative, and the work was a singular success.

Certain characteristic opera seria themes pervade the libretto. Dramas of political power, torn affections, and moral dilemmas come alive due to Handel's superb characterizations and sensitive planning. The first act is filled with a variety of types of allegro arias, in which the action of the opera is framed. These vigorous numbers set in relief the arias of the two lovers, Rodelinda and Bertarido, who poignantly long for one another in "Dove sei?" and "Ombre, piante." "Ombre, piante" is particularly lovely; a solo violin joins the passionately lamenting Rodelinda as she mourns her lost husband. Again, in Act Two, the music of the other characters sets the stage for the two lovers' arias, who are again poignant in their isolation and separateness. After an intervening aria by the ruling tyrant, the two are finally joined in a sublime duet. The third act is a brilliant dramatic coup. Often in Baroque opera, changes of scene involve a dramatic change in venue. In the earlier Baroque, this often included a change from an earthly realm to the infernal realm, with an intermediate stop in the celestial regions. As opera seria attempted to bring opera closer to French tragédie, comedy and spectacle were omitted, so a spectacular descent into the underworld was no longer a viable option. However, Handel was permitted a similar dramatic change from the earthly to the infernal, as the cast goes to seek out the imprisoned Bertarido in the depths of the dungeons of Grimoaldo, the wicked tyrant.

The strength of *Rodelinda* lies in the depth of emotion that each character feels and the realistic appraisal one is able to make of their characters. The variety of human emotion is matched only by the inventiveness of Handel's music, which carries the listener through this highly dramatic work. *—Rita Laurance*

Synopsis:

Act One. The story takes place in seventh century Milan. In a private chamber in the royal palace, Rodelinda, Queen of Lombardy, grieves over the loss of her husband, King Bertarido, who, unbeknownst to her, is still alive. Grimoaldo, Bertarido's nemesis and deposer, proposes marriage to Rodelinda, who angrily turns him down.

Grimoaldo is engaged to Bertarido's sister, Eduige, and schemes to destroy his commitment to their marriage, eying Rodelinda's eventual acquiescence. His unsavory friend Garibaldo, Duke of Turin, volunteers his assistance. Eduige enters and her disparaging of Grimoaldo falls into his plans. He informs her their relationship has ended, and after he departs Eduige declares him unfit. The duplicitous Garibaldo now envisions himself marrying Rodelinda and ascending to the throne.

On the burial ground of Lombardic Kings, Bertarido, in disguise, peruses his own grave. Rodelinda and their son Flavio appear to place a wreath at the site, but as Bertarido is about to unveil himself to them, his companion Unulfo restrains him. Garibaldo appears and threatens Rodelinda with Flavio's execution if she does not consent to marry Grimoaldo. She acquiesces, but declares she will take costly revenge against Garibaldo. The latter then reports the "good" news to Grimoaldo. Meanwhile, Bertarido worries over the difficult situation as his friend Unulfo tries to give him solace.

Act Two. Garibaldo proposes marriage to Eduige, but her reply is unclear, indicating she may still love Grimoaldo. Asked again by Grimoaldo to marry, Rodelinda consents only if he kills Flavio, since the boy would be the rightful heir to the throne. Grimoaldo is repulsed by the proposal (as Rodelinda expected), though Garibaldo sees an opening to the throne for himself, but unwisely divulges his ambitions to Unulfo.

Meanwhile, Bertarido wanders a wooded area and encounters Eduige. He tells her he merely desires Rodelinda and Flavio and cares little for the throne. Eduige, who covets the crown herself, is pleased by the news. Unulfo advises Bertarido to step forth from hiding and unveil himself. Later, after Unulfo informs Rodelinda in her royal palace that Bertarido is alive, the two reunite in a passionate embrace, an act observed by Grimoaldo when he bursts in. He assumes Bertarido is a lover of Rodelinda, since he has never met him. Bertarido identifies himself, but Rodelinda, to protect him, asserts he is lying to shield her name. Grimoaldo vows to kill him whoever he is.

Act Three. Bertarido has been imprisoned on orders of Grimoaldo, but Eduige instructs Unulfo to rescue him, giving him a prison key. Grimoaldo is hesitant to kill Bertarido, despite the prodding of Garibaldo. In his attempt to set Bertarido free Unulfo is wounded when Bertarido mistakes his friend for the executioner, striking him with a sword brought along for defensive purposes. The two depart the prison, leaving Unulfo's blood-stained cloak behind, which is soon found by Rodelinda, Eduige, and Flavio, who had planned another rescue. They believe Bertarido has been executed.

As Bertarido tends to Unulfo's wound in the palace garden, Grimoaldo appears, causing the two to hide. The usurper laments his evil acts and wishes he were merely a shepherd. He then falls asleep and soon Garibaldo finds him and attempts to kill him. But he is driven off then caught and slain by Bertarido. Rodelinda appears and is once more astonished and happy to see her husband alive. Grimoaldo is grateful to Bertarido for saving his life and thus relinquishes the throne to him and then reconciles with Eduige. *—Robert Cummings*

Recommended:

○ **Handel: Rodelinda** / Kraemer, Thompson, Robbin, Blaze, Raglan Baroque Players / 1998 / Virgin 45277

Serse (Xerxes), HWV 40 (1738)

Both of Handel's new operas for the 1737–38 season at the Haymarket had to be postponed due to the death of Queen Caroline. Handel composed the funeral music for her, and there also was a period of mourning. After the failure of *Faramondo*, Handel premiered an altogether different kind of opera. *Serse* is a comedy. It has buffo elements in the plot, in the musical style, and in the cast of characters. Elviro is a buffo bass role, an old servant who is central to the mismanagement of Serse's love affair, and who is responsible for some of the comic situations that evolve around the love plots. The opera *Serse* confused audiences and critics alike. Some called it an opera buffo, others a farce, and Burney even thought it the product of a "diseased" mind. It was a bigger flop even than *Faramondo*, although it has been revived for the modern operatic theater. Some of the music is exquisite, however. The beautiful love lyric "Ombra mai fù" later became renowned as an instrumental piece, and the duets in the opera are imaginative, individual, and original.

Serse is very unusually constructed for a Handel opera; half of the arias are not cast in the usual da capo form. There are several duets and important extended scenes involving linked numbers and recitativo accompagnato. The opera opens with an offstage aria by Romilda, accompanied by recorders, in an extended scene during which Serse becomes enamored of her. Another extended scene in Act Two has the comic servant Elviro singing a song in which he imitates the calls of street vendors. It is in this scene that he misdelivers an important love letter, thus setting the stage for many of the comic scenes to follow. Act Two is also livened by two unusual duets. In the second, the two male leads sing about their jealousy in asides to the audience. Only at the very close of this comical number do the two voices sing together. Even the argument written in the audiences' wordbook to explain the opera's plot is laced with irony and humor. In wit and feeling, this opera has been compared to *Le nozze di Figaro* and *Così fan tutte* of Mozart. *—Rita Laurance*

Synopsis:

Act One. The story is set in Abydos, in ancient Greece. Xerxes, King of Persia, becomes enamored of the singing of Romilda, daughter of Ariodate, commander of the army. He asks his brother Arsamene about the identity of the singer, but Arsamene claims not to know her. Xerxes orders him to tell the young woman that the King wants to take her as his wife. Arsamene, who is already her lover, is bewildered and declares he is too timid for the task. Xerxes decides he will do his own courting. Arsamene quickly alerts Romilda to the situation, while her sister Atalanta, who is secretly in love with Arsamene, hopes Romilda will abandon him for the King. Romilda, however, is unreceptive to Xerxes' advances, and the King prohibits his brother from attending court activities.

Ariodate receives congratulations from Xerxes on his recent victory and capture of enemy soliders. This scene is observed by Amastre, a foreign princess once betrothed to Xerxes, who is in disguise. Ariodate announces that Romilda will wed a royal family member. Amastre plots revenge against Xerxes, while Atalanta's scheme to convince Romilda that Arsamene has a lover fails.

Act Two. Elviro, Arsamene's servant, is dressed as a flower seller and is on his way to deliver a letter to Romilda expressing his master's anguish over their separation. He meets Amastre in the public square and informs her, to her dismay, of Xerxes' intentions regarding Romilda. When Elviro later encounters Atalanta, he makes his identity known to her; she tells him Romilda is in love with Xerxes and that she will deliver the letter. Xerxes observes Atalanta reading the letter, whose handwriting he recognizes as his brother's. Atalanta informs the King that it was written to her, and he is elated. He shows the letter to Romilda, but she still rejects him. The busy Elviro prevents Amastre from taking her life, and later he reveals Atalanta's claims about Romilda to Arsamene. He turns forlorn at the news.

Xerxes tells Arsamene he is back in his favor and allows him permission to marry the woman Xerxes believes he loves, Atalanta. But Arsamene informs him he is steadfast in his devotion to Romilda. Xerxes tells Atalanta that his brother does not love her, but she remains adamant in pursuing him. Xerxes asks Romilda to wed him once more, but Amastre interrupts the proposal and brandishes a sword. She is arrested but quickly released at the request of Romilda, who admires her faithfulness in love.

Act Three. Atalanta admits to her scheme, and Romilda and Arsamene are reconciled. When Xerxes presses Romilda once more to marry him, she tells him to obtain her father's consent. In a misunderstanding, Ariodate gives his permission, believing it is Arsamene whom she will marry. Romilda still refuses to marry Xerxes, who then orders the execution of Arsamene.

In the Temple of the Sun, Romilda and Arsamene appear, and their hands are joined together in marriage by Ariodate. Xerxes arrives to find that Ariodate has botched things, but his anger is temporarily detoured by the arrival of a letter denigrating him for his faithlessness. Its author is at first thought to be Romilda, but is soon divulged to be Amastre. Xerxes commands Romilda to kill Arsamene with his sword, but Amastre interrupts the proceedings and asks the King if it is betrayal he wants avenged, and he assents. She suddenly directs the weapon against him, and he then asks her forgiveness. His feelings for Amastre rekindled, he relents and countenances the marriage of Romilda and Arsamene. *—Robert Cummings*

Recommended:

○ **Handel: Serse** / Malgoire (cond.), Esswood, Hendricks, Watkinson, Cold, Grande Ecurie et la Chambre du Roy / 1995 / Sony 36941

○ **Handel: Serse** / McGegan (cond.), Smith, Malafronte, Milne, Bickley, Hanover Band / 1998 / Conifer 51312

○ **Handel: Serse** / Kubelik (cond.), Wunderlich, Topper, Hallstein, Kohn, Bavarian Radio Chorus & SO / Verona 27032

Tamerlano, HWV 18 (1724; revised 1731)

Tamerlano was the second of three Handel masterpieces which highlighted the middle years of the Royal Academy of Music. *Giulio Cesare* had been the smash hit of the 1723–24 season at the King's Theatre in the Haymarket, and *Tamerlano* began the 1724–25 opera season. Again, Cuzzoni and Senesino were the two principals, playing the lovers Asteria and Andronico. Asteria is a full-blooded female lead. A true heroine, loving daughter, and adoring lover of Andronico, she brings the opera to life. Andronico, although not as well-hewn a character as Asteria, is a good foil for her heroism and is supplied with plenty of beautiful music as a lover. The strongest character in the plot is Bajazet, whose pride antagonizes his arrogant adversary Tamerlane. Bajazet is the misused father of Asteria, and is cast as a tenor. Bajazet is the first great tenor role in the history of opera. Tenors were uncommon in eighteenth century opera, especially in heroic or prominent roles. So the new singer brought in from Italy, Francesco Borosini, was something of a novelty to the London public and immediately gained a following. The opera was very successful and played to full houses throughout its run.

As in *Giulio Cesare*, the libretto is by Nicola Haym. The opera seria conventions are written into the libretto by Haym in such a way as to allow room for dramatic manipulation on the part of Handel. When he wanted to create a more dramatic and flexible form out of the standard scenic repetitions of recitative and aria, he altered the structures of the arias. The second act of *Tamerlano* offers a perfect example. Instead of exit arias, three characters in a row are given aria settings that are not in the da capo form. Bajazet sings a cavatina, followed by a bar form aria for Andronico, and a repeated binary-form aria for Irene. Finally, the grand heroine receives a full blown da capo exit aria. The denial of convention must have been extremely startling to the audience, used to the regularity of form of the opera seria.

The orchestration of Tamerlano is again brilliant and imaginative, making use of an early type of clarinet known as the chalumeau. Handel and Rameau were the first to write for this instrument. The finale of the opera is an extended piece built up of recitatives, ariosos, and ensembles that build to the end. The climax of the opera is breathtaking, as the dying Bajazet sings to his heartbroken daughter, "Dearest daughter, weep no more." *Tamerlano* was finished with even more than Handel's characteristic speed; he composed the work in 20 days. *—Rita Laurance*

Synopsis:

Act One. The setting is Prusa (now Bursa), Turkey, 1402. The defeated Turkish Emperor Bajazete is freed by the Greek Prince Andronico outside the prison of the former. Bajazete contemplates suicide upon learning that his release was ordered by his conqueror, Tamerlano, but realizes he could bring harm to his daughter, Asteria, who is in love with Andronico. Tamerlano reveals that he is in love with her, but promises Andronico the throne in Byzantium and also the hand of his betrothed, Irene, if he will help him gain Asteria's hand.

Tamerlano proposes marriage to Asteria, using Bajazete's life as a bargaining chip. He informs her that Andronico will marry Irene. She is dismayed at Andronico's seeming disloyalty and realizes she may have to accept Tamerlano's proposal.

Bajazete refuses permission for the marriage and learns from his daughter of Andronico's treachery. But Andronico insists he still loves Asteria and is encouraged by Bajazete to resist Tamerlano. Irene arrives at Tamerlano's court, but is refused permission to see him. Andronico advises her to disguise herself as one of her own attendants bearing important news for Tamerlano. He sends his aide Leo along with her.

Act Two. Andronico learns from Tamerlano of Asteria's consent to the marriage proposal. He berates her and she counters in kind. Irene appears in disguise before Tamerlano and Asteria and chides the latter for switching affections. Tamerlano declares he will reject Asteria if she displeases him, and after he departs Asteria promises Irene she will surely lose favor with him quickly. Andronico apprises Bajazete of his daughter's decision to marry Tamerlano. He resolves to prevent the wedding, while Andronico ponders suicide in the event he loses Asteria.

As Asteria is about to join Tamerlano on the royal thrones, Bajazete prevents her. As he lies prostrate and defiant, Asteria refuses to step over him but agrees to sit beside Tamerlano if her father is removed. The guards pull Bajazete up, while he renounces his daughter. In disguise, Irene appears before Tamerlano and assails his character just after he had offered her hand to Andronico. Bajazete calls on Asteria to remain faithful to a vow of vengeance she had made on Tamerlano, or to renounce it by killing him (Bajazete). She produces a dagger and declares she would have used it on Tamerlano on their wedding day. Tamerlano orders them imprisoned.

Act Three. In prison Asteria and Bajazete possess poisons they will use if a planned escape fails. Andronico announces he will challenge Tamerlano for Asteria, his statement overheard by her, causing her to rekindle her love for him and to renounce Tamerlano. Tamerlano sentences Bajazete to death and consigns Asteria to marry a lowly slave.

Later, in the imperial hall, Leo implores Irene to replace Tamerlano on the throne. Tamerlano appears with Bajazete, then forces Asteria to serve him a cup as a slave. She inserts the poison, but Irene prevents Tamerlano from drinking it, then reveals her true identity. Tamerlano is grateful to her and renews romantic feelings for her. Asteria attempts to take the poison herself, having refused Tamerlano's order to give it to her father or to Andronico. Tamerlano orders that she be consigned to the seraglio to be raped while Bajazete watches. The latter, however, drinks the poison to be free of Tamerlano's tyranny, then curses him as he dies. As Andronico is about to commit suicide, Tamerlano intervenes and announces that Andronico can marry Asteria and rule Byzantium. Tamerlano declares that he will marry Irene. *—Robert Cummings*

Recommended:

- ○ **Handel: Tamerlano** / Pinnock (cond.), Abete, Bacelli, Pushee, Norberg-Schulz, Bonitatibus, English Concert / 2002 / Avie 1501
- ○ **Handel: Tamerlano** / Malgoire (cond.), Jacobs, Elwes, Poulenard, Ledroit, Grande Ecurie et la Chambre du Roy / 1997 / Sony 37893

CHORAL

Acis and Galatea, oratorio, HWV 49 (1718; revised 1732)

The ancient tale of *Acis and Galatea*—perhaps invented by Theocritus in the third century, B.C. but preserved and made famous by Ovid in his *Metamorphoses*—was one that occupied George Frideric Handel many times during his long career as a musical dramatist. In 1708, a few years into his Italian residency, Handel composed a dramatic cantata based on the tale (*Aci, Galatea e Polifemo*); then in 1718, while enjoying the position of composer-in-residence at Cannons, the luxurious English home of James Brydges, shortly thereafter named Duke of Chandos, he composed the first version of a much more famous work—the English oratorio (or more properly a masque—a kind of miniature opera), *Acis and Galatea*, HWV 49b, to a libretto written by John Gay. By 1732, Handel was very probably the best-known composer in England, and when a rival opera company decided to present the 1718 *Acis and Galatea*, he decided to best those rivals by mounting his own revised version of the masque at King's Theatre. For this 1732 version, Handel augmented the instrumental forces employed and added new music, some taken from the 1708 cantata. Today, however, it is usually the original 1718 version of *Acis and Galatea* that audiences are presented with, though very often the orchestra and chorus used are of sizes that would have been impossible at Cannons.

Acis and Galatea is a *pastorale* in the truest sense of the word; it is the tale of the love of a sea nymph (Galatea, soprano) for a young shepherd (Acis, tenor), and that love's destruction at the hands of the jealous cyclops, Polyphemus (bass). To these three principal parts is added the role of the kind and thoughtful shepherd Damon (tenor or countertenor). A chorus of shepherds and shepherdesses chimes in from time to time.

After the opening instrumental sinfonia, the chorus extols the pleasures of pastoral life in a gentle chorus constructed over a pedal tone. The first of many recitatives/arias is given to Galatea; the aria portion, "Hush, ye pretty warbling choir," is perhaps the most famous number from the entire masque, and, like each of the other arias in *Acis and Galatea*, is an example of da capo aria form (ABA in both music and text). After both Acis and Damon offer their own thoughts in aria form and Acis is united with his beloved Galatea, Act I concludes with the joyful duet "Happy we."

At the opening of Act II, the chorus warns Acis and Galatea of rageful Polyphemus' approach. The cyclops' first utterances are a fevered recitative and the firmly articulated aria "O ruddier than the cherry," setting the stage for a heated argument, in recitative form, between Polyphemus and Galatea. Tempers flare in two further arias, and are partly doused by Damon in the aria "Consider, fond shepherd"—a number not found in the original 1718 version. In an electric trio, Galatea and Acis' affirmations of eternal love are juxtaposed with Polyphemus' growing anger, climaxing in the violent murder of Acis—here Handel provides a passionate recitative for Acis, in which he cries out to both Galatea and his own divine parents to save him, but to no avail. Galatea's final aria, sung to the gentle accompaniment of violins and recorders, tells of Acis' new immortality, achieved by Galatea's own effort; pulsating, dotted-rhythm melismas manage to rekindle something of the innocent pastoral feel that opened the masque. *—Blair Johnston*

Synopsis:

Act One. The chorus sings of a pleasant life of dancing and hunting ("Oh, the pleasures of the plains!"). The nymph Galatea, however, finds all the beauties of nature vexing as they remind her of her absent lover Acis, a shepherd ("Hush, ye pretty warbling quire") and inflame her desire for him. Acis is making his way to her ("Where shall I seek the charming fair?"). Another shepherd, Damon, urges him instead to tend to his flocks and forget the cares of love ("Shepherd, what art thou pursuing?"). Acis pays no attention and throws himself at Galatea's feet ("Love in her eyes sits playing"). Galatea reproaches him for ever wanting to be absent from her ("As when the dove"), but they sing of their bliss ("Happy we!").

Act Two. The chorus warns Acis and Galatea that the cyclops Polyphemus is approaching ("Wretched lovers! Fate has passed"). He enters, raging that the feeble god of love has overcome him and he throws away the pine tree he uses for a walking stick and instead plucks reeds to make a pipe with which to praise Galatea's beauty ("O ruddier than the cherry"). She instead runs away, and he calls to her to share in his riches and feasts. She fiercely rejects him and he decides to use force ("Cease to beauty to be suing"). The shepherd Coridon advises him to use kindness, instead, as possession by force does not bring the full joys of love ("Would you gain the tender creature"). Acis vows to fight Polyphemus to defend Galatea and welcomes even the thought of death ("Love sounds th'alarm"). Coridon tries to dissuade him ("Consider, fond shepherd") and Galatea tries to assure him that fate will be kind to their love and that she will never yield. As the lovers promise their eternal constancy ("The flocks shall leave the mountains"), Polyphemus fumes, and finally hurls a huge rock at Acis, killing him. The chorus laments ("Mourn, all ye muses! Weep, all ye swains"), and Galatea mourns for her lover ("Must I my Acis still bemoan"). The chorus offers her some comfort, suggesting that she exert her powers to make Acis immortal in the form of a river. She does so ("Heart, the seat of soft delight"), and the chorus sings that now Acis is a god, still murmuring his love as he runs through his beloved plains ("Galatea, dry thy tears"). *—Ann Feeney*

Recommended:

- ○ **Handel: Acis & Galatea** / King (cond.), George, Ainsley, McFadden, Covey-Crump, Harre-Jones, King's Consort / 1990 / Hyperion 66361
- ○ **Handel: Acis & Galatea** / Christie (cond.), Cornwell, Agnew, Daneman, Ewing; Arts Florissants Orch. & Chorus / Teldec 25505
- ○ **Handel: Acis & Galatea** / Gardiner (cond.), Hill, Elliott, Johnson, Burrowes, White, English Baroque Soloists / Archiv 474225

Alexander's Feast, ode for St. Cecilia's Day, HWV 75 (1736; revised 1742)

During the course of 1735, Handel's fluctuating operatic fortunes dramatically turned with the success of *Alcina* and *Ariodante* at Covent Garden. However, it was now evident to Handel that real prosperity lay in the performance of oratorios, four of which had also been mounted during the same season. In January 1736, he commenced on a new English dramatic work that, although not a traditional oratorio, still shows Handel's commitment to that new, and financially promising, genre.

Alexander's Feast; or The Power of Music is based on an ode written by John Dryden to celebrate St. Cecilia, the patron saint of music, in 1697. Her feast day

(November 22) had been traditionally celebrated in England since early Restoration times, as witnessed by the settings of odes in her honor by Purcell, Blow, and others. Direct connections between the saint and Dryden's ode are few; the text makes reference to her only in its concluding pages. It was arranged for Handel into a sequence of recitatives, arias, and choruses cast in two parts by a minor man of letters, Newburgh Hamilton.

The "entertainment," as it was described, is set at the famous feast of Alexander held to celebrate the conquest of Persepolis. The musical allegory is enhanced by the inclusion at the feast of the legendary singer Timotheus; the comparison between him and Cecilia forms the climax of the work. There is little dramatic development, but Dryden's picturesque imagery allowed Handel to produce a superbly varied score that includes such famous numbers as the two bass arias "Bacchus, ever fair" (with chorus) and "Revenge, Timotheus cries." The work calls for five soloists (SAATB), chorus, and a large orchestra employing recorders, oboes, bassoons, horns, trumpets, timpani, and strings.

Completed in relative haste, *Alexander's Feast* was first performed at a well-attended Covent Garden on February 19, 1736; on that occasion it was supplemented by several concertos, including the *Concerto Grosso in C* (now known as the *Alexander's Feast Concerto*) and the *Organ Concerto*, Op. 4, No. 1. Two years after its first performance, *Alexander's Feast* achieved the unusual distinction of being published in full score by the London publisher John Walsh. *—Brian Robins*

Recommended:

- ○ **Handel: Alexander's Feast; Ode for Queen Anne** / Deller (cond.), Bevan, Sheppard, Worthley, Oriana Concert Orch. & Chorus / 1999 / Vanguard 8113
- ○ **Handel: Saul; Alexander's Feast; The Choice of Hercules** / Ledger (cond.), Allen, Tear, Donath, Tunnell, English CO / 2002 / Virgin 562118

Chandos Anthems (1717–1718)

In 1717, Handel gained a new patron, James Brydges, Earl of Carnarvon and from 1719 Duke of Chandos. Brydges had built a substantial fortune as Paymaster General to Marlborough's armies, and offered Handel residence at Cannons, his newly built palace near the village of Edgware, then a rural retreat on the outskirts of London. The Earl was a keen musical enthusiast who under the directorship of Johann Pepusch maintained a small retinue of musicians who were expected to both play and sing in addition to performing other household duties. After the turmoil of London's operatic life, Cannons must have seemed an oasis to Handel, who rewarded the Earl with a number of works that ensured a place in posterity for the name of Chandos. Principal among these are the delectable English masque *Acis and Galatea*, and the 11 anthems today known by Chandos' name.

Each anthem is a substantial and elaborate work consisting of a setting of one of the psalms (or the instance of Nos. 2, 4, and 5, a conflation of stanzas from more than one). Their musical setting follows a similar format in every instance. A short Italianate instrumental introduction, marked either "sonata" or "sinfonia" (the two terms were interchangeable during this period), is succeeded by a sequence of choral and solo vocal movements, each with its own distinctive character. They thus fall broadly into the category of the orchestrally accompanied verse anthem of Purcell's day, although their breadth and scope extends beyond anything of that period. The vocal and instrumental scoring reflect the restricted forces available at Cannons. Numbers 1 to 6 include writing for only a three-part chorus (STB), and alto parts, either solo or choral, are found in only two of the anthems, No. 7 ("My song shall be alway," Psalm 89) and No. 11 ("Let God Arise," Psalm 68). Similarly the orchestral scoring contains no viola parts, the scoring being largely restricted to an oboe, bassoon, and strings, No. 8 ("O come, let us sing unto the Lord," Psalm 95), providing the sole exception with its parts for two recorders. Conversely, the number of fine tenor arias and virtuoso obbligato parts for solo oboe suggests that these were particular Cannons strengths. Although the precise order in which Handel composed the anthems is not certain, it appears, judging from a letter written by the earl in 1717, that Handel supplied the anthems to him in pairs. Since the chapel attached to Cannons was not completed until 1720, shortly after Handel returned to London, the anthems were composed for the small church of St. Lawrence, Whitchurch, which was used by the duke until the chapel's completion. Too elaborate to enter the English cathedral repertoire, the *Chandos Anthems* represent a uniquely conceived and executed contribution to the native church repertoire. *—Brian Robins*

Recommended:

- ○ **Handel: Chandos Anthems 1–11** / Christophers (cond.), Partridge, Dawson, George, Kwella, The Sixteen Choir & Orch. / 1994 / Chandos 554

Coronation Anthems, for chorus & orchestra, HWV 258–261 (1727)

The death of George I in Germany on June 11, 1727, brought his successor George II to the British throne. In keeping with tradition, elaborate preparations were made for a magnificent coronation ceremony. Music had long played an important role at coronations, its composition generally entrusted to the organist and composer of the Chapel Royal. However, William Croft, the composer who held that post in 1727, died on August 14 of that year; on September 9, it was made known that the music for the service would be provided by Handel. The texts Handel chose for the four anthems included in the service were traditional. They included "Zadok the Priest," the anthem traditionally sung during the Anointing, "My heart is inditing," which is specific to the coronation of a queen, "The King shall rejoice," sung at the presentation of the king to the people, and "Let thy hand be strengthened," to be sung during the Enthroning and the only one of the anthems that does not call for full brass and drums. Earlier settings of all four had been used at the coronation of James II in 1685. George's coronation eventually took place in Westminster Abbey on October 11, 1727, a week later than originally planned. Handei had at his disposal 40 choristers and a huge orchestra said to have numbered 160, although some authorities doubt this figure. He rose to the occasion, exploiting the large ensemble to create magnificent contrasts of brilliant splendor in the outer sections with more lyrical passages. Only *"Zadok the Priest"* departs from this scheme, with a cumulative rise of grandeur throughout.

Rehearsals of the anthems aroused enormous public interest, but things do not seem to have gone smoothly at the coronation itself. According to contemporary reports, the standard of performance was not very high; no less a dignitary than the Archbishop of Canterbury complained of the performance of the first piece ("My heart is inditing") that "The Anthem all in confusion: All irregular in the Music." Nonetheless, the magnificence and pomp of the four anthems as a group has ensured for them a special place in the affection of the English people. *"Zadok the Priest"* in particular rapidly attained a popularity that has never waned, and the work has had an honored place in every British coronation service since that of George II. *—Brian Robins*

Recommended:

- ○ **Handel: Coronation Anthems; Musick for the Royal Fireworks** / Higginbottom, King (conds.), King's Consort, New College Choir Oxford / Hyperion 66350

Dixit Dominus, hymn in G minor, HWV 232 (1707)

When George Frideric Handel moved from northern Germany, his lifelong home, to Italy in 1706, it was for the purpose of gathering firsthand knowledge of Italian opera. However, Handel's decision to travel to Rome near the end of that first Italian year (or perhaps at the start of the next) must have been a bit counterproductive, since Papal edict had put an end to all theatrical entertainment in the city all the way back in 1677. Handel had no trouble finding employment as a composer of pure sacred music, however, and spring and summer of 1707 saw the composition of a large proportion of his wonderful Latin-texted choral works, including the large-scale *Dixit Dominus* for vocal solists, chorus, and string orchestra, HWV 232.

The *Dixit Dominus* is a musical setting in eight sections of Psalm 109, to which is added a setting of the Lesser Doxology that normally follows the reading of a psalm. Handel essentially crafted the text into a half-hour oratorio, finding, as so many Italian composers had already done, that Church authorities didn't seem to mind if one indulged in full-blown operatic style as long as the subject remained appropriate for sacred services. The lyric arias and dramatic choruses in the work are very similar to those one finds in Handel's English oratorios of many decades later, even if they show a little less aristocratic flair.

A sizable instrumental introduction, full of dramatic violin arpeggios, ushers in the opening chorus, "Dixit Dominus Domine meo." The alto (or, more properly, countertenor) aria "Virgam virtutis" is by comparison far more relaxed, while the soprano's first aria offers the opportunity for both exquisite cantabile and refined melismatic exercise. The second chorus, "Iuravit Dominus," is a striking thing, bursting forth rapidly after a mysterious opening, but then moving almost immediately back—via a very dramatic grand pause—to the chromatic quagmire of the opening; again things rush forth, this time maintaining velocity until the end. The second half of the psalm verse begun in "Iuravit Dominus" is given in the next chorus, "Tu es sacerdos." The chorus and five soloists (two sopranos, alto, tenor, and bass) join forces for the next two numbers, "Dominus a dextris" and "Iudicabit in nationibus." "De torrente in via bibet" is a very dissonant duet for two sopranos, while the final Doxology ("Gloria Patri…") moves forward along very melismatic lines. The final Amen is in the traditional fugal style. *—Blair Johnston*

Recommended:

- ○ **Handel: Dixit Dominus; Nisi Dominus; Salve Regina** / Preston (cond.), Dawson, Goodman, Birchall, Montague, Westminster Abbey Choir & Orch. / Archiv 423594
- ○ **Handel: Dixit Dominus** / Minkowski (cond.), Kozena, Massis, Fulgoni, Les Musiciens du Louvre / 1999 / Archiv 459627
- ○ **Vivaldi: Gloria; Handel: Gloria; Dixit Dominus** / Gardiner (cond.), Ross, Clarkson, Kazimierczuk, Humphries, English Baroque Soloists, Monteverdi Choir / 2001 / Philips 462597
- ○ **Händel: Gloria; Dixit Dominus** / Ohrwall (cond.), Otter, Martinpelto, Drottningholm Court Baroque Ens. / 2001 / BIS 301235

Israel in Egypt, oratorio, HWV 54 (1738)

Very few people have ever heard George Frideric Handel's sacred oratorio *Israel in Egypt* in anything like the form in which he first composed it. The story of the work's genesis is interesting: as Handel originally penned it in 1738, *Israel in Egypt* was a work in three acts, the first of which was an adaptation of the *Funeral Anthem*, HWV 264, composed the previous year on the death of his former pupil Queen Caroline. (Such wholesale borrowing from his own works—or even sometimes from other composers' works—was one of Handel's favorite time-saving tactics.) The texts of both this original and the later versions of *Israel in Egypt* were taken almost entirely from the Book of Exodus (by Charles Jennens, who also provided the libretto for the oratorio *Saul*), and tell of the Israelites' suffering in and deliverance from Egypt. The only additions are a few psalms.

At its King's Theatre premiere on April 4, 1739, *Israel in Egypt* was an utter failure. Handel had long since recognized that his English audience had lost its taste for Italian opera and forms derived from it, and throughout the 1730s he had been exploring ways to make his natural flair for musical drama commercially viable. With the first version of *Israel in Egypt*, however, one might argue that he went too far in "de-operatizing" his style; his audience had no idea what to make of the use of biblical texts in a theater environment, and the absolute predominance of the chorus meant a shortage of the solo arias that were still the only reason they came to performances. The work was, in addition, rather lengthy. Handel tinkered with *Israel in Egypt* many times—shortening it, adding arias—in an attempt to make the work a more audience-friendly one. For a 1756 performance of the oratorio, however, he decided to start more or less from scratch; it is this 1756 verison of *Israel in Egypt* that today's audiences will recognize.

Gone is the three-act work with its opening lamentation based on the 1737 Funeral Anthem. In its place is a leaner two-act oratorio that begins with music taken straight from the *Occasional Oratorio* (1746) and *Solomon* (1749). The chorus is still far more prominent, and serves much greater variety of expressive purposes, than one finds almost anywhere else in Handel's output, and the use of the six vocal soloists—two sopranos, an alto, a tenor, and two basses—is minimal. But it would not take long for this 1756 version of *Israel in Egypt* to assume a place alongside the *Messiah* as one of England's favorite choral treasures. Part One tells of the Israelites' deliverance from their Egyptian captivity at the hands of Moses; the 12 choruses that describe the miracles leading to the Israelites' freedom are among the most stunning and colorful ever written—images of hailstones, pestilence, and even the glorious parting of the Red Sea are achieved without once resorting to the kind of pictorialism that a lesser composer would relish. Part Two, Moses' Song, recounts the Israelites' victory and has room for more arias than does Part One; the two-soprano duet "The Lord is my strength" and the solo soprano aria "Thou didst blow with the wind" are particularly fine. *—Blair Johnston*

Synopsis:

Part One (Exodus). Joseph's memory has passed in Egypt, and the Israelites living under the new Pharoh's reign are made to suffer the ignominies and hardships of slavery. They cry out to God in their misery, and God responds by sending Moses and Aaron, the chosen of the Lord, to deliver Israel from Egypt. Through divine power the Nile is turned to blood, frogs pop up throughout Egypt, even in Pharoh's chambers; pestilence, plaque, locusts, darkness, and even fire-crowned hailstones are employed to convince Egypt to release the Israelites. Finally, after all of Egypt's firstborn are smitten by the Lord, Moses leads his people out of Egypt and through the Red Sea, which swallows up the pursuing Egyptians. Israel is happy in its freedom, and Moses becomes their new hero and leader.

Part Two (Moses' Song). Moses and the Israelites sing songs of praise to the Lord and recount the wonders of His triumph over Pharaoh and Egypt (all is taken from Exodus 15). *—Blair Johnston*

Recommended:

○ **Handel: Israel in Egypt** / Gardiner (cond.), Robertson, Chance, Stafford, Holton, English Baroque Soloists, Monteverdi Choir / 1995 / Philips 432110

○ **Handel: Israel in Egypt** / Parrott (cond.), Argenta, Johnson, Thomas, Evera, Taverner Choir & Players / 1990 / EMI 54018

○ **Handel: Israel in Egypt** / Cleobury (cond.), Chance, Bostridge, Varcoe, East, Brandenburg Consort / Decca 452295

Judas Maccabaeus, oratorio, HWV 63 (1746; revised 1758)

During Handel's lifetime, *Judas Maccabaeus* was one of the most popular of all his oratorios. Following its hugely successful first performance at London's Covent Garden theater on April 1, 1747, the work was subsequently revived during Handel's oratorio seasons every year until his death in 1759, with the single exception of 1749. Yet the oratorio has its genesis in one of the bleaker periods of Handel's life. In 1745 he was forced to abandon his Covent Garden season for lack of support, and he was also in ill-health. Notwithstanding, *Judas Maccabaeus* was begun in the fall of that year. The work was temporarily laid aside in favor of *The Occasional Oratorio*, quickly composed and drawing heavily from preexisting material, as Handel's loyalist contribution to the fight to put down the serious Jacobite revolution launched by the Stuarts. Only after the threat of the rebellion's success was lifted following the bloodily conclusive battle of Culloden in April 1746 did Handel again take up the score, completing it on August 11.

With its warlike story of the triumph of a Jewish hero over invading forces, *Judas Maccabaeus* formed the ideal victory celebration, and was overtly planned as such by Handel and his librettist, the Rev. Thomas Morell. Indeed the latter designed his book as "a compliment to the Duke of Cumberland upon his returning victorious from Scotland." Its main source is the first book of Maccabees, which appears in the Apocrypha. The oratorio falls into three acts, the first of which opens after one of Handel's finest overtures, with the mourning of the Israelites lamenting the death of Mattathias, the father of Judas Maccabaeus and the leader of Jewish resistance to the invading Syrians. This somber opening sequence includes one of Handel's most famous arias, "Pious orgies," with its mournful tones underpinned by dark bassoons. The Israelites are galvanized by Judas, and the remainder of the oratorio is dominated by a militaristic triumphalism illustrated through some of Handel's grandest and most stirring choruses, among which "Sound an alarm" (Act Two) and "Sing unto God" (Act Three) are notable examples. At the end of the oratorio the exploits of Judas and his forces ensure a peace guaranteed by Roman power, a moment celebrated in one of the oratorio's few moments of repose in "O lovely peace," the lovely pastoral aria sung by the Israelite Woman.

The famous number "See the conqu'ring Hero" is often associated with Judas, but was in fact originally composed for the oratorio's close relative, *Joshua* (1747); it was only later added to the present work. In keeping with the mood and scale of the work, Handel's lavish scoring includes trumpets, horns, and timpani in addition to the flutes, oboes, and the usual complement of strings. There are solo parts for soprano, mezzo-soprano, alto, tenor, and two basses in addition to the usual four-part chorus. *Judas Maccabaeus* is one of the few oratorios to have remained popular from Handel's day through to the twenty-first century. A singular hit with the Jewish population of London at the time, it remains a celebration of the Feast of Hanukkah, which commemorates the events it depicts. *—Brian Robins*

Recommended:

○ **Handel: Judas Maccabaeus** / Higginbottom, King (conds.), George, Kirkby, Birchall, Bowman, King's Consort, New College Choir Oxford / 1992 / Hyperion 66641

○ **Handel: Judas Maccabaeus** / McGegan (cond.), Butt, Thomas, Saffer, Spence, Mey, Philharmonia Baroque Orch. / 1993 / HM 907077

Messiah, oratorio, HWV 56 (1741; revised 1743)

With the arguable exception of the *Water Music*, the oratorio *Messiah* is the one work of Handel's which is universally known. Yet it was composed at a time when Handel's fortunes were at a low ebb. His final attempt to return to opera with *Imeneo* (1740) and *Deidamia* (1741) had proved a failure, and rumor even had it that, having despaired of the London public, he was preparing to leave England. Fortuitously, the clergyman and writer Charles Jennens, Handel's collaborator in *Saul*, lured Handel back to the idea of English oratorio; at much the same time, the composer received an offer from William Cavendish, Lord Lieutenant of Ireland, to take part in the following season of oratorio performances in Dublin. The libretto offered to Handel by Jennens was based around the birth and Passion of Christ. It was called *Messiah*. Handel set to work on the libretto on August 22, 1741, completing the score just over three weeks later on September 12.

The resulting sacred, non-dramatic oratorio was a first for Handel, and, although it heralded the composer's final great phase of oratorio composition, he never wrote one like it again. *Messiah* is therefore completely atypical within the context of Handel's oratorios, the majority of which relate to Old Testament or Apocryphal stories in dramatized form. As a statement of Christian faith it moves the worldly Handel closer to Bach than any other work of his, although not sufficiently to prevent contemporary accusations of operatic influences. It is also worth recalling that during Handel's day *Messiah* was more frequently performed in theaters than in churches.

Jennens divided his text into three parts, the first of which deals with the Prophecy of the Messiah and its fulfillment. The second takes us from the Passion to the triumph of the Resurrection, while the final part deals with the role of the Messiah in life after death. Handel's setting consists of the usual juxtaposition of recitative, arias, and choruses. Jennens' libretto draws across a wide spectrum of both Old and New Testament sources, but uniquely among Handel's oratorios there are no named characters. The drama is thus articulated purely through the textual message, most powerfully through the overwhelming choruses that have ensured the enduring popularity of the oratorio. The first performance took place at the New Music Hall in Dublin on April 13, 1742. It was received with huge acclaim, the *Dublin Journal* proclaiming that "*Messiah* was allowed by the greatest Judges to be the finest Composition of Musick that ever was heard." The following year the triumph was repeated at Covent Garden, when Handel added two more solos. Further revisions took place in 1745 at the famous Foundling Hospital performances, leaving all subsequent conductors with editorial problems as to Handel's "final" intentions. By the time of the composer's death in 1758 *Messiah* had already attained an iconic status it has never relinquished.

Alongside its immensely popular choruses—of which the "Hallelujah" is king—*Messiah*'s primary allure is its effective arias and recitatives for solo voices. The opening "Every Valley," sung by tenor, sets the tone for tunefulness and expressive charm, and is well-matched by the soprano's "Rejoice Greatly," the alto's "He was Despised" and the bass' "The Trumpet Shall Sound." *—Brian Robins*

Recommended:

- ○ **Handel: Messiah** / Hogwood (cond.), Preston, Elliott, Kirkby, Watkinson, Nelson, Academy of Ancient Music, Oxford Christ Church Cathedral Choir / 1991 / L'oiseau-Lyre 430488
- ○ **Handel: Messiah** / Beecham (cond.), Vickers, Tozzi, Sinclair, Vyvyan, Royal PO & Chorus / 1992 / RCA 61266
- ○ **Handel: Messiah** / Gardiner (cond.), Brett, Ross, Robbin, Johnson, English Baroque Soloists, Monteverdi Choir / 1992 / Philips 434297

Ode for St Cecilia's Day ("Song for St Cecilia's Day"), HWV 76 (1739)

Like *Alexander's Feast,* the composer's more famous work in honor of the patron saint of music, George Frideric Handel's *Ode for St. Cecilia's Day,* HWV 76, is a setting of texts written in honor of Saint Cecilia by John Dryden in 1697. Perhaps inspired by the sweeping success of *Alexander's Feast* (composed and first performed in 1736), Handel revisited Dryden's ode three years later to create a new, shorter work. The circumstances of the November 22, 1739, Lincoln's Inn Fields premiere of HWV 76 were something of an omen of things to come: the *Ode for St. Cecilia's Day* was presented as little more than a prelude to *Alexander's Feast,* and indeed the work has remained in the shadow of its sister piece ever since. The Ode is of very considerable merit, however; the three choruses contained within it are among the finest ever crafted by the composer, and the six arias are of equally high quality.

HWV 76 is properly an ode and not an oratorio; there is no plot, but rather a series of recitatives, arias, choruses, and instrumental pieces that extol the praises of the St. Cecilia (a third century martyr). Handel's score is for soprano and tenor soloists, the usual SATB chorus, and a colorful orchestra made up of strings, continuo, flute, double reeds, trumpets and timpani.

Handel's tendency to borrow music from himself and other composers is famous, and indeed, essentially all of the melodies contained in the *Ode for St. Cecilia's Day* were lifted straight from the keyboard pieces of Gottlieb Muffat's *Componimenti musicali* (published ca. 1739). However, the working-out of this pre-fab material over the course of the *Ode* is entirely Handel's own. The musical subject of Dryden's ode provides a sure footing for all sorts of musical text-painting and allusion.

The *Ode* falls loosely into two halves, each of which ends with a chorus, and which are separated by an orchestral March. The work's two-part overture was taken from, or perhaps used as the model for, the composer's own *Concerto grosso,* Op. 6, No. 5, composed around the same time. The singing begins with a recitative for tenor solo, "From harmony, from heav'nly harmony," the text of which is immediately echoed in the first of the three choruses. The soprano follows with the stunning but graceful aria "What passion cannot Music raise and quell," and the boisterous tenor counters with "The Trumpet's loud clangor," immediately taken up by the chorus.

A succession of four arias—three for soprano, one for tenor (but that one the delightful "Violins proclaim")—begins the second half of the *Ode for St. Cecilia's Day.* A soprano recitative ("But bright Cecilia rais'd the wonder high'r") prefaces the final chorus ("As from the pow'r of sacred lays" / "The dead shall live"), itself a spectacular example of Handel's choral writing. It moves seamlessly from the opening soprano solo to a purely choral climax and finale in which the composer displays his contrapuntal wizardry in a stunning double fugue. *—Blair Johnston*

Recommended:

- ○ **Handel: Ode for St. Cecilia's Day** / King (cond.), King's Consort, Sampson, Gilchrist / 2004 / Hyperion 67463
- ○ **Handel: Ode for St. Cecilia's Day** / Harnoncourt (cond.), Johnson, Palmer, Vienna Concentus Musicus / 1996 / Teldec 12319

La Resurrezione, oratorio, HWV 47 (1708)

La Resurrezione was one of Handel's earliest oratorios, and does not belong to the same genre as his later English oratorios. It was composed in Italy where the oratorio was similar in construction to the cantata, and made up of recitatives and arias which were operatic in nature. *La Resurrezione* premiered on Easter Day in 1708 at the palace of Marchese Ruspoli, a member of the Arcadian Academy and an avid patron of the young Handel. The cast was of the finest singers, the orchestra was large, and Ruspoli provided for three paid rehearsals and hired Arcangelo Corelli to direct. By the time that the young Handel composed *La Resurrezione,* he was completely at home in Italian genres and idioms, and his writing showed complete mastery of the elegant, euphonious style of melody which dominated vocal music. In addition, he had absorbed Venetian customs of orchestration, and his accompaniments were rich and varied, providing commentary on the main vocal music as well as dialogue with it.

The text for *La Resurrezione* was written by Carlo Capece, and is a dramatic telling of the story of Easter. The poetry is vivid, expressive, and even melodramatic at times. Lucifer is one of the main characters, and provides, in his robust bass arias and melodically imbued recitatives, almost comic contrast to the soprano Angel, the pious Marys, and the gallant tenor solos of St. John. Lucifer's text settings are especially striking: Handel pays special attention to assonance and long vowel sounds, giving the impression of Lucifer as a truly hissing serpent from hell. The chorus is used only twice, first as a chorus of angels glorifying God at the end of the first part, and then at the very end. However there are other portions of writing that become almost as full as a chorus—for instance when the full orchestra accompanies an aria or recitative, or when shared arias become full duets. The variety in textures is directly indebted to Italian operatic writing of the time, and Handel excels at it. One of the finest moments in the first part is when Mary Magdalene rejoices that the Lord is risen. Her soprano voice is accompanied by violins in unison with her melody; instrumental ritornellos intervene between sections, but the lightness of her aria prevails, as well as the mood of sanctity. *—Rita Laurance*

Recommended:

- ○ **Handel: La Resurrezione** / McGegan (cond.), George, Nelson, Thomas, Saffer, Spence, Philharmonia Baroque Orch. / 1997 / HM 1907027/28
- ○ **Handel: La Resurrezione** / Koopman (cond.), Laurens, Mertens, Argenta, Schlick, Mey, Amsterdam Baroque Orch. / Erato 45617

Samson, oratorio, HWV 57 (1741; revised 1742)

Samson was begun immediately after Handel had finished writing *Messiah* in 1741. Although almost all of the work was done by October of that year, he put the oratorio aside so that it could be premiered in London. It premiered at the Covent Garden Theatre in February 1743, where it had an extremely successful run of eight performances. *Samson* was staged in direct competition to the opera season at the King's Theatre, and was by far the more successful.

Handel's approach was new, having written and hired all English singers and performers. Up until this time, Handel had always had a lead castrato sing the heroic role, but he no longer had the resources in personnel that he once had. He decided to write the part for a singer who was not in the least virtuosic, but was known for his musicianship and dramatic skill: a tenor by the name of John Beard. His choice for Dalila was an actress capable of acting the part of a great seductress, Catherine Clive.

The score borrows a good deal from the music of others: Legrenzi, Telemann, Muffat, and Porta. It was hailed by the public as one of Handel's great works, and became a favorite of Londoners. The aria "Total eclipse!" in which Samson bewails his loss of sight, was known in later years to move both Handel and the London audience to tears, as Handel, spending the last ten years of his life blind, sat unseeing at his harpsichord during oratorio performances.

The libretto is taken from the Milton poem *Samson Agonistes,* as well as the biblical story from the Book of Judges. The librettist, Newburgh Hamilton, revised the poem to be a dramatic masterpiece for an oratorio. It opens with Samson in chains, having lost his strength and been blinded by the Philistines. The drama of Hamilton's libretto surrounds the transformation that takes place within Samson, as he changes from a despairing, defeated Israelite hero, into a resolved, committed, and believing instrument of retribution against the worshippers of Dagon. Each act is divided into sections in the libretto which are reflected in the score. The first act contrasts the celebrating Philistines with Samson's bleak circumstances. Trumpets and drums at the opening contrast with the soulful minor singing of the despondent Samson. Towards the end of the act Samson's transformation begins. In "Why does the God of Israel sleep?" Samson calls on Jehovah for aid. The entire closing sequence, which continues with a grand contrapuntal chorus and a solo for Samson's father, is in major, symbolizing Samson's growing inner strength. In Act II, Samson must confront first Dalila, his profligate wife, and then an emissary of the Philistines. In "Traitor to love," Dalila and Samson voice their conflicting views, and angrily spurn one another. In this oratorio Handel makes effective use of "crowd" choruses. When Harapha the champion of the Philistines arrives, crowds of Philistines and Israelites sing against one another in contrasting keys and types of thematic material. In the third act, Samson's final transformation takes place. The triumphal key of D major prevails in its exultant choruses, as the Israelites rejoice in their victory. *—Rita Laurance*

Synopsis:

In Act One, Samson, blinded and in chains, has been given a respite from his labor as a slave to the Philistines, in accordance with the customs for the feast of the god Dagon. The chorus of Philistines sings, "Awake the trumpet's lofty sound," and a Philistine man and woman alternate songs of praise. Samson expresses his despair at his condition, "Torments, alas, are not confin'd." Micah and Israelites come in and sadly observe his hopeless state, Micah lamenting, "Oh, mirror of our fickle state!" that one who had been so strong and so glorious now lies in chains. Samson, not aware of their presence, rebukes himself bitterly for entrusting the secret of his great strength to Dalila, who betrayed the secret to the Philistines, leading to his capture, blinding, and slavery. Micah greets him, and he thanks them for remaining loyal to him. He laments his blindness even more than his captivity, "Total eclipse!" and Micah condoles with him, as the Israelites contemplate the force of light, "O first created beam!" Samson again regrets having given in to Dalila's charms. Manoah comes to see his son, and Samson is desolated by the grief he has caused him. One of the men sings of the transience of human power, "God of our fathers, what is man?" Manoah describes how his son, his greatest joy once, is now his deepest sorrow, "Thy glorious deeds inspir'd my tongue." Samson laments that his downfall has let the Philistines boast that Dagon has overcome Jehovah, but hopes in Jehovah's ultimate victory, "Why does the God of Israel sleep?" Samson for himself wishes only death, though Manoah says he has hopes of being able to ransom him, and encourages him to expect heavenly rest, "Joys that are pure." The act closes with the Israelites singing of how God triumphs over death, "Then round about the starry throne."

In Act Two, Manoah, Micah, and the Israelites again attempt to comfort Samson. He thinks back on how he never drank wine, but instead succumbed to the worse temptations of lust. Manoah urges him to trust in God, "Just are the ways of God to man," but this does not ease Samson's despair or longing only to die. Micah and the Israelites pray, "Return, O God of hosts!" Dalila comes in, splendidly dressed, and attended by her maidens. Samson cries out in horror and rage as Micah tells him this. Micah tells him that she is crying, and Dalila herself says that she was afraid of his anger, but her love was strong enough to make her dare to come to him. She asks if there is anything that she can do to expiate her thoughtless treachery, and he bitterly accuses her of coming to taunt him and being as treacherous and incorrigible as all false women. She says she was guilty only of curiosity and indiscretion, and he holds some responsibility for betraying his strength to her weakness. She and a Philistine attendant compare her sorrow to a turtledove without its mate, "With plaintive notes and am'rous moan," but he responds with further accusations, "Your charms to ruin led the way." She asks him to permit her to take him to her home and tend to him, promising him her most loving care, "My faith and truth, O Samson, prove," echoed by her attendant and maidens, and follows by promising him pleasures in every sense but sight, "To fleeting pleasures make your court." He responds that he prefers imprisonment to being ensnared by her again and rejects even her plea to let her touch his hand. Finally, she responds angrily, telling him that she is considered the savior of her own country, and in their duet, "Traitor to love," each accuses the other. She and the women leave, and Micah comments that women love only themselves, "It is not virtue, valour, wit," the chorus adding that women should be subservient to their husbands, "To man God's universal law." Harapha enters, accompanied by Philistines, and mocks him. Samson challenges him to fight, and Harapha refuses an unfair advantage, "Honour and arms scorn such a foe." Samson responds with the aria "My strength is from the living God," and again challenges him, but Harapha will not fight. They defy one another, "Go, baffled coward, go." The Philistines and Israelites each sing to their respective deities, "Fix'd in his everlasting seat."

In Act Three, Harapha returns and orders Samson to show off his strength at the feast to Dagon. Samson at first refuses, despite Harapha's threats, "Presuming slave, to move their wrath!" but then, after Harapha leaves and the Israelites pray, "With thunder arm'd," he is overcome by a prophetic sensation that he should go, and when Harapha returns, he agrees, and expects to defeat his enemies, "Thus when the sun." Micah and the Israelites pray for him, "The Holy One of Israel be thy guide." Manoah returns, and they hear the sound of the Philistine celebrations, "Great Dagon has subdu'd our foe." Manoah hopes to ransom and tend to Samson, "How willing my paternal love." They hear screams, and a messenger runs on, telling them that Samson brought the temple down upon himself and the Philistines. The Israelites lament his death, though still thankful for the victory, "Ye sons of Israel, now lament," and when Samson's body is brought in, praise his deed, "Glorious hero, may thy grave," and the work concludes as a woman expresses their exultation, "Let the bright seraphim." *—Ann Feeney*

Recommended:

- ○ **Handel: Samson** / Harnoncourt (cond.), Alexander, Johnson, Kowalski, Miles, Vienna Concentus Musicus / 1993 / Teldec 74871
- ○ **Handel: Samson** / Leppard (cond.), Edwards, Baker, Langridge, Luxon, English CO, London Voices / 1993 / Erato 45994

Saul, oratorio, HWV 53 (1738)

At the end of the 1737 opera season, the Opera of the Nobility, Handel's archrival opera company, had finally gone bankrupt. However, Handel was badly in debt as well. The public seemed fed up with Italian opera as they knew it, and craved something new. In July 1738, Handel once more turned to oratorio. He began to compose the monumental and heroic story of Saul. The libretto had been put together by Charles Jennens, a very wealthy literary dilettante with many pretensions, but some talent. He played to Handel's strengths, and gave the composer many dramatic opportunities in the libretto. The characterizations are keen, and the motivations clear. Handel had a difficult time finishing this oratorio, interrupting it to compose the opera *Imeneo.*

The story of David and Saul has always been a popular one, and on the English stage it is represented by a magnificent operatic scena by Henry Purcell. As an oratorio, it was also set by the Italian Carissimi, a master of oratorio writing, by the Italian opera seria maverick Porpora, as well as by Handel's German colleague Keiser. In addition, earlier in 1738, John Christopher Smith Jr. had composed a setting called *David's Lamentations over Saul and Jonathan.* Handel is sure to have known all of these works. The tragedy of Saul is stark, and concerns his derangement, his moral failings, and his heroism. The drama is given a spiritual and magical element with the Witch of Endor and the ghost of Samuel as intermediaries into the next world. The dramatic chorus, again used as a chorus might be used in a classic Greek tragedy, moves the drama along, creates the moods, and influences the action. It is a chorus of Saul's people, who are heavily involved in his fate, and in the results of his actions. Handel composed for bass voice, tenor, and countertenor, and refrained from introducing into the score a virtuosic castrato as was common in his day. The somberness of the story required natural male voices whose depth adds to the gravity and weight of the outcome. The orchestration of *Saul* is on a grand scale, and calls for carillon, solo organ, trombones, and drums. The oratorio opens and closes with rich extended pieces made up of several interlocking numbers. The tragedy of *Saul* is filled with high drama, and although the chorus again proves the flexibility of the oratorio form, the characterizations and solo music are filled with passion, and vigor. The tableau which closes the work was called the "Elegy on the death of Saul and Jonathan," and contains all new music. Some of Handel's most moving, it features a magnificent lament and a grandiose dirge. *—Rita Laurance*

Recommended:

- ○ **Handel: Saul** / Harnoncourt (cond.), Fischer-Dieskau, Esswood, Varady, Johnson, Vienna Concentus Musicus / 1995 / Teldec 97504
- ○ **Handel: Saul** / Gardiner (cond.), Dawson, Holton, Miles, Ragin, English Baroque Soloists, Monteverdi Choir / 1991 / Philips 426265
- ○ **Handel: Saul** / Martini (cond.), Schlick, McFadden, Schwarz, MacLeod, Frankfurt Baroque Orch. / 1998 / Naxos 554361

Semele, oratorio, HWV 58 (1743; revised 1744)

Semele opened the 1744 oratorio season at Covent Garden. Composed during the summer of 1743 after the huge success of *Samson,* it is altogether a different kind of work than his other oratorios. It has a secular subject, and although performed as an oratorio comes very close to being an English opera. The many accompanied recitatives and the exclusive use of the da capo aria form give it traits from the Italian opera. The libretto is by one of England's finest dramatists of all time, William Congreve. The character of the story and the use of the language is entirely English, and the music's rhythmic and cadential feel is indebted to Handel's new language. Handel also attempts to combine in *Semele* elements of the English lyric stage, introducing traits from the semi-opera and masque.

William Congreve wrote *Semele* in 1707 as a libretto, intending it to be set by John Eccles, then a popular composer of the stage. Indeed a score for the work resides in the British museum. Newburgh Hamilton adapted the play for Handel's use, skillfully adding dramatic opportunities for the composer. The libretto was very congenial to Handel, who liked the sources from Ovid, Greek myth, and Euripides. However, the secular story, with its themes of carnal love, and the operatic music which is filled with lyric intensity, completely shocked the English. The music and the text both reflect the passion of the characters, and appeal to the sensual delight of the audience. When *Semele* premiered in Covent Garden in February 1744, it was a complete failure. Handel attempted to produce it only one more time before completely giving up on the work. The public thought of *Semele* as an opera, which it really is. *—Rita Laurance*

Recommended:

- ○ **Handel: Semele** / Gardiner (cond.), Jones, Kwella, Lloyd, Penrose, English Baroque Soloists, Monteverdi Choir / Erato 45982
- ○ **Handel: Semele** / Nelson (cond.), English CO, Ambrosian Opera Chorus / 1993 / DG 435782

Solomon, oratorio, HWV 67 (1748; revised 1759)

Solomon was one of two oratorios that Handel composed for the 1749 Lenten concert season in London (the other being *Susannah*); as was his habit, he composed the work during the relatively open months of the previous summer (May/June, 1748) when his energies were less divided by the presentation of concerts and operas. Textual similarities between *Solomon* and *Susannah* suggest their librettos—both of exceptional quality—were written by the same person; unfortunately there is no record of the author's identity. Both libretti were once thought to be the work of Thomas Morell—the author of *Jeptha, Judas Maccabaeus, Theodora,* and *Joshua*—but any close examination of the texts reveals irreconcilable stylistic disparities.

Most of the text for *Solomon* was based on scriptural passages drawn from II Chronicles and I Kings; as the title of the work makes clear, the selected passages are those dealing with the renowned King Solomon. It is possible that Handel's choice of this subject matter was his tribute to King George II of England, a generous patron, and under whose rule England enjoyed a period of comparable prosperity; but—unlike *Judas Maccabaeus,* in which case Handel wrote letters specifically outlining his intended tribute to the victorious Duke of Cumberland—there is no textual evidence to establish this as fact.

In portraying the biblical Solomon, the anonymous librettist chose to divide his work into three acts, each of which sheds a slightly different light on his subject. The first act evokes the sensual and poetic voice from the *Song of Solomon*; the king and his new wife express their mutual rapture and contentment. The Solomon portrayed here is fiercely devoted to his lone queen—far from faithful to scripture, in which he is said to have had many hundreds of wives, and half again as many concubines! The second act takes up Solomon's most famous action, namely his resolution of the dispute between two harlots, each of whom claims to be the rightful mother of a baby; by suggesting that he cut the child in half and give one part to each woman, he ferrets out their true intentions and justly resolves the case. Act three takes as its subject a visit by the Queen of Sheba. *Solomon* presents the wonders of his kingdom to her in the form of a musical masque.

Handel's score is notable for the inclusion of a full array of brass instruments, and an unusually large complement of strings, both of which lend the score a particular opulence and richness; this is often highlighted by the composer's division of the chorus into five, or sometimes eight, parts. The opening sinfonia is of unusual scope for Handel's oratorios. It has been suggested that one of the most popular excerpts from *Solomon*, namely the entrance of the Queen of Sheba from the third act, was not actually composed for the work at hand, but rather was borrowed from another unfinished project.

The first performance of *Solomon* took place on March 17, 1749, at Covent Garden and under the composer's direction. Although this was a reasonable success, and despite the consistently high quality of the libretto—drawing from Handel some of his most highly shaded melodies and characterizations—the work never gained the popularity enjoyed by a number of his other oratorios. In modern performance it is often subject to substantial cuts which, although they trim the length of performance from its full two-and-one-half hours, tend to compromise the carefully balanced structure of the work as a whole. *—Allen Schrott*

Recommended:

- ○ **Handel: Solomon** / McCreesh (cond.), Harvey, Scholl, Agnew, Gritton, Gabrielli Consort & Players / Archiv 459688
- ○ **Handel: Solomon** / Gardiner (cond.), Hendricks, Varcoe, Argenta, Johnsonn, English Baroque Soloists, Monteverdi Choir / Philips 412612

Susanna, oratorio, HWV 66 (1748)

Susanna and *Solomon* were composed as a pair of oratorios. They are very divergent in subject matter, style, content, and purpose. *Susanna* is almost a light chamber opera, and is heavily indebted to English music, especially the type of music that Handel would have heard around him in London. Many musicologists attribute its "English" sound to the influence of Thomas Arne, as well as folk music and folk idioms. The music is indebted in its rhythmic cadences to the English language, its rhythms, and speech patterns. Although there are many da capo arias, which allies this oratorio to Italian opera, the tunes are light.

The story is taken from the *Book of Daniel*, but really has the character of a folk tale, and there is ample room for levity. The subject matter of the story celebrates the joys of carnal love, and pokes fun at lechery and "purple passions." Susanna's character is exemplary; she is beautiful, virtuous, and madly in love with her husband Joachim. She is beset by two old wicked judges, the first of whom is portrayed as a guilt-ridden lecher and given to a tenor voice. The second lecher is a buffo bass role. He has no qualms about his lust, and pursues Susanna shamelessly. Handel has opportunity to write comedic music, as well as beautiful ballads and arias that are sincere, melodious, and artless. One of the highlights is the trio between Susanna and the two lecher/elders. They are each given their own accompaniment, and then their music is combined very cleverly to produce a type of divergent trio. The buffo bass forms the comic bottom, and is broadly accompanied in unison fashion, while the first elder has homophonic chords beneath Susanna's imitative prattle.

Susanna's premier evening of February 10, 1749, played to a full house, but predictions were made that it would not survive, and they were right. The English public was quite shocked at the provocative story, and confused at having their opera and oratorio mixed together in such a fashion. Although a thoroughly entertaining and sophisticated work, it is rarely heard even today. The librettist for *Susanna* is unknown. Although he wrote into the libretto a fine chamber opera, he added many ponderous choruses in an effort to keep the flavor of a traditional oratorio. Although they are somewhat out of place in this work, they are written with Handel's customary flair. *—Rita Laurance*

Recommended:

- ○ **Handel: Susanna** / Thomas (cond.), Brett, Feldman, Hunt, Minter, Philharmonia Baroque Orch. / HM 907030
- ○ **Handel: Susanna** / Neumann (cond.), Holton, Magnus, Sol, Buwalda, Cologne Chamber Choir, Cartusianum Collegium / 1999 / MDG 3320945

Theodora, oratorio, HWV 68 (1749)

On the evening of March 16, 1750, the 64-year-old Handel raised his baton in London's Covent Garden playhouse to open the first performance of a new oratorio. Unfortunately, the English public that night was underwhelmed. Whether because they disliked Handel's new kind of moralistic subject or feared that week's London earthquakes, the first audiences for *Theodora* were very thin. Some of Handel's friends thought it his most "finished, beautiful, and labor'd" work ever; nevertheless, it only ran for three performances. Later generations have discovered and rediscovered the emotional depth and intensity of Handel's *Theodora*, now acknowledged one of his finest oratorios. In it mingle his operatic gift for characterization and his masterful hand in setting the English language for its many choruses.

The subject matter of Handel's *Theodora* may have surprised its first London audiences. This work is nearly alone among his 22 English oratorios in having a non-Biblical story, and is the only one set in Christian times. The plot concerns two Christian martyrs in Antioch during the persecution of Diocletian. St. Ambrose first recorded the story of the martyrs Theodora and Didymus; later English audiences knew the tale through Foxe's *Book of Martyrs*, through Corneille's play on the subject, and especially via the novel by the eminent scientist and theologian Robert Boyle. Handel's libretto came from the pen of Rev. Thomas Morell (also librettist for his *Judas Maccabeus*, *Alexander Balus*, and *Jeptha*).

Morell gave Handel an intimate and sentimental tale of two Christian lovers who are faced with torture, rape, and death for their faith; their steadfast hope in the afterlife, and their love for one another, allow them to triumph spiritually. Handel's music brilliantly embodies their profound sense of hope despite the violence and danger of the surface events. A bullying Roman governor (Valens) threatens the heroine *Theodora*, leader of the Antiochine Christians, with multiple violation by his soldiers, and with all the torture instruments of the Inquisition, if she refuses to worship the Roman gods. In the end, both Theodora and Didymus, a Roman soldier who supports free Christian thought and tries to save her, are sentenced to death. Yet the passionate uplift of Handel's music in their arias and duets maintains a deep emotional sense of hope. His choruses of Christians (which alternate with choruses of vengeful pagans) both react to and participate in the action, reinforcing the moral (or amoral) choices of the main characters. *—Timothy Dickey*

Recommended:

- ○ **Handel: Theodora** / McCreesh (cond.), Blaze, Agnew, Smith, Gritton, Gabrieli Consort & Players / 2000 / DG 469061
- ○ **Handel: Theodora** / Christie (cond.), Berg, Daneman, Taylor, Croft, Les Arts Florissants / 2003 / Erato 43181
- ○ **Handel: Theodora** / Harnoncourt (cond.), Ortner, Alexander, Blochwitz, Kowalski, Arnold Schoenberg Choir, Vienna Concentus Musicus / 1991 / Teldec 46447

ORCHESTRAL

Music for the Royal Fireworks, HWV 351 (1749)

The War of Austrian Succession was brought to an end by the Treaty of Aix-la-Chapelle, signed in October 1748. Although England had been a somewhat reluctant participant and had gained little from the war, preparations for celebrations commenced the following month with the erection of a large wooden structure incorporating a triumphal arch in London's Green Park—the framework for a large and impressive display of fireworks. Peace was formally declared in the following February, and Handel, who had then just completed two contrasting oratorios, *Susanna* and *Solomon*, was commissioned to provide music for the occasion. Obviously, such music would have to be both grand in scale and suitable for open-air performance—this latter aspect, in practical terms, calling for a large contingent of wind and brass instruments. Handel originally intended to make use of no fewer than 16 each of trumpets and horns. However, he ran into trouble with the organizers, evidenced by a sequence of bad-tempered letters. Ultimately, he settled for something a little more "modest": 24 oboes, 12 bassoons (including a contrabassoon), nine each of trumpets and horns, three pairs of kettledrums, and an unspecified number of side drums.

Music for the Royal Fireworks consists of five movements, commencing with a suitably pompous and ceremonial Overture in the French style: a slow, dotted-rhythm introduction followed by a contrapuntal Allegro. The suite continues with a lively Bourée, a quieter movement entitled "La paix," the ebullient "La réjouissance," and a final Minuet. A second Minuet, in D minor, which seems to have been added later, was probably used by the composer as a trio section before a final triumphant return to the main Minuet in D major.

The rehearsal of *Music for the Royal Fireworks* in Vauxhall Gardens on April 21, 1749 takes a place as one of the best attended in the history of musical performance. A huge crowd, said to number in excess of 12,000, is reported to have turned up, blocking many surrounding streets and causing traffic chaos. The actual event was rather less successful; observers reported that in particular, many of the fireworks failed to impress. To make matters worse, the display set fire to one of the pavilions that formed part of the structure. A month later, the music was performed in the rather more peaceful surroundings of the Foundling Hospital. For this occasion Handel reverted to a traditional combination of strings and winds. This is the version in which the music, one of Handel's most popular works, is most often heard today, although at least two recordings have been made which employ the massive wind forces heard at the first performance. —*Brian Robins*

Recommended:

○ **Handel: Water Music; Music for the Royal Fireworks** / Savall (cond.), Le Concert des Nations / 1999 / Astrée 9920

○ **George Frideric Handel** / Pinnock (cond.), English Concert / 2000 / DG 469145

Water Music Suites Nos. 1–3, HWV 348–350 (1717)

Early in his career Handel left Germany, where he resented the limitations of his role. He left for for England, where he hoped that the more cosmopolitan musical life of the capital, subject to market forces led by fashion and popular taste, rather than princely dictate, would offer a more lucrative reception for his stage works. Despite his limited mastery of the English language, Handel made a triumphant entrée into London society. His operas were immensely successful there for a time, and it was for London that Handel composed his two most universally popular orchestral works, the *Music for the Royal Fireworks*, and the three *Water Music* suites.

Both of these were intended for outdoor performance, and were scored for ensembles with complements of woodwinds and brasses that could be heard to good advantage in open air. Moreover, each drew in some measure upon material Handel had already composed. By the time Handel composed his *Water Music* in 1717, he had been able to fully evaluate the musical trends of his adopted home. He brought to what might at first seem like a rather nondescript assemblage of nautical folk melodies, songs, and country dances what Professor H.C. Robbins Landon has described as "far more than the usual international flair; a remarkable fusion of solid German upbringing, Italian training and a thorough acquaintance with French tastes." Each piece is a miniature gem with a finely sculpted expressive point, drawing, as Landon indicates, upon the various suite components and types of orchestral writing that Handel had mastered.

English monarch King George I held a society river party, probably a sort of eighteenth century equivalent of the "photo op," on the Thames on July 17, 1717. For this event Handel composed a collection of short, festive pieces, known collectively as the *Water Music* since the publication soon afterward of a group of them as "The Celebrated Water-Musick." The original order and grouping of the pieces is not known; not all employ the supernumerary trumpets, horns, oboes, and drums suited particularly to outdoor festive events, and it seems likely that the Suite in G (which employs the softer tones of flutes and strings) was reserved for performance at the "choice supper" reported by the London *Daily Courant*, held "at Lord Ranelagh's villa at Chelsea, where there was another fine Consort of Musick, which lasted until two (am)." Of the river-festivities earlier that day, the same newspaper also recorded that "many barges with Persons of Quality attended, and so great a number of boats that the whole river in a manner was cover'd; a City Company's barge was employ'd for all the musick, wherein were fifty instruments of all sorts, who play'd all the way from Lambeth . . . the finest of Symphonies compos'd express for this Occasion, by Mr. Hendel; which his Majesty liked so well, that he caus'd it to be plaid three times in going and again in the returning."

The arrangement of the music into three suites may have been intended by Handel originally; with three keys used in the work (F, D, and G), the grouping is natural. Conductors have also ordered the pieces in other ways. —*Michael Jameson*

Recommended:

○ **Handel: Water Music; Organ Concertos** / Harnoncourt (cond.), Tachezi, Vienna Concentus Musicus / 1994 / Teldec 93668

○ **Handel: Water Music; Music for the Royal Fireworks** / Savall (cond.), Le Concert des Nations / 1999 / Astree 9920

○ **Handel: Orchestral Works** / Pinnock (cond.), Standage, Wilcock, English Concert / Archiv 463094

CONCERTO

Concerti grossi (1712–1739)

The concerto grosso was one of two forms of concerto developed during the latter part of the seventeenth century. Credit for its invention is usually given to the immensely influential set of 12 works published by Arcangelo Corelli as his opus 6 in 1712. While the solo concerto rapidly gained precedence in Italy, the concerto grosso soon became established as the favored form in England. There its combination of three (or four) fairly demanding solo parts (the concertino) with easier parts for the body of strings (the ripieno) made it an ideal vehicle for the rapid spread of professional and amateur music making that burgeoned during the eighteenth century.

Handel's contribution to this repertoire consists of two sets, one of six concertos (HWV 312–317), published in London by John Walsh in 1734 as opus 3, the other consisting of 12 concertos (HWV 319–330), and also issued by John Walsh as opus 6 in 1740. In addition, there is a further *Concerto grosso in C*, composed by Handel to preface the second part of his Cecilian choral work, *Alexander's Feast* (HWV 318). All these works are scored for the standard concerto grosso forces of two solo violins and solo cello, with ripieno parts for the normal orchestral string disposition of two violins, violas, and bass continuo. The concertos of Op. 3 and HWV 318 also have parts for pairs of oboes and bassoons, while five of the concertos of Op. 6 (Nos. 1, 2, 5 and 6) also include oboe parts, although the printed parts were considered complete without them. The opus 3 set appears to have been issued by Walsh with only the tacit authorization of Handel, who appears to have played little or no part in assembling the concertos from previously composed material. With these works, which vary from two to five movements, the publisher was no doubt looking to extend the success he had enjoyed with the issue of similar works by Corelli and Francesco Geminiani. The opus 6 concertos are a very different matter, at once Handel's most grandly conceived set of orchestral works, and unquestionably the finest of all sets of concerti grossi. All 12 were composed within the astonishingly short period of a month between September and October 1739 and issued by Walsh, who had just signed a new copyright privilege with Handel, as "Twelve Grand Concertos" on April 21, 1740. Handel's purpose in composing the concertos was to serve as interval music during his choral concert season of the winter of 1739–40, a function previously also served by the organ concertos of Opp. 4 and 7, which the composer had himself played with enormous success between the acts of his oratorio performances. As with opus 3, the number of movements varies, although most consist of five or six, opening with an imposing slowish section succeeded by an alternation of quick or moderate tempo sections. —*Brian Robins*

Recommended:

○ **Handel: Concerti Grossi, Op3 & 6** / Harnoncourt (cond.), Vienna Concentus Musicus / 1994 / Elektra 95500

Harp Concerto in B flat major, Op. 4/6 (1736)

On February 19, 1736, King's Theater in London played host to a remarkable gala musical event, of the likes of which modern Baroque aficionados can only dream. No fewer than four of George Frideric Handel's best-known full-scale concert pieces were first heard on that blustery winter evening: an *Ode for St. Cecilia's Day* for soloists, chorus and orchestra (HWV 75), served as the massive centerpiece around which were performed the *"Alexander's Feast" Concerto grosso* (HWV 318), the *Organ Concerto in G minor*, Op. 4, No. 1, and, perhaps most strikingly, a thing rather remarkable for its time: a concerto for harp and orchestra in B flat major (HWV 294, later printed as the sixth and last piece of the collection of concertos called Opus 4 that publisher John Walsh released in 1738). In the Opus 4 publication, this *Harp Concerto* was issued as a work for organ and orchestra (making it congruous with the other five works in the volume), and it is on this instrument that the work is most often played today. But a quick glance at the pared-down orchestra parts and streamlined textures—the violins are muted, bass parts played pizzicato, and the wind family is represented by two lone flutes—reveals immediately that it was originally conceived of for the quieter and gentler harp. The piece is cast in three movements, more or less following the then-emerging modern concerto fast-slow-fast ordering. As with many of the organ concertos, the orchestra is entirely subordinate to the soloist in Op. 4, No. 6. In the first movement, for instance, 46 of the 66 measures are the exclusive province of the harp; the tutti appears just four times (double that counting the repeats)—at the movement's opening and close, and to lend strength to two major internal cadences. However, unlike the organ concertos, whose keyboard parts were played by the very skilled Handel himself, the *Harp Concerto* features little in the way of virtuosic flair. Certainly there are running 16th notes galore in the first movement, but these are almost always built around repetitive Alberti bass-like figures that fall easily to the hand, not the kind of flash-and-dazzle workout that is found in, say, the Op. 7, No. 2 concerto in A major.

The transparent opening movement, with its main theme built of seven broken-up, individual gestures, gives way to the thicker, more integrated melody of the G minor Larghetto. Throughout the movement, the tutti is consumed with pondering repeated dotted figures while, each time it is given a chance, the harp/organ breaks out with improvisatory musings of a far more flexible nature.

Wholly dance-like is the concluding Allegro moderato, with its bouncing 3/8 meter and 1 + 2 metric grouping. —*Blair Johnston*

Recommended:

○ **Harp Concertos** / Brown (cond.), Robles, Academy of St. Martin-in-the-Fields / 1990 / London 425723

○ **George Frideric Handel** / Pinnock (cond.), Holliger, English Concert / 2000 / DG 469145

Organ Concertos (ca. 1735–1751)

The keyboard concerto for harpsichord or organ was a late entrant among Baroque concertos, a genre cultivated principally by Bach for his Leipzig concerts and Handel. The first occasion on which Handel combined the organ with orchestra dates back to his early Roman oratorio *Il Trionfo del Tempo e del disingano* (1707), in which he included a short sonata for solo organ and orchestra. His fully fledged organ concertos were composed many years later, and all were composed with the specific purpose of providing entr'acte music during the theater performances of Handel's oratorios. His introduction of such pieces was an astute move. Handel was a renowned organist, particularly famed for his skill as an improviser, and he quickly discovered that his appearance as a solo player during the oratorio acted as a powerful incentive to attract audiences. Between 1735, when Handel first started performing oratorios at Covent Garden, and 1751, 15 organ concertos were composed for this purpose. A 16th work is an arrangement of the *Concerto a due cori No. 3*, HWV 334, and is normally omitted from the canon. Six of the remaining 15 were published by Handel's usual London publisher, John Walsh in 1738 as opus 4, and another six posthumously in 1761 as opus 7. Of the three other concertos, that in F, HWV 295, is the popular work known as "The Cuckoo and the Nightingale" from the suggestions of bird song in the Allegro second movement.

In the first concertos to be composed, Op. 4, No. 2 in B flat, and Op. 4, No. 3 in G minor, Handel was working in what was virtually a new form, and he drew heavily on movements from trio sonatas. A number of the other concertos also find the composer drawing on his own works and those of other composers, but this applies less to the generally more assured concertos of Op. 7 than those published earlier. With the exception of the five-movement Op. 7, No. 1 in B flat, arguably the finest of the set, all the organ concertos are cast in either three or four movements, the first frequently a slowish movement of considerable grandeur. A notable feature of the Op. 7 concertos is the inclusion in all except one of a movement marked "organo ad libitum." This was the point at which Handel inserted an extemporary movement, generally filled in by today's performers with organ arrangements borrowed from other works of Handel's. With a single exception, the orchestral scoring of all the concertos is for two oboes, bassoon, strings, and continuo. That exception, Op. 4, No. 6, is a special case which was originally composed to be inserted into *Alexander's Feast* as a harp concerto, although there is evidence that it was subsequently played as an organ concerto. In keeping with the gentle, mellifluous nature of the work, Handel here replaces oboes with a pair of flutes. Handel's organ concertos were later much imitated by his English contemporaries. —*Brian Robins*

Recommended:

○ **Handel: Complete Organ Concertos** / Pinnock (cond.), Preston, English Concert / 2002 / Archiv 469358

KEYBOARD

Keyboard Suites (1720–1733)

Comparisons between the solo keyboard works of J.S. Bach and G.F. Handel more often than not cast those of Handel in an unfavorable light. Like Bach, Handel was among Europe's premier keyboardists during the early eighteenth century, but Handel's harpsichord music has very little of the profound symmetry and varnish that have made Bach's keyboard works famous, or even the simple elan found in similar works of the great Italian, Domenico Scarlatti. As a result, Handel's entries in the genre have been sadly neglected.

The reason that Handel's keyboard output would seem, at first glance, to fall noticeably below the bar set by his two worthy contemporaries is simple: Handel never intended any of it to be published, and Handel as a rule took a great deal less care with music not meant for public consumption than he did with the commercially minded operas and oratorios upon which his reputation still rests.

Handel's 25-plus harpsichord suites were probably meant for use in teaching as much as for performance, though Handel himself often played—or improvised—them for his friends, students, and employers. Two collections of suites appeared in print during his lifetime: one in 1720 (eight suites) and one in 1733 (nine). The 1720 volume was issued to counter a Dutch publisher's publication of the same works without Handel's consent; the 1733 volume may or may not have been approved by Handel, though in the preface to the 1720 volume Handel had promised to release more keyboard works to the public. There are also a dozen or more suites not published during Handel's lifetime, some of which remained unknown until the twentieth century.

For the most part, the suites are cast in the old Froberger Suite mold (allemande, courante, sarabande, gigue, etc.); sometimes a Prelude or an Ouverture is affixed to the beginning, and occasionally a fugue appears in the middle. Very often, Handel incorporates a variation form of some kind—either a sarabande or an air with variations (like the "Harmonious Blacksmith" movement of the *Suite in E major*, HWV 430, or the third movement of the *B flat major Suite*, HWV 434 that provided Brahms with the theme for his *Handel Variations*), or a chaconne that, by nature, is a kind of variation form (like the final movement of the *Suite in G minor*, HWV 432). Two of the suites in the 1733 volume, HWV 435 in G major and HWV 442 in G major, are in fact not multi-movement works, but single-movement chaconnes; HWV 442 was originally published with a prelude that turns out to have been written by another composer.

The suites are undeniably inconsistent—brilliant here, mediocre there; they are rarely truly finished products. They are also, however, evidence of Handel's fertile mind; once one gets to know them they seem to bubble over with life. It is as if Handel could not be bothered to touch up what he had written—his mind was already churning with the next thought; and by the time that next thought had been sketched he had moved on to some new project that demanded his full attention (most likely an opera or an oratorio). Handel's harpsichord suites are like a musical mixing bag, a vat into which he threw ideas without any promises or guarantees. Naturally they make for fascinating listening. —*Blair Johnston*

Recommended:

○ **Handel: The 8 Suites** / Nicholson / 2002 / Hyperion 22045

CHAMBER MUSIC

Oboe Sonata in G minor, HWV 404 (1717–1718)

The manuscript of this sonata is held in the British Library. Scored for oboe and violin or two violins, it bears the inscription "Compos'd at the Age of 14." If such is the case, it would make one of the earliest of Handel's known works. The style, which is very much that of the Corellian trio sonata, certainly points to an early work. It is cast in four brief movements. The first is a gracious, flowing Andante whose thematic material bears a strong resemblance to the trio "The Flocks Shall Come" from *Acis and Galatea*. The succeeding Allegro is, typically for such a work, a fugue. That is followed by an expressive Largo and the work concludes with a lively Allegro. It was published by London publisher John Walsh around 1730 as the second of *Six Sonatas*, Op. 2. —*Brian Robins*

Recommended:

○ **Handel: Oboe Sonatas** / London Harpsichord Ens. / 1994 / Unicorn 9153

Recorder Sonata in F major, Op. 1/11 (1725–1726)

Of the 15 or so sonatas for solo instrument and basso continuo composed by George Frideric Handel that have at various times and in various combinations been lumped together under the title Opus 1, a full third were originally composed with the recorder—really, along with the violin, the most common and popular instrument around the turn of the eighteenth century—in mind; in fact, only the violin is more fully represented in the Opus 1 collection. However, each of the five sonatas for recorder and basso continuo from Opus 1—including the *Flute Sonata in B minor*, Op. 1, No. 9, that originally saw life as a *Recorder Sonata in D minor*—is undoubtedly the product of Handel's pen, whereas a handful of the violin sonatas may well be spurious. They are all splendid examples of Handel's youthful craftsmanship, very likely composed before the composer moved to England in 1710 and at any rate not after 1720, and showing how well able the 20-some year old composer was to adapt the phenomenally popular Corelli sonata style to suit his own personal musical language.

Opus 1, No. 11 in F major (HWV 369) is the second of two major-mode recorder sonatas from the collection. At first glance, this sonata appears to be a sonata da chiesa, with the normal slow-fast-slow-fast, four-movement structure. However, the twon fast movements are very lively and dance-like. The sonata opens with a stately Larghetto in which the recorder's phrases begin on the offbeats. This leads without break into the second movement, a binary form Allegro. Both quite lively sections of the Allegro move right along with sixteenth note passages. The third movement is an unusual one. Here Handel inserts a Sicilienne in D minor, with short motives that end on the third beat of the measure. Again there is no break as the Sicilienne leads into the final Allegro, a dance in 12/8 meter that has almost the feel of a hornpipe. —*AMG*

Recommended:

○ **Handel: The Complete Sonatas for Recorder** / Koopman, Linden, Verbruggen / 1995 / HM 907151

○ **Handel: The Complete Chamber Music** / Petri, Academy of St. Martin-in-the-Fields Chamber Ens. / 2002 / Philips 470893

○ **Handel: 20 Sonatas Op1** / Nicholson, Tunnicliffe, Beckett / 1995 / Hyperion 66921

Solo Sonatas, Op. 1

Musicologists, by and large, do not complain too much about the immense difficulties in dating and categorizing the 15 or so sonatas for solo instrument and continuo that at one time or another have been lumped together as George Frideric Handel's Opus 1: that much of the composer's early chamber music has even survived is extraordinary, as Handel himself never published the works and in fact seems to have abandoned them to their fate when he moved to England in 1710. It is only due to the efforts of two commercially minded publishers that the music ever went to print. Different editions of Opus 1 appeared between 1722 and 1732, however; each contained a slightly different set of pieces, some possibly not composed by Handel, and many assigned to instruments more or less at random and with little regard for Handel's often very clear intentions on the matter. Regardless, much of the music contained within this blemished vessel displays Handel's uncanny knack for putting a new twist on very ordinary musical idioms and gestures, and in doing so filling what were rapidly becoming tired old forms with wit, surprise, and a good dose of the high-minded musical regalia for which he is so well known.

Most of the Opus 1 pieces are examples of the sonata da chiesa variety, with its four movement, slow-fast/slow-fast pairing; a few works, however, have five, six, or even seven movements, and thus tend more in the direction of the sonata da camera. Following is a brief overview of the Opus 1 works as they are now numbered.

No. 1a: a flute sonata in E minor that takes two of its movements from No. 1b and two of its movements from No. 2.

No. 1b: a flute sonata in E minor, itself a recomposition of the sonata for violin and continuo in D minor, HWV 359a.

No. 2: a recorder sonata in G minor, sharing two movements with No. 1a.

No. 3: in A major, one of three Handel violin sonatas not plagued by doubts about authenticity. This is a stunning work, almost equal in quality to the D major violin sonata (No. 13 below).

No. 4: a recorder sonata in A minor whose four movements are of somewhat large dimensions for a Handel sonata da chiesa.

No. 5: a flute sonata in G major that is really a revision of a work for oboe and continuo in F major (HWV 363a). The third movement of this sonata is shared with No. 7.

No. 6: a sonata in G minor that originally appeared in 1722 as an oboe work but survives in an autograph manuscript upon which Handel has clearly written "violino."

No. 7: a recorder sonata in C major.

No. 8: a oboe sonata in C minor.

No. 9: a flute sonata in B minor that actually was written for recorder to play a minor third higher (as HWV 367a).

No. 10: a violin sonata in G minor thought by many to be spurious.

No. 11: a recorder sonata in F major related to the Organ Concerto Op. 4, No. 5.

No. 12: another possibly spurious violin sonata, this time in F major.

No. 13: a violin sonata in D major, the high point of the whole collection. This gorgeous sonata da chiesa was not actually composed until around 1750 and wasn't included in Opus 1 until almost a century later.

No. 14: a violin sonata in A major, again very possibly not by Handel.

No. 15: another doubtful violin sonata, in E major. *—Blair Johnston*

Recommended:

○ **Handel: 20 Sonatas Op1** / Wallfisch, Nicholson, Goodwin, Tunnicliffe, Beznosiuk, Beckett / 1995 / Hyperion 66921

Jacobus Handl (Gallus)

b. 1550, Carniola, Slovenia, **d.** Jul. 18, 1591, Prague, Bohemia (Czech Rep.)

Composer: Choral

Jacob Handl was one of the most-respected and serious composers of the late Renaissance period in Austria. (He was so high minded that even his secular madrigals are in Latin.) At the same time, his music was often highly complex, chromatic, and dissonant.

His origins are a bit obscure. If his family had been Slovenian, his natal name might have been Jakob Petelin, the surname in that language meaning "rooster" as do "Handl" and the Latin "Gallus," which he also sometimes used.

The location of his education is a matter for guesswork. Scholars suggest Reifnitz itself, or perhaps a Cistercian monastery in Sticna. Around 1565, he went to Austria to make his fortune. He enjoyed staying in monasteries and lived for a while at the Benedictine abbey in Melk. He arrived in Vienna about 1568 and it is sometimes stated that during this period he became a monk. Historical records are incomplete concerning his movements, but it is known that in 1574, he was a singer in the imperial chapel of Maximilian II. Handl decided to travel more and made his way through Austria, Moravia, Bohemia, and Silesia.

In 1579 or 1580, he was appointed choirmaster to the Bishop of Olmütz (now Olomouc, Czech Republic), Stanislas Pavlovsky. He remained there for five years and then took the post of Kantor of St. Jan na Brzehu, Prague, a post he retained until death. There was a lively literary group centered on that church and it is likely that they performed secular choral music. The position also meant that Handl would sometimes appear and perform at the court of Emperor Rudolf II. Because of these contacts, Handl gained a high reputation for his literary knowledge and compositional skill.

Most of Handl's work consists of sacred Latin settings. The bulk of it is a group of 374 motets making up music for the Proper of the Time, certain Marian festivals, the Common of Saints, and several festivals from the Proper of Saints. The musical style is derived from Netherlands polyphony. He also wrote 20 masses, often on themes he had devised for motets. His secular music uses texts from Ovid, Vergil, Catullus, Horace, and other classical Roman poets.

Handl's rhythmic notation is very subtle, his textures are often very complex, and his music is full of canons. Nevertheless, as a good Counter Reformationist composer, he took care to make the words understandable. His lines often create fully triadic harmony, but there are also chromatic progressions skillfully used for emotional effect. His use of syncopations is remarkable; his rhythmic imagination is hard to match in the era or for many ages afterward. His style may represent one of the most astonishingly accomplished summations of the music of the prior century, but it did not make much mark on the much simpler early Baroque style that followed it, and it remained to the twentieth century to rediscover him. *—Joseph Stevenson*

CHORAL

Overview of Works (ca. 1580–1590)

In Handl's music, one finds a noteworthy integration of the Netherlandish and Italianate techniques and styles of the latter sixteenth century. He was as masterful a composer of polychoral music as he was a brilliant contrapuntist. Indeed, the complexity of his music seems to have earned some criticism during Handl's lifetime. From his death onward, however, his music has received almost unanimous praise. Most of the music that has come down to us—all choral music—was published during his lifetime.

The bulk of his work was for liturgical use, comprising literally hundreds of motets, 20 masses, and three Passion settings. A majority of the motets (374 to be exact) are in the four-volume *Opus musicum*, providing music for the Propers for Sundays and feast days. Sixteen of the 20 masses are distributed over four volumes of mass settings. With three exceptions, the secular works are set to Latin texts, and are contained in two collections totaling four volumes.

Regarding counterpoint, Handl's music is full of ingenious canonic writing. In general, counterpoint is an organic part of composition, not a stilted layer. As would be expected with a composer working in the Netherlands tradition, there is much borrowed material used in his masses and motets. Many of the masses are parody masses, most based on his own motets, but some on secular songs of Franco-Netherlandish contemporaries and predecessors, such as Clemens non Papa, Crecquillon, Verdelot and Lassus. In the rhythmic sphere, Handl's use of rhythmic notation earned him mention by Michael Praetorius. Striking syncopations abound in the secular choral works. Harmonically, his music sounds as thought it is informed more by the major-minor system of tonality that was to come than the modal harmony of the day. Chromaticism also plays a significant role, particularly in the setting of affective texts. Handl was quite responsive to the meaning of words, and one can find plenty of word-painting typical of the time. His proficiency with the Venetian polychoral idiom is quite notable. Imaginative sonorities and clarity are the hallmarks of his practice. The eighteenth century writers Walther and Burney both admired the four-choir, 24-voice psalm settings for All Saints' Day that close the *Opus musicum*. *—Neil Cardew-Fanning*

Recommended:

○ **Iacobus Handl-Gallus: Moralia; Harmoniae Morales (Box Set)** / Handl (Gallus): Diversos diversa iuvant, Handl (Gallus): Tempore felici multi numerantur amici / Singer Pur / Ars Musici 1262

Hanover Band

f. 1980, Sussex, England

Ensemble

The Hanover Band is a period instrument chamber orchestra based in Sussex, England. It attracted much attention early on for its individual performance style, which often puzzled critics and created controversy. Certain recordings, the Beethoven nine symphonies in particular, have managed to generate both awards and sharp criticism.

Founded in 1980 by Caroline Brown, the Hanover Band has given concerts in a variety of locations, but has resided in the Old Market Building, Hove, Sussex, since November 1998. Its first concert took place at St. Margaret's Westminster (London) on March 26, 1980, under the direction of Marie Leonhardt. In May of that year, Monica Huggett was appointed music director of the Hanover Band. In 1981, Roy Goodman became a regular conductor and over the years, other illustrious figures would guest conduct the group, such as Sir Charles Mackerras and Nicholas McGegan. By January, 1982, the Hanover Band's first recording was issued on Nimbus Records, an all-Beethoven release featuring Huggett conducting the *Symphony No. 1*, paired with the *Piano Concerto No. 1*, for which soloist Mary Verney performed on the fortepiano. This recording of the symphony, it would turn out, was the first in a set that would include all nine Beethoven symphonies issued later in the decade on Nimbus. On March 31, 1982, Sir Charles Mackerras led the ensemble in a memorable concert of music by Haydn in Westminster Abbey, marking the 250th anniversary of the composer's birth. Over the next few years, the Hanover Band issued recordings at an increasing rate and gave numerous concerts and tours abroad. They appeared in a memorable televised Beethoven concert from Whitehall on April 9, 1985, and then on May 3 initiated a six-week-long series entitled *Basically Beethoven*, from London's Queen Elizabeth Hall. The ensemble's first tour of the United States came in October, 1985. By 2002, the group had made ten such concert tours of the U.S. In 1986, Roy Goodman was appointed principal conductor of the ensemble. He led the players in many successful concerts over the years, but perhaps his greatest legacy was the completion of the Beethoven symphony cycle started by Huggett. Goodman finished the cycle in 1988 and the set received at least two major awards, the first from the Music Retailers Association (Best Box Set) in 1989, and a Record of the Year Award from *Fono Forum* (1990). Yet many critics expressed varying degrees of disapproval of the performances, largely owing to brisk tempos and what they considered unusual phrasing. In 1994, Roy Goodman stepped down as principal conductor and was succeeded by Anthony Halstead. The Hanover Wind Band was formed the following year as an off-shoot of the ensemble. Its focus has been repertory from the latter half of the nineteenth and early twentieth centuries, taking on serious as well as ragtime music. In 1999, the Hanover Band launched a one-year music education project in Brighton & Hove entitled "No Beethoven, No Beat," successfully introducing young audiences to the symphonies of Beethoven. In 2001, Halstead and the Hanover Band completed a massive recording project they began in 1995 for the label cpo that offered the complete works of Johann Christian Bach. The set is comprised of 22 discs. *—Robert Cummings*

Recommended:

- ○ **J.C. Bach: Symphonies Op9** / Halstead (cond.), Hanover Band / CPO 999487
- ○ **J.C. Bach: Symphonies Op6** / Halstead (cond.), Hanover Band / CPO 999298
- ○ **Haydn: Symphonies 9, 10, 11 & 12** / Goodman (cond.), Hanover Band / 2002 / Hyperion 55113
- ○ **18th C. British Symphonies** / Lea-Cox (cond.), Hanover Band / 2001 / ASV 216
- ○ **Haydn: Symphony 82, 83 & 84** / Goodman (cond.), Hanover Band / 2003 / Hyperion 55123
- ○ **J.C. Bach: Symphonies Concertantes Vol. 5** / Halstead (cond.), Hanover Band / CPO 999628

Howard Hanson

b. Oct. 28, 1896, Wahoo, NE, **d.** Feb. 26, 1981, Rochester, NY

Composer: Symphonic, Orchestral, Concerto, Choral

Howard Hanson was among the first twentieth century American composers to achieve widespread prominence. In contrast to the angular Stravinskian and Americana-influenced sounds that dominated American concert music prior to World War II, Hanson wrote in an unabashedly Romantic idiom influenced by his Nordic roots. Of particular importance to the composer was the music of Sibelius; however, he also acknowledged the influence of composers such as Palestrina and Bach.

After boyhood studies on the piano, Hanson studied music at the Institute of Musical Art in New York City and Northwestern University, where he earned a degree in 1916. In 1921, he became the first American to win the Prix de Rome, which provided him the opportunity to study with Ottorino Respighi, whose colorful orchestral language was clearly an influence on Hanson's own. Upon his return to the United States, Hanson was appointed head of the Eastman School of Music at the University of Rochester at the age of 28. Under the composer's guidance over the course of more than four decades, Eastman became one of the world's preeminent educational institutions. During his tenure there Hanson continued to compose prolifically; he also embarked on a career as a conductor, in which capacity he proved himself one of the great champions of American music. At Eastman, it has been calculated, he presented some 1,500 works by 700 composers. Hanson also commercially recorded a number of modern works in a series for the Mercury label in the 1950s, drawing much attention to otherwise neglected repertoire.

Hanson's most characteristic works are undoubtedly his seven symphonies. The first of these, the *"Nordic" Symphony* (1922), dates from the composer's studies in Rome. The *Second Symphony ("Romantic")*, remains Hanson's best-known work, a characteristic realization of the lush, lyric aesthetic with which is closely associated. Further notable among Hanson's symphonies are the *Symphony No. 4* (1943), awarded the Pulitzer Prize, and the *Symphony No. 7* (1977), one of a series of works inspired by the poetry of Walt Whitman. Other important works in Hanson's catalogue include The *Lament for Beowulf* (1925) for chorus and orchestra; the opera *Merry Mount* (1933), well received at its premiere and in subsequent productions, but now rarely performed; and a variety of other chamber, vocal, and orchestral works. *—Michael Rodman*

SYMPHONIC

Symphony No. 2 ("Romantic"), Op. 30 (1930)

The frequent classification of Howard Hanson as a "neo-Romantic" composer is certainly not without merit, though the case is perhaps disproportionately affected by the overwhelming success of his *Second Symphony*, which has maintained a stronger foothold in the canon than any of his other works. Still, the composer himself lists as his greatest influence—even above Respighi, with whom Hanson studied at the Academy of Santa Cecilia in Rome—the last great romantic symphonist, Jean Sibelius. Indeed, the melodic warmth and accessibility of Sibelius' *Fifth Symphony* (which itself seemed to revert to a more traditional style than had been reached in the *Fourth*) can certainly be heard in the more tranquil moments of Hanson's *"Romantic" Symphony*, though it is often interrupted by the sort of endearingly melodramatic "plot-thickenings" of Grieg.

The development of Hanson's music materials in the *Second Symphony* proceeds in a very direct manner, which is perhaps why the work has been so well-received by audiences. Take for example, the opening of the first movement (marked Adagio; Allegro Moderato): a simple stepwise ascent of a minor third is reiterated in different instrumental guises, gradually amassing volume and strength before being carried by the crash of cymbals into the next episode. Such buildups of orchestral weight and dramatic tension are set in contrast with passages of rhapsodic lyricism, in which long, arching lines float above ebbing accompanimental textures. These same characteristics are found in the subsequent two movements as well.

The second (Andante con tenerezza) begins with a simple melody doubled in harmonious thirds; this is eventually joined by a countermelody in the horn, then a high descant in the strings. Here we find Hanson employing a few harmonic surprises, albeit in an extremely conservative fashion: suspensions remain dissonant just a bit longer than we expect them to before resolving; the horn line occasionally leaps beyond its melodic mark before settling into consonance with the flutes. It is often in transitions between sections that we find Hanson stepping furthest outside of traditional tonality: as this idyllic flute episode ends, a menacing, polytonal dissonance in the bass emerges, leading to a recollection of the haunting minor third descent that began the entire work.

These opposing forces gradually find reconciliation over the course of the middle movement, though not without considerable difficulty (and a few heart-wrenching harmonic deceptions). As the third and final movement opens, a carnivalesque, *Petrushka*-like fanfare build and breaks into a subdued and pensive string passage, which itself cedes to an even more explicit allusion to Stravinsky: the insistent ostinati and heavy-handed drums that follow underscore a brass line that owes an unmistakable debt to *Rite of Spring*. This initiates yet another orchestrational snowball, which gathers thunder before finally exhausting itself and languishing in a return to the lush melody that sought repose in both the previous movements. The ease with which the ear makes these large-scale, structural connections, adds to the accessibility as well as the emotional engagement of this work. *—Jeremy Grimshaw*

Recommended:

- ○ **Hanson Conducts Hanson** / Hanson (cond.), Eastman-Rochester Pops Orch. / 1990 / Mercury 432008
- ○ **Hanson: Symphony 2; Barber: Violin Concerto** / Slatkin (cond.), St. Louis SO / 1987 / EMI 47850

Symphony No. 6 (1968)

This approximately 20-minute symphony consists of six short movements, played without pause. They are linked by a somewhat ubiquitous three-note ascending motif that appears at the outset. On the whole the work is emotionally cooler than Hanson's other, more overtly Romantic symphonies. It has, in fact, an austerity about it, which is especially evident in the three-and-a-half minute opening Andante. The three-note motif permeates this panel, bringing with it a bleakness of mood and almost desperate sense of struggle.

The second and third movements, at nearly five minutes each, are the longest of the six. The former is marked Allegro scherzando and opens with two anxious, competing snare drums and a triangle, then turns bright and colorful, without jettisoning the sense of tension and conflict. In the latter half, the music becomes more agitated, finally petering out in the closing pages. The third movement (Adagio) looks more toward the composer's Romantic side than any other. The music soars beautifully, and just when you think it is falling apart, it revives and revels in its warmth and lyrical beauty.

The two-minute fourth movement (Allegro) scurries along with a nervous, almost playful sense, slowing for a brief recollection of the motto theme. The ensuing Adagio builds slowly through somber, lower-range timbres in its first half to bring on a sense of triumph at the close of its three-minute duration. The two-minute finale takes off like an anxious bullet from the Adagio's exploding gun. It brims with energy and seems in hot pursuit of something. The "something" turns out to be the motto theme, which triumphantly returns to close out the symphony. *—Robert Cummings*

Recommended:

- ○ **Hanson: Symphonies 3 & 6; Fantasy Variations on a Theme of Youth** / Schwarz (cond.), Johnson, Baunton, Seattle SO / 1990 / Delos 3092

Symphony No. 7 ("A Sea Symphony") (1977)

Symphony No. 7 "A Sea Symphony" was Hanson's last work in the genre. Its music, valedictorian and celestial in character, and its texts, derived from Walt Whitman's *Leaves of Grass*, combine to clearly suggest a picture of a life nearing its happy end. This view hardly assumes any element of controversy with the revelation that the composer was in his 81st year when he wrote the symphony. The work is cast in three movements and generally lasts a bit less than 20 minutes. The opening panel, marked Largamente, begins quietly and mysteriously, the orchestra gradually swelling in sound until the chorus intones the words "Lo, the unbounded sea," which comprise the subtitle for this movement. The music then takes on an ethereal and somewhat triumphant character thereafter, striking the listener as more a choral tone poem than a symphony. The second movement, at about four minutes, is the shortest of the three. Marked Adagio and subtitled "The untold want," it clings to the same ethereal sense, but is somewhat bleak and much darker than the opening panel. The finale begins briskly, with swirling energy from the orchestra (Allegro molto). Shortly after the chorus enters with the words "Joy, shipmate, joy!" (again, the subtitle of the movement), the orchestra proclaims a brief and grand quotation from the composer's *Symphony No. 2 "Romantic."* The music soon turns restless, then grows quiet before majestically building as the chorus serenely and triumphantly sings about the voyage toward "unknown shores." The ending is ecstatic, conveying a sense of both confidence and joy. —*Robert Cummings*

Recommended:

- **Hanson: Symphonies 5 & 7; Piano Concerto; Mosaics** / Schwarz (cond.), Sparks, Seattle SO & Chorale / 1992 / Delos 3130

ORCHESTRAL

Merry Mount, suite from the opera, Op. 31 (1938)

That he lived in the twentieth century not withstanding, Howard Hanson was a Romantic of the purest sort. He stated that music should be "a manifestation of the emotions," and his works glow from within with passion. His most ambitious work was his opera, *Merry Mount*. Based upon a Nathaniel Hawthorne short story, it is a tale of tragic love set in Puritan New England in which a pastor becomes obsessed with a visiting woman and subsequently runs amok. The opera was first performed in 1934 to thunderous success at no less venue than the Metropolitan Opera in New York. The suite, crafted by Hanson four years later, is a set of four short pieces, all brilliantly evocative and characteristically intense. The opera's overture, a brief "Children's Dance," a mournful "Love Duet," and finally a rousing Prelude to Act II and "Maypole Dances" comprise the 16-minute suite. —*Michael Morrison*

Recommended:

- **Hanson: Orchestral Works Vol. 1** / Schermerhorn (cond.), Nashville Symphony / 2000 / Naxos 559072
- **The Composer & His Orchestra** / Hanson (cond.), Eastman-Rochester Orch. & Chorus / 1996 / Mercury 434370

CONCERTO

Serenade for flute, harp & strings, Op. 35 (1944)

On July 24, 1946, Howard Hanson married Margaret Elizabeth Nelson. As a wedding present for her, Hanson composed the *Serenade*, Op. 35 (three years later Hanson also had written the *Pastorale* for oboe, harp and strings, Op. 38 for her). A couple of somewhat darker sections provide some contrast, but the clouds lift rather quickly, leading back to the more pastoral music that dominates this work as well as the *Pastorale*.

This piece is everything a composer's wedding gift to his bride should be: ardent, romantic, and lovely. Despite the tenderness of the music, it flows along with a considerable rhythmic impulse. Using one of the special scales that Hanson sometimes devised for himself, it possesses unusual and original twists to the melodies which give it an indefinable exotic flavor. This gentle six-minute work is a genuine treasure in the flute's repertoire of short pieces, second only to Griffes' *Poem* among American contributions to that literature. —*AMG*

Recommended:

- **Great American Composers Collection** / Schwarz (cond.), Jolles, Mendenhall, New York Chamber Symphony / 2002 / Delos 3708

CHORAL

The Lament for Beowulf, for chorus & orchestra, Op. 25 (1925)

In 1921 Howard Hanson received the Prix de Rome, which gave him the opportunity to live, study, and work in Italy for three years. During a side trip to England, Hanson came across a copy of the Old English epic poem *Beowulf*, as translated by William Morris and A.J. Wyatt. Thinking that its ending would make a striking musical setting, Hanson started work on the *Lament for Beowulf* in Scotland, which was, as Hanson later wrote, "an environment rugged, swept with mist, and wholly appropriate to the scene" of the piece. Hanson continued his setting back in Rome, and completed it in 1925 just after he had returned to America and taken the post of director of the Eastman School of Music. The work was given its premiere at the 1926 Ann Arbor Festival, in a performance conducted by Hanson himself (who later recorded the work as well).

The poem, which dates to approximately 700 A.D., tells of Beowulf's killing of the monster Grendel and its mother, his long reign as King of the Geats, his mortal struggle with a dragon that ends in the deaths of both, and Beowulf's funeral rites. It is this last portion of the story that Hanson sets in his work. The composer once made reference to the "austerity and stoicism" and the "heroic atmosphere" of the poem, and it is these qualities that he emphasized in his musical setting—an imposing one for mixed chorus and full orchestra—along with the timeless quality of the poem and its humanity.

There is a dramatic stride to the orchestra prelude that opens the work. As a funeral pyre is constructed, women lament the death of their king, communicate their "sorrow careful," in music of unaffected sadness. Great words are spoken of Beowulf, and the music turns dramatic as the chorus, singing in majestic polyphony, recounts the treasures that are to be buried with him. The work ends with a eulogy of the hero, with the words of praise accompanied by lovely, peaceful music. —*Chris Morrison*

Recommended:

- **Hanson: Symphony 3; Elegy; Lament For Beowulf** / Hanson (cond.), Eastman-Rochester Orch. & Chorus / 1991 / Mercury 434302

Pierre Hantaï

b. 1964, Paris, France

Harpsichordist

French harpsichordist Pierre Hantaï began to study his instrument of choice from the age of 12 with Arthur Haas; later he continued his lessons with Gustav Leonhardt. In 1983 Hantaï scored his first major triumph through taking first prize at the International Bach-Handel Competition of Bruges in Belgium; since then, Hantaï has collected an impressive number of honors and awards.

In 1985 Hantaï founded the chamber group le Concert Français with his brothers Marc Hantaï and Jérome Hantaï and violinist François Fernandez. At the same time, Hantaï became a regular member of la Petite Bande, a period instrument orchestra led by Sigiswald Kuijken. Hantaï has also worked extensively with conductors Philippe Herreweghe and his former teacher Gustav Leonhardt. On his own, Hantaï's recordings of works of Johann Sebastian Bach have garnered him special praise from critics, in particular his two recordings of the *Goldberg Variations*, made in 1992 and 2002, respectively. But Hantaï also specializes in seventeenth century English keyboard music and in the works of Domenico Scarlatti. —*Uncle Dave Lewis*

Recommended:

- **Scarlatti 1: Harpsichord Sonatas** / Hantaï / 2002 / Ambroisie 9918
- **Scarlatti: 22 Sonates pour clavecin** / Hantaï / 2001 / Astree 8836
- **Bach: Goldberg Variations** / Hantaï / Mirare 9945

John Harris Harbison

b. Dec. 20, 1938, Orange, NJ

Composer

John Harris Harbison is among the most prominent and prolific of American composers; his highly varied and interesting output has earned him the moniker, "the great master of ambiguity." His principal works include three string quartets, three symphonies, the cantata *The Flight Into Egypt* (Pulitzer Prize, 1987), and three operas, including *The Great Gatsby* (commissioned by The Metropolitan Opera—premiered there, 1999).

Harbison was born in Orange, New Jersey, on December 20, 1938, and grew up in Princeton. While a teenager he received musical guidance from Roger Sessions, one of his formative influences, while also developing considerable skills as a jazz pianist. Other of Harbison's teachers include Walter Piston at Harvard, Boris Blacher at the Berlin Hochschule für Musik, and Earl Kim at Princeton. As influential as any teacher was Harbison's marriage to violinist Rose Mary Pederson—the inspiration for many of his violin pieces. Since 1969, he has been professor of music at the Massachusetts Institute of Technology, necessitating his becoming a "summer composer." More than 30 of his compositions have been recorded on the Nonesuch, Northeastern, Harmonia Mundi, New World, Decca, Koch, Centaur, Archetype, and CRI labels. His music is published exclusively by Associated Music Publishers.

Exceptional economy and expressive range mark Harbison's music. His works embrace elements of jazz as well as the early and late Baroque styles of Heinrich Schütz and J. S. Bach. At times, the harmonic palette brings to mind the sound of Prokofiev or the rigorous serialism of 1950s Stravinsky. He is also a practiced writer on the art and craft of composition, and was recognized in his student years as an outstanding poet, later writing the libretto for his *The Great Gatsby*.

Harbison's music first garnered national attention with the Boston Symphony Orchestra's 1976 premiere of *Diotima*, a commission by the Koussevitzky Foundation. This, his first major work for orchestra, showed him an adept symphonic composer—a talent that he then applied to a string of concerted works, such as his *Piano Concerto* (1978) (recipient of the 1980 Kennedy Center Friedheim Award), and the *Violin Concerto* (1978–80, rev. 1987), written for and premiered by Rose Mary Harbison. Other concertos came later, including one for viola (1989), oboe (1991), cello (1993), and flute (1993).

Occasionally, as in *The Most Often Used Chords (Gli accordi più usati)* of 1993, Harbison enjoys putting compositional restrictions on himself to ignite his imagination. A great percentage of Harbison's works are for voice—either solo, small ensemble, or large chorus; most notable among these are his *Mirabai Songs* (for soprano and percussion ensemble) and his operas, which (besides the aforementioned *Gatsby*) are: *Full Moon In March* (1977) and *Winter's Tale* (1974, rev. 1991).

Harbison has worked extensively as a conductor, particularly with the Cantata Singers (1969–73) and the new-music group Collage (established in 1984). He is a champion of twentieth century music, especially composers he feels have been neglected, such as Luigi Dallapiccola. *—John Palmer*

Overview of Works

The music of John Harbison reflects the eclectic approach of contemporary composers that began in the later third of the twentieth century. In this, the conveyance of a musical idea was held to be of primary importance, the means (i.e., adherence to a particular style, theory, or school) secondary. Thus, a composer in his career may be found to explore serialism in one work, minimalism in the next, and then follow that with an essay in neo-Romanticism. Typically, Harbison's output reveals a varied source of influences. The composer's formative years were against the backdrop of a cosmopolitan and open-minded upbringing. Thus, a love of Bach was compatible with Harbison's heading his own jazz band on keyboard in his adolescence. Later studies at Harvard with Walter Piston nurtured a neo-Classic bent, enhanced by a love of mid- and late-period Stravinsky. One of the elder of the current generation of composers, he felt the influence of serialism that was still mainstream in the mid-twentieth century. Thus, even within one piece, these sundry factors can be found juxtaposed, producing a Mahlerian spectrum of musical-emotional experience. Rarely is tonality totally absent from any work; it can frequently be found emerging from the jazz-oriented sections, acting as a tempering or equalizing factor rather than as protagonist or antagonist. This can be found as early as the 1961 *Duo for Flute and Piano* or in the 1991 *Three City Blocks* for band, in which the foresaid processes are threaded together by the rough-hewn urban Romanticism reminiscent of Leonard Bernstein's metropolitan forays. In his operas, Harbison uses a similarly catholic approach to the externals as well as the musical fabric. The action is often carried forward not just by the singing of the principals, but also by means of instrumental narrative, dance, pantomime, and musical narration. These characteristics can be found as early as his 1974 premiere opera *A Winter's Tale* (after Shakespeare). Even in 1999's *The Great Gatsby* (after Fitzgerald), Harbison, an accomplished poet and writer, supplied his own libretti, in the case of the latter in collaboration with M. Horwitz. Far from being an ivory tower composer, Harbison has used his art as an expression of social conscience and empathy, as evinced by the 1995 song cycle *Flashes and Dedications* written to commemorate the 50th Anniversary of the Normandy Landing, as well as that same year's *Flute of Interior Time* for voice and piano. The former was composed as part of a requiem to honor the victims of World War II, the latter as part of the Heartbeats AIDS Quilt Songbook project. In such works, the composer takes up the prophetic challenge of Copland in the 1930s for the modern composer to reconnect with the public; for Harbison, this is a social as well as artistic calling. *—Wayne Reisig*

Recommended:

- ○ **Harbison: 4 Songs of Solitude; Variations; Twilight Music** / Blumenthal, Jansen, Krug, Oudenweijer / 2003 / Naxos 8559173
- ○ **Simple Daylight, Words From Paterson** / Upshaw, Kalish, Sylvan, Boston Symphony Chamber Players / 1993 / Nonesuch 79189
- ○ **Flight into Egypt & other works** / Previn (cond.), Sylvan, Felty, Anderson, Los Angeles PO, LA Phil. New Music Group, Cantata Singers & Ens. / 1990 / New World 80395
- ○ **Harbison: Violin Concerto; Recordare** / Smith (cond.), Kelley, Wilkinson, Anderson, Geha, Emmanuel Music Orch. & Chorus / 1997 / Koch 37310
- ○ **Harbison: Samuel Chapter; Ulysses' Bow** / Previn (cons.), Pittsburgh SO / Nonesuch 79129
- ○ **Harbison: Mirabai Songs; Variations** / Felty, Rose / Northeastern 230
- ○ **Harbison: Most Often Used Chords; Flute Concerto; Symphony 3** / Miller (cond.), Bowman, Albany SO / 2000 / Albany 390

John Harle

b. Sep. 20, 1956, Newcastle-upon-Tyne, England

Saxophonist

John Harle's first instrument was the clarinet, and his teacher on that instrument was Jack Brymer. At age 13, Harle expressed to Brymer the frustration he was experiencing in trying to create the clarinet sound he wanted. Brymer suggested a switch to the saxophone, which proved a natural fit for Harle. His skills soon won him admission into the Royal College of Music in London, where he studied until 1980; he supplemented his education with two years at the Paris Conservatoire. Back in London, Harle made the acquaintance of composer Michael Nyman, joining the latter's band in 1982; Nyman eventually supplied Harle with a full-scale concerto, entitled *Where the Bee Dances*. Through his work with Nyman, Harle also gained entry into the world of film and television scores. In 1987, Harle was named professor of Saxophone and Chamber Music at the Guildhall School of Music and Drama in London. In 1988 he was the subject of a BBC2 special, "A Man and his Sax"; that same year, the score he co-wrote with Stanley Myers for the film *Prick Up Your Ears* won the Best Achievement in a Feature Film award at Cannes.

By 1991, Harle was recording for both EMI and Argo as a saxophone soloist. Harle's work for EMI reflected his standard concert programs. These included the Debussy *Rhapsodie*, Villa-Lobos' *Fantasia* and *In the Shadow of the Duke*, Harle's tribute to his idol, Duke Ellington saxophonist Johnny Hodges. Harle's Argo recordings feature works written by living composers, including Dominic Muldowney, Gavin Bryars, Luciano Berio, and Mike Westbrook, with Harle specifically in mind. In 1993, Harle composed a commercial jingle for Nissan entitled *Nissan Donna*; Jazzy B of the hip-hop group Soul II Soul remixed the tune as a single, which made it to number six on the British pop charts. Harle's performance of Harrison Birtwistle's *Panic at the Last Night of the Proms* in 1995 garnered him a great deal of positive critical attention. Since then, Harle has concentrated strongly on serious composition in addition to his saxophone playing, concertizing, and film work. In 1996 he collaborated with vocalists Sarah Leonard and Elvis Costello on the album *Terror and Magnificence*, released on Argo. The disc went into the top ten in the U.K., and was followed by a brief concert tour the following year. The following year, Harle contributed to another hit record as part of the arranging staff that worked on Sir Paul McCartney's *Standing Stone*. The year 1998 witnessed the debut of Harle's opera *Angel Magick*, based on the life of sixteenth century alchemist John Dee, with a libretto by David Pourtnoy. *Angel Magick* gained some notoriety for its introduction of full frontal nudity to the stage of the Proms.

As a soloist, Harle has toured worldwide, and claims to be the most recorded classical saxophonist in history. In 2000, Harle renewed his association with Sir Paul McCartney, arranging McCartney's *Nova*, a tribute to the ex-Beatle's late wife, for the memorial benefit album *A Garland for Linda*. *—Uncle Dave Lewis*

Recommended:

- ○ **Saxophone Concertos** / Marriner (cond.), Harle, Academy of St. Martin-in-the-Fields / 1997 / EMI 72109
- ○ **Harle: Terror + Magificence** / Harle, Edwards, Leonard, Balanescu, Balanescu Quartet, John Harle Band, London Voices / 1996 / Argo 452605

Nikolaus Harnoncourt

b. Dec. 6, 1929, Berlin, Germany

Conductor

Perhaps no single musician has ever achieved such high accomplishment across such a broad span of repertory as Nikolaus Harnoncourt. His first professional job was as cellist for the Vienna Symphony Orchestra. Almost immediately, however, Harnoncourt sought to specialize in performing music of the past upon historically correct instruments; he was one of the first professional musicians to do so. Over the course of a stunningly influential career, Harnoncourt has gradually worked forward into more modern repertories. His many awards include repeated top recording medals from at least six European countries, and a Grammophone Award for Special Achievement in 1990. His decades of recordings on the Teldec label fully encompass seven centuries of music history.

Harnoncourt considers his own life strongly influenced by an adolescence under the shadow of Nazism. He was born Nikolaus de la Fontaine und d'Harnoncourt in Berlin; his aristocratic family moved south to its ancestral mansion in Graz, Austria. After years of hardship under the Nazi regime, the Harnoncourt family fled to Salzburg in 1945. There he found his calling, and began studying the cello under Paul Grummer. No less a figure than Herbert von Karajan accepted Harnoncourt into the Vienna Symphony in 1952. However, his path was destined elsewhere. While in college, Harnoncourt became fascinated by the original Baroque instruments languishing in antique shops, and wondered why professional musicians didn't use these brilliant artifacts to produce the music of their time.

In 1953, Harnoncourt and his wife Alice founded the Concentus Musicus Wien, the first professional Baroque orchestra. They took players from the symphony, trained collaboratively for four years on early instruments, and exploded onto the European scene in 1957. Their first recording project was the Purcell *Viol Fantasias*, followed by a series of highly acclaimed recordings of the major works of Bach. In the 1970s, Harnoncourt and Gustav Leonhardt collaborated on a massive recording project of all Bach's cantatas. Meanwhile, Harnoncourt and Concentus Musicus romped through much of the Baroque literature, including Monteverdi's operas, Telemann, Rameau, and Fux. Later, he broadened his repertory to include Haydn and Mozart with Concentus Musicus, as well as masterworks from the nineteenth century operatic and symphonic repertory (including a million-selling cycle of Beethoven symphonies) with the Chamber Orchestra of Europe, the Berlin Philharmonic, and the Concertgebouw Orchestra. He taught as professor of performance practice at the Salzburg Mozarteum (1972–93), and has written three full-length books on the subject closest to his heart. *—Timothy Dickey*

Recommended:

- ○ **Haydn: Symphonies 30, 45, & 73** / Harnoncourt (cond.), Vienna Concentus Musicus / 1995 / Teldec 10016
- ○ **Monteverdi: L'Incoronazione Di Poppea** / Harnoncourt (cond.), Berberian, Esswood, Langridge, Soderstrom, Vienna Concentus Musicus / 1993 / Teldec 42547
- ○ **Bach: Motets** / Harnoncourt (cond.) / 1984 / Teldec 842663

○ **Handel: Water Music** / Harnoncourt (cond.), Vienna Concentus Musicus / 1996 / Teldec 450997987

○ **Zelenka: Hipocondrie; Trio Sonata; Overture** / Harnoncourt (cond.), Vienna Concentus Musicus / 1997 / Teldec 17386

Ofra Harnoy

b. Jan. 31, 1965, Hadera, Israel

Cellist

Canadian cellist Ofra Harnoy is one of the best-known performers on her instrument worldwide. She has given concerts on five continents and has played at the request of Charles, Prince of Wales; President Bill Clinton; three Canadian Prime Ministers; and several times for the Imperial Japanese family.

Harnoy was not born in Canada but in Israel, daughter to Jacob Harnoy, a classical record producer and compulsive record collector whose holdings run to more than 30,000 items. She received her first instruction on the cello from her father, who is a violinist; more serious studies were undertaken with Vladimir Orloff after Harnoy immigrated with her family to Canada. Harnoy made her debut in Toronto at the age of ten; at 14 she participated in the Aldeburgh Festival, where she met her idol cellist Jacqueline Du Pré and then studied for three years with Du Pré's teacher William Pleeth. In 1982 Harnoy won an International Concert Artist's Guild Award, and in 1983 *Musical America* magazine named her its "young musician of the year."

Harnoy has enjoyed the benefits of a long (by postmodern standards) association with a major label, BMG Classics, beginning in 1987. These recordings elicited considerable comment, not so much from the music involved as from the dolled-up, glamour-conscious photos on the front covers of the releases. Some critics carped about Harnoy's pop star appearance, and in doing so missed the brave stand Harnoy made for neglected and significant cello music—Harnoy recorded nearly all of the Vivaldi concertos, the mega-difficult Offenbach concerto, and works by Viotti, Myslivecek, and Lalo.

Harnoy's work for BMG Classics concluded after 15 releases in 1999, ending so abruptly that it stranded her recording of the Elgar *Cello Concerto.* A couple of years earlier Harnoy likewise broke free from the influence of her father Jacob Harnoy, who had acted as her manager. Although recordings have not figured into her later career, Harnoy has continued in teaching master classes and in concertizing, an activity she enjoys the most among her endeavors. As Harnoy once stated in an interview; "The only time I really feel that I'm making music is when I'm performing. I love feeling the vibrations of the audience, when they hold their breath through the silences, which is when I really feel a bond. It's an incredible experience." *—Uncle Dave Lewis*

Recommended:

○ **The Art of Ofra Harnoy Vol. 1** / Harnoy, etc. / Mastersound 12

○ **Vivaldi Sonatas** / Harnoy, Tilney / RCA 60430

Lynn Harrell

b. Jan. 30, 1944, New York, NY

Cellist

Lynn Harrell, born to musician parents, at the age of eight decided to learn the cello, taking initial lessons with Heinrich Joachim of the New York Philharmonic. When the family moved to Dallas, Texas, Lynn found an excellent teacher in Lev Aronson, the first to recognize his talent. Lynn says that Aronson "showed me passion, for the instrument, for music and for life." After high school Lynn entered the Juilliard School, studying with the renowned Leonard Rose. Harrell then went to the Curtis Institute for further studies with Orlando Cole, who recommended that Harrell join an orchestra as preparation for his desired solo career. Harrell consulted with his godfather Robert Shaw. At the time Shaw was the choral director of the Cleveland Orchestra under conductor Georg Szell. Shaw arranged an audition for Harrell, who, at the age of 18, won a spot in the orchestra. Two years later Mr. Szell appointed him principal cellist, a position he held until 1971.

Harrell's years at Cleveland yielded a lifelong friendship with the orchestra's associate conductor James Levine. Levine helped acquaint Harrell with a wide range of repertoire, particularly the music of the post-World War II era. Levine inspired Harrell to study all aspects of his own playing style: "I ripped it apart and built it back together again," he says. Rather than simply learning the cello parts of the orchestral pieces he played, he studied the full scores. He has maintained that habit during his solo career, studying all aspects of the accompaniment to the solo works he plays. He strongly urges string players contemplating a solo career to follow his lead and first play in an orchestra or chamber ensemble. When Szell passed-away, Harrell was 27 and felt he was ready to pursue his solo career, so he left the Cleveland Orchestra. For his first engagement in New York, the initial audience turnout was dismal. He subsisted on a small number of concerts, and managed to attract the attention of savvy New York impresarios. In 1972 he was invited to appear as soloist with the Chamber Music Society of Lincoln Center. The *New York Times* enthused, "This young man has everything." His career began to build and in 1975 it reached a decisive turning point when he won the prestigious Avery Fisher Prize, launching his solo career into the international limelight.

Subsequently, Harrell has become known as one of the world's finest cellists, performing with the leading ensembles of the world. A special part of his life is the Aspen Music Festival, where he has spent his summers performing and teaching for nearly 50 years. He is the recipient of numerous awards including the Piatigorsky Award, and the Ford Foundation Concert Artists' Award. Before Pope John Paul II and the Chief Rabbi of Rome, Harrell appeared in a 1994 Vatican concert dedicated to the memory of those who perished in the Holocaust, with the Royal Philharmonic conducted by Gilbert Levine. Harrell also appeared on the 1994 Grammy Awards broadcast, performing with Itzhak Perlman and Pinchas Zukerman. His extensive discography of over 30 recordings include the complete Bach *Cello Suites,* numerous premieres, and collaborations with the world's foremost artists. *—Joseph Stevenson*

Recommended:

○ **Beethoven: Cello Sonatas** / Harrell, Ashkenazy (piano) / 2000 / Decca 466733

○ **Cello Concertos of Haydn & Vivaldi** / Marriner, Zukerman (conds.), Harrell, Academy of St. Martin-in-the-Fields, English CO / 2001 / EMI 74734

○ **Rachmaninov: Cello Sonata; Vocalise** / Harrell, Ashkenazy / 1986 / London 414340

Roy Harris

b. Feb. 12, 1898, Chandler, OK, **d.** Oct. 1, 1979, Santa Monica, CA

Composer: Symphonic

Roy Harris became a renowned composer on the American scene in the 1940s, owing to the immense popularity of his *Third Symphony.* His mature compositions incorporated folk music or folk-inspired elements with fresh harmonies, often in orchestration that favored wind instruments, fashioning a style that could embrace a mixture of savagery, lyricism, celebration, tenderness, and rural Americana. His choral music divulged characteristics of both chant and the hymn and folk styles of his rural background.

Harris was born in Lincoln County, Oklahoma. After the family moved to the San Gabriel Valley when Roy was about five, he began showing talent on the piano. He quickly developed his keyboard talents and even learned to play the clarinet in high school. By the time he was 18, his skills on the piano and clarinet were quite advanced, but he had not yet written any music. In 1919, he enrolled in the University of California at Berkelely to study sociology, philosophy, history, and economics. He had a short-lived marriage in 1922 to a woman named Davida, and two more unsuccessful marriages before 1936.

Harris began studying composition in his college years, first with Charles Demarest and Ernest Douglas, organists both, and in 1924 with Arthur Farwell. While studying with Farwell, he wrote the Andante to a projected symphony titled, *Our Heritage.* It was premiered in 1926 by Howard Hanson and the Eastman School Orchestra and later that year performed by the New York Philharmonic Orchestra.

At the behest of Aaron Copland, Harris departed for France in 1926 to study with Nadia Boulanger. While there, he wrote the *Concerto for Piano, Clarinet and String Quartet,* his first major success. A 1929 fall in France temporarily crippled the composer, necessitating surgery in the United States and a period of convalescence for most of 1930. In 1933, Copland introduced Harris to Serge Koussevitzky, for whom he would produce his first symphony, "*Symphony 1933.*" This was the composer's greatest success to date.

In 1936, Harris married for the fourth and last time. His bride was Beulah Duffy (whom he called Johana), a pianist on the faculty at Juilliard. Harris' *Third Symphony* premiered in 1939 and became a sensation, achieving many performances and recordings. While Harris scored triumphs with succeeding symphonies such as the 1940 Fourth ("*Folksong Symphony*"), and with other works, he would never again experience success so overwhelming.

Harris' restless nature is underscored by his positions with a number of colleges and universities beginning in the late 1940s: Utah State (1948), Peabody College (1949), Chatham College (1951), Indiana University (1957), UCLA (1961), and the University of the Pacific (1963). He did produce a violin concerto in 1949, but his *Seventh Symphony* (1952; rev. 1955) was perhaps his finest work from the post-war era.

In 1958, Harris, along with Peter Mennin, Roger Sessions, and Ulysses Kay, traveled to the Soviet Union on a cultural exchange mission for the Department of State. There he conducted the Moscow Radio Symphony Orchestra in a performance of his *Fifth Symphony,* and met prominent Soviet composers, including Dmitri Shostakovich.

In the late 1950s, Harris' inspiration slowed, and even when he experienced productive periods thereafter, the results were uneven at best. *Canticle of the Sun* (1960) and "*San Francisco Symphony*" (Symphony No. 8; 1961–62) were examples of his less successful endeavors.

After the failure of his *Eleventh* (1967) and *Twelfth Symphonies* (1967–69), the composer wrote mainly choral, vocal and band music. Harris died on October 1, 1979, after a fall the previous month. *—Robert Cummings*

Overview of Works (1924–1977)

Roy Harris is one of those figures in music thought to have produced only one supreme composition, a single work that is both a masterpiece and widely popular. That work, of course, was his *Symphony No. 3* (1937), a one-movement effort of about 20 minutes' duration that became a sensation within three years of its 1939 premiere by the Boston Symphony Orchestra under the baton of Sergey Koussevitzky. The work was taken up by most other American orchestras in the 1940s and was even conducted by the more traditional-minded and Eurocentric Arturo Toscanini. Its uniquely American mixture of lyrical, pastoral, and heroic music and its powerful, colorful fugue in section four—probably the most effective of the five in the symphony—have nearly always managed to keep the work in or near the fringes of the repertory in the United States and in parts of Europe. Harris, however, would neither repeat this kind of success nor even approach it. Yet he turned out numerous worthwhile compositions in various genres. His symphonies number to 13, among which the *Fifth* (1942; rev. 1946) and the *Seventh* (1952; rev. 1955) are also strong efforts. Harris' 1961 *San Francisco Symphony* (*No. 8*) and 1969 *Pere Marquette Symphony* (*No. 12*) were less successful, religiously inspired efforts. He wrote other works in a religious vein, including his 1948 *Mass for Male Chorus and Organ*. But most of his compositions here were less significant: *Sanctus* (1935), *Rock of Ages* (1939), and others are mostly forgotten today. His efforts on patriotic texts were numerous and not without their modest successes, however. *Abraham Lincoln Walks at Midnight* (1953), for mezzo-soprano, violin, cello, and piano, is quite a compelling work, not least because of Harris' deft marrying of his music's rhythms with those in the text and also because of his subtle sense for drama and masterful instrumentation. Such chamber-sized instrumental ensembles appear in many of Harris' works, such as his piano quintet (1936) written for his wife, pianist Johana (Beulah) Duffy Harris, a work that already divulges the young composer's masterful sense for polyphonic writing. In a way, this strength—this ability to write brilliant fugal, canonic, and other contrapuntal styles of music—would become, according to some musicologists, the one feature he often pursued too zealously. In any event, Harris also produced numerous other chamber works, including the 1939 string quintet and the 1944 *Four Charming Little Pieces*, for violin and piano. Harris also composed a large output of band music. *Cimarron* (1941), which incorporates a chorus, and the *West Point Symphony* are two of his more notable efforts here. His last symphony, *Bicentennial Symphony* (*No. 13*), from 1976, was also scored for band, but is one of his least-successful efforts. Harris' piano music does not comprise a major part of his output, but contains a few significant works, including his challenging *Toccata* and his rather undemanding and charming *Children at Play*. *—Robert Cummings*

Recommended:

- ○ **I Hear America Singing** / Shewan (cond.), Roberts Wesleyan College Chorale, Wesleyan Brass Ens. / 1995 / Albany 164
- ○ **Harris: Cimarron; Piano Concerto; Elegy & Dance; Toccata** / Harris, etc. / Bay Cities 1002
- ○ **Roy Harris** / Smith (cond.), Whitney (cond.), Fulkerson, Louisville Orch. / 2002 / First Edition 5
- ○ **The Great American 9th** / Miller (cond.), Feinberg, Albany SO / 1999 / Albany 350

SYMPHONIC

Symphony No. 3 (1937; revised 1938)

"Let's not kid ourselves," Roy Harris once wrote. "My *Third Symphony* happened to come along when it was needed." At that time, American musicians and audiences had begun to throw off their deference to European musical models and were hungry for music that expressed something uniquely American. Harris' *Symphony No. 3*, conceived in an organic form that takes more inspiration from natural growth than from traditional symphonic development, and molded from indigenous musical materials, satisfied that hunger, propelling Harris to fame and heralding the beginning of a new tradition in American symphonic music. Much of the music in the *Symphony No. 3* comes from a violin concerto that Harris abandoned after the great virtuoso Jascha Heifetz refused it. The symphony itself was originally commissioned by Hans Kindler, at the time the conductor of the National Symphony Orchestra. However, after completing the work, Harris doubted the ability of the NSO to give an adequate performance, and instead presented it to Serge Koussevitzky, conductor of the Boston Symphony Orchestra, in an attempt to repair a rift between the two men. The symphony proved an adequate peace offering, and it received its premiere under Koussevitzky's baton in 1939. The work itself is nominally in one movement, but Harris identified five sections: "Tragic," "Lyric," "Pastoral," "Fugue-Dramatic," and "Dramatic-Tragic." A long, rich, rustic melody on the cellos alone opens the "Tragic" section; it is then harmonized in parallel fourths and fifths by the other strings, and finally receives a independent accompaniment. This sequence of events might be seen as a brief recounting of the early history of music. Horns enter at the beginning of the "Lyric" section, then support a broad melody in the violins which takes cues from the preceding section. After a climax with punching horns and pleading strings, the music settles into the "Pastoral" section, the longest of the five. The winds finally enter in this section, and enter a dialogue with the strings; the woodwinds play fragments, while the strings play music that swells and subsides quickly. The music seems to be pulling itself together from elemental roots, until the winds begin to play little related melodic fragments, derived from folk music, over shimmering string chords; it sounds something like the world's most beautiful hoe down. The horns then enter with boisterous melodic turns that foreshadow the subject of the "Fugue-Dramatic" section. This is one of the more famous melodies in American music, exuberant, open, airy, played on rich strings and sonorous brass, and supported by decisive timpani strokes. Harris develops this for a while in a contrapuntal fashion, but eventually the music slips into a minor-ish mode and becomes the "Dramatic-Tragic" section. This envelops a melody similar to that of the opening movement in ambiguous harmonies from the brass, and punctuation from the timpani. It eventually becomes a march, with the same texture, and some gigantic percussion eventually propels it towards a thunderous conclusion. All who wish to become familiar with American music need to acquaint themselves with Roy Harris' *Symphony No. 3*. *—Andrew Lindemann Malone*

Recommended:

- ○ **American Masters** / Bernstein (cond.), New York PO / 2003 / DG 474439
- ○ **Serge Koussevitzky** / Koussevitzky (cond.), Boston SO / 2002 / EMI 75118

Lou Harrison

b. May 14, 1917, Portland, OR, **d.** Feb. 2, 2003, Lafayette, IN
Composer: Chamber Music, Concerto

Lou Harrison is one of the most inventive and individual of American composers. His music is noted for its pervasive integration of Native American and Asian musical influences and its emphasis on melody and rhythm, often avoiding harmony altogether.

His family moved from Oregon when he was nine, and continued to move frequently around the San Francisco Bay area. The very diverse musical atmosphere of San Francisco was the primary formative force in his life. He could hear Cantonese opera; Gregorian chant; Spanish, Mexican, and Native-American music; and jazz and classical music. The San Francisco Public Library, with its strong music department, enabled him to take armloads of music home to study. He studied jazz piano, Gregorian chant, and conducting while in high school. He took Henry Cowell's course on "Music of the People of the World," further studying counterpoint and composition with Cowell.

He and John Cage both wrote percussion-dominated music and found new percussion instruments in automobile junkyards and import shops; one of their discoveries was the wonderful pitched ringing sound produced by brake drums. Harrison eventually went to the University of California at Los Angeles to work with its dance department. While there, he was a composition pupil of Arnold Schoenberg. Harrison had already developed a love of Renaissance and earlier music. He adopted the old dance form "estampie," a word he translates as "stampede" for his own stamping, highly rhythmic fast movements.

In 1943, he moved to New York where he worked as a musician and writer. It was the unhappiest period of his life; he did not like the place, and found it difficult to make a living, although he did write some 300 music reviews for the Herald Tribune from 1944 to 1947. He developed a stomach ulcer and finally had a nervous breakdown. During this period, he made the acquaintance of Charles Ives and assisted the aged composer by editing and preparing for performance Ives' *Third Symphony*, which Harrison conducted at its premiere. Ives assisted Harrison financially when needed and, when the *Third Symphony* won the Pulitzer Prize in Music, Ives gave Harrison half the money.

The 1947 nervous breakdown resulted in Harrison deciding to change his compositional style. He began to imitate the sounds of gamelan orchestra, which he had first heard at the 1939 Golden Gate Exposition. He studied Harry Partch's theoretical book *Genesis of a Music* (a gift from Virgil Thomson) and was convinced to adopt various forms of just-intonation rather than the fudged tuning of the standard 12-note scale. (He says he wishes musicians were numerically trained, so that he could say, for instance, "Cellos, you gave me a 10/9 there; please give me a 9/8 instead.")

He resumed his high productivity, returned to the West coast in 1951 to settle for life in Aptos, California, with his partner, the late William Colvig, and continued to write music sounding primarily Asian in general, often for unusual combinations of instruments. He first visited Asia in 1961 at a world music symposium. Following that, he became interested in establishing gamelan orchestras in North America, and devised an "American gamelan" made by Colvig from readily obtainable materials. He went on to write hundreds of compositions, and has often been recorded, usually by small, enthusiastic record labels. He developed a system of musical organization based around melodic shapes he calls "melodicles" and analogous rhythmic patterns ("rhythmicals") and durations ("icti controls"). He has won numerous prizes and was celebrated at 80th birthday concerts in 1997. He died in 2003 en route to an Ohio festival dedicated to performances of his works. *—Joseph Stevenson*

Overview of Works (1934–1999)

It would be difficult to identify any Western composer whose works cover a wider technical, stylistic, and even geographic span than do those of Lou Harrison. As an early champion of Charles Ives, a collaborator with John Cage, and a former student of experts as varied as American experimentalist Henry Cowell, serialist pioneer Arnold Schoenberg, and gamelan master K.R.T. Wasitodiningrat, Harrison, a composer with an intimate knowledge of various strands of musical thought, has fostered a body of works encompassing traditional Western ensembles, Eastern instruments, unique hybrids, and compositional approaches ranging from rigorous 12-tone rows to exotic microtonal scales.

Such wide-ranging interests are perhaps most at home in the inherently multicultural collection of instruments in the percussion family, and Harrison's earliest works demonstrate the composer's lifelong fascination with percussion instruments and sounds. Harrison co-composed *Double Music*, a piece for percussion quartet, with John Cage in 1941, a series of five *Canticles* for percussion ensemble during the same period, and a number of other works. These works already demonstrate Harrison's musical globehopping tendencies, utilizing a variety of instruments from around the world as well as traditional Western instruments. Harrison eventually acquired a considerable level of expertise in several nonwestern instruments, and his oeuvre includes a substantial number of works for gamelan (traditional Javanese or Balinese percussion ensemble). One of Harrison's most ambitious projects was to create, with the help of his partner William Colvig, an "American Gamelan," comprised of instruments made from commercially available materials (aluminum, tin cans, etc.) and tuned to a D major diatonic scale. Important works for this ensemble include the *Suite for Violin and American Gamelan* (1974) and an epic work entitled *La Koro Sutro* (1972), for 100-voice chorus, American Gamelan, harp, and organ. The instruments are also employed in Harrison's puppet theater piece, *Young Caesar* (1971), which eventually underwent the transformation into a full-fledged opera (with Western instruments). Harrison's works also include a number of pieces involving Korean and Taiwanese instruments integrated into Western ensembles. These included *Pacifika Rondo* (1963) and *Nova Odo* (1968); his *Music for Violin and Various Instruments* (1967) includes, among other things, a quartet of African mbiras.

Non-Western influences can be heard in a number of his works for Western instruments, such as the glimmering melodic ornamentation and playful percussion of the *Varied Trio* (1987), and the Orientalist contours in some of his larger scale works, such as the *Symphony No. 4* (1990) and the *P'i-p'a Concerto* (1997). Harrison's interest in non-Western sounds enjoys a synergistic relationship with his experiments in alternate tuning systems. Harrison is reported to have composed several microtonal works while still in high school, and later took an interest in just intonation and other tunings. (The tuning system in his *Simfony in Free Style* (1955) is so complex that the work is virtually impossible to perform live.) Harrison's experimental and multicultural attitude conveys strong political messages as well; the opera *Young Caesar* depicts a romance that is not only cross-cultural, but homosexual as well. *—Jeremy Grimshaw*

Recommended:

- ○ **Homage to Lou Harrison** / Facchin (cond.), Tammittam Percussion Ens. / Dynamic 221
- ○ **Homage to Lou Harrison Vol. 2** / Facchin (cond.), Tammittam Percussion Ens. / 2000 / Dynamic 263
- ○ **Homage to Lou Harrison Vol. 3** / Facchin (cond.), Tammittam Percussion Ens. / 2001 / Dynamic 359
- ○ **Harrison: La Koro Sutro** / Brett, Bergamo (conds.), Abel-Steinberg-Winan Trio, American Gamelan / 1988 / New Albion 015
- ○ **Harrison: Concerto for violin & percussion orchestra; Concerto for organ & percussion** / Kraft (cond.), Craighead, Shapiro, Los Angeles Percussion Ens. / Crystal 850
- ○ **Lou Harrison: Works 1939–2000** / Paiement (cond.), Winant, Andrie, McGushin, Staufenbiel, Maginnis, Miller, Brown, Cass, Brandenburg, Macomber, Gandolfi, Poplin, Rivard, Rosenberg, California Parallele Ens., UCSC Chamber Singers / 2003 / Mode 122

CHAMBER MUSIC

Canticle No. 3 for ocarina, guitar & percussion (1941; revised 1989)

The ocarina, a torpedo-shaped terra cotta flute, has a pure, primeval tone that, combined with percussion, gives this Lou Harrison score a hauntingly primitive, ritualistic feel. The five percussionists haul out tam-tam, xylophone, snare drums, bass drums, wood blocks, temple blocks, tom-toms, and maracas, as well as such exotica as teponaztli, sistrums, brake drums (both muted and suspended), metal pipes, elephant bells, cowbells, and water-buffalo bells. Amid all this—which Harrison exploits for timbral richness, not loudness—the guitar struggles to make an impact of its own, remaining absent or in the background until taking a slightly more prominent role at the end. The work falls into three large sections. In the first, the ocarina plays a little pentatonic dance, then retreats for what amounts to an extended percussion cadenza arising from the rhythm of the ocarina tune. The ocarina returns for the second part, now playing a very slow melody of short, repeated phrases deeply indebted to Native American music. Percussion instruments give the melody a shimmering halo, but again the ocarina disappears during a fast-tempo, gradually expanding percussion crescendo distantly based on the rhythm and pitches of the opening tune. Just as this section climaxes in a series of widely spaced crashes, the ocarina and guitar take advantage of a moment of silence to bring back the pentatonic tune from the beginning, the quiet percussion accompaniment now more threatening than before. Yet instead of exploding in a final percussive outburst, the music very gradually slows and fades away, leaving nothing but a slowly throbbing bass drum. *—James Reel*

Recommended:

- ○ **Harrison: Drums Along the Pacific** / Davies (cond.), etc. / 2003 / New Albion 122

CONCERTO

Concerto in Slendro, for violin, celesta, 2 tack pianos & percussion (1961; revised 1972)

Lou Harrison got his first chance to hear Asian music at its source in 1961, when he received a Rockefeller Foundation grant to travel to the East-West Music Encounter Conference in Tokyo. Harrison made the journey as a passenger on a freighter, using the long sea journey as an opportunity to explore the possibilities of pentatonic scales and to work on his *Concerto in Slendro.*

Among Harrison's compositions, the Concerto is one of those most thoroughly influenced by Asian music. This influence goes to the very basis of the work, for the "Slendro" of the title refers to one of the two main systems of tuning used for Balinese gamelans. The other system, Pelog, uses unequal intervals; Slendro is a six-note-to-the octave system, with the notes separated by nearly equal intervals. The so-called octave in this system is not really a pure one—it is actually a bit wider—so that each successive octave is a little more "out of tune" with its lower counterparts. The system is not rigid; there is no defined tuning pitch (like the Western A = 440), and each orchestra is tuned a little bit differently, lending each a characteristic sound. It is the slight out-of-tuneness of these metal percussion orchestras that results in the beat frequencies that produce the typical shimmering sound of Balinese music.

In practice, Balinese musicians select one of several five-tone modes from within the six available notes, and it is this principal that Harrison makes use of in the Concerto. The work calls for solo violin, celesta, two tack pianos, and percussion. The percussion section, consisting mainly of metallic instruments, includes an assortment of standard and non-standard sound sources—for example, galvanized garbage cans.

The Concerto is in three movements. In the dynamic first movement, marked Allegro vivo, the violin sings an ecstatic, highly ornamental line over the ensemble's distinctive timbres. The Molto adagio second movement features the violin playing very slow, long tones of a Southeast Asian cast over splashes of color from the other instruments. The work concludes with a lively syncopated Allegro, molto vigoroso. The Concerto in Slendro is one of the better distillations of Harrison's style; as is the case with most of his works, it is marked by highly attractive melodies, sparkling sonorities, vital rhythms, and almost no harmonies aside from those that occur coincidentally when melodies and figurations merge in the acoustic space.

The Concerto was premiered in Santa Cruz, California, on January 21, 1962 by violinist Zalik Kaufman and an ensemble directed by Robert Hughes. Harrison made slight revisions to the score in 1972. *—AMG*

Recommended:

- ○ **Music Of Lou Harrison** / Hughes (cond.), etc. / 1991 / CRI 613

Double Concerto for violin, cello & Javanese gamelan (1981–1982)

After completing his *Scenes from Cavafy* for baritone (in operatic style), male chorus (in Gregorian chant style), and Javanese gamelan, Harrison became interested through a commission in seeing whether the violin and violoncello would work well with the fixed tunings of the gamelan. He had a chance at UCLA to try out the first two movements of the piece with the Kyai Mendung, the first gamelan to enter the United States, and was satisfied that the combination was viable. Harrison's solution of having the violin and cello play mostly in unison with basic variation procedures, and having the gamelan proceed with its own tuning and gestures, allows the instruments to blend in heavenly and mutually supportive counterpoint.

The first movement of this double concerto, lasting slightly over eight minutes, is played "Grandly, but moderate." Two similar descending modes are played by the orchestra and when the slower unchanging line is added, the harmonic bending (especially the tritone feeling) is striking. The violin and cello join in octave unison on a middle speed melody of highly expressive emotion. The cello continues, answered from time to time by a repeated three-note gesture. The two join in unison again and expand the melody in farther registers. The violin then continues on its own to soar with an independently expressive voice above the fixed gamelan parts.

Once again, the soloists join in the melody. The tempo is then gradually increased as the intensity of emotion rises. A gradual ritardando to a single tone ends the movement.

A joyously dancing "Stampede," lasting approximately seven and a half minutes, forms the middle movement. The violin and cello introduce the continuously unraveling theme with high, middle, and deep drum accompaniment (*kendhang kalih*). The meter is mostly in a skipping triple feel with a few duple turnarounds. The soloists harmonize briefly in fourths and fifths with a "blues scale" tinge, and later engage in brilliant flashes of imitative counterpoint, but mostly continue to engage the listener by weaving a breathlessly unending line of melodic variation. This movement ends simply with a strong single accent.

The third and last movement is played Allegro moderato and lasts seven minutes. A lovely pentatonic melody in the gamelan appears at the opening like rain descending from the heavens. The violin and cello join in the melody backed by exquisite gamelan writing that imitates single gestures from the main melody and adds the sound of a thin stringed harp-like strumming. The tempo is increased slightly in the last minute of the movement for gamelan alone and then slowed down in the traditional manner. *—"Blue Gene" Tyranny*

Recommended:

○ **Harrison: Double Concerto & Trio** / Winant, King, Goldsmith, Harrison, Mills College Gamelan Ens. / Music & Arts 1073

Clara Haskil

b. Jan. 7, 1895, Bucharest, Romania, **d.** Dec. 7, 1960, Brussels, Belgium
Pianist

Romanian pianist Clara Haskil began her career as a child prodigy at the Bucharest Conservatory under Richard Robert at age 7, making her debut at the age of ten. Haskil ultimately graduated from Alfred Cortot's class at the Paris Conservatoire at 15 with the Prémier Prix to her credit. By the age of 18, however, Haskil was forced to endure the first of many physical setbacks that would hold back her career, in this case an attack of meningitis that kept her in a body cast for four years. Haskil did recover, making her New York debut in 1924 and her London debut in 1926. Although it was late in her career that her name was inextricably linked with the Mozart piano concerti, at this stage Haskil was associated with Romantic literature. Her performances of the Schumann *Concerto* in Philadelphia with Leopold Stokowski were widely praised.

With the outbreak of war, Haskil was trapped in occupied Paris, but was able to escape to Marseilles. There she survived a surreptitious surgical procedure to remove a tumor from her optic nerve, and was then smuggled to Vevey, Switzerland, where Haskil settled for the rest of her days. With war's end she resumed her career yet again, and thereafter enjoyed her greatest successes with a busy concert and recording schedule that took her around the world. Despite her amazing stamina, she proved unable to survive a fall she suffered in a Paris railway station in 1960, and died one month short of her 66th birthday.

With Haskil, musicianship came first and technical matters were irrelevant; she had enormous hands and could play a 12th in her left hand with a fingering of 2–5. Haskil reputedly had an amazing memory, and could accurately play back a piece of music she'd heard only once, even after the passage of several years, without ever having seen the score. The Clara Haskil Prize, awarded once every two years in Vevey, Switzerland, was established in 1962 as a memorial to the pianist. *—Uncle Dave Lewis*

Recommended:

○ **Mozart: Concerto 20; Scarlatti: 11 Sonatas** / Swoboda (cond.), Haskil, Winterthur SO / 2001 / DG 471214

○ **Clara Haskil** / Haskil, etc. / 1998 / Philips 456826

○ **Scarlatti: 11 Sonatas; Schubert: Sonata D960** / Haskil / 2002 / Archipel 60

Johann Adolf Hasse

b. Mar. 25, 1699, Bergedorf, Germany, **d.** Dec. 16, 1783, Venice, Italy
Composer: Opera

Johann Adolf Hasse, born near Hamburg, Germany in 1699, became one of the greatest composers of opera in his time. He is credited with composing at least 80 operas, in addition to theater works, cantatas, and sacred music. He spent much of his life traveling between Germany and Italy, holding positions of Kapellmeister in both regions simultaneously. He spent over twenty years directing the famous Dresden Staatskapelle, at the time one of the two best orchestras in all of Europe. He became a royal favorite when he came to the attention of Frederick the Great in 1742 during a performance of his opera *Lucio Papirio* (1742). Hasse spent the final ten years of his life in Venice composing sacred music. He died there in relative obscurity on December 16, 1783.

Hasse was the product of a multigenerational musical family, dating back to his great-grandfather. His early formal training was in voice, beginning when he was 15 years old. He joined his first opera company in 1718 as a tenor. During his early performing career, he also began composing. His first opera *Antioco* was performed in 1721.

Hasse first journeyed to Italy in 1722, traveling around the country before settling in Naples. While there, he furthered his studies under singer and composer Nicola Porpora, and composer Alessandro Scarlatti. He remained in Italy until 1731 when he moved to Dresden with his new wife Faustina Bordoni, a popular soprano. While there he became the *maestro di capella* for the electoral court, and in 1734 became the Hofkapellmeister of the famed Dresden Staatskapelle. He retained this position for 22 years, during which he traveled frequently to Italy to supervise performances of his operas. During his tenure with the orchestra, Hasse developed orchestra-seating arrangements that were used as models for other orchestras being established around Germany. The Dresden Staatskapelle achieved critical acclaim under Hasse's leadership. While serving in Dresden, Hasse also served as the maestro di capella for the Ospedale degli incuràbili in Venice, for whom he had probably been composing music since 1730.

Hasse was a prolific and commercially successful composer of serious opera. Between 1726 and 1733 he had over twenty of his operas performed for the Neapolitan Court in Naples, including *La Contadina* (1728), *Artaserse* (1730), and *Cajo Fabrizio* (1732). His first opera performed in Dresden was *Cleofide* (1731). Johann Sebastian Bach and his son Wilhelm, reportedly attended the performance in September of that year. The opera was based on *Alessandro nell Indie* which featured a libretto by Metastasio, who would figure prominently in many of Hasse's future works. Hasse also teamed with Dresden court poet Pallavicino for five operas that premiered between February 1737 and May 1738.

The Seven Years' War caused the Dresden court to take up residence in Warsaw (1756–62), and although it is believed Hasse visited there, he apparently spent most of his time in Italy. During this period, he traveled, composed, and produced operas for the Carnival in Venice in 1758, for the Neapolitan court between 1758 and 1760, and for the Venetian court, from 1760 to 1763.

The court returned to Dresden in 1762, whereupon Hasse returned to continue his duties as Hofkapellmeister of the Staatskapelle. He found Dresden and the ensemble decimated. He left his position in 1764 and took up residence in Vienna until 1772. During this period, Hasse continued to travel to Italy, composing and producing operatic performances. His final opera, *Ruggiero* was published in 1771. He spent his final years in Venice, composing primarily sacred music. *—Bruce Lundgren*

OPERA

Operas (1721–1771)

One of the most important opera composers of the eighteenth century, Hasse is unique among German composers for having gained a top reputation in Italy as a composer of opera seria. Although he spent most of his life as Kapellmeister at the Saxon court in Dresden, so prestigious was Hasse's name across Italy that he became widely known as "il caro Sassone" (the dear Saxon). His time was mostly divided between Dresden and Venice, but he also traveled widely throughout Italy and saw his operas performed in every major center. His career as an opera composer is strongly linked with that of his wife, the mezzo-soprano Faustina Bordoni, one of the greatest singers of the day. In addition to appearing as prima donna in many of Hasse's operas, Bordoni also pursued an independent career, most notably creating a number of leading roles in Handel's London operas.

Hasse's output includes more than 60 opere serie, many of them set to librettos by the leading poet of the genre, Pietro Metastasio. These largely conform to the strict conventions of the form, and feature noble characters whose behavior is dignified by the expression of elevated sentiments of love, fidelity, and honor. The principal vehicle for such emotions was the da capo aria, a complex construction in an ABA form which unless modified frequently ran to considerable length. Ensembles are relatively rare, and the chorus has little or no part in such operas, which also depended for their appeal upon grand staging and lavish costumes. Hasse's first operas were composed for Naples, where he was resident for about seven years during the 1720s. There he laid the first foundations for his enormous popularity, which was based above all on his ability to write graceful, melodious arias of a classical elegance. Such lyrical gifts were supported by orchestral writing that largely eschews contrapuntal complexity, remaining more concerned with clarity and elegance. Hasse was also followed clear procedures in the realm of large-scale harmonic structure, depicting particular emotions through the use of specific, clearly defined keys. In addition to serious opera, Hasse also composed a number of lighter intermezzos in a comic vein. These works, the forerunner of the opera buffa, are generally quite brief, often being inserted between the acts of the main serious opera in performance. The characters who people the intermezzo represent a wider range of social types than those of serious opera; servants and maids mix and interact with the higher-born in the manner of seventeenth century opera. Hasse also composed a substantial body of church music, much of it based on the florid Neapolitan style. Opportunities for hearing Hasse's operas today remain rare, but his *Cleofide*, first performed in Dresden to a libretto by Metastasio in 1731, has received a complete recording, while the delightful intermezzo *Scintilla e Don Tabarro* (or *La contadina*) has also been recorded. —*Brian Robins*

Recommended:

○ **Hasse: Cleofide** / Christie (cond.), Kirkby, Ragin, Visse, Mellon, Capella Coloniensis, Rheinische Kantorei / Capriccio 10193

○ **Hasse: Piramo e Tisbe** / Bolgan, San Rocco Academy Orch. (Venice) / 1998 / Mondo Musica 10100

Hans Leo Hassler

b. Aug. 27, 1562, Nuremberg, Germany, **d.** Jun. 8, 1612, Frankfurt am Main, Germany

Composer

Hans Leo Hassler was one of the most significant of the composers who brought Italian styles to Germany in the early seventeenth century. His father, Isaak Hassler, was a stonecutter and musician in Nuremberg; all three Hassler sons had music lessons from their father and became musicians. Like many other composers from north of the Alps, Hassler went to Venice to pursue his education, probably on a municipal stipend, and there met Giovanni Gabrieli and his uncle, Andrea Gabrieli, the organist of St. Mark's cathedral. Hassler became the elder Gabrieli's pupil, remaining in Venice for 18 months. By 1586, he was chamber organist to Octavian Fugger II in Augsburg. The Fuggers also hired Hassler's two brothers, and practically admitted them to the family circle. Hassler composed prolifically, and in 1591 the emperor gave him a patent to copyright his works. Hassler's fame grew so much that Moritz, Landgrave of Hesse, tried unsuccessfully to get Octavian II to "loan" Hassler to him. Meanwhile, Hassler had expanded his business interests, becoming a metals dealer and getting involved in the manufacture of mechanical musical instruments.

In 1600, Octavian II died, leaving Hassler without a job. Augsburg's town council, to keep him, gave him the job of town music director, but he went home to Nuremberg the next year to take a similar position. In 1604 he got a year's leave of absence, went to Ulm, and married the daughter of a highly placed merchant. When the year's leave expired, Hassler cut his ties with Nuremberg, became a citizen of Ulm, and in 1607 was admitted to the Ulm merchants' guild.

In 1608 Elector Christian II of Saxony commissioned Hassler to write a composition for his capital at Dresden, and appointed him as chamber organist. Soon after arriving in Dresden, he was found to have tuberculosis. No compositions are known to have been written by Hassler after 1608, but he does not seem to have cut back on his other work , and, indeed, took over the duties of the Kapellmeister. In 1612 the Electoral court visited Frankfurt am Main for the crowning of Emperor Mathias. While he was there Hassler collapsed and died.

Hassler was highly influenced by the two Gabrielis and by Orlando di Lassus. He wrote for both the Roman Catholic and Lutheran churches, although he himself was a Protestant. As a composer he was highly conservative, hewing to the highly polyphonic idiom that had been in its heyday a half century earlier. Hassler never wrote with a basso continuo, the hallmark of the new Baroque style. He used the cantus firmus technique as the basis of his polyphony; often all parts treat motives derived from the cantus firmus. He also wrote a large quantity of secular music, including Italian madrigals in five or six voices, instrumental works (also very contrapuntal), and dance songs that are highly rhythmic and homophonic. One of his best known songs was the romantic *G'mut ist mir verwirret* ("My Head is Spinning"), whose theme Johann Sebastian Bach combined with the words of Gerhardt, "O Haput voll Blut und Wunde" (O, Head all Bloody and Wounded), in his *St. Matthew Passion* to describe the sufferings of Christ on the Cross. Another popular song he wrote, *All Lust und Freud* (All Pleasure and Joy), a galliard, was adapted by Schütz in his *Psalmen Davids* and in that form is still used in Protestant services.—*Joseph Stevenson*

Overview of Works (ca. 1590–1612)

Hans Leo Hassler epitomized the Renaissance man as musician as well as anyone. His output embraced all major idioms of the time and reflected the cosmopolitan outlook that, despite the backdrop of constant wars, was reflective of the budding enlightenment of the era, at least among the learned and artistic. This may largely be attributed to Hassler's period of study in the Venice of the Gabrielis, leavening the weightier Northern European style to produce one that travels very well. A similar generosity of outlook may be found in his religious music. Hassler cultivated both Latin and Lutheran turf in his sacred music. The composer often used non-denomination-specific texts. The largely Latin motets in particular show a wide variety of style that ranges from strikingly chromatic and contrapuntal to homophony with sparse chord punctuation that is almost suggestive of lute-accompanied song. Some of the more traditional in the genre reflect Hassler's Venetian years, such as the *Missa Secunda Gloria* with its Gabrielli-influenced antiphonal passages. Others, such as the *Missa I Super Dixit Maria*, are almost Palestrinan in directness and purity of expression. The Lutheran works, in German, are similarly varied, but are marked by a retrospective bent, often utilizing the old cantus firmus technique of the mid-Renaissance. These, however, can be very expressive, as in his solemn setting of the well-known *O Haupt voll Blut und Wunden.* Hassler was equally adept in secular music. Lyrically, his madrigals and songs betray an inclination toward sunnier climes, however. Even when using German texts, these are frequently translations of Italian poetry. Curiously, these reveal a certain rhythmic deliberateness more northern in nature. In mood, they can range from the lighthearted *Tantzen und springen* to the introspective *Mein G'müt ist mir verwirret*, which uses the solemn melody of the sacred *O Haupt.* One of the most noteworthy aspects of Hassler's art—his keyboard works—may have been no more than a footnote in musicology had it not been for the discovery of their tablatures in the 1960s. These reveal a wide variety of style, mood, and technical difficulty, all the more remarkable as the keyboard was still emerging as a secular instrument to rival lute and recorder. Prior to this, even non-service writing for the keyboard, as was customary in the German countries, usually relied on the old cantus firmus practice of taking an existing ecclesiastical theme and working it into the keyboard idiom. Hassler drew upon the Italian purely instrumental genre to produce fantasias, ricercares, toccatas, and variations. Though contrapuntal, these pieces sport a rhythmic vivacity more associated with the Mediterranean. Hassler's influence on keyboard writing was to be felt well into the late Baroque period. In this, as in all of Hassler's music, it reflects the Renaissance ideal, the creative fruit of an enlightened and open mind. —*Wayne Reisig*

Recommended:

○ **Hassler: Ihr Musici** / Regensburger Domspatzen / 1992 / Essence 3011

○ **Hassler: Missa Super Dixit Maria** / Herreweghe, Europeen Ens. Vocal / HM 2901401

Franz Josef Haydn

b. Mar. 31, 1732, Rohrau, Austria, **d.** May 31, 1809, Vienna, Austria

Composer: Symphonic, Orchestral, Chamber Music, Concerto, Keyboard, Choral, Vocal, Opera

Franz Joseph Haydn is the composer who, more than any other, epitomizes the aims and achievements of the Classical era. Perhaps his most important achievement was that he developed and evolved in countless subtle ways the most influential structural principle in the history of music: his perfection of the set of expectations known as sonata form made an epochal impact. In hundreds of instrumental sonatas, string quartets, and symphonies, Haydn both broke new ground and provided durable models; indeed, he was among the creators of these fundamental genres of classical music. His influence upon later composers is immeasurable; Haydn's most illustrious pupil, Beethoven, was the direct beneficiary of the elder master's musical imagination, and Haydn's shadow lurks within (and sometimes looms over) the music of composers like Schubert, Mendelssohn, and Brahms.

Part and parcel of Haydn's formal mastery was his famous sense of humor, his feeling for the unpredictable, elegant twist. In the *Symphony No. 94 ("Surprise")* (1791), the composer tweaks those audience members who typically fall asleep during slow movements with the sudden, completely unexpected intrusion of a fortissimo chord during a passage of quietude. Haydn's pictorial sense is much in evidence works like his epic oratorio *The Creation* (1796–98), in which images of the cosmos taking shape are thrillingly, movingly portrayed in tones. By one estimate, Haydn produced some 340 hours of music, more than Bach or Handel, Mozart or Beethoven. Few of them lack some unexpected detail or clever solution to a formal problem.

Haydn was prolific not just because he was a tireless worker with an inexhaustible musical imagination, but also because of the circumstances of his musical career: he was the last prominent beneficiary of the system of noble patronage that had nourished European musical composition since the Renaissance. Born in the small Austrian village of Rohrau, he became a choirboy at St. Stephen's cathedral in Vienna when he was eight. After his voice broke and he was turned out of the choir, he eked out a precarious living as a teenage freelance musician in Vienna. His fortunes began to turn in the late 1750s as members of Vienna's noble families became aware of his music, and on May 1, 1761, he went to work for the Esterházy family. He remained in their employ for the next 30 years, writing many of his instrumental compositions and operas for performance at their vast summer palace, Esterháza.

Musical creativity may often, it is true, meet a tragic end, but Haydn lived long enough to reap the rewards of his own imagination and toil. The Esterházys curtailed their musical activities in 1790, but by that time Haydn was known all over Europe and widely considered the greatest living composer. (He himself deferred to Mozart in that regard, and the friendly competition between the two composers deepened the music of both.) Two trips to London during the 1790s resulted in two sets of six symphonies each (among them the "Surprise" symphony) that remain centerpieces of the orchestral repertoire. Haydn's final masterpieces included powerful choral works: the *Creation* and *Seasons* oratorios and a group of six masses. Haydn stopped composing in 1803, after which he prefaced his correspondence with a little musical quotation (from one of his part-songs) bearing the text "Gone is all my strength; I am old and weak." He died in Vienna on May 31, 1809. —*AMG*

SYMPHONIC

Sinfonia Concertante, H. I/105 (1792)

Originally, and more accurately, titled "Concertante," Haydn composed this essay in multiple concerto form while a visitor in London in the 1790s, the same period during which he produced his well-known "London" Symphonies. The *Sinfonia concertante* (1792), scored for oboe, bassoon, violin, cello, and orchestra, is the only real work of its kind that Haydn ever penned (though several earlier symphonies do contain extended passages for solo instruments). Haydn wrote the work at the urging of violinist and impresario Johann Salomon, who had been instrumental in bringing Haydn to London and who also played the violin part at the premiere.

The work opens with a somewhat relaxed Allegro whose dimensions, perhaps to accomodate four soloists, exceed those of the usual Classical sonata-allegro movement. The principal theme is a lively thought broken into two halves; the first reaches upward expectantly, while the second winds its way back down, sparkling with a few simple ornaments. Haydn is characteristically unpredictable in his use of sonata/concerto form: the solo instruments begin to enter well before the opening tutti has reached its end. The tutti is finally completed with a decisive tonic cadence, at which point the true solo narratives begin. Uncharacteristically for Haydn, the long development section is saturated by the minor mode. The cadenza to the first movement is the composer's own; Haydn evidently and wisely realized that for four players to successfully improvise a cadenza would have been folly.

The Andante is even more original in its formal conception than the opening Allegro. Here, the four soloists are accompanied only by strings and a reduced complement of winds. Only once, deep in the middle of the movement, do all four soloists drop out and allow the orchestra a brief interlude. The movement, mainly an extended conversation among the soloists, comes across as large-scale chamber music—so much so that the above-mentioned orchestral ritornello, though only four measures long, seems something of an unwanted intrusion into the soloists' private conversation.

There is no Menuet in the *Sinfonia concertante*, evidence that the influence of the concerto upon the work is more pervasive than that of the symphony. The finale opens with the traditional, spirited rondo theme, but before long it too delves into unconventionalities: the solo violin interrupts the texture with a decidedly operatic passage marked "Recitative, adagio." This surprising passage eventually winds its way back to the movement proper, which continues in a light, humorous manner, engaging the soloists in virtuoso pyrotechnics.

In Haydn's own time the *Sinfonia concertante* did not enjoy the immediate and enduring success of the "London" Symphonies, and in the nineteenth century it fell largely into obscurity. The twentieth century brought a renewed interest in the work, however, particularly in the decades following World War II, and it has since enjoyed a renewed life in the concert hall. *—Blair Johnston*

Recommended:

○ **Haydn: Violin Concertos; Sinfonia Concertante** / Wallfisch (cond.), Robson, Watkin, Warnock, Orch. of the Age of Enlightenment / 1996 / Virgin 61301

○ **Haydn: Cello Concerto; Sinfonia Concertante** / Norrington (cond.), Isserlis, Boyd, Wilkie, Blankenstijn, CO of Europe / 1998 / BMG 68578

○ **Haydn: Symphonies 26, 52 & 53; Sinfonia Concertante** / Wallfisch, S. Kuijken (conds.), Watkin, Robson, Warnock, Orch. of the Age of Enlightenment / 2000 / Angel 61800

Symphony No. 6 in D major ("Le Matin"), H. 1/6 (1761)

Among the first works Haydn wrote upon entering the service of the Esterházy family, the sixth, seventh, and eighth symphonies form a triptych depicting different times of day. At least that's how Prince Paul Anton Esterházy interpreted them when he suggested their subtitles. Haydn's main intention seemed to be showing off the skills of his musicians, for each symphony abounds with prominent solos.

No. 6, *"Le Matin"* ("Morning"), begins with an Adagio introduction that seems to depict a sunrise, coming up from nothing, rising in volume and pitch, and then subsiding. The main Allegro begins with a quick flute theme, followed by manic passagework for the strings with tiny interjections from the various wind soloists. The development is largely a matter of fast vibration in the strings, with the winds trying to smooth things out with the opening flute tune. The Adagio movement falls into three parts, the first—again—rising slowly out of nothing into a little violin cadenza. The concertmaster plays a patiently ascending theme derived from the opening bars, and then, in the movement's second section, offers a more ornate melody with subdued orchestral accompaniment. This melody eventually becomes a duet with the first cello. The brief third section is a mirror image of the first, the movement descending gently into silence. Some commentators have interpreted these closing bars as an homage to Corelli, and aome have suggested that this movement is a portrait of a music lesson, with the Esterházy orchestra's violinist Luigi Tomasini performing scales and other exercises; the violin is in fact so prominent here that one could almost mistake this for a portion of one of the violin concertos that Haydn wrote for Tomasini a few years later. The French-style Minuet features an elegant flute solo, which is eventually echoed by the oboes and horns. The trio section descends to the bottom of the orchestra for a witty if subdued dialogue between the bassoon and double bass. A Baroque concerto grosso seems to take over during the final, compact Allegro movement, which lavishes brief, burbling concertante roles on almost every principal player in turn. *—James Reel*

Recommended:

○ **Haydn: Symphonies 6–8** / Freiburg Baroque Orch. / HM 901767

○ **Haydn Symphonies Vol. 3** / Hogwood (cond.), Academy of Ancient Music / 1992 / L'Oiseau-Lyre 433661

○ **Haydn: Symphonies 6–8** / Goodman (cond.), Hanover Band / 2002 / Hyperion 55112

Symphony No. 7 in C major ("Le midi"), H. 1/7 (1761)

This is the second of three consecutive symphonies in which Haydn follows the course of the day. No. 6 began with an obvious evocation of sunrise, but precisely what No. 7 has to do with afternoon is unclear. What this symphony really concerns is the symphonic and operatic style of the recent past; perhaps Haydn was showing his new employer, Prince Paul Anton Esterházy, that he was well aware of the noble Baroque conventions, but was capable of adding his own personal flourishes, too. The dotted rhythms of the Adagio introduction recall the Baroque era's French overture style, the sort of music with which Bach began his orchestral suites. In the ensuing Allegro, Haydn's rhythmic structures and use of counterpoint seem equally archaic, very much something out of a Handel opera overture; yet the themes are far more strongly contrasted than in the past. Between bubbling tutti passages come elaborate solos, most prominently for two violinists answered by various other string and woodwind players. Haydn dubs the next movement Recitativo. It's an adagio movement with a tiny allegro core, a takeoff on opera seria with its sudden changes of tempo and key. It initially seems like the accompaniment to an unperformed aria, the strings drifting aimlessly upward without anything happening in the foreground. The solo violin does eventually deliver snatches of an operatic recitative, and takes an increasingly prominent role as the movement wanders along. The true slow movement, an Adagio, is a long, relaxed duet for violin and cello, with occasional flute commentary. The movement closes with an extended cadenza for the two string soloists. Next, the stately Minuet proceeds without incident until the trio section, in which solo cello and horn natter at each other from their respective corners of the orchestra. The concluding Allegro, for the first time in this symphony, uses the flute and oboe at the same time. The movement is somewhat reminiscent of a Baroque aria, with the solo instruments (nearly every principal player, by the end of the work) handling increasingly florid treatments of the bustling theme. *—James Reel*

Recommended:

○ **Haydn: Symphonies 6–8** / Freiburg Baroque Orch. / HM 901767

○ **Haydn: Symphonies 6–8** / Goodman (cond.), Hanover Band / 1991 / Hyperion 66523

○ **Haydn Symphonies Vol. 3** / Hogwood (cond.), Academy of Ancient Music / 1992 / L'Oiseau-Lyre 433661

Symphony No. 8 in G major ("Le soir"), H. 1/8 (ca. 1761)

Although Haydn's *"Morning"* and *"Noon"* symphonies (numbers 6 and 7) paid their respects to conventions of the Baroque era, his *"Night" Symphony* looks forward to the developing Classical period. There's no evidence that Haydn wrote this work with anything nocturnal in mind; the title was appended by his boss, Prince Paul Anton Esterházy. A happy, slightly irregularly phrased, lightly dancing tune eases the Allegro molto movement into action. It's really the only theme out of which Haydn constructs the movement, although he does draw variety from whirling material for full orchestra that grows out of the melody. The development passes snatches of the melody around to various orchestral soloists, and the recapitulation is upon us before we realize that the development has ended. The Andante is a tender, lyrical movement that distributes its main melody among the first-stand string players. The movement proceeds through a very mild minor-mode variation before restating the long opening section essentially as it began. The Minuet follows the evolving conventions of the time, with extremely regular phrasing and the strings and woodwinds playing off against each other in their own separate episodes. Unexpectedly the trio section turns into a miniature double bass concerto—quite a noble one, without a trace of the clownishness that would afflict the instrument beginning in the nineteenth century. The symphony's alternate nickname, *"La Tempesta,"* comes from the stormy final Presto. It begins with a quick drizzle of notes from the solo violin and then flute, and develops into an intermittent shower of sixteenth notes washing through the orchestra. With the absence of timpani, thunder is implied merely by some forceful, rapidly descending string figures. Some four decades later, Haydn would reuse many of these ideas in the storm sequence of his oratorio *The Seasons*. *—James Reel*

Recommended:

○ **Haydn: Symphonies 6–8** / Freiburg Baroque Orch. / HM 901767

○ **Haydn: Symphonies Vol. 3** / Hogwood (cond.), Academy of Ancient Music / 1992 / L'Oiseau-Lyre 433661

Symphony No. 22 in E flat major ("Philosopher"), H. 1/22 (1764)

Haydn's *Symphony No. 22 in E flat major ("Philosopher")* is a good example of a work that bridges the late Baroque and early Classical styles. Here Haydn employs the Baroque sonata da chiesa form (i.e. movements in a slow-fast-slow-fast scheme) while making use of a characteristically Classical harmonic language and phrase structure.

The stunning Adagio that opens the symphony represents a hybrid of older ritornello-style form and the emergent Classical sonata form. The main musical idea unfolds in the spirit of a chorale; this idea is first intoned by the horns and is answered, in an orchestrational oddity for the time, by the English horns. This chorale appears in several different keys as the movement progresses, eventually returning to the prevailing E flat major in a kind of recapitulation. The movement is further characterized by a profusion of Baroque delicacies, and suspensions and sequences abound.

A humorous, vivacious Presto follows, providing distinct contrast to the introspective first movement. The Classical aspect of the symphony is further underscored by a third movement in the form of a minuet and trio, the former somewhat plodding, the latter typically dance-like.

In the intriguing finale, Haydn uses a galloping 6/8 meter and hunting calls on the horn and English horn to good effect. Though perhaps unremarkable to modern listeners, the incorporation of hunting music into a symphony surely came as a shock to audiences in the 1760s.

A second, spurious version of the symphony begins with the Presto and omits the Adagio and Minuet and Trio movements. In this incarnation, an Andante—almost certainly not composed by Haydn—bridges the Presto and the finale. Though widely known during the composer's lifetime, this version cannot by any means be considered authentic.

As with most of Haydn's "nicknamed" symphonies, the "Philosopher" appellation is not the composer's own; it does, however, capture something of the work's thoughtful atmosphere. *—Blair Johnston*

Recommended:

- ○ **Haydn: Symphonies 22–25** / Goodman (cond.), Hanover Band / 2002 / Hyperion 55116
- ○ **Haydn: Symphonies 22, 86 & 102** / Rattle (cond.), Birmingham SO / 1995 / EMI 55509

Symphony No. 26 in D minor ("Lamentatione"), H. 1/26 (ca. 1768)

This D minor symphony, Haydn's 26th, was for a time erroneously associated with Christmas, but the liturgical subject it clearly relates to is rather opposite in character: the Passiontide. Indeed, Haydn not only employs themes derived from Gregorian chant, but borrows one for the second movement from the Lamentations used in the Roman Catholic Church for Holy Thursday services.

The first movement is marked Allegro assai con spirito and opens with urgency in its grim and sorrowful music. But the mood soon brightens with a theme of liturgical origin, the music here imparting a sense of lightness and elegance. After a repeat of the exposition, the development section ensues, focusing first on the darker music from the opening and overall conveying a somewhat epic character. The reprise presents the main material, but with changes, and the movement ends with an almost triumphal sense.

The second movement (Adagio) presents the aforementioned "Lamentation" theme in a mood balancing serenity with sadness: the strings sing the melody mournfully and solemnly, but with a sense of consolation, especially in the splendid warmth of the oboe writing. A second theme is soon heard, a spirited, almost playful creation presented by the strings and used mostly as an obbligato accompaniment to the main melody. Some development ensues, as well as a fair, though hardly excessive amount of repetition of previous thematic materials.

The finale is a Minuet and Trio, and would thus normally convey a lighter, brighter mood, but here, the music, while elegant and rhythmic, is a bit more serious in character than the uninitiated listener would expect. The outer Minuet sections often exude an austere manner in their elegance and a restive character in their angularity, while the inner Trio music is somewhat playful and lighter. This Haydn symphony is brief, lasting only about 15 minutes. *—Robert Cummings*

Recommended:

- ○ **Haydn: Symphonies 26, 42–44, 48 & 49** / Hogwood (cond.), Academy of Ancient Music / 1994 / L'Oiseau-Lyre 440222
- ○ **Haydn: The "Sturm und Drang" Symphonies** / Pinnock (cond.), English Concert / Archiv 463731
- ○ **Haydn: Symphonies 26, 52 & 53** / Kuijken (cond.) La Petite Bande / 1995 / Virgin 61212

Symphony No. 31 in D major ("Hornsignal"), H. 1/31 (1765)

Haydn was hired in 1761 as Vice-Kapellmeister in the musical establishment of Prince Anton Esterházy, a leading member of the Hungarian nobility. When Nicholas Esterházy succeeded to the title of Prince after the death of Anton, he had a large hunting lodge in the rural community of Suttor expanded into a great palace, Esterháza, where Haydn and the musicians he supervised (the composer was the acting Kapellmeister now) spent part of their year. It was in 1765 that Nicholas began his practice of summer residence there.

D major was a key often used for festive, celebratory music, qualities that this symphony certainly possesses. It probably was written to welcome the Esterházy retinue to the Suttor residence. D major had festive overtones because the trumpet could be played in that key, and because horns pitched in that key had a useful high range. Haydn used four horns rather than the usual two in this symphony for a richer, more heraldic sound. Haydn scholar H.C. Robbins Landon concludes that Haydn would have separated the horns into two pairs, placing them on opposite sides of the orchestra or otherwise spatially apart from each other, to play echo effects.

The symphony has strong concertante qualities; Haydn was probably showing off the talents of his musicians as Prince Nicholas was showing off his new residence. There are solos for flute, oboe, violin, cello, horn, and even the bass (a violone, not quite the same instrument as the familiar double bass, the bass viol). The symphony begins with a familiar horn call that was played by the drivers on the official postal delivery coaches to announce their arrival. The slow movement has difficult parts for cello and for violin. There is excellent and original scoring for interlocked oboes and horns in the minuet. The finale is in the form of a theme and variations. Each variation is for a different solo instrument until all the principals have had a turn, and the scope of the finale as a whole is notable. *—Joseph Stevenson*

Recommended:

- ○ **Haydn: Symphonies 31, 59 & 73** / Harnoncourt (cond.), Vienna Concentus Musicus / 1994 / Teldec 90843
- ○ **Haydn: Symphonies 31 & 45** / Mackerras (cond.), Orch. of St. Luke's / 1989 / Telarc 80156
- ○ **Haydn: Jagd-Symphonien** / Rifkin (cond.), Capella Coloniensis / Capriccio 10733

Symphony No. 43 in E flat major ("Mercury"), H. 1/43 (1772)

Scored for two oboes, two horns and strings with a bassoon continuo, Symphony No. 43 (called "Mercury" in the nineteenth century—no one knows exactly why) is one of Haydn's "chamber" symphonies—indicating not only the absence of drums and trumpets but also the style of writing. This type of symphony is usually of a lighter texture, with more lyrical themes than the so-called "grand" symphonies. Haydn would merge these characteristics to a great extent in his later symphonies, but this relatively early work maintains a distinct chamber quality. Dating from the composer's years in the service of the Esterházy family, it was most likely composed between the years of 1766 and 1772.

The thematic material at beginning of the symphony does not fall into the typical groups of two-, four- or eight-measure ideas. One of the longest Haydn ever wrote, the main theme is unabashedly lyrical and slow moving, underpinned by an unusual harmonic progression. Even the traditional tutti restatement and transition are not heavy; the orchestration is transparent with the horns working on the periphery. Once the secondary theme arrives, we find that it is really a varied restatement of the first theme, but on the dominant. The false recapitulation in the development section has something of the comic opera in it, while in the real recapitulation Haydn allows himself to dwell on the main theme even longer than in the exposition.

The second movement is luxuriant and performed mostly by the strings. Haydn spends an unusual amount of time spinning out the principle theme. Possibly because of this excess, the development section focuses not on the theme, but on a fragment consisting of three repeated sixteenth notes followed by two eighth notes that either rise or fall.

Harmonic contrast is paramount in the E flat major Minuet, which is clearly reminiscent of the Austrian Ländler. The graceful trio section begins in C minor, its first half moving to B flat (the dominant of the Minuet). This harmony does not go where we expect it to, for the second part of the trio begins again on C minor, moving eventually to E flat of the return of the Minuet. As in the slow movement, the winds are used sparingly.

Instead of a brisk, ebullient finale that might close one of the "grand" symphonies, Haydn writes for this work a Finale with a lengthy, legato theme. The coda is very unusual in that it does not end the movement with a "bang"; rather, it consists of lyrical passages that diminish both in dynamic and instrumentation, leading to a moment of silence. Haydn then calls for a final tutti passage before the finish. *—John Palmer*

Recommended:

- ○ **Haydn: Symphonies 41, 42 & 43** / Weil (cond.), Tafelmusik Baroque Orch. / 1992 / Sony 48370
- ○ **Haydn: Symphonies 42, 43 & 44** / Goodman (cond.), Hanover Band / 2002 / Hyperion 55117
- ○ **Haydn: The "Sturm und Drang" Symphonies** / Pinnock (cond.), English Concert / Archiv 463731

○ **Haydn: Symphonies 26, 42–44, 48 &, 49** / Hogwood (cond.), Academy of Ancient Music / 1994 / L'Oiseau-Lyre 440222

Symphony No. 44 in E minor ("Trauer" / "Funeral" / "Letter E"), H. 1/44 (before 1772)

This symphony acquired its nickname ("Symphony of Mourning") because Haydn in his old age requested that it be played at his funeral. It is a work of the period between roughly 1768 and 1774, when the so-called *Sturm und Drang* (Storm and Stress) style, with its dominant aesthetic of heightened emotionalism, flourished not only in Haydn's output but in Austrian music in general. The *Sturm und Drang* came from the title of a 1776 German novel, and was also applied to a German literary movement.

This emotionalism took the form of devices such as increased use of minor keys, a tendency towards stronger, even violent, contrasts in the music, restless syncopated figures in the accompaniment, and other devices, many of which had originated in Italian opera of the 1760s. The sudden interest by Austrian musicians in writing music of this sort may simply be that they saw in these new items of musical vocabulary a way to enrich and extend the expressive content of their music beyond the rather genteel "galant" style that had ruled since the end of the Baroque era.

The symphony begins with a forceful four-note motif that Haydn uses extensively. The music is unusually contrapuntal, with the high point coming in a three-part counterpoint passage in the first movement's coda. The minuet comes second, a rare format for Haydn. Like the first movement, it is severe and contrapuntal. The slow movement is similar in character to those of Handel, and the final movement maintains the learned use of counterpoint. The main theme later in the movement is treated in double counterpoint. The finale bears one of the fastest available tempo markings, but it is not light. Its energy is frenzied and threatening. It was expected at the time for minor-key works to end with a movement in the major, or at least affirm the major in a resultantly uplifting conclusion. Not here. The power Haydn has built drives inexorably to a minor-key ending of deep despair. *—Joseph Stevenson*

Recommended:

○ **Haydn: The "Sturm und Drang" Symphonies** / Pinnock (cond.), English Concert / Archiv 463731

○ **Haydn: Symphonies 42, 43 & 44** / Goodman (cond.), Hanover Band / 2002 / Hyperion 55117

○ **Haydn: Symphonies 44–47** / Janigro (cond.), Zagreb Radio SO / 1995 / Vanguard 5/6

○ **Haydn: Symphonies 26, 42–44, 48 & 49** / Hogwood (cond.), Academy of Ancient Music / 1994 / L'Oiseau-Lyre 440222

Symphony No. 45 in F sharp minor ("Farewell" / "Candle" / "Letter B"), H. 1/45 (1772)

In 1761 Haydn was engaged to work for Prince Nicolas Esterházy, one of the highest-ranking families of the Hungarian nobility. He was in charge of the musical establishment, including an orchestra of around 25 players. They divided their time between Prince Nicolas' estate in Eisenstadt (not far from Vienna) and in his great summer palace, Esterháza, near Suttor in what is now Hungary. This was quite an isolated location, and the work there generally kept Haydn's musicians away from their families for an extended period. These conditions occasioned this famous symphony's composition and first performance. According to Haydn's friend Griesinger, the Prince had decided to extend his summer stay for an indefinite time, discomfiting the musicians. So Haydn wrote the last part of the finale of the symphony so that each group of musicians ends its part at a different time. The musicians were instructed to get up, snuff out the candles on the music stands, take the written music for their parts, and leave the stage. In the end only Haydn and his concertmaster, Tommasini, were left, playing violin. (They were the only two musicians who were permitted to bring their families to Esterháza.) The Prince, according to Haydn, got the point and ordered his retinue's departure the next day.

Overall the symphony is a melancholy work. The first movement is urgent and agitated. The key of F sharp minor is a rarely used one in the eighteenth century and contributes a feeling of tension. Haydn experiments with form; the recapitulation in this movement is not literal, but continues developing the melodies. The Adagio and Minuet are also restless. *—Joseph Stevenson*

Recommended:

○ **Haydn: Surprise & Farewell** / Weil (cond.), Tafelmusik Baroque Orch. / 1999 / Sony 61700

○ **Haydn: Symphonies 31 & 45** / Mackerras (cond.), Orch. of St. Luke's / 1989 / Telarc 80156

○ **Haydn: The "Sturm und Drang" Symphonies** / Pinnock (cond.), English Concert / Archiv 463731

○ **Haydn Symphonies, 45–47, 51, 52 & 64** / Hogwood (cond.), Academy of Ancient Music / 1996 / L'Oiseau-Lyre 443777

Symphony No. 48 in C major ("Maria Theresia"), H. 1/48 (ca. 1769)

For years, this festive C major symphony was thought to have been one of those composed to honor the empress Maria Theresa on the occasion of her 1773 visit to Esterháza, the stately rural summer palace of Haydn's employer, the Hungarian Prince Nicolaus Esterházy. But more recent research has unearthed an authenticated 1769 manuscript of the symphony in the hand of Joseph Elssler, Haydn's own copyist.

This discovery also raised a question as to the scoring of the work. There are ten different versions of the trumpet and timpani parts for this symphony, none of them authenticated. The symphony in the Elssler source is scored for two oboes, two horns (C alto and F), and strings with a bassoon doubling the bass line. There is no timpani part at all. However, in 1779, Haydn very nearly lost all of his music in a great fire at Esterháza. Fortunately he had a collection of orchestra parts in his own house, and these were spared. He took them to a publisher in Vienna to have them copied into new scores and published. The resulting parts for this symphony had both a timpani part and trumpet parts doubling the high horn parts in the fast movements. The timpani part, therefore, is surely not authentically by Haydn, but seems to have been approved by him.

The work, at any rate, should not be nicknamed for the empress, but the name has stuck and will probably continue to adhere to it. Musically, the symphony has a regal sound and dignity that does entitle it to bear an empress's name. The high horn parts in C (as written) scale to dizzying heights with audacity and daring. (For that reason, this writer prefers that the work be played without trumpets, not only so as not to obscure the horns, but also to make their parts more exposed and thus to add some nervousness to the sound.) Haydn creates a veritable drama in his alternation of mood between the brightness of the parts with high horn parts and some lengthy shadowy sections.

The symphony is remarkably unified; it truly feels like a single drama in music. The second movement is quiet but intense. The Minuet and Trio contribute to the drama as well, with the latter section of the third movement having chilling low C's in basses and cellos. The finale wraps things up at a whirling pace, but chromaticism in the inner voices continues to keep the music's ultimate message in doubt before the bright conclusion. *—Joseph Stevenson*

Recommended:

○ **Haydn: The "Sturm und Drang" Symphonies** / Pinnock (cond.), English Concert / Archiv 463731

○ **Haydn: Symphonies 48–50** / Goodman (cond.), Hanover Band / 2002 / Hyperion 55119

○ **Haydn: Symphonies 26, 42–44, 48 & 49** / Hogwood (cond.), Academy of Ancient Music / 1994 / L'Oiseau-Lyre 440222

○ **Haydn: Symphonies 45 & 48** / Solomons (cond.), L'Estro Armonico / 1990 / Sony 46507

Symphony No. 49 in F minor ("La passione"), H. 1/49 (1768)

The adventurous, expressive nature of Haydn's symphonies from the mid-1760s shows the composer's desire to expand the scope of the genre beyond its traditional role as graceful entertainment for the gentry; the popular nicknames some of these works inspired, such as "Trauersinfonie" (Funeral Symphony) (No. 44) and *"La passione"* (No. 49), indicate that he succeeded. Of special significance are the symphonies in minor keys from this period: Nos. 26, 49, 39, 44, 45 and 52; they exhibit the well-honed wit that would characterize his later works. However, they also contain a harsher, more emotional language than the composer had previously employed—a language he would later abandon.

Many commentators, including Haydn himself, have attributed the composer's experimentation to his physical separation from the musical mainstream. In 1766, Haydn's patron, Nikolaus Esterházy, completed the family residence, called Esterháza, where Haydn would live and work until 1790. The palace was just far enough from Vienna to make frequent visits to the city difficult and Haydn's numerous duties made them nearly impossible. As Haydn later related to a biographer, "I was isolated from the world, no one near me could confuse and torment me, and so I had to become original." Some, however, have linked Haydn's style in this period with the contemporaneous *Sturm und Drang* (Storm and Stress) movement in literature.

Considered the most radical of the symphonies Haydn composed between 1766 and 1772, the *Symphony No. 49 in F minor* was given its nickname, "La passione," by its French publisher. For Haydn and his contemporaries, F minor was the appropriate key for somber and supernatural scenes in stage works as well as for the expression of passion in instrumental works (such as Beethoven's *"Appassionata" sonata*). Haydn produces unity in part by using F (either major or minor) as the tonic all of the movements, which are arranged in the old-fashioned, "church sonata" format—four movements in the order slow-fast-slow-fast; here, the third movement is a slow Minuet and Trio. The work is scored for two oboes, two horns, bassoon, and strings.

From the beginning of the Adagio we sense a weighty seriousness, typical of Haydn's works in the church sonata format. Contrasting dynamics do not diminish the dark atmosphere, which continues through the rest of the symphony.

The second movement, an Allegro molto in sonata form, is arguably the most "passionate" of the symphony. The opening motive leaps violently before a fiercely syncopated gesture takes over. After a modulation from the opening F minor to A flat major and a repeat of the exposition, an intense development section begins, featuring nearly full presentations of the themes from the exposition, but on the "wrong" harmonies. What is most striking is the return, in the development section, from the serene secondary theme back to the original key. Wide dynamic contrasts materialize unexpectedly throughout the movement, while passages of syncopation produce nervous energy.

Beginning with the same motive as the Allegro, the Minuet and Trio provide a welcome break from the somber atmosphere of the first two movements. The Trio provides contrast by shifting to the major mode. The closing Presto is a monothematic sonata-form movement that is thematically related to the previous movements. It is most notable for its highly concentrated melodic material. Again, Haydn does not attempt to lighten the atmosphere of the piece in any way. *—John Palmer*

Recommended:

- ○ **Haydn: Surprise & Farewell** / Solomons (cond.), L'Estro Armonica / 1999 / Sony 61700
- ○ **Haydn: The "Sturm und Drang" Symphonies** / Pinnock (cond.), English Concert / Archiv 463731
- ○ **Haydn: Symphonies 44–47** / Janigro (cond.), Zagreb Radio SO / 1995 / Vanguard 5/6
- ○ **Haydn: Symphonies 26, 42–44, 48 & 49** / Hogwood (cond.), Academy of Ancient Music / 1994 / L'Oiseau-Lyre 440222

Symphony No. 53 in D major ("L'Impériale" / "Festino"), H. 1/53 (ca. 1780)

After his highly creative and dramatic symphonies composed between 1771 and 1774, the following period (through about 1784) for Franz Josef Haydn is marked by many conservative and, indeed, less creative compositions. *Symphony No. 53* is, in fact, a pastiche of separately composed pieces of earlier periods and exists in at least three different forms. To further complicate the history, it is very unclear when the work was composed (the early date of 1774 has been all but refuted by modern scholars). Most agree that a good "soft" date for the work as it exists in symphonic form is about 1780.

Instead of the conspicuous drama of the Sturm und Drang style, the opening movement is decidedly insipid. It is unclear when the slow introduction was added, though it is reasonable to assume that it was added after the completion of the remainder of the movement. Though the opening of the movement proper is relatively uninspired in terms of form or orchestration, it contains enormous thematic density; the opening motive and its a variation on its inversion provide the melodic underpinning for the entire movement (even the second theme is a thinly veiled variation of this motive). Unable to hold himself back throughout the entire movement, Haydn subtly modulates to a distant key in the recapitulation and provides lush orchestration, perhaps to make amends for the dry opening.

The second movement is based on an old French chanson (a technique he used in other "pastiche" symphonies). Though well-constructed in terms of form, it lacks development.

The third movement is linked somewhat to the first; although relatively unobtrusive yet well composed, Haydn again cannot stifle his creative voice. In the minuet section, Haydn does a daring chromatic slide over a dominant pedal point. In so doing, he slithers into and out of harmonic regions surprisingly rapidly, which is in direct contrast with the relatively stable remainder of the movement.

The original finale, a capriccio, was crudely constructed and its attribution to Haydn is spurious, as it is markedly unlike any other movement composed by him, combined with a relatively weak melodic and harmonic character. The more common finale may have been originally the opening movement, and was almost certainly used as an independent overture to an opera in 1777. Additionally, it exists in no fewer than three distinct forms, two of which are found in separate manuscripts for this symphony. As the strongest movement of this motley symphony, this section is sprightly in nature and was used in a slightly different version in *Symphony No. 62*. In Haydn's lifetime it seems that another finale was published which is truly without merit and is certainly not by Haydn. However, some recordings after World War II utilize it despite its vapid melodic, harmonic, and formal contents. *—Nemesio Valle*

Recommended:

- ○ **Haydn: Symphonies 26, 52, 53, 82–87** / Kuijken (cond.), La Petite Bande / 2002 / Virgin 562041
- ○ **Haydn: Symphonies 53, 73 & 79** / Orpheus CO / 1994 / DG 439779

Symphony No. 59 in A major ("Fire"), H. 1/59 (ca. 1768)

Haydn composed his *Symphony No. 59 in A major*, for two oboes, two horns, and strings, during a period in which he was primarily occupied with writing operas. The symphony exhibits an unusual power and is quite strange in some places. These traits, and other such "evidence," have led some historians to suggest that the music was originally intended for the stage.

A note inscribed on a manuscript now in the northern German city of Schwerin tells us that the music was written for use between acts of the play, *Die Feuersbrunst* (The Conflagration), by Gustav Friedrich Wilhelm Grossman (1746–96), performed at the Esterházy palace in 1774 by Carl Wahr's traveling theater troupe. This performance did indeed take place in 1774, but plenty of manuscript and other evidence shows clearly that the symphony dates from, at the latest, 1769, before the play was even published. Therefore, it is likely that Haydn used the existing work for the play in 1774 and this association may be the source of its nickname, "Feuersymphonie" (Fire Symphony).

It is, in any event, a fiery work, with many traits placing it in the composer's so-called *Sturm und Drang* (Storm and Stress) group of symphonies. Without introduction, the Presto first movement opens with a theme of great intensity consisting of falling and rising scales accompanied by a driving rhythm in the violins. Wide dynamic contrasts animate a transition begins that reaches the dominant (E major) only shortly before the end of the exposition. The secondary theme, built of triplet figures in the violins, is just as intense as the first and closes over a drawn-out dominant pedal. The tension continues through the relatively brief development section, which focuses on motives from the transition and second themes, again stressing wide dynamic contrasts. When the second theme arrives in the recapitulation it occurs on the tonic with the familiar triplet figures, but the melody is completely altered; the texture and overall sound suffice bring the passage to mind. The movement ends abruptly with no coda.

Marked Andante o più tosto Allegretto, the second movement is almost entirely for strings. It features an unusual harmonic scheme, with a transition from A minor to A major over the course of the movement via excursions to C minor and C major. Haydn's light hearted Minuet is not unusual except that, in its second strain, he reverses the traditional order of events, placing the old material first and the new second. The Trio, for strings only, is in A minor. The woodwind instruments are the stars of the Finale, a curt, sonata-form movement marked Allegro assai. Both themes are short, as is the development section, which avoids the first theme. The first theme does receive some treatment, however, in the short coda. As in the first movement, Haydn surprises the listener with sudden contrasts in dynamics and orchestration. *—John Palmer*

Recommended:

- ○ **Haydn: Symphonies 31, 59 & 73** / Harnoncourt (cond.), Vienna Concentus Musicus / 1994 / Teldec 90843
- ○ **Haydn: Symphony 35, 38, 39, 41, 58, 59 & 65** / Hogwood (cond.), Academy of Ancient Music / 1992 / Decca 433012
- ○ **Haydn: The "Sturm und Drang" Symphonies** / Pinnock (cond.), English Concert / Archiv 463731

Symphony No. 60 in C major ("Il distratto"), H. 1/60 (1774)

As a featured part of the regular round of theatrical performances put on at the Esterházy court, the Carl Wahr Troupe had a brief residency every summer from 1772 to 1777. The Troupe specialized in Shakespeare performances in German translation, but also presented various other plays. As part of their 1774 season, they presented the five act comedy *Der Zerstreute* (The Absent-Minded Man), a translation of *Le Distrait* by Jean François Regnard. For this play Franz Josef Haydn composed an overture and several additional pieces of incidental music. The play, and Haydn's music, were very well received; the newspaper *Pressburger Zeitung* reported: "The connoisseurs are amazed on the one hand, whilst the rest of the public is simply enchanted. For Haydn knows how to satisfy both. From the most affected pompousness he drops into doggerel, and thus Haydn and Regnard vie with each other to see who can produce the most whimsical absentminded entertainment." At some point Haydn assembled this music into a symphony, which he titled in Italian, *Il Distratto* (The Distracted one).

The action of the play revolves around the absentmindedness of Leandre, whose forgetfulness gets him into all sorts of trouble. For this light-hearted farce Haydn created equally comical music; even in the more serious-minded (the first and fifth) of the symphony's six movements, the spirit of comedy is not far off. Here Haydn also made his most extensive use of folk songs in a symphony; such tunes can be found in movements 2, 3, 4 and 6.

The first movement is noteworthy for the several times the music gradually dies away, followed by a loud and abrupt return; these gestures are quite reminiscent of the "surprise" of Haydn's eponymous *Symphony No. 94* of 1791. The gracious second movement employs a French folk song, and features fanfare-like interruptions from the winds. After the Menuetto comes the fourth movement, Presto, and its frantic sequence of Balkan folk melodies. For the fifth movement, titled Adagio (di Lamentatione), Haydn employs a melody that may have derived from Gregorian chant; gentle arpeggios in the strings accompany this lovely tune; after a brief fanfare, the melody returns.

Haydn saves his broadest joke for the last movement, which bursts into action at a wild Prestissimo pace but grinds to an abrupt halt when the violins realize that their G strings are mistuned to F! They noisily retune, and then the music starts up again, flying forward brilliantly to the end. —*Chris Morrison*

Recommended:

- ○ **Haydn: Symphonies 60 & 91; Overture to Armida** / Orpheus CO / DG 437783
- ○ **Haydn: Symphonies Nos. 60, 70 & 90** / Rattle (cond.), Birmingham SO / 1995 / EMI 54297

Symphony No. 82 in C major ("The Bear"), H. 1/82 (1786)

In 1784, the Board of Directors of the Concerts de la Loge Olympique in Paris asked Haydn to write six symphonies for their concert series; this was the composer's first foreign commission, having spent most of his professional life in service at the Esterházy court. The Loge Olympique concerts, instituted in 1780, were among the most prestigious in France; Marie Antoinette was an occasional attendee, as were various officials from the court at Versailles. Over the next two years Haydn composed the Symphonies Nos. 82 through 87, now known collectively as the "Paris" Symphonies, for the large orchestra—the largest Haydn ever had at his disposal, featuring up to 40 violins, ten double basses, and as many as four of each woodwind—of the Loge Olympique. Despite its numbering as the first of the six, the *Symphony No. 82* was in fact the last of these works to be written; it was completed in 1786.

The first movement (Vivace assai) alternates between the festive, extroverted mood of its opening theme, and the more thoughtful, graceful tone of the second (which makes its first appearance in the strings over a quiet drone from the bassoon). Development section and recapitulation are especially inventively blurred, even by the high standards of this period of Haydn's career. The second movement isn't a true slow movement but rather an Allegretto—a theme and variations based on a theme in two parts, the first flowing, the second with a tinge of agitation.

The Menuetto third movement opens and closes with pomp and ceremony; this music frames a playful, graceful trio section in which Haydn's colorful woodwind scoring comes to the fore. The final movement is the one that provides this work its nickname, *"The Bear."* It features a rustic tune played over a comical drone, which suggested to its early listeners the sound of bagpipes and the dancing bears which frolicked to their sound at village fairs. Haydn moves from these rustic sounds into some exciting contrapuntal development that builds up to a false ending, giving him the opportunity for one last exciting drive to the real conclusion. —*Chris Morrison*

Recommended:

- ○ **Haydn: Paris Symphonies** / Kuijken (cond.), Orch of the Age of Enlightenment / 1999 / Angel 61659
- ○ **Haydn: Paris Symphonies** / Brueggen (cond.), Orch. of the 18th Century / 1999 / Philips 462111
- ○ **Haydn: Symphonies 26, 52, 53, 82–87** / Kuijken (cond.), Orch. of the Age of Enlightenment / 2002 / Virgin 562041

Symphony No. 83 in G minor ("The Hen"), H. 1/83 (1785)

The Symphony No. 83 in G minor (1785) is not as well known as its five "Paris" brethren, and yet Haydn's genius is no less in evidence in this work than elsewhere. Haydn opens the first movement directly, *sans* introduction, with a main theme that slowly outlines an unsettling diminished triad that resolves to a descending dotted-rhythm figure. After the arrival of the light, detached secondary theme in the first violins, Haydn combines it with the earlier dotted rhythm played by a single oboe, a figure that gave rise to the work's nickname, "La Poule" (The Hen). Throughout the development, which is nearly as long as the exposition, the rising triad, the dotted figure, and the secondary theme each undergo various permutations. Haydn provides all-new transitional material in the recapitulation and resolves the secondary theme to G major, whereupon G minor has breathed its last in the work.

The Andante, in E flat major, is in slow-movement sonata form—that is, it has no development section. Haydn does, however, indulge in some development at the reprise of the first theme. Detached repeated notes suggest an echo of the first movement, as do Haydn's use of grace notes and a secondary theme in B flat major.

The symphony's developmental tendencies continue in the G major Minuet and Trio, marked Allegretto. The stately, eight-measure opening theme is conventional enough, but the second part of the Minuet does not follow the traditional pattern of new material rounded off by the first theme. Instead, Haydn constructs the second part from fragments of the first while never actually stating the first theme in full. The texture lightens in the Trio, whose theme is played piano by a solo flute doubled by violins.

The monothematic 12/8 finale, marked Vivace, is a movement of boundless energy. The development section is a continuous series of triplet figures over changing harmonies, while real thematic development occurs in the recapitulation. —*John Palmer*

Recommended:

- ○ **Haydn: Paris Symphonies** / Kuijken (cond.), Orch. of the Age of Enlightenment / 1999 / Angel 61659
- ○ **Haydn: Paris Symphonies** / Brueggen (cond.), Orch. of the 18th Century / 1999 / Philips 462111
- ○ **Haydn: Symphonies 26, 52, 53, 82–87** / Kuijken (cond.), Orch. of the Age of Enlightenment / 2002 / Virgin 562041

Symphony No. 84 in E flat major ("In Nomine Domini"), H. 1/84 (1786)

Claude-François-Marie Rigoley, Comte d'Ogny (1757–90) was one of the promoters of the Concert de la Loge Olympique in Paris. Sometime in either late 1784 or early 1785, he commissioned six symphonies from Haydn, agreeing to pay 25 gold *louis d'or* for each. Such a commission attests to Haydn's widespread fame at the time. The works were not composed in their present order: Nos. 83 and 87 (and possibly 85) date from 1785 while Nos. 82, 84, and 86 are from 1786. Haydn requested that his Viennese publisher, Artaria & Co., publish the works in the following order: 87, 85, 83, 84, 86, and 82. His wish was not granted. The Paris publication of 1788 uses the present order. Four of the "Paris" symphonies are scored for one flute and two each of oboe, bassoon, and horn, with strings; in Nos. 82 and 86 Haydn adds timpani and two trumpets. It is easy to see why Haydn jumped at the commission from Rigoley, which gave him a chance to experiment and create something on an altogether larger and more public scale than the works intended for the Esterházy court.

One of the three works in the group with a slow introduction, No. 85 begins in a profound manner, contrasting full-orchestra fortissimo chords with quiet, arching passages in the strings. The introduction takes on greater rhythmic drive and then halts on the dominant before the sprightly Allegro theme enters quietly in the strings. The main body of the movement pleasingly combines Haydn's monothematic economy with a graceful accessibility. We hear a full restatement of the first theme, with the addition of the flute, before a lengthy, highly energetic transition to the dominant, B flat. Once the new key is confirmed, the a version of the first theme sounds in the woodwinds, transposed to B flat. The same theme opens the development section, every measure of which contains an element of the theme as Haydn produces a dense wash of sound that lasts longer than the exposition. In the recapitulation, Haydn alters the transitional material and does not bother with a restatement of the original dominant-key section.

The second movement, an Andante in B flat major, is serious in mood, with an extended coda that develops previous material prior to a pianissimo close. Haydn expands the traditional proportions of the Minuet with long, motivically organized themes in both parts. His wit comes to the fore in the second part, in which a varied statement of the main theme is interrupted by three beats of rest before continuing at a much lower dynamic level. The trio is light and comical, its first theme played by a solo bassoon.

In an unusual move, Haydn begins the development section of the monothematic Finale with the theme on the dominant, later including an unusual, complete presentation on the subdominant (A flat major). Even more striking is the appearance of the theme on the dominant very near the end of the movement. —*John Palmer*

Recommended:

- ○ **Haydn: Paris Symphonies** / Kuijken (cond.), Orch. of the Age of Enlightenment / 1999 / Angel 61659
- ○ **Haydn: Paris Symphonies** / Brueggen (cond.), Orch. of the 18th Century / 1999 / Philips 462111
- ○ **Haydn: Symphonies 26, 52, 53, 82–87** / Kuijken (cond.), Orch. of the Age of Enlightenment / 2002 / Virgin 562041
- ○ **Haydn: Symphonies 82–84** / Goodman (cond.), Hanover Band / 2003 / Hyperion 55123

Symphony No. 85 in B flat major ("La Reine"), H. 1/85 (1785)

Symphony No. 85 in B flat major is known as "La Reine" (The Queen). The first movement is notable for its slow introduction—typical of Haydn's processes at this point in his career—and for its main theme, which is cleverly assembled from two different elements: a sustained tone that seems to suspend itself above the texture before eventually falling, and rapidly descending scale. These elements dominate the entire movement. The development section is one of Haydn's longest, taking the rising and falling arpeggio of the secondary theme through numerous harmonies.

Haydn set the slow movement in theme and variations form, choosing as a theme a contemporary French ballad, "La gentile et belle Lisette" ("The Kind and Beautiful Lisette"). The ensuing variations are generally decorative in nature, elaborating on rather than obscuring the recognizable theme; the theme finds its way into different instruments for variety of timbre.

The third movement, a Minuet and Trio, contains some humorous expansions on the traditional format. For instance, in the Trio we hear a humorously long melodic extension in the second half that separates the new phrase from the expected rounding return of the first phrase. Although the extension acts like a transition, it only serves to make us wait for what we know is coming.

The Finale is a mingling of ternary rondo and sonata forms. The theme, first played by a single bassoon, is alternated with contrasting episodes, as is typical of a rondo; however, the second, rather lengthy episode has a developmental quality to it, so that the return to the main theme afterwards feels recapitulatory. *—John Palmer*

Recommended:

- ○ **Haydn: Paris Symphonies** / Brueggen (cond.), Orch. of the 18th Century / 1999 / Philips 462111
- ○ **Haydn: Symphonies 26, 52, 53, 82–87** / Kuijken (cond.), Orch. of the Age of Enlightenment / 2002 / Virgin 562041
- ○ **Haydn: Symphonies 85, 86 & 87** / Kuijken (cond.), Orch. of the Age of Enlightenment / Virgin 59557

Symphony No. 86 in D major, H. 1/86 (1786)

Considered by some to be the best of the "Paris" symphonies, Haydn's Symphony No. 86 maintains an unprecedented intensity from beginning to end. The slow introduction to the first movement, although relatively brief, is unusually expansive. A great change in atmosphere occurs at the beginning of the Allegro spirituoso sonata-form movement, in which the first theme begins in an unsettling manner. An outburst from the full orchestra consisting of three eighth notes finally confirms the tonic; the same outburst later does the same for the dominant (A major). The secondary theme is marked by a series of syncopated accents.

Haydn chose G major for the slow movement, labeled Capriccio and in a Largo tempo. Such a combination—a very slow tempo with a potential for profundity and a format that connotes complete structural freedom—produce a movement with very curious and astounding effects.

Sonata form permeates the Minuet and Trio. While following the traditional pattern of the minuet, Haydn takes his material through the modulations and resolutions that characterize sonata-form movements. In its lightness and measured step, the Trio resembles an Austrian Ländler.

Much as in the first movement, a series of eighth notes marks the changes in sections in the Finale, (Allegro con spirito). Here we find a merger of sonata and rondo form in which the typical central section of the rondo acts as a development section, and material that departs from the tonic on first hearing returns before the close. *—John Palmer*

Recommended:

- ○ **Haydn: Paris Symphonies** / Kuijken (cond.), Orch. of the Age of Enlightenment / 1999 / Angel 61659
- ○ **Haydn: Symphonies 85–87** / Kuijken (cond.), Orch. of the Age of Enlightenment / 1990 / Virgin 90844
- ○ **Haydn: Paris Symphonies** / Brueggen (cond.), Orch. of the 18th Century / 1999 / Philips 462111
- ○ **Haydn: Paris Symphonies** / Karajan (cond.), Berlin PO / DG 445532

Symphony No. 87 in A major, H. 1/87 (1785)

Despite its numbering in the series of "Paris" symphonies, the A major No. 87 was most likely the first of the group composed, not the last.

Like the other five *Paris Symphonies*, it is scored for a much larger orchestra than Haydn had written for in Austria, but does not employ trumpets or drums. Cast in four movements, it opens with a lively Vivace that lacks the usual slow introduction. The spirited, chipper main theme launches the movement with both a sense of energy and muscularity. The second subject, though it begins vigorously in the strings, is comparatively subdued and light, contrasting well with the main theme. After a repeat of the thematic materials, the development section begins with the second subject, now presented in a sterner vein, in A minor. The music works up some tension here before yielding to a delightful reprise of the main material.

The ensuing Adagio features a dreamy main theme where the strings are not so dominant, with flute, oboe, and bassoon sharing a good portion of the limelight. The melody varies somewhat throughout and its second subject, introduced by the oboe, is a bit livelier without breaking away from the peaceful serenity of the surrounding music. The ensuing Menuet is spirited and graceful in its outer sections, while the inner trio is playful and more intimate, and features a charming solo for oboe. The finale is a Rondo marked Vivace, its happy main theme and related material never losing their energy or color throughout. Haydn's writing divulges some imaginative contrapuntal features as he develops the main theme in the latter half of this brief movement. This A major symphony typically has a duration of 20 to 25 minutes. *—Robert Cummings*

Recommended:

- ○ **Haydn: Paris Symphonies** / Kuijken (cond.), Orch. of the Age of Enlightenment / 1999 / Angel 61659
- ○ **Haydn: Paris Symphonies** / Brueggen (cond.), Orch. of the 18th Century / 1999 / Philips 462111
- ○ **Haydn: Symphonies 26, 52, 53, 82–87** / Kuijken (cond.), Orch. of the Age of Enlightenment / 2002 / Virgin 562041
- ○ **Haydn Symphonies Vol. 11** / Drahos (cond.), Budapest Nicolaus Esterhazy Sinfonia / 1993 / Naxos 550768

Symphony No. 88 in G major ("Letter V"), H. 1/88 (1787)

Haydn's *Symphony No. 88* is a tuneful and inventive work that has rightly become a concert and recording favorite. It and its successor, the *Symphony No. 89* in F, were written in 1787 for Johann Peter Tost, a violinist in Haydn's orchestra at the Esterházy court. Tost, who was also a not-quite-trustworthy businessman, sold the publishing rights for these two symphonies, along with Haydn's Op. 54 and 55 string quartets and some other music (including one work by the composer Adalbert Gyrowetz which Tost passed off as Haydn's) to the publisher Sieber in Paris, then managed to forget to forward the 300 gulden payment to Haydn.

The early life of the *Symphony No. 88* is not well known. The work may have been premiered at Esterháza; it may also have been written with a Parisian audience in mind, as were the *Symphonies Nos. 82–87* (collectively known as the "Paris" Symphonies). No. 88 was certainly performed in London in 1789, and helped to create the enthusiastically receptive atmosphere that greeted Haydn when he traveled there two years later. The nickname "Letter V" sometimes attached to this work refers to the catalog of the Royal Philharmonic Society in London; in the nineteenth century, many of Haydn's symphonies were known by their call letters in the Society's catalog.

The symphony's first movement is brilliant and energetic, its slow introduction leading into a fast main theme. After a dramatic development section, the main themes are repeated with added woodwind commentary. Of the main melody of the Largo second movement, Johannes Brahms is alleged to have said, "I want my *Ninth Symphony* to be like this!" The melody, stated initially by solo oboe and cello, is indeed sublime, and features a rich variety of accompaniments in its many returns. One particularly dramatic punctuation comes from the full orchestra, including the surprising first appearance of the trumpets and timpani. The succeeding Minuet is stately and rhythmic; its folksy middle section is played over a bagpipe-like drone. The Finale's main theme also has a folkish cast, and it is subjected to a brief but sophisticated development with much contrapuntal play (including a canon between the upper and lower strings). A rousing coda brings the work to a brilliant conclusion. *—Chris Morrison*

Recommended:

- ○ **Haydn: Symphonies 88, 89 & 92** / Böhm (cond.), Vienna PO / 1975 / DG 429523
- ○ **Bruno Walter Edition: Haydn** / Walter (cond.), Columbia SO / 1996 / Sony 64485
- ○ **Schumann: Symphony 1; Bruckner: Symphony 4; Haydn: Symphony 88** / Furtwängler (cond.), Vienna PO / 2002 / Orfeo 559022
- ○ **Haydn: Symphonies 26, 52, 53, 82–87** / Kuijken (cond.), La Petite Bande / 2002 / Virgin 562041

Symphony No. 89 in F major ("Letter W"), H. 1/89 (1787)

Upon his return from his first trip to Paris, Haydn found an aging Prince Nicholas and thus a reduced demand for his services. Having tasted international fame, he was eager to venture forth into the world again, and at the urging of the London promoter Johann Peter Salomon, he began planning a trip to England. In the meantime, Haydn continued to compose in the service of Esterházy. It was during this comparatively slack time that he crafted the *Symphony No. 89*; it was dedicated to violinist Johann Tost, a former member of the Esterházy orchestra who had succeeded as a virtuoso in Paris. Haydn was still carrying on his close friendship with Mozart during this period, and the two would frequently spend hours together, playing music and exchanging ideas. The younger composer's influence may be heard in some of the scoring. An example would be the barking bassoon in the first movement—a device Mozart used extensively, but one not readily employed by Haydn. There is also a swirling transition at about the midpoint of this seven-minute Vivace movement which is eerie in its resemblance to passages of Mozart. The second-movement Andante is slow-stepping and stately, featuring the rhythmic surprises characteristic of Haydn but remaining harmonically conventional. The third-movement minuet is in some respects a throwback to the Baroque style, with its Bach-like horn calls, swirling continuo-like bass line, and complex counterpoint which at a few points even seems to resemble Baroque polyphony. The finale, a four-and-a-half minute Vivace assai, is full of simple stomping and effective dynamic contrasts. Although there are no exaggerated surprises or rude notes—these were not far in Haydn's future, but are not yet here—the movement has momentum, and a second theme provides a racy passage between introduction and recapitulation. The finale is one of the more ambitious that Haydn crafted up to this point, bringing the work to a satisfying conclusion. In one respect, the work represents a rebound from the less-than-ambitious "grand symphonies," numbers 82 through 87, which Haydn wrote during the Paris trip and which seem to reflect his insecurity at facing a new audience and a new culture. It is perhaps more comfortably Haydn and less self-conscious than those works. *—Michael Morrison*

Recommended:

- ○ **Haydn: Symphonies 88, 89 & 92** / Böhm (cond.), Vienna PO / 1975 / DG 429523
- ○ **Haydn: Symphonies 88 & 89** / Brueggen (cond.), Orch. of the 18th Century / 2000 / Philips 462602
- ○ **Haydn: Symphonies 26, 52, 53, 82–87** / Kuijken (cond.), La Petite Bande / 2002 / Virgin 562041

Symphony No. 90 in C major ("Letter R"), H. 1/90 (1788)

In the late 1780s, after many years of relative obscurity at the court of Prince Nicolaus Esterházy, Franz Josef Haydn would become quite a celebrity throughout Europe. The six so-called "Paris" Symphonies (Nos. 82–87), composed on a commission from the Loge Olympique Concerts in Paris in 1785 and 1786, had been big hits, and Haydn was soon to embark on the first of the London trips that would seal his fame. Claude-François-Marie Rigoley, Count d'Ogny had helped to get Haydn involved in the Loge Olympique Concerts, and he commissioned three further symphonies (Nos. 90–92) in 1788 or 1789. In these later symphonies, and certainly in the forthcoming "London" Symphonies, the composer demonstrates a complete, individual command of the orchestra and of symphonic form.

The idea of a slow introduction to the opening fast movement of a symphony is really little more than an abridgment of the slow movement that typically opened the Baroque sonata da chiesa. In the Symphony No. 90, Haydn solves the problem of unifying the introduction and the main body of the movement by allowing the subsidiary musical material of the introduction to become the main theme of the Allegro assai which follows. The movement is festive and energetic as, indeed, are most of the composer's symphonies in the joyous key of C major.

The slow movement is more reserved in tone. Although possessed of delicate lyricism, and a somber middle section in F minor, the movement as a whole seems surprisingly non-emotional, perhaps a comment on the superficial concerns of the French aristocracy for whom the work was composed. This atmosphere of restrained, distant dignity continues in the Menuet and Trio: one wishes at times for the more truly German, foot-stomping dances that find their way into other Haydn minuets. The humorous finale, cast in a monothematic sonata-allegro form, is notable for its extended coda, which begins after an unexpected turn into the remote key of D flat major. *—Blair Johnston*

Recommended:

- ○ **Haydn: Symphonies 90–92** / Goodman (cond.), Hanover Band / 2003 / Hyperion 55125
- ○ **Haydn: Symphonies 60, 70 & 90** / Rattle (cond.), Birmingham SO / 1995 / EMI 54297
- ○ **Haydn: Symphonies 90 & 91** / Kuijken (cond.), La Petite Bande / 1995 / Virgin 45068

Symphony No. 91 in E flat major ("Letter T"), H. 1/91 (1788)

The second of the group of three symphonies Haydn composed for Comte d'Ogny in 1788, the Symphony No. 91 is a veritable tour de force of symphonic writing at its Classical peak, a work full of warmth and good spirits. Haydn shows off a bit more than usual in the impressive opening movement. Following the broad lines of the introduction, the movement proper commences with a theme built in double counterpoint; the contrapuntal complexity of this principal theme increases as the exposition unfolds, adding more strands to the texture, first in the strings, then in the winds. Counterpoint continues to accrue in the development, preparing the listener for the skillful simultaneous combination of all of these lines at the end of the movement—a feat akin to, and perhaps to some degree the inspiration for, the amazing contrapuntal display in the final movement of Mozart's *Symphony No. 41 in C major*, the "Jupiter" Symphony (1788).

The second movement is an Andante theme and variations. This otherwise typical movement takes a turn towards the unexpected at its end, where a striking, trill-laden burst throughout the orchestra gives the impression of a well-oiled machine breaking down, leaving the players unsure of what to do next. The Menuet and Trio are graceful, danceable and well-mannered; the Trio is in fact a waltz, a dance just coming into its own in the last part of the eighteenth century. The finale, cast as a sonata-allegro, is virtually monothematic; though there is actually a wisp of a second subject, it never takes on real importance. The symphony ends as it began, bathed in sunlight and good humor. *—Blair Johnston*

Recommended:

- ○ **Haydn: Symphonies 90 & 91** / Kuijken (cond.), La Petite Bande / 1995 / Virgin 45068
- ○ **Haydn: Symphonies 60 & 91; Overture to Armida** / Orpheus CO / DG 437783
- ○ **Haydn: Symphonies 90–92** / Goodman (cond.), Hanover Band / 2003 / Hyperion 55125

Symphony No. 92 in G major ("Oxford" / "Letter Q"), H. 1/92 (1789)

The *Symphony No. 92* might have received its premiere at the Loge Olympique, but no one knows for sure. It was one of three further symphonies, after the "Paris" group that Haydn composed at the request of Claude-François-Marie Rigoley, Count d'Ogny.

When Johann Peter Salomon brought Haydn to London at the beginning of 1791, one of the compositions Haydn took with him was the *Symphony No. 92*, which he conducted at his first London concert on March 11, 1791. The work was reprised "by particular Desire" in concerts later in March and April. Haydn was quickly becoming the most famous musician in England, and his fame led to the receipt of an honorary doctorate degree from Oxford University. For his degree he had to compose a canon and conduct three concerts at the University. Haydn had wanted to present a new symphony to the Oxford audience, but he arrived rather late to the proceedings and, lacking rehearsal time, had to substitute a work that the orchestra's musicians already knew. So he conducted the *Symphony No. 92* at the July 7, 1791 concert at Oxford's Sheldonian Theatre at which he received his degree, which he apparently valued more than any of the other awards and distinctions he received in his long lifetime. By the early nineteenth century No. 92 had received its nickname, the "Oxford."

The strings open the symphony with a tranquil melody. A vigorous Allegro spiritoso follows, its propulsive development taking some brief turns into the minor mode. The varied recapitulation features added commentary from the winds; throughout the movement, the woodwinds offer delicate coloring. The main melody of the second movement (Adagio) is peaceful, with a touch of nobility; the purposeful stride of the central section leads to the touching return of the opening tune. Particularly noteworthy is the way the melody tentatively interrupts itself towards the end; then, once it gets going again, an ensemble of woodwinds has a short cadenza. The third movement is a sturdy and whimsical, rather quirky Minuet. In the exciting Finale, the two main themes are developed polyphonically after a series of pauses, and the movement closes in exuberant fashion. *—Chris Morrison*

Recommended:

- ○ **Haydn: Symphonies 88, 89 & 92** / Böhm (cond.) / 1975 / DG 429523
- ○ **Haydn: Symphonies 92, 94 & 96** / Szell (cond.), Cleveland Orch. / 2003 / Sony 87284

Symphony No. 93 in D major, H. 1/93 (1791)

The London-based concert promoter Johann Peter Salomon (1745–1815) was in Cologne when he heard of the death of Nikolaus Esterházy I, in September 1790; he immediately went to Vienna to secure an arrangement with Haydn, whom he had tried unsuccessfully to engage several times during the 1780s. Now freed from his commitments to the Esterházy family for the first time in 30 years, Haydn was finally prepared to seize this very lucrative and exciting opportunity. The first of Haydn's two subsequent excursions to London began in December of 1790 and was, by all accounts, a great success; he remained in London for two concert seasons, returning to Vienna in July 1792. The composer wrote six new symphonies for the concert series; these are now numbered 93–98, the first six of the so-called "London" symphonies.

The third of these, the *Symphony No. 93 in D major*, was most likely completed during the fall and winter of 1791; it was first performed on February 17, 1792 as part of Salomon's 1792 concert season. It is scored for two each of flute, oboe, bassoon, horn, and trumpet, with timpani and strings.

The introduction to the sonata-form first movement invokes a martial atmosphere that seems add odds with the waltz-like rhythm of the first main theme. This more quaint rhythmic quality wins out, however, and it also pervades the second theme. The highly modified recapitulation features solo passages for the bassoon.

The pastoral tone of the slow movement stems from the falling fifths in the opening violin melody and the relatively high tessitura of the solo bassoon part. In G major, the movement is marked Largo cantabile.

An aggressive minuet returns to D major with a forceful unison opening. Again, the bassoons have a prominent role. The Trio contrasts melodically static woodwind outbursts with a subdued theme in the strings.

Fits and starts pepper the Presto ma non troppo Finale; the second half of the theme halts abruptly before a minor mode presentation of the opening measures. Haydn's humor is at its best in this high-spirited movement: at the moment just before the reprise of the beginning of the movement, a fortissimo passage in which the full orchestra hammers away at the opening motive comes to an abrupt stop. A solo cello twice plays the same motive, piano, before being pushed aside by another fortissimo outburst from the full orchestra. *—John Palmer*

Recommended:

- ○ **Haydn: Symphonies 93–95** / Goodman (cond.), Hanover Band / 2003 / Hyperion 55126
- ○ **Haydn: Symphonies 93, 99 & 104** / Beecham (cond.), London PO / Pearl 9064
- ○ **Haydn: London Symphonies Vol. 2** / Davis (cond.), Concertgebouw / 1994 / Philips 442614

Symphony No. 94 in G major ("Surprise" / "The Drumstroke" / "Mit dem Paukenschlag"), H. 1/94 (1791)

Haydn arrived in England (his first trip ever outside Austria) on January 1, 1791, and the first of Salomon's three wildly successful concert seasons got started in

March. The *Symphony No. 94* was premiered under Haydn's direction on March 23, 1792, in the middle of the second season.

The symphony opens tenderly, with a genial, gently rocking main theme that builds up quite a head of steam as it is developed. As is the case so frequently with Haydn, the recapitulation of the opening themes is really more of an extension of their development. There is a nice passage for the woodwinds just before the movement's ending.

The symphony's nickname derives from the justly famous second movement, which is a set of variations on a sweet, naïve little tune. As the melody spins itself out, it gets quieter and quieter, dying to near silence—and then there is a sudden loud chord from the entire orchestra. There are several theories as to why Haydn inserted that "surprise" (which was actually an afterthought, and doesn't appear in his original manuscript). One account tells us that Haydn may have said, "This will make the ladies jump!" He may also have been thinking of the elderly gentlemen he saw in his audiences who, lulled by their heavy dinners and a few too many drinks, routinely dozed off once the music had begun. Also, with the overwhelming success of the Salomon/Haydn concerts, a rival concert series under the direction of composer Ignaz Pleyel (one of Haydn's former students) had begun. On one occasion Haydn admitted that he included the "surprise" not to startle the audience, but simply to make the work memorable in the face of his competition. Whatever the reason, the "surprise" is just one of the delights of this movement, which features a series of variations on the main theme—one stormy and dramatic, another sweetly decorated by the woodwinds, another propelled forward by trumpets and timpani. The movement's quiet, poignant conclusion is rather a surprise in itself.

An aggressive little minuet follows, with a graceful middle section for strings joined by a solo bassoon. The symphony concludes with a sparkling Allegro di molto finale; this, and other finales in the 12 "London" symphonies, calls for truly virtuosic playing from the strings—Salomon's players in London must have been a formidable group indeed. *—Chris Morrison*

Recommended:

- ○ **Haydn: Symphonies 93–95** / Goodman (cond.), Hanover Band / 2003 / Hyperion 55126
- ○ **Haydn: Symphonies 92, 94 & 96** / Szell (cond.), Cleveland Orch. / 2003 / Sony 87284
- ○ **Haydn: London Symphonies Vol. 2** / Davis (cond.), Concertgebouw / 1994 / Philips 442614
- ○ **Arturo Toscanini: Great Symphonies Vol. 6** / Toscanini (cond.), NBCSO / 1999 / RCA 59481
- ○ **Haydn: Symphonies 94 & 96** / Hogwood (cond.). Academy of Ancient Music / L'Oiseau-Lyre 414330

Symphony No. 95 in C minor, H. 1/95 (1791)

Composed in 1791, this symphony was first performed near the end of Salomon's 1791 concert season in London, probably in May or June. There is evidence Haydn initially paired the *Symphony No. 95* as with the *D major symphony, No. 96.*

It is unique among the "London" symphonies in its lack of a slow introduction and its minor key. Haydn may have felt the dramatic nature of C minor made a slow introduction unnecessary. It is also his only minor key symphony that includes trumpets and timpani.

The striking opening of the first movement, with its initial fortissimo outburst followed by a dotted-rhythm melody, is suffused with Sturm und Drang tension. A dynamically diverse transition, built on the opening figure, modulates to the relative major (E flat) for the secondary theme, a falling figure in the violins. Both primary and secondary themes appear in the extensive development section, but the forceful figure from the very beginning of the movement takes center stage. In fact, the tune sounds so many times that Haydn elects to omit it from the truncated recapitulation, beginning the section instead with the dotted-rhythm theme. When the second theme makes its entrance it is not on the tonic, C minor, but on C major, the key in which the movement ends.

Marked Andante cantabile (only Andante in Haydn's autograph) and in E flat major, the second movement is almost entirely scored for strings alone. The lightheartedness of the movement turns ominous as the opening theme returns in E flat minor.

While maintaining the traditional formal parameters of the minuet and trio, Haydn greatly expands the form in the third movement, in C minor. The first section of the Menuetto is twenty-two measures in length, rather than the typical eight or sixteen. After the first part closes on E flat, the second part begins in this same key with new material and rounds off with the typical restatement of the first section, but returning the harmony to C minor. The contrasting Trio is in C major and features a cello solo throughout.

Haydn closes the symphony on a bright note by setting the Finale in C major. The lively movement draws much of its forward motion from its 2/2 meter and constant eighth-note pulse in the accompanimental parts. The rapid chromatic adventures in the middle of the movement anticipate the fortissimo C minor segment near the end. *—John Palmer*

Recommended:

- ○ **Britten Conducts Mozart, Haydn, Mendelssohn & others** / Britten, English CO / 1999 / BBC 8008
- ○ **Haydn: Symphonies 93–95** / Goodman (cond.), Hanover Band / 2003 / Hyperion 55126
- ○ **Haydn: Symphonies 93, 95 & 97** / Szell (cond.), Cleveland Orch. / 1995 / Sony 67175
- ○ **Haydn: London Symphonies Vol. 1** / Davis (cond.), Concertgebouw / 1994 / Philips 442611
- ○ **Haydn: Symphonies 93–95** / Kuijken (cond.), La Petite Bande / 1993 / DG 77275

Symphony No. 96 in D major ("Miracle"), H. 1/96 (1791)

Supposedly, at the premiere of this work in London's Hanover Square Rooms in 1791, a chandelier crashed into the hall but didn't injure anyone because the audience had pressed forward to hear Haydn's new symphony. That's how the "Miracle" nickname arose, but it's attached to the wrong symphony; the "miracle" actually occurred during a performance of *Symphony No. 102.*

Symphony No. 96 opened the first "Haydn season" in London in March 1791, and the composer took pains to present himself as both a learned musician and a composer who could appeal to a wide, bourgeois audience (back in central Europe, he'd been playing to the courtly crowd). So this symphony begins with a brief Adagio, very serious yet neither heavy nor dramatic. This leads to the main Allegro matter with its mildly contrapuntal initial bars that burst into a resounding tutti. This music is busy, vibrant, and celebratory, full of sudden dynamic contrasts geared to keep the unpredictable English audience attentive. Of the 12 *"Salomon" Symphonies,* this has one of the more interesting development sections, working through the melodic fragments with greater thoroughness and variety than usual. Then after an unusual full stop comes the recapitulation, with a striking trumpet fanfare launching the coda.

The Andante varies a hesitant theme that consists of a brief ascending phrase, an equally brief descending answer, and a fairly long rumination on the terse exchange. Variety comes through orchestration rather than manipulation of the notes themselves, although the melody does sometimes benefit from a contrapuntal treatment. Otherwise, the guises range from the intimate to the pompous, with the former quality prevailing.

The Minuet alternates a brawny statement for full orchestra with a more delicate response for strings and woodwinds. As in the Andante, this answering phrase consists of short, hesitant utterances followed by a smoother, undulating passage. The trio features an oboe solo in a Ländler tune—a light one, not given the buffoonish treatment that Haydn often prefers.

The finale, Vivace assai, offers one of Haydn's lighthearted, scampering tunes for strings with occasional woodwind doubling. Things remain at a low dynamic level until the first contrasting episode, which is derived from the main theme—as will be each episode in this movement, which is a cross between rondo and sonata form. The music becomes boisterous only intermittently, including a brief minor-mode incident and the rousing if short conclusion. *—James Reel*

Recommended:

- ○ **Haydn: Symphonies 94 & 96** / Hogwood (cond.), Academy of Ancient Music / L'Oiseau-Lyre 414330
- ○ **Bruno Walter Edition Vol. 4** / Walter (cond.), New York PO / 1996 / Sony 66249
- ○ **Haydn: Symphonies 92, 94 & 96** / Szell (cond.), Cleveland Orch. / 2003 / Sony 87284
- ○ **Haydn: London Symphonies Vol. 1** / Davis (cond.), Concertgebouw / 1994 / Philips 442611

Symphony No. 97 in C major, H. 1/97 (1792)

Despite its numbering, Haydn's *Symphony No. 97* in C major (H. I:97) was the last of the six initial "London" symphonies he composed. It was first performed on May 3, 1792, in London.

It is the last in a long line of brilliant, festive "trumpet and drum" symphonies in C major. March-like rhythms and fanfare-like motives imbue the first movement with a martial atmosphere. Haydn creates a link between the first movement's slow introduction and the ensuing sonata-form structure by using the cadence from the beginning and end of the introduction to close the exposition, unifying what in other ways are decidedly disparate sections of the piece.

The slow movement, marked Adagio ma non troppo, is a set of variations in which subtle orchestral effects contribute as much to the variants of the theme as do changes in melodic shape and harmonic background.

Subtle alterations in orchestration are also a feature of the Minuet and Trio, in which none of the repeats is literal, allowing for changes in instrumentation and texture while following the traditional pattern of repetition characteristic of the minuet. Haydn's Allegretto tempo keeps the movement in the realm of the minuet as opposed to the quicker scherzo. At the close of the trio is a violin solo with the direction, "Salomon solo ma piano," most likely a gesture of thanks to the impresario who was responsible for the most fulfilling musical and professional experience of the composer's life. The isolation of this single line from the rest of the orchestra, supported by an "oom-pah-pah" accompaniment in the timpani and horns (an unusual use of tone color for the time), as well as the leaping grace notes in the horns and violins on downbeats, are evidence of Haydn's mastery of orchestration.

An amalgam of sonata and rondo forms, the Finale was originally marked Spirituoso, but after his arrival in Vienna in 1792, Haydn changed the direction to Presto assai. Section A is repeated and moves to the dominant, G major. Section B takes up the new key with horns pounding away on G naturals. After a few measures this stark accompaniment shifts to the trumpets and timpani—another case of unusual scoring. A reference to the "A" theme rounds off section B, which ends on the tonic and is repeated. The central section contains not only new material, but developmental passages based on themes from the first two sections, after which both A and B return in their original forms without repeats. Because section B in its original form ends on C major, there is no reason for any modification at its reprise, but the ensuing coda's further confirmation of the tonic is necessary as the movement closes with snippets of the A theme. —*John Palmer*

Recommended:

- ○ **Haydn: Symphonies 93, 95 & 97** / Szell (cond.), Cleveland Orch. / 1995 / Sony 67175
- ○ **Haydn: London Symphonies Vol. 2** / Davis (cond.), Concertgebouw / 1994 / Philips 442614
- ○ **Haydn: Symphonies 97 & 98** / Brueggen (cond.), Orch. of the 18th Century / 1994 / Philips 434921
- ○ **Haydn: Symphonies 88, 89 & 90** / Weil (cond.), Tafelmusik Baroque Orch. / 1995 / Sony 66253

Symphony No. 98 in B flat major, H. 1/98 (1792)

The general atmosphere of Haydn's Symphony No. 98 is drastically different from that of the first four "London" symphonies. The highly profound nature of the work may be Haydn's response to the death of Mozart (on December 5, 1791) in Vienna, while Haydn was in London. Haydn was clearly stunned, later writing to Michael Puchberg, a friend who had also been very close to Mozart, "For some time I was beside myself about his death, and I could not believe that Providence would so soon claim the life of such an indispensable man."

Haydn's scoring for the symphony is somewhat unusual, requiring one flute plus two each of oboe, bassoon, horn, and trumpet, with timpani, strings and harpsichord obbligato. A weighty, portentous introduction actually contains the main theme of the ensuing movement, but the tempo is so slow that the melody in the introduction sounds more like an outline of harmonies than a theme. Many of Haydn's slow introductions contain such references to the theme of the first movement, and his ability to present this material without it sounding like the actual beginning of the symphony is one of his greatest achievements. The first movement proper is in sonata form and boasts a muscular power that was hitherto unknown in Haydn's output.

The most striking aspect of the Symphony No. 98 is the Adagio second movement. Here we find a depth of feeling that stands in stark contrast to the lightweight slow movements of the previous "London" symphonies. Haydn's grief seems to come to the fore in the contemplative movement.

Perhaps the most notable feature of the Haydn's Symphony No. 98 is something we rarely hear: an 11-measure keyboard passage just before the end of the work, marked "Haydn solo" and accompanied by pizzicato strings. This was omitted from every edition of the piece published during the composer's lifetime except in arrangements for piano quintet and piano trio, where it is sometimes given to the violin. We know Haydn directed the "London" symphonies from the keyboard, as was common in performances of orchestral works, and the use of a harpsichord or fortepiano on such occasions was both a way of keeping the ensemble together and a nod to a stubborn tradition. By the 1790s the need for a keyboard instrument to fill in harmonies during an orchestral performance had diminished to the point that it was unnecessary—the instrument was seen more than heard—and Haydn's insertion of a solo for the instrument at the end of a large piece is one of his most humorous strokes. —*John Palmer*

Recommended:

- ○ **Haydn: Symphonies 97 & 98** / Brueggen (cond.), Orch. of the 18th Century / 1994 / Philips 434921
- ○ **Haydn: London Symphonies Vol. 1** / Davis (cond.), Concertgebouw / 1994 / Philips 442611
- ○ **Haydn: Symphonies 66, 90, 91 & 98** / Leitner (cond.), Capella Coloniensis / Capriccio 51090

Symphony No. 99 in E flat major, H. 1/99 (1793)

The first of the six symphonies Haydn composed for his second visit to England was the *Symphony No. 99* in E flat major. It was first performed on February 10, 1794, in London.

The symphony is scored for two each of flute, oboe, clarinet, bassoon, horn, and trumpet, with timpani and strings. This is the first symphony in which Haydn's usual forces are augmented by a pair of clarinets, which certainly contribute to the overall mellow tone color of the entire piece. The piece's plangent expressiveness often obscures its contrapuntal detail.

After one of Haydn's characteristic slow introductions, the sonata-form first movement sprints ahead at a Vivace assai tempo, the main theme appearing in the strings only. A repeat of the first theme with the full orchestra leads to the transition, which, as in many late works by Haydn, is significantly longer than the first theme segment. When the dominant arrives, we are treated to the first theme again, but on B flat major, suggesting this will be a monothematic movement. A true secondary theme, however, appears much later. The development section tosses about the opening measures of the main theme, sometimes in inversion and combined with other elements. When the recapitulation arrives, we hear the full orchestra, with all the material of the exposition resolved to the tonic following a significantly shortened transition.

It is very likely that the melancholy Adagio is Haydn's musical response to the death, in January, 1793, of his close friend Marianne von Genzinger. With an unusually long development section for a slow movement in sonata form, the G major movement features some fascinating reorchestration during the recapitulation of the second theme.

In the E flat major Minuet, the first section modulates to the dominant. This harmony continues as the second section opens with a rising motive that counters the falling figure of the first section—a perfect example of Haydn's predilection for long-range melodic balance. A return of the opening material rounds out the Minuet and brings back E flat major. The Trio, in the striking key of C major, is built of melodies with a much narrower range than those of the Minuet.

The Rondo Finale blazes along in a Vivace tempo and 2/4 meter. The relentless pulse pauses for a poignant moment at the middle of the movement, containing a harmonic reference to a similar passage in the introduction to the first movement. After regaining its momentum, the Rondo pushes to powerful close. —*John Palmer*

Recommended:

- ○ **Haydn: Symphonies 99 & 102** / Brueggen (cond.), Orch. of the 18th Century / 1992 / Philips 434077
- ○ **Haydn: Symphonies 97, 98 & 99** / Szell (cond.), Cleveland Orch. / 1997 / Sony 62979
- ○ **Haydn: London Symphonies Vol. 2** / Davis (cond.), Concertgebouw / 1994 / Philips 442614

Symphony No. 100 in G major ("Military") H. 1/100 (1793–1794)

In the wake of Haydn's glorious first journey to England in 1791–1792 (after three decades in Esterháza castle on a marshy plain in Western Hungary), he grew angry and dispirited back home in Vienna, where Prince Anton had moved the court. While he remained the official and fully salaried Esterházy Kapellmeister, there were no duties. Newspapers took no notice of his return or the extraordinary success abroad. His cherished Mozart had died; his Xanthippean wife behaved more mulishly than ever; and there was an unpleasant year spent with brash young Beethoven—come from Bonn to study with him—who made it plain that were Mozart still alive, he would have been first choice.

And so, when Johann Peter Salomon invited Haydn back to England for two more seasons of concerts, he was primed. Managing to finagle permission from Prince Anton (who kept him on the payroll as a trophy), he left Vienna on January 19, 1794, accompanied by his copyist and devoted factotum, Joseph Elssler. Haydn had already composed *Symphony No. 99* and portions of *100* and *101* (the latter nicknamed *Clock* by London audiences) for a new season of 12 concerts in the Hanover Square Rooms, where an expert orchestra now included clarinets. He and Salomon co-conducted—from the harpsichord and the concertmaster's chair, respectively.

His *Military Symphony* was the 1794 season's third and final premiere, on March 31—Haydn's 62nd birthday—and enjoyed a career-high success. The audience demanded an encore after the second movement, which introduced "Turkish" instruments (triangle, crash cymbals, and bass drum) heretofore heard only in the opera house. This scene was repeated at a second performance on April 7, and likewise after the repercussive finale. Conventional wisdom has held ever since that Haydn was commemorating the war-in-progress against France. But more likely he was remembering the Ottoman incursion of 1788–1790 into the Hapsburg Empire, during which Joseph II was taken ill at the front and subsequently died. Trumpet music in the second movement was an actual army call known as the Austrian General Salute.

Today, this symphony, with the exception of the slow movement, sounds exuberant, even buoyant, with characteristic flashes of humor. Yet Haydn quite seriously evoked war, as he did several years later in the Masses *In tempore belli* and *In angustiis* (aka "Lord Nelson"), and as Beethoven did thereafter in *Fidelio*, in the "Agnus Dei" of his *Missa solemnis*, and in the finale of the *Ninth Symphony*. It bears noting, beyond the percussive novelty, that the *Military Symphony* has a monothematic finale; that the exposition of the first movement (after an Adagio introduction) assigns the main theme to a flute and two oboes—unprecedented in concert music before 1794; and that the trio of the minuet has a loud, dotted ostinato passage underscored with timpani (could Giordano have remembered this in the opening scene of *Andrea Chénier*?). The *Military Symphony* has even more surprises than the so-called *Surprise* of 1791, plus greater finesse and a total mastery of means. *—Roger Dettmer*

Recommended:

- ○ **Haydn: Symphonies 100 & 104** / Brueggen (cond.), Orch. of the 18th Century / 1992 / Philips 434096
- ○ **Haydn: Symphonies 99–104** / Beecham (cond.), Royal PO / 1992 / EMI 64066
- ○ **Bruno Walter Edition: Haydn** / Walter (cond.), Columbia SO / 1996 / Sony 64485
- ○ **Haydn: Symphonies 99 & 100** / Norrington (cond.), London Classical Players / 1994 / EMI 55192
- ○ **Haydn: 6 London Symphonies** / Davis (cond.), Concertgebouw / 2001 / Philips 464707
- ○ **Haydn: Symphonies 100 & 104** / Hogwood, Academy of Ancient Music / L'Oiseau-Lyre 411833

Symphony No. 101 in D major ("Clock"), H. 1/101 (1793–1794)

Haydn again arrived in England in February 1794, and over the next few months presented another series of concerts including the premieres of his *Symphonies Nos. 99–101*. No. 101 was first performed under Haydn's direction at the Hanover Square Concert Rooms on March 3, 1794.

The first movement's opening is dramatic and hushed. When the tempo speeds to Presto, it is in a lively, rollicking 6/8 meter (very unusual for the first movement of a symphony).

The symphony's nickname comes from the "tick-tock" accompaniment that pervades much of the second movement (Andante). Bassoons and pizzicato strings provide the tick-tock at first, accompanying a graceful, slightly coy tune. There is a stormy interlude at the movement's center; then the tick-tock returns, this time played by the flute and bassoon two octaves apart.

With the third movement, probably the longest and most complex of Haydn's minuet movements, the symphony's nickname becomes doubly appropriate. Back in 1793 in Vienna, Haydn had given his patron Prince Esterházy the gift of an elaborate musical clock, for which he also wrote a set of 12 short pieces; one of those 12 pieces became the basis for this grand, ceremonious movement. The slightly comical trio section seems to evoke a not-very-talented village band, whose "wrong" notes and other quirks were often "corrected" by the symphony's later conductors and publishers. This trio may have provided some inspiration for Beethoven in a similar passage in the third movement of his *"Pastoral" Symphony* almost 15 years later.

The Finale is based on a lively tune that is subjected to a very complex development, even including a vigorous fugue at one point. As is characteristic of the London symphonies, the string section is called upon to play some extraordinarily difficult passages. *—Chris Morrison*

Recommended:

- ○ **Haydn: Symphonies 99–104** / Beecham (cond.), Royal PO / 1992 / EMI 64066
- ○ **Dvořák: Symphony 9; Haydn: Symphony 101** / Klemperer (cond.), London PO / 1999 / EMI 67033
- ○ **Haydn: Symphonies 101 & 102** / Norrington (cond.), London Classical Players / 1994 / EMI 55111
- ○ **Haydn: 6 London Symphonies** / Davis (cond.), Concertgebouw / 2001 / Philips 464707
- ○ **Toscanini: Maestro Furioso** / Toscanini (cond.), etc. / History 2031931

Symphony No. 102 in B flat major, H. 1/102 (1794)

Rapturously received at its London premiere and still regarded by critics as one of Haydn's finest symphonic works—perhaps even his best symphony—this is, curiously, one of the least performed of Haydn's last 20-some symphonies. It lacks a nickname and broad musical jokes, but that's a superficial reason for its neglect. Though it is the *Symphony No. 96* that bears the nickname "Miracle," it was actually at the premiere of this work that a chandelier crashed to the floor of the hall—inspiring shouts of "it's a miracle" when it became clear that no one had been hurt.

As is almost always the case in Haydn's "Salomon" symphonies, *No. 102* begins with a slow introduction. A soft, solemn chord for full orchestra complete with timpani roll announces an equivocal Largo string theme that seems unsure of its direction; the chord is repeated, and then the theme returns at greater length, finally displaced by an exuberant Allegro vivace that is essentially an elaboration of the introduction. Unusually for Haydn during this period, the movement's second subject is completely independent, rather than a variation of the first; though punctuated by two loud chords it is comparatively subdued, and hints at the minor. The development is one of Haydn's most extensive and dramatic, with the two themes trading off quickly and sometimes overlapping. The straightforward recapitulation is topped off with an unusually stormy coda.

After this, the Adagio brings a long moment of repose. Here appearing in F major, it can also be found in an F sharp transposition in the middle of Haydn's *Piano Trio*, H. 15/26. With its involuted main theme, which undergoes several metamorphoses, this movement carries a light melancholy that hints at something deeper in its very few brass-reinforced climaxes. The Minuet lightens the mood again, with its insouciant theme speckled with grace notes at the beginning of almost every bar. The trio section, carried mainly by the oboe and bassoon, just barely suggests the wistfulness of the slow movement, but this is swept away by the return of the first section.

The Presto finale has no room for melancholy. It's built on one of Haydn's typical quick string tunes, here interrupted by little sputters from the woodwinds. The melody enjoys a thorough development through the course of the movement, with strenuous, proto-Beethovenian moments scraping against witty episodes that could have been easily transplanted into any French opera overture written in the next five decades. Commentators, in fact, stress the junctures at which this symphony forecasts the coming of Beethoven: the forceful unisons that stop the motion of the opening movement, the conclusion of the second movement which is unusually muscular for such a gentle movement, the rather rowdy minuet, and the frequent balance between loud and soft statements in the last movement. *—James Reel*

Recommended:

- ○ **Haydn: Symphonies 99 & 102** / Brueggen (cond.), Orch. of the 18th Century / 1992 / Philips 434077
- ○ **Haydn: Symphonies 99–104** / Beecham (cond.), Royal PO / 1992 / EMI 64066
- ○ **Haydn: London Symphonies Vol. 1** / Davis (cond.), Concertgebouw / 1994 / Philips 442611

Symphony No. 103 in E flat major ("Drumroll"), H. 1/103 (1795)

The *Symphony No. 103* is Haydn's penultimate symphony, one of three that he wrote for the 1795 season of Opera Concerts in London, produced by the violinist-composer Giovanni Battista Viotti. The work was written over the winter of 1794 and 1795, and was first performed under Haydn's direction on March 2, 1795 at the King's Theatre. Later that year, after his return to Vienna, Haydn revised the symphony slightly; that new, somewhat compressed version of the work was premiered in Vienna on September 21, 1795.

The *"Drumroll"* of the title is heard at the very beginning of the symphony; as there are no dynamic markings in the score, the actual sound of the roll on the timpani depends on the particular performance. It sometimes starts loud and gradually dies out; at other times it starts quietly, then grows gradually louder, and then dies out again. In either case, the drumroll leads into a rather ominous slow opening that hints at the medieval "Dies irae" melody. The mood gradually lightens, leading into livelier music with a sweet, waltz-like theme. The development section is wide-ranging, and incorporates a startling return of the ominous opening music, complete with timpani roll, before a sparkling close.

The second movement is based on a pair of folk songs, probably of Croatian origin, that Haydn had likely heard back home in Austria. The two similar themes, respectively in the major and minor, are presented in a stately opening for the strings. Each of the tunes is subjected to a pair of variations, including a particularly dramatic one including trumpets and timpani, and a charming one for woodwinds answered by the strings. Also incorporated into the movement is a florid violin solo, written for the Opera Concerts' leader Viotti.

The Menuet third movement is laid-back, with some lovely doubling of the strings by the woodwinds in the movement's trio section. In the fourth movement, the combination of French horn calls and a sparkling violin tune heard at the opening carries the entire piece, which is unassuming, but subtle and charming. *—Chris Morrison*

Recommended:

- ○ **Haydn: Symphonies 103 & 104** / Norrington (cond.), London Classical Players / 1994 / EMI 55002
- ○ **Haydn: Symphony 100 & 103** / Mackerras (cond.), Orch. of St. Luke's / 1991 / Telarc 80282
- ○ **Haydn: Symphonies 99–104** / Beecham (cond.), Royal PO / 1992 / EMI 64066
- ○ **Haydn: 6 London Symphonies** / Davis (cond.), Concertgebouw / 2001 / Philips 464707
- ○ **Haydn: Symphonies 103 & 104** / Kuijken (cond.), La Petite Bande / 1997 / Deutsche HM 77362

Symphony No. 104 in D major ("London"), H. 1/104 (1795)

The *Symphony No. 104* was given its first performance on May 4, 1795 at London's King's Theatre. That all-Haydn concert, conducted by the composer, also included a reprise of his *"Military" Symphony* (No. 100) and was one of the greatest of his many triumphs in London during the 1790s. By this time he was not only tremendously popular, but also quite comfortable financially: a farewell concert given for his benefit shortly before his return to Austria netted him 4,000 gulden. As Haydn wrote in his diary, "One can make as much as this only in England." By August 1795, Haydn had returned to the European mainland, to his duties under Prince Nikolaus II Esterházy. His overwhelming fame in England had spread, and although he wrote no more symphonies, the 12 he wrote for London were soon being performed in Austria and all over Europe.

The dramatic, imperious opening of the first movement of the *Symphony No. 104* gives way to a high-spirited Allegro; its one main theme is extensively developed. The second movement Andante features a fairly simple, stately theme which in the course of its melodic and harmonic travels becomes quite touching, even profound. The grand Menuet third movement turns gentle in the central trio section, with some delicate work for the woodwinds.

As is the case in many of his 104 symphonies (and in a few of the 12 "London" symphonies), Haydn turns to folk music for the Finale, marked Spiritoso. The main tune of the movement is a Croatian folk song (identified as *"Oj Jelena"*) which Haydn likely encountered at his old home in Eisenstadt, where the Esterházy's winter residence was located. Coincidentally, the tune also evokes, according to some accounts, the street cries which were commonly used by vendors and hawkers in eighteenth century England. It might be that Haydn heard those street sounds during his years in London and was reminded of that old folk song. In any case, the melody is subjected to some exciting and complex development, and the symphony ends with an imposing and uplifting peroration. *—Chris Morrison*

Recommended:

- ○ **Haydn: Symphonies 99–104** / Beecham (cond.), Royal PO / 1992 / EMI 64066
- ○ **Haydn: Symphonies 100 & 104** / Brueggen (cond.), Orch. of the 18th Century / 1992 / Philips 434096
- ○ **Haydn: London Symphonies Vol. 1** / Davis (cond.), Concertgebouw / 1994 / Philips 442611
- ○ **Haydn: London Symphony; Schumann: Symphony 2** / Norrington (cond.), Stuttgart SWRSO / 1999 / Haenssler 93011
- ○ **Haydn: Symphonies 103 & 104** / Kuijken (cond.), La Petite Bande / 1997 / DG 77362
- ○ **Haydn: Symphonies 100 & 104** / Hogwood (cond.), Academy of Ancient Music / L'Oiseau-Lyre 411833

ORCHESTRAL

Notturni, H. 2/25–32 (before 1790)

It's odd that so odious a tyrant as King Ferdinand IV of Naples would choose as his instrument the lira organizzata, a strange cross-breeding of the viola and hurdy-gurdy. It had a limited range and could not be played quickly enough to produce an effect of regal virtuosity. Resembling a large viola, the lira had six to eight external strings that vibrated sympathetically with a set of little internal organ pipes (hence the adjective "organizzata," meaning "organified"). A crank drove a small bellows for the pipes, while the strings were agitated by a rotating rosined wheel; although the strings were not bowed, they could be plucked and fingering controlled their vibration. Mechanical keys linked to the pipes chose the pitches. The instrument's origins date to the tenth century, but this version of the lira would fall into oblivion by Ferdinand's death in 1825 (a cruder form remained popular as a Neapolitan street instrument). In its final decades, though, the lira organizzata was blessed with a handful of pleasant works that Ferdinand commissioned from Franz Josef Haydn.

Haydn first delivered a collection of lira concertos to Ferdinand in 1786; five of these survive. Soon, the king ordered another set of works, which Haydn designated not as concerti but as notturni. He scored them for pairs of lire, clarinets, horns, and violas, plus a "basso," presumably meaning cello. Haydn worked on various versions of these nonets between 1788 and 1792. Eight of them survive, although there may have been more. Haydn packed them into his trunk for his first visit to London in 1791, for that occasion rescoring them more practically. He replaced the two lire with flute and oboe (or two flutes; the parts may also easily be played by alto recorders, which give a fair approximation of the lira's sound), and he substituted violins for the clarinets.

Except for the first notturno, which adds an introductory march, each of the notturni falls into three movements, in a fast-slow-fast pattern (*No. 6*, however, is missing its finale). The slow movements tend not to be too leisurely; often they are marked Andante, an easy walking tempo. The finales are often quite fast, although the speed is provided by the wind and string instruments, the lire tootling along as well as they can. Unexpectedly in works designed for light entertainment, the fifth notturno ends with a fugue. The opening movements sometimes include slow, brief introductions and adhere to the sonata-allegro structure typical of Haydn's late symphonies and quartets: mostly exposition and recapitulation, sandwiching a short but inventive development of thematic fragments. This is all prime Haydn, full of firm, vigorous rhythms and strong themes. The notturni deserve to be better known, but their popularity is sabotaged by their unusual, impractical scoring—perversely, the element that provides these works their unique flavor. *—James Reel*

Recommended:

- ○ **Haydn: 8 Nocturnes** / Hacker, The Music Party / 1998 / Decca 458075
- ○ **Haydn: 8 Nocturnes** / Niesemann, Root, Archibudelli, Mozzafiato / 1997 / Sony 62878

Die Sieben letzten Worte unseres Erlösers am Kreuze (The Seven Last Words of Christ on the Cross), H. 20/1 A (ca. 1786)

The commission for *Die Sieben letzten Worte unseres Erlösers am Kreuze* (The Seven Last Words of Our Savior on the Cross) came from Cádiz in southern Spain. The bishop of the cathedral requested Haydn to compose an orchestral work for Good Friday services. As Haydn wrote in the preface to the published score, "... The walls, windows and pillars of the church were covered with black cloth and only a large lamp hanging in the center lit the holy darkness. At noon, all the doors were closed: and then the music began." Haydn's music was to provide an introduction, interludes, and an epilogue for the meditations of the bishop on the seven last sentences uttered by Christ on the Cross. All the music was supposed to be slow, solemn, and profoundly spiritual. The resulting composition was one of the most revered and most popular of works of Haydn's lifetime, a work played in the capitals of Europe and later arranged for solo piano, for string quartet, and for soloist, chorus, and orchestra.

After a Maestoso ed Adagio introduction, Haydn divides the work into seven movements called sonatas that are marked Largo, Grave e cantabile, Grave, Largo, Adagio, Lento, and Largo. Most movements are in sonata form with lyrical themes of ineffable pain and loveliness and dramatic developments of tremendous suffering and beauty. Haydn claimed that "it was not an easy matter to compose seven (slow movements) to last ten minutes each," but each of his sonatas is so intensely concentrated, so deeply moving, and so profoundly spiritual that *Die Sieben letzten Worte unseres Erlösers am Kreuze* is one of Haydn's most compelling works. The last sonata is followed by the only fast music in the work, a "Terremoto" (Earthquake) of overwhelming power. *—James Leonard*

Recommended:

- ○ **Haydn: The Seven Last Words of Jesus Christ** / Savall (cond.), Taibo, Le Concert des Nations / 1999 / Astree 9935
- ○ **Haydn: The Seven Last Words of Jesus Christ** / Kuijken SQ / Denon 78973

CHAMBER MUSIC

Baryton trios, H. 11 (1766–1778)

The baryton trios of Haydn occupy a large but little-known part of his output. The instrument they were composed for is now defunct, although copies have been revived in recent years. It is probably best described as a combination of two instruments: the viola da gamba with a broadened neck and the harp, the latter being situated behind the gamba section of the instrument. The harp strings are diagonally strung over a low bridge to those of the bowed part, with the player both bowing and plucking simultaneously. The resultant sound has a characteristically rich, dark sonority that makes the instrument particularly suited to slower moving music. It was a great favorite of Haydn's employer, Prince Nicholas Esterházy, who was an enthusiastic amateur performer on the baryton. As Prince Esterházy required a large repertoire to play, Haydn was frequently called upon to fulfill this need. For the prince, he wrote solo works; duos for two barytons; and serenades, quintets, and octets featuring the instrument. By far the largest body of surviving works, however, includes the 126 trios for baryton, viola, and cello. As the tenor-and-bass disposition of the scoring suggests, these are works that fully exploit the low register of the instrument. Most are in three movements, the first frequently an Adagio that both in length and seriousness of purpose carries the main weight of the work. Since many of the trios were composed in the late 1760s or early 1770s, these slow movements are often highly expressive, showing an uncharacteristically melancholic side to the composer and at times inflected with the dramatic Sturm und Drang (storm and stress) influences of some of the symphonies of this period. A few trios deviate from the three-movement format, one such being the *Trio in D No. 97*, a seven-movement work dating from 1771 that carries the subtitle "Fatto per la felicissima nascita di S: Ai:S Prencipe Estorhazi," in other words composed on the occasion of the prince's birthday. *—Brian Robins*

Recommended:

- ○ **Haydn Divertimenti** / Haydn Baryton Trio / 1996 / Dorian 90233
- ○ **Haydn: Baryton Trios** / Geringas Baryton Trio / 1995 / CPO 999094

Keyboard Trio in G major ("Gypsy Trio") H. 15/25 (1795)

Although their popularity continues to be vastly overshadowed by the universal success of his 12 "London" symphonies (Nos. 93–104), Haydn devoted equal energy during his two visits to London in 1791–92 and 1794–95 to trios for piano, with violin, and cello. The world-renowned Haydn scholar and chronicler Professor H.C.

Robbins Landon has pointed out that "in many ways, these trios are the most neglected works of the period, and probably of Haydn's entire output."

The piano trio genre has its origins in the Baroque trio sonata, in which a solo instrument, usually a violin, is accompanied by a keyboard instrument and a bass stringed instrument (originally a violone or viola da gamba), and there is plenty of evidence to suggest that a number of Haydn's trios began life as sonatas for keyboard with violin. We owe it to Haydn's friendship with several prominent society women that he went to such trouble over these particular works. The trios Nos. 35–37 (Haydn normally composed them in groups of three) were dedicated to the Princess Marie Esterházy, also recipient of a number of Haydn's keyboard sonatas. His next set of piano trios, Nos. 38–40, were written and published in London in 1795, and were dedicated to Mrs. Rebecca Schroeter, one of the composer's closest friends during his London sojourns. The two corresponded frequently after his return to Vienna that same year. Two installments from this set are exceptionally important works. The last, No. 40, in the uncommon key of F sharp minor, for example, bears comparison with other works in this key: the similarly dramatic *"Farewell" symphony, No. 45*, and the fourth of the Op. 50 quartets.

But the *Trio in G major, Hob. 15/25*, has good claims to be nominated as the most popular of all Haydn's piano trios. As with most of these works, it has three movements; the first is a series of variations, most of them with repeated sections, on a straightforward Andante theme heard in the violin (which often doubles the piano) at the start of the work. In the variations which follow, the basic theme is little altered although it is subjected to a certain degree of rhythmic manipulation, and there are the expected minor-key excursions to add further interest.

The central movement is in the contrasting key of E major, but it is the spirited rondo all'ongarese (in Hungarian gypsy-style) finale that has given this piano trio its popular nickname—the "Gypsy Rondo" trio. The first published edition laid considerable stress on this aspect of the work; a press announcement highlighted the last movement "in the Gypsie' stile," but the zestful melody upon which it is based is typical of the Magyar folk themes to which Haydn resorted not infrequently. This movement, however, has the special distinction of being the only Rondo finale to be found in any of his piano trios from this period. Of particular interest to the listener are the several "Minore" episodes, where the violin takes up the frenzied dance with even greater intensity. This spirited and brilliant trio ends in the expected home key of G major. *—Michael Jameson*

Recommended:

- ○ **Haydn: Piano Trios 38–40** / London Fortepiano Trio / 1989 / Hyperion 66297
- ○ **Haydn & the Gypsies** / Burman-Hall (cond.), Huggett, Lux Musica / 2000 / Kleos 5101
- ○ **Haydn: Trios 38–40** / Cohen, Coin, Hobarth / HM 901514

Pieces for flute-clock, H. 19/1–32 (1792)

Joseph Haydn produced a total of 32 individual works for a surprising variety of mechanical musical instruments and associated inventions. Taken together, these form what remains one of the least explored and least documented areas of his diverse compositional activity.

Such devices as the mechanical organ, and for more modest domestic applications, the musical clock (otherwise known as the Flötenuhr) had grown enormously in popularity during the latter part of the eighteenth century. Though extremely expensive, and usually of a very ornate and complex design, their growing acceptance amongst the wealthy classes was further evidence of the Enlightenment's call to unify the apparently polarised forces of technological progress and aesthetic sentiment in a single object that could provide pleasure and scientific fascination.

Haydn's works for both mechanical clocks and organs were written chiefly during the 17-month interlude between his great London sojourns of 1791–92 and 1794–95. In 1780, Pater Joseph Niemecz (of the Barmherzige brethren) had joined the Esterházy court as its librarian; Niemecz (1750–1806) was a skilled amateur inventor, with a keen interest in unusual musical instruments. Niemecz undoubtedly showed Haydn his mechanical organs, which formed the bottom sections of huge clocks, the mechanisms of which could activate the instruments to sound at preprogrammed intervals. Only three Niemecz organs survive, and most, if not all, had a range of approximately 3-1/2 octaves.

Haydn began to compose intermittently for mechanical organ during the last years of the 1780s, when he wrote several original pieces for a recently commissioned instrument of Niemecz's manufacture. In the years 1792–93, he completed the bulk of his output in this very unusual form. All have been published by E.F. Schmidt in *Nagel's Musik Archiv No. 1*, of 1932. It is perhaps not surprising that no fewer than 21 of these pieces are in C major, a concession which presumably reflects the technological challenges of adding every semitone half-step to the range of usable notes.

A considerable number of Haydn's works for mechanical clock were transcribed from other existing pieces. These included arrangements of the trio section of the minuet from the *Symphony No. 85* ("La Reine"), the virtuoso finale of the *"Lark" string quartet*, Op. 64 No. 5, and an aria ("La ragazza col vecchione") from Haydn's opera *Il mondo della luna*. Haydn scholar Professor H.C. Robbins Landon has suggested that several of the mechanical organ works could possibly have predated familiar versions of pieces like the final movement of the *String Quartet*, Op. 71, No. 2, and even more significantly, the famous *"Clock" symphony, No. 101* in D. In this case, though, where we might have expected Haydn to use the tick-tocking andante movement that gives the symphony its nickname, he chose, for whatever reason, to adapt the minuet movement instead. *—Michael Jameson*

Recommended:

- ○ **Flötenuhr** / Ericsson / 1993 / Bis 609

String Quartets, Op. 1, H. 3/1–4, 6; H 2/6 (1755–1759)

Just when Haydn began composing chamber music for an ensemble of two violins, viola, and cello is uncertain. Georg August Griesinger (d. 1828), one of the earliest writers on Haydn, states that the composer wrote his first string quartet in 1750 for Baron Fürnberg's quartet gatherings. Guiseppe Carpani (1752–1825), however, asserts that Haydn did not know Fürnberg until after 1752. Most recent research suggests that Haydn and Fürnberg became acquainted even later than Carpani presumed and the earliest quartets date from between 1757 and 1759.

Called Divertimento, Notturno, Sonata a quattro, Symphony, and occasionally Quartetto in the various editions, the quartets are hybrid compositions reflecting different traditions in the arrangement of multi-movement works. Haydn's Op. 1 quartets are in five movements, usually arranged in a Fast-Minuet and Trio-Slow-Minuet and Trio-Fast pattern, reminiscent of the Viennese serenade. The two exceptions are in a Slow-Minuet and Trio-Scherzo-Minuet and Trio-Fast format. All of the outer movements, as well as the first Minuets of the second and third movements, are in the tonic key, with the middle movement usually in the dominant or subdominant and sometimes in the tonic minor. That these works were meant to be light and accessible is evident in the fact that five of the six have first or last movements in either 6/8 or 3/8 meter, considered suitable for convivial, lighthearted situations.

A combination of old and new marks the first quartet of the set, in B flat major. The opening of the first movement must have sounded unusual to contemporary listeners; its main theme shows none of the slick sophistication of the Italian operatic clichés that had crept into chamber music. The abrupt contrast between unison writing and passages in harmony must also have piqued the interest of other musicians. Both of these features were to become characteristic of Haydn's output. The first movement and finale, marked Presto, are both small scale sonata-form compositions, the latter a monothematic example. In the E flat major Adagio all of the melodic material is in the first violin, as in a traditional Baroque trio sonata. The antiphonal nature of the first Trio is quite striking.

The second of the set, in E flat major, begins with a concise sonata-form movement with a diminutive development. Both the Trio of the first Minuet and the ensuing three-part slow movement are in B flat major, providing the only real tonal contrast in the piece.

In the third of the Op. 1 quartets, in D major, we find Haydn giving a nod to the Baroque church-sonata format with its arrangement of Slow-Fast-Minuet-Fast movements by beginning with an Adagio. Furthermore, the texture of the first movement resembles that of the Baroque trio sonata in its subordination of the lower parts to the role of rhythmic and harmonic accompaniment while the melodic material is distributed between the first and second violins.

Haydn returns to the traditional serenade arrangement of movements for the fourth quartet of the Op. 1 set, in G major. The central movement, Adagio, is among most expressive and extensive slow movements of Haydn's early compositions.

Brevity and tautness characterize the fifth of the Op. 1 set, in E flat major. The sonata form of the first movement is especially concise; its brevity creating an almost abrupt language with no "padding" between sections. This quartet and No. 6 did not appear in the early Paris publication entitled *Six Simphonies ou Quatuors Dialogués*.

The last of the set, in C major, may have been one of the first composed. It is somewhat less adventurous than the first five and features a fast, lively finale that is clearly meant to entertain. *—John Palmer*

Recommended:

- ○ **Haydn: String Quartets Op1** / Petersen SQ / Capriccio 10786

String Quartets, Op. 2, H. 3/7–12 (1760–1765)

Joseph Haydn is regarded as the father of the string quartet, and four of the six quartets included in his Op. 2 are among the earliest examples of their kind extant. Haydn's Op. 2 quartets were published by the Amsterdam firm of J.J. Hummel in 1765 or 1766 as *Six quatuor à deux violons, taille, et basse obligés, opera seconda* (Hoboken catalogue III 7–12), appearing alongside Haydn's Op. 1. These printings quickly sold out, and reprints of both sets were common throughout Europe well until the 1820s. Eighteenth century manuscript copies of individual quartets from these sets are abundant. The popularity of these early string quartets initially established Haydn's reputation as a published composer.

The quartets assembled in the Op. 1 & 2 sets were not originally so designated by Haydn. His title was "Cassation(s)"; "Divertimento" or "Divertimenti à quattro" are also frequently encountered in manuscript copies. Of the Op. 2 quartets, numbers 3 and 5 (Hoboken III: 9 and 11) are derived, not by Haydn, from six-part *Cassations* that originally contained parts for two horns. In these string quartet versions, the horn parts were omitted from the texture. While the absence of horns really doesn't change the musical content of these works, these versions do not respect Haydn's intentions and were compiled for commercial purposes.

The remaining four observe a five-movement pattern generally framed by a lively Allegro and faster closing Presto, with the Adagio serving as both centerpiece and the longest movement of the five. The Adagio is flanked on either side by a dance, usually a minuet. Overall, Haydn only minimally exploits interdependence between the four parts of the texture, and the lead violin generally carries the music along with the other instruments' support. Haydn is not yet deeply involved in investigating the effects of key relationships, and this music was once wonderfully described by BBC commentator Rosemary Hughes as "like a short country walk always within sight of one's own house."

Certain signifiers, however, indicate future developments are on Haydn's mind even at this early point. The *Quartet in A*, Op. 2/1 (Hob. III: 7), opens with a motto that envelops a rhythmic gesture that Haydn will develop as his contrasting idea. The dances in Op. 2/1 have a genuine folk character, perhaps suggested by Ländler, and do not reflect the usual trend towards the courtly minuet danced by the nobility. *Quartet in F*, Op. 2/4 (Hob. III 10), exchanges the Presto for the Allegro, opening the work in a fast 6/8 time. The *Quartet in B flat*, Op. 2/6 (Hob. III 12), opens with an Adagio, which is cast in variation form over a ground; Haydn then substitutes a Scherzo as the middle movement. Also worth mentioning is the meltingly beautiful Adagio of the *Quartet in E*, Op. 2/2 (Hob. III 8). In 1924 guitarist Hans Dagobert Bruger published an adaptation of this quartet which is allegedly based on an eighteenth century arrangement, and this has become a standard chamber piece for guitarists. *—Uncle Dave Lewis*

Recommended:

○ **Haydn: String Quartets Op42; 2/4&6** / Kodaly SQ / 1993 / Naxos 550732

String Quartets, Op. 9, H. 3/19–24 (1769–1770)

The composer-approved edition of Haydn's string quartets brought out by Pleyel in 1802 ignored the comparatively primitive, divertimento-like works of Opp. 1 and 2, and began with the half-dozen quartets of Opus 9. Even so, these are still not quite the sophisticated masterworks Haydn would soon be spinning out with such apparent ease. By this time Haydn was writing quite forceful, imaginative symphonies, such as *No. 49, "La passione."* But his quartets—or, as he was designating them at the time, *"divertimenti a quattro"*—were still graceful, light hearted pieces designed for the easy entertainment of a culturally superficial aristocracy (the guests of Haydn's employer, the more discriminating Prince Esterházy). Unlike Haydn's earlier efforts in the genre, all these quartets are in the now-traditional four movements rather than five. The first movements, formerly simple dance numbers, now follow sonata structure, except for No. 5, a slow theme and variations. They are marked Moderato or Allegro moderato (except for No. 6, which is Presto), thus launching a slowish-fast-slow-fast movement pattern evoking the Baroque sonata. A minuet comes second (rather than third, which eventually became the norm), and is followed by a songful, elaborately ornamented slow movement. The last movements are extremely fast and vivacious, and remarkably short. As in the Baroque sonata, it's the violin (here the first violin) that takes the spotlight, with the other instruments serving mainly as accompanists. Haydn knew that these pieces would be played by the brilliant concertmaster of his Esterházy orchestra, Luigi Tommasini, so he gave them a concertante character with frequent opportunities for small improvised cadenzas. The first three quartets are all in major keys: C, E flat, and G. The fourth is an unusual excursion into the minor, specifically D minor. The fifth is in B flat major, and the sixth is in A major. Charmingly unpretentious, these compositions are works of a great composer in a relaxed mood. *—James Reel*

Recommended:

○ **Haydn: 6 String Quartets, Op9** / Tatrai SQ / Hungaroton 31296–97

String Quartets, Op. 17, H. 3/25–30 (1771)

With these six works, Haydn finally broke decisively with the divertimento form that had characterized his Opp. 1 and 2 quartets, and lingered in Op. 9. Haydn was entering his *Sturm und Drang* period, so these quartets take on a new sense of drama and seriousness; they are no longer merely light dinnertime diversions. Haydn's shifting harmonies are more sophisticated, his melodies flirt more often with chromaticism, and the minor mode begins to creep into the music. These are not fully "mature" string quartets, though, in half the works the Minuet comes second rather than in what would become its customary third place. On the other hand, all the first movements except for that of No. 3 are now in sonata form with increasingly substantial development sections. The first violin remains the dominant voice (Haydn probably wrote these quartets with his brilliant Esterházy violinist Luigi Tommasini in mind), but the other three instruments are now making more significant contributions to the textures and share the thematic material more equally. The first quartet, in E major, remains light in spirit and rather thin in compositional technique, but No. 2 in F major is more vigorous and boasts a more involved first-movement development. No. 3 in E flat major begins with a noble theme-and-variations movement, and its other three movements include some unusual modulations. No. 4 is Haydn's only quartet in the ominous key of C minor, but has more in common with the shifting-emotion *empfindsam* style of C.P.E. Bach than with the storm and stress in which Haydn would soon specialize. No. 5 in G major and No. 6 in D major are to some degree throwbacks to Haydn's earlier quartet style; they are less emotive and less structurally complex, and the violin writing is often quite brilliant and attention-getting. *—James Reel*

Recommended:

○ **Haydn: String Quartets Op17** / Tatrai SQ / Hungaroton 11382

String Quartets, Op. 20, H. 3/31–36 (1771–1772)

Haydn's six quartets, Op. 20, were composed in 1771–72 and published in 1774 as *6 Divertimentos.* Although often dismissed as "early," the Op. 20 quartets have been described by some critics, including Sir Donald Francis Tovey, as Haydn's most important in terms of stylistic development.

The fugal finales in three of the Op. 20 quartets may reflect the growing popularity in Vienna of works in the style of the old church sonata, although Haydn's patron, Prince Nikolaus Esterházy, also enjoyed the fugue. Haydn's use of such a serious, learned technique in what are essentially galant style compositions should be viewed as a touch of humor, made all the more evident by the appearance of fugues in the finales, traditionally the most light and frivolous movements. The composer was fully aware of this unusual trait, for in his personal catalog the quartets are assembled into two groups: Nos. 5, 6, and 2 and 3, 4, and 1, separating those with fugues from those without.

More importantly, the Op. 20 quartets come in the wake of Haydn's symphonic experiments. Characteristics of Haydn's symphonies (for him a progressive idiom) that find their way into the quartets are increased harmonic tension, expanded phrase structures, themes and motives of a more personal nature, and more expressive writing, particularly in the slow movements. Possibly the most important trait of these quartets is the increased independence of the cello part. While three of the minuets appear as second movements, the other three are in third-movement position, further evidence of the encroachment of Haydn's symphonic thinking.

Although he composed it last, Haydn placed the E flat major quartet first in the published set. Haydn's handling of the instruments is at its most colorful in the first movement, in which there are antiphonal passages, duets, the grouping of three instruments in opposition to another three, and the rising of the cello part above that of the viola. Here, the minuet appears second. The slow movement of *No. 1* is one of Haydn's most personal creations. Marked Affetuoso e sostenuto and homorhythmic nearly throughout, the movement's melodic material moves from instrument to instrument, producing a deeply serious mood.

After opening with a sonata-form, Moderato movement, the quartet in C major features a C minor slow movement, Capriccio: Adagio, that is in a free-form, fantasia style with a hesitant opening. The fugal finale, Fuga a 4 soggetti (Fugue in four voices), carries the instruction sempre sotto voce (always quiet) and could also be described as a double fugue with two countersubjects.

In G minor, the third quartet finds the minuet again in second position. The fascinating, highly intricate slow movement, marked Adagio, is set in G major while the closing rondo is an essay in sprightliness. The fourth of the set, in D major, features a slow movement that is a theme and variation with coda.

In F minor, *No. 5* is the second of the set with a fugal finale, Fuga a 2 soggetti (Fugue in two voices), also with the instruction sempre sotto voce. The subject is stated first in the second violin, its archaic sound the result of both its opening leaps and its alla breve feel.

Lyricism is the primary characteristic of *No. 6*, in A major. This trait is at its finest in the aria-like slow movement, and even finds its way into the fugal finale, Fuga a 3 soggetti (Fugue in three voices). The first violin is charged with introducing the subject, which is somewhat like a peasant dance in its 6/8 meter and octave leaps. *—John Palmer*

Recommended:

○ **Haydn: String Quartets Op20** / Mosaiques SQ / 2000 / Astrée 8802

String Quartets, Op. 33, H. 3/37–42 (1781)

The six quartets of Op. 33 were published as a set in 1782 by Artaria in Vienna, but Haydn sought to earn more money by selling manuscript copies of the works prior to publication. He asked various patrons to subscribe, noting that the quartets had been composed "in a completely new, special manner." Many scholars have interpreted this to indicate that Haydn had embarked on a new style, an interpretation reinforced by the fact that these were his first string quartets in a decade. Others see merely a marketing ploy and maintain that Op. 33 is best viewed as indicating no general stylistic change. A real differences between the Op. 20 quartets and Op. 33 is that the newer pieces are not as weighty or "serious" as the earlier ones. Their triple-meter movements are marked scherzo instead of minuet, prompting contemporary listeners to refer to the set as Gli Scherzi. They are excellent examples of Classical unity and variety, filled with invention. Haydn's dedication of the published quartets to Grand Duke Paul of Russia inspired the sobriquet "Russian."

Haydn's tendency to move the primary voice from instrument to instrument comes to the fore in No. 1, in B minor. After the violin introduces the theme, the cello takes it up under a simple accompaniment in the other instruments. However, it becomes clear that the cello will only repeat one figure from the theme, as the accompaniment in the first violin becomes a new melody. Thus, theme becomes accompaniment and vice versa.

Haydn skillfully uses dynamic markings to accentuate the rhythm in the slow movement of No. 2, in E flat major. During a syncopated passage, piano markings make the off-beat notes sound as if they are echoes of the actual beats, even though nothing is played on these beats.

The coda of the first movement of No. 3, in C major, is remarkable in that it begins with the second theme then moves on to the first, cutting it off before it is "finished." This mirror-image presentation of exposition material helps balance the entire movement.

Possibly the most humorous composition by Haydn is Op. 33, No. 4 in B flat major. References to the main theme, a sustained note over changing accompaniment, occur 20 times, on different pitches, in a movement that is only 89 measures long, creating listener confusion. Haydn's humor verges on the grotesque in the finale. The main theme begins with a pickup to a three-fold repetition of a B flat in the first violin. Near the end of the movement, Haydn distorts the melody by placing the repeated B flats in different octaves, leaping ridiculously.

No. 5, in G major, was the first of the Op. 33 set Haydn composed. As in No. 3, the coda to the first movement reverses the order of the initial exposition motives.

The last of the set, in D major, features a Trio in which Haydn again plays role reversal as the cello tune becomes accompaniment for a brief violin figure. *—John Palmer*

Recommended:

○ **Haydn: String Quartets, Op33** / Mosaiques SQ. / 2000 / Astrée 8801

String Quartet No. 35 in D minor, Op. 42, H. 3/43 (1785–1786)

In one of his letters, Haydn refers to a commission from Spain for a set of short quartets, each to be in three movements. We know nothing more of the commission, nor do we know why Haydn never completed it, but it has long been assumed that the *String Quartet in D minor, Op. 42*, was composed for Spain, despite the fact that it is in four, rather than three, movements. The quartet was printed alone by Artaria in 1786.

It is tempting to equate the relative brevity of this work with simplicity, but the austere D minor quartet is anything but simple. Haydn increases the apparent size of the work by employing the old-fashioned "church sonata" style, opening with a profound slow movement. Haydn "modernizes" the work, however, by departing from the practice of writing each movement in the tonic key. Its unusual features prompted Haydn biographer Karl Geiringer to describe the quartet as "a foreign body in the firm suite of quartets up to now."

Opening with a slow movement, marked Andante ed innocentemente, the D minor quartet instantly establishes an air of ominous depth. The Allegretto Minuet and Trio, in D major, provides some relief from this bare-bones intensity, but it is over so quickly its effect is minimal. Remarkable is the extremely high register in which Haydn asks the first violinist to play several times in this movement. Some have suggested that the composer thought Spanish violinists were generally capable of playing comfortably in this register; others have pointed out that during this period Haydn tended to write high parts for the first violins in his chamber works.

The third movement, an Adagio cantabile, has confused commentators since it was published. A seductive melody begins in the first violin and continues for a much longer time than one would expect; it does not become the basis of variations, does not go through development and does not lead to a contrasting second theme. It broadens across the span of the entire movement, rounding itself out at the conclusion. Its purpose seems to be to provide lyric contrast in a work of intense dramatic action. Haydn infuses the Finale with an incredible intensity by employing the short theme in fugato passages, similar to what we hear in the Finale of his *Symphony No. 77*, of 1782. *—John Palmer*

Recommended:

○ **Haydn: String Quartets, Opp. 1, 2, 42, 103** / Tatrai SQ / 1998 / Hungaroton 31089

○ **Haydn: String Quartets, Opp. 42, 2/4,6** / Kodaly SQ / 1993 / Naxos 550732

String Quartets, Op. 50, H. 3/44–49 (1787)

Published in 1787, the six quartets of Op. 50 are dedicated to the King of Prussia, Friedrich Wilhelm II, who had succeeded his uncle in August of 1786 and had given Haydn a gold ring that same year. Despite the fact that Wilhelm II played the cello, there are no extensive solos for that instrument in the Op. 50 quartets. On the contrary, they possess the same sparse texture, equality among the parts and tight musical arguments as the Op. 33 quartets. In the Op. 50 set, Haydn achieved a masterful balance between unity and variety. Also, the composer imbued the quartets with a greater air of seriousness by abandoning the light, rondo finale. The slow movements, however, combine rondo and variation form.

Examples of Haydn's willingness to experiment abound in these quartets, beginning with his approach to sonata form in the first movement of the B flat major quartet. The modulation to the dominant is actually moved to what is really the second part of the exposition, during the secondary theme. Haydn's compositional economy is at its greatest here, for the entire first movement is constructed from a repeated note in the cello and a six-note figure in the violin.

The second quartet, in C major, contains an F major Adagio in which there is a Mozartean twist as Haydn moves the opening phrase from the second violin to the first, reharmonizing the first measure in such a way that it sounds completely new.

Haydn humorously refers to old-fashioned compositional techniques in No. 3, in E flat major. In the opening Allegro there is a false reprise, then the actual recapitulation begins, but the first four measures of the primary theme are missing. Composers of the prior generation often skipped part or all of the first theme at the beginning of the recapitulation, but by the 1780s this procedure was decidedly out of date. The real joke, however, is that after what sounds, awkwardly, like the close of the movement, there are two measures of silence, broken by a literal performance of the first four measures of the piece.

In the opening Allegro of No. 4, in F sharp minor, Haydn achieves his modulation to the relative major through sequential transpositions of the theme, not new transitional material. The quartet closes with an Allegro fugue in 6/8 that eventually relaxes into a sedate homorhythmic texture for the conclusion.

The F major quartet shows Haydn's ability to suffuse detail with importance, as an early C sharp in the cello becomes the pitch through which the modulation to the dominant begins. Haydn uses "slow-movement" sonata form in the second movement, from which the quartet derives its nickname, "Ein Traum" (A Dream).

Wit is the salient feature of No. 6, in D major. The first note is an E natural, not one of the notes of the tonic chord. Throughout the movement there are unsettling clashes between D natural and E natural, which becomes the pivotal in the modulation. *—John Palmer*

Recommended:

○ **Haydn: String Quartets, Op50** / Tatrai SQ / Hungaroton 11934–35

String Quartets, Op. 54, H. 3/57–59 (1788)

The quartets of Opp. 54, 55, and 64 date from 1788–90 and are generally referred to as the "Tost" quartets. Johann Tost was a violinist in the Esterházy orchestra who brought some of Haydn's works, including the quartets that became Opp. 54 and 55, to Paris. Haydn's six quartets from 1788 were split into two sets of three for publication; the first of these was printed in 1789 as Op. 54; the others in 1796 as Op. 55.

Haydn composed the quartets of Opp. 54 and 55 free from any obligations, making it possible for him to explore the art of composition for its own sake. The composer's isolation at the Esterházy palace in many ways prompted his unique development, and throughout the three quartets of Op. 54 Haydn becomes more experimental and adventurous. His use of the cello, for instance, breaks from tradition as he exploits the full range of the instrument. The slow movements take on a more dramatic character than those of his previous quartets, and the second of the Op. 54 set, in C major, actually contains two slow movements.

The unique nature of the Op. 54 quartets first becomes apparent in the Allegretto of No. 1, in G major. Its fleet movement, in part a result of the 6/8 meter, may stem from an earlier example by Haydn such as the "slow" movement of his Op. 33, No. 1. Also, Mozart's F major *Concerto*, K. 459 boasts such an Allegretto, featuring the same fluidity, simplicity and chromatic changes in harmony.

In C major, the second of the set contains an unusual second movement, marked Adagio. The movement consists of an eight-measure ground played four times. Over this foundation the violin performs plaintively, suggesting Hungarian Gypsy music played in a quasi-improvisatory manner, at one point creating dissonance with the accompanying voices. Haydn's sense of large-scale unification is at its best, as he uses the harmonic changes in this rubato segment as the basis of the harmonies of the Trio. The form of the Finale is enigmatic. Perhaps its most unusual trait is that it is a slow, not fast, close to the quartet, with a Presto central section that seems out of place, but whose subtle variations of the preceding material become clear after several hearings.

What is often referred to as the "conversational" characteristic of Haydn's quartet writing is prominent from the beginning of the Allegro of No. 3, in E major, where the theme is begun by the viola and second violin, only to be interrupted by the first violin; this trading continues throughout the movement. As in the slow movement of No. 2, in the second movement of No. 3 there is a passage in which the violin performs a kind of written-out rubato, creating some unusual, dissonant effects. *—John Palmer*

Recommended:

○ **Haydn: String Quartets, Op54** / Salomon SQ / 1995 / Hyperion 66971

String Quartets, Op. 55, H. 3/60–62 (1788)

Throughout the three quartets of Op. 55, Haydn exploits the various tone colors of the cello, bring it from the lower range to the higher through arpeggios. The slow movements take on a more dramatic character than those of his previous quartets and one of them, that for No. 2 in F minor, Haydn felt profound enough to open the piece.

The most impressive aspect of the first of the Op. 55 set, in A major, is the monothematic slow movement, marked Adagio cantabile. It is in "slow-movement sonata form" in that it has no central development section. It does, however, boast substantial development in its coda. The Finale, marked Vivace, begins as a cheerful rondo that takes on a degree of seriousness when the first return of the main theme evolves into a triple fugue. When, at the end, the rondo theme returns in its original form, there is the sense that the fugal segment is something of a development section.

In a highly unusual move, Haydn opens the F minor quartet, No. 2, nicknamed "Razor," with the slow movement, an Andante in an introspective double variation form. The ensuing Allegro, in F minor, has all the characteristics of the typical first movement.

The opening of the B flat major quartet, No. 3, shows Haydn's capacity to infuse the smallest detail with profound importance that is realized only later. In the first few measures there is something akin to a tug-of-war between E flat and E natural. The importance of E natural becomes clear only 15 measures later as the modulation to the dominant begins. The E natural is also a necessary element of the cello presentation of the main theme on the dominant, only a few measures later. The clash between the two notes is also part of the secondary theme, but here the E flat sounds like the "wrong" note. *—John Palmer*

Recommended:

○ **Haydn: String Quartets, Op 55** / Salomon SQ / Hyperion 66972

String Quartets, Op. 64, H. 3/63–68 (1790)

Haydn's Op. 64 quartets were were dedicated to Johann Tost, and their style is more intimate than the later quartets of Opp. 71 and 74, evident in Haydn's placement of the Minuet before the slow movement in Nos. 1 and 4. Certainly the composer felt less constrained by convention in these works than in more public genres, such as the symphony. The egalitarian texture pioneered in the earlier quartets is further refined in the Op. 64 set and the unity among the four movements of each work is also emphasized. Variation is the favored technique the in slow movements.

The recapitulation of the C major quartet features a segment stressing an A flat major chord for an unusually long time. When it finally resolves, the climax is as powerful as that at the end of the development section. The Minuet opens with an excellent example of Haydn's interplay between instruments as the cello, clearly the primary instrument for the first few beats, relinquishes the melody to the violins. In sonata form, the Finale features an exhilarating development section opening with a staggered, sequential presentation of the first theme, producing dense, four-part counterpoint.

In the second quartet of Op. 64, in B minor, Haydn looks back to his own Op. 33, No. 2, both in the opening measures, which suggest D major, and the shape of the main theme. Throughout the Adagio slow movement, Haydn uses the main idea, a four-note figure first sounding in the first violin, in a cantus firmus manner with decoration and variation happening around it.

The third of the set, in B flat major, shows Haydn at his wittiest, especially in the Finale. Irregular melodies abound in the first group of the opening Vivace assai, but after the modulation to the dominant we hear a regular, four-measure theme. In a humorous twist, this theme does not appear in the recapitulation, most likely because when it shows up in the development section it does so in full and on the tonic, thus, the development takes on the role of the recapitulation.

The recapitulation of the first movement of the G major quartet covers the main theme twice. This is in part because the theme makes a brief second appearance in the exposition and mainly because the recapitulation almost immediately moves to G minor, requiring a second statement in the major mode.

Only after a few measures of sparse, non-melodic material do we hear the principal theme of the D major quartet, played high in the stratosphere by the first violin. Curiously, this theme, when it appears in the development section, is always played in full, never fragmented. The Vivace Finale juxtaposes moto perpetuo, soloistic writing for the first violin with a passage in double fugue, placing highly contrapuntal segments next those in a more popular, homorhythmic style.

Haydn's attention to detail comes to the fore in the last of the set, in E flat major. In the first movement, a rising half-step in the violins in the ninth and tenth measures becomes the beginning of the transition as all four instruments play the same interval in measure 13. *—John Palmer*

Recommended:

○ **Haydn: String Quartets, Op64** / Tatrai SQ / Hungaroton 11838

String Quartets, Op. 71, H. 3/69–71 (1793)

After Haydn returned to Vienna in July, 1792, has was able, for the first time in many years, to compose in peace. Free of his long-standing duties as Kapellmeister for the Esterházy family, and temporarily free of contractual obligation to Johann Peter Salomon, the promoter of his visits to London, he composed his *Symphony in E flat major, No. 99* and began work on his quartets dedicated to Count Apponyi, Opp. 71 and 74. The Op. 71 quartets were intended for public, rather than private, performance, and so they have a less intimate character than those of Op. 64 or Op. 76. Bold unison passages and a greater emphasis on harmonic processes bring to mind Haydn's symphonic compositions. Haydn's first-movement introductions in these quartets are unusually terse, but still create a sense of anticipation.

The first quartet, in B flat major, departs from the style of his first "London" symphonies and contemporaneous quartets by reusing passages from the first theme group as developmental material in the opening movement. The second movement, adagio, blurs the formal lines between sonata form and the simpler minuet. The following Minuet and the lively Trio are both in B flat major, and the propulsive Vivace is a masterpiece of motivic manipulation and contrapuntal passage work.

In D major, the second of the Op. 71 set is the only quartet from Opp. 71 and 74 in which the introduction to the first movement is in a slower tempo than the main body. Haydn's clear delineation of melody from accompanimental textures is reminiscent of his symphonies from the same period. The Adagio cantabile is notable for its sustained lyricism, and the concluding rondo is marked by alternating major and minor harmonies.

The opening gesture of the third quartet—a single E flat major chord—may well have inspired Beethoven's similar gesture in his *Third Symphony.* Most notable is the second movement, in which the pattern of repetition creates a double minuet and trio format, rounded by a varied return to the first theme. *—John Palmer*

Recommended:

○ **Haydn: String Quartets Op71/1–3** / Kodaly SQ / 1991 / Naxos 550394

String Quartets, Op. 74, H. 3/72–74 (1793)

English violinist and impresario Johann Peter Salomon brought Haydn to England twice, in 1790 and 1794. The first time, he came with a selection of his most recent symphonies and string quartets. The second time, he came with symphonies and string quartets newly composed for English tastes in general and for Salomon's style in particular. Commissioned by Hungarian nobleman Count Antal Apponyi, the six string quartets Haydn composed for England were published privately in London in 1795 and publicly in London, Paris, and Vienna in 1796. When they were published as part of a complete edition of the quartets in Haydn's lifetime, the six quartets were divided into two groups of three printed as Op. 71 and Op. 74. The three quartets of Op. 74 were probably composed after the Op. 71, but in substance they are aesthetically equal. Both sets are Haydn at his mature best: rhythmically muscular, thematically cogent, structurally compelling, brilliantly witty, and sometimes incredibly soulful. The *String Quartet in C major,* Op. 74/1, starts with a vivacious Allegro moderato with a virtuoso first violin part, moves through an endlessly charming Andantino grazioso and a Minuet that is less a dance than an outburst of bad temper, and ends with a Vivace Finale that is all dance set in sonata form. The *String Quartet in F major,* Op. 74/2, starts with a powerfully argued and openly joyful Allegro spiritoso, moves through a deeply affecting Andantino grazioso and a Minuet with a barrel organ trio, and ends with a delightfully droll and contrapuntally concentrated Presto Finale. The *String Quartet in G minor,* Op. 74/3, is the best known of the Op. 74 set of quartets, no doubt because of its nickname, "The Rider." The triple-time opening Allegro moderato is tightly built and intensely rhythmic. The Largo assai is leanly lyrical and surprisingly modern for 1793. The Minuet is in the tonic major, while its Trio is in the tonic minor. The closing Allegro con brio starts in the tonic minor but, earning its nickname, rides to victory in the glorious tonic major on the last page. *—James Leonard*

Recommended:

○ **Haydn: String Quartets, Op74/1–3** / Kodaly SQ / 1990 / Naxos 550396

String Quartets, Op. 76, H. 3/75–80 (1797)

After Haydn returned to Vienna after his second journey to London in 1794–95, he all but quit composing instrumental music. The string quartet was the only instrumental genre he consistently pursued in his later years, completing the six *"Erdödy" Quartets,* Op. 76 in 1797 and the two (of a planned set of six) *"Lobkowitz" Quartets,* Op. 77, in 1799. By 1803, he had finished only two movements of another quartet, which he had published in 1806 as Op. 103. Haydn dedicated the six quartets of Op. 76 to Count Joseph Erdödy, whose exclusive rights to use the works for a period delayed their publication until 1799.

The freedom and diversity that mark Haydn's style are everywhere evident in the Op. 76 quartets, where works of vastly contrasting atmospheres are placed side by side. Haydn stresses textural contrast in the first of the six quartets of Op. 76, in G major; large, quasi-orchestral chords are set off from passages of masterful, relaxed counterpoint. The sublime second movement, marked Adagio sostenuto, is similar to Mozart's "March of the Priests" from *Die Zauberflöte.* Because of its Presto tempo, the third movement, a Menuetto, takes on the character of a genuine scherzo with a feel of one beat per measure. Innovation continues in the finale, which is in the minor mode and turns to the major only in its last few measures before the coda.

Because of its key and texture, the Quartet in D minor (No. 2), recalls Mozart's K. 421, also the second in his set of "Haydn" quartets. Because of the preponderance of the interval of a fifth, heard from the outset, the piece has earned the nickname, "Fifths." The Menuetto boasts a lengthy canon between the upper and lower strings. A rising fifth at the end of the Finale seems to counter the numerous falling fifths of the first movement, making this piece among the most tightly constructed of Haydn's quartets. Unusually, the different movements of the work do not explore different tonalities; rather, the alternate between D minor and major.

The most popular of the six Op. 76 quartets is No. 3, in C major ("Emperor"), dated September 28, 1797. This fame is the result of the second movement, a fine set of variations on Haydn's own *Emperor's Hymn*, which Haydn composed to be Austria's National Hymn. (The piece would later be appropriated by Germany for its National Hymn.) The atmosphere overall is more relaxed than that of the D minor quartet.

A stunning opening with a long melody in the first violin emerging from sustained chords in the lower strings prompted one listener, at least, to christen the B flat major quartet, "Sunrise." That the second theme of the movement is an inversion of the "Sunrise" theme seems to have gone unnoticed by the christener.

Haydn begins the fifth quartet, in D major, with an unusual variation movement that strays from the harmonic structure of the theme. Because of the importance of B minor in the work and the slow movement's key of F sharp major, this quartet may be the first example of a work built around keys related by a third.

Beginning with a set of variations that closes with a fugue, the last of the set is in E flat major. Haydn's experimentation is perhaps at it greatest in the second movement, a "Fantasia" that takes the listener on a far-reaching tonal journey. As in the G major quartet, the Menuetto is so fast that it is indeed a scherzo, the Trio of which is labeled "Alternativo." *—John Palmer*

Recommended:

- ○ **Haydn: String Quartets Op76** / Mosaiques SQ / 2000 / Astrée 8665

String Quartets ("Lobkowitz"), Op. 77, H. 3/81–82 (1799)

Haydn all but quit composing instrumental music when he returned to Vienna after his second journey to London in 1794–95. The string quartet was the only instrumental genre he consistently pursued in his later years, completing the six *"Erdödy" Quartets*, Op. 76, in 1797 and the two *"Lobkowitz" Quartets*, Op. 77, in 1799. By 1803, he had finished two movements of another, which were published in 1806 as Op. 103.

Why Haydn was unable to finish his projected set of six quartets for Prince Lobkowitz is a matter of conjecture. Some critics have suggested that the appearance of Beethoven's Op. 18 quartets during the time Haydn was composing his pieces may have caused the elder composer to feel that his work would be judged old-fashioned by comparison; however, the composition and publication dates of the various quartets by both composers lead one to question the plausibility of this suggestion.

The first of the two "Lobkowitz" quartets, in G major, is considered by many to be Haydn's finest, with especially idiomatic writing for the four instruments. The first movement demonstrates that the essence of sonata form for Haydn was the manipulation of tonal materials, not melodies. For instance, one of the themes appears on the tonic at the end of the development section; thus, in a highly unusual procedure, the development has taken on some of the responsibility for resolution normally found in the recapitulation. The crowning glory of the piece is the second movement, an Adagio with a loose sonata-form structure. Both dominant major and minor are present in the secondary themes and the recapitulation is more a variation on the exposition than a reprise. The Finale is a virtuosic dance, perhaps based on the *kolo*, a round dance from Croatia.

In F major, the second quartet of Op. 77 boasts wit and subtlety that has been likened to the *Symphony No. 99*, although the writing is in a more private, learned style. The first movement opens with a lengthy theme, fragments of which then become an accompaniment to the second theme. Motives from the transition between the two themes play the largest role in the contrapuntal development before the straightforward recapitulation closes the movement. Although the scherzo-like Minuet is in F major, the Trio is in the unexpected key of D flat major, more related to F minor than F major. The pathetic half-step relationship between D flat and the dominant, C major, becomes clear in the tiny coda. Such harmonic relationships are the type Beethoven would employ throughout his maturity. The Andante brings together elements of Variation and Rondo form wherein the returning rondo theme is varied at each repetition. The movement, in D major, is even more removed tonally from the first and last movements than is the Minuet. After the shock of the Andante's F sharps suddenly becoming F naturals in the first measure of the Finale, the listener becomes aware that the Finale is a light-hearted, relatively simple sonata-form structure. It is monothematic in that the secondary theme is a varied restatement of the first. Furthermore, the contrapuntally conceived development section is almost totally based on the first theme. *—John Palmer*

Recommended:

- ○ **Haydn: String Quartets, Op77** / Mosaiques SQ / 2000 / Astree 8800
- ○ **Haydn: Last 3 String Quartets** / L'Archibudelli / 1997 / Sony 62731

String Quartet in D minor, Op. 103, H. 3/83 (unfinished) (1803)

Haydn was in failing health when he accepted a commission in 1803 for six quartets from Count Moritz von Fries, who was also an active supporter of Beethoven. Haydn began a quartet with its less demanding inner movements, intending to write the more mentally taxing outer movements—and the rest of the set—when he felt stronger. By and by, he realized that his health would not improve, and he had the two finished movements published on their own with the announcement that they should be considered his farewell. The Andante grazioso, in B flat, is in ternary song form. The first of its three sections is a measured, patrician yet bittersweet melody carried mainly by the violins with some especially rich supporting work for the viola and cello. The initially mysterious second section is a sort of development of the first, lacking a really coherent, independent melody. It is mostly atmosphere, passing through several unexpected major and minor keys and brief moments of sharp drama. Eventually the opening melody returns in its original B flat for a full repetition of the initial section, rounded out by a lengthy coda and a few decisive chords. The Minuet is in an unexpectedly dramatic D minor, and even though the pulse is a clearly felt 3/4, the unsettled movement here toils far from its origins as a formal dance. Its phrases are alternately stern and questioning, and entirely unsettling. The trio brings on the more reassuring key of D major, but the melodic writing is highly chromatic and some of the harmonic voicing is quite full, looking ahead to middle-period and late Beethoven. The movement's severe opening section returns to close out this torso of a quartet, which would surely have been one of Haydn's most remarkable works had he been able to complete its outer movements in the same manner. *—James Reel*

Recommended:

- ○ **Haydn: String Quartets, Op77** / Mosaiques SQ / 2000 / Astree 8800
- ○ **Haydn: 7 Last Words of Jesus Christ; String Quartet, Op103** / Kodaly SQ / 1989 / Naxos 550346

Trio for 2 flutes & cello in C major ("London"), H. 4/1 (1794)

In his London notebook entry for the date November 14, 1794, Haydn wrote: "I went with Lord Abingdon to Preston, 26 miles from London, to visit the Baron of Aston—he and his wife both love music...." It was for this visit that the composer took with him as a hostess present several divertimentos for the uncommon instrumental grouping of two flutes and cello. Two of these works were published in January 1799, by Earl Abingdon's friend Teobaldo Monzani, an accomplished flute-player, who also had interests in the publishing business. The complete set of four trios are known collectively as Haydn's *London Trios*. Haydn must have been well aware of the flute's growing popularity in England, since it had become the most fashionable amateur instrument, second only to the harpsichord.

Trio No. 1 in C (Hob. 4:1) has three movements, Allegro moderato, Andante, Vivace, in the familiar fast-slow-fast pattern common to most of Haydn's trios. The work survives in Haydn's original manuscript (at the Staatsbibliothek in Berlin), but there are two alternative versions of the slow movement, and Haydn scholars have naturally concluded that the longer one, of some 45 measures in all, is in all likelihood Haydn's final definitive statement. However, the problem is an intriguing one, and the evidence is not entirely conclusive. Monzani's first published edition takes material from both Haydn texts, but it is not clear why Haydn should have gone to seemingly inordinate lengths over what is a fairly inconsequential, if delightful little piece. Even if the *London Trios* stand for little more than a great composer having fun, this first work of the set also reveals Haydn's wit and originality as much as his occasionally more serious side. This latter is felt in the terse rigor of the development section of the sonata form first movement. Although only three voices are employed, Haydn still manages to create a harmonic severity and canonic interest normally expected in much more complex music.

Like so many of Haydn's lighter pieces, however, the *London Trios* quickly fell out of vogue, and were not reintroduced to the chamber literature until 1909. Robbins Landon states by 1971, San Francisco buskers had them in their repertories, and that they "got the biggest audiences and made the most money." Robbins Landon adds, this was "a purpose for which Haydn certainly did not intend his *London Trios*, but which illustrates how music of this charm, vitality, and technical mastery will survive despite the works' temporary eclipse in the nineteenth century." *—Michael Jameson*

Recommended:

- ○ **Haydn: 6 Quartets, Op5; London Trios** / Kuijken Ens. / Accent 9283/84
- ○ **Haydn: London Trios; Divertissements** / Rampal, Rostropovich, Stern / 1982 / CBS 37786

Trio for 2 flutes & cello in G major ("London"), H. 4/2 (1794)

The second of Haydn's four trios for two flutes and cello was published along with the first one in an edition overseen by Teobaldo Monzani, a flutist who also had business interests in instrument making and publishing. Monzani was a friend of Lord Abingdon, an amateur flutist, for whom Haydn wrote this trio. The entire work takes a mere four minutes to perform and is based on the song *The Ladies Looking-Glass* or "Trust Not Too Much," which was one of the songs said to have been written by Lord Abingdon and harmonized by Haydn (Hob. 31c/17). The melody is plain and does not range too far, which makes it a perfect theme for variations, which is how Haydn treats it in the first movement of the trio. The two flutes share the bulk of the work, creating pleasant, not too complex versions of the theme, while the cello provides a simple bass line. Usually one flute has the theme or a similarly paced modified theme, and the second has a more florid or moving line to contrast. The extremely brief second movement, Allegro, is actually another variation of the song, a jaunty version with trills and even a coda attached. *—Patsy Morita*

Recommended:

- ○ **Haydn: 6 Quartets, Op5; London Trios** / Kuijken Ens. / Accent 9283/84

CONCERTO

Concertos (ca. 1756–1796)

Possibly because Haydn was not a virtuoso performer, he composed few concertos. He could, however, compose virtuosic music, but his virtuosity appears more in his chamber works and symphonies than in the concertos.

Haydn's earliest known keyboard concerto, in C and for organ or harpsichord, two oboes, and strings (*H. 18/1*), is dated 1756. It shows the 24-year-old Haydn to be a capable composer, working in the church-music style and following in the footsteps of his older Viennese contemporaries such as Wagenseil. The *Piano Concerto in D* (H. 18/11) of 1784 departs from the style of Haydn's earlier works in the genre in that it approaches the more contemporary, symphonic style of concerto composition.

The *Concerto for Trumpet in E flat* (H. 7e/1) is one of Haydn's most popular works and arguably the best known of all trumpet concertos. It was composed in 1796, just after Haydn had returned form his second trip to London. The concerto's scoring for both the solo instrument and orchestra is masterful, betraying Haydn's previous experience with the orchestra while composing the "London" symphonies.

In Haydn's personal thematic catalog he lists four violin concertos. Of these, No. 2, in D, is missing. Several violin concertos formerly attributed to Haydn have proven to be by composers such as Stamitz, Cannabich, and Haydn's brother, Michael. The three authenticated violin concertos, in C, G, and A, date from 1765–70, the early years of Haydn's tenure at Esterházy, and were probably composed for the court violinist, Luigi Tomasini, to be accompanied only by strings. The concertos in C and G were not printed until the early twentieth century; that in A in 1952. That in C is the most virtuosic of the three, with numerous double stops and high passages. Cantabile writing in the Italian style characterizes the slow middle movement and recalls Haydn's *Symphony No. 6, "Le matin."* The solo part of the concerto in G is not as technically demanding as that of the C major concerto, and the work is Baroque in conception, with a solo part consisting mostly of modulatory passages, leaving the thematic material to the orchestra. Rediscovered in only 1949, the concerto in A (often referred to as the *"Melk" Concerto*, after the monastery at which it was found) shows a more Classical-era approach in which the soloist and orchestra share the presentation of thematic material. The oboe parts heard in recordings are a hypothetical reconstruction.

The *Cello Concerto in C*, Haydn's first, was rediscovered in 1961. The only known manuscript copy is signed by Joseph Weigl (the elder), cellist in Haydn's orchestra at Esterházy from 1761–68, thus giving a rough idea of when the work was composed. Although published as a work by Haydn in 1803, the *Cello Concerto in D* was long thought to be the work of Anton Kraft, Esterházy cellist from 1778–90. One of the best known concertos for the cello, it exhibits all the wit, charm and inventiveness of the mature Haydn. *—John Palmer*

Recommended:

- ○ **Haydn: Concerti** / Marriner, Rolla, Haselbock, Dafov (conds.), Lencses, Friedrich, Kalafusz, Perenyi, Gleissner, Herder, Evrov, Sofia PO, Franz Liszt CO, etc. / 2002 / Capriccio 51102

Cello Concerto No. 1 in C major, H. 7b/1 (1761–1765)

Composed between 1761 and 1765 for Joseph Weigl, a gifted cellist in Haydn's Esterházy orchestra, this concerto was presumed lost until 1961, when it turned up the National Museum in Prague among documents originally from Radenin Castle. High virtuosity is demanded of the cellist, as in the Sixth, Seventh, and Eighth symphonies (in which Haydn provided solos especially for Weigl). What Haydn did not provide are authenticated cadenzas for the first and second movements; cellists generally employ either anonymous eighteenth century cadenzas, or those prepared since 1961.

The first movement, marked Moderato, begins with a confident, courtly theme with dotted rhythms; in contrast, the second subject is softer and more sinuous, establishing a more lyrical mood. The mildly syncopated orchestral exposition ends with Lombardic rhythms at the conclusion of the orchestral introduction. When the cello enters and takes command of the themes, it launches the first theme with a resonant C major chord, eventually presenting each melody in an increasingly ornate manner. The development engages the cellist in intense passagework derived from the primary theme, while reappearances of the second subject allow the soloist to sing more expansively. Haydn works through the theme groups in sequence twice before reaching the cadenza and a brief coda derived from the movement's opening measures.

The Adagio dispenses with the orchestra's oboes and horns, leaving the soloist to emerge from the sound of the string orchestra with a long, powerfully expressive note. The noble, somewhat melancholic, first theme requires an especially strong tone from the cello, while its answering subject calls for double stops. The movement's shadowy middle section derives from a theme almost as austere as one from a Baroque church sonata, yet encourages the cellist to play with a warm, expressive tone. The third section is an abbreviated repetition of the first one.

Last comes an Allegro molto finale which pretty much follows the ritornello form found in many Vivaldi concertos. The orchestra establishes a fleet theme that recurs, as in a rondo, throughout the rest of the movement. As in the slow movement, almost every time the cello enters, it emerges from the orchestra with a single, long note; this time, however, the long note metamorphoses into a rapidly ascending C major scale. However, while expected to execute intricate high-register passagework which includes rapid scales, the cellist also has an opportunity to interpret melodic phrases of exceptional lyricism. *—James Reel*

Recommended:

- ○ **Haydn: Cello Concertos** / Rostropovich, Academy of St. Martin-in-the-Fields / 2000 / Angel 67263
- ○ **Haydn: Cello Concertos** / Harding (cond.), Capucon, Mahler CO / 2003 / Virgin 45560
- ○ **Haydn & Vivaldi: Cello Concertos** / Marriner (cond.), Harrell, Academy of St. Martin-in-the-Fields / 2001 / EMI 74734
- ○ **Jacqueline du Pré Concerto Collection** / Barenboim (cond.), Du Pré, English CO / 2000 / EMI 67341
- ○ **Haydn: Cello Concertos; Sinfonia Concertante** / Norrington (cond.), Isserlis, CO of Europe / 1998 / BMG 68578

Cello Concerto No. 2 in D major, H. 7b/2 (Op. 101) (1783)

Dating from 1783, this concerto not only brilliantly exploits the resources of the cello, using double-stops, octaves, and high-register passagework, but also rewards the listener with music of extraordinary beauty and elegance. Perhaps composed for Anton Kraft, the principal cellist at the Esterházy court during the 1780s, the concerto was even regarded as Kraft's work. However, the discovery, in 1951, of Haydn's autograph finally settled the issue of authorship.

A more relaxed work than Haydn's effervescent *C major cello concerto*, which was composed in the early 1760s, this concerto starts with a long, rich orchestral exposition, in which the principal themes of the first movement (Allegro moderato) are presented. The first theme introduces a mood of delightful repose which is slightly modified, but not interrupted, by the pleasing chromaticism of the second theme. When the soloist reiterates the first theme, adding beautiful, and technically demanding, ornamentation, the listener is able to enjoy the balanced, mellifluous interplay between the soloist and the orchestral accompaniment. Haydn's ritornellos are lengthy, particularly the second one, but critics who bemoan the length of this movement seem to ignore the sheer esthetic pleasure that Haydn's music, in concise or elaborate form, provides. While the development section imposes a variety of technical demands on the cellist, whose left hand literally races up and down the fingerboard, this part of the movement contains many passages of enchanting lyricism.

In the Adagio, which the soloist opens opens with an expansive, almost dreamy, theme, the feeling of tranquillity is maintained. Yet, as in the first movement, what the composer conveys to the listener is not languor, but a realization that intuitions of wisdom and beauty can, and sometimes must, be savored slowly, even if that offends the impatient listener. Reminiscent of a gentle, unassuming operatic aria, the main theme is presented three times, enabling the soloist to express the main musical idea in different manners. These reiterations of the theme maintain the flow, so to speak, of the musical discourse. Once the orchestra softly restates the opening tune, the cello indulges in a quiet cadenza and leads the orchestra into a brief coda.

The final Allegro is a rondo revolving around a bright pastoral tune of an almost childlike simplicity. The cello moves through the musical landscape with jaunty rhythms and intricate passagework. On its second entrance, the pastoral theme appears in a minor mode, which gives the soloist an opportunity to perform ascending arpeggio-like figurations leading to another cadenza. The main theme regains its sunny nature for a last appearance, which surrounds virtuosic passagework for the cello. However, there is more to this movement than a fanciful blend of pastoral motifs and flashy virtuosity: the technically involved elaborations of the theme reveal musical ideas and feelings of remarkable depth and intensity. *—AMG*

Recommended:

- ○ **Haydn: Cello Concertos in C & D; Sinfonia Concertante** / Norrington (cond.), Isserlis, CO of Europe / 1998 / RCA 68578
- ○ **Haydn & Vivaldi: Cello Concertos** / Harrell, Marriner (cond.), Academy of St. Martin-in-the-Fields / 2001 / EMI 74734
- ○ **Haydn: Cello Concertos 1 & 2** / Rostropovich, Academy of St. Martin-in-the-Fields / 2000 / EMI 67263

○ **Haydn & Boccherini: Cello Concertos** / Barbirolli (cond.), Du Pré, London SO / 1998 / EMI 66948

Trumpet Concerto in E flat major, H. 7e/1 (1796)

A favorite of the trumpet repertoire and possibly Haydn's most popular concerto, this work was composed in 1796 while the composer was working on the *Creation.* In the final years of his career Haydn seemed to prefer large choral works to instrumental pieces, but he was intrigued by a request for a concerto from Anton Weidinger, the trumpeter in the Vienna Court Orchestra. The valveless trumpets of the time could play only notes derived from a fundamental pitch and its related harmonic series, and so trumpet music tended to be melodically limited. Weidinger invented a keyed trumpet along the lines of a woodwind instrument; with drilled holes in the body of the instrument, the player could easily raise the pitch in half-tone steps, enabling them to play chromatic passages. The modern trumpet has been greatly refined since Weidinger's time, but the principle remains the same. Weidinger did not perform the Concerto in public until 1800. Surviving in a single manuscript copy, this extraordinary work wasn't performed again until 1929.

Splendidly orchestrated, Haydn's Concerto fully exploits the trumpet's new technical abilities. The opening Allegro is festive and radiant, with the orchestra introducing the main themes before they're taken up by the soloist. There's a motif that initially rises, subsequently allowing the trumpet to show off its new stock of notes in the low register. This motif evolves into a fanfare-like subject, which the soloist enriches with effective trills and other ornamentation. The development section requires the trumpeter to play in different keys, which would have been impossible on a valveless trumpet. Opening with a lovely, expansive melody in siciliano style, the second movement reveals the full lyrical and expressive potential of the new trumpet. In addition, this movement, which exemplifies the consummate melodic artistry of Haydn's late works, showcases the instrument's ability to easily modulate from key to key. Written in a sonata rondo form, the concluding Allegro begins with an angular, fanfare-like theme, continuing with material which calls upon the soloist's dexterity in handling trills and other technical effects. Following a concise, brief development section which mainly negotiates primary thematic material, a recapitulation leads the trumpeter to a higher, brighter tessitura. A spirited combination of technical brilliance and musical élan, the third movement ends with a gleaming, celebratory coda. *—James Reel*

Recommended:

○ **Famous Classical Trumpet Concertos** / Marriner (cond.), Hardenberger, Academy of St. Martin-in-the-Fields / 1999 / Philips 464028

○ **Favorite Trumpet Concertos** / Marriner (cond.), Wilbraham, Academy of St. Martin-in-the-Fields / 1997 / Seraphim 69731

○ **Classical Trumpet Concertos** / King (cond.), Steele-Perkins, King's Consort / 2001 / Hyperion 67266

Violin Concerto in G major, H. 7a/4 (ca. 1769)

Haydn is credited with four violin concertos, the second of which has been completely lost. This, ostensibly the last of the series, may not be by Haydn; musicologists point out that the idiom is more old-fashioned than that of the other two survivors, which were also written in the 1760s. This could mean, of course, merely that Haydn wrote it before the others. It begins, Allegro moderato, with a flowing theme that pours out of a sharp opening chord. This winds its way smoothly through a number of closely related episodes that never completely break off into full-fledged secondary subjects. This material is introduced concisely by the orchestra, then taken up by the soloist, who gives it an even more ornate treatment. The development covers all this ground again, but now the violinist gives it a more plaintive character. The soloist leads the way through what seems to be the recapitulation, but turns out to be an extension of the development; after a pause for the cadenza, the orchestra takes charge (mostly) for the true, brief recapitulation. The Adagio movement is a moderately embellished violin aria, with an ever-so-slightly troubled middle section that flirts with minor keys and gives the soloist a much more ornate line. A small cadenza opportunity provides the bridge to a repeat of the first section, in which the orchestra now has a more prominent role. The final Allegro mimics the trilling, galloping style of C.P.E. Bach, complete with a couple of sudden orchestral shouts. The demanding solo part requires the violinist to be fleet and nimble through the course of this monothematic sonata-rondo, a typically Haydnesque finale despite the doubts of musicologists. *—James Reel*

Recommended:

○ **Haydn: Violin Concertos; Sinfonia Concertante** / Wallfisch (cond.), Orch. of the Age of Enlightenment / 1996 / Virgin 61301

○ **Haydn: Violin Concertos; Sinfonia Concertante; Symphony 26, 52 & 53** / Wallfisch (cond.), Orch. of the Age of Enlightenment / 2000 / Angel 61800

Violin Concerto No. 1 in C major, H. 7a/1 (before 1769)

The delightful *C major Violin Concerto,* like various other Haydn's concerti only relatively recently rediscovered, was composed for the well-known Italian violinist Luigi Tommasini. The exact date of composition is unknown—it has been ascribed to the year 1769, but only because it appears in a publisher's catalog for that year. No matter when it was composed, it is certainly one of the most attractive concerti (of Haydn's or otherwise) from the middle of the eighteenth century.

The opening movement is energetic and regal, as one would expect from its C major tonality, with virtuoso writing more in the Italian tradition than the northern one—the solo part has wide melodic leaps, long strings of harmonic sequences, and frequent arpeggiation. The slow movement has become somewhat famous on its own, and rightly so. It is cast in three sections, and the opening and closing sections are built on a simple rising idea in the violin part, supported by a repetitive accompaniment which crescendos to a climax along with the soloist. The central section is sweetly lyrical, with the strings providing gentle support for the violinist's musings. There is an opportunity for the soloist to insert a brief cadenza shortly before the close of the movement. The finale, a lively romp in 3/8 time, is technically quite difficult (and would have been exceedingly troublesome for violinists of the day). *—Blair Johnston*

Recommended:

○ **Haydn: Violin Concertos; Sinfonia Concertante** / Wallfisch, Orch. of the Age of Enlightenment / 1996 / Virgin 61301

○ **Haydn: Violin Concerto in G H7a/4, Haydn: Violin Concerto in C No1, H7a/1, Haydn: Concerto in F H18** / A. Oprean, J. Oprean, European Community CO / 1989 / Hyperion 88037

○ **Haydn: Violin Concertos; Sinfonia Concertante, Symphonies 26, 52 & 53** / Wallfisch, Orch. of the Age of Enlightenment / 2000 / Angel 61800

KEYBOARD

Andante with variations for piano in F minor, H. 17/6 (1793)

Franz Josef Haydn composed his *Andante con variazioni for piano in F minor* in 1793. Although he composed the works with pianist Barbara von Ployer in mind, there is reason to believe that the work was secretly dedicated to another woman altogether, Marianne von Genzinger, the woman thought to be Haydn's last great love. Genzinger was a fine pianist for whom he had already written the sublime *Piano Sonata in E flat major,* and his *Andante con variazioni* was composed shortly after Genzinger's death at 42 early in 1793. In his last letter to her, Haydn had asked her to send "the final big Aria in F minor" from his tragic opera *L'anima del filosofo* (The Spirit of the Philosopher), his setting of the Orpheus myth. In the *Andante con variazioni,* Haydn takes as one of his themes a modified version of a phrase from the final Aria "Perduto un' altra volta," the aria in which the inconsolable Orpheus, having lost his Eurydice, yearns for death. A set of double variations on a pair of themes alternating between Orpheus' theme in F minor and a consoling theme in F major, the Andante allows only two variations for each theme before the enormous and heartrending coda, a rhapsodic outpouring of grief and rage that ultimately collapses into a quiet, final leave-taking at the end. Not only is the *Andante con variazioni* the deepest and most profound set of variations for piano composed between Bach and Beethoven, it is Haydn's greatest work for piano and one of the high points of his entire oeuvre. *—James Leonard*

Recommended:

○ **Haydn: 11 Piano Sonatas** / Brendel / Philips 416643

○ **Sviatoslav Richter Plays Haydn & Mozart** / Richter / 1993 / Stradivarius 33343

○ **Sonatas & Variations** / Pletnev / 1996 / Virgin 45254

○ **Haydn: Keyboard Works** / Odiaga / 1987 / Titanic 160

Keyboard Sonatas (ca. 1765–1795)

Until Beethoven, the piano sonata was not composed as a vehicle for virtuoso technique—that was the domain of the concerto—but as entertainment for amateurs in the privacy of their homes or as an exercise for students. Haydn's earliest surviving keyboard sonatas fit into this mold and were most likely composed during the period before 1760, while he survived by teaching piano. There are about 18 complete works that range in technical and compositional complexity. The simplest of these are generally in keys such as F, C, G, and D, considered easier by inexperienced keyboard players. The pieces in B flat, E, flat, A, and E are more complex, requiring a more advanced technique. This parallel between "difficult" keys and technique supports the theory that the complexity of the work is related more to the ability of a given student than to the date it was composed. Unfortunately, some of these works have been lost because Haydn gave the manuscripts to his students without making copies. Stylistically, the early works were influenced by Haydn's Viennese contemporary Georg Wagenseil. Most of the early works are in three movements in a fast-Minuet-fast format, while four are in a fast-slow-Minuet pattern. Two have only two movements, and two others have four. Most first movements are in sonata form, although Hob. 16:5, 6, 1, and 3 are more like rounded binary form. Some contain experiments Haydn never repeated, and some, like Hob. 16:13, have a very early return to the tonic, a characteristic of many of Haydn's early pieces.

Haydn's sonatas of the 1760s demonstrate his growing compositional powers. Those from between 1766–70, Hob. 16:18, 19, and 44–46, have much larger structures. Furthermore, slower tempos give the first movements more gravity. Three of the five are in three movements and two are in three. None has a Minuet and Trio. In Hob. 16:44, in G minor, Haydn ventures into the realm of the minor mode and its expressive power while masterfully manipulating even the most banal musical material. The *Sonata in A flat*, Hob. 16:46, is notable for a weighty slow movement that contrasts contrapuntal passages with others in a homorhythmic style.

During the 1770s, Haydn composed at least 18 keyboard sonatas, published in sets of six. Of these, the Sonata in C minor, Hob. 16:20, is usually described as the best of Haydn's Sturm und Drang pieces. The set dedicated to Esterházy (Hob. 16:21–26) is generally considered the most consistently good, exhibiting a great variety of invention.

A set of three sonatas published in 1784, dedicated to Princess Marie Esterházy, is very unusual. Each is in two movements and only one movement is in sonata form. The rest are in variation form or freely composed. Some writers have suggested that Haydn was experimenting with different uses of a theme. The striking *Sonata in E flat major*, Hob. 16:49, (1789) was composed for Marianne von Genzinger, the wife of the Esterházy family physician.

Haydn's late sonatas were not composed for students. Two of these, in C major and E flat major (Hob. XVI: 50 and 52), were written in 1794–95 for Therese Jansen, a leading pianist in London who had studied with Clementi. The two sonatas give evidence not only of Ms. Jansen's formidable technique, but of the more powerful sonority of the English piano in comparison to its German and Austrian counterparts. The C major sonata, in particular, betrays its temporal proximity to Haydn's unpredictable *"London" Symphonies* and their frequent eccentricities. *—John Palmer*

Recommended:

- ○ **Haydn: Early, Middle & Late Sonatas** / Odiaga / 1994 / Albany 147

Keyboard Sonata in E flat major, H. 16/49 (1789–1790)

By the late 1780s, Haydn's works for keyboard were clearly intended for the piano as opposed to the harpsichord. His exploitation of the dynamic potential of the relatively new piano grows with each of his last sonatas.

Until Beethoven's middle-period sonatas, Classical-era works for solo keyboard were very often written for a composer's students and were intended to stress certain aspects of technique. At the time, the concerto was the vehicle for the performing virtuoso. Haydn was never a keyboard virtuoso, but had a number of students for whom he composed piano sonatas. The wide range of ability among his students accounts for the disparate levels of sophistication and technical difficulty we find among the surviving sonatas, most of which were written before 1770. Some of these works have been lost because Haydn gave the manuscripts to his students without making copies. A few of Haydn's sonatas, however, were not composed for his students.

The Sonata in E flat major, H. 16:49, was composed for Marianne von Genzinger, the wife of the Esterházy family physician. Haydn's relationship with Genzinger may have grown from a mutual affinity for things musical, but it seems certain from some the composer's letters that the relationship grew into some version of love. However, most of the composer's communications to Genzinger, although in a more relaxed style than those to others, are discreet, often discussing musical issues. Concerning the late C major sonata, Haydn referred to the second movement, an Adagio, as "quite new . . . it contains many things I shall analyze for Your Grace when the time comes; it is rather difficult but full of feeling."

The E flat major sonata is also a fairly late work, completed in 1790. It shares a certain intimate style with other works directed toward Genzinger, but is quite Beethovenian in some respects. (In general, Haydn's late keyboard sonatas are among his most forward-looking works, and perhaps those in which his influence upon Beethoven is most visible.) The first movement, in sonata form, is marked Allegro non troppo and moves forward quickly in a bouncing triple meter. Compared to those of the symphonies Haydn composed during this same period, the transition between key areas is brief. We hear a plethora of material on the secondary key, B flat major, most of which shows up in the extensive development. In the recapitulation, the transition, as usual, resolves the secondary material to the tonic. A coda develops transitional material on its way to a firm close—a procedure Beethoven would borrow from Haydn and expand upon.

The exquisite Adagio cantabile is an ABA structure in B flat major with highly decorated thematic material. Touches of the tonic minor add a melancholic feel to the movement, while numerous runs suggest that Genzinger had a formidable technique.

Haydn composed a large Minuet with two Trio sections as the finale of the E flat major sonata. Everything begins conventionally enough: the Minuet follows the traditional pattern of repetition, with the first part consisting of an eight-measure phrase that closes on the dominant. The first Trio opens with a theme built of descending scales, which contrast with the rising figures of the second part. After the Trio we hear a literal return to the Minuet, as we expect, but only the first part appears and it turns out to be a bridge to the second Trio, in E flat minor. This in turn is followed by a slightly varied reprise of the entire first Minuet section in E flat major. *—John Palmer*

Recommended:

- ○ **Haydn: 11 Piano Sonatas** / Brendel / Philips 416643
- ○ **Richter in Recital** / Richter / 1994 / Vanguard 8076
- ○ **Haydn Piano Sonatas** / Ax / 1994 / Sony 53635
- ○ **Haydn: Piano Music** / Kalish / 1987 / Nonesuch 79162
- ○ **Glenn Gould Edition: Haydn Piano Sonatas** / Gould / 1994 / Sony 52623

Keyboard Sonata in C major, H. 16/50 (ca. 1794–1795)

Until Beethoven, the piano sonata was not composed as a vehicle for virtuoso technique—that was the domain of the concerto—but as entertainment for amateurs in the privacy of their homes. Many such pieces were written for students, often as something of an exercise. Haydn had a number of students for whom he composed piano sonatas, and the wide range of ability among his students accounts for the disparate levels of sophistication we find among the over 50 surviving sonatas. Some of these works have been lost because Haydn gave the manuscripts to his students without making copies.

Two of Haydn's sonatas, the Sonatas in C major and E flat major (Hoboken XVI: 50 and 52), were not written for students, but for Therese Jansen, a leading pianist in London who had studied with Clementi. Haydn composed them in 1794–95, during his second visit to the English capital. The two sonatas give evidence not only of Ms. Jansen's formidable technique, but of the more powerful sonority of the English piano in comparison to its German and Austrian counterparts. The C major sonata, in particular, betrays its temporal proximity to Haydn's unpredictable "London" Symphonies and their frequent eccentricities. The "additive" process at the opening of the first movement is only one example.

The first Allegro is one of the most impressive monothematic sonata-form movements in Haydn's output. The first theme is a sparse articulation of the tonic triad that pauses in its sixth measure. After a transition that is significantly longer than the first theme, Haydn arrives at the dominant, G major, restating the theme, this time in double notes and accompanied by rising scales in the left hand. More scales and variations close the exposition. In the development section, the material passes through numerous harmonies while the theme is reduced to only one of its fragments—a falling octave that changes to different intervals. The recapitulation is highly modified and contains some new material. Because the secondary theme is the same as the first, there is no need to "resolve" it to the tonic, so Haydn skips ahead to the ensuing passages.

Highly expressive and technically demanding, the Adagio was clearly written for an accomplished musician. Set in the subdominant, F major, the movement is in sonata form with a brief development section. The brilliant right-hand octave passages in the second theme group contrast with the delicate, arched opening theme and attest to Ms. Jansen's technique.

Much as in the Rondo finale of Haydn's *Symphony No. 88*, the recurrent theme in the Allegro finale of the C major sonata serves as variation fodder for the intervening episodes. There are teasing moments when only part of the rondo theme returns while frequent pauses heighten the listeners' anticipation. *—John Palmer*

Recommended:

- ○ **Haydn: 11 Piano Sonatas** / Brendel / Philips 416643
- ○ **Russian Piano School: Sviatoslav Richter Vol. 6** / Richter / 1995 / Melodiya 25178
- ○ **Haydn: Piano Sonatas** / Schiff / 1998 / Telarc 17141
- ○ **Haydn: Sonatas & Variations** / Odiaga / 1986 / Titanic 156

Keyboard Sonata in E flat major, H. 16/52 (1794)

Unlike Mozart, Beethoven, Clementi, and a number of his other near-contemporaries, Haydn was not a virtuoso pianist. Haydn recognized this, once stating, "I was a wizard on no instrument, but I knew the strength and working of all." However, until Beethoven, the piano sonata was not composed primarily as a vehicle for virtuoso technique—that was the domain of the concerto—but as entertainment for amateurs in the privacy of their homes. Often, such pieces were directed toward women, who were expected to attain a moderate degree of accomplishment on a keyboard instrument in order to be "eligible for marriage." Also, many such pieces were written for students, often as something of an exercise.

Haydn composed piano sonatas for a number of different students, and the wide range of their ability accounts for the disparate levels of sophistication we find among the nearly 50 surviving sonatas, most of which were written before 1770; some of these works have been lost because Haydn gave the manuscripts to his students without making copies. A few of Haydn's sonatas, however, were not composed for his students; three of these, the Sonatas in C major, D major and E flat major (Hoboken 16: 50–52), were written for Therese Jansen, a leading pianist in London who had studied with Clementi. Haydn composed them in 1794–95, during his second visit to the English capital. The last three piano sonatas give evidence not only of Ms. Jansen's formidable technique, but of the more powerful sonority of the English piano in comparison to its German and Austrian counterparts.

The Piano Sonata in E flat major, H. 16/52, is often described as Haydn's finest work in the genre. Forming more of a cohesive whole than either of its siblings,

Haydn's E flat major sonata is exceptional in both size and scope and manipulation of tonal material.

An abundance of ideas floods the opening of the Allegro moderato, sonata-form first movement, which is a perfect example of Haydn's predilection for monothematic movements; although there are several themes in the exposition, they are all derived from the material of the first eight bars. The first genuinely new material appears at the very end of the exposition, and forms the basis for a long development.

The second movement, marked Adagio and in three-part form, is in E major, a half step above the tonic (a relationship generally referred to as "Neapolitan"). The dotted rhythm and general shape of the main theme create a strong relationship between this and the first movement.

Instead of the traditional rondo, Haydn chose to compose a fast sonata-form movement to close the piece. Again there is an abundance of material; we hear two themes in each key area. The development section visits just about all the material of the exposition, which, aside from transpositions and a few alterations to the transition, is restated in the recapitulation nearly note for note. *—John Palmer*

Recommended:

- ○ **Haydn: 11 Piano Sonatas** / Brendel / Philips 416643
- ○ **Haydn, Beethoven, Weber** / Richter / 1994 / Philips 438617
- ○ **Sonatas & Variations** / Pletnev / 1996 / Virgin 45254
- ○ **Haydn: Piano Sonatas Vol. 1** / Jando / 1993 / Naxos 550657
- ○ **Haydn: London Sonatas** / Brautigam / 1998 / Bis 994

CHORAL

Die Jahreszeiten (The Seasons), oratorio, H. 21/3 (1801)

Encouraged by the reception of *Die Schöpfung*, Baron Gottfried van Swieten and others of Haydn's circle persuaded him to attempt a second oratorio, suggesting another English model, James Thomson's *The Seasons*, a lengthy poem of 1726–30, in a German translation by Barthold Brockes. Van Swieten reduced the work to a fraction of its original size and wrote final verses. It seems Haydn was not enthused about the new project, intimating that van Swieten had become somewhat dictatorial concerning the music. Nevertheless, for the next two years the composer poured his energy into *Die Jahreszeiten*. The contrast between the two works could not have been greater: the bucolic ruminations on peasant life in *Die Jahreszeiten* are a world apart from the lofty sentiments of *Die Schöpfung*. Furthermore, the subject matter prompted the composition of four independent sections, not the highly unified musical stream of *Die Schöpfung*. These separate parts, however, are masterfully crafted, exhibiting a youthful freshness, originality and spontaneity that belie the composer's age. *Die Jahreszeiten* was first performed privately in the Schwarzenberg Palace in Vienna on April 24, 1801. A month later it received a public performance in Vienna, achieving popular success at home and abroad.

Die Jahreszeiten features three principal characters—Simon, a farmer; Hanne, his daughter; and Lukas, a country lad—joined by a chorus of country folk. After a stormy, G minor overture that banishes the last vestiges of winter before the onset of "Der Frühling" (Spring), a recitative begins in which the principal characters celebrate the passing of winter. The chorus, welcoming spring, enters in G major (a foil to the overture). Ensuing arias and choruses, with folk song-like melodies, describe nature's reawakening. At the center of the movement is a number for trio and choir (No. 6, "Sei nun gnädig"), in which an extensive Handelian fugue for the choir tells of the wonders of nature.

"Der Sommer" (Summer) opens with an instrumental introduction portraying dawn on a summer's day, complete with a birdsong in the oboe. The pastoral quality of Simon's aria (No. 10, "Der muntre Hirt"), is complemented by horn calls, after which the three soloists and choir greet the sunrise. One of the more popular numbers from *Die Jahreszeiten* is Hanne's aria (No. 16, "Welche Labung für die Sinne"), in which the woman describes the bliss of resting under a shady tree.

"Der Herbst" (Autumn) is a song of praise for a healthy harvest. In the midst of the season, however, there is time for love, as expressed in the duet between Lukas and Hanne (No. 22, "Ihr Schönen aus der Stadt").

In "Der Winter," Haydn chose not to depict the harsh, stormy aspects of season; rather, he focuses on the gray, dull, lifeless mood that stifles both nature and the mind. Soloists remark on the mist-covered mountains and the cessation of nature's growth. Lukas' aria describing a traveler lost in the snow is especially poignant. The closing chorus looks forward to new life beyond earth and contains yet another Handelian fugue. *—John Palmer*

Recommended:

- ○ **Haydn: The Seasons** / Böhm (cond.), Schreier, Janowitz, Talvela, Vienna SO / DG 457713
- ○ **Haydn: The Seasons** / Davis (cond.), Harper, Shirley-Quirk, Davies, Sillem, BBC SO, BBC Theatre Orch. & Chorus / 1999 / Philips 464034
- ○ **Haydn: The Seasons** / Gardiner (cond.), Schmidt, Bonney, Johnson, Monteverdi Choir, English Baroque Soloists / 1992 / Archiv 447282

Mass in B flat major ("Harmoniemesse"), H. 22/14 (1802)

The *Mass in B flat major* called the *"Harmoniemesse"* was Haydn's last mass and his last large-scale composition. As he had all his recent masses, he wrote it for the name day of the Princess Maria, the wife of his employer Prince Nikolaus Esterházy. Tired and with a slightly shaky hand, Haydn completed the mass for its September premiere, which he himself prepared and directed. The *"Harmoniemesse"* is scored for four soloists, full chorus, organ, strings, brass, and two pairs of woodwinds, hence the name "Harmonie," being German for the wind section. The work sets the mass text in the standard sections: Kyrie, Gloria, Credo, Sanctus, Benedictus, Agnus Dei-Dona nobis pacem. The opening Kyrie is an enormous and glorious Adagio alternating between the soloists and the chorus above the vast orchestra. The Gloria is set in three parts: an opening song of joy for soprano soloist then joined by the whole chorus, a central meditation for alto soloist followed by a hymn for chorus and orchestra, and then a return to the joyful music of the opening transformed into a double fugue. The Credo is also set in three parts: an opening march for chorus and orchestra with fanfares from the trumpets and tympani, a central mystery culminating in the word Crucifixus and fading with the chorus pianissimo, and a closing double fugue starting in G minor, but grandly ending back in the tonic major. The Sanctus is two parts: a short, slow introduction and a brief allegro conclusion of unsurpassed beauty. The Benedictus is a huge choral/orchestral dance. The closing movement fuses a radiant Agnus Dei for soloist and small orchestra with a fast and furious Dona Nobis Pacem and ends with a richly scored Adagio. *—James Leonard*

Recommended:

- ○ **Haydn: The Masses** / Guest (cond.), Young, Rouleau, Runnett, Spoorenberg, St. John's College Choir, Academy of St. Martin-in-the-Fields / 1996 / London 448518
- ○ **Haydn: Harmoniemesse; Salve Regina** / Hickox (cond.), Varcoe, Padmore, Stephen, Collegium Musicum 90 / 1997 / Chandos 0612
- ○ **Haydn: Harmony Mass; Te Deum** / S. Kuijken (cond.), Cao, Groop, Piau, Pregardien, van der Kamp, Namur Chamber Choir, La Petite Bande / 1996 / Deutsche HM 77337
- ○ **Haydn: Harmoniemesse; Kleine Orgelmesse** / Hill (cond.), George, Kendall, Russell, Wyn-Rogers, Brandenburg Orch., Winchester Cathedral Choir / Hyperion 66508

Mass in D minor ("Lord Nelson"), H. 22/11 (1798)

In the early days of August 1798, the British Admiral Lord Nelson engaged Napoleon's fleet at Aboukir Bay, near the mouth of the Nile River. Nelson's victory in what became known as the Battle of the Nile was a major breakthrough in the battle against the French. News of it traveled quickly, and Nelson became a celebrated hero.

Back at the Esterházy court, Franz Josef Haydn was putting the finishing touches to his *Mass in D minor*, the third of six masses he wrote over the years 1796 to 1802 to commemorate the nameday of Princess Marie Hermenegild, the wife of his patron Prince Nikolaus II Esterházy. Haydn had already taken note of the war against Napoleon in his *Mass in Time of War* (1796), and there are likewise allusions to the fighting in the *Mass in D minor*—Haydn's only mass in a minor key—whose original title, *Missa in angustiis*, can be translated as *Mass in Time of Difficulty or Anxiety*. The news of Nelson's victory had probably reached Esterháza by the time of the first performance of the mass, under Haydn's direction, on September 23, 1798; in September 1800, Admiral Nelson himself visited Eisenstadt on his return trip to London. While there, he heard a performance of the *D minor Mass*, which by that point was firmly associated with him—hence the nickname which has come down to us.

The atmosphere of war is evident in the opening Kyrie, especially the harshness of its trumpet and timpani fanfares. The celebratory Gloria that follows evokes the figure of Handel, with whose music Haydn had become well acquainted during his years in London earlier in the 1790s. A lovely, peaceful Qui tollis is at the heart of the Gloria, in which the bass soloist is supported by the chorus and gentle decoration from the organ (probably played by Haydn himself at the work's premiere). The Credo begins traditionally with an old church melody sung polyphonically by the chorus. Then it moves into a ravishing Et incarnatus for the soprano soloist, the usual darkening of mood as the text refers to the Crucifixion, and lastly a brightening of spirit at the Et resurrexit. A brief, restrained Sanctus follows. The portentous Benedictus dominates the second half of the mass; the anger of the hammering of the trumpets and timpani towards its end is one of the fiercest passages in all of Haydn's music. The mood changes with a sweetly flowing Agnus Dei for the vocal soloists, and the chorus takes over for the rousing Dona Nobis Pacem which concludes the work. *—Chris Morrison*

Recommended:

- ○ **Haydn: Masses** / Willcocks (cond.), Preston, Brown, Krause, Stahlman, King's College Choir / 1996 / London 448518
- ○ **Haydn: Masses** / Hickox (cond.), Varcoe, Padmore, Gritton, Stephen, Collegium Musicum 90 / 1999 / Chandos 640

○ **Haydn: Nelson-Messe; Te Deum** / Pinnock (cond.), Lott, Watkinson, Wilson-Johnson, Davies, Parle, English Concert & Choir / Archiv 423097

Mass in B flat major ("Theresienmesse"), H. 22/12 (1799)

On returning to Austria in 1795 from his second London trip, Franz Josef Haydn again took up his position with the Esterházy family. Prince Anton Esterházy had died in 1794 after largely dissolving the family's musical establishment. Haydn's new employer, Prince Nikolaus II, wanted to reestablish the musical chapel to some extent, but wasn't nearly the music lover his grandfather Nikolaus I was (Haydn had happily served the latter for close to 30 years). One of the few demands Nikolaus II made of Haydn was the annual composition of a mass to commemorate the nameday of Princess Marie Hermenegild, Nikolaus II's wife. Over the years 1796 to 1802 Haydn wrote six such masses, of which the fourth was the "Theresienmesse," written in 1799.

The Therese of the title was probably Marie Therese, the wife of Emperor Francis II. Marie Therese was one of Haydn's patronesses, and a singer who performed the soprano parts in the premieres of Haydn's great oratorios *The Creation* and *The Seasons*.

By the time of this *Mass'* composition Prince Nikolaus II's orchestra was reduced to strings, trumpets, timpani and organ; these, along with a pair of clarinets brought in from Vienna, are the only instruments featured in this relatively intimate mass. Adding to the intimacy is the extensive use of the vocal quartet, both as soloists in ensemble. They are at the forefront in the stately opening Kyrie. The extroverted, radiant Gloria has a lovely Gratias agimus tibi at its center, in which the soprano soloist is eventually joined by the rest of the soloists. The forthright and joyous Credo is followed by a short, gentle Sanctus, and a more extensive Benedictus that is almost playful in its high sprits. The most forceful portions of the work are the Et resurrexit that concludes the Credo movement, and the final section, which juxtaposes a dramatic Agnus Dei and a big, affirmative Dona nobis pacem with punctuations from the trumpets and timpani. *—Chris Morrison*

Recommended:

○ **Haydn: The Masses** / Guest (cond.), Krause, Runnett, Spoorenberg, Mitchinson, St. John's College Choir, Academy of St. Martin-in-the-Fields / 1996 / London 448518

○ **Haydn: Theresienmesse; Kleine Orgelmesse** / Hickox (cond.), Varcoe, Padmore, Watson, Stephen, Collegium Musicum 90 / 1996 / Chandos 0592

Missa brevis St. Joannis de Deo, in B flat major ("Little Organ Mass"), H. 22/7 (before 1778)

Haydn's long-time employer, Prince Nikolaus I Esterházy, was a lover of instrumental music and opera, and Haydn composed extensively in those forms for him; even though it was also part of Haydn's job to provide ecclesiastical works, he was seldom called upon to do so. Up until his cycle of great masses written for Nikolaus' grandfather in the late 1790s and early 1800s, most of the church works Haydn composed were written for people or organizations other than the Esterházys. Such is the case with the so-called *"Little Organ Mass,"* written sometime in the 1770s (as early as 1770 or as late as 1778) for the Brothers of Mercy, who ran the hospital in Eisenstadt, where the Esterházy winter residence was located. The Brothers' patron saint was St. John of God, hence the other longer title of this work, *Missa brevis Sancti Joannis de Deo*.

The forces employed in this Mass are modest: singers, two violins, organ, and continuo. This most intimate of Haydn's masses begins with a simple, beautiful Kyrie. The emphatic little Gloria that follows is not even a minute long; the Credo begins at the Gloria's fast tempo, but the mood becomes hushed and the tempo slows for the central Et incarnatus. The Sanctus is a companion to the Gloria in both mood and length. Haydn grows much more expansive in the lovely Benedictus; the florid organ part (which gives the Mass its nickname) and gentle strings provide a framework for the soprano soloist. A portentous Agnus Dei leads into a surprisingly restrained and luminous Dona nobis pacem. The latter text is normally set with faster and more extroverted music to close the mass emphatically and in an affirmative spirit. But in this particular case, Haydn chose to set the words very quietly and reverently, capturing the mood of the text even more effectively. *—Chris Morrison*

Recommended:

○ **Haydn: The Masses** / Guest (cond.), Scott, Smith, St. John's College Choir, Academy of St. Martin-in-the-Fields / 1996 / London 448518

○ **Haydn: Theresienmesse; Kleine Orgelmesse** / Hickox (cond.), Varcoe, Padmore, Watson, Stephen, Collegium Musicum 90 / 1996 / Chandos 0592

○ **Haydn: Harmoniemesse; Kleine Orgelmesse** / Hill (cond.), George, Holman, Kendall, Russell, Wyn-Rogers, Brandenburg Orch., Winchester Cathedral Choir / Hyperion 66508

Missa in tempore belli, in C major ("Paukenmesse"), H. 22/9 (1796)

In 1795, Paul Anton Esterházy's successor, Nikolaus II, decided to reform the Esterházy orchestra. In the process, he invited Haydn back to serve as active Kapellmeister—rejuvenating the purely nominal post the composer had held for the previous five years. Compared to his previous 30 years of service to the family, Haydn's new duties were still minimal, but they included the annual composition of a mass to celebrate the name day of Princess Josepha Maria in Eisenstadt, forty kilometers south of Vienna.

On the first page of his autograph manuscript of the C major mass, Haydn wrote, *"Missa in tempore belli"* (Mass in time of war). At the time, Austria was engulfed in a war with the French, and Napoleon was advancing from victory to victory unchecked. In August 1796, precisely when Haydn was at work on the C major mass, the Austrian government issued an order for general mobilization. Some writers have suggested that the baleful timpani part in the Agnus Dei reflects Haydn's reaction to the escalating military conflict; these timpani passages inspired the work's nickname, "Paukenmesse" (Timpani Mass).

Scholars are unsure of the date and place of the first performance. It may have taken place on September 13, 1796 in Eisenstadt, but there is some evidence that this was another mass, the *Missa St. Bernardi.* Some suggest it was first performed on September 29, 1797, in Eisenstadt. However, because the *"Missa in tempore belli"* formed part of a service in Vienna on the feast of St. Stephen (December 26) in 1796, it is more likely that the work was finished and given its premiere in 1796.

The *Mass in C major* is scored for soprano, alto, tenor, and bass soloists, a four-voice mixed choir and a large orchestra with paired woodwinds, trumpets and continuo (organ). Different recordings may feature varied instrumentation during some parts of the mass, as there exist two versions.

The symphonic character of the mass is evident from the opening of the Kyrie with its pulsating accompaniment in the strings and the imitations between the voices and woodwinds. After the slow introduction for chorus and orchestra closes on the dominant the soloists take over at an Allegro tempo. The climax of the movement occurs near the end, when the chorus loudly intones the only setting of Christe eleison in the whole movement on a sustained dominant seventh chord.

The divisions in the Gloria and Credo are based more on the passages of text than on musical considerations. The most poignant section of the Gloria is the "Qui tollis," where the tempo shifts abruptly from Vivace to Adagio and the key from C major to D major. A solo cello introduces the section's main theme, which is then taken up by the bass soloist. The antiphonal pairing of chorus voice parts in the "Amen" of the Gloria is only one example of the numerous textures Haydn develops throughout this rich work. Haydn's shift back to C major at the Quoniam is also very abrupt.

Haydn separates the Benedictus from the Sanctus and sets it in the tonic minor until about the midpoint, where the mode shifts to major. After the first line of the Agnus Dei the timpani enter with the quiet, rapid-fire motive that inspired the mass' second sobriquet. The dark atmosphere of the opening measures gives way to a brighter C major. Possibly reflecting the piece's historical context, nearly three-quarters of the movement is devoted to setting three words, "dona nobis pacem" (grant us peace). *—John Palmer*

Recommended:

○ **Haydn: The Masses** / Guest (cond.), Cantelo, Tear, Cleobury, McDaniel, St. John's College Choir, Academy of St. Martin-in-the-Fields / 1996 / London 448518

○ **Haydn: Missa in tempore belli; Te Deum; Grosses Te Deum** / Hickox (cond.), Varcoe, Argenta, Padmore, Denley, Collegium Musicum 90 / 1998 / Chandos 0633

○ **Haydn: Missa in Tempore Belli; Salve Regina** / Harnoncourt (cond.), Vienna Concentus Musicus, Arnold Schoenberg Choir / 1997 / Teldec 13146

Die Schöpfung (The Creation), oratorio, H. 21/2 (1798)

One of Haydn's two greatest choral masterpieces, his oratorio *The Creation* was composed during 1795, to a libretto specially prepared by the Baron Gottfried von Swieten, and based jointly upon the Book of Genesis, supplemented by appropriate sections of the Book of Psalms, and on John Milton's allegorical study of the creation and fall, *Paradise Lost.*

By this time, however, the once seemingly unstoppable Handelian cult of oratorio was rapidly becoming outmoded and unfashionable, in the face of the Enlightenment's call to reason and the rejection of religious dogma in favor of the pursuit of material objectivity. It seems not a little ironic, in retrospect, therefore, that a theme already rejected by Handel himself should provide a point of convergence for Haydn's devout religious faith and the prevailing intellectual climate of the age, engineering at the same a new-found confidence in a genre which seemed to have had its day. The scholar Hans Schnoor called this "an exceptional instance of the complete musical interpretation of the social and individual psyche," and it was doubly remarkable considering the eccentricities and idiosyncrasies which are to found peppering von Swieten's text.

The oratorio begins with one of the most futuristic episodes to be found in any pre-Romantic music. This is the famous "Representation of Chaos," which serves as a preface to the work. The unfocused harmonic textures and atmosphere of vague formlessness must have stunned Haydn's contemporaries, and the section still sounds uncanny and highly impressionistic to modern ears.

Another equally inspired moment, and one of which John Milton would doubtless have approved, comes as the chorus sings over a hushed, slowly pulsing orchestral background "And the spirit of God moved on the face of the waters. . . ."

Suddenly, incredibly, "There was light!" sing the chorus, in one of the most spine-tingling C major fortissimo eruptions to be found anywhere in music! It was a logical, natural move, and one which was wholly characteristic of late, great Haydn at the summit of his powers. There now follows one exultant outpouring after another, as the chorus of the heavenly host sing praises in honor of each successive day of creation.

Narrative or purely descriptive numbers are given over to the three soloists, named after the archangels Gabriel, Uriel, and Raphael, supported by orchestra alone. However, Haydn's expertly applied technical skills ensures that there is a pleasing balance throughout between the respective vocal and instrumental forces, as can be heard whenever chorus and soloists are heard together. Good examples of this are "The marv'llous work behold amazed" for soprano with chorus, and the trio "Most beautiful appear," which leads directly to the chorus "The Lord is Great." In this section, all three soloists and chorus are employed, with orchestra, as they are also in the most famous section of the oratorio "The Heavens are telling the Glory of God." *—Michael Jameson*

Recommended:

- ○ **Haydn: Die Schöpfung** / Karajan (cond.), Wunderlich, Fischer-Dieskau, Ludwig, Janowitz, Berlin PO, Vienna Singverein / DG 449761
- ○ **Haydn: Die Schöpfung** / Shaw (cond.), Upshaw, Murphy, Humphrey, Carter, Atlanta SO & Chorus / 1992 / Telarc 80298
- ○ **Haydn: Die Schöpfung** / Gardiner (cond.), McNair, Brown, Finley, Schade, English Baroque Soloists, Monteverdi Choir / Archiv 449217
- ○ **Haydn: Die Schöpfung** / Lamon, Weil (cond.), van der Kamp, Monoyios, Hering, Tafelmusik Baroque Orch., Tolzner Knabenchor / 1994 / Sony 57965

VOCAL

English Canzonettas (ca. 1794–1795)

Haydn was not particularly noted as a German song (lieder) composer and some of his finest songs are, in fact, the English songs he composed during his visits to London. Among these are two published groups of canzonettas composed in 1794 and 1795, respectively. All are strophic songs set to poems mostly by Anne Hunter, the widow of the famous surgeon John Hunter, who died in 1793. Haydn had come to know the Hunters during his first visit to London in 1791–92 and during the course of his second visit, the relationship between the poetess and the unhappily married composer unquestionably deepened.

The first song, "The Mermaid's Song," immediately shows a Haydn more at home with song form than in his German lieder. It has a long opening ritornello for the piano, and the piano part, although simple, is frequently independent of the voice. The second, "Recollection" is a melancholy reflection on happier times. That is followed by "A Pastoral Song," better-known as "My Mother bids me bind my hair," and possibly the best-known of the whole set. "Despair," the fourth, is generally considered to be one of Haydn's finest songs. It opens with a boldly conceived piano introduction that seems to presage Schubert. The penultimate song, "Pleasing Pain" is another pastoral that again looks back from quietly sad maturity. The last song of the first group, "Fidelity," is an impassioned declaration of faith in one of Haydn's favorite Sturm und Drang (storm and stress) modes of F minor. The second group appeared in 1795 and represents a further development in both design and richness of the piano accompaniments. The first is "The Sailor's Song," a rollicking evocation of the sea and sailors. "The Wanderer" is another minor mode song (G minor), both sentiments and music of which look forward to Romanticism. The third of this group, "Sympathy," is a translation of a text by the great Italian librettist Metastasio, while "She Never Told Her Love" is a setting of Viola's words from Shakespeare's *Twelfth Night.* It is unique among the canzonets in being through-composed and is, in the words of Haydn scholar H.C. Robbins-Landon, "a little masterpiece." The final two songs, "Piercing Eyes" and "Transport of Pleasure," return to poems by Anne Hunter, the former employing one of those deceptively simple, almost folk-like melodies of which Haydn was such a master. *—Brian Robins*

Recommended:

- ○ **Songs by Haydn** / Vignoles, Ainsley, Fink, Milne / 2002 / Hyperion 67174

Folk Song Settings (1792–1804)

During the latter part of the eighteenth century, there was a considerable vogue in England for folk songs, in particular those of Scotland. Composers of some repute not only provided accompaniments to the melodies of folk songs to meet the ever-increasing demands of domestic music-making, but also on occasions—as in the instance of Johann Christian Bach—worked them into the fabric of concertos. The most notable composers to devote themselves to what was a lucrative source of income were Haydn and Beethoven. The former produced around 400 such arrangements for two British publishers. The first was William Napier, who according to contemporary accounts was the beneficiary of an act of generosity from Haydn that averted his bankruptcy. In 1791, during the first of his highly successful visits to England, Haydn's attention was drawn to Napier's predicament and he set 100 Scottish folk-song arrangements with an accompaniment for piano, violin, and cello with little expectation of payment. So successful were these arrangements, which traded on the immense popularity of Haydn's name, that Napier was enabled to commission a second group of 50 songs, this time apparently paying him in full for both sets. The arrangements Haydn made for Napier are fairly basic, with no introductions or ritornellos and a keyboard part that was not fully written out. Those he produced several years later for the Edinburgh publisher George Thomson (who also commissioned settings from Beethoven) are considerably more sophisticated and contain quite elaborate opening symphonies and concluding passages for the accompanying trio. While the folk-song arrangements of both Haydn and Beethoven have a certain charm that casts an interesting light on domestic music-making at the end of the eighteenth century, their gentility is thoroughly out of step with an era that seeks a more authentic edge to its folk songs. *—Brian Robins*

Recommended:

- ○ **Haydn: Piano Trios & Scottish Songs** / Mackay, English Piano Trio / 1992 / Meridian 84222
- ○ **Haydn: Welsh Airs** / Dearing, Witsenburg / Preiser 90492

Das Kaiserlied ("Gott erhalte Franz den Kaiser"), national anthem, H. 26a/43 (1797)

The notion of a national anthem was unknown before the French Revolution. After all, what need was there of a national anthem when there were no nations, just geographic entities organized around a ruling dynasty? However, when the French Revolution effectively destroyed the Bourbon dynasty by beheading its king and queen, they perforce created the first modern nation. And it wasn't long before a national anthem followed: The bloodthirsty *"La Marseilles"* became the marching song for the Grande armee as it conquered continental Europe. Seeing the effect *"La Marseilles"* had on the population in general and the army in particular, the British responded with their "God Save the King," a drinking song pressed into service for the patriotic cause.

Austria was luckier in its choice of national anthem. In early 1797, Franz Joseph, Count Saurau commissioned Franz Josef Haydn, considered the greatest living Austrian composer, to write a hymn for the birthday of the Austrian Emperor Franz II. Based on a Croatian folk tune *"Zalostna Zarucnice"* (The Sad Bride), Haydn quickly wrote the tune to the words *Gott Erhalte Franz den Kaiser* (God Save Franz the Emperor) and the piece proved an immediate and lasting success. The tune is instantly memorable with deeply moving harmonies and a simple and effective rhythm. Soon, the *Kaiserlied* appeared on all manner of arrangements for every conceivable assortment of instruments and voices. Haydn himself fully realized the musical implications of the hymn as the slow movement of his *String Quartet in C major No. 3,* Op. 76. The hymn was later adapted by the German poet, anti-Semite, and anti-French nationalist Hoffmann von Fallersleben for his *Deutschlandlied,* a perversion that would surely have appalled Haydn. *—James Leonard*

Recommended:

- ○ **Wedding Hymns** / Weeks (cond.), Choir of Queen's College Cambridge, Cambridge U. Brass Choir / 1999 / Guild 7160

OPERA

Armida, H. 28/12 (1783)

Armida was the last work Haydn composed for the opera house at Eszterháza, which he ran for most of his career as part of his duties as the court's music director. Composed in 1783 and premiered in February 1784, *Armida* reflects the composer's growing interest in serious opera and reveals some innovative tendencies which might have found expression had he composed more works for the stage. Called a "dramma eroica" (heroic drama), the work is an opera seria very much in the eighteenth century tradition—a historical drama in three acts, played out through the emotions of its protagonists rather than through plot action; extended arias and recitatives (rather than ensemble finales) take center stage. Haydn felt it to be his finest opera, and of all his dramas (none of which has found a firm place in the repertory) it has been the most often performed. It had over 50 performances during his lifetime (some even outside of Eszterháza), and it has had several modern revivals, including one by Peter Sellars (1981, at the Monadnock Festival in New Hampshire).

The libretto, by Jacopo Durandi, was derived from Torquato Tasso's epic poem *Gerusalemme liberata* (Jerusalem Delivered). This particular episode of Tasso's poem, the love story of Armida, the heathen sorceress, and Rinaldo, the Christian knight, had been used other by opera composers, including Lully and Gluck. The two main characters, Armida and Rinaldo, are each given a number of extended recitatives and arias, while the secondary players are reduced to rather one-dimensional representations. The extended scenes reveal Haydn at his creative best, bringing his sense of introspective drama and his talent for orchestral subtlety to the forefront. *—Allen Schrott*

Synopsis:

Act One. The opera opens in Idreno's palace in the time of the Crusades. He tells his satraps, Armida, and Rinaldo that the crusaders are approaching, and Rinaldo vows to fight for his beloved Armida's sake ("Vado a pugnar"). When he leaves, Armida confides in Idreno that she is afraid for Rinaldo, and he assures her that Rinaldo will win. Aftet that, he says, he will give him Armida and the kingdom itself (" Se dal suo braccio"). She is still afraid, though she plans to use her magic to protect him, and prays for his safety ("Se pietade avete"). In the crusaders' camp at the base of the mountain of which Armida's castle stands at the peak, Ubaldo is momentarily overwhelmed by fear when she sends illusions of icy winds and monsters ("Dove son?") but is still determined to rescue Rinaldo from Armida's enchantments. Zelmira descends, determining that her honor forbids her to obey Armida's and Idreno's orders to entice the crusaders into a trap. When she and Clotarco see one another, they immediately fall in love, and she even offers to guide the crusaders up through a safe path ("Se tu seguir"). In Armida's rooms, Rinaldo is gazing admiringly at the warriors, but she begs him, for the sake of their love, not to let any of the Franks see him. He agrees, but before he can leave, Ubaldo enters, and with a magic shield he breaks through (but does not completely eradicate) Armida's spell over him. Ubaldo reminds him of his duty and former honor as a warrior, and he leaves. Rinaldo is ready to follow, but Armida accuses him of faithlessness, and he vows his fidelity and promises to stay with her ("Cara, saro fidele").

Act Two. Idreno tells Zelmira he plans to ambush the crusaders and refuses to listen to her protests against such a treacherous move. She warns him ("Tu mi sprezzi"), but he remains firm. Clotarco enters and asks him to agree to meet with Ubaldo to discuss a peace treaty ("Ah, si plachi"). He agrees, and Ubaldo enters. He demands the return of the warriors whom Armida's magic enticed from their camp, and Idreno responds that they left voluntarily, but have now already returned. Ubaldo goes on to demand that Rinaldo return as well, but Idreno again says that Rinaldo is acting of his free will and has always been free to leave. He professes his friendship, admiration, and desire for peace ("Teco lo guida"). Ubaldo is suspicious, but when Rinaldo comes in, he again reminds him of his former glory, and Rinaldo agrees to come with him. Armida enters, and, when he bids her farewell, collapses. He is torn, but finally leaves ("Cara, è vero"). When she revives, she is heartbroken and furious ("Odio, furor, dispetto"). In the camp, Ubaldo again urges him to remember his duty and glory rather than his love ("Prence amato"). Armida enters, begging to be allowed to stay with him, and when Ubaldo and Rinaldo refuse, she angrily calls him unfaithful ("Partiro, ma pensa"). Rinaldo wavers briefly but leaves with the crusaders.

Act Three. Rinaldo is preparing to chop down the myrtle tree that is the source of her power. Nymphs and Zelmira appear, and Zelmira begs him to return to Armida ("Torna pure al caro bene"). He refuses to listen, and Armida herself appears ("Ah, non ferir"), begging for pity. He insists on destroying the tree, and she leaves in a rage, threatening him. Furies emerge from the tree and attack him, to his terror ("Dei pietosi"), but he regains his courage and destroys it. The last scene is in the crusaders' camp. Armida, Idreno, and Zelmira enter. Armida pleads with Rinaldo once more, but he refuses to go with her immediately. In the finale, she summons an infernal chariot and tells him she will now be happy to see him among the battle's corpses. He still protests his love, but leaves with the crusaders. *—Ann Feeney*

Recommended:

○ **Haydn: Armida** / Harnoncourt (cond.), Bartoli, Pregardien, Weir, Petibon, Vienna Concentus Musicus / 2000 / Teldec 81108

Lo Speziale (Der Apotheker), H. 28/3 (1768)

On August 5, 1768, the Esterházy family celebrated the name-day of Princess Maria Elisabeth at their country estate of Esterháza. The occasion included illuminations and fireworks, balls, dinners, and plays. It appears that the presentation of this, a new opera written to inaugurate the theater, was on September 2 of that same year. It is admirably suited to a relatively small private theatrical establishment, needing only a small orchestra and four singers. The opera was a huge success (Prince Nicolas Esterházy distributed liberal cash gifts to the orchestra and the cast afterwards). It was also the first Haydn opera to be revived, in 1899, Gustav Mahler conducting, and it has continued to be well received in frequent revivals ever since.

The text was a pre-existing libretto by the Italian playwright Carlo Goldoni, which had already been set as an opera by Domenico Fischietti and Vincenzo Pallavicino. The version Haydn set was simplified and made more direct, retaining the funniest parts and those that help the plot zip along. The plot is a pretty stock affair, revolving around an old man who has a lovely young ward and wants to marry her. It includes disguises, scenes involving a fake notary, and a scene with exceptionally inventive "Turkish" music (because one of the characters disguises himself as a Turk). The opera is in two acts, with a tiny little third act added on, almost as an afterthought. Haydn was aware of the problem in dramatic interest that this caused, and so reserved some of his best music (including the Turkish scene) for that act. Unfortunately some of Act Three was lost and has had to be reconstructed. In mood the opera is light hearted. There is a mock "Sturm and Drang" aria in G minor for the character called Volpino that almost turns out to express real passion, and one comic aria in which the young lady expresses her love for Volpino in music of exceptional charm. The opera is also full of word-painting, presaging that of *The Creation*. *—Joseph Stevenson*

Synopsis:

Act One. The action takes place in an eighteenth century pharmacy in Italy. Sempronio, the Apothecary, has a foster daughter, Grilletta, whom he intends to marry, despite their vast difference in age. About the only other thing of interest to him is unusual items of news. Mengone serves as his assistant and is really the object of Grilletta's affections. He possesses little interest in the pharmacological profession and has little respect for his eccentric boss. As Mengone works and sings in the pharmacy one day, the well-to-do Volpino stops in, pretending to need prescriptions, but actually wanting to visit Grilletta. He also fancies himself a suitor of the attractive young girl. Mengone cannot be fooled by him and frustrates his intentions.

Grilletta finally enters, however, and begins teasing Volpino. Eventually he becomes angry and departs. Grilletta and Mengone declare their love for each other, but must hide their affections when Sempronio enters suddenly. Later, however, they fail to conceal their feelings toward each other when he catches them holding hands.

Act Two. Volpino comes to Sempronio to ask for Grilletta's hand in marriage, but his proposal is rudely turned down. Undaunted by the rejection, Volpino attempts to gain favor with the Apothecary by recounting an unusual story for him from France, after which Sempronio reveals his supposed adroitness at handling young women, claiming always to be a step ahead of them. Grilletta and Mengone have a minor quarrel, and she decides to teach him a lesson he won't soon forget: She consents to Sempronio's marriage proposal, realizing almost immediately she may have gone too far in her plans to punish Mengone.

Sempronio sends for a notary to perform the marriage, and Volpino shows up in disguise. Mengone soon arrives, also in disguise as a notary. Sempronio begins dictating the terms of the marriage to both notaries, as they jot down his words. Soon, however, their deception is uncovered by Sempronio, and much comical confusion ensues.

Act Three. Volpino poses as Pascha, a Turk interested in buying Sempronio's business. He has brought several of his servants along and, in actuality, hopes to abduct Grilletta. Sempronio resists his offer, and the Turks begin smashing things. In the end, the besieged Sempronio is forced to concede that Grilletta should marry a Turk. The lucky 'Turk' is not Volpino, however, but Mengone in disguise. When identities are made known, both Sempronio and Volpino realize they have been outsmarted by the two lovers in the game of love. (This short final act is shorter still in most performances, since part of Haydn's original score for it is missing, with but two numbers surviving. The libretto, as given here, is complete.) *—James Reel*

Recommended:

○ **Haydn: Lo Speziale** / Goritzki (cond.), Browner, Morino, Antalffy, German CO / 2000 / Berlin Classics 0017122

Johann Michael Haydn

b. Sep. 14, 1737, Rohrau, Austria, **d.** Aug. 10, 1806, Salzburg, Austria

Composer: Symphonic, Concerto

Michael Haydn's fame is now considerably overshadowed by that of his older brother, Franz Joseph Haydn, but he was a prolific composer who in his day was much admired. Further, the passage of time has allowed an appreciation of his music's impact upon succeeding generations; he influenced both Mozart and Schubert, and he was the teacher of such notable composers as Carl Maria von Weber, Anton Diabelli and Sigismund Neukomm.

Like Franz Joseph, Michael Haydn was born in Rohrau, in Lower Austria. Although the exact date of his birth is unknown, he was baptized on September 14, 1737. He left home around 1745 to attend the choir school at St. Stephen's Cathedral in Vienna, where he received instruction in general subjects, singing, keyboard and violin. It was at St. Stephen's that Haydn gained a reputation for his unusually clear and beautiful voice, as well as for its extremely large range of three octaves. He was dismissed from St. Stephen's when his voice broke.

In 1757, after a precarious few years (probably in Vienna), Haydn was appointed Kapellmeister to the Bishop of Grosswardein in Hungary, now Oradea, Romania. He served the Bishop until 1763, when he accepted the position of court musician and Konzertmeister to Archbishop Sigismund Schrettenbach in Salzburg, who was renowned as a generous patron of the arts. This appointment put Haydn in a position to have a profound impact on the young Mozart, who spent his formative years in Salzburg. It was also through this appointment that Haydn met the woman who would become his wife, Maria Magdalena Lipp, a singer in the archbishop's court and daughter of the court organist Ignaz Lipp. The two were married in 1768. The couple's only child, Aloysia Josepha, was born in 1770; however, she died within a year.

With the death, in 1777 of Anton Cajetan Adlgasser, the first organist at the Dreifaltigkeitskirche (Trinity Church), Haydn was appointed to the post. Concurrently, Mozart became the organist at the cathedral. When Mozart left the employ of the Archbishop Hieronymus Colloredo in 1781, Haydn took over at the cathedral as well. During the last years of his life, Haydn was frequently ill. He died in Salzburg on August 10, 1806. He was buried in the cemetery at St. Peter's, where, in 1821, his friends erected a memorial in his honor.

Haydn was an extremely versatile composer who wrote in both the stile antico, represented by the music of Fux, and in more modern styles; his masses followed the tradition of concluding the Gloria and Credo with fugues. Although he wrote a great deal of secular music for use at court (he was one of the first composers to write unaccompanied German part-songs for male chorus), Haydn made his greatest contribution in the area of sacred music. Although his compositions in this genre show the impact of the church reforms of the period, they are representative of a distinct personal voice. Joseph's reforms demanded a reduction in the number of religious services, and a simplification of those that remained. There were also edicts against the use of instrumental music in the church, and against the use of highly florid, soloistic material. Always concerned with liturgical propriety, Haydn's sacred compositions follow the guidelines of the reforms in their reduced instrumental forces, and in their frequent use of the stile antico.—*Stephen Kingsbury*

Overview of Works (1754–1805)

The lesser-known younger brother of Joseph Haydn, Michael Haydn was born in Rohrau, Lower Austria, on September 13, 1737. The earlier part of his career followed a similar pattern to that of Joseph. He was a choirboy at St. Stephen's Cathedral in Vienna, after which he joined the orchestra of the Bishop of Grosswardein in Hungary. In 1762, he was offered the post of leader of the Salzburg court orchestra by Archbishop Schrattenbach. Michael Haydn remained in Salzburg for the rest of his life, becoming friendly with the Mozart family, although Leopold Mozart (Wolfgang's father) always maintained a wary attitude toward him. He died in 1806.

Although Haydn composed in most of the leading forms of his Classical-era day, he was particularly renowned for his church music, of which he composed a substantial amount. His brother considered him a better composer of sacred music than he himself was, while Mozart is known to have copied out several of his scores and had a high regard for him. Haydn's substantial contribution to the liturgy of Salzburg Cathedral and other religious institutions in the vicinity includes two requiem masses, some two dozen other masses, and a large corpus of shorter religious works. Although widely disseminated in Catholic areas of Austria and Germany during the eighteenth and nineteenth centuries, Haydn's sacred music gradually fell into an obscurity from which it has never fully recovered. While recent years have witnessed something of a revival, our present knowledge remains too sketchy for a fair evaluation to be made. In style it combines a solid understanding of old-fashioned counterpoint (included in Haydn's training in Vienna) with more modern Italianate trends in the solo sections. Even Leopold Mozart was impressed by the fugal writing in the big *Missa Sancti Hieronymi* of 1777, telling his son in a letter that they were "worked out in masterly fashion" and that although the mass had lasted a full 75 minutes, "it was for me too short, for the music was truly well composed." In addition to sacred music, Haydn composed some 30 symphonies. In general they are weaker and less innovative than those of his brother, and closer to the more Italian style of Mozart. One, in G, composed in 1783, was indeed long able to masquerade as a work of Mozart's after the latter added a slow introduction to it and it became known as Mozart's *Symphony No. 37*. Among a smaller body of chamber music, there are three fine string quintets. Haydn's attention to stage works was far more restricted than that of Joseph; the lack of a theater in Salzburg meant that there was little impetus to compose more than a few small-scale German dramas. —*Brian Robins*

Recommended:

- ○ **M. Haydn: In Grosswardein** / Nemeth (cond.), Cser, Gergely, Karoly, Tokesi, Savaria Baroque Orch., Cantus Corvinus Vocal Ens. / Hungaroton 32005
- ○ **M. Haydn: Symphonies** / Bamert (cond.), London Mozart Players / 1996 / Chandos 9352
- ○ **M. Haydn: String Quintets** / Wiener Philharmonia Quintet / 2003 / Camerata 28013
- ○ **M. Haydn: 4 Symphonies** / Frank (cond.), Helsingborg SO / 1992 / Bis 481
- ○ **M. Haydn: Chamber Music** / Piccolo Concerto Wien / Symphonia 97154

SYMPHONIC

Symphony in A major, P 6 (ca. Aug. 1, 1771)

In part because he was a lesser figure than his brother Josef, some of Michael Haydn's works—several of the early symphonies, for example—were lost and some were misattributed, like the *Symphony in G* (P. 16), which was once listed in Mozart's canon. There are 41 surviving symphonies in Michael Haydn's output. This A major effort is based on materials found in another of his compositions, the music for the tragedy *Hermann* (1773), and possibly in another dramatic work, one whose title is believed to be *Ballo* (1770). The *Symphony in A major* is cast in four movements and scored for just two oboes, two horns, and strings. Performances today may include harpsichord to serve as continuo. The first movement is marked Allegro molto and features vigorous music whose emphatic rhythmic manner and joyous mood make it quite attractive. The second movement is a charming Minuet and Trio, while the ensuing Andante is graceful and stately. The Allegro molto finale is the liveliest and most muscular movement and provides a fittingly colorful close to this charming work. The *Symphony in A* lasts about 15 minutes in a typical performance. —*Robert Cummings*

Recommended:

- ○ **M. Haydn: Symphonies** / Bamert (cond.), London Mozart Players / 1996 / Chandos 9352
- ○ **M. Haydn: Symphonies** / Nemeth (cond.), Savaria Capella / Hungaroton 31706

Symphony in D major, P 23 (May 30, 1786)

Michael Haydn's *Symphony in D major* (Sherman 420/Perger 23) is numbered as his 32nd, and it stands out from the rest of his other 50 or so symphonies for a number of reasons. First of all, it is only cast in two movements, Vivace assai and Finale: Presto, and for many years it was assumed that part of the manuscript, held at Széchényi National Library in Budapest, had to be missing. But further study has revealed that the work is complete as it is, and it represents a rare avis among eighteenth century symphonies in that it is written in only two movements; certainly it is the only such symphony composed by Haydn. As the manuscript is dated May 30, 1786, it has been assumed that this symphony was composed for the birthday of the Prince Archbishop of Salzburg, as were several other Haydn symphonies written at or around the date of May 30. It must've been a very joyous occasion, as this is one of the most animated and exciting of Haydn's symphonies. The form of the work goes from Vivace to Presto (or from fast to faster) and is rich in surprisingly independent instrumental parts, brilliant passagework for the strings, and thundering kettledrums. —*Uncle Dave Lewis*

Recommended:

- ○ **M. Haydn: Symphonies 21, 30–32** / Goritzki (cond.), Neuss German Chamber Academy / CPO 999179

Symphony in E flat major, P 17 (Aug. 14, 1783)

This symphony was found among Mozart's papers when they were inventoried after his death; for that reason, and because the opening movement and part of the andante were written in Mozart's hand, it was thought for nearly a century to be by Mozart, and was listed in the Breitkopf & Härtel catalog as his No. 37. Subsequent authorities confused it with the symphony composed in Linz (commonly known as *No. 36*). When the true *"Linz" Symphony* became known, they continued to believe that this symphony was also written by Mozart in Linz, when in fact it was by Franz Josef Haydn's younger brother, Michael—a Salzburg composer well-known to the Mozart family. For reasons that remain unclear, Mozart added an opening slow movement of his own. Perhaps he thought the work incomplete without it, or needing "improvement." Nevertheless, the young Haydn's work was good enough to be mistaken for Mozart until 1907. Even after that date, the symphony was performed for a while under Mozart's name, and then faded from the repertory. Only with the late twentieth century revival of interest in Michael Haydn's contemporaries has this work been appreciated on its own terms. —*Joseph Stevenson*

Recommended:

- ○ **Haydn: Symphonies 26, 27 & 28** / Warchal (cond.), Slovak CO / CPO 999156

CONCERTO

Trumpet Concerto in D major (ca. 1757–1764)

This little concerto, probably composed in Salzburg in the mid-1760s, has the distinction of containing one of the highest notes (and perhaps *the* highest note) ever written for the trumpet, an F sharp two and a half octaves above middle C. The work is actually written for the clarino, a Baroque ancestor of the trumpet with a distinct construction and a special mouthpiece that emphasized the instrument's highest register and enabled the player to hit notes well above the range of a conventional trumpet. The result is a very tough trumpet part that has endeared the piece to Maurice André and other virtuoso trumpeters, they being the only players these days who have the lips for the very top notes. Beyond this special feature the *Trumpet Concerto in D major* is a pleasant piece of early Classical-period instrumental music. It is in two movements of roughly equal length, the first a singing Adagio and the second a flashily arpeggiated Allegro that contains the virtuoso thrills and room for a cadenza; the two movements total nine or ten minutes in performance. The work is perhaps at its most effective when juxtaposed with trumpet works from other periods, as an illustration of the surprising sounds that have come from the instrument at various points during its long history. —*James Manheim*

Recommended:

- ○ **Wynton Marsalis: Baroque Music For Trumpets** / Leppard (cond.), Marsalis, English CO / 1992 / Sony 42478
- ○ **Trumpet Concertos** / André, Franz Liszt CO / 1992 / EMI 69152

Jascha Heifetz

b. Feb. 2, 1901, Vilnius, Lithuania, **d.** Dec. 10, 1987, Los Angeles, CA
Violinist

Jascha Heifetz was the leading figure among the extraordinary group of Russian Jews who dominated violin playing in the second and third quarters of the twentieth century. As a technician he had no superior, and, of all the artists of his time and later, only two or three could even offer a challenge to his electrifying precision of execution. His diamond-point tone and quick vibrato afforded his playing a clarity of line that some felt was almost too perfect, even cold. Most conductors and other violinists—and audiences—felt differently and a Heifetz concert inevitably drew sell-out crowds.

Heifetz was born in Vilna, where his father Ruvim was a violinist in the city theatre. When he was three, his father bought for him a quarter-size instrument and gave him beginning instruction. By the age of five, Heifetz had advanced enough to enter the Vilna Conservatory where he began instruction under Elias Malkin. Only a year later, Heifetz made his first public appearance performing the Mendelssohn *Violin Concerto.* The six-year-old was so successful that offers for other appearances came from numerous other venues in Russia and he was hailed as a real prodigy.

When Leopold Auer, then a famous professor at the St. Petersburg Conservatory, came to Vilna in 1909, he was persuaded by Malkin to listen to Heifetz. After hearing him in Mendelssohn and Paganini, Auer embraced him and predicted for him a splendid future, urging him to come to St. Petersburg and become his pupil.

Ruvim Heifetz resigned his position, sold the family belongings, and took his son to St. Petersburg, but Auer initially failed to recognize the boy and refused him admittance to his home. By the time Auer realized his error, the Conservatory entrance deadline had passed and Jascha had to enroll in the class of an assistant. Six months later, however, Heifetz was able enter Auer's class, and thereafter his progress was astounding.

During an appearance at the International Exposition in Odessa, the reception accorded Heifetz was so explosive a police escort was needed afterward. Concerts throughout Europe followed immediately and, at an appearance with the Berlin Philharmonic in 1914, conductor Artur Nikisch declared that he had never heard violin playing such as his.

Heifetz' American debut took place at Carnegie Hall in 1917, eliciting such observations as "only the molten gold of Fritz Kreisler can be conjured up in comparison" (Herbert F. Peyser) and "He is a modern miracle" (Pitts Sanborn). The ensuing year brought triumph after triumph, with critics vying with each other to offer the most extravagant superlatives. A period of transition a few years later brought some critical reservations as Heifetz sought to move away from the overt emotionalism of his Russian training and become a more objective player. By the mid-1920s, however, a balance had been struck and once again accolades flew as critics and audiences noted a new, more mature approach to his music.

Heifetz became an American citizen, settled in California, and enjoyed the benefit of a long-term recording contract with RCA, amassing a sizeable discography over the years. Throughout his career, Heifetz favored gut strings, perhaps to temper the fine-edged aggressiveness of his attack and the enormous strength of his bowing arm. Early recordings of concertos, made mostly overseas, were gradually redone—though not supplanted—with American orchestras and in improved sound. Nonetheless, many of the earlier releases, despite their having been done in short takes required by 78 discs, still compel attention for their unsurpassed mastery. *—Erik Eriksson*

Recommended:

- ○ **Sibelius: Concerto** / Hendl (cond.), Heifetz, Chicago SO / 2002 / JVC 223
- ○ **Beethoven: Concerto** / Munch (cond.), Heifetz, BSO / 2003 / JVC 24003
- ○ **Brahms: Concerto; Double Concerto** / Reiner, Wallenstein (conds.), Heifetz, Piatigorsky, Chicago SO, RCA Victor SO / 2004 / RCA 59410
- ○ **Tchaikovsky: Concerto** / Reiner (cond.), Heifetz, Chicago SO / 2001 / JVC 9
- ○ **Heifetz Showpieces** / Heifetz, etc. / RCA 7709
- ○ **Bach: Sonatas & Partitas** / Heifetz / 1994 / BMG 0902661748

Johann David Heinichen

b. Apr. 17, 1683, Krössuln, Germany, **d.** Jul. 16, 1729, Dresden, Germany
Composer

Although Johann David Heinichen was well known and respected both as a theorist and as a composer during his lifetime, his name would not have been recognized by most classical music listeners until scholar/conductor Reinhard Goebel began championing his music during the 1990s. Since then, more and more listeners have become acquainted with Heinichen's sprightly, colorful, charming music. Heinichen's father was a pastor in Krossuln, Germany. Johann apparently was a gifted child; he claimed that he had composed and conducted sacred music in local churches before the age of 12. In 1695, Heinichen enrolled at the Thomasschule in Leipzig, which his father also had attended, studying with and impressing the composer Johann Kuhnau. Heinichen began studying law at Leipzig University in 1702, and completed the degree in 1706, moving to Weissenfels to practice. However, the law apparently held little allure for Heinichen; he began composing occasional music for Duke Johann Georg's court, and in 1709 gave up the law altogether and moved to Leipzig to write for the opera house there. Heinichen was quite successful in Leipzig, but decided he needed to learn how to write Italian opera firsthand, and abruptly left behind Leipzig for Venice in 1710. He met numerous composers in that city, including Antonio Vivaldi, and apparently picked up the Italian style quickly, writing two successful operas for the S Angelo Theater. His fame spread all the way to the Prince-Elector of Saxony, Augustus II, in Dresden. Augustus hired Heinichen to share Kapellmeister duties with Johann Christoph Schmidt at his court in 1717. Heinichen spent the rest of his life there.

Augustus II's court was an ideal situation for a composer. It boasted the greatest orchestra in Europe, for which scores of composers (including Vivaldi, Georg Philip Telemann, and Tomaso Albinoni) spontaneously wrote concerti; it employed numerous other eminent composers, like Johann Joachim Quantz, Francesco Veracini, and Jan Dismas Zelenka; and it had a patron who was determined to keep the music playing. Apart from a disastrous quarrel in the Italian opera company between Heinichen and the singers Senesino and Berselli, which eventually resulted in the dissolution of the company, Heinichen's tenure was peaceful and productive. He only wrote one opera there, but wrote much instrumental and sacred vocal music which combined elements of the Italian, French and German styles into a recognizable, coherent, personal style. His music revels in the instrumental colors the Dresden orchestra could create, and moves along with splendid rhythmic spring and vigor. If his music is occasionally too extroverted, it is a forgivable excess. While he was at Dresden, Heinichen also had the opportunity to rewrite his treatise *Der General-Bass in der Composition,* which provides much more than its title would indicate; it is a manual for composition, a discussion of the proper expression of the affections in music, and a compendium of footnotes and asides which sound like an eager professor instructing his students. It was one of the most respected texts of its day, and it is still used by scholars seeking a better understanding of Baroque performance practice. *—Andrew Lindemann Malone*

Overview of Works (ca. 1705–1727)

Born near Weissenfels, Germany, in 1683, Heinichen was a pupil at the Thomasschule in Leipzig, studying under Johann Schelle and Johann Kuhnau and later serving as Kuhnau's assistant. He also studied law at Leipzig University and for a short time was director of the *collegium musicum,* a concert-giving organization subsequently made famous by its association with Bach. After deciding to make music rather than law his profession, Heinichen traveled to Venice and Rome. In 1717, he was appointed Kapellmeister at Dresden. He remained in the post until 1729, when he was succeeded by Hasse.

Although Heinichen had several operas produced in both Germany and Venice, he is today primarily remembered for his concertos. In form they show the strong influence of the Venetian style of concerto as developed by Vivaldi. However Heinichen also assimilated French influences, forging a personal style which owes more to a dynamic rhythmic drive and colorful orchestration than to contrapuntal complexity. The relative simplicity of his harmony and melody owes much to forward-looking galant principles. The scoring of his concertos is often lavish, taking particular advantage of the fine wind players of the Dresden orchestra, one of the finest in Europe at this time. Parts for several soloists, after the fashion of the Venetian concerto for many instruments, abound in his concertos, often in exotic combinations. A *Concerto in F* (Siebel 235), for instance, has solo parts for oboe, violin, two flutes, and two horns. Although Heinichen retained the standard Vivaldian three-movement form (fast-slow-fast), for many of his concertos, he also frequently expanded them to four or more movements. The *G major Concerto* (Siebel 213) has no fewer than six movements, with the inclusion of such French dance movements as an Entrée and a Loure taking the work closer to the form of the suite than to the usual concerto form. This vital and colorful composer was long neglected but has enjoyed something of a revival in recent years, particularly at the hands of Reinhard Goebel and his Musica Antiqua Köln. *—Brian Robins*

Recommended:

- ○ **Heinichen: Dresden Concerti** / Goebel (cond.), Cologne Musica Antiqua / Archiv 437549
- ○ **Heinichen: Lamentationes; Passionsmusik** / Goebel (cond.), Cologne Musica Antiqua / Archiv 447092

Barbara Hendricks

b. Nov. 20, 1948, Stephens, AR
Soprano

Barbara Hendricks' voice—particularly suited to Fauré, Debussy, Bizet, Mozart, and works of operetta—has a warm, crystalline quality that has kept her in demand on stage and in recording studios. Her performances have embraced everything from contemporary music to popular standards, including songs of Duke Ellington and several world premieres. She has been careful with her choices of repertoire, avoiding roles that would overextend her essentially lyric instrument. Aside from music, she is deeply committed to humanitarian work, with a particular concern for refugees and those in war or poverty zones. She sang a concert in Sarajevo in 1993 while the city was being shelled, so she had to wear a bulletproof vest and helmet.

As a child, Hendricks sang in church choirs, but believing her talent for math and science would be more likely to lead to solid employment, she did not choose to study music; instead she went to the University of Nebraska and graduated with a double major in Mathematics and Chemistry. However, after singing in a community event at the Aspen Institute, she was invited to attend the summer music festival there. Doing so brought her into contact with Jennie Tourel, whose teaching—both there and at the Juilliard School—would eventually lead her into a singing career. Tourel, who was Jewish, fled France during World War II, escaping on the last boat that was allowed to leave. Hearing Tourel's descriptions of those events peaked Hendricks' interest in the plight of refugees; later, when her daughter was born, she named her Jennie after Mme. Tourel.

Hendricks' first opera role was at the Mini-Met chamber-opera arm of the Metropolitan Opera in 1973 as St. Settlement in Virgil Thomson's *Four Saints in Three Acts*. In 1974, she made her Glyndebourne debut as Cavalli's *Calisto* and was also in the world premiere of David Del Tredici's *Final Alice*. She appeared in the United States premiere of Penderecki's *Desiree* in 1976. Her first of many recordings was for EMI in the small part of the Celestial Voice in *Don Carlo* in 1978. In 1982, she debuted at the Paris Opera as Juliette in Gounod's *Romeo et Juliette* (she was also offered, but turned down, the lead of the film *Diva* that year). Her Met debut was as Sophie in Richard Strauss' *Der Rosenkavalier* in 1986, and she was awarded the title of *Commandeur des Arts et des Lettres* by the French government, the youngest ever recipient of that title. The next year she made her La Scala debut as Susanna in *Le Nozze di Figaro*. 1987 was the year when she first began to work with the United Nations High Commission for Refugees, and became a Goodwill Ambassador. In 1996, she was in the world premiere of Tobias Pickers' *The Rain in the Trees*. The Ensemble Intercontemporain commissioned *Das Erschaft der Dichter nicht* from Bruno Mantovani specifically for her, which work she premiered in 2002.*—Ann Feeney*

Recommended:

- ○ **Fauré: Mélodies** / Hendricks, Dalberto / EMI 49841
- ○ **Tribute to Duke Ellington** / Hendricks, etc. / EMI 55346
- ○ **Debussy: Mélodies** / Hendricks, Beroff / EMI 47888

Hans Werner Henze

b. Jul. 1, 1926, Gütersloh, Westphalia (Germany)

Composer: Opera, Vocal, Symphonic

Hans Werner Henze has been a prolific composer over a career spanning six decades, writing extensively in all the standard genres such as symphony, concerto, opera, and song, in a remarkable variety of styles. As he has said, "I am bored by the idea of employing approaches which I have already tried." At times in his career, his controversial political views have attracted almost as much attention as his music.

Henze started composing at age 12, even before his formal music education began at the Braunschweig State Music School, which he attended from 1942–44. From an early age, he was interested in political and social issues. His rejection of the bourgeois values of his upbringing and the Nazism that he encountered first hand probably had a large influence on his later political thinking. He served for a time in the German army in World War II and was briefly held as a prisoner-of-war. After the war, he continued his musical studies at the Institute for Church Music in Heidelberg, where he worked with Wolfgang Fortner, and at Darmstadt, where he studied with Schoenberg disciple René Leibowitz. His earliest acknowledged compositions date from this time, like the *Chamber Concerto* (1946) which was Henze's first publicly performed work. His first full-length opera, *Boulevard Solitude*, was completed in 1951.

Despite the hints of jazz and Neo-Classicism in some of that early music, Henze was strongly identified with the post-Arnold Schoenberg serial composers for several years. With his move to Italy in 1953, Henze sought to change that perception and brought to his music a new lyricism. One can hear this in his second opera, *König Hirsch*, premiered in 1956, and the *Symphony No. 4, "Il Re Crevo"* (1955), which makes use of music from that opera's second act finale. W. H. Auden and Chester Kallman, Stravinsky's librettists for *The Rake's Progress*, provided the words for Henze's fourth and sixth operas, *Elegy for Young Lovers* (1961) and *The Bassarids* (1965–66). It was around this time that Henze took his first teaching post, director of master classes in composition at the Salzburg Mozarteum.

The notorious premiere of the oratorio *Das Floss der Medusa* (The Raft of Medusa, a requiem for Che Guevara) in Hamburg in 1968, at which the work's librettist and others were arrested, brought Henze further notoriety. Interactions with German students and Italian intellectuals had motivated Henze to bring to his work an increasing political consciousness. Socialism and the New Left were very appealing to him, even more so after a year of teaching in Cuba in 1969–70, during which he led the Cuban National Symphony in the premiere of his *Symphony No. 6* for two chamber orchestras.

Voices (1973), a song cycle with texts by Ho Chi Minh, Bertold Brecht, and others, reflects Henze's political commitment and his musical eclecticism. In his later works, Henze has incorporated such disparate elements as rock and popular music, electronics, taped sounds, microtones, and extended vocal and instrumental techniques. His harrowing *Symphony No. 9*, premiered in 1997, tells the story of prisoners who escape from a German concentration camp; the Symphony is dedicated to "the heroes and martyrs of German anti-fascism."

Henze has written for many of the great performers of his time, such as Dietrich Fischer-Dieskau, Peter Pears, Julian Bream, Heinz and Ursula Holliger, and Christoph Eschenbach. He has also actively championed his own music, traveling the world to conduct and record his compositions. *—Chris Morrison*

Overview of Works

Acknowledged with Stockhausen as one of the two leading composers of postwar Germany, Hans Werner Henze's oeuvre is essentially the history of his conscious and continuous attempt to come to terms with his position as the heir of both Germany's music and politics. Always a prolific composer, Henze's earliest works from the late 1940s and early 1950s were written under the influence of Fortner and Hartmann—*Symphony No. 1* (1947)—and later Berg and Stravinsky—*Symphony No. 3*. But by his ballet *Boulevard Solitude* (1951), Henze had already formed his own style: strongly but lightly rhythmic, richly and complexly tonal, and intensely lyrical. This style suffused his works of the later 1950s and early 1960s—the dark fairy tale opera *König Hirsch* (1952–55), the lyrical opera *Elegy for Young Lovers* (1959–61), the ironic "classical" opera *Der Junge Herr* (1964), and climaxing with the tragic opera *The Bassarids* (1965) after Euripides. After the riotous political demonstrations at the premiere of his oratorio *The Raft of the Medusa* (1968), Henze turned from what he called the "bourgeois" music of his twenties and thirties to a deliberately revolutionary style in his music of the late 1960s and 1970s. Both the dramatic chamber work *El Cimarrón* (1970) and the *Symphony No. 6 for Two Chamber Orchestras* (1969) were composed in Cuba, and culminating in the opera *We Come to the River* (1974–76), Henze's musical language became much denser and his aesthetic far more directly confrontational. At the same time, however, Henze composed the severely beautiful absolute music of the string quartets *No. 3*, *No. 4*, and *No. 5* (1975–77). Without renouncing his political works of the 1960s and 1970s, Henze's music from the 1980s and 1990s was increasingly concerned with reconciling his revolutionary politics with his role as a German composer. Henze conceived both his *Seventh* and especially his *Symphony No. 9* as German symphonies. The *Seventh* (1983–84)—a four-movement work starting with a furious Allemande and ending with a desolate orchestral setting of Hölderlin's *Half Life*—takes the melodic and harmonic inheritance of Berg, Hartmann, and the young Henze to its highest point of development. The *Ninth* (1996) goes back to Beethoven's *Symphony No. 9* to create a profoundly moving, seven-movement choral-orchestral masterpiece dedicated "to the heroes and martyrs of German anti-fascism." *—James Leonard*

Recommended:

- ○ **Henze: Barcarola; Symphony 7** / Rattle (cond.), Birmingham SO / 1993 / EMI 54762
- ○ **Henze: Die Bassariden** / Dohnányi (cond.), Meyer, Paskalis, Lagger, Melchert, Vienna PO / 2003 / Orfeo 605032
- ○ **Henze: Streichquartett 1–5** / Arditti SQ / 1986 / Wergo 60114
- ○ **Henze: Songs** / Bostridge, Drake (piano) / 2001 / EMI 57112
- ○ **Henze: Scorriabanda sinfonica; Antifone; Piano Concerto 1** / Ruzicka, Tainton, NDR Orch. / 2003 / Wergo 6657
- ○ **Henze: Royal Winter Music 1 & 2** / Kres / Wergo 60126

OPERA

Boulevard Solitude, lyric drama (1951)

Though Hans Werner Henze had made forays into operatic music with his radio opera, *Ein Landarzt* (Kafka) in 1951, *Boulevard Solitude* represented his first fully realized work for the stage. A very successful piece at its premiere, *Boulevard* revealed Henze to be a highly original composer well suited to drama. Having embraced a variety of musical styles and materials during the course of his education, he brought them all to bear in a work that moved freely between sections of tonality, free atonality, serialism, and jazz-inspired music. There was enough variety to keep the audience on its toes without losing overall cohesion, and the work has inspired occasional comparisons to the operas of Alban Berg. The use of antiquated set pieces—such as the aria, recitative, and sectional ensemble—made an interesting foil to the composer's forward-looking eclecticism and became a hallmark of his operatic style.

Boulevard's success was due in no small part to the libretto (by Greta Weil), which is a retelling of the story of Manon Lescaut—already the inspiration for Puccini's *Manon Lescaut* and Massenet's *Manon*. Based on Walter Jockisch's adaptation of Antoine-François Prévost's original novel, Weil's libretto shifts the focus away from the story of Manon to that of her lover, Armand des Grieux, and thereby provides a fresh look at the events and circumstances of an already familiar story. The grim tale is set in modern-day Paris and features elements such as drug dealing and a cast of characters who could have come straight out of a prime-time soap opera. The first performance took place in Hannover on February 17, 1952. Its success pointed toward Henze's status as the foremost German composer of opera during the latter half of the twentieth century—and also toward a group of operas of several decades later that featured material drawn from everyday life (John Adams, composer of Nixon in China, was surely aware of this work). *—Allen Schrott*

Synopsis:

Scene One. The story is based on the venerable operatic tale of Manon Lescaut, but is set in Paris in the 1950s. In a railroad station waiting room in a large French city, amidst the bustle of passengers, porters, waiters, and so forth, Armand des Grieux, a young man, is sitting reading with his friend Francis, who has come to see him off. The loudspeakers announce the boarding of a train, and Francis says goodbye. Manon Lescaut and her brother, Lescaut, enter. He points her toward Armand's table. She approaches him, smiles, and asks if she can sit there, giving no sign that she recognizes Lescaut, who retreats to a bar. Armand asks if she also is going to Paris, and she tells him she is going to Lausanne to boarding school. She must be a well-born young lady, Armand says, but Manon denies this. She is just a girl with so many dreams and longings and who is so lonely.

This brings out a long speech from Armand about the lonely life of a student in Paris. He imagines elegant, beautiful ladies who ignore him. Manon plays to his fantasy; one day one of them is sure to notice him and leave him a number written in lipstick. Manon then tells him her name and continues the fantasy, picturing the two of them in the rapture of his dreams. They leave together. Lescaut, who has been unobtrusively watching them, finishes his drink in obvious satisfaction.

Scene Two. Armand and Manon are living together in his attic apartment in Paris. As they lie in bed, Manon sings beguilingly of a lovely hat she has seen in a shop. She says she will buy it today. Armand begs her not to; since he stopped attending classes, his father has cut him off. But on seeing her disappointment he decides to go to his friend Francis, who lives in the building, and borrow some money so she can have her hat.

Lescaut appears. When Manon asks what he wants, he begins, "Your two ravishing breasts...." She is shocked at this hint of incest, but he continues that he wants them for a new admirer he has found for her, one who is fat, old, and rich. Armand returns. He has overheard. He sarcastically predicts that she can become highly successful, if only she takes care to treat all her lovers cruelly. He says he will give her five minutes to make up her mind. Then, if she still wants to, she can call the fat, rich pig to his room for all he cares.

Scene Three. Manon has made her choice and is now living in the luxurious house of Lilaque Sr. But she misses Armand and writes him a note hinting they can have an affair under Lilaque's nose. Lescaut enters, angered that she is risking the continued largesse of her sugar daddy, and tears up the letter. Manon protests that he is killing all the beauty in her soul. Lescaut reminds her that he depends on her passing onto him "gifts" from Lilaque. Then, driven by his need for cash, he breaks into the old man's safe. Lilaque arrives in time to catch him at it, and in a rage throws them out of his house. If either ever returns, he says, he will call the police.

Scene Four. At the university library, Armand has returned to his studies; with Francis, he is reading the Roman poet Catullus, famous for his poems about his betrayal by a mercenary and heartless woman. Francis happens to mention that he has news of Manon, who is now with another man, having been thrown out by Lilaque for theft or embezzlement—or so the gossip says. Armand refuses to believe anything bad about Manon and declares that Lescaut must have been solely responsible. Francis shakes his head at Armand's love-blindness and leaves. Manon now appears and joins him in reading Catullus' erotic poetry, and they leave together, swearing eternal faithfulness.

Scene Five. The setting is a low-life bar. Manon has just left Armand for a richer lover, and the luckless student is attempting to buy more cocaine to forget her once again. Lescaut arrives with a new prospective client for Manon—none other than Lilaque's son—and demands to know where she is. Armand can only say that she promised to meet him there soon. While waiting, Lescaut sells Armand a small portion of the drug. Lilaque Jr. is impatient. Since seeing Manon at his father's house, he has been haunted by her image. Armand's perceptions are now altered by the cocaine, and he scarcely registers what is happening when Manon does arrive. Manon calms him down.

Soon he becomes aware that she has left with young Lilaque. She has left him a note, and he is dazed by its message: she will call for him tomorrow night. Meanwhile, for tonight, he has arranged for him to be "entertained" by one of the most beautiful girls in Paris.

Scene Six. At young Lilaque's handsome apartment, Armand and Manon are in bed. Lescaut arrives to get Armand to leave while there is still time. But a servant phones the older Lilaque. Lescaut notices that a picture in the room is a Picasso and removes it from its frame.

Lilaque's angry voice is heard from the anteroom, praising the servant for tipping him to the presence of "this rabble." Manon hides the men and attempts to seduce Lilaque when he confronts her. When he discovers the theft and the two men, Lescaut shoots him, forces the revolver into Manon's hand, and escapes. Young Lilaque rushes in and discovers them, petrified.

Scene Seven. Outside a prison, Armand hopes to have a final word with Manon, but she is led away with other prisoners without being able to say a word. Distorted images of their time together pass across the stage as the opera ends in a manic rumba rhythm. *—Joseph Stevenson*

Elegy for Young Lovers (1959–1961; revised 1987)

Elegy for Young Lovers was the first of two collaborations between Hans Werner Henze and the team of W.H. Auden and Chester Kallman—already authors of librettos for Igor Stravinsky (*The Rake's Progress*) and Benjamin Britten (*Paul Bunyon*). Approaching the two authors in 1958, Henze requested a libretto suitable for "tender, beautiful noises," and from their reply he crafted a particularly touching chamber opera.

Stylistically similar to his earlier operas—especially with respect to the use of set pieces as structural units and a tendency toward eclecticism—*Elegy* is notable for its utilization of dramatically specific instrumental colors; the timbres of solo instruments, or families of instruments, represent certain characters in much the same manner as leitmotifs. The premiere (in German translation) was in Schwetzingen on May 20, 1961, and was notable for its inclusion of Dietrich Fischer-Dieskau in the role of Mittenhofer. The first performance of the English-language version was at Glyndebourne in 1963.

The plot of *Elegy* surrounds the intertwined lives and loves of a group of travelers lodging in the Austrian Alps—in particular the love of the young couple, Toni and Elisabeth, who consummate their passionate affair by freezing to death together in a blizzard on the infamous Hammerhorn. The very separate, yet interrelated concerns of the various characters are well represented by Henze's integration of small, closed musical forms into large-scale formal designs. The writings of the character Mittenhofer—a poet—serve to foreshadow many elements of the drama; appropriately, those sections of the score in which his poetry is "read" assume a structural and thematic importance. This is also true of the music of the elderly Hilda Mack, whose tragic longing for her long-dead husband—frozen to death on the Hammerhorn—lends emotional weight to the affair of the young lovers, as well as to their fate. *—Allen Schrott*

Synopsis:

The story centers around Gregor Mittenhofer, who is a poet of considerable renown. He resides in a hotel secluded high in the Alps where, with his needs met by an entourage of support staff, he plies his trade. In fact, his employees and the others at the hotel not only provide for his day-to-day needs, but also serve as inspiration for his work; he borrows from their real lives and uses them in his writing. The Countess Carolina serves as patron and assistant to Mittenhofer; Dr. Wilhelm Reischmann, who is accompanied at the hotel by his son Toni; the poet's mistress, Elisabeth Zimmer; and Hilda Mack, a distraught and disoriented kind of Miss Donnithorne figure who is haunted by visions of her long lost husband and who continually waits for his unlikely return from a 40-year mountain excursion. Mittenhofer treats this cast of characters as his own *dramatis personae*, exploiting the varied circumstances of their existences, and their dependence on him, for his own artistic ends.

This perverse symbiosis is disrupted, however, as unexpected circumstances realign dependencies and allegiances. Mittenhofer turns bitterly jealous when Toni, the doctor's son, gains the love of the mistress, Elisabeth. When Hilda Mack, the crazed widow, learns that the body of her dead husband has been discovered, having been buried by the snow pack decades before, she suddenly snaps out of her hallucinatory world. Thus unburdened, she breaks her tethers to the mountain village and departs, leaving Mittenhofer without one of his prized and most intriguing sources of poetic material.

When it becomes clear that Elisabeth will leave the hotel with Toni, Mittenhofer asks them a final favor: to hike into the mountains and fetch for him an edelweiss bloom. After they depart, a mountaineer arrives at the hotel and informs Mittenhofer and the Countess that a fierce mountain storm is on its way. The poet and patron do not tell him that Toni and Elisabeth are hiking, and thus they are left to the mercies of the storm. Like widow Mack's husband, Toni and Elisabeth meet an icy demise. The opera ends with Mittenhofer treating this tragedy as yet another artistic commodity: he presents a new poem, entitled "Elegy for Young Lovers," with Toni and Elisabeth as its dedicatees. *—Jeremy Grimshaw*

Recommended:

○ **Henze: Elegie Für Junge Liebende** / Jones, Akina (conds.), Richard, Schudel, Fath, Hajek, Lloyd-Morgan, Berlin Chamber Opera Orch. / 1995 / Deutsche Schallplatten 1050

VOCAL

Kammermusik 1958, for tenor, guitar & 8 instruments (1958; revised 1963)

When Hans Werner Henze moved to Italy in 1953, along with his change of residence came a marked change in his musical style. While his writing up to that point had been strictly serialist—and continued to draw on serialist idioms for some time—it became much more relaxed and lyrical overall. His *Kammermusik*, written five years after the move, is an entirely typical example of his work from this period.

Henze described this song cycle with instrumental interludes as "an encounter between Germany and Greece as conjured up by a poet (Friedrich Hölderlin) whose brain was clouded by insanity and who expressed his vision in wonderful but apparently disjointed phrases." Henze carries thematic material from one atonal movement to the next, greatly transforming it along the way. *Kammermusik*, in 12 movements with a concluding Adagio, is scored for tenor voice, guitar or harp, clarinet, horn, bassoon, and strings (two violins, viola, cello, bass). Interestingly, it is dedicated to Benjamin Britten, whose good friend Julian Bream worked with Henze on preparing the guitar parts. The Adagio (Epilogue), scored for the five strings, was actually written in 1963 to honor of the 70th birthday of Josef Rufer, the man who first wrote about the 12-tone system of composition, but Henze specifically intended it to also serve as the conclusion to *Kammermusik*. All the even-numbered movements feature the poetry of Hölderlin.

Only the fourth, sixth, and final movements of the work ("Innen aus Verschiedenem entsteht," "Es findet das Aug'oft," and "Wie Bache reißt das Ende von Etwas mich dahin") are scored for the full ensemble. Movements 1 (Prefazione), 7 (Sonata), and 9 (Cadenza) are scored for the winds and strings; 2, 8, and 10 for tenor and guitar; and 3, 5, and 11 (called "tentos," after a Spanish Renaissance term for a free-form instrumental piece, usually of considerable difficulty) for solo guitar. Perhaps for this reason, complete performances of *Kammermusik* are rare. It is more common to hear separate performances of either the three movements for winds and strings, the three tentos, or the pieces for tenor and guitar (under the title *Fragments from Hölderlin*). While all the parts are fairly difficult, the writing for the tenor and guitar is especially demanding, requiring not only a wide range and formidable technique, but also a lot of expressivity. *—Dawn Culbertson*

Recommended:

○ **Guitar Recital** / McFadden / 1996 / Naxos 553401

Stimmen (Voices), songs for 2 mezzo-sopranos, tenor & 15 instruments (1973)

This collection of 22 songs, which may be played singly or in its entirety (with an intermission after No. 11), was composed in 1973 and premiered at Queen Elizabeth Hall in London, on January 4, 1974. These songs, with texts by 22 different writers, are powerful reflections on personal and social struggles in the modern world. They are orchestrated for a wide variety of instruments, percussion, and sound-making devices.

"Los poetas cubanos ya no sueñan" (The Cuban Poets Do Not Dream) for tenor and standard winds, brass, percussion (including glass chimes, shell chimes, and thundersheet), and strings, blends lilting Cuban rhythms with pointillistic writing and Edgard Varèse-like fanfare passages and massive, fast piano chords. The ending is a pounding Largo at an *ffff* dynamic level.

"Prison Song" (The Leg-Irons) (Ho Chi Minh) is written in graph notation for a mezzo-soprano (whose part is notated in relatively pitched diamond-shaped notes) and an ensemble including standard, Bengal, and Inca flutes, oboe, jew's harp, brass, piano, strings, and gong. The brass players are called upon to stamp their feet in marching tempo. The string harmonics are icy and sul tasto. The pianist slams the keyboard cover, throws marbles on the strings, and imitates the vocalist's syllables. The gong is sounded under water. ("With hungry mouth open like a wicked monster, each night the irons devour the legs of people... yet there is one thing stranger in this world: people rush in to place their legs in irons. Once they are shackled, they can sleep in peace.")

"Keiner oder alle" (No One or Everyone), for tenor, is like a Kurt Weill or Hans Eisler agitprop tune with a slight tango feel.

"The Electric Cop" is written for tenor and an ensemble including Hammond organ, four transistor radios, and green and pink balloons which are shot at by the players. ("This guy on TV who rob everything he got a thief who rob who kill a killer who kills this guy on TV... captain america tears his panties as he swings for freedom.")

Other songs are studies in polyrhythms: "The Distant Drum" ("I am not a metaphor or a symbol... it is I being maimed in the street"); "42 Schulkinder" (42 Schoolchildren) ("How far is it from Washington to Berchtesgaden... what have we learned... that it is really not so far"); two Neapolitan-inspired pieces, *"Caino"* and *"Il Pasi,"* a skewed folk song; *"Heimkehr"* (Homecoming); the lyrical and powerfully declamatory *"Grecia 1970"*; the plaintive and mythological *"Legende von der Entstehung des Buches Taoteking auf dem Weg des Laotse in die Emigration"* (Legend of the Origin of the *Tao Te Ching* During the Emigration of Lao-Tze); the neo-tango *"Gedanken eines Revuemädchens während des Entkleidungsaktes"* (Thoughts of a Chorus Girl During Costume Change), with its out-of-tune violins and quarter-tone brass glissandos; *"Das wirkliche Messer"* (The Real Knife); the droll, bitonal *"Recht und billig"* (Right and Cheap); the solid Spanish rhythms of *"Patria"* (Homeland); "Screams (Interlude)" with its terrifying cluster runs; the heartbreaking, intense "The Worker" with a humming, word-fragmenting male chorus; *"Para aconsejar a una dama"* (Advice for a Lady); "Roses and Revolutions"; *"Vermutung über Hessen"* (A Guess about Hessen); *"Schluss"* (Conclusion); and the cycling *"Das Blumenfest"* (The Flower Festival) ("I plant flowers... I destroy them ... I bury him with flowers as with drink, food, tobacco, gold and words"). *—"Blue Gene" Tyranny*

Recommended:

○ **Henze: Voices** / Kalitzke, Pelker, Lang, Musikfabrik Nrw / 1993 / CPO 999192

○ **Henze: Voices** / H. Neumann (cond.), Trexler, Vogt, Leipzig Radio SO / 1994 / Berlin Classics 0021802

SYMPHONIC

Symphonies (1947–1996)

In his symphonies, Hans Werner Henze created not only an expression of all that was truly great in German musical culture, but a living testimony of what it meant aesthetically and politically to be a German composer after the Nazis. Henze's symphonies began in the advanced but still tonal harmonic style of Fortner with the large-scale structures of Hartmann and the spiky rhythms of Stravinsky. The *Symphony No. 1* (1947) is an extremely impressive piece of work, albeit one that he later thoroughly revised, dropping one of its four movements and re-scoring it for chamber orchestra. The three-movement *Symphony No. 2* (1949) shows the influence of Berg in its almost atonal lyricism and darkly tragic tone. The *Symphony No. 3* (1950) is balletic in its rhythms and use of tempo as a means of creating structure, but it also makes use of Schoenberg's serial method of composition in its closing movement. The single-movement *Symphony No. 4* (1955) is lyrical with long, arching waves of string-soaked melodies colored by delicate use of the winds. The *Symphony No. 5* (1962) is again more balletic in nature, describing a cityscape in lean but powerful rhythms. With his *Symphony No. 6* (1969), Henze turned his back on the high art music of his earlier years in a conscious attempt to write revolutionary music. Composed in Cuba, the *Sixth* is composed in three continuous movements scored for two large chamber orchestras. Throughout the work, elements of what Henze called his "bourgeois" music are brought into conflict with Cuban folk music. The resulting work is at times absolutely clear melodically and at times immensely complex harmonically and rhythmically. The *Symphony No. 7* (1983–84)—described by Henze as "a German symphony"—is in four movements: a furiously rhythmic "Tanz" based on the German dance the Allemande; a Ruhig bewegt (Restfully moving) is a deeply moving funeral song for orchestra; a delirious Scherzo describing the sufferings of the mad poet Friedrich Holderlin; and a desolate finale that sets Holderlin's *Half of Life* as a song for orchestra. The *Symphony No. 8* (1992–93) is a lyrical and lightly rhythmic programmatic symphony in three movements based on three episodes from Shakespeare's *A Midsummer Night's Dream*. Inevitably, a *Symphony No. 9* by a German composer evokes the image of Beethoven's choral-orchestral *Ninth*'s *Ode to Joy*. In his *Ninth* (1996), Henze wrote a choral-orchestral symphony that deals with the German Vaterland and is "Dedicated to the heroes and martyrs of German antifascism." In seven alternating fast and slow movements, Henze's *Ninth* is his symphonic masterpiece: a work with gorgeous melodies and hideous harmonies, with pellucidly beautiful lyricism and infernally chaotic textures with the noblest moral and aesthetic goals and the most vile and despicable gestures. *—James Leonard*

Recommended:

○ **Henze: Symphonies 1–6** / Henze (cond.), Berlin PO, London SO / 1990 / DG 429854

Ben Heppner

b. Jan. 14, 1956, Murrayville, BC, Canada

Tenor

While Heppner considers himself fundamentally a lyric tenor, he has become an eminent Wagnerian, and his Tristan has been hailed as a worthy successor to Lauritz Melchior's. Even after his "second debut" in Wagnerian roles, he still sang the title roles of Mozart's *Idomeneo* and *La clemenza di Tito*, complete with ornamentation, and added not only lieder, but popular parlor songs to his recital repertoire. His operatic repertoire also includes Verdi, Massenet, and Puccini, and he is a noted Peter Grimes. While his voice is not as large as that of some of the heldentenors, it has a very bright, focused sound that allows it to carry through even the heavier orchestral writing in Wagner, though it also has a slight tendency to crack, particularly in the longer operas that require high notes towards the end.

Like his compatriot Jon Vickers, also hailed as Grimes and in Wagner, he grew up as a farm boy in Canada (in a town named Dawson Creek, oddly enough). He studied at the University of British Columbia School of Music, and upon graduation, began a career as a lyric tenor, winning the Canadian Broadcasting Competition award in 1979. In 1981, he made his opera debut as Rodrigo in *Otello* at the Vancouver Opera, and performed such light roles as Camille in *The Merry Widow* and Alfredo in *Die Fledermaus* with the Canadian Opera Company. However, in 1987, he returned to study, this time preparing for dramatic tenor roles, and won the first Birgit Nilsson Prize in 1988 in the Metropolitan Opera Auditions. He made his U.S. debut at Carnegie Hall that same year and his United States opera debut was at the Lyric Opera of Chicago in the small role of Walter von der Vogelweide in *Tannhäuser* in the fall season. As part of the Nilsson Prize, he made his Stockholm debut at the Royal Swedish Opera in 1989 in his first Lohengrin, later traveling with the same company to Moscow to perform the same role at the *Bolshoi*.

His La Scala debut was in 1990 as Walter von Stolzig in *Der Meistersinger*, and his Salzburg debut in 1992 as Tito in Mozart's *La clemenza di Tito*, and later that year he created the title role in William Bolcom's *McTeague* at the Lyric Opera of Chicago. In 1998, he sang his first Tristan in Seattle with Jane Eaglen as Isolde, to great critical acclaim.

His Walter on Solti's *Die Meistersinger* (Decca 452 606) is an excellent example of the lyricism that he brings to Wagner, and his recording of Richard Strauss arias on a CBC recording (SMCD 5142) makes some of the most difficult tenor scenes in the entire repertoire seem natural and fluid. His BMG recording of Italian arias (BMG 62504), while focusing on the spinto repertoire, does display his trills to advantage in the scene from *Il trovatore*.

Heppner sticks hard to his personal rule of taking every other summer off, not doing the usual festival performances, in order to spend more time with his wife and three children and to prepare for opera roles. *—Ann Feeney*

Recommended:

- ○ **My Secret Heart** / Tunick (cond.), Heppner, London PO / 1999 / BMG 0902663508
- ○ **Ben Heppner** / Abbado, Glaser (conds.), Heppner, Musser, Munich Radio Orch. / 1995 / BMG 62504
- ○ **Wagner: Lohengrin** / Davis (cond.), Terfel, Leiferkus, Heppner, Rootering, Bavarian RSO & Chorus / 1995 / RCA 62646

Victor Herbert

b. Feb. 1, 1859, Dublin, Ireland, **d.** May 26, 1924, New York, NY

Composer: Opera, Concerto

Victor Herbert was one of the most versatile and important figures in American music at the turn of the twentieth century. This Irish-born American was a busy conductor and one of the foremost cellists of his time, besides being a once-popular operetta composer. His talent as a composer should not be overstated; Herbert's music, tailored to the middle-class tastes of his era, now seems quaint, yet it is solidly crafted and durably melodic enough to merit revival.

Raised in Stuttgart, Herbert studied composition there with Max Seifritz and cello with Bernhard Cossmann. During his teens he was employed as a cellist in various European orchestras. In 1880 he joined the Eduard Strauss waltz orchestra in Vienna, but the following year he returned to Stuttgart to play in the court orchestra and study composition at the conservatory. In 1886 he went to New York with his new wife, Therese Förster, who had been recruited as a prima donna at the Metropolitan Opera. Herbert, too, got a job at the Met, playing in the orchestra. He played his first *Cello Concerto* with the New York Philharmonic Society in 1887, and premiered his *Second Concerto* there in 1894; Dvořák heard the latter work, which inspired him to write his own cello concerto.

As a conductor, Herbert was affiliated with the Boston Festival Orchestra in 1891 and the Worcester Festival from 1889 to 1891; for that organization, he composed his dramatic cantata *The Captive*. In 1893 he assumed leadership of the celebrated 22nd Regiment Band (formerly P.S. Gilmore's). From 1898 to 1904 he conducted the Pittsburgh Symphony Orchestra, there premiering several of his own pieces, including *Hero and Leander* (nearly a century later, the Pittsburgh Symphony finally recorded some of this material under Lorin Maazel). In 1904 Herbert organized the Victor Herbert New York Orchestra for light programs and high-profile benefit performances, leading more than 400 participants in concerts to raise money for the victims of the Galveston flood and later the San Francisco earthquake. He also led the fight for copyright legislation, passed in 1909, and he helped found the American Society of Composers, Authors, and Publishers (ASCAP) in 1914, serving as its vice president until his death.

Herbert's first operetta was *Prince Ananias* (1894), penned at the suggestion of the manager of the Boston Ideal Opera Company. It was followed by more than 40 others. Among the best are *Babes in Toyland* (1903; it periodically suffers loose film and TV adaptations, but its March survives intact as a pops favorite); *Mlle. Modiste* (1905; his greatest hit of the period); *The Red Mill* (1906); *Naughty Marietta* (1910); *Sweethearts* (1913); and *Eileen*, first performed as *Hearts of Erin* (1917). He also wrote two grand operas, the Wagnerian *Natoma* (1911; premiered in Philadelphia by a cast that included Mary Garden and John McCormack), and the Straussian *Madeleine* (1914). Both of them, despite high expectations and initial enthusiasm, were ultimately judged failures. He also produced the music for the motion picture *The Fall of a Nation* (1916), one of the first original symphonic scores composed for a feature film. Late in life he wrote for revues, notably the *Ziegfeld Follies*. *—James Reel*

OPERA

Babes in Toyland, operetta "extravaganza" (1903)

Babes in Toyland was patterned after the highly successful production of *The Wizard of Oz* in 1902. The producers of that show commissioned Victor Herbert and Glen MacDonough to come up with a musical extravaganza, and the plot of *Babes in Toyland* ended up with themes similar to those of *The Wizard of Oz*; it featured the wits of innocent young people overcoming grasping and wicked adult authority figures. Despite the derivation, the inventive treatment of the subject made for an enjoyable show.

The stage spectacle is one of the most powerful perennial draws in *Babes in Toyland*, for the show features all kinds of toys that come to life, as well as characters from children's fairy tales. Herbert's score is skillfully wrought and displays his intimate knowledge of classical compositional practices. His large orchestral numbers add to the show's overall magnificence, while his smaller ensembles and set pieces capture the innocence of youth, and contribute charm and delicacy to the atmosphere. Familiar songs from the show include "March of the Toys," "I Can't Do That Sum," and "Toyland."

The show first opened in Chicago, Illinois, at the Grand Opera House, on June 17, 1903. It quickly made its way to the Broadway stage, and played for almost 200 performances at the Majestic Theater. The show toured extensively and has had many revivals over the years. Two major motion pictures were made, one with Laurel and Hardy by MGM in 1934, and another in 1961 by the Walt Disney studios. There were televised broadcasts in 1955 and 1960. The strength of the score, the appeal of the story line, and the entertaining diversionary scenic effects all ensure that *Babes in Toyland* will remain popular down through the years. *—Rita Laurance*

Synopsis:

Act One. In the land of Mother Goose, a garden party is being held at the home of Contrary Mary. Flowers bedeck the stage, and Japanese garden decorations make the scene festive. The widow of the Pied Piper lives in a nearby house. There are tumblers dancing, and a chorus of the Pied Piper's children. Hilda is offering the guests lemonade, and all come up to the table to take a glass. Little Bo Peep enters in tears and breaks up the festive mood—she has lost her sheep. Hilda and the children try to comfort her by promising to help her find them. Wicked Uncle Barnaby enters and tells them that he plans to become engaged to Contrary Mary. He says that *he* is the host of the party, and they respond with skepticism. He says that he will give the Widow Piper her house, which he owns, when he gets married to Contrary Mary. But Contrary Mary loves Alan. Barnaby tries to tell them that Alan and Jane, his niece and nephew, have drowned at sea. The children decide to dunk Uncle Barnaby in his own lemonade, and he is barely rescued by Tom, the Piper's son. Tom decides to look for Alan and Jane in Toyland, for that is their likely whereabouts. He is in love with Jane and is sure they will have gone to Toyland to seek help from the Master Toymaker.

Wicked Uncle Barnaby convinces the Widow Piper to convince Contrary Mary to marry him. He agrees to give her her home free of charge plus a sack of gold pieces if she is successful. Roderigo and Gonzago come on-stage and confront Uncle Barnaby. They want to be paid for their services. They drowned Jane and Alan in the sea, or so they claim, and Uncle Barnaby hired them to do it. Smoothly he convinces them to accept stock in his chicken farm as payment instead. They exit amicably, and a vagrant gypsy comes on stage. But it is no gypsy. It is Jane, in disguise, and Alan is not far behind! They are in gypsy clothing because gypsies rescued them from their shipwreck. Hilda tells them that Tom has gone to look for Jane in Toyland, but they may be able to catch him if they hurry.

Both Barnaby and the Widow Piper try to convince Contrary Mary to marry him, but she refuses. Alan thinks that Mary is going to marry Uncle Barnaby, so plans to go to Toyland with Jane. Mary decides to run away to Toyland also, to get away from Uncle Barnaby. Alan and Jane get lost in the Forest of the Spiders. They rescue a moth from a spider's web, and the Fairy Queen decides to rescue them. She sends a bear into the forest to save them from a giant spider, and then guides them to safety.

Act Two. In the Master Toymaker's showroom, millions of toys are on display: bikes, toy trains, mechanical dolls, and anything that the imagination can fancy. The toyshop workers all join in a chorus and dance in honor of Toyland. Wicked Uncle Barnaby enters with Hilda and the Widow Piper. They have come to look for Contrary Mary. Hilda finds her first, with Tom at her side, and cautions them to hide. The Master Toymaker shows the Piper children around Toyland, and showers them with toys.

Barnaby wants to create harmful toys, but the master Toymaker has captured all evil powers in a flask. Mary and Alan finally find one another and are lovingly reunited. Barnaby release the evil spirits, but they turn on him instead of attacking the children. The Master Toymaker falls into a trance and cannot control the evil spirits. Alan is thought to be responsible for the crime and is condemned to death. He escapes from prison, but Barnaby threatens to tell on him unless Contrary Mary marries him. But then Barnaby drinks a magical glass of water that causes him to laugh continuously. The laughter subdues the evil spirits and forces them back into captivity. All discover that Alan is innocent, and the Master Toymaker comes out of his trance. *—Rita Laurance*

Recommended:

- ○ **Herbert: Babes in Toyland; The Red Mill** / Brion (cond.), Razumovsky SO / 1999 / Naxos 559025
- ○ **Herbert: Babes in Toyland; The Red Mill** / Smallens (cond.), Baker / 2002 / Decca 018729

Mademoiselle Modiste, operetta (1905)

Victor Herbert was both prolific and widely praised for his operettas and instrumental music during his lifetime, though in the latter genre his popularity sharply declined after his death in 1924. *Mademoiselle Modiste* came during one of his most successful periods, in between the 1903 *Babes in Toyland* and the 1906 *The Red Mill.* Like most of his better operettas, *Mademoiselle Modiste* contains its share of popular numbers, including "Kiss Me Again," "The Time and the Place and the Girl," and "The Mascot of the Troop." Herbert wrote the work for Fritzi Scheff, a popular soprano at the Metropolitan Opera who appeared in his earlier and less-successful operetta *Babette.* Henry Blossom wrote the libretto and would also serve as Herbert's librettist for *The Red Mill.* The story concerns Paris hat shop clerk Fifi (Mademoiselle Modiste), who is engaged to marry the son of the hat shop's owner (Madame Cecile), but Fifi is in love with the aristocrat Etienne, who cannot marry below his social class. Aided by an American millionaire (Hiram Bent), Fifi realizes her goal of becoming a singer and performs at the palatial residence of Etienne's family, thereby winning their support for her marriage to Etienne. This utterly charming operetta features a total of 15 numbers and opens with a bright and colorfully orchestrated overture. The real hit of this work is the aforementioned *Kiss Me Again,* which offers a bright, soaring melody of Romantic character that is instantly catchy. (The real title of this song is "If I Were on Stage," the words "kiss me again" not coming until the third verse. But it is the memorable refrain-like music associated with those words that have virtually renamed the song.) Some of the numbers are sung by the chorus, like the lively opening "Furs and Feathers," and many, of course, involve a soloist and chorus, such as Etienne's charming first song "The Time and the Place and the Girl." "When the Cat's Away," sung by the manipulative Madame Cecile, is delightful in its sense of humor. Like virtually all other operettas and musicals, the story of *Mademoiselle Modiste* is presented with much spoken dialogue in between numbers. Here, the work brilliantly succeeds because Herbert brilliantly manages to enliven the story's elements of romance and frustration with songs of great melodic distinction. *—Robert Cummings*

Naughty Marietta, operetta (1910)

In May 1910, shortly after the Metropolitan Opera paid Oscar Hammerstein well over a million dollars not to compete with them any longer in the production of grand opera, Hammerstein (grandfather of the later partner to Richard Rodgers) commissioned Victor Herbert, at the time the most sought-after theatrical composer in New York, to compose a light opera for his company. The resulting operetta, *Naughty Marietta,* became perhaps the great American musical theater piece of the pre-World War I era.

Hammerstein's company included the young Italian soprano star Emma Trentini and the Indiana talent Orville Harrold (this Hoosier tenor was dubbed America's "little Caruso"). For these and the company's other accomplished vocalists, Herbert produced a vocal score more demanding than those of his other operettas such as *Babes in Toyland.* Even the prima donna, for whom the title role was composed, complained to the *New York Times* during rehearsals that her part was too high. Such a public display was enough to make the composer dig in his heels and refuse to change a note. The accompanying orchestration, heavily reliant upon strings with winds for color, was perhaps Herbert's most symphonic; as with all his other operettas, the orchestration was later updated in revivals. The librettist for the work was Rida Johnson Young, a playwright making her first foray into musical theater. Later collaborations would include Herbert's final show, *The Dream Girl.* Although fairly standard, the book is more effective as a vehicle for Herbert's melodies than for its own dramaturgical strength.

The scene of *Naughty Marietta* is set in eighteenth century New Orleans, at a confluence of cultures that allowed the composer to spice his Viennese-acquired operetta style with various local colors. The score includes the sensual minstrel-inflected song "'Neath the Southern Moon" and the operatic ensemble "Italian Street Song"; chorus scenes include a gathering of townspeople and a martial number for a troop of rangers. Notable for its balance, the show features each of its six principals in one solo and at least one ensemble number. Each principal's music goes beyond mere underscoring of emotion and aids in characterization, for example delineating the title character as charming, playful, and blithe.

An obvious influence is the Viennese light opera of such composers as Franz Lehár and Johann Strauss. Several characteristic waltzes in the score, including the famous tenor song "I've Fallen in Love with Someone," demonstrate this influence. Less often observed but nonetheless present are echoes of Gilbert and Sullivan, with whose comic timing the Irishman Herbert was well familiar before emigrating to the United States.

Premiered on Broadway on November 7, 1910, the show had a run of 136 performances that was limited only because of prior contractual agreements. A 1935 film, with Nelson Eddy and Jeanette MacDonald, helped bring the score an international reputation. Though the plot has not proved durable enough to establish for the work a secure spot in the repertoire, Herbert's melodies have nevertheless guaranteed *Naughty Marietta*'s survival. *—Thomas Oram*

Synopsis:

Act One. Set in provincial, eighteenth century Louisiana, the opera opens at dawn in the Place D'Armes in New Orleans. The townspeople, going about their daily business, are pulled out of their routine by the arrival of a shipload of poor French girls sent to the province to find husbands. Into the hubbub comes the haughty young aristocrat Etienne Grandet, son of the lieutenant governor of Louisiana. Etienne is told of a mysterious voice singing a distant melody. Captain Richard Warrington and his band of rangers then enter the scene ("Tramp, Tramp, Tramp"). Captain Dick and his men, including the comic figure Simon, are bounty hunters in search of the pirate Bras Prique ("tattooed arm").

As they exit, the mysterious voice is heard singing a fragment of a melody. Marietta enters, having escaped from the ship from France, and is discovered by Captain Dick. She cannot marry, she tells him, until she meets the man who can complete this fragment she has heard in a dream. A delicate flirtation ensues, resulting only in Marietta's securing a promise from a stoic Captain Dick to hide her so that she will not be forced to marry ("It Never, Never Can Be Love"). This is done by dressing her as a boy and passing her off as the son of a puppeteer. Dick's sidekick Simon returns with a bride, Lizette, picked out, and the two comic foils engage in a song and dance.

Etienne's slave Adah enters alone, fearing aloud that her master's passion for her is disappearing ("'Neath the Southern Moon"). The puppet troupe takes the stage, and Marietta, in short pants, sings an "Italian Street Song." Witnessing the performance is Etienne, whose father's secretary announces a reward for the discovery of a Countess Marietta, escaped from her family in Italy to avoid a marriage. Also in the crowd, however, is a member of Captain Dick's band, who recognizes the "boy" as the finale concludes.

Act Two. Marietta has given up her boyish disguise, but will not admit to Etienne that she is the Countess. Neither will she attend the Quadroon Ball with him, but when she refuses his invitation, he tells her that Captain Dick is to attend with Adah. Jealous, Marietta decides to go, but by herself. An exasperated Etienne then contemplates the ways of women ("You Marry a Marionette"). When an equally jealous Adah confronts him with his attraction to Marietta, he threatens to sell the slave.

The scene then changes to the ballroom, where upper-class New Orleans is enjoying itself. Etienne and his father, Lieutenant Governor Grandet, enter, attended by Simon, who has now hired himself out as Etienne's whipping boy to achieve status, leaving Lizette to worry if she must find another husband. Marietta arrives incognito but is quickly deprived of her mask by a drunken reveler. Etienne offers to escort her home, but they come upon Captain Dick talking with Adah. The four join in a quartet ("Live For Today").

Etienne proposes to Marietta, telling her he means to sell Adah. Dick, slightly inebriated, confesses to Marietta that his resolve is crumbling ("I'm Falling In Love With Someone"). Etienne then stops the party to sell Adah to the highest bidder; the fearful girl pleads with Captain Dick to save her from the uncertainty of a new owner. When he outbids the rest, an angry Marietta acknowledges her aristocracy and accepts Etienne's proposal.

While preparations are made for a wedding, Dick frees Adah, who in her gratitude reveals that Etienne and the pirate, Bras Prique, are one and the same. When Dick moves to arrest him, proving his accusation with the tattooed arm, Lieutenant Governor Grandet insists that Simon bear the punishment for his son. As Simon is led off, Captain Dick goes in search of his men for support. Given this revealing turn of events, Marietta despairs over having made the wrong decision, even more so when Dick's voice is heard singing her fragmented dream melody complete. She rejects Etienne's approaches as Captain Dick and his men return, with a freed Simon. Marietta runs to him, and in the excitement Etienne escapes. Having finally gotten what he truly wanted, Dick lets him go. *—Thomas Oram*

Recommended:

- ○ **Herbert: Naughty Marietta** / Byess (cond.), Woods, Carter, Christopher, Fredland, Pickle, Mackus, Balach, Matsos, Meachem, Sumners, Maida, Ohio Light Opera Orch. / 2001 / Albany 432

The Red Mill, musical comedy (1906)

The Red Mill was a huge success when it premiered in 1906, going on to tally 274 performances on its first run. It was the third such consecutive success for its composer, who had suddenly become the most prominent American associated with the operetta genre. Once again, he collaborated with Henry Blossom, who had also served as his librettist on *Mademoiselle Modiste*. As with virtually all of Herbert's most successful operettas, there are several hit numbers and at least one or two of outstanding quality. In this case, "Every Day Is Lady's Day With Me" and "Moonbeams" are the most memorable songs, and of the remaining 14, "The Isle of Our Dreams," "Because You're You," and "If You Love but Me" are also enduring numbers from this delightful light work.

The story is relatively unusual for an early twentieth century operetta. Two con artist Americans in Holland, Con Kidder and Kid Conner, broke and seeking the means for passage back home, come to the aid (via impersonations and other comic high jinks) of Gretchen , whose father, the burgomaster, opposes her wish to marry Captain Christian and wants her to marry the old womanizing governor instead. In the end, after the Captain gains an inheritance, she receives her father's blessing to marry him.

The aforementioned "Moonbeams" (or "Moonbeams Shining") is a lovely song set to a waltz tempo. It is the second of two duets between Gretchen and Christian, the first being another nearly-as-memorable waltz number, "The Isle of Our Dreams." It is the old governor who delivers this operetta's other big hit, "Every Day Is Lady's Day With Me", a lively, colorful song he sings just before encountering the burgomaster's sister Bertha (an old flame), whom he decides to marry, thereby inadvertently making Gretchen's marriage to Christian easier. Other numbers of distinction in *The Red Mill* include one by Tina, the daughter of the innkeeper who becomes a part of Con Kidder and Kid Conner's plans to aid Gretchen. Tina's "Whistle It!" is witty and colorful but requires a singer with considerable dramatic ability to bring off its giddy character to proper effect. Another strong number is a ballad sung by Bertha, the "Legend of the Mill": the darkest number in the operetta by far, it has a funereal manner that would be almost appropriate for a Wagner opera. *—Robert Cummings*

Synopsis:

Act One. Two American tourists-turned-con artists are broke and in need of the financial means to buy passage back to the U.S. from the small Holland town where they are stranded. Con Kidder and Kid Conner, as they call themselves, cannot even scrape up the money to pay the bill for board at the inn where they have been staying and thus attempt to escape. Their effort is thwarted by the Burgomaster, who recommends they be jailed. The Innkeeper, however, intercedes on their behalf and arranges for them to work off their debts at the inn, Con becoming an interpreter, Kid a servant. The pair take pity on the Burgomaster's beautiful daughter, Gretchen. They devise a scheme to both extricate her from an arranged marriage to the Governor and to aid her in eloping with her true love, Captain Van Damm. The Innkeeper overhears their plans and reports them to the Burgomaster, who reacts by incarcerating his daughter in the red mill and appointing the Sheriff to stand guard there. But the resourceful Con and Kid bring off a scheme to free her.

Act Two. The scene opens at the home of the Burgomaster, a man desperate to find his daughter, for this is the day of her wedding to the Governor. He offers a substantial reward and sends a communiqué to Sherlock Holmes and Dr. Watson to enlist their aid in the search. Con and Kid intercept the telegram and disguise themselves as the famous detectives. They have the Sheriff arrested and manage to free Captain Van Damm, who had also been held captive. The Governor arrives, but his disappointment over the bride's absence quickly evaporates when he meets her wealthy aunt. Both find each other attractive and decide a marriage will soon take place, after all. Gretchen and the Captain are reunited by Con and Kid, and Con himself snares a love interest in the person of the beautiful Tina, the Innkeeper's daughter. *—Robert Cummings*

Recommended:

○ **Herbert: The Red Mill** / Thompson (cond.), Balach, Miller, King, Wannen, Woods, Woodward, Simmonds, Stinson, Meachem, Musick, Sumners, Maida, Ohio Light Opera Orch. & Chorus / 2001 / Albany 492/493

CONCERTO

Cello Concerto No. 2 in E minor, Op. 30 (1894)

The only one of Victor Herbert's instrumental works that has taken hold in the repertory is the *Cello Concerto No. 2 in E minor*. This is not altogether surprising, since before becoming known as a composer of operetta, Herbert was among the great cello virtuosi of his day. The concerto was first given at a Philharmonic-Society concert in New York under the direction of Anton Seidl in March 1894. Contemporary New York critics give some hint of the concert's success; "Mr. Herbert played with rare skill and finish, his tone is mellow and sympathetic, and his playing of his own composition gave such pleasure to the audience that he was twice recalled." Herbert later wrote: "after I had played my *Cello Concerto* in one of the Philharmonic concerts, Dr. Dvořák came back to the 'Stimmen-Zimmer'—threw his arms around me, saying before many in the orchestra—'famos! famos! Gang famos!'" Dvořák was in fact so impressed by Herbert's playing that he was inspired to write his own *B minor Cello Concerto*—one of the most famous works ever penned in the genre. Herbert's concerto has been widely admired over the years as well, but it is played less frequently than Dvořák's, owing perhaps to its prohibitive difficulty.

The impact of the work is immediate; the cello jumps out of the texture near the start of the concerto, grabbing the listener by the shirt collar with its plaintive, yet intense, melodic argument. The second movement, Lento-Andante tranquillo, is one of the loveliest of Herbert's creations; it maintains a depth of mood and bears Herbert's unique stamp in terms of modulations and melodic shape. The final movement, Allegro, contains some extremely challenging writing for the solo cello in rapid sixteenths. *—Uncle Dave Lewis*

Recommended:

○ **Herbert: Cello Concerto 2; Grofé: Grand Canyon Suite; Mississippi Suite** / Hanson (cond.), Miquelle, Eastman-Rochester Pops Orch. / 1995 / Mercury 434355

○ **Concertos from the New World** / Masur (cond.), Ma, New York PO / 1995 / Sony 67173

Philippe Herreweghe

b. May 2, 1947, Ghent, Belgium

Conductor

Belgian conductor Philippe Herreweghe, in addition to studying piano with Marcel Gazelle at the Conservatory in Ghent, concurrently studied medicine and psychiatry at the University of Ghent. During that time, he founded the Collegium Vocale of Ghent (1969). Nikolaus Harnoncourt and Gustav Leonhardt took notice of the young artist and promptly invited him and his newly organized ensemble, to collaborate with them in a recording project that would document the entire catalog of Bach cantatas. Continuing his education at the conservatory, Herreweghe studied the harpsichord with Johan Huys and organ with Gabriel Verschraegen.

Ambitious to say the least, Herreweghe formed numerous ensembles that each respectively acted as a performance vehicle for specific genres and periods of composition, resulting in numerous recordings for Harmonia Mundi. His Ensemble Vocale Elysees specialized and concentrated on, the work of Bach and his predecessors. The Ensemble La Chapelle Royale (founded with Philippe Beaussant in 1977) focused on music from the French Baroque, as well as vocal scores from the Classical and Romantic eras. The Ensemble Vocale Europeen (founded 1989) concentrated on Renaissance polyphony, while the Orchestre des Champs-Elysees (founded 1991), an original instrument ensemble, performed literature from the Classical and Romantic periods. Herreweghe divides his time in thirds and spends one with early music, one with the Romantic repertoire, and the last third with contemporary compositions. In an interview with *La Scena Musicale* (November, 1997), the conductor described his ensembles as a, "poupee russe, you know those Russian dolls that fit one inside the other. My core Baroque instruments group for Bach and German repertoire is Collegium Vocale. For bigger works and French Baroque we enlarge it to make La Chapelle Royale. For even bigger classical and romantic works we add about twenty percent more players to form the Orchestre des Champs-Elysees. This way I can conduct a large repertoire while maintaining the organic integrity of the groups as much as possible."

Herreweghe has conducted many prestigious ensembles including the Royal Concertgebouw Orchestra of Amsterdam, Berlin Philharmonic, Vienna Philharmonic, Lyon Opera Orchestra, Concerto Koln, Orchestra of the Age of Enlightenment, Ensemble Musique Oblique, and the Orchestra of St. Lukes in New York City. Herreweghe assumed the position of music director of the Festival of Saintes in 1982. The conductor, nominated for Musical Personality of the Year (1990), has received many more awards including European Musician of the Year (1991), Cultural Ambassador of Flanders with his Collegium Chorale (1993), Doctor Honoris Causa of the Leuven Catholic University (1997), and the order of Officer of Arts and Letters (1994). Herreweghe assumed the post of music director of the Flanders Philharmonic Orchestra in 1997.

Widely regarded as one of the cultural landscape's greatest champions, Philippe Herreweghe has brought a dignity and integrity to the arts that seems timeless. Confidently honest with regards to his own opinions, Herreweghe programs the repertoire that interests him, and overlooks that which does not. He tirelessly explores the work of Bach, performing many works numerous times, but approaches each effort with a studious dedication and genuine curiosity. Each time the conductor opens a score, he ponders how the music inside should be approached. Herreweghe's recordings, a discography that numbers more than 60, is highly regarded and commended for its sincerity. *—David Brensilver*

Recommended:

○ **C.P.E. Bach: Resurrection & Ascension of Jesus** / Herreweghe (cond.), Harvey, Martinpelto, Pregardien, Orch. of the Age of Enlightenment, Collegium Vocale / 1992 / Virgin 59069

○ **Rameau: Les Indes Galantes, Suites** / Herreweghe (cond.), La Chapelle Royale / HM 1951130

○ **Bach: Johannes-Passion** / Herreweghe (cond.), Padmore, Scholl, Rubens, Collegium Vocale / HM 901748

Bernard Herrmann

b. Jun. 29, 1911, New York, NY, **d.** Dec. 24, 1975, Los Angeles, CA

Composer: Film Music, Choral

The man whose name is for many synonymous with film music was born prematurely to Abraham and Ida Herrmann. Abraham, an optometrist, came from an intellectual family, while Ida was highly religious; the family's handsome brownstone was the scene of frequent arguments. At the age of five Herrmann began to suffer from Sydenham's syndrome, a neurological disorder that can affect personality development. A calm environment is needed for recovery, but Herrmann did not enjoy one. He grew up to be a nervous and aggressively touchy person who tended to alienate friends and associates.

He was also incessantly creative, composing music at an early age. At age 13 he won a hundred-dollar prize for an orchestral composition, and this settled him on a musical career. He studied with Percy Grainger at New York University, composing much music that he later destroyed. At 20 he debuted as a conductor on Broadway, leading a ballet of his own in a musical revue called "Americana." He also founded the New Chamber Orchestra.

In 1934 Herrmann began conducting and scoring for the CBS radio network. He developed a gift for quick evocation of a situation or psychological state with very short musical gestures such as a repeating note pattern, a chord, or a shift in color. Herrmann worked for Orson Welles, the young director of the Mercury Theater radio drama series. When Welles went to Hollywood to direct his debut film, *Citizen Kane*, he took along several Mercury Theater regulars, including Herrmann, who scored the film. With the *Citizen Kane* score Herrmann virtually invented a new, American film sound that stood in contrast with lush, European-derived styles.

Herrmann remained with CBS, becoming conductor of the CBS Symphony Orchestra in 1940. He championed new British and American music, giving millions their first exposure to such composers as Walton and Ives. Herrmann won an Academy Award for his second film score, that for William Dieterle's *The Devil and Daniel Webster*. Almost alone among Hollywood composers, he did all his orchestration himself, devising such novel effects as the electronic group employed in *The Day the Earth Stood Still* or the massed harps of *Beneath the Twelve-Mile Reef*. He was noted for building his scores on ostinato patterns, often based on an unstable chord. The emotional tension thus produced made Herrmann an ideal collaborator for the master of suspense, Alfred Hitchcock.

Herrmann's collaboration with Hitchcock began with the remake of *The Man Who Knew Too Much*, just after CBS eliminated its orchestra in 1955. Although of his 68 film scores, only eight were written for Hitchcock (Herrmann also supervised the naturalistic soundtrack for *The Birds*), the two were among history's greatest director-and-composer teams. Herrmann's all-string score to *Psycho*, with its nerve-raw shrieking violins for the knife attack scenes, was widely imitated.

Angrily leaving Hollywood when producers moved toward melodious scores that could yield a hit tune as an additional profit point, Herrmann moved to London, still composing film scores for Hitchcock admirers such as François Truffaut, Martin Scorsese, and Brian DePalma. He also stepped up his concert and recording activities, committing to tape his performances of many of the classical pieces he had continued to write over the years. These include a masterly symphony and an opera version of *Wuthering Heights*.

Herrmann died in Hollywood, passing away unexpectedly in his sleep on Christmas Eve after a scoring session for Scorsese's *Taxi Driver*, whose jazz-oriented music hinted at an intriguing change in direction. Commentators regard him as the greatest of American film composers or even as the greatest of any nationality, and interest in his music of all genres has shown unceasing growth since his death. *—Joseph Stevenson*

FILM MUSIC

Cape Fear (1961)

In 1962, J. Lee Thompson directed this tense psychological thriller which virtually out-Hitchcocks Hitchcock, and wisely engaged Bernard Herrmann, then the famous suspense director's favorite composer, to score it. The plot involves a released convict (Robert Mitchum) seeking revenge against the witness (Gregory Peck) whose testimony had resulted in his conviction in a sex assault case. Mitchum's character seeks to get Peck by stalking his teenaged daughter. The film culminates in a storm-drenched chase through the swamplands of Cape Fear County, NC. Herrmann's music of rapidly repeated patterns swiftly tossing from major to minor and back is chillingly effective in portraying both the external violence of nature and the psychological turbulence underlying the story. It begins with the whole horn section braying out the dark, fearful main motive of the music. An effective concert extract from the film has been devised, beginning with the film's stark opening credit music and progressing to the building tension of the stalking scenes and finally ending in the confrontation through the swamps. At the end, there is a dark uncertainty still lingering; the family's ordeal has shattered its peaceful selfimage.

Martin Scorsese's remake of the film not only paid tribute to the original film by casting Peck and Mitchum in supporting roles, but used Bernard Herrmann's music from the original film, as reworked by another great film music composer, Elmer Bernstein. *—Joseph Stevenson*

Citizen Kane (1941)

When boy-genius broadcaster Orson Welles packed up much of his *Mercury Theatre* troupe and headed for RKO studios in Hollywood, ultimately to begin his cinematic career with his greatest triumph (and suffer a slow, agonizingly inevitable downhill career from there), he took with him CBS's master composer Bernard Herrmann. The stable of Hollywood composers had, in the previous decade of sound movies, established the "Hollywood sound" (deriving ultimately from the Viennese style of Richard Strauss, Franz Schmidt, and Anton von Zemlinsky). In contrast, Herrmann had a leaner, anti-Romantic, much more fittingly American sound that exactly suited Welles' American dream-turned-nightmare tale of an idealistic young newspaper publisher who builds an immense financial empire and gathers political power at the cost of becoming the kind of corrupt mogul he originally crusaded against.

Herrmann was nominated for an Academy Award for this, his first film score. Its music has been extracted in various ways, including Herrmann's own suite, *Welles Raises Kane* (which also includes music from Welles' second film, the ill-fated *The Magnificent Ambersons*). A highlight of the score is the music which underpins the film's brilliant "breakfast montage" where a series of scenes using only body language and music conveys the slow death over a period of years of the love of Kane and his bride.

Also found in the score is an aria from a fictional opera called *Salammbo*. Herrmann wrote it in such a way that it required a strong, dramatic soprano voice (such as a Turandot or an Aida), but had it sung by a lyric soprano more suited to roles such as Mimì or Susanna to depict the undeserved starring part given to Kane's mistress. It has been recorded, as well, using a suitable voice, and is a nice parody of a late Romantic dramatic opera scene. *—Joseph Stevenson*

Recommended:

- ○ **Citizen Kane: The Classic Film Scores of Bernard Herrmann** / Gerhardt (cond.), Te Kanawa, National PO / 1974 / RCA 0707
- ○ **Citizen Kane / The Magnificent Ambersons** / unidentified orchestra / 2000 / Soundtrack Factory 33553

The Day the Earth Stood Still (1951)

Composed in June and July 1951, this was the composer's first film soundtrack after he moved to Hollywood. Herrmann chose a most unusual instrumentation for director Robert Wise's picture: electric violin, electric bass, two theremins (electronic instruments from the 1920s controlled by proximity detectors sensing hand movements), test oscillators (normally used for calibrating studio recording levels), vibraphone, four pianos, four harps, and a section of approximately 30 brass instruments. In several cues, unusual overdubbing and tape reversal techniques were also used. Edmund H. North's script, based on Harry Bates' 1940 story *Farewell to the Master*, features a humanoid alien named Klaatu, who bears a message of peaceful coexistence with other planets (the alternative is Earth's destruction), and lands his ship in the middle of Washington, D.C., accompanied by his giant robot Gort. In the "Prelude: Outer Space" cue that opens the film, starry universe visuals emerge to an audio atmosphere of steadily arpeggiating harps and pianos through which Richard Strauss-like brass calls and eerie theremin melodies sail. The next main cue is "Radar" for multiple pianos backed up by electric bass pizzicati and sustained chords on vibraphone. This music underlines the worldwide transmission of news about the saucer's landing. The powerful cue "Gort" occurs when the robot emerges from the ship to defend Klaatu, who has been shot by nervous, trigger-happy soldiers. The music is made from low piano octaves, low percussion, brass, and low theremins. "The Robot" is a similar cue later in the movie where a kindly widow returns the apparently dead spaceman to his ship, and causes his resurrection with the classic line "Klaatu barada nikto." "Space Control" is a light, mysterious cue full of bells, pianos, and a melody on electric guitar that depicts the inside of the spaceship. "Terror" is a general cue for theremins used throughout the film, including the day when Klaatu demonstrates that he has the power to stop all the engines of the world. "Farewell and Finale" underscores the final message from Klaatu's international broadcast, and repeats the initial opening music ending in a sustained major chord with odd wailing from the theremins. Herrmann's unique score was clearly ahead of its time, and prophetic of the many devices and sounds to be used for decades to follow. Herrmann's score remains a model of impressive emotional effect achieved by musically economic means. *—"Blue Gene" Tyranny*

Recommended:

- ○ **The Day the Earth Stood Still** / McNeely (cond.) / 2002 / Varese Sarabande 066314
- ○ **The Day the Earth Stood Still** / Newman (cond.) / 1993 / Fox 11010

Fahrenheit 451 (1966)

After suffering the humiliation of having his score for Alfred Hitchcock's 1966 film *Torn Curtain* tossed aside and replaced, Bernard Herrmann turned right around and set to work on a film score that many feel contains his finest work:

Fahrenheit 451, released in 1967 by Universal. The movie, which is director Francois Truffaut's sole English-language film, puts on celluloid Ray Bradbury's classic and terrifying novel of the same name—a tale of a not-so-distant future in which books, any and all books, are deemed to be subversive by a repressive mega-government. Herrmann's score proves once again that some of the finest film scoring efforts achieve their greatness by going firmly against the superficial grain of the film. The *Fahrenheit 451* score is intense, human, and deeply personal (and, as such, sometimes quite unhappy or ugly) in a cinematic world that is cold and absolutely inhuman.

What Herrmann provides is less a depiction of or even response to the elements of plot and cinematography, but more a ticket into some internal cross-section of the protagonist, Guy Montag, that finds its way to the screen only fleetingly. Beyond that, it is a musical bill of faith in the eternally unbreakable human spirit, an element that comes into the movie only at its very end. The movie often moves along in two very different layers—sight and sound (film proper) and musical score—and the effect can be overwhelming.

This duality is apparent even at the very opening of the film. Herrmann's music for the brightly-colored, strikingly cut opening credits (which are read aloud, no words on the screen, as indeed there shouldn't be as one enters a realm devoid of books) is light and airy, with harp arpeggios, tinkling percussion, and shimmering strings. The music and film would seem to have nothing at all to do with one another, and the effect is perfect. There is also a certain mysteriousness to that opening music, a hint of darkness each time the densely scored lower strings come in, sometimes with chords that have nothing to do with the music above. Here the music itself has two layers—a hint from Herrmann of things to come.

Some cues, such as *The Bedroom*, burn with passion (in this future society there is no room for romance). Others, like *Fire Engine*, just after the opening credits, in which the fireman go about their business of burning books, are terrifyingly mechanized, and at the end of the film *The Road* takes one to a warm, but pained, world within a world, where people commit books to memory with the hope that someday the precious legacy might be restored. *—Blair Johnston*

Recommended:

○ **Great Film Music** / Herrmann (cond.), National PO / 1996 / London 443899

○ **Hermann: The Film Scores** / Salonen (cond.), Los Angeles PO / 2000 / Sony 62700

Jane Eyre (1943)

Twentieth-Century Fox Films hired Orson Welles to star as Rochester in this adaptation of Charlotte Brontë's classic novel, opposite Joan Fontaine in the title role. Welles more or less took over the writing of the script and other aspects of the film, and recommended his favorite musical partner, Bernard Herrmann, for the score. It introduced Herrmann to the world of the Brontës, resulting in his opera *Wuthering Heights* written at about the same time. It is not surprising that the two projects share some of their musical material.

The film concerns a young girl from a harsh orphanage growing into an assured and loving woman. Jane is sent to be governess to Adele, a little French girl who is the ward of Edward Rochester. The action takes place in a prototypical Gothic manor, where Rochester's insane wife is kept hidden away behind a forbidden door.

The score was Herrmann's longest for films; the dark romantic film required nearly constant music. There are three main themes: Jane (in F sharp minor), Rochester (in F major), and their love (F minor, though this expansive theme goes through eight different keys). Herrmann brilliantly develops them, and a host of related subsidiary motives, linking them through motive cells. Herrmann uses a more or less standard symphony orchestra, with all the auxiliary wind instruments and the colorful addition of harps, vibraphone, chimes, organ, celesta, glockenspiel, and piano. Herrmann characteristically stresses the lower winds and brass, with prominent use of clarinets, to make a dark, smooth, brooding sound. In the 1970s the composer prepared a 13-minute orchestral movement from the music. In the 1990s, working with the best surviving version of the score (a blurry, reduced photostat) the conductor Adriano edited it into 21 sections running to nearly 70 minutes. *—Joseph Stevenson*

Recommended:

○ **Hermann: Jane Eyre** / Adriano (cond.), Slovak Radio SO Bratislava / 1994 / Marco Polo 223535

The Man Who Knew Too Much (1956)

In a rare case of a movie remake vastly outclassing its predecessor, Alfred Hitchcock redid his 1930s British hit for Paramount in the 1950s, starring the popular team of James Stewart and Doris Day.

This is one of the first fruits of a collaboration of two men who had arrived in Hollywood at about the same time: Herrmann the radio composer who was brought West with Orson Welles to score *Citizen Kane*, and Hitchcock the well-known British director who began his years in Hollywood with *Rebecca*. The movie world quickly realized that Herrmann's terse and effective music, particularly his unequaled ability to depict psychological undercurrents in the characters, enhanced Hitchcock's dark cinematic vision.

The movie begins with a stormy and tense prelude foreshadowing the intensity of the coming situation. The music for the opening credits draws much more of the audience's attention than ordinary, for under the credits you actually see the orchestra playing it! The camera moves inexorably towards the percussion row at the back of the orchestra, where an impassive percussionist stands before the pair of immense cymbals resting on their cloth-covered table. At the right moment, he picks them up, readies them and, now in close up, smashes them together at full force, thus foreshadowing the entire complex plot. *The Man Who Knew Too Much* is, in fact, a story that hinges strongly on music; the plot is dominated by two compositions not written by Herrmann. Perhaps for that reason the rest of Herrmann's score after the prelude is rather functional, serving brilliantly its purpose, but not really distinct enough for a separate concert life (other than the prelude).

The first outside bit of music is a popular song called *"Que Sera Sera."* In the story, it was one of the famous hits that Doris Day's character had in her singing career; now she uses it as a bedtime song for her son. Later in the story, that fact takes on key significance.

The most famous music of the film is by Arthur Benjamin. The Australian composer had composed the entire score of the original British version of the film, including the music to be played to the assassination scene. For that movie, Benjamin wrote the first eight minutes to what is presumably a larger work, called *The Storm-Clouds Cantata*. (The concert is disrupted by the assassin's bullet so no more of the music than that was needed.) In it, he seems to have fun needling the British genre of pastorale or nature music, like an overdone version of Vaughan Williams' *A Sea Symphony*. It builds to several waves of false climax (to keep the movie audience's tension rising) and then culminates in the full force cymbal clash. Herrmann and Hitchcock cleverly kept this music in the remake; the fact that it is in the voice of a totally different composer sets it apart and makes it more convincing as the fictional symphony concert piece.

Both Herrmann's *Prelude* and Benjamin's *Storm Clouds Cantata* have been recorded in CDs of Herrmann and Hitchcock film score collections. *—Joseph Stevenson*

North by Northwest (1959)

Bernard Herrmann's scores for such films as *The Seventh Voyage of Sinbad*, *Journey to the Center of the Earth*, *The Day the Earth Stood Still*, and *The Mysterious Island* defined the sound of fantasy, but those were almost the least of his achievements. He also worked with Orson Wells on *Citizen Kane*, with Francois Truffaut on *Fahrenheit 451*, and, above all, with Alfred Hitchcock in his series of masterpieces from the 1950s. Among these were *The Trouble With Harry*, *Rear Window*, *Vertigo*, *Psycho*, and *North by Northwest* (1959). Aside from snippets of incidental music, Herrmann composed three types of music for *North by Northwest*: chase music, suspense music, and love music. All three types of music are tonally based. The chase music's use of whole-tone scale melodies and augmented triads, the suspense music's dissonant harmonic suspensions, and the love music's yearning appoggiaturas à la *Tristan und Isolde* all have their origins in late nineteenth century Romanticism. But Herrmann's use of brilliantly syncopated rhythms and a vastly expanded percussion section gives his essentially Romantic music the coloring of conservative modernism. Each of the film's three types of music is clearly distinct. The chase music that serves as the film's Overture under the Saul Bass opening-title sequence is in nervously fast triple time with slashing strings, wailing winds, blasting trombones, and thundering tympani. The suspense music is in slow triple time, with slowly rising harmonic sequences in the low winds and strings. The love music is in Herrmann's beloved Lento amoroso tempo with long-breathed melodies for intertwining winds above throbbing cellos and basses. Herrmann rarely repeated music exactly, but rather developed the music over the course of the movie. Thus, the love music for Grant and Saint is at first tentative in the dining car sequence, more passionate in the first sleeping car sequence, and finally ecstatic in the second sleeping car sequence that closes the film. As with all of his film scores, the score for *North by Northwest* enhanced the action (chase music for the pursuit across the faces on Mount Rushmore), defined the situations (suspense music for the mutual suspicion of Grant and Mason's characters in the scene in the mansion at Glen Cove), established the relationships between the characters (the blossoming love music in the dining sequence between Grant and Saint), and often revealed the hidden feelings of the characters toward each other (the uneasy mixture of love and suspense in the scene in the Ambassador East between Grant and Saint). But Herrmann (and, of course, Hitchcock) also knew when music should be silent: the entire crop-dusting sequence was filmed almost entirely without dialogue and entirely without music. *—James Leonard*

Recommended:

○ **North by Northwest** / Johnson (cond.), London Studio Orch. / 1990 / Unicorn Kanchana 2040

Psycho (1960)

Countless movie-goers who have never heard of Bernard Herrmann nevertheless are quite capable of immediately recognizing his most famous motion picture score—the score for the 1960 Paramount film *Psycho*. Director Alfred Hitchcock's budget for *Psycho* was not very large, and Herrmann was forced to restrict himself to a relatively small instrumental ensemble. The result is a score composed entirely for string instruments that perfectly suits the stark black and white cinematography of the film. Although many feel that Herrmann crafted scores intrinsically superior to it, the *Psycho* score has been, and likely will remain, his most widely-admired and often-imitated film score.

Melody as we normally think of it is altogether absent in *Psycho*; even theme, in the proper sense of the word, only occasionally sneaks onto the scene. Instead, the music is built around strings of fragmentary motives, stacked around one another in often very dissonant ways, and raised up into a musical whole that manages to create a state of near-perpetual suspense, unresolved, unremitting, and yet, never tired or worn thin.

Some of *Psycho*'s music is active and physical. For example, the famous opening credits music, which is reused as the character of Marion Crane flees with stolen money, her face dispassionate but her mind frenzied and burning, and, of course, the infamous shower scene music, with its shrieking jabs in the uppermost register of the violins. Some of the music, on the other hand, simmers quietly to itself, tension and insanity woven by layers of agonized counterpoints: e.g. a cue called "The Madhouse," in which Norman Bates first begins to seem to us a man off his rocker. And then there is music like "Temptation" (which underscores Marion's growing desire to steal the money from her boss at the start of the film) and "The Peephole" (which underscores Norman spying on Marion), in which a kind of steady, pulsating music seems to go nowhere and yet boils inside. Even—indeed, especially—in the last bars of the score there is no resolution of the psychological or harmonic dissonance: inhuman strands of counterpoint in the high violins and violas, con sordino and pianissimo, dissolve and are replaced by a dense final sonority as Marion's car is dragged out of the swamp behind the Bates Motel.

There is a brief suite comprising the major moments of the score, plus the resolution of the film's concluding music. It is variously known as *Psycho: A Narrative for Orchestra* and *Psycho: Suite for Strings*. —*Blair Johnston*

Recommended:

○ **Herrmann: Psycho** / Herrmann (cond.), National PO / Unicorn Kanchana 2021

Taxi Driver (1976)

Herrmann's regular employment in Hollywood ended during a period when the studios decided to embrace song-oriented scores. Ironically, this trend began with Hitchcock and Herrmann's inclusion of the pop tune "Que Sera, Sera" in the film *The Man Who Knew Too Much*. The song became one of Doris Day's huge hits, and a financial bonus for the studio. In an infamous scene, Hitchcock fired Herrmann at the scoring stage for *Torn Curtain* when the composer disregarded orders to write what Hitchcock called a "beat" score. Herrmann then moved to London and became a freelance film score writer. Among the most important jobs Herrmann had were films by young directors emulating Hitchcock—Truffaut, Scorsese, and de Palma in particular. All three wisely used Herrmann to provide the classic "Hitchcock sound" and conjure his unique ability to convey psychological danger. In *Taxi Driver*, Herrmann's last score (he died the very evening he finished recording it), he brilliantly underlined Scorsese's depiction of a tense urban jungle and the dangerous mind of anti-hero Travis Bickle (Robert de Niro), who believes he can cleanse society through violence, a belief that in fact turns against him when he becomes a focus of urban terror himself.

Herrmann used his familiar harmonic vocabulary, so brilliant in evoking suspense, nightmare, and mental instability. He broke new and innovative ground by prominently incorporating urban jazz elements into the score, particularly a soaring yet strangely inhibited saxophone solo. It is in many ways Herrmann's most distinctive score, and clearly shows that the film music master, had he lived, would have continued to evolve creatively. The original soundtrack recording, with performances by a standard orchestra and a jazz ensemble, has scarcely if ever been out of print since the classic film was released. But an even more effective presentation of the orchestral side of the music was achieved by the late British arranger and film-music historian Christopher Palmer, who devised an exceptional eight-minute movement, virtually a mini-concerto for saxophone and orchestra, that unifies some of the best and most characteristic moments of this masterful score. —*Joseph Stevenson*

Vertigo (1958)

Vertigo is regarded by many as the greatest and most characteristic of Alfred Hitchcock's films. Scottie (James Stewart) is a San Francisco police detective who slips and nearly falls off a roof. A policeman who tries to rescue him falls to his death. Scottie then falls and is severely injured, but makes a full physical recovery; psychically, though, he is scarred by guilt over his partner's death and develops a severe fear of heights. In time, he agrees to help an old school friend who expresses concern that his wife, Madeleine (Kim Novak), is falling into a hereditary pattern of suicidal madness. In long, achingly lonely silent sequences set against a beautiful San Francisco backdrop, Scottie follows the woman, piecing together the details of what clearly emerges as a fatal obsession with a tragic ancestor, Carlotta Valdez. None too surprisingly for a film by Hitchcock, monstrous deception and true evil lurk beneath it all.

Herrmann's lengthy and masterful score weaves together and energizes the film and, at times, provides the main narrative force. As Scottie falls in love with Madeleine, the harmonies and orchestration become richer, the pulse-beat underlying the scene stronger. At the same time, though, the heartbeat has a slightly broken effect, a hesitation that serves two purposes: it both predicts the hopelessness that is Scottie's apparent fate and develops into a Spanish rhythm that portrays Madeleine's obsession with the tragic figure of Carlotta. Scottie's love theme, the "Carlotta" rhythm, and a third motive, the "vertigo" effect, provide the main musical material for the score. The first of these is a long, lonely theme on the violins which seemingly avoids assuming a definite shape. The second is a bizarre, violent fandango with a harsh descending line in half-steps, representing a descent into madness. The powerful "vertigo" motive is dizzying in the way it ascends and descends through two major and minor chords at the same time.

The concert suite that Herrmann drew from the score comprises three sections, each based on the most characteristic form of the three motives noted above. The composer's genius for depicting inner drama is revealed here as never before, and his score, though immensely satisfying as "pure" music, provides a striking object lesson in just how effective film music can be in the hands of so capable a craftsman. —*Joseph Stevenson*

Recommended:

○ **Herrmann: Alfred Hitchcock's Vertigo** / Mathieson (cond.), City of London Sinfonia / 1990 / Mercury 422106

CHORAL

Moby Dick, cantata (1936–1938)

American composer Bernard Herrmann is best known for his many film scores, especially those for Orson Wells and Alfred Hitchcock. But Herrmann also wrote what serious music before composing for films dominated his career: a symphony (1939–41); an opera based on Brontë's *Wurthering Heights* (1940–52); and *Moby Dick*, his dramatic cantata for two tenors, two basses, male chorus, and orchestra based on Herman Melville's novel of the same name. Begun in February 1937 and completed in August 1938, Herrmann had read Melville's book many times, but he had a more intimate connection with the subject: his father had served on two whaling ships and had often regaled his sons Bernard and Louis with stories of his adventures. Composed while Herrmann was the music director of the CBS, *Moby Dick* is written in Herrmann's resolutely tonal and romantic style. Clearly influenced by contemporary English composers such as Bax, Delius, and especially Vaughan Williams, Herrmann's *Moby Dick* is as well composed as the slightly later symphony, but less individual in style and tone. Premiered by the New York Philharmonic and greeted positively by the audience and the press, *Moby Dick* seemed to portend a career as a composer of classical music. But the success of Herrmann's music for Wells' famous broadcast of *War of the Worlds* and the subsequent acclaim of Herrmann's music for Wells' *Citizen Kane* moved Herrmann and his music to Hollywood. —*James Leonard*

Recommended:

○ **Herrmann: For the Fallen; Moby Dick** / Herrmann (cond.), London PO / 1993 / Unicorn Kanchana 2061

Hespèrion XX

f. 1974

Ensemble

Jordi Savall (born 1941), one of the world's leading players of the viola da gamba, founded the ensemble Hespèrion XX in 1974. Savall's goal—and that of cofounders Montserrat Figueras, Hopkinson Smith, and Lorenzo Alpert—was to explore lesser-known repertories of the European Middle Ages, Renaissance, and Baroque periods; their special love has been early Spanish music. The group has toured over five continents and produced well over 50 recordings (many on the Astrée Audivis label). The group's membership changes with the repertory of an individual recording or performance project, and with the particular orchestration envisioned by Savall. The list of early music luminaries who have repeatedly collaborated with Savall on Hespèrion recordings includes not only founders Figueras (soprano) and Smith (plucked strings), but also Pedro Memelsdorff (recorder), Andrew Lawrence-King (harps), Rolf Lislevand (guitar, theorbo, and vihuela), Ton Koopman (harpsichord), Bruce Dickey (cornetto), and Richard Cheetham (sackbut). Often, Hespèrion XX performs early chamber music (such as the *Fantasias* of Henry Purcell) only on a consort of viols; Savall argued famously for performance of J.S. Bach's *Die Kunst der Fugue* with this orchestration because of the transparence and clarity of the lines. For larger works (such as the Couperin *Apothéoses*), Hespèrion XX expands its instrumentation and adds singers, such as the Capella Reial de Catalunya or Philippe Herreweghe's Collegium Vocale. In performances of early Spanish music—from the *Cantigas de Santa Maria* to the *Cancionero de la Columbina* and the *Cancionero Musicale del Palacio*—the ensemble achieves a distinctly Moorish influence (as had Thomas Binkley and René Clemencic a generation before). In every repertory, Hespèrion XX combines a high level of polish and virtosity with vivid orchestrations and a vibrant sound that cares for the life of each individual tone. Even the vocal style of Hespèrion's singers sometimes mimics the characteristic pulsation of each tone in Savall's viol playing (in their recording of the Morales *Requiem*, for instance). One eminent musicologist has criticized Hespèrion XX for the romanticism of its sound; the group's dynamic performances, on the other hand, have achieved one of early music's widest and most enthusiastic audiences. *—Timothy Dickey*

Recommended:

- ○ **Purcell: Fantasias for Viols** / Savall (cond.), Hespèrion XX / 1999 / Astrée 9922
- ○ **El Cancionero de Palacio** / Savall (cond.), Hespèrion XX / 2000 / Astrée 9943
- ○ **Couperin: Les Nations** / Savall (cond.), Hespèrion XX / 2000 / Astrée 9956
- ○ **Bach: Die Kunst der Fuge** / Savall (cond.), Hespèrion XX / 2001 / Alia Vox 9818
- ○ **Victoria: Cantica Beatae Virginis** / Savall (cond.), Figueras, Climent, Costa, Ormazabal, Hespèrion XX, Capella Reial de Catalunya / 2002 / Astrée 9975

Dame Myra Hess

b. Feb. 25, 1890, London, England, **d.** Nov. 25, 1965, London, England
Pianist

Dame Myra Hess was one of the best known and most beloved of British pianists. She was a pupil of Julian Pascal and Orlando Morgan. At 12 she earned a scholarship to the Royal Academy of Music and became a pupil of Tobias Matthay, whom she viewed as her primary teacher.

She debuted at the age of 17 in Beethoven's *Fourth Concerto*, with Thomas Beecham conducting. In a departure for pianists of her era she took a special interest in chamber music, including participating in a piano duo with her cousin Irene Scharrer. She toured Europe and the United States.

She was a warm person and well liked, particularly in English-speaking countries, and visited America frequently. Her reputation was particularly enhanced by her innovative and deeply appreciated venture during World War II, the National Gallery Concerts. Wartime blackouts closed the concert halls of London. In the meantime, the National Gallery in London had been emptied of its art treasures, which were sent to parts of the country less vulnerable to German bombing. It was Hess's idea to open the Gallery to the public for concerts every day during the lunch hours.

Londoners flocked to these informal concerts. Hess arranged concerts from solo recitals to full-scale orchestral and choral music. She personally appeared more than any other artist (never asking for a fee), and got some of the finest musicians of the country to appear there. She received her knighthood as a Dame of the British Empire for this service in 1942. The effort was seen as a major boost to morale, and it is said that when the artworks were returned to the Gallery in 1946, ending the musical series, that there was considerable disappointment.

In common with many artists she adopted a wide-ranging repertory, including much music of her time, when she was younger, but focused increasingly on the great classic masters in later years. Her playing was noted for both warmth and thoughtfulness. She made numerous transcriptions, of which one in particular, Bach's chorale prelude *Jesu, Joy of Man's Desiring* from *Cantata 147*, has become an international favorite. *—Joseph Stevenson*

Recommended:

- ○ **Myra Hess** / Schwarz (cond.), Hess, London PO / 1999 / Philips 456832
- ○ **Dame Myra Hess Vol. 1** / Hess, etc. / Pearl 9462
- ○ **Piano Concertos of Beethoven & Mozart** / Boult (cond.), Hess, London PO / 2002 / BBC 4111

Angela Hewitt

b. Jul. 26, 1958, Ottawa, Ontario, Canada
Pianist

Angela Hewitt is a highly esteemed pianist, particularly noted as a Bach performer, but accomplished in an exceptionally large repertory that embraces all eras of keyboard music. The daughter of an organist, Hewitt began to study piano at age three, making a public debut at the age of four, winning a scholarship at six, and eventually adding studies in ballet, singing, violin, and recorder.

She entered the Royal Conservatory of Music in Toronto in 1964, and gave her first recital there at the age of nine. In 1973, she entered the University of Ottawa, where she studied with Jean-Paul Sevilla, a French pianist. She graduated from the University with a bachelor of music degree at the age of 18.

Hewitt slowly gained recognition in Canada and the United States, winning some noteworthy competitions, including the International Bach Competitions of Washington and Leipzig, the Schumann Competition in Zwickau, the Casadesus Competition in Cleveland, and the Dino Ciani Competition on the stage of the La Scala opera house in Milan.

Her breakthrough came with a victory at the unique International Bach Piano Competition, held in honor of the late Glenn Gould in Toronto, May 1985. This led to a Deutsche Grammophon recording of Bach solo keyboard music that won critical acclaim and established her as one of the great Bach interpreters.

Hewitt has appeared in the world's major recital venues, including Alice Tully Hall in New York, Wigmore Hall in London, the Ravinia Festival in Chicago, Salle Gaveau in Paris, Tokyo's Bunka Kaikan, Roy Thompson Hall in Toronto, and the *Sydney Opera House*. She has appeared on the concert platform with every major Canadian orchestra, all of the Australian Broadcasting Corporation's orchestra, the Japan Philharmonic, the San Francisco, Minnesota, Baltimore, Oregon, and Cincinnati Symphony Orchestras in the United States, and in London with the Philharmonia, the Royal Philharmonic, the BBC Philharmonic, and the City of London Sinfonia.

Hewitt's vast repertory includes music from Bach to Messiaen. She has done two complete recital cycles of the piano music of Maurice Ravel, and has devoted entire single-composer recital programs to Roussel, Brahms, Fauré, Chopin, Robert Schumann, Beethoven, and Brahms.

She is an avid chamber music performer, and often performs with leading singers and instrumentalists in North America and Europe. Her residence in England has not ended her close connection to Canada, and late in the 1990s she founded an organization called Piano Six, devoted to bring major Canadian piano artists to the far-flung rural communities of the vast country. (Their motto is "Keep live music alive.")

Hewitt frequently records, and since 1994 has been involved in a project with Britain's Hyperion Records label to record all the major clavier music of Johann Sebastian Bach on piano. Three of that series have been named "Editor's Choice" CDs in *Gramophone Magazine*, and her account of the *Well-Tempered Clavier* (Book One) was on two different *London Sunday Times* critics' Top Ten lists for 1998 and also won Canada's Juno Award. She has also released Granados' *Spanish Dances* on the CBC Records label and an all-Messiaen release on Hyperion.

Angela Hewitt received an honorary doctorate from the University of Ottawa in 1995 and in 1997 was given the Key to the City of Ottawa. *—Joseph Stevenson*

Recommended:

- ○ **Ravel: The Complete Solo Piano Music** / Hewitt / 2002 / Hyperion 67341/2
- ○ **Couperin: Keyboard Music Vol. 1** / Hewitt / Hyperion 6744
- ○ **Bach: English Suites** / Hewitt / Hyperion 67451/52
- ○ **Bach: Goldberg Variations** / Hewitt / 2000 / Hyperion 67305
- ○ **Bach: The Six Partitas** / Hewitt / 1997 / Hyperion 69191
- ○ **Chopin: Nocturnes** / Hewitt / 2004 / Hyperion 67371/2

Richard Hickox

b. Mar. 5, 1948, Stokenchurch, England
Conductor

Richard Hickox is one of the most active and well-known conductors in Britain, with a strong international reputation, especially for performing music of his native country. He began conducting at the age of 16 and, after studies at the Royal College of Music and Queen's College, where he was an organ scholar, founded the City of London Sinfonia in 1971, of which he has remained musical director ever since.

In 1972 he became organist and master of music at St. Margaret's Church, Westminster, remaining in that position until 1982. In 1977 he was appointed conductor of the London Symphony Orchestra Chorus, and in 1982 became the music director of the Northern Sinfonia in Newcastle-upon-Tyne. He is credited with re-establishing that orchestra as an ensemble of stature, confirmed by a highly successful tour of the United States and a complete Beethoven symphony recording cycle for the ASV label. He was associate conductor of the San Diego Symphony Orchestra from 1982 to 1985, and took the same title at the London Symphony Orchestra in 1985. He shares leadership duties with Simon Standage for Collegium Musicum '90, a period instrument group the two founded.

All this activity has made Hickox a very familiar face on the British music scene. With his various choral and orchestral ensembles he frequently appears at the major British music festivals, and at the BBC Proms Concerts. He has participated in several notable special projects, including a BBC video production of Purcell's *Dido and Aeneas* and an appearance in the Istanbul Festival leading a production of Mozart's *The Abduction from the Seraglio* inside the actual sultans' seraglio in the Topkapi Museum. He also provided music for a Ken Russell film for the BBC on the wives of great composers.

In the 1990s he increased his involvement with opera, leading new productions of Handel's *Julius Caesar* in Berlin, Walton's *Troilus and Cressida* in a live BBC broadcast of an Opera North production, and Vaughan Williams' *Pilgrim's Progress* at the Royal Opera House, Covent Garden.

He guest conducts around the world, including frequent appearances with the Los Angeles Opera and the New Japan Philharmonic in Tokyo. He has made over 150 recordings and won numerous awards, including a Gramophon Award for 1992 for his account of Britten's *War Requiem*, and three Gramophone Awards, a Diapason d'Or, the Deutsche Schalplattenpreis and a Grammy for his recording of Britten's *Peter Grimes* in 1995 on the Chandos label, probably the most honored classical recording of the last quarter of the twentieth century. His recordings appear on the ASV, Argo, EMI, and Virgin labels, and since the early 1990s he has been an exclusive Chandos artist. *—Joseph Stevenson*

Recommended:

- ○ **Grainger: Works for Chorus & Orchestra** / Hickox (cond.), Varcoe, Padmore, Thwaites, Pearson, City of London Sonfonia, Joyful Company of Singers / 1996 / Chandos 9499
- ○ **Britten: War Requiem, etc.** / Hickox (cond.), Scott, Langridge, Hill, Harper, London SO & Chorus / 2003 / Chandos 5007
- ○ **Dyson: Canterbury Pilgrims** / Hickox (cond.), Kenny, Roberts, Tear, London SO & Chorus / 1997 / Chandos 9531
- ○ **Tippet: Symphony 4; 2 Fantasias** / Hickox (cond.), O'Brien, Shelley, Koos, Verrall, Bournemouth Sinfonietta / 1993 / Chandos 9233

Hildegard of Bingen

b. 1098, Bemersheim, Germany, **d.** Sep. 17, 1179, Rupertsburg, Germany
Composer: Vocal, Choral

In the summer of 1098, a child was born to noble parents in Bermersheim, near Alzey, in modern-day Rheinhessen, and was christened Hildegard. By her own account, she was having visions at the age of five; her parents placed her in the care of a small nunnery when she was eight. Over an 81-year life-span, this remarkable woman would go on to lead the Abbey at Disibodenberg, and found two further convents of her own; she wrote three major theological works and a number of shorter treatises on natural history, herbalism, and healing, as well as the first surviving morality play and a large number of hymns and sequences. Her correspondence gave counsel and advice to many of the most prominent figures of her time, even to Frederick Barbarossa himself. She performed healings and a celebrated exorcism, and—an extremely rare privilege for a woman—took several officially sanctioned public preaching tours.

Hildebert and Mechtild, her parents, had promised this (their tenth child) to the Church's service, and gave the precocious eight-year-old as novice to Jutta of Spanheim, who led a small cell of nuns attached to the Benedictine monastery of Disibodenberg, near Bingen and the cathedral town of Mainz. Hildegard took her vows at the age of 15, and on Jutta's death in 1136 succeeded her as prioress of the small eremitic community. In 1141, God granted her a vision of flaming tongues descending upon her from heaven, and she devoted her life to following this mystic vision. Pope Eugenius III officially validated her religious visions at the Synod of Trier in 1148, and gave her permission to record them in written form. In addition to her writings, she began to attract further women to her community, and, between 1147 and 1150, she founded (against the wishes of her male superiors at Disibodenberg) a new abbey at Rupertsberg in the Rhine valley. Her ministry thrived and she established a daughter abbey at Eibingen around 1165. Four times in the 1160s she took preaching tours through the German lands, and after her death in 1179, Popes Gregory IX and Innocent IV proposed her canonization, followed by Clement V and John XXII, to no avail.

With the aid and encouragement of her monastic secretary Volmar, Hildegard began in 1141 to record her revelations; twenty-six visions comprise her first work, the *Scivias*, compiled over a ten-year period. Her prophetic and apocalyptic writings would later include the *Liber vite meritorum* (1158–63) and *Liber divinorum operum* (1163–70). In the interval between these volumes, Hildegard wrote two works on natural history (*Physica*) and medicine (*Cause et cure*), a commentary on the Rule of St. Benedict, lives of two saints, and a number of surviving sermons on sundry topics. Her interest in devotional poetry first shows up in the *Scivias*. In the early 1150s, she collected a large number of liturgical and devotional poems, each with associated music, such as the *Symphonia armonie celestium revelationum*, which also included her liturgical drama the *Ordo virtutem*. This work she continued to enlarge and embellish through her life. The "Sybil of the Rhine" also left a voluminous correspondence—some three hundred surviving letters—sending advice, prayers, teachings, encouragements, and often chastisement to popes, emperors, kings, archbishops, abbots and abbesses throughout Europe. *—Timothy Dickey*

VOCAL

Chants and Songs (ca. 1140–1179)

The name Hildegard of Bingen appears on the historical honor rolls of many disciplines: poetry, medicine, naturalism, hagiography, medieval politics and, as we are becoming increasingly aware, music. We will leave it for others to debate the true nature of her mystic visions (some believe them to have been the effect of a serious migraine condition, others accept them at face value) and instead focus on the particulars of this remarkable woman's contribution to Western music. Hildegard, like other prominent musicians of her day (1098–1179), mustn't be thought of as a composer in our modern understanding of the term—the generative process, design, and even the very notation of the music were all towards an end that most of us today, with our modern ideas and ideals, would find utterly foreign and perhaps even disconcerting. Hildegard was first and foremost a poet, a poet with a profound belief in the communicative and spiritual power of sound and tone; the monophonic (i.e. single-line, just one melody) music that she attached to her mystic poems provides an outlet for this belief. As notated, it is simple and sparse; these tunes, like most notated medieval music, are not finished compositions, but rather indications, hints if you will, by which a group of musicians might draw from their own musical expertise and produce something of value, half-notated, half-improvised. Such was the medieval way, and such was Hildegard's way.

Her music probably dates mostly from the 1140s and 1150s. She put it all together into a volume called *Symphonia armonie celestium revelationum* (Harmonious Symphonies of Heavenly Revelation). The word "symphonies" at that time was a general term for musical "sounding-together" or, to make it a little more abstract and thus probably closer to Hildegard's own meaning, a kind of "oneness." The music is not built from pre-existing chant, but it does operate in the same manner as Gregorian chant. Lovers of chant will note that Hildegard restricted herself to only two or three of the most common melodic modes.

Included in the *Symphonia* are four kinds of poetic-musical pieces, meant for the Divine Office and collectively forming a liturgical feast-cycle: 1) 43 antiphons, short(ish) pieces to be sung before and after psalm readings; 2) 18 responsories, to be sung after scripture lessons, often taking the shape of answer-response (hence the name) between a single singer and a group; 3) seven sequences, dramatic and usual lengthy poems/songs; and 4) four hymns, generally the simplest of Hildegard's works.

The music is notated in the simplest of fashions: a pitch is given for each syllable (or, in melismatic passages, multiple pitches are given for each syllable) while rhythm is left to the collective discretion of the singers, who will take the syllabic characteristics of the text as their starting-point. Hildegard's poems make frequent reference to musical instruments, which has led many to feel it appropriate to include instruments in performances of her music. *—Blair Johnston*

Recommended:

- ○ **Hildegard: O Jerusalem** / Sequentia / 1997 / Deutsche HM 77353

CHORAL

Ordo Virtutum, liturgical drama (ca. 1140–1179)

Abbess Hildegard of Bingen led an extraordinary life. Few women in medieval Europe could match single endeavors from the varied list of her accomplishments: abbess; poetess (sanctioned by the Pope); mystic; composer of music; correspondent to Frederick Barbarossa, Bernard de Clairvaux, and Eleanor of Aquitaine; scholar of medicine; astrology; ethics; and natural history. For her elite band of nuns at the Abbey of Rupertsberg, Hildegard wrote a complete liturgical cycle of ecstatic hymns, the *Symphonia*. To it she also appended a complete liturgical drama, the *Ordo Virtutum*. Hildegard's *Ordo* (a rite rather than a play) has often been called the "first Morality Play," but its intense mixture of sacred music, drama, and ritual is *sui generis*. The *Ordo Virtutum* presents a prayerful and emotional allegory of temptation, sin, and the victory of repentance, a celebration of the entire monastic ideal; its music bristles with Hildegard's characteristic melodic motifs, and with dramatic, large-scale modal shifts. The play may have been part of the 1151 consecration rites for Hildegard's new Abbey, and may also have served in the solemn (and public) liturgy of veiling the convent's new nuns.

The drama of the *Ordo Virtutum*, for which Hildegard composed both the lyrical Latin text and the music, centers on the struggles of Anima (Soul). At the beginning, this Soul (a type of Everyman) blissfully resides within the company of the Virtues, yet she hears the voice of the Devil tempting her to the world's pleasures. Hildegard's Devil character does not sing, as she thought song a purely divine ability, but he persuasively speaks and shouts. The Virtues try to support the Soul, but she leaves them, perhaps even physically running out of the church. The second large section contains an extended counterpoint between the Devil's rude words and the lyrical songs of the Virtues. All 16 of the Virtues and their Queen Humility define themselves in solo song, followed by choral celebrations of each Virtue. Often, their texts are quite sensual and the melodies lush, as the Virtue Chastity's depiction of the "king's embrace" and the centerpiece choral "Flos campi" that follows it. Soul eventually returns, repenting of her sins; the Virtues led by Victory bind the Devil in chains, while Chastity steps on his head. The play concludes with a bizarre and mystical chorus of praise, sung in unison by the Virtues, Patriarchs, and Souls Still Imprisoned in Bodies, their voices presenting the words of the wounded Christ himself. *—Timothy Dickey*

Recommended:

- ○ **Hildegard: Ordo Virtutum** / Sequentia / 1998 / Deutsche HM 77394

Hilliard Ensemble

f. 1974, Oxford, England
Ensemble

An entire class of English vocal ensembles, sometimes placed under an "Oxbridge Sound" umbrella, specializes in early music. Among the prestigious ranks of the Gothic Voices, the Tallis Scholars, Pro Cantione Antiqua, the Oxford Camerata, and the Sixteen, longevity and musical versatility place the Hilliard Ensemble in a class almost of their own. Named for the great Elizabethan miniaturist painter Nicholas

Hilliard, and not for their longtime director, the Hilliard Ensemble grew out of the musical vision of baritone Paul Hillier, a graduate of the Guildhall School of Music, and his friendships with three other singers (two of them from Oxford). Their intention was to explore the then less-heard musical riches of the Middle Ages and the Renaissance. Their musical odyssey has covered music from the eleventh to the seventeenth century, with a strong interest in late twentieth century vocal music as well. Though Paul Hillier himself left the ensemble in 1990 to take American academic positions at the University of California at Davis and then at the Early Music Institute at the University of Indiana, the core membership has remained otherwise fairly consistent: countertenor David James, tenors Rogers Covey-Crump and John Potter, and basses Michael George and later Gordon Jones.

The Hilliard Ensemble's work under Hillier's direction centered on English and "Netherlandish" music. Notable recordings include pathbreaking performances of Leonel Power and the Old Hall manuscript, a large selection of music from the Continental generations influenced by the English style; the "Contenance Angloise" (Dufay, Ockeghem, and Josquin); and excellent renditions of later English composers such as Thomas Tallis and William Byrd. As an example of their many departures from this Renaissance main road, however, the Hilliard's catalog features a musically powerful and quite controversial 1989 recording of the music of Perotin. At all times, Hillier and his singers performed almost exclusively one on a part (in contrast to the "choral" Tallis Scholars), with a characteristic full and resonant vocal production, and impeccable tuning. In addition, Hillier's individual approach emphasized historical pronunciation; he performed Latin texts by English composers, for instance, with regional Anglo-Latin dialects, thereby significantly altering the very sound of the music.

During Hillier's tenure as director, and even more spectacularly through the 1990s, the Hilliard Ensemble also devoted significant energy to the presentation of contemporary classical music. A large number of ECM label discs containing the *tintinnabuli* music of Estonian composer Arvo Pärt have featured the ensemble, as did a 1995 recording of the music of Giya Kancheli, *Abii ne viderem.* A two-disc compilation from 1996, *A Hilliard Songbook: New Music for Voices,* presented the results of several years of the ensemble's direct commissions and Hilliard Composition Prizes; among the composers represented are Morton Feldman, James MacMillan, Ivan Moody, and Joanne Metcalf. A fascinating collaboration between the Hilliard Ensemble and jazz saxophonist Jan Garbarek yielded the 1994 *Officium,* bridging the centuries with esoteric flights of saxophone improvisation above the hyper-resonant landscape of the Hilliard group singing chants and spiritual motets—a musical nexus that nearly defies description. And these certainly do not represent the final chapter in new sounds that the Hilliard Ensemble will bring into the world. *—Timothy Dickey*

Recommended:

- ○ **Machaut: Motets** / Hilliard Ens. / 2004 / ECM 1859
- ○ **Lassus** / Hilliard Ens. / 1998 / ECM 453841
- ○ **Ockeghem: Requiem; Missa mi - mi** / Hilliard Ens. / 1995 / Veritas 61219
- ○ **Perotin** / Hilliard Ens. / ECM 837751
- ○ **Pärt: Arbos** / Davies (cond.), Kremer, Dawson, James, Demenga, Hilliard Ensemble, Brass Ens. of Stuttgart State Orch. / 1987 / ECM 831959
- ○ **Gesualdo: Tenebrae** / Hilliard Ens. / 1991 / ECM 843867

Paul Hillier

b. Feb. 9, 1949, Dorchester, England

Conductor, baritone

English baritone Paul Hillier is one of the leading figures, both as a singer and conductor, in the early music movement and now makes his home in the United States, where he has shown increasing interest in new music.

As a boy he was a chorister at St. Paul's Cathedral in London. This position carries with it an opportunity to learn a wide expanse of choral repertoire, to receive a thorough musical and general education at the St. Paul's Cathedral School, and to make important lifelong contacts. After graduating from school he studied music at London's Guildhall. He returned to St. Paul's Cathedral in 1973 as its vicar-choral for one season. He was also a member of the Queen's Chapel Royal at Windsor Castle. In 1974 he made his solo recital debut at the Purcell Room in London. In the same year he co-founded the Hilliard Ensemble, becoming its music director. The ensemble soon became one of the world's best known early music vocal groups, and was much in demand for performances worldwide, making a number of bestselling and award-winning recordings. The all-male quartet specialized in Renaissance music.

In 1980–81 he taught as a visiting professor at the University of California, Santa Cruz. After that he began to spend an increasing amount of time in America. He was the Copland Colloquium Fellow at Amherst College in Massachusetts in 1984. He became more interested in New Music and tried to get the Hilliard Ensemble to branch out in that direction. That, and a wish to add female voices and engage in the more theatrical style of performance presentation, led to his leaving the Ensemble.

In 1990 he moved to the United States to become a professor of music at the University of California, Davis. He founded Theatre of Voices, an ensemble of male and female singers, specializing both in early and recent music, and performing in dynamic, theatrical stage presentations. Unlike the Hilliard Ensemble, it was planned to include a varying number of singers, depending on the demands of the performances. Theatre of Voices records exclusively for Harmonia Mundi USA, on which it has released a repertoire ranging from twelfth century chant to music of Arvo Pärt, including *Litany of the Whale* by John Cage, and the selection of early American religious music, including hymns sung in the "shaped note" tradition.

In 1996 Hillier left California to join the faculty of Indiana University, Bloomington, as director of its Early Music Institute. This is an interdisciplinary study program offering undergraduate and graduate degrees involving not just the study of ancient performance practice and musicology, but also courses in literature, fine arts, and medieval studies in other departments and schools of the university. Hillier also is conductor of Indiana University's Pro Arte Singers, its early music choir.

Since his move to the United States, Hillier has maintained his active career as a singer and conductor, appearing frequently in North America, Europe, and Japan, though he has relaxed this pace sufficiently to carry out his teaching and administrative responsibilities and also to research and write. His books include *300 Years of English Partsongs, Romantic English Partsongs, The Catch Book,* and one on Estonian composer Arvo Pärt, and he has edited of a book of collected writings of composer Steve Reich.

Hillier has won many prizes for recordings. He performs on the Harmonia Mundi, ECM, EMI, Finlandia, and Hyperion labels. *—Joseph Stevenson*

Recommended:

- ○ **Pärt: I am the True Vine** / Hillier (cond.), Bowers-Broadbent, Pro Arte Singers, Theatre of Voices / 1999 / HM 907242
- ○ **Cage: Litany for the Whale** / Hillier (cond.), Elliott, Bennett, Fullington, Owens, Riley, Theatre of Voices / 2002 / HM 907279
- ○ **Palestrina: Canticum canticorum: Spiritual Madrigals** / Hillier (cond.), Hilliard Ensemble / 2003 / Virgin 562239
- ○ **Pärt: Passio** / Hillier (cond.), George, Potter, Dawson, James, Western Wind Chamber Choir, Hilliard Ensemble / 1988 / ECM 837109
- ○ **Early American Choral Music Vol. 1** / Hillier (cond.), His Majestie's Clerkes / 2001 / Classical Express 3957048
- ○ **Monastic Chant** / Hillier (cond.), Elliott, Hargis, Bennett, Bowers-Broadbent, Rickards, Theatre of Voices / 2003 / HM 2907356/57

Paul Hindemith

b. Nov. 16, 1895, Hanau, Germany, **d.** Dec. 28, 1963, Frankfurt, Germany

Composer: Symphonic, Orchestral, Concerto, Ballet, Chamber Music, Keyboard, Vocal, Choral

A theorist, teacher, violist, conductor, and composer who is regarded by many as the foremost German composer of his generation, Paul Hindemith was one of the most central figures in music between the First and Second World Wars. Born outside of Frankfurt, Hindemith moved with his family to the city in 1902. It was here, in 1904, that Hindemith began taking violin lessons. By 1908, Hindemith became a student of Adolf Rebner, a teacher at the Hoch Conservatory in Frankfurt, who arranged for Hindemith to be awarded a free place at the conservatory the following year. Although he had long been composing, Hindemith, in addition to continuing his study of the violin, began to study composition formally. However, he was forced to leave the conservatory in 1917 when he was called up for military service. He spent most of his service as a member of a regimental band stationed about 3 kilometer from the front line.

After returning from the war, Hindemith again took to the concert stage, having switched to viola in 1919. In 1923 he was invited to join the administrative committee of the Donaueschingen Festival, a group over which he exerted an ever increasing amount of control; programming works of such composers as Schoenberg and Webern. The next year he married Gertrud Rottenberg, the daughter of the conductor of the Frankfurt Opera Orchestra, an ensemble in which Hindemith had been playing. In 1927 he received an appointment as professor of composition at the Hochschule für Musik in Berlin. In addition to maintaining an active performing career, Hindemith soon developed a strong interest in teaching, and even took on an evening class at the Volksmusikschule NeuKolln.

Early in 1934, the Nazi party began a campaign to discredit Hindemith, which culminated in a boycott of the composer's works announced by the Kulturgemeinde in November of that year. In January 1935, Hindemith was given a six-month leave from the Hochschule. However, as the boycott of his music was not endorsed by the music division of the Nazi party until 1937, Hindemith was allowed not only to return to teaching, but also to undertake a series of concert tours abroad, to have his music published, and to enter into an agreement with the government of Turkey to build an organized musical life in that country. However, in 1937, Hindemith left Germany for Switzerland, and in 1940 came to the U.S.

After a series of lecture and teaching engagements which had been arranged by friends, Hindemith took a position at Yale, teaching composition and, from 1945 to 1953, conducting the Collegium Musicum. In 1946, Hindemith became an American citizen. In 1951 he accepted a position at the University of Zurich and, after retiring from Yale in 1953, took up permanent residence in Switzerland. After retiring from his post in Zurich, in 1955, he became more active as a conductor. In November 1963, he was taken ill and transferred to a hospital in Frankfurt, where he died of acute pancreatitis. *—Stephen Kingsbury*

SYMPHONIC

Mathis der Maler, symphony (from the opera) (1934)

The neo-Classical (or perhaps more accurately, neo-Baroque) concerns of Hindemith's startling instrumental works of the 1920s converged with what Hindemith later described as a growing awareness of "the ethical imperatives of music and the moral obligations of the musician" in his opera *Mathis der Maler.* Hindemith was exploring the conflict faced by an artist in turbulent times: to honor one's obligation to the society in which he lives or to remain true only to the artistic ideals he espouses. In the story of German Renaissance painter Matthias Grünewald, Hindemith was able to comment on his own situation. His stance did not go unnoticed by the Nazis, and the symphony he extracted from the opera was premiered in Berlin in 1934 only upon the insistence of conductor Wilhelm Furtwängler. The opera itself was not heard until 1938, in Zurich, after Hindemith had left Germany.

Hindemith's inspiration for the opera came partly from Grünewald's masterpiece, the *Isenheim Altarpiece,* a paneled triptych whose structure is mirrored in the three-movement symphony. The first movement, "Angelic Concert," serves as the opera's overture and appears here intact. After serene, widely-spaced chords on strings, the horns introduce a theme based on the German folk song *"Es sungen drei Engel"* ("Three angels sang a sweet song"), which reaches a glowing climax, richly orchestrated. A faster theme introduced by solo flute and strings is given a lively contrapuntal treatment, with resourceful and highly colorful orchestration, a new neo-Romantic sound-world for Hindemith. The climax of the movement is in two parts: the folksong returns on horns, then fully fleshed out in brass; after a moment of calm, fugato strings gather the orchestra for the final brazen (and brazenly triadic!) chords, with strings chiming and bells and triangle shimmering.

The second movement is titled "Entombment," and in the opera is a brief intermezzo expressing Mathis' grief on the death of his daughter. In this spare elegy, harmonies based on fourths and fifths prevail, intervals that the composer often employed to express solemnity. Flute and oboe, over pizzicato strings, entwine in a tender lament; there is a brief outcry of grief, then a return to the quietude of the opening, with the flute offering a gesture of consolation.

The music for the lengthy finale is drawn from the opera's episode in which the temptation of St. Anthony (one of the Isenheim Altarpiece scenes) is likened to the temptations and trials of Mathis himself. A chromatic recitative for unison lower strings is the thematic foundation of the three episodes that follow, beginning with a fast section in galloping rhythm, suggesting relentless pursuit and hopeless flight. An unsettling, high trill in the violins introduces the next section, a sensuous melody for violas and cellos depicting the pleasures of the flesh offered (vainly) to St. Anthony. The turmoil of the first section returns and reaches a cadence, at which point strings begin the contrapuntally complex resolution based on the plainchant hymn *"Lauda Sion salvatorem."* Ringing "Alleluias" in the brass bring the symphony to a close. *—Mark Satola*

Recommended:

- ○ **Hindemith: Symphonic Metamorphosis; Nobilissima Visone; Mathis der Maler** / Sawallisch (cond.), Philadelphia Orch. / 1995 / EMI 55230
- ○ **Hindemith: Konzertmusik; Mathis der Maler; Concerto for 3 winds** / Belohlávek (cond.), Czech PO / 1996 / Chandos 9457

Pittsburgh Symphony (1958)

Paul Hindemith wrote the *Pittsburgh Symphony,* his sixth and final symphony, at the request of the Pittsburgh Symphony Orchestra's then-music director William Steinberg in 1958 to celebrate the 200th anniversary of the founding of the city. To accomplish this musical celebration, Hindemith included two songs associated with the city in the fabric of his work, the Pennsylvania Dutch folk song *Hab lumbedruwwel mit me lumbeschatz* in the central portion of the central movement and the contemporary folk song "Pittsburgh Is a Great Old Town" by Woody Guthrie and Pete Seeger in the final portion of the closing movement. The opening movement, Molto energico, is a mono-thematic movement that has elements of both sonata form and three-part form in its structure. The outer sections are the exposition and recapitulation of sonata form, but the central section, Piu calmo, is more of a quiet interlude between the stormy outer section rather than a development section proper. The central movement is actually three movements in one: a slow march led by the oboe and then taken up by the strings in a series of variations, an Allegro assai central section that treats the Pennsylvania Dutch folk song as a symphonic scherzo, and a closing section that unites the slow march and the scherzo in one structure. The closing movement, Ostinato Allegro moderato, is—like so many of Hindemith's symphonic finales—a passacaglia. The movement and the work reaches a climax in the statement of Guthrie and Seeger's song as a cantus firmus in the horns that drives the work to its powerful conclusion. It is interesting to note that, for all his stated antipathy to atonal and serial music, Hindemith found a way to integrate a quotation from Webern's symphony in the finale of the *Pittsburgh Symphony. —James Leonard*

Recommended:

- ○ **Hindemith: Complete Orchestral Works** / Albert (cond.), Melbourne SO / CPO 999248
- ○ **Hindemith: Symphonic Dances; Ragtime; Pittsburg Symphony** / Tortelier (cond.), BBCPO / 1997 / Chandos 9530

Symphonia Serena (1946)

Like much of Hindemith's music written after World War II, the *Symphonia Serena* (1946) combines a new preoccupation with intensely chromatic counterpoint with a wry sense of humor, a feature largely dormant in the composer's music since his departure from Germany in the 1930s. As might be expected from a composer whose own instrumental expertise fostered a special affinity with performers, Hindemith also filled his score with a multitude of felicities that could be counted on to delight players and listeners alike: witty parody, ingenious instrumental combinations, and different simultaneous tempi.

The opening movement, marked "Moderately fast," presents an appropriately serene, motto-like theme in the horns against celestial-sounding strings; a pastoral, plangent second subject appears in counterpoint in the woodwinds. The movement proceeds much like a set of variations, employing mostly the second subject in a series of episodes that highlight various sections and individual instruments of the orchestra. Particularly outstanding is the wistful treatment of the second theme by the solo violin, accompanied by chordal woodwinds, which builds to a fine contrapuntal climax at the re-entry of the first theme. There follows a remarkable sequence, again utilizing the endlessly pliable second theme on English horn and piccolo, accompanied by pizzicato strings and tuned woodblocks. The movement ends with a fugal episode that culminates in a brass-heavy peroration of the opening motto.

A miniature military march by Beethoven, the "*Yorck'sche Marsch,*" is the thematic basis for the second movement, "Geschwindmarsch by Beethoven." This scherzo is scored entirely for winds and brass. Chattering woodwinds create a shifting chromatic background for fragments of Beethoven's theme, stuttered out amusingly by horns and tuba. A trio section presents the same theme in irregular chordal phrases, with woodwinds imitating the reedy drone of bagpipes. The return of the main section presents Beethoven's march theme in its entirety, with the same élan and harmonic abandon that Hindemith employed twenty-five years earlier in his orchestral jazz parody *Ragtime (Well-Tempered).*

The third movement, "Colloquy," is an ingenious interlocking puzzle consisting of three sections, the third section a superimposition of the first two. The sections are divided by two mirror-like cadenza sequences, each featuring a dialogue between an onstage and an offstage solo instrument. Where the second movement featured winds with some percussion underpinning, "Colloquy" is scored for strings alone, divided into two groups. The first section presents chorale-like material played divisi and arco by the first string group. A cadenza for solo violin, echoed by an offstage violin, leads to the middle section, played pizzicato by the second string group. In a reversal of the previous cadenza sequence, the second cadenza features an offstage solo viola answered by its onstage colleague before the two solo violins return and usher in the final section of the movement. Here, the arco and pizzicato sections run simultaneously, providing both a striking surprise and a satisfying conclusion to this sophisticated hall of mirrors.

The entire orchestra is reunited for the finale, marked "Gay." The movement's unusually wide-ranging theme is first heard in the solo clarinet. The whirlwind interplay of this and subsequent themes results in one of Hindemith's most complex essays. During the ten or so minutes that conclude the *Symphonia Serena,* the sections and first-desk players are called upon to create a tricky contrapuntal web that climaxes, appropriately, with a return of the symphony's opening horn theme and a lengthy, complex coda that features the clarinet theme and one characterized by an insistently repeated note. The work ends with a bold fanfare.

The *Symphonia Serena* was premiered on February 2, 1947, by the Dallas Symphony Orchestra directed by Antal Dorati. *—Mark Satola*

Recommended:

- ○ **Hindemith: Symphonia Serena; Harmonie der Welt** / Blomstedt (cond.), Gewandhaus / 2000 / Decca 458899
- ○ **Hindemith: Symphonia Serena; Harmonie der Welt** / Tortelier (cond.), BBCPO / 1993 / Chandos 9217

Symphony in B flat major, for concert band (1951)

Hindemith composed his Symphony in B flat major for Concert Band (1951) on a commission from the United States Army Band. Unlike European military bands, the U.S. Army Band included a large number of saxophones in its ranks. Hindemith took full advantage of this feature, investing his three-movement work with a jazzy sound that hearkened to the composer's years as an *enfant terrible* in the 1920s.

The opening movement ("Moderately fast, with vigor") juxtaposes two main theme groups, the first marked by a rather grim declamation in the cornets and trumpets against triplet woodwind rhythms, the second by a sinuous woodwind unison from which a brass chorale of similar character emerges. Hindemith connects the two groups with a quizzical theme in the oboe and accompanying woodwinds. This theme reappears to generate the climax of the fugal middle section, in which saxophones play a prominent role. The movement climaxes in a recapitulation of the chorale.

The dialogue between saxophone and cornet that opens the middle movement, Andantino grazioso, is Weill-esque, with a suggestion of banjo accompaniment in its dolorous give-and-take. The central episode ("Fast and gay") is pure Hindemith, however, in its scurrying triple-time counterpoint and clever imitative effects. At the end of this tripartite movement, Hindemith uses a favorite trick, interlocking the first and second sections to make a third.

An abrupt four-note ascending figure forms the basis of the fugal finale, which at its climax brings back the opening trumpet and cornet theme of the first movement, another familiar Hindemithian device no less effective here for its familiarity. The concluding consonant chords, enlivened by busily piping woodwinds, stand in striking relief to the edgy harmonic language that characterizes this modest masterpiece. *—Mark Satola*

Recommended:

- ○ **Paradigm** / Corporon (cond.), Cincinnati Wind Symphony / 1994 / Klavier 11059

Symphony in E flat major (1940)

This was among the first works Hindemith composed when he settled in the United States in 1940, a refugee from Nazi Germany who would become an American citizen following the war. He started this symphony in September 1940, about the time he joined the faculty of Yale University, and completed it on December 15, that same year. The work hardly discloses a significant change in the composer's style or manner from the music he was composing when he departed Germany.

The *Symphony* is in four movements, with the last two played without break. The opening panel is marked "Very lively," and begins with a fanfare-like theme of heroic character. The music bristles with energy as the main theme permeates the musical landscape throughout. The short first movement is followed by the relatively lengthy second, marked "Very slowly." It starts off in a funereal mood, with brass and winds presenting a somber theme. The strings take it up and the music gradually intensifies, producing several climactic episodes. The third movement, marked "Lively," is really a scherzo, though the composer did not designate it as such. The music is playful and energetic, full of high spirits and humor. The finale begins with a variant of the fanfare-like theme from the first movement. As the music progresses, this theme transforms more closely back to its original guise. The whole movement is dramatic and heroic and reaches a resoundingly triumphant conclusion. *—Robert Cummings*

Recommended:

- ○ **Hindemith: Complete Orchestral Works** / Albert (cond.), Melbourne SO / CPO 999248
- ○ **Hindemith: Symphony in E flat; Nobilissima Visione; Neus vom Tage** / Tortelier (cond.), BBCPO / 1992 / Chandos 9060

ORCHESTRAL

Konzertmusik, for brass & strings, Op. 50 (1930)

In the 1920s, Hindemith's musical language matured through a series of instrumental works of increasing seriousness and accomplishment, notably the seven *Kammermusiken* (1922–27), and the three *Konzertmusiken*, Op. 48 (viola and large chamber orchestra), Op.49 (piano, brass, two harps) and Op. 50 for Brass and Strings. As the last of the series, Op. 50 was written in response to a commission from Sergey Koussevitzky for the fiftieth anniversary season of the Boston Symphony Orchestra. Koussevitzky conducted its premiere on April 3, 1931.

The work is in two movements. An emphatic unison note from the brass is answered by an upward-rushing phrase from unison strings, which launch into a brisk and rather stern chordal accompaniment for the main theme, a long-breathed, chromatic melody declaimed by unison brass, with occasional pungent harmonic underpinnings. The second theme, bracing and energetic, is stated and developed by brass alone, in virtuosic counterpoint. After a remarkable cadence featuring hieratic horn calls and a "rocket" phrase on the interval of the major third, the strings and brass reunite for further development of the second theme, with low strings repeating the opening melody underneath. After a second cadence in which string chords of stacked fourths tumble to a halt, the strings again sing the opening melody, with doleful harmonies from the brass ending the movement in a slow and melancholy mood.

Throughout the "Jazz Age" decade, Hindemith had often employed elements of jazz in his music, usually for satiric or even sarcastic purposes. In the second movement of the Op. 50 *Konzertmusik*, jazz is used as an integral part of the musical rhetoric, without being disingenuous. The cross rhythms and high spirits of jazz inform the opening moments, a fast and tricky fugato for strings, against which the trumpet sounds a five-note phrase that will prove to be significant. The brass joins in the chase, and the strings launch a breezy and fast theme. A slow middle section recalls the dolorous closing bars of the first movement, though the featured arioso for trombone is more bittersweet than melancholy. The effect here is not unlike some of the theater music of Kurt Weill, though the music is closer in spirit to the jazz inflections of William Walton (for whose jazzy yet wistful *Viola Concerto* Hindemith had been soloist at its 1929 premiere in London). The fugato section returns, though somewhat more seriously, with blue notes now becoming an indelible part of the proceedings. There is an exciting coda, with divided strings chiming the Gershwin-esque phrase, and a quick summary of the emphatic unison notes that opened the work. *—Mark Satola*

Recommended:

- ○ **Royal Eurostar** / Honeyball (cond.), London Brass Virtuosi, Philharmonia / 1996 / Hyperion 66870

Symphonic Metamorphosis of Themes by Carl Maria von Weber (1943)

In his *Symphonic Metamorphosis on Themes of Carl Maria von Weber* (1943), Hindemith pays homage to the important German early Romantic composer by adapting some of his music—works for piano duo and for the stage—as an orchestral suite. It's uncertain whether Hindemith preferred the plural or singular form of the word "metamophosis" in the title; whichever form of the word he intended, it is the key to the music. Hindemith adapts each of the extracts from Weber to serve as the theme for one of the movements, beginning the process of transformation that continues throughout each.

One of the work's highlights is the second movement, in which a "Chinese" flute theme twice receives the *Bolero* treatment. At first it is incessantly cycled in ever-richening instrumental textures, then the process repeats with "jazzy" syncopated rhythms. At times the percussion instruments take over, and different groups in the orchestra seem to go off in their own tempi, independent of the others. The third movement is notable for an awe-inspiring flute solo, while the two outer two movements are vigorous march tunes. *—Joseph Stevenson*

Recommended:

- ○ **Hindemith: Mathis der Maler; Symphonic Metamorphosis; Walton: Variations** / Szell (cond.), Cleveland Orch. / 1993 / Sony 53258
- ○ **Hindemith: Symphonic Metamorphosis; Nobilissima Visone; Mathis der Maler** / Sawallisch (cond.), Philadelphia Orch. / 1995 / EMI 55230
- ○ **Janáček: Sinfonietta; Hindemith: Symphonic Metamorphosis, Prokofiev: Symphony 3** / Abbado (cond.), London SO / 1995 / London 448579
- ○ **Bartók, Kodaly, Hindemith & Schoenberg** / Dorati (cond.), Kubelik (cond.), Chicago SO / 1998 / Mercury 434397

CONCERTO

Clarinet Concerto (1947)

Hindemith had lived in the United States for seven years and had become a citizen when clarinetist and bandleader Benny Goodman approached him about writing a clarinet concerto. Goodman enjoyed a reputation as one of America's first great crossover successes: wildly popular as a jazz artist, he was also respected for his interpretations of the Classical clarinet repertoire. In the 1940s he commissioned important new works from a number of composers, including Bartók and Copland. He premiered Hindemith's *Clarinet Concerto* on December 11, 1950.

The *Clarinet Concerto* was written at a time when Hindemith's music was marked by a distinctive, individual tonal language encompassing the entire chromatic scale. By the late 1940s, World War II had reached its end, and the composer was prosperous, financially secure, and prolific as ever. Perhaps influenced in part by these comfortable circumstances, Hindemith invested the concerto with a particular serenity and lyricism. The work is in four movements: a sonata-allegro first movement with a surprise-laden recapitulation, a brief scherzo on an ostinato, an ever-intensifying variation movement, and a vigorous rondo finale. *—Joseph Stevenson*

Recommended:

- ○ **Hindemith: Complete Wind Concertos** / Albert (cond.), Mehlhart, RSO Stuttgart / CPO 999142
- ○ **Martin Fröst plays concertos dedicated to Benny Goodman** / Shui (cond.), Fröst, Malmö SO / 1997 / Bis 893

Horn Concerto (1949)

Hindemith wrote his *Horn Concerto* for one of the greatest players in the instrument's history, the English virtuoso Dennis Brain. The composer, on vacation from his academic post at Yale, completed the work in Switzerland (which eventually became his permanent residence). The composer conducted the premiere, featuring Brain and the Southwest German Orchestra, in Baden-Baden on June 8, 1950.

Though the work is cast in three movements, as is typical of a concerto, its plan is decidely unconventional. The first two movements, both relatively short, are in fast tempi: the first is a pugnacious sonatina which restricts thematic development to a bare minimum, the second a scherzo. The finale is in three sections in a slow-fast-slow scheme. The arrangement of the movements suggests that the first two are intended to demonstrate the horn's agility, the last its most soulful qualities. Another unusual feature of the work is the inclusion in the score of a poem composed by Hindemith himself, over a section of the solo part marked "Declamation." The performer is directed to play this passage in recitative style, wordlessly "reciting" the poem—which is about the tone quality of the horn—by his or her playing. *—Joseph Stevenson*

Recommended:

- ○ **Strauss & Hindemith: Music for Horn & Orchestra** / Hindemith (cond.), Brain, Philharmonia / 2002 / EMI 67783

Der Schwanendreher, concerto for viola & small orchestra (1935; revised 1936)

Hindemith, whose interest in the viola was intense and lifelong, wrote a number of concertante works for the instrument which he often publicly performed himself and which greatly enriched the instrument's rather slender repertoire. Among the best known of these is *Der Schwanendreher*, a concerto which takes a number of folk songs as its point of departure.

The work was written on the heels of the composer's monumental, medieval-themed opera *Mathis der Maler* (1934–35); it is thought, in fact, that Hindemith's research for that work led him to the songs employed in *Der Schwanendreher*. The title of the work is shared with that of the tune that forms the basis of the finale; the "Schwanendreher" in question is a "swan-turner," a cook's assistant who turns the spit upon which a swan is roasted. (In his nearly contemporaneous *Carmina Burana* (1935–36), Carl Orff likewise bases an entire movement on the theme of roasting swans—in this case, from the animal's point of view!)

Hindemith—no slouch as a violist—casts the soloist in the role of "an itinerant fiddler who... presents everything he has brought with him from afar: songs grave and gay, and finally a dance-tune." The composer further indicates that the player might well embellish and alter the tunes according to his own fancy, which similarly describes the way he incorporates the original folk tunes into the musical fabric. *Der Schwanendreher*, an amiable and vigorous work, is a product of Hindemith's mature neo-Classical style, marked by clearer tonality and less dense polyphony than that in his music of the previous decade. *—Joseph Stevenson*

Recommended:

- ○ **Hindemith: Viola Concertos** / Albert (cond.), Dean, Brisbane Queensland SO / 1999 / CPO 999492
- ○ **Hindemith: Concertos** / Rozhdestvensky (cond.), Boguslavsky, USSR RSO / 1995 / RCA 24219

Trauermusik for viola or violin or cello & string orchestra (1936)

At one point in his career, concerned as always about the artist's proper role in society, Hindemith espoused what he called Gebrauchsmusik or "useful music," meaning music written for a practical purpose. The composition of this work is an impressive example. He was already in the London studios of the BBC one afternoon preparing a concert when word was received of the death of King George V. In the few hours remaining before the concert he wrote a substitute piece, this *Funeral Music*, with time left to have the parts copied for string orchestra, learn to play the solo viola part, and rehearse the whole thing. The wonderful thing is that the result of this very rushed labor is a fine and touching, austere and unusually serene piece of music. *—Joseph Stevenson*

Recommended:

- ○ **Hindemith: Chamber Music & Concert Music** / Albert (cond.), Dean, Brisbane Queensland SO / 1999 / CPO 999492
- ○ **Lachrymae** / Davies (cond.), Kashkashian, Stuttgart CO / 1993 / ECM 439611
- ○ **Brahms, Hindemith, Dvořák** / Strehle, Wisniewska (piano) / 1996 / Nimbus 5473

BALLET

Nobilissima visione, dance legend (1938)

According to the great dancer/choreographer Léonide Massine, the idea for *Nobilissima Visione* (Exalted Vision) was Hindemith's. As with the opera *Mathis der Maler*, the composer was inspired by art, in this case frescoes by Giotto in Santa Croce, Florence, depicting the life of St. Francis.

Nobilissima Visione is in one act with five scenes. The score's 11 numbers are closely linked by key relationships and recurrence of themes and motives. Throughout the ballet, Hindemith utilized the quite tonal melody *Ce fut en Mai*, by thirteenth century trouvère Moniot d'Arras, who had been associated with the young Francis. "Einleitung und Lied des Troubadours" (Introduction and Troubadour's [sic] Song) not only gives *Ce fut en Mai* in chorale prelude fashion, but also includes passages encountered later in the ballet, particularly in the next number, "Tuchkäufer und Bettler" (Cloth Buyers and Beggar), and the later "Festmusik." In the midst of the quick, increasingly loud, and dissonant music of "Schluss des Festes" (End of the Feast) returns that of the "Pastoral Koda" from the quiet, aria-like "Erscheinung der Drei Frauen" (Appearance of the Three Women). From beginning to end of the ballet, triple meter predominates.

A fitting example of Hindemith's neo-Classicism, *Nobilissima Visione* includes music reminiscent of the eighteenth century. "Erscheinung der drei Frauen" and "Meditation" are ornamented arias. Dance suite movements and general instrumental music are found throughout the score, notably in "Marsch" (March), "Pastoral Koda," "Geigenspiel" (Violin Playing), "Kärgliches Hochzeit" (Indigent Wedding), and "Incipient laudes creaturarum" (Begin Praising Him, All Created Things—St. Francis' "Canticle of the Sun"), a passacaglia. A nod to pseudo-antiquity marks the languid, quiet, triple-meter dance second theme of "Tuchkäufer und Bettler," with its emphasis on the second beat reminiscent of Satie's famous *Gymnopédies*. It is definitely a work from the earlier twentieth century, as the quartal/quintal harmony and dissonance affirm. A somewhat reduced pit orchestra didn't hinder the composer's characteristic orchestrations.

Despite a certain lack of box-office appeal and Massine's assertion that it was "... not really a ballet at all... [but] a dramatic and choreographic interpretation of the life of St. Francis...," *Nobilissima Visione* stayed in the active repertoire for a few decades after its London premiere on July 21, 1938. On October 14 of that year, it received its United States premiere as *St. Francis* at the Metropolitan Opera House. Prior to that, the composer made an orchestral suite from the score. He also arranged the "Meditation" for violin, viola, or cello solo with accompaniment. Unfortunately, the popularity of the suite has overshadowed the superior, organic, and masterful ballet score. *—Neil Cardew-Fanning*

Recommended:

- ○ **Hindemith: Mathis der Maler Symphony; Nobilissima Visione; Symphonic Metamorphosis** / Decker (cond.), New Zealand SO / 1994 / Naxos 553078

Theme with 4 Variations "The Four Temperaments," for piano & strings (1940)

Paul Hindemith wrote his ballet *The Four Temperaments* for piano and orchestra for choreographer George Balanchine in 1940. As a ballet, the work had to wait six years for its premiere and has since left the stage. As a concert work, however, *The Four Temperaments* premiered the same year it was written and has maintained its place in the concert hall as a type of piano concerto ever since. Based on the medieval notion that each person is dominated by a particular humor or bodily fluid—black bile for the melancholic, blood for the sanguine, phlegm for the phlegmatic, and yellow bile for the choleric—Hindemith's work treats each of these personality types as variations on a theme. Thus, the work is in five movements: "Theme," "Melancholy," "Sanguine," "Phlegmatic," and "Choleric." The theme itself is in three parts: an opening section based on a long-breathed string melody of great lyrical nobility, a faster central section that introduces the virtuoso piano soloist, and a closing section that unites piano and orchestra in a tenderly swaying Siciliano. "Melancholy" opens with a gravely double-dotted rhythm like a Baroque French overture. In "Melancholy's" central section, the strings and piano increase in tempo and tension until bursting into a slow and heavy march based on the Siciliano. "Sanguine" is a complete contrast to "Melancholy": it opens with a joyous waltz, moves into a brilliant central section, and closes with an ardent statement of the Siciliano. The following "Phlegmatic" begins dull and indifferent, becomes casual and nonchalant, and ends with a shruggingly syncopated Siciliano. The closing "Choleric" is hotheaded and zealous, with the piano and orchestra fighting for dominance in the opening section, the orchestra winning through in the central section, but not without the piano casting aspersions on its victory and a concluding Siciliano even more passionate than the opening. *—James Leonard*

Recommended:

- ○ **Hindemith: The 4 Temperaments; Nobilissima Visione** / DePreist (cond.), Rosenberger, Royal PO / 1986 / Delos 1006
- ○ **The 4 Temperaments** / Stigmer (cond.), Gimse, Kristiansand CO / 2000 / Intim Musik 68

CHAMBER MUSIC

Alto Horn (Saxophone) Sonata (1943)

When Hindemith discovered that the alto horn wasn't as common in the United States as he'd thought, he authorized substitution of alto saxophone or standard horn in this sonata. In any case, it's the same work, typical of Hindemith in every respect, except for the inclusion of a poem to be recited by the players. The opening "Ruhig bewegt" movement is a short, wistful prelude, setting a tone of pastoral nostalgia to which Hindemith will later return. Suddenly, a vigorous mini-rondo bursts in, the horn and piano trading off the primary phrases. The music lurches into a contrapuntal, metrically irregular theme; after the instruments seem to stumble into a moment of inertia, the opening theme carries the movement to a more conventional ending. The slow movement, "Sehr langsam," is short, lyrical (based on two contrasting ideas), and toward the end, almost bluesy. The finale, "Lehaft," begins not with music but with the horn player reading a poem by Hindemith, *The Posthorn (Dialogue)*. The text links the sound of the horn to the distant past, evoking "pallid yearning, melancholy longing." The pianist replies to the hornist, in part,

"Your task it is, amid confusion, rush, and noise to grasp the lasting, calm, and meaningful, and finding it anew, to hold and treasure it." The pianist then plays rapid figures possibly evoking "confusion, rush, and noise"; the horn soloist responds with a very lyrical melody, recalling the mood of the opening movement, but now in a more outgoing manner. The piano's "confusion" music intertwines with the horn's song-like material, bringing the sonata to a conclusion that is simultaneously exciting and comforting. *—James Reel*

Recommended:

○ **Hindemith: Complete Brass Works** / Topilow (cond.), Lichtmann, Summit Brass / 1990 / Summit 115

Bassoon Sonata (1938)

In the career of composer Paul Hindemith, 1938 was a reasonably productive year, for he managed to write not only this *Sonata for Bassoon and Piano,* but three other chamber works as well. That creative activity is quite amazing since that same year he uprooted himself and his family and fled the madness of Hitler's Germany, ultimately settling in the United States.

This bassoon sonata, while hardly a popular work, has attracted a fair amount of attention on the concert stage and in the recording studio. Cast in two movements, with the second containing three inner movements, the sonata is short, lasting not quite ten minutes. The opening panel is lively and features a typical Hindemithian theme: It has a quaintly jovial manner as first presented on the bassoon, but takes on a somewhat heroic, more serious character as this brief panel proceeds. The second movement presents a lovely lyrical theme on the bassoon against dreamy accompaniment on the piano. Suddenly, the music changes moods, launching into the next section—the longest in the work—a lively, playful march of great color. The pastoral closing section begins with a relatively lengthy piano solo of serene character. The bassoon finally enters, taking up the piano's theme and this attractive work soon ends in a pensive mood. *—Robert Cummings*

Recommended:

○ **Hindemith: Chamber Music** / Knardahl, Sonstevold / 1983 / Bis 159

Cello Sonata, Op. 11/3 (1919; revised 1921)

Hindemith's *Sonata for cello and piano,* Op. 11/3, is one of five sonatas in Op. 11, composed between 1917 and 1919, the beginning of his career-long fascination with the form. It is often considered the work of an "angry young man" because of its sharpness, spikiness, and general savagery. He was, naturally, appalled by what had happened to Europe during World War I, and, as with many composers at the time, his music became a means of expressing his distaste for a tradition that seemed linked to the causes of that war. The cello sonata is as much anti-Romantic as it is neo-Classical. It features two movements, each itself in two sections, full of contrasts between two themes most of the time, ranging in dynamics from *ppp* to *fff,* and featuring the uncomfortable minor second dissonance. The first movement—"Mässig schnell, Viertel-Lebhaft"—opens with that minor dissonance and a struggle between rhythm and meter, immediately setting the tone for what follows: a toccata-like frenzy. The second part of the first movement, the longer of the two, begins with an obsessive theme and another one made up of three long-short figures. The two are woven together and follow on each other, continuing the struggle between the keys of E major and F minor from the first section. The Langsam opening of the second movement provides the only glimpses of lyricism in the sonata. Again, two contrasting themes are used: one lyric and the other more march-like. The finale, Sehr lebhaft, is built from a piece of the second theme of the Langsam and seems to satirize both the Viennese waltz and the Scherzo of Beethoven's *Symphony No. 5.* A 1921 revision of the sonata tempers some of its wildness. *—Patsy Morita*

Recommended:

○ **Hindemith: Cello Music** / Markiz (cond.), Thedeen, Pontinen, Amsterdam New Sinfonietta / 1996 / Bis 816

Clarinet Sonata in B flat major (1939)

Keenly interested in the physical possibilities and idiomatic characteristics of each instrument, Hindemith made a point of exploring each on its own terms, and during the last years of the 1930s alone, he wrote sonatas for no less than a dozen instruments. He confided to a friend that his various sonatas were part of his preparation for a "great coup" that he hoped to mount the following year (but, in fact, would not realize until 1957): his monumental symphony *Die Harmonie der Welt.* Despite their seemingly pragmatic conception, the instrumental sonatas certainly merit consideration outside of the shadow of Hindemith's larger projects.

The work under consideration here, the *Sonata for Clarinet and Piano,* is no exception. The piece exemplifies the coalescence and synthesis of Hindemith's various influences and innovations, conveying a neo-Classical concern for formal balance and a rigorous approach to counterpoint, as well as a less severely constructionist—and ultimately more expressive—approach to mood and melody. The work is cast in four movements, alternating slow or moderate tempos and/or restrained energy with more lively material. The first movement, marked Allegro Moderato, assumes a leisurely pace, with the clarinet and piano trading phrases of a plaintive, long-breathed melody. The harmonic language is adventurous but always lucid, the soft contour of the melody rounding the edges of unexpected tonal trajectories and eventually circling in quietly on the movement's final harmonic center. The second movement, though thematically connected to the first, is much more nimble and the individual parts more assertive. Here the clarinet's lines are more angular and the piano's responses and accompaniment are more insistent; louder dynamics likewise serve to foil the relative repose of the first movement as well. The third movement, in turn, likewise provides a sharp contrast with its "Very Slow" tempo indication, its more dramatic and gestural lines, and its emphasis on minor modalities. The featured instrument enhances the sense of mystery and melancholy in its languorous quasi-cadenza passages, as does the constant interplay of quarter notes and triplets in both clarinet line and piano accompaniment. Hindemith includes for his final movement a "Little Rondo," in which a quirky march figure alternates with various episodes of thematic elaboration. Neither instrument rests for any length of time, but the clarinet frequently assumes an accompanimental role to the piano's more extroverted moments. The movement, and the work, end with a nonchalant reiteration of the main theme, echoed by the wryly nonplused piano. *—Jeremy Grimshaw*

Recommended:

○ **Schumann: Soireestücke; 3 Romanzen; Hindemith: Clarinet Sonata, etc.** / Leister, Bognar (piano) / Camerata 320

Double Bass Sonata (1949)

Paul Hindemith's numerous sonatas for solo instrument and piano manifest a keen interest in the special idiomatic qualities of each individual instrument. Indeed, although his output in this genre strongly favored his own "native" instruments—he was a skilled violinist and violist, and wrote a number of sonatas for both—he made a point of writing sonatas for as many instruments as possible. During an initial spurt from 1918–22, and another in the late 1930s, Hindemith's collection of sonatas for piano and solo instrument (or in a few cases, instrument alone) came to include virtually every instrument in the string, woodwind, and brass sections of the orchestra. Some instruments proved more difficult, however, and did not receive their sonata treatment from Hindemith until some time later. In composing the work under consideration here, his *Sonata for Double Bass and Piano,* Hindemith faced the challenge of writing a duo sonata in which the traditional roles of featured soloist and supporting accompaniment instrument were inverted with respect to instrumental ranges. Undertaken in 1949, the bass sonata nearly rounded out the series, which still awaited the composition in 1955 of the *Sonata for Tuba and Piano* (a project which, presumably, was late in coming, for similar musical reasons). Hindemith uses a number of techniques to spotlight the role of the normally subservient double bass, and to lend the bass/piano pair more agility. Perhaps, most notably, (to the bassist, anyhow), the composer indicates a scordatura tuning that pitches each of the four bass strings a whole step higher than normal (A-E-B-F sharp, instead of G-D-A-E); the added string tension gives the instrument a more brilliant timbre and serves to counteract somewhat the thick strings' relative sluggishness. The first movement of the work, a light and lively Allegretto, demonstrates other special techniques. The bass melody often reaches into the middle and upper ranges of the instrument, while the piano part is often placed in a somewhat higher register, and confined to a smaller range. They further avoid stepping on each others' toes by frequently engaging in hocket-like figurations; a busy, dissonant contrapuntal passage in the piano might be riddled with intermittent pauses and gaps, which the bass fills in with pizzicato punctuation. In the middle of the movement a brief melody in bass harmonics appears, its strained high tones in contrast with the sparse, and suddenly low, piano accompaniment. The second movement, a frivolous Scherzo, alternates playful bass melodies and quiet, offbeat chords with sudden furious chromatic figurations in the piano. Quite clearly, the last movement is the most substantial and the most varied: its main body, as well as the extended Molto Adagio, obsesses over a single pensive and pervasive motif consisting of an one-step upward motion followed by a brusque descent. The piano also receives an extended solo, in which spurts of angular melody surge and then expend themselves. A short recitative section marks the height of the movement's dramatic tension, leading to a final and lighthearted coda. *—Jeremy Grimshaw*

Recommended:

○ **Eugene Levinson, Principal Double Bass, New York PO** / Levinson, New York PO Principal Players / 1996 / Cala 0507

English Horn Sonata (1941)

Hindemith wrote a variety of sonatas for various combinations of instruments that paired the piano in individual efforts with the clarinet, cello, double bass, flute, oboe, saxophone, trombone, trumpet, tuba, and horn. He also wrote several sonatas each for violin and piano and for viola and piano. He fully understood the subtleties of these instruments since he could play most of them quite proficiently. This *Sonata for piano and horn,* from 1939, came during a darkly unsettling period for the composer, just after he had fled the madness of Hitler's Germany for Switzerland, from where he would depart for the United States in 1940. Yet the music of this sonata does not sound pessimistic. It opens in a moderately lively tempo (Mäßig bewegt) with one of those instantly recognizable Hindemithian heroic melodies on the horn, with the piano providing bouncy rhythmic accompaniment. The alternate theme is reflective in its lyrical warmth, and the muscular development section exhibits tension in its subtle thematic workings. The slow middle movement (Ruhig bewegt), with a noble but slightly melancholy main theme, is serene and beautiful, and dominated by the piano. The lively finale (Lebhaft) features a vigorous main theme that can suddenly turn playful. The slow-paced middle section (Langsam) is gloomy and somewhat dreamy, but the work's close is triumphant, even defiant. *—Robert Cummings*

Recommended:

○ **Thomas Indermühle Plays Britten, Haas, Hindemith** / Indermühle, Randalu (piano) / Camerata 30449

Flute Sonata (1936)

While the music of certain twentieth century composers often reflected personal or political problems—Shostakovich comes prominently to mind here—Hindemith's compositions rarely reflected any of the troubles that often plagued his life. That said, this piece, written in Nazi Germany in 1936, two years before Hindemith fled to Switzerland, is a mostly upbeat work, but its darker undercurrents and bouts of melancholy might well reflect the turmoil in the composer's homeland. "If in the next days you receive flute sonatas instead of book chapters, do have pity on the poor tortured musician, who sometimes has more than he can take of theorizing." So wrote Gertrude Hindemith to her husband's publisher on December 4, 1936—a scheduled day off from Hindemith's heavy work on a theoretical treatise. In the middle of the night, Hindemith suddenly got up and started writing a flute sonata. He finished the first movement while Gertrude was still composing her letter, finished the second on December 7, and finished the last on December 16. The moderately paced opening movement begins with a stately theme on flute that will, in the course of its deft development, spawn delightful variants and motifs. The music throughout the movement is slightly ambivalent, ultimately sounding bright but tinged with a sense of conflict, especially from the piano's often unsettled harmonies. The slow middle movement conveys a lonely sense, the piano again imparting a darker character than the dreamy flute. The lively finale opens with a joyous playful theme on flute over driving piano rhythms. The music intensifies midway through, then comes to a halt, seeming on the verge of collapse. The lively manner from the opening revives, its playfulness and cheer returning, and the work ends happily. *—Robert Cummings*

Recommended:

○ **Dufour Performs Martinü, Prokofiev & Hindemith** / Dufour, Madzar / HM 911770

Harp Sonata (1939)

Hindemith wrote his *Harp Sonata* in Switzerland in 1939, while en route to the United States, for the Italian harpist Clelia Gatti-Aldrovandi. In its three short movements, Hindemith—who had a natural understanding of nearly every musical instrument—masterfully encapsulated the spirit of the harp: its contrapuntal and harmonic independence, and its heritage as one of the oldest musical instruments.

The first movement, marked "Moderately fast," opens with an imperious chordal gesture that is both declamatory in its rhetoric and archaic in its modal harmony. The full range of the instrument is called upon in this resourcefully written sonata form movement, the character of which is noble and detached. The subsequent scherzo, marked "Lively," exploits the harp's capacity for quick filigree and lightness of texture. In the last movement, "Lied," Hindemith uses a nostalgic poem by the nineteenth century poet Hölty to create a literal "song" without words. The poem relates a dying harpist's last wish: that, after his death, his harp be placed behind the church altar as a memorial, where "at sunset" ("im Abendrot") it will sound, seemingly of its own accord—much like the Aeolian harps of antiquity. In this finale, the noble archaism of the music takes on a sad and bittersweet quality that is all the more satisfying for its ingenuousness. *—Mark Satola*

Recommended:

○ **Harfe Harp** / Steckermeier-Thiele / 1998 / Eroica 3043

Horn Sonata (1939)

Having resolved to write at least one sonata for every orchestral instrument, either solo or with piano, Hindemith began his brass series in 1939 with sonatas for horn and for trumpet. (The project would carry him well into the 1950s.) The *Sonata for Horn and Piano* is fully typical of Hindemith's work in this genre: classically balanced, with a counterpoint-based equality between the two instruments. Alone among the concise brass sonatas, though, this one lasts a bit more than a quarter-hour. The first movement, "Mässig bewegt," opens with a broad, confident horn theme over a percolating piano accompaniment. The second theme, equally spacious, is more reflective. A mysterious, step-like passage leads to an efficient development of all this material, the movement concluding with a heroic statement of the opening melody, now emphasizing its very faint Hungarian twist at the end.

The second movement, marked "Ruhig bewegt," features slow, expansive horn melodies, their romantic potential undermined by the piano's alternation between busy accompaniment and firm tread, and by the horn's sometimes wide intervallic leaps. Once a curt, recurring sputter of a motif is established, the concluding movement, "Lebhaft," again plays broad horn themes against urgent keyboard work; at times, the horn draws the piano into more introspective interludes and near the end, the piano enlists the horn in a little dance, but for the most part each instrument maintains its initial character. *—James Reel*

Recommended:

○ **Glenn Gould Edition: Hindemith: Sonatas for Brass & Piano** / Jones, Gould / 1992 / Sony 52671

○ **David Pyatt Recital** / Jones, Pyatt / 1998 / Erato 21632

Kammermusik Nos.1–7 (1922–1927)

Hindemith's series of seven works titled *Kammermusik*, written between 1922 and 1927, represent some of the composer's earliest masterworks. *Kammermusik No. 1* is designated Op. 26, Nos. 2–5 constitute Op. 36, and Nos. 6 and 7 make up Op. 46. These are exciting and iconoclastic works which sparked some controversy when they first appeared in the 1920s. Indeed, *Kammermusik No. 1* sparked a riot at its performance in Munich in 1923; booing, whistling, and chair throwing culminated in Hindemith himself taking the stage and pounding on the drums while blowing a slide whistle. The dilemma for the Munich audience was also Hindemith's: was he a young radical or a traditionalist? Was his music all style and technique, or was it music of feeling? The composer would not reconcile these disparate elements of his work until the 1930s.

Kammermusik No. 1 is a rigorous and challenging work for small orchestra, and contains elements of jazz. *Kammermusik No. 2* is a piano concerto, written with the pianist Emma Lubbecke-Job in mind. Hindemith was grateful for Lubbecke-Job's early championing of his music, insisting that she was one of only a few pianists who could play his music properly, without, in his words, "the wretched way of rubato playing and expression" that typified much early-twentieth century piano playing. Kammermusik Nos. 3–6 are concerti for violin, cello, viola, and viola d'amore, respectively. That Hindemith would write so many concerti for string instruments is not surprising, as he was an accomplished violinist and violist himself, and later took up what he called the "sport" of playing the viola d'amore. The last work in the Kammermusik series is a concerto for organ.

These seven works provide an apt summary of Hindemith's early compositional esthetic. They contain almost none of the post-Romantic tendencies found in the music of some of Hindemith's contemporaries (e.g. that of Schoenberg), but instead reflect both Hindemith's technical skill as a composer and his headlong plunge into the world of German modernist music in the 1920s. *—Alexander Carpenter*

Recommended:

○ **Hindemith: Kammermusik 1–7** / Concerto Amsterdam, Bylsma, Schroder, Klerk, Doktor / 1998 / Teldec 21773

Kleine Kammermusik, for wind quintet, Op. 24/2 (1922)

Hindemith at his most deadpan is to be found in this small, five-movement wind quintet, which was published along with the *Kammermusik No. 1*, Op. 24, No. 1, though it shares neither instrumentation nor character with its raucous, jazz-influenced companion. The sense of humor so characteristic of Hindemith in the 1920s here shares the spotlight with notably resourceful and virtuosic writing for the small ensemble.

The first movement is a march, lighthearted and civilian in nature, with much cross-rhythmic play among the instruments and a dissonant polytonality that is more comic and friendly than challenging. Hindemith had the unique ability to master in a few hours' time nearly any instrument he picked up, and his innate understanding of the woodwinds results in music so natural to the instruments that it seems almost to compose itself as it's played. The march is closed by an amiable shrug from the clarinet.

A simple waltz, wryly subverted by polytonal flights of fancy and Milhaud-like "wrong" notes, pokes fun at the sentimental fare then popular in Europe. It's followed by a fairly serious slow movement, in which a dour theme in thirds, with a prominent "Scotch snap," frames a furtive middle section featuring a quietly ominous chord sequence over which a long-breathed theme arches.

The fourth movement is almost a fragment, less than a minute in length, in which dissonant, scolding chords are separated by mini-cadenzas for each of the instruments. The finale is a swinging, swaggering march in which open fifths in the lower instruments are answered by a broad arch of theme in major and minor thirds. The demands on the ensemble are greatest here, but the music, when well-played, is exhilarating. *—Mark Satola*

Recommended:

○ **Hindemith: Horn Chamber Music** / Dullaert, Bon, Netherlands Woodwind Quintet, Pavilion Quartet / 1993 / CPO 999229

Overture To "Fliegenden Holländer," parody for string quartet (ca. 1925)

It would be unfortunate indeed to encounter Paul Hindemith's *Overture to "Fliegenden Holländer"* (Flying Dutchman) without the fair warning provided by the full title of the piece: "Overture to 'Flying Dutchman' as Played At Sight By a Second-Rate Concert Orchestra at the Village Well at 7 o'clock in the Morning." Despite the sometimes stodgy character that might be read into Hindemith's immaculately crafted and technically demanding scores, anecdotes from his acquaintances suggest he could be quite a musical cut-up when the fancy struck him. For example, his friends delighted in his "sea-lion" renditions of Chopin and Beethoven, played by slapping at the piano keyboard with his hands as if they were flippers. Likewise, Hindemith is known to have occasionally taken a break from writing his characteristically angular, modernistically virtuosic compositions by indulging in musical parody. Sadly, many of these efforts survive only in second-hand accounts, such as the now-lost *Music for Six Instruments and Page Turner*. Among those that survive, however, is Hindemith's send-up for string quartet of Wagner's classic overture, which Giselher Schubert insists in the preface to the score "is *not* a parody of Wagner's music, but rather exactly the kind of music-making described in the title." The burps and squeaks that so rudely interrupt the surface of Wagner's triumphant original are of the kind Hindemith imagines might occur under the circumstances described in the title. Intonation throughout the piece, which lasts just over seven minutes, is decidedly off, with special care taken to render the high strings' urgent repeated notes in especially strident tones. Bold leaps of octaves, fifths, or fourths, which abound in Wagner's original, are bent and stretched into overanxious ninths, apathetic sevenths, and clumsy tritones. The caricature is enhanced by the employment of exaggerated textures and articulations: notes of particular melodic emphasis are set off with maudlin portamenti, brass fanfares are intoned with loud but loose homophony, and delicate pizzicato figures skitter out of sync with each other like drunken ballerinas. In the end, the ensemble finally gives up on Wagner altogether, arriving pell-mell on a rousing and outrageous waltz. The Dutchman makes a final, haggard appearance near the end, his themes rendered in parallel lines a semitone apart and accompanied by the most disoriented meandering in the lower strings, before the piece comes to its final (but hardly conclusive) chord. *—Jeremy Grimshaw*

Recommended:

- ○ **Hindemith: Minimax; String Quartets** / Kocian SQ / 1995 / Praga 250

Quartet, for clarinet, violin, cello & piano (1938)

Hindemith wrote this quartet in the middle of a period (1933–45) that, in terms of chamber music, was otherwise exclusively devoted to sonatas for only one or two instruments. It would be tempting to link Hindemith's sonata preoccupation with his ability in this quartet to make all the instruments full partners, often operating contrapuntally, but this was actually Hindemith's standard operating procedure. This is prime and quite typical Hindemith, a work that remains underplayed solely because of its unusual instrumentation. (Hindemith also arranged it for two pianos, but only for study purposes.)

The first of the three movements, "Mässig bewegt," builds on three primarily lyrical themes and falls into three sections, in the manner of the classical exposition-development-recapitulation format. The difference here is that what should be the development section is just a polyphonic riff on the second theme. The slow movement, "Sehr langsam," is in a free ternary form culminating in a variation of the opening theme. It begins with a clarinet melody pouring slowly and thickly over a rocking 12/8 meter. Sterner stuff arrives with the second section and its nervously nattering piano chords, all building to a fortissimo climax before the varied but still austere return of the first theme. The third movement piles up three separate episodes and erects a large coda at the summit. The initial section, "Mässig bewegt," is lyrical and in moderate tempo. The second, "Lebhaft," unleashes Hindemith's contrapuntal skills in a fast 9/8 meter. Things relax in the "Ruhig bewegt" section, but after a pause, the piano launches into a veritable toccata that initiates the wild coda, marked "Sehr lebhaft." *—James Reel*

Recommended:

- ○ **Hindemith: Heckelphone Trio; Clarinet Quartet; Sonata for 4 Horns** / Villa Musica Ens. / MDG 3040537

Sonata for solo cello, Op. 25/3 (1922)

One finds in Paul Hindemith's *Sonata for Solo Cello* (Opus 25, No. 3) two particular qualities: the kind of brash gestures that characterized the composer's early works, and the idiomatic surety that each of his individual instrumental studies exemplifies. Having mastered the various instrumental idioms early on, works such as the *Sonata for Solo Cello* differ from his later undertakings in terms of style much more than in maturity.

Composed in the same year as his famous *Suite 1922* (for piano), the *Sonata for Solo Cello* is one of three sonatas for solo string instruments included in his Opus 25. (The others include a sonata for solo viola, another for viola and piano, and a *"Little Sonata" for Viola d'Amore and Piano*.) The piece was apparently quick work: four of the five movements were said to have been composed in a single day. Likewise, the practical spirit of *Gebrauchsmusik* (translated roughly, "music for use") inhabits the music in the way the lines seem to explore the contours of the instrument's capabilities. Despite his creative expediency, Hindemith's careful consideration of the instrument's "physiology" allows him to establish a continuum between execution and expression, and a stronger connection between the performer's hands and his/her head.

The five rather short movements are arranged in a somewhat symmetrical fashion: two relatively longer movements bookend the composition, while a pair of tiny fast movements surround the long, slow movement at the work's center. From the outset, the opening movement carves sharp angles, highlighted by strained double stops and extreme registral shifts. The player seems to spend much time stirring restlessly on the lower strings, despite more melodic entreaties from the upper range. The second movement, though still shadowy, is lighter on its feet, with a coy tune embellished by occasional turns and trills. The long central movement indulges in broad strokes of languorous melody, seemingly torn between launching into heartwrenching lament and succumbing to banal accompanimental figures. The fourth movement is by far the most lively, but its quick triplets expend their energy in less than a minute; the final movement turns to weightier matters, the player again grinding away at the lower strings much of the time. Here again, dark chordal sawings from the bottom range engage in dialogue with more lyrical lines in the treble area, the two finally reaching an uneasy consensus on a perfunctory pizzicato note. Hindemith thus seems to act out in the music itself his own efforts to breach the divide between the physical and the emotional. *—Jeremy Grimshaw*

Recommended:

- ○ **Prokofiev: Cello Sonata; Hindemith: Cello Sonata Op25/3, Cassado: Suite** / Starker, Planes / INA Memoire Vive 262012
- ○ **The Road To Cello Playing** / Starker, Parnassus / 1997 / Parnassus 97008

Sonata for solo viola, Op. 25/1 (1922)

"Raging tempo. Wild. Beauty of tone is of secondary importance." The notoriety of this oft-cited performance note, attached to the fourth movement of Hindemith's Sonata for solo viola, Op. 25/1 (1922), unfairly overshadows the real musical value of work as a whole. Far removed from the angry, nihilistic outlook suggested by the indication above, the sonata is a vigorous, virtuosic tour de force whose technical and expressive challenges are amply repaid in the stunning sonic result. Hindemith, a violist of considerable abilities, wrote the sonata largely for his own use; it remained in his repertoire for the duration of his performing career, and he made a recording of it in 1934.

The first movement presents two main ideas that form the basis of the entire work: a stern theme in dissonant double stops, in which the interval of an augmented fourth is prominent, and a sinuous phrase that skates lightly up and down a chromatic scale. The second movement, which follows the first without pause, rhapsodizes at length on these ideas; intense chromatic harmonies add considerable tension and stretch the musical language to the limits of tonality.

The third movement, marked "Very slowly," is no less demanding on performer and listener, but its exploration of the themes is somewhat more relaxed; consonant intervals lighten the mood of the viola's long, yearning phrases. This relative calm heightens the wildness of the tiny whirlwind that follows, in which frantic double-stopped chords are launched from a furiously repeated pedal point. The finale is, unexpectedly, an elegy of some emotional weight; the elements of the preceding movements coalesce here into a darkly tinted, powerful lament. *—Mark Satola*

Recommended:

- ○ **Igor Oistrakh & Rudolf Barshay** / Barshai / 1995 / Multisonic 310355
- ○ **Hindemith: Sonatas for viola & piano or viola solo** / Kashkashian / 1988 / ECM 833309

Sonata for solo violin, Op. 31/2 (1924)

Though composed in 1924, by which point Paul Hindemith had established himself as one of the most brilliant and brash composers of Weimar, the *Sonata for Violin Solo No. 2*, Op. 31, contains not only the sort of blocky, angular writing for which Hindemith is well known, but also demonstrates the composer's lyrical and expressive side. Like the *Sonata No. 1* from the same opus, this work was written for a violinist in the Amar Quartet, the group whose performance of Hindemith's *String Quartet No. 2* at the 1921 Donaueschingen Festival had helped launch his career. In the first movement melodic materials unfold in such a fluid fashion as to draw attention from the piece's symmetry and repetition. A recurring motive begins in the upper range and leisurely descends through a series of steps and small leaps before rising again in a kind of slow, tidal fashion. For a brief moment in the middle, this tranquil atmosphere is interrupted by rhythmic double stops, but the tidal motion then resumes, inflected with chromatic alterations and mysterious whole-tone scales. The second movement proceeds at a careful pace as well, but frequent dissonant double stops, a more angular melodic contour, and ventures into the extremities of the instrument's upper range lend it a more uneasy and dramatic mood. The third movement provides a stark contrast to the restrained pace and texture of the first two. It is entirely rendered in pizzicato, with cleverly stratified layers of melody and accompaniment and carefully crafted counterpoint that testify to Hindemith's familiarity with the physical possibilities of the instrument itself (he was an expert violinist and violist himself). His broad harmonic palette is apparent as well, the march-like interplay between "bass" notes and offbeat chords lending order to intractable chordal trajectories that skirt the edge of tonality. The fourth and final movement is constructed as a series of variations on a theme by Mozart. The tune, "Komm, lieber Mai" ("Come, beloved May"), seems to suggest that the work was inspired in part by the spring day it was conceived; indeed, at the top of Hindemith's original manuscript from 1924 appears a note in the composer's hand: "What lovely weather outside..." Despite the metrically and melodically square presentation of Mozart's theme, the movement turns out to be the most substantial of the entire sonata. Immediately with the first variation, Hindemith takes considerable license in recasting the original melody, the presence of which, at times, can hardly be detected. Here, Hindemith grants the performer opportunities for virtuosic display, with far-flung figurations and fingerboard acrobatics; at the end of the piece these are suddenly reined in, however, with an unexpected deceleration and the appearance of a serene and unambiguous cadence. *—Jeremy Grimshaw*

Recommended:

○ **Solo** / Gringolts / 1999 / Bis 1051

Sonata for 4 horns (1952)

With this work, Hindemith pays tribute to the Baroque era with music that would have been unplayable on the valveless horns of that period. Harmonically, the work is fully in line with Hindemith's mid-twentieth century techniques; this is not a pastiche or parody. The sonata is Baroque in spirit, though, and even reaches back beyond the time of Bach to harvest a Renaissance tune for the final movement. The sonata begins with a very slow, very short fugato, the intensity and dynamics building as the texture thickens. The second movement, "Lebhaft," is a virtuosic, chugging allegro that develops a little swing, enters a declamatory phase, and resumes the chugging material before resolving into a stately chorale. The finale begins with a chorale-like setting of *Ich Schell Mein Horn ins Jammerthal* ("I sound my horn in this vale of tears"), a tune published around 1520 by Arnt von Aich. The horns soon rise from the vale of tears for a series of variations: an energetic treatment; a long, mournful passage; a dancing version; and ultimately, another very brief chorale. *—James Reel*

Recommended:

○ **Hindemith: Complete Brass Works** / Summit Brass / 1990 / Summit 115

String Quartet No. 5, Op. 32 (1923)

The Amar Quartet was founded in 1920 (with Hindemith as violist) for the express purpose of premiering the composer's *String Quartet No. 2 in C major,* Op. 16, but continued on through the decade as one of the finest exponents of the modern string quartet literature. Hindemith's subsequent two quartets were composed for the Amar Quartet. The *String Quartet No. 4,* Op. 32, was written in 1923.

Fugal elements are the most prominent feature of this virtuosic score. After a four-note gesture that functions as a motivic cell for the entire work, the first movement launches into a fugue of ferocious energy, polytonal and extremely dissonant, with virtuosic writing and highly resourceful disposition of the four instruments. The middle section arrives abruptly: a rhapsodic interlude with textures of great beauty and complex harmony, in which fugal elements continue to drive the rhetoric. The opening section returns via an ingenious conception wherein the violins skirl contrapuntally in close intervals and high range as viola and cello attempt through repeated shoutings of the four-note cell to end the interlude. The lower strings finally succeed in wresting control of the music, and the movement ends with a strict fugue on the main theme.

Rhythmic superimpositions dominate the second movement, a sustained melodic meditation on the implications of the opening gesture. Even here are elements of fugal treatment, as the violins and viola enter one after another in a leisurely 12/8 signature, underpinned by walking-bass pizzicati in 4/4 from the cello. Hindemith employs what would become a favorite technique for the third movement, wherein a lengthy slow movement is followed by a small, humorous one, in this case a cheeky "Kleiner Marsch" ("Little March"). The march starts off quietly, as if heard from a distance, and builds to a fine, hysterical climax before it quickly disappears, pianissimo.

The finale is one of Hindemith's most impressive structures up to this time, a passacaglia with 27 variations on a dark, inward-turning theme sounded first by muted cello. The music begins in an air of desolation, with vague echoes of the march just completed, as if Hindemith were evoking the emptiness left in the wake of miltaristic pursuits. The variations quickly become more elaborate, demonstrating a remarkably wide range of mood and expression for so young a composer. The coda is yet another turn of the screw: a fast fugato (marked, in fact, "as fast as possible") featuring an insistently sounded low C from the viola that drives the climax much in the same way as the infamous fourth movement of the Op. 25 No. 1 solo *Viola Sonata* (1922). The last chord is a final surprise, a D flat major chord half a step up from the expected one in C major. *—Mark Satola*

Recommended:

○ **Hindemith: String Quartets 3 & 5** / Juilliard SQ / 1996 / Wergo 6283

Trombone Sonata (1941)

A tremendously difficult piano part enriches this sonata, a true duo for keyboard and brass instrument, in which the partners sometimes trade off passages of dominance. The opening Allegro moderato maestoso (among Hindemith's brass chamber works, only this and the *Tuba Sonata* bear Italian tempo markings) begins with an aggressive statement by the trombone over frantic piano passagework. The second theme pulls back; the trombone line becomes more playful, or at least less aggressive, accompanied by the piano's constant chatter. A very brief, comparatively mellow development gives way to the aggressive material—but that is suddenly interrupted by the second movement, Allegro grazioso. In the second movement, the piano introduces a tinkling theme it will proceed to vary, each variation preceded by an unchanging trombone refrain. The brief Allegro pesante is subtitled "Lied des Raufbolds" (Song of the Ruffians), and consists of two themes: the first theme is somewhat relaxed, the trombone taking long strides; the second theme is somewhat rushed, busily supported by the piano. Without any significant pause, the concluding Allegro moderato maestoso arrives with ruminating material low in the piano; this material soon becomes a march rhythm for a vigorous trombone theme. The trombone's music remains steadily declamatory over the course of the movement, while the piano part grows increasingly stormy. Both instruments come to terms in a few brief, emphatically final bars. *—James Reel*

Recommended:

○ **Glenn Gould Edition: Hindemith: Sonatas for Brass & Piano** / Smith, Gould / 1992 / Sony 52671

○ **The Virtuoso Trombone** / Lindberg, Pontinen / 1984 / Bis 258

Trumpet Sonata (1939)

Paul Hindemith's wide-ranging instrumental tastes are well known, as is his intimate knowledge of the performative, mechanical, and idiomatic properties and possibilities of each instrument for which he composed. This is certainly demonstrated in his extensive series of duo sonatas. In fact, fully half of Hindemith's compositions dating from 1939 are duo sonatas. Counted among these is the work under consideration here, the *Sonata in B flat for Trumpet and Piano.*

An established favorite in the body of brass repertoire, the *Sonata for Trumpet and Piano* was probably Hindemith's last composition of very productive year, and one of his favorite accomplishments from the period; as he wrote to a friend, "it is maybe the best thing I have succeeded in doing in recent times, and that is quite a good sign, since I do not regard any of my newest productions as of little value." The burst of creativity culminating in the *Trumpet Sonata* came at a fortunate moment, as circumstances—particularly the outbreak of World War II and the composer's subsequent emigration to the United States—would impose such difficult obligations as to prevent any compositional output until the following summer.

The work itself is cast in three movements, although in terms of length the first two together balance roughly with the last alone. One recognizes from the outset of the work's opening a clarity of thematic arrangement. The opening material, reflective of expressive marking in the score, "mit Kraft" (with strength), demarcates a sturdy melody made of more leaps than steps. This is later contrasted with a nimble figuration low in the piano, its underlying triplet feel and quick ornaments lending it a mysterious quality. The culmination of the movement occurs when these two elements fuse together: the trumpet returns to its firm opening melody at the same time as the piano works its triplet figuration into a shimmering frenzy. The moderately paced second movement conveys a vaguely march-like quality, one whose rhythmical nature is enhanced by the polychordal strands occurring separately in the treble and bass. As the movement proceeds, the trumpet and piano spin off into separate textural directions, the trumpet continuing its simple tune while the piano alternates between flowing triplet figures and angular countermelodies. As suggested by the subtitle, "Trauermusik" (music for mourning), the final movement assumes a somber tone, the emphasis on deliberate harmonic colorings and dramatic melodic iterations over intensifying accompanimental figures. The texture shifts between the overwhelming and the sparse, highlighting, on the one hand, pungent dissonances and bold lines, and on the other, pensive melodies and chordal colorings. The movement ends with a fitting musical allusion: a borrowed line from the chorale, "All Menschen müssen sterben" (All men must die). *—Jeremy Grimshaw*

Recommended:

○ **Glenn Gould Edition: Hindemith: Sonatas for Brass & Piano** / Johnson, Gould / 1992 / Sony 52671

○ **20th Century Settings for Trumpet** / Plog, Davis / Crystal 663

Tuba Sonata (1955)

Intentional metric confusion and wayward chromatic themes mark the last of Hindemith's sonatas for brass and piano. The first movement, Allegro pesante, has the piano tinkling duple figures around the tuba's heavy triple meter groans in the outer sections; the middle section lets the tuba sing more coherently in tandem with the piano. The Allegro assai, a tiny scherzo, is even more of a rhythmic free-for-all, the tuba lumbering after the scurrying piano. Most substantial is the final movement, a set of variations on an initially ill-defined theme. Just as the music begins to come together, the piano takes control with a skittish solo, followed by a measured tuba cadenza. At length, the duo variations resume, the tuba playing the melody with the piano engaging in soft, dizzying acrobatics high in the treble. This short sonata's overall effect is whimsical, another example of how even the most accomplished composers rarely take the tuba seriously. *—James Reel*

Recommended:

- ○ **Glenn Gould Edition: Hindemith: Sonatas for Brass & Piano** / Torchinsky, Gould / 1992 / Sony 52671
- ○ **Hindemith: Sonatas for Brass and Piano** / Pilafian, Korevaar / 2002 / Kleos 5118

Viola Sonata in F major, Op. 11/4 (1919)

Hindemith composed his *Viola Sonata* Op. 11, No. 4 in 1919, the same year that as a performer he switched from violin to what Lionel Tertis dubbed the "Cinderella" of instruments. That year also saw the development of what would be viewed as an Expressionistic period for the composer, his music reflecting the social, economic and political turbulence of the disastrous years after the war. The *Viola Sonata*, however, partakes little of these radical tendencies.

In this work, one can plainly discern the influences of such composers as Reger and Debussy, as well as Brahms and, to a lesser degree, Richard Strauss, and there are (obviously) unintentional similarities to the violin sonatas of Charles Ives; but the listener will not find much that sounds like the mature Hindemith. The most unusual aspect of this work is its three-movement structure: Phantasie, Theme with Variations and Finale with Variations. The opening movement is sweetly harmonic in a way that reflects the post-Romantic sensibilities of the pre-war era, with alternating rich chords and intricate figurations from the piano and, in the viola, a marked use of grace notes and trills quite uncharacteristic of the later Hindemith.

A brief cadenza leads to the first small set of variations, in which the melody (based on the opening Phantasie) is to be played "like a folksong." The harmonic language becomes more adventurous, making use of whole-note scales and occasional, mildly dissonant polytonality. Despite the stylistic eclecticism, the writing for both instruments is assured and the course of the musical argument is always of distinct interest. The last variation of the second movement is the thematic basis of the finale, wherein declamatory chords and two-handed octaves from the piano threaten to overwhelm the viola's naturally darker tone, though emphatic writing for the stringed instrument helps it to stand up to the keyboard competition. The coda is bright and exciting. *—Mark Satola*

Recommended:

- ○ **Music For Viola & Piano** / Bashmet, Richter / Olympia 625
- ○ **Hindemith: Sonatas for viola & piano or viola solo** / Kashkashian, Levin / 1988 / ECM 833309

Violin Sonata in E flat major, Op. 11/1 (1918)

Paul Hindemith is known for his keen sense of an instrument's physical nature and for his exploitation of the boundary between the bodily actions involved in making sound and the expressive or emotive elements that those sounds conjure up. This quality is especially apparent in his numerous sonatas for solo instruments or instruments with piano, which deliberately cover the gamut of instruments found in the symphony orchestra. (Indeed, this concern for intimately idiomatic writing seems to have been a more widespread interest: Hindemith's French contemporary, Darius Milhaud, undertook a similar ongoing project during his career). While Hindemith's sonata output would eventually encompass a wide range of instruments, his initial forays into the genre focused on string instruments, especially his own "native" instruments: the violin and the viola (and even a sonata for the antiquated viola d'amore, which Hindemith composed in 1922). Between 1918 and 1924, Hindemith produced three sets of sonatas, Op. 11 (1918–19), Op. 25 (1922), and Op. 31 (1924), all for strings. The first of these works, the *Sonata in E flat for Violin and Piano No. 1,* Op. 11, aptly demonstrates the young Hindemith's craftsman-like approach to composition, his studied attention to musical surfaces, and his skilled use of rhythmic tension as a dramatic device. *No. 1,* Op. 11, is cast in two parts, the first a casually conflicted juxtaposition of lively, rhythmically driving passages that bookend a more relaxed middle section. Most of the movement's musical materials spin out of the opening theme's bold dotted figures and double stops, which are introduced by the piano and taken up in the violin, and the relentless ascending scalar figurations in triplets that emerge as a foil to the opening gesture. Shifts of mood are sudden: the opening-section cadence is pompously in E flat, but is immediately followed by a delicate passage marked with *pppp.* The middle section's relative repose is occasionally disturbed by sudden dynamic outbursts, and the opening material returns in similar fashion, unexpectedly interrupting flowing triplets over a pianissimo pedal point. The harmonic language of the movement is characteristically highly chromatic and tonally ambiguous, the E flat tonic repeatedly emphasized at various points but subject to continual obfuscation. The second movement, according to Hindemith's score markings, is rendered as a "slow, solemn dance." A slow triple meter, occasionally offset with bars of duple, dominates the beginning and end. The piano part lends special weight to the second beat, giving the piece a continual iambic undertow. A slow, dynamic curve peaks at the piece's midpoint, corresponding with increased forward motion, harmonic tension, and metric unpredictability. The violin melody is both lyrical and angular, with a kind of gestural consistency that holds the work together above a sometimes turbulent harmonic flow. As the piece settles in toward its close, both piano and violin gravitate toward the tonic E flat, slowly abandoning their chromatic diversions and ending the piece on a sustained and unadorned unison. *—Jeremy Grimshaw*

Recommended:

- ○ **Hindemith: Violin Sonatas** / Kagan, Richter / Live Classics 161
- ○ **Hindemith: Complete Violin Sonatas** / Wallin, Pontinen / 1995 / Bis 761

KEYBOARD

Ludus tonalis (1942)

The role of the composer in modern society had been a concern for Hindemith even before he explored it dramatically in the operas *Cardillac der Goldschmied* (1926) and *Mathis der Maler* (1938). Hindemith's "Gebrauchsmusik" ("utility music," a term the composer disliked), written to fill a need for high-quality music that could be performed by talented amateurs, was one mainfestation of his concerns; another was his interest in the teaching of music, as evidenced in his efforts toward the organization of music education in Turkey, at the behest of that country's government, in 1937. Hindemith demonstrated his beliefs regarding the politico-ethical responsibilities of the composer when he chose to leave Nazi Germany at the end of the 1930s, eventually settling in the United States as a professor of music at Yale University. In *Ludus tonalis* (1942) for solo piano, Hindemith wove together the varied strands of his professional and artistic life up to that point. Hindemith's subtitle for the work, "Studies in Counterpoint, Tonal Organization and Piano Playing," perhaps carries a deceptive connotation of dryness or academicism. But *Ludus tonalis* ranges well beyond the stated intent of its heading, exploring matters of technique, theory, inspiration, and communication. It is in effect, a veritable catalogue of the composer's mature style, expressed in lively, imaginative, compact vignettes. While a complete performance requires nearly an hour, none of individual parts is longer than four minutes.

Ludus tonalis ("Tonal Games") is ingeniously arranged, its 12 fugues connected by interludes that modulate from the key of one fugue to that of the next. The interludes also serve as a means of thematic modulation; each propagates thematic "cells" that anticipate the material of the succeeding fugue. While the fugues are entirely contrapuntal—often ingeniously so, as when Hindemith creates the effect of three-part polyphony with just two voices—the interludes are homophonic, taking harmony and variety of expression as their major concerns. Framing the whole is a Praeludium and a Postludium; in keeping with the playful suggestion of the title, the latter is a retrograde inversion of the former.

In the Praeludium Hindemith "signs in" with cascading toccata figurations, followed by a meditative arioso and a solemn conclusion of imposing chords over a bell-like descending figure in the bass. This introduction is also a bank of the work's thematic material, which Hindemith explores throughout with great inventiveness and facility. The Interludes, virtually character pieces, are marked by individual, distinctive personalities. The third, a scherzo, is a funny promenade with a prominent, cheeky Scotch snap; the eighth is notable for its fast, chordal, hand-over-hand pianism; the ninth is quiet and introspective, recalling the composer's works of mourning. There is also a noteworthy resourcefulness in the fugues, a restrictive form that poses challenges in creating variety. The second fugue is based on an insistent repeated note from which the theme suddenly launches upward, while the jaunty ninth fugue juxtaposes an assertive grace note figure with a motive of four 32nd notes. *—Mark Satola*

Recommended:

- ○ **Hindemith: Suite "1922"; Ludus tonalis** / McCabe / 1996 / Hyperion 66824

Suite "1922," Op. 26 (1921–1922)

Whereas in the *Kleine Kammermusik* of 1921 Hindemith chuckled good-naturedly about such shopworn forms as marches and waltzes, in the *1922 Suite for solo piano*, his attitude toward the march, shimmy, Boston and ragtime is more plainly bad-tempered. In the years immediately following the First World War, Hindemith had been privately composing pastiches of popular dances of the day, but had held them back from publication, considering them mere "sports." By 1922, however, Hindemith no longer had any qualms about using popular music as a basis for serious musical statements.

In *Suite "1922"*, satire borders on sarcasm; in the opening "Marsch," the pianist is instructed to play it "rather clumsily." The writing for the piano is unusually thick and heavy with chords, especially in the left hand; as such it is almost unrecognizable as coming from one of the master contrapuntalists of the twentieth century. The rhythm is irregular, and the harmonies—built on dissonant, cluster-like explosions and angular aggregations of fourths and fifths—make for a very unmarchable march indeed.

The other dance forms are similarly undermined in the suite. The second movement, "Shimmy," is based on a dance-hall variant of the foxtrot, but makes only occasional allusions to the form, spending most of its time musing on a dour, ambiguously harmonized theme. The central "Nachtstück" anticipates Hindemith's serious and contemplative mature style—harmonically quite dark in this instance;

the central section is ethereal, with haunting motives drifting about in the upper range of the keyboard. It is succeeded by an equally unsettled "Boston"—an old American dance with similarities to the waltz. Repeated attempts to establish the requisite triple-time drift instead into tonally ambiguous (albeit fascinating) meditations. For the "Ragtime" finale, Hindemith instructs the pianist to play wildly but in strict rhythm, and to "[r]egard the piano here as an interesting percussion instrument." Dissonance reaches its maximum intensity in this loud and disturbing movement.

In 1940, Hindemith wrote to Hugo Strecker, "I think it is not necessary to reprint that awful *Suite '1922'*.... The piece is really not an honorable ornament in the music-history of our time, and it depresses an old man rather seriously to see that just the sins of his youth impress the people more than his better creations." That it continued to impress listeners, however, amply demonstrates its intrinsic value. *—Mark Satola*

Recommended:

○ **Gloria Cheng: Piano Dance** / Cheng / 2000 / Telarc 80549

VOCAL

Das Marienleben, song cycle, Op. 27 (1922–1923; revised 1935)

Paul Hindemith's song cycle *Das Marienleben* (The Life of Mary; poetry by Rainer Maria Rilke) is a complicated subject, primarily because there are two distinct versions of the work. Although it is not uncommon for works to undergo revision—indeed, many of the most famous pieces in the classical repertory have existed in more than one version—*Das Marienleben* is a special case, because each of the two versions has been vehemently championed as "authentic."

Hindemith began revising *Das Marienleben* almost immediately following its premiere, the success of which caught the composer quite off guard despite his own awareness of the work's importance ("That was not easy to do," he commented soon after completing it). He quickly set about correcting what he perceived to be technical weaknesses in the score.

In 1936 Hindemith reopened the score and began stylistic revisions, partly in preparation for the orchestration of four of the songs. These revisions also were intended to serve as a practical preamble to the first volume of his treatise *The Craft of Musical Composition, Theoretical Part* (1937). Hindemith continued his extensive reworking of the score through his American years and in 1948 published the new version, along with an introductory essay explaining the reasons for his unusual artistic act.

In both versions, *Das Marienleben* is divided into four parts, the first part dealing with the experience of Mary prior to the birth of Christ, the second leading from "Joseph's Suspicion" through Christ's birth and the flight into Egypt, the third depicting Christ's passion (and Mary's own experience of it), and the last part meditating on the death of Mary.

In the original version, Hindemith's musical language is fresh and impulsive, often expressionistic and sometimes atonal. The writing for soprano voice, while demanding and occasionally ungrateful, is melodically inventive; the accompaniment is sensitive and idiomatic to the piano, without the technical facileness that sometimes intruded into Hindemith's later work. The revised version smoothes out many of the rhythmic asymmetries of the earlier version, and imposes a harmonic system in which keys stand for characters and ideas (B for Mary, E for Christ, E flat for purity, etc.), an idea more in keeping with Hindemith's latter-day musical philosophies, but quite unlikely to be perceived by the average listener. The most aggressive changes to the score involved entirely new settings of certain portions, such as "The Annunciation." Throughout both versions of the *Marienleben* cycle, Hindemith employs Baroque formal designs, including a chorale fantasy, a theme and variations, and a ground bass.

Both versions have their felicities and weaknesses. The biggest problem with the revision is the great difference in the composer's style between the years of original composition and the final revision; these differences in aesthetic and craft are apparent and unresolved in the score. Among those who championed the earlier version were Arnold Schoenberg, who expressed his preference when the revision was first published, and Glenn Gould, who made a well-reasoned plea for the 1923 edition in his persuasive essay, "A Tale of Two Marienlebens." *—AMG*

Recommended:

○ **Hindemith: Das Marienleben; Krenek & Strauss: Lieder** / Roslak, Rideout, Marshall, Gould / 1995 / Sony 52674

○ **Hindemith: Orchestral Songs & Lieder** / Garben (cond.), Ziesak, Eisenlohr, Hannover Radio SO / CPO 999331

CHORAL

Six Chansons on poems by Rilke, for chorus (1939)

Hindemith had never been comfortable with Nazi rule in Germany and had steady problems with the regime for the five or six years he lived under it. He left for Switzerland in 1938, to stay with friends, and would eventually travel to the United States and become a citizen. While in Switzerland during this transitional period, he wrote this a cappella work based on French poems by Rainer Maria Rilke (1875–1926). Appropriately enough for the texts here, Hindemith's music seems closely akin to that of Poulenc. There are extended and quartal harmonies rooted in an essentially tonal and triadic idiom, wide vertical spacings used somewhat in the manner of substitute consonances, and a pervasive melodicism that nevertheless has a cool quality. The quartal harmonies and other effects have a vaguely medieval feel; after emigrating to the U.S. in 1940, Hindemith founded an early-music ensemble at Yale and became interested in the historical performance movement.

The texts of these poems all deal with pastoral or natural topics, and the composer scored them for a chorus of soprano, alto, tenor, and bass voices. The first chanson, "The Doe," is an attractive, slow chorus whose lovely character sounds almost religious at times. The next, "A Swan," is ethereal and soothing, while the lively, colorful character of "Since All Is Passing" makes for a convincing contrast. The fourth song, "Springtime," is one of the more romantic- and warmer-sounding of these efforts, and the succeeding "In Winter" is appropriately dark and subdued. The charming "Orchard" closes out this attractive set of pieces that, though they are little known in this capacity, would be ideal for the repertoires of student choirs based. *—Robert Cummings*

Recommended:

○ **Hindemith: Songs & Madrigals** / Berlin RSO / 1998 / Wergo 6629

○ **Westminster Choir at Spoleto Festival U.S.A.** / Flummerfelt (cond.), Westminster Choir, / Gothic 49078

His Majesty's Sagbutts and Cornetts

f. 1982, London, England

Ensemble

His Majesty's Sagbutts and Cornetts are an ensemble of wind players specializing in the performance of music of the sixteenth and seventeenth centuries on original instruments. The core of the ensemble consists of two cornetts and four sackbuts accompanied by a harpsichord or chamber organ, but the group regularly expands when the repertoire demands. The archaic spelling "sagbutt" in the name is derived from the original incarnation of His Majesty's Sagbutts and Cornetts in 1516. It was for this illustrious ensemble that composers such as Matthew Locke supplied numerous works. The modern ensemble was founded in 1982 and is directed by Timothy Roberts. The group has toured Europe and Asia and has made over 15 recordings. They have collaborated with singers such as Emma Kirkby, Catherine Bott, and Charles Daniels, and numerous period instrument conductors, including Roger Norrington and John Eliot Gardiner. The ensemble has been featured at many prestigious music festivals, such as those at Salzburg, Utrecht, and Edinburgh. Since 1995, His Majesty's Sagbutts and Cornetts has been an ensemble-in-residence at the Royal College of Music, London. *—Robert Adelson*

Recommended:

○ **Gabrieli: Canzonas & Sonatas from Sacrae Symphoniae 1597** / Roberts (cond.), His Majesty's Sagbutts & Coronets / 1997 / Hyperion 66908

○ **English Music from Henry VIII to Charles II** / Roberts (cond.), His Majesty's Sagbutts & Coronets / 1997 / Hyperion 66894

○ **Lassus: Missa ad imitationem Vinum bonum** / Skidmore (cond.), His Majesty's Sagbutts & Coronets / 1996 / ASV 150

○ **Gabrieli: Missa Pater Peccavi, Motets, & Instumental Music** / Roberts (cond.), His Majesty's Sagbutts & Coronets, His Majesty's Consort of Voices / Hyperion 67167

Ian Hobson

b. Aug. 7, 1952, Wolverhampton, England

Pianist

Scholarly, personable, fastidious, and perceptive in matters of style, Ian Hobson achieved his reputation as a pianist able to do justice to music of many periods. His thoughtful pursuit of interesting repertory has transferred itself to his work as conductor. With his own Sinfonia da Camera, as well as with other leading chamber orchestras, Hobson has offered stimulating concerts, some of which have been preparatory to recordings for the company he founded specifically to document both standard repertory and other works of unusual interest. As a long-standing music professor at the University of Illinois at Champaign-Urbana, he has made that school a center for exciting performance both during the regular academic year and as director of the Summer Music Festival.

After schooling at the Royal Academy of Music and Cambridge University, Hobson undertook further studies in the United States at Yale University. Among his distinguished teachers were Sidney Harrison, Claude Franck, and Menahem Pressler. Silver medals in the Artur Rubinstein and Vienna-Beethoven competitions preceded a first prize in the 1981 Leeds International Piano Competition. With that award, Hobson found himself fully launched on an international solo career. In addition to performing recitals, Hobson appeared with many of the world's major orchestras, including several in London, the Scottish National Orchestra (now the Royal Scottish National), the Halle, the Royal Liverpool Orchestra, the Orchester der

Beethovenhalle, the ORD-Vienna, the New Zealand Symphony, and many of America's principal symphonic ensembles. His concerto repertory, aside from more customary fare, includes the concertos of Mendelssohn's mentor, Ignaz Moscheles, and Ignace Paderewski (works now recorded by the pianist), Clara Schumann, and Henry Holden Huss. For recitals, Hobson has included in his eclectic programming works such as Brahms' *Variations for Piano*, the Chopin-Godowsky etudes, Rachmaninov's *Preludes* and *17 Etudes-Tableaux*, in addition to works written for him by contemporary composers, including Gardner, Lees, Liptak, and Ridout. Demand has grown for appearances that present Hobson as both conductor and soloist with such orchestras as the English Chamber Orchestra, the Stuttgart Chamber Orchestra, the Kibbutz Chamber Orchestra of Israel, the Indianapolis Chamber Orchestra, and his own Sinfonia da Camera. Hobson also is heard with some frequency as a partner in duo piano and piano four-hands recitals with his wife, Claude Edrei Hobson. In addition to Hobson's many other activities, he has conducted opera. Espousing repertory from Pergolesi to Richard Strauss, he performed and recorded John Philip Sousa's *El capitan* in the world premiere of a new concert edition. The production, featuring the Sinfonia da Camera and a cast of young singers, was released on the Zephyr label in early 1998. Since he founded the ensemble in 1984, Hobson has attracted world-class artists to perform with the Sinfonia da Camera. Violinists Pamela Frank, Gil Shaham, Itzhak Perlman, Elmar Oliveira, and Pinchas Zukerman; pianists Michel Block, Charles Rosen, and Menahem Pressler; clarinetists David Shifrin and Richard Stoltzman; guitarist Christopher Parkening; and singers Marilyn Horne and Nathan Gunn are but a few who have appeared during the Sinfonia's annual concert series. Aside from an astonishingly active performance and teaching schedule, Hobson has served on competition juries. At the express wish of Van Cliburn, Hobson served as a juror for both the preliminary and final rounds of the tenth Cliburn International Piano Competition in 1997. The following year, Hobson returned to Poland for the Artur Rubinstein Competition, this time multi-tasking as juror, recitalist, and orchestra conductor for the schedule's final round. *—Erik Eriksson*

Recommended:

- ○ **Moscheles: Concertos 5 & 3** / Hobson (cond. & piano), Sinfonia da Camera / 2001 / Zephyr 11901
- ○ **Godowsky's Schubert Arrangements** / Hobson / 1997 / Zephyr 11298
- ○ **Paderewski: Concerto; Polish Fantasy** / Maksymiuk (cond.), Hobson, Sinfonia Varsovia / 2002 / Zephyr 12202

Josef Hofmann

b. Jan. 20, 1876, Podgorze, Poland, **d.** Feb. 16, 1957, Los Angeles, CA

Pianist

Joszef Kazimierz (or Josef Casimir) Hofmann was one of the great pianists of all time. Both parents worked for the Krakow Theater, where his father, Kazimierz Hofmann (1842–1911) was conductor and his mother sang in light operas. His father was also a notable teacher of harmony and counterpoint and began teaching his son the basics of music, while Josef's sister and aunt both taught him piano. This resulted in Josef becoming one of the all-time great child prodigies. In fact, it is said that his facility in mathematics and science were the equal of his musical talent. By the age of seven he was touring as a pianist and composing music. At 11 he made his U.S. debut at the Metropolitan Opera House, playing Beethoven's *First Piano Concerto*. This event has been counted as one of the most sensational concerts in history.

He became a well-known figure, appearing in 42 concerts throughout the U.S. He became a cause célèbre when the Society for the Prevention of Cruelty to Children publicly protested the obviously exhausting exploitation, his father having resigned all his teaching posts in order to direct young Josef's career. The American glass-making magnate Alfred Corning Clark put up a fund of $50,000 to promote the boy's education. Fortunately, the family accepted, and Josef returned to Berlin in 1892 to study piano with Moritz Moszkowski.

However, he did not get along with Moszkowski. Instead, he auditioned for Anton Rubinstein in 1892, and the great pianist and teacher accepted Hofmann as his only private pupil. Hofmann traveled by train twice a week to Rubinstein's home in Dresden and worked strenuously with him, learning not only maturity in playing, but his musical ideals.

Hofmann debuted as a mature artist in 1894, the year of Rubinstein's death. He achieved unprecedented international success in Europe, Russia, and North and South America. He was regarded as the ideal pianist in a literal as well as a metaphoric sense; his style and technique were put before students as the goal to which they should aspire. He had a fabulous control over tonal qualities, and could erupt out of a restrained, dignified sound into a passionate emotional outburst. His repertoire was almost entirely limited to the first half of the nineteenth century (roughly, from Beethoven through Schumann and Liszt). However, he did play Rachmaninov's *Third Concerto* (which was dedicated to him).

He was the first professional musician in history to make a recording, which he did when he visited Thomas Edison's laboratories and made several cylinder recordings in 1887. He was not a prolific maker of commercial recordings, but a large number of live performance recordings was made, confirming the remarkable accounts of his playing.

In 1926 he accepted the invitation of Mary Louise Curtis Bok to become the director of the Curtis Institute of Music, which she had recently formed. He remained in that position for 12 years (1926–48), and was instrumental in forming it into one of the world's great conservatories. In 1937 he celebrated the 50th anniversary of his U.S. debut with a concert at the old Metropolitan, playing an Anton Rubinstein concerto and some of his own music. He composed over 100 works under the pen name Michel Dvorsky. He moved to California in 1938 and closed his concert career in 1945; alcoholism was a factor. However, he continued to work on improvements to piano actions and recording techniques, accounting for some of the 70 patents he held. *—Joseph Stevenson*

Recommended:

- ○ **Hofmann Plays Chopin** / Barbirolli (cond.), Hofmann, New York PO / 2002 / Urania 229
- ○ **Chopin** / Hofmann / 1995 / Nimbus 8803
- ○ **Liszt, Beethoven, Scarlatti & Schumann** / Hofmann / 1999 / Nimbus 8818
- ○ **Josef Hofmann** / Hofmann / 1999 / Philips 456835

Christopher Hogwood

b. Sep. 10, 1941, Nottingham, England

Conductor

Christopher Hogwood is one of the most prominent conductor of period-instrument performances of Classical and Baroque music. He studied classical literature in addition to music at Pembroke College, Oxford, where he obtained a bachelor's degree in 1964. His harpsichord instructors were Rafael Puyana and Gustav Leonhardt. Leonhardt, the British harpsichordist Thurston Dart, and conductor Raymond Leppard, all prominent in early music research and performance, influenced Hogwood's career path. The British Council gave him a scholarship, enabling him to spend a year in Prague at the Charles University and the Prague Academy of Music.

In 1967 David Munrow and Hogwood co-founded the Early Music Consort to undertake authentic performances of medieval music. Munrow's approach attracted fans and raised eyebrows. The performances were lively, with driving dance rhythms, and the group began to record extensively.

In 1973 Hogwood founded the Academy of Ancient Music, taking its name from a London music society and orchestra of the eighteenth century. Hogwood's group was the first British ensemble formed to play music of the Baroque and early Classical periods on original instruments, a more lightly elegant specialty than that of Munrow's group. The AAM quickly became one of the most popular and influential organizations in the "authentic performance" movement. (Hogwood now prefers the less confrontational term "historically informed performance" to "authentic.") They record frequently on Decca's imprint L'Oiseau-Lyre and have forged forward into High Classicism, releasing complete sets of Mozart and Haydn symphonies. Hogwood's interpretations are instantly recognizable, with a restrained, technically perfect style that diverged fundamentally from the glittering Baroque performances that were the norm.

Hogwood has not limited his activities to period-instrument groups or Classical and Baroque music. Since 1981 he has regularly conducted leading American orchestras, and he conducted his first opera in America in 1983, a production of Mozart's *Don Giovanni* in St. Louis. He brings to standard-instrument ensembles many of the interpretive principles he developed from his research, and often juxtaposes his Baroque and Classical interpretations with twentieth century music of the Neo-Classical style, from such composers as Stravinsky, Martinů, and Tippett.

From 1983 to 1985 he was artistic director of London's Mostly Mozart Festival at the Barbican Centre, and is conductor laureate of the Handel & Haydn Society, Boston's historic concert organization, which now includes America's leading orchestra of period instruments. He was musical director of the St. Paul (Minnesota) Chamber Orchestra from 1987 to 1992. He regularly guest conducts and has served as director for a number of festivals. In 2000, he was named principal guest conductor of the Kammerorchester Basel, taking on the same position with the Orquesta Ciudad de Granada the following year.

Hogwood has said that his busy schedule affords him insufficient time to teach, but took a step toward correcting that state of affairs in 1992 when he was named visiting professor of Early Music Performance at the Royal Academy of Music in London, and a visiting professor at King's College, London. He teaches frequently at Harvard and is an honorary professor at the University of Cambridge. Hogwood has also published several widely praised books, including a biography of Handel. *—Joseph Stevenson*

Recommended:

- ○ **Mozart: Concertos** / Hogwood (cond.), Kelly, Beznosiuk, Bond, Academy of Ancient Music / 1998 / Decca 417622
- ○ **Emma Kirkby sings Handel, Arne, Haydn & Mozart** / Hogwood (cond.), Kirkby, Lubin, Hirons, Academy of Ancient Music / 1998 / London 458084

○ **Vivaldi: Concertos** / Hogwood (cond.), Rifkin, Bylsma, McGegan, MacIntosh, Academy of Ancient Music / 1997 / L'Oiseau-Lyre 455703

○ **Handel: Messiah** / Hogwood (cond.), Preston, Elliott, Kirkby, Watkinson, Nelson, Academy of Ancient Music, Oxford Christ Church Cathedral Chorus / 1991 / L'oiseau-Lyre 430488

○ **Martinů, Stravinsky & Honneger** / Hogwood (cond.), Kammerorchester-basel / 2001 / Arte Nova 86236

○ **Mozart: Violin Concertos** / Hogwood (cond.), Standage, Academy of Ancient Music / 1997 / Decca 455721

Antony Holborne

b. 1500s, England [?], **d.** 1602, England [?]

Composer

A shadowy figure before the late 1590s, Antony Holborne was one of the most acclaimed and prolific dance composers of his period. Of his 150 works, about three-quarters of them are dances, many of them surviving in up to four different arrangements. Like many pop artists of the present day, Holborne enjoyed only fleeting acclaim. In the *New Grove Dictionary of Music and Musicians*, David Brown crisply illustrates the concept of damning with faint praise: "Although he cannot count among the major English composers of his time, he was a good artisan with a facility for producing well-written, attractive music of a sort that made him widely popular in his lifetime, but which was not of sufficient musical substance to maintain his reputation for long after his death." Yet Holborne pieces regularly appear on recorded anthologies of instrumental English Renaissance music, and to members of amateur Renaissance consorts his name is quite a familiar one. So the composer is safe from the dustbin of music history.

Despite occasional, mysterious references to a certain Holborne between 1588 and 1596, Antony Holborne did not enjoy a chance at archival immortality until 1597, when no fewer than 58 of his pieces appeared in a publication called *The Cittharn Schoole*. (Antony's brother William also saw his first and last publication in the same volume: six three-voice vocal compositions latterly dismissed as "feeble.")

Holborne contributed introductory poems to publications by Robert Morley and Giles Farnaby during the next couple of years, but no more music appeared until 1599, when 65 pieces of consort music were issued under the title *Pavans, Galliards, Almains... in Five Parts*. This made a tremendous splash, and the next year John Dowland dedicated one of his songs "to the most famous, Anthony Holborne." In a posthumous publication, Holborne was described as having been a "Gentleman usher" to Queen Elizabeth, but what this entailed is unclear.

Lute arrangements of three of Holborne's dances were published in Germany in 1600, but employment as a courier seems to have distracted him from much further composition and apparently even hastened his death, which occurred sometime between November 29 and December 1, 1602, at an unknown location. *—James Reel*

Overview of Works (ca. 1565–1600)

The musician and courtier Antony Holborne was born around 1547 and died in 1602, just months before Queen Elizabeth I. In common with so many of his Elizabethan contemporaries, Holborne was a cultivated man of wide interests. Educated at Christ's College, Cambridge, he became a lawyer and was also a lover of literature and the classics. He was a friend of John Dowland's, who in 1600 dedicated his famous song "I saw my lady weep," "To the most famous Antony Holborne." Not many other details of his life have come down to us, but a surviving letter from his widow to Sir Robert Cecil, Secretary of State to the queen, makes clear that his death was caused by a diplomatic mission undertaken on Cecil's behalf.

Holborne's music is best known through his most extensive collection, the pavans, galliards, almains, and other "short aeirs," published in London in 1599. The collection consists of 65 pieces in five parts, representing one of the largest and most important collections of dances published in Elizabethan England. In the title, Holborne makes clear that his dances "both grave, and light" are suitable for performance either by viol consort, by a group of the then-new violins, or by wind instruments, thus displaying a pragmatism typical of the period. Holborne seems to have been little troubled by the strong streak of melancholy, typified by Dowland, that played such a major part in the ethos of Elizabethan artists in various disciplines. His music is above all characterized by a tunefulness and liveliness that does not exclude sophistication or a profound mastery of craft. Although Holborne retained the generic titles of the dances of the period for a number of his pieces, many others have intriguing descriptive titles, among which *Sicke, sicke, and very sicke*, and *The fruit of love* are among the more colorful. Sometimes mistakenly regarded as a composer of light trifles, Holborne in fact exemplifies the Elizabethan spirit: he was a multi-faceted composer capable of being both entertaining, and, in pavans such as *The Funerals*, deeply moving. *—Brian Robins*

Recommended:

○ **Holborne: The Teares of the Muses** / Savall (cond.), Hespèrion XXI / 2000 / Alia Vox 9813

○ **Holborne: My Selfe** / O'Dette, King's Noyse / HM 2907238

○ **Holborne: Pavans, Galliards, Almains** / Lindberg (cond.), Dowland Consort / 1989 / Bis 469

○ **Holburns Passion** / Heringman, Pell / 1997 / ASV 173

Heinz Holliger

b. May 21, 1939, Langenthal, Switzerland

Oboist

Heinz Holliger (b. 1939) is considered one of the world's leading oboe virtuosos, as well as a noted composer and conductor. He began playing recorder at age four and piano at six. Eventually he switched to oboe, studying with Cassagnaud and Veress at the Berne Conservatory. He then moved to Paris to study oboe with Pierlot, and piano with Lefébure. In 1959 he won a first prize for oboe in the Geneva Competition, and in the same year was hired as an oboist by the Basel Symphony Orchestra. Meanwhile, he studied composition with Pierre Boulez form 1961 to 1963. His career as an international oboe virtuoso began in 1963. His tours included solo appearances, performances with his wife, the harpist Ursula Holliger, and chamber music appearances with the Holliger Ensemble, a chamber group he founded. He was appointed professor of oboe at the Staatliche Musikhochschule of Freiburg in 1965.

He quickly became known as the outstanding oboist of the time. He adopted the smoother, thinner French sound rather than the wider German quality. Even by comparison with the French sound, his tone quality is exceptionally bright. He has a deep understanding for the performance practices of all eras of music, and has garnered particular praise for his mastery of the many extended techniques related to the performance of twentieth century music. He is credited with having extended the technical range of the instrument more than any other oboist. Some of these extended techniques include harmonics, double trills, multiphonics, and glissandos. In interviews he has disputed this accreditation, saying, "I have invented nothing." He points to instances where these techniques appeared in earlier music, such as an oboe glissando in Mahler's Third Symphony, but in fact he was the first to make extensive use of these techniques. In addition, he has introduced new sounds attainable only by placing a microphone inside the instrument.

He is very alert to the need for expanding the repertoire of the instrument. He has been critical of oboists for not commissioning challenging new works. He has commissioned works from Berio, Stockhausen, Penderecki, Frank Martin, Pousseur, Henze, Krenek, Jolivet, and Lutosławski. The Lutosławski work, a double concerto for oboe, harp, and orchestra, written for Holliger and his wife, is considered a masterpiece of twentieth century literature.

Holliger began composing when he was young, and has compiled an extensive catalogue in many genres. His music is thoroughly influenced by Schoenberg, Webern and Luigi Nono. Holliger composed *The Magical Dances* for two dancers, chorus, orchestra, and tape, a work of exceptional aural density and fine nuances. He has also used Indian rhythms to represent specific poetic imagery. In *Pneuma* (1970) for thirty-six winds, four radios, organ, and percussion, he requires the performers to make specific breathing sounds into microphones, and *Cardiophonie* uses an amplified stethoscope attached to a solo wind player to add the players pulse to the music. Usually Holliger's music has a very tight internal logic caused by the strict use of serial procedures, and his musical textures can range from slow, attenuated wisps of sound to combinations of instrumental sound so thick that they practically become "white noise." His compositions are almost uniformly technically difficult to perform, and highly challenging to listen to. *—Joseph Stevenson*

Recommended:

○ **Holliger: Scardanelli-Zyklus** / Holliger, Edwards (cond.), Nicolet, Ensemble Modern, London Voices / 1993 / ECM 437441

○ **Zelenka: Trio Sonatas** / Holliger, Zehetmair, Jaccottet, Bourgue, Stoll, Rubin, Thunemann / 1999 / ECM 462542

○ **Albinoni: Adagio & Concerti** / various / DG 469607

○ **Mozart: Oboe Quartet; Divertimento, K251; Adagio, K580a** / Holliger, Baumann, Orlando Quartet / Philips 412618

Hollywood Bowl Orchestra

f. 1991, Los Angeles, CA

Ensemble

As a venue, the Hollywood Bowl can boast that it has hosted an astounding range of luminaries throughout its history. In tandem with the Los Angeles Philharmonic's perennial summer residency there, conductors ranging from Otto Klemperer to Leopold Stokowski (who actually founded the short-lived Hollywood Bowl Symphony in 1943) to Herbert von Karajan to Leonard Bernstein have stood upon its podium; Arturo Toscanini, it is said, is the only major conductor of his time not to have led a concert on its stage. Performers from outside the realm of classical music—including Al Jolson, Frank Sinatra, Simon and Garfunkel, and Mikhail Baryshnikov—have also lent a special cachet to the legendary Bowl. Australian/American composer Percy Grainger was married on its stage in 1928.

Though the Hollywood Bowl's association with the Los Angeles Philharmonic dates to 1922, the Bowl's own resident orchestra—the Hollywood Bowl Orchestra—

only came into being in 1991. Since then, under music director John Mauceri, the ensemble has distinguished itself for its spirited, always crowd-pleasing performances. Generally avoiding the weightier staples of the orchestral repertory, the Hollywood Bowl Orchestra has gained much favorable attention for its performances of film and Broadway music, light classics, and other "pops" favorites. Among the ensemble's recordings are well-received interpretations of the music of George Gershwin, Irving Berlin, and Duke Ellington. The ensemble has made several tours to Japan and a successful 1996 trip to Brazil. In the late 1990s, it began presenting live orchestral accompaniment to films clips projected on the Bowl's big screen. Mauceri and the orchestra have also made it a mission to restore classic film scores. *—AMG*

Recommended:

- ○ **Star Wars: The Sound of Hollywood** / Mauceri (cond.), Hollywood Bowl Orch. / Philips 468161
- ○ **An Evening With The Hollywood Bowl** / various conds., Pennario, Rabin, Hollywood Bowl Orch. / EMI 68860

Gustav Holst

b. Sep. 21, 1874, Cheltenham, England, **d.** May 25, 1934, London, England

Composer: Orchestral, Band Music, Choral, Opera

Known primarily for his popular orchestral composition, *The Planets*, Gustav Holst embraced a wide variety of musical models, from Arthur Sullivan, Edvard Grieg, and Wagner to the melodic simplicity of English folk music. In his maturity, he managed to merge these various influences into a rather sparse personal style that became increasingly transparent in his later years. Perhaps his greatest talent lay in the realm of choral music; his *Hymn of Jesus* stands as one of the finest works in the genre from the early twentieth century.

Holst's first instruction came from his father, Adolph, a piano teacher, who also made him take lessons on the violin and trombone; the father believed that these studies might alleviate the youth's asthma.

By age 12, the young Holst was composing, even dabbling in orchestration; in 1888, he won a prize in an amateur competition for his vocal work, *A Christmas Carol*. Thereafter he sang in the All Saints' Church choir and played violin and trombone in its orchestra. In 1892, he traveled to London and heard a Covent Garden performance of *Götterdämmerung*, led by Mahler. The experience opened up new compositional vistas for the young composer.

Holst entered the Royal College of Music the following year where he met fellow student Ralph Vaughan Williams, who would remain a close lifelong friend. Shortly after his arrival in London, Holst found that the neuritis in his right arm, which had afflicted him in his early youth, had worsened and now caused him to abandon ideas of a career as a concert pianist. In 1898, Holst left the RCM to take a position in the Carl Rosa Opera Company as rehearsal pianist and coach. He completed his Cotswold Symphony in 1900, and its premiere in April 1902 was a success. On June 22, 1901, Holst married Emily Isobel Harrison, whom he had met in a choir he had directed a few years before.

In late 1903, Holst took on a teaching position at James Allen's Girls' School, in South London. The following year he acquired a second post, the directorship of music at St. Paul's Girls' School, which he would retain until his death. He added another teaching post at Morley College in 1907, bogging him down and leaving little time for composition. Still, the *St. Paul's Suite*, written during this period (1912–13), is among his most often-performed works.

In 1914, Holst began work on what would become his most popular composition, *The Planets*. The war years were extremely productive, as the composer not only completed *The Planets*, but also wrote *Hymn of Jesus*. In spring 1918, Holst began educational work for the YMCA at its various facilities on European battlefields.

He returned to London at the end of June 1919 and took a prestigious post teaching theory and composition at the RCM in 1920. The composer's fame was not only growing domestically in the early 1920s but internationally as well, as works like the *Hymn of Jesus* were receiving regular and acclaimed performances. By 1924, Holst's health was clearly declining, and he thus lessened his workload.

Beginning in late December 1928, Holst made a series of trips abroad that included visits to France, Italy, Sicily, and the U.S. In Boston, a duodenal ulcer was diagnosed in 1932. On May 23, 1934, he underwent surgery for the ulcer, but died two days later. *—Robert Cummings*

ORCHESTRAL

Brook Green Suite, for strings (1933)

One of the last works Gustav Holst completed before his death was this *Brook Green Suite for string orchestra*. Written for the St. Paul's Girls' School where he had taught since 1905, the suite was the companion piece for his earlier *St. Paul's Suite for string orchestra* (1912–13). Named after the part of Hammersmith in which Holst lived, the *Brook Green Suite* is as easy to play as it is to hear, having been written for the school's junior orchestra. Based on folk song or folk-song-like melodies set to conservative harmonies, the suite is in three movements: a fast-ish Prelude, a beguiling slow Air, and a lightly rhythmic final "Dance." Although clearly not one of Holst's self-consciously "great" works, the *Brook Green Suite* would appeal to listeners who enjoy his earlier *St. Paul's Suite* and Benjamin Britten's later *Simple Symphony*. *—James Leonard*

Recommended:

- ○ **Holst** / Menuhin (cond.), English CO / 2003 / EMI 575981
- ○ **Holst: St. Paul's Suite** / Hickox (cond.), City of London Sinfonia / 1994 / Chandos 9270

Egdon Heath (Homage to Hardy), Op. 47 (1927)

"A place perfectly accordant with man's nature—neither ghastly, hateful nor ugly; neither commonplace, unmeaning nor tame; but like man, slighted and enduring; and withal singularly colossal and mysterious in its swarthy monotony." This quotation from Thomas Hardy's 1878 novel *The Return of the Native* appears on the score of Gustav Holst's tone poem *Egdon Heath*, which was written in 1927, dedicated to Hardy (who, at age 87, had one more year of life remaining), and long regarded by the composer as his finest work. It was commissioned by the New York Symphony Orchestra, which premiered it under the direction of Walter Damrosch at New York's Mecca Auditorium on February 12, 1928. The next day Holst led the City of Birmingham Symphony in the British premiere at Cheltenham, where the first major festival of Holst's music had taken place the previous year. Those initial performances went well, but another in London a few days later was greeted poorly by a noisy and unreceptive audience. This seems to have made Holst a bit anxious about the work, and may have led to his desire that the above Hardy quotation always appear in any explanatory program notes.

In her book on her father's music, Holst's daughter Imogen evokes the Hardy quotation in referring to the "mysterious monotony" of the tone poem, which begins with a somber melody heard first in the double basses, then taken up by the rest of the strings. A nostalgic theme in the brass and woodwinds, and a scurrying theme in the strings and oboe, work their way into the texture as well, leading to moody, twilit music and what has been described as a "strange, ghostly dance." This dark, evocative work finishes mysteriously, quietly, and somewhat inconclusively. *—Chris Morrison*

Recommended:

- ○ **Holst: Orchestral Works** / Hickox (cond.), London SO / 1996 / Chandos 9420
- ○ **Holst: The Plantets; Egdon Heath** / Davis (cond.), BBCSO / 1994 / Teldec 94541

The Planets, suite for orchestra & female chorus, Op. 32 (1914–1916)

Vaughan Williams once described *The Planets* (1914–16), by Gustav Holst, as "the perfect equilibrium" of the mystic and the melodic sides of the composer's nature. Shortly before its composition, Holst told a friend, "As a rule I only study things that suggest music to me... Recently the character of each planet suggested lots to me." Typically known as a miniaturist, Holst expanded his reputation when he wrote this work of symphonic proportions for an impossibly large orchestra. Containing seven tone poems, the composition, which is comparable in size to those by Strauss, Mahler, and Schoenberg, has become known as his biggest and most important work. Accustomed to composing only for special purposes, Holst luxuriously allowed himself everything he wanted in this work.

The Planets was composed while Holst was employed as music master at a school in Dulwich and at St. Paul's Girls' School. It was the first and only work of its kind that he produced; between 1900–14 he had written mainly choral pieces. Under the influence of Wagner, Strauss, Rimsky-Korsakov, Stravinsky, the French composers, and additional Russians, Holst started to sketch No. 1: "Mars, The Bringer of War" just as the first World War began. Insistent on the stupidity of war, with all its horrors, the composer opened *The Planets* with this movement of relentless and brutal power. The entire work bears the feel of vulgarity, pleasantly accompanied by the richness and emotional warmth of humanity.

With the exception of Earth and Pluto, each planet in our solar system has its own movement in Holst's composition. "Mars" opens the work in a broad ABA form, each section rising to a climax, concluding with a crashing unison of the entire orchestra. "Venus" follows, dissipating the brutality of the first movement, by peacefully presenting several figures and closing with a rich and calm amplification of its opening. "Mercury," which is in two keys in nearly every bar, leaves an impression of winged lightness and speed by rapidly swinging between chords. In "Jupiter" the composer sought to embody the radiant happiness of a person who enjoys life, in an ABACABA form. "Saturn" beautifully and peacefully brings old age, in a march that penetrates unlike any other work by the composer. Although Holst did not hear Dukas' *Sorcerer's Apprentice* prior to composing "Uranus," the two have remarkable similarities, particularly in the use of staccato bassoons. It is one of his supreme tuttis. This atmospheric composition closes with the delicately scored "Neptune." Meant to be a tuneless, expressionless, and shapeless pianissimo movement, the piece fades away to a close with a memorable wordless six-part female chorus.

The first complete public performance was conducted by Albert Coates on November 15, 1920. Prior to that, Adrian Boult led a semi-private rehearsal at the

Queen's Hall Orchestra in 1918. The work is also available in an excellent version for two pianos. *—Meredith Gailey*

Recommended:

- ○ **Holst: Planets; Elgar: Enigma Variations** / Boult (cond.), London PO, Geoffrey Mitchell Choir / 2002 / EMI 67749
- ○ **Holst: The Planets** / Karajan (cond.), Berlin PO / DG 439011
- ○ **Holst: The Planets** / Dutoit (cond.), Montreal SO / 1998 / London 460606

St. Paul's Suite, for strings, Op. 29/2 (1912–1913)

Gustav Holst spent a good portion of his musical life dealing with students and other non-professional musicians. In 1903 he succeeded his good friend Ralph Vaughan Williams as the director of the school orchestra at James Allen's Girls' School in London. Two years later he became musical director at the St. Paul's Girls' School, a post he kept for the rest of his life. Along with his teaching, Holst continued to compose in his spare time, and around 1907, began to explore English and Scottish folk music. Those folk tunes started making their way into compositions like the *St. Paul's Suite* for string orchestra, written in 1912–13 for his students at the St. Paul's School.

The suite opens with a slightly dark Jig, based on a memorably rustic tune. The ostinato second movement features a tender melody and an accompaniment spiced with pizzicati. A passionate modal theme, announced by the full string body and later taken up by a quiet solo violin, dominates the third-movement Intermezzo. The rousing Finale takes up the folk tune *"The Dargason"* (which Holst also employs in the finale of his *Second Suite* for military band), repeating it 30 times with harmonic and rhythmic variations. Towards the end of the movement the famous tune "Greensleeves" makes an appearance as a countermelody. *—Chris Morrison*

Recommended:

- ○ **Holst: St. Paul's Suite; etc.** / Menuhin (cond.), English CO / EMI 2227
- ○ **English Music for Strings** / Hurst (cond.), Bournemouth Sinfonietta / 1985 / Chandos 8375

BAND MUSIC

Hammersmith, prelude & scherzo for military band, Op. 52 (1930; revised 1931)

Composed in 1930 on commission from the BBC, Gustav Holst's *Hammersmith* is a two-part tone poem that creates a musical impression of the Hammersmith section of London where Holst taught school for nearly 30 years. Originally written for military band, *Hammersmith* was later transcribed for orchestra and received its premiere performance in that form in 1931. Curiously, the original and more effective version for band was not performed until 1954, 20 years after Holst's death.

The Prelude section of this work evokes the quiet river flowing, apparently unconcerned and often unnoticed, through Hammersmith. Although the use of the tuba and euphonium in the opening phrases of this section create a rather ominous setting, the Prelude carries a contemplative mood emphasized by a warmth and sensitivity which Holst rarely allowed himself in his other compositions.

The Prelude gives way to the Scherzo section, which paints a musical picture of the lively and good-natured people who populate the Hammersmith section of London. The raucous good humor of the Saturday night crowds, the street vendors hawking their wares, and the often chaotic mood of city life are all given their due in the overlapping snatches of musical lines that are passed between the instrumental sections. As the Scherzo closes, the reflective mood of the Prelude reemerges to conclude the work on a note of contentment and tranquillity.

The Lyric movement of this piece which was included in the orchestral version, but not in the original band composition was written during Holst's last illness and shows a tender austerity in its soulful solo viola line and lyrical orchestration.

The most impressionistic of Holst's compositions for band, *Hammersmith* shows the apogee of his compositional skill and understanding of the expressive capabilities of the concert band. It conveys the concert band away from the limitations of the parade field and creates a solid foundation for band repertoire to take its place as a serious musical medium. *—Corie Stanton Root*

Recommended:

- ○ **Holst: Orchestral Works** / Hickox (cond.), London SO / 1996 / Chandos 9420
- ○ **British & American Band Classics** / Fennell (cond.), Eastman Wind Ens. / 1990 / Mercury 432009
- ○ **Holst: Orchestral Works** / Lloyd-Jones (cond.), Scottish National Orch. / 1998 / Naxos 553696

A Moorside Suite, for brass band (1928)

Gustav Holst's *Moorside Suite* was the first significant twentieth century work composed specifically for brass band. Holst composed it for the 1928 National Brass Band Championships, eager to explore the possibilities of the medium, which he found less restrictive than the military band (for which he had already written his *Suites in E flat and F*). The result is a lively and elegant work that has remained in the brass band repertory ever since.

The Scherzo movement of this work has a reserved exuberance and is reminiscent of Holst's earlier work, "Fantasy on the Dargason" from the *Second Suite*. The jig-like opening theme, introduced by the trumpet line, is skillfully handed down through the sections as the harmonic complexity of the movement builds. A hunting horn call from the French horn line is answered by a seemingly distant fanfare of trumpets. As the jig returns, it is passed from the lower brasses upward, then unwinds back down through the sections to the tuba, which ends the musical statement with a clarity that is characteristic of Holst's work.

The haunting melody of the Nocturne is carried by a solo trumpet and gives a feeling of melancholy and longing. As the trombone line adds a countermelody and then echoes the opening trumpet theme, the lyrical quality of this movement echoes the sweetness of the "Venus" section of Holst's *The Planets*. The stately trumpet and French horn lines are supported by a walking bass in the lower brasses which then carry the reprise of the trumpet solo to an harmonically rich conclusion. The trumpet fanfare that opens the March section of this work is made even more brilliant than it might be by the rapid-fire snare drum line which exactly matches the rhythm of the trumpet line. Suddenly, the March comes to an abrupt halt and changes character from a lively two-step to a stately processional, then builds to a smashing finale ablaze with cymbal crashes and thunderous bass drum strikes.

First played by each of the 15 bands competing at the National Brass Band Championships of 1928, the *Moorside Suite* is not only an excellent test piece for brass band but is a lyrical and musically challenging foundation stone of brass band repertoire. *—Corie Stanton Root*

Recommended:

- ○ **Holst: Hammersmith; Moorside Suite; Suite 1 & 2** / Dunn (cond.), Dallas Wind Symphony / 1991 / Reference 39

Suite No. 1, for military band in E flat major, Op. 28/1 (1909)

Gustav Holst's *Suite No. 1 in E flat* is the cornerstone of twentieth century band repertoire. Written in 1909 for military band, it is the first significant composition to showcase the expressive range and capabilities of brass and woodwind bands. As a professional trombonist, Holst was appalled by the lack of repertoire for bands which then consisted of marches, unimaginative operatic potpourris and hackneyed arrangements of popular songs. His experience as a band musician gave Holst a distinct advantage over other composers in this medium. Instead of approaching such compositions from an orchestral perspective by simply writing pieces for an orchestra without strings, Holst's works were specifically created for wind band and offer a crispness of musical line that became the foundation of twentieth century band and drum corps style. The *Suite No. 1 in E flat* is considered the first meaningful step toward making the military band a serious concert medium. Often played by military-style bands in concert or competition, it is cleverly written to showcase the various musical colors and abilities of the wind band instruments.

The 3/4 time and stately introduction of the musical theme by the lower brasses give the Chaconne, the first of this composition's three movements, a dignified character appropriate to the Spanish dance that is its namesake. As this theme is echoed and embellished by the upper brasses and then by the woodwinds, it allows each section to show its virtuosity in turn; a requirement for military band competitions. The original theme is then overtaken by running scales in the woodwind line supported by short, percussive phrases in the brass and percussion parts. A further variation of this second theme is carried in a peaceful woodwind interlude which leads to a reintroduction of the original melody. Built from the lower brasses throughout the sections, the theme culminates with an exciting fanfare lead by the trumpet line and emphasized by the cannon-like strikes of the bass drum which are reminiscent of Tchaikovsky's *"1812" Overture*.

In the Intermezzo, Holst creates a sprightly opening melody with the woodwinds and tambourine. This theme eventually wraps itself around a variation of the folk song, *"I Love my Love"*, which is skillfully handed back and forth between the clarinet and trumpet lines. Holst's penchant for using folk songs as themes for his compositions is evident in this movement and is very effective, even in this early band work.

The March is a stirring, if somewhat typical parade-style march reminiscent of the works of John Philip Sousa. Written to be performed at the traditional walking andante meter used by military bands on the competition field or parade grounds, the brass setting of the opening melody is well balanced and elegant. As the woodwinds weave snatches of folk song melodies together in smooth succession, the brass echoes and varies these lines. With an upward modulation in key, Holst reintroduces the opening march theme, led by the trumpet line, in an irruptive and glorious fanfare that brings this piece to a spirited conclusion. *—Corie Stanton Root*

Recommended:

- ○ **Frederick Fennell** / Fennell (cond.), Eastman Wind Ens. / 1999 / Mercury 462960
- ○ **Vaughan Williams, Holst & Jacob** / Stamp (cond.), Keystone Wind Ens. / 1999 / Citadel 88137

○ **Time Pieces** / Corporon (cond.), North Texas Wind Symphony / 2001 / Klavier 11122

Suite No. 2, for military band in F major, Op. 28/2 (1911)

Gustav Holst's *Suite No. 2 in F* nicely combines Holst's abilities as a composer of band music and his penchant for the use of folk songs in classical works. Written in 1911 for military band, this piece makes use of no less that seven traditional English folk melodies. As it does in all his band music, Holst's experience as a trombonist shows through in the *Suite No. 2.* Instead of approaching band music from an orchestral perspective and writing pieces for orchestras without strings as some of his contemporaries did, Holst was able to compose pieces that are responsive to the expressive capabilities of wind bands. The *Suite No. 2* is an excellent example.

Composed in four movements, the suite opens with a march instead of closing with one as was traditional. The melodies of the folk songs *"Swansea Town"* and *"Cloudy Banks"* and an old morris dance tune are deftly passed from the woodwinds to the trumpets and lower brasses and back again, creating a swirl of melodies. In the second movement, "Song without Words," the melancholy melody of *"I Love my Love"* is introduced by a solo clarinet supported by rich chords in the lower brasses. As the other woodwinds and upper brasses are added to this slow and haunting mix, the harmony becomes increasingly complex until, one by one, the sections drop away and leave only the baritone to complete the last mournful notes.

The brief "Song of the Blacksmith," which Holst also later arranged for baritone voice and piano, serves as the scherzo movement of this suite. The lively melody is carried by the clarinets and then the upper brass, and is punctuated with dissonant, syncopated chords in the lower brass and percussion sections. All of this, emphasized by the hammer-to-anvil strikes of the blacksmith, creates an excellent musical picture of a skilled tradesman hard at work.

The last movement, "Fantasia on the Dargason," is the original version of the final movement of Holst's *St. Paul's Suite.* The "Dargason," a Renaissance dance melody best known to twentieth century audiences as "The Irish Washerwoman," is given a vigorous setting as it is passed back and forth from the trumpet line to the woodwinds and interwoven with the lyrical melody of the familiar "Greensleeves." This spirited movement concludes with a delightfully comic duet between the piccolo and the tuba.

Holst's *Suite No. 2 in F* is a jewel of band repertoire, bringing intricate musical lines and expressive use of wind band instrumentation together with the familiar melodies of well-loved folk songs. *—Corie Stanton Root*

Recommended:

○ **Frederick Fennell** / Fennell (cond.), Eastman Wind Ens. / 1999 / Mercury 462960

○ **Vaughan Williams, Holst & Jacob** / Stamp (cond.), Keystone Wind Ens. / 1999 / Citadel 88137

○ **British Wind Band Classics** / Reynish (cond.), Royal Northern College of Music Wind Orch. / 1999 / Chandos 9697

CHORAL

Choral Hymns from the Rig Veda, for chorus & orchestra, Op. 26 (1908–1914)

The years 1900 through 1912 could be thought of as Holst's "Sanskrit" period. Inspired by his Theosophist stepmother, Holst developed an interest in the religious literature and poetry of India in his mid-twenties, going so far as to learn the rudiments of the Sanskrit language at University College, London, so that he could make his own translations when he found those that were available unsuitable for his musical settings. His first effort in this vein was the opera *Sita* (1900–06); later came works like the opera *Sàvitri* (1908), the choral work *The Cloud Messenger* (1909–10), and the *Choral Hymns from the Rig Veda,* written over the years 1908 through 1912.

The *Rig Veda* is a set of over 1,000 hymns—singing the praises of the sacred plant soma and gods like Varuna, Agni, and Indra—brought by Indo-European speaking peoples into India somewhere around 1500–1000 B.C. Holst set 14 of these hymns in his four groups of *Choral Hymns,* which were fairly popular during his lifetime, but have seldom been performed since.

The first group (written in 1908–10, premiered at *Newcastle* on December 6, 1911) is scored for mixed chorus and orchestra. It opens with the primitivistic "Battle Hymn," with its repeated refrain "Indra and Maruts fight for us!" The second hymn, "To the Unknown God," begins with the chorus singing quietly in unison, and builds to a huge climax over martial rhythms. The set concludes with a "Funeral Hymn."

The second group (written in 1909, premiered at *Queen's Hall* on March 22, 1911) features women's chorus with orchestra. The mysterious "To Varuna (God of the Waters)," with its quiet, desolate opening and unusual harmonies, is followed by the lively, polyphonic "To Agni (God of Fire)" and the haunting "Funeral Chant."

The third group (written in 1910, premiered at Blackburn on March 16, 1911) combines women's chorus with harp accompaniment, the latter's rippling arpeggios backing the gentle singing of "Hymn to the Dawn." The unusual time signature of 21/8 is employed in "Hymn to the Waters." The gentle, beautiful "Hymn to Vena (Sun rising through the mist)" and increasingly elaborate "Hymn of the Travelers" (once considered by Holst for use as an overture to the opera *Sàvitri*) conclude the group.

The fourth group (written in 1912, premiered at Queen's Hall on March 18, 1914) is scored for men's chorus and orchestra, and is generally considered the most conventional and weakest of the four. The opening "Hymn to Agni" is followed by the jaunty "Hymn to Soma (the juice of an herb)." A baritone soloist, representing the spirit of a dying man, opens the first couple of verses and is answered by the chorus in the simple but effective, a cappella "Hymn to Manas." The group concludes with a "Hymn to Indra." *—Chris Morrison*

In the bleak midwinter, for chorus & organ (1904–1905)

Gustav Holst's *In the Bleak Midwinter* (1905) is a hymn specifically composed for congregational singing. Throughout his career Holst advocated writing music for the masses, as well as for the musically astute; therefore, much of the composer's repertoire—including hymns, music for military band, and numerous songs—was written with the amateur musician in mind. Many of these "lighter" compositions have stood the test of time because even though they are made of relatively simple stuff, they still bear the mark of Holst's careful and loving craftsmanship.

Around the beginning of 1905, a group of clergymen created a committee with the purpose of updating the hymn book called *Hymns Ancient and Modern.* This hymnal was considered to be old-fashioned, so new hymns were to be added. Percy Dearmer, a fellow clergyman and professor of Ecclesiastical Art at King's College in London, was named chairman of this committee. Ralph Vaughan Williams was decided upon to be the music editor, whose task was to make all final decisions on which hymns would be added. Vaughan Williams was skeptical of this duty, but accepted the post upon being promised that the work required would only take two months. In actuality, the project wasn't completed until two years later. With Holst aiding in the editing process, Vaughan Williams looked to include "the finest hymn tunes in the world." Folk tunes and traditional songs would be added, as well as songs by earlier English composers, such as Thomas Tallis. English composers of the time were invited by Vaughan Williams to create new hymns for the updated hymnal. It was soon evident that the addendum would be comparable in size to the original hymnal, so it was decided that an entirely new hymn book would be produced, under the title of *The English Hymnal.* Holst composed three original hymns based on previously gathered folk tunes for this new volume. *In the Bleak Midwinter* is set to text by Christina Rossetti and the folk tune used is known as the "Crantham," named after the town in which it was collected. It is believed that Holst actually composed the hymn while staying in this village for a short amount of time, and a cottage in the village was eventually named Midwinter Cottage.

Another new hymnal was created in the mid-1920s, entitled *Songs of Praise.* Once again Dearmer and Vaughan Williams teamed up to manage the hymnal's creation. *In the Bleak Midwinter* was also included in this new hymn book, as well as a number of other Holst hymns. The hymn was one of Holst's most popular compositions during his lifetime and remains to be well known and often performed. *—Chris Boyes*

Recommended:

○ **Carols from the Old and New Worlds** / Hillier (cond.), Theatre of Voices / HM 907079

OPERA

The Perfect Fool, Op. 39 (1918–1922)

Gustav Holst had been thinking of an opera, *The Perfect Fool,* for some years prior to its presentation in 1922. The opera is a rarity, a large-scale parody opera. It spoofs the conventions of nineteenth century opera in a diffuse structure, including a number of purely spoken passages. Even the composer's daughter, Imogen Holst, has remarked (in her article on the composer in *Grove's Dictionary*) that the text by Holst himself is "inadequate." Still, it has been observed that "there is a lot of good music locked up in this rather impossible framework."

The opera begins, oddly, with a 12-minute ballet, said to have been written to provide a sort of précis of the plot of the opera, which is rather difficult to comprehend without such help. The ballet music is written with a clarity and brilliance of instrumentation that will be instantly recognized by any listener familiar with *The Planets.* A brief opening andante featuring an invocation on trombones by a Wizard (surely a close relative of "Uranus, the Magician") opens three sparkling character dances of, respectively, "The Spirits of Earth," "The Spirits of Water," and "The Spirits of Air." The work has been a concert favorite in Britain for some time. *—Joseph Stevenson*

Synopsis:

The curtain rises on the Wizard, who summons the spirits of the elements to help him make a magic potion. The spell exhausts him and, just as he falls asleep with the cup of potion by his side, the Woman wanders by, her son the Fool in tow. She recalls the words a sage uttered when the boy was born: "He wins a bride with a glance of his eye, with a look he kills a foe. He achieves where others fail, with one word." How can this be true, she wonders aloud, if he never takes on a fight, never says a word, and always sleeps—even now?

At this moment the Wizard awakens and remembers he has not drunk the potion. When the Woman inquires, he tells her of its power: when a man drinks it, the first woman he looks at falls in love with him, and his enemies perish with a glance. The Wizard plans to take it before meeting the Princess, but, still exhausted, decides to nap until she arrives. As he sleeps, the Woman steals the potion and pours it down the Fool's throat, then fills the Wizard's cup with water.

Trumpets herald the arrival of the Princess, who has chosen this day to find the man worthy to be her husband, according to the old prophecy: that he will "do the deed that no other can do." The Wizard awakens and presents himself to the Princess. When she scoffs at his wrinkled old countenance, he produces what he thinks is the potion and drinks it with much fanfare. "All I feel," she responds, to the Wizard's dismay, "is that the joke is getting a little old—like you." He leaves, enraged. Other suitors appear—a warbling Troubadour (meant as a parody of Wagner) and an overprosaic Traveller (a Verdi send-up)—but their praises fall on deaf ears as well. Just then, the Fool awakens and catches the eye of the Princess, who immediately falls under the spell—while he falls back asleep.

A messenger arrives with terrible news: a mysterious forest fire is sweeping across the land and is nearly upon them. All flee but the Woman, the Princess, and the Fool. The latter awakens and tries to run, but the women hold him still and force him to face the Wizard, who has conjured the wall of flames. With the Fool's, glance the fire turns and engulfs the old man instead, fulfilling the potion's other promise. Soon the last part of the wise man's prophecy about the Fool is fulfilled as well—that he would "achieve where others fail, with one word": all others cannot help falling in love with the Princess, but when she asks if the Fool loves her, he simply replies "No." Having thus done "the deed that no other can do," he is, by prophecy, the only man worthy of the crown. The opera ends with the coronation—during which the Fool Prince, alas, falls asleep. *—Jeremy Grimshaw*

Arthur Honegger

b. Mar. 10, 1892, Le Havre, France, **d.** Nov. 27, 1955, Paris, France

Composer: Symphonic, Orchestral, Choral

Born in France to Swiss parents, Arthur Honegger was a major twentieth century composer whose musical style was more cosmopolitan than either French or Swiss. An almost exact contemporary of Prokofiev (1891–1953), he rivaled Poulenc as the most successful member of Les Six and was without doubt among the greatest French composers of his day. Stylistically, he was quite protean, eschewing the Impressionism of Debussy while absorbing certain features of neo-Classicism and taking on a sometimes brash and usually rugged expressive manner, always within a tonal context.

Honegger became proficient on the violin as a child, but also developed an interest in composition early on. His first work, an unorchestrated opera, *Philippa*, dates to 1903. He enrolled at the Zurich Conservatory while in his teens, where he studied composition with Friedrich Hegar and violin with Willem de Boer. He left after two years for the more prestigious Paris Conservatory in 1911, where he studied composition with Widor and Gédalge. Although he continued to take instruction on the violin there, he was clearly more interested in a career as a composer. In 1913, his family relocated to Zurich, but Honegger remained in Le Havre and commuted daily to Paris by train, perhaps one of the reasons he developed a fascination with locomotives. His first works began gaining exposure by 1916 and four years later, he and his conservatory friends Milhaud, Auric, and Tailleferre, along with Poulenc and Durey, found themselves aligned in the famous musical group called Les Six, a name coined by critic Henri Collet. Les Six was formed in reaction to Impressionism and Wagnerian ideas, but Honegger did not recognize any musical creed in his association with the group.

In 1923, Honegger composed one of his most famous works, *Pacific 231 (Mouvement symphonique No. 1)*, a work whose motoric qualities were inspired by the sounds and rhythms of a locomotive. The piece was a tremendous success and spawned many imitations. In 1926, Honegger married a young, highly gifted French pianist Andrée Vaurabourg. The two rarely lived together during their marriage, owing to the composer's need for solitude in his creative activities. On concert tours, however, they apparently shared quarters and throughout their marriage were otherwise a happy, loving couple. The 1928 *Rugby (Mouvement symphonique No. 2)* was also a success for Honegger and is another example of the composer being inspired by an extra-musical interest: he was a sports enthusiast, especially of rugby. Honegger made many concert tours in the 1930s with his wife, who would perform his piano and chamber works or serve as accompanist to his songs. His concert and compositional activity was curtailed for a year when he nursed his wife along to recovery following a serious injury in a 1935 automobile accident. During the war years, Honegger taught at the École Normale de Musique and made many trips to Zurich, where his *Symphony No. 2* (1940–41) was successfully premiered by Paul Sacher and the Collegium Musicum on May 18, 1942. Honegger remained quite prolific during these dark years, especially in the realm of film music. He wrote 11 film scores in the period of 1942–43, though some were collaborations with other composers, such as Jolivet. In 1947, on a concert tour in the United States, Honegger suffered a heart attack and thereafter his health declined, severely limiting his musical activities, with his wife tending to him in his final year. *—Robert Cummings*

SYMPHONIC

Symphony No. 2, for strings & trumpet ad lib in D major (1940–1941)

Honegger's *Symphony No. 2* was begun in 1937 as a commission from Paul Sacher of the Basel Chamber Orchestra. But the rising international tensions in the late 1930s and finally the start of the war in 1939 interrupted its progress and the "Symphonie pour cordes" was not completed until 1941 and was premiered by Sacher in 1942. As much as Vaughan Williams' *Fourth* or Shostakovich's *Seventh*, Honegger's *Second* is a war symphony. Cast as all Honegger's symphonies are—in three movements—the work charts the same course as Beethoven's *Fifth*, the course from darkness to light. The *Second* opens with a weighty Molto moderato wrenched into a bludgeoning Allegro; moves through a "somber, not to say, at times, positively hopeless" Adagio mesto; and ends in a climactic Vivace non troppo—Presto. In the closing pages, Honegger calls for a solo trumpeter ad lib who "calls forth a golden sun on the horizon. Joy conquers at last, but only at the very last moment." Honegger's language is astringent, but still tonal, his rhythms abrasive and propulsive, his forms lithe but monumental, his intentions noble, and his success complete. *—James Leonard*

Recommended:

- ○ **Honegger: Symphonies 2 & 3** / Karajan (cond.), Wesenigk, Berlin PO / 1995 / DG 447435
- ○ **Ravel: Boléro; Daphnis et Chloé; Rapsodie espagnole, Honegger: Symphony 2** / Münch (cond.), Paris Orch. / 2001 / Angel 67597
- ○ **Honegger: Orchestral Works** / Zinman (cond.), Zurich Tonhalle Orch. / 1999 / Decca 455352

Symphony No. 3 ("Liturgique") (1945–1946)

As he grew older, Honegger more and more embraced Catholicism. And as he lived through the war, the occupation, and the liberation, he wrote his *Symphony No. 3 "Liturgique"* as "the reaction of modern man against barbarity, stupidity, sufferings, mechanism, and bureaucracy." Composed between October 1945 and April 1946, Honegger described his symphony as "a drama which is enacted, if you like, between three characters, real or symbolic: misery, happiness and man. These are eternal themes. I have tried to bring them up to date." The work was premiered in August 1946 by Charles Münch in Switzerland. The "Liturgique" is scored for large orchestra and set in three movements with titles taken from the Catholic liturgy: "Dies Irae," "De profundis clamavi," and "Dona nobis pacem." As Honegger vividly described them to a friend: "Dies Irae" is "Human terror in from of divine wrath… Day of Wrath! There is a rapid succession of violent themes… there is not time to breathe, no time to think, the hurricane carries everything before it, sweeps everything away. Blindly, furiously…"; "De profundis clamavi" is "the painful mediation of man forsaken by divinity—a meditation which is already a prayer… And how hard it is to put inside human mouths a hopeless prayer!"; and "Dona nobis pacem" is "Collective stupidity as a heavy-footed march for which I wrote a deliberately idiotic theme… a feeling of rebellion dawns in the ranks of the victims… a huge clamor thrice repeated breaks from the oppressed throats… a song of peace soars above the symphony as the dove soared in the old days above the immensity of the ocean." *—James Leonard*

Recommended:

- ○ **Honegger: Symphonies 3 & 5** / Dutoit (cond.), Bavarian RSO / Erato 45208
- ○ **Honegger: Symphonies 2 & 3** / Karajan (cond.), Berlin PO / 1995 / DG 447435

Symphony No. 5 in D major ("Di Tre Re") (1950)

Honegger, identified as a member of "Les Six," was decidedly remote from the perspectives of its other members. Indeed, he and Erik Satie disliked each other's music. Honegger was more serious in his application, as much German as French in temperament, more concerned with form, more devoted (at least initially) to counterpoint than to color and harmony. Once he had passed his mid-twenties, however, he had the means to provide content as well as form and he advanced to a position of importance among twentieth century composers.

Commissioned by the Koussevitzky Music Foundation and bearing a dedication to the conductor's late wife, Honegger's *Symphony No. 5, Di tre re* (Of the three Ds) was premiered on March 9, 1951, by the Boston Symphony Orchestra under Charles Münch, who followed Sergey Koussevitzky as the orchestra's music director. The composer had begun work in September 1950, completing it in December of that year.

At 22 to 25 minutes in length, the *Fifth Symphony* is slightly shorter than the languorous *Fourth* and very different in temperament and intent. The first movement is marked Grave and opens with high-density chords moving in counter fashion, the lower ones rising as the high ones descend. Around the initial D minor chord, dissonant cadences circle, weighty and menacing. On longer lines now, the movement builds in intensity over the same measured tempo, volume rising in a restatement of the opening motive. Trumpets punctuate the climax and then a softly voiced variation emerges, and the movement works its way to a subdued close. The final note is a low D played pizzicato by cellos and double basses along with timpani.

The second movement is a sober one marked Allegretto, Adagio, a scherzo of sorts, though a cheerless one. The clarinet, along with stabbing violin figures, begins and, when the music peaks, an Adagio theme begins with mid-range strings moving above the violins. When the Allegretto starts again, it rides over a bed of 16th notes. The Adagio cuts in once more before yielding to a final return of the initial theme. The movement ends with the low D that concluded the first movement, again voiced by cellos, basses, and timpani.

With a march rhythm (Allegro marcato) sounded by the trumpets, the final movement threatens and glowers. Other instruments dart about, but cannot overpower the relentless 4/4 motion as the music drives forward with inexorable determination. Suddenly, it sounds softly, volume brought low as the pulse continues, unyielding. As the double basses drop down to the low D, the music ends. The third of the Ds in the symphony's title is sounded once more—pizzicato cellos, basses, and timpani. *—Erik Eriksson*

Recommended:

- ○ **Milhaud: Les Choéphores; Honegger: Symphonie 5; Roussel: Bacchus et Ariane** / Markevitch (cond.), Lamoureux Concert Association Orch. / 1997 / DG 449748

ORCHESTRAL

Pacific 231, symphonic movement ("Mouvement symphonique No. 1") (1923)

This work caused a sensation at its May 8, 1924, Paris premiere, ushering in a trend toward mechanistic works, a trend that influenced even giants like Prokofiev, in his *Symphony No. 2,* and the then Paris-based lesser light American composer George Antheil in his riotous *Ballet méchanique.* But *Pacific 231* (this is really the subtitle and *Mouvement symphonique No. 1* the actual title), never caught on like other sensational Paris premieres, such as Stravinsky's *The Rite of Spring.* Still, it is hardly a neglected piece today, and how many twentieth century works can approach the popularity of Stravinsky's masterpiece? *Pacific 231* depicts the mechanical movements of a train, the Pacific 231. It starts off chugging, gradually gaining momentum, a momentum the listener soon senses will turn brutal and crushing. The music gains in energy, never losing its motoric poise, its austere determination taking on the role of an unleashed force of nature, blindly wreaking its savagery to all things in its path. The music grows in intensity, melody not significant to its expressive manner here, only rhythm and headlong drive. After a powerful climax, the work ends with the locomotive elements slowing but not surrendering their all-conquering grip. *—Robert Cummings*

Recommended:

- ○ **Honegger** / Martinon (cond.), O.R.T.F. / EMI 63944
- ○ **Honegger: Orchestral Works** / Zinman (cond.), Zurich Tonhalle Orch. / 1999 / Decca 455352
- ○ **Honegger: Symphonies 1–5, etc** / Dutoit (cond.), Bavarian Radio SO / 1998 / Teldec 21340
- ○ **Honegger: Symphonies; Mouvements Symphoniques** / Luisi (cond.), Suisse Romande Orch. / 2000 / Cascavelle 6132

Pastorale d'été, symphonic poem for chamber orchestra (1920)

Arthur Honegger was one of the more prominent members of Les Six and this composition was one of his earliest successes. It would not create the sensation caused by the 1924 premiere of his *Pacific 231,* of course, but *Pastorale d'été* did receive a Prix Verley by the audience, who, as part of their concert-series duties, rated new works after their premieres. Subtitled, "Poème symphonique" and prefaced in the score with the words, "I have embraced the summer's red of morn," the work is scored for a chamber-sized ensemble consisting of strings, single woodwinds, and horn. It opens with a lovely, languorously soaring theme first given to the horn, then taken up by the strings. The instrumentation—especially for the horn, flute, and clarinet—is quite simple, but perfectly matched to the pastoral nature of the theme and overall mood in the outer sections. The middle section is lively, full of playful mischief, and colorfully orchestrated. The main theme returns to close the piece in the same peaceful, Romantic manner of the opening. *Pastorale d'été* lasts eight to ten minutes in a typical performance. *—Robert Cummings*

Recommended:

- ○ **Honegger** / Martinon (cond.), O.R.T.F. / EMI 63944
- ○ **The 4 Seasons** / Plasson (cond.), Toulouse Orch. / DG 469376

Rugby, tone poem ("Mouvement symphonique No. 2") (1928)

Arthur Honegger's *Rugby* (1928) takes a place among the composer's best-known orchestral works. *Rugby* is the second in a series of "mouvements symphoniques" that includes the popular *Pacific 231* (1923). These short, intense works took their inspiration in part from purely practical concerns: Honegger observed that orchestras often tended to turn away from modern music, preferring to stick to time-tested repertoire; by expressing his ideas in the compact "mouvement symphonique" format, he hoped to give them greater potential for success among conductors and audiences alike.

Honegger took a special interest in things mechanical and sportive, and such themes found musical expression in the "mouvements symphoniques." *Pacific 231* celebrates the power and excitement of locomotion, while *Rugby* colorfully evokes the movement and aggression of that sport. Still, Honegger was wary of music that required visual or symbolic aids and liked to think of *Rugby* as an absolute, rather than programmatic, work.

Per the suggestion of its title, there is hardly a dull moment in *Rugby.* A rapid ascending figure in the violins heralds a flurry of activity. A fast triplet figure repeats numerous times until the trombone enters with a fragment of the "sport" motive. This theme, as it were, takes a while to develop more fully; like a ball being passed about, it restlessly moves from one instrumental grouping to another. A more lyrical line emerges from the violins, but is soon swept away in a flurry of activity.

A pointillistic section features the bassoons and basses. The lyrical melody makes another brief appearance, while the "sport" motive continues to blossom. A series of dissonant block chords provide the impression of a conclusion; however, a more consonant statement takes over, as though signalling a victory, and brings *Rugby* to a powerful and enthusiastic end. *—Franklin Stover*

Recommended:

- ○ **Honegger** / Martinon (cond.), O.R.T.F. / EMI 63944
- ○ **Honegger: Orchestral Works** / Zinman (cond.), Zurich Tonhalle Orch. / 1999 / Decca 455352
- ○ **Milhaud: Les Choéphores; Roussel: Symphony 3; Honegger: Rugby; Pacific 231** / Bernstein (cond.), New York PO / 1996 / Sony 62352

CHORAL

Jeanne d'Arc au bûcher, dramatic oratorio (1935–1944)

The dramatic oratorio *Jeanne d'Arc au bûcher* (Joan of Arc at the Stake) remains the best-known and most-often-played composition of Arthur Honegger. Since its premiere in 1938, *Jeanne d'Arc au bûcher* has enjoyed both critical and popular esteem. Honegger, however, claimed that he had merely put his talents at the disposal of the immensely talented Paul Claudel, the French poet and politician who wrote the work's libretto.

In 1934, dancer Ida Rubenstein, taken with the concept of the medieval mystery play, approached Honegger with the idea for an oratorio based on life of the recently canonized Joan of Arc. But their first meeting with Claudel went poorly. The poet felt that the project was too difficult, that it was impossible to improve upon the story of the warrior maid. Yet, riding the train home, he was suddenly struck with inspiration; the libretto was complete days later.

Claudel's libretto ranges from dark humor to heartbreaking poignancy. Puns are interspersed with scriptural allusions; medieval Latin legal terms are juxtaposed with mystical images. The dramatic action flows freely, irrespective of chronology: the stake is located at a confluence of past, present, and future. In addition to the libretto, Claudel provided Honegger with scenarios detailing what should happen in the music, which the composer was later to cite in reducing his role to that of collaborator.

But Honegger rose to meet the powerful libretto. At this point in his career, he had begun writing film scores (he would compose more than 40), and *Jeanne d'Arc au bûcher* is certainly dramatic. The chorus alone runs the gamut from whispering to wordless humming, from singing exuberant folk melodies to shouting accusations at the heroine. Honegger achieved further variety by using several different groups, including speaking parts (Joan and the friar), solo voices (3 women, 2 men), and a second chorus (of children). The composer not only utilized percussion and winds skillfully, but also used new instruments (the expressive ondes martenot) and old ones in new ways (anticipating later composers such as Cage, Honegger used a prepared piano).

Composed in 1935, the oratorio did not have its premiere until May 12, 1938. However, its overwhelming reception finally guaranteed Honegger the admiration of the French artistic community, which had previously regarded him with some skepticism. Claudel and Honegger would collaborate again immediately, on the oratorio *La Danse des morts.* In 1944 they would add the Prologue to *Jeanne d'Arc au bûcher,* which compares the formless void of Genesis to the darkness enveloping France during the Hundred Years' War. The date of its addition suggests the intention of a further comparison to France during World War II.

Honegger's score caricatures various older forms in its darkly comic moments, including chant, Medieval song, Baroque ritornello, folk song, and 1930s jazz. These in turn set off soaring, lyrically expressive moments. *Jeanne d'Arc au bûcher* is one of those rare works in which both text and music rise to the occasion demanded by the lofty subject. *—Thomas Oram*

Synopsis:

Prologue. Quoting Genesis, the chorus describes the chaos enveloping France of the Hundred Years' War. God's sending of Joan is likened to His dispelling of the formless void. By the conclusion of the prologue, the comparison to another annunciation is overt: "there was a virgin by the name of Joan."

Scene One—Voices from Heaven. After an orchestral introduction, a wordless chorus culminates in a threefold cry of "Joan!"

Scene Two—The Book. Joan of Arc enters, chained, as the choral cry of "Joan" becomes the cry of Brother Dominic, a friar visiting her. She recognizes him as a Dominican, at which he professes shame at his brothers' treatment of her. Joan, ever forgiving, gracefully declares that her blood will cleanse that guilt. Brother Dominic reveals that he is carrying a book in which the events of her life have been inscribed, at which Joan confesses that she cannot read. Dominic then begins to read to Joan, in reverse, the events of her life which she will now experience.

Scene Three—Voices from Earth. Brother Dominic reads the allegations, which Joan repeats in disbelief. The chorus takes up the accusation "Heretic! Witch! Apostate!" as Joan begs to know why she deserves such slurs. A solo bass intones in Latin the charges and is joined by a tenor intoning the death sentence, punctuated by the chorus. Joan cannot believe that men of God would accuse her in such a manner. In reply, Dominic declares that they are not men at all, but beasts.

Scene Four—Joan Given Over to the Beasts. A herald tries to establish the court, but one by one the wild beasts, including a tiger, fox, and snake, refuse. Finally, the bishop Cauchon, appearing as Porcus, a pig, agrees to serve as inquisitor. An ass is appointed stenographer, and a hasty, farcical trial ensues, which climaxes in Joan, who has maintained her innocence throughout, receiving the sentence of death by flames.

Scene Five—Joan at the Stake. Joan beseeches Brother Dominic to read on. He tells her that her misfortune is the result of a game of cards. She receives the following scene as explanation.

Scene Six—The Kings, or the Invention of the Game of Cards. Heralds announce a royal game of cards, and an automated ballet-like scene begins. The King of France, with Queen Stupidity, enters. Next the King of England, with Queen Bombast, and the Duke of Burgundy, on the arm of Avarice. The necessary fourth is found in the person of Death, accompanied by Lust. Yet the actual game is controlled by the Jacks, the French nobility. Following the third game, the loser has nothing left to give and agrees to hand over Joan of Arc.

Scene Seven—Catherine and Margaret. Joan again hears voices from heaven, which urge her to action. The girl prepares to lead the Dauphin to his coronation.

Scene Eight—The King Who Goes to Rheims. A chorus of children gives way to a reunion between Heurtebise (the Windmill) and the Mother of the Barrels. Representing the two halves, north and south, of fifteenth century France, they are united as the people celebrate. A clerk announces the arrival of the royal procession. As the triumph swells, Joan cries out that all this was her doing. Brother Dominic reproves her, claiming that the author is God. Joan replies, "God with Joan!"

Scene Nine—The Sword of Joan. Again the celestial voices address Joan, who while admiring the beauty of Normandy longs for the Lorraine of her childhood. Brother Dominic asks whence she got her sword, and Joan replies that she must show him Lorraine for him to understand. The folk-like chorus evokes this past, and Joan declares that it was here that she first heard the voices and received her sword, "whose name is not Hatred, but Love!"

Scene Ten—Trimazo. The book is now finished, the scene is again at Rouen. Joan attempts to sing the folk melody from Lorraine, but there is no escape any longer.

Scene Eleven—Joan of Arc in the Flames. Abandoned to her fate, a fearful Joan is comforted by the Virgin. Joan refuses to sign a confession forced upon her by the inquisitors. She fears that the flames are her bridal gown, but the Virgin declares that death is her ultimate triumph over her persecutors. She breaks her chains as the chorus joins with the heavenly voices and the Virgin to confess that "greater love hath no man than this—to give his life for those he loves." *—Thomas Oram*

Recommended:

○ **Honegger: Jeanne D'Arc Au Bûcher** / Baudo (cond.), Herzog, Rodde, Chateau, Jankovsky, Kuhn Children's Chorus, Prague SO / Supraphon 0557

Le roi David, oratorio ("Psaume symphonique") (1921; revised 1923)

King David originated as music for a play, styled a "dramatic psalm," by Rene Morat in 1921. Honegger set about recasting the music as a formal oratorio with full orchestra. In that form it has been successful ever since, despite its unusual demands for performing forces. Its origins are reflected in its form, which is in 27 smaller segments collected into three major sections, and interlinked with spoken narration. All the incidents of the great Hebrew king's life are recounted: Part 1 follows the shepherd boy David through his battles, including his triumph over Goliath and his conflict with King Saul. The brief second section is his coronation and a dance before the Ark. The final movement chronicles his troubled reign, including the incident with Bathsheba and the revolt of Absalom (which call forth two separate and moving songs of penitence). The conclusion, a flowing alleluia sung against a chorale, is deeply affecting. Along the way there are dances, barbaric marches, and the virtual invention of the musical style that would emerge in Hollywood biblical epics. *—Joseph Stevenson*

Synopsis:

Part One. The setting is Israel, approximately 1000 B.C.E. The narrator describes God's anger with Saul and command to the prophet Samuel to go look for a new king among Jesse's sons. In the "Cantique du berger David" (Song of David the Shepherd), he declares his confidence in God. The chorus praises God ("Loue soit le Seignuer"). The narrator goes on to describe David's killing Goliath and thus defeating the Philistine army, and the women going out to greet him, singing his praises ("Chant de Victoire"). The song ends with a declamation that Saul has slain thousands and David tens of thousands. The narrator says that Micah, Saul's daughter, fell in love with David, and that God sent an evil spirit into Saul so that while David was playing the harp for him, Saul tried to kill him. David bewails his persecution but still puts his faith in God ("Ne crains rien"). The narrator goes on to describe David's flight into the desert, joining the community of prophets, and his prayers to God for peace and safety ("Ah, si' j'avais des ailes de colombe"). The prophets sing of the transience of human life ("L'homme ne de la femme"). David prays for God's pity ("Pitie de moi, mon Dieu, pitie"), but still anticipates singing joyful songs of praise. The narrator describes David entering Saul's camp, but instead of killing him, taking his spear and water jug as a sign that he would not strike God's anointed. The Philistines return, David among them, and the chorus sings that under God's protection, they have no fear ("L'eternel est ma lumière infinie"). Saul is unable to receive any vision from God and so he seeks out the Pythoness (the Witch of Endor). She raises the ghost of the angel Samuel ("Om! Om! Par le feu et par l'eau"), and Samuel tells Saul that he will be defeated and killed. After the battle, a messenger brings David Saul's crown and bracelet, and David weeps for him and for his son Jonathan, who had been his friend. The soloists and chorus lament Saul's death and Israel's defeat ("Ah! Pleurez Saul").

Part Two. The narrator declares that David has become king of Israel, and the women sing and dance before the Ark of the Covenant ("Chantez, mes soeurs, chantez"), celebrating the freedom that David has brought them. The soldiers and priests join in the celebrations ("Jehovah! Jehovah!"), and David dances in celebration before the Ark. An angel sings that a descendant of David will reign over all the nations ("David, ce n'est pas toi le roi"), and a choir of angels sing "Alleluia."

The chorus rejoices in David's kingship ("De mon coeur jaillit un cantique"). The narrator says that David became the greatest of all the kings, but one evening he walked on the roof of his palace and from there saw Bathsheba, Uriah's wife, bathing. The narrator tells how David had Uriah killed in battle and took Bathsheba for his own wife, but that God punished him by killing their infant son. In the "Psaume de penitence" (Penitential Psalm), the chorus begs for forgiveness. The narrator says that God sent Nathan to David to denounce his crime, and the chorus again begs for mercy ("Je fus concu dans le peche"). The narrator describes the further turmoil in David's family, a brother has raped his sister, and another brother killed his sibling. Absalom, another son raised a revolt, and David again fled to the desert. David remains confident in God's help ("Je leve mes regards vers la montagne"). The narrator says that Absalom's army was defeated and Absalom himself killed in the forest of Ephraim, and the women's chorus celebrates ("La chansom d'Ephraim"). The narrator describes David's tears for his son, though he still thanks his army and praises God ("Je t'aimerai, Seigneur, d'un amour tendre"). However, the narrator describes David's becoming proud of his power and ordering a census (against God's decree), and so God sent a plague. The choir prays for help ("Dans cet effroi"). After the plague passes, David builds the magnificent Temple of Jerusalem, and has Solomon, his son by Bathsheba, crowned king. The narrator describes David's thanking God for his life, and the angel and chorus sing of David's offspring (Jesus) who will give life to all God's people ("Dieu te dit"). *—Ann Feeney*

Recommended:

○ **Honegger: Le Roi David** / Abravanel (cond.), Watts, Davrath, Preston, Sorenson, Utah SO, University of Utah Chorus / 1991 / Vanguard 4038

○ **Honegger: Le Roi David** / Dutoit (cond.), Eda-Pierre, Tappy, Collard, Valere, Instrumental Ens., Philippe Caillard Chorale / Erato 45800

Hong Kong Philharmonic Orchestra

f. 1895, Hong Kong

Ensemble

Without doubt, the Hong Kong Philharmonic Orchestra is one of the most important performing ensembles in Asia. While the HKPO has roots that date back to 1895, it came into existence as a viable entity under its current name in 1957. Yet it did not become a professional performing ensemble until 1974.

The orchestra was formed in 1895 and gave its inaugural concert that year under the baton of George Lammert. It disbanded the same year, but re-formed in 1903 and began giving concerts again. Once more it ceased, remaining idle until 1907, when Denman Fuller took over as conductor. Concerts were given irregularly and the players were amateurs, though the level of talent was considered relatively high and enthusiasm among the public was strong. For the next several decades, the orchestra sporadically performed under different conductors with no apparent serious intention by management of converting the players to professionals or the operations to a more regular schedule.

After World War II, the ensemble was reorganized and called the Sino-British Orchestra. Its conductor was talented violinist Solomon Bard, who helped shape the players into a quite talented ensemble, yet the orchestra's concerts always featured only native artists. That would change during the tenure of Bard's successor, Shanghai conductor Arrigo Foa, who assumed duties when Bard stepped down in 1953. Foa first attracted Hungarian pianist Louis (Lajos) Kentner, who collaborated with him in a performance of the Beethoven *Piano Concerto No. 3.* Near the end of 1957, the orchestra took its current name, splitting with the Hong Kong Philharmonic Society. Foa remained its music director. In 1962, the HKPO began performing in Hong Kong's newly constructed city hall. In 1969, Lim Kektjiang was appointed to succeed Foa as music director. It was owing to his initiative that the orchestra turned professional in 1973. Its size of 27 players, however, limited it mostly to the more lightly scored early Classical and Baroque repertory. Kektjiang was succeeded by Hans Gunter Mommer in 1975, who encouraged a more European sound and oversaw the orchestra's gradual increase in size. Mommer resigned in 1978 amid morale problems and difficulties with players, who now numbered 78. Chinese conductor Ling Tung was appointed music director that same year, but in a short time developed a strained relationship with the HKPO members, many of whom resigned or were dismissed. Tung resigned in 1981 and the orchestra was without a permanent conductor until 1984, though many prominent guest conductors were engaged, including Maxim Shostakovich, who had recently defected from the Soviet Union with his son Dmitry. In fact, Shostakovich was appointed to serve as principal guest conductor in 1982. American Kenneth Schermerhorn assumed the post of music director in 1984. Two years later, the HKPO made a successful concert tour of the Republic of China. Schermerhorn made several highly praised recordings with his new orchestra, including one of the Villa-Lobos *Choros 8 & 9.* In 1989, David Atherton assumed the podium duties and the orchestra, having already achieved much prestige under the leadership of Schermerhorn, continued to live up to its reputation as one of the finest orchestras in Asia. Atherton made a series of well-received Stravinsky recordings with the orchestra. The HKPO's music director in the new century was Samuel Wong, who made a critically successful recording with the orchestra of the *Turandot Suite* and other works by Ferruccio Busoni. In 2002, the HKPO consisted of 89 members and performed its regular concerts in the Hong Kong Cultural Center. *—Robert Cummings*

Recommended:

○ **Bright Sheng** / Wong (cond.), Gondek, Qiang, Hong Kong PO / 2002 / Naxos 8555866

○ **First Contemporary Chinese Composers Festival 1986** / Schermerhorn, Tang (conds.), Banowetz, Rippon, Hong Kong PO / 1995 / Marco Polo 223915

○ **DU Mingxin: Great Wall Symphony** / Jean (cond.), Hong Kong PO / 1994 / Marco Polo 223939

Jascha Horenstein

b. May 6, 1898, Kiev, Ukraine, **d.** Apr. 2, 1973, London, England
Conductor

A champion of modern music and an intellectual and philosophical conductor of a sort not much encountered any more, Jascha Horenstein moved to Vienna with his family at age six. He went on to study violin with Adolf Busch, Indian philosophy at the University of Vienna, and music at the Vienna School of Music. By 20 he had already decided to become a conductor and left Vienna for study in Berlin, where he conducted the Schubert Choir and became an assistant to Furtwängler. In 1924, he made his debut with the Vienna Symphony Orchestra, conducting Mahler's then-little-known *First Symphony.* From 1925 to 1928, he conducted the Berlin Symphony Orchestra, and in 1929, as guest conductor, he led the Berlin Philharmonic Orchestra in the premiere of Alban Berg's *Lyric Suite.* As a young man he made the acquaintance of Schoenberg, Webern, Stravinsky, Rachmaninov, Richard Strauss, Busoni, and Janáček, and frequently programmed their music for the rest of his life.

On Furtwängler's recommendation, Horenstein was appointed director of the Düsseldorf Opera in 1929, and remained there until, as a Jew, he was forced to leave Nazi Germany. In the 1930s he lived in Paris and traveled extensively, conducting in Brussels, Vienna, and the USSR, visiting Scandinavia with the ballets russes, and touring Australia and New Zealand. He settled in the U.S. in 1942, became U.S. citizen, conducted many of the leading orchestras of both North and South America and was one of four conductors, including Toscanini, to conduct the newly-formed Palestine Symphony Orchestra. Though in great demand from the 1930s onwards, Horenstein did not actively seek a permanent conductorship; he appeared to prefer to work on his own terms.

After the Second World War, Horenstein returned to Europe and lived in Lausanne, Switzerland. Highlights of his renewed European career came in 1950, when he introduced Berg's opera *Wozzeck* in Paris, and in 1959, when his performance of Mahler's *Eighth Symphony* for the BBC did much to stimulate a Mahler revival in Britain. After 1964, when he presented Busoni's *Doktor Faust* in New York, he gave many concerts in London with the London Symphony Orchestra and in Manchester with the BBC Northern Symphony Orchestra. In his later years, he appeared frequently at London's Covent Garden.

From Furtwängler, Horenstein learned the importance in searching for the metaphysical rather than theoretical meaning of music, and that outlook coincided with his own interest in Eastern philosophy. As a conductor, Horenstein greatly admired Stokowski for his broad repertoire and the sense of occasion he brought to every performance. He was intolerant of routine performances, even from the greatest orchestras, and in rehearsal, he would run through large sections of a work to establish coherence and continuity before proceeding to finer details of interpretation. In the words of his assistant Lazar, "[t]he exceptional unity and cohesion that characterized his performances arose from the way he controlled rhythm, harmony, dynamics and tempo so that each individual moment might achieve the most vivid characterization, but the overall line and cumulative effect would not be lost."

In the early days of the LP record, Horenstein was widely known for his recordings of the Viennese masters, particularly Mahler and Bruckner, and derived inspiration from the interpretations of his idols, Nikisch, Walter, and Furtwängler. Before he was 30, he had recorded Mahler's *Kindertotenlieder* and Bruckner's *Seventh Symphony.* Shortly before his death, he said that "[o]ne of the greatest regrets in dying is that I shall never again be able to hear 'Das Lied von der Erde.'" *—Roy Brewer*

Recommended:

○ **Horenstein conducts Strauss, Wagner, Mahler & Schönberg** / Horenstein (cond.), Foster, Bamberg SO, Southwest German Radio Orch. / 1996 / Vox 5529

○ **Dvořák: Symphony 9; Wagner: The Flying Dutchman Ov.; Siegfried-Idyll** / Horenstein (cond.), Royal PO / 1989 / Chesky 31

○ **Mahler: Symphony 9 / Kindertotenlieder** / Horenstein (cond.), Baker, London SO, Scottish National Orch. / 2001 / BBC 4075

○ **Mahler: Symphony 6** / Horenstein (cond.), Stockholm PO / 1989 / Unicorn Kanchana 202425

Marilyn Horne

b. Jan. 16, 1934, Bradford, PA
Mezzo-Soprano

Marilyn Horne was one of the most admired singers of her generation, and was a major factor in the bel canto revival of the 1960s. While she was especially associated with the works of Rossini and Handel (she persuaded the Metropolitan Opera to mount *Rinaldo* for her in 1984, making it the first time the house had ever performed a Handël opera), she was no less adept in Vivaldi and Bellini operas, lieder (especially Mahler), French roles such as Fidès in Meyerbeer's *Le Prophete* and the title role of Thomas' *Mignon*; she even took on some Verdi roles, but public reception for those was mixed. Her highly flexible and powerful voice had a certain metallic quality that was especially effective in trouser roles, particularly the martial ones, such as *Rinaldo* and *Tancredi*—earning her the sometime nickname of "General Horne." She possessed an extraordinary range, and in concert even performed Brünnhilde's Immolation Scene.

Horne's father was an amateur singer and her first teacher. Her professional debut was at the age of four—at a picnic rally for Franklin Delano Roosevelt's presidential reelection, where she sang "Believe me, if all those endearing young charms," and received a can of soda as her salary!. As her vocal potential became clearer still, she began studies with Edna Luce, whom she credits for the extraordinary breathing technique formed the foundation of her bel canto excellence. In 1951, she was awarded a scholarship to the University of Southern California, Long Beach, sang part-time in the noted Roger Wagner Chorale, and also participated in Lotte Lehmann's master classes. In 1954, she made her opera debut as Hata in *The Bartered Bride* with the Guild Opera Company, and came to national fame by providing the singing voice for Dorothy Dandridge in the film *Carmen Jones.*

In 1956, she went to Europe to continue her studies and, in 1957, joined the opera company at Gehenkirchen, Germany, as a soprano. There she sang such lyric soprano roles as Mimi in *La Bohème,* Amelia in *Simon Boccanegra,* and Tatiana in *Eugene Onegin.* She returned to the United States in 1960, and made her San Francisco debut as Marie in Alban Berg's *Wozzeck.* The next year, she made her New York debut at the American Opera Society, singing a concert performance of Bellini's *Beatrice di Tenda* in a cast featuring another singer making her New York debut, Joan Sutherland. The two of them became *the* soprano/mezzo pairing for bel canto operas such as *Norma, Semiramide,* and *Anna Bolena.* In 1969, she made her La Scala debut as Neocles in Rossini's *The Siege of Corinth*, and her Met debut as Adalgisa in *Norma* followed in 1970. In 1982, the Rossini Foundation awarded her its first Golden Plaque, acclaiming her as "the greatest Rossini singer in the world." In 1999, she announced her retirement from classical music. From 1960 to 1976, Horne was married to the African-American conductor Henry Lewis (They met while in college; he was in the orchestra for *The Bartered Bride*, and upon hearing her powerful low register emerge from the chorus, he leaned over to ask a friend "who's that tenor?"). *—Ann Feeney*

Recommended:

- ○ **Recital** / Scimone (cond.), Horne, I Solisti Veneti / Erato 063014069
- ○ **Marilyn Horne Recital** / Horne, etc. / 2004 / Decca 000214402
- ○ **The Golden Voice** / Horne, etc. / 2003 / Decca 000151202
- ○ **Rossini: Semiramide** / Bonynge (cond.), Sutherland, Horne, Rouleau, Fyson, London SO / 1986 / Decca 425481

Vladimir Horowitz

b. Oct. 1, 1903, Berdichev, Russia, **d.** Nov. 5, 1989, New York, NY
Pianist

A pianist of legendary fame and stature, Vladimir Horowitz was born in Kiev, Ukraine. His mother, herself a professional pianist, provided his first instruction at the piano and was the first to recognize his extraordinary talents; he studied further at the Kiev Conservatory. His first public appearance was a recital in Kiev on May 30, 1920, and in 1922 he gave a series of 15 concerts in Kharkov for which he was paid in food and clothing. Although Russia was still reeling from the revolution of 1917, Horowitz fashioned successful concert tours in major cities such as Moscow, Leningrad, and Kiev—marking the beginning of a performing career of unflagging and spectacular success.

His first international appearance came with his 1926 trip to Berlin, soon after which followed concerts in Paris, London, and New York. Further appearances in the United States solidified his reputation as an exceptional virtuoso, and the country which was to become his adopted home embraced him warmly. He was invited to the White House to play for President Hoover in 1931, and in 1933 he married Wanda Toscanini—the daughter of the famous conductor Arturo Toscanini, who would soon conduct Horowitz and the New York Philharmonic Orchestra in performances of the Beethoven piano concertos. Horowitz permanently settled in the United States in 1940 and achieved citizenship in 1944.

Wanda Toscanini assumed a gentle stewardship of her new husband, who was in fragile physical and emotional health. Often seized with an irrational fear of failure, Horowitz found the life of touring threatening to his equilibrium. He withdrew from the concert stage for several periods during his life, and made only rare appearances after 1970. When Horowitz did schedule a concert, it often took the persuasive powers of his wife and friends to keep him from canceling at the last minute. His nagging, and often overpowering, insecurity led him to seek shock therapy in 1973, but though he seemed to achieve some benefit from treatment, he was never free of anxiety when playing in public. The one exception to this trend was when he appeared as accompanist to another artist, which he often did with baritone Dietrich Fischer-Dieskau, cellist Mstislav Rostropovich, and violinist Isaac Stern. Because of his long absences from the concert stage, Horowitz's popularity was largely sustained by his recordings.

Perhaps the most significant single event in Horowitz's long career was his long-overdue return to the Soviet Union (his first since his departure in the 1920s) for a series of concerts in 1986. The resulting tour became a major political event, coinciding as it did with an era of new understanding between the United States and the Soviet Union, and it resonated powerfully with Soviet audiences. Revitalized by the Soviet tour, Horwowitz signed a new contract with Sony; the contract included provisions for recording him at home on his favorite piano. He made his last such recording on November 1, 1989; on November 5 he died of a massive heart attack.

As a performer, Horowitz had huge resources of speed and power, and a clean articulation. His performances were brilliant, exciting, and often mystifying to those who found his technique enigmatic (he played, for instance, with unusually straight fingers, laying them nearly flat on the keys). Though his performances were frequently criticized for their willfulness and self-indulgent nature, there was an undeniable charisma to his playing that endeared him to most everyone who heard him. *—AMG*

Recommended:

- ○ **Horowitz Rediscovered** / Horowitz / 2003 / RCA 50749
- ○ **Horowitz Plays Rachmaninoff** / Horowitz / RCA 7754
- ○ **Horowitz: Piano** / Coates (cond.), Horowitz, London SO / 2002 / Andante 2980
- ○ **Chopin: Piano Music** / Horowitz / 2001 / RCA 68008
- ○ **Horowitz Plays Scriabin** / Horowitz / 2003 / Sony 90445
- ○ **Horowitz Plays Scarlatti** / Horowitz / 2003 / Sony 90414
- ○ **Horowitz Plays Schumann** / Horowitz / 1998 / Philips 456838

Mieczysław Horszowski

b. Jun. 23, 1892, Lemberg (Lvov), Poland, **d.** May 22, 1993, Philadelphia, PA
Pianist

Polish-born pianist Mieczysław Horszowski performed his last recital at age 99, slightly more than a year before his death in 1993. His recording career went back to the age of cylinders, and the traditions of playing he represented were even older than that, dating back to the early Romantic era. He was taught to play the piano by his mother, a student of one of Chopin's students, and his main teacher, Theodor Leschetizky, was a protégé of Czerny. Horszowski was playing (and transposing) Bach inventions at age five; at eight he was presented to the public as a prodigy, and at ten he began his formal career. He played for Fauré and perhaps Saint-Saëns in 1905 and made his U.S. debut, at Carnegie Hall, the following year. It was also during 1906 that he met the youthful Pablo Casals and Arturo Toscanini, who became lifelong friends and collaborators. Horszowski was especially noted as a chamber music pianist and became a fixture of Casals' Prades Festival for many years.

Interrupting his high-flying career to pursue a humanities degree at the Sorbonne in Paris from 1911 to 1913, Horszowski moved to Milan during the war and remained there until 1939, touring internationally. As World War II broke out he was appearing in Brazil, and instead of returning to Europe he headed for the U.S., where he remained for the rest of his life. Horszowski quickly found performing opportunities with Toscanini's NBC Symphony, and he began teaching at Philadelphia's Curtis Institute in 1942. He was a fixture of New York's recital scene, performing complete cycles of Beethoven's piano works and Mozart sonatas and concertos, and he appeared at the White House in 1961 and 1978. Horszowski was the first person to record while playing the first known piano constructed, an instrument built in 1720 by Bartolomeo Cristofori and housed in the collection of the Metropolitan Museum of Art in New York. In 1981, at age 89, Horszowski married for the first time; his wife was Italian pianist Beatrice Costa. His eyesight declined, which put an end to his concerto and chamber music performances, but he continued his solo recital career, performing from memory. At the Curtis Institute he taught an impressive roster of students, including Anton Kuerti, Murray Perahia, and Richard Goode. Horszowski played a range of music but focused on Bach, Beethoven, and Chopin, and even in his last years he essayed difficult works like Beethoven's *Diabelli Variations*. *—James Manheim*

Recommended:

- ○ **Horszowski Plays Schumann, Chopin & Bach** / Horszowski / 1992 / Nonesuch 79264
- ○ **Horszowski Plays Chopin** / Horszowski / Pearl 9108
- ○ **Bach, Beethoven, Chopin & Schumann** / Horszowski / BBC 4122

Hans Hotter

b. Jan. 19, 1909, Offenbach am Main, Germany, **d.** Dec. 6, 2003, Grünwald, Germany
Bass

Hans Hotter was one of the twentieth century's greatest singing actors. Indeed, he was often compared to the Russian bass-baritone Feodor Chaliapin in histrionic ability as well as vocal endowment. Like the Russian, he was tall, able to bring the authority of his six feet four inch frame to the Wagnerian roles in which he came to specialize. After the retirement of Friedrich Schorr in 1943, Hotter came to be considered the supreme Wotan in Wagner's *Ring of the Nibelung* tetrology.

Hotter trained as an organist and choirmaster, but found his vocal gifts pushing him in the direction of a singing career. He made his debut as the Speaker in Mozart's *Die Zauberflöte* at the age of 20 in the small theatre at Opava. Following contracts in Prague, Breslau, and Hamburg, he was invited to Munich in 1938 and remained associated with that company for much of his subsequent career. In Munich, he came in close contact with composer Richard Strauss who, much impressed with Hotter's singing and acting, composed three roles specifically for him, beginning with the Commandant in *Friedenstag* (Freedom's Day) which had its premiere in Munich in 1938. Following that, Strauss wrote for Hotter the part of Jupiter in *Die Liebe der Danae* (The Love of Danae). Hotter sang the dress rehearsal for a much-delayed production at Salzburg just before all theatres were closed in 1944. In *Capriccio*, Strauss' final opera, Hotter appeared as Olivier at the 1942 premiere.

With the cessation of World War II hostilities, Hotter's career took him abroad, first to London in 1947 where, among other roles, he performed Wotan in stagings given in English; he remained a revered artist in England for as long as his long career continued. In 1950, he made an impressive debut at New York's Metropolitan Opera as the protagonist in Wagner's *Fliegende Holländer*. His immense voice and baleful appearance made a profound effect upon both critics and audiences as yet more comparisons to Chaliapin were invoked. After only a few seasons, however, his Met career came to a halt when general manager Rudolf Bing sought to steer him in the direction of secondary parts. The rest of the opera world was only too happy to hear him perform the great Wagnerian and Strauss roles in which he was incomparable and he was a welcome guest in San Francisco and Chicago.

Vienna was one of several European venues to benefit from his appearances in roles he seldom undertook in the United States. Roles such as Don Basilio in *Barbiere di Siviglia* and King Phillip in Verdi's *Don Carlo* were two especially memorable interpretations.

Throughout the 1950s and on through the last of his public appearances in 1972, Hotter's voice was increasingly prone to unsteadiness at full volume. Acute hay fever bedeviled him during summer engagements such as those at the Bayreuth Festival. Still, his performances remained riveting even in vocal decline and Georg Solti chose him for his *Ring* recording even after he was significantly past his prime.

While better known as an operatic personality, Hotter was a magnificent interpreter of German lieder (he in fact enjoyed performing this music more than opera) and made many recordings of the repertory over a three-decade span. His interpretive genius and ability to scale back his huge voice suited this kind of singing superbly, and the reissue on CD of his best song recordings has won the enthusiasm of a new generation of followers. *—Erik Eriksson*

Recommended:

- ○ **Hotter Lieder Recital** / Hotter, Moore / 2000 / Testament 1198
- ○ **Hotter singt Loewe Balladen** / Hotter, Raucheisen / Preiser 90301
- ○ **Wagner: Tristan und Isolde** / Karajan (cond.), Hotter, Vinay, Weber, Unger, Bayreuth Festival Orch. & Choir / 2002 / Urania 218

Houston Symphony Orchestra

f. 1913, Houston, TX
Ensemble

Houston, Texas, is one of the major port cities of the United States (despite being several dozen miles away from the Gulf of Mexico and connected to it only by bayous and canals), a center of the U.S. petroleum industry, and the headquarters of the American space agency, NASA. The city's "can do" spirit shows itself in the interrupted history of what grew from a small, nearly amateur, orchestra to one of the best U.S. orchestras.

The person who is most responsible for the birth, rebirth, and development of the Houston Symphony Orchestra was a remarkable woman named Ima Hogg. She was the spark plug of a group of civic leaders in 1913 who formed a Symphony Society to establish a regular local orchestra. Until then, Houston had relied on touring orchestras to fill its taste for symphonic music.

In the beginning, it was an ill-paid group of part-time players. Accounts differ as to how large a group and how ill-paid: the authoritative *New Grove Dictionary* says there were 35 musicians paid from an annual budget of $1,500 while the orchestra's own publicity says there were 33 with a budget of $2,500. At any rate, the orchestra was not paid well enough to survive World War I. The first conductor was Julian Paul Blitz (1913–16), who was succeeded by Paul Berge who led the ensemble until it disbanded in 1918.

However, Ms. Hogg's organization remained in existence, and it increased sponsorship and regular appearances of several American orchestras in the city.

The Depression era might have seemed a poor time to try again, but a new orchestra was formed in 1930. (The orchestra officially observes 1913 as its birth year.) It held on, despite the country's financial problems, under the musical leadership of Uriel Nespoli (1931–32) and Frank St. Leger (1932–35).

The orchestra was transformed into a fully professional orchestra by Music Director Ernst Hoffman (1936–47), and attained high standards, which were still more improved by his successor Efrem Kurtz (1948–54). Kurtz introduced Houston to some of the finest new music of the era, including works of Ives, Honegger, Bartók, and Shostakovich.

The orchestra has continued a policy of hiring well-known and established musicians as music director. Ferenc Fricsay served briefly in 1954, followed by Leopold Stokowski (1955–61) and Sir John Barbirolli (1961–67). The next director, André Previn (1967–69) was only beginning his stellar conducting career, but already had been a major jazz and popular pianist for a decade. Then Lawrence Foster (1971–78), Sergiu Comissiona (1979–88) and Christoph Eschenbach (1988–99) continued the Symphony's consistent artistic growth. Since the days of Kurtz and Stokowski, the HSO has continued its support for newer music. Hans Graf was appointed music director in 2000.

It obtained its current home, Jesse Jones Hall, in 1966. Ima Hogg continued to exercise her leadership until her death in 1975. By that time, the orchestra had become (in 1971) a full-time, 52-week orchestra and become acclaimed as one of America's finest. It plays over 200 concerts annually, records frequently, and has a radio program on Houston Public Radio.

A sub-ensemble, the Houston Symphony Chamber Players began appearing in 1993, using the principals of the orchestra, with Eschenbach appearing as conductor and pianist. It specializes in the Classical and contemporary eras, and carries on its own tours, in addition to the HSO's long tradition of touring. *—Joseph Stevenson*

Recommended:

- ○ **Bruckner: Symphony 6** / Eschenbach (cond.), Houston SO / 2000 / Koch International Classics 7484
- ○ **Rouse: Symphony 2; Flute Concerto; Phaethon** / Eschenbach (cond.), Wincenc, Houston SO / 1997 / Telarc 80452
- ○ **Violin Concertos by Adams & Glass** / Eschenbach (cond.), McDuffie, HSO / 1999 / Telarc 80494

Alan Hovhaness

b. Mar. 8, 1911, Somerville, MA, **d.** Jun. 21, 2000, Seattle, WA
Composer: Symphonic, Avant-garde, Orchestral, Concerto

Alan Hovhaness, one of the most prolific composers of the twentieth century, left behind a legacy of hundreds of works, including more than 60 symphonies, numerous choral works, ballets, and operas, and all manner of chamber music. Hovhaness, born of Scottish and Armenian descent in 1911, took an early interest in composition, and by the age of 13 had composed two operas. After studies at the New England Conservatory with Frederick Converse, Hovhaness made a favorable impression with his first acknowledged symphony, *Exile*, when it was performed by the BBC Symphony in London in 1939. The works of Hovhaness' early period both reflect the influence of Renaissance music and utilize the harmonies of the late nineteenth century. During the 1930s the composer developed an interest in Indian music, which became one of the most pervasive influences upon his own works from that time on. In 1942 he received a scholarship to the Berkshire Music Center at Tanglewood, where he attended composition seminars led by Aaron Copland (assisted by Leonard Bernstein). The experience, unfortunately, was less than positive, since both Copland and Bernstein were highly critical of Hovhaness' music. The ridicule he experienced led Hovhaness to leave Tanglewood early. Discouraged, he destroyed many of his early works. Serendipitously, though, the composer's return to Boston was followed by a meeting with the Greek painter and psychic Herman DiGiovanno, who convinced him to study the music of his Armenian ancestry. Further immersion in Armenian church music led Hovhaness to the works of Komitas Vartabed, a priest and composer who died in 1936 and whom Hovhaness described as the "Armenian Bartók." Hovhaness' discovery of Armenian music had a direct effect upon his own works, which became more rhythmically and contrapuntally active and began to reflect the improvisatory nature of Armenian church melodies.

During the 1940s Hovhaness furthered his study of the Armenian culture, playing organ at an Armenian church and learning the Armenian language, and took a further interest in the Eastern philosophies. The growing success of his music in the 1950s led to several important grants and commissions; a grant from the National Institute of Arts and Letters in 1951 allowed him to move to New York. After composing *Ardent Song* (1954), a ballet score for Martha Graham, Hovhaness toured the Far East. Still shunned by the mainstream musical establishment of the time, he continued to receive recognition from without, including Guggenheim Fellowships in 1953, 1954, and 1958. A commission from the Houston Symphony, the *Symphony No. 2* ("Mysterious Mountain"; 1955) provided Hovhaness his first popular success. The work was auspiciously premiered by Leopold Stokowski, and the redoubtable Fritz Reiner made a highly regarded recording of it with the Chicago Symphony.

After receiving a Fulbright Fellowship in 1959, Hovhaness again toured the East and was the first Western composer invited to participate in the music festival in Madras, India. He was also received warmly in Japan, where he made television appearances and conducted his music with the Tokyo Symphony. During a return to Asia in 1962 on a Rockefeller Grant, Hovhaness studied the ancient court music of Japan and Korea.

The aural result of the composer's immersion in Eastern culture is a musical language invested with a sense of mysticism and spirituality. Among his voluminous catalogue, Hovhaness' colorful orchestral works have maintained the greatest popularity among audiences; notable examples include the *Symphony No. 17* ("Symphony for Metal Orchestra"; 1963); *And God Created Great Whales* (1970), which incorporates recordings of actual whale "songs," and the *Symphony No. 50* ("Mount St. Helen's"; 1982). *—Kristen Grimshaw*

SYMPHONIC

Symphony No. 2 ("Mysterious Mountain"), Op. 132 (1955)

The *Symphony No. 2 ("Mysterious Mountain")* is without a doubt Hovhaness' best-known and most popular work. The work was commissioned by Leopold Stokowski, one of the composer's most consistent advocates, and premiered by the Houston Symphony on its first program under the legendary conductor. The concert was telecast nationwide, and Stokowski subsequently featured the work during guest appearances with many of America's leading orchestras. However, the disproportionate success of "Mysterious Mountain" is probably chiefly attributable to a 1958 RCA Victor recording of the work by the Chicago Symphony under Fritz Reiner. Though the work has been recorded a number of times, the Reiner recording has scarcely waned in popularity and has remained in print for over 40 years.

The *Symphony No. 2* is notable for a pervasive sense of spiritual serenity. The first of its three movements alternates between richly consonant hymnlike passages and calm, gentle instrumental solos; throughout, the peaceful mood is never broken. The second movement is a double fugue: the first subject is pentatonic, its development resembling the polyphonic techniques of Renaissance masters like Josquin Desprez; the second subject is quite vigorous and provides the only moments of agitation in the entire work. (This material, indcidentally, appears in more primitive form in Hovhaness' 1936 *String Quartet No. 1*). Eventually the two subjects come together in a majestic, awe-inspiring climax. The third movement returns to the calm, peaceful mood of the opening. A melody, barely audible at first, is repeated rather ominously at an ever-increasing dynamic level until it peaks in a full climax. The Symphony ends with an epilogue that expresses an exquisite spiritual rapture—a passage, the composer maintained, that came to him in a dream. *—Walter Simmons*

Recommended:

○ **Hovhaness: Symphony 2; Prokofiev: Lieutenant Kijé; Stravinsky: Divertimento** / Reiner (cond.), Chicago SO / 1995 / RCA 902661957

○ **Hovhaness: Mysterious Mountains** / Schwarz (cond.), Royal Liverpool PO / 2003 / Telarc 80604

Symphony No. 6, for small orchestra ("Celestial Gate"), Op. 173 (1959)

Of the more than 60 works that Hovhaness has designated "symphonies," the *Symphony No. 6 "Celestial Gate"*, scored for chamber orchestra, is one of the most concise, most thoroughly integrated, and most consistently inspired. Although it did not appear on recording until the early 1970s, it has gradually grown in popularity, benefiting from several fine recorded performances since the advent of the compact disc.

The *Symphony No. 6* comprises one multi-sectional movement lasting approximately 20 minutes. Its tone is consistently reverent and beatific, with even fewer contrasts in mood than are found in the *Symphony No. 2, "Mysterious Mountain."* Like the *Magnificat*, Op. 157, the *Sixth Symphony* may be seen as a consummation of Hovhaness's preoccupation with the materials that concerned him during the 1950s: mysterious pizzicato murmurings in the strings, increasingly unrelated to the prevailing tonality; hymnlike string passages, now including seventh chords; deliberately chaotic episodes, in which groups of instruments play similar passages simultaneously without being coordinated rhythmically; chant like incantations featuring trumpet and other instrumental solos; fervently celestial effects produced by dividing the string sections into sub-groupings; and dance like passages in Armenian style. In addition the central thematic idea of the work is a modal melody of unusual poignancy, less obviously rooted in Armenian melos. This melody is subjected to considerable contrapuntal development, while remaining within a consonant, diatonic, modal framework. Hovhaness has indicated that the work was influenced by Korean traditional music as well as by his usual Armenian sources. *—Walter Simmons*

Recommended:

○ **Hovhaness: Celestial Gate and Other Orchestral Works** / Werthen (cond.), I Fiamminghi / 1995 / Telarc 80392

○ **Hovhaness: Symphonies 6 & 25; Prayer Of St. Gregory** / Hovhaness (cond.), Polyphony Orch. / Crystal 807

Symphony No. 50 ("Mount St. Helens"), Op. 360 (1982)

As is the case with most of his works, Hovhaness' *Symphony No. 50* is dominated by long, Eastern-influenced melody, dance music of the Himalayas and Caucasian mountains, and evocations of Chinese, Korean, and Japanese art and music. But it is the image of the mountain, Hovhaness' most enduring fascination, both literally and figuratively, that takes center stage here—in this case, Mount St. Helens. Hovhaness reportedly witnessed the great volcano's 1980 eruption, and over the course of its three movements, this symphony attempts to capture the serenity of the location before that event, the violence of the eruption itself, and then finally the miracle of creation that volcanism represents—the very remaking of the Earth's surface. The first movement is devoted to the mountain itself—one of the most serene and beautiful in the world before its eruption. The second movement depicts nearby Spirit Lake, where visitors could see the entire mountain reflected in the waters surface. The eruption, which took the top third of the mountain off, and buried Spririt Lake entirely under ash and dust, finally occurs in the third movement. As one might expect, it is one of the most awesome orchestral outbursts in all of music. However, the climax soon gives way to a more celebratory tone, very much in keeping with Hovhaness' view of mountains as symbols of upward reaching spirit. *—Joseph Stevenson*

Recommended:

○ **Hovhaness: Mysterious Mountains** / Schwarz (cond.), Royal Liverpool PO / 2003 / Telarc 80604

○ **Hovhannes Collection Vol. 2** / Schwarz (cond.), Seattle SO / 1993 / Delos 3711

AVANT-GARDE

And God Created Great Whales, for orchestra & taped whale sounds, Op. 229/1 (1970)

Hovaness' *And God Created Great Whales* (1970) combines orchestral sounds with recorded whale songs, including those of the humpback whale and the bowhead. The work begins with rustlings from the string orchestra, quasi-aleatoric (i.e. chance-derived) sounds created by the rapid asynchronous repetition of brief phrases in the strings in what Hovhaness calls "free non-rhythm chaos." Out of this swirling comes a stentorian, pentatonic tune in the brass (suggestive, according to the composer, of "undersea mountains") and a subsequent gentle theme in the strings, leading into the first of four sections of whale songs. In between these songs the trombones and violins imitate the whale sounds through long glissandi. Tuned percussion and harp create a gentle shimmer at one point, picked up by the winds. After more whale songs and rustlings from the strings, the work builds to a loud and forceful coda.

The work was commissioned by André Kostelanetz and the New York Philharmonic. Kostelanetz, one of the composer's most fervent champions, did much to popularize Hovhaness' music via concerts and recordings, and he led the premiere of *And God Created Great Whales* in New York on June 11, 1970. *—Chris Morrison*

Recommended:

○ **Hovhaness: Mysterious Mountain; And God Created Great Whales** / Schwarz (cond.), Seattle SO / 1994 / Delos 3157

ORCHESTRAL

Alleluia and Fugue for strings, Op. 40b (1941)

The *Alleluia and Fugue* (1941), one of Hovhaness' earliest works for string orchestra, is a companion to the *Psalm and Fugue* of the same year. The richness of its textures—the violins are divided into six parts, the cellos into two—owes a great debt to choral music of the Renaissance, as well as more modern works like the similarly Renaissance-inspired *Fantasia on a Theme of Thomas Tallis* by Ralph Vaughan Williams.

The Alleluia is modal, with dense, flowing polyphony that gradually becomes more intense. The five-voice Fugue begins in the cellos and travels throughout the strings. Its tone is restrained, almost pastoral at first, eventually progressing to an almost ecstatic peroration. *—Chris Morrison*

Recommended:

○ **Hovhaness: Mysterious Mountain; And God Created Great Whales** / Schwarz (cond.), Seattle SO / 1994 / Delos 3157

○ **Hovhaness: Celestial Gate** / Werthen (cond.), I Fiamminghi / 1995 / Telarc 80392

Armenian Rhapsody No. 2, for strings, Op. 51 (1944)

The second of Hovhaness' three *Armenian Rhapsodies*, all written in the 1940s for string orchestra, depicts a church festival; after solemn services, the congregants dance joyously in a monastery courtyard. The slow first half is based on the *dagh*, or Armenian sacred song, "Krisdos Paratz Takavorn" (Christ, King of Glory). After a somber, majestic introduction, a faster melody breaks out and is canonically developed. The music recedes into the depths of the cellos and violas, whereupon the dancing begins. In this second section, an Armenian peasant song kicks off over a pizzicato version of the *dagh* and then an even livelier folk dance arrives to join in a polyphonic finale of obsessively repeated motifs. *—James Reel*

Recommended:

○ **Hovhaness: Armenian Rhapsodies 1, 2 & 3; Symphony 38; Concerto 10** / Schwarz (cond.), Seattle SO / 1997 / Koch Schwann 374222

Armenian Rhapsody No. 3, for strings, Op. 189 (1944)

Hovhaness wrote three works designated *Armenian Rhapsody* in 1944. This was a period in Hovhaness' career when he had begun to acknowledge his Armenian heritage in his music. All three are unusual in Hovhaness' output in using actual Armenian folk music.

Hovhaness had organized an amateur string orchestra to raise money for wartime charities. For its first concert (June 17, 1944) he included two of his compositions, which became the basis for this rhapsody. He connected the two pieces with an interlude based on a song he remembered his father singing. The first traditional song, "My Heart is Shattered" is a Good Thursday hymn tune. The second is a secular folk song, "By the Fountain." Hovhaness said that in the brief six-minute span of this rhapsody is a "miniature history of Armenia in three arcs of sound." The first is a cry of the soul of the people, the second is the harp of exile, and the third is a dream of a village fountain, finally dissolving into nothingness. *—Joseph Stevenson*

Recommended:

○ **Hovhaness: Armenian Rhapsodies 1, 2 & 3; Symphony 38; Concerto 10** / Schwarz (cond.), Seattle SO / 1997 / Koch Schwann 374222

○ **Hovhaness: Symphony Etchmiadzin; Armenian Rhapsody 3** / Hovhaness (cond.), Royal PO / Crystal 804

Celestial Fantasy, for strings, Op. 44 (1935–1944)

The *Celestial Fantasy*, completed in 1944, derives from music Hovhaness originally wrote as early as 1935. He dedicated the *Fantasy* to the saint and poet Nerses Shnorhali, who led the Armenian Church around the year 1100. Marked "noble and heroic" in the score, the piece begins in the low strings with a darkly impressive hymn of a rather Armenian cast. After some development of the hymn theme a four-voice fugue evolves naturally out of the polyphony that preceded it, and builds to a rapturous conclusion. *—Chris Morrison*

Recommended:

- **Hovhaness: Mysterious Mountain; And God Created Great Whales** / Schwarz (cond.), Seattle SO / 1994 / Delos 3157
- **Hovhaness: Celestial Fantasy** / Stratton (cond.), Slovak Radio SO Bratislava / 1998 / Dorian 93166

The Holy City, for trumpet, chimes, harp & strings, Op. 218 (1966)

Alan Hovhaness composed the short orchestral work, *Holy City*, in 1965. Inspired by St. John's vision in the Book of Revelations and scored for trumpet, chimes or bells tuned in A, harp, and strings, the work was commissioned by Arthur Bennett Lipkin through the Committee to Further American Contemporary Music. Lipkin conducted its premiere in Portland, Oregon, on April 11, 1967, and recorded the work soon thereafter.

The unique sound world of *Holy City* draws on the composer's ancestral roots (he is of Scots-Armenian descent) and from a lifetime of contact with musics of Asia and India. Other clear influences are old church chorales, the ancient church modes, and polyphonic music of the Netherlands Renaissance style.

Swirling arpeggios from the harp and glissandos (or slides) from the strings open the piece in a mysterious and unsettled fashion. Later a peaceful theme in the strings, in Hovhaness's best hymn-like style, is combined with an arching trumpet melody; these are framed by slow, somewhat dissonant string canons and punctuations from the harp and chimes. *—Chris Morrison*

Recommended:

- **Hovhaness: The Holy City; Psalm & Fugue; Symphony 17; Khrimian** / Clark (cond.), Gecker, Manhattan CO / 1995 / Koch International Classics 7289

CONCERTO

Prayer of St. Gregory, for trumpet & string orchestra, Op. 62b (1946)

The Prayer of St. Gregory, a five-minute work for trumpet and strings, began life as an intermezzo in Hovhaness' opera *Etchmiadzin*, composed in mid-1946, and premiered in New York in October of that year. The present excerpt, described by Hovhaness as "a prayer in darkness," was soon extracted as a separate work, and is one of his most popular short pieces. The personage referred to in the work's title is St. Gregory the Illuminator, who at the beginning of the fourth century brought Christianity to Armenia. This calm work, in a moderate tempo, begins with gentle string chords, chorale-like, in Hovhaness' unmistakable modal melodic and harmonic vein, over which a slow trumpet melody gradually unfolds itself. *—Chris Morrison*

Recommended:

- **Music for Organ, Brass & Percussion** / Woods (cond.), Murray, Empire Brass / 1990 / Telarc 80218
- **Hovhaness: Prayer of St. Gregory; Symphony 22; etc.** / Schwarz (cond.), Butler, Seattle SO / 1997 / Delos 3700
- **Hovhaness: Mountains & Rivers without End; Prayer of St. Gregory; etc.** / Clark (cond.), Gekker, Manhattan CO / 1994 / Koch International Classics 7221

Leslie Howard

b. Apr. 29, 1948, Melbourne, Australia

Pianist

Known as a Liszt specialist, this Australian pianist trained in his native country and later settled in England, where he devoted himself to concert performance, teaching, and scholarly writing mostly all focused on the music of Liszt. Among his many impressive achievements is the recording of the composer's complete solo piano works, including many not heard since the Liszt was alive and performing. Much honored, Leslie Howard has shared his extraordinary understanding of Liszt with students at a number of master classes where his erudition and ease help him convey the essence of Liszt's style. Despite his close identification with Liszt, Howard has recorded works by others composers, proving himself especially persuasive in the music of Franck, Rubinstein, and his fellow countryman Percy Grainger. In his native Melbourne, Howard studied with Donald Britton, June McLean, and Michael Brimer before making his debut with the Melbourne Symphony Orchestra in 1967. He began teaching at Monash University in 1970 and moved to England in 1972. There he undertook further piano training with Noretta Conci and studied composition with Franco Donatoni. Master classes in Siena with Guido Agosti added further polish to his piano technique. As he began to perform extensively in Europe and Australia, he acquired a reputation as a virtuoso artist whose approach was guided by a scholarly mind. He also became an instructor at the Guildhall School of Music beginning in 1987. Two years before, Howard had begun his monumental project which would result, at its completion in 1999, in 94 CDs holding the complete solo piano works of Liszt, including music prepared by the pianist from Liszt's unpublished manuscripts. The result prompted the issuance of a Special Grand Prix du Disque honoring the massive accomplishment. This acknowledgement was in addition to no fewer than five other awards of the regular Grand Prix du Disque given in recognition of Howard's special place in the classical recording industry. Throughout, Howard has enjoyed the support and encouragement of Hyperion Records. Howard has served as President of the British Liszt Society and is an honorary member of the Istituto Liszt in Bologna, Italy. For the inauguration of the latter organization, Howard played a drawing room concert as director Rossana Dalmonte explained the aims of the new organization. Performing on a restored 1860s vintage Steinway, Howard included pieces as varied as the *Sarabande und Chaconne* from Handel's *Almira* to *Weinen, Klagen, Sorgen, Zagen*. His having been chosen for the occasion was evidence of the status he enjoys among Liszt scholars. Included in the 1999 Queen's Birthday Honors list, Howard was appointed a Member of the Order of Australia for his services to the arts. In 2000, Howard was honored by Hungary by being given the Pro Cultura Hungarica Award. A regular lecturer on radio and television, Howard is also a member of the London Beethoven Trio together with violinist Catherine Manson and cellist Thomas Carroll. Among other interesting items in Howard's large discography are a two-CD set of works by Rubinstein, a recording of Tchaikovsky sonatas, and two twin CD sets of the complete piano and orchestra works of Liszt recorded with the Budapest Symphony Orchestra and directed by Karl Anton Rickenbacher. Howard's recordings of music by Rachmaninov are also of fine quality. *—Erik Eriksson*

Recommended:

- **Liszt: Hungarian Rhapsodies** / Howard / 1999 / Hyperion 67418/9
- **Liszt: Piano Music** / Rickenbacher (cond.), Howard, Budapest SO / 2001 / Hyperion LISZT1
- **Liszt: The Late Pieces** / Howard / 1991 / Hyperion 66445

Elgar Howarth

b. Nov. 4, 1935, Cannock, Staffordshire, England

Conductor

Elgar Howarth is one of the most conspicuous figures in modern English musical life, managing to maintain a multifaceted career as a conductor, composer, arranger, and instrumentalist. As such, he is a throwback to an earlier time when a musician was fluent in all facets of his craft, much like his versatile namesake, Sir Edward.

Howarth was the son of a brass band conductor. Thus, his musical training was early, and at ten, he joined his father's ensemble, graduating to principal cornetist at 14. Howarth furthered his musical education at Manchester University and later the Royal Manchester College of Music, majoring in composition at the latter. There he met fellow student and kindred spirit Peter Maxwell Davies, with whom he formed the Manchester New Music Group. Upon graduation, he began his career in earnest as trumpeter at the Royal Opera House and moved through a number of ensembles, some very worthy, among them the Royal Air Force Band, the Royal Philharmonic Orchestra, the Philip Jones Brass Ensemble, and conductorship of the Grimethorpe Colliery Band. The latter was notable for Howarth's expanding the repertoire beyond the traditional band fare. An appearance with the London Sinfonietta in Italy drew the attention of Ligeti, who engaged Howarth to conduct the Stockholm premiere of the former's *Le grande macabre*. Howarth's predilection for the less-trodden path may be seen through the succession of his projects: Harrison Birtwistle's *Mask of Orpheus* (1986), *Gawain* (1991), *The Second Mrs. Kong* (1994); the major British premiere of Carl Nielsen's *Maskarade* (1990); and numerous orchestral and instrumental works by Ligeti, Birtwistle, Previn, Keuris, Gloria Coates, and Lumsdaine to name but a few from his broad repertoire that ranges from these composers back to Haydn and Mozart.

As a bandsman, Howarth's interest is truly catholic, his acclaimed recordings ranging from Sousa to band works by the above mentioned composers to the "discovery" of early twentieth century British band composer William Rimmer. Howarth's arrangements for band include numerous Wagner adaptations and a remarkable transcription of Mussorgsky's *Pictures at an Exhibition*.

Although it is as an interpreter that he is best known, Howarth is a prolific composer and exhibits the versatility and tonal inclination that marks the English school. As may be expected, his brass band works are extensive, including the Copland-esque *Legends*, the reflective, Satie-like *American Dream*, as well as the more extrovert *Fireworks* and *Concerto for Trumpet and Brass Band*. Among his orchestral works are concerti for trumpet and trombone. Many of his compositions appear under the pseudonym of W. Hogarth Lear. It is also worth noting that Howarth, with a few others, provided the trumpet parts to the Beatles' 1967 recording *Magical Mystery Tour*. *—Wayne Reisig*

Recommended:

- ○ **Birtwistle: The Triumph of Time; Ritual Fragment; Gawain's Journey** / Howarth (cond.), Philharmonia Orch. / NMC 88
- ○ **Sousa: Marches** / Howarth, Bashford, Parkes, Harris (conds.), Philip Jones Brass Ens., Grenadier Guards Band / 2004 / Universal 000217902

Herbert Howells

b. Oct. 17, 1892, Lydney, Gloucestershire, England, **d.** Feb. 24, 1983, Oxford, England

Composer: Choral

Herbert Howells decided at a young age that he wanted to compose music and then sought out musical training. His most important teacher was the cathedral organist at Gloucester, Herbert Brewer, and he became Brewer's assistant. At the age of 20, he entered and won an open scholarship competition at the Royal College of Music.

His main teachers were Charles Wood in counterpoint and Charles Villiers Stanford in composition. He is said to have been Stanford's favorite pupil and Stanford conducted Howells' *Piano Concerto No. 1* at a Queen's Hall concert in 1913. Meanwhile, Howells' *Mass in Dorian Mode* was sung in Westminster Cathedral. In 1916, his piano quintet became the first work to be published under the Carnegie Trust.

He obtained a position as a sub-organist at Salisbury Cathedral, but had to give it up because of ill health, which had already kept him out of military service during World War I. He was not expected to live, but did recover and in 1920 was able to resume his career. He started teaching composition at the Royal College of Music in 1920.

His compositional style quickly emerged: it is in the tradition of modal, folk-based music that is sometimes called "English pastoralist," continuing the trends of Elgar and Ralph Vaughan Williams. His imagination was often stimulated by particular places and by people he knew. This holds true even for his large body of church music, which was not inspired by religious sentiments ("I am not a religious man any more than Ralph was," he once said). It is probable that he wrote so much church music simply because he liked choral writing and his style is rich and melodic.

Although he wrote a substantial amount of fine instrumental and orchestral music, his choral and other vocal music is considered the work most likely to keep his memory alive. His masterwork is usually considered to be the *Hymnus paradisi*, a quasi-requiem he wrote out of the grief suffered when he lost his nine-year-old son in 1938. It is a visionary work, with the kind of deep but quiet feeling that is also associated with Frederick Delius.

He received other teaching appoinments as well. After Holst's death in 1934, Howells was chosen to succeed him as director of music at St. Paul's School and in 1954, he was named King Edward VII Professor of Music at the University of London. He was made Commander of the British Empire in 1953 by Queen Elizabeth II. He retired from his St. Paul's position and the University of London post in 1964, but retained his professorship at the Royal College of Music and held classes there almost right up to his death at the age of 90. *—Joseph Stevenson*

CHORAL

Choral Works (1909–1978)

From his early *Three Choral Anthems* composed between 1918–20, which includes his first characteristic masterpiece, *A Spotless Rose*, through to his magnificent final anthems *Come My Soul* and *Sweetest of Sweets*, both written in 1976, Howells' choral music is lucid yet luminous, deeply sensual in texture but profoundly spiritual in effect, often more modal than tonal, and always sensitive to both the specific words and to the formal structure of the text. Howells four supreme masterpieces for chorus are his *Requiem* (1936), his *Hymnus Paradisi* (1936–38), *An English Mass* (1955), the motet *Take Him, Earth, for Cherishing* (1964), and a setting of the *Stabat Mater* (1965). Both the *Requiem* and the *Hymnus Paradisi* were written after the death of his son, Michael, of meningitis in 1935. Prior to that, Howells had been a capable but not especially inspired or profound composer. But, for all its horror, Michael's death unlocked Howells' heart, and the result was music of searing spiritual intensity and unfathomable emotional depth. The *Requiem* is an a cappella choral work of concentrated austerity and the *Hymnus Paradisi for soprano, tenor, choir, and orchestra* is arguably Howells' masterpiece. At over three-quarters of an hour, the music moves from sorrowful tenebrous darkness to consoling, radiant light. Although the work was composed in the 1930s, it was not premiered until the 1950 Three Choirs Festival at the insistence of Vaughan Williams. *An English Mass* sets the ordinary of the mass and is scored for chorus and orchestra with prominent part for organ. In its fusion of conservative twentieth century English tonality, late Tudor-period English modality, and its exquisitely expressive writing for much-divided chorus, *An English Mass* rivals Vaughan Williams' own a cappella mass setting from 30 years earlier. Howells final choral masterpiece is his setting of the *Stabat Mater* text for tenor, chorus, and orchestra. Inspired by Michelangelo's *Pietà*, Howells' *Stabat Mater* is darkly scored and agonizingly harmonized for much of its length and only achieves a troubled serenity and unclouded radiance in its final bars. *—James Leonard*

Recommended:

- ○ **Howells: Choral Works** / Spicer (cond.), Finzi Singers / 1996 / Chandos 9458
- ○ **Complete Morning and Evening Canticles of Howells Vol. 1** / Millinger (cond.), The Collegiate Singers / 2000 / Priory 745

Like as the Hart Desireth the Waterbrooks (Psalm 42), anthem (1941)

Snowed in at Cheltenham while London was under a nearly constant air assault in January 1941, Herbert Howells composed feverishly during the first two weeks of the year. Though he titled the resulting choral works simply *Four Anthems*, it is clear from his writings that he originally conceived of the set as anthems "in time of war." Though the set (which also includes *O Pray for the Peace of Jerusalem*, *We Have Heard With Our Ears*, and *Let God Arise*) has been welcomed as a whole into the prestigious canon of the Anglican anthem, it has been the third in the set, *Like as the Hart Desireth the Waterbrooks*, which has become the most enduring. Written in the span of a single day (January 8, 1941) *Like as the Hart*, for SATB chorus and organ, is a simple but at times mysteriously foreboding setting of the first three verses of Psalm 42.

That the score demands a "quiet intensity" is clear from the outset. After a placid introduction played by the organ, the bass voices enter with a remarkably lyrical melodic line, giving the lie to the contention that Howells had no ear for melody. Though the piece is consistently tonal, the composer occasionally colors both harmony and melody with pointed chromaticism, as here. The full chorus then enters, with great effect, on the plea "When shall I come to appear before the presence of God," slowly dying away from a loud peak to a quiet conclusion in E minor. The middle section of the piece follows, with the alto voices taking the solo for "My tears have been my meat"; again the full chorus dramatically joins in with a louder section. The tenors then take the melody, in counterpoint with the sopranos; gradually the basses and altos are added, and the section ebbs to a close. An organ interlude serves to swell the music into the final section, in which the original bass melody returns, this time against a soprano countermelody. The interplay of the lines is prolonged, accentuating the already-extended nature of the melodic lines. Again the chorus joins together for an impassioned peak, as several parts of the text are recapitulated; then as the organ drops out, the chorus is left to conclude with a protracted cadence, which, in E major, surprisingly gives a hopeful twist to the work. The final chord is sustained for a long time, after which the organ recapitulates the cadence, further prolonging the mood.

Herbert Howells often jokingly referred to himself as the reincarnation of a Tudor-era church composer; in *Like as the Hart Desireth the Waterbrooks* he made a strong contribution to the modern Anglican anthem tradition. *—Thomas Oram*

Recommended:

- ○ **Masters of English Church Music** / Rutter (cond.), Marshall, Cambridge Singers / 1995 / Collegium 301
- ○ **Howells: Requiem; Take Him, Earth, for Cherishing** / Robinson (cond.), Farrington, King's College Choir / 1999 / Naxos 8554659

Magnificat and Nunc Dimittis (St. Paul's Cathedral) (ca. 1950)

Herbert Howells began to seriously compose music for the church in 1944, when he served as the choir director at the King's College in Cambridge. Howells was asked to compose a setting of the Magnificat and Nunc Dimittis for performance in St. Paul's Cathedral. The *Magnificat and Nunc Dimittis for St. Paul's Cathedral for chorus* (1950) was completed by Howells on December 26, while he was at home in London. The composition of this work was greatly influenced by the cathedral in which it was to be performed. Howells noted that *St. Paul's* had a "prolonged echo." The composer then decided to employ a slowly moving harmonic rhythm, so that no more than two subsequent harmonies would be heard together at any time. In any other less reverberant setting, this work would perhaps seem dull, but in *St. Paul's* each sound lingers for such a long period of time that an air of "levitation" is present. Howells was aware of the problem of acoustics in church music throughout his life, because of his familiarity with the Gloucester Cathedral, in which a sound will reverberate for around five seconds. He attempted to incorporate his knowledge of the acoustics of buildings and the dramatic effects that could be produced into his church music. *—Chris Boyes*

Recommended:

- ○ **Howells: Requiem; Take Him, Earth, for Cherishing** / Robinson (cond.), Farrington, King's College Choir / 1999 / Naxos 8554659
- ○ **Howells: St. Paul's Service & Other Music** / Scott (cond.), St. Paul's Cathedral Choir, Dearnley / 1998 / Hyperion 22038

Requiem (1932)

Howells' only son, Michael, died at age nine in 1935 from meningitis. In search of some emotional and spiritual release and consolation, Howells the following year completed an a cappella *Requiem*, mostly in English, for mixed choir and soloists; he had begun the piece before his son's illness, but it nevertheless seems strongly marked by the composer's tragic experience. Howells withheld the work, "for personal reasons," until 1980. This requiem should not be confused with Howells' related *Hymnus Paradisi* of 1938, which uses some of the same material and was published in 1950.

For this piece Howells provided a limited organ accompaniment for rehearsal, specifying that it could be used in performance only "if absolutely necessary." In any case, the setting of Psalm 23 should always be unaccompanied. He also allowed the first, second, third, and sixth movements to be performed separately as anthems or introits.

The music's style is harmonically rich and deeply Romantic, but restrained—in the manner of Fauré's *Requiem* but with a more pointed sense of grief and loss.

The first section is a melancholy setting in English of the Sarum "Salvator mundi" text. Toward the end, the choir splits into two antiphonal units, an effect Howells will frequently employ through the rest of the *Requiem*. Next comes a setting of Psalm 23, "The Lord is my shepherd," an austere treatment that begins with solos for soprano and alto (or countertenor). Third comes the first of two settings of the Requiem Aeternam; this is a desolate version for antiphonal choirs.

Howells' setting of Psalm 121 ("I will lift up mine eyes") opens with a baritone solo answered and shortly taken over by the choir, in peaceful, pastoral music concluding with a brief solo for tenor. The second Requiem Aeternam proceeds from a hushed, mournful beginning (vaguely reminiscent of the opening of Samuel Barber's contemporaneous *Adagio for Strings*), builds very gradually to a glowing climax at the light-bathed words "et lux perpetua luceat," and gently subsides in a long diminuendo.

The final section, "I heard a voice from heaven," alternates very briefly tenor, baritone, and soprano solos with the full chorus. It is truly haunted music that at one point acquires an almost bluesy edge, but dies away into a blessing for the dead, who rest in their labors. *—James Reel*

Recommended:

- ○ **Vaughan Williams: Mass in Gm, Te Deum; Howells: Requiem; Take Him, Earth** / Best (cond.), Chance, Salmon, Best, Coxwell, Corydon Singers / Hyperion 66076
- ○ **Cathedral Classics** / Warland (cond.), Malek, Newhouse, Olson, Palermo, Thompson, Dale Warland Singers / 1994 / American Choral 120

A Spotless Rose (1919)

The second of three Carol-Anthems for unaccompanied mixed chorus composed in 1918–20, *A Spotless Rose* is typical of the early choral works of English composer Herbert Howells. Taking the lithesome wistfulness and melodic purity of Elgar, the deep sensual nostalgia and warm choral writing of Delius, the agnostic spiritual exaltation of Vaughan Williams, and combining these with his own modally inflected harmonies and his lucid yet luminous textures, Howells created his first characteristic masterpiece. It also prefigured his future path as a composer: although Howells also composed many superb songs and several large-scale orchestral pieces, he was the most prolific composer of music for the English church in the twentieth century. *—James Leonard*

Recommended:

- ○ **Faire is the Heaven** / Rutter (cond.), Cambridge Singers / 1988 / Collegium 107
- ○ **Nativitas** / Higginbottom (cond.), Cave, New College Choir Oxford / Erato 19350

Take Him, Earth, for Cherishing, motet on the death of President Kennedy (1964)

The English composer Herbert Howells is best known for his works written in the tradition of English choral music. His brief motet for unaccompanied mixed choir, *Take Him, Earth, for Cherishing* (1964), composed after the assassination of President John F. Kennedy, is typical of Howells' mature style: tonal but modernist, lucid but atmospheric, deeply expressive but not specifically religious. The motet's profound sense of public loss combined with its exalted personal spirituality makes it one of the most affective works composed in honor of Kennedy and one of Howells' most immediately attractive works.

A short time after the assassination, Howells was given a commission to write a choral motet to be performed at a memorial service for Kennedy, which would be held at a later date at the Washington Cathedral. From that time until the following May, the motet did not have a title because the composer had not chosen a suitable text for this memorial work. Howells decided to use a Latin text that he had previously set in the sketches of *Hymnus Paradisi* (1938), the first piece that the composer worked on after the premature death of his young son, Michael, in 1935. The same sections of text were subsequently removed from the earlier work. Howells discovered the text, which was written by Prudentius, in Helen Waddell's English translation of *Medieval Latin Lyrics*. *—AMG*

Recommended:

- ○ **Howells: Requiem; Take Him, Earth, for Cherishing** / Robinson (cond.), Farrington, King's College Choir / 1999 / Naxos 8554659
- ○ **Vaughan Williams: Mass in Gm; Te Deum; Howells: Requiem, Howells: Take Him, Earth, for Cherishing** / Best (cond.), Corydon Singers / Hyperion 66076

Bronisław Huberman

b. Dec. 19, 1882, Czestochowa, Poland, **d.** Jun. 16, 1947, Corsier-sur-Vevey, Switzerland

Violinist

Bronisław Huberman was one of the towering figures among violinists of his generation. Yet despite lavish praise from Fürtwangler, Toscanini, Walter, and other major conductors and artists, he remained a controversial artist throughout his career, owing to his highly individual style of interpretation and to a technique that, while not weak or unimpressive, lacked the consistency in difficult passages of the finest virtuosos.

Huberman was the son of a law clerk who was a good amateur musician himself. As a young child, Huberman showed remarkable talent, giving his first public concert at age seven. He studied with Michalowicz and Rosen, then at the Warsaw Conservatory with Isidor Lotto, all before he reached the age of ten. In Berlin, Joachim was impressed with the youth's talent, but not disposed toward teaching prodigies. He referred him to Markees, but it was, by Huberman's own assessment, his study in Berlin with Charles Grigorovich that honed his talents. At the age of 11, he gave a successful concert tour of Holland and Belgium and soon afterward gained the support of arts patron Count Zamoyski in Paris and singer Adelina Patti in London. The former presented him with a Stradivarius and the latter, after some wrangling, allowed him to play at some of her final concerts. At a January 1896 concert in Vienna, Huberman astonished Brahms with a performance of his violin concerto and by his late teens, he had scored numerous successes throughout Europe. He had even given one hugely successful tour of the United States in 1896–97. In 1902, following a lengthy suspension of concert activity, Huberman suffered a great loss with the passing of his father, who had given up his law clerk position and sacrificed much else for his son's career. Huberman soon resumed concertizing with numerous successful tours. His only marriage came in 1910, to actress Elza Galafrés. Their union lasted but four years and produced one child, Johannes (born 1911). At the outbreak of World War I, Huberman was briefly interned, but he remained active throughout the next two decades, curtailing his schedule in 1933 with the rise of the Nazis. In the 1920s, Huberman became an active supporter of the Pan-European movement, even writing several essays later published in a book entitled *Vaterland Europa* (1932). He refused to play any concerts in Germany from 1933 on and in 1935 helped found the Palestine Symphony Orchestra (which in 1948 became the Israel Philharmonic Orchestra). Toscanini was engaged to lead this ensemble of mostly Jewish refugee musicians in their 1936 inaugural concert. Huberman went on tour that same year and during a concert given in New York's Carnegie Hall, his Stradivarius violin was stolen. (In 1985, the thief confessed his deed and two years later the instrument was recovered, but four decades after Huberman's death.) The purloined violin was a relatively minor misfortune for Huberman during the turbulent 1930s: a 1937 plane crash rendered him incapable of playing for over a year. In November 1938, he successfully returned to the concert stage in Egypt, and the following month he appeared as soloist with the Palestine Symphony Orchestra for the first time in his career. After a tour of Europe in 1939, Huberman relocated to New York, where he lived until the end of the war. Following cessation of hostilities, he took up residence near Lake Geneva, Switzerland. In 1946, he became ill and was unsuccessfully treated in Italy for six months. Huberman died in Corsier-sur-Vevey, Switzerland, in 1947. *—Robert Cummings*

Recommended:

- ○ **Concert & Recital Recordings** / Barzin (cond.), Huberman, Friedman, National Orchestral Association Orch. / 1998 / Arbiter 115
- ○ **Violin Concertos of Beethoven & Tchaikovksy** / Szell, Steinberg (conds.), Huberman, Vienna PO / 1999 / Naxos 110903

Huelgas Ensemble

f. 1971, Basel, Switzerland

Ensemble

The Huelgas Ensemble, directed by its founder Paul van Nevel, began as the result of a previous generation's work in early music performance, led by, among others, Thomas Binkley and David Munrow. Remarkably, after more than 30 years, the Ensemble retains a sense of excitement, innovation and discovery, long after the mass recording industry and the New Age movement co-opted the esoteric sounds of the Middle Ages and Renaissance. When van Nevel, active at the Schola Cantorum Basilensis, founded the ensemble in 1971, a rediscovered instrumentarium of cornettos, sackbuts, recorders, and crumhorns were being jubilantly applied to early music performances. The Huelgas Ensemble then sat at the center of the movement towards "authentic" performance practices, and its interpretations were strongly influential. As the scholarly and performative norms for Medieval music have changed, so has the sound of Huelgas, most prominently depicted in its increased vocalizations. But the Ensemble has retained a mantle of eccentricity and innovation.

Nearly every aspect of director van Nevel's performances has been subject to experimentation over his career. From the group's inception, reliable and evocative ornamentation was a goal for both instrumentalists and singers. The ensemble constantly upsets expectations through scoring and orchestration. A 1994 program of *Music for King Janus of Nicosia* presents some pieces at half or less the expected tempo, losing the text, but richly extending the pungency of dissonances. In the same year, Huelgas released a recording of the Lassus *Lagrime di San Pietro* juxtaposed with a performance by an all-vocal ensemble led by Philippe Herreweghe. A 1999 recording dedicated to Alexander Agricola includes some striking chromatic manipulations of the so-called "Secret Chromatic Art." At all times, Paul van Nevel's approach to his repertory has been fearlessly innovative, despite criticism both from scholars and from other performers.

Another area of van Nevel's musical boldness, that of musical repertory, has been perhaps the ensemble's greatest contribution to our musical world. The director's scholarly interests lead him towards little-known manuscripts—the Turin manuscript (1985), the Naples collection of "*l'Homme Armé*" Masses (1990), the Huelgas Codex (1999)—and less-appreciated composers—Gombert (1993), Constanzo Festa (1994), Mattheus Pipelare (1996), Pierre de Manchicourt (1998), Matteo da Perugia (1998), and Alexander Agricola (1999). The Huelgas Ensemble brought out the only "complete works" recording of Johannes Ciconia as early as 1982, has given world premiere recording of the Brumel *"Earthquake" Mass*, and undertook a fascinating collaboration with the Portuguese singers of Fado called *Tears of Lisbon*. In each case, the lively and compelling performances have stretched musical boundaries. *—Timothy Dickey*

Recommended:

- ○ **Rore: Missa Praeter rerum seriem; Motets** / Nevel (cond.), Huelgas Ens. / HM 901760
- ○ **Ciconia: Complete Works** / Nevel (cond.), Huelgas Ens. / 1997 / Pavane 7345
- ○ **Tears of Lisbon** / Nevel (cond.), Rocha, Manuel, Antonio, Huelgas Ens. / 1996 / Sony 62256
- ○ **Dufay: O gemma, lux** / Nevel (cond.), Huelgas Ens. / HM 901700

Monica Huggett

b. May 16, 1953, London, England
Violinist

Monica Huggett has evolved from a hardworking fixture of the historical performance movement to a true star of the Baroque violin, essaying virtuoso works like the Bach sonatas and partitas and founding her own performing group. Huggett was born in London and educated at the Green School for Girls, moving on to the Royal Academy of Music and intending to pursue a career as a conventional violinist. The first time she played a Baroque violin, however, she felt an immediate connection with the instrument. She studied with several of the major figures who brought historical-instrument performances into the mainstream of concert life, including Sigiswald Kuijken, Gustav Leonhardt, and Ton Koopman, the last named of whom became something of a mentor. The two worked together to found the Amsterdam Baroque Orchestra in 1980, and Huggett became the group's leader. Later, both musicians became involved with the Portland (OR) Baroque Orchestra in the U.S.

Steadily, Huggett began to make more solo appearances in concert and on recordings. Her set of the Bach sonatas and partitas for solo violin was named an Editors' Choice by *Gramophone* magazine in December 1997, and her 2001 set of Biber's spectacular violin sonatas was especially widely praised: "This is a disc that merits the attention of anybody who appreciates the highest flights of violin playing, from whatever period," raved the *Telegraph*. Huggett was notable for the chronological range of the repertory she performed; she played everything from Renaissance consort music to Beethoven's *Violin Concerto*, selecting appropriate instruments for each. She was adventurous in terms of the concepts of her recordings; *Haydn and the Gypsies*, a 2001 disc exploring the influence of Romany music on Haydn and other composers, was a notable example. After making guest conducting appearances with the Orchestra of the Age of Enlightenment and the European Union Baroque Orchestra, Huggett founded her own ensemble, Sonnerie, in the mid-1990s. That group likewise made frequent successes with unfamiliar repertoire; its 2003 disc *The World's First Piano Concertos*, featuring works by J.C. Bach, Abel, Hayes, and Hook, was both attractive and challenging in its assertion of a new dividing line between piano and harpsichord repertoire. Between concert tours, Huggett serves as professor of Baroque violin at her alma mater, the Royal Academy of Music. *—James Manheim*

Recommended:

- ○ **Biber: Violin Sonatas; Nisi Dominus; Passacaglia** / Huggett, Guthrie, Sonnerie Ensemble / 2001 / ASV 203
- ○ **Leclair: Concertos** / Huggett, Guimond, Arion / Atma 2143
- ○ **Haydn & the Gypsies** / Burman-Hall (cond. & piano), Huggett / 2000 / Kleos 5101
- ○ **Bach: Sonatas & Partitas** / Huggett / 2004 / Virgin 562340

Johann Nepomuk Hummel

b. Nov. 14, 1778, Pressburg, Austria (Slovakia), **d.** Oct. 17, 1837, Weimar, Germany
Composer: Concerto, Chamber Music, Keyboard

Johann Nepomuk Hummel (1778–1837) was an important composer from the late Classical period, known primarily for his solo piano compositions and piano concertos. In recent years, however, attention has been given to his chamber music, operas, and sacred works. He tended to write long-breathed melodies, often used Alberti bass accompaniments and dotted rhythms, and favored the sonata-allegro and rondo forms. Among his greatest works in the keyboard genre are the *Sonata in A Flat, for piano 4 hands*, Op. 92, and the *Sonata in F Sharp*, Op. 81. His Mass, Op. 111, and some of his cantatas are also important works. Hummel wrote a highly-regarded three-volume treatise on pianism, entitled *A Complete Theoretical and Practical Course on the Art of Pianoforte Playing*.

Hummel was born on November 14, 1778, in Bratislava (then Pressburg), Slovakia. Young Johann's first musical studies came on the violin at the behest of his father, a player of string instruments himself, and director of the local Imperial School of Military Music. By the age of five Hummel could play the violin with proficiency. But he would abandon it in favor of the piano, on which he developed an astonishing technique by age six.

When the family moved to Vienna in 1786, Johann studied with Mozart, with whom he lived for two years. After concert appearances throughout Europe at age ten, Hummel and his father traveled to London, where they settled temporarily. Johann met Clementi there, and took private instruction from him.

Hummel returned to Vienna in 1793 and began studies with Albrechtsberger. Now 14, the young composer largely turned away from the concert stage, in favor of teaching and composing. Among his works were a set of variations for piano in 1794, and, four years later, two sonatas for piano and violin, and one for piano and viola. But he struggled with opera: *Il viaggiator ridicolo* (1797), and *Don Anchise* (c. 1800) were left incomplete. He did, however, finish *Dankgefühl einer Geretten* (1799).

His *Piano Trio in E Flat* and the *Variations in G on a Romance by Méhul* came in the early years of the next century, and he completed his opera *Le vicende d'amore* in 1804. Soon more operas would come, as well as his Concerto in G, for piano and violin. His first major appointment came in April, 1804, when he accepted the post of Concertmaster to Prince Nikolaus Esterházy at his Eisenstadt court. Hummel also wrote several masses, including the Mass in E Flat (1804), and Mass in D (1808); and he composed a Te Deum (1806), and two Salve Reginas. More operas came, too: *Der vereitelten Ränke* (1806) and *Mathilde von Guise* (1810; revised in . 1821).

In May, 1811, Hummel was dismissed as Kapellmeister in a controversy and returned to Vienna to focus on composition. Two years later he married Elizabeth Röckel. Late the following year, at his wife's behest, he launched a concert tour in Vienna, scoring triumph after triumph. He subsequently toured Germany and Europe with great success, sometimes also assuming the role of conductor.

Hummel accepted the Kapellmeister posts in Stuttgart (1816) and Weimar (1819). This was a most productive period for him, as many of his best works appeared, including the *Trio for Piano, Violin, and Cello*, Op. 83 (1819), the *Sonata in A Flat, for piano four hands*, Op. 92 (1820), and two "birthday" cantatas for the Duke (1823 and 1827).

By 1832, Hummel's health was in decline, and he frequently took leave of his Kapellmeister duties in Weimar because of sickness. He died on October 17, 1837. *—Robert Cummings*

Overview of Works (1797–1836)

Hummel (1778–1837) has been considered primarily a keyboard composer. But, he also composed in almost every other genre, including opera, sacred and chamber music, songs, and cantatas. He produced no symphonies, however. Despite his versatility, his most impressive works are still to be found in the keyboard realm and in the chamber genre involving piano. Unlike Beethoven, Hummel did not embrace the burgeoning Romantic movement.

Hummel wrote many operas and singspiels, though the scores to a number of them have been lost. *Mathilde von Guise* was composed in 1810 and revised 11 years later. Yet, for all the skill found here and in many of his other operas, Hummel was not particularly innovative in the genre, and his operas have never gained currency. The same can be said of his sacred music, which includes several masses. His songs have fared little better, though his output was not large.

In the keyboard realm Hummel is best known for his concertos and sonatas. The *Piano Concerto in B minor*, Op. 89 (often designated his third), opens with a beguiling theme on the piano more than vaguely reminiscent of the famous melody in the first movement of Mozart's *Symphony No. 40*. The Op. 85 *Piano Concerto in A minor*, features a lengthy orchestral introduction in the first movement Allegro Moderato that contains several attractive themes, the first of which is nearly as striking as the one that opens the B minor concerto. There are seven published piano concertos in Hummel's catalog, one with violin, and also a *Concertino*. An unpublished *Piano Concerto* dates from the 1790s.

Of particular note among Hummel's six piano sonatas is the *F sharp minor*, Op. 81, whose slightly Beethoven manner features a dramatic and atmospheric opening and many keyboard effects, such as the glissando-like runs in the first movement. The Largo middle panel features a quite memorable long-breathed, serious theme of dark character.

Among his chamber works, the Op. 83 *Piano Trio* and Op. 87 *Quintet*, scored for piano, violin, viola, cello, and double bass (the same as Schubert's *Trout*) are notable. The *Quartet in E flat* is a solid four-movement work that divulges Hummel's considerable skills in woodwind writing. If his Op. 2 *Flute Sonata* is decidedly Mozartean, his A major Op. 64 *Flute Sonata* is in a more muscular Classical tradition. The *Trio for flute, cello and piano in A major*, Op. 78, is quite attractive and features a memorable theme, with seven deftly-crafted variations. *—Robert Cummings*

Recommended:

- ○ **Hummel: Complete Piano Sonatas Vol. 3** / Keene / 2001 / Newport 60163
- ○ **Hummel: 3 String Quartets, Op30** / Delme SQ / 1992 / Hyperion 66568
- ○ **Hummel: Piano Trio 1, 5 & 7** / Borodin Trio / 1997 / Chandos 9529
- ○ **Hummel: Bassoon Concerto in F major** / Dini-Ciacci (cond.), Gonella, Finotti, Italian International Orch. / 1999 / Naxos 554280
- ○ **Hummel: Piano Works** / Shelley / 2000 / Chandos 9807

CONCERTO

Piano Concerto in A minor, Op. 85 (ca. 1816)

Even into the twenty-first century, Hummel's music is being assessed and reassessed, always with the view that his genius has been consistently underrated. His piano concertos are among his greatest accomplishments, and he might have excelled in the symphony too, had he not taken to heart so seriously his rivalry with Beethoven. Hummel's *Second* and *Third* piano concertos are undoubtedly his most popular, though even they have enjoyed paltry few recordings and relatively meager representation in the concert halls.

The A minor *Second* is cast in three movements: a lengthy Allegro moderato is followed by a very brief Larghetto and a substantial Rondo (Allegro moderato). The first movement opens with a long orchestral introduction wherein the striking main theme is immediately presented by the strings, a theme whose character is both restless and heroic, looking back toward the darker side of Mozart as well as to the contemporary grandiosity of Beethoven. An alternate melody follows, a jovial, proud creation introduced by the flute. When the piano enters, it gives a lighter treatment to the thematic material that is lighter in touch, but not in emotional expressivity. Hummel's development is full of deft elaborations and brilliant piano writing. His orchestration will recall Beethoven's throughout this movement, but his music has an individuality and great beauty, even if his contrapuntal skills fall a bit short of his great rival's.

The short second movement Larghetto serves as a kind of pleasant interlude between the two larger outer panels. The theme here is delicate and graceful in its Classical sweetness, its music having an almost mesmerizing serenity making one wish it would linger beyond its lovely five minutes. The Rondo finale follows without pause, the piano introducing a somewhat exotic rhythmic theme that gradually picks up momentum and richer textures. The music is striking here, the melody instantly sticking in the mind, so much so as to make the alternate material initially sound less interesting by contrast. The more subdued music that alternates with this theme is revealed upon second and third hearing, however, to be just as finely imagined as the opening theme. In the end, this concerto must be assessed as standing on about the same plateau as Beethoven's first two piano concertos. *—Robert Cummings*

Recommended:

- ○ **Hummel: Piano Concertos in A Minor & B Minor** / Thomson (cond.), Hough, English CO / 1987 / Chandos 8507

Piano Concerto in B minor, Op. 89 (Oct. 1819)

Hummel's piano sonatas are generally considered his most compelling compositions, in particular the *Sonata in F sharp*, Op. 81, and the *Sonata in A flat for piano, four hands*, Op. 92. But his piano concertos also stake out an important corner of his output, with the *Second* and *Third* probably standing as his finest. The *Piano Concerto No. 3 in B minor* consists of three movements and has an almost identical structure to that of the *Second*. The opening panel is a lengthy Allegro moderato and there follows a subdued, short Larghetto, after which comes the Vivace finale, which finally breaks the pattern of the *Second*, whose closing movement is an Allegro moderato Rondo. The *Third*'s first movement begins with an orchestral introduction that presents an intense, somewhat heroic main theme played by the winds, a theme whose direct manner has immediate appeal, sounding almost like a lost Beethoven melody. An alternate theme of playful, almost carefree character soon appears. When the piano enters, it does not reprise the main theme in the manner of Beethoven with his contemporary *"Emperor" Piano Concerto*. Hummel leaves statements of it to the orchestra, compensating with brilliantly inventive keyboard writing, whether in the deft presentation of the alternate theme or in the sublime development section. The second movement is a subdued Larghetto, featuring a lengthy introduction by horns that present the lovely main theme. The ensuing piano's rendition of it is vastly superior in its imaginative sense of intimacy and sweetness. The keyboard writing throughout the central panel is touching, especially in the final statement of the main theme. The Vivace Finale follows without pause, the piano presenting the playful main theme as Hummel once again creates an utterly memorable tune. Allusions to the main theme from the first movement appear amid later material, but the mood remains buoyant and light right up to its colorful ending. In sum, one must assess this nearly 40-minute piano concerto as at least a minor masterpiece, deserving of far greater attention than it has gotten. *—Robert Cummings*

Recommended:

- ○ **Hummel: Piano Concertos in A Minor & B Minor** / Thomson (cond.), Hough, English CO / 1987 / Chandos 8507
- ○ **Hummel: Piano Concertos 2 & 3** / Pal (cond.), Chang, Budapest CO / 1993 / Naxos 550837

Trumpet Concerto in E or E flat major, WoO 1 (Dec. 8, 1803)

In 1803 the famed Viennese trumpeter Anton Weidinger requested from Johann Nepomuk Hummel a new concerto for his keyed trumpet, a recently developed instrument that allowed the player to produce far more chromatic notes than had previously been possible. The imposing figure of Haydn must have been prominent in Hummel's mind as he undertook the commission. He had just succeeded Haydn as Kapellmeister at the Esterházy court—a position Haydn had held for some 30 years—and counted himself among the elder composer's good friends. Moreover, it was Haydn who seven years earlier had written the first concerto for Weidinger's keyed instrument. In the end, Hummel's work proved equally as successful as Haydn's, and Weidinger subsequently played it throughout Europe.

The concerto opens with a celebratory Allegro con spirito that is notable for a few unusual modulations, likely included to show off the instrument's expanded capabilities. Not only is the soloist given a thorough workout, but the orchestral support is similarly spirited; the writing for the woodwinds is particularly effective. A plaintive Andante follows, and the work concludes with a sprightly Allegro that includes much brilliant writing for the soloist.

One final note: the concerto exists in two different forms. The work was originally written in E flat major, though either Hummel or Weidinger (or possibly both) made a less frequently played version in E major. *—Chris Morrison*

Recommended:

- ○ **Telemann, L. Mozart, Vivaldi & Hummel** / Karajan (cond.), Andre, Berlin PO / 1998 / EMI 66961
- ○ **Trumpet Concertos** / Leppard (cond.), Marsalis, National PO / 2001 / Sony 89862

CHAMBER MUSIC

Piano Quintet in E flat major/minor, Op. 87 (Oct. 1802)

This quintet, written in 1802 at a time when Hummel and Beethoven were vying for the attention of Viennese audiences, might be regarded as the foundation stone of the entire tradition of compositions for piano quintet in the nineteenth century. It led directly to the composition of Schubert's *"Trout" Quintet* of 1819, with which it shares the instrumentation of piano, violin, viola, cello, and double bass; Schubert's quintet was written for a group of players who were performing Hummel's piece and wanted another work for the same forces. The persistence of Hummel's quintet over 17 years of rapid musical change testifies to its popularity in the composer's day, although it, along with most of the rest of Hummel's oeuvre, was forgotten after his death. Revivalists who have unearthed it have discovered a work with the composer's proto-Romantic musical language fully in place. The quintet is in four movements, with E flat minor and E flat major contending interestingly for dominance in all but the slow (major) third movement. The wide harmonic range of Beethoven's middle-period works was not his invention; it was in the air at the time, and Beethoven's achievement was to bring a new concision to complicated harmonic structures. Hummel's opening movement has many of the Beethovenian trademarks: a four-note motive that weaves its way through all the instruments and appears in various harmonic guises, a plethora of third relationships and flat supertonics and submediants, and an effective integration of pianism with a chamber grouping. The movement opens in E flat minor and goes to A flat major for a lyrical second subject before dropping down to the expected relative major of G flat. The movement is a large one with splashes of harmonic color that are nicely woven with motivic material to recall earlier sections of the music. The quintet's second movement is an E flat minor scherzo with a lyrical trio section in a slower tempo and a contrasting accent pattern. The third movement, consisting of a group of harmonically ambiguous chords followed by a simple ornamented melody, is essentially an introduction to the final rondo. Though the work is sometimes marked by blankly periodic structures that Beethoven would have gleefully demolished, it is well worth the closer acquaintance that composers of its own time would have had. *—James Manheim*

Recommended:

○ **Hummel, Schubert, Schumann: Piano Quintets** / Schubert Ens. of London / 1996 / Hyperion 22008

Violin Sonata in D major, Op. 50

Hummel has been one of music history's great underdogs, suffering in the giant shadow cast by Beethoven. In the latter decades of the twentieth century, however, his music was rediscovered and many of his scores are now viewed as worthy to stand with Beethoven's. His piano concertos and chamber music have especially garnered attention, and this sonata—written for violin (or flute) and piano—is one of his better-crafted, more popular efforts. Cast in three movements, the work is short, lasting about 15 minutes, with the opening panel nearly as long as the other two combined. Marked Allegro con brio, the first movement presents a jaunty main theme first given to the violin (or flute, in the alternate scoring), which is then taken up by the piano. A more relaxed second theme appears, after which the development section shows the opening melody to have a more muscular, more intense side. Still, the first movement remains largely light and a quite similar mood prevails in the ensuing Andante. It has a livelier manner than its marking suggests, although its music is mostly relaxed and playful. The Rondo Pastorale finale may offer the most catchy music, its main theme a chipper creation of memorable character and its writing for both instruments full of color and excitement. Both the violin and flute versions are equally effective, though it appears the flute rendition is the more often recorded. *—Robert Cummings*

Recommended:

○ **Hummel: Rondo brillant; Sonata in D; Variations, etc.** / Adorjan, Lee, etc. / 1998 / Erato 25596

KEYBOARD

Piano Sonata No. 2 in E flat major, Op. 13

This is an early sonata in Hummel's fairly sizable output, but it already divulges its composer's keyboard mastery. It is clearly in the Classical mold, and while it is not imitative, its themes would not sound out of place in a Beethoven sonata. Yet its structural features probably owe as much to Mozart as to Beethoven. That said, the first movement's main theme bears a striking resemblance in both its notes and mood to the first part of the melody in the Mozart *Symphony No. 41*'s finale. Still, what Hummel makes of it is closer in spirit to Beethoven than to Mozart.

The greatest immediate difference between Hummel and Beethoven is the former's more delicate, somewhat less heroic manner. The ten-minute first movement (Allegro con brio—"Alleluia") brims with sunshine and energetic joy. The Adagio middle panel opens with a relatively somber introductory passage, after which the music turns sweet with some of the composer's loveliest lyrical writing. The Allegro con spirito finale exhibits Hummel's deft rhythmic skills, as well as his colorful sense of humor. Even if his contrapuntal skills were not as fully developed here as they later became, this nearly half-hour work is surely among Hummel's largely neglected but eminently worthy efforts. *—Robert Cummings*

Recommended:

○ **Hummel: Piano Works** / Shelley / 2000 / Chandos 9807

Piano Sonata No. 3 in F minor, Op. 20

Hummel was appointed concertmaster at the Eisenstadt Court of Prince Nikolaus Esterházy in 1804, a post that was, in effect, tantamount to Kapellmeister, owing to the declining Haydn's inability to fulfill his duties. Despite the taxing demands of the position, Hummel, who officially became Kapellmeister in 1809, was inspired to write much distinctive music during these years, including many masses, operas, chamber works, sonatas, and other piano compositions. The *Piano Sonata No. 3* reflects his growing sense of confidence and effectively mines his ever-reliable thematic creativity. The first of the sonata's three movements is marked Allegro moderato—Adagio—Allegro agitato. It opens with a strikingly dark theme, barrenly scored, which quickly turns lively and somewhat anxious. The second subject and subsequent thematic material are masterfully wrought, as is Hummel's imaginative, often intense development of it. The reprise is especially compelling in its darker, agitated manner and brilliant close. The middle panel, marked Adagio maestoso, has, as its maestoso tag suggests, a majestic character both in its serene, stately main theme, and in its gorgeous keyboard writing. The finale (Presto—Ancor piu presto), at about five minutes, is the shortest movement, but, as one might surmise from its Presto marking, it is full of bustling energy. While it lacks the thematic appeal of the previous movements, its colors and rhythmic drive offer ample rewards for the listener. *—Robert Cummings*

Recommended:

○ **Hummel Piano Sonatas, Vol. 3** / Hobson / 1989 / Arabesque 6566

Engelbert Humperdinck

b. Sep. 1, 1854, Siegburg, Germany, **d.** Sep. 27, 1921, Neustrelitz, Germany
Composer: Opera

Though Engelbert Humperdinck wrote a great deal of music in a variety of genres, he is best remembered for a single opera, *Hänsel und Gretel* (1893), based on the familiar fairy tale. Humperdinck's musical style is infused with elements of the German folk tradition, but the composer's primary influence was clearly the music of Wagner; indeed, Humperdinck worked as an assistant to the older master for a time, even providing extra music for a scene change in the premiere staging of Wagner's *Parsifal* in 1882. It is possible that Humperdinck's music remains, uncredited, as part of the score that has come down to posterity.

Following a conventional education at Paderborn, Humperdinck entered the Cologne Conservatory at the age of 18 and began studies in voice and composition. While a student there, he was the winner of the Mozart Stipend of Frankfurt in 1876; with the aid of its financial award, he went to Munich to study first with Franz Lachner and then with Rheinberger at the Royal Music School. While enrolled there (1877–79), he won an award from the Mendelssohn Foundation of Berlin, following which he traveled to Italy and had the fortune to meet up with Wagner in Naples.

Written to a libretto by Humperdinck's sister Adelheid Wette (who added characters and scenes to expand the little story to operatic dimensions), *Hänsel und Gretel* was first presented in Weimar in December of 1893; it was quickly taken up in opera houses all over Europe, representing the perfect antidote to the chill, veristic winds blowing out of Italy at the time. Ostensibly a work for children, the opera has always found favor with audiences of all ages thanks to its odd blend of fable-like innocence and Wagnerian weight. Humperdinck's succesful blending of a children's story with his own, rather monumental, orchestral world has made *Hänsel und Gretel* the only post-Wagnerian work to be considered a succesful synthesis of the German master's style.

During the course of his musical career, Humperdinck supplemented his compositional activities with turns as a music editor, critic, and, at various times, a music teacher; Wagner's son Siegfried was one of his pupils. His other works, particulary the pleasant 1880 *Humoreske for orchestra in E major*, find occasional performances today. In the 1960s and 1970s, Humperdinck's name was again on the lips of the public; in this case, however, "Engelbert Humperdinck" was the new persona (chosen from a music dictionary) of a pop balladeer formerly known as Arnold Dorsey, fondly or not-so-fondly remembered for his stagey rendition of "Release Me." The two, needless to say, are not related. *—AMG*

OPERA

Hänsel und Gretel (1893)

The genesis of this opera was unusual and more than a little fortuitous. Humperdinck's sister wanted to put on a show for a family children's party and hit on the idea of dramatizing the Grimm Brothers' tale of *Hänsel und Gretel*. She asked her brother if he would write a little music for her project, and he happily provided some musical numbers. The entertainment went off so well that the composer decided to expand what he had written into a three-act opera.

He was fortunate also that he sent the completed score to Richard Strauss, who immediately recognized its excellence. Strauss conducted the work's premiere, and it vaulted instantly into fame; within a year there was scarcely an opera house in the entire German-speaking world that had not performed it. The opera was also produced in English in London, and the English company took their production across the Atlantic to New York as early as October of 1895.

Technically, the work is an intriguing construction according to Wagnerian music drama principles. There are plenty of harmonic and orchestral devices inspired by Wagner, yet *Hänsel und Gretel* does not make an impression of being at all Wagnerian in terms of solemnity, seriousness, or excessive length. The familiar tale fits well with the musical universe originally developed by the colossus of the *Ring* cycle to represent a supernatural world. Though the story is elaborated with a few additional characters, it is clearly comprehensible even to young people with no prior exposure to opera. *Hänsel und Gretel* is regarded as the leading children's opera in the repertoire.*—Joseph Stevenson*

Synopsis:

Act One. In Peter's cottage, Hansel is sitting binding a broom and Gretel is knitting. She sings a folk song to herself ("Suse, liebe Suse") about geese who are too poor to afford shoes. They are tired and hungry, but Gretel reminds Hansel that, to use their father's words, when need is at its worst, God holds out a helping hand ("Wenn die Not auf's"). They stop work to play ("Griesgram hinaus"), first pretending they are sweeping their troubles out the door, then dancing ("Brüderchen, komm tanz' mit mir"). They dance wildly, ending up sprawled on the floor, out of breath. Gertrude enters just then and scolds them. As she does so, she knocks over the jug of milk, and sends them out to pick strawberries, as that was all that they will have for supper. She tells them not to come back until the basket is full or she will beat them. When they scurry out, she gives into despair over their poverty ("Da liegt nun") and cries herself to sleep, her head on the table. Peter is heard singing in the distance, proclaiming that hunger is the best chef of all. He comes in, tipsy, and when he wakes her up, Gertrude scolds him in turn. He answers that it was a festival day, and he sold all his brooms for a good price, and shows her the food he brought home. For a moment, they dance around in celebration, and then he asks where the children are. She narrates their naughtiness and says she sent them into the woods. He is horrified, as at night, the woods are haunted by the witch, who lures children into her house made of gingerbread and candy, and then bakes them into gingerbread children. Gertrude runs to find the children and Peter follows her, stopping to grab his bottle. In the woods, Gretel sings a folk song ("Ein Männlein steht im Walde") and the two children eat all the strawberries they had gathered. They realize they are lost and it is too dark to find the way back, and begin to panic. The Sandman comes in ("Der kleine Sandmann bin ich"), and he drops his magic sand in their eyes so they can go to sleep. Before they do so, they sing a prayer about their guardian angels ("Abends, will ich schlafen gehn") and when they are asleep, the angels come and watch over them.

Act Two. The next morning the Dew Fairy sprinkles dew from a flower onto the children's eyes ("Der kleine Taumann") and they wake up. They playfully imitate the birds they hear ("Ti-re-li-re-li") and are surprised that they had the same dream about being watched over by angels. As the mist clears, they see the gingerbread house and are amazed ("Von Kuchen und Torten ein Häuslein"). Hansel begins to break off a piece and eat. The witch calls out, asking who is nibbling at her house, briefly frightening the children, but when it is silent again, they decide it was the wind. The witch comes out and throws a rope over Hansel. They almost escape, but she uses her magic stick to cast a spell that freezes them ("Hokus, pokus, Hexenschuss"). She puts Hansel in a cage and goes inside. Hansel whispers to Gretel to pretend to obey the witch, and she returns with goodies to fatten Hansel, who is too thin. He pretends to be asleep and she orders Gretel to do the housework, and gloats over her plan to cook Gretel; she will tell her to see if the oven is hot, and then when Gretel bends over, push her in. She rides around on her broom in a frenzy of excitement ("Hopp, Galopp, mein Besengaul!"). She makes Hansel put out his tongue and then show her his finger, but he holds out a stick instead, convincing the near-sighted witch that he is still too bony. Gretel covertly picks up the wand and repeats the spell, releasing Hansel when the witch isn't looking. When the witch tells her to look in the oven, she pretends not to understand and asks to be shown how. The witch bends over and the two push her in triumphantly. They dance around in celebration and then ransack the house for sweets. The oven suddenly explodes with a bang, which partially frees the other children who have been turned into gingerbread ("Erlöst, befreit"), and Hansel and Gretel break the spell. They all sing and dance ("Die Hexerei ist nun vorbei"). Peter and Gertrude rush in, too late to do anything but point out not one but two morals: that the wicked are caught in their own traps ("Kinder, schaut das Wunder an!") and that God helps when the need is greatest ("Wenn die Not auf's"). *—Ann Feeney*

Recommended:

- ○ **Humperdinck: Hänsel & Gretel** / Runnicles (cond.), Ziesak, Larmore, Behrens, Schafer, Bavarian RSO / 1994 / Teldec 94549
- ○ **Humperdinck: Hänsel & Gretel** / Karajan (cond.), Schwarzkopf, Grummer, Metternich, Felbermayery, London PO / 1999 / EMI 67145
- ○ **Humperdinck: Hänsel & Gretel** / Eichhorn (cond.), Fischer-Dieskau, Moffo, Ludwig, Auger, Munich Radio Orch. / 1999 / RCA 252812

Peter Hurford

b. Nov. 22, 1930, Minehead, Somerset, England

Organist

Trained in both music and law, Peter Hurford has enjoyed an enviable reputation for both his organ playing and his musical scholarship. The latter has produced not only revised ideas about performance of early music, but also different notions about the construction of the instruments upon which such music ought to be played. His extensive recordings for the Decca label (earlier, London Records in the United States) have passed into the realm of the legendary and his live performances have attracted positive reviews, as well as stimulating numerous discussions regarding performance practice and the art of organ building.

After initial studies with Harold Darke, the famous and much-respected English organist and composer, Hurford read both music and law at Jesus College, Cambridge University, graduating with dual degrees. Through study in Paris with the blind French organist André Marchal, Hurford explored the music of the Baroque period, with a particular emphasis on J.S. Bach and the French masters, and he acquired something of his teacher's brilliance as an improviser. His own singular notions of authentic performing style also took form at that time and were soon regularly implemented before the public once he had received an appointment as music master at St. Albans Abbey in 1958. There, he experimented, rebuilt the organ to comply with his convictions, and soon began to attract the attention of other English organists unsatisfied with the traditional and often heavy-handed Baroque style customarily heard in English churches. By 1963, Hurford's stature made possible the immediate success of the International Organ Festival he devised for St. Albans. There, organists and organ scholars were able to gather to hear and discuss performances and share scholarly findings regarding performance style, registration, repertory, and audience building. Winners of competitions at the St. Albans Festival have included such international virtuosos as Gillian Weir and Thomas Trotter. Many a competitor counted himself fortunate to have received an autographed copy of Hurford's recordings of Bach's complete organ works. After decades at St. Albans, Hurford resigned to fulfill the demand for solo performances. By that time, his recordings had made his name a familiar one even to those who had not heard him in live performance. In addition to his concert appearances, Hurford began to devote time to teaching and made himself a welcome visiting scholar in numerous venues, especially in England and the United States. After having worked out his ideas during several decades of lecturing and performance, Hurford assembled them in written form in his book *Making Music on the Organ*, published in 1988. The simple, direct title conceals a wealth of carefully considered issues and effective solutions to them. Hurford also achieved some renown as a composer of organ works and choral pieces. Mostly dating from his St. Albans years, some of them are flowingly lyrical while others are joyously animated. All reflect Hurford's skill and inclinations as an improviser. Hurford's largest recording project was putting on disc the complete organ works of Bach, a project that began in the 1970s. The full set is still available (now in remastered sound) along side a smaller, two-disc set of highlights. Another double-disc set of organ masses by Couperin is also a seminal issue. Hurford's often-brisk tempi and variety of registration decidedly changed organ performance; both sets demonstrate why. *—Erik Eriksson*

Recommended:

- ○ **Handel: Organ Concertos** / Hurford / London 414604
- ○ **Saint-Saëns: Symphony 3; Carnaval des animaux** / Dutoit (cond.), Roge, Hurford, Ortiz, Kampen, Bell, Pay, McGee, London Sinfonietta, Montreal SO / 1991 / London 430720
- ○ **Bach: Great Organ Works** / Hurford / 1994 / London 443485

Karel Husa

b. Aug. 7, 1921, Prague, Czechoslovakia

Composer: Band Music, Chamber Music, Orchestral Music

Karel Husa is an important composer, the bulk of whose career took place in the last half of the twentieth century. While he is generally ranked in the second tier among his contemporaries, his standing may change for the better in the coming decades. His expressive language, although sometimes employing serial techniques and other advanced methods, is far from difficult: Husa's rhythms and use of ostinatos impart sinew and drive to his music, and his orchestration is always assured and colorful. Among his important compositions are his *Fantasies for Orchestra* (1956), *Third String Quartet* (1968), *Music for Prague 1968*, and the ballet *The Trojan Women* (1980–81).

Karel Husa showed talent early in his childhood, learning to play both the violin and piano. He enrolled at the Prague Conservatory in 1939, in part to avoid being drafted into the occupying German Army. There he studied composition with Jaroslav Ridky, and conducting with Metod Dolezil and Pavel Dedecek. His Op. 1 *Sonatina*, for piano, dates from his student years, as well as his first big work, *Overture for Large Orchestra*, Op. 3.

After taking further courses with Ridky following the war, Husa traveled to Paris in 1947 to study with Arthur Honegger. He also studied composition with Nadia Boulanger and conducting with Jean Fournet. In the coming years, his career would be split equally between composing and conducting duties. His *First String Quartet* (1948) received the 1950 Lili Boulanger Prize and helped to establish his name internationally.

Cut off from his homeland by the Communist takeover in 1948, Husa accepted a faculty position with Cornell University in Ithaca, New York, in 1954 to teach composition and to lead the student orchestra. He also took on many guest conducting appearances with orchestras in the United States, Europe, and Asia, and accepted a post as conductor of the Ithaca Chamber Orchestra. He might have stayed in Europe a while longer, but by now he had a wife and two daughters to support. Besides, as it turned out, he found the the Cornell post was much to his liking, remaining in it until his retirement in 1992.

In 1959, Husa became an American citizen, and by that time many of his works were appearing on concert programs in his adopted country and abroad. Then-recent compositions include his *Divertimento for Brass Ensemble and Percussion* (1958), actually a transcription of four pieces from his 1955 *Eight Czech Duos*, for piano four-hands. The 1960s might have been Husa's most successful decade: in 1964 he received a Guggenheim fellowship, and five years later his *Third String Quartet* was awarded a Pulitzer Prize. In addition, his *Music for Prague 1968* has become his most often-performed work.

Husa remained quite active in the field of composition over the next several decades, writing most of his music at a cottage he had purchased along Cayuga lake. Among his compositions from the 1970s are *Two Sonnets from Michelangelo* (1971) and *Fresco for Wind Ensemble* (1975). Some impressive commissions came in the 1980s: *Concerto for Orchestra* (1986) was written for Zubin Mehta and the New York Philharmonic Orchestra; and the *Concerto for Trumpet and Orchestra* (1987–88) met the commission of Sir Georg Solti and the Chicago Symphony Orchestra. Husa's 1993 *Violin Concerto* was written for another New York

Philharmonic commission. In 1995, the composer received what was perhaps his most cherished honor, the Czech Republic's State Medal Award of Merit, First Class, given by President Vaclav Havel. *—Robert Cummings*

Overview of Works

Karel Husa was born in Czechoslovakia, trained in Paris, and has spent most of his creative life in the United States. All three places have influenced his compositional career. First educated at the Prague conservatory, Husa was awarded a scholarship to study composition in Paris under Nadia Boulanger and Arthur Honegger. His *String Quartet No. 1* (1948) and *Symphony No. 1* (1953) were composed in Paris and showed the influence of his teachers as well as other trends in postwar composition, particularly the neo-Classicism of Hindemith and Stravinsky. In 1954, he became a member of the music faculty of Cornell University in New York and his music began to incorporate American influences as well. His best-known works—*Music for Prague 1968*, based on his reaction to the Soviet suppression of the Prague, and *Apotheosis of This Earth* (1970) on ecological themes—were both scored for concert band, and both incorporate the momentum-generating ostinatos of Honegger and the aleatoric principles of Cage in context of Husa's own gesturally dramatic and rhythmically powerful style. *—James Leonard*

Recommended:

- ○ **Husa: Divertimento; Fantasies for Orchestra; Trojan Women** / Husa (cond.), Paris Orch. of Soloïsts / 1995 / Phoenix USA 128
- ○ **Husa: SQ 2 & 3; Evocations** / Long Island Chamber Ens., Fine Arts Quartet / 1990 / Phoenix USA 113
- ○ **Husa: Violin Sonata; Piano Sonata 2; 12 Moravian Songs** / Oliveira, Oei, Rodgers, Basquin, Martin / 1995 / New World 80493

BAND MUSIC

Music for Prague 1968, for concert band (1968)

Although he had been an American citizen for a decade, a fierce stirring of pain, anger, and patriotism for the besieged land of his birth set Karel Husa's pen in motion. The result was *Music for Prague* (1968), along with *Apotheosis of this Earth*, the composer's most celebrated works. Although not a tone poem, the composer gives the listener a gripping account of the invasion and conquest of the Czech capital in that year of seemingly universal tragedy, made all the more eloquent by implication rather than delineation. For the Western musical world, Husa became a modern Sibelius, *Prague* his own grimly defiant *Finlandia*. The work's final triumph would be long in coming but eventually complete. The work was commissioned by the Ithaca College Concert Band and premiered by that ensemble under Kenneth Snapp on January 31, 1969. There soon followed an orchestral arrangement which the composer gave with the Munich Philharmonic in that city one year later to the day. But the work would not be heard (understandably) in his homeland until 1989. With the fall of the old regime and the election of Vaclav Havel, Husa returned to give the Czech premiere of *Music for Prague* in that city with the Czech Philharmonic Orchestra.

As with many of his other works, the composer, as eloquent with word as with tone, has provided insightful notes to *Music for Prague*, and the interested listener is urged to read them on the recording jacket or the preface to the score. The three-movement work begins softly, nebulously (as so often with Husa), yet discordant, as though an unspecified anxiety was descending upon a metropolis as it goes about business as normal. Suddenly there is a brass alarum. A smattering of an old medieval Czech hymn tries to rise. Snare drum tattoos break out; as in Shostakovich's *Leningrad Symphony*, the former heroes are now the oppressors. A solo piccolo, said by Husa to be a bird call, a symbol of liberty, closes the first movement. The following one opens with Mussorgskyan bell chords, but here there is no rejoicing, forced or otherwise. Rampant long-held siren like tones and an anguished wandering melody evoke barren nocturnal streets. The finale opens with a muffled side drum; flecks of pitched percussion glint and vanish. A sharp unmuffled snare tattoo and brash fanfare announces a vigorous and ironic section of nervous counterpoint, grows to a forte, and moves inexorably forward until checked by resolute declamatory brass. Chaos ensues, and the scene is repeated to carry through as the coda. It could be considered an open ending, for at the time of its composition, vindication—social and personal—would be a long time in coming. *—Wayne Reisig*

Recommended:

- ○ **Eastman Wind Ens.** / Hunsberger (cond.), / 1989 / CBS 44916

Dmitri Hvorostovsky

b. Oct. 16, 1962, Krasnoyarsk, Siberia, USSR

Baritone

Known for captivating song recitals, lyrical performances of Verdi baritone roles, and, not least of all, his striking silver hair, Dmitri Hvorostovsky has enjoyed an A-list career since he emerged in the early 1990s. His brilliant, yet deceptively dark-hued voice is the embodiment of chiaroscuro, and the combination of vocal polish and emotion that he brings to his performances has made him an audience favorite.

Having grown up, studied, and debuted (as Marullo in *Rigoletto*) in his hometown of Krasnoyarsk, he took top honors at the 1987 Glinka National Competition, the 1988 Toulouse Singing Competition, and then the 1989 Cardiff Singer of the World competition. The last of these, in which he edged out both the meteoric Bryn Terfel and Monica Groop for the win, launched him into the spotlight and led to his western operatic debut, as Yeletsky in Tchaikovsky's *The Queen of Spades* in Nice. The next several years brought debut recitals in London and New York, his Italian debut as Eugene Onegin at the famous La Fenice, and engagements at Covent Garden, the Metropolitan Opera, the Chicago Lyric Opera, and the Berlin State Opera. His first solo recording contract, with Philips, began in the early 1990s, as well; the artistic and commercial success of his first several CDs, and the explosion of his operatic and concert schedule around the world, sent his career into high gear.

Although he is closely identified with the roles of Eugene Onegin and Yeletsky (*The Queen of Spades*), Hvorostovsky's operatic repertory is centered on Italian works more so than Russian; in the early 2000s, he began to explore new Russian territory, like Prokofiev's *War and Peace*, but in general he feels Russian roles call for a gruffer, less lyrical voice than his. He is known best for his performances as the elder Germont in *La traviata*, Posa in *Don Carlos*, Don Giovanni, and Rossini's Figaro. However, as a recitalist, Hvorostovsky has always been intensely focused on Russian song, making moody, dramatic works of Rachmaninov, Tchaikovsky, Rimsky-Korsakov, Glinka, and Mussorgsky the centerpieces of his performances. With his longtime collaborator Mikhail Arkadiev at the piano, Hvorostovsky has established himself as one of the finest singers of that repertory anywhere in the world. The special nature of that collaboration was honored by Russian composer Georgy Sviridov in 1995, when he dedicated his vocal poem *Petersburg* to Hvorostovsky and Arkadiev; the two have remained champions of his music. *—Allen Schrott*

Recommended:

- ○ **Kalinka: Russian Folk Songs** / Korniev (cond.), Hvorostovsky, St. Petersburg Chamber Choir / 1998 / Philips 456399
- ○ **Songs & Dances of Death** / Gergiev (cond.), Hvorostovsky, Kirov Orch. / 1994 / Philips 438872
- ○ **My Restless Soul** / Hvorostovsky, Arkadiev (piano) / Philips 442536
- ○ **Tchaikovsky & Verdi Arias** / Gergiev (cond.), Hvorostovsky, Rotterdam PO / 1990 / Philips 426740

Jorma Hynninen

b. Apr. 3, 1941, Leppävirta, Finland

Baritone

Jorma Hynninen is one of the most important figures in contemporary Scandinavian music and in music administration, a champion of new compositions who has not only made them a focus of the venues where he has acted as artistic director, but also given them life in riveting musical and dramatic performances. While considerably less well known outside of Scandinavia, he has been praised worldwide for his roles in the standard operatic repertoire and is considered one of the best performers of his day of Tchaikovsky's *Eugene Onegin*, Wolfram in *Tannhauser*, and Posa in Verdi's *Don Carlo*, as well as an accomplished lieder and song performer, with his warm, flexible voice, and strong vocal and physical acting abilities.

He studied at the Sibelius Academy in Helsinki with Matti Tuloisela and Antii Koskinen, and after graduating, went to Rome to study with Luigi Ricci. He won the Lappeenranta song competition in 1969 and made his opera debut with the Finnish National Opera in the same year as Silvio in Leoncavallo's *Pagliacci*. He made his Paris debut in *Pelléas et Mélisande* in 1980, the year of his New York debut in a Carnegie Hall recital. Also that year, he became artistic director of Finland's Joensuu Song Festival, holding that position for 11 years. His Met debut was in 1984 in *Don Carlo*, the same year in which he became the artistic director of the Finnish National Opera, a post he held until 1990. Two years later, he was named artistic director of the Savonlinna Festival, one of the world's most prestigious music festivals. While maintaining this responsibility, he continues to sing worldwide, including contemporary and Romantic-era Scandinavian music, German lieder, and Tchaikovsky, Wagner, and Mozart, and the more lyric Verdi roles. The Sibelius Academy appointed him professor of the arts in 1990 and professor of singing in 1997.

Hynninen has created the title roles of Rautavaara's *Thomas* in 1985 and *Vincent* (based on the life of Vincent Van Gogh) in 1990, Sallinen's *The Red Line* in 1978, *The King Goes Forth to France* in 1984, and *Kullervo* in 1990, and Merikanto's *Juha* in 1978. He has also recorded other contemporary music, such as Dallapiccola's *Il Prigioniero*, popular love songs, and spirituals. *—Ann Feeney*

Recommended:

- ○ **Sibelius Songs** / Segerstam (cond.), Hynninen, Tampere PO / Ondine 823
- ○ **Hynninen: Profile of a Great Career** / Hynninen, etc. / 1999 / Ondine 944

I

Jacques Ibert

b. Aug. 15, 1890, Paris, France, **d.** Feb. 5, 1962, Paris, France

Composer: Chamber Music, Orchestral, Concerto, Vocal

Though Jacques Ibert is best remembered for a handful of orchestral bonbons in the manner and spirit of Ravel, his output encompasses nearly every genre and bears testament to a musical language characterized as much by unmistakable craftsmanship as by picturesque color. Ibert trained at the Paris Conservatory under Paul Vidal; as a student, he showed great promise and took a number of the Conservatory's awards. Following military service in World War I, Ibert travelled to Italy as a recipient of the Prix de Rome; there, he composed what was to become one of his most popular works, the orchestral suite *Escales* (1922). This "travelogue in tones," which depicts touristy locales in Italy, Tunisia, and Spain, has come to be regarded as representative of the "Ibert sound": breezy, good-humored, and evocative. Still, Ibert was far from a "one-note" composer of chronically pleasant music. Another of his works written in Rome, *La ballade de la geôle de Reading* (The Ballad of Reading Gaol, 1920), is a tone poem based on Oscar Wilde's far-from-cheery reflection upon life in prison; it was the work, in fact, that first brought the composer to widespread attention. Though most of Ibert's works for the stage remain relatively little known, both the one-act opera *Angélique* (1926) and the *Don Quixote*-themed ballet *Le chevalier errant* (1935) have enjoyed continued currency. More popular still, and indeed, one of Ibert's most enduring creations, is the colorful, comical *Divertissement* (1930) fashioned from the composer's incidental score to Labiche's *The Italian Straw Hat*. Reflecting the farcical frenzy of the story, Ibert's score is a comic panoply that includes everything from jazz elements to Viennese waltzes to the "Wedding March" from Mendelssohn's *Midsummer Night's Dream*. Among Ibert's other works, the *Concerto da camera* (1935) for alto saxophone and 11 instruments stands out as one of a handful of genuine mainstays of the saxophone repertoire. Like a number of his "serious" contemporaries, Ibert also ventured from time to time into film scoring; his most conspicuous efforts in this realm include music for Orson Welles' 1948 version of *Macbeth* and the "Circus" sequence from Gene Kelly's *Invitation to the Dance* (1952). *—Michael Rodman*

CHAMBER MUSIC

Entr'acte, for flute or violin & harp or guitar (1937)

Ibert's brief but brilliant *Entr'acte* is one of his most well-recognized works and a direct product of his love for Spanish literature and music. In 1935 Ibert wrote incidental music for a French production of Pedro Calderón's *El médico de su honra*. The entr'acte of that music was published that same year for flute or violin and guitar or harp. It has been transcribed for and recorded with many other instruments since its original publication. It opens with a breathless, whirling dance with propulsive accompaniment, inspired by flamenco guitar music. The opening is then repeated after the briefest of pauses, the music vividly calling to mind a dancer as he or she improvises a variation on the theme. That image of an animated dancer, showing off his or her footwork, continues in the following serenade-like solo for the guitar. That, in turn, leads into a cadenza for both instruments and a final, brief statement of the theme, ending, so obviously, with the dancer's arms in the air and a final stamp of the feet. *—Patsy Morita*

Recommended:

○ **Music, My Love** / Rampal, Laskine (harp) / 1989 / CBS 45548

Histoires, for saxophone (or flute) & piano (1933)

Six of these ten charming little pieces, originally written for the piano by Ibert, were arranged in 1933 for flute and piano by Marcel Moyse.

For "La meneuse de tortues d'or..." (The Leader of the Golden Tortoises), the sweet, droll melodic line expressing the movement of the "slowpoke" is totally given over to the flute, but other than that, few additions or changes are made to the piano original except for an occasional doubling of a bass figure in octaves. The scoring of the music for the two separate instruments does, however, make the feeling of the piece more "doux et mélancolique" (sweet and melancholy). "Dans la maison triste" (In the Sad House), with its elusive three-part mini-story is also enhanced by this same instrumental separation, especially in the easier-to-follow 1940s-romantic-mystery-film-score chromatic lines in the first part. Similarly, the staccato crystalline chords that accompany "La cage de cristal..." (The Crystal Cage ...) are beautifully distinguished from its childlike melody.

"Le petit âne blanc..." (The Little White Donkey...) is transposed a half step higher than the piano original to G major, which makes the piece more playable on the flute and makes the timbre somewhat lighter. The charming melody is given over to the flute. Moyse distributes the notes of the little "hee-haw" dissonances between the two instruments (simultaneously, an upward figure for the flute and a downward figure for the piano), which makes their timbre sharper and more contrasting. He retains the more densely chorded "hee-haws" as in the original, and later doubles the top notes with the flute, making these dissonances more poignant and delightful. To the coda, Moyse has added a major-scale run not in the original but which makes for a more effective cadence against the sustained piano chords.

"La marchande d'eau fraîche..." (The woman Who Sells Fresh Water) is an especially effective arrangement which allows the piano to continue the lovely patterns made of alternating fourths in both hands, while the flute picks up the melody. This gives the music a more "liquid" texture than the piano original, where the pattern must be stopped in the right hand in order to play the melodies.

Likewise, in "Le cortège de Balkis..." (The Balkis Procession), the flute is given most of the melodic material, which frees the line to truly be "free and brilliant" as well as "supple and nonchalant." The timbre of the flute itself here suggests the oriental dance and march of the music. The separations of the often contrasting articulations of the piano and flute also create more colors. *—"Blue Gene" Tyranny*

Recommended:

○ **The French Saxophone** / Savijoki, Rahkonen & Surala (pianos) / 1982 / Bis 209

Trois Pièces brèves, for wind quintet (1930)

These three attractive, modest, and brightly orchestrated chamber works are scored for flute, oboe, clarinet, horn, and bassoon. They possess the charm and sense of humor of much of the composer's œuvre, such as the *Histoires*, which includes the well-known *Little White Donkey* (*Le petit âne blanc*) and the musical farce *Angélique* (1926) in the spirit of Offenbach. The works also evoke direct emotions associated with the countryside and simple mythological scenes.

The first "brief" piece, of approximately two-and-a-half minutes' duration, is marked Assez lent in tempo and is performed at a moderately lively clip, like music for a farce. The punctuated high dissonances of the introduction which descend into a tongue-in-cheek imitation of a banal vaudeville, or perhaps operetta or tiny march band's opening, make the ears immediately sit up and take notice. The bassoon and horn then pump out an elegantly modulated version of a Gilbert and Sullivan-type accompaniment, and the clarinet plays a lively springtime tune answered by grace-note bird calls in the oboe. The flute interweaves a fast line with little earnest accents concluding the melody. A bridge on somewhat more serious chords alerts the listener that something out of place may be happening, but the music never relents its energetic push. The flute plays chromatic, almost atonal, lines and then sustains a note by itself before coming in with a lively triple meter theme almost like a waltz. The bridge, back in duple meter and pulsing, reappears with the oboe this time signaling that all may not be jolly. But a comment by the flute brings the tonality back around to the introductory tonality. The first theme is heard again played by the clarinet and then the flute with tiny comments by the bassoon. The clarinet chimes in with the waltz theme and then a quick, flashy "let's have a big hand for the performers, folks"-type coda ends the piece.

The second piece is a gentle pastoral in Andante tempo without a hint of the plaintive, of slightly over a minute and a half's duration. The movement opens with two lyrical lines in an extended counterpoint for flute and clarinet. The horn and bassoon then sustain a warm, bourdon-like drone in the bass while the oboe, and then the clarinet and flute, create a flowing texture above the sustaining tones. The whole ensemble cadences on a tender major harmony.

The third and last piece unfolds in an Allegro tempo. The main theme in fast duple time winds about in rotating figures and is similar to a sailor's piping tune, or perhaps a spirited village dance with high stepping movements. The basic pattern of the tune first occurs on the lower steps of a major mode and is then repeated on the higher tones with a flat seventh step throwing the mode into wild abandon in the Mixolydian mode. The coda deliberately speeds up to create a comically "showy" conclusion. *—"Blue Gene" Tyranny*

Recommended:

- ○ **French** / Philadelphia Woodwind Quintet / 2001 / Boston 1061
- ○ **French Music for Wind Ensemble** / Athena Ens. / 1991 / Chandos 6543

ORCHESTRAL

Divertissement, for chamber orchestra (1929–1930)

The cultural scene of the 1920s was infused by a spirit—part relief, part jubilation—in which entertainment could be enjoyed guilt free, unfettered by the sobriety, austerity, and destruction that had attended the recent Great War. Dance and theater enjoyed a creative explosion, and composers of every musical persuasion participated, producing perhaps more incidental and theater music and ballet scores than at any other time since; scarcely any composer of note escaped the decade without having produced his or her share of such works.

Ibert's *Divertissement* is drawn from the incidental score the composer produced for the farcical nineteenth century Labiche play *The Italian Straw Hat.* Labiche's comedy, a classic of its type, recounts the adventures of a nervous bridegroom on his wedding day as he attempts to save a woman's honor by searching for a replacement for a hat he inadvertently ruined, all the while concealing his frantic mission from his intended bride, her suspicious father, and the entire wedding party. Along the way, disguises, unlikely deceptions, misunderstandings, and mistaken identities propel the action to ever greater frenzy before a tidy resolution.

The confluence of periods in the *Divertissement*—a genre with roots in the Baroque applied to a nineteenth century comedy by a twentieth century composer—is reflected in the parodistic pastiche that informs the work's six sections. In addition to Ibert's "own" music, references to other styles, both sly and blatant, abound. By the end, the astute listener has made his way through a thicket strewn with blues and jazz, music hall tunes, spiky modernist dissonance, Viennese waltzes, and the *Wedding March* from Mendelssohn's music for *A Midsummer Night's Dream.—AMG*

Recommended:

- ○ **Fête à la Française** / Dutoit (cond.), Montreal SO / 1989 / London 421527
- ○ **Ibert: Divertissement; Escales; Chausson: Symphony** / Mata (cond.), Dallas SO / 1994 / Dorian 90181

Escales (Ports of Call), suite (1922)

Jacques Ibert enjoyed a major sensation when his *Escales* was premiered in 1924. As a sumptuous, brilliantly orchestrated work depicting sunny climes in perfect postcard music, Ibert's suite follows in the steps of such predecessors as Saint-Saëns' *Suite algérienne* (1880), Chabrier's *España* (1883), Debussy's *Ibéria* (1905–08), and Ravel's *Rapsodie espagnole* (1907).

In the span of about 15 minutes, *Escales* retraces a voyage Ibert himself might have made while he was in the Navy during World War I, cruising the Mediterranean. The first movement, "Rome-Palermo," evokes the sights and sounds of these major Italian centers with a melody of appropriate regional flavor. "Tunis-Nefta" brings the sailors ashore in Northern Africa; timpani and pulsing strings provide a hypnotic beat while an oboe imitates the chromatic improvisations of local reed instruments. "Valencia," a whirling dance scene, brings the suite to a close with a portrayal of Spanish culture at its liveliest.*—Joseph Stevenson*

Recommended:

- ○ **Roussel: Bacchus et Ariane; Ibert: Escales; etc.** / Ormandy (cond.), Philadelphia Orch. / 1996 / Sony 62644

CONCERTO

Concertino da camera, for alto saxophone & 11 instruments (1935)

By the 1930s many of France's leading composers were jazz besotted, and Ibert was no exception. His saxophone concertino not only appropriates jazz's most characteristic instrument, but employs plenty of syncopation and, in the slow section, some bluesy material. Still, this is not crossover music, but a classical piece inspired by a few specific pop trends of the day.

The brief work begins with an Allegro con moto entering with a raucous blast from the small ensemble of strings and winds. The soloist quickly bursts in with a percolating tune that eventually makes way for a second subject that croons in the saxophone's high register. Here and in the very brief development section, Ibert maintains a close, complex interplay between the soloist and the little band; indeed, the saxophone is reduced to noodling in the background when the strings take over the second subject.

The Larghetto is a lonely, bluesy solo that sends the saxophone gliding oh-so-gradually up and down its entire range, with the strings entering at length to provide simple support for the sax's balladlike material. Eventually the woodwinds provide their own paraphrase of the theme, followed by a string statement. Without a break, the concluding Animato molto arrives with jittery material over which the saxophone dances and hovers. One of the soloist's main themes is lyrical but still syncopated. The concertino's only cadenza arrives near the end, a free riff on tiny fragments of the movement's main, sewing-machine theme; soloist and ensemble offer a bright restatement of this main theme in full, scampering to an upbeat conclusion. *—James Reel*

Recommended:

- ○ **Saxophone Concertos** / Marriner (cond.), Harle, Academy of St. Martin-in-the-Fields / 1997 / EMI 72109
- ○ **Creation** / Marsalis, Orpheus CO / 2001 / Sony 89251

Concerto for cello & 10 wind instruments (1925)

Although the contrast may seem irresistible, there have been few concertos for string instruments with wind backing. Kurt Weill's serious, extended *Violin Concerto* is the most familiar, and its 1925 premiere in Paris may have inspired Jacques Ibert to write his own *Concerto for Cello and Winds* that year. Ibert's modest piece is more of a concertino, clocking in at only about 12 minutes and not taking time to develop the materials to any great depth. It also hints at why string solos against wind ensembles aren't more common; the balance here is difficult, and Ibert often just gives up and moves the soloist to the background, giving the "accompanying" ensemble more prominence than one would expect in a concerto.

It begins with a Pastorale: Allant. The woodwinds set the country scene with a tender, gently flowing theme soon taken up by the cello. But almost immediately the horn intrudes with a fanfare that sends the cello into burping little convulsions. The woodwinds take the lead through the rest of the movement, which, after a seemingly disorganized transition, returns to the opening material, now harmonically unsettled.

Romance: Souple begins with chattery woodwind phrases that call the movement's heading into question, but the cello arrives with a more lyrical, long-lined melody. Again, the winds attempt to dominate the proceedings, and their quietly humorous, syncopated material momentarily pushes the soloist aside. The cello returns with solo utterances blending both the movement's principal elements, concluding with an eloquent restatement of its romance melody that almost but not quite wins over the incurably perky winds.

Gigue: Animé is exactly what the title announces, a fleet pseudo-Scottish affair that quickly devolves into very mild, slightly jazzy parody. A sequence of quiet exchanges of passagework between the cello and individuals from the wind ensemble leads to a motoric little cello cadenza and a wind-dominated coda based on the gigue tune. *—James Reel*

Recommended:

- ○ **Ibert: Oeuvres Variées** / Clark (cond.), Rosen, Lucarelli, Manhattan CO / 1996 / Newport Classic 85598
- ○ **Concertos for Cello & Winds** / Baumer (cond.), Thedeen / 2002 / BIS 1136

Flute Concerto (1932–1933)

"In my concertos I have allotted the instruments the types of themes which correspond to their particular tone qualities and respect their expressive possibilities." This statement of Jacques Ibert's certainly applies to his *Flute Concerto,* written over the years 1932–33. The work was dedicated to Marcel Moyse, who was the featured soloist in its premiere performance, under Philippe Gaubert's direction, in Paris on February 25, 1934. Both Moyse and Gaubert, incidentally, were students of the great French flutist and teacher Paul Taffanel, for whom many of the greatest French flute works were written.

Ibert's *Concerto* was dedicated to Moyse, who didn't play it often. In fact, the work lay neglected for many years due to its perceived difficulty. The opening Allegro is based on a perky first theme with a neoclassical shape, and a slower, more languorous second theme. Throughout, the flute is kept constantly busy. A sweet, lyrical Andante follows, the flute's long-breathed song accompanied by gentle strings. The longest of the work's three movements is the last, a jazzy Allegro scherzando with a virtuoso solo cadenza; this Finale is such a challenge for flutists that it became a test piece at the Paris Conservatoire. *—Chris Morrison*

Recommended:

- ○ **60 Years, 60 Flute Masterpieces** / Dutoit (cond.), Galway, Royal PO / 1999 / RCA 63432

Symphonie concertante, for oboe & string orchestra (1948–1949)

Ibert is best-known as a perfumed Impressionist (*Escales*) and a parodist (*Divertissement*), so this gritty oboe concerto will surprise those who know only his most popular works. It was composed in 1949 for Paul Sacher, founder and conductor of the Basel Chamber Orchestra, whose many commissions sometimes drew the day's leading composers into unexpected moods; Honegger's *Symphony No. 4,* for example, is uncharacteristically sunny. Ibert's *Symphonie concertante,* in contrast, begins grimly.

In the opening Allegro con moto, the low strings introduce a sharply angular theme, whereupon the high strings churn and roil until the oboe finally enters with a tune in lighter spirits. After a dour string intrusion, the oboe presents a dancing tune that the strings manage to corrupt upon their return. The movement continues in this contrasting manner; even when the oboe introduces an airy melody in the style of Poulenc, the strings soon begin slashing at it. The development continues this pattern of oboe and strings appropriating each other's material and altering its character. The cadenza noodles mainly with the oboe's first theme, which is derived from a few notes of the strings' opening motif. The briefest of codas finishes off the movement.

The thematic relationships are more obvious in the Adagio, ma non troppo. In a lengthy introduction, the strings play an unsettled motif, beginning with harsh sobs and spreading into a long-lined lament. The oboe offers its own version of this music, which the strings then appropriate for a jagged variation. The soloist returns with a lyrical elaboration of a portion of the theme, but the movement has now reached the peak of its arch and descends backwards through the material that has already been presented.

The finale, Allegro brillante, also springs from two contrasting themes, although unlike in the slow movement, these are completely independent of each other. The strings burst in with rapid, urgent passagework, which the oboe answers with an angular, syncopated theme. Its second melody is more spacious, but wanders up and down the staff, as if it has lost the key. The strings become preoccupied with combinations of and elaborations on their opening passagework and the angular theme, while the oboe applies itself to fast runs and trills, silencing the strings for two brief, abortive cadenzas. The strings embark on a fugal treatment of the angular theme, but this soon falls apart and the work ends with the oboe joining in a quick survey of the movement's basic materials. *—James Reel*

Recommended:

- ○ **John de Lancie, Philadelphia Orchestra's Former Solo Oboist** / de Lancie, Previn (cond.), London SO / 2002 / Boston 1045
- ○ **Strauss: Oboe Concerto; Ibert: Symphonie concertante; Françaix** / de Lancie, Previn (cond.) / 1991 / RCA 7989

VOCAL

Chansons de Don Quichotte et Chanson de Sancho (1932)

These songs were written for a 1932 film on the story of Don Quixote, directed by Georg W. Pabst and starring the great Russian bass, Feodor Chaliapin. Unbeknownst to Ibert, he was only one of five composers approached by the producers, who also secured submissions from Marcel Delannoy, Manuel de Falla, Darius Milhaud, and Maurice Ravel; each composer thought his music was to be used in the film. The dishonest circumstances of the "competition," and the fact that his songs were chosen over those of Ravel, whom he greatly admired, were embarrassments to Ibert. It also angered Ravel, who considered a lawsuit against the producers. He eventually dropped the action, however, and the two composers remained close friends.

Ibert's *Quatre Chansons* were written to sixteenth century French poems by Ronsard and Alexandre Arnoux, but the extensive use of guitar, reed instruments, and metric asymmetry lend them a distinctly Spanish flavor. Together, they do a remarkable job of capturing both the story and the spirit of Don Quixote, who is the first-person "voice" of all four songs. The first and last songs of the group, "Chanson du départ" and "Chanson de la mort," are in the style of free and speech-like recitatives; in the first, we are introduced to Quixote's unique perspective on the world: his lady lives in a grand castle, fortified against vice and which one may only enter if he has proved himself worthy. The last is a tender farewell by Quixote's to his faithful sidekick, Sancho; although dying, Don Quixote is going somewhere pure and without lies. The middle two songs, "Chanson à Dulcinée" and "Chanson du Duc," are more vigorous and rhythmic. Number two is an anthem of impatient love; each hour is a day, each minute an hour in which he cannot see his Dulcinée. The third is an ode to the purifying and elevating effects of love, delivered in the noblest of melodic styles. *—Allen Schrott*

Recommended:

- ○ **José Van Dam** / Nagano (cond.), Van Dam, Lyon Opera Orch. / 1992 / Virgin 59236

Nobuko Imai

b. Mar. 18, 1943, Tokyo, Japan
Violist

Nobuko Imai has been a leading viola player since the early 1990s. She studied at Tokyo's Toho Gakuen Music School before continuing her training in the United States at both Yale University and the Juilliard School. Following her graduation from Juilliard, she triumphantly vanquished all competitors to win the highest prizes at the Munich and Geneva international competitions. She is a former member of the prestigious Vermeer Quartet, known for sharp performances of the Mozart and Beethoven chamber repertoire. Since leaving this ensemble, she divides her time between performing as a soloist with the world's major orchestras, such as the English Chamber Orchestra, the London Symphony Orchestra, the London Philharmonic, and the Dallas Symphony Orchestra, and teaching at the German Detmold School of Music and the Utrecht Conservatory in the Netherlands. She returns regularly to her native land where she serves as artistic adviser of Casals Hall in Tokyo. She also continues to be active in chamber music, performing alongside such greats as Gidon Kremer, Yo-Yo Ma, Midori, Itzhak Perlman, András Schiff, and the late Isaac Stern.

The violist's superb discography includes more than 30 releases on labels such as BIS, Chandos, EMI, Hyperion, and Philips. In 1996 she was awarded the leading Japanese prize for music, the Suntory Hall Prize. She is known for an innovative approach to her instrument, and her unique accomplishments include creating viola adaptations of works for cello from the classical repertoire. Even in her early days as a student she was known for sparks of technical brilliance; when her class was going through an intense study of Bach, attempting to come as close as possible to the composer's original intentions, it was Imai that came up with the idea of the string players use Baroque bows instead of modern bows with their modern instruments. She also brings this focus into her involvement with contemporary music, naturally. Always an enthusiast for new works, her discography includes a collaboration with the Japanese avant-garde composer Toru Takemitsu, who created a work specifically for the violist focusing on the unique characteristics of the instrument. Commercial success rarely follows an artist's involvement with contemporary music, but Imai's collection of twentieth century pieces for viola and piano released on BIS, including the work by Takemitsu, was a best seller in Japan. She has also premiered works by George Benjamin, Duncan McTier, and David Horne. Another aspect of her ambitious career are events involving cultural exchange. In 2000 she initiated and assisted in the production of a concert series held at both the Concertgebouw in Amsterdam and in Tokyo which featured Japanese and Dutch early and contemporary music, celebrating the relationship between the two countries which has existed for more than four centuries. Also in 2000 she founded an institution called the East West Baroque Academy, where young music professionals are able to gain experience in authentic early music style and performance practices. *—Eugene Chadbourne*

Recommended:

- ○ **Viola on Stage** / Imai, Pontinen (piano) / 1996 / BIS 300829
- ○ **Viola Bouquet** / Imai, Pontinen (piano) / 1996 / Philips 446103
- ○ **Hindemith: Sonatas for Solo Viola** / Imai / 1992 / Bis 571
- ○ **Schnittke: In Menoriam; Viola Concerto** / Markiz (cond.), Imai, Malmo SO / 1989 / Bis 447

Eliahu Inbal

b. Feb. 16, 1936, Jerusalem, Israel
Conductor

Israeli conductor Eliahu Inbal has become known to many worldwide for both his concert performances and his numerous recordings, including the complete symphonies of several composers. In Europe, however, Inbal is nearly as well known as a conductor of opera, with interests running from the Italian bel cantists through works of the twentieth century. Nor has he ignored the symphonic works of his own time; a number of important original works and reconstructions have been premiered under his preparation and direction. Given his broad repertory, it is not surprising that few of his interpretations may be said to surpass all others, but his technical control and sensitivity to colors make the majority of his work highly commendable. Inbal attended Jerusalem University where he studied the violin, but thereafter he directed his training toward conducting. He participated in conducting classes led by the legendary and iconoclastic Romanian maestro Sergiu Celibidache at Hilversum and pursued further courses in conducting at the Paris Conservatoire. In 1963, Inbal's growing proficiency was recognized when he won the Guido Cantelli Prize at Novara. For the next two years, the young conductor concentrated his work in Italy, winning appreciative notices from critics and gaining increasing approval from the Italian public. Inbal's 1965 conducting debut in England, however, came not in the opera house, but in the concert hall when he led the London Philharmonic Orchestra. His success with the L.P.O. led to engagements with other English orchestras and to his eventual acquisition of joint British citizenship. Continuing to balance concert and opera work, Inbal made his debut in Bologna in 1969, leading a performance of Strauss' *Elektra.* A production of Verdi's *Don Carlo* at Verona the same year added to Inbal's reputation as a conductor able to draw together the strands of a sometimes-diffuse score. In 1971, he led a concert performance of Cherubini's *Anacréon,* the work's first French-language hearing since 1803, the year of its premiere. In 1984, Inbal was appointed chief conductor at the Teatro la Fenice in Venice, remaining in that position until 1989. Undertaking an unusually stressful assignment in 1986, Inbal conducted productions of two Verdi operas, *Stiffelio* and *Aroldo,* on the same day, receiving acclaim for the orchestral performance despite indifferent singing from the casts. Meanwhile, Inbal's other life proceeded apace with his engagement as chief conductor of the Frankfurt Radio Symphony Orchestra, the ensemble with which he would make a noteworthy series of recordings. Inbal remained at that post until 1990 and in 1996 was named the orchestra's conductor laureate. Presiding over several world premieres, Inbal received particular recognition for his performance of Juan Allende-Blin's edition of Debussy's uncompleted *La chûte de la maison Usher* given in 1977. That same year saw the first performance of Xavier Benguerel's *Concerto for percussion.* In 1982, Inbal presented the premiere of Isang Yun's first violin concerto. Among

Inbal's achievements in the recording studio are the complete symphonies of Mahler, Bruckner, and Shostakovich, as well as releases of the complete orchestral works of Ravel, Scriabin, Schumann, and Berlioz. A recording of Donizetti's *Maria de Rudenz* issued on Mondo Musica is distinguished by the conductor's grasp of the composer's transitional style. In 1990, Inbal was honored with the French Ordre des Arts et des Lettres and in 1996 he was made an honorary member of Italy's Orchestra Sinfonica Nazionale della RAI. —*Erik Eriksson*

Recommended:

- ○ **Schönberg: Die Jakobsleiter; Webern: Concerto; 6 Pieces** / Inbal (cond.), Hauptmann, Lewis, Azesberger, Gahmlich, RSO Frankfurt / Denon 78977
- ○ **Berlioz: Te Deum** / Inbal (cond.), Lewis, Eisenberg, RSO Frankfurt / Brilliant 99999/9
- ○ **Shostakovich: Symphony 14** / Inbal (cond.), Vienna SO / 1995 / Denon 78821

Mikhail Ippolitov-Ivanov

b. Nov. 19, 1859, Gatchina, Russia, **d.** Jan. 28, 1935, Moscow, Russia
Composer: Orchestral

A Russian composer of orchestral works and operas influenced by Caucasian and Georgian folk music, Mikhail Ippolitov-Ivanov was born with the simple Ivanov as his last name. He later added his mother's maiden name to distinguish himself from a music critic with a similar surname. He formed his aesthetic in the 1880s under the influence of Rimsky-Korsakov, Balakirev, and Russian folk music, and his style never changed much even though he lived and worked into the 1930s. He was a capable yet rarely individual composer, a sort of Glazunov with a more highly developed interest in ethnic music (part of which probably came under state "encouragement" after the Revolution).

Ippolitov-Ivanov entered the St. Petersburg Conservatory in 1875, studying under Nikolai Rimsky-Korsakov, and graduated in 1882. That year he became conductor of the symphony orchestra and director of the music school in Tiflis (later Tbilisi), Georgia, in the region of the Caucasus mountains. During his 11 years there he became enamored of the area's folk music, which colored his own works with quasi-Oriental melodies and rhythms. A recommendation from Tchaikovsky obtained Ippolitov-Ivanov a post as composition professor at the Moscow Conservatory from 1893 to 1906; in the latter year he began serving as the institution's director. His star pupil at the conservatory was Reinhold Glière. Ippolitov-Ivanov also served as conductor of the Russian Choral Society from 1895 to 1901 (but most of his major choral works postdate that tenure), and of the Mamontova Opera in Moscow from 1899 to 1906. After his 1922 retirement from the Moscow Conservatory, Ippolitov-Ivanov spent 1924–25 reorganizing the Georgian State Conservatory, formerly the Tbilisi School. In 1925 he returned to Moscow to become the principal conductor at the Bolshoi Theater. He oversaw the premieres of a number of Rimsky-Korsakov's operas, including *The Tsar's Bride*, and he supervised an important revival of Mussorgsky's *Boris Godunov*. In 1931 he also completed Mussorgsky's unfinished opera *Marriage*.

Ippolitov-Ivanov's 11 years in the Caucasus led to the lifelong interest in Georgian folk music that inspired several of his orchestral compositions, including two suites of *Caucasian Sketches* (the first being the composer's only lasting hold on the concert hall, thanks to its "Procession of the Sardar"), an *Armenian Rhapsody* (1909), and the symphonic poem after a verse by Mikhail Lermontov, *Mtsyri* ("The Novice," 1922). His folk music interests extended well to the west, as well; he wrote orchestral suites on Catalan and Finnish themes. He also composed string quartets, a violin sonata, and a symphony, but most of his orchestral works were highly programmatic, the subjects careening from *On the Volga* (1910) to *Episodes in the Life of Schubert* (1929) and *Year 1917*. These pieces were seldom performed after the mid-twentieth century, even in the Soviet Union; likewise, his seven operas did not remain popular. So far, Ippolitov-Ivanov seems doomed to be a one-hit composer. —*James Reel*

ORCHESTRAL

Caucasian Sketches, suite, Op. 10 (1894)

Ippolitov-Ivanov is far from being the only composer in musical history to be remembered almost entirely on the basis of just one of his many works. Nevertheless, on those very few occasions that Ippolitov-Ivanov's name is mentioned at all, it is almost invariably in connection with his *Caucasian Sketches* (1894); even then, a lone movement, the glittering festive tableau "Procession of the Sardar," is often singled out.

A student of Rimsky-Korsakov, whose distinctive flair for exotic orchestration he inherited, Ippolitov-Ivanov graduated from the St. Petersburg Conservatory in 1882, quickly securing the directorship of the orchestra and conservatory of Tbilisi (Tiflis), the Georgian capital. During the seven years he spent in this remote mountainous region, Ippolitov-Ivanov undertook a detailed study of indigenous Georgian folk music, whose distinctive melodies and sonorities, now decked out in extravagant orchestral colors, are a central presence in *Caucasian Sketches*. The four movements—"In a Mountain Pass," "In a Village," "In a Mosque," and "Procession of the Sardar"—require little explanation, and Rimsky-Korsakov himself would hardly have disapproved their decorous orchestration. Although it is virtually unknown and almost never heard in the concert hall, Ippolitov-Ivanov further explored Georgian themes in a second Caucasian suite, subtitled "Iveria," published in 1896. This work was completed after the composer had returned to Moscow; though entirely characteristic, it lacks the populist feel of the *Caucasian Sketches*. —*Michael Jameson*

Recommended:

- ○ **Khachaturian & Ippolitov-Ivanov: Orchestral Works** / Glushchenko (cond.), Fisher, Woodrow, BBCPO / 1994 / Chandos 9321
- ○ **Kodály: Galánta & Marosszék Dances; Ippolitov-Ivanov: Caucasian Sketches** / Rodzinski (cond.), Royal PO / 2002 / Westminster 471267

John Ireland

b. Aug. 13, 1879, Inglewood, Cheshire, England, **d.** Jun. 12, 1962, Rock Mill, Sussex, England
Composer: Keyboard, Chamber Music, Band Music

John Ireland was a conservative British composer whose music developed from a style that looked backward towards Beethoven, Brahms, and other Classical and Romantic influences, and forward towards a post-Romantic manner, rich in lyricism, but having absorbed Impressionist and Neo-Classical elements. He is best known for his chamber music, solo piano compositions, and his songs. Yet, even in these genres, he was not consistent. In the orchestral realm he composed relatively few works, though several were of high quality, including the *Piano Concerto in E flat* and *A London Overture*. Ireland wrote not a single symphony or opera, and produced a single cantata, *These Things Shall Be*, a work which he came to dislike. In the end, Ireland must be assessed an important composer, who at his best could stand with his countrymen and contemporaries Vaughan Williams and Walton.

John Ireland was born near Manchester. As a youth he exhibited musical talent early, despite his parents' involvement in the literary world. They had many friends who were writers, including Ralph Waldo Emerson. This literary connection would surface later in many of Ireland's songs, many being settings of poems by Thomas Hardy, A.E. Housman, John Masefield, Christina Rosetti, and other English poets. At the age of fourteen he entered the Royal College of Music and shortly afterward suffered the loss of both parents. At the RCM he studied piano (with Frederick Cliffe), organ, and composition. In the latter realm, his teacher was the difficult but thorough Stanford, with whom he began study in 1897.

Ireland wrote a fair number of compositions during his student years, but later destroyed most of them. One work of significance from this period that has survived, though, was the *Sextet for Clarinet, Horn and String Quartet* (1898). After Ireland ended his studies with Stanford in 1901, he worked as an organist and choir director. He served in that dual capacity at St. Luke's Church in Chelsea, beginning in 1904, holding the post until 1926.

Ireland's *Phantasie Trio* (1906) and his *Violin Sonata No. 1* (1908–09) helped establish his reputation. The influence of Impressionism was taking hold of him in the early part of the new century, though largely affecting his piano works. Ireland composed his orchestral piece, *The Forgotten Rite*, in 1913, a work that reflected his interest in pagan mysticism. In the period 1915–17 he produced his *Violin Sonata No. 2*, regarded by many as among the greatest chamber works to emerge from wartime England.

Ireland took a faculty post in composition at the RCM in 1923. Over the years, his students there would include Britten, Searle, and Moeran. In 1927, the composer married, but only briefly, the ceremony subsequently being annulled and thus swiftly ending a most unpleasant episode in his personal life.

Ireland left the RCM in 1939, but continued composing, turning out works like the brilliant *Fantasy-Sonata* for clarinet and piano in 1943. After he composed the film score for *The Overlanders* in the years 1946–47, however, he wrote nothing more. It has been said that Ireland led a relatively uneventful life, landing no conducting post, traveling very little, never startling his audiences with a bold new composition, or exhibiting outrageous personal behavior. He was a self-critical, introspective man, haunted by memories of a sad childhood. He spent the latter part of his retirement in Rock Mill, Sussex, where he purchased a converted wind mill in 1953 and died nine years later. —*Robert Cummings*

KEYBOARD

The Holy Boy, prelude (1913)

John Ireland's short piano work *The Holy Boy* is subtitled "A Carol of the Nativity." Composed on Christmas day in 1913 and published as the third of the composer's *Four Preludes for piano*, the work eventually became one of his best-known compositions and has been heard in a variety of alternative arrangements, including one for cello and piano made in 1919 and another for string orchestra from the early 1940s. The "holy boy" of the title was Bobby Glasby, a chorister at St. Luke's Church, Chelsea, where Ireland worked as an organist and choirmaster from 1904 to 1926. The easy rocking triple meter, melodic grace, and peaceful, hymn-like atmosphere of this three-minute composition—as well as its relative technical simplicity—have made it a favorite. So popular did it become in England that a portrait of "The Holy Boy" is part of the John Ireland Memorial Window in the Musician's Chapel of London's Church of the Holy Sepulchre; the window also features a portrait of Ireland himself and of a couple of the composer's favorite places. *—Chris Morrison*

Recommended:

○ **Ireland: Downland Suite; Bridge: Suite for String Orchestra, etc.** / Garforth (cond.), English CO / 1984 / Chandos 8390

CHAMBER MUSIC

Cello Sonata in G minor (1923)

When Ireland wrote his *Cello Sonata*, he had already had great success with his two violin sonatas and a piano sonata. This sonata would also prove to be a critical success for him. It had been three years since he finished the piano sonata, and he had written nothing else in the form before beginning the sonata for cello. It was completed in time for an early April premiere by Beatrice Harrison and would become the only piece he produced during the entire year. It provides both the cellist and pianist with challenges in technique and interpretation. The sonata begins with a movement marked Moderato e sostenuto, using two themes that contain motives that reappear throughout the sonata. The movement has a troubled character, although it ends in the major, and a sparer sound than his earlier works. Its brief citations of Ireland's songs perhaps give hints to the reason for the nature of the movement. It quotes a motif associated with passionate love used throughout the song cycle *Marigold*, and a passage from *The Trellis*, a song about secret love. The E flat major second movement, Poco largamente, has a more sentimental nature that moves without break into the final Con moto e marcato, a return to G minor and the wilder, more impassioned temperament. A few musicologists related the sonata to Ireland's other works associated with paganism and the rawness of nature, going so far as to name specific places in England as the inspiration. Regardless, there is no denying that the spirit of the sonata is a major element of its success. *—Patsy Morita*

Recommended:

○ **Ireland: Chamber Works** / Mordkovitch, Brown, Georgian / 1995 / Chandos 9377

○ **Ireland: Violin Sonata 1; Trio 2; Cello Sonata in G minor** / Lloyd Webber, Hope, McCabe / 2004 / ASV 4009

Fantasy-Sonata for clarinet & piano in E flat (1943)

Composed in 1943 and first performed in February 1944, Ireland's *Fantasy-Sonata for clarinet and piano* was one of his last major works. The chamber music medium often displays the music of this conservative yet individualistic English composer to best advantage, and the *Fantasy-Sonata*, like much of Ireland's music, is both lyrical and densely concise. As was that of Benjamin Britten, Ireland's music was sometimes loaded with references intended for a small circle of friends; commentator Fiona Richards has identified links between the *Fantasy-Sonata* and the orchestral *Satyricon* overture of 1946, and has suggested that the work contains allusions to Ireland's attraction to younger men. ("I should like to call it 'The Song of Gito—the boy in the Satyricon—but, of course, *I dare not*," Ireland wrote in a letter. The *Satyricon* was a long comic poem from the court of the Roman emperor Nero that depicted a homosexual love triangle.) Clearer to the average listener, however, are the work's origins in the midst of World War II. Ireland was forced to flee the island of Jersey at the beginning of the war as German troops approached, abandoning a pastoral idyll that had often served to inspire him compositionally. The *Fantasy-Sonata*, about 15 minutes long, falls into three distinct sections corresponding roughly to the movements of a Classical sonata. The final section, rather than resolving musical questions, turns dark and pounding, with sharp, unsettling accents in the clarinet part; the music up to that point has been calm and reflective with Ireland's usual admirable mix of Brahmsian motivic concision and impressionistic scene-painting over long piano ostinatos. Ireland wrote the work for a specific clarinetist, Frederick Thurston, and the clarinet writing is idiomatic and attractive. It's a fine recital work that will give attendees something to chew on. *—James Manheim*

Recommended:

○ **English Music for Clarinet & Piano** / de Peyer, Pryor (piano) / 1987 / Chandos 8549

Violin Sonata No. 1 in D minor (1908–1909; revised 1917)

"People of the older school regard me as a revolutionary, while the rising generation look on me as an old fogey, so one pleases nobody but oneself," John Ireland once reflected. The *Violin Sonata No. 1 in D minor*, indeed, is an innovative work within a late Romantic framework, but it is not revolutionary in spirit. It is an early work by this English composer, less well known than his *Violin Sonata No. 2* of 1917. Completed in 1909, the *Violin Sonata No. 1* had as its impetus a prize competition established by W.W. Cobbett of encyclopedia fame. Ireland's sonata took first prize over 133 other entries, and the work was published in 1911. But it had to wait two more years for its first performance; Ireland at the time was little known. The composer thought enough of the work to revise it twice, once in 1917 and once in 1944.

The most striking characteristic of the *Violin Sonata No. 1* is its extreme variability of mood, with emotional shifts spilling freely over the boundaries of what are otherwise straightforward structures. The first movement is in a clearly delineated sonata form, with opening material in the tonic D minor and a shift to the relative major during the exposition. Yet everywhere the music is subject to subtle and unexpected shadings. Ireland makes use not only of Grieg's characteristic shifts from major to minor, which suffused English concert life at the time, but of a variety of other harmonic twists and turns that show the composer's awareness of Debussy without taking on an Impressionist atmosphere. The movement ends with a coda that is as unsettled as what has gone before. The second movement, labeled a Romance, opens tunefully but veers in a chordal central section to a harmonically remote region that suggests Ireland's long interest in the supernatural. The sonata's finale, at six minutes just over half the length of the other two movements, is a cheerful and straightforward rondo, close to the Brahmsian chamber music Ireland wrote as a young man in its tendency to develop contrasting episodes out of the opening material. There is a quality of youthful experimentation about the sonata as a whole, but it is a rich piece of late Romantic chamber music, unfairly forgotten by those who saw the music of the early twentieth century as an inexorable march toward serialism. *—James Manheim*

Recommended:

○ **Ireland: Chamber Works** / Mordkovitch, Brown / 1995 / Chandos 9377

○ **Ireland: Violin Sonata 1; Trio 2; Cello Sonata in G minor** / Hope, McCabe / 2004 / ASV 4009

Violin Sonata No. 2 in A minor (1915–1917)

John Ireland's *Sonata No. 2 in A minor for violin and piano* is, quite simply, one of the most important works composed in Britain during World War I—this is war music to the core, full of violence and destruction, of anguish and ghastly militarism, but more important, of hope. Ireland himself was not sure that he had remained within the bounds of musical good taste when composing the piece—many friends heard him worrying that he had "gone too far." But after the work's very successful 1917 premiere his fears were forgotten: the work was immediately added to the then very small list of genuine British chamber music triumphs. Both performers at the premiere wore military dress, not because they sought to drive home the ideas of the piece, but because they were in active service and had had to get special leave to give the concert.

There is no tone painting per se in the sonata; nor is there a story line. The war that then engulfed Britain manifested itself in Ireland's music in general rather than specific terms, and in doing so lent greater power and durability to his efforts. First and foremost, this is well-written music: the two players work hand in hand from start to finish, lyric lines are beautifully crafted, and the architectural drama would be immediately appreciated by a composer from a century earlier who had never even imagined such a thing as World War I. There are three movements: 1. Allegro, 2. Poco lento quasi adagio, 3. In tempo moderato—Con brio.

Martial-sounding quartal/quintal harmonies fill the opening of the aggressively-paced first movement; great sweeps of motion build to a crashing climax that dissolves away into a hushed, pianissimo, F major second subject—a mirage of tranquility, imagined, not real, that is soon fractured by the strangled, pedal point-driven development. (There is some echo of the Brahms *Violin Sonata No. 3* first movement development, though how Ireland thought about any relation between the two pieces is anyone's guess.)

As the Poco lento begins, we must wait a while to hear the real theme of the movement; first there is a gasping opening thought that spans the whole range of the violin in short order, shifting and chromatic. The actual theme, by contrast, radiates a warm E flat major light. The finale shifts gears several times, moving from the declamatory moderato to a Con brio that is exactly twice as fast, then back and forth between the two several more times until the fortissimo blast of holy A major calls an end to the piece (and probably, in Ireland's mind, the war as well). *—Blair Johnston*

Recommended:

○ **Ireland: Chamber Works** / Mordkovitch, Ian Brown / 1995 / Chandos 9377

BAND MUSIC

A Downland Suite, for brass band (1932)

This leading composition for brass band is a direct outgrowth of Britain's famous National Brass Band Competitions. The year 1932 was one of the biggest years of this historic contest, which began in 1860. Ireland, one of the leading composers of the "English pastoralist" generation (a loose group of composers who often found their inspiration and their style in English rural folk music) was goaded into writing this suite by Harry Mortimer, one of the country's leading bandleaders. "You people don't bother about brass bands," he said to Ireland, who responded to the implied challenge by writing this, his first piece for brass band, for use as the year's mandatory test piece. Ireland creates a variety of moods in the piece, ranging from the expected pastoral outdoorsy mood suggested by the title, to an inward-looking slow movement, and including in the minuet some very non-brass-like "indoors" music. The final movement contains a trick: Ireland deliberately misnamed the music, which is not a rondo at all but is a perpetual motion interrupted only for one grand statement of the theme of the Elegy movement. *—Joseph Stevenson*

Recommended:

- ○ **Ireland: Downland Suite; Bridge: Suite for String Orch., etc.** / Garforth (cond.), English CO / 1984 / Chandos 8390
- ○ **English Music for Brass** / Honeyball (cond.), London Brass Virtuosi / 2002 / Hyperion 55070

Heinrich Isaac

b. ca. 1450, Flanders, **d.** Mar. 26, 1517, Florence, Italy

Composer: Vocal, Choral

While Josquin Desprez is unquestionably the major figure of the middle Renaissance period, there are many other outstanding names that deserve attention. Above all, the music of Heinrich Isaac—another exceptionally versatile composer of the Franco-Flemish school—stands out from this particularly rich period of musical composition.

Born around the same time as Josquin, Isaac (ca. 1450–1517) is likewise a composer whose early life remains obscure. After 1480 he is known to have been in Florence in the service of Lorenzo the Magnificent, a member of the powerful ruling Medici family; Lorenzo was responsible for Isaac's appointment as organist of the cathedral. Following the fall of the Medicis in 1497, he was appointed court composer to the Emperor Maximilian I in Vienna and Innsbruck, but his heart remained in Florence, to where he made frequent return journeys before finally settling there three years before his death in 1517.

Isaac was typical of his time in his travels to and from Italy, and his large body of compositions reflects to an unusual degree the cosmopolitan nature of the international Franco-Flemish school of the age; his secular works show him to have been equally at ease with German, Italian or French song. The Italian songs are strongly influenced by the frottola, a kind of simple, light song that largely avoided polyphony in favor of catchy dance rhythms. Many of them were doubtless composed for the frequent Florentine carnivals; their relatively small number is likely due to the religious fanatic Savonarola's wholesale destruction of "profane" repertoire in the aftermath of the downfall of the Medicis. One such Isaac song, "Ne più bella di queste," celebrates the city that held such an inescapable fascination for him; it ends with the words, "all the earth sings and laughs in Florence and says Florence is paradise." Among Isaac's German songs, "Innsbruck, ich muss dich lassen" is perhaps the best known; it too is simple in style, with predominantly homophonic writing and an elegant melancholy that looks forward to the era of the madrigal.

Depending on which authority one consults, Isaac is said to have composed anything between ten and thirty masses, a discrepancy that significantly illustrates just how little attention has so far been devoted to this aspect of his work. In contrast to those of most of his contemporaries, many of Isaac's sacred works employ a rich six-part palette, a format he adopted in the *Missa de Apostolis*. This is one of the masses composed during Isaac's service at Maximilian's court, and, in common with Austrian practice at the time, it omits a polyphonic setting of the Credo, and alternates polyphony with plainsong in the remaining sections of the Ordinary. Despite such telescoping it is an expansive work, amply demonstrating the composer's love of contrasting sonorities, long melodic lines, and—when compared with Josquin—less tightly organized polyphony. During a sojourn in Konstanz around 1507, Isaac began the composition of a huge cycle of Mass *Propers*; these appear in the monumental three-volume *Choralis Constantinus*, the first known integral set of music for the propers for the whole ecclesiastical year. On Isaac's death his student Ludwig Senfl set about completing it; it was not published until 1555. *—Brian Robins*

Overview of Works (ca. 1470–1517)

Isaac, a Fleming by birth, spent his best years serving the splendid courts of Medicean Florence and the Holy Roman Empire. Along the way, he proved himself a master of all regional dialects of composition, and versatile across all national styles and forms. This is most obvious in his secular compositions: around 35 French- and Dutch-texted works apply the most current traditions of Northern counterpoint to the most popular "hits" of the day; many are witty polyphonic reworkings of monophonic or polyphonic originals, including *Le serviteur, J'ay pris amours* (twice), and *De tous biens plaine*. For Italian patrons, his writing not only fed a then-fashionable Francophilia, but also contributed to local genres such as the Florentine carnival songs (*La battaglia, Donna, di dentro*); he further arranged Italian popular songs (*Fortuna desperata* five or six times). Though he eschewed the graceful courtly tradition of the "Burgundian" chanson, his German songs include both four-voiced love songs in high style, and popular song arrangements in French *rustique* style.

Isaac's 36 surviving Mass Ordinary cycles divide equally between two styles. Sixteen use the cantus firmus techniques popular in French and Italian lands, taking as models French chansons (for instance, masses on *Comme femme* and *Quant j'ay*), motets (*Argentum et aurum*), and sacred chants (*Salva nos*, likely written on the death of Lorenzo di Medici). The *varietas* of his cantus firmus writing includes melodic elaboration, ostinato, canonic imitation, and sequential writing over long-note Tenors; imitation pervades his textures. On the other hand, he contributed at least 20 plainchant *alternatim* masses to the Hapsburg Chapel after 1496. These masses for four to six voices each serve a particular feast (Easter and Christmas) or class (Apostles, Martyrs), and alternate vocal movements with plainchant or organ improvisations. Once again, the vocal writing includes a veritable compendium of cantus firmus styles and techniques.

The crowning achievement of this composer, however, must be the *Choralis Constantinus*, a series of nearly 100 Mass Proper cycles, covering the liturgical year. The Cathedral of Konstanz commissioned 25 cycles, for the highest feast days, from him in 1508. These became the middle *Choralis* volume, while he wrote the 48 cycles for Sundays through the year (vol. 1) and a further 25 festal cycles (vol. 3) apparently for the Imperial Chapel. Each cycle contains four motets for four to six voices: the Introit, Alleluia or Prosa, Sequence, and Communion Proper to the occasion. The appropriate chant in Imperial usage is omnipresent in these pieces, subjected to all the manifold devices of Northern contrapuntal ingenuity; at the same time, his fertile imagination shows in nearly madrigalian text sensitivity, and expressive modal harmonic progressions. Many of these motets must have been previewed during his Florentine tenure; a further 52 unaffiliated motets survive, spanning his career. These include settings of plainchant, five-voiced tenor motets in the tradition of Regis, and occasional pieces such as *Quis dabit capiti meo aquam* on the death of Lorenzo, and *Quid retribuam*, a thanksgiving text to Pope Leo X. *—Timothy Dickey*

Recommended:

- ○ **Isaac: Optime pastor; Virgo Prudentissima; etc.** / Nies (cond.), Munich Dommusik / 1999 / Christophorus 77218
- ○ **Isaac: Missa Paschalis** / Rombach (cond.), Ens. Officium / 2004 / Christophorus 77267
- ○ **Isaac: La Spagna** / Col (cond.), Pandolfo, Tamminga, Odhecaton / 2002 / Bongiovanni 5607

VOCAL

Innsbruck, ich muß dich lassen, song for 4 voices (ca. 1510–1517)

Heinrich Isaac visited the quaint Tyrolean town of Innsbruck on at least three occasions. In September 1484, civic documents show him completing a stay there, apparently to accept a new and prestigious position serving the Medici in Florence. Later, during his long service to the Emperor Maximilian I, Isaac spent time in Innsbruck in February 1500 and December 1501. It is thus somewhat fitting that this great and peripatetic contemporary of Josquin Desprez would leave as one of his best-known pieces a sentimental lament for his departure: *Innsbruck, ich muß dich lassen* ("Innsbruck, I must leave you"). He composed at least two settings of the song, possibly on different occasions. Both eschew the now-traditional Germanic barform, in favor of a simple strophic form of aabccd.

One version of this song survives in manuscript form only, in Basel and Munich; it follows the compositional customs of the polyphonic German Tenorlied. The melody is in the tenor voice, with a supporting bass and a "Contratenor Altus" above, which imitates the melody quite closely. A discant contrapuntal part may have been added to this three-voice combination later. The second version was included in a collection of German songs printed in 1539; this is the setting most often associated with the "Innsbruck" title. In this version, Isaac places the melody in the uppermost voice, supported by the other voices in a texture of chordal homophony; this possibly reflects the composer's experience of Italian music. Whether he himself wrote the simple melody, or whether he adapted a popular tune current in Innsbruck, Isaac's lied was brought into the Lutheran chorale repertory as *O welt, ich muß dich lassen*, and became the basis of later chorale settings by J.S. Bach. The melody lived on in two of the organ preludes of Johannes Brahms (including one of the last pieces of music of that composer's life), and remains an emblem of the town today. *—Timothy Dickey*

Recommended:

- ○ **Oh Flanders Free** / Capilla Flamenca / 2000 / Naxos 554516

La morra, song for 3 voices (ca. 1492)

The courts of northern Italy in the late fifteenth century strove mightily against one another for the services of the best-trained foreign composers of music; the likes of Josquin Desprez, Heinrich Isaac, Alexander Agricola, and Loyset Compère, were highly prized for the luster with which they could adorn a noble's cultural retinue. A number of these composers, notably Isaac, Agricola, and Johannes Martini, apparently spent quite a bit of effort crafting pieces in the genre of the instrumental fantasia; many even refer in their obscure titles to members (often female) of the noble court society. Isaac's *La morra* (or *La mora*) was an extremely popular contribution to this tradition; nearly 20 copies survive in manuscripts across Europe, some suggesting text, some perhaps adapted for wind ensemble, some intabulated for lute or keyboard.

In form, *La morra* begins gently, much in the style of French and Italian secular "art" song popular in Medicean Florence. Soon, however, the composer's fancy takes flight, and small motivic patterns—both in imitation between voices, and in sequence (frequently fourfold) among them—dominate the musical surface. The tenor voice seems to vary in function between full participation in the counterpoint, and holding (*tenere*) a central melody around which the other voices spin. The title and original context for the piece remain somewhat enigmatic. A number of early sources give an Italian text incipit, "Donna gentile," but with no complete text. The more common title *La morra* could either refer to the well-known political figure and cultural patron Ludovico il Moro, Duke of Milan, or perhaps to a 1492 Spanish victory over the Moors at Granada, an event celebrated throughout Catholic Europe. *—Timothy Dickey*

Recommended:

○ **Ottaviano dei Petrucci: Harmonice Musices Odhecaton** / Fretwork / 2001 / HM 907291

CHORAL

Missa de Apostolis, for 4 voices

When Heinrich Isaac took up the prestigious post as Court Composer to the Holy Roman Emperor Maximilian I around 1497, the local style and specific liturgy of the Imperial Court demanded a new type of composition from him: the Austro-German Alternatim Mass. His previous musical employment in the brilliant (but worldly) environs of Medicean Florence called for stylish mass settings based upon popular French love songs. The Imperial custom, on the other hand, required that the mass celebration on high feast days be adorned with polyphonic music based upon the appropriate sacred chant of the Catholic liturgy. In both styles, Isaac left numerous mass settings of the highest compositional quality and wit. The three mass cycles surviving under the title *Missa De apostolis* (Mass for the feast of an Apostle) apparently were intended for these more solemn Imperial rites.

The Rite of the Diocese of Passau, observed by the Imperial chapel, gives a specific series of chants for the feast of an Apostle, and these chants provided the compositional basis for polyphonic elaboration in Isaac's three masses. Each cycle—one for four voices, one for five, and one for six—contains four movements: Kyrie, Gloria, Sanctus, and Agnus Dei; this court did not usually sing the Credo in polyphony, though Isaac composed a large number of isolated Credo settings which might have been inserted. Local custom also called for only certain subsections of the movements to be set; the alternate verses would either be sung by the choir in unadorned plainchant, or might be spoken by the priest during an organ improvisation upon the chant.

Though thus comprising a series of fragmentary musical settings, Isaac's three masses on the "De apostolis" chant show the riches of his musical imagination. His most common technique is known as Cantus fractus, a practice which differentiates the chant-bearing voice by means of longer note values. The well-known chant melody is thus highlighted in the texture. But the composer passes this chant freely between voices from one movement to the next, once (in the six-voiced Sanctus) even dividing phrases of the chant between voices midstream. Many movements (Kyries especially) open with imitation in several voices upon the chant's incipit, building intensity and rhythmic drive gradually to the end. The *Apostles' Masses* also contain quite a number of skillful canonic passages, including canonic repetition of the chant melody between two (or three) voices, close canonic imitation of a contrapuntal voice, one instance of a double canon (the five-voiced *Quoniam*, which contains both types at the same time), and two crab canons, wherein a pair of voices simultaneously sings the chant melody forwards and backwards. *—Timothy Dickey*

Recommended:

○ **Isaac: Missa de Apostolis** / Phillips (cond.), Tallis Scholars / 2002 / Gimell 23

Sharon Isbin

b. Aug. 7, 1956, Minneapolis, MN

Guitarist

Described by the Boston Globe's Michael Manning as a musician who plays "beyond virtuosity," guitarist Sharon Isbin has been a consistent challenge for critics, who struggle to find the right superlative that would do justice to her exquisite playing. "In her hands," wrote Anne Midgette in The New York Times, "the guitar takes on the precision of a diamond, each note a clear, shining facet that catches, prism-like, a glimpse of the spectrum." In essence, a performance by Isbin is like a painting by Vermeer: a formally impeccable and inexhaustible work of art. A Renaissance woman of the guitar, Isbin performs worldwide at famous venues and commissions new work from distinguished American composers (more than any other guitarist) for her instruments, collaborates with a wide variety of musicians, and indefatigably searches for new music to play. As a child, Isbin wanted to be a scientist like her father. However, she started guitar lessons at the age of nine (the family was living in Italy at the time) and found her vocation. Her teachers included Andrés Segovia and harpsichordist Rosalyn Tureck. With Tureck, Isbin worked on the first performance edition, for guitar, of J.S. Bach's *Lute Suites*. This project eventually resulted in a critically acclaimed disc. In 1989, Isbin founded the guitar department at the Juilliard School of Music and became that institution's first professor of guitar. Isbin's recordings have consistently been assessed as groundbreaking musical events. In 1995, her disc was the first ever American guitar concert presented to a Russian cosmonaut during a rendezvous between the space shuttle Atlantis and the Russian spaceship Mir. *Journey to the Amazon*, performed with Brazilian percussionist Thiago de Mello and saxophonist Paul Winter, earned Isbin a Grammy nomination in 1999. She received a Grammy in 2001 for her *Dreams of a World: Folk-Inspired Music for Guitar*. Significantly, this was the first classical guitar Grammy in 28 years. In 2002, Isbin got another Grammy for her extraordinary performance of concerti by Christopher Rouse and Tan Dun. The concerti featured on this world-premiere disc were dedicated to Isbin. Spanning various styles, genres, and periods, Isbin's other recordings include Aaron Jay Kernis' *Double Concerto* (with violinist Cho-Liang Lin), *Rodrigo: Concierto de Aranjues*, and *Sharon Isbin Plays Baroque Favorites for Guitar*. The last-named album features a truly astounding performance of a transcription of Bach's *Violin Concerto in A minor*. *—Zoran Minderovic*

Recommended:

○ **Sharon Isbin's Greatest Hits** / Foster, Wolff (conds.), Isbin, St. Paul CO / 2002 / Virgin 62075

○ **Bach: Complete Lute Suites** / Isbin / 1989 / Virgin 59503

○ **Road to the Sun** / Isbin / 1990 / Virgin 59591

○ **Sharon Isbin** / Tang (cond.), Isbin, Gulbenkian Orch. / 2001 / Teldec 81830

Israel Philharmonic Orchestra

f. 1936, Tel Aviv, Israel

Ensemble

The 110-member Israel Philharmonic Orchestra, often described as Israel's foremost cultural asset and regarded by many as the "Orchestra of the Jewish People," has emerged in its relatively short life as a world-class ensemble.

Central European musical traditions made their way to the Middle East from the time of the first mass migration of Jews to Turkish-controlled Palestine in the 1880s. Following Turkey's defeat in World War I, the Balfour Declaration designated part of Palestine as a "national home for the Jewish people," which resulted in an increase of Jewish settlement in the area. Institutions of musical education were established as the Jewish population grew. As scores of Jews fled Nazi persecution in the 1930s, the population grew ever greater. One of that number was violinist Bronislav Huberman, who arrived in 1933 and immediately urged the leading Jewish orchestral players in Germany, many of whom had lost their jobs, to come to Palestine. Huberman brought together a number of musicians as the Palestine Orchestra. Conductor William Steinberg helped organize and prepare the orchestra; the premiere concert took place under the baton of Arturo Toscanini on December 26, 1936. The ensemble began touring almost immediately with appearances in Cairo and Alexandria. When the Israel's independence was proclaimed in 1948, the group was renamed the Israel Philharmonic Orchestra.

The Philharmonic had no permanent conductor for nearly the first forty years of its existence; it was instead led by a succession of prominent guest conductors. This exposure to a remarkable array of leading *maestri* lent the orchestra a certain flexibility and versatility, but at the cost of attaining cohesion and a consistent sound. However, two names dominate its history: Leonard Bernstein (1918–90) and Zubin Mehta. Bernstein began conducting the orchestra nearly from the time he rocketed to fame during the 1940s, and led the historic concert at Beer-Sheva in 1947 just after the Israel Defense Forces took the site. He also conducted an important concert at the Lebanese border and, following the 1967 war, led the legendary Mount Scopus performance of Mahler's *Symphony No. 2* in celebration of the capturing of Jerusalem. His 40-year association with the Philharmonic was deep, committed, and intense, even though he never held an official position with the orchestra.

Mehta was appointed music advisor to the orchestra in 1968 and, in 1977, became its music director. In 1981 he was named music director for life. He demonstrated continued commitment to the orchestra even as he received more prominent appointments, including the music directorships of the Los Angeles and New York Philharmonics.

The orchestra is a true "philharmonic" in the traditional sense, meaning that it is a cooperative owned by its musicians. The Philharmonic performs concert series in its home city of Tel-Aviv and in Haifa and Jerusalem, and makes frequent appearances elsewhere. Its main venue is the Mann Auditorium in Tel-Aviv, a hall with whose acoustics have often proven especially problematic for recording companies.*—Joseph Stevenson*

Recommended:

- ○ **Bernstein: Judaica** / Bernstein (cond.), Harrer, Theuring, Ludwig, Caballe, Vienna Choir Boys, Israel PO, New York PO / 1999 / DG 463462
- ○ **Smetana: Ma Vlast** / Mehta (cond.), Israel PO / 1994 / Sony 58944
- ○ **Israel PO—60th Anniversay Gala Concert** / Barenboim, Mehta (conds.), Shaham, Zukerman, Stern, Vengerov, IPO / 1997 / BMG 68768

Steven Isserlis

b. Dec. 19, 1958, London, England
Cellist

Steven John Isserlis is one of the leading internationally ranked cellists. He plays a wide range of repertory and is noted for using gut strings and a great deal of vibrato. He is the grandson of Russian composer and pianist Julius Isserlis and can trace his family tree back to connections with both Karl Marx and Felix Mendelssohn.

He spent most of his teenage years (1969–76) as a pupil of Jane Cowan at the International Cello Centre. He describes her teaching method as both "total immersion" and "very holistic." For instance, she required the students to read Goethe's *Faust* in order to understand Beethoven better and memorize *Racine* to know the sound of the French language when playing French music. During his last two years at the Cello Centre he lived at her house in Scotland three times a year for eight-week stretches.

After finishing at the International Cello Centre, he went to study in the United States at Oberlin College in Ohio with Richard Kapuscinski (1976–1978). During this period, he made his debut in London in 1977. After graduation from Oberlin, he began to establish what has become one of the major cello careers. He has played with many of the leading orchestras and conductors in the world, including the London Symphony, Berlin Philharmonic, Los Angeles Philharmonic, Philadelphia Orchestra, Czech Philharmonic, the Philharmonia, and the London Philharmonic under such conductors as John Eliot Gardiner, Michael Tilson Thomas, Christoph Eschenbach, Roger Norrington, Colin Davis, and Vladimir Ashkenazy. He is also very active as a chamber player. In 1991, he founded a regular trio with violinist Joshua Bell and pianist Olli Mustonen, and frequently gives recitals with pianist and fortepianist Melvyn Tan. Other frequent partners have been Stephen Kovacevich, Tabea Zimmermann, Pamela Frank, and Stephen Hough.

He performs the major cello repertory from before Bach to current times. When he plays Classical- or Baroque-era works, he is likely to do so with "period instrument" ensembles. He uses his own cello (sometimes with a slight change in set-up) on such occasions rather than a Baroque cello. However, he often practices for such concerts with a Baroque or Classical bow to get an idea of the likely phrasing and articulation.

One of the most famous late twentieth century works for cello and orchestra, John Tavener's *The Protecting Veil*, was written for him, and he gave it its first performance in London in 1989 and its American debut in Boston in 1993. He also recorded its first release, on Virgin Classics, a recording that won a Gramophone Award. In 1992, he received the Piatigorsky Artist Award, and in 1993 got the Royal Philharmonic Society's Instrumentalist of the Year Award. Other composers who have written new music for Isserlis include Elizabeth Maconchy, Howard Blake, and Robert Saxton. Isserlis has recorded the Elgar concerto, Britten's *Cello Symphony*, Bloch's *Schelomo*, and Tchaikovsky's *Rococo Variations*, which he played in the composer's original version, and received wide acclaim for them.

He was an exclusive artist on the Virgin Records label, going back to the days when it was a large independent company, and continued with it for several years after it was acquired by EMI. He now has an exclusive contract with BMG Classics with plans to release major contemporary cello works and standard works on the RCA Victor Red Seal label.

He has increased his teaching activities and gives master classes at the Manchester Cello Festival, and since 1996, when he succeeded Sandor Végh as artistic director of the International Musicians Seminar in Cornwall, England, he has taught and given master classes there annually. *—Joseph Stevenson*

Recommended:

- ○ **Fauré: Complete Works for Cello** / Isserlis, Devoyon (piano) / 1995 / RCA 68049
- ○ **Rachmaninov, Franck: Cello Sonatas** / Isserlis, Hough, Evans / 2003 / Hyperion 67376
- ○ **Haydn: Concertos; Sinfonia Concertante** / Norrington (cond.), Isserlis, CO of Europe / 1998 / BMG 68578
- ○ **Tavener: The Protecting Veil; Britten Suite 3** / Rozhdestvensky (cond.), Isserlis, London SO / 2000 / Virgin 61849
- ○ **Boccherini: Concertos & Sonatas** / Kangas (cond.), Isserlis, Cole, Ostrobothnian Chamber Orchest / 2000 / EMI 562202
- ○ **Concertos by Bloch & Elgar** / Hickox (cond.), Isserlis, London SO / 1994 / Virgin 61125

Eugene Istomin

b. Nov. 26, 1925, New York, NY, **d.** Oct. 10, 2003, Washington, DC
Pianist

American pianist Eugene Istomin, known more for his poise and refinement than for heaven-storming bravura, made himself an important figure both as a solo artist and as a chamber player of rare discretion and musicality. His trio with violinist Isaac Stern and cellist Leonard Rose was recognized for the directness and honesty of its interpretations, always heartfelt. As was true for other pianists, winning the Leventritt Award opened doors for Istomin at a relatively early age. He returned from his first European tour in 1950 a well-established artist and continued to involve himself in music activities of high purpose.

Under the tutelage of Kiriena Siloti, Istomin was prepared for entry into the Curtis Institute where his instructors included such rigorous concert pianists as Mieczysław Horszowski and Rudolf Serkin. At 18, he won two important awards, both leading to appearances with orchestras ranking among America's top five. With the Philadelphia Youth Award, he won an engagement with the Philadelphia Orchestra directed by Eugene Ormandy. Istomin's performance of Chopin's *Second Piano Concerto* was awarded high praise by both the audience and critics. The more prestigious Leventritt Award resulted in a performance of the Brahms *Piano Concerto No. 2* with Artur Rodzinski and the New York Philharmonic, an occasion for which he won further accolades from listeners and press alike. With these two successes, offers from other major American orchestras followed and his career moved forward quickly as both an orchestral soloist and a recitalist. Performances with the Busch Chamber Players were applauded and his first recording, Bach's *D minor Concerto* played with the Busch ensemble, created something of a stir in chamber music circles.

Istomin's European tour of 1950 found him performing with major French orchestras and giving recitals in Switzerland and Italy. It also introduced him to the Pablo Casals Festival in Prades. For each of the following years, he appeared at the French festival, frequently together with the great cellist. Istomin was much appreciated by Casals, who pronounced him "destined for a great career." When Casals established a new festival in San Juan, Puerto Rico, the young pianist became one of its leading artists, once again proving himself a superior collaborator. Critic Howard Taubman described him as a "revelation," praising his singing tone and noting, "not once did he forget that he was part of an intimate chamber music group."

Once Istomin had completed his first European tour, subsequent trips were planned and he performed throughout Europe and America. In 1956, he embarked upon an extended junket to the Far East, giving some 30 concerts through the joint sponsorship of the Sangyo Keizai Shimbun and the American National Theatre and Academy's International Exchange Program. Once again, the reviews were enthusiastic as were the responses of audiences throughout the tour.

Istomin assembled the Istomin/Stern/Rose Trio in 1961, prevailing upon two colleagues with whom he felt an ease and musical kinship. The three made a number of praiseworthy recordings, concentrating on late Classical and Romantic-age composers. Several recording made during the Prades Festivals of the early 1950s have seen release on CD. Istomin also made recordings for the Reference label in the 1990s, all reflecting the pianist's thoughtful musicality and attention to detail.

Istomin's connection with Pablo Casals continued even after the cellist/humanitarian's death when, in 1975, the pianist married Casals' widow, Marta. *—Erik Eriksson*

Recommended:

- ○ **Beethoven: Piano Trios** / Stern, Rose, Istomin / 1995 / Sony 64513
- ○ **Beethoven: 3 Sonatas** / Istomin / 1996 / Reference 69

Charles Ives

b. Oct. 20, 1874, Danbury, CT, **d.** May 19, 1954, New York, NY
Composer: Symphonic, Orchestral, Chamber Music, Keyboard, Vocal, Choral

Charles Ives was the son of George Ives, a Danbury, Connecticut bandmaster and a musical experimenter whose approach heavily influenced his son. Charles Ives' musical skills quickly developed; he was playing organ services at the local Presbyterian church from the age of 12 and began to compose at 13. Ives' rural, rough-and-tumble childhood was revisited vividly and repeatedly in the music he composed as an adult.

In 1894 Ives entered Yale to study music, and his father died at age 40 from a heart attack. Professor Horatio T. Parker was not at all interested in encouraging Ives' experimental style. Ives dutifully learned the basics, creating an interesting but conventional *Symphony No. 1* as his graduation thesis in 1898. After barely managing to earn his diploma, Ives moved with a couple of his fraternity buddies to an apartment in New York City. He became organist at Central Presbyterian Church and composed his first large-scale attempt to reflect the spirit of America, the *Symphony No. 2*. In off hours Ives worked on his wild, highly dissonant and ragtime-influenced *Piano Sonata No. 1*, making a din that his roommates described as "resident disturbances."

In 1902 a friend introduced Ives to the insurance agent Julian Myrick. They co-founded the first Mutual Life Insurance office in Manhattan. Through his hard work and easy ability to communicate with customers, Ives would become a very wealthy insurance executive. In 1906 he married Harmony Twichell, a woman from a prominent New England family. Ives continued to compose his music on commuter trains, in the evening, and on weekends, writing what pleased him without worrying what the outside world might think of it. In order to check details of orchestration, Ives hired out theater orchestras to rehearse his scores. In 1910 Ives gave New York Philharmonic conductor Gustav Mahler a score and parts to his *Symphony No. 3, "The Camp Meeting."* Mahler tried it in rehearsal after returning to Vienna, but died before he could perform it.

In the 1910s, Ives would produce several of his most important masterworks, the *Symphony No. 4*, the *Orchestral Set No. 1: "Three Places in New England,"* the *String Quartet No. 2*, and the massive *Piano Sonata No. 2, "Concord, Mass., 1840–1860,"* commonly referred to as the *Concord Sonata*. With the beginning of America's involvement in World War I, Ives raised funds for the war effort, supported an unsuccessful constitutional amendment prohibiting a declaration of war without the support of two-thirds of the populace, published a manual (*Surveying the Prospect*) that for years served as a bible for the insurance industry, and composed at an astounding pace. In October 1918 Ives suffered a severe heart attack that nearly killed him. In 1921 he published the *Concord Sonata* and in 1922 followed it with *114 Songs*, containing songs dating from 1888 to the eve of publication. These editions were sent out free to anyone who wanted them, and many copies wound up in the wastebaskets of music conservatories.

In 1924 pianist and new music enthusiast E. Robert Schmitz made an appointment with Ives to buy insurance, but left instead with a copy of the *Concord Sonata*. He introduced the work to Edgard Varèse and to Henry Cowell, who became Ives' strongest advocate. Soon Ives' music began to appear on concert programs, and when Cowell launched his *New Music Quarterly* in 1927, Ives helped back the project financially. But that same year Ives confided to Harmony that he'd somehow lost the gift that compelled him to write music.

In 1930 Ives and Myrick both decided to retire, and from this time forward Ives concerned himself with revising existing works. Ives' eyesight was beginning to deteriorate, so he had huge Photostats made of his scores and also made recordings to work from. Composers Cowell, John J. Becker, and Lou Harrison helped Ives create legible scores of his music, instituting a scholarly tradition of Ives editing that continues to this day. In January 1939, pianist John Kirkpatrick performed the complete "Concord" in a recital so successful that even critics distrustful of modern music gave it rave reviews. In 1947 Ives was awarded the Pulitzer Prize in music for his *Symphony No. 3*, completed nearly 40 years earlier. With Ives' death in May 1954 his musical legacy became top priority for a generation of biographers, researchers, and performers.

Ives' early works expertly channel European influences into totally fresh constructs; mature works make use of quotation, collage techniques, spatial redistribution of instrumental groups and soloists, metric modulation, homegrown forms of pitch organization and dense, massed blocks of clustered chords. The difficult idiom of many of his pieces has denied Ives the mass appeal of Copland and Gershwin, and he can be an acquired taste. Some critics and conductors, mainly European, discount the value of his innovations, concluding that Ives was an amateur who didn't know what he was doing. By the turn of the twenty-first century renewed researches into Ives' theoretical approach revealed that he certainly did know what he was doing, and he has much to teach us yet today in terms of fresh ideas and techniques. *—Uncle Dave Lewis*

SYMPHONIC

Symphony No. 2 (1900–1902; revised 1909)

This five-movement, immensely likeable work, filled with direct quotations drawn from various corners of American musical life, was first assembled around 1900 from a group of Ives' early church preludes and secular overtures, with development sections and orchestrations added in 1907–10. Ives continued to tinker with the work from time to time for the rest of his life. This symphony predates, by almost 30 years, the work of American nationalist composers such as Roy Harris, Aaron Copland, and Virgil Thomson.

The first movement is in an Andante moderato tempo. A beautiful fugato, at first solemn and romantic but soon turning playful (with a bit of the fiddle tune "Pig Town Fling"), opens the work. A hint of Stephen Foster's "Massa's in de Cold Cold Ground" makes its way into the lovely counterpoint. "Columbia the Gem of the Ocean" suddenly appears out of nowhere but fits in perfectly. A slight, delightful ragtime passage with pizzicati forms a transition section. The music again becomes grand and full before thinning out to a lovely, small string group.

A sweet oboe solo provides a segue into the second movement, which opens with a high-spirited setting of Henry Clay Work's tune "Wake Nicodemus", set for the winds and brass and echoed by the strings as the music modulates through several keys. The well-known revival hymn "Bringing In The Sheaves," played in a minor key but in a jolly rhythm, appears as a second subject amidst continual modulations of the first theme. Some lovely pastoral writing with modal gestures against a drone, as in Beethoven's *Pastoral Symphony*, leads into a lyrical setting of the old college hazing tune "Where O Where Are the Verdant Freshmen?"; then fragments of the previous tunes are entered into the constant modulation scheme and full tunes are recapitulated as the movement continues. The development soon moves into triplets combined with offbeat snare drum accents as the intensity builds. Much of the opening material is repeated and the hymn "Hamburg" is added in the brass to bring the movement to a grand conclusion with a snatch of lively rhythm.

The third movement, Adagio cantabile, quotes "Beulah Land" in a cello solo, as well as "America the Beautiful" ("Materna") and the hymns "Missionary Chant" and "Nettleton." As in the other movements, there are brief passages of raw, strong open fifths and parallel movement of chords recalling the early New England psalmody tradition and its homegrown harmonization. There are even moments of nineteenth century Romantic orchestral style.

The relatively brief fourth movement, Lento maestoso, reorchestrates and extends material from the first movement in a grand style. Even "Columbia the Gem of the Ocean" now has a rolling, dramatic accompaniment. Ending on an unresolved dominant seventh chord, the fourth movement seems like an introduction to the fifth and last movement.

A fiddle tune quickly moves into Foster's "Camptown Races," and some lovely orchestration recalls the mood of the first movement. Reveille, "Wake Nicodemus," "Pig Town Fling", and "Columbia" are played together for a bang-up ending. *—"Blue Gene" Tyranny*

Recommended:

- ○ **Ives: Symphonies 2 & 3** / Bernstein (cond.), New York PO / 1998 / Sony 60202
- ○ **Ives: Symphonies 2 & 3** / Tilson Thomas (cond.), Concertgebouw / 1982 / Sony 46440

Symphony No. 3: The Camp Meeting (1904; revised 1909)

Charles Ives' *Third Symphony*, subtitled "The Camp Meeting," originated in a trio of organ works written for services at Central Presbyterian Church in New York City in 1901–02. Ives scored them for orchestra in 1904, and revised the whole significantly in 1909–11. The *Third* is the most atypical of Ives' five symphonies. Scored in a classical manner with strings and a few winds, this is a clear and uncluttered reminiscence of nineteenth century America as prismatically viewed through some of its traditional hymn tunes.

The first movement, "Old Folks' Gatherin'" (Andante maestoso), quotes the hymn tunes *Azmon*, *Erie* (that is, "What a Friend We Have in Jesus"), and *Woodworth* ("Just As I Am"). Wandering strings set the pace for what follows; a patchwork of hymn tunes drifting through an unpredictable, constantly changing harmonic orientation. After a climax is reached, a quiet passage opens with oboe and flute over hushed, distant strings. Ives reintroduces part of the middle section, and settles down to a quiet coda, ending the movement almost imperceptibly.

The second movement, "Children's Day" (Allegro) opens with strings in two parts over Haydnesque eighth notes in the horns. "There is a Fountain Filled with Blood," "Happy Land," "Naomi," and "There's Music in the Air" all are heard, although one could swear "Aloha Oe" is also peeking through the texture. As this is a movement depicting children at play, Ives is playful himself, weaving hymn tunes into one another in a somewhat tongue-in-cheek manner, and using parts of tunes to imitate the sound of other hymns.

The third movement, "Communion" (Largo), has its roots in a communion piece originally scored for unison chorus, organ and strings. It is much darker in tone than the others, and "Azmon" and "Woodworth" return from the first movement. As the third movement relates strongly in content to the first, it provides a psychologically satisfactory close to the work as a whole.

Ives added about two dozen "shadow" parts to this symphony, where instruments play pianissimo in the shadow of the principal voices. Ives had stricken these from his manuscripts, and the fair ink copy made by Carl Pagano in 1946, which led to Lou Harrison's 1947 edition of the symphony, did not retain these details. They were not included until the Ives Society edition of 1990. In performance, they make a difference, particularly at climax points.

The *Third Symphony* of Ives was first heard under Lou Harrison at a League of Composers concert in New York City on April 5, 1946. Later that year, the work was awarded a special citation by the New York Music Critics' Circle, and on May 5, 1947, it won Ives the Pulitzer Prize for music. Ives, then 72 years of age, gave away the $25,000 cash award, stating "prizes are for boys and I'm all grown up." *—Uncle Dave Lewis*

Recommended:

- ○ **Ives: Symphony 3, etc.** / Sinclair (cond.), Northern Sinfonia / 2003 / Naxos 8559087
- ○ **Ives: Symphonies 2 & 3** / Bernstein (cond.), New York PO / 1998 / Sony 60202

○ **Ives: Symphonies 2 & 3** / Tilson Thomas (cond.), Concertgebouw / 1982 / Sony 46440

Symphony No. 4 (1910–1916; revised 1919)

Ives' *Fourth Symphony* is conceived on the largest scale of all his completed orchestral works. Begun in 1910, the first stage of work on the *Fourth* was complete by 1916. This early version was likely in three movements only, with the opening movement included as an unnumbered "Prelude" and the "Hawthorne Concerto" in the place of the current second movement.

Between 1919–22 Ives completely recast the second movement into the "comedy" that it is now, using the piano piece *The Celestial Railroad* as sort of intermediary between the "Concerto" and "comedy." The third movement is an orchestration of the first movement of Ives' *String Quartet No. 1* (1898). In 1922–23, a full ink score of the first three movements was prepared, but the fourth movement had to wait until 1943 when John J. Becker completed this part of the score under Ives' supervision.

The *Fourth Symphony* calls for an enlarged orchestra augmented with chorus, an extra battery of percussion, organ, and four-hand quarter-tone piano with options for saxophones and theremin. While the orchestra retains the main stage, the chorus and percussion is placed throughout the auditorium, achieving a spatial separation that is difficult to transmit via recording. The work requires three conductors, and Ives provides extensive cues in the score to facilitate this.

Ives "aesthetic program" for the *Fourth Symphony* is "that of a searching question of 'What' and 'Why' which the spirit of man asks of life." The question is stated in the first movement, Prelude: maestoso where the chorus sings an altered setting of the hymn "Watchman, Tell Us of the Night" over a background suggestive of universal space and mystery. The first answer, Allegretto, Ives described as a "comedy" in the transcendental sense; it is a dazzlingly complex collage of tune quotations, representing the confusion of urban existence. Ives punctuates this movement with bizarre effects, including at one point a series of tremolandi heard throughout the entire orchestra. In the third movement, Fugue, the stoic reserve of religious life as Ives knew it is presented as the second answer to the question. In the final movement, Largo, the distant percussion enters quietly and is joined by the orchestra engaging in a battle between tonally centered material and discordant, "universal" sounds. The chorus enters singing a wordless, peaceful passage that quells down the whole texture until just the percussion is left, providing the final, transcendental answer to Ives' question.

The first two movements were premiered at Town Hall in New York City under Eugene Goosens in January, 1927. Composer Jerome Moross arranged the first and third movements for a New School performance conducted by Bernard Herrmann in 1933. Otherwise, the premiere of the whole work did not occur until 1965 under Leopold Stokowski, José Serebrier, and David Katz at Carnegie Hall with the American Symphony Orchestra. *—Uncle Dave Lewis*

Recommended:

○ **Ives: Symphonies 2 & 4** / Serebrier (cond.), London PO, John Alldis Choir / 1999 / BMG 63316

○ **Ives: Symphonies 1 & 4; Hymns** / Tilson Thomas (cond.), Chicago Orch. & Chorus / 1991 / Sony 44939

○ **An American Journey** / Tilson Thomas (cond.), San Francisco SO / RCA 63703

A Symphony: New England Holidays ("Holidays Symphony") (1917–1919)

Referring to his *New England Holidays*, an assemblage of four orchestral works written between 1903 and 1913, Ives stated that "they are separate pieces and can be thought of and played as such. These four together were called a symphony, and later just a set of pieces. . . . " Taking a jab at critics who were appalled at his brash style, Ives further explained his reasons for viewing the work in this way: "I was getting somewhat tired of hearing the lily boys say 'This is a symphony? Mercy!'" Like so many of Ives' works, *New England Holidays* finds its inspiration in nostalgic recollections of the composer's childhood. Each of the four constituent tone poems takes as its title a different holiday that evoked for the composer memories with specific musical associations.

The first movement, "Washington's Birthday," portrays a midwinter barn dance, complete with strains of "Turkey in the Straw" and "Camptown Races." In his own notes that accompany the score, Ives describes it thus: "The village band of fiddles, fife and horn keep up an unending 'break-down' medley, and the young folks 'salute their partners and balance corners' till midnight; —as the party breaks up, the sentimental songs of those days are sung half in fun, half seriously, and with the inevitable 'adieu to the ladies' the 'social' gives way to the grey bleakness of the February night."

The second movement, "Decoration Day," recalls the holiday once set aside to honor Civil War veterans (since replaced by Memorial Day). After the crowd gathers at the square, the processional embarks for the cemetery to the tune of "How Firm a Foundation." The assembly's arrival at its destination is marked by the playing of "Taps," combined with strains of "Nearer My God to Thee." This somber moment is contrasted by the peppy parade back into town, accompanied by Ives' raucous reinterpretation of the "Second Connecticut National Guard March."

The third movement, "The Fourth of July," calls for various pyrotechnic feats on the part of the orchestra. Ives' impression of this holiday takes shape as a complicated combination of well-known marches and tunes as well as newly composed material, offset by odd beats and assembled into a spirited, mischievous whole. Characteristically, Ives makes use of much nineteenth century musical material with patriotic associations: "Yankee Doodle," "Battle Hymn of the Republic," "Columbia, Gem of the Ocean," and "Battle Cry of Freedom," all make prominent appearances during this schizophrenic, multilayered celebration.

"Thanksgiving," which brings *New England Holidays* to a close, attempts, as Ives explains, to portray "the sternness and strength and austerity of the Puritan character" in its stubborn polytonality and forceful texture. Though "Thanksgiving" makes reference to several hymns, one in particular receives added emphasis in a setting for chorus. As the movement reaches its climax, the voices exclaim: "Oh God, beneath Thy guiding hand our exiled fathers crossed the sea; and when they trod the wintry strand, with prayer and psalm they worshipped Thee." *—Jeremy Grimshaw*

Recommended:

○ **Ives: 3 Places in New England; New England Holidays; etc.** / Zinman (cond.), Baltimore SO & Chorus / 1996 / Argo 444860

○ **Ives: New England Holidays; etc.** / Tilson Thomas (cond.), Spector, Chicago SO & Chorus / 1992 / Sony 42381

Universe Symphony (1911–1928)

Charles Ives (1874–1954) began his last symphony in 1911 and continued working on it through 1915 when he broke off composition. He took it up in 1927, stopped again the following year, but kept adding "a few notes" until three years before his death in 1954. According to composer Larry Austin, "There are 36 extant sketch pages which I believe are definitely part of the *Universe Symphony*, including completed music, musical sketches and fragments, and detailed narrative and graphic descriptions concerning the form, continuity, and transcendental aesthetic of the work." From this, Austin has elaborated a symphony in three continuous movements: "Past," representing chaos to formation of the Waters and Mountains; "Present," depicting the Earth and the Firmament and the evolution in Nature and Humanity; and "Future" portraying Heaven and the rise of all to the Spiritual. In Austin's realization, the work is scored for large symphony plus an enormous percussion section usually divided into several smaller orchestras. Although critics are divided on the success of Austin's realization, most agree that the opening 24-minute percussion introduction is wholly unlike anything in Ives' entire output and the remainder sounds like a pastiche or a parody of Ives' style. *—James Leonard*

Recommended:

○ **Ives: Universe Symphony; Symphony 2** / Stern (cond.), Rundfunk-Sinfonieorchester Saarbrucken / 2003 / Col Legno 20074

ORCHESTRAL

Central Park in the Dark (1906; revised 1936)

Central Park in the Dark (1906), like many of Ives' works, is comprised of multiple independent layers of sound. As in its companion work, *The Unanswered Question*, strings provide a slow, impassive sonic layer. However, in place of *The Unanswered Question*'s transcendental call-and-answer between trumpet and woodwinds, the woodwinds and pianos in *Central Park* slowly construct a collage of popular and pop-influenced tunes—the most recognizable being "Hello Ma Baby"—above this string undercurrent. As Ives writes in the notes that accompany the score, "This piece purports to be a picture-in-sounds of the sounds of nature and of happenings that men would hear some 30 years ago (before the combustion engine and radio monopolized the earth and air), when sitting on a bench in Central Park on a hot summer night." The ever-present backdrop of the strings embodies the silence and murmur of nature, interrupted by the trolley car, a casino, the fire engine, and a band of street musicians, all represented by the rest of the ensemble. As these sounds die away, the texture recedes to the hushed sounds and silence of the night. *—Jeremy Grimshaw*

Recommended:

○ **Ives: Holidays Symphony; Central Park in the Dark** / Tilson Thomas (cond.), Chicago SO / 1992 / Sony 42381

○ **Ives: The Unanswered Question** / Bernstein, Vacchiano, New York PO / 1998 / Sony 60203

Orchestral Set No. 1: Three Places in New England (1913–1914; revised 1929)

Ives assembled his *Orchestral Set No. 1*—best known by its subtitle, *Three Places in New England*—in 1913–14. The first movement, "The Saint-Gaudens in Boston Common" (1914) was inspired by a bas-relief by sculptor Augustus Saint-Gaudens displayed in Boston, Massachusetts. The sculpture memorializes the first African-American regiment in the Union Army during the Civil War. Ives' somber sonic impression is based on a three-note figure common to both "Old Black Joe" and "Jesus

Loves Me." By way of a preface, Ives wrote a poem that begins with the words "Moving-Marching-Faces of Souls," though he never recast *Saint-Gaudens* into a song.

The second movement, "Putnam's Camp, Redding, Connecticut," represents Ives' boyhood memory of two bands marching into town, each playing different music, and the resulting clash of sonorities. Along the way there is a dream sequence in which the boy in Ives' program dozes off and envisages General Israel Putnam's regiment marching toward him. In the midst of this sonic dream world, a metrically contrasting march enters the texture, carrying the listener seamlessly into the next "conscious" section. As is common in Ives' music, "Putnam's Camp" was partly synthesized from two earlier works, the *Country Band March* (1903) and *Overture and March: 1776* (1904).

The concluding movement, "The Housatonic at Stockbridge" (1913–14), may have begun as an orchestral song in 1908. (Ives later made a reduction of the song for voice and piano.) Of its incarnation in *Three Places*, Ives wrote: "the upper strings, muted, [are intended] to be listened to separately or subconsciously as a kind of distant background of mists seen through the trees or over a river valley." The waters of the Housatonic River gather speed and force, and this texture builds to a powerful climax before settling into the prior, "subconscious" material.

When conductor Nicolas Slonimsky asked Ives for a work to program with his Boston Chamber Players, the composer willingly ignored his already large corpus of music for small orchestra, instead rescoring *Three Places* within the means of Slonimsky's ensemble. The work was premiered at Town Hall in New York City on January 10, 1931. Slonimsky subsequently performed *Three Places* in Europe, where it was enthusiastically received and did much to establish Ives' reputation outside the United States.

For the work's publication in 1935, Ives and Slonimsky added doublings to the chamber orchestra score, and the work soon became best known in this third version. A subsequent edition of the work, edited by James Sinclair and premiered in 1974, combines the 1935 edition with Ives' original orchestration. The original full-orchestra version of *Three Places* remained unheard until 1993. *—Uncle Dave Lewis*

Recommended:

○ **Hanson Conducts Ives, Shuman & Mennin** / Hanson (cond.), Eastman-Rochester Pops Orch. / 1991 / Mercury 432755

○ **Ives: Three Places in New England; New England Holidays; They Are There!** / Zinman, Baltimore SO / 2004 / Decca 000340202

Orchestral Set No. 2 (1909–1915; revised 1925)

Charles Ives did not intend for his *Orchestral Set No. 2* to be a follow-up to the famous first set, *Three Places in New England*. His notes indicate that by 1911 he'd completed the first two movements, and that the third was written in the fall of 1915. The finished grouping of these three movements wasn't assembled until 1919, whereas *Three Places* was put together around 1914. Ives' *Orchestral Set No. 2* premiered under Morton Gould in Chicago in 1967.

The *Orchestral Set No. 2* is scored for a very large orchestra and chorus, rivaling the scale of the *Fourth Symphony*. The first movement, entitled "An Elegy to Our Forefathers," was originally conceived as an "Overture to Stephen Foster" and undertaken around 1909. It includes quotations from such familiar Foster fare as "Old Black Joe" and "Massa's in de Cold, Cold Ground," but also snatches of African American spirituals such as "Nobody Knows the Trouble I've Seen." Bathed in dark hues of thick, mysterious orchestral color, this movement is the most touching of Ives' forays into African American song. Conductor Leopold Stokowski attempted to point up this element of the work by asking composer Hershy Kay to add a unison chorus to this movement in 1970. While the added choral part doesn't sound out of place in this context, Ives never intended it, and this addition has to be considered spurious.

The second movement, "The Rockstrewn Hills Join in the People's Outdoor Meeting" is based on the *Four Ragtime Dances* of 1902; some of the same material also appears in the fourth movement of the *First Piano Sonata*. This piece is a full throttle, no-holds-barred send-up of ragtime rhythm; it contains some of Ives' most trenchantly dissonant writing for the strings and brass in the center section. Bells ring in the climax, consisting of a wonderfully sour rendering of "Bringing in the Sheaves" before the music quiets back down. Despite the outdoor setting indicated by the title, this is urban music—big and ugly.

The final piece, "From Hanover Square North, at the End of a Tragic Day, the Voice of the People Again Arose" memorializes an event that occurred on a train platform in New York City on Friday, May 7, 1915. Ives records in his *Memos* how the atmosphere on that day was thick with apprehension at the news that a German Submarine had torpedoed the Lusitania, meaning war was imminent. As Ives waited along with a crowd at the Third Avenue "El," "In the Sweet Bye and Bye" broke out among some of the workers, and soon the whole crowd picked it up. As the train arrived, the magic remained; no one spoke, and some were still singing the tune while boarding. In Ives' score, he utilizes the large orchestral forces at his disposal and unison chorus to perfectly capture the tension and claustrophobia of this scene. *—Uncle Dave Lewis*

Recommended:

○ **Ives & Ruggles** / Dohnányi (cond.), Cleveland Orch. / 1995 / London 443776

The Unanswered Question (I & II), for trumpet, winds & strings (1906; revised 1930)

One of Ives' most striking and original works, *The Unanswered Question* (1906) is the first half of a diptych titled *Two Contemplations* (which is rounded out by the well-known *Central Park in the Dark*). As with much of Ives' music, *The Unanswered Question* is marked by a deep philosophical undercurrent. The musical discourse unfolds among three distinct entities. A small ensemble of strings provides a hymnlike yet ethereal foundation with a warm, glacially paced chorale. A solo trumpet provides a recurrent "eternal question of existence," a short, enigmatic motto which is mockingly answered each time—except, significantly, for its last appearance—by an increasingly shrill and belligerent quartet of flutes. In performance, the three musical entitities, each with a distintive melodic and rhythmic profile, are spatially separated, enhancing the sense of philosophical distance among them.

Throughout his insular, unconventional compositional career, Ives continued to experiment with the superimposition of several layers of seemingly disparate musical materials, sometimes resulting in textures of near-unimaginable complexity. This technique indeed became one of the most distinctive hallmarks of his music, reaching its zenith of sophistication in works like the *Orchestral Set No. 2* (1909–15) and the *Symphony No. 4* (1909–16). *—AMG*

Recommended:

○ **John Adams conducts American Elegies** / Adams (cond.), Orch. of St. Luke's / 1991 / Nonesuch 79249

○ **Ives: The Unanswered Question** / Bernstein (cond.), Vacchiano, New York PO / 1998 / Sony 60203

CHAMBER MUSIC

Scherzo: Over the Pavements, for piccolo, clarinet, bassoon, 3 trombones, piano & percussion (1907–1913; revised 1913)

Ives at the time worked for Mutual Insurance Company and was, in his spare time, making some of the most remarkable stylistic advances in music history. This work would, for all its brevity, turn out to be one of his most important pieces for its treatment of rhythm and tempo.

Ives later wrote that it began when he made an observation from the front basement window where he shared a bedroom with another young businessman in an apartment on Central Park West that its denizens called "Poverty Flat." He saw and heard the people going past, mostly in "all different steps." Horses, with their distinctive rhythm, also passed, and sometimes a trolley car drowned them all out. "I was struck with how many different and changing kinds of beats, times, rhythms, etc., went on together—but quite naturally."

Ives wrote down some of these rhythms in a piece he called *Take-Off #3: Rube Trying to Walk 2 to 3!*. In a period of a few years, Ives polished the idea into a somewhat longer piece, which he eventually titled *Over the Pavements*. (A scrap of *Rube Walking* was also used in the short song *1, 2, 3*.) *Over the Pavements* is Ives' first wholly realized and successful essay in continuously separate streams of music in different rhythms, the concept that would occupy him in the future more than any other.

Ives described *Over the Pavements* as "also a kind of take-off of street dancing." It begins with a perky 3/8 meter clarinet tune over a bassoon in 2/8. Polyrhythms then pile up to six streams in different beats and in many cases in different keys, and a ragtime rhythmic undercurrent is established. The piece is more than just a takeoff, and more than just a technical exercise. It neatly tickles the ear with its experimental rhythmic tricks while the descriptive impulse of the piece provides a lift. It has great forward momentum and maintains a sense of fun throughout. Just when it seems that there is no real way to end this cascade of busy forward rhythms Ives does so: there is a sudden shift to a 2/8 oom-pah rhythm and a textbook cadence on a C major chord, its hilarity compounded by the fact that the stream of preceding music is so polytonal as to be, in effect, atonal. *—Joseph Stevenson*

Recommended:

○ **Remembrance** / Reynolds (cond.), Detroit Chamber Winds / 1993 / Koch 7182

String Quartet No. 2 (1911–1913)

Charles Ives' 1896 *Quartet No. 1*, much of it based on American hymn tunes, was the product of a 21-year-old student. By the time he returned to the quartet form a decade later, his style had grown much more complex and dissonant. The earliest sketches of the *Quartet No. 2* date from as early as 1907, but most of the work on it took place in the early 1910s. As so often happened with Ives' music, after the quartet was completed in 1913, it sat on a shelf for many years. Not until May 11, 1946, was it given its first public performance in New York.

The *Quartet No. 2* is a programmatic work in which the instrumentalists depict four men who, in the composer's words, "converse, discuss, argue (in re 'Politick'), fight, shake hands, shut up—then walk up the mountain side to view the firmament!" The first movement, titled "Discussions," gives the listener a flavor of the seriousness of these discussions. The movement is mostly slow, occasionally passionate, with the trademark Ivesian references to popular songs like "Dixie," "Marching Through Georgia," and the composer's favorite, "Columbia, the Gem of the Ocean."

The discussion becomes more animated in the second movement, "Arguments." This movement began as a 1907 sketch inspired by lively conversations in which Ives took part at "Poverty Flat," the apartment he shared with friends. As the movement progresses there are several abrupt changes of pace, and the conversation becomes quite cacophonous in spots. The second violin, which Ives dubs "Rollo" in the score, attempts a Romantic-style cadenza but is drowned out by his interlocutors. Once again there are numerous quotations, this time including bits of Tchaikovsky, Brahms, and Beethoven's "Ode to Joy" theme.

Nearly static, dissonant chords introduce the third movement, "The Call of the Mountains." The music unfolds slowly, but starts to build in strength. Furious tremolos break out, but calm returns. The instruments gradually move to the upper limits of their registers as the four ascend the mountain, and the work ends quietly and mysteriously. *—Chris Morrison*

Recommended:

○ **American Originals** / Emerson SQ / 1992 / DG 435864

Violin Sonata No. 3 (1913–1914)

When looking at a collage, we have the benefit of being able to see all the seams—where one layer ends and another begins; thus we can distinguish the various components and try to decipher their meaning. The problem with Charles Ives is that his collages are aural rather than visual, and we can't always see the scissor work. What sounds like a harsh cacophony to the listener is often an eclectic collection of symbols or icons—references to outside ideas that are packed with semantic baggage. Such is the case with the third sonata for violin and piano. The first movement contains four sections; the opening Adagio begins with expansive quartal harmonies in the piano that set the stage for violin's stark melody. The subsequent Andante is more tuneful, waxing rhapsodic before returning to the refrain tune with which the Adagio had ended. An Allegretto precedes the return of the Adagio, this time featuring a moving quote from the Robert Lowry hymn "I Need Thee Every Hour." The second movement, marked Allegro, draws upon the rowdy sounds of ragtime, combined and contrasted with more somber references to hymns such as "Oh Happy Day." The third movement once again recalls Lowry's "I Need Thee Every Hour"—fragments of its melody appear here and there as thematic material. As the tune is finally assembled for a stirring chorus, the listener familiar to American hymnody recalls Annie S. Hawkes' corresponding text: "I need Thee, oh, I need Thee;/Every hour I need Thee!/Oh, bless me now, my Savior;/I come to Thee!" *—Jeremy Grimshaw*

Recommended:

○ **Ives: Violin Sonatas 1–4** / Thompson, Waters / 2003 / Naxos 8559119

Violin Sonata No. 4 ("Children's Day At the Camp Meeting") (1900–1916; revised 1939)

Though the last of Ives' violin sonatas to be completed, "Children's Day at a Camp Meeting" was the first to be published (1915). For the revised edition of 1942, Ives removed the fourth movement, which he had appropriated—typically, without explanation or apology—for the Sonata No. 2. Not only does the sonata's descriptive subtitle provide some suggestion as to Ives' source of inspiration, but the composer himself also provided a detailed narrative to accompany the music. The first movement, a lackadaisical march, recalls the famous stories of how Ives' father, George, sharpened his children's musical ears by having them sing a tune simultaneously in different keys. The movement itself portrays Ives and his boyhood companions marching about and deliberately singing off-key; tunes like "Tell Me the Old, Old Story" and "Work, for the Night is Coming" well up among remembrances of the young Ives practicing one of his father's organ fugues. The outer Adagio sections of the second movement, both based on "Jesus Loves Me," frame a raucous middle section which recalls the point during the religious service at which restless boys were excused to "throw stones down on the rocks in the brook!" Appropriately, and with the composer's characteristic humor, this section is marked "Allegro (conslugarocko)." The final movement recalls the march-like feel of the first with its evocations of "Shall We Gather at the River?" This hymn appears prominently elsewhere in the composer's music, including in the *Symphony No. 4* (1909–16) and the powerful vocal setting *At the River* (1916). *—Jeremy Grimshaw*

Recommended:

○ **The American Album** / Meyers, Schub / 1996 / RCA 68114

○ **Ives: Violin Sonatas 1–4** / Thompson, Waters / 2003 / Naxos 8559119

KEYBOARD

Piano Sonata No. 1 (1901–1909; revised 1919)

Charles Ives' *Sonata No. 1* has its genesis in improvisation: upon leaving Yale in 1898, Ives moved into a flat in New York City with some of his fellow graduates. There was a piano, and Ives spent many hours pounding out what his roommates referred to as "resident disturbances." Ives stated that most of the *Sonata* was written in 1900–04. The second movement incorporates the "First Ragtime Dance" for theater orchestra of 1899, also known as "In the Inn." The fourth movement contains the last music written for the sonata in 1911, although Ives further overhauled the fifth movement in 1914–17. At some point, Ives had a clear ink copy made of the Sonata, loaning it to a friend. This score was never returned and has been lost.

The "finished" formal scheme would be 1) Adagio con moto, 2a) Allegro moderato-Andante, 2b) Meno mosso con moto ("In the Inn"), 3) Largo-Allegro, 4a) no tempo given, 4b) Allegro-Presto, 5) Andante maestoso. At about 42 minutes, this is Ives' longest work for the piano, and is written at such a level of difficulty that few pianists undertake it. One pianist who became strongly identified with the Ives *Sonata No. 1* was William Masselos, who premiered it on February 17, 1949, recorded it in two variant versions in 1950 and 1967, and helped edit the *Sonata*'s first two editions. Masselos' collaborator in these publications was composer Lou Harrison, forced to work without the lost fair copy; certain sections of this work are incomplete save for some practically illegible sketches. Ives left only a hint of what he had in mind for this *Sonata*; "[it's] mostly about the outdoor life in Connecticut villages in the [18]80s and [18]90s." Not to second-guess Ives' intentions, but there is clearly a lot of New York City in this work as well, particularly in its liberal use of ragtime rhythm and even a boogie-woogie styled left hand part in the last movement. There are some amazing, even mind-boggling, technical innovations achieved throughout the whole work, for example the opening chromatic and contrary ostinato, which is counterpoised with single notes falling from the treble range; just like something out of Schoenberg's 12-tone piano music. Also worth noting is the passage which opens "In the Inn" where a frantic, rushing figure stated in sixteenth note quintuplets are played against a 3/4 accompaniment stated in 4/4 bars.

William Masselos once wrote "(The *Sonata No. 1*) always seems like an inspired improvisation, with each performance having a character quite its own. I can never predict how I will play it on any given night." Indeed, the *Sonata* contains so many ideas and shifts through them so rapidly that different details come to light with each listening. So Ives' *Sonata No. 1* is still essentially unfinished, but true to the improvisational spirit in which it was conceived. *—Uncle Dave Lewis*

Recommended:

○ **Ives: Piano Pieces** / Henck / Wergo 60101

Piano Sonata No. 2: Concord, Mass., 1840–60 (1911–1915; revised 1921)

Charles Ives' *"Concord" Sonata* has come to be recognized as perhaps the greatest of American piano works. Largely composed over the years 1911–15, it contains some of the most radical experiments in harmony and rhythm of its time. Pianist John Kirkpatrick, long associated with the music of Ives, gave the work its historic first performance at New York's Town Hall on January 20, 1939.

While working on the initial publication of the sonata in 1919, Ives wrote his *Essays Before a Sonata*, in which he discusses the genesis and content of the work. He described the sonata as his "impression of the spirit of transcendentalism that is associated in the minds of many with Concord, Mass., of over a half century ago, ...undertaken in impressionistic pictures of [Ralph Waldo] Emerson and [Henry David] Thoreau, a sketch of the Alcotts, and a Scherzo supposed to reflect a lighter quality which is often found in the fantastic side of [Nathaniel] Hawthorne." Ives' interest in American literature, pursued during his student days at Yale, was reawakened by his wife Harmony (whom he married in 1908) and became integral to the sonata.

The monumental, dissonant beginning of the "Emerson" movement creates the impression of a vast struggle. The famous four-note motto from the opening of Beethoven's *Fifth Symphony* emerges (as it does elsewhere in the work), representing, according to Ives, "the Soul of humanity knocking at the door of the Divine mysteries." Thick, almost orchestral sonorities dominate this longest of the sonata's four movements. Towards the end a viola makes a ghostly two-measure appearance. Ives never felt this movement to be entirely finished; numerous variants exist, and he later created a new work, *Four Transcriptions from Emerson*, which develops some of its ideas further.

The "Hawthorne" movement acts as a scherzo, with wild flurries of notes, a couple of brief lyrical episodes, and hints of hymn tunes and a country band. At one point, Ives directs the pianist to use a 14 3/4" piece of wood to sound an enormous tone cluster. All this is meant to evoke what the composer called Hawthorne's "wilder, fantastical adventures into the half-childlike, half-fairylike phantasmal realms."

The peaceful third movement, "The Alcotts," serves as a respite. Here Ives meditates on the calm of Concord's streets and the "trials and happiness of the family." Beethoven's *Fifth* reappears, this time transformed into a nostalgic tune, as Ives imagines one of the Alcotts playing on "the little old spinet-piano Sophia Thoreau gave to the Alcott children."

For the closing "Thoreau" movement, Ives creates a portrait of "an autumn day of Indian summer at Walden." The constant use of the piano's pedals creates an almost impressionistic atmosphere as the slow, enigmatic music unfolds, only raising its voice on a couple of occasions. An ostinato bass line pervades much of the second half of the movement. Thoreau's instrument, the flute, appears briefly with a lyrical melody symbolizing "a mist heard over Walden Pond." The movement ends quietly. *—Chris Morrison*

Recommended:

○ **Ives: Sonata 2** / Kalish, Baron / 1977 / Nonesuch 71337

Three Quarter-Tone Pieces, for 2 pianos (1923–1924)

This work is scored for two pianos tuned a quarter-tone apart, Ives taking his inspiration from a whimsical childhood memory of two matronly sisters who played their Sunday School classes that way. In 1923, Ives sold insurance to the pianist E. Robert Schmitz. Casually learning of Ives' interest in microtonality, Schmitz informed him about a two-manual quarter-tone piano lately designed by another pianist, Hans Barth. Interested, Ives completed the *Three Pieces* by the end of 1924. Barth and Sigmund Klein premiered the "Chorale" at Chickering Hall on February 8, 1925, along with an explanatory talk given by Schmitz. Ives' own comments, entitled "Some Quarter-tone Impressions," appeared in print a month later. The "Largo" remained unperformed until Barth and another pianist premiered it in the Ballroom of the Plaza Hotel in New York, April 9, 1929. Barth repeated the "Chorale" at his two-manual quarter-tone instrument at Carnegie Hall on February 23, 1930. The whole work was not heard until 1967, when Stuart Lanning and George V. Pappastavarou, the latter editing the work from manuscript, recorded the *Three Pieces* for CBS.

Of the three pieces, the opening "Largo" is the most enigmatic, and the overall mood is darkly mystical. At one point, a slowly syncopated figure gains speed and volume and is followed by fortissimo glissandi. As the overtones of the glissandi resonate in the air, Ives introduces some quiet, tentative quarter-tone chords in the middle register of the piano, resulting in a three-dimensional texture. Unlike many of Ives' works, this piece doesn't seem to contain a single reference to previously composed music.

The "Allegro" is an Ivesian "comedy" which opens with a couple of his trademark dissonant chords and launches into some jaunty ragtime figures. About this piece, Ives felt that "from a pure quarter-tone harmonic standpoint it doesn't amount to much," but as a jazzy and clangorous romp it's a delight. Ives seems to take particular pleasure in having the two pianists exchange quick, chromatically rising and falling chord sequences and "out-of-tune" arpeggios. A figure from his 1911 song *"The Se'er"* appears and is battered around a bit.

The "Chorale" is the longest of the three and the most "conventional"; it is the only one of the group that appears to have a previous history. In 1909, Ives sketched a Chorale for quarter-tone string ensemble that provided his model. While only a scrap of the original survives, Ives left indications in the margins of his manuscript as to how the piano piece could be re-scored for strings. Composer Alan Stout undertook this challenge and the results first appeared in print in 1974. "My Country 'tis of Thee" is heard near the end of the middle section, and outside of a brief buildup in the low register, this piece is hymn-like and peaceful throughout. It provides a serene close to the world of Ives' keyboard output. *—Uncle Dave Lewis*

Recommended:

○ **Ives: Quarter-Tone Pieces; Messiaen: Visions de l'Amen; etc.** / Bouwhuas & Zeeland (pianos) / 1992 / Channel Classics 4592

Three-Page Sonata, for piano (& optional glockenspiel) (Sep. 1905; revised after 1924)

For Charles Ives, dissonance was a sign of strength and machismo. During one concert, when the audience began verbally expressing its distaste for one of his works, he reportedly stood and chastised the crowd, admonishing people to "open your ears and listen like a man!" He had little patience for the musically unadventurous. The same attitude appears in a note Ives attached to a copy of his *Three-Page Sonata* from 1905, which indicated that the piece was "made mostly as a joke to knock the mollycoddles out of their boxes and to kick out the soft ears." Despite its title (which merely refers to the manuscript space occupied by the original sketches), the *Three-Page Sonata* is a substantial work, cast in three brief but challenging movements. The first, Allegro Moderato, weaves musical references to Bach (the letters of the name translating, in the German notation system, as the notes B flat-A-C-B), into a densely dissonant and polyrhythmic web. Meters continually change and gestures continually misalign; twice, the right-hand figure divides the beat into six notes, while in the same amount of time the left-hand executes five. The effect is one of continual disorientation. The middle movement, a languorous Andante, continues the intermusical references by quoting the melody from *Ever of Thee*, a piece by Bach's teacher Carl Foeppl. The third and final movement takes the form of a clumsy, discombobulated march. Its opening fanfare follows an angular chromatic contour; in fact, the melody portentously takes the form of a 12-tone row. Polyrhythmic layering here is used with comic excess, growing ever-more convoluted until, with a sweeping crescendo, the march is suddenly interrupted by an off-kilter ragtime passage. The march eventually resumes, but is interrupted once more by the doodling ragtime figure before returning for the flashy final cadence. For decades, the *Three-Page Sonata* existed only in sketch form, snatches of it dispersed among the papers that survived him. It wasn't until 1949, before Ives' death but probably without his supervision, that composer Henry Cowell prepared a published edition of the sonata. The 1975 critical edition of the piece prepared by John Kirkpatrick, curator of the Ives Collection at Yale, replaced Cowell's version as the definitive performance score. It also informed the lively and thoroughly unmollycoddling recording of the work prepared in 1999 by David Berman. *—Jeremy Grimshaw*

Recommended:

○ **Ives: Piano Music** / Deutsch / 1993 / Vox 5089

Variations on "America," for organ (1891–1892; revised 1902)

Even after his move in 1899 from Connecticut to Manhattan—to become an insurance actuary, and, nine years later, to co-found a trailblazing agency—Ives continued to play the organ in Protestant churches until 1902. A generation later, Virgil Thomson and Leo Sowerby followed his lead, by no means common among American composers. Although Ives composed for the organ as a young man, including a sonata he once likened to Mendelssohn's, only four works survived—all written between 1888 and 1897. The 17-year-old composer introduced the second of these, originally called "Variations Etc. on National Hymn," at Brewster, New York on July 4, 1891. Before he submitted it for publication, young Ives jettisoned the "Etc." (a band-like introduction, a roller-coaster coda, and two bitonal Interludes), but retained five tongue-in-cheek variations that follow a soft, solemn statement of "America" (aka "God Save the Queen"). When publishers predictably rejected it, the piece went into a drawer with a great deal else composed between 1890 and 1928—some works finished, many more incomplete. (By 1930, heart disease, diabetes, and a progressive deterioration of the nervous system left Ives unable any longer to hold a pen).

In 1949, with the composer's cooperation, organist E. Power Biggs reassembled all the materials for publication. In December 1962, he included *Variations on "America"*—now the official title—on a program dedicating the new organ in Lincoln Center's Philharmonic Hall (since rebuilt inside and renamed Avery Fisher Hall). Enter William Schuman, who had become the new Center's president in January 1962. He wrote later on that "by the time the piece was over, I knew I simply had to transcribe it . . . to make as effective an orchestral piece as I could devise without changing any of the musical materials." Broadcast Music Inc. commissioned the task, and it was introduced on May 20, 1964, by the New York Philharmonic conducted by André Kostelanetz.

Schuman stated that he took no liberties with Ives' harmonies or melodies: "all remain exactly as they were in the original." But he needed to invent percussion parts and, since the original registration "was rather inexact," chose "registers which would fit the orchestral timbres I had selected." He did not, however, consider his orchestral version to be "Ives transcribed by Schuman" but rather "Ives/Schuman."

After a rollicking introduction based on segments of the melody, "America" is played very softly by the brass with col legno strings and percussion. The winds dominate an étude-like first variation, complete with flute descants. Variation 2 is woozily sentimental until a barber-shop cadence appears midway and again at the end. Variation 3 contains the first surviving example of Ives' polytonality, a loopy pizzicato waltz in 6/8 time. Variation 4 is a kind of minor-key polonaise, except that tambourine and castanets add a Latin flavoring. Variation 5 is brief and quasi-Baroque before giving way to a marching band and the restored coda. *—Roger Dettmer*

Recommended:

○ **American Masterpieces** / Ormandy (cond.), Philadelphia Orch. / 1997 / Sony 63034

VOCAL

114 Songs (1888–1921)

Charles Ives privately funded the printing of his *114 Songs* in 1921. The oldest song included, "Slow March," is dated 1888; the rest date from virtually every year up to the time of publication. Some of the songs were newly arranged for voice & piano, or condensed from other sources explicitly for inclusion in the volume during 1920–21. Ives' initial motivation was solely to be able to hold a book of his own songs in his hands, but in the "Preface" to the *114 Songs*, Ives refers to other motivations that had occurred to him in the interim: "(It) was undertaken primarily in order to have a few clear copies that could be sent to friends who have been interested enough to ask for copies of some of the songs. It contains plenty of songs which have not been and will not be asked for."

A bit more than half of Ives' known output of 200 songs are represented in this collection. Among the best known items included are "Evening," "Charlie Rutlage," "Ann Street," "Serenity," "The Cage," "The Children's Hour," and "Memories." A few songs are sub-grouped into sets that are related thematically; for example "Old Home Day," "In the Alley," "A Son of a Gambolier," "Down East," and "The Circus Band" are grouped together as "Five Street Songs and Pieces." Stylistically the *114 Songs* cover the breadth of Ives' musical terrain, from the endearingly simple to the mind-bogglingly complex; songs such as "The Collection" are straightforward enough to be appropriate for church use, while other pieces, like "from 'Paracelsus,'" contain piano parts absolutely blackened with notes and voice parts full of ungainly intervals, sometimes as wide as a minor tenth. The extremes of both consonance and dissonance, stillness and cacophony are all present, and each bears Ives' unmistakable stamp of personality.

Interwoven with this musical diversity is an equally characteristic variety of expressive purpose. Ives' good-natured wit, irreverent humor, genuine sentimentality, and political and philosophical leanings are all well represented in his choices of texts, and each is wedded to music of surprising flexibility. One need only examine the smile-inducingly brief "1, 2, 3"—which manages to make pithy patriotic commentary out of a mere sentence of text—and the sprawling "Housatonic at Stockbridge"—the lyrical expansiveness of which puts Ives on par with the any song composer in history—to see how open-minded and individual Ives was in his approach to text setting.

Many writers have stated that the *114 Songs* are the most important group of art songs ever written by an American composer. In an age where Tin Pan Alley material is often elevated to the level of art song in recitals and recordings, this has become more difficult to defend. However, there is no another collection of songs quite like the *114* of Ives. Ives wrote, "this package of paper, uncollectible notes, marks of respect and expression, is now thrown, so to speak, at the music fraternity, who will for this reason feel free to do dodge it on its way—perhaps to the waste basket." Indeed, that's exactly where many copies of the rare first edition of this work ended up. However, the reputation of Ives' *114 Songs* has improved considerably since then, and in 2001 MUSA announced the publication of *129 Songs*, which is the first critical edition of *114 Songs*, plus 15 others, edited by H. Wiley Hitchcock. *—Uncle Dave Lewis*

Recommended:

○ **Charles Ives: Songs** / de Gaetani, Kalish / 1976 / Nonesuch 71325

○ **Songs of Charles Ives and Ernst Bacon** / Boatwright, Kirkpatrick / 1994 / CRI 675

○ **The Complete Songs of Charles Ives Vol. 1** / Ohrenstein, Bush, Hart, Helmrich, Sperry, Vallecillo-Gray, Sharp, Blier / 1992 / Albany 077

○ **The Complete Songs of Charles Ives Vol. 2** / Ohrenstein, Bush, Hart, Helmrich, Sperry, Vallecillo-Gray, Sharp, Blier / 1993 / Albany 078

○ **The Complete Songs of Charles Ives Vol. 3** / Ohrenstein, Bush, Hart, Helmrich, Sperry, Vallecillo-Gray, Sharp, Blier / 1993 / Albany 079

○ **The Complete Songs of Charles Ives Vol. 4** / Ohrenstein, Bush, Hart, Helmrich, Sperry, Vallecillo-Gray, Sharp, Blier / 1994 / Albany 080

Ann Street, song (1921)

Charles Ives was a master of short, evocative pieces, and this statement is equally true of his songs. Among his nearly 150 songs, some of the best are pithy statements that are over practically before they begin. "Ann Street" depicts one of the shortest thoroughfares in New York City, in one of the shortest songs on record. Although there are songs in Ives' output that take fewer pages and have shorter verses, this one, over in about 30 seconds, is exceptionally terse.

Nevertheless, the 20-measure song is full of description and incident. The words are by a New York newspaper poet named Maurice Morris. Ives dated the song 1921 and published it in his collection of *114 Songs*. The song is in his late advanced style, with wild effects and clangorous harmonies. It has no time signature, though it is measured.

It begins with a long-held bass A, designated in the score as Broadway. Sudden rushes of arpeggios and dense treble chords in two measures seem suddenly to populate the famous thoroughfare with traffic.

The singer describes little Ann Street, "... width of same, ten feet." A few tinkly measures hint as its short length and minimal width, and then the harmonies grow thicker and more complex as its normal rush of business is depicted. Three dissonant measures of held tremolando chords suspend motion; Ann Street's traffic has to stop where "Nassau crosses Ann St.," as an unsung note appears in the score. Then the song comes to a stop as abruptly as the real-life street does.

The ending usually gets a laugh in a recital. In the end, the mood of the little song is one of lightly ironic whimsy. *—Joseph Stevenson*

Recommended:

○ **The Complete Songs of Ives Vol. 4** / Sharp, Blier (piano) / 1994 / Albany 080

○ **Charles Ives Songs** / de Gaetani, Kalish (piano) / 1976 / Nonesuch 71325

The Cage, song (1906; revised 1914)

This is the song version published in 1922 of a work Ives wrote in 1906. It is perhaps better known as a piece for small orchestra, "In The Cage," released by Ives in 1932 as the first movement of the *Set for Theatre Orchestra*, S. 20.

This work belongs to a category of short Ives pieces that the composer called "take-offs." As early as his college days at Yale Ives entertained friends, roommates, and fraternity brothers with piano improvisations that depicted events of the day (things like a football game, a lecture, or the traditional fraternity pledge night festivities). His friends were amused by their sound effects and didn't really stop to worry about whether what they were listening to was actual music or just Charlie playing around at the piano, but Ives jotted down the most successful ideas to emerge from these take-offs. Ives kept up this habit when he was an aspiring young businessman in Manhattan in the decade after his graduation from Yale in 1908. He and a few other young men lived in a succession of apartments they called "Poverty Flats" but which were in reality pretty comfortable lodgings.

One of his roommates was David Twichell, son of New Haven, Connecticut's most prominent clergyman. Through Rev. Twichell, a young exile from China, Bart Yung, came to live there. (Yung's father was a revolutionary who had been compelled to flee China.) One day Ives, Yung, and another roommate, George Lewis, visited Central Park Zoo, where the saw a leopard pacing restlessly back and forth in its cage. Bart joked, "Is life anything like that?" Ives transformed the quip into a short poem that first depicts the leopard, then transforms Yung into "a boy who had been there three hours." The song is essentially an epigram in music, built on radical new chords piled up in the interval of the fourth rather than the conventional thirds. Also remarkable is the repeated introduction to the piano part, a succession of chords of durations lasting (in terms of sixteenth notes) the sequence of 8-6-4-3-2-1. This shortening of the length of each chord has an uncanny claustrophobic effect. "The Cage" is one of Ives' most effective ultra-short pieces. *—Joseph Stevenson*

Recommended:

○ **Charles Ives Songs** / de Gaetani, Kalish (piano) / 1976 / Nonesuch 71325

○ **Complete Songs of Ives Vol. 3** / Sperry, Vallecillo-Gray / 1993 / Albany 079

Charlie Rutlage, song (1920–1921)

Despite the late date of this song, it showed that even though Ives had been writing some of the world's most radical music for over a decade, he still found occasion to compose music within (or at least close to) the standard tonal system, in straightforward rhythms (one at a time!). The text for this relatively long song is from John A. Lomax's *Cowboy Songs and Other Frontier Ballads*. It tells the story of a cowboy who has just died. In fact, it could be an elegy or remembrance of the cowboy Charlie Rutlage, spoken by one of his range-riding friends.

The song begins in a loping cow or horse gait "in moderate time," as the speaker wishes he could find "a resting place within the golden gate." He recalls other cowpunchers who died before Charlie. The tempo picks up and the rhythms begin to go off kilter. Chords begin to acquire extra, dissonant notes and scramble restlessly among keys. The speaker shifts from song to speech, rhythmically notated but without note heads. The piano begins to obsess on the old folk song "Whoopie Ti Yi Yo" in four-beat patterns, but the bass line has turned chromatic and has shifted to a three-beat pattern.

As the music gets "faster and faster—louder and louder," the piano breaks into wild cascades as the narrator tells how the herd turned and caused Charlie's horse to fall, crushing him. Crash chords are played at this point, with both fists striking clusters of keys. The music resumes the cowboy rhythm, but evens out to quiet chords that lead to a radiant ending in pure B flat major. The narrator says his final prayer for Rutlage: "I hope he'll meet his parents, will meet them face to face, and that they'll grasp him by the right hand at the shining throne of grace."

It is important to note that Ives set the direct and naïve cowboy language in the song without the slightest hint of condescension. The final revival-camp imagery of the poem (which is reflected in Ives' harmonies) comes through as an utterly sincere wish in Ives' music, as well as in the presumed thoughts of the original cowboy author of the poem. Therefore, it is imperative for the singer to resist the temptation to try out a dialect accent on this song.

This song is a wonderful introduction to Ives. Its capturing of an authentic American folk voice, its easy command of complex rhythms, its fine melodic qualities, and its sudden introduction of harshly modern sounds at just an appropriate point give a nice picture of what Ives is about. It was actually performed twice, in the winter of 1924 and in 1932, when Hubert Lipscot sang it to Aaron Copland's piano accompaniment as part of a well-chosen set of Ives songs. It brought down the house and had to be repeated. *—Joseph Stevenson*

Recommended:

○ **Ives: When The Moon** / Sylvan, Feinberg / 2000 / Decca 466841

○ **The Voice of America** / Ramey, Jones / 2003 / Decca 000047802

General William Booth Enters into Heaven, song (1914; revised 1934)

Of Charles Ives' more than 200 songs, *General William Booth Enters Into Heaven* is one of the best known, and certainly one of the most musically ambitious. The stirring song is a setting of the poem by the same name, penned by Vachel Lindsay in 1912. The poem, which became very popular and brought considerable notoriety to its author, is an ode to William Booth, founder of the Salvation Army. In it, Lindsay imagines Booth marching into the hereafter at the head of a large army consisting of lepers, drunks, and other downtrodden folks, of which "each slum had sent its half-a-score the round world over." These "vermin-eaten saints with mouldy breath" march as a procession in drills before the pearly gates, and, as they enter in, Jesus appears, his outstretched hand healing them of their ills.

Ives' brash musical style is a perfect match for Lindsay's uncompromising imagery (which William Butler Yeats praised for being "stripped bare of ornament").

The setting is both emotionally evocative and pictorial. At the beginning of the song, before the entrance of the singer, the piano plucks a series of dissonant chords; their strict rhythms and attacks accurately depict the bass drum to which General Booth's band marches, while the uneasy harmonies suggest the grotesquerie of the parade as described by Lindsay. In fact, Ives' musical renderings of the narrative often border on caricature, a kind of exaggeration that serves ultimately to drive home the intensely spiritual message behind the musical and poetic imagery. When the "big voiced lassies" play their banjos and work themselves into a delirium of hallelujahs, Ives' sends his singer and accompanist into a similar state of spiritual and musical fervor; likewise, the motley band of "bull-necked convicts" and "loons with trumpets" are met with a grandiose degree of musical heraldry as they march "Onward, upward, thro' the golden air!" Ives characteristically includes in his broad palette of musical materials liberal quotations from familiar musical sources. The most prominent of these is a repeated refrain, interpolated throughout the song, which is taken from the Salvation Army hymn tune known as "Fountain." The refrain, which often finds itself juxtaposed with Lindsay's most unsavory images, poses the question "Are you washed in the blood of the Lamb." These parenthetical asides poignantly highlight a familiar Christian metaphor by placing side-by-side the unsightly image of Jesus' suffering with that of Booth's weary followers. Ives further seems to revert the message outward to the listener by rendering the refrain with a sudden change of tonal orientation. This imperative is driven home when, at the end of the piece, as Booth's troops are healed and welcomed into heaven and the piano's drum beats fade into silence, the refrain appears once again as a lingering question. *—Jeremy Grimshaw*

Recommended:

- **Complete Songs of Ives Vol. 3** / Sharp, Blier / 1993 / Albany 079
- **Love's Secret** / Gramm, Cumming / 1996 / VoxBox 5129
- **Songs of Ives & Bacon** / Boatwright, Kirkpatrick / 1994 / CRI 675

Like a Sick Eagle (1920)

Although Ives is famous for painting nostalgic pictures of happy memories in his life, he almost never wrote music in direct response to his life's tragedies; this work is an exception. It stems from the most devastating event of his marriage—the miscarriage of his wife's first pregnancy, mere months after they were married. The pregnancy was followed by an emergency hysterectomy, ending both their hopes for a household of children (although they did adopt in 1916).

The text is from Keats' sonnet "To the Elgin Marbles," and is a despairing recognition of personal mortality: "Each... God-like hardship tells me I must die, like a sick eagle looking towards the sky." Ives first set it on April 20, 1909—just nine days after the operation.

Ives would sometimes conceive music in response to a poem, but then realize it as an instrumental piece. Later, when compiling his *114 Songs*, he reworked many of these into songs, and reduced the instrumental parts for piano. This appears to be the origin of the two versions of "Like a Sick Eagle": first a sketch, then a working-out of the idea as a chamber piece for voice or English horn (later changed to basset-horn) with flute, strings & piano, and then a song for voice & piano in 1920.

Ives assigned the instrumental version to his *Set No. 1 for orchestra*, Kv 27, a six-movement suite of short pieces of which "Like a Sick Eagle" is the fourth. He also considered assembling a *Set no. 5*, a three-movement suite to include "Like a Sick Eagle" as its first movement.

Ives marked the instrumental version "Draggingly Voice intones words with English horn (not like singing)." In the song version he wrote "Very slowly, in a weak and dragging way." In the instrumental part, he also inserted plus marks in the melody line and explained them in the following direction: "The ++ over and between the notes means that between 1/2-tones a slide through a 1/4-tone may be made, and between whole tones, through a 1/3 tones. This, done in a certain way, gives a more desolate sound...."

The directions "not like singing" and the direction to use a glide through microtones in effect duplicates Arnold Schoenberg's Sprechstimme effect.

The song itself is entirely chromatic and essentially atonal. The result comes as close as anything can to capturing the feeling of deep despair. *—Joseph Stevenson*

Recommended:

- **Charles Ives Songs** / de Gaetani, Kalish / 1976 / Nonesuch 71325
- **Charles Ives Songs** / Alexander, Crone / 1984 / Etcetera 1020

Tom Sails Away, song (1917)

America's entry into World War I in April 1917 pulled Ives away from composing. Until then, he had undertaken a punishing schedule, building his highly successful insurance business in New York by day (making himself a multi-millionaire in the process) and composing at night until exhaustion prevented more work. But in 1917 he wrote little music aside from four songs that seem to have been directly inspired by the war. He devoted the rest of his free time to political activities.

When Ives compiled numerous songs into the self-published *114 Songs* he grouped this song with "In Flanders Fields" and "He is There" (later retitled "They are There!") in *114 Songs* as *Three Songs of the War*. This is the least jingoistic of the three, and has an accessible nostalgic melody, even though it ranges chromatically away from a main key. The text is by Ives, and begins with the highly characteristic phrase, "Scenes of my childhood are with me...." In evocative word painting Ives describes the time near the end of daylight when Daddy should return home from the mill. "But today! In freedom's cause Tom sailed away for over there, over there, over there!" The music uses Ives' brand of impressionism, with misty pedal-held chords in the piano at the beginning. The harmonies are highly chromatic and create a dreamy mood. The music presses faster as the factory whistles blow. They run down the hill to meet Daddy, but there is a sudden quiet moment, then the music leaps into the song's only loud passage, on the words that reveal Tom has left for war. The music quickly fades out. The inevitable quotation from Cohan's popular song "Over There!" becomes a slow, sad chant. Then the misty held chords of the opening return to the mood of the original mood of the song in a typical Ives epilogue. "Tom Sails Away" is one of Ives' most moving songs. It also has the extramusical sad association with its position in Ives' output, for it comes near the end of his ability to creative output. *—Joseph Stevenson*

Recommended:

- **Ives & Crumb** / de Gaetani, Kalish / 1987 / Bridge 9006
- **Frederica von Stade** / Von Stade, Isepp / Gala 339

CHORAL

The Celestial Country, cantata (1898–1899; revised 1901)

This early cantata from 1902, lasting approximately 39 minutes, was written shortly after Ives' graduation from Yale University, and it was partly inspired by the cantata *Hora novissima* (1893) by Ives' teacher Horatio Parker who was very academic in his composition and teaching methods, but nevertheless very accomplished in his chosen style. The text for *The Celestial Country* is based on Henry Alford's "Forward be our watchword," which Ives considered to be a translation of Bernard of Morlaix's Latin poem "Rhythm of the Celestial Country." The chorus represents pilgrims, and the instrumental accompaniment tries to distract them from their journey.

Although *The Celestial Country* is more traditional than Ives' later work (an early experimental work which he never showed to Parker), there are some lovely instrumental melodies in the "introductions" and "preludes" to various sections which are accompanied by an organ harmonized in elaborate chords of stacked thirds (apparently a later addition after the first and only performance under Ives' direction on April 18, 1902 at the Central Presbyterian Church in New York City). However, Ives was known by this time for adding complex harmonies during the usual church services. This tonal complexity is found at the outset with the "Introduction Before No. 1," which is followed by "No. 1: Prelude, Trio, and Chorus" for strings and chorus: "Far o'er yon horizon Rise the city towers, Where our God abideth, that fair home is ours." The choruses are often very energetic, and contain some unusual, quickly shifting meters of 3/4 and 4/4, as well as quick and unusual harmonic shifts. Often performed as a separate composition is "No. 4: Intermezzo for String Quartet." This beautifully lyric piece is a simple, unadorned Romantic composition in the late nineteenth century American ballad style, which concludes on an unresolved chord to be followed by a brief "Interlude After No. 4" for organ and cello that wanders through quiet but dense chords to the final cadence. In the terrifying "Introduction to No. 7," with its massive organ harmonies followed by loud tympani and brass and an earnest but heavy-handed chorus finale that has some "moments," one can hear Ives suppressing his own creativity in order to produce something of that period. Disappointed by the moderate reception that the work received, Ives quit his position as the church organist and began to sell insurance for a living and following his true muse on weekends and whenever he could (still producing an astonishing amount of music). *—"Blue Gene" Tyranny*

Recommended:

- **Ives: Celestial Country; Silence Unaccompanied** / Armstrong (cond.), St. Olaf Choir &Chamber Ens. / 2002 / Linn 203

Processional: Let There Be Light (I), for chorus & organ (1901; revised 1907)

Charles Ives' *Processional: Let There Be Light*, a brief piece for voices (or alternately, trombones) and organ, was composed in 1901, during the composer's tenure as organist at Central Presbyterian Church in New York. The work is a setting of a short text by Rev. John Ellerton, one troped from the creation account in *Genesis*: "This is the Day of Light: Let there be Light Today." Although the piece lasts less than three minutes in performance, Ives uses his rich harmonic palette to encapsulate the breadth of his subject matter. There is a great deal of Ives' characteristic harmonic friction here, emblematic of the spiritual connotations that the composer and his New England contemporaries attached to dissonance/consonance relationships. Indeed, the overall contours of the work seem to be demarcated by carefully spaced pillars of stable octaves, between which the composer ventures into various degrees of harmonic complexity. Although an underlying melody is usually apparent, the tune sometimes bears the weight of thick layers of tone clusters. This spectrum, ranging from pure octave consonances to brash and unwieldy chromaticisms, evokes the polarity of forces, the light separating from the darkness, described in the scriptural account and suggested in Ellerton's text. *—Jeremy Grimshaw*

Recommended:

○ **Triton's Journey** / Triton Trombone Quartet / 1997 / Bis 884

Psalm 67 (1894; revised 1898)

Charles Ives' ten psalm settings belong to the early part of his career (ranging roughly from 1888 to 1902) from the time of his service as a boy organist in Danbury, Connecticut, to his resignation as organist from Central Presbyterian Church in New York City. Of these, his setting of number 67, written in 1894, is the most famous; the text, taken from the King James Version, begins "God be merciful unto us, and bless us." Ives utilizes a bi-tonal combination right from the start, stacking a C major triad in the sopranos and altos over G minor in the tenors and basses. Ives utilizes subtle alterations, mostly in the soprano and alto parts, to keep the harmony under control, something he would hardly see fit to do in later music. By the line "Let all the people praise thee" Ives twists the polytonal harmony around to achieve a standard cadence of the kind common to nineteenth century church music. With the phrase "O let the nations be glad and sing for joy," Ives introduces a brief canonic section in which the minor key becomes the dominant factor, but soon returns to his prior scheme and recaps the section beginning "Let the people praise thee." Ives referred to Psalm 67 as a sort of "enlarged plainchant"; the last lines "and all the ends of the earth shall fear him" is set in a chant-like declamation on the two chords which begin the piece. Psalm 67 concludes its three minutes in a feeling of repose and quietude.

This was apparently the last new work Ives shared with his father before his death. George Ives felt this work was "best suited for use in church" of his son's early choral compositions and had a "dignity and sense of finality." Psalm 67 disappeared into Ives' portfolio of compositions until 1937, when conductor Lehman Engel premiered it with his group, the Madrigal Singers, at the WPA Theater of Music in New York City. A CBS broadcast of the piece soon followed; public response was favorable enough to merit publication of the piece and the issuance of it on a 78-rpm record.

The work has become a choral standard, and is still startling in its harmonic resemblance to popular choral music of the 1960s. Indeed, Psalm 67 may have provided a direct harmonic model for that style; it was known to Fred Waring through his assistant Robert Shaw and was programmed at one point by the Pennsylvanians chorus. Echoes of its sound may be heard in a wide range of pieces recorded by the choruses of Ray Charles (the choral conductor, not the Rhythm and Blues artist), Randy Van Horne, and sacred composer Gene Puerling. *—Uncle Dave Lewis*

Recommended:

○ **Like As A Hart** / Flummerfelt (cond.), Westminster Choir / Chesky 138

J

Christiane Jaccottet

b. May 18, 1937, Lausanne, France, **d.** 1999, Geneva, Switzerland
Harpsichordist

Swiss harpsichordist Christiane Jaccottet came from a musical family and began studying piano at the age of four. She continued her studies at the Conservatory at La-Chaux-de-Fonds and then the Viennese Musical Academy. At the age of 20, she won a competition sponsored by ARD Television in Munich. She developed her approach to performing on period instruments under Gustav Leonhardt. In 1964, she won the Soloist's Prize from the Swiss Music Society, and the following year she won the prize for harpsichord and basso continuo at the First International Music Competition in Bruges. She has toured the United States, Candada, Europe, and Australia, and has performed at major international music festivals. Her collaborators have included Heinz Holliger, Aurèle Nicolet, Michel Corboz, and Frank Martin. From 1975 until her death in 1999, she was a professor at the Geneva Conservatory. Jaccottet participated in over 100 recordings; especially notable are her interpretations of the Bach *English Suites* and Frank Martin's harpsichord concertos. —*Robert Adelson*

Recommended:

- ○ **Bach: English Suite 1; Toccatas** / Jaccottet / 1994 / Point Classics 265029
- ○ **Bach: Goldberg-Variationen; 4 Duette** / Jaccottet / 1990 / Pilz 160127
- ○ **Bach: Das Wohltempierte Klavier, Teil 1, Vol. 1** / Jaccottet / 1989 / Pilz 160121

Paul Jacobs

b. Jun. 22, 1931, New York, NY, **d.** Sep. 25, 1983, New York, NY
Pianist

Paul Jacobs was one of the most brilliant of American pianists. Although his approach to music was intellectual, this did not prevent his interpretations from being touching and honest in feeling, as well as being exceptionally clear in execution and delineation of formal elements. He was especially well known for his crystalline approach to Debussy.

Jacobs, who grew up in the Bronx, was already a proficient pianist before he was ten. He avidly read and played through vast quantities of piano music, borrowing everything he could get from the New York Public Library system. He studied at the Third Street Music School Settlement and then at the Juilliard School with Ernest Hutchenson. He gave major New York recitals while still a teenager and played in major new music ensembles, including the Composers' Forum.

He moved to Europe in 1951, remaining there nine years. He became a familiar figure among the serial-oriented avant-garde of the time, attending the summer sessions at Darmstadt and often performing with Pierre Boulez's Domaine Musical. He was the first to perform the complete solo piano music of Arnold Schoenberg, which he recorded for the Véga label.

Jacobs continued his active participation in the new music scene when he returned to the United States in 1960. Aaron Copland said "[h]e brings to his piano playing a passion for the contemporary, and a breadth of musical and general culture such as is rare."

His recitals were predominantly devoted to the most recent music, although he also played Baroque harpsichord music, having come to love the sound of the instrument through his involvement in performances of Elliott Carter's *Double Concerto for Harpsichord and Piano with Two Orchestras*.

He frequently gave premieres, including works of Stockhausen, Boulez, Berio, Henze, Messiaen, Sessions, Carter, and many others. He also became known for the clarity and emotion he gave to the late Beethoven & Schubert sonatas. He played with the leading new music ensembles on the New York scene, such as the Contemporary Innovations series organized by Gunther Schuller, the Contemporary Chamber Ensemble, and the Fromm Fellowship Players.

In 1962, Leonard Bernstein appointed him the official pianist of the New York Philharmonic, and in 1974, added official harpsichordist to Jacobs' title. Jacobs remained in those positions until his death.

He was an active teacher, and although he taught frequently at Tanglewood, the Mannes School, and the Manhattan School of Music, his lasting affiliation was at Brooklyn College of the City University of New York, beginning in 1968, also remaining there until death. He was by all accounts exceptionally energetic, constantly organizing concerts and lecture series. He tended to stay in New York, rather than undertake the life of a touring concert virtuoso.

He recorded for several labels. Among his most cherished LPs were the fifteen released on the Nonesuch label, including music of Schoenberg, Debussy, Stravinsky, Carter, Messiaen, Ravel, Thompson, Bartók, Mozart, and Beethoven, and especially the original piano music of Ferruccio Busoni, recorded between 1976 and 1979. (Although some of these recordings were reissued when Nonesuch revived as a compact disc label, the highly regarded Busoni series' rights reverted elsewhere and remained out of print for nearly twenty years until they reappeared on the Arbiter label in 2000, along with some of his other hard-to-find piano recordings.)

Sometime before April 1982, he began suffering from exhaustion and other symptoms of what was called the "mystery disease" that appeared to afflict the homosexual male community. Shortly before his death in 1983, the disease was named AIDS, and Jacobs was one of its first prominent artist victims. —*Joseph Stevenson*

Recommended:

- ○ **Legendary Busoni Recordings** / Jacobs / 1979 / Arbiter 124
- ○ **Debussy: Préludes** / Jacobs / 1997 / Nonesuch 79474
- ○ **Schoenberg: Piano Music** / Jacobs / 1975 / Nonesuch 71309

René Jacobs

b. Oct. 30, 1946, Ghent, Belgium
Conductor, Countertenor

René Jacobs has been highly successful in a unique dual career as a countertenor and conductor, specializing in vocal music of the Baroque period.

He was a chorister in the Cathedral of his home town of Ghent. Also the home of conductor Philippe Herreweghe, Ghent was a center of the movement to restore older music to the repertoire in authentic style performances. Jacobs studied classical philology at the University of Ghent while continuing his studies of singing in Brussels. He became acquainted with the Kuijken brothers (leading Baroque instrumentalists), Gustav Leonhardt (a top conductor on the authentic instruments scene), and Alfred Deller (a pioneering countertenor). They advised him to continue preparing for a singing career and correctly analyzed his voice as suitable for extension into the countertenor range. Jacobs' interest in Baroque music stems in part from his vocal type: many leading Baroque operatic roles were written for high male voices, either natural altos (countertenors) or artificial (castrati). Jacobs' growing fame as a countertenor led him to become a scholar of Baroque vocal music.

In 1977 he began an association with the Harmonia Mundi France record company, starting with performances with the Concerto Vocale. His early Harmonia Mundi records included vocal chamber music by Cesti, d'India, Ferrari, Marenzio, Lambert, Guéderon, and others.

Soon afterwards his studies led him to conducting. Among his recordings and live performances, many of which were the first performances of these works in centuries, are Cesti's *Orontea*, Cavalli's *Xerxe and Giasone*, Monteverdi's *L'Incoronazione di Poppea* and *Il Ritorno d'Ulisse in Patria*, Handel's *Flavio* and *Giulio Cesare*, Gluck's *Le Cinese* and *Echo und Narziss*, Mozart's *La Finta Semplice*, and Conti's *Don Chisciotte in Sierra Morena*. He performed in the complete operas of Monteverdi for the Salzburg Festival. As a conductor, he frequently appears with the Concerto Köln, the Orchestra of the Age of Enlightenment, Akademie für alte Musik Berlin, the Nederlands Kamerkoor, and the RIAS-Kammerchor.

He has made over a hundred recordings and won many of the major classical music record awards as both conductor and singer, including the Edison Award, Vivaldi Prize, the Gramophone Award, the Deutscher Schallplattenpreis, and the International Record Critics Award.

In 1991 he was appointed artistic director of the opera programs of the Festwochen der Alten Musik of Innsbruck, and teaches Baroque interpretation at the Schola Cantorum Basiliensis. —*Joseph Stevenson*

Recommended:

- ○ **Monteverdi: Il Ritorno d'Ulisse in Patria** / Jacobs (cond.), Hill, Visse, Hunt, Hogman, Concerto Vocale / HM 2901427/29

- **Graun: Cleopatra & Cesare** / Jacobs (cond.), Dawson, Vermillion, Williams, Popken, RIAS-Kammerchor, Cologne Concerto / HM 2901561/63
- **Telemann: Orpheus** / Jacobs (cond.), Ziesak, Poulenard, Roschmann, Kiehr, RIAS-Kammerchor, Berlin Academy for Early Music / HM 2901618/19
- **Cavalli: La Calisto** / Jacobs (cond.), Bayo, Ragon, Visse, Keenlyside, Concerto Vocale / HM 2901515/17
- **René Jacobs, countertenor** / Jacobs, Junghanel, Kuijken, Kimura, Verelst, Concerto Vocale / HM 2908033

Jacopo da Bologna

b. 1300s, Bologna, Italy (?), **d.** 1386 (?), Aragon, Spain (?)

Composer

An Italian composer and theorist, Jacopo da Bologna exerted a profound influence on the major figures of fourteenth century Italian music (known as Trecento music). Thirty-four vocal compositions can be securely attributed to him, including the earliest-known three-part, non-canonic Italian madrigals. His madrigal *Non al suo amante* is the only extant musical setting of a poem by the great Petrarch (1304–74) by a contemporary. Jacopo is also the author of a treatise on mensural notation in the French manner, *L'arte del biscanto misurato secondo el maestro Jacopo da Bologna.*

Although he held important positions in powerful courts, no biographical documents have survived. Only the barest information can be gleaned from references to living persons and events in his songs. He was apparently employed by the Visconti family of Milan from 1339 to 1360, save for a brief period spent at the court of Mastino II della Scala in Verona, around 1350. He left no traces after 1360, although the court of Aragon in Spain employed a dancing master of the same name between 1378 and 1386.

The texts of Jacopo's songs depict courtly matters and events. Several of his contemporaries, primarily Giovanni da Cascia and Piero, wrote songs with near-identical subject matter (composers were apparently competing with each other for courtly favors!). The copious references to living persons found therein establishes a fairly reliable chronology of Jacopo's works.

Jacopo composed at a time when polyphonic techniques were in their infancy. His musical settings show a clear stylistic evolution over the years, indicating a conscious effort to develop and refine his craft. The early madrigals, mostly in two parts, are characteristic of "primitive" polyphony: quasi-improvisational writing containing many perfect consonances over a plodding tenor, mostly in long notes. The three-part writing from this period is rudimentary at best, with two upper voices in parallel motion above the tenor. The polyphony of his later works shows much greater control and sophistication. The voices are more balanced and independent, motivically related through improved imitative techniques. More attention is paid, too, to the overall shape of the piece, with carefully worked-out formal divisions which underline the text.

Manuscript evidence indicates that his works were widely circulated in northern Italy and Tuscany, and highly regarded long after his death. His ideal of melodic suavity, his refined artistry, and theoretical scholarship were immensely influential throughout the fourteenth century. *—Natalie Boisvert*

Overview of Works

The flowering of Italian musical composition in the age of Petrarch and Giotto was led by the three northern composers: Maestro Piero, Giovanni da Cascia, and Jacopo da Bologna. Jacopo, like the others, seems to have taken native vernacular traditions—in his case preeminently the madrigal—and codified a strong musical tradition about them. Jacopo's 34 surviving works comprise 25 madrigals for two voices, seven madrigals and cacce for three voices, a single lauda (the incomplete *Nel mio parler di questa donn' eterna*), and a Latin motet (*Lux purpurata raddiis*) in praise of his Milanese patron Luchino Visconti.

Some eclecticism of practice in his works may be due to his interest in music theory; Jacopo was one of the few composers of his time to leave theoretical writings in prose. It may also stem from his exposure to the music of the French "Ars nova," as seen in his unique tritextual madrigal *Aquil' altera*, or in his fetching use of the technique of hocket to represent the cooing of a turtledove in *Fenice fu'e vissi.* Jacopo, Piero, and Giovanni da Cascia apparently participated in musical contests among themselves when residing together at the Veronese court, composing a madrigal cycle together, and setting a group of texts with similar hidden references to local figures in Milan and Verona. Throughout his life, he seems to have sought a suavity of melodic writing (which would stylistically help to pave the way for Francesco Landini and Bartolino da Padova).

In Jacopo's hands, the Italian Trecento madrigal evolved its classic form. Two or more tercets—the lines containing either seven or eleven syllables—are followed by a "Ritornello" in a contrasting meter; both voices carry this text. The most common procedure sets each line of text to a phrase consisting of a held consonance, followed by a flowering of long and rapid melismatic writing, a burst of syllabic declamation, and a final melismatic approach to the cadence. Examples of the balance between syllabic and melismatic music may be seen in Jacopo's *In su bei fiori* and *Un bel sparver.* In other madrigals, he experimented with closer motivic relationships between the two voices; this is the case in his famous contemporaneous setting of Petrarch's *Non al suo amante*, and more clearly in the similarly well-known *Fenice fu'e vissi.* Another frequent stylistic trait of Jacopo's (which would also resurface in the music of Landini) is a transition melody in a single voice which links two phrases, as seen in *O cieco mondo.* *—Timothy Dickey*

Recommended:

- **Jacopo da Bologna** / PAN, Ens. Project Ars Nova / 2001 / Ars Musici 1274
- **Codex Faenza** / Posch (cond.), Unicorn Ens. / 1998 / Naxos 553618

Leoš Janáček

b. Jul. 3, 1854, Hukvaldy, Moravia (Czech Rep.), **d.** Aug. 12, 1928, Moravská Ostrava, Czechoslovakia

Composer: Opera, Orchestral, Concerto, Keyboard, Chamber Music, Choral, Vocal

Leoš Janáček (1854–1928) is regarded as the greatest Czech composer of the early twentieth century. In his early works, which included the opera *Sárka* (1888), and numerous vocal and instrumental works, Janáček followed a traditional, Romantic idiom, typical of late nineteenth century music. Having completed *Sárka*, however, Janáček immersed himself in the folk music of his native Moravia, gradually developing an original compositional style. Eschewing regular metrical phrasing, Janáček developed a declamatory method of setting the voice that follows the natural rhythmic patterns of the Czech language. Characteristically, Janáček allowed these patterns to inform the music itself. In addition, Janáček's harmonies, forms and orchestration are highly idiosyncratic. His music favors repetitive patterns, often set in stark contrast to longer, more lyrical, lines, or large blocks of sound. Dramatic effects are attained with minimal thematic or contrapuntal elaboration. The result is music of great rhythmic drive, sharp contrasts, and an intricate, montage-like texture. Exemplifying Janáček's radical stylistic transformation is his tragic opera *Jenůfa* (1904), based on a story of jealousy, murder, and innocence.

At first unknown outside of Moravia, where he was recognized primarily as a teacher, conductor, and champion of folk music, Janáček first gained national and international fame with the Prague production of *Jenůfa* in 1916. The success of *Jenůfa* in Prague tremendously energized the composer, who, in his sixties, experienced an astonishing creative surge, composing several masterpieces. Janáček's euphoric state of mind could be attributed to two factors. First of all, after the foundation, in 1918, of the Czechoslovak state, Janáček became a national celebrity. The second, and perhaps more important, factor, was Janáček's affection for Kamila Stösslová, a considerably younger married woman. While his ardor was not reciprocated, Janáček's passion for Kamila undoubtedly simulated his creativity. Janáček's modern fame rests on his four last operas, *Kát'a Kabanová* (1921), *The Cunning Little Vixen* (1924), *The Makropulos Affair* (1926) and the posthumously premiered *From the House of the Dead* (1930). What makes these works outstanding is Janáček's profound dramatic sense, which allows his operas, in spite of their brevity, to effectively communicate a complex plot. The dramatic effect is heightened by the composer's ability to adapt his music to the tonal and rhythmic characteristics of the Czech language. The last four operas in particular are perfectly paced for the right dramatic impact. In addition, Janáček drew on the inner resources of music and speech to convey complex feelings and emotional states to his listeners. Janáček's extraordinary power in translating profound psychological insights into music truly comes to the fore in The *Makropoulos Affair*, based on a work by Karel Capek, a story about a woman with the gift of eternal youth. In 1926, Janáček, whose early interest in Moravian folk music developed into an effort to grasp Slavic musical traditions in their totality, composed his *Glagolitic Mass*, a work aiming to express the profound spiritual bonds underlying the seemingly disparate cultural traditions of the Slavic nations (the term "glagolitic" refers to one of the early alphabets of Old Slavic). During his final creative period, Janáček also composed a small number of exceptional chamber works, including the two string quartets and the *Sinfonietta.* In addition to his work as a composer, Janáček actively contributed to his country's musical life as a teacher, critic, and organizer. Founder of the Brno Organ School (later to become the Brno Conservatory), director of the Czech Philharmonic Orchestra, teacher at the State Conservatory of Prague, and initiator of many musical festivals, Janáček greatly enriched Eastern European music education and culture. *—Zoran Minderovic*

OPERA

The Cunning Little Vixen (Príhody Lisky Bystrousky) (Jan. 22, 1922–Oct. 10, 1923; revised 1924)

The story of the Cunning Little Vixen originally appeared in the Czech newspaper *Lidove Noviny* (Popular Daily), as prose written by staffer Rudolf Tesnohlidek to accompany drawings by Stanislav Lolek. Leos Janáček was a regular reader of *Lidove Noviny*, and when the story came out in serialized form in 1920, he recognized its potential for operatic treatment. Janáček's housekeeper wrote in her memoirs that she had introduced Janáček to the serial, but the truth of this claim has been disputed.

The idea of composing a work on a story based in the natural world happily coincided with Janáček's 1921 purchase of a house in the country (a luxury which, until then, he had been unable to afford), and once he had adapted the libretto, work went swiftly. By January 1924, the opera was complete, and it premiered in Brno on November 6 of that year. Janáček modified Tesnohlidek's story considerably, condensing it, shifting its chronology, and changing the ending. The libretto contains some chronological impossibilities and confusing references as a result of Janáček's manipulations; characteristically, Janáček cared more for the spirit of the story than the letter of logic.

The work is difficult to stage convincingly, since there are adult singing roles for the fox, for another fox who becomes her husband, and for a badger, a dog, some chickens, and other animals, all on the same stage, with a a variety of human characters who observe and even capture Sharp-Ears. In the immensely touching final scene, Sharp-Ears has died, and her latest cubs carry on with the same sort of endearing comic antics as her mother did. Janáček had a unique penchant for offbeat operatic subjects. In this case he was surely led to this story by an ardent love of nature that pours from every measure of this magical score. It may play clumsily on stage, but when you hear a recording you can stage it in your imagination. *The Cunning Little Vixen* is perhaps this composer's most lovable work.

Janáček's score makes extensive use of motivic variation, as he maneuvers his speech melodies into different, related forms to suggest parallels between parts of the story. For example, the mournful melody played when the Vixen is captured in the first act recurs to color the penultimate scene's human longings. But the score of *The Cunning Little Vixen* is distinguished primarily by its brilliance and sunniness. Textures are light and bright; sometimes, as in the Ballet of the Blue Dragonfly, they seem almost transparent. Humor is embraced along with pathos, and the deceptions of the Vixen are treated with the same sense of affectionate play as her forays into love and sensuality. Even the death of the Vixen seems graceful: it is rendered simply with a cymbal-gunshot and a brief silence, The final scene, in which the Forester meditates on the cycle of life, is fearlessly optimistic. *The Cunning Little Vixen* is one of Janáček's freshest and most vital works. *—AMG*

Synopsis:

Act One. The opera opens up in a wooded glen near Brno in the summer, about 1920. The tired Forester decides to lie down on the grass for a brief nap. There is much activity around him, from the singing of the cricket and grasshopper to the antics of the frog, who pursues a mosquito. The frog's presence arouses the interest of Bystrouska, the Vixen, who begins to chase him. In his efforts to escape he wakes the Forester, who immediately captures the Vixen. He takes her home for his children's amusement. There the Vixen is harassed by a horny dog and by the teasing of the children. She also observes with disgust the servitude of the hens to the cock. Bystrouska sets a trap for the cock and kills him. The forester attempts to punish her, but she bites her way free of the encumbering leash and escapes.

Act Two. The Vixen returns to her forest neighborhood and tosses the Badger out of his cell, but only after enduring a considerable beating from the feisty foe. It is now winter, and the Forester, Priest, and Schoolmaster play a game of cards at the Inn, the former taunting the latter about rumors in the neighborhood of his possible marriage. But the Schoolmaster turns the tables, poking fun at the Forester over letting the Vixen escape. After the Priest and Schoolmaster depart, the Innkeeper, Pasek, reprises the subject of the Vixen. The Forester, irked that the animal had outsmarted him, leaves to find her. A little while later in the woods, with the Priest and the tipsy Schoolmaster in the area, he shoots in vain at the Vixen Spring. In her burrow, the Vixen brags to the Fox about her recent exploits and escape. After sharing a recent kill by the Fox—a rabbit—the two declare their love for each other and decide to marry.

Act Three. In autumn, Harasta, a poultry dealer and poacher, walks through the forest and discovers the remains of a rabbit. The Forester comes along and, admonishing Harasta not to poach, notices the dead rabbit, determining that its demise was the work of Bystrouska. He lays a trap for the cunning creature, but the Vixen finds it later while she is playing with her cubs. She and the Fox deride the Forester for his feeble attempt to catch them. They hear Harasta approaching, carrying a basket of poultry. The Vixen feigns an injury and cleverly lures Harasta away from his haul. She and her family dine on the chicken, but the angry poacher begins shooting wildly. One of his bullets mortally wounds the Vixen.

At the Inn, the Schoolmaster curses his luck that he did not win the hand of a certain village girl, Terynka, and the Priest, now stationed at a new parish, bemoans his lot in a letter about loneliness. The Forester, too, stews about his advancing age and soon departs. As in the opening scene, he takes a nap in the wooded glen, but now he dreams of a Vixen who looks like Bystrouska. He reaches out for her but seizes a frog instead, who, it turns out, is the grandson of the frog who awakened him in the first act. *—Robert Cummings*

Recommended:

○ **Janáček: The Cunning Little Vixen** / Mackerras (cond.), Popp, Novak, Blachut, Jedlicka, Vienna PO / 1986 / Decca 417129

○ **Janáček: The Cunning Little Vixen** / Neumann (cond.), Hajossyova, Benackova, Novak, Prusa, Czech PO / Supraphon 103471

From the House of the Dead (Z mrtvého domu) (Feb. 18, 1927–Jun. 20, 1928)

From the House of the Dead was the last opera of Czech composer Leos Janáček. Even for a composer with a track record of making great operas out of unusual material, it was an especially odd choice for an opera. Based on Dostoyevsky's novel of the same title, *From the House of the Dead* is almost unrelievedly grim, almost without character development, almost without dramatic action in any conventional sense, and for the first time in any opera since Monteverdi, almost completely without a female character. And yet it succeeds brilliantly both as a story and as music, capping Janáček's career with one of his masterpieces.

Set in a Siberian prison camp in the middle years of the nineteenth century, *From the House of the Dead* is in three acts. But while each act is concluded by a wonderful *coup de théâtre*, the essential structure of the opera comprises a series of monologues by the various characters describing their crimes and punishments. Equally important, however, is the role of the chorus. Like Beethoven's *Fidelio*—another prison opera—the chorus is as much a character in the drama as any of the soloists. Janáček's music for *From the House of the Dead* is an unusually extreme example of his late style: hard, harsh, aggressively modernist in its harmonies, brutal and frenetic in its rhythms, but essentially lyrical in its themes and melodies. Although these themes and melodies are terse and often elusive, they are always absolutely pertinent for the expressive needs of the character and always stunningly lyrical in their effect. Janáček's scoring is of chamberlike transparency, with a prominent part for the percussion section that includes chains, appropriately enough for a prison opera. Although left not quite complete at his unexpected death in 1928, the score of *From the House of the Dead* is perfectly performable in the state Janáček left it. *—James Leonard*

Synopsis:

Act One. This episodic, almost plotless story takes place around 1860 and is set in a Siberian prison located near the Irtysh River. In the opening scene the prisoners enter the compound's courtyard and discuss the new inmate, who soon arrives. His name is Alexander Petrovic Gorjancikov, a nobleman imprisoned for political reasons. When the prison governor learns the reason for his incarceration during an interrogation, he orders him beaten.

A captured eagle, with an injured wing, is both taunted and admired by the prisoners in the courtyard. Soon the governor directs the prisoners to work; about half of them depart for supervised tasks on the outside, the remainder staying behind to do chores inside. Among the latter group is Skuratov, a former cobbler, whose singing and dancing angers fellow inmate Luka Kuzmich. When the former falls to the ground exhausted from his wild play, the latter begins recounting his experiences in prison. He tells of inciting a riot among the prisoners and how during the uprising he killed a cruel officer. For his part in the action he was merely flogged. At this point, Gorjancikov is brought back, weak and bloody from his beating.

Act Two. It is summertime, a year later. The prisoners are at work on a boat near the bank of the Irtysh River. Gorjancikov offers to teach the Tartar boy, Alyeya, to read and write. The workday soon ends, and food is brought in by the locals as presents (it is Easter Sunday); the Governor arrives with the Priest, who blesses the meal before the two depart. While the prisoners dine, Skuratov gives an account of his murder of the wealthy watchmaker his girlfriend, Luisa, was pressured to marry.

After they have eaten, the prisoners stage two plays, Kedril and Don Juan and The Miller's Beautiful Wife. Later, Gorjancikov and Alyeya are drinking tea, and the quarrelsome Small Prisoner starts a fight because he resents Gorjancikov's refined manner. He attacks Alyeya, though, wounding him severely in the head.

Act Three. In the prison hospital, Gorjancikov stands watch over the delirious Alyeya. Cekunov is nearby, which draws the wrath of the dying Luka. She rails about Cekunov's sycophantic ways with Gorjancikov. Sapkin recounts an incident about an interrogating policeman who nearly yanked his ears off. The demented Skuratov cries out for his sweetheart.

It is night, and the hospital room is quiet until Siskov begins telling a brutal story at the behest of Cerevin. The story concerns his former friend, Filka Morozov, and his girlfriend, Akulka. Filka declares he has deflowered her and will not marry her, but Siskov does, believing she is innocent. Told otherwise by Filka, he beats her on their wedding night, but soon determines that she is a virgin after all. He later learns from her that she is still in love with Filka, and he kills her. Luka dies as Siskov ends his tale, a tale in which he viewed Luka as Filka.

The next morning Gorjancikov is taken to the Governor who, drunk, declares his release. Alyeya, somewhat improved, enters, and the two bid their farewells. As Gorjancikov departs, the prisoners set the eagle free, its wing having fully recovered. *—Robert Cummings*

Recommended:

○ **Janáček: From The House Of The Dead** / Neumann (cond.), Blachut, Novak, Berman, Jindrak, Czech PO / Supraphon 102941

Jenůfa (1894–1903; revised Oct. ??, 1903)

Jenůfa eventually became Leoš Janáček's greatest triumph, in terms both of its artistry and of the advance it generated in the composer's reputation. The triumph was slow to come in both cases. Janáček first encountered the play *Jeji pastorkyna*

("Her Foster Daughter"), by Gabriela Preissova, sometime in the early 1890s, and began working on the opera in earnest in 1894. However, the work was not completed until 1903. The delay was partly caused by Janáček's busy schedule; during this period, he held teaching posts at three institutions, organized exhibitions and concerts, and prepared folk song editions. The prolonged sickness and eventual death at age 20 of Janáček's only surviving child, Olga, also doubtless slowed the composition of the opera. (During her last days, Olga asked her father to play *Jenůfa* on the piano, a request he gladly granted.) Yet the best explanation is that *Jenůfa* seems to have pushed Janáček toward a reconsideration of how to create drama and how to portray character in music. The intense work that resulted from this long creative effort remains preeminent in Janáček's oeuvre.

The play's Moravian setting doubtless helped to inspire Janáček, and the plot teems with dramatic moments. Briefly, Jenůfa is expecting Steva's baby, but after a quarrel the jilted Laca slashes Jenůfa's cheek, rendering her unappealing to Steva. Jenůfa's powerful stepmother the Kostelnicka persuades Laca to marry Jenůfa; Laca balks when he hears that Jenůfa has just had Steva's baby, so Kostelnicka tells him the baby has died, and drowns it herself in a fit of shame and desperation. At Jenůfa and Laca's wedding feast, someone finds the baby; Jenůfa admits it is hers, and Steva is disgraced. Kostelnicka begs forgiveness and freely gives herself up to the law; Laca, impressed by Jenůfa's bravery, offers to join her in a new life.

Musically, *Jenůfa* marked the first time Janáček based an entire work on his principle of the melodic curves of speech. This principle was based on a devotion to realism in musical portrayal, and indeed many of these melodies were reduced by Janáček from actual conversations. As a result, there are very few long, broad melodies in *Jenůfa* (although Jenůfa's "Ave Maria" is a notable exception); instead, words and phrases are repeated often and throughout. This feature lends an obsessive feel to the score—very much attuned to the material, and imparting a dramatic immediacy that strikes hardest at moments of the most import, such as Kostelnicka's confession and the cathartic finale that follows. Janáček also uses some of the speech melodies as motives; one of these, representing guilt, appears in the opera over and over, each time with additional impact. *Jenůfa* was premiered in Janáček's home city of Brno in 1903, but took over a decade to reach the opera house in Prague; after a long struggle, the premiere in the Czech capital was a rousing success, and led to international performances and deserved acclaim for the work and its composer. *—Andrew Lindemann Malone*

Synopsis:

Act One. Outside a mill, Jenůfa is pregnant by Steva and is anxiously waiting to hear whether the local draft board will give him a deferment so that they can marry before her condition shows. Laca, Steva's stepbrother, teases her over Steva, and Burya scolds her for being absentminded. The boy Jano runs in, thanking her for teaching him how to read, and she promises him more books. The Miller scolds Laca for mocking Jenůfa, and when he comments on her beauty, Laca bursts out in a fit of ill-concealed jealousy. When they hear Steva has received deferment, Jenůfa is overjoyed, but Laca is disappointed. Steva comes in, drunk and accompanied by villagers and recruits, and dances wildly with Jenůfa. The Kostelnicka comes in and rebukes him for his drunkenness and wildness, and she recalls her own wretched life with a violent drunkard before his death. She insists that Steva remain sober for one year before he can marry Jenůfa, to her step-daughter's dismay, and sends him to sleep it off. Steva and Jenůfa are left alone, and he laughs when she begs that they marry immediately. When he leaves, drunkenly rhapsodizing over her beautiful face, Laca, who has overheard, first taunts her and then tries to kiss her. In their struggle, he slashes her face with his knife.

Act Two. In the Kostelnickas' house, six months later, Jenůfa has borne the child while the Kostelnicka has told everyone that she is in Vienna. She gives Jenůfa a sleeping potion and waits for Steva, whom she has sent for, to persuade him to marry Jenůfa. She is ready for the possibility that he will not, and intends to ask Laca in that case. When Steva comes, he freely admits that he has behaved badly and offers to support the child financially, but he has never wanted her as a mother-in-law and no longer wants Jenůfa now that she is disfigured by the knife scar. In any case, he is now engaged to Karolka. Despite her anger and pleas he leaves, and Laca comes to ask for news about Jenůfa and express his remorse for having injured her. He says he loves her and wants to marry her, but is unable to face the idea of raising Steva's son as his own. The Kostelnicka desperately tells him the baby died. When he leaves, she rushes outside with the child. When Jenůfa wakes up, she looks for the child and suddenly imagines she is falling into a frozen pit. She prays, and when the Kostelnicka returns, she tells Jenůfa she was asleep for two days, during which the baby died. Laca returns and Jenůfa unenthusiastically agrees to marry him. When the wind blows a window open, the Kostelnicka thinks she sees Death looking inside.

Act Three. Two months later, it is Jenůfa's wedding day, but she is downcast and the Kostelnicka is agitated. Laca arrives, and left alone with her, he expresses his love, and she expresses gratitude, but nothing else. Steva and Karolka arrive; he is uncomfortable while she is chattering. Jenůfa's friends sing a wedding song and they kneel for Grandmother Burya's blessing. The ceremony is interrupted by shouts from outside, and Jano runs in, crying that a baby's body has been found in the river. The Kostelnicka frantically tries to keep Jenůfa from going to see the corpse, but Jenůfa runs outside and returns, screaming that they have taken her baby from its grave. The villagers immediately think she has killed it, and, despite Laca's attempts to protect her, demand that she be stoned. The Kostelnicka then confesses to the crime, and Jenůfa, realizing that the Kostelnicka thought she was helping her, forgives her and raises her to her feet. The Mayor leads the Kostelnicka away, and Jenůfa turns to Laca, freeing him from his promise of marriage, as she has now been publicly disgraced, and telling him that she intends to leave the village. He insists that he wishes to remain at her side, and realizing that now they both deeply love one another, they leave together. *—Ann Feeney*

Recommended:

- ○ **Janáček: Jenůfa** / Haitink (cond.), Mattila, Silja, Hadley, Silvasti, Randova / 2002 / Erato 45330
- ○ **Janáček: Jenůfa** / Mackerras (cond.), Söderström, Ochman, Dvorsky, Randova, Popp / 1985 / Decca 414483
- ○ **Janáček: Jenůfa** / Vogel (cond.), Jelinková, Krásová, Blachut, Zídek / Supraphon 3331

Kát'a Kabanová (1919–1921)

Written between 1919 and 1921, the text for this sixth Janáček opera was written by the composer and based on the stage drama *The Storm* (1859) by the great Russian realist Alexander Nikolaievich Ostrovsky (1823–86). The basic story is that of a pure soul, Kát'a, who finds herself caught in a world between the "samodurs" (despotic rulers) or rich reactionaries of the merchant class who have absolute authority over others, and their lackeys and hangers-on—including Kát'a's lover and husband, who accept cruel treatment because they have hope of taking over the power and wealth after the deaths of the tyrants. As in most of Janáček's vocal writing, the vocal lines are built around the melodic curves of speech created by thought and emotion. The words are not forced to conform to symmetrical melodies that would disturb their natural inflection as found in ordinary speech. Janáček, democrat and humanist, before writing the opera even went on a pilgrimage to Hostyn and "spent the night there bitten by insects, experienced a storm, trampled on sleepy pilgrims in the dark. But the masts on the Volga loomed high and the waters of the Volga in the moonlight were as white as the heart and soul of Kát'a." Even written in a tonal style, the clear lines and Slavic colors of Janáček's dynamic style create a unique sound landscape, like the music of Mussorgsky and Borodin and Glinka meeting a twentieth century Czech mind passionately interested in psychology, truth, and human freedom. *—"Blue Gene" Tyranny*

Synopsis:

Act One. Scene One. Kudjras invites Glasa to join him in admiring the Volga river, but she finds nothing special about the sight. As they are arguing over the worth of the view, Kudjrash notices the merchant Dikoj coming toward them. Dikoj is accompanied by his nephew Boris, whom he is bitterly scolding. When Dikoj has left, Boris tells Kudrjash the story of how he became dependent upon the abusive Dikoj; if he ever acts disrespectfully toward him, Boris and his sister lose their inheritance. Boris also whispers that he has fallen in love with a married woman, Kát'a Kabanová. Kabanicha, the young Varvara, Tichon, and Tichon's wife Kát'a are spotted coming along. Kabanicha is scolding her son Tichon that he obviously prefers his wife to his mother and insisting that he should go all the way to the Kazan market for her if he loved her. Kát'a takes offense and storms off into the house. Kabanicha continues her tirade awhile, then also retires. Now Varvara lays into Tichon for not standing up to his mother. He then wanders off to get drunk.

Scene Two. In the Kabanov household, Kát'a and Varvara are sewing. Kát'a talks about the changes in her personality since her marriage. All the joys of her young heart have faded, while a host of sinful desires have taken their place. Varvara encourages Kát'a in these desires. Alone with Tichon, Kát'a begs him not to go to Kazan. She is afraid something terrible will happen during his absence. Kabanicha dictates to Tichon commands that are meant for Kát'a, including "No gazing at young people." Tichon is deeply puzzled by all this but goes along with it anyhow.

Act Two. Scene One. Kát'a, Kabanicha, and Varvara are in the alcove, working at their embroidery. It is late afternoon. Kabanicha chastises Kát'a for not being more upset at Tichon's departure. When Kabanicha leaves the room, Varvara offers Kát'a a key for the garden, should she wish to have a secret meeting there. Varvara also promises that if she sees Boris, she'll tell him to meet Kát'a at the gate. Kát'a's crisis of conscience is short lived; she vows to meet Boris that very night, whatever the consequences.

Scene Two. It is nighttime on an overgrown bank above the garden. Kudjrash is singing to himself on a little guitar. Boris arrives, nervous, explaining that he was told by a girl to meet Kát'a here. Varvara is heard singing as she approaches. She tells Boris to be patient, then slips away with Kudjrash. When Kát'a comes out of the darkness toward him, trembling with fear, he begs not to be sent away; she hesitates, then throws herself on his neck, crying, "You are my life!" Kudjrash and Varvara return as Káťa and Boris retreat to the garden. When one o'clock rolls around, Varvara calls the party to a close.

Act Three. Scene One. Inside a ruined building, Kuligin and Kudjrash are taking shelter from the rain. Two weeks have passed. They notice with interest the remnants of murals depicting hell. Dikoj arrives, also seeking shelter. He doesn't quite grasp Kudjrash's quasi-scientific explanation of the nature of storms, holding to his belief that storms are divine punishments. When the rain stops, they all leave. Varvara appears, as does Boris. Distant thunder can be heard, and Káťa comes rushing in, followed by Kudjrash. She is frenetic with guilt. When Kabanicha and Tichon arrive, she throws herself at their feet, spills out a desperate confession, then flees into the storm.

Scene Two. It is dusk, at a lonely spot near the Volga. Tichon, with Glasa, is searching for Káťa by lantern light. Varvara and Kudjrash appear to one side of the scene. They agree to run off to Moscow together. Káťa appears. Her monologue, unheard by the others, expresses her regret at her confession and her desire to see Boris once more before she dies. Boris, by lucky accident, hears her call. He announces that Dikoj is sending him to Siberia, and she says that Tichon has turned to drink and beats her. When the moment comes to part, Káťa asks Boris to give alms to every beggar he sees in repentance. They embrace one final time, and Boris reluctantly goes away. Now Káťa throws herself into the river; she is seen by a passerby and Glasa and Tichon try to rescue her, but it is far too late. Tichon accuses Kabanicha of destroying Káťa and throws himself, sobbing, over the wet corpse, which Dikoj has spitefully laid out on the riverbank as he says "Here is your Katerina." —*Donato Mancini*

Recommended:

- ○ **Janáček: Káťa Kabanová** / Mackerras (cond.), Soderstrom, Dvorsky, Jedlicka, Svehla, Vienna PO / 1989 / Decca 421852
- ○ **Janáček: Káťa Kabanová** / Mackerras (cond.), Benackova, Kopp, Kundlak, Straka, Prague National Theater / Supraphon 32912632

The Makropulos Case (Vec Makropulos) (Nov. 11, 1923–Dec. 3, 1925)

In this work Janáček gave the operatic world one of the great roles for dramatic soprano. It is based on a story by pioneering Czech science-fiction writer Karel Capek (who invented the word "robot," by the way); the tale grows from the idea of a longevity serum. In the story, set in 1922, the fascinating opera singer Emelia Marty is interested in finding a will that figures in an inheritance lawsuit because attached to it is a document with the secret of the serum her father, the alchemist Hieronymous Makropulos, had tried on her 321 years earlier, when she was 16. The opera is about the recovery of the document, the unraveling of her secret, and her decision whether or not to prolong her life another 300 years. It is a unique tale, told with deft characterization and a human touch in Janáček's unique style, making use of unusually brief melodies which permit the telling of strong drama faster than in most other composers' operas. It takes a little getting used to Janáček's terse melodic style (which at critical moments often broaden into lovely lyrical outpourings), but this opera proves as fascinating as its heroine. —*Joseph Stevenson*

Synopsis:

Act One. In Dr. Kolenaty's law offices, his clerk, Vitek, is filing papers and muses on the case of Gregor versus Prus, in inheritance case which has been unresolved since 1827. Baron Prus died without any acknowledged legitimate children and without a written will, but the Gregor family claims to be his descendants and rightful heirs, rather than Jaroslav Prus, the other claimant, and descendants of the "Mach Gregor," whom the Baron said he would make his heir. Albert Gregor comes in to ask about any progress. They are interrupted by Vitek's daughter Kristina's arrival. She hopes to become a singer and raves about the great Emilia Marty. Dr. Kolenaty himself enters, bringing Emilia Marty with him. She says that she is interested in the Gregor versus Prus case herself, and when Dr. Kolenaty starts to summarize it, shows as much command of the details as he possesses. She tells them that the missing heir is Ferdinand Gregor, the old Baron Prus' son by Ellian MacGregor, an opera singer. When they ask for any kind of proof, she says that the Baron's lost will, leaving the estate to Gregor, are mixed among the love letters now in Jaroslav's possessions, and Kolenaty is sent to fetch them, though he is dubious that this is the breakthrough she claims it is. Alone with her, Gregor tells her he loves her and asks for more information about his parents. She rejects him, but does ask him to give her any documents, written in Greek, that he might find among the family papers. Kolenaty returns, saying that Emilia was right, but Prus, who comes with him, asks for further proof. Emilia says she has this as well.

Act Two. At the opera house, staff gossip about Emilia. Janek, Jaroslav's son, and Kristina appear, and she flirts with him, but tells him that her career as a singer must come first. Prus enters, looking for Emilia, and Janek and Kristina are overwhelmed by Emilia's presence when she enters. She is irritable, however, and insists on paying Gregor for some jewelry he had given her and asks Janek and Kristina if they have "enjoyed heaven" together, though she says it's never worth it. Count Hauk-Sendorf enters and exclaims at the resemblance between Emilia and a Spanish singer, Eugenia Montez, who had once been his mistress. When she left him, he lost his mind. She seems oddly moved and sings to him in Spanish. She then sends everyone away and Prus questions her about her real name. He wonders why the initials keep "E.M." keep recurring: Ellian MacGregor, Eugenia Montez, Emilia Marty, and the name of the mother in the original documents about Prus' son, Elina Makropulos. He shows her another packet of papers, which he has not opened yet, and she asks to buy them. He leaves, and Gregor returns, again telling her he loves her. She begs him to steal the papers for her, if he truly loves her as he says he does, and he becomes violent and threatens to kill her. She shows him a scar on her neck from another man's murder attempt, and falls asleep as he continues his avowals of love and he leaves. Janek enters, and she now asks him to steal the papers. He is just about persuaded but Prus interrupts. He dismisses Janek and agrees to give her the papers, unopened, if she will sleep with him that night.

Act Three. In her hotel bedroom, Emilia and Prus are dressing. Prus gives Emilia the packet, though he says that she lay in his arms like a cold, dead thing, and she examines it; the contents are indeed what she was hoping for. One of Prus' servants comes to tell him that Janek has killed himself over his hopeless love for Emilia, but she is completely indifferent. Hauk-Sendorf comes to ask her to go to Spain with him, and she agrees, but when the rest of the cast comes in, with a doctor, the doctor leads him off. Kolenaty accuses her of forging the letters proving Gregor's claim; the handwriting is exactly the same as hers. She contemptuously tells him it was indeed Ellian MacGregor who wrote the letter and goes off into another room to finish dressing and have a drink, and they search her luggage. She returns, drunk, and tells Gregor that she is his great-great-great-great grandmother. She was born in Crete in the 16th century, and her father, Hieronymus Makropulos, was Emperor Rudolf's physician. He promised the Emperor an elixir that would prolong his life for 300 years, and Rudolf insisted that she drink it, to prove that it was not poisoned. After she drank it, she fell unconscious and her father was arrested. However, she awakened and since then, has had dozens of different identities. One of these was Ellian MacGregor, and she bore Prus a child, Ferdinand, Gregor's ancestor. Now she will age and die unless she drinks more of the elixir; she had lost the formula and has finally found it in the packet she obtained from Prus. She begins to wither physically, and her mind wandering, prays in Greek, and they begin to believe her story. Now that she has the recipe, and can prolong her life yet again, she has no wish to do so. Life has meaning only if it has an end. She gives the recipe to Kristina, who burns it, and Emilia dies. —*Ann Feeney*

Recommended:

- ○ **Janáček: The Makropulos Case** / Mackerras (cond.), Soderstrom, Blachut, Jedlicka, Krejcik, Vienna PO / 1991 / London 430372
- ○ **Janáček: The Makropulos Case** / Gregor (cond.), Zidek, Berman, Tattermuschova, Koci, Prague National Theatre / Supraphon 108351

ORCHESTRAL

Lachian (Lasské) Dances (1924)

Despite the late publication date, Janáček had actually done most of the work on the *Lachian Dances* back in the late 1880s and early 1890s, when he was studying and collecting the folk music of his native Lachian region. This accounts for the more conventionally Romantic approach to the music, setting it apart from such highly individual masterpieces of Janáček's old age as *Taras Bulba* and the *Sinfonietta*. Still, these dances bear Janáček's thumbprint; they are more rough-hewn, less exuberant than Dvořák's *Slavonic Dances* (on which they are modeled), with the melodies blurted out in shorter phrases linking the music as closely to song or Czech speech as to dance.

The first movement, generically titled "Ancient I," combines a ceremonial wedding dance (Starodávny) with a more turbulent "club dance." The use of violins in their highest register and the graceful deployment of woodwinds show the strong influence of Dvor˘ák's ideas about orchestration. The second movement, "Blessing's Dance," is another ceremonial wedding dance (Pozehnany), this one more bumptious with a strong, four-beat rhythmic figure reminiscent of American Indian music. The "Smith Dance" is a tumultuous piece incorporating timpani thuds and sharp chords meant to imitate a blacksmith at work. "Ancient II" is an essentially stately dance, with hints of the sweeping string writing and chugging rhythms that characterize Janác˘ek's mature work. The title "Celadensky" signifies that the swift, gopak-like fifth movement comes from the Lachian villages of Celadná and Dymák. The concluding "Saw Dance" (Pilky), its prancing outer sections surrounding a swirling center, is derived from a dance associated with autumn preparations for the coming winter. —*James Reel*

Recommended:

- ○ **Janáček** / Huybrechts (cond.), London PO / 1996 / London 448255
- ○ **Janáček: Lachian Dances; Suite; Idyll** / Rybar (cond.), Jilek (cond.), Czech State PO / Supraphon 111520

Sinfonietta ("Military" / "Sokol Festival") (1926)

In 1925, Leoš Janáček sat in an idyllic park on a sunny day and listened to a full-dress military band deliver a lovely performance. Afterward, he became intrigued with the idea of composing some military band fanfares of his own; when the organizers of the Sokol gymnastic festival asked him for "some music," he took the opportunity, and wrote a work entitled *Military Sinfonietta* and dedicated "To the Czechoslovak Armed Forces." Later, Janáček dropped the "Military" designation, and the work is now simply known as the *Sinfonietta.* The great conductor Vaclav Talich led its premiere performance in Prague on June 26, 1926. The patriotism that the military band had inspired found expression in the program Janáček eventually devised for the work, which depicts various scenes from Janáček's adopted home city of Brno in the aftermath of the declaration of Czech independence on October 28, 1918. The first movement features fanfares for orchestral brass; there are actually several increasingly quick themes which develop out of the original fanfare before the Maestoso conclusion, but all of them use the interval of the fifth prominently enough to be instantly recognizable as fanfares. The second movement depicts the castle Spilberk, with its underground dungeons, now controlled by the Czech people. It begins with a dance theme on oboes, accompanied by swirling 32nd notes, but soon introduces a lyrical theme. Both themes are sent on a wild ride of a development which unexpectedly comes to rest, with quiet, pastoral murmurings in the strings and harp supporting lyrical melodies. The dance theme returns to close the movement. The third movement, a depiction of Brno's monastery, features a lyrical theme, but this is interrupted as it is being passed around the orchestra by grim trombone fanfares and arching sprays of notes in the piccolo and flute. The trombone seems to triumph with a burlesque version of the lyrical theme, but the lyrical theme makes one last appearance, delicate and serene. The streets of Brno after liberation are the subject of the fourth movement; Janáček uses a fanfare-like theme as a call to virtually nonstop motion, broken up only by humorous tempo shifts and early entrances in the brass and bells. Brno's town hall is depicted in the triumphal fifth movement. Three flutes play a sad variant of the first fanfare, which is then developed slowly in the winds over a contrasting accompaniment of rushing strings. The work ends with a massive return of the fanfares and a gigantic coda, the brass accompanied by ecstatic orchestral swirls, proclaiming the joy of Czechoslovakia. The *Sinfonietta* is perhaps Janáček's finest orchestral work, and one of the most vibrant and life-affirming works ever written. *—Andrew Lindemann Malone*

Recommended:

- ○ **Czech Philharmonic Orch.** / Belohlavek (cond.), Czech PO / 1990 / Chandos 8897
- ○ **Janáček: Sinfonietta; Bartók: Portraits; The Miraculous Mandarin** / Abbado (cond.), Berlin PO / 1994 / DG 445501
- ○ **Janáček** / Mackerras, Vienna PO / 1996 / London 448255

Suite for string orchestra (1877)

A work from Janáček's early period, the *Suite* for string orchestra stands out as a reflection of Victorian musical taste: genteel, lightweight, sensibly balanced. Not encountered are the large mood swings which characterize his later works. The few surprises that pop up now and then are of a more controlled and modest sort. But the work does have merit in its ability to charm, convey sincere expression, and to imply irony.

Leoš Janáček composed the *Suite* at the age of 23, when the young musician was developing his art, and during a time of relative poverty. Near the end of his studies at the Prague Organ School, Janáček became the conductor of the Brno Music Society in 1876. Several months later, he presented the *Suite* to his collegues, and on December 2, 1877, it was premiered under the composers' direction.

Originally, Janáček had thought of the movements of the work in Baroque terms, naming the six movements Prelude, Allemande, Sarabande, Scherzo, Air, and Finale respectively. On further consideration, the composer dispensed with the Baroque references after realizing the movements did not correspond with the old dance forms.

The opening bars suceed in getting the listener's attention with a powerful unison theme carried in the low strings. The initial angst melts away with the introduction of a delicate melody played by the first violins, which seem to gently pierce through the dark clouds. The 20 or so bars that follow remind one of a more mature Janáček, with the high fluid melody rising above a stream of busy pentatonic figures in the accompaniment. The new theme presented in the second half is now a stately march, somewhat reminiscent of a school alma mater.

The cellos and contrabasses take a break in the second movement. This bit of writing shows Janáček at his most expressive and transparent as he puts the high strings in a vulnerable position. The movement appears simple and straightforward in writing, but tests the intonation of the players.

The third-movement Andante is a simple, bucolic melody, possibly folk song inspired. A bit unexciting for Janáček, the movement comes across as perhaps a product of his student days.

The fourth movement, Presto comes to stir up some nervous activity in D minor with a scherzo reminiscent of Beethoven. A middle section provides some calmer moments, but the fast scherzo returns in abbreviated form to end on a D major chord.

The lower strings are featured more in the fifth movement, in this slow and meditative piece. It almost seems to signal a deeply reflective time in the composer's life. The center of the piece builds modestly. The movement ends in much the way it started.

The sixth movement completes the suite cycle in a satisfying way. In two sections, the piece contrasts a melancholic B minor melody with what could be described as a fragment of a hero's theme, pulling the listener out of self-reflection. There appears to be an element of irony in Janáček's choice of materials, which adds to the tension and to the enjoyment of the *Suite* for string orchestra. *—Franklin Stover*

Recommended:

- ○ **Janáček** / Marriner (cond.), Los Angeles CO / 1996 / London 448255
- ○ **Portals in Time** / Mottl (cond.), Brno CO / 2001 / Klavier 11116

Taras Bulba, rhapsody (1915–1918)

Janáček began this work in 1915, completing it on March 29, 1918. František Neumann conducted the premiere at Brno on October 9, 1921. It is scored for double winds and trumpets, plus piccolo, English horn, contrabassoon, standard brass, strings, harp, organ, timpani, and four percussion. His admiration of pre-Soviet Russia in the early years of World War I led to the composition of *Taras Bulba,* based on the fifteenth century Cossack hero of Nikolai Gogol's "gruesome story" published in 1839.

Taras and his sons, Andrey (or Andri) and Ostap, were sent to besiege the Poles at Dubno, whose voyvode had a daughter Andrey loved in their school days. Seeing her, he defected, whereupon Janáček's rhapsody begins, and so does Jaroslav Vogel's detailed analysis in a still-definitive biography, paraphrased here.

The Death of Andrey. "Sweetly and sadly" the English horn depicts Andrey's inner conflict, followed by his fear of being discovered. The distant sounds of organ and bells "express the prayers and anguish of the besieged" (Janáček's own words). Andrey finally finds his beloved, leading to a "passionate" love scene that starts with the oboe. Amid sounds of fighting outside, a loud, ominous trombone motif tells the son that his father is near. When Andrey joins the battle as a Pole, he comes face to face with Taras; with eyes guiltily downcast. He dismounts and is mortally wounded by his father, who gallops off.

The Death of Ostap. An abrasive string ostinato interrupts a soft, slow harp passage several times, until a two-bar motif in the bass introduces another battle on horseback. Now it is Ostap's turn to die. Captured, he is taken to Warsaw where the Poles dance "a wild mazur[ka] of victory," related to the battle motif earlier in this movement. Ostap, hideously tortured (the E flat clarinet shrieks over fortissimo string tremolos), cries out to his father who has infiltrated the onlookers and pushed forward (the trombone motif from movement 1), but just as suddenly vanishes, to the crowd's amazement. The movement ends with the beheading of Ostap.

The Prophecy and Death of Taras Bulba. After cutting a swath through Polish forces Taras, too, is finally captured and sentenced to death by burning. Nailed to a tree, he laments his lost freedom. This develops into "a mournfully majestic melody over undulating sextuplets in the lower strings, as though Taras were thinking, for the last time, of his leaderless warriors while the flames leap higher. . . ." The enemy dances "a wild krakoviak" around him, but his pain is eased by the daring escape of his warriors, who leap on horseback into the River Dnyster. Alone, as fanfares echo in the distance, Taras has a vision of his people and their "indomitable strength." Bells and organ "herald a majestic apotheosis of Russia," whose soaring new melody is "like the arch of a rainbow of peace, spanning the earth." *—Roger Dettmer*

Recommended:

- ○ **Janáček** / Mackerras (cond.), Vienna PO / 1996 / London 448255
- ○ **Janáček: Glagolitic Mass; Taras Bulba** / Ancerl (cond.), Czech PO / 2002 / Supraphon 3667
- ○ **Janáček: Taras Bulba; Jealousy** / Jilek (cond.), BRNO State PO / Supraphon 1521

CONCERTO

Concertino (1925)

Leoš Janáček's *Concertino* for piano, two violins, clarinet, French horn, and bassoon was proximally inspired by the pianist Jan Herman's performance of his *Diary of One Who Vanished*; the performance instilled in Janáček the desire to write a concerto for piano, and he would eventually dedicate the score to Herman. The *Concertino* dates from Janáček's exceptionally fertile last years, and Janáček wrote that "the whole thing comes from the youthful mood of the [wind] sextet *Mladi.*" This would explain why, according to Janáček, the *Concertino* depicts nature scenes, featuring the young Janáček interacting with talking animals, in each of its four movements. Janáček combines this childlike subject matter with concertante piano writing, references to classical form, and clear-headed programmatic writing to craft a small masterpiece.

The first movement, which suggests sonata form, depicts a hedgehog struggling to get into his lair after Janáček and his friends have blocked off the entrance; the hedgehog is represented by a rising theme with a frustrated closing turn, played on the piano and echoed on the horn. This theme metamorphoses into a kinder theme built on the turn, but the hedgehog still cannot get in, and after a charming development section the movement closes with the first theme.

A squirrel darts from tree branch to tree branch in the second movement, represented by quick piano chords broken by long rests and accompanied by a scampering clarinet; even when Janáček cages the squirrel, it cannot stop running, as is shown by a new theme with two chords jumping down onto a long trill. The third movement, a study of night birds, transforms the three-note descending motif from the second movement into a march-like theme for its outer sections and a lyrical, springlike theme—played in arching wind lines and supported by the violins—for its middle section.

A fourth movement brings all the animals together for a discussion, and features a descending motif, a retort, and a gallop theme in friendly competition with each other. The piano, acting as observer, manages to combine all the themes into a rousing climax which is eventually rejoined by all the woodland creatures. It is impossible not to respond to the 71-year-old Janáček's carefree evocation of youth, particularly with a work as well-crafted as this *Concertino*. *—Andrew Lindemann Malone*

Recommended:

○ **Janáček: Piano Works** / Firkusny, Bavarian RSO / 1997 / DG 449764

○ **Netherlands Wind Ens.** / Fischer (cond.), Berman, / 1995 / Chandos 9399

KEYBOARD

In the mists (V Mlhách) (1912)

Janáček revealed a very private and sensitive side of his musical personality when he composed *In the Mists*, a collection of four pieces for solo piano. Written in the winter of 1912–13, the work came four years after the composer's much longer collection, *On an Overgrown Path*. *In the Mists* has an feeling of introspection about it, as it were an entry in the composer's musical "journal"; it lives up to its name by maintaining an air of distance, as if the piano were at times lost in a bank of clouds. *In the Mists* is not a showcase for pianistic pyrotechnics—in fact it makes few technical demands of the performer—but it requires a light, rhapsodic touch and close attention to the halting nature of its delicate phrases.

The first piece (Andante cantando) features a simple, yet haunting, theme that is notable for its occasional tonal ambivalence; the underlying accompaniment—fluid, but constantly in motion—adds an element of impatience. A more turbulent contrasting section juxtaposes a rigid, chorale-like figure, against a wave of ascending scales to create dramatic tension.

A nebulous, permissive quality pervades the second piece of the set, which seems to grant the performer free rein over interpretation. A quiet, noble theme and a much faster, rhythmically ambigious figure alternate in a somewhat conversational manner—though at times their interaction seems more competitive than polite.

The main tune of the third piece (andantino)—a simple, yet beautiful seven-bar melody in G flat major—is almost the sole focus of this short piece. It is stated in a number of keys, making its way through a graceful harmonic arch, before a brief melodic digression prepares the way for a restatement in the original key.

Reminiscent of an extemporaneous Gypsy doina, the melodies of the fourth piece fluctuate widely in pace and mood. The left hand, which plays a rather obsessive two-note figure, figure behaves like a stummed chord at the start of a doina, wherein the soloist (right hand) adds melodic flourishes. *—Franklin Stover*

Recommended:

○ **Janáček: Piano Works** / Firkusny / 1997 / DG 449764

○ **Janáček: A Recollection** / Schiff / 2001 / ECM 461660

On the Overgrown Path (Po zarostlém chodníčku) (1900–1911)

On the Overgrown Path is a very private musical statement that emerged at the same time Janáček was writing two highly public works, the operas *Osud* (Fate) and *Jenůfa*. He was recovering from the death of his daughter, Olga, and the 15 pieces in this piano suite serve as a sort of emotional diary. The music, typically of Janáček's mature works, bears the strong influence of Moravian folk songs and dances, although Janáček employs folk elements in so personal a manner that the pieces cannot be said to be in "folk style." Melodies occur in short, sometimes gasping breaths, often with simple, repetitive left-hand accompaniment, as in songs. However, the music's erratic, improvisational nature sometimes allows the accompaniment material to break away and take control of a few measures. The rhythms and phrase lengths are irregular, as in Moravian folk music, and the frequent use of tremolo derives from the sound of the cimbalom. The pieces are brief (two to four minutes long), intimate, often brooding or melancholy, and occasionally disturbing. Janáček had ten pieces published as *Book I* in 1911, and appended titles to make them more commercially appealing; as evocative as they are, the titles were inspired by the music, rather than vice versa. Five more pieces constitute *Book II*; only the first two are complete, and all of these lack titles. *Book I* begins with the nostalgic "Our Evenings," which is followed by the mercurial and brighter "A Blown-Away Leaf." "Come With Us" is a tender polka; "The Madonna of Frydek" alludes to pilgrims visiting a shrine in that village, but is dominated by a simple tune that becomes more assertive upon each repetition. "They Chattered Like Swallows" depicts talkative girls with a quick, repeated figure that constantly veers into the minor mode. "Words Fail," with its frequent interruptions and changes of mood, has been interpreted both as a parody of a stutterer and an imitation of sobbing; the downcast mood suggests the latter. The tender "Good Night!" combines elements of lullaby and love song. "Unutterable Anguish" is how Janáček described the long period of his daughter's illness; the short, repeated figures initially imply distraction and nervousness, sometimes rising to small climaxes. Janáček described "In Tears" as "crying with a smile," and the childlike tune takes some unexpectedly fretful harmonic turns. "The Barn Owl Has Not Flown Away" alludes to the superstition that when someone is about to die, a barn owl lurks at the house; fluttering arpeggios alternate and eventually overlap with a resigned chordal melody. *Book II* consists of an unsettled, questioning Andante, a bereft Allegretto, a quietly obsessive Più mosso, a dramatic and agitated Allegro propelled by constant tremolos, and a jagged and folkish Vivo. *—James Reel*

Recommended:

○ **Janáček: Piano Works** / Firkusny / 1997 / DG 449764

○ **Janáček: A Recollection** / Schiff / 2001 / ECM 461660

Piano Sonata ("Zulice, 1.X.95" / "From the Street, 1 October, 1895") (1905–1906)

This work was the composer's direct reaction to an event he witnessed, a peaceful demonstration calling for a new Czech university that left a worker stabbed to death by a repressive bayonet. Janáček was deeply affected, and wrote his only piano sonata on an impulse. The work is highly dramatic and original, having been written without any concern to make it properly pianistic. Originally it comprised three programmatic movements, each one in sonata form. After its premiere the composer, in a fit of depression, destroyed the manuscript and threw the pieces into the Vltava River. The first two parts were reconstructed from copies with the help of the performer who premiered it. What has survived are two brief movements, of similar length, in E flat minor. In the first, entitled "Foreboding," con moto, the first subject begins calmly with a wistful motive that is soon reiterated more intensely, with a cascade of octaves in the bass that ends fortissimo in a double trill. The next bar begins pianissimo, introducing the gentler second subject which is partly overlapped by echoes of the first. The brief development works into an anguished climax that leads to the reprise. The movement concludes pianissimo. In the second, "Death," Adagio, the exposition is monothematic, a slow and melancholic contemplation based on a simple four-note motive of pensive character. The development gathers momentum, with spasmodic contributions of the left hand. The development works the motive into a frenzy of repeated chords leading to the reprise. The piece closes very softly. This is one of the most concentrated and emotionally charged piano works of the century. *—Hector Bellman*

Recommended:

○ **Janáček: Piano Works** / Firkusny / 1997 / DG 449764

CHAMBER MUSIC

Capriccio ("Vzdor" / "Defiance") (1926)

One of the most original works in the piano literature is Janáček's *Capriccio* for piano left-hand, flute/piccolo, and six brass instruments. The work was written shortly after a trip the composer took to England, where several of his chamber works had been performed. Composed between June to October 1926, the *Capriccio* was the result of a commission from pianist Otakar Hollmann, who lost the use of his right arm while in the Great War. At first, the idea of composing such a work for a left-handed pianist did not particularly interest Janáček, who was quoted as saying, "to write for the left hand... would be childishly gratuitous. More reasons were necessary." Therefore—perhaps to provide his own "reasons"—Janáček chose the unusual instrumentation at hand, creating a very unique and flexible sonority as well as a wonderful solo vehicle for the pianist. Janáček subtitled the work "Vzdor" (or "Defiance"), in reference to Hollmann's enduring will to perform and refusal to succumb to his disability. Others have suggested that the choice of instrumentation was in a sense, an act of defiance; indeed, Janáček followed few traditional practices in composing his *Capriccio*.

Capriccio appeared between the modernistic *Concertino* of 1925, and the popular *Sinfonietta* of 1926. In four movements, it remains somewhat of an oddity not only in the field of chamber music, but in Janáček's output as well.

The first movement, marked Allegro, presents an energetic melody in the piano, which is then transferred to the trombone and trumpet in turn. The tune is accompanied by a somewhat off-kilter oompah-band accompaniment, that sometimes veers into humorously low ranges of pitch.

The second movement divides the ensemble more discretely into groups; the piano is given center stage for the presentation of a gentle theme, only occasionally punctuated by brass inflections. The trombone then joins the piano for a rather frenetic duet, which is followed by the first entrance of the flute. Having been reserved until the middle of the second movement, the introduction of this new instrumental color is striking and effective.

The third movement is notable for its deliberate contrasting of a light-hearted tuba solo and a more sorrowful strain in the trumpet. These two temperaments struggle for control throughout the movement.

The final movement, marked Andante, is the most diverse. Begins with a duet for flute and piano, the texture soon gives way to a much more active texture featuring lively brass and keyboard flourishes. However, the piano leaves the rest of the ensemble behind and shifts the mood toward introspection during an extended, tonally dark solo. The entire ensemble then rejoins and ends the work with a lively counterpoint of triplets. *—Franklin Stover*

Recommended:

- ○ **Janáček: Piano Works** / Firkusny, Bavarian RSO / 1997 / DG 449764
- ○ **Janáček** / Atherton, Crossley, London Sinfonietta / 1996 / London 448255

Mládí (Youth), suite for wind sextet (1924)

Janáček composed his great wind sextet *Mladi* in 1924 in the month of his 70th birthday. Also referred to as the youth sextet, the work figured into the period between the *Piano Concertino* and the orchestral *Danube*.

This was clearly a splendid time in the life of the composer. With many recent successes, a celebration was held in Janáček's honor to crown the septuagenarian's accomplishments. Performances of his music were undertaken. Even a bust of the composer was unveiled in his native Moravia. Having thus achieved a sort of celebrity status, Janáček produced the highly original sextet for winds best known as *Mladi*, Youth, a term that has been taken different ways.

Youth, as Janáček defined it (in this context), referred to childhood memories, with particular emphasis on the third movement of the sextet which recalls a tune the composer heard as a boy. A broader meaning of youth in a discussion about Janáček refers us to the last ten or so years of the composer's life, wherein his most inspired and youthfully inspired work unfolded.

Clearly one of his finest chamber works, the score of *Mladi* bubbles forth with great enthusiasm and fresh ideas. Interestingly, when Janáček was working on the sextet, he was also at work on *The Makropoulos Case*, an opera that features a young looking but chronologically ancient heroine. So, the theme of youth and regeneration appears to figure in Janáček's work, either as a programmatic aside or as a central theme, as in one of his stage productions.

The sextet was arranged for the usual woodwind quintet, but with the bass clarinet added. There are four contrasting movements. In the third movement (con moto), the flute player switches over to the piccolo and plays the *March of the Blueboys*. Janáček had originally sketched this movement out several weeks before tackling the sextet, having arranged it for piccolo and piano. The origin of this march is uncertain. Biographer Malcolm Rayment once wrote that the term *blue boys* referred to a group of boy choristers at a monastery in Brno, a monastery the young Janáček sang at. Guy Erismann, in writing on *Mladi*, reported that the march has its origin with a Prussian Army band. Apparently, the Prussians had occupied Brno in 1866; Janáček would have been twelve years old at the time, old enough to remember the melody. *—Franklin Stover*

Recommended:

- ○ **Janáček** / Bell, Harris, Eastop, Gatt, Pay, Craxton / 1996 / London 448255
- ○ **20th Century Wind Quintets** / Michael Thompson Wind Quintet / 2000 / Naxos 553851

Pohádka (Fairy Tale), for cello & piano ("The Story of Tsar Berendyey") (1910; revised 1912)

This is the earliest surviving instrumental duet by Janáček. It is in a free sonata form and might well have been named "Sonata" or "Sonata-fantasy," but Janáček's penchant for drama emerges here. The piece is inspired by Vasily Zhukovsky's poem *The Tale of Tsar Bendvei*, which itself is a modern poetic adaptation of old heroic tales. The plot involves a young warrior-prince who finds himself taken by the king of the underworld. He has to triumph in tests of valor and magic, and is aided in this by the king's daughter, who has fallen in love with Bendvei. Janáček was a late bloomer, musically, and although he was approaching 60 when he wrote the piece, he was still developing his most familiar late style. Nevertheless, the work abounds with the very short melodies which are Janáček's thumbprint, allowing for brisk, effective musical story-telling. *—Joseph Stevenson*

Recommended:

- ○ **Janáček: Chamber Works** / Schiff, Pergamenschikow / 1993 / London 440312
- ○ **Platinum Janáček** / Gregor-Smith, Wrigley / 2002 / ASV 8509

String Quartet No. 1 ("Kreutzer") (1923)

Leoš Janáček's *String Quartet No. 1* is subtitled "The Kreutzer Sonata," after the story by Leo Tolstoy upon which it is based; the title of Tolstoy's story, of course, is taken from Ludwig van Beethoven's ninth violin sonata. This was not the first work Janáček wrote based on this Tolstoy story; a piano trio from 1908 is now lost. According to Josef Suk, who led the premiere of the quartet on October 17, 1924, Janáček wished with this work to protest the tyranny of men over women; in the story, a female heroine seeks refuge from an unhappy marriage in the arms of an amoral seducer, and dies tragically after doing so. Although Janáček did not attempt a line-by-line re-creation of Tolstoy's story, the music clearly suggests certain programmatic correspondences. The first movement seems to depict the heroine's unhappy situation, with a yearning, almost questing theme bracketed by agitated figures; a pastoral theme that follows breaks up and then suddenly cuts off, yielding to an even more passionate version of the yearning theme. The second movement takes the approximate form of a Czech polka, and introduces a theme which seems to belong to the seducer; this theme has to contend with both agitated ponticello and quiet, private music, but keeps popping back up, as suave as ever. The third movement begins with a canonic duet between first violin and cello; the music they play recalls the gorgeous second subject of the first movement of Beethoven's *Kreutzer Sonata*. Even this music, however, is broken up by spasms of dissonance in the other two instruments, suggesting doubts and fears. These are realized in a violent middle section in which the violin and cello trade hysterical phrases, before collapsing into a somewhat uneasy intimacy again. The fourth movement begins slowly and sadly, and after the music speeds up, it seems all too eager, and winds itself up too tightly. The middle section of the third movement reappears, transformed, and the music reaches a wrenching climax, followed by a pathetic coda. Janáček's passion for the rights of women is as evident here as his typically sensitive use of programmatic material and his impeccable craftsmanship, making the "Kreutzer Sonata" a memorable quartet. *—Andrew Lindemann Malone*

Recommended:

- ○ **Janáček: String Quartets** / Panocha Qt. / Supraphon 02152131
- ○ **Janáček: String Quartets; Berg: Lyric Suite** / Juilliard Qt. / 1996 / Sony 66840

String Quartet No. 2 ("Listy duverné" / "Intimate Letters") (1928)

"I consider the last decade of his life: his country independent, his music at last applauded, himself loved by a young woman," Milan Kundera wrote of Janáček, "his works become more and more bold, free, merry. A Picasso-like old age." The woman was Kamila Stösslová, wife of an antiques dealer encountered during the World War I, 38 years his junior. And while she may have loved him in a general way of being flattered, tolerant, amused, uncomprehending, his passion seems to have been largely unrequited. Thus, a measure of teasing irritant stimulated Janáček's final years, provoking his last and greatest works. One catches glimpses of Kamila in the adulterous heroine of *Káťa Kabanová*, the wily wisdom of the *The Cunning Little Vixen*, and the charismatic but distant allure of the deathless Emilia Marty, heroine of *The Makropulos Case*, while the virile directness of the *Sinfonietta* and the barbaric splendors of the *Glagolitic Mass* are immediate responses to a fascination becoming increasingly obsessive. Though he may have drawn upon an early, now lost, piano trio, the completion of the *String Quartet No. 1*—inspired by *The Kreutzer Sonata*, Tolstoy's tale of adultery and jealous murder given wing by music—in just a little over a week (October 30–November 7, 1923) is testimony to an erotic frenzy. By the time of its composition, Janáček was writing to Kamila nearly every day, and in his last year kept a journal devoted to her. Nevertheless, he seems to have attempted to free himself from the tyranny she held over his imagination with the male-dominated *From the House of the Dead*—which Kundera rated, with Berg's *Wozzeck*, as "the truest, the greatest opera of our dark century"—though it is indicative that he interrupted that work's composition between January 29 and February 19, 1928, to give voice to the *String Quartet No. 2*, originally titled "Love Letters" but, for discretion's sake was re-christened "Intimate Letters." Its four movements are a drama of volatile, fluctuating emotion, from the opening rush of excited expectation through brusque turns of impetuosity, questioning, and caressing tenderness. The second movement is a passionate meditation veering from doubt to joy, while the third expands the mood of questioning to confront it with a passionate declaration. The final movement is a rondo in which the returns of a frenzied dance enclose shifts from ecstasy to despair, ending with triumphant assertion. Janáček died the following August 12. *—Adrian Corleonis*

Recommended:

- ○ **Janáček: String Quartets** / Panocha Quartet / Supraphon 02152131
- ○ **Love Letters** / Kubin Quartet / Supraphon 3349

Violin Sonata (1914–1915; revised 1922)

Janáček began writing his only mature violin sonata in 1914. He worked on it during the Great War, and gave it the final touches for its premiere only in 1922. It is a short and concentrated work, in the typical late style of the composer, based on short motives, swift changes of tempo, and intense emotional expression. The work has four movements. The first, con moto, is passionate and lyrical. It opens with an intense ascending phrase of the solo violin, followed by a tense lyrical melody accompanied by piano tremolos. The development builds to an anguished climax that leads to the reprise. The second movement, Ballade, con moto, is a warm melody based on a simple motive of folk flavor, supported by the piano's broken chords. The third movement, Allegretto, is a very peculiar two-minute scherzo. The finale, Adagio, opens and closes in desolation. The central section grows to a tense climax and then resignedly subsides into the opening material. *—Hector Bellman*

Recommended:

- ○ **Janáček: Concertino; Violin Sonata; Po Zarostlém Chodmicku** / A. Schiff (cond.), Musiktage Mondsee / 1993 / London 440313
- ○ **Janáček, Debussy, Ravel, Nielsen: Violin Sonatas** / Tetzlaff, Andsnes / 1995 / Virgin 45122

CHORAL

Glagolitic Mass (Msa glagolskaja) (1926–1927)

Leoš Janáček's magnificent *Glagolitic Mass* (or *Slavonic Mass*) had its origins in 1907, when the composer began sketching out a Latin mass for chorus and organ. Janáček had nearly finished three sections of the work (the Kyrie, Credo, and Agnus Dei) when he set it aside. He did not return to it for almost 20 years. This period of inactivity on the mass involved an attempt on the composer's part to redefine, in his most personal terms, the meanings of the mass texts. Janáček sometimes would ponder the reformulation of a traditional idea, such as the mass proper, for great stretches of time.

When the composer returned to the mass, he began with a change of text. Janáček settled on a ninth century Slavonic mass, used in ancient times in his native Moravia. The ancient Slavonic style of script, known as glagolitic, was incorporated into the title of his mass to help date the text, to connect the composer with his Moravian roots, and to honor the Greek influence of the past. The *Glagolitic Mass* had little to do with organized religion in the composer's mind, however, and was not intended for liturgical use. Janáček's mass was conceived as a paean to Nature, and a tribute to humanity. In 1928, Janáček was quoted as saying that "I wanted to portray the faith in the certainty of a nation, not on a religious basis, but on a basis of moral strength which takes God for witness."

In August of 1926, Janáček drafted an expanded version of the *Glagolitic Mass* in Luhačovice, a small Moravian town to which the composer retreated for summer vacations. There, he combined the old 1907 mass with the new (or rather, ancient) Slavonic text, and composed new material. Around the time the organ Intrada was being composed, Janáček's copyist was on hand putting together a legible copy of the score. The *Glagolitic Mass* was completed in December of 1926. But when Janáček learned that a premiere was forthcoming, he revised it yet again, watering down some of the more complicated sections. The work was finally given its world premiere on December 5, 1927, and achieved overnight success.

An inferior version of the mass has been perfomed and recorded many times over. Charles Mackerras, conductor and Janáček specialist, set out to locate the original score and to reconstruct it as closely as possible to what Janáček wanted. In 1994 the restoration was completed, and the work has been returned to its original luster with an amazing performance by Mackerras and the Danish National Radio Symphony. *—Franklin Stover*

Recommended:

- ○ **Janáček: Missa Glagolitica; Diary of One Who Disappeared** / Kubelik (cond.), Lear, Hafliger, Rossel-Majdan, Crass, Bavarian RSO / 2002 / DG 463672
- ○ **Janáček: Missa Glagolitica; Kodaly: Psalmus Hungaricus** / Mackerras (cond.), Cold, Kiberg, Stene, Svensson, Danish RSO / 1994 / Chandos 9310
- ○ **Janáček: Missa Glagolitica** / Mackerras (cond.), Soderstrom, Novak, Drobkova, Hora, Czech PO / Supraphon 103575
- ○ **Janáček: Missa Glagolitica; Sinfonietta** / Bakala (cond.), Domaninska, Brno Radio SO / 2002 / Supraphon 3613

VOCAL

Ríkadla (Nursery Rhymes) (1925–1926)

Czech composer Leoš Janáček is most famous outside the Czech Republic for his orchestral works, his string quartets, piano cycles, and operas. But inside the Czech Republic, he is especially revered for his vast number of choral pieces for diverse ensembles. Composed throughout his career, Janáček's choral works have furnished countless Czech choral groups with material. Perhaps the most charming series of choral works are the *18 Nursery Rhymes for Mixed Chorus and Ten Instruments* (1925–27). Late in life, Janáček was happily nostalgic for his youth, and several works from his final years are based on his recollections. He found the texts for the *Nursery Rhymes* in the illustrated children's section of the *Lidove noviny* newspaper. He wrote the first eight numbers in 1925 for three mezzo-sopranos and expanded these with ten more in 1927. All the numbers are childlike, but not childish, full of fun and whimsy. As befits a polyglot society, the *Nursery Rhymes* are in Czech, Slovak, and Ruthenian. And as befits a composer who—along with Mussorgsky—was supremely gifted in turning texts into melodies that follow exactly the contours of the spoken word, each is supremely singable. Interestingly, the first number recalls the folk song sung at the opening of the third act of Janáček's great opera *Jenůfa*. *—James Leonard*

Recommended:

- ○ **Janáček: Hradcany Songs & Other Choruses** / Veselka (cond.), Jilek, Czech PO / Supraphon 3295
- ○ **Janáček: Choral Music** / Wood (cond.), Williamson, New London Chamber Choir, Critical Band / 1997 / Hyperion 66893

Jenö Jandó

b. Feb. 1, 1952, Pécs, Hungary

Pianist

If the artistic identities of some performers are bound up with the recording companies that preserved their music-making—Artur Rubinstein with RCA Red Seal, for example, or Yo-Yo Ma with the crossover-friendly incarnation of Sony/CBS—then the face of the Naxos label and its repertory-based, high-volume, low-budget ways may well be pianist Jenö Jandó. Jandó was born in the southern Hungarian city of Pécs on February 1, 1952. His mother taught him to play the piano, and he went on to study at the Liszt Academy in Budapest. When he was 18 he took third place in the prestigious Beethoven Piano Competition in Vienna, bringing his name before audiences beyond Hungary. He won the Sydney (Australia) International Piano Competition in 1987, but he didn't become a familiar figure to U.S. album buyers until after the founding of Naxos by the German-born, Hong Kong-based entrepreneur Klaus Heymann in the late 1980s.

Jandó was one of the first artists to emerge from Naxos' efforts to record Eastern European artists on a larger scale than any organization outside the former East bloc had previously done. A Hungarian contact sent a tape of Jandó's playing to the company, and he was picked for one of the new company's showcase products: a complete recording of Beethoven's 32 piano sonatas. Jandó followed those up with complete tours through Mozart's piano sonatas and concertos, Bach's entire *Well-Tempered Clavier*, Bartók's piano concertos, and the comparatively rarer Haydn keyboard sonatas. Jandó continued to explore the heart of the traditional repertory, delving into Schubert's sonatas and undertaking a mammoth survey of Bartók's complete piano music. He has also performed chamber music, inclining toward Hungarian compositions, and he serves as accompanist to his wife, mezzo soprano Tamara Takács.

What suited Jandó so well to the Naxos operation? He is an ideal jack-of-all-classical-trades. His familiarity with the piano literature is wide, and his musical memory is legendary: though he always brings scores of the works he is to play with him to a recording session, he simply lays them to one side and performs from memory. Like Glenn Gould, Jandó is given to humming along with his own playing—a tendency his producers forestall by placing an unlit cigarette in his mouth. Jandó has expressed the amibition to cap off his career by recording a second complete Beethoven sonata set—something previously undertaken only by a select group of the keyboard elite. *—James Manheim*

Recommended:

- ○ **Haydn: Sonatas, Vol. 1** / Jandó / 1993 / Naxos 550657
- ○ **Liszt: Hungarian Rhapsodies, Vol. 1** / Jandó / 1998 / Naxos 554480
- ○ **Beethoven: Bagatelles & Dances, Vol. 1** / Jandó / 1999 / Naxos 553795
- ○ **Bartók: Concertos 1–3** / Ligeti (cond.), Jandó, Budapest SO / 1994 / Naxos 550771
- ○ **Bartók: Piano Music, Vol. 1** / Jandó / 2001 / Naxos 554717
- ○ **Mozart: Sonatas, Vol. 1** / Jandó / 1991 / Naxos 550445

Clément Janequin

b. ca. 1485, Châtellerault, France, **d.** 1558, Paris, France

Composer: Vocal

Among the great composers of his age (for example, Isaac, Josquin, Taverner, Willaert, Morales), Clément Janequin looms as something of a sport, a master storyteller, an audacious joker, a lover of the bawdy anecdote, an imperishable tone poet, a keen observer who turned street cries to music through the medium of the chanson. While his contemporaries practiced flowing contrapuntal austerities and exquisite charm, Janequin's onomatopoeic glees are alive with a sensation of the actual that lends him a close kinship to his great contemporary, François Rabelais, and has kept his music in performance from his time to now. Ezra Pound traced Janequin's art to a sensibility born with troubadour poet Arnaut Daniel, embodying so vivid a line that the famous *Chant des oiseaux* in Gerhart Münch's transcription for solo violin (reproduced as the body of Pound's *Canto LXXV*) retained the geste "not of one bird but of many." And yet, despite the enormous international avidity for his work, his life is sparsely documented and remains largely conjecture. He may have been a pupil of Josquin's as his work is grounded in masterly contrapuntal technique. From 1505 he was known to have been in the service of Lancelot de Fau, a well-appointed man-of-affairs who became Bishop of Luçon in 1515, and who seems to have retained Janequin until his death in 1523. In that year, Janequin is found in the service of Jean de Foix, Bishop of Bordeaux, who employed him in a number of minor and poorly remunerative clerical posts, which establish his admission to the priesthood. Janequin's work is known to have circulated in manuscript as early as 1520, while the four volumes of chansons issued by Paris publisher Pierre Attaingnant in the 1530s spread his fame across Europe. One of Janequin's most remarkable, effective, and popular chansons, *Guerre*, was composed to celebrate Francis I's victory over the Swiss at the Battle of Marignan in 1515. That monarch's passage through Bordeaux in 1530 was marked by the almost equally tumultuous *Chantons, sonnons trompettes*. In 1532 he appears in Angers among a circle in thrall to Clément Marot, whose verses Janequin set. In 1548 he is inscribed as a student of the university at Angers, probably as a prerequisite to further promotion, and in 1549 as a student of the university of Paris. In the 1550s he entered the service of Henri II as *chanter ordinaire du roi* and, at last, *compositeur ordinaire du roi*. *—Adrian Corleonis*

VOCAL

Chansons and Other Vocal Works (ca. 1520–1555)

French chansons can easily be distinguished from Renaissance madrigals by their dance-like rhythms, frequently repeated notes, and strict adherence to the cadences of the French language. Unlike the madrigal, chansons are popular in style, their appeal lying more in their intrinsic harmonic and rhythmic qualities, and the skill with which the words are set, than on elaborate counterpoint or ornamentation.

Janequin was one of two leading masters of the French chanson, the other being Claudin de Sermisy (ca. 1490–1562). There is, in fact, little to distinguish them in terms of musical skill. The larger proportion of Janequin's 280 chansons—mostly in four parts—are on the subject of romantic love, often unrequited and occasionally telling a story—the "narrative" or "program" chanson. His lively, if somewhat naïve, realism will probably continue to make him more attractive than many of his contemporaries.

Janequin's delightful pieces reflect a simple pleasure in "word painting" and even caricature, as shown by such titles as "Le chant des oiseaux" (the song of the birds) and "Le caquet des femmes" (women's chatter). One of the most famous, "La Guerre," written to celebrate the French victory at the battle of Marignano (1515), was frequently performed with the addition of instruments to provide the required warlike effects.

The popularity of the French chanson continued throughout the sixteenth century, as shown by the immense number published, but did not survive the spread of concerted music throughout Italy and Northern Europe in the seventeenth century. By then a new generation of European composers had consigned the French songsters to a footnote in musical history. Fortunately, however, the recent revival of interest in early music has resurrected examples of their wit, charm and lyricism. Chansons can be interpreted more freely than madrigals and, provided the original words are followed in modern interpretations, can sound effective on appropriate instruments, such as flutes and recorders, as well as voices. *—Roy Brewer*

Recommended:

- ○ **Janequin: Le Chant des Oyseaulx** / Clement Janequin Ens. / HM 901099
- ○ **Janequin: Elegiac & Picturesque Songs** / Patenaude (cond.), Les Petits Chanteurs de Mont-Royal / Analekta 23184
- ○ **Janequin: Le Verger de Musique** / Fabre-Garrus (cond.), A Sei Voci / 1996 / Astree 8571
- ○ **Janequin: La Chasse et autres chansons** / Clement Janequin Ens. / HM 901271

Il estoit une fillette, chanson for 4 voices (ca. 1540)

Those singers and listeners who know the sixteenth century French chanson composer Clément Janequin only through lengthy, programmatic, onomatopoetic chansons like *La chant des oiseaux*, *La chasse*, and *La guerre* will find a slim, straightforward lyric thing like the four-voice chanson *Il estoit une fillette* (ca. 1540) to be unusual terrain indeed. The witty, humorously bawdy love text of *Il estoit une fillette* is set as a series of short, "simple" phrases—square, four-bar units, each immediately repeated to new text, and then a final eight-bar phrase that is repeated without a change of text. *Il estoit une fillette* is almost entirely homophonic, and the few points at which one or another of the four voices decides to shoot off on its own have more the effect of clever localized push-and-pull between the singers than of polyphony in the normal sense; imitation is certainly not part of Janequin's game plan in *Il estoit une fillette*. Quite a change, indeed, from a sprawling, 250-bar imitative effort like *La chant des oiseaux*, but, in its own way, just as colorful and charming. *—Blair Johnston*

Recommended:

- ○ **Janequin: Le Verger de Musique** / Fabre-Garrus (cond.), A Sei Voci / 1996 / Astree 8571
- ○ **The Ancient Miracles** / Augsburg Ens. for Early Music / 1995 / Christophorus 77178

Réveillez vous, cueurs endormis, chanson for 4 voices ("Le chant des oiseaux") (ca. 1520)

Clément Janequin, famous in his own day, remains so today for his hundreds of delightful French chansons. While the dramatic *La guerre* may have been more widely known during Janequin's lifetime, the whimsical *Le chant des oiseaux* (Song of the birds) composed around 1520 is now the most famous of them all. Janequin was fond of onomatopoeic effects—singers making sounds rather than words—in his chansons, and in *Le chant des oiseaux* that fondness prods the composer, appropriately enough, to write many passages in which the singers do not so much sing as make bird-calls to one another!

Le chant des oiseaux, or *Réveillez vous*, as it is more properly titled (after its incipit), is, like all save a very few of Janequin's chansons, written for four voices and was first published by the legendary Parisian printer Pierre Attaingnant in 1528. It has five clearly delineated sections of music, each of which makes a strong cadence at the end, and each of which, save the last as compared to the fourth, is longer than the one preceding it; each section grows progressively more full of bird-call sounds.

After the brief opening portion of music, each section commences with the same little cell of bass-tenor quasi-imitation. Examples of the bird-call sounds that have made this chanson so famous and which make it so fun to sing are: "huit huit huit huit," "fi ti fi ti frr," "oyti oyti trr," "turri turri qrr" and, in dense imitation in the final section, "coqu coqu coqu." *—Blair Johnston*

Recommended:

- ○ **Janequin: Le Verger de Musique** / Fabre-Garrus (cond.), A Sei Voci / 1996 / Astree 8571
- ○ **French Chansons** / Scholars of London / 1994 / Early Music 550880

Antonio Janigro

b. Jan. 21, 1918, Milan, Italy, **d.** May 1, 1989, Milan, Italy
Conductor

Italian-born conductor and cellist Antonio Janigro is best known to contemporary audiences for his many recordings with the chamber orchestra I Solisti di Zagreb, an ensemble he founded in 1954. Staples of the record-store Baroque section for many years, they helped build the enormous popularity that has since come to the music of Vivaldi and his contemporaries, and they still hold up well as widely available reissues. Janigro came to Baroque music fairly late in life, however. His recordings as a conductor capped a musical career touched by two world wars.

Janigro once described the atmosphere of his childhood as musical but tragic. He was born in 1918 in Milan to a pianist father whose career had ended when he lost an arm to a sharpshooter in World War I. Janigro started out on piano but switched to the cello at age eight, winning admission to the Verdi Conservatory a year later. At age 11 he performed for Pablo Casals, who recommended Janigro for admission to the prestigious Ecole Normale de Musique in Paris. Studying there in the mid-1930s, he had Casals and Nadia Boulanger as teachers, Dinu Lipatti and Ginette Neveu as classmates, and Stravinsky as an eminence. His repertoire as a performer would range from early music to brand-new compositions. Practicing his cello on a train from Paris to Milan, Janigro was heard by a talent agent, and his career was launched.

After a promising start as a recitalist, Janigro took a vacation to Zagreb, Yugoslavia, just as World War II broke out. Essentially stranded, he began a new career as professor of cello at the Zagreb Conservatory. He continued to tour internationally and to teach cello after the war, with a stint at the conservatory in Düsseldorf, Germany, from 1965 to 1974. In Yugoslavia, however, he worked increasingly often as a conductor. At the behest of the government he formed the Zagreb Radio and Television Symphony Orchestra, serving as its conductor from 1954 to 1964. Taking advantage of Yugoslavia's relative independence from the Soviet domination, he also conducted several top Western European orchestras, but his most extensive touring came with I Solisti di Zagreb. That group, although not affiliated with the historical performance practice movement, offered crisp readings of Baroque orchestral works that sharply diverged from the bloated symphony performances that were the norm at the time. Despite international renown, Janigro continued to make Zagreb his home until just before his death in 1989. *—James Manheim*

Recommended:

- ○ **Janigro; Cello Favorites** / Janigro, Beltrami (piano) / 1988 / Vanguard 80
- ○ **Haydn: Symphonies 44–49** / Janigro (cond.), Zagreb RSO / 2004 / Artemis 1495
- ○ **Beethoven: Cello Sonatas** / Janigro, Demus (piano) / 2003 / Vanguard 1218

Byron Janis

b. Mar. 24, 1928, McKeesport, PA
Pianist

Byron Janis (b. 1928) became one of the most brilliant of his generation of American pianists before his career was cut short by illness. At the age of seven he was taken to New York, becoming a pupil of Adele Marcus, then of Joseph and Rosina Lhévinne. In 1943 he made his professional debut playing Rachmaninov's *Piano Concerto No. 2* with the NBC Symphony Orchestra in New York, with Frank Black conducting. In 1944 he repeated the same concerto in Pittsburgh with thirteen-year-old Lorin Maazel conducting the Pittsburgh Symphony Orchestra. Vladimir Horowitz was in the audience, and subsequently invited Janis to study with him. Then Janis embarked on a successful career as a concert pianist, including a 1948 tour to South America, and a 1952 tour of Europe.

In 1960 Janis was chosen as the first American artist to be sent to the Soviet Union, opening a newly formed Cultural Exchange between the USSR and the United States. The result was a brilliant Mercury Living Presence LP that is an all-time classic, pairing the Rachmaninov *First* and Prokofiev *Third* concertos. Aided by exemplary sound recording, the Prokofiev in particular is still regarded by many connoisseurs as the work's finest recorded interpretation. In 1995 the CD version won the Cannes Award for Best Reissue. He interrupted his career in the late 1960s at the onset of an illness, and temporarily resumed it in 1972. Soon however, his concert appearances became more rare.

Meanwhile, in 1967 he had discovered the manuscripts of two previously unknown Chopin waltzes in Paris, and in 1973, two variations of them, also in Chopin's hand, at the Yale Library. This led to a 1978 French television documentary, *Frédéric Chopin: A Voyage with Byron Janis*, in which he detailed the difficulties in determining the authentic versions of Chopin's music.

In 1985 he was invited to perform at the White House. On that occasion he publicly disclosed the nature of the illness that had hampered him for nearly 20 years: psoriatic arthritis affecting his wrists and hands. The ailment had not prevented him from continuing to play piano well, but it often made it impossible to play to his former high standard.

In the meantime, he devoted much of his energy to teaching, composing, and humanitarian concerns. He became Ambassador of the Arts for the Arthritis Foundation, often playing in fund-raising concerts. He is Chairman of the Global Forum Arts and Culture Committee. He composed the musical theme for the Global Forum on Human Survival in Oxford, England, held April, 1988. With lyrics by Sammy Cahn, it became the song *The One World*. Janis's music is primarily in the Pop style, and includes a musical version of *The Hunchback of Notre Dame*. In 1989 he composed the score for Turner Network Television's 1989 major documentary on Gary Cooper. He is on the faculty of Manhattan School of Music, and works on the Board and Music Advisory Committee for Pro Musicus, an international organization devoted to helping young artists. *—Joseph Stevenson*

Recommended:

- ○ **Prokofiev: Piano Concerto 3; Rachmaninov: Piano Concerto 1; etc.** / Janis, Kondrashin (cond.), Lawrence (cond.), Moscow Philharmonic SO / 1994 / Mercury 434333
- ○ **Rachmaninoff: Piano Concertos 2 & 3** / Janis, Dorati (cond.), London SO, Minneapolis SO / 2004 / Mercury 4706392
- ○ **Moussorgsky: Pictures at an Exhibition, etc.** / Janis, Dorati (cond.), Minnesota Orch. / 1994 / Philips 434346
- ○ **Great Pianists: Byron Janis I** / Janis / 1998 / Philips 456847

Gundula Janowitz

b. Aug. 2, 1937, Berlin, Germany
Soprano

Janowitz's voice was regarded as one of the most beautiful of its time, with a rich, creamy timbre that was ideal for the more poetic and serene operatic roles, such as the Countess in *Le nozze di Figaro*, and particularly Strauss heroines such as the Countess in *Capriccio*, Ariadne, Arabella, and the Marschallin. She was also celebrated for her Verdi, particularly Elisabetta in *Don Carlo*, Amelia in *Simon Boccanegra*, and Aida. Some critics found her performances lacking in flamboyance, calling her tepid, but others found them elegantly understated, relying on the music and the line rather than histrionics.

She studied voice at the Graz Conservatory, winning a competition to make her opera debut in 1960 as Barbarina in *Nozze* at the Vienna State Opera and beginning a lifelong association with that house. Later that year, she made her Bayreuth Festival debut as a flowermaiden in *Parsifal*. She began to sing leads at the VSO, including, at Herbert von Karajan's urging, the Empress in Strauss' *Die Frau ohne Schatten*, at the age of 27. (Karajan had a habit of urging singers into heavy repertoire, often to their detriment; however, her fine technique and caution kept her voice from suffering.) Her Glyndebourne debut came in 1964, as Ilia in Mozart's *Idomeneo* (with a new young Italian tenor, Luciano Pavarotti, singing Idamante). She made her Metropolitan Opera debut in 1967 as Sieglinde in Wagner's *Die Walküre*. Her Covent Garden debut was not until 1976, as Donna Anna in *Don Giovanni*.

Throughout her career, she was as engaged with concerts and recitals as with operatic performances, becoming especially acclaimed for her renditions of Strauss' *Four Last Songs*. She retired from the stage in 1990, though she still gave the occasional concert. *—Ann Feeney*

Recommended:

- ○ **Gundula Janowitz** / Karajan, Leitner (conds.), Janowitz, Gage, Berlin PO / 2001 / Decca 467910
- ○ **Mozart: Concert Arias** / Boettcher (cond.), Janowitz, VSO / 1996 / DG 449723

Mariss Jansons

b. Jan. 14, 1943, Riga, Latvia
Conductor

Mariss Jansons was one of the finest conductors to emerge from the former Soviet Union in the last quarter of the twentieth century. Jansons was born while Riga was under military occupation by the Germans who seized it in 1941, a year after its forcible annexation by the U.S.S.R. His father was Arvid Jansons (or Yansons) (1914–84), the leading Latvian conductor to emerge under the Soviet system after the Baltic nation was retaken by the U.S.S.R. in 1945.

Mariss studied violin, piano, and conducting at the Leningrad Conservatory, graduating with honors. In 1969 he began training in Vienna with conductor Hans Swarowski and in Salzburg with Herbert von Karajan. In 1971 he won the International Herbert von Karajan Foundation Competition in Berlin. He began to work with the Leningrad Philharmonic Orchestra in 1973 when music director Yevgeny Mravinsky invited him to become associate conductor.

In 1979 he became music director of the Oslo Philharmonic. Under his leadership it came to international attention as one of the finest and most exciting of major world orchestras. In 1985 he was promoted to principal conductor of the Leningrad Philharmonic under music director Yuri Temirkanov. Jansons has conducted both great orchestras on several international tours to great acclaim. After the fall of the Soviet State, as Russia's second city reverted to its original name, the Leningrad Philharmonic was renamed the St. Petersburg Philharmonic. He conducted it in Europe, North America, and Japan, and led the Oslo Philharmonic on tours to even more music centers of Europe, the U.S., and Japan.

He has guest conducted many of the world's major orchestras. For Chandos Records he led the Oslo orchestra in a complete Tchaikovsky symphony cycle, and led many Shostakovich symphonies for EMI. His reputation is particularly strong as a conductor of great twentieth century symphonic classics, including composers such as Bartók, Honegger, Prokofiev, Rachmaninov, Ravel, Weill, Sibelius, Respighi, Dukas, and Mahler. His recording of Shostakovich's *Seventh Symphony* with the Leningrad Philharmonic won an Edison Award in 1989.

In 1995, the Pittsburgh Symphony Orchestra announced Jansons' appointment as its eighth music director, effective in 1996. He has led it on successful tours, including a five-city, seven-concert tour of Japan in 1998, a tour of west coast U.S. cities and an international tour in 1999.

In 1995 King Harald V of Norway appointed Jansons Commander with Star of the Royal Norwegian Order of Merit, the highest Norwegian honor ever given to a person not of Norwegian descent, for his services to Norway as director of the Oslo Philharmonic. He was given honorary membership in Britain's Royal Academy of Music in 1999 and in Vienna's Gesellschaft der Musikfreunde in 2001. In 2003, he was named chief conductor of the Bayerischer Rundfunk Orchestra. *—Joseph Stevenson*

Recommended:

- ○ **Honegger: Symphonies 2 & 3; Weill: Symphony 2** / Jansons (cond.), Zimmermann, Berlin PO, Oslo PO / 2002 / EMI 575658
- ○ **Shostakovich: Symphony 7** / Jansons (cond.), Leningrad PO / 1995 / EMI 49494
- ○ **Svendsen: Symphonies 1 & 2** / Jansons (cond.), Oslo PO / 1988 / Capitol 749769
- ○ **Shostakovich: Symphonies 6 & 9** / Jansons (cond.), Oslo PO / 1995 / Capitol 54339

Keith Jarrett

b. May 8, 1945, Allentown, PA
Pianist

One of the most significant pianists to emerge since the 1960s, Keith Jarrett has had a career with several phases. He gained international fame for his solo concerts, which found him spontaneously improvising all of the music without any prior planning; but he has also led a couple of dynamic quartets/quintets, performed classical music, and later played explorative versions of standards with his long-time trio. Although his tendency to sing along with his piano now and then is distracting, Jarrett continued to grow as a powerful improviser after decades of important accomplishments.

Jarrett started on the piano when he was three, and by the time he was seven he had already played a recital. Jarrett was a professional while still in grade school. In 1962, he studied at the Berklee College of Music and then started working in the Boston area with his trio. He moved to New York in 1965, and spent four months with Art Blakey's Jazz Messengers. As a member of the very popular Charles Lloyd Quartet (1966–69), Jarrett traveled the world and became well known; he also began doubling occasionally on soprano saxophone (which he would utilize through the 1970s). Between 1969 and 1971, he was with Miles Davis' fusion group, playing organ and electric keyboards.

Upon leaving Davis, Jarrett permanently swore off electric keyboards. He had cut sessions as a leader for Vortex (1967–69) and Atlantic (1971), but starting in November 1971, he recorded extensively for ECM, an association that continued into the 2000s. In the 1970s, Jarrett led two groups: an exciting unit with Dewey Redman, Charlie Haden, Paul Motian, and occasional percussionists (often Guilherme Franco); and a European band with Jan Garbarek, Palle Danielsson, and Jon Christensen that recorded the popular "My Song." In addition, starting in 1972, Jarrett began his famous series of improvised concerts, which resulted in such popular recordings as *Solo Concerts*, *Köln Concert*, and the mammoth *Sun Bear Concerts*. By the 1980s, Jarrett was performing and composing classical music as much as jazz, playing a variety of keyboard instruments and a variety of music ranging from Bach to Pärt. He has worked with recorder player Michala Petri, violinist Gidon Kremer, and conductor Dennis Russell Davies. Jarrett's own compositions include several works for soloist and orchestra and works for piano, clavichord, and organ. Of his classical recordings, his Handel *Keyboard Suites* have been hailed as the best on record. *—AMG*

Recommended:

○ **Handel: Suites for Keyboard** / Jarrett / 1995 / ECM 445298

○ **Mozart: Concertos; Adagio & Fugue** / Davies (cond.), Jarrett, Stuttgart CO / 1999 / ECM 462651

○ **Spheres** / Jarrett / 1985 / ECM 1302

Neeme Järvi

b. Jun. 7, 1937, Tallin, Estonia

Conductor

Neeme Järvi is one of the busiest stars on the international conducting scene. Brought up within the USSR's system for developing musical talent, Järvi studied percussion and conducting at the Tallinn Music School. He made his debut as a conductor at the age of eighteen. From 1955 to 1960 he pursued further studies at the Leningrad Conservatory, where his principal teachers were Nikolaï Rabinovich and Yevgeny Mravinsky.

From the early 1960s, Järvi took a leading role in the musical life of his homeland. In 1963 he assumed the directorship of the Estonian Radio & Television Orchestra, his first important post. He also founded the Tallinn Chamber Orchestra, and for thirteen years was the chief Conductor of Opera House Estonia in Tallinn. From 1976 to 1980 he was chief conductor and artistic director of the Estonian State Symphony Orchestra, then in its infancy. By the late 1970s his fame had spread throughout the Soviet Union and Eastern Europe, and he received favorable notices for his appearances in the West. He made history by leading the first performances of Strauss' *Der Rosenkavalier* and Gershwin's *Porgy and Bess* ever given in the USSR.

While with the ESSO Järvi developed a particular interest in unearthing and performing neglected repertory by both little-known and important composers. He was a particular champion of the Estonian composers Eduard Tubin and Arvo Pärt. In 1979 he premiered Pärt's *Credo*, a work that represents a turning point in that composer's stylistic evolution. Järvi, recognizing the importance of *Credo* (which incorporates biblical texts), presented it without first navigating through the usual channels of the Communist Party or the Composers' Union. The resulting controversy and official disfavor induced Järvi to emigrate. He was permitted to leave Estonia in 1980; within a month of his departure, he made his debut performances with the Boston Symphony, the Philadelphia Orchestra, and the New York Philharmonic. He quickly received important appointments: principal guest conductor of the City of Birmingham Symphony Orchestra in England (1981–83), music director of the Royal Scottish Orchestra (1984–88), music director of the Gothenburg (Sweden) Symphony Orchestra (from 1982), and principal guest conductor of the Japan Philharmonic.

In 1990 he assumed the post of music director of the Detroit Symphony Orchestra. With that ensemble he has made 30 of some 100 recordings on the Chandos label. Järvi has also recorded for Bis, Deutsche Gramophon, and Orfeo; his various recording projects include cycles of orchestral music by Sibelius, Prokofiev, Shostakovich, Tubin, Brahms, Schumann, Shostakovich, and others. Järvi's children have made their mark on the musical world as well: son Paavo is gaining an international reputation as a conductor and holds posts as principal guest conductor of the Stockholm Philharmonic and the City of Birmingham Symphony Orchestra; Kristjan is the founder and conductor of the Absolut Ensemble of New York City; and daughter Maarika is principal flutist with the RTVE Symphony Orchestra in Madrid. Järvi announced his decision to step down from his Detroit post in 2005. He has also served as principal conductor of the New Jersey Symphony. *—Joseph Stevenson*

Recommended:

○ **Borodin: Orchestral Works** / Jarvi (cond.), Sporsen, Gothenburg SO / DG 435757

○ **George Chadwick** / Jarvi (cond.), DSO / 2002 / Chandos 10032

○ **Busoni: Orchestral Works** / Jarvi (cond.), Bradbury, BBCPO / 2002 / Chandos 9920

○ **Stenhammar: Serenade** / Jarvi (cond.), Gothenburg SO / 1985 / BIS 310

Paavo Järvi

b. Dec. 30, 1962, Tallin, Estonia

Conductor

The elder son of Estonian/American conductor Neeme Järvi, Paavo Järvi has achieved much, including appointment as the 12th music director of the Cincinnati Symphony Orchestra. Although a musician of broad interests and a resident of the United States for the greater part of his life, he has continued to champion the music of his native Estonia in live performances and on disc. Blessed with directing gifts that transcend mere talent, Järvi is among the handful of younger conductors regarded as true successors to the great maestros of the past. Born in Tallin, Estonia, Järvi began his studies in conducting and percussion at the Tallin School of Music. At the time 17, his father moved to the United States with the rest of his family and Paavo entered the Curtis Institute of Music, where his instructors in conducting were Otto-Werner Mueller and that doyen among conducting teachers, Max Rudolf. At the Los Angeles Philharmonic Institute, Järvi studied with Leonard Bernstein. The younger Järvi's abilities quickly manifested themselves enough to lead to guest engagements with such orchestras as the New York Philharmonic, the Munich Philharmonic, the Berlin Philharmonic, the London Philharmonic, the Orchestra of the Age of Enlightenment, the Philharmonia Orchestra, the Philadelphia Orchestra, the San Francisco Symphony, the Los Angeles Philharmonic, the Orchestra della Scala, the Orchestra dell'Accademia di Santa Cecilia, the Vienna Symphony, the St. Petersburg Philharmonic, the Orchestre Philharmonique de Radio France, the Orchestre National de France, the Israel Philharmonic, the Tokyo Symphony, and the NHK Symphony. While bearing the family name may have gotten him a hearing, Paavo Järvi's own brilliance prevailed in shaping scores and drawing quality performances from the widely diverse orchestras he faced. He was engaged as principal guest conductor by the Stockholm Philharmonic and the Birmingham Symphony Orchestra and earned praise for the manner in which he filled both posts. In September 2001, Järvi assumed the musical directorship of the Cincinnati Symphony Orchestra, succeeding Jesús López-Cobos. His debut in that post was preceded by release on Telarc of a C.S.O. disc conducted by Järvi holding Berlioz's *Symphonie fantastique* and the *Love Music From Roméo et Juliet*. Already established as a presence in the recording studio, Järvi had recorded discs for Virgin Records with both the Stockholm Philharmonic and the Birmingham Symphony Orchestra. His 20-some recordings include orchestral works by Stenhammar, Sibelius' *Kullervo* and the *Lemminkäinen Suite*, works by Bernstein, a disc of cello concertos with Truls Mørk, and a disc devoted to orchestral works by Estonian composer Lepo Sumera. Among other Estonians championed by Järvi were Erkki-Sven Tüür, Udo Kasemets, and Eduard Tubin, together with the better-known Arvo Pärt. With the Estonian National Symphony Orchestra, Järvi has recorded a group of orchestral works by Pärt, as well as Sibelius' solitary opera, *The Maiden in the Tower*. Along the pathway to his Cincinnati position, Järvi amassed an enviable collection of worldwide reviews for both his live performances and recordings. *Guardian* critic Tim Ashley, commenting on the conductor's "powerhouse" reading of Mahler's *Symphony No. 6* with the BBC Philharmonic, wrote: "An overwhelming achievement: one of the great conducting careers of the twenty first century is now, unquestionably, under way." Allan Kozinn, writing in *The New York Times*, noted Järvi's ability to draw from the Philadelphia Orchestra "a truly stunning sound... with a warmth and fullness that recalled the orchestra's years with Stokowski and Ormandy, but has not been typical of its sound lately." *—Erik Eriksson*

Recommended:

○ **Sibelius: Kullervo** / P. Järvi (cond.), Mattei, Stene, Stockholm PO, Estonian National Male-Voice Choir / 1997 / Virgin 45292

○ **Prokofiev: Romeo and Juliet** / P. Järvi (cond.), Cincinnati SO / 2003 / Telarc 80597

○ **Erkki-Sven Tüür: Exodus** / P. Järvi (cond.), Van Keulen, Birmingham SO / 2003 / ECM 000099302

Siegfried Jerusalem

b. Apr. 17, 1940, Oberhausen, Germany

Tenor

Trained in Essen as a bassoonist, Siegfried Jerusalem studied to become a singer and quickly worked his way through lyric roles into dramatic and, eventually, heroic parts. He grew into the heaviest Wagner protagonist just as the situation was becoming desperate; the shortage of viable singers for these daunting roles was compromising the ability of the world's major opera houses to mount the works of the essential Wagner canon. Handsome, slender, youthful in appearance, and a highly credible actor, Jerusalem filled the need with a voice that was firm and true, if somewhat dry and lacking ultimate heldentenor thrust. So crucial was he to

Wagner performances, nevertheless, that he was engaged not only for as many house performances as he could manage, but also for numerous recordings. If any singer was indispensable during the years of Jerusalem's prime, it was he.

After 17 years as a successful orchestral bassoonist, Jerusalem became convinced that he wished to retrain and become a professional singer. He studied singing at Stuttgart, initially as a baritone, before making his debut at Stuttgart in 1975 as the First Prisoner in *Fidelio*. After singing there in a number of small roles, he accepted an engagement in Aachen and then sang in Hamburg. His first Wagner role, Lohengrin, was heard in several German theaters, including Berlin. While still singing Mozart and other medium-weight roles, Jerusalem made his first appearance at Bayreuth in 1977, singing Froh in the second year of Patrice Chéreau's hotly debated *Ring*. He also sang the role of the young sailor in *Tristan*.

In 1978, Jerusalem joined the Berlin Deutsche Opera. The year following, he was back at Bayreuth for the title roles in *Parsifal* and *Lohengrin* and Walter in *Die Meistersinger*. His continuing involvement with the Bayreuth Festival found him advancing to Siegmund in 1983, to Siegfried in 1988, and to Tristan in 1993. He offered his wily, well-sung Loge there for the first time in 1994.

Meanwhile, the tenor's debut at the Metropolitan Opera took place on January 10, 1980, as Lohengrin. His career there remained somewhat quiescent until he returned as Loge in 1987. His Siegfried in the Metropolitan *Ring* during the 1990 and 1991 seasons was broadcast on television, but was not part of the Deutsche Grammophon recording under Levine as he was already taping the *Ring* with Haitink and, only slightly later, with Barenboim.

Covent Garden had beckoned in 1986 and Jerusalem made his debut there as Erik. Chicago engaged him for its *Ring* cycle in the mid-1990s. The tenor's celebrated Lohengrin was committed to disc in 1991 with Claudio Abbado and the Vienna Philharmonic. In addition to such standard non-Wagnerian fare as *Die Zauberflöte* (Tamino), operas such as Korngold's *Violanta* and *Die Königen von Saba* were recorded with Jerusalem in the leading tenor roles. Operetta, too, was an attraction and Jerusalem was featured in Willi Boskovsky's recording of Lehár's *Die Land des Lächelns* (Land of Smiles).

Aside from his steadfast work in the opera house, Jerusalem has sung both recitals and numerous concert performances with orchestra. He has made highly accomplished recordings of Mahler's *Das Lied von der Erde* with both Barenboim and Levine, Haydn's *Die Jahreszeiten* with Marriner, Schoenberg's *Gurrelieder* with Chailly, and Mozart's *Requiem* with Helmuth Rilling. *—Erik Eriksson*

Recommended:

- ○ **Wagner: Parsifal** / Barenboim (cond.), Stoy, Van Dam, Jerusalem, Meier, Berlin PO / 1991 / Teldec 74448
- ○ **Wagner: Das Rheingold** / Levine (cond.), Morris, Ludwig, Jerusalem, Moll, Metropolitan Opera Orch. / 1989 / DG 445295
- ○ **Great Tenor Arias** / Janowski, Chmura (conds.), Jerusalem, Mende, Prey, Munich Radio Orch. / 1998 / Sony 60526

Sumi Jo

b. Nov. 22, 1962, Seoul, South Korea

Soprano

A coloratura soprano who in the late 1990s became one of the most noticed new names on the international operatic circuit, Sumi Jo was a discovery of the flamboyant German conductor Herbert von Karajan. A striking beauty, she owed her initial celebrity in part to video: the conductor arranged for her a prominent role in his *Karajan in Salzburg* video production.

Sumi Jo was born in Seoul, South Korea, in 1962. After studying both voice and piano from a young age, she dropped out of Seoul National University in 1983 to travel to Italy for study at the Accademia di Santa Cecilia in Rome. Among her teachers were Carlo Bergonzi and Grannila Bonelli. She graduated in 1985, with a concentration in keyboard as well as voice and over the next few years took top voice competition prizes in several countries, attracting the attention of Karajan. Her operatic debut came as Gilda in Verdi's *Rigoletto* in 1986, and two years later she performed in *Un Ballo in Maschera* under Karajan's baton. In the 1990s and early 2000s she was ubiquitous, singing in major capitals on nearly every continent. She won a Grammy award in 1993, and among her many recordings, her several portrayals of Mozart's vocally treacherous Queen of the Night in *Die Zauberflöte* have been especially noteworthy. In 2000, she began to see the fruits of Richard Bonynge's mentorship, refining her bel canto technique and preparing for a Carnegie Hall recital in February 2001. *—AMG*

Recommended:

- ○ **Sumi Jo Sings Mozart** / Montgomery (cond.), Jo, Bennett, Black, Barritt, Tunnell, English CO / 1996 / Erato 14637
- ○ **Bel Canto** / Carella (cond.), Jo, Arevalo, English CO / Erato 17580
- ○ **Auber: Le Domino Noir** / Bonynge (cond.), Jo, Cachemaille, Ford, Bastin, English CO / 1992 / London 440646

Eugen Jochum

b. Nov. 1, 1902, Babenhausen, Bavaria, Germany, **d.** Mar. 26, 1987, Munich, Germany

Conductor

German conductor Eugen Jochum is considered by many to have been the foremost Bruckner conductor of the mid- to late twentieth century; he producing many outstanding recordings of Bruckner's symphonies (as well as worthy interpretations of a great many other composers). He also left to posterity a number of written articles on the interpretation of that composer.

Musical studies began in early childhood (both of Eugen's brothers, Otto Jochum and Georg Ludwig Jochum, went on to become successful musicians in their own right), and Jochum attended the Augsburg Conservatory until he was 20 years of age. He enrolled in the Munich Academy of Music as a composition student of Hermann von Waltershausen, but soon diverted his energies to conducting (working with Siegmund von Hausegger). He worked as a rehearsal assistant at the Munich National Theater, and, after a successful Munich debut in 1926, was invited to join the conducting staff at the Kiel opera. In 1926, having developed a sizable operatic repertory, he moved to Mannheim (1929–30) and then to Duisburg (1930–32). Although relatively young, he was asked to serve as music director for Berlin Radio in 1932, and while in that city built an association with the Berlin Philharmonic Orchestra which would led to many guest conductor appearances in the following decades.

Jochum became music director of the Hamburg opera (and, along with that title, principal conductor of the Hamburg Philharmonic) in 1934, remaining at that post until 1949—effectively avoiding Nazi interference with his musical activities. During the 1930s, Jochum continued to champion a number of contemporary composers who had been officially banned by the Nazi party (such as Hindemith and Bartók), though his great love remained the late Romantic repertory.

After forming the Bavarian Radio Symphony Orchestra in 1949, Jochum spent the 1950s developing that organization (in conjunction with his new role as music director for Bavarian radio) and building his stature as a guest conductor around Europe; his Bayreuth debut was in 1953, and he took partial charge of the Concertgebouw Orchestra in Amsterdam from 1961–64. He conducted the Bamburg Symphony orchestra from 1969 to 1973, and was appointed conductor laureate of the London Symphony Orchestra for the 1978–79 season. From 1950 on Jochum served as the president of the German chapter of the International Bruckner Society.

Jochum's conducting was marked by a fluent, lyric approach (which nevertheless proved capable of drawing tempestuous results from his players when necessary). Above all else he valued a rich, warm sound perfectly suited to the music of Bruckner and Wagner, though recordings show a wealth of insight into the music of other German masters, notably Beethoven, Bach, and Haydn. Jochum died in 1987, after a decade of semi-retirement. *—Blair Johnston*

Recommended:

- ○ **Orff: Carmina Burana** / Jochum (cond.), Fischer-Dieskau, Janowitz, Stolze, Schoneberger Sangerknaben, German Opera Orch. & Chorus / 1995 / DG 447437
- ○ **Bruckner: Te Deum; motets** / Jochum (cond.), Hafliger, Wagner, Lagger, Holm, Stader, Berlin State Opera Chorus, Berlin PO & Chorus, Bavarian Radio Chorus / 1999 / DG 457743
- ○ **Bruckner: Symphony 8** / Jochum (cond.), Berlin PO / 1999 / DG 463263

John Alldis Choir

f. 1962, London, England

Ensemble

The John Alldis Choir was a durable British choral ensemble especially notable for its performances of modern music. John Alldis was a music student at Cambridge who won a scholarship as a Choral Scholar to King's College, Cambridge, where his chorus master was Boris Ord. Choral Scholars are male students who has passed a rigorous competitive audition to sing in the famous Chorus of King's College. Those who pass receive a Cambridge education in return for singing at the daily King's College Chapel services. After his graduation he formed the John Alldis Choir in 1962, which originally comprised 16 professional singers.

They made their concert debut in London in 1962 in a program that included the world premiere of Alexander Goehr's *A Little Cantata of Proverbs*; in the same year they also premiered Malcolm Williamson's *Symphony for Voices*, a work requiring virtuoso singing and exceptionally detailed ensemble blend. These performances were highly successful, and the Chorus became much in demand.

Prior to 1966, the London Symphony Orchestra had no permanent choral organization. A financially uncertain organization until its reorganization in the late 1950s, the orchestra engaged one or another available choir to sing with it when needed, sometimes under the name "London Symphony Chorus." In 1966, the LSO decided to form a permanent choral group, and engaged Alldis to assemble it as its first music director. He remained with this Chorus through 1969, when he took a similar position with the London Philharmonic Choir. In 1972, he also took on the leadership of the Danish State Radio Chorus.

Meanwhile, he maintained the organization of the John Alldis Choir. In 1967, the choir participated in the first European performance of Stravinsky's *Requiem Canticles*, conducted by Pierre Boulez and prepared by Alldis. From 1968 through roughly the 1970s, they were active in recording studios, mostly participating in opera recordings, particularly with RCA and Decca (London) records. For these studio dates, Alldis would hire additional singers as required by the producer and conductor of the sessions. *—Joseph Stevenson*

Recommended:

- **Mozart: Requiem** / Davis (cond.), Donath, Minton, Davies, Nienstedt, John Alldis Choir, BBCSO / 1998 / London 460607
- **Hovhaness: Majnun Symphony** / Hovhaness (cond.), Hill, Wilbraham, Sax, John Alldis Choir, London National PO / Crystal 803

Anthony Rolfe Johnson

b. Nov. 5, 1940, Tackley, England
Tenor

British tenor Anthony Rolfe Johnson is among the best known operatic stars in the world. He has a high, brilliant voice and is known for his very wide repertory in opera, oratorio and other works with orchestra, and art song. He has appeared with every major British opera company, and most of the world's leading houses, and has an extensive catalog of recordings.

His professional operatic debut was at the Glyndebourne Festival Opera in the role of Fenton in Verdi's *Falstaff*. The beginning of his notable career as a singer of the great tenor roles by Benjamin Britten began with a performance of *Albert Herring* with the English Opera Group. He sang the Male Chorus in *The Rape of Lucretia* for the English National Opera. In 1983, he sang his first performance as Aschenbach in *Death in Venice*, a co-production of the Geneva Opera and Scottish Opera, and has also performed the role at the Metropolitan Opera in New York. He was Peter Quint at the Brussels Opéra La Monnaie in *The Turn of the Screw* and sang his first *Peter Grimes* in 1994 with the Scottish Opera, repeating the role at the Glyndebourne Festival, the Metropolitan Opera, Munich, Tokyo, and the Savonlinna Opera Festival in Finland. In a London revival of *Gloriana* he sang the role of Essex. He recorded *Grimes* under the direction of Bernard Haitink on an EMI CD set, and with Kent Nagano conducting sang the role of Captain Vere in *Billy Budd* in Erato's premiere recording of the opera's original four-act version. In addition, he participated in the Teldec Recording of the *War Requiem* with Kurt Masur conducting.

He is also known for his interpretations of Bach, Handel, Joseph Haydn, and Wolfgang Mozart. He frequently sings the Bach Passions, masses, Magnificat, and many of the Cantatas, and most of the great Handel oratorios.

He has sung major Mozart operatic roles, including Don Ottavio (*Don Giovanni*) with the English National Opera and the Royal Opera; the title role of *Lucio Silla* (La Scala Milan); Tamino in *The Magic Flute* (London); Tito (*La Clemenza da Tito*) at the *Metropolitan*; and *Idomeneo* (Opéra de Paris). His Handelian operas include *Semele* and *Alcina* at Covent Garden.

Some of his other roles include Florestan (Beethoven's *Fidelio*); Ulysses (Monteverdi's *Il Ritorno d'Ulisse in Patria*); Stravinsky's *Oedipus Rex* and Tom Rakewell (*The Rake's Progress*); and Debussy's *Pelléas* at La Monnaie. He created the role of Polixenes in the world premiere of Philippe Boesman's *The Winter's Tale*.

He has appeared in concert with the greatest orchestras including the Chicago Symphony Orchestra under Solti, the New York Philharmonic under Rostropovich, the Berlin Philharmonic conducted by James Levine, the Cleveland Orchestra under Simon Rattle, and the Boston Symphony under Seiji Ozawa. Other conductors he has worked with include Rozhdestvensky, Masur, Haitink, Abbado, Tennstedt, Mackerras, Gardiner, Giulini, and Harnoncourt.

His many recordings include *Oedipus Rex*, *Peter Grimes*, *The Rake's Progress*, *Billy Budd*, *Fidelio*, *Samson*, *Die Zauberflöte*, *Idomeneo*, *La Clemenza di Tito*, Haydn's *Creation* and *The Seasons*, several Handel oratorios, and the Evangelist parts in both Bach Passions, as well as numerous song recitals (including entries in Graham Johnson's Hyperion series of complete Schubert songs). *—Joseph Stevenson*

Recommended:

- **Britten: Songs** / Johnson, G. Johnson (piano) / 2001 / Hyperion 55067
- **Bach: Advent Cantatas** / Gardiner (cond.), Argenta, Johnson, Bar, Lang, Monteverdi Choir, EBS / 1992 / DG 463588
- **Song Cycles & Songs by Vaughan Williams, Warlock, Butterworth & Gurney** / Johnson, Willison (piano) / 2001 / EMI 574785

Graham Johnson

b. Jul. 10, 1950, Bulawayo, Rhodesia (Zimbabwe)
Pianist

British pianist Graham Johnson has established a reputation as a leading accompanist through his collaborations with the world's foremost vocal artists. Born in Rhodesia, Johnson attended the Royal Academy of Music in London. There he met the accompanist Gerald Moore, whose influence was instrumental to Johnson's own career. After graduation Johnson pursued further studies with Geoffrey Parsons, another respected figure in the world of vocal accompaniment. Fresh out of school, Johnson received a high-profile career boost when the tenor Peter Pears selected him as the official accompanist for his first master classes at Pears' and Benjamin Britten's annual Aldeburgh Festival. During periods when Britten—Pears' longtime accompanist—was ill, Pears frequently called upon Johnson as a replacement. In 1975 Walter Legge, the impresario and EMI records producer, selected Johnson to accompany his wife, soprano Elizabeth Schwarzkopf. By this time it was clear that Johnson was on track to become one of the most prominent figures in his field.

In search of creative new ways to explore the art song repertory, Johnson founded *The Songmakers' Almanac* in 1976. With the approval and guidance of Gerald Moore, Johnson formed the Almanac to seek out neglected piano/vocal works and to build recitals incorporating several singers. Over a quarter of a century Johnson planned and accompanied over 150 Almanac recitals. In addition, he regularly presented summer recital cycles for the London South Bank and Wigmore Hall series and was invited by Alte Oper of Frankfurt, Germany, to give a seven-part cycle of music on texts by Goethe.

One of his most frequent partners is his Royal Academy classmate Dame Felicity Lott. He has also partnered with some of the most distinguished singers of the second half of the twentieth century, including Victoria de los Angeles, Peter Schreier, Marjana Lipovsek, Felicity Palmer, Anthony Rolfe Johnson, Elly Ameling, Tom Krause, Jessye Norman, Dame Margaret Price, Arlene Auger, and Brigitte Fassbaender. He is best known internationally for his recordings of Schubert's complete lieder on Hyperion Records with such singers as Dame Janet Baker, Philip Langridge, Stephen Varcoe, Thomas Hampson, Lucia Popp, Thomas Allen, Ian Bostridge, and a number of his regular collaborators. Johnson's other recordings include the songs of Hahn, Bizet, Britten (including his realizations of *Purcell*), Gounod, Ireland, and Mendelssohn. His numerous honors include multiple Gramophone Solo Vocal Awards.

Johnson appears frequently on the BBC. In addition to performing a traditional accompanist's role, he has written and served as presenter in programs explaining the songs of Schubert, Poulenc, Liszt, and Shostakovich. He is professor of accompaniment at London's Guildhall School of Music and is a fellow of Guildhall and of the Royal Academy of Music. He has given master classes in Finland, New Zealand, and the United States. *—AMG*

Recommended:

- **Hyperion Schubert Edition** / various / 1997 / Hyperion 200
- **Sweet Power of Song** / Lott, Murray, Williams, Solodchin, Johnson / 2000 / EMI 74206
- **An 1827 Schubertiad** / Layton, Johnson, Dawson, Finley, Banse, Gibbs, Schade, Robinson, Asti, Holst Singers / 2000 / Hyperion 33036

André Jolivet

b. Aug. 8, 1905, Paris, France, **d.** Dec. 20, 1974, Paris, France
Composer: Chamber Music, Concerto

André Jolivet (1905–74) was French music's most sophisticated primitivist. While conducting advanced experiments with rhythm and sonority, Jolivet also found inspiration in the magic arts of equatorial realms and the "primitive" aspects of such instruments as the flute and percussion. He declared that he was dedicated to "restoring music's original ancient sense, as the magical and incantatory expression of the religiosity of human communities."

Interested in drama, painting, and literature in his youth, Jolivet eventually turned to music, studying cello and music theory at Notre Dame de Clignancourt. At 15, he wrote a ballet, and designed its set and costumes. His parents, who were artists, urged him to take up teaching, a more secure profession than composing. Nevertheless, in 1928, after a brief pedagogical career, Jolivet began an intense study of compositional technique under Paul Le Flem. In 1930, Jolivet fell under the spell of avant-garde composer Edgard Varèse, under whose influence he became especially aware of the potential of percussion in chamber and orchestral compositions. Jolivet's early works, which include a dense, atonal String Quartet and an Andante for String Orchestra, demonstrate his intimacy with the techniques of Béla Bartók, Arnold Schoenberg, and Alban Berg. In 1935, Jolivet helped found a contemporary chamber-music organization, *La Spirale*. The next year, this evolved into La *Jeune France*, dedicated to fostering modern French music; Jolivet's partners in this endeavor were Olivier Messiaen, Daniel Lesur, and Yves Baudrier. During his service in the French Army in World War II, Jolivet grew interested in primitive religion and magic, and this intellectual quest soon informed his style. Jolivet's intellectual preoccupations can be compared to Varèse's emphasis on Pythagorean number ratios as a basis of harmony and other musical components. In Jolivet's case, the results, as evidenced by the piano suite *Mana*, are simultaneously exotic and esoteric.

In 1943, Jolivet was named music director of the Comédie-Française, where he remained until 1959; this motivated him to develop a still adventurous, and more direct, expressive melodic style, exemplified by the virtuoso *Concertino for Trumpet, Strings, and Piano* (1948; recorded by such luminaries as Maurice André and Wynton Marsalis, and the Flute Concerto of 1949, recorded by Jean-Pierre Rampal. A love-hate relationship with the Neoclassicism of the 1930s led him to experiment with the futuristic, electronic Ondes Martenot, for which he wrote a concerto in 1948, and with complex orchestrations, that evoke the sounds of Africa, East Asia, and Polynesia.

Jolivet wrote concertos for the traditional solo instruments (piano, violin, cello), but he also delighted in unusual sonic combinations. Besides frequently enlisting the Ondes Martenot, he produced such concoctions as *Messe pour le jour de la paix for voice, organ, and tambourine*; and *Rhapsodie à Sept* for clarinet, bassoon, trumpet, trombone, percussion, violin, and double bass.

Jolivet served as president of the Concerts Lamoureux from 1963 to 1968; from 1965 to 1970, he was professor of composition at the Paris Conservatory. At his death, Jolivet was regarded, with Messiaen, as one of the leading figures in contemporary French music. *—James Reel*

Overview of Works (1920–1973)

André Jolivet was one of those maverick figures in art whose works did not necessarily reflect a clearly defined pattern of growth or faithfully follow a school of thought. Yet his music, especially after 1945, is recognizably his own unique mixture of ancient styles with exotic, sometimes ethnic elements. He also retained a measure of harshness in his expressive language from his earlier years, when his music divulged the influence of Edgard Varèse, one of his teachers.

Typical of works from that early phase was his 1934 *String Quartet*, certainly one of his more challenging compositions for the listener. Jolivet never embraced serial composition and his atonal music must ultimately be regarded as a passing phase. Thus, the quartet can hardly be called representative of his chamber music, the genre that produced some of his most popular and approachable works. His 1944 *Chant de Linos for flute and piano* (or for flute, string trio, and harp) is a dark, atmospheric work that shows the composer's affection for the flute. He had already written *Five Incantations for flute* (1935), a work that divulges both the exotic and primitive sides of his style and whose brilliant scoring never leaves the listener with the feeling the solo flute sounds barren or wanting for accompaniment.

Jolivet's 1949 *Concerto for Flute and Orchestra* is one of his more popular large works. In three movements, with the Allegro Risoluto finale beginning without pause after the Largo second movement, the concerto features some beautifully lyrical writing in both the Andante Cantabile—Allegro Scherzando first movement and in the Largo. Jolivet's *Trumpet Concerto* from the previous year divulges a neo-Classical character. The *Concerto for Ondes Martenot* (1947) and *Concerto for Piano and Orchestra* (1950) are two examples of his most exotic and appealing music from any period. The latter contains elements of African, Asian, and even Polynesian music, and features Jolivet's often spicy rhythmic side.

Jolivet, like Orff, had a penchant for use of percussion in his music, often writing scores requiring a large number of percussion instruments. *Cérémonial, hommage à Varèse* (1968), for six percussion instruments, and *Heptade* (1971), for trumpet and six percussion instruments, divulge this colorful, if not fully convincing tendency. His music for solo piano occupies a significant part of his output, too. Jolivet's 1945 *Piano Sonata*, in fact, was a landmark work for him in that it forged elements from his earlier difficult style with his more accessible wartime manner to yield what many consider the first major composition in his mature style. Also of note is *Mana* (1935), six pieces for piano that exhibiting a fairly difficult expressive language. It was highly praised by Messiaen, who would, like Jolivet, become a member of a musical group called "Jeune France." *—Robert Cummings*

Recommended:

- ○ **Oeuvres pour Piano** / Mefano / Adda 581042
- ○ **Musique Concertante** / Petit (cond.), etc. / REM 311234

CHAMBER MUSIC

Chant de Linos, for flute & piano (1944)

Jolivet composed his *Chant de Linos* as a competition piece for the Paris Conseratory in 1944. In 1945, he replaced the original flute and piano version with one scored for flute, harp, and string trio. Jolivet, who was interested in the evocation of ritual in his music, wrote that a "chant de linos" was an ancient Greek mourning chant, with wailing and dancing. Appropriately, the music is based on a six-tone scale that suggests antiquity: G, A flat, B, C sharp, D, F, and G. Other unusual modes are used in the course of the 11-minute work. The introduction is a recitative-like cadenza. This is followed by the funeral lament, a plaintive section with a polyphonic texture. A more agitated section suggests the wailing and dancing. Another cadenza introduces the second major section of the piece, a wild dance in 7/8. *—Joseph Stevenson*

Recommended:

- ○ **Paris** / Pahud, Le Sage / 1997 / EMI 56488

CONCERTO

Concertino for trumpet, strings & piano (1948)

One of "my ballets for trumpet," as Jolivet dubbed the present work and his *Trumpet Concerto No. 2*, the *Concertino* was composed in 1948 (and has in fact been choreographed). This ten-minute work is in four sections; the propulsive vigor of its opening minutes, with its dark comedy and jazzy syncopations, leads into a more languorous central section. The energy builds once again, with lively rhythms and a slight hint of jazz, and the work concludes with a brilliant coda. During and after World War II Jolivet, spurning the worldwide retreat from general audiences engaged in by many of his major contemporaries, turned toward a newly accessible style. He added Bartók's motoric rhythms to a set of stylistic influences that included Messiaen and Varèse, cultivated a basically tonal harmonic framework, and continued to pursue exotic sounds. The present *Concertino* neatly encapsulates all these traits. *—AMG*

Recommended:

- ○ **Trumpet Concertos** / Lopez-Cobos (cond.), Nakariakov, Lausanne CO / 1993 / Teldec 90846

Flute Concerto (1949)

Jolivet's *Flute Concerto* (1949) is a work that to some extent reconciles the composer's dissonant, aggressive style of the 1930s with his more melodic and accessible aesthetic of the early 1940s. Jolivet had already explored the flute's potential in *Chant de Linos* (1944), and he brought that knowledge to the *Flute Concerto*, which has been described by one commentator as "sometimes lyrical, sometimes piquant and capricious."

The first movement opens with a melancholy Andante cantabile introduction. The flute spins out a dissonant line, while the string accompaniment becomes increasingly tense and blustery. The tempo quickens to Allegro scherzando; the atmosphere remains agitated, though music of a brighter character breaks the surface from time to time. The brief, somber Largo is followed by an Allegro risoluto finale; indeed, "resolute" is a good description for this lively but stern movement. A miniature cadenza brings the work to a propulsive close. *—Chris Morrison*

Recommended:

- ○ **French Orchestral Works** / P. Järvi (cond.), Wiesler, Tapiola Sinfonietta / 1993 / Bis 630
- ○ **Flute Master Pieces** / Jolivet (cond.), Rampal, Lamoureux Concert Association Orch. / Erato 45839

Trumpet Concerto No. 2 (1954)

The jazz influence, which is one of several important elements of André Jolivet's music, comes to the fore in the *Trumpet Concerto No. 2* of 1954, which the composer described as one of "my ballets for trumpet" (the other being the *Concertino for Trumpet, Strings and Piano* of 1948). Jolivet's scoring here is quite unusual and hints at the jazz inspiration: two flutes, clarinet, English horn, two saxophones, piano, double bass, and no fewer than 14 different percussion instruments. The concerto opens quietly with a subgroup of those percussion instruments, joined by the trumpet soloist playing with a mute. That music alternates with livelier dance-like material in the first movement. The bluesy second movement, Grave, once again features muted trumpet. A simple tune works against a harsher, percussion-laden accompaniment in the final movement, marked Giocoso. There is even a passage for just the percussion in the middle of the movement, which is heavily syncopated and makes for a lively conclusion. *—Chris Morrison*

Recommended:

- ○ **Trumpet Concertos** / Soustrot (cond.), Pays de la Loire PO / 1987 / Disques Pierre Verany 788011

David Jolley

French Horn player

The genesis and success of the Orpheus Chamber Orchestra can be attributed at least in part to the involvement of founding hornist David Jolley. A hornist can never really hope to attain anything like the fame of a high-profile concert pianist or violinist, or that of an opera star, but Jolley is about as successful a brass soloist as there is.

He attended the Juilliard School for both undergraduate and graduate studies. His career was boosted while still in its infancy when Jolley won the Concert Artist Guild Award and then took top prize at the Heldenleben International Horn Competition; international prominence was not long in coming. In addition to his many performances and recordings with the Orpheus group and his activities as a horn soloist, he has collaborated over the years with a number of well-known chamber groups and organizations, including the Guarneri String Quartet, the Beaux Arts Trio, the American String Quartet, and the Chamber Music Society of Lincoln Center. As can be said of so many modern virtuosos, David Jolley has spent a great deal of his musical energy on contemporary music: John Harbison and George Perle, among others, have composed brand-new pieces for him to play. He has also found time to teach at the Manhattan School of Music, the North Carolina School of the Arts, the Hartt School of Music, and Queens College. *—Blair Johnston*

Recommended:

- ○ **Strauss: Horn Concertos** / Mayer (cond.), Jolley, Israel Sinfonietta / 1999 / Arabesque 6733
- ○ **Wilder: Music for Horn** / Jolley, Pilafian, Oei, Kay / 1995 / Arabesque 6665

Niccolò Jommelli

b. Sep. 10, 1714, Aversa, Italy, **d.** Aug. 25, 1774, Naples, Italy

Composer

Niccolò Jommelli was an innovative opera seria composer with an extraordinary dramatic flair. He altered the contemporary opera seria, involving the orchestra in an ever greater dramatic role, and coming up with innovative ways of arriving at this result. When Jommelli arrived on the scene, Italian opera was dominated by the virtuosic solo singer, and drama was of secondary or even tertiary importance. The public went to hear their favorite singer or composer, and was enthralled by the vocal acrobatics of the virtuosi of the day. Steady streams of groups of secco recitative and exit arias, an aria which was placed at the end of the scene to encourage applause so that the singer could come back on stage, were the building blocks of opera seria, and had little connection with valid dramaturgy. Jommelli and others wanted to change that. Jommelli's compositions tended to use more obbligato recitative, which involved the orchestra as a dramatic partner with the singer. In his later life, he also wrote ensembles and choruses, which had completely gone out of vogue in Italy. His largest ensemble, the final trio in *Fetonte*, was an entire action scena derived from the action ensembles of comic opera, and included a varied texture of trio, chorus, solos, arioso, and obbligato recitative, as well as programmatic orchestral music. Elements of his style include harmonic and melodic daring, full use of his orchestral resources, mingling of aria and declamation, and a liberal use of chromaticism. His orchestral writing, which included dynamics and the crescendo effect and secondary themes in the dominant, directly influenced the Mannheim symphonists.

Contemporary Neapolitan composers that influenced him include Hasse and Leo, both of whom also altered the form of the opera seria for good. Jommelli's first successes were comic operas, but his serious operas were very successful also. It was from Hasse that he learned to write obbligato recitative instead of the recitative semplice that dominated Italian opera at the time. The dramatic possibilities of the orchestra were attractive to Jommelli, and he began to experiment with his resources.

In 1741 Jommelli set a text by Metastasio, the opera *Ezio*. It was a singular success, and commissions from Bologna, Venice, Turin, and Padua followed. In 1743, on the recommendation of his colleague Hasse, Jommelli was hired as musical director of the Ospedale degli Incurabili in Venice. For the girls there he wrote oratorios, motets, masses, and choral works. However opera was still his first love.

In 1749 he became *maestro coadiutore* to the papal chapel, and he composed much sacred music. But he also received commissions for operas from many major cities, for Rome was an international center. One of the most important commissions of his career came at this time, from the city of Vienna. Jommelli set the opera *Achille in Sciro* for the Viennese court. Metastasio, the king of opera seria librettists, was the court poet in Vienna at the time, and he was so impressed that Jommelli was a court favorite in Vienna for a time. In 1753 Jommelli received an offer to move to Stuttgart, where the Duke was particularly fond of Italian opera and French spectacle. There he was given complete control over his operatic productions, and given almost unlimited resources. He had the best singers and instrumentalists in all of Europe. He developed his obbligato recitative, wrote with great formal variety, and created dramatically complex and alive scenes and acts. Unfortunately, by the time he died, the lighter styles of the opera buffa had taken hold of the public imagination, and his operas were no longer popular. *—Rita Laurance*

Overview of Works (1737–1774)

One of the greatest, but most-neglected opera composers of the eighteenth century, Jommelli was born in the Italian town of Aversa in September 1714. His early training was in Naples; there he came into contact with a number of the leading composers of the day, most notably Hasse. It was also in Naples that Jommelli started his composing career with two comic operas. The production of his first serious opera, *Ricimero rè de' Goti* (Rome, 1740) placed his career on solid foundations, and he rapidly established himself over the next few years with productions of new works in Bologna, Venice, Turin, Ferrara, and Padua. After spells in Venice (where he was appointed musical director of the Ospedale degli incurabile girls' conservatory) and Rome, he went to Vienna and then Stuttgart, where he was appointed chief musical director at the court.of the Duke of Württemburg. Now at the height of his fame, Jommelli enjoyed some of his greatest triumphs in Stuttgart, before returning to Naples for the final years of his life, where he died in 1774.

Jommelli's operatic style developed from a diverse range of influences, a number of them gathered during his travels. From Hasse he learned the importance of accompanied recitative, a telling device used to special effect by the German to heighten moments of dramatic tension. In Vienna, Jommelli's contact with such early symphonists as Dittersdorf and Wagenseil had a considerable influence on his orchestral writing, which in the mature operas attains a richness of texture foreign to most Italian operas of the period. In turn, the big orchestral crescendos of the Mannheim orchestral style in Germany is credited to Jommelli's influence. This concentration on orchestral technique was further enhanced in Stuttgart, where a strong French influence introduced Jommelli to the brilliant orchestration, ballets, and ensembles familiar from composers such as Rameau. Jommelli's mature style is thus an amalgam of various influences allied to his own distinctive gift for melody and brilliant theatrical sense. With all these features, along with a reduction of the hegemony of bravura display that had become a feature of Italian opera seria, Jommelli, along with composers like Tommaso Traetta, played a major part in operatic reform, a role too frequently ascribed solely to Gluck. His more than 80 operas include both serious and comic works, but it is the former that occupy such an important place in operatic history. Mostly based on heroic mythological or historical topics (a number were set to librettos by Pietro Metastasio, the poet who created the paradigm for the genre), this extensive output includes such masterpieces as *Il Vologeso* (Stuttgart, 1766) and *Armida abbandonata* (Naples, 1770), both among the few operas of Jommelli's to have been revived in good modern recordings (although the latter is currently unavailable). In addition to his operas, Jommelli composed a substantial body of church music, and a rather smaller amount of orchestral music. His sacred works mostly date from his earlier Neapolitan period, and unsurprisingly show the strong influence of the florid style of Neapolitan church music. *—Brian Robins*

Recommended:

- ○ **Jommelli: Didone Abbandonata** / Bernius (cond.), Kendall, Roschmann, Borst, Taylor, Stuttgart CO / 1995 / Prfep 381953
- ○ **Jommelli: Miserere; 5 Duetti Sacri** / Pozzer, Manci / 2000 / Nuova Era 7330
- ○ **Jommelli: Requiem; Veni Sponsa Christi** / Frontalini (cond.), Modavia SO / Bongiovanni 2215
- ○ **Jommelli: Lamentations of Jeremiah** / Rousset (cond.), Lanceron, Mouyren, Lesne, Gens, Seminario Musicale / 1996 / Virgin 45202

Dame Gwyneth Jones

b. Nov. 7, 1936, Pontnewynydd, Wales, England

Soprano

Dame Gwyneth Jones has achieved remarkable success throughout her vocal career. Best known for her performances of Turandot and the role of Brünnhilde, she has brought an attractive stage presence, total musicianship, a highly controlled voice, and thorough emotional and dramatic involvement to all of her appearances.

Gwyneth Jones was born to Edward George and Violet Webster Jones in 1936, in Pontnewynydd, Wales. Her studies with Arnold Smith and Ruth Packer at the Royal College of Music in London were made possible by a scholarship from the County Council. She also studied at the Accademia Musicale Chigiana in Siena, at Herbert Graf's International Opera Centre in Zurich, and with Maria Carpi in Geneva. Jones' professional debut, as a mezzo-soprano, was the role of Annina in *Der Rosenkavalier* with the Zurich Opera in 1962. Shortly afterwards, she noticed her voice moving upward, which allowed her to sing her first soprano role of Amelia in *Un Ballo in Maschera*. She was also heard singing Lady Macbeth for the Welsh National Opera and the Royal Opera, and heard filling in for Leontyne Price and Régine Crespin at Covent Garden. After performing roles such as Santuzza, Desdemona, Donna Anna, Aida, and Tosca, she made appearances at the Vienna State Opera, La Scala, and at principal opera houses in Berlin, Paris, Hamburg, and Rome. On the experiences she commented, "It has given me a special thrill to be accepted at the source—Verdi and Puccini at La Scala, Mozart and Beethoven in Munich and Vienna, and Wagner at Bayreuth."

Shortly after Jones made her 1966 American (New York) debut as the title role in Cherubini's *Medea*, she married Till Haberfeld, a director, with whom she had one child. She achieved American success with her performance of *Fidelio* with the San Francisco Opera and for her Metropolitan Opera debut as Sieglinde in *Die Walküre* on November 26, 1972. One of Jones' greatest achievements was doing all three Brünnhilde roles in the summer of 1975 at the Bayreuth centennial *Ring Cycle* under Pierre Boulez and Patrice Chéreau. Jones entered a phase of her career when at the 1984 Los Angeles Olympics, she gave her first performance of Turandot, a role she had learned from her former teacher Dame Eva Turner. This feat was regarded as one of the greatest triumphs of the later portion of Jones' career, during which she became known as the world's finest interpreter of this role. She also took on the roles of Minnie in *La Fanciulla del West*, the widow Begbick in *Mahagonny*, and the mother in *Hänsel und Gretel*. Jones continued the same energetic performance schedule she began early in her career well into her sixties; in 1999 she had 70 opera and concert performances planned. She was made a Dame of the British Empire, received the German Cross of Merit, and is a Kammersängerin of both the Vienna and Bavarian Operas. *—Meredith Gailey*

Recommended:

○ **Strauss: Die Ägyptische Helena** / Krips (cond.), Schreier, Glossop, Jones, Thomas, Vienna State Orch. & Chorus / 1999 / RCA 69429

○ **Wagner: Götterdämmerung** / Solti (cond.), Nilsson, Fischer-Dieskau, Ludwig, Popp, Frick, Watts, Jones / 1997 / London 455569

Martin Jones

b. Feb. 4, 1940, Witney, England

Pianist

Martin Jones is an elegant and gifted pianist who has recorded a wide swath of literature for the Nimbus label. Jones studied at London's Royal Academy of Music with Guido Agosti, Guy Jonson, and Gordon Green and in 1968 received the Dame Myra Hess Award given by the Musicians' Benevolent Fund in the U.K. Also in 1968 Jones made his debuts at Queen Elizabeth Hall in the South Bank Centre of London and in New York's Carnegie Hall. In 1971 Jones accepted the post of pianist-in-residence at Cardiff University, which he held until 1988. At about that time Jones began his series of recordings for Nimbus.

Since 1988, Jones has recorded the entire piano catalogs of Debussy, Grainger, Szymanowski, Mendelssohn, Stravinsky, Korngold, Brahms, and Mompou in addition to anthologies of works of other composers. With all this recording activity, one would think Jones is never outside the recording studio. But on the contrary, he is exceedingly well traveled, performing mostly in Britain but also in Australia, Canada, and the U.S., where he frequently sits a judge on several world-class piano competitions. Jones is often heard on the BBC, and he may be heard playing the piano solos in the soundtrack of the film *Howard's End*. *—Uncle Dave Lewis*

Recommended:

○ **Szymanowski: Piano Music** / Jones / 1999 / Nimbus 1750

○ **Grainger: The Complete Piano Music** / Jones / 1997 / Nimbus 1767

○ **Korngold: The Piano Music** / Jones / 2003 / Nimbus 5705

Scott Joplin

b. Nov. 24, 1868, Marshall, TX, **d.** Apr. 1, 1917, New York, NY

Composer: Keyboard, Opera

Ragtime was the direct predecessor of jazz, and Scott Joplin was ragtime's greatest composer. Born in 1868 near the Texas-Louisiana border, he was the son of a former slave who played the fiddle. He grew up in Texarkana, TX, and showed musical promise from an early age. As a young man he sang in vocal groups and had some classical piano training from a local German immigrant—studies that manifested themselves in the explicitly classicizing ambitions of many of Joplin's mature piano rags.

Joplin lived in St. Louis from about 1885 to 1893, scratching out a rough living in local bars and clubs. In 1894 he led a band at the Columbian Exposition in Chicago—essentially a world's fair—and formed the Texas Medley Quartette, which performed in vaudeville shows. Joplin moved back to Missouri, to the town of Sedalia, and embarked on further musical study at the George R. Smith College for Negroes. Beginning in 1895 he composed music for publication, and in 1899 his *Maple Leaf Rag* (named for a social organization called the Maple Leaf Club and published by Joplin's indefatigable supporter John Stark) became a national hit and a defining moment for the young genre of ragtime. The piece touched off a ragtime craze that would not subside for well over a decade. Joplin went on to publish more than 40 rags, many of them just as well wrought as his signature composition, but his imitators outstripped him in popularity and financial success.

Joplin's goals later in his career lay in the direction of a fusion of ragtime and classical music, and the impossibility of achieving this grand ambition lent his final years a tragic cast. Even early in his career he had staged a ballet, *The Ragtime Dance*, and a ragtime opera, *The Guest of Honor*. Neither was successful, a fact that continually frustrated him. Except for an instrumental interlude from the ballet that was later published separately, the music for both works has been lost. Joplin moved to New York in 1907, and by the early 1910s was becoming ill with syphilis. Depressed by his lack of success on the concert stage, Joplin pushed ahead with an unstaged concert performance of his second opera, *Treemonisha*, in 1915; set among blacks in the rural South, the opera exalted the values of education and progress. But this work, too, attracted little attention, and the composer's death in 1917 was not much noticed.

Fifty-seven years after his death, Scott Joplin finally became a household name after his music (most notably *The Entertainer*) was used by Marvin Hamlisch in his score for the popular film *The Sting*. Some of the credit for the revival of his music is due to 1950s biographer Rudi Blesh, and to pianist Joshua Rifkin's classical-styled performances and recordings of Joplin rags that followed in the 1960s. Rifkin brought to Joplin's rags the grace and subtlety that the composer himself had intended for them, helping to rescue ragtime from the realm of flashy "novelty" piano performance. In the years following Hamlisch's score, Joplin's music has achieved the classic status of which he dreamed. *Treemonisha* has been revived by several major opera companies, and the rags are fixtures of classical recitals and popular piano performances around the world. *—AMG*

KEYBOARD

Bethena, waltz (1905)

Of Joplin's 50-some pieces for solo piano, only six are waltzes—a surprise, given the waltz's popularity among the home pianists likely to snatch up Joplin's sheet music at the time. Certainly his best waltz is *Bethena*, one of two published in 1905 when Joplin was perfecting his mature style (the piece's partner is the more innocuous *Binks' Waltz*). This is a rag waltz, laying right-hand syncopations onto a 3/4 meter. The construction is elaborate: a graceful, wistful refrain (its germ heard in the brief, wide-ranging introduction) alternates with four contrasting sections, all separated by little, surprisingly chromatic interludes. The first contrasting section is closely related to the main theme, but the second is more rag-like; the third—having skipped the refrain—is a haunting minor-mode episode; the fourth, again intruding before the refrain can return, brightens the mood. The main melody finally returns, closing the piece with tender nostalgia. *—James Reel*

Recommended:

○ **Joplin: Marches, Waltzes & Rags** / Albright / 1993 / MusicMasters 67102

The Cascades (1904)

In early 1904, Joplin took a brief trip to Arkansas to visit relatives. After stopping off in Sedalia, MO, Joplin returned to St. Louis just in time for the opening of the St. Louis World's Fair on April 30. One of the main attractions of the Fair was the Cascades Garden, a series of artificial waterfalls, rapids, lagoons, and fountains that ran down the main thoroughfare. In quick time, Joplin composed the rag *The Cascades*, which was published soon thereafter and was heard often at the Fair itself in subsequent weeks. Joplin's publisher, John Stark—a man often given to enthusiasm and high-flown language—labeled this rag "The Masterpiece of Scott Joplin" on the cover of its sheet music. In an advertisement he continued: "Hear it, and you can fairly feel the earth wave under your feet. It is as high-class as Chopin and is creating a great sensation among musicians."

Dedicated to the now-unknown banjo players Kimball and Donovan, *The Cascades* is another of Joplin's works which bears a bit of a resemblance to his biggest hit, *The Maple Leaf Rag*. In particular, the first two melodies are roughly patterned after the equivalent sections in *Maple Leaf*. But *The Cascades* has its own charm: it is an extroverted and tuneful work, and its lighthearted opening strain has a lilting, music box quality which some have heard as an evocation of the flowing waters of the Cascades Garden. *—Chris Morrison*

Recommended:

○ **Joplin: Piano Works** / Hyman / 1988 / RCA 57993

The Easy Winners (1901)

Scott Joplin had lived in St. Louis on and off through the 1880s and early 1890s. But after the success of *The Maple Leaf Rag*, Joplin decided to make the permanent move, from his hometown of Sedalia to St. Louis, in the spring of 1901. He was a big hit in his new home right from the start. Among the works he wrote in 1901 was the rag *The Easy Winners*, which, unusually for Joplin, he chose to publish himself (in October of that year). Why his usual publisher, John Stark, didn't publish the rag isn't known for certain—one guess is that Joplin may have been trying to get Stark's attention after he had passed on publishing Joplin's ballet *The Ragtime Dance*.

In any case, many commentators believe *The Easy Winners*, which is something of a celebration of the sporting world, particularly horse racing, to be one of Joplin's greatest rags. Certainly it was once one of his most popular; it was one of only four Joplin pieces (the others being the *Maple Leaf*, *Gladiolus*, and *Original* rags) to be recorded before the year 1940. *—Chris Morrison*

Recommended:

○ **The Red Back Book** / Schuller (cond.), New England Conservatory Ragtime Ens. / 1985 / EMI 47193

○ **Joplin: Piano Works** / Hyman / RCA 7993

Elite Syncopations (1902)

1902 saw the issue of four new rags from Scott Joplin, who, seeking a better commercial outlet for his music, had moved from Sedalia, MO (today home to the annual Scott Joplin Festival), to the city of St. Louis about a year earlier. Three of these new pieces have since become standards of the genre: *The Ragtime Dance*, all-time favorite *The Entertainer*, and *Elite Syncopations*.

All ragtime music is rhythmically charged—forward-thrusting, syncopated—but there is a particular bounce to the step of *Elite Syncopations*, a frequent intrusion of unusual and quite wry off-beats (they are also quite graceless when played badly, as they all too often are) into the flow. Hence its title. *Elite Syncopations* is built, as are all of Joplin's pieces, from several tuneful strands. Throughout the first of them, which comes back several times, Joplin slides around chromatically, first up and then, in a charming little offbeat filler at the end of the opening phrase, back down. Towards the end of the piece we move from the F major that has thus far been home base to B flat major, never to return—lovers of Viennese waltzes and many polkas will find this last-hour shift to another key quite familiar, and once again we have to marvel at how closely Joplin's ultra-American music follows the venerable dance traditions of Europe. —*Blair Johnston*

Recommended:

○ **Joplin: Piano Works** / Hyman / 1988 / RCA 57993

The Entertainer (1902)

For those living in America (and many other parts of the world) in the mid-70s, Scott Joplin's rag *The Entertainer* was almost ubiquitous. After decades of relative neglect, it seemed as though Joplin's music, and ragtime in general, had surpassed even the stature it had enjoyed during Joplin's own lifetime. How did this come about? A small-scale Joplin revival was already underway around 1970 when composer/conductor/educator/author Gunther Schuller was given a copy of *The Red Back Book*, a 1909 publication of ragtime orchestrations put together by Joplin's publisher, John Stark. Schuller liked what he found and put together the New England Conservatory Ragtime Ensemble to perform and record some of those arrangements. The recording sold very well and won a Grammy Award. Film director George Roy Hill came across this record and thought that Joplin's music would be the perfect accompaniment for his next film, *The Sting*, which went on to be a huge success worldwide. Marvin Hamlisch arranged Joplin's music for the film; the music won the Academy Award for best film score and the soundtrack recording was a top ten bestseller. Hamlisch's version of *The Entertainer*, which served as the film's main theme, was likewise a huge hit and won a Grammy for Best Pop Instrumental Performance. In his Grammy acceptance speech, Hamlisch called Joplin "the real new artist of the year." By that time, Joplin's name and music were everywhere familiar and such was his newfound fame that Joplin received a posthumous Pulitzer Prize in 1976.

The origins of *The Entertainer* date back to Joplin's first big success, *The Maple Leaf Rag*, in 1899. The money Joplin made from that rag enabled him to move to St. Louis, MO, where he temporarily gave up playing piano publicly and devoted himself to teaching and composing. He started to look to more ambitious forms and, in the years 1901 and 1902, produced the ballet *The Ragtime Dance* and the opera *A Guest of Honor*. Both were large failures, and Joplin was forced back to writing the more financially rewarding piano rags. But the experience Joplin had gained in working in larger forms showed in the greater sophistication of his new rags. One of those new works was *The Entertainer*, written in late 1902 and dedicated to James Brown and his Mandolin Club.

The admittedly infectious sequence of melodies and the slightly wistful quality underlying the work's high spirits, made *The Entertainer* a hit right from the beginning. Joplin's publisher, John Stark even tried to capitalize on *The Entertainer*'s popularity by setting its famous opening melody to words in "Oh You Tommy." It is also said that in 1920s New Orleans, watermelon street hawkers would use the beginning of that same melody in shouting out "Watermelons, they're wet, they're cold." —*Chris Morrison*

Recommended:

○ **Complete Rags of Scott Joplin, Vol. 1** / Kirby / 1997 / VRD 2004

Eugenia (1906)

In 1905–06, Joplin published four piano pieces named after women; his marriage had been in trouble for a while and it was rumored that at least one of these pieces—*Leola*—was named for a girlfriend. The inspiration of *Eugenia* remains unknown; Joplin's pieces were often given titles that had more to do with the arbitrarily selected cover illustrations than the character or background of the music. At any rate, *Eugenia* is a rather sensual piece as rags go, its first theme slithering chromatically up and down the scale. The second strain dips gently into the minor mode without dampening the music's happy nature, the third strips off some of the syncopation, and the fourth turns mock-noble, as if Sarastro had just cakewalked in from *The Magic Flute*. Throughout, Joplin toys with harmonic instability. If *Eugenia* was one of Joplin's lovers, she obviously left him unsure of where he stood. —*James Reel*

Recommended:

○ **Euphonic Sounds** / Bolcom / Omega 3001

Gladiolus Rag (1907)

After his divorce in 1906, Joplin spent the next several months traveling. He visited many of his old stomping grounds—St. Louis, Chicago, and Texarkana. Then, around July 1907, he settled in New York and began serious musical activities again, performing frequently and composing energetically in the various hotels and rooming houses at which he stayed. He sought out a publisher for some of those new compositions, and the Jos. W. Stern Company, which had published works by several other African American composers, bought two of Joplin's rags in short order. One of these was the *Gladiolus Rag*, copyrighted on September 24, 1907.

The piece looks back in many ways to Joplin's *Leola* (1905), with which it shares some ideas, and beyond that to Joplin's first great success, the *Maple Leaf Rag* (1899). But a new maturity is in evidence. The new rag is more adventurous harmonically than its predecessors; it is among the first of several later Joplin pieces to show a distinctly Chopinesque lyricism; and its final strain is a particularly grand one that looks forward to the active left-hand parts of Joplin's last rags. The "Gladiolus" is among Joplin's best-known pieces. —*Chris Morrison*

Recommended:

○ **Euphonic Sounds** / Bolcom / Omega 3001

Magnetic Rag (1914)

By 1914, ragtime was considered old-fashioned and a commercial liability. Yet this, Joplin's final rag (he would die two years later of syphilis), seems anything but antiquated. Although Joplin's inspiration had fallen off in his previous few rags, the *Magnetic Rag* is a fine valedictory statement, an ambitious and optimistic piece with a bit of pensiveness, all packed into about three and a half minutes. A very brief, highly chromatic introduction gives way to an irrepressibly happy tune. The second strain goes into the parallel minor, darkening the proceedings without slackening the pace. Happy days are here again in the third strain, with its wayward melody and harmony. Tension returns in the next section, as the relative minor hints at some silent movie villainy. But the first theme arrives to save the day and the piece ends in high spirits, with Joplin tossing in one more playful episode of find-the-key chromaticism in the little coda. —*James Reel*

Recommended:

○ **Elite Syncopations** / Piano Roll / 2003 / Shout! Factory 30156

Maple Leaf Rag (1899)

The *Maple Leaf Rag*, published in Sedalia, MO, in 1899, was the first of Scott Joplin's piano pieces to be issued with his name, and his name only, listed as the composer. *Original Rags* of 1896 is, of course, earlier, but, according to its original title page and the records of the U.S. copyright office, it is a collaboration between Joplin and another man, and, however much diehard Joplin fans might wish it to have been otherwise, it very probably was, in fact, a collaboration. (Similarly, even today, most Joplin rags cannot be found in their original forms; they have almost always been "arranged" by somebody, for example Gunther Schuller or, in the preparation for using Joplin's music in the film *The Sting*, Marvin Hamlisch.) The *Maple Leaf Rag* was Joplin's best-known work throughout his short lifetime, and has remained among the leaders of the pack since. Joplin earned one cent for every *Maple Leaf Rag* sold, a publishing contract that might not sound very promising, but nevertheless managed to get him through some lean times.

The *Maple Leaf Rag* is in many ways the prototypical Joplin rag, and a large number of the rags he later wrote are mere imitations of it (a trap fallen into by many best-selling authors, to be sure!). It is in A flat major, filled with syncopations and bouncing left-hand accompaniment ideas, and follows a standard fixed-form dance-piece pattern: a handful of mildly contrasting ideas, the first of which operates as something of a refrain, are pitted against one another, there is a trio in an alternate key (in this case D flat major), and finally, a little coda built from a new strain of melody (just barely new, mind you) brings it home. There is throughout *Maple Leaf Rag* the slightest tinge of chromaticism (something found in most of Joplin's fine works), and, more vitally, an infectious tunefulness that together raise it above the ordinary, now-forgotten rag music of Joplin's contemporaries. —*Blair Johnston*

Recommended:

○ **Joplin: Piano Works** / Hyman / RCA 7993

Pine Apple Rag (1908)

In 1908 a new publishing house, Seminary Music in New York (which inhabited the same building as the firm that launched Irving Berlin's career), jumped on the robust Scott Joplin bandwagon; among the first Joplin piano rags issued by the newcomer was *Pine Apple Rag*, today a favorite of countless listeners who recognize it as one of the items used by composer Marvin Hamlisch and director George Roy Hill in the 1973 film *The Sting*.

Pine Apple Rag takes up the same reworked European dance blueprint as nearly all Joplin's other rags—a four-bar introduction (which in this case introduces the actual main theme, something that not all the introductions do), an opening tune that returns for another go after a second idea has run its course, and then a change of key and a pair of new thoughts. There are moments in *Pine Apple Rag* that rival, in terms of sheer infectiousness, the best that Joplin, or any other ragtime musician, ever wrote. The second strain is one of them: it is syncopated through and through, the individual off-beat accents jelling together as boisterous little groups of three eighth notes against the common-time rhythmic backdrop. The final, coda-type phrase grows from a chromatically-altered harmony that, while hardly groundbreaking in a global sense (considering what, halfway around the world, the likes of Scriabin, Schoenberg, and Mahler were up to in 1909), is striking in its own rag-ish way. —*Blair Johnston*

Recommended:

○ **Joplin: Rags & Waltzes** / Blumenthal / 1994 / Pavane 7317

The Ragtime Dance, stoptime two-step (1906)

There are actually two items in the Scott Joplin catalog by the name *The Ragtime Dance*. One is a stage work for dancers and musical ensemble—something of a ballet, though hardly in the *Sleeping Beauty* or *Coppelia* sense—composed in 1899 almost immediately after the publication of *The Maple Leaf Rag*, and the other is a piano rag in the usual and by now familiar manner. The little piano rag, which was published in 1906, is based on music from the earlier ballet work, but, quite unlike its dancehall sister, it lasts just three or four minutes and fills just a few pages of paper. *The Ragtime Dance*, meaning the solo piano version, was among those pieces selected for use in the 1973 film *The Sting*; but, like several of the other rags heard in the movie, it appeared in an extensively re-arranged guise, and so today its original form is sometimes not always recognized for what it is.

The Ragtime Dance is one of the genre's biggest charmers. It opens with a slithering introduction in octaves, proceeds to ponder a happy tune in parallel sixths, and ends with some downward-slipping chromatic parallel thirds. What everyone always remembers about *The Ragtime Dance* is the moment when Joplin asks the pianist to vigorously stomp the floor in rhythm!

Virtuoso violinist Itzhak Perlman included *The Ragtime Dance* in his 1976 album (and the corresponding sheet music volume of Joplin transcriptions for violin and piano), where he and pianist André Previn joyously stomp and saw away together. *—Blair Johnston*

Recommended:

○ **The Red Back Book** / Schuller (cond.), New England Conservatory Ragtime Ens. / 1985 / EMI 47193

Solace, Mexican serenade (1909)

Scott Joplin's *Solace* is a wonderful example of musical hybrid. Joplin was of course one of the kings of ragtime music, but here is something that he himself described as "A Mexican Serenade for piano"—certainly not an apt description for an item in true rag style! But the fact of the matter is that *Solace* is really not much more authentically Mexican than it is genuine ragtime. This is a four-minute gem of a habanera, which, as one might divine from the word, has roots in Havana. There is also in *Solace* something of the tango form, which, though distantly related to an African folk dance tradition, is more recently of the same Latin extraction as the habanera. *Solace* is, then, a true musical mish-mash—it is also a very lovely piece of Americana—familiar to millions by way of the 1973 movie *The Sting*.

As happens in Joplin's rags, several catchy little tunes, only a few of which were used by Marvin Hamlisch in *The Sting*, work together to make up *Solace*; the last of them, with its shiny, pulsing Caribbean dissonances, is especially comely. Fans of Georges Bizet's *Carmen* are invited to sit back, listen to *Solace*, and enjoy the same gently rocking habanera rhythm as is heard throughout the Frenchman's famous *Habanera* (actually it is not properly "his," since he actually adapted it from a folk tune). It is remarkable that a piece of music exists that allows us to draw a comparison between Georges Bizet and Scott Joplin. *—Blair Johnston*

Recommended:

○ **Joplin: Rags & Waltzes** / Blumenthal / 1994 / Pavane 7317

OPERA

Treemonisha (1911)

In May 1911, Scott Joplin published, at his own expense, the vocal score of his opera, *Treemonisha*—a venture quixotic, visionary, and obsessive. Unable to secure backing for its production, Joplin eventually rehearsed a cast, rented a hall in Harlem, and accompanying on piano, presented a single concert performance of *Treemonisha* in 1915, to incomprehension and derision. Disappointment broke him, while the ravages of syphilis brought on periods of deepening melancholy and dementia.

Sung in a foreign language, *Treemonisha* could become a repertory item. In English, Joplin's libretto is chock-full of redundancies, miscalculations, and embarrassing puerilities. *Treemonisha*'s father, rejecting a conjuror's "bag o' luck," utters this immortal poeticism as the music soars:

It may be worth it's [sic] weight in diamonds rare,
Or worth the earth to you.
But to me, it aint [sic] worth a possom's [sic] hair,
Or persimmons when they're new

Despite these verbal plunges, the score looms as dramatic music of a high order. The captivating overture is overlong, as is Monisha's ballad describing how the infant Treemonisha was discovered beneath a tree. Joplin resorts too often to the dominant seventh for dramatic tension. His prosody often highlights inessential words (confirming that he knew exactly what he wanted musically). His command of satire is shaky, Parson Alltalk (never addressed by name) conducts a prayer meeting whose rapt hymnody would not be out of place at a Southern Baptist revival. Nonetheless, his episodes are well paced and studded with numerous *coups de théâtre:* the surreally waltzing *Frolic of the Bears* ("Enter eight bears. Bears begin frolicking."), the incandescent ragtime dance *We're Go'in Around*, and above all, the mysterious, powerful final number *A Real Slow Drag*. Time and again, Joplin's music evokes an archetypal vision of rural Eden (*Superstition*, *We Will Rest Awhile*, *Aunt Dinah Has Blowed the Horn*), though not without its serpents. While his idiom owes far more to the popular music of his day than to European models, he molds it with great suppleness and operatic amplitude, nowhere more splendidly than in the extended, riveting finale of Act Three. It is an American classic, flawed but indispensable.

The vocal score was republished in 1971—Joplin's orchestration is lost—and the work's belated premiere was given January 28, 1972, in Atlanta by the music department of Morehouse College, with Robert Shaw conducting the Atlanta Symphony in an orchestral arrangement by T.J. Anderson. For a lavish Houston Grand Opera production in May 1975, Gunther Schuller prepared his own recension of the score—subsequently recorded by Deutsche Grammophon—which played on Broadway that year to enthusiastic audiences for a run of nine weeks. *—Adrian Corleonis*

Synopsis:

Act One. The action takes place in September 1884 on an Arkansas plantation run by former slaves. An old con man, or "conjuror" as he is called, Zodzetrick, is scolded by Ned and his daughter Treemonisha for his swindling ways. She is the only educated inhabitant of the area and poses a threat to Zodzetrick and his ilk. Afterwards, Treemonisha decides to make a wreath out of leaves, like the ones she notices the other girls wearing. She approaches a tree and her mother, Monisha, warns her to stay away from it: it is a sacred tree, the tree where she found Treemonisha as a baby. Her daughter obliges and goes off to find another tree, from which to take the leaves. Parson Alltalk arrives to preach to the locals, and during his sermon, Zodzetrick and his sidekick Luddud kidnap Treemonisha. A party of men go in search of her in the woods. Her friend Remus is among the searchers and he takes scarecrow attire with him to frighten the kidnappers.

Act Two. A gathering of conjurors in the forest is attended by Zodzetrick and Luddud, along with their captive, Treemonisha. They decide she is a menace to their dubious profession and must be punished. As they are about to toss her into a wasp's nest, Remus, dressed as a scarecrow, drives them off, the conjurors believing he is the devil. Treemonisha thanks Remus for his timely rescue and the two head back home.

Act Three. Treemonisha and Remus arrive back at the plantation, closely followed by Zodzetrick and Luddud, now in the custody of the local posse. A beating as punishment for the two is proposed by the men, but Treemonisha intercedes and asks that they only be reprimanded then released. Ned takes it upon himself to admonish the conjurors to change their ways and then they are freed. Treemonisha receives praise from the neighbors who have observed her wise and rational ways. They propose to make her their leader and she agrees to serve them in that role. *—Robert Cummings*

Recommended:

○ **Joplin: Treemonisha** / Schuller (cond.), Nance, White, Balthrop, Allen, Houston Grand Opera Orch. & Chorus / 1975 / DG 435709

Josquin Desprez

b. ca. 1455, St. Quentin, France (?), **d.** Aug. 27, 1521, Condé-sur-l'Escaut, France
Composer: Choral

"Master of the notes," Martin Luther called him. To contemporary prelates, Josquin was an adornment worthy of a world-class court; to music publishers, his was the name that assured sales; and other composers claimed his tutelage to improve their own image. Josquin's music is regarded as one of the great treasures of Western culture. Furthermore, in his compositions, music historians have seen a crucial link in the development of the Renaissance "Central Musical Language." And yet, a reliable biography of this pivotal figure has remained maddeningly elusive. As of the year 2000, the edifice of the textbook biography was overthrown by new archival discoveries. At least three prominent musicians of his time were called "Josquin"; the presence of another in Milan has bewildered "our" Josquin's biographers by suggesting a 1440 birth date and a surprisingly mediocre early career in Italy. (Similar confusion would ensue from the discovery of two Elizabethan playwrights named William Shakespeare.) The Josquin who would cast his mythic shadow across the centuries was born in the 1450s, in northern France or Hainaut (present-day Belgium), son of Gossard Lebloitte. Despite strong family ties and, later, an inheritance in Condé, Josquin's path took him south to Aix-en-Provence, where he joined King René d'Anjou's court as a singer. The young musician began his career as early as 1475 in a prosperous (and Italophile) court establishment, surrounded by a supportive courtiers' "network." After René's death in 1480, most of his singers were retained by his nephew, King Louis XI of France; Josquin may have served Louis from 1480/81 to 1483. This position may have provided an opportunity for Josquin to meet to the King's renowned *Premier chapellain*, Johannes Ockeghem. By 1484, Josquin had become a commensural familiar (personal servant, as well as singer) to Ascanio Sforza, brother to the Duke of Milan. Not only did this bring Josquin into the orbit of one of the most splendid courts of Quattrocento Italy, but Ascanio's elevation to the Cardinalate likely brought his familiar to Rome (August 1484 till 1487, returning to Milan in 1488–89). Josquin's relationship to this generous and well-connected patron continued into the next century as attested by printed attributions of music to "Josquin d'Ascanio" in 1504 and 1509. His next musical appointment, however, was to the Papal Choir in Rome, from June of 1489 until at least 1495. Two new expectative benefices in Thérouanne and Cambrai, close to his homeland, were among his immediate compensations. His location around the turn of the century is currently unknown, though this period saw a surge in the dissemination of his music, in manuscripts from centers such as Rome, Milan, and Brussels/Mechlin, but also in Petrucci's revolutionary musical press in Venice. After a brief, but highly lucrative, tenure as *Maestro di cappella* for the Duke of Ferrara from 1503–04, the aging Josquin-hero passed into semi-retirement back in Condé. The collegiate church of Notre-Dame in Condé accepted him as provost in May 1504, and he purchased a new house in August, remaining till his death in 1521. During this time, he was ordained a priest and maintained some level of activity as a composer; as late as 1520, he presented a volume of chansons to Holy Roman Emperor Charles V. Josquin's will bequeathed his home to the collegiate church, to endow his stipulated obituary services: Marian "Salve" services on Saturdays throughout the year and on Marian feast days, and the singing of his own Pater noster and Ave Maria in front of his house during all general liturgical processions. And with the profuse laments of his contemporaries, the creation of his legend began. —*Timothy Dickey*

CHORAL

Absalon, Fili Mi, motet for 4 parts (1497)

The images of David weeping for his son Absalom, Jacob desiring his grave when confronted with the blood-stained clothes of his son Joseph, and possibly Job in his misery, are all conflated in the text of an extraordinarily emotional motet, *Absalon, fili mi*. A late (and possibly untrustworthy) printed source calls the great Josquin Desprez its composer, and music historians for years have lauded it and sought possible occasions for its writing, such as the memorial service for Philip the Fair, son of the Emperor Maximilian, in 1506. A strong case has also been made on stylistic grounds, however, for attribution to Josquin's contemporary, Pierre de la Rue. Whichever man may be credited with *Absalon*, the powerful character of the music remains.

The motet is scored for four voices, but in an extremely low register: the final chord contains a B flat below the contemporary bass clef! The mensuration (time signature) in the earliest reliable source is also slow and somewhat unusual. The key signature uses more flats than any other piece by Josquin, and more are introduced as the composition proceeds. In fact, the final line of text, describing the mournful desire to "descend into Sheol, weeping," is sung to a motif of a falling-third interval; this motif repeats sequentially and descends by fifths into the harmonic depths from B flat, to E flat, A flat, D flat, and finally to G flat, a truly unheard-of sonority for the time. Then the entire progression repeats. This passage would have absolutely stunned any culturally competent listener in the Renaissance; it still wields its affective power today. —*Timothy Dickey*

Recommended:

- ○ **Josquin: Missa "La sol fa re mi"; motets** / Ruhland (cond.), Munich Capella Antiqua / 1998 / Sony 60362
- ○ **Josquin: Missa L'homme armé; Ave Maria; Absalom fili mi** / Summerly (cond.), Oxford Camerata / 1998 / Naxos 553428
- ○ **Josquin: Motets & Chansons** / Hillier (cond.), Hilliard Ens. / 1996 / Virgin 61302

Ave Maria . . . virgo serena, motet for 4 parts (1497)

A version of Josquin Desprez's *Ave Maria*, perhaps his most famous composition and certainly his most often sung today, appears at the head of the first volume of motets ever printed (1502); its composition occurred during the composer's service at one of several French and North Italian courts. Apparently written some time between 1476 and 1497; this motet expounds with classic elegance the stylistic ideals of the Italian Renaissance and provides one of the best examples of its style, power, and beauty. The structure of Josquin's musical setting corresponds to the text in a lucid way. Twentieth century theorists use the term "syntactic imitation" to describe the characteristic musical structure of High Renaissance vocal pieces. Each musical phrase corresponds to a phrase of text, and points of imitation frequently expose these phrases. Moments of structural articulation arrive at cadences, where two or more voices rest on perfect intervals. Within this style of composition, Josquin wrote a motet of classic balance. The opening section declaims the four phrases of text, in order. Clear and unobstructed imitation of each phrase (as if in a litany) occurs dramatically from the highest voice to the lowest; the imitated melody resembles a Gregorian chant version of "Ave Maria." Though the phrases of this section are completely balanced in length, the counterpoint increases in density, producing a strong climax at the first juncture where all four voices sing together. This climax quickly gives way to an imperfect, deceptive cadence. Josquin treats each strophe of the main body of the poem as a syntactic unit unto itself, roughly comparable and balanced in length with the others. Local details often relate directly to the affect of a portion of text, such as the sudden expanse of complete homophonic harmony at the text "solemni plena gaudio." Immediately following this moment comes the text "coelestia, terrestria . . . ," and the music builds in climbing melodic lines and dense syncopation of rhythms, as if literally evoking the sense of the text's filling of heaven and earth. Whereas at the beginning of the motet the regularity of imitation articulated the phrases, in the middle verses the articulation largely comes from contrasts in texture. Even as the painter may draw upon a simple repertory of postures in which to cast a figure, the basic textures used by Josquin are few but sharply contrasting. Duets alternate with one another (a characteristic and favorite textural gambit of Josquin's), and with a texture of duet plus an accompanying third voice. Each strophe is further punctuated by structural cadences which bring the large sections of music to temporary repose; the lengthier the repose and the greater the degree of "perfection" in the harmony, the more powerful the punctuation. Thus the composer locates each structural cadence in a progression of increasing power, saving the strongest, most perfect cadence (consisting only of fifths and octaves) for the very end—the prayer which Josquin sets to a slow-moving, completely homophonic texture, set apart from the preceding music by an arresting pause. The physical unity of musical sound, embodying the spiritual unity of prayer, combined with the reflective comfort of slow-moving and untroubled consonance, completes the act of worship which has been the rhetorical goal of the text. —*Timothy Dickey*

Recommended:

- ○ **Josquin: Missa Malheur me Bat** / Wickham (cond.), Clerks' Group / 2002 / Gaudeamus 306
- ○ **Magnificat** / Chanticleer / 2000 / Teldec 81829

De profundis, motet for 4 parts (ca. 1500–1521)

Since the time of Pope Innocent III, the Catholic Church had used seven particular psalms to mark moments in the liturgical year of the gravest solemnity and repentance. Among the most evocative of these Penitential Psalms, number 129 in the Vulgate (130 in the English Bible), *De profundis clamavi ad te, Domine* ("Out of the depths I cry unto thee, O Lord"), speaks of the pervasiveness of exiled Israel's sin, the depths of her degradation, and above all, the shining hope of redemption at the hands of the God of mercy. The Church recited all seven Penitential Psalms as an act of contrition and desire for pardon throughout the season of Lent. "De profundis," with the "Miserere mei, Deus" (Psalm 50/51) also became part of the requiem liturgy and the various funeral offices. Josquin composed two settings of this text. The earlier, for five voices, was apparently intended to memorialize a particular period of mourning; an inscription in a contemporary printed source explains that the triple canon in the piece symbolizes the mourning of all three estates of the realm. Sheer sonic effect, rather than symbolism per se, characterizes the later version, for four voices. The motet's structure and proportions are "classical," proceeding in long-breathed and clearly delineated grammatical segments (the archetypal Josquin motet, in this sense, being his four-voiced *Ave Maria*). Passages of alternating duets are interspersed with more climactic full textures, often employing imitation to mark the advent of a new textual idea. But within this mature and assured classicism, Josquin presents the text in a deeply emotional fashion. He chooses the most mournful mode (or key) possible in his day, the Phrygian (this mode also appears in such severe pieces as the *Missa Pange Lingua* and his setting of the other funeral psalm, *Miserere mei, Deus*). The rhythmic progress of the motet proceeds in an irrevocable duple meter, as if meant for an actual funeral procession. The most striking element is the literal profundity of the vocal ranges. All four voices are written at the bottom of their capacity: the soprano takes a full 20 measures to reach even a middle pitch G (significantly, on the text "hear my cry!"), and the opening melody of the bass drops to the depths of a low G. Only the weeping of King David over his son in the motet *Absalon, fili mi* comes close to evoking this vocal color. And yet, the Psalm speaks of hope, and Josquin's setting concludes with a "Gloria Patri," which is not merely liturgically correct, but also serves as a powerful acknowledgement on the part of the Church—sung in the fullness of Josquin's contrapuntal texture—of her hope, "World without end, amen." —*Timothy Dickey*

Recommended:

- ○ **Musical Book of Hours** / Blachly (cond.), Pomerium / 1998 / Archiv 457586
- ○ **Josquin and his contemporaries** / Kirkman (cond.), Binchois Consort / Hyperion 67183

Faulte d'argent, song for 5 parts (ca. 1475–1520)

World-famous musician Josquin Desprez retired to his hometown of Condé in 1505 and wrote songs. After 30 years of service to kings and dukes, popes and cardinals, in which time he composed at least 100 motets and three books' worth of masses, Josquin seems to have developed a late fascination with the canonic chanson. In this miniature genre, he challenged himself to create effortless counterpoint despite the severe canonic strictures. Chansons only slowly filtered into manuscript collections, later breaking on the European scene in large posthumous anthologies printed by Susato and Attaignant. Unfortunately, this pattern of sources makes it nearly impossible to discover a chronological order for these works, as important as they are to the chanson's development. There is only one five-voiced canonic chanson attributed to Josquin in a source dating from his lifetime: *Faulte d'argent*. It could thus represent one of his earliest essays and has been seen as central to understanding his "late" chanson style.

Though *Faulte d'argent* is quite brief, in it Josquin displays both a masterful command of local detail and an elegant formal structure. He bases the piece on a popular *chanson rustique*, well known in other chanson settings, and even French secular theater. The lighthearted tune serves as cantus firmus in the contratenor voice, and in canon a fifth below in the second tenor. Josquin does subtly manipulate his disposition of these preexisting materials. The popular melody repeats its own first phrase to conclude a four-line stanza, yielding a closed musical structure. For text, on the other hand, Josquin truncates the much longer original poem, concluding the first three lines of his single stanza with a later line; the lighthearted opening that complains about the state of having no money becomes a more serious ironic comment about Woman ("The woman who sleeps will wake for money"). One highly perceptive analysis of the music reveals how Josquin reflects the literary process of this punchline. Though the opening stands firmly in G dorian mode, Josquin quickly inserts several confusing cadences on D. The tonal ambiguity only resolves at the very end, with strong final cadences on D, just as the irony of the text only coalesces at its end. Josquin's musical punchline is underscored by a convergence of repeated musical motives. Nicolas Gombert quoted from this very chanson in his lament on Josquin's death, and it is also featured in Richafort's *Requiem Mass*. *—Timothy Dickey*

Recommended:

○ **Chansons** / Clement Janequin Ens., Elements Ens. / HM 290838

El grillo, song for 4 parts (ca. 1505)

Secular composition in sixteenth century Italy was dominated by the madrigal; the musical ancestors of this genre include two other vernacular genres, the lauda and the frottola. Italian popular religion fostered the growth of the lauda, which paired simple texts in Latin or Italian with similarly simple musical textures; the frottola served as its secular counterpart. In the hands of Bartolomeo Tromboncino, the most prolific fifteenth century composer of frottole, common features of the repertory included closed refrain forms, a simple, often homophonic texture, and lighthearted vernacular text. Josquin Desprez, who spent many years working in Italy, produced three frottole, of which *El Grillo* is today the best known (though there is still some question as to the accuracy of the attribution).

The jovial text speaks of the "splendid singer," the Cricket; this has sometimes been supposed to refer to one of Josquin's musical colleagues, the singer Carlo Grillo (whose last name translates as "cricket"). Josquin's musical setting is often illustrative, as in the instance in which two voices literally "hold a long note" as suggested by the text. (Other works in Ottaviano Petrucci's printed collection of frottole, in which *El Grillo* appears, imitate the cat, the swan, and the crane.) Pairs of voices playfully alternate their calls for the Cricket to "laugh, sing, and drink." The verses of the poem, set primarily chordally, are richly endowed with double entendres that describe the Cricket's erotic prowess. *—Timothy Dickey*

Recommended:

○ **Music of the Italian Renaissance** / Rumsey / 1994 / Naxos 550615

○ **Chansons** / Clement Janequin Ens., Elements Ens. / HM 290838

In te Domini speravi, frottola or motet for 4 parts (ca. 1500–1521)

Josquin's curious little piece on the Latin and Italian text *In te, Domine, speravi, per trovar pieta* stands at the juncture of several different genres of fifteenth century musical composition. The earliest published source for the piece is a 1504 anthology by Ottaviano Petrucci of the frottola, a lighthearted genre of Italian secular music; *In te, Domine* does resemble many such pieces in its lively character and chordal style. The text, however, most easily lends itself to a sacred reading: "In Thee, O Lord, have I trusted, that I may find mercy." And the musical style of the frottola closely matches a genre of Italian vernacular devotional music, sung in processions and paraliturgical praise services, known as the lauda. Josquin's *In te, Domine*, in fact, opens with music for the first few measures almost identical to a Paduan lauda preserved in a Capetown manuscript, with vernacular devotional text "A questa aspra penitentia." Further complicating the generic situation is the existence of several manuscript versions with sacred Latin texts instead of Italian, implying an attempt to elevate the piece to motet status (in a late Medieval hierarchy of genres!). Finally, an anecdotal account of an 1547 event in Josquin's life suggests the politics of courtly patronage as a possible context for the composition. Josquin, the vignette says, once became impatient while waiting to receive his wages from an early employer, Cardinal Ascanio Sforza. To gently prod the Cardinal, he composed the frottola *El Grillo*, about a cricket who sings for love (even when he has no food?), and also a sycophantic *In thee, O Lord, do I place my trust*. While the anecdote may be entirely apocryphal, the spunky little piece of music it associated with the story has been charming listeners since Josquin's day. *—Timothy Dickey*

Recommended:

○ **A Songbook for Isabella** / Thorby (cond.), Wilkinson, London Musica Antiqua / 2003 / Signum 39

○ **The Italian Lute Song** / Baird, McFarlane / 1996 / Dorian 90236

Inviolata, integra et casta es, motet for 5 parts (before 1502)

A wealth of early sixteenth century copies, printed editions, and even lute and keyboard intabulations, attest to the popularity of Josquin's five-voiced motet *Inviolata, integra et casta es, Maria*. The motet (in three parts) takes as its text a plainchant sequence for the Ladymass, which deals with Mary's immaculate person: the first part praises her, the second asks for her prayers, and the third again extols her (following the form of "O virgo prudentissima"). The surface of the motet displays a rich variety of detail: duets contrasted with antiphonal passages and fuller imitative sonorities, chordal textures with bursts of individual virtuosity, predictable cadences with surprising contrapuntal progressions. Witness, for instance, the textural sweep of the third section (O benigna), which begins with three homophonic litany-like invocations, moves to quicker waves of repetition on the word "inviolata" (reminiscent of the opening?), then broadens the rhythmic pacing of the four lower parts and allows the superius voice to take melodic flight. Beneath the apparently accessible surface, however, lies a rigid canonic structure and deep numerological symbolism. A plainchant associated with the text "Inviolata" (possibly following the Ambrosian rite of Milan) sounds in the two tenor voices in canon, at the distance of a melodic fifth; the rhythmic pace, however, remains roughly equivalent to that of the other three voices. The temporal distance within the canon decreases gradually: three units of time in the first section, two in the second, and one in the last. In Josquin's time, a listener familiar with the plainchant would immediately appreciate the obvious climax achieved by the gesture; its inner logic may still be felt. The overall proportions of the piece, innately satisfying, may also allude to the Golden Section. Furthermore, the number 12, which in Medieval numerology refers to the 12 stars on the crown of the woman in the Apocalypse (thus representing a crowned Blessed Virgin), also features prominently in Josquin's motet: 12 repetitions of the word "inviolata" at the opening (and six in the last section), 12 measures of rest before the entry of the final voice, and 12 measures of rest before the entry of the cantus firmus in the second section. *—Timothy Dickey*

Recommended:

○ **Josquin: Motets, Antiphons, Sequences** / Higginbottom (cond.), New College Choir Oxford / 1997 / Meridian 84356

○ **Musical Book of Hours** / Blachly (cond.), Pomerium / 2003 / Archiv 000040902

Mille regretz, song for 4 parts (1480s)

In Josquin's *Mille regretz*, the dramatic and expressive potential of the polyphonic chanson, which will emerge so fruitfully in the hands of Clément Janequin and Orlando di Lasso, is already becoming evident. The rigidity of the venerable *formes fixes*, which had been codified in the 1300s, had allowed composers of these elegant poetic texts to complement the text with music which was beautiful, but often quite subordinate. The ideals of the coming sixteenth century, however, would seek music which more directly reflected the sense of its text. Anticipating the future here as clearly as he ever did, Josquin set the tender anguish of this love song with fittingly affecting music.

The entire chanson is in the Phrygian mode, always evocative of solemnity or mourning due to its prominent half-step motion; the principal vertical progression is plagal (like the "Amen" of a hymn), which also carried sorrowful connotations in Josquin's time. Though moments of imitative counterpoint punctuate the music (as at "Qu'on me verra"), the textures generally retain a stark simplicity. Contrasts in texture heighten the affect of the text: observe the power of the simultaneous singing of "J'ay si grand deuil," followed by pathetic duos on "et peine douloureuse." The final chordal repetitions of "brief mes jours definer" bespeaks the poetic speaker's reluctance to admit the inevitable numbering of his days without the Beloved. *—Timothy Dickey*

Recommended:

○ **Carlos V** / Savall (cond.), Capella Reial de Catalunya / 2000 / Alia Vox 9814

○ **Music for Joan the Mad** / La Nef / 1992 / Dorian 80128

Missa de Beata Virgine (before 1514)

"In my opinion... finer music cannot be created." Thus spoke Glareanus, a contemporary music theorist, about Josquin's *Missa de Beata Virgine*. All discernable accounts from the time suggest that for the sixteenth century, this was the most popular of all Josquin's considerable output, and it found its way into more manuscript collections than any other. Its name comes from the paraphrased Gregorian chants beneath the surface—instead of a single unifying cantus firmus, a full set of mass chants suitable for any of the great feasts of the Virgin—and from three brief interpolations of Marian devotional texts into the Gloria, including a musical pun: the text "Mariam coronans" set to a chordal style often marked with fermatas, known as "coronae." The construction of each mass movement on the basis of a different chant, quite a rarity, also poses some challenge to the unity of the cycle. Not only are the different chant models in different modes (keys), but the techniques of composition vary from close imitation (as in the opening of Kyrie) to single-voice cantus firmus (as in Sanctus). It is also the case that the last three movements, by means of a musical canon, shift to five-voice texture from the four voices of Kyrie and Gloria. This has led to the suggestion that the Mass may merely be a compilation. Nevertheless, the Mass delivers to the ear an elegant completeness and maturity.

Among the many elements of Josquin's consummate mature style are the supple arches of his melodies, the careful crafting of rhythms (especially seen in sequences) to create satisfying conclusions to a movement, and the perfection of text/music relationships. But more telling than these is the powerful impregnation of the entire musical substance by the sound of the chant models (a feature that comes to its most complete fruition in the *Missa Pange lingua*). *—Timothy Dickey*

Recommended:

○ **Josquin: Missa de Beata Virgine; Jean Mouton: Motets** / Hillier (cond.), Theatre of Voices / 1998 / HM 907136

○ **Josquin: Missa de Beata Virgine; Motets à la Vierge** / Fabre-Garrus (cond.), A Sei Voci / 1995 / Astree 8560

Missa di dadi (before 1514)

Painted altarpieces in the fifteenth century, though placed directly on a church's altar table, often contain a surprising array of secular images and objects; in a like manner, Josquin's early four-part *Mass N'aray je jamais* borrows a secular French love song (by Robert Morton) as a unifying device. In each of the five movements of this Mass, the tenor voice sings the liturgical text to the melody of the love song. Already by the middle of the century, this was becoming a common practice in the polyphonic settings of the mass popular in the more prestigious cathedrals and noble chapels of Western Europe. But the *Missa di dadi* (Mass of the dice) of Josquin's includes a second—and more blatantly "secular"— element in its structure: the first printed edition (1514) puts images of pairs of dice over the music at sectional breaks! The dice are superficially related to the proportional transformations of the cantus firmus. Kyrie I and II, where the cantus firmus is sung twice as slow as the original love song, both are marked with dice showing a "two" and a "one." The two halves of the Gloria movement, with 4:1 and 8:1 augmentation respectively, both show dice of "four" and "one;" the Credo has "six" and "one" for its dice throws, and 6:1 augmentation. But the very last dice open the Sanctus, a "five" and "one." In the rules of many medieval gambling games, a total of six or twelve was an automatic victory—"game over." Josquin, then, overwrites the secular image of gambling onto the whole worship service of the Mass, until the Sanctus, the most holy moment when the priest elevates the Host just prior to the Communion. For a member of a late medieval congregation, this was indeed the moment of victory. Josquin also imbues this "throw" of the dice with numerological symbolism: it is the seventh pair of dice, and its five spots may commemorate the five wounds of Christ. Furthermore, after this, the cantus firmus changes. For the first three and a half movements, the tenor has borrowed only the first line of the love song, which says, "Won't I ever have something better?" But after the Sanctus breakthrough, Josquin consummates the moment by quoting the song in its entirety. There to the end, the lover in the chanson and the singers in the choir both may sing "I am yours, and will remain so." People living in an age of the "separation of church and state" often find such a mingling of sacred and secular difficult to comprehend. But for the educated musicians of Josquin's time, and their noble patrons, even the lyrics of a popular song and the image of gambling could add a richness to the symbolism of a worship service. *—Timothy Dickey*

Missa "Hercules Dux Ferrariae" (before 1505)

A fifteenth century composer writing a mass setting could choose from a number of borrowed musical elements for purposes of structural unity, including excerpts from Gregorian chant, polyphonic motets, popular songs, or even a sogetto cavato—a contrived and abstract subject for a cantus firmus. An early and famous example of the latter comes from the pen of Antoine Busnois, who composed the motet *In hydraulis* around a threefold repeating pattern of three notes. Perhaps the most famous such contrivance is Josquin's mass setting whose cantus firmus derives from the vowel sounds of the name of his patron the Duke of Ferrara. "Hercules, Dux Ferrariae" yields the musical tones "re ut re ut re fa mi re" which in turn provide the scaffolding for the entire five-movement mass. Each movement is based upon at least one threefold statement in the tenor voice of the resultant tune, on the climactic sequence of pitches D, A, and octave D. For instance, in the Kyrie, each of the three sections of the movement contain eight measures of tenor rest and one statement of the tune, in succession. Some movements vary the scheme in clever ways: the Benedictus contains three short duets, each based on a single cantus firmus phrase, and the Hosanna is structured around one full statement at double speed, and one at quadruple speed without the intervening rests—a stunning climax. In the final Agnus Dei, only a single, drawn-out statement is used, but the soprano voice also anticipates each phrase an octave higher.

The musical character of the other three voice parts is uniquely compact and direct, often with long sections consisting of short repetitive motives (such as the opening of the Sanctus). This may have been an intentional effort to highlight the overweening flattery of Duke Ercole intrinsic to Josquin's conception. The conceit of such flattery in a piece of worship music is such that one contemporary singing group (Pomerium) performs it with the tenors singing not the mass text, but the Duke's name itself! *—Timothy Dickey*

Recommended:

○ **Desprez: Missa Hercules dux Ferrariae; Motets & Chansons** / Blachly (cond.), Richards, Duer, Pomerium / 2003 / Glissando 43

○ **Desprez: Missa Hercules Dux Ferrariae** / Fabre-Garrus (cond.), A Sei Voci, Labyrinthes Ens. / 1997 / Astree 8601

Missa "L'homme armé" sexti toni (1502)

A contemporary theorist credits Antoine Busnois with composition of the tune *L'homme armé* (The Armed Man). The jaunty tune contains evocations of trumpet calls, and the text translates roughly: "Fear the armed man; word has gone out that everyone should arm himself with an haubregon [chainmail coat] of iron." This little piece, which seems to refer to a crusade against the Turks—and may have particular relevance to Busnois' patron Charles the Bold, Duke of Burgundy—became the single most popular borrowed melody for the composition of masses in the Renaissance period. Including those of Busnois, who wrote at least one such mass and perhaps six more, Ockeghem, and Palestrina, over 30 *L'homme armé* masses survive. Two by Josquin Desprez were written by 1502; the earlier but more intellectually virtuosic, is subtitled *super voces musicales*, as it presents the borrowed tune on every musical voice (pitch) of the scale in turn.

Josquin takes as his precompositional scaffolding a mild elaboration of the *L'homme armé* tune, and quotes this as a cantus firmus underlying each movement of the Mass; however, though the notes remain the same, each time he manipulates the structure in new and clever ways. The Kyrie movement gives the cantus firmus to the tenor voice, centered on the pitch C, one time through. The Gloria and Credo each move the cantus firmus tune up one pitch (to D and E, respectively); both also give the structural voice twice through, once forwards, and once in retrograde motion. In the Sanctus, the tenor sings the *L'homme armé* melody beginning on F; on the jubilant text "Hosanna," the note values are diminished such that the structural function is masked. Agnus Dei I continues the climactic rise to the pitch G; Agnus Dei II begins as if the cantus firmus is present on "A," but proceeds to a freely composed trio. Agnus Dei III places the now-familiar tune in extremely long notes sung by the highest voice, beginning on "A," with an indication instructing the soprano to "sing without ceasing"—that is, without rests. The other three voices in this movement sing tight, motivic, imitative passages around the climactic top voice.

The intellectual complexity of the Mass is heightened by a number of manipulations Josquin performs on the mensuration (rhythmic organization). The very first sounds heard in the first Kyrie present the *L'homme armé* tune in imitation between three voices, but as a mensuration canon: each voice interprets the notes in a different time signature. Later, in the freely composed Benedictus, Josquin completes a separate mensuration canon in each of the three duos. And every time that the outer three voices are singing in duple meter, the cantus firmus remains in its triple meter, creating a delightful polyrhythm.

As mentioned above, this *L'homme armé Mass* is only one in a long lineage. Ockeghem reacted to the Busnois' original *L'homme armé Mass* by trying to make his own setting more complex and clever than the music of the elder master; here Josquin Desprez leaps into an emerging contest of compositional skills, and trumps all comers. *—Timothy Dickey*

Recommended:

○ **Josquin: "L'homme armé" masses** / Phillips (cond.), Tallis Scholars / 1989 / Gimell 454919

○ **Josquin: Missa L'homme armé; Ave Maria; Absalom fili mi** / Summerly (cond.), Oxford Camerata / 1998 / Naxos 553428

Missa "La Sol Fa Re Mi" (before 1502)

A cantus firmus in the fifteenth century commonly borrows the tune from an excerpt of Gregorian chant (such as "Ecce ancilla Domini"), or from a popular song in the vernacular (the perennial favorite being "L'Homme Armé"); a composer of a mass would then quote this tune in each movement, perhaps varying the rhythm or ornamenting it. A rarer option is the *sogetto cavato*—an abstract musical subject made up for the occasion. In the 1501 collection of masses by Josquin Desprez printed by Petrucci lies an outstanding example of this technique: the *Missa La Sol Fa Re Mi*.

The particular group of intervals underlying this mass gives it its name. La, sol, fa, re, and mi are the Medieval solmization syllables for the pitches A, G, F, D, E. One of Glareanus' quasi-historical vignettes (in 1547) suggests that Josquin arrived upon this sequence by imitating a certain king whose phrase for unwanted courtiers was always, "Lascia fare mi" ("Leave me alone.") Whether or not this is true, virtually every moment of the mass derives from this little five-note phrase, either beginning on the pitch A, or, in a different hexachord system, on E. It is heard at various speeds as a cantus firmus in the tenor (as in the Credo), as a migrant cantus firmus in other voices (Kyrie I and Christe), as a subject of imitation (Hosanna I), and even as the subject of canon and rhythmic transformation (Agnus Dei I and III; here also the pacing of the cantus firmus accelerates till the end of the movement, using the aural tag as a vehicle for the climax). In Josquin's earlier *Missa "Faisant Regretz,"* he had attempted the task of centering an entire five-movement mass upon a single short phrase; he allowed himself the leeway, however, of transposition. In this mass, in over 200 repetitions of the little five-note phrase, only once (the end of the Christe) does it diverge from A and E, yielding a remarkable, almost Impressionistic, unity of harmonic color to the whole. *—Timothy Dickey*

Recommended:

- ○ **Josquin: Missa La sol fa re mi; motets** / Ruhland (cond.), Munich Capella Antiqua / 1998 / Sony 60362

Missa "Pange Lingua" (1514)

Josquin Desprez has enjoyed the highest esteem both of his contemporaries (Martin Luther called him the "Master of the Notes"), and of music historians since his day. A generation before him, the music of Dufay presented developing ideals of equal-voiced polyphony and of large-scale formal balance; later, Ockeghem exploited more of the imitative style and rhythmic intensity. But in Josquin (and his close contemporary Obrecht) the so-called "Netherlandish" style of the High Renaissance reached an early plateau. He composed fluently and well in every contemporary genre of music, sacred and secular. Of his 18 reliably attributed masses, the *Missa Pange lingua* deserves its high popularity, both for the beauty of individual moments, as well as for the elegance of its formal design.

A prominent biographer confidently calls this the "last Mass composed by Desprez," but no contemporary data can reliably date it. Scholars, judging by stylistic criteria and by the fact that this mass does not appear in Petrucci's third volume of Josquin's masses (published in 1514), generally concur in placing it late in his oeuvre. The Mass takes its name from the Corpus Christi hymn *Pange lingua* of St. Thomas Aquinas. This melody, with its strong initial half-step motion and graceful arch, becomes the unifying force in Josquin's composition. While heretofore, the common compositional framework used a borrowed melody in a single voice cantus firmus (such as his own masses on *L'ami baudichon* and *L'homme armé*), Josquin in this Mass takes the hymn melody and infuses it into the musical substance of the entire piece. The elegant motto openings of each major movement stem from the hymn's first phrase. In addition, this phrase is echoed in many subtle ways. For example, Josquin inserts echoes consisting of small intervals, using vocal imitation manifested through the plangent half-step. There are also frequent ornamental sections which follow ending cadences. Several movements, such as the Kyrie and Agnus Dei III which frame the cycle, derive their entire cadential and formal structure from the phrases of the hymn. And yet, with such complete impregnation of the work by the substance of the chant model, Josquin hardly misses an opportunity to enhance with symbolism and text-painting his presentation of the Mass Ordinary text. In the Gloria, for example, at the text "Qui tollis peccata mundi," Josquin thins out the texture to a severe canon, which stands out from the preceding moments. And the texture shifts instantly to a contrasting and introspective affect upon the cry "miserere nobis." Josquin's moments of greatest compositional reserve, such as the stillness of "Et incarnatus est," or the bare canonic structure which opens the Benedictus, do not represent emotional withdrawal, but rather a greater serenity, on the one hand, and a feeling of expectancy, on the other. Josquin treats the "Agnus Dei" supplications as the cycle's clear culmination, and he evokes this prayer with complex subtlety, beginning with a threefold (triune?) half-step imitation and concluding with a manipulation of the very perception of time through a web of simultaneously sounding rhythmic levels: the now-familiar tune appears in the soprano voice floating at half-speed above the supporting voices, and all voices gradually relax into a languorous imitative mantra of the final prayer, "dona nobis pacem" grant us peace. The ineffable motion of the spirit which results from our auditory experience connects us to this masterpiece across time. *—Timothy Dickey*

Recommended:

- ○ **Josquin: Missa Pange Lingua** / Peres (cond.), Clement Janequin Ens., Organum Ens. / HM 901239
- ○ **Josquin: Missa Pange Lingua** / O'Donnell (cond.), Westminster Cathedral Choir / 1992 / Hyperion 66614

Nymphes des bois/Requiem aeternam/Deploration de la Mort de Jehan Ockeghem, lament (1497)

Johannes Ockeghem composed a unique obituary ballade, *Mort tu as navre*, on the death of the elder Burgundian musician Binchois, incorporating Latin text excerpted from the requiem mass into a laudatory French chanson. And when Ockeghem, the "tresorier... et chief d'ouvre" of music himself, died in 1497, Josquin Desprez paid tribute to him in like manner, with *Nymphes des bois*.

The French text adapts a poem of deploration by Jehan Molinet, in which nymphs and goddesses are called to join the "skilled singers of all nations" in mourning for the loss of such a musician. Josquin, Brumel, Pierchon (Pierre de la Rue), and Compère are called by name to weep great tears; Josquin's uniquely powerful music certainly gives justice to the sad occasion.

The very musical style of the piece betrays little of the musical character usually associated with Josquin. Moments of imitation and voice-painting (such as the repeating notes calling for "trenchant cries" and the dramatic shift towards flat notes for the text "treasurer of music," a reference perhaps both to Ockeghem's musical mastery and his official position of Treasurer of St. Martin in Tours), while present, are few and brief. Unrelenting long-note textures pervade all five voice parts, with few conclusive cadences to soften the momentum. In fact, such relentless drive, and the indistinct, overlapping, and dramatically low vocal registers, pay homage to the style of the earlier master (known for his bass voice, and for his low textured compositions). Also archaic is the long-note tenor cantus firmus, which he here quotes from the requiem mass. Ockeghem had adopted a similar device in his Binchois lament, but here Josquin transposes the borrowed chant melody into the most mournful Phrygian mode. All five voices finally rest on the refrain, the requiem prayer "Requiescat in pace. Amen." *—Timothy Dickey*

Recommended:

- ○ **Josquin: Missa Hercules dux Ferrariae; Motets & Chansons** / Blachly (cond.), Pomerium / 2003 / Glissando 43
- ○ **Ockeghem: Missa Ecce Ancilla Domini** / Wickham (cond.), Clerks' Group / 2001 / ASV/Living Era 223

Salve Regina, motet for 5 parts (ca. 1500–1521)

An eleventh century bishop may have been the author of the first text and music for *Salve Regina*, creating the devotional lyric as a processional chant for the use of Crusaders. Tradition suggests that St. Bernard of Clairvaux added the intimate closing lines to the poem. It was also apparently used as a processional chant for the Feast of the Assumption of the Virgin. By the time of Josquin Desprez, the liturgical plainchant *Salve Regina* was well-ensconced as one of the most popular antiphons to the Virgin Mary; many parishes, including those under Roman observance, sang this piece as a final prayer at the close of Vespers each day for the entire season of Pentecost (through summer until the beginning of Advent). Though a motet such as this likely saw liturgical use, motet singing for private devotion and entertainment was also common; a Ferrarese ambassador in Rome reports hearing a *Salve Regina* by Josquin sung while the Pope was at the table eating dinner.

Josquin composed two motets based on the music and text of the popular Marian chant. An earlier version for four voices may date from around 1480 during his service in French-speaking lands, or later with Cardinal Ascanio Sforza. In it, the upper two voices proceed in a canonic relationship, the superius voice following the altus at a close interval of time and echoing the altus' elaboration and paraphrase of the plainchant melody. At the same time, the lower two voices are also in canon, yielding a tour de force of the composer's tight control over the development of his material. This canonic procedure relates to Josquin's early canonic chanson experiments, such as *Basiez moy* and *En l'ombre d'ung buissonet*.

A presumably later five-voiced setting of the same text is much more expansive and long-breathed by comparison. Considerably longer, the second setting is divided into three *partes*, or sections, following the main grammatical divisions of the text. The chant melody this time appears in its entirety only in one voice: transposed up an octave and placed in the superius. The lower three voices proceed in free counterpoint beneath this paraphrase, though they often (characteristically for Josquin) echo small motifs from the melody. The fifth voice sings only ostinato repetitions of the first four notes of the chant: "Salve!" (or Hail!) As is the case in the *Missa Hercules Dux Ferrariae* and the clever motet *Illibata Dei Virgo nutrix*, the underlying structure of this motet is hidden in these repetitions. The ostinato takes seven measures to sing (Josquin was certainly not above a numerological reference to the Seven Joys of the Virgin Mary), and then is performed down a fourth; this takes place six times in the prima pars, twice in the secunda, and four times in the tertia. This provides for the motet an utterly rational basis underlying a surface fluidity of beautifully shifting textures and melodies. *—Timothy Dickey*

Recommended:

- ○ **Josquin: Motets, Antiphons, Sequences** / Higginbottom (cond.), New College Choir Oxford / 1997 / Meridian 84356
- ○ **Josquin: Messe Ave Maris Stella; Motets a la Vierge** / Fabre-Garrus (cond.), A Sei Voci / 1993 / Astree 8507

Marcel Journet

b. Jul. 25, 1867, Grasse, France, **d.** Sep. 5, 1933, Vittel, France

Bass

A rare example of the classically defined bass-baritone, Marcel Journet's sinuous and powerful voice encompassed both the bass and baritone registers. Journet was one of the last of that elegant school of French bass singing that largely disappeared with his death. Journet came close to matching the exceptional polish of his predecessor Pol Plançon while wielding sufficient power to excel in the heaviest Wagnerian parts. He was an exemplary Méphistophélès in Gounod's *Faust* as well as an authoritative exponent of such Italian baritone roles as Scarpia and Tonio, as well as the Wagnerian heroic baritone depths of Hans Sachs and Wotan. Counter to most voices, Journet's lightened somewhat in timbre and rose in tonal center as he aged. As his recording of *Faust* reveals, he was still in magnificent voice in his mid-sixties.

After vocal studies with Seneghetti and Vittel at the Paris Conservatoire, Journet made his debut in Béziers in 1891, singing the role of Balthasar in Donizetti's *La favorite*. He was engaged by the Monnaie in Brussels from 1894 to 1900, also appearing in other theaters, including Paris. In London, he introduced himself in

1897 as the Duke of Mendoza in *Inez Mendo*, whose composer was Baron Frédéric d'Erlanger, although it was publicized as though by Frederic Regnal. The opera received mixed reviews, but Journet won positive notices in a London season which also offered the likes of Eduard de Reszke and Pol Plançon. He also presented his Landgraf in *Tannhäuser* and, next season added the King in *Aida*, Sparafucile, Colline, and the Commendatore, increasing his profile and gaining more positive press. By 1901, Journet was alternating Méphistophélès with Plançon and sharing the stage with the great bass in three operas, including *Les Huguenots*. In 1902, the year of Caruso's London debut, Journet sang Raimondo to the tenor's Edgardo. Journet's next Wagner role in London was Heinrich in a 1904 *Lohengrin*.

Meanwhile, Journet had initiated a relationship with the Metropolitan Opera in New York. On December 22, 1900, he appeared as the King in *Aida* and continued for eight seasons, essaying no fewer than 38 roles. During his first season, he was applauded for his "smooth, sonorous, extensive and well-placed voice." Although Journet's participation in Meyerbeer's *Le Prophète* in December of 1902 did not excite the critics (only Schumann-Heink's Fidès did), the bass-baritone continued make gains in the estimation of critics and audiences alike. In November 1904, he was a virile Escamillo to Olive Fremstad's bewitching Carmen. The Father in Mascagni's *Iris* proved a splendid vehicle for him in 1907.

In the period after Journet's Metropolitan association, he returned to New York with the Chicago Opera to sing a superb Bishop in Février's *Monna Vanna* at the Lexington Theater. His Frère Laurent in Gounod's *Roméo et Juliette* was regarded as a model of beautiful, modulated, masterful singing. During his Chicago seasons with the company, Journet sang Lothario in *Mignon*, Colline, Méphistophélès, Ennius in Massenet's *Cléopâtre*, Phanuel in *Hérodiade*, Gondebaud in *Grisélidis*, the Comte in *Manon*, the Prior in *Le jongleur de Notre-Dame*, Leporello, Zacharie in *Le prophète*, and Zuniga.

After leaving Chicago, Journet sang principally in Europe, frequently at La Scala (1917 to 1928) where in 1924 he created the role of the sorcerer Simon Mago in Boito's *Nerone*. He also appeared at the Teatro Colón in Buenos Aires from 1916 to 1918 and again in the 1920s. *—Erik Eriksson*

Recommended:

○ **Complete Solo Gramophone Recordings, 1909–1933** / Journet, Ansseau, Cozette, Heldy / 1998 / Marston 52009

○ **Marcel Journet** / Journet, etc. / 1998 / Nimbus 7894

Juilliard Quartet

f. 1946, New York, NY

Ensemble

The Juilliard emerged from a Coast Artillery jazz band in 1945, when founder Robert Mann recruited army buddies Robert Koff, also a violinist, and cellist Arthur Winograd to play chamber music. In 1946, they approached William Schuman, the Juilliard School's new president, who urged them to find a violist their own age. Raphael Hillyer was recommended by a senior Boston Symphony colleague and modern-music advocate Eugene Lehner, who became the Juilliard's mentor in 1946. Although never formally tenured, the new Quartet taught at the school between engagements, which mushroomed despite a mixed reaction to their leaner-than-customary tone, rhythmic incisiveness, and onstage physicality. In 1948, they played the first U.S. cycle of Bartók's string quartets at Tanglewood, and the next summer performed all four by Schoenberg.

In 1949, Columbia (later CBS Masterworks, now Sony Classical) Records, for which the current personnel still record, signed the Juilliard to a long-term, non-exclusive contract. Their first Bartók and Schoenberg LPs were taped during the mono era. They also recorded chamber music by Berg, Fine, Cage, Mennin, Copland, Schuman, and Webern, along with Mozart, Beethoven, and other "standard" classicists. Later on they championed Elliott Carter in particular (Sony published his four quartets and piano-violin *Duo* on two CDs in 1991). During the Juilliard's 50th-anniversary season it featured new music by Diamond, Babbitt, Shapey, Wuorinen, and Dutilleux. But the Juilliard has never neglected Bach (*The Art of the Fugue*), Haydn, Schubert, Mendelssohn, Schumann, Brahms, Dvořák, Janáček, Hindemith, Prokofiev, Shostakovich (including the two piano concertos in 1999 with Yefim Bronfman and the Los Angeles Philharmonic), Verdi, Sibelius, Smetana, Franck, Chausson, Lerdahl, Wolpe, Martino, Glenn Gould, Gershwin, and Barber's *Dover Beach*. Only Charles Ives is missing. However, the complete Beethoven quartets, Mozart quintets and "Haydn" quartets, Bartók, and Carter have anchored the Juilliard's disc repertory.

Mann stayed on longest, 51 years as first violinist, until he yielded in 1997 to Joel Smirnoff, the group's second violinist, who had succeeded Earl Carlyss (1966–86). Winograd was the first defector from the original four, in 1955. Cellist Claus Adam replaced him until he, in turn, was replaced by a pupil, Joel Krosnick, in 1974—the Quartet's elder statesman at the start of the new millennium. Violinist Robert Koff left in 1958. Isidore Cohen came next, but quit in 1966 to lead the Beaux Arts Trio. In 1968, Hillyer resigned after a blowup with Mann, and was replaced by violist Samuel Rhodes, second in seniority to Krosnick. Ronald Copes became the new second violinist in 1997.

At their namesake school, the Juilliard has mentored the Emerson, Tokyo, Concord, American, Manhattan, La Salle, Lark, and New World String Quartets between their worldwide tours. The Juilliard was named resident quartet at the Library of Congress in 1962. *—Roger Dettmer*

Recommended:

○ **Janáček & Berg** / Juilliard Quartet / 1996 / Sony 66840

○ **Beethoven: The Early String Quartets** / Juilliard Quartet / 1983 / CBS 37868

K

Dmitry Kabalevsky

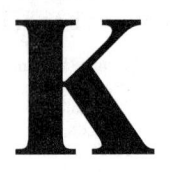

b. Dec. 30, 1904, St. Petersburg, Russia, **d.** Feb. 14, 1987, Moscow, Russia
Composer: Keyboard, Orchestral, Concerto, Symphonic, Opera
The music of Russian composer and teacher Dmitri Kabalevsky was hailed by Communist authorities as the finest incarnation of their artistic vision. Born in St. Petersburg in 1904, he lived during a notoriously difficult time for composers in that country. In 1918, Kabalevsky moved with his family to Moscow, where he studied at the Scriabin Music School. At the age of 18, Kabalevsky began to compose, primarily for the piano. His early pieces were studies for his young students, a practical facet of his compositional output which would remain with him throughout his career. He entered the Moscow Conservatory in 1925, studying piano with Goldenweiser and composition with Miaskovsky, the latter being particularly influential on Kabalevsky's developing musical outlook. By the end of the 1920s Kabalevsky was gaining notoriety as a composer; in 1928 the premiere of his *First Piano Concerto* launched him into the forefront of Soviet composers, while at the same time, the charming C major *Sonatina for piano* brought him international acclaim.

From his appointment to the composition faculty of the Moscow Conservatory in 1932 to his death in 1987, Kabalevsky produced a steady stream of works which sought to embody Soviet musical ideals through the use of diatonic tonality and accessible structural contours. He is perhaps best known for the overture to his opera *Colas Breugnon* (1936) which Arturo Toscanini conducted worldwide in the 1940s and 1950s. His suite *The Comedians* (1940), is another well-known work, while the *Piano Concerto No. 2* (1935) is likely his finest purely musical achievement. A series of concertos for young players (Violin 1948, Cello 1949, and the *Third Piano Concerto* of 1952) has greatly enriched the literature for student soloists. Kabalevsky's *Requiem*, Op. 72, completed in 1962, is a memorial to those who lost their lives during World War II. The text is based on a poem written by Robert Rozhdestvensky.

In addition to his compositional activities, Kabalevsky was a frequent contributor to pedagogical magazines and he held positions on various State educational bodies. Kabalevsky joined the Communist Party in 1940; by 1941 he received the Medal of Honour from the Soviet government for his musical prowess. During World War II, Kabalevsky wrote several inspirational songs and battle hymns. In 1942, his *Great Homeland*, and *Avengers of the People* were written to inspire heroism and patriotism. Kabalevsky's popular *The Taras Family* (1947) used music from the opera *In the Fire.* It became a success in spite of the 1948 party decree on music, probably because Kabalevsky's music had become more lyrical in nature. Kabalevsky was one of the few well-known Soviet composers who escaped the infamous 1948 condemnation of composers by the Central Committee of the Communist Party. (The scapegoats, including Prokofiev, Shostakovich, Khachaturian, and Miaskovsky were censured for indulging in "decadent formalism.")

Later in life, Kabalevsky became more involved in choral music. Kabalevsky continued to be a force in musical education. He was elected the head of the Commission of Musical Esthetic Education of Children in 1962, as well as being elected president of the Scientific Council of Educational Esthetics in the Academy of Pedagogical Sciences of the U.S.S.R. in 1969. Kabalevsky also received the honorary degree of president of the International Society of Musical Education. *—Blair Johnston*

KEYBOARD

Piano Music for Children

Although Dmitry Kabalevsky was many things (pianist, composer, writer, administrator, Soviet patriot, etc.), it is perhaps for his work as a teacher of, and composer for, children that he is best known today. Kabalevsky's children's piano music fills many volumes and was composed over a nearly five-decade period from about 1925 to 1971; most are short pieces or little sets of variations that Kabalevsky put together into larger collections over the decades (the most famous being the *30 Children's pieces*, Op. 27, and the *24 Pieces for Children*, Op. 39); all of these were reprinted, with some new additions, as a 13-volume anthology entitled *Piano Music for Children and Youth* (1970–73). It is a worthy and most useful little repertory.

The simplest of Kabalevsky's children's piano music is written in a lean melodic style, with just two or maybe three voices, or perhaps some simple chord figurations in the left hand. Kabalevsky's great achievement in this area was to produce fresh, exciting pieces that fully and respectfully exploit their young players' capacity for expression—here one never smells the kind of musical condescension that infects so much music for children—but avoid the kinds of intricacies and stretches that a small hand might find both discouraging and painful. Some of the well-known Op. 27 pieces are: "Ditty," "A Little Prank," "War Dance," "Fairy Tale," "Sad Story," "Snow Storm," "Old Dance," and the wonderfully open-ended "A Dramatic Event." In Op. 27 Kabalevsky also begins to introduce the young players to more advanced names like Etude and Scherzo.

But there is also intermediate-level material, the best-known of which are the two *Sonatinas*, Op. 13, of 1930–33 and the *Six Preludes and Fugues*, Op. 61, of 1958–59. The *Sonatinas* are quite like Kabalevsky's bona-fide piano sonatas, just watered a little down for smaller hands—the same prickly, Prokofiev-derived rhythms and articulations fill the pages, and some of the harmonies are bound to throw the young student who has thus far been raised on Clementi and Mozart for a loop. The *Preludes and Fugues*, Op. 61, grow more demanding even as one makes one's way through them: the first is in two voices and is really quite simple, but No. 6, with its four-voice fugue, is tough to play clearly and might bring sweat to the brow of even a professional!

The following is a list of Kabalevsky's most important children's piano music: *Collection of Children's Pieces*, Op. 3; *Two Sonatinas*, Op. 13; *Four Little Pieces*, Op. 14; *30 Children's Pieces*, in three books, Op. 27; *24 Pieces for Children*, Op. 39; *Easy Variations*, Op. 40; *Five Easy Variations on a Russian Folk Song*, Op. 51; *Four Rondos*, Op. 60; *Six Preludes and Fugues*, Op. 61; *Spring Games and Dances*, Op. 81; *Recitative and Rondo*, Op. 84; *Ten Sets of Variations*, in 3 books, Op. 85; *Variations on Folk Themes*, Op. 87; *Children's Dreams*, Op. 88; and *35 Easy Pieces*, Op. 89. *—Blair Johnston*

Recommended:

○ **Classical Fun** / Gresko / 1994 / Atma 9723

Piano Sonata No. 3 in F major, Op. 46 (1946)

Dmitry Kabalevsky's *Piano Sonata No. 3* was completed in 1945 as the horrors of World War II in the Soviet Union were finally coming to a close. In the composer's words, "The Sonata lacks a concrete program, yet two themes, two major images: youth and war, prevail here. The collision of those themes and the final triumph of youth sums up the plot of the work!" As such, this sonata made excellent propaganda material for the Soviet state, but it reflected Kabalevsky's true feelings about the war experience as well. Each movement of this spirited, well-crafted sonata brings a confrontation of some kind between youth and war. The Allegro con moto first movement opens with two representations of youth, a bright, quick, almost impetuous theme which trips lightly over the keyboard, followed by a less irrepressible but still lively theme that contains some witty play with rhythms. When the exposition ends, the development begins almost immediately to subject the "youth" themes to the perils of war, welding the formerly high-flying themes to diabolical, motoric rhythms and assailing them with crashes and attacks from the left hand. The themes struggle to break away, but the war music continues to hold sway until suddenly the recapitulation begins and the war music subsides entirely. A nervous mood nonetheless hangs over the recapitulation, and the first theme must fight off one more challenge of war in the coda, which ends slowly and quietly. The second-movement Andante cantabile follows a similar blueprint. It opens with a graceful, wistful theme in triple meter, which is played in two slightly different versions before strife starts to creep in. Subtle dissonances crop up, and become less and less subtle each time they are played; there emerges a sudden predilection for the minor mode. Here, though, when the opening theme comes back, the crashes and explosions of the central section now serve as elaborating devices for an embellished repetition of the first section, suggesting that war has somehow given maturity to youth. An Allegro giocoso closes the sonata, beginning with music that is close in form, if not spirit, to Shostakovich's toy-shop music, with jaunty rhythms and equally jaunty melodies. One of these recalls Richard Strauss' *Till Eulenspiegel*, and truly Kabalevsky seems enamored of such merry pranks. Here war takes the form of a one-to-the-bar waltz which whirls and storms until it loses its composure entirely, and yields to a spirited reprise of the opening themes. *—Andrew Lindemann Malone*

Recommended:

- ○ **Prokofiev: Sonata 7; Toccata; Barber: Sonata; Kabalevsky: Sonata 3; Fauré: Nocturne** / Horowitz / 1990 / BMG 60377
- ○ **Hommage à Werner Haas** / Haas / 2001 / MDG 6421086

ORCHESTRAL

The Comedians, suite for small orchestra, Op. 26 (1940)

In 1938, Dmitri Kabalevsky provided incidental music for a play produced by the Central Children's Theater in Moscow, entitled *Inventor and Comedian.* The score is light and witty and its expressive language quite direct, as was expected in Stalin's Soviet Union at that time. But here Kabalevsky was aiming at young audiences and had good reason to write tuneful, rather simple music. The play's plot deals with a traveling group of entertainers who are more clowns than comedians.

Two years later Kabalevsky extracted ten numbers from the score for his suite *The Comedians,* which would become his most popular work, with only the overture to his opera *Colas Breugnon* even remotely rivaling it. His effort was quite successful in distilling the work's best moments into a 15-minute suite, which he scored for small orchestra. The first number is the Prologue, a light and effervescent piece featuring colorful orchestral writing, the xylophone in particular enhancing the playful, mischievous atmosphere.

The Galop comes next; it is probably the most famous single number Kabalevsky ever wrote. Many a man and woman on the street know this galloping, descending, rhythmic tune, which again is colorfully punctuated by the xylophone. The music is joyous and witty, quite effectively capturing the tumbling actions of the clownish entertainers. The ensuing March is slow and amusing in its drunken gait, while the Waltz that follows is lithe and gossamer, subtly giddy and colorful.

"Pantomime" struggles to get going, it seems, remaining in the lower ranges of the orchestra and prodded in its laggardly manner by the snare drum at the outset. Its glum theme sounds like a parody of a funeral march. The Intermezzo is light and, in contrast to the previous number, scored mostly for the upper ranges of the orchestra. The "Little Lyrical Scene" is gentle and sweet, but features a melody which, especially when taken up by the horn, sounds Romantic and heroic. The delightful and very Russian-sounding Gavotte follows, masking the French origins of this dance form.

Next is a busy and colorful Scherzo whose main section alternates with somewhat exotic music of calmer demeanor. The Epilogue closes the work with the most boisterous sounds in the suite. Its ecstatic and brilliantly-scored ending seems to be the perfect orchestral incarnation of hysterical laughter.

All ten numbers in this suite are short, but Kabalevsky clearly demonstrates that his brevity of expression does not reduce the artistic impact of the music. While it is light, it is seriously light and must be judged a masterpiece of its type. *—Robert Cummings*

Recommended:

- ○ **Russian Orchestral Works** / Ormandy (cond.), Philadelphia Orch. / 1996 / Sony 62647

Spring (Vesna), symphonic poem, Op. 65 (1960)

Kabalevsky's brief symphonic poem is a waltz, not quite as grand or lush as Ravel's *La valse,* but still very much in a post-Romantic vein, even though he completed it in 1960. It begins with a solo flute playing a wandering melody, the first spring breeze. The violins and then the other instruments join in on an understated waltz beat, while the oboe, and then the flute again, float above. The poem continues on in much the same way, building to a couple of false climaxes with the full orchestra and dipping in and out of a minor mode, as if the new season were teasing with its approach. Finally *Spring* arrives in full bloom, and the waltz takes on more earnestness. Once it settles in, however, it rests on its laurels, and the poem returns to the calm and quiet to finish. *—Patsy Morita*

Recommended:

- ○ **Kabalevsky: Cello Concertos; Spring** / Golovschin (cond.), Moscow SO / 1997 / Naxos 553788
- ○ **Kabalevsky: Symphonies 1 & 2; Spring** / Tjeknavorian (cond.), Armenian PO / 1998 / ASV 1032

CONCERTO

Cello Concerto No. 1 in G minor, Op. 49 (1948–1949)

Dmitri Kabalevsky wrote his *Cello Concerto No.1* in 1948 and 1949. It is the middle piece in a trilogy of concertos that he wrote for young Russian musicians, to whom he dedicated a large part of his life's energy and compositions. The Op. 48 is a violin concerto and the Op. 50 is a piano concerto. The *Cello Concerto No. 1* was premiered in 1949, by Svyatoslav Knushevitsky, a young student to whom the piece was also dedicated. The orchestra was a student group from the Moscow Conservatory. The piece was received with much acclaim, as were the other two concertos in the trilogy. Kabalevsky was very popular with Russian audiences, composing music that was pleasing to the ear, and did not stray far from convention. Kabalevsky did, however, draw criticism from some because he generally rejected the direction new music was taking.

This concerto is in G minor and comprises three movements. The first is a march-type Allegro that begins with pizzicato in the string sections. They provide a steady pulse over which the cello enters, arco, with a striking melody that contains at once an energetic, melodic tension and a lyrical melodic release as the line soars into the upper register. The contrasting theme in this movement sounds less like a march and has almost a singsong quality about it. There is a brief cadenza toward the end, and the cello part becomes more virtuosic, as ascending double stops and passagework in octaves create an exciting peak before the movement ends in a surprisingly quiet manner.

The second movement is an elegiac Largo that Kabalevsky wrote in dedication to fallen Russian soldiers. The melody, although in B major, is based on a melancholy Russian folk song, and the movement is structured so that the cello part plays several lyrical stanzas of the melody. The solo part is accompanied by muted strings and there is a striking duo between the cello and the horns. Eventually the cello reaches a solo cadenza and the key is transformed from major into minor. This movement, like the first, has a very quiet ending.

The final movement is an Allegro Molto containing a set of variations based on another well-known Russian song. A lyrical clarinet line begins the movement before the cello enters with an emphatic melody. The melody slips quickly between agitation and lyricism, and during the lyrical parts various winds and brass in the orchestra take turns playing the melodic material from the cello's opening. This movement contains many beautiful, expressive moments that are peppered with variations of the more agitated material from the opening. The cello part is at times more virtuosic than in the previous two movements, growing in intensity until very fast notes lead to a spirited close. *—Emily Stoops*

Recommended:

- ○ **Kabalevsky: Cello Concertos; Spring** / Golovschin (cond.), Rudin, Moscow SO / 1997 / Naxos 553788
- ○ **Daniel Shafran, cello** / Kabalevsky (cond.), Shafran, Russia PO / 1952 / Omega 1026
- ○ **Shostakovich: Cello Concerto 1; Kabalevsky: Cello Concerto 1** / Ormandy (cond.), Ma, Miller, Philadelphia Orch. / CBS 37840

Cello Concerto No. 2 in C major, Op. 77 (1964)

Of Dmitry Kabalevsky's six instrumental concertos, a body of work that includes three piano concertos, a pair of cello concertos and the one violin concerto, all composed over a span of nearly 40 years, half are explicitly meant for the education and enjoyment of young performers. The other three, however, are a different matter: the first two piano concertos and the *Cello Concerto No. 2 in C minor/major,* Op. 77, of 1964, while by no means extreme in difficulty, have a grittiness to them—a full-blooded drama quite absent in the markedly lighter youth concertos. If the *Second Piano Concerto* is Kabalevsky's finest instrumental creation, the *Cello Concerto No. 2,* many feel, comes in a close second.

The concerto has three connected movements: 1. Molto sostenuto—Allegro molto e energico, 2. Presto marcato, 3. Andante con moto—Allegro. The orchestra is of average size and, except for the inclusion of a saxophone, standard in makeup. A scruffy timpani roll, a contrabass line whose only support is an occasional thunk from the lowest strings of the harp, and a "sonorous" (Kabalevsky's marking, in fact) pizzicato solo cello tune make for an ear-catching start, and soon the flutes, enthralled, take up the soloist's idea. But just as we are starting to feel comfortable in this opening musical paragraph, Kabalevsky shifts gears, and a scrambling Allegro, driven by mini-arpeggios, takes off on a journey of its own. The sudden shift from the Andante's C minor to the E minor home-base of the Allegro is anything but Classical, and Kabalevsky decides to let us have it again—this time in reverse—when a brief reprise of the opening Andante is made. It is in fact not so much a reprise as it is a transition to the movement's cadenza, which itself is used to make the transition from the first movement into the second.

The lengthy Presto marcato is a stubborn, prickly affair that can't decide between 3/8 and 2/4 time and so devotes large sections of music to each. Again transition to the following movement is made via cadenza; this time the cello gets some help from the timpani and cymbals.

For the quick music of the final movement Kabalevsky revives the flying mini-arpeggios of the first movement. But this Allegro stuff has to contend with a series of more tranquil episodes (one of which is heard at the beginning of the movement), and in the end it is quietude, in the shape of a wholesome C major harmony (colored by the inclusion of the non-harmonic tone D) in the strings and a calm 32nd note rustling from the solo cello, rather than action that prevails. *—Blair Johnston*

Recommended:

- ○ **Kabalevsky: Cello Concertos; Spring** / Golovschin (cond.), Rudin, Moscow SO / 1997 / Naxos 553788
- ○ **Russian Soul** / Shafran, Leningrad PO / 2002 / Cello Classics 1008

○ **Kabalevsky: Violin Concerto: Cello Concerto 2** / Thomson (cond.), Wallfisch, London PO / 2002 / Chandos 10011

Violin Concerto in C major, Op. 48 (1948)

A great deal of Dmitry Kabalevsky's best-known music is either music written expressly for children to play or music that might appeal directly and immediately to the musical sensibilities of a child—cheery, energetic stuff possessed of square rhythms and an apparently simple lyricism. Some pieces, like the *Violin Concerto in C major*, Op. 48, of 1948, are both. The *Violin Concerto* is the first of three instrumental concertos composed by Kabalevsky during the late 1940s and early 1950s and dedicated to the Soviet youth (the others are the *Cello Concerto No. 1* and the *Piano Concerto No. 3*), and was first performed in fall of 1948 by 18-year-old violinist Igor Bezrodny—not exactly a child, certainly, but the piece is not exactly a simple one either. It seems that Kabalevsky had in mind that each of these three concertos would serve as a model of an advanced study piece for young players, something more elegant (and in line with current Soviet musical policy) than the usual stuff student performers hone their skills on. Today the piece is nearly as often played by bona fide virtuosi as by students—a trend started immediately after the piece was premiered by David Oistrakh, who felt it an attractive enough piece to deserve professional-level performance and took the job upon himself—and stands alongside the Khachaturian *Violin Concerto* of eight years earlier as a memento of those composers who fully embraced the accessible, tuneful Soviet music-making ideal of the 1940s and 1950s.

Kabalevsky's *Violin Concerto* is in three relatively brief movements. Snappy rhythms, a main theme with a persistent hemiola, and a cantando second theme in G minor make for a compact, cadenza-less sonata-allegro form first movement (Allegro molto e con brio). The Andante cantabile middle movement is in three clear sections; when the "A" music, with its steadily plodding accompaniment and interesting harmonic twists, returns at the end, the soloist abandons the theme to the orchestra and takes up a flowing obbligato instead. Room is found in the rambunctious Vivace giocoso last movement for a short, transparent cadenza. *—Blair Johnston*

Recommended:

○ **David Oistrakh** / Kabalevsky (cond.), D. Oistrakh, U.S.S.R. State Orch. / 2002 / Classica d'Oro 2013

○ **Meeting in Moscow** / Pletnev (cond.), Shaham, Russian National Orch. / DG 457064

SYMPHONIC

Symphony No. 2 in C minor, Op. 19 (1934)

Kabalevsky is best-known in the West for such sprightly, witty pieces as *The Comedians* and the *Colas Breugnon Overture*, and perhaps for the lyrical *"Youth" Concerto* for piano. His symphonies are surprisingly dour by comparison, but the *Second* nevertheless comes across as fairly positive and certainly extroverted, despite its C minor key. It was written and premiered in 1934. As befits a Soviet work, its subject, stated by the composer, is mankind achieving his salvation by taking an active part in the reconstruction of his society.

The first movement, Allegro quasi presto, is in sonata form, taking off from nattering, ultimately beefy scherzando material full of busy passagework and a more tender but still quick theme winding through the winds and strings over a palpitating, unsettled accompaniment. The development section varies the main ideas concisely, giving way to a long crescendo building from a quiet bassoon solo and culminating in an impassioned statement of the movement's first theme. The recapitulation revisits the opening section in an entirely straightforward way, then leads into a virtuosic coda.

The Andante non troppo is an elegy that first offers an artless flute solo over a restless, mildly dissonant string accompaniment. Once the strings have expanded this material to a climax with brass reinforcement, the oboe enters with a melancholy melody, the string accompaniment now simpler and more elegiac. A chromatic, processional section for pizzicato strings ushers in a gradual crescendo and after the inevitable climax, the opening flute material leads the way to the end of the movement, with the clarinet recalling the second theme just before the close. The concluding Prestissimo scherzando is a rondo that applies a quiet, perpetual-motion treatment to an essentially pastoral tune; jubilant, militaristic outbursts constitute the intervening episodes. Toward the end, these two elements contend for supremacy; the happy moto perpetuo theme barely gets in the last word, accommodating the optimistic finale expected of Soviet symphonies of this period. *—James Reel*

Recommended:

○ **Kabalevsky: Symphonies 1 & 2; Spring** / Tjeknavorian (cond.), Armenian PO / 1998 / ASV 1032

OPERA

Colas Breugnon (Kola Bryun'yon), Op. 24/Op. 90 (1936–1938; revised 1953)

Kola Bryun'on: Master iz Klamsi (Colas Breugnon: Master of Clamecy), was Kabalevsky's first opera. His interest in the novella of the same name by French writer Romain Rolland prompted Kabalevsky to approach the author concerning an operatic interpretation. Rolland gave Kabalevsky his consent and told the composer he could interpret the novella as he wished. However, Rolland was disappointed in the libretto because much of the Burgundian setting had been eliminated.

Consisting of a prologue and three acts, *Colas Breugnon* was first performed at the Maliy Opera Theater, St. Petersburg, on February 22, 1938, and was published as Kabalevsky's Op. 24. Kabalevsky undertook major revisions to *Colas Breugnon* in 1953, but was not satisfied with his efforts until 1969, when he republished the opera as his Op. 90. This version received its first performance on April 16, 1970, also at the Maliy Opera Theater, and received the Lenin Prize in 1972. The *Overture* is a concert favorite in Russia and occasionally appears on concert programs in the United States.

Even without the distinctively Burgundian elements of Rolland's story, Kabalevsky's music for *Colas Breugnon* is infused with French flavor. Kabalevsky did not quote French melodies directly, but, after intense immersion in the study of French folk music, he succeeded in imparting a general spirit of French music to the score. For instance, the beginning of Act One is a chorus for women harvesters, *Cherez les gustoy* (Through the thick woods), the melodies of which resemble French popular songs.

Kabalevsky borrows from a wide variety of forms and styles throughout *Colas Breugnon.* In Colas' tongue twister, *Vskapïvat, vspakhivat* (To dig, to plough), Colas lists his various skills to Mademoiselle de Termes, constantly returning to the main theme in rondo fashion. When the leading female character, Selina, sings of cowardice in *Luga vecherniye myagki* (The evening meadows are soft), Kabalevsky accompanies her with a waltz, perhaps in a comment on the Russian perception of Austria. The drunken Curé of Act One and the delirious, deathly ill Colas in Act Two are given music that evokes Mussorgsky in mood and style, especially in the eerie dance in which Colas attempts to exhaust himself to the point of death. Later in the second act, when Colas and Selina meet unexpectedly, their reminiscences are accompanied by a return of the harvesting song from the opening of the first act, reminding us of their earlier amorous intentions.

One of the most significant changes made between Kabalevsky's original conception and his 1969 version occurs at the end of the opera. After the Duke smashes all of Colas' sculptures, Colas exacts vengeance, but not through violence, as in the first version, but through his art—by mocking the Duke with a statue. *—John Palmer*

Synopsis:

Prologue. Colas drinks and introduces the series of reminiscences.

Act One. In the vineyards, women are harvesting the grapes and singing ("Cherez lesh gustoy"). Colas and Selina exchange flirtatious insults, and when he leaves, she wishes he wouldn't let some teasing drive him off ("Noch i dien"). She falls asleep, and when Colas returns, he puts his arms around her. He turns to leave, but Gifflard, who wants Selina for himself, interrupts and provokes a quarrel. They are interrupted by the news that the Duke, with a troop of new soldiers, is returning. Outside the castle, the Duke obliviously wonders why his return seems to have frightened the townsfolk. Chamaille calls for music, and Mademoiselle de Termes, who has accompanied the Duke from Paris, notices Colas, who is in the ensemble, approvingly. She coyly asks him about his accomplishments, and he happily boasts that he can successfully turn his hand to nearly everything ("Vskapïvat, vspakhivat"), pointing out that he has sculpted the elegant fountain. She invites him into the Duke's castle to show her his other masterworks, as Selina watches jealously. She sings a ballad of a cowardly warrior ("Luga vechernye myagkt") and Gifflard takes the opportunity to denigrate Colas to her. When Colas swaggers back and invites her to dance, she refuses. Jacqueline, who is secretly in love with Colas, offers herself as a partner instead. Colas returns inside the castle, and annoyed by the sound of his playing and the flirtatious laughter she hears, Selina leaves with Gifflard.

Act Two. In Colas' workshop, much later, with Jacqueline and Colas married, though unhappily, with one grandchild, he and Robinet return to work on a sculpture of Selina. They are interrupted by the arrival of the Duke and Gifflard, and Colas hides the sculpture, but Gifflard uncovers it, and the Duke seizes it for his collection. Colas comforts himself with the thought that his masterwork will be kept safely, at least. Chamaille comes in, pursued by some angry parishioners, and he and Colas drink together, Colas performing a drinking song ("Za Provansom") and Jacqueline and Robinet singing as well. The light mood is interrupted by the sound of a *Dies Irae* being sung by mourners, who inform them that the Duke's soldiers have carried the plague back with them. Jacqueline and the others flee, taking the granddaughter with them, but Colas defies fate and stays. Later, he is ill and delirious, imagining his impending death ("Noch tianetsia"). He begins to dance, but falls to the ground, hallucinating the sight of stars and sound of music. Chamaille comes in, expecting to find him dead, but helps him revive with his bottle of wine. Robinet returns, reporting that the soldiers have burnt everything in the town, but he did manage to save Colas' wooden flute. Chamaille tries to prepare Colas for the news that both Jacqueline and his granddaughter were infected and are dying, and Colas determines to see them, though his heart is far more set on the little girl. The two of them found shelter in a stranger's house, and Jacqueline tells Colas she has always loved him and envied him his easygoing laughter. She is dying but their granddaughter is recovering, and when Jacqueline dies, Colas vows to take care of the child ("Slavnaya zverushka"). Outside her house, Selina and Colas encounter one another, and converse shyly. Selina breaks the awkwardness by demanding a kiss and telling him how she truly did love him ("Ya lyubila tebya"). He does not wish to repeat the past, and is skeptical about whether love would have lasted, and after another kiss, he leaves. However, when he hears that the Duke and Gifflard are continuing to tyrannize the town, he decides to confront them.

Act Three. From the castle, the Duke watches the completion of the burning of the town. Gifflard, still resentful of Colas, tells the Duke that Colas is leading an uprising, and in retaliation, they set out to destroy all his works. When Colas enters, he is dismayed to hear that even the sculpture of Selina has been smashed, but recovers his good humor, laughing and telling the Duke he will have his revenge on the feast day of St. Martin. In the next scene, the townsfolk are dancing and singing in honor of the saint, and the Duke and his guests make a grand appearance for the unveiling of Colas' sculpture detailing his proud achievements. The people sing of their city's beauty ("O slavny grad Clamsi") and the cloth covering the sculpture is ceremoniously lifted. The statue features the Duke in full regalia, but sitting backwards on a donkey. The Duke and his guests, furious and shocked, rush back into the castle, and Colas tells the laughing, exultant crowd his philosophy that the only flaw of human life is that it is too brief. *—Ann Feeney*

Recommended:

- ○ **Mussorgsky: Pictures at an Exhibition; etc.** / Reiner (cond.), Chicago SO / 1994 / RCA Victor 61958
- ○ **Kabalevsky: Piano Concertos 2 & 3; Colas Breugnon Overture; The Comedians** / Sinaisky (cond.), BBCPO / 2003 / Chandos 10052

Mauricio Kagel

b. Dec. 24, 1931, Buenos Aires, Argentina
Composer

Born in Buenos Aires, Argentina, Kagel proved to be one of the most versatile, creative, and witty composers to come of age in the second half of the twentieth century. He studied piano, theory, violoncello, organ, singing, and conducting, and was self-taught as a composer. Kagel also studied philosophy and literature extensively during his college years, and his career eventually included film and drama.

His early career found Kagel filling positions that drew upon all of these interests. After having served in the early 1950s as advisor to the Agrupación Nueva Musica of Buenos Aires and one of the founders of the Cinémathèque Argentine, he took a position in Colón as conductor of the Chamber Opera and Theater. He conducted new music concerts with the Rhineland Chamber Orchestra in the late 1950s before serving as visiting lecturer in Darmstadt. The 1960s found Kagel in the United States, where he undertook a lecture tour and taught briefly at the University of Buffalo. He then returned to Europe, where he lectured at the Berlin Film and Television Academy before filling Stockhausen's shoes as the director of the Institute of New Music at the Rheinische Musikschule. He was also a presence at the West German Radio electronic music studio, and produced several of his own films and plays. Of course, one finds much bleed between categories and genres when looking at a given work by such a jack-of-all-trades. His plays and films often utilize musical forms as their underlying structures; likewise, his concept of "instrumental theater" insists on the importance of not only the musical sounds produced but also all the physical actions executed by the players. His post-structuralist leanings demand that he constantly elude labels such as "Dadaist" or "anticomposer," on the one hand, or a modernist, on the other; his aesthetic does not emphasize the dismantling of traditions and the building of new ones, but rather a constant and pervasive reevaluation of what constitutes music *now.*

Fittingly, then, one can find in Kagel's output elements ranging from serialism to expressionism to musique concrète to Dada to aleatoria. Even his earliest works exhibit this experimental attitude. *Palimstesos* (1950) utilizes word dissociation and metamorphosed speech patterns, ideas that were further explored a few years later in *Anagrama* (1955–58). In this latter piece, a Latin palindrome provides the generative musical material; the sounds of words become a compositional device, while the meaning of the words is downplayed or even distorted. In addition, the letters of the words employed inform the pitches used, since many of the letters correspond to musical notes.

Many of his works also employ musical collage techniques, such as his *Music for Renaissance Instruments* and the music for the film *Ludwig van.* The influence of Satie, Cage, (and perhaps Partch?) can be seen in *Der Schall* and *Unter Strom,* two chamber pieces which call for a variety of archaic, invented, or "nonmusical" (i.e. cash registers, horns, etc.) instruments. Again, however, these sounds are not thrown together with reckless abandon; as Kagel himself stated, "An essential aspect of my work is strict composition with elements which are not themselves pure." *—Jeremy Grimshaw*

Overview of Works

"An essential aspect of my work," explained Argentinean-German composer Mauricio Kagel, "is strict composition with elements which are not themselves pure." Among the first generation of composers free to assess and integrate the various strands of music developed over the course of the twentieth century—neo-Classicism, serialism, indeterminism—Kagel has created a body of work that variously embraces both structure and post-structuralism, formalism and anarchy. Several of Kagel's earliest works utilize 12-tone methods, but do so in a rather self-conscious manner; some scholars read into the serial methods in works such as his string sextet (1953) and *Anagrama* (1958), an underlying irony meant to challenge the parametric control exercised by serial methods. Most of Kagel's best-known works involve music in conjunction with other kinds of media, a practice established early in his career with the musical and visual work *Musica para la torre* (1952). Kagel developed an approach to performance that has been referred to as "instrumental theater," in which the instrumentalists convey—through gestures, choreography, and interaction—certain ideas about the circumstance of performance. A kind of deconstruction of the performance circumstance characterizes *Sur scéne,* a multimedia work from 1960, and *Exotica,* a chamber work for non-Western instruments from 1972, both of which challenge lingering colonialist and elitist paradigms implied by Western music and culture. *Match,* from 1964, involves a kind of competition between a pair of cellos, with a percussionist providing play-by-play. His film *Hallelujah* (1968) documents a musical performance using a set of instructions ordered and executed in an indeterminate manner. So important is the visual element to Kagel's works that a number of his pieces are primarily visual and his credits include a number of additional films. The most well-known of these is perhaps *Ludwig van,* created in 1970 as a complex musical and visual musing on the music of Beethoven. Other films take on musical subjects as well, including Brahms and Handel in *Variationen ohne Fuge* (1972), and Schubert in *Aus Deutschland* (1980). A strong historicist tendency is likewise apparent in Kagel's "anti-opera" from 1970, *Staatstheater.* Virtually every number in the work transgresses its own conventions and the work as a whole conveys a strong anarchistic and non-conformist message. Some of Kagel's later works seem less confrontational or at least more subtle in their subversive intent. His works from the last two decades of the twentieth century lean toward neo-tonality, even as they employ pastiche techniques. Kagel's *Sanct-Bach Passion* (1985) is more of an homage than a parody, and works from the 1990s such as *Fanfaren* for four trumpets (1993), the *String Quartet No. 4* (1993), and the chamber orchestra cycle *Die Stücke der Windrose* (1994) utilize relatively familiar harmonic languages. *—Jeremy Grimshaw*

Recommended:

- ○ **Kagel: Heterophonie; Improvisation ajoutée** / Gielen (cond.), Zacher, Frankfurt Radio SO / 2001 / Wergo 6645
- ○ **Mauricio Kagel** / Le Sage, Tharaud, Bernold, Marder, etc. / 2003 / Aeon 311
- ○ **Kagel: 1898; Music for Renaissance Instruments** / Flittard (cond.), Brugense Collegium Instrumentale / 1998 / DG 459570
- ○ **Kagel: Pan; String Quartets 1–3** / Arditti SQ, Wiesner / 2000 / Disques Montaigne 782129
- ○ **Kagel: 5 Stücke der Windrose; Phantasiestück** / de Leeuw (cond.), Schoenberg Ens. / 2001 / Disques Montaigne 782140
- ○ **Kagel orchestral works** / Kagel (cond.), etc. / 2000 / Col Legno 20502
- ○ **Kagel: Chamber Works** / Art pour l'art / CPO 999577

Vasily Kalinnikov

b. Jan. 13, 1866, Voin, Russia, **d.** Jan. 11, 1901, Yalta, Russia
Composer: Symphonic

Like those of his Belgian contemporary Lekeu and his older countryman Mussorgsky, the story of Vasily Kalinnikov is a tragically short one in which a handful of works gives a tantalizing glimpse of what may have been.

Born is the village of Voin in the province of Orlov, Kalinnikov was the son of a cleric who also held the position of local police chief. The elder man was musically inclined, playing guitar and accordion as well as singing in the church choir. Young Vasily learned the latter instrument on his own and with the help of the village doctor, later adding the violin to his accomplishments. Further on he joined the church choir, learning the basics of music theory in the process and becoming the choir conductor at 14. Kalinnikov resolved to make music his career.

At 18 and with the most tenuous of financial resources, Kalinnikov set out for Moscow to study music at the conservatory, transferring to the Philharmonic Music School a half year later. While there, he bolstered his meager income by taking a course in bassoon, which resultantly enabled him to play in various orchestras as bassoonist, violinist, or timpanist. He also took on work as a music copyist.

Having graduated, Kalinnikov held various teaching posts and was assistant conductor at an opera company. However, the delayed effects of the strain of holding multiple positions during his student years undermined his health and he contracted tuberculosis. For this the composer traveled south, meeting Tchaikovsky in 1892. He received praise from the older man when he showed him the score of his own orchestral suite. This encouragement was a morale boost for the ailing young composer and he began work on his *First Symphony in C minor.* Completed in 1895, it was performed by the Russian Music Society in 1897. By that year, Kalinnikov had also completed his *Second Symphony in A flat*, this despite consumption of the throat compounding his health problems. The following year he completed the symphonic poem *The Cedar and the Palm* and received a commission to provide incidental music for a production of Tolstoy's *Tsar Boris*, for which he completed a substantial amount of music. But the young man's skein was running out and he succumbed to his illness on January 11, 1901, too frail to attend a performance of his Prologue to *Boris*.

In the centenary year of his birth recordings of the two symphonies led to the discovery of Kalinnikov by the public. While his premature passing is to be lamented, the small body of works which he left are very enjoyable exercises in late Russian Romanticism. Although these pieces are unmistakably Slavic in flavor, they seem to escape the brooding and gloom so omnipresent of his time and place in the arts, all the more curious given the external misery of his life. As such, Kalinnikov's work, especially the symphonies, are a happy if lesser known addition to the Russian orchestral literature. *— Wayne Gerard Reisig*

Overview of Works (1884–1900)

Kalinnikov was only beginning to establish his reputation when he died of tuberculosis only two days before his 35th birthday. His publisher estimated that Kalinnikov's premature demise had increased the value of his music tenfold, and more than one musicologist has speculated that, had he lived a normal lifespan, Kalinnikov would have become one of Russia's greatest composers. As it turns out, interest in his music has waxed and waned over the past century; Kalinnikov's works enjoy periodic vogues, more on disc than in concert, only to fall again into neglect.

This is unfortunate, for Kalinnikov's few works suggest an extraordinary talent. His two symphonies show him to be more structurally assured than Tchaikovsky, and more melodically distinctive than, say, Balakirev or Glazunov. Kalinnikov favored a Slavic style of writing, but generally avoided the exoticism and rich colors of Rimsky-Korsakov. He was fond of strong accents, cross rhythms, movement into unexpected keys, thematic transformation, and engaging melodies built largely from seconds and thirds.

In Russia he is known primarily as a choral composer, his output including 15 a cappella choruses setting texts by Russian poets and choral arrangements of Russian folk songs, as well as religious works and pieces for children's choirs. This music is virtually unknown in the West, and his piano pieces, songs, and sole string quartet fare no better.

The two works that represent Kalinnikov to the widest public are his symphonies, composed between 1895 and 1897. The first is the more popular of the two, with its generous Slavic lyricism, but the second shows a less rote approach to form. Slow sections are tender, and fast sections are ebullient without falling to the charges of vulgarity often leveled against Tchaikovsky. Both symphonies are sunny and lyrical, as are most of his other compositions, colorfully orchestrated in the manner of Borodin, the composer Kalinnikov most closely resembles. *—James Reel*

Recommended:

○ **Kalinnikov: Tsar Boris; etc.** / Jancsovics (cond.), Budapest SO / Marco Polo 223135

SYMPHONIC

Symphony No. 1 in G minor (1894–1895)

Vasily Kalinnikov is one of the lesser known members of that tragic yet august company of "what if?" composers. Succumbing to tuberculosis at 34, he managed to leave behind a handful of completed enjoyable works which come as an unexpected delight, or at the very least a diversion, to lovers of Tchaikovsky, Borodin, Rachmaninov, and the other Russian symphonists. Most conspicuous are his two symphonies, pleasant outings in late Russian Romanticism, unclouded and cheery, sleigh rides rather than treks. The *Symphony No. 1 in G minor*, despite some obvious flaws, was a decided success at its 1897 premiere by the Russian Music Society. Performances in Vienna, Berlin, and Paris followed in rapid succession and the frail young musician seemed posed for better things, having at that time completed his *Second Symphony* as well.

The chief attraction of the *G minor Symphony* is its font of engaging, typically Russian melody, as well as some rather novel ideas. What works against the composition is an essentially textbook approach to symphonic form. But the complaint is largely confined to the opening movement, and, at that, given the perspective of time and circumstance at that point in Kalinnikov's life, it should not deter. From the start the symphony commences with a bluff, likable theme such as a burly peasant might hum to himself while plying his labor. This is contrasted with a lyrical second theme which, curiously, sounds as though it could be an extension of the first one, which may have been the composer's intent. However, the material is not worked skillfully enough, with too much verbatim repetition. Even the Tchaikovskian climaxes are robbed of their vigor and effect by overexposure. The second movement, however, is another matter, a study in muted half-shaded beauty. In song form, the main theme is incanted against a hypnotic ostinato of two eighth notes. A solidly peaceful feeling of reverie pervades, contrasted with a more earthly lyrical theme before its return. The following scherzo too is striking, utilizing a stomping Brucknerian gait to support its Slavic themes. The trio is almost long enough to be a movement in itself, more exotic in mood; a suggestion of Borodin's orientalism peers through the bars. In the finale, the two main themes of the opening movement make an appearance before each of the corresponding new ones, each organically derived from the former, a rather novel approach to cyclic procedure. The overall sound is more grandiose than that of the opening movement in its emulation of the German Post-Romanticism of Mahler and Strauss, although it is difficult to say how familiar Kalinnikov may have been with these Western models given the brevity of his life span. Whatever the case, Kalinnikov's *First* is, but for its few flaws, a charmer, its defects bested by its freshness and overall happiness. *— Wayne Reisig*

Recommended:

○ **Kalinnikov: Symphonies 1 & 2** / Kuchar (cond.) / 1995 / Naxos 553417

○ **Kalinnikov: Symphonies 1 & 2** / Jarvi (cond.), Scottish National Orch. / 1997 / Chandos 9546

Symphony No. 2 in A major (1895–1897)

Even as his *First Symphony* was making the rounds of Europe, Kalinnikov was completing his *Second*. What is even more remarkable is the artistic growth which took place in this brief period. Where the *First Symphony* boasted a plethora of "big tunes," to which it owed its early success, these were handled in somewhat lackluster outer movements. By the time its successor was completed in 1898, the ailing composer was nonetheless cheerily plying his craft with assurance and ease. The themes are attractive and melodious, their treatment is imaginative as well as symphonic. The term "sweep," the quality of a natural unfolding in motion, serves admirably here. Had Kalinnikov been granted a longer span, he could have been a great symphonist linking the era of Tchaikovsky with that of the post-Revolution composers, even going beyond national borders. And to boot, it is very enjoyable.

While suffused with typically Slavic melody, Kalinnikov was not adverse to looking towards Western models. The opening movement recalls that of Brahms' *First Serenade* in mood; there are some Wagnerian harmonic turns, as well as some Brucknerian processes (according to Vladimir Horowitz there was a Bruckner cult early on in Russia). The symphony commences with a broad, majestic introduction from which the happy main theme derives by diminution. Likewise is the slightly more pensive second theme skillfully derived from its predecessor. The third theme, a very Russian Trepak, is so short as to be almost a punctuation but will play a more important role as the work progresses. The development, where "padding" is wont to occur, shows instead great invention and variety. In the recapitulation the third theme is given more prominence. In the coda there is a reminiscence of the second theme by the horn before the last big *finis*. In the second movement, the English horn's plaintive theme accompanied by "strummed" harp and strings evokes a bardic, medieval atmosphere, which is contrasted with the lush exoticism of the second theme. There is a climax built on a Bruckner-like sequence, with the overall mood one of serenity and resignation, perhaps the only indication of the composer's reflection on mortality. The scherzo features a swinging triplet rhythm, martial yet frolicking, recalling that of Bizet's *Symphony in C*, the chattering woodwinds providing some sardonic humor. The trio, with the reappearance of the English horn, looks back to the slow movement. In the finale, festivity prevails as previous themes are woven into the fabric. The Trepak theme of the first movement makes a conspicuous reappearance while the grandiose opening theme reemerges in the development. Most striking in the recapitulation is the appearance of syncopation curiously premonitory of Gershwin. The recall of the symphony's opening theme sets the coda in motion and the work concludes on a joyous note, a hearty affirmation of life from one well aware of its preciousness. *— Wayne Reisig*

Recommended:

○ **Kalinnikov: Symphonies 1 & 2** / Kuchar (cond.) / 1995 / Naxos 553417

○ **Kalinnikov: Symphonies 1 & 2** / Jarvi (cond.), Scottish National Orch. / 1997 / Chandos 9546

Gilbert Kalish

b. Jul. 2, 1935, Brooklyn, NY

Pianist

Equally at home in classroom and concert hall, pianist Gilbert Kalish has introduced audiences to a range of modern works that are now considered standards of the repertory. A solo artist who has released over 100 recordings, he is likewise noted for his roles in chamber music ensembles and for his collaborations as accompanist with soprano Dawn Upshaw, cellist Joel Krosnick, and above all, mezzo soprano Jan de Gaetani. Born in New York City, Kalish attended Columbia University. His B.A. from Columbia in 1956 was augmented by studies at the Berkshire Music Center and the Marlboro Festival, and by an honorary doctorate from Swarthmore College in 1987. Kalish has been nominated for three Grammy awards and has received a host of other awards, including the Paul Fromm Award, bestowed by the University of Chicago in recognition of his advocacy of the music of our time.

Kalish's commitment to new music led him to become a founding member of the Contemporary Chamber Ensemble in 1962, and his musical partnership with de Gaetani began not long after that. In 1969 Kalish joined the Boston Symphony Chamber Players, and he has performed with many of the world's top string quartets over the years. His solo career flourished; he has performed recitals in most of the major musical capitals, and he is a familiar face at such recurring events as New York's Mostly Mozart festival. Especially noted for his performances of Ives' piano music (the *"Concord" Sonata* in particular), Kalish has given world premieres of works by Ives and also of pieces by many of the other big names in American music of the twentieth century: Elliott Carter, Copland, George Crumb, and David Diamond, to name a few.

Professor (since 1970) and chair of the performance faculty at the State University of New York at Stony Brook, Kalish straddles the academic and public realms in his teaching and has become immensely influential as an educator. He gives several master classes a year around the U.S. and Canada, often accepts guest faculty appointments, and from 1968 to 1997 he was on the faculty at the Tanglewood Music Center. Kalish has recorded for the Nonesuch, Arabesque, Desto, and New World labels, among others, traversing mainstream classics, well-known modern works, and world premieres with equal enthusiasm. His recording of Stephen Foster's songs with de Gaetani on Nonesuch is a perennial bestseller. *—James Manheim*

Recommended:

○ **Charles Ives** / Kalish, Baron, Graham / 1977 / Nonesuch 71337
○ **In The Shadow Of World War II** / Kalish, Krosnick / 1996 / Arabesque 6682
○ **Songs By Stephen Foster** / de Gaetani, Guinn, Kalish / 1987 / Nonesuch 79158
○ **Haydn: Piano Sonatas** / Kalish / 1987 / Nonesuch 79162

Giya Kancheli

b. Aug. 10, 1935, Tbilisi, Georgia, U.S.S.R.
Composer: Symphonic

After the fall of the Soviet Union, Giya Kancheli (b. 1935) emerged into international fame as one of the country's composers who resisted the official pressure to conform to an approved realist style. Georgia has its own unique religious, folk, and classical music traditions. Georgian composers, and those of other "exotic" republics, were encouraged to add their regional traditions to the approved Russian style of classical music as a way of appealing to the nationalism of all major Soviet regions.

Thus, Kancheli was able to study his musical roots as well as Western techniques when he entered the Tbilisi Conservatory in 1959. He studied composition with Il. Tuskiya and remained there until 1963. After graduation, Kancheli began working as a freelance composer. He did not take an academic position or join a Soviet musical organization to support himself. He composed popular music in the Georgian folk style as well as a large amount of film music.

Meanwhile, he developed his own classical and symphonic styles, working toward an ideal that combined avant-garde ideas with elements of the most ancient Georgian religious and folk music, though it should be noted that he never directly quotes material in his concert works.

He wrote at least 38 film scores between 1964 and 1995 for Georgia-Film Studio and for Mos-Film, the main Russian studio. He found that Communist Party arts and music officials did not pay much attention to the style of film scores, and so he was frequently able to use some of his newest musical thought in these works. In addition, he wrote a considerable amount of incidental music for the director Robert Sturua and in 1971 became the music director of Sturua's own Rustavili Theater. His opera, *Music for the Living* (1984), was written in collaboration with Sturua.

A look at Kancheli's catalogue shows a change in the character of the titles of his compositions. The period ending in 1982 shows abstract titles predominating. Kancheli had joined fellow Russian composers like Shostakovich, Gubaidulina, Schnittke, Pärt, and Artyomov in cloaking his agenda in musical symbolism. But as openness (glasnost) became a Soviet policy, the works gained more overt titles, such as *Bright Sorrow* and *Life without Christmas*. In 1990, the first significant Western recording of Kancheli works was released, including the *Third Symphony* and the *Sixth Symphony*, both of which were widely praised.

There is a clear influence from Shostakovich in the opening ten minutes of the *Third Symphony*, including the parody a military march. The *Sixth Symphony*, which seems concerned with ominous, oppressive silence, had a clear relationship to the long, slow opening movement of Shostakovich's own Sixth. Yet, there was a striving for religious ecstasy that set Kancheli's music apart from Shostakovich's. In addition, there are elements drawn from indigenous and historic Georgian music, with trance-like drones and strange, otherworldly orchestration, often featuring the alto flute, an idea consciously borrowed from American jazz arranger Gil Evans. Kancheli's tendency toward even, treading motions is based on his great fondness for the conclusion of Stravinsky's *Symphony of Psalms*, and orchestrational styles learned from film composers Michel Legrand and Nino Rota are also present in Kancheli's music.

In 1991, following the collapse of the U.S.S.R., Kancheli left the political uncertainties of his homeland and settled for a few years in Berlin, and then moved on to Antwerp in 1995. Like his late colleague Schnittke, Kanchelli uses multiple styles that can often be unpredictable. Prominent performers, particularly Latvian violinist Gidon Kremer, frequently perform his music, and it has been frequently recorded. *—Joseph Stevenson*

Overview of Works

Giya Kancheli's mature style divulges a sense of tragedy, loneliness, and desperation in music that is often slow and threadbare in its presentation of conventional melodic materials. In his orchestral scores, there is much quiet music over which violent outbursts can occur, or there is soft music of fragmentary character that can grow steadily to form recognizable melodic ideas, as in his *Lament* (subtitled "Music of Mourning in Memory of Luigi Nono") from 1994. His works are generally tonal and often use Georgian folk elements. They can also exhibit a liturgical or medieval chant-like character, as in much of his *Symphony No. 3* (1973), a well-crafted, riveting work with long sections of unrelieved gloom. There are seven symphonies in his output, the *First* composed in 1967 and the last in 1986. The *Fourth* ("In Memoria di Michelangelo"; 1975) and *Fifth* ("In Remembrance of My Parents"; 1977) have received high praise for their deep sense of tragedy where, especially in the latter work, there are long, quiet sections often juxtaposed with powerful outbursts. The *Symphony No. 1*, cast in two movements, is somewhat uncharacteristic in the sustained fast tempos of the first movement, though the tense and grim manner of the whole work reflect much of the composer's mature style. The *Second ("Canticles")*, from 1970, is colorful and shows further advancement in expressive language (and an allusion to Stravinsky's *Petrouchka* in the Allegro middle panel?), while the *Sixth* (1977) may be his finest symphony. It begins modestly with a quiet Georgian folk lament and imaginatively progresses toward a powerful march at the close. The *Seventh*, divulging a polystylistic character akin to Schnittke's, is complex and less successful. Kancheli wrote *Mourned by the Wind for Viola and Orchestra* in 1989 and later transcribed it for cello and orchestra. The original version of this powerful work is perhaps more gripping, the viola seeming to desperately cry out quite effectively and appropriately in certain passages, where the more mellow cello merely sounds passionate. Kancheli's lone opera, *Music for the Living* (1982–84), on texts by Robert Sturua, has had some success and achieved a prestigious production in Weimar by the German National Theater in 1999. His most important choral works include *Light Sorrow* (1985), an anguished piece commemorating children killed during World War II. The 1994 *Exil* (Exile) is one of several works in which Kancheli uses tape quite imaginatively—others include the compelling *Night Prayers* (1992), for string quartet. *Exil* is scored for soprano and chamber ensemble and uses texts from psalms and several poems. Its music has a lovely, tortured beauty in its vocal writing and an overall ghostly sense to the work itself. The orchestral work *Rokwa* and *Styx for Viola, Chorus, and Orchestra*, both appeared in 1999. *—Robert Cummings*

Recommended:

○ **Kancheli: Abii ne viderem** / Davies (cond.), Kashkashian, Pschenitschnikova, Tevdorashvili, Hilliard Ens., Stuttgart CO / 1995 / ECM 445941
○ **Kancheli: Symphonies 6 & 7** / Kakhidze (cond.), Tbilisi SO / 2001 / Beaux 2026
○ **Kancheli: Symphony 3; Light Sorrow** / Kakhidze (cond.), Tbilisi SO / 2003 / Beaux 2010
○ **Kancheli: Exil** / Jurowski (cond.) / 1995 / ECM 447808
○ **Kancheli: Mourned By The Wind; Light Sorrow** / Werthen (cond.), Springuel, Ford, Hayes, Fiamminghi, Cantate Domino Chorus / 1997 / Telarc 80455
○ **Kancheli: Caris Mere** / Davies (cond.), Kashkashian, Brunner, Garbarek, Deubner, Tevdorashvili, Stuttgart CO / 1997 / ECM 449198
○ **Kancheli: Magnum Ignotum** / Kakhidze (cond.), Rostropovich, Flanders PO / 2000 / ECM 462713
○ **Kancheli: Lament** / Kakhidze (cond.), Kremer, Deubner, Tbilisi SO / 1999 / ECM 465138

SYMPHONIC

Symphony No. 4 ("In Commemoration of Michaelangelo") (1975)

Commissioned by the U.S.S.R. Ministry of Culture, Kancheli's *Symphony No. 4* was written in 1974 in anticipation of the 500th anniversary of the birth of Michelangelo the following year (another noteworthy Russian work written for the occasion was Shostakovich's *Suite on Verses of Michelangelo Buonarroti*, Op. 145). Kancheli's symphony was given its first performance in Tbilisi on January 13, 1975, by the Georgian State Symphony Orchestra conducted by Dzhansug Kakhidze. It won the U.S.S.R. State Prize in 1976, and also became the first of Kancheli's works to receive significant attention in the West when the Philadelphia Orchestra gave its U.S. premiere in 1978 under the direction of Yuri Temirkanov.

Church bells, both on and off stage, play an important role in this single-movement symphony (marked Largo). The bells are heard solemnly tolling at the work's beginning, eventually joined by long sustained tones from the orchestra. This bare texture builds into an ominous and grandiose crescendo. One of the hallmarks of Kancheli's 1970s style—slow, quiet, mournful music which is interrupted abruptly by loud chords and blasts—is prominent here. After a particularly violent eruption, a soothing nursery tune quietly emerges, played by two harps and a celesta. But those loud interruptions continue, leading into stormy scherzo-like music which, it has been suggested, represents Michelangelo's flight from Pope Julius II in 1505. A strange, ghostly folk song now appears in the strings—in 1971 Kancheli had become the music director of the Rustaveli Theatre in Tbilisi, where he came into contact with Georgian folk music and musicians. Another bell-laden eruption follows, but the last few minutes of the symphony are very spare in texture. A quiet ticking sound and distant bells fade into silence. *—Chris Morrison*

Recommended:

- ○ **Kancheli: Symphonies 4 & 5** / Kakhidze (cond.), Georgian Festival Orch. / 1992 / Nonesuch 79290

Jean-Jacques Kantorow

f. Oct. 3, 1945, Cannes, France
Violinist

Better known in Europe than in North America, Jean-Jacques Kantorow is a noted violinist who has made a transition to conducting, administration, and teaching. Of Russian ancestry, Kantorow was born in Cannes, France, in 1945. He showed talent in childhood and enrolled at the Nice Conservatory and then, at 13, at the Paris Conservatory, where he took home a top prize in 1960. Throughout the 1960s he remained one of Europe's most consistent competition prize-winners, and his performance career became worldwide in scope. He recorded much of the standard concerto repertory, and of his more than 130 recordings, dozens remain available. Kantorow has been primarily associated with the Denon label.

Among the many figures in the musical world who hailed his playing was Glenn Gould, who called Kantorow a "staggering" talent and the most original violinist he had ever heard. His playing, noted the *Grove* dictionary, "combines the best features of the French and Russian schools."

Kantorow grew into conducting as an orchestra leader, serving in that capacity with the Orchestre de Paris in 1977 and 1978, and with the Netherlands Chamber Orchestra (1978–1984). He became principal conductor of the Auvergne Chamber Orchestra in 1985 and of the Ensemble Orchestral de Paris in 1993. He also held substantial conducting engagements with various ensembles outside France, including the Netherlands Chamber Orchestra, the BBC Chamber Orchestra, and Finland's Tapiola Sinfonietta and Helsinki Chamber Orchestra, serving as artistic director of the Helsinki group. Increasingly his career has been rounded out with major teaching positions at conservatories in Strasbourg and Rotterdam and at the Conservatoire National Supérieur de Musique de Paris. *—James Manheim*

Recommended:

- ○ **Le Chevalier de Saint-Georges** / Thomas (cond.), Kantorow, Bernard Thomas CO / Arion 68093
- ○ **Kantorow & Gifford** / Kantorow, Gifford (guitar) / 1992 / Droffig 3
- ○ **Pärt: Summa** / Kantorow (cond.), Laivuori, Soderblom, Talka, Vartiainen, Tapiola Sinfonietta / 1996 / Bis 834

William Kapell

b. Sep. 20, 1922, New York, NY, **d.** Oct. 29, 1953, King's Mountain, CA
Pianist

William Kapell was one of the most promising American pianists of the postwar generation, producing a few recordings that have attained legendary status after his untimely death.

He studied in New York with Dorothea Anderson la Follett, and then at the Philadelphia Conservatory with Olga Samaroff. He went to the Juilliard School when she relocated there. He won the Philadelphia Orchestra's youth competition and the Naumberg Award in 1941. He debuted in New York through his prize from the Naumberg Foundation; this debut recital won him the Town Hall Award for the outstanding concert of the year by an artist under 30.

A national recital career quickly developed, leading to a recording contract with RCA Victor's Red Seal records. One of his enthusiasms was for the recently composed *Piano Concerto in D flat major* by Soviet composer Aram Khachaturian, which he frequently played. Because it is an extroverted and flashy work, he gained a reputation as a specialist in such music. His recorded legacy shows that he performed in the appropriate style from graceful renditions of Mozart to powerful Prokofiev.

After World War II, he expanded his touring to cover the world. It was on his return from a tour of Australia that his airplane crashed into King's Mountain near San Francisco. *—Joseph Stevenson*

Recommended:

- ○ **William Kapell Edition** / Kapell, etc. / 1998 / RCA 902668442
- ○ **Khachaturian: Concerto; Prokofiev: Concerto 3** / Dorati, Koussevitzky (conds.), Kapell, BSO, Dallas SO / 1998 / RCA 902668993
- ○ **Rachmaninoff: Concerto 2; Rhapsody on a Theme of Paganini** / Reiner, Steinberg (conds.), Kapell, Robin Hood Dell Orch. / 1998 / RCA 902668992
- ○ **William Kapell** / Dorati, Steinberg (conds.), Kapell, Dallas SO, Robin Hood Dell Orch. / 1999 / Philips 456853

Herbert von Karajan

b. Apr. 5, 1908, Salzburg, Austria, **d.** Jul. 16, 1989, Anif, near Salzburg, Austria
Conductor

Herbert von Karajan was among the most famous conductors of all time—a man whose talent and autocratic bearing lifted him to a position of unprecedented dominance in European musical circles. He was born on April 5, 1908 in Salzburg, Austria, to a cultured Austrian family of Greek descent (their original name was Karajannis). His musical training began at the Mozarteum Conservatory in Salzburg where he studied piano with Franz Ledwenke, theory with Franz Zauer, and composition with Bernhard Paumgartner, who encouraged Karajan to pursue conducting. Karajan graduated from the conservatory in 1926, and continued his studies at the Vienna Academy of Music and Performing Arts, where he studied piano with Josef Hofman and conducting with Alexander Wunderer and Franz Schalk. Karajan's conducting debut came on January 22, 1929, with the Mozarteum Orchestra in Salzburg. Consequently, the young maestro directed a performance of Strauss' *Salome* at the Salzburg Festspielhaus, and was named principal conductor of the Ulm Stadttheater, where he remained in that capacity until 1934.

The next fourteen years saw the young conductor's reputation grow rapidly. He was named music director of the Aachen Stadttheater (1934–42), had his debut at the Vienna State Opera (1937), and accepted a position with the Deutsch Grammophon Gesellschaft (1938–43). In 1939, Karajan was appointed conductor of the Berlin State Opera, and director of the Preussiche Staatskapelle Symphony concerts. In 1948, he was appointed for life, to the position of director of the Chorale Society at the Society of the Friends of Music, in Vienna.

In 1948, Herbert von Karajan also served at the Vienna Symphony Orchestra, the Philharmonia Orchestra, and La Scala, before succeeding Wilhelm Furtwängler as the music director of the Berlin Philharmonic Orchestra—a union that would cement his reputation as one of the world's premier conductors. In 1955, Karajan brought that orchestra to the United States on the first of many international tours. The decade that followed saw Karajan accept several appointments, including those to the Salzburg Festival and the Vienna State Opera. In 1967, Karajan had his Metropolitan Opera debut, conducting a performance of Wagner's *Die Walküre*, and the same year, founded the Salzburg Easter Festival. In 1968, the Herbert von Karajan Foundation was founded to support the research of "conscious musical perception."

Herbert von Karajan was awarded the "Ring of the Province of Salzburg," Golden Grammophone, Arts Prize (Lucerne), Grand Prix International du Disque, Gold Medal of the Royal Philharmonic Society, German Golden Disc Prize, UNESCO International Music Prize, Olympia Prize of the Onassis Foundation, and multiple Grammophone awards, among others. He was elected to an honorary senate seat at the University of Salzburg. The maestro was also recognized with honorary degrees from a host of universities.

Karajan, along with Akio Morita and Norio Ohga (president and vice-president respectively, of Japanese Sony Group), unveiled and presented the Compact Disc Digital Audio System in 1981. In 1982, Karajan founded Telemondial S.A.M. with Dr. Uli Markle, in an effort to document the maestro's illustrious legacy on videotape and laser disc, and to help broaden the scope of "musical expression," through the use of modern technology. In 1984, Karajan recorded the complete Beethoven symphonies with film adaptation, made possible by his own Telemondial. In 1988, Deutsch Grammophone released a collection of one hundred "masterworks" recordings made by the conductor. Herbert von Karajan's discography is impressive to say the least, and will certainly endure in musical arenas, as some of the most valued interpretations of the repertoire available. Herbert von Karajan, often referred to as "general music director of Europe," died in Salzburg of heart failure July 16, 1989. *—David Brensilver*

Recommended:

- ○ **Mahler: Symphony 9, Kindertotenlieder, Rückert-Lieder** / Karajan (cond.), Ludwig, Berlin PO / DG 453040
- ○ **Wagner: Der fliegende Holländer** / Karajan (cond.), Van Dam, Moll, Moser, Hofmann, Berlin PO / EMI 47054
- ○ **Tchaikovsky: Symphony 6** / Karajan (cond.), Berlin PO / 1998 / London 460609
- ○ **Verdi: Requiem** / Karajan (cond.), Freni, Ludwig, Ghiaurov, Cossutta, Berlin PO / 1992 / DG 437473

○ **Strauss: Zarathustra; Don Juan; 4 Last Songs, etc.** / Karajan (cond.), Tomowa-Sintow, Bell, Schwalbe, Berlin PO / 2003 / DG 000020202

Sigfrid Karg-Elert

b. Nov. 21, 1877, Oberndorf am Neckar, Germany, **d.** Apr. 9, 1933, Leipzig, Germany

Composer

German composer and organist Sigfrid Karg-Elert, though not widely known, had a prodigious output, having composed his greatest bulk of work for the organ and harmonium. A reappraisal of his work began with a series of ambitious recording projects in the 1990s, cataloguing his most important contributions.

The composer's father, Johann Karg, a book dealer, rarely saw his family. Constantly on the move, the family lived in many areas throughout German-speaking Europe. Karg-Elert was the youngest of 12 children. Nonetheless, in spite of these hardships, his great musical aptitude was recognized early on. Traveling through Leipzig, the boy tried out for a position with the choir of Saint John's Church, which began his musical training. At 12, he composed a cantata, and soon thereafter began private piano lessons. In 1896, composer Emil von Reznicek obtained three years of tuition free study at the Leipzig Conservatory for the budding musician. There, he studied with Carl Reinecke, Salomon Jadassohn, and others. He supported himself during this time playing in cafes and playing now and then with regional orchestras.

Karg-Elert's *Piano Concerto*, performed by himself as soloist, won him additional free training at the Leipzig Conservatory, enabling him to graduate fully from the institution. This was arranged by piano virtuoso Reisenauer, who also convinced Karg-Elert to embark on a recital tour of Germany. However, it was composition that interested him, and on his return to Leipzig, he took up advanced composition study with Teichmuller at the conservatory. He was later appointed head of the master class at the Magdeburg Conservatory in 1902.

Not happy at Magdeburg, he left teaching altogether and concentrated full-time on composition. Around 1904, he met Edvard Grieg, who recommended his work to several publishers, notably Novello and Carl Simon, the Berlin publisher and harmonium specialist. The publication of his work resulted in gaining the backing of influential performers and composers of the day. Busoni, Kreutzer, and Reger performed his work, and encouraged the creation of new ones.

In 1915, Karg-Elert enlisted in the army, and played various instruments in the regimental bands. At this time, he composed his solo works for flute and clarinet. He returned to Leipzig in 1919 to teach at the Leipzig Conservatory once more. A rather dark time in the composers' life intervened between 1920 to about 1926. He was being criticized by some of his peers for not being nationalistic enough, and too cosmopolitan. The era of heightened national pride caused Karg-Elert to feel like a stranger in his own country, and he was even branded as a Jew, although he was not.

Karg-Elert composed over 250 pieces for organ, 100 pieces for the harmonium d'art (developed by French instrument-maker Mustel), numerous chamber works, and he completed several theoretical works. His theory of *Harmonologie* developed original approaches to practical theoretical considerations. *—Franklin Stover*

Overview of Works (1895–1932)

Sigfrid Karg-Elert was a little-known figure until the latter twentieth century, when some of his many compositions were recorded. His output mainly consists of works for the keyboard—for (in order of dominance) organ, harmonium, and piano. He also wrote a fair amount of chamber and choral music, songs, and orchestral music. Stylistically Karg-Elert was generally conservative, though he did briefly dabble in atonal writing. His music is often complex and features fairly sophisticated, typically chromatic harmonies. Ultimately, however, he remained an eclectic partial to Romanticism throughout most of his career.

Karg-Elert's early organ music divulges the influence of Bach, as heard in his *66 Choral Improvisations* (1908–10). The 1908 *Chaconne and Fugue Trilogy with Choral* features brilliant contrapuntal writing throughout and makes deft use of a Bach motif. Yet there is little that is actually Baroque in either of these two works, Bach's presence in the former piece being felt largely in the forms chosen—sarabande, canon, chaconne—and in the latter, both in his imaginative counterpoint and, of course, in use of the motif. As his career progressed, Karg-Elert developed his organ style more freely, moving toward a more abstract kind of expression. Still, his admiration for Bach and for the forms he used would be felt as late as 1931, when he composed the *Passacaglia and Fugue on B-A-C-H*.

Not surprisingly, Karg-Elert's harmonium works are closer in spirit to his organ music than his piano compositions. The harmonium output is still largely ignored—not least because of the instrument's passé status—but it nonetheless contains many gems, foremost among which is the *Sonata No. 2* (1909–12). It is a huge work of elaborate structure whose material he reused in the aforementioned *Passacaglia and Fugue on B-A-C-H*. Also of note are the 1905 *Phantasie and Fugue* and the 1906 *Sonatina No. 3*.

The piano compositions clearly come from the same pen as the other keyboard works, but are quite different, especially in their wide-ranging moods. The *Five Bagatelles* from 1902 are quite light and sunny in mood, while the 1920 *Hexameron*, comprised of six pieces, is also optimistic and good natured, though a Debussyian influence is noticeable. But Karg-Elert could be quite serious in his piano compositions, as evidenced by the 1914–20 Scriabin-esque *Piano Sonata No. 3 "Patetica"* and the 1922 *Partita*, a 20-minute work whose playful manner features greater depth than one might think from one hearing.

Karg-Elert's orchestral music includes a relative handful of works, among which are two piano concertos (from 1900 and 1913, respectively) and the *Sinfonia Brevis* (1897), all of some interest, but not on the level of his solo keyboard compositions. His vocal output includes lieder, as well as choral and sacred works, the latter realm including a *Mass in B minor*. Again, the music is well crafted here, but appears to lack the mastery often found in his keyboard music. *—Robert Cummings*

Recommended:

○ **Karg-Elert: Organ Works, Vols. 1–4** / Stockmeier / CPO 999019
○ **Karg-Elert: Piano Works, Vol. 1** / Breidenbach / CPO 999683
○ **Karg-Elert: Compositions for Harmonium** / Jacobs / 1990 / CPO 999051
○ **Karg-Elert: Cathedral Windows** / Fagius / 2000 / BIS 1184
○ **Chamber Music** / Schneeberger, Grimmer / Jecklin 686

Gary Karr

b. Nov. 20, 1941, Los Angeles, CA

Bassist

There have been only five notable solo double-bass virtuosos in the past two-and-a-half centuries—remarkable for an instrument developed before 1600 and refined ever since. Gary Karr is the most recent and widely famous of these rare players, virtually the Yo-Yo Ma of the cello's big brother. Domenico Dragonetti (1776–1846) came first, playing an instrument built by Amati in 1611. Giovanni Bottesini (1821–89) followed, after him Franz Simandl (1841–1912), and then Sergey Koussevitzky (1874–1951), who played the 1611 Amati until he traded his bow for a baton in 1908. In 1924, Koussevitzky moved from a post-Russian base camp at Paris to Boston, where he conducted one of the three greatest U.S. orchestras until his retirement in 1949—eight years after Karr's birth into a family that had been playing the double-bass for seven generations. Karr's paternal grandfather, father, an uncle, two cousins, and he (starting at age nine) played concurrently in Los Angeles-area orchestras until Gary entered UCLA, where he studied briefly with Herman Reinshagen before transferring to Northwestern University for study with Warren Benfield, then to The Juilliard School where Stuart Sankey became his principally credited mentor (he studied on the side, however, with mezzo-soprano Jennie Tourel, and cellists Gabor Rejto, Leonard Rose, and Zara Nelsova).

He made his professional debut in 1961 with Thor Johnson (then Director of Orchestral Activities at NU after 11 years in Cincinnati) and the touring Chicago Little Symphony. Leonard Bernstein's Young People's Concerts with the NY Philharmonic in 1962 were his breakthrough, however—the same year he made his solo recital debut in Carnegie Hall. After that concert, Koussevitzky's widow, who had attended, phoned him and made him a gift of her late husband's 1611 Amati. He played the historic instrument exclusively until recently, when luthier James Harn built a new one for him "of remarkable craftsmanship, beautiful wood, and superior power even to the Amati." But he still records on the 1611 Amati, and performed most of his concerts on it before officially retiring from the stage five months before his 60th birthday—during the June 2001 convention at Indianapolis of the International Society of Bassists (which Karr founded in 1967).

As a worldwide performer and TV personality, as a teacher for more than half of his public lifetime (including a videotape called *BASSically Karr*), and as the author of three textbooks on double-bass history and technique, Karr has been an indefatigable champion. In addition to master classes wherever he has played, he presides for four weeks annually at Karr Kamp, a summer school on the University of Victoria campus in British Columbia, where he makes his home. He established an eponymous Foundation in 1983 to preserve a collection of fine instruments for use without cost by gifted young musicians. Furthermore, he has commissioned more than 50 works, both concertos and solo concert pieces, from composers including Paul Ramsier, Hans Werner Henze, John Downey, Gunther Schuller, Lalo Schifrin, and Robert Rodriguez.

Three things have characterized Karr's career beyond the achievements listed above (more can be learned from his own website and BASSically.net). One is a career-long interest in children—their pleasure and growth as listeners. Another is the sense of humor typified by puns in his promotional materials, and some stand-up comedy during certain kinds of performances. The third is his musical ecumenism: he has been as natural playing Christmas melodies and non-classical music (a CD of spirituals and Stephen Foster, for example) as he is in re-creating Bach's *Cello Suites*. *—Roger Dettmer*

Recommended:

○ **Super Double-Bass** / Karr, Lewis (piano) / Lim 7

Vesselina Kasarova

b. Jul. 18, 1965, Stara Zagora, Bulgaria
Mezzo-Soprano

An exceptionally talented mezzo-soprano who stood out even in an era with no shortage of them, Vesselina Kasarova emerged as a popular favorite in the late 1990s, both as a recitalist and as an operatic specialist in the bel canto works of Mozart, Rossini, Bellini, and Donizetti. Born in the medium-sized city of Stara Zagora in Bulgaria's center, Kasarova attended music school there, majoring in piano rather than voice. She dreamed of a vocal career, however, and auditioned at the national Academy of Sofia. She was accepted and blossomed rapidly as a singer, joining the company of the National Opera of Sofia even before her graduation in 1989.

Kasarova's international debut came at the 1991 Salzburg Festival in Austria, where she appeared as Annio in Mozart's *La Clemenza di Tito* under the baton of Sir Colin Davis. In the autumn of that year, she appeared as Rosina in Rossini's *Il Barbiere di Siviglia* at the prestigious Vienna State Opera. Through the 1990s she appeared at many of the world's major opera houses, broadening her reach into the deeper sound of the late nineteenth century and into the French repertoire. She also has given recitals and performed vocal concert works throughout Europe. She has recorded for RCA Red Seal, and in 1996 received a Grand Prix du Disque award for a French song recital disc that included the Berlioz *Les Nuits d'été* cycle. In 2003 she made an unusual move for an operatic artist by recording an album of Bulgarian folk music, *Bulgarian Soul*. *—AMG*

Recommended:

- ○ **Mozart Arias** / Davis, Mikorey (conds.), Kasarova, Dresden Staatskapelle / 1997 / RCA 902668661
- ○ **Massenet: Werther** / Jurowski (cond.), Vargas, Kasarova, Kotoski, Schaldenbrand, German Symphony Orch, Berlin / 1999 / RCA 7432158224
- ○ **A Portrait** / Kasarova, etc. / 1996 / BMG 68522
- ○ **Bulgarian Soul** / Delibozov (cond.), Kasarova, Schweizer-Sekulinova, Sofia Soloists Chamber Ens, Cosmic Voices from Bulgaria / 2003 / RCA 57736

Kim Kashkashian

b. Aug. 31, 1952, Detroit, MI
Violist

If anyone has "made" the viola in the latter part of the twentieth century, it has been American violist Kim Kashkashian. Born in Detroit and of Armenian extraction, Kashkashian studied the viola with Karen Tuttle and legendary violist Walter Trampler at the Peabody Conservatory of Music in Baltimore.

Kashkashian has been a staunch proponent of commissioning new works for her instrument. The list of composers who have written works especially for her reads like a "Who's Who" of contemporary composition: Arvo Pärt, Tigran Mansurian, Peter Eötvös, Krzysztof Penderecki, Paul Chihara, Sofiya Gubaidulina, Linda Bouchard, Giya Kancheli, and György Kurtág are all among them. A frequent flyer at the Marlboro Music Festival, Kashkashian was strongly influenced in her approach toward commissioning new music for chamber combinations in her role as assistant to one of the festival's organizers, violinist Felix Galimir. It was also at Marlboro that Kashkashian met pianist Robert Levin, with whom she frequently performs and records; other public events at which Kashkashian can regularly be seen include the Salzburg, Lockenhaus, and Stavenger festivals in Europe. Kashkashian's musicianship has been well represented on recordings through her association with Germany's ECM label in a happy collaboration that is, in 2004, close to entering its third decade.

Kashkashian has written eloquently about the neglect of the viola and the reasons her instrument has been consigned to second-class status for so long. The instrument she terms "the much-maligned viola" has a first-class champion who works to broaden the range of technique, advocacy, and repertoire for the instrument. Kim Kashkashian teaches at the New England Conservatory of Music. *—Uncle Dave Lewis*

Recommended:

- ○ **Bartok: Concerto for viola; Movement for viola & orchestra** / Eotvos (cond.), Kashkashian, Netherlands Radio CO / 2000 / ECM 465420
- ○ **Lachrymae** / Davies (cond.), Kashkashian, Stuttgart CO / 1993 / ECM 439611
- ○ **Kancheli: Abii ne viderem** / Davies (cond.), Kashkashian, Pschenitschnikova, Tevdorashvili, Hilliard Ensemble, Stuttgart CO / 1995 / ECM 445941
- ○ **Hindemith: Sonatas for viola/piano & viola alone** / Kashkashian, Levin (piano) / 1988 / ECM 833309

Julius Katchen

b. Aug. 15, 1926, Long Beach, NJ, **d.** May 29, 1969, Paris, France
Pianist

A child prodigy of startling promise, Julius Katchen matured into a solo and chamber music pianist of broad interests and probing artistry. His death from cancer at age 42 denied a discerning public the presence of a pianist especially well-equipped to penetrate to the center-most meanings of those works he favored.

Born to a musical family, Katchen was instructed in the musical arts from his earliest years. His grandmother, formerly a faculty member at the Warsaw Conservatory, was his first piano instructor, while his grandfather taught him theory (his mother, a pianist, had trained at the Fontainebleau School of Music and had made concert appearances in both Europe and America). In 1937, Katchen presented himself to Eugene Ormandy and requested that he be permitted to play for him. Ormandy was sufficiently impressed to engage the lad for an appearance with the Philadelphia Orchestra. The October 21, 1937, concert found Katchen performing Mozart's *Concerto in D minor* to high praise. Following this glowing reception, the 11-year-old pianist was invited to perform at a pension fund concert with the New York Philharmonic the following month. Critic Lawrence Gilman was moved to recall the debut of Josef Hofmann as a prodigy a half century before. "His fingers are fleet, his conceptions clear and intelligent," wrote Gilman of Katchen. "He has a musicianly feeling for the contour and flow and rhythm of a phrase and a sense of what is meant by Mozartean style." A New York recital a year later brought even more enthusiastic praise for the youth's musical understanding.

Before his career advanced, however, Katchen's parents chose to place a hold on further public appearances and enroll him instead at Haverford College, where he majored in philosophy and English literature. His break, Katchen often insisted, developed in him the intellectual curiosity that fed his interest in the more mentally challenging works in the repertory.

A fellowship extended by the French government permitted Katchen to travel to Paris in 1946; that cosmopolitan city became his home for the remainder of his life and he lost no time in making himself a formidable presence there and in the rest of Europe, respected for his commanding interpretive thoughtfulness and virtuoso technique. He undertook several highly successful tours of the Continent, winning acclaim in each center he visited. Decca Records signed him to an exclusive contract and he began recording a bracing cross-section of the repertory with Brahms always at the core. He presented concert performances of Brahms' complete solo piano works in New York, London, Amsterdam, Vienna, and Berlin and was heard with major orchestras in the two piano concertos. In addition to solo appearances, Katchen often took part in chamber music performances, again concentrating on Brahms, but certainly not neglecting other aspects of an extensive personal repertory. Ned Rorem and Benjamin Britten were just two contemporary composers to benefit from Katchen's advocacy. To say, as some have, that Katchen never achieved the success in America that was his in Europe fails to account for the far greater portion of his mature years that were spent on the Continent where other cultural stimulations prompted his most involved and productive work. His tragic death was keenly felt on both sides of the Atlantic. *—Erik Eriksson*

Recommended:

- ○ **Julius Katchen** / Katchen / 1998 / Philips 456856
- ○ **The Art of Julius Katchen, Vol. 1** / Gamba (cond.), Katchen, London SO / 2004 / Decca 460822

Peter Katin

b. Nov. 14, 1930, London, England
Pianist

Although his early career seemed centered on Mozart and Beethoven, pianist Peter Katin became known as a great interpreter of Romantic keyboard literature, which he played with a serene warmth and big tone. He started playing when he was four years old. He had been studying privately with Harold Craxton before he was granted early admission to study with Craxton at the Royal Academy of Music at the age of 12, rather than the normal age of 16. He also credits Clifford Curzon, Claudio Arrau, and Myra Hess as being great influences in his musical life: "...I learned more in three long afternoons than I ever learned anywhere else." He gave his debut recital, a program that ranged from Scarlatti to Scriabin, at Wigmore Hall in 1948. His first concerto performance was Beethoven's *Concerto No. 4* with the London Symphony in 1951. Enthusiastic critical response led to many more orchestral engagements, most featuring Romantic concertos, beginning with the Tchaikovsky *Piano Concerto No. 2* for his first appearance at the Proms in 1952 and Rachmaninov's *Concerto No. 3* for his second the next year. Christopher Seaman, Paavo Berglund, George Cleve, and Owain Arwel Hughes are just a few of the conductors he worked with in his career. In the late 1960s, Katin undertook more comprehensive study of certain composers, such as Chopin, Schubert, Schumann, Debussy, Liszt, and Grieg, often presenting recitals comprising a single composer's works. His diligent study also led to his writing his own program notes and recording performances on historical instruments, such as one Chopin used on his last visit to London. Most of his recordings are of the solo piano works of those composers he studied. His career as a soloist gave him few opportunities to perform with others, although in the 1970s he did accompany Victoria de Los Angeles in three recitals, and he did form a piano trio in 1997. He taught privately in addition to holding positions at the Royal Academy of Music (1956–59), the University of Western Ontario (1978–84), and the Royal Conservatory of Music since 1992. His students included Gordon Fergus-Thompson, Howard Shelley, and Philip Fowke. In 1998 he was able to relive his debut recital, 50 years later to the day, at Wigmore with a very simliar program. By 2004, he had essentially given up performing in public, primarily due to a damaged tendon in his right hand. —*Patsy Morita*

Recommended:

○ **Schubert: Impromptus** / Katin / 1994 / Athene 5

○ **Katin Plays Chopin, Vol. 1** / Katin / Olympia 186

○ **Katin: A Liszt Recital** / Katin / Olympia 199

Martin Katz

b. Nov. 27, 1945, Los Angeles, CA

Pianist

Martin Katz is a veteran and highly respected American collaborative pianist. He has been performing for over 30 years, accompanying such stars as Marilyn Horne, Kathleen Battle, Kiri Te Kanawa, Frederica von Stade, and José Carreras. He has appeared on many of the world's leading recital stages, and recorded for many of the major record labels. As a scholar, he has prepared editions of Baroque- and bel canto-era operas that have been performed at the Metropolitan Opera and other prominent venues. The 1998 winner of Musical America's "Accompanist of the Year" award, Katz is currently the Artur Schnabel Professor of Music at the University of Michigan, where he teaches vocal repertory, ensemble piano, and vocal coaching, and often conducts the university's opera productions.—*Joseph Stevenson*

Recommended:

○ **Voyage à Paris** / Von Stade, Katz / 1995 / RCA 902662711

○ **Serenade** / Daniels, Katz / 2000 / Virgin 45400

○ **Barber, Bernstein, Bolcom** / Horne, Katz, Harada, Isomura, Ikeda, Oundijian, Tokyo String Quartet / 1998 / RCA 902668771

Ani Kavafian

b. May 10, 1948, Istanbul, Turkey

Violinist

Ani Kavafian is one of the most respected of American violinists, particularly in the field of chamber music and in the more modern repertory. Her father was born in Bulgaria to the family of an Armenian refugee from the notorious suppression of the Armenians by the Ottoman Empire in 1914 and 1915. Her father, in turn, left Bulgaria, fleeing the Communist government there and settling in Turkey. Her father was the principal violist of the Istanbul State Symphony Orchestra, where he met Ani's mother, a member of the first violin section.

Ani recalls that there was no particular anti-Armenian sentiment in Istanbul when she was a young girl, but that it reappeared during anti-Greek riots that broke out in 1956 over the issue of independence of Cyprus. The Kavafian family left Turkey and settled in Detroit.

By then, Ani's younger sister Ida had been born (Oct 29, 1952). Ani had a strong interest in learning piano and studied that instrument, but recalled that she used to always put her ear against the door to her mother's practice room just so she could hear the violin. Beginning in 1957, the two girls began taking violin lessons from Ara Zerounian and later from Mischa Mischakoff. Ani recalls Mischakoff as a tough teacher who particularly stressed accuracy of intonation. Once, she says, he took her violin, untuned the strings, played her music perfectly in tune, then handed it to her and demanded she do the same: "No excuses! No matter what your open strings are doing you should be able to adjust."

In 1966, she went to New York to enter the Juilliard School, where she studied with Ivan Galamian. It is to this teacher that she attributed the development of her sound which, she says, was "pretty but very small" when she first came to him, and credits Sally Thomas as establishing a solid technical foundation through frequent drills.

Sister Ida followed the same career path, arriving at Juilliard in 1969, and the two have frequently performed together in various forms of chamber music. Ani made her debut that year at Carnegie Recital Hall. Her European debut was in Paris in 1973.

She and Ida have both established leading violin careers. Ani toured widely in the 1970s, appearing with the world's leading orchestras. She has appeared at the White House three times and on television frequently. She joined the faculties of the Manhattan School of Music and Mannes College of Music in the 1980s.

In 1979, she joined the Chamber Music Society of Lincoln Center. She became the senior member of that organization (which later also included Ida). Although she loves the standard repertory (particularly the Mozart, Brahms, and Mendelssohn concertos), Ani is best known for twentieth century music. She also is especially fond of the Bartók second and Shostakovich first concertos, the concerto of Samuel Barber, and that of Korngold. She often plays the Khachaturian concerto, but one gets the impression that this is because of the Armenian connection to that work. She has premiered Henri Lazarof's *Concerto for violin and string orchestra* and Tod Machover's *Concerto for hyper violin and orchestra* (using a violin as input to a computer to produce extended sounds).

She is married to Bernard Mindich, an artist. Their son, Matthew, is a promising cello student. Ani Kavafian owns the 1736 instrument known as the Muir-Mackenzie Stradivarius. —*Joseph Stevenson*

Recommended:

○ **Brahms: String Quintet in G; Clarinet Quintet** / Shifrin, Kavafian, Kavafian, Trampler, Sherry, Tenenbom / 1994 / Delos 3066

○ **The 3rd Tucson Winter Chamber Music, 1996** / Kavafian, Suk, Kanka, Phelps, Holek, Kluson, Rejto, Votapek / Arizona Chamber 96202

Ida Kavafian

b. Oct. 29, 1952, Istanbul, Turkey

Violinist

Though born in Istanbul, Ida Kavafian is of Armenian lineage. She is the sister of violinist Ani Kavafian and has often performed with her sibling. The two have appeared together on the *Today Show* and *CBS Sunday Morning*. As both a soloist and a member of chamber groups such as Tashi and the Beaux Arts Trio, Ida Kavafian has appeared on many recordings for major labels, including RCA and Philips.

Born in Turkey, Ida Kavafian moved with her family to the United States in 1956. She showed musical talent very early on and began instruction on the violin at age six with Ara Zerounian in Detroit. She later studied with Mischa Mischakoff, then enrolled at the Juilliard School of Music in 1969, where she studied with Oscar Shumsky and Ivan Galamian. In 1973, Kavafian traveled to Lisbon and took first prize at the Vianna da Motta International Violin Competition. Two years later, she graduated from Juilliard with a master's degree and then co-founded the now-celebrated chamber group Tashi, which consists of Peter Serkin on piano, Fred Sherry on cello, Richard Stoltzman on clarinet, and of course, Kavafian on violin. They would make many notable recordings over the years, including one of Messiaen's *Quartet for the End of Time*, for RCA. Kavafian concurrently established a career as a soloist, debuting in New York in 1978 with Serkin accompanying, and in London in 1982. Her first major appearance with her sister was at Carnegie Hall in 1983, which, like the debut concerts, received positive notices. Kavafian expanded her career to include performance of jazz compositions when she went on an international tour with an ensemble led by Chick Corea in 1983–84. From 1989 until 1993, Kavafian was an Artist Member of the Chamber Music Society. She became a member once again in 1996, a post she retained through 2002. She was a member of the Beaux Arts Trio from 1992 to 1998 and still performs regularly with the group. Kavafian co-founded *Opus One* in 1998, a piano quartet whose other members are pianist Anne-Marie McDermott, violist Steven Tenenbom (Kavafian's husband), and cellist Peter Wiley (also a former member of the Beaux Arts Trio, who joined the Guarneri Quartet in 2001). In 2002, Kavafian was on the faculty at the Curtis Institute and Mannes College of Music. She and Wiley live in Connecticut, where they also find time to breed show dogs. Kavafian's repertory is broad, encompassing compositions by Mozart, Beethoven, and Mendelssohn, as well as new works by Wuorinen, Ruth Crawford, and Toru Takemitsu, the latter having composed a concerto for her, which she premiered. —*Robert Cummings*

Recommended:

○ **Rorem: Winter Pages; Bright Music** / Kavafian, Kavafian, Sherry, Serkin / 1992 / New World 80416

○ **Messiaen: Quartet for the End of Time** / Tashi / 1988 / BMG 7835

Rudolf Kempe

b. Jun. 14, 1910, Niederpoyritz, Saxony, Germany, **d.** May 12, 1976, Zurich, Switzerland

Conductor

One of the great unsung conductors of the middle twentieth century, Rudolf Kempe enjoyed a strong reputation in England but never quite achieved the international acclaim that he might have had with more aggressive management, promotion, and recording. Not well enough known to be a celebrity but too widely respected to count as a cult figure, Kempe is perhaps best remembered as a connoisseur's conductor, one valued for his strong creative temperament rather than for any personal mystique.

He studied oboe as a child, performed with the Dortmund Opera, and, in 1929, barely out of his teens, he became first oboist of the Leipzig Gewandhaus Orchestra. His conducting debut came in 1936, at the Leipzig Opera; this performance of Lortzing's *Der Wildschütz* was so successful that the Leipzig Opera hired him as a répétiteur. Kempe served in the German army during World War II, but much of his duty was out of the line of fire; in 1942 he was assigned to a music post at the Chemnitz Opera. After the war, untainted by Nazi activities, he returned to Chemnitz as director of the opera (1945–48), and then moved on to the Weimar National Theater (1948–49). From 1949 to 1953 he served as general music director of the Staatskapelle Dresden, East Germany's finest orchestra. He then moved to the identical position at the Bavarian State Opera in Munich, 1952–54, succeeding the young and upwardly mobile Georg Solti. During this period he was also making guest appearances outside of Germany, mainly in opera: in Vienna (1951), at London's Covent Garden (1953), and at New York's Metropolitan Opera (1954), to mention only the highlights. Although he conducted Wagner extensively, especially at Covent Garden, Kempe did not make his Bayreuth debut until 1960. As an opera conductor he was greatly concerned with balance and texture, and singers particularly appreciated his efforts on their behalf.

Kempe made a great impression in England, and in 1960 Sir Thomas Beecham named him associate conductor of London's Royal Philharmonic. Kempe became the orchestra's principal conductor upon Beecham's death the following year, and, after the orchestra was reorganized, served as its artistic director from 1963 to 1975. He was also the chief conductor of the Zurich Tonhalle Orchestra from 1965 to 1972, and of the Munich Philharmonic from 1967 until his death in 1976. During the last year of his life he also entered into a close association with the BBC Symphony Orchestra.

Interpretively, Kempe was something of a German Beecham. He was at his best—lively, incisive, warm, expressive, but never even remotely self-indulgent—in the Austro-Germanic and Czech repertory. Opera lovers prize his versions of *Lohengrin*, *Die Meistersinger*, and *Ariadne auf Naxos*. His greatest recorded legacy, accomplished during the last four or five years of his life, was the multi-volume EMI set of the orchestral works and concertos of Richard Strauss, performed with the highly idiomatic Dresden Staatskapelle. These recordings were only intermittently available outside of Europe in the LP days, but in the 1990s EMI issued them on nine compact discs. *—James Reel*

Recommended:

- ○ **Rudolf Kempe** / Kempe (cond.), Berlin PO, Royal PO, Vienna PO, Munich PO / EMI 75950
- ○ **Strauss: Orchestral Works** / Kempe (cond.), Frager, Rosel, Damm, Hoelscher, Dresden Staatskapelle / 1999 / Angel 73614
- ○ **Brahms & Mendelssohn** / Kempe (cond.), Royal PO / 2002 / Testament 1278

Wilhelm Kempff

b. Nov. 25, 1895, Jüterbog, Germany, **d.** May 23, 1991, Positano, Italy
Pianist

One of the twentieth century's most important pianists, Wilhelm Kempff found warmth in Beethoven where many others discovered only stress and passion. Concentrating on the composers of the late Classical and early-to-middle Romantic periods, Kempff achieved graceful, amiable results while not neglecting the sterner core of this music. His nobility of purpose was everywhere evident, made manifest through lucid textures, an adherence to a flowing legato, and tonal shading. In addition, he was a composer whose oeuvre included two symphonies, four operas, songs, and solo piano works.

Trained first by his Lutheran church musician father, Kempff studied privately before entering Berlin's Hochschule für Musik at age nine. In 1914, he traveled to Potsdam for further studies at the Viktoriagymnasium before returning to Berlin to finish his work at the Hochschule and enroll at the university. At age 20, Kempff served as organist and pianist on a tour of Germany and Scandinavia by the Berlin Cathedral Choir. A successful 1917 piano recital at the Berlin Singakademie led to an engagement the following year with the Berlin Philharmonic, the first of innumerable collaborations with that august ensemble. During the 1920s and 1930s, he toured South America and Japan, as well as many parts of Europe, adding to his reputation for uncompromising musicianship and personable interpretation. At the same time, he taught, serving first as director at the Stuttgart Musikhochschule from 1924 to 1929 and, later, as piano instructor at Potsdam's Mamorpalais for the decade before World War II. The war kept his activities confined to Germany, but with its end, Kempff once more resumed a busy performance schedule.

England and America heard Kempff only later. In London, the public, including a large number of German émigrés, applauded him upon his first appearance there in 1951. Not until 1964 did New York hear the pianist in person, although by then his many Deutsche Grammophon recordings had already established his stature for Americans. Indeed, Kempff's long and fruitful relationship with that label had brought to the market a long list of desirable recordings, among them the complete Beethoven piano concerti; the sonatas; a relaxed, but rewarding survey with Wolfgang Schneiderhan of the Beethoven violin sonatas; and various collections of Schubert, Schumann, Chopin, and Brahms. *—Erik Eriksson*

Recommended:

- ○ **Beethoven: Sonatas 14, 17 & 23** / Kempff / DG 469618
- ○ **Schubert: Wanderer Fantasy; Impromptus** / Kempff / DG 453672
- ○ **The Complete 1950's Concerto Recordings** / Kempff, etc. / 2002 / DG 474024
- ○ **Schubert: The Sonatas** / Kempff / DG 463766
- ○ **Mozart: Concertos 8, 23 & 24** / Leitner (cond.), Kempff, Berlin PO / 1999 / DG 457759
- ○ **Complete 1950s Solo Recordings** / Kempff / 2003 / DG 000085502

Nigel Kennedy

b. Dec. 28, 1956, Brighton, England
Violinist

"Kennedy," as he chose to be known for a time, is an individualistic and undeniably talented violinist who has emerged as one of the bona fide stars of the rich generation that came of age in the last quarter of the twentieth century. He has made a point of discarding what he sees as the conservative, staid traditions of classical concertmaking, and his personality may be summed up as flamboyant.

Born in 1956, Nigel Kennedy started playing the violin when he was five. He attended the Sir Yehudi Menuhin School in England, and later moved to New York to study at the Juilliard School with the famous teacher Dorothy DeLay. Kennedy made his debut in London in 1977, playing Mendelssohn's *Concerto in E minor*, as standard a work as could be desired. In his early broadcast appearances he exhibited a standard educated English accent. Later, when he adopted the image of a punk musician, his accent shifted to Cockney.

As his concert career grew, he was signed to a recording contract with Britain's EMI label. His first recording of Elgar's *Violin Concerto* was the 1985 Gramophone Record of the Year and rose to the top of the charts in England, selling over 300,000 copies. He exceeded even that mark with his Vivaldi *Four Seasons* disc, that even in the face of the stacks of other recordings of that warhorse work eventually won a listing in the Guinness Book of World Records as the best-selling classical recording of all time.

Kennedy began to add jazz improvisations as encores to his concerts. His concert demeanor and dress became more and more unconventional as he cultivated a carefully scruffy appearance that evoked Britain's punk rock scene. The violinist's new, decidedly nontraditional image proved to have wide appeal, boosting his sales and putting several more CDs at the top of the bestseller charts. Going further and further with his attempts to shake up the classical establishment, Kennedy did crossover performances and took on various eccentric mannerisms. His new ways included trashing hotel rooms in the fashion of a rock star. In 1992 he proclaimed that he was tired of playing "dead guys' stuff" and ceased performing.

He spent the time playing privately with friends and writing, but then edged back into playing with virtually unpublicized appearances at places like Oxford and Cambridge. He returned to the concert stage officially in 1997, and it was at this time that he asked to be called simply "Kennedy." He had written a concerto based on the music of Jimi Hendrix and frequently performed it with his band, "The Kennedy Experience." EMI elected not to release Kennedy's rock performances, but he found a congenial home for his new experiments on the increasingly crossover-oriented Sony label. Rumors that he had given up classical music entirely, or left EMI, turned out to be untrue; new classical releases, including a remake of the Elgar concerto, have appeared on that label alongside the Hendrix album. In 2003 Kennedy (now using his first name once again) returned to Vivaldi's *Four Seasons* and announced a new focus on Baroque repertoire.

Early in his career Kennedy played the "Cathedrale" Stradivarius violin, but at the beginning of the 1990s he bought a lovely blond-colored Guarneri del Gèsu instrument known as the "Lafont"—the instrument on which the Tchaikovsky *Violin Concerto* was premiered. *—Joseph Stevenson*

Recommended:

- ○ **Vivaldi: The Four Seasons** / Kennedy, English CO / 1997 / EMI 56253
- ○ **Walton: Violin & Viola Concertos; Vaughan Williams: The Lark Ascending** / Rattle (cond.), Previn (cond.), Kennedy, Royal PO, Birmingham SO / 2004 / EMI 62814
- ○ **Kennedy's Greatest Hits** / Kennedy, etc. / 2002 / EMI 57330

Aaron Jay Kernis

b. Jan. 15, 1960, Philadelphia, PA
Composer

Aaron Jay Kernis' musical character emerged early and has remained essentially constant throughout his career: he is a composer with eclectic interests (both musical and non-musical), a theatrical, dramatic bent, and an uncompromising attitude toward his art. Kernis' style is accessible and popular (perhaps because he has avoided academe), and his music is widely played.

Kernis began his musical training on the violin, and at the age of 12 began to teach himself piano. He studied for one year (1977–78) at the San Francisco Conservatory with John Adams, and then completed a degree in 1981 at the Manhattan School of Music, studying composition with Charles Wuorinen and Elias Tanenbaum. In 1983 Kernis received a Master's degree from Yale, where he had studied with Jacob Druckman among others. That year, Kernis came to national attention with *Dream of the Morning Sky*, premiered at the Horizons Festival by the New York Philharmonic: when Zubin Mehta, the conductor, had some difficulty with a passage, the 23-year-old Kernis advised him to "just read what's there." The piece already showed important elements of Kernis' style: brilliant, effective orchestration, a basically diatonic background, and an offbeat non-musical inspiration (in this case, a pantheistic poem by N. Scott Momaday).

Like other American composers such as David Del Tredici or Christopher Rouse), Kernis has made frequent reference to music of the past. Kernis has generally used earlier eras for inspiration: the Medieval era (as in the first string quartet, 1990's *Musica Celestis*, which is partly a reaction to the music of Hildegard von Bingen), and the Renaissance and Baroque (the second string quartet, the 1998 Pulitzer Prize winner *Musica Instrumentalis*, uses the *Fitzwilliam Virginal Book* and Bach's keyboard suites as springboards). Kernis does not use pastiche in reclaiming this music; rather, he uses forms (such as the sarabande or gigue) or a generally modal language to recall it indirectly. As Kernis has written: "I feel a greater kinship with music of past centuries that with that of our century, but at the same time feel vehemently that we cannot return to the past musically (as some neo-romantics and neo-modernists have tried to do) but must carry the present, past and future with us at all times." In addition to early music, Kernis has used modern popular forms, most notably salsa (*Salsa Pasada* (1996) for guitar and strings, and *Concierto de "Dance Hits"* (1999) for orchestra) and early American pop (*America(n) (Day)Dreams* (1984) for mezzo-soprano and chamber ensemble).

The extra-musical inspirations of Kernis' works have been even more wide-ranging than the musical ones. The texts he has set include those by William Blake (*Songs of Innocence* [1989] for high voice and piano) and Gertrude Stein (*Six Fragments of Gertrude Stein* [1979] for soprano and flute), as well as various religious texts. The Persian Gulf War provided the impetus for the *Second Symphony* (1991), a protest against American actions which received some harsh criticism; mosaics at Ravenna in Italy inspired in a series of three major instrumental pieces.

Though Kernis is best known for his extravagantly colorful instrumental and vocal writing, especially involving large orchestra, his most popular work is probably *Air*, for violin and piano (later arranged several times for different forces), written for the violinist Joshua Bell. Kernis comments that "[i]t contains many hymn- or chant-like elements, and though rooted in E major, it retains a kind of plaintive quality more reminiscent of minor or modal tonalities. Formally, it combines a developing variation form with a simple song form." *Air* can perhaps be seen as a pure distillation of Kernis's compositional concerns through the 1980s and 1990s. *—David McCarthy*

Overview of Works

If a thread is to be found running throughout the dizzying plurality of musical styles found throughout the twentieth century, it is perhaps the cycle of division and cohesion of stylistic trends. Schoenberg, for example, followed the seemingly polar paths of both Wagner and Brahms; a century later, composers as wide-ranging as, say, Frederic Rzewski, John Corigliano, and John Adams would all share a tendency to freely and unproblematically borrow from the various and sometimes conflicting musical styles and ideals that preceded them. It is no surprise, then, that in the works of Aaron Jay Kernis, who serves as a suitable representative for the first generation of composers born into postmodernism (he was born in 1960 and was, in fact, a student of John Adams), one finds such a wide range of styles and methods. His works, which touch on a wide variety of genres and instrumentations, aptly reflect the landscape—both musical and cultural—of America in the last decades of the twentieth century and the beginning of the twenty-first. His earliest works reflect the aesthetics of procedural control inherited from the high serialists, as well as the early minimalists. *Morningsongs* (1983), a work for baritone and large instrumental ensemble, has been described as a "process" work with its economic presentation of pitch materials and structural rigor. Subsequent works exhibit a less-rigid organization of musical materials and even a kind of expressive or dramatic kind of formalism. For example, the episodic, disjointed structure of *Love Scenes* (1987), set to poems by Anna Swir, reflects the progress of the narrative it accompanies. Later works "loosen" even further in terms of their loyalty to mood and drama, rather than formal scheme or procedure. Perhaps it is this conscientious shedding of accreted pretension that so endeared audiences to his music of the late 1980s and 1990s. Covering a wide variety of genres and instrumentations, his works from this period have received numerous accolades. The integration of programmatic concept and formal design that forms the core of his *Symphony in Waves* (1989) conveys a deeply felt expressivity that overshadows the comprehensively intertwined structural layers at work in the piece. A strong emotional focus energizes his series of politically oriented pieces from the 1990s, which together form a kind of orchestral cycle on the tragedy of war (specifically, the contemporaneous war taking place in the Persian Gulf). These works include *Symphony No. 2* (1991), a smaller chamber work *Still Movement with Hymn* (1993), *Colored Field* (1994), and *Lament and Prayer* (1996). Kernis has successfully approached more lighthearted topics as well, demonstrating the ease with which he traverses "high" and "low" art in such pieces as the chamber piece for string quartet and guitar, *100 Greatest Dance Hits* (1993). Another work for string quartet, his *Quartet No. 2* (1998) made him the youngest winner of a Pulitzer Prize in Music. *Goblin Market* (1995), a setting of the story by Rossetti, represented Kernis' first attempt at music for the stage. *—Jeremy Grimshaw*

Recommended:

- ○ **Kernis: Colored Field; Still Movement With Hymn** / Neale (cond.), Frank, O'Riley, Neubauer, Giacobassi, Brey, San Francisco SO / 1996 / Argo 448174
- ○ **Kernis: Chamber Music** / Eberli Ens. / 1999 / Phoenix USA 142
- ○ **Kernis: Air; Double Concerto; Lament & Prayer** / Zinman (cond.), Wolff (cond.), Bell, Isbin, Lin, Frank, Minnesota Orch., Saint Paul CO / 1999 / Argo 460226
- ○ **Kernis: Colored Field; Musica Celestis; Air** / Oue (cond.), Moerk, Minnesota Orch. / 2001 / Virgin 45464

Istvan Kertész

b. Aug. 28, 1929, Budapest, Hungary, **d.** Apr. 16, 1973, near Tel Aviv, Israel
Conductor

An inordinately gifted conductor, István Kertész died at age 43 in a tragic drowning off the Israeli coast. He had already reached full maturity as a musician, proving his worth in opera, oratorio, and the symphonic repertory. His interests were wide-ranging, including works from the Classical and Romantic periods and large portions of twentieth century music.

Beginning with private lessons in childhood, Kertész studied piano and violin. He continued with violin training at the Ferenc Liszt Academy in Budapest, adding composition under the supervision of such teachers as Weiner and Kodály. He pursued his conducting studies with László Somogyi, at the same time benefiting from studying the performances of Otto Klemperer, who was then working at the Hungarian State Opera. In 1953, Kertész was appointed resident conductor at Györ, two years later transferring his activities to Budapest, where he was hired as coach and conductor. Following the political uprising and Soviet response in 1956, Kertész moved with his family to Germany, subsequently acquiring German citizenship.

From 1958 to 1963, Kertész was general music director at Augsburg. His British debut took place with the Royal Liverpool Philharmonic Orchestra in 1960, followed by appearances with the London Symphony Orchestra in 1961. His American debut came with a tour with the NDR Symphony Orchestra in 1961, during which he made a positive impression on American audiences and critics alike. An appointment as general music director in Cologne came in 1964 and 1966 brought both a Covent Garden debut, directing *Un ballo in maschera*. A global tour with the London Symphony Orchestra led to his succeeding Pierre Monteux as LSO principal conductor in 1966. In 1971, he became music director of Cologne's Gürzenich-Orchester, a position he held until his death two years later.

Kertész was decidedly non-interventionist as a conductor. With scrupulous attention to the composer's directions, his interpretations were more remarkable for sound musicianship than for striking individualism. Still, his performances often held high drama, and he was intentional about advocacy of works he believed in, which, in light of his broad interests, were numerous. At Cologne, he presented the German premiere of Verdi's *Stiffelio* as well as Mozart's *La clemenza di Tito* (a work he recorded in its first complete edition on disc).

For Decca, Kertész recorded a superb *Bluebeard's Castle* with Christa Ludwig and Walter Berry, still unsurpassed after several decades. His complete recordings of the Dvořák, Brahms, and Schubert symphonies still enjoy honorable places among the best versions committed to disc. The first Western recording of Kodály's *Háry János* (the complete opera) was made with the London Symphony under Kertész's direction. The Decca label coupling of Dvořák's *Requiem* and Kodály's *Psalmus Hungaricus* is another fitting tribute to a superb artist too soon departed.

In addition to Bartók, Kertész was an indefatigable champion of works by Stravinsky, Henze, and Britten. Britten's *Billy Budd* was first presented to German audiences under Kertész's baton and he directed the first performance of the War Requiem heard in Vienna. For Ravinia Festival audiences, Kertész directed the War Requiem with the Chicago Symphony Orchestra & Chorus shortly before his death. With soloists Phyllis Curtin, Robert Tear, and John Shirley-Quirk, the conductor's shattering interpretation left audience members limp. *—Erik Eriksson*

Recommended:

- ○ **Dvořák: Symphony 9** / Kertesz (cond.), London SO / 1998 / London 460604
- ○ **Bartók: Bluebeard's Castle** / Kertesz (cond.), Ludwig, Berry, London SO / 1999 / Decca 466377
- ○ **Shostakovich: Symphony 5; Kodaly: Peacock Variations** / Kertesz (cond.), London SO, Orch. de la Suisse Romande / 2003 / Testament 1290

Aram Khachaturian

b. Jun. 6, 1903, Tbilisi, Georgia, **d.** May 1, 1978, Moscow, U.S.S.R.
Composer: Ballet, Orchestral, Concerto, Symphonic, Chamber Music, Keyboard

Although he was indicted (along with Shostakovich, Prokofiev, and a number of other prominent Soviet musicians) for "formalism," in the infamous Zhdanov decree of 1948, Aram Khachaturian was, for most of his long career, one of the Soviet musical establishment's most prized representatives. Born into an Armenian family, in Tbilisi, in 1903, Khachaturian's musical identity formed slowly, and, although a tuba player in his school band and a self-taught pianist, he wanted to be a biologist, and did not study music formally until entering Moscow's Gnesin Music Academy (as a cellist) in 1922. His considerable musical talents soon manifested themselves, and by 1925 he was studying composition privately with Gnesin himself. In 1929, Khachaturian joined Miaskovsky's composition class at the Moscow Conservatory. Khachaturian graduated in 1934, and before the completion, in 1937, of his postgraduate studies, the successful premieres of such works as the *Symphony No. 2 in A Minor "With a Bell"* (1935) and, especially, the *Piano Concerto in D flat Major* (1936) established Khachaturian as the leading Soviet composer of his generation. During the vicious government-sponsored attacks, in 1948, on the Soviet Composers' Union (in which Khachaturian, an active member since 1937, also held an administrative function) Khachaturian took a great deal of criticism. However, although he was officially censured for employing modernistic, politically incorrect musical techniques which fostered an "anti-people art," Khachaturian's music contained few, if any, of the objectionable traits found in the music of some of his more adventuresome colleagues. In retrospect, it was most likely Khachaturian's administrative role in the Union, perceived by the government as a bastion of politically incorrect music, and not his music as such, which earned him a place on the black list of 1948. Nevertheless, Khachaturian made a very full and humble apology for his artistic "errors" following the Zhdanov decree; his musical style, however, underwent no changes. Khachaturian joined the composition faculty of the Moscow Conservatory and the Gnesin Academy in 1950, and that same year he made his debut as a conductor. During the years until his death in 1978 Khachaturian made frequent European conducting appearances, and in January of 1968 he made a culturally significant trip to Washington, D.C., conducting the National Symphony Orchestra in a program of his own works. Khachaturian's characteristic musical style draws on the melodic and rhythmic vitality of Armenian folk music. Although not adverse to sharp dissonance, Khachaturian never strayed from a basically diatonic musical language. The Piano Concerto and the *Violin Concerto in D Minor* are truly Romantic works, virtuosic, clear, and unaffectedly expressive, remaining therefore popular and frequently performed composition. Of course, many neither of these works matches the popularity of the famous "Sabre Dance" from the ballet *Gayane*, which made Khachaturian a household name during World War II. His other works include film scores, songs, piano pieces, and chamber music. The degree of Khachaturian's success as a Soviet composer can be measured by his many honors, which include the 1941 Lenin Prize, for the Violin Concerto, the 1959 Stalin Prize, for the ballet *Spartacus*, and the title, awarded in 1954, of People's Artist. *—Blair Johnston*

BALLET

Gayane (1941–1942; revised 1957)

Aram Khachaturian's ballet *Gayane*, variously spelled "Gayne," "Gayaneh," and "Gayané," had its premiere at the Kirov Ballet on December 9, 1942, in wartime. The ballet's story concerned a young woman named Gayane living on a collective farm of which her father is the chairman. Gayane helps entrap a spy bent on stealing Soviet geological secrets. That clunker of a Communist plot may explain why recordings of the entire ballet have been hard to find in recent decades, even though *Gayane* spawned one of the last of the great orchestral warhorses, the *Sabre Dance*. Originally part of a suite of ethnic dances in the ballet's second act, the *Sabre Dance* is an irresistible piece of fun that's known and loved far beyond the confines of classical music fandom. Its appeal partly derives from its combination of a highly dissonant element, an alternation between major and minor sevenths with full-blown, hell-for-leather, stomp-your-feet forward motion.

The neglect of the rest of Khachaturian's music is a shame, for the ballet has many noteworthy moments of folkloric flavor beyond the *Sabre Dance*. The story resolves itself in praise for the friendship among the various peoples of the Soviet Union, a development that gave the Georgian-born and Armenian-begotten Khachaturian plenty of room to explore the rhythms and textures of Central Asian folk music. Two of the other dances in the Act II set evokes a group much in the news, the Kurds, and in general *Gayane* did much to inspire a folkloristic strain in postwar Soviet music even as its composer suffered condemnation at the hands of Stalinist cultural thugs. *Gayane*, whose music Khachaturian created for Russian ballerina Nina Anisimova, enjoyed several revivals in the years after its composition, and each time Khachaturian tinkered with the score. One indication of the music's riches and its popularity in its own day is that the composer extracted three orchestral suites from the music during and after the ballet's composition. *—James Manheim*

Recommended:

- ○ **Gayaneh (Complete Ballet)** / Kakhidze (cond.), USSR Radio & TV SO / Russian Disc 11029

Spartacus (1950–1954; revised 1968)

The dates in the headnote pertain to the complete ballet itself, not to the four suites Khachaturian extracted from it. The first three were written in the period of 1955–57 and the last in 1967, just as he was about to revise the complete ballet. Precisely why he devoted so much energy to this work is not clear.

Perhaps part of the reason is that its story of slaves rebelling against oppressive rulers was just the what the Soviet musical czars were looking to promote in their art, an allegory of the proletariat struggling against their bourgeois overlords. Spartacus was a Thracian warrior who led a slave revolt against Rome, beginning in 73 B.C. After the seizure of Mount Vesuvius, set up as their fortress, they were defeated in bloody battle by Licinius Crassus and Pompey in 71 B.C. Six thousand captured slaves were subsequently crucified on the Appian Way, including *Spartacus*.

The four suites extracted from the ballet consist, respectively, of five, four, five, and four numbers, and contain well over half the music from the complete work, which has over 50 numbers. The suites often incorporate music from several numbers into one movement.

Much of the music in both the ballet and its suites has that far-Eastern flavor that Khachaturian was famous for, as in *Dance of an Egyptian Girl* (No. 2 in Suite No. 3), or that rollicking saber-dance style, as heard in the *Dance of the Pirate* (No. 4 in Suite No. 2). Among the most famous music sections in the ballet is the love of Spartacus and Phrygia, which has an exoticism in its romance, a sort of slick quality to its appeal, that would not make it seem out of place in a 1950s big-screen love story.

Even though virtually none of the music is an attempt at profundity, there is a certain amount of grimness in it, as can be heard in *Call to Arms, Spartacus' Uprising* (No. 4 in Suite No. 4). In the end, this ballet, unpretentious and melodic, must be ranked a success. To those who admire the exotic, colorful, and folk-flavored style of Khachaturian, *Spartacus* and its offshoots will offer substantial rewards. *—Robert Cummings*

Synopsis:

This ballet's 12 scenes have been staged in both three- and four-act versions. The story takes place in the Ancient Roman Empire, around 73 B.C.

Scene One. Licinius Crassus, commander of the Roman Army, launches a successful attack against relatively weak resistance and is victorious. Among his captives are Spartacus, a Thracian warrior, and his lover Phrygia.

Scene Two. Spartacus and Phrygia are separated at the slaves' market and sold.

Scene Three. At a feast and orgy at Crassus' villa, guests taunt the new slave girl Phrygia. Crassus orders that gladiators be brought in and fight to the death for the amusement of his guests and for his own pleasure. Two are led in blindfolded and are forced to fight, one being felled rather quickly. When the winner's mask is removed, he is revealed to be Spartacus, who is repulsed in the knowledge he was used as a pawn, forced to fight to the death with a fellow slave.

Scene Four. Spartacus incites an uprising among the gladiators and they manage to break free of their Roman captors.

Scene Five. Along the Appian Way, the former slaves march, their ranks swelling with peasants and others eager to join their rebellion against Roman rule. Spartacus is elected leader of the slave rebels.

Scene Six. Spartacus goes to Crassus' villa in search of Phrygia and finds her there. The two share an ecstatic reunion, but soon must hide from guests, among whom is Aegina, Crassus' scheming courtesan.

Scene Seven. While Crassus and Aegina are enjoying a feast in his honor, they are given news that Spartacus and his rebel hordes are about to attack the villa. The celebration ends quickly and all attempt to flee.

Scene Eight. The rebels capture Crassus, and when he is brought before Spartacus, he allows the Roman commander to challenge him in combat. In the struggle, Spartacus handily emerges the victor and can slay Crassus, who has lost his sword in the contest. But he spares him, sensing Crassus' defeat will bring him humiliation.

Scene Nine. Crassus is mortified, but is able to rebound with the support of the unscrupulous Aegina. He determines that Spartacus must be defeated at all costs.

Scene Ten. In his victorious camp, Spartacus and Phrygia enjoy a blissful union, but their happiness is threatened with the news that Crassus' huge army is advancing toward them. Spartacus remains firm in his resolve to defeat Roman tyranny, and is thus quite willing to do battle with Crassus. Some of his rebels, however, abandon him. The battle nears and Spartacus senses a tragic end to the insurrection.

Scene Eleven. Using wine and courtesans, Aegina entraps the rebels who have fled the conflict, and they are taken captive by Crassus' Army.

Scene Twelve. The Roman Army surrounds the rebel forces and crushes them in battle. Spartacus is killed when soldiers crucify him with their spears. Phrygia finds his body and pledges to make his name live long in the memory of all people. *—Robert Cummings*

Recommended:

- ○ **Khachaturian: Spartacus** / Jurowski (cond.), RIAS-Kammerchor, Berlin German SO / Capriccio 10817/18

ORCHESTRAL

Masquerada, incidental music (1943)

The drama *Masquerade* by the short-lived Russian playwright and poet Mikhail Lermontov (1814–41)— once controversial due to its sharp commentaries on Russian society—has served as inspiration for music on many occasions, providing the subject matter for several operas and at least one ballet. Aram Khachaturian followed the example of his famous countryman Alexander Glazunov in writing incidental music to accompany the stage action for *Masquerade.* Khachaturian's score was prepared for a production by the Vakhtangov Theater; it had its premiere on June 21, 1941. The music proved popular, and in 1944 the composer extracted a suite of five pieces from the score for concert performance.

Khachaturian's music is rather lighter in tone than the play itself. He employs occasional irony in depicting the gaiety of Russian social life in the early nineteenth century, but otherwise eschews the darkness of the play in favor of tuneful, light-hearted music with an occasional inflection of Russian folk styles. The orchestration is big and splashy. One portion of the incidental score, "Nina's Song," had some independent success in Russia but is not included in the suite, which begins with the apparently carefree but vaguely sinister Waltz. The slightly sentimental Nocturne, a splashy Mazurka, and a touching Romance that shares in some of the Nocturne's sentimentality follow, and the suite concludes with a lively Gallop. The most familiar of these excerpts is probably the opening Waltz, which was played at the 1978 funeral services for Khachaturian in the Grand Hall of the Moscow Conservatory. *—Chris Morrison*

Recommended:

- ○ **Khachaturian: Piano Concerto; Gayaneh Ballet Suite; Masquerade Suite** / Järvi (cond.), Scottish National Orch. / 1987 / Chandos 8542
- ○ **Khachaturian: Masquerage Suite; Kabalevsky: The Comedians; Tchaikovsky: Capriccio Italien** / Kondrashin (cond.), RCA Victor SO / 1999 / BMG 633022

CONCERTO

Piano Concerto in D flat major (1936)

Although Aram Khachaturian is revered in the Soviet Union for a large body of music, his fame in the West is based largely on a mere handful of works, among which is the *Piano Concerto* (1936). The concerto's widespread appeal is at once understandable, given its virtuosic flair, honest, unabashedly passionate melodic sense, and rich orchestration, all in the Russian Romantic manner of Tchaikovsky and Rachmaninov.

The opening movement of the concerto is cast in a somewhat loose sonata form, the impatient main theme developing almost immediately upon its appearance. Out of this sonic mass the secondary material arises and evolves into a powerful, cerebral monologue for the soloist before the furious development leads into an exuberant, headstrong cadenza. The primary theme returns in force as the subject of the coda. The second movement begins with a dignified melody, introduced by the bass clarinet. The dramatic heart of the movement is the middle section, a potent combination of oriental flavoring and turbulent Russian drama that builds to an ecstatic climax. The movement is rounded out by a return of the introductory material. The far-reaching, virtuosic Allegro brillante finale is built around contrasting themes and an outrageous, bravura cadenza. The concerto comes to a close with the return, on a grand scale, of material from the first movement. *—Graham Olson*

Recommended:

- ○ **Khachaturian: Violin Concerto; Piano Concerto in D flat Major** / Oborin, Mravinsky (cond.) / Praga 250017
- ○ **Khachaturian: Piano Concerto; Prokofiev: Piano Concerto 3** / Atamian, Schwarz (cond.), Seattle SO / 1994 / Delos 3155

Violin Concerto in D minor (1940)

The particular élan that characterizes Aram Khachaturian's concerti has no doubt contributed to their continued popularity, and indeed, the *Violin Concerto* (1940) takes a place among the staples of the twentieth century violin repertoire. The concerto bears the unmistakable stamp of its composer in its characteristic rhythmic drive and rich, folk-infused melodies. The first movement begins with a fierce, energetic figure, played in unison, that eventually evolves into the rustically lyrical second subject. The intoxicating Andante sostenuto second movement, redolent of the undulating, gradually unfolding style of ashugs (Armenian folk musicians), has a free-flowing, semi-improvisatory feel. Based largely on material from the first movement's secondary theme, the highly folk-influenced finale takes the form of a vigorous Armenian country dance in which the solo violin figures prominently with unrelenting, fiery virtuosity.

Khachaturian wrote the *Violin Concerto* for David Oistrakh, the dedicatee of so many mid-century Russian violin concerti. Oistrakh was the soloist at the work's premiere on November 16, 1940. *—Graham Olson*

Recommended:

- ○ **Prokofiev & Khachaturian** / Monteux (cond.), Kogan, Boston SO / 2000 / RCA 63708
- ○ **David Oistrakh in Prague** / Kubelik (cond.), Oistrakh, Prague SO / Praga 256007
- ○ **Khachaturian & Kabalevsky: Violin Concertos** / Jarvi (cond.), Mordkovitch, Scottish National Orch. / 1990 / Chandos 8918

SYMPHONIC

Symphony No. 2 in A minor ("Symphony with Bells") (1943; revised 1944)

Safely ensconced in the Composers' Union retreat in Ivanovo with the likes of Prokofiev and Shostakovich, Khachaturian was nevertheless deeply affected by World War II while it raged to the west. In the summer of 1943, he translated the war and the feelings it inspired in him into a symphony, which he described as "a requiem of wrath, a requiem of protest against war and violence." It's a massive work, consuming about 50 minutes when performed uncut. Khachaturian tinkered with it over the years and eventually reversed the order of the inner movements, so the sequence varies with the vintage of the recording.

The opening Andante maestoso—Allegro agitato begins stridently, with a bit of clanging from the orchestral bells that give the work its subtitle, but it immediately falls into the Technicolor, Armenian-flavored style familiar from Khachaturian's ballet *Spartacus.* A mournful section develops, carried mainly by the strings, and is repeatedly thrown into contrast with the alarming gesture from the movement's opening bars. Despite passages of high drama, the movement ends with a long, gradual fade-out.

The Allegro risoluto (sometimes heard third rather than second) is a scherzo arising from an agitated rhythmic figure, which serves as an ostinato moving through the various orchestral sections during the sinister dance of the movement's outer segments. The very brief middle section is more lyrical; Khachaturian said it symbolized "rest after hard labor."

The Andante sostenuto justifies Khachaturian's use of the word "requiem" more than any other movement. It's based on the distinctively Armenian folk song "Vorskan akhper," wherein a mother learns the story of her son's heroic death. The mourning reaches a peak of intensity, after which the *Dies Irae* from the medieval mass for the dead plays at half speed in the strings. The concluding movement, Andante mosso—Allegro sostenuto, looks ahead to victory, but a grim victory. Brassy, somewhat garish, and usually turbulent, the movement ends with the alarm bell providing a clanging reminder that the people must remain vigilant even in triumph. *—James Reel*

Recommended:

- ○ **Khachaturian** / (cond.), Vienna PO / 1996 / London 448252
- ○ **The Symphony Of The Air** / Stokowski (cond.), Symphony of the Air / 1994 / EMI 65427

CHAMBER MUSIC

Sonata-Fantasy, for solo cello in C major (1974)

The *Sonata-Fantasy for cello solo in C major,* written in 1974, is one of several works for solo instruments dating from Khachaturian's last years; others were the *Sonata-Monologue for violin* (1975) and *Sonata-Song for viola* (1976). Better known among instrumentalists than among the general public, all are notable for how they combine a highly expressive language with fixed musical procedures. Beginning on low C, the instrument's lowest note, the *Sonata-Fantasy* in short order outlines two recurrent elements: an open tonic-fifth pair (C and G at the beginning), which may be stated vertically or horizontally by the cello, and a flat supertonic or submediant (D flat at the beginning) that sharply disturbs the diatonic feel and may be hinted at or agonizingly emphasized. Khachaturian manipulates these elements, rather than traditional tonic and dominant harmonies, to generate a sonata-like structure. He moves to a songful section built on a low G-D pair in the cello but then destabilizes the music with gradually more intense E flats, leading into the equivalent of a classical development section. The structure is both tight and spare in its outlines, leaving plenty of room for the "fantasy." Khachaturian's cello takes on a variety of moods. The melodic material often tends toward a texture reminiscent of religious chant—a frequent practice on Khachaturian's part even if he is better known for experimenting with the folk rhythms of his native Armenia. The result is a deeply felt, lyrical piece that rewards repeated hearings, strongly recommended for people who know Khachaturian only through the *Sabre Dance* from the ballet *Gayane.* Like that little orchestral chestnut, the *Sonata-Fantasy* develops viscerally appealing music from an abstract kernel. The work lasts about 13 minutes in performance. *—James Manheim*

Recommended:

- ○ **Works for Solo Cello** / Bengtsson / 1995 / Danacord 425
- ○ **Cello** / Penny / 1997 / Tall Poppies 103

Trio for clarinet, violin & piano in G minor (1932)

Khachaturian was still a student of Miaskovsky at the Moscow Conservatory in the early 1930s when he wrote this trio for clarinet, violin, and piano, and yet it displays the same rhythmic and harmonic devices that mark his mature works. What first distinguishes Khachaturian's *Clarinet Trio* from nearly all others written earlier, such as Mozart's, Beethoven's, or Brahms', is his use of the violin rather than the mellower-sounding viola or cello. The higher-sounding string instrument becomes more of a partner to the clarinet, sharing the melodic duties throughout the piece. In three movements, the trio displays Khachaturian's trademark use of cross-rhythms, folk songs, and harmonies that could be thorny at some times or bitter-sweet at others. The opening Andante con dolore, molto espressione is a duet for the clarinet and violin, almost improvisational, with the piano accompaniment adding a complex layer seemingly in rhythmic conflict with the other instruments. It takes extremely skilled ensemble players to make it sound right. The middle Allegro is very obviously modeled on folk dances, with rich color and precise rhythms. The Moderato finale is a set of variations on an Uzbekistani folk song, effectively contrasting the timbres of the instruments and showing off the clarinet as a folk instrument. Prokofiev was so impressed with this piece that he was able to see that it was performed and published in Paris soon after it was completed. *—Patsy Morita*

Recommended:

- ○ **Bartók; Françaix; Khachaturian** / Melos Ens. / 1998 / Angel 72646
- ○ **Kodaly; Khachaturian; Bolcom; Durufle** / South African Chamber Music Society / Koch 920462
- ○ **Eimer Trio** / / 1994 / Dynamic 60

KEYBOARD

Toccata in E flat minor (1932)

Khachaturian composed his *Toccata* in 1932, while he studied composition with Miaskovsky at the Moscow Conservatory. Khachaturian's work shows the blending of local color with the greater "Russian" school, a blend supported by the Soviet ideology on music education. The *Toccata* is pianistic and brilliant in its use of the piano, while aspects of its melodic and rhythmic material are traceable to Armenian folk music.

A powerful rhythmic drive establishes itself from the very beginning of the *Toccata*, which begins Allegro marcatissimo. Khachaturian repeats four-beat rhythmic units (a single measure of 4/4) four times each, accelerating from single quarter notes to a dotted eighth note figure to bundles of sixteenth notes. With each repetition he moves to another harmony, but the rhythm remains insistent, and the melodic material consists almost exclusively of leaps of a fourth and a third. Thus, rhythm becomes the salient feature of the opening section. Sustained block chords break the motion and prove to be part of a transition to a new section that begins first with triplet repeated notes and moves to a swirling triplet figure. Repetition again takes over as leaps of various sizes become the only variable melodic material. After a few harmonic changes and some rapidly descending arpeggios the triplet flourish begins again, eventually crashing to a halt after more descending arpeggios land in the low bass.

The central section, marked Andante espressivo, provides a drastic contrast to the beginning of the piece. Expressive flourishes in the left hand employ modal scales evocative of Armenian folk music. Again, repetitive figures in the right hand dominate the texture, which reduces to a single repeated note as the opening tempo resumes in preparation for the return of section A.

Khachaturian skips the first few measures of the A section and makes a few other alterations during its reprise, but the bulk of the material is there, now fitted with a strong close based on the beginning of slow section. *—John Palmer*

Recommended:

- ○ **Uncommon Encores** / Paperno / 1992 / Cedille 7
- ○ **The Historic Recordings** / Cherkassky / 2001 / Ivory 72003

King's Consort

f. 1980, Cambridge, England

Ensemble

The King's Consort was founded at Cambridge University in England by Robert King, at the time a 20-year-old student. At first, the King's Consort consisted only of a small choir and band, but its concerts attracted such acclaim and positive critical notices that by 1982, King was able to establish the Consort as a full-time professional orchestral ensemble based out of London. In the five years that followed, the King's Consort toured widely and made a small number of recordings for Meridian and IMP. In 1987, King made the acquaintance of Hyperion Records founder and president Ted Perry. From this point forward, the King's Consort has recorded exclusively for Hyperion, a partnership that has been witnessed on more than 75 releases, the combined sales of which exceed a million copies. The King's Consort has recorded all of the odes, welcome music, anthems, and services of Henry Purcell, and its recordings of George Frideric Handel's operas and oratorios are likewise justly celebrated, having been awarded numerous recording prizes. By spring 2003, the King's Consort had completed recording all of Antonio Vivaldi's sacred music and was in preparation to perform the same service for Claudio Monteverdi. King has made much headway into researching the lesser-known regions of Baroque sacred literature and as a result, the King's Consort has recorded works of such lesser-known composers as Johann Adolf Hasse, John Blow, Sebastian Knüpfer, and Johann Schelle. One of the King's Consort's most outstanding projects is a reconstruction of the musical program of the *Coronation of King George II*, a significant political event that occurred in 1727. As the King's Consort has recorded to such a prolific extent, it is easy to lose sight of the fact that it also tours worldwide, having appeared in the Far East, both North and South Americas, and in every country in Europe. *—Uncle Dave Lewis*

Recommended:

- ○ **Vivaldi: Sacred Music, Vol. 10** / King (cond.), Choir of the King's Consort, The King's Consort / 2004 / Hyperion 66849
- ○ **Handel: Judas Maccabaeus** / Higginbottom, King (conds.), George, Kirkby, Birchall, Bowman, King's Consort, New College Choir Oxford / 1992 / Hyperion 66641
- ○ **Purcell: Hail! bright Cecilia** / King (cond.), Choir of New College Oxford, The King's Consort / 1989 / Hyperion 66349

King's Singers

f. May 1, 1968, Cambridge, England

Ensemble

While the first concert given by the King's Singers officially took place on May 1, 1968, their roots actually date to 1965 when 14 choral students at King's College (Cambridge) formed a group called Schola Cantorum Pro Musica Profana. Three of the original members of the King's Singers were a part of that ensemble: Alastair Hume (countertenor), Simon Carrington (baritone), and Brian Kay (bass). The Schola Cantorum group produced a private recording of poplar songs, but more importantly yielded an offshoot sextet taking the name Six Choral Scholars From King's College, which became the precursor to the King's Singers. Joining Hume, Kay, and Carrington in the ensemble were three other singers from King's College: Martin Lane, Neil Jenkins, and Richard Salter. This latter trio, however, did not stay on. Their replacements were Nigel Perrin (countertenor), Alastair Thompson (tenor), and Anthony Holt (baritone).

In 1968, the sextet debuted under the name of the King's Singers at London's Queen Elizabeth Hall. All were graduates of King's College except for Holt and Perrin, the latter graduating in 1969. Holt, however, had received his choral training at Christ's Church Oxford. The vocal style established by the group from its earliest days mixes madrigal-like singing with a sort of barber shop quartet manner that divulges other, more-modern American styles associated with groups like the Four Freshmen. Their repertory includes a broad range of music from the works of Janequin and Josquin Desprez to that of Gilbert and Sullivan, from Japanese folk songs to Berio and Penderecki, and from sacred to popular music. By 1971, the King's Singers had drawn considerable attention in England and began making their first recordings. *By Appointment* and *The King's Music* appeared in 1971 and 1972, respectively, the former a collection of British folk songs and the latter devoted to music from the last quarter of the Middle Ages. After these initial efforts, the group returned to the recording studio with regularity, usually turning out several titles each year. By 2002, they had made over 60 recordings, most of which remain available or periodically become available through reissues.

In the 1980s, the King's Singers had experienced its first personnel changes and by the end of that decade, three new members were in place: Jeremy Jackman, Robert Chilcott, and Colin Mason. Alastair Thompson, Nigel Perrin, and Brian Kay had departed, but their exit was no indication of any internal problems or artistic decline. Indeed, the group's popularity remained high, bolstered by a heavy touring schedule that even included an appearance on Johnny Carson's *Tonight Show*. Then-recent recordings, like their *All at Once Well Met: English Madrigals* (1985) and *Beatles Connection* (1986), had achieved impressive sales. Over the years, despite personnel changes and an ever-widening repertory, the group continues to grow in artistic stature, making concert appearances with some of the most prominent singers and artists (Domingo and Te Kanawa) and drawing works from leading composers (Richard Rodney Bennett, Ligeti, and Maxwell Davies). In addition, at the Royal College of Music, they serve as Prince Consort Ensemble in Residence. Since 1968, there have been 11 changes in personnel, one featuring two replacements. After 1997, no member from the original group remained. In 2002, the King's Singers was comprised of Robin Tyson (countertenor), David Hurley (countertenor), Paul Phoenix (tenor), Gabriel Crouch (baritone), Philip Lawson (baritone), and Stephen Connolly (bass). Tyson was the last new addition, joining the ensemble in January, 2001. Some of the group's later recordings include *De Janequin aux Beatles* (1999) and *Fire—Water* (2000). *—Robert Cummings*

Recommended:

- ○ **Madrigal History Tour** / King's Singers, Musicke Instrumental Consort / 2004 / EMI 85714
- ○ **Renaissance** / King's Singers / 1993 / BMG 61814
- ○ **A Little Christmas Music** / Hickox (cond.), Te Kanawa, King's Singers, City of London Sinfonia / 1989 / EMI 49909
- ○ **Annie Laurie: Folksongs of the British Isles** / Barrueco, King's Singers / Angel 754904

Alexander Kipnis

b. Feb. 13, 1891, Zhitomir, Ukraine, **d.** May 14, 1978, Westport, CT
Bass

Alexander Kipnis represented for many the very model of a bass singer, with a voice deep, round, and solid. Although a native Ukrainian, he studied predominantly in Germany; perhaps because of this he specialized in the major bass roles of Wagner, Mozart and Strauss. Kipnis also became one of the most respected lieder singers of his age and made numerous recordings which keep his memory very much alive.

Born in extreme poverty in a Ukrainian ghetto, Kipnis was able to learn music and perform at the local synagogue; later he moved to a slightly more prosperous temple in Bessarabia (in Moldavia). When he returned to Ukraine, he became a jack-of-all-trades with a small theatrical troop, working in the crew as well as acting and singing. When he was 19, he entered the Warsaw Conservatory, intending to become a band conductor. However, he still sang in synagogues to provide himself with an income, and in 1912, at a teacher's encouragement, he left Warsaw for Berlin to study singing (as well as to avoid conscription into the Russian army).

When World War I broke out, the Russian Kipnis was arrested and jailed. A German colonel, whose brother was an opera impresario, heard him sing and had Kipnis audition for him (in jail!); the singer was subsequently engaged by the Hamburg Opera. Under supervision, Kipnis was permitted to both study and fulfill his contract. Following two years in Hamburg, he was engaged by the Royal Opera in Wiesbaden where he built an impressive repertory. By the end of the war, Kipnis' reputation had spread well beyond Germany, and he began performing throughout Europe.

In 1922, he traveled to the United States as a member of the Wagner Festival Company and was shortly thereafter engaged by the Chicago Civic Opera Company; there he continued to sing major roles for nine seasons (also during this time becoming an American citizen). Despite being a true bass (rather than the bass-baritone more typical of the role), he undertook the demanding role of Wotan in Wagner's *Ring Cycle*.

During this time Kipnis also attracted attention for his recital performances. The *New York Times* described him as "not only one of the greatest contemporary operatic basses but also one of the foremost living masters of the lied."

Upon leaving the Chicago opera, Kipnis returned to Germany to become principal bass with the Berlin State Opera and a leading artist at the Bayreuth and (later) Salzburg festivals. This same period also found him at the Glyndebourne Festival and Covent Garden in England and at Argentina's Teatro Colón. With Hitler's rise in Germany, Kipnis, a Jew, transferred his performing activities to Austria. When the Anschluss took place, Kipnis moved to America, where he remained for the rest of his career.

His Metropolitan Opera debut came on January 6, 1940, in *Parsifal*. Critic Olin Downes commented, "Mr. Kipnis immediately won the favor of his audience. He invested the role with the utmost significance." Kipnis remained at the Met for seven seasons, where his primary roles were King Marke in *Tristan und Isolde*, Arkel in *Pelleas et Melisande*, Hermann in *Tannhäuser*, Hunding in *Die Walküre*, Hagen in *Götterdämmerung*, and Sarastro in *Die Zauberflöte*. He also sang *Boris Godunov* in the original Russian while the rest of the cast sang in Italian. Kipnis retired in 1946, and undertook a distinguished second career as a voice teacher.

Kipnis was married to Mildred Levy of Chicago for 53 years. Their son, Igor, is a well-known harpsichordist. *—AMG*

Recommended:

- ○ **Opera Arias & Songs** / Bowers (cond.), Kipnis, Bergh, Bibb / 1996 / Sony 62354
- ○ **Russian Arias and Songs** / Berezowsky (cond.), Kipnis, Dougherty, Victor Orch. / Preiser 89946
- ○ **Alexander Kipnis sings Brahms & Wolf** / Kipnis, Moore, Bos, Wolff / Preiser 89204

Igor Kipnis

b. Sep. 27, 1930, Berlin, Germany, **d.** Jan. 24, 2001, Redding, CT
Harpsichordist

Igor Kipnis, the son of the great Russian bass singer Alexander Kipnis (1891–1978), was for some years America's leading harpsichord and fortepiano player. Unsurprisingly, he was exposed to music from his earliest days. His father was singing with the Berlin Opera when Igor was born. For the next eight years the family mostly moved about Europe, wherever Alexander's career took them. The Kipnis family moved to the United States in 1938 when Alexander joined the roster of the Metropolitan Opera.

Igor's mother's side of the family is also musical. His grandfather Heniot Levy was the head of the piano department at the American Conservatory in Chicago, and gave Igor some of his early keyboard lessons.

Much of the music in the house came from his father's 78-rpm record player and an extensive collection of lieder and opera aria disks. Igor himself got the record collecting bug and decided to buy Edwin Fischer's famous recording of the complete *Well-Tempered Clavier* by Bach, a set of five albums, costing 90 dollars. Although this was an astronomical sum for a boy in the 1940s, Igor worked to earn the money, then found that the last volume contained two more 78s as a filler. These presented the *English Suite No. 2* played on harpsichord by Wanda Landowska. The sound of the instrument fascinated him.

However, Igor had little thought of becoming a musician, although he had developed fine keyboard skills. He majored in social relations at Harvard and wanted to work in radio or TV production or the record industry. He finally had a chance to play a harpsichord when taking a course on Handel with composer Randall Thompson. "Nothing happened, however, until 1957," he wrote, "when my parents imported a small instrument for me to fool around with after work."

At the time he oversaw cover design and wrote program notes for Westminster Records, having briefly worked at WMCA, New York's top-40 radio station, as record librarian, and was writing reviews for the *American Record Guide*. Meanwhile, he had studied harpsichord with Thurston Dart. He debuted as a freelance harpsichord player, in addition to his other jobs, in 1959, mostly playing harpsichord continuo, including some recordings of Baroque trumpet music with Richard Kapp.

From this a notable international recording and touring career grew. He recorded over 81 albums, including around 60 solo discs. He taught and played at the Berkshire Music Center at Tanglewood (1964–67), Fairfield University in Connecticut (1971–77), and the Festival Music Society in Indianapolis. He added the fortepiano (precursor of the piano) to his instruments, making his first appearance playing it in Indianapolis. He was involved in radio as a frequent guest on the syndicated record review program "First Hearing" and for three years hosted his own WQXR radio program, "The Age of Baroque" and a syndicated series, "The Classical Organ." He published several editions of Baroque keyboard music, and enjoys writing record reviews for leading American publications.

His harpsichord repertoire included an enormous quantity of Baroque- and Classical-era music, but also a copious amount of the music for harpsichord that has been written since the revival of the instrument in the 1920s. This included works by Falla, Rochberg, Rorem, McCabe, Curtis-Smith, Locklair, Kolb, Salzman, and Richard Rodney Bennett.

In 1995, he formed the Kipnis-Kushner Piano Duo with Karen Kushner, which toured internationally. *—Joseph Stevenson*

Recommended:

- ○ **Scarlatti: Keyboard Sonatas** / Kipnis / 2001 / Angel 74281
- ○ **The Anna Magdalena Bach Notebook** / Kipnis, Luxon, Blegen, Meints / 1981 / Nonesuch 79020
- ○ **The Young Beethoven** / Kipnis / Epiphany 1

Leon Kirchner

b. Jan. 24, 1919, New York, NY
Composer: Chamber Music, Avant-garde

A dominant figure in American music throughout most of the twentieth century, composer Leon Kirchner (b. 1919) has written a large quantity of music which, although stylistically tied to the work of Arnold Schoenberg and the Second Viennese School, remains powerfully individual in expression, and free of the systematic use of 12-tone techniques. In addition, he has proven himself to be a formidable pianist, and a skilled conductor of his own works and the established classics.

Born in Brooklyn, Kirchner received most of his musical education in southern California. Piano lessons began at the age of four, and Kirchner's early compositions, written in his teens, gained the notice of composer Ernst Toch at Los Angeles City College (where Kirchner was studying at the time), who recommended that Kirchner study with Schoenberg at the University of California Los Angeles. After taking a BA from the University in 1940 Kirchner began graduate work with Ernst Bloch at Berkeley, though a period of study in New York with Roger Sessions during 1942, and three years of military service would postpone the completion of a master's degree until 1949.

He had already been awarded, in 1948, a Guggenheim Fellowship, and in 1949 he was honored by that foundation a second time. During the early 1950s, Kirchner served on the faculty of the University of Southern California Los Angeles, after which in 1954, he accepted an appointment with Mills College in Oakland. He joined Harvard University in 1961, eventually succeeding Walter Piston as the Walter Bigelow Rosen Professor of Music. In addition to his activities as a composer, Kirchner was active as a conductor and pianist at Harvard, as well as with numerous professional orchestras, until his retirement in 1989. He has received many awards and honors throughout his long career, including two New York Music Critics Circle Awards (for his first two string quartets, in 1950 and 1960, respectively), the 1967 Pulitzer Prize for his *Third String Quartet*, and, in 1994, the Kennedy Center Friedham Award. Since the 1960s he has been a member of both the National Institute of Arts and Letters, and the American Academy of Arts and Sciences.

Despite the wide variety of influences Kirchner was exposed to during his student years—or perhaps because of it—his music is consistently original in both content and language. His music is very chromatic, usually in a linear fashion, while a love of irregular rhythm adds a piquant metric flavor to his work. The intervallic content of Kirchner's language and the manner in which intervallic/harmonic units are employed throughout a given work bespeak the influence of Schoenberg, though Kirchner has never been a strictly serial composer in any sense of the word. His consummate craftsmanship is most apparent in the three string quartets. Kirchner remained active during the 1990s, the *Music for Cello and Orchestra*, premiered by Yo-Yo Ma and the Philadelphia Orchestra, being perhaps the most famous work composed in that decade.—*Blair Johnston*

Overview of Works

While the twentieth century in music is often seen as a hodgepodge collection of disparate and variously rigid stylistic camps, a number of composers have taken paths less governed by partisan trends. The oeuvre of composer/performer/conductor/teacher Leon Kirchner reflects this kind of attitude; his works demonstrate his decided avoidance of allowing the "idea, the precious ore of art, [to become] lost in the jungle of graphs, prepared tapes, feedbacks, and cold stylistic minutiae." Perhaps the relatively modest scope of his compositional output owes in part to his activity in other areas, such as performing, teaching, and conducting. On the other hand, his extensive experience at either end of the baton, as well as his various studies under Schoenberg, Sessions, and Bloch, contribute to the acute expressive intuition that overshadows technical method in his works. Chamber and solo works comprise the lion's share of Kirchner's works list. His skill as a pianist is reflected by solo piano works such as a piano sonata (1948), *A Moment for Roger* (1978), *Five Pieces* (1987), and *For the Left Hand* (1995). Kirchner's string quartets, though all dating from early in his career, stand out as well; the *Quartet No. 3* (1966) won a Pulitzer Prize. Vocal works have been less prominent; in fact, all of Kirchner's vocal music from the 1940s and 1950s, including song settings of Lorca and Whitman, remained unpublished a half century later. Published vocal works include the choral piece *Words of Wordsworth* (1966); *The Twilight Stood*, a song cycle on texts by Dickinson (1982); and the emotionally charged "duo-drama" for soloists, chorus, and orchestra, *Of Things Exactly as They Are* (1997). Aside from the *Sinfonia* (1951), the *Toccata* (1955), and two works bearing the title *Music for Orchestra* (1969, 1989), all of Kirchner's orchestral works from the 1950s to the 1990s are concertos. The two piano concertos, from 1953 and 1963, benefit from Kirchner's ability to blur the boundary between the virtuosic and the expressive (that is, to employ the latter in the service of the former, while not diminishing its profile). Other concertos feature strings, save the *Music for Flute and Orchestra* from 1978. Kirchner has composed only one opera, *Lily* (1973–76), after Saul Bellow's *Henderson, the Rain King*. Despite the opera's obscurity, however, it has produced two spin-off pieces: a non-staged arrangement for soprano, chamber ensemble, and tape (1973), and the solo flute work *Flutings for Paula* (1973). —*Jeremy Grimshaw*

Recommended:

- ○ **Kirchner Historic Recordings** / Mitropoulos (cond.), Fleisher, Neikrug, Shapiro, Rubin, Kirchner, New York PO, Washington Chamber Soloists, Lenox Quartet / Music & Arts 1045
- ○ **Kirchner: Complete String Quartets** / Boston Composers SQ / 1994 / Albany 137
- ○ **Kirchner: Concerto; Trio; 5 Pieces; Music For 12** / Kirchner (cond.), Kalish, Eskin, Lowe, Boston Symphony Chamber Players / 1989 / Nonesuch 79188

CHAMBER MUSIC

Piano Trio No. 1 (1954)

Under a commission from the Elizabeth Sprague Coolidge Foundation, Schoenberg disciple Leon Kirchner produced a volatile, expressionistic piano trio to celebrate the 50th anniversary of the Coleman Chamber Series in Pasadena, CA. The first of its two movements begins with an expansive cello theme, opening what has been aptly but anonymously described as a "perpetual variation on certain motive and harmonic fragments, in a sort of 'stream-of-consciousness' unfolding." The mood changes every few bars, often setting the two string instruments in opposition to the piano. A short crescendo marked "Wild!" erupts into an appassionato section, which relaxes into a lyrical passage disrupted by a piano crescendo marked "Coming from nowhere, almost out of control." Marcato sections alternate with calmer, quieter music, all yanked around by little accelerandos and ritards. The second movement is less mercurial. Marked Largo, it begins with simple material: tense, creeping music for the strings alternating with more open, almost childlike material for the piano. All three instruments join for a cautiously slow interplay, with time out for a short, agitated piano cadenza about two-thirds of the way through. The music then toughens and grows in nervous anger, ending with a sharp, decisive piano chord and pizzicato double and triple stops in the strings. —*James Reel*

Recommended:

- ○ **Kirchner: Concerto; Trio; 5 Pieces; Music For 12** / Kirchner (cond.), Kalish, Eskin, Lowe, Boston Symphony Chamber Players / 1989 / Nonesuch 79188

AVANT-GARDE

String Quartet No. 3 (1966)

The *String Quartet No. 3* for strings and tape is the work for which Leon Kirchner received the Pulitzer Prize in 1967. It is a single-movement work, lasting about 17 and a half minutes, but there are three distinct sections within that movement, nearly equal in length, which, despite the modern sound, have some characteristics of traditional forms. Kirchner said "I set out to produce a meaningful confrontation between 'new' electronic sounds and those of the traditional string quartet." What occurs is not necessarily a confrontation in the hostile sense, but more of an active dialogue between two musical instruments: the string quartet and the tape. For the greater part, either one or the other is voicing the musical thoughts; there are only a few places where they are heard together and even then, one usually dominates over the other. The work opens with the string quartet offering two rising gestures, followed by the tape in a metronomic tapping. From there they begin testing each other, responding to and imitating the gestures and harmonies each one makes. The section ends with a tape cadenza that bubbles off and sounds tones, deep twangs, and sighs while the strings play quiet harmonics and glissandi at the discretion of the performers. The middle section is left to the quartet alone. It is also in three sections, giving it a fast-slow-fast structure. Here the quartet is broken into its individual voices. Many of the gestures played by each instrument echo those of the tape, but there are also moments of lyric melody. The section ends with a contrapuntal discussion among the four instruments before a pause introduces the finale. Here the quartet and tape again begin the dialogue, the tape making tapping noises similar to those at the beginning of the work. The strings are slightly more independent of each other. At one point, the cello imitates the low, singular notes of the tape, then the first violin whizzes off on its own thought, which is eventually picked up by the others. Shortly after that, it is imitated in a solo by the tape just before strings close the piece in a sparse, suspended chord with gentle pulsing above it. Kirchner composed the 11 tape cues on a Buchla synthesizer, with the assistance of his former student, composer Morton Subotnick. The work was premiered in January 1967 by the Beaux Arts Quartet. —*Patsy Morita*

Recommended:

- ○ **American String Quartets, 1950–1970** / Concord SQ / 1995 / VoxBox 5143

Emma Kirkby

b. Feb. 26, 1949, Camberley, England

Soprano

English soprano Emma Kirkby is one of the leading proponents of Renaissance and Baroque vocal music. Having begun her vocal studies with Jessica Cash at Oxford University (while studying classic literature), she made her 1974 concert debut in London; she has been regarded as an early music specialist from the beginning. She made her first tour of the United States in 1978; tours to all of the major music capitals of the world have followed. Especially noteworthy was a tour of the Arabian states with lutenist Anthony Rooley.

She has been a member of the Academy of Ancient Music, The London Baroque, The Taverner Players and the Consort of Musicke. In her collaborations with these groups she has increased the public awareness of correct Baroque performance practice while carefully avoiding pedantry; she brings a great deal of drama and musicianship to her performances. Besides the lute songs of the Renaissance era, Kirkby is well known for her performances of the cantatas and passions of Bach and the choral music of Monteverdi. Though she has rarely appeared on the operatic stage, she had great success as Dorlina in Handel's *Orlando* and in the title role of Scarlatti's *Giuditta*.

Kirkby's voice is a very light, lyric soprano of unusual sweetness. She has excellent control of the voice and is able to sing without any vibrato—a quality that many practitioners of early music prefer. Her recordings give an excellent view of the range of her repertoire—at times even expanding on it, since she has recorded several operas which she has not sung on stage, including Purcell's *Dido and Aeneas*, Monteverdi' Orfeo, Handel's *Orlando* and Hasse's *Cleofide*. —*Richard LeSueur*

Recommended:

- ○ **Dr Arne at Vauxhall Gardens** / Goodman (cond.), Kirkby, Morton, Parley of Instruments / 1987 / Hyperion 66237
- ○ **Emma Kirkby Collection** / Kirkby, etc. / 1987 / Hyperion 66227
- ○ **Beach: Chanson d'amour** / Kirkby, Romantic Chamber Group of London / 2000 / Bis 1245
- ○ **Vivaldi: Opera Arias & Sinfonias** / Goodman (cond.), Arfken, Kirkby, Brandenburg Consort / 1994 / Hyperion 66745
- ○ **Handel: Messiah** / Hogwood (cond.), Preston, Elliott, Kirkby, Watkinson, Nelson, Academy of Ancient Music / 1991 / L'oiseau-Lyre 430488

Ralph Kirkpatrick

b. Jun. 10, 1911, Leominster, MA, **d.** Apr. 13, 1984, Guilford, CT

Harpsichordist

Harpsichordist/clavichordist/scholar Ralph Kirkpatrick was, by the time of his death, recognized as much for his scholarship and work on behalf of composer Domenico Scarlatti as for his estimable performing career. His interests extended well beyond Scarlatti, however. His performing repertory embraced a majority of

Bach's keyboard works and much French music written for the clavichord, and even extended into the realm of music written for the virginals.

Kirkpatrick began music lessons with his mother at age six and graduated from Harvard University with a bachelor's degree in fine arts in 1931. During his studies there, he had made his first appearance as a harpsichordist in Cambridge in 1930. At Harvard, he had won a John Knowles Paine Traveling Scholarship which he applied toward additional studies in Europe, first in France (1931–32), then in England and Germany. While at the Bibliothèque Nationale in Paris, he undertook harpsichord instruction with Wanda Landowska and studied music theory with Nadia Boulanger. The summer months of 1932 were spent in England where Kirkpatrick studied with Arnold Dolmetsch. The following year, he traveled to Germany where he worked briefly with Heinz Tiessen and Günther Ramin. In 1933–34, Kirkpatrick was an instructor at Salzburg's Mozarteum.

Further opportunities were afforded through a Guggenheim Fellowship awarded in 1937. Equipped with this funding, Kirkpatrick was able to advance his research into performance of seventeenth and eighteenth century chamber music in France, Germany, and England. He compiled source materials, assembled treatises on performance practice, and made a close study of ornamentation issues. Shortly thereafter, he initiated his explorations into the music of Domenico Scarlatti, examining great quantities of unpublished material found in Italy, Spain, and Portugal.

In 1940, Kirkpatrick was appointed visiting lecturer and instructor in harpsichord performance at Yale University. Later, he was made a full professor and remained at Yale until 1976 as a fellow of Jonathan Edwards College. The final stage of Kirkpatrick's academic career was spent as the first Ernest Bloch Professor of Music at the University of California at Berkeley.

After a successful Berlin performance of Bach's *Goldberg Variations* in 1933, Kirkpatrick enjoyed a major performing career throughout Europe and America. On a radio broadcast from New York City in 1946, he made his first appearance as a clavichordist, and he subsequently performed publicly on fortepianos and their immediate successors.

Kirkpatrick's volume *Domenico Scarlatti*, published in 1953, won a reputation as the most comprehensive, most thoughtfully organized study of that composer's music to date. His published editions of Scarlatti's sonatas were likewise regarded as major accomplishments in scholarship. His cataloging system, listing a total of 555 sonatas, was considered an important advance over that of Alessandro Longo, whose edition of Scarlatti was published by Ricordi in 1913.

In addition to numerous sound recordings, Kirkpatrick left several performances on video, the most prominent among them assembled in an hour-long program entitled *Ralph Kirkpatrick Plays Bach*. Among his many other published items is a charming commentary on clavichord performance appearing in the July 1981 edition of *Early Music* as "On Playing the Clavichord."

Subsequent performers on early keyboard instruments may have achieved a greater fluidity of execution, but Kirkpatrick's playing was always imbued with integrity and conviction born of exhaustive study. His place among the most significant of those who have specialized in keyboard music of the Baroque and early Classical periods is assured. *—Erik Eriksson*

Recommended:

○ **Well-Tempered Clavier, Book 1** / Kirkpatrick / 2000 / DG 463601

○ **Scarlatti: 53 Sonatas** / Kirkpatrick / Urania 4222

Evgeny Kissin

b. Oct. 10, 1971, Moscow, Russia

Pianist

Although the U.S.S.R.'s system of identifying and training musically talented youngsters produced amazingly precocious pianists on a regular basis, Evgeny Kissin stood out from the rest for a talent far surpassing that of the usual Wunderkind. He has become, seemingly without difficulty, one of the finest adult pianists on the world's concert stages. His life was marked by early milestones. At two, he began playing and improvising at the piano. At six he was admitted to the Gnessin School of Music for Gifted Children. Anna Pavlovna Kantor was his teacher at the Gnessin School, and she remained his only teacher, even traveling and living with his family. At ten, he debuted playing *Mozart's Piano Concerto*, K. 466, with the Orchestra of Ulyanovsky. His first solo recital was in Moscow at age 11. In March, 1984, when he was 12, he played both Chopin concertos in the Moscow Conservatory Great Hall with Dmitri Kitaenko conducting the Moscow State Philharmonic, which also became his first recording.

An appearance at the 1987 Berlin Festival, where he played Tchaikovsky's *First Piano Concerto* with the Berlin Philharmonic under Herbert von Karajan, was his debut in the West. He was then 16 and was hailed as a remarkable and mature artist. Recording contracts with western companies were soon to follow. He returned to Western Europe for a 1988 tour with the Moscow Virtuosi, Vladimir Spivakov conducting. In the same year he debuted at the BBC Promenade Concerts with David Atherton conducting, and closed out the year at the traditional Berlin Philharmonic New Year's Eve concert under Karajan.

The two Chopin concertos were the vehicles for his American debut with Zubin Mehta and the New York Philharmonic. Ten days later he followed this with a sensational New York recital debut at Carnegie Hall. Predictions of a major piano career were common, and have since been entirely borne out.

His amazing finger dexterity and power are coupled with an electrifying stage personality. His performances are dramatic and beautifully judged, musically. He tours widely, and his records are eagerly awaited. He appeared on the 1992 Grammy Awards ceremony, and in 1995 became the youngest person ever awarded the Musical American Instrumentalist of the Year. In 1996, the Russian government granted him the Triumph Award for Excellence, one of its highest honors for culture. In 1997 he was the first ever to give a solo piano recital as one of the BBC Proms concerts. The more-than-6,000 seats of the hall were sold out. *—Joseph Stevenson*

Recommended:

○ **Evgeny Kissin** / Kissin / 2002 / RCA 63884

○ **Prokofiev: Concertos 1 & 3** / Abbado (cond.), Kissin, Berlin PO / 1994 / DG 439898

○ **Chopin: Concertos 1 & 2** / Kitaenko (cond.), Kissin, Moscow PO / Brilliant 92118/2

○ **Tchaikovsky: Concerto 1; Shostakovich: Concerto 1** / Spivakov, Gergiev (conds.), Kissin, St. Petersburg Orch. / Brilliant 92118/1

○ **Kissin Plays Shostakovich** / Kissin, etc. / RCA 7947

Carlos Kleiber

b. Jul. 30, 1930, Berlin, Germany, **d.** Jul. 13, 2004, Munich, Germany

Conductor

Carlos Kleiber was one of the legendary conductors of his time, famous for his infrequent, but supreme interpretations of a limited repertory. The New York Times called him "the most venerated conductor since Arturo Toscanini." Carlos Kleiber was born in Berlin, but was raised in Argentina. He was interested in music from an early age, despite opposition from his famous father, the conductor Erich Kleiber. Carlos settled in Europe in 1952 to become a répétiteur at the Theater am Gärtnerplatz in Munich. He made his debut conducting Millöcker's *Gasparone* in Potsdam in 1954. He attained another repétiteur position in 1956 at the Deutsche Oper am Rhein in Düsseldorf and was promoted to conductor in 1958. From 1964 to 1966 he was a conductor at the Zürich Opera, then first conductor at the Württemberg State Theater in Stuttgart (1966–68). From 1968 to 1978 he was a conductor at the Bavarian State Opera in Munich.

During this period he made notable guest appearances. His British debut was conducting Berg's *Wozzeck* at the Edinburgh Festival in 1966. His Vienna debut was leading *Tristan und Isolde* in 1973, and he debuted at Bayreuth conducting the same work. In 1974 he appeared for the first time at Covent Garden and La Scala, in both cases conducting Richard Strauss's *Der Rosenkavalier*. His American debut vehicle was with Verdi's *Otello* in San Francisco. He made his debut at the Met in 1988. Subsequently, he also appeared as a conductor of orchestral concerts, including performances with the Chicago Symphony, the Vienna Philharmonic, and the Berlin Philharmonic.

After Kleiber gave up his position in Munich, he did not enter into another permanent relationship with an orchestra or opera house, preferring instead to make rare guest appearances. Kleiber was a tireless perfectionist who possesses a remarkable intensity in rehearsal and performance. He produced performances of refined, polished execution that strip away everything but the composer's purest intentions. Kleiber released only a few recordings, but each one is considered a masterpiece of interpretation. His repertory came primarily from the Classical and Romantic repertoire, including Beethoven, Brahms, and Mozart symphonies and overtures. Among the highlights of his career were his interpretations of opera, including *Der Rosenkavalier*, and Johann Strauss' *Die Fledermaus*. His repertoire also included waltzes and other lighter works, which he performed on the Vienna Philharmonic's New Year's concerts. Some of his opera productions, and a documentary of his rehearsal and conducting technique, are available on video. A very private man, he avoided public appearances and press interviews. He became a naturalized Austrian citizen in 1980. *—Joseph Stevenson*

Recommended:

○ **Beethoven: Symphonies 5 & 7** / Kleiber (cond.), Vienna PO / 1995 / DG 447400

○ **Verdi: La Traviata** / Kleiber (cond.), Cotrubas, Domingo, Milnes / DG 000311436

○ **1992 New Year's Concert** / Kleiber (cond.), Vienna PO / 1992 / Sony 48376

○ **Beethoven: Symphony 6** / Kleiber (cond.), Bavarian State Opera Orch. / 2003 / Orfeo D'Or 600031

Erich Kleiber

b. Aug. 5, 1890, Vienna, Austria, **d.** Jan. 27, 1956, Zurich, Switzerland

Conductor

Erich Kleiber decided to become a conductor while still a student at the Prague Conservatory after hearing Gustav Mahler conducting his *Sixth Symphony*. As choirmaster at the German Theater in Prague, he made his conducting début in

1911 directing the music for a stage comedy. A composer in his student years, his works include violin and piano concertos, orchestral and chamber works.

Following a series of appointments as conductor at Darmstadt, Barmen-Eberfeld, Düsseldorf, and Mannheim, he became general music director of the Berlin State Opera in 1923. In addition to the mainstream repertory, Kleiber introduced unfamiliar works such as Schoenberg's *Pierrot Lunaire*, Janáček's *Jenůfa*, Bittner's *Das Rosengärtlein*, and, after an astounding 132 rehearsals, gave the first U.S. performance of Berg's *Wozzeck* in 1924. His U.S. debut as an orchestral conductor was with the New York Philharmonic Orchestra in 1930.

As conductor of the Berlin Philharmonic Orchestra and a friend of Alban Berg, Kleiber was planning a Berlin performance of the five symphonic interludes from Berg's opera *Lulu*, but, incensed by the Nazi regime's hostility to atonal music and growing political interference in his choice of programs, he resigned his Berlin post in 1934, left Germany, and appeared as guest conductor in London, Prague, Brussels, Buenos Aires, Amsterdam, and Salzburg. In 1939, Kleiber took up residence in Buenos Aires and became an Argentine citizen. He conducted opera at the Teatro Colón, trained the Buenos Aires Symphony Orchestra and toured extensively in South America with various orchestras. From 1943 he was with the Havana Philharmonic Orchestra, leaving for Europe in 1948.

In postwar Europe, Kleiber was ready to return to his roots. In 1951, he accepted the position of conductor at the Berlin State Opera, then located in the Communist sector of East Berlin, and from 1950 to 1953 conducted at London's Covent Garden opera house. Once again, however, he became dissatisfied with the atmosphere of repression and resigned his Berlin post in 1955. Before his relatively early death, he appeared as guest conductor of orchestras in London, Vienna, Cologne, Stuttgart, and other European centers.

Despite his early enthusiasm for twentieth century music, Kleiber is best remembered for minutely rehearsed and finely balanced interpretations of Beethoven, Mahler, and Bruckner. Even when in Berlin, where much of the Classical and Romantic repertory was familiar to the performers, he usually called five rehearsals before a concert. A perfectionist by nature, he insisted on complete faithfulness to the score. In his words, "[t]here are only two enemies of good performance: one is routine and the other improvisation."

Kleiber's recorded performances are confined mainly to the last ten years of his life when under contract to Decca. His Beethoven *Fifth Symphony* has been called the finest recorded interpretation of this much-recorded work. His son Carlos, himself a distinguished conductor, made an equally celebrated recording of the same work in 1975. Nevertheless, Erich Kleiber was never satisfied with his own interpretation of Beethoven's Third (*"Eroica"*) Symphony, and would not allow Decca to release it. After his death, a performance by the Vienna Philharmonic Orchestra became available on CD, as did the *Rosenkavalier* he recorded in 1954. *—Roy Brewer*

Recommended:

- ○ **Beethoven: Symphonies 2 & 6** / Kleiber (cond.), London PO, Berlin Opera Orch. / 2001 / Dutton 9716
- ○ **Erich Kleiber Conducts Vol. 2** / Kleiber (cond.), Berlin PO, Czech PO, Bavarian State Orch. / Preiser 90287
- ○ **Erich Kleiber** / Kleiber (cond.), London PO, Vienna PO, Czech PO, North German RSO / EMI 75115
- ○ **Wagner: Das Rheingold** / Kleiber (cond.), Janssen, List, Svanholm, Sattler / 2002 / Gebhardt 36

Otto Klemperer

b. May 14, 1885, Breslau, Germany, **d.** Jul. 6, 1973, Zurich, Switzerland
Conductor

German conductor Otto Klemperer attended the Hoch Conservatorium in Frankfurt-am-Main, studied violin and piano at the Klindworth-Scharwenka and Stern Conservatories in Berlin, and composition with the German composer Pfitzner. He made his début in Berlin in 1905, where he conducted fifty performances of Offenbach's *Orpheus in the Underworld*, not a work that would now be identified with Klemperer's serious and profoundly personal approach to music.

Shortly afterwards, he visited Gustav Mahler in Vienna and impressed the composer by playing a scherzo from a Mahler symphony by memory at the piano. With Mahler's personal recommendation, Klemperer was appointed choirmaster and conductor at the German Opera in Prague. He held this post for three years, during which he returned to Vienna to assist in rehearsals for Mahler's later symphonies. Again with Mahler's help, he became conductor at the Hamburg Opera in 1910. There followed a succession of appointments in Barmen (1913), Strasbourg (1914–16), Cologne (1916–24) and Wiesbaden (1924–27) and visits to Barcelona, Rome, the U.S.S.R., and the U.S. between 1920 and 1936.

In 1927, he was engaged as director of the Kroll Opera House in Berlin, where he remained until 1931 when political pressures and financial difficulties forced its closure. In addition to better-known operas, Klemperer introduced new works which ran counter to the Nazis' idealized view of German culture, such as Schoenberg's *Die glückliche Hand* and *Erwartung*, Hindemith's two operas, *Cardillac* and *Neues von Tag*, and Janáček's *From the House of the Dead*. Indeed, Klemperer was then noted more for his interest in contemporary music than for his interpretations of the mainstream Classical and Romantic repertory on which, in later life, he concentrated almost entirely.

After a highly successful series of London concerts in 1929, Klemperer returned to Germany in 1931 to conduct the Berlin State Opera. As a Jew, he was in danger of persecution and, though honored with a gold medal for his "outstanding contribution to German culture," a German newspaper of the time sourly commented "[h]is whole outlook ran counter to German thought and feeling."

Klemperer was dismissed in 1933 and fled with his family first to Austria and later to Switzerland. While there, he was appointed conductor of the Los Angeles Philharmonic Orchestra and lived in California from 1935 to 1939 during which he also conducted the New York Philharmonic and Philadelphia Symphony Orchestra. In 1937, he helped to reorganize the Pittsburgh Symphony Orchestra, though refused to become its conductor.

Following a brain tumor that left him partially paralyzed, his career faltered. In 1940, Klemperer became a U.S. citizen, but his sufferings were increased by a manic depressive state characterized by recurring cycles of exhilaration and depression. In 1951, an accident at the Montreal airport forced Klemperer to conduct from a chair. To prove himself competent, he hired an orchestra to perform a concert of works of his own choice at Carnegie Hall. It was a success but, after an argument with American immigration authorities, Klemperer returned to Europe where he continued conducting in Italy, Sweden, Switzerland, and France.

The peak of Klemperer's career came in 1959 with the Philharmonia Orchestra, based in London. When attempts were made to disband the orchestra in 1964, its members appointed him president, and the orchestra was reconstituted. As the New Philharmonia, the group reached new heights in the Beethoven cycles during the early 1960s. In the same period he conducted at Covent Garden Opera House. *—Roy Brewer*

Recommended:

- ○ **Beethoven: Symphony 9** / Klemperer (cond.), Ludwig, Lewis, Berry, Giebel, London PO / 1996 / Testament 1332
- ○ **Otto Klemperer** / Klemperer, etc. / IMG Artists 75465
- ○ **Bach: St. Matthew Passion** / Klemperer (cond.), Fischer-Dieskau, Schwarzkopf, Pears, Ludwig, Philharmonia Orch. / 2001 / EMI 67542
- ○ **Klemperer: Die Kroll-Jahre** / Klemperer, etc. / Symposium 1042
- ○ **Bruckner: Symphony 4** / Klemperer (cond.), London PO / 2004 / EMI 62816
- ○ **Mahler: Symphony 2** / Klemperer (cond.), Ferrier, Vincent, Concertgebouw / 2001 / Archipel 33
- ○ **Wagner: Orchestral Music** / Klemperer (cond.), London PO / 2002 / EMI 67896
- ○ **Mahler: Symphony 9; Wagner: Siegfried Idyll** / Klemperer (cond.), Vienna PO / Living Stage 34705

Walter Klien

b. Nov. 27, 1928, Graz, Austria, **d.** Feb. 11, 1991, Vienna, Austria
Pianist

Of the generally named great pianists of the twentieth century, Austria's Walter Klien is one of the least known. He studied with Josef Dichler and Arturo Benedetti Michelangeli in the 1940s and was awarded two third-place prizes at the International Busoni Piano Competitions of 1951 and 1952. Nonetheless, Klien did not make his debut in the United States until 1969, concertizing most frequently in Europe. Most of Klien's recordings were made in Vienna for the American Vox label; in some cases Klien performed as part of a four-hand duet with his friend and fellow Austrian Alfred Brendel. Klien also backed up violinists Arthur Grumiaux and Wolfgang Schneiderhan in violin and piano works.

Throughout his life, Klien recorded several sets for Vox that encompass the entire known keyboard output of certain composers, including Mozart, Brahms, and Schubert. His Schubert recordings are particularly exceptional, and are widely considered on a par with or better than the series made by Alfred Brendel—lean, clean, and refined, yet expressive and deeply felt. Vox' reputation as a low-budget classical label almost assured that Klien's performances would remain undervalued during his lifetime; however, not long after Klien died, there was a sharp reversal in his critical fortunes. Although Klien's overall legacy is extraordinarily consistent and in itself rewarding, it is his Schubert cycle that represents Klien at his best. *—Uncle Dave Lewis*

Recommended:

- ○ **Schubert: Sonatas, Vol. 1** / Klien / 1996 / VoxBox 5173
- ○ **Mozart: Sonatas, Vol. 1** / Klien / 1991 / Vox 5026

Hans Knappertsbusch

b. Mar. 13, 1888, Elberfeld, Germany, **d.** Oct. 25, 1965, Munich, Germany
Conductor

Hans Knappertsbusch was one of the most renowned and beloved conductors of the German Romantic repertoire in the middle twentieth century. Although he grew up playing and loving music, his parents objected to the notion of a musical career. Thus Knappertsbusch studied philosophy at Bonn University. In 1908, however, he entered the Cologne Conservatory and took conducting courses with Fritz Steinbach.

Knappertsbusch began his career as a staff conductor at the Mülheim-Ruhr Theater (1910–12) and then as opera director in his home town of Elberfeld. Equally important to his development were his forays into the temple of Wagnerism. He spent several summers as an assistant to director Siegfried Wagner and conductor Hans Richter at the Bayreuth Festival and took part in the Netherlands Wagner Festivals in 1913 and 1914. After the end of World War I Knappertsbusch worked in Dessau and Leipzig, and in 1922 he was asked to succeed Bruno Walter as music director of the Munich Opera.

Knappertsbusch's personality was easygoing; he was notably free of the restlessness and undue ambition that often attended a rising career such as his. He was content mainly to stay in Munich, with the result that he never became as well-known as many of his colleagues. In any case, Munich fully appreciated Knappertsbusch's talents, and he was named conductor for life. However, he refused several demands made by the Nazis and was fired from his lifetime post in 1936. He conducted a memorable Salome in Covent Garden in 1936 and 1937, and made some guest appearances elsewhere in Germany, but was content to maintain a low profile during the Nazi regime. He left Germany after the Munich debacle, settling in Vienna where he frequently conducted the Philharmonic and the Vienna State Opera. Knappertsbusch's career was again affected by the Nazis when Germany took over Austria over in 1938, but he was mostly able to steer clear of trouble.

Knappertsbusch gained a reputation for broad, magisteral performances of Bruckner and, more and more, seemed emerge as the representative of the traditional style of unhurried Wagner performances. He was famous for disliking rehearsals, often cutting them short; his orchestral players maintained that this was not the result of laziness, but of complete security in his interpretation and trust of the players. His performances were therefore not rigidly preconceived, but instead had a remarkable freshness and spontaneity.

When the Bayreuth Festival reopened in 1951, Knappertsbusch worked closely with Wieland Wagner on orchestral matters (though the conductor was known to dislike the director's spare, revolutionary stage productions). Perhaps Knappertsbusch's most notable recording is his stereo account of Wagner's *Parsifal* from the Bayreuth stage. *—Joseph Stevenson*

Recommended:

- ○ **Wagner: Götterdämmerung** / Knappertsbusch (cond.), Schwarzkopf, Varnay, Weber, Hongen, Bavarian Festival Orch. / 1999 / Testament 4175
- ○ **Bruckner: Symphony 8; Wagner: Siegfried Idyll; Preludes** / Knappertsbusch (cond.), Munich PO / 2001 / DG 471211
- ○ **Wagner Gala** / Knappertsbusch (cond.), Flagstad, Nilsson, London, Vienna PO / 2000 / Decca 458238
- ○ **Knappertsbusch: Maestro Energico** / Knappertsbusch (cond.), Schneiderhan, Rohn, Grehlinger, Troester, Vienna PO, Berlin PO / 2003 / Documents 205230

Oliver Knussen

b. Jun. 12, 1952, Glasgow, Scotland

Composer: Opera

Oliver Knussen's composing and conducting careers began with early successes, and he has continued to be active in both fields since. His early compositions were influenced by the Russian and American traditions of orchestral writing. A large proportion of these early pieces were also composed with 12-tone and serial techniques. His later music uses detailed harmonic and rhythmic structures to create complex but clearly defined textures, with fine orchestral color. In all of his work, an accessible sound world is united with highly thought-out structural details.

Knussen was born into a musical family and as a child spent time at London Symphony Orchestra rehearsals, where his father was principal double bass. Oliver was thrown into prominence early in life, when at the age of 15 his *First Symphony* was performed in London. His precocity as a conductor was demonstrated at the same time when the illness of the scheduled conductor forced Knussen onto the podium. Two weeks later the work was performed in New York under Daniel Barenboim.

Knussen's first composition teacher was John Lambert, a student of Nadia Boulanger, and then from 1970 to 1973 he studied with Gunther Schuller in Tanglewood and Boston. Schuller's influence is evident in the expressionist character of the *Second Symphony* (1970–71), which sets verses by the poets Georg Trakl and Sylvia Plath. Other influences in this period appear in the *Concerto for Orchestra* (1970) which incorporates jazz and the Charleston.

After the spotlight on Knussen receded, rumors abounded that his success was not entirely based on merit, and performances dwindled. He himself felt that early exposure was a mixed blessing and that the smaller pieces he wrote at the time of the *First Symphony* were more interesting. This trend was evident in his chamber pieces of the 1970s, which were slightly more radical than the larger symphonies, notably *Coursing* (1979) for chamber orchestra.

In the early 1980s Knussen's compositional energies were concentrated on two large-scale projects which he termed fantasy operas, settings of children's books by Maurice Sendak, who became the librettist: *Where the Wild Things Are* (1979–83), and *Higgledy Piggledy Pop* (1984–90). These works use varied compositional resources, including layers of contrasting rhythms (polyrhythms) and very subtle orchestral colors, to create a range of refined textures. Many styles are also present, from jazz to Mozart references.

Shortly afterwards, the composer became attracted to music on a more miniature time frame, for example in the orchestral *Flourish with Fireworks* (1988). This work is in a line of pieces which use subtle references to the works of older composers. *The Whitman Settings*, for soprano and orchestra, although originally composed for voice with piano in 1991, were written as the composer was attracted to four unusually short poems of Walt Whitman.

Knussen's conducting career has encompassed a wide-ranging repertoire, and he specializes in the works of contemporary composers. He has been the music director of the London Sinfonietta (an ensemble which also frequently perform his own music) and the artistic director of Aldeburgh Festival from 1992 to 1998. In that same period, he was principal guest conductor of the Residentie Orchestra), The Hague. In 1989 he was appointed associate guest conductor with the BBC Symphony Orchestra and from 1986–90 was the coordinator of contemporary music activities at the Tanglewood Music Centre. He was named a commander of the British Empire in 1994 and the following year signed an exclusive contract with Deutsche Grammophon to record contemporary music; many of those albums have won awards. *—Rachel Campbell*

Overview of Works

After his *Symphony No. 1* was premiered by the London Symphony Orchestra when the composer was only 15 years old, Oliver Knussen became one of the most watched young composers in Great Britain and eventually, one of the most admired. His works have followed a compositional trajectory moving from strict 12-tone procedures to more varied (but no less rigorous) methods, all the while maintaining a kind of non-tonal consonance and directness that suggests such varied influences as Mahler, Mussorgsky, Berg, Schuller (one of his teachers), and Britten. The precocious *Symphony No. 1* (1967), the *Concerto for orchestra* (1970), and the chamber-orchestral song cycle comprising the *Symphony No. 2* (1971, on texts by Trakl and Plath), show a deft skill with utilizing the expressive possibilities of tonal ambiguity within serial contexts—as demonstrated by the glowing A major triad that emerges from the chromatic pall of the *Symphony No. 2*'s fourth movement. Subsequent works involve smaller and more malleable collections of generative pitches. *Ophelia Dances* (1974), for chamber ensemble, takes as its impetus the enigmatic three- and four-note pitch collections of "Sphinxes" from Schumann's *Carnaval*. The *Symphony No. 3* (1973–79) takes up similar concerns on a broader and more varied scale, combining them with an interest (influenced by Elliott Carter) in complex rhythms. Among Knussen's most beloved works are his "fantasy operas" on children's stories by Maurice Sendak, *Where the Wild Things Are* (1983) and *Higglety Pigglety Pop!* (1984, rev. 1999), as well as the spin-offs from these works: *Songs and a Sea Interlude* (1981, for soprano and orchestra), *The Wild Rumpus* (1983, for orchestra), and *The Way to Castle Yonder* (1990, for orchestra). Both operas, like much of his mature oeuvre, are built upon strict manipulations of "all interval" tetrachords (groups of four notes whose collective relationships represent every possible interval), a method producing sonorities reminiscent of Mussorgsky and Stravinsky. These he presents in operatic contexts that draw on stylistic allusions both old and new, from jazz combo to quotations from *Boris Godunov* (in *Wild Things*). In addition to his important orchestral/vocal works, song cycles figure prominently in Knussen's oeuvre as well. Early pieces of note include the *Rosary Songs* (1972) and *Trumpets* (1975), both on texts by Trakl. Later works include the *Late Poems*; an *Epigram of Rainer Maria Rilke* (1988), which uses an uncharacteristically intuitive compositional scheme; and the more rigorously constructed *Whitman Settings* (1991). *—Jeremy Grimshaw*

Recommended:

- ○ **Knussen: Higglety Pigglety Pop!; Where the Wild Things Are** / Knussen (cond.), Hardy, Wilson-Johnson, Richardson, Saffer, London Sinfonietta / 2001 / DG 469556
- ○ **Knussen: Horn Concerto; Whitman Settings; Way to Castle Yonder** / Knussen (cond.), Tuckwell, Constable, Shelton, Collins, London Sinfonietta / 2003 / DG 000141002
- ○ **Knussen: Variations; Songs without Voices; etc.** / Serkin / Virgin 59308

OPERA

Where the Wild Things Are, Op. 20 (1979–1983)

Oliver Knussen is an important English conductor and composer who in his music uses an "advanced" late twentieth century style. His music is characterized, frequently, by energy and muscularity. He has written two children's operas based on two famous illustrated books by Maurice Sendak. They are clattery, modernistic scores, yet children do seem to like them.

Where the Wild Things Are is a story similar to Ravel's *L'enfant et les sortilèges* in some respects. A boy, Max, is sent to his room, having been called a "wild thing." Here, his imagination takes him to the land of the Wild Things, where he is crowned king by a sextet of very wild-looking wild things (to amusing quotations of the Coronation Scene from Mussorgsky's *Boris Godunov*), and then back again.

Many adults thought the book much too wild: too approving of wildness, too scary in its illustrations of the six hulking, toothy monsters (well, five are hulking, the goat wild thing is small, and five are toothy, the rooster wild thing has a wicked beak rather than wicked teeth.) Similarly, some think the music too wild and advanced for children. But the book appealed broadly to children, probably because confronting and mastering one's own internal and external "wild things" is very much a part of childhood. And the music no doubt does too, because children at that age have simply not learned that they are not supposed to like modernist classical music. What they have is an understandable story, and music that goes along with it. *—Joseph Stevenson*

Synopsis:

Scene One. In the upstairs hallway of his house, a little boy, Max, dressed in a wolf suit, plays roughhouse-style with his teddy bear, toy soldiers, and other objects.

Scene Two. Max is playing dead, but suddenly he becomes frightened by a noisy shadow on the wall. The image is that of his mother, who is running the vacuum cleaner. She scolds him for his naughty behavior, but he pays little attention to her admonishing words. He kicks the vacuum cleaner and defies her until she orders him to his bedroom, with no supper.

Scene Three. Max begins fantasizing in his room, seeing first a forest, which then appears on-stage, and soon a sailboat atop calm waters. He hops aboard.

Sea Interlude No. 1. Max sails the high seas and eventually spots a sea monster, which he magically makes disappear. He now sees an island.

Scene Four. Max sets foot on the island, hearing strange noises in the distance. The sounds are emanating from caves, out of which charge the Wild Things—odd-looking creatures that could pose a threat to Max, he decides. He simply halts their advance with his enchanted stare.

Scene Five. Max makes the water vanish and the sky darken, with bolts of lightning striking. The Wild Things surround him and crown him their King.

Scene Six. Max begins leading the Wild Things in a dance, and their movements become frenzied as they swing from trees. The head of one of the creatures falls off, and Max becomes perturbed. He orders the creatures to bed without supper. They protest but eventually fall asleep.

Scene Seven. Max removes his crown and longs for home and his mother.

Scene Eight. He goes quietly to his boat, being careful not to disturb the sleeping monsters. They hear him nevertheless, and half-beg and half-threaten him not to leave. He ignores their wishes and departs, and the island and the Wild Things gradually disappear as he sails off.

Sea Interlude No. 2. Max navigates the seas again, but gradually the forest reappears and he steps onto land.

Scene Nine. Max is standing in his bedroom, the forest also having gradually faded. He sees a tray of food in the corner, and its aroma draws his attention quickly. "Is it still hot?" he wonders. He tastes it and finds that it is. *—Robert Cummings*

Recommended:

- ○ **Where the Wild Things Are** / Knussen (cond.), Hardy, Richardson, King, Gallacher, London Sinfonietta / 1985 / Arabesque 6535
- ○ **Knussen: Higglety Pigglety Pop!; Where the Wild Things Are** / Knussen (cond.), Wilson-Johnson, Richardson, Saffer, King, London Sinfonietta / 2001 / DG 469556

Zoltán Kocsis

b. May 30, 1952, Budapest, Hungary
Pianist

Eminent Hungarian pianist and composer Zoltán Kocsis began his studies on piano at the age of five and entered the Béla Bartók Conservatory of Music in Budapest at age nine. At 15 Kocsis transferred to the Ferenc Liszt Academy of Music, studied composition with Pál Kadosa and György Kurtág, and received his diploma at 19. His appointment to the teaching staff of the Liszt Academy was practically instantaneous. By this time Kocsis was already a seasoned veteran of the concert circuit, making his American debut in 1971 and appearing in London in 1972. Kocsis is known for his participation in summer music festivals around the world, such as in Salzburg, Edinburgh, and at the Prague Spring Festival. Interestingly, Kocsis had yet to perform in Africa or South America in 2004.

Kocsis' career as a recording artist began in a scattershot fashion with various releases on the Hungaroton, Harmonia Mundi, and Japanese Denon labels. In 1980 he signed an exclusive contract with Philips Classics, reportedly still in force 25 years later, although the company itself has since been subsumed into Decca Music Group. For Philips, Kocsis has recorded the complete piano music of Bartók, including the concerti and selected works of Debussy, Beethoven, and Johann Sebastian Bach. Although Kocsis' Bach playing has been singled out for especial praise by critics, the music of Bartók is central to Kocsis' activities as a whole. Kocsis co-compiled with musicologist Laszlo Somfai the Hungaroton multi-LP set *Bartók at the Piano*, issued as part of the centenary observances for Bartók in Hungary—this contains all of Bartók's commercially recorded output. Kocsis has also orchestrated several of Bartók's works the composer had intended to transcribe into orchestral form, but never got around to the task. Over the years, Kocsis has maintained a close relationship with composer György Kurtág and has premiered many of his works in Hungary. Kocsis is also a perceptive critic and journalist whose articles on music have regularly appeared in the Hungarian magazine *Holmi* for more than 20 years.

Kocsis' original efforts at musical composition are less known in America than in Europe, where his works are played by Ensemble Modern and his own group, the New Music Studio of Budapest. In Hungary Kocsis is also renowned as a conductor, and in 1997 was named the musical director and chief conductor of the Budapest Festival Orchestra. Kocsis has ushered the ensemble into a post-Cold War sensibility, discarding outdated state-proscribed formulas of programming and giving the Hungarian premieres of previously suppressed works by everyone from Charles Ives to Tchaikovsky. Kocsis is also regularly seen on Hungarian television, giving concerts and talking about music. Outside of Central Europe it is difficult to access Kocsis' work as a composer and conductor, but that does not make it less significant—in his native land, Kocsis is held in a similar regard to that once accorded to the late Leonard Bernstein in America. *—Uncle Dave Lewis*

Recommended:

- ○ **Orchestrations by Kocsis of Debussy & Ravel** / Kocsis (cond.), Hajnoczy, Hungarian National PO / Hungaroton 32106
- ○ **Piano Duets of Mozart, Ravel & Brahms** / Kocsis, Ranki / Hungaroton 11646
- ○ **Haydn Piano Music** / Kocsis / Hungaroton 11618
- ○ **Zoltán Kocsis** / de Waart (cond.), Fischer (cond.), Kocsis, Budapest Festival Orch. / 1998 / Philips 456874
- ○ **Kocsis Plays Bartók** / Kocsis / Denon 7813

Zoltán Kodály

b. Dec. 16, 1882, Kecskemét, Hungary, **d.** Mar. 6, 1967, Budapest, Hungary
Composer: Orchestral, Chamber Music, Choral, Opera

Hungarian composer Zoltán Kodály is today remembered as much for his contributions to the fields of ethnomusicology and music education as he is for his own musical creations. Born in 1881, Kodály was the son of a local railway station master and amateur violinist who provided a rich musical environment for his child. Young Zoltán's early exposure to the German classics was tempered by an interest in the folk heritage of his native land; in 1900, after graduating from the Archiepiscopal Grammar School in Nagyszombat, he enrolled simultaneously at Budapest University (where he studied Germanic and Hungarian literature) and at the Budapest Academy of Music. Composition studies at the Academy were fruitful for Kodály, and he took a diploma in the subject in 1904. In 1905 he received a second diploma in music education, and in 1906 Kodály crowned his academic career with a Ph.D. earned for his thorough structural analysis of Hungarian folksong. During the preparation of this dissertation Kodály went on the first of many excursions into rural Hungary to record and transcribe authentic folk music, and in doing so built a strong and lasting friendship with Béla Bartók (who was engaged in the same practice at the time, and with whom Kodály would go on to publish several collections of Hungarian folk music).

Kodály's debut as a composer came in October of 1906 with a successful performance of his orchestral poem *Summer Evening* (Nyári este) at the Academy of Music. Two months later Kodály left Hungary for the first time, having received funding from the Academy for a period of study in Berlin and Paris. Upon his return in 1907 he was appointed to the faculty of the Academy, eventually succeeding his teacher Koessler as professor of composition (and becoming Dohnányi's assistant when the latter was appointed director of the Academy in 1919). With the creation of the New Hungarian Music Society in 1911, Kodály firmly established himself alongside Bartók and Dohnányi as a powerful force in Hungary's developing musical culture.

Kodály produced a steady stream of music (his most famous works being the opera *Háry János* from 1927 and the orchestral suite from that opera) and important educational works (which have collectively become known to music educators as the Kodály method, and rank in significance alongside similar contributions by Orff and Dalcroze) until his death in 1967. In later years he made frequent concert tours during which he appeared as a conductor of his own music, though he never abandoned what he himself considered to be his primary work: the collection and systematization of Hungarian folk music and culture, and a corresponding assimilation of that body of work into a new Hungarian artistic aesthetic (a goal also shared by his friend Bartók). In the years after the Second World War he was honored by countless academic, musical, and political organizations around the globe; in 1961 he served as president of the International Folk Music Council, and, in 1964, as honorary president of the International Society of Music Educators. —*Blair Johnston*

ORCHESTRAL

Dances of Galánta (Galánti táncok) (1933)

Despite the prominence of folk music in his career, Kodály was a type of artist/scholar—an omnicompetent musician who composed fastidiously crafted chamber works richly colored by a fascination with French music, Debussy in particular, that were accepted by an international public long before they were embraced by his countrymen. He did not come to prominence in his native land until his *Psalmus Hungaricus*, given its premiere in 1923, took the audience by storm and went on to performances around the world. The first version of his opera *Háry János* (1926) met even greater success. The pattern of cosmopolitan influence and international acceptance, coupled with incomprehension and hostility at home, is paralleled in the career of his exact contemporary, the Polish composer Karol Szymanowski. But Szymanowski came to Polish folk music late in life, seizing upon it as a basis for a major stylistic turning point; Kodály grew up in the provinces, hearing folk music all around him. Beginning in 1905, he began collecting folk songs, eventually notating over 4,000 examples and publishing landmark scholarly articles on his discoveries. Among them was the gulf between authentic folk song, usually modal, and folk music overlaid by popular European dance idioms spiced with flamboyant gypsy ornamentation—verbunkos music. Before Kodály and Bartók, authentic Hungarian folk music was overshadowed by verbunkos music, which had come to be accepted as the national Hungarian idiom. Even Liszt, seduced by the brilliance of gypsy musicians, was moved by it, and much of the material included in his *Hungarian Rhapsodies* is verbunkos in origin. Kodály's family moved to the village of Galánta before he was two and remained there for some seven years. Thus, when he was commissioned for a work by the Budapest Philharmonic Society in 1933 to commemorate its 80th anniversary, Kodály turned to his origins. Curiously, most of the material of *Dances of Galánta* is verbunkos-related, though its companion piece, the *Marosszék Dances*, employs authentic folk tunes. After an evocative flourish, a series of dances—the sultry and insinuating giving way to the exhilarating and scintillant—brilliantly conceived in opulent, glowing orchestral sonorities, place *Dances of Galánta* shoulder to shoulder with such ripe masterpieces as Falla's *Nights in the Gardens of Spain* and Dukas' *La Péri* while looming as perhaps the last and finest composition in the mold of Liszt's *Hungarian Rhapsodies*. Kodály conducted the Budapest Philharmonic at its premiere on December 19, 1934. —*Adrian Corleonis*

Recommended:

- ○ **Dorati Conducts Kodaly & Bartok** / Dorati (cond.), Hungarica Philharmonia / 1990 / Mercury 432005
- ○ **Janáček: Sinfonietta; Taras Bulba; Kodály: Dances** / Ormandy (cond.), Philadelphia Orch. / 1996 / Sony 62404

Dances of Marosszék (Marosszéki táncok) (1930)

Kodály composed the piano version of this work in 1927 and decided its colorful, folk-inspired music would adapt well to a larger setting. The 1930 orchestral rendition, while not a standard repertory item, is the more popular of the two versions of the work today. Kodály, like his compatriot and friend Bartók, devoted much time to the collection and arrangement of folk music. The six tunes used here he collected from Marosszek, a town in the Szekely region of eastern Hungary. He revealed that the folk sources of these dances are Transylvanian and date back several centuries. The piece opens with a catchy theme whose ethnic character exudes a colorful exoticism and passion. Eventually, Kodály works the music into a more intense, fiery manner, after which he introduces the next theme, a livelier and equally colorful tune. But the opening melody soon returns, now in a bigger, more epic guise. Then several more themes follow, with the main one reappearing between them. Kodály presents the material with a fine sense for contrast and color, playful and carefree music, for example, being followed by dramatic, exotic, and almost frenzied music. A mood of festivity and merriment closes out the work in grandly colorful style. This piece typically has a duration of 12 or 13 minutes. —*Robert Cummings*

Recommended:

- ○ **Dorati Conducts Kodály & Bartók** / Dorati (cond.), Hungarica Philharmonia / 1990 / Mercury 432005
- ○ **Kodály: Dances of Galánta; Háry János Suite; Psalmus hungaricus** / Fricsay (cond.), Berlin Radio SO / DG 457745

Summer Evening (Nyári este) (1906; revised 1929)

Kodály's first significant orchestral work (not including an overture he'd written for his school orchestra in 1898) was *Summer Evening*, composed in 1906 and first performed at a music academy graduation concert. Kodály heavily revised the work in 1929 at the suggestion of Arturo Toscanini, who conducted it the following year with the New York Philharmonic. This is the version heard and recorded today.

It's an idyll for chamber orchestra—no percussion or brass, except for the horns that are blended into the woodwind section. Despite its evocative title, the piece carries no particular program. Kodály noted simply that "it was conceived on summer evenings, amid harvested cornfields, by the ripples of the Adriatic." Not the loose rhapsody the title implies, this music is firmly hung on an elaborated sonata form.

At the very beginning, the English horn sings out the work's most important theme: long, soft, expressive, and flowing. This is taken up by the strings, then presented in several variant forms, interlacing brief woodwind solos with more forceful statements by the string section. After this mini development comes a new motif, a soft, short, fluid two-bar phrase offered by oboe, then flute, and soon strings bringing it to a crescendo. Kodály now brings on the rest of his thematic material more quickly: first, a melody in the violins containing a couple of very Hungarian-sounding twisting triplets, and then a sharply marked figure in the oboe, immediately repeated by full orchestra, that ends with a quick upward flourish. Kodály next subjects all these themes to a full development so intense that it hardly seems nocturnal anymore. The mood eventually relaxes for a loose recapitulation of the four themes, unwinding into a soft, atmospheric conclusion. —*James Reel*

Recommended:

- ○ **Kodaly: Symphony; Summer Evening; Hungarian Rondo** / Butt (cond.), London Philharmonia Orch. / 1995 / ASV 924
- ○ **Kodály: Hungarian Rondo; Summer Evening; Suk: Serenade** / Orpheus CO / 1996 / DG 447109

Variations on a Hungarian folksong, "The Peacock" ("Felszállott a páva") (1937–1939)

As admirers of Kodály are aware, the composer was well known for his work in ethnomusicology. The *Peacock Variations* fall into this vast realm of the composer's output, using a melody that has Hungarian and possibly Mari roots and apparently dating back over 1,500 years, as the composer asserted in a brief note about the work in 1966. The melody was used in a popular Hungarian folk song entitled *Fly, Peacock*.

The Peacock Variations opens with a brief, slow introduction based on the tune, after which the oboe takes up the melody, enhancing its exoticism and songful, lively character. There follow 16 variations and a finale, the whole piece lasting about 25 minutes. The first three variations (marked, respectively, Con brio, Staccato leggiero, Appassionato) are lively and very short, the last having a rollicking, especially colorful manner. The next (Poco calmato), also a mere half-minute or so, is subdued, but the music quickly fills with tension in the ensuing variant (Appassionato), only to turn tranquil again in the sixth (Calmato).

The Vivo number seven is jolly and bright, and could almost be mistaken for the more folkish music of Vaughan Williams. The next variation (Piu vivo) is also much in that same chipper vein, but contrast is again strongly felt in number nine, among the most lyrical and lovely of the variations, the music here soaring to the swirling caresses of the clarinet. The next variant (Molto vivo) is chipper, featuring pizzicato strings and jaunty winds.

The English horn and strings impart rich exoticism in the following variation (Andante espressivo), and that same character is retained but greatly intensified in the ensuing Adagio, which, at over three minutes, is the longest and probably darkest of the 16 variations. Number 13 (Tempo di marcia funebre) also has a grimness to its funereal tread, but the generally lighter character of the work returns with the following variation (Andante), which summons images of the peacock in flight, with deftly dreamy writing for the piccolo.

Lively music finally returns with the jolly and bright number 15 (Allegro giocoso) and the ensuing stately 16th variation (Maestoso). The piece closes with its longest section, the finale. Here much of the work's thematic ideas reappear in different guises in generally lively and colorful orchestration, crowning this charming composition with a mixture of triumph and folklike festivity. —*Robert Cummings*

Recommended:

- ○ **Bartok: Concerto for Orch.; Kodaly: Peacock Variations** / Leinsdorf (cond.), Boston SO / 1999 / RCA 63309
- ○ **Antal Dorati; Rafael Kubelik** / Dorati (cond.), Chicago SO / 1998 / Mercury 434397

CHAMBER MUSIC

Cello Sonata, Op. 4 (1909–1910)

Kodály was already an avid folk music collector when he began writing this sonata, and the work's melodies are redolent of Hungarian folk song, while the harmonies evoke the Impressionism of Debussy. Kodály intended this sonata to fall into the usual three movements, but he withheld the first, with which he was never satisfied. About a decade later, he fashioned a new first movement, but felt it didn't fit stylistically with the older material, so he left the sonata in two-movement form.

The opening Fantasia (Adagio di molto) begins with a meditative recitative for solo cello. The piano eventually creeps in and spurs the cello on to the main sonata-form matter of the movement. Kodály does not quote folk songs here, but he liberally employs fourths in his melodies, which are characteristic of Hungarian music, and he gives the work a rhapsodic nature, full of rubato. Also, the piano often finds itself imitating the undampened sound of the cimbalom. At the end, it's the piano that quotes the initial theme.

Kodály credited Beethoven as the inspiration of the animated main theme of the Allegro con spirito, but its repetitive patterns, modal harmonies, occasional use of drones in the cello, and stamping exuberance are straight out of Hungarian folk dance. Here the cello and piano are true partners, trading off the primary material. The dance rises to an exuberant conclusion, but after a brief pause the piano leads the cello into a long reminiscence of the Fantasia's opening theme, bringing the work full circle. *—James Reel*

Recommended:

○ **Kodály: Music for Cello** / Kliegel, Jando / 1996 / Naxos 553160

○ **Kodály: Works for Cello** / Varjon, Perenyi / Hungaroton 32196/8

Duo for violin & cello, Op. 7 (1914)

Zoltán Kodály's *Duo for violin and cello,* Op. 7, was composed at the start of World War I (1914), but not played in public until a full decade later when it was heard in Salzburg as part of the 1924 ISCM Festival. In the century since its birth it has become a cornerstone in the scant repertoire for violin and cello duo—a miniature ensemble that has been heartily neglected by composers. The Kodály *Duo* is in fact bested in popularity only by the Ravel *Sonata for violin and cello* of 1920–22.

The *Duo*'s three movements follow the traditional fast-slow-fast plan. As one would expect, the first movement (Allegro serioso, non troppo) is full of rhapsodic folk-music gestures that gush forth from the one instrument and then the other (Kodály was, after all, Bartók's comrade-in-arms in fusing together central European folk music and traditional art music). The solo cello ushers in the central Adagio movement, and then the violin joins in with great, fluctuating passion. The finale begins with a wandering, rhetorical Maestoso e largamente, ma non troppo lento; one can easily hear the instruments' gestures as words rather than abstract musical cells. After this introductory section, a sparkling Presto—the body of the movement—takes off. *—Blair Johnston*

Recommended:

○ **Starker plays Kodály** / Starker, Gingold / 1987 / Delos 1015

○ **Face à face** / Capucon, Capucon / 2003 / Virgin 45576

○ **Music for a Glass Bead Game** / Delmoni, Rosen / 1997 / John Marks Records 15

Sonata for solo cello, Op. 8 (1915)

Kodály's *Sonata for solo cello* of 1915 is perhaps the first major work for unaccompanied cello after Bach's six great suites of almost 200 years earlier. The sonata, in three movements totaling about half an hour, synthesizes many of the musical interests Kodály was exploring at this early time in his career. Since becoming a professor of composition at Budapest's Royal Academy of Music in 1908, most of his compositions had been chamber works for strings; the *Cello Sonata* is perhaps the most ambitious of the early string works. The sonata exhibits Kodály's interest in the music of Claude Debussy, which he had encountered while studying in Paris a couple of years before. Hints of the style of Béla Bartók, Kodály's good friend, can likewise be discerned. The sounds and inflections of Hungarian folk music also play a prominent role; Kodály was passionately interested in the folk music of his native land and several years earlier had started taking regular trips around the country, many with Bartók, collecting, recording, and transcribing folk songs and dances.

Kodály was declared unfit for military service in World War I; during those years he worked with a volunteer group put in charge of defending the chief monuments in Budapest, while continuing his studies in Hungarian folk music and composing. Due to the war, the sonata, once completed, had to wait three years for its first performance. The cellist to whom the sonata is dedicated, Jenö Kerpely, gave that premiere in Budapest on May 7, 1918.

The sonata begins with a very serious-minded Allegro maestoso ma appassionato, featuring big gestures and alternating between anger and acquiescence. The second movement, Adagio con grand' espressione, begins with a dark, meandering melodic line accompanied by occasional resonant pizzicati. After a much more aggressive central section, the music slows again and works its way to a spare and haunting conclusion. With the third movement, Allegro molto vivace, the listener is plunged into the world of Hungarian folk music. This headlong, vigorous, and diverse movement is full of virtuoso passages featuring pizzicati, double stops, and fast repeated notes and runs, and makes for an exciting conclusion.

In a 1921 article titled "The New Music of Hungary," Béla Bartók wrote of this sonata: "No other composer has written music that is at all similar to this type of work... Here Kodály is expressing, with the simplest possible technical means, ideas that are completely original. It is precisely the complexity of the problem that offered him the opportunity of creating an original and unusual style, with its surprising effects of vocal type; though quite apart from these effects the musical value of the work is brilliantly apparent." *—Chris Morrison*

Recommended:

○ **Starker plays Kodály** / Starker / 1987 / Delos 1015

○ **Shostakovich: Cello Concerto 1; Kodály: Sonata for Cello Solo** / Wispelwey / 1999 / Channel Crossings 15398

String Quartet No. 1, Op. 2 (1908–1909)

A study trip to Paris in 1907 brought the young Kodály into close contact with the music of Claude Debussy, and the French Impressionist's string quartet exerted a profound structural influence on Kodály's first quartet. Yet Kodály's work also looks ahead to the his intense interest in developing a distinctive Hungarian style even when not quoting indigenous tunes.

The entire four-movement, 40-minute work derives from a single thematic germ—but not exactly the theme in the slow introduction (Andante poco rubato) to the first movement (Allegro). Kodály had written half the movement when he noticed his original theme's resemblance to a folk song that begins "Down went the sun in its own course." "So I subsequently placed the folk song as a kind of password at the beginning of the movement," Kodály later wrote, "but the work itself did not originate from the song and I did not set to work with the intention of treating the folk song in sonata form, for I knew at the very outset that this is impossible."

The plaintive folk song calls out from the cello, high chords from the other instruments providing atmosphere. This material is in F sharp, but the main matter of the Allegro arrives in the distantly related C minor, as if Kodály were trying to set the folk music apart from his original work as distinctly as possible. The cello, again, announces the passionate main theme, with staccato violin accompaniment. An unsettled, remote transition leads to a second theme and its subsidiary material—much more cheerful than the first theme, even prancing at times. With all the motifs arising from the same material, the development section could seem monochromatic, but Kodály reworks everything imaginatively yet smoothly. Near the end of the reprise, after some turbulent runs, a snippet of the first theme emerges as a lugubrious march.

The Lento assai, tranquillo finds the violins playing a broad, gentle melody, which the cello sometimes adorns with pizzicato. The long central section is oddly complex; it begins with a leisurely fugato, which gives way to a pizzicato double fugue that ultimately melds with the first fugal subject. The viola eventually escorts the Lento's opening melody back into the proceedings with tremolo commentary from the other instruments, and the movement gradually fades away.

The brief Presto begins with fast, restless material that initially sounds more Czech than Hungarian; the central section features a more easygoing theme with a nervous, staccato accompaniment and sudden key changes. The tonal surprises continue when the first section returns to stumble through some unconventional key changes.

The final movement begins with a playful Allegro introduction that recalls elements of the first and third movements. The movement's main matter (Allegretto semplice) arrives with a measured, courtly tune with five witty, animated variations hewing to the key of C major. The fourth variation is actually by Emma Sándor, the composer's future wife, to whom the quartet is dedicated and on whose birthday (March 17, 1910) the work was premiered. *—James Reel*

Recommended:

○ **Kodály: String Quartets 1 & 2** / Kodaly Qt. / Hungaroton 12362

String Quartet No. 2, Op. 10 (1916–1918)

Kodály's second quartet is only half as long as his first, but integrates elements of Hungarian folk music more smoothly and intricately than its predecessor. Here, the intervals and modal harmonies of Hungarian music are essential to Kodály's style, but Kodály's complex treatment of rhythm and his employment of mild dissonance take folk music only as their starting point; this is clearly art music, not a pastiche of folk tunes. Particularly in the second movement, Kodály favors bagpipe-like ostinatos and appoggiaturas characteristic of folk song and dance.

The first and shorter of the two movements, marked Allegro, begins very much in French Impressionist style, but within a few bars the melody is beginning to employ more Hungarian intervals and a hint of a pentatonic scale. Still, the music remains more chromatic and harmonically unsettled than would be Kodály's standard within a few years. The meter is a rocking, Siciliano-like 6/8 and 9/8, and the sonata structure is essentially monothematic, each subject arising from the same melodic root.

The second movement is almost two in one. It begins with an Andante (Quasi recitativo), serving as a long bridge to the fast music that follows. When the 4/4 Allegro giocoso finally kicks in, the players are thrust into a dance suite, employing six different and highly contrasted motifs with strong Hungarian flavor; some are rather subdued, others are highly vigorous. Still, the music's ebb and flow remains free, though always with a strong rhythmic propulsion. Kodály also makes liberal use of pizzicato, suggesting a variety of folk instruments. Early critics mistook the style as Romanian, but Kodály clearly was evoking gypsy and Hungarian folk music. *—James Reel*

Recommended:

○ **Kodály: String Quartets 1 & 2** / Kodaly Qt. / Hungaroton 12362

CHORAL

Missa Brevis (1942–1944)

The Russian Army was besieging Nazi-occupied Budapest when Kodály put the finishing touches on this powerful work, which he had begun two years earlier in 1942 as a solo organ mass. Kodály, hidden in the cellar of a Budapest convent, then reworked it for chorus and organ, soon thereafter producing a third version, for chorus and orchestra, which was premiered in early 1945. Under the circumstances, it's surprising that Kodály imbued the work with so few of his characteristic Hungarian touches, but he clearly intended this *Missa Brevis* to be an act of spiritual supplication rather than a gesture of nationalism. The organ sonorities remain evident in the work's opening bars, not just because an organ is incorporated into the texture, but because the block-like brass and woodwind writing evokes organ registration. The substantial orchestral "Introitus" leads without pause to the subdued choral entry in the "Kyrie," the choir alternating phrases with high, suppliant utterances by the trio of soprano soloists.

A tenor solo announces the more celebratory "Gloria," in which the chorus soon gains dominance, although the bass, contralto, and ultimately tenor appropriate the morose, central "Qui tollis peccata mundi" section for themselves. The tenor also heralds the generally bright and uplifting opening of the "Credo," which is nevertheless mainly a choral movement. The music turns slow and dour in the "Et incarnatus est" section, alluding to the crucifixion, but becomes jubilant for the "Et resurrexit," recounting the resurrection. The "Sanctus" begins with very slow, pastoral woodwind and organ writing, followed by the ethereal entry of the women's chorus. The movement flows in waves of crescendos and decrescendos, and looks ahead to the rapt choral writing Kodály's countryman Miklós Rózsa would soon be producing for Hollywood Biblical epics. The ensuing "Benedictus" remains on a more consistently restrained level, except for an intense climax halfway through. A dark, earnest series of "Qui tollis peccata mundi" solos by the tenor and contralto, echoed by the chorus, begins the "Agnus Dei." This plea for mercy and peace plateaus on a powerful climax, then subsides, eventually leading to some eerie work from the soprano trio and a heavy, grim "Dona nobis pacem" at the end. That's not the true end, though; Kodály wraps things up with an assertive "Ite Missa est," concluding with hope and grandeur. *—James Reel*

Recommended:

○ **Kodály: Missa Brevis; Janáček: Mass in E flat ; Otce nás** / Cleobury (cond.), Gilchrist, King's College Choir / 1995 / EMI 65587

Psalmus Hungaricus, oratorio, Op. 13 (1923)

A November 1923, concert celebrating the 50th anniversary of the merging of the towns of Buda, Pest, and Óbuda unveiled one interesting and two exceptional works. The interesting item was the *Festival Overture* by Dohnányi, who conducted the concert; the masterpieces were Bartók's *Dance Suite* and Kodály's *Psalmus Hungaricus*. Kodály's work draws from a sacred text for a secular occasion; it's largely homophonic, eschewing the heavily polyphonic models of religious music of the Renaissance and Baroque periods. And although Kodály never quotes Hungarian folk songs here, he does incorporate many modal turns of phrase that make the work's national origin unquestionable.

Rather than writing a celebratory work, Kodály chose to examine Hungary's immediate, tragic past and distasteful present. The music reflects the nation's difficult years during and after World War I, and the text makes the connection clear, if in a subtle way; it's a free Hungarian translation of Psalm 55, "Give ear to my prayer, o God," in which sixteenth century poet, preacher, and translator Mihály Vég draws a parallel between the sorrows of King David and the suffering of the Hungarians under Turkish occupation. Thus, the *Psalmus Hungaricus* neatly encapsulates two and a half millennia of political distress.

A short orchestral prelude setting the Hungarian tone leads to a brief, subdued choral narrative. The solo tenor soon takes over, passionately singing "Oh, that I had wings like a dove." The chorus offers the tenor a brief respite from this aria of operatic proportions, but he returns with more declamatory material; upon naming the sinners who plot the downfall of innocents, he is joined by a wordlessly lamenting female chorus, their cries and the tenor's material swelling to the climactic choral assertion that "God shall hear, and afflict them." This subsides and the tenor returns with a dramatic monologue that carries the movement almost to its end, when the chorus joins in again with a strenuous outburst. The second movement begins without pause, but in a more reflective mode, with a shimmering undercurrent of harp and pizzicato strings and extended solos for various instruments, particularly clarinet and violin. The tenor returns with a long, flowing nocturnal treatment of "But reassure my heart," which balances tenderness and ardor just as a love aria would. The chorus then takes command in the final movement, which is intermittently militaristic; it's also defiant, even in its quieter interludes. The work ends, however, with a hushed prayer. *—James Reel*

Recommended:

○ **Sir Georg Solti: The Last Recording** / Solti (cond.), Daroczy, Budapest Festival Orch. / 1998 / London 458929

○ **Bartok: Cantata Profana; Kodaly: Psalmus Hungaricus** / Dorati (cond.), Simandy, Hungarian State SO / Hungaroton 31503

OPERA

Háry János, Op. 15 (1926; revised 1937)

Although not well known on stages in America or Western Europe, Zoltán Kodály's opera *Háry János* has been an institution in the composer's native country of Hungary since its premiere in 1926, and it continues to receive regular performances in Budapest and elsewhere. Despite the special connection the opera has with the soil from which it sprouted, Western audiences would find much to appreciate: the rustic exoticism of Kodály's folk evocations is entertaining, and the score, while perhaps not the weightiest in all of opera, has much in its orchestral and stylistic synthesis to recommend it.

Called "A Song Play in Five Adventures," the opera takes its story from a tale by poet Johann Grey. The opera depicts the various yarns spun by the title character, a beloved war veteran and local curiosity who enjoys entertaining his fellow townsfolk with stories of his many adventures. These are, of course, fabricated, but he recalls them with such vivid detail that eventually Háry himself fails to discern autobiography from fiction. The townsfolk, so amused by his wild claims, play along with him as he invents his past adventures.

The score that Kodály provides to accompany Háry János' imaginings is filled with local stylistic color as well as brilliant orchestral effect. The whole of the work begins with what may be the only (and is certainly the most convincing) orchestral depiction of a sneeze: a quivering, ascending inhalation followed by an enormous and percussive explosion. According to longtime local legend, a sneeze at the beginning of a story is a sign of its truthfulness. Sneeze completed, Háry proceeds to describe his various encounters. The images and events described are rendered with pictorial charm. Hungarian elements appear prominently throughout, particularly the use of borrowed folk melodies and idioms, as well as the use in several scenes of the cimbalom. Kodály also demonstrates his skill and cleverness at other kinds of borrowings as well. Worthy of particular note is the music for the scene "The Battle and Defeat of Napoleon," which parades around in a clumsy caricature of a march and which employs a sly distortion of the French national anthem *La Marseillaise*. (This scene has been compared to Prokofiev's later military music parody in *Lieutenant Kijé*.) While the opera may not grace Western stages frequently, it is known to many through its reincarnation as a concert suite programmatically encapsulating the story in five movements: "Prelude: The Fairy-Tale Begins"; "The Viennese Musical Clock," a Hungarian folk-themed song; the aforementioned "Battle and Defeat of Napoleon"; a lively Intermezzo based on the folk dance *Verbunkos*; and the final "Entry of the Imperial Court." *—Jeremy Grimshaw*

Synopsis:

Prologue. The story is set in early nineteenth century Hungary. The brief Prologue features Háry (Háry is the surname of the main character) entering an inn where he is well known for wildly embellished stories about his past. When the subject of Napoleon is raised by a student, Háry replies that he once took the dictator prisoner.

Adventure One. Near the Galician/Russian border, Ilka, Háry's fiancée, is ogled by a Hungarian guard. She warns him to stop; otherwise she will alert Háry to his brutish behavior. Háry later appears and inquires after her whereabouts. After being told of the direction she was traveling, he goes off in pursuit of her.

Later, when Háry learns that the Austrian Empress is being held in the Russian guardroom, not permitted to cross the border, he seizes the guardroom and drags it over into Hungarian territory. After the Empress emerges, a Russian guard complains that he will get into trouble when the building is found on Hungarian soil. Following an unsuccessful attempt by the Austrian diplomat Ebelasztin to drag it back, Háry grabs hold of it again and returns it to the Russian side.

Adventure Two. At the Imperial Palace in Vienna, Ebelasztin exhibits obvious hostility toward Háry and sends him to riding school. There he is presented with the wildest horse in the stable, Lucifer, which he handily tames after a rooftop adventure with the animal. The Austrian Empress is impressed with Háry's skills, but the mood is dampened soon when all learn that Napoleon has declared war on Austria and that Háry, now a Captain in the Army, will have to depart for battle. He kisses Ilka goodbye.

Adventure Three. On the battlefield, Háry, now a Colonel, stands firm in his resolve to face the oncoming French troops, when General-Blood-and-Thunder orders the army to withdraw. Háry pulls out his sword, and the motion creates a powerful draught that blows over the advancing French soldiers. Napoleon is driven to his knees, then captured by the heroic Háry. The new Colonel is celebrated by his fellow soldiers for his bravery in battle, and Ilka and Marie-Louise, the Empress' daughters, fight over him.

Adventure Four. In Háry's Vienna quarters, Marie-Louise, in the company of her mother, expresses a desire to marry Háry. Soon a grand procession to celebrate Háry is led in by the Emperor, who offers the hero half his empire and palace. At a feast that follows, Háry is uneasy and does not eat. He declares he will not marry Marie-Louise, his choice being Ilka instead, and asks that his only reward be an early discharge from the army in order that he may return home and marry her. Ilka enters, forlorn, but soon she learns of Háry's intentions. Háry offers praise to the Emperor, and when his nemesis Ebelasztin arrives in chains, he sets him free.

Epilogue. In the same inn that appeared in the Prologue, Háry concludes his story with his marriage to Ilka. She has now died, and thus no one is left to verify his story. —*Robert Cummings*

Recommended:

- **Kodaly: Háry János** / Ferencsik (cond.), Nagy, Csanyi, Solyom-Nagy, Gregor, Hungarian State Opera Orch. & Chorus / 1995 / Hungaroton 12837

Charles Koechlin

b. Nov. 27, 1867, Paris, France, **d.** Dec. 31, 1950, Le Canadel, Var, France
Composer

Though his reputation as a composer has remained rather isolated in the decades since his death, Charles Koechlin enjoyed a prominent place in the French music scene in the first half of the twentieth century. Born in Paris on November 27, 1867, Koechlin began formal musical studies at the Paris Conservatory in 1890. His teachers there included Massenet and Fauré; the latter ultimately proved the greatest influence upon Koechlin's uncomplicated but colorful, mildly Impressionistic style. In 1918, Satie welcomed him into Les nouveaux jeunes, a short-lived collective of young French composers (including Roussel and Milhaud) that ultimately metamorphosed into Les Six.

In his lifetime, Koechlin was more widely known for his work as a theorist and teacher than for his own music. His writings include a multi-volume treatise on orchestration, one of the most extensive of its kind. Among his students were two members of Les Six, Germaine Tailleferre and Francis Poulenc, as well as film and television composer Lalo Schifrin. Koechlin's skill and reputation as an orchestrator were considerable. Saint-Saëns, Fauré, and Debussy entrusted to him the orchestration of a number of their own works, including most of Debussy's first ballet, *Khamma* (1911–12). Koechlin traveled widely as a lecturer on music, including three tours in the United States. After a career that encompassed every aspect of French musical life, he died in Le Canadel, France, on New Year's Eve, 1950.

While Koechlin's music is not as distinctive in its dramatic, structural, or formal profile as that of contemporaries like Debussy or Ravel, it nonetheless bears the stamp of an unusual personality. Many of his works are conspicuously sectional and almost improvisatory in the manner in which they unfold; his melodies in particular tend toward unrestricted, continual motion. Harmony and instrumental color are generally at the fore in Koechlin's music, which is perhaps most effective in the way it creates exquisitely shaded atmospheres. The composer wrote prolifically and for nearly every medium—except, tellingly, for the operatic stage—but carved out a quirky compositional niche that remains unique. Prefiguring multiwork "literary" cycles like American composer David Del Tredici's *Alice in Wonderland* series, Koechlin produced seven interrelated works based on Kipling's *The Jungle Book.* Perhaps unexpectedly, given his sober, messianic appearance, he also harbored a virtual mania for the cinema, which he translated into a number of works inspired by various silver-screen personalities. He celebrated the icons of Hollywood's Golden Age in works like *Five Dances for Ginger* [Rogers] (1937) and *Epitaphe de Jean Harlow* (1937), but his most stimulating muse was apparently English-German actress Lilian Harvey (1906–68). Initially flattered by Koechlin's *hommages,* which included more than a hundred works, including two "Lilian Albums," Harvey eventually grew uneasy with his seeming obsession. She also enjoys a place of honor in what is likely the most famous (if not generally familiar) of Koechlin's works, the *Seven Stars Symphony* (1933). Neither astrological nor astronomical in inspiration, the symphony is instead a suite of tone poems, each an evocative portrait of a leading screen figure of the day: Douglas Fairbanks, Harvey, Greta Garbo, Clara Bow, Marlene Dietrich, Emil Jannings, and Charlie Chaplin. —*Michael Rodman*

Overview of Works (1890–1950)

Like Liszt's catalog, Koechlin's is vast, labyrinthine, and complicated by transcriptions and self-borrowing; while like Reger's, a single opus number may signify an extensive body of work (e.g., the *20 Chansons Bretonnes for Cello and Piano,* Op. 115). The sheer variety of his work ranges from extensive albums for solo instruments (e.g., the *96 Chants de Nectaire for Flute* which comprise Opp. 198, 199, 200) to large symphonic works of stunning, tumultuous complexity. The fact that a number of Koechlin's most ambitious works remain unpublished and unheard (e.g., the late symphonic poem *Le Docteur Fabricius*) makes any just assessment of his oeuvre difficult. Koechlin came of age in *fin de siècle* Paris as his teacher and friend, Fauré, was entering his richest period and Debussy, followed by the young Ravel, was affecting a suavely ravishing revolution. Koechlin's work is colored by this ambience with an art nouveau charm heard in his copious early mélodies, though it never deserted him and informs many of his many chamber works—for instance, the delicious *Quintet "Primavera"* for flute, harp, violin, viola, and cello (1936)—and the several collections of the 1930s inspired by actors and actresses: the two *Albums pour Lilian,* the *Seven Stars Symphony* (with movements depicting Douglas Fairbanks, Lilian Harvey, Greta Garbo, Clara Bow, Marlene Dietrich, Emil Jannings, and Charlie Chaplin), or the *Epitaphe de Jean Harlow* for flute, saxophone, and piano. As a prominent theorist, Koechlin avidly followed the unprecedented developments in the music of his era, while his own late Romantic vein is overlaid by a polymodal/polytonal Modernism—supported by masterly contrapuntal thinking—lending his mature work a luminous, curiously timeless aura in which music's entire past seems radiantly alive and fraught with strange glimpses into a boundless future. This is nowhere more effective than in the orchestral *Offrande Musicale sur le nom de BACH,* whose piquantly evocative atmospheric splendors are suffused with Gothic eeriness. He knows, too, how to achieve large effects with disarmingly simple means, as in the symphonic poem *Le buisson ardent,* in which a spiritually regenerative windstorm is suggested largely by an exploration of the whole tone scale. Koechlin's *summa* and testament is undoubtedly *Le livre de la jungle.* This cycle of symphonic poems was assembled from works composed between 1899 and 1940, prompted by a lifelong admiration for Kipling's *Jungle Books,* in which the diaphanously glowing early style of the vocal works, augmented by aquarelle-like orchestral color, is jostled by the satire of *Les Bandar-Log,* flanked by two imposing orchestral monodies, and surmounted by the seemingly chaotic *La course de printemps,* one of the most richly complex orchestral works of the twentieth century. For all its formal daring and wealth of invention, the fatal weakness of Koechlin's music is its lack of memorable melody, though one can hardly deny him the title of master melodist in his shaping of long, supple, and fluent lines if their ultimate effect is too often more hypnotic than gripping. —*Adrian Corleonis*

Recommended:

- **Koechlin: Danses pour Ginger Rogers** / Sharon / 2000 / Arcobaleno 9438
- **In Search Of Charles Koechlin** / Foucheux, Petit, Gardiens de la Paix de Paris, Nice PO, RTF Orch. / Skarbo 3924
- **Koechlin: Horn Sonata; Morceau De Lecture; 15 Pieces; Sonneries** / Tuckwell, Blumenthal / 1996 / ASV 716
- **Koechlin: Heures Persanes** / Henck / Wergo 60137
- **Koechlin: Le Livre de la Jungle** / Segerstam (cond.), Rheinland-Pfalz Philharmonic / Marco Polo 223484
- **Koechlin: Le Saxophone Lumineux** / Mondelci, Stott / 2002 / Chandos 9803

Joonas Kokkonen

b. Nov. 13, 1921, Iisalmi, Finland **d.** Oct. 2, 1996, Järvenpää, Finland
Composer: Symphonic, Choral, Opera

Finnish composer Joonas Kokkonen helped in several ways to foster the musical vitality his country has recently exhibited. He was the teacher of such composers as Aulis Sallinen and Paavo Heininen, and he laid much organizational groundwork for Finland's modern concert life through his executive work with a variety of musical organizations. It is tempting, therefore, to regard him as the link between Sibelius and the Finnish composers of today; he was active from the late 1940s through the late 1980s. His style, however, was his own. Kokkonen's best-known work was the religious opera *Viimeiset kiusaukset* (The Last Temptation). After its premiere in Helsinki in 1975, the work was performed at numerous major opera houses, including the Metropolitan in New York.

Born in Iisalmi, Finland in 1921, Kokkonen attended the University of Helsinki. His musical education was completed at Finland's top music school, the Sibelius Academy, where he taught from 1950 to 1963. His works include, in addition to *Viimeiset kiusaukset,* four symphonies and other orchestral works, choral and solo vocal works, chamber music, and works for solo piano. The *Sinfonia da camera* of 1962 was one of the first of his works to win performances outside of Finland. Kokkonen spent most of his life in the town of Järvenpää near Helsinki, where Sibelius had also lived; his home was designed by Finnish architect Alvar Aalto.

Kokkonen's music fell into the sequence of dominant stylistic molds that ruled musical fashion in the twentieth century: he was by turns a neo-classicist, a serialist, and a neo-tonal Romantic. Several distinctive turns of his career bespeak his independent musical mind, however, and thus the continuing influence of his music. His neo-classic chamber works of the 1950s are economical pieces, often rigorously developed from a single cell introduced at the outset. And, having adopted serialism in the early 1960s, Kokkonen was unusually quick to turn away from it, with both his Symphony No. 3 (1967) and Symphony No. 4 (1971) giving signs of a more accessible style to come. —*James Manheim*

SYMPHONIC

Symphony No. 2 (1961)

This tragic and dramatic symphony is one of the most important works utilizing twelve-tone technique to come from a Nordic country. Joonas Kokkonen used the technique for only a relatively brief period during his career, but his first two symphonies are a pair of dark, gripping symphonies in the tradition of Alban Berg's expressive masterpieces.

Kokkonen wrote in a tonal neo-Classical style until nearly the end of the 1950s, when chromatic elements began to enter his music, and he adopted the twelve-tone technique. Normally, he would a composition sit for awhile after its completion so that the next time he revisited the same form or genre he could approach it from a fresh perspective. In this case, though, working with the 12-tone system in his *Symphony No. 1* generated so many fresh ideas that Kokkonen was compelled to go directly to a new symphony, even though he also had sketched out other pieces, including some that were facing deadlines on commission. From August 1960 through January 1961 Kokkonen lived in Herrlieberg, Switzerland, on Lake Zürich and the Glörnisch Alps on a UNESCO arts scholarship. He said that the lake and its surroundings awakened some of the traditional Finnish elements of nature imagery in the music, though he said there is "as much of Lake Pielavesi and its hills as there is of Lake Zürich," and went on to add also to the music's inspiration Herttoniemi, in Helsinki, where he lived in the two months needed further to complete the work. After all this, he said "... the experiences offered by nature, however powerful they may have been, did not affect the composition of the symphony."

The symphony is a 21-minute work in the same form as Saint-Saëns' *"Organ" Symphony:* two pairs of linked movements. The first movement, Adagio non troppo, begins quietly in woodwinds, but immediately establishes a sense of loss and aimlessness. The melodic forms of the music are not disjunct, and despite their sometimes unexpected wide leaps, generally flow smoothly and sadly.

The second movement, Allegro, follows without pause. It is in rapid, skittering rhythms, serving the function of a scherzo. It alternates between toccata-like double time and a mechanically rotating, triple rhythm. Over these incessant rhythms there are several attempts to establish yearning, lyrical lines, but the movement ends by tailing off into a couple of scattered notes.

The third movement Andante starts in a lonely mood with the English horn and bass clarinet. This is the tragic heart of the symphony, and it rises to a searing conclusion, then moves without pause to a brief but violent concluding movement, Allegro vivace, before fading out on a 12-note chord. *—Joseph Stevenson*

Recommended:

○ **Kokkonen: 4 Symphonies; Requiem** / Vänskä (cond.), Lahti SO / 1991 / BIS 849/850

CHORAL

Erekhtheion (1969–1970)

Perhaps because it was to be part of a public occasion, composer Joonas Kokkonen, who was then in the midst of a stylistic shift from atonal, twelve-tone music back toward tonality, wrote this lovely and thrilling cantata in a completely tonal idiom. The 16-minute work is part of a Finnish tradition established by Jean Sibelius, who wrote a cantata for the Helsinki University Ceremonies of 1897. Important academic occasions in Finland ever since have often included the performance of a specially composed cantata. Tauno Nurmala, rector of Turku University, requested this cantata from Kokkonen and poet Arvi Kivimaa for the 50th anniversary of the University. The shape of the cantata is in line with Nurmala's requests for a four movement work: sublime, noble, relaxed, and humorous.

The theme of the cantata is a familiar metaphor for learning: light, expressed as the coming of spring and summer. This would be a particularly effective subject, as the celebrations were set for the February 28 anniversary of the founding date, and also Kalevala Day and Finnish Culture Day. The making of a "sun temple" for knowledge in various fields is referred to in Kivimaa's poem as the "birth of Erekhtheion in Pohjola's land." The metaphor refers to the temple of Athena Polias, the Erechtheion, on the Acropolis in Athens, which had rooms on different levels to accommodate use by different religious groups.

The cantata's first movement, called "Erekhtheion," evokes the idea of a Nordic Erekhtheion. This is elevated and beautiful music, recalling the past and Greek Classical ideal, opening with a baritone solo. Woodwinds suggest the aulos, the leading wind instrument of Greece, whose music was essential in religious ceremonies. The second movement, "Hahmo" (Shape), introduces an important treading figure on timpani, and the regular rhythms suggest the realization in concrete shape of the ideal expressed in the first part. "Aikamiesten tanssi" (Adult [men's] Dance) is, fittingly, a light-hearted piece, cast in the sort of irregularly divided beats often found in the music of Greece and other Balkan countries. Finally, in "Tämä Maa" (This Land) the treading rhythm reappears as part of an invocation for the continuance of enlightenment in Finland. The music rises to a powerful and rousing conclusion that avoids any traces of bombast. *—Joseph Stevenson*

Recommended:

○ **Kokkonen: Complete Works Vol. 3** / Vänskä (cond.), Vihavainen, Grönroos, Lahti SO / 1991 / BIS 498

OPERA

The Last Temptations (1975)

The 1975 premiere of *The Last Temptations* (Viimeiset Kiusaukset) gave Joonas Kokkonen immediate success and recognition not only from the Finnish public, but from international musicians as well. The opera is based on a play of the same name, by the composer's cousin, Lauri Kokkonen. The play, well known in Finland, revolves around the last night in the life of Paavo Ruotsalainen, a nineteenth century lay preacher who traveled as an evangelist, frequently leaving his wife and son starving at home. Much of the opera follows the recollections and hallucinations that Ruotsalainen has as he lies dying, and considers whether his life has prepared him for entry into Heaven. Only the opening and final scenes are based in reality, with spoken, rather than singing, parts in both scenes. Unlike other Finnish operas that have been staged outside the country, no matter where it is performed, *The Last Temptations* has only ever been produced in the original Finnish, retaining its own ethnic identity despite the more universally understood issues. Kokkonen wrote the demanding role of Ruotsalainen for the bass Martti Talvela. The conductor of the premiere and countless subsequent performances, Ulf Söderblom, has said of the music, "As a soundscape, the score of *The Last Temptations* is infinitely rich;" that "what lies at the heart of Kokkonen's world of sound" is "inherent Finnishness combined with ultimate refinement." The music pleases not only musicians, but audiences as well. It represents Kokkonen's neo-Romantic style, which relies much less on 12-tone techniques and more on clear timbres and melodies. In the opera, there is some dissonance, as Kokkonen carefully matches the music to the emotion of the drama, but there are also references to Finnish hymns. Kokkonen extracted selections from the first act of the opera as *Four Interludes* for orchestra, which have become popular in their own right. *—Patsy Morita*

Recommended:

○ **Viimeiset kiusaukset ("The Last Temptations")** / Auvinen, Buohonen, Lehtinen, Talvela, Söderblom, Savonlinna Opera Fest. Orch. / Finlandia 104

Yolanda Kondonassis

b. ca. 1965, Norman, OK

Harpist

American harpist Yolanda Kondonassis is one of the world's most famous players of her instrument.

At home in Oklahoma, she turned to music early, starting piano at the age of three. This was a matter of family talent coming down to her; Yolanda's mother was also a pianist and carefully watched her development. On a trip to Chicago at the age of nine, Yolanda saw the window display of the Lyon & Healy music store, one of the world's leading manufacturers of harps. The loveliness of the display appealed to her, and she asked for harp lessons as well. She did not give up piano, but studied both instruments through high school.

She says the piano was "neck and neck" with the harp as her ultimate choice. The choice was made by a several factors. One was that she had a facility for developing the particular muscles that are used in harp playing (and virtually nothing else). Another was that she loved the sensation of creating the music directly by her own fingers on the strings. And she felt that she could contribute more as a harpist.

At age 14, she began boarding at the Interlochen Arts Academy. Her higher education was at the Cleveland Institute of Music. Her teacher there was Alice Chalifoux, the principal harpist of the Cleveland Orchestra. Kondonassis obtained both her bachelor's and master's degrees at Curtis.

A competition win gained her a young artists' debut prize as a soloist with Zubin Mehta and the New York Philharmonic. She obtained regular employment as an orchestral harpist (and has held this job with the Cleveland Orchestra, the St. Louis Symphony, the San Francisco Symphony, and the Atlanta Symphony). In 1987 she won the top prize in the Affiliate Artists National Auditions, which enabled her to tour for five years. She developed a type of program she called "informances," where she plays music, makes light commentary, and also interacts with the audience.

She plays all the regular harp repertory, and has recorded much of it. Her *Sky Music* CD was one of the Ten Best Classical CDs of 1996 in the estimation of the *New York Daily News.* Her recording of the Mozart *Flute and Harp Concerto* with the English Chamber Orchestra was released in 1997. She has recorded major twentieth century works featuring the harp by Salzedo, Ginastera, Miyagi, and Hovhaness. She has also made transcriptions (including one of Vivaldi's *Four Seasons*), commissioned new works, and has begun to compose in her own right. Among the composers who have written music for her are George Rochberg and Donald Erb. She is interested in contradicting the stereotyped idea of the harp as an "angelic," "heavenly," or "impressionistic" instrument; one of the movements of the sonata Erb wrote for her is called *Dirty Rotten Scherzo.*

Kondonassis also has an academic career, and is now the head of the harp departments at both the Cleveland Institute of Music and the Oberlin College Conservatory. She is married to Michael Sachs, the trumpet soloist of the Cleveland Orchestra. *—Joseph Stevenson*

Recommended:

○ **Music of Alan Hovhaness** / Werthen (cond.), Kondonassis, Zukerman, Leisner, Flanders Fiamminghi Orch. / 2000 / Telarc 80530

○ **The Romantic Harp** / Kondonassis / 2003 / Telarc 80581

○ **Scintillation** / Kondonassis / 1993 / Telarc 80361

Ton Koopman

b. Oct. 12, 1944, Zwolle, Netherlands

Conductor, Organist, Harpsichordist

By his twenties, Antonius "Ton" Koopman was already carving a musical niche for himself in which he would rise to become one of the world's most prominent performers in the early music movement. Koopman was born in the Dutch town of Zwolle in 1944. After what he describes as a "classical education," he went to Amsterdam to study organ (with Simon C. Jansen), harpsichord (with Gustav Leonhardt), and musicology. Koopman's musical interests from the outset centered upon the re-creation of older musics on their original instruments in a thoroughly researched historical performing style. He founded his first Baroque orchestra in 1966, followed by an exuberant career (40 years and counting) of mingled performance, conducting, and scholarship.

As a keyboardist, Ton Koopman has appeared on the most prestigious concert stages of five continents and has produced an extensive discography on Erato, Philips, Sony, Teldec, and other labels. He has concertized on many of the greatest historical organs throughout Europe. He plays harpsichord while leading the Amsterdam Baroque Orchestra & Choir (both of which he also founded), in addition to giving regular guest performances with professional orchestras throughout the world. He has taught harpsichord at the Sweelinck conservatory, serves as a professor of harpsichord at the Hague's Royal Conservatory, and is an honorary member of the Royal Academy of Music in London. Koopman's first international prizes—a pair of Prix d'Excellence—came for his performances on organ and harpsichord.

Koopman's work as a conductor of early music has garnered him a wealth of further awards, including two Edison Prizes, a 3M Prize, a Deutsche Schallplattenpreis, a French Grand Prix du Disque and Prix Hector Berlioz, Grammy nominations in both the U.S. and Britain, and the Silver Phonograph from the Dutch recording industry. Much of his recorded work has been with the period instrument ensemble the Amsterdam Baroque Orchestra, which he founded in 1979. Together, Koopman and the Amsterdam Baroque have produced scores of recordings; Biber, Charpentier, Handel, Mozart, Purcell, and Vivaldi have been featured, though Koopman is best known now for his massive projects with recording the music of J.S. Bach. Between 1994 and 2004 he conducted and recorded the entire corpus of Bach's cantatas; other projects have included the complete Bach organ works and Passions (including Koopman's own reconstruction of the lost *Markuspassion*). Finally, Koopman maintains an incredibly active schedule as guest conductor, as well as a lengthy publishing career. *—Timothy Dickey*

Recommended:

○ **Wassenaer: 6 Concerti Armonici** / Koopman (cond.), Amsterdam Baroque Orch. / Erato 75395

○ **Buxtehude: Organ Works** / Koopman / 1989 / Novalis 150048

○ **Bach: Easter Oratorio; Magnificat** / Koopman (cond.), Amsterdam Baroque Orch. & Chorus / 1998 / Erato 23416

Erich Wolfgang Korngold

b. May 29, 1897, Brünn, Austria, **d.** Nov. 29, 1957, Hollywood, CA

Composer: Opera, Film Music, Keyboard, Chamber Music, Orchestral, Concerto

Erich Wolfgang Korngold's career bridged astonishing gaps in history and music—from the final years of Imperial Austria, when he was hailed as "a new Mozart," to Hollywood in the heyday of the studio system, to the darkened era of postwar Europe. In Vienna of the 1920s, his name evoked the best that engagingly melodic, tonal music had to offer in the concert hall or the opera house; in Hollywood he was synonymous with the swashbucklers of Errol Flynn. Born in Brünn, in Moravia (now Brno, Czechoslovakia) he was the son of Dr. Julius Korngold, one of the most influential music critics in Vienna. Korngold was beating time with a spoon by the age of three, playing basic melodies at age five, and composing at age six. He was encouraged by Gustav Mahler to pursue his musical studies, and his teachers included Alexander Von Zemlinsky. He'd written a Piano Sonata in D minor and a ballet entitled *The Snowman* before he was ten, and at 13, he saw his second piano sonata premiered by Artur Schnabel. He wrote his first two operas, *Der Ring des Polykrates* and *Violanta*, in his teens, and in 1920, at 23, Korngold completed his most celebrated operatic work, *Die tote Stadt*; it was an immediate hit in Austria and Germany, and quickly entered the repertory of opera companies around the world.

The 1920s saw Korngold add theatrical music to his activities—his adaptation of Johann Strauss' *Eine Nacht In Venedig* was a worldwide success, as was his Strauss pastiche, *Waltzes In Vienna*. In 1929, Korngold was commissioned by the producer Max Reinhardt to work on a new stage production of *Die Fledermaus*. Reinhardt was pleased with the results and impressed with Korngold's work; three years later, when Warner Bros. studios engaged Reinhardt to adapt his stage version of *A Midsummer Night's Dream* into a film, he engaged Korngold to arrange Felix Mendelssohn's music for the movie. The resulting film was a financial failure, but the studio was impressed with what Korngold had done with the music. He was offered a contract, which he accepted after some slight hesitation.

His first film score, for *Captain Blood* (1935), delighted both the studio's executives and millions of filmgoers—Korngold's music added a richness to the sweeping tale of heroism and triumph over injustice that startled viewers with its inventiveness, adding an extra dimension to the drama, and excitement and beauty of the movie. Over the next two years, Korngold turned in dazzling musical scores for *Anthony Adverse* (1936), *Green Pastures* (1936), and *The Prince And The Pauper* (1937).

In late 1937, he returned to Vienna in hope of premiering a new operatic work, but the growing Nazi influence over politics and art made it impossible for Korngold and his family (all of whom were Jewish) to remain. In early 1938, he accepted a new contract offer from Warner Bros. and got himself and his family to America just before Germany annexed Austria. Korngold spent the next nine years in Hollywood among the movie colony's artistic elite, able to pick and choose his films and always doing superb work. Korngold turned in a dozen memorable scores that defined elegance in film music—from costumed adventures like *The Sea Hawk* (1940) to serious drama such as *Kings Row* (1942).

Following the end of World War II, he returned to Austria and got a harsh reception from a populace resentful of his years in Hollywood, and derision from critics over his melodic, tonal music. Korngold lived his final years comfortably in California, in near complete artistic eclipse. *—Bruce Eder*

OPERA

Die tote Stadt (The Dead City), Op. 12 (1920)

Much admired by Berg, Puccini, and countless others, Erich Wolfgang Korngold's *Die tote Stadt* (1920), the composer's most enduring work and one of the finest operas of its period, lies at the watershed between German Romanticism and the emergent Neue Sachlichkeit (New Realism) that reached its peak in the 1920s. An epic tale based on Georges Rodenbach's *Bruges-la-Morte* (1892) and originally developed under the working title *Der Triumph das Lebens* (The Triumph of Life), the opera calls for musical forces of Brobdingnagian proportions. In addition to the principal vocalists, three separate choruses, and eight offstage sopranos, the score makes use of bass trumpet, two harps, a massive assortment of percussion (including tuned and untuned bells), a wind machine, four keyboards, a mandolin, and two onstage bands, all supplementing a full-blown symphony orchestra with triple woodwinds and a mammoth brass section. In fact, the opera's very scale—and the attendant expense—has been the principal factor precluding more frequent productions.

The size of the ensemble readily lends itself to the extraordinarily rich and sumptuous orchestration for which Korngold was renowned, here as much an integral dramatic element as it is in the operas of Strauss. The epic, heroic cast of the music seized the hearts and minds of the public immediately after the opera's simultaneous premieres in Hamburg and Cologne. Puccini's reaction to the music was to pronounce Korngold "the strongest hope for new German music"; for a time thereafter, Korngold was saddled with the sobriquet "the Viennese Puccini."

The story is a multi-layered psychological drama focusing on a man named Paul who is obsessed with the memory of his deceased wife, Marie. He encounters a woman, Marietta, who is the image of Marie. This encounter causes Paul to have a series of disturbing visions which causes him to question his devotion to his dead wife. The city of Bruges, to which the opera's title refers, provides a backdrop of darkness and death for the haunting story.

Throughout his life, Korngold was drawn to complex themes, and the psychological intensity of *Die tote Stadt* inspired him to create music of a highly mystical quality, capable of transporting the listener to a different place and time. The composer was both a brilliant melodist and an imaginative orchestrator, qualities which are evident throughout *Die tote Stadt*. The famous "Marietta's Lied" (Marietta's Song) is among the most exquisitely beautiful arias in all of twentieth century opera and it is often performed by the world's leading sopranos. Equally moving is the nostalgic "Pierrot's Tanzlied" (Pierrot's Dance Song) for baritone voice, which appears in Act Two. *Die tote Stadt* was highly successful in the years following its composition, with performances throughout Europe and at New York's Metropolitan Opera. In the middle of the century, Korngold's music was labeled by many critics as too conservative, and *Die tote Stadt* was seldom performed for several decades. In recent years, the opera has been well represented on major recordings and has been produced occasionally at a number of leading opera houses throughout the world. *—AMG*

Synopsis:

The scene is set in Bruges, Belgium, late in the nineteenth century. The vision portrayed in the last two acts portrays events which will occur, it is thought, several weeks after those of Act One.

Act One. In the somber home of Paul, late in the day. Brigitta, the housekeeper, enters with Frank, telling him of the disturbing, morbid change Paul has recently gone through. Frank remarks that he has never known Paul to behave in any strange way. She shows him the portrait Paul keeps of his adored dead wife Marie. When Paul arrives, he and Frank talk of Marie. Paul swears she is alive and says that he saw her that very morning as he sat daydreaming down by the water—it was a woman who had Marie's perfect likeness. Warning Paul against such dangerous mental games, Frank leaves. Soon afterwards, the woman arrives; she is a stunningly beautiful, uninhibited dancer named Marietta. She enjoys the obvious signs of wealth in Paul's home. They wrap her in one of the dead woman's shawls, and Marietta plays a sad song on the lute that deeply moves Paul. Discovering the portrait of the dead woman on the wall, she realizes what is being done to her. Angered, she leaves for her rehearsal while Paul begs her to stay. As night falls, Paul hallucinates that he is speaking with Marie, who questions the depth of his devotion to her: "Life comes to claim you, a new love beckons." Paul's hallucination gives way to a vision of Marietta.

Act Two. Paul's vision is set on a lonely quai in Bruges, late in the evening. He is making his confession, accompanied by the bells of Bruges, of an intense desire for Marietta, whose house he is near. Brigitta passes, following a procession of Beguines; she has quit Paul's service and joined a religious order out of horror at Paul's sinful disloyalty to Marie. Frank arrives, also on his way to Marietta's house; they quarrel jealously, and Frank runs off, the friendship broken. A moon rises as a lantern-lit boat appears on the canal, carrying Marietta's companions and Count Albert, who are singing of her graces. She appears with Gaston, and they all sing "Down with Bruges, and down with all it stands for!" As part of the spontaneous merrymaking, they start to act out a resurrection scene, with Marietta as the central figure. Paul, who has been observing from the shadows, rushes forward in outrage: "You, a resurrected woman? Never!" He grabs Marietta and her friends rush forth to protect her, but she dismisses them, saying that she will deal with him in her own way. In a fit of passion Paul accuses her of depravity and, to wound her, confesses that he was drawn only by her resemblance to Marie. When Paul sinks down, spent by his outburst, Marietta, her vanity hurt, exacts revenge by seducing him; they go, at her request, back to Paul's house to "drain the cup of love."

Act Three. Paul's vision continues. The setting is Paul's house, the next morning. Marietta is gloating before the portrait of Marie. She hears a procession of children in the distance, singing "O Saviour, sweet and mild/receive thy loving child." Paul, who had gone out before she awakened, returns and is outraged to find her in the shrine. He tries to drag her out, but before he manages to do so he gets caught up in contemplation of the religious procession outside. He is moved to prayer, sinking down to his knees. Marietta mocks him for his piousness and prepares to seduce him again, intending to defile the shrine ("How attractive you are in your saintly mood. Kiss me, my darling."). They quarrel until Marietta performs an unforgivable sacrilege: she removes the braid of Marie's hair that Paul keeps in the crystal shrine, mocks him with it, puts it around her neck, and dances seductively. This is all too much for Paul, who throws her to the ground and strangles her to death with the braid, exclaiming morbidly that "now she is exactly like her—Marie!" Here the vision ends, Paul wakes up, realizes that it was all a fantasy and that no time has passed. Brigitta announces that Marietta has returned to fetch her umbrella. Although she takes this as an indication that she should stay, Paul just looks at her blankly until she leaves, coquettishly greeting Frank, who has returned, on her way out. Paul discovers he is at last free of his obsession and Frank invites him to leave Bruges, the "City of Death." He accepts, looking forward to a bright new life. *—Donato Mancini*

Recommended:

○ **Korngold: Die tote Stadt** / Leinsdorf (cond.), Schmidt-Gaden, Luxon, Kollo, Prey, Munich Radio Orch. / 1975 / RCA 7767

○ **Korngold: Die tote Stadt** / Segerstam (cond.), Leidland, Bergstrom, Tobiasson, Sunnegardh, Swedish Opera Orch. / 1997 / Naxos 660060-61

FILM MUSIC

The Adventures of Robin Hood (1938)

Though it was called by Korngold biographer Brendan G. Carroll "...the high-water mark of motion picture scoring," Korngold nearly failed to write this score. The story opens on the night of January 22, 1938, in Vienna. Korngold was attending a concert given by the pianist Robert Kohnen, who was playing the composer's *Piano Sonata No. 3* when a telegram arrived, asking Korngold if he could be in Hollywood within 12 days to score *Robin Hood*. Korngold left Vienna three days later and arrived in Hollywood in early February. When he first saw a cut of the movie, he rejected the commission to write for it, believing it to be too much of an action picture for him to work with. He believed himself to be much more in tune with psychological and atmospheric storylines such as *Anthony Adverse*, which he had completed for Warner Brothers two years earlier. His aversion to action pictures was principally that it was too difficult to write music of worth which could be heard above the on-screen noise of the frequent action scenes. But fate took a hand and changed Korngold's mind.

Some days later, at the same time that entreaties poured out of Warner Brothers' offices for him to reconsider, it became apparent to Korngold that Austria was about to be subsumed into Hitler's Greater Germany and that he (Korngold) was, therefore, unlikely to be able to return home. He promptly began scoring the movie, a task which was completed in seven short weeks, barely a month before the film was released. But for the arrival of that telegram, Korngold may well have ended up in the gas chambers—as the unfortunate pianist from that January concert did.

Korngold used his earlier "Miss Austria" theme from *Rosen aus Florida* in the score and also some of the material from his *Sursum Corda*. The studio orchestra dubbed the score (humorously, but without rancor) "Robin Hood in the Vienna Woods"—a characterization which is much more obvious in the suite the composer later arranged from it. This is the most prestigious of all Korngold's movie projects and is today recognized as one of the most apt and celebrated of all film scores. Unusual for the time, the studio arranged a radio broadcast of practically the entire score just a week before releasing the film, having recognized the tremendous worth of the music. Later that year, Korngold won his second Oscar (this time awarded to him, unlike the *Anthony Adverse* Oscar that was given to the studio), presented by Jerome Kern, a composer he greatly admired. He was paid the surprising sum of $12,500 for the commission—significantly more than practically any other film composer of the time—and *Robin Hood*, along with *The Sea Hawk*, remains today one of the first routes through which listeners are introduced to his music. *—Tim Mahon*

Recommended:

○ **Robin Hood; Requiem for a Cavalier** / Korngold (cond.) / 1987 / Facet 8104

Captain Blood (1935)

Korngold's work on the music for Michael Curtiz's *Captain Blood* (1935) was a "second job" of sorts for the composer. He completed the score in the remarkably short span of three weeks—and then, working only at night—since his daytime hours were occupied with the music for Alexander Hall's *Give Us this Night* (1936).

Despite the rush that attended its creation, *Captain Blood*'s score bears no evidence of anything but the composer's most professional and imaginative effort. The studio provided an orchestrator to assist Korngold, over the classically trained composer's vehement objections. However, the assistant, Hugo Friedhofer, proved himself a skillful craftsman and a valuable asset, and he and Korngold thereafter collaborated on a regular basis.

Captain Blood marks a milestone in Korngold's career, since it is his first fully symphonic film score. When the original 119 minutes of the film was shortened to 95, much of Korngold's music was likewise discarded. Still, the high point of the movie's final print, the duel scene, is accompanied by one of the composer's greatest orchestrations, based on a passage from Liszt's tone poem *Prometheus*. *—Tim Mahon*

The Sea Hawk (1940)

Erich Wolfgang Korngold's score to *The Sea Hawk*, a 1940 Warner Bros. action film, represents a peak of Hollywood "Golden Age" film scoring. Nearly 40 years later it proved to be a work of unexpected influence.

In 1940, when Korngold chose to work on *The Sea Hawk*, he had already written outstanding scores for Errol Flynn's films *The Adventures of Robin Hood* and *Captain Blood*. The story of *The Sea Hawk* has elements of both pictures, plus the ambience of another Warner costume hit, *The Private Lives of Elizabeth and Essex*. (In fact, sets and costumes for that film were still around and were used in this film.) In it, Flynn plays British sea captain Thorpe, based on the historical Sir Frances Drake. Thorpe has the combined qualities of the heroic pirate Captain Blood and of Robin Hood, for Thorpe's plundering of the rich, arrogant Spaniards is motivated by devotion to the British throne and by his hatred of tyranny and injustice. The film also had a superior script. Korngold wrote 106 minutes of music for its 126-minute length. He used the full Warner Bros. orchestra of 54 players, plus exotic percussion instruments in the sequences set in Panama.

The music is lushly romantic, full of sweeping themes and stirring action. *The Sea Hawk* incorporates many of the signature aspects of Korngold's style: a dramatic use of chromaticism, an abundance of memorable melodies, and the use of leitmotives, beginning with the bright fanfare that opens the film. One particularly beautiful melody, the lute song for the character Marie, was later recycled by the composer for use in his *Five Songs for voice and piano, Op. 38*. Korngold's typically imaginative use of orchestral color is evident throughout the score. Korngold employed four assistants to orchestrate the score according to his sketches and under his supervision. Korngold received his fifth Academy Award nomination for the score.

There are two versions of the finale of the film, one for the British release (including a wartime patriotic speech by Queen Elizabeth) and a shorter American version.

The most common concert arrangement of the music includes the opening titles, a lyrical section that includes the love music and song (the melody of which Korngold had composed when he was 14), and the American version of the finale.

The appearance of Korngold's music for *The Sea Hawk* on RCA Victor's *Classic Film Score* series in the 1970s attracted the attention of George Lucas. When he engaged John Williams to score the first *Star Wars* film, he asked him to compose (instead of modernistic "sci-fi" sounds or the recent song-oriented sound track style), a Romantic swashbuckler score like *The Sea Hawk.* Williams' success in recapturing Korngold's style effected a new respect in Hollywood for this kind of symphonic score. *—Joseph Stevenson*

Recommended:

- ○ **Korngold: The Sea Hawk & Other Film Music** / Previn (cond.), London SO / DG 471347
- ○ **The Sea Hawk: The Classic Film Scores of Korngold** / Gerhardt (cond.), National PO / 1989 / RCA 7890

KEYBOARD

Piano Sonata No. 2 in E major, Op. 2 (1910)

Erich Wolfgang Korngold composed his *Piano Sonata No. 2 in E major,* Op. 2, in 1910 when he was 13 years old, two years after completing his unpublished *Piano Sonata No. 1.* It was premiered the following year in Berlin by Artur Schnabel, who continued to champion the work. Written in the floridly emotional style of the Viennese *fin de siècle,* the work is in four large movements, all of which demand a virtuoso technique from the pianist. The opening Moderato is strikingly exuberant and harmonically inventive. The following Scherzo, marked Allegro impetuoso, is tremendously difficult, while its central Trio is a parody waltz. The following *Largo marked con dolore* is set in deeply tragic C minor with a brief climax in C major before returning to the tragic mood of its start. The closing Finale, marked Allegro vivace, is intensely joyful and brings the work to an end with a return to the theme of the opening Moderato. *—James Leonard*

Recommended:

- ○ **Korngold: The Piano Sonatas** / Tozer / 1995 / Chandos 9389

CHAMBER MUSIC

Piano Trio in D major, Op. 1 (1910)

Erich Wolfgang Korngold composed his *Piano Trio in D major,* Op. 1, in 1910 when he was 13 years old. Dedicated "To my beloved Father," the Trio was the composer's first published score. Korngold wrote it while under the tutelage of Alexander Zemlinsky, and the work was premiered in Berlin and New York in November 1910. Written in the highly expressive language of the Viennese *fin de siècle,* the *Piano Trio* is in four large movements. The opening Allegro non troppo, con espressione is intensely lyrical and extremely lyrical. The following Scherzo is lightly humorous with a Trio of great Viennese charm. The Trio is written in an almost cyclical form, the coda ingeniously repeating and providing a reworking of the work's opening theme. The following Larghetto is darker and filled with longing. The closing Finale is bright and cheerful with virtuoso writing for all three instruments. Strauss is said to have heard the Trio and remarked that it was an astonishingly assured composition "for one so young," and reviews expressed astonishment at the quality and maturity of the 13-year-old composer's skill and imagination. Finely crafted and owing much to the traditions of Brahms and Strauss, the Trio is nonetheless Korngold's through and through. The lyrical tunes, coupled with a thoroughly modern harmonic language, provide a bellwether for Korngold's then-emerging style. *—AMG*

Recommended:

- ○ **Korngold: Trio & Suite** / Czech Trio / 1998 / Supraphon 3347
- ○ **Korngold: Piano Trio; Ives: Piano Trio** / Pacific Art Trio / 1987 / Delos 1009

ORCHESTRAL

Much Ado about Nothing, incidental music, Op. 11 (1918–1919)

At the age of 20, Korngold (one of music history's most amazing child prodigies) had already been a famous name to Viennese concertgoers for years when he produced his incidental music for a production of Shakespeare's play at the Burgtheater in Vienna. Although it was scored for a chamber orchestra, due to the space requirements of the theater, Korngold simultaneously prepared a five-movement suite for a somewhat larger orchestra, which immediately became popular in the concert halls.

Korngold's style is late Romantic, but firmly tonal, with an exceptional skill and imagination at orchestration. One of the unusual features of this score is its use of the harmonium (the reed pump organ). It also sports virtuoso horn writing in the raucous "hornpipe" that concludes it. The longest movement (at only a little over five minutes) is the overture, a fast piece that could serve as a model for its use of the classical sonata form and its superb development section. The remaining movements are delightful brief character pieces. *—Joseph Stevenson*

Recommended:

- ○ **Korngold: Symphony; Much Ado about Nothing Suite** / Previn (cond.), London SO / DG 453436

Sinfonietta in B major, Op. 5 (1912)

Prominent Viennese music critic Julius Korngold must have known exactly how Leopold Mozart felt. Just as the elder Mozart had watched the astonishing development of his son Wolfgang, Julius saw his own son Erich Wolfgang developing musical talents so rapidly and spontaneously that the boy fully lived up to his middle name. Erich burst on Vienna as child who stood out even among the great *Wunderkinder* of history. When he was 11 he wrote an opera, *Der Schneeman* (The Snowman), that was performed at the Vienna Opera House in 1910. Although the eminent composer Alexander von Zemlinsky did the orchestration, young Korngold watched him do it, and that seems to have been all he needed in the way of orchestration lessons. The great conductor Arthur Nikisch conducted the boy's first overture when Erich was 14.

By that time Erich was writing this *Sinfonietta.* The modest title conceals what is no less than a full-scale (45-minute) symphony for large orchestra. In it Korngold's mature style is present, nearly completely formed. It is in the key of B (in German notation, the key of H), a tonality that is especially bright because of its five sharps. In the future, Korngold would prefer such keys; his other symphony is in F sharp.

Korngold's formal sense and control over his material is utterly astonishing. The entire work is based on a single theme, making prominent use of what the composer called "The Motif of the Cheerful Heart." (An upbeat attitude is also characteristic of Korngold's music and is certainly the dominant feeling of this *Sinfonietta.*) This motive is three upward perfect fourths (for instance, B, E, A). His rich harmonization is already well ahead of its time. While his contemporaries were deserting tonality in order to use all 12 chromatic notes, Korngold wrote in a kind of extended polytonality, using all 12 notes as adjuncts to a central tonality.

The layout of the *Sinfonietta* is that of a standard symphony with a scherzo and trio placed second among the four movements. The dreamy slow movement, with delicate and thoroughly refined orchestration, is especially haunting, and the finale is breathtaking in the way its climaxes are judged and timed—it is one of those pieces that simply carries an audience away with it.

The great conductor Felix Weingartner premiered the *Sinfonietta* on November 30, 1913, with the Vienna Philharmonic Orchestra. Many great conductors took it up, including Richard Strauss. *—Joseph Stevenson*

Recommended:

- ○ **Korngold: Sinfonietta; Violin Concerto** / Litton (cond.), Mathe, Dallas SO / 1995 / Dorian 90216
- ○ **Korngold: Orchestral Works, Vol. 1** / Albert (cond.), Nordwestdeutsche Philharmonie / CPO 999037

CONCERTO

Violin Concerto in D major, Op. 35 (1937; revised 1947)

In 1906, the then-nine-year-old Erich Wolfgang Korngold's cantata *Gold* elicited from Gustav Mahler the response "A genius!" Korngold went on to become one of the most prolific composers of his generation, writing in every serious genre and making a particularly strong impact as a composer of operas, receiving unanimous acclaim for his *Violanta* of 1916, and repeating the success with his *Die tote Stadt,* staged triumphantly in both Hamburg and Cologne during 1920. But in 1934, Korngold settled in Hollywood, where he renewed his associations with the theatre director Max Reinhardt, and went on to become the most celebrated of a generation of European émigré composers who are best remembered for their film scores.

Korngold's most popular movie scores included *King's Row, The Seahawk, Anthony Adverse,* and *Robin Hood.* But despite the acknowledged quality of his works for the silver screen, it would be idle to pretend that these served greatly to enhance Korngold's repute as a "serious" composer. What did help enormously in this regard was the support and patronage of great artists, among them the celebrated violinist Jascha Heifetz, for whom Korngold composed his *Violin Concerto in D major,* Op. 35, during 1945. Other key orchestral works by Korngold included a cello concerto for Piatigorsky, and a brilliantly accomplished symphony in F sharp minor.

The violin concerto is an unashamedly romantic work, with a vibrantly cinematic character, begging the lie that no "hack" celluloid composer could write a work that not only ranked as one of the best concertos of its time, but also retained the populist feel of a Hollywood movie in the unforgettable contouring of its thematic material. The concerto comprises three movements. In the first (Moderato mobile), the soloist enters almost at once, with a lush, broadly stated melody that is quintessential Korngold. The music moves steadily forward into a faster-moving episode, with constant reminders of the opening ideas, and making searching demands on the soloist as a result of its highly rhapsodic style. The movement also includes a virtuoso cadenza and a final coda of arresting power. The central movement (Romanze) brings the required contrast, in a delicately scored piece in which the soloist reflects at length on material of a touchingly nostalgic coloration. A powerfully assertive mood prevails once again with the arrival of the finale (Allegro assai vivace), whose angular, strongly motoric rhythms serve as reminder that Korngold came from the same creative stable as Schoenberg and Zemlinsky (his childhood mentor), while also being a modernist in the sense of being fully able to write in a totally original, independent manner. Again, the movement calls for outstanding technique and fearless virtuosity, but a more relaxed and lyrical central episode again brings the required contrast. The closing section, a thrilling pyrotechnic tailpiece, again imposes severe technical demands on soloist and orchestra alike. *—Michael Jameson*

Recommended:

- ○ **Korngold: Concerto; Rózsa: Concerto; Tema con variazioni; Waxman: "Carmen" Fantasy** / Wallenstein (cond.), Heifetz, Los Angeles PO / 1994 / RCA Victor 61752
- ○ **Barber & Korngold** / Previn (cond.), Shaham, London SO / 1994 / DG 439886

Serge Koussevitzky

b. Jul. 26, 1874, Vishny-Volochok, Russia, **d.** Jun. 4, 1951, Boston, MA
Composer: Chamber Music, Concerto
Conductor

Sergei Aleksandrovich Kusevitskii (known in the West by the French spelling of his name, Serge, Koussevitzky) was one of the great conductors of the twentieth century American orchestral scene and a champion of newer music. Born into a rural Russian-Jewish family of amateur musicians, young Sergei made a little money playing trumpet at weddings and fairs in a small wind ensemble. He moved to Moscow at the age of 14, accepting Christian baptism because Jews were otherwise barred from having careers. Choosing to study double bass, he won a scholarship to the Moscow Philharmonic Society's school and became one of history's great virtuoso double-bassists. He joined the Bolshoi Theater Orchestra in 1894 and began touring as a double bass soloist in 1896. He wrote some compositions to enlarge the small repertoire of solo pieces for the instrument, even enlisting the assistance of Reinhold Glière to write a concerto for himself. Meanwhile, he closely studied the great conductors he encountered as an orchestra player and at concerts, particularly Arthur Nikisch.

On September 8, 1905, Koussevitsky married Natalya Ushkova, daughter of a wealthy tea merchant. Soon thereafter, he gave up the regular grind of theatrical orchestral playing and toured full time. In 1907, he had his first experience in conducting with a student orchestra. He was satisfied enough with his skill that he hired the Berlin Philharmonic to let him conduct at a public concert on January 23, 1908. The appearance was so successful it led to his engagement as guest conductor.

In 1909, Koussevitzky went into music publishing, establishing the firm known in the West as *Editions Russe de Musique*, and organized his own symphony orchestra. In 1910, he took the orchestra up and down the Volga River on a chartered steamboat, bringing symphonic music to places where it had scarcely been heard of before, repeating the tours in 1912 and 1914. As a publisher and conductor, he championed the works of Scriabin, Stravinsky, Medtner, Rachmaninov, and Prokofiev.

During the difficult years after the 1917 Bolshevik coup and the subsequent civil war, he continued to conduct in Moscow through 1920, when he permanently left for the West. He presented a series of concerts called Concerts Koussevitzky in Paris, again featuring new music: Ravel, Honegger, Stravinsky, and Prokofiev. These concerts included the world premiere of the Ravel orchestration of Mussorgsky's *Pictures at an Exhibition*; it soon became a concert staple in both Europe and America.

In 1924, Koussevitsky was chosen as music director of the Boston Symphony Orchestra. With the BSO, he continued his tradition of championing the new music he found around him, thus giving vital exposure to great American composers, such as Copland, Barber, Bernstein, Carter, Hanson, Harris, and a host of others over the years. During the 1931 season, he commissioned a series of commemorative works for the orchestra's fiftieth anniversary, yielding a treasury that included Stravinsky's *Symphony of Psalms* and Ravel's *Piano Concerto in G*. Beginning in 1935, he annually brought the orchestra to the summer Berkshire Festival, organized by Henry Hadley in 1934, becoming its music director and making it part of the BSO's operation. Koussevitzky established the Berkshire Music Center (now Tanglewood Music Center) in conjunction with the festival in 1940, making it into one of the premier American educational institutions where young musicians could polish their craft and network. After his wife died in 1941, Koussevitsky set up a foundation to commission works in her memory. Britten's opera *Peter Grimes* was one of the first works that resulted.

Until his death in 1951, he continued to direct both the Boston Symphony Orchestra and Berkshire Festival, recording frequently. *—Joseph Stevenson*

Recommended:

- ○ **Copland: Appalachian Spring; Symphony 3** / Koussevitzky (cond.), Douglas, BSO / 1998 / Dutton 5021
- ○ **Serge Koussevitzky** / Koussevitzky (cond.), BSO, London PO BBCSO / 2002 / EMI 75118
- ○ **Koussevitzky conducts Prokofiev** / Koussevitzky (cond.), BSO / Pearl 9487
- ○ **Koussevitzky: Maestro Risoluto** / Koussevitzky (cond.), BSO / 2001 / History 205260

CHAMBER MUSIC

Valse Miniature, for double bass & piano, Op. 1 (ca. 1901–1905)

Before Serge Koussevitzky took up publishing and conducting, he was a double bass player. To supplement the sparse solo repertoire for that instrument, he composed several small pieces plus—with the help of Glière—a concerto. The first of the small pieces was the *Valse Miniature* for double bass and piano published as his Opus 1. The title says it all: Koussevitzky's work is in fact a tiny waltz for double bass. Although having a Russian melody of no special distinction and exhibiting no particular compositional skill, Koussevitzky's *Valse Miniature* as well as his handful of other works have remained in the still-sparse repertoire of double bass players. *—James Leonard*

Recommended:

- ○ **Eugene Levinson, Principal Double Bass, New York PO** / Levinson, New York PO Principal Players / 1996 / Cala 0507

CONCERTO

Double Bass Concerto, Op. 3 (1905)

Serge Koussevitzky is remembered as a significant conductor with a vital interest in the music of his time, but he started out as a touring double-bass virtuoso. Sometime between 1902 and 1905 (sources vary), just before he turned his attention to conducting, he composed a concerto for his instrument—possibly with the help of Reinhold Glière, although this is disputed. And the work, instead of following the most progressive tendencies of its time (as one might expect, judging from Koussevitzky's later tastes in composers), is a ripe example of Russian Romanticism.

Koussevitzky dedicated the concerto to his fiancée and gave its premiere in Moscow; he played it subsequently in Germany, Paris, and Boston. But the score remained in manuscript even though the composer operated his own publishing company, and it went unplayed once Koussevitzky permanently put aside the bass in 1929, shortly after recording the concerto's Andante movement with the Boston Symphony. Several years after Koussevitzky's death, conductor Alfredo Antonini brought the work to light, and it has since become a staple of the limited double-bass concerto repertory.

The concerto falls into the conventional three movements, beginning with an Allegro that opens with a declamatory, Tchaikovsky-like theme succinctly stated by the orchestra, and answered by a short bass recitative. The soloist takes up the opening motto, presenting it lyrically yet passionately. The solo line seamlessly threads its way into related material sounding very much like passages of the Dvořák *Cello Concerto*, and eventually offers a songful second subject. Koussevitzky dwells on this Dvorákian material without providing a full development, then fashions a modest bridge to the Andante, which sounds much like an aria from a Tchaikovsky opera. Here, for the first time, the composer periodically takes the instrument into its lower range, but only briefly, usually in the course of weaving the melody up and down the staff. For the most part, Koussevitzky exploits the instrument's middle and upper ranges, where it projects better, and is careful not to let the woodwind-tinged orchestration overpower the bass (which is not a loud instrument, despite its size). A full pause precedes the third movement, another Allegro, which begins with the same declamatory theme as the first movement. The bass picks up this melody more ardently than before, and adheres to its contours more closely than before as it proceeds through a loose, rhapsodic restatement of the opening movement. *—James Reel*

Recommended:

- ○ **Diamond, Porter & Koussevitzky** / Antonini (cond.), Karr, Oslo PO / Citadel 88133

Stephen Bishop Kovacevich

b. Dec. 17, 1940, San Pedro, CA
Pianist

A highly regarded pianist featured in the Philips label's "Great Pianists of the 20th Century" series, Stephen Kovacevich is particularly known for his original approach to the standard classical repertoire. Prominent in his repertoire is the music of such composers as Bach, Mozart, Beethoven, Schubert, Schumann, Grieg, Brahms, and Bartók, but he is also an acclaimed interpreter of contemporary music, including Tippett's *Piano Concerto* and Richard Rodney Bennett's concerto (which was dedicated to Kovacevich). Born Stephen Bishop, he added his Croatian mother's surname, Kovacevich, in 1975, just in time to avoid confusion with popular singer-songwriter Stephen Bishop. Later in his career, however, he decided to use just the Croatian surname. He played his first concert in San Francisco, at the age of 11. When he was 14, he played Ravel's *Piano Concerto in G Major* and Schumann's *Piano Concerto in A Minor* with the San Francisco Symphony Orchestra. In 1959, Kovacevich went to London, where he studied with Dame Myra Hess. A highly influential teacher, Myra Hess recognized and encouraged Kovacevich's affinity with Beethoven's music, particularly the works form his late period. On his London debut, in 1961, Kovacevich played Beethoven's *"Diabelli" Variations* to enthusiastic reviews. Following his London triumph, Kovacevich embarked on a brilliant international career, performing with many major orchestras and making numerous acclaimed recordings, including legendary performances with Martha Argerich and Jacqueline du Pré. Kovacevich, who has played all of Mozart's concertos, is also known for his acclaimed series of Schubert's and Beethoven's sonatas. A particularly memorable performance is his interpretation of Brahms's *Piano Concerto No. 1*, with Sawallisch, which received the 1993 Gramophone Award. He has an exclusive recording contract with EMI International. In 1984, Kovacevich started a conducting career, and has since conducted the Australian Chamber Orchestra and the Irish Chamber Orchestra. Also known for his support of contemporary composers, Kovacevich commissioned Stephen Montague's *Southern Lament* and performed the premiere at the Cheltenham International Music Festival in 1997. Also a teacher, Kovacevich has published a scholarly edition of Schubert's piano music. *—AMG*

Recommended:

○ **Beethoven: Sonatas, Opp81a & 106** / Kovacevich / 2003 / EMI 57520

○ **Brahms** / Kovacevich / Philips 411137

○ **Schumann & Grieg Concertos** / Kovacevich / Philips 412923

Alfredo Kraus

b. Sep. 24, 1927, Las Palmas, Canary Islands, **d.** Sep. 10, 1999, Madrid, Spain

Tenor

A leading lyric tenor of his generation, Alfredo Kraus parlayed his vocal and artistic gifts into one of the longest and best managed careers in recent memory. Always careful—both in choice of roles and in the regulation of his performing schedule—not to overextend himself, he achieved a degree of consistency and longevity that kept him active professionally well into his sixties, always applauded for his youthful tone and delivery. Among his vocal assets were an admirable top extension—which included an enviable D above high C—a warm tone, and an instinctive feel for the shape of phrases, especially in French repertory. He, Carlo Bergonzi, and Nicolai Gedda were noted for their style, refinement, and musicianship in an era when, especially in Italian opera, tenors often neglected such qualities. He starred in the title role of Viladamot's 1959 film *Gayarre*, a biography of the famous Spanish tenor.

While he studied music as a youngster, Kraus had no intention of becoming a professional singer, until friends and family began encouraging him to do so. In taking up vocal studies, Kraus avoided heavier repertory and focused on the bel canto tenore di grazia parts that he knew were right for his voice. At the age of 28, he won first prize at the Geneva Competition, and a representative of the Cairo Opera, who was present at the auditions, offered him the role of the Duke in *Rigoletto*; he made his professional opera debut at the Cairo Opera in that role in 1956. His great success there was followed by equally gratifying appearances in Venice, Turin, and Barcelona, and in 1958, he appeared in *La Traviata* with Maria Callas in Lisbon—*the* Lisbon *Traviata*. In 1959, he sang Arturo in *I Puritani* for the first time, made his La Scala and Covent Garden debuts, followed by his Metropolitan Opera debut in 1965 and Salzburg debut in 1968. In Rome, he sang his first *Werther*, a role that, like Arturo, was to become one of his signatures.

Aside from his fine sense of the musical nuance and phrasing, his portrayal of the mentally unstable, morbid, masochistic, and manipulative character of Werther has been acclaimed as one of the most effective and insightful readings ever. During the 1980s, he began to limit the number of his performances even further (at the peak of his career, he never sang more than 50 in a year), and started to turn his attention to teaching, although even in the 1990s he still had an active performing schedule. Kraus died on September 10, 1999, after an extended illness. *—AMG*

Recommended:

○ **Auber: La Muette de Portici** / Fulton (cond.), Laforge, Aler, Anderson, Kraus, Monte Carlo PO / 2002 / EMI 575257

○ **Alfredo Kraus of Spain** / Kraus, etc. / Montilla 2011

○ **Great Opera Tenors: Alfredo Kraus** / Kraus, etc. / 2000 / D Classics 70664

Joseph Martin Kraus

b. Jun. 20, 1756, Miltenberg-am-Main, Germany, **d.** Dec. 15, 1792, Stockholm, Sweden

Composer

Joseph Martin Kraus was born in the town of Miltenberg, on the Main River near Frankfurt. Kraus' family encouraged his early interest in music, and at age 12 sent him to study in the nearby city of Mannheim. They also expected him to follow the more germane pursuit of Law in the hope he would obtain a job in the German government. This he did in Mainz and Erfurt; but it was at the University of Göttingen in the 1770s that Kraus made the decisive break with a government career. At Göttingen, Kraus fell in with a literary cadre devoted to the school of "Sturm und Drang" (storm and stress), a proto-Romantic faction belonging to the eighteenth century, inspired by the early works of Goethe. Kraus engaged in writing and publishing short stories representative of this literary approach.

Swedish exchange students suggested Kraus petition the court of King Gustav III in their home country. The opera-loving King had established the first Academy of music in Sweden upon his accession in 1771, but had found native talent slow to develop, and was reaching out to musicians of other nations to help improve the quality of performances at the opera house he had built. After two years of hardship in Stockholm, Kraus' 1780 opera *Prosperina* gained him a conductor's job with the Royal Opera House. Part of his training involved a four-year sojourn to the capitols of Europe in order to study current trends, a condition that Kraus was happy to accept.

It was during this period of travelling that Kraus composed all but one of his symphonies, upon which his posthumous reputation largely rests. It appears Kraus wrote a total of 15 symphonies; 12 are known to exist. His best known work is the *Symphony in C minor*, a stormy, aggressive, and vibrantly rhythmic work. Kraus' symphonies were well enough regarded in their time to achieve publication, although some editions bear the name of a better known composer and not Kraus'. At one point, Kraus journeyed to Esterháza to meet his idol, Joseph Haydn. Upon conducting Kraus' work, Haydn remarked that "the symphony (Kraus) wrote here in Vienna especially for me will be regarded as a masterpiece for centuries to come."

His tour of duty ended, Kraus was now required to return to Stockholm and attend to the musical needs of the King. Gustav III was nowhere near as enamored of instrumental music as was Kraus, and Kraus was obliged to spend most of his years in Stockholm writing opera, opera inserts, incidental music, and arias. Like Haydn, Kraus found opera an uncomfortable match for his talent, but he persevered. In 1782, he was named chief conductor of the Opera and educational director of the Academy. In 1792, Gustav III was assassinated, and Kraus memorialized his patron with a *Funeral Symphony* and a fine setting of the *Requiem Mass*. Kraus himself expired in Stockholm later that same year at the age of 36.

Kraus was remarkably productive, his brief lifespan yielding over 200 works including the symphonies, five operas, concerti, chamber works, and songs. After his death, his works were forgotten, but in the last part of the twentieth century they came back with a vengeance, especially in Sweden where Kraus is regarded as the most significant figure in Swedish music in the later eighteenth century. As Kraus' international profile evolves, it may become so that, after two centuries of neglect, Haydn's prediction for this ever young composer will come to pass. *—Uncle Dave Lewis*

Overview of Works (1775–1792)

Joseph Martin Kraus is one of the great composers of the late eighteenth century, a composer who wrote in both the *Sturm und Drang* style and in the severest high classical style, a composer of great breadth and balance, but above all, a passionately expressive composer whose best works equaled those of Haydn and Mozart.

Kraus' oeuvre falls into three periods: his early years in Germany in the intellectual climate of the university town of Gottingen, his first years in Sweden in the enlightened court of Gustav III, and his final years in Sweden through the death of Gustav III. In his early German years, Kraus wrote brilliant three-movement symphonies in the Mannheim style and facile piano sonatas in the latest style. When he moved to Sweden, he had his first success with the opera *Proserpina*, a work rooted in high Classical style, but much more intensely expressive. This was followed by a superb series of symphonies, including the fiery *Symphony in C sharp minor* (1783) admired by Haydn. While on a grand tour of Europe under the auspices of Gustav III, Kraus befriended Gluck in Paris and wrote the exhilarating *Symphony in E flat major* (1784) for that city's superb orchestra. His magnum opus is the six-hour tragic opera *Aeneas i Cartago* (1782), which was not premiered in his lifetime. In his later years in Sweden, Kraus' style became more contrapuntal, but no less expressive, as in his splendid series of six string quartets. In Kraus' final year, Gustav III was assassinated, and the state commissioned a symphony and a cantata for his funeral services. The *Sinfonie funèbre* (1792) is a four-movement work for strings, low winds, trombones, and tympani of greatest restraint and deepest sorrow. The *Funeral Cantata* (1792) is a work of highest drama and utmost fury. Kraus died of tuberculosis nine months later, and his funeral music was played at his graveside. *—James Leonard*

Recommended:

○ **Kraus: 4 Symphonies** / Concerto Koln / Capriccio 10396

○ **Kraus: Sonatas** / Despres / 2003 / Naxos 8555771

○ **Kraus: String Quartets. Vol. 1** / Joseph Martin Krauss Qt. / 2000 / Cavalli 224

Lili Kraus

b. Apr. 3, 1905, Budapest, Hungary, **d.** Nov. 6, 1986, Asheville, NC

Pianist

Born in Budapest, in 1905, to an impoverished Hungarian mother and Czech father, Kraus entered the Academy of Music there as a piano major at age eight. Taught by Kodály and Bartók, among others, she graduated in 1922, with top honors. Kraus then attended the Vienna Konservatorium to study with Eduard

Steuermann and Schnabel, from whom she took master classes. Starting in 1925, became a teacher there herself for six years. In the 1930s, she toured both as soloist and as the recital partner of violinist Szymon Goldberg, with whom she recorded Beethoven and Mozart sonatas for British Parlophone in 1935 and 1937, along with solo reperoire. Her other specialties included Chopin, Haydn, Schubert, and Bartók.

When Kraus married philosopher Otto Mandl, they converted to Catholicism, living in Italy until the cloud of Nazism compelled them to move to the Dutch East Indies. While touring in 1942, Kraus, her husband, and their two children were arrested in Indonesia, and sent to separate prisoner-of-war camps on Java for nearly three years. They survived principally because the Japanese knew her name and her recordings. A Japanese conductor reputedly provided food as well as musical scores until their rescue by British forces. For two years Kraus played in Australia and New Zealand (where she became a British subject), and in South Africa too, before returning to England in 1948, where she resumed her career before debuting in the U.S., in 1949. She also resumed recording, albeit with second-class Viennese orchestras and conductors for Vox, mainly, in concertos by Mozart and Beethoven, but later on for Vanguard in the U.S. During the 1966–67 season, she performed 25 of Mozart's 27 concertos in New York City on a single series, and the next season played his complete keyboard sonatas.

A nonstop talker who designed her own concert gowns, Kraus was never ranked as a virtuoso even before World War II, but she *was* a notably distinguished interpreter. Those who heard her before and after the war confided sadly that something had forever changed. She never stopped playing, however—always forthrightly, even brusquely, in some repertoire. Texas Christian University at Fort Worth appointed her artist-in-residence in 1968, and she became a regular juror at the Cliburn International Competitions. She tried to instill in her pupils the same enthusiasm that sustained her as a public concert artist until 1982, an intensity that unnerved some of the shy and introverted studnets. At various U.S. piano competitions, regular observers labeled her a surrogate stage mother, as she endlessly exhorted and lobbied. But she taught and cherished her pupils, emulating the teachers from her childhood.

In 1978, the Austrian government awarded Kraus the Cross of Honor for Science and Art. Remaining a British subject, she taught in Texas until her retirement in 1983. She maintained a home in Asheville, North Carolina, where she died in 1986. *—Roger Dettmer*

Recommended:

○ **Kraus Plays Mozart** / Moralt (cond.), Jorda (cond.), Kraus, VSO, Pro Musica CO / 1993 / Vox 5510

○ **Les Rarissimes de Lili Kraus** / Kraus / 2004 / EMI 62831

Fritz Kreisler

b. Feb. 2, 1875, Vienna, Austria, **d.** Jan. 29, 1962, New York, NY
Composer: Chamber Music
Violinist

Violinist Fritz Kreisler was one of the most beloved and best known of early recording era musicians. His burnished tone and patrician phrasing were quintessentially Viennese, and the warmth of his playing won him devoted followers wherever he appeared. So great was his fame and the affection in which he was held that he survived a blaze of controversy when he revealed in 1935 that many of the short pieces he had performed as "transcriptions" of such composers as Couperin, Vivaldi, and Pugnani were, in fact, his own work. While the critics fumed, the public expressed little concern and continued to pack his concert appearances.

Kreisler was the son of a famous surgeon, a good amateur musician who gave young Fritz his first violin lessons. Kreisler made his public debut at seven in a collection of short works. Shortly thereafter, he was permitted to enter the Vienna Conservatory despite a policy that no one younger than 14 be accepted. After three years of study with Joseph Hellmesberger, he was awarded a gold medal.

Kreisler was sent to Paris for further studies with Delibes and Massart. At the age of 12, he won the Premier Grand Prix de Rome gold medal competing against 40 other players, all of whom were at least 20 years of age.

In 1888, Kreisler sailed to the United States for a concert tour with pianist Moriz Rosenthal, earning many complimentary reviews. When he returned to Vienna, he applied to the Vienna Philharmonic for a position but was turned down. Feeling discouraged, he resolved to abandon music and chose to pursue a career in medicine. After several years, he rejected that course and began the study of painting. First in Paris, then in Rome, he worked toward mastering his technique, but soon this, too, became tiresome. He returned to Vienna and enlisted in the army.

A full year as a soldier was sufficient to cause yet more rethinking and Kreisler resigned his commission and returned to the study of violin. He spent eight weeks in country solitude readying himself for his return to the concert stage. His "second debut" in Berlin was successful, but widespread acclaim came during several American tours between 1901 and 1903. In the United States, he was hailed as one of the foremost violinists of his time and, soon after, Europe followed suit in recognizing his extraordinary artistry.

In 1910 in London, Kreisler gave the premiere performance of Elgar's *Violin Concerto*, a work dedicated to him.

While vacationing in Switzerland in 1914, Kreisler received the news that Austria was at war. Returning to his native country, he rejoined his former division, now stationed in Galicia. An attack by the Russians resulted in an injury and his discharge with high honors. Wishing to help his country, Kreisler embarked on a lengthy concert tour of America. The United States' entry into the war, however, put him in the awkward position of being an ex-Austrian officer aiding what was now an enemy nation. Negative reaction obliged him to withdraw from concertizing and retire to Maine to pass the remaining period of hostilities.

At his return to the New York concert stage in 1919, however, he was given a tumultuous reception. He took up residence in Berlin for ten years beginning in 1924. With the Anschluss in 1938, he moved to France, but returned to the United States before the Nazi invasion and lived his remaining years in America, where he gave his final public concert in 1947. He continued to perform on broadcasts until 1950. *—Erik Eriksson*

Recommended:

○ **Fritz Kreisler Plays Kreisler** / Kreisler, etc. / 1996 / BMG 68448

○ **Complete Concerto Recordings, Vol. 1** / Blech (cond.), Kreisler, Berlin State Opera Orch. / 2000 / Naxos 110909

○ **Beethoven: Violin Sonatas** / Kreisler, Rupp (piano) / Pearl 9400

Overview of Works (ca. 1905–1935)

Fritz Kreisler infused his original compositions with the qualities that made him personally popular: warmth, charm, wit, and bittersweet sentimentality. Most of his scores are small, colorful pieces for violin and piano, what critic Harold Schonberg described as "transfigured salon music." They may be modest, but they are neither simple to play nor simple-minded. Kreisler employed the same kinds of abrupt modulations, misplaced accents, and cross rhythms that marked the music of Richard Strauss. As a composer, Kreisler kept pace with the trends among the leading conservative composers of his time and Viennese heritage.

Kreisler wrote a *String Quartet in A minor* in an early-Straussian mode and two melodic operettas, *Apple Blossoms* and *Sissy*, in the manner of Franz Lehár and Oscar Straus. (The 1936 film *The King Steps Out* is nothing more than song arrangements by Dorothy Fields of existing Kreisler pieces.)

The cadenzas he prepared for concertos by Mozart, Viotti, Beethoven, and Brahms were crafted especially for his own playing style: aristocratic yet sweet-toned, and technically challenging. Kreisler's original pieces, on the other hand, are more circumspect in terms of technique. Many do pose challenges, but the main point is to maintain an ingratiating, *gemütlich* style.

This is particularly true of the charming Viennese pieces for which he is best remembered: the humorous and sparkling *Caprice Viennois*, and the waltzes *Liebesfreud*, *Liebesleid*, and *Schön Rosmarin*. Kreisler originally passed off *Liebesfreud* and *Liebesleid* as "rediscovered" manuscripts of Joseph Lanner, the waltz-band leader who worked with Johann Strauss I. In fact, the bulk of Kreisler's original music first appeared under the names of obscure, long-dead composers; Kreisler admitted to the ruse in 1935, saying that he thought it would be unseemly for his name to appear so many times on his own programs. Now they are listed as "in the style of" the composers to whom Kreisler made the attributions—as if such figures as Pugnani, Porpora, Dittersdorf, and Francoeur had identifiably individual styles that could be imitated. In truth, each piece is in one of Kreisler's two pseudo-Classical styles: noble, formal items designed to emphasize his singing line (the "W.F. Bach" *Grave*, the "Martini" *Andantino*), and technical showpieces (the "Pugnani" *Praeludium and Allegro*).

Kreisler also showed off his technique in such character pieces as *Tambourin Chinois*, *La Gitana*, and the *Recitativo and Scherzo-Caprice*, as well as in his many legitimate transcriptions of works by the likes of Falla, Albéniz, and Dvořák. *—James Reel*

Recommended:

○ **The Kreisler Album** / Perlman, Sanders / 2003 / EMI 62601

○ **Kreisler Plays Kreisler** / Kreisler, etc. / 1996 / BMG 68448

○ **The Kreisler Album** / Bell, Coker / 1996 / London 444409

○ **Kreisler: Famous Violin Transcriptions** / Sitkovetsky, Canino / Orfeo 48831

CHAMBER MUSIC

Liebesfreud (Love's Joy), Liebesleid (Love's Sorrow), for violin & piano (before 1910)

Fritz Kreisler was one of the twentieth century's most celebrated violinists, with a touring career that began in 1887 after he quit taking lessons at the Paris Conservatory at the age of 12. He might have been excused for thinking that they had nothing more to teach him, for he had already shared in the school's first prize that year. Kreisler practiced very little and never took another violin lesson, but his was a talent both gigantic and absolutely natural.

In Kreisler's day the concerts given by a touring violin virtuoso had a more popular tone than they would today; typically the program would include a number of short pieces that would please the crowd and let the performer show off technique or milk a few extra drops of sentiment. Kreisler, a gifted composer whose works in the styles of various earlier eras fooled even top musicologists until he owned up to the hoax in 1935, wrote many of these showpieces for himself. Without a doubt the two most popular are this *Liebesfreud* ("Love's Joy) and its companion *Liebesleid* ("Love's Sorrow"), both for violin and piano. Simple pieces with little syncopations that open out into vibrato-drenched passages that are like big teardrops, they still appear on the recordings of many a violinist, even as the performance environment that gave birth to them has largely faded away. *—AMG*

Recommended:

- ○ **The Kreisler Album** / Bell, Coker / 1996 / London 444409
- ○ **Szeryng plays Kreisler and other Treasures** / Szeryng, Reiner / 1995 / Mercury 434351
- ○ **Tango Song and Dance** / Mutter, Orkis / 2003 / DG 000005802

Praeludium and Allegro in the Style of Pugnani, for violin & piano (1910)

Liebesleid, *Liebesfreud*, and *Caprice viennois* may well be the most widely known and dearly beloved of Fritz Kreisler's many short pieces for violin and piano, but of all those pieces, it is without a doubt *Praeludium and Allegro* that an aspiring young student violinist will most ardently desire to sink his or her teeth into. *Praeludium and Allegro* is one of those Kreisler works originally attributed to eighteenth century composers when first published in 1905 (in this case, the obscure Italian violinist/composer Gaetano Pugnani); these works have come to be collectively described as pieces "in the style of...," though even that can be somewhat misleading, as Kreisler's original intent, in 1905, was to convince people that he had found a bunch of old, unknown manuscripts and arranged them freely in his own style—the result is a true stylistic hodgepodge.

Praeludium and Allegro is, as its title indicates, a piece in two sections. The first is a firm declaration, in quarter notes, whose stern manner softens just a little as the section progresses but reasserts itself at the dramatic close. The second is a quick-paced affair in 16th notes, eventually building up to a flash-and-dazzle quasi-cadenza, over a rumbling dominant pedal-point in the bass register of the piano, and a strong-willed, double-stop-ridden final issue of the theme. *—Blair Johnston*

Recommended:

- ○ **The Kreisler Album** / Bell, Coker / 1996 / London 444409
- ○ **Encore!** / Midori, McDonald / 1992 / Sony 52568

Schön Rosmarin, for violin & piano (before 1905)

Fritz Kreisler found it amusing (and, happily enough, entirely beneficial to his career) to bend the truth when it came to questions of musical authorship; critics and historians still love to pull out and dust off the ethical debate that raged when, in 1935, Kreisler admitted that he himself had composed most of the delightful miniatures for violin and piano that he had for decades been passing off as arrangements of other composers' works (Kreisler could never understand how anybody had actually been taken in by his ploy). Fewer people remember, however, how a quarter of a century earlier it had come to light that three pieces for violin and piano—then known, and still sometimes referred to, as the *Three Old Viennese Melodies* (First published in 1905), of which *Schön Rosmarin* is the third—credited to nineteenth century composer Josef Lanner were actually penned by Kreisler. When, exactly, Kreisler wrote these three delightful musical truffles is unknown; they were certainly well-established parts of his own performing repertory when, on September 15, 1910, Kreisler first copyrighted them in his own name.

Lanner was famous almost exclusively for his Ländler and his waltzes, and *Schön Rosmarin* is an example of the latter, cast by Kreisler in three musical paragraphs. Listening to Kreisler himself playing the piece, one is struck by the amazing elasticity of rhythm throughout the opening Grazioso passage—filled with leggiero running eighth notes (marked piano by Kreisler) that every so often make room for a delightful Luftpause after one or another of several upward melodic gestures. In the more robust middle section (forte, meno mosso), Kreisler's famous "detached" style of bowing is put on display as the broken-up hemiola gestures—making two measures of 3/4 meter into one large measure of 3/2—unfold. As this meno mosso moves forward, Kreisler allows the music to move away a little bit from otherwise ever-present G major for the first and only time; with his characteristic simplicity of approach and good-naturedness, however, he almost immediately slides right back into the home key with a final, pianissimo toss-off of the hemiola melody (typically, Kreisler himself ignores the dynamic change). A literal reprise of the opening Grazioso draws a conclusion that embodies, perfectly, the essence of latter-day Viennese *gemütlichkeit*. *—Blair Johnston*

Recommended:

- ○ **The Kreisler Album** / Bell, Coker / 1996 / London 444409
- ○ **Kreisler Plays Kreisler** / Kreisler, Lamson / 1996 / BMG 68448

Gidon Kremer

b. Feb. 27, 1947, Riga, Latvia

Violinist

Gidon Kremer's technical brilliance, inward but passionate playing, and commitment to both new works and new interpretations of old works have made him one of the most respected violinists in the world today. Kremer was born on February 27, 1947, in Riga, Latvia, which was then part of the Soviet Union. Kremer's parents were both symphony violinists, and, as with so many virtuosi, Kremer's gift was apparent almost immediately after a violin was put in his hands. His grandfather, Georg Bruckner, concertmaster of the Riga Opera, is credited by many with having guided the development of Kremer's formidable talent. He won the first prize of the Latvian Republic at age sixteen, and entered the Moscow Conservatory to study under the legendary violinist David Oistrakh.

Oistrakh taught Kremer for eight years, and eventually offered him a position as an assistant after he graduated. By that time, however, Kremer had already won numerous violin competitions (most notably the 1970 Tchaikovsky Competition, which he won over the also extraordinary Vladimir Spivakov), and his star was rising as a soloist; indeed, the teacher sometimes served as the student's accompanist, for Oistrakh was launching a conducting career at the time. Around that time, Kremer was denied permission to travel abroad. Allowed to leave the country in 1975, Kremer became a sensation in the West, when the star German conductor Herbert von Karajan in 1976 proclaimed Kremer the greatest violinist in the world after recording the Brahms violin concerto with him.

He eventually became one of the proudest advocates for the music of Soviet composers such as Alfred Schnittke, Sofia Gubaydulina, and Arvo Pärt.

Kremer kept apartments around the world after his exile, but became particularly fond of a town in Austria called Lockenhaus. He founded the Lockenhaus Chamber Music Festival there in 1981, but ended the festival in 1990, deciding to stop before the task became too exhausting. As a violinist, Kremer has never settled for the status quo. Always a champion of the new and the rare, he has rhetorically asked "Why ride the same old warhorses to success?" In the late 1990s, he created the punningly named Kremerata Baltica with a group of young Latvian players; the group's recordings of Pärt and Astor Piazzolla placed them out in front of two of the hottest trends of the twentieth century's end.

Kremer enjoys thumbing his nose at conventional wisdom, regularly creating radical reinterpretations of the classics. Sometimes these have created controversy, as in his 1980 recording of the Beethoven *Violin Concerto* with somewhat bizarre cadenzas by Schnittke. Whatever critics mey say, Kremer's performances are never boring. He disdains virtuosity for virtuosity's sake, but is nonetheless one of the most technically proficient violinists in the world. His playing tends toward a thoughtful austerity rather than the extroversion of a Jascha Heifetz, but when he is in top form he is a mesmerizing performer. *—Andrew Lindemann Malone*

Recommended:

- ○ **Hommage to Piazzolla** / Kremer, etc. / 1996 / Nonesuch 79407
- ○ **Silencio** / Klas (cond.), Kremer, Grindenko, Kremerata Baltica / 2000 / Nonesuch 79582
- ○ **Nono: La lontanaza; Hay que caminar** / Kremer, Grindenko (piano) / DG 000140902
- ○ **Gubaidulina: Offertorium; Hommage to T.S. Eliot** / Dutoit (cond.), Kremer, BSO / DG 427336

Ernst Krenek

b. Aug. 23, 1900, Vienna, Austria, **d.** Dec. 23, 1991, Palm Springs, CA

Composer: Opera, Choral

A study of Viennese-born composer Ernst Krenek's prodigious output is rather like a study of twentieth century music in microcosm. Krenek moved with ease through the various aesthetic and stylistic changes that marked that turbulent century, taking what he considered the best features of each and fusing them into a new language all his own. Born in August of 1900, Krenek began musical training at the age of six, and later studied privately with Franz Schreker in Vienna before enrolling for formal training with the same at the Berlin Conservatory in 1920.

Krenek's music of the early 1920s (including the *Symphony No.1* from 1921 and the first two string quartets) is chromatically charged and rather angst-ridden; however, a 1924 trip to France, during which he was exposed to the more utilitarian, entertaining aspects of Parisian music (and Stravinsky's neo-Classicism in particular) encouraged him to explore a more accessible style. In 1927 the opera *Jonny spielt auf*, which fuses jazz idioms to Krenek's own brand of tonality, made Krenek a household name; the work was such a popular success that it eventually received performances in over a hundred cities in eighteen different languages.

From 1925 to 1927 Krenek lived in Kassel and Wiesbaden, serving as assistant manager of those city's operas. After returning to Vienna in 1928 Krenek began questioning his own musical aesthetic, and, upon meeting Alban Berg and Anton Webern, made a serious study of the Second Vienesse School's 12-tone techniques. By 1931, when he began composing the opera *Karl V* (in celebration of the unifying virtues of Catholicism, as opposed to the degeneration of Germanic society in the 1930s), Krenek was convinced of the merits of serial composition; the opera stands as his first thoroughly dodecaphonic work. Nazi officials were not oblivious to the political subtext of the opera, and the planned 1934 Vienna premiere of the work was cancelled by the authorities. Krenek visited the United States in 1937, and when Hitler invaded Poland, Krenek was expelled from Austria and moved across the Atlantic permanently.

Krenek divided the remainder of his life between active composition (he remained prolific until his death in 1991) and teaching duties (first at Vassar College in New York, and later at Hamline University in Minneapolis and as guest professor/lecturer at many other American institutions). Krenek was an American citizen from 1945 on.

In the 1950s and 1960s Krenek began to explore electronic composition (e.g. *Spiritus intelligentiae Sanctus* for voices and electronic sounds in 1956), and also aleatoric (chance) music (e.g. the 1957 work *Sestina*). During the last decades of his life Krenek scrupulously avoided all compositional "trends" and "systems," choosing instead to rely on his own musical wits.

In 1992, one year after his death, Krenek's remains were transferred to the city of Vienna, where in later years he had come to be honored as befits a musician of his stature. —*Blair Johnston*

Overview of Works (1921–1988)

In the long career of the prolific Austrian-American composer Ernst Krenek, most of the major trends of twentieth century music can be discerned. Works like the two early *Concerti Grossi* (1921 and 1924) were written under the influence of French neo-Classicism. His colossal *Symphony No. 2* (1922) follows the in the path of the monumental works of Bruckner and Mahler. His opera *Jonny spielt auf* (1925–26) fuses the verismo of Puccini with, as Krenek put it "the condiments of jazz." After the income he earned from the enormously successful *Jonny* allowed him to move to Vienna in the late 1920s, Krenek cultivated a lushly melodic and richly harmonic style reminiscent of Austrian Romanticism at its height, as in his song cycle *Reisebuch auf den österreichischen Alpen, Der Wein* (1929). But by the early 1930s, Krenek began to utilize Schoenberg's serial method of composition. This great work of this period, his political opera *Karl V* (1930–33), was so musically advanced that it could not receive its intended premiere in the increasingly repressive Vienna of the 1930s and was instead premiered in Prague in June 1938. After Germany annexed what it called the Sudentenland later that same year, Krenek fled Europe for the United States. Most of his works from the 1940s and early 1950s, such as the *Symphony No. 5* (1949) and the *Symphonic Elegy for Strings* (1946), were written using strict serial technique, but this technique did not obscure Krenek's deeply expressive lyricism. In the later 1950s and 1960s, Krenek began incorporating elements of chance into his technique, and works like *Horizon Circled* (1968) move from serial to aleotoric techniques. At the same time, Krenek even began exploring tape as a medium for musical expression in works such as *San Fernando Sequence* (1963). Despite this plethora of styles, however, Krenek's own identity as a composer with deep roots in the lyrical Romanticism of Austria is always audible. —*James Leonard*

Recommended:

- ○ **Krenek: Chamber Music For Strings** / Recherche Trio / 1994 / CPO 999197
- ○ **Krenek: Symphony 2** / Zagrosek (cond.), Leipzig Gewandhaus Orch. / 1997 / London 452479
- ○ **Krenek: String Quartets** / Petersen Quartet / 2003 / Capriccio 67015
- ○ **Krenek: Symphony 1 & 5** / Ukigaya (cond.), Hannover Radio SO / CPO 999359
- ○ **Krenek: Symphony 3; Potpourri** / Ukigaya (cond.), Hannover Radio SO / CPO 999236
- ○ **Krenek: 12-Tone Miniatures** / Blumenthal / 1997 / Gallante 1016
- ○ **Krenek: Complete String Quartets** / Sonare Qt. / MDG 4280

OPERA

Jonny spielt auf, Op. 45 (1925–1926)

Jonny spielt auf was an immense success at its premiere in Leipzig in February 1927. Yet, within the decade, Krenek was forced to flee from central Europe, his work banned by the Nazis.

After studies in Vienna with Franz Schreker, Krenek followed his teacher to Berlin in 1920 where he continued to work with him at the Academy of Music. In Berlin, Krenek became friendly with a number of musicians and composers of progressive leanings and, in doing so, gradually distanced himself from the lush, post-Romanticism of Schreker. From 1925 to 1927, Krenek served theaters in Kassel and Wiesbaden as conductor and composer. While his first opera *Der Sprung über den Schatten* employed jazz effects amidst an atonal score, he next turned to a more tonal context for *Jonny spielt auf*, perhaps to fashion a more congenial and accessible vessel for the jazz-flavored atmosphere of the libretto. This was the "jazz age" on the continent as well as in America and the public was eager to hear works which employed the new idioms.

For all its success in Germany and Austria, however, *Jonny* did not appeal to audiences in either Paris or at the Metropolitan Opera in 1929. The need to employ a white singer in black face for the title role was at least partly to blame. In Paris and at the Met, audiences were somewhat more sophisticated about authentic jazz and were less accepting of a score that offered only the trappings, but not the substance of real jazz.

The notion of a black musician as protagonist was not met with favor by the National Socialists either, and the enormous response given the work initially dwindled in the face of demonstrations, first erupting in Vienna in the winter of 1927–28. Nazi supporters protested the "introduction of Jewish-Nigger filth" to the operatic repertory and, subsequently, other venues were subject to outbreaks of violence. In 1938, Krenek's was declared *entartete Musik* (forbidden music), due in no small part to this score. That same year, the composer left for America where he taught (from necessity) and composed (largely for his own satisfaction), acquired citizenship in 1945, settling finally in California in 1947.

Although without doubt a period piece, *Jonny* has been the subject of renewed interest as the result of performance and recording projects exploring the vast amount of music suppressed by the Nazis. Dated in its use of jazz elements, the score nonetheless remains striking, its characters interesting, as well as quirky. The struggle of the real hero, the composer Max, to overcome his indecision, to integrate love of nature with a drive toward new expression in music, provides a viable text. Krenek's score fleshes out the story, providing for a satisfyingly provocative theatrical experience. Max finally departs for America with his beloved Anita, as Jonny once more strikes up on his jazz fiddle. A new time has arrived. —*Erik Eriksson*

Synopsis:

Part One, Scene One. High on a glacier's edge, Max, a composer, is struggling to climb the mountain when he meets the singer Anita, lost and frightened by the glacier's isolation. She pleads with him to take her back to her hotel, to the company of others. Max agrees, hoping to induce her to return some other time so that she can "see that it is beautiful."

Scene Two. The second scene shows the two now in love, he desiring her constant companionship, but she feeling constrained by his attentions. He gives her the manuscript of a new opera, but she doesn't wish to travel to Paris to sing it. Rather, she wishes that he would turn from the pursuit of fame and remain with her.

Scene Three. The scene opens to reveal a Paris hotel where a jazz band is playing. Jonny, a black musician, hopes that his liaison with the chambermaid Yvonne will give him access to the room of Daniello, whose violin he covets. Anita returns from the opera and prepares to return to Max, but is beset by Jonny, to whom she almost yields before being rescued by Daniello. Subsequently, Daniello seduces her while Jonny steals his violin and hides it in Anita's banjo case.

Scene Four. Despite a night of love, Anita prepares to return to Max. Daniello, his pride wounded, plans to get even, asking her for a ring as a remembrance. He discovers that his violin is missing and calls for the hotel's manager. The manager dismisses Yvonne, who knows nothing of what has happened. Anita hires Yvonne on the spot and begins to escort her away. Daniello slips Anita's ring to Yvonne, telling her to give it to Max. Jonny, meanwhile, resigns as house musician.

Part Two, Scene Five. Max is agonizing over Anita's delayed return, feeling that she is "slipping away" from him.

Scene Six. Max dreams that Anita will return and, when she does arrive, they reveal to each other their polarizing differences. He is not comfortable with the tumultuous world of people, while she believes that Max's steadfastness is really indecisiveness. Moreover, she is convinced that he must somehow find his own confidence. Yvonne, not grasping Daniello's purpose, gives Anita's ring to Max. Surmising how Daniello came into its possession, Max hastily departs for the comforting solitude of his beloved glacier. Jonny, who has followed Anita and Yvonne, appears and removes the stolen violin as Yvonne looks on, perplexed. Jonny tells her that all of value is now his. "The old world created it, but does not know what to do with it any longer."

Scene Seven. Max stands on the glacier where he wishes to end it all, but the voice of the glacier bids him "return to life... be not afraid!" Hearing Anita's voice through a loudspeaker at a nearby hotel, Max is again drawn to her. Jonny's music is heard on the radio, and Daniello, recognizing the sound of his instrument, summons the police.

Scene Eight. Jonny is running from the authorities. He drops his train ticket on the street, where it is soon found by the police.

Scene Nine. Jonny places the violin with Max's luggage. In the meantime, Max has resolved to accompany Anita to America, where she has a new job, but when the violin is discovered, Max is arrested. Daniello relates his vengeful plot to Anita. When he attempts to prevent the distraught Yvonne from going to the police, Daniello falls backward onto the tracks under an approaching train.

Scene Ten. Jonny is waiting outside the police station, looking to seize the violin once more. He assures Yvonne that he will free Max and climbs into the police auto taking Max to an interrogation. Max suddenly concludes that his plight has come about due solely to his passivity and he resolves to return to the train station. Jonny overcomes the police and the car disappears from sight.

Scene Eleven. Anita is waiting anxiously at the station. Max breathlessly arrives and leaps onto Anita's train as the chorus sings "The new time is nigh." *Jonny spielt auf*—Jonny strikes up the melody as the station clock turns into the globe and the crowd dances around it. The principal characters now all sing "So, Jonny has played for us to dance." As the opera concludes, Jonny emerges from between the curtains a final time to play his violin. —*Erik Eriksson*

Recommended:

○ **Krenek: Jonny spielt auf** / Hollreiser (cond.), Popp, Equiluz, Lear, Stewart, Vienna State Opera Orch. / 1993 / Vanguard 8048

○ **Krenek: Jonny spielt auf** / Zagrosek (cond.), Kruse, St. Hill, Korn, Weichert / 1993 / London 436631

CHORAL

Lamentatio Jeremiae Prophetae, Op. 93 (1941–1942)

The *Lamentatio Jeremiae Prophetae for chorus*, Op. 93, by Austrian American composer Ernst Krenek is, on the one hand, one of the most austere and severe works composed in the twentieth century, and on the other hand, one of the most emotionally and spiritually moving works of the twentieth century. Written in November 1941 when Krenek was living in exile in the United States, having left his beloved Austria after the rise of the National Socialists, Krenek's *Lamentatio Jeremiae Prophetae* (Lamentations of the Prophet Jeremiae) is a elegy for his lost homeland couched in the language of the Biblical prophet's lament for the fall of Jerusalem. Krenek had been studying the music of Ockeghem, and his *Lamentatio* is steeped in the linear counterpoint and floating rhythm of the late medieval period. At the same time, however, Krenek's harmonic language was suffused with the serial method of Schoenberg and the combination of the influences of Ockeghem and Schoenberg can be heard in every bar of the work. Setting texts he chose himself from the Book of Jeremiah, Krenek's a cappella work is arranged in three large sections that are subdivided into smaller subsections. The choral writing ranges from monody to 20 separate parts, but it is nevertheless always clear and lucid. —*James Leonard*

Recommended:

○ **Krenek: Lamentation of the Prophet Jeremiae** / Creed (cond.), RIAS-Kammerchor / HM 901551

Franz Krommer

b. Nov. 27, 1759, Kamenice u Trebice, Moravia, **d.** Jan. 8, 1831, Vienna, Austria
Composer: Concerto

Franz Krommer was considered a strong rival of Beethoven in the early nineteenth century, his string quartets especially being held in high esteem: more than a few contemporaries compared them with those of Haydn. In the decades following Krommer's death in 1831, however, his reputation faded, in large part because of the increasing dominance of Beethoven. Another factor that has hampered Krommer's popularity over the years is the variable appearance of his name. Instead of the German Franz Krommer, it is often stated as František Kramár, a Czech form of the name. Sometimes, however, both the German and Czech forms are combined, yielding the quaint Krommer-Kramár.

Born in the Moravian town of Kamenice (Kamenitz), Krommer divulged unusual talent early on and began studies in 1774 on the violin and organ with his uncle, Anton Matthias Krommer, composer and choirmaster at Turan. Through his uncle, Krommer became the temporary organist at Turan in 1777 or 1778. From his years of study with his uncle until about 1785, Krommer also took it upon himself to learn theory and composition. He traveled to Vienna in 1785, but could find no steady work during the year or so he spent there. He obtained an appointment as a violinist in the Court orchestra of the Duke of Styrum in Simontornya (now part of Hungary), in about 1786. Although Krommer's earliest surviving works appear to date to the early 1790s, some may actually come from this period since he typically sought publication years after composition. In 1788, Krommer was appointed music director of the Duke's orchestra, but he departed the post in 1790 to become concertmaster at the Pecs Cathedral. He would also take on assignments at two smaller courts nearby as concertmaster, beginning in 1793. He returned to Vienna in 1795, where as a composer with a growing reputation, he is thought to have taught composition for the next three years. In 1798, he was appointed concertmaster at the court of Duke Ignaz Fuchs, where he remained until 1810. This dozen-year period would prove a fertile one for Krommer, with the publication of his earliest symphonies, concertos, and nearly 50 of his more than 70 string quartets. In 1811, Krommer accepted the appointment of ballet concertmaster at the Vienna Hoftheater. Four years later, he accepted the post of Kammertürhüter (Chamber door guardian) to Emperor Franz I, which required much travel. Krommer accompanied the Hapsburg ruler to various European cities in France and Italy over the next two years. In 1818, Krommer was elevated to the rank of court composer and director of chamber music under Franz I, succeeding Leopold Kozeluch. He served in this post until his death in 1831. During this final period, his creative output declined: though the last several of his approximately ten symphonies appeared, he wrote but a handful of string quartets and other compositions. Stylistically, Krommer's music reflected the spirit of Haydn and Mozart rather than that of Beethoven. He wrote an array of compositions in most genres, but produced no operas or lieder. —*Robert Cummings*

CONCERTO

Clarinet Concerto in E flat major, Op. 36 (1803)

The two versions of Franz Krommer's name exist because, in common with many Bohemian composers of the time who found favor in Western countries, "František Vincenc Kramar" Germanized his name to Franz Vincenz Krommer. After a long stretch of dues-paying (mostly involving jobs in the wilder, eastern provinces of Hungary), he found favor in Vienna, around 1795, and became a favorite composer of Emperor Franz I, who named him court composer. By the time this concerto was written, he was widely famous in Europe and sometimes ranked with such geniuses as Mozart and Haydn; later, some would elevate him to a status similar to Beethoven's.

This concerto appeared in print in 1803. It is in the form of a standard Classical concerto, with a first movement that is long because it has a double exposition, one with orchestra only and the other featuring the soloist. Despite the form, there are ample anticipations of coming Romantic styles. These include a yearning second movement that begins with an astonishing pre-echo of Donizetti's bel canto operatic aria "Una furtiva lagrima."

The orchestra is relatively large, with a full standard woodwind section in twos, a pair of horns, and even brass and timpani, which were rare for wind concertos at the time. The opening Allegro movement is serious, with a mood similar to Mozart's *Prague Symphony* and a sense of the heroic. The Adagio movement is in song form, resembling an operatic aria of the time, and leads directly into a Rondo finale in moderately fast tempo. The proto-Romantic qualities of the music are most evident in the frequent and dramatic shifts to minor keys, which occur throughout.

The concerto is not a virtuoso work. Krommer's intent seemed to be to showcase the clarinet's strengths as a lyrical instrument, and the piece is indeed especially pretty. Even if Krommer no longer ranks with the giants of the Classical era, this concerto is nevertheless well worth hearing as a strong representative of the wind concerto in the age of Beethoven. —*Joseph Stevenson*

Recommended:

○ **Mozart & Krommer: Clarinet Concertos** / Faerber (cond.), Kam, Wurttenberg CO / 1998 / Teldec 21462

Concerto for 2 clarinets & orchestra in E flat major, Op. 35 (Feb. ?, ? 18??)

Franz Krommer (1759–1831) was a highly prolific composer who wrote a substantial number of string quartets and other works that were highly regarded at the time. But he made arguably far more daring advances in his superb wind music, whether in the form of serenades and other lighter genres for mixed wind ensemble or in a series of splendid clarinet concertos. Krommer's *Concerto for two clarinets in E flat*, Op. 35, dates from just a decade after Mozart's *Clarinet concerto*, but in style and idiom, it could hardly be more different. The orchestration, particularly in the majestic opening movement (Allegro) is calculated to create maximum effect, and even if some of the effects come straight from the opera stage, the solo writing for the two clarinets is both entertaining and ingenious. Neither part is more difficult or exposed than the other, and for much of the time both players are heard in close dialogue. The central Adagio already has a Beethovenian *gravitas* about it, but here again, Krommer demonstrates that from Mozart he had learned much about the clarinet's more somber and elegiac tonal possibilities. Next comes the finale, a lively Rondo, which imposes testing demands on the soloists through many bravura passages, at times exploiting almost the whole range of the clarinet. This impressive yet genial double concerto, with its martial gestures and fine vocalized solo lines, undoubtedly made a powerful impression upon two early German Romantic composers, Weber and Spohr, both of whom wrote extensively for the clarinet. —*Michael Jameson*

Recommended:

○ **Krommer & Rossini: Works for Clarinet & Orchestra** / Faerber (cond.), Meyer, Wurttemberg CO / 1988 / EMI 49397

○ **Kramár & Krommer: Clarinet Concertos** / Pesek (cond.), Mares, Hlavac, Prague CO / 2003 / Supraphon 3748

Concerto for 2 clarinets & orchestra in E flat major, Op. 91 (ca. 1815)

The second of Krommer's concertos for two clarinets is musically more advanced than his first. The *Concerto in E flat major*, Op. 91, was written sometime around 1815, about the same period in which Weber wrote his clarinet works. It shares features with Weber's works, such as full use of the instrument's range, graceful ornamentation, and passages that range from legato to staccato to long, sustained trills. The opening Allegro is unusual in that the clarinets begin with the orchestra for a brief introduction of the main theme, which is followed by a developmental section for orchestra alone before the clarinets present the true exposition. The minor key, middle movement, Adagio, starts out sounding very much like a Classical period funeral march. That mood is broken when the clarinets enter and create a sweet duet. The final movement, like the last movement of Weber's *Clarinet Concerto No. 2*, is given the tempo marking Alla Polacca; however, Krommer does not use this to indicate a mazurka-like rondo movement. It is in 3/4 meter and is lively, containing more ornamentation than the other movements, but the melodies do not have that emphasis on the second beat that a mazurka would have. And although the first and second tutti sections are identical, there is really nothing else that would mark the movement as a rondo. Throughout the concerto, Krommer's writing for the two soloists is very much in the bel canto spirit, with their parts working together as dialogue and duet, demonstrating why Krommer's wind concertos are generally held to be his best works. —*Patsy Morita*

Recommended:

- ○ **Krommer & Rossini: Works for Clarinet & Orchestra** / Faerber (cond.), Meyer, Wurttemberg CO (Heilbronn) / 1988 / EMI 49397
- ○ **Krommer: Concertos for 2 Clarinets & Orchestra** / Hauschild (cond.), Klocker, Wandel, Stuttgart SWRSO / 1996 / Koch Schwann 310772

Kronos Quartet

f. 1974, Oakland, CA

Ensemble

No one seems quite clear as to whether they're a classical group with jazz and populist leanings, or a populist band with classical expertise. Whatever their methods and motivation, the Kronos Quartet has blurred musical categories for decades and attracted interest from audiences who never knew what a string quartet was. Respected as one of the most charismatic and innovative ensembles performing today, Kronos was founded at Mills College in 1974 by violinist David Harrington. By the end of the 1970s, Hank Dutt (viola), John Sherba (violin), and Joan Jeanrenaud (cello) rounded out the group's permanent personnel. Since then, Kronos has aggressively commissioned new music, including over 450 of their repertory of 600 pieces. This unprecedented commissioning project has been credited with reviving and revitalizing a stagnating medium.

The ensemble made a quick impression with guest appearances on recordings by Warren Benson, Dane Rudhyar, and David Grisman before cutting their own debut on the Sounds Wonderful label in 1982. Since then, Kronos has recorded over thirty albums for Nonesuch, receiving six Grammy nominations and one award, for Best New Composition (*Different Trains* by Steve Reich). Kronos specializes in works of the twentieth century, ranging from jazz pioineers Ornette Coleman and John Zorn to Jimi Hendrix, Webern, and Bartók. The group has devoted entire albums to diverse figures such as Theolonious Monk (*Monk Suite*, 1985), Bill Evans (*Music of Bill Evans*, 1986), Alfred Schnittke (*The Complete String Quartets*, 1998), and Philip Glass (several, including *Dracula*, 1999). For their recording *Black Angels* (1990), the quartet provided spirited, effective accompaniment to a scratchy, decades-old recording of American iconoclast composer Charles Ives singing one of his own songs.

Kronos has been profiled on the television show *CBS Sunday Morning*, produced their own syndicated radio program that combined interview and performance segments, and been nominated for Grammy awards on a regular basis. In 1999 Joan Jeanrenaud began a sabbatical leave, and before it was over she had resigned, no longer wishing to maintain Kronos' active travel, performance, and rehearsal schedule. Jeanrenaud was replaced by Jennifer Culp. The quartet's *Nuevo* album of 2003 was a striking, genre-crossing survey of the music of Mexico. —*Ron Wynn*

Recommended:

- ○ **Black Angels** / Kronos Quartet / 1990 / Nonesuch 79242
- ○ **Feldman: Piano & String Quartet** / Takahashi, Kronos Quartet / 1993 / Nonesuch 79320
- ○ **Adams: John's Book Of Alleged Dances; Gnarly Buttons** / Adams (cond.), Kronos Quartet, London Sinfonietta / 1998 / Nonesuch 79465
- ○ **Kronos Quartet: 25 Years** / Kronos Quartet, etc. / 1998 / Nonesuch 79504
- ○ **Nuevo** / Kronos Quartet, Warner, Conte, Flores, Cafe Tacuba / 2003 / Nonesuch 79649
- ○ **Mugam Sayagi: Music of Franghiz Ali-Zadeh** / Kronos Quartet, Ali-Zadeh / 2005 / Nonesuch 79804

Rafael Kubelik

b. Jun. 29, 1914, Bychony, Czechoslovakia, **d.** Aug. 11, 1996, Lucerne, Switzerland

Conductor

A top conductor of large orchestral works of the late nineteenth century, Rafael Kubelik was born near Prague in 1914. The son of violinist Jan Kubelik (1880–1940), he studied violin, piano, composition, and conducting at the Prague Conservatory. He made his debut before the Czech Philharmonic Orchestra at age 19, and in 1939 became the music director of the National Opera in Brno, Czechoslovakia. In 1941, he became the music director of the Czech Philharmonic Orchestra, a post he held until 1948. In 1948, with the establishment of a Communist dictatorship in Czechoslovakia, Kubelik left his homeland and became an exile for the next 40 years.

Kubelik's three years with the Chicago Symphony Orchestra, beginning in 1950, were frustrating. A persuasive rather than a dictatorial figure and a diplomat rather than a martinet, he lacked the ability to control the orchestra. Additionally, Kubelik's musical sensibilities had been shaped in the early twentieth century rather than the late nineteenth, as had been the case with his immediate predecessors, and he programmed far too much modern music for the taste of critics and subscribers. Kubelik was fortunate that his appointment coincided with the orchestra making its first move into long-playing records for the Mercury label. Among his two dozen recordings with the Chicago Symphony Orchestra was a riveting performance of Mussorgsky's *Pictures at an Exhibition* and one of Smetana's *My Fatherland*. Ultimately the fit just wasn't right between Kubelik and the orchestra, and he gave up the appointment.

Kubelik served for three years, from 1955 through 1958, as music director of the Covent Garden Opera in London, where he conducted the British premieres of Janáček's *Jenůfa* and Berlioz's *Les troyens*. From 1961 until 1979, he was music director of the Bavarian Radio Symphony in Munich, with which he also recorded extensively (for Deutsche Grammophon), and was the principal conductor of the Metropolitan Opera in New York during the 1973–74 season as well. He was a most-welcomed guest conductor in Chicago on many occasions throughout his later career, appeared with virtually all of the world's major orchestras, and recorded extensively in England, America, and Germany. In 1973, he became a Swiss citizen.

Rafael Kubelik embodied a tradition of robust post-Romantic music-making that was ideally suited to the recording medium as well as the concert hall. He was celebrated as a master of rich orchestral color, which was brought out most vividly in the late Romantic and post-Romantic scores for which he was most popular. This included much of the Russian repertory and virtually all of the nationalist music of the era, especially the work of his fellow countrymen Antonin Dvořák, Leoš Janáček, and Bedřich Smetana. He recorded the latter's *Má Vlast* at least four times on as many different labels, the last at a live performance in Prague during 1990 at a concert commemorating the liberation of the country from Communist rule released on the Supraphon label. The sheer number of his recordings that remain in print, and their equal distribution between the "historical" and modern sections of classical music departments, speaks volumes about his enduring popularity and the validity of his performances and interpretations. His complete Beethoven and Mahler cycles remained in print for many years. Although relatively little of his operatic work was preserved on record, the small number of these are also well-regarded, especially his *Rigoletto*.

With the fall of the Communist dictatorship, Kubelik, who had been intermittently ill for several years, returned to Czechoslovakia for the first time in four decades with the intention of resuming composing full-time. As it was, he had authored five operas, several symphonies, and various works for soloist and orchestra, vocal works, and chamber pieces. —*Bruce Eder*

Recommended:

- ○ **Smetana: Symphonic Poems** / Kubelik (cond.), Czech PO / 2002 / Classica d'Oro 1062
- ○ **Smetana: Má Vlast** / Kubelik (cond.), Czech PO / 1990 / Supraphon 111208
- ○ **Mahler: Symphony 1** / Kubelik (cond.), Bavarian RSO / 2000 / Audite 95467
- ○ **Smetana: Má Vlast** / Kubelik (cond.), Chicago SO / 1996 / Mercury 434379
- ○ **Janáček: Missa Glagolitica** / Kubelik (cond.), Lear, Hafliger, Rossel-Majdan, Crass, Bavarian RSO & Chorus / 2002 / DG 463672
- ○ **Dvořák: Slavonic Dances; Overtures; Symphonic Poems** / Kubelik (cond.), Bavarian RSO / DG 469366

Friedrich Kuhlau

b. Sep. 11, 1786, Uelzen, Germany, **d.** Mar. 12, 1832, Copenhagen, Denmark

Composer

Friedrich Kuhlau is generally remembered for his piano music, particularly because of its pedagogical value. His sonatas and sonatinas are not difficult and offer musical an excellent training ground for the more challenging works of Beethoven. Yet his music can also stand on its own, as his *Piano Concerto in C*, from 1810, and many other solo keyboard works amply demonstrate. While the concerto is not on the level with Beethoven's last three, it is a composition of considerable artistic merit. His flute works are also of generally high quality, featuring fine writing that demonstrates a grasp of the instrument's expressive range. Kuhlau wrote operas and other dramatic works, most of which are finely-crafted; the best of them fully on the level of his piano music.

Friedrich Kuhlau was born in the North German town of Uelzen, near Hannover. His father was a musician in a military band, and of necessity often had to relocate his family. After moving to Lüneburg when he was seven, Friedrich slipped on ice in the street and sustained an injury to his right eye, causing blindness in that eye for life. At 14, he finished his schooling in Brunswick at the Katharineum-gymnasium, and having shown unusual musical talent throughout his childhood, he began composition studies in Hamburg with Schwenke.

Over the next several years, Kuhlau composed some songs and chamber music, and in 1804 began regularly appearing as a concert pianist. Many of his works at this time and throughout his whole career were written for flute, and for years it was believed that Kuhlau was himself a fine flutist. He could not play the instrument, however, but wrote works for it to earn money.

In 1810, Kuhlau traveled to Copenhagen to flee the invading troops of Napoleon. He had completed his *Piano Concerto* earlier that year and his performances of it helped him obtain an appointment as a non-salaried musician in the Danish Court in 1812. He supported himself by giving recitals and teaching music. Two years later, he wrote the score for the singspiel *The Robber's Castle*, which was a huge success. Around this time, his parents and younger sister joined him, all of whom he had to support.

After taking a high-paying post as singing teacher at the Royal Theater in the years 1816–17, Kuhlau left it, eventually obtaining another with the Court, which required him to compose works occasionally. One of them would be his opera *The Magic Harp*, which was a failure owing mainly to its controversial libretto. His next opera, *Elisa* (1820), fared as poorly.

Kuhlau traveled to Vienna in 1821 (for four months) and in 1825, at which time he befriended Beethoven. The year before, his opera *Lulu* had premiered in Hamburg with great success. After returning to Copenhagen, Kuhlau wrote the incidental music to Boye's play, *William Shakespeare*, and scored another success. Still supporting his parents, he worked diligently, turning out another opera in 1827, *Hugo and Adelheid*, which failed.

In 1828, Kuhlau was given an honorary professorship that yielded substantial remuneration for him. The same year saw the premiere of his *The Elf's Hill*, a singspiel that was a huge success. A series of tragedies ensued: Kuhlau lost both parents in 1830, and the following year his house burned down, the composer suffering a resultant chest ailment that afflicted him until his death. *—Robert Cummings*

Overview of Works (1803–1830)

Friedrich Kuhlau (1786–1832) was a German composer whose career flowered in Denmark following an abrupt departure from his homeland in 1810, owing to the occupation by Napoleon's troops. He is best known for his piano music, though he wrote operas, songs, and a fair number of chamber works. Several of his many piano sonatas and sonatinas, for both solo and piano four-hands, have etched out a place in the repertory and served as teaching instruments to amateur pianists, since their technical demands are relatively few.

One of the composer's earliest important works was his *Piano Concerto in C major*, Op. 7. Written in 1810, Kuhlau's work shows the influence of the giant he greatly admired, Ludwig van Beethoven, who had by that time already composed all his concertos. Kuhlau's C major concerto features a long first movement (a typical feature in many of the composer's opening movements), an attractive Adagio middle panel, and a Rondo finale, marked Allegro.

None of Kuhlau's operas have entered the repertory, despite music which is generally imaginative and well crafted. His first, *The Robbers' Castle* (1815), and his fourth, *Lulu* (1824), were received enthusiastically at the outset, but *The Magic Harp* (1817), *Elisa* (1820), and *Hugo and Adelheid* (1827) were failures. Kuhlau did not succeed in his operas largely because the texts he selected were weak. Much of his vocal writing is good and might have served him well with different, more dynamic librettos.

He did have some genuine successes on the stage, though. Probably Kuhlau's greatest was his incidental score for *The Elf Mound*. While there are echoes of Beethoven, especially in the big overture, the work is dramatically effective in its frequent use of Danish folk music. The overture is quite popular in Denmark, viewed by the citizenry much the way the Finns regard *Finlandia*.

Among Kuhlau's more enduring piano works are the *Three Easy Sonatas*, Op. 59 (1824) and *Three Sonatinas*, Op. 60 (1824), charming, unpretentious works of some substance. He also wrote some attractive variation works, including the *Variations on a Danish Folksong*, Op. 30 (1820) and *Ten Variations on a Theme From Der Freischutz*, Op. 48 (1822).

Kuhlau composed a fair number of popular works for the flute, an instrument, contrary to long-held belief, that he could not play. His 1827 sonata for flute and piano, the so-called *Grande sonate concertante*, Op. 85, is one of his finest chamber compositions. Kuhlau's finely imagined piano quartets, in *C minor*, Op. 32 (1820), *A major*, Op. 50 (1822), and *G minor*, Op. 108 (1833), began receiving some renewed interest in the latter half of the twentieth century, both in concert and on recordings.

Kuhlau also wrote a large number of songs, their scoring often favoring a quartet of male voices, as in the *Nine Songs*, Op. 82 (1827) and the *Eight Songs*, Op. 89 (1826). While his compositions in this genre are often compelling, like his operas, they are ultimately not particularly memorable. *—Robert Cummings*

Recommended:

- ○ **Kuhlau: Sonatas, Variations & Rondos, Vol. 1** / Brigandi / Nuova Era 7379
- ○ **Kuhlau: Sonatas for Flute & Piano** / Grodd, Napoli / 2002 / Naxos 555346
- ○ **Kuhlau: Overtures** / Schoenwandt (cond.), Danish Radio SO / 1998 / Chandos 9648
- ○ **Kuhlau: Flute Quintets 1–3** / Rafn, Sjoegren, Rasmussen, Johansen / 1995 / Naxos 553303
- ○ **Kuhlau: Complete Violin Sonatas** / Bratchkova, Meyer-Hermann / CPO 999363
- ○ **Piano Music** / Ponti / Unicorn Kanchana 9110

Johann Kuhnau

b. Apr. 6, 1660, Geising, Germany, **d.** Jun. 5, 1722, Leipzig, Germany
Composer: Keyboard

A German Baroque composer and keyboard player, Johann Kuhnau was a man of many gifts. A learned intellectual, a writer on music, linguist, philosopher, author of a satiric novel, and successful lawyer, he is remembered today mostly for his keyboard compositions. Kuhnau, however, was an important and influential voice in the German Baroque, particularly in Leipzig, where he was Bach's immediate predecessor as Kantor at the Thomasschule. He came from a family of musicians and showed an early aptitude for the art. Kuhnau studied music throughout his youth, was a chorister at the Kreuzschule in Dresden, and became a fine organist, but he entered the University of Leipzig as a law student, getting his degree in 1688. In 1689 he married, and over the course of the years had eight children. The years that followed, from 1689 until 1699, were very successful. He was well respected as a musician, particularly as a performer on the organ and as a teacher of music, and his law practice thrived. He wrote his satirical novel, entitled *Der Musicalishe Quack-Salber* (The Musical Quack), and he studied mathematics, Hebrew, and Greek, French, and Italian.

In 1701 Kuhnau was appointed Kantor at the Thomaskirche and Leipzig University's director of music. He taught music, directed performances, and composed. His competition in those years included the young Telemann, who entered law school in 1701. Telemann founded a collegium musicum, a musical performance association, to rival that of Kuhnau, and even encroached upon some of Kuhnau's duties as Kantor. Kuhnau suffered from severe ill health in his later years, and the city of Leipzig even offered Telemann Kuhnau's position in the event of the latter's death. Johann Friedrich Fasch and Melchior Hoffmann were also active in Leipzig and also numbered among Kuhnau's rivals; in the case of the former, who had been Kuhnau's pupil, the sting must have been especially acute. Nevertheless, Kuhnau was widely admired by his contemporaries and successors, and many German composers of the early eighteeth century either studied with him or otherwise showed his influence.

Kuhnau composed sacred music, secular vocal music, and keyboard music, but all that remains of his output are his keyboard music and his sacred cantatas. The *Biblische Historien* (Biblical Histories), his last set of keyboard works, are his most famous compositions; these are programmatic works that depict episodes from the Old Testament. They are extremely complex and inventive texturally. Also included in his keyboard works is a set of seven dance suites called the *Neue Clavier Übung*; both these and the *Biblische Historien* are notable for their incorporation of instrumental-music devices into keyboard music. Kuhnau's sacred cantatas likely had some influence upon Bach's own Leipzig works in the form. *—Rita Laurance*

Overview of Works (ca. 1683–1722)

Though often remembered merely as Bach's predecessor as cantor of the famous Thomasschule in Leipzig, Johann Kuhnau (1660–1722) was a considerable composer in his own right. His family originally hailed from Bohemia, but the Counter Reformation forced them to leave. Kuhnau therefore received his initial musical training in Dresden, where it seems probable he came into contact with the elderly Heinrich Schütz, an encounter that provides a direct link between Schütz and Bach, the two greatest exponents of German Protestant Baroque sacred music. Subsequently, Kuhnau studied music in Italy and law in Leipzig. One of the last great musical polymaths, he was also a mathematician, a theorist, a linguist, and the author of a novel (*Der musicalische Quack-Salber*, 1700) satirizing the superficial musical trends of his day. In 1684, he was appointed to the organ post at the Thomaskirche, and became cantor in 1701 following the death of the incumbent Johann Schelle. Kuhnau remained in the post until his own death 21 years later.

Kuhnau's musical output largely reflects his training as a keyboard player and his duties as cantor. His published keyboard works, which include two volumes of suites (*Neuer Clavier-Übung*, 1689 and 1692), and two of sonatas (*Frische Clavier Früchte*, 1696, and the *Biblischer Historien*, 1700), all precede his appointment as cantor in Leipzig. The suites, which the title (Keyboard Study) and composer's preface show to have a didactic purpose, follow the pattern established during the seventeenth century: an opening prelude (or praeludium as Kuhnau terms it) followed by a group of dances, generally in the standard sequence of allemande, courante, sarabande, and gigue. The *Biblischer Historien* are an interesting example of a genre popular in the late seventeenth century—the pictorial description of biblical and other events through instrumental music. (Biber's *"Mystery" [or Rosary] Sonatas for violin* are the most famous example.)

Kuhnau wrote a considerable body of sacred music which, unfortunately, has suffered almost complete neglect until recent years. These works are mostly cantatas and motets, but Kuhnau also composed a large-scale *St. Mark Passion*, first given in 1721; it signals the introduction of such works to the Holy Week literature in Leipzig—an innovation triumphantly capitalized upon by his successor.

Paradoxically, Kuhnau's cantatas display many of the Italianate operatic traits of which he was so critical in his theoretical writings. However, his word-setting is meticulously observed and carefully molded to the German language, thus following closely a characteristic of the sacred works of Schütz. In form they follow a close alternation of recitative and short aria or arioso sections in which instrumental ritornellos frequently imitate the vocal line. Orchestral scoring is often modest, but works such as the festive Ascension cantata, *Ihr Himmel jubilirt von oben* (1717), are more lavishly scored; in this instance two recorders, three trumpets, and timpani join the strings. —*Brian Robins*

Recommended:

- ○ **Kuhnau: Sacred Music** / King (cond.), King's Consort / 1998 / Hyperion 67059
- ○ **Kuhnau: Neue Clavier-Übung, Vol. 1** / Micheli / 2000 / Dynamic 265

KEYBOARD

Biblical Sonatas (ca. 1690–1700)

Johann Kuhnau (1660–1722) is often remembered for little more than having been Bach's predecessor as cantor of the Thomasschule in Leipzig; however, recordings issued in recent years have demonstrated that his music is highly worthy of consideration in its own right. Following musical training in Dresden (where he probably came into contact with the aging Heinrich Schütz) and Italy, Kuhnau trained as a lawyer at the University in Leipzig. One of the last great musical polymaths, he was also a linguist, mathematician, and the author of a satirical novel, *Der musicalische Quack-Salber* (The Musical Quack, 1700) in which he lampooned the superficiality of "modern" music.

Published in 1700, the *Musicalische Vorstellung einiger biblischer Historien* (Biblical Sonatas) form the last of four sets of keyboard music issued by Kuhnau before he turned principally to sacred music following his appointment as cantor in Leipzig in 1701. The publication consists of six sonatas headed with the titles of Old Testament biblical stories. The sonatas are overtly programmatic in a manner popular among late seventeenth century composers. The titles given to the sonatas are: I. "The Combat between David and Goliath"; II. "The Melancholy of Saul Assuaged by Means of Music"; III. "The Wedding of Jacob"; IV. "Hezekiah Dying and Restored to Health"; V. "Gideon the Saviour of the People of Israel"; and VI. "The Tomb of Jacob." Not content with providing titles, Kuhnau also wrote under the opening bars of each short movement a detailed description of what it was intended to convey to the listener. Many of these pictorial depictions (the shuddering tremolo at "The trembling of the Israelites at the appearance of the Giant" (Sonata I/2) are today more likely to be viewed as quaint rather than graphic, but such musical painting played an important part in Baroque rhetoric and would also have made a deeper impression on listeners better versed in the Old Testament than most people are today.

Musically, the sonatas are of importance for the various elements of French (the improvisatory "broken-chord" style for Jacob's burial [Sonata VI/4]), Italian (the toccata-like writing in Gideon's battle against the Midianites), and German keyboard writing that would see its paradigmatic synthesis in the keyboard works of Bach. One of the most impressive sections is Kuhnau's depiction of Saul's melancholy in the opening of Sonata II, a deeply-felt movement whose odd harmonic progressions and chromaticism show the composer as equally at home in the "fantastic" style as Heinrich Biber is in his *"Mystery" (or Rosary) Sonatas* for violin. Kuhnau names no specific keyboard instrument for the performance of the sonatas. They are suitable for both organ and harpsichord; performers often choose to alternate between the two in a complete performance. —*Brian Robins*

Recommended:

- ○ **Kuhnau: Biblical Sonatas** / Butt / HM 907133

Sigiswald Kuijken

b. Feb. 16, 1944, Dilbbek, Belgium
Conductor, Violinist

Sigiswald Kuijken has been a pioneer in performing and teaching Baroque violin technique. He and his brothers were all exposed to early instruments as youngsters. Sigiswald and Wieland intuitively taught themselves how to play the viola da gamba. Sigiswald studied violin at the conservatory in Bruges, then in Brussels with Maurice Raskin, earning his degree in 1964. After doing his own research into Baroque performance practice, Kuijken began playing Baroque works on the violin without using a chinrest or shoulder rest and, in fact, not using his chin at all to hold the instrument. He began teaching this method, and others quickly adopted it. Kuijken performed with the Alarius Ensemble between 1964 and 1972, and then at the encouragement of the Deutsche Harmonia Mundi label and Gustav Leonhardt, founded his own orchestra, la Petite Bande, to perform Baroque and Classical works. He has traveled throughout Europe, North America, Australia, China, and Japan with la Petite Bande, and together they have recorded works by Lully, Pergolesi, Mozart, Haydn, Bach, and Geminiani. He also undertook more independent projects with others, such as his brothers Wieland and Barthold, Gustav Leonhardt, Robert Kohnen, Anner Bylsma, Frans Brueggen, and René Jacobs. In 1986, he and his brother Wieland founded the Kuikjen String Quartet with François Fernandez, Marleen Thiers, and sometimes joined by violist Ryo Terakado, specifically to perform Classical period quartets and quintets. That same year, Kuijken conducted the inaugural concert in London of the Orchestra of the Age of Enlightenment. Kuijken taught Baroque violin at the Koninklijk Conservatorium in The Hague (1971–96) and at the Koninklijk Muziekconservatorium in Brussels (since 1993). He is frequently invited to teach at the Royal College of Music in London, Salamanca University, and the Accademia Chigiana in Siena, among other schools. In the late 1990s, he began doing more conducting of modern orchestras in works of Mendelssohn, Schumann, and Brahms. Ongoing projects include the sonatas of Mozart, plus Mozart's and Debussy's chamber music with his brothers. —*Patsy Morita*

Recommended:

- ○ **C.P.E. Bach: Die Auferstehung und Himmelfahrt Jesu** / Kuijken (cond.), Genz, Schwabe, Genz, La Petite Bande / Hyperion 67364
- ○ **Bach: Motets** / Kuijken (cond.), La Petite Bande / Accent 9287
- ○ **Mozart: Violin Sonatas** / Kuijken, Devos (keyboard) / Accent 9175
- ○ **Bach: Sonatas & Partitas** / Kuijken / 1990 / Editio Classica 77043
- ○ **Haydn: Symphonies 26, 52, 53, 82–87** / Kuijken (cond.), Orch. of the Age of Enlightenment, La Petite Bande / 2002 / Virgin 562041
- ○ **Telemann: Paris Quartets** / Kuijken, Kuijken, Leonhardt, Kuijken / Sony 63115
- ○ **Bach: Musical Offering** / S. Kuijken, B. Kuijken, Leonhardt, W. Kuijken / 1997 / Sony 63189

Wieland Kuijken

b. Aug. 31, 1938, Dilbeek, Belgium
Gambist, Cellist, Viol Player

Wieland Kuijken is widely regarded as one of the most influential pioneers in the twentieth century revival of the viola da gamba and early cello. Born to a musical family near Brussels, he began studies on the cello at the Conservatory at Bruges in 1952. He then attended the Brussels Conservatory, winning the Prix d'Excellence in 1962. His musical activities as a student in Brussels were varied and included performance with the contemporary music ensemble Musiques Nouvelles. At the same time, he began to teach himself the viola da gamba, and from 1959 to 1972, he performed with the Alarius Ensemble, an ensemble devoted to performances of French Baroque music. Soon thereafter, the name "Kuijken" became synonymous with stylistically accurate performances of Baroque music thanks to concerts with his brothers Sigiswald (violin) and Barthold (flute) in the Kuijken Early Music Group. Specializing in the bass viol, Wieland Kuijken has performed and recorded a large repertoire as both a continuo player and soloist. His recordings of Bach, Marais, and Forqueray have garnered critical acclaim, and his repertoire encompasses music by composers as late as Mozart and Boccherini. He has taught at the conservatories of Antwerp, Brussels, and the Hague, and has been a featured performer at festivals of early music such as Flanders, Saintes, and the English Bach Festival. Aside from his brothers, notable collaborators have included Alfred Deller, Frans Brueggen, Jordi Savall, and Gustav Leonhardt. —*Robert Adelson*

Recommended:

- ○ **French Flute Music of the 18th Century** / B. Kuijken, W. Kuijken, Kohnen / Accent 67909
- ○ **Haydn: Trios Vol. 2** / B. Kuijken, S. Kuijken, W. Kuijken / Accent 68641
- ○ **Sainte Colombe: Concerts à deux violes esgales, Tome II** / Savall, W. Kuijken / 2002 / Naive 9933
- ○ **Couperin: Concerts Royaux** / B. Kuijken, W. Kuijken, Kohnen / Accent 23153
- ○ **Rameau: Pièces de clavecin en concerts** / B. Kuijken, S. Kuijken, W. Kuijken, Kohnen / Accent 9493

Erich Kunzel

b. Mar. 21, 1935, New York, NY
Conductor

Erich Kunzel was dubbed the "Prince of Pops" by the *Chicago Tribune* in 1977 and has gone on to become one of the most successful *Billboard* Classical/Crossover recording artists in history. He was born in New York and raised in Connecticut. He attended Dartmouth College, where he decided on music as a career. He earned degrees at Dartmouth, Harvard, and Brown and went to Hancock, Maine, to study conducting with Pierre Monteux.

His professional conducting career began with the Santa Fe Opera in 1957. He also became a personal assistant to Pierre Monteux. Kunzel attracted the attention of another renowned teacher of conductors, the Cincinnati Symphony Orchestra's music director Max Rudolf, who invited Kunzel to become a resident conductor with the orchestra. One of the duties of that position was to lead concerts in the "Eight O'Clock Pops" series. He debuted with the Cincinnati Symphony in October, 1965, leading one of the pops concerts and showed an immediate affinity for this kind of presentation. Kunzel had not considered this area of music as his career objective, but quickly decided he liked it. Arthur Fiedler, noting Kunzel's work, invited him to guest conduct his Boston Pops Orchestra in 1970. He has been invited back to the Boston Pops every year under Fiedler and his two successors John Williams and Keith Lockhart, and has made over 85 appearances with the original Boston Pops orchestra and taken it on tour.

Kunzel made recordings with labels associated with the Vox record company while making the "Eight O'Clock Pops" even more of a favorite in Cincinnati. In 1977, the board of the orchestra decided to follow the organizational example of the Boston Symphony Orchestra and constitute a Cincinnati Pops Orchestra as a separate sub-organization using members of the main orchestra, and appointed Kunzel its conductor. Five years later he was also appointed pops conductor of the symphony orchestra in nearby Indianapolis in 1982. He has gone on to conduct over 200 pops concerts there and many more in Detroit, Toronto, Minnesota, and Naples, Florida. He holds the records for attendance at Chicago's Ravinia Festival and Cleveland's Blossom Music Festival—over 22,000 in each venue.

In the 1980s, Telarc records, the U.S.'s largest audiophile label, began recording in Cincinnati and included the Pops in its program. Beginning with the legendary *Straussfest* recording, they produced an unprecedented series of audio spectaculars including classical repertory, Broadway, popular song albums, and movie score compilations. Kunzel has recorded 100 releases, including 70 on Telarc. Fifty of them have been on the *Billboard* charts. He has been the *Billboard* Top Classical/Crossover Artist of the year several times, including an unprecedented four years in a row. He was won the Grand Prix du Disque in Europe, the Award for Classical Album of the Year 1989 from the Japan Record Association, Sony's Tiffany Walkman Award, and four Grammy nominations.

He often appears on television, most prominently in Fourth of July and Memorial Day concerts with the National Symphony Orchestra of Washington, D.C., playing on the Mall in an annual PBS television broadcast. He has played in the Fourth of July series annually since 1990. The 1996 appearance was the largest PBS audience ever for a musical event and drew nearly a million people to hear the concert live.

Kunzel has taught on the faculties of Brown University and the University of Cincinnati College-Conservatory of Music. He has conducted opera performances with the Cincinnati Opera and the Canadian Opera Company. He has received numerous awards and recognition, including the 1994 Presidential Medal for Outstanding Leadership and Achievement from Dartmouth and the 1995 Salvation Army "Others" Award. *—Joseph Stevenson*

Recommended:

○ **Grofé: Grand Canyon Suite; Gershwin: Catfish Row** / Kunzel (cond.), Tritt, Berens, Ruder, Snyder, Cincinnati Pops Orch. / 1987 / Telarc 80086

○ **Aaron Copland: Lincoln Portrait; Old American Songs** / Kunzel (cond.), Milnes, Hepburn, Cincinnati Pops Orch. / 1987 / Telarc 80117

○ **The Magical Music of Disney** / Kunzel (cond.), Stoll, Chertock, Patterson, Wolfley, Cincinnati Pops Orch. / 1995 / Telarc 80381

○ **Ein Straussfest** / Kunzel (cond.), Keyes, Cincinnati Pops Orch. / 1985 / Telarc 80098

○ **Time Warp** / Kunzel (cond.), Cincinnati Pops Orch. / 1984 / Telarc 80106

○ **Fantastic Journey** / Kunzel (cond.), Cincinnati Pops Orch. / 1990 / Telarc 80231

Joan La Barbara

b. Jun. 8, 1947, Philadelphia, PA
Vocalist
Joan La Barbara is recognized as one of the foremost exponents of new music for voice. A native of Philadelphia, La Barbara studied at Syracuse University with Helen Boatwright in the late 1960s, moving to New York University to obtain her bachelor's degree. As La Barbara was dutifully practicing scales and attending classes in the conservatory, the musical world around her was a welling spring of avant-garde experimentation, and it wasn't long before La Barbara found a place in it as a performer. She made her debut in 1971 singing with Steve Reich and Musicians at Town Hall in New York, and in 1974 she also joined the Philip Glass Ensemble. La Barbara's earliest compositions likewise date from this time; they are collected on the Lovely Music release *Voice Is the Original Instrument*.

Over the years La Barbara has developed a wide variety of unusual vocal techniques, such as glottal sounds, grunts, clicks, multi-phonic voicings, falsettos, and circular singing. La Barbara often performs on her own, with the aid of, or without, the use of electronics, of which she is regarded as a pioneer. La Barbara is also an effective improviser and interpreter who has collaborated with some of the top contemporary composers, among them David Tudor, David Behrman, John Cage, Phill Niblock, Robert Ashley, and Morton Feldman, whose *Three Voices* is dedicated to La Barbara. She has also worked with jazz artists such as guitarist Jim Hall and arranger Don Sebesky, writers and visual artists ranging from Kenneth Goldsmith to Judy Chicago, and La Barbara's voice is a key element in several works by composer Morton Subotnick, whom she married in 1979.

La Barbara's talents as a composer and performer have taken her by 2004 through seven releases, some of which were on her own label, Wizard Records; currently her work appears most commonly on the Mode, New Albion, and New World labels. In addition to her achievements in music, La Barbara is also respected for her work on behalf of arts organizations, and she served as vice president of the Board of Directors of the American Music Center for most of the 1980s. She is a longtime host of the Other Voices, Other Sounds radio program on NPR and, unusually, has provided the voice of the alien baby in the movie *Alien Resurrection* (1997). *—Uncle Dave Lewis*

Recommended:

- ○ **Voice is the Original Instrument** / La Barbara / 2003 / Lovely Music 3003
- ○ **La Barbara: Shamansong** / La Barbara, Kirkpatrick / 1998 / New World 80545
- ○ **Singing Through** / La Barbara, Winant, Stein, Evans / 1990 / New Albion 035
- ○ **Feldman: 3 Voices for Joan La Barbara** / La Barbara / 1989 / New Albion 18

Katia and Marielle Labèque

b. Hendaye, France
Duo Pianists
The two Labèque sisters are Basque in origin, having been born on the southwest coast of France near the Spanish border. Katia and Marielle are a sharply contrasted, yet highly communicative piano team. While their joint reputation was won initially through the performance of unusual repertoire, they have not neglected traditional works for two pianos.

The sisters received initial instruction from their Italian mother, an accomplished piano teacher, who began lessons when her daughters were three and five years of age. Madame Labèque had been born in Tuscany, in Torre del Lago, where Puccini's estate was located. The girls' father was a doctor from Landes. Following the preparation provided by their mother, the sisters entered the Paris Conservatoire where both of them took First Prizes. Upon graduation in their mid-teens, the two undertook performance of contemporary music, works by Berio, Boulez, Ligeti, and Messiaen, much to the surprise (if not the consternation) of those who had previously guided their careers. Indeed, during their first decade or so of public performance, this was the music for which they became best known. Each has commented that older audiences came to their concerts hoping to hear Mozart or Schubert and instead were treated to music that struck them with shocking effect. While a certain notoriety came with this performance repertoire, true celebrity arrived when their two-piano recording of Gershwin's *Rhapsody in Blue* sold over a half million copies in 1981. Previously, Gershwin's famous piece had been regarded in Europe as too lightweight to be taken seriously as concert fare.

As their reputation as a duo-piano team grew, the sisters enjoyed collaborations with many of the world's leading conductors, among them Riccardo Chailly, James Conlon, Sir Colin Davis, Charles Dutoit, Jesús López-Cobos, Seiji Ozawa, Sir Simon Rattle, Esa-Pekka Salonen, the late Giuseppe Sinopoli, Leonard Slatkin, and Michael Tilson Thomas. They have performed with most of the world's most prestigious orchestras in Amsterdam, Berlin, Boston, Chicago, Cleveland, Dresden, Leipzig, London, Los Angeles, Milan, New York, Philadelphia, and Vienna.

As recitalists, the Labèques have appeared at most of the world's most important music festivals. These encompass, among many others, the Berlin Festival, Ohio's Blossom Festival, the City of London Festival, the Edinburgh Festival, the Hollywood Bowl, the Maggio Musicale Fiorentino, New York's Mostly Mozart Festival, the Proms at London's Royal Albert Hall, Chicago's Ravinia Festival, and Tanglewood. In addition to covering Europe and the United States, the sisters have toured extensively in Asia.

The Labèques' personal attractiveness hastened their involvement with television production and they can boast of numerous appearances on broadcasts originating from Great Britain, Germany, Austria, Holland, Japan, and the United States. Their participation in the Washington D.C. gala, *Piano Grand!* in 2000 was viewed throughout America and in many other parts of the world. The Labèques have recorded extensively for EMI, Philips, and Sony, both duo recitals and concertos, the latter with several of the world's great orchestras. Their jazz-flavored recording, *Love of Colours*, has also been well-received. Katia has recorded several straight jazz albums, three of them with guitarist John McLaughlin.

The sisters moved from their London residence in 1993 and now live in a Tuscan palazzo (formerly owned by the Medici) in which several pianos are housed. For a Bach Celebration with Musica Antiqua Köln in 2000 and subsequent appearances with Il Giardino Armonico, the Labèques commissioned two Silbermann instruments of mid-eighteenth century design on which to perform music of that period. *—Erik Eriksson*

Recommended:

- ○ **España!: Katia & Marielle Labèque** / K. & M. Labeque / 1994 / Philips 438938
- ○ **Encore!** / K. & M. Labeque / Sony 48381
- ○ **The Debussy Album** / K. & M. Labeque / Philips 454471

Alexandre Lagoya

b. Jun. 21, 1929, Alexandria, Egypt, **d.** Aug. 24, 1999, Paris, France
Guitarist
Alexandre Lagoya was one of the foremost guitarists of the twentieth century. Born in Alexandria, Egypt, to a Greek father and Italian mother, he began serious study of the guitar as a prodigious eight-year-old at the local conservatory. In 1948, he relocated to Paris and studied guitar with Jean Saudry and composition with Brazilian composer Heitor Villa-Lobos. By this time, he was already a veteran of the recital stage with more than 500 concerts to his credit. Lagoya later studied with Andrés Segovia during summers at Siena. It was here, in 1950, that he met his future wife, virtuoso guitarist Ida Presti. The couple married in 1952 and decided to forego their largely successful solo careers in order to form a duo. Their decision was risky: Segovia and others were still pressing for wide acceptance of the guitar as a solo instrument; moreover, repertory for duo guitarists was practically nonexistent. The pair initially played transcriptions of keyboard works by Bach, Debussy, Falla, and others, but they eventually drew commissions from prominent composers. Mario Castelnuovo-Tedesco wrote a *Concerto for two guitars* for them, as well as the *Preludes and Fugues*. Additional works came from Joaquín Rodrigo, André Jolivet, and others. The two made numerous recordings during the 15 years of their partnership and gave an estimated 2,000 concerts. Presti died in 1967 from complications of lung cancer. Her premature passing was a devastating blow to Lagoya: he withdrew from performance, but took on a professorship at the Paris Conservatory in 1969. Starting in 1960, he had taught a summer course in guitar at the International Academy of Music in Nice with his wife, an activity he continued after her death. Among his students at the Nice Academy was the now-famous

Canadian guitarist Liona Boyd. Lagoya resumed his solo career in 1972 and also returned to the recording studio. His friendship with composer/pianist Claude Bolling resulted in the latter's *Concerto for classic guitar and jazz piano trio* in 1979, which he later recorded with Bolling. Lagoya remained active throughout the 1980s and for most of the following decade, though he retired from his posts at the Paris Conservatory and Nice Academy in 1994. —*Robert Cummings*

Recommended:

- ○ **Rodrigo: Concierto de Aranjuez** / Almeida (cond.), Lagoya, Michel, Monte Carlo National Opera Orch. / 1994 / Philips 442392
- ○ **Romantic Guitar** / Lagoya, Presti / 1994 / Belart/Karussell 450146

Michel-Richard De Lalande

b. Dec. 15, 1657, Paris, France, **d.** Jun. 18, 1726, Versailles, France
Composer: Choral

A younger contemporary of Jean-Baptiste Lully (1632–87), Michel-Richard de Lalande taught music to the daughters of Louis XIV. He eventually became master of the king's chamber music and later director of the royal chapel. He composed ballets and other instrumental works, but is best known as the leading composer of the French grand motet.

Lalande was one of 15 children born to Michel Lalande and Claude Dumourtiers. Little is known about his early life, but it is certain that at about the age of nine he became a member of the royal church of St. Germain-l'Auxerrois, in Paris; when his voice changed at age 15, he left the group. Lalande played several instruments and auditioned, unsuccessfully, as a violinist for Lully's opera orchestra. He was also an excellent keyboard player and gave harpsichord lessons to the daughter of Maréchal de Noailles, who recommended the young teacher to Louis XIV for his two daughters. As an organist, Lalande found work at four churches in Paris: St. Louis, Petit St. Antoine, St. Gervais, and St. Jean-en-Grève.

In 1683, Lalande became one of four musicians to divide the duties of the royal chapel under Louis XIV. Each of the four (Coupillet, Collasse, Minoret, and Lalande) was responsible for one quarter of the year. It seems the king favored Lalande, and as each of the other three musicians retired, Lalande assumed his duties. By 1714, he was the sole director of music at the royal chapel. In 1685, Lalande had been made *compositeur de musique de la chambre,* his duties shared with Collasse and Pierre Robert. As these composers died, Lalande garnered more responsibility until 1709, when he was the only composer for the king's chamber. Also, in 1695, after a similar process, Lalande became *maître de musique de la chambre.* Lalande was paid well and lived a life of relative luxury.

Lalande married singer Anne Rebel in 1684 and their two daughters, Marie-Anne (b. 1686) and Jeanne (b. 1687) enjoyed the patronage of Louis XIV. Both died of smallpox in 1711; the king sponsored a memorial service the next spring in their honor. After Louis XIV died in 1715, Lalande began to transfer his court duties to his students, eventually requesting that his salary be decreased and that the chapel return to the four composer arrangement of previous years. In 1722, Lalande's wife died; in 1723 he married Marie-Louise de Cury (1692–1775), with whom he had one daughter. Lalande died of pneumonia in 1726 and was buried in the church of Notre Dame de Versailles.

Lalande is best known today for his *grands motets,* composed for the royal chapel. These works resemble the German cantata in style, with alternating solo arias, ensembles, and polyphonic choruses. The motets are composed for three "choirs": a small group with one singer per part, a full chorus, and an orchestra. Lalande's approach to such compositions changed during his tenure at the royal chapel: his earlier works are organized somewhat loosely without clear divisions between sections; these were modified later by the composer into delineated segments of syllabic recitative contrasting with set arias, choruses, smaller ensembles, and instrumental passages. His choruses became more polyphonic, usually in five parts, and his orchestral parts more independent of the vocal lines. The 1729 posthumous version of his *De profundis* provides an excellent example. Often, a motive established in the opening instrumental symphonie becomes the subject of the ensuing choral fugue, as in "Hostem repellas longius," from Lalande's *Veni Creator Spiritus* of 1684 (rev. 1722). Striking harmonies in Lalande's *Pange lingua* reveal him to be as adventurous a composer as any in France. —*John Palmer*

Overview of Works (1680–1725)

One of the most important court composers during the reign of Louis XIV, Michel-Richard de Lalande (1657–1726) gained considerable power as the successor of Jean-Baptiste Lully. In his early days, his ambitions were thwarted by the hegemony enjoyed at court by Lully, but from 1683, when he was appointed one of four alternating sous-maîtres at the Chapelle Royale, Lalande gradually accumulated many of the most prestigious court posts at Versailles: *surintendant de la musique de chambre* (1689), *maître da la chambre* (1695), *compositeur de la musique de chambre* (1709), and *maître de la chapelle* (1714). After the death of Louis XIV (1715), Lalande progressively released his posts to pupils and relatives.

Lalande composed both sacred and secular works, but he is known above all for his works in the grand motet style developed by Lully and others. Invariably a psalm setting, the grand motet consists of a varied and flexible alternation of choral and solo or solo ensemble numbers punctuated by brilliant orchestral ritornelli. It was the grandest ceremonial form of sacred music heard at Versailles and other major establishments in France. Frequently lavishly scored for trumpets and timpani, the grand motet was brought to its peak by Lalande, whose 70-odd works in the form served as a model for later French Baroque composers such as Jean-Philippe Rameau.

Lalande's mature motets generally comprise from ten to fifteen sections. Following an opening orchestral introduction (or simphonie), soloists and both "petit" (chamber) and full choirs proclaim the chosen text, thus providing works in which contrast is effected by ever-changing textures, coloration, and tempos. The juxtaposition of homophonic and contrapuntal choruses provides a further element of contrast to works that sought to praise both a temporal and a divine God. As in the works of Charpentier, there is often an element of Italianate brilliance and éclat to be found in Lalande's sacred works, but the most famous of all his motets is the deeply-felt *De profundis,* a work performed at the funeral of Louis XIV at Saint-Denis, and one that remained in the repertoire of the famous *Concert Spiritual* throughout the remainder of the eighteenth century.

In addition to his sacred music, Lalande composed a smaller corpus of stage music (his *Ballet de la jeunesse* is an important precursor of opéra-ballet) and a substantial body of orchestral music, of which the *Symphonies pour les Soupirs du Roy* is the best-known example. Consisting of nearly 500 pieces arranged into some 30 suites, the *Symphonies* were, as the title suggests, designed as table music to accompany the king's (both Louis XIV and Louis XV) ceremonial dinner, which was held in public at ten each night. The short pieces that make up the suites are mostly dance movements, often entitled "air" and feature a variety of scoring from strings alone to more lavishly orchestrated pieces including wind instruments and, on occasions, trumpets and timpani. —*Brian Robins*

Recommended:

- ○ **Lalande: Grand Motets** / Schneebeli (cond.), etc. / 2002 / Virgin 545531
- ○ **Lalande: Symphonies pour les Soupers du Roy** / Reyne (cond.), Ens. La Simphonie du Marais / HM 901303
- ○ **Lalande: Music for the Sun King** / Skidmore (cond.), Ex Cathedra Chamber Choir and Baroque Orch. / Hyperion 67325

CHORAL

De profundis, grand motet (1689)

Lalande was an organist and composer under Lully's direction at the Chapelle Royal of King Louis XIV in Versailles. His *De Profundis* is based on Psalm 129 ("Unto the depths...") and bears some resemblance to the somber outlines of a requiem mass. Yet, whatever the subject, eighteenth century French Baroque church music rarely sounds as remote and solemn as that of earlier composers, such as Byrd and Palestrina.

In fifteenth- and sixteenth century polyphonic style, voices sing harmonically and mainly in counterpoint, but by the eighteenth century this was being replaced by a greater emphasis on melody and the vocal line. Indeed, parts of this work could easily be taken to be a Baroque opera! It is quite long for its place and time and is scored for six soloists, organ, small choir, and instrumental ensemble.

The humanistic lightness and gracefulness found in Lalande's secular music for the royal chamber is never far away, especially in the recitatives "Quia apud Dominem" for contralto and flute and "Sustinit anima mea" for soprano and oboe. The woodwind and string writing is transparently beautiful throughout. —*Roy Brewer*

Recommended:

- ○ **Lalande: motets** / Skidmore (cond.), Ex Cathedra Chamber Choir and Baroque Orch. / 1995 / ASV 141

Edouard Lalo

b. Jan. 27, 1823, Lille, France, **d.** Apr. 22, 1892, Paris, France
Composer: Concerto, Opera, Chamber Music, Ballet

Author of the popular *Symphonie espagnole* for violin and orchestra, a work which captivates the listener with its melodic charm and great passion, Lalo was a major composer of orchestral and chamber music at a time when French musicians were dominated by an impulse to compose for the theater. His lesser known, but by no means little accomplished, works include the powerfully emotional *Cello Concerto in D minor,* a work which aptly makes use of the instrument's expressive potential, and the ballet, *Namouna.*

Lalo left home at the age of 16 because his father did not want him to be a professional musician. He studied the violin at the Paris Conservatoire, also learning composition privately. While supporting himself as a violinist, performing and giving lessons, Lalo also composed. His early works, published in the 1840s, include pieces for the violin. In the 1850s, Lalo became an important member of a movement to revive chamber music in France. By the mid-1850s, he had already composed two piano trios, which show a considerable mastery of that form. In 1855, Lalo helped found the Armingaud Quartet; this ensemble was created to promote the music of Haydn, Mozart, Beethoven, Schumann, and Mendelssohn. Lalo, who was the quartet's violist and second violinist, composed a string quartet in 1859, thus enhancing his stature as a composer of chamber music. In 1865, Lalo married Julie Bernier de Maligny, a singer who eventually became a leading performer of his songs.

Nevertheless, Lalo wished to compose for the stage, and in 1866 he started writing *Fiesque*, an opera based on Friedrich Schiller's play *Fiesko*. While Lalo was pleased by his opera, the Paris Opera decided against producing this work. However, despite this setback, Lalo's career flourished. The creation, in 1871, of the *Societe Nationale de Musique*, whose program was to promote the works of contemporary composers, provided Lalo with an impetus to continue composing for the orchestra. Thus, during the 1870s, Lalo composed several impressive works, including a *Violin Concerto in F major*, the famous *Symphonie espagnole*, the *Cello Concerto*, and the *Fantaisie norvegienne* for violin and orchestra.

In 1875, Lalo started work on *Le Roi d'Ys*, an opera based on a Breton legend. Feeling that his work was nearing completion, Lalo offered it to the Opera in 1881. Once again, theaters refused to produce Lalo's work; however, perhaps wishing to somehow compensate the composer, the Opera asked him to compose a ballet. During 1881 and 1882 Lalo wrote *Namouna*, based on a story from Casanova's *Memoires*, and the ballet was performed in 1883 to a less-than-appreciative audience. Throughout the 1880s, however, Lalo continued promoting *Le Roi d'Ys*. The opera was finally performed at the Opera-Comique in 1888, and the reception was extremely favorable. Following this belated triumph, Lalo embarked on several new projects, including *Neron*, a pantomime, which was performed in 1891. A new opera, *La jacquerie*, remained unfinished. *—Zoran Minderovic*

Overview of Works (ca. 1848–1889)

Lalo left home at 16 to live by his wits in Paris; he survived by giving lessons on stringed instruments, performing in orchestras and, from 1855, playing viola and second violin in the Armingaud Quartet. Bohemian life and a haphazard education delayed the impulse to compose, and only as he approached 30 did Lalo begin to publish romances, as did many composers who would become better known for better works—Berlioz, for instance, or Gounod, Bizet, and Chabrier. His marriage to the contralto, Julie de Maligny, in 1865 prompted a continued spate of drawing room fare on poems by writers ranging from those now forgotten to Hugo, Musset, Lamartine, and Silvestre. Some early pieces for violin and piano—with titles such as *Espérance* and *Insouciance*—fall into this category, though two piano trios, the *Violin Sonata*, *Cello Sonata*, and *String Quartet*, composed through the decade of the 1850s, are testimony to his high seriousness, his embrace of Romanticism (Berlioz and Schumann, in particular), and a certain deficit of resourcefulness in the development of his ideas. Lalo hit his stride as a composer only with the composition of the unperformed *Fiesque* (1866–68)—an opera hampered by an involved libretto, though propelled by rich, powerful music upon which he would draw for other works throughout the remainder of his career, e.g., the balletic *Divertissement* (1872) and the pantomime with chorus, *Néron* (1891). *The Violin Concerto in F* (1873) and the *Symphonie espagnole* for violin and orchestra (1874), both championed by Sarasate, brought Lalo to prominence in works of a symphonic breadth, virile candor, and vivacious melody which would continue to distinguish the works of his maturity—the *Cello Concerto* (1877), the *Fantaisie norvégienne* for violin and orchestra (1878), and the orchestral *Rapsodie norvégienne* (1879), which share the use of Norwegian folk melodies, and the *Concerto russe* for violin and orchestra (1879), which utilizes Russian folk melodies. Bringing this series of great concertos to a disappointing close, the *Piano Concerto* (1888–89), though not without striking ideas, is merely pompous and labored. On the other hand, the *Piano Trio No. 3* (1880) looms as one of Lalo's most splendid works, while the orchestration of its *Scherzo* (1884) reveals its essentially symphonic conception. But the most vibrant springs of Lalo's imagination seem to have been tapped only by drama, color, a touch of the exotic—as in the *Symphonie espagnole* or, above all, the opera *Le Roi d'Ys* (1875–88), based on a Breton folk legend (the one which inspired Debussy's *La Cathédrale engloutie*), and the ballet, *Namouna* (1881–82) which, though the Corfu-set scenario is generic fluff, Lalo invested with character, an unusual rhythmic animation, and preternatural charm. A similar vivacity lurks at the heart of his *Symphony* (1886), whose scherzo and Adagio are drawn from earlier music, while the outer movements proceed from sonata-form logic. Among several smaller works also piquantly spiced are the *Fantaisie-ballet* for violin and orchestra (1885) on themes from *Namouna* and the compelling *Guitare* for violin and piano. *—Adrian Corleonis*

Recommended:

- ○ **Lalo: Symphony in G minor** / Butt (cond.), Royal PO / 1990 / ASV 709
- ○ **Lalo: 3 Trios** / Salomone Trio / 2001 / Meridian 84437

CONCERTO

Cello Concerto in D minor (1877)

For the many who know Edouard Lalo only as the composer of the warhorse *Symphonie espagnole* for violin and orchestra, it is surprising to learn that he is the author of over a half-dozen other vehicles for soloist and orchestra (and all kinds of other works, operatic, orchestra, chamber, and sacred, as well), including two other violin concertos and an absolutely unknown piano concerto. The only one of these other concerto-type works to have earned any kind of reputation at all is the *Concerto for cello and orchestra in D minor* composed in 1877, a favorite of student cellists that is nevertheless surprisingly and wonderfully colorful in a master's hands. Lalo was a better and more thoughtful composer than historians usually allow, and although the work sometimes veers towards the trite, the *Cello Concerto* is not short of charms.

Though a Frenchman, Lalo was of Spanish descent; Spanish idioms fill the three movements of the *Cello Concerto*, here subtly, there blatantly. The Allegro maestoso first movement is prefaced by a Lento introduction in which the cellist ponders the coming movement in recitative style—there is no traditional orchestral exposition here. The body of the movement is built around three elements: a firmly chiseled tune first offered by the soloist, an unshakable descending accompaniment theme, and a gorgeous, dolcissimo second theme, during which the descending accompaniment theme takes on a new tenderness but does not dissolve. The second movement is an intermezzo that alternates between lyric Andantino con moto music and sprightly Allegro presto music. After a brief introduction (which temporarily moves into the unlikely realm of B flat minor and gives an advance copy of one of the upcoming themes), the last movement takes the shape of a robust rondo. *—Blair Johnston*

Recommended:

- ○ **Ravel, Lalo, Enescu** / Silvestri (cond.), Navarra, Czech PO / 2000 / Supraphon 3514
- ○ **Rostropovich Live** / Rostropovich, etc. / Russian Disc 11101
- ○ **Saint-Saëns: Cello Concerto 1; Fauré: Élégie; Lalo: Cello Concerto** / Cassado, etc. / Vox 8143
- ○ **Pierre Fournier** / Martinon (cond.), Fournier, Lamoureux Concert Association Orch. / 1999 / DG 457761

Concerto russe, for violin & orchestra, Op. 29 (1879)

Composer Edouard Lalo sometimes falls chronologically and/or stylistically between pillars of high Romanticism, such as Wagner and Brahms, and the first musical generation of twentieth century composers, which included fellow Frenchmen Debussy and Ravel. Having garnered the favor of a number of important performers, particularly the famous violinist Pablo de Sarasate, he composed several important works for violin and orchestra in the 1870s, including the *Concerto in F major* (1874), the famous *Symphonie espagnole* (1975), as well as the piece under consideration here, the *Concerto russe for Violin and Orchestra* (1879). Despite his French nationality, many observers hear Lalo's style as a kind of synthesis of Germanic form and balance and Russian, Scandinavian, or Spanish color. Modern listeners are tempted to simply reduce this to a general interest in the exotic, and more than one scholar has noticed strong affinities between the vibrant physicality of the *Symphonie espagnole* and the rhythmic drive in the faster portions of the *Concerto russe*. Whatever stylized geographic associations one derives from the tunes and textures, though, the ruling aesthetics in the *Concerto russe* are high Romantic lyricism, opulent expressiveness, and virtuosic flair. However, Sarasate chose not to perform it, leaving the premiere to Martin Marsick.

The concerto is cast in four movements, beginning with the slow prelude that leads directly into the Allegro first movement. The prelude alternates stately brass fanfares with brief but dramatic responses from the soloist. The violin responses grow increasingly difficult and expressive, with bowed quadruple stops and rising chromatic quintuplets suddenly catapulted to shimmering accented notes, before finally indulging in a short roller-coaster cadenza. This leads to the movement proper, its minor-mode melody at once more tuneful and more compelling. The movement proceeds in alternating fits of busy angst and more staid repose, with strong and evocative emphases on offbeats and less-than-subtle orchestrational effects. The second movement, subtitled "Chants russes," provides a stark contrast to the aggression of the first. A serene chordal accompaniment provides a hushed undercurrent for the soloist's gentle, plaintive melody. Movement three, identified as an Intermezzo, assumes a humorous herky-jerky character with soft, staccato chords disrupted by noisy off-beat accents. This serves as a springboard for the violin's furious fingerwork and acrobatic leaps across octaves. The fourth movement begins with a slow but forceful introduction, which leads into a nimble Vivace finale. Also bearing the subtitle "Chants russe," the movement's dotted rhythms and hemiolas lend the orchestral accompaniment a rhythmic drive and exotic vibrancy, while the quick triple-meter tune readily takes on ornamental flourishes and extroverted gestures appropriate to a late nineteenth century concerto finale. *—Jeremy Grimshaw*

Recommended:

- ○ **Lalo: Concerto; Overture; Scherzo** / Tortelier (cond.), Charlier, BBC PO / 1999 / Chandos 9758
- ○ **Lalo: Symphonie Espagnole; Concerto Russe** / Valek (cond.), Poulet, Prague Radio SO / 1995 / Praga 250062

Symphonie espagnole, for violin & orchestra in D minor, Op. 21 (1874)

This concerto-like work is one of the favorite large-scale violin works of the Romantic era. Its colorful Spanish quality and its flowing, attractive melodies, along with its copious display of violin tricks, have kept it before a public that has largely forgotten the other works of its composer.

Stimulated by Pablo de Sarasate's playing of his *First Violin Concerto* in 1874, Lalo decided to write another concerto, this time paying tribute to Sarasate's Spanish nationality and his own Spanish descent. Lalo tailor-made the new *Symphonie Espagnole* to fit Sarasate's playing style, which was innovative for stressing a bright, light attack rather than the powerhouse style that had characterized earlier violinists. It is likely that Sarasate collaborated with Lalo in the details of the violin part, for it features the singing line and effervescent arpeggio and scale work that was a trademark of his playing and which are featured in Sarasate's own recital music. Sarasate played it for the first time in Paris on February 7, 1875. It immediately pleased the audience, and happened to hit in the middle of a vogue for Spanish music recently touched off by Bizet's opera *Carmen*.

It has frequently been said that it is not a concerto or a symphony at all, although it does have elements of symphonic form. It is really a suite, whose five movements add up to the dimensions of a symphony, about 30 minutes.

The first movement, Allegro non troppo, opens with a full-orchestra statement of a theme that stresses a typical 2/4 + 6/8 Spanish rhythm. The violin then states a main theme in triplets. The soloist also introduces a second subject, which is the main material for the development, where it acquires the triplets of the other subject. The coda has a brief development of the first subject.

The second movement, Scherzando; Allegro molto, is a sparkling fast Spanish waltz, which follows an introduction featuring bright pizzicato writing for the orchestral strings. The outer portions of the three-part form are in the Spanish rhythm called the seguidilla. The middle part of this movement is rhapsodic, with frequent shifts of tempo.

Lalo made the symphony a five-movement work by adding an Intermezzo as the third movement after the premiere. It is, in effect, a second scherzo, though in a slower tempo. It has a nice use of the contrast between minor and major modes. Unfortunately, for some years many violinists adopted the practice of omitting this movement. That is a shame, for the sultry second subject is one of the nicest themes in the symphony.

The true slow movement is the sultry and romantic fourth movement, Andante, with a dark and soulful mood.

The finale is a rondo whose main subject sets off a series of dazzling episodes. Lalo begins the movement with a nice trick to raise anticipation: he repeats an accompaniment many times until the violin inserts the theme. After that the movement continues in dance-like mode until the brilliant conclusion. *—Joseph Stevenson*

Recommended:

- ○ **Lalo: Symphonie Espagnole, Etc.** / Martinon (cond.), Oistrakh / 1997 / Testament 1116
- ○ **Artist Profile: Leonid Kogan** / Kondrashin (cond.), Kogan, London PO / 1993 / EMI 67732
- ○ **Lalo & Saint-Saëns** / Lopez-Cobos (cond.), Chee-Yun, London PO / 1997 / Denon 18017

OPERA

Le roi d'Ys (1875–1888)

Best known outside France for his *Symphonie espagnole* (1874), Edouard Lalo was recognized in his own country almost entirely for his opera *Le roi d'Ys* (The King of Ys). Lalo began setting Edouard Blau's libretto, about the legendary Breton city, in 1875. After the Théâtre-Lyrique rejected the opera in 1878 and the Paris Opéra did the same in 1879, Lalo extracted several numbers from the work and performed them in concert. In 1886, he completely revised the work and tried once again to find a company to stage it; two years later, the Opéra-Comique finally agreed to produce the opera. The premiere was nearly a disaster: The management of the Opéra-Comique (performing in the Théâtre des Nations) oversold the house, causing such a commotion that the audience did not quiet down until the beginning of the second act. Still, those who managed to find seats enjoyed what they heard, enthusiastically applauding and calling for encores. *Le roi d'Ys* became Lalo's most successful work for the stage, achieving its 100th performance at the Opéra-Comique by the following June.

The opera would have been more appropriately named "Margared d'Ys," for the King has a very small role and is not pivotal to the story. Margared, on the other hand, is onstage throughout the opera and is a character of tremendous depth, torn between succumbing to her own passions and doing what is right for others. In the manner of Wagner's Ortrud, Margared redeems herself through self-sacrifice at the end of the opera. Lalo created the role of Margared for his wife, the singer Julie de Maligny, though she never actually performed it. She did, however, perform several of the arias in concert.

Other characters are more predictable. Mylio and Rozenn have no hidden agendas, and their music is consistent from scene to scene. Karnac's music is sinister from the outset, belying his verbal assurance that he is now an ally of the King. St. Corentin functions as a *deus ex machina*. Both musically and dramatically, the two couples, Margared and Karnac, and Mylio and Rozenn, are juxtaposed in a manner similar to the way Wagner draws the "good" and "bad" couples in *Lohengrin*.

The overture unfolds along the lines of early nineteenth century models, functioning as a preview of what is to come. References to music associated with Mylio, Rozenn and the people of Ys (along with a quote from *Tannhäuser*) make up the material, which receives wonderfully transparent orchestration. Indeed, throughout the entire opera the orchestration is clear and subservient to the melodic lines, which are generally simple and diatonic. Lalo uses instrumental color as a backdrop for the vocal parts, increasing the importance of the orchestra in the large ensembles.

In *Le roi d'Ys* Lalo writes in a chromatic idiom that is more akin to music of Liszt than that of Wagner. Forceful 6/8 meters, a favorite of the composer, underline the most dramatic sections. Some of the choruses suggest an echo of Breton folk songs, which Lalo surely learned from his Bretonese wife (who also may have brought the legend of Ys to her husband's attention in the first place). Although *Le roi d'Ys* contains certain characteristics of traditional grand opera, this highly individual work marks a new direction in French music of its time. *—John Palmer*

Synopsis:

The action takes place in the legendary Breton city of Ys, engulfed by the ocean centuries ago.

Act One. Margared, the daughter of the King of Ys, is engaged to Karnac, a former enemy of the King. At the engagement celebration Margared tells her sister, Rozenn that she is in love, not with Karnac, but with Mylio, an old friend who now lives in a distant land. Unbeknownst to Margared, Rozenn, too, loves Mylio, and his heart belongs to Rozenn. Mylio surprises everyone by returning to Ys in the middle of Margared and Karnac's engagement ceremony. Once Margared learns that Mylio is back, she rejects Karnac and refuses to go ahead with the wedding. Karnac, threatening vengeance, curses the city of Ys and once again becomes the enemy of the King.

Act Two. Margared finally realizes that Mylio is not in love with her, but with her sister. She becomes furiously jealous. The King promises Rozenn's hand in marriage to Mylio if Mylio is able to defeat Karnac in an upcoming confrontation. Mylio is victorious, but gives credit for his achievement to the intervention of St. Corentin, the patron saint of Ys. After a long victory parade has passed, the defeated, distraught Karnac enters. Margared tries to console him, offering to join with him in a quest for revenge. As Margared mentions her plot to open the floodgates that separate the city from the surrounding sea, the nearby statue of St. Corentin overhears their conversation and warns her against taking any such action.

Act Three. The King is upset that Margared is missing from the wedding ceremony of Rozenn and Mylio. Margared had wanted to attend, but Karnac awakened her jealousy and convinced her to carry out her plan of opening the sluices. When Margared finally arrives at the ceremony she tells everyone that Karnac has opened the floodgates and the city will be destroyed. Mylio leaves, returning later and stating that he has killed Karnac, but was too late to prevent him from opening the sluices and allowing the seawater to rush into the city—all is lost.

Margared speaks to the people of Ys, telling them that the sea desires a sacrifice and that she must be the one, because she and Karnac, who is already dead, devised the plot to open the floodgates and destroy the city. From a high ledge, she throws herself into the sea. Satisfied by Margared's death, St. Corentin appears and spares the city, sending the waves back to the ocean. *—John Palmer*

Recommended:

- ○ **Lalo: Le roi d'Ys** / Jordan (cond.), Hendricks, Courtis, Ziegler, Villa / Erato 45015

CHAMBER MUSIC

Piano Trio No. 3 in A minor, Op. 26 (1880)

Chamber music in France through the mid-nineteenth century remained a special taste, composed for and performed within small but devoted enclaves while the center of musical gravity—success, fame, money—in Paris remained the Opéra. From 1855, Lalo played viola and later, second violin, in the Armingaud Quartet, which was to achieve high renown, while the composer augmented an already intimate knowledge of string technique. Composed through the 1850s, the bulk of Lalo's works in the chamber medium—the string quartet, violin sonata, cello sonata, and two piano trios—are a notable addition to this almost clandestine resurgence, combining a classical concision of form with the occasional boldness of a budding dramatist and a vein of whimsy beholden to Mendelssohn and Schumann, though not entirely free from echoes of the salon.

Composed in 1880, the *Piano Trio No. 3*, on the other hand, is a mature work whose high seriousness embraces brioso lift, architectural tension, and lyric warmth bespeaking the Lalo of the legend-inspired grand opera *Le roi d'Ys* (1875). Merely flirting with profundity, the first movement Allegro appassionato nevertheless works its attractive materials with compelling élan to a substantial development through which the Romanticism of an earlier era—virile candor, or a sort of grand naïveté—looms untouched by the gilding, calculation, and irony with which a later generation would appropriate Romantic means (as, for instance, the manner in which the formulas of bel canto opera are parodied in the Gilbert and Sullivan operettas). The second movement Presto, in its bounding, impassioned vivacity—set off by a chorale-like processional in the piano piquantly accompanied by plucked strings—is the high point of the score and looks forward to the more vigorous parts of the ballet *Namouna*, which would follow over 1881–82. Recognizing its worth, Lalo orchestrated this movement as a Scherzo in 1884, with particular emphasis on rich brass sonorities, which earned him the glib charge of Wagnerism. An achingly spun melody for violin unfolds in the extensive "Très lent" third movement over solemn chords and rising to moments of somber anguish and resolving in a passion-spent calm. And the festive final Allegro molto bubbles with joyous ardor, though it remains overshadowed by the balletic Presto. If the balance between the movements is somewhat uneven, Lalo's *Piano Trio No. 3* is nonetheless his richest chamber work and the one in which the composer is familiar from his better-known music, albeit in the domain of pure music and shorn of exotic elements. *—Adrian Corleonis*

Recommended:

○ **Lalo: 3 Trios** / Salomone Trio / 2001 / Meridian 84437

○ **Mendelssohn & Lalo: Piano Trios** / Gryphon Trio / Analekta 23127

BALLET

Namouna (1881–1882)

"Among too many stupid ballets," Debussy wrote at the turn of the century, "Lalo's *Namouna* is something of a masterpiece." Such an estimation is well in keeping with the score's glowing color, melodic richness, rhythmic verve, and overall vibrancy. And Debussy confirms his admiration by breezily alluding to its sérénade in the Assez vif et bien rythmé movement of his own *String Quartet*. Given the constraints under which *Namouna* was composed, one can only marvel at its wealth of ingratiating invention.

In 1879, perhaps as a consideration for having refused his opera, *Le roi d'Ys*, the newly appointed director of the Paris Opéra, Auguste Vaucorbeil, commissioned a ballet from Lalo for production in November, 1881. The fashioning of a scenario led to delays, with the chore being passed between the critic, Henri Blaze de Bury, the librettist, Charles Nuitter, and the choreographer, Lucien Petipa. Not until July, 1881, did Lalo have something in hand to compose to. Set on Corfu, the slender story of a slave girl passed between two wealthy playboys on the turn of a bet took on, chez Lalo, not only exotic color, but character and depth of feeling. The strain of rushing led to his hemiplegic stroke on December 10. The unrelenting Vaucorbeil moved to have the work completed by another hand, but Lalo rallied and, after an appeal to the Minister of the Interior, and with Gounod's help filling in the orchestration, he completed *Namouna*. Meanwhile, a hostile press had already set about denouncing the unheard *Namouna*, as "Wagnerian"—an absurd charge routinely leveled at any music of symphonic scope. *Namouna*'s premiere on March 6, 1882, was unsympathetically received, very likely because, striving for antiphonal effects, Lalo had groups of instruments not only in the pit, but on stage and in the front boxes. When these were placed together in the pit after the third performance, audience objections thinned, but *Namouna* was allowed a disappointing run of 15 performances.

The "Valse de la cigarette," in which Namouna rolls a cigarette for her lover, provoked a sensation. And several Moroccan melodies, heard at the 1878 World Exhibition, were employed to piquant effect. Sensing that he'd given some of his best inspiration to *Namouna*, Lalo salvaged a great deal of it in two suites, recomposing and reorchestrating much of the music. Individual numbers were also exquisitely arranged—the Andantino for violin and orchestra, and the Sérénade for strings—while some of the score's most winning melodic materials were worked into a ravishing *Fantaisie-ballet* for violin and orchestra. *—Adrian Corleonis*

Recommended:

○ **Lalo: Namouna** / Robertson (cond.), Monte Carlo PO / 2001 / Naive 4907

Constant Lambert

b. Aug. 23, 1905, London, England, **d.** Aug. 21, 1951, London, England

Composer: Concerto, Choral

Constant Lambert was born the son of painter George Washington Thomas Lambert in London. Isolated in infirmaries for long spells as a child due to poor health, Lambert used this time to read voraciously and intensively study music. In 1922, Lambert won a scholarship to the Royal College of Music in London, where he studied composition with Ralph Vaughan Williams (whom Lambert admired but did not emulate) and George Dyson (whom Lambert loathed). Early on, Lambert made friends with composers William Walton and Philip Heseltine (aka Peter Warlock), and made some arrangements from Walton's *Façade*.

The influence of Walton's approach can be seen in very early Lambert works such as the children's fable *Mr. Bear Squash-you-all-flat* (1924). However, it was the music of Liszt and Duke Ellington that made the deepest impact on Lambert. Jazz inflections can be found in many of the pieces Lambert wrote before 1931, including the *Piano Concerto* (1924), *Concerto for Plano and Nine Players* (1931), *Piano Sonata* (1928), and the short *Elegiac Blues* (1927) Lambert wrote in memory of the ill-fated vaudeville diva Florence Mills. Russian motifs and the example of Stravinsky also had a great impact on Lambert, and his ballet *Romeo & Juliet* (1927) was the first work by a British composer to be staged by the ballets russes. Lambert's infatuation with Chinese-American silent movie queen Anna May Wong led to the composition of his delicate *Eight Poems of Li-Po* (1927). In 1928, Lambert composed *The Rio Grande*, scored for chorus, piano, brass, strings, and percussion. This work proved a huge success, but helped establish the image of Lambert as a composer of entertaining yet insubstantial music.

After his more serious subsequent efforts failed to gain a foothold with the public, Lambert turned to music criticism and wrote *Music Ho!: A Study of Music in Decline* (1934), a pessimistic and vitriolic tome that foretold a bleak future for twentieth century concert music. This book is still seen as a most vital and valuable tool for study in the art music of the 1920s and 1930s. By the late 1930s, Lambert was building a reputation as a conductor, and from then on his output as a composer slackened. He was strongly associated with ballet and co-founded the Vic Wells Company with Ninette de Valois. Lambert conducted at the Royal Ballet, Covent Garden, at the Promenade Concerts and at International Society for Contemporary Music concerts in England. By the 1940s, he was one of the most prominent conductors in England and well known internationally through recordings and his popular ballet *Horoscope* (1937). However, this work even more firmly established Lambert as a neo-Classical triviality in the minds of his peers and among critics who knew nothing of Lambert's 1920s compositions. Lambert finally returned to serious composition in 1951 with the scandalous three-act ballet *Tiresias*, which was so "hot" that its premiere was censored. Lambert's publisher, Oxford University Press, rejected it. This came as a final, sour blow to the pessimistic composer, who promptly died two days short of his 46th birthday, the result of an undiagnosed diabetic condition aggravated by years of hard drinking. Lambert came from the same generation of British musicians that produced Walton, Tippett, Warlock, and Spike Hughes; however, his music is stylistically nothing like these composers. In Lambert's jazz works he can be seen as a predecessor of the serious, large-form pieces written by jazz composers such as Keith Jarrett and Chick Corea starting in the 1970s. His other music is likewise inspired, original, and well worth rediscovering. *—Uncle Dave Lewis*

CONCERTO

Concerto for piano & 9 players (1930–1931)

For the self-aware composer coming of age in the wake of the Great War, the achievement of what Busoni called "a comprehensive certainty of style" had become acute. The precocious Constant Lambert, who had composed a ballet for Diaghilev at the age of 19, was an intimate of the circle surrounding the mysterious Dutch composer, Bernard van Dieren, which included Philip Heseltine (known to all lovers of English song as Peter Warlock), Cecil Gray (now forgotten but an influential critic in his day and a closet composer of great interest), Sorabji, Bliss, Walton, and the Sitwells. Nearly all of them followed Busoni in the close charting and assessment of the chaotic musical riches of their era—Heseltine/Warlock and Sorabji as music critics, van Dieren in *Down Among the Dead Men*, a covertly influential volume of essays, Gray with systematic thoroughness in several books, and Lambert in the engaging, scintillantly perceptive, and pessimistic *Music Ho!—A Study of Music in Decline* (1934). Given this preoccupation, it is hardly surprising that, despite abundant invention, staggering technical resourcefulness, lavish color, and an evident sympathy with pop and jazz, an air of *arrière pensée* clings even to Lambert's most inspired music. The *Rio Grande for Piano, Orchestra, and Chorus* (1926), for instance—often referred to as England's answer to Gershwin's *Rhapsody in Blue*—though attractively shot through with pop elements carried with exuberance and panache, lacked the visceral appeal to become a viable crossover work, though its embrace of pop and season of acclaim raised expectations which his acerbic later works were to disappoint. Chief among these were the *Piano Sonata* (1928–29) and the *Concerto for Piano and Nine Instruments* (six winds, cello, double bass, percussion) in which a strong tinge of jazz—used by other composers as a facilely upbeat leavening—colors the music with the melancholy morbidity of a hangover. Its tone is frenetic high jinks recalled in a sickness more spiritual than physical, though one is reminded that Lambert was both alcoholic and often in poor health. Composed in 1931, it is dedicated to the memory of his boon companion, Peter Warlock, who had committed suicide in December 1930. To a friend, during its composition, he writes, "My musical St. Vitus dance gets worse and worse. My new concerto has now got out of 11/8 only to get into 13/8." In three movements, the music is incisively substantive, if often rebarbative, its mock-gaiety grotesquely disturbing, and the haunting blues of its Intermède profoundly moving. *—Adrian Corleonis*

Recommended:

○ **Lambert: Piano Concerto & Sonata; Li-Po Poems; Mr. Bear Squash-you-all-flat** / Friend (cond.), Brown, Nash Ens. / 1995 / Hyperion 66754

CHORAL

The Rio Grande, for piano, chorus & orchestra (1927)

Also famous as a journalist on the subject of music, Lambert had an eclectic compositional viewpoint. This is his most famous composition. Composed in 1927, it is an early specimen of British concert music making use of jazz idioms. It is a combination of piano concerto and cantata for mezzo-soprano, brass, strings, a large percussion section, chorus, and obbligato piano. The text is by Sacheverell Sitwell, a member of a rather experimental-minded artistic circle in which Lambert (as well as Walton, Lord Berners, and Warlock) took part. The poem itself depends upon associative word-play more than on meaning or emotion. It is not a portrait of the river that flows through Colorado and New Mexico to form the U.S. border with Mexico. Instead, the poem seems more concerned with a South American carnival. Nevertheless, the musical material is predominantly North American, making much use of African-American elements. Still, there is a habanera and a trace of samba. It opens with a bouncy fanfare-like burst of exuberance from all forces, then settles into a remarkable cadenza for percussion and piano. The middle is slow and romantic, becoming a torrid habanera. A cakewalk boosts the tempo to repeat the opening material. The coda uses blues harmonies and a humming chorus, then piano and percussion wind the work down. The mood of the piece is definitely more U.S. urban than anything Latin-American. It is exhilarating, in mood a kind of nostalgic evocation of the Roaring Twenties. The work offers enjoyable listening, but may for American listeners of the present day seem somewhat less innovative or remarkable than British writers appear to think. —*Joseph Stevenson*

Recommended:

- ○ **Constant Lambert: Summer's Last Will and Testament; The Rio Grande; Aubade Héroïque** / Lloyd-Jones (cond.), Burgess, Cookson, Lees, English Northern Philharmonia / 1992 / Hyperion 66565
- ○ **Constant Lambert Vol. 2** / Lambert (cond.), Ripley, London Philharmonia Orch. / Pearl 0069

Francesco Landini

b. ca. 1325, Florence, Italy, **d.** Sep. 2, 1397, Florence, Italy

Composer

Francesco Landini was the most celebrated musician in the first school of polyphonic music in Italy. Landini was born in Fiesole on the outskirts of Florence, the son of Jacopo del Casentino, a painter and student of Giotto. A childhood bout with smallpox left him blind, and he took refuge in music; he reputedly played several instruments, but mastered the organ. Landini was famed for his ability on the organetto, a small portative organ that was pumped with one hand and played with the other. In the two surviving portraits of the composer, Landini is shown with this instrument. Landini is also a featured character in a 1389 *romanza* by Giovanni da Prato; in it the "sweetness and harmony" of Landini's organetto playing is said to have been capable of charming the birds down out of the trees. He most likely studied with Jacopo da Bologna and Giovanni da Cascia and was largely based in Northern Italy before 1365. He helped build the organs installed in the St. Annunziata and Florence cathedrals in 1379 and 1387 respectively. Landini was named choirmaster at the church of St. Lorenzo in Florence in 1365, a post that he held until his death in 1397.

Landini was the most popular musician in Italy in the fourteenth century, and 154 works are known to have been written by him, constituting more than a quarter of all surviving polyphonic music from the Italian trecento. Of his pieces, all but 14 are two and three-part ballate, a loose form of song perhaps following French models, with a refrain or ritornello. Some of these ballate were very popular; the ballata *Questa fanciulla, Amor* is found in five different manuscripts, including some that set the music to sacred texts. *Orsu, gentili spiriti* is mentioned by name in the da Prato *romanza*. The short phrases and catchy rhythm of *Ecco la primavera* seem to project a popular, uncultivated feel, and all of Landini's surviving music is based on secular subjects. Fragments of sacred motets ascribed to Landini are known, but their authenticity remains unclear. He also wrote 12 works known as "Madrigali"; these are not sixteenth century madrigals but more resemble an expanded form of conductus. A French virelai, *Adiu, adiu, dous dame* and a *Pesch*, or fishing caccia, *Cosi pensoso*, round out his known works.

Landini's music is rhythmically very free, incorporating bits of hocket, syncopation, and allusions to dance steps. There are florid figurations in some parts that are clearly intended as instrumental rather than vocal, and in his late works Landini sometimes includes an untexted part that appears to have an accompanimental function. The harmonic feature that bears his name, the "Landini" or "under-third" cadence (in which the melodic line drops briefly to a third before the final note), appears commonly throughout his works, but also can be found in earlier French works. After Landini however, the under-third cadence appears with greater frequency, and it became a key element in Italian music of the fifteenth century. Composers of later generations believed that this figure originated with Landini himself. Landini was also a noted improviser and poet, and is believed to have written many of his own texts. Contemporary accounts also allude to his skill as a philosopher and astrologer. —*Uncle Dave Lewis*

Overview of Works (ca. 1350–1397)

In the century of Petrarch and Boccaccio, the vibrant musical culture of Florence culminated in the works of the blind organist Francesco Landini. More than one quarter of all surviving music from all of Trecento Italy is his; his music represents nearly half of the contents of the massive retrospective collection of Florentine music, the *Squarcialupi Codex*. Landini's music shows not only the prolific flowering of Italian traditions—as seen in the music of Maestro Piero, Giovanni da Cascia, Jacopo da Bologna, and the Florentines Donato and Gherardello—but also a growing synthesis with the compositional and notational traits of the French style of Philippe de Vitry (though very few individual pieces of his are datable). In general, Landini's music is known for the grace and "dolcezza" of his melodies, and for a deeper sense of tonal coherence. The cadential ornament which uses an "under-third" beneath the cadence pitch, though employed widely by his contemporaries, is sometimes called the "Landini cadence."

The majority of Landini's surviving works (all of which are secular) are ballate for either two or three voices. The term Ballata indicates an Italian vernacular refrain form ultimately derived from a dance song, the counterpart to the French Virelai. Though monophonic ballate were eagerly cultivated earlier in the century, Landini seems to have been a pioneer in the cultivation of this form in polyphony. Nearly all of his ninety-one ballate for two voices are texted in both voices after the fashion of the Italian madrigal, and many contain lengthy opening and closing melismas (egg. *Ochi dolenti mie, L'anitca fiamma*).

The fifty additional works for three voices betray more characteristics of French musical styles: most often only a single voice is texted, the more flowing Italian melodies give way to more rhythmic complexity, French meters are more common, and the French practice of "open" and "closed" cadence pairs appears (*Po' che partir convien* provides a good example). A few of these three-voiced pieces present more complex mingling of the two influences, such as the famous *Questa fanciull' amor*.

In addition to his prolific essays in the Ballata form, Landini composed one French-texted virelai (*Adiu, adiu, dous dame*), ten madrigals, one Italian caccia (the canonic *Cosí pensoso*), and possibly as many as four political motets. Seven of the madrigals are for two voices, and follow the conventions for that term in the thirteenth century (as opposed to the "Madrigal" of the later Renaissance). Both voices are texted—poetic lines of a standard seven or eleven syllables—and the first and last syllables of each line receive long, graceful melismas. One of the madrigals for three voices is in the form of a Caccia, with its three voices each derived from the "chase" of canonically following voices. The other two three-voiced madrigals again betray French motet techniques: one polytextual, and the other—*Sí dolce non sonó*—with an isorhythmic tenor. Some of Landini's manifold poetic texts—on an extremely wide range of subjects from the erotic to the political—must be his own, though none have been proven. —*Timothy Dickey*

Recommended:

- ○ **Second Circle** / Anonymous 4 / 2001 / HM 907269
- ○ **Landini: Ballate** / Nova Camerata / Tactus 321201
- ○ **Landini & Italian Ars Nova** / Lesne, Alla Francesca / 1992 / Opus 111 609206
- ○ **Landini & His Time** / Alba Musica Kyo Ens. / 1993 / Channel Classics 5793

Wanda Landowska

b. Jul. 5, 1879, Warsaw, Poland, **d.** Aug. 16, 1959, Lakeville, CT

Harpsichordist, Pianist

Perhaps the single most influential popularizer of the harpsichord in the twentieth century, Wanda Alexandra Landowska began playing piano at the age of four. She had lessons with Jan Klecynski, entered the Warsaw Conservatory where she studied piano with Aleksander Michalowski, and studied in Berlin with Moritz Moszkowski. In Berlin, she also studied composition, but admitted that she was put off by the textbook rules that bound the early stages of study in that craft.

She had a strong predilection for the music of Bach in her earliest piano recitals. She began to tour widely as a pianist and, increasingly, as a harpsichordist. In 1909, on a tour of Russia, she played for the elderly writer Count Lev Tolstoi, who took a keen interest in her views of classical music performance. Her husband, writer Henry Lew, assisted her in her intense study of musical style and interpretation of the seventeenth and eighteenth centuries. She focused on reviving the harpsichord as a living concert and recital instrument, becoming an ancestor of the "original instruments" and "authentic performance" movements of the twentieth century. In 1912, she commissioned the Pleyel piano manufacturing firm to construct the first of many harpsichords built to her specifications.

In 1913, after being invited by Kretzschmar to give a harpsichord seminar at the Berlin Hochschule für Musik, she became trapped in Germany when World War I began. She and her husband were granted limited freedom as "civil prisoners on parole" for the duration as Russian subjects (Poland at the time was a province of Russia). After their release at the end of the war, her husband was killed in an automobile accident in Berlin. Soon after, she played the continuo part in a performance of Bach's *St. Matthew Passion* in Basel, the first time in that century that the harpsichord was used in the performance of the great work. Landowska had become convinced that only the harpsichord was truly appropriate to the Baroque and early Classical periods. She began teaching at the Basel Conservatory in 1919 and then returned to teach in Paris. She toured the United States for the first time in 1923, taking four Pleyel harpsichords with her. On this tour, she appeared with Leopold Stokowski and the Philadelphia Orchestra, making her first acoustic recordings. (She had previously made piano rolls.)

She established L'Ecole de Musique Ancienne in St.-Leu-la-Forêt, near Paris, in 1925. She appeared in concerts in Paris, sometimes still playing piano. She commissioned from Manuel de Falla a masterpiece of modern harpsichord literature, the *Concerto for harpsichord and chamber ensemble*, and then another one, Francis Poulenc's *Concert champêtre for harpsichord and orchestra*.

When the Germans invaded France, Landowska fled her establishment, leaving behind many harpsichords and a library of 10,000 volumes. She reached Banyuls-sur-mer, in the Pyrenees, and managed to get passage to the United States in 1941. She gave a concert of harpsichord music in New York on February 2, 1942, and returned to teaching as her main occupation. She toured widely and was particularly noted for her performance of Bach's *Goldberg Variations*. She found a new home in Lakeville, CT, and recorded a highly acclaimed collection of the complete *Well-Tempered Clavier* at the age of 70. She lived a few weeks past her 80th birthday.

Her playing was vigorous, rhythmic, and colorful. She had a predilection for a very strong-voiced, richly colored instrument that is questioned today by some; it is opined that this was a reaction against the instrument's general reputation for being dry and colorless. She developed modern harpsichord technique, which permits a considerable degree of legato playing despite the instrument's nature as a producer of individually plucked notes. *—Joseph Stevenson*

Recommended:

- ○ **Landowska plays Bach** / Landowska, Bigot (cond.) / Pearl 0169
- ○ **The Well-Tempered Clavier, Book I** / Landowska / 1987 / RCA 6217
- ○ **Bach: Goldberg Variations; Italian Concerto** / Landowska / 2001 / Classica d'Oro 3008
- ○ **Landowska Plays Handel & Mozart** / Landowska / Classical Collector 150042
- ○ **Landowska Plays Scarlatti, Bach & Handel** / Landowska / Pearl 0106
- ○ **Landowska Plays Haydn & Mozart** / Landowska / Pearl 9286

Jean Langlais

b. Feb. 15, 1907, La Fontenelle, France, **d.** May 8, 1991, Paris, France

Composer: Choral

Blind from the age of two, this composer, organist, and influential teacher studied at the Institution des Jeunes Aveugles (National Institute for the Young Blind) in Paris. Langlais' harmony teacher was Albert Mahaut, a former pupil of César Franck. He studied piano with Blazy and organ with André Marchal, who was also blind.

In 1930, Langlais won the *premier prix* in organ in Marcel Dupré's class at the National Conservatory. In 1934, he won a composition prize in Paul Dukas' class and, like Messiaen, was one of the composer's last students.

Langlais studied improvisation with Charles Tournemire and received the *Grand Prix d'Exécution et Improvisation des Amis de l'Orgue* in 1931. He became organist for St. Pierre de Montrouge. During this time, Langlais composed his first works, the organ pieces *Trois poèmes évangéliques* (1932) and the *24 pièces* (1933–39). In 1945, he joined the staff of the Institution des Jeunes Aveugles, where he was to remain for 40 years teaching and conducting the choir. Following in the steps of Franck and Tournemire, he became a professor at the prestigious organ tribune of Sainte-Clotilde in Paris, a position he held for the next 42 years. His immediate postwar compositions include the organ suites, his first *Organ Concerto* with orchestra (1949), and the famous choral *Messe solennelle* (1951), one of 13 masses composed by Langlais. The other most performed masses are the *Missa in Simplicitate* for chorus and organ (1953) and the impressive *Missa Salve Regina* for three solo vocalists, unison chorus, two organs, and eight brass (1954). The vast majority of Langlais' 254 compositions are on religious themes, although there are several concertos, organ symphonies, and individual secular pieces. Many pieces incorporate Gregorian themes that are varied with great originality and surrounded with expressive and splendid modal harmonies.

In 1952, Langlais visited the United States for the first time and proceeded to give approximately 300 recitals and hold many master classes there in the succeeding years. He composed numerous pieces for Americans, including an *American Suite* for organ (1959) and his *Solemn Mass "Orbis factor"* for chorus and organ, which was premiered in Washington, D.C., in 1969.

Between 1961 and 1976, Langlais taught French and foreign students at the Schola Cantorum in Paris. His later compositions include choral and organ works and chamber pieces for trumpet. *—"Blue Gene" Tyranny*

Overview of Works (1932–1989)

Jean Langlais was the most prolific major organ composer after Bach and he dabbled in chamber and orchestral music, too. Such a huge corpus written over a long life stylistically varies, but the differences have less to do with career chronology than with the melodic sources. Langlais drew thematic inspiration from three areas: Gregorian chant, folk tunes, and original melodies. In everything he wrote, Langlais remained conscious of his place in the so-called "St. Clotilde Tradition"; as organist at the Basilica of St. Clotilde, he followed in the footsteps of such predecessors as César Franck and Charles Tournemire. The bulk of Langlais' works are religious, either in inspiration or as music intended for actual liturgical use (the *Medieval Suite* of 1947, for instance, takes the traditional form of the French organ mass). Langlais also wrote free rhapsodies and small character pieces (such as the *24 Pieces for Harmonium or Organ* of 1933–39 and the *Organ Book* of 1956). And he naturally took a more abstract approach to his handful of chamber works (most of which involved woodwinds or trumpet, sonorities akin to those of the organ).

The Gregorian-based music tends to be religious, plushly harmonized, and often polymodal, with sonorous climaxes. Among these works are *Three Gregorian Paraphrases* (1933–34), showing the strong influence of his teachers Paul Dukas and Tournemire, and *Nine Pieces*, Op. 28 (1942–43), five of which are based on chant and chorale themes and four of which employ original melodies, still in the manner of Dukas and Tournemire. A more difficult work in terms of demands on the listener as well as the performer is *Offering to a Soul* (1979), written upon the death of Langlais' first wife. This grief-laden diptych uses simple, even austere settings of Gregorian chants from the requiem and burial service, but incorporates more complex music as well, including at least one theme derived from the Braille-alphabet spelling of his wife's name.

The folkloric material tends to be his most accessible, although the later pieces take on the gnarled, quiet, and abstract style that characterized his mature, wholly original works. The *Folkloric Suite*, Op. 61 (1952), largely draws from the music of Brittany, Langlais' native region, and includes one of only three examples of the composer's fugal writing. The very late *Eight Songs of Brittany* (1975) also pay homage to Langlais' French-Celtic origins, but now the modal melodies are surrounded by dissonant harmonies.

Boisterous, rhythmically driven, and harmonically unpredictable from the beginning, his music based on original themes became even more complex and violent from the 1960s. A benign, accessible example of this is his 1948 *Suite Française*, paying tribute to French music of the seventeenth and eighteenth centuries. The *Triptyque* (1957) introduces more angular themes and counterpoint, but concludes with Langlais' characteristic exuberance. Carrying this further are the *Poem of Life*, *Poem of Peace*, and *Poem of Happiness* (1965–67), with their free-ranging, improvisatory themes and astringent harmonies. *—James Reel*

Recommended:

- ○ **Langlais: Suite Médiévale; Cinq Méditations sur l' Apocalypse** / Mathieu / 1995 / Naxos 553190
- ○ **Klingende Vergangenheit: Jean Langlais Improvisation** / Langlais / Motette 10371

CHORAL

Messe Solennelle (1951)

The blind French organist Jean Langlais commented that he had thought about his *Messe Solennelle* (Solemn Mass) for 12 years before actually composing it over 13 days in November 1949. His first setting of the Mass ordinary, the 20-minute work is scored for a four-part mixed chorus and two organs (alternately, for organ and brass). The *Messe Solennelle* combines bold organ writing, grounded in the French tradition, with fairly standard choral writing within an adventurously colorful harmonic landscape. Langlais himself played its premiere in 1950.

The Kyrie begins with a slow and mysterious introduction, the pedal subtly bringing in the plainsong melody around which Langlais evolves the movement. As the tenor repeats and develops the chant melody, other parts are added. In the tripartite Christe section, as a freer rhythm builds momentum, the full chorus sings striking melismatic passages. The movement concludes with forceful, impassioned statements of the Kyrie; this modal section concludes, surprisingly, in the major, setting a pattern for the cadences of the work. In this movement, as in the rest of the work, the composer wisely controls his occasionally bold dissonances and parallelisms by limiting them to inner voices.

The chant introit to the Gloria betrays the origin of the second movement's melodic material: from *Mass XIII* of the *Gregorian Kyriale*. In fugal style the chorus enters: bass, tenor, alto, and soprano. Imitation is constant throughout this highly polyphonic movement, as the voices come together only near the end of phrases; Langlais accelerates the pace to the end, with stretto passages building to the conclusion. Characteristic of both the movement and the entire work is the frequent contrast of choral statements with organ commentary, as Langlais creates an ever-evolving melodic and rhythmic dialogue.

In the Sanctus/Benedictus and Agnus Dei, the melodic motives are newly composed and not based on chant any longer, but Langlais' treatment of them is the same. The Sanctus begins with a serpentine melody in the organ that slowly ascends before giving way to a majestic, forceful choral statement of "Sanctus" (Holy). The movement is set almost word by word, and again there is a crescendo to the climax: unison singing grows to six parts, for an exuberant "hosanna." The Benedictus, which immediately follows, is more restrained, a slowly moving duet of the soprano and alto at the octave, accompanied in the organ by the distinctive voix celeste. As the "hosanna" returns, so does the music of the previous section, with which it concludes.

The Agnus Dei, like its predecessors, emerges from sonic depths to build slowly to its climax, utilizing fugal style. In concert, this common aspect of the *Messe Solennelle* begins to seem too much; spaced out within the liturgy for which it was written, however, it would rather unify the work. However, the difficulty of the latter all but precludes such use. Yet in the bittersweet chromaticism of "miserere nobis" and the ascending excitement of the concluding "dona nobis pacem," it is easy to forgive this foible. *—Thomas Oram*

Recommended:

○ **Most Sacred Banquet** / Hancock (cond.), St. Thomas Choir of Men and Boys / 1996 / Koch International Classics 7228

Paul Lansky

b. Jun. 18, 1944, New York, NY

Composer: Avant-garde

A pioneer in the field of computer music, Paul Lansky was formally educated first at Queens College, then at Princeton University, and studied under such teachers as George Perle, Hugo Weisgall, Milton Babbitt, Earl Kim, and Edward Cone. He was the horn player for the Dorian Wind Quintet, and has worked for such schools as the Mannes School of Music, Swarthmore College, and Princeton University, as well as being visiting professor for several other universities. He has won several awards, including a Columbia-Princeton Electronic Music Center commission, National Endowment for the Arts Fellowship, and an American Society of Composers, Authors, and Publishers award, to name a few.

Lansky's music is primarily written for the computer. To this end, he has written his own software in order to write his music, and has received recognition for this program, called CMIX. In addition, as a major writer on music, he has been published many times in *Perspectives of New Music*, bringing him recognition as a theorist and writer.

His music cannot be pigeonholed. The style of his works changes radically from piece to piece, including everything from folk song in pieces like *Folk-Images* to the 12-tone technique, such as in his *String Quartet*. His work in the latter style brought him a wider audience, especially in his collaboration with Perle in the late 1960s and early 1970s. Lansky also experiments with timbre as a structural element, and has made many references to the styles of popular and folk music, as well as jazz.

In 1979 most of Lansky's music was for electronic tape alone. *Six Fantasies on a Poem by Thomas Campion* was written as a pointed break from his other styles of writing. The piece was conceived and completed primarily using LPC synthesis techniques, which manipulate the original timbre on the reference tape to produce the sounds required for the complete work. Many of the pieces that followed *Six Fantasies* use the timbre of the human voice for manipulations.

Much of Lansky's music has been based upon the spoken human voice; not upon the words spoken necessarily, but rather their timbre, tone, and rhythm. To this end, many of his pieces (including *Small Talk* and *Conversation Pieces*) are based originally on conversations between him and his wife, Hannah MacKay. He adds to the vocal implications already present simple acoustic sounds from orchestral instruments and the piano, and, using the computer, combines them to create timbres otherwise impossible, yet somehow familiar.*—Michael Blostein*

Overview of Works

Paul Lansky insists outright that, in contrast to the perceived traditions of classical music consumption, the vast majority of his compositions exist primarily, and often exclusively, as *recorded* rather than *performed* works. Likewise, though Lansky himself was trained in the Ivy League and continued his career as professor at Princeton University, his compositions wreak havoc on the term "classical music," both in terms of their methods and their style. On the one hand, Lansky's pieces utilize methods of production one might associate with electronic work of Stockhausen, Babbitt, and Boulez; on the other, he employs such advanced electronic technology and methodology to create music with dazzling surfaces, engaging narratives, and accessible forms.

His earliest compositions reflect the influence of his training. *mild und leise*, from 1973, takes its title from Isolde's words at the beginning of the famous "transfiguration" scene from Wagner's *Tristan and Isolde*; having studied with George Perle, Lansky created this electronically generated work by applying Perle's "12-tone tonality" theory to the opera's famously problematic "Tristan chord." (*mild und leise* would later gain notoriety by being sampled in Radiohead's hit song *"Idioteque."*) While this and other early electronic works dealt with purely synthesized timbres, Lansky soon developed a fascination with more human sounds, and soon turned his attention to manipulating sounds from the real world through highly advanced computer methods. Lansky's works demonstrate a particular fascination with human speech, and a number of pieces explore the boundary between the semantics of speech—that is, what the words mean—and the pure sound of speech. Each of his *Six Fantasies on a Poem by Thomas Campion* (1979), for example, applies a different set of filters and effects to the sound of Lansky's wife reading Campion's words. *The Lesson*, from 1989, takes as its raw material a recording of one of Lansky's former professors talking about famous composers; the speech is virtually indecipherable underneath Lansky's computer manipulations, causing the ears to enjoy the sheer contours and exaggerated harmonics of the words. *Idle Chatter* from 1985 and its musical sequels, *just_more_idle_chatter*, *notjustmoreidlechatter*, and *Idle Chatter Jr.*, string together countless tiny snippets of conversation, each bit shorter than a single syllable, layering them into lush chord progressions and mapping them onto an undulating drum track. A few works take their inspiration from other environmental noises, such as the freeway noises in *Night Traffic* (1990).

Although the overwhelming majority of his compositions are realized through electronic means and exist primarily as recordings rather than performable scores, Lansky's oeuvre also includes a number of pieces for traditional acoustical instruments. These include his *String Quartets No. 1* (1967) and *No. 2* (1971), and a much later work for the same forces entitled *Ricercare* (2000); his virtuosic *Three Moves for Marimba* from 1998; several works for guitar, including *Semi-Suite* from 1998 and *Crooked Courante* from 1997; and a handful of works for small chamber ensembles or instruments with tape, such as *Stroll* (1998) and *Values of Time* (1987). *—Jeremy Grimshaw*

Recommended:

○ **Lansky: Smalltalk** / Mackey, DeRosa / 1990 / New Albion 030
○ **Lansky: Things She Carried** / tape / 1997 / Bridge 9076
○ **Lansky: Table's Clear, Night Chatter, etc.** / tape / Bridge 9035
○ **Lansky: More than Idle Chatter** / tape / Bridge 9050
○ **Lansky: Ride** / tape / 2000 / Bridge 9103
○ **Lansky: Conversation Pieces** / tape / 1998 / Bridge 9083

AVANT-GARDE

Six Fantasies on a Poem by Thomas Campion, for computer synthesized tape (1978–1979)

It speaks to his skill and creativity as a composer that Paul Lansky's *Six Fantasies on a Poem by Thomas Campion*, though composed in the earliest stages of modern computer technology, manages to draw attention away from the (now-dated) electronic means by which it was created and instead focus the ear on its sometimes startling musical shapes. Following Milton Babbitt's maxim that nothing has a shorter shelf life than a "new" electronic sound, *Six Fantasies* initiates what for Lansky will become a lifelong project: the employment of electronic sound manipulation not so much as a tool for creating yet-unheard sound, but rather introspectively, as a means of exploring the sonic environment of everyday human experience.

Campion's poem, originally published in 1602 as "Rose cheekt Lawra," takes as its subject Petrarch's famed muse. Her beauty, Campion tells us, resonates with a "silent musick" that far transcends the "dull notes we sing" with our voices. Likewise, the composer was attracted to Campion's poetry because of its attention to sonic contour, as well as semantic content. Indeed, the composer insists, he saw in Campion (himself a composer as well as a poet) a common interest in the relationship between the spoken and the sung word. "Speech and song are commonly considered different and distinct—as apples and oranges," Lansky observes. "It is my feeling, however, that they are more usefully thought of as occupying opposite ends of a spectrum, encompassing a wealth of musical potential." Rather than setting Campion's text as a song, Lansky uses a recording of the poem (as read by his wife and frequent collaborator, Hannah MacKay) as raw materials for digital manipulation. Each of the six fantasies approaches the same four stanzas of poetry but with different tools and techniques. One of the most important is a computing technique known as Linear Predictive Coding, which involves predicting a given moment of sound data according to algorithms that consider the sound date previous to it. In telecommunications field this has a purely pragmatic use, as a means of storing huge quantities of sound data in as small a digital space as possible; in the musical realm, however, the parameters of this technique can be adjusted and exploited to drastically alter the sonic shape of the input sound. Within two decades of the *Six Fantasies*, Linear Predictive Coding would become a ubiquitous tool for composers of electronic music. Lansky applies it and a variety of other effects (including various reverberation envelopes and digital sound filters) in order to "read" the poem according to six of Laura's (or perhaps MacKay's) aspects, each corresponding with the title of one of the six fantasies: her voice, her presence, her reflection, her song, her ritual, and her self. This last fantasy, appropriately, renders the text without layers of opaque effects, leaving the words to be understood at once clearly and with the added perspective of the previous sonic explorations. *—Jeremy Grimshaw*

Recommended:

○ **Lansky: Fantasies & Tableaux** / tape / 1994 / CRI 683

Idle Chatter, for computer synthesized tape (1985)

"To my ear," says groundbreaking electronic composer Paul Lansky, "speech and song are not mutually exclusive: there is music in speech, and speech in song." After initially taking an interest in the otherworldly possibilities of computer-generated sounds while studying at Princeton in the 1960s, Lansky eventually turned his attention to the possibilities of using computers to alter and manipulate the sounds of everyday situations and interactions. Composed in 1985, *Idle Chatter* is an intricate but surprisingly listenable experiment in speech as music. Lansky uses multiple layers of altered, spliced, and concatenated speech fragments to create a dizzying web of almost-words. "The texture is designed to make it seem as if the words, rhythms, and harmonies are understandable," explains Lansky, "but what results ... is a musical surface with a lot of places around which your ear can dance while you vainly try to figure out what is going on."

It is fortunate that the surface of this music is lively enough to distract us from our disorientation. Lansky's aural microscope focuses on little bends, turns, and inflections that our ears aren't used to hearing as independent sounds, and the brain struggles to hear the barrage of noises as sentences—as if we were at a noisy party trying to follow a single exchange from among the din of multiple simultaneous conversations. As with many of Lansky's speech pieces (including such *Idle Chatter* offspring as *just_more_idle_chatter*, *Notjustmoreidlechatter*, and *Just Idle Chatter Jr.*), a remarkable thing happens a few minutes into the piece: the ear eventually abandons the task of looking for syntax and grammar in Lansky's busy terrain, and suddenly the web of speech snippets glimmer as pure noises. The foreground material sounds vaguely like some kind of rubber band orchestra, with blurping, twanging voice fragments bubbling left and right across the stereophonic spectrum. These percussive sounds are set against a scrim of airy, sustained voices, looped and stretched into broad swaths of background harmony. In this regard *Idle Chatter* almost sounds like Steve Reich's *Tehillim* or *Desert Music*: Lansky's interlocking patterns of percussive syllables stand in for Reich's marimbas and keyboards, while the sinuous voice loops in the upper ranges evoke Reich's pensive strings and singers.

There are no players here, though, unless one counts the IBM 3081 mainframe computer on which the piece was created. Such a mixture of the human and the mechanical would perhaps seem a little too Orwellian for some tastes, but Lansky makes a point of letting us know that a living, breathing person is at the controls. Rather than coercing his speech manipulations into intractable serialist systems or angular dissonances, Lansky organizes them into ethereal but surprisingly friendly tonal harmonies —which only emerge as such when we let go of the words as such and relax our minds and ears enough to listen in the abstract. *—Jeremy Grimshaw*

Recommended:

○ **More than Idle Chatter** / tape / Bridge 9050

Mario Lanza

b. Jan. 31, 1921, Philadelphia, PA, **d.** Oct. 7, 1959, Rome, Italy
Tenor

Dubbed "the greatest voice of the twentieth century" by Arturo Toscanini, Mario Lanza was one of America's most successful singers and movie stars in the years immediately following World War II. Born Alfredo Arnold Cocozza, he was the son of Italian immigrants, adopting his stage name from the masculine form of his mother's maiden name, Maria Lanza. From the age of 15, he studied to be a professional singer, later signing to the Columbia Artists Management agency as a concert singer; however, his career took a left turn in 1943, when he was drafted into the U.S. Army. Billed as "the Service Caruso," Lanza performed for his fellow infantrymen and also sang in the production *Winged Victory*; upon his return from duty, he relocated to New York, where he performed concert dates and appeared on radio. One of his audition tapes found its way to MGM's Hollywood studios, and after MGM chief Louis B. Mayer subsequently saw Lanza perform live, he signed the singer to a seven-year contract.

After making his first—and final—appearance on the professional opera stage in 1948 in the New Orleans Opera's production of *Madama Butterfly*, Lanza made his MGM debut the following year in *The Midnight Kiss*, scoring a hit with the soundtrack's "Celeste Aida" (from Verdi's *Aida*). *The Toast of New Orleans* followed, launching his first million-selling hit, "Be My Love." In 1951 Lanza starred as his idol in the biopic *The Great Caruso*, scoring another million seller with "The Loveliest Night of the Year." In 1951 he mounted his own CBS radio series, and the following year starred in *Because You're Mine*; the title song, penned by Sammy Cahn and Nicholas Brodszky, earned an Academy Award nomination, and became Lanza's third and final million-selling effort.

After completing the music for the MGM production of *The Student Prince*, Lanza walked out on the project; by allowing the studio to retain rights to the recordings, he was able to avoid a breach of contract lawsuit, with the single "The Drinking Song" rising to the top of the U.S. charts. In the wake of his walkout Lanza became a recluse, disappearing from the limelight for over a year while battling addictions to food, alcohol, and tranquilizers; he also faced a series of battles with the IRS. Finally, in 1956 he resumed his film career in the Warner Bros. production *Serenade*; however, the next year, disillusioned with American life, he moved to Italy, settling in Rome to star in 1958's *The Seven Hills of Rome*. That same year Lanza toured the U.K., making one final film, *For the First Time*. He died in 1959 of a heart attack; his passing was later rumored to have been a Mafia hit ordered following his refusal to perform at the request of mob boss Lucky Luciano, but these allegations have never been substantiated, and in fact have been refuted by the Lanza family. *—AMG*

Recommended:

○ **Mario Lanza–Don't Forget Me** / Lanza, etc. / RCA 61420

○ **Lanza: Greatest Hits** / Sinatra (cond.), Callinicos (cond.), Lanza, RCA Victor SO / 1995 / BMG 68134

○ **Legendary Mario Lanza** / Lanza, etc. / BMG 91305

Jaime Laredo

b. Jun. 7, 1941, Cochabamba, Bolivia
Violinist, Violist

Jaime Eduardo Laredo y Unzueta quickly became one of the world's most important violinists in the 1960s, known for his solo and chamber music performances and his organizational leadership. He has appeared with over a hundred orchestras in the Americas and Europe and has made dozens of recordings, winning several awards, including the Deutsche Schallplatten Prize, the Gramophone Award, and several nominations for the Grammy, which he won in 1991 for Best Chamber Music recording.

He began playing violin at the age of five. By seven, his talents were so evident that his family relocated to the United States to advance his musical training. At the age of eight, he gave his first full recital. His professional debut was with the San Francisco Symphony Orchestra. Recalling other talented child violinists who had debuted in the same place, *The San Francisco Examiner* said, "In the 1920s it was Yehudi Menuhin, in the 1930s it was Isaac Stern; and last night it was Jaime Laredo." In San Francisco, he studied with Antonio de Grassi and Frank Houser. He went to Cleveland to study with Josef Gingold and attended the Curtis Institute in Philadelphia, where his teacher was Ivan Galamian.

In May 1959, he won the Queen Elizabeth of Belgium Competition and debuted in October, 1960, at Carnegie Hall. During the first few years of his active international career as a soloist, the great conductor George Szell took time from his other activities to coach Laredo in repertoire.

In 1960, he married the Detroit-born pianist Ruth Meckler, who continued her career under the name Ruth Laredo after they divorced in 1974. He remarried, to cellist Sharon Robinson, and with pianist Joseph Kalichstein, they founded the Laredo-Robinson-Kalichstein Trio, becoming one of the world's leading chamber music ensembles. He and Robinson make their home in Vermont, where he has frequently participated in the Marlboro Festival.

Laredo founded, and is artistic director of, New York's Chamber Music at the 92nd Street Y series and is a member of the Chamber Music Society of Lincoln Center, two of the most important performance series for chamber music in the U.S. Close friend and eminent violinist Alexander "Sascha" Schneider asked Laredo to carry on his pet project, the New York String Seminar and Orchestra, which attracts young string players from throughout the U.S. during the Christmas season. In addition, in 1994 he accepted the position of jury president of the Indianapolis International Violin Competition at the personal request of the competition's founder, Josef Gingold.

In the 1970s, Laredo also began a notable conducting career. He frequently conducts both the St. Paul and the Scottish Chamber Orchestras and in the 1999–2000 season became music advisor for the Vermont Symphony Orchestra.

His commissions for new works forward the repertoire of the L-R-K Trio and duos for him and his wife. Indiana-based composer David Ott composed *Conversations*, a duo work, as well as a *Triple Concerto*, which the Trio performed with the Indianapolis Symphony under Raymond Leppard. In addition, Ned Rorem composed a *Double Concerto for violin, cello, and orchestra* for him and Robinson, which was premiered in Saarbrücken.

In addition to solo concerto performances, he has recorded other notable multi-soloist works such as Mozart's *Sinfonia concertante* and *Concertone*. Although he has appeared on major labels such as RCA and CBS/Sony, some of his most notable releases are on the American independent labels Dorian and Arabesque. For the former, he has released an acclaimed set of Schubert's complete violin and piano music with pianist Susan Brown and on Arabesque the Trio recorded the complete trios and sonatas of Dmitry Shostakovich and Maurice Ravel. *—Joseph Stevenson*

Recommended:

○ **Schubert: The Works for Violin & Piano** / Laredo, Brown / 1990 / Dorian 90137

○ **Bach: Violin Sonatas** / Gould, Rose, Laredo / 1994 / Sony 52615

Ruth Laredo

b. Nov. 20, 1937, Detroit, MI, **d.** May 25, 2005, New York, NY
Pianist
American pianist Ruth Laredo achieved considerable prominence as a concert pianist in the 1970s and 1980s and has remained active in her career into the new century. Her recordings of Rachmaninov and Scriabin's piano works were considered milestones by some and in the case of the latter composer, may well have been instrumental in the revival of his piano music in the last decades of the twentieth century.

Laredo (née Meckler) showed unusual musical talent as a child. She later enrolled at the Curtis Institute, where she studied under Rudolf Serkin. Her first performance with an orchestra provided her with instant credentials in the classical world: she appeared in 1962 at Carnegie Hall with Leopold Stokowski conducting the American Symphony Orchestra. She would later take part in another high-profile debut when she appeared with the New York Philharmonic Orchestra led by Pierre Boulez. She has had many stunning concert successes in the U.S. and Europe throughout her career, but some will contend her greatest contributions have come in the recording studio. With the release in 1971 of LP recordings of etudes, preludes, and the complete sonatas of Alexander Scriabin, Laredo drew much critical acclaim, not only for her enlightening performances, but for her bold choice to turn her attention to this then rather-neglected corner of the repertory. An even more important recording project followed: in 1975, CBS Masterworks released the first in a series of seven LPs by Laredo, devoted to the complete solo piano music of Sergey Rachmaninov. By 1981, the series was complete, giving Laredo the distinction of being the first pianist to have conquered this Mount Everest. Moreover, critical response was generally very favorable and the effort helped Laredo achieve nearly front-rank standing among the world's piano virtuosos. While she continues to record, mostly with smaller labels and focusing on the music of Bach, Beethoven, Mozart, Mendelssohn, and many others, Laredo has expanded her career to include other interests. She wrote a column for *Piano Today* magazine, occasionally appeared as a critic on New York's WQXR radio's *First Hearing*, and served as a correspondent on NPR's Morning Edition. In July 1996, Laredo turned her attention to jazz, giving a concert with jazz pianists Marian McPartland and Dick Hyman at New York's 92nd St. Y. She also appeared in Woody Allen's *Small Time Crooks* (2000), where she is shown giving a recital playing Rachmaninov. Early in her career, Laredo married the well-known violinist Jaime Laredo. Their union produced a daughter, Jennifer. Ruth Laredo was long a resident of New York City. *—Robert Cummings*

Recommended:
- ○ **Scriabin: Complete Sonatas** / Laredo / Nonesuch 73035
- ○ **Rachmaninov: Complete Solo Piano Music Vol. 1** / Laredo / 1993 / Sony 48468

Jennifer Larmore

b. Jun. 21, 1958, Atlanta, GA
Mezzo-Soprano
Jennifer Larmore is an outstanding American mezzo soprano who parlayed operatic success in Europe into international stardom during the 1990s. Known for excelling in the coloratura roles of Rossini and Handel, she has also moved into the early nineteenth century bel canto repertory, as well as the operas of Mozart and Richard Strauss. Especially since 2000, Larmore has been a very active recitalist, and she has recorded widely for the Harmonia Mundi, Teldec, and Deutsche Grammophon labels.

Originally from Atlanta, Larmore studied at the Westminster Choir College, and then privately with John Bullock and Regina Resnik. She made her professional debut at Santa Barbara's Music Academy of the West as Rosina in Rossini's *The Barber of Seville*—appropriate, considering that Rosina has since become her signature role, one that she has performed more than 500 times. Three years later, a last-minute audition led to a contract at the Nice Opera. There, her vocal talents, energetic acting, and natural beauty quickly established her as an emerging star, and during the next decade she performed dozens of leading roles with major European houses.

In the mid-1990s Larmore returned to the United States, making her Chicago Lyric Opera debut in 1993, winning the prestigious Richard Tucker award in 1994, and debuting as Rosina at the Metropolitan Opera in 1995. Since then she has been a regular attraction at the Met, singing everything from Handel's *Giulio Cesare* to Humperdinck's *Hänsel und Gretel.* With her frequent collaborator Antoine Palloc, she has made several international recital tours, including appearances in Amsterdam, Paris, Madrid, Hong Kong, and London, as well as most major American cities.

Larmore's *Giulio Cesare* on Harmonia Mundi (with René Jacobs), *L'étoile*, a collection of French arias, and *Call Me Mister*, a celebration of mezzo soprano "pants" roles, are notable among her recordings. A particularly unique venture has been her satellite radio program *Backstage with Jennifer Larmore*, on which she proves herself a witty and insightful interviewer and commentator. *—Allen Schrott*

Recommended:
- ○ **L'Étoile: French Arias** / Billy (cond.), Larmore, Vienna RSO / 2003 / Teldec 87193
- ○ **Call Me Mister** / Larmore, Welsh National Orch. / 1996 / Teldec 10211
- ○ **Monteverdi: L'incoronazione di Poppea** / Jacobs (cond.), Dery, Laurens, Coen, Larmore, Concerto Vocale / HM 901330
- ○ **Rossini: Il Barbiere di Siviglia** / Lopez-Cobos (cond.), Ramey, Hagegård, Corbelli, Larmore, Lausanne CO / 1993 / Teldec 74885

Alicia de Larrocha

b. May 23, 1923, Barcelona, Spain
Pianist
Alicia de Larrocha's greatest contribution as a musician has been her unrivaled advocacy of Spanish and Catalonian piano music. Her interpretations of the music of Albéniz, Granados, Falla, Mompou (a lifelong friend who dedicated several works to her), and Montsalvatge are universally described as brilliant, authentic, and masterful in tonal color, texture, and rhythm. She is also highly regarded for her recordings of Mozart and French Impressionist music. She began her career before the age of six with a solo recital, followed by her orchestral debut at the age of 11 performing Mozart's *"Coronation" Concerto* (K. 537) with the Orquesta Sinfónica de Madrid. She studied with Frank Marshall at his Academia Marshall and also studied music theory with Ricardo Lamote de Gignon. Her adult career began in 1940, but she did not make any international tours until 1947, when she first toured Europe. In 1953, she premiered Montsalvatge's *Concierto breve*, which is dedicated to her, and also made her first visit to England. Her first appearance in the U.S. was in 1955 with the Los Angeles Philharmonic. Since then she has performed around the world, working with such artists as Victoria de Los Angeles, Montserrat Caballé, the Guarneri and Tokyo String Quartets, Sir Colin Davis, Rafael Frühbeck de Burgos, Kent Nagano, and Gerard Schwarz. She even performed Poulenc's *Concerto for two pianos* with the composer at the second piano. In addition to her performing, she took on the directorship of the Academia Marshall in 1959. Her recordings, particularly of Albéniz and Granados, have received numerous prizes, including Grammys, the Edison Prize, the Grand Prix du Disques, and the Deutsche Schallplatten Prize. She herself has been awarded the Paderewski Memorial Medal and the Principe de Asturias prize, among others, and has been recognized for her talents by the city of Barcelona, the Spanish and French governments, and UNESCO. *—Patsy Morita*

Recommended:
- ○ **Albéniz: Iberia; Granados: Goyescas** / Larrocha / 1996 / London 448191
- ○ **The Art of Alicia de Larrocha** / Larrocha, etc. / 2003 / Decca 000018002
- ○ **Mozart: Concerto for 2 Pianos; Sonata for 2 Pianos** / Previn, Larrocha, Orch. of St. Luke's / 1995 / RCA 902668044
- ○ **Mozart: Piano Sonatas** / Larrocha / 1992 / RCA 60454

Lars-Erik Larsson

b. May 15, 1908, Åkarp, Sweden, **d.** Dec. 27, 1986, Hälsingborg, Sweden
Composer: Concerto
It would be hard to imagine a busier professional life than that of Lars-Erik Larsson, whose activities in composition, education, and broadcasting were a cornerstone of Swedish musical life in the twentieth century. Curiously, Larsson never settled on a single style of composition, switching easily among different approaches at various points in his life.

Larsson was born in 1908 in Akarp. Studies in organ, composition, and conducting culminated in a series of youthful works that highlighted him as a composer worth watching. *En spelmans jordafaerd* for violin and piano (1928) and the *Symphony No. 1* (1927–28) were written in an attractive Nordic style reminiscent of Sibelius, and they garnered not only public and professional appreciation, but also a state composer's grant which allowed him to study with Alban Berg in Vienna and Fritz Reuter in Leipzig in 1929–30. Upon his return to Sweden, Larsson earned his daily bread teaching in Malmö and Lund, writing music criticism for the *Lund Dagblad* and coaching at the Royal Theatre in Stockholm.

Larsson's year on the Continent alerted him to some of the recent developments in music. These were reflected in works written after his return, such as the *Ten Two-Part Piano Pieces* of 1932, which contained the first 12-tone music written in Sweden; but it was a bracing, somewhat athletic brand of neo-Classicism that blossomed most fully in Larsson's works, beginning with the *Sinfonietta*, which was premiered to acclaim at the 1934 ISCM Festival. Other works in this style followed, including the *Little Serenade for Strings* (1934), the *Concert Overture No. 2* (1934), the *Divertimento No. 2* (1935), and the *Piano Sonatina* (1936). More adventurous but less immediately successful were Larsson's *Symphony No. 2* (1937) and his opera *Princessen av Cypern* (The Princess from Cyprus; 1930–37), both of which were withdrawn shortly after their premieres (the *Symphony No. 2* was revised in the 1960s and has since re-entered the repertoire).

In 1937, Larsson began his fruitful association with Swedish radio, composing, conducting, and producing programs for broadcast and thereby influencing the musical tastes of thousands of Swedish listeners. One of his most interesting innovations from this association was the "lyrical suite," which he developed with Hjalmar Gullberg and Pontus Boman. In such works as *Dagens stunder* (1938), Larsson and his collaborators combined music and poetic recitation in a new and interesting way that was quite different from the old nineteenth century melodramas. During this period Larsson also composed music for films and theater; and when the Second World War broke out, he wrote the *Obligationsmarschen*, which in a Norwegian version was taken up as music of inspiration by the Norwegian resistance movement.

After World War II, Larsson embarked on another important musical mission as administrator of Sweden's state-run amateur orchestras, for which he wrote 12 attractive *Concertinos*, Op. 45. These works, with solo parts for all the major string instruments, as well as the major wind instruments and piano, were written for players of moderate ability. It's interesting to note that the *Concertinos* are more than a little reminiscent of another "practical musician"—Paul Hindemith.

At the end of his life, Larsson ventured into distant stylistic realms with a handful of works written in a highly individual version of serialism, in which clusters of notes, or "interval piles," are arranged in groups. These serious and austere works were nevertheless written cheek-by-jowl with some of his most accessible and romantic music. Larsson died in 1986, having retired from his astonishingly busy career ten years earlier. *—Mark Satola*

Overview of Works (1927–1980)

Swedish composer Lars-Erik Larsson is musically best known for his lighter neo-Classical works, such as the *Little Serenade for Strings*, and historically best-known as the first Swedish composer to use serial techniques in his works. Between these two extremes, however, lies a more complex compositional career, one that moved from Nordic Romanticism to neo-Classicism to his own brand of serialism, but one that was also informed by Larsson's innate lyricism and elegant sense of structure. His earliest works, the *Symphony No. 1* (1927–28) and *Concert Overture* (1929), are clearly in the heroic Sibelian style that dominated Scandinavian composing in the 1920s and 1930s. But Larsson sought to shake off this style by introducing elements of warm neo-Classicism in works such as *Divertimento No. 1* (1932) and his still popular *Little Serenade for Strings* (1934). And Larsson went further yet by traveling to Vienna to study with Berg, whose influence can be heard in the *Symphony No. 2* (1936–37) and his monumental four-act opera *The Princess From Cyprus* (1930–37). Both works were coldly received at their premieres, however, and were then withdrawn by the composer. Larsson worked for the Swedish radio from 1937–47 and while there, he concentrated exclusively on music for broadcasting. In the best of these works, the *Pastoral Suite* (1938) and *The Disgraced God* (1940), Larsson reverted to the graceful lyricism of his pre-Berg works. In the middle and late 1940s, Larsson returned to more dramatic instrumental works with his powerful *Symphony No. 3* (1944–45) and especially his weighty *Music for Orchestra* (1948–49). Some of the most often-performed works of this period were the Hindemithian cycle of 12 concertinos for solo instruments and small orchestra. In the late 1950s, Larsson developed his own style of serial composition based on groups of intervals in works like the austere *Adagio for Strings* (1960) and the *Orchestral Variations* (1962–63). Yet only a little later, Larsson composed the genial and gracious *Lyrical Fantasy for Orchestra* (1966). In his later works, Larsson amalgamated all his styles into a purer style of great lyrical warmth coupled with deeper intimacy. *—James Leonard*

Recommended:

- ○ **Larsson: God in Disguise** / Warren-Green (cond.), Lander, Kohn, Jonkoping Chamber Choir, Jonkoping Sinfonietta / 2002 / Intim Musik 82
- ○ **Larsson: Piano Music** / Palsson / 1996 / Bis 758
- ○ **Larsson: Symphonies 1 & 2** / Frank (cond.), Helsingborg SO / 1989 / Bis 426
- ○ **Larsson: Förklädd Gud; Symphony 3** / Frykberg (cond.), Hagegård, Nordin, Helsingborg SO / 1989 / Bis 96

CONCERTO

Concertinos for solo instruments & string orchestra, Op. 45 (1955–1957)

Immediately after World War II, Larsson found himself in charge of Sweden's state-supported amateur orchestras. He was distressed to discover how little good music was available at the amateur level, but didn't rectify the situation until a half-decade after his tenure in the government post had ended. Between 1953 and 1957, Larsson turned out a dozen concertinos suitable for performance by amateur orchestras and their principal players. He wrote one work for each of the instruments found in the standard brass quintet, woodwind quintet, and string quartet, adding the double bass and piano for good measure. He neglected, however, the tuba, harp, and tympani/percussion. They are short, ranging from about seven minutes (the *Trumpet Concertino*) to 15 (that for piano), hovering for the most part around 12, and require small forces and only modest skill. The solo parts are not entirely simple; music teachers and similarly competent players were often engaged as principals in the Swedish provinces, so the solos require technical facility, though not virtuosity. All the concertinos follow the standard three-movement, fast-slow-fast pattern with final movements sometimes returning to material from a work's opening. And except for the neo-Classical piano concertino and a general nod to Hindemith's similar but much more difficult *Kammermusik* series, they all display Larsson's Romantic side rather than venturing into the more austere and abstract styles Larsson also employed throughout his career. Perhaps because of their reputation as "easy" music, the concertinos have not been taken up with any enthusiasm by professional musicians outside Sweden, aside from university and conservatory professors and their students desperate for fresh material.

The numbering of the concertinos, incidentally, does not reflect their order of composition. Larsson grouped together the woodwind pieces, then the brass, then strings, and finally piano. The *Flute Concertino*'s outer movements are perky yet pastoral, while the central Arietta has an oriental air. The *Oboe Concertino* begins with a faux archaic Allegro and continues with a mildly melancholy Andante, but ends playfully. The *Clarinet* and *Horn Concertinos* are two of the more Hindemithian works in the set, with their firm rhythms and meandering solo lines. The *Bassoon Concertino* plays its teasing melodies off harmonies that unsettlingly flirt with the minor mode. The *Trumpet Concertino*, first to be written, is the shortest and most playful of the group aside from its very lyrical slow movement. The *Trombone Concertino* seems at least slightly satirical, with its pompous utterances in the outer movements, although the slow movement is bluesy. The *Violin Concertino* sounds in certain passages like Bartók's lighter, folk-inspired pieces; the faint Hungarian flavor remains and darkens in the *Viola Concertino*, although the last movement goes slightly Celtic while the *Cello Concertino* alludes to Swedish folk music in its finale. The *Double Bass Concertino* is the most solemn and forthright work in the collection, while the *Piano Concertino* is motoric and sparkling. *—James Reel*

Recommended:

- ○ **Orchestral Works of Lars-Erik Larsson** / Matson (cond.), NY Scandia Symphony / 2002 / Centaur 2607

Pierre de la Rue

b. ca. 1460, Tournai, Flanders (Belgium), **d.** Nov. 20, 1518, Courtrai, Flanders (Belgium)

Composer

In an age when professional musicians flung themselves from court to international court seeking the most lucrative salary and perquisites, Pierre de La Rue's temperament was marked more by loyalty and hard work. Unlike many of his contemporaries in the so-called "Josquin generation" of musicians, La Rue may never have followed the talent drain from the North to Italy, and once he had slowly worked his way up into one of the finest musical establishments in Europe, he stayed. This consummate professional musician, ordained to the deaconate, wrote copious amounts of music (30 or more masses, with at least two dozen motets and an equal number of chansons) while apparently caring for the poor in the name of Christ.

La Rue's birth in Tournai cannot be documented because of the destruction of that city's records in World War II, but his early positions of employment have been rediscovered. The earliest record calls him a tenor (adult) at St. Goedele in Brussels in 1469–70, indicating a birthdate in the early 1450s. The tenor "Pieter vander straten" then proceeded to St. Jacob's in Ghent (during 1471 and 1472) and Onze Lieve Vrouw in Niewpoort (leaving by 1477). He is known to have worked at an unknown church in Cologne at some point, and may have spent some time between 1482 and 1485 at the Cathedral in Siena, Italy. The Italian employment, however, seems questionable on musical grounds, as few traces of Italian styles appear in his music, and no Italian manuscript sources from the time contain any pieces by him. In 1489, at any rate, La Rue began serving a confraternity in 's-Hertogenbosch, from which he would move in 1492 to his "tenured" position with the Hapsburg-Burgundian chapel.

Emperor Maximilian I took La Rue into the chapel he was rebuilding for his son Philip the Fair, Duke of Burgundy (1493–1506). He served Philip throughout his reign, then sang for Philip's widow Juana in Spain until 1508. After this time, La Rue remained in Hapsburg service, as court singer for Marguerite of Austria in Mechlin from 1508 till 1514 and then briefly for the future Emperor Charles V himself. During this service, he seems to have travelled somewhat, meeting Isaac, Févin, and probably Josquin on trips to Spain; Alexander Agricola sang with him in Philip's chapel from 1500–06. He also continued composition apace; Marguerite held his music in especially high esteem, comissioning two elaborate manuscript volumes of his masses as well as including many of his chansons in her personal chansonniers. After a quarter century of Hapsburg service, La Rue retired to Courtrai in 1516, made his will later that year, and died in 1518. His epitaph lauds his musical service (erroneously read to include Hungary and Ireland), but also commemorates his virtue. *—Timothy Dickey*

Overview of Works (ca. 1485–1516)

Pierre de La Rue, like Heinrich Isaac and Jacob Obrecht, lived in the shadow of Josquin. His music, thus, is less well understood on its own merits, and more often seen in the negative. By comparison to his contemporaries, he was not as constructivist as Obrecht, not as facile with manifold national styles as Isaac, and not as concerned with textual nuance or tonal focus as Josquin; he is not as concerned as Josquin with the articulation of rhetorically potent musical structure through cadence planning and rhythmic drive (the Josquin comparisons perhaps stem from his lack of concern with trendy Italian styles). Positively speaking, his music is marked by the individuality of the vocal lines and the complex interactions between them. His music is strongly driven by imitation, often to the point of ostinato repetitions or canonic scaffolding. Duo passages punctuate the form more often than grammatical cadences. He is freer in his employment of dissonance, and in the use of dark and brooding vocal textures. In all these, the musical features, and La Rue's careful compositional hand are foregrounded.

La Rue, the consummate craftsman, left from his prolific pen nearly 30 each of masses, motets, and chansons. Among the masses, some are unified by the fifteenth century's cantus firmus technique, with borrowed melody commonly presented once per movement. He may, however, undergird such a simple structure with significant levels of canonic artifice, such as in a mass on the famous "*L'Homme armé*" tune which climaxes in a four-in-one mensuration canon in the final Agnus. In other masses (such as *Missa Sancta Dei genitrix*), an excerpt from the model may serve for an ostinato; La Rue also composed several cycles based upon a liturgically apt succession of chant models (the *Easter Mass*, the *Missa da Feria*, and the *Missa de Beata Virgine*). This is also the case with the *Requiem Mass*, a work famous for its darkly radiant colors and surprisingly low vocal textures. Only one known "parody" mass by this composer survives, an extraordinary work on many counts: the *Missa Ave sanctissima Maria*, derives its six voices throughout by canon from three, while parodying a motet model itself a six-in-three canon.

The motets and chansons are most often in four voices, with similar characteristics. Imitative writing dominates, with the exception of *O salutaris hostia*, an Elevation motet remarkably in the chordal style of the Milanese motetti missales. His penchant for canonic structures again is evident, as with the three-part canon in one of the few six-voiced motets, *Pater de coelis Deus*. A famous setting of *Absalon, fili mi*, attributed to Josquin, has been re-ascribed to La Rue on the stylistic grounds of its imitative technique, radical harmonic pattern, and extremely low voicing; it seems especially close in style to his chanson *Pourquoy non*. Though some of the Chansons follow the fixed forms (*Pourquoy tant me fault*), more jettison the poetic rigidity in favor of a freer musical form and more smooth, unbroken flow (*Il viendra le jour*). His adaptation of Ockeghem's *Fors seulement* uses his characteristic imitative motives to undermine the poetic form. In general, the secular works adopt a similar level of gravitas to their sacred counterparts. La Rue's patron Marguerite of Austria valued both his masses and chansons, and commissioned personal manuscript volumes in which to preserve and showcase them; five hundred years later, his music is finally undergoing rediscovery. *—Timothy Dickey*

Recommended:

- ○ **LaRue: Chansons from the Album of Marguerite of Austria** / Kalmanovitz (cond.), Corvina Consort / Hungaroton 32018
- ○ **LaRue: 2 Masses** / Sanvoisin (cond.), Ars Antique de Paris / 2000 / Naxos 554656
- ○ **LaRue: Missa De Sancta Anna; Lamentatione Jeremiæ** / Moll (cond.), Scola Discantus / 1996 / Lyrichord 8021
- ○ **LaRue: Requiem, etc.** / Visse (cond.), Ensemble Clément Janequin / HM 901296
- ○ **LaRue: Missa de Feria; Missa Sancta di genitrix** / Gothic Voices, Page (cond.) / 1998 / Hyperion 67010

Lily Laskine

b. Aug. 31, 1893, Paris, France, **d.** Jan. 4, 1988, Paris, France

Harpist

The daughter of Russian immigrants to Paris, harpist Lily Laskine was drawn into music by both parents. Her mother was a pianist, and she took up the piano at first. But she took more strongly to the harp, and soon she was practicing the instrument, at her mother's behest, for six hours a day. All one needs to play the harp, Laskine once said, is good fingers and a sacrificed childhood. At age eight, after some jawboning on her mother's part opened the doors, Laskine started lessons with Paris Conservatoire professor Alphonse Hasselmans, and three years later she enrolled at the venerable music school. By 1906 she had won the conservatory's top prize, and she formally embarked on her career at 13, never taking another harp lesson but continuing to absorb music and its lore throughout her life.

What made Laskine a figure strongly identified with the harp over much of the world was her catholic interest in its entire literature, regardless of genre boundaries. She refused to be categorized as a recitalist and sought out opportunities to play wherever they might be found. In 1909, she became the first female member of the Paris Opéra Orchestra, on any instrument. She remained at the Opéra until 1926, also performing with concert series orchestras such as that of the Lamoureux Association and with an orchestra led by conductor Sergey Koussevitsky. In the 1930s Laskine made several European tours and began her recording career, which included both classical and popular releases. She was heard on records with Edith Piaf, Maurice Chevalier, and other greats of French popular song, and she contributed to many film scores. In 1979 she won the Grand Prix du Film Musical for her work on the score for *La Leçon de Musique*.

A duet partner of French flutist Jean-Pierre Rampal for several decades, Laskine continued to perform and record until late in life. Several harp concertos were written for her, and she uncovered unknown historical works for harp such as Gossec's *Symphonie concertante for two harps*. Laskine served as professor of harp at the Conservatoire from 1948 to 1958, in which year she was made a Chevalier of the Legion of Honor. *—James Manheim*

Recommended:

- ○ **Sakura: Japanese Melodies for Flute and Harp** / Rampal, Laskine / CBS 34568
- ○ **Mozart: Concertos for Flute, Flute & Harp** / Paillard, Guschlbauer (conds.), Rampal, Laskine, VSO, Jean-Francois Paillard Chamber Orch. / Erato 45832
- ○ **Harpe Passion** / Laskine, etc. / 2003 / EMI 585201
- ○ **Flute & Harp** / Rampal, Laskine / Erato 45837

Orlande de Lassus

b. 1532, Mons, Hainaut (Belgium), **d.** Jun. 14, 1594, Munich, Germany

Composer: Choral, Vocal

Renaissance composer Orlande de Lassus was born in Mons and got his start as a choirboy. An often disputed story has the child Lassus kidnapped three times on account of his beautiful singing voice; the only certainty is that by 1544 he had joined the service of Ferrante Gonzaga, Viceroy of Sicily. A stopover in Mantua allowed Lassus to absorb prevailing Italian influences. Lassus spent less than a year in Sicily and transferred to Milan for the remainder of the 1540s. He often used an Italian form of his name, Orlando di Lasso. In 1551, Lassus was made choirmaster at St. John of Lateran in Rome, but remained only until 1553, being succeeded by Palestrina. Lassus returned to Mons in 1554, receiving word that his parents were ill, but upon his arrival found them already dead and buried. In 1555, Lassus' first book of madrigals and a collection of various secular works appeared simultaneously in Antwerp and Venice, thus beginning his status as a one-man industry of musical publications. Lassus' work accounts for three-fifths of all music printed in Europe between 1555 and 1600.

In 1557, the German Duke Albrecht V engaged Lassus' services as a singer at the court in Munich. Lassus' status was upgraded to Kapellmeister in 1561. His position enabled considerable travel, and Lassus made frequent trips to Venice, where he met and made friends with the Gabrielis. Judging from the wide range of settings, both sacred and secular, coming from Lassus in these years, it is apparent he was asked to supply music for a wide variety of events at the court of Duke Albrecht. The flood of published editions, both authorized and not, of Lassus' music during this time established him as the most popular composer in Europe, and in 1574 he was made a Knight of the Golden Spur by Pope Gregory XIII.

In 1579, Duke Albrecht V died, and the longstanding extravagance of his court left his successor, Duke Wilhelm, with little choice but to make deep cuts in the entertainment budget. This had a direct and negative affected on Lassus' fortunes, but nonetheless he declined an offer in 1580 to relocate to the Court at Dresden. By the late 1580s, the number of new pieces Lassus undertook began to slow down. In the months before his death, Lassus succeeded in bringing to life his last great masterwork, the *Lagrime di San Pietro*, in itself a summation of the highest forms of Renaissance musical art. He died at about the age of 62, and in 1604 his sons published an edition of his collected works entitled *Magnus opus musicum*. This was used as the basis for the first modern edition of Lassus' music, published in Leipzig between 1894 and 1926.

Among his key works, the *Sibylline Prophecies* (1553) and *Penitential Psalms* (1560) reflect the influence of Italian mannerism. While later music contains occasional chromatic alterations, mature Lassus works favor a unique style that combines an intensely dramatic sense of text painting, nervous and excited rhythmic figurations, and glorious, rolling counterpoint. Late works demonstrate a concern for terseness in expression, and texts are realized in a highly compressed state. No verifiable instrumental music is known from Lassus, and his masses are generally considered unfavorably in light of Palestrina's achievement in that realm. But his other works—motets, madrigals, French chansons, and German lieder—are considered second to none in the context of the late Renaissance, and several of his secular songs were known from king to peasant in the second half of the sixteenth century. *—Uncle Dave Lewis*

Overview of Works (ca. 1565–1594)

The letters of Lassus to his patron the Duke of Bavaria, flitting wittily between four languages, are a speculum mirroring his musical character. His French birth, Italian training, and German employment exposed this most cosmopolitan composer to all contemporary musical styles and accents. He wrote prolifically and well in every major genre, leaving more than 500 motets, around 60 masses, 102 Magnificat settings, 200 madrigals, 150 chansons, and 90 German lieder. The only constant features over such a wide repertory are Lassus' close concern for the expression of his texts and the dazzling variety of his technique.

His enormous catalog of motets, from simple didactic duos and trios to antiphonal eight-voiced works, are often considered the cornerstone of his accomplishment. His texts span a wide gamut from liturgical/Biblical excerpts through humanist and classical sources ("Dido's lament," "Dulces exuviae"), to ceremonial and occasional pieces in praise of his patrons and all manner of lighter and comic texts such as Latin drinking songs. The motets fall into rough chronological groups: the inventive and polished counterpoint of the 1550s and 1560s (with Rore and Italian fashions an early influence), the greater emphasis on declamation in the 1570s and 1580s, and concluding with the dense textures of, for example, *Musica Dei donum optimi*. Throughout the genre, his music shows a remarkable "rhetorical" power, especially through sharply profiled, epigrammatic motives and a careful directionality of harmonic motion.

In mass composition, Palestrina often eclipses him, though Lassus' masses demonstrate the same virtuosic creativity. Most of his settings parody motets (especially his own), chansons (favoring Gombert), and madrigals (Arcadelt, Rore, Palestrina). His attitude to his models, though quite sensitive to style, uses them more often as seasoning to his own music than as stock. Around 40 of his responsorial magnificat settings similarly parody a variety of polyphonic models. His pen also left a number of syllabic Missae Breves (including a breathlessly short mass for a court hunting-day morning), two requiems, four Passion narratives and other Holy Week music, penitential *psalms*, litanies, festal hymns and prospers, and fully 13 settings of the Nunc dimittis.

Nine publications of his sole authorship preserve his varied Italian madrigals. With discriminating literacy, he favors Petrarch in a large number of "serious" settings, but he covers the spectrum from light *villanesche* to declamatory settings betraying a knowledge of Marenzio to the penitential severity of the Lagrime cycle. His affective and stylistic range when setting his native French, likewise, is demonstrated by comparing the imitative texture of the famous *Suzanne ung jour*, the rhetorical control over homophony in *Bon jour, mon coeur*, and the singularly frigid chromaticism of *La nuit froide et sombre*. His chanson texts contain some serious love poetry, but dip often into earthier (even licentious) topics. In both chanson and madrigal, the music frequently opens with an imitative exordium, proceeding to lighter motivic banter. His (later) German-language settings include both sacred works (such as psalms) in a traditional cantus firmus style, and secular lieder in a more "advanced" style. *—Timothy Dickey*

Recommended:

- ○ **Lassus: Penitential Psalms** / Brown (cond.), Henry's Eight / 1998 / Hyperion 67271
- ○ **Lassus: Requiem; Magnificat** / Turner (cond.), Pro Cantione Antiqua / 2004 / DHM 60153
- ○ **Lassus: Patrocinium Musices** / Nevel (cond.), Cabre, Laethem, Caals, Van Altena, Currende, Concertino Palatino / Accent 8855
- ○ **Lassus: Chansons** / Visse (cond.), Bellocq, Clement Janequin Ens. / HM 1951391
- ○ **Lassus: Sacred Choral Music; Missa ad imitationem vinum bonum** / Skidmore (cond.), West, His Majesty's Sagbutts & Cornetts, Ex Cathedra / 1996 / ASV 150
- ○ **Lassus: Moduli Quinis Vocibus** / Herreweghe (cond.), Collegium Vocale, Hannover Boys Choir Soloists / 2001 / Astrée 10887
- ○ **Lassus** / Hillier (cond.), Hilliard Ens. / 1998 / ECM 453841
- ○ **Lassus: Missa Osculetur me** / Phillips (cond.), Tallis Scholars / 2002 / Gimell 18

CHORAL

Lamentationes Hieremiae, for 5 voices

The rhythms of Hebrew funereal verse pattern give pattern to the plangent poetry of the prophet Jeremiah's lament over the holy city of Jerusalem, fallen through sin to the Babylonians. The Catholic Church appropriated verses from Lamentations for the mournful and most penitential *sacrum triduum*, the Holy Days leading up to Easter. The tripartite night office of Matins for Maundy Thursday, Good Friday, and Holy Saturday consists of three nocturns, each containing three chanted psalms, and three Lessons selected from the Lamentations. The affective texts and solemn liturgical occasion attracted composers through the fifteenth and sixteenth centuries; Morales, Victoria, Isaac, La Rue, Palestrina, and Tallis all composed at least one setting. Orlando de Lassus set a selection of these texts for four vocies in the early 1580s and published a rich five-voiced setting in 1585, written for the monastery of Benediktbeuern.

Lassus chose three verses from each Lesson, creating a structure of interlocking "perfections": three services, three lessons, three verses each. This structure is framed by "punctuation" texts, which function like formal rhetorical devices. Each Lesson begins with an *incipit*, to introduce the mode and "to render the ears and mind of the listener attentive to the song" (in Burmeister's words); each concludes with a refrain from Hosea, "Jerusalem, turn to the Lord your God," reiterating the pentitential drive of the liturgy. Each verse, furthermore, opens with a single Hebrew letter: the original text was an acrostic poem (Aleph, Beth, Gimel), and Jerome's Vulgate translation (as well as some modern English ones) retained the acrostics at the head of each verse. Lassus, conventionally, provides related introductory musical passages rich in imitation and invention for each acrostic. These serve both the musical purpose of modal introduction and the aesthetic one of solemnity and ornamentation—much like the illuminated capitals in a lavish presentation manuscript.

Though this work is less exhuberant in text painting than his madrigals, and less chromatically daring than the *Prophetiae Sibyllarum*, Lassus carefully wields his tonal weaponry for powerful rhetorical effect. He generally holds to full five-voiced textures, allowing harmonic progressions to bear the weight of textual representation. A descending harmonic sequence at the end of the "vigilavit iugum" section, for instance, evokes the text's powerless descent ("hands from which I am unable to rise"); other examples include the subtle poignancy of sudden bass descents in "O vos omnes" and at the word "silence" in "Bonus est Dominus." Though the vocal tessituras do not noticeably change over these progressions, a sense of motion is unavoidable; the motion is not a linear melody, but, in a sense, linear harmony within Lassus' modal system. His peregrinations (via accidentals) from extremely "sharp" harmonies (E major) to extremely "flat" (E flat) are always anchored, however, by a firm cadential structure, which favors the more "sorrowful" plagal motions, until the Lessons begin to speak of mercy in texts for the hours just before Easter sunrise. Without recourse to the mannered experimental style popular among the madrigalists of his day, Lassus fashions a Lamentations cycle which poignantly evokes the austerity, the pathos, and the hidden hope of Holy Week. *—Timothy Dickey*

Recommended:

- ○ **Lassus: Hieremiae Prophetae Lamentationes** / Herreweghe (cond.), Ens. Vocale Europeen de la Chapelle Royale / HM 901299

Masses (ca. 1565–1594)

So prolific was Orlando de Lasso in other areas of composition (particularly the motet, of which he composed over 500), and so adept was he at meeting new textual imagery with creative musical embodiments, that his masses are sometimes considered a secondary aspect of his musical career. "The unchanging text [of the Ordinary liturgy]," one prominent scholar has suggested, "does not seem to have stirred the composer's imagination as profoundly as the varying texts of the motets." The later twentieth century saw renewed interest in Lasso's masses, however. Indeed, considered on their own, these works demonstrate an impressive variety of style and compositional approach; despite the shadow cast over them by the rest of Lasso's extensive output, these works constitute an important part of the repertoire of sacred vocal music that has been passed down to us from the latter half of the sixteenth century.

Lasso's masses all date from the late 1550s, by which time he had accepted employment in Munich at the court of the Duke of Bavaria. As he would retain this position until his death in 1594, his entire output in the mass genre—comprising some 70 works in total—is linked to the Bavarian court. The majority of Lasso's masses are known in modern parlance as "parody masses"; that is, masses based on musical materials that are borrowed or derived from a preexisting piece of vocal polyphony. Many of Lasso's masses take as their borrowed source material the composer's own motets. For example, his *Missa Locutus sum* is a complex six-voice work from 1587 that is based on a six-voice motet Lasso had composed nearly 20 years earlier. Sources for other parody masses include a number of other motets by Lasso himself, as well motets, French chansons, and Italian madrigals by other composers—including such prominent figures as Palestrina (*Io son ferito ahi lasso*), Willaert (*Qui la dira*, *Rompe di l'empio cor*), and Rore (*Qual donna attende*, *Scarco di doglia*, and others). These works demonstrate a reconciliation between, on the one hand, the lush vocal sonority and compositional unity inherent in the parody mass genre, and on the other, Lasso's tendency toward evocative and carefully rhetorically text expression.

His mass output includes a number of less substantial works, categorized as missae breves. These works, concise in their musical materials and text declamation, include some parody masses (often borrowing from source that themselves are polyphonically streamlined and/or syllabic) as well as some plainchant-based works. One of the most curious of the shorter masses is the *Missa venatorum* or *Jäger Mass*, a work that executed the liturgical texts as expeditiously as possible so that the men of the court could be done with church and spend the rest of the day hunting. The popularity during his lifetime of some of Lasso's shorter masses, well-crafted as they may be, seems until relatively recently to have distracted attention from his more venerable contributions to the mass repertoire. *—Jeremy Grimshaw*

Recommended:

- ○ **Lassus: Missa Osculetur me** / Phillips (cond.), Tallis Scholars / 2002 / Gimell 18
- ○ **Lassus** / Hillier (cond.), Hilliard Ens. / 1998 / ECM 453841

Motets (ca. 1565–1594)

Orlando di Lasso stands as one of the most prolific composers of the sixteenth century, and while his ocuvre includes pieces in virtually every genre of the day—including mass movements and cycles, madrigals, and chansons—he is best known for his huge body of motets. Indeed, the *Magnum opus musicum*, a collection of his works that his sons published in 1604 as a tribute to their father after his death (in 1594), contains over 500 motets. Among these one finds pieces covering a broad spectrum of style and function, from relatively simple two-voice works meant for training pupils, to grand ceremonial motets for up to ten voices, composed to commemorate important occasions in the Bavarian ducal court in Munich, where he was employed for most of his career.

A stylistic chronology is difficult to derive from Lasso's huge motet output (largely because the publication prepared by his sons arranged the works according to number of voices rather than date of composition or publication). Nonetheless, scholars have recognized at least two broad periods in the development of Lasso's motet style. In the first two decades of his career (roughly to the early 1570s), one observes a careful balance between lucid (though often adventurous) harmonic trajectories, evocative text expression, and clarity of text delivery. The famous *Penitential Psalms*, a cycle of five-voice motets composed for Duke Albrecht in the late 1550s, stand as a fine exemplar of these qualities. Scholars have noted in these works both Lasso's ability to evoke the general mood of a text through his general musical framework of texture and harmony, as well as his ability to set off certain words or ideas in clever pictorial fashions. Indeed, Lasso's biographer Samuel Quickelberg, writing on the *Penitential Psalms*, praised the composer's ability to "describe an object almost as if it were before one's eyes." Another prominent observer of the time, Joachim Burmeister, considered Lasso's motets in terms of rhetorical strength, going so far as to identify in Lasso's *In me transierunt* (a motet published in 1562) a long inventory of musically realized rhetorical devices, which for him embodied Lasso's ability to compel his listener's minds and hearts. The term "musica reservata" appears frequently in connection with Lasso's work from this period, referring variously to his skill at musical pictorialization, his mastery of advanced harmonic procedures, and the sophistication of his overall style.

The later decades of Lasso's career saw something of a change in style (though again, chronological ambiguity and stylistic diversity problematize this claim). As the rustic Italian song styles of the villanella, villanesca, and later, the canzonetta, became increasingly popular, Lasso seems to have sometimes adopted a style in which short chordal sections in unadorned text declamation would alternate with brief and unassuming imitative passages. More assured of his stylistic maturity, however, works from the last years of his life (such as the magnificent six-voice motet *Musica Dei donum optimi*), demonstrate a culmination of Lasso's craftsmanship and expressive gift. *—Jeremy Grimshaw*

Recommended:

- ○ **Lassus: Moduli Quinis Vocibus** / Collegium Vocale, Knabenchor Hannover / Astrée 7780
- ○ **Lassus: Penitential Psalms** / Brown (cond.), Henry's Eight / 1998 / Hyperion 67271

Prophetiae Sibyllarum . . . chromatico more singulari confectae, motet collection for 4 voices

For the sixteenth century humanist, Christianity was tied to Antiquity through hidden strands that included mythology, magic, cosmology, and alchemy. The Ancients were credited with a fabulous wealth of hidden knowledge secretly passed down through carefully guarded channels. Exemplifying this secret knowledge are the messianic prophecies of the Sibyls, a prime instance of the Renaissance Christian reverence toward ancient mystic voices. Thus, Michelangelo painted five of the Sibyls alongside several Old Testament prophets on the ceiling of the Sistine Chapel. Orlande de Lassus' *Prophetiae Sibyllarum*, based on Latin writings inspired by the Sibyls, differs from the rest of his oeuvre by virtue of its incredible harmonic language and intricate voice leading. Furthermore, in the spirit of the humanists' interest in occult knowledge, the *Prophetiae Sibyllarum* were performed for select insiders only, and were not published until after the composer's death.

An exact composition date is not known. However, evidence suggests that in the early 1550s Lassus would have been witness to the great debate about chromaticism taking place at the time, and as a young composer of barely 20 years, sided with more musically progressive parties. A Latin print of the *Sibylline Prophecies* was released in 1555, suggesting that perhaps the harmonically and intellectually ambitious Lassus combined his interest in radical chromaticism and Christian mysticism to produce the *Prophetiae Sibyllarum* in the middle or late 1550s. So extreme was the experimentation found in these settings that Lassus seems to have abandoned it.

Following a prologue, there are musical renditions of verses by each of 12 Sibyls. The musical prologue, while explaining the chromatic style in which the subsequent prophecies will be set, follows a dizzying harmonic trajectory in which virtually every word is accompanied by a move to an unexpected chord. At the same time, the individual voices proceed in a more or less logical melodic fashion. However, it should be pointed out that modern singers face the challenge of singing in just intonation (as opposed to equal temperament, the current tuning system used in Western classical music). Sung in a "modern" fashion, the work drastically slides out of tune. The extreme chromaticism of this composition has prompted certain scholars to suggest links between music and alchemy. After all, the alchemist also practices chromaticism—the Greek word *chroma* means "color." A successful alchemical transfiguration was signaled by particular observable changes in the color of the mixture. The analogy between alchemy and Lassus' *Prophetiae Sibyllarum* seems compelling: only when the intricate individual lines are carried out accurately and with intonational precision does the chromaticism take on the desired harmonic hue. *—Jeremy Grimshaw*

Recommended:

- ○ **Lasso: Prophetiae Sibyllarum** / Junghanel (dir.), Cantus Colln / 2002 / Deutsche HM 77854
- ○ **Lassus** / Hillier (dir.), Hilliard Ens. / 1998 / ECM 453841

VOCAL

Lagrime di S Pietro (Tansillo), madrigal cycle

Orlando di Lassus published his first books of madrigals later in life, but obviously composed many either during, or in memory of, his travels in Italy in the 1540s and 1550s. He generally favored settings of Petrarch's poetry, using sensitive and starkly expressive musical gestures to convey a very close reading of his text. He published the *Lagrime di San Pietro* (the "Tears of St. Peter"), on the other hand, in the last year of his life, completing the cycle of compositions six weeks before his death and possibly thinking of death while writing this dolorous, but farsighted, cycle of *Madrigali spirituali*. This important madrigal sub-genre (pioneered by Palestrina) used the techniques of madrigal composition to set vernacular sacred texts, apparently for amateur performance in private chambers. The vernacular texts sometimes rearranged popular love songs, substituting the Virgin Mary for the Beloved, but were often freely composed devotional lyrics. A strong penitential cast to the entire repertory reflects the severity of Counter-Reformation piety. Lassus' cycle sets 20 *ottave* from a contemporary cycle of poems, followed by a single Latin stanza. The 20 stanzas of Italian poetry come from a longer (though incomplete) poetic cycle by Luigi Tansillo. The form of each is *ottava rime*, the classic eight-line Italian stanzaic form, with rhyme scheme ABABABCC; the severe and pessimistic set describes the contrition of St. Peter as an old man, as he remembers his betrayal of Christ. The first six stanzas use a variety of images to describe the old man's recollected painful moment (described in Luke 22:61–62) when, after Peter's denial, Jesus turned and their eyes met. Stanzas seven and eight quote the rebuke he imagined in Christ's gaze at that moment. The six following recall Peter's desperate escape from these eyes and the flooding of his own with tears. Stanzas 15 to 20 speak in the first person of the despair which he felt then and which still, near the hour of his death, makes him feel unworthy of salvation. Appended to this selection is a single Latin stanza, which serves the same function as a figure in an altarpiece painting whose eyes look outward—to make the drama personal for the viewer. The voice of Christ Himself is evoked in this final stanza, asking all who pass by to consider the suffering He endured, and His greater suffering at humankind's ingratitude. Lassus' cycle of three times seven stanzas, set for a lush seven-voiced texture, displays both an almost atomistic concern for local motifs and an innovative large-scale tonal arch over the entire cycle. The seven voices offer a variety of textures, often counterpoising antiphonal groups. In contrast to the floridity of his earlier madrigal style, these late pieces conjure up small images in the text by means of much smaller motifs and much subtler tonal motions. But at the same time, the Lagrime as a set build powerfully on one another through key relationships. The first 15 *madrigali* move gradually through related keys (each key thought at the time to carry its own intrinsic emotional affect) in glacially increasing intensity. Madrigals 16 to 20 in the cycle shift suddenly and affectively to the "flat" side of the tonal spectrum, the more mournful and despairing; the specific line of text upon which the shift occurs is "O vita troppo rea, troppo fallace" ("O wicked, deceptive life!"). The final Latin stanza receives the most evocative tonal treatment, even venturing into outright chromaticism in its dramatic concluding pathos. *—Timothy Dickey*

Recommended:

- ○ **Lassus: Lagrime di San Pietro** / Herreweghe (cond.), Ens. Vocal Europeen / HM 901483
- ○ **Lassus: Lagrime di San Pietro** / Nevel (cond.), Huelgas Ens. / 1993 / Sony 53373
- ○ **Lassus: Lagrime di San Pietro** / Picotti (cond.), Capella Ducale Venetia / 2003 / CPO 999862

Giacomo Lauri-Volpi

b. Dec. 11, 1892, Lanuvio, Italy, **d.** Mar. 17, 1979, Valencia, Spain

Tenor

The intense, sometimes febrile art of Giacomo Lauri-Volpi seemed, during his early prime, a natural extension of his voice—powerful, edgy, and possessed of a rapid, nervous-sounding vibrato. Described as "a law unto himself" by soprano Maria Carbone, Lauri-Volpi eventually settled into a somewhat more measured (though scarcely less competitive) artistry and may be considered one of the most important Italian tenors of his age. He continued to sing well into his sixties, although by that time, mere loudness was the primary attraction. An intelligent man behind the temperamental façade, he wrote perceptively of his own singing and that of other contemporary artists.

Following studies at Rome's Accademia di Santa Cecilia with Enrico Rosati and Antonio Cotogni, Lauri-Volpi made his stage debut in Viterbo in the role of Arturo in Bellini's *I Puritani.* He sang that 1919 production under the name of Giacomo Rubini. The following year, he introduced himself to Rome, singing the role of Des Grieux in Massenet's *Manon* (opposite the famous Rosina Storchio) as Giacomo Lauri-Volpi. His La Scala debut came in 1922 as the Duke and he remained an important singer there throughout the 1920s and 1930s.

Lauri-Volpi first appeared at the Metropolitan Opera on January 26, 1923, as the Duke, opening a decade-long relationship with that house singing, among other roles, the first American performance of Rodolfo in Verdi's *Luisa Miller.* He sang in the November 16, 1926, American premiere of *Turandot,* Calaf being a perfect match for his firm legato and brilliant top notes. The tenor's debut had brought a positive verdict from veteran critic W.J. Henderson who deemed his voice of "excellent quality," but questionable health held more comprehensive evaluation at bay. Subsequent seasons brought a greater appreciation of his gifts, although he never won the level of acclaim that greeted him in his native country. At the end of the 1932–33 season, he was not re-engaged.

The tenor's debut at Covent Garden in 1925 as Andrea Chénier found the tenor's "top notes and Italian vulgarities" pleasing those in the gallery but not many others. Apparent fee problems kept Lauri-Volpi away from London until 1936, when he returned as the Duke in *Rigoletto* and refused, perhaps because of a tepid reception, to take even a single curtain call. As Radames and Cavaradossi, the tenor had better fortune, being well-received in both roles and, in the latter, showing his ability to out-sing a too-loud orchestra. His high fees, however, precluded a reengagement.

Seasons at Paris and at the Teatro Colón in Buenos Aires brought generally positive reviews. Among honors in Italy were his assignment of the title role in Boito's *Nerone* to open the Teatro dell'Opera in Rome in 1928 and his engagement for the role of Arnold in La Scala's centenary mounting of *Guillaume Tell.* From the mid-1930s on, Lauri-Volpi's performances took place primarily in Italy and Spain. Although he retired at 67, he occasionally appeared at public occasions to sing an aria or two, most notably at Barcelona when, at age 80, he sang "Nessun dorma" from *Turandot.*

Lauri-Volpi wrote five volumes of memoirs and singing treatises, his two final publications, *Voce parallele* (1955) and *Misteri della voce umana* (1957), being the best-known and most influential. He was remembered by the public and colleagues alike as an uneven, but often electrifying singer. *—Erik Eriksson*

Recommended:

○ **Giacomo Lauri-Volpi** / Lauri-Volpi, etc. / 1993 / Nimbus 7845

○ **Lebendige Vergangenheit: Giacomo Lauri Volpi** / Lauri-Volpi, etc. / Preiser 89012

Henry Lawes

b. Jan. 5, 1596, Dinton, Wiltshire, England, **d.** Oct. 21, 1662, London, England

Composer

Henry Lawes is remembered, if at all, as the elder brother of now famous William Lawes and the composer for Milton's *Comus.* Readers of English poetry may recall the several fond tributes to Henry Lawes scattered through the works of Milton, Herrick, Carew, Waller, and a number of lesser poets, yet during his life it was Lawes' name and reputation as the composer to their verses that presented an attractive cover for *their* work. And when Ezra Pound, in a climactic moment of *The Pisan Cantos,* indicts the refrain "Lawes and Jenkyns guard thy rest/Dolmetsch ever be thy guest," it is Henry Lawes who is invoked, along with his fellow composer to the courts of both Charles I and Charles II, John Jenkins. Henry Lawes composed well over 400 songs to become the most celebrated lyric composer of his age: his relative neglect represents an important large gap in the knowledge of seventeenth century English music. Henry Lawes was born in Dinton, Wiltshire, in 1596, the year Shakespeare's *King John, The Merchant of Venice,* and Part I of *Henry IV* were first staged. Lawes' early life is a matter of conjecture—he *may* have been a chorister at Salisbury Cathedral, he *may* have studied music with Coprario, he *may* have befriended Milton around 1630. John Egerton, Earl of Bridgwater, *may* have become his patron as early as 1615, but by 1620 Lawes was moving in court circles. Firm dating begins with his becoming a "pistoler" of the Chapel Royal January 1, 1626, and Gentleman the following November 3. January 6, 1631, he joined Charles I's cadre of musicians "for the lutes and voices," by which time his reputation at large would have been made by manuscript circulation of his voluminous production of songs. He *may* have been instrumental in the commissioning of Milton to write *Comus,* a masque privately performed by Lawes and the Bridgwater children at Ludlow Castle September 29, 1634, to celebrate the Earl's elevation to Lord President of the Council of Wales, and from the music of which only five settings by Lawes survive. The Civil War claimed William Lawes at the Battle of Chester in 1645, but Henry seems to have thrived during the Commonwealth as music teacher to remaining Loyalists. With the Restoration, Lawes resumed his former posts, and his anthem *Zadok* the priest was sung at Charles II's coronation, April 23, 1661. *—Adrian Corleonis*

Overview of Works (ca. 1635–1661)

English composer Henry Lawes (1596–1662) occupies an important place among English songwriters. He was appointed one of the composers of the Chapel Royal and in 1631 became one of Charles I's musicians for "lute and voices." Lawes collaborated in a number of court masques, either with his brother William (*The Triumphs of the Prince d'Amour*) or others. On the *Restoration* in 1660, Lawes composed the anthem *Zadok the Priest* for the coronation of Charles II.

Although Henry Lawes composed church, theater, and instrumental music, his overwhelming importance lies in his abilities as a composer of songs, both sacred and secular. Two collections stand out among the former: the *Choice Psalms* of 1648, which were dedicated to Lawes' soon to be executed royal master Charles I; and the *Select Psalmes of a New Translation,* the words of which were verse translations by two poets with whom Lawes closely worked at court: Thomas Carew and George Sandys. Set for five voices and "symphonies of violins, organ, and other instruments," they were obviously designed for chamber use in secret during the Commonwealth. Some, such as the extended *My Soul the Great God's Praises Sings,* however, belong to the tradition of the verse anthem, while others, like the beautiful *Sitting By Streams* are five-part settings with instrumental ritornellos.

Lawes' secular songs vary in design from dramatic cantatas, of which the most famous is his Ariadne's lament *Theseus, O Theseus,* to simple strophic settings often in verse and refrain form. The former, although Lawes draws upon and adapts to his own needs the declamatory Italian style, bears little resemblance to Monteverdi's famous setting, being rather a discursive narration of events rather than Monteverdi's bold, grand scena. The simpler songs show a considerable gift for lyric charm and great skill in setting the English language. Many were composed to pastoral texts by such Cavalier poets as Carew and Herrick and, as in a song like *Chloris Now Thou Art Fled Away,* tap into a vein of gentle, wistful nostalgia. Others, such as *This Mossy Bank,* are set in the dialogue form popular among composers during the seventeenth century. Perhaps most moving of all is the *Pastoral Elegie to the Memory of My Deare Brother, William Lawes,* composed following the death of the latter at the Siege of Chester in 1645. Henry Lawes also tapped into a lighter vein in his secular songs, composing a number of catches and humorous part-songs, of which *The Angler's Song* set to words by Izaak Walton is a good example. *—Brian Robins*

Recommended:

○ **Sitting by the Streams** / Rooley (cond.), Consort of Musicke / 1993 / Hyperion 66135

William Lawes

b. May 1, 1602, Salisbury, England, **d.** Sep. 24, 1645, Chester, England

Composer: Orchestral

William Lawes, son of a lay vicar at Salisbury Cathedral, showed (like his older brother Henry Lawes) musical promise at any early age. He found an early patron in Edward Seymour, Earl of Hertford, who brought the young chorister to his Wiltshire estates to study music with his private music master, the renowned John Coprario. William likely met the future King Charles I (r. 1625–49) through Coprario. William and his brother were both named musicians "in ordinary for the lutes and voices" for Charles' court; the honor came to William in 1635, though it appears he was composing personally for the King at least as early as 1633. While in Charles' service, Lawes contributed vocal and instrumental music to the life of the court, as well as music for the Masques popular in Caroline England. William Lawes went with the King to Oxford in 1642 and enlisted in the royalist army (a portrait in Oxford depicts him in Cavalier garb). Though for his safety Lawes was made a commissary in the King's personal guard, he suffered a fatal gunshot wound while relieving the siege of Chester in 1645. King Charles reputedly mourned for Lawes as the "Father of Musick."

Though none of William Lawes' music appeared in print during his lifetime, his brother released certain of his psalm settings and sacred canons in the *Choice Psalms* of 1648, and the influential published collections of John Playford beginning around 1650 furthered both the dissemination and popularity of his music. He wrote prolifically and idiomatically for the consort of viols. His suites and fantasias meld the fluidity of late Renaissance counterpoint with the more "mannered" chromatic colors of the late madrigal; he did in fact know some of the works of

Marenzio and Monteverdi. His other chamber music (especially involving violins), on the other hand, displays an early Baroque idiom of paired strings and basso continuo. Some scholars of his music speculate that this Italian style reached him though Coprario's tutelage.

Despite his large instrumental output, and an even greater number of secular songs and Anglican anthems surviving from his pen, William's greatest legacy may have been his dramatic music. Between the years 1633 and 1641, he contributed music to at least 25 courtly Masques and other dramatic productions. The English courtly Masque at this time comprised a composite art form with music, dance, drama, and scenery, comparable to the Lullian *Ballet de cour* in France. Early in the century, Ben Jonson and Inigo Jones were leading collaborators in the Masque. The genre climaxed in the spectacular *Triumph of Peace* (1634) by James Shirley, to which William Lawes contributed music. His achievement in stage music made possible the later work of Matthew Locke, John Blow, and eventually Henry Purcell himself. *—Timothy Dickey*

ORCHESTRAL

Fantasia-Suites (ca. 1630–1645)

William Lawes (1602–45) was the most important English composer between Orlando Gibbons and Henry Purcell. Born in or near Salisbury, he received his early musical training from John Coprario, later joining Prince Charles' musical retinue. When the prince succeeded to the throne as Charles I, both Lawes and his brother Henry became an important part of the king's musical establishment. Lawes' devotion to his monarch was such that on the outbreak of the Civil War he took up arms in the Royalist cause, tragically meeting his death at the Siege of Chester.

While his brother excelled in the composition of vocal music, William Lawes' greatness as a composer rests principally with his instrumental chamber works, which include compositions for viol consort, a form favored in England for well over a century, and music for the more modern and increasingly popular violin. The so-called fantasia-suites fall into the latter category. These form two groups, each consisting of eight "setts," as Lawes termed them, cast in three movements: a "Fantazia" followed by two dances, an Almaine and a Galliard. One group is scored for violin, bass viol, and keyboard (chamber organ), the other for two violins, bass viol, and chamber organ. That the two sets were intended to complement each other is clear from the key sequence Lawes follows, which is identical in each group.

The influence of the Italophile Coprario (who changed his original name from John Cooper) is in evidence in the use of Italianate ornamental figurations, but in general terms the sets inhabit an introverted, at times elegiac world very different from the brilliant and better-known Royal Consort suites. The main emotional weight of the fantasia-suites falls on the opening movements, although Lawes ensures that we are aware that these are serious chamber works by adding a slow and sometimes extended coda to the concluding galliard. While the violin writing at times recalls early Italian Baroque techniques, the construction of Lawes' music, with its terse motifs, is far removed from such models.

In the opening fantazias in particular, the composer often uses fragmentary material that constantly undergoes changes of mood and rhythm, at the same time employing an astonishing freedom in the skillfully wrought counterpoint and interchange of material between the instruments. The organ parts are particularly notable, attaining a degree of emancipation that is far removed from the keyboard's role as a continuo instrument. More than anything, these works reveal Lawes as an audacious innovator, a free romantic spirit constantly able to surprise the listener with an odd melodic twist or unexpected harmonic progression. *—Brian Robins*

Recommended:

- ○ **Sonatas for Violin & Continuo** / Egarr / HM 901493
- ○ **Lawes: Fantasia Suites** / Purcell SQ / 1994 / Chandos 0552

Andrew Lawrence-King

b. 1959, Guernsey, England

Harpist

Like many of England's finest musicians, Andrew Lawrence-King began his career in choir school, serving as head chorister for the Cathedral and Parish Church of St. Peter Port, Guernsey. He took an organ scholarship to Cambridge University, where he read mathematics, but finished his studies in organ and voice at the London Early Music Centre. A party at a harpmaker's house gave the opportunity for Lawrence-King to own his first early harp, modeled after a Medieval Irish instrument. Without any modern teachers of historical harp performance available, he proceeded to teach himself the technique by studying historical sources, literary, iconographical, and musical. He discovered the "perfection" of plucked instruments, which can play both melody and polyphony.

Since then, Lawrence-King has performed with many of the leading early music ensembles in the world, playing continuo and as harp soloist with Hesperion XX, Tragicomedia (which he founded with Stephen Stubbs in 1988), the Harp Consort, and with Christopher Page's Gothic Voices, Paul Hillier's Theatre of Voices, Stephen Stubbs, Ton Koopman, Andrew Parrott, and Paul O'Dette. In addition, he conducts Baroque orchestras throughout Europe. He has been awarded the 1992 Erwin Bodky Award (Cambridge, MA, Society for Early Music), the 1996 American Handel Society Prize (for his recording of *Alcina*), the 1997 Noah Greenberg Award from the American Musicological Society, and the 1998 Echo Klassik Prize for Best Early Music Recording. The Akademie für Alte Musik in Bremen appointed Lawrence-King professor of harp and continuo; in his spare time, he earned the Yachtmaster Certificate from the Royal Yachting Association. Over 100 recordings of music spanning more than 500 years bear the imprint of his artistry.

Improvisation lies at the heart of Andrew Lawrence-King's approach to performing early instrumental music. Though music history clings to its notated sources, he argues that the unwritten traditions of Medieval and Renaissance instrumentalists may be recovered and brought to audiences in a vital way; he has compared his type of improvisation to the vitality of jazz, which follows an "emotional logic" more than a formal one, and which stretches, yet remains within, clear stylistic boundaries. Both the harp and early keyboard instruments have been excellent vehicles for his music, both able to mingle tone colors and effortlessly shift from melodic use to polyphony (he numbers them among the "perfect instruments"). His creative approach shows especially well in a series of collaborative recordings with Paul Hillier and with the work of his ensemble the Harp Consort, founded in 1994 of all continuo improvisers, with group improvisation its aesthetic goal. *—Timothy Dickey*

Recommended:

- ○ **The Harp of Luduvíco** / Lawrence-King / 1992 / Hyperion 66518
- ○ **Missa Mexicana** / Lawrence-King (cond.), Harp Consort / 2002 / HM 907293
- ○ **Miracles of Notre Dame** / Lawrence-King (cond.), Harp Consort / 2003 / HM 907317
- ○ **Treasures of the Spanish Renaissance** / Hill (cond.), Lawrence-King, O'Donnell, Van Der Beek, Westminster Cathedral Choir / 1993 / Hyperion 66168
- ○ **Jácaras!** / O'Dette, Lawrence-King, O'Brien, Estevan, Player / 1998 / HM 907212

Jean-Marie Leclair

b. May 10, 1697, Lyon, France, **d.** Oct. 22, 1764, Paris, France

Composer: Chamber Music, Opera

The French violinist and composer Jean-Marie Leclair (often referred to as "the elder" to distinguish him from a younger brother who went by the same name) is remembered for an effective synthesis of his own Parisian musical heritage with the Italian sonata style brought into vogue by Corelli.

Born in 1697 to a French lacemaker and cellist, Leclair was considered a master of both the violin and his father's lacemaking trade by the time he reached adulthood. His skill as a dancer earned him a position with the Lyons Opera (1716 or perhaps a little earlier), and in the next few years it is probable that he either lived in or was a frequent visitor to Paris (an assumption scholars base on a 1721 Parisian musical publication which included ten of Leclair's violin sonatas). By 1723 Leclair had convinced Joseph Bonnier, one of France's wealthiest aristocrats, to publish his Opus 1 collection of violin sonatas, which were received with great admiration by the Parisian musical establishment.

Around 1726 Leclair found his way to Turin to study with violinist-composer G.B. Somis, as well as to compose ballet interludes (now lost) for opera productions at the Teatro Regio Ducale. A second opus of violin sonatas was published in 1728, and during that same year Leclair made his debut as a violinist at the Concert Spirituel. Performances of his own music in London, Kassel (where Leclair engaged in a musical "duel" with famed Italian violinist Pietro Locatelli) and Paris earned Leclair a reputation as one of the leading figures of the new French school of violinist-composers. Formal recognition came in 1733 with an appointment to the musical court of Louis XV, to whom Leclair dedicated his third opus of violin sonatas as a display of gratitude.

Leclair divided his time between a number of court appointments for the remaining decades of his life, including positions at The Hague, at the court of Orange in the Netherlands, and in the service of the Duke of Gramont (a former pupil of the composer). The official investigation of Leclair's suspicious death in 1767 incriminated both his nephew and his second wife (the couple had lived in separate households since 1758), but neither was ever formally charged with his murder.

Leclair took the Italian sonata da chiesa and the sonata da camera and infused them with a stylistic elegance derived largely from the ballet music of Jean-Baptiste Lully. Fittingly, he composed almost exclusively for the violin (he did compose one opera in 1746, but the work never entered the Parisian repertory). His significance as a teacher of the violin, however, is perhaps greater than his place in the annals of composition: with a string of pupils including notable French violinists L'abbé le fils, Jean-Josephe Rudolphe, and Pierre Gaviniès, Leclair can truly be called the father of the modern French violin school.*—Blair Johnston*

CHAMBER MUSIC

Trio Sonatas for 2 violins & continuo, Op. 4 (1731–1733)

Although today Leclair's solo sonatas and concertos are his best-known works, in his day it was his concertos, his sonatas for two violins, and his trio sonatas that made him famous. The six *Trio Sonatas,* Op. 4, are his only published original works in the form (his Op. 13 trio sonatas borrowed heavily from his other works). They are written for two violins and continuo and date from sometime around the early 1730s. Having studied broadly, Leclair was able to combine the melody of the Italian violin school, the counterpoint of the Germans, and the stylized dances of the French tradition in these works, sounding at times like Lully, Vivaldi, Handel, or even Purcell, to name just a few. The sonatas represent the fading of the Corellian distinction between the sonata da chiesa and sonata da camera that occurred after 1700. Gavottes and sarabandes are mixed with fugues and double fugues in Leclair's trio sonatas. In his *Abhandlung von der Fuge,* Friedrich Wilhelm Marpurg reproduced the double fugue of the *Sonata No. 3 in D minor,* and he regarded Leclair's counterpoint equal to that of Handel, Telemann, and Bach. The violin parts of Leclair's trio sonatas are not used so much for technical display as they are in the solo sonatas and concertos, but for experimentation in melody and harmony. This is where you find the idiosyncratic effects of Leclair's absorption of the styles of others. The final Allegro movement of the *Sonata No. 2 in B flat* is even more sophisticated than his other works in this respect. As a set, these are some of the finest, final examples of the trio sonata form from the Baroque period. *—Patsy Morita*

Recommended:

○ **Leclair: Sonates en Trio, Op4** / London Baroque / HM 901617

Violin Sonatas, Book I, Op. 1 (1723)

While in Turin, as ballet master to the court, Leclair also studied the violin with one of the great Italian masters of the instrument, Giovanni Battista Somis, a meeting of French and Italian that would play a crucial part in forging Leclair's own musical style.

At the age of 25, Leclair had published the first of his sets of sonatas for violin and continuo in Paris. Consisting of the customary 12 works, his Op. 1 obviously had considerable success since it was republished on no less than four occasions. Each of the sonatas is cast in four movements and opens with either a quick or slow movement that is generally followed by several stylized dance movements. The sonatas had already achieved the fusion of Italian brilliance with French elegance and "weight" that can be readily discerned in the expansive opening Largo of the eighth of the set, a *Sonata in G,* the gentle pathos of which is typical of so much of the composer's music. Also, here is the double-stopping that was such a feature of the composer's own playing (he was especially renowned for playing them perfectly in tune) and the left-hand tremolo that is another characteristic trademark of the composer's style. This is succeeded by a Vivace full of brilliant Italianate figuration calling for rapid bowing and (again) double stopping. Two of the sonatas, in E minor and C, were indicated by Leclair as also being suitable for the flute. With the sonatas of Op. 1, Leclair announced himself as one of the outstanding composers for his instrument. *—Brian Robins*

Recommended:

○ **Leclair: Premier Livre de Sonates** / Biondi, Alessandrini, Monteilhet, Naddeo / 1992 / Arcana 39

○ **Leclair: Sonatas Opp. 1 & 2** / Kuijken, Kohnen / Accent 58435

Violin Sonatas, Book II, Op. 2 (ca. 1728)

In 1728, Jean-Marie Leclair returned to Paris from Turin, where he had been ballet master, and during the course of his journey, he gave a violin concert with the great Italian virtuoso Pietro Locatelli. This led to the famous observation that while Locatelli, all Italian fire, "played like a devil," Leclair, who was noted for the purity of his tone, "played like an angel." In the same year, Leclair brought out the second of his sets of violin sonatas (the first had appeared in Paris six years earlier). Comprising the customary 12 sonatas, this second publication is in general easier to play than the demanding sonatas of Op. 1, as was made explicit by their composer: "I have taken care to compose sonatas that are within the capabilities of persons of greater or lesser skill." Missing, therefore, are the difficult passages of double-stopping, high-lying passagework that characterized the first publication. They are replaced by a combination of lyrical purity and highly expressive writing that contains Italian brilliance and French elegance, as can clearly be heard in the first of the sonatas in E minor, one of two works in the publication also suitable for performance on the flute. Cast in five movements, it opens with a deeply felt and noble Adagio. The *Sarabande* (iii) also taps into a rich vein of lyricism, while the finale is a brilliant Italianate display of fast passagework. *—Brian Robins*

Recommended:

○ **Sonatas Opp1 & 2** / Kuijken, Kohnen / Accent 58435

Violin Sonatas, Book III, Op. 5 (ca. 1734)

Jean-Marie Leclair was the most famous of a family of musicians who hailed from Lyons. He became one of the foremost violinists of his day, renowned for the beauty of his tone, an ability to play double stops in perfect tune, and his mastery of both French and Italian styles. The latter was gained during a stay in Italy, during which Leclair studied with eminent Italian violinist Giovanni Battista Somis.

The *Sonatas (12) for Violin and Continuo,* Op. 5, the third such set, were published in 1734. Here, as elsewhere in Leclair's output, is demonstration of the fusion of French and Italian he effected with such skill. Here, the programmatic genre elements so popular among his French contemporaries are largely missing. And although extremely demanding, the showy virtuosity of such Italian contemporaries as Locatelli is also largely missing, replaced by the pathos of the harmonies, greater contrapuntal interest, and above all, a graceful melodic tenderness that is entirely French. The sonatas are cast in four movements, opening with either a quick or slow movement. The sonatas of Op. 5 include perhaps the most famous of all Leclair's sonatas, that in C minor, the sixth of the set. Known as "Le tombeau," possibly because it was played at the composer's funeral, but also because its dramatic opening Grave resembles the type of genre piece known as the tombeau, a kind of musical elegy. *—Brian Robins*

Recommended:

○ **Leclair: Sonatas Vol. I** / Convivium / 1999 / Hyperion 67033

○ **Leclair: Violin Sonatas** / Terakado, Rousset, Suzuki, Uemura / Denon 75720

Violin Sonatas, Book IV, Op. 9 (ca. 1743)

Jean-Marie Leclair was the most famous French violinist of the early part of the eighteenth century and the outstanding composer of concertos and sonatas for the instrument during his lifetime. His early training, however, was not as a violinist, but as a dancer. It was in this capacity that he went to Turin in 1722 as ballet master, a stay during which he was encouraged as a violinist by the Italian virtuoso Giovanni Battista Somis. The contact had a crucial effect on the development of Leclair's compositional style, which combines an innate French sense of elegance with fiery Italianate virtuosity in unique fashion.

The 12 sonatas of Op. 9 were the last of his four sets of solo sonatas to be issued by Leclair during his lifetime (a fifth appeared posthumously in 1767). As such, it may be seen as summation of his sonata style. It includes both extremely demanding works, such as the *Sonata No. 9 in E flat,* and easier pieces, such as *No. 7* in G, that eschew the arsenal of virtuoso trickery developed by Leclair (this last work was written with the flute in mind; it is marked "Qui peut se jouer sur la Flûte Allemande"). The former, in Leclair's favored four-movement form, opens with a movement marked Corente a la Francese and manages to combine the composer's characteristic elegance with strong rhythmic momentum. In the final movement, Leclair pulls out all the stops in a display of virtuosity that includes multiple double-stopping (a device he was famed for playing in perfect tune), very high sequential figuration, and long slurs, an Italian technique hardly employed in French music. *—Brian Robins*

Recommended:

○ **Leclair: Sonatas For Violin** / Sonnerie Trio / 1984 / ASV 106

OPERA

Scylla et Glaucus, Op. 11 (1746)

Scylla et Glaucus is Jean-Marie Leclair's only opera; he was better known as a composer of concertos and instrumental music. Cast in the form of the tragédie en musique developed by Lully during the seventeenth century, it also owes much to similar works by Lully's great successor, Jean-Philippe Rameau. By the time *Scylla* received its first performance at the Paris Opéra on October 4, 1746, the form was already becoming outdated, threatened by both the newly evolving form of opéra-ballet and the increasingly popular Italian comic opera. Doubtless this accounts for its limited success despite a strong cast that included some of the leading French singers and dancers of the day. *Scylla* received a total of 18 performances, after which it was dropped, not to be revived again in its entirety until John Eliot Gardiner performed the work in 1979.

The opera is cast in the traditional tragédie en musique form: a Prologue followed by five acts. The libretto by d'Albaret is based on episodes from Books 10, 13, and 14 of Ovid's *Metamorphosis.* The Prologue takes place in the Temple of Venus, where the goddess turns to stone a group of maidens who deny her deity, thus foreshadowing the ending of the opera, which is one of only a handful to defy the eighteenth century convention of a happy conclusion. The opera itself tells the story of the rivalry between the nymph Scylla and the sorceress Circe for the love of the sea-god Glaucus; this conflict reaches its tragic outcome when Scylla, driven to madness by Circe, is petrified and left to stand for all time in the Straights of Sicily, her siren followers an eternal threat to sailors.

While the form of *Scylla et Glaucus* might have been old-fashioned, and the general approach indebted to Rameau, its music was neither outmoded nor derivative. Leclair received much of his musical training in Italy, where he was exposed to the influence of Locatelli and others. Consequently, to a far greater degree than with Rameau, the writing, while remaining recognizably French, is full of Italianisms. These are particularly apparent in the opera's brilliant orchestral scoring; the "thunderclap" symphony in the Prologue—a dazzling piece of Vivaldian virtuosity—and the powerful orchestration of the climactic final act are excellent examples. Yet, as Eliot Gardiner has pointed out, perhaps the most surprising aspect of *Scylla* is the quality of the vocal writing by a composer who had little experience in the genre.

The sheer beauty of Scylla's arias contrasts strongly with those of Circe, whose formidable and fully developed character is one of the most remarkable features of this fine work. *—Brian Robins*

Synopsis:

Prologue. The Sicilian people worship in the temple of Venus. They are interrupted by the Propoetides, young women from Amanthus, who enter the temple and deny Venus' divinity. The annoyed goddess punishes them by turning them to stone, after which the congregation celebrates in "Que digne fils du plus grand des vainqueurs," actually a thinly veiled tribute to King Louis XV of France.

Act One. In a forest, Scylla, a nymph, is alone and ponders her fear of love ("Non, je ne cessarai jamais de fuir tes dangereuses chaînes"). A sylvan and a shepherd try to court her ("Loin de nos retraites"), but she is unmoved by their words of love. Glaucus, a marine god, enters and, he, too, tries to woo Scylla. But this only makes her angry, which surprises Glaucus. Determined to win Scylla, Glaucus decides to ask for help from the sorceress Circe.

Act Two. In Circe's palace, which is filled with strange animals altered by Circe's spells, Circe's magic has warned her that a rejected lover is on his way to the palace. She feels apprehensive and vulnerable. As she feared, she becomes attracted to Glaucus when he arrives. She feigns interest in Glaucus' cause and promises to help him with her magic, gathering her minions around her. But over the next few minutes, she and her magicians cast a spell on Glaucus, making him fall in love with Circe ("Amours dont le prix"). However, when Glaucus' friend, Licas, comes to Circe's palace to inform Glaucus that Scylla now longs for him, the spell is broken by the mention of Scylla's name. Glaucus rushes quickly from the palace to meet Scylla, leaving behind the seething Circe, who swears that she will have revenge.

Act Three. The action takes place at a seashore. Scylla is completely in love with Glaucus and believes he is not with her at the moment simply because he is fickle ("Serments trompeurs, tendre langage"). When Glaucus arrives, Scylla suggests that he has fallen for Circe, but Glaucus assures her that this is not so and that his love is true. Scylla is embarrassed at her behavior and confesses her love for Glaucus ("Que le tendre amour nous engage"). Sea gods appear to celebrate Glaucus and Scylla's love ("Dieu charmant, réspondez à notre impatience"). The crowd sees a cloud descending upon them and believe Cupid is hidden within it. Unfortunately, it contains Circe, the sight of whom sends the sea gods running in fear. Circe, still in love with Glaucus, tries once again to win him for herself, threatening terrible consequences if he does not submit to her.

Act Four. The setting is the ash-covered countryside surrounding Mount Etna. Thus far, Glaucus has been able to deflect Circe's amorous advances, and she relates her disappointment in the aria "Reviens, ingrat mais cher amant." Finally, in desperation, she tells Glaucus that she will kill Scylla if he does not accept her love. The threat hits its mark, and Glaucus swears he will cease loving Scylla if Circe promises not to hurt her. Just as Glaucus is about to leave with Circe, Scylla enters. Glaucus and Scylla begin a tearful duet in which Glaucus tries to explain the situation. Circe, angered and sickened by the scene, pretends to be merciful and selfless, and in her aria "Allez, couple fidèle," she gives her blessing to the loving couple, claiming to have been moved by their devotion to one another. Once Glaucus and Scylla have gone, Circe reveals her plan for revenge.

The scene changes as Mount Etna begins erupting. Under a full moon, Circe calls on the gods of the underworld. During a raucous, demonic display of power and hate, the gods and Circe call out for Hecate, the goddess of spells and incantations. At this, the moon, the symbol of Hecate, becomes dim and eventually falls from the sky. A large crack appears in the earth, from which emerges Hecate. Dramatically, she gives to Circe an herb she has picked from the banks of the river Phlegeton, which runs through Hades. Circe is to use it to poison Scylla.

Act Five. Near a fountain, preparations have been made for a celebration. Scylla tells Glaucus that she is pleased to know she has his love, but she is still uneasy about the threat posed by Circe. Glaucus tries to calm her by explaining that Circe poses no danger to them, but Scylla is not convinced. A crowd gathers to participate in a celebration of the anniversary of Sicily's liberation from the terror of the Cyclops. As the festivities take place around him, Glaucus thanks Cupid for bringing him and Scylla together ("Chantez l'Amour, chantez ses douces flammes"). Glaucus then shows Scylla a fountain, explaining that in its waters he first saw her reflection. Unknown to either of them, the waters of the fountain have been poisoned by Circe's herb, and staring into them makes Scylla go mad and faint. Glaucus and the others nearby believe Scylla has died, but she awakens at the sound of her name and, confused, runs off. Glaucus tries to follow Scylla, but his way is blocked by the sudden appearance of Circe, astride a dragon and declaring that Scylla has drowned. Circe then creates a re-enactment of Scylla's death.

The scene changes to the Straits of Sicily, with the whirlpool of Charybdis on the Italian side and a siren-shaped rock surrounded by monsters on the Sicilian side. The monsters around the rock howl. Glaucus is despondent over the loss of Scylla. Circe notes that Scylla has been turned to stone to memorialize her anger, in part as a warning to others.*—John Palmer*

Recommended:

○ **Leclair: Scylla & Glaucus** / Gardiner (cond.), Robertson, Brown, Crook, Dubosc, English Baroque Soloists / Erato 98518

Ernesto Lecuona

b. Aug. 7, 1896, Guanabacoa, Cuba, **d.** Nov. 29, 1963, Tenerife, Canary Islands

Composer: Keyboard

Ernesto Lecuona has often been hailed as the greatest composer from Cuba. A sort of Latin Gershwin, he was both versatile and prolific, writing over 400 songs, 170-odd piano pieces, 37 orchestral works, 11 film scores, and numerous zarzuelas, ballets, and an opera. He wrote in an approachable, often popular style, especially in his songs, and exhibited Latin and Afro-Cuban elements in his music. In some of his later compositions, he wrote in a more serious, somewhat neo-Classical style. Lecuona was born in Guanabacoa, Cuba, a suburb of Havana. All five children in the Lecuona family were musically gifted, four as pianists and one son as a violinist. Young Ernesto was given piano lessons by his older sister, Ernestina. He gave a public recital at the age of five and was in every respect a child prodigy: he was composing at the age of 11 and went on to graduate from Havana's National Conservatory—where he studied piano and composition—before his 17th birthday. He traveled to New York City for his American debut the following year, giving a well-received concert at Aeolian Hall. He then decided on further musical studies, taking instruction from Joaquin Nin, and in France, from Maurice Ravel. In the 1920s and 1930s, Lecuona wrote a number of popular songs and piano pieces. In the latter genre, his *Malagueña*, from his *Andalucía Suite for piano* (1927), became an instant hit and is still probably the composer's most famous piece, whether in its original piano form, its song version, or in its countless other instrumental arrangements. Lecuona also formed a dance band called Orquesta Cubana, which mainly performed arrangements of popular Cuban dance pieces and songs. The group quickly became well known and made many tours of the United States, Europe, and South America. Ironically, Lecuona was not the band's pianist: that role was left to Armando Fichin Oréfiche, a skilled artist and composer in his own right who also did some of the group's musical arrangements. Beginning in 1931, Lecuona began writing film scores, turning out three that year alone: *Under Cuban Skies*, *Free Soul*, and *Susana Lenox*, all for MGM. He also wrote many zarzuelas during this period, including *Rosa la china* (1932). In 1934, following a lengthy bout of pneumonia, Lecuona withdrew from the band on the advice of doctors. The group was thereafter known as the Lecuona Cuban Boys and still made many numerous and successful tours. Lecuona continued to compose and perform, of course, producing a variety of works that included more film scores, especially during the war years. He received an Academy Award nomination for Best Song in the 1942 Warner Bros. film *Always in My Heart*. One of his more popular postwar film efforts was for the 1947 movie *Carnival in Costa Rica*. After the war, Lecuona seldom performed as a pianist, though he remained active in composition. He returned to Cuba after living for a long period in New York City. He left his homeland again, however, in 1960 following the Communist takeover, determined not to return until the Castro regime was ousted. He established homes in New York City and Florida. Among his many accomplishments was the co-founding (with composer Gonzalo Roig) of the Havana Symphony Orchestra. Lecuona was one of the few composers who was successful in several genres, arguably becoming the quintessential crossover musician long before the term existed. *—Robert Cummings*

Overview of Works (ca. 1915–1955)

The music of Ernesto Lecuona is as much a picture postcard of pre-Revolutionary Cuba as the waltzes of Strauss collectively are of old Vienna. Sun-drenched and easeful, it hearkens back to a happier, possibly idealized time. Although it would seem glib to label him as a "classical Desi Arnaz," he does seem to straddle two worlds of music, as indeed have Leroy Anderson, Gershwin, and Bernstein, to name a few, and like them, does so very well. The most conspicuous part of his oeuvre is his piano music, himself a prodigy on the instrument, and the germinal versions of some of his best-known works were spawned from the keyboard. This owes more to the post-Liszt era nationalists such as Granados than then-current trends, probably to the ire of some contemporary progressives. This mattered little for it provided a foothold on to the international stage and an enthusiastic public following. Best known among the piano works are his 1928 treatment of the seemingly timeless *Malagueña*, in which the reiterated high keys delineated the open strings of a guitar, and the equally evocative *Andalucía* of 1930, which a decade later provided a swing-era hit with the lyrics "The Breeze and I." Among Lecuona's songs proper, the best-known is undoubtedly *Siboney* (1939) with its languidly hypnotic samba rhythm, along with *Desengano* with lyrics by de Galarraga, and adaptations of *Malagueña* and *Andalucía*. Intriguingly walking a line between art song and Latin popular, this section of his body of work drew international attention and led to work with Hollywood, perhaps the best-known of these collaborations being his music for the 1942 film *Always in My Heart*. Lecuona's output also includes a substantial amount of orchestral music, including *Rapsodia negra for piano and orchestra* (1943) and his orchestral suite of 1945. For the most part,

Lecuona entrusted most of the orchestration of his piano pieces to assistants (it should be remembered that Liszt also did the same at times). Lecuona's music, up to a point, had largely drawn its distinctiveness from its national flavor while treading traditional turf in its reliance on tonality and traditional harmony and melody. One can sense, however, inquisitiveness on the composer's part, for his last years were marked by a stretching out into more modernistic realms of expression manifested in some chamber works. Most ambitious was a large-scale opera (he had written two smaller-scale works in the 1920s) entitled *El Sombrèro de Yarey.* It remained unfinished at his passing in 1963. Lecuona was one of the last cultural representatives of a national era, yet without even trying he was a visionary in that he, along with other Western-hemisphere composers, effortlessly removed preconceived stylistic boundaries. *—Wayne Reisig*

Recommended:

- ○ **Lecuona: Complete Piano Music Vol 1.** / Bartos (cond.), Tirino, Polish National SO / 1995 / Bis 754
- ○ **Always in My Heart** / Domingo, Holdridge / 1997 / Sony 63199
- ○ **Lecuona: María la O** / Romeu (cond.), Sanchez, Romeu, Guerrini, Ayala, Orquesta Sinfonica Nacional / 1995 / Egrem 122
- ○ **Lecuona: The Ultimate Collection** / Lecuona / RCA 902668671

KEYBOARD

Andalucía, suite ("Suite Española") (ca. 1927)

For much of the last century, Ernesto Lecuona's piano suite *Andalucía* was the hidden source of a variety of musical compositions and performances. Its fiery finale, *Malagueña,* exists in several arrangements for guitar, became a popular song with a text by Marian Banks, and showed up for years on easy listening LPs by the likes of Andre Kostelanetz and the 101 Strings. Other pieces from the suite also appeared with added English texts, and no doubt Lecuona himself popularized the music during his years in New York as leader of the band Lecuona's Cuban Boys. But the original work, written around 1927, was largely forgotten outside of Cuba until pianist Thomas Tirino began to revive the music of the "Cuban Gershwin" in the late 1990s. What Tirino revealed, to growing acclaim at first centered on South Florida, was a splendid six-movement concert showpiece that fused dynamic pianism rooted in Romantic virtuosity, Spanish and gypsy folk rhythms, and Lecuona's own unerring melodic sense. The six movements evoke various Spanish sounds and scenes, alternating lyrical pieces with dance rhythms topped by spectacular runs. *Gitanerías* is a flamenco-influenced piece, while *Alhambra,* an evocation of Spain's Moorish-era palace, is one of several pieces that reveals Lecuona's familiarity with impressionist idioms. All in all, *Andalucía* (also known as the "Spanish Suite" or "Suite Española") fully lives up to the Gershwin comparison: it is classical piano music enlivened by popular vigor and informed by a distinctive compositional intelligence. *—James Manheim*

Recommended:

- ○ **Danzas Cubanas** / Ferman / 1998 / Talent 44
- ○ **Lecuona: Complete Piano Music Vol. 1** / Tirino / 1995 / Bis 754

Danzas afro-cubanos (1930)

Sorting out the various pieces Lecuona labeled Afro-Cuban dances is difficult; a couple are thought lost, several have been grouped into different piano albums, and others are scattered in various arrangements, some more legitimate than others. A core group of dances in this style, however, was published as a piano suite in 1930; the set is characteristic of all the pieces Lecuona wrote under the "Afro-Cuban" title. The rhythms tend to be lively and strongly marked, and are derived from the popular music of Cuba's black population—a colorful blend of Latin and African sounds, employed in a salon style that doesn't condescend to the source material. "La conga de media noche" is a fast piece evoking late night conga lines; it begins quietly, the dynamics swelling and receding several times. The climax is extremely loud, but the movement ends with a triple-pianissimo glissando into the piano's upper reaches. "Danza negra" is a very marcato piece in moderate tempo, with thick, sharply punched-out chords dominating the central section. "...Y la negra bailaba!" falls along similar lines, equally jittery and a bit faster, but with less-pounding rhythms. "Danza de los ñáñigos" ("Dance of the Mulattos") is slightly more relaxed, at least in terms of tempo, and ends very quietly after some boisterous passages. "Danza lucumí" swings along with strong accents on the last beat of the bar, while the brief "La comparsa" depicts the approach and withdrawal of a carnival procession, with revelry at the central climax. *—James Reel*

Recommended:

- ○ **Lecuona: Piano Music Vol. 3** / Tirino / 1996 / Bis 794

Danzas Cubanas

Ernesto Lecuona wrote sets of Cuban dances for piano at various stages of his long career. There is a group of Afro-Cuban dances, another of Cuban dances of the nineteenth century, and yet another of *danzas cubanas típicas.* The set of six pieces designated simply as *Danzas Cubanas* are brief pieces, in the neighborhood of two minutes apiece in duration. They bear descriptive titles rather than names of dances themselves: 1. *No hables más* (Don't Say Any More), 2. *No puedo contigo* (I Can't Go with You), 3. *Ahí viene el chino* (Here Comes the Chinese Man), 4. *¿Por qué te vas* (Why Are You Leaving?), 5. *Lola está de fiesta* (Lola at the Party), and 6. *En tres por cuatro* (In 3/4 Time). As the titles suggest, these are songs without words, easy to imagine with added texts and of a piece musically with the more famous Lecuona pieces from the Andalucía set that are equally well known in instrumental and vocal versions. Especially pleasing is *Ahí viene el chino,* a bit of musical orientalism thought out independently of, and much more subtly than, U.S. representations of Chinese music. The piano writing of the *Danzas Cubanas* generally features light ornamentation around a clearly stated tune—if Lecuona is, as one so often hears, the Cuban Gershwin, then these pieces are closer to the Gershwin *Songbook* than to the *Preludes.* Long forgotten outside Cuba, the *Danzas Cubanas* owe their rediscovery to the pioneering Florida pianist Thomas Tirino. *—James Manheim*

Recommended:

- ○ **Lecuona: Piano Music Vol. 3** / Bartos (cond.), Tirino, Polish National Radio SO / 1996 / Bis 794

Reinbert de Leeuw

b. Sep. 8, 1938, Amsterdam, Netherlands

Conductor

Reinbert de Leeuw is a triple-threat artist, internationally known as a conductor, composer, and keyboard player. He studied at the Amsterdam Conservatory, taking piano and music theory with Jaap Spaanderman, while also learning composition with Kees van Baaren in The Hague. In 1963 he became a member of the faculty of the Royal Conservatory of The Hague.

He has been a political activist, and he jointly composed (with Peter Schat, Jan van Vlijmen, Mischa Mengelberg, and Louis Andriessen) an anti-imperialism multimedia opera called *Reconstruction,* given at the Holland Festival in 1969. He has published a book with J. Bernlef on U.S. composer Charles E. Ives. He also composed a symphonic work called *Abschied,* and *Hymns and Chorales* for two electric guitars, 15 winds, and electronic organ.

He has a special interest in the music of Erik Satie. His piano interpretations of Satie's piano music, played intensely and more slowly than usual, have been recorded on the Philips label, and for the 1973 and 1974 Holland Festivals collaborated with the Contemporary Dance Foundation of Koert Stuyf and Ellen Edinoff on productions featuring music of Satie. He appeared performing the music for the film *Satie and Suzanne—The Passion of a Lifetime,* a filmed dance performance by Veronica Tannent. As an essayist he is known for articles in the Dutch magazine *De Gids* under the collective title *Musical Anarchy.* *—Joseph Stevenson*

Recommended:

- ○ **Satie: Early Piano Works** / Leeuw / 1998 / Philips 462161
- ○ **Leeuw: Antigone** / Leeuw (cond.), Mahe, Netherlands Radio CO / N.M. Classics 92036
- ○ **Andriessen: Mausoleum; Hoketus** / Leeuw (cond.), Barick, Van Tassel, Bakunin, Hoketus Ensemble / Donemus 20
- ○ **The Ligeti Project Vol. 1** / Leeuw, Aimard, Masseurs, Schoenberg Ensemble, ASKO Ensemble / 2001 / Teldec 83953

Giovanni Legrenzi

b. Aug. 12, 1626, Clusone, Italy, **d.** May 27, 1690, Venice, Italy

Composer

As in the worlds of literature, technology, and business, often the most inventive musical pioneers are overshadowed by their successors. This is certainly the case with Legrenzi, whose name is known to relatively few but whose musical influence is almost impossible to overestimate. His pupils included Vivaldi and possibly Caldara, he was a major influence on Alessandro Scarlatti, and his sonatas formed the basis for what was to become the modern format, marked by clear distinctions between the movements and specific tempo indications giving performers more direction and less discretion. He mastered both the trio sonata (*sonata a tre*) as well as the *sonata a due* (sonata for two instruments). Typically, the bass is the background for the other instruments, though in many of the *sonatas a due,* the violin and bass take almost equal roles. These sonatas often featured fugues with carefully crafted sequences and deft changes of theme from tonic to dominant, features that were to become hallmarks of the modern sonata. His cantatas, too, were seminal, with a particularly strong influence on the works of Alessandro Scarlatti. They are also masterly in their use of themes and figures, and show a wide freedom of structure in the disposition of recitative, arioso, and aria passages. Like many of his contemporaries, he excelled in vocal music as well as instrumental, and composed many operas as well as cantatas, though few have remained in the repertoire. He came from a musical family and first studied music with his father. In 1645, he took the position of organist at Santa Maria Maggiore in Bergamo, near Clusone. Like many composers, he entered the priesthood, in 1651. He left Bergamo for the more musically prestigious court of Ferrara, where he was named to the position of *maestro di cappella* at the Accademia dello Santo Spirito, a position he held from 1657 until 1664. He enjoyed great success as both composer and choir master. He left Ferrara at some point in 1665 and little is known about the positions he held or even where he lived until 1670, when he became the *maestro di coro* at the Ospedale dei Derelitti. (Literally named hospitals, "ospedale" were more a cross between boarding homes and conservatories, which specialized, as the names suggest, in the education of orphaned or abandoned girls. Many prominent composers were very closely affiliated with these, most famously, Vivaldi and the Pieta.) In 1671, he also took the post of *maestro di cappella* at the oratory of the Congregazione dei Filippini. In 1681, Legrenzi became *vice maestro di cappella* at San Marco, succeeding Antonio Sartorio in that position, and in 1683, he became *maestro di coro* at the Ospedale dei Mendicanti. His most prolific years of opera composition began in 1681, during which he produced at least two major works a year. In 1685, he was promoted to *maestro di cappella* at San Marco and with this promotion, returned the majority of his attention to sacred music. *—Ann Feeney*

Overview of Works (ca. 1655–1690)

Giovanni Legrenzi, well-known and acclaimed in his day, is today viewed as typical of the mainstream of the high Baroque era. He tilled most major musical fields of his day—sacred, vocal, instrumental, opera—in the predominant highly contrapuntal style with emphasis on harmonic rather than melodic activity. Legrenzi's consistency may be attributed, in part at least, to his lifelong pursuit of sought-after positions. It was, after all, the age of patronage and one relied on the approval of a beneficent employer. In his religious works, Legrenzi shows the influence of his mentor Cazzati. In motets and psalm settings, he utilized the concerto style for smaller vocal forces and employed chorus soloists and instruments for masses and vespers. Sometimes Legrenzi hearkens back to the older Venetian school with multi-choir writing. Remarkable among this output is the *Mass* of 1689, which seems to tap unusual harmonic resources. Similar innovation is more omnipresent in Legrenzi's instrumental works, particularly his sonatas. Again, it is the process rather than the themes or styles that is worthy of attention. Most are for various combinations of strings and continuo; some expand to as many as six parts and have lead to the theory that there was an eye toward orchestral performance. These would have a great influence on later works in the form by Vivaldi and Bach. Esteemed for his sacred and instrumental works, in the field of opera one finds what would have seemed Legrenzi's least distinguished part of his output. Yet he seemed to surprise the public with his facility and the pleasing results in his theatrical works. He came fairly late to the medium in 1662 with *Nino il giusto*, hitting his stride in the mid-1670s and favoring the comedic mock-heroic style so popular at the time. In their time, *Pausania*, *Germanico sul Reno*, *La divisione del mondo*, *Totila*, and *Giustino* were popular and well regarded by colleagues and public. While he broke no significant new ground, Legrenzi became more adept at his craft within his selected scope as he went through his long-spanned (by contemporary standards) life. This is surely not a criticism, for some composers, such as Mozart and Brahms, do not so much break new ground as bring a style to a state of perfection. Ironically, the Baroque style would reach its apotheosis decades later in the work of an "anachronism," Johann Sebastian Bach. But at his best (which was virtually a lifelong state), Legrenzi was tastefully in step with his time and an important representative of the Northern Italian School. — *Wayne Reisig*

Recommended:

- ○ **Legrenzi: Sonate e Motetti** / Klikar (cond.), Prague Musica Antiqua / Supraphon 3185
- ○ **Legrenzi: Il Cuor umano all'incanto** / Ens. Legrenzi / Tactus 621201

Franz Lehár

b. Apr. 30, 1870, Komorn, Hungary, **d.** Oct. 24, 1948, Bad Ischl, Austria
Composer: Opera, Orchestral

The most prominent figure of the early twentieth century Viennese operetta revival, Franz Lehár ranks among history's greatest composers in the genre. He was known above all for his international success *Die lustige Witwe* (The Merry Widow). That work kicked off a vogue for Viennese operetta in America. He expanded the genre by introducing more serious subjects in such works as *Eva*. *Die lustige Witwe* had the dubious honor of being Hitler's favorite stage work of all time, but its merits are greater than this recommendation indicates. Dramatic and vigorous, full of life, it is original and full of melodic invention. The libretto is unusually good, and the story full of romance and wit.

Lehár's ancestry included a typically Central European ethnic mix: his father, a composer, horn player, and bandmaster of note, had roots in the Czech-German Sudetenland, and his mother was Hungarian. The young Franz studied violin and entered the Prague Conservatory at age 12. He studied instrumental performance and composition, and in 1888 was hired as a violinist in a Rhineland theater orchestra. He was drafted into the military, beginning a long career as a military bandmaster, following in his father's and uncle's footsteps. Lehár composed marches, waltzes, and dances, and, after a new post brought him to Vienna from Budapest, tried his hand at operetta. He became music director of the Theater an der Wien in 1902, but his first operettas, with the exception of *Der Rastelbinder* (The Tinker), were not terribly successful. Lehár was a second choice as composer for the *Merry Widow* libretto, but the runaway success of that work established for him a permanent place on the world's stages.

Der Mann mit den drei Frauen (The Man with Three Wives), *Der Graf von Luxemburg* (The Count of Luxembourg), and *Zigeunerliebe* (Gypsy Love) were all given in 1908 and cemented Lehár's success. And as Lehár became better known, his stage works became ever more ambitious, and he began to draw on the musical resources of contemporary grand opera, particularly the works of Puccini, in his scores. During the First World War he again conducted music for the military. After the war, Viennese opera declined in popularity as new kinds of popular music took over the scene, including blues and American popular dance tunes. Instead of acknowledging defeat, Lehár tried to incorporate these new elements into the Viennese genre. The result was more successes. His success in the 1920s was also due to the famous tenor, Richard Tauber, who could handle Lehár's increasing challenging vocal roles. Two of Lehár's best operettas from the postwar period include *Der Zarewitsch* (The Tsarevitch) of 1927 and *Das Land des Lächelns* (The Land of Smiles) of 1929. Lehár also began composing film scores and producing filmed versions of his operettas. *Giuditta*, based upon the biblical story of Judith, was his final opera, produced in 1934. Written for the Vienna Staatsoper, its dramatic content and music helped blur the distinction between serious opera and the lighter genre, which was on the wane. An ambitious work, it was broadcast by 120 radio companies. Lehár remained in Vienna during the Second World War, even though his wife was Jewish. He remained aloof from politics, and thus briefly attracted the attention of Allied anti-fascist investigators after the war. *—Rita Laurance*

OPERA

Friederike, operetta (1928)

Franz Lehár's *Friederike* is an example of so-called "biographical operetta," a genre popular in the early decades the twentieth century. Typically, such works take the form of Romanticized anecdotal accounts in which a historical figure is the protagonist in a bittersweet love affair. Lehár had previously essayed the genre in *Paganini* (1924–25), which takes as its starting point the famous violinist's employment in Lucca.

Choosing the poet Goethe as the subject matter for an operetta was a daring move. Lehár was enthusiastic about the original libretto by Fritz Löhner and Ludwig Herzer, for he felt the story of Goethe's romantic attachment to Friederike Brion, a pastor's daughter in Alsace-Lorraine, was perfect material for musical treatment. As word of the enterprise spread through Berlin, reactions to the project appeared in local publications. Intellectuals and cabaret fans thought the scenario ridiculous, while most of the public looked forward to the new production. The controversy helped to sell out the house when *Friederike* was premiered at the Metropol-Theater on October 4, 1928.

Friederike is representative of the last phase of the "silver age" of operetta, which is marked by a tendency toward the sphere of "serious" opera and symphonic music, subject matter of the type then popular in cinema, and vocal writing influenced by Puccini. *Friederike*'s orchestration is refined in its use of colorful contrasts, it musical characterizations precise. The vocal writing is unabashedly lyrical, perhaps because Lehár was certain of the abilities of the performers who were to give the premiere.

The composer tailored the part of Goethe to the voice of Richard Tauber, the famous Austrian tenor who had become the composer's most renowned interpreter and whose voice and stage presence almost ensured the success of Lehár's later works. Tauber once claimed that he and Lehár were brothers "without the luxury of a blood relationship." Lehár was thus able to compose very ambitious parts for the tenor, and a typical "Tauber song" developed, featuring a dramatic, upward initial thrust that others came to imitate. Such songs in *Friederike* include "O Mädchen, mein Mädchen" and "O wie schön, wie wunderschön." Interestingly, there is evidence that Tauber was at first hesitant to play the part of Goethe. He of course ultimately assumed the role, and the decision proved to be a boon to his career.

Friederike is one of Lehár's most passionate scores, and, aside from songs for the title character (played at the premiere by the celebrated Käthe Dorsch), most of the numbers went to Tauber. Although critics hated *Friederike*, the public loved it, and within a year it was playing in houses throughout Europe. *—John Palmer*

Synopsis:

Act One. Outside the parish house in Sesenheim on Whitsunday 1771. An afternoon service, accompanied by organ music, is being held in the nearby church. The daughter of Pastor Jacob Brion, Friederike, enters with village children. She is infatuated with Goethe, a young student who has been a guest at the house numerous times. Her parents meet her, and together they drink coffee in the garden. Friederike's mother expresses her hope for a permanent relationship for her daughter as news arrives that Goethe and his friends are on their way to Sesenheim. Salomea, Friederike's older sister, asks Friederike if Goethe has already kissed her. Friederike tells her that Goethe has been wary of kissing ever since a Strasbourg girl kissed him and wished bad luck on everyone who kissed him afterward.

Students from Strasbourg enter the house, but Lenz is still missing and everyone present goes out to meet him. Thus, Goethe arrives to find the parish house empty except for "Mamsell Riekchen," who has stayed behind to wait for him.

The group returns with the shy Lenz, who has with him a lamb, about which the others tease him. Goethe, in a quiet moment alone, takes out a notebook and begins to write some verses that have just come to him—lines that would become famous as the "Heidenröslein" (The Wild Rosebud). The act closes with a country feast at which everyone dances and Goethe kisses Friederike despite the Strasbourg girl's curse.

Act Two. The bourgeois salon of Madame Schöll in Strasbourg, August 6, 1771. Madame Schöll has invited her nieces from Sesenheim, as well as Goethe and other students, to be her guests. Salomea is now engaged to the serious Weyland, who warns Goethe not to have an affair with Friederike. Goethe tells Weyland that he will soon be in a position to establish a household and offer Friederike a home, because he has just received a position in Weimar. However, Goethe learns from Captain Knebel, the Duke's ambassador, that he will be accepted in Weimar only if he remains unmarried. Goethe considers rejecting the position. Weyland then tells Friederike not to make things difficult for Goethe. Friederike understands, and begins to act distant and coquettish, which offends Goethe, who leaves with Knebel for Weimar without a word to Friederike.

Act Three. Outside the Sesenheim parish house, September 25, 1779. A vintage festival slowly gets underway as young people ask Friederike to dance. She refuses, warning the young boys and girls that they may "lose their hearts while dancing." Lenz, whose presence in the town was formerly overshadowed by Goethe, now spends as much time as possible around Friederike, trying to win her affections. However, he also courts Salomea when she returns from Strasbourg, having had an argument with her husband, Weyland. Weyland arrives shortly after Salomea, expresses his love for her, and the two are reconciled. In the evening, Goethe and the Duke of Saxe-Weimar stop in Sesenheim on their way to Switzerland. Friederike has waited eight years to see Goethe again, but the poet, plagued by memories, has only a few moments to speak with Friederike. She knows she did the right thing when she let Goethe go eight years earlier, saying, "Goethe belongs to the whole world, thus also to me!" The Duke and Goethe depart quickly, leaving the saddened Friederike behind. *—John Palmer*

Recommended:

- ○ **Lehár: Operettas** / Fuchs, Stader, Kalenberg, Pawels, Wolff, Chor des Bayerischen Runfunks / 2004 / EMI 85997
- ○ **Franz Lehár: Friederike; Schön Ist Die Welt** / Wallberg, Donath, Dallapozza, Fuchs, Finke, Munich Radio Orch. / 1995 / Kaiserliche Operette 863442

Giuditta, opera (1933)

Premiered in January 1934, *Giuditta,* Lehár's last operetta, is generally viewed as his finest, greater even than his most popular, *The Merry Widow* (1905). Lehár himself was partial to *Giuditta,* not least because he designed the work from the beginning on a grand scale, attempting to bridge the worlds of opera and operetta. In many respects, he succeeded, but *Giuditta* ends up not quite as either, landing in a limbo suspended between the two that has partially sabotaged its acceptance with both performers and the public. The story concerns the beautiful but married Giuditta who takes up with the attractive army captain Octavio in North Africa, only to endure a breakup in their relationship when he is transferred and refuses to desert. Giuditta then becomes a dancer in a nightclub and Octavio does finally desert, but when a reconciliation years later fails, the story ends sadly, though not quite tragically. With slightly darker music and a more grimly powerful ending, the work might have become a full-fledged opera in spite of its plentiful dialogue. Like Lehár's best efforts, *Giuditta* contains many fine numbers. In Scene 1, Octavio's "Freunde, das Leben, Ist Lebenswert!" (Comrades, this life is the life for me), is dramatic and exotic, divulging supposed African ethnic elements that are really Lehár's own ersatz creations. The Scene 2 duet between Giuditta and Octavio, "Schön Wie Die Blaue Sommernacht" (Blue as the summer sky above), also displays an exotic character and conveys a slick, *Carmen*-like sensuality in its music. Another popular number in *Giuditta* is "Du Bist Meine Sonne" (You are my sun), Scene 3, No. 11, sung passionately though sweetly by a yearning Octavio. Giuditta's Scene 4 "Meine Lippen, Sie Kussen So Heiss" (On my lips every kiss is like wine), is alluring, if light, again more slick than emotional, but quite effective within the context of the story. Many of the numbers in the work, as one might gather, are love songs or songs of hope for a better life. A complete performance of *Giuditta* will generally last a bit over one-and-a-half hours, though with some of the dialogue trimmed (but including all the music), *Giuditta* can be accommodated on a single 80-minute CD. *—Robert Cummings*

Recommended:

- ○ **Lehár: Giuditta** / Bonynge (cond.), Hadley, Atkinson, Busher, Itami, English CO / 1997 / Telarc 80436
- ○ **Lehár: Operettas** / Cloe, Jung, Munchner Chor / 2004 / EMI 85997

Der Graf von Luxemburg, operetta (1909; revised 1937)

Lehár's *Der Graf von Luxemburg* (The Count from Luxembourg; 1909) is one of three operettas the composer produced in a three-month period following the failure of his *Der Mann mit den drei Frauen* (The Man with Three Wives). Of the three new works, *Der Graf von Luxemburg* and *Zigeunerliebe* (Gypsy Love) became international hits.

Johann Strauss Jr. set the libretto of *Der Graf von Luxemburg* in 1897, under the title *Die Göttin der Vernunft* (The Goddess of Reason); it was, in fact, his last operetta. Alfred Maria Willner, Robert Bodanzky, and Leo Stein (actually L. Rosenstein) adapted the earlier libretto, by Willner and Bernhard Buchbinder. Strauss had reluctantly composed the work only to fulfill a contract, which resulted in a work that soon vanished from the stage, prompting several artists to later tinker with the libretto.

The story of *Der Graf von Luxemburg,* in which a Count who is in need of money consents to a marriage of appearances to a woman he never sees, stands on flimsy dramatic legs. However, the youthful vigor and sensuous melodies of Lehár's score overshadow the libretto's faults, and the operetta was an immediate success, in part because of an excellent cast. The work ran for 299 continuous performances in Vienna. By 1911 it had spread through theaters in Germany and soon after created a frenzy in London and Paris.

In Lehár's treatment, the dramatic clash between money and marriage has its musical parallel in the work's contrast of Parisian inflections and Slavic flavors, especially in the dance-like music that accompanies Basil Basilowitsch. Lehár's use of dance rhythms has all the power evident in his *Die lustige Witwe* (The Merry Widow; 1905). In particular, the moderato waltz tempo plays a much larger role in *Der Graf von Luxemburg* than in the earlier work. In *Der Graf von Luxemburg,* music in this tempo accompanies most of the communication between René and Angèle, who, although married, must remain apart. Soon after they are wed, while separated by an easel, the moderato waltz in "Sie geht links, er geht rechts" (She goes left, he goes right) serves as a premonition of their impending mutual attraction. The tempo becomes prominent in the second act, when the two fall in love, not yet knowing that they are actually married. Their duet, "Lieber Freund, man greift nicht nach den Sternen" (Dear friend, one does not reach for the stars) is an excellent example, as is Angèle's earlier solo, "Soll ich, soll ich nicht?" (Should I or shouldn't I?) In "Lieber Freund," the sense of anticipation is heightened by the pause at the beginning of each measure, creating an atmosphere of capricious unrest in the circular melody.

Other characters, too, are characterized by their music. March rhythms mark the two buffo characters, Hans and Veit, most notably in the second number of the operetta, "Wir bummeln durchs Leben" (We loiter through life). Groaning sounds from the orchestra accompany the lusty old Basil in his "Packt die Liebe" (Love stows away). Also, in Basil's "Ein Löwe war ich im Salon" (I was a lion in the salon), Slavic overtones are heard in the stormy orchestral backdrop to a fiery polka.

Lehár's *Der Graf von Luxemburg* in its original version premiered at the *Theater an der Wien* in Vienna on November 12, 1909. A revised version appeared in 1937. *—John Palmer*

Synopsis:

Act One. The action takes place in Paris. The painter Armand Brissard is at work in his studio, while his girlfriend, Juliette Vermont, would much rather go with him to a masked ball. Brissard's friends, also painters, show up in a boisterous mood with their models, intending to have a festive banquet in Brissard's studio. Juliette sings "Ich bring' dir, bring' dir, Bübchen" (I'll bring you, bring you, boys). Only one person is missing from the happy crowd, the Count René of Luxembourg. At this point René, already masked, enters triumphantly ("So liri, liri, lari"). After him come three gentlemen in masks, among them the Prince Basil Basilowitsch, who wishes to have an important conversation with René. Basilowitsch is in love with the prima donna at the Paris opera, Angèle Didier, whom Basilowitsch has trained and educated at his expense and now wants to marry. Angèle is indebted to the Prince and believes she must not say no to him. However, Angèle is a commoner, and Basilowitsch is afraid that the Czar will withhold his consent. So, he has come up with a plan: Angèle will marry the Count of Luxembourg, who Basil knows is perpetually in financial straits. After three months the couple will divorce, and then the Czar will have to consent to the perfectly legitimate union. For this, Basil offers René a sum of 500,000 francs under the condition that he remain quiet and, for the duration of the marriage, give up his name. René agrees to the plan. In order to avoid having René and Angèle see one another, an easel is requested, and René and Angèle take places on either side of it. Soon the wedding ceremony is over and the rings are exchanged, all without the married couple seeing each other, while we hear the duet "Sie geht links, er geht rechts" (She goes to the right, he goes to the left). They part, saying, "wiedersehen."

Act Two. In Angèle's palace, three months have passed. This evening, Angèle says her farewell in order to marry Basil in the morning, after her divorce. René and Brissard have come to the official farewell; they have spent the entire three months outside of Paris. Earlier today, René saw Angèle for the first time, at the opera. He introduces himself as Baron Reval and entreats Angèle to abandon the "rational" marriage to Basil and to be with him in the duet "Lieber Freund, man greift nicht nach den Sternen" (Dear friend, one does not reach for the stars). To his great surprise Brissard meets his girlfriend Juliette, who cannot forgive him for leaving town so suddenly. In the duet "Mädel klein, Mädel fein" (Little girl, exquisite girl), Brissard consoles Juliette by solemnly swearing he will marry her. Basil cannot wait for the next day and announces to his guests that his marriage to Angèle will take place today. At this, Brissard comes forward and announces, ironically, that Angèle is already married. This is of no help to Basil, who must now reveal that until tomorrow morning Angèle is the wife of the Count of Luxembourg and that he has paid for this arrangement. Angèle declares disparagingly that a man who would sell his name for money must be despised. René, hearing Angèle's last words, reveals himself as the "Marriage Prince." Everyone is flabbergasted. But, when René turns to leave, Angèle hurries after him.

Act Three. The setting is the vestibule of the Grand Hotel. René loves Angèle, but he must, in order to keep his word, recognize her as Basil's bride. However, under the influence of champagne, he forgets all his good intentions, takes Angèle in his arms, and joins her in the duet "Es duftet nach Trêfle incarnat" (It smells like clover incarnate). They are surprised by a stately, older woman, the Countess Kokozow, who has come to Paris to remind Basil of his promise of marriage. Nothing can come from the two situations. The Countess quickly hides behind a folding screen. When the Count enters, believing he will embrace Angèle, he pulls aside the folding screen and the Countess grabs him around the throat. In order that René not betray Basil, Basil must release him from his promise. Now, all the correct married people may kiss each other. *—John Palmer*

Recommended:

- ○ **The Count of Luxembourg** / Wordsworth (cond.), Smith, Jenkins, Davies, Nicoll, Fitchew, Rice, Stirling, Bunning, Richard, Bull, DeVan, Harrison, Jagusz, Lang, Marandola, McCord, Meanley, Tierney, Walker / 1997 / Jay 1271
- ○ **Lehár: Operettas** / Mattes (cond.), Fuchs, Stader, Cloe, Datz, Grabenhorst, Jung, Kalenberg, Kiss, Moeller, Pawels, Wichartz, Wiedenhofer, Wolff, Glyndebourne Festival Chorus, Chor des Bayerischen Runfunks / 2004 / EMI 85997

Das Land des Lächelns (The Land of Smiles), operetta (1929)

Though best known for the "Tauber tune," (the romantic hit *"Dein ist mein ganzes Herz"*), this work (also known as *The Land of Smiles*) is filled with a wide variety of music, from Mi's soubrettish melodies to hints of Orientalism to pensively amourous tunes, as well as the standard Viennese waltzes. The bittersweet plot, with its sad but not tragic ending, allowed Lehár to add more musically and dramatically serious elements (as with *Giuditta*). While in its first appearance *"Dein ist mein ganzes Herz"* is a passionate expression of romantic devotion, the melody later serves almost as a leitmotif when the action turns tragic; it is somewhat reminiscent of "Du bist der Lenz," reprised at Siegmund's death in *Die Walküre* as a love song that briefly returns to evoke the sadness of lost love. The work originally premiered in 1923 in Vienna as *Die gelbe Jacket* (The Yellow Jacket). It ran for about 100 performances, but 1929 reworking, with a new cast and new music, captured audiences both at the Berlin premiere and worldwide. The two leads, Richard Tauber and Vera Schwarz, had plenty of star appeal, and the new numbers, including *"Im Salon zur blau'n Pagode," "Bei inem Tee a deux,"* and of course, *"Dein ist mein ganzes Herz,"* added even more to the operetta's charm and light exoticism. The work has firmly remained in the operetta repertoire ever since, though in the late twentieth and early twenty-first centuries, some of the cultural concepts can be uncomfortable to audiences. *—Ann Feeney*

Synopsis:

Setting: Vienna and China, 1912

Act One. A ball is taking place at Count Lichtenfels' home, celebrating Lisa's victory in a riding contest. Lisa finds such events are boring her ("Gern, gern war ich verliebt"). Count Gustl proposes to her, now that he has enough money to marry on, but she refuses, as she has fallen in love with Prince Sou-Chong, a Chinese diplomat. Sou-Chong has just sent her a gift, a magnificent statue of the Buddha. Lisa and Gustl agree to remain friends, and he still has hopes of winning her love ("Es ist nicht das ersternal"). Sou-Chong arrives, and, while waiting to be announced, muses that her house seems to be the holiest place he knows, so much so that he trembles when he enters it. He is deeply attracted to her, but fears that for her he is just an exotic curiosity, and so keeps his feelings hidden behind his smile ("Immer nur lacheln und immer vergnugt"). He and Lisa enjoy a cup of tea together ("Bei einem Tee à deux"), and at her request, he describes the process of courtship in China, to her friends ("Von Apfelbluten einen Kranz"). As he portrays a young man singing to the woman he loves, he turns to Lisa. He receives a message that his father died, and that he must return to China to assume the role of Prime Minister. When he finds Lisa to say goodbye, she tells him of a song that has enchanted her ("Ein Lied, es verfolgt"), and he admits that he is leaving his heart behind. She suggests that he take it with him, instead, and to his delight, says that she will gladly follow him to China.

Act Two. In Beijing, Sou-Chong, in a majestic ceremony, is given the yellow jacket signifying his new role ("Dschinthien wuomen ju chon ma goa can"). Lisa has come to China with him, and they are deeply in love ("Wer hat die Liebe"). Mi, his very Westernized sister, sings, albeit with spirit, of the restrictions placed upon her by the old-fashioned court ("Im Salon zur blau'n Pagode"). She is immediately attracted to Gustl, who has come in pursuit of Lisa, and they talk about the different ways of saying ("I love you"). although love is the same the world around ("Meine Liebe, deine Liebe"). Tschang, uncle of Sou-Chong and Mi, reminds Sou-Chong that according to tradition, he must take four wives. Sou-Chong reassures Lisa that his entire heart belongs to her ("Deine is mein ganzes Herz"). Lisa, already disenchanted, suddenly feels homesick when she sees Gustl ("Ich mocht wieder einmal"). She watches the wedding processing bringing the four brides and tells Sou-Chong that she will return to Vienna. He refuses to permit it, though she tells him that by giving orders, he has turned her love to hate ("Mit welchen Recht?"). He gives orders forbidding her to leave the palace, and alone, he is horrified and mourns over their lost love ("Ihr Gotter sagt"), giving a locket she gave him as an offering to the Buddha.

Act Three. Lisa is confined in the women's quarters, and slaves try to cheer her up. Gustl bribes his way in, saying that they can escape through the temple. Mi is glad for Lisa, and excited to be defying the rules, but privately desolated at Gustl's departure ("Zi, zig, zig, zig, ih!"), and they bid one another goodbye ("Wie rasch verwelkt") with bittersweet affection. When Lisa and Gustl are about to leave, they find Sou-Chong blocking the doorway. However, at Lisa's reminders of their past love and pleas to allow her her freedom ("Dieselbe Sonne, die uber Europa scheint"), he gives in, asking Gustl to watch over her. He then turns to comfort Mi, telling her they will both hide their sorrow under their smiles. *—Ann Feeney*

Recommended:

- ○ **Léhar: Das Land des Lächelns** / Marzalek (cond.), Wunderlich, Fahberg, Cologne Radio Orch. / Gala 329
- ○ **Lehar: 2 Operettas** / Ackermann (cond.), Schwarzkopf, Gedda, Kunz, Loose, London PO / Angel 67529
- ○ **Léhar: Das Land des Lächelns** / Bonynge (cond.), Hadley, Atkinson, Gustafson, Itami, English CO / 1996 / Teldec 80419

Die lustige Witwe (The Merry Widow), operetta (1905)

With the possible exception of Johann Strauss' Die Fledermaus, Franz Lehár's *The Merry Widow* is the best known of all Viennese operettas. The score overflows with melodies—not just waltzes, but can-cans, marches, and mazurkas—and the plot is a perfect mix of fun and slightly bittersweet romance. And, in the end, at least one pair of lovers is both wiser and happier.

Hanna, the "merry widow" of the title, provides the sole economic support for the fictional country of Pontevedro by way of an inheritance from her wealthy old husband. The Pontevedro legation in Paris is desperate at the thought that Hanna will marry again—a Frenchman, no less—and persuades Danilo, an old Pontevedran flame of hers, to try and woo her. Hanna is of course fully aware that her suitors are after her money; however, after various complications, Hanna and Danilo discover that they are truly in love with one another and are reunited.

The operetta's two most famous numbers are Hanna's "Vilja-lied" (a song about a woodland sprite), and the "Merry Widow Waltz." Like the operetta itself, both numbers are deceptively simple, combining guilelessness and exquisite craftsmanship in a manner that well explains their enduring popularity. *—Ann Feeney*

Synopsis:

Act One. In the Pontevedro (a fictional Balkan country) legation in Paris, the aristocratic Pontevedrans and Parisian guests are celebrating the birthday of the prince. Vicomte Cascada proposes a toast ("Verehrteste Damen und Herren"). Meanwhile, Camille is paying court to Valencienne, though she half-heartedly protests that she is and intends to remain a respectable wife. Njegus announces, to great anticipation, the arrival of Hanna Glawari, a Pontevedran woman of humble birth but great wealth, due to her marriage to an elderly banker who conveniently died and left her a fortune. The Baron, aware of Pontevedro's dire financial straits, intends for her to marry a Pontevedran, to keep her fortune in the country. She makes a glamorous entrance ("Bitte meine Herr'n"), but as the men pay her extravagant attention, she is fully aware that her wealth is the attraction. She invites all present to come to a Pontevedranstyle party at her house the next evening. The Baron has quietly sent for Danilo, who was reluctantly forced to come from the nightclub Maxim's. He tells the Baron he is perfectly willing to work all day for his country, but his evenings are his own, to spend with the lovely grisettes who entertain at the cabarets ("Da geh' ich zu Maxim"). As the guests go into another room, he falls asleep on a couch. Hanna, returning, hears his snores and recognizes him. In Pontevedro, they had been in love, but his guardian had forbidden him to marry Hanna, a poor, humbly-born woman, and so she married the banker, instead. Both are embittered, and when she taunts him that her wealth has made her acceptable to the aristocracy, he insists he has no interest in her or her wealth. She sweeps out, and the Baron tells Danilo his plan, and Danilo refuses. In the ballroom, the dance is ladies choice, and Danilo introduces his bevy of grisettes. Hanna chooses Danilo, the only man not clamoring for the dance, and to make the men's motives clear, he ascertains that the dance is his to dispose of, and offers it to any man who will donate ten thousand francs to charity. Nobody accepts the offer, and Hanna and Danilo end up partners.

Act Two. At Hanna's house, entertainers perform a traditional kolo dance. Hanna sings about a wood spirit who entranced a wandering hunter ("Es lebt' eine Vilja"). The Baron and Njegas discuss the rumor that Hanna has her eye on Camille, and when Njegas says another rumor has it that Camille is in love with a married Pontevedran woman, and the Baron, dismissing the woman's husband as an idiot, thinks the man could be persuaded to give up his wife to Camille to prevent Hanna from marrying a foreigner. Danilo has been avoiding Hanna, but when she confronts him, insists that he is just showing his heritage in the cavalry by reconnoitering ("Dummer, dummer, Reitersmann"). The French and Pontevedran men discuss the difficulty in understanding women ("Ja, das Studium der Weiber"). Camille continues to court Valencienne, and writes on her fan, "I love you." She writes, "I am a respectable wife" on the other side in response, and gives it to him. She suggests that he marry Hanna, but he insists that he loves her ("Wie eine Rosenknospe"). She does permit him a final meeting in the summerhouse. Njegus tells the Baron that Camille and a woman are in the summerhouse, and the Baron peers through the keyhole, only to recognize his own wife. To save Valencienne's reputation, Hanna slips in through a back door and Valencienne slips out. Hanna and Camille make a grand exit, and announce their engagement. Hanna teases Danilo by describing her excitement ("Eine flotter Ehestand"), and he responds by telling the story of a prince who, unable to express his love for a princess, saw her marry another ("Es waren zwei Königskinder"). He storms off to Maxim's and Hanna is triumphantly certain that he still loves her.

Act Three. Hanna has replicated a nightclub, knowing that that is Danilo's favorite setting. Valencienne and the cabaret girls perform a cancan ("Ja, wir sind es"). Danilo petulantly forbids Hanna to marry Camille, and she tells him she was in the summerhouse with Camille to protect another woman's reputation. They sing a tender love duet ("Beijedem Walzerschritt") and dance. The Baron finds Valencienne's fan, with Camille's declaration of love written on it, and is convinced she is unfaithful. He declares he considers himself divorced and proposes to Hanna. Hanna accepts, but casually adds that the terms of her late husband's will mean she loses every penny should she remarry. The Baron promptly withdraws his offer, and Danilo, knowing that now she will understand he loves her, not her money, proposes himself. She accepts this offer, and clarifies the terms of the will: the money will transfer to the ownership of her new husband. The Baron is consoled when Valencienne indignantly points out the words on the reverse of the fan, "I am a respectable wife," which he had not even noticed. *—Ann Feeney*

Recommended:

○ **Lehár: Die lustige Witwe** / Gardiner (cond.), Terfel, Bonney, Skovhus, Studer, Vienna PO / 1994 / DG 439911

○ **Lehar: Two Operettas** / Ackermann (cond.), Schwarzkopf, Gedda, Kunz, Loose, London PO / Angel 67529

○ **Lehár: Die lustige Witwe** / Matacic (cond.), Schwarzkopf, Gedda, Equiluz, Wachter, London PO / 2000 / Angel 67367

Paganini, operetta (1924–1925)

Paul Knepler, a Viennese publisher, sent Franz Lehár the libretto for *Paganini* (then entitled *Hexenmeister* [Wizard]), anonymously. Knepler intended to set the text himself, but eventually came to realize the task was beyond him; Lehár was immediately taken with the subject matter and set to work before he had even drawn up a contract with the author. Lehár required fourteen months to compose the score; during this period, he called on Béla Jenbach to make some finishing touches to the text.

Lehár tailored the part of Paganini for the voice of Richard Tauber, the famous Austrian tenor who had become the composer's standard interpreter. Unfortunately, Tauber was unavailable for the Vienna premiere of *Paganini,* on October 30, 1925. This was probably part of the reason for the operetta's lukewarm reception in Vienna. Lehár convinced Tauber to participate in the Berlin premiere of January 30, 1925. Both Lehár and Tauber triumphed that evening, and the production was sold out for the next three months.

Lehár's 28th completed work for the stage, *Paganini* is typifies the last phase of the "silver age" of operetta; representative qualities include: adopting the aura of "serious" opera and symphonic music, subject matter that one also finds in the cinema of the time, and vocal writing influenced by Puccini. The *buffo* numbers, such as the dance song, "Einmal möcht' ich was Närrisches tun" (Just once I would like to so something crazy), reveal a more sophisticated treatment than in Lehár's earlier works, and the *arioso* tenor numbers are more lyrical. Element's of the composer's Slavonic style emerge in Paganini's "Gern hab' ich die Frauen geküsst" (I've enjoyed kissing ladies). The use of pentatonic and whole-tone elements may derive from Lehár's study with Dvořák and Fibich, or from similar devices in Puccini's *Madame Butterfly* and Turandot.

Lehár's *Paganini* is one of many so-called "biographical operettas" that were popular in the first part of the twentieth century. In these anecdotal, romanticized accounts, historical figures become the central figures in theatrically bittersweet love affairs. Before making his name as a touring virtuoso, Paganini was indeed employed in 1801 as a violinist in the recently established "National Orchestra" of Lucca. The town, however, experienced financial difficulties and disbanded the orchestra not long after. In 1805, Napoleon assigned the Principality of Lucca to his sister, Elisa Bacchiocchi, who in 1806 invited *Paganini* to join the court chamber orchestra as second violinist. After this ensemble, too, met its demise, *Paganini* joined the ruling family's string quartet and began instructing the young prince and conducting operatic performances. In 1809, citing personal reasons, *Paganini* left his employment in Lucca and began his life on the road. Lehár and Knepler's central figure presents the contemporary stereotype of the Romantic artist and his noble mission: he does not want to belong to any woman; he must live only for his art. As in many stylized artist "biographies" of the era, *Paganini,* the demonic artist, rejects a life of comfort for a nomadic existence as a defiantly independent creative soul. *—John Palmer*

Synopsis:

Act One. Paganini, accompnied by Bartucci, his impresario, visits the tiny Principality of Lucca and the townspeople have a chance to hear the master's sensational violin playing. The audience members are of divided opinion concerning what they consider to be a "musical sorcerer." The women all swoon when they hear Paganini play, but the men are more skeptical, and wish he would "go to hell." In the village tavern the mayor, Pimpinelli, provides a meal for the town's Hunting Society and her royal highness, Princess Anna Elisa Bonaparte, Napoleon's sister. Pimpinelli is disgusted that the Princess has chosen an ordinary public place at which to dine.

From a distance, Princess Anna Elisa hears Paganini's playing, and is immediately enthralled. Paganini enters and begins throwing coins to the townspeople while praising his native land, "fair Italy." At first, the Princess was hypnotized by only Paganini's violin playing, but now she is intoxicated by his personal charm. She comments that he is quite young, yet a great master, whereupon he relates that he tells his greatest secrets only to his violin. It seems Paganini is on his way to getting what he wants when Bartucci announces that Prince Felice has barred Paganini from performing in Lucca. Paganini, confused and angered by what he considers an irrational decision, begins to pack up his belongings. All the while, the Princess speaks of the hot fire burning inside her, noting that, "A man like that is worth a little sinning."

Pimpinelli meets the beautiful Bella Giretti, prima donna of the Royal Opera House. Considering himself a "Don Juan," Pimpinelli expresses his intentions to her. Bella, who is currently the Prince's mistress, participates wholeheartedly in the flirtation. The Princess Anna Elisa and Paganini meet a second time, but they are interrupted by passers-by. When Prince Felice arrives from a hunt he and the Princess argue over the cancellation of Paganini's concert. Anna Elisa threatens to make public the affair between her husband and Bella Giretti if he does not allow Paganini to perform in Lucca. The Prince, seeing no other alternative, retracts his earlier ban on the concert. The Princess is pleased that she may finally hear Paganini's "sweet playing."

Act Two. During the past six months, Paganini has been appointed both court conductor and musical director of Lucca's Opera. Numerous artists have gathered to play a game of cards, during which Paganini gambles away his prized Stradivarius. Pimpinelli, the winner, promises to return the violin in exchange for Paganini's secret to conquering the opposite sex. Paganini tells him that he has always enjoyed kissing women. He never considers whether it is the proper thing to do, he simply takes them and kisses them, for that's why they exist. With this new method, Pimpinelli hopes to achieve "his goals." Paganini then sings a love song he has composed for the Princess Anna Elisa.

Pimpinelli tries again with Bella Giretti, who admits, "I would like to do something crazy just once." Bartucci is upset that Paganini is pursuing the Princess, but the violinist genuinely loves her. The Princess, however, is a little unsure, asking Paganini "how many sweet red lips" he has already kissed. To this he responds that no one loves her as he does.

Court gossip abounds and rumors even reach Paris, where Napoleon, in a rage, sends Graf Hedouville to Lucca with orders that Paganini is to leave the town without delay. The enraged Princess refuses to be separated from her lover and demands that this order be nullified. Although he is truly in love with Anna Elisa, Paganini still has thoughts of other women, one of whom is Bella Giretti. Paganini is unable to resist Bella's charms and dedicates to her the love song he had originally written for Anna Elisa. The Princess is about to banish Bella from the court when Bella shows her the love song from Paganini. Anna Elisa swears vengeance and, as the concert begins, orders Graf Hedouville to arrest Paganini while he is playing. Everyone at court is very curious about the goings on and they prod Pimpinelli for information. Bella tries to warn Paganini but he ignores her and continues playing, once again mesmerizing Anna Elisa, who falls in love with the violinist all over again. She pledges her love to him in front of the entire court before leaving with him.

Act Three. At the smuggler's tavern, "Zum rostigen Hufnagel" (The Rusty Hobnail), smugglers are gambling and drinking when a knock is heard. Its is

Pimpinelli and Bella, who ask for lodging for the night. Momentarily, Paganini appears, prepared to be smuggled across the border that night by the assembled group of criminals. Bartucci unexpectedly arrives, and Paganini tells him that his only true love is the violin. Bella tries to dissuade the musician from his course of action and attempts to change his mind about his feelings for his violin. She is not successful, and must settle for Pimpinelli: "Better the mayor than no man at all." Disguised as a street singer, the Princess Anna Elisa has followed Paganini to the tavern; she sings a song. Paganini recognizes her voice and, while leaving, tells her, "No other woman stands between us, but you must nevertheless leave, for I must be alone." Anna Elisa responds with, "You can't belong to any woman who holds you in her loving arms. Art alone must be your mistress, you belong to all the world." *—John Palmer*

Recommended:

○ **Lehár: Paganini** / Boskovsky (cond.), Rothenberger, Miljakovic, Gedda, Zednik, Kusche / 1996 / EMI 65968

Schön ist die Welt, operetta (1930)

Schön ist die Welt is a revision of Lehár's earlier effort from 1914, *Endlich Allein*, and is one of the six operettas he wrote specifically for the tenor Richard Tauber. The libretto is by Ludwig Herzer and Fritz Löhner, and the work was first produced at the Metropol-Theater, Berlin, in December 1930. Its Vienna premiere was in December 1931. *Schön ist die Welt* uses the well-worn theatrical device of mistaken (or in this case, hidden) identity as the basis for its central love story, that between Crown Prince Georg and Princess Elizabeth von und zu Lichtenberg, who are betrothed by arrangement. By straining against the arranged marriage, they end up truly in love. As is the case with most of Lehár's stage works, the trivial plot is enlivened by the beauty, expressivity, and innate characterization of his music, which transcended the genre of operetta. The most memorable numbers include Georg's "Liebste, glaub' an mich" (the signature "Tauber-lied") and the harmonically adventurous and catchy tango "Rio de Janeiro" (performed by Mercedes del Rossa, the center of a peripheral romance). Lehár's inclusion of mandolins and banjo in the orchestration add a special color to the score. *—Allen Schrott*

Recommended:

○ **Lehár: Schön ist die Welt** / Lehar (cond.), Dermota, Kern, Niessner, Emmerich, Vienna PO / History 203152

Der Zarewitsch, operetta (1927)

Der Zarewitsch is representative of the last phase of the "silver age" of operetta. It takes on an aura of serious opera and symphonic music, it includes subject matter that one also finds in the cinema of the time; and the vocal writing shows the influence of Puccini. Lehár's orchestration is refined in its use of colorful contrasts, and the stage roles are precisely characterized musically. The vocal writing in *Der Zarewitsch* is unabashedly lyrical, perhaps because Lehár was certain of the quality of the performers he would have for the work's first performance.

The success of Lehár's *Paganini* of 1925 prompted the composer to continue in the direction of historical drama, producing first *Der Zarewitsch* and then, soon after, *Friederike. Der Zarewitsch* is based on a Polish play of the same name, by the playwright Gabryela Zapolska, which Lehár had seen in Vienna in 1917. From the original play Béla Jenbach (1871–1943) and Heinz Reichert developed a libretto, which was offered to Lehár in 1925. Evidently, the composer rejected the book, which was then offered to Mascagni, who wrote nothing, then to Eduard Künneke. Lehár eventually changed his mind and decided to set the text.

Jenbach and Reichert glossed over some of the unpleasant historical facts contained in Zapolska's play, which is loosely based on the life of Czar Peter the Great's son, Alexei. Very early in the eighteenth century, Alexei left Russia with a Finnish woman, intending to live in Italy. Advisors convinced Alexei to return to his homeland, but he was promptly put on trial by his father and sent to prison, where he eventually died. In Jenbach and Reichert's version, the Czar-to-be leaves his lady, Sonja, in Italy to take up his duties in Russia.

Lehár tailored the part of the Zarewitsch to the voice of Richard Tauber, the famous Austrian tenor who had become the composer's standard interpreter and whose voice and stage presence almost ensured the success of Lehár's later works. Tauber once claimed that he and Lehár were brothers, "without the luxury of a blood relationship." Lehár was able to compose very ambitious voice parts for Tauber, and a typical "Tauber song" developed, featuring a dramatic, initial upward thrust that others came to imitate. Such songs in *Der Zarewitsch* are "Es steht ein Soldat am Wolgastrand" (There stands a soldier on the bank of the Volga) from the first act and "Willst du?" (Do you want to?), from Act Two. Tauber later claimed *Der Zarewitsch* was his favorite role.

Lehár found Berlin audiences more responsive to his Romantic voice than the Viennese and relocated to Berlin shortly before beginning *Der Zarewitsch.* Commissioned by the Deutsches Künstlertheater, *Der Zarewitsch* received its premiere there on February 21, 1927. Although the work may not have the continuous melodic flow of Paganini, it does possess some excellent numbers, among them Sonja's "Einer wird kommen" (Someone will come) and the first-act duet for Marscha and Ivan, "Dich nur allein, nenn' ich mein" (You alone I take for mine). "Warum hat jeder Frühling, ach, nur einen Mai?" (Why does every spring have but one May?), a duet for Sonja and *Der Zarewitsch* at the beginning of the third act, is a melodically splendid vehicle for both singers, especially the tenor.

Most of these numbers would fit well into any of Lehár's late operettas and bring nothing to the particular atmosphere of *Der Zarewitsch.* Lehár established the local color of the operetta's Russian milieu through orchestration, including balalaikas, and the use of the Neapolitan sixth chord and various church modes to create an "exotic" flavor. *—John Palmer*

Synopsis:

Act One. At the palace of the Czar, a few curious women of the Russian aristocracy inspect the simple, Spartan room of the Zarewitsch while on a tour guided by the Grand-Duke. The Zarewitsch, the Grand-Duke's nephew, leads a completely secluded life and is averse to all women. Also, he doesn't know that his footman, Ivan, is married and that Ivan's wife, Marscha, despite the fact that it will create a difficult situation, is visiting the castle. Marscha is very jealous and intends to make a scene with her husband ("Dich nur allein, nenn' ich mein"). The Grand-Duke returns, eagerly engaged in a conversation with the Ministry President concerning a very important diplomatic mission. For political reasons the Zarewitsch must soon marry. In order to familiarize the Zarewitsch with the company of women, the Ministry President has prevailed upon the dancer Sonja, clothed as Tscherkesse, to go to the Zarewitsch. The Zarewitsch enters and, as always, is sad and full of melancholy ("Es steht ein Soldat am Wolgastrand"). Sonja is led in, and the Zarewitsch, thinking she is a man, demands that she turn around, whereupon he recognizes that a woman stands before him. Full of indignation, the Zarewitsch wants to show Sonja the door, but her pleading stirs him and he allows her to stay with him. In order to have some peace in front of the Ministry President, Sonja is to give the appearance that she is the Zarewitsch's sweetheart, even thought she is really just a good friend. To play out the comedy in a genuine fashion, he orders champagne and sweets and the two of them sing their "Champagne Song" ("Champagne ist ein Feuerwein"). But the Zarewitsch's amusement soon disappears, as Sonja becomes tired. He "allows" her to come again the next day.

Act Two. Sonja and the Zarewitsch act out their comedy further. Smirking, the Grand-Duke finds here and there little intimate things belonging to a woman, such as a dainty slipper, a hairslide and bows, and greatly embarrasses the Zarewitsch with them. The Zarewitsch has become so familiar with Sonja that he forbids her to continue dancing with his troops. In the future she is only to be there for him, an issue they discuss in the duet ("Hab' nur dich allein").

It is time to prepare the parade. In a bad mood, the Zarewitsch dresses, trying not to think about the speech he is supposed to give before the officers. Again and again Sonja enters his mind ("Willst du?"). Sonja has brought along her friends to show them the castle and the park. Everyone looks at her in wonder and envy during "Wenn der Heimat Lieder erklingen." The Grand-Duke appears. He is afraid that the Zarewitsch could actually fall in love with Sonja and orders her to give the Zarewitsch an account of her dark past, otherwise she must lose him. Trembling, she promises to tell him. As the head steward announces that the future wife of the Zarewitsch is about to enter, the Zarewitsch declares that he does not wish to listen to the orders of the Czar and the Grand-Duke cannot change his mind. The Grand-Duke then grasps at his last straw. He tells the Zarewitsch that Sonja has something to confess regarding her history. Deeply hurt, the Zarewitsch pushes Sonja back. But her love is great and she falls to her knees and confesses that she feels only love for him and fears that she will lose him. Shaking, the Zarewitsch takes her in his arms.

Act Three. The lovers have fled to Naples to enjoy a brief period of happiness ("Warum hat jeder Frühling, ach, nur einen Mai?"). The Grand-Duke and his officers have come after the Zarewitsch to remind him of his duty. Once again the Zarewitsch refuses his duty and says he would rather renounce the throne and his rank than be chained to a woman he does not love. Then, the Grand-Duke turns to Sonja and demands from her a sacrifice: she must, of her own free will, leave the Zarewitsch. Sonja recognizes that this would be the best for both the Zarewitsch and for Russia, and promises to do so. With words that tear her heart to shreds she swears to the Zarewitsch to relinquish his and her happiness as a sacrifice to a nobler goal. The Zarewitsch is incapable of giving an answer, as he has just received a telegram informing him of the death of the Czar. The officers salute their new Czar as he allows Sonja to clothe him in his coat and helmet. Once more he takes her in his arms before he leaves to do his duty. Sonja is left alone. *—John Palmer*

Recommended:

○ **Lehár: The Czarevitch** / Bonynge (cond.), Gustafson, Hadley, Itami / 1996 / Telarc 80395

○ **Lehár: Operettas** / Mattes (cond.), Friedauer, Streich, Gedda, Reichart / 2004 / EMI 85997

Zigeunerliebe (Gypsy Love), operetta (1909; revised 1943)

Lehár's *Zigeunerliebe* (Gypsy Love; 1909) is one of three operettas the composer produced in a three-month period following the failure of his *Der Mann mit den drei Frauen* (1908). Of the three new works, *Zigeunerliebe* and *Der Graf von Luxemburg* (The Count of Luxembourg) became international hits.

Zigeunerliebe, with a book by Alfred Maria Willner and Robert Bodanzky, is the story of a young woman, Zorika, who is engaged to Jonel, but is unsure of her feelings toward him. She is at the same time fascinated with the adventurous Gypsy violinist, Józsi. Zorika recalls the popular belief that, if a bride drinks of the water of the Czerna River, she will be able to see the future. After taking a handful of the water, Zorika falls asleep and dreams of a less-than-perfect future with Józsi. When she awakens, she decides to spend her life with Jonel.

Few of Lehár's other scores are as melodically inventive, harmonically daring, and instrumentally colorful; no other score, by Lehár or anyone else, uses Hungarian and Gypsy folk music in such a convincing manner. The libretto is marked by a wide range of dramatic affect, from yearning and doubt to conceit and pretension, from unbounded lust to restrained intimacy. Characters are driven by genuine passion, and their music is fittingly earnest. The Romanian and Hungarian setting of *Zigeunerliebe* further allowed Lehár to infuse the score with what many perceived as a Balkan flavor, which is really more Hungarian than Romanian.

Many numbers from the operetta became famous, including Zorika's czárdás, "Hör' ich Cymbalklänge" (I hear the sound of cymbals) and Zorika and Józsi's duet, "Es liegt in blauen Fernen" (It lies in the blue distance). Józsi's numbers with czárdás characteristics, "Welche hier von allen würde mir gefallen" (Which of all these would please me?) and "Ich bin ein Zigeunerkind" (I am a Gypsy child), are also audience favorites. As in *Der Graf von Luxemburg*, the moderato waltz tempo plays an important role, particularly in Zorika's "Gib mir dort vom Himmelszelt" (Give me, from the vault of heaven) and Jonel's "Zorika, Zorika, kehre zurück" (Zorika, Zorika, come back), both of which are marked by a Balkan flavor derived from their rhythms and instrumentation. *Zigeunerliebe* occasionally ventures into the sonic realm of "serious" opera. When Zorika drinks from the river Czerna and slips into her dream, for example, Lehár ventures into the harmonic waters that Wagner had navigated with his Rhinemaidens. In the end, however, he always finds his way back to the lively language which characterizes his music.

Contemporary critics and theater managers recognized the Puccini-like tendencies of *Zigeunerliebe*, especially evident in the soaring vocal lines, lush, Romantic orchestration, and the love-story setting free from the comic elements and frivolity of the composer's *Der Graf von Luxemburg* or *Die lustige Witwe*. In contrast to these works, *Zigeunerliebe* is marked by a spirit by melancholy and fantasy.

The original version of the operetta was premiered at the Carltheater in Vienna on January 8, 1910. For a London run that began in July 1812, Lehár added several numbers, including the popular drinking song, "Liebe und Wein" (Love and wine). In 1943, near the end of his life, Lehár revised *Zigeunerliebe* as the opera *Garaboncíás diák* (The Wandering Scholar) for the Hungarian State Opera in Budapest. *—John Palmer*

Synopsis:

The action takes place in a mountainous region of Romania, not far from the Hungarian border, at the beginning of the nineteenth century. The first act is set outside Peter Dragotin's hunting castle on the banks of the river Czerna; the second in a tavern; the third in Dragotin's hunting castle.

According to an old legend, a woman who is engaged to be married will be able to see the future if she drinks from the river Czerna. Zorika, daughter of the landowner Peter Dragotin, is engaged to Jonel Bolescu, a boyar like her father. Zorika's conscience, however, is plagued with doubts. She is not sure she is in love with Jonel and has nowhere to go for advice, for on every side she finds people who practice no restraint when it comes to love. Her father continually pesters the landowner Ilona von Körörsháza, who for her part makes eyes at the Józsi, a Gypsy violinist. Zorika finds herself much more fascinated with the hot-blooded Gypsy than with Jonel, who seems too docile to her. Confused, she wants to know what her future holds she leaves her engagement celebration and takes a walk to the Czerna to drink a handful of the river's water. The song of a water-nymph lulls Zorika to sleep.

While sleeping, Zorika has a dream of her life two years hence in which she has been disowned by her family because she has married Józsi, who has no love for her and treats her terribly. Zorika also discovers that her husband is a fan of "free love." She lives "without peace and quiet," and, in addition to enduring her shame, she must travel alone through strange lands. When Zorika wakes, she ponders the meaning of her horrible dream. Viewing the dream as a warning, Zorika determines not to give in to the temptation of the adventurous Józsi. Instead, she will happily give herself to the sweet, trustworthy Jonel. She is certain that a gentle, quiet life with him is preferable to a wild existence with the mysterious Gypsy violinist. Zorika runs back to her engagement celebration and into the arms of the waiting, happy Jonel. *—John Palmer*

ORCHESTRAL

Gold und Silber-Walzer, Op. 79 (1902)

Lehár was the bandmaster of the 26th regiment in Vienna when he was asked by the Princess Metternich to compose "something especially fine" for her "Gold und Silber" gala ball given on January 27, 1902, in the Sophiensäle. This commission continued an old Viennese tradition, dating back to Lanner and Johann Strauss the Elder, of the so-called "name waltz," which received its title from the important occasion at which it was premiered. The "name waltz" would be given as the first piece of the evening, an instrumental concert work to set the mood before the dancing began.

Although the waltz was to achieve international fame as "Gold and Silver" balls became popular throughout Europe, England, and America, and quickly gained fame for its composer, apparently that first evening it made little impression on the crowd. Every one was dressed in some variety of the theme colors, the ceiling was painted silver with golden stars, and arc lamp lighting highlighted golden palms with silver trunks. But people were antsy and began dancing and talking excitedly right away, drawing attention away from the music. Although the piece was given one encore, it received little notice in the papers. However, the composition was soon published by Chmel in Austria, was eventually distributed by the English firm of Bosworth and Co., and became a hit.

Within this style, Lehár's waltz is an ideal example of thematic balance and emotional contrast. The first theme ascends and descends within a small range of tones and begins the work with a warm tone colored with birdcall-like grace notes in the woodwinds on beats two and three. A triangle adds a "silvery" quality, and harp arpeggios help the music flow elegantly.

Suddenly, there is a minorish theme which rushes along in the lower string range. An atmosphere of anxious excitement is evoked, accentuated by the trilling winds and the drum rolls. This brief storm begins to subside quickly.

A few staccati as the tempo slows down in anticipation of the main theme. This third theme, 32 measures long in C major, enters with a pickup, and gradually sweeps its way gently upward with dips and turns. It is richly romantic, Viennese, and continental, and floats among the harp arpeggios with constantly singing confidence. At the end there is a gently retreating diminuendo with a glint in its eye.

Suddenly, the fourth motif enters with a clash of cymbals. This is a bright, lively theme with unison winds answered by the strings. A distant hunting call in the horns leads into a subdued, pastoral fifth motif played by pizzicato strings and horns. Then the sixth motif enters with drum rolls. This coda is replete with ascending trumpet arpeggios in a Wagnerian style (evidently a joke on "Das Rheingold"), and "serious" diminished and minor harmonies resolving into bright major chords. Repeated chordal accents and drum rolls bring the piece to a grand, symphonic conclusion. —"Blue Gene" Tyranny

Recommended:

○ **Lehár: Waltzes** / Boskovsky (cond.), Vienna Johann Strauss Orch. / 2001 / EMI 74735

Lotte Lehmann

b. Feb. 27, 1888, Perleberg, Germany, **d.** Aug. 26, 1976, Santa Barbara, CA
Soprano

"If she had been born in Texas they would have called her a gusher, so impulsively did she pour out her voice in an exuberant, generous flood." The opening words of recording producer Walter Legge's appreciation go a long way toward explaining the Lotte Lehmann phenomenon. Richard Strauss wrote three roles with her extraordinary voice and personality in mind and she sang the premieres, gathering still more fans into the orbit of her art. While opera was the primary outlet for her talents, she made many magnificent lieder appearances, notably in the decade before her 1951 retirement. A number of favorite songs made their way to disc.

Lehmann was a Prussian by birth, but she captured the Viennese and gave of herself unreservedly as though she had been born one of them. A self-assured individual, she nonetheless had her battles with colleagues (especially those who sang the same roles as she) and occasionally found herself the victim of unfortunate timing. Her recordings still sell in significant numbers years after they were made.

Lehmann's father was a town government official who intended that his daughter have a thorough education, one which would prepare her for a career in teaching. Instead, in a high school in Berlin where the family had moved, she applied her unmistakable intelligence to the writing of poetry (an interest that remained her entire life) rather than being conscientious about her studies. This independence would manifest itself throughout her career.

Having sung from childhood, Lehmann was enthusiastic when a neighbor made possible an audition which led to vocal study at the Royal Academy of Music. Upon finishing there, she became a private pupil of Mathilde Malinger, who devoted herself to preparing Lehmann for a serious career.

A three-year contract at the Hamburg Opera began inauspiciously, with small parts and tepid notices. Then, when conductor Otto Klemperer had to find a replacement for the role of Elsa in *Lohengrin*, Lehmann was asked to attempt the part. A period of intensive study brought her a triumph on opening night. Lost in Elsa's character, she gave the first of countless performances both vocally thrilling and dramatically absorbing. Quickly, other roles, including those in the French and Italian repertories, were assigned to her and, when an official from the Vienna Court Opera heard her one evening, she was engaged for that theater.

In Vienna, she achieved her highest measure of fame, steadily undertaking all the great roles that would be associated with her: Sieglinde, Leonore in *Fidelio*, and the Marschallin. Strauss selected her to create the Composer in *Ariadne auf Naxos*, the Dyer's Wife in *Die Frau ohne Schatten*, and Christine in *Intermezzo*. She made a debut in 1924 at Covent Garden, performed between 1928 and 1934 at Paris, and joined the Chicago Opera in 1930. Her Metropolitan Opera debut in 1934 as Sieglinde drew a ten-minute ovation at her first curtain call.

When the Nazis came to power in 1933, Lehmann renounced her native country, and resettled in Vienna. Upon news of the Anschluss, she moved on the United States and applied for citizenship there. After leaving the Met in 1945, she sang a final season at the San Francisco Opera before retiring from the stage. She continued to make recital appearances until 1951 when she retired from singing and devoted herself to teaching, writing, and painting.

Although Lehmann never quite mastered her breath control, her exquisite, inimitable sound and instinctively imaginative phrasing made her one of the recording era's most treasurable singers. *—Erik Eriksson*

Recommended:

- ○ **Lehmann Sings 26 Lieder** / Weissmann (cond.), Lehmann, Ulanowsky, Berlin State Opera Orch. / 1994 / GSE Claremont 785057
- ○ **The Complete RCA Victor Recordings, 1947–49** / Armbruster (cond.), Lehmann, Ulanowsky, RCA Victor CO / 2000 / Romophone 81033
- ○ **Lebendige Vergangenheit: Lotte Lehmann** / Lehmann, etc. / Preiser 89189
- ○ **The New York Farewell Recital** / Lehmann, Ulanowsky (piano) / 1993 / VAI Audio 1038

Sergei Leiferkus

b. Apr. 4, 1946, Leningrad, USSR
Bass

Russian-born bass Sergei Leiferkus has proven himself authoritative in many areas of the repertory. He was among the first of the Soviet artists of the 1980s to have established himself as an important singer in the West, as well as in his own country. In addition to opera, he has excelled in recital and concert work. His sturdy, almost brazen timbre and incisive phrasing make a bold effect and his instrument's dark coloring makes it possible for him to effectively assume such bass parts as that of the soloist in Shostakovich's *Symphony No. 13 (Babi Yar)*. After studies in Leningrad, Leiferkus was engaged by the Maliy Opera Theatre in 1972, remaining with that company as a principal singer until 1978. His debut at Leningrad's Kirov took place as Prince Andrei in 1977. As an increasingly important figure among that theater's growing roster of world-class singers, Leiferkus assumed such roles as Don Giovanni and Rossini's *Figaro*. His Western debut came not in an opera house, but rather on the concert stage when he appeared in 1980 with the Berlin Philharmonic under Kurt Masur. In 1982, he appeared at the small but well-known Wexford Festival singing the Marquis in Massenet's rather obscure *Grisélidis*. He was invited back for the title role in Marschner's *Hans Heiling*, the Fiddler in Humperdinck's *Königskinder* and Boniface in another Massenet rarity, *Le jongleur de Notre-Dame*. Leiferkus established other ties in the British Isles, performing *Yevgeny Onegin* and *Don Giovanni* for the Scottish Opera, essaying Zurga and Escamillo for the English National Opera and Zurga and Scarpia for Opera North. His debut at the Royal Opera took place as the Count di Luna in a 1989 production of *Il trovatore*. Subsequent roles there included Prince Igor, Iago, Onegin, Telramund, Scarpia, and Ruprecht in Prokofiev's *Fiery Angel*. With the Kirov company, Leiferkus toured England in 1987, performing both Onegin and Tomsky in Tchaikovsky's *Pique Dame*. The Glyndebourne Festival invited Leiferkus to repeat Tomsky in 1992; the same year, the baritone made his Metropolitan Opera debut as Onegin. Among his other nearly 50 roles are Mazeppa, Telramund, Pizarro (all three recorded), the elder Germont and Anckarstroem in *Un ballo in maschera* (a role that won him outstanding reviews at San Francisco in 2000). He has sung in such other venues as the Wiener Staatsoper, La Scala, the Teatro Colón, the Bastille Opera in Paris, and the Netherlands Opera in Amsterdam. Besides Glyndebourne, Leiferkus has sung opera performances at the Salzburg Easter Festival, at Edinburgh, and at Bregenz. Leiferkus has made a series of excellent song recordings for both Conifer and Chandos. The first disc of his complete cycle of Mussorgsky songs was nominated for a Grammy, while Volume Two won a 1997 *Cannes* classical award, and three volumes from the set were honored with a Diapason d'Or that same year. The singer's recital appearances have been acclaimed in both America and England. Leiferkus has appeared several times at Lincoln Center and at the Frick Collection and has sung memorable programs at Covent Garden and Wigmore Hall. In addition to other recitals at Tanglewood, the Wexford Festival, the Kozerthaus in Vienna, and the Cologne Philharmonic, Leiferkus has conducted master classes at the Britten-Pears School at Aldeburgh, England. *—Erik Eriksson*

Recommended:

- ○ **Glinka: A Farewell to St. Petersburg** / Leiferkus, Skigin / 1996 / Conifer 51264
- ○ **Mussorgsky Songs** / Leiferkus, Skigin / 1995 / Conifer 51229
- ○ **Rachmaninov: Songs** / Leiferkus, Shelley / 1995 / Chandos 9374

Erich Leinsdorf

b. Feb. 4, 1912, Vienna, Austria, **d.** Aug. 11, 1993, Zurich, Switzerland
Conductor

Erich Leinsdorf was one of the most respected (if not always well-liked) European-born conductors and music directors to achieve prominence in America after World War II. He was an acclaimed operatic conductor, whose recordings of *Turandot* and *Madama Butterfly* from the late 1950s remain among the most popular in the catalog; his reputation as a conductor of orchestral music hasn't survived quite as well.

He was born Erich Landauer in Vienna, Austria, and by the age of five was enrolled in a local music school. He studied music at the University of Vienna and the Vienna Conservatory, making his conducting debut at the Musikvereinsaal upon graduation. Leinsdorf became the assistant conductor of the Workers' Chorus in Vienna in 1933, and a year later successfully auditioned before Bruno Walter and Arturo Toscanini at the Salzburg Festival, where he was appointed Toscanini's assistant.

Leinsdorf's American debut took place at the Metropolitan Opera when he conducted Wagner's *Die Walküre* on January 21, 1938. His success with Wagnerian operas led to his appointment at the Met in 1939 as head of the company's German repertoire. While at the Met he began to develop a reputation as a strict taskmaster, requiring increased rehearsal time from his singers and extremely precise fidelity to the written score from musicians; although audiences generally appreciated the results, many of the performers he worked with resented his demands.

He took American citizenship in 1942. The following year he was appointed music director of the Cleveland Orchestra, but was soon inducted into the United States Army. Discharged in 1944, he returned to the Met. During 1945 and 1946, he also conducted the Cleveland Orchestra on several occasions, and returned to Europe where, as one of a group of major Austrian-born conductors who had no connections with the Nazis, he was engaged to conduct the Vienna Philharmonic. He found his reception in his home city, destitute in the immediate wake of World War II, to be less than entirely cordial.

By 1947, Leinsdorf was back in the United States as music director of the Rochester Philharmonic Orchestra in upstate New York, a post he held until 1955. Leinsdorf served as music director of the New York City Opera for part of 1956, before returning to the Met as a conductor and musical consultant. In 1962, Leinsdorf acceded to one of the most prestigious musical posts in America, succeeding Charles Munch as music director of the Boston Symphony Orchestra. Leinsdorf's tenure at Boston was extremely productive, but stormy. He found the political considerations of a music directorship—juggling the demands of individual musicians, their unions and existing work and rehearsal rules, and the board of directors—to be a distraction from his musical goals. Leinsdorf also became known for open criticism his musicians' educational shortcomings, and of errors made by his fellow conductors and by editors of musical scores.

He resigned the Boston post with the 1968–69 season, happy, in his own words, to have exited with his health intact. Leinsdorf conducted opera and concert performances throughout the United States and Europe for the next two decades. In 1978, he took up his first permanent post in Europe, becoming principal conductor of the Berlin Radio Symphony Orchestra, a post he held until 1980. In 1976, he published *Cadenza: A Musical Career*, a memoir as notable for its candid, brutally honest assessments of himself and his fellow musicians as for its biographical contents. *—Bruce Eder*

Recommended:

- ○ **Beethoven: Symphony 9; Schoenberg: Survivor from Warsaw** / Leinsdorf (cond.), Varon, Patterson, Domingo, Milnes, BSO / RCA 63682
- ○ **Korngold: Die tote Stadt** / Leinsdorf (cond.), Schmidt-Gaden, Luxon, Kollo, Prey, Munich Radio Orch. / 1975 / RCA 7767
- ○ **Puccini: La Bohème** / Leinsdorf (cond.), Moffo, Merrill, Tucker, Tozzi, Rome Opera House Orch. / 1998 / RCA 63179
- ○ **Portraits in Sound** / Leinsdorf (cond.), Concert Arts Symphony Orch. / EMI 65205

Leipzig Gewandhaus Orchestra

f. 1743, Leipzig, Germany
Ensemble

Both Dresden and Leipzig, Saxony's leading cities, claim to have Europe's oldest permanent orchestra, although Norway insists on Bergen's "Harmonien" being the oldest. While both German cities had municipal music as far back as the sixteenth century, the Dresdner Staatskapelle (created in 1548 as a court orchestra) can claim an unbroken history. Dresden was principally an operatic center, however, whereas Leipzig specialized in choral and instrumental music, the latter led by concertmasters. Only vocal music, secular or sacred, had "conductors." Local partisans insist the Collegium Musicum, founded by Telemann and extended by his successor

Johann Sebastian Bach, was father of the orchestra that played its fist concert on March 11, 1743, in the Gewandhaus—a garment mart—although it didn't become the Gewandhausorchester officially until 1781. Notable concertmasters included Bartolomeo Campagnoli and Karl Matthaï, who presided consecutively from 1797 to 1835, when Mendelssohn was named *Dirigent.*

He was the first conductor to use a baton, to lead both choral and concert music, and to double the size of the orchestra (salaries, too). His 1841 revival of the *St. Matthew Passion* was the cornerstone of a Bach renaissance. Mendelssohn also sponsored contemporary music—the world premieres of three symphonies by his friend Schumann plus *Das Paradies und die Peri*, Schubert's long-lost *Ninth Symphony*, his own *Scottish Symphony* and *Violin Concerto.* He invited Liszt and Berlioz as guest conductors (despite his dislike of the latter's *Symphonie fantastique*). Mendelssohn's premature death, however, in 1847 precipitated a crisis. Julius Rietz, newly appointed by the Leipzig Opera, was deputized (with Niels Gade and concertmaster Ferdinand David to assist), but continued at the opera until double-duty exhausted him in 1854. By then Leipzig had commissioned a statue of Mendelssohn, unveiled in front of the "new" Gewandhaus he had inaugurated in 1840. The Nazis removed this in 1936, but the concert hall survived until Allied bombs destroyed it in 1943.

In 1860, Carl Reinecke followed Rietz for 35 conservative years, although he was devoted to Brahms, and invited Wagner, Tchaikovsky, Grieg, and Strauss to guest-conduct their works. His successor in 1895 was Artur Nikisch, one of the world's leading conductors (along with Mahler and Toscanini), who also accepted leadership of the Berlin Philharmonic in 1897. He continued to conduct both orchestras until his death in 1922, when Wilhelm Furtwängler followed, likewise in Berlin as well as Leipzig (where Charles Munch was concertmaster from 1926 to 1932). However, after seven years, he left the Gewandhaus to become a permanent guest conductor in Vienna.

By then the orchestra numbered 100, double the size of Mendelssohn's, which welcomed Bruno Walter as their new conductor. However, he was a Jew, so the Nazis forced his resignation in 1933 and installed Hermann Abendroth, who became conductor in 1934 and continued until the war disrupted musical life.

Herbert Albert took over for three postwar seasons (1946–49) before Franz Konwitschny rebuilt the orchestra, then playing in the great hall of the zoo that was later remodeled as a congress hall. He remained music director until his death in 1962 (while rehearsing in Belgrade). Before Kurt Masur came in 1970, Leipzig had two more leaders: the Czech Václav Neumann (1964–68), and Heinz Bongartz from Dresden.

During Masur's 27-year tenure, Leipzig built a "third" Gewandhaus (with two concert chambers, the larger one seating 1,900), which opened on October 4, 1981. Although Masur became music director of the NY Philharmonic in 1991, he stayed with Leipzig until 1997–98, then handed the baton to Herbert Blomstedt, Tilson Thomas' predecessor in San Francisco, and before that the leader of state radio orchestras in Copenhagen, Stockholm, Hamburg, and Tokyo. *—Roger Dettmer*

Recommended:

- ○ **Hindemith: Symphonia Serena; Harmonie der Welt** / Blomstedt (cond.), Suske, Funke, Freiberger, Jacklin, Gewandhaus / 2000 / Decca 458899
- ○ **Beethoven: Complete Overtures** / Masur, Marriner (cond.), Gewandhaus, Academy of St. Martin-in-the-Fields / 1993 / Philips 438706
- ○ **Goldschmidt: Der gewaltige Hahnrei; Mediterranean Songs** / Zagrosek (cond.), Alexander, Ainsley, Kraus, Wottrich, Berlin RSO & Chorus, Gewandhaus / 1994 / London 440850
- ○ **Mendelssohn: Elias** / Sawallisch (cond.), Ameling, Schreier, Rotzsch, Adam, Gewandhaus / 1993 / Philips 438368

Ute Lemper

b. Jul. 4, 1963, Münster, Germany

Vocalist

Ute Lemper is a multifaceted singer/actress closely associated with the Berlin cabaret style of songs and the music of Kurt Weill. Although she has appeared in a number of movies, she has generally focused on vocal concerts or on roles in musicals. Some of her admirers have asserted that the marketing of her recordings under the umbrella of classical or semi-classical music has hampered their sales, yet most have been commercial successes (and in some cases best sellers), especially those containing the music of Weill.

Exposed to music in her childhood through her opera-singer mother, she veered away from classical music and developed a fondness for American jazz and popular music. She first studied piano and dancing at age nine. She later studied voice and furthered her musical education in Berlin, Salzburg, and Cologne. She also took acting lessons in Vienna at the Max Reinhardt Seminary. At age 16, she joined the punk music group the Panama Drive Band and, true to her broad artistic tastes, soon began taking on roles in Chekhov and Fassbinder plays at the Staatstheater Stuttgart. Her first important stage effort was the 1983 Vienna production of Andrew Lloyd Webber's *Cats*, where she played the roles of Grizabella and Bombalurina on an alternate basis. In 1985, she landed the lead role in the Berlin production of the *Peter Pan* musical comedy. The following year turned out to be a pivotal period in her career: She played Sally Bowles in a touring production of *Cabaret* staged in Rome, Paris, Lyon, and Dusseldorf, and began to develop a strong interest in the music of Weill. That same year, she won the prestigious French Moliere Award as Best Actress in a Musical for her work in the Paris staging of *Cabaret.* In 1987, she appeared in a New York production based on the life and music of Weill. Her first major recording was released that same year on the German label Bayer, *Ute Lemper Sings Kurt Weill.* Other successful recordings soon followed, including several more Weill CDs, one in 1991 of *The Three-Penny Opera*, and further volumes of his songs in 1993. She also recorded a pop album, released in 1991, entitled *Crimes of the Heart.* While Lemper focused heavily on the music of Weill in the cabaret genre, she also sang and recorded songs by Hollaender, Nelson, and several others, which appeared on recordings in 1996 and 1997. Meanwhile, Lemper was making inroads into film, too: she appeared as Marie-Antoinette in Pierre Granier-Deferre's 1989 film *L'Autrichienne* and in Peter Greenaway's 1990 *Prospero's Books.* Michael Nyman, who had written the music for the Greenaway film, wrote his *Six Celan Songs* for Lemper in 1990, who performed them to critical acclaim. In 1992, Lemper left Germany and eventually settled in New York, where she now lives with her husband, comedian David Tabatsky, whom she married in 1994. They have two children, Max (born 1994) and Stella (born 1997). Lemper has received numerous awards, including *Billboard's* Crossover Artist of the Year for 1993–94. Her work also includes her portrayal of Velma Kelley in the 1997 London production of *Chicago* and the album *Punishing Kiss*, released in 2000, featuring songs by Weill, Philip Glass, Elvis Costello, and others. She also appeared with critical success at the 2000 Covent Garden Festival in a production of Weill's *Die sieben Todsünden.* *—Robert Cummings*

Recommended:

- ○ **Lemper Sings Kurt Weill** / Lemper, Meyer, Rautenberg / 1988 / London 425204
- ○ **Berlin Cabaret Songs** / Ziegler (cond.), Lemper, Cohen, Matrix Ensemble / 1997 / London 452849

Leningrad Philharmonic Orchestra

f. Dec. 25, 1882, St. Petersburg, Russia

Ensemble

The Leningrad Philharmonic Orchestra has roots dating to 1882, when it was formed for the Court of Tsar Alexander III and called the Imperial Music Choir. Its inaugural concert was given on December 25, 1882, and most of its performances for the next two decades were for Court purposes. The first music director, G. Flige, served from 1882 until 1907, by which time the orchestra was staging public concerts. Under its next director, G. Varlikh, who took the podium in 1907, the orchestra began performing music by contemporary non-Russian composers such as Richard Strauss, who led the group in concert in 1912. After the Bolshevik Revolution of 1917, the orchestra members renamed the ensemble the State Orchestra. Serge Koussevitzky succeeded Varlikh that same year and the orchestra began performing in the Pavlovsky Vokzal concert hall. It was under Emil Cooper, music director from 1920 to 1923, that the orchestra began receiving state support and started performing in the Great Hall of the Philharmonic, formerly the Court Assembly concert hall.

Cooper presided over many spectacular concerts, including one of Beethoven's *Symphony No. 9* featuring nearly 500 performers. Valery Berdyaev and well-known Soviet conductor Nicolai Malko succeeded Cooper. The orchestra was now known as the Leningrad Philharmonic Orchestra, carrying the name of its resident city, which had changed from Petrograd to Leningrad in 1924. By the late 1920s, the LPO had developed the reputation as the Soviet Union's finest orchestra. It attracted many famous conductors during this time, including Bruno Walter, Ernest Ansermet, and Hans Knappertsbusch. Malko was succeeded by Alexander Gauk in 1930. He remained only three seasons, but introduced many new compositions by Russian composers like Prokofiev, Shostakovich, and Miaskovsky. Austrian conductor Fritz Stiedry served as music director from 1934–37, further developing the orchestra's accuracy and precision. His departure in 1937 came as a result of the developing political turmoil in Europe.

Yevgeny Mravinsky was appointed music director in 1938 and would serve a half century in that capacity. He probably introduced as many famous contemporary compositions as any conductor of his time. He premiered many by Shostakovich, including his *Symphony No. 5*, as a guest conductor in 1937, and the *Sixth* in November 1939. He also introduced the Prokofiev *Sixth* in October 1947 and numerous other compositions by Soviet composers. He made many recordings of works by Tchaikovsky, Prokofiev, Shostakovich, and other Russian composers, but usually avoided the studio, preferring the "live concert" venue. Because of the war, the Leningrad Philharmonic was evacuated to Novosibirsk in 1941, where it performed until its 1944 return. It suffered a noticeable decline in its ensemble skills in the postwar era, owing to the death of some of the orchestra personnel and to defections, but Mravinsky, assisted by Kurt Sanderling, gradually rebuilt the LPO and by the late 1960s, it was once again considered a world-class ensemble. Many tours abroad in the 1970s confirmed this judgment. In the last decade or so of Mravinsky's tenure, he was largely inactive, allowing assistant conductors to lead the orchestra. Upon his death, Yuri Temirkanov was appointed music director. In 1991, when the city of Leningrad reverted to its old name of St. Petersburg, the orchestra was renamed the St. Petersburg Philharmonic. *—Robert Cummings*

Recommended:

- ○ **Evgeny Mravinsky** / Mravinsky (cond.), London PO / EMI 75953
- ○ **Shostakovich: Symphony 7** / Jansons (cond.), London PO / 1995 / EMI 49494
- ○ **Hindemith: Symphony Die Harmonie Der Welt; Honegger: Symphony 3** / Mravinsky (cond.), London PO / 1995 / Melodiya 0316
- ○ **Tchaikovsky: Symphonies 4, 5 & 6** / Mravinsky (cond.), London PO / DG 419745

Sarah Leonard

b. Apr. 10, 1953, Winchester, Hampshire, England

Soprano

Soprano Sarah Leonard is a leading singer of twentieth century and contemporary music. She received her early training at the Guildhall School of Music and Drama, London, after which she joined the BBC Singers and the Endymion Ensemble. In 1988 she performed the role of Drusilla in Monteverdi's *L'incoronazione di Poppea* under Richard Hickox on Virgin—one of her few recordings of repertory works. She has worked extensively with the Hilliard Ensemble and the Michael Nyman Band, and, beginning in 1994, with pianist Malcolm Martineau on his series, "A Century of English Song," which was released in several volumes on the Somm label. In 1997 she sang the premiere of Helmut Lachenmann's Das Mädchen mit den Schwefelhölzern, a work she later recorded on Kairos. Leonard has also appeared with the Ensemble Modern, Klangforum Wien, the Royal Concertgebouw Orchestra, the Birmingham Symphony Orchestra, the London Symphony, and the San Francisco Symphony. Her other recordings include music of Luigi Nono, György Ligeti, Kurt Weill, and Howard Skempton. *—AMG*

Recommended:

- ○ **Alexander Goehr** / Knussen, Leonard, Chance, Shelton, Wallace, Richardson / 2003 / NMC 96
- ○ **A Century of English Song Vol. 3** / Leonard, Martineau, Viera / 2000 / Somm 224

Ruggero Leoncavallo

b. Mar. 8, 1857, Naples, Italy, **d.** Aug. 9, 1919, Montecatini, Italy

Composer: Opera, Vocal

Ruggero Leoncavallo is remembered almost exclusively for his opera *I Pagliacci*, which—along with Mascagni's *Cavalleria rusticana*—has become the hallmark of the late nineteenth century verismo style. Leoncavallo studied composition at the Naples conservatory and literature at Bologna University; this dual passion for music and poetry would lead the young composer to seek a unity between the two disciplines in the manner of Richard Wagner, whose music would come as a revelation.

His first operatic efforts were thwarted by ill fortune: a production of his student work, *Chatterton*, fell through after the impresario made off with the money Leoncavallo himself had furnished to cover the costs. However, after several years of scraping by as a café pianist, he was introduced to the influential publisher Giulio Ricordi, who bought the rights to *Chatterton* and engaged Leoncavallo as a librettist. While this signified a temporary improvement in the young man's circumstances, the creative alliance between Leoncavallo and Ricordi proved frustrating. Ricordi declined his next opera, *I Medici*, and his attempts at a libretto for Puccini's *Manon Lescaut* led to irreconcilable creative differences.

These combined misfortunes instilled in Leoncavallo a singular desire for operatic success, which he channeled into his masterpiece, *I Pagliacci*. Modeled on Mascagni's *Cavalleria*, *Pagliacci* was an instant sensation at its premier in 1892. From that point onward, Leoncavallo enjoyed fame and wealth, although the success of this work was never to be repeated.

In 1897 Leoncavallo produced a setting of *La Bohème* that was meant to rival that of Puccini, but, although it pleased the public somewhat, Puccini's finer and more sophisticated work quickly outstripped Leoncavallo's in popularity. Subsequent reworkings of *Chatterton* and *I Medici* proved to be dismal failures in Italy, but *I Medici* sufficiently impressed the Kaiser of Germany to gain a commission for a new work, *Der Roland von Berlin* (1904), which enjoyed modest success in Berlin. However, Leoncavallo never again gained his footing in Italy, where his works formed a succession of spectacular failures and tepid successes.

The advent of recording technology was fortuitous for Leoncavallo, who conducted *I Pagliacci* in the first complete recording of an Italian opera. He also accompanied Enrico Caruso in a recorded performance of the song, "Mattinata," which has become his most popular work after *Pagliacci*. *—AMG*

OPERA

Pagliacci (1892)

Late in 1891, Leoncavallo set out to compose an opera similar to, but surpassing, Mascagni's *Cavalleria rusticana*, one of the primary examples verismo (lusually translated as "realism"). Within five months, Leoncavallo had completed *Pagliacci* (The Clowns), his second opera, but his first to be performed. It made him famous overnight, achieving such a success that his 20 other works for the stage are all but unknown in comparison. By the end of 1893, *Pagliacci* had played everywhere from Mexico to Moscow.

The text of *Pagliacci*, by the composer, is based on one of the cases encountered by Leoncavallo's father, a police magistrate in Naples. The actual case concerned a middle-aged actor who murdered his unfaithful wife, to which Leoncavallo added elements from the *commedia dell'arte*, such as the traveling actors, and naturalist ideas. He took the finished score to the Sonzogno publishing firm, which arranged the first performance, at the Teatro dal Verme in Milan, on May 21, 1892.

Consisting of a Prologue and two acts, *Pagliacci* is a short opera. Leoncavallo initially cast the entire drama in a Prologue and one act, but the ecstatic reception of climactic aria "Vesti la giubba" (Put on your costume) prompted the composer to drop the curtain after it on subsequent nights, reserving the ensuing "play within a play" for the second act. "Vesti la giubba," with its heart-rendering "Ridi, Pagliaccio, sul tuo amore infranto!" (Laugh and be merry, though your love betrayed you), has become the most famous number from the opera and obligatory for star tenors.

Although in *Pagliacci* Leoncavallo makes no attempt to deny Italian origins of the opera, he does draw on the French opéra lyrique and makes moderate use of Wagnerian Leitmotiv. The latter is evident in the static musical symbols for clowns: Canio's motive of doubt and the motive representing the love of Nedda and Silvio. This mixture of elements from different styles allows Leoncavallo to speak with a unique voice. Leoncavallo sets his sordid subject matter to melodic material of high quality and great variety, ranging from the simplest, folk song-like tunes to Canio's extremely passionate and lyrical "Vesti la giubba."

The fine line that can exist between fantasy and reality is the point of the second act, in which Canio, aware of his wife's infidelity, transfers his anger into the comedy in which he plays a part. The audience on the stage believes Canio is a great actor, while we know that his rage is real. Only when real deaths occur do the viewers onstage understand the "reality" they are witnessing. Leoncavallo then shatters this "reality" by having Tonio, as he does in the Prologue, address us, letting us know that what we have seen is a play and urging us to go home, for "the comedy is finished!"

Recordings or performances in which the character of Canio delivers the line "the comedy is finished," are incorrect and the result of tenor vanity. *—John Palmer*

Synopsis:

The action takes place in Montalto, in Calabria, southern Italy, on 15 August 1865.

Prologue. During the orchestral Prelude, Tonio steps in front of the curtain and addresses the audience. He speaks of the drama that is about to unfold, telling the audience it is based on actual events. Explaining that what we are about to see applies to us all, he notes that "we all wander around in the same light ... believe me, just as you are filled with lust and passion, so a heart beats inside a clown." With the words, "Let the play begin!," the curtain rises.

Act One. It is the Christian feast of the Assumption of Mary into heaven. During the celebration the people gather in the village square to watch Canio's recently arrived troupe of actors. Trumpets, shouts, and playing children make such a racket that Canio can hardly make his introduction and announcement heard: "We have prepared an excellent play today." Tonio springs from the troupe's wagon and tries to help Nedda, Canio's wife, down the ramp. However, the jealous Canio punches Tonio. The crowd teases the enraged Tonio, who wishes to bring down the "donkey," Canio. Tonio is willing to play the clown on stage but not in real life. Canio tells Nedda that it is his love for her that makes him jealous, and if he finds her "with another man, that's the end, little girl." A group of musician passes on their way to vespers and the people evacuate the village square, leaving Nedda alone to sing her "Birdsong." Tonio notices the solitary Nedda on the stage and tries to approach her once again, but Nedda drives him away with a whip. Tonio finally realizes that Nedda despises him and that he will get nowhere with her. In the meantime, Silvio, a young farmer, has come over the wall in search of Nedda, whom he wants to convince to run off with him. Tonio witnesses the lovers' conversation and sets off to bring Canio from the tavern. When Canio arrives, Silvio manages to escape back over the wall. Canio then turns on Nedda, using force to make her give the name of her lover. Beppo, one of the troupe's actors, reminds everyone that a show is about to begin and that the audience has already assembled. Canio, left behind and distraught, realizes the show must go on and that he must act the clown, smiling and laughing, because that is how he earns his living. After his "Vesti la giubba, e la faccia infarina" (Put on your costume and paint your face), the curtain falls.

Act Two. The "play within a play" begins. Silvio is among the assembled audience despite the fact that he has been warned of Canio's anger. Silvio and

Nedda plan to flee after the show. On stage, Colombina (played by Nedda) sits at a table in a room waiting for Harlequin (Beppo), with whom she plans to elope and leave her husband, Pagliaccio (Canio). Harlequin sings a serenade from behind the stage. With a basket filled with items to sell, Taddeo (Tonio) enters the room and begins to confess his love for her. However, Harlequin appears and Taddeo leaves, quickly, amusing the onstage audience. As Nedda and Harlequin sing a happy duet, Harlequin senses Pagliaccio's arrival and jumps out the window, repeating the words Silvio said to Nedda when they parted earlier in the evening. Pagliaccio enters and demands to know the name of Colombina's lover, just as Canio had demanded of Nedda only shortly before. Soon, Canio is no longer playing Pagliaccio, and his anger takes over and leads to a great outburst. The audience applauds the excellent "acting" while Nedda continues to play her role. Beppo, behind the scene, notices the mounting danger, but is held back from intervening by Tonio. Canio threatens to kill Nedda if she does not give the name of her lover, then picks up a knife from the table and stabs her. Dying, she cries out for Silvio. Silvio runs onto the stage to help, only to be stabbed by Canio. Canio, exhausted, allows himself to be apprehended as Tonio turns to the audience offstage, telling them, "Go home, the comedy is over." *—John Palmer*

Recommended:

- ○ **Mascagni: Cavalleria Rusticana; Leoncavallo: Pagliacci** / Patane (cond.), Pavarotti, Freni, Wixell, Sax, National PO / 1988 / London 414590

VOCAL

Mattinata, song (1904)

Leoncavallo's charming "Mattinata," whose title translates as "Morning Song," is a greeting from a lover to his beloved. He calls to her to awaken and to come down to him. The dawn is dressed in white, giving joy to the earth. The narrator asks the object of his affections to likewise dress and give joy to him: "Ove non sei, la luca manca, ove tu sei, nasce l'amor!" ("Where you are not, the light cannot shine, where you are, love is born!").

The music is appropriately cheerful; the keyboard provides an accompaniment of swift major-key arpeggios and scales, calling for a light touch on the part of the pianist. The vocal line follows the same pattern for most of the song; the last lines of the setting receive a more operatic treatment, including higher and longer-held notes.

The song, written to Leoncavallo's own text, quickly became a recital and concert favorite among tenors; it is, however, occasionally sung by baritones, mezzo-sopranos, and sopranos. Its popularity is such that it has attained the status of a folk song in the composer's native Italy. *—Ann Feeney*

Recommended:

- ○ **Very Best of Jussi Björling** / Grevillius (cond.), Björling, etc. / 2003 / EMI 75900
- ○ **Romantica** / Gamba (cond.), Pavarotti, London PO / 2002 / Decca 470331
- ○ **Caruso: The Complete Recordings Vol. 2** / Caruso, etc. / 2000 / Naxos 110704

Gustav Leonhardt

b. May 30, 1928, Amsterdam, Netherlands

Harpsichordist, Conductor, Organist

Though participants in the "authentic performance practice" movement might insist otherwise, the search for the old is really a search for the new. This statement certainly captures the spirit that Dutch keyboardist Gustav Leonhardt began bringing to his early music performances in the 1950s. His style was characterized not by a rigorous observance of rules, but by the intuitive, almost spiritual connection it tried to establish with the music—a kind of authenticity that sought validation not so much from a rigorously academic accuracy (though Leonhardt is by no means historically careless) as from its having an "authentic" effect on the listener.

Born in Amsterdam in 1928, Leonhardt learned cello and piano before entering the Schola Cantorum in Basel to study organ and harpsichord with Eduard Müller. After graduating in 1950, he undertook a year of musicological studies before accepting a position at the Vienna Academy. Shortly thereafter, he returned to his home town, where he assumed a position at the Amsterdam Conservatory that he would keep for decades thereafter.

His first public performance took place in 1950, when he performed J.S. Bach's *The Art of the Fugue* for a Viennese audience. This marked the beginning of a legendary and influential career that would take him to performance venues all over the world, setting stylistic and interpretive standards for keyboard music dating from the early 1500s to the late 1700s. His treatment of the works of Couperin, Froberger, and Frescobaldi were pivotal in affecting a shift in Baroque performance practice from the motoric to the malleable.

Beginning in the 1950s, he also established the Leonhardt Consort, a group applying his same performance ideals to chamber works; during his career he also demonstrated great skill in conducting early choral and operatic works. Along the way, he tutored an entire generation of the most vibrant and stylistically varied early music figures, including Christopher Hogwood, Pierre Hantaï, and Ton Koopman.

When Leonhardt speaks of "correct" style, certain parameters are clear, while others leave much to be read between the lines. The use of the proper instrument, for example, is crucial to Leonhardt: one should not play a piece from a particular country and a particular time on an instrument from a different region and century (and of course it goes without saying what problems he might have with playing eighteenth century music on a twentieth century Steinway). His discussion of style, however, is quite flexible—or at least elusive: "I cannot say it's a secret, but it's almost impossible to describe in words.... Essentially, it must be based on a dynamic wish." Though he does consult primary sources to justify his sound—which falls somewhere between the rubato sound of Landowska and the robotic sound of her immediate successors, he insists that the truest "rules" about the music he plays are to be discovered through the playing itself. *—Jeremy Grimshaw*

Recommended:

- ○ **Bach: The Goldberg Variations** / Leonhardt / 2003 / Artemis 1281
- ○ **Valls: Missa Scala Aretina; Biber: Requiem** / Leonhardt (cond.), Elwes, Piau, van der Kamp, Cordier, Sluis, Nederlandse Bachvereniging / 2002 / DHM 77842
- ○ **Bach: Inventions & Sinfonias** / Leonhardt / 1999 / Sony 61869
- ○ **Scarlatti: Sonatas** / Leonhardt / 1999 / Sony 61820
- ○ **J.S. & C.P.E. Bach: Harpsichord Concertos** / Leonhardt / 1997 / Sony 63188
- ○ **Telemann: Paris Quartets** / B. Kuijken, S. Kuijken, Leonhardt, W. Kuijken / Sony 63115

Léonin

fl. ca. 1150–1201, **d.** ca. 1201

Composer: Vocal

Léonin, or Magister Léoninus, is identified through a thirteenth century English source, Anonymous 4, as the composer and compiler of the *Magnus Liber organi de gradali et antiphonario pro servitio divino.* This massive work originally consisted of musical settings for the entire church year, feast days and Saints days, with two-voice polyphonic responses for each scripture reading. The *Magnus liber* was compiled about 1170, and was utilized first by the choir of the Cathedral of Notre Dame, still under construction at the time the book appeared. This music is known in four major manuscripts; *Wölfenbuttel 677 (W1)* and *1099 (W2)*, *Codex Florenz*, and *Codex Madrid*, the last named containing a condensed version of the *Magnus liber. W1*, though chronologically the "youngest" of these late thirteeth century manuscripts, is believed to contain the music which is closest to Léonin's original concept.

Anonymous 4 refers to Léonin as "optimus organista," and in his work he employed a two-part polyphonic texture which Léonin termed *Organum Duplum*; the tenor was the "principal voice" (*vox principalis*), generally intoning long syllables drawn from plainchant, and an "organizing voice" (*vox organalis*) which added freely rhythmic melismata up above. Léonin usually alternated these passages with discant sections, where the tenor and organizer would move more or less together in a note-per-syllable pattern. Sections of chant not set by Léonin would be sung out by the choir in unison, and sometimes the choir would read along with the tenor during the discants. But the organizing and principal parts were sung by expert vocalists who were placed at the center of the choir.

As construction of the huge sanctuary progressed at Notre Dame, the desirability of added "triplum" and even "quadruplum" parts to the *Magnus liber* became an issue; the text of the work began to change under other hands, most famously those of Léonin's alleged pupil Perotin. It is apparent in the *Florenz*, *W2*, and *Madrid* sources that long sections of the *organalis* seen in *W1* have been wiped away in favor of new, and more elaborate material. That's why it's difficult to separate out specific pieces within the *Magnus liber* as being safely within the camp of Léonin and his school, apart from 13 responses intended for the Canonical Hours and 32 responses to specific masses. In the original work, more than a hundred pieces would have been preserved in *Organum Duplum*. Some scholars have suggested Léonin as a possible author of some of the three-voice organa, though Anonymous 4 states otherwise.

Léonin was also known as a poet, and is said to have written a rendering of the first eight books of the Holy Bible in verse. In the late twentieth century, a scholar proposed that Léonin was likely the author of a salacious book concerning carnal behavior among the clergy which appeared in the 1180s. While Perotin's settings in the *Magnus liber* are more frequently performed, Léonin's achievement in compiling the book is on a par within Western sacred music with the Lutheran hymnal or Bach's cantata cycle. Although Léonin died more than eight centuries ago, scholars are yet engaged on an enthusiastic search for Léonin, including details about his life and his status as one of the first great composers in western music history. *—Uncle Dave Lewis*

VOCAL

Magnus Liber Organi (ca. 1150–1200)

Literally "big book," the term *Magnus Liber* refers generally to a body of compositions associated with the establishment of the Cathedral of Notre Dame in the late twelfth century. The *Magnus Liber* is not a particular book, however, but rather a large repertory of compositions found in a number of medieval manuscripts, all of them supposedly traceable to an original collection created by the composers at Notre Dame. The most prominent of these, Léonin and Pérotin, are generally credited with developing the techniques of composition that would eventually give rise to what is perhaps the most prominent feature of Western art music: the interaction of multiple voices to create harmonies, or polyphony. The music associated with the *Magnus Liber* is thus, according to one authoritative scholar, "perhaps the greatest single achievement in medieval music."

Although some mention of polyphony appears in earlier writings, such as those of Guido of Arezzo (eleventh century), the music of the *Magnus Liber* represents the establishment of a large body of polyphonic pieces used regularly in liturgical or paraliturgical settings. Though the various contributions of the authors of the music in the *Magnus Liber* repertory is not clear (Léonin and Pérotin were probably joined by several others in the preparation of the original collection), Léonin is generally known (and described by later writers, such as Anonymous 4) for his mastery of the organum. This initial type of polyphony is comprised of two voices, one singing the traditional plainchant line of the liturgy, the other singing the newly composed "organal" line. Two types of two-voice organum appear in the *Magnus Liber*. The first, often referred to as "organum purum," is characterized by long melismas or melodic flourishes in the organal voice, sung above long-sustained notes in the plainchant voice, or tenor (from the Latin "tenere," meaning "to hold"). The other type of organum is known as "discant," and is characterized by a tenor voice moving through the original plainchant melody at a much quicker pace, nearly equal to that of the tenor voice; this would usually be applied to more florid passages of the original chant. Such coordination required new developments in rhythm, which also set apart the Notre Dame School as particularly important in the development of Western music.

Organa were composed for the responsorial chants of the liturgy (that is, those chants in which a soloist alternates with a choir, such as the Gradual), and were applied only to those parts of the chant originally sung by a soloist. Thus in practice, singers of Léonin's music would perform a Gradual by singing the soloist's part in two-voice organum, alternating with a choir singing their passages in unison. Pérotin is recognized for expanding the practice of organum to three or even four voices, and also helping develop extended discant passages into independent compositions called "clausulas." Eventually, the added music of the clausula was given additional text, which marked the creation of the most important musical development of the subsequent century, the motet. *—Jeremy Grimshaw*

Recommended:

○ **Mystery of Notre Dame** / Orlando Consort / Archiv 453487

Raymond Leppard

b. Aug. 11, 1927, London, England

Conductor

Raymond John Leppard, one of the foremost British conductors of the twentieth century, has also been a film score composer and a leading scholar and conductor in the movement to restore older music to the stage in performances of authentic style.

Although he was born in London, he was raised in the resort town of Bath. He graduated from Trinity College, Cambridge, in 1952. There, his teachers were Hubert Middleton and Boris Ord. While at Cambridge, he studied harpsichord and viola, was a choral conductor, and became music director of the Cambridge Philharmonic Society. His professional debut was in 1952 in London's Wigmore Hall, as a conductor.

He specialized in music of the seventeenth and eighteenth centuries, often conducting from the harpsichord as he provided inventive, even witty realizations of the harpsichord continuo parts. He also conducted in British opera houses, still socializing in Baroque and Classical era music. In 1957, he became a lecturing fellow at Trinity, remaining in that position until 1967. In 1959, he debuted at Covent Garden in a production of Handel's *Samson*, marking the bicentenary of that opera. He first appeared at the Glyndebourne Festival in 1962 and at Sadler's Wells in 1965.

During all this time, he had formed an association with the Goldsborough Orchestra, which later became the English Chamber Orchestra. Many of his early concert recordings and appearances were with the E.C.O. In the meantime, he embarked on two major fields of endeavor outside performing and teaching: film score composition and editing of Baroque operas. He wrote a large number of film scores, including the classic *Lord of the Flies* (1963). His last score was *Hotel New Hampshire* (1985). He edited operas of Monteverdi and Cavalli and his first such edition was a realization of Monteverdi's *L'incoronazione di Poppea*, which he conducted at Glyndebourne in 1962. His editions of these operas and his conducting them brought them back to the public often for the first time in 300 years and was a tremendous boost to the movement to bring back Baroque opera and other music of composers of the century before Bach.

However, Leppard is not a part of what is called the "authentic" or "period" instrument movement, working with the instruments that can be found in the world's opera orchestras of today. The period instrument adherents find points to criticize in his willingness to transpose vocal parts particularly of leading male roles from alto singers to male voice range, his restructuring of the libretti to more modern dramatic tastes, and the general richness of the orchestration. He answers these criticisms in his book *Authenticity in Music*. As many of his editions are published, they remain the basis for many modern productions of such works as Monteverdi's *Orfeo* and *Il ritorno d'Ulisse in patria* and Cavalli's *L'Ormindo, La Calista*, and *L'Orione*. The Italian government has honored him with the title of Commendatore for his services in bringing early Italian music back to the repertory.

Meanwhile, he expanded is activities into the standard repertory. He was principal conductor of the BBC Northern Symphony Orchestra (now the BBC Philharmonic) (1973–80). His American debut was in 1969 with the Westminster Choir and the New York Philharmonic in a concert during which he played and conducted the Haydn *D major harpsichord concerto*. His theatrical debut in the U.S. was at the Santa Fe Opera in 1974, leading *L'Egisto*. He also conducted a memorable revival of Virgil Thomson's *The Mother of Us All* at Santa Fe and debuted at the Metropolitan Opera in 1978 leading Britten's *Billy Budd*.

He settled in the United States in 1976 and became principal guest conductor of the Saint Louis Symphony Orchestra (1984–90). His major orchestral appointment was as music director of the Indianapolis Symphony Orchestra (1987), where he stepped down at the expiration of his latest contract in the early 2000s. His avowed purpose was to keep this 87-piece, full-time orchestra the same size (which he considers ideal for Classical repertory and that part of the Romantic and twentieth century repertory that adheres to neo-Classical symphonic tradition) and make it the best "Classical orchestra" in the world.

He has made more than 170 recordings in Britain and the U.S. on many major and independent labels, including EMI, London, Lyrita, and Koss Classics, and has won virtually every international recording prize. In Indianapolis, he has created a warm, elegant sound to add to his recognized virtues of clarity of line, lightness of rhythmic touch, and superb phrasing. *—Joseph Stevenson*

Recommended:

○ **Tippett: Fantasia Concertante; Symphony 3** / Leppard (cond.), Barstow, BBCSO / BBC 9140

○ **Prokofiev: Peter & the Wolf; Britten: TheYoung Person's Guide to the Orchestra** / Leppard (cond.), New Philharmonia Orch. / 1995 / EMI 185

Oscar Levant

b. Dec. 27, 1906, Pittsburgh, PA, **d.** Aug. 14, 1972, Beverly Hills, CA

Pianist

Levant wore several hats—most famously as a concert pianist from 1932 until 1958—in a bizarre career that began as a Broadway musician in the mid-1920s, segued to Hollywood in 1929, and ended in self-deprecating, chain-smoking eccentricity on radio and TV.

The son of Ukrainian-Jewish blue-collar parents, he was precocious at an early age, although not a prodigy. After his father's death in 1922, his mother moved the family to New York, where Oscar continued his keyboard instruction with Zygmunt Stojowski, an esteemed countryman of Paderewski (for whom Levant played privately). Although Broadway, booze, drugs, and women preoccupied him, he managed to attend concerts and opera regularly. In 1928, Oscar moved to Hollywood, repeating a role in *The Dance of Life* that he had played on Broadway in the movie's source-work, *Burlesque*. A year later, Levant was composing film music when he met, and became a bosom friend of, George Gershwin, the most influential person in his life. Their shared ethnic background along with Levant's innate shyness bonded them: he never tried to upstage Gershwin, who expected to be the center of attention wherever he appeared and invariably performed.

In 1929 alone, Levant scored six films, but tapered off after 1930, when his concert career gathered momentum. He did, however, write a cameo opera in 1936 for *Charlie Chan at the Opera*, and the next year scored *Nothing Sacred* starring Carole Lombard. By then Levant had studied composition for a year with Joseph Schillinger at Gershwin's urging, and in 1935–37 with Arnold Schoenberg. Oscar started composing seriously in 1932 with a *Piano Sonatina* that Copland invited him to premiere at Yaddo, then a *Sinfonietta* (1934), *Nocturne for Orchestra* (1936, "To Arnold Schoenberg"), and a two-movement *String Quartet*. In 1937, following Gershwin's shockingly premature death, Levant began *Suite for Orchestra*. The middle-movement, Dirge—Andante, he dedicated "In Memory of George Gershwin," and conducted the premiere himself in Pittsburgh at Fritz Reiner's invitation in 1939. On the same program Levant played the Gershwin *Concerto in F*, by then his signature work, along with *Rhapsody in Blue* and the *Second Rhapsody*. In 1939 he married actress June Gale, the mother of his three daughters, who survived him.

In 1940, Levant resumed his film career as Bing Crosby's sidekick in *Rhythm on the River*, and also debuted as a regular "panel expert" on the long-running radio show, Information Please. He composed *Overture 1912 (alias Polka for Oscar Homolka)* and *Caprice for Orchestra*, then in 1941 the *Piano Concerto*, his magnum opus and last major composition, combining Gershwinesque turns and Schoenbergian atonalism. In 1942, Levant became a leading Columbia Masterworks artist (recording with conductors Reiner, Ormandy, Mitropoulos, Morton Gould, and Kostelanetz) while he concertized widely as the highest-paid soloist of his day. That year he also published his first book, *A Smattering of Ignorance*.

In 1945, Levant returned to films, starting with *Rhapsody in Blue*, a Gershwin biopic in which he played himself. The last was *Cobweb* in 1955, an insane asylum melodrama wherein art imitated life. Already in the 1940s, Levant's chronic substance abuse accelerated to a point that the American Federation of Musicians temporarily banned him from union stages for canceling performances. On television talk shows in the 1950s and after, beginning with his own, he became so unpredictably slanderous that another ban was threatened. Nonetheless, between repeated hospitalizations, he appeared sporadically in concert as late as August 1958. In his last years he wrote two more books, *The Memoirs of an Amnesiac* and *The Unimportance of Being Oscar*. —*Roger Dettmer*

Recommended:

- ○ **Oscar Levant** / Levant, Columbia Concert Orch. / Pearl 0105
- ○ **Levant—Plays Gershwin** / Levant / Sony 47681

Robert Levin

b. Oct. 13, 1947, Brooklyn, NY
Pianist

Robert Levin is both a pianist and musicologist, serving in the latter role as a teacher of composition, Mozart scholar, and writer of numerous articles on music. As a performer, he is most closely associated with the compositions of Mozart, which he plays on fortepiano in recordings, but usually on piano in concert. He has also completed several important compositions by Mozart, as well, most notably the *Requiem*. Beethoven has occupied a significant chunk of his repertory, too, Levin having recorded all the piano concertos. He has also been an advocate for modern composers, including Harbison and Denisov.

Despite his immense keyboard gifts as a child, he initially decided to primarily focus on composition, studying in New York with composer Stefan Wolpe from the 1957–61. He then took piano instruction from Louis Martin over the next three years, also in New York City. Concurrent with this activity, Levin studied composition under Nadia Boulanger and piano with Alice Gaultier-Léon at the Fontainebleau Conservatoire Américain in France (1960–64). It is remarkable that all this advanced training took place while Levin was still in high school. Levin went on to Harvard and following graduation, was appointed head of music theory at the Curtis Institute in 1968, upon the recommendation of Rudolf Serkin. Two years later, he took on a professorship at S.U.N.Y., Purchase, which he concurrently held until he departed his Curtis post in 1973. He would remain at Purchase until 1986, but again take a second position during his tenure there, this at the Fontainebleau Conservatoire, from 1979–83, on the invitation of former teacher Boulanger. While Levin had been making impressive strides in his pedagogical profession, his keyboard career had advanced only modestly during the nearly two decades following his graduation from Harvard. He had given public concerts with reasonable frequency from childhood, but his first major appearance would not come until his Alice Tully Hall recital in 1987, after which he enjoyed a nearly meteoric rise. Yet Levin was hardly turning away from his teaching career at this point: he had accepted a post at the Freiburg Staatliche Hochschule für Musik the year before, holding the post until 1993. By that time, he had launched his recording career. The first issue in his highly praised Mozart fortepiano concerto series, with Christopher Hogwood and the Academy of Ancient Music, was issued in 1994 on L'oiseau-Lyre. He had appeared in chamber music recordings as early as 1986 (with Kim Kashkashian on viola) and in the Mozart *Concerto for Three Pianos* with his friends Malcolm Bilson and Melvyn Tan. Levin's eighth release in his own Mozart concerto series came in early 2001. He has been widely praised for the performances, particularly for his imaginative, improvised cadenzas, a once-popular performance practice that some have credited him with restoring to tradition. Levin has also made a mark with his set of the five Beethoven piano concertos (also played on fortepiano), which he recorded between 1996 and 2000. His version of Mozart's *Requiem* was premiered in 1991 in Stuttgart at the European Music Festival, conducted by Helmuth Rilling. Perhaps Levin's most famous Mozart essay was his 1998 *Who Wrote the Mozart Four-Wind Concertante?* In 1993, Levin left his post in Freiburg and accepted a professorship at Harvard, where he served as a Dwight P. Robinson Jr. Professor of the Humanities. —*Robert Cummings*

Recommended:

- ○ **Beethoven: Concerto 4; Symphony 2 (Chamber Versions)** / Levin, Watkin, Isserlis, Hanson, George, Howard / 2003 / Archiv 474224
- ○ **Mozart: Concertos 5, 14, 16** / Hogwood (cond.), Levin, Academy of Ancient Music / 1999 / Decca 458285
- ○ **Beethoven: Concertos 3 & 4** / Gardiner (cond.), Levin, Revolutionnaire et Romantique / 1998 / Archiv 457608
- ○ **Beethoven: Concertos 1 & 2** / Gardiner (cond.), Levin, Revolutionnaire et Romantique / Archiv 453438

James Levine

b. Jun. 23, 1943, Cincinnati, OH
Conductor

Conductor and pianist James Levine is one of the powerhouse figures of the classical music scene today. As a child he undertook both piano and the violin; he was so accomplished on the violin that at the age of ten he played Mendelssohn's second violin concerto at a Cincinnati Symphony Orchestra youth concert. He studied piano at various summer music festivals before enrolling at New York's Juilliard School, where he took conducting courses with Jean Morel and continued piano studies with Rosina Lhevinne. Further conducting studies included work at the Aspen Music Festival and with the American Conductors Project, a program run by the Baltimore Symphony Orchestra, after his Juilliard graduation in 1964.

George Szell of the Cleveland Orchestra then invited him to become an apprentice. At the conclusion of this term, he became an assistant conductor of the orchestra from 1965 to 1970. In 1973 he became the music director of both the Ravinia Festival (the Chicago Symphony's summer series) and of the Cincinnati May Festival. His debut with the Metropolitan Opera Company of New York also came in a summer festival appearance; on June 5, 1971, he conducted Puccini's *Tosca*.

In 1973, following the sudden departure of music director Rafael Kubelik over artistic differences, the Metropolitan Opera appointed Levine its principal conductor. In 1975 the position was redesignated "music director." Although Kubelik was the first conductor ever to have been given that title at the Metropolitan, he did not remain there long enough to actually exercise the wide responsibilities it implies; Levine was effectively the first music director of the Met. In 1986 his position was further expanded to "artistic director," which implies control over all aspects of the stage presentation, not just the music.

Levine's tenure at the Metropolitan has been one of the longest such associations between an opera company and its chief conductor, providing the company with one of its greatest and most stable periods. His season planning has been outstanding, and the Metropolitan Opera Orchestra owes its reputation as a world-class ensemble to his leadership.

He began in 1975 to appear regularly at the Salzburg Festival in Austria, where his performances of Mozart were highly esteemed, and proved himself an excellent Wagnerian in his appearances at the Bayreuth Festival beginning in 1982. However, his guest conducting availability has been limited: he considers the artistic leadership of the Metropolitan to be a full-time, year-round job. When time allows, he performs as a pianist in chamber music and as an accompanist for singers.

Levine commands a wide repertoire in opera and also in the concert hall, ranging from Bach, Haydn, and Mozart to Iannis Xenakis. He is known for an open and engaging personality which appears in his rehearsals as well, but this does not prevent him from conducting them with businesslike efficiency. In 1996 the Metropolitan conducted a televised celebration of 25th anniversary of Levine's first performance there in the form of a gala. So many singers agreed to appear that the event lasted over eight hours—conducted entirely by Levine. He has produced a large number of recordings with the Metropolitan Opera and other opera houses, as well as orchestral recordings with the Chicago Symphony and other great orchestras. He is also noted as a pianist who has accompanied many of the world's top vocalists and participated in several chamber music recordings. In 2004, Levine became music director of the Boston Symphony Orchestra. —*Joseph Stevenson*

Recommended:

- ○ **Tchaikovsky: Ballet Suites** / Levine (cond.), Kuchl, Bartolomey, Vienna PO / DM 437806
- ○ **Wagner: Die Walküre** / Levine (cond.), Norman, Morris, Ludwig, Moll, Metropolitan Opera Orch. / DM 423389
- ○ **Kathleen Battle Sings Mozart** / Levine (cond.), Battle, Metropolitan Opera Orch. / 1997 / DM 439949
- ○ **Dvořák: Symphonies 7 & 9** / Levine (cond.), Chicago SO / 2001 / BMG 68013

Richard Lewis

b. May 10, 1914, Manchester, England, **d.** Nov. 13, 1990, Eastbourne, England
Tenor

One of England's most famous tenors, Richard Lewis used his strong lyric instrument wisely in a broad repertory, achieving his greatest success in opera and concert work. Lewis was entrusted with the premieres of several important works, gaining a positive reputation abroad first through recordings and, subsequently, in live performance. Indeed, his became a name recognized worldwide during a period in which many British artists lived and performed in artistic insularity. Remarkably versatile, Richard Lewis offered a soft-edged voice large enough to approach some heavier roles, although he was heard at his best in lyric parts and was especially noted for his lovely mezza voce singing. The latter quality contributed to his reputation as the finest Gerontius of his time.

Born in Manchester to Welsh parents, Lewis began training as a boy soprano at age 12. After winning first prize in 13 competitions, he was invited to record for Parlophone. His voice broke before the recordings could be made, however, and he withdrew from singing for the next four years. At 16, Lewis abandoned his schooling to take on an office position. Though a dreary job, it afforded Lewis the time to pursue the private study of music. Over the next several years, he achieved three gold medals in his board examinations and eventually won a scholarship to the Royal Manchester College of Music, where he studied for four years under the famous English bass Norman Allin. In 1941, he was invited to join the Carl Rosa Opera Company with which he toured the English north country until he was called into service. Stationed in Brussels for nine months, he enjoyed opportunities to perform both there and in Norway, where he was later posted.

After the war's end, Lewis traveled to London to seek performing opportunities and after completing his scholarship, transferred to the Royal Academy of Music where Allin was now an instructor. Engagements came quickly thereafter: the male chorus in Britten's *Rape of Lucretia* for both the Glyndebourne Festival and Covent Garden in 1947 and essaying Tamino, Alfredo, and Peter Grimes at the Royal Opera House that same season. During the years following at Covent Garden, Lewis sang the premieres of Walton's *Troilus and Cressida* (Troilus), Tippett's *The Midsummer Marriage* (Mark), and Tippett's *King Priam* (Achilles), as well as Hoffmann, Don José, Captain Vere (*Billy Budd*), Gherman (*Pique Dame*), and Aron in the first English production of Schoenberg's *Moses und Aron.* Over more than a quarter century at Glyndebourne, the tenor ranged over an even broader field, singing roles from Nero in Monteverdi's *L'incoronazione di Poppea* to Tom Rakewell in *The Rake's Progress* with (among others) Florestan and Bacchus in between.

Lewis made his debut with the San Francisco Opera in 1955 and for a number of seasons proved his worth in such diverse roles as Don José, Troilus, the False Dimitri, Pinkerton, Herod, Eisenstein, Jeník, Des Grieux (Massenet), Alwa in Berg's *Lulu*, and the Captain in the same composer's *Wozzeck.* Lewis was the Aron for the first American stage production of *Moses und Aron* in Boston in 1966. Lewis' many recordings include a noble Idomeneo, a live taping of the premiere of *The Midsummer Marriage*, excerpts from *Troilus* (with Walton conducting and Schwarzkopf as Cressida) and two remembrances of his affecting Gerontius (the second with Barbirolli conducting and Janet Baker as the Angel). *—Erik Eriksson*

Recommended:

- ○ **Beethoven: Symphony 9** / Klemperer (cond.), Ludwig, Lewis, Berry, Giebel, London PO / 1996 / Testament 1332
- ○ **Mozart: Idomeneo** / Busch (cond.), Nilsson, Lewis, Jurinac, Poell, Glyndebourne Festival Chorus & Orch. / 2001 / Urania 182

Cecile Licad

b. May 11, 1961, Manila, The Phillippines

Pianist

One of the most outstanding concert artists in the world is pianist Cecile Licad. Born in the Philippines, Licad began her studies on piano at the age of Three with her mother and made her public debut in Manila at the tender age of Seven. At 14, Licad played for pianist Rudolf Serkin, who upon hearing her exclaimed "when I was her age, I could not touch what she is doing." Licad was soon packed off to the Curtis Institute of Music in Philadelphia, where she studied with Serkin, Seymour Lipkin, and Mieczysław Horszowski. In 1980 Licad was awarded the prestigious Leventritt Award, even though she hadn't competed for it and the competition itself had been dormant for several years.

Her recording career began promisingly enough, with Licad's early CBS recordings of the Rachmaninov *Piano Concerto No. 2* and the Saint-Saëns *Piano Concerto No. 2* invading the *Billboard* classical charts. After her work with CBS ended in 1989 with a splendid album of Schumann's piano music, she recorded some chamber music with Nadja Salerno-Sonnenberg for EMI, also appearing with the latter at Lincoln Center. In the mid-'90s Licad recorded two discs of Chopin and Ravel for the MusicMasters label that represented some of her best recordings. But even as Licad was winning unqualified raves for her work in the concert hall, changing economics in the classical music market sank MusicMasters, taking her recordings along with it.

In 2003 Licad made a stunning comeback in the record market with a magnificent recording of piano music by American composer Louis Moreau Gottschalk for the Naxos label. All along Licad has continued to tour and give concerts even as competition among soloists for a shrinking number of engagements is growing tighter by each season. One good example of Licad's toughness, however, is that in 2003 she was playing an outreach concert in Tuguegarao City, in the northern province of Philippines, and decided to take a side trip to view the Banaue rice fields. Licad and her company were trapped by a series of mud slides; however, she managed to slog through a couple of miles of knee-deep mud in order to make it to a helicopter, just in time to catch her 8 a.m. flight from Manila to her next engagement in Madison, WI.

About a Licad concert, a *Washington Post* reviewer once wrote "every sound she made was beautiful, every note and phrase the result of intellect warmed by emotion." Indeed, Licad is so good that she makes you forget the composer and luxuriate in the warmth and deep feeling elicited by her playing alone—she could probably bring one to tears with a Czerny etude. Anyone who is foolish enough to stipulate that all the greatest concert artists belong to the past and that "they just don't make them like that anymore" has never heard Cecile Licad play. *—Uncle Dave Lewis*

Recommended:

- ○ **Gottschalk: Piano Music** / Licad / 2003 / Naxos 8559145
- ○ **Ravel: Piano Works** / Licad / 1998 / MusicMasters 67172
- ○ **Schumann: Carnaval; Papillons; Toccata** / Licad / 1990 / Sony 45742

György Ligeti

b. May 28, 1923, Discöszentmáton, Romania

Composer: Keyboard, Chamber Music, Choral, Orchestral, Vocal, Avant-garde

György Ligeti is one of the most important avant-garde composers in the latter half of the twentieth century. He stands with Boulez, Berio, Stockhausen, and Cage as one of the most innovative and influential among progressive figures of his time. His early works show the influence of Bartók and Kodály, and like them, he studied folk music and made transcriptions from folk material. In *Apparitions* (1958–59) and *Atmosphères* (1961), he developed a style forged from chromatic cluster chords that are devoid of conventional melody, pitch and rhythm, but instead grow into timbres and textures that yield new sonic possibilities. The composer referred to this method as "micropolyphony." In *Aventures* (1962), Ligeti devised a vocal technique in which the singers are required to make a full range of vocalizations, cries and nonsense noises to fashion a kind of imaginary, non-specific drama, but with rather specifically expressed emotions. Ligeti is almost alone among progressive composers from the latter twentieth century who have written popular and widely performed music.

Ligeti was born on May 28, 1923, in the Transylvanian town of Dicsöszentmárton, Romania and grew up in Kolozsvar, Klausenburg. At the age of 14, he began taking piano lessons and soon wrote his first composition, a waltz.

Because he was a Jew living under the Nazi-puppet regime in Hungary, Ligeti was forbidden university study and thus enrolled in the Kolozsvar Conservatory in 1941, and began studies with Ferenc Farkas, a Respighi pupil. Later, in Budapest, he also studied with pianist-composer Pál Kadosa.

In January, 1944, Ligeti was arrested and sent to a labor camp where he remained imprisoned until 1945. Other family members were sent to Auschwitz, where only his mother survived. Ligeti graduated from the Budapest Academy of Music in 1949 and began an extended period of study of folk music.

In the years of 1950–56, he served as a professor at the Budapest Academy. His music was largely unadventurous during this period, owing to restrictions by the Hungarian Communist regime. Ligeti and his wife fled their homeland during the Revolution in 1956, settling in Vienna. Ligeti began studying and composing at the Cologne-based Electronic Music Studio from 1957 to 1959, producing the influential *Artikulation* (1958), one of his first electronic works.

Other important progressive works followed, such as the orchestral composition, *Apparitions* (1958–59) and *Atmosphères* (1961). In 1959, Ligeti began serving as visiting professor at the Academy of Music in Stockholm and also started teaching courses at Darmstadt.

His choral work Requiem (1963–65) was another success, as were *Ramifications* (1968–69), for string orchestra or twelve solo strings, and *Clocks and Clouds* (1972–73). In 1972, Ligeti became Composer in Residence at Stanford University and the following year took on a professorship at the Hamburg Academy of Music. Ligeti composed his opera *Le Grand Macabre* in the period 1975–77, but revised it in the 1990s, with the final version completed in 1997. It has become one of his most popular large works.

In 1982, the composer's mother died. That same year saw a return of Ligeti's health after a period of five years' sickness. In the 1980s the composer forswore further composition in the realm of electronic music. Ligeti retired from his post as professor of composition at the Hamburg Music Academy in 1989. In the 1990s, he spent much time on the aforementioned second version of *Le Grand Macabre.*

Ligeti has received his share of awards and prizes, including the 1986 Grawemeyer Prize and the 1996 Music Prize of the International Music Council. *—Robert Cummings*

KEYBOARD

Continuum, for harpsichord (1968)

Ligeti's *Continuum* (1968) is a short work indeed: according to the composer, all the notes in this single prestissimo movement must be played within the span of four minutes. The work is written for harpsichord, as much because the required speed would be nigh impossible to achieve on the heavier action of piano as because of the fact that the composer calls for two separate manuals. The hands play continuously at this furious pace in a manner that renders single sonorities imperceptible; instead, the sonic flurry blurs into a "continuum." *—Umberto Posarelli*

Recommended:

○ **Ligeti: Continum; Zehn Stück für Bläserquintett; Artikulation** / Vischer / 1988 / Wergo 60161

○ **Ligeti Edition Vol. 6** / Chojnacka / 1997 / Sony 62307

Etudes for piano, Books 1–3 (1985–1995)

In his series of etudes for solo piano (*Book I*, 1985; *Book II*, 1988–93; *Book III*, 1995–present; with a possible *Book IV*), Ligeti has drawn upon a host of styles and influences that have contributed to his own unique sound world. In these etudes one can hear elements of the 1950s and 1960s avant-garde of which Ligeti was so prominent a part, along with the complex polyrhythms of African music, the Indonesian gamelan, jazz, and the composers of the past and present who have explored the limits of piano technique—Scarlatti, Chopin, Schumann, Liszt, Nancarrow, and many others. The great pianist Alfred Brendel has gone so far as to say, "You need three or five hands to play Ligeti."

The jagged, aggressive *Disorder* leads off *Book I*. It is followed by *Open Strings*, a study based on the interval of the fifth, which is very lyrical at first, but becomes faster and more dissonant as it goes. *Blocked Keys* skitters nervously about the keyboard, and *Fanfares* develops out of a repeating ostinato figure. The fifth piece, *Rainbow*, is a mellow nocturne not far from the world of jazz pianist Bill Evans; the piece is even marked "con eleganza, with swing." *Book I* concludes with *Autumn in Warsaw*, a tribute to a city and country that had long supported Ligeti's music. The delicate passagework, made up of several different lines traveling at different speeds, was inspired by his interest in how polyrhythms are deployed in various forms of African music.

After a break of several years during, which he composed his *Piano Concerto*, Ligeti returned to the etude cycle with *Book II*, which features works of even greater complexity than *Book I*. The title of the opener, *Galamb borong*, is ersatz Indonesian; the complex rhythms of the gamelan are mapped onto the whole-tone scales of Claude Debussy, who was himself fascinated by the Indonesian gamelan. *Metal* is playful and jazzy, with an almost barrelhouse quality to the rhythm. *Vertigo* is a very challenging piece, with its constant swirl of scales up and down the keyboard. *The Sorcerer's Apprentice* bears no relationship to the Paul Dukas piece of the same name; its rapid repeating notes are a contrast to the elegant, spacious *In Suspense* that follows it. *Interlacings* is another rhythmically complex piece. A series of unpleasant experiences in the Santa Monica area in 1993 led to *The Devil's Staircase*, a jagged and unrelenting piece that ends with a thundering chord. *Book II* ends with *Infinite Column*, inspired by the Brancusi sculpture of the same name. Its series of loud, upward-striving scales is a great challenge to the pianist; Ligeti in fact originally conceived this piece, as the score states, "for player piano (ad lib. living pianist)." Inspired by the *Studies for Player Piano* by Conlon Nancarrow, Ligeti has authorized arrangements of many of the etudes, including all of *Book II*, for that instrument. Those arrangements are quite effective in their own right, especially in the ferocious torrent of notes found in *Infinite Column* or *Vertigo*.

Ligeti sees the etudes as an ongoing series. He has already completed several pieces for *Book III*, including the very peaceful *White on White* (1995), which never quite settles on one tonality, but is nonetheless quite diatonic and, despite the restless ending, quite lovely. "For Irina" and *Etude No. 17* were also composed in 1995. *—Chris Morrison*

Recommended:

○ **Ligeti: Etudes, Books 1 & 2** / Biret / 2003 / Naxos 8555777

Musica ricercata, for piano (1951–1953)

Although known primarily for his sound-mass compositions (such as *Lux Aeterna*, which was featured in Stanley Kubrick's film, *2001: A Space Odyssey*) and the use of so-called micropolyphony, György Ligeti spent his later years obsessed with the piano, eventually embarking on an extended series of etudes for the instrument. These grand achievements were not without precedent, however, as can be seen in his *Musica Ricercata*, for piano, of 1953. This early work, written before his flight from Hungary, establishes his affinity for the keyboard, and acknowledges the influence of Béla Bartók, whose *Mikrokosmos* exhibits a similar progressive approach to composition.

Musica Ricercata comprises 11 individual pieces, the first of which includes only two pitch values (and their octave equivalents); each subsequent piece adds another pitch, so that by the last in the set all twelve pitches are brought into play. This systematic adding of pitches to the tonal mix is the binding formal element in the set—one that forces Ligeti to look to other elements, such as rhythm, register, and dynamics, for the development of musical interest.

Ligeti travels widely through the *Musica Ricercata* in his explorations of style and technique. The first piece heralds the pitch A with much bravura, building up thundering octaves and dizzying ostinati, before finally landing on a sustained D, as if to create a cadence. The second piece uses three chromatic neighbor tones to create a study of dissonance and drama. The third shifts gears completely, evoking Bartók in its jaunty treatment of a triad containing both the major and minor thirds. The fourth piece is a waltz-like dance, evoking the ghost of Mahler, perhaps, in the combination of thirds and chromatic runs over a static accompaniment. The fifth piece, using six pitches, combines a Beethovenian recitative-like passage with more dissonant, lamentoso themes. The sixth work, using a full seven-note diatonic complement, again evokes the folk music world of Bartók. The next study, one of the most substantial (four minutes in duration), unfolds a beautiful song over a fast ostinato in the left hand that is reminiscent of piano music by Samuel Barber or Alberto Ginastera, though it is doubtful such influences would have been explicit. The eighth piece is an exuberant Eastern European dance in an asymmetrical meter. The ninth is explicitly dedicated to Bartók, though it does not try to evoke his music in any obvious way; it is a poignant, concentrated work. The tenth piece, using 11 pitches, is a humorous, biting score that harmonizes diatonic material with various dissonances; a repeated cluster that is pounded out near the end points forward to Ligeti's later post-tonal, textural music. The final, most substantial work of the set is an intricate contrapuntal study dedicated to Girolamo Frescobaldi, seventeenth century master of the polyphonic ricercare form—perhaps the inspiration for the work's title. *—Jim Harley*

Recommended:

○ **Ligeti Edition Vol. 3** / Aimard / Sony 62308

○ **Ligeti: Complete Piano Music Vol. 2** / Ullen / 1998 / BIS 983

CHAMBER MUSIC

Six Bagatelles for wind quintet (1953)

These six pieces were originally part of a collection of 12 bagatelles composed for piano between 1951 and 1953. In 1953, Ligeti transcribed six of the bagatelles for a wind quintet comprised of flute, oboe, clarinet, horn, and bassoon. With the exception of the second and fifth bagatelles, these are quick, spirited little pieces. They reflect Ligeti's economical approach to composition, as a minimum number of notes are used to maximum effect. The bagatelles are often texturally sparse, with most of the notes either played staccato or strongly accented to create cool but insistent music. The dynamics change frequently, sometimes several times in each bar, and the instruments are often called on to play muted, adding different colors to each piece. Ligeti's bagatelles employ some harsh dissonances and complex ideas; however, they are also very moving and accessible little chamber pieces that explore both the expressive and the purely musical potential of a limited amount of material.

These pieces are very short: most are under two minutes in duration, and none are over three. The first bagatelle, Allegro con spirito, is comprised of only four pitches yet is amazingly varied in expression and is motivically inventive. The second bagatelle is a passionate, anguished Lamentoso. The third is quick, but with longer cantabile melodies juxtaposed with quiet staccato figures. Bagatelle number four is exuberant and strongly accented, while number five, dedicated to the memory of Béla Bartók, begins as a spare adagio, but soon becomes more vivacious as dotted rhythmic figures are added. The final bagatelle is like a wild, frenetic race, and the penultimate measures are marked "as though insane"; but the piece ultimately ends with a soft, muted horn solo. *—Alexander Carpenter*

Recommended:

○ **Ligeti: Chamber Music** / London SO Winds / 1998 / Sony 62309

○ **Debussy, Ligeti, Janáček** / Cassen, Lefevre, Nessi, Olle, Guyot / HM 911624

String Quartet No. 1 ("Métamorphoses nocturnes") (1953–1954)

Ligeti's *String Quartet No. 1* was written in Budapest in 1953–54, but not premiered until May 8, 1958, by the Ramor Quartet in Vienna. By that time Ligeti had already left the Soviet-controlled Hungary for the West and had been introduced to music that had only barely penetrated the Eastern bloc; including the music of Stockhausen and Boulez, the advent of serialism, and the electronic music studios. Ligeti's own progress as a composer put him far beyond the influence of Kodály, Bartók, and the Hungarian nationalism that permeated most of his work in Budapest. He has returned to these influences more and more explicitly, for example in the *Piano Études* of the 1980s and 1990s. Bartók's influence on Ligeti's music is twofold, and includes his sophisticated sense of rhythm and motivic development, and also his lifelong use of folk song and folk-influenced musical materials. Ligeti's *Musica ricercata for piano*; their offspring, the *Six Bagatelles for wind quintet*; and the *String Quartet No. 1* show these influences most clearly.

Although the *String Quartet No. 1* is ostensibly a one-movement work lasting over 20 minutes, this single movement makes up many sections of disparate character. The piece opens with a stepwise melody (G-A-G sharp-A sharp) accompanied by chromatic scales. A second theme is angular, staccato, and aggressive. Closer attention to these two apparently disparate sections, however, reveals similarities in their melodic contours, which are based on the relatively simple chromaticism of the opening motif. New ideas and textures succeed one another throughout the piece, typically in fast-slow-fast alternation (another Bartók technique), but the melodic characteristics of each section may be traced to the piece's opening. Variation of rhythm provides the piece with much of its sense of progression, with somewhat amorphous passages giving way to the quick irregular meters of a dance form; there are also other stylistic parodies of folk music. Use of biting dissonance (one of the reasons the composer's more advanced work was not officially supported) occurs throughout; the second section features passages of parallel minor seconds. Ligeti's ear for unusual timbral possibilities is already at work in this early piece. High harmonic glissandi near the end of the work may presage the distinctive sound of *Apparitions* and the later pieces for which Ligeti came to be known. *—Robert Kirzinger*

Recommended:

- ○ **Ligeti: String Quartets; etc.** / Arditti SQ / 1996 / Sony 62306
- ○ **Ligeti: String Quartet 1; San Francisco Polyphony; etc.** / Voces Intimae SQ / Bis 53

Trio for horn, violin & piano ("Hommage à Brahms") (1982)

Ligeti's *Trio for violin, horn, and piano* was completed in 1982 and premiered on August 7 of that year. Apart from some smaller works, including *Hungarian Rock* (chaconne) and *Passacaglia ungherese* for harpsichord, Ligeti had composed very little since completing *Le Grand Macabre* in 1977. The extreme eclecticism and physical scope of the opera seem to have cast the composer into a compositional crisis: what does one write when one has just finished writing everything? As many composers before him had done, Ligeti turned to music history and other musical cultures for an answer. Though Ligeti had never been averse to history, his more explicit turn in that direction is reflected in the chaconne and passacaglia forms in the 1978 harpsichord pieces and in the final scene of *Le Grand Macabre*, which itself is a passacaglia. In the late 1970s and early 1980s, Ligeti gained inspiration from many sources, but most particularly from study of sub-Saharan African drumming and from research into fractal procedures in mathematics. In 1980 Ligeti also discovered the music of American expatriate composer Conlon Nancarrow (1912–97), whose multi-layered, complex studies for player piano closely paralleled Ligeti's rhythmic interests at the time.

Ligeti also became interested in the music of Chopin and Schumann, particularly in their use of rubato and hemiola (a subverting of the predominant rhythmic pattern with a different division of the beat). The idea of a melodic line carrying its own distinct rhythmic burden became one of the main concerns of the *Trio for violin, horn, and piano.* Ligeti had another, even more specific influence in the horn trio of Brahms Op. 40 (1865). Ligeti's musical language, having emerged from the vex of a writer's block, is paradoxically purified and direct in its presentation of ambiguous rhythmic cross-relations and skewed harmonic clichés, such as several versions of the common "horn fifths" motif. In the first movement the violin and horn engage in a duet of two tempos, but the relationship between the two is relatively exact. The horn is the main melodic instrument, soaring in high, fast runs. In spite of the apparent complexity of the melodic language, the harmonic profile of the movement, and of the piece as a whole, is surprisingly diatonic. After the circumspect first movement, the motoric but dancing rhythms of the second and third movements show the results of Ligeti's knowledge of the musics of Africa and the Caribbean, and of Nancarrow. The second movement is in an eighth note pulse that is further subdivided into groups of three plus two plus three. Ligeti manipulates the groupings of this pattern to produce seemingly different tempos among the three instruments, a technique he took even further in the *Six Piano Études* of the following year. The third movement begins with a stuttering rhythmic unison that gradually goes out of phase. A lyrical, legato section succeeds this material with differing phrase lengths among the instruments. The final movement is a lament based loosely on the sorrowful, descending funeral chants of several Eastern European cultures. Again, the varying phrase lengths are an important expressive aspect of the music.

The *Trio for violin, horn, and piano* led directly to the *Études for piano, Book I* of 1985 and to the *Piano Concerto* of 1985–88. Portions of all three works share virtually the same concerns, and reuse very specific gestures and modes of expression, just as Ligeti reused those ticking clocks and harmonic clouds throughout his earlier music. *—Robert Kirzinger*

Recommended:

- ○ **Ligeti Edition Vol. 7** / Aimard, Gawriloff, Neunecker / 1998 / Sony 62309
- ○ **Brahms & Ligeti: Horn Trios** / Danish Horn Trio / 2001 / Chandos 9964

CHORAL

Lux aeterna (1966)

Ligeti's mysterious and beautiful *Lux aeterna* (1966) for 16-part mixed chorus primarily varies between two textures: a surface of sustained, multi-timbral clusters that arise from polyphonically accumulated long tones, and short sustained consonant sonorities that give the effect of whispering.

Moving outward from a shared unison tone, the voices act individually to amass and develop close tetrachords which slowly modulate until reaching another unison (or octave) center. The work bears several remarkable features; for example, the word "Dominum" is first heard sung by three basses in falsetto voices, like an androgynous chorus of angels. The work demands excellent breath control from the singers; several entrances occur on high tones at piano and pianissimo dynamics, while other passages employ tones that must be sustained for extended periods (these notes are always doubled by at least one other voice so that subtle staggered breathing is possible). The work ends with the four altos on a major-second interval that dies out to nothing, followed by seven tacet measures which create a meditative silence to balance the work's restrained intensity.

Like *Atmosphères* (1961) for orchestra, *Lux aeterna* moves away from the pointed rhythmic style of Ligeti's earlier folkloric vocal music and angular orchestral works toward an even, smoothly developed surface texture. The eight-minute *Lux aeterna* is perhaps most familiar as the "voice" of the monolith in Stanley Kubrick's film *2001: A Space Odyssey*; on its own, however, it suggests a pervasive universal presence rather than mere widescreen bigness. *—"Blue Gene" Tyranny*

Recommended:

- ○ **Ligeti: A Cappella Choral Works Vol. 2** / Edwards (cond.), London Sinfonietta Voices / 1996 / Sony 62305
- ○ **Ligeti: Kammerkonzert; Ramifications; Lux aeterna; Atmospheres** / Gottwald (cond.), Stuttgart Schola Cantorum / 1988 / Wergo 60162

Requiem (1963–1965)

The works of György Ligeti often seem to take as an auxiliary aim the obsolescence of terms normally used to identify—and distinguish—the various parameters of music, such as melody, harmony, rhythm, and especially texture. In this regard, his work is presaged by the perpetually unfamiliar soundscapes of Edgard Varèse and finds certain resonance with the transparent surfaces of minimalism, as well as the Penderecki's tone clusters and Stockhausen's obscure timbres. To varying degrees, it echoes in the electronic and microtonal experimentation of the twentieth century's end. Ligeti's *Requiem*, which he began composing in 1963 and finished two years later, in many ways bears the edgy, modernist characteristics general to his most prominent works. At the same time, as the title suggests, it also positions itself in relation to musical tradition, as if applying the composer's pioneering sonorities to the service of "expression," in a more visceral and subjective manner than modernism usually admits. Perhaps the most striking feature of the work, which is scored for two choirs, orchestra, and two soloists (soprano and mezzo-soprano) is its vibrant, quivering surface. The individual parts comprising his chromatic clusters are often too close to each other to be individually discerned, but their motion adds a distinctive, acoustical glimmer. Melody, then, is generally subsumed by the work's texture, but contributes crucially to its character. This technique also becomes a variant in and of itself, as the pace of the work and the character of the various liturgical sections or texts are often established by the register and relative opacity of the contrapuntal clusters. One startling effect, perhaps inspired by the creepy bass intonations of Vaèse's *Nocturnal* from a few years before, is the use of two low men's voices in near unison, their pitches offset enough to create a hauntingly beating effect. Likewise, when one of the high female solo voices breaks through the thick chromatic pall of the orchestra and chorus, the lucidity of her line is cast in brighter relief. These contrasts, coupled with extremes of dynamics and articulation, reach their apex in the carefully disjointed Dies Irae. Thus, despite Ligeti's unique and complex musical language, the ultimate result of his work is not entirely different in principle from the large-scale requiems of previous centuries, which projected grandeur, intensity, and intimacy through the careful deployment of their vocal and instrumental forces. *—Jeremy Grimshaw*

Recommended:

- ○ **Ligeti: Requiem; Aventures; Nouvelles Aventures** / Gielen (cond.), Schubert, Poli, Ericson, Bavarian Radio Chorus / 1985 / Wergo 60045

ORCHESTRAL

Atmosphères (1961)

Atmosphères has been heard by its largest audiences through the excerpts of the work used by movie director/producer Stanley Kubrick in his film *2001: A Space Odyssey* (along with Ligeti's *Lux Aeterna*).

Composed in 1961 for large orchestra without percussion, *Atmosphères* makes an indelible first impression with a subdued five-octave chromatic chord utilizing every note in this massive span and employing each instrument of the orchestra in its realization. As section after section drops away, flutes, clarinets, and horns are left sounding a bright, piercing tone cluster. Prismatic voices from high strings sounding in quickly pulsing clusters lead a remarkable array of timbral effects. Cadences with the same contours moving at differing tempi, heaving brass players breathing volubly through their horns, and sheets of slithering instrumental voices in highest registers are among other arresting devices employed here by Ligeti.

The work scarcely hints at forward movement. Rather, the listener hears an all but motionless series of sound evolutions unfolding at various moments. It is, if not a revelation of music in all of its aspects, a study in orchestral timbre, all the more effective, all the more spectacular because of its being employed with such a sizeable number of instruments. It successfully demonstrates the contemporary colors available to the symphony orchestra without reliance upon peripheral electronics. Scarcely any doubt can exist over what attracted Kubrick: it was the perfect realization in sound of his visual exploration of outer space.

Although first responses to the work were muted, especially from those of the avant-garde, *Atmosphères* prevailed with the public who desired contemporary music to which they could feel some attraction. Indeed, this work can be regarded as clearing a pathway for minimalist composers of a later period who likewise explored (and sometimes exploited) timbral effects which gradually evolve throughout works composed for orchestra or large ensemble. *—Erik Eriksson*

Recommended:

○ **Ligeti Project Vol. 2** / Nott (cond.), Berlin PO / 2002 / Teldec 88261

○ **Ligeti: Kammerkonzert; Ramifications; Lux aeterna; Atmospheres** / Bour (cond.), Mitteldeutschen RSO / 1988 / Wergo 60162

VOCAL

Aventures, for 3 voices & 7 instruments (1963)

In the late 1950s, Ligeti worked at the Studio for Electronic Music of the West German Radio in Cologne. He had the chance to immerse himself in the techniques of the avant-garde, including the unusual uses of the human voice being championed by composers like John Cage and Luciano Berio. One concept that particularly interested him was the replacement, in vocal works, of conventional texts by nonsense syllables and sounds. Ligeti went on to use such texts in several works, notably in *Aventures* and its sequel *Nouvelles Aventures. Aventures* was given its first performance under Friedrich Cerha's direction in Hamburg on April 4, 1963, and was later championed and recorded by composer-conductor Bruno Maderna. A portion of the work, as well as other Ligeti music, appeared memorably in the score for Stanley Kubrick's film *2001: A Space Odyssey.*

Aventures is scored for soprano, contralto, and baritone soloists, accompanied by an ensemble of flute, French horn, cello, bass, percussion, piano, and harpsichord. Although it isn't readily apparent in the listening, Ligeti has written that the three singers are each playing five roles simultaneously, acting out a scenario involving five emotional states—humorous, ghostly-horrific, sentimental, mystical-funereal, and erotic. The singers are called on at different points to shriek, grunt, laugh, breathe loudly, whisper, murmur, and otherwise create all sorts of curious sounds—including the extremely wide leaps of pitch that Ligeti has referred to as his "supercooled expressionism"—all to a text of nonsense sounds created by the composer according to what he called a "secret formula." The instrumentalists also employ extended techniques, and their music is supplemented by the sounds of twanging elastic bands, a paper bag being inflated and popped, and wooden furniture being hit by a stick. The 12-minute work was intended to be, at least in part, humorous, although the musical surface is rather eerie and intimidating. Ligeti himself recognized that listeners might grow weary of lengthy works in this style, so he cut *Aventures* off after a contralto solo, and only "completed" the work with *Nouvelles Aventures* in 1965. *—Chris Morrison*

Recommended:

○ **Ligeti: Vocal Works** / Salonen (cond.), Bryn-Julson, Taylor, Ebrahim, Philharmonia / 1996 / Sony 62311

○ **Ligeti: Aventures** / Boulez (cond.), Manning, Thomas, InterContemporain Ens. / 2002 / DG 471608

Nouvelles aventures, for 3 voices & 7 instruments (1962–1965)

While at Cologne's Studio for Electronic Music of the West German Radio in 1957, Ligeti was exposed to a number of new musical styles and approaches—including novel approaches to voices and text setting—by the likes of Luciano Berio and John Cage. Revisiting his early fascination with language (as a child, he had invented an imaginary land called Kylwiria with its own language), Ligeti created the outlines of a new language using a "secret recipe," which involved associating particular vowel sounds with the notes of the chromatic scale. He first employed this new language in his *Aventures* (1962) for three singers (soprano, contralto, and baritone) and seven instrumentalists (flute, French horn, cello, bass, percussion, piano, and harpsichord). At that point Ligeti was unsure how long a piece in such an unusual style would be acceptable to an audience, so he ended *Aventures* rather abruptly. Later he revisited his work, and completed its sequel *Nouvelles Aventures* in 1965. It was first performed, under Andrzej Markowski's direction, in Hamburg on May 26, 1966, and both pieces were later championed by conductor Bruno Maderna.

There are no recognizable characters in either *Aventures* or its sequel. Ligeti uses a series of five emotional states—humorous, sentimental, erotic, etc.—and moves from one to another very quickly and abruptly. The various episodes of *Nouvelles Aventures* have descriptive titles, such as "Gossips" and "The Demonic Clocks." The latter employs what Ligeti has called his "meccanico" style, in which different rhythms and speeds are heard simultaneously. There is also a "Grand Hysterical Scene" which, however brief, pays tribute to the familiar mad scenes from operas like Donizetti's *Lucia di Lammermoor.* And all sorts of odd sounds punctuate the "action," such as the ripping of paper and silk, a carpet being beaten, and the destruction of bottles and a pile of dishes.

Nouvelles Aventures is in two sections. The texture of the first is very fragmentary. Short, abrupt interjections from the singers are heard, with a variety of grunts, panting, whispering and so on mixed in. The second section is much faster in tempo, though similar in approach at first. Then a slow quasi-chorale is heard, interrupted violently by shouting and short interjections from the instrumentalists. One hears laughing, whispering, glass breaking, and all kinds of mysterious rustlings. The listener doesn't quite know whether to cower in fright or laugh out loud. Perhaps both responses are equally appropriate. *—Chris Morrison*

Recommended:

○ **Ligeti: Aventures** / Boulez (cond.), Manning, Thomas, InterContemporain Ens. / 2002 / DG 471608

○ **Ligeti: Requiem; Aventures; Nouvelles Aventures** / Cerha (cond.), Markowski (cond.) / 1985 / Wergo 60045

AVANT-GARDE

Poème symphonique, for 100 metronomes (1962)

The premiere of the "musical ceremony" *Poème symphonique* (for 100 metronomes, ten performers, and conductor) was quite a scandal, and the piece itself has become a landmark of the twentieth century avant-garde. Ligeti himself left a very amusing account of that first performance, in which he acted as conductor.

The performance was scheduled as the final event of the Courses and Concerts of New Music of the Gaudeamus Foundation in Hilversum, the Netherlands, to take place at an official reception at Hilversum's City Hall on September 13, 1963. Unaware of the scope of the event, which was to include television coverage and speeches by local politicians and dignitaries, Ligeti proceeded with his preparations. Each of the metronomes had to be unpacked, wound down, and set up in a banquet room, a process which took so long that Ligeti barely had time to put on his tuxedo. After platitudinous speeches by the Mayor of Hilversum and others on the value of the arts to society, Ligeti and the ten performers entered the room. They wound the metronomes and set the speeds (all 100 are set at different speeds). Then, after a few minutes, Ligeti gave the signal, and the players started the metronomes and left the stage. After the half hour or so duration of the performance, the confused audience, which before the event had been given no idea of what to expect, set up a loud protest. The television coverage, which was to air the following day, was cancelled at the request of the Hilversum Senate. Only six years later was Ligeti himself allowed to see the footage.

In the composition, which was written in 1962, Ligeti was exploring a concept that continues to fascinate him: the combination of different musical lines at different rhythms and tempos. The fact that one hundred metronomes are called for is somewhat arbitrary; Ligeti knew that many metronomes would be needed to get the effect he desired, but never imagined that a hundred would actually be made available to him.

Despite the oddness of the concept, the *Poème symphonique* is quite interesting from a musical standpoint. The clicking of the metronomes is chaotic at first. As some of them run down, regular rhythmic patterns start to emerge. There is also an increasing amount of silence to be heard amongst the ever-diminishing ticking. The patterns seem to cohere gradually until, eventually, the metronomes wind down and only one is left, ticking away by itself, then silence. *—Chris Morrison*

Recommended:

○ **Ligeti Edition Vol. 5** / Charial / Sony 62310

Christian Lindberg

b. Feb. 15, 1958, Stockholm, Sweden

Trombonist

Christian Lindberg is perhaps the first classical trombonist to maintain a successful full-time performing career as a soloist. Though now considered among the instrument's foremost exponents, he actually took up the trombone fairly late, only starting playing at age 17 after hearing recordings by the great jazz trombonist Jack Teagarden. By 19, Lindberg was the principle trombonist of the Royal Opera Orchestra in Stockholm. But he left that position after just a year, saying he was bored playing in an orchestra. After further studies in Stockholm, London, and Los Angeles, Lindberg began his solo career. He established himself very quickly, and now plays about 100 concerts per year all over the world. He has won many major competitions, gives frequent lectures and masterclasses, and holds the honorary title of Prince Consort Composer at London's Royal College of Music.

Lindberg has been very active in expanding the repertoire for his instrument, having premiered over 60 new concertos and arranged or transcribed over 100 other works for the trombone. Composers such as Alfred Schnittke, Michael Nyman, Toru Takemitsu, Christopher Rouse, Luciano Berio, and Arvo Pärt have written pieces for him. One of his most frequent collaborators has been composer Jan Sandström, who wrote his *Motorbike Concerto* for Lindberg (and which Lindberg performs in costume, as he does other pieces).

Lindberg's debut recording, *The Virtuoso Trombone,* was released in 1983, and he has since released over 50 other albums for several labels. He has also branched out into conducting and composing; his first composition was *Arabenne,* for trombone and strings. Lindberg lives on the Stockholm coastline with his wife and four children. *—Chris Morrison*

Recommended:

- ○ **All the Lonely People** / Vanska (cond.), Lindberg, Tapiola Sinfonietta / 1993 / Bis 568
- ○ **The Romantic Trombone** / Lindberg, Pontinen / 1985 / Bis 298
- ○ **The Criminal Trombone** / Lindberg, Pontinen / 1987 / Bis 328
- ○ **American Trombone Concertos** / DePreist (cond.), Lindberg, Malmo SO / 1993 / BIS 628
- ○ **The Solitary Trombone** / Lindberg / 1988 / BIS 388

Jakob Lindberg

b. Oct. 16, 1952, Djursholm, Sweden

Lutenist, Theorbist

Swedish lutenist Jakob Lindberg began his studies on the guitar after being inspired by the music of the Beatles. His guitar teacher, Jörgen Rörby, introduced him to the lute, which he went on to study at Stockholm University and the Royal College of Music in London. His studies with Diana Poulton and Carlos Bonell in London further focused his interests on performing Renaissance and Baroque music on period instruments. Among the rare instruments he uses is one of the few extant lutes by the Augsburg maker Sixtus Rauwolf (ca. 1595). He has made an extraordinary number of recordings for Bis, often presenting lute music that has never before been recorded. The repertoire he has championed includes lute music by Scottish composers; Italian music for the chitarrone; and chamber music by Vivaldi, Haydn, and Boccherini. He is the first lutenist to have recorded the complete solo lute music by John Dowland and he has received critical acclaim for his interpretations of Bach's music for solo lute. In 1985, he formed the Dowland Consort, specializing in music of the Elizabethan and Jacobean periods, particularly that of Dowland and Weiss. Lindberg has performed as a continuo player on the theorbo and arch lute with many of the most active period nstrument ensembles, including the English Concert, Taverner Choir, the Purcell Quartet, Monteverdi Choir, Chiaroscuro, the Orchestra of the Age of Enlightenment, and the Academy of Ancient Music. He is a frequent collaborator with singers such as Emma Kirkby, Anne Sofie von Otter, Nigel Rogers, and Ian Partridge. For the Royal Swedish Opera at the Drottningholm Court Theatre, he has directed several Baroque operas from the chitarrone, including Purcell's *Dido and Aeneas* in 1995 (where he co-directed the production with Andrew Parrot) and Jacopo Peri's *Euridice* in 1997. Lindberg made his solo recital debut at the Wigmore Hall in 1978, and since then has toured Europe, Japan, Mexico, Russia, Australia, Canada, and the United States. He teaches at the Royal College of Music in London, where he succeeded Diana Poulton as professor of lute in 1979. Richard Popplewell's *Variations on Brigg Fair* for solo lute (1988) was composed for Lindberg. *—Robert Adelson*

Recommended:

- ○ **Dowland: Galliards & Fancies** / Lindberg / 1994 / BIS 300824
- ○ **Spanish Guitar Music** / Lindberg / 1999 / Bis 899
- ○ **Vivaldi: Complete Works for Italian Lute** / Lindberg, Huggett, Sparf, Drottningholm Baroque Ens. / 1985 / Bis 290
- ○ **Boccherini: Guitar Quintets** / Lindberg, Drottningholm Baroque Ens / 1992 / Bis 597

Lindsay String Quartet

f. London, England

Ensemble

This British string quartet, founded at the Royal Academy of Music in London, has gained a worldwide reputation for its rare intensity, an intensity matching or surpassing that of any other contemporary quartet. While this fiery approach has occasionally led the ensemble into patches of questionable intonation, its often-breathtaking realization of thrice-familiar scores has endeared it to audiences seeking something more than polite re-creation. Aside from traditional repertory, the quartet has demonstrated a fervent involvement with the music of its own day, having gained a special identification with the quartets of Sir Michael Tippett, one of which it commissioned. A long-term and imaginative relationship with ASV Records has assured the group's continuing strong presence internationally.

The Lindsays, as they are often called, came together in 1966 under the supervision and mentoring ear of Sidney Griller. The original complement consisted of Peter Cropper, Michael Adamson, Roger Bigley, and Bernard Gregor-Smith. After having captured every available Royal Academy of Music award for quartet performance, the quartet was awarded a Leverhulme scholarship to Keele University. There, working with former Hungarian Quartet member Alexandre Moskowsky, the group assumed the name of university founder Lord Lindsay. The quartet members studied the music of the Classical and post-Classical periods with members of the Amadeus Quartet and explored the ensemble music of Bartók with Sándor Végh and Vilmos Tatrai, among others.

The quartet was a prizewinner in the Liege Competition in 1969, gaining an important measure of international recognition. Three years later, Michael Adamson was replaced by Ronald Birks as second violinist. In 1972, the Lindsays were offered a residency at Sheffield University. Another residency followed at Manchester University in 1979. The first of several tours of the United States and Canada was undertaken in 1981, further enhancing the quartet's reputation. In 1984, the Lindsay Quartet initiated a series of annual festivals at Sheffield University; three years later, they began performing some of these programs in London.

Another change of personnel occurred in 1986 when Bigley left and was replaced by Robin Ireland. Following that, the quartet advanced in balancing the homogeneity needed in small ensemble while giving heed, even celebrating, the uniqueness of each individual player. This reconciling of elements, which might seem to be in opposition, has given the Lindsays much of their collective tang.

The Lindsay Quartet's performances of the Beethoven quartets, the late ones particularly, have represented for many a benchmark by which to measure other contemporary ensembles. The quartet's public performances and recordings of works by Dvořák and Bartók have likewise been hailed as exemplary. For Mozart's quintets, the ensemble has been joined by Patrick Ireland, father of Robin Ireland. Tippett's quartets have been a central part of the Lindsay repertory, the *Quartet No. 5* having been commissioned by them.

Few artists or ensembles have ever enjoyed the closely collaborative relationship with a recording company that marks the Lindsay Quartet's association with ASV. With that company, the quartet has been able to commit to disc those interpretations attaining full ripeness, thus preserving, in nearly every instance, a performance that adds illumination to an important score. This legacy has grown to be one of the most important in the annals of recorded chamber music. *—Erik Eriksson*

Recommended:

- ○ **Brahms & Mendelssohn: String Quartets** / Lindsay SQ / 1990 / ASV 712
- ○ **Beethoven: Quartets Vol. 7** / Lindsay SQ / 2001 / ASV 1117
- ○ **Haydn: Quartets, Op20/2, 5 & 6** / Lindsay SQ / 1999 / ASV 1057
- ○ **Schubert: Quartets 8 & 13** / Lindsay SQ / 1987 / ASV 593
- ○ **Tippett: String Quartets** / Lindsay SQ / 1996 / ASV 231

Dinu Lipatti

b. Mar. 19, 1917, Bucharest, Romania, **d.** Dec. 2, 1950, Geneva, Switzerland

Pianist

Dinu Lipatti is regarded as a legend among twentieth century pianists. Alfred Cortot thought Lipatti's playing "perfection," while Clara Haskil once wrote to him, "How I envy your talent. The devil take it. Why must you have so much talent and I so little? Is this justice on earth?" Was it justice that such a talented musician had such a short life? Both Lipatti's parents were musicians: his father was a violinist who had studied with Sarasate and Flesch, his mother a pianist. They, and Lipatti's godfather Georges Enescu, nurtured his talents early. Lipatti attended the Bucharest Conservatory, working with Floria Musicescu from 1928 to 1932. Cortot was one of the judges at the 1934 Vienna International Piano Competition, where Lipatti was awarded second prize. Cortot, who thought Lipatti should have won first prize, resigned from the jury and took Lipatti to Paris to study with him and his assistant Yvonne Lefébure. Lipatti also studied conducting with Charles Münch and composition with Nadia Boulanger and Paul Dukas. Lipatti recitals and concerts in Paris in the late 1930s secured his reputation as a performer. He was known for his self-discipline and thoroughness, taking years to learn a concerto before performing it in public. Those who heard him play assumed that either he had studied the music with a composer's eye or he instinctively knew how to make whatever he played sound so obviously what the composer intended, whether it was Bach or Schubert or Ravel. He returned to Bucharest in 1939 to spend the war years teaching, composing, and writing criticism. Just before the end of the war, he was diagnosed with a rare form of leukemia. His illness was relieved somewhat by new medicines in 1946, enough for him to make recordings for Columbia at his home in Geneva. He took a post teaching at the Geneva Conservatory in 1949 and also recorded the Schumann *Piano Concerto* with Herbert von Karajan in London. The next year, however, he had to cancel tours of Australia and North and South America and cut back his European performance engagements. Just three months before his death at the age of 33, he gave one last recital in Besançon, fortunately recorded for posterity, his playing still unsurpassed despite his illness. *—Patsy Morita*

Recommended:

- ○ **Lipatti: Chopin; Brahms; Ravel** / Lipatti / EMI 63038
- ○ **Lipatti, 1947** / Galliera (cond.), Lipatti, London PO / Enterprise 300
- ○ **Last Recital** / Lipatti / 1994 / EMI 65166
- ○ **Dinu Lipatti Plays Grieg & Schumann** / Karajan, Galliera (cond.), Lipatti, London PO, Philharmonia / 2001 / Dutton 9719
- ○ **Dinu Lipatti** / Lipatti, etc. / 1998 / Philips 456892
- ○ **Chopin Waltzes** / Lipatti / 2004 / EMI 62820

Eugene List

b. Jul. 6, 1918, Philadelphia, PA, **d.** Mar. 1, 1985, New York, NY
Pianist

A pianist who has reshaped the repertory of the instrument, Eugene List manifested his gifts early and at age 12 had already made his orchestral debut with the Los Angeles Philharmonic. A teacher-imposed hiatus led to a more disciplined approach to his art and thereafter his progress was steady and sustained. His comprehensive musical interests led him to program the works of many composers outside the mainstream, as well as little-known works by already established composers. His devotion to the piano oeuvre of Louis Gottschalk was documented by several recordings.

Born to parents who were Russian émigrés, List lived his childhood in Los Angeles, where his family had moved when he was a year old. At age five, List began piano studies with his mother, later entering the Sutro-Seyler Studios in Los Angeles for more advanced training. His successful debut with the Los Angeles Philharmonic was followed by a family bus trip back to Philadelphia, where the young pianist was entered in a competition for a scholarship to study with Olga Samaroff. List won the competition and was accepted as Samaroff's pupil with the agreement that he would be withdrawn from further public performances until she felt he was ready. Meanwhile, his enrollment at the advanced Philadelphia High School provided an outstanding academic education. During his final year at the school, List entered a Philadelphia Orchestra competition, performing Beethoven and Schumann concertos and winning by unanimous vote. His award included a performance with the orchestra during a December 12, 1934, youth concert, an occasion on which he gave the American premiere of the Shostakovich *Piano Concerto No. 1*. After a summer in Austria devoted to further study with Samaroff, List entered Juilliard's graduate school and on December 19, 1935, made his New York debut with the New York Philharmonic, once more performing the Shostakovich concerto. The reviews were complimentary, but were stronger still for his New York recital debut in January. Praising the comprehensiveness of his art, Samuel Chotzinoff noted his "naturally beautiful" tone and his assured and often brilliant technique. List subsequently toured extensively, appearing with leading orchestras and in recital. He became a popular figure in radio broadcasting and won first prize in the Rising Musical Star series. In 1942, he played the United States premiere of Carlos Chávez's piano concerto with the New York Philharmonic directed by Dimitri Mitropoulos. The same year, he entered the Special Services Division of the United States Army. During his tour of duty, he was called upon to perform at the postwar Potsdam conference when Harry Truman served as his page turner. Upon discharge from the Army in 1946, List toured seven European countries and, together with his wife, violinist Carroll Glenn, made tours of the occupied countries under United States Army auspices. The couple helped organize the American Music Center in Berlin, a project created to foster better relations through music.

An advocate for many non-repertory works, List became an especially eloquent proponent of the music of Edward MacDowell and Louis Gottschalk; for the latter composer, he performed, collated, and recorded works (some very obscure), leading a Gottschalk revival. List was also a compelling performer of the grand Romantic-age works and the music of George Gershwin. In addition to his performing career, List edited the complete works of Stephen Foster and taught at both the Eastman School of Music and New York University. *—Erik Eriksson*

Recommended:

- ○ **Gottschalk: Piano Music** / Abravanel (cond.), List, Utah SO / 1993 / Vanguard 91447
- ○ **Gershwin: Rhapsody in Blue; An American in Paris** / Kunzel (cond.), List, Cincinnati SO / 1981 / Telarc 80058

Franz Liszt

b. Oct. 22, 1811, Raiding, Hungary, **d.** Jul. 31, 1886, Bayreuth, Germany
Composer: Keyboard, Concerto, Orchestral, Symphonic, Vocal, Choral, Chamber Music

Liszt was the only contemporary whose music Richard Wagner gratefully acknowledged as an influence upon his own. His lasting fame was an alchemy of extraordinary digital ability—the greatest in the history of keyboard playing—an unmatched instinct for showmanship, and one of the most progressive musical imaginations of his time. Hailed by some as a visionary, reviled by others as a symbol of empty Romantic excess, Franz Liszt wrote his name across music history in a truly inimitable manner.

From his youth, Liszt demonstrated a natural facility at the keyboard that placed him among the top performing prodigies of his day. Though contemporary accounts describe his improvisational skill as dazzling, his talent as a composer emerged only in his adulthood. Still, he was at the age of eleven the youngest contributor to publisher Anton Diabelli's famous variation commissioning project, best remembered as the inspiration for Beethoven's final piano masterpiece. An oft-repeated anecdote—first recounted by Liszt himself decades later, and possibly fanciful—has Beethoven attending a recital given by the youngster and bestowing a kiss of benediction upon him.

Though already a veteran of the stage by his teens, Liszt recognized the necessity of further musical tuition. He studied for a time with Czerny and Salieri in Vienna, and later sought acceptance to the Paris Conservatory. When he was turned down there—foreigners were not then admitted—he instead studied privately with Anton Reicha. Ultimately, his Hungarian origins proved a great asset to his career, enhancing his aura of mystery and exoticism and inspiring an extensive body of works, none more famous than the *Hungarian Rhapsodies* (1846–85).

Liszt soon became a prominent figure in Parisian society, his romantic entanglements providing much material for gossip. Still, not even the juiciest accounts of his amorous exploits could compete with the stories about his wizardry at the keyboard. Inspired by the superhuman technique—and, indeed, diabolical stage presence—of the violinist Paganini, Liszt set out to translate these qualities to the piano. As his career as a touring performer, conductor, and teacher burgeoned, he began to devote an increasing amount of time to composition. He wrote most of his hundreds of original piano works for his own use; accordingly, they are frequently characterized by technical demands that push performers—and in Liszt's own day, the instrument itself—to their limits. The "transcendence" of his *Transcendental Etudes* (1851), for example, is not a reference to the writings of Emerson and Thoreau, but an indication of the works' level of difficulty. Liszt was well into his thirties before he mastered the rudiments of orchestration—works like the *Piano Concerto No. 1* (1849) were orchestrated by talented students—but made up for lost time in the production of two "literary" symphonies (*Faust*, 1854–57, and *Dante*, 1855–56) and a series of orchestral essays (including *Les préludes*, 1848–54) that marks the genesis of the tone poem as a distinct genre.

After a lifetime of near-constant sensation, Liszt settled down somewhat in his later years. In his final decade he joined the Catholic Church and devoted much of his creative effort to the production of sacred works. The complexion of his music darkened; the flash that had characterized his previous efforts gave way to a peculiar introspection, manifested in strikingly original, forward-looking efforts like *Nuages gris* (1881). Liszt died in Bayreuth, Germany, on July 31, 1886, having outlived Wagner, his son-in-law and greatest creative beneficiary. *—Michael Rodman*

KEYBOARD

Album d'un voyageur, for piano, S. 156 (1834–1836; revised 1840)

Album d'un voyageur consists of three sections. The first, *Impressions and Poems*, is comprised of seven pieces, the middle five of which were revised and incorporated into the trilogy, *Années de Pèlerinage*. The First Year, "Suisse," S. 160, represents impressions of his travels in the period 1835–39 with his lover, Marie d'Agoult. The second section, *Flowers of Melody from the Alps*, consists of nine untitled pieces, the second and third of which were also reworked for use in the *"Suisse" Années*. The final section is comprised of three paraphrases.

Many of the pieces in the first section are preceded by quotations from Byron's *Childe Harold*. The first item, "Lyon," is dedicated to the philosopher Lamennais, who led a group of insurgent weavers in nineteenth century Lyon. A heroic march represents the struggle for social justice for the oppressed workers. The music is by turns rousing, violent, and passionate. "Le Lac de Wallenstadt" (The Lake of Wallenstadt) is a tranquil work that depicts the peaceful, bucolic scene of the lake, with the soothing rustling of its waves and its peaceful surroundings. "Au bord d'une source" (Beside a spring) offers a pastoral setting again, however, the tempo is livelier, but still unhurried. "Les cloches de Genève" (The bells of Geneva) may have less to do with the sound of bells than with the birth of Liszt's daughter Blandine, with its Romantic theme and brilliant writing. "La Valée d'Obermann" (The Valley of Obermann) is a deeper work and was inspired by the character from the 1804 novel of the same name by Etiene Jeane Senancour. Obermann wanders the country disconsolate over his misfortunes. The music depicts his depressed state of mind at the outset, but grows hopeful and promising as the work progresses. The "Chapelle de Guillaume Tell" (The Chapel of William Tell) tells of the famous Swiss hero. A hymnlike melody at the outset grows intense, but the music then turns triumphant and glorious. The exultant mood subsides, but the piece still ends in a positive vein. "Psaume," the last item in the first set, is a fairly literal arrangement of Psalm 42, from the setting of Louis Bourgeois (1510–61).

The nine short pieces comprising the second section are less significant, though the aforementioned *"Suisse"* items, "Le mal du pays" (roughly translated as "homesickness" or "depression") and "Pastorale," are important works. The former effectively depicts gloomy and unhappy feelings; the latter is devoted to bucolic moods. The fifth and eighth items here are based on melodies by Ferdinand Huber, and the remainder on Swiss folk material.

The first piece in the last set, "Ranz de Vaches," is based on a Swiss melody (as arranged by Huber), typically played by an Alphorn. The second item, "Une soir dans les montagnes," is another work dealing with pastoral subjects, the middle section featuring a powerful thunderstorm. The main theme is based on a melody by publisher Ernst Knop. The last piece, "Ranz des chèvres," is also based on a theme by Huber. *—Robert Cummings*

Recommended:

- ○ **Liszt: Album d'un voyageur** / Howard / Hyperion 66601

Bagatelle sans tonalité, for piano, S. 216a (1885)

In the mid-twentieth century, Liszt's piano music was unfairly viewed by many as generally flashy and virtuosic, often saccharine in its Romantic demeanor and only rarely of harmonic, rhythmic, or melodic interest. When his neglected and previously unpublished late works finally began appearing, and when musicologists also started to reevaluate his middle-period output, his artistic worth was not only upgraded, but his influence on succeeding generations of composers was finally recognized.

Bagatelle sans tonalité is one of the first pieces to explore atonality and probably the first by a major composer. It clearly anticipates Schoenberg and the Second Vienna School, as well as other modernist movements. The piece humorously begins as the music seems to playfully hesitate, almost awkwardly, in mapping out its course, a sense of mischief seeming to hover above the proceedings. The mood remains amusing throughout, subtly so even when the music threatens to turn serious as it builds up with a rising series of chords. In the end, the impression left is one of colorful, playful music clothed in odd-ball writing where notes stumble and caress by turns. For all this charming three-minute work's supposed modernism, first-time listeners unaware of the *Bagatelle's* title will likely not notice its atonality. *—Robert Cummings*

Recommended:

○ **Alfred Brendel 3** / Brendel / 1999 / Philips 456733

○ **Alfred Brendel plays Liszt** / Brendel / Vox 5172

Ballade for piano No. 2 in B minor, S. 171 (1853)

Though the composer provided no subtitle, this work's inspiration was Bürger's poetic ballad *Lenore*. In the *Second Ballade* Liszt surpasses the music of his *First*, his only other work in the genre. The earlier piece is fairly direct and uncomplicated, with a lovely main theme and an attractive march-like second subject. Without doubt, it is worthy of greater attention on the recital stages and may be a more compelling work to some ears than its sibling. The B minor, however, is considerably more substantial—at about 15 minutes it is twice the length of the first ballade, and its formal design and scope are conceived on a far grander scale. It is also the more popular of the two ballades, many pianists having taken up the work in the latter part of the twentieth century.

An ominous theme in the lower register opens the work, at once setting the groundwork for that menacing dark music so typical of the composer throughout his career. It's as if some grand evil is lurking around the corner. A lovely second subject is soon heard, marked allegretto and making for a contrast that could hardly be more diametrical. Both themes are heard again before there is any development.

In the middle section the music turns militaristic and brilliant. Here there are virtuosic fireworks and titanic struggles, suggesting a good-versus-evil scenario. Themes are transformed brilliantly afterward, especially near the close, as a glorious, almost operatic-sounding melody is presented; it turns out to be a variant of the grim opening idea. The piece ends softly, with echoes of the alternate theme resonating in a gentle soothing sound. Liszt had originally written a bigger, more bombastic ending, but changed it before publication (1854). He dedicated the piece to Count Karl von Leiningen. *—Robert Cummings*

Recommended:

○ **Vladimir Horowitz 2** / Horowitz / 1999 / Philips 456844

○ **Horowitz at the Met** / Horowitz / 1992 / RCA 63314

Consolations, for piano, S. 172 (1849–1850)

Liszt's six *Consolations* date from 1849–50, near the beginning of the most productive period in the composer/pianist/conductor's career. Inspired by a set of poems of the same name by historian Joseph Delorme (under the pseudonym Charles Sainte-Beuve), these diminutive compositions convey a mood of unfulfilled hope. As is evident from the sequence of keys and moods, the *Consolations* were conceived and are best played as a single entity, though they are frequently performed individually on recital programs.

The first *Consolation*, Andante con moto, serves as an introductory meditation and establishes the predominant E major tonality of the entire group. It ends on an incomplete measure that segues directly to the first bar of the second piece.

The second *Consolation*, Un poco più mosso, is a lilting work that recalls the composer's many song transcriptions. The primary melody is presented in four different ways, each accompanied in a different fashion, increasing the impression of harmonic complexity. To achieve this effect, Liszt uses one of his favorite keyboard devices, dividing the melody between the hands.

The third *Consolation*, Lento placido, was inspired by the nocturnes of Chopin and has long enjoyed the greatest popularity of the pieces in the set. It features a right-hand cantilena over a broken-chord accompaniment in the bass line, lending the whole a flowing, lyrical texture. The lovely melody, simple and elegant, is often expressed in soaring open octaves in the treble. A one-measure cadenza provides additional interest at the close of this charming piece.

The highly chordal texture of the fourth *Consolation* is almost hymnlike in the impression it makes. Based on a theme supplied by the Grand Duchess Maria Pavlovna of Russia, the slow and sustained melody has a purposely ambiguous meter that adds to the contemplative mood.

The fifth *Consolation* was once circulated by an English publisher under the title "Eugenie," with no reference to Liszt's own designation, Andantino. This piece effects a return to the key of E major in preparation for the collection's conclusion. The continuously singing melody is distinctly vocal, while Liszt's use of parallel thirds and sixths suggests the influence of Mendelssohn. The simple statement of the theme and a brief but lyrical coda make this one of Liszt's most ingratiating piano works.

The last and longest of the *Consolations*, marked Allegretto, departs, at least temporarily, from the mood of the other five pieces. The wide-ranging melodic line is supported by a flowing bass accompaniment. Though the piece is uplifting for most of its length, the 16-bar coda recalls the somber yet gently consoling quality present in the previous *Consolations*. The final two bars return to the 4/4 meter of the first *Consolation*, and the cycle thus comes full circle. *—Corie Stanton Root*

Recommended:

○ **Liszt: Piano Works** / Bolet / Decca 467801

○ **Liszt: Sonatas; Elégies; Consolations; etc.** / Howard / 1991 / Hyperion 66429

En rêve, nocturne for piano, S. 207 (1885)

Liszt's brief piano composition *En rêve* (Dreaming) was written in 1885. Composed in the last period of his life, it is a work of great beauty despite its modest proportions, and shows Liszt's compositional style in its most polished and mature form. While much of Liszt's later work is mournful in character, this piece has an uplifting quality and lyrical sense of line. True to its title, the piece has a dreamlike quality expressed in a lilting melody and supported by a flowing, broken-chord accompaniment in the left hand. As with several other late Liszt pieces, the harmonic structure of this work foreshadows the tonal experiments of the twentieth century, but its mood is reflectively peaceful. The lovingly placed embellishments in the melodic line add an ethereal sense to this charming and personal work. Less than two minutes in length, this piece is a diminutive gem. *—Corie Stanton Root*

Recommended:

○ **Art Of Alfred Brendel Vol. 4** / Brendel / 1996 / Philips 446924

○ **Liszt: Sonata in B minor; Paganini Etudes; etc.** / Watts / 2001 / Seraphim 74504

Études d'exécution transcendante (Transcendental Etudes), for piano, S. 139 (1851)

The date of composition of this collection might arguably stretch back to 1826, when the 15-year-old Liszt fashioned a collection of piano pieces called *Étude en douze exercices*. He intended to expand the dozen to 48; however, he reworked them into the 1838 version of the *Transcendental Etudes*. During the period 1851–52, Liszt revised the 12 pieces once more, now known as *Études d'exécution transcendante*. The 1838 and 1852 sets are quite similar, the former not necessarily appreciably more difficult than the latter.

The first etude, "Preludio," is brief, typically Lisztian and serves the purpose of a prelude or introduction in the sense that it is a sort of warming-up exercise for the performer. The second, in A minor, marked Molto vivace, carries no subtitle. It is a stormy and brilliant piece, anxious one moment, uplifting the next, but muscular in its fleetness.

"Paysage" (Landscape) is a serene, lovely piece, whose repetitive theme appears in a descending pattern. It builds up and reaches an ecstatic climax in the latter half. This is the least difficult of the 12 etudes. In contrast, the fourth, "Mazeppa," inspired by Victor Hugo's 1828 poem, *Les Orientales*, offers formidable challenges to the performer. After angering the husband of a Polish noblewoman, Mazeppa is tied to a wild horse and dragged all the way to Ukraine. He is released, eventually to lead a Cossack uprising. This etude is manic at the outset, featuring a colorful theme, part-march, part-gallop. Liszt subjects it to a brilliant series of variations.

The fifth etude, "Feux Follets" (Will-o'-the-wisps), is a delicate, fleet piece of playful, wayward character that tests the performer's technique not just in terms of speed, but in dynamics and nuances of coloration. The next entry, "Vision," is somber but ominous in its arpeggiations and tremolo effects. Is it the *Dies Irae* theme that Liszt alludes to throughout? Perhaps—Busoni claimed it depicted Napoleon's funeral. "Eroica" shares the same key as Beethoven's *Eroica Symphony No. 3*, but its theme is not so much heroic as it is dignified and noble.

"Wilde Jagd" (Wild Hunt) is aptly named, as the mood of this dramatic piece, marked presto furioso, lives up to its title by changing from savage to subtle, from furious to furtive, all to brilliantly portray a hunting scene, as typified in the music of German Romantics going back to Weber. "Ricordanza" (Remembrance) is a lovely piece whose focus is nostalgia. It features a beautiful Andantino theme, described by Busoni as evoking the image of a person perusing cherished old love letters.

The tenth etude, unnamed and marked Allegro agitato molto, begins with notes rapidly cascading downward, but it quickly begins a passionate, anxious theme. The music is mostly restless and becomes furious at the end. "Harmonies du soir" (Evening Harmonies) features a beautiful melody that evokes a blossoming of strong passions. The final entry, "Chasse-neige" (Snowstorm) depicts deepening snow. The music is, however, more tempestuous than a snowstorm would usually suggest.—*Robert Cummings*

Recommended:

- ○ **Liszt: Complete Sonatas** / Arrau / 1997 / Philips 456339
- ○ **Liszt: Piano Works** / Bolet / Decca 467801
- ○ **Sviatoslav Richter à Prague** / Richter / Praga 356020-34
- ○ **Liszt: Transcendental Studies** / Howard / 1989 / Hyperion 66357

Etudes d'exécution transcendante d'après Paganini, for piano, S. 140 (1838–1840)

This is the early version of the better known *Grand Etudes of Paganini,* S. 141 of 1851. These six Études are actually transcriptions of six of Paganini's *Caprices* for violin solo. In the early nineteenth century, the Italian violinist Paganini made an incredible impression throughout Europe by raising violin technique to a level deemed impossible by all prior standards. The *Caprices* were Paganini's written compendium of his technical accomplishments. Liszt set himself the goal of accomplishing a similar task for the piano, and appropriately used Paganini as his compositional impetus. Unlike the *Twelve Etudes* Op. 6, though, this is no student work, but Liszt's own compendium of his innovations in piano technique. Although he followed the musical form of the caprices exactly, Liszt expanded the texture to orchestral dimensions. Beginning where Chopin left off in his *Etudes* Op. 10 and Op. 25, Liszt raised piano virtuosity to levels previously unimagined. The result was a unique and brilliant style attainable only by the greatest virtuosos. This earlier version of the Paganini *Etudes* was probably unplayable by anyone but Liszt at the time of its composition, and remains only rarely attempted today. The later, revised version (S. 141) is technically easier, and thus generally more effective in performance, and is therefore the version usually heard. Regardless, it is this early version that established Liszt as the preeminent piano virtuoso of his time and revolutionized piano composition forever. —*Steven Coburn*

Recommended:

- ○ **Liszt: Complete Sonatas** / Arrau / 1997 / Philips 456339
- ○ **Jorge Bolet 2** / Bolet / 1999 / Philips 456814
- ○ **First Russian Recordings (1934–1938) Of Emil Gilels** / Gilels / The Piano Library 235
- ○ **Liszt: Complete Paganini Etudes** / Howard / 1998 / Hyperion 67193

Fantasie & Fugue über den Choral "Ad nos, ad salutarem undam", for organ, S. 259 (1850)

The fourth in a series of "illustrations" based on Giacomo Meyerbeer's *Le prophète* (1849), Liszt's *Fantasy and Fugue "Ad nos, ad salutarem undam"* for organ is a massive work requiring the better part of three-quarters of an hour to perform. The *Fantasy and Fugue* is neither a direct transcription of music from the opera nor an operatic fantasia or paraphrase in the usual sense of the word; rather, it is a wholly independent composition based on a brief chorale melody used in Meyerbeer's work.

The *Fantasy and Fugue* falls into three large sections that collectively form a kind of ambiguous, large-scale sonata design in C minor. The harmonic language is marked by a high density and chromaticism that clearly pave the way to the masterful *Piano Sonata in B minor* (1854) and the *Prelude and Fugue "B.A.C.H."* (1855). Liszt uses diminished seventh chords and augmented triads with particular abundance.

The work unfolds in a process of virtually nonstop development after the initial statement of the chorale melody. Appropriately, Liszt alters Meyerbeer's theme so as to produce a number of melodic tritones, which are harmonically "composed out" as the piece progresses by means of the aforementioned diminished and augmented chords, as well as through transitional passages based on the whole-tone scale. The first of the sections is a colorful fantasia, agitated and harmonically restless. A marziale section in A flat major, based on the second phrase of the chorale melody, offers a brief respite from the incessant modulations of the opening, though it, too, is soon diverted to a number of secondary keys. The harmonic dissolution which ends the opening section is followed by a lengthy Adagio in F sharp major, which offers several expressive variations on the chorale theme. The whole-tone passages that link the variations are an extraordinary innovation for 1850, and one can clearly see the degree to which Liszt's music influenced the experiments of Debussy and Scriabin a few decades later.

An exciting flurry of activity, requiring some deft footwork from the organist, follows, after which the Fugue begins. In typical Lisztian fashion, the Fugue has little to do with traditional academic voice leading, though the imitations and stretto passages are quite cleverly constructed. The Fugue leads directly into a reprise of the marziale music, and the work comes to an end with a glorious rendition of the chorale melody in C major.

Shortly after the work's composition, Liszt also produced a version for piano solo (S. 624). —*Blair Johnston*

Recommended:

- ○ **Liszt Organ Music** / Fagius / 1992 / Bis 170

Grand Galop chromatique, for piano, S. 219 (1837; revised 1886)

This attractive dance work is usually programmed as a dazzling showpiece on disc or as an encore in the concert hall, and while it is the kind of fare that helped stereotype Liszt as the Romantic school's chief exponent of virtuoso piano music, it is a well-crafted, worthwhile piece. It is light and jovial, in no way pretentious, and conveys a festive sense amid much colorful and difficult writing for the piano. The work begins with a lively fanfare-like announcement, quite the same as that which opens Chopin's *Valse Brilliante.* The energetic main theme follows—an amusing, busy creation that playfully rises into the upper register—then yields a second subject whose emphatic chords at the outset serve to underscore the fun and celebration. The thematic material deftly takes on different guises without breaking the merriment and then later on, the second subject turns utterly rollicking. The ending is pure Lisztian virtuosity, but in its showmanship still manages to capture the ear as notes fly, fingers and wrists blur, and tempos turn manic. The piece lasts about four minutes and will appeal to those who have a special fondness for Liszt's operatic transcriptions and paraphrases. —*Robert Cummings*

Recommended:

- ○ **Liszt: Piano Works** / Bolet / Decca 467801
- ○ **Liszt: Dances & Marches** / Howard / 1994 / Hyperion 66811/2

Hungarian Rhapsodies, for piano, S. 244 (1846–1885)

According to Charles Rosen, the *Hungarian Rhapsodies* represent "the least respectable side of Liszt." Their charm lies not in their musical invention, but in their dazzling expansion of the range of expression possible on the piano, or, as Rosen puts it, "the various noises that can be made with a piano."

When Liszt visited Hungary in 1839, he had been away from the country for 13 years. This visit, plus another in 1840, prompted the production of ten volumes of piano pieces between 1840 and 1847 based on Hungarian themes. In 1851–53, Liszt published 15 of these works as the *Hungarian Rhapsodies,* composing and publishing four more in 1882–86.

While in Hungary, Liszt transcribed numerous melodies performed by indigenous gypsy bands. By using these "ancient" melodies in his *Hungarian Rhapsodies,* Liszt saw himself as immortalizing the Hungarian race. Actually, many of the tunes Liszt rhapsodized were written by contemporary Hungarian composers and had become popular outside the cities. Like most tourists, Liszt didn't care. He also didn't care that the blatantly flashy, non-musical piano passages in all of the *Rhapsodies* prompted the contempt of Schumann and Chopin.

The large-scale organization of Liszt's *Hungarian Rhapsodies* derives from the multi-sectional nineteenth century *verbunkos.* The *Verbunkos* is a Hungarian dance style derived from the method of recruiting troops in Hungary in the eighteenth century. It features at least two contrasting sections: the slow *lassu,* or *lassan,* and the fast *friss,* or *friska.* Liszt varies the number and order of these in the various *Rhapsodies,* in some cases linking the sections, in others, creating a stream of unrelated ideas in the traditional fashion of a rhapsody.

In the second of Liszt's *Rhapsodies,* we hear one *lassu* followed by one lengthy *friss,* all prefaced by a brief introduction. Typically, the sudden changes of material interrupt what would otherwise be a constant race to the end. While the *lassu* maintains the opening key of C sharp minor until its very close, the *friss* is generally in the major mode, closing on F sharp major.

Liszt's approach to the *lassu/friss* structure is somewhat different in Rhapsody No. 13, in A minor. In the opening *lassu,* he puts two motives from the second melody through developmental treatment. This leads to a climax, a concept far removed from the gypsy style of music performance. Liszt makes conspicuous use of one Hungarian scale, with a raised fourth degree, while other Hungarian scales appear in Nos. 16 and 17, both beginning in minor keys.

Western art music also permeates Rhapsody No. 14, in F minor. The piece begins with a somber melody with a distinctive rhythmic pattern. In the *friss,* the same tune and rhythm appear in thick chords, smoothing over the sudden changes that are typical of the traditional *verbunkos.*

The eleventh Rhapsody adheres more closely to the "gypsy style." Opening with a lento a capriccio, the piece gradually accelerates through three sections, the first of which is a typical *verbunkos,* the next two evoking the style of the Hungarian *csárdás.* —*John Palmer*

Recommended:

- ○ **Liszt: Hungarian Rhapsodies** / Cziffra / 1976 / EMI 56228

Deux Légendes, for piano, S.175 (1863)

Liszt composed both of these *Légendes* in 1863; they appeared simultaneously in Budapest and France in 1866.The two *Légendes* are entitled "St. François d'Assise: La Prédication aux oiseaux" (St. Francis of Assisi preaching to the birds) and "St. François de Paule marchant sur les flots" (St. Francis of Paola walking on the waters). Both, as the titles suggest, are descriptive of events said to have occurred in the lives of the two saints.

In the first Légende, St. Francis stops along his travels at the sight of a large gathering of birds, deciding to deliver a sermon to them. As he begins preaching, they surround him, coming down from trees, and all remain near him until he finishes and blesses them. Liszt brilliantly incarnates this scene on the piano, offering yet another example of a sort of rudimentary or early Impressionism. He would come even closer to foreshadowing Debussy with "Les jeux d'eaux à la Villa d'Este" (The Fountains of the Villa d'Este) from the Third Year of the *Années de Pèlerinage.*

The music in the first Légende begins in the upper register with shimming and fluttering sounds, along with little chirps, that vividly depict the presence and activities of birds. An ethereal melody represents them, while the sermon is given sublime music. Save for one grandiose outburst near the end, the piece remains calm and peaceful throughout, ending with the twittering sounds of birds heard at the opening.

The second Légende deals with St. Francis of Paola, who, lacking the fee to board a ferry to cross the Straits of Messina, uses his cloak and staff as a makeshift sailing apparatus. He then stands on his garment and guides it with his staff, crossing the waters and arriving ahead of the boat and its astonished passengers. Liszt depicts St. Francis with a glorious theme, underpinned by rippling harmonies that represent unruly waters. As the impoverished saint begins crossing, the music becomes tense, the rippling sounds turning gradually into hostile harmonies that threaten to sink him. St. Francis seems to teeter on the brink of disaster as he struggles to stay afloat, the waters tossing him about as if incited by a violent storm. But his strong faith saves him, and the glorious theme rings out as he reaches the other side. The ending is serene and glorious, with not the slightest trace of bombast. Again, as in the previous piece, the music is brilliantly descriptive, but much more dramatically so here. This is Liszt at his finest. *—Robert Cummings*

Recommended:

- ○ **Liszt: Légendes; Trauer-Gondel; etc.** / Brendel / Philips 410040
- ○ **Liszt: Sonata; Legends; Scherzo & March** / Demidenko / 1992 / Hyperion 66616

Liebestraum, 3 notturnos for piano, S. 541 (1843–1850)

Franz Liszt loved crafting solo piano transcriptions of lieder and other kinds of voice/piano songs (but, then again, he loved making solo piano transcriptions of just about anything), and he didn't limit himself to just the standard catalog of Schubert favorites; often he took his own songs to the re-arranging room. The three *Liebesträume* for piano, S. 541, the third of which is the famous *Liebesträum* that seems to be on every pianist's encore list and every romantic piano music CD sampler, are such items—they and their song equivalents were in fact published simultaneously in 1850. Liszt's songs, including these, are unjustly neglected, but the *Liebesträume*—or one of them, anyway—never have been.

The three *Liebesträume,* which Liszt also called notturnos (nocturnes, in English), are based on the following three songs: 1. "Höhe Liebe," S. 307, to a text by Johann Ludwig Uhland and probably composed in 1849, 2. "Gestorben war ich," S. 308, likewise Uhland and 1849, 3. "O Lieb, so lang du lieben kannst," S. 298, with a text by Ferdinand Freiligrath and first sketched by Liszt nearly six years before the other two.

In the piano versions, as in his other piano transcriptions, Liszt moves in and out of the original musical text as he feels need to—here is a passage virtually identical to the parallel one in the lied, but over there is a far more soloistic episode that would seem altogether out of place in a song. A handful of mini-cadenzas (of the type, not coincidentally, found in Chopin's nocturnes) pop up in each *Liebestraum,* usually to bridge one section of music to another.

Two of the S. 541 pieces, No. 1 and No. 3, are in the warm, ingratiating key of A flat major, a favorite tonal location of nocturne composers. No. 2 is set in E major. All are sewn from the smoothest melodic silk and the kind of rich, semi-chromatic harmonies so beloved of middle-Romantic composers. But it isn't hard to see, or rather hear, why No. 3 is universally known and the other two are only infrequently heard. Its gently-arcing six-bar phrases and throbbing repeated notes, and that glowing, completely unexpected modulation to B major after the opening paragraph of music, make it a miniature masterpiece. *—Blair Johnston*

Recommended:

- ○ **Liszt: Piano Works** / Bolet / Decca 467801
- ○ **Chopin & Liszt** / Stott / 1995 / Conifer 51753
- ○ **Liszt: Liebesträume & Other Song Transcriptions** / Howard / 1992 / Hyperion 66593

Mephisto Waltzes, for piano (1856–1885)

Franz Liszt's intense devotion to the Christian faith was perhaps the cause (or more appropriately, the foil) for his preoccupation with the legend of Faust, and the character of Mephistopheles in particular. Perhaps this is because his boyhood idol, the great violin virtuoso Nicolò Paganini, was popularly rumored to be in league with the devil. Motivations aside, "Mephisto" provided Liszt with a great deal of musical inspiration. In all, he composed four *Mephisto Waltzes* (the fourth of which he left incomplete), as well as a *Mephisto Polka.*

The first *Mephisto Waltz* is actually the second of *Two Episodes from Lenau's "Faust",* S. 110 (1861), titled "The Dance at the Village Inn." It is by far the most familiar of the four waltzes, and is popular in two contemporaneous versions by Liszt, one for orchestra, one for piano. Striking and well-crafted, it is noteworthy not only for its own dramatic impact, but also for its advanced chromatic idiom, which would so decisively influence composers like Richard Wagner.

The second waltz dates from 1881, during a period in which the composer developed an increasingly experimental language, including innovations that prefigured by decades similar elements in the music of Debussy and Bartók. Though this waltz is by no means one of the more "advanced" of Liszt's late works, it is demonstrably more adventurous than the first *Mephisto Waltz.* The composer loved to provide surprise endings, and does so here: as the waltz nears its conclusion, the music builds to a violent whirlwind of activity in the key of E flat major, only to change course without warning and land upon onto the notes F and B, the "strange" interval of a tritone which for centuries was designated "the devil in music."

Though less popular than the first two, the third waltz (1883) is no less masterful. It was originally conceived for the piano, and indeed, no other instrument could provide the sheer percussive violence which is so integral to the work. Cast in a key with six sharps—perhaps just to make it seem more demonic!—the waltz opens with a five-measure phrase, one of the most extraordinary passages in tonal music to that point: the tetrachord C sharp—E sharp—A sharp—D sharp is hammered out in fortissimo arpeggiated figures, only to immediately stall on a sustained D sharp, after which the real motion of the piece begins. Unlike the first waltz, which has a syncopated, seductively lyrical middle section, the third waltz offers the listener little respite from its unrelenting fury, demonstrating Liszt's demonic sense at its most potent.

The work that Liszt had planned on recasting into the fourth waltz, *Bagatelle sans tonalité* (Atonal Bagatelle), dates from 1885, the year before his death. Evidence suggests that Liszt intended to provide a central section of completely different character and content, so the work in its extant form, first published in 1956, cannot be considered definitive. *—AMG*

Recommended:

- ○ **Liszt: Favourite Piano Works** / Bolet / 1995 / London 444851
- ○ **Liszt Waltzes** / Howard / 1986 / Hyperion 66201

Nuages gris (Trübe Wolken), for piano, S. 199 (1881)

Franz Liszt's short, two-page piano piece *Nuages gris* (Grey Clouds) is, among certain circles, a very famous piece of music. Outside those circles, which are inhabited mostly by musicologists and theorists fascinated by the amazing modernity of Liszt's late music, it is essentially unknown. One rarely hears it played, and the reason for its obscurity on the one hand is probably the same as the reason for its limited fame on the other: it is, for 1881, a bizarre piece of music, and audiences today are as baffled by it as audiences in the 1880s would have been had they ever gotten a chance to hear it (they did not—Liszt was writing for himself in the 1880s, and himself alone). When Liszt's late music started trickling out of publishing houses during the early twentieth century, many musicians were simply amazed by how progressive the aged Liszt had been. Throwing traditional laws of harmony and voice-leading to the wind, he created in pieces like *Nuages gris* music that is bitingly dissonant, and, perhaps even more striking, utterly "non-Lisztian" in texture.

Nuages gris bears a two-flat key signature, and it is in fact in G minor. But this is not a functional G minor as those in the nineteenth century would have understood it—the music unfolds in multiple simultaneous layers (one at the very start, two for most of the piece, and three during the last several bars), each of which seems to care not one whit what the others are doing. A two-bar mini-theme is played twice by the right hand at the beginning; it is then played twice more as a tremolo in the bass register and rises up like a gust of soggy air. Soon, the tremolo takes the form of a repeating oscillation between pitches B flat and A natural, above which the right hand plays a series of descending augmented chords that often clash harshly with the underlying tremolo. Later on, the initial two-bar theme is taken over by the left hand as the right hand offers a thin countermelody.

The most startling music, however, is that at the end. The B flat/A natural oscillation returns (now no longer in tremolo form) in the left hand, which also plays a new form of the augmented chord idea heard earlier; the right hand plays a line that slowly rises up, chromatically one half-step at a time, until finally reaching a pair of complex seven-note chords that have nothing whatever to do with G minor (or, from a traditional view, any other key), but nevertheless are its closing cadence—if you can call it that. The tempo of *Nuages gris,* Andante, may be relaxed, but not much else in it is. *—Blair Johnston*

Recommended:

- ○ **Chopin, Liszt** / Richter / 1994 / Philips 438620
- ○ **Early Recordings Vol. 2** / Fiorentino / 1999 / APR 5582

Paganini Etudes, for piano ("Grandes Etudes de Paganini"), S. 141 (1851)

Liszt assembled the first version of this set of six pieces in 1838 when he composed five works based on Paganini's *24 Caprices for solo violin,* Op. 1. He added a sixth, the so-called *Grand fantasia de bravura sur la clochette* (1831–32), after being inspired by Paganini's concert appearances in Paris in 1831. This piece was placed third in the collection and given the nickname "La Campanella." It is based on the last movement of Paganini's Op. 7 *Violin Concerto, in B minor.*

In 1851 Liszt reworked the six pieces and designated them the *Grandes études de Paganini*. Because of its popularity and grandstanding potential, it brought Liszt both fame and scorn. It was music like this that had damaged the reputation of Liszt as a composer, yet he never intended it to be anything more than light, entertaining music that would dazzle audiences owing to its great difficulty. Liszt dedicated this collection to the virtuoso pianist and composer, Clara Wieck Schumann, wife of Robert Schumann.

The first item, *Preludio et Etude*, features many scales, arpeggios, and tremolos to showcase the colors of the various performance techniques. For all its obvious virtuosic demands, the piece does have thematic charm. The next item, *La Capriciosa*, is based on Paganini's *Caprice No. 17* and features all manner of pyrotechnics, including cadenza-like writing, with octave passages and scales in tenths played with hands crossed. The theme is a sort of nonchalant, simple one, delivered by jaunty chords, whose regular pauses are filled in with a healthy dose of acrobatics.

La Campanella (The Little Bell) is the third item here and probably the most popular of the six. In the 1838 version, it was written in A flat minor, but Liszt enharmonically respelled it to G sharp minor. Its busy theme, enmeshed in nearly continual filigree and devilish difficulties, has a charm in its fantasy-like atmosphere and bell-like sonorities. Liszt demands much subtlety in the dynamics to capture the delicacy and color of the source music. The fourth, in E major, is a study in arpeggios that also features many trills. Delicacy and nuance of dynamics, in fact, are also key elements in bringing this piece off effectively. The next, *La Chasse* (The Hunt), is based on Paganini's *Caprice No. 9* and quite vividly paints the picture its title suggests, replete with horn calls and a sense of adventure in its joyful theme. The sixth, in A minor, features the famous melody found in the *Caprice No. 24* that Rachmaninov used in his popular work for piano and orchestra, *Rhapsody on a Theme of Paganini*, and Brahms used in his *Variations on a Theme of Paganini* for piano. Here Liszt presents the theme, then offers some variations to display additional pianistic challenges. It must be said that his variations are not particularly distinctive, even as light music. Still, there is no short supply of color and Lisztian flair here. *—Robert Cummings*

Recommended:

- ○ **Liszt: Paganini Studies; Schubert March Transcriptions** / Hamelin / 2002 / Hyperion 67370
- ○ **Russian Piano School** / Merzhanov / 1995 / Russian Compact Disc 16209
- ○ **Liszt: Complete Paganini Etudes** / Howard / 1998 / Hyperion 67193

Piano Sonata in B minor, S. 178 (1851–1853)

There are only three works in Liszt's vast output which are entitled as belonging to any sonata form: the *Faust Symphony*, the *Dante Symphony*, and the *Sonata in B minor for piano*. It will readily be seen that this is the only work he wrote in an absolute sonata form.

However, he made the sonata form his own in this innovative and unique work in one movement. Wagner described the work as beautiful "beyond all conception" and "sublime." In it, Liszt presents what is considered by most commentators as his finest example of the musical technique of continuous "thematic transformation," which was to have a profound effect on the future of music—especially as taken up by Wagner and used as the basic musical means by which he constructed all his later operas, especially the great *Ring of the Nibelung* tetralogy.

This one-movement sonata makes the impression of a free, unbridled fantasia, virtually an improvisation. But in reality the whole work is tightly constructed from the music of the sonata's introduction. From that introduction he develops, first, three striking and powerful themes, then a passage sounding like a religious chorale. The final main section not only demands the utmost in piano technique to deal with its prestissimo tempo, but also employs elements of all the themes which have been spun out of the opening. Ultimately, in an eloquent concluding Andante, Liszt returns to the earliest versions of the main musical material and recedes into silence. Full of Romantic fire and spontaneity as the sonata may be, it also fits, depending on how one listens to it, into either the pattern of a single sonata-allegro-form movement (with exposition, development, recapitulation, and coda), or the four-movement structure of a traditional sonata (opening movement, slow movement, scherzo, and finale). Thus this work remains an enduring masterpiece even in the estimation of those listeners who tend to find Liszt's music overblown. In the *Sonata in B minor*, Liszt, the great radical, connected himself convincingly with the sonata tradition.

The sonata dates from 1854, shortly after the Princess Carolyn Sayn-Wittgenstein, with whom the composer lived, had convinced Liszt to quit touring as a pianist and concentrate on composition. The pianist and musicologist Alfred Brendel, among others, has claimed for years that the sonata is related to the Faust legend. While such an interpretation may actually fit the structure and emotional spirit of the work, it must be regarded with a measure of skepticism. Some musicologists have also argued that the piece is autobiographical, and point out that such a view would not exclude a Faustian interpretation. *—AMG*

Recommended:

- ○ **Martha Argerich 2** / Argerich / 1999 / Philips 456703
- ○ **Vladimir Horowitz 2** / Horowitz / 1999 / Philips 456844
- ○ **Schumann & Liszt: Piano Works** / Pollini / 2001 / DG 471358
- ○ **Liszt & Scriabin** / Pogorelich / 1992 / DG 429391
- ○ **Liszt: Sonata in B minor; 2 Études en concert** / Arrau / 2001 / Philips 464713
- ○ **Liszt: Piano Concertos & Sonata** / Richter / 1995 / Philips 446200

R.W.-Venezia, for piano, S. 201 (1883)

Richard Wagner, a good friend of Liszt's, died on February 13, 1883, in Venice. The great composer's death deeply affected Liszt, and in that year he composed two pieces in Wagner's memory, *Am Grabe Richard Wagners* (At the Grave of Richard Wagner) and *R. W.-Venezia* (R. W.-Venice). Most likely, *R. W.-Venezia* was the first composed of the two; the piece was first published in the multi-volume *F. Liszt:* Musikalische Werke, printed in Leipzig between 1907 and 1936.

Liszt begins *R. W.-Venezia* with a lugubrious bass line that outlines an augmented triad; the resultant lack of tonal direction pervades the piece. Chords begin to rise over this recurring bass pattern; these, too, come to rest on augmented triads. A slow crescendo builds to a fanfare, with repeated chords, that appears on three different harmonies. The consecutive appearances of these three harmonies—B flat major, D flat major and E major—outlines a diminished triad and may be Liszt's reference to Wagner's harmonic style. After this outburst, a falling line outlines the same augmented triad that opens the piece; however, now Liszt includes a B flat that slides chromatically down to A natural, mingling anguish with the unsettling lack of direction.

Unlike most of Liszt's works with foreboding, pensive beginnings, *R. W.-Venezia* does not proceed toward triumph, and makes no attempt to do so. Its ends without a sense of closure—the music simply stops, on a C sharp played *pp*, and we are left to ponder where we have been. *—John Palmer*

Recommended:

- ○ **Art Of Alfred Brendel Vol. 4** / Brendel / 1996 / Philips 446924
- ○ **Liszt: The Late Pieces** / Howard / 1991 / Hyperion 66445

Transcriptions, Fantasies, and Paraphrases on Works by Other Composers

Transcriptions and arrangements for piano of numerous types of music were common in the nineteenth century. In the absence of recordings, such publications often gave audiences an otherwise unavailable opportunity to hear new music. In addition to writing transcriptions of operas, ballets, and orchestral works, pianist/composers often created fantasies on popular tunes, and audiences enjoyed comparing one virtuoso's interpretation with another's.

Liszt excelled in all these areas, and his unparalleled skill at the piano enabled him to transcribe orchestral music for the keyboard with unsurpassed and still startling accuracy. His transcriptions of Beethoven symphonies were well-known to nineteenth century audiences and have recently been revived after decades of neglect. Although the writing remains pianistic throughout his works of this sort, the sound is genuinely orchestral in effect. Among Liszt's piano transcriptions of orchestral works, those of the nine Beethoven symphonies and Berlioz's *Symphonie fantastique* are the best known. Liszt also turned to the orchestral music of Schubert, arranging some of his waltzes in the *Soirées de Vienne*. Several of Bach's organ works also were transcribed for piano, but these are perhaps not as successful as other Liszt arrangements. The *Prelude and Fugue in A minor* nevertheless survived the transfer very well.

Best known among Liszt's arrangements are his *Hungarian Rhapsodies*, piano fantasies based on Hungarian Gypsy tunes; similar to the 19 *Hungarian Rhapsodies* is the *Rhapsodie espagnole*, an arrangement of Iberian melodies. The *Hungarian Rhapsodies* are organized like the multi-sectional nineteenth century *verbunkos*, a Hungarian dance style derived from the Hungarian army's method of recruiting troops. It features at least two contrasting sections—the slow *lassu*, or *lassan*, and the fast *friss*, or *friska*. Liszt varies the number and order of these in the various Rhapsodies, in some cases linking the sections, and in others creating a stream of unrelated or loosely related ideas in the traditional fashion of a rhapsody.

In addition to extemporizations on popular and folk melodies, Liszt produced a number of operatic fantasies. These consist of assembled variations on numbers from individual operas and are best described as showpieces—flights of virtuosity. The most popular of Liszt's operatic transcriptions are those of the *Faust* waltz (From Gounod's *Faust*), and works based upon Mozart's *Don Giovanni*, Bellini's *Norma* and *Sonnambula*, Verdi's *Rigoletto* and *Simon Boccanegra*, and the overture from Rossini's *William Tell*. Liszt's admiration for Wagner is clear in his lush transcription of Isolde's transformation at the close of *Tristan und Isolde*, an arrangement Liszt entitled *Isolde's Liebestod*. The polonaise from Tchaikovsky's *Eugene Onegin* and the Sarabande and Chaconne from Handel's *Almira* also received Lisztian treatment.

Song transcriptions form the single largest subgroup of Liszt's arrangements of works by other composers. Between 1840 and 1850 he set 50 songs by Schubert alone, exercising admirable restraint and maintaining the elegant simplicity of the originals. Liszt's arrangement of "Die Forelle" is one of the best examples; in it the melody and accompaniment merge into a continuous flow as the melody moves from hand to hand. Liszt also arranged vocal pieces by Schumann and Rossini, including Schumann's *"Weihnachtslied"* and Rossini's *Soirées musicale.* Six practically unknown songs by Chopin received such an informed treatment that they end up sounding like Chopin's own *Nocturnes.*

Among Liszt's piano transcriptions of orchestral works, those of the nine Beethoven symphonies and Berlioz's *Symphonie fantastique* are the best known. Liszt again culls from Schubert, arranging some of his waltzes in the *Soirées de Vienne.* Several of Bach's organ works also were transcribed for piano, but these are not as successful as other of Liszt's arrangements, although the *Prelude and Fugue in A minor* survived the transfer very well. *—John Palmer*

Recommended:

- ○ **Liszt Transcriptions of Berlioz, Chopin, Saint-Saëns** / Howard / 1990 / Hyperion 66346
- ○ **Liszt at the Opera** / Howard / 1990 / Hyperion 66371
- ○ **Franz Liszt: Opera Transcriptions** / Thibaudet / 1993 / London 436736
- ○ **Liszt: Transcriptions from the Operas of Richard Wagner** / Wehr / 1994 / Connoisseur Society 4199

Die Trauer-Gondel (La lugubre gondola I), for piano, S. 200/1 (1884)

This is the first of the two pieces usually listed as *La lugubre gondola* (The Lugubrious [funeral] gondola). It is one of several works Liszt wrote relating to the death of Wagner (1813–83), who was his son-in-law, but only two years his junior. Liszt wrote that near the end of 1882, while staying with Wagner in Venice, he had a premonition that Wagner would die there and that his body would thus be born be a funeral gondola through the streets. Wagner, in fact, did die in Venice the following February. The first *Lugubrious gondola* is one of Liszt's darkest, most morbid piano works, coming at a time in his career when his keyboard compositions were turning barren in their writing, bleak in mood, and showing little of the virtuosity for which he had become so famous. The piece has barcarolle-like features, but the rocking accompanying figure in the left hand is gloomy and desolate, while the theme imparts an ethereal lonesomeness in its descending, dark phrases. Its mood is not sad as much as utterly depressing, bordering on despair in its feeling of loss. This is a deep composition with highly imaginative harmonies and a deft, vivid sense for mood. Lasting about five minutes, it is one of the composer's inventive efforts from his last years. *—Robert Cummings*

Recommended:

- ○ **Schumann & Liszt: Piano Works** / Pollini / 2001 / DG 471358
- ○ **Liszt: The Late Pieces** / Howard / 1991 / Hyperion 66445

Unstern! Sinistre, disastro, for piano, S. 208 (1886)

In three languages, the title means *Dark Star: Sinister, Disastrous.* Liszt's last period contains several works which are among the most advanced and radical music anyone had written to that point, not excluding that of Liszt's son-in-law, Richard Wagner. The dissonances of this darkly glittering piece are remarkable. An unwary listener would be apt to place them among the works of the twentieth century's most important innovators. The dissonances are practically unresolved; the tension is continuous. Before Debussy, Liszt employs the whole tone scale harmonically, to produce a series of augmented triads. Both the scale and this sort of harmony open many possibilities. At the end, organ-like sonorities portray the prayers of a terrified humanity. *—Joseph Stevenson*

Recommended:

- ○ **Pollini Plays Liszt** / Pollini / DG 427322
- ○ **Liszt: The Late Pieces** / Howard / 1991 / Hyperion 66445
- ○ **Art Of Alfred Brendel Vol. 4** / Brendel / 1996 / Philips 446924

Weihnachtsbaum, for piano, S. 186 (1873–1876; revised 1882)

Weihnachtsbaum (Christmas Tree) occupies an unusual place in Liszt's output. Unlike many of his earlier piano compositions, it is not difficult or complex, not the kind of fare a virtuoso pianist looks for to impress audiences. Neither is this collection of 12 pieces fraught with the kind of gloom or grandiose religiosity found in music from his late years. A parallel comes to mind in the twentieth century from Prokofiev: his Op. 65 *Music for Children,* which also consists of 12 piano pieces, is rather simple of execution as well, and direct in its mode of expression.

Liszt composed these pieces in 1874–76 and dedicated them to his granddaughter, Daniela von Bülow. They are simple and straightforward, and in that sense typical of much of his piano writing at the time. However, their moods are upbeat and celebratory, placing them almost in a category by themselves. The first entry, "Altes Weihnachslied" (Old Christmas Carol) is joyous and colorful. It, like many of the items here, is based on a Christmas carol.

The next piece, "O Heilige Nacht! Weihnachtslied Nach Einer Alten Weise" (O Holy Night!: Christmas Song on an Old Theme) is solemn and has a simple religious air about it. "Die Hirten an der Krippe" (The Sherpherds at the Manger) returns to the lighter, more joyful mood of the first piece. "Adeste Fideles: Marsch der Heiligen Drei Könige" (Adeste Fideles: March of the Three Holy Kings) uses the famous Christmas carol tune and presents interesting variants that change the mood to the more serious.

The fifth piece here, "Altes Provenzalisches Weihnachtslied" (Old Provincial Carol) is lively in its evocation of joyful sentiments, and sounds as though it could have come from the Classical period. "Abendglocken" (Evening Bells) conjures sonorities of bells, but gently so. In great contrast to the last piece, this composition sounds modern, almost Impressionistic.

"Scherzoso: Man zuendet die Kerzen des Baumes An" (Lighting the Candles on the Tree at Last) is a brief and ecstatic piece, full of energy and childlike expectation. "Carillon" presents more bell-like sonorities, and it appears that Octavio Pinto imitated its frothy, rapid chords in his "Run, Run" from *Scenes from Childhood,* for piano. "Schlummerlied" (Slumber Song) evokes the images of a child or loved one sleeping peacefully in its calm mood and comforting music.

The last three pieces are not associated with Christmas, but, according to Humphrey Searle, with some aspect of Liszt's relationship with Princess Carolyne Sayn-Wittgenstein, the woman the composer almost married some years earlier. "Ehemals" (In Days Gone By) is slightly melancholy, but never lapses into that late Lisztian gloom. This piece is believed to depict Liszt's first meeting with the Princess. "Ungarisch" (In Hungarian Style) begins in boisterous joviality, then goes on to suggest defiance and national pride. "Polnisch" (In Polish Style) begins in a reflective vein, then turns lively and colorful. Its ending is brilliant and full of joy. These last two pieces are thought to be musical characterizations of Liszt and Princess Carolyne, respectively.

Liszt published *Weihnachtsbaum* in Berlin in 1882. He also arranged this collection for duet and made a version of the second piece for tenor, female chorus, and organ. *—Robert Cummings*

Recommended:

- ○ **The Art Of Alfred Brendel** / Brendel / 1996 / Philips 446920
- ○ **Liszt: Weihnachtsbaum; Via Crucis** / Howard / 1990 / Hyperion 66388

CONCERTO

Piano Concerto No. 1 in E flat major, S. 124 (1835; revised 1849)

The genesis of Liszt's Piano Concerto No. 1 in E flat major dates to 1830, when the composer sketched out the main theme in a notebook. It wasn't until the 1840s, however, that Liszt actually commenced work on the concerto. As a neophyte in the art of orchestration—his output to that point consisted almost entirely of keyboard music—Liszt enlisted the assistance of his pupil Joachim Raff in providing the work an instrumental skin. Liszt completed the concerto in 1849 but made a number of revisions over the next several years. The final version of the work dates from 1856.

The concerto's three main sections—Allegro maestoso, Quasi adagio-Allegretto vivace-Allegro animato, and Allegro marziale animato—are joined seamlessly into a single large-scale structure. The opening statement, characterized by a bold, almost martial chromatic descent, contains the essential elements from which all subsequent thematic material is derived. The piano enters with a dramatic passage in characteristic Lisztian octaves, after which the main theme reappears in a more tranquil guise. The second subject in introduced in the piano, after which a dialogue between piano and clarinet ensues. The sweetness of the mood suddenly gives way to intensity as the main theme makes a dramatic, almost angry reappearance.

The second section begins with a quiet cantabile melody in the muted strings. After the piano takes up the theme, the mood grows restive with mercurial, dramatic statements from the orchestra that alternate with quasi-improvisatory passages in the piano. The tempo picks up as the flute, and then oboe and clarinet, take up the theme. Lyricism gives way to a more lighthearted spirit, signaled by a pair of delicate strokes on the triangle. (The prominence of this instrument in the latter portion of the work, in fact, elicited derisive commentary from a number of critics. Eduard Hanslick, for example, leapt on this feature in describing the work as Liszt's "Triangle Concerto.") The piano introduces a lively, playful theme in its upper register; other instruments gradually join the texture as the triangle continues to chime in with jovial comment. The mood darkens with the reappearance of the concerto's opening theme, as though to suggest a return to that musical sequence of events. Instead, the piano introduces the final section, which commences with a sped-up version of the cantabile theme from the second section. Other earlier themes reappear in various guises as the triangle continues to add its color throughout. Alternating between intricate passagework and thunderous octaves, the concerto draws to a close in the bravura manner with which Liszt is so closely associated. *—Robert Cummings*

Recommended:

- ○ **Chopin: Concerto 1; Liszt: Concerto 1** / Abbado (cond.), Argerich, London SO / DG 449719
- ○ **Liszt: Piano Concertos & Sonata** / Kondrashin (cond.), Richter, London SO / 1995 / Philips 446200
- ○ **Svjatoslav Richter in Prague** / Ancerl (cond.), Richter, Czech PO / Praga 256002
- ○ **Liszt: Concertos 1 & 2** / Ormandy (cond.), Entremont / 1992 / Sony 48167

Piano Concerto No. 2 in A major, S. 125 (1839; revised 1849)

Liszt began work on his *Piano Concerto No. 2* in 1839 and initially completed it in 1857. Further revisions were made over the course of the next few years and a final version was fashioned in 1861, with its publication in 1863. Like the first piano concerto, it is cast in a single movement although, unlike its sibling, the sections comprising it are numerous and less distinct, prompting some musicologists to view it as a symphonic poem with piano. W.F. Apthorp subtitled the concerto, "The life and adventures of a melody." His description is quite appropriate because, also like the *First*, the whole of this concerto derives from its opening melody, which, over the course of the work's 20 or so minutes, yields many transformations and variations. This is also a more intimate composition than the first, and, ironically, more bombastic, as well.

The main theme is a long-breathed melancholy melody, first presented by the woodwinds. The piano enters in a modest, almost tentative way, playing filigree as the strings sweetly deliver the theme. The piano's deferential role ends with a dramatic, rippling plunge that keeps the instrument in the bass regions to introduce a menacing, rhythmic theme. The orchestra joins the grim proceedings, but the piano then incites further sonic mayhem with octave passages and other virtuosic fireworks. The orchestra takes over to punctuate the episode with a dramatic climax, after which the melody is played by a solo cello, accompanied by the piano. The piano then plays a variation on the melody, joined soon by the strings as the emotional pitch heightens. This section ends with sweetly descending scales and expectant swirls in the piano's upper register. This precedes bombastic chords from the piano, as the brass section blares out a variant of the theme. After a dreamy passage in the strings, the music intensifies and the piano breaks into furious octaves. A further buildup leads to another episode where the brass, now abetted by the piano, deliver a march-like variation of the opening melody. The music gradually winds down and the piano plays a straightforward rendering of the ubiquitous main theme, after which the woodwinds play in kind. This passage ends with the same kind of sweet, delicate cascading of notes that closed out the first extended slow section. Liszt invests the concerto's final episode with all manner of pianistic and orchestral fireworks.

For all the brilliant variations and transformations of the *Second Concerto*, its music does not seem to arrive at a resolution resulting from some logical musical sequence. It is well crafted, but hardly profound. The work was premiered in Weimar on January 7, 1857, with the work's dedicatee, Hans von Bronsart, as soloist and Liszt conducting. *—Robert Cummings*

Recommended:

○ **Liszt: Piano Concertos; Piano Sonata** / Richter, Kondrashin (cond.), London SO / 1995 / Philips 446200

○ **Liszt: Music for Piano & Orchestra Vol. 2** / Howard, Rickenbacher (cond.), Csurgay / 1998 / Hyperion 67403

Totentanz, for piano & orchestra, S. 126 (1847–1862)

As many may already know, Liszt's output was enormous, his list of works taking up page after page in reference catalogs. Yet, its size is not quite as it appears, for the composer wrote many versions of the same piece. One such example is *Totentanz* (Dance of death), which exists in two versions for piano and orchestra and one for solo piano. The two orchestral renditions are similar, but have very clear differences, too, with the latter version being the better known by far. It opens with crashing dark chords on the piano, over which the orchestra plays the *Dies Irae* theme (Andante), the ancient melody used in the Roman Catholic requiem mass. After some thrilling pyrotechnics on the piano and further renditions of the theme, there follow six variations, the first three of which are short, lasting less than a minute each. The final three are all substantial, each with a duration of more than three minutes. The fifth (Vivace), featuring a brilliant fugato and cadenza, may be the finest for sheer drama, though the mostly Lento-paced fourth is mesmeric in its mixture of innocence and dark mysticism. Of course, Liszt supplies a spectacular close to the work which, despite a measure of bombast, is a more dramatic and effective denouement than heard in any of his concertos or other piano/orchestral works.

The first version of *Totentanz*, nicknamed "De Profundis," is usually heard in the Busoni edition from 1919, which may contain revisions from 1853. It opens softly and darkly, with the piano silent, the gong ominously rumbling with restraint. The first three variations appear almost the same way here, but then the order of the variants changes, and Liszt adds a seventh. Moreover, music from the fourth variation in the later version does not appear here, but Liszt presents a lengthy slow section after all variations are heard with the "De Profundis" theme. Here, he also introduces thematic ideas that would appear in *Thoughts on Death* from his piano collection *Harmonies Religious and Poetic*. The ending to the early version differs greatly from the later *Totentanz*, too, not least in its brass-dominated bombast. In the end, both versions are convincing, but the latter rendition is clearly superior both for its more convincing structural properties and better writing. *—Robert Cummings*

Recommended:

○ **Liszt: Piano Works** / Fischer (cond.), Bolet, London SO / Decca 467801

○ **Alfred Brendel plays Liszt** / Gielen (cond.), Brendel, VSO / Vox 5172

○ **Zimerman Plays Chopin & Liszt** / Ozawa (cond.), Zimerman, BSO / 1998 / DG 459053

ORCHESTRAL

Symphonic Poems (1847–1883)

Liszt wrote all 13 of his symphonic poems for orchestra and transcribed all for two pianos and most for piano, four hands. Only one, *Orpheus*, appears to exist in a version for organ. Liszt was an influential figure with his symphonic poems and helped establish it as a new form, but contrary to what some have written, he did not invent the symphonic poem.

His first was *Ce qu'on entend sur la montagne* ("What one hears on the mountain," 1848–54), after a Victor Hugo poem. The work was revised twice, with the first two versions being orchestrated by composer Joachim Raff. It is a restive piece with inner conflicts that are finally resolved, the music ending in a serene mood. The pattern of composition here was much the same for about a half-dozen of the ensuing Liszt symphonic poems: Raff (and Conradi in *Tasso*) did the orchestration for the early drafts, though Liszt himself scored the final versions. *Tasso: lamento e trionfo* (1847–54), after Byron, was based largely on a hymn tune of folk origin, from which Liszt fashioned many brilliant variations. The third, *Les Préludes* (after Lamartine, 1848–54), is the most popular by far—but also, some would argue, the weakest. Sourced in a three-note motif, the music is both colorful and bombastic, full of drama and Lisztian angst. *Orpheus* (1853–54) came next, with relatively subdued music, while *No. 5, Prometheus* (1850–55) is heroic and gentle, featuring a brilliant fugal section. *Mazeppa* (1851–54), after Hugo, followed, based on Liszt's *Transcendental Etude No. 4* and retaining that work's sense of fury, suffering, and final triumph. The seventh, *Festklänge* (1853), as its title suggests, is festive, and the ensuing *Héroïde Funebrè* (1849–54) is, not surprisingly, funereal in mood, but contains a Hungarian folkish flavor, too. Speaking of Hungarian flavors, *Hungaria* (1854) (*No. 9*), based on Liszt's own 1840 *Heroic March in Hungarian Style*, deftly mixes heroic and funeral march music that divulges the ethnic character of Liszt's Hungary. *Hamlet* (1858), after Shakespeare, followed, a largely gloomy but compelling effort that may well rank as one of Liszt's finest symphonic poems. *No. 11, Hunnenschlacht* ("Battle of the Huns"; 1857), after von Kaulbach, is also considered by many to be among his finest. Stormy and full of conflict—with two themes locked in struggle in the dramatic development section—the work ends in triumph. *Die Ideale* (1857), after Schiller, was the only symphonic poem Liszt did not arrange for piano, four hands. It is a mostly subdued and subtle creation, as is his last symphonic poem, *Von der Wiege bis zum Grabe* (From the Cradle to the Grave), which came in 1881–82, about 25 years later. It is a dark, intense work of profound character, stylistically quite unlike the other symphonic poems. In the end, the piano and organ transcriptions, while not without merit, cannot stand up to the orchestral versions of these works. *—Robert Cummings*

Recommended:

○ **Liszt: Symphonic Poems** / Budapest Piano Duet / 2003 / Hungaroton 41005

○ **Liszt: Complete Symphonic Poems** / Joo (cond.), Budapest SO / Brilliant 9938

○ **Liszt: Complete Symphonic Poems for 2 Pianos Vol. 1** / G. Mangos, L. Mangos / 1993 / Cedille 014

○ **Liszt: Symphonic Poems** / Mehta (cond.), Berlin PO / 1997 / Sony 66834

○ **Liszt: Symphonic Poems** / Halasz (cond.), Katowice RSO / 1991 / Naxos 550487

Orpheus, symphonic poem, S. 98 (1853–1854; revised 1861)

Orpheus is the fourth of Liszt's 12 symphonic poems, written during his tenure as Grand Ducal Director of Music Extraordinary at Weimar. While conducting a performance of Gluck's *Orfeo ed Eurydice* at the Weimar Court Theatre in 1854, he decided to compose a prelude and postlude to *Orfeo*; these were performed with the opera on February 16, 1854. Though the postlude remains little known and was in fact lost for many years, the prelude survives as the symphonic poem *Orpheus*.

The plot of the opera itself had little to do with the creation of Liszt's tone poem; it merely provided the impetus for the composer's preoccupation with the title character. Liszt had previously seen an Etruscan vase at the Louvre which pictured the mythological Orpheus singing and playing his lyre, taming the wild animals around him. This image fascinated the composer, who saw Orpheus as a symbol of the civilizing influence of music and the arts upon mankind's baser instincts.

Orpheus is unlike Liszt's other symphonic poems in that it portrays no conflict, failure, or victory; instead it takes on the quality of a tonal "stream." The main theme, introduced on horns and harps (in imitation of Orpheus' lyre), is explored and developed in the horns and cellos and is eventually juxtaposed against a contrasting motive introduced by a solo violin. A pious, devotional chord progression brings the work to a hushed close. *—Margaret Godfrey*

Recommended:

○ **Liszt Tone Poems** / Frühbeck de Burgos (cond.), Wolters, Berlin RSO / 1999 / Bis 1117

***Les Préludes*, symphonic poem, S. 97 (1848–1854; revised 1861)**

Liszt was the virtual inventor of the symphonic poem (or tone poem), a form in which a literary or other nonmusical source provides a narrative foundation for a single-movement orchestral work. Liszt's symphonic poems, however, were not exclusively dependent on their source material: The composer's goal was more to distill the essence of the poetic concept in music than to exactly recreate it. *Les préludes* (1848–54) is the third, and by far the most popular, of the 12 symphonic poems Liszt wrote during his tenure as Grand Ducal Director of Music Extraordinary at Weimar. All 12 works are dedicated to Princess Carolyne Sayn-Wittgenstein.

Despite the suggestion of its title, *Les préludes* is by itself a complete, freestanding work. Long before it reached its final form, however, Liszt had envisioned it in another context. In 1844–45, he composed a cycle for male choir and piano, *Les quatre elements*, based on poems of Joseph Autran. Liszt planned to introduce the four choruses, which depict the earth, north winds, waves, and stars, with an overture. In the following years, he set aside the choruses while continuing to revise this introductory movement. As it became independent of its original purpose, Liszt stopped referring to it as an "overture," and by 1854 it had became a full-fledged work in its own right. Liszt derived the title from an ode by French poet Alphonse de Lamartine, "Méditations poetiques," which describes the life of man from youthful love through the harsh realities of work and war and finally to self-acceptance. An excerpt from the poem accompanies Liszt's score: "What else is our life than a series of preludes to an unknown song, whose first and solemn notes are intoned by death?"

Though *Les préludes* was not specifically inspired by Lamartine's text, its final version faithfully reflects the shifting mood sequences of each section of the poem. The musical discourse unfolds in parallel to the themes in the text without providing a direct translation of its elements. A single three-note motive provides the main glue, its various permutations and transformations reflecting the many and varied moods of each section. Another theme, a distant cousin of the original motive, eventually emerges, providing an element of contrast as it also undergoes transformation. *Les préludes* ends with a return to the three-note motive in its original form, as well as to the contemplative, questioning mood of the opening. *—Margaret Godfrey*

Recommended:

- ○ **Liszt: Complete Tone Poems Vol. 1** / Haitink (cond.), London PO / Philips 438751
- ○ **Rimsky-Korsakov: Scheherazade, etc.** / Dorati (cond.), London SO / 1998 / Mercury 462953

SYMPHONIC

***Faust Symphony*, S. 108 (1854–1857; revised 1861)**

After first encountering Goethe's *Faust* in 1830, Liszt ruminated for years on the idea of creating a musical work based on the play. It was not until he heard an 1852 performance of Berlioz's *The Damnation of Faust* that he was inspired to begin serious work on what was to become his *Faust Symphony*. The first version of the work (1854), for a small orchestra without brass, was substantially shorter than its final form. Over the next three years, Liszt expanded the symphony, eventually adding the final chorus in 1857.

Unlike the more episodic and narrative *Dante Symphony* (1855–56), the *Faust Symphony* is structured along more purely musical lines. Each of its three movements is a character portrait, of Faust, Gretchen, and Mephistopheles, respectively; together, they were regarded by Liszt as three of his finest tone poems. The first movement, "Faust," is cast as a sonata-allegro. Faust's theme, consisting of broken augmented triads, uses all 12 tones of the chromatic scale, anticipating the rise of 12-tone and other atonal techniques that were still decades in the future. In spite of the extreme economy of its material, the movement is nearly 30 minutes in duration, demonstrating Liszt's process of thematic transformation as it spans a remarkable variety of moods that evoke Faust's complex character.

"Gretchen," is slow, meditative and delicately scored. Liszt here continues the process of thematic transformation with material derived from the previous movement. Finally, in keeping with the negative and mocking character of Mephistopheles, the third movement is a grotesque parody of the first and uses only one new theme, appropriately borrowed from Liszt's own *Malédiction*, S. 121.

Liszt added the choral ending to the work only after having completed the *Dante Symphony*, which likewise has this feature. In the *Faust Symphony*, the text is the *Chorus mysticus* which ends Part II of the play. *—Steven Coburn*

Recommended:

- ○ **Liszt: Faust Symphony** / Horenstein (cond.), Mitchinson, BBC Singers, BBC Northern SO / Music & Arts 4744
- ○ **Liszt: Faust Symphony** / Bernstein (cond.), Riegel, Boston SO, Tanglewood Festival Chorus / DG 447449
- ○ **Liszt: Faust Symphony** / Dausgaard (cond.), Elsner, Danish Radio Chamber Choir, Danish Radio SO / 2000 / Chandos 9814

VOCAL

***Songs* (1839–1884)**

Liszt's music proliferates like a force of nature, nowhere more apparently than in his vast and varied catalog of songs—80 items ranging from the 1839 setting of Bocella's "Angiolin del biondo crin" (prompted by his daughter, Blandine) to "Und wir dachten der Toten" to a poem by Freiligrath in 1884, two years before his death. Though Liszt worked quickly, often producing an elaborate composition in a few hours, he had frequent second and even third thoughts, and many of the songs were so extensively revised that succeeding versions loom as new compositions. The task of sorting through such abundance has discouraged their inclusion by lieder recitalists. Liszt's songs also make an index to the stylistic uncertainties facing the Romantic composer. Such early songs as *Im Rhein* (Heine, ca. 1840), *Die Loreley* (Heine, 1841), *Der du von dem Himmel bist* (Goethe, 1842), *Oh! quand je dors* (Hugo, 1842), *Über allen Gipfeln ist Ruh* (Goethe, ca. 1848), for instance—all subsequently revised—draw upon the bel canto operatic style current in that era, many notable moments of which (the sextet from Donizetti's *Lucia de Lammermoor*, for instance, or the *Réminiscences de Norma*, after Bellini's opera) he transcribed for solo piano. The piano accompaniments of these early songs are often overloaded, while the vocal lines (e.g., in *Über allen Gipfeln* offers a particularly egregious example) often devolve into wandering melismas. The ideal balance of youthful efflorescence, ecstaticism, and narrative shapeliness was struck in the *Tre Sonetti del Petrarca* (1843–64), though it is indicative that their outsized gestures have found far wider acceptance in the transcriptions for solo piano Liszt fashioned from them in the late 1840s. During his Weimar years, 1848–61, Liszt began not only to prune and streamline former works, but, with a number of devoted singers at his disposal, to experiment, pushing the expressive domain of song into new territory. His best songs break new ground: *Jeanne d'Arc au bûcher* (Dumas, 1845) is almost an operatic scene, the three songs from Schiller's *Wilhelm Tell* (ca. 1845) are Alpine tone poems with vocal obbligato, *Die drei Zigeuner* (Lenau, 1860) is a frank narrative, while such things as *Vergiftet sind meine Lieder* (Heine, 1843), *Die Vätergruft* (Uhland, 1844), *Ein Fichtenbaum steht einsam* (Heine, 1860), or *Es muss ein Wunderbares sein* (Redwitz, 1852) prefigure the compact richness of Hugo Wolf. The songs of his old age are too often spare, wan, and crabbed. *—Adrian Corleonis*

Recommended:

- ○ **Liszt: Lieder** / Schmiege, Sulzen / 1998 / Orfeo 440981
- ○ **Liszt: 16 Lieder** / Shirai, Holl / Capriccio 10294
- ○ **Toujours l'Amour: Lieder von Liszt** / Egel, etc. / FSM Adagio 97215
- ○ **Liszt: Lieder** / Fischer-Dieskau, Barenboim & Demus / 2000 / DG 463508
- ○ **Liszt: Orchestral Songs** / Korodi (cond.), Tokody, Takacs, Molnar, Solyom-Nagy, Hungarian State SO / Hungaroton 12105

***Sonetti di Petrarca*, song cycle, S. 270 (1843–1864; revised 1864)**

Like so many of the composer's works, Franz Liszt's *Tre sonetti di Petrarca* (1838–39; 1861) only assumed their final form after many decades of recomposition and revision. Indeed, several different versions for various types of voice with piano exist, as does a version for piano alone. Therefore, one cannot necessarily say that there is a "final" version of the *Sonetti*—rather, one is greeted with a spectrum of pieces that reflect Liszt's continually changing attitude toward both his own music and Petrarch's deeply sentimental poetry.

Around 1838 or 1839 Liszt composed the initial version of the *Sonetti*, for tenor (and a high one at that, with a range extending to high C sharp) and piano. Liszt originally presented the *Sonetti* in the following order (the numbers corresponding to those assigned to Petrarch's sonnets): No.104, No.47, and No.123. Of the settings, No. 47 is perhaps the weakest, with its barely covered structural seams and occasionally rambling narrative. Already at this early stage, though, the other two songs show an intimate understanding of Petrarch's rather erotic verse, as evidenced by their charged atmosphere and rich melodic sense.

The *Sonetti* remained unpublished for many years, during which time Liszt crafted the first solo piano version. The piano version was published in 1846—about the same time that the version for tenor and piano appeared in print—but in 1858 Liszt recrafted the piano version and included it in the second book of *Années de pèlerinage*. It is in this form, in fact, that the *Sonetti* are today best known.

The *Sonetti*, in their 1858 incarnation, are surely among the most splendid of the mid-nineteenth century piano works. Although Liszt had not entirely repaired the flaws of No. 47, both Nos. 104 and 123 are lovely and idiomatic; the music comes forth from the piano so naturally that many are unaware of its vocal origins. Liszt does not suppress the ebullience of his youthful attitude towards love, but rather augments and clarifies his vision in the 1858 version. Like much of the second book of *Années de pèlerinage*, the *Sonetti* show a strong affinity for the sleek melodic contours of Italian opera. (It is interesting to note that Liszt reversed the order of the first two *Sonetti* for the 1858 version, significantly streamlining the dramatic narrative of the group as a whole.)

The most substantial revision came in 1865, when Liszt chose to transcribe the original vocal version for lower voice. Now intended for baritone or bass, this "final" version of the *Sonetti* provides a stark contrast to each of its predecessors. Here, Liszt has greatly simplified the textures, removing much of the exuberant emotion which so characterized the earlier versions, and has replaced his youthful optimism with something approaching the grim austerity of his later works. *—Blair Johnston*

Recommended:

○ **Fischer-Dieskau Edition** / Fischer-Dieskau, Demus / 2000 / DG 463500

○ **Of Ladies and Love . . .** / Schade, Martineau / Hyperion 67315

CHORAL

Choral Works (1845–1885)

Although Liszt produced his first sacred choral work, the lost *Tantum ergo*, in 1822, he did not begin writing such pieces consistently until the 1840s. In 1834, he expressed his ideas on the composition of sacred music: "It must be devotional, strong and drastic—uniting on a colossal scale the theater and the Church. . . ." Two of Liszt's earliest, large-scale sacred works, the oratorios *Die Legende von der heiligen Elisabeth* (The legend of Saint Elizabeth), and *Christus*, are clear attempts to realize this aim.

Liszt worked on his *Elisabeth* in 1857–62, setting a libretto by Otto Roquette for four soloists, chorus, orchestra and organ. Depicting the life of Hungary's Saint Elizabeth, the oratorio incorporates the Catholic plainchant used on her feast day along with Hungarian popular tunes and hymns. From the plainchant Liszt extracted a short motive, which he used as the symbol of the cross in many of his sacred pieces; other leitmotifs appear throughout the six movements. Though the work as a whole is not seen as one of his best, the Miracle of the Rose scene is a particularly fine excerpt.

Christus, at over four hours in length, is indeed colossal. Composed between 1863 and 1867, it is in three parts that take as their subject, respectively: the birth of Jesus; Jesus' Sermon on the Mount, miracles, and entry into Jerusalem; and Jesus' death and resurrection. The second part of the oratorio is generally regarded as the best; it extracts a great breadth of drama from the events of Jesus' life, from the delicately scored, restrained Sermon on the Mount and the stormy, violent segment in which Jesus walks on the waves.

The *Missa solemnis zur Einweihung der Basilika in Gran* (Mass for the consecration of the basilica in Gran) of 1855 is Liszt's first setting of the mass. Thick and unabashedly Romantic, it owes a debt to Beethoven's *Missa solemnis*. Liszt's *Hungarian Coronation Mass* (1867) was composed in three weeks for Franz Joseph's crowning as King of Hungary. Simpler than the *Missa solemnis*, the *Hungarian Mass* incorporates Hungarian melodies and features a plainsong-like Credo and a lyrical violin solo in the Benedictus. Liszt composed several psalm settings, the most celebrated of which is Psalm XIII, for tenor, chorus and orchestra (1855).

Liszt's secular choral works are less important than his sacred. An uncharacteristic *Festkantata* of 1845, written for the unveiling of a Beethoven monument in Bonn, garnered initial praise but quickly disappeared from the repertory; a second cantata on Beethoven appeared in 1870. Several fine compositions for four-voice male choir and piano exist, and the cantata, *Hungaria 1848*, contains references to the *Rákócky March*. *—John Palmer*

Recommended:

○ **Liszt: Psalms** / Forrai (cond.), Lelkes, Reti, Jambor, Margittay, Hungarian State SO / Hungaroton 11261

○ **Liszt: Sacred Choral Music** / Fasolis (cond.), Zanasi, Crivellaro, Balducci, Rausch, Labusch, Choir of Radio Svizzera / 1997 / Naxos 553786

○ **Liszt: Sacred Choral Music** / Ugrin (cond.), Molnar, Borza, Inhoff, Kovacs, Nagy, Hungarian State Choir / Hungaroton 31103

○ **Liszt: Missa Solemnis** / Ferencsik (cond.), Kincses, Gregor, Takacs, Margittay, Budapest SO / 1994 / Hungaroton 11861

○ **Liszt: Missa Coronationalis** / Lehel (cond.), Kincses, Lehotka, Gulyas, Polgar, Takacs, Budapest SO / Hungaroton 12148

○ **Liszt: Legend of Saint Elizabeth** / Joo (cond.), Marton, Kovats, Solyom-Nagy, Gregor, Hungarian State SO / Hungaroton 12694

○ **Liszt: Choral Works** / Best (cond.), Trotter, Melrose, Corydon Singers / 2000 / Hyperion 67199

○ **Liszt: Cantatas & Hymns** / Ferencsik (cond.), Lehotka, Solyom-Nagy, Melis, Andor, Budapest SO / Hungaroton 31960

Christus, oratorio, S. 3 (1859–1863)

Following immediately on the heels of the composer's somewhat disappointing oratorio on the subject of St. Elisabeth, Franz Liszt's grand oratorio *Christus* is an altogether more successful effort. Composed to a text drawn from biblical and liturgical sources by the composer himself, *Christus* is a massive, three-part celebration of the life and works of Christ scored for an ensemble requiring soprano, alto, tenor, baritone, and bass soloists, chorus, organ, and full orchestra.

The three sections of the oratorio correspond to the Christmas story, the life and miracles of Christ, and the Passion. Following a brief introduction, the work begins with a musical depiction of the angels heralding the birth of Christ. This is followed by the liturgical hymn *Stabat mater speciosa*, and then two purely instrumental numbers, including a delightful tutti depiction of the Magi on their way to Bethlehem. The second part begins with three choral sections depicting Jesus' times in Jerusalem, and, following a stormy orchestral interlude that portrays the miracle of Jesus walking on water, ends with rousing cries of "Hosanna." The third part begins with a musical dialogue between Christ—represented, as tradition demands, by a baritone—and the orchestra. A *Stabat mater* and an Easter hymn for children's chorus pave the way for a massive Resurrection scene, which Liszt vividly paints with a colorful orchestral palette.

Like most of Liszt's choral music, *Christus* has not been regularly performed by professional ensembles, and its demands are far beyond the capabilities of all but the most extraordinary amateur groups. Nevertheless, *Christus* contains some of the finest moments anywhere in the music of Liszt, and devotees of the composer's work continually hope for a revival of this forgotten treasure. *—Blair Johnston*

Recommended:

○ **Christus Oratorio** / Dorati (cond.), Kincses, Polgar, Hock, Solyom-Nagy, Hungarian State SO / Hungaroton 12831

Psalm 13, Herr, wie lange, for tenor, chorus & orchestra, S. 13b (1855–1863; revised 1878)

In the mid-1850s, Liszt was at the height of his powers. He had put aside his career as a traveling virtuoso in 1848 to become Kapellmeister to the Duchy of Saxen-Weimar, where he had an orchestra, chorus, and opera house at his disposal. Ensconced with his mistress, Princess Carolyne Sayn-Wittgenstein, in Weimar's Altenburg, the luxurious villa that accompanied his position, his creative work took on a new focus. His writing for orchestra took on a new assurance as the spate of masterpieces continued unabated—the piano sonata (1852–53), the orchestral poem, *Orpheus* (1854), the *Prelude and Fugue on BACH for Organ* (1855), the imposing *Gran Mass* (1855), and above all, the *Faust Symphony* (1854). Liszt's personal life was no less unbelievably crowded. In addition to hosting the artistic elite of Europe at the Altenburg (including the young Brahms), he began giving piano lessons in autumn 1853 to the modestly talented but highly intelligent, sensual, and beautiful Agnès Street-Klindworth—daughter of the notorious Georg Klindworth, Metternich's spymaster—then in her late twenties. By late 1854, they had become lovers, though Liszt was aware that her mission in Weimar was to gather intelligence for her father.

Amid this tangle of affairs, Liszt pursued composition through summer 1855, working on his *Dante Symphony* and choral music for Johann Gottfried von Herder's play, *Prometheus Unbound*. "I broke off from the score of my *Prometheus* choruses to write [*Psalm 13*]," Liszt remarked to a correspondent, "which came to me out of abundance of the heart." His expressiveness possessed an unaccustomed grandeur, though it can seem theatrical; the sanguine nature of *Psalm 13* has much in common with Rossini's *Stabat Mater* and Verdi's *Requiem*. Set in German, the tenor asks in a *supplicante* phrase, "How long wilt thou forget me, O Lord?" Taken up by the chorus, the dialogue reaches an impassioned climax before continuing in a religioso episode—"Consider and hear me, O Lord"—similar in its rhapsodically lyrical imploration to the piano sonata's cantando espressivo. A furious allegro agitato protests that the Psalmist's enemies may prevail, to subside in a fugato hymn of praise—"But I have trusted in thy mercy"—worked to an allegro impetuoso apotheosis. *—Adrian Corleonis*

Recommended:

○ **Liszt: Psalms** / Forrai (cond.), Reti, Hungarian State SO, Budapest Chorus / Hungaroton 11261

CHAMBER MUSIC

Am Grabe Richard Wagners, for string quartet & harp ad lib, S. 135 (1883)

As most of his admirers are aware, Liszt had a penchant for writing several versions of the same piece. Often, one version is expanded or contains additional music, or conversely, is pared down. But Liszt also simply transcribed the source music for a different instrument or instruments, as is the case here with *Am Grabe Richard Wagners* (At the Grave of Richard Wagner). He originally wrote the piece for piano solo, then transcribed it for organ and also for string quartet with optional harp. Of course, the latter version here, with four or five instruments instead of one, would of necessity require some expansion upon the piano original, but its music, nutrified but not fattened, remains in spirit and structure quite the same. Liszt uses a theme in its opening from his own choral work, *The Bells of Strasbourg Cathedral*, from the movement "Excelsior!" Wagner used the same theme in the opening of his last opera *Parsifal*. The mood of *Am Grabe Richard Wagners* is hushed and gentle, bleak but hopeful, hopeful in the many rising contours of the thematic material. In the ending, Liszt uses *Parsifal*'s bell motif as a final tribute and farewell to Wagner. The string quartet version here is marginally warmer than its piano counterpart and more effective in pointing up the thematic connections between the composers. *—Robert Cummings*

Recommended:

○ **At the Grave of Richard Wagner** / Takahashi, DeCray, Kronos Quartet / 1993 / Nonesuch 79318

Tasmin Little

b. 1965, London, England
Violinist

Tasmin Little is a versatile and appealing English violinist who has left few musical stones unturned in her young, but busy, career. As a concerto soloist, a recitalist, a chamber musician, and even as a scholar and television producer, she has proved that her interests know few boundaries, and, especially in England, she has become somewhat of a celebrity.

Little studied at the Yehudi Menuhin School and the Guildhall School of Music, where she was a gold medal winner. She later studied privately in Toronto with Lorand Fenyves. 1988 marked two important debuts: a recital at London's Purcell Room with the pianist Piers Lane (who has remained a frequent chamber music partner), and her solo debut with the Hallé Orchestra. During the 1990s, Little built a solid international reputation, often working with Kurt Masur, Simon Rattle, Vladimir Ashkenazy, Andrew Davis, and other renowned conductors, and presenting unusually personable recitals in which she engages directly with the audience in discussion of the music.

During the same period, Little began a prodigious recording career, appearing on excellent issues from EMI, Chandos, Decca, Virgin, and Hyperion. The real breadth of her repertory comes into focus when examining her discography, which includes a range of concertos (Brahms, Bruch, Delius, Dvořák, Lalo, Sibelius, Walton, and others); chamber works by Debussy, Poulenc, and Ravel; and a variety of miniatures. She has been particularly associated with the music of Frederick Delius, about whom she produced a television documentary (BBC2's *The Works*). She was awarded the Diapason d'Or for her recording of Delius' sonatas, and the Delius Society published her scholarly paper on the composer's *Violin Concerto*.
—Allen Schrott

Recommended:

- ○ **Bruch: Scottish Fantasy; Lalo: Symphonie espagnole** / Handley (cond.), Little, Scottish National Orch. / 2002 / EMI 575802
- ○ **Lloyd: Works for Violin & Piano** / Little, Roscoe (piano) / 1990 / Albany 029
- ○ **Pärt: Tabula Rasa, etc.** / Studt (cond.), Little, Roscoe, Aldwinckle, Bournemouth Sinfonietta / 1994 / EMI 65031
- ○ **Elgar: Violin Sonata; Bax: Violin Sonata 2** / Little, Roscoe (piano) / 2000 / Gmn.com 113

Andrew Litton

b. May 16, 1959, New York, NY
Conductor

Identified early as a gifted musician, Andrew Litton trained in America and then established himself as an outstanding conductor in England before returning to the United States to assume the directorship of a major orchestra, the Dallas Symphony. As one of only a small handful of American-born, American-trained artists to hold an important podium position in the United States, Litton has endured a greater-than-customary-degree of scrutiny. While few of his interpretations have been found definitive, his preparedness and high competence have proven rewarding. He has enjoyed the additional benefit of conducting in a remarkable concert hall and recording for a company that has afforded him and his orchestra extraordinarily vivid sound. At New York's Juilliard School of Music, Litton studied conducting under Swedish maestro Sixten Ehrling and piano under Nadia Reisenberg. Demonstrating exceptional ability, he won the Bruno Walter Scholarship for further study with Edoardo Müller and Neeme Järvi and with Walter Weller in Austria. Winning the 1982 Rupert Foundation International Competition in England provided Litton a debut conducting the BBC Symphony Orchestra later that same year and generous exposure to British audiences. Litton served first as associate conductor, than as assistant conductor under Mstislav Rostropovich with Washington's National Symphony Orchestra from 1982 to 1986. There, he learned much, especially from the man he describes as his "first and only boss." While Litton missed the opportunity to work with Kiril Kondrashin in Amsterdam when the famous Russian conductor died in 1981, he gained numerous insights about Shostakovich from Rostropovich. Litton has expressed his belief that Shostakovich was the twentieth century's great symphonist, capturing the struggles of living in modern times. After his years with the N.S.O., Litton conducted widely throughout the United States and Europe before being appointed principal conductor and artistic advisor of England's Bournemouth Symphony Orchestra in 1988. He remained there, earning high marks from English critics and the approval of English audiences while attracting worldwide attention through a series of recordings. In 1994, Litton was appointed music director of the Dallas Symphony Orchestra while becoming conductor laureate in Bournemouth. Meanwhile, Litton undertook several opera assignments, making his Metropolitan Opera debut in 1989 leading a production of *Yevgeny Onegin*. When the Glyndebourne Festival production of *Porgy and Bess*, originally conducted by Simon Rattle, was revived at Covent Garden in 1992, Litton was chosen to lead it. He also conducted performances of *Salome* and *Falstaff* for the English National Opera. In Dallas, Litton has stepped into the comprehensive role played by an American music director with clear understanding of his responsibility for not only conducting stimulating performances, but also playing a key role in fundraising. His outgoing personality has been an asset in meeting the people of the Dallas and convincing them that their orchestra is an enhancement central to a vital community. Litton points with some pride to an endowment increase over seven years from 19 million to 70 million dollars. Under Litton, the Dallas Symphony became the first major orchestra to broadcast a live concert via the Internet. Litton has expressed the belief that this medium can break down prejudices about concert works and afford listeners an opportunity to respond and comment immediately. He is enthused over critics no longer having the final word. Among Litton's recordings are discs devoted to Shostakovich, Mahler, Elgar, and Tchaikovsky.
—Erik Eriksson

Recommended:

- ○ **Elgar: In the South; Serenade; Enigma Variations** / Litton (cond.), Royal PO / 1995 / Virgin 61255
- ○ **Liebermann: Symphony 2 / Flute Concerto** / Litton (cond.), Davidson, Zukerman, Dallas SO & Chorus / 2000 / Delos 3256
- ○ **Dallas Space Spectacular** / Litton (cond.), Dallas SO / 1998 / Delos 3225
- ○ **Litolff: Concerti Symphonique 3 & 5** / Litton (cond.), Donohoe, BBC Scottish SO / Hyperion 67210

Julian Lloyd Webber

b. Apr. 14, 1951, London, England
Cellist

Julian Lloyd Webber is known as a cellist who is always willing to expand the horizons of the instrument's world. The son of composer William Lloyd Webber and brother of composer Andrew Lloyd Webber, he studied with Douglas Cameron and Joan Dickson, and at the Royal Conservatory of Music in London, and also spent some time in Geneva with Pierre Fournier. His London debut was in 1971, in a recital, followed in 1972 by his concert debut performing the *Cello Concerto* of Arthur Bliss. His recording of that same work marked the first of what are now over 50 premiere recordings of works for the cello, many of them written for him. The Guildhall School of Music named him professor of cello in 1978, and he made his American debut in 1980 in New York. He wrote an account of his career in 1984, entitled *Travels With My Cello*, which happens to be the "Barjansky" Stradivarius, made around 1690. In appearances around the world, he has given premieres of concertos by Rodrigo (*Concierto como un Divertimento*, 1982), Malcolm Arnold (1989), Gavin Bryars (*Farewell to Philosophy*, 1995), and Philip Glass (2001, recorded in 2004 with the Royal Liverpool Philharmonic and Gerard Schwarz). He has worked with many English orchestras and conductors, such as the London Symphony, Yehudi Menuhin, Sir Neville Marriner and the Academy of St. Martin-in-the-Fields, James Judd and the Philharmonia Orchestra, but also more international artists, such as Maxim Shostakovich and Vaclav Neumann and the Czech Philharmonic. In his more adventuresome collaborations he has worked with Elton John, Cleo Laine, and even formed his own ensemble, ¡Bossa Nova! Lloyd Webber's recordings include the collections of shorter pieces and transcriptions *Cello Moods*, *Cradle Songs*, and *Cello Song*, and a retrospective of his work for Philips/Universal, *Made in England*, released in 2003.
—Patsy Morita

Recommended:

- ○ **Byars: Farewell to Philosophy** / Judd (cond.), Lloyd Webber, Haden, English CO, Nexus / 1996 / Point 454126
- ○ **Gentle Dreams** / Lloyd Webber, etc. / 2003 / Philips 000167802
- ○ **Delius & Grieg: Complete music for cello & piano** / Lloyd Webber, Forsberg (piano) / 1998 / Philips 454458
- ○ **Cello Moods** / Lloyd Webber, etc. / 1999 / Philips 462588

George Lloyd

b. Jun. 28, 1913, St. Ives, Cornwall, England, **d.** Jul. 3, 1998, London, England
Composer: Symphonic, Keyboard

George Walter Selwyn Lloyd's career was completely destroyed by ill health and a shift in critical favor, but was revived again when audiences that had by then had enough sterile modernism happily embraced him as "the modern composer who writes tunes." His formal school studies were seriously interrupted by rheumatic fever, but he did receive composition lessons from Harry Farjeon. At 19 he heard his *First Symphony* premiered, leading to two more symphonies and two operas produced in the 1930s. He received acclaim as one of the most promising young British composers.

With the outbreak of World War II Lloyd enlisted in the Royal Marines. A gunner, he served on a cruiser on the Murmansk convoy route. In 1942 a faulty torpedo reversed directions and blew up his ship. He was below decks at the time, and witnessed his mates drown in oil. He was rescued from the frigid Arctic waters. "My whole nervous system seemed burned out," he said, describing his post-traumatic shock syndrome. He recovered his health slowly in Switzerland after the war. He wrote music, with difficulty, coming to terms with his wartime experiences in his *Fourth* and *Fifth Symphonies*. The former is a kind of portrayal of denial: After a grim symphonic journey, the final movement is a succession of trivial marches. "When the funeral is over the band plays quick cheerful tunes," he said of its forced cheerfulness.

He wrote an opera, *John Socman*, whose hero is a soldier at the battle of Agincourt. The opera foundered on backstage battles among the opera company. And in the 12-tone dominated world of new music, Lloyd's tonal, melodic music had, as Lloyd was told to his face, "no contemporary significance." "My health went skew-whiff again," Lloyd said, as he realized nobody wanted to play his music. He quit music and started raising produce (first carnations, then mushrooms). Music emerged again in his life as a hobby. In this non-pressured context, Lloyd looked forward to rising at 4:30 to compose for three hours before work. As he and his wife Nancy built a successful business, he began to amass a catalog of new music. However, he continued to reject 12-tone music. "I did study the blessed thing in the Thirties. I thought it was a cock-eyed idea that produced horrible sounds. It made composers forget how to sing." The BBC returned his music unread.

In the 1970s Gavin Henderson, administrator of the Philharmonia Orchestra, began to take interest in his music and talked it up. The BBC in 1969 accepted Lloyd's *Eighth Symphony* for performance, although they didn't get around to actually playing the thing for eight years. Audiences sat up and took notice on that evening in 1977: here was a modern composer, clearly British and clearly speaking of modern times, but in an entirely tonal style and with good, understandable tunes.

All around the world, composers were returning to tonality after the 30-year detour down the 12-tone road. A large audience appreciated his steady adherence to his musical principles. Three of his symphonies were recorded on the British Lyrita label after his *Sixth Symphony* was premiered at the *Proms* of 1981.

Peter Kermani, a New York music lover, then interested the Albany Symphony Orchestra in New York in Lloyd's music. The orchestra commissioned Lloyd's last two symphonies. The Albany Record label ultimately recorded all his operas and concertos, other major works, and his late masterpiece, *Symphonic Mass*.

After suffering some heart trouble, he resumed work on a *Requiem*, which, like Mozart's, proved to be his final work, completed three weeks before his death. *—Joseph Stevenson*

SYMPHONIC

Symphonies (1932–1989)

George Lloyd (1913–98) was undoubtedly one of the most remarkable British symphonists of his era, and until widely recognized as a composer of stature late in life, certainly the least appreciated. After studying with Harry Farjeon and William Lovelock at Trinity College, London, Lloyd's initial success came in 1932 when he conducted his *First Symphony* with an amateur orchestra in Cornwall. A second followed in 1933, and after the enthusiastic reception accorded to Lloyd's first opera, described as "spontaneous, melodious and dramatic," his *Symphony No. 3* impressed the composer John Ireland. Following Ireland's recommendation to the BBC, Lloyd was invited to conduct it on air in November 1935.

Throughout World War II, Lloyd served as a Royal Marines bandsman. He was one of only four survivors of an accident in which his vessel was accidentally struck by its own torpedo. Lloyd was seriously injured, but continued to compose, producing his next two symphonies in Switzerland between 1946 and 1948. This time, both were rejected by the BBC, and for the next few years, he devoted himself largely to opera.

Lloyd's *Symphony No. 8* (1961–65), widely considered his finest, marked a watershed when first broadcast in 1977, and during the last two decades of his life, Lloyd enjoyed great success worldwide. As Lewis Foreman has written, Lloyd's music "with its wide-spanning lines and traditional tonal harmony became for many an icon of anti-modernism." A further five symphonies were premiered by Edward Downes, and Lloyd produced his last two symphonies (Nos. 11 and 12) for the Albany Symphony Orchestra in 1985 and 1989 respectively. George Lloyd's symphonies stand out as traditional, melodic compositions, almost unparalleled amid an age of extreme modernism. As Foreman concludes, all are "characterized by their dramatic treatment and superb ear for textures... Almost all of his works have been recorded." *—Michael Jameson*

Recommended:

- ○ **Lloyd: Symphony 8** / Lloyd (cond.), London PO / 1997 / Albany 230
- ○ **Lloyd: Charade; Symphony 3** / Lloyd (cond.), BBCPO / 1992 / Albany 090

KEYBOARD

Works for Piano (1966–1989)

George Lloyd was known for works in the large Romantic forms—symphony, opera, and chorus-and-orchestra extravaganza. In a way, then, his solo piano works stand apart from the rest of his output. There are seven (plus two for two pianos), and all, except for the 23-minute *An African Shrine*, are shorter pieces. Lloyd's piano music dates from later in his career; he learned the instrument only when British pianist John Ogdon began to champion his works in the 1960s. *An African Shrine* was written for Ogdon in 1966. The work evokes the disturbances that engulfed several of the new African countries in the 1960s. Its score is headed with a program that in form but not in content is of the Romantic era: "Scene: A lonely road. A deserted shrine. A woman kneels weeping. As the armies of the world pass by, she prays."

That description points to the sense in which Lloyd's piano music, though smaller in scale, is of a piece with the rest of his output. The irrepressibly melodic Lloyd is wrongly tagged as a reactionary. True, he made a fine standard bearer for all those audiences repelled by serialist orthodoxy. But he was more eclectic than neo-Romantic, and some passages in his piano pieces, when the moment demands it, sound as dissonant as music of any modernist.

Like *An African Shrine*, Lloyd's shorter piano works are programmatic in a novel way. *The Aggressive Fishes* (1972) was inspired by biologist Konrad Lorenz and his investigations of violence in the animal kingdom; it does indeed evoke a sudden flurry of activity in a calm and colorful aquarium, but there is an edge to the aggressive moments that does not bespeak the pastoralist Lloyd's detractors deride. The 1972 suite entitled *The Transformation of That Naked Ape* gently mocks the book named in its title, and even the short, entirely tonal lullaby *Intercom Baby* (1987) somehow manages to suggest the presence of the titular modern technology within a conventional context. Perhaps Lloyd's most delightful piano score is *The Road Through Samarkand* (1972). That work deploys a century's worth of orientalisms in imagining a group of young British Hare Krishnas. "With burning hearts they danced their way from Calais to Calcutta, but what did they find?" wrote Lloyd in his program. In his piano music, as elsewhere, George Lloyd may have been a conservative, but he was hardly the kind that longed for a vanished world, musical or otherwise. *—James Manheim*

Recommended:

- ○ **Lloyd: Piano Concertos 1 & 2** / Lloyd (cond.), Roscoe, BBCPO / 1991 / Albany 037
- ○ **Lloyd: Piano Concerto 3** / Lloyd (cond.), Stott, BBC PO / 1989 / Albany 019
- ○ **Lloyd: Piano Concerto 4** / Lloyd (cond.), Stott, London SO / 1988 / Albany 004

Pietro Antonio Locatelli

b. Sep. 3, 1695, Bergamo, Italy, **d.** Mar. 30, 1764, Amsterdam, Netherlands
Composer: Concerto

Locatelli was one of the leading Italian violinists and composers in the first half of the eighteenth century. At one time, he was known as the "Paganini of the eighteenth century" due to his 12 concertos and 24 caprices for violin. Although he was known primarily as a virtuoso violinist in the early part of his life, his abilities as a composer were far more important. Stylistically, Locatelli worked within the conservative forms of the composers of the Roman school (Corelli, for example), but incorporated many of the more progressive elements of the Venetian school (Vivaldi, above all). He wrote mostly sonatas and concertos for string instruments, although there is a set of flute sonatas, and a lost concerto for wind instruments with strings. With the exception of those flute sonatas, Opus 2, which occasionally have three movements, his other works were almost exclusively in the older four-movement format. Locatelli also made the written-out cadenza a standard part of his violin concertos, an innovation from the earlier practice of exclusively improvised cadenzas. In general, though, his style was a consolidation of existing trends, yet still original in the beauty and resourcefulness of its harmonies.

Very little is known about Locatelli's early life and training, other than that he held a post as violinist in Bergamo until 1711. By 1712, he was in Rome, probably studying with Giuseppe Valentini, Corelli's rival. During the subsequent years, Locatelli worked exclusively as a violinist, particularly at the basilica of St. Lorenza in Damaso, Italy. In 1725, he was appointed virtuoso da camera of Mantua, a position which allowed him free rein to travel as a virtuoso.

In 1729, Locatelli moved permanently to Amsterdam, where he devoted his attention to teaching and composing with an occasional concert tour. He was also involved in importing Roman violin strings and in publishing. By his death in 1764, Locatelli had been successful enough to leave behind a considerable estate, as well as a compositional legacy that remained fairly current until the beginning of the next century. *—Steven Coburn*

Overview of Works (ca. 1720–1760)

Locatelli's fame as a violinist was legendary, it having been said that while his great French rival Leclair played "like an angel," Locatelli played "like the devil." With the exception of a set of *12 Flute Sonatas*, published as Op. 2 in 1732, most of his works were composed for his own instrument, although his first publication (in 1721) was a set of 12 concerti grossi. These show the influence of the Corellian type of concerto, although their longer movements are more expansive than those of the Roman master. In 1732, Locatelli published in Amsterdam his important and influential *L'arte del violino*. A set of 12 violin concertos was issued as Op. 3, each cast in the typical Vivaldian three-movement form, some of the concertos being of the *da chiesa* type opening with a slow Largo movement (Nos. 4, 5, and 6), while others conform to the more traditional fast-slow-fast pattern. What makes the concertos of Op. 3 truly original, however, are the extraordinarily demanding sections for solo violin termed by Locatelli as capriccios and inserted into the concluding pages of the first and last movements of the sonatas, thus acting as a kind of extended (some nearly as long as the movement itself) cadenza. Taken as a whole, the concertos represent a compendium of the possibilities of violin technique at the time, including such effects as playing in very high positions, frequent trills and double stopping, and difficult bowing devices such as slurred staccatos. Locatelli's Op. 4 (1735) is perhaps more musically interesting. Consisting of a group of six "symphonies" called *Introduttioni Teatrale* and six concertos, Op. 4 represents a considerable advance on his earlier works with much longer movements whose rhythmic verve and wealth of musical ideas look forward to the Classical era. In his Op. 6, published in Amsterdam in 1737, Locatelli returns to his own instrument in a set of 12 sonatas for violin and continuo. Cast in the three- (rather than four) movement form, the sonatas are also progressive in outlook, particularly in regard to their harmonies, which in their simplicity look forward to the pre-Classical idiom. Locatelli's two final groups of concertos (Op. 7 and Op. 10) carry such traits further forward in three-movement works that betray many typical elements of galant style, such as concluding minuets. *—Brian Robins*

Recommended:

- ○ **Locatelli: Violin Sonatas Op6** / Locatelli Trio / 1990 / Hyperion 66363
- ○ **Locatelli's Opus 4** / Wallfisch (cond.), Raglan Baroque Players / 1997 / Hyperion 67041
- ○ **Locatelli: Concertos Op7** / Bezzina, Baroque Ens. of Nice / Adda 581118
- ○ **Locatelli: Sonatas Op8** / Isserlis, Locatelli Trio / 1996 / Hyperion 67021
- ○ **Locatelli: Flute Sonatas Op2** / Il Ruggiero / Tactus 691202

CONCERTO

The Art of the Violin: 12 Concertos & 24 Caprices, Op. 3 (before 1733)

Though its music is unknown except to a very few Baroque specialists and an even fewer violinists, Pietro Antonio Locatelli's *L'arte del violino, Op. 3* (The Art of the Violin) (1733)—12 concertos for solo violin, strings, and basso continuo—is truly one of the most extraordinary works for violin ever conceived and penned, and as it turned out, a work that informed and continues to indirectly inform composers the world round. Locatelli was a master violinist, as were most of the Italian concerto composers, and the volume of concerti grossi released in 1721, as Op. 1, had elevated him from well-known virtuoso to famous virtuoso/composer. With *L'arte del violino,* Op. 3, he moved the role and technique of violin playing, and the solo concerto as a genre, into a whole new realm. Locatelli dedicated *L'arte del violino* to the Venetian patriarch Girolamo Michiel Lini, for whom he had performed while staying in the city and of whose orchestra Locatelli remarked upon the skill and "unparalleled size."

Ignoring, for the moment, the wonderful style and impeccable form of the Op. 3 concertos, the first thing one notices, when a performance of a concerto from *L'arte del violino* begins, is how extraordinarily difficult the solo violin part is, but this can hardly prepare one for the shock to come: at the end of the first and third movements of each of the concertos, just before the final tutti, Locatelli inserts a capriccio, or caprice, for unaccompanied solo violin. There are 24 in all, of fiendish and unprecedented technical difficulty. If the idea of *24 Caprices for solo violin* rings a bell for violin lovers, it might be mentioned that it was after discovering a copy of Locatelli's *L'arte del violino* in Genoa that Paganini began to work on his own *24 Caprices for solo violin.* Paganini even quotes one of Locatelli's (from the first movement of the *Concerto in E major,* Op. 3, No. 4) in his very first caprice. Locatelli's caprices, when performed at all, are usually extracted from the concertos and played as self-standing virtuoso truffles. When heard in this fashion one cannot enjoy the remarkable way that they sprout from the dramatic conclusions to the quick movements of the concertos. The manner of the solo concerto cadenza, especially, but not exclusively, the violin cadenza, was codified by Locatelli in ways only touched upon by earlier composers, like Vivaldi and Corelli. The effects on both concerto format and violin technique were far-reaching indeed.

The 12 concertos in Op. 3 are all constructed after the by-then venerable model of Torelli's solo concerto in three movements, but Locatelli's creative interplay between the soloist and the tutti ensemble goes beyond anything that earlier concerto composers had devised. His constant surprises and clever ensemble effects, though perhaps not striking to a modern audience, were a delight to audiences of his day. *—Blair Johnston*

Recommended:

- ○ **Locatelli: L'Arte del Violino** / Wallfisch (cond.), Kraemer, Raglan Baroque Players / 1994 / Hyperion 66721
- ○ **Locatelli: The Art of the Violin Vol. 1** / Kehr (cond.), Lautenbacher, Mainz CO / 1990 / Vox 5018

12 Concerti Grossi, Op. 1 (before 1721)

Italian-born violinist and composer Pietro Locatelli was probably not a student of Arcangelo Corelli, as some historians have claimed, but his indebtedness to the elder Italian is nevertheless very marked. In fact, the large-scale format of Locatelli's very first published volume of music, the *12 Concerti grossi,* Op. 1 (published in 1721 and 1729 by the Amsterdam-based publishing house of Estienne Roger, who no doubt exerted some influence on the shape that Locatelli's first opus would take), is patterned directly after Corelli's bestselling *Concerti grossi,* Op. 6, right down to the division into eight concerti da chiesa and four concerti da camera and the inclusion of a Christmas concerto as the eighth piece. Beyond this mimicking of surface design, Locatelli's Op. 1 set displays the kinds of stylistic similarities to Corelli's music that we would expect in the music of someone whose teenage years were spent travelling with one of Corelli's former students. When one begins to turn the pages of the volume, however, it becomes clear that this is the same distinctive-voiced Pietro Locatelli who a few years later would release the very sophisticated *L'Arte del violino,* Op. 3. If in Op. 1 we are perhaps not afforded as much of a glimpse into Locatelli's developing bag of tricks as we might like, we can still take immense enjoyment in what are, without a doubt, twelve of the better Italian concertos penned by members of the first post-Corelli generation.

The usual division of musical forces into a tutti group and a solo group (or concertino) is made in Opus 1; somewhat unusually, Locatelli includes a viola, sometimes two, in the concertino group. Although, in general, we can speak of *concerti da chiesa* and *da camera* (merely the four-movement sonata da chiesa and multiple-dance-movement sonata da camera ideas applied to a larger ensemble) in Op. 1, Locatelli often embroiders these two traditional formal designs. The first three concertos of the set, in F major, C minor, and B flat major, are cast not in the plain four movement slow-fast-slow-fast of the normal sonata da chiesa but rather in five movements: in the first concerto there is an extra fast movement at the opening, while the second and third each have an additional fast movement at the end. The concerto Op. 1, No. 7 in F major is truncated rather than expanded, the opening slow movement being omitted to produce something more in the vein of the three-movement Venetian concerto form. The Christmas Concerto (Op. 1, No. 8 in F minor) is a stunning seven-movement thing that ends with a Pastorale very appropriately written in the parallel major.

Although in the four *da camera* concertos (Nos. 9–12) Locatelli marks only the allemande and sarabande movements with their dance-form titles (one gigue is also so marked in No. 11), it is very clear that many of the other movements are also of dance origin, or at least dance inspiration. The Largo andante of Op. 1, No. 10 in C major is something of a siciliano, while the closing movement of the last piece in the set, Op. 1, No. 12 in G minor, is sewn of the same compound-meter stuff used to make gigues.

Both the Christmas Concerto and the Concerto in B flat major, Op. 1, No. 3, are special treats. In Op. 1, No. 3, Locatelli explores the same repetitive staccato-type slow movement that Vivaldi often wrote in his instrumental works; the brief finale of the same concerto is a rowdy outburst in 2/4 meter that bustles along atop energetic syncopations. *—Blair Johnston*

Recommended:

- ○ **Locatelli: Concerti Grossi Op1** / Wallfisch (cond.), Kraemer, Raglan Baroque Players / 1995 / Hyperion 66981/2

Matthew Locke

b. ca. 1621, Exeter, England, **d.** Aug. 1677, London, England

Composer

A composer central to the musical life of turbulent mid-seventeenth century England, Matthew Locke learned music as a choirboy at Exeter. A 1648 manuscript that Locke subtitled *When I was in the Low Countreys* has been cited as evidence he was employed by the court of Prince Charles, who was then living in exile as a refugee from the English Civil War. By the time Locke is known to have returned to England in 1651, he had probably adopted the Catholic faith favored by Charles himself.

By 1653, Locke had begun to establish himself as a force on the English stage. That year he may have collaborated with Christopher Gibbons on the music for John Shirley's masque *Cupid and Death.* In 1656, Locke joined forces with playwright William Davenant and several others in compiling what might be regarded as the first English opera, *The Siege of Rhodes.* Locke also contributed music for revivals of Shakespeare's plays, including *The Tempest, Henry VIII* and *Macbeth.* During this time, Locke began to cultivate a reputation for composing instrumental music; he was a close associate of composer John Playford, contributing to the latter's publications *Courtly Masquing Ayres* and *The Dancing Master.*

In 1660, Charles II was restored to the English throne after eleven years of Commonwealth. Locke was then named private composer-in-ordinary to the King. Among his tasks was to supervise a consort of eight string players which, in emulation of French court practice, was expanded into a mini-orchestra of 24 violins in 1662. That year Charles II married Catherine of Braganza, and Locke was appointed her private organist. Locke played both in the chapels where Catherine worshipped and in her apartment, sometimes with a small band of chamber players. During the 1660s Locke continued to write music for the London stage, although he moved, along with the entire court, to Oxford in 1665 in order to escape the Black Death, then raging in the city. Thus began an association with Oxford and its university music school that produced the best of Locke's sacred vocal music, most of which survives in manuscripts copied by Edward Lowe, then head of Oxford's music department. Locke's work at Oxford continued happily until 1672, when he became embroiled in an ugly and very public dispute with composer and Trinity College graduate Thomas Salmon, most of which was played out in the press.

In 1673, Locke published *Melothesia*, a volume of keyboard music which contains a detailed method of figured-bass continuo playing, the first such treatise written in English. Locke died at the age of about 56 in the summer of 1677; his tasks with the court band of Four and Twenty were taken over by the teenaged Henry Purcell. Purcell composed a fine ode in Locke's memory, and was made the gift of a large manuscript volume containing the chamber music that Locke had seen fit to preserve.

Much of Locke's music is highly chromatic and dissonant; he was stubbornly committed to his conception of what constituted English style, and once commented that "I never yet saw any Forain Instrumental Composition worthy an English mans Transcribing." He favored long phrases of irregular length, and there are many harmonically unstable and wandering passages in which Locke seems openly to defy stylistic preconceptions of the early Baroque. Locke's instrumental music, in particular that for "broken consort," is some of the most important music of its kind written in the seventeenth century. His vocal and theater music is less known, but all of Locke's work is significant, and his topsy-turvy music provides a splendid counterpoint to the constant upheavals of the England of his day. *—Uncle Dave Lewis*

Overview of Works (ca. 1665–1677)

One of the most important and versatile English composers of the seventeenth century, Matthew Locke (ca. 1621–77) was a chorister at Exeter Cathedral. During the Civil Wars his name occasionally appears among musicians in Charles I's circle. In 1648, he was in the Netherlands where he may have met the exiled future Charles II. On Charles' Restoration in 1660, Locke acquired three important court posts, later supplemented by his appointment as organist to Queen Catherine (like the composer, a Catholic), and other marks of royal favor.

Locke's extensive output includes music in every genre of his period. He played an important role in attempts to establish English opera, a goal which—as a chauvinist who once declared that he "never yet saw any Forain Instrumental Composition... worthy an Englishman's Transcribing"—would have been close to his heart. In 1656, he was one of several composers to provide the music for William Davenant's *The Siege of Rhodes*, often cited as the first English opera. The music is unfortunately lost, but Locke's music for another music drama *Cupid and Death* survives. It is an example of the post-court masque, with spoken dialogue and dances; Locke added music to a preexisting score by Christopher Gibbons for the work's revival in 1659.

After the Restoration, Locke continued to compose music for theater, most notably the instrumental music he provided for an operatic version of *The Tempest* (a score that remained popular throughout the eighteenth century, when it was frequently misattributed to Purcell), and *Psyche*, which the composer pointedly published under the title of "The English Opera." *Psyche*, inspired by Lully's tragédie-ballet of the same name, includes music by both Locke and the expatriate Italian Giovanni Battista Draghi. It incorporates dances and spoken dialogue, Locke's contribution being some of the finest dramatic music in English music theater before that of Purcell.

The best of Locke's instrumental music also bears comparison with anything written by English composers during the seventeenth century. Pride of place must go to his superb collection of six viol consort suites published under the title of *Consort of Fower Parts*, noble works that occupy a major place in the long and distinguished history of English music for the viol. Locke's instrumental chamber works also include *The Broken Consort*, six suites scored for the more modern combination of violins, bass viols, theorbos, and organ. Other instrumental publications include *Melothesia* (1673), Locke's only major keyboard collection, and *Tripla concordia* (1677), a set of trios for two violins and bass viol.

Locke's chauvinism apparently did not extend to Italian sacred music. While in the Netherlands he copied a group of Latin motets, the influence of which is clearly apparent in his own Catholic church music, of which the large-scale motet *Super flumina Babylonis* is a particularly fine example. More surprisingly, Locke also composed a substantial body of music for the Anglican church which skillfully combines elements of English and Italian styles. *—Brian Robins*

Recommended:

- ○ **Locke: Anthems, Motets & Ceremonial Music** / Higginbottom (cond.), Parley of Instruments, New College Choir Oxford / 1990 / Hyperion 66373
- ○ **Locke: The Broken Consort** / Holman (cone.), Parley of Instruments / 1995 / Hyperion 66727
- ○ **Locke: Consort of 4 parts** / Savall (cond.), Hespèrion XX / 2002 / Astrée Naive 9921
- ○ **Locke: Psyche** / Pickett (cond.), Robson, Gooding, Bell, New London Consort / 1995 / L'Oiseau-Lyre 444336

Carl Loewe

b. Nov. 30, 1796, Löbejün, Germany, **d.** Apr. 20, 1869, Kiel, Germany
Composer: Vocal

Referred to as "the North German Schubert" during his life, Carl Loewe, like his Austrian counterpart, developed the Romantic ballad for voice and piano into a powerful art form. An excellent singer, he undertook numerous tours performing his own works. Known mostly for his solo songs, Loewe also composed six operas, 17 oratorios, and numerous cantatas, string quartets, and piano works.

Loewe's earliest training was from his father, a schoolmaster, and he sang in the church choir at Cöthen. At age 12, having already published some songs and instrumental pieces, he entered the Gymnasium at Halle, in Thuringia, where the headmaster continued his training. Jerome Bonaparte, the King of Westphalia, heard Loewe sing and was sufficiently impressed to award the boy an annual stipend, enabling Loewe to continue studying music. This support ended abruptly in 1813, when Jerome was deposed; however, the chancellor of the Gymnasium came to Loewe's aid and helped him matriculate in theology at Halle University.

During 1819–1820, Loewe toured Germany, becoming *Kantor* and professor at the Stettin Gymnasium and seminary. In 1821, he was appointed Director of Music at Stettin, a position he would hold until 1865. His marriage to Julie von Jacob in 1821 lasted only two years; in 1826 he married Auguste Lange, a singer from Königsberg who often performed Loewe's songs in concert. Between 1820 and 1830, he was especially productive, completing some of this most popular songs and ballads, several piano sonatas, and his first opera, *Rudolf der deutsche Herr*. Most notable from this era are his settings of Byron's *Hebrew Melodies*.

By 1835, Loewe was famous throughout German-speaking lands as a conductor and composer as well as a singer. He began to tour internationally in 1844; from Loewe's letters home, it is clear that the trip was a success, bringing him a great deal of acclaim. A trip to London in 1847 was not as successful. In later years, he visited Scandinavia and France. Loewe suffered a stroke in 1864 and had to resign his post at Stettin the next year; he died in Kiel, after another stroke.

Loewe was first and foremost a composer of vocal music; even his *Sonata for Piano in E major*, Op. 16, contains a song for tenor as the slow movement (a setting of *Adolf an Adele*). His Op. 1, consisting of three ballads, reflects his varied tastes for poetry: *Edward* is by an anonymous Scottish poet, *Der Wirthin Töchterlein* is by Uhland, and his *Erlkönig* is, of course, by Johann Wolfgang von Goethe, whom Loewe met in 1819 or 1820. The last of these is frequently contrasted with Schubert's famous setting; indeed, the choice of G minor as the key, an agitated piano accompaniment, and use of a recitative-like ending, all make for striking similarities. Loewe's daughter would later state that her father saw Schubert's setting and wished to compose a better one; however, such a scenario is very unlikely.

The narrative Romantic ballad required departure from the standard strophic forms that had dominated the German lied during the late eighteenth century. Loewe addressed this issue by using through-composed forms or modified strophic forms—contrasting arioso with dramatic, accompanied recitative—as we find in *Der Wirthin Töchterlein*.

Loewe's settings of Byron's *Hebrew Melodies* showcase all of the composer's strengths. His writing for the piano is idiomatic and independent of the voice part without being obtrusive. Quick but masterful key changes often highlight moments of drama in the texts. *Tom der Reimer* and *Der Asra*, both dating from 1863, are often cited as his best ballads. *Hiob* is considered his best oratorio, while *Emmy* is arguably his finest opera. *—John Palmer*

VOCAL

Lieder (ca. 1810–1864)

Loewe was almost as prolific a composer as Schubert and Schumann, producing 17 volumes of ballads over his lifetime and hundreds of other songs, including settings of Goethe, Rückert, Grun, and Freiligrath texts, as well as translations of folk ballads and Shakespeare. Also like Schubert and Schumann, he was deeply committed to creating psychological and dramatic insight into the characters of his songs. In his setting of Herder's translation of the Scottish poem "Edward," the contrast between the two characters' agitation—the mother's excitement and pseudo-innocence, and the son's dulled, almost numbed responses before he finally admits to murder—makes it one of the most insightful versions that any composer created. However, in stark contrast to them, Loewe (who was one of the few lieder composers who was also a trained and accomplished singer) devoted nearly all of his attention to the vocal part, rather than creating a true partnership between voice and accompaniment. Even in the songs where the piano plays a major role in establishing a dramatic setting or a mood, the effect is one of the voice briefly moving out of focus, rather than sharing focus with the piano. While nearly all his ballads are through-composed, he still reflected their folk origins by using repeated themes and occasionally using clearly delineated stanzas, though in many cases the themes are so subtly repeated that they are more apparent on the printed page than in the performances. Typically, the longer a text he had to work with, the more successful the lied. Loewe was perhaps more at home in oratorio, opera, and symphony, which larger-scale works allow much more time to unfold a situation and characterizations. His extended ballad *Archibald Douglas* (also a Scottish text) is practically a miniature opera and creates commensurate dramatic demands on the interpreters, particularly with his heavy use of repetition to express the aging Douglas' longing for his homeland. Most lieder composers had an affinity for the supernatural and he was no exception; aside from *Der Erlkönig*, his admirable settings of *Herr Oluf* (which such varied composers as Spontini and Wagner both admired greatly) and *Walpurgisnacht* (another Wagner favorite) that reflect the terrifying side of the supernatural, *Irrlichter* (from his Op. 62) perfectly captures the mischievous and playful nature of the supernatural figures. *—Ann Feeney*

Recommended:

- ○ **Loewe: Lieder & Balladen Vol. 10** / Ziesak, Garben / 1998 / CPO 999543
- ○ **Loewe: Lieder & Balladen Vol. 11** / Groop, Garben / 1999 / CPO 999612
- ○ **Loewe: Lieder & Balladen Vol. 14** / Moll, Garben / CPO 999414

London Brass

f. 1986, London, England
Ensemble

The London Brass was founded largely from the membership of the renowned Philip Jones Brass Ensemble upon that group's disbandment in 1986. Appearing most often as a ten-piece ensemble, the group has adapted its performing forces to the needs of the works at hand, and at times reduces to the more traditional brass quintet format.

Making one of their primary objectives the promotion of new music, London Brass has commissioned works from Richard Rodney Bennett, John Lunn, Dominic Muldowney, Nigel Osborne, Michael Nyman, Mark-Anthony Turnage, Mike Gibbs, Django Bates, Paul Hart, Carla Bley, and Deidre Gribbin. The ensemble's members welcome cutting-edge, experimental pieces such as Jay Arden's *Bayo's Way*, for electronic tuba and ensemble; according to trombonist David Purser, "This is a piece we had written to showcase the extraordinary techniques that Oren Marshall has developed using guitar pedals and amplifier. It's not an easy piece to listen to, but it has always been a great success with our audiences."

As Ensemble in Residence at the Royal College of Music in London, the members of the London Brass have a variety of teaching and coaching duties. They also conduct master classes and other educational activities outside of Britain, particularly in Norway and Germany.

The London Brass boasts several expert arrangers among their membership who have produced transcriptions of works by composers from nearly all eras of Western music, including J. S. Bach (*Brandenburg Concerto No. 3*), Witold Lutosławski (*Variations on a theme by Paganini for piano duet*), Brahms, Elgar, Ravel and others who wrote little or no music for brass ensemble. Particularly impressive are Chris Mowat's arrangement of Edward Elgar's *Introduction and Allegro* and Richard Bissill's transcription of Franz Liszt's famous *Second Hungarian Rhapsody*. (Arrangements by the London Brass are published by Brass Wind Publications.) In concert, these excellent transcriptions are juxtaposed with performances of authentic brass music, both old and new. The group also performs much earlier music, especially late Renaissance and early Baroque works with choir; works by Schütz and Gabrieli figure prominently in their annual programming.

As of the 2000/2001 season the membership of the London Brass included Andy Crowley, Paul Beniston, John Barclay, and Anne MacAneney on trumpet, Lindsay Schilling, Richard Edward, and David Purser on trombones, Richard Bissill on horn, Oren Marshall on tuba, and David Stewart on bass trombone. Each of them leads a busy career apart from the London Brass, taking up such diverse pursuits as solo engagements, orchestral positions, chamber music, and faculty positions at London conservatories. Among them are principal players from the English Chamber Orchestra, the London Sinfonietta, and three (horn, trumpet and trombone) from the London Philharmonic Orchestra, as well as soloists from some of London's best known jazz orchestras. They spend two or three months of each year touring, recording and enjoying one another's company as London Brass. *—John Palmer*

Recommended:

- ○ **The Royal Golden Jubilee** / Westminster Abbey Choir, London Brass, Llandaff Cathedral Choir / 2002 / Griffin 4034
- ○ **Music for Royal Occasions** / London Brass, Llandaff Cathedral Choir / 2002 / Griffin 4037

London Philharmonic Orchestra

f. Oct. 7, 1932, London, England
Ensemble

Sir Thomas Beecham founded the London Philharmonic Orchestra in 1932 with assistance from arts patrons Robert Mayer and Samuel Courtauld. Consisting then of 106 players and giving more than 70 concerts yearly, the ensemble immediately established itself as a major orchestra. On October 7, 1932, its inaugural concert took place at Queen's Hall, with Beecham conducting. The orchestra began making recordings in 1933, but their number remained scarce until the 1950s. In 1936, the LPO made a highly successful tour of Germany, giving one concert in Berlin in the presence of Adolf Hitler. Financial difficulties beset the orchestra by 1939, prompting Beecham to help raise money. Soon, however, he resigned and relocated to the United States for a stint with the Seattle Symphony Orchestra, though he maintained ties to the orchestra. Adrian Boult, Malcolm Sargent, and Basil Cameron shared podium duties until 1945. In 1947, the LPO formed the London Philharmonic Choir and named Eduard van Beinum, long associated with the Amsterdam Concertgebouw, as principal conductor. Van Beinum had a successful but brief reign and was succeeded in 1951 by Adrian Boult. Under his leadership, the LPO began recording heavily and would continue to do so thereafter, becoming one of the most heavily recorded ensembles among the world's major orchestras, with hundreds of LP and (then later) CD titles issued by various major labels. American William Steinberg succeeded Boult in 1958, but served only two seasons, leaving the orchestra once more without a principal conductor. John Pritchard was appointed his successor in 1962 and effected many important changes in the orchestra personnel and repertory. In 1966, Bernard Haitink succeeded Pritchard and had a tenure longer than any previous or subsequent conductor, serving until 1979. Georg Solti was appointed principal conductor that year, holding the post until 1983, at which time he took on emeritus status, thereby maintaining ties to the orchestra. East German conductor Klaus Tennstedt became principal conductor in 1983. Another, but far younger, German conductor, Franz Welser-Möst, succeeded him in 1990 and led an often controversial tenure. Still, his concert tour of South Africa was a great success, as were several recordings. Kurt Masur, took the reins as principal conductor in September 2000. The LPO regularly performs in Royal Festival Hall, London. *—Robert Cummings*

Recommended:

- ○ **Beethoven: Symphony 2; Missa Solemnis** / Beecham (cond.), McCallum, Nash, Baillie, Falkner, Jarred, Richardson, London PO / EMI 5
- ○ **Elgar: Violin Concerto** / Handley (cond.), Kennedy, London PO / 2002 / EMI 575139
- ○ **Schubert: Symphony 9** / Boult (cond.), Baker, London PO / 2004 / EMI 62792
- ○ **Banks: Seven, suite** / Dixon (cond.), Banks, London PO / 2004 / Naxos 8557466

London Symphony Chorus

f. 1966, London, England
Ensemble

The year 1966 was a major watershed in the history of the London Symphony Orchestra. The oldest of London's full-sized orchestras, founded in 1904, it had never possessed a permanent venue of its own and had long been in uncertain financial and artistic shape. In that year, the Corporation of the City of London committed to building the new Barbican Arts Centre and chose the London Symphony Orchestra (which had seen a vast improvement in standards in a short time) as its permanent residential orchestra. Also in 1966, the London Symphony Chorus was formed as a complement to the LSO. (Prior to then, recordings and concerts featuring a group designated "London Symphony Chorus" usually had an ad hoc chorus, or a chorus provided by such organizations as the Ambrosian Singers, a core group of hundreds of available professional singers.)

The London Symphony Chorus comprises over 200 amateur singers from all walks of life. Although it works closely with the London Symphony, it is not organizationally a part of the orchestra (which is a self-governing co-op of its members). The chorus is, instead, a separate self-governing group, whose members choose nine elected representatives to administer it.

In addition to appearing regularly in concerts with the LSO, the chorus is free to appear with other orchestras. The heart of its repertoire is the wide range of twentieth century choral music, including Mahler's three choral symphonies, Elgar's *The Dream of Gerontius*, Britten's *War Requiem*, Janáček's *Glagolitic Mass*, and Walton's *Belshazzar's Feast*. It has made over 90 recordings, including Richard Hickox's recording of *War Requiem* (winner of the Grand Prix du Disque), Bernstein's *Candide*, and Britten's *Peter Grimes* (the latter two both Grammy Award winners).

It has a commissioning program, which has resulted in the writing of such works as Tavener's *The Myrrh Bearer* and Sir Peter Maxwell Davies' *The Three Kings*, a Christmas cantata. It appears in major festivals, and frequently undertakes tours to all parts of the world. *—Joseph Stevenson*

Recommended:

- ○ **Vaughan Williams: A Sea Symphony** / Hickox (cond.), Roberts, Marshall, London Symphony Chorus, London PO / 1990 / Virgin 90843
- ○ **Berlioz: Requiem; Te Deum** / Davis (cond.), Kynaston, Dowd, Tagliavini, London SO & Chorus / 2001 / Philips 464689

○ **Britten: War Requiem, etc.** / Hickox (cond.), Scott, Langridge, Hill, Harper, London SO & Chorus / 2003 / Chandos 5007

○ **Handel: Messiah** / Davis (cond.), Harper, Watts, Shirley-Quirk, Pearson, London SO & Chorus / 1993 / Philips 438356

○ **Prokofiev & Rachmaninoff** / Muti, Previn (conds.), Reynolds, Arkhipova, London SO & Chorus / 1999 / EMI 73353

○ **Handel: Messiah, Arias & Choruses** / Boult (cond.), Sutherland, Malcolm, Bumbry, McKellar, London SO & Chorus / Decca 467401

London Symphony Orchestra

f. 1904, London, England

Ensemble

Formed in 1904 by a group of 46 musicians who had resigned from London's Queen's Hall Orchestra because of change in policy, the London Symphony Orchestra (LSO) is an ensemble of "firsts." It was the first orchestra in England to set up a self-governing administrative structure, the first to tour North America, and the first to accept commercial sponsorship. Known as one of England's most gifted and versatile ensembles, it is the resident orchestra at London's famous Barbican Centre. This and the fact that the LSO tours extensively; has provided music for countless films, radio broadcasts, and television productions; and records prolifically has helped to consolidate the group's reputation as one of the world's leading orchestras.

During the late nineteenth and early twentieth century, London musicians worked on a strictly freelance basis, finding work where they could for the highest possible fee. In 1904, Henry Wood, conductor of the Queen's Hall Orchestra, decided that he could no longer tolerate the chaos of the situation and hired players as full-time employees with a small but guaranteed wage for about 100 scheduled performances a year. Many of the best musicians, who were in great demand and who stood to lose a significant portion of their earnings through this restriction, resigned from Wood's ensemble and formed their own, self-governing orchestra.

Soon after its creation, the LSO invited Hans Richter to be its first conductor. He accepted the position on the condition that the orchestra increase its number to at least 100 players. Although Richter conducted a great many of the orchestra's concerts during his eight-year tenure, the group also attracted numerous other distinguished conductors to the podium. These included Nikisch, Steinbach, and Elgar. In so doing, the LSO promoted the idea of guest conductors in English musical society.

Two years after its foundation, the orchestra played its first concerts outside England; two concerts in Paris. Under the direction of Nikisch in 1912, the LSO became the first British orchestra to tour North America, presenting 28 concerts in 21 days, beginning and ending with performances in New York's Carnegie Hall.

Over the next 50 years, the LSO was lead by a number of gifted and distinguished conductors including Sir Thomas Beecham, Albert Coates , Sir Hamilton Harty, Josef Krips, Pierre Monteux, Istvan Kertesz, André Previn, and Claudio Abbado. All of these men, in addition to the many guest conductors and artists invited to work with the LSO, left their marks on the orchestra; shaping and honing the virtuosity of its players into an ensemble of great sensitivity and versatility.

The orchestra's association with the film industry began in 1922 when Walter Wanger, head of United Artists, hired the LSO to play for the presentation of silent films at Covent Garden's Opera House. Since then, the ensemble has provided music for numerous films including the *Star Wars* series for which the LSO won a platinum disc.

The LSO's connection with the BBC goes back to 1924 when Ralph Vaughan Williams conducted the orchestra in the premiere broadcast performance of his *Pastoral Symphony.* The LSO was the unofficial orchestra in residence for the BBC until the formation of the BBC Symphony in 1930 and has continued to broadcast concerts and provide background music for many BBC productions.

When Michael Tilson Thomas replaced Abbado in 1987, he set about securing the organization's financial as well as musical future by encouraging the LSO to accept corporate sponsorship. Conducted by Sir Colin Davis since 1995, the London Symphony Orchestra has long enjoyed its well-deserved reputation as a pioneer in several areas of British orchestral history and is a highly versatile and distinguished world-class ensemble. *—Corie Stanton Root*

Recommended:

○ **Rózsa, Gould, Menotti, Lavry** / Amos (cond.), Percy, Carter, McGrath, Arbuckle, London SO / 2000 / Kleos 5103

○ **Liszt: Dante Symphony; Tasso** / Botstein (cond.), London SO / 2003 / Telarc 80613

○ **LSO: Salzburg Festival (1973–1977)** / Böhm (cond.), Szeryng, Gilels, London SO / 2003 / Andante 4030

○ **Zappa: London SO, Vols. 1 & 2** / Nagano (cond.), Ocker, Mann, Wackerman, London SO / 1995 / Vack 1252

George London

b. May 5, 1919, Montreal, Quebec, Canada, **d.** Mar. 23, 1985, Armonk, NY

Bass

George London was one of the most celebrated singing actors of his generation, with an imposing stage presence. In addition to excelling in a wide range of roles, from Mozart's Don Giovanni to Wotan to Scarpia to Escamillo, he was the first North American singer to appear on the stage of Moscow's *Bolshoi Theater,* where in 1960 he triumphed in arguably the greatest Russian male role, Boris Godunov.

London began his vocal training after his family moved to Los Angeles, when he was 15. He made his operatic debut as Doctor Grenvil in Verdi's *La traviata* at the Hollywood Bowl, and for a while sang with Frances Yeend and Mario Lanza in the Bel Canto Trio. In 1949, he decided to make his career in Europe, and after an audition with Karl Böhm, joined the Vienna State Opera, where he made his debut as Amonasro, and was an overnight success. He remained a favorite there throughout his career, and was named a Kammersänger.

He made his Bayreuth Festival debut the year it reopened, 1951, as Amfortas, and he also appeared there in the title role of *The Flying Dutchman.* In 1962, he sang the complete *Ring* in Cologne, under the direction of Wieland Wagner.

In 1966, one of his vocal chords became paralyzed, and he retired from singing. However, he remained very active in the musical world. In 1971, he established a foundation for young singers (a list of just the most prominent award recipients includes Renée Fleming, Kathleen Battle, Jerry Hadley, Barbara Hendricks, James Morris, and Dawn Upshaw).

He also served as artistic administrator of the Kennedy Center for the Performing Arts (Washington, D.C.) from 1968 to 1971, and executive director of the National Opera Institute from 1971 to 1976, as well as the director of the Washington Opera from 1975 to 1979. In 1975, in Seattle, he staged the first-ever complete *Ring Cycle* in English. *—Ann Feeney*

Recommended:

○ **Of Gods and Demons** / London, etc. / 1996 / Sony 62758

○ **George London** / London, etc. / Preiser 90543

○ **Mussorgsky: Boris Godunov** / Melik-Pashaev (cond.), London, Arkhipova, Ktitorov, Ivanov / 2002 / Sony 52571

Jesús López-Cobos

b. Feb. 25, 1940, Toro, Spain

Conductor

Born in Toro, Spain, Jesús López-Cobos was educated at the universities of Granada and Madrid, earning a doctorate in philosophy at the latter institution in 1964. In his student days, López-Cobos led a student chorus with such success that he decided to undertake full-time musical studies, first earning a degree in composition from Madrid in 1966. He then studied conducting with Franco Ferrara in Italy. In 1968, López-Cobos won first prize at the Besançon international conducting competition, and as a student of Hans Swarowsky he took his degree in conducting at the Vienna Academy in 1969. That same year, López-Cobos gave his debut concert as a symphony conductor in Prague, and as an opera conductor at La Fenice in Venice.

López-Cobos first led the Deutsche Oper Berlin in 1970, and would serve as general musical director for that company from 1981 to 1990. During that time, López-Cobos led Wagner's *Ring* cycle on tour in Japan in 1987; the tour marked the first time the whole Ring cycle had been staged in that country. In the 1970s and 1980s, López-Cobos also led opera productions at Covent Garden, San Francisco, the Vienna Opera, La Scala, and he Metropolitan in New York. López-Cobos was named principal guest conductor of the London Philharmonic and served there from 1981 to 1986. Also, from 1984 to 1989, he served as principal conductor and artistic director of the Spanish National Orchestra.

In 1986, López-Cobos was named principal conductor and music director of the Cincinnati Symphony; he added the Lausanne Chamber Orchestra to his musical directorships in 1990. With Cincinnati he would embark on an extensive recording schedule with Telarc, resulting in recordings of works by Respighi, Ravel, Richard Strauss, Wagner, Bruckner, Mahler, Falla, Bizet, Franck, and Dukas. Among these, his recording of the Mahler *Symphony No. 9* has been singled out as a critical favorite, and his complete recording of Albéniz's *Iberia* in the Arbos and Surinach orchestrations is apparently unique in the catalog. His repertory is rich with works of the late nineteenth and early twentieth centuries. López-Cobos has also recorded with the Lausanne Chamber Orchestra for Denon and Teldec.

López-Cobos has led the usually homebound Cincinnati Symphony on several tours, including one to Puerto Rico in 1998 and the first West Coast tour in the orchestra's history in 1992. His annual appearances with the Cincinnati orchestra at Carnegie Hall in New York regularly sell out the house. In 1997, López-Cobos led the ensemble in its first coast-to-coast telecast on PBS, featuring pianist Alicia de Larrocha. In 1996, the Cincinnati College-Conservatory of Music awarded López-Cobos an honorary doctorate in music.

In 2001, Maestro López-Cobos became conductor emeritus in Cincinnati. He also ended his association with the Lausanne Chamber Orchestra in 2000. López-Cobos continues as Permanent Conductor of the Orchestre Français des Jeunes, a Paris-based summer workshop for student musicians. —*Uncle Dave Lewis*

Recommended:

- ○ **Turina & Debussy** / Lopez-Cobos (cond.), Cincinnati SO / 2001 / Telarc 60574
- ○ **Albeniz: Iberia** / Lopez-Cobos (cond.), Cincinnati SO / 1998 / Telarc 80470
- ○ **Respighi: Church Windows; Brazilian Impressions; Roman Festivals** / Lopez-Cobos (cond.), Cincinnati SO / 1994 / Telarc 80356
- ○ **Falla: The Three-Cornered Hat, etc.** / Lopez-Cobos (cond.), Quivar, Cincinnati SO / 1987 / Telarc 80149

Yvonne Loriod

b. Jan. 20, 1924, Houilles, France
Pianist

Yvonne Loriod is a remarkably talented pianist, well known for her performances and recordings of twentieth century piano literature. Her playing is marked by its rich colorfulness and her keen sense of rhythm. Loriod's early musical training was with her godmother Madame Eminger-Sivade. As a youngster, with her teacher's support, she would present monthly recitals of works from the Classical, Romantic, and Modern periods. Before she entered the Paris Conservatoire, she had learned Bach's *Well-Tempered Klavier*, Beethoven's sonatas, the works of Chopin and Schumann, and Mozart's concertos. At the Conservatoire, she studied with Isidor Philipp, Marcel Ciampi, and Lazare Lévy for piano, as well as studying chamber music, piano accompaniment, and fugue, and taking composition with Messiaen and Milhaud. By the time she left the school, she had won seven premier prix. In another remarkable feat, she performed 22 of Mozart's concertos in a single week with the Lamoureux Orchestra, conducted by Pierre Boulez, Bruno Maderna, and Louis Martin. She first performed with Messiaen in 1943 for the premiere of his *Vision de l'amen*. She would go on to perform and record all of his works featuring the piano, and eventually became his second wife in 1961. Her American debut was the world-premiere performance of Messiaen's *Turangalila Symphony* with Leonard Bernstein and the Boston Symphony Orchestra in 1949. Schoenberg, Bartók, Barraqué, and Boulez were a few of the other composers whose works she often performed and recorded. She and Boulez premiered Boulez's *Structures, Book 2*, in 1961 at Donaueschingen. Loriod's recordings brought her 12 Grand Prix du Disque awards. She taught both at the Paris Conservatoire (1967–89) and at Darmstadt. She also edited Messiaen's massive *Traité de rythme, de couleur et d'ornithologie*. Loriod continued to perform through the 1990s and could be found adjudicating at competitions, including the triennial Concours Olivier Messiaen, and participating in various Messiaen festivals in the early 2000s. —*Patsy Morita*

Recommended:

- ○ **Olivier Messiaen** / Boulez (cond.), Loriod, InterContemporain Ensemble / 2000 / Disques Montaigne 782131
- ○ **Messiaen: Réveil des Oiseaux; 3 Petites Liturgies de la Présence Divine** / Nagano (cond.), Loriod, Loriod, Hery, Griffet, Sendrez, France, France / Erato 12702

Louis Lortie

b. Apr. 27, 1959, Montreal, Quebec, Canada
Pianist

French-Canadian pianist Louis Lortie achieved international recognition by his mid-twenties. His strong, yet sensitively crafted playing has served him well in a repertory of considerable breadth, with a concentration on composers from the late Classical period to the early twentieth century. Through a particularly fruitful association with his record company, he has been able to preserve on disc many of his most impressive interpretations and to enjoy a wide audience for his artistry.

After studying with Yvonne Hubert, Lortie made his first professional public appearance as soloist with the Montreal Symphony Orchestra. He was then 13 years old and, wisely, elected not to pursue a concert career immediately. After winning first prize in Canada's two premiere competitions, the Canadian National Music Competition and the CBC National Competition when he was 16, he made what he considers his official debut with the Toronto Symphony in 1978 and joined the orchestra in a subsequent tour of Japan and the People's Republic of China. While in his early twenties, Lortie moved to Baltimore in order to work with Leon Fleisher and to expand his knowledge of the piano literature.

In 1984, Lortie was first prizewinner of the Busoni International Competition and a prizewinner as well at the Leeds Piano Competition. Along the way, he had traveled to Europe, living for a time in Paris, Florence, and Vienna. Following his exposure to European culture and the recognition resulting from his successes in competition, Lortie began to undertake a more extensive number of concert engagements and made his first recording in 1986.

Within the first few years of an active career, Lortie performed throughout the United States, Canada, and Europe. His engagement calendar included dates with such orchestras as the Cleveland Orchestra, the San Francisco Symphony, the Houston Symphony, the Dallas Symphony, the Saint Louis Symphony, the Los Angeles Philharmonic, the BBC Philharmonic, the Royal Scottish National Orchestra, the Deutsche Symphonie Orchester, and the Orchestre National de France. With the latter ensemble he performed on tour. Recital tours in Italy became yearly occurrences and, under the auspices of the Australian Broadcasting Corporation, Lortie was well-received throughout an extensive tour of Australia.

Over the course of a number of summers, Lortie performed with the Montreal Symphony in program series devoted to a single composer. Complete cycles of the 32 Beethoven sonatas have been given in London, Toronto, Berlin, and Milan. Acknowledging one of his London appearances, the *Daily Telegraph* described Lortie as "one of perhaps half a dozen pianists who is worth dropping everything to go and hear."

Few pianists have enjoyed such a long-term and mutually satisfying relationship with a recording company as that existing between Lortie and Chandos. Lortie has been afforded the opportunity to preserve his interpretations of composers extending from Mozart to Ligeti. Among them is his collection of the complete piano works of Ravel, a set that has received several awards. His recordings of Chopin's *Preludes and Etudes* are also of particular interest.

Having found exposure to a variety of performing traditions of great value, Lortie has taught at the piano institute at Imola, Italy, when his schedule has allowed. That school's philosophy is congenial to him and he has been pleased to work with advanced students similarly interested in a concert career.

In 1992, Lortie was honored by being made an Officer of the Order of Canada. —*Erik Eriksson*

Recommended:

- ○ **Ravel: Concertos; Fauré: Ballade** / Frühbeck de Burgos (cond.), Lortie, London SO / 1989 / Chandos 8773
- ○ **To the Distant Beloved** / Lortie / 2000 / Chandos 9793
- ○ **Mozart: Sonata K448; Andante mit Variationen; Schubert: Fantaisie D940** / Lortie, Mercier / 1993 / Chandos 9162
- ○ **Liszt: Works for Piano & Orchestra Vol. 1** / Pehlivanian (cond.), Lortie, Residensie Orch. The Hague / 2000 / Chandos 9801

Albert Lortzing

b. Oct. 23, 1801, Berlin, Germany, **d.** Jan. 21, 1851, Berlin, Germany
Composer: Opera

Albert Lortzing is remembered chiefly for his 1837 opera *Zar und Zimmermann*, but he also wrote other works of artistic merit, including the operas *Undine* (1845) and *Rolands Knappen* (1849). His greatest strength lay in the realm of comic opera, where he developed a style that fused elements from the French opéra-comique genre with those of the German singspiel. When he ventured into more serious subject matter, as in his opera, *Regina* (1848), he often lost his way. Lortzing also wrote a small number of orchestral and choral works.

Lortzing was born on October 23, 1801, in Berlin. His parents were amateur actors, thus drawing their precocious only child (a sister died in infancy) to the stage. Young Albert's first love, however, was music, and he showed remarkable talent for it in his early childhood. He would begin composing small pieces and eventually take piano lessons from J. H. Greibel. He also took instruction in theory from Rungenhagen.

Lortzing's father sold the family tannery business in 1812 to take up acting professionally with his wife, while young Albert continued studying composition (largely on his own), as well as violin and cello. He also began taking children's parts on the stage. Over the next several years, the family moved to a number of locales: Bamberg (1813), Strasbourg (1814), Bonn (1817), and elsewhere. Lortzing had already written several ambitious scores by 1817, including music for the Kotzebue play *Der Schutzgeist*. In 1820, he wrote the *Andante maestoso con variazioni*, for horn and orchestra. Other significant compositions followed, and the composer also began courting an actress, Rosina Regina Ahles, whom he married on January 30, 1823.

Lortzing continued his acting, singing, and composing careers, appearing in plays, often with his wife and parents, and turning out works like the 1829 *Die Himmelfahrt Jesu Christi*. A string of singspiels from 1832, including *Der Pole und sein Kind* and *Szenen aus Mozarts Leben*, all use music from other sources.

Lortzing wrote his first comic opera, *Die Beiden Schützen* in 1835, staged two years later with great success in Berlin and other German cities. His greatest success came next, however, with the aforementioned *Zar und Zimmermann*; it was performed the same year, but achieved widespread success beginning in 1839. Other notable operas followed, too—*Der Wildschütz* (1842), for example—while Lortzing continued singing and acting. By now he was a dissatisfied producer, covetous of a conducting post. In 1844, he got his wish, becoming Kapellmeister at the Leipzig Stadttheater. But he did not perform well in the post and was dismissed in 1846. Immensely popular from his operas, however, he quickly received the appointment as Kapellmeister at the Theater an der Wien, where his new opera *Der Waffenschmied* was premiered in May that year. But, as in Leipzig, Lortzing began experiencing setbacks: he was unable to get *Regina* performed (and never did in his lifetime), and was dismissed in September of that year.

Lortzing took up his last directorship in April, 1850, at the Friedrich-Wilhelmstadt Theater in Berlin. His last opera was premiered in Frankfurt am Main in January 1851; he died the following day from a stroke, leaving his wife and 11 children in financial difficulty. *—Robert Cummings*

OPERA

Der Wildschütz (1842)

Lortzing's operas, however popular they remain in their native Germany, have not traveled well to other world venues. Their hearty simplicity contains a certain heaviness that appeals to Germans, but not many others, acclimated to more subtle, more finely crafted operatic works.

Born to a father who was an actor and a member of an amateur theater society, young Albert likewise evinced an early interest in the stage. When the family leather business fell on bad times, both parents entered stage work professionally. Albert, too, undertook dramatic and comedic parts and began to compose incidental music at the request of whichever management the family was working for at the moment. In 1837, his opera *Dir beiden Schützen*, written two years earlier, brought him a widespread success.

Der Wildschütz (The Poacher), premiered on New Year's Eve, 1842, at the Municipal Theatre in Leipzig, is consistent with the stylistic markings that place all of Lortzing's operas in a singular category. For the most part, he furnished his own libretti, in this case one freely adapted from a comedy by August von Kotzebue. While the humor is usually direct and innocent, it is also regional and often naïve to an almost sophomoric degree. What sets *Der Wildschütz* apart, however, is a higher level of character differentiation. The title figure, Baculus the schoolmaster, is drawn with considerable craft and perception, as well as with a vigor that invites the listener's attention and sympathy. In the music itself, too, one finds more variety and less reliance on one foursquare tune and chorus after another. Still, Lortzing's technical limitations are unavoidable. Lacking formal training—or even the opportunity to study privately at length—his musical foundations were necessarily very basic. Perhaps, the verdict should note that he did remarkably well with what he had.

Wildschütz has both abundant humor and charm. Baculus, an elderly schoolmaster, is engaged to the lovely—and much younger—Gretchen. She is thoroughly honest about having sacrificed romance for security. When Baculus is dismissed for poaching on the lands of the Count of Eberbach, he urges Gretchen to plead with the Count that he be forgiven (he was caught trying to shoot a buck to provide Gretchen with venison for their guests). Baroness Freimann arrives disguised as a student in order to investigate a Baron her brother wishes her to marry. She offers to approach the Count in the guise of Gretchen (a woman impersonating a man impersonating a woman!). The Count takes a liking to her, as does the Baron. After innumerable machinations, the Baron offers 5,000 thalers to Baculus if he renounces his claim to the supposed Gretchen, and Baculus agrees, rejoicing in newfound wealth in his aria "Fünftausend Taler!" The Baroness reveals all and agrees to marry the Baron. Since it was discovered that Baculus had shot his own donkey and not a buck, he is forgiven. *—Erik Eriksson*

Synopsis:

Act One. The old schoolmaster Baculus celebrates his engagement to his ward, Gretchen, in a festive gathering with his neighbors. The only problem is that Gretchen is not in love with Baculus, but is marrying him only for security. Complications arise when a messenger from the Count of Eberbach delivers a note to Baculus stating that he is being dismissed from his job as schoolmaster because he was caught poaching on the Count's property. At the time, Baculus was intent on having venison for dinner but had to run when he was caught redhanded. Fearing for his future, Baculus asks Gretchen to go before the Count and plead for clemency. Gretchen agrees to do so without hesitation, which upsets Baculus because he knows the Count is a ladies' man.

In the midst of the heated discussion between Baculus and Gretchen about the Count, the Baroness Freimann and her maid enter. They are dressed as traveling students to enable the Baroness, who is the Count's widowed sister, to spy on Baron Kronthal. The Baron is also recently widowed, and the Count wants his sister to marry him. Gretchen and Baculus tell the Baroness of Baculus's dismissal, and the "student" Baroness decides to go to the Count in place of Gretchen, whose clothing she will wear. Baculus is glad to have this "student" intercede on his behalf instead of his fiancée, and accepts the proposition.

The Count enters with a hunting party that includes Baron Kronthal. Despite Baculus' entreaties, the Count will not forgive the poacher, although he is attracted to the woman he believes is Gretchen—and whom he does not recognize as his sister. Devising a plan to get closer to the young woman, he invites everyone to his castle the next day for his birthday celebration.

Act Two. The setting is the Count's castle. Later that evening, the Countess of Eberbach is occupied with reading aloud from Sophocles's *Antigone*, which she does often. Later, she receives (feigned) amorous advances from Baron Kronthal, who, unbeknownst to her, is her brother (they have been separated since they were children). Hoping to influence the Countess to speak to her husband in his favor, Baculus pretends to be well-versed in ancient Greek tragedy. The Count enters and finds Baculus, and, in a rage, prepares to throw him out. However, there is a terrible storm outside, and the Count lets Baculus remain in the castle. Disguised as Gretchen, the Baroness enters and receives the attention of both the Count and Baron Kronthal.

A game of billiards ensues, in which the Count and Baron Kronthal compete for "Gretchen." As the situation is on the verge of getting out of control, the lights go out. Unexpectedly, the Countess enters, which annoys her husband because Baron Kronthal is now free to take the lead in the competition. After intense negotiations undertaken right under the nose of the jealous Count, Kronthal offers Baculus 5,000 thalers for the hand of his fiancée.

Act Three. In the garden of the Count's palace, the next day, a birthday celebration for the Count is in full swing. When Baculus brings the real Gretchen before Baron Kronthal and asks for the sum of 5,000 thalers, as offered, the Baron refuses. He does not want this Gretchen, but the apparently "false" Gretchen he met the previous evening. This false Gretchen shows up and reveals that she is actually the Baroness Freimann. Now the pieces begin falling into place. The Baroness announces that she is the sister of the Count and that she is prepared to marry Baron Kronthal. Kronthal, in turn, reveals that he is the brother of the Countess. When the Count learns that the animal Baculus shot on his property was not a deer but Baculus' own donkey, the Count forgives the poacher. As all rejoice in their clear consciences, the curtain falls. *—John Palmer*

Recommended:

○ **Lortzing: Der Wildschütz** / Klee (cond.), Schreier, Mathis, Soffel, Hornik, Berlin RSO / 1995 / Berlin Classics 0011432

Zar und Zimmermann (1837)

Lortzing was the most important German composer before Wagner to write his own librettos. He preferred to draw his material from obscure plays or other sources, avoiding the well-trodden path through the classics. Regarding the selection of subject matter, Lortzing once wrote, "I would make no other general rule, except not to grasp at easily accessible classical pieces.... Forgotten sources, like *Der Bürgermeister von Saardam*...one can make something of them." It was from *Der Bürgermeister von Saardam, oder Die zwei Peter* by Georg Christian Römer (1766–1829) that Lortzing developed his comic opera *Zar und Zimmermann* (The Czar and the Carpenter). Römer in turn based his comedy on earlier French sources; it had its premiere in 1822 in Berlin. From Römer, Lortzing took the first two acts almost intact, some sections word for word, but greatly modified Römer's third act, especially the ending, in which the Czar, Lefort, Peter, and Marie sail away from Saardam.

Zar und Zimmermann was Lortzing's second comic opera; the first was *Die beiden Schützen*, composed in 1835 but produced only in early 1837. The success of his first effort prompted Lortzing to forge ahead with another work based on the youth of Peter the Great. Historical facts inform Lortzing's *Zar und Zimmermann*. In 1697, Peter the Great (ca. 1672–1725) did indeed leave Russia accompanied by his friend and advisor Lefort for adventures abroad. The two stopped in the Netherlands port town of Zaandam, on the river Zaan, to learn the art of shipbuilding. They stayed in Zaandam only eight days. Peter's wanderlust drew him to Amsterdam, where he signed on with the Dutch East India Company for four months of work.

Zar und Zimmermann premiered on December 22, 1837, at the Stadttheater in Leipzig. Lortzing, a well-rounded musician indeed, sang the role of Peter Ivanov, and Lortzing's mother played the role of Widow Browe. Although *Zar und Zimmermann* received a warm reception at its premiere, it was its first Berlin performance two years later that proved to be its springboard to great success.

As in earlier German comic operas, dialogue advances the plot between musical numbers. Sometimes dialogue is even interpolated into the numbers themselves, as in Marie's "Die Eifersucht ist eine Plage" (Jealousy is a Plague), from Act I, in which Ivanov gives spoken responses as Marie tries to quiet his jealousy.

Van Bett is a classic buffo bass, derived from Rossini's Bartolo in *Il barbiere di Siviglia*. One of Lortzing's most amusing strokes comes in Van Bett's "O sancta justitia, ich möchte rasen" (Sacred Justice, I Would Rage), in which the low F natural he fails to produce finally appears in the bassoon. One of the finest ensembles from the opera also involves Van Bett: at the beginning of Act Three, he attempts to rehearse a chorus. The incompetent singers constantly misunderstand their conductor, enter incorrectly, and blame Van Bett. Overall, the integration of the opera's various elements into a continuous whole is remarkable. The party in Act Two is, in Lortzing's words, "high-comedy, stupid," and shows Lortzing at his best, writing for a combination of *buffo* parts intermingled and alternating with solo segments. Throughout *Zar und Zimmermann*, Lortzing's musical articulation of his characters is exemplary. The aged moan, while the young speak with optimistic vigor. *—John Palmer*

Synopsis:

Act One. At a shipyard in Saardam, in order to learn the art of shipbuilding, Czar Peter the Great has disguised himself as a carpenter and is using the name Peter Michaelov. Another Russian working at the shipyard, Peter Ivanov, has befriended the Czar, unaware of his true identity. Peter is in love with Marie, the mayor's niece. Peter is very jealous of Marie's other suitors, but she tries to calm him ("Die Eifersucht is ein Plage" [Jealousy is a plague]). General Lefort, the Russian ambassador, informs the Czar that the Czar's sister has been fomenting unrest in Moscow. After sending Lefort back to Moscow the Czar expresses his rage ("Verrathen! von euch Verrathen! [Betrayal! From you, betrayal!]). The mayor, Van Bett, a jolly fellow, enters ("O sancta justitia, ich möchte rasen"). He has been instructed to uncover a masquerading foreigner called Peter who happens to be working at the shipyard. Once he asks to see all of the people working for Widow Browe, the master carpenter, the mayor realizes that many of the workers are named Peter, but two, Michaelov and Ivanov, are foreigners. He decides Ivanov is the most suspicious of the two. Lord Syndham, the English ambassador, enters and offers Van Bett £2,000 if he will disclose Peter's plans regarding England. Because of this, Van Bett thinks that Ivanov is a very important person, and begins to treat him with respect. When Ivanov returns he is confused by the major's new attitude, and during a duet between the men ("Darf ich wohl den Worten trauen" [May I trust your words]), Van Bett even offers his niece's hand in marriage to Ivanov if the Russian will divulge his plans. Marquis de Chateauneuf, the French ambassador, enters and deduces that Peter Michaelov is the Czar and establishes contact with him during the preparations for the wedding of Widow Browe's son.

Act Two. The wedding feast for Widow Browe's son is taking place at an inn. The Marquis de Chateauneuf and General Lefort have disguised themselves as sailors and make plans with the Czar. To create a distraction, Chateauneuf sings ("Lebe wohl, mein flandrisch Mädchen" [Farewell, my Flemish girl]). Syndham, now dressed as a Dutch sailor, enters and quizzes the mayor about any information he may have. A sextet ensues ("Zum Werk das wir beginnen" [Work that we begin]) during which Van Bett and Syndham attempt to approach Ivanov. Across the room Chateauneuf is in the midst of achieving his diplomatic goals in a conversation with the Czar. As part of the wedding feast, Marie sings her bridal song ("Lieblich röthen sich die Wangen" [My cheeks sweetly blush]), but a Dutch officer and a few soldiers interrupt the festivities with orders to interrogate all foreigners. Confusion reigns as all three ambassadors are revealed and Syndham discloses that Ivanov is the Czar of Russia while Chateauneuf makes the same announcement about Michaelov.

Act Three. The setting is the great room of the town hall. Van Bett still believes Ivanov is the real Czar, and has put together a choir to rehearse a cantata in his honor ("Den hohen Herrscher würdig zu empfangen" [A worthy reception for the Nobel lord]). Marie is unhappy because she feels that marriage to Ivanov, whom she believes is the Czar, is now not possible, but the real Czar tells her that everything will be all right. The Czar then finds himself alone and ponders his lofty existence ("Sonst spielt' ich mit Scepter, mit Krone und Stern" [Otherwise, I played with scepter, crown and star]). Maria and Ivanov then sing a duet ("Darf eine nied're Magd es wagen" [May a lowly maiden dare?]); Marie addresses Ivanov as the Czar, which befuddles the young man, but as the duet closes the two end up declaring their mutual love. Marie leaves, and the real Czar returns, upset that the harbor has been blockaded. Syndham, however, has given Ivanov a note guaranteeing safe conduct and has placed a yacht, sailors and cash at his disposal. In exchange for the note the Czar gives Ivanov a document which he is not to open for an hour. When Chateauneuf and Lefort arrive they leave with the Czar and head for the harbor. Poor Ivanov is left behind to have Van Bett bestow upon him the deputation of honor. Van Bett still speaks to Ivanov as if he is the Czar and joins him in a comic clog dance. When those assembled hear cannon fire they open the doors of the hall, revealing the properly uniformed Czar standing on a ship as it leaves the harbor. When Ivanov tears open the document the Czar gave to him, he discovers that he has been made Imperial Overseer and that the Czar has given him permission to marry Marie. Everyone rejoices as the Czar sings a farewell. *—John Palmer*

Recommended:

- ○ **Lortzing: Zar und Zimmermann** / Wallberg (cond.), Popp, Prey, Kraus, Krenn, Munich Radio Orch. / Pilz Acanta 42424

Los Angeles Guitar Quartet (LAGQ)

f. 1980, Los Angeles, CA

Ensemble

The Los Angeles Guitar Quartet (LAGQ) became the world's leading guitar ensemble in the 1990s.

The group's origins lay with the great guitar player and teacher Pepe Romero, who formed four of his students into a guitar quartet in 1980. Romero was himself a member of one of the premiere guitar quartets, Los Romeros, made up of members of his family. When he became a teacher at the University of Southern California, he passed the Los Romeros tradition on to the LAGQ.

In 1990 three of the original members, Scott Tennant, John Dearman, and William Kanengiser, accepted Andrew York, already a well-known guitarist and composer, as a member of the LAGQ.

Since then their popularity has soared. They recorded for the GHA and Delos record labels and in 1998 became exclusive artists for Sony Classics. Their first release for the label, titled *L.A.G.Q.*, entered the *Billboard Magazine* classical-crossover charts in the Top Ten.

The performing style of the quartet is energetic, with strong showmanship and personality. To the small repertory of original four-guitar music they have added a series of acclaimed and intricate arrangements of classical music, but also feature jazz and world music in their concerts and on their recordings.

This inventive and eclectic program-making has resulted in wide acclaim. Their Delos album *Labyrinth*, for instance, includes Andrew York's *Pacific Coast Highway*, Aaron Copland's *Simple Gifts Variations*, Sousa's *Black Horse Troop March*, and Count Basie's *Jumpin' at the Woodside*. Their Delos discography includes a number of albums each representing a side of their repertory: *Evening in Granada* focuses on one of the guitar's staples, Spanish music. *For Thy Pleasure* emphasizes Baroque and earlier music in transcriptions. *Wild Mountain Thyme*, however, is a collection of Celtic folk music, and includes a guest steel guitar artist.

The LAGQ has appeared nationwide on radio (St. Paul Sunday Morning) and television (*Evening at Pops*, *Today Show*, and *Breakfast with the Arts*). They tour widely, including highly successful visits to Europe and Asia. *—Joseph Stevenson*

Recommended:

- ○ **Evening In Granada** / Los Angeles Guitar Quartet / 1993 / Delos 3144
- ○ **Best of L.A.G.Q.** / Los Angeles Guitar Quartet / 1998 / Delos 1607
- ○ **L.A.G.Q.** / Los Angeles Guitar Quartet / 1998 / Sony 60274

Los Angeles Philharmonic Orchestra

f. 1919, Los Angeles, CA

Ensemble

By the end of the twentieth century, the Los Angeles Philharmonic had established itself as one of the world's leading orchestras. Like other ensembles on the West Coast of the United States, it has served as an important forum for contemporary music.

The Los Angeles Philharmonic was founded in 1919 by Los Angeles multimillionaire and avid amateur musician William Andrews Clark Jr. The orchestra's first music director was Walter Henry Rothwell. Rehearsals began on October 13, and the first concert was October 24 at Trinity Auditorium in downtown Los Angeles. The next year the Philharmonic moved into The Temple, a church built in 1907 and renamed Philharmonic Auditorium. Despite the name change, the hall remained a place of worship, and the orchestra had to plan its activities around those of the church. The Philharmonic benefited from the attraction that California held for European expatriates; following Rothwell, its music directors were Georg Schnéevoigt (1927–29), Artur Rodzinski (1929–33), Otto Klemperer (1933–39), Alfred Wallenstein (1943–56), and Eduard van Beinum (1956–59).

In 1945 Leopold Stokowski had founded the Hollywood Bowl Symphony for the summer concerts at the Hollywood Bowl, a striking art-deco outdoor concert shell in a lovely natural amphitheater. That orchestra disbanded two years later, and the Los Angeles Philharmonic replaced them as the regular orchestra for this series; though many American orchestras offer summer concerts, few have as high a profile in the cultural lives of their cities as this one did (and still does). In 1962 Zubin Mehta began his long and productive tenure as music director, which lasted until 1978. He burnished the sound of the orchestra, and initiated a successful series of recordings. He was succeeded by Carlo Maria Giulini (1978–84), who brought his strong identification with the Classical repertory to the orchestra. He was succeeded by André Previn, who had a successful tenure from 1985 to 1989.

In 1964 the LAPO moved into a new home, the Dorothy Chandler Music Pavilion in downtown Los Angeles. The hall was shared with the Civic Light Opera Association and other concert and theater companies, a situation that grew uncomfortable and limiting for the Philharmonic.

In 1990, the orchestra followed the lead of the Boston Pops by making an organizational distinction between its winter concerts and his summer series by founding the Hollywood Bowl Symphony Orchestra as a separate entity from the Los Angeles Philharmonic. John Mauceri was appointed its music director. In concerts, and on recordings the HBSO stresses its identification with the film capital.

The LAPO gives an annual 30-week winter season. The LAPO's music director since 1992 has been Esa-Pekka Salonen, an exciting young Finnish conductor whose programming is built around the great established classics of the twentieth century, some new music, and a solid representation of established repertoire. A new permanent home for the orchestra, Walt Disney Hall, featuring a striking design, and titanium and brushed stainless steel exterior, was inaugurated in October 2003. *—Joseph Stevenson*

Recommended:

- ○ **Adams: Naïve and Sentimental Music** / Salonen (cond.), Tanenbaum, Los Angeles PO / 2002 / Nonesuch 79636
- ○ **Hermann: The Film Scores** / Salonen (cond.), Los Angeles PO / 2000 / Sony Classical 62700
- ○ **Prokofiev: Alexander Nevsky Cantata; Lieutenant Kijé Suite** / Previn (cond.), Cairns, Los Angeles PO / 1987 / Telarc 80143

- ○ **Shapero: Symphony for Classical Orchestra; 9-Minute Overture** / Previn (cond.), Los Angeles PO / New World 80373
- ○ **Gershwin, Bernstein, Barber** / Bernstein, Troyanos, Edeiken, Los Angeles PO, Israel PO / DG 427806

Victoria de los Angeles

b. Nov. 1, 1923, Barcelona, Spain, **d.** Jan. 15, 2005

Soprano

Victoria de los Angeles was one of the finest lyric sopranos in the decades after World War II. She was born Victoria Gómez Cima. She learned to sing and play piano and guitar while still in school. She entered the Conservatorio de Liceo in Barcelona to study piano and singing. Victoria completed the six-year program in three years, graduating with full honors at the age of eighteen. Her membership in the Conservatory's Ars Musicae gave her wide exposure to the art song repertory and Baroque and Renaissance music.

De los Angeles debuted in a song recital at the Palay de la Musica Catalana. Her operatic debut was also in Barcelona, at the Gran Teatro de Liceo, singing the Countess in Mozart's *Marriage of Figaro.*

Her national and international breakthroughs occurred after she won the Geneva International Singing Competition in 1947. She was immediately booked for performances in Madrid, singing in *Manon* and *La Bohème* opposite Beniamino Gigli before returning to Barcelona. There she moved into Germanic roles, adding *Freischütz, Lohengrin,* and *Tannhäuser* to her portrayals. The Geneva Competition had also brought her to the attention of the BBC, which brought her to London to sing the part of Salud in Manuel de Falla's *La Vida Breve* in 1948, when she signed an exclusive contract with EMI. This association lasted thirty years and included at least 21 full-length opera recordings, 25 solo recitals, and appearances on 40 other EMI releases.

Her first Paris appearance was in 1949, as Marguerite in Gounod's *Faust,* a role she repeated as her Metropolitan Opera debut in 1951. She debuted in Covent Garden in 1950, once again singing Mimì in *La Bohème,* which was one of the roles most closely associated with her. She sang regularly at both the Met and Covent Garden. Wieland Wagner asked her to sing in a new production of *Tannhäuser* opening the Bayreuth Festival for 1961.

She sang in most of the major houses of the world, touring in South Africa, the Middle East, Australia, East Asia, and Latin America (where she was a frequent guest artist at the Teatro Colón in Buenos Aires). She performed with such great conductors as Thomas Beecham, Herbert von Karajan, Georg Solti, Pierre Monteux, Carlo Maria Giulini, Charles Münch, Zubin Mehta, and Rafael Frühbeck de Burgos.

She had a wide vocal and dramatic range, singing in operas as diverse as *Carmen, The Barber of Seville, Acis and Galatea, Pelléas et Mélisande, Die Meistersinger, Simon Boccanegra, Dido and Aeneas, La Traviata,* and *Madama Butterfly.* In one evening, she sang both the roles of Nedda in *I pagliacci* and Santuzza in *Cavalleria rusticana.* As a recitalist, her vast and wide repertory embraced not only the central German and French Romantic and twentieth century eras, but had a strong representation of early music. In addition, she often added Spanish and Catalan folk songs to her solo recitals.

Besides having a lovely, warm, and dark tone, she was always noted for the intelligence of her portrayals and musical choices. She closely monitored her own singing. She retired from the operatic stage in 1969, after an exceptionally successful portrayal of Verdi's Desdemona in Dallas, though she returned to Covent Garden as Carmen in 1978.

However, she continued singing recitals. As time passed, she lowered the number of her appearances, yet reviews continued to stress the purity of her voice. She was heard to say that the moment she heard a wobble in her voice she would "shut up the shop." One of her last appearances was in connection with the 1992 Olympic Games in Barcelona, where she still exhibited characteristic vocal purity. *—Joseph Stevenson*

Recommended:

- ○ **The Very Best of Victoria de los Angeles** / Los Angeles, etc. / 2003 / EMI 75888
- ○ **The Fabulous Victoria de los Angeles** / Los Angeles, etc. / 2001 / Testament 1246
- ○ **The Early Recordings, 1942–1953** / Los Angeles, etc. / 1996 / Testament 1087
- ○ **Songs of Spain** / Los Angeles, etc. / EMI 66937
- ○ **Puccini: Madama Butterfly** / Santini (cond.), Bjoerling, Los Angeles, Sereni, dePalma, Rome Opera Orchestra & Chorus / 1990 / EMI 63634

Felicity Lott

b. May 8, 1947, Cheltenham, England

Soprano

English soprano Felicity Lott began her musical studies on the violin and piano, but she did not entertain the idea of a musical career until after completing a degree in French at the Royal Holloway College. Having studied voice during college, she auditioned for the Royal Academy of Music, and spent the next four years there. Her debut came in London as Seleuce in Handel's *Tolomeo,* but she first came to public attention in 1975 when she stepped in as Pamina in *Die Zauberflöte* at the English National Opera, where she also sang Natasha in Prokofiev's *War and Peace* and Roxane in Szymanowski's *King Roger.* In 1976 at the Royal Opera, Covent Garden she continued this thread of modern opera in Henze's *We Come to the River* and Britten's *A Midsummer Night's Dream.* The following year, she sang Anne Trulove in *The Rake's Progress* at Glyndebourne and Jennifer in Tippett's *Midsummer marriage* at the Welsh National Opera. Perhaps even more important was singing the Countess in Strauss's *Capriccio* for the Glyndebourne Touring Company; this was the first of many Strauss roles she was to make her own.

Lott also undertook roles from the standard repertory, including Poppea in Monteverdi's *L'incoronazione di Poppea,* the Countess in *Le Nozze di Figaro,* Fiordiligi in *Così fan tutte* and Xiphares in *Mitridate, ré di Ponto.* She had great success in French opera, especially as Charpentier's *Louise,* Blanche in Poulenc's *Dialogues des Carmelites* and the Woman in *La voix humaine.* She eventually added more Strauss roles to her repertoire, including both Octavian and the Marschallin in *Der Rosenkavalier,* Christine in *Intermezzo* and *Arabella.* She has sung at all of the major opera houses around the world, including Lyric Opera of Chicago, San Francisco, the Metropolitan, Hamburg, Dresden, Vienna, Paris Opera, and Munich. Her Mozart roles have remained central in her performing schedule.

Lott is also very active as a recitalist. She is one of the original members of the *Songmaker's Almanac,* a group created by pianist Graham Johnson to explore all areas of song literature. She and Richard Jackson have been admired for their performances of Wolf's *Italianisches Liederbuch.* She is also well known for her interpretations of the songs of Francis Poulenc and has recorded nearly all of the songs appropriate for female voice. Her performances of Schumann's *Frauenliebe und -leben* and Berg's *Sieben frühe Lieder* are also highly acclaimed. Her recital programs are unusually varied and often contain little-known pieces, and are much anticipated by audiences. She also appears regularly with major orchestras around the world. Her concert repertoire includes the second and fourth symphonies of Mahler, the oratorios of Bach, Handel, Mendelssohn, and, of course, the *Four Last Songs* of Strauss.

When Felicity Lott began performing, her voice was a medium sized lyric soprano with a strong lower register. As she has matured, the voice has taken on darker hues which have enabled her to be able to fulfill all of the demands of the great Strauss operas for which she is justly famous. She has excellent control of the entire dynamic range and a wonderful feel for the long phrases of Mozart and Strauss. She is an excellent actress and is careful to create a complete character in her performances.

Lott is married to the actor Gabriel Woolf. She became a Commander of the British Empire in 1990, and was knighted as a Dame Commander of the British Empire in 1996. *—Richard LeSueur*

Recommended:

- ○ **Poulenc: La Voix humaine** / Jordan (cond.), Lott, Suisse Romande Orch. / HM 901759
- ○ **Felicity Sings Schubert** / Lott, Johnson / Carlton 2016
- ○ **Wolf: Italienisches Liederbuch** / Lott, Johnson, Schreier / 1994 / Hyperion 66760
- ○ **Strauss: Orchestral Songs Vol. 2** / Järvi, Paling (conds.), Lott, Scottish National Orch. / 1993 / Chandos 9159
- ○ **Strauss: Four Last Songs; Closing Scene from Capriccio; Orchestral Songs** / Järvi (cond.), Lott, Scottish National Orch. / 2003 / Chandos 10075

Louisville Orchestra

f. Nov. 2, 1937, Louisville, KY

Ensemble

The Louisville Orchestra is a major American symphony orchestra, widely known for its unique commissions of new music and for its recordings on its own label. Despite its durable musical traditions, the Kentucky city had no permanent orchestra until November 2, 1937, when the Louisville Civic Arts Association formed the Louisville Civic Orchestra, an ensemble of 54 paid but part-time musicians. The first music director was the English-born American conductor Robert Whitney. The original venue was Memorial Auditorium. Whitney enlarged the orchestra and brought it to full-time (though partial-year) status and in 1947, renamed it the Louisville Philharmonic Orchestra. The orchestra was known for the top-name soloists it engaged, and, over the ten-year period, had accumulated a $40,000 deficit.

Whitney and Louisville mayor Charles P. Farnsley envisioned an innovative change of direction in the orchestra's policies designed to distinguish the orchestra and to eliminate the deficit. The expensive guest soloists would have to go. In their place, the orchestra's programs would include new works commissioned by the orchestra. The first such premiere was Spanish composer Joaquin Rodrigo's *Quatro*

Madrigales Amatorios, played in the orchestra's home at the time, Columbia Auditorium. Some of the Louisville-commissioned recordings appeared on such major labels as Columbia and Mercury. In fact, the Louisville Orchestra's performance of William Schuman's ballet *Judith* was the first domestic orchestral recording made and released by Mercury. In technique and sound this rare recording shows a developmental stage of the label's famed "Living Presence" sound. In 1953 the commissioning series was given financial support by a major grant from the Rockefeller Foundation to record all the newly commissioned works and release them on the orchestra's own record label, known as First Edition Records. Over the years, the label has released hundreds of recordings of works by over 250 composers.

Whitney retired after thirty years in 1967. He was succeeded by Jorge Mester (1967–79), Akira Endo (1980–82), Lawrence Leighton Smith (1983–94) and Max Bragado-Darman (1994–97). The orchestra was nominated for several Grammy Awards, and under Smith played at Carnegie Hall and the Kennedy Center in Washington.

An interim period began in 1997 with the appointment of three conductors pending search for a new music director. Uriel Segal conducted the regular concert series, Robert Bernhardt the pops series, and Robert Franz the educational and the "LG&E New Dimensions" series. Segal was named music director during the course of the 1998–99 season.

The Orchestra endured several years of deficits during the 1980s and early 1990s, but returned to a budget in the black in 1996–97. It plays several series of concerts a year: major symphony concerts, pops, light classics, "New Dimensions," and the children's series "orKIDStra." Its summer venue is at the Louisville Zoo and, in addition to playing the regular concerts and children's concerts in its regular home, it performs at the campus of Indiana University Southeast in New Albany, Indiana. It also functions as the orchestra for the Louisville Ballet and Louisville Opera. *—Joseph Stevenson*

Recommended:

- ○ **Villa-Lobos** / Mester, Whitney (conds.), Louisville Orch. / 2003 / First Edition 16
- ○ **Ginastera** / Mester, Whitney (conds.), Louisville Orch. / 2003 / First Edition 15
- ○ **Mennin** / Mester, Whitney (conds.), Starker, Louisville Orch. / 2003 / First Edition 13
- ○ **Crumb** / Mester, Gilbert (conds.), Louisville Orch. / 2002 / First Edition 8
- ○ **Hovhaness** / Whitney (cond.), Dahlin, East, Nossaman, Dales, Johnson, Louisville Orch. / 2002 / First Edition 6
- ○ **Cowell** / Mester, Whitney (conds.), Louisville Orch. / 2001 / First Edition 3
- ○ **Harrison** / Whitney (cond.), Dahlin, Bingham, Louisville Orch. / 2003 / First Edition 14

Fernando de Lucia

b. Oct. 11, 1860, Naples, Italy, **d.** Feb. 21, 1925, Naples, Italy

Tenor

Fernando de Lucia was one of the bridges between nineteenth and twentieth century styles, a link that is reflected, appropriately enough, in his career. He began his career as a lyric tenor, verging on *tenore di grazia*, but by the end of the century he was well established as a verismo tenor. He also taught some of the most prominent tenors of the first half of the twentieth century, including Ivan Petroff, Enzo de Muro Lomanto, and Georges Thill. Like his contemporary Enrico Caruso (he sang at Caruso's funeral), he had an almost baritonal timbre and rather limited top, and particularly in his verismo roles he was most often compared to Caruso.

He studied voice at the Naples Conservatory, where his teachers included Vincenzo Lombardi. His opera debut was in the title role of Gounod's *Faust* in 1885 at *the* Teatro San Carlo. In 1887, he made his London debut at the Drury Lane Theatre, though his London triumphs were not to come until 1893 and his Covent Garden debut as Canio in Leoncavallo's *Pagliacci.* This established him as a favorite at that house. 1893 also marked his Metropolitan Opera debut, though he sang only one season there. His verismo roles had taken a toll on his voice and by 1909, he had greatly reduced his stage appearances. He gave his last performance, in the title role of Mascagni's *L'amico Fritz*, in 1917, though he continued to make recordings. Though many of these show some wear on his voice and much of the material was transposed down, even the late recordings show his profound sense of musical style in both the bel canto and verismo schools. *—Ann Feeney*

Recommended:

- ○ **Fernando de Lucia** / Lucia, etc. / 1994 / Symposium 1149
- ○ **Fernando de Lucia** / Lucia, etc. / 2003 / Nimbus 7911

Alvin Lucier

b. May 14, 1931, Nashua, NH

Composer: Avant-garde

A trailblazing force in psycho-acoustic music, avant-garde composer and performer Alvin Lucier was born in Nashua, New Hampshire in 1931; educated at Yale and Brandeis, he also spent two years in Rome on a Fulbright Scholarship before returning to Brandeis in 1962 to teach and conduct the university's chamber chorus. His breakthrough composition, *Music for Solo Performer (1964–65) for Enormously Amplified Brain Waves and Percussion*, was the first work to feature sounds generated by brain waves in live performance; biological stimuli played an increasing role in Lucier's subsequent work as well, most notably through his notation of performers' physical movements. Acoustical phenomena, meanwhile, was the subject of 1970's landmark *I Am Sitting in a Room*, in which several sentences of recorded speech were simultaneously played back into a room and re-recorded there dozens of times over, the space gradually filtering the speech into pure sound. 1980's *Music on a Long Thin Wire* was a further extension of Lucier's fascination with the physics of sound—a conceptual piece featuring a taut 50-foot wire passed through the poles of a large magnet and driven by an oscillator, the amplified vibrations yielded beautifully ethereal results. A professor at Wesleyan University from 1970 onward, Lucier in his later works additionally included a number of sound installations as well as works for solo instruments, chamber ensembles, and orchestra. *—Jason Ankeny*

AVANT-GARDE

I Am Sitting in a Room (1970)

"I am sitting in a room, different from the one you are in now." So begins one of the masterpieces of twentieth century music, merging processed music, minimalism, and self-reference into an utterly amazing work. The instructions for producing the piece are, in fact, the piece itself. The composer sits and describes what will happen, and then it happens. Lucier tapes these instructions (about 80 seconds' worth), tapes it, replays that tape into the room, tapes that, plays the second tape into the room, and so on. Little by little, the "natural resonant frequencies of the room" erode the source material, softening hard edges, blurring boundaries between words. Different rooms will, presumably, give different results depending on their individual architectural properties. After ten or 12 repetitions, the listener already has difficulty distinguishing individual words, though the rhythmic pattern remains. But, and this is one of the cruxes of the work, all is not entropy. As the text becomes indecipherable, elements of undeniably musical tones emerge from nowhere, as though they were embedded in the original speech and only came to light after the surface structure was eliminated. Indeed, small melodies can actually be heard and the effect is absolutely magical. Fifteen minutes into the composition, Lucier's speech has become a hazy cloud of wavering, bell-like tones interrupted by the occasional sibilance, the latter generated by the composer's stutter, which adds an element of poignancy to the piece's conception. Halfway through, no aspect of the speech can be gleaned except a rough cadence; instead, the listener has been transported to a sound world so a far removed from the initial text as to leave one both baffled and awash in wonder. *I Am Sitting in a Room* is a unique, extraordinary idea/composition, a landmark among late twentieth century avant-garde music and a touchstone for a generation of composer/theoreticians. It's a rare combination of sensual beauty and intellectual rigor, and should be heard by anyone interested in contemporary music. *—Brian Olewnick*

Recommended:

- ○ **Lucier: I Am Sitting in a Room** / Lucier / Lovely Music 1013

Music on a Long Thin Wire (1977)

Alvin Lucier seems to think along different planes than most people, and whereas many composers are thought of as having redefined the boundaries of music as an aesthetic abstraction, Lucier's works continually redefine music as an acoustical phenomenon. A cursory survey of his output sees him as a kind of musical mad scientist; a deeper reading reveals an intriguing mind that gracefully, carefully, and convincingly combines music with physics, design, electrical engineering, psychology, and performance art. His experiments don't find their validation in the conceptual world, but in the physical one, creating for the listener an experience that is both intellectually challenging and viscerally engaging. Joan la Barbara calls it "supermusic."

So from the same composer who once wrote a piece for an ensemble consisting of oboe, chest of drawers, the Atlantic Ocean, and the Federal Bureau of Investigation, came in 1977 a composition for a single piece of wire. Lucier originally used three- to four-foot-long wires, but gradually lengthened them over the course of several performances. "A short length of wire," said the composer, "would look like a laboratory experiment, but if you thought of it as a sound sculpture, your imagination could take that wire down the length of the room." Commissioned by the Crane School of Music at SUNY Potsdam, the "score" instructs the performer to stretch the wire across the length of the performance space, tensioning it over bridges at either end. Both ends of the wire are connected to the output of an amplifier, which drives the wire with a sine wave oscillator. A magnet is placed so that the wire runs between its poles. When the wire is electrified, the current running through it interacts with the magnetic field lateral to it. Microphones connected to the bridges pick up the vibrations, which are amplified. The performer controls the power going through the wire, "producing nodal shifts, echo trains, noisy overdrivings," and a variety of other sonic phenomena.

According to the composer, the idea behind this piece is "an interest in the poetry of what we used to think of as science." He further explains: "I always thought that the world was divided into two kinds of people, poets and practical people, and that while the practical people ran the world, poets had visions about it.... Now I realize that there is no difference between science and art." Accordingly, a full grasp of the rather complicated electroacoustic processes going on isn't essential to "understanding" the piece; in fact, Lucier often goes to great lengths to build some sort of explanation of the piece into the piece itself. The text of his famous *I Am Sitting in a Room* is made up entirely of a rundown of the acoustical transformations that the spoken text will undergo over the course of the piece. A fascinatingly self-referential aspect of *Music on a Long Thin Wire* is that the listener can watch the sound as he listens to it. The performer is instructed to "light the wire so that the modes of vibration are visible to the viewers." Thus, as different frequencies and amplitudes are passed through the wire, the same waveforms that strike our ears appear right in front of our eyes. *—Jeremy Grimshaw*

Recommended:

○ **Lucier: Music on a Long Thin Wire** / Lucier / 1979 / Lovely Music 1011

Christa Ludwig

b. Mar. 16, 1924, Berlin, Germany
Mezzo-Soprano

Christa Ludwig was one of the most admired mezzo-sopranos of her generation, with a wide repertoire of both lieder and opera. She brought a fine sense of musicianship as well as drama to her performances. Her roles ranged from Dorabella in *Cosi fan Tutte* to Brangane in *Tristan und Isolde* and Clytemnestra in *Elektra*, and she was the creator of the role of Claire in Gottfried von Einem's *Besuch der alten Dame*. Her technique and upper register were solid enough to let her sing the Marschallin in *Der Rosenkavalier* and the Dyer's Wife in *Die Frau ohne Schatten*, parts almost exclusively sung by sopranos—though she did retreat from plans to sing Isolde and Brunhilde. She was also a noted lieder performer, especially of Mahler.

Her parents (tenor Anton Ludwig, who later became a stage director, and mezzo-soprano Eugenie Ludwig Besalla) were both singers, and her first vocal studies were with her mother, who also taught her piano, flute, and cello. Her first performances were in 1954, at the age of 17, singing operatic arias she had learned from growing up in the theater. She made her operatic debut as Prince Orlofsky in Strauss' *Die Fledermaus* in 1946, at the Frankfurt State Opera, where she was a member of the company until 1952. She then moved to Darmstadt to study acting with the director Gustav Sellner. After two years, she and her mother (who was still teaching her) moved to Hanover, where she began to sing leading roles such as Carmen, Ortrud, and Kundry. Her Salzburg debut was in 1954 as Cherubino, and followed by her 1955 debut in the same role at the Vienna State Opera, at the invitation of Karl Böhm, where she sang for more than 30 years. In 1957, she sang with Elisabeth Schwartzkopf, who encouraged her husband Walter Legge, the famous producer, to sign Ludwig with EMI records. Ludwig's United States debut was in 1959 in Chicago, as Dorabella. In the 1970s, she went through a vocal crisis due to menopause, and she took some of the most demanding roles out of her repertoire and began to give more attention to songs. Again she challenged the typical views of repertoire, and sang material, such as *Winterreise*, that is most often associated with male voices, especially baritones. Working with Leonard Bernstein, she developed a special affection for Mahler (whose music Bernstein championed when Mahler was relatively obscure.)

She was married to bass Walter Berry from 1957 until 1971, and their son, Marc Berry, is a popular song composer. She has a wide recorded legacy; among the best of her material is a *Das Lied von der Erde* under Bernstein (Sony SMK 47589) and a Brangane in *Tristan und Isolde*, with Vickers as Tristan and Dernesch as Isolde, under von Karajan (EMI CMS7 69319-2).*—Ann Feeney*

Recommended:

○ **The Very Best of Christa Ludwig** / Ludwig, etc. / 2003 / EMI 85099

○ **Tribute to Vienna** / Ludwig, Spencer (piano) / RCA 62652

○ **Les Introuvables: Christa Ludwig** / Ludwig, etc. / EMI 64074

○ **Beethoven: Symphony 9** / Klemperer (cond.), Ludwig, Lewis, Berry, Giebel, London PO / 1996 / Testament 1332

○ **Wagner: Das Rheingold** / Levine (cond.), Morris, Ludwig, Jerusalem, Moll, Metropolitan Opera Orch. / 1989 / DG 445295

Jean-Baptiste Lully

b. Nov. 28, 1632, Florence, Italy, **d.** Mar. 22, 1687, Paris, France
Composer: Opera, Ballet, Choral

Clearly the most successful musician of his time, in terms of power and financial wealth, Jean-Baptiste Lully was almost singularly responsible for the shape of French opera during the seventeenth and eighteenth centuries. Born Italian, he died a wealthy Frenchman at the early age of 54. Although most remembered for his opera compositions, he was also a talented violinist and dancer. His business sense and, some say, unscrupulous manner, made him one of the most powerful musicians in all of France, if not Europe. His patron and friend King Louis XIV further cemented Lully's position at the top of Europe's musical elite. Lully's operas remain his legacy, but he also composed over 30 ballets, motets, incidental music, dances, and marches.

Lully was born the son of a miller who lost custody of him after his mother died. While in his early teenage years, Lully was taken to France by the Chevalier de Guise in March 1646. He served as a musician and page in Mlle de Montpensier's court until she was exiled, in 1652, to her estate at St. Targeau for her role in the Fronde. During his service with the Montepensier court, Lully was schooled in guitar, violin, and dance. His talents brought him to the attention of the young King Louis XIV. After his release from the Montepensier court, Lully joined the King's court, as a composer and dancer. He became the leader of a small string ensemble formed by the King. Lully's prestige at the court, as well as throughout France, grew even more when he was appointed the Superintendent of Music and subsequently, the Master of Music for the Royal Family.

When Lully began composing opera in the 1670s, Italy was the center of great opera. Opera in France was in its infancy. Lully's operas, which were based on Italian models but with French libretto, helped popularize the art form. He composed one a year between 1673 and 1680, and then again between 1682 and 1686. Besides being the premier opera composer in Paris at the time, Lully ensured his exalted position by securing patent rights which would ultimately allow him to determine what opera could be performed and severely limiting performances of operas he himself had not approved of. These patent rights, obtained from librettist Pierre Perrin who had been jailed for debt problems, were for the sole right to form the Royal Academy of Music. Lully bargained with Perrin for those rights, paying off his debts and providing him with a lifetime stipend. Lully formed the Royal Academie in March 1672. A year later, in April 1673, restrictions were passed that limited productions performed outside of the academie's auspices to no more than two singers and six players.

Lully was naturalized a French citizen in December 1661. On July 24, 1662, he married the daughter of his mentor and royal chief musician, Michel Lambert. King Louis XIV attended Lully's wedding to Madeleine Lambert and became the godfather of their eldest son. In 1681, Lully was granted Lettres de Noblesse and named one of the Secretaires du Roi. During a performance celebrating the recovery of the King from an illness, Lully accidentally hit his foot with his conducting staff. An infection resulted, and it ultimately killed him. When Lully died in 1687, he left his wife, six children, and an estate with an estimated value of 800,000 livres, a value more than 500 times the annual salary of an average court musician. *—Bruce Lundgren*

OPERA

Operas (1663–1687)

Jean-Baptiste Lully's style and influence as an operatic composer grew directly out of his experience with ballet. From 1652, when he first arrived at the court of Louis XIV as a violinist and dancer, to 1672, he composed music for the court spectacles. During the 1660s, in collaboration with the great playwright Molière, he founded a new form, the comédie-ballet; more dramatic than the highly formalized court ballet, the comédie-ballet introduced comic spoken dialogue alongside dance, chorus, and solo vocal airs. The genre marked an important step forward toward what had increasingly become Lully's objective—the creation of a wholly French style of opera. His opportunity to do so soon presented itself when he gained control over the newly formed royal Académies d'Opéra (founded by the poet Pierre Perrin). Lully's appropriation of the royal patent gave him absolute hegemony, a power he wielded ruthlessly until his death in March 1687.

The first of Lully's operas, *Cadmus et Hermione* appeared in April 1673. Like all but two of the composer's stage works, it has a libretto by Philippe Quinault. Although many of the elements of *Cadmus* had been apparent in earlier stage works, it marks the invention of a totally French form of opera, the tragédie lyrique; this form would remain a powerful benchmark for nearly a century, frequently stiffening resistance against the pan-European dominance of Italian opera.

Lully's tragédies lyriques were five-act works prefaced by an allegorical or mythical prologue; the prologue was invariably an obsequious glorification of the king. In both the prologue and opera proper, the action proceeded through a flexible blend of recitative, chorus, and air. The importance of the chorus distinguished the French form from its Italian siblings, as did the close modeling of the musical style on the French language; this was especially apparent in the two main types of recitative: declamatory, free récitatif simple, and the lyrical récitatif mesuré. Another important distinction from Italian opera was the inclusion of a divertissement in each act, allowing for an extended ballet—a near-obligatory component of French opera through the nineteenth century. Finally, the subject matter adhered to mythological themes; no fewer than five of the librettos Quinault prepared for Lully are drawn from Ovid's *Metamorphosis* alone. Although Lully's earlier operas such as *Cadmus et Hermione*, *Alceste* (1674), and *Thésée* (1675) retained subplots and even elements of comedy typical of seventeenth century Venetian opera, Lully and Quinault increasingly sought to "purge" their operas of such extraneous material. *Atys* of 1676 was the first to do so, marking a new phase in which the deepening of character becomes as important as the element of brilliant spectacle. *—Brian Robins*

Alceste, ou Le triomphe d'Alcide, LWV 50

In March 1672, Lully took over the exclusive royal patent of the Académie d'Opéra from the poet Pierre Perrin. This gave Lully total control over operatic activity at Versailles and in Paris, marking the start of a period that would witness the production of 13 operas over the next 15 years. *Alceste* was the second of these operas, termed by their composer tragédies en musique. All conform to the standard form of a prologue featuring allegorical characters and obsequious praise of the monarch, followed by five acts. The librettist of *Alceste* (and indeed all but two of Lully's operas) was the poet Philippe Quinault, who, in keeping with French seventeenth century theatrical tradition, fashioned his book on a Classical theme, the subject, in this instance, being drawn from Euripides' Alcestis. "A rehearsal of *Alceste* was enthusiastically received by the king and his courtiers in November 1673, but the first public performance was accompanied by a cabal of musicians and poets opposed to Lully's ever-increasing power."

All Lully's tragédies en musique consist of a flexible juxtaposition of the French recitative he had developed after carefully observing the declamation of the French language in the lyric theater, and arias following the long tradition of the air de cour, the two constituents often alternating seamlessly. The character of Lully's operas is therefore markedly different from Italian opera, which at this period was increasingly being divided into clearly demarcated "closed" sections—recitative and aria. Three other crucial elements mark the difference between Italian opera and those of Lully: the inclusion of dance in interpolated divertissements, and the important role given to the orchestra and chorus, the latter by this stage absent in Italian opera.

Following the Prologue in which Louis XIV is praised for his military exploits, the story of *Alceste* follows that of the noble actions of Queen Alcestis, who, in response to a call from Apollo, is prepared to achieve immortal glory by going to Hades in the place of her mortally wounded husband, Admetus. She does so and her funeral obsequies are performed in one of Lully's most impressive tableaux (Act Three), a huge pantomime featuring the chorus and dance. The following act, set on the banks of the River Acheron, contains a famous air for Charon, the boatman of the Styx, and some of Lully's most colorful dramatic effects. In the final act, and in keeping with the convention of happy endings, Alcestis is released from Hades by Hercules, who acting the part of deus ex machina allows the royal couple to remain together. Despite the cabal mounted against it, *Alceste* was a success, its heroic and spectacular effects winning the day. Nevertheless, it is not today considered one of Lully's best operas. *—Brian Robins*

Synopsis:

Prologue. The story is set in ancient Greek mythological times. The Nymphs of the Seine, of the Tuileries, and of the Marne offer praise to French King Louis XIV for his exploits in battle, and all yearn for his triumphant return to Paris.

Act One. In Iolcos, Thessaly, Lycomedes, once a suitor of Alceste, abducts her at her wedding to Admetus. She is taken aboard a ship, which is soon under siege by a violent storm. But Lycomedes is successful in the kidnapping venture largely because of the storm, which hampers pursuit by Admetus, and his forces, among whom is Hercules, also once a suitor to Alceste.

Act Two. On the island of Scyros, the armies of Admetus and Lycomedes clash, with the latter suffering defeat. Hercules rescues Alceste, but Admetus is fatally wounded in battle. Alceste comes to him as he is dying and the two deliver sweet farewells. Apollo appears, however, and announces that anyone choosing to die in the place of Admetus will be granted immortal glory.

Act Three. The scene is at a grand monument constructed by the Arts. Alceste has agreed to sacrifice herself to save Admetus, and her funeral soon follows. Hercules cannot bear to lose Alceste and decides that he will enter Hades to retrieve her. He asks Admetus to release her from their relationship so that he (Hercules) can wed her. Desperate to see her brought back, Admetus agrees.

Act Four. Hercules departs on his mission in a boat, while Alceste enters the underworld to spend eternity. Soon, Hercules arrives and appeals for Alceste. Proserpina is moved by his words and pleads with Pluto to allow Alceste to return with Hercules. He grants the request.

Act Five. Hercules is greeted as a great hero and conqueror of death by a large crowd, which includes Admetus. The latter meets with Alceste and as they are preparing for a sad farewell, Hercules announces that as a conqueror on the battlefield and in underworld, he will also conquer his own hungers by allowing Admetus to reunite with Alceste, after all. There follows a great celebration. *—Robert Cummings*

Recommended:

○ **Lully: Alceste** / Malgoire (cond.), La Grande Ecurie, La Chambre du Roy / Astrée 8527

Atys, LWV 53

Atys, Lully's fourth full-length opera (or tragédie en musique), was first performed at the theater at St. Germain-en-Laye on January 10, 1676. The first public performance took place at the Paris Opéra in April that year. For reasons that have not been established, it became known as "the king's opera." More importantly, it marked a major development in the history of the tragédie en musique as established by Lully and his regular librettist Philippe Quinault. In their earlier collaborations—*Cadmus et Hermione*, *Alceste*, and *Thésée*—Lully and Quinault, while aspiring to the pure style of French Classical lyric theater, had not totally abandoned certain elements of Venetian opera, with its subplots and burlesque characters. *Atys* marks the beginning of a new phase in which all extraneous elements are purged in order to concentrate on the drama of the central plot. This was achieved without foregoing the brilliance of spectacle which formed an integral part of part of French opera.

As with all of Quinault's librettos for Lully (11 in all), the story is drawn from classical literature—in this case from Ovid's *Fasti*. It tells of the tragic love of Atys and the gentle river nymph Sangaride; their love is doomed by the opposition of Cybèle, Queen of the Gods, who also loves Atys. In the powerful and tragic denouement of the opera, Atys, driven temporarily mad by Cybèle, stabs Sangaride. Overcome with remorse when restored to sanity, Atys tries to kill himself, but is restrained by Cybèle, who instead transforms the stricken lover into a pine tree. Thus she too loses the man she loves. The opera ends in tragic mourning—a tone unique among Lully's operas and rare among seventeenth and eighteenth century operas, which, however tragically structured, invariably turn at the last to a satisfying happy ending.

Atys follows the tradition of tragédie en musique by being cast in five acts prefaced by a prologue. As was customary, the Prologue introduces a series of allegorical characters whose principal function is the glorification of Louis XIV, here praised as a hero by Time and a chorus of the Hours of Night and Day. Unlike Italian opera of this period, from which the chorus had disappeared, the chorus plays a major role not only in the prologue, but as participants in the drama itself. The chorus also allows for another essential feature of French operas, namely dance passages, which form the centerpiece of the divertissements introduced into each act. *Atys* includes one of the most famous of all Lully's divertissements: the famous sommeil (or sleep scene) (Act Three) in which Cybèle invokes the god of Sleep to announce her love to Atys in a dream, contrasting the pleasant dreams that he will experience if he returns her love with the nightmare of the baleful dreams he will suffer if he rejects her. *—Brian Robins*

Synopsis:

Prologue. The story is set in ancient Phrygia. The god of Time, the goddess Flora, and other mythical powers and figures give praise to King Louis XIV. (Paying to tribute to the King was a common practice in French operas of the day.) Hercules, Antaeus and other famous warriors then present a pantomime of their various battles and, following a ceremonious pronouncement on art presided over by the goddess Iris, at the behest of the goddess Cybèle, a grand celebration caps the prologue.

Act One. Standing on a sacred mountain dedicated to Cybèle, Attis confides in Idas that he has fallen in love, though he claims to be impervious to romance altogether when he congratulates the object of his affections, Sangaride, on her upcoming wedding. Little does he realize that Sangaride is also in love with him. She reveals this to Doris, stating she is enamored of Attis rather than of her fiancé, Celaenus, King of Phrygia and son of Neptune. Sangaride and Attis soon divulge their mutual feelings of love to each other, but conceal them when the Phrygians assemble to praise Cybèle on her arrival from on high in a chariot.

Act Two. In Cybèle's temple, Celaenus reveals thoughts of insecurity about Sangaride's feelings toward him, asking Attis to confirm that she loves him. The latter tells him merely that she will perform her duties as his wife. Cybèle informs Celaenus that she has selected Attis as the Great Sacrificer, then confides in Melisse that she is in love with Attis. Little Zephyrs and a crowd of many nationalities give praise to Attis as the Great Sacrificer.

Act Three. In the Great Sacrificer's palace, Idas and Doris warn Attis that Sangaride intends to confess her love for him to Cybèle. Attis worries over the situation and after they leave, feels himself growing tired, unaware that Cybèle has enlisted the aid of the god of sleep to inform him of Cybèle's love for him in a dream. This is conveyed to him as he sleeps, as well as a sense that rejecting Cybèle would be dangerous. Attis awakens in an anxious state and is immediately confronted with Cybèle's offer of love. But Sangaride enters seeking discharge from her commitment to Celaenus. Attis does not allow her to divulge their own mutual love to Cybèle, leaving her bewildered and the goddess suspicious.

Act Four. At the River Sangarius palace Sangaride, misinterpreting Attis' intention, tells Doris and Idas that Attis has lost interest in her, and she determines to refocus her attentions on Celaenus after all. But later, after mutual accusations of infidelity, Attis and Sangaride reconcile. The gods, though, approve the marriage of Sangaride and Celaenus, but in his powerful role as the Great Sacrificer Attis will not sanction it.

Act Five. Cybèle and Celaenus berate Attis and Sangaride for their defiance. Cybèle summons the (underworld) Fury Alecto to punish them. He arrives and renders Attis mad, who chases and kills Sangaride under the illusion she is monster. Cybèle restores his sanity, and he then grieves over his horrible deed. Later, Cybèle confesses to Melisse that the punishment may have been unduly harsh. Suddenly Attis stumbles along, dying from a self-inflicted stab wound. But Cybèle cannot allow him to die and so transmutes him into a pine tree that she pledges to love eternally. —*James Reel*

Recommended:

- ○ **Lully: Atys** / Christie (cond.), Laurens, Fouchecourt, Deletre, Ragon, Les Arts Florissants / HM 901257

BALLET

Ballets and Other Stage Works (1652–1687)

When the young Florentine Giovanni Battista Lulli arrived in Paris in 1646 to serve as a valet to Louis XIV's cousin Mlle de Montpensier, no one could have predicted the glittering career he would enjoy at court. It was a career based largely on stage works, culminating in the series of 11 operas, or tragédies en musique that were produced largely in collaboration with the poet Philippe Quinault. By the time he left Mlle de Montpensier's employ in 1652 to take up a post at the royal court, Lulli had become an accomplished violinist and dancer. Ambitious and unscrupulous, Lulli soon advanced at the court and was appointed *compositeur de musique instrumentale* by the king only a year after arriving at Versailles. In this capacity, Lully (who changed his name when he became a naturalized French citizen in 1661) was responsible for composing the music for court ballets, works which despite the name also included danced choruses and solo vocal numbers (airs de cour). These highly stylized court ballets took the form of a series of "entrées" featuring mythological scenes and characters, and involved the active participation of the king and his court in addition to Lully himself. Glorification of Louis was indeed a major constituent of these spectacles. In the *Ballet Royal de la Nuict* of 1653 (a collaborative work involving several older composers but not Lully himself), for example, Louis appears as the triumphant Sun, victor over the Frondists. Lully soon took over the composition of the airs as well as dances, and his ballets increasingly often took on dramatic qualities. In addition, Lully had taken over the training of the *petits violons*, an offshoot of the larger *24 violons du Roi*, introducing a type of disciplined playing that marked an important advance in the development of the orchestra. During the 1660s, Lully developed a new kind of ballet in collaboration with the great playwright Molière, the so-called *comédie-ballet*, which included spoken comedy in addition to the dances, airs, and choruses. The series opened with *Le mariage forcé*, first given at the Louvre in 1664, and culminates with the most famous, *Le bourgeois gentilhomme* (1670), the last of the composer's collaborations with Molière. During this period Lully also continued to continued to compose court ballets, but his mind now increasingly turned to opera. In 1672 he embarked on the great series of tragédies lyriques, mostly in collaboration with Quinault. It would be nearly ten years before Lully returned to ballet in 1681 with *Le triomphe de l'amour*, a large-scale work with no less than 20 entrées, also produced in collaboration with Quinault. In his final years, Lully produced two further nonoperatic works, a one-act divertissement, *Idylle sur la paix* (1685), with a libretto by Jean Racine, and *Le temple de la paix* (1685), his final ballet. —*Brian Robins*

Recommended:

- ○ **Lully: L'Orchestre du Roi Soleil** / Savall (cond.), Kraemer, Le Concert des Nations / Alia Vox 9807
- ○ **Lully: Les divertissements de Versailles** / Christie (cond.), Daneman, Bazola, Lallouette, Shaham, Arts Florissants / 2002 / Erato 44655
- ○ **Lully: Ballet Music for the Sun King** / Mallon (cond.), Arcadia Baroque Ens. / 2000 / Naxos 554003

CHORAL

Sacred Music (1664–1687)

The young Florentine Giovanni Battista Lulli arrived in Paris in 1646, taking up a position at Louis XIV's court at Versailles six years later. Over the next 35 years Lully (he changed his name on taking up French nationality in 1661) established himself as the most powerful musician serving under the king, ruthlessly gaining over French music control as absolute as that of the Sun King himself. The focus of his work during these years was on dramatic music, initially on the sung and danced ballets that stood at the heart of magnificent court display, later on tragédies lyriques, the form of French opera invented by Lully and his favored librettist, Philippe Quinault.

In addition to his dramatic works, Lully also composed a substantial, but far less known body of sacred music for the chapel of the French court and religious establishments in Paris. These fall almost exclusively into one of two categories, the grand motet and the petit motet. Both draw on either complete settings of psalms, or texts assembled from various psalms. Although vastly different in scale, Lully's two types of motet share in common a far greater reliance on his Italian roots than is the case with his stage music, for which he established a style that has come to be recognized as quintessentially French.

All the surviving 11 petit motets are chamber works composed for three voices and simple basso continuo accompaniment (two also call for a solo violin). Most call for three soprano voices, lending credence to the belief that they were composed for the nuns at the Dames de l'Assomption convent, in the rue St.-Honoré in Paris—a convent known for the quality of its singing. In these short pieces, cast in two or more sections, Lully's skillful imitative writing shows a clear debt to the sacred works of the important Roman composer Giacomo Carissimi, who was also probably the teacher of Lully's contemporary, Marc-Antoine Charpentier.

By contrast, the grand motets are large-scale ceremonial works composed for important feast days (the only times high mass was performed at Versailles). In contrast to his role of innovator in opera, Lully inherited the grand motets, a form which depends on a sequence of contrasting movements that include orchestral "symphonies" and ritornellos (passages for both small [chamber] choir and full choir), and solo airs and ensembles. These follow each other without interruption, thus creating a tapestry of ever-changing color, sonority, and weight. Lully composed some 20 grands motets, the first of which, a *Miserere* composed in 1664, immediately displays his mastery of the form and became a particular favorite of the king's. Other particularly impressive examples include the splendid *Te Deum* of 1677, written to celebrate the victories that preceded the Peace of Nijmegen, and the powerful and intensely moving *Dies Irae* of 1674, a work that alone destroys the image of Lully as a cool, dispassionate composer. —*Brian Robins*

Recommended:

- ○ **Lully: Te Deum; Misesrere; Plaude laetare** / Niquet (cond.), Le Concert Spirituel / 1994 / FNAC 592308
- ○ **Lully: Grands Motet Vol. 2** / Niquet (cond.), Le Concert Spirituel / 2000 / Naxos 554398

Radu Lupu

b. Nov. 30, 1945, Galati, Romania

Pianist

Romanian pianist Radu Lupu has enjoyed an outstandingly successful career. Born in the final year of World War II, he began studies on the piano at the age of six, and after only six years of study made his public recital debut; this garnered attention in Soviet musical circles and eventually landed him a scholarship to the Moscow Conservatory, where he worked under the great Heinrich Neuhaus.

In 1966 Lupu won the prestigious Van Cliburn Competition. Usually such a triumph would move a young pianist to abandon formal training and embark on a full-scale professional career, but Lupu chose instead to remain at the Conservatory for another few years and hone his already remarkable skills. Only when honored with the top prize at the Leeds International Piano Competition in 1969 did Lupu disengage himself once and for all from student life and take up the role of traveling virtuoso; in the next few years he made appearances in all of the major musical capitals of both Europe and the United States.

As can be said of many of his compatriots, Radu Lupu has made a musical home for himself in the rich nineteenth century repertoire—Schubert, Schumann, Beethoven, and Brahms especially. But he has never hesitated to stray to either side of this self-prescribed pasture—his Mozart touch is shining when called upon (witness his chamber collaborations with violinist Szymon Goldberg), and he endows performances of modern works with an honesty and intelligence not always offered by top-rank virtuosi. —*Blair Johnston*

Recommended:

- ○ **Radu Lupu** / Previn (cond.), Lupu, London SO / 1999 / Philips 456895
- ○ **Schubert: Impromptus** / Lupu / 1999 / Decca 460975
- ○ **Mozart: Sonata for 2 Pianos K448; Schubert: Fantasia in F Minor** / Perahia, Lupu / 2003 / Sony 93015
- ○ **Schubert: Military Marches; Variations; Grand Duo** / Barenboim, Lupu / 1997 / Teldec 17146

Witold Lutosławski

b. Jan. 25, 1913, Warsaw, Poland, **d.** Feb. 7, 1994, Warsaw, Poland

Composer: Symphonic, Orchestral, Concerto, Chamber Music, Vocal, Keyboard

Lutosławski was the leading progressive figure in Polish music of the second half of the twentieth century. Born in Warsaw, he showed an exceptional musical talent at an early age, with his first compositions dating from 1922. He studied piano, violin and composition (with Witold Maliszewski, a pupil of Rimsky-Korsakov), graduating from the Warsaw Conservatory in 1937. Two years, at the beginning of World War II, Poland was occupied by the Nazi Germany; and Nazi repression included censorship on artistic expression. Lutosławski survived the difficult war years as well as the subsequent Stalinist period by writing for radio, film, and theatre. In addition, he arranged folk-songs and composed music for children.

Considered too formalist, his concert music was rarely performed. His first substantial orchestral work, *The Symphonic Variations* was premiered in 1939. It is a work firmly rooted in tonality with a folk-like theme that is varied in a kaleidoscopic way. His first stylistic period culminated in the folk-influenced, three-movement *Concerto for Orchestra* (1954).

With the cultural thaw which started in the late 1950s, his reputation began to grow, at home and abroad, as did his compositional style, with 12-tone techniques appearing in *Funeral Music* (1958). In this work, Lutosławski continually resolves ascending scales with semi-tone intervals that tend to anchor tonal centers within keyless regions. In *Jeux Vénitiens* (1961), Lutosławski took his first step into a "limited aleatory music"— after hearing a performance of John Cage's *Concerto for Piano* in 1960. Lutosławski's elegant *String Quartet* (1964) utilizes four rhythmically independent strands simultaneously, yielding wonderfully dense and elastic textures. In the *Live pour orchestra* (1968) the work's four main sections are connected by controlled aleatory passages. Most of his subsequent works were orchestral, fully chromatic, orchestrated in a manner suggesting Debussy and Ravel, and consistently develop an opposition between aleatory and metrical textures. Lutosławski went on to compose nearly twenty major orchestral works, including *Symphony No. 3* (1982), for which he was awarded the prestigious Grawemeyer Award, and his final *Symphony No. 4* (1992), commissioned and premiered by the Los Angeles Philharmonic.

He also composed works for distinguished soloists, such as Dietrich Fischer-Dieskau, (*Les espaces du sommeil*), Heinz and Ursula Holliger (*Concerto for Oboe and Harp*), Anne-Sophie Mutter, (*Chain II*), Mstislav Rostropovich (Cello Concerto), and Krystian Zimmerman (*Piano Concerto*). Lutosławski's extensive experience conducting his own works helped him to refine his musical language, his later works becoming more lyrical and harmonically transparent. *—James Harley*

SYMPHONIC

Symphony No. 2 (1966–1967)

While Lutosławski's *Symphony No. 2* is regarded as a less challenging work for the listener than his 1947 *First*, which was received poorly by Communist Party arts meddlers, it can hardly be classed as easy listening. Cast in two movements, the first subtitled "Hesitant" and the second "Direct," the work is austere, if colorfully scored, and structurally unconventional, veering away from the exposition-development-reprise pattern and other forms typically found in traditional symphonies in favor of a more episodic or, to use the composer's term, open structure. Yet, especially for its time, it cannot be called avant-garde, either—indeed, it has quite recognizable, if difficult themes.

"Hesitant" opens with an extended passage of what seemingly begins as big brass-dominated fanfares, but what soon deteriorates into roiling, discordant music struggling to find direction. The mood then turns relatively calm, but the music appears uncertain of its direction. Gradually, amid much delicate but busy instrumental activity, the thematic material unravels, without, however, shedding its sense of indecision or generally unsmiling mood. The scoring is brilliantly imaginative throughout, conveying a sense of the primitive. Note, in particular, the growling brass and winds at the close of the movement.

"Direct," as the listener would surmise, presents its material more directly and imparts a more resolute sense of shaping its structure and trajectory. That said, it begins mysteriously, the orchestra wandering and roiling in its lower ranges. Soon the accrued tension finds partial release when sonorities rise higher and take on a brighter mood. But tension continues to grow, with several dissonant brass outbursts and frenetic, driving strings and winds. Even when things seem to herald calm, the music soon begins to spew energy again: a menacing piano dazzles in its dissonant fanaticism, inciting the orchestra to a fury of rhythmic drive and sonic mayhem. But the close is relatively calm, even if the music divulges an undercurrent of unresolved tension. *—Robert Cummings*

Recommended:

- ○ **Lutosławski: Symphony 2; Chantefleurs et Chantefables; Piano Concerto** / Salonen (cond.), Los Angeles PO / 1996 / Sony 67189
- ○ **Lutosławski Orchestral Music** / Lutosławski (cond.), Katowice Polish Radio Orch. / 2000 / Angel 73833

Symphony No. 3 (1972–1973)

Witold Lutosławski is known as one of the great orchestral composers of the latter half of the twentieth century. His music is rooted in the Classical-Romantic tradition as well as the spirited character of Eastern European predecessors such as Bartók, Prokofiev, and Szymanowski. Along the way, though, he introduced a number of innovations in keeping with the avant-garde tendencies of his Polish compatriots. He managed to strike a balance, somehow, between novel, even aleatoric textures, chromatically expressive melodies, wide-ranging rhythms, and a clear formal balance that conveyed an engagingly dramatic narrative. His *Symphony No. 3* is the most ambitious, and possibly the most successful, example of his style.

Lutosławski struggled for many years with this score. Begun in the early 1970s as a prestigious commission for the Chicago Symphony Orchestra, he finally delivered the completed score in 1983. In discussions on its genesis, Lutosławski has tended to focus on his own difficulties in working through Poland's period of Martial Law, a difficult time for those engaged in artistic expression. There are "martial" elements in the piece, particularly in the aggressive brass motives that impose themselves at various points, but this work is not programmatic, or possessed of a literal narrative.

One of the composer's main concerns was to find a way to incorporate lighter, more melodic passages into his work. His *Symphony No. 2* (1967), for example, is built primarily from blocks of dense textures; there is very little line to the piece. *Symphony No. 3*, by contrast, is much more nuanced, both in the variety of materials and in the formal design. The piece unfolds as one continuous movement, but a number of sections can clearly be heard. The brass shout a call-to-arms to launch the symphony, but the music quickly dissolves into a nebulous wash.

The work proceeds in an episodic fashion, with the attention shifting abruptly from one texture to another. The brass continue to interject, and at last an extended transition pushes toward a more substantial section. A toccata-like, contrapuntal string texture casts a Beethovenian shadow, and one can hear vestiges of the sonata allegro form in this passage, with the strings leading into a more lyrical "second theme." These elements are developed in succession, intercut with passages featuring the brass. Along the way, there are a few triumphant moments for full orchestra. The final culmination leads to what Lutosławski calls an Epilogue. This section constitutes a grand crescendo, building from the bottom up, with more and more instruments entering until the entire orchestra erupts in a final lyrical outpouring. The coda is brief, winding its way quickly downward, ending with one last gasp.

Symphony No. 3 represents the pinnacle of Lutosławski's achievement. The various families of instruments are all featured in one fashion or another, complementing very well the talents of a great orchestra such as the Chicago Symphony. New to Lutosławski's style is the lyricism which is evident throughout the work, set against his more characteristic orchestrational brilliance and rhythmic vitality. The formal construction is impressive, too; the thematic elements are carefully developed, and the harmonies, though non-tonal, are often sonorous and built from triadic superpositions. Lutosławski completed this symphony at the mature age of 70 and would complete one more. *—Jim Harley*

Recommended:

- ○ **Lutosławski: Symphonies 3 & 4** / Salonen (cond.), Los Angeles PO / 1994 / Sony 66280
- ○ **Essential Lutosławski** / Lutosławski (cond.), Berlin PO / 1999 / Philips 464043

Symphony No. 4 (1993)

Lutosławski's *Symphony No. 4* is cast in two continuous movements and lasts about 20 minutes. Like other symphonies and orchestral works by the composer, it employs limited aleatoric or chance elements, thus making each performance different. The work is generally considered one of Lutosławski's more approachable compositions, featuring a healthy measure of lyricism and less dissonance than is often the norm. Still, it will strike some listeners as densely woven and difficult.

The symphony mysteriously opens with strings playing sustained chords and the harp seeming to wander in the darkness. The clarinet then floats a lovely, if reticent melody above the drone-like background, and is joined near the end by the flute, the phrase ending on an ethereal ascent. While the music that follows features several lively passages, the overall character of the movement remains mysterious, even eerie in the string writing, while also divulging an undercurrent of tension in tempos that are generally slow or lacking a sense of thrust.

The second movement, marked Allegro, begins about seven minutes into the work and contains livelier music, though there are many moderately or slowly paced passages. Lutosławski uses the same melodic material presented in the opening panel, but imaginatively transforms it into many guises. There is less lyricism here, but a greater sense of development, as well as more colorful scoring: hear the playful central episode dominated by piccolo that deftly seems to imitate chirps or peeps, or the intense music on strings and brass that follows.

Again, there is an air of mystery, almost a ghostly Shostakovian sense, in this lengthy movement, but also a restless, conflicted character. Near the end the music seems to be peacefully fading into a playful netherworld when it revives and ends harshly, though with a triumphant defiance. *—Robert Cummings*

Recommended:

- ○ **Lutosławski: Symphonies 3 & 4** / Salonen (cond.), Los Angeles PO / 1994 / Sony 66280
- ○ **Lutosławski: Symphony 4; Partita for Violin & Orchestra** / Wit (cond.), Polish RSO / 1996 / Naxos 553202

ORCHESTRAL

Funeral Music, for strings (1954–1958)

For those familiar only with the early music of Lutosławski—such as the widely admired *Concerto for Orchestra*—or with the later symphonies and "Chain" pieces, the *Musique funèbre* ("Funeral Music in memoriam Bela Bartók") for string orchestra (1958) will be something of a surprise. The early folk-like music—relating strongly to the music of Bartók and of a great Polish predecessor, Karol Szymanowski (1882–1937)—was conservative by necessity, since the repressive Communist government regnant after World War II allowed very little in the way of artistic freedom. But something of a political "thaw" set in after 1956, and Lutosławski was one of dozens of Polish composers who responded by radically exploring avant-garde developments. The result is Lutosławski's only important 12-tone work. *Musique funèbre* doesn't sound as dry or doctrinaire as most of the other serialist music from its time, but it takes an expressive performance to bring out its unique power.

The work comprises four sections (each titled in Lutosławski's beloved French), the last three of which proceed to the next without pause. The lugubrious, flowing "Prologue," an homage to the first movement of Bartók's *Music for Strings, Percussion and Celesta*, lays out the 12-tone row in strict canon. The first version is played by two solo cellos in canon at the half note, the second stated a few bars later by solo viola. As each row is made up only of the intervals of semitone and tritone, it gives the entire movement a singular harmonic palette which, due to the constant and consistent up-down jumping of such a linear series, often gives the impression of moving in sequences. After the entire string orchestra has joined in, the movement reaches an extended climax by stretching out into broader rhythms and by limiting the pitches in use to only F and B; it then quickly dies out on those two notes.

The "Métamorphoses" that follow, which have a theme-and-variations quality to them, seem to get faster and faster, though in fact the rhythmic values just get smaller and smaller—the movement's tempo never actually changes. The music's linear intervals are more various in this movement, with richer and more interesting harmonies the result; as in the first movement, moments of stasis are achieved by carefully timed repetitions of important pitch groups.

The drama of the "Métamorphoses" builds and builds until it reaches its effective climax, the "Apogée" movement. The rough concentration of this music, marked fff, is achieved by using massive 12-note chords (a preview of Lutosławski's later style): variety comes from the masterful use of widely differing registers and rhythmic durations, making each sonority sound different from its neighbors. The music then rapidly climbs down from the heights and, at the "Epilogue," gathers into a powerful unison statement of the 12-tone row from the opening movement. After the restatement of some material from the opening, the music dies out, with a solo cello sifting four final pitches until each is left behind, like a ghost. *—Russell Platt*

Recommended:

○ **Lutosławski Orchestral Music** / Lutosławski (cond.), Katowice Polish Radio Orch. / 2000 / Angel 73833

○ **Lutosławski: Symphony 4; Partita for Violin & Orchestra** / Wit (cond.), Polish Radio SO / 1996 / Naxos 553202

CONCERTO

Cello Concerto (1966–1970)

Starting around the middle 1950s, Lutosławski began to incorporate unusual sounds and playing techniques into his works. Among these were aleatorics, or chance elements. Lutosławski first encountered the use of chance in the works of John Cage, and, inspired by that encounter, developed what he called "controlled chance" or "limited aleatoric technique"—the employment of short sections of chance-derived sounds within a larger composition. In a description which also provides an apt metaphor for his *Concerto for Cello and Orchestra*, in which limited aleatorics are used, Lutosławski said that the chance element "grants the musicians a touch of self-determination within the otherwise hierarchical, authoritarian organization of conductor and orchestra."

The *Cello Concerto* was written for and dedicated to Mstislav Rostropovich, for whom Lutosławski also wrote the *Novelette* of 1978–79. Rostropovich took part in the work's premiere, along with the Bournemouth Symphony and conductor Edward Downes, on October 14, 1970. At that time Rostropovich's dissident status within the Soviet Union was well known, and Lutosławski and members of his family had likewise suffered at the hands of the Soviets. These events must have had some influence, despite Lutosławski's statements to the contrary, on the dialectic of the *Concerto*, in which the cellist plays the traditional but innovatively modified role of individual hero in conflict with the orchestra (representing the state or society).

This concerto, in four linked movements, begins with an Introduction, a soliloquy for the cello in which repeated D tones are broken by short, abrupt phrases. After about four minutes, the orchestra finally enters with a loud interruption from the brass instruments. There are four such eruptions in the second movement, Episodes, during most of which the cello carries on a dialogue with members of the orchestra. The slow Cantilena third movement features a lyrical cello solo over a somewhat ominous accompaniment. The intensity builds to near chaos, and in the Finale the cello is, as it were, set upon by the orchestra. After an aggressive back-and-forth between soloist and orchestra and a harsh sustained chord, the cello takes control and leads the way to the resolute ending. *—Chris Morrison*

Recommended:

○ **Dutilleux & Lutosławski: Cello Concertos** / Lutosławski (cond.), Rostropovich, Paris Orch. / Angel 67868

○ **Lutosławski: Cello Concerto; Novellettes** / Wit (cond.), Bauer, Katowice Polish Radio Orch. / 1998 / Naxos 553625

Chain 2, dialogue for violin & orchestra (1984)

After the crowning achievement of his *Symphony No. 3*, Witold Lutosławski searched for new forms to explore. He had spent much of his career working to perfect the single-movement symphonic form, but by the mid-1980s, his attention had shifted toward chamber music and the solo voice. He had, in fact, composed his *Partita for violin and piano* in 1984, and in that piece had developed new means for sustaining melodic lines with sparse textures and harmonies that were more suitable for a chamber setting. The opportunity to write something for the phenomenal Anne-Sophie Mutter no doubt served as inspiration for Lutosławski's *Chain 2, dialogue for violin and orchestra*, composed just a year after the Partita. Apart from featuring the violin, however, there is little resemblance between the two pieces, a remarkable fact considering their chronological proximity.

Chain 2 takes its title from a technique Lutosławski had developed earlier in his career, but which had preoccupied him in the 1980s. The notion of the "chain" derives from the overlapping of distinct materials. For example, a phrase launched by the violin may be picked up in midstream by woodwinds, while the violin then drops out. Then another instrument may enter playing something new, and so on. In this way, the musical flow is perpetual, and new elements can be continuously introduced. In essence, this chain technique is a form of counterpoint, but extends a considerable relational freedom, including the possibility for simultaneous tempi, an innovation Lutosławski was happy to explore. However, this technique does not form the main focus of the whole piece. Instead, Lutosławski created four distinct movements, the first and third being related, and the second and fourth also bearing a resemblance to each other. The chain technique is most prominent in the first and third movements, which are both performed as a structured ad libitum. In Lutosławski's music, this means that while the music is fully notated, the conductor does not keep time, but cues the entrances for the different players, who then proceed at their own pace outside of any metrical divisions. This allows the violin soloist, in particular, to perform freely, as if in a cadenza, able to give full expression without needing to be precisely synchronized with the orchestra. The opening movement is indeed rhapsodic in character, followed by a lively, scherzo-like second movement. The third is slow and deeply lyrical, while the finale is brilliant and quick, as one might expect.

While exploring new means of shaping his music, Lutosławski also looked back tothe Baroque, to the concerto tradition shaped by Corelli, Vivaldi, and perhaps Mozart. The tone is certainly lighter than a Romantic concerto, and in *Chain 2* this is underscored by the chamber orchestra. Indeed, compared to his intensely dramatic *Cello Concerto* from 1970, *Chain 2* is a paragon of balance and refinement. *—Jim Harley*

Recommended:

○ **Lutosławski: Partita; Chain 2; Stravinsky: Violin Concerto** / Lutosławski (cond.), Mutter, BBCSO / 2002 / DG 471588

Concerto for Orchestra (1950–1954)

With the close of World War II, the musical life of Poland experienced something of a renaissance, in which Lutosławski played a significant role. After marrying in 1946, however, he was forced to spend much of his composing time creating "functional" music—music for theatre and film, children's songs, and arrangements of folk and popular tunes—to support his growing family. His more serious works encountered resistance from the Stalinist regime in Poland; his *First Symphony* (1947) was banned for a time for "formalism."

Partly as a result of his own interest and partly due to the influence of the cultural commissars, Lutosławski turned to folk music for inspiration in many of his works of the late 1940s and early 1950s. This was the case with the *Concerto for Orchestra*, which was commissioned by conductor Witold Rowicki, to whom the work is dedicated, who wanted a new composition for his recently created Warsaw National Philharmonic Orchestra (founded in 1950). Written over a five year span, the *Concerto* was premiered by Rowicki and his orchestra in Warsaw on November 26, 1954. Lutosławski called the *Concerto* "the only serious piece" among his folk music inspired works.

The influence on Lutosławski's *Concerto* of Béla Bartók's *Concerto for Orchestra* of just a few years before is hard to ignore. The themes in both works are folk-like and attractive, their settings employ some dissonance but are still accessible, and the manipulation of the orchestra in both cases is highly virtuosic. There are other more specific similarities, too, like the arch-form (a form Bartók used often) of Lutosławski's first movement and the chorale theme of his third movement, which is virtually a quotation of the chorale theme from the second movement of the Bartók work.

The Lutosławski *Concerto* is in three movements. The lively opening Intrada is built on a repetitive, pounding F sharp from the timpani and basses, over which short melodic phrases (apparently derived from a popular melody from Mazovia) multiply. Gossamer textures open the second movement, Capriccio notturno e Arioso. The Arioso opens with a trumpet fanfare, and turns stormy before the darker-textured return of the opening Capriccio theme. The final movement, Passacaglia, Toccata e Corale, is longer than the first two combined. The quirky bass line of the Passacaglia supports a series of variations that become increasingly ominous and grandiose. After the Passacaglia theme quiets and ascends into the upper reaches of the orchestra, the Toccata takes a variant of that theme and whips up considerable excitement. The Corale, with its evocation of the Bartók *Concerto*, begins sedately, but also builds up steam as the theme is passed around within the orchestra. The coda builds from a rumbling piano to a grand fanfare and ends brilliantly, again in a manner reminiscent of Bartók's work. *—Chris Morrison*

Recommended:

- ○ **Lutosławski Orchestra Works** / Lutosławski (cond.), Katowice Polish Radio Orch. / 2000 / Angel 73833
- ○ **Bartok & Lutosławski: Concertos for Orchestra** / Davis (cond.), Stockholm PO / Finlandia 14909

Dance Preludes for clarinet & orchestra (1955)

Lutosławski described the *Dance Preludes* as his "farewell to folklore"; in the middle 1950s he stopped writing works inspired by Polish folk music (like the *Concerto for Orchestra*), and adopted a more dissonant style informed by the European avant-garde. Written over the years 1954 and 1955, the *Dance Preludes* were premiered in Warsaw on February 15, 1955. Lutosławski subsequently rearranged them twice: in 1955 for clarinet, string orchestra, harp, piano, and percussion, and in 1959 for flute, oboe, clarinet, bassoon, French horn, and string quartet.

The five *Preludes* are uniformly light-hearted and melodic, each of them only a minute or two in length. The first, third, and fifth are quick and lively, whereas the second and fourth are slower in tempo and more melancholic in tone. *—Chris Morrison*

Recommended:

- ○ Lutosławski, **Blake, Seiber** / Litton (cond.), King, English CO / 2002 / Hyperion 55068

Piano Concerto (1987)

Although Lutosławski was a concert pianist for five years of his career, he did not get around to writing a piano concerto until his last decade, a time when his music was mellowing. The work is in four continuous movements and features greater emphasis on melody and less on aleatoric counterpoint, an element found in many of his previous large compositions.

Cast in four sections, the opening panel serves as a sort of introduction, presenting the materials from which the succeeding movements spring. It begins in a haze of trills and swirls, an air of mystery and playfulness immediately evident. The piano enters delicately in the upper register, maintaining the ethereal mood. Tension gradually accrues, and the piano erupts, provoking the orchestra to violently spring to life just in time for the start of the second movement.

The driving second movement begins menacingly in the bass register, swirling upwards, taking on a Bartókian sort of rhythmic spring, both on the keyboard and then in the orchestra. The music mixes playfulness with a queasy sense of risk, of danger lurking around the corner. The latter moments are eerie as the music slowly fades. The composer's aleatoric contrapuntal procedures are in evidence more so in the second movement than in any other.

The third movement also begins on the piano, the music slowly taking shape, initially seeming to struggle to find its lyrical way in the long piano solo that dominates the first half. The orchestra finally enters, imparting a sense of tension with its softly trilling strings. The piano erupts in the latter half, drawing out hazy brass proclamations and anxious string activity. The music turns calm until the start of the finale.

The theme for this final movement is delivered throughout by the orchestra and is made up of short phrases filled out by rests. The music, then, has a sort of stop-and-start character in its creepy opening. The piano's material is derived from the main theme and is imaginatively integrated with the orchestra's music. The finale has a somewhat episodic character as tension builds and variants come and go. The piano writing is dazzling throughout and the presto ending is thrilling. *—Robert Cummings*

Recommended:

- ○ **Lutosławski: Symphony 2; Chantefleurs et Chantefables; Piano Concerto** / Salonen (cond.), Crossley, Los Angeles PO / 1996 / Sony 67189
- ○ **Lutosławski: Partita; Chain 2; Piano Concerto** / Lutosławski (cond.), Zimerman, BBCSO / 2002 / DG 471588

Variations on a theme of Paganini, for piano & orchestra (1941–1978)

Although he was the slowest of twentieth century Poland's stellar composers to develop, Lutosławski proved to be the most distinctive, most individual, least manneristic, ultimately the greatest of his countrymen after Chopin—this in the terminal 35 years of his long life. The German occupation of Poland in 1939, soon after his graduation from the Warsaw Conservatory (with diplomas in piano and composition), limited Lutosławski's artistic growth by driving him and his contemporaries underground. With public concerts banned, he and Andrzej Panufnik formed a two-piano team that played surreptitiously in Warsaw's cabarets for the duration of World War II. Between them they composed or arranged some 200 works, of which only Lutosławski's variations on the *24th Capriccio* of Paganini survived, and was published in 1949. Lutosławski developed at his own tempo—mostly largo, sometimes mesto. Following a folk-music period, and a brief flirtation with 12-note mantras, he took up "chance" music, stimulated by a broadcast of John Cage's *Piano Concerto.* Before a fourth and final period of sharpened individuality, indeed of utter mastery, he'd become the world's leading composer of aleatoric (or "chance") music.

It was during the transition from Lutosławski's third to last period, whilst writing the *Third Symphony* (1972–82)—after *Mi-parti* in 1976, but before the severally delayed *Novelette* Rostropovich requested for Washington, D.C.—that Felicja Blumenthal asked him, in 1977, to please write something for piano and orchestra. The solo concerto he finally produced in 1987 hadn't yet taken form in his mind, and so he reworked the two-piano *Paganini Variations* of 1941 for one piano and orchestra.

This newer version, however, which Mme. Blumenthal introduced on November 18, 1979, with Brian Priestman conducting the former Florida Philharmonic of Miami, was no mere transcription. It is variations on variations on variations (the original form of Paganini's *Capriccio* that also fascinated Liszt, Brahms, Casella, Rachmaninov, and Blacher). In Lutosławski's vivacious, virtuosic second version, a dozen of them fill a nine-minute span. Material originally divided between duo-pianists at two keyboards is assigned first to the soloist, then to the orchestra, except in the theme itself and Variations X and XI. Not all are antic, however; in Variation V, before midpoint, high spirits yield to a Poco lento of pensive beauty. The kaleidoscopic orchestra includes four horns, three each of trumpets and trombones, tuba, tubular bells, and other wood and metal percussion instruments plus harp—all of them adding spice to the composer's voluptuous sonorities. *—Roger Dettmer*

Recommended:

- ○ **Duo Piano Extravaganza** / Zinman (cond.), Argerich, Concertgebouw / 1995 / Philips 446557
- ○ **Safri Duo** / / 1995 / Chandos 9398

CHAMBER MUSIC

Mini Overture, for brass quintet (1978)

Witold Lutosławski is known primarily for his orchestral works, which have established him as one of the twentieth century's major compositional voices; along the way, though, he wrote some important chamber works, and a collection of miniatures. These pieces were often memorials, or tailored to the needs of a specific occasion (sometimes as gifts); his *Mini Overture* is one of these. Written as a 50th-birthday tribute for Ursula, wife of Philip Jones, leader of the renowned Philip Jones Brass Ensemble (PJBE), it was premiered by that group in Lucerne, Switzerland, in March of 1982. While only three minutes in length, this piece has transcended the occasion of its composition to become a popular addition to the brass ensemble repertory.

While the PJBE comprised ten players, Lutosławski chose to score his piece for the more traditional brass quintet: two trumpets, horn, trombone, and tuba. He had never written for such an ensemble before, though the brass are often featured in his orchestral music. (He later wrote a couple of very short fanfares for brass ensembles.) Nonetheless, he penned a highly idiomatic work.

Fashioned into a tiny sonata form lasting about two and a half minutes, the *Overture* uses two compact and contrasting themes: the first is propulsive and long-limbed, while the more tranquil second theme area (about 40 seconds into the work) is formed in a layered manner from a single motif. The sound of the work is unusually euphonious and conservative—given Lutosławski's frequent use of aleatoric counterpoint, and other more adventurous techniques—alternating between fast, choppy phrases featuring repeated tones, sharp articulations, and short chromatic runs; there are periodic moments of repose, with long-held tones and a concentrated lyricism. There is also a great deal of thematic layering, with different instruments carrying on contrasting material at the same time. The *Mini Overture* is a sharply-etched gem that exploits the colors and sonorities of the brass quintet to great effect. Such birthday presents are to be cherished, no doubt! *—Jim Harley*

Recommended:

- ○ **Heavy Metal** / Stockholm Chamber Brass / 1992 / Bis 544
- ○ **PJBE Finale** / Philip Jones Brass Ens. / 1987 / Chandos 8490

String Quartet (1964)

This string quartet of 1964 is one of Lutosławski's finest chamber works. It is also the work in which he took his interest in aleatoric procedures the farthest. Typically, and mistakenly referred to as chance music, aleatoric music as practiced by Lutosławski allows the performers to make some of the choices usually dictated by a composer. Lutosławski used to liken his approach to the mobiles of Alexander Calder, wherein fixed shapes can move and assume new relationships with each other. In this case, the length of the various sections can differ, and the four string parts are unsynchronized and independent of each other.

The quartet is a succession of such mobiles for each of the four players. There are points where they are loosely coordinated, but for the most part the players are independent of one another and play their parts as a continuous stream. Players are called upon to make their own decisions regarding lengths of pauses, and how to execute accelerandos and ritenutos. They must not attempt to coordinate with each other. The parts are so independent that the composer did not even write them into a score; he simply composed the four parts independently. His wife, Danuta, did devise a practical and clever way to assemble the four parts into a score without making the false impression that the parts should align.

The quartet begins with an extended soliloquy for the first violin. A recurring pattern (repeated octave Cs) is established. This recurs throughout the movement, and is an audible signal that a player has reached the end of an aleatoric section. This "signal" is developed, recurring in a different pattern each time it appears. The composition is also based on a strict method of pitch organization. The "signal" motive ultimately is distorted into a dissonance, pushing the quartet to a climactic point. The aftermath of the climax creates a bleak soundscape, marked Funèbre (funereal). Having devised a system of composition that virtually guaranteed a different result each time, the composer remarked to the LaSalle Quartet at a rehearsal shortly before the premiere, "Keep it just the same!" *—Joseph Stevenson*

Recommended:

○ **Lutosławski: String Quartet** / Kronos Quartet / 1991 / Nonesuch 79255

○ **Lutosławski, Urbanner, Berio** / Alban Berg SQ / 1997 / EMI 56363

VOCAL

Chantefleurs et Chantefables (Songflowers and songfables), for soprano & orchestra (1991)

Chantefleurs et Chantefables ("Songflowers and Songfables") is one of the most gracious and affecting works of Lutosławski's last years. It was premiered at the London Promenade Concerts on August 8, 1991 by soprano Solveig Kringleborn and the BBC Symphony Orchestra, with the composer conducting.

Chantefleurs et Chantefables makes no use of aleatoric counterpoint until the fast-moving final song. Until then the piece is highly conservative, both in its softly dappled textures, reminiscent of Debussy, and in its tonally-derived harmony. It is not, however, unoriginal. Although the work never uses functional harmony per se, triads, seventh chords, bitonal, quartal, and added-note chords are used freely and unambiguously, while in more rhythmically active sections the composer uses arpeggiation-like figures to tactfully explore a fuller use of chromatic possibilities. Temporary centers of pitch are established gently through repetition or through orchestrational emphasis. Quintuple meter (5/8, 5/4) is used frequently in both fast and slow contexts, giving the rhythms a floating-world quality.

The poetry, of course, deserves special mention, not least since it concludes Lutosławski's longtime love affair with the French language. Robert Desnos wrote some of the most important French verse of the first half of the century, prized for its deft and easy mixture of dream and reality, the innocent and the surreal, the concrete and the abstract. The composer felt that the structures of Desnos' poems invited musical settings; he had used some previously for another masterpiece, *Les Espaces du sommeil* (1975) for baritone and large orchestra. Beneath the childlike imagery of the *Chantefleurs* verses, Lutosławski sometimes brings out dark undertones, in places you might expect (the angelica poem) and in places you might not (the tale of the flower and the bull).

There are nine songs, each subtly different from the others. The first and third, made from poems of six lines, both use slight rhythmic differentiations in the two violin parts to establish a hazy mood, offset by twinkling tones of piano and bells in "La Belle-de-Nuit," sharp brass chords in "La Véronique." "La Sauterelle" is a deft scherzo based on the little interval of the major second, mimicking the grasshopper's jumps; its companion piece, "L'Eglantine, l'Aubépine et la Glycine" (The Dogrose, the Hawthorn and the Wisteria) uses another narrowing device—good old strophic form—until the final line, when a bird keeps whamming itself into the poor flowers and the form cracks open. "La Tortue" (The Tortoise) and "L'Alligator" are humorous nursery tales, "La Rose" and "L'Angélique" rapturous lyrics of timeless beauty. The finale, partially aleatoric, is a change, its "three hundred million butterflies" descending on the poor towns of Châtillon in scampering, jazzy bass lines. *—Russell Platt*

Recommended:

○ **Lutosławski: Symphony 2; Chantefleurs et Chantefables; Piano Concerto** / Salonen (cond.), Upshaw, Los Angeles PO / 1996 / Sony 67189

Les espaces du sommeil, for baritone & orchestra (1975)

Long a fan of the French Surrealist writers, Lutosławski first set their poetry to music in the *Trois Poèmes d'Henri Michaux* (1961–63); he returned to the Surrealists in the early 1970s when the renowned baritone Dietrich Fischer-Dieskau asked him for a composition. The text Lutosławski chose was *Les espaces du sommeil* (Sleep's Spaces), from the volume *Corps et biens* by Robert Desnos (1900–45), the Paris-born poet and early Surrealist who was known for writing much of his work in a quasi-hypnotic state. Desnos was also a resistance fighter in World War II who died of typhus at the Theresienstadt concentration camp; Lutosławski later returned to Desnos' work for the song cycle *Chantefleurs et Chantefables* (1990). Fischer-Dieskau sang the premiere of *Les espaces du sommeil*, with the Berlin Philharmonic conducted by Lutosławski, in Berlin on April 12, 1978.

Lutosławski liked what he called the "musical attitude" of Desnos' poem, as well as its mixture of concrete and dream-like imagery. His setting is itself dream-like, its orchestral textures mostly delicate and evanescent; the vocal line is lyrical for the most part, with some hints of sprechstimme. One can hear an influence of the French Impressionist composers Claude Debussy and Maurice Ravel, an influence also evident in later Lutosławski works like the *Double Concerto for oboe and harp* (1979–80) and the *Symphony No. 3* (1981–83).

Early in *Les espaces du sommeil* the repeated gentle phrase "In the night" recurs with varying imagery. Amidst these images, "there is you"; the concept of "you," always ambivalent and loosely understood, becomes central to the work—the elusive link between the conscious and the subconscious ("elusive in reality and in dream"). Narrative attempts to give more concrete definition to the character of "you" are interrupted by tense, sometimes violent, outbursts from the orchestra, which seem to destroy any chance of understanding. In the end it is the night, and sleep, that return in the restored musical calm; alongside them is "you"—omnipresent in both night and day. *—Chris Morrison*

Recommended:

○ **Lutosławski: Symphonies 3 & 4** / Salonen (cond.), Shirley-Quirk, Los Angeles PO / 1994 / Sony 66280

○ **Essential Lutosławski** / Lutosławski (cond.), Fischer-Dieskau, Berlin PO / 1999 / Philips 464043

KEYBOARD

Folk melodies, 12 easy pieces (1945)

Lutosławski worked after World War II at Radio Poland, where in the course of his everyday activities he wrote music of various kinds—including children's music and even popular songs. These 12 piano pieces, essentially arrangements of Polish folk melodies, were written in 1945 and were commissioned and issued by the Polish government's music publishing office PWM (Polskie Wydawnisctwo Muzyczne). The tunes were taken from a contemporary collection of Polish folk music, and each piece was based on a song from a different region of Poland. By the late 1950s, they had been made compulsory for Polish piano students by the government, with the result that nearly all Polish musicians not only know but have played these works. Lutosławski stated that he didn't consider the *Folk Melodies* suitable for concert performance, but he later arranged several of them for string ensembles. Others have arranged them for guitars and other instruments. Lutosławski's harmonizations of these essentially diatonic tunes show commonalities with other folk-based music he was composing at the time, which ultimately had roots in Bartók's example rather than in socialist realist strictures (which the *Folk Melodies* preceded by several years anyhow). *—James Manheim*

Elisabeth Lutyens

b. Jul. 9, 1906, London, England, **d.** Apr. 14, 1983, London, England

Composer

An uncompromising radical in a musical culture marked by "schools," Elisabeth Lutyens was one of the first British composers to adopt serialist ideas. Her life was as unconventional as her music. Born in 1906, she announced (at age nine) her decision to become a composer. She studied music in Paris, falling under the spell of Debussy, and then moved on to the Royal College of Music in London in 1926. Lutyens hated the music of Elgar and the other gigantist symphonists of the age, and she derided the works of the British pastoralists as "cowpat music." But, like the early 12-tone composers, she admired Brahms. At one point she set the entire biblical Book of Job in Brahmsian musical language. At the RCM, Lutyens joined with a small group of female students devoted to modern music. She encountered the works of Britten and was influenced by Renaissance music and its continuous flow. By the time she composed the *Concerto for Nine Instruments* (1939), she was working in a quasi-serial style.

In 1933 Lutyens married singer Ian Glennie and had three children, but five years later she left him for BBC producer Edward Clark, who tried but failed to push the network toward contemporary music programming. After Clark quit his job, Lutyens became the breadwinner of the family (she had brought her children with her). For much of her life she supported them by writing film and television scores such as that for *Dr. Terror's House of Horrors* (1966). From time to time she supplemented the family income by renting out rooms; one of her boarders was poet Dylan Thomas.

After World War II, as she fully developed her personal serial-influenced language, she began to build an audience, earning the nickname "12-Note Lizzie" from traditionalists. Her setting of the Rimbaud poem "O Saisons, O Châteaux" (1947) was among her first major successes. Her opera *Infidelio* (1954) had to wait two decades for a performance, but lean modernist works such as *Six Tempi* (1957) and *Music for Orchestra II* (1962) won admirers. As British audiences warmed to modern music and Lutyens herself shifted to a somewhat lighter, more evocative style in such works as the choral *Essence of Our Happinesses* (1968), she was acclaimed as a pioneer. In 1969 she was made a Commander of the British Empire. The major works of Lutyens' last years were operas: *The Numbered* (1967), *Time Off? Not a Ghost of a Chance* (1968), and *Isis and Osiris* (1970). *—James Manheim*

Overview of Works (1937–1982)

Elisabeth Lutyens maintained that her style developed in complete isolation from and unawareness of the continental trends in music. It is therefore tempting to speculate if her formative years as the daughter of a well-known English architect may have influenced her in the evolution of her approach to serialism. More verifiable an influence was her student exposure to early English Baroque string fantasias with their rigorous counterpoint, premonitory of later Baroque. This texture was applied to what is regarded as her first major work, the striking *Chamber Concerto No. 1.* The said technique, coupled with an intense chromatic language that stops just short of atonality, laid the groundwork for her mature style, toward which she would doggedly evolve despite externally compromising circumstances. This period saw Lutyens explore myriad avenues, perhaps the byproduct of her working in film and radio to make ends meet for her family. Thus, the intense yet objective chamber concerto is contrasted with the contemporary neo-Romantic subjectivity of the *Three Symphonic Preludes* and further contrasted with the neo-Classicism of the various concertos from the 1940s for sundry instruments and combinations; the latter would seem to bear earmarks of Stravinsky and Les Six, save Lutyens' word that she was unaware of these trends. With the new decade, Lutyens began to investigate a lean, stark mode of expression commencing with the 1950 *Concertante for Five Instruments.* Applied to this was the serial language she had naturally evolved. At this point, the composer began to work in something of an isolated environment, Britain being less receptive to the innovations of the Second Viennese School. Yet Lutyens began producing what is, for some, her most definitive music. Leaning more heavily into vocal idioms, she produced her opera *Infidelio* and tapped into the literature of Wittgenstein and Chaucer for choral works. Curiously, in the instrumental works of this period, more of a lyrical approach seems to pervade. These trends continued into the mid-1960s, a watershed for the composer. In step with a more populist ethic, her music became less dense and less harmonically forbidding. Lighter textures and judicious use of silences (recalling, of all people, Bruckner and his pauses) may be heard in the choral *The Essence of Our Happinesses,* which drew on John Donne and Middle Eastern literature for its text. Here, the wind-blown ethereal approach seems admirably suited to the meditative subject matter. The same building blocks are used in a more animated mode of utterance in the 1967 theatrical *Time Off? Not a Ghost of a Chance!,* which seems to combine the ethic of *Zarathustra* with Walton's *Façade* as it draws a wry bead on man's place in the cosmos. Other operas of the period, *The Numbered* (1965) and *Isis and Osiris* (1969), dealt with much more fatalistic topics. Lutyens' output slowed until her death in 1983. *— Wayne Reisig*

Recommended:

- ○ **Elisabeth Lutyens** / Montgomery (cond.), Jane's Minstrels / 1993 / NMC 11

Anatol Konstantinovich Lyadov

b. May 11, 1855, St. Petersburg, Russia, **d.** Aug. 28, 1914, Polinovka, Russia

Composer: Orchestral, Keyboard

Anatol Konstantinovich Lyadov (the last name is often spelled "Liadov") was the son and grandson of noted conductors who led musical ensembles at the Mariinsky Theater and the St. Petersburg Philharmonic, respectively. The young Lyadov showed exceptional talent and was admitted to the Conservatory. While admiring his native talent, his main teacher, Nikolai Rimsky-Korsakov, was forced to expel him for unexplained absences. He was later permitted to take the graduation exams, and passed them easily. He became a noted professor and ethnomusicologist (publishing over 120 folk songs). He married in 1884, a match that gave him considerable wealth and a large estate at Polinovka.

His music is beautiful, exceptionally skilled and imaginative, with an impressionistic mood (though not the Debussyian style that word usually denotes). He was said to be shy and diffident. Either because of exceptional lack of confidence or laziness he was incapable of completing more than a few large-scale works. He wrote some piano pieces and songs, a few choruses, and about a dozen small but evocative orchestral works, some of which were fragments from his unfinished opera *Zoryushka.* His inability to finish a commission from Diaghilev to write the score for a ballet, *The Firebird,* led, famously, to its being given to the young Igor Stravinsky and launching that composer to international fame. *—Joseph Stevenson*

Overview of Works (1873–1914)

Russian composer Anatol Konstantinovich Lyadov's tremendous talent as a composer was severely compromised by his inability to write a cohenrent piece that lasted more than a quarter hour. His most popular works—the brief but evocative tone poems *Baba-Yaga* (1891–1904), *The Enchanted Lake* (1909), and *Kikimora* (1909)—are all based on Russian folk tales and all of their forms are dependent on those tale's narrative structures for their coherence. Writing in the style of the Mighty Handful—Balakirev, Mussorgsky, Borodin, Cui, and especially his teacher and later friend Rimsky-Korsakov—Lyadov's best music has the extraordinary orchestral color and the rhythmic vivacity of their music, but entirely lacks their epic scope and dramatic depth. At his best, he is charming and exciting; at his worst, he is facile and superficial. Toward the end of his life, Lyadov seemed to be reaching beyond the shallowness of his earlier works to a greater emotional depth and larger musical structures in his symphonic poems *From the Apocalypse* (1910–12) and *Nénie* (1914). But his premature death in August 1914 prevented him from consolidating his explorations. *—James Leonard*

Recommended:

- ○ **Liadov: 3 Symphonic Sketches; Russian Folksongs** / Nikolayev (cond.), Moscow Conservatory SO / Saison Russe 288144
- ○ **Liadov: Enchanted Lake & Other Orchestral Works** / Batiz (cond.), Mexico City PO / 1989 / ASV 657
- ○ **Lyadov: Orchestral Works** / Sinaisky (cond.), BBCPO / 2001 / Chandos 9911
- ○ **Liadov: Orchestral Works** / Gunzenhauser (cond.), Slovak PO / 2001 / Naxos 555242
- ○ **Russian Fairy Tales** / various / Brilliant 92138

ORCHESTRAL

Baba-Yaga, Op. 56 (ca. 1891–1904)

Nearly a decade since he first conceived the idea, Lyadov, the Oblomov of Russian composers, finally completed his three-and-a-half-minute tone poem *Baba-Yaga* in 1904. The archetypal Russian witch, Baba-Yaga is a small, gnomish creature whom Mussorgsky had previously depicted in music in "The Hut on Hen's Legs" from his *Pictures at an Exhibition.* Lyadov's "Picture from a Russian Folk-Tale" is set for large, late Romantic orchestra with numerous winds, brass, strings, a vast percussion section, and of course, the contrabassoon taking the witch's part. A pseudo-spooky evocation of the supernatural à la Dukas' contemporaneous *Sorcerer's Apprentice,* Lyadov's *Baba-Yaga* is clearly the basis of many of Hollywood's witches, but especially the Wicked Witch of the West from *The Wizard of Oz* with its shrieks in the woodwinds, its glissandos in the trombones, its chromatic runs in the strings, and its xylophone and bass drum. *—James Leonard*

Recommended:

- ○ **Russian Fantasy** / Pletnev (cond.), Russian National Orch. / 1998 / DG 459059
- ○ **Lyadov: Orchestral Works** / Sinaisky (cond.), BBCPO / 2001 / Chandos 9911

Enchanted Lake, Op. 62 (1909)

Although this work drew its inspiration from one of the legends of the "Kalevala"—the epic collection of Finnish poems that moved Sibelius to compose his more famous quartet of orchestral pieces—it was also inspired by the lakes and pastoral scenery of Lyadov's own native Russia. The *Enchanted Lake* is an approximately seven-minute work of gentle descriptive character, more the product of a Rachmaninovian post-Romanticism than of Debussy's then-fashionable Impressionism.

That said, it still portrays a vivid nature scene in splendidly imaginative orchestration—orchestration that is somewhat scaled-down in the elimination of trumpets, trombones, and percussion. The work begins quietly and lazily, the various instruments and sections of the orchestra chiming in by turn, as if the sun were rising and rousing them from a peaceful sleep. Sonorities slowly pulsate and often quiver and murmur—especially in the strings—the whole conveying an obsessive sound world that seems to come in gentle, soothing waves. Tension soon develops in the central portion, however, but portends nothing threatening, only perhaps a sense of yearning. In the latter moments the music returns to the serenity and quiet of the opening, and gently undulating strings gradually fade to bring on the lovely, peaceful ending. *—Robert Cummings*

Recommended:

- ○ **Music For Quiet Listening Vol. 2** / Hanson (cond.), Eastman Philharmonia / 1997 / Philips 434390
- ○ **Lyadov: Orchestral Works** / Sinaisky (cond.), BBCPO / 2001 / Chandos 9911
- ○ **Russian Fantasy** / Pletnev (cond.), Russian National Orch. / 1998 / DG 459059

Kikimora, Op. 63 (1909)

Lyadov apparently had a thing for witches: in his brief and desultory career as a composer, he wrote not one but two tone poems for orchestra depicting witches. The first is *Baba-Yaga* from 1904, a short and pseudo-spooky "picture from a Russian folk tale," and the second is *Kikimora,* a longer but still pseudo-spooky folk tale. Both are scored for full, late Romantic orchestra with a huge percussion section, including the obligatory xylophone, a prerequisite for evoking rattling skeletons. Like *Baba-Yaga,* the main body of *Kikimora* is a Presto replete with chromatic scales, woodwinds wails, and brass blasts. But unlike *Baba-Yaga, Kikimora* has a dark and moody Adagio introduction with the bleakness and despair of Rachmaninov and the harmonic vagueness of Debussy. Thus, although *Kikimora* is for the most part merely a re-write of *Baba-Yaga,* its introduction shows that Lyadov could be more than a procurer for witches. *—James Leonard*

Recommended:

- ○ **Music For Quiet Listening Vol. 2** / Hanson (cond.), Eastman Philharmonia / 1997 / Philips 434390
- ○ **Lyadov: Orchestral Works** / Sinaisky (cond.), BBCPO / 2001 / Chandos 9911
- ○ **Igor Markevich** / Markevitch (cond.) / 1995 / Testament 1060

Eight Russian Folksongs, Op. 58 (1906)

An avid collector of Russian folk music, Lyadov arranged eight indigenous pieces into an orchestral suite of about 15 minutes. Together, these *Eight Russian Folksongs* stand as the composer's signature work, perhaps along with the little tone poems *Kikimora* and *Baba-Yaga*. The orchestration is colorful but never garish, relying many times on woodwind solos and pizzicato string effects. The first dance is really a song: "Religious Chant" quietly begins undulating in the woodwinds with what sounds like a Russian Orthodox melody. The tune repeats several times over the course of two minutes, with variety provided by different, subtle countermelodies and an orchestration that shifts from winds to strings and back. "Christmas Carol" is cheerful, but still low key, following the same structural and instrumental pattern as the first piece, except that now, Lyadov introduces a closely related second subject in the middle. "Plaintive Song" or "Lament" is exactly that, featuring a solo cello quietly backed by members of the string section, all of which gathers to carry the movement through its second half with very subtle wind coloring near the end. In "Humorous Song," a buzzing effect in the strings underlies a perky, flute-dominated tune. "Legend of the Birds" ornaments a slightly ominous melody with fleeting, bird-like figures in the woodwinds; the center of this piece is the first truly loud music in the suite. "Cradle Song," for strings, offers a spare, quiet tune over a gently rocking figure. "Round Dance" scampers in on pizzicato strings imitating domras and balalaikas, with the piccolo playing the sparkling main theme. "Village-Dance Song" is an extroverted finale, deploying the entire orchestra, including brass, for a fast but not overbearing celebration. *—James Reel*

Recommended:

- ○ **Lyadov: Orchestral Works** / Sinaisky (cond.), BBCPO / 2001 / Chandos 9911

KEYBOARD

Works for Piano (1876–1914)

Unfortunately, Russian composer Anatol Lyadov (1855–1914) composed piano music like he composed everything else: slowly and with much procrastination. Although said to be a virtuoso pianist and a tremendously gifted composer with a terrific command of counterpoint, Lyadov was also too lazy to complete any extended piano works, and in his total oeuvre of 43 published piano pieces from every stage of his career, every single one is either of miniatures or sets of miniatures. Some are virtuoso studies: the *Etude in A flat*, Op. 5, (1881), and *Etude in C sharp minor*, Op. 40, (1897); some are contrapuntal studies: the *Three Canons*, Op. 34, (1894) and the *Two Fugues*, Op. 41 (1896); some are character pieces: *Two bagatelles "La douleur" and "Pastoral,"* Op. 17, (1887), the *Four Pieces: Grimace, Tenebres, Tentation, and Reminiscences*, Op. 64, (1909–10) and Lyadov's most-often-played piano work, *Musical Snuffbox*, Op. 32, (1893); some are brief dance suites: *Two Pieces, Waltz and Mazurka*, Op. 9, (1883), and *Three Ballet Numbers*, Op. 52, (1901); but, with the exception of two sets of variations, *Variations on a Theme by Glinka*, Op. 35, (1894) and *Variations on a Polish Folk Theme*, Op. 51, (1901), which are themselves sets of miniatures, none of them last more than six minutes in performance. Within the scale Lyadov set for himself, his piano miniatures are charming, but given the talent and ability they demonstrate, it is regrettable he did not work harder. *—James Leonard*

Recommended:

- ○ **Liadov: A Piano Anthology** / Poroshina / 1995 / ESS.A.Y. 1045
- ○ **Liadov: Marionettes, etc.** / Coombs / 1998 / Hyperion 66986
- ○ **Liadov: Piano Miniatures** / Duphil / Marco Polo 220416

Musical Snuffbox, Op. 32 (1893)

For over a century countless piano students have had occasion to encounter this charming trifle. Anatol Konstantinovich Lyadov (sometimes spelled Liadov or Liadoff) was at his best writing short pieces because he was notoriously lazy and undisciplined. He rarely kept at a large-scale composition for the length of time needed to finish and polish it. However, he was a talented and imaginative composer, capable of producing beautiful sound pictures, and left several brief pieces such as this one.

From the late eighteenth century, snuffboxes were highly popular among upper-class Europeans. We often read, for instance, that Mozart was given a snuffbox by this or that member of royalty or nobility after performing or writing a composition for them, and perhaps wonder what he did with all of them. (The answer is that such gifts were usually stuffed with gold coins and were designed to preserve the polite fictions that the high-born individual was not descending to the level of commerce by actually paying for something and that the composer was not a hired servant. In addition, the snuffboxes were often made of gold and silver and could readily be sold for additional cash with no offense taken.) Many snuffboxes had musical mechanisms inside; these were expensive and highly popular in Mozart's time among the wealthy. It is likely that Lyadov had such an ornate and charming bauble in mind when he wrote this piano piece for his son Mikhail in 1893.

The piano imitates the sound of a music box by limiting itself to the relatively small range of notes that would be contained in such a device, placed in the high register of the piano to give the music a tinkly sound. The piece is in the form of a delicate little waltz, not too slow, and marked in the score "Automaticamente" ("Automatically"). Its lightness seems to suggest a rococo scene, although the waltz itself is not authentic to that era in music.

In 1897, Lyadov outdid himself in charm by creating an orchestrated version of the piece. It uses only the flutes and clarinets of the orchestra, plus glockenspiel and harp, preserving the special delicacy and lightness of this two-minute marvel. *—Joseph Stevenson*

Recommended:

- ○ **Dolly Suite & Narnia Suite** / Batiz (cond.), Mexico City PO / 1996 / ASV 6182
- ○ **Vladimir Sofronitsky Vol. 17** / Sofronitsky / Arlecchino 174
- ○ **Stephen Hough: The Piano Album** / Hough / 1998 / Virgin 61498

M

Yo-Yo Ma

b. Oct. 7, 1955, Paris, France
Cellist

Yo-Yo Ma is among the finest cellists of his generation, and a musician of unusually broad appeal. His great success is no doubt due to an easygoing, friendly stage personality in addition to his fine, adventurous musicianship.

Indeed, Ma appears to have music in his blood: his mother was a singer in Hong Kong, his father a conductor, composer, and teacher. Although he had his first cello lessons at age four, memorizing two bars of Bach's *Cello Suites* every day, he had initially studied the violin, then the viola. When he was seven, the family moved to New York so that Yo-Yo could study with Janos Scholz. At the age of eight, Ma appeared on American television on "The American Pageant of the Arts," in a concert conducted by Leonard Bernstein. He joined the junior department of the Juilliard School as a pupil of Leonard Rose. However, he left Juilliard in 1971, questioning whether he would continue with his cello studies despite international recognition while still in his teens.

Ma eventually enrolled at Harvard, where teachers, including composers Leon Kirchner and Earl Kim, gave him confidence to continue. The most important turning point, though, was a trip to the Marlboro Festival, where he heard the great cellist Pablo Casals perform. Says Ma, "The commitment behind each note, the belief he had, was a wonderful example."

In 1978 Ma won the Avery Fisher Prize, establishing himself as one of a very few genuine superstars in classical music. Since then, he has appeared with nearly all of the world's great orchestras and conductors. He also is active in chamber music, often in a piano trio with Young Uck Kim and Emanuel Ax; Ma and Ax won a Grammy award for their recording of the Brahms *Cello Sonatas*. In 1982 Ma was invited to appear in the inaugural concert of the London Symphony Orchestra's new concert hall at the Barbican Centre in London, where he played in the presence of Queen Elizabeth II. He has won numerous Grammy awards, recording such diverse music as Brazilian bossa nova, Argentine tango, American roots and bluegrass, and the soundtrack for *Crouching Tiger, Hidden Dragon*. In 1998 he founded the Silk Road Project, to explore the exchange of musical ideas that occurred along the trade route. His CDs of the early 2000s have touched on both traditional and crossover repertory, with two albums of Vivaldi's music recorded with keyboardist and conductor Ton Koopman emerging as successful examples of the former, and the *Obrigado Brazil* CD becoming another crossover best seller.

Playing a Montagnana cello and the "Davidov" Stradivari previously used by Jacqueline du Pré, Ma produces a relatively lean and focused, though warm, tone, with a tight, fast vibrato. His performances are a unique blend of rhapsodic and seemingly spontaneous music-making; at the same time, his playing is tempered by intellectually rigorous analysis and forethought. He places great importance on not repeating performances from the past, either those of other artists or his own. *—Joseph Stevenson*

Recommended:

- ○ **Yo-Yo Ma: Solo** / Ma / 1999 / Sony 64114
- ○ **Concertos from the New World** / Masur (cond.), Ozawa (cond.), Ma, Perlman, New York PO, BSO / 2004 / Sony 93072
- ○ **Yo-Yo Ma & Bobby McFerrin: Hush** / Ma, McFerrin (voice) / 1992 / Sony 48177
- ○ **Soul of the Tango** / Ma, Calandrelli, Stott, Console, Agri / 1997 / Sony 63122
- ○ **The Cello Suites Inspired by Bach** / Ma / 1997 / Sony 63203
- ○ **Rachmaninoff, Prokofiev: Cello Sonatas** / Ma, Ax (piano) / 2003 / Sony 90397
- ○ **Silk Road Journeys** / Ma, Silk Road Ensemble / 2001 / Sony 89782

Lorin Maazel

b. Mar. 6, 1930, Neuilly, France
Conductor

Born to American parents in Neuilly, France, conductor Lorin Maazel displayed musical maturity at an early age. Educated in the United States, he studied conducting with Vladimir Bakaleinikov, as well as violin and piano in Pittsburgh. Maazel's conducting career was underway by the tender age of seven, when the legendary Arturo Toscanini invited him to lead the NBC Orchestra in New York. Subsequently, young Maazel directed a series of New York Philharmonic performances at Lewisohn Stadium. In 1939, he conducted the Interlochen Orchestra at the World's Fair in New York, and the Los Angeles Philharmonic at the Hollywood Bowl, sharing the podium with Leopold Stokowski. Maazel's Cleveland Orchestra debut was in 1943, beginning what would become a historic relationship. In 1946, he enrolled in the languages, mathematics, and philosophy departments at the University of Pittsburgh. Concurrently, Maazel was a member of the Pittsburgh Symphony's violin section. In 1951, Maazel traveled to Italy as a Fulbright Scholar to the study music of the Baroque period, and enjoyed success conducting many leading European orchestras.

In 1972, the celebrated Cleveland Orchestra appointed Maazel its fifth music director. He remained in this capacity for a decade. Maazel has since served as music director of several prestigious orchestras, including the Deutsch Oper Berlin, Berlin Radio Symphony, and Orchestre National de France, in addition to serving as principal guest conductor of the Philharmonia Orchestra in London. He has been the conductor for the Pittsburgh Symphony, and the Bavarian Radio Symphony since 1988, and 1993 respectively. Maazel holds the distinction of being not only the youngest to ever conduct at Bayreuth, but the first American. In fact, when he conducted Wagner's *Ring* at Bayreuth, Maazel became the first non-German to do so. The maestro has conducted virtually all of the world's leading orchestras, including the New York Philharmonic, Chicago Symphony, Boston Symphony, and more. He has vast and impressive experience directing opera, appearing at such prestigious houses as the Salzbug, Lucerne, Paris, and Metropolitan operas. He has also conducted at La Scala and Covent Garden, as well as serving as artistic director (and general manager) of the Vienna State Opera from 1982–84.

Maazel has received numerous awards and distinctions, including the Comande's Cross of Merit of the Federal Republic (Germany), Legion of Honor (France), Commander of the Lion (Finland), and was made an honorary member of the Israel Philharmonic in 1985. He has received the Grand Prix du Disque award ten times, and been given numerous honorary degrees from various universities. His popularity and influence were undeniable when the United Nations named him Ambassador of Goodwill.

Maazel has championed the use of television and film, himself writing film adaptations for such landmark works as Gustav Holst's *Planets*, and Vivaldi's *Four Seasons*. He has also written operatic film music for Mozart's *Don Giovanni* and Bizet's *Carmen*, directed by Joseph Losey and Francisco Rossi, respectively. For these efforts, Maazel has been awarded several international prizes.

Throughout his career, Maazel has recorded extensively, continuously adding to a discography that is highlighted by recordings of the complete symphonic output of Beethoven, Mahler, Rachmaninov, and Sibelius. In addition to an ever-flourishing conducting career, Maazel maintains his dedication to composition. The 1996 recording of his concertos for cello, flute, and violin, with Rostropovich, Galway, and the composer as soloists respectively, is indicative of Lorin Maazel's timeless devotion to musical creativity. *—David Brensilver*

Recommended:

- ○ **Lorin Maazel Conducts R. Strauss** / Maazel (cond.), Bavarian RSO / 1999 / RCA 63265
- ○ **Berlioz: Symphonie Fantastique** / Maazel (cond.), Cleveland Orch. / 1982 / Telarc 80076
- ○ **Mussorgsky: Pictures; Night on Bald Mountain** / Maazel (cond.), Cleveland Orch. / 2001 / Telarc 60042
- ○ **A Portrait of Lorin Maazel** / Maazel (cond.), Gilels, New Philharmonia, Berlin PO, London PO / 1999 / D Classics 70592

Edward MacDowell

b. Dec. 18, 1860, New York, NY, **d.** Jan. 23, 1908, New York, NY
Composer: Keyboard, Concerto, Orchestral

At the beginning of the twentieth century, MacDowell was regarded as the single most important composer in the American canon. Future developments in

American music dented that reputation, and his music went into a long eclipse, although its influence is strongly felt in the incidental music composed for American radio programs and animated cartoons of the 1930s. MacDowell's supporters are many, including eminent pianists such as André Watts and Constance Keene. They decry the neglect of MacDowell's works, and perhaps justly so; many are outstanding in quality, particularly the *Sketches* and the *"Keltic" Sonata*, the latter being an exploration of MacDowell's own Scots-Irish roots.

Edward MacDowell was born in New York City, the son of a milkman and his musically inclined spouse. At eight, MacDowell began piano lessons with a boarder in the home, Juan Buitrago. Through Buitrago, the boy MacDowell met pianist and international concert star Teresa Carreño, who also provided MacDowell with instruction and encouragement. In the late nineteenth century, the only way for a promising American musician to obtain a musical education was to travel to Europe. MacDowell and his mother made the trip to Paris in April 1877, MacDowell enrolling into the Paris Conservatoire. In 1878, MacDowell heard Nikolai Rubinstein in the first Tchaikovsky piano concerto, and with that, he decided to abandon Paris and study in Germany. He went first to Stuttgart, then Wiesbaden, and finally to Frankfurt where he studied with Joachim Raff and concertized in the presence of Franz Liszt. MacDowell began to take in piano pupils of his own, and one of them, Margaret Nevins, became MacDowell's wife in 1884. On Liszt's recommendation MacDowell began to pursue composition rather than performance, and his *First* and *Second Modern Suites* were widely successful on first publication, with Carreño helping to spread the word through her frequent programming of these works.

In 1888, Benjamin Johnson Lang, a close family friend, encouraged MacDowell to resettle in Boston, then the center of concert life in America. From this time until 1896 MacDowell enjoyed his greatest successes and patronage, and it is during this time that MacDowell wrote most of his music: the *Second Piano Concerto, Indian Suite, Sonata Tragica*, most of his songs, and the *Woodland Sketches*. This last named work contained both *To a Water Lily* and *To a Wild Rose*, both destined to become staples of American piano repertoire and known to every student.

In 1895, the MacDowells purchased a farm in Peterborough, New Hampshire, so that the nervy MacDowell could concentrate effectively on his work. In 1896, MacDowell was named head of the newly established music department at Columbia University, an important academic position at a major liberal arts college. MacDowell quickly won the admiration of his colleagues and students through his boundless energy and enthusiasm. However, in 1902 Columbia elected a new president, Nicholas Murray Butler, who did not share MacDowell's vision and sought to eliminate the music department altogether. This instituted a heated conflict between Butler and MacDowell that mainly served to undermine the health of the short-tempered composer, which was further aggravated by MacDowell's being run down in 1904 by a cab on the New York City streets. That year, MacDowell resigned from Columbia, and afterward his health began to decline rapidly. He died on the Peterborough farm on January 23, 1908 at age 47. In accordance with MacDowell's own wishes, MacDowell's widow later converted the farm into an artist's colony, which has become the best-known and most respected environment of its kind in the United States. *—Uncle Dave Lewis*

KEYBOARD

Idyls after Goethe, Op. 28 (1887; revised 1901)

Edward MacDowell was one of the most important American composers of his generation. Trained in Germany and hailed throughout Europe as a virtuoso pianist, his music hardly sounded American, as these six works attest. Often, his works had a Germanic or French or even Norwegian character. Here, a mixture of those influences can be heard in music that is light and fantasy-like. The first of the Edward *Idyls*, "In the Woods," carries the parenthetical instructions to the performer of "Lightly, almost jauntily." It is light music, to be sure, but not unserious. It has a French, almost Franckian character in its carefree manner, yet also divulges an intimacy of expression: while the music has a jauntiness, it is gentle and demure, having a feline pounce rather than a stomping gait. The ensuing "Siesta," to be played "Slowly, swayingly," is sedate and dreamy and has nothing of Spain in its warm, rather cosmopolitan character. "To the Moonlight," marked "With breadth and tenderness," follows. Not surprisingly, it has a nocturnal manner in its soothing sweetness, although one mild eruption from the bass register occurs in the latter half. The ensuing "Silver Clouds" ("Smoothly, placidly") continues the gentle mood, this time imparting a playful sense of joy, the music oblivious to all woes and frustrations. The fifth, "Flute Idyll" ("Lightly, joyously"), is similar in mood to "Silver Clouds," making one wonder, despite its good music, why MacDowell did not insert it elsewhere and offer some sense of contrast. The concluding "Bluebell" ("Lightly, daintily") has a somewhat wistful quality in its playful music and an engaging fluff in its sweet nonchalance. *—Robert Cummings*

Recommended:

○ **MacDowell: Piano Music, Vol. 2** / Barbagallo / 1998 / Naxos 559011

New England Idyls, Op. 62 (1901–1902)

Several autobiographical details are embedded within the *New England Idyls*, which Edward MacDowell wrote in 1902 while serving as professor of composition at Columbia University. The pieces, among MacDowell's finer short piano works, were actually written at the cabin the MacDowell family used as a summer home at Peterborough, NH, where years later MacDowell's widow Marian set up the famous MacDowell Colony for artists.

Each of the *New England Idyls* is brief, between one and three minutes in length, and unpretentiously atmospheric and tuneful. Most are not particularly demanding for the pianist. As was the case with the earlier *Sea Pieces*, Op. 55 (1896–1998), MacDowell included short poetic epigraphs with each of the ten *Idyls*.

The set begins with the gentle nostalgia of "An Old Garden," and moves to the languorous "Mid-summer" and the more somber "Mid-winter" with its sudden flashes of brilliance. "With Sweet Lavender" is quiet and delicate, and "In Deep Woods" is one of MacDowell's numerous short portraits of the woods around Peterborough. For the "Indian Idyll" the composer borrows a melody he found in American scholar Theodore Baker's work on Native American music (which also provided some of the themes for MacDowell's orchestral *"Indian" Suite*). The solemn grandeur of "To an Old White Pine" is followed by the large Romantic gestures of the eighth of the ten *Idyls*, "From Puritan Days," whose motto in the score is simply "In Nomine Domini" (In the Name of God). The rollicking, lively "The Joys of Autumn" closes the set. But just before that, comes the penultimate Idyl, "From a Log Cabin," which may have been a portrait of MacDowell's Peterborough home. The poem-motto he included with it in the score was later borrowed by MacDowell's wife for his tombstone:

A house of dreams untold,
It looks out over the whispering tree-tops
And faces the setting sun.

—Chris Morrison

Recommended:

○ **MacDowell: Piano Music, Vol. 1** / Barbagallo / 1998 / Naxos 559010

Piano Sonata No. 3 in D minor ("Norse"), Op. 57 (1898–1899)

All four of MacDowell's piano sonatas are to some extent programmatic, and the third, dedicated to Norwegian composer Edvard Grieg, is appropriately subtitled "Norse," taking inspiration from old Norse legends. MacDowell established the setting with some original verse published with the score:

Night had fallen on a day of deeds
The great rafters in the red-ribbed hall
Flashed crimson in the fitful flame
Of smoldering logs;
And from the stealthy shadows
That crept 'round Harald's throne
Rang out a Skald's strong voice
With tales of battles won:
Of Gudrun's love
And Sigurd, Siegmund's son.

Despite appearances, this is not Wagner's *Ring* cycle in piano reduction, but a sense of high drama and a theatrical flair can be found throughout the work. The first movement ("Mesto, ma con passione") begins lurking at the bottom of the keyboard, a primary theme striving upward. The melody becomes perspiringly heroic and MacDowell runs his material through a series of strenuous battle scenes offset by more reflective passages.

The slow movement is evocatively marked "Tristamente, ma con tenerezza." Its initial theme, very much in the style of Grieg's more serious keyboard pieces, rises chordally through a series of passionate little climaxes. The score eventually takes on a glittering filigree that becomes quite florid and impassioned, but the music ultimately subsides into something more bittersweet, delicately harmonized in the manner of Debussy except for some steely chord progressions near the end. The third movement, Allegro con fuoco, opens in a celebratory mood, but quickly moves into more strenuous material full of ringing chords and fast runs. The movement settles into a lyrical midsection (evoking "Gudrun's love?"), but the virtuosic clangor returns, only to dribble out in fatigue and fall back into the ominous bass rumblings of the sonata's beginning, evoking in its descent the opening figure of Franz Liszt's *Sonata in B minor* before ending with a few ringing chords. *—James Reel*

Recommended:

○ **Macdowell: Piano Music Vol. 2** / Barbagallo / 1998 / Naxos 559011

○ **MacDowell & Griffes Vol. 2** / Tocco / Gasparo 232

Piano Sonata No. 4 in E minor ("Keltic"), Op. 59 (1900)

Thought by many to be the finest of MacDowell's solo piano works, the *"Keltic" Sonata* was composed in 1901 and dedicated, as was its predecessor the *Piano Sonata No. 3* (subtitled "Norse"), to Edvard Grieg. A motto on the front page of the score was derived from the works of William Sharp, who under the nom de plume of Fiona MacLeod wrote many novels and other works based on Irish folklore and who contributed much to the late nineteenth century revival of interest in Ireland in which MacDowell took part. The motto gives a sense of the music to follow:

Who minds now Keltic tales of yore,
Dark Druid rhymes that thrall;

Deirdre's song, and wizard lore
Of great Cuchullin's fall.

The medieval Irish tales that underlie the *"Keltic" Sonata* derive from stories in the *Ulster Cycle*. Briefly summarized, the stories tell of Deirdre, the daughter of King Conchobar's harpist. The King fell in love with Deirdre and married her. But she loved another and ran off with him. They sought the help of the half-god/half-man Cuchullin, who was immensely strong yet mortal. King Conchobar attacked, Cuchullin fought bravely but was killed, and Deirdre winds up committing suicide.

The heroic opening movement, marked "With great power and dignity," features a grand opening theme with thick chords and a quieter, enigmatic second theme. A powerful development follows, with rippling figures running up and down the keyboard. The movement effectively evokes the dramatic setting of the story. With the second movement we move to Deirdre. This sublime and fanciful piece, marked "With naïve tenderness," reminds one of the best of MacDowell's many character pieces. The music critic Lawrence Gilman, who was MacDowell's first biographer, felt that the sonata's third movement, "Very swift and fierce," was "MacDowell's loftiest flight." This violent music, full of difficulties for the pianist, depicts the death of Cuchullin. Although MacDowell included few specific programmatic references in the sonata, a two-note motive heard here may suggest the call of the bird that lands on Cuchullin's shoulder as he dies. After a brief slow meditation, a final flurry of notes brings the sonata to a forceful conclusion. *—Chris Morrison*

Recommended:

○ **Griffes: Preludes; Roman Sketches; MacDowell: Piano Sonata 4** / Tocco / 1984 / Gasparo 231

○ **MacDowell: Piano Works** / Mandel / 2000 / Phoenix USA 148

Sea Pieces, Op. 55 (1896–1898)

Edward MacDowell composed his *Sea Pieces* on summer holidays between 1896 and 1898; they were published as Op. 55 in the latter year. At this stage in his life, MacDowell was happily engaged in the hard work of establishing a music department at Columbia University, and the style of the *Sea Pieces* suggest a sense of recreation and amusement. A poetic excerpt prefaces each piece; MacDowell likely provided these as well.

The eight pieces are "To the Sea," "From a Wandering Iceberg," "A. D. MDCXX," "Starlight," "Song," "From the Depths," "Nautilus," and "In Mid-Ocean." It's difficult to not lavish too much praise on MacDowell's work here: from a purely pictorial standpoint, the *Sea Pieces* are superbly successful, as you can literally smell the sea air from the opening bars. Waves crash, and sea birds hover over the horizon. In musical terms, the score is laid out with splendid clarity, and sounds very well on the piano; however, it is by no means easy to play, save perhaps "Nautilus"—a fairy scene that adds contrast in an otherwise implacably sea-going set of pieces.

Some chord voicings are fairly modern sounding for the 1890s, as is the case with many late works of MacDowell. However, rather than providing a sense of foreshadowing, MacDowell's harmonic craft provides an aura of timelessness to the work, making it both difficult to tie to a specific chronological period and "built to last." Among many unusual passages in the *Sea Pieces* is the fifth-based decrescendo at the end of "A. D. MDCXX." *—Uncle Dave Lewis*

Recommended:

○ **MacDowell: Piano Music, Vol. 1** / Barbagallo / 1998 / Naxos 559010

Sonata Eroica, in G minor ("Piano Sonata No. 2"), Op. 50 (1894–1895)

American composer Edward MacDowell's four piano sonatas represent, to most of those relative few who are at all familiar with his now largely abandoned music, the most involved, weighty, and high-aspiring musical thoughts the man had to offer; and he does not fall so short of those aspirations as his total historical neglect might imply. MacDowell himself seems to have felt the *Sonata No. 4 in E minor*, Op. 59 (the *"Keltic" Sonata*), to be his greatest achievement, but the second sonata, the *Sonata eroica in G minor*, Op. 50 (counterpart to the *Sonata tragica* five opus numbers below it) of 1894–95, offers a good challenge for the distinction.

The *Sonata eroica* was composed about a year before MacDowell, who was becoming increasingly famous in his homeland and throughout Europe, joined the faculty of Columbia University in New York City. At Columbia he was charged with the unfriendly task of creating an entire department of music where none existed. The sonata, however, is not the kind of music that today we associate with American academicians—it has far more in common with the piano music written by the wandering virtuosi of a generation or two earlier and with that of Edvard Grieg, who collectively were the composers who generally appealed most to MacDowell. It is free-spirited in a high-flying Romantic way, poetic without necessarily being particularly salon-ish, passionate without necessarily plunging too deeply into the depths of the human soul. It is surprisingly skillful and refined.

MacDowell has written a traditional four-movement sonata, and he places the scherzo in the second-movement slot as had been fashionable ever since Beethoven's *Ninth Symphony*. The first movement is marked "Slow, with nobility" at the opening, but, as happens so frequently in music of the day, fast music is just around the corner. The elf-like scherzo is in B flat minor and follows a course determined by successive 16th note bursts. The bass register of the piano periodically makes a syncopated throbbing sound throughout the E flat major slow movement ("Tenderly, longingly, yet with passion"). The finale is speedy and sets rigidly-articulated gestures against broad, flowing lyric ideas; a G major coda brings the *Sonata eroica* to a dolcissimo close. *—Blair Johnston*

Recommended:

○ **Griffes: De Profundis; Piano Sonata; MacDowell: Piano Sonata 2** / Tocco / 1994 / Gasparo 233

○ **Macdowell: Piano Sonata 2; 12 Virtuoso Etudes** / Fierro / 1989 / Delos 1019

Woodland Sketches, Op. 51 (1896)

Edward MacDowell published his *Woodland Sketches* Op. 51 in 1896 through the New York branch of his German publisher Breitkopf and Härtel. Perhaps inspired by his move to a farm in Peterborough, N.H.—later to become the MacDowell colony—and its peaceful woodland surroundings, these ten short pieces for piano have remained the composer's best-known works.

"To a Wild Rose" (No. 1) and "To a Water Lily" (No. 6) are the most frequently played of the set, included in countless editions of primary level piano collections. These gentle works, with their mildly impressionistic harmony and simple rhythmic profile, are both easy and satisfying to play; the harmonic richness of these works has flattered many beginner pianists! "To a Wild Rose" is based on a tune sung by the Brotherton Native American tribe. "To a Water Lily" is played almost entirely on the black keys of the piano, and some difficulty reading is encountered when the notation branches out to three staves instead of the usual two.

Of the rest, the most significant is probably No. 8, "A Deserted Farm." MacDowell presents the minor-key tune in a stark and simple harmonization; at times, the texture pares down to a single melodic voice. The piece captures a barren landscape where home and hearth once stood. This bare texture and relative lack of adornment looks forward to the vernacular American style of the 1930s—unusual in so conservative a composer as MacDowell.

Also mostly in the minor, but a good deal more colorful, is "Will o' the Wisp" (No. 2), which hints at the impish flickering of fireflies. "At an Old Trysting Place" (No. 3) is a sentimental tune spelled out in straightforward harmony, evoking a hymnlike nostalgia; at just 35 measures, this is the shortest *Woodland Sketch*. "In Autumn" (No. 4) begins with brilliant, rising octaves and settles into a dance-like texture reminiscent of Grieg. "From an Indian Lodge" (No. 5) is the most austere piece of the set; while it does not try to evoke Native American melody as in "To a Wild Rose," it is a pictorial work representing the resolute determination of Native Americans themselves, stated in octaves and underscored with crabbed, sometimes discordant chords (it is marked "sternly, with great emphasis"). "From Uncle Remus" (No. 7) is a character piece with the buoyant spirit of minstrel song, but is without its rhythmic syncopation—sounding more Scottish than African American. "By a Meadow Brook" (No. 9) is etude-like and makes up for the simplicity of "To a Wild Rose" in virtuosic sprays of color. "Told at Sunset" (No. 10) serves to summarize the whole set, incorporating parts of "The Deserted Farm" and "From an Indian Lodge," although a stately march tune dominates the first half. *—Uncle Dave Lewis*

Recommended:

○ **MacDowell's Woodland Sketches** / Nielsen, Beinema, Groot, Heijtmajer, Jong, Jonge, Mutter / Basta 9038

○ **Schumann: Piano Concerto; MacDowell: Woodland Sketches; Piano Concerto 2** / Cliburn / RCA 60420

CONCERTO

Piano Concerto No. 2 in D minor, Op. 23 (1884–1886)

MacDowell composed this work in 1884 and 1885, and played the first performance with Theodore Thomas and his eponymous orchestra in Chickering Hall, New York City, on March 5, 1889. The accompaniment is scored for two each of winds and trumpets, four horns, three trombones, timpani, and strings. In *American Music since 1910*, Virgil Thomson cited MacDowell as "our nearest to a great composer before [Charles] Ives. His short works for piano still speak to us." Let us add that the *Second Piano Concerto* remains among the most popular of way too few staples in the concerto genre by American composers. Only Gershwin's *Concerto in F*, composed 40 years after, enjoys a comparable status in the repertory, followed distantly by Aaron Copland's single endeavor (1926), and Samuel Barber's lone essay.

MacDowell was 15 when his mother took him abroad to study—at the Paris Conservatoire for three years (where Debussy was a fellow student), then in Stuttgart and Frankfurt for three years (where Joseph Raff was his composition professor and Carl Heymann his piano pedagogue). In 1881 the Darmstadt Conservatory made MacDowell its chief piano instructor. In 1882 he took his *First Piano Concerto* to Liszt, who advised him to concentrate on composition, and persuaded the Leipzig firm of Breitkopf & Härtel to publish *Modern Suites Nos. 1 and 2*, thereby establishing MacDowell here and abroad as the first notable "American" composer.

He returned briefly to the U.S. in 1884, to marry, then returned to Germany. On his honeymoon he sketched what became the scherzo in this concerto, which was completed at Frankfurt and Wiesbaden. Grieg (to whom MacDowell dedicated one of his four piano sonatas) is reflexively cited along with Liszt as a major influence on MacDowell's music. But the *Second Piano Concerto*, not to deny its own voice or expertise, is plainly in the tradition of Saint-Saëns' *Second*, especially the scherzo movement. MacDowell absorbed more during his unhappy years at Paris than he may consciously have realized.

What stands out in the first movement is the organic relationship of themes throughout—the lengthy Larghetto calmato introduction, the impassioned subjects of a Poco più mosso con passione section (in sonata form), and a quiet coda that echoes the opening reveal obvious and suble linkages to the attentive listener. The brief, fleet, frolicsome Presto giocoso second movement is a rondo in 2/4 time, with a roller-coaster main subject and two more that are rhythmically sprung (the second one anticipates the second subject of the finale, which is also related to the main theme of movement one). Like the first movement, the third and final movement begins slowly, with a variant of the former's main subject. It becomes a triple-meter Molto allegro whose principal theme is introduced by winds before the piano takes over. A calm patch near the end ties it to the coda of the opening movement. Really, the whole is a masterful construction, with impassioned themes only a smidgen less memorable than Grieg's, or Rachmaninov's and technical fireworks befitting an American who had impressed Europe's best. *—Roger Dettmer*

Recommended:

- ○ **Schumann: Piano Concerto; MacDowell: Woodland Sketches; Piano Concerto 2** / Reiner (cond.), Cliburn, Chicago SO / RCA 60420
- ○ **MacDowell: Piano Concertos 1 & 2; 2nd Modern Suite** / Brabbins (cond.), Tanyel, BBC Scottish SO / 2001 / Hyperion 67165

ORCHESTRAL

Suite No. 2 ("Indian"), Op. 48 (1891–1895)

The 1890s were years of good fortune and hard work for Edward MacDowell: he had recently returned to the United States, and from his home base in Boston, he soon earned himself a reputation as one of the nation's brightest musical stars. His concert tours as a pianist took him around the country, but he still found plenty of time to compose his own music—which, after all, is what he was really interested in (he never planned on a virtuoso piano career)—and most of his best-known pieces, including the *Suite No. 2 for orchestra, Op. 48*, were written around this time.

The *Suite No. 2*, which was very famous in its day but has, like the rest of MacDowell's music, faded almost completely from the collective musical memory, carries the subtitle "Indian" on account of the composer's use of Native American folk tunes throughout its five movements. (In his preface to the score, MacDowell remarks upon the "occasional similarity" of these themes to Northern European themes, which he takes as evidence in favor of a shared cultural heritage—an interesting, if not entirely anthropologically sound, belief.)

Although the five movements properly bear no individual titles, MacDowell allows that concert programmers might desire such titles and offers the following suggestions: 1. "Legend," 2. "Love Song," 3. "In War-time," 4. "Dirge," 5. "Village Festival." The entire suite lasts about a half-hour.

The E minor first movement begins "Not fast; with much dignity and character" and opens with a firm, fortissimo call from the horns, unaccompanied. As one might expect, quicker music arrives momentarily to carry the movement through to its end. "Love Song" is a tender 6/8 meter thing in which the woodwinds sing a tune that is saturated by the so-called Scottish snap, which, despite its name is a rhythmic gesture common in North American folk music. The quick third movement is "rough" and "savage," to quote the composer, while the fourth movement "Dirge" is appropriately slow and mournful. For the finale, MacDowell created a fleet-footed movement—almost Mendelssohnian in its quick-paced, leggiero sweetness—that turns back to the E of the first movement, now, however, in the major. *—Blair Johnston*

Recommended:

- ○ **Farwell, Hadley, Herbert, MacDowell, Parker** / Krueger (cond.), Royal PO / 2003 / Bridge 9124
- ○ **MacDowell: Suites 1 & 2; Sea Pieces** / Johnson (cond.), Bohuslav Martinů PO / 1997 / Albany 224

Guillaume de Machaut

b. ca. 1300, Machaut, Champagne (?), France, **d.** Apr. 13, 1377, Rheims (?), France
Composer: Vocal, Choral

Generally acclaimed the greatest composer of the fourteenth century is Guillaume de Machaut, born in Champagne around 1300. In the early 1320s he entered the service of John, Duke of Luxembourg and King of Bohemia, who secured for Machaut various ecclesiastical posts, documented in a series of papal bulls. One of the most important was a canonry at Rheims Cathedral, although there is no evidence that Machaut was ever a practicing clergyman or even particularly pious; indeed, most of his music is secular. He remained in John's service until the latter's death at the Battle of Crécy in 1346, after which his continuing association with high nobility enabled him to travel freely. Around 1350 Machaut found a new patron in Charles, King of Navarre and pretender to the French throne.

Like so many other medieval composers, Machaut was both musician and poet. His works are preserved to a degree astonishing for the fourteenth century: there are manuscripts for hundreds of poems and some 145 musical works. The poems are particularly fascinating for the light they shed on Machaut's own life and times; they record such events as the Black Death, which ravaged Europe in 1348 and 1349, and the Siege of Rheims in the early part of the Hundred Years' War. On a happier level his poetry reveals a love of falconry, riding, and the beauties of the French countryside. In some respects a conservative who built on existing traditions, such as the isorhythmic motet and even the monophonic trouvère song, he was, however, a composer of rare versatility whose music covers a range much wider than that suggested by his most famous work, the Messe de Nostre Dame (Notre Dame Mass).

The fame of that work has tended to obscure Machaut's secular works; his songs are his most characteristic pieces. Lyrical in spirit, with a new emphasis on melody in the top or cantus line, they nevertheless contain considerable subtleties in their manipulation of musical and verbal refrains. One of the most popular of the so-called formes fixes of the day was the virelai, a principal feature of which is that words and music have refrains that do not coincide with each other. Most of Machaut's virelais are monophonic, showing the continuing influence of the trouvères. These represent the most approachable side of his art, particularly in as happy an example as the delightful "Foy Porter." Two other song forms Machaut cultivated were the rondeau and the ballade. A particularly striking example of the latter is "Dame, de qui toute ma joie vieni," a song of infectious rhythmic vitality in praise of the poet's lady. Set polyphonically for four voices, this ballade, like the virelai mentioned above, has three strophic stanzas. The musical form of this and other ballades is A-A-B-C, the last section being a verse refrain.

The celebrity of the *Messe de Nostre Dame* probably owes much to its place in musical history as the first extant complete mass setting by a single composer. It is however possible that (as with Bach's *Mass in B minor*) its individual sections were not composed with a view to complete performance, a supposition supported by the work's diversity of styles and absence of thematic unity. Complex isorhythms are applied to all four parts in the shorter-texted sections (Kyrie, Sanctus and Agnus Dei), while the Gloria and the Credo are monosyllabic. The title, incidentally, refers not to Notre Dame in Paris, but the great cathedral of Rheims, the coronation place of the kings of France and, as already mentioned, the location of Machaut's canonry. *—Brian Robins*

VOCAL

Ballades (ca. 1330–1365)

Among the polyphonic chansons found within the surviving output of Guillaume de Machaut—which includes virelais, rondeaux, and ballades—the ballade repertory is the largest, and also exhibits the widest variety of structural and textural variation. Of the known ballade texts (all written by Machaut himself, whose reputation as a poet was at least as great as that of his music), 42 survive with the music intact, and 40 of these are arranged in semi-chronological order within one collection. That volume offers unique insights into Machaut's formal experimentation and into his overall compositional development.

In his first ballade, "S'Amour ne fait par," both voices are composed according to isorhythmic principles borrowed from the Ars Nova motet of the earlier fourteenth century. Machaut appears to have recognized the difficulty with which these ideas aligned with the ballade form, for after this initial song isorhythm is abandoned. Other anomalous works are a double ballade (for three voices) and the two triple ballades (for four), which employ multiple, simultaneously sung texts, again in the manner of the motet; the three-voice canon that occurs in one of the triple ballades is unique within Machaut's oeuvre. Some unique structural variations appear as well, as in the five ballades that repeat both, rather than just the second, of their constituent musical sections. Still, a fairly regular pattern emerges from Machaut's ballade repertory as a whole, one which more or less defined the ballade as one of the formes fixes of the Ars Nova period. This form, usually articulated within a two- or three-voice texture, can be depicted by the shorthand "aa'bC." Here, "a" is the first musical section, "b" is the second, and "C" is the refrain, the capital letter indicating a refrain of both music and text. The first completion of "a" arrives at an open ending—that is, it does not cadence on the expected tonal center. This section is repeated with a new text couplet and a "closed" ending ("a'"). A new musical section, "b," sets a new couplet. The stanza then closes with a refrain (C), which often borrows the closing gestures from the "a" section. Machaut usually composed his ballade texts as three stanzas (thus articulating a musical form of aa'bCaa'bCaa'bC), with the same rhyme scheme applying to each stanza. This affords a close and easily audible association between poetic form and musical structure.

The subject of Machaut's polyphonic songs, in the tradition of the monophonic secular songs of the trouvères, is usually courtly love. The speaker's unrequited love finds voice in elegant metaphors and romantic hyperbole. In *Nes que on porroit*, for example, the first stanza describes the speaker's intense desire, which can be described "no more than one can count all the stars"; in the second stanza the speaker attempts to suppress his grief; and the final stanza finds the speaker "languish[ing] piteously" out of unrequited desire. *—Jeremy Grimshaw*

Recommended:

○ **Dreams in the Pleasure Garden** / Orlando Consort / 1998 / Archiv 457618

Hoquetus David, for 3 voices (ca. 1360)

The hocket, a device commonly employed in medieval and early Renaissance music, involves the interruption of a melodic line with rests and the distribution of a melody's notes between two or more instruments or voices. The term is etymologically related to the word "hiccup," and a hocket can indeed often sound like a rhythmic disruption, or hiccup. Most often the hocket is found in the midst of a vocal motet or chanson. There are a few instrumental hockets, however, one of which is the *Hoquetus David*—Guillaume de Machaut's only instrumental composition, which likely dates from the 1360s. Why the work was written is unknown, although it may have been somehow associated with the coronation of Charles V in Reims in 1364; Charles had spent some time at Machaut's house three years earlier and was one of his several patrons.

The work's title derives from the source of the tenor part of this three-part piece, the melisma on "David" from Machaut's Alleluia verse "Nativitas gloriose virginis." Machaut does not specify the instruments to be used in his *Hoquetus*, which is among the earliest known polyphonic instrumental pieces. In sound it resembles a fanfare, with the alternating notes giving something of the effect of an antiphonal call-and-response. The angular quality of the piece, and its occasional dissonance, has inspired several modern composers, including Peter Maxwell Davies, who made an arrangement of the work for soprano and ensemble in 1971. *—Chris Morrison*

Recommended:

○ **Music of the Gothic Era** / Munrow (cond.), London Early Music Consort / Archiv 471731

Rondeaux (ca. 1330–1365)

Though it would be overstating the case to credit Guillaume de Machaut with the invention of the poetic form of the rondeau, one can safely attribute to Machaut the standardization and dissemination of certain stylistic traits that would characterize this and other polyphonic secular song traditions throughout the latter half of the fourteenth century and the first several decades of the fifteenth. As derived from Machaut's 21 musical settings, the polyphonic rondeau combines a bipartite musical form with a refrain-based poetic scheme. This overall poetic form is often described as "ABaAabAB," where the letters refer to sections of text, and capitals indicate a refrain.

The standard polyphonic rondeau form calls for two, three, or four voices; only one of these executes the poetic text, which, like most of Machaut's chansons, usually deals with a romantic subject. The textless parts, it is widely presumed, would have been performed by instruments. (Thus, the term polyphonic chanson is somewhat misleading). The sung line, or cantus, proceeds in relatively quicker note values against the slower-moving tenor, which in about half of the surviving rondeaux is joined in its accompanimental role by a contratenor. In a handful of rondeaux an additional upper voice, or triplum, counterpoints the cantus line at a higher rate of speed than the other accompanimental voice(s).

Machaut was not only the composer of these works but the poet as well. (Indeed, a number of his songs survive only as texts). It is not surprising, then, to see the high level of integration between poetic and musical form in his polyphonic songs in general and the rondeaux in particular. 17 of the 22 rondeaux utilize an eight-line rhyme scheme that corresponds with the overall structural divisions outlined above. One rather straightforward example is the two-voice rondeau *Quant j'ay l'espart*, whose eight poetic lines align exactly with the aforementioned ABaAabAB formal structure. A few other rondeaux foreshadow later poetic developments in the rondeau by fitting additional poetic lines within one or both musical sections. In *Rose, liz*, for example, each occurrence of the "a" music corresponds with two poetic lines, while the "b" section accommodates only one. Even more elaborate poetic developments were undertaken by subsequent composers; still, the general form of the rondeau as "codified" by Machaut remained intact for nearly a century after the composer's death. *—Jeremy Grimshaw*

Recommended:

○ **Dreams in the Pleasure Garden** / Orlando Consort / 1998 / Archiv 457618

○ **The Mirror of Narcissus** / Page (cond.), Gothic Voices / 1988 / Hyperion 66087

Rondeau: Ma fin est mon commencement, for 3 voices (ca. 1330–1365)

Though arguably atypical of his rondeau practice in particular and his song style in general, Guillaume de Machaut's *Ma fin est mon commencement* is one of his best-known works. This should come as no surprise, as fans of early music seem to prefer pieces that stand out of a genre and propose new methods of composition and new modes of listening to compositions typifying a genre. The ingenious construction of *Ma fin* gives a glimpse of the composer at his wittiest and most resourceful, while at the same time managing to fulfill the expectations of the ars nova aesthetic and also respecting the stipulations of the rondeau form.

One of the 21 surviving rondeaux by Machaut, *Ma fin* exhibits the bipartite musical form and poetic layout that one would expect. The rondeau was often presented in an "ABaAabAB" form, where "a" and "b" (upper or lower case) represent the two musical sections and capital letters represent the refrain text. A refrain text fills out both musical sections, followed by a new text set to the first musical section, then a repetition of the first half of the refrain text and music, then new text lines are set to the first and second musical sections, followed by a return of the full refrain. Within this standard rondeau form, however, Machaut introduces a rather elaborate performance trick—elaborate to listeners, that is, for notational games and musical puns were fairly common among medieval and Renaissance composers. Nevertheless, the craftiness of *Ma fin* is quite unusual and would perhaps be lost on the lay listener were it not for the clue provided by the composer, who was also an esteemed poet, in the opening lines. The text of the refrain states that "My end is my beginning, and my beginning my end." In the lowest voice, or tenor, this text refers to the palindromic nature of the musical line, which, whether read forward from the beginning or backwards from the ending, articulates the exact same sequence of notes and durations. In fact, Machaut originally provided the singer with the first half of the line only, and instructed him simply to sing it forward then backward. The melody sung by the triplum (or "third voice"), when turned around, is exactly the same as the music sung by the cantus (which sings in the same general range as the triplum and above the tenor). In fact, in the original sources, one singer read a line of music left to right while the other read the same line in the opposite direction. This creates a uniquely unified musical structure in which the music occurring above the palindromic line of the tenor is symmetrical across a double axis: the first half of the triplum's melody is a mirror image of the last half of the cantus', while the cantus' first half mirrors the triplum's last. *—Jeremy Grimshaw*

Recommended:

○ **Dreams in the Pleasure Garden** / Orlando Consort / 1998 / Archiv 457618

○ **Machaut: Messe de Notre Dame** / Hillier (cond.), Hilliard Ens. / 1989 / Hyperion 66358

Virelais

Within Guillaume de Machaut's chanson output, his virelais stand out in several regards. While most of his other chansons are polyphonic, the virelais are mostly monophonic, and virtually all of them exhibit a simplified approach to melody. Also, a wide range of poetic possibilities can be accommodated by the musical form, whereas the poetic and musical structures in the rondeaux and ballades, for instance—at least Machaut's—are less flexible (though subsequent composers would initiate new formal developments). Perhaps most importantly, the virelai was less established as a "fixed form" at the beginning of the fourteenth century, still malleable enough that Machaut's stamp would leave a deep impression.

Machaut in fact disliked the term virelai, preferring instead to use the label chanson baladée. This may reflect a familial connection to the ballade, which shares with the virelai the utilization of triple-stanza poetic forms. In fact, some scholars suggest that the virelai was seen by Machaut and his contemporaries simply as a ballade framed by a different type of refrain. Machaut's preference for the term chanson baladée may also point up a connection to the Italian ballata, which utilizes a formal scheme identical to that of the virelai and which also originated as a monophonic dance song.

The form of the virelai can be described as "AbbaA," where the letters stand for text sections and capital letters indicate a musical refrain. Within the tripartite poetic form of the virelai Machaut uses a wide variety of line groupings and rhyme schemes. The monophonic virelai "Loyaute weil tous jours," for example, utilizes three-line stanzas in the "a" section, while the "b" section accommodates only two lines. Conversely, *"En mon cuer"* contrasts extended seven-line stanzas in the "a" sections with the brevity of the "b" sections' three-line stanzas.

Perhaps the most distinctive aspect of the virelais, however, is the melodic style Machaut employs. While his other chansons are characterized by lyrical melodic lines spun out to dramatic lengths with elaborate melismas, Machaut's virelais tend towards a simpler, more syllabic approach to text declamation and expression. While one occasionally finds figuration within the virelais melodies, rarely does a particular syllable occupy more than two or three notes. Rather, the focus seems to be on the simple shape of the melody and the clear projection of the text. *—Jeremy Grimshaw*

Recommended:

○ **Dreams in the Pleasure Garden** / Orlando Consort / 1998 / Archiv 457618

○ **The Mirror of Narcissus** / Page (cond.), Gothic Voices / 1988 / Hyperion 66087

CHORAL

Messe de Nostre Dame, for 4 voices (ca. 1364)

Since its inception just after Christ's earthly ministry, the Christian Church has memorialized His sacrifice and atonement in the Eucharistic celebration of the mass.

This ritual, central to the life and teaching of the Church, creates a sacred moment of communion between God and His people. The mass was not the first Catholic rite to attract musical polyphony, but as early as the fourteenth century, the unchanging words of the *Mass Ordinary* began to receive more elaborate musical settings. To solemnify major feasts, scribes collected musically linked pairs of mass movements, as well as larger groups such as the *Tournai Mass*, the *Toulouse Mass*, the *Sorbonne Mass*, and the *Barcelona Mass* (probably written for the Papal court at Avignon). One other complete polyphonic *Mass Ordinary* survives as the first composed by one individual: the *Messe de Notre Dame* of Guillaume de Machaut.

Frustratingly little historical evidence exists regarding the composition of Machaut's *Mass*. Some commentators have even doubted that Machaut composed its six movements as a single unit, though he included them as a unit in some of the earliest manuscripts of his collected works. From the dates of these manuscripts, and from musical similarities to other later works of his, the *Messe de Notre Dame* appears to date from the early 1360s. The attractive suggestion that Machaut composed the mass to celebrate the coronation of King Charles V in Reims Cathedral (where Machaut was serving as canon) in May 1364 unfortunately has no historical basis; similarly groundless is the suggestion that he wrote the mass as a prayer for peace during the English siege of Reims in 1359–60. A moderately more plausible hypothesis comes from text in Machaut's will that suggests he provided music for a Saturday Ladymass sung at the Cathedral weekly on behalf of the faithful departed.

Musically, Machaut's *Mass* shows signs both of unity and of disjunction. Three movements (Kyrie, Gloria, and Credo) are in the Dorian mode, while the final three (Sanctus, Agnus, and *Ite Missa est*) take the F mode. He sets the wordiest pair of movements, the Gloria/Credo, in a terse, homophonic style, only becoming more expansive in their concluding "Amens." All four other movements follow the conventions of the isorhythmic motet, applying rigorously repetitive rhythmic structures to their plainchant tenor melodies, and frequently to other voices. Complex contrapuntal devices of hocket, syncopation, and sequence further vivify these movements. *—Timothy Dickey*

Recommended:

- ○ **Machaut: Messe de Notre Dame** / Peres (cond.), Organum Ens. / HM Franc 901590

Motets (ca. 1330–1360)

The 23 motets by poet/composer Guillaume de Machaut embody many of the stylistic and technical characteristics of the fourteenth century motet. Nonetheless, certain particular aspects of Machaut's motets set them apart from those of his Ars Nova colleagues, and within his body of works in this genre one finds a considerable amount of stylistic and structural multiplicity. Though comprising only a fraction of the 140 surviving works by Machaut, the motets demonstrate the composer's masterful integration of music and poetry, while at the same time suggesting his skill in manipulating the complex and sometimes esoteric constructional principles of Ars Nova isorhythmic composition.

One of the most conspicuous ways in which many of Machaut's motets differ from those of his contemporaries is the language in which the texts are written. While works by other composers favored Latin texts, Machaut only employed Latin texts exclusively in six motets (the well-known *Bone pastor* being one example) and utilized both Latin and French texts in two motets (for example, *Quant vrais amour*). Machaut even occasionally replaced the standard plainchant-derived tenor with one derived from a secular French (rather than sacred Latin) source.

For the most part, Machaut's motets exhibit the general structural traits of the fourteenth century isorhythmic motet, which, with its highly complex proportional relationships and meticulous construction, has been compared to the elaborately constructed stained glass windows of medieval French cathedrals: though requiring an incredible amount of intricate artistry, a window may be situated so high above the viewer that its details are hidden from view. Likewise, the details of an Ars Nova motet seem to be meant primarily for the ears of the connoisseur and/or Deity. Composed for three or four voices (triplum, duplum, tenor; the occasional fourth performer sings contratenor), the motet is characterized by the simultaneous singing of different texts in the upper voices set against slow-moving material in the lower voice(s). Machaut's motets are constructed upon an isorhythmic framework in which the tenor (sometimes in tandem with a contratenor) sings a line comprised of long durations organized into rhythmic repetitions called taleas and pitch repetitions called colors. These concurrent patterns usually align in simple ratios (one color for every two taleas, for example}. However, Machaut creates a more elaborate framework: in many of his motets, two repetitions of the pitch cycle correspond with three of the rhythmic cycle (see *Lasse! je sui en aventure*).

Machaut frequently makes his complex constructions somewhat audible by organizing the upper voices in repeating rhythmic and/or pitch patterns as well, utilizing special figuration and hockets (syncopations between voices) to articulate structural points. These points are often constructed so as to align with particular ideas in the texts, which themselves are also frequently intertwined in highly complex ways: a word or idea highlighted musically in one voice might align with and lend new meaning to a word in another voice, creating a complex matrix of textual and musical meaning.*—Jeremy Grimshaw*

Recommended:

- ○ **The Mirror of Narcissus** / Page (cond.), Gothic Voices / 1988 / Hyperion 66087
- ○ **Dreams in the Pleasure Garden** / Orlando Consort / 1998 / Archiv 457618

Sir Charles Mackerras

b. Nov. 17, 1925, Schenectady, NY

Conductor

Sir Charles Mackerras (b. 1925) is known for his broad repertoire, expertise in Czech music, and use of period, performance practices with modern orchestras. Born an American, he was taken to Australia as an infant by his family. He studied oboe, piano, and composition at New South Wales Conservatorium, Sydney. He joined the Sydney Symphony Orchestra as an oboist in 1945, and in that year also conducted the orchestra for the first time.

Mackerras traveled to Europe in 1947 and became a member of the Sadler's Wells opera company orchestra. While in England, he won a British Council Scholarship to become a conducting student of Vaclav Talich at the Academy of Fine Arts in Prague. During his studies in Czechoslovakia, he developed a lifelong interest in the music of Slavonic composers, especially Leoš Janáček. After his formal training, he returned to Sadler's Wells, where he made his London debut leading Johann Strauss' *Der Fledermaus*, and remained on the company's conducting staff until 1954. In 1951 he conducted the British premiere of Janáček's opera *Káťa Kabanová* (1919–21).

Following his engagement as principal conductor of the BBC Symphony Orchestra in 1954–56, Mackerras guest conducted *orchestras* in Britain and throughout Europe. In 1963 he conducted at Covent Garden for the first time, leading Shostakovich's opera *Katerina Ismaylova* (the revised version of *Lady Macbeth of Mtsensk*); thereafter, he conducted frequently at the house. From 1966 to 1970 he was the first conductor at the Hamburg State Opera. In 1970 he assumed the position of music director at Sadler's Wells, which changed its name to the English National Opera in 1974. Mackerras returned to Australia in 1973 to conduct the inaugural concert of the new Sydney Opera House and also conducted the production of Mozart's *The Magic Flute* during that opening year. He made his Metropolitan Opera debut in 1974 with Gluck's *Orfeo et Eurydice*.

Mackerras' reputation as a specialist in the music of the Classical era began with his Sadler's Wells production of Mozart's *The Marriage of Figaro* in 1965, in which he used the results of the burgeoning research into authentic performing styles to perform appogiaturas correctly, and to have the singers ornament their parts in accordance with the practices of Mozart's day. These and subsequent performances and recordings have been highly influential in shaping the current approach to earlier music, as have Mackerras' editions of Handel's music. Meanwhile, Mackerras has thoroughly researched the music of Janáček (the published editions of which were unusually prone to errors) and both produced and recorded accurate editions of the Czech composer's music. *—Joseph Stevenson*

Recommended:

- ○ **Janáček: Glagolitic Mass; Kodaly: Psalmus Hungaricus** / Mackerras (cond.), Cold, Kiberg, Stene, Svensson, Danish National RSO & Choir / 1994 / Chandos 9310
- ○ **Martinů: The Greek Passion** / Mackerras (cond.), Tomlinson, Davies, Field, Jonasova, BRNO State PO / Supraphon 3611
- ○ **Mozart: Così fan tutte** / Mackerras (cond.), Smith, Corbelli, Hadley, Lott, Scottish CO / 1994 / Telarc 80360
- ○ **Kaleidoscope** / Mackerras (cond.), London SO / 1995 / Mercury 434352
- ○ **Dvořák: Rusalka** / Mackerras (cond.), Fleming, Heppner, Kusnjer, Hawlata, Czech PO / 1998 / London 460568
- ○ **Dvořák: Slavonic Dances** / Mackerras (cond.), Czech PO / 1999 / Supraphon 34222031

Catherine Mackintosh

b. May 6, 1947, London, England

Violinist

Catherine Mackintosh has been one of the most active violinists on the English early music scene. She studied violin with Aurea Pernel and Silvia Rosenberg at the Royal College of Music, London. During her student years, she studied chamber music with Kenneth Skeaping and sang in Roger Norrington's Schütz choir. She was then awarded a three-year scholarship (1967–69) to attend the European Seminars of Early Music in Bruges, where she performed on the early violin and viola, the viola d'amore, and the viol. In 1969, she helped found the Consort of Musicke and also joined the English Consort of Viols. In 1973, she became the first concertmistress of the Academy of Ancient Music, a position she held until 1987. With this orchestra, she made important recordings under the direction of Christopher Hogwood, including Handel's *Messiah*, the complete Mozart symphonies, and Vivaldi's

L'estro armonico and the *Four Seasons* (sharing the solo parts in these concertos with Alison Bury, John Holloway, and Monica Huggett). In 1984, Mackintosh founded the Purcell Quartet, with which she recorded trio sonatas by Lawes, Purcell, Biber, Corelli, Handel, and Leclair. That same year, she became co-concertmistress with the Orchestra of the Age of Enlightenment, with which she made the first recording on period instruments of Vivaldi's concertos for viola d'amore. In 1997, she recorded the Bach violin sonatas with Maggie Cole. Mackintosh is an influential teacher of the early violin, having trained a new generation of period-instrument string players. She has taught at the Royal College of Music, London (1977–99), and at the Royal Scottish Academy of Music and Drama (from 1988). *—Robert Adelson*

Recommended:

- ○ **Vivaldi: Viola d'amore Concertos** / Mackintosh, Orch. of the Age of Enlightenment / 2004 / Hyperion 55178
- ○ **Handel: Italian cantatas & trio sonatas** / Purcell SQ, Mackintosh, Boothby, Bott, Weiss, Manson, Woolley, Kershaw / 1998 / Chandos 620
- ○ **Biber: Sacro-profanum** / Purcell SQ, Wistreich, Mackintosh, Hunt, Harvey, Boothby, Isserlis, etc. / 1997 / Chandos 0605

James Maddalena

b. 1954, Lynn, MA
Baritone

American baritone James Maddalena commands a large and varied repertoire of roles, from Monteverdi to contemporary opera. His performance of the role of Richard Nixon in the world premiere of John Adams' *Nixon in China* at the Houston Grand Opera won him an international audience. The performance broadcast nationally on the PBS *Great Performances* series won an Emmy Award and the recording of the opera for Nonesuch won a Grammy Award. Maddalena is a frequent collaborator with director Peter Sellars and sang major roles in Sellars' controversial stagings of the Mozart-Da Ponte operas (the Count in *Le nozze di Figaro* and Guglielmo in *Così fan tutte*). He also appeared in the Sellars production of *Nixon in China* at the Netherlands Opera, the Edinburgh Festival, the Brooklyn Academy of Music, the Washington Opera, the Frankfurt Opera, at Australia's Adelaide Festival, and in Paris. In 1991, Maddalena created the role of the Captain in John Adams' *The Death of Klinghoffer* in the world premiere at the Théâtre de la Monnaie in Brussels. *Klinghoffer* was then produced at the Opera de Lyon, the Brooklyn Academy of Music, the San Francisco Opera, and at the Vienna Festival prior to being recorded by Nonesuch (with Kent Nagano conducting). Maddalena also sang in the world premiere of *Harvey Milk* with the Houston Grand Opera, as well as the subsequent production with San Francisco Opera (recorded by Teldec with Donald Runnicles conducting). In 2001, he performed the role of Gideon March in Adamo's *Little Women* at the Houston Grand Opera. On the concert stage, Maddalena has performed with Boston's Handel & Haydn Society, the Orchestra of the Accademia di Santi Cecilia in Rome, and the San Francisco Symphony. He sang in the premiere of Elliot Goldenthal's oratorio *Fire, Water, Paper* with the Pacific Symphony (recorded by Sony Classical) and in the world premiere of John Harbison's *Four Psalms* with the Chicago Symphony Orchestra. *—Robert Adelson*

Recommended:

- ○ **Robert Moran: The Dracula Diary** / Holmquist (cond.), Connelly, Maddalena, Grove, Very / 1994 / BMG 62638
- ○ **Nixon in China** / Waart (cond.), Hampson, Sylvan, Friedman, Maddalena, Orch. of St. Luke's / 1988 / Nonesuch 79177

Bruno Maderna

b. Apr. 21, 1920, Venice, Italy, **d.** Nov. 13, 1973, Darmstadt, Germany
Composer: Chamber Music

Italian composer and conductor Bruno Maderna was one of the preeminent figures in contemporary European music in the mid-twentieth century. Born in Venice, Maderna was a child prodigy who played hot violin in a local combo and made his conducting debut at La Scala at age 12. By 1935 the course of Maderna's career was redirected by Italian fascists, who sent the talented child out to tour the capitals of Europe as a symbol of the superiority of the fascist order. Maderna was rescued from this depressing situation by prominent Veronese fashion designer Irma Manfredi, who took the now-adolescent professional musician under her wing and provided for his education.

By the age of 20 Bruno Maderna had already earned his degree in composition from the Conservatory of Rome and returned to Venice to continue under composer Gian Francesco Malipiero. Under Malipiero, Maderna began to master the complexities of serial composition, but this was interrupted by his conscription into the fascist army. By 1943 Maderna had deserted, and in 1945 he turned up fighting on the side of the partisans. At war's end, Malipiero helped to get Maderna a teaching job at the Venice Conservatory. He supplemented his income by making transcriptions of Baroque music for the publisher G. Ricordi, composing pop tunes, and creating scores for radio drama and some rather undistinguished Italian films.

In 1948 Maderna took a conducting class with legendary maestro Hermann Scherchen and through him probably got to know Wolfgang Steinecke, the founder of the Darmstadt Festival. Maderna had already met composer Luigi Nono at Ricordi, and would meet Luciano Berio in Milan after leaving the Venice Conservatory in 1952. Steinecke engaged Maderna as a conductor at the Darmstadt Festival, a post that made Maderna a celebrity in postwar European avant-garde and one that he would hold until the end of his days. With Berio, Maderna co-founded the Studio Fonologia Musicale of the RAI in 1955, a major electronic music facility which hosted composers such as John Cage, Francesco Donatoni, Henri Pousseur, Niccolò Castiglioni, Luc Ferrari, and others.

As the 1950s gave way to the 1960s, Bruno Maderna's work as a composer began to take a back seat to his activity as a conductor. He was named principal guest conductor with the Chicago Symphony Orchestra, appeared frequently with the Julliard Ensemble and was musical director for two years at the Berkshire Music Center in Tanglewood. He also spent a great deal of time in the recording studio and produced many fine albums of contemporary music, although in concert Maderna was equally well known for conducting the symphonies of Mahler and other well-worn repertoire of the Viennese classics. Perhaps this had some effect on Maderna's personality as a composer as well, for by the end of his life he'd turned his back on the serial aesthetic espoused by the Darmstadt Festival and his colleague Pierre Boulez. This phase of Maderna's career is experienced in his opera *Satyricon* (1973), the orchestral piece *Quadrivium* (1969) and in his never-finished series of pieces blanketed under the title "Hyperion" (1964–1973), unofficially an opera but officially a "lyric (drama) in the form of a spectacle."

When the end came for Maderna at age 53, it did so swiftly—he was diagnosed with lung cancer during the rehearsals for *Satyricon* which premiered in March 1973, and dead by that November. His celebrity in America was so short-lived that by 2004 Maderna's name was largely forgotten there, but not so in Europe, where he is yet regarded as one of the giants of postwar modernism. *—Uncle Dave Lewis*

Overview of Works (1937–1973)

"I grow more and more aware that one must not be consistent in one's life, particularly if one is a composer or an artist," Bruno Maderna once observed. His large and influential body of work demonstrates the composer's belief that, by exploring various compositional techniques—but subscribing to none exclusively or inflexibly—one could circumscribe a musical essence transcending any particular school or practice. One favorite source of variety in Maderna's works is a broad and deep knowledge of musical history that mingles freely with the modernist climate of the composer's training and career. Aside from numerous outright transcriptions and arrangements of works by composers as stylistically and chronologically disparate as Josquin, Monteverdi, Vivaldi, Offenbach, and Weill, a number of works weave old and new elements together. The early orchestral work *Introduzione e passacaglia "Laudi Sion Salvatorem"* (1942), for example, demonstrates a sophisticated approach to the ideals of neo-Classicism, while *Composizione No. 2 for orchestra* (1950) quotes a truly "classical" melody from ancient Greece. At the same time, one detects a concern for highly rigorous organization in virtually all of Maderna's mature works—inherited in motivic terms from the Second Viennese School and in structural terms from the Darmstadt circle—and apparent in works such as the chamber cantata *Vier Briefe* from 1953. In fact, as scholar Rossana Dalmonte has observed, although many of Maderna's pieces from the 1950s and early 1960s derive their compositional parameters from elaborate precompositional apparatuses, no single method or doctrine predominates. Later pieces, such as the *Concerto for oboe No. 1* (1962) and the chamber work *Serenata per un satellite* (1969), even introduce elements of chance into their performative realizations. Overriding Maderna's various compositional practices is a concern for compelling musical expression that seems somewhat at odds with modernism's austere aesthetics. This is apparent in the compelling lines of vocal works such as his solo songs on *Verlaine* (1947); the settings of Auden, Garcia Lorca, and Hölderlin found in the various stage and concert versions of *Hyperion* (1964–66); the late opera *Satyricon* (1973); and the "radio opera" from 1962, *Don Perlimplin* (one of several scores for broadcast media). His melodic expressivity couples with a concern for novel sound surfaces, as in the multiple shifting orchestral strata of *Aura* (1972) or the parallel universes of *Musica su due dimensioni for flute and tape* (1952), one of Maderna's numerous pioneering electronic and electro-acoustic works. *—Jeremy Grimshaw*

Recommended:

- ○ **Bruno Maderna for Strings** / Arditti SQ / 1999 / Disques Montaigne 782049
- ○ **Maderna: Orchestral Works** / Tamayo, Zender, Madernas (cond.), SWF SO Baden-Baden, Netherlands Radio CO / 2000 / Col Legno 20503
- ○ **Bruno Moderna** / Gorli (cond.), Arciuli, Zoboli, Bellocchio, Caiello, Giuseppe Verdi Orch. Milan / 2002 / Stradivarius 33574

CHAMBER MUSIC

Quadrivium, for percussion quartet & orchestra (1969)

This work, translated from the Latin as "crossroads," is scored for four percussionists and four orchestral groups, and was originally written for the Royan Festival.

The orchestral groups are made up of strings, woodwinds and brass, and the percussionists have available a large array of relatively non-pitched instruments (claves, cymbals, bell trees, woodblocks, gongs, timbales, ratchets, quiro, tambourines, etc.) as well as tuned percussion, including two vibraphones, two xylophones, two marimbas, two glockenspiels, and two sets of tubular bells. Each percussionist is associated with one of the four orchestral groups.

The score is written in an open, indeterminate style providing materials for live structuring and decision making during performance (in the tradition of Earle Brown's *Available Forms*). The conductor stands at a "crossroads" as it were, continually selecting details that make up the progression of the music, the sound complexes, and the entry point for each of the groups. The distribution of the instruments is guided by the traditional Venetian concept of the imitative polychoral or echoing style of Baroque composers such as the Gabrieli's.

Many fascinating and colorful timbres—from the transparent to the overpowering—are the result of the various combinatory decisions. And, of course, the combinations of the given material are different for every performance. Some sections are formed with a considerable amount of silence and occasional small touches of widely distributed sounds. Other passages give vent to wild gestures among the brass segueing into dense, quietly floating harmonies among the strings. At other times, flights of poly-melodic tuned percussion remind one of the massed bird songs of some of Messiaen's pieces. There are also dense string and woodwind passages with furious trills and tremolos, followed by intense blasts from the percussion while the strings sustained massive tone clusters.

Given all the possibilities, Maderna's sense of clarity and rich timbral writing still comes through. *—"Blue Gene" Tyranny*

Serenata per un satellite (1969)

This imaginative work in graphic notation was dedicated to Umberto Montalenti, the director of the European Operative Center for Space Research in Darmstadt, Germany, where the satellite named "Boreas" was launched on October 1, 1969. The score is written in an open style that allows the performers to begin reading at several points; the method of approach to these starting points is usually decided by the players or a coordinator (conductor) prior to performance.

At first glance, the score appears to be a fanciful, almost cartoonish, representation of the frenzied path of an out-of-control satellite, or perhaps to resemble time-lapse photos of the intersecting paths of several satellites. However, the work's internal organization easily reveals itself. There are three groups of staves in five directions each, drawn left to right and at various oblique and partially intersecting angles (like an unfolded pentagram). The lines of two of the groups are connected and the third group consists of five isolated musical fragments scattered about the page. Each of these elements has its own fixed tempo a quarter note equals 42 beats per minute when it appears in a horizontal line, 92 beats per minute when part of a descending oblique line, and 132 beats per minute its line appears at an ascending oblique angle. Thus, some "satellites" seem to zip across this musical sky like shooting stars.

Two staves at the very bottom of the score appear to be unconnected to any of this action. They are marked "as fast as possible, *ff*, never holding back the tempo." These appears to furnish an analog for some sort of constant electrical pulse, like the carrier wave for a radio signal or perhaps a data stream emitted by a passing satellite. The pitches at the beginning of each staff give certain gestures that are opened up and varied as the line progresses.

Maderna states that the piece should last from four to 12 minutes, and that "it can be played by violin, flute (also piccolo), oboe (also oboe d'amore or musette), clarinet... marimba, harp, guitar, and mandolin (playing what they can) all together or in solos and in groups, improvising, in short, but with the notes written on the paper." However, many realizations of this piece have used other instrumental combinations; one recorded performance employed two flute/piccolo players, clarinet, bass clarinet, soprano, alto and baritone saxophones, standard percussion and Latin American percussion, electric guitar, piano, harp, and string quartet. Both exacting (in tempi, at points of intersection, etc.) and poetic approaches to the score would seem to be acceptable, and both have been tried. *—"Blue Gene" Tyranny*

Recommended:

- ○ **Bruno Maderna** / Borgonovo, Lazzara, New Music Studium / Dynamic 174
- ○ **Piano & Percussion in the XXth Century** / Facchin (cond.), Orvieto, Maioli, Tammittam Percussion Ens. / 1997 / Dynamic 2010

Albéric Magnard

b. Jun. 9, 1865, Paris, France, **d.** Sep. 3, 1914, Baron, Oise, France

Composer

Lucien Denis Gabriel Albéric Magnard was a highly individual and inventive composer who, rather than embracing the new French trend of impressionism, extended his highly Romantic, post-Wagnerian style into Classical forms. His very touchy, misanthropic personality led to his being largely overlooked in his own lifetime, waiting until the end of the twentieth century before he started to attain wide appreciation.

His father was Francis Magnard, a journalist who became editor of *Le Figaro*, France's top newspaper, from 1879 to his death in 1894. Magnard's mother died when he was young. He had an easy, upper middle-class background in which musical training for social (not professional) attainment was standard. Eventually, he turned against the ease of his station, not hesitating to show his contempt for his bourgeois class, and seemingly choosing the rougher path whenever the opportunities arose.

After finishing secondary school he lived a monastic life for a while at Ramsgate Abbey in England, did a tour of military service as an officer, and then entered law school back in France. Although he had not demonstrated proficiency at an instrument or as a composer, he decided to make music a career, turning down offers of jobs in journalism from his father or from other journalists who obviously wanted to curry favor with the powerful elder Magnard.

Like many young Frenchmen of the time, Magnard made the pilgrimage to Wagner's theater and shrine at Bayreuth, Bavaria, where he was duly bowled over by *Tristan und Isolde*. Incidentally, the name he preferred is only coincidentally Wagnerian; it was his godfather's name.

Magnard entered the Conservatoire and studied with Dubois and Massenet. He didn't like either teacher, but he did graduate with first prize in harmony. He met César Franck and studied for four years with Vincent d'Indy. He was highly influenced by their music, which showed a tendency to mix Wagnerian harmony with Classical forms and to rely on cyclic themes (i.e., main musical ideas that recur from one movement to later ones) in their construction. Magnard adopted this sort of form, but initially wrote thickly over-orchestrated music, exemplified by his *First Symphony*.

He also wrote a one-act opera, *Yolanda*. It was premiered in 1892 in Brussels, while the *First Symphony* was first heard in Angers in 1894. He had to endure not-so-quietly whispered innuendos that these works could not make it on their own merits, but were produced solely to curry favor with his powerful journalist father. He did not endure these rumors gracefully, and he developed even more of a tendency to humorlessness and lack of tact and social grace.

In 1894 his father died. Seemingly in reaction to this blow, he wrote his *Chant funèbre*, a work of powerful but severely restrained emotions that seemed to clarify his artistic direction. In 1896, he became a counterpoint teacher at the Schola Cantorum. In the same year he married Julia Creton, and set to work on his *Second Symphony*. At the time of his marriage, he wrote for her to play a piano suite called *Promenades*, which is a rare light-hearted piece from his pen, happily recalling places in Paris they enjoyed together.

Magnard alienated a segment of the public by his reaction to the Dreyfus affair-polarized France. Magnard, disgusted with the Army's blatant anti-Semitism, publicly resigned his reserve commission.

In 1900, he wrote an opera, *Guercoeur*, a post-Wagnerian work set in legendary times. During his life it received only two separate concert performances of one individual act each. It was not produced on stage or heard in its entirety until April 1931, by which time some parts of it had gone missing and had to be reconstructed by Magnard's friend, the composer Guy Ropartz.

Failure to get *Guercoeur* produced further embittered Magnard. In addition, he began to go deaf. Much as in the case of Beethoven, this made his exterior even more forbidding. It prompted him to retreat to the quiet and security of his country estate at Baron. In a major career miscalculation, he fired his publisher because he thought it was unseemly to advertise and publicize himself. He self-published his music thereafter. Without an agent and publisher to promote and network his music, he lost opportunities for performance and began to be forgotten except by his strongest advocates. Still, his chamber music received some performance. Another opera, *Bérénice*, was performed at the Opéra-Comique in 1911, but again fell flat with an unprepared public.

In August 1914, when World War I began, Magnard sent his wife and children west for safety, but he remained at Baron for a while. On September 3, he was working in his study, alone in the house, when he spotted a troop of German cavalry riding on his estate grounds. He seized his old Army rifle and shot two of them dead from his upstairs window. The Germans returned fire and burned down the house, where his body was later found in the ashes. Also lost in the fire were all existing materials for the opera *Yolanda*, the full score of two acts of *Guercoeur* and a new set of 12 songs. *—Joseph Stevenson*

Overview of Works (1887–1914)

The signal fact of Magnard's catalog is that, apart from an early song and piano piece, it contains but 21 works—including three remarkable operas (to his own libretti), four powerful symphonies, and five richly concentrated chamber works. In this, he is only a bit less fastidious than his contemporary, Paul Dukas, with his scant dozen masterpieces. Magnard also recalls Chausson in having been independently wealthy, having begun his composition studies with Massenet only to shift his allegiance to Franck (though he was actually taught by Franck's disciple, d'Indy), and in the manic-depressive intensity of his works. His official Op. 1, the *Trois Pièces pour piano*, and the soon-to-follow *Suite d'Orchestre dans le style ancien*, are characteristic products of d'Indy's teaching in their reliance on such scholastic procedures as canon, fugue, chorale, and formal rigor. The *Six Poèmes en musique*, on the other hand, in their ambition and elaborate writing for the piano, bear the mighty impress of Berlioz and Wagner—it was, after all, a hearing of *Tristan und Isolde* at Bayreuth in 1886 which decided Magnard on a career as a composer. Dating from the late 1880s, those apprentice works are rounded off with the one-act opera, *Yolande* (1891), which essays a mediaeval legend with youthful ardor—unfurled with many of the characteristic gestures of his music to come—and the tightly coiled *First Symphony* (1889–90). With the collection of seven glowing, atmospheric piano *Promenades* (1893) he hits his stride. Composed during his courtship of Julia Creton, who became his wife in 1896, they mark a rare moment of equilibrium—veering from crisply brisk to ecstatically serene—matched by the high-strung gaiety of the *Quintet for Piano and Winds* (1894). If the orchestral *Chant funèbre* (in memory of his father, 1895) and the *Ouverture* (1895) are austere and overlong, and the *Hymne à la justice* looms as generic Magnard, the *Second, Third,* and *Fourth* symphonies (1893, 1896, 1913) hit the mark with unerring formal concision constraining a tremendous emotional turbulence to a Beethovenian effect of new wine in old bottles. Here, we encounter the ever-recurring gamut of Magnard's expressiveness—the celebrated brusquerie making for startlingly immediate lift, the obligatory formal fugue, moments of swaying, ecstatic syncopation, the folk dance-inspired rhythmic audacities of his scherzi, the mordant bite of his woodwind scoring, the cyclic recall of themes, a final blazing chorale signifying triumph—coalescing in an overall impression of what Paul Landormy termed "violent meditation." The composer's own description, "enthusiastic pessimism," is made explicit in the grand, testamentary operas, *Guercoeur* (1897–1901) and—the richest throw of Magnard's art—*Bérénice* (1905–09). With the operas, the through-composed *Quatre Poèmes en musique* (1902), and the orchestral *Hymne à Vénus* (1904), we enter the feminine-dominated inner sanctum of Magnard's being. The chastely lyrical *Violin Sonata* (1901), the contrapuntally taut *String Quartet* (1902–03), the elaborately developed *Piano Trio* (1904–05), and the explosive *Cello Sonata* (1908–10) are major contributions to the chamber music repertoire but, given their preternatural intensity, a special taste. *—Adrian Corleonis*

Recommended:

- ○ **Magnard: Quintette; Trio** / Keller, Demenga, Graf, Oprean, Flieger, Schmid, Schmid / Accord 200102
- ○ **Magnard: Œuvres orchestrales** / Stringer (cond.), Luxembourg SO / 2002 / Timpani 1067
- ○ **Magnard: Symphonies 2 & 4** / Sanderling (cond.), Malmo SO / 1998 / Bis 928
- ○ **Magnard: Symphonies 1 & 3** / Sanderling (cond.), Malmo SO / 1998 / Bis 927

Gustav Mahler

b. Jul. 7, 1860, Kalischt, Bohemia (Czech Rep.), **d.** May 18, 1911, Vienna, Austria
Composer: Symphonic, Vocal, Choral

"Imagine the universe beginning to sing and resound," Mahler wrote of his *Symphony No. 8, the "Symphony of a Thousand."* "It is no longer human voices; it is planets and suns revolving." Mahler was late Romantic music's ultimate big thinker. In his own lifetime he was generally regarded as a conductor who composed on the side, producing huge, bizarre symphonies accepted only by a cult following.

Born in 1860, in Kalischt, Bohemia, he came from a middle-class family. He entered the Vienna Conservatory in 1875, studying piano, harmony, and composition in a musically conservative atmosphere. Nevertheless, he became a supporter of Wagner and Bruckner, both of whose works he would later conduct frequently, and became part of a social circle interested in socialism, Nietzschean philosophy, and pan-Germanism. Around 1880, he began conducting and wrote his first mature work, *Das klagende Lied*. Mahler's conducting career advanced rapidly, moving him from Kassel to Prague to Leipzig to Budapest; he was usually either greatly respected or thoroughly despised by the performers for his exacting rehearsals and perfectionism. In 1897 he became music director of the Vienna Court Opera and then, a year later, of the Vienna Philharmonic. Mahler's conducting career permitted composition only during the summers, in a series of "composing huts" he had built in picturesque rural locations. He completed his first symphony in 1888, but it met with utter audience incomprehension. He reserved this time for symphonies, all of them large-scale works, and song cycles. In *Das Lied von der Erde* (The Song of the Earth), he merged the two forms into an immense song-symphony. The Viennese public largely failed to understand his music, but Mahler took their reactions calmly, accurately predicting that "My time will yet come." Meanwhile, his autocratic ways as a conductor alienated musicians. In 1901, the press and the musicians essentially forced his resignation from the Philharmonic. He married a young composition student, Alma Schindler in 1902, and they soon had two daughters. By 1907 Mahler was increasingly away from Vienna, conducting his own works, and thus he resigned from the opera as well. Just after accepting the position of principal conductor of New York's Metropolitan Opera, but before leaving Vienna, Mahler's older daughter, aged four, died from scarlet fever and diphtheria, and he learned he himself had a defective heart valve. In New York, he was impressed by the caliber of talent and quickly gained audience approval. In 1909 he became conductor of the New York Philharmonic, which he found much more agreeable than the opera work by this time. The following year, he had a triumphant premiere of his massive *Symphony No. 8* in Munich. Despite the professional successes, his personal life suffered another blow when his and Alma's marriage began having problems. They stayed together, and after he became ill in February 1911, she saw to it that he made it back to Vienna, where he died on May 18.

The conductors Bruno Walter, Otto Klemperer, Willem Mengelberg, and Maurice Abravanel kept Mahler's legacy alive, and Mahler's are now among the most recorded of any symphonies. His frequent incorporation of vocal elements into symphonic writing brought to full fruition a process that had begun with Beethoven's *Symphony No. 9*, demonstrating his music's firm roots in the Germanic classical tradition. However, it was his huge tapestries of shifting moods and tones, ranging from tragedy to bitter irony (often explicitly indicated in performance directions), from café music to evocations of the sublime, that portended a century in which multiplicity ruled. *—AMG*

SYMPHONIC

Das Lied von der Erde, symphony for alto (or baritone), tenor & orchestra (1908–1909)

Although seemingly a set of songs with orchestra, this is for all intents and purposes Mahler's ninth symphony. *Das Lied* represents a refinement and concentration of the means and expression of the *Eighth Symphony*. In *Das Lied*, the same contrapuntally oriented style prevails, but the thinner textures make it seem more pronounced. Also, the more intimate and personal nature of much of the writing is a direct response to the private musings of the Chinese poems rather than a major stylistic upheaval.

Das Lied is an integrated symphonic whole, as the six songs are organized into four parts analogous to symphonic movements. Mahler's harmonic and expressive language is so powerful that he was able to create a progressive effect that unite these songs into a single semantic and artistic entity.

"Das Trinklied vom Jammer der Erde" (The Drinking Song of Earth's Sorrow). The first song is a hybrid of strophic song and sonata form. It stands by itself, not only formally, but in its black, uncompromising defiance of grief in the face of mortality. The powerfully sweeping opening is contrasted with an ethereal central section, but eventually culminates in a weird and shrieking evocation of Man's fate.

"Der Einsame im Herbst" (The Lonely One in Autumn). This resigned song evokes the mists of Fall as the poet grieves over the loss of summer and life. The thin textures and wandering lines perfectly capture bitter loneliness.

"Von der Jugend" (Of Youth). This and the next two songs comprise the "scherzo" of the symphonic structure. They are all shorter, lighter in tone, and nostalgic in mood. Here, memories of young people drinking tea is captured with light and airy pentatonic lines, invoking the innocence and carefree attitude of youth.

"Von der Schönheit" (Of Beauty). A romantic scene. The gentle innocence of the girls is depicted with a delicately moving Andante. At the appearance of the horsemen there is a sudden military outburst in the orchestra, while the voice accelerates into a breathless melody, effectively portraying the maidens' fluttering hearts.

"Der Trunkene im Frühling" (The Drunk in Spring). In spite of a longing central passage, this song is mostly comic in its evocations of nature and a young man's drunken reeling. Mahler here uses an astonishing variety of harmonic and orchestral effects.

"Der Abschied" (The Farewell). There are two separate poems here. The first depicts a solitary figure waiting for a friend to come for a last farewell, the second is the farewell itself. By far the longest movement of the work, Mahler precedes each poem with a lengthy orchestral section, also making this the most instrumentally oriented movement. The first is longing and plaintive, repeated in part after the voice finally enters. The second is a long and moving funeral march, culminating in a huge and tragic climax. In the final stanza, as the poet looks back at life, Mahler composed a resigned and expansive coda. *—Steven Coburn*

Recommended:

- ○ **Mahler: Last Works** / Kubelik (cond.), Baker, Kmentt, Bavarian RSO / Originals 806
- ○ **Walter Conducts Das Lied von der Erde** / Walter (cond.), Thorborg, Kullmann, Vienna PO / 2001 / Dutton 9722
- ○ **Horenstein** / (cond.), Hodgson, Mitchinson, BBC Northern SO / 2000 / BBC 4042
- ○ **Mahler: Das Lied von der Erde** / Klemperer (cond.), Wunderlich, Ludwig, New Philharmonia, Philharmonia / 1998 / EMI 66944

Symphony No. 1 in D major ("Titan") (1884–1888; revised 1893)

Mahler's *First Symphony* was originally conceived as a tone poem in two parts. Loosely based on Jean Paul's novel *Titan*, the structure was this: Part I: "From the Days of Youth," Music of Flowers, Fruit and Thorn—1. Spring and No End; 2. Flowers; 3. In Full Sail; Part II: "The Human Comedy"—4. "Stranded!" Funeral March in the Style of Callot; 5. D'all Inferno al'Paradiso (From Hell to Heaven). These titles were accompanied by more extensive programs describing the metaphorical content of each movement. In Jean Paul's *Titan* we have a youth gifted with a burning artistic desire that the world has no use for, and who, finding no outlet or ability to adapt, gives way to despair and suicide. Mahler apparently saw himself in this figure, as he described this work as autobiographical in a very loose sense. On the other hand the music, some of which Mahler actually accumulated from various earlier works, contradicts this program in so many ways, especially in the triumphant conclusion, that Mahler later withdrew it. He eventually came to scorn the application of specific programs to his symphonies in general.

Beyond Mahler's suppression of the program, there were other changes made before the symphony achieved its final form: the orchestra was expanded and the original second movement, entitled "Blumine" (Flowers) was dropped. This movement, the only surviving piece from Mahler's incidental music to Scheffel's *Der Trompeter von Säkkingen*, although having thematic ties to the rest of the symphony, is stylistically different, being scored for a much smaller orchestra.

The primary source material for the remaining movements of the *First Symphony* is Mahler's *Lieder eines Fahrenden Gesellen* (Songs of a Wayfarer). The material of these songs, specifically the first and second, is not only quoted but also used as thematic material in the symphony, creating additional programmatic implications. Mahler's *First Symphony* is a stunning achievement for so young a composer, and despite its convoluted genesis is a fully mature, integrated and highly effective work.

The first movement, Langsam Schleppend (Slow and Dragging), opens with an introduction invoking nature, eventually with cuckoo calls and distant fanfares. The principal theme is from the song "Ging heut' morgens übers Feld" (I Went Out This Morning Through the Fields) and is developed in a standard sonata form. The second movement, Kräftig bewegt (Strongly moving), is a lusty and hearty Austrian Ländler replete with yodels and foot stomping. The slower and wistful Trio conjures feelings of nostalgia and longing. Based on a woodcut depicting animals carrying a hunter to his grave, the third-movement funeral march, Feierlich und gemessen (Solemnly and measured), is deeply ironic. Mahler uses the folk song "Frère Jacques" in a lugubrious minor, played by a muted double bass solo. The central Trio is an evocation of tawdry Viennese cabaret music.

Mahler's original program for the Stürmisch bewegt (Stormy) finale called the movement's dramatic opening "the sudden outburst of a wounded heart." After a long and violent beginning invoking the torments of hell, including a vehement march derived from the first movement, the music subsides into a yearning theme. After a return to the march, Mahler interrupts the mood with a transformative fanfare that eventually leads to a triumphant conclusion. *—Steven Coburn*

Recommended:

- ○ **Mahler: Symphony 1; Songs of a Wayfarer** / Kubelik (cond.), Bavarian Radio SO / 1999 / DG 460654
- ○ **Mahler: Symphonies 1 & ; Lieder eines fahrenden Gesellen** / Walter (cond.), Columbia SO / 1994 / Sony 64447
- ○ **Mahler: Symphony 1** / Solti (cond.), Chicago SO / 1984 / London 411731

Symphony No. 2 in C minor ("Resurrection") (1888–1894; revised 1903)

Mahler's *Second Symphony* represents a step in the direction of expansion from the *First*. Its enormous resources—huge orchestra, soprano and alto soloists, chorus, and organ, as well as its epic theme of death and resurrection—represent Mahler at the pinnacle of his earlier heaven-storming style and aesthetic. The transformative theme employed here will eventually become the common thread of every subsequent symphony. It is quintessential Mahler and covers a vast panorama of style and emotion, culminating in one of the most breathtaking and moving conclusions in the symphonic repertory.

Just like the *First Symphony*, Mahler's *Second* began life as a single-movement tone poem, *Todtenfeier* (Funeral Rites). At one time Mahler commented that this tone poem represented the funeral of the hero from his *First Symphony*. Sometime in 1893 Mahler decided to expand *Todtenfeier* into a symphony. He began by composing an Andante and expanding his recently composed *Wunderhorn* song *Des Antonius von Padua Fischpredigt* (Antony of Padua's Sermon to the Fish) into an orchestral scherzo. At this point Mahler struggled to find a sufficiently powerful ending to balance the already massive symphonic torso. He solved the problem when he discovered Klopstock's chorale *Resurrection*. Having created the progression from the death of *Todtenfeier*, now the first movement, to the resurrection theme of the Finale, Mahler bridged the gap with another *Wunderhorn* song, "Urlicht" (Primeval Light). He used this song entire, with voice, and excluded it from the published collection of *Wunderhorn Songs*. The structure was now complete. It is the crowning glory of Mahler's earlier works and his most popular composition.

Allegro maestoso. This massive and unusual movement is in a hugely expanded sonata form. The sharp contrast between the funeral march material and the hymnlike lyrical second subject set the theme for the entire symphony.

Andante moderato. The dance structure alternates a folk-like and melodic Ländler with two more agitated Trios. The Ländler, according to Mahler's original program, represents the "image of a long-dead hour of Happiness," while the Trios recall death.

In ruhig fliessender Bewegung (Quietly Flowing). This movement carries the same theme as the song from which it is derived—the futility and pointlessness of life. The St. Antony song pervades the main sections, while the Trios represent, respectively false joy and sentiment.

"Urlicht." In a subtle breakthrough, Mahler does a complete spiritual reversal on the preceding sardonic Scherzo. "Urlicht" is a rapt hymn of deep beauty, powerful enough in its brevity to change the bitter mood of what has come so far to the latent hope of what will follow.

Im Tempo des Scherzos. Wild herausfahrend. (In Scherzo tempo, Wildly driven). The opening is a "cry of disgust" for the plight of humankind, but shortly gives way to a spacious and haunting evocation of nature and the last trumpet awakening the dead. This is expanded into a typical march that culminates in a return to the "cry of disgust," before finally giving way permanently to the "Resurrection" chorale and the triumphant conclusion. *—Steven Coburn*

Recommended:

- ○ **Mahler: Symphony 2** / Klemperer (cond.), Baker, Harper, Bavarian RSO / 1998 / EMI 66867
- ○ **Mahler: Symphony 2** / Slatkin (cond.), Peck, Battle, Forrester, St. Louis SO / 1983 / Telarc 80081
- ○ **Abbado Conducts Mahler & Debussy** / Abbado (cond.), Gvazava, Larsson, Lucerne Festival Orch. / 2004 / DG 000339702
- ○ **Mahler: Symphonies 1 & 2** / Tennstedt (cond.), Mathis, Soffel, London PO / 2000 / EMI 74182
- ○ **Mahler: Symphonies 1 & 2; Lieder eines fahrenden Gesellen** / Walter (cond.), Forrester, Cundari, New York Philharmonic / 1994 / Sony 64447
- ○ **Mahler: The Symphonies** / Solti (cond.), Hillis, Zakai, Buchanan, Chicago SO / 1991 / London 430805-14

Symphony No. 3 in D minor (1893–1896; revised 1906)

This is Mahler's longest symphony, in six movements and lasting nearly two hours. Mahler's concept of the symphony as a world unto itself finds its complete exposition here in the highly diverse styles and elements, creating problems of continuity and coherence that he did not completely solve. The primary theme of the *Third* is Nature and Man's place therein, and its principal literary inspirations are *Das Knaben Wunderhorn* (as in the previous symphony) and Nietzsche. As in the *Second Symphony*, Mahler added words and voices to expand his means of expression and used material from one of his earlier *Wunderhorn Songs*. The original program ran like this: "The Joyful Knowledge: A Summer Morning's Dream." I. Pan Awakes: Summer Marches In; II. What the Meadow Flowers Tell Me; III. What the Creatures of the Forest Tell Me; IV. What Night Tells Me (Mankind); V. What the Morning Bells Tell Me (the Angels); VI. What Love Tells Me; and VII. The Heavenly Life (What the Child Tells Me). Ultimately, Mahler dropped the seventh movement and used it as the core around which he built the *Fourth Symphony*. The sum of this program represents Mahler's cosmological hierarchy at this point in his life and the *Third Symphony* as a whole is his most specific example of "world building" in artistic terms.

Kräftig. Entschieden. (Strongly and Confidently). This is the single longest sonata-form movement ever written. Mahler sets bizarre, primordial, and harsh brass and percussion rumblings depicting Pan's awakening in opposition to pastoral music of bird calls and light fanfares over tremulous strings and woodwind trillings. These elements are transformed into the ultimate example of Mahler's symphonic military marches. The entire movement covers a vast soundscape of imagery, from bold, assertive proclamation to harsh and grotesque fugal passages, to despairing outcries, to a lighthearted and popular sounding march tune.

Tempo di Menuetto. (Minuet Tempo). This is a light and folk-like dance movement in the style of the comic *Wunderhorn Songs*. It stands in sharp contrast to the weighty first movement.

Comodo. Scherzando. Ohne Hast. (Moving, Scherzo-like, Without Haste). This movement quotes extensively from Mahler's song *Ablösung im Sommer* (Relief in the Summer) about a dead cuckoo. Its comic vein is interrupted twice, once by a sentimental posthorn solo, and later by a dramatic outburst symbolic of the great god Pan's intrusion into the peaceful summer.

Sehr langsam. Misterioso. Durchaus ppp. (Very Slow, Mysterious, Pianissimo Throughout). Here Mahler moves into a more metaphysical realm by setting Nietzsche's "Midnight Song" in this slow and haunting movement.

Lustig im Tempo und keck im Ausdruck. (Happy in Tempo, Saucily Bold in Expression). Boys and women's voices are used here to sing this angel's song about the redemption of sin from *Das Knaben Wunderhorn*. Mahler imitates church bells to delightful effect in this innocent and uplifting movement.

Langsam. Ruhevoll. Empfunden. (Slow, Peaceful, Deeply Felt). A majestic and awesome Adagio concludes the symphony in a hymnlike paean on love. It rises to a powerful climax as "Nature in its totality rings and resounds." *—Steven Coburn*

Recommended:

- ○ **Mahler: Symphony 3** / Abbado (cond.), Norman, Hetzel, Holler, Vienna PO / DG 410715
- ○ **Mahler: Symphony 3** / Tilson Thomas (cond.), George, DeYoung, San Francisco SO / 2002 / San Francisco Symphony 3
- ○ **Mahler: Symphony 3** / Salonen (cond), Salamunovich, Sauer, Chalifour, Larsson, Los Angeles PO / 1998 / Sony 60250

Symphony No. 4 in G major (1892–1900; revised 1901)

This symphony represents a culmination and distillation of the previous three. It is the shortest of Mahler's symphonies, with a reduced orchestra, and a style consciously archaic in its evocation of classical models. Yet it is redolent of the *Wunderhorn* aesthetic that imbues this entire period of Mahler's career. The entire symphony, in fact, grew out of the final movement, which Mahler originally composed for his orchestral song collection on poems from *Das Knaben Wunderhorn* (The Young Boys' Magic Horn). Mahler originally planned to use this song, "Das himmlische Leben" (Heavenly Life), as the Finale for his *Third Symphony*, but withdrew it, probably because its theme was so similar to that of the fifth movement. At any rate, the other three movements were extrapolated from this long and joyful folk song and were calculated to culminate in its childlike vision of heaven. This in part explains the relatively lighter mood of the symphony as a whole as well as its tendency toward a more classical balance in its style, proportions, and scoring. In spite of the greater popularity of the *Second Symphony*, which in some ways is more typically Mahlerian, the *Fourth Symphony*, although lacking the barn-storming climaxes and extremes of emotion, was his best composition to date and entirely more refined and subtle in expression and technique.

Bedächtig. Nicht eilen. (Moderately, not rushed). From the very outset we have Mahler's evocation of nature, with sleigh bells and bird calls leading into a flirtatious melody, so unlike the pretentious horns of the *Third*. There are dark moments later in the movement, but they appear as if through the veil of childhood's vision, unreal and imagined. The movement is in a clear sonata form.

In gemächlicher Bewegung. (Leisurely moving). This was originally called "Freund Hein spielt auf" (Friend Hein strikes up), representing a sinister character out of German folklore roughly analogous to the "Pied Piper." His fiddle (as opposed to a pipe) is brilliantly depicted by Mahler with the use of a violin purposely tuned a full step up to give it a fiddle sound. The movement itself is a wryly grotesque Scherzo alternating with more earthy Ländler-like Trios.

Ruhevoll. (Peacefully). Beginning as a gentle lullaby, the principal form of the movement is an alternation of this peaceful opening with a more searching and anguished theme. An impassioned variant of this theme leads to a series of brief variations in quickening tempos followed by a reprise of the opening. A sudden and ecstatic climax ensues and leads directly to the quiet coda.

Sehr behaglich. (Comfortably). The song for soprano is "Das himmlische Leben," and depicts a child's view of heaven in this folklike setting. Ingenuous melodies alternate with a hymnlike stanza representing the child's occasional awe. An animated interlude that recurs between many of the stanzas is the source for the opening of the first movement, but in the symphonic context it functions as a cyclic reference backward to that movement. *—Steven Coburn*

Recommended:

- ○ **Mahler: Symphony 4; Songs of a Wayfarer** / Szell (cond.), Raskin; Cleveland Orch. / 1991 / Sony 46535
- ○ **Mahler: Symphony 4** / Reiner (cond.), Casa, Chicago SO / 2000 / RCA 63533
- ○ **Mahler: Symphonies 2 & 4** / Abbado (cond.), Von Stade, Hetzel, Vienna PO / DG 453037
- ○ **Mahler: Symphony 4; Berlioz: Le Corsaire** / Barbirolli (cond.), Harper, BBCSO / 1996 / BBC 4014
- ○ **Mahler: Symphony 4** / Haenchen (cond.), Coku, Martinova, Netherlands PO / 1994 / Laserlight 14139

Symphony No. 5 in C sharp minor (1901–1902)

Mahler kept revising the orchestration of this work until his death. He conducted the first performance with the Gürzenich Orchestra in Cologne on October 18, 1904. It is scored for quadruple winds, six horns, four trumpets, three trombones, tuba, timpani, three other drums, metal and wood percussion, harp, and string choir.

He'd begun the *Fifth Symphony* at Maiernegg in 1901—writing the third, first and second movements in that order, after a death-obsessed song, "Der Tambours'gsell," and the *Kindertotenlieder* cycle ("on the death of children"). After nearly bleeding to death the previous winter (from an intestinal hemorrhage), Mahler's symphonic orientation underwent a profound change. During his recovery he immersed himself in the complete works of Bach.

A new appreciation of counterpoint was born, but not yet a mastery of orchestral balances or effects—as subsequent events were to prove. Beginning with *No. 5*, he applied this new passion (which he called "intensive counterpoint") to five purely instrumental symphonies without *Wunderhorn* associations. Like the *Resurrection Second* and the first version of *No. 1* (with the Blumine slow movement later abandoned) Mahler cast his *Fifth Symphony* in five movements that fall naturally into three parts.

The first begins in C sharp minor with a funeral march, of measured tread and austere (Movement I). A sonata-form movement follows, marked "Stormily, with greatest vehemence" (Movement II), which shares themes as well as mood with the opening.

The second part (which Mahler composed first) is a scherzo: "Vigorously, not too fast" (Movement III)—the symphony's shortest large section, but its longest single movement. This emphatically joyous, albeit manic movement puts forward D major as the work's focal key. Although its form has remained a topic of debate since 1904, rondo and sonata-form elements are both present.

Part Three begins with a seraphic Adagietto: "Very slowly" (Movement IV). This is indubitably related to the Rückert song Mahler composed in August 1901, *"Ich bin der Welt abhanden gekommen"* (I have become lost to the world . . . I live alone in my heaven, in my loving, in my song). A Rondo-Finale: "Allegro giocoso, lively" (Movement V) concludes the symphony, although Mahler devised a form far removed from classic models. While sectional, in truth episodic, this too has elements of sonata form. To weld its diverse components into a unity he wrote four "fugal episodes," with a D major chorale just before the final Allegro molto.

Mahler's search for a new vocabulary caused him no end of orchestration problems. Before his death in 1911 he had made several versions, the original of which was published in 1904. C.F. Peters failed, however, to emend either mistakes or revisions in the first pocket score, although they reengraved orchestral parts (at Mahler's expense) to include his first set of corrections. Not even Erwin Ratz's "first critical edition" of 1964 was the last word. Revisions Mahler made just before his terminal illness didn't come to light until the "second critical edition," by Karl Heinz Füssl, published just around 1989. *—Roger Dettmer*

Recommended:

- ○ **Mahler: Symphony 5** / Abbado (cond.), Berlin PO / 1993 / DG 437789
- ○ **Mahler: Symphony 5** / Barbirolli (cond.), New Philharmonia / 1998 / EMI 66962
- ○ **Mahler: Symphony 5; Das Lied von der Erde** / Tennstedt (cond.), London PO / 2001 / EMI 74849

Symphony No. 6 in A minor ("Tragic") (1903–1904; revised 1906)

As with his *Fifth Symphony*, this work is exclusively instrumental. It is also Mahler's most "Classical" symphony in its form and layout. Although the *Sixth Symphony* has no specific program, much has been written about the "tragic" aspects of the work that gave rise to its subtitle, which, by the way, was withdrawn by Mahler before publication. The prevailingly dark mood is not unusual for Mahler, but there is no transformation into a glorious ending or peaceful resignation. It is his only symphony to end unremittingly in the minor. As for the autobiographical elements, it is known from Alma Mahler's memoirs that it may have been Mahler himself upon whom three hammer strokes of fate fall in the Finale, which seems strangely prophetic of the following year when Mahler lost his Vienna Opera position, lost his daughter, and was diagnosed with heart disease. The song quotes, Ländlers, country tunes, bird calls, and military marches are all gone. In their place is a powerful and stark contrapuntal texture, certainly not devoid of soaring melodies and lush harmonies, but lacking in the referential styles of the early symphonies. The entire symphony is unified by a motto theme that consists of a major moving to minor triad over a characteristic rhythm. It carries particular significance in the Finale, as it is linked with the aforementioned hammer strokes of fate. Many commentators believe this to be Mahler's most cohesive and tautly organized symphony.

Allegro energico, ma non troppo. Heftig, aber markig. (Not too fast. Vigorous, but marked). This is a standard sonata form with repeated exposition. The opening theme is harsh and marchlike, while the sweeping second subject, written specifically as a portrayal of Mahler's wife, Alma, is in sharp contrast. The themes are developed imaginatively, and the movement closes triumphantly with the "Alma theme."

Scherzo. Wuchtig. (Forcefully). This movement is usually performed second, but Mahler seems to have always placed it after the Andante. This is the first of Mahler's really diabolical scherzos. It is a bizarre, grotesquely stamping dance full of percussive strokes and shrieking woodwinds. This alternates with a strange little trio to which Mahler gives the marking Altväterisch (Old-fashioned). It is full of rhythmic ingenuity in its timid and hesitant manner.

Andante moderato. (Moderately moving). Alma reported in her memoirs that this pastoral and nostalgic movement was a musical depiction of their children at play. It is simple in form, and rather yearning and plaintive in mood.

Finale. Sostenuto. (Sustained). This huge sonata-form movement is one of Mahler's most epic in scope and conception. It nearly dwarfs the rest of the symphony and certainly represents its cornerstone, both structurally and emotionally. It opens with an impressionistic sweep that extends out to the somber introduction. After this, the main material is a powerful march that three times rises to exultation, only to be overcome by the motto theme and each of the three hammer strokes. The movement concludes with a long and mournful coda, unremitting to the end. *—Steven Coburn*

Recommended:

- ○ **Mahler: Symphony 6; Kindertotenlieder** / Karajan (cond.), Berlin PO / DG 457716
- ○ **Mahler: Symphony 6** / Tilson-Thomas (cond.), San Francisco SO / San Francisco Symphony 0001
- ○ **Mahler: Symphony 6** / Neumann (cond.), Czech PO / Supraphon 1977
- ○ **Mahler: Symphonies 6–8** / Tennstedt (cond.), London PO / 1992 / EMI 64476

Symphony No. 7 in E minor ("Song of the Night") (1904–1905)

In his *Seventh Symphony*, Mahler returned to the five-movement pattern: two large, outer movements flank three shorter inner ones. Exclusively instrumental, it not only is without the programmatic trappings of the earlier ones, but does not have even the biographical implications of the *Sixth*. It is his most purely abstract work. Perhaps because of this it seems to lack the compelling drive and conviction of all the other symphonies—it remains his least understood and least popular work. Even so, it is also in some ways his most original work. Mahler's orchestration reached a new height of creativity, and virtually every measure is full of fantastic and innovative combinations. Also, the degree of harmonic experimentation in the first movement goes beyond anything Mahler had done before, and became a model for many subsequent composers. The three inner movements are all subtle stylizations of Romantic genre pieces and open up new expressive possibilities and combinations. Only the Finale seems artificial and forced in its bustling counterpoints, and in spite of a valiant effort, fails to conclude the symphony convincingly.

Langsam (Slow). This intense and driven sonata form carries over some of the harsh and wailing bitterness of the *Sixth*, but there are also moments of ethereal beauty in the development. The most interesting feature, technically, is Mahler's extensive use of melodies and harmonies based on the interval of a fourth, which lend the music a mysteriously unsettling and abstract quality.

Nachtmusik. Allegro moderato. (Night Music. Moderately fast). This weird movement directly evokes and almost satirizes some of Mahler's earlier Romantic mannerisms. The opening horn call, directly followed by an extended and static passage of complex bird stylizations is an example. This alternates with an absurd and improbable march tune, which juxtaposes popular harmonies with eerie militaristic figures, and quotes several times from the march from the first movement of the *Third Symphony*.

Scherzo. Schattenhaft. (Shadowy). This Scherzo is in the same diabolical mode as that of the *Sixth Symphony*, but is subtler and more haunting in its fleeting harmonies and irregular rhythms. The movement is dominated by eerie and slippery figures that alternate with a grotesque waltz. A slow, but equally weird waltz forms the basis of the Trio, which, unusual for Mahler, only occurs once in its entirety.

Nachtmusik. Andante amoroso. (Night Music. Amorously moving). This movement is a truly romantic and genial serenade. Tender and longing themes are enmeshed in a texture dominated by harp, guitar, and mandolin, lending it its stylized serenade atmosphere. In spite of this obvious stylization, the entire movement is full of charm and grace, and is one of Mahler's most immediately attractive compositions.

Rondo-Finale. Tempo I (Allegro ordinario). (An Ordinary Allegro). Despite Mahler's best efforts at creating a rousing Finale, the rather uninspired themes and their forced development simply make this movement, for all its bluster, rhythmic activity and instrumental virtuosity, less than effective. It is generally considered Mahler's weakest movement. *—Steven Coburn*

Recommended:

- ○ **Mahler: Symphony 7** / Horenstein (cond.), New Philharmonia / 2000 / BBC 4051
- ○ **Mahler: Symphony 7** / Abbado (cond.), Berlin PO / 2002 / DG 471623
- ○ **Mahler: Symphony 7** / Tilson Thomas (cond.), London SO / 1999 / RCA 63510
- ○ **Mahler: Symphony 7; Das Knaben Wunderhorn** / Solti (cond.), Chicago SO / 1985 / London 414675

Symphony No. 8 in E flat major ("Symphony of a Thousand") (1906–1907)

Gustav Mahler completed his *Symphony No. 8* in E flat, "Symphony of a Thousand," in 1906. The name "Symphony of a Thousand" was not the composer's idea but an impresario's. It was written for the largest ensemble yet conceived, consisting of three sopranos, two contraltos, tenor, baritone, bass, double choir, boys' choir, orchestra, and organ. The work's premiere took place on September 12, 1910 at the Exposition Concert Hall in Munich. Mahler conducted a cast totaling (himself included) 1,003 performers. The reviews were glowing, making the premiere easily the triumph of his artistic career. It is an incredible thing to make so many musicians work together and make any sort of sense, from both the perspective of a conductor and a composer. No one really thought this sort of thing was possible before Mahler went ahead and proved it a viable act. His contributions were such that they shaped the nature of artistic courage in the modern era.

The work is under 90 minutes in duration and in two parts. The first part is a medieval Catholic hymn, *Veni creator spiritus*. It is the briefer of the two movements and generally praises God with robust vigor. The declaration of faith is of course clear and implicit. It is also constantly choral in delivery and amazingly clear, with no polyphonic jams to speak of. The second part of the symphony is a setting of the final movement from Goethe's *Faust*. This part is more of a secular cantata, featuring the soloists more prominently. Its first section is an adagio followed by a scherzo, and then a finale. Other than the almost nocturnal opening of the second part, there is little music in this work that is mysterious; it is mostly very direct and never murky. In the manner of Goethe, the second part is openly romantic, somewhat pastoral, and clearly Germanic. Mahler rarely lets the texture thin out much, and manages to keep the variety of soundscape and the interest of the listener consistent. At the end of the twentieth century, it was not unusual to attend live performances of this piece, in spite of the enormity of the cost to stage such a work. Some writers contend that it was the great choral document of the twentieth century, just as Beethoven's *Ninth Symphony* is the choral document of the nineteenth century. This is not actually the case, insofar as the musical language of *Symphony of a Thousand* is still firmly entrenched in late nineteenth century tonality. It is however a great work. The amount of ideas that Mahler can process simultaneously is astounding. It is the combination of certainty and wonder that makes this work succeed. *—John Keillor*

Recommended:

- ○ **Mahler: Symphony 8** / Solti (cond.), Auger, Popp, Harper, Kollo, Chicago SO / London 414493
- ○ **Mahler: Symphony 8; Schoenberg: Die Jakobsleiter** / Gielen (cond.), Daus, Weingartner, Marc, Michaels-Moore, SWF SO / 2001 / Haenssler 93015

Symphony No. 9 in D major (1908–1909)

Where *Das Lied von der Erde* ended with gentle resignation, here Mahler attacks death head-on with music of profound violence and irony. The grim character of the music, certain cryptic phrases Mahler marked into the drafts of the symphony, and the recurring use of an unusual motive and chord progression from Beethoven's *"Les adieux" Sonata*, Op. 81, have led commentators to believe that this symphony is autobiographical, a kind of "farewell" symphony. Since Mahler immediately proceeded to the composition of his *Tenth Symphony*, though, this interpretation is without real merit. It seems sufficient to accept that death, once again, is simply an obsessive theme.

Musically, what is new in this symphony is a synthesis of the sharp-edged style of the *Sixth* and *Seventh* with the rarefied, contrapuntal technique of *Das Lied*. Combined with Mahler's increasingly advanced harmony and sophisticated thematic development, the result is music that is more closely allied with the expressionism of Schoenberg than with Mahler's earlier romanticism. At times it approaches a complete collapse of tonality, blurring traditional thematic and tonal differentiations in a totally modernistic way.

Andante comodo (Moving). This powerful and devastating movement begins innocently enough with gentle figures in the strings, harp, and horns and expands into a beautifully resigned, sighing theme. Soon it is interrupted by a chromatic and despairing theme. These two ideas alternate in various forms, rising to several great climaxes. The movement culminates in a complete transfiguration of the opening motives into a nearly cacophonous collapse. It never recovers as solo instruments seem to wander aimlessly before the final resignation of the coda.

Im Tempo eines gemächlichen Ländlers (In a leisurely Ländler Tempo.) This dance movement alternates a quirky and awkward Ländler devoid of charm with a tawdry Waltz, clearly meant to evoke cheap, popular styles as a metaphor for the pointlessness of life. These two ideas intermingle in increasingly complex ways, only interrupted once by a more gentle, nostalgic Trio.

Rondo. Burleske. Allegro assai. Sehr trotzig (Very fast and defiantly.) This is ostensibly a Scherzo, but has the proportions and weight of a Finale. It is also Mahler's most modern movement, consisting of intensely complex and dissonant linear counterpoint. There are alternations with some grotesque band music, but these only add to the insanely off-balance and violently ferocious general style. This wild pandemonium is interrupted suddenly by a transcendent section reminiscent of the beginning of the symphony. It slowly expands into a passionate melody for the strings before finally returning to the diabolical. The ending is defiant and grim.

Adagio. Sehr Langsam und noch zurückhaltend (Very slow yet still held back.) The violence of the preceding movement is transformed into a calm, if bitter, acceptance. A hymnlike passage of stately character seems to express Mahler's deepest yearnings. This alternates with a somewhat spare, rarefied section in barest counterpoint that seems to express emotional exhaustion. A big and tragic climax, highlighted by a fanfare transfigured from the first movement leads to the resigned and quiet coda. *—Steven Coburn*

Recommended:

- ○ **Mahler: Symphony 9** / Karajan (cond.), Berlin PO / DG 439024

- ○ **Mahler: Symphony 9** / Walter (cond.), Columbia SO / Sony 64452
- ○ **Mahler: Symphony 9; Wagner: Siegfried Idyll; Strauss: Metamorphosen** / Klemperer (cond.), New Philharmonia / 1999 / EMI 67039
- ○ **Mahler: Symphony 9** / Barbirolli (cond.), Berlin PO / 2002 / EMI 67926
- ○ **Mahler: Symphony 9** / Abbado (cond.), Berlin PO / DG 471624

Symphony No. 10 in F sharp minor (1910)

Mahler left a substantially complete first movement of his tenth symphony, marked Adagio and published a few years after his death. It is a meditative, tragic movement, rising to a screamingly dissonant chord pierced by a high trumpet note. Mahler died after sketching out the rest. Musicologist Deryck Cooke discovered around 1960 that the composer had written at least a melodic line from the beginning of the second movement to the end, sometimes with detailed indications of instrumentation and harmony, sometimes with less information, sometimes with nothing but the melodic line. He used this sketch to produce a "performing version" in which to Mahler's material he added, where needed, countermelodies, harmonies, and orchestration. Later Cooke redid his completion, using a larger orchestra. The interior of the symphony comprises two scherzos divided by a movement called "Purgatorio," based on the accompaniment to one of his early *Wunderhorn* songs. The first scherzo is grotesque, the second more dramatic, with a great deal of good humor. The fourth movement ends with a muffled bass drum stroke, an effect Mahler observed at a New York City fireman's funeral procession. The final movement is a struggle movement, faster in tempo, not yielding easy answers, and reprising the screaming chord of the first movement. Is this completed version valid? Many conductors, including arch-Mahlerite Leonard Bernstein, did not think so. This writer accepts it as fascinating listening which is never less than at least a good imitation of Mahler, and frequently coming close to the genuine article. *—Joseph Stevenson*

Recommended:

- ○ **Mahler: Symphony 10** / Slatkin (cond.), St. Louis SO / 1995 / RCA Victor 68190
- ○ **Mahler: Symphony 10** / Rattle (cond.), Berlin PO / 2000 / EMI 56972
- ○ **Mahler: Symphony 10; Walton: Partita for Orchestra; Stravinsky: Firebird Suite** / Szell (cond.), Cleveland Orch. / 2001 / Sony 89415
- ○ **Mahler: Symphony 10** / Lopez-Cobos (cond.), Cincinnati SO / 2000 / Telarc 80565

VOCAL

Kindertotenlieder (1901–1904)

The heartbreaking poems that Mahler used here were written by Friedrich Rückert out of grief after the loss of his own two children. Although one of Mahler's own daughters died three years after their completion, it is absurd to make any connection. The songs were more likely set in memory of Mahler's beloved younger brother (lost in childhood), who shared the same name as Rückert's son—Ernst.

These songs, unconditionally specified as a set to be performed together, are a far cry from the *Wunderhorn* songs of the previous decade. In anticipation of his later style, Mahler reduced the orchestral texture to thin, solo, contrapuntal lines, only rarely combining for dynamic effect. The voice part is no longer the scalar and triadic folk-style, but now has become part of the contrapuntal fabric. The range of emotion is extreme, as before, but now it is distilled, becoming all the more poignant and effective. The entire cycle is almost unremitting in its anguish and darkness, relieved only twice by way of consolation.

"Nun will die Sonn' so hell aufgeh'n" (Now Will the Sun Rise as Brightly). This deeply moving and bleak song tells of a sunrise that can no longer bring comfort. The barren and chromatic lines perfectly capture stunned grief, the interplay between minor and major offers only irony.

"Nun seh'ich wohl, warum so dunkle Flammen" (Now I See Well Why Such Dark Flames). Here, the grief-stricken father remembers his children's eyes as premonitions of their death. The bitter sadness of the opening is offset by the gentle consolation of the lush accompaniment of the central phrase, only to return to the opening music at the end.

"Wenn dein Mütterlein" (When Your Dear Mother). Set in an ironic imitation of folk song style, the large intervals and repetitive patterns of the vocal line portray the painful memories that habitual actions provoke.

"Oft denk' ich, sie sind nur ausgegangen" (Often I Think They Have Only Gone Out). Mahler uses the subtle interplay between major and minor to illustrate the illusion that the children have only gone out for a walk. The final stanza, set to stunningly beautiful music, offers the consolation that they have gone to another place, where they will one day be reunited with their parents.

"In diesem Wetter, in diesem Braus" (In This Weather, in This Torrent). Here in the final song, the father recalls the storm on the day of the funeral, set to the only fast and aggressive music of the set. This turbulence gives way in the final stanza to the realization that the children have found rest, set to the only really gentle music in the entire cycle. *—Steven Coburn*

Recommended:

- ○ **Mahler Lieder: Des Knaben Wunderhorn** / Kempe (cond.), Fischer-Dieskau, Berlin PO / 2001 / EMI 67557
- ○ **Mahler: Symphony 9; Kindertotenlieder; Rückert-Lieder** / Karajan (cond.), Ludwig, Berlin PO / DG 453040
- ○ **Mahler: Lieder eines fahrenden Gesellen; Kindertotenlieder; Rückert-Lieder** / Bohm (cond.), Fischer-Dieskau, Berlin PO / 2000 / DG 463516
- ○ **Mahler: Kindertotenlieder; Mendelssohn: Songs; etc.** / Walter (cond.), Ferrier, Vienna PO / 1998 / EMI 66963

Lieder aus Des Knaben Wunderhorn (1892–1898)

This collection of ten songs is the culmination of Mahler's many settings from *Das Knaben Wunderhorn* (The Young Boy's Magic Horn), a collection of German Folk Poetry. They are usually performed as a set, often also including the two later Wunderhorn songs, "Revelge" (Reveille) and "Der Tambourg'sell" (The Drummer Boy), since their poetic origin and performance requirements are so similar. There is no cyclical connection or sequence to the songs—they stand alone, each having its own unique affect, scoring, and conception. Representing Mahler's mature style, the songs cover a vast range of moods and topics, from grim and ironic tragedy to fairy tales. Unlike his *Wunderhorn* settings for voice with piano, these are truly symphonic in scope and technique, and the composer eventually expanded several of them into symphonic movements.

"Der schildwache Nachtlied" (The Sentry's Night-song). A sentry is killed on duty while he is distracted by dreams of his sweetheart. Mahler casts the story as a ghostly dialog between the sentry and his girl, alternating between military drums and fanfares and sustained melodic passages.

"Verlor'ne Müh" (Wasted Effort). A young girl unsuccessfully attempts to seduce a boy in this charming and witty dialog. It is set as a Ländler and often sung as a duet.

"Trost im Unglück" (Solace in Sorrow). Another humorous and lively dialog between two lovers, this one is more raucous and full of military orchestral effects. It is usually sung as a duet.

"Wer hat dies Liedlien erdacht?" (Who Made Up This Little Song?). This is yet another comic love song, with the protagonist pining away for his love. The shortest and simplest of these songs, it is a Ländler with a yodeling vocal line always doubled in the orchestra.

"Das irdische Leben" (Earthly Life). Here Mahler depicts a starving child who waits in vain for the grain to be harvested and milled. Cast as a chilling dialog between child and mother, the cruel inevitability of death is portrayed in the perpetual motion of the orchestra.

"Des Antonius von Padua Fischpredigt" (Antony of Padua's Sermon to the Fish). This is a parody on the unchanging nature of human behavior. Mahler here uses perpetual motion in the orchestra to illustrate the purposeless busyness of life.

"Rheinlegendchen" (Rhine Legend). Here is another charming Ländler, in this case telling a fairy-tale about a golden ring tossed into the Rhine.

"Lied des Verfolgten im Turm" (Song of the Prisoner in the Tower). A political prisoner sings of freedom, while his lover, outside the prison, mourns him in contrasting lyrical passages.

"Wo die schönen Trompeten blasen" (Where the Beautiful Trumpets are Blowing). Mahler again used contrasting materials in this touching song about a dead soldier's ghost visiting his beloved. Muted and hushed fanfares alternate with a gentle Ländler depicting the soldier and the girl, respectively.

"Lob des hohen Verstandes" (In Praise of Lofty Intellect). This is an absurd and comical song in which a donkey judges the singing of two birds. In spite of its humor, it is a biting satire of human self-importance. *—Steven Coburn*

Recommended:

- ○ **Mahler: Des Knaben Wunderhorn** / Abbado (cond.), Quasthoff, Berlin PO / DG 459646
- ○ **Mahler: Lieder eines fahrenden Gesellen; Kindertotenlieder; 5 Lieder** / Klemperer (cond.), Ludwig, London PO / 2001 / EMI 74738
- ○ **Mahler: Symphony 9/; Wunderhorn-Lieder** / Haitink (cond.), Norman, Shirley-Quirk, Concertgebouw / 2001 / Philips 464714
- ○ **Mahler: Des Knaben Wunderhorn** / Szell (cond.), Schwarzkopf, Fischer-Dieskau, London SO / 2000 / Angel 67256

Lieder eines fahrenden Gesellen, song cycle (1883–1885)

This is Mahler's first completely mature work. It is also his first full-fledged orchestral song cycle, a genre Mahler was eventually to bring to its height. Unlike its two predecessors, Berlioz's *Nuits d'été* (Summer Nights) and Wagner's *Wesendonck-Lieder* (Wesendonck Songs), Mahler's cycle was intended from the beginning as orchestral. Despite the fact that it was first sketched with piano and published this way as an alternative, the orchestral version is clearly superior. The texts are all by Mahler, although they were inspired by the collection of German folk poetry entitled *Das Knaben Wunderhorn* (The Young Boy's Magic Horn); they depict a "Spring Journey" of a young man who has lost his love to a rival. Stylistically, all the elements of Mahler's early work are present: folklike melodies, the invocation of nature through bird calls and open textures, an intensely dramatic and dark Allegro, and a grim military march. Also present is Mahler's lifelong juxtaposition of the love of life and nature with despair, emptiness, and death. Anticipating his later harmonic complexities, none of these songs end in the same key as they began—a procedure called "progressive tonality."

In "Wenn mein Schatz Hochzeit macht" (When My Sweetheart Has Her Wedding), the protagonist mourns the loss of his love to a rival and attempts to find solace in nature. The first part, in which the lover mourns, is written in a simple and moving folk-Slavic style. This gives way in a central, faster section to the invocation of nature through imitation bird calls, always incorporated into the musical fabric of the accompaniment. A return to the opening mournful music ends the song bleakly.

In "Ging heut' morgens übers Feld" (I Went Out This Morning Through the Fields), the protagonist sets out on a cheerful walk in the country, only to eventually remind himself of his lost love. This is also in a folkish style, with scale-derived melodies and hints of Austrian yodeling. The accompaniment begins with simple open textures, only to give way to a flowing and contrapuntally rich texture. Towards the end, the almost ecstatic quality of much of the song gives way to a wistful melancholy.

"Ich hab' ein glühend Messer" (I Have a Glowing Knife) describes the metaphorical knife the sweetheart plunged into the lover's breast with her betrayal. In what would become Mahler's typical diabolical style, the song features muted trumpets, tremolo strings, and snarling brass. The tortured and aggressive quality of the music perfectly depicts the lover's angst.

in "Die zwei blauen Augen" (The Two Blue Eyes), finally, the protagonist goes out in the night to find peace under the linden tree (a durable Romantic metaphor for death), to the accompaniment of a funeral march the likes of which only Mahler could compose. This march eventually fades into a more folklike style, but it remains colored by its original harmonies. A poignant and grim return to a single repeated phrase of the march concludes the song. *—Steven Coburn*

Recommended:

- ○ **Mahler Lieder** / Furtwängler (cond.), Fischer-Dieskau, London PO / 2001 / EMI 67557
- ○ **Mahler & Zemlinsky: Lieder** / Gardiner (cond.), Otter, NDRSO / DG 439928
- ○ **Mahler: Lieder** / Fischer-Dieskau, Bernstein (piano) / 1991 / Sony 47170
- ○ **Mahler: Lieder** / Kubelik (cond.), Fischer-Dieskau, Bavarian RSO / 2000 / DG 463516
- ○ **Mahler: Lieder** / Bernstein (cond.), Hampson, Vienna PO / DG 431682

Rückert Lieder (1901–1902)

These five songs were published together with "Revelge" and "Der Tambourg'sell" as *Seven Last Songs*, and were not intended as a cycle. This is illustrated by the lack of connection between the songs and by the different combinations of instruments. Although often performed together, there is no particular order. Mahler conceived all but one of these songs for orchestral accompaniment; he wrote "Liebst du um Schönheit" for piano accompaniment. Unlike Mahler's earlier "Wunderhorn" songs, these songs are, with one exception, completely in the lyrical lied style. The folk song element of Mahler's earlier songs is entirely absent.

"Blicke mir nicht in die Lieder," scored for single winds, horn, harp, and strings without basses, is a somewhat ephemeral setting of a maiden's presumed modesty. The flowing accompaniment and the ingenuous vocal line create the light mood and the playful orchestral ending reflects the maiden's feigned innocence.

"Ich atmet' einen linden Duft" uses in addition to the winds, three horns, harp, celesta, violins, and violas. It is a delicate and evocative setting of a summertime scene. The vocal line moves in lyrical duet with various woodwind solos over an undulating string accompaniment. Unfortunately the play on the words "Lind" (delicate) and "Linde" (lime-tree), which is the point of the poem, is lost in translation. The arpeggios of the celesta illustrate the piquancy of the lime-tree's scent in the introduction and coda.

"Ich bin der Welt abhanden gekommen" is surely Mahler's finest song. The first of Mahler's compositions based on a "world-weary" theme (*Das Lied von der Erde* being the largest example), this song is rich in lush, late-Romantic harmonies and beautiful melodic lines. The mournful violin solo between the second and third verses is reminiscent of parts of the *Kindertotenlieder* composed at about the same time. In spite of this and other moments of anguish, the song is generally imbued with a mood of quiet acceptance and resignation. The scoring consists of double woodwinds without flutes and with English horn, two horns, harp, and full strings.

The one song that is not a lyrical lied is "Um Mitternacht." The epic and philosophical text of this song is reflected in the rather austere, hymn-like setting for full winds, brass, timpani, harp, and piano. As the singer contemplates human destiny, the orchestra accompanies with broadly moving contrapuntal lines. A grand brass chorale underlines the casting of mankind's fate into God's hands for the climactic ending. Less a song, and more a symphonic ode, "Um Mitternacht" seems almost too big for a solo vocal setting. The last verse in particular is reminiscent of Mahler's great choral/orchestral symphonies.

In a completely different vein is "Liebst du um Schönheit." Originally conceived with only piano accompaniment, this is an intimate and beautiful love song composed by Mahler specifically for his wife, Alma. The vocal line is simple, yet highly expressive, and the accompaniment is subtle and unobtrusive. The standard orchestration by Max Puttmann is appropriately simple, if not entirely characteristic. *—Steven Coburn*

Recommended:

- ○ **Mahler Lieder** / Fischer-Dieskau, Barenboim (piano) / 2001 / EMI 67557
- ○ **Mahler & Zemlinsky: Lieder** / Gardiner (cond.), Otter, NDRSO / DG 439928
- ○ **Mahler: Symphony 9; Kindertotenlieder; Rückert-Lieder** / Karajan (cond.), Ludwig, Berlin PO / DG 453040
- ○ **Mahler: Lieder** / Bohm (cond.), Fischer-Dieskau, Berlin PO / 2000 / DG 463516
- ○ **Mahler: Lieder** / Barbirolli (cond.), Baker, New Philharmonia / 1999 / EMI 66996

CHORAL

Das klagende Lied, cantata (1878–1880; revised 1892)

Despite the current enthusiasm for Mahler, this is his least-known large-scale work. The composer identified it his Op. 1; but, though he commenced his composition studies aged eighteen, Mahler was 41 before it was premiered in 1901, and even then only the first part, "Waldmärchen" (a woodland legend) was played. Originally called "Märchen in drei Abteilungen" (legend in three parts), the second and third sections were revised in 1893, and in 1898 Mahler prepared a retitled final version, substantially rewritten. This is the one usually performed, though some conductors tend to omit the second part.

Das klagende Lied is scored for soprano, alto and tenor soloists, choir, and orchestra. Though it cannot be said to equal Mahler's better-known works, it comes close in many ways to the song cycle *Des Knaben Wunderhorn*, and bears unmistakable hallmarks of the mature composer. It certainly deserves a better fate than a tenuous survival as a Mahler curiosity.

The grim tale of posthumous revenge appears in various guises elsewhere in central European folklore (Dvořák's symphonic poem *The Wood Dove* has a somewhat similar source). The poem, based on a retelling of the story by Ludwig Bechstein, is by Mahler himself. The original version of "Waldmärchen" told the story of two brothers who go in search of a forest flower, the reward for finding it being the hand of the queen. The elder brother murders the younger who finds a red flower "as beautiful as the queen."

Mahler later replaced this with a more elaborate reworking of the story. A minstrel passing through a wood finds a bone from which he fashions a flute. When he plays it, he hears a melancholy song in which a dead knight accuses his brother of murdering him in order to marry "a little flower of beautiful hue." The minstrel wanders far and wide and eventually arrives at a castle where the elder brother is celebrating his marriage to the queen. The guilty king snatches the flute from the minstrel and puts it to his lips, only to hear his brother's voice accusing him of his violent death. The queen sinks to the ground and the wedding feast ends in chaos.

The work has much of the power and inventiveness of Mahler's better-known scores, including some striking resemblances to parts of the Fourth Symphony; yet comparisons are not easy. It is operatic in style and, while identifiably "Mahlerian" from the outset, Wagner's influence is strong, especially in the choral and orchestral writing. Some of the finest passages are those in the first part, where the atmosphere of fairy tale is magically conveyed.

It has been suggested that the reason the composer returned obsessively to the work was a sense of guilt following the suicide of his younger brother, Ernst, in 1874, but this writer can detect no such autobiographical clues. *—Roy Brewer*

Recommended:

- ○ **Mahler: Das klagende Lied** / Hickox (cond.), Blochwitz, Finnie, Rodgers, Hayward, Bournemouth Sinfonietta / 1994 / Chandos 9247
- ○ **Mahler: Das klagende Lied** / Tilson Thomas (cond.), George, Leiferkus, Moser, DeYoung, San Francisco SO / 1997 / RCA 902668599

Mischa Maisky

b. Jan. 10, 1948, Riga, Latvia

Cellist

Born in 1948 in Riga, the capital of then Soviet (and now independent) Latvia, Mischa Maisky started studying the cello at the age of eight. An immensely talented student, he entered the Riga Conservatory. Discouraged by the rigid curriculum, however, he moved to Leningrad (now St. Petersburg) in 1965. That year, he not only won the Soviet Union's national cello competition, but also had an acclaimed debut with the Leningrad Philharmonic. In 1966, Maisky won a prize at the International Tchaikovsky Competition in Moscow. One of the jurors for the Tchaikovsky Competition was the great cellist Mstislav Rostropovich, who invited

Maisky to study with him at the Moscow Conservatory. Maisky developed rapidly under Rostropovich's tutelage, launching a concert career in the Soviet Union. Maisky's career was threatened, however, when his sister decided to emigrate to Israel. As a relative of a person who wanted to leave the country, Maisky was targeted for harassment by the government. When he bought a tape recorder on the black market, he was arrested and sentenced to 18 months in a labor camp. After his release, Maisky was called to do his military service. Since an exemption given to developing artists was out of the question, he entered a mental hospital to avoid military service. Finally, the Soviet authorities allowed him to emigrate with the stipulation that he pay back the entire cost of his education. The Mayor of Jerusalem, Teddy Kollek, made headlines by getting a rich American to pay Maisky's alleged debt to the U.S.S.R. In 1972, Maisky left for Jerusalem. Zubin Mehta, conductor of the Israel Philharmonic Orchestra, subsequently engaged Maisky to participate in the orchestra's upcoming American tour. The following year, Maisky won the Gaspar Cassadò International Cello Competition in Florence, also making his Carnegie Hall debut with the Pittsburgh Symphony Orchestra conducted by William Steinberg. After the concert, an anonymous fan gave Maisky an instrument made by the eighteenth century Venetian master Domenico Montagnana. Maisky has played that cello ever since. Despite his extraordinary success as a performing artist, Maisky still felt the need to study with a more experienced musician. Consequently, in 1974, he approached the celebrated Russian cellist Gregor Piatigorsky, who lived in Los Angeles, and became Piatigorsky's last student. Maisky is thus the only cellist to have studied with both Rostropovich and Piatigorsky. Maisky made his London debut in 1976 in a series of orchestral concerts, beginning with the Royal Philharmonic Orchestra. His London recital debut was in 1977. His partner then was pianist Radu Lupu, who had accompanied him in a Moscow recital nearly a decade earlier. A powerful and polished soloist, Maisky is also known as an artist who gladly shares the podium with colleagues. For example, commenting on his London recital with Lupu, *The London Daily Telegraph* praised the performers' "finely tempered and mutually responsive" phrasing. In 1995, after an absence of 23 years, Maisky played in Moscow. In great demand as a chamber player, Maisky has performed with a number of extraordinary musicians, including Vladimir Ashkenazy, Gidon Kremer, Peter Serkin, and Martha Argerich. Maisky and Argerich recorded Bach's *Sonatas for viola da gamba and harpsichord* (played on their modern equivalents, cello and piano), winning the Record Academy Prize of Tokyo and the French Grand Prix du Disque. Maisky also won these prizes for his performance of the Bach *Six suites for solo cello.* Acclaimed for his renditions of concertos by Haydn and Schumann, Maisky is the only cellist to have received a Deutsche Grammophon offer to record Bach's complete works for the cello. *—AMG*

Recommended:

- ○ **Franck, Debussy: Cello Sonatas** / Maisky, Argerich (piano) / EMI 63577
- ○ **Schumann: Cello Concerto, etc.** / Maisky, Argerich, Orpheus Chamber Orchestra / 2000 / DG 469524
- ○ **Après un rêve** / Maisky, Hovora (piano) / 1999 / DG 457657
- ○ **Maisky & Argerich Live in Japan** / Maisky, Argerich (piano) / 2001 / DG 471346

Gian Francesco Malipiero

b. Mar. 18, 1882, Venice, Italy, **d.** Aug. 1, 1973, Treviso, Italy
Composer: Orchestral

Extremely prolific, highly uneven, and tremendously influential, Gian Francesco Malipiero came to be regarded—even by other Italian composers—as the most original musical mind of his day and place. His music fused modern techniques with the stylistic qualities of early Italian music.

In his youth Malipiero briefly enrolled as a violin student at the Vienna Conservatory, and also studied in Venice and Bologna (where he obtained a diploma in composition from the G.B. Martini Music School in 1904). In 1913 he traveled to Paris, where he was influenced by French Impressionism, with its fondness for enriching harmonies with sixths, ninths, and elevenths. He was also transformed by attending the premiere of Stravinsky's *Rite of Spring*, which so caused him to rethink his aesthetics that he suppressed all the music he'd written to that time. Yet, something of a paleo-nationalist, Malipiero found even greater inspiration in Italian Baroque polyphony, which he had discovered on his own and begun transcribing from library manuscripts as early as 1902. His academic interests also led him to accept intermittent teaching and administrative appointments. In 1921 he became professor of composition at the Parma Conservatory for two years. Later he was director of the Instituto Musicale Pollini at Padua, and in 1939 he became director of the Liceo Benedetto Marcello in Venice.

Malipiero initially produced works that, although often harmonically dense and oddly structured, reflect the spirit of seventeenth and eighteenth century Venetian music. His compositions are characteristically contrapuntal, with some dissonance resulting from the counterpoint. What is usually judged to be his best music bases its tonality on free use of diatonic material, although Malipiero employed chromaticism more aggressively in his old age.

Malipiero's principal works, among the hundreds he churned out during his long career, include the operas *L'orfeide* (1918–22) and *Venere prigioniera* (Captive Venus, 1957); the cantata or "mystery" *San Francesco d'Assisi* (1922); the oratorio *La Passione* (1935); and about a dozen free-form symphonies, only seven of them numbered. Among his other orchestral works are *Pause del silenzio* (1917), a response to World War I, which deeply traumatized him even though he was a noncombatant; *Impressioni dal vero* (Impression of Truth, 1910–22); and *Fantasie di ogni giorni* (Fantasy of Every Day, 1954). His chamber works include seven string quartets, of which the first, *Rispetti e strambotti* (Regards and Folderol, 1920), has circulated more widely than any of his other compositions.

Much of this work is characterized by varying degrees of Expressionism, dissonance, and modality. Malipiero's most original and cohesive period was 1917–29, although certain pieces from his predominantly diatonic middle period, such as the *First Violin Concerto* (1932), have found greater audience favor, using as they do a rather aimless lyricism that replaced the more focused agony of his earlier work. His compositions from the late 1940s on became more chromatic, subdued, and meandering. Malipiero also made important contributions to musical scholarship. He edited the complete works of Monteverdi, a widely criticized yet pioneering endeavor. He also collaborated on a collected edition of the works of Vivaldi; edited works of Corelli, Frescobaldi, and others; and wrote many articles for scholarly journals. *—James Reel*

Overview of Works (1904–1971)

While Malipiero's works were strongly influenced by the seminal composers of his day, as well as earlier composers, especially Monteverdi and Vivaldi, he was nonetheless one of the most creative musical thinkers of the early twentieth century, combining external influences and his own innovations to produce striking and thought-provoking compositions. While most of his compositions are in direct rebellion against and rejection of nineteenth century Romanticism, he frequently hearkened back to early music, particularly Monteverdi, whom he greatly admired (and whose work he helped bring back to the forefront of musical attention), and plainsong. He was thoroughly modernistic in his avoidance of traditional themes and thematic buildup, showing the influence of both the meditative Debussy and the more brash Stravinsky, to name just the most prominent. Aside from his creativity within individual works, his musical output spans nearly every form, such as piano works, ballets, songs, symphonies, operas, cantatas, and chamber works. While he was not as thorough about the destruction of his early works as he declared, they are not as individualistic and experimental as he later became; while striking and effective, his *Poemetti lunari*, for example, clearly show the influence of Debussy's piano works in their impressionistic colorations and avoidance of traditional thematic structures. As for most European composers, World War I not only disrupted his career but traumatized his life, and the sense of agitation and stark tragedy are reflected in his compositions from around this time. His 1918–19 opera-ballet *Pantea* uses a dancer for the protagonist and a backstage chorus and soloist whose music is almost wordless to suggest a grief that has gone beyond normal articulation or operatic expression. In contrast, however, he paid homage to Monteverdi in his 1920 opera *San Francesco d'Assisi*, which is marked at times by a formal directness of expression. *San Francesco* marks a change in his approach and style, one in which he returned more and more frequently to early music for inspiration. He broke away from formal stage structures, as well, in such works as his 1929 *Torneo notturno*, a series of brief operas that also combine song and silent expression. (Compare these to Puccini's far-more traditional *Trittico*, from roughly the same time period.) He often juxtaposed brief fragments of elaborate, Renaissance-Baroque type polyphony and counterpoint with overtly modern devices and symbolism and wrote direct tributes to earlier composers, such as his 1920 piano *Omaggio a Claude Debussy* and 1932 *Omaggio a Bach*. *—Ann Feeney*

Recommended:

- ○ **Malipiero: String Quartets** / SQ of Venice / 1996 / Dynamic 168/1-2
- ○ **Malipiero: L'Orféide** / Scherchen (cond.), Olivero, Maggio Musicale Fiorentino Orch. & Choir / 1996 / Tahra 897
- ○ **Malipiero: Orchestral Music** / Maag (cond.), Veneto PO / 2001 / Naxos 555515
- ○ **Malipiero: I Capricci di Callot** / Marschik (cond.), Sabrowski, Kjellevold, Kiel PO / CPO 999830
- ○ **Malipiero: I Dialoghi** / Molinini (cond.), Naviglio, Balducci, Braconi, Cappelluti, New Philharmonia / 2002 / Stradivarius 33620
- ○ **Malipiero: Endecatode** / Cardi (cond.), Vernizzi, Chiara, Caianiello, Freon Ens. / 2003 / Stradivarius 33664
- ○ **Malipiero: Grottesco; Cello Concerto; Dialogo 1; Ricercari** / Garbarino (cond.), Palm, Orch. del Festival di Villa Marigola / Nuova Era 6998
- ○ **Malipiero: Piano Music** / Terekiev / Nuova Era 7150

ORCHESTRAL

Sinfonias Nos. 1–11 (1933–1969)

Malipiero was one of the first Italians in over a century to produce significant symphonic music, and his success in the genre brought him great respect from his contemporaries, including Luigi Dallapiccola, who called him "the greatest Italian composer since Verdi." His first symphony, *"in quattro tempi come le quattro stagoni"* (1933), was written at the end of his acclaimed "vintage years" of 1917–29; symphonies would represent his most significant works for the next 20 years. Malipiero stated that the Italian symphony is a free kind of poem; several sections follow one another capriciously only obeying those mysterious laws that instinct recognizes," and his works illustrating this, departing from the Austro-German formal tradition. Without purposeful tonal and thematic processes to move the music forward, his work depended upon strength of well-developed musical imagery. Except for No. 3 *"delle campe"* (1945), his early symphonies *No. 2 "elegiaca"* (1936), *No. 4 "in memoriam"* (1946), *No. 5 "concertante, in eco"* (1947), *No. 6 "degli archi"* (1947), and *No. 7 "delle canzoni"* (1948)} all exhibit this "Italian" character. The *Fifth* features two pianos so prominently in the orchestra that it almost becomes a double concerto.

Sixteen years elapsed between the composition of Malipiero's seventh and eighth symponies; this was motivated by the composer's fear of the number seven, and the need to "escape from the fascination of the orchestra." The development of his style in the interim is clear. His works of the 1930s and 1940s (No. 1–7), were frequently modal and diatonic while his later works moved toward atonality with greater chromaticism and sharper dissonance; these are: *No. 8 "Symphonia brevis"* (1964), *No. 9 "dell'achime"* (1966), and *No. 10 "atropo"* (1967). His last symphony was *No. 11, "delle cornamuse"* (1969). The subtitle *"delle cornamuse"* ("of the bagpipes") refers to the oboe, a cor anglais, and bassoon, which created a droning bagpipe-like sonority. *—Meredith Murphy*

Recommended:

○ **Malipiero: Symphonies 5, 6, 8 & 11** / Almeida (cond.), Moscow State SO / 1994 / Marco Polo 223696

Francesco Onofrio Manfredini

b. Jun. 22, 1684, Pistoia, Italy, **d.** Oct. 6, 1762, Pistoia, Italy

Composer: Concerto

Francesco Onofrio Manfredini was born during a particularly fertile period for the production of great composers. Born within 16 months of him were Rameau, Walther, Handel, Johann Sebastian Bach, and Domenico Scarlatti. Against the glare of these first-magnitude stars (and the not much older Telemann and Vivaldi), the lesser but noteworthy talent of Manfredini is easy to overlook.

His father was a trombonist in the parish church of Pistoia. He was sent to Bologna as a teenager to study violin with Giuseppe Torelli and counterpoint with Perti. In 1700, the 16-year-old Manfredini went to Ferrara to take a job as first violinist in the Church of the Holy Spirit. In 1704, the orchestra of Bologna's church of San Petronio was reconstituted. Since its dissolution was the reason Manfredini had left Bologna in the first place, he returned and joined it, also becoming a member of the Accademia Filarmonica. He published a set of concerti in 1704.

In 1707, as Manfredini was preparing to visit or move to Venice, a friend named Aldrovandini, with the intent of traveling to Venice with him, accidentally drowned on his way to joining Manfredini. It's not clear whether Manfredini went ahead with his planned trip, nor is much known about Manfredini's doings for the next 20 years. There is speculation that he joined the court of Prince Antoine I of Monaco. During these years, he published additional sets of incidental music, a group of 12 *Sinfonie da chiesa*, and 12 concerti. He also wrote an oratorio, *Tommaso Moro*. In 1724, he returned to Pistoia to become *maestro di cappella* of St. Philip's Cathedral there. Shortly afterwards, he published four oratorios, presumably all written in the years 1725–28. He remained in that post until his death 35 years later.

Manfredini was not a prolific composer, or if he was, an undue amount of his work has been lost, but there are 43 published instrumental works, nine oratorios (music lost), and a couple of unpublished works. Although he lacks a distinctive personal "sound," his instrumental music is attractive, with the group of six posthumous sonatas (London, 1764) being the best representation of his talents. Unfortunately for his reputation, he became something of a symbol for the mediocre, run-of-the-mill Baroque composer in the 1970s when musicologist H.C. Robbins Landon wrote an article, "A Pox on Manfredini," intended to decry the record companies' trend of recording the "complete music" of Baroque composers, no matter how unimportant. While Landon's main point was not ill-taken, he did unnecessarily disparage Manfredini's music. *—Joseph Stevenson*

CONCERTO

12 Concerti Grossi, Op. 3 (before 1718)

The most famous concerto grosso from Francesco Manfredini's Op. 3 set of 12 is undoubtedly the last one, a Christmas concerto subtitled "Pastorale per il Santissimo Natale." This is inarguably a lovely concerto, featuring melodies imbued with a contemplative rapture, skillful interweaving of the two solo violins, and a suitably joyous final movement with a surprising, hushed ending. It is a shame, however, that the attention paid to this concerto has obscured the other 11, which make for equally pleasant and intriguing listening, even if they do not have the benefit of Yuletide associations. The whole set was published in 1718, with a dedication to Prince Antoine I of Monaco; Manfredini may have been serving at his court as maestro di cappella (chief musician). He had gone there from Bologna, where he had learned composition from Giuseppe Torelli and Giacomo Antonio Perti. His concerti reflect these lessons: the structure of these compositions based on the trio sonata form and the distribution of music to the players generally reserves the virtuoso passages for the soloists while the full orchestra intersperses brief comments. The first four concerti are ripieno concerti, for orchestra alone, while the second and third groups of four feature one and two violin soloists, respectively. Besides having no soloists, the ripieno concerti also differ from the other concerti in that (except in the third) they have no slow movements as such, just slow, modulatory links between fast movements. Thus, these concerti often feel like miniature suites, an impression reinforced by their profusion of dance finales. The second concerto, for example, feels quite vibrant despite its A minor key signature, with buoyant rhythms, spirited melodies, and tempi that vary from allegro to presto. The violin parts of the solo concerti often reflect Manfredini's study of his illustrious Venetian contemporary Antonio Vivaldi. While Manfredini never spotlights the violin quite as much as Vivaldi, he certainly lets the violin take over movements, as in the slow movement of the eighth concerto, which unexpectedly jumps to a Presto tempo midway through and then closes with a slow, gripping violin soliloquy. The two-violin concerti tend to be the longest and most innovative, as in the 11th concerto. The first movement of this C minor concerto features a grim eighth note motif in the orchestra that the soloists seem to be trying to escape by constant movement and which shapes the orchestral contribution throughout. The two violins soar and accompany one another in the reflective, luminous Adagio that follows; a Phrygian cadence leads into a vigorous jig, introduced by the two violins, which closes the concerto. Manfredini's *12 Concerti Grossi*, Op. 3 are pleasingly varied and unfailingly fluent, and make good listening for anyone wanting to explore a byway of Baroque music. *—Andrew Lindemann Malone*

Andrew Manze

b. Jan. 14, 1965, Beckenham, England

Violinist

Andrew Manze has emerged as one of the leading violinists in the early music movement. He specializes in music from between 1610 and 1830. His education began at Cambridge, where he studied Classics. He then moved on to music studies at the Royal Academy of Music in London and at the Royal Conservatory in The Hague, studying with both Simon Standage and Marie Leonhardt. Manze then joined the Amsterdam Baroque Orchestra, remaining there until 1993. The following year he began collaborating with harpsichordist Richard Egarr. One of their major releases presented a 1712 collection of violin sonatas by the French composer Jean-Féry Rebel. Meanwhile, Manze formed the group Romanesca, with harpsichordist John Tell and lutenist Nigel North; the trio specialized in music of the seventeenth century. In 1996 Manze was appointed associate director and concertmaster of the London-based Baroque group The Academy of Ancient Music. In the 2003–2004 season, he became music director of The English Concert.

Manze is well-known in Britain for his broadcast work. He has become a popular "presenter" on BBC radio, and made his debut with the *BBC Promenade Concert* in 1998. That concert was televised nationally, with Manze playing concertos by Pergolesi, Bach, Vivaldi, and Mozart, and introducing the public to the enthusiasm and directness of the new ways of performing Baroque and Classic music.

Recording for the French Harmonia Mundi label, Manze won Gramophone, Edison, and Cannes Classical awards for his recording with Romanesca of Biber's flashy and mystical violin sonatas. His playing of Vivaldi's newly discovered "Manchester" sonatas won the *Premio Internazionale del Disco Vivaldi Antica Italiana*. His album *Phantasticus* won the Cannes Classical Award and a Diapason D'Or. The later award was also given to his recording of Schmelzer's violin sonatas. Manze was named the 1998 Classical Artist of the Year.

Manze is in demand as an expert in Baroque music interpretation. He serves as a performance advisor and director for the European Community Baroque Orchestra, gives master classes, and has been visiting professor at the Royal College of Music in London. He is also a busy soloist on the international concert scene, appearing in one season with the Zurich Chamber Orchestra, the Swedish Chamber Orchestra, the Orchestra of the Age of Enlightenment, the Canadian early music group Tafelmusik, and the Berlin Philharmonic.

He is known for his freedom of ornamentation, bringing an improvisatory excitement to his concerts. Manze lives with his wife (also a violinist) in England's Cotswolds region. *—Joseph Stevenson*

Recommended:

○ **Andrew Manze Portrait** / Manze, Egarr, Linden, Balding, Academy of Ancient Music (UK), Romanesca / 2000 / HM 2907278

○ **Biber: Violin Sonatas** / Manze, Romanesca, North, Toll / 2002 / HM 2907344/45

○ **Telemann: 12 Fantasias for Violin Solo; Gulliver Suite for 2 Violins** / Manze, Balding / 1995 / HM Franc 907137

○ **Vivaldi: Concert for the Prince of Poland** / Manze (cond.), Academy of Ancient Music (UK) / 2002 / HM 2907230

○ **Bach: Solo & Double Violin Concertos** / Manze, Podger, Academy of Ancient Music (UK) / 1997 / HM 2907155

○ **Handel: Complete Violin Sonatas** / Manze, Egarr / 2001 / HM 2907259

Marin Marais

b. May 31, 1656, Paris, France, **d.** Aug. 15, 1728, Paris, France
Composer: Chamber Music

Marais was the preeminent bass viol player in turn-of-the-seventeenth century France. Although he composed four operas, he is primarily remembered for his some 600 compositions for various combinations of bass viols. These works were in the French tradition of collections of various pieces, rather than the Italian concertos and sonatas. The collections, ranging from seven to 41 pieces each, consist primarily of dances, fantasies, chaconnes, rondeaux, tombeaux, and pièces de caractère. These last are short, colorful works including descriptive titles such as *Les voix humaines* and *Cloche ou carillon.* There is even one work that is meant to describe an operation for the removal of a bladder stone. Marais intended these pieces to be played on any instruments, but they are in fact idiomatically suited for the bass viol and represent the finest collection of pieces for that instrument. Among Marais' numerous other compositions, his *Pieces en trio pour les flûtes, violon, et dessus de viole* (Trios for flute, violin and highest viol) of 1692 was the first published set of trio sonatas in France.

Marais spent his entire life in Paris. Little is known of his childhood other than his having studied with Sainte-Colombe, the most prominent violist and teacher at the time. In 1679, he became the "Regular Violist for the King," a position he held until his retirement in 1725. Marais also studied composition with Lully and subsequently worked with him throughout his career as a violist in his ensemble. Lully probably encouraged Marais to compose his four operas, *Alcide* (1693), *Ariane et Bacchus* (1696), *Alcione* (1706), and *Sémélé* (1709). All four are rather typical five-act tragedies very much in Lully's style, and seemed to have been considerably successful, *Alcione* being staged as late as 1771. It is as the greatest and most important composer for the bass viol, however, that Marais is remembered today. *—Steven Coburn*

Overview of Works (ca. 1685–1725)

One of the greatest of all viol players, Paris-born Marin Marais (1656–1728) represents the culmination of the great school of French performer/composers that included his master Sainte-Colombe. Brilliantly gifted as a performer, he soon gained a post at the court of Louis XIV, where he may have studied under Lully. In 1676, he became a member of the orchestra that performed Lully's operas, thoroughly assimilating the style of his tragédies lyrique. This influence Marais put to effective use in four operas of his own: *Alcide* (1693), composed in collaboration with Lully's son Louis, *Ariane et Bacchus* (1696), *Sémélé* (1709), and, most notably, *Alcyone,* first given at the Paris Opéra in February 1706. *Alcyone,* the only one of Marais' operas to have been revived, reveals him as an even more colorful and imaginative orchestrator than Lully, anticipating the bold strokes of Rameau. The work became especially famous for its dramatic storm scene, and was the subject of a number of revivals during the course of the eighteenth century.

However, it is for his over 500 pièces de violes—collected in five published books—that Marais is justly celebrated. These reveal a meticulous approach to detailing such matters as fingering, bowing, and ornamentation, leaving his work a paradigmatic guide for all viol players. The five books include works for one, two, and three bass viols.

The first, published in 1686 with a dedication to Lully, was the first published by a Frenchman to include a basso continuo part. The remaining four appeared respectively in 1701, 1711, 1717, and 1725. Each book contains pieces that the performer is expected to arrange into suites according to key. While many are in the usual dance idioms that make up instrumental suites from the time, there are also examples of the sorrowfully expressive plainte, tombeaux—written to commemorate a death (those composed as a tribute to Sainte-Colombe [Book 2] and Marais' own son [Book 5] being particularly moving examples)—and the character pieces so popular among French Baroque composers. This group includes evocations of bells (*Cloches ou carillon,* Book 2), a bizarre account of an operation to remove a gallstone complete with spoken commentary (*Le tableau de l'opération de la taille,* Book 5), and *Le Labyrinthe.* The last-named is Marais' longest continuous movement, a superbly constructed rondo describing a metaphysical journey through a labyrinth and the final joy at solving its riddle. More conventionally, there are countless other pieces scattered across the five books that consistently display Marais' elegant refinement, and, above all, ability to exploit the most expressive and eloquent characteristics of the viol. *—Brian Robins*

Recommended:

○ **Marais: Alcione Suites** / Savall (cond.), Le Concert des Nations / 2000 / Astree 9945

○ **Marais: The Suite to Suit Strange Tastes** / Palviainen, Luolajan-Mikkola, Polho, Suihkonen, Battalia Continuo Group / 1997 / Marquis 81207

○ **Marais: Pièces de viole, Book 2** / Savall, Smith, Gallet / 2002 / Astree 9978

○ **Marais: La Gamme** / Medlam (cond.), London Baroque / 2000 / HM 1951105

○ **Marais: Suites for viola da gamba & continuo** / Quintana, Cremonesi / HM 905248

○ **Marais: Pièces de viole** / J. Hantai, P. Hantai, Verzier / 1997 / Virgin 45266

○ **Marais: Viol Music for the Sun King** / Spectre de la Rose / 1995 / Naxos 553081

○ **Marais: Pièces de Viole, Book 5** / Savall, Koopman, Smith / Astree 7708

CHAMBER MUSIC

Le Tableau de l'opération de la taille, for viola da gamba & continuo (1725)

Although clearly a product of the French Baroque, when descriptive and programmatic instrumental pieces were common, Marin Marais' *Tableau de l'opération de la taille* (Picture of the Surgical Operation) from his *Fifth Book* of pieces for the viola da gamba is in a class of its own. Not only does it explicitly depict an operation for the removal of gallstones in all its gruesome details, it appears that Marais meant to have spoken aloud the words which appear in the score describing each stage of the process. Apparently, Marais himself underwent such an operation, and he did not intend for his work to be taken as a joke but rather as a serious and harrowing work of pictorial musical art. With its moans and groans, its sighs and shivers, and its excruciating climax, Marais' *Tableau de l'opération de la taille* is an extremely effective piece of musical theater. *—James Leonard*

Recommended:

○ **Marais: Le Labyrinthe & autre hitoires...** / Pandolfo, Meyerson / 2000 / Glossa 920404

○ **Maris: Pièces de viole, Book 5** / Kuijken, Kohnen, Uemura / Accent 78744

Variations (Couplets) on Les folies d'Espagne, for viola da gamba (or flute) & continuo (1701)

Although immensely popular in his own time, the vast majority of music from Marin Marais dropped from the repertoire soon after his death, and he remained an almost completely unknown figure until the early music revival of the later half of the twentieth century. This precipitous decline had less to do with the range and quality of his music than that he wrote for the viola da gamba, a stringed instrument like the cello, which the violin completely superseded as the standard stringed instrument. The vast majority of Marais' music—over 700 pieces—was written for the gamba, an instrument upon which he was acknowledged to be the supreme master. But of all of those pieces—the joyful, the melancholy, the funny, the militant, the sophisticated, the simple, the abstract, the descriptive, the programmatic, the funeral works, and the celebratory works—only one held its place in the repertoire after Marais' death: *Les folies d'Espagne.* Published as part of Marais' second book of pieces for the gamba published in 1701, *Les folies d'Espagne* is an enormous set of 32 variations on a Spanish dance, familiar to many by the name *La Folia.* The word *folies* in the title refers not to the English word follies—that is, foolishness or silliness—but rather to the highly imaginative and even fantastic approach that the composer took to the Spanish theme. Indeed, *Les folies* is astoundingly imaginative: the variations or couplets have the whole emotional range of Marais' music in them. Equally important, however, is the compositional skill with which Marais creates his variations. From simple but beautiful melodies to extraordinarily difficult virtuoso writing, from tunes with chordal accompaniment to complex counterpoint, from the lowest to the highest points on the gamba's range, Marais' *Les folies d'Espagne* is a tour de force of his abilities as a composer and performer. Oddly, though, *Les folies d'Espagne* retained its place in the repertoire because it also exists in a transcription for flute. Although this arrangement is clearly inferior to the gamba original, it did allow the work to continue to exist in the repertoire for the quarter of a millennium until the early music revival. *—James Leonard*

Recommended:

○ **La Folia** / Savall (cond. & viol), Lislevand, Cocset, Estevan, Behringer, Gonzalez-Campa / 1998 / Alia Vox 9805

○ **Tous les matins du monde** / Savall (cond & viol.), Lislevand, Behringer / Alia Vox 9821

○ **Marais: Pièces de viole, Book 2** / Savall, Smith, Gallet / 2002 / Astree 9978

○ **La Folia** / Purcell Quartet / Hyperion 67035

Alessandro Marcello

b. Aug. 24, 1669, Venice, Italy, **d.** Jun. 19, 1747, Padua, Italy
Composer: Concerto

Much of what is known about Alessandro Marcello comes not from his few compositions, but from his professional career and social activities as a member of Venice's nobility. Both he and his more famous brother Benedetto studied law and were members of the city-state's high council. Alessandro was educated at the Collegio di S. Antonio, then joined the Venetian Arcadian society, the Accademia degli Animosi in 1698, and served the city as a diplomat in the Levant and the Peloponnese in 1700 and 1701. After returning to Venice, he took on a series of judiciary positions while dabbling in a number of creative endeavors. He was responsible for paintings found in the family palaces and parish church and, after joining the literary society, the Accademia della Crusca, published eight books of couplets, *Ozii giovanili*, in 1719. That same year, he was named head of the Accademia degli Animosi, and as such, he did much to expand its collection of musical instruments, many of which are now in Rome's National Museum of Musical Instruments. Marcello's compositional output is small, consisting of not much more than a dozen each of chamber cantatas, violin sonatas, and concertos. Most of his works were published under the pseudonym "Eterio Stinfalico," which is one of the reasons why it wasn't known until the mid-twentieth century that Bach's *Keyboard Concerto in D minor*, BWV 974, was a transcription of Marcello's *Oboe Concerto in D minor*, and even so, both the Bach and the *Oboe Concerto* are still often attributed to Benedetto Marcello. His cantatas dealt primarily with pastoral subjects and contained topical references, and, befitting his station in society, were clearly intended for Venice's and Rome's best singers, including Farinelli, Checchino, Laura and Virginia Predieri, and Benedetto's student, Faustina Bordoni. His instrumental works reflect a knowledge and understanding of the differences in French, Italian, and German music of the time, including choices of instruments for both the solo and continuo parts and use of ornamentation. Of all of his works, what is best known is the Adagio from the *Oboe Concerto*, which has become a staple of wedding music collections. *—Patsy Morita*

Overview of Works (1708–1740)

Alessandro Marcello was one of two (the other is the better-known Benedetto) noble-born Venetian brothers trained by their father and later admitted to the Accademia dell'Arcadia in Rome. Both brothers became able, dilettante composers who, because of their status, published little. Alessandro's best-known work is a fine *Concerto for oboe in D minor* published in 1716 and long ascribed to his brother. It is cast in the usual three movements, an Andante e spiccato that develops from an angular opening; an affective, romantic Adagio; and a final Presto featuring much interplay between soloist and orchestra. That the concerto achieved widespread dissemination in its time is evidenced by the fact that it was one of the Venetian concertos Bach chose to transcribe, in this instance, for harpsichord, BWV 974. The sole set of Alessandro Marcello's extant is a group of six concertos issued under the title of *La cetra* without a date, although it was probably published some time during the 1730s. All cast in three movements, they are specifically intended (according to the title page) for an orchestra consisting of two flutes or oboes, six violins, two violas, two cellos, double bass, bassoon, and harpsichord. Also unusually specific for the period are Marcello's dynamic instructions. Although cast in the standard three-movement form, the concertos neither conform to the typical fast-slow-fast pattern of the Venetian concerto, nor can any of them be described as a concerto for a specific solo instrument, the parts being equally disposed between the principal players. The mood is often turbulent and intense, marking Marcello out as a highly individual composer rather than one who slavishly followed Venetian fashion.

Several cantatas, some elaborately published and some in manuscript, for voice and continuo are not notable for their music qualities. Although written for well-known Italian singers, they rely on pastoral caricatures and particular local and personal references. *—Brian Robins*

Recommended:

- ○ **Marcello: "La Cetra" Concertos** / Standage, Collegium Musicum 90 / 1995 / Chandos 563
- ○ **Marcello: Oboe Concertos** / Marcon (cond.), Venice Baroque Orch. / 1998 / Arts 47505

CONCERTO

Oboe Concerto in D minor (1716)

Alessandro Marcello was the elder of two bothers, born to a noble Venetian family. Like Albinoni, they were dilettante musicians who were able to choose a freelance career rather than regular employment. Possibly for this reason, neither Alessandro nor his brother published a substantial amount of music, but both were entirely serious musicians of considerable capability. It is likely that a substantial body of manuscript works by both brothers has been lost. Alessandro's largest collected body of works is a set of concertos published under the title *La Cetra* sometime between 1730 and 1740. They were issued under the pseudonym of Eterio Stinfalico, probably to disguise his noble background.

His most famous work is however the present concerto, first published in Amsterdam around 1717 among a miscellaneous collection of concertos by the famous publishing house of Jeanne Roger and Le Cène. In the usual three movements, the concerto adopts a style similar to that frequently encountered in Albinoni's oboe concertos. The outer movements are gracefully lyrical; the opening Allegro attains an elegiac beauty far removed from the drive and energy of Marcello's Venetian contemporary Vivaldi. The central movement is a deeply-felt Adagio which aspires to genuine pathos. J.S. Bach obviously appreciated the work's special qualities; it was one of a number of Venetian concertos he transcribed, in this instance for solo harpsichord (BWV 974). *—Brian Robins*

Recommended:

- ○ **Recorder Concertos by Marcello, Vivaldi, Telemann & Naudot** / Sillito (cond.), Petri, Academy of St. Martin-in-the-Fields / Philips 412630
- ○ **Concerti per Oboe** / Angerer (cond.), Lencses, Southwest German CO / 1996 / Carus 83114
- ○ **Baroque Oboe Concertos** / Messiter, Guildhall String Ens. / 1990 / RCA 60224

Benedetto Marcello

b. Aug. 1, 1686, Venice, Italy, **d.** Jul. 24, 1739, Brescia, Italy

Composer: Chamber Music

Before the early years of the twentieth century, any list of significant Western composers from past eras would have included the name of Benedetto Marcello. Through his advocacy of a return to the proportional values and simplicity of ancient Greco-Roman civilization, Marcello helped set the stage for the Classical era in Western music, soon to unseat the aesthetic norms of the Baroque in which Marcello lived and worked. Nonetheless, controversy and confusion surrounding his works and history have considerably dimmed Marcello's star. Many of the instrumental works once believed by Marcello are actually by others. Composer Alessandro Marcello was Benedetto's older brother, and some of Alessandro's music has been misattributed to Benedetto. Various instrumental pieces attributed to Marcello are merely instrumental arrangements of his Psalmi, in some cases made decades after his death.

Marcello was what eighteenth century chroniclers called a "dilettante"; not a dabbler as in the current vernacular, but an aristocrat who also pursued musical composition as a sideline. Born in Venice, Marcello served the Venetian Republic as a magistrate from about 1708 until 1728, when he was exiled to the resort city of Pula, now in Croatia. In 1738 Marcello was appointed to his final position as chief financial officer of the city of Brescia, but died after less than a year in this job on or around his 53rd birthday.

Marcello was best known in his day through his massively influential eight-volume publication *Estro poetico-armonico* (1724–26), popularly known as the "Psalmi." It is a collection of 50 psalm settings for male voices. Marcello's sacred vocal music was revered by most of his contemporaries as representing the supreme example of contrapuntal technique, and he was in use in teaching through the end of the nineteenth century. Scarcely less popular was his treatise, *Il teatro alla moda* (1720), a satire that skewered the opera world of his time. Marcello wrote nearly 400 cantatas, some so well known that they exist in up to 25 contemporary manuscript copies, in addition to oratorios, operas, and nearly 100 small chamber works for singers. His surviving instrumental catalog is less generous, mostly consisting of keyboard sonatas, but also containing a few sinfonias and concertos. All of Marcello's instrumental music was composed by 1710 or thereabouts; the set of 12 concerti published as Marcello's "Op. 1" in 1708, including the work transcribed by Johann Sebastian Bach as BWV 981, is lacking its first violin part. *—Uncle Dave Lewis*

Overview of Works (1704–1734)

Benedetto Marcello was one of two dilettanti composer brothers born into a noble Venetian family. Seventeen years younger than his sibling Alessandro, Benedetto held important civil posts in the Venetian Republic after training in law. Notwithstanding, Marcello also managed to pursue a career as a composer and teacher (among his pupils were the famous soprano Faustina Bordoni and the composer Baldassare Galuppi). He also gained some fame as a writer and satirist, his best known literary work being *Il teatro alla moda* (1720), a savage critique on contemporary opera conventions and still considered important primary source material.

Marcello's first publication was a set of six concertos, issued in 1708 as his opus 1. Scored in five parts for a solo, or concertino violin and strings, they are spirited works in the Venetian tradition. In keeping with many concertos of the period, they alternate between da chiesa (church) style, with serious slow introductions and a following fugal allegro, and the da camera (chamber) form with a quick opening movement. A later concerto of Benedetto's that has achieved some fame is a brilliant virtuoso work in D, also composed for five-part strings. Among other orchestral works are a group of sinfonias, mostly in three-movement form and which show evidence of having been adapted from concertos. Better known than the concertos and sinfonias is Marcello's Op. 2 (1712), a set of sonatas for recorder and continuo bass. In four movements, and containing relatively few excessive technical demands, they remain popular among students of the instrument. During the 1730s, Marcello turned to the cello sonata, a genre for which there was a vogue at the time. There are two sets—one for cello and continuo published in Amsterdam in 1732, the other for two cellos and bass issued around 1734. Stylistically, they show little advance on the recorder sonatas, but feature a number of the more eccentric harmonic traits for which Marcello had a fondness. The same might be said to apply to his keyboard sonatas, which were never published, but have recently been established as a conjectural "Op. 3."

Marcello's vocal output is dominated by a set of 50 psalm settings paraphrased in the vernacular and set in cantata form. Published in eight installments over a two-year period as *Estro-poetico-harmonico*, they achieved widespread popularity throughout Europe. Recently an impressive *Requiem in the Venetian Style* has also achieved notice. Still virtually unexplored is a large body of secular chamber cantatas, a genre to which Marcello contributed some 200 works. While no operas have been attributed to him, he did compose several dramatic works in the more modest serenata form, theater pieces designed for private performance on celebratory occasions. Among them is one commissioned for the birthday of the Habsburg Emperor Charles VI in 1725. *—Brian Robins*

Recommended:

- ○ **Marcello: Estro poetico-armonico** / Junghanel (cond.), Cantus Colln / HM 901696
- ○ **Marcello: Sonatas for Harpsichord** / Loreggian / 2001 / Chandos 671
- ○ **Marcello: Concerti Grossi, Op1** / Frontalini (cond.), Kannas CO / Bongiovanni 5550/1
- ○ **Marcello: O Signor chi sarà mai; Io sempre t'amerò** / Mertens, Balconi, Zadori, Mey / HM 1903048
- ○ **Marcello: Canzone & Cantates** / Ledroit, Spieth / Solstice FY 108

CHAMBER MUSIC

Recorder Sonatas, Op. 2 (1712)

Although known primarily for his large output of enthusiastically received vocal compositions, these early *suonate* with basso continuo vividly demonstrate the melodic invention and rhythmic variation in the Venetian style for which Marcello became appreciated.

A description of two of the middle sonatas will give some idea of Marcello's original perspective on elements inherited primarily from the Gabrielis. Both sonatas feature movements that contrast highly in mood and tempi.

The Sonata V in G major opens with a beautifully written three-part canon in a slow triple meter in a Largo tempo. The top two lines are in the higher treble registers with the bottom line in a moderate cello range. With suspended non-harmonic tones creating an unstated tension, and the sighing patterns in the melody, this lovely movement describes a heavenly yet somewhat plaintive atmosphere.

After a full perfect cadence, the music suddenly launches into a common time (4/4) Allegro that converts the previous sighing tones into lively skipping figures. Toward the end, the harmony rises upward by a series of diminished-seventh chords (a device used several centuries later in the Romantic period) toward another perfect cadence. The next movement, a 3/4 Adagio in the relative minor key of E minor, is built on a variation of patterns in the first movement, but is different enough to not be a rondo-like recapitulation. The mood is again quickly modulated in the following G major Allegro which is a gigue in 12/8 that takes the duple sighing pattern and translates it into a happy triplet gesture.

The harmony in all of these movements is consistently tonal although always changing and dynamic. However, Marcello does occasionally veer off and bend the ear a bit; for example, by creating a kind of faux-chromatic harmony in minor key passages by using the minor IV of IV (for example, in the first movement progression E minor, A minor, D minor [or F major], B major, E minor).

The Sonata VI in C major opens, in an Adagio non troppo tempo, with a French-overture type melody in a staggered rhythm with a declarative yet pleading quality. This is immediately followed by a sprightly, joyous three-part canon. The melody creates bright dissonances through many accented non-harmonic anticipations and suspensions. After a powerful cadence, the music continues without pause into an undulating motion in A minor. This movement has a pastoral feeling with a subtle texture of regret, and closes with a resigned diminuendo. An abrupt transition occurs again as a trumpeting theme in an Allegro giusto 3/4 shines its light. The texture soon transforms into floating undulations and scale runs, followed by quick changes from minor to major and a positive final cadence. *—"Blue Gene" Tyranny*

Recommended:

- ○ **Italian Recorder Sonatas** / Petri, Malcolm / Philips 412632
- ○ **Italian Recorder Sonatas: Frans Brüggen, Vol. 2** / Bylsma, Brueggen, Leonhardt / 1995 / Teldec 93669

Luca Marenzio

b. 1553, Coccaglio, Italy, **d.** Aug. 22, 1599, Rome, Italy

Composer: Vocal

Over some twenty years, Marenzio wrote more than 400 madrigals and around 80 villanelles, published in 23 books, as well as many sacred works, including about 75 motets. As a court musician with powerful patrons, he exercised considerable influence over the composers of his own time and the succeeding generation, notably Claudio Monteverdi (1567–1643). Marenzio also gained an international reputation in the period of transition between the austere vocal styles of the late Renaissance and the colorful "new music" of the Baroque. The madrigals reflect the growing confidence, freedom of subject and passionate expression that characterize Monteverdi's own essays in the genre, ranging from light pastorals to sonnets and love songs, with all the variety and imagination of his great Italian contemporary. As Alec Harman and Anthony Milner wrote in the 1988 edition of their *Late Renaissance and Baroque Music*, "Marenzio is the summation of practically all the previous trends in the madrigal."

By the end of the sixteenth century, the "normal" sacred and secular madrigals of the late Renaissance were being replaced by works more suited to public performance, and with greater emphasis on humanistic and literary concepts, such as love and contemplation. Due to the changes in style and substance taking place by the late sixteenth century, the madrigal in four to six parts, with or without instruments, flourished, and became a vehicle for dramatic new developments.

Marenzio was probably a pupil of Contino in Brescia. He moved to Rome in 1574, and remained there until 1586, serving cardinals and other wealthy patrons, including Luigi d'Este. In 1557, he went to Verona, where he served Ferdinando de Medici in Florence for a year, and composed the instrumental music for the Duke's wedding celebrations. Later, he was a member of the Duke of Bracciano's household until 1593, also entering the service of Cardinal Cinzio Aldobrandini. In 1594, he held a Vatican apartment; the following year, he visited Polish court. Marenzio returned to Rome in 1598.

Marenzio's consummate skill in musical "word painting," especially in the madrigals, was much admired by the cognoscenti of his time. Some works, such a the great madrigal cycle *Si quel dolor* (Books 13 and 22) contain mysterious and somber thoughts expressed in powerfully evocative chromatic sounds, while the lighter *Bacci soave et carri* cycle belongs more to the risky territory of Western lovemaking manuals, being a musical exploration of kissing in its many varieties. The Concerto della donna, a choir of young ladies of Ferrara led by the composer, is well represented in the six-part pieces for voices in Book 6. The predominantly pastoral villanelles have a charmingly unselfconscious, open-air feeling about them.

As it took more than 200 years for Monteverdi's reputation to be reestablished, it is, perhaps, not surprising that a composer whom John Dowland called "the most famous Luca Marenzio" is still not widely known, though as a mainstream composer of his time he has been the subject of some attention in academic circles; however, the important thing about this music is not only its technical mastery, but also its drama and potency, and the way in which it comes alive in a convincing performance. In 1949, the musicologist Alfred Einstein described Marenzio as "the embodiment of artistry in its purest form . . . art for art's sake" and "a dreamer and a sensualist for connoisseurs." *—Roy Brewer*

VOCAL

Madrigals (1577–1599)

Marenzio's madrigals, composed throughout his creative life, are the basis for his lasting reputation. Preferring a five-voice texture (especially in his earlier works), he produced ten books of such madrigals, usually choosing texts of a pastoral nature. There are a further seven books containing six-voice madrigals and two more with four-voice works. Eleven books of madrigals were printed between 1580 and 1590; eight more appeared in 1591–99.

Marenzio's early madrigals tend to be bright in sound and contrapuntaly uncomplicated, with numerous parallel thirds, tenths, and sixths; his later works take on a more chromatic, polyphonically dense character—qualities reflected in his choices of more serious poems. Marenzio is a representative of what Claudio Monteverdi called the *seconda pratica* (second practice), in which the expressive needs of the text were considered more important than the "rules" of musical composition. In order to express fully feelings suggested by a text, composers employed a richer and more ostentatious musical palate than the composers of the older *prima pratica*, including using dissonance more freely.

Like most of his contemporaries, Marenzio tended to set pastoral poetry; he drew many of his texts from *Il pastor fido*, a play by Giovanni Battista Guarini. Nearly all of his secular works are strophic, with a poetic scheme of AABCC for each strophe. Contemporaries commented on Marenzio's style by complimenting its "good air and fine invention."

Marenzio made great efforts to illustrate even the minutest details of a text in his music. A good example is *Due rose fresche* (Two fresh roses), from his fifth volume of five-voice madrigals (1585): Marenzio begins with a duet for the "two fresh roses," but at the phrase "tra duo minori egualmente diviso" ("divided equally between two younger ones"), we hear the text distributed among two pairs of voices; when these pairs reach the word "equally," the setting becomes homophonic. The word "paradiso" receives a conspicuously ascending line, and when the text refers to the first of May there is musical reference to a maypole dance.

Continuous polyphony is a salient feature of the five-voice *Madonna mia gentil* of 1580. A good example of a six-voice work from the period is *Cantate ninfe* (1581), in which three pairs of voices move through contrasting polyphonic and homophonic passages. In the more expressive works we hear augmented triads and ninth chords such as that setting "my dark days and my grievous nights" in *O voi che sospirate* (1581).

In his last decade, Marenzio's music became more chromatic and dissonant as he chose more serious texts. For example, in his five-voice setting of Petrarch's *Solo e pensoso* (Alone and thoughtful) (1599), the beginning of the poem, in which the protagonist walks alone "with measured, slow and dragging steps," is set to long notes that ascend chromatically over more than an octave before chromatically descending. Also, his later works tend to be for a group with two tenors instead of two sopranos, producing a darker sound. Marenzio admitted to searching for text with a "melancholy gravity," best exemplified by his *O fere stelle* (1588). *—John Palmer*

Recommended:

- ○ **Marenzio: Madrigaux à 5 et 6 voix** / Jacobs (cond.), Concerto Vocale / HM 1901065

Igor Markevitch

b. Jul. 27, 1912, Kiev, Ukraine, **d.** Mar. 7, 1983, Antibes, France
Conductor

Igor Markevitch was a leading conductor, known for brilliant performances, especially of twentieth century music. He was also a composer who attracted some interest in his own day. His parents left Kiev when he was two years old. Markevitch was brought up in Vevay, Switzerland. He took piano lessons from his father and then with Paul Loyonnet and also started to compose. The pianist Alfred Cortot saw some of his piano compositions and recommended that the boy study in Paris. In 1925 he enrolled in Cortot's piano class at the École Normale de Musique. He studied harmony, counterpoint, and composition with Nadia Boulanger. The ballet impresario Sergei Diaghilev commissioned him to write a piano concerto and a ballet. The concerto premiered in London in 1929, but Diaghilev's death in August of that year caused Markevitch to stop work on the ballet, instead recycling materials from it into a cantata, premiered with great success in Paris on June 4, 1930. Later that year, another new work, a *Concerto Grosso*, received even greater acclaim. The ballet, *Rébus*, was first staged in December 1931, and was hailed as a great composition. The next ballet, *L'envol d'Icare* (June 1933), was once again highly praised. But after this Markevitch began to receive criticism for his use of unrelieved dissonance and his novel use of instruments.

Meanwhile, Markevitch had begun to conduct, debuting on the podium with the Amsterdam Concertgebouw Orchestra in 1930. He studied conducting with Hermann Scherchen in 1935. His composing activities dropped off as he increased his conducting. He spent World War II in Italy, having acquired Italian citizenship. In 1944 he was appointed music director of the Maggio Musicale Orchestra in Florence. He began conducting full time, coming into demand as a guest conductor, and held a variety of directorships or principal conducting appointments with the Stockholm Symphony Orchestra (1952–55), the Montreal Symphony Orchestra (1956–60), the Havana Philharmonic Orchestra (1957–58), the Concerts Lamoureux of Paris (1957–61), the Spanish Radio and Television Orchestra (1965–69), the Monte Carlo Orchestra (1967), and the orchestra of the Accademia di Santa Cecilia in Rome (1967–72). His American debut was with the Boston Symphony Orchestra in 1955. He also began giving conducting master classes, especially in Monte Carlo, from 1969.

He was known for his performance of the Russian repertory and twentieth century music. He had a quick temper, reflected in his music in sharp emotional shifts, yet the music was meticulously prepared and nearly always followed the composer's directions with exceptional care. In the late 1990s his recordings came back into demand in re-release, and even his compositions were finding a small but interested market and were praised anew for their originality. *—Joseph Stevenson*

Recommended:

- ○ **Igor Markevitch** / Markevitch (cond.), London SO, New Philharmonia, Lamoureux Concert Association / 2002 / EMI 75124
- ○ **Tchaikovsky: Symphony 4–6** / Markevitch (cond.), London SO / 1993 / Philips 438335
- ○ **Milhaud: Les Choéphores; Honegger: Symphonie; Roussel: Bacchus et Ariane** / Markevitch (cond.), Rehfuss, Moizan, Bouvier, Nollier, Lamoureux Concert Association / 1997 / DG 449748
- ○ **Stravinsky: Le Sacre du Printemps** / Markevitch (cond.), Philharmonia / 1997 / Testament 1076
- ○ **Igor Markevitch** / Markevitch (cond.), Nicolet, Arkhipova, Ilosfalvy, Ales, Berlin PO, Symphony of the Air, Lamoureux Concert Association, USSR SO / 2003 / DG 000085602

Neville Marriner

b. Apr. 15, 1924, Lincoln, England
Conductor

Rivaled only by Nikolaus Harnoncourt, Neville Marriner was one of the most important of the early figures who spearheaded the reawakening of modern interest in Baroque and early Classical music. In the 1950s, he founded Academy of St. Martin-in-the-Fields, the first British early music ensemble to find a large international audience. Marriner has since become one of the most popular conductors in the world, acclaimed for his interpretations of composers from Bach to Britten.

Marriner was first taught the violin as a child, by his father, and attended the Royal College of Music, beginning at age thirteen. Wounded during World War II, he met future collaborator Thurston Dart during his hospitalization. In 1948 he became professor at the Royal Academy of Music. As well as joining the Martin String Quartet as second violin, he formed a violin-and-harpsichord duet with Dart, and their performances led to the formation of the Jacobean Ensemble, an early music group that recorded the Purcell trio sonatas in 1950. Around this time, he began studying conducting with Pierre Monteux at Monteux's school in Maine. Marriner's reputation in general music circles also grew; in 1956 he was appointed principal second violin with the London Symphony Orchestra.

A turning point came in 1959, when Marriner was asked to supply music for the church of St. Martin-in-the-Fields, in London's Trafalgar Square. Marriner formed a chamber orchestra which he named the Academy of St. Martin-in-the-Fields. The group's work attracted the attention of the Decca imprint L'Oiseau Lyre, which recorded its performance of Couperin's *Les Nations*. Favorable reviews and unexpectedly robust sales of this recording led to more recordings for L'Oiseau Lyre and its sister label Argo, and by the end of the 1970s the Academy of St. Martin-in-the-Fields had become the best-selling chamber orchestra in recorded music's history. The group expanded from thirteen players to twenty or more, and performed Classical symphonic works and twentieth century British music as well as Baroque material. The sound of Marriner's Academy recordings is crisp, with an extremely bright sound, using period performance standards with modern instruments. Marriner's name remains closely associated with the Academy of St. Martin-in-the-Fields, and the group now has more than 300 recordings to its credit. These include the soundtrack for the 1984 film *Amadeus*, for which Marriner selected, arranged, and directed works of Salieri and Pergolesi, in addition to Mozart.

In 1969 Marriner he organized the Los Angeles Chamber Orchestra, and he later took this orchestra on a tour of Europe. Additionally, he served as a guest conductor with leading U.S. orchestras, and in England held an appointment as conductor of the Northern Sinfonia, based in Newcastle. In the late 1970s and early 1980s, he spent most of his time in the U.S., primarily as music director and conductor of the Minnesota Orchestra. After being knighted in 1985, Marriner went back to Europe, conducting of the Stuttgart Radio Symphony Orchestra from 1986–89. Since then, he has conducted around the world, including at the Opéra de Lyon, and continues to record.

His conducting is known for its vitality and brightness, as well as precise ensemble technique, a reflection of his violinist days. In a 1991 interview he said of his style: "I was never a potentate swinging a scepter, but was always in a dialogue with my musicians." *—AMG*

Recommended:

- ○ **Mozart: Symphonies 35 & 41** / Marriner (cond.), Academy of St. Martin-in-the-Fields / 2004 / EMI 85696
- ○ **Bach: Brandenburg Concertos; Orchestral Suites** / Marriner (cond.), Szeryng, Holliger, Rampal, Petri, Academy of St. Martin-in-the-Fields / 2002 / Philips 470934
- ○ **Rossini: String Sonatas** / Marriner (cond.), Lord, , Academy of St. Martin-in-the-Fields / 1995 / London 443838
- ○ **The Best of the Academy** / Marriner (cond.), Bennett, Sillito, Vigay, Davies, Academy of St. Martin-in-the-Fields / 2003 / EMI 585624
- ○ **Mozart: Symphony Nos. 25, 26, 27, 29 & 32** / Marriner (cond.), Academy of St. Martin-in-the-Fields / 1991 / Decca 430268
- ○ **Vaughan Williams Favorites** / Marriner (cond.), Academy of St. Martin-in-the-Fields / 1995 / Philips 442427

Wynton Marsalis

b. Oct. 18, 1961, New Orleans, LA
Trumpeter

As jazz has become more frequently considered "America's classical music," its roots have become a subject of interest for an increasingly broad audience. With one foot in the European classical tradition and the other in the sounds of Jelly Roll Morton, Duke Ellington, Louie Armstrong, and their successors, trumpeter and composer Wynton Marsalis has been a prominent figure in an ongoing movement that has brought jazz music to the forefront of American culture.

Marsalis was born into a musical family, in the musical town of New Orleans, on October 18, 1961, and was already demonstrating his proficiency on the trumpet in his early teens. His early musical experiences reflect the wide-ranging interests of his later years: during high school he participated in marching band, jazz band, funk groups, and classical ensembles. After finishing high school, Marsalis was accepted into the Juilliard School of Music. His virtuosity must have been apparent from the start; shortly after his arrival in New York City, he became a member of Art Blakey's Jazz Messengers, and his own self-titled debut album was released soon after in 1982.

Marsalis became a household name in 1987, when he helped initiate the Jazz at Lincoln Center program. It was with this organization that Marsalis became the country's foremost jazz curator; in addition to performing some new works (including Marsalis' own), the Lincoln Center Jazz Orchestra recreated numerous legendary jazz works, often using transcribed charts and notated solos taken from surviving recordings of the original artists. Such musical resurrection infuses performances with what some might see as an odd irony: a tradition based on intuitive, in-the-moment improvisation, being faithfully re-executed note by note! At any rate, such projects aspire to raise jazz to the same arena of esteem as musical works of the classical tradition, placing both within the musical museum of the concert hall.

Other efforts have attempted a fusion of classical and jazz traditions. In 1997, he became the first composer to receive a Pulitzer Prize in music for a work of jazz orientation, his "epic oratorio," *Blood on the Fields*. Composed in 1994, this musical commentary on slavery garnered wide praise from the press (it was named one of the top ten highlights of the musical year by *Time* magazine). In 1998, Marsalis contributed to a musically ecumenical undertaking by the Lincoln Center ensembles entitled MARSALIS/STRAVINSKY. Commissioned jointly by the Chamber Music Society at Lincoln Center and Jazz at Lincoln Center, Marsalis' *A Fiddler's Tale* retold the story of Stravinsky's *L'histoire du Soldat*. In Stravinsky's original, a soldier on his way home from duty sells his soul to the devil; in Marsalis' recasting, which takes inspiration from Stravinsky's appropriation of early twentieth century jazz idioms, a musician sells his soul to a record producer.

In addition to jazz and "crossover" projects, Marsalis is respected as a performer of classical repertoire: *In Gabriel's Garden*, recorded with the English Chamber Orchestra, included J.S. Bach's *Brandenburg Concerto No. 2*, and Mouret's *Rondeau* (Marsalis' recording of which was chosen as the new theme music for PBS' *Masterpiece Theater*) are both notable releases. A subsequent release, *Classic Wynton*, rendered music from the Baroque to Contemporary, including a previously unreleased recording of twentieth century composer Alan Hovhanhess' *Prayer of Saint Gregory*.

The 1990s saw Marsalis also heavily involved in educational efforts, including frequent demonstrations at public schools; he won a Peabody Award in 1996 for his video series, "Marsalis on Music." Such efforts prompted one national magazine to identify him as among the 25 most influential people in America. His massive 2002 work for chorus, orchestra, and jazz band, *All Rise*, included such diverse elements as a massive fugue for strings and traces of Cuban and Argentine rhythms. *—Jeremy Grimshaw*

Recommended:

- ○ **Trumpet Concertos** / Leppard (cond.), Marsalis, English CO, National PO / 2001 / Sony 89862
- ○ **In Gabriel's Garden** / Newman (cond.), Marsalis, Bennett, Black, Lin, English CO / 1996 / Sony 66244
- ○ **On the Twentieth Century** / Marsalis, Stillman (piano) / 1993 / Sony 47193
- ○ **Wynton Marsalis: All Rise** / Salonen (cond.), Marsalis, Smith, Goines, Printup, Pearson, Los Angeles PO, Lincoln Center Jazz Orch. / 2002 / Sony 89817

Frank Martin

b. Sep. 15, 1890, Geneva, Switzerland, **d.** Nov. 21, 1974, Naarden, Netherlands

Composer: Chamber Music, Concerto, Choral, Orchestral, Vocal

Martin's long, quietly productive career reflected a quest to reconcile creative imperatives with stylistic integrity in an era of unprecedented technical challenges, experiments, and fragmentation. A conventionally trained musician would have been less liable to brook such challenges as an ethical dilemma or to see in them an almost paralyzing array of possibilities, while Martin, the tenth child of a Calvinist pastor, felt both keenly. Martin began composing at eight, was overwhelmed by a performance of Bach's *St. Matthew Passion* at ten, and by his 16th year knew that music was his destiny. While formally studying mathematics and physics at his parents' behest, he pursued music privately with the distinguished Swiss composer Joseph Lauber, who introduced him to the rudiments of piano, harmony, and composition. Martin became an able interpreter at the piano and harpsichord and, in later life, proved well enough equipped to make a definitive recording of his difficult *Preludes for piano*. In 1918 Martin moved to Zurich, then on to Rome and Paris, returning to Geneva in 1926 with the experience of jazz hot in the ear. A meeting that year with Émile Jaques-Dalcroze, founder of eurhythmics, went hand-in-hand with exploration of Hindu and Bulgarian rhythms, issuing in the orchestral triptych *Rhythmes* (1926) an element of rhythmic *nervosité* as a persistent feature of his music. Modal and serial elements also informed his work without being slavishly adopted. That the fairly prolific Martin achieved his first characteristic work—the secular oratorio *Le vin herbé* (1938–41)—only as he passed his 50th year owes as much, perhaps, to the German-dominated insularity of Swiss musical life as to the search for an ideal purity of utterance. The impact of Debussy and Ravel, for instance, was brought to bear only during the Great War through the revelations of Swiss conductor Ernest Ansermet, who performed Martin's *Les dithyrambes* in 1918 and became a champion of his work, making several classic recordings of it. Recognition came in the form of teaching posts, directorship of the Technicum Moderne de Musique, president of the Swiss Musicians' Union 1943–1946, a composition class at the Cologne Hochschule für Musik 1950–57, and commissions (e.g., by Geneva Radio for the oratorio *In terra pax* for broadcast on armistice day). In 1943 he married his third wife, Maria Boeke, and in 1946 moved with her to Amsterdam, and later to Naarden. Masterworks flowed from his pen between concert tours that carried his music worldwide. *—Adrian Corleonis*

CHAMBER MUSIC

Four Short Pieces for guitar (1933; revised 1955)

Originally composed in 1933 for Spanish guitarist Andrés Segovia, Swiss composer Frank Martin's *Four Short Pieces for Guitar* also exist in versions for piano and, unlikely as it may seem (and it seems even more unlikely after one has heard the originals), full orchestra. Both alternate versions date from around the same time as the original. True to their title, they collectively take only about eight minutes to perform. But they make up for their slight builds with genuine lyric charm and quasi-Baroque formal grace, and they deserve their place in the modern guitarist's repertory.

The first of the four pieces, Prélude, is flexible in tempo, moving from the opening Lent to quicker musical paragraphs (Plus vite, or Vite) and then back and forth again. It is in B minor but is quite chromatically colored, and the whole of it spins out from a single opening gesture in 12/8 time. No. 2, Air, is marked Lent et bien rythmé and moves along charming, modal C sharp major lines (there are four sharps in the key signature, but Martin insists on the major tonic rather than the C sharp minor that one would expect from a four-sharp key signature). The main dance idea is lightly syncopated, and prefers to display itself quietly, but there is a short-lived forte climax near the end. The third piece, Plainte, is a thick-textured, steady-pulsed dance that accelerates as it moves towards its conclusion (Sans lenteur becomes Quasi allegro and then finally Vite) until there is in the final measures nothing but a rapid sextuplet tremolando on the lowest note of the instrument. Comme une Gigue, No. 4 (Con moto), moves back to the modified B minor tonality of the first piece; it is in 6/8 time but has a built-in cross rhythm (three-against-two) that manages to work itself so deeply into the music that the entirety of the middle section is written in 3/4 time. The final bars are made Plus lent très déclamé, fortissimo, to draw a firm closing cadence. *—Blair Johnston*

Recommended:

- ○ **Nocturnal** / Bream / 1993 / EMI 54901

CONCERTO

Ballade for cello & small orchestra (1949)

Frank Martin was one of the leading Swiss-born composers of the generation that emerged prior to the Second World War. The basis of his forms and expression is neo-classicism, but within that context he used various innovations in twentieth century notions of harmony and tonality. Among his most important series of compositions is the set of one-movement works with solo instrument called *Ballades*.

Unlike nineteenth century works with that title, Martin's *Ballades* are not especially melodic. The *Ballade for Cello* was originally written for piano accompaniment and later orchestrated for a chamber group. In the orchestral version Martin often pits the warm, low voice of the cello against the thinner, high sound of the oboe. The piece exploits the cello's wide range and its capacity for double-stopping. The work is tonal, with harmonies made more tart by the addition of pointed dissonances. The 15-minute work builds up in tension, but soon subsides to a static conclusion. *—Joseph Stevenson*

Recommended:

- ○ **Martin: Ballades** / Bamert (cond.), London PO / 1995 / Chandos 9380

Ballade for flute & small orchestra (1939)

Over the course of his career Frank Martin produced a series of pieces he called Ballades, all one-movement works featuring a solo instrumental part. The *Ballade for flute and piano* is one of the earliest such entries in his catalogue. Like all but two of the Ballades, it was written first with a piano accompaniment and later orchestrated. Martin originally composed the Ballade as a compulsory piece for a flute competition; the particular musical challenge it poses for the performer is the negotiation of the composer's typical wide melodic leaps while retaining a lyrical, legato line. The work further tests the performer's abilities throughout the instrument's entire range; the section that focuses on the low register is particularly striking, with an effective ostinato in the accompaniment. The Ballade is neoclassical in its orientation and tonal (though marked by chromatic coloration) in its harmonic language, and has remained one of the most popular shorter works in the twentieth century flute repertoire. *—Joseph Stevenson*

Recommended:

- ○ **Martin Interprète Frank Martin** / Ameling, Rehfuss, Willoughby, Martin / Jecklin 563

○ **Jeanne Baxtresser, Principal Flute, New York PO** / Baxtresser, etc. / 1997 / Cala 0512

○ **Martin: Ballades** / Bamert (cond.), London PO / 1995 / Chandos 9380

Ballade for alto saxophone, strings, piano & percussion (1938)

The *Ballade for saxophone and piano* is the first in a series of similarly titled works by Frank Martin, each of which features a different instrument in a prominent role. This work, nearly 15 minutes long, has the dimensions of a single-movement concerto. The particular instrument called for is the alto saxophone, whose solo repertoire at the time was rather slender. Martin deftly explores the instrument's still-emerging possiblities—using it, for example, in the far reaches of what was then its upper range. Though much of the rhythmic activity in is marked by syncopation, the composer makes no overt reference to the saxophone's associations with jazz and popular music. Martin makes notable use of dissonant sonorities in the work, lending considerable harmonic spice. Like most of the Ballades, this one was first written with piano accompaniment and later orchestrated. *—Joseph Stevenson*

Recommended:

○ **Martin: Ballades** / Bamert (cond.), Robertson, London PO / 1995 / Chandos 9380

Concerto for 7 wind instruments & string orchestra (1949)

This Swiss composer's music tends to be tartly neo-Classical, often using a reduced orchestra. Obviously this 1949 work, where the entire wind section is oboe, clarinet, horn, trumpet, trombone, bassoon, and flute, is one of these. The work begins with an allegro movement, starting with a motto theme which serves to introduce each of the seven solos, in the order listed above. Following that, the movement effectively contrasts a lyrical theme appearing first on clarinet, then a bolder theme (trombone). The movement ends with another instance of the seven instruments playing, in the same order as at the start. The second movement is a theme and variations, marked adagietto, on a pensive theme. The final movement, Allegro vivace, is a rondo with development of the main themes. The first theme has the character of a scherzo; the whole movement is full of life. This work was an immediate success. *—Joseph Stevenson*

Recommended:

○ **Frank Martin** / Jordan (cond.), Suisse Romande / 1991 / Cascavelle 3026

○ **Frank Martin** / Ansermet (cond.), Suisse Romande / 1996 / London 448264

Harpsichord Concerto (1951–1952)

Composed for soloist Isabelle Nef, Martin's harpsichord concerto finds the inherently bright solo instrument lurking in the shadows. This is sinister music and perhaps the first harpsichord concerto to take up a fully twentieth century aesthetic, rather than mimic (and poke fun at) eighteenth century conventions, as do the concertos of Falla and Poulenc. The first movement, Allegro commodo, presents a mysterious motif creeping along the keyboard with minimal orchestral accompaniment. The orchestra soon carries the theme more assertively, the staccato wind and brass passages and pizzicato strings mimicking the plucked sound of the harpsichord. The orchestra introduces a new section, dark and slow, with the soloist offering nattering commentary that devolves into a long series of trills. The two main thematic ideas fold into each other in the ominous development section, with the soloist and orchestra now sharing equal duties. A brief harpsichord solo, not really a full cadenza, turns what was in the 1950s thought to be the generic Baroque "sewing machine" style into a dark ostinato, whereupon Martin recaps the main themes that loosen and gradually wind down. The remaining sections are played attaca. Woodwinds begin the Adagio with a mysterious theme, vaguely Middle Eastern, but evoking a vague feeling of cultural alienation rather than depicting a specific exotic place. The harpsichord lays a rhapsodic filigree over this material, soon introducing a dour, implacable footstep figure that eventually marches through the orchestra. The music's tempo and volume gradually increase (Poco più mosso), but this long crescendo backs away from a full climax. After further swelling and contraction, the score eases into a roiling, full cadenza for the soloist that seems to be partly modeled on the cadenza in the first movement of Bach's *Brandenburg Concerto No. 5*, but here the music is in minor mode and threatening. At the end, the harpsichord offers a chordal statement of the main Adagio theme, which the orchestra then picks up in a very brief, sardonic Tempo di valsa. *—James Reel*

Recommended:

○ **Frank Martin dirige Frank Martin** / Martin, Jaccottet, Rosin, Benda, Lausanne CO / 1989 / Jecklin 529

CHORAL

Mass (1922–1926)

Given that Frank Martin's most important formative musical experience was hearing the *St. Matthew Passion* of Johann Sebastian Bach at the age of ten, it makes sense that he would eventually try his hand at writing for the double choir Bach used in that work. Yet Martin's *Mass for double choir* looks even further back for musical inspiration, to Renaissance polyphony and to plainsong church modes. The work itself is lovely, simple, and devotional. Martin apparently wrote it in 1922 and revised it in 1926, with no thought of public performance; it had its premiere in 1961. The opening moments of the Kyrie set the mood for the rest of the piece: there is a plainsong-like line in the altos, soon joined imitatively by the remainder of one choir. When the full choir takes up the line, there is a startling sense of space suddenly explored. High, harsh outbursts on the word "Kyrie" also set the pattern of tension occurring in the upper registers and relaxing in the lower. Like the Kyrie, the Gloria takes full advantage of the antiphonal and polyphonic possibilities offered by the use of two choirs. Phrases rise from quiet and low to strong and high, never more memorably than in the opening "Gloria in excelsis." The closing "In gloria dei Patris" goes against the grain by featuring sweet high notes and a lovely melisma in the sopranos. The Credo is primarily homophonic, using entrances in sequence for dramatic effect—as in the layered, dissonant outbursts on "Crucifixus" or the subsequent solemn, painfully measured tones of "passus, et sepultus est." Both the Sanctus and Benedictus begin with short motives in the lower voices which become the bases of their respective settings; the "Osanna in excelsis" in the Sanctus winds voices in and out in compound meter, providing a modest yet powerful vision of eternity, while the second "Osanna" is simpler but no less effective. The Agnus Dei uses a few repeated chords in the second choir as the basis for melody in the first, until just before the end when both choirs join together and homophonically pronounce the "dona nobis pacem" like a blessing, ending on a G major chord. It is hard to imagine that Martin's *Mass for double choir* went unperformed for so long, for it has now been recognized as one of his most purely lovely (and most popular) compositions. *—Andrew Lindemann Malone*

Recommended:

○ **Cathedral Classics** / Warland (cond.), Dale Warland Singers / 1994 / American Choral 120

ORCHESTRAL

Petite symphonie concertante, for harp, harpsichord, piano & 2 string orchestras (1944–1945)

The Swiss composer Martin is noted for compositions of tight formal logic and an austere formal surface which, in the better pieces, an underlying energy and passion often seem to seek to break. This composition is based on slow material which is stated near the beginning. This gradually increases in speed until the solo instruments add rhythmic propulsion.

The combination of harp, piano, and harpsichord is an unusual one; their sounds don't really blend, and there are problems of balance. The harpsichord is moderate in volume and dynamically inflexible, while the harp is both quiet and highly nuanced in tone and timbre. The pianoforte, on the other hand, takes its very name from its wide dynamic range. Martin overcomes these problems by making the very disparity of touch and dynamic response a part of the structure of his score. The solo instruments amplify and color each others' solos, while the strings are often plucked to act as extensions of the two plucked solo instruments (harp and harpshichord). Moods of intensely driven rhythm alternate with a tense, expectant melody and finally add up to a dashing conclusion. There are sounds of the Baroque toccata mixed with the twentieth century elements of this unique-sounding score. *—Joseph Stevenson*

Recommended:

○ **Frank Martin** / Ansermet (cond.), Suisse Romande / 1996 / London 448264

VOCAL

Six Monologues aus Jedermann, for baritone & piano (1943–1944)

Precocious, brilliant, dapper, and proud, Austrian poet Hugo von Hofmannsthal was not yet 40 when, on the eve of World War I, spurred by collaboration with Richard Strauss, his multifaceted genius reached white heat in the libretti for such very different works as *Elektra* (1909), *Der Rosenkavalier* (1911), the first version of *Ariadne auf Naxos* (1912), and, in 1911, the rewriting of the medieval English morality play *Everyman* as a Modern parable. But not until the war ended, and its devastations—physical and cultural—became apparent, was Jedermann's existential questioning felt to be apposite. When Strauss, theater director Max Reinhardt, conductor Franz Schalk, and Hofmannsthal established the Salzburg Festival just after the war, the latter's *Jedermann* was chosen as its centerpiece, receiving its premiere August 22, 1920, staged by Reinhardt on the steps of the Salzburg Cathedral, where it has been performed since annually. Drawing upon the Hecastus (1549) of Hans Sachs for sundry details, Hofmannsthal fashioned from *Everyman* what he called a *Märchen*—a fairytale—of stark power as Death confronts the representative rich man, Everyman (Jedermann), in the midst of his feasting and wealth with the terrible question "what shall speak for him before the face of God?" For the Calvinist minister's son, Frank Martin, this held an immediate appeal as World War II engulfed Europe, and from Jedermann's vicissitudes, as he struggles for salvation, Martin culled six monologues, which, at the request of Swiss baritone Max Christmann, he set in 1943 for baritone (or alto) and piano to reflect, in a unique, tonally expanded, tense, often eerie, dissonantly declamatory idiom fraught with psychological acuity, the faces of angst: surprised terror, hysteria, resigned exhaustion, an anguished protest against extinction, a tortuous recognition of sin and confession, and, at last, a despairing prayer. The cumulative effect is crushing as no saccharine vision of hope or celestial voice crowns Jedermann's growing self-discovery. The premiere was given by Christmann on August 6, 1944, at Gstaad, with Martin accompanying. In 1949 the composer orchestrated the *Monologes*, in which version the sudden offbeat tympani strokes of approaching judgment, heard throughout, are particularly effective. In either version, the *Monologes* became part of the Salzburg Festival performing tradition, with Dietrich Fischer-Dieskau, recorded several times over the years, as a divinatory proponent. There also exists a classic recording of Martin accompanying baritone Heinz Rehfuss in the *Monologes*. *—Adrian Corleonis*

Recommended:

- **José Van Dam** / Nagano (cond.), Van Dam, Lyon Opera Orch. / 1992 / Virgin 59236
- **Martin: Petite Symphonie Concertante; etc.** / Jordan (cond.), Cachemaille, Suisse Romande / 2002 / Apex 48687

Malcolm Martineau

b. Feb. 3, 1960, Edinburgh, Scotland

Pianist

Although most closely identified with Welsh bass baritone Bryn Terfel, with whom he has appeared and recorded to striking effect, Malcolm Martineau has established himself independently among the cream of singers and instrumentalists from the British Isles and beyond. One of a remarkable third generation of accompanists following the great Gerald Moore, Martineau combines a comprehensive technique, unfaltering musicality, and the ability to collaborate at the highest level with artists of widely varying temperaments and approaches. He has wisely made his way in an area of musical endeavor once regarded as highly unpromising and has become something of a star in doing it. Martineau, in the British expression, read music at St. Catherine's College at Cambridge, England. In 1981, he continued his studies at the Royal College of Music, where he primarily worked with Joyce Rathbone, but also studied with Geoffrey Parsons, that paragon among all other post-Moore accompanists. Engaged as an accompanist for the Walther Grüner International Lieder Competition, Martineau was himself a winner, having been chosen as best accompanist. He played for the winner of the lieder award at the Cardiff Singer of the World Competition in 1989 and that event turned out to be unexpectedly fortuitous: the first-place singer was Terfel and the two artists would subsequently appear together often with the international spotlight trained on them. The following year, he was an accompaniest at the Elly Ameling Competition, once again working with the winning artist. At the Britten-Pears School at Aldeburgh, Martineau has accompanied in master classes given by such luminaries as Elisabeth Schwarzkopf, Suzanne Danco, Joan Sutherland, Kurt Equiluz, and Ileana Cotrubas. Under his own name, he has presented two important series on song. At St. John's Smith Square in London, he offered a series on the complete songs of Debussy and Poulenc and at London's venerable Wigmore Hall, he conducted a series devoted to Benjamin Britten's vocal works. Both series were broadcast by the BBC. Martineau has, in addition to appearing at many of the most important British festivals, performed at the Salzburg, Vienna, and Aix-en-Provence festivals as well as on tours throughout North and South America. Recitals have taken him to most major European cities, Amsterdam, Paris, Munich, Berlin, and Milan among them. The list of singers for whom he has provided accompaniment is extensive and multinational: Dame Janet Baker, Felicity Lott, Sir Thomas Allen, Sarah Walker, Frederica von Stade, Tom Krause, Amanda Roocroft, Barbara Bonney, Anne Sofie von Otter, John Mark Ainsley, Susan Graham, Joan Rodgers, Della Jones, Olaf Bär, Karita Mattila, and Simon Keenlyside among them. In addition, his performances with instrumentalists are equally convincing. He has collaborated with clarinetist Emma Johnson in both live performance and recording. Examples of Martineau's flexibility in recorded performance may be found in his work with such different artists as Susan Graham and Terfel. With Graham, the accompanist recorded a recital of songs by Ned Rorem, an American composer with high regard for both French elegance and American simplicity. With Graham's luminous singing and direct diction, Martineau offers exemplary interplay, neither overstated nor too acquiescent. For the far more extroverted Terfel, Martineau is ever responsive to the broad dynamics favored by the singer. In discs devoted to Schubert lieder, English songs, Schumann's *Liederkreis*, Op. 39, and *Ballads and Romances*, he supports his singer's vivid interpretations, often finding real magic, especially in the disc devoted to English song. *—Erik Eriksson*

Recommended:

- **Songs by Debussy** / Maltman, Martineau (piano) / 2003 / Hyperion 67357
- **The Vagabond** / Terfel, Martineau (piano) / 1995 / DG 445946
- **Susan Graham at Carnegie Hall** / Graham, Martineau (piano) / 2003 / Erato 60293

Giovanni Martinelli

b. Oct. 22, 1885, Montagnana, Italy, **d.** Feb. 2, 1969, New York, NY

Tenor

Martinelli remains a legend of stamina and longevity in the opera world, particularly for a heroic tenor, a type of voice not always associated with longevity. He made his opera debut in 1908 and sang his last performance in 1967. His voice was not, by contemporary accounts, as huge as that of most heroic tenors, but he had such strong focus and projection that he more than compensated for this perceived shortfall. Particularly at the Met, Martinelli was considered Caruso's successor in the more dramatic roles, as Gigli was in the more lyrical ones. Martinelli had a strong sense of legato phrasing, powerful breath control, and a distinctive timbre, although some listeners found it overly metallic. Martinelli made more use of rubato than what would be permitted in post-1970s practice, but unlike most heroic tenors of any era, he generally sang, rather than slurred, grace notes.

The eldest of 14 children (which may well have been a driving force behind developing such a strong voice!), Martinelli) sang in the church choir and played the clarinet. When Martinelli was 17 and serving in the military, his powerful voice drew the attention of an officer who arranged for him to study with Maestro Mandolini, a noted teacher in Milan. Martinelli's opera debut in 1908 was as the messenger in *Aida*. In 1910, Martinelli sang the title role of Ernani at La Scala, and was promptly invited to audition for the Italian premiere of *La Fanciulla del West* (which had premiered at the Met with Caruso.) After some hesitation over his lack of experience, Puccini and Toscanini chose him, and later, according to one story, he was Puccini's choice for the world premiere of *Turandot*, but the Met management would not release Martinelli from his contract.

In 1912 he made his Covent Garden debut as Cavaradossi in *Tosca*, and his Met debut in 1913—the first of an eventual 663 performances at the Met. 1913 was also the year of the posthumous premiere of Massenet's *Panurge*, in which Martinelli sang Pantagruel. In 1915 he sang Lefebvre in the premiere of Giordano's Madame *Sans-Gene*, and in 1916, created the role of Fernando in Granados' *Goyescas*. Martinelli began to increase his repertoire to include most of the Italian and French dramatic roles—Canio, Otello, Samson, Radames, Manrico, Don Jose in *Carmen*, Alvaro in *La Forza del Destino*, Eleazar in *La Juive*, Vasco da Gama in *L'Africaine*, Arnold in Rossini's *William Tell*.

In the 1920s, Martinelli's home town of Montagnana built a theater to be named after their "two tenors" (the other being Aureliano Pertile). Much of Martinelli' s career was focused in the United States, and it was not until 1937 that he returned to Covent Garden. In 1939, he sang *Tristan und Isolde* in Chicago with Kirsten Flagstad. In 1945 he stopped singing staged operas at the Met, but still participated in various benefit recitals. His last "full" role was as Samson in Philadelphia in 1950, but in 1967, he sang the Emperor in a Seattle production of *Turandot*.

Nimbus has re-released many of Martinelli's early HMV and Victor recordings (on NI 7804), which include arias from many of his most important roles and the famous excerpts from *La Forza del Destino* with di Luca, Ponselle, and Pinza. Pearl has released extended excerpts from complete opera productions that feature Martinelli, including a set with material from *Simon Boccanegra* and *Otello*. *—Ann Feeney*

Recommended:

- **Prima Voce: Martinelli** / Martinelli, etc. / 1989 / Nimbus 7804
- **Lebendige Vergangenheit: Giovanni Martinelli** / Martinelli, etc. / Preiser 89062

Donald Martino

b. May 16, 1931, Plainfield, NJ

Composer

Donald Martino is one of the most highly regarded American composers to emerge from the post-World War II era's fascination with mathematically directed musical structures. Even so, his music maintains a communicative dimension that is particularly evident in his flair for exciting solo instrumental parts. At the age of nine, Martino began studying clarinet, saxophone, and oboe. In high school he decided to become a professional clarinetist and started composing at the age of 15. In 1948, he began studies at Syracuse University where he took composition lessons with Ernst Bacon. After obtaining his bachelor of music degree in 1952, he went on to graduate school at Princeton University, where his initial plan was to study history. Composition soon became more appealing, and he switched to a master of fine arts program. His main teachers there were Roger Sessions and Milton Babbitt, and he was soon awarded a Koussevitzky Fellowship. After obtaining his degree in 1954, he received a Fulbright Scholarship and went to Italy to study with Luigi Dallapiccola. Dallapiccola's mature and highly expressive 12-tone style was influential to the emerging Martino.

On his return to the United States in 1956, Martino taught at the Third Street Music School Settlement in New York City, taking additional work playing jazz and writing arrangements. In 1959, he obtained a professorship at Yale University, which he held for ten years while teaching summers at Tanglewood. Throughout this period, the expressive aspects of his music became increasingly pronounced as he grew confident enough to add personal elements to the systematic 12-tone style he had used from the beginning of his career. This development is a result of his growing admiration for Romantic-era composers. He says that he responds "very powerfully" to Chopin, Schumann, and Verdi, but that it is Brahms and Beethoven to whom he turns "as a model of creation." In 1969 he accepted the chairmanship of the composition department at the New England Conservatory of Music in Boston. In 1974, he won the Pulitzer Prize in Music for his chamber work *Notturno*, for flutes, clarinets, violin, viola, cello, and piano. He founded Dantalian, Inc. in 1978 to publish his own music. In addition to his music in an advanced classical idiom, he wrote numerous jazz compositions, 178 harmonizations of chorales by J.S. Bach, and a series of transcriptions for clarinet and piano. He is also the inventor of the Stringograph, an aid to composers and arrangers for writing string parts. In 1980 he was named the Irving Fine Professor of Music at Brandeis University. In 1983 he moved to Harvard University as a professor of composition, and was appointed to the Walter Bigelow Rosen Chair in 1989. He has won three Guggenheim fellowships, and in 1987, was named a Fellow of the American Academy of Arts and Sciences. *—Joseph Stevenson*

Overview of Works

Donald Martino has generally been viewed as being among the more progressive composers of the latter twentieth century. He is often attacked by certain tradition-minded critics for clinging to serialism, a method they consider devoid of further yield or one that never did deliver a worthwhile yield. Yet, while he has used serial techniques—hardly anything new when he began to compose in the 1950s—he has employed them with his own imaginative modifications, sort of in an Italianate spirit, evidenced in the "singing" quality he imparts, even in densely woven and highly dissonant works. Moreover, Martino, especially in his later works, avoids sounding academic or cold, managing to infuse color and a sense of freshness and invention into them.

His first works, not surprisingly, show a young Martino searching for a style. His clarinet sonata (1950–51) divulges the influence of Paul Hindemith and also makes use of jazz elements, in the end producing an interesting but not distinctive work. Better, but far from masterful, is the Bartókian violin sonata from 1954. His advancement toward more radical expressive means turned toward 12-tone methods after study with Roger Sessions and Milton Babbitt in the mid-1950s. His 1958 *Piano Fantasy* delved into serial techniques, but lacked individuality. The *Trio for Clarinet, Violin, and Piano* (1959), however, showed stronger, more vital character. His piano concerto (1965) and *Mosaic for Grand Orchestra* (1967) exhibit greater development in his expressive language, to be sure, but it was the 1973 *Notturno*, for chamber ensemble, that revealed his mastery. It is a three-movement chamber work divided into 19 sections, whose mostly slow music features a subtle manipulation of sound-blocks from which emerge attractive thematic ideas that are then deftly drawn into larger, typically polyphonic washes of sound. The work was awarded a Pulitzer Prize in 1974, the same year Martino produced his *Paradiso Choruses*, for which he used Italian texts by Dante. The "Inferno" movement is appropriately quite dissonant and harsh, "Paradiso" is warmer and brighter, and coming emotionally right between their moods is "Purgatorio." Martino's 1983 *String Quartet No. 4* also received a major award, the Kennedy Center Friedheim Competition's first prize (1985). Among his later compositions of note are his alto saxophone concerto (1987) and his *12 Preludes for Piano* (1991), the latter collection divided into two parts—six preludes each—and featuring powerfully atmospheric writing within moods that are often gloomy (*No. 2*) or sinister (*No. 5*). His violin concerto (1996) divulges his talent and imagination for both melody and contrapuntal writing while exploring new ground in harmony and rhythm.

Performances of Martino's later works have included premieres of *Variazioni Sopra un Soggetto Cavato* for solo clarinet on February 5, 1998, with the composer as soloist, and *Three Sad Songs* on April 16, 1998, at the Library of Congress with Samuel Rhodes on viola and Thomas Sauer on piano. *—Robert Cummings*

Recommended:

- ○ **Martino: Solo & Chamber Works** / Weisberg (cond.), Kalish, Zukofsky, Baron, Bloom, Rutgers U. Contemporary Chamber Ens. / 1995 / CRI 693
- ○ **Notturno** / Sollberger, Shulman (conds.), Holzman, Devendra, Smylie, Thimmig, Speculum Musicae, Columbia U. Group for Contemporary Music / 1995 / Albany 168
- ○ **Martino: A Jazz Set** / Core Ens. / 1996 / New World 80518

Jean Martinon

b. Jan. 10, 1910, Lyon, France, **d.** Mar. 1, 1976, Paris, France

Conductor

In the words of one of his biographers, conductor Jean Martinon's performances "were distinguished by a concern for translucent orchestral textures, and sustained by a subtle sense of rhythm and phrasing." Occasionally, "he stressed a poetic inflection at the expense of literal accuracy."

Martinon's first instrument was the violin; he studied at the Lyons Conservatory (1924–25), then transferred to the Paris Conservatory, where he won first prize in violin upon his graduation in 1928. He subsequently studied composition, with Albert Roussel, and conducting, with Charles Munch and Roger Desormière. Until the outbreak of World War II, Martinon was primarily a composer. His early substantial works include a *Symphoniette for piano, percussion, and strings* (1935); Symphony No. 1 (1936); *Concerto giocoso for violin and orchestra* (1937); and a wind quintet (1938). At the start of the war he was drafted into the French army. Taken prisoner in 1940, he passed the next two years in a Nazi labor camp. There, he wrote *Stalag IX (Musique d'exil)*, an orchestral piece incorporating elements of jazz; during his internment, he also composed several religious works, including *Absolve, Domine* for male chorus and orchestra, and *Psalm 136 (Chant des captifs)*, the latter receiving a composition prize from the city of Paris in 1946.

Upon his release from the Nazi camp, Martinon became conductor of the Bordeaux Symphony Orchestra (from 1943 to 1945) and assistant conductor of the Paris Conservatory Orchestra (from 1944 to 1946), then associate conductor of the London Philharmonic (from 1947 to 1949). He toured as a guest conductor as well, although his U.S. debut did not come until 1957, with the Boston Symphony giving the American premiere of his *Symphony No. 2*. Although he devoted as much time as he could to composing in the early postwar years—producing a string quartet (1946), an "Irish" Symphony (1948), the ballet *Ambohimanga* (1946), and the opera *Hécube* (1949–54)—he was increasingly occupied with conducting, working with the Concerts Lamoureux (from 1951 to 1957), the Israel Philharmonic (from 1957 to 1959), and Düsseldorf Symphony Orchestra (from 1960 to 1966). In 1963, he succeeded Fritz Reiner as head of the Chicago Symphony. Martinon's tenure there was difficult. In five seasons, he conducted 60 works by modern European and American composers, and made a number of outstanding LPs for RCA, mostly of bracing twentieth century repertory in audiophile sound. Chicago's conservative music lovers soon sent him packing.

Martinon jumped at the chance to take over the French National Radio Orchestra in 1968; working with this ensemble, he recorded almost the entire standard French repertory for Erato and EMI. His earlier Erato efforts that focused on such secondary but nevertheless interesting figures as Roussel, Pierné, and Dukas, whereas EMI assigned him integral sets of the Saint-Saëns symphonies and the orchestral works of Debussy and Ravel, among other projects. In 1974, he was appointed principal conductor of the Residentie Orkest in The Hague, but he died before that relationship could bear much fruit.

Martinon resumed his career as a composer around 1960, writing his *Violin Concerto No. 2* (1960) for Henryk Szeryng, his *Cello Concerto* (1964) for Pierre Fournier, and his *Symphony No. 4 ("Altitudes")*, composed in 1965, for the 75th anniversary of the Chicago Symphony. He acknowledged Prokofiev and Bartók as strong influences on his scores, which meld Expressionism with French Neoclassicism. Martinon continued composing into the 1970s, but he seldom recorded any of his own music, with the notable exception of the *Violin Concerto No. 2* for Deutsche Grammophon. *—James Reel*

Recommended:

- ○ **Ravel: Orchestral Works** / Martinon (cond.), Paris Orch. / 1995 / EMI 68610
- ○ **Saint-Saëns: Symphony 3; Danse macabre; Poulenc: Organ Concerto** / Martinon (cond.), Alain, O.R.T.F. / Erato 55001
- ○ **Honegger** / Martinon (cond.), Puig-Roget, Maurane, O.R.T.F. / EMI 63944

João Carlos Martins

b. Jun. 25, 1940, São Paolo, Brazil, **d.** 1981

Pianist

A child prodigy, Brazilian pianist João Carlos Martins began studying the piano with José Kliass at the age of eight. The following year, he won a competition sponsored by the Bach Society of Brazil. Soon thereafter, the legendary Alfred Cortot proclaimed: "With this kind of tone, with the ability of his fingers, he could become very important for the history of piano playing." At the age of 18, he was among the first Latin Americans to be invited to participate in the prestigious Casals Music Festival in Puerto Rico. International attention grew in 1961 when, at 20, he gave a performance of the 48 Preludes and Fugues from Bach's *Well-Tempered Clavier* (a work that later became one of his specialties) in his debut concert in Washington, D.C. During the 1960s, he performed as a soloist with major orchestras throughout the United States and Europe. After a soccer injury in 1969, Martins gave up the piano for several years. During that period, he tried a number of other careers, including banking, managing prizefighters, and construction. He eventually returned to the piano, but not to the exclusion of other activities. In 1981, he was named Brazil's secretary of culture. Between 1979 and 1998, he devoted himself to recording Bach's complete works for keyboard on the Concord Concerto and Labor Records labels. In the meantime, while visiting Bulgaria, Martins was the victim of a random attack by thugs, receiving injuries to his skull and brain, causing the loss of use of his right arm. Therapy in the next few years brought back much movement, but an operation in early 2000 rendered his hand essentially useless. Instead of retiring completely from the piano, Martin turned to recording the complete repertoire for the left hand. The series began with a disc of Ravel's concerto,

Saint-Saëns' *Etudes*, and Brahms' transcription of the Bach *Chaconne* in June 2001. —*Robert Adelson*

Recommended:

- **Bach: Well-Tempered Clavier Book 1** / Martins / 1996 / Concord 42018
- **The Essential Bach** / Djurov (cond.), Martins, Sofia Soloists / 1998 / Concord 42054
- **Vivaldi: The Four Seasons** / Martins, Corvisier (piano) / 1996 / Concord 42022

Bohuslav Martinů

b. Dec. 8, 1890, Polička, Czechoslovakia, **d.** Aug. 28, 1959, Liestal, Switzerland
Composer: Symphonic, Chamber Music, Concerto, Orchestral, Opera, Choral, Ballet
Along with Leoš Janáček, Bohuslav Martinů was one of the twin giants of Czech music in the twentieth century, a composer with a distinctly individual voice and a versatility that led him to excel in every medium from stage works to symphonies to string quartets. Martinů was born in the Moravian town of Polička. Starting violin lessons at the of seven, he gave his first recital when he was 15. By the age of ten he had written his first compositions; his juvenilia include songs, piano music, symphonic poems, string quartets, and ballets. In 1906, he entered Prague Conservatory, but reading and the theater diverted Martinů from his studies, and he was finally expelled for "incorrigible negligence" in 1910.

However, he continued composing. Exempted, as a teacher, from military service, Martinů produced many works during the World War I, including the patriotic cantata *Czech Rhapsody* (1918). Although this work and two ballets, *Istar* (1918–21) and *Who is the Most Powerful in the World?* (1922–23), gained favorable attention. Martinů felt the need for additional training. Returning to the Conservatory, he studied composition Josef Suk, later working in Paris with Albert Roussel, whose muscular, rhythmically vigorous music eventually influenced Martinů's own.

Martinů's music was well received in post-war Paris. Like many of his contemporaries, Martinů absorbed the influence of jazz, as evidenced in such works as the ballet *La revue de cuisine* (1927), which also incorporates South American rhythms, and the one-act opera *Les larmes du couteau* (The Tears of the Knife; 1928). In 1930, Martinů's constant desire to learn more led him to the music of Corelli, Vivaldi, and Bach, signaling a new concern with rhythmic continuity and contrapuntal technique.

Following the resounding success of his opera *Juliette* in Prague in 1938, World War II forced Martinů to flee his adopted home of Paris. After spending nine miserable months in the south of France, the composer and his wife made their way to Spain, and then to America, in the early months of 1941. For the duration of the war, the composer lived in various cities in the Eastern United States, surviving on commissions and producing five symphonies by 1946.

Though Martinů had planned to return to Czechoslovakia after the war, injuries and health problems prevented him from traveling. He eventually regained his health, however, producing such works as the *Sixth Symphony* (1951–53), widely regarded as a masterpiece, two of operas for television, and many chamber compositions. Martinů became an American citizen but spent much time in Europe: one of his final teaching positions was at his alma mater, the Czech Conservatory. His late scores, produced mainly in Italy and Switzerland, include striking orchestral works like *The Frescoes of Piero della Francesca* (1955), *The Rock* (1957), and *The Parables* (1957–58); he also produced an ambitious four-act opera, *The Greek Passion* (1956–59). The composer died in Liestal, Switzerland, on August 28, 1959.

Harry Halbreich's catalogue of Martinů's music, to which the composer did not assign opus numbers, lists nearly 400 compositions. Well established in the repertoire, Martinů's best works confirm Martinů's status as an important twentieth century composer. —*Michael Rodman*

SYMPHONIC

Symphony No. 1, H. 289 (1942)

Though he had composed a wealth of chamber, ballet, and operatic works, the purely symphonic form did not interest the Czech-born Martinů before 1942, because he had not felt "sufficiently prepared" for its challenges. This, his first attempt in the genre—written at the age of 52—shows that his awareness of his own abilities was indeed keen, and that his many years of experience were well digested when he set about sketching the *Symphony No. 1*. The work led a charmed existence from the start: having been in the United States for less than a year, Martinů received funding from the Koussevitzky Foundation (they would eventually commission Martinů's next five symphonic works), and the work was premiered by Serge Koussevitzky and the Boston Symphony Orchestra on November 12, 1942. Koussevitzky remarked to a group of critics that "you cannot change a single note ... it is a classical symphony"; the premiere was an outstanding success, moving Virgil Thompson, music critic for the *New York Herald Tribune*, to remark that Martinů was the successor to his compatriot Smetana.

Martinů utilized several unifying devices to make a cohesive whole of the four movements, while at the same time finding a surprising amount of variety within his material. The opening bars of the first movement, for example—a *dissonant* shimmer suspended over an ostinato bass—appear also in the third movement, returning the listener to his first impression. The main melodic material of the first movement is carried by the violins, supported by a highly rhythmic cello part. The quiet, consonant ending to the movement complements the mysterious introduction, creating a sense of dynamic balance.

The second movement is in three parts; the middle section is devoted to lyrical expression, while the outer sections are devoted to displays of power and speed. In these outer sections, one perceives a march just over the horizon as the brass section takes center stage. The lyrical mid-section relies on the solo voice of the oboe. The third movement begins with a brooding melody in the cellos and basses; with the introduction of winds and the incessant thumping of repeated bass notes in the piano, the tension rises. As with the second movement, a plaintive solo—this time for the English Horn—forms the basis for a contrasting middle section.

The finale is hard-driving and rhythmic throughout—the sheer kinetic energy rarely lets up. The ending is among the most boisterous and exciting to found in a twentieth century symphonic work. —*Franklin Stover*

Recommended:

- **Martinů: Symphony 1; Double Concerto** / Belohlavek (cond.), Czech PO / 1991 / Chandos 8950
- **Martinů: Symphonies 1 & 6** / Fagen (cond.), National SO / 1997 / Naxos 553348

Symphony No. 4, H. 305 (Apr. 1, 1945–Jun. 14, 1945)

The years Martinů spent in America between 1941 and 1953 weren't happy ones; the combination of political events in Czechoslovakia, the turmoil of World War II, and Martinů's residing in a country he found less than congenial depressed his spirits considerably. Nevertheless, he managed to keep up his usual prolific pace of composition. In his first five years in America he had produced fully 25 new pieces, and the spirit of optimism upon the end of the war brought Martinů a new burst of creativity; the *Symphony No. 4*, one of Martinů's most engaging and mellow orchestral works, was born of this spirit. Dedicated to Helen and Bill Ziegler, the Symphony was written over the months of April–June 1945, mostly in New York and partly at Martinů's summer home near South Orleans, Massachusetts, on Cape Cod. It was first performed on November 30, 1945, at Philadelphia's Academy of Music, by the Philadelphia Orchestra under Eugene Ormandy.

A soft Impressionistic rustle opens the first movement, Poco moderato–Poco allegro, leading into a playful woodwind motif which has been characterized as "like bird music." The movement has no development section as such, but features a constant metamorphosis of a couple of brief ideas, leading into a grand coda. The scherzo-like second movement starts with a rollicking tune that makes its way from the bassoon to the trumpet and right around the orchestra. Between the two presentations of this lively music is a mellow, almost Dvořák-like trio section featuring Martinů's characteristic rhythmic playfulness.

A hint of restlessness and anxiety underlies the mysterious, and quite beautiful, third movement (Largo). A more expansive and relaxed theme appears and leads to the one loud climax of the movement. The sense of anxiety returns, but is dispelled in the calm coda. There is likewise a note of unease in the opening theme of the Poco allegro final movement. This restlessness alternates with a broad, rich string tune; these two ideas are developed, the tension between the two is resolved and brighter spirits ultimately prevail. —*Chris Morrison*

Recommended:

- **Martinů: Memorial to Lidice; Field Mass; Symphony 4** / Belohlavek (cond.), Czech PO / 1993 / Chandos 9138
- **Martinů: Symphonies 3 & 4** / Neumann (cond.), Czech PO / Supraphon 1967

Symphony No. 5, H. 310 (1946)

Having not written his *First Symphony* until age 51, in 1942, Martinů then proceeded to write one every year until 1946. He composed the *Symphony No. 5*, which was originally inspired by the Red Cross but in the end dedicated to the Czech Philharmonic, between January and May of 1946. Rafael Kubelik led the Czech Philharmonic in the work's premiere at the First Prague Spring Festival, on May 28, 1947. After *No. 5*, Martinů didn't return to the symphony form until 1953 and the *Fantaisies symphoniques* (also known as his *Sixth Symphony*).

The multifaceted and mercurial nature of the *Symphony No. 5* to some extent mirrors Martinů's own state of mind at the time. Filled with great hope for the future at the end of World War II, in September 1945 Martinů was offered something of a dream teaching post—a professorship in the Master Class of Composition at the Prague Conservatory. He immediately accepted the position, but ended up having to wait until November 1946 for a reply from the Conservatory. In the meantime, he was given the chance to lecture at the Berkshire Summer Music School at Tanglewood, Massachusetts; it was in the months before he began teaching there that he wrote the *Symphony No. 5*.

Like the *Symphony No. 3* that preceded it and the *Fantaisies symphoniques* that came later, the *Fifth Symphony* is in three movements. A three-note motif heard at the beginning of the work becomes the basis of the first movement, which is in five sections, alternating fast and slow tempos. There is a haunting quality in the movement's slower sections that is, however, dispelled by the lively, bucolic music of the faster ones. After the sparkling opening of the second movement Larghetto, a flute takes an extended solo over pulsating strings. The movement as a whole is rather playful, and more of a scherzo than a slow movement (it is meant to fulfil both functions). The finale begins with a poignant Lento. The body of the movement, largely Allegro, borrows both thematic material from the first movement as well as its strategy of alternating fast and slow sections. The movement turns aggressive at times, but is for the most part a lively and optimistic conclusion. *—Chris Morrison*

Recommended:

○ **Martinů: Symphonies 1, 3 & 5** / Ancerl (cond.), Czech PO / Multisonic 310023

○ **Karel Ancerl** / Ancerl (cond.), Toronto SO / 2002 / EMI 75091

Symphony No. 6 ("Fantaisies symphoniques"), H. 343 (1951–May 26, 1953)

The first of the late orchestral works of Martinů, the *Symphony No. 6*, "Fantaisies symphoniques," is truly awe-inspiring. Commissioned by Charles Münch of the Boston Symphony in 1951, Martinů completed the work two years later, a remarkably long gestation period for a composer of Martinů's fluency. But the concentration of the work and the freedom of the development was both a challenge and a goal for him, and he assiduously applied himself to its realization. In the *Fantaisies symphoniques*, Martinů takes the slow-fast-slow, three-movement form of Debussy's *Three Nocturnes* and *La mer* and the glittering orchestral palate of Les Six and imbues them with his own elusive symphonic procedures. Each movement grows out of the same three-note motif that emerges out of the blooming, buzzing confusion of the trills of the winds and strings at the work's start, and each movement develops the motif in radically different ways. The opening movement contrasts blocks of music moving at different tempos through different textures. The central movement is a scherzo of sorts, developing the motif in airborne colors racing over the bar lines. The closing movement grows through intensities and rhythms to a final cadence that vertically expands the three-note motif as three huge and quiet chords spread over the range of the orchestra. *—James Leonard*

Recommended:

○ **Charles Munch** / Munch (cond.), BSO / EMI 75477

○ **Martinů, Janáček, Suk** / Belohlavek (cond.), Czech PO / 1990 / Chandos 8897

○ **Martinů: Symphonies 5 & 6** / Jarvi (cond.), Bamberg SO / 1988 / BIS 402

CHAMBER MUSIC

Chamber music (1900–1959)

Of Bohuslav Martinů's nearly 400 compositions, chamber music accounts for some 60, including seven string quartets, three violin sonatas, three cello sonatas, two piano quintets, a host of other sonatas, and miscellaneous works. Although best known for orchestral and choral music, Martinů once said "I am always more myself in pure chamber music."

Martinů's first composition, at age ten, was a string quartet titled *The Three Riders* which was good enough to help get him into the Prague Conservatory years later. A violinist, Martinů played in quartets as a youth and joined the Czech Philharmonic after his unsuccessful tenure as a Conservatory student. Early chamber compositions like his *String Quartet No. 1* (1918) betray an infatuation with French Impressionism.

Martinů lived in Paris from 1923 to 1940, soaking in a wide range of musical influences. The spirit of Stravinsky hangs over his *Quartet for clarinet, horn, cello, and side drum* (1924); studies with Albert Roussel influenced the *String Quartet No. 2* (1925); and jazz makes its way into the *Violin Sonata No. 1* and *Sextet* (both 1929). Many of the chamber works of those years were brief studies, like the *Piano Trio No. 1* ("Five Short Pieces" [1930]), which Martinů regarded as a watershed in terms of his contrapuntal abilities. The more ambitious *String Sextet* (1932) won him the Elizabeth Sprague Coolidge prize of $1,000. One of Martinů's greatest chamber works, the dramatic *String Quartet No. 5* (1938), was inspired by a sometimes stormy affair with composer/conductor Vítezslava Kaprálová. The upheaval of world events also crept into works like the *Cello Sonata No. 1* (1939); Martinů was able to stay in Paris just long enough to hear its premiere in May 1940. Three weeks later, he fled the city, later emigrating to America.

Despite low spirits due to the war and the difficult transition to American life, Martinů continued to compose prolifically. The *Piano Quartet No. 1* (1942) was premiered at the Berkshire Music Center in Massachusetts, where Martinů's patron Serge Koussevitzky had gotten him a teaching job. Other acquaintances inspired new music: the *Rossini Variations* (1942) were written for cellist Gregor Piatigorsky; the *Five Madrigal Stanzas* (1943) were dedicated to that noted amateur violinist Albert Einstein; and Fritz Kreisler was the dedicatee of the *Czech Rhapsody* (1945).

After a fall from a balcony in July 1946, Martinů's output dropped off briefly. The *String Quartet No. 7* (1947) and *Piano Trio No. 2* (1950) are both informed by Martinů's love of the music of Haydn. He was still capable of writing quickly: the attractive *Cello Sonata No. 3* (1952) took a mere three weeks. After a dozen years in America, in 1953 Martinů finally moved back to Europe and remained there, save for one more brief American trip, for the rest of his life. Ambitious choral and orchestral works dominate those last years. Weakened by cancer, Martinů completed a charming nonet as a sort of valedictory just months before his death in August 1959. *—Chris Morrison*

Recommended:

○ **Martinů: La Revue de Cuisine; Nonet; 3 Madrigals** / Dartington Ens. / 1998 / Hyperion 22039

Czech Rhapsody, for violin & piano, H. 307 (1945)

After his forced emigration from Europe in 1941, Czech composer Bohuslav Martinů settled in the United States. In addition to symphonies and other works, Martinů wrote one new work for violin every year, starting with 1941's *Concerto da camera* for violin and string orchestra with piano and percussions. After the Allied victory in Europe in spring 1945, Martinů's thoughts turned back toward his Czech homeland, and he composed his *Czech Rhapsody* (H. 307) from July 9 through 15 of that year on Cape Cod, MA. A virtuoso piece, it was dedicated by Martinů to the great violinist Fritz Kreisler. Writing to his friend Milos Safranek on July 10, Martinů remarked on the *Czech Rhapsody* "... it is a form I thought that I would not be doing again, and it is quite demanding...." Starting with a slow introduction, the *Czech Rhapsody* moves through four sections—a fantasy, a dance, an adagio, and finally a rapturous conclusion based on the polka. This *Czech Rhapsody* should not be confused with a work for soloist, chorus, and orchestra that Martinů immediately wrote after the end of World War I and the founding of the Czech Republic. *—James Leonard*

Recommended:

○ **Martinů: Nocturnes; Piano Trios 2 & 3** / Bekova Sisters / 1998 / Chandos 9632

Duo for violin & cello No. 2 in D major, H. 371 (Jun. 28, 1958–Jul. 1, 1958)

The extremely prolific Czech composer Bohuslav Martinů rarely stopped writing music. Even after he had been diagnosed with cancer in 1958, he continued to compose copiously, completing his last opera *The Greek Passion* and his oratorio *The Prophecy of Isaiah* in the year before his death. But despite these major works and his increasing ill health, Martinů found time to compose numerous chamber works, including his second *Duo for Violin and Cello* (H. 371). Written in four days between June 28 and July 1, 1958, the *Duo in D major* gives no sign that its composer was a dying man with only 13 months to live. Like all of Martinů's music, the *Duo* is essentially lyrical with long, gorgeous melodies that defy gravity as well as the bar line and, like most of Martinů's music, the *Duo* has lightly sprung rhythms in its outer movements that draw as much on Renaissance materialists as on modernist composers. But in its central Adagio, Martinů's melodies seem particularly poignant and his harmonies seem especially affecting, almost as if even the resolutely sanguine Martinů was musically acknowledging his own mortality. *—James Leonard*

Recommended:

○ **Double Play** / Barton, Warner / 1999 / Cedille 47

Five Madrigal Stanzas, for violin & piano, H. 297 (Nov. ??, 1943)

Physicist Albert Einstein was responsible not only for the theory of relativity, but for these 11 minutes of music by Martinů. Both men were professors at Princeton during World War II and Martinů discovered that Einstein was a decent enough violinist to play Mozart sonatas with pianist Robert Casadesus. Martinů wrote his *Five Madrigal Stanzas* especially for this duo, which apparently played the music in private recitals, dedicating the score to Einstein.

Martinů had become enamored with madrigal form in 1922, when he heard English madrigals performed in Prague. Between 1937 and 1959, he wrote three sets of madrigals for voices and four instrumental works incorporating "madrigal" into their titles. Third in the instrumental series, the *Five Madrigal Stanzas* have nothing to do with the form of English or Italian madrigals, but they do echo the contrapuntal nature of Renaissance vocal music. Bearing in mind Einstein's modest musical abilities, Martinů held this music to slow-to-moderate speeds and kept the violin writing simple. The piano part, in contrast, is quite challenging, tailored to Casadesus' skill. The madrigal's linear independence was ideal for these mismatched players. In general, the pieces reveal the influence of Czech folk song, although these are not song transcriptions. The first item, Moderato, gives the violin a simple but very lyrical melody, which the piano underlines with busy yet delicate material. The Poco allegretto is much more angular, particularly in the sputtering piano part. The Andante moderato offers the most songful violin music so far, with spare piano chords gently marking the beat. The piano creates an illusion of speed in the Scherzando, poco allegro, darting around the violin's staccato material and occasional trills. The concluding Poco allegro is especially playful, using the same techniques as the Scherzo, but with the occasional "wrong-note" chord in the piano. *—James Reel*

Recommended:

○ **Martinů: La Revue de Cuisine; Nonet; 3 Madrigals** / Benson, Butterworth / 1998 / Hyperion 22039

Four Nocturnes for cello & piano, H. 189 (1930)

During the 17 years Martinů spent in Paris (from 1923 to 1940), his music underwent many stylistic evolutions. Around 1929, he became very interested in chamber music and, along with a variety of trios, quartets, and sextets, he composed a large number of brief studies for pairs of instruments. The cello seems to have caught his fancy in 1930 as he wrote, along with the four nocturnes, a set of six pastorales, and the suite miniature for cello and piano. The nocturnes—significantly subtitled *Four Études for Cello with Piano Accompaniment*—hint at Martinů's newfound love of Baroque music, as well as his increasing interest in the folk music of his Czech homeland. Strangely, only the second of these four pieces is conventionally nocturne-like, slow and mysterious. The other three are rather extraverted and fast in tempo. The first, with its unusual rhythms, has a rough, folk-music flavor. Its puckish, sly humor is quite a contrast to the ambitious second nocturne and at eight minutes, it is by far the longest of the four. Dramatic opening chords alternate between piano and cello, leading into a lovely, gentle central section for both instruments. After a short transition in the lowest register of the cello, the opening chords return, but mellowed a bit the second time through. Slow, agitated arpeggios from the piano and a long-breathed cello melody lead into a lighter, folk-inflected section in the third piece. Cello pizzicati open the fourth, with staccato accompaniment in the piano; momentum builds with the second theme in bowed cello and the pizzicati return to close the cycle. *—Chris Morrison*

Recommended:

- ○ **Martinů: Works for Cello & Piano, Vol. 2** / C. Benda, S. Benda / 2000 / Naxos 554503
- ○ **Martinů: Nocturnes; Piano Trios 1 & 2** / Bekova Sisters / 1998 / Chandos 9632

Sonatina for clarinet & piano, H. 356 (Jan. 20, 1956)

Martinů maintained his optimistic musical spirit despite his double exile. As a Czech composer living in Paris he found himself cut off from his homeland when Hitler occupied Czechoslovakia in 1938, then had to flee Europe itself when Germany invaded France. Finally, living in the United States, he was again cut off from home when his homeland fell to a Soviet-dominated puppet-regime takeover in 1948. His style contains a neat blend of Dvořák's good humor and melodic gift, Janáček's terseness and fast musical action, and Stravinsky's neoclassicism. This blend is well represented in this charming and extroverted ten-minute piece.

The first movement is twice as long as either of the two others, but since it is divided into two clearly marked sections, the effect is a suite-like structure. The first movement is a test of rhythmic coordination, with complex cross rhythms between the different players' parts. The second movement uses the entire compass of the clarinet in a flowing melody. The third movement features dazzling trills and other showy techniques. In a tricky effect to bring off, Martinů keeps the clarinet part an eighth note ahead of the piano part in the counterpoint that dominates the music. *—Joseph Stevenson*

Recommended:

- ○ **Recital 1** / Wright, Batlle / 1998 / Boston 1023
- ○ **Saint-Saëns, Martinů, Rabaud, Bjelinski, Ladmirault** / Bach, Edwards / Crystal 735

Violin Sonata No. 2, H. 208 (1931)

The second of Martinů's three numbered violin sonatas emerged from the middle of Martinů's French phase. The composer lived in Paris for most of the 1920s and 1930s, and fell under the influence of Albert Roussel, whose motoric rhythms would throb through Martinů's scores for the rest of the Czech composer's life. Subtle wit marks much of this short work, without producing a blatantly comic effect. The first movement derives from two main motifs, a broad yet, for Martinů, typically angular melody first played by the violin over a spidery piano accompaniment reminiscent of Hindemith, and an equally characteristic chugging or rapidly sawing figure. These elements mix and match and shift from one instrument to the other over the course of their development, sometimes combining for an almost neo-Baroque effect. The Larghetto begins in the same manner as the first movement, with the violin and piano maintaining clearly independent voices. Indeed, the piano takes an extended solo before the violin returns for the movement's central section, still another lyrical-angular string melody over dry, busy piano figures; it offers little contrast with the material that opens and then closes the movement. A galloping but not too fast piano figure announces the concluding Poco allegretto, the violin soon picking up the skipping, jagged motif. The rhythmic figure, almost immediately becoming more a pogo stick ostinato than a gallop, holds steady in one instrument or the other throughout the movement. Martinů toys with this material without seriously varying it or introducing contrasting passages, merely having the violin present the tune especially emphatically at the end. *—James Reel Recommended:*

- ○ **Martinů: Madrigal Stanzas; Violin Sonata 2 & 3** / Suk, Hala / Supraphon 110099
- ○ **Martinů: Czech Rhapsody; Violin Sonatas 1, 2 & 3** / Kotkova, Mulligan / Studio Matous 00452131

Violin Sonata No. 3, H. 303 (1944)

Twice as long as Martinů's preceding violin sonata from more than a decade earlier, and having roughly the proportions of the symphonies he was writing at the time (he'd just finished his third), Martinů's *Violin Sonata No. 3* is one of his darkest, most dramatic duo works. This is not surprising; the sonata dates from 1944, when Martinů had exiled himself to the United States and Europe was still clawing its way through the horror of World War II. A stern piano chord and a shower of keyboard passage work announce the first movement, Poco allegro. The violin soon enters and together the instruments produce music that couldn't be mistaken for anyone else's; the violin offers an essentially lyrical yet nervous (often hovering in a high register) and sometimes angular melody over a chugging piano ostinato, producing an effect of steady, fast physical movement. Contrast arrives with fierce, jagged material for the violin, soon giving way to a more contemplative theme. The lyrical and the motoric vie for supremacy through the remainder of this sonata-form movement, the motoric aspect emerging victorious. Lyricism has its chance in the Adagio, which begins with the violin carefully picking its way stepwise up and down the scale over mysterious piano chords. A simple but big-hearted falling motif emerges as a mini climax in this section. The movement continues along these lines, the violin exotically winding up and down the scale then sawing through the path, then retracing its steps more tenderly and with great care. The Scherzo launches with a frantic piano introduction, soon giving way to a strongly syncopated violin tune that's quite lighthearted compared to what has come before. The two instruments play tag with a brief phrase and proceed through a more conventionally stressed version of the opening melody. This is repeated at the end, but in between comes a noodling trio section and a long, percolating crescendo and decrescendo. The final movement begins with a ruminative, haunting Lento; without breaking the mood, this at length gives way to a syncopated Poco allegro section that builds and releases tension in terraced steps. In the final pages, the movement breaks into an implacable Allegro vivo, becoming increasingly grim the faster it gets. *—James Reel*

Recommended:

- ○ **Martinů: Madrigal Stanzas; Violin Sonatas 2 & 3** / Suk, Hala / Supraphon 110099
- ○ **Martinů: Works for violin & piano, Vol. 2** / Matousek, Adamec / Supraphon 3412

CONCERTO

Cello Concerto No. 1, H. 196 (1930; revised 1939)

Around the year 1930, Martinů, having written several recent works in a style evocative of Czech folk music, came under the spell of the concerti grossi of Baroque-era composers like Handel and, especially, Arcangelo Corelli. He started incorporating elements of that style into his own music; the initial manifestation of this was the first of the three versions of the *Cello Concerto No. 1*, scored with chamber orchestra accompaniment. The concerto was written in Martinů's hometown of Policka between August and September 1930. Gaspar Cassadó, the work's dedicatee, premiered this version of the work in Berlin on December 13, 1931. In 1939 Martinů revisited it, rescoring it for a full symphony orchestra. This version was dedicated to, and premiered by, Pierre Fournier, who presented the work often over the ensuing 15 years. But in 1955 Martinů, then living in Nice, Italy, happened on a radio broadcast of the concerto from Paris and, dismayed by what he heard, decided to rescore it once again, thinning out the orchestration. Once again Fournier was the dedicatee; he continued to perform the work often and revised the concerto's third movement cadenza. This final version of the concerto has gone on to become one of Martinů's most popular works.

The first movement, Allegro moderato, opens with a bold, striding, confident main theme. A more lyrical second theme of a Czech hue ensues, in which the cellist interacts with various solo woodwinds. These two themes are developed, with the cellist kept constantly busy. A lonely clarinet introduces the second movement, Andante moderato, joined by bassoon, trumpet and other winds. The cellist enters with a gently melancholy melody that sets the tone for the entire movement, one of Martinů's most lovely inspirations. The finale begins with a lively and propulsive, rhythmically playful Allegro. The tempo slows to an Andantino briefly with a return of the ambience of the slow second movement; this leads into a brief cadenza for the soloist and a brilliant conclusion. *—Chris Morrison*

Recommended:

- ○ **Dvořák Martinů: Cello Concertos** / Neumann (cond.), Chuchro, Czech PO / Supraphon 3093
- ○ **Martinů: Cello Concertos** / Neumann (cond.), May, Czech PO / 2001 / Supraphon 3543

Double Concerto for 2 string orchestras, piano & timpani, H. 271 (1938)

Although he had lived in Paris for several years, Martinů kept in close contact with many in his homeland of Czechoslovakia. In July 1938 he had returned to Prague for the annual Festival of the Sokols; two months later he and his wife were invited to spend some time at conductor Paul Sacher's mountain retreat in Schönenberg, Switzerland. Sacher, who had supported Martinů and his music for years, had requested a work for the Basle Chamber Orchestra; Martinů began work on the *Double Concerto* for Sacher, and continued work on it in Switzerland.

It was there that Martinů learned of the Munich Pact, which allowed the Nazis to enter the Sudetenland. By October the Nazis had entered Czechoslovakia. As Martinů described the time, "With anguish we listened every day to the news bulletins on the radio, trying to find encouragement and hope that did not come. The clouds were quickly gathering and becoming steadily more threatening. During this time I was at work on the *Double Concerto*, but all my thoughts and longings were constantly with my endangered country." In 1939, Martinů was moved to volunteer for the Czech army, but health problems precluded his service. He completed the *Double Concerto*, whose emotional tenor he later linked to the circumstances of its creation: "Its notes sang out the feelings and sufferings of all those of our people who, far away from their home, were gazing into the distance and seeing the approaching catastrophe. It is a composition written under terrible circumstances, but the emotions it voices are not those of despair but rather of revolt, courage, and unshakable faith in the future." The concerto was given its premiere in Basle by Sacher and the Basle Chamber Orchestra on February 9, 1940.

The concerto is one of Martinů's most unyielding and dissonant works. Even in its quieter moments there is a stern, implacable quality. The polyphonic exchanges between the two string orchestras are reminiscent of the concertos of the Baroque era, which had been such an influence on Martinů's style through the 1930s. The *Double Concerto* is in three movements, the first an agitated Poco allegro with an aggressive motoric rhythm. The anguished second-movement Largo opens with a declamatory motif; the drama of the movement turns briefly introspective with a piano solo, but the tense polyphony of the string orchestras gradually builds to a return of the declamatory opening and a meandering coda, as though the music had spent itself. The third movement Allegro returns to the motoric rhythms of the first; once again, after a brief moment of quiet, a relentless crescendo builds to a final return of the second movement's declamatory motif. *—Chris Morrison*

Recommended:

○ **Martinů: Orchestral Works** / Conlon (cond.), Heisser, Planes, Nat Orch. of France / 1998 / Teldec 24238

Oboe Concerto, H. 353 (1955)

One of his late works, Martinů's oboe concerto lacks movement headings, but it is by no means the thorny, highly intellectual sort of 1950s music that might suggest. It's quite traditional, both in terms of its fast-slow-fast structure and in terms of the composer's personal aesthetic; the style is instantly recognizable as Martinů's: broad, wistful melodies soar over percolating rhythms with the orchestral piano providing particular color. The first movement begins with a fairly quick, bright, perambulating introduction, a characteristic Martinů ostinato that here stretches out and relaxes. The oboe enters with a measured, pastoral melody that grows more wistful as it continues. The orchestra introduces a moment of agitation, which nudges the oboe into perkier material. The soloist picks up the animated orchestral theme from the movement's beginning and eases the section toward its conclusion. The slow second movement starts with a long, dark theme primarily for strings. The oboe wanders in with a distressed, chromatic melody over a shimmering piano accompaniment. The strings offer a broader, reassuring passage, but the oboe returns in as great distress as before, the piano again underpinning what otherwise would pass for a cadenza. At last, the oboe joins the strings in a slow, elegiac version of the movement's opening theme. A rumbling piano launches the last movement's jittery folk dance, the oboe bouncing over orchestral ostinatos and then, after an agitated orchestral build-up, enjoying a full cadenza. The orchestra returns, initially bright and animated, but veering into darker material before the oboe dances the score back into the light toward an upbeat, sometimes whimsical coda.

Oboists around the world immediately took it up as a new addition to their standard repertoire. Martinů wrote the concerto for Czech oboist Jiri Tancibudek, who asked to keep the manuscripts with the cadenzas. The score, published after Martinů's death, was, therefore, missing these. Comparing the published version with his manuscript, Tancibudek noticed an unusual amount of other errors in it. In the 1980s, he and James Brody at Indiana University published a list of corrections with some interpretational suggestions. *—James Reel*

Recommended:

○ **Martinů: Oboe Concerto; Harpsichord Concerto; Piano Concerto 3** / Neumann (cond.), Sequrtd, Czech PO / 2002 / Supraphon 3622

ORCHESTRAL

Frescoes of Piero della Francesca, H. 352 (Feb. 20, 1955–Apr. 13, 1955)

In May 1953, Martinů left America, where he had spent 12 relatively unhappy years. He returned to Europe, reestablishing connections with family and friends and spending the next few years in France, Switzerland, and Italy. Much of his music of this period is vocal/choral, but he was drawn back to writing for the orchestra for the first time since leaving America as a result of a trip he took to Perugia in the spring of 1955. Travelling down the Tiber Valley, Martinů saw Piero della Francesca's *The Resurrection* in Borgo San Sepolcro. Later, in Arezzo, he spent much time with Piero's ten-panel series *The Proving of the True Cross*. Inspired by the themes and style of these visual works, Martinů composed the three *Frescoes of Piero della Francesca* for conductor Rafael Kubelik, who led the premiere at the Salzburg Festival on August 28, 1956.

Frescoes of Piero della Francesca is not for the most part directly illustrative of Piero's frescoes; Martinů was more interested in capturing their essence and general ambiance. The first of the pieces, Andante poco moderato, is connected to two of Piero's depictions of the Queen of Sheba: in one she kneels at a bridge, the wood of which will later be used to build Christ's cross; the other depicts her bowing before King Solomon. A gentle impressionistic shimmer from harp, muted strings, and horns leads into a quasi-Baroque figure from a trio of violins. More lyrical and tempestuous ideas are added to the mix, and a quiet English horn and muted strings lead the way to a recapitulation and a quiet close.

A vision of the sleeping Emperor Constantine, in which an angel shows him a cross in the sky, signaling his coming defeat of the Emperor Maxentius in battle, informs the Adagio. The mysterious opening evokes Constantine's dreams. A solo viola sounds the call to battle, which rages musically before a gentle interlude and coda with quiet drum taps.

The final Poco allegro conflates two of Piero's battle paintings, one in which Constantine, cross in hand, defeats Maxentius, the other depicting the defeat of the army of Chosroes, the Persian king who had stolen the Cross from Jerusalem. A heavily syncopated theme rocks between two, then three notes. The music alternates between forceful drama and a more pensive theme in the strings until the mood gradually calms, leading to a peaceful coda. *—Chris Morrison*

Recommended:

○ **Martinů: Symphony 5; Paraboly; Frescoes of Piero della Francesca, etc.** / Ancerl (cond.), Czech PO / 1992 / Supraphon 111931

OPERA

Recké pasije (The Greek Passion), H. 372 (Feb. 20, 1956–Jan. 8, 1957; revised Feb. 9, 1958)

In Nikos Kazantzakis' novel *Christ Recrucified*, Martinů found an operatic subject that at first seemed to defy his abilities in scale and scope. But this highly original retelling of the Crucifixion of Christ—set on a Greek island during a period of Turkish occupation—so inspired Martinů with its fusion of social justice and religious symbolism that he overcame his doubts and produced *The Greek Passion*. This would be the composer's last opera, and, fittingly, it offers some of the composer's greatest and most profound music. Martinů initially wrote the opera over a period of six months in 1956. But after two aborted offers for performance—first by Rafael Kubelik, then by Herbert von Karajan—he rewrote it, finishing this second version on January 15, 1959, only months before his death on August 28. It was first performed in Zürich in June 1961.

The Greek Passion is a deeply religious work centered around the mounting of a Passion Play in the small Greek village of Lykovrissi. Martinů based his vocal themes on Greek folk songs and church music, giving the work an undeniable authenticity. The orchestration is vivid and highly colorful. The opera is in four acts. In Act One, villagers are picked to perform in the spring Passion play. In Act Two, these villagers begin to take on the personalities of their characters in response to the rest of the villagers' persecution of a group of refugees. In Act Three, the villager playing Christ renounces his former life to work for justice for the refugees. Part of the text is spoken rather than sung here. At the climax of the opera in Act Four, the Christ character is murdered by the reigning sacred and secular powers. His death is marked by a passage of beautiful eight-part choral writing, full of power and majesty. *—James Leonard*

Synopsis:

Act One. It is Easter, sometime in the early 1900s. As the villagers of Lykovrissi, Greece, leave the church, the priest Grigoris appoints various members of the community to play parts in the next year's Passion Play. As he does so, he also announces that certain sinners will put an end to their ways; Kostandis, the café owner, for example, is to stop cheating customers by thinning the coffee with barley and to stop beating his wife. The role of Mary Magdalene is assigned to Katerina; Jesus to Manolios, though he declares that he is not worthy; Judas to Panait; and the disciple John to Michelis. Grigoris blesses them and leaves, and the players contemplate the responsibility given to them; they must, to honor their roles, lead lives worthy of Christ's companions. Lenio, Manolios' fiancée, comes in to find Manolios and asks him to name their wedding day. He is distant, not even looking at her, and to her dismay, pays more attention to distant chanting from a church service than to her. Fotis, another priest, leads in a group of refugees from another village, fleeing from the Turkish invasion, and asks that they be allowed to settle there. Fearing a threat to his own influence, Grigoris looks for an excuse to turn then away, and when one of them dies of hunger during the conversation, he claims that she had cholera and demands that they leave. Katerina is visibly interested in catching Manolios' attention, and Panait, who wants to court her himself, watches jealously. Manolios advises Fotis to take the refugees to a nearby mountain, where they can at least find fuel, and they leave.

Act Two. The merchant Yannakos has offered his donkey for the procession of Jesus into Jerusalem, happily telling the animal of how it will be greatly honored next year, though he is already intimidated by the moral responsibility he now holds. Katerina tells him that last night she had a dream in which Manolios appeared to her in the form of an archangel. Ladas suggests to Yannakos that they buy any jewelry the refugees have brought with them. Yannakos advances Ladas money, but predicts they will be more than willing to sell in exchange for food. At the spring, Katerina and Manolios meet. She tells him of her dream, but despite his growing attraction, he turns away. On the mountain, the refugees prepare their new settlement, dedicating a gate and foundations. Yannakos, who had come on his errand, watches at first with derision, then with growing awe and gives them Ladas' money. An old man leaps into one of the pits, declaring that a human sacrifice is necessary for the village's prosperity. Fotis welcomes Yannakos, who admits that he had come to take advantage of their situation. As they converse, the refugees cry out in shock that the old man is dead. Fotis says that he sees a strong future for their new home.

Act Three. In Manolios' hut, he asks Nikolio, apprentice to Yannakos, to play his pipe, and then falls asleep, dreaming of his upcoming role in the play and hearing the voices of Lenio, Grigoris, and Katerina, the latter personifying sensual temptation. Yannakos accuses him of merely going through the motions of the play, saying that his mind is on his upcoming marriage. A woman dressed in black appears, and Manolios first thinks that she is Mary, then sees that she is Katerina. He awakens, and Lenio comes in person. She wants him either to name a date for their wedding or release her from the engagement. He neither refuses nor agrees, and says he is going to the village. She leaves, but returns shortly afterwards, and she and Nikolio embrace. She passionately says that he is her salvation and that if he leaves her she will lose her soul, but he tries to extricate himself by saying she must forget about him. On the road, Katerina is taking supplies for the refugees and meets Yannakos. She confides that she dreams of the scene in which she, as Mary Magdalene, washes Jesus' feet and wipes them with her hair. He is sympathetic, having undergone a spiritual conversion after his experience. The villagers, led by Grigoris, are angry at Manolios, who seems to be taking his role as Jesus too personally and has begun to preach. After hearing him convince a farmer to give part of his harvest to the poor, and a woman's comment that he preaches with Jesus' own eloquence, Grigoris is determined to run him out of the village. Michelis announces that Lenio has received her father's permission to marry Nikolio instead. To Nikolio's astonishment, Manolios does not demand to fight over this.

Act Four. At the wedding, Grigoris interrupts the festivities with his demand that Manolios be driven from the village, like an animal that could spread infection to the rest of the herd. However, the other actors in the Passion Play say that they will not support this, and Grigoris announces that they must be driven away, as well. Manolios himself enters and says that though he was tempted by thoughts of the flesh, he is now purified and reaffirmed. The refugees enter, starving and asking for food. When Manolios says that it is their Christian duty to offer charity to their needy brothers and sisters, Grigoris leads the villagers against him, and Panait kills him. As the refugees, Katerina, and Lenio pray, Fotis leads his people onward. *—Ann Feeney*

Recommended:

○ **Martinů: Greek Passion** / Mackerras (cond.), Tomlinson, Davies, Field, Jonasova, BRNO State PO / Supraphon 3611

CHORAL

Gilgames (The Epic of Gilgamesh), oratorio, H. 351 (Dec. 23, 1954–Feb. 16, 1955)

Czech composer Bohuslav Martinů composed *Gilgames* (The Epic of Gilgamesh) in Nice, France, in 1954 and 1955. Part oratorio, part cantata, and part symphony, this is a work in three sections scored for soprano, tenor, baritone, bass soloists, mixed chorus, orchestra, and speaker. Based on the ancient Sumerian text from three millennia before the birth of Jesus, Martinů's work treats the oldest question to trouble humanity: "What happens after we die?" The first part of the work deals with the meeting of Gilgamesh, the legendary King of Ourouk, and Enkidu, the man who would later become his best friend. The second part describes the death of Enkidu and Gilgamesh's shattering response. The third part, entitled "Invocation," is Gilgamesh's vision of the world beyond. As in the original, Martinů's Gilgamesh does not describe his vision; when asked what he saw, all he can say is "I saw. I saw." With the sibilant whispering of the chorus, the strange sounds of the percussion, the angular beauty of the vocal melodies, *Gilgames* is a powerfully haunting work of extraordinary and eerie effects that mysteriously but mercilessly impart Martinů's strange, barbaric, and ultimately supernatural vision. *—James Leonard*

Recommended:

○ **Martinů: Epic of Gilgamesh** / Kosler (cond.), Kusnjer, Vele, Depoltova, Margita, Karpisek, Slovak PO / 2002 / Naxos 555138

BALLET

La Revue de Cuisine (Kitchen Revue), jazz suite & ballet, H. 161 (1927)

Bohuslav Martinů's first few years in Paris were a real eye-opener for him. The Paris of the 1920s was, of course, one of the most remarkable and diverse artistic centers of all time, and Martinů encountered a wider range of music and art than he ever had before. Seemingly everything he saw and heard, from Impressionist music to jazz to avant-garde theater, made its way into his own prolific output of the time. In the year 1927 alone he created three new ballets—*Le Raid merveilleux, On Tourne!* (Shoot!), and *Pokušení svatouská* (Temptation of the Saintly Pot). The last-named became Martinů's first great success when it was premiered in Prague—by the Group of Jarmila Kröschlová conducted by Martinů's good friend Stanislav Novák—under its revised title *La Revue de Cuisine* (The Kitchen Revue).

In *La Revue de Cuisine* the dancers play kitchen utensils. As the curtain rises, the marriage of Pot and Lid is threatened by rival Twirling Stick. Pot initially succumbs to Twirling Stick's sweet talk. In Pot's absence, Dishcloth tries to strike something up with Lid, who is subsequently challenged to a duel by Broom. Pot eventually tires of Twirling Stick and wants to return to beloved Lid, but Lid has disappeared. An enormous foot suddenly appears and kicks Lid back on stage. Pot and Lid return to one another, and Twirling Stick's affections move to Dishcloth.

The ballet's music reflects Martinů's early flirtation with jazz and popular styles, which also informs later works like the *Three Sketches in Modern Dance Forms for piano* (1927), the orchestral piece *Le Jazz* (1928), and the *Violin Sonata No. 1* (1930). The music of Igor Stravinsky, almost an unavoidable influence on musicians of that time, is also a significant element (Martinů had actually been accused by some of plagiarizing Stravinsky in the orchestral work *Half-Time* of 1924). Martinů's ensemble for *La Revue de Cuisine*—a chamber group made up of violin, cello, clarinet, trumpet, bassoon, and piano—inevitably calls to mind a work like Stravinsky's *L'Histoire du soldat* (1918).

Martinů's score features a lively opening Prologue, as well as a comically dramatic Tango (the music has its dark elements, which are undercut by the actions on stage and act as an ironic commentary on it). The jazz element comes to the fore in the Charleston, and the march that serves as a Finale reprises the opening music. *—Chris Morrison*

Recommended:

○ **Martinů: Works Inspired by Jazz & Sport** / Rauch, Dlouhy, Formacek, Sadlo, Belcik, Junek / Supraphon 3058

Giuseppe Martucci

b. Jan. 6, 1856, Capua, Italy, **d.** Jun. 1, 1909, Naples, Italy

Composer: Keyboard, Vocal, Symphonic, Concerto

Giuseppe Martucci was an influential teacher and leader of the group of Italian composers determined to break away from the dominance of opera in their country's musical life.

His father was a bandmaster who gave him his early music lessons. He made his debut playing piano at the age of eight; his sister Teresa, who was on the same program, was even younger. In 1867, he began studies at the Naples Conservatory, taking piano with Beniamino Cesi and composition with Paolo Serrao. However, his father, seeing the boy's talent at the keyboard blossom to an astonishing degree, decided to cash in and pulled him out of the Conservatory at the age of 15 to start a concert career in 1871. He was successful and was noted for the unusual seriousness and breadth of his performances. Rather than the popular Romantic knucklebusters, he played the established great classics from Bach and Scarlatti to Liszt and frequently accompanied cellist Alfredo Carlo Piatti. But when he attained adulthood and independence from his father, he applied for a job teaching at Naples Conservatory, was appointed professor, and virtually quit concert touring. He took up the baton in 1881. He helped establish the new permanent symphony orchestra in Naples and did much to promote the important composers of Northern Europe, especially Wagner, whose work he led in concert and whose opera *Tristan und Isolde* he was the first to conduct in Italy (Bologna, June 2, 1888). He had moved to Bologna in 1886 to take the leadership of the Liceo Musicale Bolognese orchestra. His 16 years at its helm are still counted by many as a high point in the city's rich musical history.

It is not surprising that his career as a composer parallels his life as a performer. His first 44 opus numbers are practically all typical Romantic piano fluff. With his *Piano Quintet*, Op. 45, Martucci shows a sudden and drastic elevation of his aims and quality. His outstanding qualities are his lyrical gift and his sense of lighthearted fantasy. These are attributes that are more suited to short music and, indeed, his shorter works of the post opus 45 works are perhaps his best music. However, his larger scale works, including concertos, symphonies, and full-scale chamber music compositions, show a noble purpose with a similar sort of lyricism, but a sometimes self-conscious struggle to find the right form. His finest large orchestral work is his *Symphony No. 2*, which composer Gian Francesco Malipiero called "the starting point of the renaissance of non-operatic Italian music." *—Joseph Stevenson*

KEYBOARD

Notturno No. 1 in G flat major, Op. 70/1 (1891)

The Italian composer Giuseppe Martucci made his reputation in his lifetime as conductor, pianist, and composer. In his *Notturno* for piano (or orchestra) No. 1, Op. 70, he successfully combined all three. The work was originally for solo piano which the composer premiered, was arranged for orchestra by the composer in 1888, and premiered by him later that same year. A dreamy and romantic work, the *Notturno* is small in ambition and scale but nonetheless melodically attractive and highly effective in his orchestral setting. *—James Leonard*

Recommended:

○ **Martucci: Complete Orchestral Works** / D'Avalos (cond.), London PO / 1990 / ASV 408

○ **Busoni: Turandot Suite** / Muti (cond.), La Scala Theater Orch. / 1993 / Sony 53280

VOCAL

La Canzone dei ricordi, song cycle for soprano & orchestra (1898)

Giuseppe Martucci was the only major Italian composer of his generation to eschew the writing of opera. He instead concentrated on the abstract forms of the symphony and piano concerto. The closest he ever got to writing an opera was in his song cycle *La Canzone dei ricordi* (The Song of Memory). Originally conceived as a work for voice and piano, the work found its final form and highest expression in this arrangement for soprano and orchestra. A lushly Wagnerian setting of seven poems by Rocco Pagliera, Martucci's *La Canzone dei ricordi* is held together more by its mood of intense yearning than by melodic and harmonic leitmotifs. Although historically significant as the first Italian orchestral song cycle, *La Canzone dei ricordi*'s intensely lyrical musical expression indicates that Martucci might have been a great opera composer had he turned his mind to it. *—James Leonard*

Recommended:

○ **Martucci: Complete Orchestral Works** / D'Avalos (cond.), Yakar, London PO / 1990 / ASV 408

○ **Martucci & Respighi** / Lopez-Cobos (cond.), Balleys, Lausanne CO / 1998 / Claves 509807

SYMPHONIC

Symphony No. 2 in F major, Op 81 (1899–1904)

Alone among the major Italian composers of his generation, Giuseppe Martucci devoted himself almost exclusively to the composition of instrumental music. Among his most important works are the two piano concertos and the two symphonies. Of these, the *Second Symphony in F major* (1904) is his masterpiece. An expansive four-movement work, the *F major Symphony* is tonally advanced, skillfully structured, intensely lyrical, and brilliantly orchestrated. Premiered on December 11, 1904, under the direction of the composer, the symphony received its second and third performances under Toscanini, who kept Martucci's works in repertoire. With its motivically organized opening Allegro moderato, its Mendelssohnian Scherzo, its emotionally effective Adagio ma non troppo and its exciting fugal finale, Martucci's *Second Symphony* is arguably the best symphony ever composed by an Italian. *—James Leonard*

Recommended:

○ **Toscanini conducts Martucci** / Toscanini (cond.), NBCSO / Iron Needle 1352

○ **Martucci: Symphonies 1 & 2** / Malaysian PO, Bakels (cond.) / 2002 / BIS 1255

CONCERTO

Piano Concerto No. 2 in B flat minor, Op. 66 (1884–1885)

Sometimes called "the Italian Brahms," Giuseppe Martucci abjured the traditional Italian fascination with opera for a musical career as a conductor, pianist, and composer. His two symphonies and two piano concertos all demonstrate his allegiance in what he called "absolute music." His *Second Piano Concerto in B flat minor*, Op. 66, (1884–85) is a massive work in three movements. The opening movement, Allegro giusto, alone is more than 20 minutes long and contains three themes, an extensive development section, and an enormous cadenza. The central movement, Larghetto, has two contrasted themes which reach their climax in a section which recalls the piano recitative central movement of Beethoven's *Fourth Piano Concerto*. The closing movement, Allegro con spirito, is a brilliant virtuoso work for both soloist and orchestra ending in resounding triumph. The *Second Piano Concerto* was premiered on January 31, 1885, with the composer as the soloist. *—James Leonard*

Recommended:

○ **Martucci: Complete Orchestral Works** / D'Avalos (cond.), Caramiello, Philharmonia / 1990 / ASV 408

Pietro Mascagni

b. Dec. 7, 1863, Livorno, Italy, **d.** Aug. 2, 1945, Rome, Italy
Composer: Opera

Though regarded by casual opera followers as a one-work composer, Pietro Mascagni wrote other operas of interest and some quality. Aside from *Cavalleria Rusticana*, the winsomely comic *L'amico Fritz*, the wrenchingly dramatic *Iris*, and *Il Piccolo Marat* attest to a diversity of mood and manner. Still, Mascagni's first opera was so successful that subsequent efforts simply could not equal that initial triumph. His embrace of Mussolini's Fascist regime seemed self-serving during the 1920s and 1930s; at the end, it left Mascagni discredited and impoverished.

Although his parents had conceived for their son a career in law, Mascagni did receive some private training. However, when he began to study with the director of the newly formed Istituto Musicale Livornese, his father forbade further musical studies until a bachelor uncle interceded to offer young Pietro a home and means to finance his training. When Mascagni arrived at the Milan Conservatory, he remained only two years before embarking on an unsettled career as an orchestra member and occasional conductor of touring operetta companies. Upon marriage to Lina Carbognani in 1889, he settled in Puglia as a music instructor.

To a competition mounted by the music publisher Sonzogno, Mascagni submitted his third opera, *Cavalleria Rusticana*, in February 1890. At its Roman premiere on May 17, an unprecedented success propelled the composer from provincial hopeful to newly minted maestro. The following year, Mascagni enjoyed a more muted achievement with *L'Amico Fritz*. *Silvano* brought a return to verismo in 1895, although its reception was less positive than that accorded *Iris*, a substantial success in 1899 with a hyper-intense Oriental theme. Recurrently, the composer turned to themes of loss when choosing his libretti, recalling the desolation he felt at his mother's death when he was but 10 years old. An illicit relationship with Anna Lolli, begun in 1903, lasted until Mascagni's death in 1945.

Mascagni continued to compose in the new century, completing *Isabeau* in 1911, *Parisina* in 1913, *Lodoletta* in 1917, and *Il piccolo Marat* in 1921. As with the overblown *Nerone*, written in 1935 to please the regime, Mascagni often explored the outer limits of vocal possibility with punishing tessituras and unrelentingly high volume. He appeared occasionally as a conductor, more positively in Italy than in an ill-conceived American tour in 1902–03. *—Erik Eriksson*

OPERA

L'amico Fritz (1891)

First performed on October 31, 1891, at the Teatro Costanzi in Rome, *L'amico Fritz* is Mascagni's second most popular opera and is still staged with some frequency in Italy. Although fans expected another *Cavalleria rusticana*, and initially expressed their disappointment at not receiving one, the qualities of *L'amico Fritz* eventually won over its potential detractors. Some, including Gustav Mahler, who gave a performance of the opera in Hamburg in 1892, considered *L'amico Fritz* superior to *Cavalleria* in many ways.

L'amico Fritz is strikingly different; having launched the verismo school with *Cavalleria*, Mascagni here made a complete stylistic about-face. But this was at least in part because of the commission Mascagni received in early 1891 from the Teatro Costanzi in Rome; the management asked the composer to deliver an opera on a light, entertaining subject. After some searching, Mascagni chose a French comedy by Emile Erckmann and Alexandre Chatrian, *L'Ami Fritz*, which had been published in 1864 and adapted for the stage in 1872. The story was further transformed into a libretto by P. Suardon (an anagram for the famous writer, N. Daspuro), who maintained the fundamental ingredients of the original: Fritz Kobus, a wealthy, confirmed bachelor, lives on his estate in Alsace. The Rabbi David (changed to a physician during Italy's Mussolini years), a persistent matchmaker, is determined to get Fritz to marry. Partly through David's plotting, Fritz falls in love with Suzel, the daughter of his steward, and asks her to marry him.

So, absent is *Cavelleria*'s stark realism, charged eroticism, and blistering, brief, and frenetic segments of music. Instead, *L'amico Fritz* offers a subdued, idyllic atmosphere that makes it irresistible and charming. The first performance was a triumph; several numbers were repeated and there were innumerable curtain calls. Within a year of the premiere, *L'amico Fritz* played across Europe.

The characters are exquisitely drawn. The most colorfully illustrated of these is Suzel, a shy person capable of emotional outbursts. Her romance from Act One, "Son pochi fiori," is especially impressive, its melody looking forward to Puccini's *Manon Lescaut*. Suzel's second-act ballad, "Bel cavalier," is notable in that each of its four verses rises a step above the previous one, increasing tension, and her anguished "Non mi resta che il pianto," from Act Three, has become a concert favorite. Fritz is the next most carefully drawn character; his growing love becomes clear in his impassioned "Quale strano turbamento!" from the second act as well as the Act Three romance, "O amore o bella luce del cuore!" As is the case with most of Mascagni's tenor parts, the tessitura is uncommonly high—a challenge for even the finest singers. Rabbi David's sturdy, serious personality comes across in the stately setting of his "Per voi, ghiottoni inutili," from Act One, and in the chorale-like, third-act duet with Suzel, "Faceasi vecchio Abramo," in which they discuss a Bible story.

Alsatian folk songs arranged for an off-stage chorus create local color, while Mascagni portrays the pastoral setting in Suzel's "Son pochi fiori" and her "Cherry" duet with Fritz in Act Two. Beppe's gypsy background becomes apparent in the violin solo that serves as his introduction. *—John Palmer*

Synopsis:

Act One. Fritz is disparaging the institution of marriage in conversation with the Rabbi David, who has just arranged another marriage and is asking Fritz to guarantee the dowry. His friends Federico and Hanezo, also confirmed bachelors, come to wish him a happy birthday. David leaves to deliver the news, and Fritz declares his intention to be a friend always to everyone, but never a married man. Caterina announces Suzel, the daughter of one of his tenants, who comes with flowers for him ("Son pochi fiori"), and he invites her to join them for their meal. Beppe, a gypsy, comes and sings a song about Fritz's benefactions ("Laceri, miseri, tanti bambini") despite his embarassed protests. When Suzel leaves, David says that he will be arranging a marriage for her soon, but Fritz protests that she is still a child, and continues to disparage matrimony. David defends the institution and furthermore bets ownership of a vineyard with Fritz that he will marry some day. A group of orphans whom Fritz has befriended approaches, playing instruments, and Fritz tells David that he already has children; the two go out to greet them.

Act Two. In an orchard, Suzel picks cherries while the chorus sings offstage. She sings a ballad, "Bel cavaliere," about a knight, and Fritz comes out to listen. In the Cherry Duet, "Suzel, buon di," they share their delight in the beautiful morning. David and his other friends join them, and David guesses from Fritz's glances and words that he is smitten with Suzel. He stays behind to talk with her when the others go off. He asks Suzel to draw water from the well for him and also asks her to tell the biblical story ("Faceasi vecchio Abramo") of how Abraham's servant prayed that God would show him the right wife for Isaac by letting the first one to offer to draw water be the chosen woman, and how Rebecca thus came to marry him. When Fritz and the others return, she runs off in confusion. David tests Fritz by declaring his intention of finding a husband for her immediately. Fritz is strangely annoyed, and when they leave, he realizes he is beginning to fall in love ("Quale strano turbamento"). He decides to leave immediately, and when Suzel hears the news, she bursts into tears.

Act Three. Fritz has come back, unable to make himself forget Suzel; everywhere he finds reminders of love. Beppe comes to visit and diagnoses Fritz's glumness as a sign that he is in love. He sings him a love song he wrote when he himself was sadly in love, "O pallida, che un giorno," and Fritz becomes still more perturbed. He asks Beppe to leave and reflects on love, finally deciding to surrender ("Ed anche Beppe amo . . . O amore, o bella luce del core"). David comes in and tells him he has arranged for Suzel's marriage to a wealthy young man. Fritz snaps that he will not consent and stomps off. Suzel comes in, and David tries to comfort her, but leaves her alone. She expresses her persistent sadness ("Non mi resta che il pianto"), and when Fritz returns, she confides that she is marrying only because her father wishes to secure her future. She pleads with him to ask her father not to agree to the marriage, saying that she would rather be alone and trust in God's care than to marry someone she doesn't love. He asks if she loves another, and when she feebly denies it, he declares his own love for her. They embrace happily ("Io t'amo"), and when David and his friends come in, Fritz admits he has lost the bet. David gives the vineyard to Suzel for her dowry and declares his intention of marrying off the other two confirmed bachelors, as all repeat Fritz's words about the power of love: "O amore, o bella luce del core." *—Ann Feeney*

Recommended:

○ **Mascagni: L'amico Fritz** / Gavazzeni (cond.), Freni, Pavarotti, Sardinero, Pudwell, Royal Opera House Orch. Covent Garden / 2000 / Angel 67373

○ **Mascagni: L'amico Fritz** / Mascagni (cond.), Tagliavini, Tassinari, Latinucci, Meletti, Turin RAI SO / 2003 / Warner Fonit 4661818

Cavalleria rusticana (1890)

Along with Leoncavallo's *I Pagliacci* (1892), *Cavalleria rusticana* (Rustic Chivalry) is the primary example of Italian verismo (literally, "truthism" or "realism"). *Cavalleria rusticana* was both the best and worst thing that happened to Mascagni, for its success—never to be repeated—weighed upon the composer all his life.

Giovanni Verga's (1840–1922) play *Cavalleria rusticana* was staged for the first time in 1884 to great acclaim. That same year, Mascagni saw the play in Milan, but considered using it as the basis of an opera only four years later, when he learned of the publisher Sonzogno's competition for a one-act opera, in 1888. (Mascagni claimed that his wife sent Sonzogno the score of *Cavalleria rusticana*, when he had planned to submit another work.) The composer commissioned Giovanni Targioni-Tozzetti (1859–1934) to write a libretto and Targioni-Tozzetti sought help from Guido Menasci. The two finished the libretto by December 1888; Mascagni completed the score about six months later. Awarded the first prize in Sonzogno's competition, Mascagni's *Cavalleria rusticana* premiered on May 17, 1890, at the *Teatro Costanzi* in Rome. Its success was immediate and unparalleled, it was translated into several languages and performed throughout the world within a year.

Mascagni stated his desire to remain close to Verga's original, and this is generally the case. However, Targioni-Tozzetti and Menasci made one important dramatic change. In Verga's, play, Santuzza disappears after she fulfills her dramatic function in her conversation with Alfio. At the end of the opera, she returns to center stage and faints.

There are significant parallels between *Cavalleria* and the hard-hitting realism and expressive music of Bizet's *Carmen.* Both take jealousy as the primary dramatic motivation, and both have Mediterranean settings with an emphasis on local color; Mascagni produces the latter by using a Sicilian dialect in Turiddu's serenade during the innovative orchestral *Prelude* (innovative primarily for its inclusion of this central sung passage). The key of F major, traditionally a "rustic" key, dominates the *Prelude.*

Leitmotives serve an important function in *Cavalleria.* The most powerful of these is the lugubrious theme accompanying Santuzza's entrance and reappearing at several climactic moments. Among these are "Mala Pasqua," in which Santuzza berates Turiddu and at the tragic ending of the piece, suggesting that the theme represents cruel fate rather than Santuzza. Musical illustration of a different type occurs in Alfio's entrance aria, in which the unsettling rhythms and malign melody belie the wonderful world he describes. Alternating recitative and arioso convey myriad feelings in the duet for Turiddu and Santuzza ("Tu qui, Santuzza?").

In some aspects of the formal organization of *Cavalleria,* Mascagni takes a step backward. This is most apparent in the composer's use of set "numbers," which Verdi had almost abandoned in the recent *Otello* (1887). This traditional plan allowed Mascagni to communicate his ideas more directly and create a series of continuous scenes in which characters could express their individual passions. *—John Palmer*

Synopsis:

Scene One. The action takes place in what was the present day, in a Sicilian village on Easter morning. During an orchestral prelude Turiddu, from behind the curtain, sings a Siciliana in praise of Lola, "O Lola, bianca come fior di spino" (Lola, fair as flowers smiling in beauty). After Turiddu waxes poetic about her lips and cheeks, the curtain rises on a crowd of villagers streaming into their colorfully adorned village church, its ringing bells calling everyone to the early morning Easter service. Santuzza, a young peasant girl, steps up to Lucia's house and asks where Turiddu may be lingering. Lucia, Turiddu's mother, is surprised and answers that Turiddu is in Francoforte purchasing wine. Santuzza, however, knows that Turiddu is at the house —she saw him in town only last night. Santuzza confesses to Turiddu's mother that her son has behaved badly to her; she feels terrible and ashamed and wants to leave town. Santuzza knows he is not out shopping for wine, because she saw him on his way to visit Lola, with whom he is in love, even though she is married to Alfio. Lola has won over Turiddu and has caused him to be unfaithful to Santuzza. Alfio, as yet, know nothing of his bride's infidelity.

Alfio comes home singing a spirited wagoner's song and happy about the rest he will get on the holiday. Santuzza asks Lucia to be quiet about the affair and begs her to pray for her. She waits alone at the church, hoping to see Turiddu. When Turiddu appears, Santuzza asks him where he has been. She does not believe he went to Francoforte to purchase wine and aggressively questions him. Turiddu wants to explain himself, but as he begins to realize he has been found out, his shame drives him to shout at Santuzza. With a threatening voice he tells her he will not be her slave. The passionate exchange is brought to a halt by the appearance of Lola, who suddenly enters singing a lighthearted song. She infuriates Turiddu by asking him about Alfio, scoffs at Santuzza and leaves them both behind in an agitated state. In vain, Santuzza resumes entreating Turiddu, asking him not to leave her. He pushes her away from him and runs after Lola. When Alfio enters, Santuzza reveals to him his wife's infidelity. Santuzza's news unleashes Alfio's rage, and he swears bloody revenge on his betrayer. Santuzza realizes, too late, what she, in her despair, has done.

A powerful orchestral intermezzo divides the opera into two scenes.

Scene Two. It is now full daylight, and the sun has completely risen. The people of the village stream out of the church. Turiddu wants to be away from the crowd and invites his friends to join him for a drink. Lola, too, will come along. As the group sings songs and passes mugs around, Alfio enters the scene. He refuses the wine Turiddu offers him. Everyone senses that something unpleasant is about to happen, and the women leave, taking the frightened Lola with them. As the two men embrace, Alfio bites Turiddu on the ear—the traditional Sicilian method of challenging someone to a duel. Suddenly, remorse wells up inside Turiddu, and he convinces himself to be courageous. He declares that he must live for his Santuzza and that his death will be a dagger in her heart. Alfio, unmoved, tells Turiddu he will meet him in the orchard. Turiddu calls to his mother, asking for her blessing and protection for Santuzza if he does not return. Lucia does not understand, and her son walks outside. Excited, Santuzza runs to Lucia. The two women embrace as other women rush in from outside exclaiming, "Turiddu is murdered!" Santuzza and Lucia faint. *—John Palmer*

Recommended:

- ○ **Mascagni: Cavalleria Rusticana; Leoncavallo: Pagliacci** / Gavazzeni (cond.), Pavarotti, Varady, Cappuccilli / 1988 / London 414590
- ○ **Mascagni: Cavalleria Rusticana** / Karajan (cond.), Bergonzi, Cossotto, Allegri / 1999 / DG 457764
- ○ **Mascagni: Cavalleria Rusticana** / Bychkov (cond.), Norman, Giacomini, Hvorostovsky / 1991 / Philips 432105

Iris (1898; revised 1899)

Luigi Illica (1857–1919) was contracted in 1894 to create a libretto for the composer Alberto Franchetti focusing on the Japanese legend of the flower lover. Franchetti changed his mind about the opera, and after three years, Illica offered the book to Mascagni, who agreed to take on the project if it were to be published by Giulio Ricordi, the man who foolishly had turned down *Cavalleria rusticana* a few years earlier.

The success of *Cavalleria* weighed heavily upon Mascagni, who tried to remove himself from the style of his most popular offspring. In *Iris* he found the opportunity to expand his orchestral palette and make the most of the exotic imagery afforded by Illica's libretto, which demonstrates a genuine knowledge of Japan. Beginning in June 1896, Mascagni worked very slowly and deliberately on the score. He wrote that he had never before been so possessed by a work, and that he intended to compose "real music, not... some buffoonery of oddities and scenes over a contrabassoon or bass pedal." It quickly became his most widely accepted work aside from *Cavalleria*, playing at La Scala in Milan, with slight revisions, two months after its premiere in Rome on November 22, 1898. By 1902 the opera had been given throughout Europe and South America and staged in New York, under Mascagni's baton.

Musically, *Iris* is breathtaking. Mascagni's orchestration, including gongs, celesta, glockenspiel, and chimes, made a strong impression on Puccini, as you can hear in *Madama Butterfly*. *Iris* opens with an impressive prologue depicting the sunrise that betrays the influence of Wagner in the gradually rising thematic material in the orchestra, culminating in a moving choral hymn to the sun. Osaka's serenade in Act One, "Apri la tua finestra," is a true test of vocal mastery in its high tessitura and key changes. Aside from Iris' "Ho fatto un triste sogno," it is the best-known number from the opera. Music for all-female ensembles predominates, two examples of which are the chorus of laundresses, who sing while Iris tends to her garden in the first act, and the chilling, non-texted passages for the geisha at the beginning of the second act. Throughout the opera, Mascagni creates an "exotic" atmosphere his contemporaries would have associated with Japan. A harp conveys the delicate sound of the samisen Iris plays in Act Two while modal passages in the strings sound during the puppet show in Act One. Mascagni flavors the score with whole-tone scales, an exoticism that is a fundamental characteristic of Debussy's music, also influenced by Eastern sounds. *—John Palmer*

Synopsis:

Act One. A chorus sings as the sun proclaims itself to be life and warmth, light, and love ("Son Io! Son Io, la vita"). Iris emerges from the cottage she shares with her father, recalling a terrible dream she had ("Ho fatto un triste sogno"): her doll was ill, and she took it into the mysteriously silent garden, which suddenly filled with threatening monsters. Now she greets the sun, and holds her doll up to do the same. She runs back inside as her father calls, and Osaka and Kyoto, who have been observing her, come out of hiding. Osaka insists that Kyoto obtain her for him. They leave, and Iris leads her blind father Il Cieco into the sunshine to sit and pray on his Buddhist rosary. Young women come to the brook and sing as they wash their laundry ("Al rio! Al rio!"); Iris sings as she waters her plants ("In pure stille"); and Il Cieco prays ("Tu mi hai tolto la vista"), thankful for Iris' companionship. They hear strolling entertainers, and Iris draws closer to watch. Kyoto and Osaka have arranged for the puppet show, which portrays Dhia cruelly treated by her father ("Misera! Ognor qui sola!"). The girls in the audience react indignantly, as if the show were real. Osaka sings the role of Jor, son of the Sun, calling lovingly to Dhia ("Apri la tua finestra"), who dies and joins him in the heavens. Iris is so moved that she comes close enough that when the geishas dance, their movements hide her kidnapping. Kyoto leaves a note and money for Il Cieco, and the players leave with their captive. Il Cieco calls to Iris, and as he frenziedly tries to search for her, falls to the ground. Some peddlers hear his cries, come to help him and also find the note, which says she has gone to the Yoshiwara (the prostitutes' district). Believing she has gone freely, he curses her, and goes after her in a rage, as the peddlers reverently guide him.

Act Two. In Kyoto's brothel, Iris is asleep. Kyoto scolds the geishas and sends them away as Osaka enters. He watches her in an agony of desire ("Crea in quegli occhi"). Kyoto advises him to win her affections with coaxing and presents. They leave, and Iris wakes up. Seeing the lavish surroundings, she imagines that she has died and is in paradise. She finds paint and paper, and tries to draw flowers and the sky, but the images seem menacing to her ("Io pingo... pingo"). Osaka comes in and pays her extravagant compliments, ("Oh, come al tuo sottile corpo"); she naively thinks he is Jor. He tells her that he will teach her and says his true name is Pleasure. She is alarmed, ("Un di ero piccina") because a priest showed her a screen depicting a woman enveloped by an octopus, and told her the octopus that was killing her as she smiled was pleasure, which is death. She begs to go back her father, but he ignores this and brings in presents ("Or dammi il braccio tuo"). All she wants is her home. Osaka becomes bored and leaves her to Kyoto. Kyoto has the geishas dress her in a nearly transparent robe and, when she tries to run away, orders her to obey and threatens to throw her into the darkness below. She begs him not to hurt her, and to keep her calm, he gives her the puppet doll of Jor, which she happily plays with, singing the ("Apri la tua finestra"). When she is prepared, he displays her in the window to the excited crowd ("Oh, maraviglia delle maraviglie"). Osaka, seeing her from outside, is newly excited and calls out, declaring that he still desires her and regretting his previous indifference ("Iris, son io!"). Il Cieco emerges from the crowd and she calls to him, stretching out her arms. He furiously throws mud at her, and deranged with grief, she throws herself into the deep sewer.

Act Three. Ragpickers poke into the ditch with hooks, one singing to the moon ("Ad ora brunae tarda"). Their hooks catch first on a pile of weeds and then on a rock, and then they see a glimpse of something gleaming. It is Iris, still in the dress, which they begin to pull off, thinking her dead. She shivers, and they run away. In a reverie, she asks "Why? Why?" Osaka, Kyoto, and Il Cieco respond, each in an arioso about his own egoism in how he used her, each arioso ending "Such is life, goodbye." She still cannot comprehend why such terrible things have happened to her ("Ancora il triste sogno") and again asks why. The sun appears and begins to illuminate and warm her with its rays, and she exclaims in an outburst of joy that it has not abandoned her and dies exclaiming at its beauty. The chorus again personifies it ("Ancor! Son Io, la Vita") and as the sun summons them to her as a fellow flower, flowers burst into bloom around her corpse, turning the ditch into a field of blossoms, and raising her on their stems towards the sun. *—Ann Feeney*

Recommended:

- ○ **Mascagni: Iris** / Patane (cond.), Domingo, Pons, Tokody, Giaiotti, Munich Radio Orch. / 1989 / CBS 45526

Jules Massenet

b. May 12, 1842, Montaud, Loire, France, **d.** Aug. 13, 1912, Paris, France

Composer: Opera, Vocal

Today Jules Massenet is best known for the operas *Manon and* Werther and the solo violin *Méditation*, from *Thaïs*. During his lifetime, however, Massenet was one of the most prolific and celebrated operatic composers on earth. The public anxiously awaited his output, and Massenet became both wealthy and famous practicing his craft. His legacy endures because of his ability to create music which portrays the intimacy of human relationships and the emotions and conflicts that arise from them. His gift for melody is reflected in a variety of arias that are among the most beautiful in the French operatic repertoire. He was also a brilliant orchestrator, a skill which allowed him to capture the moods and colors of a wide variety of places and eras. In addition to opera, Massenet composed songs, oratorios, ballets and orchestral works, as well as chamber music and works for solo piano.

Massenet was born in Montaud, France, to the family of a struggling metal worker. At the tender age of 10, he was admitted to the Paris Conservatory, where he studied with famed operatic composer Ambroise Thomas. In 1863, Massenet won the Prix de Rome, a prize which allowed him to travel and study in Italy. There the young man experienced the sounds and textures of the region and began to compose in earnest. While in Italy, Massenet met Liszt, who introduced him to his future wife, Mademoiselle Sainte-Marie.

Massenet's first opera, a one-act entitled *La Grand' Tante* (The Great Aunt), was produced (with only moderate success) at the Opéra-Comique in 1867. In 1877 Massenet's *exotic opera Le Roi de Lahore* (The King of Lahore) had a highly successful premiere at the Paris Opera, marking the beginning of his ascendancy as France's most prolific and celebrated operatic composer.

In 1878, his former teacher, Thomas, invited him to become a professor at the Paris Conservatory. Massenet achieved considerable success as a teacher, influencing an entire generation of French composers, including Gustav Charpentier and the song composer Reynaldo Hahn.

A highly prolific composer, Massenet worked continuously throughout his life, completing a great deal of music in addition to his 25 published operas. His approximately 250 songs often reflect the same melodic ingenuity and expressiveness that define his operatic works. Massenet composed several song cycles, including *Poéme d'Avril* (April Poem), which is often identified as the first French song cycle. Among the most famous of his solo songs are *"Ouvre tes yeux bleus"* (Open your blue eyes) and "Si tu veux, Mignonne" (If you wish it, sweetheart). The composer's *First Orchestral Suite* (originally entitled *Symphony in F*) premiered in 1867. This was the first of seven suites by Massenet, with programmatic subjects ranging from Alsace (*Scènes alsaciennes*, 1882) to Hungary (*Scènes hongroises*, 1871), and from Shakespeare (*Scénes dramatiques*, 1875) to Fairyland (*Scènes de féerie*, 1881). The most famous of his orchestral suites, *Scénes pittoresques* (Picturesque Scenes), was first performed in Paris during March of 1874. *Massenet* also composed several ballets, including *La Cigale*, *Espada*, and *Les Rosati*. In addition to *Marie-Magdeleine*, his oratorios include *Ève* (1875) and *La Terre promise* (The promised land, 1900). He wrote a considerable amount of incidental music for plays, including Sardou's *Le Crocodile* (1886) and Racine's *Phèdre* (1900). His only piano concerto was first performed in 1903 and receives occasional modern performances. *—Robert Barefield*

OPERA

Le Cid (1885)

Jules Massenet's *Le Cid* represented a turning point for the composer as he realized that grand opera was not his most effective medium. The sixth opera of his to have been performed, it is based on a drama by the seventeenth century French playwright Pierre Corneille. It relates the story of the eleventh century Spanish military hero El Cid, Rodrigo Díaz de Vivar. With a libretto representing the combined efforts of three writers (Edouard Blau, Adolphe d'Ennery, and Louis Gallet), the work was premiered at the Paris Opéra on November 30, 1885. The theatre provided a cast of preeminent Meyerbeer specialists, among them the period's most accomplished lyric/dramatic tenor singing the French repertory, Jean de Reszke (Polish) and the two finest basses of the time, his brother Edouard and the elegant Pol Plançon. The de Reszke brothers had enjoyed success in Massenet's previous grand opera, *Hérodiade*. They, together with Plançon sang at the Metropolitan Opera premiere of *Le Cid* in 1897, but the opera was performed there only seven times. Massenet wrote only one more grand opera (*Le Roi de Lehore*), choosing instead to devote himself to more intimate subjects.

The opera boasts an imposing overture whose emphatic effect is unlike the lush, somewhat feverish quality of Massenet's customary orchestral writing. Some dramatic scenes work well, for example Rodrigue's knighthood investiture where he addresses his sword in the broad and assertive aria, "O noble lame étincelante." The agitated music accompanying the duel between Rodrigue and Gormas yields effectively to a solemn requiem intoned by the mourners who gather. The protracted springtime ballet episode amply meets the requirement that grand opera include both dance and spectacle. Based upon the dances of Spain's provinces, Massenet's introduction of the "Castillane," "Andalouse," "Aragonaise," "Aubade," "Catalane," "Madrilène," and "Navarraise" reveal his exceptional gifts as an orchestrator in music lush, brilliant, and exotic. Both Chimène's lament, "Pleurez, pleurez, mes yeux," a lyric aria close to Massenet's best standards and the Rodrigue/Chimène duet that follows are finely crafted. Before battle, Rodrigue sings the most celebrated piece from the score, the moving invocation "O souverain, o juge, o père," an aria encountered not infrequently in concerts and recorded recitals. *—Erik Eriksson*

Synopsis:

Act One. The story is set in eleventh century Spain. Because of his fearless exploits in battle, the young Rodrigue will be rewarded by knighthood. The proud Count de Gormas will also receive distinction from the monarch when he is appointed the guardian to the King's son. Rodrigue is in love with Gormas' daughter, Chimène, and the Count grants permission for him to marry her. Though the King's daughter, the Infanta, has also declared her love for Rodrigue, she has decided to withdraw her interest in him because he is not of royal lineage.

On the day Rodrigue is knighted at the church, the King, who remains outside, appoints Don Diègue, Rodrigue's elderly father, as the guardian of his son, passing over Count de Gormas. The Count becomes livid at the news and challenges Don Diègue to a duel. Though their confrontation does not result in violence, the old man is mocked and humiliated. Rodrigue appears finally and, spurred on by his father, vows to take revenge against the culprit who dishonored him, unaware that he is Chimène's father. When he learns his identity, he decides he cannot back down.

Act Two. Rodrigue proposes a duel to the Count to settle the matter, and de Gormas is killed. Chimène is devastated by the news of her father's death and soon learns, to her utter dismay, that his killer was Rodrigue. She calls for justice at court in the matter, but finds there is disagreement as to the guilt of Rodrigue, some finding he was understandably provoked to take action, others feeling he should be executed. The proceedings are suddenly interrupted, however, when a Moorish emissary presents a proclamation of war. Don Diègue convinces the King to allow his son to lead the Spanish armies, and Rodrigue announces that he will return and accept whatever fate awaits with regard to the slaying of the Count de Gormas.

Act Three. Rodrigue visits Chimène to offer his farewell, and the two renew their love for each other. But she declares her forgiveness is contingent upon his victory over the enemy. Before departure for battle, certain officers inform Rodrigue that defeat is unavoidable, and they desert. Alone, the unwavering Rodrigue prays for victory in battle and becomes confident of ultimate triumph when he sees a vision of St. James.

Act Four. News is delivered to Rodrigue's father by the deserting officers that his son has been killed. Both Don Diègue and Chimène are heartbroken by the revelation. But their grief is short-lived; the King arrives with Rodrigue to reveal that the latter has led Spanish forces to victory. The King then turns to Chimène for her decision in the matter of her father's death. She is hesitant and cannot bring herself to offer the forgiveness she feels in her heart. Rodrigue threatens to take his life and begins to reach for his sword. She hurries over to him and prevents the action. The two are reunited and the opera ends happily. *—Robert Cummings*

Recommended:

○ **Massenet: Le Cid** / Queler (cond.), Domingo, Plishka, Gardner, Ingram, NY Opera Orch. / 1976 / CBS 79300

Hérodiade (1881; revised 1884)

While addressing the same story—more or less—as Richard Strauss' *Salome*, Massenet's work, written nearly a quarter century earlier, employs both a different perspective and a notion of sensuality far removed from that embodied in the German composer's obsessed teenager. The variance in titles is instructive. Strauss focused on *Salome*, Massenet (despite what he labeled his opera) on the entire central assortment of characters. Strauss' John the Baptist despises Salome with the fervor of an unwavering prophet. Massenet's Jean loves Salomé, however much he wishes he did not. Strauss' Herodias is a scold, unremittingly antagonistic toward the husband who lusts after her acknowledged daughter. Massenet's Hérodiade is not only the title character, but a woman anguished and perplexed by her husband's eye for the youthful Salomé, a girl she doesn't know is her daughter.

The music, too, differs enormously. National origin and public taste of course play a huge part. While Massenet's score is alternatingly voluptuous and fragrantly sensual in a fashion appreciated by the French, Strauss' work breaks new ground in its overt, grisly sexuality, every element of it blatantly echoed in his immense and unrelenting orchestra.

Although Massenet's score was completed by May 1881, a planned production at La Scala fell through. With the path seemingly open to the Paris Opéra, Massenet gathered courage and presented his opera to the new Director, Auguste-Emmanuel Vaucorbeil, himself a composer. With their first meeting, Massenet realized that the Opéra was closed to him. The directors of Brussels' Théâtre de la Monnaie, however, were only too happy to commit to a production. Several hundred opera enthusiasts made the trip from Paris for the premiere, which was further honored by the presence of the Belgian Queen. *Hérodiade* was presented a remarkable 55 times at the Monnaie in that first season alone. Soon thereafter, it was presented at many of Europe's other important houses before finally reaching Paris in 1884, where it was offered in Italian.

Strauss' *Salome* quickly overtook *Hérodiade* in public favor in the new century, despite the vociferous receptions accorded Massenet's opera during its first several decades. By the late twentieth century, *Hérodiade* was a curiosity, revived only occasionally, seldom in America.

Still, the public has remained aware of *Hérodiade* both through recordings and for two arias favored by singers for recitals and concerts. Salomé's "Il est Doux, Il est Bon" and Hérode's "Vision Fugitive" are both memorable examples of French aria, both languorous and effective vehicles for singers with sensuous instruments and an elegant approach to interpretation. Jean's Act-Four aria likewise is an inspired and well-crafted moment, not unknown to followers of French vocal art. The fortunes of *Hérodiade*, like those of most of Massenet's other operas and French opera in general, rise and fall with the availability of artists who sing the French language expressively and who possess voices of strength, beauty and refinement. *—Erik Eriksson*

Synopsis:

Act One. At dawn in a courtyard of Hérode's palace, a shouting match erupts among merchants of different tribes as they prepare for the day's market. Phanuel, a Chaldean, calms them by exhorting them to save their energies for the overthrow of their Roman oppressors. Salomé emerges from the palace, and Phanuel is startled to see her. Though known to Phanuel as Hérodiade's daughter, she admits to him that she has been seeking the mother she has never known and that she has been comforted in her distress by Jean (John the Baptist). She confides that she loves him. Hérode enters. Not finding Salomé among the court dancers, he rhapsodizes about how she fascinates him. Hérodiade appears, highly agitated. She has been threatened by Jean. She demands his head, but Hérode refuses, wishing instead to use Jean's authority over his people to help overthrow the Romans. Jean appears and curses Hérodiade. Salomé returns to confess her love to Jean. He urges her to think rather upon heavenly things and leaves, as Salomé sinks to the ground.

Act Two. The first tableau is set in Hérode's bedchamber. He insists that his slaves dance to remind him of Salomé's beauty. He takes a draught to invoke a vision of his desire, but Phanuel arrives and chides him for his weakness when his kingdom needs his leadership. The Tetrarch believes, however, that Roman rule will be overturned.

As the second tableau opens, Hérode speaks to his people at a public square, urging them to rise against the Roman presence. The Roman proconsul, Vitellius, arrives and heeds the demands of the crowd, telling them that their just wishes will be honored. Jean enters followed by a body of Canaanite women – and Salomé. Hérode indicates her presence to Phanuel. Hérodiade observes Hérode's discomfort and tells Vitellius that Jean is a man who dreams of power. The proconsul orders his arrest as Hérode, unable to remove his eyes from Salomé, is led away by Phanuel.

Act Three. The first tableau takes place in Phanuel's residence as the Chaldean contemplates the prophet's true nature. Hérodiade comes seeking advice. If only she could find her lost child, she would be consoled. When Phanuel informs her that Salomé is that child, she can conceive of her only as her rival. Phanuel dismisses her with a curse, "You are a woman only. Never a mother!"

At the beginning of the second tableau, Salomé enters the temple, fatigued and distraught. She prays for Jean to be saved, then collapses. Hérode enters. Salomé spurns him, protesting that she loves another, "more magnificent than the heroes." Hérode angrily swears vengeance on her and her "fatal love."

For the unveiling of the Tabernacle, the crowds press into the temple. Priests insist upon the death of Jean, who is then brought before Hérode. The Tetrarch, who seeks to use Jean for his own purposes, declares that a madman cannot be condemned. Jean summarily rejects Hérode's offer of help. Salomé moves forward, and, at the feet of the Baptist, declares that she wishes to share his fate. Hérode, now recognizing that Jean is his rival, condemns both to death.

Act Four. Alone in a darkened temple vault, Jean first rejoices at the thought of becoming a martyr but then thinks of Salomé and wonders whether he has really been chosen by God – or is just a man whose faith has been disturbed by love for a woman. Salomé enters and is received by Jean, who believes that death can bring transfiguration of their love. When the High Priest arrives to take Jean away to his death, Salomé is pulled from him, having been pardoned by Hérode.

The second tableau reveals a banquet room at the residence of Vitellius where Roman victory is being celebrated. The proconsul enters with Hérode and Hérodiade, followed by Phanuel. Salomé wrests herself from the guards and pleads for Jean's life. Her tears touch the heart of Hérodiade, who is about to grant her request when the executioner enters with his blade covered in Jean's blood. Salomé hurls herself at Hérodiade, attempting to slay the woman she believes has commissioned the Baptist's death. But Hérodiade shouts "Mercy!" and reveals that she is her mother. Salomé cries furiously that if she indeed was born by her "odious thighs," Hérodiade must take back her blood and her daughter's life. She turns her dagger on herself and falls lifeless as the crowd shouts "Jour d'horreur"–Day of Horror! *—Erik Eriksson*

Recommended:

○ **Massenet: Hérodiade** / Plasson (cond.), Hampson, Heppner, Fouchecourt, Van Dam, Toulouse Capitole Orch. / 1995 / EMI 555378

Manon (1882–1883)

The libretto for this work, by playwright Henri Meilhac (1831–97) and journalist Philippe Gille, is based on the novel, *L'histoire du chevalier des Grieux et de Manon Lescaut,* by Abbé Prévost (1697–1763), published in 1731. Earlier musical interpretations of the novel include a ballet by Halévy of 1830, an opera by Michael Balfe of 1836, and Auber's opera of 1856. Puccini's *Manon Lescaut* appeared in 1908. Meilhac and Gille's libretto conforms to the original more than does Auber's, and most of their changes are made with the drama in mind. For instance, they reduce the number of times Manon leaves des Grieux from three to one; Lescaut is changed from Manon's brother to her cousin; and Manon's death takes place on the way to Le Havre, not in Louisiana.

In 1882, Massenet and his collaborators finalized the form of the libretto, which the composer then set in piano/vocal format. Orchestration was completed in the summer of 1883. *Manon* was first performed on January 19, 1884, at the Opéra-Comique in Paris. Although the opera received a mixed reception by critics, the public loved it, and it remained in the repertory of the Opéra-Comique until 1959, with over 2000 performances. By late 1885, *Manon* was playing in New York.

Massenet was aware of Opéra-Comique director Léon Carvalho's tendency to alter the works premiering at his establishment. To combat this, Massenet had the score of *Manon* printed before rehearsals began. Nevertheless, the composer himself later made some changes, adding Manon's Gavotte in 1884 and changing the same number to the "Fabliau" ten years later.

Manon is less impressive as a whole than as a succession of striking numbers. Retaining the novel's eighteenth century setting, the opera offers noisy crowd scenes, passionate duets, and tense melodramas that certainly pleased Opéra-Comique patrons. Fortunately, the traditions of French Opéra-Comique formed a good fit with Prévost's eighteenth century novel.

Variety is at the heart of *Manon.* Spoken dialogue, such as Guillot's "Hôtelier de malheur," from the first act, alternates with several different types of melodrama. Some of the melodrama sections employ the traditional spoken dialogue set against a simple, sustained orchestral backdrop, such as the Count's "Bravo, mon cher, succès complet!" in the St. Sulpice scenes in the third act. Other melodrama passages blatantly make use of important motives from the opera, such as Brétigny's "Jamais plus doux regard n'illumina plus gracieux visage" in the first act, which incorporates Manon's theme. Recitatives vary from those that conform to the prosody of the text to others that are more song-like, such as Lescaut's "Mademoiselle est ma cousine," from Act Two.

Massenet adroitly conveys the essence of the drama through music. For example, Manon's first aria, "Je suis encore tout étourdie," perfectly characterizes the young Manon in its hesitancy. "N'est-ce plus ma main," which closes the third act, boasts a scintillating, erotically charged violin gesture at the moment the lovers touch. Perhaps most impressive are the Cours-la-Reine scenes, which are connected in rondo fashion, supporting the shifting of focus from one character to another and then back. *—John Palmer*

Synopsis:

Act One. The action takes place in Amiens, in Paris and on the roads to Le Havre in the first half of the eighteenth century, around 1730. In the large courtyard of an inn in Amiens, Guillot and Brétigny, accompanied by the actresses Pousette, Javotte, and Rosette, impatiently call to an innkeeper for food and drink. Finally, the innkeeper shows up and tells them that the afternoon bread is being brought in, and they begin discussing the menu and enter the dining room. A bell rings as numerous travelers arrive with bags, and people from the city fill the courtyard to gawk at the arrivals. In the crowd is Lescaut with two guards; he has just come from gambling in order to meet his 15-year-old cousin, Manon, who is on her way to join a cloister, under her parents' orders. When Manon enters, she reveals that this is her first time away from home ("Je suis encore tout étourdie").

Another ring of the bell makes the crowd disperse and head for the carriage. Momentarily, Manon is left behind as Lescaut leaves to fetch her luggage. Guillot comes out of the dining room and into the courtyard to find the innkeeper, who still has not brought him any wine. When he sees Manon he is transfixed. He introduces himself to Manon, telling her that he has a lot of money and would gladly give her some if she would say a few sweet words to him. Manon rejects Guillot and his friends laugh at him. Guillot then puts his coach at Manon's disposal, telling her it will leave in a few moments. As Guillot tells her this, Lescaut returns, warns Manon about being led astray, then runs back to his poker game. Brétigny and the women call out from the dining room about the delay.

Thoughtfully, Manon sits down on a bench, noting that life simultaneously entices and oppresses her. Grieux, having missed his coach, finds Manon in her confused, pensive state. He believes that in no way should such vibrant beauty be allowed to wither behind the walls of a cloister. Manon finds herself powerless against such words of wooing, and the two ride off in Guillot's coach. Lescaut returns and accuses Guillot of abducting his cousin, but the innkeeper clears up the situation by informing them that Manon has left with another man. As Brétigny mocks Guillot's bad luck, Guillot swears revenge, and Lescaut raves about family honor, the curtain falls.

Act Two. At Grieux and Manon's apartment in the rue Vivienne, Paris, Grieux writes a letter to his father, the Count des Grieux, asking permission to marry Manon. After reading the letter back to Grieux, Manon wonders why it is not enough that they simply remain lovers. Grieux notices a bunch of flowers and jealously asks Manon who gave them to her. Manon replies that an unknown person tossed them through the window. The servant announces the arrival of two soldiers, one of whom is Lescaut and the other, in disguise, is Brétigny, who also has designs on Manon. As Lescaut begins to rage about his family's honor, Grieux shows him the letter concerning his proposed marriage to Manon. This calms Lescaut but angers Brétigny, who surreptitiously tells Manon that Grieux will be abducted that night by his father's henchmen. If she insists on escaping with Grieux, Grieux's father will disinherit his son, leaving him penniless. If, however, she abandons Grieux, she will share the Brétigny fortune. Manon convinces herself that she is not worthy of Grieux and that she should accept Brétigny's offer. She sings a farewell to the domestic life she has come to treasure and tries to hide her torment from Grieux, who tells her of the pleasant life they will have together. There is a knock at the door. When Grieux answers it, he is abducted.

Act Three. Lescaut, the three actresses, Guillot, and Brétigny are on the Cours-la-Reine. The actresses ignore Guillot, who taunts Brétigny because he refused Manon's wish to have members of the Opéra perform in his home. After Manon enters with Brétigny, she overhears an exchange between Brétigny and the Count des Grieux, who relates that his son is taking holy orders and will give his first sermon later that day at St. Sulpice. Manon questions the Count about his son as Guillot brings in the Opéra ballet company to impress Manon. Manon is not interested and requests that her coach take her to St. Sulpice, once again humiliating Guillot.

The scene changes to the parlor of the seminary at St. Sulpice. At the church, women speak highly of the new abbé. The Count tries to talk his son out of completing his holy orders, offering to give him some of his inheritance. Grieux is unmoved, for this is the only way to forget Manon. He leaves to take his orders. Manon enters and asks to see Grieux. When he appears he angrily asks her to leave. She asks him to forgive her and remember their previous love. After touching Manon, Grieux gives in and the two run off again.

Act Four. Lescaut, the actresses, and others gamble at the Hôtel de Transylvanie. Lescaut cheats, and Guillot recites satirical verses about the Regent. Manon enters with Grieux, whose inheritance is almost gone; he is trying to make money at the gambling table. Guillot involves Grieux in a game and accuses Grieux of cheating. Guillot leaves and returns with the police, who arrest Grieux and Manon, pleasing Grieux's father.

Act Five. The setting is the road to Le Havre. Grieux has been freed from jail, but Manon is being deported to the colonies. On the way, Lescaut and Grieux bribe one of the escorts so that they may speak with Manon. Grieux and Manon are left alone. Manon bags for forgiveness while reminiscing over past events. Exhausted, she dies in Grieux's arms. *—John Palmer*

Recommended:

○ **Massenet: Manon** / Pappano (cond.), Gheorghiu, Alagna, Patriarco, Van Dam / 2000 / EMI 57005

○ **Massenet: Manon** / Rudel (cond.), Sills, Gedda, Souzay, Bacquier / 1988 / Angel 69831

Thaïs (1892; revised 1898)

The opera *Thaïs* is generally considered one of Massenet's finest works, although it is not as well known today as his *Manon* and *Werther*. Based on the popular novel by Anatole France, the opera's libretto was written by Louis Gallet. It is set in fourth century Egypt and tells the story of a Cenobite monk, Athanaël, who is obsessed with the beautiful courtesan, Thaïs. He sublimates his longing by converting her to Christianity and delivering her to a monastery. He then realizes that he has lost her forever.

Massenet composed the opera for the American soprano Sibyl Sanderson, who had previously achieved success in performances of his *Esclarmonde*. The first performance took place at the Paris Opera on March 16, 1894. The vibrant score, with its mysticism and oriental influences, reveals Massenet's brilliance as an orchestrator. The opera features a major ballet in Act Two. The juxtaposition of religious fervor and erotic tension inspired Massenet to compose some of his most sublime melodies, including the famous *Méditation* for solo violin, which first appears as a musical interlude in Act Two. The theme returns more than once in the opera and is used in the final duet between Thaïs and Athanaël. The desperate monk returns to the monastery where he has previously led Thaïs in order to confess his love for her. He finds her near death, focusing only on her future life in heaven. *—Robert Barefield*

Synopsis:

Act One. Outside their huts in fourth century Egypt, the Cenobites pray for the absent Athanaël, whom they consider one of God's elect. He comes in, refusing food, and says that Thaïs, the beautiful courtesan and priestess of Venus, has corrupted Alexandria ("Hélas! enfant encore"). He says that he himself, while still a boy, had been tempted by her, but that God saved him. He wants to convert her, but Palemon gently warns him against becoming involved with the world. The Cenobites pray ("Prions que les noirs démons"). Athanaël falls asleep and dreams of Thaïs. Awakening, he feverishly prays to be the one to save her ("Toi, qui mis la pitié"). Palemon repeats his warning, with a hint of reproach, but Athanaël leaves as the monks pray. Outside Nicias' luxurious house, Athanaël asks to speak with Nicias. The servant threatens to beat him away, but seeing his calm, commanding demeanor, he bows and obeys. Athanaël contemplates the worldly, beautiful city, calling angels to cleanse it. Nicias enters, with his arms around Crobyle and Myrtale, and greets him affectionately as an old friend. Athanaël asks whether he knows Thaïs, and Nicias laughingly answers that he has spent a fortune on her but she is still leaving him; tonight is their last feast as lovers. Athanaël says he will bring her to join a convent, and Nicias, still greatly amused, warns that Venus might avenge herself. Athanaël asks for suitable garments, and the slaves dress him, though he violently refuses to remove his hairshirt. They laugh and comment that he is quite handsome, and Nicias urges him to enjoy the experience, while he prays ("Ne t'offense pas de leur raillerie"). Thaïs and Nicias' guests come in, and he and Thaïs exchange a sweetly ironic farewell. Athanaël tells her he has come to teach her contempt of the flesh, and she alluringly teases him that he should not give the lie to the flame in his eyes, but should love ("Que te fait si sévère." He flees as she begins to disrobe.

Act Two. Thaïs is alone and finds her life empty, though she looks into her mirror, asking for reassurance that she will always be beautiful ("Dis-moi que je suis belle"). Athanaël enters, praying that her charm will not defeat him, and she greets him coquettishly. He tells her he intends to conquer her and bring a love that will provide unending happiness. His fervor unsettles her, and she agrees to listen, though she burns incense to Venus as she listens ("Vénus, invisible et présente"). He suddenly tears away his elaborate robe, telling her he curses the flesh and the death that possesses her. She collapses, moaning that she fears death, and begs him to give her life. Outside, they hear Nicias returning for one last kiss, and she tells Athanaël to send him away. He responds that he will wait on her doorstep, and she hysterically answers that she will remain what she is, that she does not want Nicias, Athanaël, or his God. Outside, after an interlude, Thaïs emerges and tells him that his words remained in her heart and illuminated her soul. He tells her that he will take her to a nunnery and orders her to destroy her possessions. She agrees, but wishes to spare an ivory statue of Eros, the god of love, saying that love is a rare virtue ("Considère, o mon père"), but when he hears it was a gift from Nicias, he violently breaks it. Nicias and his fellow revelers come in, drunk. Having won a great fortune at gambling, Nicias calls for dancing. A dancer called The Charmer enters, and she performs as Croybale and Myrtale sing ("Celle qui vient"). Athanaël comes out of Thaïs' house, and they assume that Thaïs seduced him, but he tells them he made her God's bride and will take her away. They become angered and are about to stone him, but Nicias distracts them by throwing gold. As they leave, Thaïs' house burns.

Act Three. Athanaël leads Thaïs on foot through the desert. They arrive at an oasis, and she asks to rest, but he orders her to break and destroy her flesh and atone for her sins. She submits, but falls down. He softens and helps her to sit, kisses her bleeding feet, and brings her fruit and water. She tells him her life is his ("Baigne d'eau mes mains"), and he repeats her words. The nuns enter, singing, and Athanaël tells Albine, the mother superior, that he is entrusting Thaïs to her. He bids her farewell and exaltedly exclaims that she is beautiful. As he watches them leave, he repeats that he will never see her again. Back with the Cenobites, Palemon worries that since his return, 20 days before, Athanaël seems to have been destroyed. He emerges and confesses ("Demeure auprès de moi") that he now thinks of nothing but Thaïs' beauty. Palemon cannot help him, and when Athanaël sleeps, he sees Thaïs repeating her alluring words. He calls to her and then sees an image of her dying in the convent. Desperately gasping that he wants her ("Thaïs va mourir"), he rushes out. In the convent garden, Thaïs lies dying but tranquil. Albine reflects that Thaïs' devout penances have destroyed her body. Athanaël comes in and Albine greets him respectfully as Thaïs' spiritual father. She and the nuns move aside, and he collapses next to her. Thaïs awakens and recognizes him. She recalls how he brought her to spiritual redemption, but he tells her that he remembers only her mortal beauty, even saying that when he spoke of spiritual love, he lied. Oblivious to his words, she imagines the heavens opening to receive her as he desperately says she belongs to him and he loves her. As she dies, he collapses in despair, crying out for pity. *—Ann Feeney*

Recommended:

○ **Massenet: Thaïs** / Abel (cond.), Fleming, Hampson, Sabbatini, Vidal, Bordeaux Aquitaine National Orch. / 2000 / Decca 466766

○ **Massenet: Thaïs** / Maazel (cond.), Milnes, Gedda, Sills, Murray, New Philharmonia / 1995 / EMI 65479

Werther (1891)

Premiered in Vienna, in February 1892, under the direction of Hans Richter, Massenet's *Werther* has proven an enduring work, one of the composer's most tightly constructed and dramatically urgent. The libretto was fashioned by writers Georges Hartmann, Edouard Blau, and Paul Millet, after Goethe's *The Sorrows of Young Werther*. The serviceable text worked to keep the focus on the insistent love of the protagonist and the object of his passion.

Ironically, not only was *Werther*'s premiere conducted by a figure most closely associated with Brahms and Wagner, but it is in Germany that the opera has found ongoing favor—even though critics and audiences there have often taken issue with treatment of their revered Goethe by French composers. At the premiere, the title role was undertaken by the famous Belgian tenor Ernest van Dyck. For its 1894 American premiere in Chicago (a touring performance by the Metropolitan Opera), *Werther* was sung by the legendary Jean de Reszke. The appeal of the melancholy *Werther* was so strong that Italian baritone Mattia Battistini persuaded Massenet to provide for him a revision suitable for baritone. Rather than rewriting most of the *Werther*'s vocal lines, Massenet simply wrote alternatives for certain higher-lying phrases.

Massenet has been accused of having been a limited composer, writing within a narrow emotional and expressive framework. Yet, for *Werther*, he located and fixed himself on the very marrow of his hero's despair. The drama, while manifested in outward action, is primarily internal. Werther falls undeniably in love with the 20-year-old Charlotte. She senses the stirrings of love as well, but feels bound to honor her betrothal to Albert, an engagement planned by her mother. Werther cannot suppress his desire. The love which blossomed in summer still demands expression in autumn even after Charlotte is married. Its denouement takes place in winter, to the accompaniment of the Christmas carol first heard as the children rehearse it in July.

While the music serves the drama in compellingly straightforward fashion, two set pieces have become favorite moments, often excerpted as concert items. Charlotte's "Letter Scene" at the beginning of Act Three is a despairing meditation on passion versus responsibility. Werther's aria later in that same act, "Pourquoi me," is anguished questioning, all the stronger for its not becoming an operatic rant full of theatrical outbursts. Sung by a great artist, it can be heartbreaking.

Massenet was not unwilling to bow to public demands for spectacle and overcooked orchestration, but in *Werther* he remained true to Goethe's youthful drama written more than a century before. Massenet's restraint serves Goethe well. The feelings of the doomed pair boil more intensely for being contained until impending death allows them ultimate abandon. Werther's death brings him surcease, but for Charlotte, only a future of emptiness. *—Erik Eriksson*

Synopsis:

Act One. The opera opens in the garden of the Bailiff's house. It is July, sometime in the 1780s. The Bailiff, a widower, sings a Christmas carol with six of his children. Schmidt and Johann, friends of the Bailiff, drop by to remind him to join them later for an evening at the Raison d'Or. Sophie enters, and conversation turns to the melancholy Werther and to Albert as a possible future husband for her older sister, Charlotte.

After everyone leaves, Werther enters quietly and contemplates the summer's eve. Charlotte enters, dressed for a ball and accompanied by the Bailiff and the children. While awaiting her escort, she is introduced to Werther, who subsequently goes off with her to the ball. Sophie, who has remained behind, is about to leave when Albert arrives after having been away for six months. He speaks of his love for Charlotte and hers for him.

Werther and Charlotte later return from the ball, and the young poet declares his love for her. Suddenly the Bailiff greets Charlotte with the news that Albert is back. Werther is in despair upon learning that it is Albert who has been chosen by Charlotte's mother to be her daughter's betrothed. In anguish, he cries, "Another, her husband!" and the act ends.

Act Two. On a Sunday afternoon in the fall of the same year, Johann and Schmidt are seated outside the tavern, offering praise for the wine and the fine day. Albert and Charlotte, married now for three months, stroll by and enter the church nearby. Werther, observing from a distance, is deeply regretful over having lost Charlotte. Albert emerges from the church and sympathizes with Werther's feelings; Werther, moved, tells him that he will be faithful to them both. When Charlotte comes from the church, Werther is unable to resist once more expressing his love. She tells him, however, that she belongs to another and that he must leave and not return until Christmas. Sophie tries to invite him to the pastor's wedding anniversary celebration, but Werther rejects her offer. Leaving, he vows never to return. Albert, realizes from Sophie's comments that Werther is still in love with Charlotte.

Act Three. At Christmas Eve in Albert's house, Charlotte thinks of Werther, rereading his letters to her and realizing that she loves him. Torn between her passion and her sense of responsibility, she is chilled by the tone of his last letter to her. Quite suddenly, Werther appears in the study, pallid and disconsolate. He has returned, he tells her, at the appointed time, but time has not diminished his love. They recall the times in which they sang and read together and Werther recites a poem: "Why awaken me, o breath of spring?" Charlotte pleads with him to stop, and, with painful resolve, declares that he must see her no more. Werther rushes off, telling her, "My grave opens!"

Albert then enters, noting that Werther has been seen and wondering about the open door to the street. Calling Charlotte, he inquires about her highly agitated state. A letter is brought by a servant, and Albert reads it aloud. Werther has written that he is leaving on a long journey and requests of Albert the loan of his pistols. Albert coldly tells Charlotte to give them to him. She removes the pistols from the desk and hands them to the servant. Realizing, after Albert's departure, the import of Werther's request, she takes her cloak and rushes forth in search of him.

Act Four. Following an orchestral interlude, Charlotte is seen arriving at Werther's study. She finds him lying on the floor, having inflicted on himself a mortal shot. Weakly, he asks her forgiveness, while she protests that she is the one in need of forgiveness. He asks that she call no one. Rather, he implores her to give him her hand, saying that he is happy to die telling her of his adoration. She loves him, she tells him, kissing him, avowing that they will put all else aside as their souls join together. Werther weakens but harkens to the children's carols floating in the Christmas Eve air, hearing in them a message of hope and forgiveness. Charlotte tells him that he must not die, but Werther replies that death is overtaking him and that he wishes to be buried beneath the lime trees in the graveyard. Charlotte faints at the feet of Werther's lifeless body. *—Erik Eriksson*

Recommended:

○ **Massenet: Werther** / Jurowski (cond.), Vargas, Kasarova, Kotoski, Schaldenbrand, Berlin SO / 1999 / RCA 7432158224

○ **Massenet: Werther** / Thill, Cohen (cond.), Vallin, Feraldy, Paris National Opera Theater Orch. / 2000 / Naxos 110061-62

VOCAL

Elégie: O doux printemps d'autrefois (1866)

Having survived a bout of cholera in Paris, the convalescent 23-year-old Massenet eased back into normal life by composing his Opus 10, *Dix pieces de genre* for piano. A "chip from the workbench" proved to be more than that and took on a life of its own, for often a trifle created in a moment of relaxation can reveal more of its creator's essence than many a more ambitious work. In this case it was the piece which went on to become the famous *Elégie*, later arranged for cello as instrumental music to de Lisle's play *Les Erinnyes*. It gained even greater renown as a song for voice and piano, *O doux printemps d'autrefois* (O spring of days long ago blooming and bright), to words by Louis Gallet.

The melody of the *Elégie* seems to have cried out for words from the beginning and is a study in deeply felt yet restrained Romanticism, of resigned longing for the past. In structure and mood it is reminiscent of Chopin's E minor prelude, with which it shares a common key (in most arrangements). The main phrase consists of a yearning octave leap and sighing descent, and on this germinal idea the song is built. A brief excursion into the relative major aspires to relieve. Toward the end there is an intriguing suggestion of bitonality but this tension quickly resolves back to melancholy to close this perfectly formed miniature. *—Wayne Reisig*

Recommended:

○ **French Song Recital** / Cole, Stephens / 1993 / Delos 3131

Kurt Masur

b. Jul. 18, 1927, Brieg, Silesia (Poland)

Conductor

Kurt Masur's tenure with the New York Philharmonic in the 1990s superficially seemed a throwback to the days when American orchestras always looked to the European continent when naming their conductors. In fact, the appointment was both unusual and forward-thinking. Born in Brieg, Silesia (in modern-day Poland) in 1927, Masur is one of the most respected conductors of his generation and is well known for his human rights activities.

Masur studied cello and piano while at the Breslau Music School from 1942 to 1944. After the war he found himself in the Soviet-occupied zone of Germany, which became the German Democratic Republic (DDR) or East Germany. His education then continued at the Leipzig Hochschule für Musik, where he studied piano, composition, and conducting (1946–48). His professional career began as a coach and assistant conductor in the Halle Landestheater. He then became Kapellmeister of the Erfurt City Theater (1951–53). Next, he was his appointed as Kapellmeister of the Leipzig Opera Theater. (1953–55).

His first orchestral position came with the Dresden Philharmonic (1955–58). He then returned to opera, becoming Generalmusikdirektor of the Mecklenburg State Theater in Schwerin (1958–60). One of his most important appointments came in 1960, when he took the post as Senior Director of Music at the Berlin Komische Oper, where he worked with the famous director and producer Walter Felsenstein. He returned to the Dresden Philharmonic as its music director (1967–72). In 1970 he became Gewandhauskapellmeister of Leipzig, a position of high prestige ever since the Gewandhaus Orchestra had been led by Wilhelm Furtwängler, Bruno Walter, and indeed Felix Mendelssohn. He remained at the Gewandhaus through 1996, during one of the most important stretches in the orchestra's history. Together they made numerous recordings for the East German state recording company, many of which became generally available in the West only during the 1990s. He also took the orchestra on significant foreign tours, and in 1975 he became a professor at the Leipzig Academy.

Masur was and remains a frequent guest conductor with the world's leading orchestras. His U.S. debut came in 1974, when he led the Cleveland Orchestra and also took the Gewandhaus Orchestra on its first American tour. His New York Philharmonic debut took place in 1981.

Masur became outspoken in his opposition to DDR policies, and in 1989 he played a central role in the growing demonstrations against Communist rule. As a result he was awarded several of Germany's highest civilian honors, and his profile in the West was raised still further.

In 1991 Masur was appointed music director of the New York Philharmonic. Although the orchestra was in fine form when he took it, he was been credited with sharpening its precision, creating a more incisive sound. Masur and the Philharmonic recorded extensively on the Teldec label. Under his tenure, the orchestra resumed its historic series of live national radio broadcasts, becoming the only orchestra in the United States with such a program in place. In 1999, the orchestra's "Messages for the Millennium" project commissioned works by Thomas Ades, John Corigliano, Hans Werner Henze, Giya Kancheli, and Kaija Saariaho, and in June of the following year, Masur and the Philharmonic completed their fifth European tour.

In 1996 he stepped down from his position with the Gewandhaus, which elected to give him the title of Conductor Laureate—the first time it had bestowed that honor. Since 1992, he has held the lifetime title of Honorary Guest Conductor of the Israel Philharmonic Orchestra. In September 2000, Masur assumed the position of Principal Conductor of the London Philharmonic Orchestra. At the end of his contract with the New York Philharmonic in 2002, Masur became music director of the Orchestre National de France.

Masur also holds honorary degrees from the Breslau Academy of Music, the Cleveland Institute of Music, Colgate University, Hamilton College, Indiana University, the Juilliard School, Leipzig University, the Manhattan School of Music, the University of Michigan, Westminster Choir College, SUNY Binghamton, and Yale University. *—Joseph Stevenson*

Recommended:

- ○ **Beethoven: Overtures** / Masur (cond.), Gewandhaus / 2004 / Universal Classics 000173902
- ○ **Brahms: Symphony 1; Tragic Overture** / Masur (cond.), New York PO / 2002 / Apex 44351
- ○ **Mahler: Symphony 7** / Masur (cond.), Gewandhaus / 1992 / Berlin Classics 0020582
- ○ **Beethoven: Symphony 9** / Masur (cond.), McNair, Heilmann, Nes, Weikl, Gewandhaus / 2003 / DG 473846
- ○ **Bruch/Mendelssohn: Violin Concertos** / Masur (cond.), Vengerov, Gewandhaus / 1993 / Teldec 90875
- ○ **Bruch: Complete Symphonies** / Masur (cond.), Accardo, Gewandhaus / 1998 / Philips 462164

Eduardo Mata

b. Sep. 5, 1942, Mexico City, Mexico, **d.** Jan. 4, 1995, Xochitepec, Morelos, Mexico
Conductor

Eduardo Mata was an internationally known conductor. He conducted a wide repertoire and was particularly recognized for twentieth century music, particularly of Latin American composers.

He began studying guitar when he was about eight years old. In 1953, he enrolled in the National Conservatory of Music, studying with Rodolfo Halffter and Jose Moncayo. From 1960 to 1963, he was in the composition workshop of Carlos Chavez and Julián Orbón. After winning a Koussevitzky Fellowship, he traveled to Tanglewood where he continued his studies in composition under Gunther Schuller and in conducting from Max Rudolf and Erich Leinsdorf.

In 1965, he became the permanent conductor of the Guadalajara Orchestra while also taking an appointment as head of the Music Department at the University of Mexico. Most of his compositions were written in the 1960s, before his conducting career began to dominate his time. They consist of several chamber works including a well-regarded cello/piano sonata, *Improvisations* (1966) for two pianos and strings, and three symphonies.

He resigned from the Guadalajara position in 1972 when he was appointed principal conductor of the Phoenix Symphony Orchestra in Arizona. He remained in that position until he was offered the position of music director of the Dallas Symphony Orchestra in 1977.

Although Dallas is the major financial, business, and arts center of the American Southwest, at the time its orchestra was in shaky condition. It had closed for the third time in its history in 1974, due to an insurmountable deficit. A new organization plan had reopened it, under the temporary leadership of American Louis Lane, billed as its "guest conductor." Lane had just achieved, for the first time, a full-time, 52-week contract for the musicians, deemed essential to establishing the security needed to attract worthy players. Mata brought the orchestra to what commentators referred to as its second "golden age," referring to the previous golden age of conductors Antal Dorati (1945–49) and Walter Hendl (1949–58). He lifted the orchestra to unexpectedly high standards, and made a number of digital recordings with it for Pro Arte, RCA Victor, Delos, Telarc, and Dorian.

At the helm of the Dallas Symphony, he participated in the planning of its acoustically excellent concert hall in the Meyerson Symphony Center and led the first concerts in the hall. The recordings made there with Dorian Records are counted among the finest.

As a conductor, he was controversial. He was youthful for such an important position, and was sometimes criticized for inconsistency in interpretation—criticisms that became less frequent over the years. He had a penchant for deliberate tempos, but produced a rich, detailed, and transparent orchestral sound.

He was also the principal guest conductor of the New Zealand Symphony and artistic director of Solistas de Mexico, and guest conducted widely, including appearances in London, Berlin, Rotterdam, Philadelphia, Chicago, Cleveland, and San Francisco. He stepped down from his Dallas position in 1993 and was succeeded by American conductor Andrew Litton. With the Simón Bolívar Symphony Orchestra of Venezuela, he and Dorian Records launched a fruitful series of recordings of Latin-American orchestral compositions, concentrating on such composers as Antonio Estévez, Ginastera, Villa-Lobos, and Revueltas. The series continued after he was killed when the private plane he piloted went down near Cuernavaca Airport on January 4, 1995. A high school in Dallas has been renamed after him, and the state of Oaxaca (Mexico) established an "Eduardo Mata Autumn Festival" in his honor.—*Joseph Stevenson*

Recommended:

- ○ **Chávez: Complete Symphonies** / Mata (cond.), London SO / 1992 / Vox 5061
- ○ **Respighi** / Mata (cond.), Dallas SO / 1993 / Dorian 90182
- ○ **Music Of Latin American Masters** / Mata (cond.), Simon Bolivar SO, Cuarteto LatinoAmericano / 1995 / Dorian 98102
- ○ **Orbon, Villa-Lobos, Estevez, Chavez** / Mata (cond.), Simon Bolivar SO / 1994 / Dorian 90179

Edith Mathis

b. Feb. 11, 1938, Lucerne, Switzerland
Soprano

Edith Mathis has had one of the leading international vocal careers of the twentieth century and was particularly well known for her Mozart and Strauss roles. She studied at the Lucerne Conservatory and made her stage debut there as the Second Boy in Mozart's *Die Zauberflöte*. After singing in Zürich, she joined the Cologne Opera in 1959. Remaining with the company until 1963, she began singing the major repertory roles. She also made guest appearance during these years at the Hamburg State Opera, Glyndebourne (where she first appeared in 1962 singing Cherubino in Mozart's *Marriage of Figaro*), and the Salzburg Festival opera.

In 1963, she joined the Deutsche Oper, Berlin. Her Covent Garden debut was in 1970, as Susanna. She went on to sing in the major opera houses of the world, including the Bavarian State Opera in Munich, the Vienna State Opera, the Metropolitan Opera in New York, and the Opéra de Paris. She sang regularly at the Salzburg and Munich Festivals.

Among her other roles were Zerlina in *Don Giovanni*, Marzelline in *Fidelio*, and Mélisande in Debussy's *Pélleas et Mélisande*, and Pamina in the *Magic Flute*. She was considered outstanding in the role of Sophie in Strauss' *Der Rosenkavalier*. As the list of roles indicates, she had a bright voice suggesting youth and freshness, and she was regarded an excellent actress. Other roles with which she was particularly associated include the Marschallin in *Der Rosenkavalier*, the Countess in *Le Nozze di Figaro*, and Agathe in *Der Freischütz*.

Mathis is also a highly regarded oratorio and recital singer, known for direct, simple expression of the classic lieder repertory, and is also highly regarded as a Bach singer, as well as singing the oratorios of Joseph Haydn and numerous works of Mozart and Handel.

She has made many recordings and received numerous recording prizes, including the Prix Mondial du Disque. Other honors include the Hans-Reinhard-Ring from the Swiss Society for Theater, the Arts Prize of the city of Lucerne, the Buxtehude Prize from the Senate of Lübeck, and the Mozart Medal of the Mozarteum in Salzburg. In 1979 the Bavarian government declared her a Bayerische Kammersangerin. —*Joseph Stevenson*

Recommended:

- ○ **Schubert: Complete Songs, Vol. 21** / Mathis, Johnson (piano) / 1994 / Hyperion 33021
- ○ **Loewe: Lieder & Balladen, Vol. 5** / Mathis, Garben (piano) / CPO 999334

Karita Mattila

b. Sep. 5, 1960, Somero, Finland
Soprano

In the 1990s, the Finnish soprano Karita Mattila established herself as one of the world's leading operatic sopranos. Coming to early attention as a prize-winning singer adept at the more lyric roles in the repertory, she developed the qualities of a dramatic soprano as well, with an especially warm and grand voice. She is a tall, blond, and striking woman with excellent stage presence and acting skills.

She studied voice at the Sibelius Academy in Helsinki. While still a student, she won one the first prize of the Lappeenranta Competition in 1981. This led to her professional debut at the Savonlinna Opera Festival, where she sang Donna Anna in Mozart's *Don Giovanni*. In 1983, she became the first Cardiff Singer of the World.

She was now ready to enter the international opera world. Once again she debuted in one of the great Mozart roles: Countess Almaviva in *Le nozze di Figaro* at La Monnaie Opera in Brussels. While not exclusively singing Mozart, she became best known for her work in his operas. She chose Donna Elvira (another role in *Don Giovanni*) for her British and American debuts in 1985; these were at the Scottish Opera and Washington, D.C. Opera, respectively. She made her Covent Garden and Paris debuts the next year as Fiordiligi in *Cosi fan tutte*, and also added Pamina and Ilia to her operatic repertory.

She continued to make international appearances, but found that her career was leveling out in the early 1990s. She went into a period of introspection and she came to the realization that full vocal maturity was leading her into a different quality. She took the time needed to restudy and retrain it for its new, rich, and weighty quality.

After that, she re-emerged with a striking new capacity to sing roles such as Eva in *Die Meistersinger* and Chrysothemis in Richard Strauss' *Elektra*. She sang the Wagnerian role of Elsa in *Lohengrin* in her debut at San Francisco in 1996. But the role in which she had her greatest triumphs was that of Elisabeth of Valois in Verdi's *Don Carlos*, a level of acclaim that was matched by her stunning appearance as Janáček's *Jenufa* at the Hamburg Opera in 1998. She has proven especially effective in Slavonic operas; in addition to *Jenufa* she is noted for her performances as both of Tchaikovsky's greatest heroines, Tatyana in *Eugene Onegin* and Lisa in *Pikovaya Dama* (*Queen of Spades*), which she sang at the Metropolitan Opera in 1995.

Other roles she has sung are Emma in Schubert's *Fierrabras*, Musetta in *La bohème*, Puccini's *Manon Lescaut*, and Amelia in Verdi's *Simon Boccanegra*. In 2000, her first performance as Leonora in Beethoven's *Fidelio* (Metropolitan Opera with James Levine conducting) won accolades.

When she appears in lieder recitals, she regularly receives great acclaim, especially in Sibelius songs. Her stage presence allows her to appear effectively in the increasingly popular large-scale outdoor arena events, where she is not hesitant to use electronic amplification.

She holds her performances down to between 45 and 60 performances a year, believing that this represents for her the right mixture of work and rest to keep her voice in good shape. This means that she has come to restrict her performances to leading music venues like New York, Paris, London, and Salzburg. "Not the crappiest places in the world, are they?" she laughs.

Karita Mattila has been an active recording artist, with releases on the Philips, Ondine, Bis, and EMI labels, and has recorded popular songs as well as classical and operatic selections. *—Joseph Stevenson*

Recommended:

- ○ **Karita Mattila Live in Helsinki** / Saraste (cond.), Mattila, Finnish RSO / 2000 / Ondine 968
- ○ **Janáček: Jenufa** / Haitink (cond.), Mattila, Silja, Hadley, Manning, Choir & Orch. of the Royal Opera / 2002 / Erato 45330
- ○ **Grieg & Sibelius Songs** / Oramo (cond.), Mattila, Birmingham SO / 2004 / Warner 80243

John Mauceri

b. Sep. 12, 1945, New York, NY
Conductor

Conductor John Mauceri commenced early piano studies with his Sicilian-born grandfather. A prolific student, he received many honors before entering Yale College, where Mauceri majored in music theory and composition. After a year at Yale's graduate school, Mauceri was appointed music director of the Yale Symphony Orchestra and remained on the faculty for 15 years, leading many premieres. In 1978, he developed a department of music theater at New York University, now rated as one of the finest of its type in the U.S.

Mauceri was invited to Tanglewood as a conducting fellow in 1971 and studied with Bruno Maderna, Colin Davis, Seiji Ozawa, Gunther Schuller, and Leonard Bernstein, whose assistant he became a year later and worked with until Bernstein's death. Mauceri's professional debut was at Wolf Trap Farm in 1973, where he conducted Gian Carlo Menotti's *The Saint of Bleecker Street*. Subsequent seasons saw him in charge of a vast number of new opera productions worldwide. In 1979, he became music director of the Washington Opera and between 1987 until 1993, he also served as music director of the Scottish Opera. Since 2000, he has been director of the Pittsburgh Opera. He is one of the most sought after opera conductors in the world and also writes and lectures widely on opera and musical theater. Of especial importance are Mauceri's studies of late nineteenth century performance practice, which have called into question many long-established traditions in the interpretation and staging of operas by Verdi, Wagner, and others.

Mauceri also guest conducts many of the world's leading orchestras and has an extraordinarily fruitful association with Broadway, where he has directed many productions. He has also received countless international awards for his work in musical theater and for his restorations and arrangements of classic film scores, which have been heard across the world. In 1991, the Hollywood Bowl Orchestra was created for him by the Los Angeles Philharmonic Association, with an initial 15-CD recording contract on the Philips label. Mauceri has also made important recordings with London/Decca, including highly acclaimed stage works by Kurt Weill, a composer with whom he is strongly identified. *—Michael Jameson*

Recommended:

- ○ **John Mauceri: Greatest Hits** / Mauceri (cond.), Shaham, Horne, McNair, LuPone, Hollywood Bowl Orch. / 2001 / Philips 468686
- ○ **Korngold, Schreker, Eisler** / Mauceri (cond.), etc. / London 452664
- ○ **Korngold: Between Two Worlds** / Mauceri (cond.), Frey, Berlin RSO, Berlin SO / 1995 / London 430170

Nicholas Maw

b. Nov. 5, 1935, Grantham, Lincolnshire, England
Composer

Nicholas Maw, one of the most highly regarded British composers of his generation, has written music in a language greatly influenced by the expressionistic style closely associated with Arnold Schoenberg. Still, it is misleading as well as unduly dismissive of Maw's singular mode of expression to categorize him simply as Schoenbergian, or even as expressionistic. Maw's music, with its opposition and blending of 12-tone and tonal principles, is better regarded as the multiply influenced but cohesive creation of a wholly original creative voice.

Maw, born in Grantham, Lincolnshire, England on November 5, 1935, received his early formal training at the Royal Academy of Music in London (1955–58). There he studied composition with Lennox Berkeley and harmony and counterpoint with Paul Steinitz. With financial help from the French government and the Lili Boulanger Prize, Maw pursued further studies in Paris with famed pedagogue Nadia Boulanger, with whom Berkeley had also studied. It was during his time in Paris that Maw studied under former Schoenberg pupil Max Deutsch, who influenced his exploration of 12-tone techniques.

In 1962, at the age of 26, Maw wrote *Scenes and Arias* for orchestra and three women's voices, the work which established him as a composer of some consequence. Since then, he has composed operas, sonatas, and chamber, vocal, and choral works, but remains best known for his orchestral music. From 1973 to 1987 he worked on the immense symphonic poem *Odyssey*, generally regarded as his greatest creative achievement. Maw's other orchestral music includes popular works like *Spring Music* (1983), *The World in the Evening* (1988), *Shahnama* (1992), and the *Violin Concerto* (1993).

The composer's smaller works include three string quartets (1965, 1982, and 1993–94), *Life Studies* (1973) for chamber ensemble, and *Personae IV, V, VI* (1985–86) for piano. His first two operas, *One Man Show* (1964) and *The Rising of the Moon* (1970), use comedy to convey underlying social and political commentary.

Maw's academic career began with a post as resident composer at Trinity College, Cambridge (1966–70). In 1972, he served briefly as a visiting lecturer in composition at Exeter University and later held positions at Yale University and Bard College in New York. He has achieved considerable popularity in both his native country and his adopted U.S. home. He has been a particular favorite of the British Broadcasting Company, which has commissioned music from him on several occasions; other commissions include works for the Academy of St. Martin-in-the-Fields, the Philharmonia Orchestra, the Royal Opera House, and the Royal Philharmonic Orchestra. A recording of *Odyssey* by Simon Rattle and the City of Birmingham Symphony Orchestra was nominated for a Grammy award in 1992. *—Bruce Lundgren*

Overview of Works

The works of Nicholas Maw are frequently described as essential to the "neo-Romantic revival" or an "attempt to reconnect with the Romantic tradition that was broken with the onset of Modernism." Maw himself has said, "There was a break in the natural tradition around 1914, for obvious social and political reasons. . . . It seems that I am trying to regain that tradition." That said, his works have an appeal to much wider audiences than the music of, say, Philip Glass, and, in a way, Maw's work is less well known than Glass' because he is so traditional, and, therefore, doesn't generate the same amount of artistic debate. Maw has written in every genre, with his best-known works being his operas and orchestral pieces. Maw's earliest works—such as the *Sonatina for flute and piano* and *Six Chinese Songs*—are student efforts and show the conflict between what was expected of a composer in the 1950s (serial, atonal music) and what his own instinct told him he wanted to write (more melodic, harmonically centered music). His acknowledged breakthrough work, *Scenes and Arias* (1962, revised 1966), is a lush, lyrical set of pieces for three female voices and orchestra, rooted in two central chords and the intervals of the seventh and ninth. This led to the comedy operas *One Man Show* (1964, revised 1966 and 1970) and *The Rising of the Moon* (1967–1970), both compared to the works of Britten and Richard Strauss. A third opera, *Sophie's Choice*, was premiered in 2002, and again, Maw's score was praised for its lyricism and expression. Maw's other breakthrough work is the 90-plus-minute orchestral *Odyssey* (1972–1987), displaying extended and self-generating melodies. A *Violin Concerto* composed in 1993 for Joshua Bell has also been well-received. Between these large-scale works are many smaller works, all of which demonstrate Maw's skill at using traditional forms (such as the sonata and passacaglia, and even the tone row), harmonies that tend to either allude to tonality through atonal means or allude to atonality through tonal means, and rich melodic ideas. Among these are *La vita nuova for soprano and chamber ensemble*; *Roman Canticles for voice, flute, viola, and harp*; the three string quartets (1965, 1982, and 1994–1995); the *Piano Trio*; *Sonata for solo violin*; *American Games for symphonic winds*; and *Dances Scenes for orchestra*, to name just a few. *—Patsy Morita*

Recommended:

- ○ **Maw: Hymnus; Little Concert; Shahnama** / Cleobury (cond.), Daniel, BBC Concert Orch., Britten Sinfonia / 1999 / ASV 1070
- ○ **Maw: Violin Concerto** / Norrington (cond.), Bell, London PO / 1999 / Sony 62856
- ○ **Maw: Odyssey; Dance Scenes** / Rattle, Harding (conds.), Thomas, London PO, Birmingham SO / 2003 / EMI 585145
- ○ **Maw: Ghost Dances; La Vita Nuova; Roman Canticle** / Kendall (cond.), Sharp, Pelton, 20th Century Consort / 1997 / ASV 999
- ○ **Maw: Serenata Notturna** / Boughton (cond.), Wallfisch, English String Orch. / 1996 / Nimbus 5471

John McCormack

b. Jun. 14, 1884, Athlone, Ireland, **d.** Sep. 16, 1945, Dublin, Ireland
Tenor
John McCormack, one of the most popular singers of his generation and the very archetype of the Irish tenor, was born in Athlone, Ireland. Without the benefit of prior training, he won the National Music Festival in Dublin in 1903 and thereafter continued his studies as a member of Dublin's Cathedral Choir. In 1905, he went to Italy to train with Vincenzo Sabatini; in the following year, he made his first appearance on the operatic stage in Savona, Italy (in the title role of *L'amico Fritz*) under the name Giovanni Foli. His official debut, as Turiddù in *Cavalleria rusticana*, took place at Covent Garden on October 15, 1907. Over the next several years he appeared there regularly in such operas as *Rigoletto, Don Giovanni, Il barbiere di Siviglia, Faust, Roméo et Juliette, La bohème*, and *Madama Butterfly*. He debuted in America in a Manhattan Opera House *La Traviata* in 1909 and thereafter appeared in a number of Metropolitan Opera productions. Both in London and New York he held the stage with such *dive assolute* as Luisa Tetrazzini and Nellie Melba. In 1914 he was slated to participate in a star-studded *Don Giovanni* in Salzburg, along with Lilli Lehmann, Geraldine Farrar, and Feodor Chalyapin; unfortunately, the outbreak of World War I meant that what should have been a legendary production had to be called off.

By the middle 1910s, McCormack, aware of his own limitations as an actor, abandoned the operatic stage and devoted himself to a career as a recitalist. In this milieu he attained even greater fame; though his sensitive interpretions of Handel, Mozart, and Romantic lieder were greeted with general enthusiasm, it was his sincere performances of folk songs and popular ballads that captured the hearts of the public. From the second decade of the twentieth century he also enjoyed remarkable success as a recording artist; on the strength of his recordings, some have held him up as as the only tenor of his era with a gift to rival that of Caruso.

In the later stages of his career, McCormack parlayed his still-considerable reputation into occasional film roles, most notably as the lead (opposite Maureen O'Hara) in the early talkie *Song O' My Heart* (1929) and as himself in the British *Wings of the Morning* (1937). Though he had become an American citizen in 1917, he spent his last decades in Dublin and died there. *—AMG*

Recommended:

- ○ **I Hear You Calling Me** / McCormack, etc. / 2004 / Living Era 281
- ○ **McCormack In Song** / McCormack, etc. / 1993 / Nimbus 7854

Audra McDonald

b. Jul. 3, 1970, Berlin, Germany
Vocalist
Born in California into a musical family, soprano Audra McDonald received her classical vocal training at the Juilliard School, graduating in 1993. Since then, she has pursued a successful career in both classical voice and musical theater. She made her Carnegie Hall debut singing selections from Gershwin's *Porgy and Bess* with the San Francisco Symphony under the direction of Michael Tilson Thomas in a concert televised internationally and recorded for BMG Classics. She has also performed with the Cleveland Orchestra under Leonard Slatkin, the Philadelphia Orchestra under Marin Alsop, and the Boston Pops under Keith Lockhart. She sang at the 1999 BBC Proms with Simon Rattle and also performed in the Divas at the Donmar series in London. On Broadway, she has won Tony Awards for featured roles in *Ragtime* (1998), *Master Class* (1996), and *Carousel* (1994). Her recordings include discs of songs by Harold Arlen, Leonard Bernstein, and Jerome Kern. *—Robert Adelson*

Recommended:

- ○ **I Was Looking at the Ceiling and Then I Saw the Sky** / Adams (cond.), Gershon, Muenz, Mutru, McDonald / Nonesuch 79473
- ○ **Bernstein: Wonderful Town** / Rattle (cond.), Hampson, Atkinson, McDonald, Criswell, Birmingham Contemporary Music Group, London Voices / 1999 / EMI 56753

Ronn McFarlane

b. 1953, West Virginia
Lutenist
Ronn McFarlane is one of the principal interpreters of music for the Renaissance lute. This sets McFarlane apart from many players who study the lute in addition to the guitar, or those who play lute music on the guitar. McFarlane is mainly devoted to the lute only, and he has mastered a variety of different lutes of diverse courses from discrete historical periods.

Born in West Virginia, McFarlane initially studied the guitar, even played in a few rock and blues groups while taking a course of study in classical guitar at Shenandoah University in Winchester, VA. McFarlane ultimately dropped out of the pop bands and completed his training in classical guitar at the Peabody Institute, where he would also teach for a time afterward. Among his own teachers were Paul O'Dette, Roger Harmon, and Pat O'Brien. McFarlane decided to give up the guitar altogether in favor of the lute in 1978. Not long after he was among the co-founders of the group the Baltimore Consort, which soon became the best-known American period instrument group in the world thanks to a generous touring schedule and an extremely popular series of releases on the Dorian label.

Although some members have been in and out of the Baltimore Consort over the years, McFarlane has remained a constant member within the group. Yet he has recorded and concertized on his own far more prolifically than any other member in the Baltimore Consort. McFarlane has recorded six CDs for Dorian, including such popular discs as *A Distant Shore, The Renaissance Lute*, and *The Scottish Lute*. He has also recorded three more backing honey-toned soprano Julianne Baird and another accompanying tenor Frederick Urrey. In 1996 McFarlane was awarded an honorary doctorate from his alma mater, Shenandoah University, for his work in popularizing the lute and universalizing its appeal. *—Uncle Dave Lewis*

Recommended:

- ○ **Art of the Lute: Best of Ronn McFarlane** / Cudek, McFarlane / 2003 / Dorian 90022
- ○ **The Scottish Lute** / McFarlane / 1990 / Dorian 90129
- ○ **John Dowland** / McFarlane / 1991 / Dorian 90148
- ○ **The Renaissance Lute** / McFarlane / 1994 / Dorian 90186

Nicholas McGegan

b. Jan. 14, 1950, Sawbridgeworth, England
Conductor, Harpsichordist
Nicholas McGegan has done more for the early music movement in America than nearly anyone else, and his tireless explorations of the byways of Baroque opera have put many fascinating works into the concert hall and onto recordings. He studied piano at London's Trinity College of Music, and learned to play the flute while he was there, but entertained no special desire to study historical performance. When he entered Corpus Christi College in Cambridge, however, one of the courses required for a music degree was professor Nicholas Shackleton's acoustics course. This course often met in the professor's home, which contained both a large collection of eighteenth century wind instruments and a tenant named Christopher Hogwood. Hogwood, of course, was then one of the leading lions of the period-instrument Baroque movement in England, so McGegan could not have been in a better position to learn about it. Although he had been studying twentieth century music, one day he picked up a Baroque wooden flute and never looked back. During the 1970s, McGegan became one of the bright lights of England's starry period-instrument scene, playing the flute as well as harpsichord and fortepiano with all the major period instrument groups in England, especially Hogwood's Academy of Ancient Music. He became director of early music at the Royal College of Music in London in 1976.

In 1979, McGegan made the fateful decision to accept a three-month artist-in-residence position at Washington University at St. Louis. McGegan's teaching and performance caused quite a stir at the university, and numerous renewals of the initial term followed; McGegan has said that during this time he became "more American-based than European-based." In 1985, McGegan became music director of the Philharmonia Baroque Orchestra, which previously had been a players' co-operative without a leader. McGegan ended the orchestra's "Birkenstock period," but the ensemble still places a premium on collaboration and creativity under McGegan's direction. It has become the finest period instrument group in America and one of the finest in the world since McGegan took it over, going from giving 12 concerts a year on subscription to 50, and making numerous recordings under McGegan's direction.

In 2000, McGegan became Music Director Laureate of the PBO, which allows him to direct more international performances while staying involved with the PBO. One of the international positions this very busy conductor holds is Artistic Director of the Gottingen Handel Festival, the oldest festival for Baroque music in the world. He also performs and records quite often with Hungary's Capella Savaria. McGegan has also founded the Arcadian Academy, a chamber offshoot of the PBO, which records extensively and tours througout the U.S. and Europe. In addition, he serves as the Baroque Series Director for the St. Paul Chamber Orchestra and as an advisory board member for the University of Maryland Handel Festival and London's Handel House.

Despite, or perhaps because of, his academic credentials and background in period performance, McGegan's performances exemplify joy and fun, rather than sober scholarship. He has compared the PBO to a "jazz band" in terms of its ability to play together and play with spirit, and the comparison rings true when listening to the PBO live or on record—or, indeed, when listening to any of McGegan's performances. Although he is primarily identified with Handel, he has played repertoire stretching into the nineteenth century, and has brought the same sense of fun to all of it. *—Andrew Lindemann Malone*

Recommended:

- ○ **Handel: Atalanta** / McGegan (cond.), Polgar, Gregor, Bandi, Bartfai-Barta, Philharmonia Baroque, Savaria Capella / Hungaroton 12612

- ○ **Handel: Giustino** / McGegan (cond.), Kohler, Chance, Minter, Padmore, Savaria Capella, Freiburg Baroque / HM 907130
- ○ **Handel: Opera Arias, Vol. 1** / McGegan (cond.), Minter, Greer, Philharmonia Baroque / 2001 / Classical Express 3955183
- ○ **Corelli: Concertos, Vol. 1** / McGegan (cond.), Philharmonia Baroque / 2001 / Classical Express 3957014
- ○ **Rameau: Orchestral Suites** / McGegan (cond.), Philharmonia Baroque / HM 907121

Sylvia McNair

b. Jun. 23, 1956, Mansfield, OH
Soprano
Sylvia McNair is a globe-trotting American soprano with an unusually clear and brilliant sound on the lighter side of the vocal spectrum. She sings a wide range of operatic and concert music, including Mozart (her specialty), Baroque operas of Handel and Monteverdi, modern works by Stravinsky and Britten, and songs of Gershwin and Jerome Kern. Although her operatic career has centered mostly on European houses, she has made selected appearances at New York's Metropolitan Opera, and, particularly since winning the Marian Anderson award in 1992, she has been a dedicated recitalist both in America and abroad. Her many recordings for the Philips and Deutsche Grammophon labels are consistently excellent, and they have been the cornerstone of her success with American audiences.

McNair was born in Mansfield, OH, the daughter of an amateur choral conductor and a piano teacher. She took lessons on both the piano and violin as a child, and continued intensive studies on the violin into her early twenties. McNair credits this early and thorough introduction to music as contributing to her success as a singer. After a bachelor's degree at Wheaton College, she entered the master's program at Indiana University, where she got her first taste of operatic singing in the university's renowned training program. After completing the young artist's program at the San Francisco Opera, she made a swift entry into the professional world, performing at the 1982 Mostly Mozart Festival, singing a range of roles with the St. Louis Opera (1983–1989), and making debuts in Santa Fe, Vienna, Amsterdam, and Berlin.

From the beginning, McNair has been associated with Mozart's Pamina (*The Magic Flute*) and Ilia (*Idomeneo*), and Monteverdi's Poppea (*L'incoronazione di Poppea*), but it was her Anne Trulove in Stravinsky's *The Rake's Progress*, at Glyndebourne in 1989, that launched her into the international spotlight. Since that time she has enjoyed an unbroken chain of critical and musical successes around the world, steadily praised for the beauty, intelligence, and uncommon exactness of her performances. Her work with conductor John Eliot Gardiner has established her as a fine singer of Baroque music, able to negotiate the intricacies of period ornamentation without sacrificing vocal color. Likewise, her concerts and recordings with Robert Shaw, Seiji Ozawa, Bernard Haitink, Kurt Masur, and Neville Marriner show her at ease in everything from Mozart's sacred choral works to Mahler's *Symphony No. 2* —*Allen Schrott*

Recommended:

- ○ **The Echoing Air: Music of Henry Purcell** / Hogwood (cond.), McNair, O'Dette, Steele-Perkins, Standage, Dreyfus, Academy of Ancient Music / 1995 / Philips 446081
- ○ **Love's Sweet Surrender** / Marriner (cond.), McNair, Brendel, Josefowicz, Academy of St. Martin-in-the-Fields / 1997 / Philips 446712
- ○ **Mozart: Mass in C minor** / Gardiner (cond.), McNair, Beznosiuk, Johnson, Montague, EBS, Monteverdi Choir / Philips 420210
- ○ **Rêveries** / McNair, Vignoles (piano) / 1997 / Philips 446656

Colin McPhee

b. Feb. 15, 1900, Montreal, Canada, **d.** Jan. 7, 1964, Los Angeles, CA
Composer: Concerto, Symphonic, Keyboard
Born in Montreal, Colin McPhee was a distinctive and imaginative composer, ethnomusicologist, pianist, and writer, most noted for absorbing the sounds of Balinese music into his own compositions. He came to the USA to study at the Peabody Institute in Baltimore, where his composition teacher was Gustav Strube (1867–1953). He returned to Canada to study piano with Arthur Friedheim in Toronto. The Toronto Symphony gave his *First Piano Concerto* a world premiere in 1924. He left Toronto for Paris to study piano with Isidore Philipp, and composition with Paul Le Flem.

Even McPhee's early music has a marked tendency to use layers of ostinati. When he first heard cylinder recordings of Balinese music he was entranced. He married Jane Belo, an anthropologist (and graduate student of Margaret Mead). They traveled to Bali, where Jane built a home in the hill country. McPhee vigorously notated the melodies and rhythmic devices of every gamelan he heard. He is credited with saving a number of gamelans that were likely to go out of existence, and of resurrecting some older instruments and styles. The couple adopted a child, Samphi, who later became a member of a Balinese dance troupe that toured the United States.

He worked for the rest of his life on a serious study, *Music in Bali*, which was published posthumously in 1966. He also wrote transcriptions for Western instruments, and original compositions full of the sound, melodies, and rhythms of gamelan music. The most famous of these, *Tabuh-Tabuhan*, for orchestra, was premiered during a trip he made in the summer of 1936 to Mexico, conducted by Carlos Chávez.

McPhee and his wife sold their house, left Bali, and divorced in 1939. In the early 1940s McPhee lived in a large brownstone in Brooklyn, shared with other artists and literary figures such as Leonard Bernstein and Benjamin Britten among many others. McPhee, Britten, and Bernstein are said to have fought all the time over who got to play the grand piano. Britten and McPhee participated in the first recording of McPhee's *Balinese Ceremonial Music* for two pianos and flute in 1941. The strain of Balinese sounds that runs through Britten's music clearly originated with McPhee.

In the later 1940s, McPhee, lonely for his beloved Bali, slipped into an alcohol-deepened depression, and his output drastically declined. He pulled himself out of the depths and produced new compositions in the 1950s. In 1958 he was appointed professor of ethnomusicology at UCLA, and he became an esteemed jazz critic.

Howard Hanson's recording of *Tabuh-Tabuhan* on the now legendary Mercury Living Presence disc of 1956 excited many music lovers and caught the ears of young American composers. Within a decade, some of them had taken the idea of layers of repeated ostinati that marks the music of McPhee and Bali, and from it created American minimalism. —*Joseph Stevenson*

CONCERTO

Concerto for piano & wind octet (1928)

McPhee is primarily known as the reluctant Modernist who went native in Bali—and as the composer of a rich handful of lusciously kinetic, gamelan-inspired works—though his Balinese adventure did not commence until 1931, as he turned 31. A persistent composer from his teens, nearly all of his early music is lost, including numerous piano and chamber works, two piano concertos, and a symphony. Thus, the fortuitously surviving *Concerto for Piano and Wind Octet* provides a rare glimpse the young McPhee before his ultimately defining embarkation. McPhee began his career, after studies with Liszt's pupil Arthur Friedheim, as a concert pianist and it is hardly surprising to find him testing the stylistic waters through the medium of the piano concerto. Friedheim, no doubt, gave a fillip to McPhee's essential Romanticism—his first piano concerto had been titled *La Mort d'Arthur*—though the neo-Classicism of Stravinsky's *Wind Octet* (1923) and the *Concerto for Piano and Wind Instruments* (1924) generated an immediate vogue which was difficult to ignore by the later 1920s. McPhee is audibly indebted to the latter works, but what is remarkable about his own *Concerto for Piano and Wind Octet*, composed in 1928, is the individual profile emerging, from the opening bars, from the neo-Classic manner of brittle smart-alecking. It is nearly impossible not to hear the work retrospectively, as diffidence, whimsy, irony, and vaguely vast portent looming across a darkening horizon in search of some rare, unexampled richness. The second movement Chorale—an homage to his Schola Cantorum tradition passed on through studies with Paul Le Flem between 1924 and 1926—resembles an ancient ritual revisited through an ear poised between sensuous *décadence* and the faddishly acerbic blandishments of Modernism, which win out in the motoric last movement, though not without an occasional backward glance. The three compact movements, playing together a little over a quarter of an hour, provide an engagingly telling conspectus of the young McPhee at the compositional crossroads with a barely suppressed exoticism about to blossom. —*Adrian Corleonis*

Recommended:

- ○ **Colin McPhee** / Davies (cond.), Drury, Takagi, Brooklyn PO / 1996 / MusicMasters 67159

Tabuh-tabuhan, for 2 pianos & orchestra (1936)

Canadian composer Colin McPhee lived in Bali for nearly all of the 1930s, studying and absorbing the music there. Its influence on him was such that certain elements found their way into virtually every piece he wrote thereafter. The sound of the famous gamelan orchestras relies on gongs, flutes, drums, and metallic keyboard instruments. Short patterns played in longer durations provide both the beat and the harmonic underpinning of this music. The higher instruments often play the same material as the bass but in faster, whirling patterns. Syncopated drums and cymbals are a striking feature, particularly in the more modern styles.

This three-movement, approximately 20-minute piece strikingly imitates the gamelan sound. McPhee adds a sub-ensemble of two pianos, celesta, xylophone, marimba, glockenspiel, and two Balinese gongs at the nucleus of his orchestra, similar to a concertino group in a Baroque concerto grosso. Formally, the work is described as a toccata, and musical patterns recur and predominate; it has clearly been an influence on some of the minimalist compositions written decades later. It was first played in Mexico City by Carlos Chavez and the Orquesta Sinfónica del Estado de México. The title is a complex Balinese word referring to various drumbeats. The first movement, Ostinatos, and the final movement, Finale, are fast, rhythmic, and consistently Oriental in sound, although western ideas of repetition and structure do exist. The middle movement, Nocturne, is a gentle piece with genuine, lullaby-like melodies, particularly on the flute. This is an exceptionally original and attractive piece of music, one of the most famous works by any Canadian composer. *—Joseph Stevenson*

Recommended:

- ○ **Tabuh-Tabuhan** / Pauk (cond.), Espirit Orch. / 1997 / CBC 5181
- ○ **Hanson Conducts McPhee, Sessions & Thomson** / Hanson (cond.), Clatworthy, Eastman-Rochester Orch. & Chorus / 1992 / Mercury 434310
- ○ **McPhee, Ung & Harrison** / Davies (cond.), Oldfather, Basquin, American Composers Orch. / 1995 / Argo 444560

SYMPHONIC

Symphony No. 2 ("Pastorale") (1957)

Flirtation with the art and music of the mysterious East goes back at least to Félicien David's vastly influential symphonic ode *Le Désert* (1844)—and parodied, with the entire orientalizing vogue, in Offenbach's *Ba-ta-clan* (1855)—though the adaptation of ethnic oddments in such things as Borodin's *In the Steppes of Central Asia* and *Prince Igor* remained largely sportive until Debussy's originality was given a decisive fillip by Javanese gamelan at the 1889 Paris Exposition. By the turn of the century, the search was on for authentic folk music, fast disappearing under the urban pressures of railway expansion, telegraphic communication, and faddishness. Vaughan Williams in England, Grainger in England and Scandinavia, Bartók and Kodály in Hungary and Transylvania, did extensive field work collecting folk songs that directly influenced composition. In the early 1920s, Szymanowski turned to Polish folk music of as the basis of a creative renewal. But it was left to Colin McPhee to find—or invent—himself through intimate contact with Balinese gamelan and musical tradition. Born with the century, McPhee spent his early years working through Romantic gestures inherited from his piano teacher, Liszt pupil Arthur Friedheim, and absorbing Stravinsky's neo-Classicism, both of which proved to be compositional cul-de-sacs. Hearing a primitive recording of gamelan music proved a revelation, and McPhee departed for Bali in 1931. Gamelan is an elaborate ensemble of percussion instruments in use throughout the islands of Indonesia—gongs, chimes, and other metallophones—whose traditional use employs sinuous melody as a device for organizing exuberantly pressing rhythmic patterns. The transformative effect of this music upon McPhee is recorded in his memoir, *A House in Bali* (1946):

"At first, as I listened . . . the music was simply a delicious confusion, a strangely sensuous and quite unfathomable art, mysteriously aerial, aeolian, filled with joy and radiance. Each night the music started up I experienced the same sensation of freedom and indescribable freshness."

Returning to the United States in 1939, McPhee realized this romanticized vision of Bali in a handful of piquant, poignant, driving evocations, of which the most famous was the orchestral toccata *Tabuh-tabuhan* and the most subtle and exquisite, the *Symphony No. 2*—a commission from the Louisville Symphony completed in 1957. In three movements (Moderato Misterioso, Elegy, and Molto Energico), the symphony is a fantastically glowing fantasy of sophisticated primitivism of all mystery, "delicious confusion," and beguiling melody whose languor is relieved by erotically throbbing ostinati. *—Adrian Corleonis*

Recommended:

- ○ **Tabuh-Tabuhan** / Pauk (cond.), Espirit Orch. / 1997 / CBC 5181

KEYBOARD

Balinese Ceremonial Music, for 2 pianos (1934–1938)

While Canadian composer Colin McPhee lived in Bali for the decade of the 1930s, he was so enamored of the music of the island's local percussion orchestra, the gamelan, that it shaped his entire compositional style. His Balinese musician friends were, for their part, intrigued when his piano arrived. As described in his book, *A House in Bali*, they were puzzled by the thick-sounding Western-style chords, but they quickly were impressed by the way one or two people at the keyboard could imitate the multi-layered simultaneous patterns of their own music. While in Bali, McPhee made over 40 direct transcriptions of Balinese gamelan compositions. Back in New York in 1941, McPhee recorded these three (which conveniently fit on the two sides of a 78-rpm record). His partner was the young British expatriate composer, Benjamin Britten. The set of transcriptions comprises three works, arranged in a typically Western fast/slow/fast suite. Since Balinese music with its patterns was an inspiration for minimalism (which McPhee, who died in 1964, did not quite live to witness) this music sounds surprisingly more modern. *—Joseph Stevenson*

Recommended:

- ○ **Britten & McPhee** / Goldstone & Clemmow / 1998 / Olympia 648

Nikolay Medtner

b. Jan. 5, 1880, Moscow, Russia, **d.** Nov. 13, 1951, London, England

Composer: Keyboard, Vocal, Concerto

Russian composer Nikolai Karlovich Medtner (or Metner) was born to parents of German descent who had lived in Russia for several generations. The family background was musical; his mother's brother was Fedor Gedike (Theodore Goedicke), a minor Romantic composer and professional pianist. He received early piano lessons from his mother and was entered into the Moscow Conservatory's junior classes at the age of twelve, winning a gold medal when he completed his keyboard training in 1900. He studied privately with Sergei Taneyev, but largely taught himself composition. Taneyev encouraged him to consider composition as a career.

Nevertheless he went on tour as a pianist and received the Rubinstein Medal in Vienna. He gradually devoted more time to composition, but still performed, and in 1909 he was invited to join the conservatory faculty as a piano professor. A quiet person, he did not enjoy teaching, and resigned after a year, partly for that reason and partly to have more time for composition. In 1910, the wealthy conductor Sergei Koussevitzky invited Medtner to join the editorial board of his new music publishing firm, Editions Russe. He also made the acquaintance of Sergei Rachmaninov the same year. The two composer-pianists became close friends.

Medtner moved to Germany, but was repatriated when World War I broke out, with Russia and Germany on opposite sides. He felt it necessary to accept another teaching post in Moscow. In 1919 he married Anna Medtner (née Bratenshi), who had been the wife of his brother; the two of them suffered during the civil war and repression that followed the Bolshevik coup of 1917. In 1921 they were granted permission to tour abroad. They landed in Germany; aside from a 1927 tour they would never see Russia again. After a tour of the United States in 1925, they settled in Paris, which had the most important Russian emigré colony in Europe.

Medtner's music was harmonically adventurous, but had a Romantic aesthetic that was out of fashion in trendy Paris. Other locales welcomed his music more readily: he was acclaimed in the United States and Canada, and especially in England. His 1935 book *The Muse and Fashion*, published by Rachmaninov in Paris, expressed his disillusionment with modern music. The same year, Medtner moved to England. Failing health compelled him to give up concertizing in 1944, but he was able to make some classic recordings of his piano music through an arrangement set up by a newly formed Medtner Society, supported by the Maharajah of Mysore. These are outstanding examples of his superb playing technique and of his compositional intentions. He also made recordings of his songs, accompanying soprano Elisabeth Schwarzkopf. Medtner died at the end of a series of the heart attacks that gradually incapacitated him.

His output includes a few pieces of chamber music, over a hundred songs, and a large quantity of piano music, including a "Concert-Piece" and three concertos for piano and orchestra, his only works with orchestra. While there is a Russian flavor to his music, it really falls into the line of Schumann and Brahms, and he adopted the latter's interest in thematic unity. His canons and other contrapuntal works were well-planned, with inventive rhythms distinguishing the different lines. His harmonies tend to be low in the keyboard, giving his music a dark, brooding quality. He had strong opinions about the role of art, assigning it an almost religious role, and there is perhaps a spiritual purity to his music.Medtner was largely overlooked during the largely anti-Romantic twentieth century, but his music has recently enjoyed a sudden resurgence of interest. *—Joseph Stevenson*

KEYBOARD

Works for Piano (1894–1945)

The piano figured as prominently in the output of Nikolay Medtner (1880–1951) as it had in the oeuvre of Chopin. The former composer, of course, has never approached the latter's popularity, but he has developed a loyal though small following who would insist on his inclusion as a major figure in piano literature. That view might be extreme, but charges that Medtner's music was nothing more than warmed-over Rachmaninov and that it favored German rather than Russian traditions are certainly misinformed, not least because they are obviously contradictory.

There are 100 songs and a handful of chamber works in Medtner's output, but the rest was written for piano or for piano and orchestra. And even the songs and chamber music, with one exception, involve the piano. At the core of Medtner's keyboard works are his 14 sonatas. Most are in one movement and are short. The earliest, the Op. 5, in F minor, is an exception to both rules: cast in four movements, it lasts a half hour or more and is one of the stronger efforts in the series.

Among the finest of the sonatas is the G minor, Op. 22 (1910), a work that began receiving some currency in the later twentieth century. Perhaps better still is Medtner's *Sonata in E minor*, Op. 25/2 (1911), generally regarded as his greatest large composition for solo piano. Also long and complex, this work exemplifies many of the stylistic traits that set Medtner apart from Rachmaninov. Cast in one movement, it consists of inner sections or sub-movements, but musicologists are confused as to exactly how many there are or even specifically where their borders lie. The themes and harmonies here may exhibit a superficial similarity to Rachmaninov's, but the music is more Classical in style and involves contrapuntal activity to a far greater degree. Moreover, it is less lush-sounding, less emotional, and more intellectual.

Medtner was not always as dry-sounding as the above description might suggest: his one-movement *Sonata Reminiscenza*, the first work in the *Forgotten Melodies*, Op. 38, features two quite beautiful melodies in a rich Romantic vein. Other works such as the *Sonata-Idyll* (ca. 1937), Op. 56, the composer's last piano sonata, have a lighter and somewhat less complex nature, using relatively direct expressive language.

Medtner wrote three piano concertos, *No. 1 in C minor*, Op. 33, spanning the war years 1914–18, *No. 2 in C minor* (1920–27) finished a decade later, and the last (1940–1943), in E minor, appearing in the era of World War II. Each lasts around 35 minutes and features a multi-movement structure. The *Third* has a most interesting appearance, with massive outer movements surrounding a brief Interludium which connects to the finale without pause. All three concertos began gaining a foothold in the repertory and with the public in the late twentieth century, in part, ironically, because of their seeming likenesses to Rachmaninov's music. *—Robert Cummings*

Recommended:

- ○ **Medtner: Piano Sonatas** / Hamelin / 1998 / Hyperion 67221/4
- ○ **Demidenko plays Medtner** / Demidenko / 1993 / Hyperion 66636
- ○ **Piano Works Of Nikolai Medtner, Vol. 1** / Tozer / 1992 / Chandos 9050

Arabesques, Op. 7 (1901–1904)

The *Arabesques* here are early compositions, and while they are not among Medtner's better-known or more rewarding works, they are nonetheless worthwhile efforts. All are similar in certain respects and each requires a formidable technique, as well as a good measure of interpretive insight. Like so much of Medtner's piano music, the three pieces are heavily chromatic and each is written in a minor key. Each *Arabesque* begins in a sort of pastoral or serene mood and gradually develops tension. The third one in G minor is the most rhythmically charged and dissonant of the trio and will probably strike the listener as the most dramatic. The second, A minor, is also a well-crafted work and shows much interesting development by Medtner. When the *Arabesques* are recorded at all, the pianist usually chooses the second or third, and each is generally performed in three to four minutes. *—Robert Cummings*

Recommended:

- ○ **Medtner: Complete Solo Piano Recordings, Vol. 2** / Medtner / 1999 / APR 5547
- ○ **Medtner: Piano Concertos 2 & 3; Arabesque; Tale In F** / Medtner / 1993 / Testament 1027

Four Fairy Tales (Skazki), Op. 26 (ca. 1912)

Nikolay Medtner wrote a number of shorter works he called "skazka," better translated into English as folktale rather than fairy tale, since the Russian stories he had in mind do not always deal with enchanted beings or magic. In fact, most of the 38 works do not refer to a specific story, and he used the title in much the same way "legend" was used by Dvořák. The four skazki in Op. 26 were written around 1912, when Medtner was trying to make a name for himself amongst Moscow's musical leaders. No. 1 in E flat major, marked Allegro frescamente with a Giocoso central section, has a happy, almost pastoral melody set against a rolling accompaniment. The left hand plays constant triplets while the right plays above, somewhat like a Mendelssohn song without words. No. 2 is also in E flat major, but this time it's a bouncy game of tag where the right hand scurries around and the left hand leaps to catch it. No. 3 in F minor has the tempo indication Narrante a piacere, or narrating at pleasure. A single, clear voice throughout the piece briefly turns into a waltz before going back to the story. The final skazka is a longer, more complex piece. Whereas in the first three there were no more than two different moods expressed, this one is more like Medtner's sonata movements where themes and motives are used in a variety of ways to convey contrasting moods. Here, one measure contains both scherzando and tranquillo markings, while a little further on there are the markings risolute, poco giocoso, and disinvolto in successive measures. The melody switches between hands and the texture of the accompaniment changes to further transform melodic motives. The overall effect is a story that starts quietly and calmly and eventually ends exultantly. Even if Medtner didn't have magical stories in mind when he composed these, they are enchanting in their own right. *—Patsy Morita*

Recommended:

- ○ **Medtner: Complete Solo Piano Recordings, Vol. 1** / Medtner / 1998 / APR 5546
- ○ **Binns Plays Medtner** / Binns / Pearl 9628

VOCAL

Songs (1896–1951)

An inordinately modest man, Nikolay Medtner lacked the outward drive that might have made him a more prominent figure. Forced into exile thrice, first from his native Russia to Germany, thence to France, and finally to England, Medtner sculpted his own compositional identity owing much to his forebears, but mostly relying on his inner sense of the appropriate. Rejecting late Romantic notions of Gesamtkunstwerk, Medtner believed that music was about music alone and this conviction is heard in his many songs. Believing that his music needed to be in and of itself, Medtner provided no undergirding of text in his songs. The accompaniments do not rise and fall with the meaning of the poems he set and do not musically echo the psychological import of the words. Rather, the piano part pursues its own logical course, not unmindful of what the words are saying, but not bound to them as is found in the lieder of Hugo Wolf, for example. Medtner was selective in his choice of texts, however, utilizing poetry of high quality. Whether he composed as he did because he was attracted to strong literary works or whether he chose the texts he did because of his musical convictions is not entirely clear. Comparisons to Brahms in this one aspect only are not misleading. On the whole, however, he was a very different personality. Although Medtner wrote his final song in 1944, the rest of his lyric works were composed between 1902 and 1929, the time of life in pre-Revolutionary Russia and Germany. His gifts as a concert pianist are reflected in his songs, in accompaniments that are often elaborate and always elegantly wrought. He frequently alternates rhythmic pulses between the right hand and left and each example reflects an admirable polish. Medtner's first song was to a text by Pushkin and his first published trio of songs to poems by Lermontov, Pushkin, and Goethe. Although his German heritage was filtered through more than a century of Russian residency, Medtner was enthusiastic about such other German poets as Heine (three poems for Medtner's Op. 12), Nietzsche (five texts set in 1910), and Eichendorff (three poems in Medtner's Op. 46). While Pushkin was set most often, Medtner also composed to texts by two lesser-known, but superb Russians: Fet and Tyutchev. *—Erik Eriksson*

Recommended:

- ○ **Nikolai Medtner: Songs** / Tozer, Andrew / 1994 / Chandos 9327

CONCERTO

Piano Concerto No. 3 in E minor ("Ballade"), Op. 60 (ca. 1940–1943)

Composed in London, the *"Ballade" Concerto* is a rhapsodic work consisting of three continuous movements without break that are fairly homogenous in their style and content. The work is a piano-and-orchestra ballade on a grand scale whose structure breaks the mold of the traditional concerto. The horns open the first movement (Con moto largamente) with a plaintive theme of repeated tones and falling thirds which serves as a unifying link between the movements of the concerto. The piano answers with a more chordal secondary theme marked by melodic leaps, and a third, lyrical theme is introduced by the strings; both are developed later in the concerto. Two cadenzas by the piano and several restatements of the themes round out the exposition. The movement has no clear-cut development or recapitulation sections. Instead, the entire concerto is an extended "development" of the initial themes and their offspring, with each successive phrase expanding further upon the subjects. The remainder of the first movement focuses on derivations of the third theme, though the other two subjects occasionally surface. The piano introduces and explores an enchantingly simple descending melody, and a short cadenza leads directly into the second movement. The brief Interludium begins with a vigorous variation based on the concerto's two opening themes. The soloist explores the descending theme from the first movement, and a dramatic climax develops into the opening of the third movement. The energetic Finale, Allegro molto, eroica, introduces and rhapsodically develops two themes that are reminiscent of the first and second opening subjects of the concerto, respectively. A new episode, andante con moto tranquilo, introduces a triadic phrase that becomes the centerpiece of the movement. There follows a chronological, abbreviated recapitulation of all the themes of the concerto. Ultimately, the opening theme is reestablished as the thesis of the work. An optimistic, tranquil coda concludes the ballade by comparing the first theme with the last. *—David Kent*

Recommended:

- ○ **Medtner: Piano Concerts 2 & 3** / Maksymiuk (cond.),Demidenko, BBC Scottish SO / 1992 / Hyperion 66580
- ○ **Medtner: Piano Concerts 1 & 3** / Ziva (cond.), Scherbakov, Moscow SO / 1999 / Naxos 553359

Zubin Mehta

b. Apr. 29, 1936, Bombay, India

Conductor

Conductor Zubin Mehta was born in Bombay (now Mumbai), Maharashtra state, India on April 29, 1936. He is an adherent of the Parsi religion. His father was Mehli Mehta, a violinist who was the founder and conductor of the Bombay Symphony Orchestra. At the age of 18, after considering a career in medicine, Zubin entered the Vienna Academy of Music, learned to play the double bass in order to join the Academy's orchestra, and took conducting lessons from Hans Swarowsky. He graduated from the Academy in 1957 and made his professional debut in Vienna, guest conducting the Tonkünstler Orchestra. In a London appearance in 1961, Mehta became the first Indian to conduct a major British orchestra. A victory in the first international conductors' competition organized by the Royal Liverpool Philharmonic Orchestra led to a one-year appointment as their assistant conductor. After completing his year-long tenure, Mehta was engaged to conduct the Vienna Philharmonic Orchestra, and made another important and successful guest conducting position with the Philadelphia Orchestra.

Guest appearances with the Montreal and Los Angeles symphonies both led to permanent positions; in 1960 he became music director in Montreal and associate conductor in Los Angeles. Thus Mehta became one of the first of a new breed of conductors sometimes called the "jet set," who are able to maintain two (or even more) principal conductorships of major orchestras by means of frequently flying between the cities involved.

Mehta's accomplishments in Los Angeles, where he became musical director in 1962, were particularly striking. In just a few years he was able to turn the lackluster ensemble into one of the nation's finest orchestras, and, still under 30 years of age when he was appointed, he became the youngest music director of any "major" U.S. orchestra. An exuberant, extroverted performer and person, he possessed a genuine star quality; soon, he conducted the orchestra on a notable series of excellent recordings for London (Decca) Records. Mehta made his operatic debut at the Metropolitan Opera in New York on December 29, 1965, and in 1967 he resigned his position in Montreal, and forged a new relationship with the Israeli Philharmonic Orchestra, eventually becoming its chief music adviser in 1970. In 1971 he conducted the Los Angeles Philharmonic on the soundtrack of Frank Zappa's film *200 Motels*.

In 1978 he resigned his Los Angeles post to succeed Pierre Boulez as music director of the New York Philharmonic Orchestra. After the rather ascetic, ultramodern Boulez, Mehta's interest in lush Romanticism, and a more traditional repertoire made for a favorable impression, and a long and successful relationship with the orchestra. However, by the time of his resignation in 1991, a little of the bloom had faded from his relationship with the critics, some of whom seemed to be put off by the more "Hollywood" aspects of his style and personality.

In 1990 Mehta was asked to conduct the first of the now-legendary *Three Tenors* concerts. Mehta proved a highly appropriate choice, being one of the few conductors with the charisma to match the well-practiced stagecraft of the three star tenors. The concert was a huge success, with a worldwide television audience, and enormous record sales. When the phenomenon was repeated in 1994 from Los Angeles, Mehta again conducted.

Since 1998, Mehta has been music director of the Bavarian State Opera in Munich. That year, his path intersected with that of U.S. President Bill Clinton, as former Clinton associate Susan McDougal, who went to jail rather than testify against the president, was accused of embezzling $150,000 from the Mehta family, for whom she had worked for several years. He made several tours with the Bavarian State Opera and kept up a busy schedule of guest conducting appearances into the new century. *—Joseph Stevenson*

Recommended:

- ○ **Orff: Carmina Burana** / Mehta (cond.), Jo, Skovhus, Kowalski, London PO & Chorus / 2001 / Apex 41377
- ○ **Mahler: Symphony 2/ Schmidt: Symphony 4** / Mehta (cond.), Ludwig, Cotrubas, Vienna PO / 1994 / London 440615
- ○ **John Knowles Paine** / Mehta (cond.), New York PO / 1989 / New World 80374
- ○ **Puccini: La Fanciulla del West** / Mehta (cond.), Domingo, Milnes, Lloyd, Howell, Royal Opera House Orch. / DG 419640

Etienne-Nicolas Méhul

b. Jun. 22, 1763, Givet, Ardennes, France, **d.** Oct. 18, 1817, Paris, France
Composer

Méhul was the greatest French symphonist before Berlioz and an important and prolific composer of opéras comiques. His musical style came out of Gluck's tradition of opera and Haydn's and early Beethoven's tradition of choral and instrumental writing. Méhul went beyond these influences, though, particularly in the realm of orchestration. His use of large forces and novel and striking effects anticipated Berlioz. The more colorful aspects of his instrumentation were always a result of the drama of the opera and never gratuitous. Méhul also developed certain other techniques such as the reminiscence-motif, which was to have a great influence on Weber and, later, Wagner. His harmonies could also be striking and unusual, but were generally less effective on a larger scale, where he remained quite conservative.

Méhul's only important teacher was Jean-Frédéric Edelmann, with whom he began studies in 1779. During the next decade, he produced two sets of piano sonatas and taught keyboard for a living. There is almost no other music surviving from this period to chart Méhul's early development. It was likely that he wrote much, though, for his first surviving opera, *Cora* (1786), is assured and well written. His next opera, *Euphrosine* (1790), however, literally made him famous overnight. *Adrien* (1791), never performed until 1799 for political reasons, and *Stratonice* (1792) followed. In the latter, Méhul created an intentionally antique style to capture the setting of the drama, a particularly romantic technique. The comedy *Le jeune sage et le vieux fou* (1793) was Méhul's last opera for many years to be unaffected by the impending political crisis in France. The remaining operas of the 1790s, *Horatius Coclès* (1794), *Mélidore et Phrosine* (1794), *Le jeune Henri* (1797), and *Ariodant* (1799), all contain political overtones and a "republican" message. During this period, Méhul also composed numerous anthems and instrumental works for the Institut National de Musique. This activity eventually brought him to Napoleon's notice, for whom he composed several works after 1800, including the opera *L'irato* (1801) and the *Chant national du 14 juillet 1800*, an important forerunner of Berlioz's *Requiem*.

Méhul turned to a series of minor comedies over the next years. The only important opera to emerge from this decade was *Joseph* (1807), probably his greatest. After this, Méhul turned to symphonic composition for a brief time, producing two extraordinarily successful works in 1808–09, and a series of Napoleonic cantatas (1810–11). His opera *Les amazones* (1811) failed, however, and Méhul, disenchanted with the fall of the First Empire and the reorganization of the Conservatoire, produced no other major works until the successful *La journée aux aventures* in 1816. Although Méhul's works are seldom performed today, his influence on Berlioz, Beethoven, Mendelssohn, and Weber was profound, and he stands as one of the most important composers of the early Romantic movement in France. *—Steven Coburn*

Overview of Works (1782–1816)

Méhul was a leading figure among a group of composers sometimes called the "Paris school"—Grétry, Gossec, Dalayrac, Monsigny, Le Sueur—whose careers straddle the French Revolution. Apart from two early collections of keyboard sonatas and many songs composed throughout his career, Méhul's oeuvre mainly consists of a large number of opéras comiques and several ballets, a mass intended for Napoleon's coronation (not used, and of which only a vocal score remains), a number of revolutionary choral odes, and four symphonies. As a teenager in Paris, a hearing of Gluck's *Iphigénie en Tauride* awakened Méhul to the possibilities of dramatic music and he followed Gluck's example in realizing dramatic truth through precise declamation and orchestral resourcefulness (Berlioz cites Méhul twice in his *Treatise on Instrumentation*). After several unperformed "practice" operas, *Euphrosine, ou Le Tyran corrigé* was produced at the Comédie Italienne on September 4, 1790, and scored a large success, the duet "Gardez-vous de la jalousie" becoming an instant hit and carrying Méhul's name across Europe. According to Berlioz, who admired Méhul as a continuator of the school of Gluck, and who devoted some 15 pages to him in *Les Soirées de l'orchestre* (1852), "having heard the 'jealousy' duet Grétry exclaimed: 'It's enough to break open the roof of the house with the skulls of the audience!' The *mot* is not excessive." Pared from five acts to three in 1795 and retitled *Euphosine et Coradin*, it remained in the repertoire for 40 years. Between 1790 and 1807 hardly a year passed without one or more of Méhul's opéras comiques, less often operas, produced in Paris—*Cora* (1791), *Stratonice* (1792), *Le Jeune sage et le vieux fou* (1793), *Horatius Coclès* (1794), and so on. Today, these are known, if known at all, from their overtures, that to *Le jeune Henri* (1797) remaining persistently popular. *Joseph* (1807), owing to its quasi-religious atmosphere and high level of inspiration, merits revival. Among the odes, the *Chant national du 14 juillet 1800*, with its three instrumental ensembles and three choirs, anticipates the spatial effects of Berlioz's *Requiem*, while the stirring *Chant du départ* (1794) has often been called a "second Marseillaise." Beethoven, who closely followed Méhul's work, adapted the trumpet calls and thematic recall from of the latter's *Héléna* (1803) in *Fidelio*. The four extant completed symphonies date from 1809–10, *No. 1* in G minor and *No. 2* in D claiming a place between Haydn's last symphonies and Beethoven's first two with their rhythmic vivacity, compact pomp, and frigid grandeur. *—Adrian Corleonis*

Recommended:

- ○ **Méhul: Complete Symphonies** / Swierczewski (cond.), Lisbon Gulbenkian Foundation Orch. / 1989 / Nimbus 5184/5
- ○ **Méhul: Overtures** / Sanderling (cond.), Bretagne Orch. / 2002 / ASV 1140

Dame Nellie Melba

b. May 19, 1861, Burnley, near Richmond, Australia, **d.** Feb. 23, 1931, Sydney, Australia
Soprano

Melba was one of the most admired singers of her era, both for the beauty of her voice and for her phenomenal technique. While her recordings were both late in her career and misleading as to the size of her voice (ironically, the reason her voice sounds minuscule on many of her recordings is because it was in fact large enough that to avoid tonal distortions, the sound engineers had her stand far away from the recording equipment), they nonetheless do capture something of technique and voice. Her acting ranged from non-existent to wooden, and she frequently indulged in diva behavior, but generally it was only her snubbed colleagues who objected. She also conducted her personal life with a gusto that the tabloids of today would delight in. And, of course, there are the two dishes named after her—Melba toast and Peach Melba.

Though she came from a musical family, she did not begin seriously thinking about a singing career until she was in her twenties; in the mid-1880s, she left her husband and went to Melbourne to study with Mary Ellen Christian and Pietro Cecchi in Melbourne, where she gave her first concerts. (Born Helen Porter Mitchell, she took her stage name from the name of the city.) In 1886, she went to Paris to study with Mathilde Marchesi, and nine months later made her operatic debut as Gilda at the Théâtre de la Monnaie in 1887, followed by performances of Lakmé and Ophelie in Thomas' *Hamlet*, all of which were great successes with critics and public. She was especially admired for the coloratura fireworks of mad scenes, and made her Covent Garden debut in *Lucia di Lammermoor* in 1888. This performance was not as well-received as her other debuts, but the next year, with the powerful sponsorship of Lady de Gray and her fine performance of Juliette, she established herself firmly with the company, returning every season until 1908, and continuing to make appearances there until her retirement. She made her Paris Opera debut in 1899 as Ophelie. Lucia was the role of her La Scala debut in 1893, as well as her Met debut in the same year. In 1896, she unwisely took on the role of Brunhilde in Wagner's *Siegfried*, but realizing she could ruin her voice's flexibility and coloratura by continuing, she immediately dropped the role. In 1898, she formed her own touring company, the Melba Grand Opera Company, and she later formed the Melba-Williamson company, which toured Australia.

Herman Bemberg wrote an Arthurian opera, *Elaine*, for her and the de Reske brothers, and she recorded one aria from it, but otherwise the work faded into obscurity after her retirement, and Saint-Saëns' *Hélène*, also written for her, entered even deeper obscurity. While it was not written for her, she appeared in the premiere of Mascagni's *I Rantzau* (only slightly less obscure during the middle and late twentieth century). She wasn't the jinx that this list might suggest—on the contrary, she bullied the management of Covent Garden and the Met into introducing Puccini's *La bohème* into the repertoire, even sweetening the deal with a promise to sing some of her showpiece mad scenes from *Hamlet* and *Lucia* after the end of the opera, to make sure the audience left happy. She studied *La bohème* with Puccini himself.

She began her formal teaching career in Melbourne in 1915, was made a Dame of the British Empire in 1918, and gave her farewell recital at Covent Garden in 1926. —*Ann Feeney*

Recommended:

- ○ **Nellie Melba: 1904 London Recordings** / Melba, etc. / 2002 / Naxos 8110738
- ○ **Nellie Melba** / Melba, etc. / 1997 / Nimbus 7890

Lauritz Melchior

b. Mar. 2, 1890, Copenhagen, Denmark, **d.** Mar. 18, 1973, Santa Monica, CA
Tenor

Lauritz Melchior was the first of the great Wagnerian heldentenors (heroic tenors) to sing on records, and he was the first operatic tenor to sing on radio. His recorded legacy is considered a benchmark for all subsequent Siegfrieds and Tristans. One can only imagine what a legacy was lost when he and his wife fled Germany in 1939; his home there was subsequently occupied and looted by both German and Russian soldiers and a collection of unpublished recordings was used for target practice. Contemporary reviews performances indicated that he was frequently lax in keeping rhythms, and many of his debuts were not completely successful, but he had a long operatic career.

Melchior started singing at an early age, when a boarder in his father's house who was a voice teacher gave Melchior and the other children in the family singing lessons. He often accompanied his sister (who was blind) to the opera, and from her reactions he learned how dramatically powerful a voice can be, even without stagecraft. Like many Wagnerian and heroic tenors, he started his career as a baritone (and very briefly as a bass), first studying privately with Paul Bang, and after he turned 21, studying at the Copenhagen Royal Opera School. His unofficial debut was in 1912 as Germont in *La traviata* with a tiny touring company, the Zwicki and Stagel Opera Company, and he made his official debut in 1913 as Silvio in *I Pagliacci* at the Royal Opera. He remained there for several seasons, first in comprimario roles, and later in major roles, beginning what looked like a solid career as a Verdi baritone when singing di Luna in *Il trovatore* and the elder Germont in *La traviata*.

A colleague heard him take an unwritten high C in *Il trovatore* one evening and told the directors of the Royal Opera she heard the foundation of a heldentenor in Melchior's voice. The management agreed and made arrangements for him to restudy his voice with the tenor Wilhelm Herold. He made his debut as a tenor in 1918 as Tannhauser, again at the Copenhagen Royal Opera. However, he was still uncertain of his technique and voice. In 1919, a wealthy patron encouraged the conductor Henry Woods to audition him, and he had his London debut at the Proms in 1920. He came to the attention of another patron, Hugh Walpole, the noted author, who provided Melchior with a generous allowance to further his studies as well as support his family. His Covent Garden debut was in 1924 as Siegmund. He auditioned for Siegfried Wagner (the son of the composer) and made his Bayreuth debut in 1924 as Parsifal. He continued to take leading roles there, including the legendary 1930 *Tristan und Isolde* under Toscanini, who dubbed him "Tristanissimo," until shortly before World War II. His Metropolitan debut was in 1926 as Tannhauser and he sang there regularly until 1950, when one of Rudolf Bing's first actions as general manager was to decline to renew his contract. This was partly for extra-musical reasons, including a predilection for practical jokes and appearing on "low brow" venues such as radio comedy and variety shows with Fred Allen and Bing Crosby, and partly for a growing disinclination to attend lengthy rehearsals.

After this dismissal, Melchior retired from the stage, though he continued to appear in films and operettas, sang on the radio (including a broadcast of the first act of *Die Walkure* from Copenhagen on his 70th birthday), and as part of his own touring music company. —*Ann Feeney*

Recommended:

- ○ **Wagner: Tristan und Isolde** / Reiner (cond.), Flagstad, Melchior, Janssen, List, London PO / 2000 / Naxos 110068-70
- ○ **Lauritz Melchior** / Melchior, etc. / Preiser 89032
- ○ **Melchior** / Melchior, etc. / 1990 / Nimbus 7816

Felix Mendelssohn

b. Feb. 3, 1809, Hamburg, Germany, **d.** Nov. 4, 1847, Leipzig, Germany
Composer: Symphonic, Orchestral, Concerto, Keyboard, Chamber Music, Choral, Vocal

Far from the troubled, coarse libertine that has become an archetype of the Romantic composer, Felix Mendelssohn was something of an anomaly among his contemporaries. His own situation—one largely of domestic tranquility and unhindered career fulfillment—stands in stark contrast to the personal *Sturm und Drang* familiar to his peers. Mendelssohn was the only musical prodigy of the nineteenth century whose stature could rival that of Mozart. Still, his parents resisted any entrepreneurial impulses and spared young Felix the strange, grueling lifestyle that was the lot of many child prodigies. He and his sister Fanny were given piano lessons (he also studied violin), and both joined the Berlin Singakademie. Carl Friedrich Zelter, director of the Singakademie, became Mendelssohn's first composition instructor. Even in his youth, Mendelssohn moved with natural grace among the circles of influence in society, politics, literature, and art. Although he did spend some time at the University of Berlin, most of his education was received through friendships and travel. Mendelssohn's advocacy was the single most important factor in the revival of Bach's vocal music in the nineteenth century, most famously realized in the 1829 performance of the *St. Matthew Passion* at the Berlin Singakadamie. He did some touring as a pianist with Ignaz Moscheles, then took the position as music director in Düsseldorf from 1833 to 1835, which involved conducting both the choral and orchestral societies, preparing music for church services and later, becoming intendant for the new theatre. Tension with the theater owner caused him to resign some of his duties, and he began looking for a new post. In 1835, Mendelssohn became municipal music director in Leipzig, where he also would conduct the Gewandhaus Orchestra. He would raise the level of the still-thriving ensemble to a new standard of excellence. In 1838, he married Cécile Jeanrenaud, enjoying an idyllic marriage and family life that was quite unlike the stormy romantic entanglements which profoundly affected such composers as Berlioz, Chopin, and Liszt. He was in demand as a conductor, spent some time as royal composer and music director in Berlin, but remained committed to musical life in Leipzig. He was even able to establish a new conservatory in the city, which is still a well-respected institution.

Mendelssohn was a true Renaissance man. A talented visual artist, he was a refined connoisseur of literature and philosophy. While Mendelssohn's name rarely arises in discussions of the nineteenth century vanguard, the intrinsic importance of his music is undeniable. A distinct personality emerges at once in its exceptional formal sophistication, its singular melodic sense, and its colorful, masterful deployment of the instrumental forces at hand. A true apotheosis of life, Mendelssohn's music absolutely overflows with energy, ebullience, drama, and invention, as evidenced in his most enduring works: the incidental music to *A Midsummer Night's Dream* (1826–42); the *Hebrides Overture* (1830); the *Songs Without Words* (1830–45); the Symphonies Nos. 3 (1841–42) and 4 (1833); and the *Violin Concerto in E minor* (1844). While the sunny disposition of so many of Mendelssohn's works has led some to view the composer as possessing great talent but little depth, his religious compositions—particularly the great oratorios *Paulus* (1836) and *Elijah* (1846)—reflect the complexity and deeply spiritual basis of his personality. —*AMG*

SYMPHONIC

12 Sinfonias for string orchestra (1821–1823)

In 1819, Mendelssohn began studying theory and composition with Karl Friedrich Zelter (1758–1832). Zelter, a friend of Johann Wolfgang von Goethe, was intent on teaching the young Mendelssohn the contrapuntal style of Bach and the formal practices of Mozart. For Zelter, Mendelssohn composed 13 symphonies for string orchestra in 1821–23.

Mendelssohn and Zelter consecutively numbered the first ten of them, leaving two others and a single movement in C minor unnumbered. These last three pieces are now designated Nos. 11–13. The first six of the symphonies show Mendelssohn attempting to master the rhetoric of the Viennese Classical style, with an occasional movement infused with the contrapuntal style of Bach.

The seventh string symphony, in D minor, and the eighth, in D major, reflect clear advances in Mendelssohn's understanding of the counterpoint of Bach and Handel and the Classical-era language of Haydn and Mozart. In the first movements of both we find an emphasis on polyphony; this is especially pronounced in No. 8, which also reveals Mendelssohn's familiarity with Haydn's works. The first movement begins with a slow introduction in the tonic minor (D minor) and the outer movements are monothematic. Numerous passages evoke the sound of *The Magic Flute*. In the slow movement, Mendelssohn produces a dark atmosphere by leaving out the violins, while the lively trio section points forward to his later works. A few days after completing the *D major Symphony* Mendelssohn added woodwinds to the score and substituted another Trio.

Nos. 9–13 were all composed in 1823. The first of these, in C major, is an impressive work. In the lively, monothematic first movement, a simple melody receives masterful Mozartian development. Again, the movement is preceded by a slow introduction in the minor mode. Mendelssohn explores various string colors in the second movement, dividing material between high and low strings. The light-hearted Scherzo gives way to a Trio based on a Swiss yodeling tune. The finale contains three contrasting ideas, one fugal, one lyrical and one rhythmically driven. Another Swiss folk song appears in the Scherzo of No. 11 (it was composed while Mendelssohn's family was vacationing in Switzerland). In the first movement of No. 12 we find Mendelssohn trying to combine the polyphonic practices of Bach with that of Mozart and developing a unique mode of expression. He tried a similar procedure in the isolated movement in C minor, which melds a triple fugue with sonata-form development. *—John Palmer*

Recommended:

- ○ **Mendelssohn: The String Symphonies** / Goodman (cond.), Hanover Band / 2004 / RCA 60427
- ○ **Mendelssohn: 12 String Symphonies** / Pople (cond.), London Festival Orch. / 1991 / Hyperion 66561

Symphony No. 2 in B flat major ("Lobgesang"/"Hymn of Praise"), Op. 52 (1840)

The standard numbering of Mendelssohn's symphonies and their opus numbers are unreliable as guides to the order of composition. This symphony, composed for the 1840 celebration of the 400th anniversary of the invention of printing from movable type, was actually the last of Mendelssohn's five symphonies. "Lobgesang" means "Song of Praise." It is an immense work. In its 70-minute length it rivals its clear predecessor, Beethoven's *Symphony No. 9*, and Mendelssohn directed that its four movements be played without pause. The first half hour is designated "Sinfonia," and includes three movements: an allegro with introduction, a scherzo, and an adagio religioso. A trombone theme from the introduction is a binding element appearing in various guises throughout the symphony. The 40-minute choral section is, true to the title of the work, a multi-section cantata in praise of the Lord. There is a finely judged dramatic flow of tension giving way to thrilling release in this huge finale. It is easy to see why this serious-minded work is not exactly a concert favorite, but there is much in it that is fine, and it deserves more frequent hearings. *—Joseph Stevenson*

Recommended:

- ○ **Mendelssohn: Symphony 2** / Masur (cond.), Frischmuth, Bonney, Schreier, Wiens, Gewandhaus / 1989 / Teldec 244178

Symphony No. 3 in A minor ("Scottish"), Op. 56 (1842)

Mendelssohn's *Symphony No. 3 in A minor*, Op. 56, is the last symphony the composer completed. Mendelssohn's letters show that his first inspiration for the symphony came in 1829, during his first visit to England. After some sketching, Mendelssohn set aside the piece until 1841, when disappointments in his life placed him in a mood similar to that he experienced in England 12 years earlier. The early conception and sketching may account for the squarness of some of the themes. The piece was completed on January 20, 1842; it was first performed on March 3, same year, in Leipzig, and was published in 1843. After a successful performance of the symphony in England in 1842, Mendelssohn received permission to dedicate it to Queen Victoria.

Each movement is to move immediately to the next without pause, setting it apart from Mendelssohn's other symphonies. To the tempo markings of each movement Mendelssohn adds directions reflecting the character of the music, which conveys Mendelssohn's impressions of the Scottish landscape.

Opening with a restrained, Haydn-esque slow introduction, the first movement moves suddenly to an Allegro un poco agitato tempo with a main theme that is treated with variation technique. The orchestration is among Mendelssohn's most dense; curious and exhilarating modulations open both the development section and coda. The development section is concise and effective. When the main theme returns in the recapitulation and the introduction returns in the coda, the themes are underpinned with a counter-theme in the cellos. The coda also contains the famous chromatic "wave," played by the strings.

The cheerful Scherzo, marked Vivace non troppo, is derived from Scottish folk music, which is a surprise, since in 1829 Mendelssohn complained that such sounds gave him "a toothache." It stands in stark contrast to the thick first movement and is in sonata form. The movement fades and dissolves to prepare for the ensuing Adagio.

Resignation reigns in the third movement, an Adagio cantabile in A major. A clear reference to Beethoven appears in the low strings, which play a motive resembling the theme of the Allegretto of Beethoven's *Seventh Symphony*. Reminiscences of Beethoven's Op. 74 string quartet also appear. Beautifully orchestrated, the movement is in two major sections separated by returning material.

Folk melodies appear again in the Finale, an unusually powerful and militant movement for Mendelssohn. A leaping, aggressive theme in the violins begins the movement, appropriate for Mendelssohn's direction, Allegro guerriero (Fast and warlike). Fragmentation technique propels the development section as themes are layered and treated contrapuntally. After the recapitulation we do not hear a coda with thematic references to the exposition. Instead, Mendelssohn shifts to a Maestoso coda, in which we hear new material and the theme from the introduction, which is again taken through variations and now conveys an air of triumph after the "battle." The symphony closes in A major. *—John Palmer*

Recommended:

- ○ **Mendelssohn: Symphony 3; Midsummer Night's Dream** / Maag (cond.), London SO / 2000 / Decca 466990
- ○ **Mendelssohn: Symphonies 3 & 4** / Abbado (cond.), London SO / DG 427810

Symphony No. 4 in A major ("Italian"), Op. 90 (1833)

In early 1833, Mendelssohn completed his *Symphony No. 4 in A major*, published posthumously as his Op. 90. He started the piece in Italy in 1832 and finished it in Berlin. It was first performed in London on March 13, 1833, and has since been Mendelssohn's most popular symphony. The composer gave the piece its nickname, "Italian."

Somewhat dissatisfied with the *Symphony in A major*, Mendelssohn planned to revise it before publication; this never occurred however, and the piece was published as it stood after his death. The composer noted that in the symphony he tried to convey his personal impressions of the art, nature, and people of Italy. Musically, it is a more tightly-controlled, original work than his previous symphonies; the opening theme is among the most famous in all music.

Mendelssohn's signature orchestral textures are evident from the very beginning: pulsing woodwinds create a harmonic background for the simple, horn-call theme in the violins. The rapid pace and fragmentary nature of the theme keep the music from falling into predictable rendering of the 6/8 meter. Two more themes appear before the development section, in which we hear fugato treatment of the main theme, the transitional theme and new melodic material in the minor mode. The recapitulation is not literal; everything is varied. In the coda, the minor-mode theme from the development returns, but the movement closes on A major.

Ignaz Moscheles contended that the main theme of the second movement, an Andante con moto in D minor, contains the melody of a Czech pilgrim song; others claim it is a rendition of Karl Friedrich Zelter's "Es war ein König in Thule." Cast in D minor, the elegant movement has two major sections arranged in an ABAA' pattern, the contrasting B section emphasizing A major. The closing, quiet, pizzicato bass notes convey a sense of resignation.

The third movement, Con moto moderato, is a fairly conventional minuet and trio in A major, possibly inspired by Johann Wolfgang von Goethe's humorous poem, *Lilis Park*. In the coda, the melody of the trio section tries, unsuccessfully, to assert itself over that of the minuet.

Mendelssohn entitled the Finale, "Saltarello," which is a lively Neopolitan dance featuring hopping and jumping; the fast main theme conveys the leaping aspect of the dance. The movement's high point is the central development, in which Mendelssohn creates a continuos crescendo from pianissimo to fortissimo. Near the close we hear a reference to the main theme of the first movement, but on A minor, the key in which the movement ends. *—John Palmer*

Recommended:

- ○ **Mendelssohn: Symphonies 3 & 4; "Hebrides" Overture** / Szell (cond.), Cleveland Orch. / 1991 / Sony 46536
- ○ **Mendelssohn: Symphonies 3 & 4** / Abbado (cond.), London SO / DG 427810
- ○ **Schubert: Symphony 8; Mendelssohn: Symphony 4** / Blomstedt (cond.), San Francisco SO / 1999 / Decca 460643
- ○ **Mendelssohn: Symphony 4; Schumann: Symphony 2** / Sinopoli (cond.), Philharmonia / 1998 / DG 459049
- ○ **Schubert: Symphonies 5, 8 & 9; Mendelssohn: Symphonies 4 & 5** / Toscanini (cond.), NBCSO / 1999 / RCA 59480

Symphony No. 5 in D major/D minor ("Reformation"), Op. 107 1830; revised 1832)

Mendelssohn composed his *Symphony No. 5 in D major ("Reformation")*, Op. 107, for the centenary of the Augsburg Protestant Confession. Perhaps less well-known than the third and fourth symphonies, it nevertheless offers much to interest those absorbed by Mendelssohn's rediscovery of the musical past, by his noteworthy religious odyssey, or by the more general confluence of Christianity and musical Romanticism.

In December of 1831 the "Reformation" symphony was to have been played in Paris by the Conservatoire orchestra. The players felt it contained too much counterpoint and was lacking in melody, however, and refused to play it. The work was first performed in Berlin in 1832, but it was not published until 1868. Mendelssohn was not proud of the piece, calling it "a fat, bristly animal" and "a complete misfit."

The symphony seems to suggest a program depicting the evolution toward Protestantism in Germany. Mendelssohn first introduces the "Dresden Amen" (a setting of the word "Amen" by J.G. Naumann [1741–1801] that still appears in hymnals) at the end of the slow introduction to the first movement, and it soon reappears at the close of the development section. (Wagner would use the same melody in *Parsifal*.) The Finale is based on Martin Luther's *Ein feste Burg is unser Gott* (A Mighty Fortress Is Our God), and contains a further reference to the "Dresden Amen," which becomes a unifying device.

In the slow introduction to the first movement, the "Dresden Amen" appears twice in the strings, separated by a leaping figure in the woodwinds, and persists until the beginning of the Allegro con fuoco. The Allegro shifts to D minor and begins with an idea similar to a theme from Haydn's *Symphony No. 104* which covers the rising fifth of the "Amen" with a leap instead of a scale. The secondary theme is also derived from the "Amen" motive. Mendelssohn ends the sonata-form movement in D minor.

The second movement could not be more different from the first. Resembling band music, the lively scherzo begins with a dotted inversion of the "Amen." A more literal reference occurs in the subdued trio section. The third movement, marked Andante and in G minor, is chiefly for the strings. Fragments of the "Amen" appear in the first violin melody, and the movement closes with a reference to the second theme of the first movement.

Mendelssohn moves without pause from the third movement to the Finale, which begins with an introductory instrumental chorale based on a streamlined version of *Ein feste Burg*, first appearing in the flute. Marked Allegro vivace, the Finale proper is in sonata form and 6/8 time, featuring a secondary theme that is an inversion of the main theme of the first movement's Allegro con fuoco section. Counterpoint is prominent in the development section, which treats the second verse of Luther's chorale, using it as a cantus firmus. At the end of the raucous coda, Mendelssohn gives a last, loud variant of the chorale for the whole orchestra. *—John Palmer*

Recommended:

- ○ **Franck: Symphony; Mendelssohn: Symphony 5** / Maazel (cond.), Berlin RSO / DG 449720
- ○ **Mendelssohn: Symphonies 4 & 5** / Abbado (cond.), London SO / DG 415974

ORCHESTRAL

Calm Sea and Prosperous Voyage, overture in D major, Op. 27 (1828)

This is the fourth of Mendelssohn's seven overtures and was written before the similarly maritime *Hebrides Overture*, Op. 26. It was composed in 1828 and inspired by a pair of poems (*Calm Sea* and *Prosperous Voyage*) by Goethe, who very much liked young Mendelssohn's orchestral setting. The same poems were used by Beethoven to produce a short choral work with the same title.

Mendelssohn meant to create an unorthodox form comprising two pictures, though in performance the "Calm Sea" portion sounds like a conventional slow introduction to a fast overture. One musical idea pervades the whole composition, generating the main motive of the opening section and both main themes of the "Prosperous Voyage" section. In mood, the music moves from the depressed feelings of the opening (a "calm sea" was a disaster for merchants in the days of sailing ships), where a slow chordal accompaniment in strings support anxious woodwinds, to the activity and optimism of the second section, where plucked strings depict the sails snapping to and the flute part gains a hopeful melody. Cellos take up a fine melody as the ship makes forward progress. Finally, it ends in an Allegro maestoso coda expressing celebration on sighting land, which is where Mendelssohn allows his poetic imagination to be swamped by conventionality, with insincere brass and timpani. On the other hand, the overture is remarkable for its wide rhythmic variety. *—Joseph Stevenson*

Recommended:

- ○ **Mendelssohn: Overtures** / Abbado (cond.), London SO / DG 423104
- ○ **Mendelssohn: Overtures** / Marriner (cond.), Academy of St. Martin-in-the-Fields / Capriccio 10708

Fair Melusina, overture in E major, Op. 32 (1833; revised 1835)

A medieval French romance, first recorded in 1387 by Jean d'Arras, tells of a water sprite, or mermaid, named Melusine (in English, Melusina). She is able to render her fishy bottom half human for several days at a time to go about on land. She is able to marry Count Raymond of Poitiers, but only on the condition that he never see her on Saturdays, as that's when she must resume her mermaid form. Eventually, of course, Raymond does spy on her one Saturday, with dire results according to a few versions of the story. However, most versions are, so to speak, watered down. Mendelssohn was captivated by the tale and wrote a concert overture on the subject. The music does not narrate a specific sequence of events, but, like Tchaikovsky's later *Romeo and Juliet*, simply evokes certain characters and situations from the story. The first section employs a gracefully burbling theme introduced by clarinets, suggesting Melusine and her natural environment. There soon follows a long, turbulent passage relating to the storm and stress of life among humans, which subsides into a less strenuous melody under which the rhythm of the more violent section remains. That rhythm, incidentally, is derived from the fluid, watery figure in the overture's opening bars. Mendelssohn subjects all this material to a substantial development. The final section returns to the gentler music of the opening, which gradually slows, thins, and trickles away. *—James Reel*

Recommended:

- ○ **Mendelssohn: Overtures** / Abbado (cond.), London SO / DG 423104
- ○ **Mendelssohn: Die schöne Melusine; Schubert: Symphony 4; Schumann: Symphony 4** / Harnoncourt (cond.), Berlin PO / 1996 / Teldec 94543

The Hebrides, overture in B minor ("Fingal's Cave"), Op. 26 (1830)

Mendelssohn composed and then revised this music between 1829 and 1832, conducting its first performance on May 14, 1832, for the London Philharmonic Society. The French critic Émile Vuillermoz wrote during the 1930s that "Mendelssohn was handsome. Mendelssohn was rich. Mendelssohn was intelligent, sensitive, refined, elegant, and endowed with all the advantages of home and a family life." But Vuillermoz neglected to say that he was the earliest full-blown genius in the history of Western music (more so than Mozart or Schubert), that he was seldom secure about the product of his genius, and that he very likely worked himself to death in his 39th year.

Felix sketched ideas for a Hebridean piece on a trip to England and Scotland during his 20th summer. The day before visiting sea caves on the island of Staffa, he wrote the B minor main theme for an "Overture to a Lonely Isle," as he called the first version—a birthday present to his father, completed in Rome on December 20, 1830, one and a half years later. He revised this, however, in 1832 (as *Die Hebriden*, dedicated to the pianist Ignatz Moscheles), the version first performed with the London Philharmonic Society. But that wasn't the last version: immediately after the premiere, he further revised what finally was called *The Hebrides Overture*, although published in 1835 as *Fingal's Cave*.

The music belies its long gestation, causing even such a pooh-bah as Sir Donald Francis Tovey to assume that Mendelssohn was musically fluent to the point of glibness in one of the silliest analyses in his overrated lexicon. It was Tovey who persuaded subsequent pooh-bahs to single out "the roar of the waves rolling into the cavern, the cries of sea-birds, and perhaps almost more than anything else the radiant and telescopic clearness of the air when the mist is completely dissolved or not yet formed."

That first theme sketched in 1829 constantly reforms itself with every repetition, over a stretch of 46 bars, before yielding to the D major second theme for cellos and bassoons that Tovey (getting it right) called "quite the greatest melody that Mendelssohn ever wrote." A development section follows, then a reprise that concentrates on the glorious second theme, and finally a coda that ends with three soft, unison Bs on pizzicato strings and timpani under a B held by the solo flute. *—Roger Dettmer*

Recommended:

- ○ **Mendelssohn: Symphony 4; Hebrides Overture** / Szell (cond.), Cleveland Orch. / 1997 / Sony 63251
- ○ **Mendelssohn: Overtures** / Abbado (cond.), London SO / DG 423104
- ○ **Mendelssohn: Symphony 4; A Midsummer Night's Dream** / Wordsworth (cond.), London SO / 1994 / Virgin 61131

A Midsummer Night's Dream, incidental music, Op. 61 (1843)

Mendelssohn's incidental music for *A Midsummer Night's Dream*, Op. 61, was completed 16 years after he wrote the *Overture*, Op. 21. The consistency of style and musical unity between them belie the disparate dates of composition. The overture was by an incredibly musically gifted youth of 17, and the incidental music was by the music director of Prussia's King Friedrich Wilhelm IV's Academy of the Arts and the Leipzig Gewandhaus Orchestra.

A Midsummer Night's Dream had always been a favorite of Felix and his sister, Fanny. The commission for the remaining music came from the King, for a Potsdam production of the play, one of several commissions for theatrical music Mendelssohn received while in this post. The producer of the play was Ludwig Tieck, one of the translators of the definitive German version of the play, the same version that the Mendelssohns had enjoyed and absorbed thoroughly as their own.

The incidental music consists of 14 sections, including the overture. There are vocal sections and instrumental movements. The vocal selections include the song "Ye spotted snakes" and the melodramas "Over hill, over dale," "The Spells," "What hempen homespuns," and "The Removal of the Spells." The melodramas served to enhance Shakespeare's text. The remaining sections are primarily cues. The music combines the traditional forms and structures of Classical music with the feeling and expression of the Romantic era. Throughout the sections, Mendelssohn sprinkles themes and motives pulled from the earlier overture to create coherence.

The instrumental movements, Scherzo, Intermezzo, Notturno, and the "Wedding March," are usually excerpted with the overture for orchestral concert performance. The Scherzo appropriately introduces the fairy-world of Act Two with rapid, running passages in the woodwinds, similar to the string passage in the opening of the overture, both set in a minor mode. The rest of the orchestra joins the woodwinds in a Classical sonata-form movement. Several small motives are repeated, up and down, then down and up the scale, to form the development section. The Intermezzo represents the confusion encountered as Hermia awakes, with a swirling melody buffeted about by the orchestra. The rustic players enter jauntily, represented by the bassoons and ending the Intermezzo in the major. A German Romantic horn melody is the theme of the Notturno. The music evokes the dreams of the couples as Puck puts right his previous mischief. The "Wedding March" opens with that oh-so-familiar trumpet fanfare, fitting for the Duke of Athens' wedding. Two trio sections are separated by the opening theme; the final occurrence of the main theme includes twittering flutes and strings, suggesting the fairies' part in the matchmaking. The "Finale" returns to the overture for most of its sparkling material, ending with the same four woodwind chords that begin the entire work.

Although some consider Mendelssohn's work to be lightweight and uninspired, the entirety of *A Midsummer Night's Dream* proves otherwise in its inventiveness in reviving his older material and in its expression. *—Patsy Morita*

Recommended:

- ○ **Mendelssohn: A Midsummer Night's Dream** / Previn (cond.), Wallis, Watson, London SO / 1977 / EMI 574981
- ○ **Mendelssohn: Symphony 3; Midsummer Night's Dream** / Maag (cond.), Vyvyan, Lowe, London SO / 2000 / Decca 466990

Ruy Blas, overture in C minor, Op. 95 (1839)

This overture is the result of a request to Mendelssohn from the Leipzig Theatrical Pension Fund, a charity that Mendelssohn liked to support. They intended to mount a benefit performance of Victor Hugo's *Ruy Blas*, and asked him for an overture and a song for the production. Mendelssohn obliged with a choral song, but initially demurred as to the overture; having read the play he privately decided that it was "quite ghastly" and politely told the Pension Fund people that he did not have time to write an overture. Then he thought the situation over and realized that he had left the impression that he could not write an overture in the space of a few months. His competitive nature flared up, and he wrote the overture in three days. The overture is a blood-and-thunder affair of generalized Romantic era emotionalism, with a troubled introduction, a furious opening theme, a tense second subject, and a lot of violence in working out. Bombastic? Unusually for Mendelssohn, absolutely yes. But it is effective and a good curtain raiser. Incidentally, Mendelssohn never changed his mind about the play, and preferred to call this work the "Theatrical Pension Fund Overture." *—Joseph Stevenson*

Recommended:

- ○ **Mendelssohn: Overtures** / Abbado (cond.), London SO / DG 423104
- ○ **Mendelssohn: Symphony 3; Overtures** / O. Dohnányi (cond.), Slovak PO / 1989 / Naxos 550222

CONCERTO

Capriccio brillant, for piano & orchestra in B minor, Op. 22 (1832)

Written during the composer's second visit to England, Felix Mendelssohn's *Capriccio brillant*, Op. 22, is a charming example of the composer's pianistic art. The Andante introduction is a gentle, unassuming melody with a light touch of melancholy, enriched by a discreet arpeggiated accompaniment. This reflective, languid mood is suddenly shattered by the Allegro con fuoco, which starts with a nervous, kinetic cascade of arpeggios that eventually leads into the rather square, marchlike principal theme. As a contrast to this theme, which is reiterated by both piano and orchestra, Mendelssohn introduces the truly capriccioso segments of the work, energetic bursts which are not easily defined as fully developed musical ideas. Nevertheless, the solo part, which showcases octaves, chromatic runs, and dizzying arpeggios, never lapses into technical display for its own sake. Mendelssohn's fluid virtuosity, even when listeners wonder where it might lead, possesses a truly satisfying charm which amply compensates for the work's conventional harmonies and predictable thematic development. *—Zoran Minderovic*

Recommended:

- ○ **Mendelssohn: Piano Concertos 1 & 2; Capriccio Brillant; Rondo Brillant** / Foster (cond.), Hough, Birmingham SO / 1997 / Hyperion 66969
- ○ **Brahms, Mendelssohn & Schumann** / Ormandy (cond.), Serkin, Philadelphia Orch. / 1992 / Sony 48166

Piano Concerto No. 1 in G minor, Op. 25 (1831)

Mendelssohn, precocious and prodigious, wrote five works for piano and orchestra between the ages of 21 and 29. He began the first of them, the *Capriccio brilliant*, in 1830, but did not complete it until 1832. He composed the *G minor Concerto* in the interim, on a visit to Munich, where his frequent companion was Delphine von Schauroth, the daughter of a baroness. "She is an artist, and very cultured, whom everyone adores," he wrote to his cherished sister Fanny. "Ministers and counts trot around her like domestic animals in the hen yard; artists, too, and other cultivated persons.... In short, I made sheep's eyes."

The concerto took shape in 1831 before and after morning calls on Delphine. Again to Fanny: "She composed a passage... that makes a startling effect," without specifying which one. Felix dedicated the work to Delphine, but assured Fanny that he did not love her. But then Mendelssohn didn't quite love his wife Cécile, either, when they were wed in 1837. Passion and joy developed later on, reversing the more common conjugal pattern.

He played the premiere himself in Munich on October 17, 1831, and often thereafter, with great success far and wide. Yet it was a performance by Liszt in Paris that made the work truly famous. A legion of young pianists took it up—so obsessively that Berlioz, in *Evenings with the Orchestra*, wrote tongue-in-cheek of an Érard piano on which 31 contestants played the music competitively. He claimed that the instrument refused to quit playing the music until it was chopped into pieces and burned.

While Mendelssohn's model was the 1821 *Konzertstück* by Carl Maria von Weber, his indebtedness does not reduce the merits of his *G minor Concerto*, any more than Grieg's indebtedness to Schumann detracted from their stylistically related piano concertos in A minor. The melodic vocabulary and harmonic syntax are pure Mendelssohn, already a master at 17 and by 22 a consummate individualist.

This fast, fiery first movement begins with an uprushing, chromatic crescendo for the orchestra. The piano enters with staccato octaves that change themselves into the principal subject. The orchestra takes over and embellishes the main theme until the piano counters with a new, palpitantly lyrical subject. Both are developed rhapsodically, followed by a proud and virtuosic reprise. A fanfare leads without pause to the second movement, an E major Andante, song-structured, of tenderness and poignance that verge on melancholy. The principal theme is sung by violas, then cellos, with bassoons and horns in support. When this ultimately fades into silence, another fanfare heralds an ebullient rondo finale, Molto allegro e vivace, whose main theme is introduced by the piano. At the close, Mendelssohn ties everything together by recalling the lyrical second subject of the opening movement. *—Roger Dettmer*

Recommended:

- ○ **Mendelssohn: Piano Concertos; Violin Concerto** / Ormandy (cond.), Serkin, Philadelphia Orch. / 2002 / Sony 89842
- ○ **Mendelssohn: Piano Concertos** / Blomstedt (cond.), Thibaudet, Gewandhaus / 2001 / Decca 468600
- ○ **Mendelssohn: Piano Concertos** / Shelley (cond.), Bowes, London Mozart Players / 1993 / Chandos 9215

Piano Concerto No. 2 in D minor, Op. 40 (1837)

Felix Mendelssohn's *Piano Concerto No. 2 in D minor*, Op. 40 (1837) was premiered by the composer, to much acclaim, at the 1837 Birmingham Festival. In comparison with the *Piano Concerto No. 1 in G minor*, Op. 25 (1830–31), the *Second Concerto* is somewhat subdued, lacking the irrepressible verve and impatience of the earlier work. Nevertheless, this works exhibits all the admirable characteristics of Mendelssohn's writing for piano and orchestra: dramatic themes, engaging virtuosity, and moments of reflective, even mysterious, calm. While the solo part unmistakably assumes a central role, Mendelssohn never relegates the orchestra to mere accompanimental figuration: instead, it figures prominently in presenting the main themes and complementing the piano with sensitive coloration. The Concerto opens with the orchestra presenting a simple, triadic theme; in Mendelssohn's hands, however, this deceptive simplicity translates into a mood of seriousness, immediately engaging the listener. This atmosphere is dispelled by the brightness of the charming second theme, which introduces an atmosphere of lightness and transparence. The second theme, almost narrative in quality, reappears in a number of guises, exemplifying Mendelssohn's extraordinary ability to imaginatively reiterate a particular musical idea. The second movement opens with a piano solo that develops into an emotional labyrinth. Mendelssohn creates a hypnotic atmosphere of tranquil meditation, mystery, and melancholy. As the movement progresses, this mood transforms into a subtle dialogue between piano and orchestra. The third movement displays the scherzando qualities so typical of Mendelssohn's concertante works. Breathless, energetic, and somewhat fragmented, the finale exploits the brilliance and virtuosic possibilities of the piano to the fullest, deftly interspersing this effervescent flow with moments of soul-searching tranquility.*—Zoran Minderovic*

Recommended:

- ○ **Mendelssohn: Piano Concertos; Violin Concerto** / Ormandy (cond.), Serkin, Columbia SO / 2002 / Sony 89842

○ **Mendelssohn: Piano Concertos** / Blomstedt (cond.), Thibaudet, Gewandhaus / 2001 / Decca 468600

○ **Mendelssohn: Piano Concertos** / Markiz (cond.), Brautigam, Nieuw Sinfonietta Amsterdam / 1994 / Bis 718

Rondo brillant, for piano & orchestra in E flat major, Op. 29 (Jan. 29, 1834)

Although a fine virtuoso pianist himself, German composer Felix Mendelssohn (1809–47) composed his *Rondo brillant*, Op. 29, for his former teacher and later colleague Ignaz Moscheles. Written in 1834 when Mendelssohn was 25, the *Rondo brillant* is his most technically difficult work for piano and orchestra, demanding strength, dexterity, and stamina from the pianist, all characteristics Moscheles had demonstrated in his own virtuoso works for piano and orchestra. Without introduction and with an almost abrupt ending, Mendelssohn's *Rondo brillant* seems concerned more with pianistic virtuosity than with compositional virtuosity. With its truly brilliant main theme, its charming but still driven secondary themes, and its galloping rhythms in the orchestra, the *Rondo brillant* literally gives the impression of the pianist as rider mounted on a racing stallion. Although the virtuosity of the *Rondo brillant* was soon surpassed by the super-virtuosity of Liszt and the later Romantics, Mendelssohn's work remains more delightful than many of the more elaborate works. *—James Leonard*

Recommended:

○ **Mendelssohn: Piano Concertos; Capriccio Brillant; Rondo Brillant** / Foster (cond.), Hough, Birmingham SO / 1997 / Hyperion 66969

○ **Felix Mendelssohn-Bartholdy** / Markiz (cond.), Brautigam, Nieuw Sinfonietta Amsterdam / 1995 / Bis 713

Violin Concerto in E minor, Op. 64 (1844)

What today's talking heads on the radio habitually call "the Mendelssohn Concerto," as if there had been only one, was actually the last of at least eight, including two each for piano, violin, and two pianos, most of them in minor keys. On July 30, 1838, the composer wrote to Ferdinand David, his concertmaster at Leipzig: "I would like to write a violin concerto for you next winter. One in E minor goes through my head, and the beginning will not leave me in peace." By then, however, his celebrity throughout Europe led to overwork, by no means advantageously. Responding to David's queries in 1839, Mendelssohn replied: "It is very nice of you to press me for a violin concerto! But it is not an easy task. You want it to be brilliant, [yet] how is someone like me to manage that?"

In 1840, Prussia acquired a new monarch, Friedrich Wilhelm IV, an impractical visionary already half mad. He summoned Germany's most famous composer and outlined grandiose plans for Berlin that eerily prefigured Hitler's. The Mendelssohn family, which had moved to the capital in 1811, urged Felix to come home from Leipzig, where he had conducted the Gewandhaus Orchestra since 1835. When the king's scheme collapsed, Mendelssohn had wasted two of the sadly few years left him to live. For this reason more than any other, he did not complete the E minor violin concerto until 1844, six years after starting it.

He was not free to conduct the premiere, which the Danish composer Niels Gade led in his stead on March 13, 1845, with David as soloist. Despite the work's appearance of spontaneity, several calculated departures from standard procedure surprised and delighted the Saxon cognoscenti. Dispensing with the usual double exposition, Mendelssohn has the violin spin out a lyrical main subject, Allegro molto appassionato, beginning in the second measure. This passionate melody is the concerto's most recognizable feature, but equally attractive is the way Mendelssohn develops, out of this unorthodox opening, a structure in which soloist and orchestra intertwine flexibly and variously, rather than simply standing in flashy opposition to one another. Mendelssohn assigns the second subject to flutes and clarinets, but let the first one dominate the development. Then, instead of a solo cadenza after the reprise, he inserts one ahead of it instead. A held B natural on bassoon connects to the C major Andante movement (an A-B-A structure, with an agitated center in A minor), and there is no pause after this movement, either. A transitional passage in E minor for the soloist with string accompaniment leads to a sonata-rondo finale in E major that goes like the wind—Allegro molto vivace—music whose blithe ardor belies its date late in its composer's life. After the *Violin Concerto*, *Elijah* would be Mendelssohn's last work with orchestra. The work is a pillar of the violin concerto repertoire, programmed in concerts great and small hundreds of times each year. *—Roger Dettmer*

Recommended:

○ **Brahms & Mendelssohn: Violin Concertos** / Kondrashin (cond.), Oistrakh, USSR SO / 2002 / Classica d'Oro 2015

○ **Favourite Violin Concertos** / Haitink (cond.), Grumiaux, Concertgebouw / 1994 / Philips 442287

○ **Mendelssohn & Sibelius: Violin Concertos** / Jansons (cond.), Chang, Berlin PO / 1998 / EMI 56418

○ **Mendelssohn & Beethoven: Violin Concertos** / Norrington (cond.), Bell, Salzburg Camerata / 2002 / Sony 89505

KEYBOARD

Three Fantasies or Caprices for piano, Op. 16 (Sep. 4, 1829–Nov. 13, 1829)

The *Three Fantasies or Caprices*, Op. 16, were composed during one of Mendelssohn's many trips to Britain. While there, Mendelssohn performed Beethoven's *Fifth Piano Concerto* and a symphony of his own, marking the beginning of his fame in England. The Op. 16 Fantasies have their origin in a visit Mendelssohn made to the estate of a business acquaintance of Mendelssohn's father. The Taylor family had three daughters, and for each one Mendelssohn composed a Fantasie. Legend has it that the first was inspired by a bouquet of carnations and roses, the second by small flowers shaped like trumpets that one of the girls wore in her hair, and the third by a brook. The pieces were published as *Trois fantaisies ou caprices* in Vienna in 1829.

No. 1, in A minor, was completed on September 4, 1829. The piece is in ternary form, with slow outer sections in A minor and a central, 6/8 section in A major. Marked Andante, the opening segment is based on an arching melody that traces the A minor triad at the beginning. Quiet and reserved, it disintegrates into non-thematic arpeggios and other figures that serve as an introduction to the Allegro vivace. The most interesting aspect of the fast middle section is a tremolo octave accompaniment figure in the right hand that continues through the change back to A minor and the return of the Andante theme, now played by the left hand.

No. 2, in E minor, is dated November 13, 1829, and entitled Scherzo. Its rhythmic feel and texture are similar to that of the song *Neue Liebe, Op. 19a, No. 4*, composed not long after the Fantasie. After beginning the piece with an intense, repeated-note figure, Mendelssohn runs through the same material twice, varying it the second time around and closing on E major.

Mendelssohn finished the third of the set, in E major, on September 5, 1829. The piece resembles some of the composer's *Songs Without Words* in that it has a melody in the highest register and a moving bass line with accompaniment figures in the middle register, usually played by the fingers of the right hand not busy with the melody. Varied returns of the melody are separated by virtuoso flourishes as the piece remains in E major throughout. *—John Palmer*

Recommended:

○ **Mendelssohn: Piano Music** / Artymiw / Chandos 8326

○ **Mendelssohn: Piano Works, Vol. 3** / Frith / 1997 / Naxos 553186

Fantasy for piano in F sharp minor ("Sonate écossaise"), Op. 28 (ca. 1833)

Exactly when Mendelssohn composed his *Fantasia in F sharp minor* ("Sonate écossaise"), Op. 28, has not been determined. We know that the final manuscript was completed on January 29, 1833. However, letters from Mendelssohn to his sister suggest that the piece, then titled "Sonate écossaise" (Scottish Sonata), was written as early as 1828, linking it with Mendelssohn's conception of his *Scottish Symphony* and *Hebrides overture*. What has puzzled some, however, is that if the *"Sonata écossaise"* originated in 1828, it could not have been inspired by Mendelssohn's 1829 trip to Scotland. This does not really present a problem, because pieces entitled "Écossaise" ("Scottish" in French) and based on a Scottish country dance had been popular in Europe for many years by 1828. When Mendelssohn had the *Fantasia*, Op. 28, published in 1834 in Bonn, he suppressed the original title.

The *F sharp minor Fantasia* is generally considered one of the best examples of Mendelssohn's virtuoso works for the piano. It has all the marks of the composer's later "Scottish" works, including chords with open fifths, open harmonies, pedaling that creates a fuzzy effect, and powerful, dissonant crescendos.

Mendelssohn builds the *Fantasia* on simple, elegant themes that can be taken easily through various harmonies and transformed. In three movements, each at a faster tempo than the previous one, the *Fantasia* resembles Beethoven's *Sonata quasi una fantasia*, Op. 27, No. 2 (*"Moonlight" Sonata*) in its overall format and minor key. The material of the *Fantasia*, however, is nothing like Beethoven's.

The first movement is in a loose sonata form and begins with introductory, ascending and wide-ranging arpeggios. The ensuing Andante is melancholy in character with a simple, eight-measure theme. Quiet arpeggios return to lead to the secondary theme in the relative major. Flashy arpeggios and octaves, marked Con moto agitato, form the central section. The recapitulation begins fortissimo, the first theme played an octave higher and over a driving, chromatic bass. In the coda, the main theme reappears, unharmonized and played with the pedal open.

Mendelssohn casts the second movement, Allegro con moto, in A major. A scherzo in form, the quaint movement features some thematic transformation of the main theme in the second half of the scherzo. After the charming trio, with its simple melody in octaves, the scherzo material is repeated note for note, with an extension.

Marked Presto, the finale is a fiery sonata-form movement in F sharp minor. After rapid, plummeting scales the exposition maintains a high energy level, even during the cantabile second theme. The development juxtaposes rapid scales and a rising figure in the left hand derived from the main theme. When the second theme appears in the recapitulation it is resolved to F sharp, but is still in the major mode. The coda further develops the rising figure from the development section and closes the piece in F sharp minor. *—John Palmer*

Recommended:

○ **Live at Wigmore Hall** / Demidenko / 1998 / Hyperion 22024

Organ Sonatas, Op. 65 (1844)

As the foremost figure in the nineteenth century revival of the music of Johann Sebastian Bach, it is hardly surprising that Mendelssohn should have turned to the Baroque master's own instrument, the organ, throughout his career. Mendelssohn's six *Organ Sonatas*, Op. 65 (1844) came into being as the result of a commission for a group of voluntaries of average difficulty; the project quickly evolved into these sonatas, which make considerable demands indeed on the player. (Mendelssohn himself was an accomplished performer on the instrument.)

Each of the sonatas, save one, is based on a chorale motive. The Sonata No. 1 in F minor, for example, takes the melody *Was mein Gott will, das gescheh' allzeit* as material for its opening movement, further using its chordal progressions as the basis for the entire work's harmonic structure. As with the trio sonatas of Bach and his contemporaries, this piece follows a logical sequence of keys, moving inexorably toward a triumphant restatement of the principal theme after a fugato section which opens in F minor and progresses into the major mode by the close.

The Sonata No. 2 in C minor is the only work in the group to avoid chorale references entirely. The Sonata No. 3 in A major uses a march theme that Mendelssohn had originallly written for the wedding of his sister Fanny in 1839. This is followed by a fugue in the minor mode, in which a new chorale melody replaces the conventional repetition of fugal material. This theme also receives fugal treatment before the work ends with a restful Andante tranquillo postlude.

The Sonata No. 4 in B flat major opens with a bipartite Allegro in which flowing and highly rhythmical elements are juxtaposed and sometimes subtly combined. The second movement, Andante religioso, was originally titled "March," though this designation was removed prior to publication. An Allegretto in a pastoral triple meter fulfills the role of a scherzo before the sonata ends in a blaze of glory with a movement marked Vivace e maestoso, which also incorporates a complex fugal episode.

The penultimate Sonata No. 5 in D major is a reflection on a chorale attributed to Mendelssohn himself. The last of the group, the Sonata No. 6 in D minor, is in three substantial movements. The first, based on *Vater unser im Himmelreich*, presents five variations on this theme, each of which reflects the evolving devotional sentiments of the original German text. Perhaps reflecting Mendelssohn's strong Anglophiliac sympathies, the finale reaches its impressive climax with a setting of the well-loved English hymn *When I survey the wondrous cross*. *—Michael Jameson*

Recommended:

○ **Hans Fagius** / Fagius / 1980 / Bis 156

Six Preludes & Fugues for piano, Op. 35 (1827–1837)

Mendelssohn's motivation in writing the *Six Preludes and Fugues* was, as he expressed to his sister Fanny, to impose a strict discipline upon his piano writing after having produced several series of *Songs without Words*. From the results, it is also clear that he was trying to find a newly Romantic voice for the fugue at a time when it was widely considered an out-of-date, archaic means of musical expression. The composer Anton Reicha had suggested a method steeped in complete tonal freedom; others simply imitated the model of Johann Sebastian Bach in examples that lacked the older master's originality and artistry.

Mendelssohn was especially successful in shaking his fugues free of the ghost of Bach, who nonetheless remained one of his most important influences. In the Preludes and Fugues, Mendelssohn's essentially Romantic character exists side by side with a learned but fresh contrapuntal sense. Given the improvisatory character of the keyboard prelude, even in the time of Bach, Mendelssohn was free to indulge his pianism and imagination in the Preludes of Op. 35. The third of these is a blazing Capriccio, while the fifth resembles nothing so much as one of the composer's *Songs without Words*.

A number of the Fugues are particularly striking. In the first, a powerful crescendo climaxes in a free chorale before ending softly; even when the fugue subject returns in inversion, there is no sense of mere academic display. The third is a splendid, varied display of contrapuntal mastery, while the sixth is characterized by a particular virtuosity and brilliantly articulated rhythms. *—Joseph Stevenson*

Recommended:

○ **Mendelssohn: Piano Works Vol.1** / Frith / 1995 / Naxos 550939

○ **Mendelssohn: Songs without Words & Other Piano Favorites** / Jones / 1994 / Nimbus 7704

Rondo capriccioso, for piano in E major, Op. 14 (ca. 1830)

Opinions differ on the date of composition for Mendelssohn's *Rondo capriccioso*, Op. 14. Some suggest he composed the work in 1824; if this is the case, it is the most advanced work he had composed at the time. Also, publication dates of both 1827 and 1830 dot the literature. The most recent research shows that the *Rondo capriccioso* was finished by 1828, but lacked the introductory Andante section. Two years later Mendelssohn revised the piece, possibly as a gift for Delphine von Schauroth, a pianist from Munich. The autograph of this version, dated June 13, 1830, includes both the Andante and Presto. The piece is still popular among pianists, in part because it sounds more difficult to play than it actually is.

The *Rondo capriccioso* is in two parts: an Andante in 4/4 meter and E major, and a Presto in 6/8 meter and E minor. In subsequent works, such as the *Capriccio* in E minor and the Andante cantabile and Presto agitato, Mendelssohn uses this same format. The piece also presages Mendelssohn's linking of slow movements to fast finales in the *Capriccio brilliant*, Op. 22, and the *Serenade und Allegro giocoso*, Op. 43. The progression from major to minor also occurs in the *"Italian" symphony*.

In their tendency to descend through the tonic triad, the themes of the two movements are related. The cantabile setting of the Andante, with repeated chords in the left hand and an initially arching melody in the right, is very songlike. This passes quickly, though, as the tune becomes increasingly embellished, culminating in plunging octaves, played fortissimo. The texture quickly thins as rising scales introduce the Rondo, marked Presto. Some have found in the opening of the minor-mode Andante section a hint of Weber, but the rhythmic drive of the melody, gradually increasing in speed, and its beginning on the third beat, are pure Mendelssohn.

The Presto has all the lilt and fire of the *Overture to a Midsummer Night's Dream*. The B theme is not very original, but the Rondo passages are electrifying. Flashy arpeggios act as links between sections, one of which, at the center of the movement, is in E major and presents rhythmic fragments of the Rondo theme in developmental fashion. After a transposed reprise of the G major episode, resolving it to the tonic, the key shifts back to E minor for the final appearance of the Rondo theme and a raucous closing passage. *—John Palmer*

Recommended:

○ **Mendelssohn: Piano Concertos; Rondo** / Perahia / 1975 / Sony 42401

○ **Mikhail Pletnev: Hommage à Rachmaninov** / Pletnev / DG 459634

Sonatas and Other Works for Piano (ca. 1820–1847)

Mendelssohn wrote a considerable amount of piano music aside from his famous *Lieder ohne Worte*. Like the *Lieder ohne Worte*, most of these pieces are shorter, intimate forms. The differences between these pieces are vast.

The *Sonata in G minor*, Op. 105, (1821) is one of Mendelssohn's earliest works. His debt to Haydn is clear in the monothematic first movement. While not particularly inventive, the piece shows the 11-year-old Mendelssohn's grasp of musical procedures and forms. The *Sonata in E major*, Op. 6, is from March 1826 and demonstrates the considerable growth of the composer's powers. Lyrical themes fit easily into a deftly composed sonata form first movement. Typically, the second movement is a scherzo, but with a touch of Mendelssohnian fugue. The piece also features cyclical repetition of themes. A year later, he composed the less interesting *Sonata in B flat major*, Op. 106, which was not published until 1868. Its first movement resembles that of Beethoven's *"Hammerklavier" Sonata*, in part because of the fugue in the development.

Originally conceived as a sonata, the *Fantasia in F sharp minor*, Op. 28, was probably written in 1828. When it was published in 1834, Mendelssohn suppressed his original title, *"Sonate écossaise"* (Scottish Sonata). It is in three movements, each at a faster tempo than the previous one, thus resembling Beethoven's *"Moonlight" Sonata*. The first movement is in sonata form and built of simple, elegant themes that can be taken easily through various harmonies and transformed. Considered one of the best examples of Mendelssohn's virtuoso works for the piano, the *Fantasia* has the characteristics of later "Scottish" works.

The *Rondo capriccioso* was finished by 1828, but lacked the introductory Andante section, which was added by June 1830. It is the earliest example of Mendelssohn beginning a work with a slow movement in a major key and then moving to the tonic major for a concluding fast movement. Mendelssohn uses this same format in several subsequent piano works, such as the *Capriccio* in E minor and the *Andante cantabile* and *Presto agitato*. The two movements of the *Rondo capriccioso* are thematically related.

The *Three Fantasies or Caprices*, Op. 16, were composed during one of Mendelssohn's many trips to Britain. They were completed between September 4 and November 13, 1829. The first is notable for Mendelssohn's recasting of the main theme at the beginning of the recapitulation, while the third resembles one of his *Songs Without Words*.

Mendelssohn's three *Capriccios*, Op. 33, are more disparate in mood than those of Op. 16. Two agitated works surround a more relaxed, wandering piece. Most interesting are the slow introductions to each, which are strikingly original.

Mendelssohn composed the six *Preludes and Fugues*, Op. 35, over several years. Typical of the set is the pair in E minor. The fugue, from 1827, increases in tension until a chorale-like passage interrupts the fugue, while the prelude, from 1837, resembles some of the more vigorous *Songs Without Words*. *—John Palmer*

Recommended:

○ **Mendelssohn: Piano Works Vol. 1** / Frith / 1995 / Naxos 550939

- ○ **Mendelssohn: Songs without Words** / Rev / 1997 / Hyperion 22020
- ○ **Mendelssohn: Piano Music** / Perahia / 1984 / CBS 37838
- ○ **Mendelssohn: Songs without Words & Other Piano Favorites** / Jones / 1994 / Nimbus 7704
- ○ **Mendelssohn: Complete Piano Music** / Jones / 1997 / Nimbus 1772
- ○ **Mendelssohn: Piano Music** / Artymiw / Chandos 8326
- ○ **Mendelssohn: Songs without Words** / Nagy / Naxos 550316
- ○ **Mendelssohn: Works for 2 Pianos and 4 Hands** / Duo Egri & Pertis / Hungaroton 31855
- ○ **Mendelssohn: Complete Works for Piano 4 Hands** / Mrongovius, Uriarte / 2001 / Arts 47622
- ○ **Mendelssohn: Piano Music** / Chiu / 2004 / HM 3957117

Songs without Words, for piano, Books 1–8 (1829–1845)

The idea of a "Song without Words" may have originated between Mendelssohn and his sister, Fanny, when they were children. It is somewhat ironic that fruits of their childhood games became very popular among the European public, and that Mendelssohn's reputation as a composer for the keyboard would be built, in part, upon these tiny pieces. These events are directly related to the rise of the piano as the predominant instrument for home music-making.

Mendelssohn first refers to "Lieder ohne Worte" (Songs without Words) in a letter to his sister of December 1828. He composed them initially for family and friends, but by 1832 decided to revise and publish these miniatures. Six sets of *Lieder ohne Worte* were printed during the composer's lifetime and each volume was dedicated to a woman. After Mendelssohn's death, two more volumes appeared that included pieces the composer had rejected from earlier sets.

Only five of Mendelssohn's 36 *Lieder ohne Worte* received titles from the composer. Of these five, three are entitled "Venezianisches Gondollied" (Venetian Gondolier's Song): Op. 19, No. 6; Op. 30, No. 6; and Op. 62, No. 5. All are in minor keys and, like the barcarolle, are in 6/8 meter with melancholy melodies and wave-like accompaniments. However, their songlike qualities are clear in their treble melodies and arpeggiated accompaniments.

Mendelssohn's first set of *Lieder ohne Worte*, Op. 19, was first published in London in 1832 as "Melodies for the Pianoforte." Like all the other sets, it begins with a "solo" lied, with the melody in the soprano. Also outstanding is No. 3, "Jägerlied" (Hunter's Song), which features a horn-call figure associated with hunting.

The next six volumes of *Lieder ohne Worte*—Op. 30 (1835), Op. 38 (1837), Op. 53 (1841), Op. 62 (1844), Op. 67 (1845), Op. 85 (1850), Op. 102 (n.d.)—were published in Bonn. The second volume, Op. 30, is unusual in that it begins as a solo lied, but takes on characteristics of a duet in its middle section. In the sixth piece of Op. 38, "Duetto," we find a perfect example of Mendelssohn spreading the accompaniment between the hands. As the soprano and tenor melodies alternate, the accompaniment moves from high to low register. The fifth piece of Volume IV, "Volkslied" (Folksong), boasts parallel fifths in the right hand and "horn fifths" in the homophonic section that give it a folk song flavor. In Mendelssohn's fifth volume, Op. 62, four of the six pieces are in major keys and there are a variety of song types, including examples of the solo lied, duet and partsong. Op. 62, No. 2, vacillates between three and four melodic lines, while Op. 67, No. 5 is clearly constructed like a partsong. *—John Palmer*

Recommended:

- ○ **Mendelssohn: Songs without Words** / Rev / 1997 / Hyperion 22020

Variations sérieuses, for piano in D minor, Op. 54 (1841)

Mendelssohn wrote three sets of piano variations in 1841, but this was the only group published during his lifetime; it is regarded as the finest of the three, and, indeed, it remains Mendelssohn's most-often performed substantial piano work. The solemn theme, despite a few anachronistic harmonic excursions, evokes Baroque keyboard music, and reminds us of Mendelssohn's admiration of J.S. Bach. There follow 17 miniature variations packed into little more than ten minutes. What they lack in length they make up for in their wide range. The first evokes a solemn Bach harpsichord *Invention*. After that, the texture becomes slightly denser, and by the third variation Mendelssohn summons an urgency almost reminiscent of Beethoven. What follows is a miniscule scherzo, which leads to a quick chordal treatment. Later variations hold a Brahmsian power or are fleet and virtuosic or launch a sober little canon or break into song. Throughout, the mood is exactly as advertised: serious, without a trace of the elfin spirit that marks many of Mendelssohn's most popular works. The piece culminates in a short series of resounding, highly dramatic variations that abruptly give way to a few quiet concluding chords, returning in the final seconds to the mood of the opening bars. *—James Reel*

Recommended:

- ○ **Alfred Brendel 3** / Brendel / 1999 / Philips 456733
- ○ **Schumann: Papillons; Carnaval; Mendelssohn: Variations Serieuses** / Sofronitsky / Urania 4205

CHAMBER MUSIC

Cello Sonata No. 1 in B flat major, Op. 45 (1838)

Felix Mendelssohn's *Sonata for Cello and Piano No. 1 in B flat major*, Op. 45 was composed in October, 1838, during the composer's tenure in Leipzig. Although its popularity is overshadowed by that of its sibling, the *Sonata for Cello and Piano No. 2*, Op. 58, it readily exemplifies the composer's fluid, elegant handling of string instruments, and his ability to wring interesting material from standard forms.

Written in a comfortable tessitura for the cellist and fully utilizing the sonorities of the lower strings, the first movement introduces a relaxed atmosphere in which Mendelssohn's natural melodic facility at once comes to the fore. The piano provides more than mere accompaniment, assuming the role of an equal to the cello, while never overshadowing that instrument's natural cantabile voice. The movement follows a classical sonata form, never straying from expected harmonic developments; still, the music's effectiveness confirms that, in hands as capable as Mendelssohn's, predictability and logical development present their own expressive possibilities.

The second movement, an Andante, opens with the piano. The movement's primary theme consists of punctuated phrases that suggest a playful, whimsically enigmatic, spirit. This mood eventually yields, without fundamentally changing the character of the theme, to a feeling of drama, enabling the piano to display a certain measure of virtuosity.

Although the principal theme of the final movement recalls elements from the first movement, the mood here is of breezy lightness. In accompanying the melodic line, the piano engages in a pleasant jocosity while never threatening to overpower the cello. *—Zoran Minderovic*

Recommended:

- ○ **Mendelssohn: Works for Cello & Piano** / Isserlis, Tan / 1994 / BMG 62553
- ○ **Mendelssohn: Complete Music for Cello** / Lester, Tomes / 2000 / Hyperion 55064

Cello Sonata No. 2 in D major, Op. 58 (1843)

Mendelssohn was briefly between jobs when he wrote the second of his two cello sonatas; he was making the transition from handling musical matters for the King of Prussia to assuming the directorship of the new Leipzig Conservatory. The attendant stress of this period is hardly reflected in this sonata, which the composer wrote for his brother Paul, a cellist. The first movement, Allegro assai vivace, begins with a surging, confident melody for the cello, underpinned by a pressing piano accompaniment. The keyboard then presents its own statement of the theme, the cello now relegated to the background. The piano remains dominant during the introduction of the more lyrical but still impulsive second subject, but the cello eventually gets its turn at an extension of the tune. Unwary listeners might gather that Mendelssohn is here launching a third subject, but the cello is clearly playing the flowing outline of the melody the piano has just broached. Indeed, the instruments will be treated as equals throughout most of this sonata, and often each is allowed a virtuoso flourish. Mendelssohn develops his themes sequentially and neatly, with an almost circumspect ardor that never subordinates one instrument to the other.

The second movement, Allegretto scherzando, opens with a whimsical tune in the piano that is quickly taken up pizzicato by the cello. The melody becomes a bit more lyrical when played arco, but *Mendelssohn* reserves real songfulness for the second theme, which the cello sings out over a palpitating piano accompaniment. The movement continues with a repeat of the first section that turns uncharacteristically gruff before a brief reprise of the second theme, again in the cello. The instruments quietly slip away, playing fragments of both melodies.

The Adagio begins with graceful piano arpeggios that follow the chord structure of the aria "Es ist vollbracht" from Bach's *St. John Passion*, reflecting Mendelssohn's lifelong devotion to the music of the German Baroque master. The piano recedes into the background as the cello offers an aria of its own, which grows more ardent and recitative-like as it progresses. Before long, the cello is playing its aria over the piano's chorale-like arpeggios; at the very end, the piano offers its own treatment of the cello's theme. Cellist Coenraad Bloemendal has proposed reading this movement as "a programmatic representation of the competing religious forces that coexisted in Mendelssohn's mind"—the "Lutheran" piano part overlapping and ultimately embracing what Bloemendal describes as the cello's "cantorial chant."

The extensive finale, Molto allegro e vivace, begins with hectic yet low-key material that recalls the composer's famous *Spinning Song*. All of this sonata-form movement's thematic elements are spun from the material of the first several measures. Mendelssohn does not vary or develop this material so much as use it to put the two instruments through accelerating, arduous runs, culminating in a final section that creates a dazzling effect without descending to vulgarity. *—James Reel*

Recommended:

- ○ **Mendelssohn: Works for Cello & Piano** / Isserlis, Tan / 1994 / BMG 62553
- ○ **Brahms & Mendelssohn: Cello Sonatas** / Starker, Sebok / 1996 / Mercury 434377

Octet for strings in E flat major, Op. 20 (1825)

In 1825, when Mendelssohn completed his *Octet, Op. 20*, he had already produced his first numbered symphony a year earlier, but the octet is more sophisticated and may safely be considered a full blown symphony, even though written for only eight string players. Mendelssohn's own words, written on the autograph score in his own hand, are proof of this: "The Octet must be played in the style of a symphony in all parts; the pianos and fortes must be precisely differentiated and be more sharply accentuated than is ordinarily done in pieces of this type."

Not merely a doubled quartet, the piece is a true octet in which counterpoint, texturing, and harmonic complexity are every bit as sophisticated as in any symphony. In four movements, the work unfolds like a symphony, with a brilliant first movement allegro giving way to a marvelously dreamy second movement andante. A third movement scherzo is chamber-like in its texture and transparency but, again, symphonic in scope and size. It in fact develops a near-diabolical complexity due to Mendelssohn's brilliant use of eight voices instead of four or even fewer. The presto finale opens with outright bizarre chuffing from the cellos, but explodes immediately into a vigorous romp which plunges ahead, barely taking a breath, to a large, truly symphonic finale.

The piece is particularly significant in Mendelssohn's career as it was one of two singularly brilliant works considered to be a signpost of his genius in his teenage years. (The other work thus identified is the equally brilliant *Overture to A Midsummer Night's Dream.*) It was also the first string octet to be written as a true eight-part work and to this day remains the finest work in that form extant. It bridges the gap between Mendelssohn the chamber composer and Mendelssohn the symphonist in a particularly effective way.

The third movement scherzo was subsequently scored for full orchestra by the composer and presented to the London Philharmonic Society in 1829 as a separate, complete work. *—Michael Morrison*

Recommended:

- ○ **Beethoven: Septet; Octet; Mendelssohn: Octet; Schubert: Octet** / Melos Ens. of London / 1997 / EMI 69755
- ○ **Mendelssohn & Gade: Octets for Strings** / L'Archibudelli, Smithsonian Chamber Players / 1992 / Sony 48307

Piano Trio No. 1 in D minor, Op. 49 (1839)

Mendelssohn completed the *Piano Trio No. 1 in D minor*, Op. 49, on September 23, 1839. For piano, violin and cello, the Trio was published the next year and has since been recognized as one of the composer's best chamber works and is one of his most popular. It is a lively, melodic piece that is satisfying to perform. After his initial work on the Trio, Op. 49, Ferdinand Hiller, a pianist and friend of Mendelssohn, suggested the composer revise the piano part to make it more brilliant. It was this piece that prompted Schumann, in a review, to assert that "Mendelssohn is the Mozart of the nineteenth century, the most illuminating of musicians...."

Without introduction, the cello states the songlike main theme of the first movement against a syncopated accompaniment in the piano. Later, the violin joins the cello with a distorted version of the theme. Variations of the theme fill the transition to the second subject, an arching melody on the dominant that is also introduced by the cello. Mendelssohn fragments and layers both themes in the development, which does not stray very far from D minor, the key on which the movement closes. In the recapitulation, Mendelssohn adds a violin counter-melody to support the return of the main theme.

The piano introduces the second movement, Andante con moto tranquilo, with the melody in the right hand and the accompaniment divided between the hands, as in a number of Mendelssohn's *Songs Without Words* (especially Op. 62, No. 1). Below this, the bass line in the piano walks along methodically and must be carefully balanced with the accompanimental figure and the melody. After the piano states the lyrical, eight-measure theme, the violin repeats it with a counterpoint in the cello.

Mendelssohn's *Scherzo* is concise and light. As in the Andante, the piano first states the main theme, which begins to reduce itself to fragments almost immediately. A rhythmic germ from the first theme permeates the movement, except in the more lyrical central section, the theme of which resembles material from the first movement.

After its first few pages, the Finale begins to sound heavy handed, largely because of the busy piano part. All types of keyboard writing occur in the movement, from close-position chords to swirling arpeggios and chromatic octaves. The cantabile moments are refreshing, as is the shift to D major shortly before the close. *—John Palmer*

Recommended:

- ○ **David Oistrakh Collection, Vol. 9** / Oistrakh, Oborin, Knushevitsky / Doremi 7790
- ○ **Mendelssohn: Piano Trios 1 & 2** / Borodin Trio / 1985 / Chandos 8404

Piano Trio No. 2 in C minor, Op. 66 (1845)

Completed and published in 1845, the *Piano Trio No. 2 in C minor*, Op. 66, is invariably compared to its older sibling, the *Piano Trio No. 1 in D minor*, Op. 49, written six years earlier. The later work is more complex, employing themes that are less song-like and more amenable to intense development. Also, the *Trio in C minor* is a more detailed work that rewards repeated listening. Mendelssohn dedicated the *Piano Trio in C minor* to Louis Spohr (1784–1859), who played through the piece with the composer at least once.

Marked Allegro energico e fuoco, the first movement begins with a segmented theme consisting of rising and falling arpeggios and scales. Its generic components make the theme very flexible and well suited to sonata form and to contrapuntal elaboration, which occurs frequently in the movement. The secondary theme is much more broad than the first and makes an important appearance in the coda. Harmonically, the Allegro is subdued and dark, with Mendelssohn progressing from C minor through G flat major, C flat major, and A flat minor, with occasional returns to C minor to remind us of the primary key.

Mendelssohn cast the second movement, Andante espressivo, in the relative major, E flat. Its subdued main theme, played first in block chords in the piano, sets the tone for the whole movement.

The G minor Scherzo resembles that of Mendelssohn's *Octet*, Op. 20, but is less refined. Formally, it is unusual. The Scherzo, a frenetic, although quiet, bundle of energy in G minor, gives way to a lyrical Trio in G major. After the Trio has run its course, a significantly shortened reprise of the Trio forms a link to the return of the Scherzo, which is itself abbreviated.

C minor reappears at the beginning of the Finale, marked Allegro appassionato and in 6/8 meter. (Brahms would later quote the main theme in the Scherzo of his *Piano Sonata in F minor*, Op. 5.) The short, modular theme, first stated in the cello, lends itself to Beethovenian development. In the midst of the development section, Mendelssohn inserts the theme of a chorale, *"Vor deinen Thron,"* presented almost literally and mingled with statements of the first theme. Mendelssohn was perhaps following the example of Beethoven, who uses a chorale in his *Piano Sonata in C major*, Op. 2, No. 3, to impart a sense of profundity. In the case of Mendelssohn, we are left to ponder the reason for this incongruous addition. When this chorale tune returns in the coda, it is given massive, symphonic treatment and is completely detached from the first theme. *—John Palmer*

Recommended:

- ○ **David Oistrakh Collection, Vol. 9** / Oistrakh, Oborin, Knushevitsky / Doremi 7790
- ○ **Mendelssohn: Piano Trios,** / Grieg Trio / 1996 / Virgin 61312

String Quartet No. 1 in E flat major, Op. 12 (Sep. 14, 1829)

Mendelssohn's *String Quartet No. 1* in E flat major, Op. 12, was brewing in his mind during a visit to Coed-du, the estate of the Taylor family, a business acquaintance of Mendelssohn's father. The Quartet was completed on September 14, 1829, and published later that year.

In general, it is more lyrical than the earlier *String Quartet in A minor*, Op. 13, and is more controlled and masterfully composed. However, the influence of Beethoven is still clear. As in the *Quartet in A minor* the *String Quartet No. 1* features the cyclic recurrence of themes. The slow introduction, Adagio non troppo, to the first movement is similar to that of Beethoven's *String Quartet in E flat major*, Op. 74 ("Harp"), but the ensuing Allegro non tardante is stylistically unlike music by the older composer. The material is song-like in this sonata-form structure, into the beginning of the development of which Mendelssohn works a new theme that, in a procedure mirroring Beethoven, appears in the coda. Mendelssohn's master stroke in the movement is in the contrast between the main theme at the beginning of the movement and its reprise at the start of the recapitulation. At the outset of the Allegro, the harmony is somewhat vague and there isn't a tonic chord in root position for several measures. At the beginning of the recapitulation, however, Mendelssohn underscores the theme with a strong E flat in the cello from the beginning. Paradoxically, however, this firm presentation of the main theme enters pianissimo and is not introduced by a dominant chord, making it a very anticlimactic moment. Mendelssohn replaces the expected scherzo with a canzonetta. This amiable movement is popular apart from the quartet. An Andante fills the third spot in the quartet. It is a brief movement with two aggressive, recitative-like passages marked con fuoco.

The Andante leads without break into the lively finale, much of which is in G minor. The "new theme" from the development section of the first movement appears both in the middle of the finale and the coda, which contains a near complete reprise of the coda of the first movement. The appearance of the first-movement coda seems inevitable as Mendelssohn alternates the finale's main theme with the "new theme" from the first movement, just as he does with the "new theme" in the coda of the first movement. Ending the first and last movements of a multi-movement work with the same music was not a new idea for Mendelssohn; he had used the same procedure in his *Piano Sonata in E major*, Op. 6, composed in early 1826. *—John Palmer*

Recommended:

- ○ **Mendelssohn: Quatuors Opp12 & 13** / Mosaiques Qt. / 1998 / Astree 8622
- ○ **Mendelssohn: Complete String Quartets** / Coull Qt. / 1994 / Hyperion 44051/3

String Quartet No. 2 in A minor, Op. 13 (Oct. 26, 1827)

Despite its higher opus number, the *String Quartet No. 2* in A minor, Op. 13, was composed almost exactly two years before the *String Quartet No. 1* in E flat major, Op. 12. Although it was completed on October 26, 1827, the *A minor Quartet* was not published until 1830, a year after the *Quartet in E flat.*

In the introduction to the first movement is a quote from Mendelssohn's song *Ist es wahr?*, the first line of which is "Is it true you are waiting for me in the arbor by the vine-clad wall?" Because of this, some writers have suggested the piece derives from Mendelssohn's emotions concerning a youthful love affair. A much more powerful and significant presence in the quartet, however, is that of Beethoven. After the introduction, the first movement bursts into a passionate sonata-form structure in which the material is treated in counterpoint. A dissonant transition leads to a secondary theme, group, made up of three themes. The development section is frantic, and after the recapitulation, there is more development in the coda.

The pensive slow movement is marked Adagio non lento. The *Ist es wahr* figure from the first movement appears in the first section, as does a quote from the Cavatina of Beethoven's *String Quartet*, Op. 130. Its central, fugal segment is clearly a reference to the fugue in the middle of the slow movement of Beethoven's *Quartet in F major*, Op. 95. Not only are the subjects very similar, but the fugue in both cases begins in the viola and is answered by the second violin. As in the Beethoven, the fugal material alternates with the beginning of the movement, but in the Mendelssohn the two sections are less disparate and come together at the end.

Of the four movements in the Op. 13 Quartet, the third, an Intermezzo, is the least indebted to Beethoven. It has a more lyrical sound than many of Mendelssohn's scherzos, and the contrasting central section is filled with youthful liveliness.

Mendelssohn's "recitative" introduction to the Finale is a blatant imitation of the same procedure in Beethoven's *String Quartet in A major*, Op. 132, where it gives way, attacca, to the ensuing Allegro finale. Mendelssohn's recitative even includes detached chords like those in Beethoven's. The development section contains reminiscences of the recitative introduction and the fugue of the second movement, which returns yet again in the coda. Mendelssohn brings the listener full circle by closing with a reprise of the Adagio introduction to the first movement, stretching the melody of *Ist es wahr.* Here, the first violin makes a continuous line from reminiscences of the introduction to the main theme of the finale, the second-movement fugue and the main motive of the first movement, unifying the entire piece and making clear the relationships between the themes. *—John Palmer*

Recommended:

- ○ **Mendelssohn: Quatuors Opp12 & 13** / Mosaiques Qt. / 1998 / Astree 8622
- ○ **Mendelssohn: String Quartets, Opp12 & 13** / Juilliard SQ / 2001 / Sony 89733

CHORAL

Elijah (Elias), oratorio, Op. 70 (Aug. 11, 1846; revised 1847)

The immediate success of *Elijah* (1846) may in some way be regarded as inevitable, given the confluence of elements central to Mendelssohn's being as a composer: his cultish following in Victorian England, his lyric and dramatic gifts, his devotion to the genius of Bach and to his own ideals of religious music. The Mozartian fluency that was usual in Mendelssohn's compositional process gave way during the creation of *Elijah* to constant, extensive reworkings of the musical materials as he divined the possibilities of the biblical texts. After nearly ten years of intermittent collaboration with librettist Julius Schubring, an invitation sent to Mendelssohn in June 1845 from the committee of England's Birmingham Festival provided the composer with the necessary impetus to have the project completed in time for a premiere there in August of the following year. The long-anticipated first performance was prepared amid great ceremony. After two full rehearsals in London, the entire contingent of performers, numbering nearly 400, was bundled onto two chartered trains which ran to the festival site. The performance met every expectation as an unqualified triumph.

In a brief but dramatically crucial introduction, Mendelssohn sets the stage for the remainder of the work: the prophet Elijah foretells of the drought which is to plague the people of Israel. Later, the terrified cries of the people to the idol Baal are repeatedly greeted with stunningly bleak, Godless silences. This skillful use of the ensemble in the illustration of the text is again evident in the chorus "Thanks Be to God," which ends the first section. Here the drought is relieved amid surging arpeggios in the strings, while the bright, kinetic sonorities of the brass and the chorus suggest the deliverance and spiritual triumph of the people. The operatic analogies which might be drawn from *Elijah* extend even to Mozart. The terzetto for women's voices "O Lift Thine Eyes," for example, at once evokes the spirit of the Three Ladies from *The Magic Flute.* In what is perhaps the oratorio's most famous aria, "It is Enough," an almost Baroque gravity predominates, heightened by the darkly scored sarabande rhythm that underpins Elijah's desolate plea. In the expertly crafted passages that abound in fugal writing and four-part chorales, Mendelssohn again acknowledges his lifelong debt to the music of Bach. The composer's own gift of song is evident in several of the arias; "If with All Your Hearts" demonstrates a particular expansiveness. In choruses such as "He, Watching over Israel," the effect resembles nothing so much as a lied set for the entire chorus.

After the work's premiere, Mendelssohn made extensive changes to the score, noting, "I am right not to rest till such work is as good as it is in my power to make it; even though very few people care to hear about such things, or notice them, and even though they take very much time; yet the impression such passages, if really better, produce in themselves and on the whole work, is such a different one, that I feel I cannot leave them as they now stand." He did not, in fact, allow the publication of the score until the revisions were complete. It is this final version which remains not only Mendelssohn's last completed work of this scope, but perhaps also the work that best reveals those elements—steadfast religious faith, an affinity with his musical forebearers, and an unerring dramatic sense—which remained central during the relatively brief but prodigious span of his career. *—Michael Rodman*

Recommended:

- ○ **Mendelssohn: Elijah** / Sawallisch (cond.), Ameling, Schreier, Rotzsch, Adam, Gewandhaus Orch. / 1993 / Philips 438368
- ○ **Mendelssohn: Elijah** / Herreweghe (cond.), Groop, Ainsley, Salomaa, Collot, Champs Elysees Orch., Chapelle Royale, Collegium Vocale / HM 901463
- ○ **Mendelssohn: Elijah** / Daniel (cond.), Terfel, Fleming, Ainsley, Watkin, Orch of the Age of Enlightenment / 1997 / London 455688

Die erste Walpurgisnacht, cantata, Op. 60 (Feb. 13, 1832; revised 1842)

Mendelssohn's relationship with Johann Wolfgang von Goethe was both complex and problematical. An approximate contemporary of Mozart, Goethe revered that composer's work to the extent he understood it but found no favor in the Romantic thrashings of Beethoven, for example, even though he himself was a linchpin in the evolution of Romanticism. Having most likely never heard of the 12-year-old Mendelssohn in 1821, Goethe was persuaded to meet him by a mutual friend, Carl Friedrich Zelter, who was also Mendelssohn's musical advisor. Zelter, a composer of modest gifts, had himself attempted to set Goethe's *Die erste Walpurgisnacht* (The First Witches' Night) to music as early as 1799, but had given up, realizing that the task was beyond him. Upon discovering the young Mendelssohn, Zelter believed he had found someone with the talent to finish the job. Believing also that Mendelssohn's early emulation of Mozart's style would endear him to Goethe, he urged the project forward. It would be an exaggeration to say the two collaborated; Mendelssohn's view of the poem was shallow in the extreme and his music, brilliant nonetheless, reflects only the theater of it, ignoring Goethe's underlying meaning. That Goethe's profundities might be beyond a 12-year-old apparently occurred only to Mendelssohn himself, and the work was not finished in any version until 11 years later, in 1832, the year Goethe died. It was not performed until 1842, after extensive revision and rethinking. Goethe, it is presumed, would not have approved. In any event, the music itself is brilliant. Nearly 36 minutes in length, the work is in effect a set of nine seamlessly connected songs based upon the text of the poem. Scattered among alto, tenor, baritone, bass, and choir, these are preceded by a feverish ten-minute overture. The piece little resembles the Witches' Sabbath movement of Berlioz's *Symphonie fantastique*, created at about the same time: listeners expecting sonic pyrotechnics will be disappointed, but those wishing to hear how Mendelssohn brings musical dimension to Goethe's darkly philosophical work will realize that his settings are effective and even chilling. As a footnote, it is interesting to consider that Mendelssohn also revered Beethoven's work, and whereas the latter in his *Symphony No. 9* crafted a heaven-storming work based upon a more or less superficial poem, Mendelssohn here created a much less ambitious work based upon a much more profound piece of literature. One wonders whether he felt Beethoven's ghost peering over his shoulder, and whether such a specter might have contributed to his taking 21 years to finally finish and perform the work. *—Michael Morrison*

Recommended:

- ○ **Mendelssohn** / Dohnányi (cond.), Krause, Laubenthal, Sramek, Lilova, Vienna PO / 1999 / Decca 460236
- ○ **Mendelssohn: Symphony 3; Die erste Walpurgisnacht** / Dohnányi (cond.), Krause, Garrison, Cairns, Wells, Cleveland Orch. / 1988 / Telarc 80184

Paulus (Saint Paul), oratorio, Op. 36 (Apr. 18, 1836)

Felix Mendelssohn's massive oratorio *Paulus* (1836) is based on the story of Saul, the zealous Pharisee who, after a dramatic encounter with the risen Christ, turns from a fanatical enemy of Christians into the most influential apologist of the Christian faith. Using the New Testament, particularly the Gospels and the Acts of the Apostles as sources, Mendelssohn wrote his own version of Paul's story. While the influence of Bach and Handel are at once evident in Mendelssohn's score, *Paulus* is by no means a replica of the Baroque oratorio. Mendelssohn expressed his ideas with great contrapuntal facility and clarity, with a technical competence rivaling the expertise of the great Baroque masters, but his counterpoint is fresh and original, and the writing fluent and elegant.

The oratorio's overture, as well as a significant section of the first choral number, is based on the chorale "*Wachet auf, ruft uns die Stimme*" (Awake, cries to us the voice). Like Bach, Mendelssohn uses chorales to express deep, fundamental religiosity. Mendelssohn's articulation of musical symbols is highly individual, expressing the composer's personal view of Christianity. While the choruses in *Paulus* may seem quite conventional, for example, Mendelssohn's use of different voice combinations to present particular characters is both innovative and highly effective. To the consternation of some of Mendelssohn's contemporaries, the voice of Christ at the most dramatic moment of the oratorio—when the Savior addresses Saul directly—is portrayed by a four-part women's choir. Critics excoriated Mendelssohn for giving the fateful words "Saul, why persecutest thou me?" to women's voices, remaining blind to the sheer emotional power of this moment.

Mendelssohn's Christ, whose voice is distant, mysterious, and yet tremendously powerful, possesses an otherworldly, spectral quality, suggesting the infinitesimal closeness and infinite remoteness of God. Mendelssohn uses powerful musical symbolism to suggest the idea of Christ's dual (i.e. human and divine) nature. Following a masterful dramatic progression, Saul's breath-taking dialogue with Christ takes the entire work to its highest emotional plane. This, of course, does not mean that the rest of the narrative, the chronicle Saul's life as the Christian Paul, lacks dramatic interest, for it encompasses both the titanic struggles of a contested faith and intimations of God's unfathomable being and limitless power. In adding exquisite instrumental coloration to the oratorio's soulful arias, Mendelssohn expresses an extraordinary spectrum of religious feeling, from dark doubt to radiant certainty. Ending with a powerful double fugue, *Paulus* is a beautiful, profound musical tribute to one of the founders of the Christian tradition. *—Zoran Minderovic*

Recommended:

- ○ **Bartholdy: Paulus** / Herreweghe (cond.), Goerne, Markert, Diener, Taylor, Collegium Vocale, Champs Elysees Orch. / HM 901584
- ○ **Bartholdy: Paulus** / Rilling (cond.), Schmidt, Banse, Danz, Schade, Czech PO / 1995 / Haenssler 98926

Psalms, motets, anthems, and other sacred choral music (1822–1847)

Part and parcel of Mendelssohn's long effort to remake himself as a Christian was a vigorous engagement with sacred choral music, much of it informed by his encounter with the music of J.S. Bach and even earlier composers. This effort bore its finest fruit in the two great oratorios, *Elijah* and *Paul*, but also manifested itself in delightfully various ways in smaller choral forms such as the motet, anthem, and psalm setting.

Mendelssohn's earliest known psalm setting, that of No. 56, dates from 1822. The first one published was *Psalm 115*, Op. 31, for soloist, chorus and orchestra, completed and printed in 1830. Formally, Op. 31 is like a Bach cantata, and its first movement begins with a vigorous double fugue with moments of homophonic interruption. The ensuing duet, "House of Israel," in 6/8, is a fluid piece with excellent part-writing, and provides a strong contrast to the bass solo, "The Lord shall increase you." The final section is elegiac and profound. As in most of Mendelssohn's sacred choral works, the strongest sections are those for the chorus. It is interesting that his musical depiction of mystical experience is nonexistent—something Mendelssohn himself acknowledged.

Psalm 42, Op. 42 (1837), and *Psalm 95*, Op. 46 (1838), are more experimental than Op. 31, but not necessarily more successful. The high point of Psalm 42 is the soprano solo, "For my soul thirsteth for God," with an oboe obbligato. In Psalm 95, normally heard in its revised version of 1841, Mendelssohn changes the order of the verses, beginning with the sixth. The first section rocks between E flat and C major and contains an impressive canonic passage. After a duet, a chorus begins that makes cyclic references to the first movement. The final movement, which reprises music from the first, is a later addition.

Although Mendelssohn's setting of Psalm 100 is his most popular, that of Psalm 114, *"When Israel out of Egypt Came,"* Op. 51, is perhaps his most impressive. Scored for double chorus and orchestra, Psalm 114 was completed in August 1839. It is in six connected parts, the first of which functions as the main theme in a sonata-form movement, the second and third as contrasting themes, the fourth as a transitional passage, the fifth as the return of the main theme and the sixth a double fugue on previous themes. Also impressive are the three unaccompanied psalms of Op. 78.

Of Mendelssohn's motets, *Tu es Petrus* (1827) is the largest. This and *Hora est* (1828) are purely liturgical music, written at a time when Mendelssohn was studying the strict linear writing of sixteenth century Italian composers of church music. The five-part chorus *Tu es Petrus* has moments of parallel seconds and sevenths, and the parts of the orchestra are treated with similar independence. Like much of Mendelssohn's sacred music, the work ends with a fugue. A fugue also closes the last of the *Three Motets for female chorus and organ*, Op. 39, completed in Rome on December 31, 1830, at about the time Mendelssohn wrote the *Three Sacred Pieces*, Op. 23.

The *Three English Church Pieces*, Op. 69 and the *Six Anthems*, Op. 79, are among Mendelssohn's last works. Op. 69, for unaccompanied soloists and chorus, includes settings of the Nunc dimittis, Jubilate, and Magnificat texts, and the writing for voices is striking. The anthems of Op. 79 are brief, austere works for double chorus that are simple and elegant. *—John Palmer*

Recommended:

- ○ **Mendelssohn: Choral Works** / Herreweghe (cond.), Reyghere, Huys, Chapelle Royale, Collegium Vocale / 2003 / Classical Express 3951142
- ○ **Mendelssohn: Chöre** / H. Neumann (cond.), Leipzig Radio Choir / 1996 / Berlin Classics 0092782

VOCAL

Songs (1819–1847)

Although Mendelssohn composed nearly 100 songs in his career, they have never entered the Romantic song repertory the way that those by his colleagues Schubert, Schumann, Brahms, or even Franz and Loewe have. This is not because Mendelssohn was a poor songwriter—in fact many of them are quite beautiful; his songs simply did not embrace the musical and poetic elements that drove the lied to the height of its popularity in the nineteenth century. To Mendelssohn, the song was still what it was to Haydn and Mozart—a charming trifle not to be taken too seriously. Nevertheless, they are graceful, natural, and wonderfully well-written for the voice, and, while they are not in the same artistic league as, say, Schubert's, they are also not deserving of dismissal simply because of their conservative nature.

Mendelssohn began composing songs as a boy (the earliest known example is an "Ave Maria" of 1820), but did not publish any until 1828. This first publication, *Twelve Songs*, Op. 8, actually contains three songs by his sister, Fanny. "Hexenlied" (Witches' Song) is the most impressive of the set. Unlike Mendelssohn's other early songs in 6/8 (of which there are many), it has an unusual amount of fire, appropriate for Ludwig Hölty's text. "Frühlingslied" (Spring Song) and "Im Grünen" (In the Green) are lively, original pieces.

The songs of Op. 9, published in 1830, are not as interesting as those of Op. 8. However, the melody of *"Frage"* (Question) appears in Mendelssohn's *String Quartet in A major*, Op. 13. *"Wartend"* (Waiting) shows Mendelssohn responding to details of the text, while "Frühlingsglaube" suffers from comparison with Schubert's setting of the same verses. Most notable about the *Six Songs*, Op. 19a (1834), is "Das erste Veilchen" (The first Violet), with phrases of varied length and a piano part with significant melodic interest. Among these Biedermeier-style settings there are two of poems by Heinrich Heine, one of which, "Neue Liebe" (New Love), is a very imaginative, varied-strophic piece with an independent accompaniment that gradually grows in strength. Two of Mendelssohn's most popular songs, "Auf Flügeln des Gesanges" (On the Wings of a Song) and *"Suleika,"* were published as part of his Op. 34 (1837). *"Frühlingslied"* is the gem of Mendelssohn's *Six Songs*, Op. 47 (1840) and features a lilting melody. Op. 57 (1843), the last set of songs to appear during Mendelssohn's lifetime, contains another attempt at Goethe's "Suleika," but is otherwise of little interest.

Of the songs published after Mendelssohn's death (Opp. 71, 84, 86, 99, 112), three from Op. 71, "An die Entfernte" (To the Distant One), "Auf der Wanderschaft" (Travelling) and the solemn "Nachtlied" (Night Song) are fine songs, composed in 1847. *—AMG*

Recommended:

- ○ **Mendelssohn: Lieder** / Fischer-Dieskau, Sawallisch / 1993 / EMI 648272
- ○ **Mendelssohn: Songs & Duets, Vol. 2** / Daneman, Asti, Loges / 2001 / Hyperion 67137

Rafael Méndez

b. Mar. 26, 1906, Jiquilpan, Michoacán, Mexico, **d.** Sep. 15, 1981, Encino, CA

Trumpeter

Known as the "Heifetz of the Trumpet," Rafael Méndez was one of 15 children in his family. His father, Maximino, conducted a family orchestra in which Rafael played cornet. Emigrating to the United States at the age of 20, Méndez settled in Detroit. By day, he worked in an automobile factory and by night, would play with local bands and orchestras. He was unable to play after being hit in the face by a swinging door while at the Fox Theatre in 1932. Méndez returned to Mexico, where his father helped him rehabilitate his playing. When he returned to Detroit, he met bandleader Rudy Vallee, and Méndez became a member of his radio orchestra, moving to New York City in 1934. Three years later, he was offered a job in Los Angeles for KHL radio, where he was a frequent soloist and where he began composing and arranging. Over the course of his lifetime, Méndez made over 300 compositions and arrangements for the trumpet. Between 1941–49 Méndez was first trumpet in the MGM studio orchestra, which gave him the opportunity to perform as featured soloist at the Hollywood Bowl. He also recorded numerous 78 rpm records for small labels, such as Coast, Azteca, and Eleayz. Méndez was signed as a Decca recording artist in 1945, and over the next 20 years, he recorded a dozen records. When Méndez left MGM, he turned to touring and performing, often with student and amateur ensembles as well as professional groups, and to acting as music director for such radio and TV stars as Roy Rogers and Red Skelton. Méndez retired from performing in 1975 due to respiratory problems. *—Robert Adelson*

Recommended:

○ **Legendary Trumpet Virtuosity of Rafael Méndez Vol. I** / Mendez, etc. / Summit 177

Willem Mengelberg

b. Mar. 28, 1871, Utrecht, Netherlands, **d.** Mar. 21, 1951, Chur, Switzerland
Conductor

Dutch conductor Willem Mengelberg was born March 28, 1871, in Utrecht. His early education was in his native city, where he studied under the tutelage of Richard Hol, Henri Wilhelm Pertri, and Anton Averkamp. Mengelberg continued his studies with Franz Wullner and Adolf Jensen in Cologne where he earned prizes as a pianist, violinist, and conductor. In 1891, Mengelberg assumed the directorship of the Lucerne City conservatory. It would not take long for the young conductor to garner an excellent reputation, and in 1895 became the music director of the prestigious Concertgebouw Orchestra, where he would serve until 1945. Concurrently, Mengelberg served as chief conductor of the Amsterdam Toonkunst Choir, an ensemble he found invaluable, marshaling his resources to perform such chorale masterpieces as Bach's *St. Matthew Passion*.

In 1902, Mengelberg met and befriended the great Gustav Mahler, and consequently became a devoted champion of the legendary Austrian composer's music. During his time, Mengelberg was widely respected as a foremost interpreter of Mahler's scores. In 1920, in celebration of the Concertgebouw's 25th season, he led the orchestra in a cycle that presented all of Mahler's symphonies. From 1907–20, Mengelberg served as the director of the Frankfurt Museum concerts, and in 1921 became the conductor of the New York International Symphony Orchestra, which he would conduct until 1929. From 1922–30, Mengelberg was the principal conductor of the New York Philharmonic, and for the 1928–29 season shared the podium with Arturo Toscanini, a relationship that was strained and led to Mengelberg's return to Amsterdam. He was an avid supporter of contemporary music, and conducted the premieres of many notable works by such influential composers as Zoltan Kodaly, Darius Milhaud, Henk Badings, Paul Hindemith, Bela Bartok, Max Reger, and Ottorino Respighi.

Mengelberg's discography is extensive, and is represented by a host of renowned orchestras including the BBC Orchestra, Berlin Radio Orchestra, Paris Radio Orchestra, New York Philharmonic, and of course the Concertgebouw Orchestra. The conductor's popularity was widespread, and was exemplified by Richard Strauss' dedication of his *Ein Heldenleben*, to the Dutch conductor. In an unfortunate incident, Mengelberg was deemed a Nazi sympathizer, and was eventually exiled to Switzerland for six years. Consequent to his exile, his tenure at the Concertgebouw Orchestra was revoked, and the Gold Medal of Arts and Sciences he had been awarded was withdrawn and reclaimed by Queen Wilhelmina. While Mengelberg was banned from his native Holland, he did receive requests to conduct elsewhere, including the Soviet Union. The conductor could not accept such offers however, as his passport had been surrendered to the Dutch government. Willem Mengelberg undoubtedly was an important figure in music. His dedication to the work of Mahler and advocacy for the artistic output of his contemporaries solidified his reputation and established his career as one of the most influential of his time. *—David Brensilver*

Recommended:

○ **Willem Mengelberg** / Mengelberg (cond.), Concertgebouw / 2002 / Andante 2966

○ **Mengelberg Conducts Beethoven & Schubert** / Mengelberg (cond.), Concertgebouw / 2003 / Naxos 8110864

○ **Mengelberg Conducts Liszt, Berlioz, Weber** / Mengelberg (cond.), Concertgebouw / 2002 / Naxos 8110853

○ **Mengelberg: Maestro Appassionato** / Mengelberg (cond.), Gieseking, Vincent, Concertgebouw / 2000 / History 205257

○ **Mengelberg: Maestro Appassionato** / Mengelberg (cond.), Gieseking, Bustabo, Szekely, Zimmermant, Concertgebouw / 2000 / History 205253

Peter Mennin

b. May 17, 1923, Erie, PA, **d.** Jun. 17, 1983, New York, NY
Composer

Peter Mennin spent most of his life working within the academic environment and his music, in the American symphonic tradition, speaks from a broad neo-Romantic imagination. Mennin began his studies at Oberlin College, and upon completing military service in the early 1940s, he obtained his bachelor's, master's and Ph.D. (1947) degrees at the Eastman School.

During these years he composed three of his eight symphonies (1941, 1944, 1946); an *Alleluia* (1941) for chorus; *Four Songs* (1941) for soprano and piano on texts by Emily Dickinson; *Concertino* (1944) for flute, strings and percussion; the *Folk Overture* (1945) for orchestra; *Sinfonia* (1946) for chamber orchestra; and the first *String Quartet* (1941). In 1945 he won the first Gershwin Memorial Award for his *Symphony No. 2* (1944).

The *Symphony No. 3* (1946) from Mennin's younger years shows many of the techniques that he would explore in later works—asymmetrical melodies of great lucidity and rhythmic invention, a bright clarity of orchestration and line, dramatic climaxes, and the use of chromatic inflection. Mennin's *Concertato* "Moby Dick" (1952) for orchestra is a dramatic work inspired by a reading of Herman Melville's classic novel. Mennin's intention was to create a depiction of the emotional impact of the book rather than a musical description of isolated incidents. The main motif appears in many variations throughout the piece. Towards the end, a beautiful and strangely archaic sounding chord accumulates. Trumpet and wind solos call through this texture, and resolve on a major chord. Other instrumental works created during these ten years were his *Fantasia (Canzona and Toccata)* (1947) for strings; the *Symphony No. 4 (The Cycle)* (1948) and *Symphony No. 5* (1950); *Canzona* (1951) for band; the *Concerto for Violoncello* (1956); the *String Quartet No. 2* (1951); and the *Five Piano Pieces* (1949). His late instrumental works include the *Symphony No. 6* (1958); *Symphony No. 7* (1963); his final symphony, *Symphony No. 8* (1973); the *Concerto for Piano* (1958); *Canto* (1963) for orchestra; and *Sinfonia* (1971) for orchestra; the *Sonata Concertante* (1959) for violin and piano; and the *Piano Sonata* (1967).

Mennin also composed several beautiful pieces for chorus during 1948–49, including *A Song of the Palace*, *Crossing the Han River*, and *The Gold-Threaded Robe*, which had texts by Kiang Kang-Hu (1948). Also from that period are *Tumbling Hair* (1949) with text by e. e. cummings, *Bought Locks* (1949) with text by Martial, and *The Christmas Story*, a larger work for soprano, tenor, chorus, brass quintet, timpani and strings. His last vocal works include the *Cantata de virtute* (1969) for narrator, solo voices, chorus, children's chorus, and orchestra, and *Voices* (1976) for low voice, piano, harp, harpsichord, and percussion.

After spending a year in Europe in 1957–58, Mennin was appointed the director of the Peabody Conservatory where he remained from 1958 through 1962. He then became president of the Juilliard School of Music. During his career he received awards from the American Academy of Arts and Letters and the Guggenheim Foundation among many others, and served as chairman of the National Music Council and president of the Naumberg Foundation. *—"Blue Gene" Tyranny*

Overview of Works (1941–1983)

Like Samuel Barber, American composer Peter Mennin had a rather meager output, but one that was fairly consistent in its level of inspiration. Unlike Barber, though, he showed virtually no sense of humor in his music, almost always divulging a serious, often austere expressive manner. He was meticulous in his work, consuming much time to produce a single composition, and sometimes, as in his early efforts (*Symphony No. 1* and *Quartet No. 1*), renouncing the finished product. At the heart of Mennin's output are his nine symphonies, spanning exactly four decades (1941–81).

Actually, Mennin recognized only seven of these symphonies, the *Second* having been premiered but ignored thereafter by its composer. The three-movement *Third* (1946), while still exhibiting some immaturity, already divulges Mennin's penchant for counterpoint and grimness of expression, though it is comparatively colorful. The *Fourth* (1947–48), subtitled "The Cycle," also in three movements, is a choral work. Supplying his own text, the composer fashions a piece here filled with anxious energy and a sense of desperation. After his three-movement 1950 *Fifth*, Mennin's style turned somewhat more dissonant with the *Sixth* (1953) and *Seventh* (1963), which while not atonal, exhibited a harsher, more complex expressive language. The latter work is a one-movement masterpiece of variation composition. His last two symphonies (1973 and 1982–83, respectively) are also tougher works, but quite rewarding ones too. Actually, the three-movement *Ninth* is not as unyielding as the powerful *Eighth*, having a slow movement that is quite approachable. Mennin must be ranked with Sessions, Diamond, Creston, and William Schuman as among the greatest American symphonists.

But he also wrote other important orchestral music, too. His cello concerto (1956), though reflecting his more advanced expressive idiom, is a masterwork deserving of greater attention. For chilling drama and a sense of ineluctable doom, Mennin's *Concertato "Moby Dick"* (1952), a ten-minute work roiling with anxious powerful sonorities, would be hard to surpass. Despite its title, though, it is not a programmatic piece. In fact, the only programmatic work in his output is his 1969 *Cantata de virtute "Pied Piper of Hamelin."* All else is abstract in nature. Perhaps this is one of the reasons Mennin composed so few songs, turning out but one large effort, *Voices* (1975), on texts by Thoreau, Melville, Whitman, and Dickinson. He suppressed his 1941 collection of four *Songs on Texts By Dickinson*. Mennin's chamber and instrumental works are paltry in number and include two quartets (1941 and 1951), *Sonata Concertante for Violin and Piano* (1959), and a piano sonata (1963). They, too, divulge the composer's serious expressive manner and deftly wrought contrapuntal writing. His list of choral works is a bit more substantial. Along with the symphony and cantata mentioned earlier, he wrote several shorter pieces, including *Four Chinese Poems on texts by Kiang Kang-Hu* (1948); *Two Choruses: Bought Hair and Tumbling* (1949; e.e. cummings); and, among others, *Reflections of Emily, for boys' chorus, harpsichord, piano, and percussion* (1978; Dickinson). —*Robert Cummings*

Recommended:

○ **Mennin: Symphonies 5 & 6; etc.** / Miller (cond.), Albany SO / 1997 / Albany 260

○ **Mennin: Symphonies 8 & 9; Folk Overture** / Badea (cond.) Columbus SO / 1989 / New World 80371

Gian Carlo Menotti

b. Jul. 7, 1911, Cadegliano, Italy

Composer: Opera, Chamber Music

Gian Carlo Menotti may be the greatest composer of American opera in the twentieth century. This kind of assessment often comes under challenge: his conservative style and traditional methods have led many to view him as a sentimental composer whose expressive language, while showing moments of inspiration, is ultimately boring and without appeal. Yet, his melodies are often memorable and some advanced techniques are indeed employed in his scores, such as the 12-tone music in his 1963 opera *The Last Savage*. Moreover, he has always been a skillful orchestrator, favoring transparency and clarity, and has treated the voice effectively, making it the musical heart of his operas. Menotti is unusual in that he has written all his operas' librettos and is considered one of the most gifted librettists of the twentieth century. He had also written instrumental music, ballets, and choral works.

Menotti was born into an affluent family. His mother, Ines, was a good musician who often hosted small concerts and recitals at the family villa. Young Gian Carlo attended with enthusiasm and began showing musical talent of his own. At the age of eleven he wrote two operas, *The Death of Pierrot* and *The Little Mermaid*. Two years later he entered the Milan Conservatory. At 16, he departed for the United States with his mother, who, with support from family friend Arturo Toscanini, saw to his enrollment at the Curtis Institute of Music. There he began study with Rosario Scalero and met lifelong friend and fellow composer, Samuel Barber. Menotti would live with the Barber family in Pennsylvania much of the time during these formative years.

He graduated from Curtis in 1933 and soon began work on his first opera, *Amelia al Ballo*. It was premiered at Curtis in 1937 with such success that it was taken up by the Metropolitan Opera the following year. *The Old Maid and the Thief* followed, his first opera in English and the first opera written for radio broadcast.

Menotti had little success with opera during the war years, though he did write his *Piano Concerto in F* and *Sebastien*, a ballet. His opera *The Medium* was premiered in May 1946, and had a run on Broadway during the following season, paired with his one-act comedy, *The Telephone*, that catapulted Menotti to nationwide fame. *The Consul*, the composer's first full-length opera and Pulitzer Prize winner, was premiered in 1950. Its story originally was intended for a Hollywood film, one of many unproduced scripts he wrote for MGM.

In 1950, NBC commissioned Menotti to write *Amahl and the Night Visitors* for television production. Since its 1951 premiere, it has received many television performances and become his most widely-known opera. Further successes also followed, like *The Saint of Bleecker Street* (1954).

In 1958, Menotti established the now-world renowned Spoleto Festival. As director, he found its duties demanding and his output slowed, though he finally turned out *Labyrinth* and *The Last Savage* in 1963. He stepped down as Spoleto's director in 1967, though he remained its president. Perhaps his most significant work during this period was the 1968 science-fiction opera, *Help, Help, the Globolinks*.

Menotti established Spoleto USA at Charleston, South Carolina, in 1977 and served as its director until 1993. He has remained active in composition in his later years, with works like the 1986 television opera *Goya*, which he revised in 1991. His last opera was *The Singing Child*, in 1993.

Menotti became director of the Rome Opera House in 1993 and has lived in East Lothian, Scotland. —*Robert Cummings*

OPERA

Amahl and the Night Visitors (1951)

Samuel Chotzinoff, music director at NBC, commissioned Menotti to compose an opera for television broadcast at Christmas time in 1951. (In 1939, Chotzinoff had commissioned from Menotti *The Old Maid and the Thief*.) The first opera written for television, *Amahl and the Night Visitors* has become the most frequently performed opera of all time, with over 500 performances annually across the world.

Menotti's inspiration for *Amahl and the Night Visitors* sprang both from his own childhood and from his viewing of Hieronymous Bosch's *The Adoration of the Magi* at New York's Metropolitan Museum of Art. In Italy, children receive gifts not from Santa Claus, but from the Three Kings who in the New Testament visit the baby Jesus. After Menotti moved away from Italy, he forgot about the Three Kings concept until he saw the Bosch painting, began to hear music, and conceived the story. This happened in November 1951, and the opera was ready for broadcast on the evening of December 24, 1951. It was first performed on stage on February 21, 1952, directed by the composer.

Menotti has confessed that he "hardly thought of television at all" while composing *Amahl and the Night Visitors*: "As a matter of fact, all my operas are conceived for an ideal stage." Menotti's story focuses on Amahl, a young handicapped boy, and his mother, who are visited by three Kings—Balthazar, Melchior, and Kaspar—on their way to find Jesus. The Kings stay the night, during which Amahl's mother tries to steal some of the Kings' gold and is caught in the act. Melchior suggests that she keep the gold, because the child they are visiting will rule his kingdom with love, not riches. Amahl's mother gives back the gold, wishing she had something to give of her own. Amahl offers his crutch as a gift and suddenly is able to walk. He decides to follow the Kings so that he himself may give his crutch to the Christ child.

The inspirational story of *Amahl and the Night Visitors* is certainly one of the reasons for its unparalleled popularity. Just as important, however, are its brevity, its lack of scene changes, and the exploitation of its limited musical forces. In addition to strings, Menotti calls for two oboes and one each of flute, clarinet, bassoon, trumpet, and horn. Percussion, harp, and piano round out the score. Diatonic and highly melodic, the music is continuous throughout, the text set according to the flow of spoken English. Portions of the work are often performed separately, particularly the pleasant Introduction, the March of the Kings as they approach Amahl's home, and the lively Shepherd's Dance.

Organized in "numbers," *Amahl and the Night Visitors* gives each principal a chance to shine, either in a solo or an ensemble. Examples are the "Good Night" duet for Amahl and his mother and Kaspar's "This is My Box." Humorous moments fill the score, some springing from Amahl's need to repeat everything he says to Kaspar because the King is hard of hearing—a characteristic suggested to Menotti by his brother's reminiscences of a costumed king of their boyhood in Italy. —*John Palmer*

Synopsis:

The action takes place in Palestine at the time of the birth of Jesus. After a Prelude the curtain rises to reveal Amahl, a 12-year-old disabled boy, sitting outside his tiny house and playing a happy melody on his shepherd's pipe. From inside the house, Amahl's mother calls to him, telling him it is time to go to bed. A typical child, Amahl would rather stay outside and avoids entering the house until the last possible moment. Once he has come into the house with the help of his crutch, he tells his mother about a bright star (the star of Bethlehem) he sees in the sky. A typical mother, she tells him he is lying and does not look for herself. Instead, she begins lamenting their impoverished existence. Even though he is treated badly by his mother, Amahl tries to comfort her as the two sing a duet in which they tell each other good night.

The sound of voices comes from somewhere outside the house and awakens Amahl. The boy struggles to the window and sees three kings, Balthazar, Kaspar, and Melchior, making their way toward the house. When Amahl tells his mother what he sees, she again accuses him of lying. She is very surprised when the three men show up with their page and ask to enter the house. After Amahl's mother lets them into the house, the Three Kings sit down on a bench and begin a conversation with Amahl and his mother. In "This is my box," Kaspar shows Amahl and his mother a great collection of jewels in a box, but Amahl is more interested in the king's tasty licorice, some of which he gives to the boy.

In an ensemble the Three Kings explain that the bright star in the sky is leading them to a Child. As they finish, shepherds arrive and dance a boisterous ballet. When the dancing shepherds take their leave and say their farewell, the music of the opening Prelude returns briefly. The kings, their page, and Amahl then go to sleep, while Amahl's mother remains awake, wishing she had some of the kings' wealth. She attempts to take a few of Kaspar's jewels, but the page catches her in the act and immediately informs the kings. This awakens Amahl, who attacks the page with his crutch, trying to make him free his mother. Melchior intervenes and forgives Amahl's mother as the music of the Prelude returns once again.

The Kings prepare to leave. Amahl, fascinated with their story of the Child they seek, offers them his crutch as a gift for the Child. Suddenly, Amahl is able to walk. General amazement leads to a lively quintet in which the kings decide to take Amahl with them so he himself may give the crutch to the Child. As the shepherds sing in the distance, Amahl plays his pipe, performing the same tune as he does at the beginning of the opera. —*John Palmer*

Recommended:

○ **Menotti: Amahl and the Night Visitors** / Schippers (cond.) / 1952 / RCA 6485

The Consul (1949)

The Consul premiered on March 1, 1950, at Philadelphia's Schubert Theater; this functioned as a test run for the Broadway premiere of March 15, 1950, at the Ethel Barrymore Theater, which subsequently ran for 269 performances. The phenomenally successful work was eventually staged throughout Europe, translated into a dozen languages, and awarded the 1950 New York Drama Critics' Circle Award for best musical play, as well as the Pulitzer Prize for Music.

The Consul is set in a totalitarian state in which John Sorel is a political dissident, fighting for a democratic government. The secret police force him to leave the country and Magda, his wife, must obtain a visa to leave the country and join him. Insurmountable bureaucracy in the form of a stone-faced Secretary and piles of paperwork cause frustrating delays at the consulate, where there seems to be no Consul. During the ensuing months, Magda's baby and mother-in-law die and she learns from a messenger, Assan, that her husband, after hearing about the baby's death, is returning to take Magda with him. Magda, knowing that her husband will be captured if he returns, writes a note to him stating that she is going to kill herself, eliminating the need for him to risk his life. As she commits suicide by gas inhalation in her home, John enters the consulate and is apprehended by the secret police.

In 1950, Eastern European nations were preventing their citizens from crossing their borders and in the United States, the McCarron Act prevented foreigners with "questionable" political views from entering the country. Even if someone were to leave an oppressive, totalitarian regime, the chances of entering the perceived Utopia of the United States were slim. The countless forms, endless waiting, denial of movement, and political oppression portrayed in *The Consul* struck a chord with many viewers—especially Europeans.

As in most of Menotti's works, the musical material is predominantly tonal, with some modal inflections. However, there is considerably greater use of dissonance, evident from the very beginning of the opera. Menotti described *The Consul* not as an opera but as a "music drama," confirming his affinity with Wagner—in approach if not style; this is clear also in his belief that opera descended from the ancient Greek conception of theater, in which music, movement, and language were united. Thus, an opera should not be a string of arias, but must consist of a heightened recitative, with phrases that heighten the import of the words. Clearly, there is nothing new in this idea—and there is nothing new in Menotti's attempt to achieve his goal. Nevertheless, the composer's fusion of word and sound is effective. The most impressive number is Magda's aria, *To this we've come: that men withhold the world from men*, a passionate denunciation of the reduction of people to numbers that closes the second act.*—John Palmer*

Synopsis:

The action takes place in Magda Sorel's home and in a consulate in a large, unnamed city in Europe, in "the present."

Act One. Magda Sorel's meager and decaying apartment

The curtain rises on the dark and vacant interior of Magda's apartment; the windows are open. From the café below comes the sound of a recording of a French popular song. The orchestra plays stridently as John Sorel quickly enters the apartment. He falls to the living room floor. A member of a group of "freedom fighters," John was wounded when a meeting of the group was raided by the secret police. From the other side of the living room a surprised Magda, John's wife, and John's Mother enter and attend to John. When the police arrive at the apartment, however, John must hide.

The police, having found nothing, leave the apartment, and John comes out of hiding. He tells his wife and mother that he must find his way to another country and that Magda should go to the consulate and apply for a visa.

At the consulate, Magda and John's mother wait and endure endless bureaucracy. Although Magda begs the Secretary to let her see the Consul, the Consul never appears. Other people at the consulate are experiencing the same problems, and Magda talks with some of them, particularly the Magician Nika Magadoff.

Act Two. The consulate

Through the windows pours, once again, the recording of the French popular song. Magda sleeps and has a terrible nightmare as John's mother sings a lullaby to Magda's very sick baby. The calm is shattered as a rock breaks one of the windows. This is a signal for Magda and John's mother to send for Assan, a glass cutter, who is supposed to have information about John. Before Assan arrives, however, a member of the secret police shows up and upsets Magda. Assan then tells Magda that her husband is hiding in the mountains. As this transpires, Magda's baby dies.

Later, the Magician performs magic tricks and hypnotizes the people in the waiting room, making them dance a waltz. Magda again tries her luck with the Secretary and ends up in a violent argument, which leads to her aria "To this we've come." After the solo, the Secretary tells Magda she may see the Consul after he is finished with his current visitor. When this visitor leaves, Magda sees that it is the agent from the secret police and she falls to the ground, unconscious.

Act Three. The consulate

Everyone assembled is still waiting. One of the group, Vera Boronel, actually succeeds in securing the papers she needs. While this is happening, Assan tells Magda that her husband now plans to come back home. Frightened and confused, Magda writes a note for her husband that contains what she believes will be a solution to their problems. She sends Assan off with the note, then leaves the consulate quickly, forgetting her purse. Unexpectedly, John arrives, and he is immediately arrested. John asks the Secretary to call his wife, which the Secretary says she will do as soon as possible. At home, Magda prepares to commit suicide by inhaling gas so that John need not return home. In the process, she experiences fantastic hallucinations involving John, John's mother, and all the people she saw in the waiting room at the consulate, whom the Magician leads in a dance of death. Just as Magda dies, the telephone in the apartment rings. *—John Palmer*

Recommended:

○ **Menotti: The Consul** / Hickox (cond.), Murray, Bullock, Fritz, Otey, Spoleto Festival Orch. / Chandos 97062

Help, Help, the Globolinks!, children's opera (1968)

This playful opera, though today performed almost exclusively in English, was first performed in German as *Hilfe, Hilfe, die Globolinks* at the Hamburg Staatsoper, the house that commissioned it, on December 21, 1968. It was not performed in English until August 1, 1969, at the Santa Fe Opera (a house known for premiering new works). The opera combines ominous elements with comedy, but there are no real moments of horror; as Menotti declared, the Globolinks are "sinister, but with a touch of humor." The sound effects that portray these villains are more bizarre than menacing (and to a contemporary audience, may be more reminiscent of bad science fiction movie and television effects than anything else) and the Globolinks themselves are so campy that they might well have emerged from an episode of the *Batman* television series or *The Avengers* (the originals in both cases). Emily's music, though, is imbued with the sincere naïveté of other children in Menotti operas, such as *Amahl*, with her direct lyricism and hints of poignancy. The interplay between Madame Euterpova and the other characters, particularly Dr. Stone, is broad farce both dramatically and vocally, with an almost Rossinian sense of exaggeration at times. (While Madame Euterpova is something of a mouthpiece for Menotti, declaring that the world has forgotten how to sing and how to value music, he also makes her faintly ridiculous and egotistical to keep her from becoming too preachy.) Aside from its entertainment value, the opera stands as a kind of musical manifesto for Menotti. He was concerned that the new interest in electronics and radical experimentation in music would replace melody and accessible music drama, so it is no coincidence that the Globolinks are represented by bizarre electronic noises and can be stopped only by music, which is represented by that most traditional of instruments, the violin. *—Ann Feeney*

Synopsis:

Libretto by the composer

Cast: Emily, a student; Tony, the bus driver; Madame Euterpova, the music teacher; Dr. Stone, the dean; Timothy, the custodian; Penelope Newkirk, the geometry teacher; Mr. Lavender-Gas, the literature teacher; and Dr. Turtlespit, the science teacher

Setting: Near a boarding school

Time: 1960s

In the prologue, the overture is interrupted by a public announcement, reporting that unknown flying objects have landed, bringing the alien Globolinks. Parts of the country are already under their control.

Along a country road, the Globolinks are seen leaping around when a school bus appears with all the children asleep inside. A sudden blast of light stops it, and Tony wonders why the engine has died. Emily wakes up, asks what has happened, and, seeing Tony's nervousness, becomes frightened. The other children wake up and the Globolinks advance, making bizarre electronic noises. Tony frightens them away with the horn. Another public announcement brings the news that the Globolinks are immune to every weapon except the sound of music. Tony and the children call for help, but without any effect. They realize they are trapped and are afraid of what will happen when the battery dies. Tony asks if any of the children brought their instruments, but they have all forgotten theirs, except for Emily, who brought her violin. She is horrified to think that she is the one who has to go out alone and come back with help, but Tony tells her to be brave: his advice, "Let music clear your path," is echoed by the children. She leaves slowly, promising to save them and asking them to pray for her as she plays her violin.

In Dr. Stone's office, he and Timothy worry about where the children are. Timothy tries to call but the phone is dead. They reflect that it's been a terrible day and call one another idiots for their various miscommunications. Timothy tells Dr. Stone (with some glee) that his troubles aren't over yet because Madame Euterpova is waiting for him. She starts to make a dramatic entrance, but he asks her to refrain, as he has a splitting headache. She retreats and sweeps back in, melodramatically insisting that she is quitting and demanding her wages. She denounces everything in the country, informs him that her "astral body is sensitive, emotional, and passionate," and tells him that the children have all left their instruments behind during vacation instead of taking them home to practice as they had promised. She goes on to accuse him of not knowing music or its power, tries to get him to sing, argues about the meaning of "la," and storms out, though on the doorstep she turns back to tell him she still loves him, news that does not noticeably cheer him up. He flops onto the coach and turns on the radio. The latest announcement says that when anyone is touched by a Globolink, he or she will turn into one within 24 hours, and that repeating the music is the only defense. He shuts the radio off and dozes. Three Globolinks enter, one of them finally touching him. He springs up, hits the buzzer, and Timothy runs in. When it becomes clear that Dr. Stone can't speak, and can only make Globolink-type noises, Timothy shouts for help and the other teachers run in. Madame Euterpova tells the other teachers of the Globolink invasion and says they must rescue the children. Fortunately, they all play musical instruments, and Madame Euterpova tries to get Dr. Stone to sing, though he can barely manage the note "la," which he repeats pathetically. Timothy comes in with his tuba, which confuses Madame Euterpova, but when she hears it, calls it a musical cannon. Telling Dr. Turtlespit that just because he is a science teacher he doesn't have to be a pig, Mr. Lavender-Gas that just because he is a literature teacher he doesn't have to be a pompous ass, and Miss Newkirk that just because she is a geometry teacher she doesn't have to be a square, Madame Euterpova effectively orders them to elect her as leader, and they march off as she encourages them, "Let the trumpet blaze." Dr. Stone follows them.

Back at the bus, the children and Tony nervously watch for Emily's return. They try to sing to keep their spirits up, but the Globolinks advance. The children panic too much to sing, but the Globolinks are suddenly dispersed by the sound of musical instruments as the teachers advance, singing triumphantly, "We're coming." The teachers ask where Emily is, and when they are told she has gone for help, Dr. Turtlespit suggests that since Dr. Stone is now part Globolink, he might be able to track her. Dr. Stone hurries off, and they follow. In an alarming landscape, Emily is wandering alone: "I still can't find the way." She is playing her violin, surrounded by Globolinks. She falls down in exhaustion, and a Globolink picks up her violin, but drops and breaks it. She wakes up and is desperate, but Dr. Stone comes in, still singing "la," but unable to say anything else, to her hurt confusion. He then turns completely into a Globolink and flies off. The teachers and children come in with their instruments, and Emily tells them that Dr. Stone has turned into a Globolink. Madame Euterpova philosophically decides she'll have to seek a husband elsewhere, terrifying the men, but for now turns her attention to lecturing the children on the value of music. Miss Newkirk interrupts her gleefully, telling her that just because she is a music teacher she doesn't have to be a bore, and Madame Euterpova accepts the admonition and leads them off, each playing an instrument. A small Globolink jumps onstage and watches them go. *—Ann Feeney*

Recommended:

○ **Menotti: Help, Help, the Globolinks!** / DeMain (cond.), MacKenzie, Madison Opera / 1998 / Newport Classic 85633

The Medium (1945)

This work, arguably Menotti's most famous serious opera (though he called it a "musical drama"), is a study in contrasts: Monica's almost folk-like lyricism and Baba's tortured, heavy, and often modal music; Toby's silence and his expressiveness; fraud and reality; and most of all, the contrast between the world of reality, where paranormal phenomena can be faked, and the world of Baba's fevered imagination. In his notes to the original complete recording, Menotti commented that "[Baba] has no scruples... until something happens which she herself has not prepared... [this] drives her almost insane with rage." Like another twentieth century opera, Britten's *The Turn of the Screw*, the drama is driven by the demands that the inexplicable creates in the observer's mind, in which something can be neither explained nor comprehended and so the protagonist is driven to doubt not only his/her sanity, but the nature of reality and reliability of the senses. Both works also explore the nature of innocence. The paranormal is associated with too much knowledge of the world and sin, corrupting and destroying children and innocence.

Menotti first thought of a work of this nature in 1936 when he joined some friends at a séance at which the friends desperately hoped to contact the spirit of their dead daughter. Menotti himself was skeptical about the experience, but the pathos of his friends' heartfelt belief struck him deeply; this experience is practically relived during the séance for the Gobineaus. The work premiered at the Brander Matthews Theater at Columbia University in May, 1946, commissioned by the Alice M. Ditson Fund. Menotti revised it shortly thereafter. The revised version was first produced with the comic opera *The Telephone*, which Menotti expressly wrote as a curtain raiser for this occasion. (The pair together is yet another study of contrasts: an unflaggingly light work set firmly in reality leading to the much darker and more ambiguous work.) It moved to the Ethel Barrymore Theatre in May, 1947, and ran for over 200 performances, relatively short for a Broadway run, but impressive for such a dark, operatic work without any blockbuster features such as dance numbers or striking sets. In 1951, Marie Powers starred as Baba in a film many critics consider a classic of film, let alone filmed opera. It was also a success in Europe, where the pairing of *The Medium* and *The Telephone* was sponsored by the U.S. State Department as an example of American culture. The dramatically intense and correspondingly rewarding role of Baba has attracted many of the great operatic singing actresses, including Regina Resnik and Renata Scotto, as well as Powers. *—Ann Feeney*

Synopsis:

Act One. In a squalid room, Toby, a deaf mute, fashions a costume for himself. Monica, daughter of Baba (known as Madame Flora), cautions him that her mother will beat him if she finds him going through her possessions. The door at the bottom of the stairs closes noisily, and before the children can replace the items, Baba angrily upbraids them for not having readied her apartment for the séance due to begin momentarily. When Monica asks her where she has been all night, Baba tells her she has been on the doorstep of a client all night, frightening the woman into paying what she owed. Monica and Toby prepare their devices for the séance. When the doorbell rings, Toby takes up his position behind the puppet theater, Monica leaves, and Baba sits down to a game of solitaire.

Two old clients, Mr. and Mrs. Gobineau, enter with a Mrs. Nolan, who has come with them to establish contact with her departed daughter, Doodly. Baba announces that the time to begin has arrived, Mr. Gobineau locks the doors and the three visitors sit down with her at the table. The lights are off and only a candle illuminates Baba as she begins to moan, indicating that she is entering a trance. Monica appears as Doodly and Mrs. Nolan speaks to her. Monica advises her to give away all of her daughter's possessions save for a little gold locket. As Mrs. Nolan replies that there was no such locket, Monica disappears. The Gobineaus then ask to speak to their son, who always laughs for them, and Monica responds with giggles. Suddenly, with a gasp, Baba looks about the room in terror, demanding, "Who is there?" She rises quickly, turning on the lights and asking who touched her. While the others ask why she should be afraid of "our dead," she orders everyone out of her room.

Monica enters to discover what happened. Madame Flora tells her that there will be no further séances, for in the midst of her trance she felt "a cold, cold hand" clutching her throat. She frantically grabs the curtain of the puppet theater, thinking it was Toby, but finding him huddled inside, she pulls him out and accuses him of having touched her. Monica protests and draws Baba away. She sits down and Baba rests at her feet, head in Monica's lap as Monica soothes her with her song of the Black Swan. Suddenly, the voice of Doodly and the laughter of the baby boy assault Baba. She forces Toby to search the room, then to join her on her knees as she prays, clutching her rosary.

Act Two. Days later, Toby has been performing a puppet show for Monica. As he tries to express his love, Monica helps him, telling him that his is the most beautiful voice in the world. Baba comes up the stairs and Monica darts to her room. Baba attempts to get Toby to confess that he touched her throat, promising Monica's hand if he will only admit that he did it. Furious at having no response, she seizes her whip and begins to beat him until she is interrupted by the doorbell. Monica enters to comfort Toby as Baba receives the Gobineaus and Mrs. Nolan. Baba admits she is a fraud and returns their money, informing them that there will be no more séances. Despite being shown all the tricks, her visitors object, all claiming that Monica's voice was not what they heard. Baba orders them to leave, shouting after them, "Fools!"

Baba decides that Toby must go, but when Monica tells her that she, too, will leave, Baba locks her in her room. Assailed by voices again, she begins to drink, begging God's forgiveness and falling into a stupor. Toby returns to the room, but cannot make his presence known to Monica. He opens the lid of the trunk, but it falls noisily, awakening Baba. Toby hides in the puppet theater as Baba demands to know who is there. She draws a gun from a desk drawer, and when the theater's curtain moves, she fires. A rivulet of blood runs down the curtain as Toby's lifeless body topples into the room. Monica pounds on her door. Baba unlocks it and when Monica sees Toby lying dead, she runs down the stairs, crying "help." Baba bends over Toby, whispering hoarsely, "Was it you?" *—Erik Eriksson*

Recommended:

○ **Menotti: The Medium** / Schippers (cond.), Powers, Italian RSO / VAI Audio 1162

The Old Maid and the Thief (1939)

First broadcast on April 22, 1939, Menotti's *The Old Maid and the Thief* was commissioned two years earlier by Samuel Chotzinoff, music director at NBC. In February 1941, the Philadelphia Opera Company staged the work, which was broadcast on television in May 1943. Contrary to popular belief, *The Old Maid and the Thief* was not the first radio opera. Several screen versions of *The Old Maid and the Thief* exist, and the work is still staged regularly.

Menotti often visited the home of his friend, Samuel Barber, in West Chester, PA. Enchanted by what he perceived to be a typical, sleepy American town, Menotti was fascinated to learn, through family gossip, of the sordid stories that brewed behind the quiet façades along the oak-lined streets. He thought an opera on such a tale would represent "the American scene." Menotti's characters, however, are stock commedia dell'arte figures. Laetitia is bright, energetic, and outspoken. The itinerant Bob is handsome, carefree, and gets what he wants; while the older, lonely women, Miss Todd and Miss Pinkerton, are simply amusing. After Miss Todd takes in a young stranger, Bob, she and her servant Laetitia are attracted to him and convince him to stay for a while. Rumors of an escaped convict in the area make them believe the mysterious man they shelter is a thief. Ironically, the women begin stealing both money and liquor as presents for Bob, hoping these will make him stay with them. When things become too complicated, Miss Todd decides to go to the police and turn in the "thief" staying with her. While she is gone, Laetitia convinces Bob to take Miss Todd's car and leave town with her.

The concept of a radio opera is un-operatic in that it eliminates entirely the visual aspect of the art form. For the original broadcast Menotti included a narrator who explained to the invisible audience the various scene changes, which could, therefore, be as "complicated" and drastic as desired or imagined.

Although he had not been speaking English for very long, Menotti felt he could create his own libretto. He had wanted to set English for quite some time: "I thought that because of its greater sharpness and greater variety of sounds, it offered to the musician much greater rhythmic possibilities than Italian." Conventional and fluid, Menotti's music makes the opera immediately accessible. Laetitia's aria in the sixth scene, "What a curse for a woman is a timid man," is the most popular number from the hour-long opera and is performed often in solo recitals. Menotti's popular piano piece, *Ricercare and Toccata on a theme from The Old Maid and the Thief*, elaborates a theme from the third scene of the opera. *—John Palmer*

Synopsis:

Scene One. The action takes place in an American town (Menotti's model was West Chester, PA). After the overture, the curtain rises on Miss Todd's parlor. It is a rainy afternoon, and soon Miss Pinkerton enters to have tea and talk with Miss Todd. As they discuss their lonely lives they reminisce about the men they have loved. Laetitia, the servant, says that a man at the door wants to speak with Miss Todd alone. Miss Pinkerton decides it is time to leave, and a young man enters the house. Calling himself Bob, he explains that he is a beggar and needs a place to stay and eat. Miss Todd thinks it a fine idea that he stay the night in her home and tells him to change out of his wet clothes and into a dry bathrobe she has provided.

Scene Two. The next morning, Miss Todd enters her kitchen, where Laetitia is already washing dishes. The two women discuss Bob and learn that they each like him and want him to stay for an extended time, regardless of what their neighbors might say.

Scene Three. Moments later, Laetitia enters Bob's room with breakfast. Bob is very pleased at this special treatment, and while having his breakfast in bed he is easily persuaded to stay with Laetitia and Miss Todd for one week. However, Laetitia advises him that when he encounters any of the neighbors, he must introduce himself as Miss Todd's cousin from Australia; otherwise, they will spread rumors. Miss Todd calls to them, interrupting Laetitia's flirtation.

Scene Four. Miss Todd walks down the street on her way to the market. She runs into Miss Pinkerton, who warns her that a criminal has escaped from the local jailhouse. When she describes the man, Miss Todd realizes that the fugitive could be Bob. When Miss Pinkerton brings up the subject of the man staying in Miss Todd's home, Miss Todd explains that he is her cousin from Australia, then leaves quickly for home.

Scene Five. Once she is back home, Miss Todd tells Laetitia Miss Pinkerton's story about the escaped convict. They feel they cannot call the police because they would have a hard time explaining why Bob was in their home in the first place. Eventually, they decide to keep him there until he can safely leave. Miss Todd tell Laetitia she will take money from the Women's Club treasury and give it to Bob to make him stay.

Scene Six. A week has passed. Laetitia is ironing Bob's clothes as she exclaims, "What a curse for a woman is a timid man." She wishes Bob would show some romantic interest in her and has tried on several occasions to make her interest obvious to him.

Scene Seven. Miss Pinkerton arrives to find Miss Todd sitting on her porch. Miss Pinkerton tells Miss Todd of a number of recent robberies in the neighborhood and says that the weekly collection at church has disappeared. With an accusing tone, she probes Miss Todd about her "cousin" from Australia. Miss Todd informs her that Bob is sick.

Scene Eight. Bob is busy packing his things. He is bored with his life and wants to sees new places and have new experiences. Laetitia enters with his breakfast and tries to talk him into staying. Bob suggests that some alcoholic beverage might change his mind.

Scene Nine. Miss Todd and Laetitia talk in the parlor about Bob's need for liquor. Miss Todd is a leader in the local Prohibition Group and feels it inappropriate that she should be seen purchasing alcohol. The two women decide to rob a liquor store during the night.

Scene Ten. At two o'clock in the morning Miss Todd and Laetitia break into a liquor store, making off with a case of gin and smashing bottles all around them.

Scene 11. Miss Pinkerton pays another visit to Miss Todd to inform her that the liquor store has been robbed. Certainly, she says, the detective assigned to the case will find the perpetrator. Miss Pinkerton hears the inebriated Bob singing loudly in his room, and Miss Todd says he has a fever. Miss Pinkerton leaves, and Miss Todd and Laetitia rush to tell Bob about the detective.

Scene 12. The two women enter Bob's room and find him on the floor, completely drunk. When they tell him he has to leave, he protests that he has done nothing wrong. They explain that they have been stealing to help him, but Bob still will not leave. Miss Todd decides to go to the police and tells Laetitia to watch over Bob.

Scene 13. Laetitia confesses her feelings for Bob and tells him she wants to steal Miss Todd's car and leave town together. Noting that "a woman can make a thief of an honest man," Bob agrees to the plan and steals everything possible in Miss Todd's home.

Scene 14. Miss Todd comes home to an empty, robbed house and faints in a chair. The curtain falls. *—John Palmer*

The Saint of Bleecker Street (1954)

Like *The Consul* (1950), *The Saint of Bleecker Street* is a full-length, serious work. Unlike several of Menotti's earlier dramas, especially *Amahl and the Night Visitors* and *The Telephone*, *The Saint of Bleecker Street* features more characteristics of traditional opera. It is in three acts, has a large cast, including a chorus, and a large orchestra. The subject matter is very serious and touches on religious experiences, violence, and murder. Suggestions of incest also appear in the story. Furthermore, it does not have a happy ending. One of Menotti's inspirations for the opera was a painting of a nun by Menotti's friend, Milena Barilla, who later committed suicide.

The Saint of Bleecker Street was first performed on December 27, 1954, at the Broadway Theatre in New York. The composer directed the stage production of the opera's initial run of 92 performances, which was unsuccessful only in comparison with the reception of his earlier works. *The Saint of Bleecker Street* received the New York Drama Critics Circle Award for best play (Menotti's second), the Music Critics Circle Award for best opera, and the Pulitzer Prize in music (his second) in 1955.

The Saint of Bleecker Street is set in contemporary New York City, in the Italian community in and around Bleecker Street. Menotti's libretto concerns the young Annina, who every Good Friday develops stigmata on her hands. Her possessive brother, Michele, fights to keep the miracle-hungry neighbors away from her and to prevent her from becoming a nun. When Michele's mistress, Desideria, accuses him of being in love with his sister, he stabs her in the back. Very ill, Annina take the nun's veil in a ceremony at her home and dies in the process.

Annina's supposedly genuine visions are belied by the very frivolous style of her music, which resembles popular song. Menotti's failure, intentional or not, to separate Annina musically from the appropriately cheesy musical description of life on Bleecker Street lends support to Michele's assertion that his sister is simply a sick woman experiencing hallucinations, not a saint. That the Roman Catholic Church would capitalize on Annina's predicament makes the scenario even more repulsive. Appropriately, the priest, Don Marco, has music that is no more elevated than anyone else's. Most impressive is the character of Desideria, Michele's mistress, whose powerful entrance at the end of Act II steals the show. As in *Amahl and the Night Visitors*, a large part of Menotti's score for *The Saint of Bleecker Street* is devoted to choral music. A group of women argue and sing the "Stigmata" chorus in the first act and an even larger chorus enlivens the Mulberry Street scene as the crowd prepares for the San Gennaro procession.*—John Palmer*

Synopsis:

The action takes place in the Italian neighborhood surrounding Bleecker Street in New York City in 1954.

Act One. A cold water flat on Good Friday afternoon. The young Annina, resting in her bedroom, has supposedly received stigmata, as she does every Good Friday. Don Marco, a priest, sits outside Annina's bedroom debating with others whether or not Annina will be able to cure the sick. Maria Corona has brought her mute son along to be healed, but she has waited for such a long time she is becoming impatient.

Don Marco has gone into Annina's room to retrieve her. He and two women help Annina into a chair. Dressed completely in black, she is nearly unconscious. As the crowd kneels around her, Annina wakes up, having a vision of the crucifixion. Terrified, she screams and passes out, her hands opening to reveal the bloody stigmata in her palms. All those in the room begin to shout "stigmata" and attempt to touch her hands. When Maria Corona pushes through the crowd, Michele, Annina's brother, enters the room and tells everyone to leave. Once they are gone, Michele picks up his sister and returns her to her bedroom.

However, Don Marco has remained behind, and when Michele comes out of the bedroom the two begin to argue about Annina. Michele tells the priest that he does not believe Annina's visions are real. Don Marco believes that Michele is competing with God for his sister, and Michele cannot win. Don Marco leaves and Michele lies down to rest.

The scene changes to Mulberry Street in Downtown New York. Every September a procession honoring the martyrdom of San Gennaro, the patron saint of Naples, passes through downtown New York. A crowd gathers on Mulberry Street to witness the procession. In a nearby vacant lot Annina and one of her friends, Carmela, fix the angel costume of a little girl who will take part in the procession. After the restless little girl and other children on the lot leave, Carmela tells Annina that she has changed her mind about entering a convent with her. Instead, she will marry a man named Salvatore. Annina is not angry. She releases Carmela from her vow and wishes her happiness, but Carmela confesses she is apprehensive. An old woman who has been eavesdropping tells Carmela that marriage is not exactly a ride in the park. Annina breaks in, describing a vision she had in which she once asked the Archangel Michael if she could see the "gates of paradise," whereupon the angel showed her the gates of heaven.

Maria Corona and her son enter and tell Annina a few people are coming to force Annina to take part in the procession, despite her brother's refusal. Many in town feel Michele has no right to deny them the stigmatized Annina and her healing powers. Maria Corona says her son, once completely mute, has begun to speak since he touched Annina. He can now say "mama." Michele enters and makes Maria leave. Michele and Annina discuss her visions, Michele explaining that they are simply hallucinations. Annina, however, is convinced that they are sent to her from God. Michele admits he does not want her to enter the convent because he needs her and fears losing her.

When Annina and Michele hear the procession approaching, Annina suggests they hide. Michele, however, is determined to stand his ground, but the men who enter beat him and chain him to a fence. They then grab Annina and carry her off on their shoulders, her arms outstretched as if tied to a cross. Michele's mistress Desideria finds Michele and frees him, at which point he faints.

Act Two. Eight months later in an Italian restaurant on Bleecker Street. Carmela and Salvatore pose for photographs at their wedding party. The couple dance as Annina and Don Marco sit at a table while Michele and a sailor sing a song in the couple's honor. Waiters enter with a cake and the wedding guests follow them into the next room. Distressed, Desideria comes into the restaurant looking for Michele. She tells him that she is the only one in the neighborhood who was not invited to the wedding and it is because she is sleeping with Michele. Now even her mother has banished her, and Desideria feels it only appropriate that Michele show his love by bringing her to the wedding with him. Michele agrees, and the two enter the wedding celebration.

Don Marco, however, stands in their way, and the argument between them attracts the attention of the other guests. When Salvatore accuses Michele of stirring up trouble, Annina then comforts Michele with caresses, causing Desideria to accuse Michele of being in love his sister, not with her. As Desideria laughs, Michele tells her to take back her accusation, then stabs her in the back. Michele runs off as Annina holds Desideria in her arms until Desideria dies.

Act Three. Several months later, Michele, sought by the police, is still at large. Annina, very ill, wants to take her holy orders at home, and Don Marco awaits permission to perform the ceremony.

In Annina's flat, women recite the Agnus Dei from the Catholic mass. Annina, dressed in black, sits in a chair while Don Marco stands before the altar. After Don Marco learns the church has approved Annina's investiture, Carmela helps Annina into the next room, where she changes into Carmela's old wedding dress.

During the investiture ceremony, Annina lies face down on the floor underneath a shawl. Don Marco christens her Sister Angela, and the shawl is removed and rearranged as a nun's habit. Michele forces his way in and begs his sister not to leave him, but it is too late. As Annina approaches Don Marco to accept the symbolic wedding ring, she collapses. Don Marco places the ring on her finger as Annina dies. *—John Palmer*

Recommended:

○ **Menotti: The Saint of Bleecker Street** / Hickox (cond.), Howard, Stephen, Hernandez, Spoleto Festival Orch. / 2002 / Chandos 9971

The Telephone (L'amour à trois) (1946)

After the first performance of Menotti's *The Medium* on May 8, 1946, at Columbia University, Menotti and producers Efrem Zimbalist Jr. and Chandler Cowles approached Lincoln Kirstein and suggested that *The Medium* run on Broadway as a part of the Ballet Society's opera season. Kirstein agreed, but insisted that Menotti provide a short curtain raiser to complement *The Medium.* In a few weeks, Menotti completed *The Telephone, or, L'amour à trois,* a 20-minute work billed as an opera buffa in one act.

The two operas were first performed together on February 18, 1947, at the Heckscher Theater in New York City, before a run of 211 performances began on May 1, 1947, at the Ethel Barrymore Theater on Broadway. The tremendous contrast between the two works seems to have helped, not hindered, their success.

The Telephone is arguably the most accessible of Menotti's works, which in general are accessible indeed. Lighthearted and entertaining, it is an excellent vehicle for a capable soprano actress with moments of coloratura and numerous comic opportunities. The opera has been broadcast on radio and television on innumerable occasions. It was translated into several languages soon after its premiere and was given on stages behind the Iron Curtain in the 1960s.

Lucy spends much of her time on the telephone. When Ben, her boyfriend, visits her intending to propose marriage, the telephone rings repeatedly, interrupting Ben every time he is about to pop the question. At one point he even attempts to destroy the phone, "in self-defense." Eventually, the audience and Ben realize that the telephone is not only Lucy's means of remaining connected to the world, but also a shield against the unknown, a type of defense mechanism. Ben decides to penetrate this shield by leaving Lucy's apartment and using a pay phone at a nearby diner to get through to her. Once Ben has Lucy's undivided attention, he asks her to marry him. Lucy agrees, but reminds him never to forget her telephone number.

Compared to *The Consul, The Telephone* is constructed with a very conventional harmonic and melodic language. There are set numbers, such as Lucy's telephone argument with George and her conversation with a friend, Margaret, which is also rounded by a return to its opening material. Arioso-like moments of recitative, in which Ben tries to have a conversation with Lucy, are interrupted by more melodic outbursts such as a wrong number and Lucy's sudden desire to call for the correct time. Ben's part mainly provides the springboard into Lucy's extended numbers and features only one significant solo, when he decides he must destroy the phone. *—John Palmer*

Synopsis:

As the opera opens at Lucy's apartment in the 1940s, Ben gives Lucy a package and tells her that he has to leave within the hour on a business trip. He has something he wants to tell her. But just as he begins to propose, the telephone rings, and it is a call from Lucy's friend Margaret. This sparks a lively conversation ("Hello? Hello?") in which Lucy asks after all their mutual acquaintances, including pets, while Ben nervously watches the time. When Margaret hangs up, Ben starts his proposal again, but the phone again interrupts, this time with a request for a wrong number. Ben comments that time is getting short, but Lucy decides to place another call, this one to find out the exact time. After this important matter is concluded, Ben starts his proposal from the beginning, but the phone rings yet again; this time it's a call from George. He and she promptly quarrel, and he calls her names and then hangs up. She bursts into tears and Ben tries to comfort her ("Listen, Lucy"). She goes into the other room to get a handkerchief and Ben grimly eyes his rival ("What can a man do?"), calling it a monster with two heads and countless umbilical cords. He tries to cut the wires but the phone rings, attracting Lucy into the room. She tells Ben that she has to call her friend Pamela right away to tell her about the quarrel with George. She makes the call ("Hello, this is Lucy… It all began") and tells the saga of the quarrel while Ben agonizes ("I've waited hour after hour"). He leaves while she is still on the phone, saying that there's only one thing he can do. After she hangs up, Lucy notices Ben's disappearance and wonders what he had on his mind and why she suddenly feels so depressed. The phone rings and it is Ben. When she asks where he is, he answers that he is right next to her ear, and proposes. She gladly accepts but tells him there is one thing he must never forget. In the final duet ("My number"), he promises. *—Ann Feeney*

Recommended:

○ **Menotti: Operas** / Balaban (cond.) / Pearl 0122

○ **Happy Endings: Comic Chamber Operas** / Radcliffe (cond.), Ommerle, Holmes, New York Chamber Ens. / 1995 / Albany 173

CHAMBER MUSIC

Instrumental Music (1930–1996)

Some musicologists think of Gian Carlo Menotti only in terms of his operatic contributions. Yet he has composed a fairly substantial and important body of choral music, as well as a significant, if somewhat slender instrumental output. Among his most important instrumental works is the 1952 *Concerto for Violin and Orchestra.* Cast in three movements, the work, not surprisingly, shows the songful nature of the composer. The first movement features a tense and dark main theme, while the ensuing Adagio finds the violin singing in its middle ranges as it spins out a lovely melody. The perky Allegro vivace finale offers a playful main theme and mischievously colorful orchestration. Menotti's single-movement *Fantasia for Cello and Orchestra* (1976) is also a worthwhile creation. Again, the cello allows the composer to express his songful side though, as in the violin concerto, where there is much color to the brilliant orchestration. Less successful is the composer's *Symphony No. 1 in A Minor, "The Halcyon"* (actually, his only symphony) from 1976. *Apocalyse* (1951), a three-movement work with inner sections, has an epic grandeur and sense of both the apocalyptic and angelic in its music. It has managed to attract some attention in the latter twentieth and early twenty-first centuries. The *Triplo Concerto a Tre* is another worthwhile effort. Cast in three movements, the work divulges a slightly Stravinskyian character in its unusual scoring for nine soloists and orchestra. The lovely Lento Molto middle panel is framed by generally playful Allegro movements. Naturally, a good many of Menotti's orchestral scores are sourced in his operas, such as the 1951 *Amahl and the Night Visitors*: Introduction, March, and "Shepherd's Dance." Other examples include *The Telephone: Lucy's Aria* (1946) and *The Medium: Monica's Waltz* (1945). Most of his opera music adapted to the orchestral realm requires a vocal soloist, as in his *The Consul: Magda's Aria* (1949) and *The Medium: Babba's Aria* (1945). In all of these cases, the work reflects the mood of the music as it appears in the opera, in the end taking a slice of the work and transporting it into the concert realm. Menotti's musical recycling of his operas has spilled over into other areas of composition: his lone piano work is an attractive selection of easy pieces based on *Amahl and the Night Visitors.* In the chamber music realm, Menotti's *Cantilena and Scherzo for Harp and String Quartet* (1977) features lovely themes and skilled writing for the strings, not that the harp is slighted, though Menotti seems to favor the sweeter, more sustainable tones of the string quartet. A 1996 *Trio for Violin, Clarinet, and Piano* is also a worthwhile composition. —*Robert Cummings*

Recommended:

- ○ **Menotti: Apocalypse; Sebastian; Fantasia** / Hickox (cond.), Wallfisch, Spoleto Festival Orch. / 2001 / Chandos 9900
- ○ **Menotti: Violin Concerto; Death of Orpheus; Muero porque no muero; Oh llama de amor viva** / Hickox (cond.), Roberts, MacDougall, Koh, Spoleto Festival Orch. / 2000 / Chandos 9979

Susanne Mentzer

b. Jan. 21, 1957, Philadelphia, PA
Mezzo-Soprano

American mezzo-soprano Susanne Mentzer is an international opera star, known for a strong, bright stage presence and agile lyric voice that has made her a natural for the leading travesti (trousers) roles. She is also active as a concert and recital singer.

Raised in her home town of Philadelphia, she moved to Santa Fe, NM, and finished her last two years of high school there. This led to ushering at the famous Santa Fe Opera Festival, which awakened an interest in classical singing.

She enrolled in the University of the Pacific in Stockton, CA, as a music therapy major. Her music teachers immediately spotted her vocal potential and her flair for the stage, and sent her as an apprentice at the Aspen Music Festival after her first college year. Despite her rookie status, she beat all the rest of the competition for the trousers role of Nicklausse in Offenbach's *Les Contes d'Hoffmann*, which, she says, got her "really hooked on opera."

She transferred to the Juilliard School of Music in New York City, where she studied with Norma Newton. Her professional stage debut was as Albina in Rossini's *La donna del lago* with the Houston Grand Opera in 1981. She made an acclaimed European debut in 1983 at Cologne as Cherubino in Mozart's *Le nozze di Figaro*.

She rapidly established a strong European reputation, singing Rosina in *The Barber of Seville* at Covent Garden in 1985. Despite her growing fame in trousers parts (Octavian in Strauss' *Der Rosenkavalier*, Cherubino, Idamante, Sextus, the Composer in *Ariadne auf Naxos*, and others), she also enchanted audiences as Dorabella in *Così fan tutte* and in the soubrette part of Zerlina in *Don Giovanni*, which she sang in 1987 at La Scala in Milan under the baton of Ricardo Muti—a portrayal available on video.

In 1987, as she was starting a family, she returned to the United States as a residence and base of operations. She made her Metropolitan Opera debut as Cherubino in 1989. When she started rehearsals, she recalls, her son Benjamin was four months old and still being breast-fed, so she was "feeling not very man-like."

She has developed into a natural successor to Marilyn Horne in the great coloratura mezzo roles of the bel canto era, such as Adalgisa in Bellini's *Norma*, and the growing interest in Baroque opera led to great acclaim in the title role of Handel's *Giulio Cesare* at the Bastille Opéra in Paris, where she has also sung Debussy's *Pelléas et Mélisande*. Among her other roles are Romeo in *I Capuleti e i Montecchi*, Giovanna Seymour in *Anna Bolena*, Marguerite in *La damnation de Faust*, the title roles of Offenbach's *La Périchole* and Ravel's *L'Enfant et les sortileges*, Rossini's *Cenerentola*, and Purcell's *Dido and Aeneas*, and Concepcion in Ravel's *L'heure espagnole*.

In concert, she has sung in major works of Bach, Beethoven, Debussy, Falla, Mahler, Handel, Stravinsky, Ravel, Mozart, Floyd, Bruckner, Berlioz, Berg, and Pergolesi. Her growing number of recital programs tend to feature innovative mixes of art songs, operatic arias, and American folk songs, with an interest in vocal music by women composers. Mentzer has recorded for Philips, Telarc, Virgin, Decca, Erato, Arabesque, and Angel/EMI. She frequently sings in benefits for charities related to the care of AIDS patients, including an annual "Jubilate" concert in Chicago. —*Joseph Stevenson*

Recommended:

- ○ **Eternal Feminine** / Mentzer, Rutenberg (piano) / 2001 / Koch 7506
- ○ **Haydn: Desert Island; Arianna & Naxos** / Golub (cond.), Mentzer, Aler, Huang, Schaldenbrand, Padova CO / 1998 / Arabesque 6717
- ○ **Mozart: Idomeneo** / Davis (cond.), Constable, Hendricks, Mentzer, Alexander, Bavarian RSO & Chorus / 1991 / Phillips 422537

Sir Yehudi Menuhin

b. Apr. 22, 1916, New York, NY, **d.** Mar. 12, 1999, Berlin, Germany
Violinist

The legendary violinist Yehudi Menuhin was the eldest child of Russian-born Hebrew scholars who met in Palestine, emigrated to New York City, and moved to San Francisco soon after their son's birth. After just three years of violin study, Yehudi made a legendary debut at age seven with the local symphony. His Carnegie Hall debut three years later, in the Beethoven *Violin Concerto*, garnered praise that likened him to Mozart as a prodigy, whereupon the family (which now included sisters Hephzibah and Yaltah) lived gypsy-like in hotels wherever Yehudi was engaged at enormous fees. But the child's talent was instinctive. As Fritz Kreisler was to remark later on, "Because the young Menuhin had anticipated so early and so much of what nature had given him, I foresaw that he would have great difficulties." And he did.

When an eminent elder colleague requested a scale after the boy had played Lalo's *Symphonie espagnole* flawlessly, Menuhin wrote in his autobiography, *Unfinished Journey*, "I groped all over the fingerboard like a blind mouse.... I played the violin without being prepared for violin playing." He began recording early on (playing among other works Elgar's *Violin Concerto* at 16, with the composer conducting) and continued to concertize, making a world tour of 73 cities during his 19th year. At the end, however, he felt "tired, indifferent, and sad," and in 1936 began an 18-month sabbatical. Menuhin resumed playing in 1938, but never after with the sublime confidence of his preadolescent years.

During World War II he gave more than 500 concerts for Allied and American troops, but stirred a hornet's nest of controversy as the first major Jewish artist to perform in postwar Germany. Likewise, after the Six Day War in the Middle East, he was vilified for performing charity concerts in Arab countries. Increasingly he devoted himself to the training of young artists, both near London (which became his home in 1952) and at Gstaad, Switzerland. Also in 1952 he went to India, became a disciple of yoga, and a colleague of sitarist Ravi Shankar. He recorded with Shankar, as he did subsequently with jazz violinist Stéphane Grappelli. In the middle 1950s Menuhin took up conducting, but was no better schooled than he had been as a child violinist—and he was conspicuously less successful despite having made a steady stream of recordings begninning in 1958. At age 82 he was guest conducting the Warsaw Symphony on tour when he suffered a fatal heart attack in Berlin.

Menuhin was named Chevalier of the Légion d'honneur in 1948, to the British knighthood in 1965, and to a Lordship in 1993. For his work on behalf of peace worldwide, he was named ambassador of goodwill to UNESCO in 1992. His dedication to the "minds and hearts" of young musicians well may be remembered after his pre-adult celebrity has faded to black. Menuhin married twice, fathered four children, and played frequent recitals with sisters Hephzibah (1920–81), starting in 1930, and years later with Yaltah (1922–2001), notably at the Bath Festival he founded and directed in the 1960s. —*Roger Dettmer*

Recommended:

- ○ **Elgar, Delius: Violin Concertos** / Boult, Davies (cond.), Menuhin, New Philharmonia, Royal PO / 1993 / EMI 64725
- ○ **Beethoven: Violin Sonatas** / Menuhin, Kentner (piano) / 2001 / EMI 74804
- ○ **Bach: Sonatas & Partitas, Vol. 1** / Menuhin / 2001 / Naxos 110918
- ○ **The Young Yehudi Menuhin** / Enescu (cond.), Menuhin, Balsam, Paris SO / 1991 / Biddulph 046

Saverio Mercadante

b. Sep. 17, 1795, Altamura, Italy, **d.** Dec. 17, 1870, Naples, Italy
Composer: Concerto, Opera

Saverio Mercadante was a prolific composer of opera during the nineteenth century, and was influential in his day for his "reformed" operas of the 1840s. Reacting to excesses in both bel canto style and grand-opera effects, he purposely restrained himself from those tendencies to arrive at a more effective drama on stage. These reforms were critical for the kinds of operas Verdi pursued early in his career.

Mercadante was born in Naples and studied with Niccolò Zingarelli between 1816 and 1820. While some of his earliest music was for various instrumental ensembles, he began to compose operas around 1819. With an opera buffa in Rossini's style, *Elisa e Claudio* (1820), his seventh opera, Mercadante achieved notice in Italy, and he followed that work with many others.

From 1829 to 1830, Mercadante lived in Spain and Portugal, where he continued to compose. With no long-term contracts emerging at the time, Mercadante returned to Italy. He served as maestro di cappella at the Cathedral in Novara from 1833 to 1840, and it was then that Mercadante reconsidered his approach to opera. His "reformed" style begins with his most famous opera, *Il giuramento*. In this work he avoided any effects that did not serve the drama directly, and purposely varied the forms used in set pieces. This prevented his resorting to strings of da capo arias or diva-based scenas. Such self-imposed restrictions were part of Mercadante's style for the rest of his career.

In 1839 Mercadante became director of the Liceo musicale in Bologna, and in 1840 he was offered the post that his teacher Zingarelli had held in Naples. He took the post in Naples and remained there for the rest of his life. While his compositional output during the latter part of Mercadante's career lessened, it was nonetheless impressive for the workmanship present in the later works. For a while Verdi associated with Mercadante, but the two parted company soon after Mercadante assisted the younger composer with finding singers for a production of *Macbeth* in Naples in 1848. Soon Verdi's career eclipsed that of Mercadante, and the dramaturgy that Verdi pursued was regarded as more effective than that of the older Mercadante. While Mercadante's reputation declined, his operas are nonetheless interesting for the quality of the music in them. Mercadante also was a prolific composer of religious music, and those compositions bear consideration for their refined and elegant style. *—James Zychowicz*

CONCERTO

Flute Concerto No. 2 in E minor, Op. 57 (1814)

Saverio Mercadante gained success and renown as an operatic composer during his lifetime, but at present, his best-known work is a student work, the *Flute Concerto No. 2 in E minor*, Op. 57. Dating from 1813, when he was studying at the conservatory at Naples, it is modeled on a French concerto of the day but displays an effortless Italianate lyricism, confident use of the received forms, and even a few unexpected touches along the way. Listening to this concerto makes one wonder why the rest of Mercadante's output has been so neglected. The Allegro maestoso first movement belies its imposing title with its graceful first and second themes, which the flutist then elaborates in normal double-exposition sonata form. Mercadante's writing for the flute is idiomatic and is nicely highlighted by the strings-led accompaniment, lending credibility to the idea that Mercadante may have had himself in mind as the flute soloist. The development stretches the flutist's capacities even further, culminating in a long, wide-ranging cadenza before an uneventful recapitulation. Imposing minor chords open the Largo second movement, followed by jarring, angry rushes in the lower strings; the quiet transition from minor to major sounds like a snatching of victory from the jaws of defeat, and throws the warm, tastefully ornamented melodies of the following sonatina-form movement into greater relief. This work's fame, however, rests on its final movement, titled "Rondo russo: Allegro vivace scherzando." The Russian theme is piped by the flute with a bit of a galop to it, accompanied by sharp little chirps in the orchestra. This is an extremely catchy theme, and it is no surprise that Mercadante does not stray far from it, even incorporating bits of it into otherwise unrelated episodes as the rondo speeds towards its conclusion. The *Flute Concerto No. 2 in E minor* may not be an undiscovered masterwork, but it is eminently pleasing music, made by a composer whose works deserve wider circulation. *—Andrew Lindemann Malone*

Recommended:

- ○ **Italian Flute Concertos** / Giuranna (cond.), Graf, Padova e del Veneto CO / Brilliant 974552

OPERA

Operas (1807–1859)

Saverio Mercadante's worthwhile contribution to the repertory of opera has been obscured since his death. Even during his lifetime, he first had to vie for recognition with the already-established Rossini and the emerging Bellini. With the former's retirement and the latter's untimely death, Mercadante for a time in the late 1830s and early 1840s finally won recognition as Italy's leading opera composer (even before Donizetti, over whom he repeatedly won jobs and commissions). However, these years were concluded by Verdi's rapid ascendance.

Mercadante was educated at the Naples Conservatory and, unusually for an Italian composer of the early nineteenth century, had a strong interest in instrumental music. This early talent as an instrumental composer would lead him to refine operatic orchestration and to raise the orchestra from its characteristically accompanimental status.

His first opera, *L'apoteosi da Ercole* (1819), gave the young composer the opportunity to write for a group of singers who had worked extensively with Rossini. The opera was better liked for its performers than composer; but as with most operas of its period, it reflected the political status of the time: its celebration of the monarchy won for Mercadante important royal approval.

This quickly became something of a liability after the revolution in Naples. In 1821, however, the facile Mercadante won international approval with *Elisa e Claudio*, his seventh opera. That this opera semiseria subtly propounded libertarian rights surely helped it succeed, so much so that Mercadante was invited to Vienna. The warm welcome wore off, however, when the three operas he composed there proved him not to be the "next Rossini" expected by the Viennese public.

Embittered by the experience, Mercadante composed several operas that perversely disregarded popular operatic convention; *Ipermestra* (1825) best represents these advances. Mercadante rejected the existing Metastasian libretto in favor of a more prosaic text, which he set with extended declamatory passages instead of vocally challenging cabalettas. *Donna Caritea* (1826), however, then set aside these reforms and was widely acclaimed.

His accumulated achievements won for him a prestigious church position in Novara, for which he at first shelved operatic composition; his return to the form saw great results. *Il giuramento* (1837) is his most lasting success. In this first of five successful "reform" operas, Mercadante put dramatic progression ahead of bel canto concerns; the prima donna does not even receive a solo aria! Its succession of many short sections broke up the traditional arrangement of "set-pieces." "Vicino a chi s'adora," the quartet and chorus concluding the first act, contains marvelous ensemble writing. In this and the four operas that followed, especially *Elena da Feltre* (1839), are found the qualities admired in mature Verdi, but before that composer had even started.

Health problems and Verdi's successes hastened Mercadante's decline from popularity in the 1850s. His last success, *Virginia* (1866), was actually composed years earlier. Though Mercadante did not possess the extraordinary melodic gift of a Rossini or Bellini, he was often hampered by poor librettos, and deserves more regard than just as a stepping-stone to Verdi. *—Thomas Oram*

Recommended:

- ○ **Mercadante: Il Bravo** / Aprea (cond.), Perry, Domenico, Antonucci, Zanni, Italian International Orch. / Nuova Era 6971
- ○ **Mercadante: Rosa, Mercadante: Les Soirées Italiennes, Mercadante: Pensiero sopra Sorrento; etc.** / Harper (cond.), Kenny, Miles, Matteuzzi, Ford, Miricioiu, Magee / 1999 / Opera Rara 206

Robert Merrill

b. Jun. 4, 1917, New York, NY, **d.** Oct. 23, 2004, New Rochele, NY

Baritone

American baritone Robert Merrill, born Moishe Miller in Brooklyn on June 4, 1917, wavered—in genuine New Yorker fashion—between a professional baseball career and one in opera before being pushed into vocal studies by his mother. During an intensive period of study with vocal coach Samuel Margoles, Merrill worked as a pop singer at a Catskills resort to gain experience; he occasionally included the famous "Largo al factotum" from Rossini's *Il Barbiere di Siviglia* in his programs, earning great applause. Undiscouraged by his failure to win his first Metropolitan Opera audition, he continued to sing; two years later, auditions director Wilfrid Pelletier asked him to try again. This time he was ready; as a winner of the Metropolitan Auditions of the Air, he made his Metropolitan Opera debut on December 15, 1945, as Germont *père* in *La Traviata*, opposite the Violetta of Licia Albanese and Richard Tucker's Alfredo. It was a role he was also privileged to sing under Arturo Toscanini.

Despite immediate audience popularity and the enthusiasm of Met management, Merrill pursued his career cautiously, staying with less demanding parts—Renato in *Un Ballo in maschera*, Rodrigo in *Don Carlo*, Valentin in *Faust*, and Marcello in *La bohème*—until he felt prepared for such larger roles as the Count di Luna in *Il Trovatore*, Barnaba in *La Gioconda*, Amonasro in *Aida*, and, eventually, Iago in Verdi's *Otello*. Large or small, nearly everything he sang made an indelible impression. For instance, his Marcello for Sir Thomas Beecham's 1956 recording of *La bohème*, with de los Angeles and Björling, brings interest and character to a part often eclipsed by the principals. Gradually, his repertory broadened to include some 20 roles, and over a career of 30 years, he was heard at the Met 750 times. Merrill's most notable foreign appearances were both as the elder Germont (a mainstay)—in Venice in 1961, and at London's Covent Garden in 1967.

Escamillo, in *Carmen*, has been one of Merrill's most spectacular characterizations—one which, at the Met, he came to own, so to speak; he recorded the role in 1959 opposite the legendary Carmen of Risë Stevens, with Jan Peerce as Don José. Fritz Reiner conducted. Five years later he repeated his triumph in another *Carmen* for Herbert von Karajan, with Leontyne Price and Franco Corelli. Among other superstar recordings from the Met's Golden Age, Merrill's lustrous baritone graced major roles in *Il Barbiere di Siviglia*, *Cavalleria Rusticana*, *I Pagliacci*, *Il Trovatore*, *Rigoletto* (twice), *La Traviata*, and Sir Georg Solti's 1962 *Aida* with Leontyne Price, Rita Gorr, and Jon Vickers—often cited as among the half-dozen or so greatest takes on this oft-recorded perennial. In addition to the Beecham recording, he also appeared in a notable disc version of *La bohème* opposite Anna Moffo and Richard Tucker, conducted by Erich Leinsdorf. It goes without saying that his work was a vital part of what made the Met's Golden Age so golden; he was highly valued there for his vigorous, powerful, and technically unshakable singing, if not for his acting skills (which were never a priority). In 1993, he was awarded the United States Medal of Arts.

Merrill recalls, as an eight-year-old, having been let in to the outfield to see Babe Ruth play. "Well, he was the Caruso of baseball and I never forgot that feeling." Appropriately, in 1986, for the Yanks' opening game at Yankee Stadium, Robert Merrill became the first person ever to *both* sing the *Star Spangled Banner* and throw out the first ball. *—Adrian Corleonis*

Recommended:

- ○ **Arias** / Downes (cond.), Merrill, New SO of London / 2004 / Decca 000214502
- ○ **Lebendige Vergangenheit: Robert Merrill, Vol. 2** / Merrill, etc. / 2001 / Preiser 89534
- ○ **Bizet: Carmen** / Merrill, etc. / 1964 / RCA 7981
- ○ **Rossini: Il Barbiere di Siviglia** / Leinsdorf (cond.), Merrill, Corena, Peters, Tozzi, Metropolitan Opera Orch. / 1987 / RCA 6505
- ○ **Puccini: La bohème** / Beecham (cond.), Björling, Los Angeles, Merrill, Tozzi, R.C.A. Victor Orch. & Chorus / 2002 / Angel 67753

Tarquinio Merula

b. ca. 1594, Cremona, Italy, **d.** Dec. 10, 1665, Cremona, Italy
Composer

The date for the birth of Tarquinio Merula is guesswork stemming from the fact that he received his confirmation on April 23, 1607, and 12 is the customary age for that. He seems to have been a contentious person and was frequently in trouble, but is recognized as one of the most progressive Italian composers of the early Baroque.

His first post appears to have been as organist of San Bartolomeo, a Carmelite Fathers' church in Cremona. He was engaged to serve as organist of Santa Maria Incoronata in Lodi on October 22, 1616, to a three-year contract. He renewed his contract in February, 1620, but left Lodi in January, 1621. It was most likely because he got a better job, because he next shows up in Warsaw as organist of church and chamber to Sigismund III, King of Poland.

He returned to Cremona in 1624, where he received a part-time position as provisional maestro di cappella for Laude della Madonna services. This meant that he led music at the main altar of the cathedral on Saturdays and during vigils devoted to the Virgin Mary. This was transformed into a permanent appointment in 1627. In 1628 he took an additional post, as organist of the collegiate church of Saint Agatha.

He moved to Bergamo in 1631, as maestro di cappella of Santa Maria Maggiore, where Alessandro Grandi, his predecessor, had died of the plague. He was faced with the job of rebuilding the cappella. On December 29, 1632, he was fired for "indecency" towards some of the choir boys. He threatened to sue to recover his salary, but the church officials threatened to turn the matter over to criminal authorities, and he dropped the suit and issued an apology in April, 1633.

He returned to Cremona again. He was held in high enough esteem as a musician that they demoted his successor and re-instated him as permanent maestro di cappella for the Lauds of the Madonna. The good feeling this evidenced did not last long: he began disagreeing with his superiors over salary and the scope of his job, and left after two years.

He moved back to Bergamo, and in 1638 was maestro di cappella and organist at the Cathedral next to Santa Maria Maggiore. It is customary for the choir of the latter to take part in some services at the cathedral, but in 1642 they issued an order forbidding their musicians and singers from performing under Merula's direction.

All of this did not prevent the Pope from honoring him with the Order of the Golden Spur, and from receiving election to the prestigious Accademia dei Filomusi of Bologna. The restless Merula again returned to Cremona in 1646, becoming maestro de cappella of the Marian Lauds again and organist of the cathedral. He finally found stability, holding these positions until his death nearly 20 years later.

Merula was an innovator in music. He wrote some of the first solo motets with string accompaniment, introduced bass ostinato patterns into his psalm settings, and was among the composers developing the form of the ritornello and an ABB design that became common in Italian music throughout the 1600s. He is also one of the first to use the formula of recitative followed by aria, which became the norm for solo cantatas of that era. His most significant works are his canzonas, but he also advanced the form and technique of instrumental music in several sets of sonatas and in keyboard music. *—Joseph Stevenson*

Overview of Works (ca. 1624–1665)

If one were to describe the works of Tarquinio Merula in terms of the twentieth century, one would say that they were avant-garde. His music bears witness to an exciting time of experimentation and refinement, particularly in relation to the newer Venetian styles of the time. Merula's oeuvre includes ensemble and keyboard music, as well as sacred and secular vocal music. It is an important part of the repertoire of Baroque music of the first half of the seventeenth century.

For quite a while in the twentieth century, Merula was known primarily for his instrumental works. Of these, his ensemble canzonas are his most outstanding contributions. Four collections were published in Venice between 1615 and 1651, and follow the development of that form as it gradually merged with sonata to become sonata da chiesa. Merula was one of the leaders in idiomatic writing for violin. Regrettably, too few of the organ and harpsichord works survived. Those that have come down to us were mostly in manuscript, and have affinities with Frescobaldi and Michelangelo Rossi.

Merula's multi-voiced sacred concertos are stylistically similar to those of Giovanni Gabrieli. Organizing principles of major minor tonality, rather than modality, are much in evidence, with parts written along harmonic, rather than melodic, lines. Formal structures are clear and succinct. Vocal lines for the fewer-voiced motets often have a fine, instrumental quality, frequently with ample divisions and ornaments. Merula was a pioneer in utilizing strings in the accompaniment of solo motets. He turned his attention to composing psalm settings for Vespers and masses in the mid-1630s. Some of these use ostinato basses: one whole mass setting is composed upon the Ruggiero, while the romenesca is used for a setting of *Beatus vir.*

The six surviving volumes of secular vocal music include monodies, dialogues, and accompanied madrigals. By the 1630s, as the novelty of the stile recitativo had worn off, composers such as Merula, Luigi Rossi, and Carissimi were finding ways to achieve more balance between harmony and formal structure, declamation and expression. Merula's arias are usually in triple meter, and show stylistic similarity to those of Grandi and Berti. Some of the accompanied madrigals of the 1630s are even divided into recitative and aria sections, foreshadowing the later Baroque cantata. Ostinato basses are a common feature. *—Neil Cardew-Fanning*

Recommended:

- ○ **Merula: Arie e Capricci a Voce Sola** / Savall, Koopman, Duftschmid, Lawrence-King, Figueras, Lislevand / 2000 / Astree 9964
- ○ **Merula: Complete Works for organ** / Cera / Tactus 591301
- ○ **Merula: Canzoni, Mitetti, Sonate** / Ensemble Fitzwilliam / Valois 4641
- ○ **Merula: Canzoni e Sonate** / Collegium Pro Musica / 1999 / Dynamic 191

Claudio Merulo

b. Apr. 8, 1533, Correggio, Italy, **d.** May 5, 1604, Parma, Italy
Composer

Claudio Merlotti Latinized his name to Merulo (the original Italian form means blackbirds and Merulo is the Latin version). He is not related to Tarquinio Merula (ca. 1595–1665), but Jacinto Merulo (1595–1650), a minor composer of Parma, may have been a grandnephew. He studied with Tuttovale Menon (an expatriate French composer/teacher) and Girolamo Donato. He became organist of Brescia Cathedral in 1556, signing a five-year contract. Nevertheless, when the post of organist of St Mark's in Venice opened up in 1557, he competed for the position and won it, beating out Andrea Gabrieli, among others.

His reputation as a brilliant organist spread quickly and he initiated a series of Sunday afternoon concerts in the basilica. He was highly regarded by the church and the Doge, which rewarded him with regular pay increases. He remained there for 30 years. During that period, he established a printing and publishing business, issuing his own music and books of madrigals by Philippe Verdelot, Costanzo Festa, and others. He was entrusted with composing the music for some of the most important events of his time, including the state visit of Henry III of France in 1574 and the marriage of Francesca de' Medici and Bianca Cappello in Florence in 1589.

Unexpectedly, he left Venice in 1584. The next solid evidence of his whereabouts shows that by 1586, he had been hired as organist to the Duke of Parma; it is likely that at some point before then he worked for the Duke of Mantua. In 1587, he added the job of organist of the Parma cathedral to his post with the Duke. If he had left Venice to improve his position, he succeeded. He added a third post in 1591, as organist to the wealthy Steccata family.

He remained famous for his skills as an organist and was widely regarded as the best player of his age. He was a skilled teacher and a thoughtful student of keyboard technique. He studied the actions of the finger and codified exercises intended to give fluidity and evenness among the fingers, an important development in keyboard technique.

On April 25, 1604, Merulo woke up with a sharp pain in his lower abdomen. The symptoms that were recorded describe a classic case of appendicitis and ensuing peritonitis. He died after a week of great pain. He was buried in Parma Cathedral next to the composer Cipriano de Rore after the honor of a state funeral.

Merulo typified the growth of instrumental music during the late Renaissance. He developed a personal keyboard style, basing his melodies on vocal music. He invented new approaches to embellish melodies that lifted this from a set of mechanical and predictable formulas to a much more artistic part of keyboard performing. He even used written-out ornaments as formal devices: by repeating one ornament, especially devised for a particular piece, he added unity to it. He built pieces on an alternation of rather formal counterpoint with passages giving the impression of improvisation and a chance to display virtuosity in performance. This virtuoso spirit is quite unusual for his age. Wild flights in one hand against held chords in the other, free dissonance sometimes ignoring rules of voice leading, and other effects are sometimes astonishingly anticipating the mood of the Romantic era. His innovations were a principal source of the keyboard style of the Baroque. In addition, he wrote some very good motets and madrigals. *—Joseph Stevenson*

Overview of Works (ca. 1565–1600)

Claudio Merulo (1533–1604) was born with the surname Melotti but referred to himself as Merulus and da Correggio before finally settling upon Merulo. Born in Correggio and believed to have been trained there, he is remembered as a Venetian polyphonist whose career coincided with the most productive period of the Renaissance. Merulo was celebrated for his facility in virtually all musical forms as well as for his virtuoso technique in organ playing. He contributed to the keyboard technique of later eras in his use of specified fingerings. His gifts as an organist figured significantly in his compositions, many of which were written for the instrument.

In 1557, he was appointed organist at the Basilica San Marco in Venice, a position he held for 27 years. During this time, he was also called upon to write secular works such as the *Tragedia* (1574), an intermedio set to a text by Frangipane. In 1584, he left San Marco and by 1586 was employed by the Duke of Parma as organist. From 1566 to 1571, Merulo was engaged in the editing and printing of music, issuing some 35 volumes of madrigals and secular songs by a number of composers. His intimacy with the works of others gained during this period likely flavored his composing, leading to the advances that marked his own later work.

Merulo's works divide themselves into six principal categories. First are the ricercari, several volumes of which were published in Venice between 1567 and 1608. His toccatas were mainly works of his later life and were published in Rome between 1598 and 1604. His organ masses published in 1568 are core works in his oeuvre, as are his Latin masses (1573), canzoni (published beginning in 1592), and madrigals both sacred and secular beginning in 1562. In 1565, one of his madrigals was performed at the wedding of Alessandro Farnese, son of the Duke of Parma. Those madrigals written for five voices represent nearly half of his works in that genre and demonstrate an airier, more buoyant texture than the works of his predecessors and contemporaries. Contrary to the common belief that the modern harmonic system was born at a single stroke with the invention of opera, many madrigals of the late sixteenth century display nearly tonal passages, and Merulo's are primary among these.

While his choral works and madrigals were fluently and imaginatively wrought, his compositions for keyboard, especially organ, were his most singular and lasting legacy. In the development of both the toccata and the ricercare, the quasi-improvisatory genres that were central to the differentiation of purely instrumental genres from vocal models, his was a major role. Embellishment was heightened, pointing the way toward the style that flourished during the Baroque period. He broke from uninterrupted polyphony to interject passages of freer, more improvisational character and he did not decline to utilize discordant tonalities from time to time. *—Erik Eriksson*

Recommended:

- ○ **Merulo: Missa Apostolorum; Toccata; Magnificat** / Andreo (dir.), Munoz, Gregor Grupo Vocal / 1995 / Naxos 553420
- ○ **Merulo: Toccate d'intavolatura d'organo** / Tasini / 1999 / Aura Classics 0430

Mady Mesplé

b. Mar. 7, 1931, Toulouse, France

Soprano

Mady Mesplé is a fine French lyric coloratura soprano who was active from the late 1950s through the 1980s. Her operatic career was centered on the core coloratura roles from Verdi's *Rigoletto*, Offenbach's *Tales of Hoffmann*, Rossini's *The Barber of Seville*, Donizetti's *Lucia di Lammermoor*, and Mozart's *The Magic Flute*, but she is best remembered for the title role in Delibes' *Lakmé*. Many consider her EMI recording of that signature role to be definitive. She also excelled in performances of new works, and as a recitalist.

Mesplé was born in Toulouse in 1931. She attended the local music academy, winning prizes in both singing and piano, and in 1953 she made her stage debut in *Liège*, as Lakme. She then added Lucia and The Queen of the Night to her resumé with the Belgian National Opera, and in 1956 she joined the Opéra-Comique in Paris. 1958 marked her debut at the Opéra de Paris, where she sang Constance in Poulenc's *Dialogue of the Carmelites*, Oscar in Verdi's *Un ballo in Maschera*, and multiple roles in Ravel's *L'enfant et les sortileges*.

During the 1960s Mesplé branched out into newer music. Charles Chaynes composed his *Four Poems of Sappho* for her, and in 1963 she premiered Gian Carlo Menotti's opera *The Last Savage*. She was also the first to sing the French version of Hans Werner Henze's *Elegy for Young Lovers* in 1965, and Pierre Boulez chose Mesplé for his performances of Schoenberg's *Jacob's Ladder*.

Mesplé's discography is split fairly equally between French operetta (especially Offenbach), opera, and recital literature. Although her *Lakmé* eclipses her other operatic recordings in recognition and popularity, her *Werther* (with Georges Prêtre on EMI) and *Guillaume Tell* (with Lamberto Gardelli, also on EMI) are also worth a listen. Her most notable song recording is of the complete songs of Ravel with Dalton Baldwin, Gabriel Bacquier, and José van Dam. *—Allen Schrott*

Recommended:

- ○ **Delibes: Lakmé** / Lombard (cond.), Mesplé, Benoit, Linval, Soyer, National Opera Theatre Orch. & Chorus / 2002 / EMI 67745
- ○ **Vive Offenbach!** / Rosenthal (cond.), Mesplé, Quillevere, Hamel, Burles, Monte Carlo PO / EMI 774088

Olivier Messiaen

b. Dec. 10, 1908, Avignon, France, **d.** Apr. 27, 1992, Clichy, France

Composer: Keyboard, Chamber Music, Symphonic, Concerto, Orchestral, Choral, Vocal, Opera

Olivier Messiaen was a French composer, organist, teacher, and ornithologist whose music is distinguished by his deep devotion to Catholicism, exoticism, and nature. At the age of 11 he entered the Paris Conservatoire, studying organ and improvisation with Marcel Dupré and composition with Paul Dukas. In 1930, he became the principal organist at La Trinité Cathedral in Paris, a post he held for more than 40 years. His distinguished teaching career is marked by appointments in Darmstadt (1950–53), his famous courses in harmony and analysis at the Paris Conservatoire beginning in 1947, and his appointment as professor of composition there in 1966. His impressive list of students includes Boulez, Stockhausen, and his second wife, keyboardist Yvonne Loriod, among many others.

In synthesizing an individual style, Messiaen discovered in the music of Debussy the properties of "exotic" modes such as the whole-tone and diminished scales, calling them "modes of limited transposition." The inherent symetricalities of these modes enabled Messiaen to create progressions and melodies free of the tonic-dominant polarity of traditional tonal music, while remaining independent of the 12-tone system as well. Messiaen was gifted with a strong sense of "synaesthesia" or hearing in colors. He often described his music in terms of "color progressions," also equating key signatures and collections (sets) of pitches with specific colors. At an early age, Messiaen developed a strong interest in rhythm, particularly fostered by Stravinsky's *The Rite of Spring*. His rhythmic investigations ranged from Gregorian chant, to ancient Greek poetic meters, to Indian raga, to gamelan music. He soon left regular metric divisions behind, although repetition remained an integral part of his rhythmic vocabulary. All of these elements are explained in great detail in his 1944 publication, *Technique de mon langage musical* (Technique of my musical language).

In 1940, while a prisoner of war of the Germans, Messiaen composed *Quatuor pour la fin du temps* (Quartet for the End of Time). The quartet's unique instrumentation of piano, clarinet, violin, and cello was written for, and premiered by Messiaen and three fellow inmates while in detention; it became one of the great chamber works of the twentieth century. Messiaen was one of the first composers to apply serial techniques to parameters other than pitch (such as duration, register, and dynamics) in *Mode de valeurs et d'intensités* (1949) for solo piano. His interest in plain chant and rhythm led him to the ancient Greeks and Hindus, where he discovered processes such as nonretrogradable, additive, and subtractive rhythms. The *Turangalila-symphonie* of 1948 is the most synthetic of his early works. It features rich orchestration, imaginative use of tonal colors, Hindu rhythms, and a formal scheme that unfolds in large, block-like structures. Also of note here is one of the earliest uses of the Ondes Martenot, an electronic instrument capable of producing eerie glissandi, as well as monophonic melodies. Messiaen had a deep love of birdsong, and spent much time in the wild making extensive transcriptions, many of which would surface in his works, most notably in an arresting orchestral passage in *Chronochromie* (1960) and the monumental *Catalogue d'oiseaux* (Catalog of the Birds) (1958) for solo piano. His large body of organ music, composed primarily during his tenure as organist at the Sainte Trinite Cathedral, is highly idiomatic, colorful in harmony and registration, and rhythmically ingenious. From 1950, his *Messe de la Pentecote* (Mass of the Pentecost) is a collection of improvisations that he shaped into a composition. His only opera, St. Francis d'Assise, was completed in 1983. *—Todd McComb*

KEYBOARD

Le banquet céleste, for organ (1928; revised 1960)

Le banquet céleste is an excellent example of Messiaen's musical aesthetic as it applies to the organ: it features thick, warm texture, and long, relaxed phrases. The work is largely atmospheric in its musical intent; the strongest emphasis is placed on harmony. Messiaen's vertical sonorities are modally organized, though they also includes conventional tonal triads. The piece unfolds so slowly—though only 25 measures long, it lasts about six minutes at the tempo prescribed by the composer—that there is no strong sense of beat. As musicologist Roger Nichols notes, Messiaen "forces us to rethink our notion of time, so that we hear the logic of harmony and melody but without feeling ourselves tied to a mundane beat."

With *le banquet céleste*, the young Messiaen (the composer was 20 when he wrote this work) creates a kind of Impressionistic soundscape, paying homage to Debussy but at the same time forging the foundations of his own musical language. The composer's style evolved to include on a regular basis the static modal harmonies that give *Le banquet céleste* its sense of suspended time. *—Alexander Carpenter*

Recommended:

- ○ **Messiaen: Complete Organ Music Vol. 1** / Ericsson / 1988 / Bis 409
- ○ **Olivier Messiaen: La Nativité** / Thiry / 2004 / Calliope 4928

Cantéyodjayâ, for piano (1949)

Even those who know very little about the music of Olivier Messiaen might well know of three elements that color a great many of his pieces: his Catholic faith, birdsong, and a deep interest in Indian rhythms. It is the last of these three that we find saturating the music of *Cantéyodjayâ*, a piano piece Messiaen wrote

while teaching at the Tanglewood music center in the summer of 1948. The title *Cantéyodjayâ* is taken from the Sanskrit name for the particular rhythm cell that begins the work, and here and there throughout the music Messiaen includes little titles that comment on the music, sometimes in clever, language-bending ways (a word like *doubléafloréalîla* is of course a bastard child of two languages). The work might seem to be a very freely composed one, even one that sounds like an improvisation, and the range of textures, dynamics, and speeds at which the music unfolds is great indeed. There is, however, a certain kind of concrete design followed. *Cantéyodjayâ* is structured, after the opening *cantéyodjayâ* portion, around a collection of "refrains" and "couplets"—three of each, to be precise. They interact little with one another, instead taking turns and collectively forming a 12-minute musical mosaic. At the end, the opening *cantéyodjayâ* music returns to lead the way to a finish in which the two hands run from each other to the opposite ends of the keyboard, as if magnetically repelled.
—Blair Johnston

Recommended:

- ○ **The Ocean that Has No West and No East** / P. Serkin / 2000 / Koch International Classics 7450
- ○ **Messiaen: Piano Music, Vol. 3** / Austbo / 1999 / Naxos 554090

Catalogue d'oiseaux, for piano, Books 1–7 (1956–1958)

Not until French composer Olivier Messiaen was in his mid-40s did his lifelong passion for ornithology manifest itself in his compositions with startling originality. Over the course of the mammoth, seven-book cycle *Catalogue d'oiseaux* (Catalogue of Birds), the songs of 77 distinct birds unfold in a series of 13 movements totaling nearly three hours of solo piano music.

Messiaen's love of nature, as displayed in the cycle (each movement not only has a title bird but also an actual French geographic region assigned to it), is nearly matched by his love of musical arch form. Both within movements and across books, Messiaen inscribes a rough symmetry: occasionally passages reoccur palindromically; more often blocks of sound mirror one another over a central axis. The first and last books both contain three movements, the third and fifth two apiece, and the second, fourth, and six books a single movement each.

Catalogue d'oiseaux begins with "Le chocard des alpes" (the Alpine chough), not only depicting the bird, but also its mountainous surrounding, in several lengthy sections of colorfully dissonant chords. The call of the raven is juxtaposed with the chough, and long silences, a favorite tool of Messiaen, abound. "Le loriot" (the golden oriole) follows with a marked contrast to "Le chocard"; indeed, contrast characterizes the succession of movements throughout the work. The oriole's repetitive song takes on virtuosic extremes, homage (along with the title pun) to the work's premiere performer, Messiaen's second wife, Yvonne Loriod. The homage is one of love as Messiaen's harmonies recall harmonies from his earlier *Cinq Rechants*. The final piece of the book, "Le merle bleu" (the blue rock thrush), is a forceful and jubilant setting.

The tranquil "Le traquet stapazin" (the black-eared wheatear) comprises the second book; the movement programmatically moves from sunrise to sunset. The third book contains two shorter pieces: "La chouette hulotte" (the tawny owl) and "L'alouette lulu" (the woodlark). Each piece depicts night, the former as terrifying, the latter as peaceful.

The fourth book contains the seventh and central movement, "La rousserolle effarvatte" (the reed warbler), at over half an hour the longest movement. Like the fourth movement and like Messiaen's earlier *Reveil des oiseaux*, it outlines more than a day of birdsong, with dozens of birds heard.

The shortest movement, "L'alouette calandrelle" (the short-toed lark) follows, recalling "Le loriot" with its simple evocation of the songs of larks. "La bouscarle" (Cetti's warbler) closes the fifth book with an evocation of a river as well as the bird.

"Le merle de roche" (the rock thrush), another nocturnal setting, comprises the sixth book; Messiaen literally renders the elusive bird with silences, disguising the bird's motive. Book VII concludes the cycle, recapitulating birdsongs similar to earlier movements, with the dodecaphonic "La buse variable" (the buzzard), the playful "Le traquet rieur" (the black wheatear), and "Le courlis cendre" (the curlew), a stark depiction of the French coastline.

Messiaen's richly intricate music demands to be listened to actively; by extension the composer subtly requires a more active audience for birds and their songs.
—Thomas Oram

Recommended:

- ○ **Messiaen: Catalogue d'oiseaux; La Fauvette des jardins** / Ugorski / DG 000048102
- ○ **Messiaen: Catalogue d'oiseaux; Petites esquisses d'oiseaux** / Austbo / 1997 / Naxos 553532-34

Quatre Études de rhythme, for piano (1949–1950)

Olivier Messiaen insisted that one did not need to understand the generative processes at work in his music in order to enjoy it, noting: "Real music, beautiful music—you can listen to it without understanding it: you don't need to have studied harmony or orchestration. You must *feel* it." The four Études de rhythme (1949–50) for piano demonstrate some of the most rigorous musical processes to be found anywhere in Messiaen's music. Still, these processes serve to create music that draws attention to its almost geographic contours while concealing a rigid, systematic underpinning. Though composed separately, the four pieces in the collection form a complete unit and, according to the composer, should always be performed thus.

The Études are bookended by the closely related "Île de Feu I" and "Île de Feu II." Both take their inspiration from Papua and New Guinea, which merged into a single entity in the same year that Messiaen commenced work on the Études. "Île de Feu," which translates as "Island of Fire," not only describes the volcanic activity of New Guinea but also suggests the spiritual "violence of the magic rites of the region." "Île de Feu I" is constructed upon a refrain that remains virtually unchanged with each repetition but that is continually combined with different accompanimental textures—now jarring drum sounds, now fluttering, strikingly realistic bird calls. Between statements of the refrain, the performer engages in episodes that grow increasingly virtuosic and complex, finally culminating in an audacious white-note glissando in the right hand that occurs simultaneously with an ascending black-note scale in the left. The second movement, "Mode de valeurs et d'intensités," goes to organizational extremes from which Messiaen later retreated somewhat, but that presaged the total serialism techniques of composers like Boulez and Stockhausen. Taking the pitch-focused dodecaphonic techniques of Schoenberg a step further, Messiaen composed "Mode de valeurs et d'intensités" using a system that governed not only pitch, but also note duration, articulation, dynamic level, and register. These various characteristics—36 pitches, 24 durations, 12 articulations, and 7 dynamic levels—are carefully combined, so that register (high, middle, or low) determines duration of a particular note. As a result, a given pitch has a different length, attack, and loudness according to the octave in which it is sounded. The overall effect is a scattered texture continually punctured and punctuated, producing a sonority Stockhausen described as "music of the stars."

A prime example of Messiaen's rhythmic explorations can be found in the third movement, "Neumes rythmiques." Taking its name from the pre-notational glyphs scribbled above chant texts to remind medieval singers of melodic contours, the movement similarly combines and recombines a series of modular rhythms into various strings. These variations occur within seven episodes, each of which is preceded by a refrain. The material of the refrain remains the same, but with every restatement each constituent duration is elongated by a sixteenth note. This kind of additive rhythmic process relieves these rhythmic figures of their superimposed metrical grid, turning them into independent musical gestures. Each episode is followed by one of Messiaen's signature figures: a musical palindrome built on a prime number. The work closes with the second "Island of Fire" movement, in which the intensity and violence of the original theme is varied and compounded.
—Jeremy Grimshaw

Recommended:

- ○ **Legendary Busoni Recordings** / Jacobs / 1979 / Arbiter 124

Livre d'orgue (1951)

Olivier Messiaen was first and last an organist—at the age of 23, Messiaen became organist at L'Église de la Trinité in Paris, and kept the job until he died in 1992. Considering this, it is fitting that the key features of his music should be poured out in full in the works he composed for his "home" instrument. So it is with the *Livre d'orgue* (Organ Book), a set of seven pieces written in 1951. In it, one finds hearty portions of serialism (an occasional bedfellow of Messiaen), complex games using exotic rhythms, birdsong, and freewheeling chromatic ecstasy. Messiaen kindly provided little descriptions at the head of each of the seven pieces of the *Livre d'orgue*, explaining in part how each piece is organized.

No. 1, Reprises par interversion, is built around three Hindu rhythms that take shape as a single line of disjunct melody runs the full course of the manuals and pedals. There are four sections in the piece, the last three of which present the same music as the first but reorganized and reordered.

No. 2, Pièce en trio I moves into a much richer, fuller world; here Hindu rhythms are again employed, and underneath the title are words from St. Paul's first letter to the Corinthians: "For now we see through a glass, darkly..." Homophony is explored for the first time at the start of *No. 3, Les mains de l'abîme*, triple-fortissimo and harmonically dense. The center of the piece is, however, floridly polyphonic.

No. 4, Chants d'oiseaux, as its title indicates, is all about birdsong. Messiaen at several points reduces the score to just a single staff for some ornate, cadenza-like treble solos. *No. 5, Pièce en trio II* is again inscribed with a quote from St. Paul: "For of him, and through him, and to him, are all things..."

No. 6, Les yeux dans les roues is a blistering, loud 16th note moto perpetuo, while *No. 7, Soixante quatre durées*, is "64 chromatic durations, 32nd notes from 1 to 64—inverted in groups of four from the outside in, forwards and backwards in alternation—treated as a retrograde canon; and all populated with birdsong"—one of the most astonishing examples of rhythmic complexity in all of music.
—Blair Johnston

Recommended:

○ **Messiaen par lui-même** / Messiaen / EMI 67400

Livre du Saint-Sacrement, for organ (1984)

This 18-movement work marked Messiaen's return to the organ after nearly a decade of absence. A commission from the American Guild of Organists, the *Livre du Saint Sacrement* is a huge work, approximately two hours in duration—Messiaen is said to have been apologetic about the length—and is deeply religious. As musicologist Gillian Weir notes, the work is based on a theological plan: the first four movements are "acts of adoration before Christ," the next seven describe Christ's life, and the final seven refer to transubstantiation and Communion. The *Livre du Saint Sacrement*, true to form for Messiaen, contains birdsong, plainchant melodies, mixtures of tonal and modal material, chromatic harmonies, and wide, angular lines. The music is also profoundly descriptive and evocative—particularly as Messiaen narrates the life of Christ, from the gentle Nativity scene to the fierce fortissimo representation of the Resurrection. The more abstract final movements are carefully colored and structured to illustrate Christ's presence in the event of Communion. *—Alexander Carpenter*

Recommended:

○ **Canticum: French Organ Music** / Hakim / 1998 / EMI 72272

Messe de la Pentecôte, for organ (1949–1950)

Olivier Messiaen's *Messe de la Pentecôte* (Pentecost Mass) for organ falls right in the middle of his stylistic development. It is a summation of techniques he used in improvising music for services at La Trinité in Paris, such as Greek and Hindu rhythms, and unusual combinations of stops, and it gives a foretaste of ideas that he would expand greatly in his later works, such as birdsong and the octatonic scale. It is not a mass consisting of the usual movements of the mass ordinary, but music to accompany those parts of the mass that are otherwise silent: the processional, the offertory, consecration of the Host, Communion, and the recessional.

The first impression of the work is that it is atonal, but closer examination reveals elements of plainsong and modal harmony. The opening "Entrée: Les langues de feu" (The Tongues of Fire), refers to the feast day itself and uses Greek rhythms contrapuntally to suggest lapping flames. Next is the "Offertoire: Les choses visibles et invisibles" (Things Visible and Invisible) featuring sharp, staccato Hindu rhythms and profound, resonating layers of sound punctuated by a Klaxonlike effect. The central "Consecration: Le don de sagesse" (The Gift of Wisdom) contrasts a plainsong motive with the Hindu rhythms. The timbres of the organ make the songs of the cuckoo, nightingale, and blackbird realistic in the atmospheric "Communion: Les oiseaux et les sources" (Birds and Springs). The final "Sortie: Le vent de l'Esprit" (The Wind of the Holy Spirit) employs a numerical technique in which the rhythm of the two lines of music, in contrary motion, increases and decreases incrementally, keeping the organist's hands flying over the keyboard. The song of the skylark is heard, along with the octatonic scale, which Messiaen referred to as his "Mode 2," used to simulate the power of the Holy Spirit, especially in the final chord that, including the bottom pedal point, covers nine octaves. *—Patsy Morita*

Recommended:

○ **Things Visible and Invisible** / Crozier / Delos 3147

La Nativité du Seigneur, 9 meditations for organ (1935)

According to Messiaen, *La Nativité du Seigneur* represented a musical coming-of-age for the young composer. The organ became for Messiaen became a self-contained orchestra, capable of endless variety and limitless expression, but also transcended the orchestra in terms of the possibilities of duration, resonance, and timbre. Timbre, in fact, is central to the work, and, as musicologist John Milsom points out, what appears on paper to be music dominated by melodic and harmonic concerns within a carefully constructed contrapuntal texture instead turns into "flashes of color and light... an astonishing display of fireworks" when performed. The work consists of nine "meditations," foreshadowing the symbolic nine-movement structure of the *Méditations sur le mystère de la Sainte Trinité* of 1969. Musically *La Nativité* is significant, for it represents the first explicit use of Messiaen's famous chromatic modes, the "modes of limited transformation" to which the composer draws attention in the work's preface. As a whole, the work is a mixture of the beautiful and the bizarre: the density of timbre is at once breathtaking and overwhelming, and the sheer variety of registration makes for a piece that is not always easily accessible. It represents a step for Messiaen toward the later, decidedly esoteric and atmospheric pieces of the late 1940s and 1950s. *—Alexander Carpenter*

Recommended:

○ **Messiaen: The Complete Organ Music Vol. 2** / Ericsson / 1989 / BIS 410

○ **Olivier Messiaen: La Nativité** / Thiry / 2004 / Calliope 4928

Vingt Regards sur l'enfant Jésus, for piano (1944)

Olivier Messiaen's *Vingt Regards sur l'Enfant Jésus* (Contemplations of the Infant Jesus) are a towering specimen of twentieth century pianism. The work lasts more than two hours on those rare occasions when performed—as Messiaen intended the pieces to be—as a complete cycle. Written in 1944 and premiered the following year by Messiaen's wife Yvonne Loriod, whose masterful early performances and recordings of Messiaen's piano works did tremendous amount to bring his music to a wider audience in the 1950s and 1960s, the *Vingt Regards sur l'Enfant Jésus* plunge into the raw depths of Messiaen's Christian faith; the scintillating and frighteningly (but exhilaratingly) virtuosic fast movements prove once again how primal and joyful Messiaen's religion was to him, and the slow movements touch the sublime in ways that perhaps no composer of Western sacred or sacred-inspired music since J.S. Bach has managed with quite the same steadfast selflessness.

In this composition Messiaen created perhaps the quintessential twentieth century Christmas suite for piano. In it, he contemplates virtually all the figures associated with the story of the Nativity, and with many of the theological implications of the same event. Some of the movements are tender; others are full of roaring power, as Messiaen turns his attention to cosmic implications.

The *Vingt Regards* are brilliantly chromatic music; the work is, for many, the high point of Messiaen's so-called early period (which is usually considered to have ended with the *Turangalîla-symphonie* of 1946–48). A number of symbolic musical motives appear throughout the score, creating a basic-level cyclicism; the most important of these is the God theme that we first hear in the very slow No. 1 "Regard du Père" and which then returns to prominence every few movements—specifically, every five. The *Vingt Regards* are built as four groups of five pieces, but there are many other numerological schemes employed that overlap with that basic pentastyle design—Messiaen himself explained some of these meaningful uses of number in a preface to the score. The score falls into two halves, the first of which features the electrifying fugal outburst of No. 6, "Par Lui tout a été fait," and the second of which concludes with the magnificent musical and spiritual peroration of No. 20, "Regard de l'église d'amour"—a true peroration that recalls and reshapes many of the events of the past two hours, and music of extraordinary power. *—Blair Johnston*

Recommended:

○ **Messiaen: Vingt Regards sur l'Enfant Jésus** / Beroff / 1987 / EMI 569668

○ **Angela Hewitt plays Messiaen** / Hewitt / 1998 / Hyperion 67054

Visions de l'Amen, for 2 pianos (1943)

Oliver Messiaen completed *Visions de l'amen*, for two pianos, in 1943. The previous year he had been released from a German prison camp in Silesia, where he wrote his most famous work, *Quartet for The End of Time.* Having returned to Paris, he discovered his wife Claire was dying in a hospital. It was under these circumstances that he wrote many of his finest works, including *Visions de l'amen.* This work's premiere took place on May 10, 1943, in Paris. Messiaen performed along with the piece's dedicatee, Yvonne Loriod. Like most of his works, this one reconciles his devout Roman Catholicism with ecstatic visions of the cosmos and of nature. Without an orchestral palette to paint the enormous chords in different colors, the composer is obliged to find different ways to illustrate the seven different visions represented here in seven movements over the course of about 48 minutes. This level of inventiveness is something that Messiaen handles easily, and there are no points in the work where the methods of presentation become boring or predictable. The first movement, "Amen of the Creation," involves one pianist providing the bell-like accompaniment while the other pianist plays the Amen theme. They are independent of one another. In the second movement, "Amen of the Stars, of the Ringed Planet," the performers are manipulating the music the other is playing, and so on for the rest of the work. No idea repeats.

The premiere of *Visions de l'amen* included brief program notes by the composer that explained the four meanings of amen. One meaning is one of creating; of saying let it be done. Another meaning is to accept God's will, and a third meaning is to agree to willingly exchange, either between God and his disciple, or between two other parties. The final meaning is to recognize that what is, is eternally. Some listeners may find a few or all of these ideas remote. They are mystical priorities forged in Messiaen's spiritual certainty. Listening to the work itself lends great weight to these ideas, regardless of the listener's personal instincts. *Visions de l'amen* is not meditative music at all; it is explosive, rhapsodic, and cosmic. There is no single fabric of sound for the listener to focus on to and ponder. It is representative of a pantheon of ideas within a monotheistic framework. Unlike most avant-garde composers of the twentieth century, Messiaen never sounds as though he is feeling around in the dark for an image or an idea or a sound. Like Wagner, he knew exactly what he wanted, and though this is generally regarded as a sure way to make something that already exists, something original emerges. In this respect, a colleague of Messiaen has been quoted before as saying "I wish I could be as sure of anything as Messiaen is of everything." The risk factor that is necessary for any form of art to work is something completely apart from this composer. One might suspect that if no one listened to or liked his music he would not change a thing about it. The reason it works is similar to why Wagner's music dramas work; the pieces are simply too full of well-articulated ideas, blended into a diverse and personal aesthetic cosmology. It may be argued that some of his works are not as good as others, simply too turgid and inward to be communicative, but in the case of *Visions de l'amen* the marvel of this mystic's inner world is displayed successfully. It is certainly not the way for every artist to approach work or life, but the Messiaenic catalog prevails. —*John Keillor*

Recommended:

- ○ **Messiaen: Visions de l'Amen** / Double Edge / 1992 / New Albion 045
- ○ **Messiaen: Visions de l'Amen** / Osborne, Roscoe / 2004 / Hyperion 67366

CHAMBER MUSIC

Quatuor pour la fin du temps, for violin, cello, clarinet & piano (1940–1941)

This work is one of the most significant and famous chamber music compositions of the twentieth century. In his early thirties, Messiaen was already known as one of the most brilliant and individual young French composers and organists. It was at Verdun that his army unit was captured during the German Army's lightning advance in 1940. Two members of Messiaen's company were also musicians: cellist Etienne Pasquier and clarinetist Henri Akoka. As the latter had his clarinet, Messiaen wrote a piece for him, which became the third movement of this quartet. The soldiers were transferred to Stalag VIII-A outside Görlitz, Silesia. Pasquier was assigned as a cook, enabling him to keep well fed and smuggle extra food to Messiaen. Messiaen met another musician, Jean Le Boulaire, a violinist who also had his instrument. Pasquier hoarded money he got by selling extra potatoes and was permitted to buy a cello from a local instrument maker. Messiaen wrote a trio for them, which became the fourth movement. Messiaen discovered a piano in a corner of a hut used as a church. He quickly wrote the quartet and the four musicians premiered it on January 15, 1941, before an audience of several thousand prisoners and the camp Kommandant and his staff. "Never was I listened to with such rapt attention and comprehension," Messiaen wrote. The keys to the piano were sticky, and the musicians had to overcome the cold, but Pasquier says it is not true—as the composer remembered—that he had only three strings on his cello, adding that it simply can't be played on fewer than the standard four. The quartet meant freedom for the players. The Germans thereafter listed them as musician-soldiers. The Wehrmacht's bureaucracy took this to mean they were noncombatant bandsmen, and released them back to France.

Messiaen, a devout Catholic, drew his title and musical imagery from Revelations 10:1-7, concerning the Angel that announces the end of time. It is thought that hunger resulted in kinesthesia, Messiaen's ability to see musical sounds as visual colors, and intensified his interest in bird calls. The eight movements are: "Liturgy of Crystal" (a blackbird's call surrounded by trills, translated to a "religious plane" as the harmonious silence of Heaven); "Vocalise for the Angel Who Announces the End of Time"; "Abyss of Birds" (where the eternity of birdcalls overcomes and Abyss of Time); "Interlude"; "Eulogy to the Eternity of Jesus" (featuring an "infinitely slow" and majestic cello solo); "Dance of Frenzy for the Seven Trumpets" (a remarkable movement written entirely in unison); "Tumult of Rainbows for the Angel Who Announces the End of Time"; and "Eulogy to the Immortality of Jesus," a timeless violin solo that ascends in register as Christ (and Mankind) ascend to the Father. —*Joseph Stevenson*

Recommended:

- ○ **Messiaen: Quatuor pour la Fin du Temps** / Tashi / 1988 / BMG 7835
- ○ **Messiaen: Quatuor pour la Fin du Temps** / Shaham, Chung, Wang, Meyer / 2000 / DG 469052
- ○ **Messiaen: Quatuor pour la Fin du Temps** / Boeykens, Groslot, Korosec, Dieltiens / HM 7901348

SYMPHONIC

Turangalîla-symphonie (1946–1948; revised 1990)

Olivier Messiaen's *Turangalîla-Symphonie* (1948) was commissioned—without restrictions to instrumentation or length—by Sergey Koussevitzky for the Boston Symphony Orchestra. Consequently, *Turangalîla* is scored for a large orchestra with a solo piano part, and makes use of the Ondes Martenot—an early electronic instrument—for eerie glissandi and sustained melodic gestures. The work is written in ten movements and lasts in excess of 75 minutes. It was premiered by Leonard Bernstein and the BSO in 1949. Though *Turangalîla* is Messiaen's most popular orchestral work, it is often mistaken for his most typical; its secular subject material and relatively sparse use of bird songs makes it unique in his orchestral oeuvre. Along with the song cycles *Harawi* (1945) and *Cinq Rechants* (1948), *Turangalîla* is the second of a three-work cycle inspired by the "Tristan" myth. Compiled by Messiaen, the title is derived from Sanskrit and collectively means love song, and hymn to joy, time, movement, rhythm, life, and death.

Turangalîla contains many themes that relate to each of its ten movements, but there are also four larger, cyclic themes that recur throughout the work. The first cyclic theme is based on thirds and is most often played by fortissimo by the trombones. Messiaen refers to this as the "statue theme," metaphoric for the oppressive brutality of ancient Mexican monuments. The second "flower" theme is heard pianissimo in the clarinets, alluding to the colors of flowers. Messiaen considers the third "love" theme to be the most significant of the four. The fourth theme is a chain of chords that undergoes rhythmic, contrapuntal, and registral transformations.

Messiaen uses three rhythmic "characters" that function in contrapuntal augmentation (attackers), diminution (victims), and unchanging (observers) note values. He also makes extensive use of non-retrogradable rhythms, or rhythmic units that are the same forwards as backwards. Relating to architecture and other decorative arts, non-retrogradable rhythms are ordered around a central axis where two equivalent halves meet.

Turangalîla also displays Messiaen's vivid sense of orchestral color. The woodwinds are grouped in threes and have extensive solos, dense contrapuntal webs, bird songs, and highly colored harmonic collections. The brass are led by the trumpets, especially the brilliant piccolo trumpet in D, along with three trumpets in C, cornet, four horns, three trombones, and tuba. The string section is generally heard as a homogeneous group, with the exception of the ninth movement, where 13 individual string parts play independently of the orchestra. The percussion writing emphasizes pitched and metallic instruments such as xylophone, glockenspiel, celeste, gongs, and vibraphone. Coupled with the piano, the percussion section forms an orchestra within an orchestra, and bears a likeness to the Balinese gamelan. The solo piano part is concerto-like in scope, including fiery displays of virtuosity in the cadenzas, several bird songs, and its role as part of the gamelan percussion orchestra. The piano part was written for and dedicated to his wife Yvonne Loriod, as was the Ondes Martenot part for her sister Jeanne Loriod.

Turangalîla is also a study in contrasts: melismatic contrapuntal strands contrast with sustaining, block-like sonorities moving in homorhythm; loud and arresting orchestral sound with passages of near inaudibility; dense chromaticism with the major mode; mystery with ecstasy; and brightness with darkness. —*AMG*

Recommended:

- ○ **Messiaen: Turangalîla Symphony** / Chung (cond.), Y. Loriod, J. Loriod, Bastille Opera Orch. / DG 431781
- ○ **Messiaen: Turangalîla-Symphonie; Lutosławski: Symphony 3** / Salonen (cond.), Crossley, Murail, London PO / 1986 / CBS 42271
- ○ **Messiaen: Turangalîla-Symphonie** / Chailly (cond.), Thibaudet, Harada, Concertgebouw / 2003 / Decca 000047636

CONCERTO

Concert à quatre, for flute, cello, piano & orchestra (1990–1992)

In the last two years of his life, French composer Olivier Messiaen devoted most of his energies to the creation of his final large-scale work for orchestra, *Éclairs sur l'au delá*. Somewhere along the line, Messiaen received a commission from oboist Heinz Holliger for a new work, and Messiaen began to comply with this request even as *Éclairs sur l'au delá* was still in progress. When death came to Messiaen on April 27, 1992, *Éclairs sur l'au delá* was as yet unperformed, but the score was complete. In the case of the Holliger commission, by now titled *Concert à quatre*, Messiaen had produced four movements, of which the first and third movements were complete, but the second and fourth remained only in sketch form.

The second movement, it turned out, was an arrangement of an already existing piece, the *Vocalise-étude* originally composed in 1939 for voice and piano. Messiaen's widow, pianist Yvonne Loriod, fleshed out the sketches for the fourth movement Rondeau adding some of Messiaen's characteristic birdcalls for good measure. Composer George Benjamin, a former student of Messiaen, completed the orchestration with some advice from Holliger. It is called *Concert à quatre* as there are actually four soloists involved in the concerto, namely oboe (played originally by Holliger), cello (premiered by Mstislav Rostropovich), flute (played by Catherine Cantin), and piano (Loriod). One of the most striking things about the *Concert à quatre* is the fact that it embraces tonality with such enthusiasm—the "Vocalise" movement hearkens back to the world of the French Impressionists. While the *Concert à quatre* has its moments of explosiveness and violence, the overall feeling of the work is relaxed, as though Messiaen laid his pen aside after a day, and a life's work, done well, drifting off into a daydream from which, sadly, he was never to wake up. —*Uncle Dave Lewis*

Recommended:

- ○ **Messiaen: Concert à Quatre** / M-W. Chung (cond.), Rostropovich, Holliger, Loriod, Cantin, Bastille Opera Orch. / 1995 / DG 445947

Sept haïkaï, for piano, 13 winds, 6 percussion & 8 violins (1962)

Olivier Messiaen drew little distinction between his work as a composer and his interest in ornithology. The titles of several works advertise their feathered subject matter, and the list of birds whose calls turn up in one or more of Messiaen's pieces contains literally hundreds of entries. In *Sept Haïkaï: esquisses japonaises* (Seven Haiku: Japanese Sketches) from 1962, no less than 25 species are represented.

The combination and integration of these unique gestures within this work stand as evidence of Messiaen's deep belief that the song of a bird is not a just a mating or warning call—some noise or alert of pure utility; rather, it is pure (perhaps the purest) music, created by nature as such. The numerous birdcalls are intertwined with other processes at work in the *Seven Haiku.*

An elaborate incorporation of Indian tâlas can be found shaping the rhythmic figurations that comprise the Introduction. Messiaen's approach to rhythm finds many concordances in Indian music, particularly with regards to the idea of additive rhythm. In many works, Messiaen's rhythmic gestures defy the gridlike boundaries of the steady meters that house them, growing instead from their own internal divisions—expanding and contracting by eighth- or sixteenth notes, or strung together end to end in modular fashion without concern for whether they add up to nice round beat-numbers.

In the Introduction to the *Haiku*, rhythmic complexity occurs on vertical as well as horizontal planes, as the woodwinds and piano execute the same collection of tâla figures forwards and backwards simultaneously. One also finds an underlying melodic-rhythmic structure that hearkens back to the fourteenth century isorhythmic motet of Vitry and Machaut. In fact, the terms "talea" and "color," used to describe the respective rhythmic and melodic repetition schemes that constitute Ars Nova isorhythm, are frequently invoked to describe similar processes at work in Messiaen's music.

The instrumentation for which the piece was written lends itself to all manner of sonic evocations of Japan. The eight vibratoless violins that appear in the second movement ("Le parc de Nara et les lanternes de pierre") and return in the fourth ("Gagaku") imitate the chordal accompaniment of the *sho*, a Japanese mouth organ. The fourth movement also finds Messiaen replicating the sound of the *hichiriki* by combining its western cousin, the oboe, with the trumpet and horn; likewise, the piccolo and clarinet stand in for the *woteki*, a kind of flute. Throughout, a variety of tintinnabula add a rhythmic, ceremonial quality.

To these evocative references must be added the numerous birdcalls that permeate the piece. In addition to the mixed choruses of calls in the winds and brass, the dramatis personae for the third movement ("Yamanaka Cadenza") includes the Narcissus Flycatcher, the Grey-headed Bunting, and the Starlet, each of whom is represented by a piano cadenza. In both the third and the sixth movement ("Les oiseaux de Karuizawa"), the trumpet plays the prominent role of the Japanese Bush Warbler. More subtle bird references can be found in the fifth movement, "Miyajima et le torii dans la mer," continuing into the sixth. Messiaen is often found speaking of alliances between certain aural pitches and visual colors. As Malcolm Troup has pointed out (*The Messiaen Reader* [Faber and Faber, 1994, p. 427]), while Messiaen in the preface identifies eight birds as being represented in this section, only half are represented by their songs; the rest are present only in the mysterious musical painting of their plumage. *—Jeremy Grimshaw*

Recommended:

○ **Olivier Messiaen** / Boulez (cond.), Jones, Cleveland Orch. / DG 453478

○ **Messiaen** / Leeuw (cond.), Donohoe, Netherlands Wind Ens. / 1994 / Chandos 9301/2

ORCHESTRAL

L'Ascension, 4 meditations (1932–1933)

Although it may well be better known in its version for organ, Olivier Messiaen's *L'Ascension* of 1932–33 is the most famous of his early orchestral scores (early in this case meaning pre-*Turangalîla-symphonie*). Messiaen had in 1931 been appointed organist at L'Église de la Trinité, and by 1935 an organ version of *L'Ascension* had been finished; in truth, the work's conception seems to lie midway between the two media: one passage may seem wholly orchestral in design and execution (even in the organ version), while another may have trickled from Messiaen's fingers as he sat at his beloved La Trinité organ. That is not to say that the orchestral version of the work is anything but masterfully and magnificently scored, only to say that, try though he might, at that point in his life Messiaen could not wholly disassociate his music from the organ-bench upon which so much of it was first played. One major difference between the two versions must be noted: the third movement of the organ version is a completely different piece of music than the third movement of the orchestral version.

In the orchestral version, the four meditations, each of which testifies to the depth of Messiaen's Catholic faith, are: 1. "Majesté du Christ demandant sa gloire à son Père," 2. "Alléluias sereins d'une âme qui désire le ciel," 3. "Alléluia sur la trompette, alléluia sur la cymbale," and 4. "Prière du Christ montant vers son Père." Each movement has attached to it a sacred quotation. The first movement is marked Très lent et majestueux (Very slow and majestic), and is scored entirely for the wind instruments, who speak out boldly and clearly. No. 2 begins in like fashion (though now Bien modéré, clair), but soon allows entry to the strings; when the opening music of the movement is reprised after a very flexibly-written middle portion, the winds are reinforced in dramatic fashion by the full contingent of strings, triple-forte. The third movement hustles and bustles along, Vif et joyeux (Fast and joyfully), beginning with a trumpet fanfare and then bursting into a veritable *perpetuum mobile* into which the cymbal figures prominently (as one would expect from the title). The solemn, slow final meditation is a complete contrast. *—Blair Johnston*

Recommended:

○ **Messiaen: Turangalîla Symphony; L'ascension** / Wit (cond.), Katowice Polish Radio Orch. & Chorus / 2000 / Naxos 554478–79

Eclairs sur l'au-delá (1988–1992)

Olivier Messiaen's *Eclairs sur l'Au-Dela* (Illuminations of the Beyond) was commissioned in 1987 by the New York Philharmonic Orchestra. It is a vast work, written for a 128-piece orchestra (including ten each of flutes and clarinets and a veritable platoon of percussion instruments) and cast in 11 movements collectively lasting over an hour. The titles of the individual movements, with one exception, are taken from the book of *Revelations*, and collectively represent the Messiaen's reflections on what awaits a soul passing from this world to the next. The work represents a celebration and a synthesis of all the musics Messiaen loved to write: music of the stars, music praising God, and bird song, to name but three.

"Apparition du Christ glorieux" (Apparition of Christ in Glory), the first movement, is written solely for symphonic winds, which play a broad, stately theme in complete unison, only occasionally becoming louder to emphasize the end of a phrase. This instrumentation gives the movement an ethereal yet grand sound, which finds a culmination in the long, loud, bright chord that ends the movement. From there, the music moves along different avenues in each movement. Some movements emphasize bird songs: "L'Oiseau-lyre et la Ville-fiancee" (The Lyrebird and the Bridal City), the third movement, is taken up entirely with the music of the superb lyrebird, and the ninth movement, "Plusieurs Oiseaux des arbres de Vie" (Many Birds From the Tree of Life), features 18 simultaneous bird songs on 18 solo woodwinds. Others feature Messiaen's rhythmic cycles, like "Les Elus marques du sceau" (The Elect Marked With a Seal), the fourth movement, which underpins more bird song with three simultaneous cycles in the strings, gongs, and bells; and the sixth movement, "Les Sept Anges aux sept trompettes" (The Seven Angels With Seven Trumpets), which features a Judgment Day melody on the horns, trombones, and bassoons played over an expanding and contracting rhythmic cycle.

Messiaen's passion for star-music comes to the fore in the second movement, "La Constellation du Sagittaire" (The Constellation of Sagittarius), which uses string glissandi to represent galactic nebulae, and in "Les Étoiles et la Gloire" (The Stars and Glory), the eighth and longest movement, which builds itself on a motif composed of ascending tritones until it finally reaches a chorale-coda, the only time in the work the entire orchestra plays together, praising God.

But the emotional heart of the work is in two movements written for strings. "Demeurer dans l'Amour" (Abide in Love), the fifth movement, has a long, slow melody played on muted violins, supported by violas and cellos. The melodic line seems to be straining upward, and the violins acquire a searing yet glistening tone as they move up to a high register. The instrumentation is almost the same, but the mood is entirely different, in the last movement, "Le Christ, lumiere de Paradis," or "Christ, Light of Paradise." Here the violin melody moves in such a way that it seems to stand still, accompanied by the lower strings, with a halo drawn around it by a triangle constantly tinkling in the background.

Messiaen's vast work draws to a close on a chord similar to that which ended the first movement, a broad, supremely luminous, restful and fulfilled chord, with the triangle promising the divine. It is a fitting end to an astonishingly diverse and resourceful work that is unified by the sheer energy and vitality of Messiaen's devotion. *—Andrew Malone*

Recommended:

○ **Messiaen: Éclairs sur l'au-delà** / Chung (cond.), Bastille Opera Orch. / 1994 / DG 439929

Et exspecto resurrectionem mortuorum (1963–1964)

Messiaen's *Et expecto resurrectionem mortuorum* (I Await the Resurrection of the Dead) is for an instrumental ensemble of 18 woodwinds, 16 brass, and a metallic percussion ensemble. The work was commissioned by André Malraux, the French Minister of Cultural Affairs. At Malraux's request, *Et expecto* received a private premiere in the Sainte-Chapelle in Paris before the public premiere in front of General de Gaulle in the Chartres Cathedral. The stained glass lining both cathedrals created a fitting aura in which to witness the work, although Messiaen also envisioned it being performed outdoors at the foot of mountain ranges, which he hoped would enhance the music's monumental, timeless, and natural imagery. Although Messiaen acknowledged the existence of death and suffering—himself a prisoner of war in Silesia—he refused Malraux's request to write a requiem commemorating the outbreak of the two World Wars and those who died. Instead, he wrote *Et expecto* to emphasize his belief in the Resurrection. In contrast to *Chronochromie* (1960), Messiaen's previous large-scale work which imagines a natural world of birds, mountains and motionless time, *Et expecto* looks ahead to a world that is to come.

The piece unfolds from five large, block-like sections, each relating to quotations from the Catholic Scriptures. The first begins with a monophonic prayer theme emerging from the lowest depths of the orchestra. The second section revolves around three motives: a six note, "lightning flash"—the first four notes of which are related by retrograde to the prayer theme—which is transformed into vertical chords, questions and answers heard in the woodwind duets, and a chorale led by the trumpets. The third section is also a three part structure. Here Messiaen used two bird songs, including the Amazonian uirapuru—traditionally heard at the moment of death—to symbolize Christ's inner voice waking the dead from their sleep; signaling an impending resurrection. The virtuosic singing of the calandra lark symbolizes celestial joy and the gift of agility. The bird songs are heard in the full ensemble of woodwinds, the ringing of the tubular bells, and then as massive orchestral chords. In the fourth section, the crashing of tam-tams, heard in recurring cells of three strokes, represents the moment of resurrection as bells ring, trumpets chant, and the lark sounds from the woodwinds. In the final section, prayer melodies from the first section and a long sequence of colorful chords form the closing chorale. *—AMG*

Recommended:

- ○ **Messiaen** / Leeuw (cond.), George, Donohoe, Netherlands Wind Ens. / 1994 / Chandos 9301/2
- ○ **Messiaen: Chronochromie; La Ville d'en haut; Et exspecto** / Boulez (cond.), Cleveland Orch. / 1995 / DG 445827

CHORAL

O sacrum convivium! (1937)

This short communion motet for unaccompanied choir (or four soloists), though an early work, is pure Messiaen in its harmonic richness (F sharp major, yet progressing through unusual intervals) and its sense of gradual motion derived from plainchant. The phrasing is in very stretched-out patterns based on speech rhythms. It begins pianissimo and remains at low dynamic levels, except for a forte outburst on the words "et futurae gloriae nobis pignus datur"; the motet then recedes back into quiet ecstasy. The text in English translation is: "O sacred feast/in which Christ is taken/the memory of his passion is renewed/the mind is filled with grace/and a promise of future glory is given us/Alleluia." The work is in Messiaen's "early style" but already has elements of his later developments, primarily in the open rhythm of its diatonically based, yet not easily classifiable, harmonies and its clear, transfixing modular constructions. *—James Reel*

Recommended:

- ○ **A Rose in Winter** / Warland (cond.), Dale Warland Singers / 1997 / d'Note 1022

VOCAL

Poèmes pour Mi, song cycle for soprano & piano (1936–1937)

Although several smaller vocal works precede it, Olivier Messiaen's *Poèmes pour Mi* (1936) stands as his first major song cycle and his first vocal work to be orchestrated. Originally written for soprano and piano, the work appeared in an orchestral version in 1937. It was dedicated to the composer's first wife, violinist Claire Delbos; "Mi" was his nickname for her. Like his later song cycle *Chants de terre et de ciel* (1938), which was written after the birth of their son and is concerned with the themes of family and parenthood, *Poèmes pour Mi* is a sentimental and deeply personal work that explores the spiritual aspects of marriage. The cycle consists of two books containing nine songs: four in the first book, five in the second. The theme of the first book is the preparation for marriage while the second book is concerned with marriage as a sacrament, a spiritual union. The text for the cycle, as with all of Messiaen's vocal works, was written by the composer. Throughout the work, dramatic declamations depicting the trials and terrors of the natural world are balanced by brief and quiet forays into the intimacies of the couple's relationship.

Poèmes pour Mi was written during a time of experimentation in which Messiaen began to explore different rhythmic systems. Greek and Indian meters and rhythmic patterns are in evidence, and foreshadow the significance that rhythm was to have in all of his later music. Canons between the singer and ensemble help the singer to grasp his complex rhythmic language. The piano version is also free of a time signature and bar lines, allowing the performers a greater rhythmic flexibility for shaping the floating melodic lines. The influence of plainchant is heard in the cumulative intensity of the melismas that end each sentence of text. The harmonic language falls consistently within Messiaen's tonal/modal universe, often resulting in subtle colorings that suggest polymodality rather than the more densely chromatic language of his later instrumental works like *Chronochromie* (1960), or the more synthetic hybrid found in the *Turangalila-Symphonie* (1948). *—Alexander Carpenter*

Recommended:

- ○ **Olivier Messiaen** / Boulez (cond.), Pollet, Cleveland Orch. / DG 453478
- ○ **Messiaen: Harawi; Poemes pour Mi** / Negro / 1975 / Bis 86

OPERA

Saint François d'Assise (1975–1983)

Messiaen, though a lifelong lover of opera, was particular about the genre and doubted from the start his ability to write a good opera. As of 1975, he had not written a large-scale vocal work since *La Transfiguration de Notre-Seigneur Jésus-Christ*, completed in 1969. Messiaen claimed throughout his life that in the history of opera there were perhaps only ten true masterpieces, the rest suffering from musical, or, more likely, dramatic flaws. Though he insisted that he had no gift for opera, Messiaen was persuaded to compose *Saint François d'Assise* as a commission for the Paris Opéra.

Messiaen chose to write an opera on the subject of Saint Francis as an alternative to a Passion based on Christ that he felt unworthy to undertake. The opera is a huge work, one which took Messiaen four years to compose and another four to orchestrate. Completed in 1983, it is over four hours long, with a 2,000-page score. Its orchestral and choral forces are enormous, and the work is nearly impossible to accommodate in most theaters. The work consists of eight "Franciscan scenes," with three each in the opera's first two acts, and two in the last. Musically, the opera represents a coming together of many of the disparate techniques from Messiaen's entire œuvre, including bird song, repetition, plainchant, 12-tone composition mixed with triadic harmony, and the use of modes. In all, it is an almost impossibly diverse work, a mixture of declamatory and lyrical vocal writing, and of sparse angular passages and brilliant, lush choral writing. This opera was, in Messiaen's view, his life's work, and he knew, as his health was failing in the mid-1980s, that he would not be able to create anything comparable to it before he died. *—Alexander Carpenter*

Synopsis:

Act One. The action takes place in various Italian churches in the thirteenth century. In Act One, the first scene, "La croix" (The Cross), Francis is traveling with Leon and tells him that perfect joy is found in suffering when one accepts it as a meditation upon and communion with the sufferings of Christ on the cross. In the second, "Les laudes" (The Lauds), Francis and the monks pray and Francis recites his famous poem, "Lodi delle creature," praising God for the creation of their brother the wind, their sister the water, their mother the earth, and the other works of nature. He also sings of his desire to love the outcast in the person of a leper. In the last scene, "Le baiser au lepreux" (The Kiss to the Leper), a Leper bitterly condemns the pain and rejection he is suffering because of his disease. Francis emerges and tells him that he must find happiness in offering his pain as penitence, but the Leper angrily tells him how the monks try to keep from vomiting when they see him. The angel sings to them that God is love and that those who live in love live in God and God in them. Francis asks the Leper to forgive him for not having loved him enough, and kisses him. The Leper suddenly leaps up, transformed into a young, healthy, well-dressed young man, and dances for joy. When he breaks down in tears that he is unworthy of being healed, Francis says that he, too, is unworthy. They pray, and the choir sings that to those who have loved much, all is forgiven.

Act Two. The second act opens with "L'ange voyageur" (The Wandering Angel). The Angel, wrapped in a magnificent robe that only the audience can perceive, comes to the monastery door and asks questions of the monks. Brother Elie is in no mood to discuss theology and curtly tells the Angel to leave, but Brother Bernard emerges and speaks to the Angel, and the Angel blesses him. In the next scene, "L'ange musicien" (The Angel Musician), Francis is praying and the Angel plays heavenly music to him. Francis is so overwhelmed by its beauty that he faints, and when three other monks come and revive him, he says that the music nearly carried his soul away. The last scene is "Le prêche aux oiseaux" (The Sermon to the Birds). Francis and Brother Massée enter, and Francis tells him the names of the various birds, calling each their brother or sister. They sit and Francis has a vision of New Caledonia, an island "like an exclamation point," where the colors gleam like those of an opal. The birds sing in a *petit concert des oiseaux*, their voices represented by various instruments, and he preaches to them, telling them of all the gifts God has given them and to praise their creator. He blesses them and, after a moment of silence, the birds sing again in the *grand concert des oiseaux*, then form a cross in the sky before they disappear. As they leave, Francis tells Brother Massée that the birds give them an example; they own nothing and yet God feeds them. If one searches only for God's kingdom and its justice, one will receive everything else.

Act Three. The last act takes place in two scenes. In the first, "Les stigmates" (The Stigmata), Francis is praying outside. He asks Jesus for two favors: the first is to be allowed to feel the same pain Jesus felt during the Passion, and the second to be allowed to feel the same love that enabled Jesus to accept such suffering. The chorus sings in response that in order to love Jesus, one must become him, enduring the same wounds and suffering. Francis wonders if he is even worthy, and the chorus sings of the divine nature of God. As the chorus calls to him, Francis receives the stigmata, wounds replicating those of Jesus. The chorus continues that many desire the heavenly kingdom but few agree to bear the cross, and that if Francis will carry the cross, it will carry him. He is rapt in ecstasy. In the last scene, "La mort et la nouvelle vie" (Death and New Life), Francis is dying inside the church, with the monks gathered around him. He bids farewell to all temporal things, including the monks, the churches he has known, and the birds. Francis blesses God for having created death to be our sister. Three of the monks sing a prayer. The Angel appears, but is visible only to Francis, repeating the words from "Le baiser au lepreux." The Leper, too, appears, and the Angel says that the Leper died a holy death and they have come to lead Francis to paradise, going on to tell Francis that he will hear the music of the invisible. The Angel and Leper disappear, and as Francis calls out to God to blind him with his overwhelming truth, he dies. Brother Léon says that he has departed like a friendly silence, or a tear, or a butterfly. They leave, reverently carrying the body away. A blinding light shines where Francis' body lay, and the chorus sings that from pain, weakness, and ignominy, God resurrects strength, glory, and joy. *—Ann Feeney*

Recommended:

- ○ **Messiaen: Saint François d'Assise** / Nagano (cond.), Ortner, Upshaw, Van Dam, Aler, Halle Orch. / 1999 / DG 445176
- ○ **Messiaen: Saint François d'Assise** / Ozawa (cond.), Van Dam, Senechal, Eda-Pierre, Riegel, Paris National Opera Theater Orch., Paris National Opera Orch. / 1998 / MS 1193

Metropolitan Opera Orchestra

f. 1883, New York, NY
Ensemble

Though the first season of the Metropolitan Opera came in 1883–84, efforts to found the New York-based company began in 1880, led by the Morgan and Vanderbilt families. Its first season was launched with Henry Abbey as company manager and Auguste Vianesi as music director and conductor. Vianesi's tenure was short-lived. The Opera's board appointed its secretary, Edmund Stanton, to contract singers appropriate for German opera, which he ably did. He also engaged Wagner protégé Anton Seidl to become music director and conductor in 1886.

Seidl worked well with the singers, and also helped shape the orchestra into a first-rate ensemble. Irish-American composer Victor Herbert, then one of the finest cellists in Europe, joined the orchestra in 1886. His wife, Therese Herbert-Förster, had been engaged to sing at the Met by Stanton. Solid and talented though the orchestra was in its early days, it was the singers, of course, who drew the attention. Indeed, some were making over 50,000 dollars per year by the late 1890s, where orchestra players earned one-tenth that amount and less. Even in the 1930s orchestra members typically were offered starting salaries of less than 10,000 dollars, far less than that of the singers, but substantially more than most orchestras in the United and States and Europe were paying personnel.

In 1908, Toscanini made his debut at the Met. He would serve as music director for seven years, and arguably his tenure resulted in stronger musicianship in the orchestra's ranks, even though he did not always have full control. Indeed, Toscanini shared the podium for two years with Gustav Mahler and for another with Sicilian conductor Francesco Spetrino. The orchestra was then, as it had been throughout its early years, comprised largely of players from Germany. Gradually it would draw on other European nationalities and even employ a fair number of American players.

On December 25, 1931, the Metropolitan Opera began radio broadcasts, which have endured to this day. In this venue, the orchestra's role in performance became more conspicuous, since the audience could obviously not see the action, but only hear the music. Television broadcasts began on March 10, 1940, featuring excerpts from various operas. The next one would not take place until November 29, 1948, with a performance of Verdi's *Otello*. Television broadcasts have endured up to the current day, with semi-regular appearances on the PBS network.

In the war and postwar eras, the orchestra was led by some of the greatest conductors of the day, like George Szell, a regular from 1942 to 1946, and Fritz Reiner, music director from 1949 to 1953. By this time the orchestra was probably the finest opera house ensemble in the world. At least some of their success could be credited to the dynamic directorship of Rudolf Bing, who held the post from 1950 to 1972. Under his leadership not only did the number of subscribers more than triple, but, by general consensus, artistic standards of the individual singers, chorus, and orchestra rose considerably.

In 1986, James Levine took over as artistic director and has held the post into the new century. He has made a number of successful recordings with the Met organization, which returned to the recording studio after a several-decades long absence. The orchestra has been called upon to perform in a number of new works, including modern ones like Glass' *The Voyage* (1992) and Harbison's *The Great Gatsby* (1999), as well as early twentieth century masterpieces like Busoni's *Doktor Faust* and Prokofiev's *The Gambler*, both in the 2000–01 season. *—Robert Cummings*

Recommended:

- ○ **Battle & Domingo Live** / Levine (cond.), Battle, Domingo, Wray, Metropolitan Opera Orch. / DG 445552
- ○ **Maestro of the Met: James Levine & Friends** / Levine (cond.), Pavarotti, Upshaw, Domingo, Bartoli, Metropolitan Opera Orch. / 1995 / DG 449229
- ○ **Levine's 25th Anniversary Metropolitan Opera Gala** / Levine (cond.), Terfel, Fleming, Domingo, Ramey, Metropolitan Opera Orch. / DG 449177

Edgar Meyer

b. Nov. 24, 1960, Oklahoma City, OK
Bassist

Edgar Meyer emerged in the 1990s as one of the world's most talented string bass players, at home, remarkably, in both the classical repertory and in bluegrass. He is also a composer whose works achieved wide diffusion in the late 1990s; they served as cornerstones in the efforts of Sony to forge new audiences for classical music by offering compositions with a direct, accessible musical language.

Born in Oklahoma City, Meyer was the son of a bass player. When he was two or three years old he started imitating his father by holding a broom, pretending it was a bass. He started learning on a real instrument at five years old, taking lessons from his father. The instrument was a 1933 bass made in Czechoslovakia and in use, hanging from someone's ceiling, as a flower planter. Meyer has said that he grew up with the bass as his primary means of personal expression, and became committed to the instrument so early that he is unable to remember a time when he was not playing it. Later he studied with Stuart Sankey, but still credits his father as his primary teacher. He attended Indiana University, studying with James Buswell. Meyer won numerous competitions and from the beginning forged a crossover career, playing with classical musicians as well as popular and country acts. What steered him toward country music was his encounter, in his early twenties, with the virtuosic and complex progressive bluegrass music of the 1980s, as exemplified by such performers as Sam Bush, Jerry Douglas, and Béla Fleck. He has toured and/or recorded with Garth Brooks, Mary Chapin Carpenter, Hank Williams Jr., Emmylou Harris, James Taylor, Lyle Lovett, Reba McEntire, Travis Tritt, the Chieftains, the Indigo Girls, Yo-Yo Ma, Paul Shaffer and the CBS Orchestra, Joshua Bell, and Mark O'Connor. From 1986 to 1992 he was a member of a progressive bluegrass band called Strength in Numbers.

He began to compose around 1990, primarily to write down things that had emerged from "noodling around" and improvising, wanting to "codify" them into pieces. He was a regular performer at the Santa Fe Chamber Music Festival from 1985 to 1993, and six of his earliest compositions were intended for performance there. He has composed a double bass concerto, a bass quartet, a work called *Trout Variations* (based on the Schubert song), a string trio, a violin concerto (premiered and recorded by Hilary Hahn), and a double concerto for bass and cello. Much of his music is influenced by bluegrass and traditional American folk styles. In the late 1990s and early 2000s, Meyer became an important participant in the American-flavored crossover albums of cellist Yo-Yo Ma.

Meyer records exclusively for Sony. He is married to violinist Connie Heard; they have one son. He has been a member of the Chamber Music Society of Lincoln Center since 1994, and in that same year became the first bassist to win the Avery Fisher Career Grant.*—Joseph Stevenson*

Recommended:

- ○ **Meyer: Bottesini Concertos** / Wolff (cond.), Meyer, Ma, Bell, St. Paul CO / 2002 / Sony 60956
- ○ **Bach: Unaccompanied Cello Suites 1, 2 & 5** / Meyer / 2000 / Sony 89183
- ○ **Music for Two** / Meyer, Fleck / 2004 / Sony 92106
- ○ **Heartland: An Appalachian Anthology** / Bell, Ma, Meyer, Taylor, O'Connor, Marshall, Mock, Fleck / 2001 / Sony 89683

Sabine Meyer

b. Mar. 30, 1959, Crailsheim, Germany
Clarinetist

The breadth of clarinetist Sabine Meyer's repertoire is matched by her dedication to collaborations with other, equally skilled musicians. She received her first music lessons from her father, clarinetist Karl Meyer, and then went on to study with Otto Hermann in Stuttgart and Hans Deinzer in Hannover. She was 16 when she made her professional debut. She joined Munich's Bavarian Radio Symphony Orchestra for a time, then in 1982, Herbert von Karajan created something of an international stir by appointing her as solo clarinetist for the Berlin Philharmonic, going against the orchestra's tradition of not admitting female musicians. However, she only remained with the orchestra for a year, as the demand grew for her to perform as soloist with other orchestras and chamber ensembles. In addition to having performed with more than 80 professional orchestras in Germany and her regular appearances throughout Europe, North America, and Japan, her work has taken her to Brazil, Africa, Israel, and Australia. Meyer's chamber music partners have included Barbara Hendricks, Gidon Kremer, Tabea Zimmermann, Heinrich Schiff, Oleg Maisenberg, Lars Vogt, the Vienna String Sextet; the Hagen, Cleveland, and Alban Berg quartets; and the Tokyo String Quartet, with whom she toured in 2001–2002. In 1983 she formed the Clarone Trio with her brother, Wolfgang Meyer, and her husband, Reiner Wehle, and in 1988 the Bläserensemble Sabine Meyer. With the Trio, she has recorded with jazz clarinetists Eddie Daniels and Michael Riessler. Meyer's recordings had garnered six ECHO awards from the Deutsche Phonoakademie as of 2003, the most for any one classical artist at the time. Her recordings include most of the standard concerto, solo, and chamber music repertory for clarinet, but she has worked assiduously with contemporary composers to present new works as well. The award-winning album *Modern Works for Wind Ensemble* features works by Denisov, Hosokawa, Castiglioni, Obst, and Raskatov, and she has also premiered pieces by Harald Genzmer, Marc-André Dalbavie, and Manfred Trojahn. In 1993 Meyer was appointed professor at the Lübeck Academy of Music. She makes a specific emphasis on solid technical training for her students to aid their tone quality. What little time she has left after all her performing, recording, and teaching engagements she spends with her husband and two children in Lübeck, where she also raises horses. *—Patsy Morita*

Recommended:

- ○ **Dvořák & Myslivecek: Serenades for Wind Instruments** / Meyer, Munich Wind Ensemble / 1995 / EMI 55512
- ○ **Mozart, Debussy, Takemitsu** / Abbado (cond.), Meyer, Berlin PO / 1999 / Angel 56832
- ○ **Weber: Clarinet Concertos; Concertino; Clarinet Quintet** / Blomstedt (cond.), Faerber (cond.), Meyer, Dresden Staatskapelle, Wurttemberg CO / 2003 / EMI 67989
- ○ **Brahms, Berg: Works for Clarinet and Piano** / Meyer, Vogt (piano) / 2003 / EMI 557524

Giacomo Meyerbeer

b. Sep. 5, 1791, Vogelsdorf, Germany, **d.** May 2, 1864, Paris, France

Composer: Opera

Giacomo Meyerbeer (1791–1864) was a major figure in French opera in the first half of the nineteenth century. In fact, he had become recognized as Europe's leading active composer of opera by the 1830s and 1840s. He also wrote German and Italian operas with some success, *Il crociato in Egitto* being a prominent example in the latter vein. Meyerbeer was known to create unusual combinations of sound in brilliant and striking orchestration, and he introduced many innovations in opera. *Robert le diable*, *Les Huguenots* and *L'africaine* are among his finest operas. Meyerbeer was born on September 5, 1791, in Vogelsdorf, near Berlin. He showed talent at an early age, and studied piano with Franz Lauska. His skills developed quickly, and at age eleven he made his concert debut in Berlin. He subsequently studied composition with B.A. Weber.

His first work for the stage was the 1809–10 ballet *Der Fischer und das Milchmädchen*. Shortly after its premiere, he went to Darmstadt to study with Abbé Vogler, whose students then included, among others, Carl Maria von Weber. After nearly two years of instruction, during which he wrote two operas and numerous other works, Meyerbeer left for Munich, ready to test his skills as a composer and performer. It was there that his second opera (but first surviving), *Jephtas Gelübde*, was unsuccessfully premiered in December, 1812. Other works for the stage would follow, but none with success.

Yet his keyboard career was moving in the opposite direction; he received many accolades and was considered one of the leading virtuosos of the day. In November 1814, Meyerbeer departed Munich for Paris. Two years later he traveled to Rome, and for the next nine years, made Italy his home, turning out a half-dozen operas, including *Romilda e Costanze* (1817), and *Il crociato in Egitto* (1824), probably his most successful stage effort of that time. He traveled to Paris in 1825, confident he could conquer Parisian operatic audiences with the same success he had achieved in Italy. His first great success there came with *Robert le diable*; the 1831 premiere was a sensation, receiving acclaim not only in Paris but throughout Europe in subsequent performances. Five years later he scored another triumph with his opera *Les Huguenots*. Meyerbeer met the admiring Wagner in 1839, and helped to mount his *Rienzi* and *The Flying Dutchman*.

In 1842, Meyerbeer became the Prussian General Music Director in Berlin, also serving as Court composer and director of music at the Court. His opera *Les Huguenots* premiered in 1842, providing him with yet another success. Owing to a dispute, he stepped down as General Music Director in 1848, but kept his duties at Court. Meyerbeer began to look toward Paris once more and in 1849 his opera *Le prophète*, a work he had begun in 1836 and finished in 1840, scored another success. In his final years Meyerbeer worked on an opera he had begun in 1837, *L'africaine*. He finished it only in 1864, but did not live to see its 1865 premiere. He died on May 2, 1864. *—Robert Cummings*

OPERA

L'africaine (1864)

L'africaine was Meyerbeer's final opera. It was in production at the time of his death, and the renowned musicologist Fétis was asked to oversee the final touches before the premiere. The work is a grand opera in the heroic manner and contains many romantic elements popular with the audiences of the day. There are no fewer than three love triangles, a prison, a sleep scene, a sinister and vengeful African or Indian, storm-tossed ships that end up wrecked on an exotic continent, Indian natives and Brahmin rituals, trees with a poisonous fragrance, and self-sacrificing lovers who die by that fragrance.

The opera was premiered at the Paris Opéra on April 28, 1865. The work was a popular triumph and was performed in opera houses until the early twentieth century.

The libretto was inspired by a poem called "Le mancenillier" (The Manchineel Tree) by Millevoye, telling of a tree with a poisonous fragrance and a pair of lovers. Although Meyerbeer and Eugène Scribe, his librettist for the work, began the opera in 1837, they quickly set it aside to work on *Le Prophète*. When that work was done they again turned to *L'africaine* but yet again set it aside, finally finishing a first draft in 1843. However, even that was rewritten and reworked. The action in the original libretto took place in Africa and Spain, but the final revision, begun in 1857 placed the story in Portugal, made the lead character Vasco da Gama, and had the "Africans" now hailing from India or Madagascar. References to Brahmin rituals and Indian gods were never taken out, although Fétis titled the opera "L'africaine" after the character of Sélika. In the original libretto, she had been an African queen who had been sold into captivity by slavers. Scribe died in 1861, and Meyerbeer had more than one other librettist help him complete the work. Then Meyerbeer himself passed away in 1864, leaving the finishing touches to those in charge of the production.

L'africaine contains some of Meyerbeer's most beautiful music, and love is the predominant motive for all of the music making. Inès is immediately set up as the romantic lead in Act One of the opera; she is given passionately florid melody and coloratura solos. Her "Romance" characterizes her ardor for the valiant Vasco as heroic, and it is their love which is bound to triumph through the trials of the opera. However, Act Two is devoted in part to establishing the relationship between Sélika, the Indian queen, and Vasco. She adores him and sings him an exquisitely erotic *sommeil* song while he lies sleeping and vulnerable in the prison of the Inquisitor. Later, when she saves Vasco's life, she and Vasco enjoy what amounts to a love duet. Finally, in Act Four, their love is mutually recognized in an Indian wedding ceremony. They have a passionate duet, after which Sélika realizes that she must relinquish Vasco. Her self-effacement and self-sacrifice forces her to give up her life for her beloved's happiness, and the opera closes with the ecstatic death of Sélika as she inhales the toxic perfume of the manchineel trees and suffers visions of her beloved's return.

The Inquisitor, Don Pédro, and the colorful character of Nesuko who invokes the Indian gods against the sailors, are adequate villains for the piece. The feeling of the original poem with the image of a poisonous fragrance comes through strongly at the close of the opera, and one feels that the entire work is something of a metaphor. *—Rita Laurance*

Synopsis:

Act One. Two years previously, two ships had set out from Portugal to tour the African coast, but they have not been heard from since. Vasco da Gama was one of those serving on the ships, and his fiancée Inès, the daughter of the admiral Don Diego, has been left behind in Lisbon to grieve. As the opera opens, the Admiral has called his daughter to him. As she is preparing to go, she tells her servant Anna of her hopes that Vasco is still alive and of her tender memories of their final moments together. However, when she meets with her father, he tells her that it is his feeling that Vasco da Gama has been lost forever. He wants her to marry Don Pedro, the head of the Royal Council. Inès mourns for the loss of her beloved.

The Royal Council of Portugal convenes, and while they are meeting, a soldier arrives. It is Vasco da Gama. He is the only survivor of the shipwreck. He has brought with him two African slaves, and wants to convince the council to send another expedition. He believes that there is a land beyond Africa, and that the appearance of the slaves proves it. Don Pedro, in an effort to discredit his rival, tells the council that Vasco is blaspheming against the Bible. After all, no lands beyond Africa are mentioned in the Old Testament. He convinces the Council that Vasco is insane, and when Vasco insults them for refusing to fund another expedition, they have him imprisoned.

Act Two. In the prison cell of Vasco da Gama, he is asleep next to the two slaves. They are Sélika and Nélusko, and they come from Madagascar. Sélika is the queen of their country, and both were captured by African slave traders and sold to da Gama. Sélika is madly in love with Vasco, but knows of his affections for Inès. She sings him a lullaby as he lies sleeping, and Nélusko is in turn jealous of Vasco. He tries to murder the sleeping sailor, but Sélika intervenes.

Don Pedro and Inès arrive at the prison cell. Inès has married Don Pedro in order to secure Vasco's freedom. They come with the news that the King of Portugal has agreed to finance Vasco's expedition, with Don Pedro at its head. Vasco gives Sélika to Inès as a gift, and Don Pedro takes Nélusko with him to be his guide. When Vasco discovers that Inès has married Don Pedro, he is completely despondent.

Act Three. Don Pedro has brought Inès and her servants with him. All of the sailors and servants are happily at work, out on the open sea. Little do they know, but Nélusko is guiding their ships into a coral reef, where they will all be destroyed and drowned. Don Alvar tries to tell Don Pedro of their danger. Two of their ships have already been lost. However, a storm is brewing, and Nélusko convinces them that only he can guide their ships to safety. He frightens the crew with stories of the god of storms, promising disaster and death, and threatens them with beatings.

Another ship is ahead of them, commanded by Vasco da Gama. He has also set out on the same expedition, although he has not been financed by the government. He comes aboard Don Pedro's ship and tries to warn them that they are headed for disaster, but Don Pedro considers Vasco his sworn enemy, and so refuses to be advised by him. He orders his men to kill Vasco, but Sélika takes Inès hostage, threatening to kill her if Vasco is not released. When Don Pedro doesn't kill him, Sélika puts down her weapon, only to be outfoxed by Don Pedro. He threatens to kill Sélika and Nélusko as well. The violence of the storm intervenes, and the boat is stranded on a coral reef. Natives of Madagascar take control of the boat, and murder most of those aboard. When they find Sélika, they bow before their queen and offer up a prayer.

Act Four. Sélika is honored as Queen of Madagascar, but forced to take a pledge to kill any foreigners trespassing on their land. Inès and her women are led into a grove of sweetly scented trees whose poisonous fragrance will put them to sleep forever. Vasco is brought before Sélika, and the people want him killed. In order to save his life, Sélika tells all that they are married. Thinking that Inès is already dead, Vasco agrees to the marriage, and he and Sélika go through with the marriage ritual. He also has begun to reciprocate her love for him, and they have a tender duet.

Act Five. Although the other Portuguese women have succumbed to the poisonous fragrance of the mancanilla trees, Inès has managed to escape to the gardens of the queen. There, Vasco finds her, and is overcome with tenderness and love. Sélika is at first jealous, and seeks revenge against the two lovers. But after seeing them together for a while, she decides to let them return to Portugal. She has Nélusko lead them to their ship, and then meet her under a large manchineel tree. As Vasco and Inès leave, Sélika inhales the poisonous fragrance, and is carried away by an ecstatic vision of being reunited with Vasco. As the poison takes hold of her system, Nélusko returns, only to find his beloved Sélika dying. Her people join them just as he takes her in his arms, and resolves to die with her.—*Rita Laurance*

Recommended:

○ **Meyerbeer: L'africaine** / (live: 1973) / Perisson (cond.), Domingo, Verrett, Caballe, Estes / 1999 / Gala 100605

○ **Meyerbeer: L'africaine** / (live: 1977) / Albrecht (cond.), Milnes, Arroyo, Rydl, Hermann, Bavaria Radio Orch. / 2001 / Myto 11235

Dinorah (Le pardon de Ploërmel) (1859)

Dinorah, or The pardon of Ploërmel, is one of Giacomo Meyerbeer's few forays into the world of the opéra-comique. The music and the libretto were almost completely his own creation. He had help from two librettists at its inception, but he expanded the initial one-act opera into a three-act work entirely on his own. The original libretto was by Barbier and Carre, and was derived from an old Breton legend about the pardon of the Blessed Virgin. Meyerbeer set the libretto, and then presented it to Perrin, the director of the Paris Opéra-Comique, who suggested that he expand it.

The resultant work is stunningly imaginative. It contains magical elements, a pastoral setting, dazzling vocalizing, and a plot worthy of a grand opera. The opera belongs to that nineteenth century genre which places the prima donna as the central force behind the story and music. Nevertheless, the story gave Meyerbeer ample opportunity for ensemble pieces as well. The two male protagonists, Hoël and Corentin, are often found in trio with Dinorah's virtuosic soprano coloratura. However, the plot also gives rise to duos containing a buffo element. The orchestrations contain storm music, delicate accompaniments, virtuosic duos with the voices, and dramatic effects. The pastoral setting is given a religious backdrop, as the people celebrate the feast of the Virgin and even close the opera in prayer. Meyerbeer used the chorus to open each act and set the stage for the story, but leaves the main body of the story telling to the three protagonists. He also composed a pastoral tableau for small choruses at the beginning of Act Three that acts as a point of repose before the dramatic conclusion to the opera.

Meyerbeer's *Dinorah* was so popular with the public that it remained in the repertoire of the Opéra-Comique of Paris until the end of the nineteenth century and beyond. By 1900 it was gaining popularity internationally. The incredible coloratura vocalizing of Dinorah is used to depict the imbalance of her mind, her light personality, and to cement her importance as the central character in the opera. The most famous number in the opera is known as the "Shadow Song" and occurs in the second act. Dinorah dances a mazurka with her shadow in the light of the moon. The elegant melody of Dinorah's vocal solo is elaborated with virtuosic fioritura. As a cloud passes over the moon, Dinorah's shadow disappears, and she sings a reflective middle section, full of sad, elegiac-like reverie. When her shadow returns, she goes back to her lively singing and dancing, closing the number with a brilliant cadenza to equally brilliant wind accompaniment. —*Rita Laurance*

Synopsis:

Act One. The goatherd Hoël has been gone for a year, having left his bride-to-be, Dinorah, who's family lost everything during a violent storm. Hoël had been told that after a year a treasure would be revealed to him, with which he hoped to help Dinorah. Dinorah went mad out of grief at his seeming desertion, and has been seen wandering the woods with a pet goat ever since. As the curtain rises, choruses of peasants in the village of Ploermel are praying to the virgin, celebrating the annual pilgrimage to the chapel.

Hoël has returned to the village to claim the secret treasure. Because of her madness, he does not recognize Dinorah anymore, who is ranting about the town. Corentin, a vagrant musician, has been living in his deceased uncle's cabin, and has been experiencing visitations of spirits and ghosts in his dreams. He and Dinorah dance for a while, and then fall asleep in the cabin. They are awakened by a loud rap on the window, and Dinorah exits in fright. It is Hoël, who wants to enlist the aid of the unsuspecting musician in finding the treasure. According to tradition, the first to touch the treasure will die. They both drink, and Corentin agrees to the adventure. According to Hoël, they must follow a magic goat with a bell around its neck. They both decide that Dinorah's goat is the magical one in the directions, and they set out after her, while she wanders about the fields.

Act Two. The act opens with a drinking chorus for the villagers. The unhappy Dinorah enters and dreamily dances with her shadow, thinking that it is a person. At midnight, Corentin and Hoël descend into a magical valley called Val Maudit, where the treasure is supposedly hidden, at the base of a tree that spans the dangerous ravine. Corentin is too frightened to walk along the tree over the ravine, so Hoël goes on ahead of him. The deranged Dinorah enters, singing about the magical treasure. She tells Corentin that the first to touch the treasure will die, and Corentin realizes that he is being used. Dinorah climbs onto the tree spanning the ravine in order to follow her lost goat, but just then a flash of lightning hits the tree, and girl and tree both go crashing into the swirling rivers below. Hoël recognizes Dinorah at last, and dives into the waters to save her.

Act Three. The storm has subsided, and all is calm. A gentle pastoral scene, featuring a hunter, a haymaker, and a pair of shepherds, serves as a divertissement to open the act. Corentin enters, followed by Hoël with Dinorah in his arms. Thinking that she is dead, Hoël repents, and tells all that love is much more important than riches. However, Dinorah miraculously revives. As she recognizes Hoël, her sanity is restored. The hymn to the Virgin is sung by the chorus and a procession leads the pair to the altar where they are finally married. —*Rita Laurance*

Recommended:

○ **Meyerbeer: Dinorah** / Judd (cond.), Pini, Smith, Jones, Oliver, Plessis, Earle, Caley, Cook, Philharmonia / 1993 / Opera Rara 5

Les Huguenots (1836)

Having been catapulted to pan-European fame by the success of his *Robert le diable* in 1831, Meyerbeer was already a household name when he completed his second work for the Paris Opéra, *Les Huguenots.* If *Robert* marked Meyerbeer's triumphant entrance onto the European music scene, the success of *Les Huguenots* after its premiere at the Opéra on February 29, 1836, simply confirmed that he had his finger on the pulse of the musical times.

Despite its positive popular reception, *Les Huguenots* did not fare consistently well in the contemporary press. *Les Huguenots* received mixed or negative reviews from virtually every Parisian music critic and from some writers and musicians from outside France. Some critics panned Eugène Scribe's libretto; Henri Blaze de Bury and Robert Schumann were outraged by what they saw as Scribe's profanation of the serious religious subject matter of the St. Bartholomew's Day massacre with his inclusion of the love story between Raoul and Valentine as the opera's centerpiece. Hector Berlioz, however, praised the libretto's dramatic seriousness (with the exception of Act Two). Other critics addressed Meyerbeer's music. Castil-Blaze objected to Meyerbeer's distortion of the French language in his musical setting of the text and his inability to develop themes. Although not particularly impressed by Meyerbeer's melodic gift, Berlioz applauded his orchestration, citing five examples from *Les Huguenots* in his *Grand traité d'instrumentation et d'orchestration.*

The opera begins with a high woodwind chorale rendition of Martin Luther's hymn *Ein' feste Burg ist unser Gott.* This tune returns throughout the opera: near the end of Act One, when the pious Marcel sings it while the Duke of Nevers interjects to lure Raoul to drink, when Marcel brings the tune back again in Act Three, and in Act Five when an offstage chorus of women sings a chorale-style harmonization of the melody, punctuated by commentary from Marcel. Orchestrational novelties and text painting highlight Meyerbeer's score. The Act One drinking song ("Bonheur de la table") is laced with cymbals and piccolo that, perhaps through their Janissary associations, conjure images of spirited hedonism. A cadenza for solo viole d'amour announces Raoul's romance in Act One ("Non loin des vieilles tours") and underscores the intimacy of his declaration of love as it accompanies him throughout, allowing only occasional interjections from the orchestra. In Marguerite's Act Two aria ("O beau pays de la Touraine"), the strings of the orchestra, with rolling arpeggios, become the "gentle stream," and the flutes chirp like the warblers and ring-doves of which she sings. And although a far cry from the extravagance Bizet would later conjure in his portrayal of the gypsy Carmen, the tambourine and triangle evoke the ethos of Romany in the otherwise staid Act Three gypsy dance. The virtuosic vocal flourishes and cadenzas, notably for Urbain's first entrance—a typical ternary (ABA) form air—in Act One, and for Marguerite's Act Two scene, are features without which no French grand opera would be complete. —*Jennifer Hambrick*

Synopsis:

Act One. The opera opens at the house of the Count de Nevers, a prominent member of the Catholic aristocracy. He has invited a group of guests to a banquet in honor of his upcoming marriage. A Huguenot has been included in the party, much to the astonishment of everyone present. The Count reminds them that the King is seeking a reconciliation between the Protestants and Catholics of the land. He urges them to welcome his friend, who turns out to be Raoul de Nangis. The stag party gets underway, and the count and his friends decide to take turns telling stories of their amorous conquests. When they ask Raoul to go first, he tells of a beautiful woman whom he rescued recently, and with whom he has fallen deeply in love. Her identity remains a mystery to him, and he does not know if he will ever see her again.

Marcel, Raoul's faithful servant, arrives. He is a staunch Huguenot and is shocked that Raoul is keeping company with a group of Catholics. Raoul is embarrassed when Marcel embarks on a rousing Huguenot song. However, the song is interrupted by the arrival of the valet of the Count, who brings the news that a lady has arrived. When the count goes to meet with her, his friends all gather at the window and watch, for they assume it is the count's latest amour. None of his Catholic friends recognizes the lady, but Raoul recognizes her as the unknown beauty whom he helped to rescue the other day. He is filled with revulsion at the thought that she is the count's mistress. The lady has brought a request to the count that he call off the wedding. The request is from Marguerite de Valois, the Queen of France, so the count has agreed.

Next, a note comes for Raoul. It asks him to agree to be led blindfolded to an unknown destination. The rest of the company recognize the letterhead as that of Marguerite de Valois, and are all deeply impressed. They begin to fawn on Raoul, and pay him extravagant compliments. He, on his part, thinks that it must be some kind of a joke, but agrees to the terms of the letter in order to amuse the rest of the company. As the curtain falls, he is blindfolded and led away.

Act Two. Marguerite de Valois and her ladies are playing on the grounds of the château of Chenonceaux. One of the ladies is Valentine, the fiancée of the Count of Nevers, and the unknown beauty whom Raoul rescued. She has just returned from the count's house where she has been released from her wedding promise. Marguerite is delighted. Now the two lovers can be wed, for Valentine is as deeply in love with Raoul as he is with her. Valentine, however, says that her father will never agree to it, for he is the Count de St. Bris, the leader of the Catholics. Queen Marguerite assures Valentine that she will personally make sure that all goes well, for both she and the King want to help resolve the differences between the Catholics and Protestants. Marguerite and her ladies bathe and relax in the river, and Raoul is led in to them blindfolded. After Marguerite dismisses her ladies, she asks Raoul to accept the daughter of the head of the Catholic nobles as a bride, and he agrees to the marriage.

Groups of Catholic and Protestant nobles are brought in and the Queen announces that she has a plan to reconcile the differences between the Catholics and Protestants. She has arranged an alliance through marriage between the two factions. However, when Valentine is brought in as the prospective bride, Raoul suddenly refuses to marry her. He has seen her outside the house of the Count of Nevers and thinks that she is the Count's mistress. Valentine is visibly shaken by this rejection, and the Catholic and Protestant nobles renew their words of hatred toward one another.

Act Three. Along the Seine, crowds of people celebrate the Sabbath. Count de Nevers and Valentine are again about to be married. Catholic and Huguenot soldiers mill about, creating tension in the crowd, while a band of gypsies plays music for their amusement. After the wedding, Valentine remains behind in the chapel to pray, while Marcel delivers a message to Count de St. Bris. It is from Raoul, who challenges the Catholic leader to a duel. The Catholics are still angry with Raoul for having rejected Valentine, and they plot revenge against him. Valentine warns Marcel to bring a company of armed men. When Raoul and his men arrive, a street fight breaks out, ending only when the Queen arrives.

Act Four. Valentine is back at the home of the Count de Nevers, musing on her circumstances. Raoul arrives, and Valentine must hide him from the rest of the household. St. Bris and a group of Catholic nobles are busy plotting a massacre of all the Huguenots. When de Nevers refuses to join them, he is taken prisoner. Monks bless their daggers, and the nobles go off into the night. Valentine at last confesses to Raoul that she loves him, but their conversation of love is interrupted by the sounds of the slaughter in the streets. Raoul, wanting to try to save some of his fellow Huguenots, leaps from the window.

Act Five. Raoul tries to warn the Huguenot leaders of the massacre, but many have already been killed. He and Marcel take refuge in a churchyard, and Valentine joins them. De Nevers is killed because he tried to defend some Huguenots, and now she is free to marry Raoul. Just as the two are blessed, a group of Catholics rush in and begin shooting the Protestants in the church. Raoul and Valentine escape to the street, only to be shot by Valentine's own father. As the opera closes, the people are heard calling for more bloodshed and killing. *—Rita Laurance*

Recommended:

○ **Meyerbeer: Les Huguenots** / Bonynge (cond.), Sutherland, Arroyo, Tourangeau, Vrenios, Ghiuselev, Bacquier / 1991 / Decca 430549

○ **Meyerbeer: Les Huguenots** / (live: 1971) / Märzendorfer (cond.), Gedda, Shane, Tarres, Diaz, Scovotti / Myto 961141

Le Prophète (1849)

Le Prophète is one of Meyerbeer's major works written for the Paris stage. It premiered there at the Theâtre de L'Opéra on April 16, 1849, to public and critical acclaim. The libretto is by Eugène Scribe, that master of the effective French drama, and its basis is the history of one John of Leyden, a fanatic who took control of the city of Münster in 1534. Jean of Leyden was crowned the emperor of Germany by his followers and held the city against the local bishop for over a year. The direct source for the libretto seems to have come from an account of the event by Voltaire in his *Essai sur les moeurs.* This opera has been called one of Meyerbeer's strangest. It is the portrait of a fraud and demagogue, of a man who begins his career with no religious or political interests whatsoever, but becomes the "Prophet" and leader of the radical and rebelling Anabaptists. His charisma leads their forces to victory until finally his own people betray him. The religious and political subject matter make this a truly French Romantic grand opera of the nineteenth century. The relationships between the characters turn the story into a powerful psychological drama as well. John of Leyden's love for his fiancée Berthe and his love and betrayal of his mother are central forces in his evolvement.

The opera took Meyerbeer and Scribe 14 years to complete. The earliest sketches were begun in 1835, and Meyerbeer began to concentrate exclusively on his new opera in 1838. By 1841 the score was complete enough to begin planning the first production, but Meyerbeer couldn't get the singers that he wanted for the lead roles. Toward the end of 1847, the opera finally went into production, but it took two years of more revisions and adjustments in the production before the premiere took place.

At its premiere, critics likened the portrait of the Anabaptists to French socialists of the time and thought that the revolutions of 1848 had inspired the libretto. Hunger riots in Paris, the fall of the Citizen King, the May revolution—all these were fresh in the public's memory. In truth, revolutionaries are depicted negatively in the opera. Although rebelling against the injustices of the feudal system, the Anabaptists are licentious, greedy, and bloodthirsty, and their leaders are false. Meyerbeer developed the relationships between Jean, his mother, and his fiancée to enrich the story and to soften its effect.

Meyerbeer takes up the entire first two acts with the exposition of the plot. The historical circumstances and the relationships between the characters are all outlined before the "Prophet" comes to power in Act Three. The high point of the opera is the coronation scene in Act Four, as Jean's fanatical followers crown him emperor in the local cathedral and he has his mother kneel before him in submission. *—Rita Laurance*

Synopsis:

Act One. In front of Count Oberthal's Castle in Dordrecht, Holland, peasants celebrate peaceful pastorale. They dance and revel, and picnic on the lawn. Berthe, one of the peasant girls, looks forward to her marriage with Jean de Leyde, but must first seek the Count's approval of the match. Fides, Jean's mother, arrives on the scene, ready to take Berthe to the engagement party. Three Anabaptist rebels enter preaching sedition and the overthrow of the feudal system. The peasants gather round and the Anabaptists lead them in rousing songs. Nevertheless, the peasants are easily dispersed and the Anabaptists easily chased away by the soldiers of the Count. Berthe and Fides plead with the Count to allow the marriage to go forward, but the Count finds Berthe attractive and decides to take her for himself. He takes both women hostage, while the rest of the peasants watch on helplessly. After he has gone, the Anabaptists return, this time preaching to more receptive ears.

Act Two. At Jean's Inn, villagers are dancing and carousing. Some Anabaptists enter and decide that Jean resembles a portrait they know back in Westphalia of King David, the Prophet. Jean, anxiously awaiting the arrival of his mother and Berthe, turns to the Anabaptists in conversation. He tells them of a disturbing vision that he has had recently, in which he was proclaimed the Messiah and worshipped, but rejected and damned by God. The Anabaptists decide that Jean should be their leader, for the vision seems real enough, but he refuses, saying that a simple life is all that he desires. Berthe enters breathless. She has escaped Count Oberthal and his men, but they are close behind, and she needs somewhere to hide. Count Oberthal enters soon afterwards and threatens Jean that, if he doesn't relinquish Berthe, his mother Fides will be executed. In a horrible, nightmarish pantomime, Jean returns his beloved to her captor, and saves his mother's life. Nevertheless, the tormented Jean wants revenge against the Count. He turns to the Anabaptists and offers to join them in their rebellious quest. He agrees to be their Messiah and leader, and they all leave together.

Act Three. The Anabaptists have an armed camp back in Westphalia, and have won victory after victory under Jean's leadership. They have taken many nobles prisoner, and now they want their blood. Count Oberthal is captured nearby and he, too, is threatened with execution. However, Jean is now sick of bloodshed, and stays his execution. Oberthal brings the news that Berthe is free, and somewhere in the city of Munster. Although he is tired of warring, Jean resolves to take the Anabaptist forces and lead them on a final siege of the city. They have mutinied once, but Jean quickly brings them under control. He has turned out to be a naturally charismatic leader, whose personality infects those around him with the spirit of their cause.

Act Four. The Anabaptists have taken the city of Munster, and all of the citizenry hail Jean as a divine being, a Prophet, and a Messiah. Jean's mother, Fides, is now a beggar on the street. She finds Berthe and tells her that the Anabaptists and their prophet have killed Jean; for this is what she thinks has happened. Berthe vows revenge for her beloved, and plans to assassinate this so-called prophet of the Anabaptists. In the Cathedral of Munster, preparations have been made for an elaborate coronation ceremony in which Jean's divine origins will be acknowledged. All is going well, and Jean is processing up the altar, when Fides recognizes her son. She calls out to him and he sees her. He is about to acknowledge her when he realizes that the Anabaptist's myth about the divine origins of their prophet will then be in jeopardy. At first, his followers threaten to kill Fides, but Jean denies her to them and insists that she is mad. He offers to let them kill him if he is really a false prophet as she claims. In order to save his life, Fides must kneel before him and deny that he is her son. In another somber and moving pantomime, mother is made subject before her offspring, and completely humiliated. His followers rejoice in the miracle that they have just witnessed: their prophet has performed an exorcism and healed a madwoman, and their new Prophet has been crowned as a holy man.

Act Five. The city of Munster is again under siege, this time by imperial forces. The three Anabaptist leaders decide that the time has come to betray Jean, in exchange for their own freedom. Fides, meanwhile, must warn Jean of Berthe's intention to assassinate the Prophet. She is still angry at her humiliation, but loves Jean because he is her son. At their reconciliation, Fides forces her son to kneel before her in the same act of submission that he forced upon her in the previous act. They are finally reunited in love and forgiveness, and Jean promises to renounce his role as the leader of the Anabaptists. Berthe discovers the two, and the three are happy and together again, but it is too late. The Imperial forces have arrived at the gates of the castle, and when Berthe realizes that Jean is the demagogue of the Anabaptists, and that it is he whom she seeks to murder, she kills herself. Jean decides that if he must fall, he will take everyone else with him. He tells his mother to look out for herself, and prepares a final feast.

In the great hall of the castle, Jean and his followers celebrate a dissolute bacchanal. They revel, drink, and enjoy their final moments in desperate gaiety. As the Imperial army arrives, Jean orders everyone locked in the castle, and the castle blown to high heaven. After the explosion, the castle collapses in a blazing inferno that takes everyone with it, the Imperial army along with drunken Anabaptists. *—Rita Laurance*

Recommended:

○ **Meyerbeer: Le Prophète** / Lewis (cond.), Horne, Scotto, Bastin, Taylor, Royal PO / 1976 / CBS 34340

Robert le diable (1831)

Few premieres have made a greater splash in the musical world than that of Giacomo Meyerbeer's *Robert le diable* on November 21, 1831, at the Paris Opéra. Meyerbeer had already composed a number of successful Italian operas during his nine-year stay in Italy (1816–24). The positive reception of one of them, *Il crociato in Egitto*, after its first performance in Paris at the Théâtre-Italien (1825), had made Meyerbeer famous throughout Europe. But by all contemporary accounts, the première of *Robert le diable* was nothing short of sensational. Meyerbeer replaced Rossini as the leading opera composer of Europe. F.J. Fétis, in his *Revue musicale* (1831), called *Robert* a "masterpiece," and in 1841 Wagner wrote in the *Dresdener Abendzeitung* that the opera was "deathless." In an article for the *Revue et Gazette musicale de Paris* (1835), Berlioz singled out Meyerbeer's orchestration as a laudable quality of *Robert le diable*, and included excerpts from the opera as examples of good orchestration in his *Grand traité d'instrumentaiton et d'orchestration* (1855). In 1852, however, Berlioz would condemn Meyerbeer's opera to the realm of "very dull French opera" in his *Soirées d'orchestre.*

Perhaps some of the contemporary popular fascination with *Robert le diable* was aroused by the theme of damnation that is the centerpiece of Eugène Scribe's libretto and to which Meyerbeer gives musical voice. Meyerbeer frequently reinforces the demonic character of Bertram, the devil and the father of Robert, through his orchestration. In the Act One recitative between Bertram and Robert ("Courage ta nouvelle conquête"), Bertram's statements alternate with octave passages scored for double bass, horns, bassoons, and clarinets. In Act Three, Bertram is accompanied by the murky combination of bassoon, bass trombone, ophycleide, and pizzicato double basses as he tells Robert of the magical branch on the tomb of Santa Rosalia ("Dans ce lieu qu'on ne saurait franchir"). Meyerbeer also musically reinforces the dramatic action. In Act One, tremolos and trills in the strings and brief scalar flourishes in the flute and oboe musically depict Robert rolling the dice in his infernal game of chance. In Act Two, a trumpet call-to-arms and Isabelle's arpeggiated vocal line suggest impending battle ("La trompette guerrière vient de retenir"). In Act Four, Meyerbeer accompanies Robert's breaking of the magical branch with the otherworldly sound of the tam-tam. All of Meyerbeer's orchestrational and dramatic felicities are wrapped up at the end of each act by a grand chorus, the final act ending in a chorus of general thanksgiving for Robert's allegiance to the forces of good. *—Jennifer Hambrick*

Synopsis:

Act One. Robert, Bertram, and a group of knights are reveling long into the night. A minstrel present is asked to amuse the company with a song, and he launches into a ballad about the infamous Robert le Diable. He was born the child of Berthe, the Duchess of Normandy, and a fiend from hell, who seduced her. The singer goes on to say that in his maturity, Robert grew so wicked and debauched that the people of Normandy drove him from his lands with the promise that he never return. He left for Sicily, where he met and fell in love with the Princess Isabelle. The knights of Sicily also would have destroyed him, but for the intervention of Bertram, who goes in the guise of a valiant knight, but is really Robert's satanic father. He has become Robert's permanent companion, and hopes to win his soul for the glory of hell. Robert is outraged. He reveals his identity and orders the minstrel executed. He is saved, however, because the minstrel's fiancée turns out to be none other than Robert's sister Alice. Just as Robert is imbued with all of the wicked vices, so Alice is virtuous and pure. Alice brings Berthe's will, which she said Robert was to read when he felt himself worthy of it. Berthe, an extremely devout woman, also begged Alice to protect Robert as best she could from the evil that would surely try to take hold of him. Robert tells her of his love for the Princess Isabelle, and she offers to take a note to her. For the moment, her protective love has helped him, but soon Bertram entices him to spend the rest of the night gambling with his comrades. Robert loses all that he possesses, including his armor.

Act Two. Back at the Sicilian palace, Isabelle laments Robert's absence. She is despondent, for her father has pledged to marry her to the Prince of Grenada. Alice enters with the letter from Robert, and Isabelle's faith in him is restored. Robert soon follows, and the two have a tender and loving reunion. Isabelle tells him of her engagement to the Prince of Grenada, and Robert vows to meet his rival in single combat at the coming tournament. Isabelle equips him with new armor, and then exits. Bertram arrives and tells his son that the Prince of Grenada wants to meet him in a nearby wood, instead of at the tournament. Robert leaves, and the tournament begins. Confused by her lover's absence, Isabelle reluctantly bestows armor on the Prince of Grenada.

Act Three. On the misty mountains of St. Irene, Raimbaut, the minstrel, has a rendezvous with his beloved Alice. However, the evil Bertram again intervenes. He throws Raimbaut a bag of gold and tells him to leave Alice, for now he can have any woman he might want. They sing a duo together, and Bertram gloats over his easy victory. He communes with the spirits of hell. Alice arrives looking for Raimbaut, but hears infernal spirits chanting the name of Robert le Diable. She hears the fiends tell Bertram that, unless he has possession of Robert's soul by midnight, he will be lost to him forever. When Bertram emerges from the cave in which he is sequestered, he finds Alice, and threatens her unless she promises to keep quiet about what she has heard and seen.

Robert comes to seek Bertram's aid in overcoming his rival in love. Because he was not at the tournament, he was unable to meet the Prince of Granada in combat. He asks Bertram what to do to recover his lost pride. Bertram convinces him to commit sacrilege, by taking a sacred branch from the tomb of St. Rosalie. Although Robert knows that he will be eternally damned, he agrees to the plan.

At the tomb of St. Rosalie, Bertram summons up the spirits of nuns who have been consigned to eternal damnation. They rise from the dead and dance an erotic bacchanal in the graveyard. When Robert arrives, they try to seduce him and ply him with drink. They lead him to the magic branch of St. Rosalie, and when he plucks it, millions of fiends are released, lightning crashes, thunder rolls, and the earth trembles. The spirits dance around him in a hideous dance, exulting over his lost soul.

Act Four. At the palace, Alice enters to warn Isabelle of the terrible dangers Robert is facing. Gifts from the Prince of Grenada arrive, and the court is astir with the preparations for the wedding. Robert arrives, and with the power of the magic branch, throws the entire court into a deep sleep. Isabelle alone is allowed to remain conscious, and he begs her to go away with him. When she asks him about the branch, he confesses that its power is from hell. She throws herself at his feet and begs him to repent. Her pleading moves him; he breaks the branch, restoring the court. However, the knights of the court recognize him, and take him prisoner.

Act Five. At the cathedral of Palermo, all is ready for the wedding of the Princess Isabelle to the Prince of Grenada. The desperate Robert again seeks Bertram's advice. He is about to yield to Bertram his soul when he hears heavenly chanting from inside of the cathedral and again stops. The Prince of Grenada was unable to enter the church because he is controlled by infernal forces. Robert, after overcoming the temptations offered to him by his father, enters in his stead. Robert has managed to escape eternal damnation within the period allotted to Bertram, so he is saved. Bertram is sent back to hell where he belongs, and Isabelle and Robert are happily married. *—Rita Laurance*

Recommended:

○ **Meyerbeer: Robert le Diable** / Palumbo (cond.), Ciofi, Mok, Surian, Colaianni, Italian International Orch. / 2000 / Dynamic 368/1-3

Arturo Benedetti Michelangeli

b. Jan. 5, 1920, Brescia, Italy, **d.** Jun. 12, 1995, Lugano, Switzerland
Pianist

One of the most enigmatic performers of the twentieth century, Arturo Benedetti Michelangeli was also one of the most compelling and, paradoxically, one of the least-heard pianists of his generation. Michelangeli was famous for having canceled nearly as many performances as he gave, and he committed little of his vast repertory to disc.

Michelangeli has born on January 5, 1920 in Orzinuovi, Italy. His father was a dedicated amateur musician who introduced young Benedetti to the art. After early studies on the violin, Michelangeli took up the piano, entering the Milan Conservatory at the age of ten. Four years later the young pianist graduated with top accolades.

In 1939 Michelangeli's concert career began in earnest after he claimed top honors at the International Piano Competition in Geneva. Of his triumphant performance at the competition, no less a luminary than the great Alfred Cortot exclaimed, "A new Liszt is born!" Service in the Italian Air Force during World War II interrupted Michelangeli's career; taking the stage again at war's end, however, he soon earned a place among the top performers of the day.

The 1950s and 1960s were a busy time for the pianist, who divided his time between a hectic concert schedule and various teaching appointments. In 1960 Michelangeli performed Beethoven's *"Emperor" Concerto* in Vatican City for the Pope. A triumphant 1964 appearance in Moscow reportedly had the audience in an uproar, and in 1965 Michelangeli became one of the first Western artists to concertize extensively in Asia.

In 1968 Michelangeli went into voluntary "exile" from Italy, angered at the government for impounding his pianos after a company in which he was a partner went bankrupt. Although Italy remained his official residence, he resided in Switzerland for the rest of his life.

In the 1970s and 1980s he made fewer and fewer concert appearances, owing both to consistent health troubles and his growing aversion to public display. During a performance in Bordeaux in October 1988 he suffered an aortic aneurysm onstage; nevertheless, he resumed performing the following season. He gave his last public performance in 1990 and died five years later died from the chronic medical problems that had plagued him since childhood.

Michelangeli regarded the life of a concert pianist as one of labor. His own schedule included upwards of ten hours of practice a day; he suggested to his pupils that they cease practicing only when the pain in the fingers and shoulders became too great for them to continue. Michelangeli took his role as a mentor very seriously; he held various teaching positions in Italy and throughout Europe, and included Martha Argerich and Maurizio Pollini among his pupils. A generous man, he funded each and every one of his students out of his own income, maintaining that music is an inalienable right for those who have the gift.

To many Michelangeli's playing was the ideal blend of technique and uncanny musical depth. His subtlety, revealed in such masterly recordings as Brahms' *Paganini Variations*, is in restraint and detachment—calculated to temper power and fury, not to replace it. His performances of Mozart, Haydn, and Scarlatti are particularly esteemed.

Michelangeli never wholly embraced life as a concert artist. He felt that to pour such adulation on a performer was a disgrace, and that it distracted the performer from the very essence of his duty. A deeply private man, Michelangeli had a tendency to distort the truth during interviews, making it difficult for musicologists and historians to build an accurate portrait of his life; he will likely remain a fascinating, little-understood man.—*Blair Johnston*

Recommended:

- ○ **Debussy: Images; Children's Corner; Préludes** / Michelangeli / 1998 / DG 459033
- ○ **The First Recordings (1939–1943)** / Ansermet, Galliera, Pedrotti (conds.), Michelangeli, La Scala Theater Orch., Suisse Romande / Grammofono 2000 78675/76
- ○ **Beethoven: Concertos 1 & 3** / Giulini (cond.), Michelangeli, Vienna SO / DG 449757
- ○ **Mozart: Concertos 13 & 23; Haydn: Concerto 11** / Stoutz, Caracciolo (conds.), Michelangeli, Zurich CO / 2004 / EMI 62824
- ○ **The Art of Arturo Benedetti Michelangeli** / Giulini, Garben (conds.), Michelangeli, VSO, North German RSO / DG 000001602
- ○ **Scarlatti, Beethoven, Clementi, Chopin** / Michelangeli / BBC 4128
- ○ **Arturo Benedetti Michelangeli** / Gracis (cond.), Michelangeli, London PO / 1999 / Philips 456901
- ○ **Schumann, Brahms, Bach-Busoni** / Michelangeli / 2004 / EMI 62757

Midori

b. Oct. 25, 1971, Osaka, Japan
Violinist

Midori was born in Osaka, Japan, and from the age of three studied violin with her mother, Setsu Goto. She made her concert debut in Osaka at six. In 1981, she went to the United States to work with the renowned Dorothy DeLay at the Aspen Music School, continuing her studies with DeLay at the Juilliard school in New York. Midori made her debut as a special guest soloist at the New York Philharmonic's New Year's Eve concert in 1982, when she was ten. She charmed the crowd profoundly: a group of collectors loaned her an original Stradivarius instrument, and conductor Zubin Mehta was impressed enough to take her on the orchestra's Asian tour the next year. The same year, she signed with CBS Masterworks (now Sony Classics), and her international career was launched. Appearances with the Berlin Philharmonic, the Boston Symphony, the Chicago Symphony, the Cleveland Orchestra, the Philadelphia Orchestra, and the London Symphony followed, establishing her as a seasoned professional. At fourteen, she landed on the front page of the *New York Times* after a performance with the Philharmonic in Central Park—often underestimated as classical music venue, but nevertheless appreciated by many classical music lovers in the U.S.

Although her child prodigy days are over, Midori has remained a distinctive and electrifying performer, her energy undiminished. Often associated with Mehta, she has worked with other conductors and orchestras worldwide. The combination of her slight stature with her enormous virtuosity makes for a surprising and often captivating stage presence, in spite of a somewhat limited repertoire. However, Midori is actively exploring the recital repertoire, making her recital debut at Carnegie Hall in October of 1990; that concert is available in video as well as audio form, and offers an ideal introduction to her meticulous and pleasing stage personality. In 1996 and 1997, she toured the Far East with the Vienna Philharmonic. Among Midori's numerous awards are a Grammy nomination in 1990 (for her recording of the over-the-top Paganini Caprices), Japan's Crystal Award, The National Arts Award from Americans for the Arts in 1998, and the Encore Award from the Arts and Business Council, Inc. In addition to her activities as a prominent virtuoso, Midori has also founded and nurtured Midori and Friends, a nonprofit organization providing educational experiences and concerts for underprivileged and hospitalized children. Her other activities include campaigning for the restoration of arts programs in U.S. schools. In 2005, Midori wrote about her experiences on tour in Asia in a weblog published on the Arts Journal site. —*Steven Coburn*

Recommended:

- ○ **Tchaikovsky: Violin Concerto; Shostakovich: Violin Concerto 1** / Abbado (cond.), Midori, Berlin PO / 2004 / Sony 93088
- ○ **Mendelssohn, Bruch: Violin Concertos** / Jansons (cond.), Midori, Berlin PO / 2003 / Sony 87740
- ○ **Elgar & Franck Sonatas** / Midori, McDonald (piano) / 1997 / Sony 63331
- ○ **Mozart: Sinfonia Concertante; Concerto for Violin & Piano** / Eschenbach (cond.), Midori, Imai, NDRSO / 2000 / Sony 89488SACD

Luis de Milán

b. ca. 1500, Valencia, Spain, **d.** ca. 1561, Valencia, Spain
Composer

Luis de Milán, a Spanish composer and poet, is important as a composer of music for the vihuela; as well as writing solo works for the instrument, he employed it in an accompanimental role in songs. Little is known of Luis de Milán's life. He spent most of his adulthood in the Spanish coastal city of Valencia, engaged at the ducal court; his connections with the court seem to have dissolved around 1538, not long after he began publishing his works. Milán enjoyed royal patronage after retiring from the Valencia court, however, and his *El cortesano*, printed in 1561, is dedicated to Philip II of Spain.

Milán published a significant amount of music; one of the earliest of these publications is a parlor-game book entitled, *El juego de mandar*, printed in 1535 in Valencia. His most important volume by far is his *Libro de música de vihuela de mano intitulado El maestro* (Valencia, 1536); containing instrumental and vocal pieces in succession, it provides valuable insight into the nature of improvisational playing that lutenists of the time may have used as preludes to songs. A good example is "Fantasia No. 9," which prepares for the ensuing vocal piece by moving, several times, to a cadence in both of the modes of the song; this sets the modes of the song in listeners' ears before it even begins.

The 40 fantasias in *El maestro* are free in structure and contain both homophonic and polyphonic passages. Typically for his time, Milán attached no specific meaning to the term "fantasia" and applied it to seemingly any instrumental piece for solo vihuela. The fantasias are clearly sectionalized, and their polyphonic segments are usually free rather than imitative. Milán's facility on the vihuela is evident in the virtuoso runs and ornaments that appear throughout the fantasias.

Milan transposed the various modal scales to different starting pitches, requiring an unusual use of accidentals for the time. More interesting still is his combination of modes in a single piece, such as "Fantasia No. 14." Also, "Fantasia No. 27" features striking chromatic writing, with augmented unisons and triads; among the songs, both "Durandarte" and the soneto *Nova angeleta* (text by Petrarch), contain bold cross-relations—the simultaneous sounding of two versions of the same note (E natural and E flat, for example).

The vocal works contained in *El maestro* include 12 villancicos (six in Castillian and six in Portuguese), four romances and six sonetos. Of the 12 villancicos, ten are "double versions"; five of these are relatively simple in texture, though the singer is directed to ornament the voice part. In each of the second versions of these, however, the vihuela part is much more elaborate and the voice part is to be sung as written; Milán clearly conceived of the vihuela as an equal "voice" in these works.

Interestingly, Milán was among the first documented users of the term *sonada*, although he did not do so to indicate a type of composition; in his usage, it connoted the "sound" or "style" of the piece—the fifth and sixth pavans in *El maestro*, for example, have an Italian "sonada." *—John Palmer*

Overview of Works (ca. 1530–1560)

The Spaniard Luis (Luys) de Milán was the first great composer for the vihuela, the predecessor of the modern guitar. He apparently spent most of his life at court in Valencia, for it was there that all his music was published, starting with *El juego de mandar* (1535) and ending with *El cortesano* (1561), the latter dedicated to Philip II. He is best remembered for his *Libro de música de viheula de mano intitulado el maestro* (1535), dedicated to John III of Portugal. Consisting of 40 free fantasies, *El maestro* is the first published collection of vihuela music and contains the first written indication of tempos in Western music. Written in the tablature used in later vihuela sources, albeit with the lowest line used to represent the lowest run of the instrument, *El maestro* also includes a musical line in red in the tablature. Although it seems likely that this was intended to be sung, some authorities claim Milán included it to serve as a ground for the fantasies. Milán's writing blends homophony with polyphony, usually simple imitation but occasionally fairly strict. The virtuosity of the player was emphasized in fast ornamental runs, chordal sequences, and arpeggios but all the pieces demand a high degree of sensitivity to Milán's highly nuanced music in order to succeed. In addition to the instrumental fantasies, *El maestro* contains 12 villancicos with six in Spanish and six in Portuguese, accompanied by the vihuela. *—James Leonard*

Recommended:

- ○ **Milán: El Maestro, songs & vihuela solos** / Heringman, King / 1998 / ASV 183
- ○ **Milan: El Maestro** / Figueras, Smith / 2002 / Astree 9976
- ○ **Fantasía: Music by Luys Milán** / Moreno, Quinteiro / 2003 / Glossa 30110

Zinka Milanov

b. May 17, 1906, Zagreb, Croatia, **d.** May 30, 1989, New York, NY
Soprano

With her stately stage deportment and unflappable sense of her own greatness, Milanov was one of the last great divas, quick to tell the story of admirers who came to see her in *La Gioconda* just to hear her float her famous pianissimo B flat at the end of the first act. She was and remains one of opera's cult figures.

She was born Zinka Kunc (koontz) and used that name until she married actor Predrag Milanov in 1937. In Croatia, she studied with Milka Ternina and later with Fernando Carpi in Prague. Her opera debut was as Leonora in *Il trovatore* in Ljubljana in 1927, and became a lead soprano with the Zagreb Opera, often traveling to sing in other parts of Europe. In 1936, Milanov had her big break when she sang Aida under Bruno Walter in Vienna. Walter was immediately taken by her voice and recommended her to Toscanini for his Salzburg performance of the Verdi *Requiem*. (According to one story, Toscanini became irritated with her phrasing and told her, in Italian, "If you had musicianship to equal your voice, you would be the greatest singer in the world." Milanov's Italian not being fluent at that point, and already with a healthy ego, she heard just the "greatest singer in the world," and bowed, responding with a heartfelt "Thank you, maestro," much to the orchestra's bewilderment.) She made her Met debut in 1937 as Leonora in *Il trovatore*, and was soon one of the house's most beloved sopranos, singing 298 performances there. Her Chicago debut was in 1940 as Aida. Her La Scala debut was not until 1950 as Tosca, and her Covent Garden debut even later, again as Tosca, in 1956. She gave her farewell performance in 1966 as Maddalena di Coigny in *Andrea Chénier* at the Met. In 1977, she began her career as a teacher at the Curtis Institute in Philadelphia.

She was famous off stage for her *bon mots*. When a fan told her after a performance that her voice was "pure silver," she immediately responded, "Gold. It was pure gold." Another soprano who sang Tosca and mildly injured herself in the last-act leap from the battlements was told, "Darling, I knew that role was too high for you." Her sense of humor did not, however, extend to tolerating *lèse-majesté*. When Lily Tomlin, the comedian, was asked by a reporter who her understudy was, and answered, "Uhhh... Zinka Milanov!," instead of taking it as a tribute to her wit, Milanov sued for "damage to her professional reputation."

Among her recordings, the RCA *Il trovatore* (GD 86643) displays her voice at its formidable best. While the coloratura is imprecise, and her phrasing sometimes unincisive, the power and lushness she possessed at her peak are well captured here. *—Ann Feeney*

Recommended:

- ○ **Zinka Milanov** / Milanov, etc. / 1990 / RCA 60074
- ○ **Puccini: Tosca** / Leinsdorf (cond.), Milanov, Warren, Corena, Monreale, Rome Opera House Orch. / 1999 / RCA 63305
- ○ **Verdi: Aida** / Perlea (cond.), Bjoerling, Milanov, Warren, Barbier, Rome Opera House Orch. / 1968 / BMG 6652

Darius Milhaud

b. Sep. 4, 1892, Aix-en-Provence, France, **d.** Jun. 22, 1974, Geneva, Switzerland
Composer: Ballet, Chamber Music, Keyboard, Concerto, Orchestral, Symphonic, Vocal, Choral, Musical Theater

One of the more prolific composers of the twentieth century, Darius Milhaud was born to a Jewish family in southern France during the last decade of the nineteenth century. He learned the violin as a youth. Studies at the Paris Conservatoire from age 17 on gave the young composer opportunity to work with some of the most prominent French composers and theorists of the day, including Charles Marie Widor, Vincent d'Indy and André Gedalge, and allowed him to focus on developing his skills as a pianist.

While serving as an attaché at the French delegation in Rio de Janeiro during the First World War, Milhaud began a long and fruitful association with poet Paul Claudel (who was at that time a Minister at the delegation), several of whose plays Milhaud would go on to provide with incidental music (*Proteé*, 1919; *L'annonce fait à Marie*, 1934) and who, in turn, would supply libretti for many of Milhaud's compositions (e.g. the opera *Christophe Colomb* of 1928).

After returning to Paris in 1919 Milhaud was adopted into the circle of "Les Six," a group of progressive French composers brought together under the guidance of Jean Cocteau. However, like any such artificial collection, Les Six was quick to dissolve, and during the 1920s Milhaud adopted an assortment of new musical influences (notably jazz, which the composer first discovered during a trip to the U.S. in 1922, and which features prominently in much of his subsequent music).

Milhaud composed, performed, and taught ceaselessly during the 1920s and 1930s, only abandoning his homeland in late 1939 after all hope of resisting the German advance vanished. Settling in the United States, Milhaud accepted a teaching position with Mills College in Oakland, California, and continued to compose prolifically. From 1947 he combined his American teaching duties with a similar position at the Paris Conservatoire, remaining at both institutions until 1971, when his poor health forced him into retirement (Milhaud had suffered from a serious, paralyzing rheumatic condition since the 1920s; in later years he was only mobile through the use of a wheelchair). He died in Switzerland three years later.

Milhaud's musical output is impressive, both in terms of quantity and quality. The numbers alone are staggering for a twentieth century composer: nine operas, 12 ballets, 12 symphonies (in addition to six chamber symphonies), six piano concertos (one of them a double concerto), 18 string quartets, and about 400 other compositions in almost every conceivable form and instrumentation. The most frequently discussed feature of his musical language is polytonality (the simultaneous use of multiple tonal centers), though Milhaud was familiar with and fluent in any number of twentieth century "techniques." A skillful contrapuntist, Milhaud composed two string quartets (Nos. 14 and 15, both from 1949) which may also be performed simultaneously as an octet. *—Blair Johnston*

BALLET

Le boeuf sur le toit, Op. 58 (1919)

Milhaud spent the years of World War I assisting poet Paul Claudel, who was then France's ambassador to Brazil. After the war, Milhaud returned to Paris, Brazil-besotted. He soon couldn't help but assemble, in his words, "a few popular melodies, tangos, maxixes, sambas, and even a Portuguese fado and [transcribe] them with a rondo-like theme recurring between each successive pair." The structure is even more ingenious than Milhaud's description suggests; the rondo theme appears 12 times, cycling through 12 different keys rising in minor thirds. This strict harmonic scheme did not prevent Milhaud from using polytonality throughout, adding a comic tension to the lively score. There's nothing the least bit academic about the result, which, for all its Brazilian character, also carries the boozy smell of the French music hall. Milhaud named the piece *Le boeuf sur le toit* (The Bull on the Roof) after a Brazilian popular song and initially subtitled it "Cinéma-Symphonie," explaining that he hoped it might be used to accompany a Charlie Chaplin film. But poet/provocateur Jean Cocteau immediately appropriated it for an absurdist stage production he conceived, set in a Prohibition-era American speakeasy (*The Nothing-Doing Bar*) and performed in slow motion by the Fretellini acrobats and clowns from the Médrano Circus. In Cocteau's scenario, a barman serves a bizarre mix of clientele, including fashionable society characters, a boxer, a black dwarf, and a redheaded woman dressed as a man. A policeman arrives, whereupon the barman and his patrons transform the establishment into an innocent milk bar. The copper continues his surveillance, though, so the barman turns on an overhead fan and decapitates him. The cross-dresser does a parody of Salome's dance with the policeman's head, the patrons wander off into the night, and the barman reassembles and revives the policeman, presenting him with the evening's bill. Understandably, *Le boeuf sur le toit* is almost never presented according to Cocteau's plan anymore and is most often heard as a concert piece. (In the 1980s, however, Swiss director Adrian Marthaler contrived his own quasi-Brechtian treatment for television.) Milhaud was never quite sure what to make of what Cocteau did with this score, protesting in his autobiography that "I, who hated comedy... had only aspired to create a merry divertissement in memory of the Brazilian rhythms that had so captured my imagination." *—James Reel*

Recommended:

- ○ **Dorati Conducts Satie, Milhaud, Auric, Françaix & Fetler** / Dorati (cond.), London SO / 1994 / Philips 434335
- ○ **Darius Milhaud Plays and Conducts** / Milhaud (cond.), Orchestre de Theatre des Champ-Elysees / 1993 / EMI 54604

La création du monde, Op. 81 (1923)

Milhaud discovered American jazz in a 1920 visit to London, where he encountered Billy Arnold's Novelty Jazz Band in a Hammersmith dance hall. By the time he arrived in New York two years later for a series of engagements, he was claiming that European composers, including himself, were strongly influenced by American jazz (even though the only evidence available consisted of very short pieces by the likes of Satie, Auric, and Stravinsky). In New York, he haunted Harlem clubs and bought as many jazz records as he could. Upon his return to Paris, Milhaud was primed to write a lengthy, jazz-inspired score and saw his chance in a collaboration with Swedish producer Rolf de Maré, designer Fernand Léger, writer Blaise Cendrars, and choreographer Jean Börlin. The subject was nothing less than the creation of the world, as seen through African myth. Léger based his scenery and costumes on African art, and Milhaud took his inspiration from the African American music then in the air: jazz. He created a score for 17 solo instruments, including saxophone, and made liberal use of syncopation and near-chaotic counterpoint with the feeling of jazz improvisation (all the notes were written out, however). The score falls into five sections performed without breaks, always underlined by percussion instruments (here including the piano) that evoke both African drums and American jazz styles. The more animated the music becomes, as in the fugal second section, the more frenetic, syncopated, and outwardly jazzy it grows. The slower, quieter passages early on have less to do with African or American styles, aside from the occasional blue note. Throughout, Milhaud makes liberal use of polytonality, as is the case with all his mature music. The curtain rises on darkness, through which can be dimly perceived in inchoate mass of human bodies. Soon, the African gods of creation, Mzamé, Mebère, and Nkwa materialize and through their incantations, various forms of life begin to emerge from the mass of bodies: trees, animals, and ultimately a man and woman. The couple performs a sassy, syncopated dance of creation; the music becomes gentler and the man and woman are left alone on-stage to welcome the first spring. *—James Reel*

Recommended:

- ○ **Honegger: Symphonies 2 & 5; Milhaud: Le Creation du Monde; Suite Provençale** / Munch (cond.), Boston SO / 1199 / RCA 60685
- ○ **Darius Milhaud Plays and Conducts** / Milhaud (cond.) / 1993 / EMI 54604
- ○ **New World Jazz** / Tilson Thomas (cond.), New World Symphony / 1998 / RCA 902668798

L'homme et son désir, Op. 48 (1918)

This is a charming, energetic, witty, and engaging score particularly notable for a style of scoring that was unprecedented. Its sound has remained in many ways unique over the decades since its composition.

Darius Milhaud (1892–1974) was turned down for military service during World War I for health reasons. Thus he continued a promising career as a composer. When he was 21, he had collaborated with the poet Paul Claudel, and in 1915, turned to Claudel's treatment of the classic Greek tragedy the *Oresteia* for *Les choëphores* (The Libation Bearers). In 1916, Claudel received an appointment as France's ambassador to Rio de Janeiro (then capital of Brazil) and took Milhaud along as a secretary. *L'homme et son désir* is one of the first fruits of his exposure to Brazilian culture. It is based on the African-based rhythms of the country, and is a precursor of his best-known scores, *Le boeuf sur le toit* (infused with South American urban dance ambience) and *Le création du Monde* (his response to U.S. jazz).

L'homme et son désir is based on a scenario by Claudel. It is an allegorical dance drama (he called it a "poème plastique") about Night, Sleep, Image (Memory), and Desire (or Illusion). It takes place in a jungle at night, ruled by the moon. The hero is the Sleeping Man, his natural primitive powers now latent. He dances in his sleep the themes of Exile and Desire. A woman is drawn to this dance. The Man unwraps her veil, enveloping himself in it as he does so. They move to the side of the stage as the Hours of Night depart and the Hours of Dawning enter.

Virtually everything about the music and the musicians is a new idea. Milhaud places the ensemble "stereophonically" to create spatial effects, and uses five groups of instruments: one group of oboe, harp, double bass, and trumpet; another of four more winds; a string quartet; a percussion section of 15 instruments; and a vocal quartet that sings without words, becoming an instrumental sound. At various times Milhaud either blends these disparate elements into fresh new combinations or keeps them separate, with their own rhythms, melodies, and pulse, to create different planes of sound. The percussion section often plays in remarkable cross-rhythms, creating a cushion of drumming under the melodies. Indeed, here Milhaud lifts the percussion to the most important role it ever occupied in a Western classical piece, entrusting important sections of the score to percussion alone, and several more parts where percussion is the dominant orchestral voice. The music is usually lively, with a haunting spirit of primitive mysteries, but ends in a passage of exceptional tenderness but for a few distant drumbeats from the world of Night to conclude the music. *—Joseph Stevenson*

Recommended:

- ○ **Milhaud: Pacem in Terris** / Abravanel (cond.), Utah SO / 1993 / Vanguard 8067

CHAMBER MUSIC

La Cheminée du Roi René, suite for wind quintet, Op. 205 (1939)

Darius Milhaud's seven-movement suite for wind quintet *La Cheminée du Roi René* (The Chimney of King René) was taken from music written for Raymond Bernard's 1939 film *Cavalcade d'Amour.* The film consists of three love stories set in the court of fifteenth century French regent René d'Anjou (1409–1480), and the sequences were set musically by three composers: Milhaud, Arthur Honegger, and Roger Desormière. Milhaud had always held a fascination with King René, his chivalric code, and the legendary jousts that were associated with his court. Milhaud was a native of Aix-en-Provence, where King René's court and castle were located. He had also studied some of the musical manuscripts from King René's reign, but little of anything of this is to be found in *La Cheminée du Roi René*; the music is all Milhaud's and is written in his most immediate and forthright idiom.

The seven-movement plan is thus: (1) "Cortège" (Procession), (2) "Aubade" (Morning Serenade), (3) "Jongleurs" (Jugglers), (4) "La Maousinglade," (5) "Joutes sur L'Arc" (Jousts on the Arc), (6) "Chasse à Valabre" (Hunting at Valabre) and (7) "Madrigal-Nocturne." These movements range in length from less than a minute to just about three minutes; many listeners hearing *La Cheminée du Roi René* without benefit of a score may well not realize that they are hearing a small suite rather than a single, uninterrupted work. Altogether *La Cheminée du Roi René* takes about 13 minutes to play, and the mood is so similar from movement to movement there is little to single out for comment. However, "La Maousinglade" with its gentle, swaying oboe-driven Sarabande, sticks in the memory long after it is heard. There is a hint of Renaissance-styled ornamentation in "Joutes sur L'Arc," and a hint of the hunting-horn is heard in "Chasse à Valabre"; towards the end of this movement there is a short passage of Milhaud's bi-tonal thorniness thrown for comic relief between the clarinet and bassoon. The pensive and strongly Neo-Classical "Madrigal" brings this short suite to a quiet and restful close.

La Cheminée du Roi René is not only one of Milhaud's best known works; it is one of the most popular chamber suites of the twentieth century. No self respecting wind quintet would consider doing without it in their repertoire, and it is programmed with relentless fervor on classical music radio in the United States and doubtless elsewhere. *—Uncle Dave Lewis*

Recommended:

- ○ **Best Of The NY Woodwind Quintet, Vol. 2** / NY Woodwind Quintet / 1996 / Boston Skyline 139
- ○ **Milhaud: Music For Wind Instruments** / Athena Ens. / 1991 / Chandos 6536

Duo concertant, for clarinet & piano, Op. 351 (1956)

There is a certain paradoxical quality to the music of Darius Milhaud, a disjunction between the lighthearted sentiments to which the composer seemed continually drawn and the meticulous craftsmanship he exercised in conveying them. Likewise, the rather systematic manner in which he expanded his oeuvre—he wrote a series of concertos for virtually every Western orchestral instrument, and made good on his early and curious promise to compose exactly 18 string quartets—not only resulted in a very tidy catalog, but also in a thorough and keen sensitivity toward the idiomatic expressive qualities of each instrument for which he wrote. It is no surprise, then, that although Milhaud is not quite a household name, he is well represented in the standard repertoire lists of virtually every Western instrument. In the canon of clarinet music, Milhaud's *Duo concertant* for clarinet and piano enjoys regular appearances in recitals and has appeared on several recordings. Its owes its popularity to a mixture of virtuosity and sheer pleasantness; on one hand, it never resorts to sentimental pandering, or on the other, to empty pyrotechnics. Milhaud's characteristic harmonic twists, curious chromatic inflections, and momentary tonal diversions ultimately serve to add subtle, modern nuances to a lucid and unassuming expressivity. Milhaud had already familiarized himself with the possibilities of the clarinet/piano duo in his *Sonatine*, Op. 100 (1927), the *Eglogue-Madrigal*, arranged from his *Four Sketches* in 1941, and the *Caprice*, Op. 335 (1954). Accordingly, the *Duo concertant* exudes a breezy confidence in exploiting the clarinet's nuances of ornament and articulation and in moving between a clear solo-accompaniment format and more integrated, polyphonically oriented textures. Cast in a single movement lasting around eight minutes, the piece begins in a moderate tempo with a jaunty, fanfare-like theme in the clarinet. Initially, the piano provides a simple chordal accompaniment, but as the piece progresses, the two instruments increasingly tread on each other's territory; as gestures in the piano's treble range come to the fore, the clarinet meanders into curious polytonal counterpoint or echoes its initial fanfares in the background. In the lyrical middle section, the clarinet is given the full spotlight, the plaintive melody underscored by steady but sometimes poignantly dissonant chords in the piano. The playful fanfare-like material from the opening returns to close the work, ending with a quick flourish of virtuosic aplomb. *—Jeremy Grimshaw*

Recommended:

○ **Moonflowers, Baby!** / Cohler, Gordon / Crystal 733

Sonatina for clarinet & piano, Op. 100 (1927)

Milhaud marked his 100th opus not with the expected monumental work, but with a modest sonatina for clarinet and piano. It's no simpering salon piece, though; bracketing a largely tranquil slow movement are two movements marked Très rude, rather dissonant (through the use of polytonality), and usually energetic. The first movement contrasts dry, fast music dominated by ninth chords in the piano with more lyrical, expressive passages for the clarinet undercut by syncopations and sour chords in the keyboard, all ending quite loudly. A plaintive clarinet melody dominates the slow movement until the piano takes control in the central section, goading the clarinet into a climax; this subsides and after a return to the movement's first theme, the section quietly ends. The short, strident third movement sends the clarinet soaring over the hyperactive piano; the music becomes more aggressive toward the end, the time signature constantly changing, but it all concludes with the unexpected affirmation of a brilliant C major chord. *—James Reel*

Recommended:

○ **Copland & Les Six: Works for Clarinet & Piano** / Soames, Drake / 1992 / Clarinet Classics 01

Suite for violin, clarinet & piano, Op. 157b (1936)

Perhaps the most striking aspect of the musical oeuvre of Darius Milhaud is its sheer breadth: he composed for just about every imaginable combination of Western instruments and his sometimes transgressive attitudes toward musical tradition and stylistic boundaries produce works in which feigned Baroque elegance might be juxtaposed with crass jazz send-ups. In this regard, Milhaud's *Suite for Violin, Clarinet, and Piano* stands as a prime example. Relying, somewhat ironically, on the concept of the traditional instrumental suite, with its multiple movements of contrasting topics or moods, Milhaud elaborates on several distinct musical ideas and draws on his wide-ranging stylistic interests along the way. The first movement, bearing the title "Ouverture," immediately establishes a piquant Latin feel (reflecting, as do other of his pieces, the influence of Milhaud's two years' residence in Brazil several years earlier). The strong, underlying syncopation is punctuated by aggressive articulations such as rolled chords in the piano and strident bowings on the violin. After a contrasting central section in a more lyrical vein, the bold gestures and syncopations from the beginning return to round out the movement. The second movement, "Divertissement," utilizes intricate and playful imitative textures, as well as Milhaud's signature polytonal techniques. The violin and clarinet begin with an imitative duet largely based on a single rising and falling motif; after their initial duet, they alternate in gentle duets with the piano before playing in tandem in a "call and response" fashion. The piano then steps into the foreground and recalls the imitative passage from the opening, while the violin and clarinet assume a deliberately unidiomatic accompanimental role. In the spirit of its title, "Jeu" (French for play), the third movement is a boisterous folk dance based on a hearty and relentless rhythm. Featuring the clarinet and violin, the movement is an exercise in caricature; on the one hand, the violin happily juxtaposes with gritty foreground fiddling (complete with squealing attacks and intonational inflections) against the clarinet's secondary line; on the other, one hears folksy strumming behind the clarinet's lead melody. The fourth movement, "Introduction et final," begins with a somber introductory passage held in check by the intermittent tolling of a repeated octave in the lowest register of the piano. Listeners familiar with the introduction of Milhaud's ballet *La création du monde* will recognize that this kind of melodramatic pall is simply a foil for the lighthearted music to follow, and indeed, the slow introduction soon cedes to the bright melody, square phrases, and easy pace of the finale proper. The lucidity and regularity of this last section, of course, is occasionally thrown slightly off kilter with odd harmonic swerves and the kind of so-called "wrong-note" polytonal writing for which Milhaud is famous, finally culminating in a kind of jazzy cowboy tune that brings the movement and the suite to a close. *—Jeremy Grimshaw*

Recommended:

○ **Milhaud: Chamber Works** / Ens. Polytonaal / 2001 / Channel Classics 13998

String Quartets (1912–1952)

The string quartets play a curious role in Darius Milhaud's compositional oeuvre. In June 1920, he stated in print his desire to compose exactly 18 string quartets during his career, and made good on his word: by that time he had already composed five quartets, and over the course of the next three decades he would compose exactly 13 more (as well as a handful of other works for string quartet exhibiting various forms and bearing other titles). They seem to have served as a kind of exercise for him, a musical diary of sorts. He frequently asserted that after composing a dramatic work or vocal piece, he would return to the string quartet in an effort to rediscipline his compositional sensibilities, rein in his lyricism, and infuse his desire for experimentation with an equal measure of control and balance. In this same vein, he used his body of quartets as a distillation of his compositional development as well as a kind of microcosm of his output as a whole. Interestingly, as biographer and friend Paul Collaer points out, Milhaud borrows a theme from his Op. 1 (the unpublished *Poèmes de Francis Jammes*) for use in his first quartet; nearly 40 years later, as Milhaud fulfills his promised quartet quota, the same theme returns to fill out the cycle in the *Eighteenth Quartet*.

The quartets take on a variety of shapes and attitudes. The first three, composed during what could perhaps be considered the composer's early period, are in three, five, and two movements, respectively. The most striking of this group is the third; its somber twin movements, both marked Très lent, were penned during the war years in memory of Léo Latil, a close friend of Milhaud's who was killed in battle. The addition of a soprano and a text by the deceased adds a particular emotional depth to this work. Various circumstances and topics inspired the next several quartets, including Milhaud's well-known diplomatic sojourn in Brazil (the *Fourth Quartet*, Op. 46, in 1918), the completion of several large-scale operas and ballets (the challenging *Seventh Quartet*, Op. 87, from 1925), and the birthday of an important patroness (the *Tenth Quartet*, Op. 218, from 1940). The *Twelfth Quartet* (Op. 252) from 1945, coming as it does after the end of the war, seems to demonstrate markedly less stress and tension than the middle quartets; composed in tribute to Gabriel Fauré, the piece exhibits the sense of balance and serenity that Milhaud so admired in Fauré's work. Among the later quartets the most notable are perhaps the *Thirteenth Quartet* (Op. 268), composed during a trip to Mexico at the invitation of Carlos Chávez, the curious *Fourteenth* and *Fifteenth* (Opp. 46 and 64, respectively), which can be performed separately or simultaneously as an octet, and the moving *Dix-huitième Quartet* (Op. 308), dedicated to the memory of the composer's parents. At the end of this last quartet, Milhaud left the following note: "COMPLETED: the eighteen string quartets, 1912–1951." *—Jeremy Grimshaw*

Recommended:

○ **Milhaud: Integrale des Quatuors à Cordes** / Parisii Qt. / 2002 / Naive 4900

KEYBOARD

La muse ménagère, suite, Op. 245 (1944)

Darius Milhaud wrote *La muse ménagère* (The Household Muse) in Oakland, CA, in 1944 as a tribute to his wife, Madeleine. It is a set of 15 short pieces for piano solo that are so brief, in fact, that the whole set lasts less than 22 minutes. *La muse ménagère* is written in a straightforward, direct, and uncomplicated style which is nonetheless clearly of the modern era. The program of *La muse ménagère* is drawn from Milhaud's own home environment and is a deeply personal work that fairly beams with the love and respect that Milhaud felt for Madeleine. Madeleine Milhaud was a famous actress in France before the Second World War, working on several projects with her husband and creating the part of the narrator in Honegger's opera *Le roi David*. Once in California, Madeleine Milhaud obtained a post as an instructor in Mills College's French Theater program, and took on the unenviable task of staging the French Classics utilizing American students whose grasp of French was limited. In addition to all this work, Madeleine continued to make a home for herself and her husband. As Milhaud recalled, "life is hard for Madeleine here: there are no servants in the United States except at wages higher than the salaries of University professors. Madeleine has to cope with it all unaided: cleaning, buying provisions, cooking and washing-up, and we have a constant stream of visitors. She also acts as chauffeur for me (the diabetic Milhaud by this time was confined to a wheelchair) and has to snatch a few moments here and there for her own work and reading. You see the title of the little piano suite I wrote for her, *La muse ménagère*, is no fanciful allusion."

Individual titles of the 15 pieces are as follows, 1. "La Mienne" (My Own), 2. "Le Réveil" (Getting Up); 3. "Les Soins du ménage" (Household Chores); 4. "La Poésie"; 5. "La Cuisine"; 6. "Les Fleurs dans la maison" (Flowers in the House); 7. "La Lessive" (Washing); 8. "Musique ensemble"; 9. "Les Fils Peintre" (this refers to Milhaud's son Daniel, studying painting at the time); 10. "Le Chat" (The cat); 11. "Cartomancie" (Fortune-Telling); 12. "Les Soins au malade" (Nursing the Sick); 13. "La Douceur des soirées" (Giving Parties); 14. "Lectures Nocturnes" (Reading at Night) and 15. "Reconnaissance á la Muse" (Gratitude to the Muse).

La muse ménagère was published as Milhaud's Op. 245 and was relatively little known until NPR Classical radio programmers began to feature it as regular broadcast fare in the 1980s. Milhaud also created a chamber suite from this score that is practically never played. The work has since gained a strong following as its graceful lilt and understated charm is immediately appealing. *La muse ménagère* has also found acceptance among feminist theorists as a genuine and unbiased celebration of femininity, rare for a work by a male composer. *—Uncle Dave Lewis*

Recommended:

○ **Milhaud: Piano Music** / Tharaud / 1995 / Naxos 553443

Trois Rag-caprices, Op. 78 (1922)

Darius Milhaud composed his *Rag-Caprices* for piano a year before the premiere of his groundbreaking ballet *La création du monde*, so it is only expected that the pieces should reflect many of the rhythmic and harmonic ideas that would so prominently emerge in the later and much more well-known work. In this tiny trio of short pieces, Milhaud's playful approach to melodic writing, his characteristic use of polytonal harmonies, and his stylized appropriation of jazz rhythms and gestures are all evident. The first movement, "Sec et musclé," begins with a breezy melody presented chordally in the right hand above a slightly inconsistent bass pattern. The two hands operate in separate harmonic planes, with the treble material initially in F sharp and the walking bass in C sharp. Milhaud takes his occasional harmonic detours, indulges in unexpected melodic flourishes, and sometimes disrupts the rhythmic regularity of the accompaniment. A brief middle section momentarily waxes lyrical before returning to the opening material. The second time around, however, Milhaud adds incessant chord reiterations that are intermittently and rudely interrupted by sudden punches of staccato dissonant chords. The second movement, "Romance (Tendrement)," indulges in a lush, plaintive melody accompanied by simple chords and coy chromatic inflections. One may feel compelled to remain on guard for some kind of subversion of the tranquil mood but, as is often the case with Milhaud, the sentimental might turn just as easily toward the sincere as the ironic. The third movement, "Précis et nerveux," follows an angular trajectory, with numerous simultaneous layers: contrary motion between bass and treble lines, alternating chords in the left and right hands across a polytonal axis, and harmonically ambiguous but virtuosically gaudy gestures suddenly emerge from the composite texture. The busy chordal and melodic material is reined in by an insistent descending leap in the bass, which ultimately takes control before dropping to its lowest octave and bringing the movement and the piece as a whole to a delightfully off-kilter close. *—Jeremy Grimshaw*

Recommended:

○ **Milhaud: Piano Music** / Bolcom / 1975 / Nonesuch 71316

Saudades do Brasil, Op. 67 (1920–1921)

French composer Darius Milhaud's *Saudades do Brazil* is a suite of 12 dances for piano. In English, the title roughly translates to "Fond Remembrances of Brazil"; according to Milhaud, it was "inspired by South American rhythms and not based on folk music." Many writers assert that Milhaud began this suite in 1918 while still serving in Brazil as secretary to the French Ambassador, Paul Claudel. However, Milhaud places the beginning of his work on this suite in Denmark during the summer of 1920, where he was working under Claudel in a similar capacity. Max Eschig published the *Saudades* in 1922 in two volumes as opus 67, with Milhaud's orchestration of same appearing as opus 67b in 1923.

When Milhaud first arrived in the United States in 1940 he frequently performed the *Saudades* in personal appearances with American orchestras. This was partly due to the fact that *Saudades do Brazil* was one of only three orchestral scores available to Milhaud in the U.S. when he arrived. The work did enjoy some popularity mid-century, and Milhaud made a splendid recording of it with the Concert Arts Orchestra in Hollywood in 1958.

Each of the 12 *Saudades* averages about two minutes in length, with "Copacabana" being the longest at nearly two-and-a-half minutes and "Paineras" the shortest at just over a minute. There are basically two types of *Saudades*: those featuring a Brazilian dance rhythm played in the left hand against a slow, simple melody in the manner of Satie played in another key, and those which bring the rhythm to the fore, with both hands work together playing polytonal chords on the beat. "Sorocaba," "Botafago," "Leme," "Corcovado," "Paineras," and "Paysandu" belong to the first group; "Gavea," "Ipanema," "Sumare," and "Laranjeiras" the second, with "Copacabana" and "Tijuca" combining both approaches. "Copacabana" is somewhat reminiscent of Ravel, with its rapid-fire rhythms and widely spread polychords. In "Ipanema," dedicated to Artur Rubinstein, dissonant ninths fan out from cluster chords in the center of the keyboard. "Tijuca," dedicated to pianist Ricardo Viñes, seems to have found the widest acceptance among these pieces, transcribed by violinist Claude Levy in 1925 and by cellist Maurice Maréchal in 1933. It is a strange piece, darkened by clusters in a way Charles Ives would admire. In "Sumare" the right-hand melody is harmonized in open fourths, and the jazzy tincture of the "Viennese fourth" is heard several times. Overall the pieces are in ternary form; sometimes the middle section is very short, as in "Sumare." "Ipanema" is in three non-repeating sections with a coda.

Much has been made of Milhaud's extensive use of polytonality at this juncture. In *Saudades do Brazil* Milhaud uses polytonal combinations mostly to add harmonic color to the Brazilian rhythms he here so expertly adapts for the piano. The orchestration softens the bite of the tone clusters, at least in comparison to the piano version. Otherwise the *Saudades do Brazil* loses nothing of its charm or energy in the orchestral equivalent. *—Uncle Dave Lewis*

Recommended:

○ **Aantonio Barbosa, Pianist** / Barbosa / 1992 / Connoisseur Society 4190

Scaramouche, for 2 pianos, Op. 165b (1937)

Milhaud's *Scaramouche*, Op. 165b, takes its name not from the fictional character created by Rafael Sabatini, but from the Théâter Scaramouche, headed by Henri Pascar. The Théâter Scaramouche specialized in productions aimed at children; in May 1937 Milhaud contributed some music to Charles Vildrac's adaptation of Moliéré's *Le medécin volant* (The Flying Doctor). That same summer Milhaud was under pressure to produce a number of works for the Paris International Exposition; among them was a request for a piano duo for Marguerite Long and Milhaud's old friend Marcelle Meyer. Milhaud recycled two of the cues from *Le medécin volant* to form the outer movements of the suite, and for the slower middle movement extracted a piece written for Jules Superville's 1936 play *Bolivar*. The finished structure is as follows: 1. "Vif," 2. "Modéré," 3. "Brazileira" (Mouvement de Samba). Milhaud was quite facile at assembling pieces in this way, and was unnerved to note that the suite wasn't falling into place as easily as he'd hoped; Milhaud later remarked "it gave me enormous trouble."

Nonetheless, *Scaramouche* was ready in time for Marcelle Meyer and Marguerite Long to play it at the Paris Exposition. To Milhaud's dismay, it attracted immediate attention, and the publisher Deiss approached Milhaud with hopes of securing the rights. Milhaud at first resisted, thinking it too slight to merit publication, but Deiss persisted, and Milhaud finally caved in. A 78-rpm record of Meyer and Long playing *Scaramouche* was made and helped spread the word, and Meyer programmed the work at concerts given in Paris in 1943 during the German occupation.

As time went on, *Scaramouche* became something of a *bête noire* for Milhaud; it proved so popular over time that he found himself returning to it repeatedly in order to create new arrangements for publishers. The versions for clarinet and saxophone are best known apart from the original, but *Scaramouche* also exists in arrangements—not all by Milhaud—for concert band, wind sextet, chamber trio, three guitars, and even 16 saxophones. Jascha Heifetz transcribed "Modéré" and "Brazileira" for the violin; most unusually, the "Brazileira" was converted into a pop song, complete with added lyrics.

The bright, tumbling opening to "Vif"—sometimes bitter with bi-tonal effects, yet strongly diatonic—pricks up the ears right from the start; it resembles an out-of-tune Parisian street piano. The "Modéré" is graceful and understated, with a gentle, falling motion reminiscent of much popular music. The "Brazileira" is like an outtake from Milhaud's *Saudades do Brasil* of 1921, and is so close to that folk idiom that it could easily be mistaken for the "real" thing. Programmers of classical radio programs resort to the charms of the *Scaramouche* often; it grabs your attention, delivers the goods, and gets out the door—all in just eight minutes. *—Uncle Dave Lewis*

Recommended:

○ **Milhaud Plays & Conducts** / Milhaud / 1993 / EMI 54604

○ **Milhaud: Music for 2 Pianos** / Coombs, Pizarro / Hyperion 67014

CONCERTO

Concertos (1913–1969)

While Darius Milhaud is famous for composing prolifically in virtually every musical genre, the breadth of his musical swath is perhaps best demonstrated by the incredible variety of instruments for which he composed concertos. His works for one or more solo instruments and orchestra (or chamber orchestra) number around 40, and include so many instruments as to render their inventory alliterative: featured soloists include piano, percussion, harp, harpsichord, harmonica, violin, viola, and even vibraphone. He even composed a *Symphonie Concertante* (1959) for several soloists and ensemble, to cover all the instruments he had theretofore left out. Most of these works, particularly their outer movements, are tastefully flashy and virtuosic, utilizing Milhaud's characteristically bitonal harmonic progressions to create multiple planes upon which the soloist and ensemble can interact. Polytonality is utilized both as a dramatic and a dramaturgical device, sometimes heightening expression within the composite harmony and at other moments serving to delineate the musical "characters" within the concerto.

Pieces for solo piano and orchestra constitute the lion's share of Milhaud's concerto output. Between 1933 and 1955 he composed five numbered piano concertos, most of which are fairly accessible and unproblematic—at least for the listener; Milhaud had a sinister habit of occasionally writing deceptively lyrical figures that fell on the keyboard in such a way as to demand virtuosic but largely inaudible—and thus thankless—acrobatics to execute. He also penned several pieces that do not bear the title "concerto" but that nonetheless feature a solo piano with orchestra; the most noteworthy of these are the *Cinq études* from 1920 and the *Suite Concertante* from 1952. Also deserving mention are the two numbered concertos for two pianos (1941 and 1961, respectively), as well as the *Suite* Op. 300 and the *Concertino d'automne*.

Milhaud composed several soloistic works for string instruments, including three numbered violin concertos and other works with solo violin. The emotionally involved inner movement of the *Second Violin Concerto* (1946) sets that work apart from the busy virtuosity of the other pieces in this category. The *Viola Concerto No. 1* (1929) has a certain historical significance, having been commissioned for performance by Paul Hindemith; still, its successor (*Viola Concerto No. 2* from 1954) is arguably more engaging. Milhaud penned two concertos for cello as well—though, like many of Milhaud's concertos, these are rarely programmed today.

Notable among Milhaud's numerous other concertos is the well-known percussion concerto from 1929, a groundbreaking and virtuosic work employing no less than 16 percussion instruments. Much lesser known—and sadly so—is the *Concerto for Marimba, Vibraphone, and Orchestra* from 1947. The outer movements of this work feature dizzying harmonic circuitry, while the inner movement is perhaps among the most heartfelt and poignant passages in all of Milhaud's oeuvre. Among his remaining concertos are the curious *Suite anglaise* for solo harmonica (1942), several concertos for wind instruments, the *Concertino d'hiver* for trombone (1953) and the *Symphonie Concertante* for solo trumpet, horn, bassoon, and contrabass. *—Jeremy Grimshaw*

Recommended:

- ○ **Milhaud: Cello Concertos; Saint-Saëns: Cello Concerto 1** / Westerberg (cond.), Drobinsky, Swedish Radio Orch. / 2001 / Doron 3035
- ○ **Milhaud & Radanovics** / Theis (cond.), Zivkovic, Osterreichische Chamber Symphony / 1995 / Musicaphon 56809
- ○ **Milhaud: Orchestral Music** / Froment, Kontarsky, Milhaud (conds.), Koch, Johannesen, Koster, Seemann, Mattern, Mallach, Luxembourg Radio Orch. / 1994 / Vox 5109

Le carnaval d'Aix, fantasy for piano & orchestra, Op. 83b (1926)

In his introduction to Darius Milhaud's autobiography *A Happy Life*, Christopher Palmer finds the composer's meticulously crafted yet irrepressibly sunny style deeply rooted in his native environs. Milhaud was born in southern France and, according to Palmer, "the outline of the strong, rugged Provençal hills was engraved on his subconscious… Aix, in one form or another, is rarely absent from [his] music." *Carnaval d'Aix*, from 1926, is one of a handful of works in which the composer makes this connection explicit. Despite the title, however, the work was inspired not only by memories of Provence, but by the composer's wanderings abroad as well. Built as a continuous string of scenes drawn from his ballet *Salade* from 1924, the piece imagines a group of traditional Commedia dell'Arte characters from the Italian theater. However, having previously taken in the sights and sounds of Brazil during a time of diplomatic service there, Milhaud imagines the troupe costumed as if for Carnaval, but somehow transported across the Atlantic to the composer's homeland of Aix-en-Provence. Although artfully crafted, *Carnaval d'Aix* is not one of Milhaud's most imposing works, even given his generally lighthearted musical disposition. During the time of its composition, Milhaud was receiving increasing attention abroad and had begun to receive offers for engagements to play his own music with various prominent orchestras (he premiered the *Carnaval* with the New York Philharmonic, under the baton of Willem Mengelberg). Though a competent pianist, he did not consider concert performance his forte. And while Milhaud surely exaggerated somewhat on the side of self-deprecation, he was self-conscious enough about his pianistic abilities for such concerns to have informed his *Ballade for piano and orchestra*, Op. 61, which he also performed during his tours abroad. Likewise, of the *Carnaval d'Aix* Milhaud wryly explained that "As I was no virtuoso, I had to compose *for myself* an easy work which would give the audience the impression that it was difficult." The hallmarks of Milhaud's style are present: the curious chromatic diversions, subtle but poignant use of dissonance within tonal contexts, polytonal complexes, and especially, vibrant rhythms inspired by jazz and South American music. Of course, Milhaud puts virtuosity to the purposes of expressive nuance rather than sheer pyrotechnics even in his most challenging works. Accordingly, what the *Carnaval d'Aix* lacks in technical complexity on the part of the soloist, it makes up for in energy and charm. *—Jeremy Grimshaw*

Recommended:

- ○ **Milhaud** / Corp (cond.), New London Orch. / 1992 / Hyperion 66594

Concerto for percussion & chamber orchestra, Op. 109 (1929–1930)

This work, only seven minutes long, creates the impression of an important piece of music despite its brevity. It is written for a single percussion player seated at, more or less, a jazz drum set, although the work is only marginally uses jazz idioms. It begins with an arresting repeated note theme, after which the soloist enters playing a virtuoso part involving a remarkable number of percussion instruments. Throughout the concerto, the percussion instruments and the rest of the orchestra operate as equal partners, copying each other's melodic outlines and rhythmic patterns, punctuating each other's thoughts with color. The first movement continues in the militant mood of the opening call to attention, with a more fragmentary, leaping subsidiary theme. The forcefulness of the opening ideas begin to fade away into the second half of the work, which is quiet, mysterious, reminiscent of a tropical rain forest. The melodies are slow and mysterious, featuring muted brass solos, but the drum patterns remain fast while remaining in quiet balance with the mood of the orchestra. Only a couple of quotations of the opening militant figure intrude on this dark, haunted mood, which soon fades away. A cornerstone of the percussion repertoire and intriguing listening. *—Joseph Stevenson*

Recommended:

- ○ **Virtuoso Percussion Music** / Kuisma (cond.), Norrkoping SO / 1974 / Bis 149

ORCHESTRAL

Suite française, Op. 248b (1944)

Unlike his more popular *Suite Provençale*, which takes its inspiration from a single province of France, Darius Milhaud's *Suite Française* offers a whirlwind tour of several French regions. Its five brief movements were commissioned by an American publisher as easy pieces for wind ensemble; this was published as Milhaud's Op. 248 and the subsequent expansion for full orchestra is designated Op. 248b.

Beginning with the Atlantic coastal regions, "Normandie" is a jaunty march with a hummable melody that ultimately picks up strong accents well off the beat. A fragment of the tune spins off into a brief counter-subject that provides a moment of polytonality when it's played against the main theme in a different key. "Bretagne" is slower—lugubrious, even—with the bass instruments moaning over a forlorn, sentimental melody in the treble. Milhaud's grim, mildly dissonant harmonization of the tune feels desolate and a little threatening. "Ile-de-France" is full of bustle around a melody of almost childlike simplicity; Paris lies at this region's heart and the "Limoges" movement from Mussorgsky's *Pictures at an Exhibition* lies in this movement's inspiration. "Alsace-Lorraine" is the suite's second slow movement, not as dour as "Bretagne" but even more nostalgic. This region was long a source of dispute between France and Germany, changing hands over the years, and Milhaud's depiction of the region becomes increasingly threatening and dissonant, until the melody finally rings out in a confident, brassy peroration. "Provence," taking music from Milhaud's own beloved region, is the sunniest, most playful, and most rhythmically challenging movement. It's a rondo with a fast, scatterbrained main theme alternating with a fife-and-tambor segment typical of the countryside and a slower, slightly more romantic subject—both of these interludes derived from the principal melody. *—James Reel*

Recommended:

- ○ **Milhaud Conducts Milhaud** / Milhaud (cond.), New York PO / 2001 / Dutton 9711
- ○ **Milhaud: Scaramouche; Le Bal Martiniquais; Paris; etc.** / Pretre (cond.), Monte Carlo PO / 2001 / EMI 74740

Suite provençale, Op. 152a (1936)

Darius Milhaud is known for his keen sense of balance—his ability to infuse his experimental tendencies with an appropriate measure of restraint. Likewise, his playful, post-Dada persona finds a partial foil in the composer's devout Jewish identity. Such balance plays out in his compositional output as well: often, as an exercise in compositional discipline, he would compose a technically demanding, detailed chamber work on the heels of a lyrically ambitious vocal or operatic work. In this regard, Milhaud's *Suite provençale* serves as a microcosm of the composer's style and oeuvre. Its eight movements alternate rousing marches and fanfares with more somber and introspective themes, creating a work that, though characteristically austere and emotionally somewhat disengaged in its individual moments, creates a dramatic framework in which emotions held at arm's length nonetheless draw in the listener and focus one's sensibilities.

The work takes inspiration from eighteenth century Provençal themes, several of which are woven into the textures of the various movements. Among these are themes by André Campra, a French composer active in the late 1600s and early 1700s who, like Milhaud, hailed from Aix-en-Provence. Though this work draws on numerous historical topics and sounds, it would be only partially accurate to call it neoclassical. Here, Milhaud does utilize familiar musical ideas, but employs them for their immediately evocative properties, not simply for their referential possibilities.

The fanfare that begins the work ("Animé") is surprisingly rousing, the polytonal resistance between the upper and lower brass adding a dramatic edge rather than the sneer of pastiche. This partitioning is realized in the rhythms too, with some instruments following a straightforward beat while others anxiously leap forward with continual syncopations.

The pensive strings and winds of the second movement ("Trés modéré") recall the opening strains of Milhaud's *La Création du Monde*. Its cadential resolutions are heightened by familiar, but still effective, techniques. As the cadence approaches, polytonal distances increase. Likewise, resolutions to tonic chords are often punctuated further by the employment of two leading tones, both a lowered and a raised seventh, which combine in shimmering dissonance before resolving to the tonic root.

Similar textural and temporal juxtapositions characterize the rest of the work. Gestures are sometimes exaggerated, as in the absent downbeats and overheavy upbeats that drive some of the subsequent march materials, but never to the point of grotesquerie. Rather, such intentionally awkward structures have a propulsive effect, one that is enhanced by Milhaud's innovative and extensive use of percussion instruments. Likewise, the last movement juxtaposes harmonically meandering contrapuntal materials with a clearly evocative fife and drum texture, whose familiar surface is moiréd with grumbling dissonances in the bass and stuttering offset rhythms.

Still, one doesn't get a sense of parody or self-effacement from this music, but a sense of multidimensionality, where uncommon harmonic and rhythmic practices are employed to highlight those points that traditional rhythmic and harmonic structures tend to emphasize. Neoclassic shapes are retained while their edges and surfaces are ornamented with modern musical language. *—Jeremy Grimshaw*

Recommended:

○ **Milhaud: Scaramouche; Le Bal Martiniquais; Paris** / Prêtre (cond.), Monte Carlo PO / 2001 / EMI 74740

○ **Milhaud: Symphonies 1 & 2; Suite Provençale** / Plasson (cond.), Toulouse Orch. / DG 435437

SYMPHONIC

Symphonies and Chamber Symphonies (1917–1958)

Milhaud composed six chamber symphonies and 12 orchestral symphonies over the course of his long career. The former were all composed between 1917 and 1923 and represent some of Milhaud's best early works. They are all, in a sense, miniatures—not one of these works is over six minutes long—and are remarkably varied and unique, with each one scored for different instrument combinations. Formally, all six chamber symphonies are cast in a three-movement, quasi-sinfonia form, though only the first two really follow the fast-slow-fast arrangement of movements typical of the sinfonia. These works are comprised of complex, well-thought out relationships between instruments, with a strong emphasis on melodic concerns (typical of Milhaud). The instruments are treated, as a rule, soloistically, and the texture tends to be polyphonic. Themes are presented quickly and barely have time to develop in these short pieces; however, Milhaud's melodies are engaging and the orchestration is colorful yet clear. While among Milhaud's chamber music his 18 string quartets are better-known and perhaps more significant works, the chamber symphonies nonetheless exemplify his early style and clearly reflect his many years of experience as a violinist in chamber ensembles.

Milhaud was strongly influenced by the German symphonic tradition, and by the music of Beethoven, Mahler, and Mozart in particular. He did not begin composing full-scale symphonies until 1939, determining to wait until he had matured (he was nearly 50) before attempting to add his own music to the legacy of the German masters. Milhaud's symphonies strongly reflect his unique personality and musical values, eschewing much of the then still-dominant Romantic symphonic esthetic and Modernist trends and turning instead towards a Mozartean, Classical model for his work. There is more stasis than high drama in these works, as melodies are not played off against each other in an allegorical struggle, but rather are simply juxtaposed or repeated, with new melodies often appearing in lieu of development. Polytonality is an important feature of these symphonies, and there are blocks in these works wherein one hears seemingly unrelated fragments in juxtaposition; however, the musical fabric is ultimately held together by Milhaud's relentlessly diatonic melodies. These symphonies are not the psychological behemoths of the Romantics and early Moderns; they are works of clarity, with transparent orchestration, thoughtful melodies, and balanced phrases. This is not to say that Milhaud's symphonies lack emotion, but rather they are emotionally controlled and tasteful. They are also evocative and moody, often suggesting mystery, nostalgia, or childlike joy.

Milhaud wrote more symphonic music after his *Twelfth Symphony* was finished in 1961, in response to a number of commissions; however, these are not numbered as symphonies, but were instead designated by the name of the place that gave him the commission. These later works are also smaller in scale and scope than the symphonies. *—Alexander Carpenter*

Recommended:

○ **Milhaud: Complete Symphonies** / Francis (cond.), Basel Radio SO / CPO 999656

○ **Milhaud: 6 Little Symphonies; etc.** / Milhaud (cond.), Luxembourg Radio Orch. / 1994 / Vox 5109

VOCAL

Songs and song cycles (1909–1964)

Though a few of Milhaud's songs find their way into recital halls on a fairly frequent basis, a substantial number are relatively unknown. This is surely due to an abundance of material rather than to low quality, and while a thorough survey of the composer's considerable song output is impossible here (his catalog lists 265 individual pieces, comprising 64 opus numbers), a look at a few pieces from various styles offers at least a glimpse into Milhaud's development as a musical renderer of poetic texts.

Biographer and friend Paul Collaer roughly divided Milhaud's songs into four broad categories: the lyrical, the dramatic, the melodies, and a handful of songs influenced by the composer's Jewish heritage. Since Milhaud's compositional character seemed to assume a rather decided trajectory early on, some mostly early examples from each group may give listeners an idea of what to expect from the composer's song output as a whole.

The *Trois poèmes de Lucile de Chateaubriand* from 1913 exhibit traits familiar in the popular perception of Milhaud. Sentiments are light, harmonic language is playfully fluid, and rhythms are self-consciously misaligned, with straightforward eighth and quarter note figures in the piano bass and voice set against perpetually syncopated triplet figures in the right hand. Also representing the lyrical category are a pair of famously curious works, the *Machines agricoles* (1919) and the *Catalogue de fleurs* (1920). The latter depicts a would-be gardener waiting out the spring rain, leafing aloud through a seed catalog, and plotting out the coming season's flora; the former is a musical setting of lines from a farm equipment brochure, with bucolic pastoral strains cleverly associated with utilitarian lines such as "The three-in-one plough-seeder-trencher has stanchions and special girders to support the weight of the seed box."

Among the more dramatic works are the lamentational *Alissa* from 1913, a setting of long excerpts from André Gide's *La porte étroite*, and *Les soirées de Petrograd* (1919), a series of episodes depicting Revolution-era Russia. Also in this category one finds several evocative settings of texts by Paul Claudel and Léo Latil, both close friends of the composer. *Tristesses* (1956), a song cycle of 23 songs on poems by Francis Jammes, figures prominently in Milhaud's later output.

Collaer uses the term "melody," his third category, specifically to describe songs on symmetrically constructed texts, using as examples the *Poésies de Catulle*, composed in 1923 for voice and violin, and the five *Child Poems* (1916), on English texts by Rabindranath Tagore. The last category of songs and song cycles find inspiration in Milhaud's deep-rooted Jewish faith. Of particular personal importance to the composer were his *Poèmes juifs*, a collection of eight songs from 1916, that address various aspects of Jewish life and identity. Similarly close to the composer's heart is the *Liturgie comtadine* (1933), a setting of five songs of Rosh Hashanah. *—Jeremy Grimshaw*

Recommended:

○ **Milhaud: Selected Songs** / Steinberg, Abramowitsch / Music & Arts 1024

CHORAL

Service sacre pour le samedi matin, Op. 279 (1947)

This composition by one of the twentieth century's important Jewish composers is a highly non-traditional work, religiously and historically speaking. It was commissioned by the Temple Emanuel-El of San Francisco, CA. (Milhaud had been a resident of the Bay Area since fleeing occupied France at the outset of World War II.) The two major non-traditional elements are the use of polyphonic textures (Jewish music is traditionally single-voiced) and the use of instruments for a liturgical text, particularly one designed for the Sabbath morning services.

Milhaud's style was strongly based in polyphony, often so strongly that he often put different voices in different keys at once. The melodic content of the *Sacred Service* is based on older modes derived from traditional Jewish music. The style of the melodies reflects the traditional cantillation of Hebrew texts. He does this by effective ornamentation of the main curve of the melodies.

Most importantly, his music reflects a deep and thoughtful faith. Despite the use of polyphony and instruments it strongly evokes the long tradition of Jewish worship. Its emotional content is joyful, full of love and caring. *—Joseph Stevenson*

Recommended:

○ **Milhaud: Service Sacré pour le Samedi Matin** / Milhaud (cond.), Rehfuss, Paris National Opera Theater Orch. / Accord 201892

MUSICAL THEATER

Les Choéphores, incidental music, Op. 24 (1915)

Darius Milhaud was living in Brazil when he completed *Les Choéphores* (The Libation Bearers) in 1916. This work forms the middle part of Milhaud's Orestian trilogy, written in collaboration with the poet Paul Claudel. *Les Choéphores* is set for vocal soloists, chorus, orchestra, and a battery of percussion instruments; it is divided into seven scenes: "Funeral Clamor" (Vocifération funébre), "Libation," "Incantation," "Omens" (Présages), "Exhortation," "Justice and Light" (La Justice et la Lumière), and "Conclusion." As is the case with Berlioz's *La Damnation de Faust*, the work is neither wholly opera nor cantata, but combines elements of both forms.

The work is dedicated to Charles Koechlin, and some of the orchestral writing recalls the latter's rich, otherworldly textures. Chords used in the "Incantation" also betray Debussy's influence, and Milhaud certainly could not have escaped the example of Richard Strauss' *Elektra*. However, Milhaud's conception is still highly original.

The instrumental content of *Les Choéphores* favors a nebulous and slightly tart polytonal combination of keys, sometimes resulting in orchestral tone clusters. His vocal writing for both chorus and soloists goes through long passages that are independent of the orchestral compliment, which provides an emotional backdrop for the action. Though Milhaud's harmonic language is sometimes impressionist-derived, his outlook is more expressionist and dramatic in style. The "Libation" section is scored for chorus alone, recalling the ghostly sound of Anton Webern's choral writing, the men supporting the women with wordless vowels.

The most unusual feature of *Les Choéphores* is in "Omens" (Presages), "Exhortation," and "Conclusion," where the orchestra is silent and the chorus is accompanied by percussion only. About this Milhaud wrote: "(These) scenes create a difficult problem for the composer; they are savage, cannibal as it were. The lyrical element in these scenes is not musical. How was I to set music to this hurricane? I finally decided to make use of a measured speech, divided into bars, and conducted as if it were sung." These parts feature a single chorus member, who recites the majority of the text as the rest of the chorus responds with syllables such as "ho" and "ha." A choral soloist with acting ability can make a lot of this part. The extensive use of percussion in this section pre-dates even Antheil's *Ballet Mécanique* by nearly a decade; Milhaud continued this practice into his ballet *L'Homme et son Désir* (1918).

The work was not heard until 1927, when Milhaud led the premiere of *Les Choéphores* at the *Paris Opera*. While not new, *Les Choéphores* was still considered shocking by the standards of its own era. A debate opened up in the Paris newspapers about the relative merits of *Les Choéphores*, with conservative critics rejecting it out of hand as the work of a madman. As time has moved forward, there are few doubts about the sincerity of Milhaud's vision, yet *Les Choéphores* is not often revived. Conductor Leonard Bernstein proved one of the few champions of this work. *—Uncle Dave Lewis*

Recommended:

- ○ **Milhaud: Les Choéphores; Roussel: Symphony 3; Honegger: Rugby; Pacific 231** / Bernstein (cond.), Boatwright, Babikian, Zorina, Jordan, New York PO, New York Schola Cantorum / 1996 / Sony 62352

Sherrill Milnes

b. Jan. 10, 1935, Downers Grove, IL
Baritone

The Verdi baritone is almost a vocal type in and of itself. These roles require outstanding breath control as well as the ability not only to sing strong high notes, but to sing for extended periods in the upper part of the baritone range. Milnes had both of these, and for a while even considered a career as a Wagner tenor rather than a baritone. His timbre was not to all tastes, but his vocal gifts, musicality, and powerful stage presence made him the leading baritone at the Met, where most of his career was focused.

He came from a musical family, and his mother was his first teacher. As often happens in such families, he learned to play not only the piano, but many other instruments, both in the string and the brass families. He studied at Drake and at Northwestern University, anticipating a career as a music teacher rather than as a performer, and sang in the Chicago Symphony Chorus under the legendary Margaret Hiller, also playing bass in a jazz band on the side. He also studied for a period with famed soprano Rosa Ponselle, and was an apprentice at the Santa Fe Opera, known for launching new artists as well as works. In 1960, he successfully auditioned for the Boris Goldovsky Opera Company, one of the most renowned touring companies in the United States, and made his opera debut with them as Masetto in Mozart's *Don Giovanni*. He remained with them for five years, singing many of the major Verdi baritone roles, as well as graduating to the title role of *Don Giovanni*, and also appearing at other opera houses such as the Baltimore Opera in 1961. In 1964, he appeared at the New York City Opera as Valentin in *Faust*, and made his Italian debut at the Teatro Nuovo in Milan. The next year he gave his first performance at the Met as Valentin, opposite Montserrat Caballe in her Met debut role. In 1967, he created the role of Adam Brant in Levy's *Mourning Becomes Electra*. His Vienna State Opera debut in 1970, in the title role of Verdi's *Macbeth*, brought him to international fame. He made his Chicago debut in 1971 as Posa in Verdi's *Don Carlo* as well as his Covent Garden debut as Renato in *Un ballo in maschera*.

During the 1980s, he underwent a vocal crisis, and made relatively few operatic appearances afterwards (having more or less reached retirement age) though he remained active as an oratorio singer and recitalist, as well as a conductor.

His Iago on the recording of *Otello* with James Levine (BMG GD 82951) verges on being over the top, but is nonetheless one of the most vivid recordings of that role. A recital CD on Decca (443 929) of materials largely from early in his career shows off his fine top notes as well as strong technical facility. *—Ann Feeney*

Recommended:

- ○ **Rossini: Il barbiere di Siviglia** / Levine (cond.), Constable, Gedda, Milnes, Sills, London SO / 2003 / EMI 85523
- ○ **Verdi: Il Trovatore** / Mehta (cond.), McCarthy, Price, Domingo, Milnes / 1998 / RCA 7432139504
- ○ **Verdi: Otello** / Levine (cond.), Domingo, McCarthy, Scotto, Milnes / 1998 / RCA 7432139501
- ○ **Verdi: Otello** / Mehta (cond.), Price, Domingo, Milnes, Plishka, New Philharmonia / 1973 / RCA 01052

Nathan Milstein

b. Dec. 31, 1904, Odessa, Russia, **d.** Dec. 21, 1992, London, England
Violinist

Although Nathan Milstein hailed from Odessa, the cradle of Russian violin playing, his personal style was more classical and intellectual in approach than many of his colleagues. By the middle of the twentieth century he had become one of the most renowned violinists in the world, and he did as much as anyone else to imbue Bach's solo violin partitas and sonatas with the rather mystical aura they have presently. Milstein began to study violin at the age of seven. His first teacher was Pyotr Stolyarsky, who remained with him through 1914. Milstein's last recital as a Stolyarsky pupil included another promising student, the five-year-old David Oistrakh. Milstein then went to the St. Petersburg Conservatory to study with Leopold Auer.

Milstein began his concert career at age ten in Odessa, and soon after he played Glazunov's concerto with the composer conducting. He continued to tour the Soviet Union for the next five years. During this time, Milstein made numerous joint appearances with Vladimir Horowitz, and Horowitz's sister Regina also joined them as Milstein's accompanist. In 1925, Milstein and Horowitz were encouraged by government officials to make a concert trip outside of Russia; Milstein would never return. Milstein recalled in his memoirs that the dramatic "grand manner" of Horowitz immediately made the pianist a star, while Milstein, a much more reserved person, did not have such immediate success. In 1926, he went to Brussels to consult with and discuss matters of interpretation with the great violinist and teacher Ysaÿe.

He made his American debut with Leopold Stokowski and the Philadelphia Orchestra in 1929, and made his New York debut in 1930. He soon established his base there, eventually becoming a United States citizen in 1942. He may not have become a concert-hall idol like Horowitz, but he had a strong musical reputation and was always in demand. When Arturo Toscanini ended his tenure as music director of the New York Philharmonic in 1936, he asked for Milstein as soloist in his final concert. After World War II Milstein made his home primarily in London, teaching master classes around the world. He was widely regarded as a sympathetic and approachable teacher.

He also established a major recording career and remains best known for his landmark recordings of the complete solo works of J.S. Bach, becoming a pioneer of the Bach solo violin literature at a time when few players programmed these pieces, and he eschewed more superficial works that were a primary part of the violin soloist's repertory. His 1950s recording of the Bach solo partitas and sonatas on the American Capitol Records label are exemplary traversals of that great cycle and are still counted as classics of recording art. Milstein maintained a remarkably long career, keeping the muscular strength and fluid joint motion he needed until his retirement at the age of 83, acquiesced to only after he broke his arm in a fall. *—Joseph Stevenson*

Recommended:

- ○ **Milstein-Balsam: 1953 Library of Congress Recital** / Milstein, Balsam (piano) / 1996 / Bridge 9066
- ○ **Milstein Encores** / Milstein, Firkušný, Pommers, Bussotti / 1999 / Angel 66872
- ○ **Art of Nathan Milstein** / Milstein, etc. / 1993 / EMI 64830
- ○ **Bach: Sonatas & Partitas** / Milstein / DG 457701

Marc Minkowski

b. Oct. 4, 1962, Paris, France
Conductor

Marc Minkowski was one of the most promising conductors to emerge in the 1990s, having carved out a niche for himself (and his hand-picked ensemble, Les Musiciens du Louvre) in the lesser-known works of the French and Italian Baroque. In the competitive fields of early music and historical performance, he has garnered considerable critical acclaim and managed to bring works of relative obscurity to the attention of wider audiences.

Minkowski began his career as a bassoonist, becoming a baroque specialist during his tenure with such ensembles as Les Arts Florissants, the Clemencic Consort of Vienna, and La Chapelle Royale. His interest in conducting flourished during studies with the highly respected French conductor Charles Bruck at the Pierre Monteux School in Hancock, Maine. After taking first prize at the first International Early Music Competition in Bruges (1984), Minkowski founded his own early instrument ensemble, Les Musiciens du Louvre, with which he has made the bulk of his recordings.

His biggest successes have come in the realm of dramatic music, where his revivals of works by Gluck, Lully, Purcell and Handel have drawn attention to his text-oriented dramatic sense. This same approach has borne similar fruit in the oratorios and choral works of Handel, which he has made a staple of his repertory.

Minkowski and Les Musiciens du Louvre signed an exclusive contract with Deutsche Grammophon's Archiv Produktion label in 1994, and in 1997 they joined forces with the Orchestre de Chambre de Grenoble. *—AMG*

Recommended:

○ **Rameau: Dardanus** / Minkowski (cond.), Ainsley, Gens, Kozena, Courtis, Musicians of the Louvre / 2000 / Archiv 463476

○ **Handel: Ariodante** / Minkowski (cond.), Otter, Dawson, Podles, Croft, Musicians of the Louvre / Archiv 457271

○ **Hippolyte et Aricie** / Minkowski (cond.), Laplenie, Zylberajch, Gens, Middenway, Musicians of the Louvre / Archiv 445853

Minnesota Orchestra

f. 1903, Minneapolis, MN
Ensemble

The Minnesota Orchestra, one of the leading American orchestras, has often been referred to as the "orchestra on wheels" because of its extensive touring. Its first tour occurred in the spring of 1907, a mere three and a half years after its formation. National tours soon led to world tours. When not on tour, the Orchestra's home was at the Minneapolis Auditorium until 1930, when they moved to the Northrop Auditorium at the University of Minnesota. The Orchestra's present home, Orchestra Hall, was constructed on the site of the original Minneapolis Auditorium and opened in 1974.

The Minnesota Orchestra was known as the Minneapolis Symphony Orchestra throughout much of its existence. The change in name reflects its evolution from a local metropolitan orchestra to one embraced by the entire state of Minnesota. The Minnesota Orchestra, like so many others, has its roots in local, amateur choral and instrumental ensembles. Emil Oberhoffer, director of the Philharmonic Club ensemble, sought the funds to found a permanent orchestra. With a group of the Danz Orchestra to form the core of the orchestra, his efforts came to fruition with the inaugural performance of the 60-member Minneapolis Symphony Orchestra on November 5, 1903.

The Orchestra has had nine music directors since its inception. The first, Emil Oberhoffer, directed the Orchestra until 1922. During his 19-year tenure, he oversaw the development of the Orchestra into a nationally acclaimed and well-traveled ensemble. Upon Oberhoffer's retirement, Henri Verbrugghen was selected to lead the Orchestra. Under his direction, the Orchestra performed its first radio broadcast in 1923, and made their first recordings. Besides expanding their classical repertoire, he introduced new music by the avante-garde of the time: Schoenberg, Stravinsky, and Honegger. Shortly after completing the 1930–31 season, Verbrugghen was stricken with a cerebral hemorrhage.

Verbrugghen's successor was Eugene Ormandy. His talent and drive, which earned him acclaim as a "young genius," likened to Toscanini and Stokowski, is credited with seeing the Orchestra successfully through America's great depression. Ormandy stayed with the Orchestra only a few short years. He left in 1936 and was replaced by Dmitri Mitropoulos.

Under Mitropoulos the Orchestra furthered its exploration of progressive music, particularly that of Schoenberg, Berg, and Krenek. But they also featured such Romantics as Schumann and Mendelssohn. Although Mitropoulos was criticized for his rather unorthodox programming, paying little heed to audience desires or balance between traditionalists and progressives, he succeeded in earning a worldwide recognition for the Orchestra.

Mitropoulos left the Orchestra in 1949 and was replaced by Antal Dorati. During his 11 years with the Orchestra, Dorati programmed performances with local choruses, directed their first television appearances, and, in 1957, led them on a world tour to Europe, the Middle East, and India, sponsored by the State Department.

Stanislaw Skrowaczewski assumed the role of director when Dorati left in 1960. Under Skrowaczewski, the Orchestra expanded both its membership and its season, now performing 50 weeks a year. During his tenure, in 1968, the Minneapolis Symphony Orchestra became The Minnesota Orchestra. He presided over numerous special events, including the 1965 concert at the United Nations on Human Rights Day and Stravinsky's guest appearance in 1966. The Orchestra was rewarded twice with the ASCAP award for programming of contemporary music.

Sir Neville Marriner became the seventh director in 1979. Marriner led the Orchestra through extensive recordings and, in 1980, began national weekly radio broadcasts. He turned the directorship over to Edo de Waart in 1986, who in turn relinquished the role to Eiji Oue in 1995. Osmo Vänskä was name music director in 2003. The Orchestra remains "the orchestra on wheels" with a European tour completed in the 2000 season. *—Bruce Lundgren*

Recommended:

○ **Kernis: Colored Field; Musica Celestis; Air** / Oue (cond.), Moerk, Minnesota Orch. / 2001 / Virgin 45464

○ **Mahler: Symphony 1; Rachmaninoff: Isle Of The Dead** / Mitropoulos (cond.), Minnesota Orch. / 1996 / Sony 62342

○ **Glazunov: The Seasons** / de Waart (cond.), Minnesota Orch. / 1993 / Telarc 80347

Drew Minter

b. Jan. 11, 1955, Washington, DC
Countertenor

American Drew Minter is one of the world's leading countertenors and is active in early music (the natural era of that type of voice), but also in contemporary music.

He began performing at the age of nine as a boy treble in the Washington National Cathedral in the nation's capital. He graduated from Indiana University's School of Music in 1977. By then he had already won a prize in the 's-Hertogenbosch International Singing Competition in 1976. He joined the Collegium Musicum Budapest and in 1977 shared in its prize in the Bruges Early Music Competition. He also received Martha Baird Rockefeller and Fulbright study grants. He continued his musical studies at the Hochschule für Musik in Vienna, winning his performer's diploma in 1979.

He won a prize in the 1981 Erwin Bodky Competition. Entering the Bruges Early Music Competition in 1983, he won a prize as a soloist. He continued his vocal and musical studies with Myron McPherson, whom he cites as his principal instructor.

Minter is a founding member of the Newberry Consort, Trefoil, and of My Lord Chamberlain's Consort, a vocal and plucked-string band, in which he both sings and plays early harps. Other ensembles with which he regularly performs include the Washington, D.C., vocal chamber music group Ensemble Five/One, the Folger Consort, and the early music vocal ensemble Pomerium. In addition, he has sung with such groups as Les Arts Florissants, the Academy of Ancient Music, Philharmonia Baroque Orchestra, the Freiburger Baroque Opera, Tafelmusik, and the Handel and Haydn Society. He has appeared at festivals such as BAM's Next Wave, the Boston Early Music Festival, and the Spoleto, Regensburg, and Edinburgh Festivals and the Handel Festivals of Hallé, Karlsruhe, Maryland, and Göttingen.

In addition to this active schedule of concert and recital appearances, he is highly active on the early operatic stage. He has sung leading roles in opera for the Opéras of Nice, Marseilles, Toulouse, and Brussels, and the BAM, Wolf Trap, Berkshire, Omaha, Santa Fe, Boston, Washington, Skylight, and Glimmerglass opera companies or festivals.

In 1994, Minter began a second career as an opera stage director, and has over 20 productions to his credit. As a singer or a director (or both) he has participated in productions of over two dozen Handel dramatic works. He directs them based on deep research of the acting methods and stage practice of the era. He also sings many Handel oratorios and other vocal/choral works, estimating that he had sung *Messiah* over 200 times in his career as of the year 2000.

Minter has made over 50 recordings and two films, including Peter Sellars' production of *Giulio Cesare* (as Tolomeo) and in a biography of the life of Abbess Hildegard von Bingen. He contributes regularly to *Opera News* magazine.

He also is widely known as a teacher. He conducts master classes and lessons on interpretation of early vocal music, the instrumental technique of early harps, and dramatic interpretation and staging of Baroque opera, including a class that discusses both the physical gestures and musical ornamentations well known to all Baroque opera singers. He has taught as a guest professor at Vassar and Smith Colleges, and is a regular teacher at the Amherst Early Music workshops. He has also prepared his own realization of Purcell's *Dido and Aeneas*. *—Joseph Stevenson*

Recommended:

○ **Elizabethan Songs** / Minter, O'Dette (lute) / 2001 / Classical Express 3957023

○ **Purcell Songs** / Minter, Springfels, O'Dette, Meyerson / 1992 / HM 7907035

○ **Handel: Opera Arias Vol. 1** / McGegan (cond.), Minter, Greer, Philharmonia Baroque / 2001 / Classical Express 3955183

Shlomo Mintz

b. Oct. 30, 1957, Moscow, Russia
Violinist

After a heady burst of international celebrity, Russian-born violinist/violist/conductor Shlomo Mintz has settled into his mature years, making solo appearances primarily as a violinist and conducting orchestras, both chamber-sized and those of full symphonic proportions. More intimate chamber music also engages his attention with some frequency. Mintz studied in Israel with Ilona Feher beginning in 1964, continuing in her care until 1973. His professional debut took place in 1968 when he performed with the Israel Philharmonic Orchestra directed by Zubin Mehta. In 1973, the young artist left his country for the United States (and a Carnegie Hall debut) to continue his studies with the celebrated Dorothy DeLay at the Juilliard School of Music, strengthening his technique and seasoning his interpretive skills. An extensive European tour in 1977 brought recognition in numerous venues as Mintz performed with leading orchestras directed by many of the finest conductors. A series of recordings for Deutsche Grammophon followed. First, a 1980 release of the Mendelssohn and Bruch concertos with Claudio Abbado leading the Chicago Symphony Orchestra and the two Prokofiev concertos with the same forces. Two years later, an all-star Vivaldi *The Four Seasons* placed Mintz in the company of Itzhak Perlman, Pinchas Zukerman, and Isaac Stern. A few years later, DG released a recording of the Sibelius and Dvořák concertos with James Levine and the Berlin Philharmonic; a disc of Franck, Debussy, and Ravel sonatas; and a recording of the Paganini caprices. From 1989 to 1993, Mintz served as conductor of the Israel Chamber Orchestra, also leading such larger symphonic ensembles as the Rotterdam Philharmonic Orchestra and the Israel Philharmonic Orchestra. In 1994, Mintz was engaged as music director of the Limburg Symphony Orchestra in Maastricht, while still continuing to perform as a guest soloist around the world. A 2001 performance of the Mendelssohn violin concerto in St. Louis, for example, drew a loud and prolonged ovation. A member of the Golan/Mintz/Haimovitz Trio, Mintz also plays recitals, often with his trio colleague Itamar Golan, and sometimes with Georges Pludermacher. Mintz has received recognition for his recordings, having been awarded a Grand Prix du Disque on several occasions. His Vivaldi series for MusicMasters recorded with the Israel Chamber Orchestra was well received when it came on the market in the early 1990s. Recognition also came in 1984 with an award of the Premio Accademia Musicale Chigiana. Mintz performs on two distinctive instruments, each noted for its burnished tone. His violin is a Guarneri del Gesù dated 1700, while his viola is by Carlo Giuseppe Testore from 1696. *—Erik Eriksson*

Recommended:

- ○ **Paganini: 24 Capricci** / Mintz / DG 415043
- ○ **Prokofiev: The Violin Concertos** / Abbado (cond.), Mintz, Chicago SO / DG 410524

Dimitri Mitropoulos

b. Mar. 1, 1896, Athens, Greece, **d.** Nov. 2, 1960, Milan, Italy

Conductor

Conductor Dimitri Mitropoulos stood apart from the European traditions that dominated first-rank American orchestras for much of the twentieth century. After attending the Athens Conservatory, where he studied piano and composition, his opera *Béatrice* was presented there. The French composer Saint-Saëns was in the audience, and was so impressed that he arranged a scholarship that enabled the 24-year-old to study composition with the Belgian composer Paul Gilson and piano with Busoni in Berlin. Busoni persuaded him to abandon composition and concentrate on becoming a conductor.

From 1921 to 1925, Mitropoulos assisted Erich Kleiber at the Berlin State Opera and on Kleiber's recommendation, was appointed conductor of the Hellenic Conservatory Symphony Orchestra in Athens. In 1927, he became conductor of the Greek State Symphony Orchestra and in 1930 was engaged to conduct the Berlin Philharmonic Orchestra, where he instituted the practice of conducting from the piano.

In 1937 Mitropoulos succeeded Eugene Ormandy as musical director of the Minneapolis Symphony Orchestra in 1937. He became a U.S. citizen in 1946, and remained in America until 1959. After 12 years in Minneapolis, he was invited to share the conductorship of the New York Philharmonic Orchestra with Stokowski, becoming its conductor when Stokowski resigned in 1950. Mitropoulos resigned the post after sharing the podium with Leonard Bernstein, his co-principal conductor, in the Orchestra's 1958 tour of Latin America. From 1954, he was a dynamic force as Bruno Walter's successor at New York's Metropolitan Opera, where he introduced many new operas, including ones by Richard Strauss and Samuel Barber.

Mitropoulos never conducted his own works, but considered his best composition to be a Concerto Grosso written in 1929. His lived simply and took little part in social activities. His conducting style was passionate, highly-charged and demonstrative; he had a phenomenal memory and rarely used a baton. The American composer and music critic Virgil Thomson once described him as "oversensitive, overweening, over brutal, over intelligent, underconfident and wholly without ease.... His personal excitement borders on hysteria and he distorted music with nervous passion." Whether or not this judgement was true, or fair, he programmed much modern music and particularly admired Schoenberg and the Second Viennese School, such as Webern and Berg, as well as twentieth century American and British composers. His recording of Mahler's *First Symphony* made with the Minneapolis Symphony Orchestra in 1941 was the first ever made in the U.S. of that work, and Mitropoulos was awarded the American Mahler Medal of Honor in 1950 for his work in promoting the composer's music. He died while rehearsing Mahler's *Third Symphony* with Toscanini's famous La Scala Orchestra. *—Roy Brewer*

Recommended:

- ○ **Berg: Wozzeck** / Mitropoulos (cond.), Ross, Farrell, Dorow, Lloyd, New York PO / 1997 / Sony 62759
- ○ **Schoenberg: Pelleas & Melisande; Scriabin: Symphony 5** / Mitropoulos (cond.), New York PO / Music & Arts 967
- ○ **Great Conductors of the 20th Century: Dimitri Mitropoulos** / Mitropoulos (cond.), New York PO, Cologne WDR SO / 2003 / EMI 75471
- ○ **Mitropoulos: Maestro Spiritoso** / Mitropoulos (cond.), Rubinstein, Graudan, New York PO, NBCSO, Minneapolis SO / 2003 / TIM 220829

Anna Moffo

b. Jun. 27, 1935, Wayne, PA

Soprano

American lyric-dramatic soprano Anna Moffo rose quickly to become one of the world's best-known opera singers in the 1950s and remained a leading star into the 1970s. Her parents were Nicolas Moffo and Regina (Cinti) Moffo. Anna made her singing debut at the age of seven in a school assembly with *Mighty Lak' a Rose*. She sang frequently in her town and surrounding regions. Possessing notable beauty to go along with her voice, she was offered a chance to audition for Hollywood. She elected music instead, winning a four-year scholarship to study at the Curtis Institute of Music in Philadelphia. Her teacher there was Eugenia Giannini-Gregory.

She won the Young Artists Auditions in 1955. A Fulbright Scholarship the same year enabled her to travel to Italy and study at the Accademica di Santa Cecilia in Rome with Luigi Ricci and Mercedes Llopart. To help support herself she worked as an X-ray technician and typist. She debuted on stage as Norina in *Don Pasquale* (Donizetti) at Spoleto. Her warm, lyric voice and full tone attracted much attention, while her slim, attractive figure and beautiful stage appearance suited her to visual media. She was engaged to sing the title role of Butterfly by television director Mario Lanfranchi. This 1956 broadcast made her an instant star in Italy, and gained her international fame. She sang other Italian television opera productions, including *Lucia di Lammermoor* and *La fille du régiment*. She made her French debut in 1956, singing Zerlina (Mozart's *Don Giovanni*) at Aix-en-Provence. She appeared throughout Italy, and debuted at Teatro alla Scala in *Falstaff* in 1957. She first appeared in America as Mimì in *La bohème* at the Lyric Opera of Chicago. In the same year she married Lanfranchi.

On November 14, 1959, she first sang at the Metropolitan Opera in what was to be one of her most important roles, Violetta in Verdi's *La traviata*. In 1960 she began to host a program about opera on Italian television, *The Anna Moffo Show*, which continued until 1973. She was voted one of the ten most beautiful women in Italy. In the 1960–61 season she sang three roles at the Met: Gild in *Rigoletto*, Adina in *L'Elisir d'Amore*, and Liù in *Turandot*, with Franco Corelli and Birgit Nilsson. She was a major vocal recording artist on the RCA Victor label.

Some of her other important roles were Pamina (*The Magic Flute*), Luisa Miller, Debussy's Mélisande, a sparkling rendition as the heroine in Offenbach's operetta *La Périchole*, and all four leading female parts in the same composer's *Les contes d'Hoffmann*. She sang at the major European opera houses, and was most associated over her career with the parts of Violetta (which she sang over 900 times) and *Lucia di Lammermoor* (500 performances). She appeared in filmed and videotaped operas, but also in non-operatic dramatic films, including the prize-winning *Una storia d'amore*.

In 1972 she and Lanfranchi were divorced and she married Robert Sarnoff, the chairman of RCA. By 1974 she had sung 220 performances in 18 operas at the Met. She had allowed herself to be pushed into making too many commitments and in that year she suffered a severe vocal collapse, which kept her off the stage for two years. When she returned, she focused more on lyrical parts, but soon was able to expand to the more dramatic roles by Verdi (Leonora in *Il trovatore*, for instance) and in 1991 added Bellini's *Norma*. In 1999, the Met honored her with a gala celebrating the 40th anniversary of her debut. *—Joseph Stevenson*

Recommended:

- ○ **Canteloube, Villa-Lobos, Rachmaninoff** / Stokowski (cond.), Moffo, American SO / 1965 / RCA 7831
- ○ **Arias** / Serafin (cond.), Moffo, Rome Opera House Orch. / 1999 / BMG 635302
- ○ **Humperdinck: Hänsel & Gretel** / Eichhorn (cond.), Fischer-Dieskau, Moffo, Ludwig, Auger, Munich Radio Orch. / 1999 / RCA 252812
- ○ **Verdi: La Traviata** / Previtali (cond.), Merrill, Moffo, Palma, Tucker, Rome Opera House Orch. & Chorus / 1997 / RCA 902668885

Kurt Moll

b. Apr. 17, 1938, Buir, Germany

Bass

A true bass voice is a relative rarity in the operatic world (though not as rare as a true contralto), and all too often, even the major candidates "gravel out" at the bottom of their ranges instead of singing, or have a tendency to bark or at least overuse sprechstimme while singing. Kurt Moll is one of the basses known for *singing* every note of his roles, even the lowest notes for Osmin in *The Abduction from the Seraglio*. The richness and sonority of his voice and sensitivity to the inflections of both music and text make him one of the foremost performers of Wagner bass roles, especially King Mark in *Tristan and Isolde* and Gurnemanz in *Parsifal*, perhaps his most acclaimed role. He is also known for his lieder singing, and is especially admired for his renditions of Brahms' *Four Serious Songs*. He and Hermann Prey have championed the songs of Loewe, a song composer greatly overshadowed by Schubert and Schumann.

He first studied at the Cologne Hochschule für Musik, and while a student, made occasional appearances in small roles at the Cologne opera, though his official debut was not until 1961, as Lodovico in *Otello*. He sang at most of the small opera houses in Germany during the 1960s, slowly rising to larger parts and more prestigious houses. He joined the Hamburg Staatsoper in 1970, the same year of his Salzburg debut, and he made his Bayreuth Festival debut in 1974 as Fafner in *Das Rheingold*. His La Scala debut was also in 1974 as King Mark in *Tristan and Isolde*, and his Covent Garden debut was the next year as Caspar in *Der Freischütz*.

In 1982, he first began to perform Russian roles, first singing Pimen in *Boris Godunov* at the Vienna State Opera, and adding the title role of that opera to his repertoire in 1983, also at the Vienna State Opera. He has been cautious about adding new roles, repeatedly turning down Wagner's Wotan and Hans Sachs, as they are written (particularly Hans Sachs) in a higher tessitura, closer to bass-baritone than bass, and so might require the kind of pushing that could damage his voice.

He credits conductor Herbert von Karajan for guiding him to many of his most telling musical and dramatic insights, and recorded both his Gurnemanz (DG 413 347-2) and Baron Ochs (DG 423 850-2) under von Karajan; though both these recordings have some less than ideal aspects, the casting of Moll and his performances are not among the flaws. *—Ann Feeney*

Recommended:

○ **Kurt Moll: Famous Opera Arias** / Eichhorn (cond.), Moll, Munich Radio Orch. / 1982 / Orfeo 9821

○ **Schubert: Lieder for Bass** / Moll, Garben (piano) / 1982 / Orfeo 21821

○ **Mozart: Die Zauberflöte** / Solti (cond.), Jo, Schmidt, Heilmann, Moll, Vienna PO / 1991 / London 433210

Johann Melchior Molter

b. Feb. 10, 1696, Tiefenort, Germany, **d.** Jan. 12, 1765, Karlsruhe, Germany
Composer: Concerto

Composer Johann Melchior Molter was born in the Thuringian-Saxon region where his father, Valentin Molter, was a teacher and Kantor in the town of Tiefenort. After early training with his father, he enrolled at the Gymnasium in Eisenach, where J.S. Bach had studied. In Eisenach, Molter heard music by Telemann, who founded the court orchestra there only a few years earlier. In 1717, he found employment in Karlsruhe as a violinist at the court of Margrave Carl Wilhelm of Baden-Durlach. The following year, he married Maria Salome Rollwagen, with whom he had eight children. In 1719, Molter was allowed to travel to Italy to absorb the compositional styles that had spread throughout Europe, spending three years in Venice and Rome. After his return to Karlsruhe, he was appointed court concertmaster. In addition to directing the sacred music at the chapel, Molter directed the operatic productions in the margrave's theater. Molter's compositions range from chamber music to orchestral works and oratorios. It is likely that he composed operas during this period, but no operatic or other vocal compositions by Molter survive. In 1733, when the war of the Polish Succession began, the margrave dissolved his court and fled to Basle in exile, leaving Molter without employment. In 1734 Molter accepted the post of concertmaster at the court of Duke Wilhelm Heinrich of Saxe-Eisenach. Three years later, after the death of his wife, Molter returned to Italy, where he explored the work of a new generation of composers such as Pergolesi, Leo, and Sammartini. When he returned to Eisenach, he married Maria Christina Wagner. In 1741, Duke of Saxe-Weimar dissolved the Eisenach court orchestra after the death of Duke Wilhelm Heinrich. Molter then returned to Karlsruhe, where he composed and taught at the Gymnasium. In 1747, the new margrave of Baden-Durlach, Carl Friedrich, asked Molter to reorganize his court's musical establishment. Molter entered an extraordinarily prolific period in his career, composing a large body of instrumental music in the new galant style. Molter continued in this post for another 18 years until his death. Like his contemporaries Hasse, Quantz, and Graun, Molter contributed much to the development of instrumental music in eighteenth century Germany. His extant works include 172 symphonies, 73 concerti, 22 concertini (for three instruments), 12 concerti for orchestra, 14 overtures, 66 sonatas, 28 flute duets, 14 solo cantatas, and six violin sonatas. These works reveal influences from the French and Italian composers he heard on his travels, as well as Telemann, Bach, and the composers of the Mannheim School. He was particularly fond of experimenting with new sound colors. He wrote for the flauto d'amore, the flauto cornetto, and the harp, and he was among the first composers to use the recently invented clarinet and chalumeau. His clarinet concertos are some of his only works to have been performed and recorded in modern times. *—Robert Adelson*

CONCERTO

Trumpet Concerto No. 1 in D major (ca. 1750)

Molter wrote three concertos around 1750 for Carl Pfeiffer, the court trumpeter of the Margraves of Baden-Durlach in Karlsruhe—Molter's own longtime employers. If the technical demands of the first concerto indicate Pfeiffer's skills, the trumpeter seems not to have had any extraordinary facility in the extreme high register, where Molter treads with care, but did have superb breath control and was able to play long phrases with few rests. Molter made no provision for cadenzas. The orchestra makes a stately, almost Handelian entrance in the opening Allegro, followed by the trumpet, with its more ornamented version of the theme. In typical Baroque fashion, the orchestra briefly responds; the soloist offers a short, flashier variation on the theme; and after another orchestral passage, all forces join for a concluding section that essentially repeats the opening material. The Adagio is another processional piece, not much different in character from the first movement. The pattern of orchestral solo interplay is similar, as well, but now the trumpet's material is broader and more lyrical. The concluding Allegro is lighter and more playful and finds the orchestra far less subservient. Indeed, the trumpet now emerges for a few bright, colorful statements, but does not enjoy any long solo passages and is sometimes enveloped and muted by the orchestral fabric. *—James Reel*

Recommended:

○ **The Art of the Baroque Trumpet, Vol. 1** / Sparf (cond.), Eklund, Drottningholm Court Baroque Ens. / 1996 / Naxos 553531

Trumpet Concerto No. 3 in D major

Johann Melchior Molter's *Trumpet Concerto No. 3 in D major* is numbered as such only to distinguish it from two others that he also wrote for Carl Pfeiffer, the court trumpeter of the Margraves of Baden-Durlach. An autograph score exists for this concerto, dating from around 1740, but the orchestra instruments are not indicated, and there are no surviving parts. Because Molter had to rebuild the court orchestra at one point, there is documentation for what small forces were at his disposal: violins, violas, a bass viol and a cello, double basses, flutes, oboes, clarinets, bassoons, horns, trumpets, and tympani, with him conducting from the harpsichord. This and the surviving parts for the *Trumpet Concerto No. 1* are used to help determine instrumentation here. The first and third movements have no tempo marking, but are assumed to be taken at an Allegro tempo, while the middle movement is marked Andante cantabile. The concerto has trademarks of the galant style—generally simpler lines and less ornamentation—but also marks of the German interpretation of the Italian style of Vivaldi and Tartini: each movement beginning tutti and the lean proportions of the fast-slow-fast movements. The opening Allegro is also Italianate in sound, with the continuo providing a steady, repeated-note accompaniment to the frothy trumpet and higher strings. That same formula is used in the second movement, in the relative key of B minor, although the upper strings also join in accompanying the trumpet's aria. In the final movement, the trumpet and whole orchestra take turns being the featured performer in a pleasant, sprightly dance, more like the concertato style works of earlier in the Baroque. *—Patsy Morita*

Recommended:

○ **World of Baroque** / Schmidt-Gertenbach (cond.), Sauter, Istropolitana Capella / 1999 / EMI 56921

Federico Mompou

b. Apr. 16, 1893, Barcelona, Spain, **d.** Jun. 30, 1987, Barcelona, Spain
Composer: Keyboard, Chamber Music

Mompou was a Catalan composer of lyric songs and piano miniatures whose music is characterized by Impressionist elegance, simple and direct melody, and the haunting, deep emotions of folk music.

Mompou studied piano at the Conservatorio del Liceo in Barcelona and gave his first concert at the age of 15. Three years later, with a letter of recommendation from composer Granados, he went to Paris to study piano and harmony. While there, he wrote his first piano pieces, the Impresiones intimas (1911–14).

He became very taken with Debussy and the modern French composers, especially the spare melodiousness of Erik Satie. Mompou characterized this Satie quality in his music as "recomençament" (starting over at the beginning), a return to a kind of fundamental, basic state of realization. In emulation of Satie, Mompou adopted his method of scoring (in many of the piano works) by eliminating bar lines and key signatures, and (like Bartók and other composers) placing accidentals only before the notes to which they immediately apply. He also picked up the idea of inserting unusual and often illogically humorous comments, directions, and surreal images in the score, which actually serve to suggest the mood of a passage more adequately than the normal emotional and articulation markings—some of Mompou's directions were *"Chantez avec le fraîcheur de l'herbe humide"* and *"Donnez des excuses."*

When World War I broke out, Mompou returned to Barcelona, where he continued composing from 1914–21. His works at that time include the song *L'hora grisa* (1915) to words by Blancafort, and the piano sets *Pessebres* (1914–17), *Scènes d'enfants* (1915–18), *Cants mágics* (1917–19), *Fêtes lointaines* (1920), and *Charmes* (1920–21). *Suburbis* (1916–17) contains musical portraits of people encountered during Mompou's long walks. They were richly orchestrated by Manuel Rosenthal in 1936. In *El carrer, el guitarrista i el cavall* (The road, the guitarist and the old horse) a trumpet tune suggests the slow progress of a cart loaded with stone drawn by a weary horse "with large, sad eyes." An old man grinds a (wonderfully imitated) barrel organ. Gitane I and Gitane II draw portraits of two female gypsy friends, La Fana and La Chatuncha, through teasing dance music. *La cegueta* expresses gentle empathy for "the little blind girl" whose slow, uncertain walk is expressed by mirrored patterns. In *L'home de l'Aristó* (The ariston player) we hear a jolly pieces played again by the wandering beggar musician.

In 1921 Mompou returned to Paris where he remained 20 years, and then returned permanently to Barcelona. He was made a Chevalier des Arts et des Lettres by the French government, and elected to the Royal Academy of San Jorge in Barcelona and of San Fernando in Madrid.

The creation of many piano sets extended over large time spans: the 12 *Cançons i dansas* (1921–28, 1942–62), the ten *Préludes* (1927–30, 1943–51), *Variaciones sobre un tema di Chopin* (1938–57), the brilliant and evocative *Paisajes* (1942–60), and *Música callada* (1959–67).

Several of his significant songs include the *Comptines I–VI* (1931, 1943), *Combat del somni* (1942–48), and *Llueve sobre el rio, Pastoral* (1945). His works for chorus are the *Cantar del alma* (1951) with text from St. John of the Cross, and Improperios (1963) for chorus and orchestra. *—"Blue Gene" Tyranny*

KEYBOARD

Cançones i danses (1921–1962)

The *Cançons i danses* of Federico Mompou fall chronologically into two groups; Nos. 1–4 were written in Paris and date from 1921–28, and Nos. 5–14 were written in Barcelona between 1942–62. All are written in a two-part structure (perhaps inspired by Lizst's *Hungarian Rhapsodies*) constructed around a Catalan melody; in each case the tune is introduced in the slow first part, and then combined with a dance in the second part. Mompou originally intended them as separate works to be played singly or in related pairs, for example nos. 1 & 2, 5 & 6, etc. No. 13 is for solo guitar, and some pianists omit it in recordings of the set. Conversely, guitarists have transcribed some of the other *Cançons i danses* that were intended for piano.

The benign spirit of Erik Satie hovers over much of this music, especially in the first four items; the first *Cançon i danse* almost sounds like a *Gymnopédie* with a Spanish accent. Many of the dance sections of these pieces have the same limpid quality of the opening Cançons, the major exception being the popular No. 5, where Mompou breaks into an exuberant and brightly colorful Spanish dance.

The *Cançons i danses* were among the first works of Mompou to gain wide acceptance among concert pianists; important early recordings of single items were made in the 1940s and 1950s by Artur Rubinstein, Arturo Benedetti Michelangeli, Gustavo Soriano, and the composer, who recorded the whole work in 1975. The music is evocative, poetic, and immediately attractive. In the United States, the *Cançons i danses* are growing in popularity, and are sometimes used as end-of-the-hour "filler" music on Classical radio stations. *—Uncle Dave Lewis*

Recommended:

○ **Mompou: Piano Music, Vol. 1** / Maso / 1998 / Naxos 554332

Charmes (1920–1921)

The Catalan composer Federico Mompou was a master whose independent nature led him to eschew conventional methods of musical study. He tended to favor the French school, in particular the music of Satie, though his style divulges elements of Debussy and Ravel. Oddly, he is best-known for his arrangements of popular songs, but his original compositions are obviously worthwhile, as evidenced by these six short pieces, which all exhibit the above-mentioned French influences.

What is unusual about Mompou here is his penchant for slow tempos: only the fifth, "Pour évoquer l'image du passé," has anything approaching a lively tempo. The set's first work, "Pour endormir la souffrance," features simple harmonies and a playful, long-breathed Debussyian theme that is heard four times, after which the piece quietly ends. The ensuing "Pour pénétrer les âmes" is glacial in its slow-moving manner. It is more about atmosphere than melody, textures than structure. The music sounds from a haze, gloomy and floating, amid dark gray clouds.

The third, "Pour inspirer l'amour," sounds relatively lively by contrast; its middle section, in fact, exhibiting much cheer and a measure of animation in its bell-ringing sonorities. The outer sections are sedate and lovely in their Satie-tinged barrenness. "Pour les guérisons" presents a theme whose similarity to Chopin's famous *Funeral March* is obvious. It is as if Satie took the theme, bleached it of its ominous drama, slowed its fateful tread, and distorted its balanced contour, the whole sounding ethereal, dark, and weird. The aforementioned "Pour évoquer l'image du passé" is bright and playful, with notes swirling around an attractive though emotionally neutral theme. The central episode features dramatic, Debussyian chords, which quickly yield back to a gentle reprise of the main theme. The last piece, "Pour appeler la joie," begins with a lively bright theme, but then slows its pace, never regaining its lost momentum. All these works are fairly direct, featuring piano writing whose textures are light and whose challenges to the performer are modest. Each piece lasts between one and three minutes, the whole collection having a duration of ten to twelve minutes. *—Robert Cummings*

Recommended:

○ **Piano Icons for the 21st Century** / Riu / 2000 / Linn 111

Impressions intimes (1911–1914; revised 1959)

While the name of the Catalan composer Federico Mompou (1893–1987) remains largely obscure, he began making inroads with pianists and some listeners in the late twentieth century. His music is mostly for piano and is typically written in an intimate and subdued style. *Impressions intimes* (Intimate Impressions) is not only an appropriate name for this collection of nine pieces but one that sums up the character of Mompou's keyboard output in general. The composer lived in Paris for many years, and his music contains a fascinating mixture of French and Spanish (including Catalan) influences: it merges the quiet intimacy of Fauré with the quirky, unexpected simplicity of Satie and the regionalist experimentation of Falla. The *Impressions intimes* were Mompou's first published work, but they contain in miniature many of the traits of his later music.

The first piece here, "Plany I," is melancholy and subdued, gentle and dark, seeming almost listless in its glacial pacing and sparse textures. "Plany II" is marginally brighter but also slow-moving and gloomy. A noticeable mood shift comes in "Plany III," where the playfulness and sunny atmosphere contrast effectively with the gray skies from the previous pieces. But its half-minute length suggests a fragile happiness. "Plany IV" is fast and anxious, sounding like nervous Rachmaninov.

"Ocell triste" returns to the gentle gloom of the opening pieces, only now in a more expansive mode, this three-minute piece being one of the longer efforts in the set. "La barca" is dark and sinister, but its gentleness prevents its black clouds from producing dangerous storms or bolts of lightning. "Bressol" sounds Debussyan, the music swelling from gentle caresses to chordal statements of relative grandeur. Not surprisingly, "Secret" is subdued and intimate in its melancholy. "Gitano" closes the set with a gentle joy, again recalling Debussy in some of the chords. One must assess Mompou's music here as original and significant at the least, and masterful at best. *—Robert Cummings*

Recommended:

○ **Spanish Fireworks** / Larrocha / 1989 / London 417795

○ **Mompou: Cançiones y danzas; Impressiones intimas** / Romero / 1996 / Koch 7185

Música callada (1959–1967)

The primary masterwork of Catalan composer Federico Mompou's late years is *Música Callada* (Silent Music), a piano suite consisting of 28 pieces arranged in four books of 9, 7, 5, and 9 movements. Most of the pieces occupy just two or three lightly scored pages of music, and the dynamic level only rarely exceeds mezzo piano. *Música Callada* sometimes breaks into brief, wistful dance phrases; otherwise the music is best characterized as containing only the barest indication of a pulse. Although the work is extremely economical in its means, it is not easy to play. On the contrary, *Música Callada* represents a test of concentration and restraint over extended periods.

About *Música Callada*, Mompou once wrote, "its mission is to reach the profound depths of our soul and the hidden domains of the vital force our spirits. This music is silent ('callada') as if heard from within." *Música Callada* represents a forward development from the work of Satie, yet was written in an era during which the so-called "International Serial style" was all the rage in Europe. However, Mompou was no shrinking violet in terms of modernity; *Música Callada* often contains bitter polytonal combinations and textures so scantily applied that the music often seems to float in the air. Nonetheless, the work attracted little attention upon its first publication, and was only appreciated beginning in the 1990s.

Unlike most art music of the 1960s, *Música Callada* is peaceful in tone and makes an excellent choice for the purpose of relaxation. Those who enjoy challenging listening will also find interest in Mompou's use of additional color in the form of biting dissonances. *—Uncle Dave Lewis*

Recommended:

○ **Mompou: Música Callada** / Henck / 1995 / ECM 445699

Preludes Nos. 1–4 (1927–1930)

More than most other composers, Mompou's art defies description, if only because it is so unlike anyone else's. Walter Starkie's entry on Mompou in the fifth edition of *Grove's Dictionary of Music and Musicians* (1954), for instance, resorts to quotations from Debussy, Enoch Soames, and Sir Thomas Browne to suggest his music's mixture of the sophisticated and primitive, hieratic and childlike, recondite and popular, spare simplicity, and incantatory repetitiveness, and so on. While nearly all of Mompou's work takes the form of sets of piano miniatures, the *Ten Préludes* make almost an index to his art, despite—or because of—their having been composed in two sets separated by more than a dozen years. The first four occupied Mompou, a slow confectioner, from 1927 to 1930, while the second group was not started until 1943. To Starkie's conspectus one might add that, in their melding of the familiar and strange, their knowing naïveté, they suggest meditations upon *Alice in Wonderland*. And while Mompou is not concerned with form in a formal sense, he is intensely concerned to strike a keenly suave balance between concealing and revealing. The *Prélude No. 1*, for instance, opens with the mien of a plangent lament only to turn oddly noncommittal by its end. The second suggests a keening song for cornemuse framing a dance fraught with the seriousness of children at play. Does *No. 3* resonate to the cracked bells of a surreal dimension? The chorale-like *Prélude No. 4* begins with confident faith to lose itself in doubt—the chorale returns, but with an oddly disconsolate air. —*Adrian Corleonis*

Recommended:

○ **Spanish Songs & Dances** / Larrocha / 1994 / BMG 62554

Preludes Nos. 5–10 (1943–1951)

Composed between 1943 and 1951, Mompou's *Six Préludes* are usually grouped with an earlier set of four and continuously numbered. An air of the strange and surreal clings to them all, though the later group is brighter in tone, despite evidence that Mompou had discovered late Scriabin just prior to their composition and found in him a kindred spirit. The *Prélude No. 5*'s vocal melody cries out for lyric explication, seeking to confide something sad and strange: the interruption of a rude dance makes the eloquently mute return of the almost speaking melody the more poignant. Playing over four minutes, the *Prélude No. 6*, for the left hand alone, is the longest of the ten—the serenade of a demented lover beset by cracked notes, thwarted passion, and nameless absurdities. *No. 7*, with its peremptory downward plunges and silvery mirages, mimics Scriabin at his most oracular. *No. 8*, in odd contrast, might almost be the transcription of a wistful 1940s popular song but for the promiscuous twining of its melodic tendrils and ascending dissolution. Though it plays barely two minutes, the *Prélude No. 9* is a vehement sigh of nostalgia for a world glimpsed in hallucinatory visions. The *Prélude No. 10* begins with a hopeful peal only to look back and lose heart, setting the seal on Mompou as a master of musical ambiguity. If unprogrammatic and inexplicit, the implicit volatility of emotions suggested by Mompou's *Préludes* possesses a power of suggestion, of fascination, looming beyond music to become—as the composer fully intended—a sort of magic that awakens a primordial, immemorial nostalgia in the penumbra of our being. Mompou remained an agile pianist into old age; hence his 1974 recording of the *Préludes* possesses unique authority. —*Adrian Corleonis*

Recommended:

○ **Mompou: Complete Piano Works, Vol. 1** / Pontremoli / 2001 / Centaur 894

Variations sobre un tema de Chopin (1938–1957)

Variations on a Theme of Chopin is one of maverick Catalan composer Federico Mompou's largest piano compositions. He originally started writing it for cello and piano, following a suggestion in 1938 from cellist Gaspar Cassadò. He abandoned the effort, but eventually turned out four variations that he oddly titled *Three Variations*. In 1957, Mompou completed this version, which like the others is founded upon the famous theme from Chopin's *Prelude in A major No. 7*, Op. 28.

There are 12 variations, the first of which leaves this slow, beautiful theme unaltered; however, it adds some curious harmonies almost as if Mompou is poking fun. The second variation, lively and carefree, imparts a sudden sense of brightness, while the next returns to the warmth and intimacy of the original theme. The fourth may be the most distant variation, sounding almost like a different theme in its subtle beauties. The ensuing variation is playful, coming across as mostly a sped-up version of Chopin's melody. The sixth is mysterious and troubled, while the next is deliciously light and colorful in its brevity. The slow and dreamy eighth variation would sound almost like a new theme but for a few quite recognizable snatches of the original melody. The ninth is stately and graceful in its serene manner and the tenth, at over three minutes, is the second-lengthiest and perhaps most colorful, even quoting the alternate theme in Chopin's *Fantasie-Impromptu*, Op. 66. The penultimate variation is initially mysterious and gentle, but transforms into a more grandiose manner, while the four-minute concluding one, the longest, deftly juxtaposes fast and slow music in its first part ("Galope") and turns serene and sweet in its Epilogue. —*Robert Cummings*

Recommended:

○ **Mompou Plays Mompou** / Mompou / EnSayo 9726

CHAMBER MUSIC

Suite compostelana, for guitar (1962)

Dedicated to the legendary Andrés Segovia, this colorful six-movement suite incorporates traditional Spanish guitar sounds and modes, as well as a twentieth century harmonic sensibility.

The "Preludio" (Prelude) opens with a traditional rotating guitar picking figure with the melody notes on the lower line alternating with a repeated inverted pedal point tone in the upper register. The beautiful modal scale sets a strange, ancient, yet romantic, mood. Eventually this pattern reaches the lowest, highly resonant octave. Some rich, modern modal chords (built in fourths) follow. When the rolling patterns begin again, the modal scale has been replaced by eerie chromatics of a disjunctive, constantly wandering nature. However, the patterns soon find their former evocativeness expressed through a modal scale in the sub-dominant key in which the piece concludes.

"Coral" (Chorale) evolves its somber, touching harmonies at a slow Lento tempo. The music gives the impression of contemporary chording mostly by accenting non-harmonic tones on the main counts and resolving them into standard triads on the softer beats, although there are places where unresolved minor ninths stand out. The mood is intimate, reflective, sad, yet lyrical.

The tender, sweet main theme of the "Cuna" (Cradle Song) gently flows along in sets of two notes in a close interval to each other, accompanied by a simple arpeggio on the first beat. The middle section has a cantabile feeling like a subdued chorale, a reflective moment. The initial theme and motion returns to cadence on a simple major chord.

The "Recitativo" (Recitative) creates a strange atmosphere, difficult to ascribe to a specific emotion. The employment of the rarely used Locrian mode (which contains the "forbidden" tritone as one of its primary intervals) with dissonant chords interspersed has something to do with this unsettled state. There are also a few measures that sound like a mocking children's song. Nevertheless, this movement in a "Lento molto espressivo e cantabile" tempo has a haunting quality.

The theme of the "Canción" (Song) is a melancholy waltz in A minor that proceeds in the pure minor mode until encountering subtle chromatic modifications that express restrained passion. The middle bridge also contains undulating motion that resolves briefly in a new mode (Dorian instead of Aeolian), but the beginning theme is fully recapitulated at the close.

The "Muñeira" is a "doll's dance" in an Allegro con moto tempo with a lilting 6/8 dance feel and a skipping accent on the fifth beat that seems to lend a slight artificial jerk to the doll's motion. The melody is played over pedal point chords and descending lines in the middle voice. In the middle section, dissonant intervals of the "ho-ho" variety add a comic and slightly grotesque characteristic to the image before things get straightened out again and the main theme comes back with fuller major harmonies and a bravura ending with pesante, fortissimo "rasgueado" (strumming). —*"Blue Gene" Tyranny*

Recommended:

○ **Laureate Series: Guitar** / Goni / 1997 / Naxos 553774

Stanisław Moniuszko

b. May 5, 1819, Ubiel, Belarus, **d.** Jun. 4, 1872, Warsaw, Poland

Composer: Opera

Although this composer never achieved quite the fame abroad that he enjoyed in his native Poland, Stanisław Moniuszko is scarcely unknown elsewhere in the world. His opera *Halka* became a national treasure in the composer's native country and is known today by many world listeners through recordings. One orchestral work, four examples of incidental music, and two string quartets stand in isolation among the composer's 24 operas, choral scores, and more than 270 songs. Clearly, Moniuszko found his ideal means of expression in the human voice. Moniuszko was born on a small estate to a former Polish army captain and a musical mother. The couple moved to Warsaw in 1827 to assure a proper musical education for their precocious son. Later, finances dictated a move to Minsk. When money became more abundant, young Stanisław was sent to the Singakademie in Berlin. There, opera and choral performances seized his imagination and prompted a decision to become a composer. After his return to Poland and subsequent marriage, Moniuszko set himself to the composing of operettas, first for amateur companies and soon for professional theaters. In Warsaw, Moniuszko made the acquaintance of the poet Wolski, who provided him with a libretto based upon a Polish folk story. The resulting opera, *Halka*, then in two acts, was an immense success at Wilno in 1848. Intrigues kept the work from Warsaw for exactly a decade, but introduction there of the four-act version on January 1, 1858, made the composer a national hero and he was soon thereafter appointed conductor at the Warsaw Opera, a position he held until his death. *Halka*, although rooted in traditional forms, acknowledged the new world of Wagnerian Leitmotifs and won the admiration of many in Germany and Austria, especially Wagner disciple Hans von Bülow. A decade after the premiere, the work had been heard in translation in Berlin, Prague, Vienna, Moscow, and other prominent venues. Other significant operas followed; some such as *Hrabina* (The Countess) and *Straszny Dwór* (The Haunted Manor) were much appreciated, though without the overwhelming acclaim accorded *Halka*. Moniuszko's two final operas were not successful. Many of Moniuszko's songs became almost as popular as *Halka*, lovely in their own right and regarded as icons of Polish culture. —*Erik Eriksson*

Overview of Works (1834–1872)

Stanisław Moniuszko is primarily remembered for his operas and other vocal music, which make up the bulk of his oeuvre. He is to Polish musical nationalism what Smetana was to Bohemia and Glinka was to Russia. His operas—particularly *Halka* (1846–1947), *The Raftsman* (1858), *The Countess* (1959), and *The Haunted Manor* (1861–1964)—use stories about Polish people and customs and utilize traditional Polish musical idioms to create what became the basis of Polish opera. Moniuszko used dance forms—the polonaise, mazurka, and krakowiak—throughout his scores, even using the dance rhythms in vocal parts. Otherwise, his operas owe a great deal to grand opera for their overall scene structure and use of the chorus. The music of Auber was influential in Moniuszko's scene structure, as was Weber's in the choral parts, while the lyricism of Rossini can be heard in his arias. Many of the arias and songs from the operas have achieved almost the status of folk songs in Poland. Moniuszko's next most important works are his 360 songs. These, again, are respected as much for their place in Polish musical tradition as for their music.

Because they utilize texts by Polish poets, they are as popular as ever in Poland, if unknown outside the country. The remainder of his output includes five masses and two Requiems, eight cantatas, concert overtures, two string quartets, and an amount of salon music for piano, typical of the era. Perhaps the most noteworthy of his non-operatic works is the *Bajka* concert overture. *—Patsy Morita*

Recommended:

- ○ **Moniuszko: Overtures** / Satanowski (cond.), Bydgoszcz Filharmonia Pomorska / CPO 999113
- ○ **Moniuszko: Canons** / Soltysik, Minkiewicz, Kusiewicz, Szmyt / 2000 / Dux 182
- ○ **Moniuszko: Piesni (Songs)** / Kryger, Jankowska / 2002 / Dux 362
- ○ **Moniuszko: The Haunted Manor** / Kaspszyk (cond.), Toczyska, Nowacki, Szmyt, Kruszewski, Polish National Opera / 2003 / EMI 57489
- ○ **Moniuszko: Religious Songs** / Rappe, Hiolski, Kozlowska, Kusiewicz, Malanowicz / 2001 / Accord 97

OPERA

Halka, opera (1846–1847; revised 1857)

While relatively little known outside Poland, *Halka*—arguably the first major Polish grand opera—is practically a national opera in its own country, comparable to Smetana's *The Bartered Bride* in Czech lands. It combines distinctly Polish elements, most notably in the dances but also in some of the vocal portions, such as Stolnik's Act One polonaise and Jontek's Act Two aria, with a standard and even conventional Italianate structure and lyricism. Like some contemporary Italian operas, it was originally considered too politically problematic, with the result that the composer had to change it to reduce the potentially inflammatory themes.

Moniuszko himself asked poet Wlodzimierz Wolski to write a libretto based on his poem, which was itself based upon a short story by Kazimierz Wojicki. Because of the above-mentioned problems with the plot, even though the work was finished in 1847, it was not presented at the Wielki Theater as planned, but in a concert performance in Vilnius. It was given a staged performance in 1854. Two years later, Moniuszko revised the piece for the first time, adding vocal and orchestral music and changing Jontek, originally for baritone, to a tenor role. In 1857, he further revised it, changing it from two acts to four and adding considerably more material. This final revision was staged at the Wielki Theater in 1858, where, ironically, it was so successful that the composer was appointed principal conductor to acknowledge his accomplishment. It soon spread to theaters throughout Poland and also had brief successes in theaters around Europe, though it did not enter the regular repertoire as it had in Poland. *—Ann Feeney*

Synopsis:

Act One. The action takes place in southern Poland in the late eighteenth century. In the drawing room of Stolnick's manor house near Kraków, an engagement party is in progress. Stolnick's daughter, Zofia, is to be married to Janusz, a young nobleman. The party guests toast the couple and wish them happiness before retiring to an adjacent room. When Stolnick, Janusz, and Zofia are left alone, the two young people ask Stolnick for his blessing, but before he can answer they all hear a voice from outside the house. It is the young peasant girl Halka, whom Janusz has used and abandoned, thinking he would never hear from her again. Stolnick and Zofia leave Janusz alone with his guilt over his treatment of Halka and the fear of how this will affect his relationship with Zofia. Halka, not yet knowing about Janusz's relationship with Zofia, enters the room. She asks him about his plans concerning her, but Janusz does not give a clear answer. Instead, he hurriedly arranges a later meeting elsewhere and rushes Halka out of the house, fearing that someone will find her there. Janusz returns to the celebration, where the noblemen sing a drinking song before Stolnick leads another toast in Janusz and Zofia's honor. In the first version of the opera, the drinking chorus closes the act.

Act Two. Halka loiters in the garden of Stolnick's manor, unable to leave because she knows Janusz is inside the house. She unexpectedly meets the mountaineer Jontek, who is in love with her. Jontek tells Halka about Janusz's relationship with Zofia and his plans to marry her—he has, in fact, betrayed Halka. Jontek hopes his news will convince Halka to return to the village with him. Halka, very confused and frantic, runs to the door of the house and knocks. Janusz answers and becomes angry at Jontek for disrupting the engagement party. At this, Halka faints. Jontek berates Janusz for betraying and deserting Halka, who, now awake, tells Janusz that he is the father of her child. A crowd begins to gather around Janusz, Jontek, and Halka, who repeats her news. Janusz convinces the crowd that Halka is simply insane and orders Dziemba, his father's steward, to get rid of the uninvited guests.

Act Three. In Halka's village in the Tatra mountains, a congregation disperses after a Vespers service and the people begin to discuss Janusz's upcoming marriage. Members of the group then begin to dance in anticipation of the wedding festivities. Jontek and Halka enter and tell of the horrible events of the evening at Stolnick's manor house. The crowd sympathizes with them. Suddenly, someone in the crowd sees a black crow fly past. Halka is mortified, for this is certainly a bad sign. When she hears the sound of a wedding procession in the distance, she becomes even more upset.

Act Four. A musician performs a lively melody on his pipe in a square in front of the village church. Jontek asks the musician to play a morose tune to accompany him as he sings of his despair over Halka. As Janusz and Zofia's wedding procession passes, Zofia notices the despondent Halka and questions her about her grief, not knowing at all who Halka is. As Halka tries to explain the situation to Zofia, the wedding procession begins to enter the church, cutting off Halka's story. Jontek and Halka once again discuss Janusz; Jontek tries to persuade her that Janusz is an awful, deceitful person unworthy of her, but Halka confesses that she still loves him. Halka decides to burn down the church, but when she hears the choir singing inside in the church she changes her mind. Even though her child has starved to death because of Janusz's neglect, she still wants to be with him. Halka next decides to commit suicide, and she rushes to the edge of a cliff and throws herself off of it as Jontek tries to stop her. Jontek returns to the church as the wedding procession begins to leave the building. He confronts Janusz and tells him of Halka's violent death. Dziemba orders the members of the procession to sing in praise of Janusz and Zofia. *—John Palmer*

Recommended:

- ○ **Moniuszko: Halka** / Satanowski (cond.), Ochman, Zagorzanka, Hiolski, Ostapiuk, Polish National Opera Orch. & Chorus / CPO 999032

Meredith Monk

b. Nov. 20, 1942, Lima, Peru

Composer: Opera, Vocal

Singer, composer, filmmaker, and choreographer Meredith Monk is a pioneer in what is now called "extended vocal technique" and "interdisciplinary performance." Her early musical training included piano, some music theory, voice, and Dalcroze Eurythmics. The vocal arts have been an important part of her family's history: "I'm the fourth-generation singer in my family. I came from an Eastern European Jewish background, with my mom being a professional radio singer and jingle singer."

In 1964, Monk graduated from Sarah Lawrence College, where she studied composition with Ruth Lloyd and Glen Mack, voice with Vicki Starr, and vocal and chamber music with Meyer Kupferman; she also participated in opera workshops directed by Paul Ukena and Bessie Schoenberg. Dance was prominent in her studies as well. After college, Monk found herself neglecting her voice until one evening she sat at a piano and began vocalizing without words; she found the voice had "limitless colors and textures."

Between 1965 and 2000 she composed over 80 works, the apparent influences of which run the gamut of musical expression. "Bartók was someone I loved as a young woman, and also Stravinsky. And then I'm a person who loves music from the '20s and '30s, and there's a jazz singer that I love named Mildred Bailey." She also credits Janis Joplin and Joni Mitchell for providing her with meaningful examples of expressiveness. For Monk, linking her vocalizing to movement was a natural extension of the performance experience, "... doing the movement was a way of me finding my own territory, so to speak, of finding my own identity."

In 1968 Monk founded The House, a company dedicated to a interdisciplinary performance; ten years later she formed the Meredith Monk Vocal Ensemble to perform her vocal compositions. Most of her recordings are available on the ECM New Series. Monk's feature length film, *Book of Days*, aired on PBS, has appeared on international film festivals and was chosen for the 1991 Whitney Biennial. Her *Atlas: an opera in three parts*, which was commissioned by the Houston Grand Opera, The Walker Art Center, and The American Music Theater Festival, premiered in February 1991, and has toured the United States and Europe; a recording was released in January 1994.

Other performances include a 1993 concert at Merkin Hall which included the world premieres of Monk's *St. Petersburg Waltz*, *Volcano Songs* (Duets), and *New York Requiem*. A new site-specific work, *American Archeology #1: Roosevelt Island*, was first performed in September 1994, and performances of *Volcano Songs* (a solo music/theater/dance work) were staged in New York City, the Portland Art Museum in Oregon, and Hancher Auditorium in Iowa City. Monk's 1998 musical theater piece, *Magic Frequencies*, toured the United States to critical acclaim; described as "a science-fiction chamber opera," this sparsely scored and sophisticated piece reveals Monk's lifelong fascination with, and investigation of, time travel and transformation.

Monk has received numerous awards, including two Guggenheim Fellowships, a Brandeis Creative Arts Award, three Obies (including an award for Sustained Achievement), two Villager Awards, a Bessie for ASCAP Awards for Musical Composition, and the 1992 Dance Magazine Award. In 1995, Monk won a MacArthur "Genius" Award. Her 1991 film, *Ellis Island*, won the CINE Golden Eagle Award. Alan Kriegsman of the *Washington Post*, writes, "When the time comes, perhaps a hundred years from now, to tally up achievements in the performing arts during the last third of the [twentieth] century, one name that seems sure to loom large is that of Meredith Monk. In originality, in scope, in depth, there are few to rival her." *—John Palmer*

OPERA

Atlas, for 18 voices & large ensemble (1991)

Although Meredith Monk had been composing theatrical and semi-theatrical vocal works for two decades, *Atlas*, from 1991, represents her first real foray into the world of opera. During the 1970s Monk had developed a unique palette of extended vocal techniques, and had combined it with choreography, film, and other media. In 1979 she presented the multi-movement vocal work *Dolmen Music*, featuring members of a recently formed ensemble trained in Monk's style. The director of the Houston Opera heard *Dolmen Music*, invited Monk to instruct some of his singers for a 1985 performance of the piece, and opened the door for the subsequent commission of *Atlas* by the opera company. Even then, the genre had to strain a bit at its edges to encompass Monk's distinctive multimedia style; likewise, the composer applied her polymath talents to a degree rarely encountered in the opera world, devising the score, training the singers, as well as singing alongside them, and participating extensively in the choreography and visual design of the work.

The opera's plot line is drawn, quite loosely, from the life of Alexandra David-Néel, a noted nineteenth century explorer and Orientalist (and, for a brief period, professional opera singer). David-Néel's story is not treated historically, however, but metaphorically: the protagonist of Monk's opera, Alexandra Davies, sets out like her namesake on a journey to a distant place, but this trip turns out to be metaphysical rather than geographical. The opera's first act, "Personal Climate," begins with a teenaged Davies choosing traveling companions and embarking on her journey. In "Night Travel," a middle-aged Davies and her companions travel to the ends of the Earth. In "Invisible Light," Davies, now advanced in years, attains spiritual awakening. These three acts make up 24 scenes, each of which is built on a distinctive and characteristically lucid musical pattern, often a simple bass line or chord progression. Aside from a few unusual colors, such as the shawm and the glass harmonica, the ten-member instrumental ensemble remains largely unobtrusive throughout, primarily serving to establish the patterns to which the voices gradually add additional layers of patterned counterpoint. Little text is used to convey the plot; rather, the singers, who also double as dancers and mimes, act as flexible, organic instruments, painting each scene with unexpected timbres, curiously incongruous syllables, and subtle expressive inflections that combine with the visual elements to create an integrated artistic whole. *—Jeremy Grimshaw*

Recommended:

○ **Monk: Atlas** / Hankin (cond.), Een, Geissinger, Osborne, Wheeler, etc. / 1993 / BMG 1491

Mercy, for 6 voices, 2 keyboards, percussion, violin & theremin (2001)

There is something to be said about the mere presence of narrative in music. In some of his later works, Debussy used vague titles (like *Images*) to depict not this or that particular scene, but simply to convey the *idea* of depiction. Later in the twentieth century, Philip Glass' collaborations with Robert Wilson made narrative out of autistic stammering and, Terry Riley, after borrowing from hodge-podged mythologies in his earlier works, began writing pieces (the *Abbeyozzud* series) based on untold tales from a nonexistent book. Meredith Monk's multimedia work *Mercy*, which she created in collaboration with visual artist Ann Hamilton, treads just this sort of terrain, with an engaging balance of dramatic ambiguity and emotional acuity: aside from the title, few textual cues as to its "plot" are to be found anywhere in the work; rather, the artists combine a montage of mostly wordless music and image to create what they describe as "a meditation on the quality of mercy throughout history and a humanistic demand for mercy in troubled times."

The work was originally conceived for stage and received its premiere in the summer of 2001 at Duke University. The original production involved a group of singers trained in the improvisatory practices and extended techniques of Monk's unique vocal style, a small instrumental ensemble, dance, mime, and video projections. For the recording of the work released the following year, Monk revised the score substantially and added clarinet parts performed by Bohdan Hilash. The resulting work proceeds in Monk's characteristically episodic fashion, with simple, mostly diatonic patterns to which multiple layers of vocal counterpoint are successively applied—though in this work Monk does offer new ideas, including some stunning moments of microtonal inflection that hover between speech and song. In absence of the visual element that originally accompanied the music, Monk might have been expected to include extensive notes about the dramatic contours of the piece, if not an outright "synopsis." Instead, beyond the cryptic track listings for the 14 sections of the piece ("Masks," "Shaking," "Woman at the Door," etc.), the notes include only a series of video stills taken from the projections: blurry, solarized close-ups of a face in various states of agony and ecstasy. "Liner notes [were] planned," Monk explained elsewhere, "but in the end, it was felt that the music, with these images, speaks for itself in a clear and unequivocal way." *—Jeremy Grimshaw*

Recommended:

○ **Monk: Mercy** / Monk, Geissinger, Gonzalez, Hollenbeck, Easter, etc. / 2002 / ECM 472468

VOCAL

Book of Days (1985)

"In most of my music...I try to express a sense of timelessness," Meredith Monk explained. "*Book of Days* is very much about the transparency and relativity of time—the sense that you can see one period through another and the sensation that everything could be happening concurrently." Like many of her multimedia works, *Book of Days* does not follow a contiguous or coherent narrative, but rather weaves together various disparate visual and narrative strands together in non-chronological fashion, the whole held together largely by Monk's engaging musical score. As the film jumps across and juxtaposed characters and elements spread across centuries, the delicate polyphonies, unusual vocal techniques, and undulating textures of Monk's music offer a context of continuity and concentration within which her images can coalesce.

Monk first conceived of the project in 1984 as two separate ideas: a film portraying the life of a young Jewish girl in the fourteenth century and a vocal concerto featuring her own signature ensemble. After the vocal concerto received its premiere at Carnegie Hall in February 1985, Monk began to explore the possibility of combining it with her ideas for the film. During the ensuing months Monk made a number of other changes to fit the score to the visual imagery, turning it into a piece primarily featuring her vocal ensemble augmented only by a handful of additional voices and a few distinctive instruments: organ, hurdy gurdy, bagpipe, hammer dulcimer, cello, and synthesizer. In combining the aural and visual elements, Monk sought "a way for the music to combine with the images so that the rhythms would give each medium a richness and luminosity, and yet help them to maintain independence. I wanted the whole film to sing." The narrative dissonance of the young girl's futuristic visions, and of the anachronistically self-conscious intrusion of the camera into everyday medieval life, is ultimately sublimated by Monk's proto-minimalist pulses and the singers' virtuosic and unpredictable gestures.

In 1990, Monk undertook to alter the score yet another time in preparation for the work's premiere audio recording. Because the film treated time so freely, Monk was neither tethered by sequential musical scenes nor limited to the musical materials in the movie. She thus reworked some passages, and even inserted a number of entirely new numbers to give the piece its own musically logical shape—or, as the composer described, to make it a "film for the ears." *—Jeremy Grimshaw*

Recommended:

○ **Monk: Book of Days** / Monk, Hankin, Een, Arnold, etc. / 1990 / ECM 839624

Dolmen Music, for 6 voices, cello & percussion (1979)

"After classical voice training and experience as a folk and rock singer," Meredith Monk wrote in 1981, "I realized that I wanted to create vocal music that had the personal style and abstract (as well as emotional) qualities that come into play in the creation of painting or dance." Monk pursued this vision throughout the late 1960s and 1970s, developing a broad repertoire of unique vocal techniques and improvisatory practices, and, eventually, training a handpicked ensemble of like-minded singers. In 1979, a year after establishing her ensemble, Monk presented *Dolmen Music*, a groundbreaking six-movement work for vocal sextet, cello, and percussion.

Much of Monk's success owes to her refusal to compose "in the abstract"—that is, her entire oeuvre resists the idea of a given melody over a given series of chords; rather, she conceives of a line sung by a *particular* voice, with its specific and unique qualities, against a highly specialized textural or timbral background or in counterpoint with similarly distinctive voices. This approach thus conflates composition with improvisation, as the musical work gradually emerges through intimate musical interaction with the performers. In her notes to *Dolmen Music*, Monk even enumerates the vocal qualities that inspired the piece: the agility of one singer, the astounding range of another, the deep resonance of yet another.

As in many of Monk's works, *Dolmen Music* betrays only hints of narrative. The title itself is taken from the word for "a prehistoric monument consisting of two or more upright stones supporting a horizontal stone slab," like those of Stonehenge. Some of the work's individual movements have somewhat pictorial titles, but Monk avoids giving her singers decipherable words; one occasionally hears the expressive contours of speech, but the "words" are made of nonsense phonemes that directly evoke poetic imagery (as in the incessant, wordless patter of the third movement, "Rain") or sheer emotional content (as in the second movement, which is built almost entirely of elastic, nasal incantations of the two syllables in its title, "Wa-Ohs"). Occasionally, the singers take on the voices of mysterious animals, machines, or specters, the vocal hues following simple repeated diatonic figures that gradually expand into intricate, undulating contrapuntal textures. *—Jeremy Grimshaw*

Recommended:

○ **Monk: Dolmen Music** / Monk, Een, Goodman, Walcott, Lockwood, etc. / ECM 825459

Turtle Dreams, for 4 voices & 2 electronic organs (1980)

By the time Meredith Monk created *Turtle Dreams* in 1983, the vocal ensemble she had hand-picked a few years before and trained in her unique singing style had become established as one of the most distinctive sounds in the new music arena. The work exploits the unusual expressive breadth of this group of singers by building a series of tableaus on repeated melodic patterns, which the singers adorn with all manner of vocal dressing, from arching, lyrical lines and pensive ostinati to whispers, burbles, and whoops. The work is clearly inspired by the minimalist movement that began to pervade popular culture in the 1980s (and perhaps even directly inspired, at least in its narrative content, by minimalist pioneer La Monte Young's series of works collectively titled *The Tortoise, His Dreams and Journeys*), but Monk's imaginative timbres and expressive effects lend her proto-minimalist patternings a distinctive element of color and emotion.

In its full multimedia form, the music is combined with carefully designed visual elements. The singers, in unassuming costumes by Yoshio Yabara and accompanied at various points by organ, piano, synthesizer, and didgeridoo, execute subtle, minimalist choreographies—mostly while staring distantly forward and moving together in a row. Footage of the singers performing is set in visual counterpoint with video of a live turtle exploring a number of different real and superimposed landscapes: he meanders through his own swampy habitat, finds himself in an urban terrain, and is even enlarged to gargantuan proportions as he roves the surface of the moon. *—Jeremy Grimshaw*

Recommended:

○ **Monk: Turtle Dreams** / Een, Goodman, Walcott, Langland, Eastman, Lockwood, Monk / ECM 811547

Pierre Monteux

b. Apr. 4, 1875, Paris, France, **d.** Jul. 1, 1964, Hancock, ME

Conductor

Pierre Monteux had one of the longest musical careers in memory, exceeded perhaps only by Pablo Casals and Leopold Stokowski. He retained a youthful appearance (and a full head of black hair!) well into old age, and he was well loved by colleagues and audiences alike.

He started violin studies at the age of six and then entered the Paris Conservatoire at the age of nine. He made his conducting debut in Paris at the age of 12. He was a co-winner of the first prize for violin in 1896, with the great violinist Jacques Thibaud. He served as principal violist in the Opera-Comique, and was also assistant conductor and concertmaster of the Concerts Colonne.

In 1894 he joined the Quatuor Geloso as a violist and was priviledged to participate in the performance of a Brahms quartet in the composer's presence. In 1908 he became conductor of the Orchestre du Casino in Dieppe and in 1911 founded a series called the Concerts Berlioz. In the same year, he began a historic association when he was hired by Diaghilev to conduct his ballets russes. He led the premieres of Ravel's *Daphnis et Chloe*, Debussy's *Jeux*, and Stravinsky's *Petrushka* and *Rite of Spring*, the last of which caused a notorious audience riot.

In 1914, when war broke out, he was called to military service. He received a discharge in 1916 and travelled to the United States, where he obtained a conducting post at the Metropolitan Opera that lasted until 1919. At that point he was engaged to conduct the Boston Symphony Orchestra. Taking up the post in 1920, he walked into a labor dispute, with his musicians on strike; by the time the strike was settled, the concertmaster and 30 other musicians had left. Monteux had to rebuild the orchestra—a difficult task, but an opportunity for Monteux to mold the orchestra according to his own taste; ever since then, the Boston Symphony Orchestra has been known for its French sound and its expertise in French and Russian repertoire. He remained in Boston through 1924, gaining a reputation as a supporter of modern music. He brought to America not only Stravinsky and the French composers, but such others as Respighi, Vaughan Williams, and Honegger.

In 1924 he began a ten year association with the Amsterdam Concertgebouw. He was a good fit with the orchestra's other conductor, Willem Mengelberg, who had a Romantic-era style, and who specialized in traditional repertoire and Dutch composers. In addition, Monteux founded the Orchestre Symphonique de Paris in 1929, and the Ecole Monteaux, a coaching school for young conductors in 1932.

In 1936 he returned to the United States as conductor of the San Francisco Symphony Orchestra, staying in that position through the 1952 season. During World War II he obtained American citizenship and transferred his Ecole Monteux to his new hometown of Hancock, Maine, where Erich Kunzel, Neville Marriner, and André Previn were among his students. He guest conducted and recorded extensively, and in 1961, at the age of eighty-six, accepted the musical directorship of the London Symphony Orchestra.

RCA Victor recorded him extensively in stereo, not only in Debussy, Ravel, Milhaud, Stravinsky, and the like, but also in Beethoven and Brahms; Monteux was especially noted for his performances of these composers' music, to which he brought an unusual charm and lyrical quality.

He strove for transparency of sound, precision, light and springy rhythms, and that elegance that seems particularly associated with French music. *—Joseph Stevenson*

Recommended:

○ **Monteux's Berlioz** / Monteux (cond.), Paris SO / Music & Arts 762

○ **Rimsky-Korsakov** / Monteux, etc. / RCA 61897

○ **Franck: Symphony; Stravinsky: Petrouchka** / Monteux (cond.), Chicago SO, BSO / 1999 / BMG 63303

○ **Pierre Monteux** / Monteux (cond.), BSO, SO, NDRSO, Danish RSO / EMI 75474

Monteverdi Choir

f. 1964, Cambridge, England

Ensemble

The Monteverdi Choir, a British ensemble with roots in the early music movement, did much to bring that music alive for general audiences. In recent years the group has broadened its repertoire beyond early music and has become one of the world's most renowned choral ensembles.

The 1950s witnessed a sudden growth of interest in Baroque and earlier music, but to many, this wave of the early music movement tended toward a careful, academic quality in performances, with often dry and ascetic results.

In March of 1964 John Eliot Gardiner, then an undergraduate at Cambridge University, formed the Monteverdi Choir for a performance of Monteverdi's *Vespers* of 1610 (the *Vespro della beata Vergine*) at King's College Chapel at Cambridge. His aim was to bring out the passion and color of Italian music within the solid British choral tradition. The choir made its debut in London with a 1966 appearance in Wigmore Hall.

Since then the Monteverdi Choir has expanded its expertise in both directions from its base in the Baroque era, achieving a large and broad repertory. Often appearing with the English Baroque Soloists (a period-instrument orchestra founded by Gardiner), the choir is famous for rich, committed performances with a strongly vital rhythmic sense and amastery of style of various eras.

It has performed and recorded Renaissance and early Baroque music (by composers such as Schütz, Gabrieli, Gesualdo, Carissimi, Campra, and Leclair), more familiar Baroque music (all of Bach's major choral works, most of Purcell's semi-operas, several Handel oratorios), Classical era masterworks (Mozart's *Requiem* and *Mass in C minor*, Haydn's *Die Jahreszeiten* (The Seasons), Mozart's *Thamos, König in Ägypten* incidental music, Beethoven's *Missa Solemnis*), Romantic repertory (Berlioz's *Roméo et Juliet*, the choral music of Schubert, Verdi's *Requiem* and *Falstaff*, Brahms' *Ein Deutsches Requiem*, Léhar's *The Merry Widow*), and the modern era (Britten's *Spring Symphony*, Kurtág's *Songs of Despair*, and music of Percy Grainger).

The choir frequently tours. One of its most notable trips, in 1989, marked its 25th anniversary and included a performance of the Monteverdi *Vespers* in St Mark's Basilica in Venice, the acoustic environment Monteverdi had in mind when he composed the work. In 1996 the group participated in the inaugural Lincoln Center Festival in New York, where it joined Gardiner's *Orchestre Révolutionare et Romantique* in Beethoven's *Symphony No. 9* and *Missa Solemnis*. It has presented a series of concerts exploring little known chorus-and-orchestra masterworks by Robert Schumann, which it subsequently recorded.

The Monteverdi Choir has recorded for DG Archive, Philips, Erato, Decca (London) and EMI. *—Joseph Stevenson*

Recommended:

○ **Handel: Messiah** / Gardiner (cond.), Brett, Ross, Robbin, Johnson, EBS, Monteverdi Choir / 1992 / Philips 434297

○ **Shütz: Die sieben Worte Jesu Christi am Kreuz; 4 Dialogues** / Gardiner (cond.), McCulloch, Cook, Harrhy, Thomas, Davies, Monteverdi Choir, Sagitarii Collegium, London Bach Society Choir / 1975 / Cantate 57615

○ **Danny Boy – The Music Of Percy Grainger** / Gardiner (cond.), Robertson, Charlesworth, Backes, Jenkin, Monteverdi Choir & Orch. / 1996 / Philips 446657

○ **Handel: Hallelujah** / Gardiner (cond.), Nicholson, Watkinson, Ross, Monteverdi Choir, EBS / 1997 / Philips 456502

Claudio Monteverdi

b. May 15, 1567, Cremona, Italy, **d.** Nov. 29, 1643, Venice, Italy

Composer: Opera, Choral, Ballet

If one were to name the composer that stitches the seam between the Renaissance and the Baroque, it would likely be Claudio Monteverdi—the same composer who is largely and frequently credited with making the cut in the first place. The path from his earliest canzonettas and madrigals to his latest operatic work exemplifies the shifts in musical thinking that took place in the last decades of the sixteenth century and the first few of the seventeenth.

Monteverdi was born in Cremona, Italy, on the 15th of May, 1567. As a youth his musical talent was already evident: his first publication was issued by a prominent Venetian publishing house when he was 15, and by the time he was 20 a variety of his works had gone to print. His first book of five-voice madrigals, while bearing a dedication to his Cremonese mentor Ingegnieri, succeeded in establishing his reputation outside of his provincial hometown, and helped him find work in the court of the Duke Gonzaga of Mantua. His compositions from the Mantuan period betray the influence of Giaches de Wert, who Monteverdi eventually succeeded as the *maestro di cappella*. It was around this time that Monteverdi's name became widely known, due largely to the criticism levied at him by G.M. Artusi in his famous 1600 treatise "on the imperfection of modern music." Artusi found Monteverdi's contrapuntal unorthodoxies unacceptable and cited several excerpts from his madrigals as examples of modern musical decadence. In the response that appeared in the preface to Monteverdi's fifth book of madrigals, the composer coined a pair of terms inextricably tied to the diversity of musical taste that came to characterize the times. He referred to the older style of composition, in which the traditional rules of counterpoint superseded expressive considerations, as the *prima prattica*. The *seconda prattica*, as characterized by such works as *Crudi Amarilli*, sought to put music in the servitude of the text by whatever means necessary-including "incorrect" counterpoint-to vividly express the text.

In 1607, Monteverdi's first opera (and the oldest to grace modern stages with any frequency) *L'Orfeo*, was performed in Mantua. This was followed in 1608 by *L'Arianna*, which, despite its popularity at the time, no longer survives except in libretti, and in the title character's famous lament, a polyphonic arrangement of which appeared in his sixth book of madrigals (1614). Disagreements with the Gonzaga court led him to seek work elsewhere, and finally in 1612 he was appointed *maestro di cappella* at St. Mark's Cathedral in Venice.

His earliest years at Venice were a rebuilding period for the cappella, and it was some time before Monteverdi was free to accept commissions outside his duties at the cathedral. In 1616 he composed the ballet *Tirsi i Clori* for Ferdinand of Mantua, the more-favored brother of his deceased and disliked ex-employer. The following years saw some abandoned operatic ventures, the now-lost opera *La finta pazza Licori*, and the dramatic dialogue *Combattimento di Tancredi e Clorinda*.

The 1630s were lean musical years for Monteverdi. Political battles and an outbreak of the plague left him without commissions from either Mantua or Venice. However, with the opening of Venetian opera houses in 1637, Monteverdi's operatic career was revived. A new production of *L'Arianna* was staged in 1640, and three new operas appeared within two years: *Il ritorno d'Ulisse in patria*, *Le nozze d'Enea con Lavinia*, and *L'incoronazione di Poppea*. This resurgence preceded his death by just a few years: he passed away in Venice in 1643. *—Jeremy Grimshaw*

OPERA

Combattimento di Tancredi e Clorinda, dramatic cantata (ca. 1638)

Stage works with music, such as mysteries, moralities, sacred dramas, and masques, have a long history. *Combattimento*—partly ballet and partly acting—was, however, a novel concept for its time. It was composed for a private entertainment at the Palazzo Giralmo Moncenigo in 1624 on the occasion of an aristocratic wedding, and performed by musicians from St. Mark's, where Monteverdi was *maestro di cappella*. The work was not published until 1638. Described by Monteverdi as a dramatic cantata, it is set to a classical text by Tasso (verses 52–68 of *Canto XII* of *Jerusalem Delivered*). In his introduction to the score he states that all details of both action and words should be strictly observed by the singers, actors, and instrumentalists. (i.e., not dictated solely by the music). The narrator (testo) who describes and comments on the events portrayed remains detached from the action, and is instructed to sing clearly and articulate correctly. Sound recordings of *Combattimento* are bound to be less than satisfactory by omitting, as they must, the visual aspects of the work.

The orchestra is small: a quartet of strings, contrabass, and harpsichord. Tancredi, a Christian knight, has fallen in love with Clorinda, a Saracen warrior. She has attacked and burned a Christian fort and, not recognizing her in armor, Tancredi pursues her as she returns from the assault. Thinking she is a man, he challenges her to mortal combat. This is the point at which the cantata begins. After the narrator has announced the theme of the story, the orchestra immediately launches into a galloping pursuit in 6/8 time and the narrator begins his description of the phases of the fight. Before an orchestral sinfonia, a beautiful inspiration called "Invocation to Night," a tremolando passage, is heard. This new device of rapidly repeated slurred notes, or stile concitato (agitated style), is used by Monteverdi to convey one of the three qualities of human emotion named by the Greek philosophers: agitated, soft, and moderate; even the narrator is required to quickly speak some of the lines to achieve a similar effect. Evidence of Monteverdi's determination to emphasize such connections is also found in his Preface. Music, he said, is represented by the soft (*molle*) and temperate, and he intends to introduce new devices to represent it: the string tremolo and string pizzicato. Both soon became commonplace in music. In the middle of the battle the combatants rest, their exhaustion reflected in the music, which is headed *Guerra*, when they return to the fight. At last Clorinda falls dying. She forgives him and asks for Christian baptism. He fetches water from a stream, raises the visor of her helmet and recognizes her. As he baptizes her she sings a last rising phrase and dies. *—Roy Brewer*

Synopsis:

The story is set during the First Crusade, 1095–1099. Several key events take place in this cantata before the narrator begins by describing Tancredi's pursuit on horseback of Clorinda. Tancredi is a Christian knight in love with the Saracen maiden Clorinda, who was raised a Muslim against the wishes of her Christian mother. Attired in armor and other male military accoutrements of Medieval times, Clorinda and a fellow warrior have just attacked and burned a Christian fortress. It is in her flight from this triumph on foot that Tancredi begins his pursuit of her, believing she is a pagan male insurgent.

The knight soon dismounts his horse and begins combat with the determined Clorinda. The fighting is fierce and exhausting from the outset, the pair needing to rest for a time before resuming their grim contest. During this break, Tancredi asks his opponent to reveal his name. But Clorinda merely responds by claiming responsibility for destroying the Christian fortress. The fight resumes with renewed vigor by both combatants, but Clorinda is finally struck down. She remains conscious in her death throes and asks Tancredi for his forgiveness. She also requests that he baptize her into Christianity. Tancredi procures water from a stream nearby and hurries back to the fallen, now contrite warrior. He lifts the visor of her armor to discover to his horror that his opponent is not a male warrior, but his beloved and beautiful Clorinda. He carries through with the baptism, and then Clorinda dies, uttering the words "... I go in peace." *—Robert Cummings*

Recommended:

- ○ **Monteverdi: Il Combattimento; Lamento della Ninfa; Madrigali** / Harnoncourt (cond.), Equiluz, Hollweg, Schmidt, Vienna Concentus Musicus / 1984 / Teldec 843054
- ○ **Monteverdi: Il Combattimento di Tancredi e Clorinda** / Christie, Les Arts Florissants Orch. & Chorus / 1998 / HM 7901426

La favola d'Orfeo (1607)

Monteverdi's *Orfeo* is one of the seminal works in the canon of Western music, the first great opera. When it was first given on February 24, 1607, in a room in the ducal palace at Mantua, the history of the genre dated back less than a decade. The direct model for *Orfeo* was one of the earliest operas, Jacopo Peri's Eurydice, first performed in Florence in 1600—although dramatic settings of the legend of Orpheus and Eurydice including music dated back at least a century earlier, stemming from the Renaissance fascination with Greek antiquity. The opera was commissioned by Francesco Gonzaga, the son of the Duke of Mantua (Monteverdi's first patron), for the Carnival season of 1607, and was given before the membership of the Accademia degli Invaghiti, one of the many artistic academies that played a major role in Italian cultural life.

The libretto for *Orfeo* was the work of Alessandro Striggio, who based his version of the legend largely upon Ovid's *Metamorphosis*. It opens with an allegorical prologue in which Music pays compliments to the audience, particularly the ruling Gonzaga family, and then introduces Orpheus. The whole of the prologue is bound by an instrumental ritornello, also heard in the opera itself, that symbolizes the power of music, a topic important to most early operas based on the legend. The drama is then unfolded throughout five short acts which move from a pastoral scene in which Orpheus and Eurydice are celebrating their wedding day with a group of shepherds, through to the great dramatic turning point marked by the arrival of a Messenger giving the stunned assembly news of Eurydice's death. Joy now turns to lamentation and mourning, followed in the third and fourth acts by Orpheus' journey to the underworld to reclaim Eurydice—the centerpiece of which is the great aria "Possente spirto," Orpheus' plea to the underworld. The published version of the score gives alternative versions, one a simple melodic outline, the other elaborately ornamented—a uniquely important piece of contemporary documentary evidence of how embellishment was employed. The music throughout shows Monteverdi mixing both the new recitative style that inspired the birth of opera with older forms such as the madrigal (heard among the shepherds), and danced airs, all at the service of the central drama. Despite the use of some closed forms, the greatness of *Orfeo* lies in its total fulfillment of the objectives of the founding fathers of opera: the expression of a natural sequence of events in which the music is at the service of the words and of dramatic veracity.

The preservation of the first published edition of the score (Venice, 1609) gives full details of the instrumentation, thus providing further unusual performance insights for this period. The large body of instruments includes strings (violins, viols), brass and wind instruments (cornetti, recorder, clarino trumpet, four trombones), and a huge continuo grouping that includes a double harp, two chittarones (large continuo lutes), two small "flue" (pipe) organs, and a regal organ. *—Brian Robins*

Synopsis:

Prologue. The action begins with the allegorical figure of Music, who sings, flattering the audience with praise, and declares her powerful nature before introducing the story of Orfeo (Orpheus). She demands silence, and the opera begins.

Act One. In pastoral setting, the nymphs and shepherds are gathered. A shepherd announces the forthcoming marriage of Orfeo to Euridice, and the chorus, with the aid of a nymph, call upon Hymen, god of marriage. They're giving thanks that Orfeo, who was indifferent to Eurydice, has had a change of heart. Orfeo enters with Eurydice. They praise each other to the skies, while another shepherd encourages them to dance and sing. All are rejoicing: after the storm, the sun shines, after the bitter frosts of winter, spring.

Act Two. Orfeo is with the shepherds in the woods, which are the haunts of Pan. Together they muse over the combatant joys and sorrows of courtship. At the shepherds' request, Orfeo sings a song contrasting these, whereupon a messenger arrives. He bitterly announces Eurydice's death by snakebite. She died, he says, calling out "Orfeo!" Disconsolate, Orfeo vows to descend into Hades and rescue his beloved from death. The messenger laments that he had to bear such news, the "knife-blade that has bled dry the loving heart of Orfeo." Shepherds raise a prayer, seeking consolation in their grief.

Act Three. Orfeo is in Hades, on the banks of the river Styx; the goddess Speranza (hope) has led him this far, but can take him no further. He begs her to stay with him, but she goes, and the boatman, Charon, steps forth to bar his way. "I shall never let any body of flesh and blood into my boat," he says. To win his pity, Orfeo sings a song expressing his grief ("Possente spirito"), but Charon cannot afford pity. Orfeo calls to the people of the underworld to give him back his beloved, and they send Charon to sleep. Orfeo ferries himself across as the chorus of infernal spirits raise a praise to the unconquerable power of human effort.

Act Four. Proserpina, daughter of Demeter, pleads with Pluto, Lord of the Underworld, to allow Eurydice to return to life. Despite professional reservations, Pluto consents, moved both by her zeal and by the eloquence of Orfeo's musical pleas. The catch, however, is that Orfeo must leave the infernal regions without once looking back upon Eurydice; if he fails, the promise is revoked and Eurydice will forever be returned to the Underworld. The spirits dutifully carry out Pluto's orders, expressing concern that Orfeo won't fulfill his requirement. Almost immediately, anxious that he's being tricked, Orfeo looks back to see whether Eurydice is following him; a darkness descends, and the spirits send Eurydice back to Hades before his very eyes. A chorus rises, praising self-control as the highest of virtues; Orfeo conquered Hades, but in the end was conquered by his own passions.

Act Five. In a pastoral setting, as at the opera's beginning, Orfeo is alone, singing laments: "I have not enough tears to suffice." The compassionate Echo responds; he thanks her for her kindness, then sings a song of praise to Eurydice. Apollo, sensitive to the laments of his son, descends in a cloud, singing, and whisks Orfeo away due to his heedless emotionalism. Together they ascend to Heaven, where Apollo promises they will see Eurydice's likeness in the stars. A chorus rises, and they commend Orfeo for his belated obedience, singing that the rewards of grace come to those who sow in sorrow. *—Donato Mancini*

Recommended:

- ○ **Monteverdi: L'Orfeo** / Gardiner (cond.), Otter, Chance, Dawson, His Majesty's Sagbutts & Cornetts, English Baroque Soloists / Archiv 419250
- ○ **Monteverdi: L'Orfeo** / Medlam, Rogers (conds.), Edwards, Kirkby, Laurens, Potter, Varcoe, Kwella, London Baroque, London Cornett & Sackbut Ens. / 1993 / EMI 64947
- ○ **Monteverdi: L'Orfeo** / Haïm (cond.), Dessay, Bostridge, Agnew, Gens, Le Concert D'Astree, European Voices / 2004 / Virgin 45642

L'incoronazione di Poppea (1642)

Among the landmarks of early opera, this was the first one based on historical incidents. The story of Nero and Poppea was well known to seventeenth century audiences, and they would probably have been familiar with Tacitus' account of the facts, with the tragedies of Seneca, and with the story of his life. Thus this masterwork of Monteverdi's old age was also quite accessible to Venetians of the day.

L'Incoronazione di Poppea was Monteverdi's largest and grandest work, premiered in Venice at the Saints Giovanni e Paolo Theater. There are a large number of closed forms—arias and instrumental pieces—that break up the flow of recitative. The composer uses instrumental ritornelli and musical motives to bind together diverse forms into larger cohesive units.

The characters in the plot are also diverse. There is a comic couple, there is the scheming Ottavia who is angered at her rejection by Nero, and there is Seneca, a noble philosopher who must die for his beliefs. There is the lovelorn Otho, weak and rejected by Poppea. And finally there are Nero and Poppea, the anti-hero and heroine. Both the librettist Busenello and Monteverdi skillfully describe each character's psychology in music and verse. The flirtations of the comic pair are contrasted with the passion of Nero and Poppea. And the sad resignation of Otho makes a vivid counterpart for the jealous vengefulness of Ottavia.

Monteverdi casts each role in a particular vocal range. Usually the male lead would have been played by a castrato, making Nero and Poppea both sopranos. Ottavia, by contrast, is a mezzo-soprano, and the nurse, a protector of Poppea, is a dark contralto. The part of Seneca is intended for a noble bass voice. And the instrumentation shifts. Nero is accompanied by the harpsichord or the regal, and Poppea by the lighter lute. Seneca's weighty voice sings to the accompaniment of the organ, and the assembled divinities to the heavenly harp.

The final scene is a beautiful illustration of the power of contrasts. Nero and Poppea are rejoicing at their coming nuptials in a passionate duet; their two soprano voices set off the lower one of Ottavia as she sings an extended lament upon leaving Rome. The weight of the music, its somber sadness, and its dramatic, tragic recitative style contrast starkly with the lovers' rejoicing. The coronation ceremony is introduced with full orchestral fanfare and a ceremonial chorus. The opera closes with another duet for Poppea and Nero, this one extremely passionate, an expression of love fulfilled.

The source for the libretto was Tacitus, a Roman historian. Both Tacitus and Suetonius told the story of the life of Nero, and both were at alive at a time when they could have gotten firsthand accounts from those who had witnessed the events of Nero's reign. Busenello did not include in his libretto the atrocities committed by Nero, nor his cold-blooded execution of his mother because of her objection to his love for Poppea. Poppea's motives for wanting to ascend the empress's throne are never impugned. Instead, the theme of the story is of love conquering all, even if the basis of that love is immoral. The nobility of Seneca is a potentially disturbing setback to this theme but is easily dismissed, and Nero and Poppea's love is the only and highest good that remains. *—Rita Laurance*

Synopsis:

Prologue. Fortune, Virtue and Love appear. Fortune and Virtue debate which of them is more powerful until Love silences them, claiming to be the greatest of all. As proof, he offers the story of Nero and Poppea.

Act One. Nightime. Otho, former lover of Poppea, discovers that he's been cuckolded by the emperor Nero. He expresses an astonished grief at her betrayal, she who so recently vowed her love, and leaves. The soldiers on guard, awakened by Otho, gossip about Nero's promiscuities and the cunning deceits of his advisor Seneca. At dawn, Nero and Poppea appear. She is begging him not to leave her. But Nero can't risk discovery of the affair until Octavia, his jealous wife, has been banished. He bids Poppea an affectionate farewell. Arnalta, Poppea's nurse, enters and warns her against Octavia's retribution, which could strike at any moment, but Poppea's confidence is unshaken.

The scene changes to the Palace, where Octavia is alone, decrying Nero's infidelities and the subservience of women. Her nurse enters, who advises her to take a lover, but Octavia refuses to risk Nero's punishment. Seneca arrives with one of her pages, offering further flattery, which she also rejects. The page ridicules the philosopher's deceits. Alone, Seneca is visited by the goddess Pallas Athena, who warns him he is in mortal danger, but death holds no terror for the philosophical Seneca. Nero arrives, announcing his plan to wed Poppea. Seneca warns him against the folly of the act and is dismissed after a heated debate.

Poppea arrives with Otho. She insinuates that Seneca considers himself the real power behind Rome. Outraged, Nero orders Seneca's suicide and leaves, saying "today you will have proof of the power of Love." Seething with jealousy, Otho comes forward, reproaches Poppea her cruel indifference. He pulls himself together, and offers his hand to the fair Drusilla, a companion of Poppea's who's long been in love with him.

Act Two. In the garden of his villa, Seneca is visited by Mercury, who wants to prepare him gracefully for death. Liberto, Captain of the Guard, arrives to convey Nero's irrational command. The grieving members of Seneca's household prepare his suicide bath.

Back at the palace, the Page indulges in love play with the Lady in Waiting. Nero enters with Lucan, singing praises of Poppea's beauty.

In another part of the palace, Otho, alone, is admonishing himself for his thoughts of murdering Poppea. Octavia summons him; she commands him to slay her rival, threatening to have him tortured to death if he doesn't obey. Elsewhere, Drusilla, with the page and the nurse, is gloating over her newfound happiness with Otho. When the servants leave, tormented Otho accosts Drusilla, tells her of his forthcoming crime, and asks her to borrow some women's clothing for his disguise. She agrees, only too glad to be rid of a rival.

The scene changes to the garden of Poppea's residence. She is with Arnalta, who is growing tired of her incessant talk of marriage to the Emperor, although she is careful to add "Don't forget me." Poppea falls asleep. Soon after, Love descends from the sky. He vows to protect her from Otho. Enter Otho, disguised in Drusilla's clothing. He creeps towards her sleeping form, and raises the sword to strike, but Love knocks it from his hand at the last moment. Awakened by the clatter, Poppea glimpses a figure she takes for Drusilla fleeing from the garden.

Act Three. In the imperial throne room, Drusilla is jubilant that her rival will soon be gone when Arnalta and Lictor arrive, pointing the accusing finger. As Nero enters, Arnalta tells him all. Drusilla pleads her innocence until threats of torture make her rescind; she prefers to take the blame upon herself than betray Otho. Nero orders her death, but Otho intervenes with his own confession, implicating Octavia as well. The Emperor spares them both, praises Drusilla's selflessness, but condemns Otho to exile. Drusilla, however, announces that she intends to stay with her beloved. For Nero, the news is good: he at last has an excuse to repudiate his wife. Poppea arrives with Arnalta. All rejoice.

Elsewhere, Octavia, alone, bids a bitter farewell to Rome. In the throne room, Nero and Poppea are rejoicing as the Counsels and Tribunes arrive from Heaven to crown the new empress. Love and Venus watch from above; Love has triumphed. *—Donato Mancini*

Recommended:

- ○ **Claudio Monteverdi: L'Incoronazione Di Poppea** / Harnoncourt (cond.), Berberian, Esswood, Langridge, Soderstrom, Vienna Concentus Musicus / 1993 / Teldec 42547
- ○ **Claudio Monteverdi: L'incoronazione Di Poppea** / Gardiner (cond.), Bott, Holman, McNair, Fink, Backes, English Baroque Soloists / Archiv 447088
- ○ **Claudio Monteverdi: L'Incoronazione Di Poppea** / Hickox (cond.), Augér, Bowman, Jones, Hirst, London Baroque Sinfonia / 1990 / Virgin 90775

Il ritorno d'Ulisse in patria (1640)

In 1637, *San Cassiano*, the first public opera house in Europe, was established in Venice. Hitherto restricted to performance within the confines of courtly palaces, opera now became a genre enjoyed by a broader audience. Among those to make an early contribution to public opera was Claudio Monteverdi, the aging maestro di cappella of St. Mark's, Venice. Between 1640 and 1643 he provided three new operas for Venice; the music for one, *Le nozze d'Enea in Lavinia* is now lost. The other two, *Il ritorno d'Ulisse in patria* and *L'incoronazione di Poppea*, are among his greatest works. In subject matter the two operas are diametrically opposed, *Il ritorno* being a celebration of faithful conjugal love while *Poppea* depicts the victory of amoral lust and naked power over the virtuous.

Il ritorno d'Ulisse in patria (The Return of Ulysses to his Homeland) was the earliest of these three operas. It was first performed in 1640, probably at the *SS Giovanni e Paolo* theater. The libretto was specifically written in an attempt to persuade Monteverdi to return to opera, a genre he had not addressed for some years. The author, Giacomo Badoaro, based his plot on the episode in Homer's *Odyssey* which relates the story of the return of the Greek hero Ulysses to his home country after many years absence at the Trojan Wars. However, the central character of the opera is not Ulysses but his stoical wife Penelope, who during the years of her husband's absence has deterred several potential suitors. The opera introduces us to three such suitors. They are eventually vanquished by the disguised Ulysses, who reveals his true identity only at the end of the opera.

The opera is cast in three acts, with an allegorical prologue in which the scene is set for the following drama. In keeping with the conventions of Venetian public opera that prevailed until the end of the seventeenth century, the large cast list includes comic as well as serious characters, the former given specific comic scenes in addition to mixing with the serious characters. The suitors themselves are revealed as absurd characters and treated in an ironic manner that serves to point up their gross contrast to the noble object of their courting.

Monteverdi's music, while retaining the objective of the founders of opera to convey strong affections through the power of the text, has moved far beyond the Renaissance influences heard in his *Orfeo* of 1607. Here he utilizes a flowing, flexible sequence of recitative, arioso, and aria to produce an opera whose grand sweep conveys much to the unfolding of the Greek drama upon which it is based. *Il ritorno* was a great success, receiving ten performances in Venice before being taken on tour to Bologna. It was revived in Venice the following year, an usual distinction in an era that constantly sought new dramatic works. *—Brian Robins*

Synopsis:

Prologue. The story is set in mythological ancient Greece, on the island of Ithaca, just after the Trojan War. Time, Fortune, and Love demonstrate their mastery of Human Frailty.

Act One. At the royal palace, Penelope bemoans the prolonged absence of her husband Ulisse as her attendant Ericlea listens. This melancholy opening stands in contrast with the following flirtatious exchange between Melanto, Penelope's maid, and her lover Eurimaco—who, it it learned, is part of a usurpation conspiracy to force Penelope to accept a suitor in place of Ulisse.

The Phaeacians return the sleeping Ulisse to the shores of Ithaca, defying Nettuno's command. After discussing the Phaeacians' punishment with Jupiter, Nettuno turns them into a rock. Ulisse awakens and is met by the goddess Minerva, who informs him of his whereabouts and of the plot against his kingdom and wife. She instructs him to enter his court in disguise as a beggar. Minerva then departs for Sparta to enlist the aid of Ulysses' son Telemaco.

Meanwhile, Melanto exhorts Penelope to select a suitor from one of the three chief conspirators. But she is steadfast in her refusal to betray Ulisse. In the countryside, Ulisse, in beggar's disguise, meets Eumete, his old servant, but does not divulge his identity to him. He tells Eumete that Ulisse will soon return.

Act Two. Minerva returns with Telemaco, and later Eumete greets him warmly in a grove. Telemaco instructs him to go to Penelope and assure her that Ulisse will soon return. Casting off his beggar's disguise, Ulisse reveals his identity to Telemachus, and the two acknowledge the supremacy of the gods over man. Ulisse tells him to go to his mother; he will join them shortly after in beggar's disguise.

At the palace Penelope turns away the three suitors—Antinoo, Pisandro, and Anfinomo—despite their attempts to charm her. Eumete reaches the palace and informs Penelope of the imminent arrival of Telemaco and (possibly) of Ulisse himself. But she is skeptical of his revelations, though the suitors, who overhear them, are not. At first they plot to murder Telemaco, but they renounce their scheme when an eagle flies overhead, which they interpret as a bad omen. They decide instead to continue their attempts to woo Penelope.

Minerva tells Ulisse that when he uses his bow against the suitors, she will enable him to strike them down. Telemaco arrives at the palace and joins his mother in a happy reunion. He informs her that Ulisse will soon return. Ulisse, dressed as a beggar, arrives at the palace with Eumete, and both are ridiculed by the suitors. Iro, an opponent of Ulisse, engages him in a fight and is badly beaten. Penelope welcomes the victorious beggar and announces that she will accept the suitor strong enough to string the bow of her husband. The three men each try and fail miserably, but Ulisse succeeds and then, calling upon the gods, slays the trio.

Act Three. Iro commits suicide, and the ghosts of the suitors are sent to hell by Mercury. Having lost her lover Eurimaco when the suitors were slain, Melanto pleads with Penelope to take action against the beggar. But Eumete reveals that he was actually Ulisse. Penelope is incredulous at the revelation.

Though Nettuno is reluctant at first, he and the other gods, Minerva and Giunone, restore Ulisse to power. Penelope continues to believe the beggar was not Ulisse and remains skeptical for a time even after he appears, shorn of his disguise. The couple are reunited, and the opera ends happily. *—Robert Cummings*

Recommended:

- ○ **Monteverdi: Il Ritorno D'Ulisse in Patria** / Jacobs (cond.), Visse, Hunt, Hogman, Prégardien, Concerto Vocale / HM 901427-29
- ○ **Monteverdi: Il Ritorno D'Ulisse In Patria** / Harnoncourt (cond.), Egmond, Esswood, Equiluz, Rogers, Vienna Concentus Musicus, Junge Kantorei / 1993 / Teldec 6019

CHORAL

Beatus Vir, motet (ca. 1640)

By 1613, when appointed *maestro di capella* at the cathedral church of St. Mark in Venice, Monteverdi had completed his opera, *Orfeo*, the magnificent *Vespers* of 1610, and a great deal of other church music; he was well established as a preeminent composer in the "new style" of the early Baroque. In Venice, he continued to revitalize church music in two great collections, *Selva morale e spirituale* (1640) and *Messa a quattro voci* (published in the year of his death, 1651), from which this setting of Psalm 112 is taken. There are few better examples of the way sacred music was being released from the emotional boundaries of Renaissance polyphony into the light and color of early Baroque humanism. Just as the *Vespers* it shows a freedom from liturgical and musical conventions of the time; but the composer was confident that this quality, coupled with the technical perfection achieved in his nine books of madrigals and other music, was the best way to keep music and poetry alive in the spirit of prayer. The work, for double choir, strings and organ, is in free concertante style. Monteverdi's setting is operatic in feeling and clearly inspired by his own sensuous madrigal *Chiome d'oro* (Golden Hair). The opening phrases, alive with simple joy, melodic grace, and sweet reason, are followed by a more reflective middle section in which the parlando (recitative-like) nature of the music is retained with no lessening of its dramatic impact. Towards the end, a slowing of tempo and broadening of harmony remind us that this is indeed a hymn of praise, and the vigor of the opening flourishes is transformed into a fervent, elaborated ritornello for choir and orchestra and a jubilant Amen. *—Roy Brewer*

Recommended:

- ○ **From Monteverdi to Vivaldi** / Parrott (cond.), Kirkby, Covey-Crump, Thomas, Taverner Consort, Choir & Players / 2003 / Virgin Classics 562167
- ○ **Venice Preserved** / Bassano (cond.), His Majesty's Sagbutts & Cornetts, Gentlemen of the Chappell / 1990 / ASV 122

Lamento d'Arianna, madrigal (ca. 1614)

Monteverdi's *Lamento d'Arianna* has been a cornerstone of his fame both in his own time and in ours. In its original form, Monteverdi composed this lament as a dramatic focal point within his opera *Arianna*. As such, it graced the 1608 wedding festivities of Prince Francesco Gonzaga of Mantua and Duchess Margherita of Savoy. Several ambassadors and other witnesses of this first performance testified to the special power of Monteverdi's music for the *Lamento*. Monteverdi himself later wrote that this piece was the "most essential part" of the entire opera and a particular challenge to his powers of invention. He published it as a separate entity in 1623 (twice), arranged it once for choral ensemble, and composed a sacred monody (the "Pianto della Vergine" from the 1641 *Selva morale e spirituale*) on its music. *Ariadne's Lament* further spawned an entire genre of lament music in the seventeenth century and sparked vibrant theoretical debates regarding the power of music to imitate human emotion. After his death, the *Lamento* was one of the earliest "revivals" of Monteverdi's music, as early as the 1780s; its first printing was in 1868 Paris. The composer's own arrangement of the *Lamento* as a five-voiced madrigal has helped fuel the piece's ongoing popularity from the twentieth century into the twenty-first.

Monteverdi apparently considered his madrigal arrangement, known by its opening Italian text "Lasciatemi morire," important enough that he placed it at the very beginning of his *Sixth Book of Madrigals* (1614). Historians have suggested that an unknown Venetian nobleman convinced the composer to re-set his *Lamento* into the more accessible medium of a bourgeois madrigal. Whether or not that was the case, Monteverdi skillfully translated his most famous solo song into an affective choral idiom. He deleted the original opera's interjected choral commentaries, instead setting just the four parts of Ariadne's own music; he retained the emotionally charged melodic gestures in the upper voice and allowed the lower four voices to share in her plaintive music. Each of the madrigal's four parts thus reflects the shifting affects of the operatic original. In the first strophe, the abandoned lover Ariadne uses frequent chromaticism in her cry to be left alone to die; the second and third sections showcase even more violent despair, in often wild leaps of tritones and melodic sevenths. Ariadne's reluctant conclusion that no one answers her tears in the final section draws the singers into passionately low registers and mournfully "flatward" tonal areas. *—Timothy Dickey*

Recommended:

○ **Monteverdi: Lamento d'Arianna; Madrigals** / Christie, Jacobs, Junghanel, Linden, Muller-Molinari, Concerto Vocale / HM 7901129

○ **Cathy Berberian sings Monteverdi** / Harnoncourt (cond.), Berberian, Vienna Concentus Musicus / 1995 / Teldec 10032

Madrigals, Book 1 (1587)

Monteverdi wrote his first madrigals in 1583 and by the end of his life had written some 250. While the sixteenth century madrigal maintained a balance of homophonic and contrapuntal writing, new stylistic features started emerging toward the end of the century. These distinctive features include declamatory (recitativo) elements and ornamental dissonances.

Fine examples of the traditional madrigal with four to six parts by composers such as Palestrina, Andrea Gabrieli, and Marenzio continued to influence later composers, despite the radical changes taking place in Italian music during the seventeenth century. The nine books of Monteverdi's secular madrigals published between 1587 and 1651 are fully representative of a steady and purposeful move away from the earlier forms of the stile antico (old style) towards a more colorful and dramatic approach, which is more closely related to public performance and theatrical interpretation than to private music-making. However, Monteverdi did not simply turn his back on the past. His first Book shows a clear continuity of stylistic development from Marenzio and, though not yet fully confident in handling five voices, the 20-year-old composer shows a firm grasp of counterpoint, with hints of the "new music" in his melodious underlining of the text and polyphonic interweaving of parts. What is more, the emotional element is already strong. Monteverdi is skillful in creating formal patterns from musical motifs with similar rhythms, as in the agile *Ardo, si, ma non t'amo*, *Ardi o gela a tua vegla*, and *Arsi e alsi a mia voglia* (all from Book One). A bold use of dissonance is also evident and points towards the innovative approach that Monteverdi would later take in order to bring out the inner meaning of the words. This is based on a musical interpretation of the ancient concept of "the four humors"—the theory that certain bodily fluids control a person's moods and emotions. In later works Monteverdi was to invent specific musical devices, such as tremolo and pizzicato strings to represent them. If, as is desirable, the Madrigal Books are studied in numerical sequence, Book One can be regarded as an initial step in fully appreciating the scope and direction of an extraordinary body of work. *—Roy Brewer*

Recommended:

○ **Monteverdi: Madrigals, Book 1** / Longhini (cond.), Delitiae Musicae / 2002 / Naxos 8555307

Madrigals, Book 2 (1590)

Monteverdi's *Second Book of Madrigals* is an ambitious project in a number of ways. Though the composer was only in his late teens or early twenties when the pieces that comprise the collection were composed, the book nonetheless demonstrates the honing of his textural and contrapuntal skills, the deepening of his expressive range, and the expansion in scope of his musical treatments.

Indeed, the first madrigal in Book II, *Non si levav*, is more than twice as long as the largest piece in his first madrigal collection, and, while full of the poignant imagery that characterizes the late Renaissance madrigal, demonstrates a keener attempt at overall form, cohesion, and expressive essence. The setting of the bipartite text by Torquato Tasso is early morning, just before sunrise; we see a pair of lovers lounging around after an amorous encounter, exchanging embraces, kisses, and sighs, and postponing their parting. A series of ascending lines corresponds with the word "dawn" in the first line of the poem, and some quick scalar figures accompany the image of morning birds spreading their feathers in the first sunlight. The lover's embrace, "like Acanthus," is painted by similarly entwined melodic lines in contrary motion. Monteverdi has a sense for the larger picture as well as local details: the opening material returns to round out the end of the first half, and appears again in the middle of the second, giving a sense of overarching cohesion. Still, it is the musical moment that steals the listener's attention from broader issues, and Tasso provides numerous other opportunities for madrigalistic tone painting. (Nine of the 20 texts in Book II are his; the remainder are taken from other well-known poets like Guarini and Bembo, as well as from a few more obscure figures like Casoni and Gottifredi.) Monteverdi's treatment of Tasso's well-known *Ecco mormorar l'onde*, for example, contains one musically evocative image after another: the lower voices sing from the depths of the "murmuring waves"; twisting melismas portray the breeze; and of course, the word "cantar" ("to sing") aligns with florid figuration in the upper voices, moving in lush parallel thirds. Perhaps to avoid an air of precocity, throughout the second book of madrigals Monteverdi frequently tips his musical hat to his noted predecessors and prominent contemporaries. *Non si levav* borrows musical material from *Non vidi mai dopo notturna*, a setting of Petrarch from Luca Marenzio's first book of four-voice madrigals (1585). *Cantai un tempo*, which closes the collection, takes as its model Cipriano de Rore's *Cantai, mentre ch'i arsi* from nearly a half-century earlier. And certainly Monteverdi's exploitation of the lower voice range (as in the opening of *Ecco mormorar l'onde*) suggests the influence Giaches de Wert. Still, the innovative and perspicacious ear for expression and poetic nuance that becomes so explicit in the later books can be detected already in Monteverdi's publication from 1590. *—Jeremy Grimshaw*

Recommended:

○ **Monteverdi: Secondo Libro de Madrigali** / Alessandrini (cond.), Cavina, Bertini, Maletto, Naglia, Concerto Italiano / 1994 / Opus 111 3011

Madrigals, Book 3 (1592)

Shortly after Vincenzo Gonzaga took the ducal seat at Mantua in 1587, he set about putting in place in his court a musical establishment that could compete with the one at nearby Ferrara. As exemplified by the famous female vocal ensemble of Ferrara, the *concerto di donne*, the Italian madrigal had changed over the course of the previous decade or so from an amateur pastime for singing nobility to an enterprise requiring professional cultivation and a high level of virtuosity. As part of his effort to establish the artistic validity of his court, Gonzaga hired Claudio Monteverdi, a young up-and-coming musician/composer to play violin in the court ensemble. Within two years of his taking the position, Monteverdi produced his *Third Book of Madrigals*. The contents of the collection at once look back on his earlier style, reflect the influence of the Mantuan musical milieu, and exemplify the spreading popularity of Ferrarese musical trends. Influence of the famous singing ladies of Ferrara can be found in the frequent use of florid upper-voice duets and trios. Indeed, these passages not only evoke the Ferrarese singers; they were probably written to be sung by Duke Gonzaga's prized Mantuan knock-off of the *concerto di donne*. The Mantuan ladies developed their own reputation for virtuosic singing as well as for their highly dramatic delivery. Their ear for rhythmic and dynamic nuance was enhanced by the use of facial expressions and pantomime, and Monteverdi's new madrigals certainly gave them plenty of material to work with. Following his Mantuan elder Giaches de Wert, Monteverdi's approach to expression became less concrete in its depictions—melismas on "breeze," an ascent on "sky," etc.—and more concerned with the human, emotional interpretation of the texts. Of course, traces of Monteverdi's earliest style can be found in the third book. The first piece, *La giovinetta pianta*, recalls his first publication from 1584, a collection of light, three-voice canzonettas. Its sentiments are tender but not overbearing, and the imagery is often vivid but never visceral. Frequent passages of homophonic declamation, and shifts between various combinations of three (out of five) voices lend the piece a lighter air. Compare this, however, with the tension and angst that accrues over the course of the last madrigal of Book III, *Rimante in pace*. A dialogue between lovers Thyrsis and Phyllis, it begins with a resonant five-voice texture that lingers languorously around an A major chord on Thyrsis' words "Stay here in peace." The word "sospirando" ("sighing") send ripples across the harmonic stasis, however, and in a characteristic madrigal gesture, a rising line on "sospiran" is interrupted by a short pause—perhaps a dramatic gasp?—before falling on the final syllable "-do." The rich harmonic palette utilized in setting the rest of the dramatic text likewise carries a gravity and poignancy not as prevalent in earlier works. The performance is no longer meant to entertain singers in a parlor, but to touch the hearts of an assembled audience. *—Jeremy Grimshaw*

Recommended:

○ **Monteverdi: Terzo Libro** / La Venexiana / 2002 / Glossa 920910

Madrigals, Book 4 (1603)

The years surrounding the turn of the seventeenth century represent a sort of fissure in the terrain of music historiography. The honored legacies left by Willaert and Josquin had been upstaged somewhat by the extreme expressivity of madrigalists like Rore and Gesualdo, and Monteverdi would soon expand the composer's expressive palette in drastic new ways. And, of course, opera was then in its embryonic stage, with Peri, Cesti, and the other members of the Florentine musical intelligentsia planting the seeds for centuries of musical drama. Innumerable smaller musical works can be found that look forward to the Baroque while at the same time retaining technical and aesthetic souvenirs from the Renaissance. Monteverdi's *Fourth Book of Madrigals* (its full title is "The Fourth Book of Madrigals of Claudio Monteverdi, Master of Music to his Most Serene

Highness, the Duke of Mantua") falls into this category, reminding us that, in the history of music, the border between old and new is almost always a rather fuzzy one.

Not only do the pieces in this collection dovetail stylistically; but they also represent a larger chronological span than simply the duration of their year of publication. The first piece in the 1603 collection, *"Ah dolente partita,"* had appeared six years earlier in a collection of pieces by various composers. The dedication that prefaces the book honors Duke Alfonso of Ferrara and mentions his recent and untimely death, which had occurred in 1597. We know that some of the pieces in the published collection of 1603 had been circulating prior to that date in manuscript copies, because Giovanni Maria Artusi mentions them in his highly critical treatise, *The Imperfection of Modern Music*, of 1600. Artusi finds particular compositional "faults" in *"Anima mea perdona,"* and *"Che se tu sé il cor mio"* from *Book Four*, as well as the famous *"Cruda Amarilli"* from *Book Five* (1605).

Artusi's complaints in all three cases relate to the harmonic and contrapuntal extremes that Monteverdi utilizes to portray the sense of the poem more vividly. While Artusi clings to time-honored rules of compositional practice, Monteverdi can here (and in the next book) be seen looking for ways to transcend the traditional rules of musical craft in order to place the music under the aesthetic authority of the text. Monteverdi was rather particular about his texts; many of the poems are taken from Guarini's famous *Il Pastor Fido*, and others are by Tasso and Arlotti. Appropriately, Monteverdi's musical settings reflect a deep reading and interpretation of the poetry. Thus the unprepared suspensions and leaps to dissonances that Artusi found offensive in this and subsequent collections are not arbitrary musical gimmickry, but rather expressive devices that intersect with and comment upon the text in new and meaningful ways. *—Jeremy Grimshaw*

Recommended:

○ **Monteverdi: Madrigals. Books 4 & 5** / Rooley (cond.), Consort of Musicke / 1997 / L'Oiseau-Lyre 455718

Madrigals, Book 5 (1605)

Although the Venetian publisher Riccardo Amadino put Monteverdi's (in)famous *Fifth Book of Madrigals* to print in 1605, some works in the collection had been circulating earlier. We know that Giovanni Maria Artusi had a copy of *"Cruda Amarilli"* on hand, because his 1600 *The Artusi, or Imperfections of Modern Music*, singles out the work as a particularly prevalent example of turn-of-the-century musical decadence. Especially objectionable to Artusi was Monteverdi's treatment of dissonance. Turning from the kind of carefully controlled counterpoint that found its culmination in the likes of Palestrina, Monteverdi employed shocking intervallic relations of sevenths and ninths that defied traditional methods of preparation and resolution. Monteverdi's reply to Artusi appears in the preface of the *Fifth Book of Madrigals*, and serves as a crucial historical document in defining the musical ideals of the emerging Baroque period. In it, Monteverdi explains that his purpose in utilizing new harmonic techniques was not simply to break rules, but to transcend them, in order to achieve a richer palette of musical expression. This new style, which he famously termed the seconda prattica, employed an expanded harmonic language that was better equipped to deliver the emotional nuances of a given text than the strict polyphonic formulae of the older style prima prattica. The opening gesture of *Cruda Amarilli* (a notable example of Monteverdi's new uses of dissonance), for example, is not arbitrarily problematic. The intervallic motion of the voices is carefully designed to emphasize the "cruel" nature of the title character. Likewise, the harshest dissonances of the piece preface the line "alas, bitterly do you teach." The text for *Cruda Amarilli*, and several of the other 18 madrigals in Monteverdi's fifth book, is taken from a popular subject of late sixteenth century madrigalist treatment, Giovanni Battista Guarini's *Il Pastor Fido*. This verse play provides Monteverdi with the opportunity to present several miniature dramas in a semi-connected fashion, utilizing the thinned out texture and refined vocal focus that reflected the operatic experiments of the time. Certainly the brand of tone painting and dramatic declamation found in the fifth book hints at the emotional color Monteverdi would soon demonstrate in his first opera, *Orfeo*. Despite the inevitably blurry border between the Renaissance and the Baroque, the fifth book of madrigals continues to be seen by many as an important turning point. *—Jeremy Grimshaw*

Recommended:

○ **Monteverdi: Madrigals Books 4 & 5** / Rooley (cond.), Consort of Musicke / 1997 / L'Oiseau-Lyre 455718

Madrigals, Book 6 (1614)

Appearing in 1614, *Book Six of Madrigals* was Monteverdi's first publication after his taking the illustrious position of *maestro di capella* at St. Mark's cathedral in Venice. Many of the pieces in the collection, including *Misero alceo* and *Presso un fiume*, were popular enough to have been circulating widely before the 1614 printing. Like the previous book from 1605, the sixth book of five-voice madrigals contains the older style of polyphonic a capella pieces along with the newer type of "concertati" madrigals for voice and continuo. Considered as a whole (an approach that modern scholarship increasingly favors), the sixth book can be divided into two large and similar sections; each begins with an a capella section for five voices, followed by a set of madrigals with basso continuo. The entire book ends with a larger-scale madrigal for an expanded vocal ensemble of seven voices with basso continuo. The format and ordering of this book is particularly poignant, as it highlights a sentiment particularly close to Monteverdi. Each of the two sections begins with and is structured around a lament cycle. The first is the famous lament from Monteverdi's 1608 Mantuan opera, *Arianna*. While the opera proper no longer survives (except in the form of a few scattered libretti without music, and in multiple arrangements of the lament), first-hand accounts describe the work as a whole—and this lament in particular—as having a profoundly emotional effect on the audience. In addition to its appearance here in Book VI, the lament spread widely in manuscript copies, was pirated in a 1619 publication, and was released as a monodic piece in 1623. By the 1620s, the lament as a genre was well-established, and virtually every "respectable" home owned a copy of the *Lamento d'Arianna*. As it appears in Book VI, the lament cycle from *Arianna* is followed by an a capella setting of Petrarch's *Zefiro torna*. Two basso continuo madrigals, *Una donna fra l'altre and A Dio* and *Florida bella*, conclude the first section. Fittingly, the lament that begins the second half of the book has special ties to the opening cycle. Bearing the incipit "Incenerite spoglie," this six-part madrigal serves as a lament for Caterina Martinelli, the singer whom Monteverdi himself had been grooming for the title role in *Arianna* until her untimely death from smallpox; it even quotes a few passages directly from the music Martinelli was supposed to have sung. This lament cycle is followed by another Petrarchan a capella setting, *Ohimè il bel viso*, and three madrigals with basso continuo. In this case, the continuo madrigals are all short dramatic scenes of dialogues or strophic variations from texts by Marino. The same poet provides the text for the finale of the book, *Presso a un fiume tranquillo*. *—Jeremy Grimshaw*

Recommended:

○ **Monteverdi: Il sesto libro dei madrigali** / Acciai (cond.), I Solisti del Madrigale / Nuova Era 7165

Madrigals, Book 7 (1619)

A comparison of Monteverdi's *Seventh Book of Madrigals* with his earlier volumes demonstrates the important developments taking place in the madrigal repertory during the first decades of the seventeenth century. His first four books had contained works for five-voice, a cappella ensembles only. Book five had contained mostly madrigals for five voices, but had concluded with a group of madrigals for five voices with basso continuo, and one for an expanded vocal ensemble with basso continuo and other instruments. Following this trend, the sixth book contained a similar ratio of concerted to a cappella pieces. Finally with the seventh book, Monteverdi discards the older performance forces completely. It contains none of the old-style five voice unaccompanied madrigals, and all the works in the collection call for basso continuo, some with other instruments as well. Also, aside from a few pieces for four-, five-, or six-voice accompanied ensembles, the collection is comprised entirely of pieces for few voices—duets, trios, and a couple of solos.

This trend seems to be a natural outgrowth of the values espoused in the famous preface to the fifth book, where Monteverdi had defended his unorthodox contrapuntal practices as attempts to more accurately and vividly express the images, ideas, and sentiments of the text. In Book VII, with fewer voices to give notes to and with an instrumental ensemble covering the harmonic and contrapuntal bases, the vocal lines are freer to devote themselves more fully to declamation and expression. This ideal is further enhanced in pieces such as the *lettere amorosa Se i languidi miei sguardi*, which bears the marking *senza battuta*, or "without beat," and which, with the designation *in genere rappresentativo*, would have been performed with dramatic theatrical gestures.

The "less theatrical" pieces nonetheless still convey Monteverdi's depth of emotion as well. His tenor-duet setting of Guarini's *Interrotte speranze* utilizes one of the composer's favorite harmonic effects, one that appeared with particular frequency in the fourth book: the divergence of unison lines into shimmering dissonances, painting with bold strokes sentiments such as a "weak heart" or "fervent ardor." Exercising a bit of poetic license, Monteverdi cuts and splices the words of the last stanza, so that one singer follows the text of the first line ("I am sending you a big handful of harsh and heartless torments") while the other interjects bitterly with "cruel lady," taken from a later line. Six of Guarini's characteristically emotive texts appear in the collection, as do several by G.B. Marino. Such evocative settings exemplify what is perhaps the *Settimo libro*'s strongest link to the Italian madrigal tradition: amorous or heartbroken sentiments full of poignant, musicable images. *—Jeremy Grimshaw*

Recommended:

○ **Monteverdi: Combattimento di Tancredi e Clorinda; Madrigals, Book 7** / Clemencic (cond.), Clemencic Consort / HM 5901426

○ **Monteverdi: Madrigals, Book 7** / Alessandrini (cond.), Concerto Italiano / 1992 / Arcana 66

Madrigals, Book 8 ("Madrigali guerrieri, et amorosi") (1638)

Monteverdi's *Eighth Book of Madrigals* is a monumental tome, containing nearly 40 individual works. The madrigals in Book VIII are culled from Monteverdi's work of the previous two decades. The pieces are carefully arranged into particular sequences, suggesting that the book be examined as a whole work rather than an arbitrarily-ordered collection. Many of the pieces in the collection are in "genere rappresentativo" as opposed to the madrigals "senza gesto" (without gesture), indicating that the performance of the book would have been at times highly theatrical. The overall ordering of the book follows the pair of adjectives in the title. The first half is comprised of "madrigali guerrieri" (warlike madrigals); the second is made of "madrigali amorosi" (amorous madrigals). Each subdivision of the book is marked by a madrigal for larger-than-normal vocal and instrumental forces. After the sinfonia (for 2 violins, viola da brazzo, and basso continuo) that introduces the whole book, the subsequent prologue begins the "guerrieri" section. A pair of six-voice madrigals with a smaller instrumental ensemble segues into the next section, which contains several duets and trios "without gesture." The subsequent piece, *Combattimento di Tancredi e Clorinda*, tells the story of a tragic battle in which Tancredi deals a fatal blow to Clorinda before lifting her visor and realizing, for the first time, that she is a fair maiden rather than a male foe. It is in this piece that we first see an important innovation of Monteverdi's: the stile concitato. Consisting of rapid, prolonged repetitions of single notes, this "agitated style" underscores poignant images such as the comparison of the combatants to "two rival bulls full of burning anger." To the performers the composer provided some rather detailed suggestions: "Clorinda should enter on foot and carrying a weapon, followed by Tancredi, also armed, and atop a horse.... The movements and gestures of the singers should be determined by the requirements of the poetry—not too much, not too little." The Combattimento is followed by a ballo, which includes singing, pantomime, and dancing. The second half of the book closely mirrors the format of the first. A prologue is followed by a group of "senza gesto" madrigals, which in turn lead to a group of more theatrical pieces. Here we find the famous *Lament of the Nymph*, a heart-wrenching soprano solo with mournful sidelines by a male trio, over a relentless four-note ground bass. Adding to the drama of the piece is the composer's instruction that the soprano exercise rhythmic license to accentuate the harsh melodic dissonances, while the remainder of the ensemble observes tempo strictly. The book then ends with another elaborate piece, the *Ballo delle ingrate* (Ballet of the Ingrate Women). For this number, scenery must be built showing "the mouth of Hell, with four openings on either side spewing flames, from which the Ingrates enter in pairs." Monteverdi instructs further that "The Ingrates should wear gray costumes decorated with teardrop shapes." (This must have been quite a spectacle, particularly since in an early performance the chief ingrate was played by the Duke of Mantua in drag!) As the sullen souls emerge from hell, they warn the women listening to heed the amorous entreaties of their suitors: "Those who oppose love and arm themselves with cruelty ... will see how it burns and pains when their elegance and beauty fade ... [despite the] false remedy of creams and ointments." The closing line of the madrigal encompasses the overarching theme of the entire book, and the idea behind much of the late madrigal repertory: "Learn pity, ladies!" *—Jeremy Grimshaw*

Recommended:

- ○ **Monteverdi: Madrgali guerrieri et amorosi** / Prague Madrigal Singers / Supraphon 32942
- ○ **Monteverdi: Madrigals, Book 8** / Marcante (cond.), Il Ruggiero / Tactus 561305

Madrigals, Book 9 (1651)

The majority of Monteverdi's 250 secular madrigals were published in eight books between 1587 and 1638. Book Eight, the last to be published in his lifetime, followed the Seventh Book after a gap of nearly 20 years and is divided into two sections containing works that date from the 1620s and early 1630s. Books Eight (again) and Nine were issued together in two large volumes in 1651, eight years after Monteverdi's death, and comprise a retrospective collection of works from earlier Books. Although Book Nine continues to appear in some writings and record catalogs, it can usefully be considered together with Book Eight as containing the fruits of the composer's long pursuit of technical perfection, and showing the development of his theories of how the classical Greek concept of "the whole man," and the four "humors" representing human moods and emotions—sanguine, phlegmatic, choleric, and melancholic—can be expressed in music. How far Monteverdi took the traditional madrigal, with its balance of counterpoint and homophony, away from its established conventions is indicated in Book Eight by the inclusion of *Il ballo del ingrate* (1608) and *Il Combattimento di Tancredi e Clorinda* (1624), both stage works and both markedly different from anything easily identifiable as a sixteenth century madrigal. In these, Monteverdi introduces bold technical devices, such as the quickly-repeated notes in *Il Combattimento* and the pizzicato strings in *Il ballo delle ingrate*, both innovations for their time. For example, in *Il Combattimento*, where a warlike spirit of agitation is conveyed by whole notes divided into 16 repeated sixteenth notes (tremolo) on a single note. Other effects equally novel for their day are more difficult to bring off, such as where a soprano is required to use tempo rubato, while the rest of the ensemble keeps strict time, the resultant passing discords sounding strangely disturbing. However, the normal madrigal with four to six parts continued to fascinate Monteverdi, and Books Eight and Nine contain many fine examples of polyphonic writing in the "old style" of Palestrina and Marenzio. The more orthodox Volume Two containing Book Nine has a larger number of pieces. The concerted works for a few voices and continuo belong to the period 1630 to 1635 and use techniques developed in duets from the Seventh Book (1619). The sexy *Ardo e sospirir, O sia tranquill'il mare*, a magnificent study in loneliness, and the *Lamento della Ninfia*, a triptych with the main part set over a four-note ground bass and framed by an introduction and conclusion setting the scene, are among the finest, and contain strikingly realistic word painting. The older style is heard to perfection in a setting of Petrarch's sonnet *Hor ch'el ciel e la terra*. At a time when solo vocal music predominated—especially in Italy—Monteverdi chose to write adventurously for vocal and instrumental ensembles and by the end of his life had written some of the finest works in the genre. It is almost incredible that it was not until the mid-twentieth century that their full glories were again revealed. *—Roy Brewer*

Recommended:

- ○ **Monteverdi: Madrigali e Canzonette a due e tre voci, libro IX** / Sarti, Farolfi, Sorelli, Agosti, Marelli, Burattin / Rivo Alto 8918

Missa et salmi, concertati, e parti de capella (ca. 1650)

In 1650, seven years after Claudio Monteverdi's death, a collection of his works entitled *Missa a quattro voce, et Salmi, concertati, e parti de cappella* was published in Venice. This followed the *Selve morale e spirituale* from 1640, but both works are thought to contain works composed during a broad span of time, the earliest of them possibly dating to shortly after Monteverdi's appointment as choirmaster at Venice's St. Mark's Cathedral. Like the *Selve*, the works in the 1650 collection represent a broad spectrum of stylistic approaches, reflecting Monteverdi's various renown (and employment) as a composer of music for court, church, and stage. They likewise reflect the long tradition of musical excellence that Monteverdi was hired to maintain. Bearing the weight of his institution's tradition, Monteverdi's sacred works in the decades prior to his death straddle the division (which he had been central in defining) between the harmonically conservative prima prattica and the more explicitly expressive seconda prattica. Likewise, while a number of the works published with the *Messa et Salmi* are crafted in a polyphonic, polychoral, and/or concerto style familiar to St. Marks, Monteverdi also demonstrates a desire to infuse his devotional works with the innovations forged in the area of vocal monody.

The four-voice mass is rendered, for the most part, in the stile antico favored by musical conservatives at the time. It usually observes a steady binary meter, distributes syllables in a rather unhurried fashion and generally avoids extended passages of fast rhythms. The parts tend to proceed in stepwise fashion and sometimes align for chordal declamations; dissonances are kept under control (according to rules codified by Willaert and Zarlino). This conservatism, however, serves to highlight Monteverdi's occasional stylistic deviations and progressive text expression. The piece also dates itself beyond the sixteenth century in its employment of basso continuo to fill out the harmonies.

Still, the antiquarian tendencies of the four-voice mass in the collection stand in stark contrast to the techniques that appear elsewhere in the collection. The concerto *Laetatus sum*, for example, demonstrates a slew of modern compositional developments. This setting of *Psalms 121* and *122* is scored for six voices and two violins (the combination of voices and instruments warranting the "concerto" designation in this period). The entire psalm proper is delivered above a relentlessly repeating chord progression. The sometimes florid text declamation, and the interaction of the instrumentalists and selected voice parts, resemble similar textures in Monteverdi's later madrigals, while the underlying ostinato recalls the insistence of Monteverdi's famous *Zefiro torna* in particular. Having mastered the emerging innovations of the secular realm, Monteverdi's last collection reflects both his ties to tradition and his willingness to adapt new techniques for sacred use. *—Jeremy Grimshaw*

Scherzi musicali a tre voci, arias & madrigals (1607)

Monteverdi published two collections under the title *Scherzi musicali*, one in 1632 consisting mainly of solo songs with continuo, and the collection under present consideration, which dates from 1607. This was a period of both intense activity and great pressure for Monteverdi, the year which saw the production of his epoch-making opera *Orfeo*, but also one in which Monteverdi, underpaid by the court in Mantua and nursing an ailing wife (Claudia Monteverdi died on September 10, 1607), was experiencing great unhappiness. Two years prior to these events Monteverdi had issued another seminal work, his *Fifth Book of Madrigals*, a set which clearly established the composer as being in the forefront of radical moves that were guiding music toward the new Baroque style, the seconda prattica. In the preface to that book Monteverdi had mounted a spirited defense of his radicalism in the face of an attack by the conservative theoretician Giovanni Maria Artusi. The subject again taken up in the preface of the *Scherzi musicali*, which was written not by Monteverdi himself, but his brother Giulio Cesare. In this immensely important document Giulio clearly defines the differences between the old and new musical styles, which he terms the prima prattica and the seconda prattica, naming the representative composers of each. He goes on claim that the *Scherzi musicali* includes several works in modern French manner, which may be defined as the airy, dance-like pieces which characterize many of the works in the publication.

It consists of 18 works scored for three voices and continuo, which according to the composer's preface are intended to be played by three viols and chittarone (a large lute), harpsichord or similar continuo. The character of the collection is immediately established in the opening song, *"I bei legami,"* with its hemiola rhythms, a type of syncopation much employed by Monteverdi in his lighter pieces. Many of the songs of the *Scherzi musicali* inhabit the same pastoral world as the madrigals of *Book Five*; they include such popular songs as *"Vaghi rai"* and *"Dolci miei sospiri."* —*Brian Robins*

Recommended:

- ○ **Monteverdi: Scherzi musicali a tre voci** / Vartolo (cond.), Concerto delle Dame di Ferrara / 1998 / Naxos 553317

Selva morale e spirituale, mass & motets (1640)

Although Monteverdi is best known for his innovations as a composer of madrigals and operas, the church positions he held, first at Mantua, then at the musically famous Cathedral of St. Mark in Venice, provided ample opportunities to establish his skill as a composer of sacred works. A large portion of Monteverdi's church music from Mantua survives in a large collection from 1610, and his years in Venice must have produced an even larger body of sacred music. As large as they are, the two compilations of Venetian works—the *Selve Morale e Spirituale*, printed in 1640 under the composer's supervision, and a 1651 publication released posthumously—stand only as samples of numerous works. As evidenced by the *Selve Morale e Spirituale*, his output in the idiom covers a broad range of chronological styles, and his more modern sacred pieces often reflect the compositional practices being developed in his secular works. A series of disagreements with his Mantuan employer, Duke Gonzaga, had led the composer to seek work elsewhere, and in 1613 he was appointed *maestro di cappella* at St. Mark. His charge was to reestablish the legendary artistic reputation that St. Mark had earned in the sixteenth century under the direction of "Messer Adrian, Messer Ciprian, e'l Reverendissimo Padre Isepo" (Adrian Willaert, Cipriano de Rore, and Isepo Zarlino). He ordered new music to be printed, hired instrumentalists to play regularly for certain feasts, and sought new singers, particularly castrati, to augment the cappella's ensemble. Traditionally, St. Mark observed its own unique rites and followed a liturgical year that honored numerous saints of particular importance to Venice. What the *Selve Morale e Spirituale* appears to be, then, is a collection of works in a wide variety of styles, representing Monteverdi's output of Venetian sacred music, from which various combinations of individual pieces may be extracted and fashioned into the appropriate and liturgically complete services for various occasions. (The pieces happen to be arranged within the collection to provide a complete Vespers sequence, though they may or may not have ever actually been performed in this combination.) Within the collection, one finds older musical styles widely dispersed among more modern pieces: sacred madrigals, a Marian lament, and psalm settings in the stile concertato are found side-by-side with a rather antique mass and several *salmi spezzati*—a rather simple and old-fashioned kind of psalm setting using two choirs. The compositional styles demonstrated by Monteverdi in his secular works occasionally find their way into his sacred pieces. The *Salve Regina* is full of quasi-madrigalistic text expression, with carefully crafted dissonances and chromaticisms highlighting the most poignant images in the text. The *Magnificat* calls for eight vocal lines and two instrumental obbligati, and features at its focal point a collections of duets separated by a stile concertato ritornello. The music for *Beatus vir* is in fact recycled from *Chiome d'oro*, a madrigal from Monteverdi's *Seventh Book of Madrigals*. Thus in borrowing from and expanding upon the stylistic innovations of his secular works, Monteverdi brought into his church music a new depth of expressive possibilities. —*Jeremy Grimshaw*

Recommended:

- ○ **Monteverdi: Selva Morale e Spirituale** / Bernius (cond.), Stuttgart Baroque Orch., Stuttgart Chamber Choir / FSM Adagio 91109

Vespro della beata vergine, for chorus & instruments (1610)

The historical interest of this work is almost as great as its inherent qualities. *Vespers* are part of the daily Offices, or Canonical Hours, of the church, music for the Offices including psalms (with antiphons), hymns, and canticles, as well as chanted lessons (with responsories). Although inspired by the Church Office, Monteverdi's *Vespers* in many ways transcends the original concept, perfectly exemplifying the transition between austere Renaissance polyphony and sheer Baroque splendor. Monteverdi makes his characteristic contribution to sacred music in a bold, almost operatic, style, complete with daring stereophonic and echo effects, and includes a suite of instrumental dances, concerti sections for both voices and orchestra, and a love song. To what extent this is liturgical music is debatable in view of the choice of texts, which some in Monteverdi's time considered blasphemous. Completed in 1610, the *Vespers* was written for the court of the Gonzaga family in Mantua, where Monteverdi was employed from 1590 to 1612, and dedicated to Pope Paul V. But the composition's true home is undoubtedly the cathedral of St. Mark in Venice, where Monteverdi was appointed *maestro di cappella* in 1613. Indeed, the *Vespers* could well have been conceived with its echoing spaces, galleries, balconies, organ, and choir lofts in mind.

The sections contain striking contrasts, but the unity and continuity of Monteverdi's grand design is maintained theatrically as well as musically. The overture, for choir and orchestra, is manifestly operatic, and close to that of Monteverdi's first opera, *Orfeo*—an upsurge of joyous energy, interposed by an orchestral toccata and ending with a jubilant Alleluia. The instrumentation (cornets, sackbuts, a variety of single and double reeds, recorders, strings, organ, and harpsichord) is, with the exception of the instrumental ritornelli, mainly intended to contribute to the formal structure of the choral sections, coloring the choir in the manner of organ stops, as in the "Dixit Dominus," "Laetatus sum," "Audi, coelum," and the beginning and end of the closing *Magnificat*, the climax of the whole work. The ways in which Monteverdi treats the cantus firmus by incorporating it into the counterpoint of the choral writing, as in "Dixit Dominus" (Psalm 109), is not found in earlier choral literature, nor is the flowing, unfettered parlando (recitation) style used in "Nigra sum," a metrically free poem with allusions to the biblical *Song of Solomon*. The concerto "Due Seraphim" is probably the most interesting section in the *Vespers*. It is set for two "answering" voices—a sort of singing competition for angels—and almost exceeds the limits of human vocal technique. The choral writing is also demanding in its splendor and complexity, much of it in six, seven, and, as in the psalm "Laudate pueri," eight parts; yet the simplicity of the two-part hymn *Ave Maris stella* is also among the many treasures of this magnificent work.

It has not been easy to arrive at satisfactory modern performing editions of the *Vespers*, and interpretations differ in important details. The title page of the first edition is inscribed "ad Sacella sive Principum Cubicula accomodata Opera" (for use in princely rooms and chapels)," but unfortunately several modern editors have attempted to regard it as a vast choral work, ignoring the comparatively small forces needed to realize its grandeur. This work was little known and not recorded until the 1930s, when musicologists and scholars, such as Nadia Boulanger, researched the puzzles and complexities of authentic Baroque performance. —*Roy Brewer*

Recommended:

- ○ **Monteverdi: Vespro della Beata Vergine** / Alessandrini (cond.), soloists, Concerto Italiano / 2004 / Naïve 30403
- ○ **Monteverdi: Vespro della Beata Vergine** / Savall (cond.), soloists, Capella Reial de Catalunya / 1999 / Astrée Naïve 9936
- ○ **Monteverdi: Vespro della Beata Vergine** / Gardiner (cond.), soloists, His Majesty's Sagbutts and Cornetts, Monteverdi Choir, English Baroque Soloists / Archiv 429565
- ○ **Monteverdi: Vespro della Beata Vergine** / Christie (cond.), soloists, Les Arts Florissants Orch. & Chorus / 1998 / Erato 23139

BALLET

Ballo delle ingrate (1638)

The *Ballo delle Ingrate* (Ballet of the ungrateful women) is one of the more substantial works in Monteverdi's *Eighth Book of Madrigals*, published in 1632 (titled *Madrigali Guerrieri ed Amorosi* [Madrigals of Love and War]). The collection is divided into two sections, the so-called "war" madrigals (in the main more allegorical than military) occupying the first half of the publication, those more overtly concerned with love the second. By the time of the publication, the madrigal had been transformed out of all recognition (largely at the hands of Monteverdi himself); *Book 8*, Monteverdi's first publication of madrigals for nearly 20 years, includes works of a disparate nature composed over a long period in different places and for varied purposes. Each section includes an extended dramatic work, the *Combattimento di Tancredi e Clorindi* in the instance of the "war" madrigals, the present work forming the conclusion to the pieces concerned with love.

The *Ballo* was first performed in Mantua on June 4, 1608, when it formed part of the wedding celebrations commissioned by the Vincenzo Gonzaga, Duke of Mantua (Monteverdi's first patron) on the occasion of the marriage of his son Francesco to Marguerite of Savoy. (Among other works performed was Monteverdi's lost opera, *Arianna*, the only surviving part of which, the famous "Lament of Ariadne," is also included in the *Eighth Book*). While building upon the dramatic foundations of *Orfeo* (1607), the *Ballo* is a highly original work that has little in common with the fashionable French court ballets of the period. The framework for the dance is provided by a dramatic plot sung in the recently evolved stile recitativo that Monteverdi had employed with such success in *Orfeo*. The drama, the text of which was written by the librettist of *Orfeo*, Ottavio Rinuccini, is set at the mouth of hell and directly addressed to the ladies of the audience by Venus. The ensuing action illustrates the fate of those who reject the forces of love. At the entreaties of Venus and Cupid, eight ingrates are allowed by Pluto to appear at hell's mouth as a dreadful example to those who would similarly deny love, the pathos of their dance juxtaposed with powerfully declaimed recitative culminating in the intensely moving lament of one of the ungrateful women, "Aer sereno e puro" (Clear, pure air) as they are ushered back to the darkness of hell. The instrumental accompaniment detailed on the title page calls for five violes da braccia (treble and tenor viols), harpsichord, and chittarone, a large continuo lute. *—Brian Robins*

Recommended:

- ○ **Monteverdi: Madrigali guerrieri ed amorosi** / Jacobs (cond.), Concerto Vocale / HM 901736/37
- ○ **Monteverdi: Il ballo delle ingrate; La Sestina** / Christie (cond.), Les Arts Florissants Orch. & Chorus / HM 7901108

Montreal Symphony Orchestra

f. 1934, Montréal, Quebec, Canada

Ensemble

The Montreal Symphony Orchestra (MSO), equally known as l'Orchestre symphonique de Montréal (OSM), was established in 1934. Over the years it has grown in stature to become, particularly under the long and fruitful leadership of Charles Dutoit, one of the world's outstanding orchestras.

The MSO was founded by a group of ambitious local music lovers in the cultural center and largest city of Quebec. In the beginning, the orchestra succeeded in securing the financial support of the provincial government, a vital element to its longevity. The first concert took place in January 1935, and the program included, among the classics, a work by Canadian composer, Calixa Lavallée. Soon after, Wilfrid Pelletier, originally from Montreal but then working at the Metropolitan Opera in New York, was appointed the first Music Director. In his five years, Pelletier launched a matinée series for young people, and outdoor summer concerts on Mount Royal, the wooded hill that dominates the city (and gives it its name). In 1940, Pelletier was succeeded by Désiré Defauw, and Pelletier is commemorated to this day by having the orchestra's concert hall at the Place-des-Arts complex named after him.

Throughout the next couple of decades, various well-known conductors visited Montreal to work with the orchestra, including Pierre Monteux, Bruno Walter, Leonard Bernstein, and even Igor Stravinsky. In 1957, composer-conductor Igor Markevitch became Music Director, and it was during his tenure that the orchestra gained full professional status. He was succeeded by the young Zubin Mehta, who took the MSO on its first European tour. Franz-Paul Decker took over in 1967, followed briefly by Rafael Frühbeck de Burgos, and then, in 1977, by Charles Dutoit.

It has been under the direction of this Swiss-born Dutoit that the MSO has achieved true international status. Dutoit has taken the orchestra on numerous tours throughout North and South America, Europe, and Asia. Since 1982, the MSO has given acclaimed annual performances at Carnegie Hall, and has also appeared at the Hollywood Bowl and Tanglewood. In addition, Dutoit's recording contract with Decca/London has resulted in a long list of award-winning discs. The MSO's 1984 recording of Ravel's *Bolero* went platinum; other issues have garnered Grammy awards and a number of other prizes. Their series of Berlioz recordings have been particularly acclaimed.

The MSO continues to receive provincial and national support for its operations, and it serves as a major cultural ambassador, not only for Montreal, but for Quebec and Canada as well. At the same time, the local population remains dedicated to the orchestra, and the annual performances at the historic Notre Dame Basilica in Old Montreal are popular with both young and old. *—Jim Harley*

Recommended:

- ○ **Berlioz' Les Troyens: Grand Scenes** / Dutoit (cond.), Edwards, Quilico, Dubosc, Voig, Montreal SO / 1998 / London 458208
- ○ **Chausson Album** / Dutoit (cond.), Juillet, Montreal SO / 2000 / Decca 458010
- ○ **Ravel: Boléro** / Dutoit (cond.), Montreal SO / 1999 / Decca 460214
- ○ **Holst: The Planets** / Dutoit (cond.), Montreal SO / 1998 / London 460606

Xavier Montsalvatge

b. Mar. 11, 1912, Gerona, Spain, **d.** May 7, 2002, Barcelona, Spain

Composer: Vocal

Catalonian composer Xavier Montsalvatge began violin lessons at the age of nine, around the same time as his father's death and his move to Barcelona to live with his grandfather. This move later allowed him to attend the Barcelona Conservatory and numerous concerts that greatly influenced him. His teachers at the conservatory were Francisco Costa for violin and Enrique Morera and Jaume Pahissa for composition. He himself became a teacher at the school in 1933. His first important works were the 1934 *Tres impromptus for piano*, for which he won the Rabell prize from the Patxot Foundation, and the *Suite burlesca*, for which he won the Pedrell prize in 1936. Rejecting the legacies of Wagner and Richard Strauss that dominated in Spain at the time, he was instead attracted to the works of Les Six and Stravinsky and made his first trip to Paris around 1934. He also soon began writing musical criticism for local papers, eventually writing for the weekly publication *Destino* for more than 30 years, as well as for *La mati* and *La Vanguardia*. The 1940s were fruitful years for Montsalvatge. He began a series of teaching jobs in prominent schools in Barcelona. He met fellow Catalan composer Federico Mompou in 1942. He married Elena Pérez de Olaguer in 1947 and a son was born in 1949. Compositions from the period include 19 ballets for the Paul Goubé/Yvonne Alexander company and the *Album de habaneras*, songs he had collected in the West Indies. *Cinco canciones negras* of 1945–46, also with a West Indian influence, and his first opera, *El gato con botas* (Puss in Boots), remain his most popular works. A daughter was born in 1952, and the next year, both Henryk Szeryng and Alicia de Larrocha asked for concertos from him. Through the next decades, he continued to write, teach, and compose, producing works in nearly every genre and winning numerous awards and honors along the way. In the 1980s, he wrote an autobiography that was published in both Spanish and Catalan, and in 1989, a piano competition was founded in his name. He retired from his official positions in the early 1980s, but continued composing into the 1990s, becoming one of the most respected composers of twentieth century Spain. *—Patsy Morita*

Overview of Works (1933–1993)

By the end of his long-spanned life, Xavier Montsalvatge had become very much a man in step with the times. Early on, he eschewed the Austro-German schools of atonality and serialism and was revered by the academics even in his native Spain. He often opted for Les Six, Stravinsky, and various national/ethnic groups as sources for inspiration. As will be seen, this presented a curious reversal of the usual process. For the first identifiable period in his works (i.e., from the 1930s on), Montsalvatge evolved a sort of nationalistic Neo-Romanticism from his embracing of tonality coupled with a profound influence of African American music, both of the North American tradition and that of Cuba and the West Indies. Add to this an uncanny sense of vivid yet never heavy orchestration and the result was a festive nationalism reminiscent of the rise of the various schools a half century before. Yet this was no mere reactionary stance, as the drawing on the sundry Western popular and folk idioms was quite unlike anything from the earlier era. Typical of this period is the *Canciones negras for violin and piano* of 1946, as well as the less nationalistic *Poema concertante for violins and orchestra* (1951), the *Concerto breve for piano and orchestra* (1953), and the *Partita for orchestra* (1958). Overlapping this period in the 1940s and 1950s, Montsalvatge tilled what could be called a children's garden, producing a series of works in various media. A unifying characteristic is the use of simplistic yet engaging melodies against a skittish, chromatic accompaniment. Typical of this are his piano works, which run the gamut from the knotty *Sonatina for Yvette* (although for his five-year-old daughter, it would seem to require training beyond most children's grasps) to the delightful *Noah's Ark*, a suite of pieces each describing one of the seafaring Biblical animals. In the spectrum of this body of work, it recalls the ethic Bartók espoused in his similar piano output. From the late 1960s onward, Montsalvatge, ever his own man, reinvestigated and embraced the 12-tone system at a time when it was beginning to be questioned as the touchstone for serious composition. Yet even in this idiom, the composer was able to preserve his identity through strong suggestions of tonality in his use of tone-row construction and his application of Hispanic flavor through color and rhythmic devices. *— Wayne Reisig*

Recommended:

- ○ **Montsalvatge: Cuarteto Indiano** / Indiano Quartet / Columna Musica 63
- ○ **Montsalvatge: Orchestral Works** / Leaper (cond.), Gran Canaria PO / 1999 / ASV 1060
- ○ **Montsalvatge: Piano Music** / Meshulam / 1998 / ASV 1022
- ○ **Montsalvatge: Una voce in off** / Ros-Marba (cond.), Comas, Liceu / Columna Musica 87
- ○ **Montsalvatge: Barcelona Blues** / Voronkova, McClure, Garriga, Barrera / Columna Musica 54
- ○ **Montsalvatge: Works for Violin & Piano; Cello & Piano** / Voronkov, Gokcen, Martins, McClure / Columna Musica 42

VOCAL

Canciones negras (1945–1946)

In this, his most often-performed song cycle, Montsalvatge found inspiration not in his native Catalonia, but in the music of the West Indies, across which he draped only a thin veil of Spanish style. The set's first song is its longest: "Cuba dentro de un piano" (Cuba on a Keyboard), setting a poem by Rafael Alberti. The languorous, lyrical habanera is a nostalgic evocation of when "the Bay of Cadiz was paradise" and "the Cuban spell was among the reeds and marshes of my land." The piano accompaniment takes on slightly sour, wrong-note harmonies when the singer complains that money (presumably American) spoiled it all, and the "si" became "yes." "Punto de Habanera (Siglo XVIII)" (Humorous Flirtation) sets Néstor Luján's lighthearted poem about a ripe young eighteenth century maiden, dressed in a billowing white hoop skirt and being ogled by sailors. Montsalvatge's music is gentle and playful, again ending with ironic little dissonances. Nicolás Guillén's "Chévere" concerns a black worker who "wields a flashing knife" and becomes "a blade himself," slicing at shadows and moonlight, making an unsuccessful stab at singing, and then going "straight after his woman." Montsalvatge's music does not reflect the violent personality depicted in the poem, but it is slow, dark, and, just before the end, mildly dissonant, barely suggesting an unpleasant end for the girlfriend. "Canción de cuna para dormir a un negrito" (Cradle Song to Put a Little Negro to Sleep) is a poem by Idefonso Pereda Valdés in which a mother assures her child that in sleep, he is no longer a slave and that if he gets enough rest, his master will make him a groom and buy him a fancy uniform. The vocal line is soothing, but the accompaniment provides an unsettling, Milhaud-like polytonal reminder that this is not a conventional, innocent lullaby. "Canto negro" (Negro Song), with text by Nicolás Guillén, is a lively but light-stepping observation of blacks singing and dancing in the jungle, with happy cries of "Yambambó, yambambé." The voice and piano version of the songs was written in 1945, with Montsalvatge's orchestration appearing four years later. *—James Reel*

Recommended:

○ **Very Best of Victoria de Los Angeles** / Frühbeck de Burgos (cond.), Los Angeles, Societé des Concerts du Conservatoire / 2003 / EMI 75888

Douglas S. Moore

b. Aug. 10, 1893, Cutchogue, NY, **d.** Jul. 25, 1969, Greenport, NY

Composer: Opera

Moore was born into a family who traced their ancestors back to the first settlers in the north fork of Long Island in 1640. Thoroughly imbued with a love of rural and pioneer life, his works celebrate those subjects in a rich tonal harmonic language.

Moore began writing popular songs at an early age, collaborating with classmate playwright Archibald MacLeish, and at Yale wrote tunes such as "Goodnight Harvard" and "Naomi, my Restaurant Queen," while undertaking composition studies with Horatio Parker. He graduated in 1917, served in the Navy until 1919, and continued writing pop tunes with John Jacob Niles, later collected as *Songs My Mother Never Taught Me.*

In Paris, Moore's studies with Vincent d'Indy influenced his harmonic style. In 1921, he joined the Cleveland Museum, organizing a concert series and playing the organ, and studied with Ernest Bloch.

He began writing for orchestra such works as *Four Museum Pieces* (1923) and *The Pageant of P.T. Barnum* (1924), a picturesque and tuneful set of five portraits describing events and people in the life of the (in)famous showman. In 1926, Moore became a teacher at Barnard College at Columbia University, then in 1940 was made head of the music department, where he remained until retiring in 1962.

His works include incidental music for Shakespeare's *Twelfth Nights* and *Much Ado about Nothing,* chamber music, and orchestral works. In 1935, Moore wrote his first of ten operas, *White Wings.* The operas are notable for their fine musical characterizations, clear vocal lines, and excellent sense of timing. There immediately followed *The Headless Horseman* (1936) and *The Devil and Daniel Webster* (1938), which is a staple of the American opera repertory. Moore then scored three films in the 1940s, as well as writing in other genres, then wrote *Giants in the Earth,* for which he won the Pulitzer Prize in 1951. Moore's popular opera *The Ballad of Baby Doe* (1956) is written in a vivid and forthright American style. His last operas all have remarkable orchestrations.

Moore was the founder of many composers' organizations, and president of both the National Institute and the American Academy of Arts and Letters. He received five honorary degrees and a Guggenheim Fellowship. *—"Blue Gene" Tyranny*

OPERA

The Ballad of Baby Doe (1956; revised 1958)

Begun with a 1953 commission from Colorado's Central City Opera House Association, Douglas Moore's *The Ballad of Baby Doe* has frequently been called the most "nearly perfect" American opera. Additional assistance from the Koussevitzky Foundation was essential to the work's completion, but it was the Colorado company which put the project into motion. With the premiere at Central City in July 1956, audiences understood that a significant work had been added to the rather small collection of American operas of enduring value. It is based on a true story about the fate of Horace Tabor, who became one of the richest men of his time after striking a silver lode in Leadville, Colorado. He was later ruined when the United States switched from the silver to the gold standard.

For his undertaking, Moore had librettist John Latouche, who shared with the composer the exacting research needed to create a work that would ring true. Latouche visited the *Leadville opera house,* spoke with those who still recalled Baby Doe (she lived until 1935), and examined campaign speeches by William Jennings Bryan in order to create an oration that would sound authentic (Bryan had never visited Leadville). Moore studied the melodies heard in the mining towns of the 1880s to put the stamp of believability on his own themes. While the story is "true," it is not factual in every detail. For example, Augusta Tabor died in 1895, the year before the election that doomed silver as a monetary standard.

The result is an opera replete with characters more fully developed than usual. Horace Tabor, in words and music, emerges as a man both proud and tender. His first wife, Augusta, could easily have been presented as a termagant, but is allowed the full dimensions of a woman wronged and angry but still in conflict over her feelings. Baby Doe has courage, intelligence, a not insubstantial moral compass and undying loyalty. The unfolding of their story engages the listener, for they are all personalities with whom the audience can empathize in some personal way.

Musically, *Baby Doe* imposes no barriers to immediate understanding, while steadfastly avoiding the obvious. The craftsmanship is apparent upon first hearing and the themes and orchestration invite a sympathetic reaction. Baby's "Silver Aria" has become a favorite audition piece for young sopranos, affording them a means to display vocal quality, range, shading, and interpretive skills. In the context of the opera, it provides one of those enchanting moments listeners hope for but are often denied in operas of the late twentieth century.

The title role is now indelibly linked with Beverly Sills, who starred in the New York City Opera's production in 1958. Some tend to believe that it was she who sang the role at its Central City premiere, but there it was Dolores Wilson. The Horace Tabor of the Colorado production appeared in New York. Walter Cassel reprised his definitive portrayal, fortunately captured on recording along with Sills' career-advancing Baby Doe. Martha Lipton repeated her stern and imposing Augusta. Over the next two decades, *Baby Doe* was performed at the NYCO 35 times in 11 seasons. *—Erik Eriksson*

Synopsis:

Act One. Scene one is set in Leadville, Colorado, on a summer's eve in 1880. Next to the Tabor Opera House where Horace and Augusta Tabor and the rest of the town's society people are attending a concert, girls from the saloon and miners are talking animatedly. Tabor, it seems, is about to buy yet another mine and the discussion surrounds the fact that he owns much of the town already. When the concert ends, Tabor and his friends join the tavern crowd. Augusta interrupts to chastise them for their lack of dignity. The party returns to the opera house save for Tabor who stays briefly, encountering a new arrival. He provides Baby Doe with directions to the Clarendon Hotel.

Scene two takes place later that same evening as Augusta bids her friends good-night and departs for their hotel apartment. Tabor, lingering to enjoy a cigar, observes Baby Doe at a hotel window, singing. He moves to the window, and clearing his throat, makes his presence known. He expresses his enchantment with her, takes her hand and kisses it. When Augusta summons him, the two bid each other a quiet good night.

In scene three, some weeks have passed and Augusta happens upon a check for the Matchless Mine lying on Tabor's desk. She notices a pair of white gloves and is at first delighted until she finds a note to Baby Doe and realizes that the gloves are not for her. She confronts Horace, demanding that the affair be terminated. He refuses, defending Baby Doe. Augusta, incensed, tells him he's gone too far, and leaves.

Scene four finds Baby Doe in the hotel lobby ready to take leave of the town. She tells her mother in a letter that although she and Horace love each other, because he is married she "must give him up." Augusta enters, insisting that the affair cease. She berates Tabor and informs Baby Doe that there have been other women, but Baby Doe defends him. Finally, however, Augusta believes that she has prevailed and leaves with a determined goodbye. Baby Doe tears up the letter and Tabor enters. She tells him she is staying and they are seen going upstairs together.

Scene five takes place in Augusta's apartment where friends have come to urge her to act. She tells them she will remain silent, but with the news that Horace plans a divorce, she resolves to create a scandal.

The sixth scene takes place three years later at the Willard Hotel in the nation's capital. A crowd awaits the just married couple amidst discussion of gold versus a bimetal policy. Tabor argues for silver before Baby sings her "Silver Aria." Baby's mother, Mrs. McCourt, informs the priest that both Horace and Baby were divorced and the cleric leaves together with other guests. Only the arrival of President Arthur stems the flow.

Act Two. In Scene one, ten years later, at the Governor's Ball, Baby is still avoided by Augusta's friends, although their husbands bow to Tabor's position and importance. Augusta comes to warn Baby that silver is in decline and that Horace's fortune is imperiled. Tabor furiously dismisses her, requesting of Baby that she always retain ownership of the Matchless Mine.

Scene two takes place two years later (1895) as friends play cards and note Tabor's evaporating wealth. He arrives seeking a loan and support for pro-silver Presidential candidate William Jennings Bryan. Denied both, Tabor irately replies that silver made them all and that he will remain loyal to it.

The third scene is set at the Matchless Mine (1896) where a political rally is about to feature candidate Bryan.

In scene four, following the election in which Bryan has lost, Augusta is visited by Mrs. McCourt asking help for the now-ruined Horace and Baby Doe. Augusta refuses, reluctantly admitting to herself the pain over losing a man she still loves.

The fifth and final scene finds Horace in 1899, aged and in precarious health, wandering distractedly on stage of the opera house, recounting his life, and visited by ghostly figures. Despairing that he is dying a failure, he sees Bay Doe led in by the stage doorman to assure him that she is taking him home. Telling her, "You were always the real thing, Baby," he expires. The light on him gradually fades, and Baby is seen in front of the Matchless Mine, avowing her everlasting loyalty. *—Erik Eriksson*

Recommended:

- ○ **Moore: The Ballad of Baby Doe** / Buckley (cond.), Sills, Bible, Cassel, NYC Opera Orch. / 1999 / DG 465148
- ○ **Moore: The Ballad of Baby Doe** / Moriarty (cond.), Taylor, Blaisdell, Raven, Steele, Central City Opera / 1997 / Newport Classic 85593

The Devil and Daniel Webster (1937–1938)

In 1936, *The Saturday Evening Post* published Stephen Vincent Benét's short story *The Devil and Daniel Webster*, it would become Benét's most popular story. Throughout 1936 and 1937 Benét and Douglas S. Moore collaborated on an opera, based on Benét's story, that was to carry the same name. Moore's opera was first performed on May 18, 1939, in New York by the American Lyric Theater Company at the Martin Beck Theater. Moore scored the work for either a large orchestra, with paired woodwinds or for a smaller group with single winds. This option has contributed to its frequent performance.

In a 1953 interview, Moore said, "Mr. Benét and I have classified *The Devil and Daniel Webster* as a folk opera because it is legendary in its subject matter and simple in its musical expression." Whether one classifies the work as an opera, a folk opera, or a musical, it is an unusual piece. In one act, it has no overture, and much of the spoken dialogue is accompanied in the manner of a melodrama. There are no traditional set pieces, but contrasting sections result when, in highly emotional moments, the creators employ verse and appropriate music to set it. Throughout, the voice parts dominate the texture, making for very clear text declamation. The Devil's strident fiddle playing in "Young William was a thriving boy" is clearly influenced by Stravinsky's *L'histoire du soldat*.

Moore emphasized local color and thus the folk flavor of the opera by including such traditional American music as a country square dance and ballads. The local sense is reinforced by placing the scenario in a specific city and time: Cross Corners, New Hampshire, in the 1840s.

Benét's libretto revolves around the ancient story of a person who sold his soul to the Devil. In this case, that person is Jabez Stone, who at the opening of the piece is at his wedding reception. Daniel Webster, the Secretary of State, arrives, as does a stranger named Mr. Scratch. From a box Mr. Scratch brings with him escapes a moth that pleads for help because he, like Jabez, has sold his soul to the Devil. Jabez admits that he sold his soul when he was impoverished and saw no other way to survive. When Webster calls for a trial, Scratch assembles a jury from hell, hoping he will win. A passionate, clever speech from Webster, however, persuades the jury and Jabez reclaims his soul.

A critic for *The Saturday Review* noted that *The Devil and Daniel Webster* "does not, either in whole or in part, remind us of any European composer." This stems, at least in part, from Moore and Benét's choice to use what Benét described as "casual, everyday speech." More importantly, Moore set out to provide an accurate setting of the prosody of colloquial speech, thereby making both the language and the music idiomatic and purely American. *—John Palmer*

Synopsis:

The action takes place in the house of Jabez Stone in Cross Corners, New Hampshire, during the 1840s.

The curtain rises to reveal a wedding reception for the farmer Jabez Stone and his wife Mary. With uncanny energy, Jabez has risen from abject poverty as a farmer to become a state senator for the district in which Cross Corners is nestled. His popularity has prompted some in politics to suggest he run for governor of New Hampshire. Even the Secretary of State, Daniel Webster, has elected to appear at Jabez's wedding.

When Webster enters, the attempt to celebrate his arrival is brought to a halt when the Fiddler begins to have problems with his violin and exclaims that "the very Devil" must have somehow made his way into the instrument and rendered it useless; the Fiddler cannot figure out what is wrong. At this moment, Mr. Scratch steps in, claiming to be an old friend of Jabez and telling everyone that he is a lawyer from Boston. He offers to repair the Fiddler's instrument, and while doing so he plays a strident accompaniment to his solo, 'Young William was a thriving boy." As the ballad becomes unpleasant and Scratch sings of death, Webster becomes angry, eventually putting a stop to Scratch's performance.

The Fiddler, too, is upset, and he begins to fiddle with a mysterious box that Scratch has brought with him. When he opens the box, a small creature, someone's soul, flies out and begs for help, claiming that both it and Jabez have sold their souls to the Devil. Most of the wedding guests are repulsed by this news, but both Mary and Webster remain with Jabez, who has a confession. He has indeed sold his soul to the Devil; he did so in order to escape poverty and experience prosperity. The problem is, today he must pay his debt to the Devil. Webster seems to think an amusing story will make Jabez feel better ("I've got a ram, Goliath"), while Mary prays for her new husband ("Now may there be a blessing").

Webster has an idea: there must be a proper trial to decide the case. Scratch, whose real identity is now clear, may choose both judge and jury, but they must be American. Although Scratch fills the room with dead villains and various outlaws, the jury finds for Jabez after Webster gives a speech about the value of freedom and leading one's own life; it appeals to the self-centered, free-spirited jurors. Now that Jabez's soul is once again his own, Webster grabs Scratch and asks the crowd to drive him out of town. *—John Palmer*

Recommended:

- ○ **Moore: The Devil & Daniel Webster** / Patterson (cond.), Stephens, Guyer, Steele, Woods, Kansas City Symphony / 1996 / Newport Classic 85585

Gerald Moore

b. Jul. 30, 1899, Watford, England, **d.** Mar. 13, 1987, Penn, Buckinghamshire, England

Pianist

Gerald Moore is generally considered the finest recital accompanist of the twentieth century. Known for his boundless facility and an unfailing ability to adapt to—and elicit the best from—his various musical partners, he was in constant demand for over 30 years, and he is represented on a huge number of fine recordings.

English-born, Moore began his musical education at the local Watford School of Music, where his piano teacher was Wallis Bandey. The family moved to Canada in 1913, at which point he took up studies with Michael Hambourg. He made his first stage appearances, both as a soloist and as an accompanist in Canada.

Moore returned to England in 1919; his teacher, Hambourg, referred him to his son, Mark Hambourg, for further study, and Moore began to make frequent appearances in England. In 1921 he accepted a recording contract with the EMI company, remaining with them his entire career. The composer, conductor, and pianist Sir Landon Ronald suggested to Moore that he had an exceptional talent as an accompanist and should concentrate on that art. In 1925 the eminent tenor John Coates asked Moore to become his permanent accompanist; Moore says that he learned the craft of accompanying from his work with Coates. They made their first joint appearances in 1926. Moore soon became sought-after as an accompanist.

His impeccable piano technique was characterized by a beautiful, singing legato touch and lovely, very flexible tone color that was partly the result of masterful use of the pedals. Most important, he was highly empathetic to his recital partners' musical personality. Soon, international artists such as Pablo Casals, John McCormack, Hans Hotter, Maria Gerhard, Feodor Chaliapin, and Elisabeth Schumann made sure they could engage Moore when they appeared in England, or even have him with them on tours. It is not an exaggeration to say that Moore's acceptance of an offer to accompany a new artist was a major indication of the newcomer's promise. He was especially known for his song accompaniment, and made frequent and memorable appearances and recordings with Dietrich Fischer-Dieskau, Elisabeth Schwarzkopf, Janet Baker, Kathleen Ferrier, and many others.

While Moore was a master of the duo-piano sonata repertory, he did not form any permanent duo-piano partnership. He came more and more to concentrate on song recitals, and became a master of the repertory. Moore prompted wide exploration of the more neglected songs of Wolf, Schubert, and Richard Strauss, and participated in recordings of virtually all of the literally hundreds of songs by these masters. During World War II Dame Myra Hess, who had founded a series of lunchtime concert in the National Gallery (which had been emptied of its precious artwork as a safeguard against bomb damage), invited Moore to participate by giving illustrated lectures about the art of accompanying. He proved to be a highly engaging lecture personality, somehow projecting devotion to the highest artistic ideals in down-to-earth, unpretentious terms. After the war, he continued lecturing, making highly successful world-wide lecture tours.

He taught master classes in song interpretation. He published a book derived from his lecture material, *The Unashamed Accompanist* which is an engaging combination of forthright discussion of interpretation, mixed with autobiographical (even gossipy) material about working with some of the great stars of the classical music world. In addition, he published teaching books on accompanying and interpretation.

Moore retired from the concert stage in 1967, but continued to be active in the recording studio for some years. He is credited with having raised the status of the accompanist to that of a true musical partner with the soloist. *—Joseph Stevenson*

Recommended:

- ○ **Tribute to Gerald Moore** / Moore, de Los Angeles, Schwarzkopf, Fischer-Dieskau, Baker / 2003 / EMI 67994
- ○ **Unashamed Accompanist** / de Los Angeles, Moore / 1999 / Testament 1176
- ○ **Schubert: Winterreise** / Fischer-Dieskau, Moore / 2004 / EMI 62787
- ○ **Wolf: Lieder-Recital** / Schwarzkopf, Moore / 1995 / EMI 65749

Cristóbal de Morales

b. ca. 1500, Seville, Spain, **d.** Sep., 1553, Marchéna, Spain

Composer

Though his masses and motets brought him international fame, and Morales is today regarded as the most important Spanish ecclesiastical composer of the

Renaissance, his career is well documented through his employment as a singer—including a decade in the papal choir—and *maestro de capella* of several prominent cathedrals. If there is hardly a single anecdote to lend personal color to a life spent in such exalted occupation, several things may be inferred. Foremost, there is pride in having been born in Seville, one of the great European cultural centers; pride in getting a thorough education (though there is no record of university study) for Morales claims to have mastered the Trivium and Quadrivium of the medieval curriculum; pride in his mastery of Classical—rather than ecclesiastical—Latin; and pride in his fluent technique—likely learned from Francisco de Peñalosa and Pedro de Escobar—which he turned to a contrapuntally elaborate, polyphonically rich, and suavely elevated utterance—anticipating (perhaps influencing) and rivaling that of Palestrina—in his 21 masses, more than 100 motets, and two sets of Magnificats. Clearly, Morales was omnicompetent and ambitious. He became *maestro de capella* at the Avila cathedral in 1526, moving on to Plasencia (at nearly double the salary) in 1528. Apparently, he was well regarded: in 1530 he was granted a month's leave to attend his sister's wedding and a substantial amount toward her dowry. Overstaying his visit, his salary was temporarily suspended and he resigned in December 1531. He next appears in the papal choir in Rome in September 1535, a post he held for the next decade, singing beside Arcadelt and Festa in the Sistine Chapel (whose frescos Michelangelo had completed in 1512) and before the crowned heads of Europe as part of the pope's retinue. His tenure was marked by increasing stints of illness. In 1544 two lavishly printed volumes of masses announced Morales' genius and his availability. Despite generous salary and vacations, he sought more remunerative employment, and when the pope conferred favors on less distinguished members of the choir, he resigned, leaving Rome in 1545 to return to Seville, where he taught Francisco Guerrero. In that year he became *maestro* of the primatical cathedral in Toledo, where he again fell ill, renouncing his post on August 9, 1547. He served as *maestro* to the Duke of Arcos at Marchena from 1548 to 1551. An unhappy term as *maestro* at Málaga Cathedral ended with Morales' death in the fall of 1553. —*Adrian Corleonis*

Overview of Works (ca. 1538–1553)

Morales, now considered by many the greatest Spanish composer of Renaissance church music since Victoria (1548–1611), was maestro di cappella at the cathedrals of Avila and Plasencia, and served at the Papal Chapel in Rome from 1535 to 1545. On returning to Spain he served at the cathedrals of Toledo, Marchena, and Málaga. The sixteenth century Spanish theorist Juan Bermudo called him "the light of Spain in music." He left little secular music and his posthumous fame rests entirely on 22 masses, 16 magnificats, and more than 80 motets.

Morales carried on in the established traditions of Franco-Flemish polyphony, and his music has a strong affinity with Nicolas Gombert (1495–1560), a highly regarded Flemish composer of sacred music. Like Gombert, Morales used clearly articulated divisions and transparent sonorities. The masses and motets include a variety of compositional techniques comparatively new to the Spanish religious music of the period, such as cantus firmus arrangements of French and Spanish songs and canons.

Modern listeners may find Morales' sober style less accessible than much of the late Renaissance church music represented in present-day recordings, though after his years in Rome Morales' works became increasingly Italian in character. The rediscovery of the masses through recordings, such as the *Missa Si bona suscepimus* by the Tallis Scholars (Gimell CDGIM 033), should help reinstate the high reputation in which Morales was held during his lifetime. —*Roy Brewer*

Recommended:

- ○ **Morales: Requiem; Lamentabatur Jacob** / Mallavibarrena (cond.), Jorda, Musica Ficta / 2000 / Cantus 9627
- ○ **Morales: Missa Queramus cum pastoribus** / O'Donnell (cond.), Westminster Cathedral Choir / 1993 / Hyperion 66635
- ○ **Morales: Missa Si bona suscipimus** / Phillips (cond.), Tallis Scholars / 2000 / Gimell 33

Ivan Moravec

b. Nov. 9, 1930, Prague, Czechoslovakia

Pianist

Although scarcely unknown to a broader audience, Czech pianist Ivan Moravec is considered by many to be a connoisseur's artist. Certainly, his performances are anything but routine, his firm, pearlescent legato reminding some of the great Dinu Lipatti. His singular touch, he has stated on several occasions, was a matter of necessity after an ice-skating fall at age ten that left him with a neck and spine injury. Thus, the intelligent use of his hands formed the basis for a sound decidedly unlike that of any of his younger colleagues. Growing up in a household where music was valued and a constant presence, Moravec began piano lessons at age seven. Since his father was an amateur violinist, the youth was already familiar with chamber works by Mozart, Beethoven, and Brahms and did not have to be forced to practice. The years of World War II were difficult ones, even though public music performances continued. After the war, Moravec made his formal debut, a small recital on a radio broadcast in 1946. He underwent further training with Madame Tepánova-Kurzová, the daughter of Professor Kurz who had taught Rudolf Firkušný, before a momentous break materialized in 1957. Moravec was invited to attend Arturo Benedetti Michelangeli's master classes in Arezzo—and the invitation came from Michelangeli himself. Moravec learned more about surmounting the mechanical reality of his instrument and producing a flowing legato sound from the iconoclastic Italian. Although his lessons at the keyboard were brief, Moravec spent a great deal of time with Michelangeli drinking wine and discussing music. Moravec made his London debut in 1959 and his New York debut in 1964, when he performed with George Szell and his superbly disciplined Cleveland Orchestra. That first New York appearance presaged subsequent American tours through which Moravec developed a following among those who valued musical integrity, beautiful sound, and a devotion to a conservative but full repertory. As one might expect, two Czech composers, Smetana and Dvořák, hold a central position among those he plays regularly. Considered one of the foremost Chopin artists of the day, Moravec also counts Mozart, Beethoven, Schumann, Brahms, Debussy, and Ravel among his other favored composers. A frequent, though reluctant visitor to the recording studio, Moravec has placed on disc many performances prized by discerning listeners. He has expressed his distaste for recording in brief takes, insisting that he is unable to play short stretches for patching. His best work, he feels, is the result of working through an entire work start to finish. It was a non-professional recording, actually, that opened the door to a productive recording career; a friend taped a 1956 Prague recital before leaving Czechoslovakia and passed it about in the West. When a copy came to the attention of the co-founders of the Connoisseur Society, they invited Moravec to come to the United States in 1962 to make the first of what would become a legendary series of recordings. Moravec has also developed a reputation as a piano's best friend. He spends time with a technician in each venue, sharing specific observations about the voicing, encouraging that technician to make adjustments that will enhance the quality of sound not only for his own use, but also for other pianists who will approach it in the future. —*Erik Eriksson*

Recommended:

- ○ **Brahms: Piano Concerto 1** / Belohlavek (cond.), Moravec, Czech PO / Supraphon 1993
- ○ **Moravec Plays Debussy & Chopin** / Moravec / 1993 / Vox 5103
- ○ **Moravec Plays (Box Set)** / Moravec / 2001 / Supraphon 3580
- ○ **Moravec Plays Mozart** / Moravec / 2001 / Supraphon 3581
- ○ **Moravec Plays Chopin** / Moravec / 2001 / Supraphon 3583

Federico Moreno Torroba

b. Mar. 3, 1891, Madrid, Spain, **d.** Sep. 12, 1982, Madrid, Spain

Composer: Chamber Music, Opera

The multitalented Spanish musician Federico Moreno Torroba began his musical studies with his father, José Moreno Ballesteros, who was an organist and teacher at the National Conservatory of Music in Madrid. Moreno Torroba eventually attended the Conservatory, studying composition with Conrado del Campo. His earliest compositions were for orchestra, such as the *Cuadros castellanos* (c. 1920), but he soon moved to writing operas using Spanish styles and subject matter; in the mid-1920s he turned his attention to the zarzuela, the traditional form of Spanish comic opera. His first zarzuela was *La mesonera de Tordesillas* (1925); he went on to write almost 80 such works in his long career, perhaps the best known of which is *Luisa Fernanda* (1932). He also became a champion of the form as a conductor and impresario. At one point he managed three different opera houses, and in the 1930s and 1940s he led a touring company which performed zarzuelas all over the world.

Guitar music was another major focus of Moreno Torroba's career. He was the first to respond to the young Andrés Segovia's request for new guitar works by modern composers, producing his *Nocturno* and *Suite castellana* for him in 1926. He went on to write many more works for Segovia over the next four-plus decades, and for other guitarists like the flamenco master Sabicas and the guitar quartet Los Romeros. By the end of his life he had composed over 100 works for the guitar, many of them strongly influenced by Spanish folk music.

In 1975, at age 84, Moreno Torroba became the president of the *Sociedad de Autores Españoles*. He continued composing right to the end of his life, even producing an opera at age 90, *El Poeta* (1980), for tenor Plácido Domingo, with whose parents Moreno Torroba had worked decades earlier. —*Chris Morrison*

CHAMBER MUSIC

Guitar Music (1924–1982)

The long-lived Federico Moreno Torroba is renowned in his native Spain for his numerous zarzuelas despite a decline in their popularity after 1960. Abroad, however, he is better known for his many guitar compositions. Though he himself was not a guitarist, he became attracted to the instrument after he developed a close friendship with Andrés Segovia in the 1920s. The first and one of the most successful works written for Segovia was the 1924 sonatina, which the virtuoso guitarist premiered in Paris in 1925. It consists of three movements, the first a light and joyful Allegretto that features two principal themes, the second one having a more lyrical character in contrast to the jauntier nature of the first. The middle panel is a lovely Andante whose Spanish flavors permeate the whole movement. The lively finale brims with colors from its typically Spanish rhythms and perky themes. There are two later guitar sonatinas (both from 1956, the second entitled *Sonatina II*) by Torroba that are attractive, but somewhat less successful. Torroba's guitar music displays the composer's partiality toward nationalist and often toward folk elements. He was a musical conservative who never soaked up cosmopolitan styles, choosing instead to imbue his works with a sense of his homeland's music, always investing it with melody. The 1926 *Nocturno* certainly displays these qualities in music whose nocturnal character sounds more heated and passionate than dark or lonely. The *Seises Piezas características* (*Preámbulo, Oliveras, Melodía, Los Mayos, Albada, Panorama*) from 1931 display Torroba's Spanish soul in even finer music, each work here at least a minor masterpiece and the collection as a whole as popular as the 1924 sonatina. *Los Mayos* (No. 4) and *Albada* (No. 5) are especially characteristic of the composer's nationalistic musical persona, the latter piece deftly mixing folklike and neo-Classical elements. Torroba's 1980 *Sonatina "Trianera"* for guitar quartet displays much Spanish color, too, not least in the use of castanets in its guitar/orchestra version, also from the same year. Yet the work, though it features fine writing and lots of fireworks, is not wholly satisfying. Among his better-known compositions for guitar and orchestra is the 1960 *Concierto di Castilla*, another tuneful, well-crafted effort of nationalist character. Other works in this genre include the colorful and rhythmically attractive *Concierto en flamenco* (1962) and the rarely encountered interesting pair of works for guitar quartet and orchestra, the *Concerto ibérico* (1976) and *Tonada concertante* (1982), the latter effort dating to the year of Torroba's death and attesting to his strong creative powers at that late stage in his career. Most of his large output for guitar and orchestra appears irregularly, if at all, in the concert hall and on recordings, though revival of some of it began in the latter twentieth century. —*Robert Cummings*

Recommended:

○ **Music of Federico Moreno Torroba** / Russell / 1996 / Telarc 80451

OPERA

Works for the Stage (1912–1980)

In a sense, Federico Moreno Torroba had two compositional careers: away from his native Spain, he is known largely for his guitar works, while at home, his zarzuelas distinguish his name. He had a string of successes in the latter genre early on with *La Marchenera* (1928), *Azabache* (1932), *Luisa Fernanda* (1932), and *La chulapona* (1934). He experienced some success in such late works as the 1960 *Baile en Capitania*, but for the most part, he produced fewer and less-successful zarzuelas after the 1930s. The two 1932 zarzuelas cited above were not the only ones the prolific Torroba wrote that year, he also turned out *La mujer de aquella noche* and *El aguaducho*. By 1966, he had written over 80 zarzuelas. His catalog also contains two operas, nine ballets, and various orchestral and instrumental works. Yet of the many zarzuelas, only two have retained any significant currency, the aforementioned pair, *Luisa Fernanda* and *La chulapona*. Their librettos were written by Federico Romero and Guillermo Fernández Shaw. Both are relatively lengthy and *Luisa* has two acts and *La chulapona* three, making them quite oversized for zarzuelas, which are typically short, one-act affairs. *Luisa Fernanda* is set in 1868 Madrid amid insurrection and intrigue and offers a familiar story: Luisa is committed to marry the wealthy Vidal Hernando, but really loves Javier. In the end, the former, knowing her true feelings, releases her to marry Javier. The music is colorful and full of Spanish flavors and the vocal and orchestral writing are brilliant and imaginative. There are many attractive vocal numbers here, including Javier's "Romanza, De este apacible rincón de Madrid" and Vidal's "Luche la fe por el triunfo." The setting for *La Chulapona* is 1893 Madrid and the story is similar to *Luisa Fernanda*'s: two women, Manuela and Rosario, vie for the same man, José Maria. In the end, Manuela steps aside to allow Rosario, pregnant with José Maria's child, to marry him. Again, the music is very colorful, from its opening orchestral introduction to the vocal numbers, like José Maria's "Romanza, Tienes razon, amigo," and the duet near the end between Manuela and Rosario, "No es que te quiera besar." The dance music is also charming, particularly in the Act Two, Scene Three flamenco dance numbers, "Bulerias" and "Tanguillo." If *La Chulapona* has fewer catchy melodies than *Luisa Fernanda*, it is nonetheless as dramatically effective. Torroba's two bona fide operas came at the opposite ends of his career: *La virgen de Mayo*, dates to 1925, while *El poeta* was written in 1980. The latter work achieved some popularity, mainly owing to the appearance of Plácido Domingo in the title role, but neither has gained currency. Torroba's ballets, which include the *Fantasia de Levante* (1957) and *Don Quijote* (1970; rev. 1982), are generally well-crafted, colorful works perhaps worth revival even if their level of inspiration is below that of the better zarzuelas. —*Robert Cummings*

Recommended:

○ **Moreno Torroba: Luisa Fernanda** / Perez, Vela, etc. / Montilla 67

Thomas Morley

b. ca. 1557, Norwich, England, **d.** Oct., 1602, London, England

Composer: Vocal

Thomas Morley, though born the obscure son of a Norwich brewer, rose over the course of his life to centrality in nearly every aspect of Elizabethan musical culture. Though no records of his early training survive, he apparently studied with William Byrd, as the dedication of his theoretical treatise *A Plaine and Easie Introduction to Practicall Musicke* (1597) calls Byrd his "Master." His professional career included service at the Cathedral of Norwich (1583 to July 1587), a Bachelor's degree in Music from Oxford in 1588, service as organist at St. Paul's in London from 1589, and a position as Gentleman of the Chapel Royal as of 1592. From 1593 until his death (apparently in 1602), he presented a total of eleven musical publications—compositions, arrangements, and writings—which brought him to the forefront of national attention. He may have been friends with Shakespeare.

Many of his own compositions, especially those for the Church, betray the influence of his teacher Byrd. A small number of Latin motets, and a selection of Anglican anthems abound in severe (and well-wrought) counterpoint; three full Anglican services and a setting of the Funeral Sentences, however, display more clarity and simplicity of texture. His keyboard works and consort music demonstrate skill and fluency in an inherited idiom.

The most influential of Morley's varied musical activities was his effort on behalf of the madrigal; indeed, he was a prime force in the adoption of this quintessential Italian form into the world of Elizabethan England. In 1595 he printed a volume, with parallel English and Italian editions, of canzonets and one of balletts, adapting and arranging these lighter Italian pieces by Anerio and Gastoldi to English usage; these were followed by two more anthologies of Italian music in 1597 and 1598. A large number of his own English madrigals were also printed; many of which are artful rearrangements of Italian models, such as *Sing we and Chant It*, which expands Gastoldi's *A lieta vita*, while others broach original themes in the style, including his best-known madrigal *April is in my Mistress' Face*, from the first book of madrigals of 1594. His very last publication, the *Triumphs of Orianna* (1602), presents a collection of his own and others' madrigals which honor the Queen. Throughout these works, Morley concentrates on lighter forms, avoiding the more "serious" devices of word-painting and chromaticism.

In addition to his work as organist, church composer, madrigalist, editor, and music printer, he assumed the Crown Monopoly on music printing first awarded to Byrd. In 1597 Morley authored a "Practicall" treatise on the notation and composition of music ("that in our vulgar tongue which of all other things hath been in writing least known to our countrymen"). The volume is passionate and quite readable, demonstrating its author's deep researches into the development of music, especially Italian music, and his desire to make his knowledge available to the public. —*Timothy Dickey*

Overview of Works (ca. 1590–1602)

The English composer Thomas Morley was born in either 1557 or 1558, spending much of the earlier part of his life in Norwich, where he became Master of the Choristers in 1583. He was a pupil of William Byrd, whom he emulated by developing a range of interests that included those of theorist, editor, printer, and business man in addition to being a prolific composer. His abilities were widely respected by his contemporaries. The composer Thomas Ravenscroft speaks of Morley after his death, as "he who did shine as the Sun in the Firmament of our Art."

Morley's extensive list of compositions includes both sacred and secular vocal works, along with solo and instrumental consort works. He is, however, best known for providing the impetus for the flowering of the madrigal in England after its late arrival from Italy. Morley's own contribution to the madrigal is to be found principally in his *Madrigalls to Foure Voyces*, published in 1594 and the first anthology of English madrigals to use the term. Like most of the English madrigalists, Morley preferred a lighter form than that generally adopted by Italian composers, and many of those included in the 1594 collection have gently amorous, pastoral subject matter. Among the most famous of Morley's madrigals are *April is in my mistress' face, Why sit I here complaining,* and *Besides a fountain.* This adoption of lighter forms and the general eschewal of more overt madrigalisms such as word painting greatly influenced English madrigal composers. Morley also cultivated two other forms allied to the madrigal (and indeed at times almost indistinguishable from it), the canzonet and ballett, both of which were also indebted to Italian models. Both are again essentially light forms, in particular the balletts, which, as the name suggests, are lively pieces in dance rhythms that the composer suggested were intended to be danced or sung. The two and three-part *Canzonets*, published respectively in 1595 and 1593, include some of Morley's most exquisite works. Among them are the three-part *Deep lamenting*, a rare occasion on which the composer attempted true madrigalian intensity in the Italian sense, and such miniature jewels as *Miraculous love's wounding*, and *When loe by breake of morning*. The two-part *Canzonets* book also includes nine two-part fantasies for viols, among the few instrumental works Morley published. In addition to his own madrigals, Morley also compiled several collections of Italian madrigals and one of English madrigals, the latter the famous *Triumphes of Oriana*, issued in honor of Elizabeth I in 1601.

Morley's sacred music forms a less familiar and less extensive part of his output. It includes both service music and anthems for the Anglican Church and Latin motets, leading to the supposition that he had Catholic sympathies at least at some stage during his life. Exceptional are the verse anthem *Out of the deep*, and a burial service, the first of its kind. *—Brian Robins*

Recommended:

- **Joyne Hands** / Musicians of Swanne Alley / Virgin 59032
- **The English Madrigal School** / Deller (cond.), Deller Consort / 1994 / Vanguard 2533
- **Morley, Inglott & Parsley** / Nicholas (cond.), Taylor, Choir of Norwich Cathedral Choir / Priory 396

VOCAL

Madrigals and Canzonets (ca. 1593–1597)

Morley was the youngest of William Byrd's contemporaries. He was the first genuine English madrigalist, and laid the foundations of what is now known as the English Madrigal School. Since the reign of Henry VIII (1509–47), musicians from Italy and the Netherlands who visited or lived in England had made the secular vocal and instrumental music of other parts of Europe popular among cognoscenti. Morley's contribution was to create specifically English forms of the madrigal and canzonet. His taste lay in cheerful subjects, which he treated with an exquisitely light touch. In his case there is little difference between English madrigals and canzonets, and it should be mentioned that, though "canzonet" is derived from "canzona"—Italian for a song—it was also used for small instrumental pieces in two or more "voices" (i.e. melodic lines).

Morley certainly anglicized the madrigal, but his debt to Italy was considerable. He edited and transcribed several volumes of Italian madrigals with new English texts and, though he was no slavish imitator, the Italian influence is clearly present in the 100 or more madrigals and canzonets he wrote. Their fresh, playful nature made them extremely popular in the reign of Elizabeth I, and many have been transcribed or adapted for various combinations of instruments and/or voices. In the seventeenth century, Morley's madrigals began to appear in alternative versions for voice and lute. Some, such as *Aprill is in my mistris face* and *Now is the month of maying*, are often performed today, and occasionally misidentified as being "traditional" music which, in this form, they are not.

The replacement of earlier styles such as motets, fantasias, and "In Nomines" by less sober music—even lively dance tunes—can be found in Morley's 12 two-part Fantasias, of which nine are used in the first book of canzonets (1595). Light and airy as these pieces are, high standards of musicianship had to be upheld. The florid Italian style in which singers often added their own embellishments to the composer's score was not tolerated. Although, as Morley explains in his famous treatise *A Plaine and Easie Introduction to Practicall Musicke* (1597), a degree of freedom was permissible. For example, in "light musicke such as Madrigals, Canzonetts, Pavins and Galliards... you may draw out your cadence or close to what length you will."

For obvious reasons Morley has long been revered in England, but present-day recordings have allowed his gentle voice to be heard all over the world. *—Roy Brewer*

Recommended:

- **Joyne Hands** / Musicians of Swanne Alley / Virgin 59032

Aprill Is in My Mistris Face, madrigal for 4 voices (1594)

The madrigal appeared late in England, the most formative influence on its development there being Thomas Morley. It was Morley who actively propagated the Italian school, particularly in its lighter form. One of his major publications, *The Triumphs of Orianna* (1601), presented works dedicated to Elizabeth I by 23 English composers. *Aprill Is in My Mistres Face*, which appeared in *Madrigalls to Foure Voyces* in 1594, is typical of the English type of madrigal pioneered by Morley. The text is taken from Vecchi's *Nel vis'ha un vago Aprile* (In her face she has a charming April). Consisting of only four short lines and taking only about a minute and a half to perform, it is distinguished by a line-by-line flexibility that builds to a stress on the final disillusioned sentiment: "But in her heart is cold December." The opening is light and jaunty, delicately textured and with an almost rippling rhythm. The penultimate line brings in a far longer, more legato line, and the first phrase of the last line, "but in her heart," is repeated frequently, building emphasis and creating the musical climax. *—AMG*

Recommended:

- **English & Italian Renaissance Madrigals** / Hilliard Ens. / 1999 / Virgin 61671
- **The English Lute Song** / Baird, McFarlane / 1988 / Dorian 90109

It Was a Lover and His Lass, for voice, lute & bass viol (1600)

The quintessential Shakespeare song, "It was a lover and his lass" first appeared in Thomas Morley's *First Book of Ayres or Little Short Songs; to sing and play to the Lute with the Base Viol*, published in 1600. The song comes from Act Five, Scene Three of *As You Like It*, where it is sung by the two pages, apparently not to the satisfaction of its auditor Touchstone, who afterwards expresses the hope that "God will mend their voices." It seems possible that Morley and Shakespeare may have had direct contact, although there is no direct evidence to support such a claim. Although it has since been set by a number of other composers, none have captured the same evocative feel of the song, which remains one of the most famous and popular settings of a Shakespeare song. *—Brian Robins*

Recommended:

- **Shakespeare's Musick** / Pickett (cond.), Musicians of the Globe / 1997 / Philips 446687
- **Shakespeare Songs** / Deller (cond.), Dupré, Deller Consort / HM 195202

Now Is the Month of Maying, madrigal for 5 voices (1595)

This charming madrigal is perhaps the best known of all English madrigals, and is the prototype of the pastoral-style madrigal, complete with references to nymphs, springtime, and dancing, and slightly suggestive references to games.

One factor that makes this madrigal so popular is the way that the frequent use of unison and simple harmonics makes the words very easy to understand, in contrast to a number of the English writers, who probably assumed that the listeners knew the text and so had less need to make the writing "transparent." The harmonics, too, are quite simple, and the repetitious melody is easy both to remember and to sing. But while this piece is quite simple, it is also very finely crafted, with a good deal of art going into the creation of the pastoral atmosphere. It seems to evoke perfectly the Tudor world of sophisticated gentlemen and ladies enthusing about an idealized simple, pastoral life of nymphs and shepherds, creating an artificial, but charming, image of rural life. *—Ann Feeney*

Recommended:

- **Flora Gave Me Fairest Flowers** / Rutter (cond.), Cambridge Singers / 1987 / Collegium 105
- **The English Madrigal School** / Deller (cond.), Deller Consort / 1994 / Vanguard 2533
- **All at Once Well Met: English Madrigals** / King's Singers / 1987 / EMI 49265

Sing Wee and Chant It, madrigal for 5 voices (1595)

Elizabethan England, though it spurned the French and defeated the Spanish Armada, embraced the popular culture of Catholic Italy. Italian poetry and music throughout the late sixteenth century had won a position of favor within English courtly circles. Then a single publication—Nicholas Younge's 1588 *Musica Transalpina*—altered the course of English musical history. It presented for public consumption for the first time a complete collection of Italian secular pieces "Englished" or supplied with English texts. The book's popularity fully launched the brief but intense reign of the English madrigal. Thomas Morley, in the first generation of English madrigalists, went beyond mere translation of Italian texts and re-created the spirit of Italian music in his new compositions. Morley and his contemporaries at first composed few authentic madrigals; it would fall to Thomas Weelkes and John Wilbye to bring the "serious" madrigal genre to fruition. Instead, they concentrated on two lighter genres. The simple pastoral Italian canzonetta became the English canzonett, and the balletti of Gastoldi translated into Thomas Morley's balletts.

Sing Wee and Chant It is perhaps Morley's most famous ballett. It is the fourth piece in his 1595 publication *The First Book of Balletts to Five Voices*. Morley himself acknowledges his debt to Giovanni Giacomo Gastoldi, crediting Gastoldi with the earliest known music in this genre. Morley claims the Italians danced to the sound of voices, which explains the generic title. Gastoldi's own *Balletti a cinque voci con li suoi versi per cantare, sonare, e ballare* appeared in England in 1591, gaining considerable popularity. Morley modeled his own 21-piece collection of balletts on Gastoldi's 21 pieces, going so far as to translate a number of the Italian's texts and adapting his music. *Sing Wee and Chant It* is Morley's adaptation of Gastoldi's first balletto, *A lieta vita*. Gastoldi follows a common form, setting his light, strophic text in two parts, each half ending with a quick "fa la la" and repeats. Likewise, Morley takes a light (even inconsequential) English adaptation of the Italian text and sets it to a quick triple-time dance. Each half of *Sing Wee and Chant It* contains two brief verses in simple homophony and a "fa la la." However, Morley expands his "fa las" in greater contrapuntal artifice. In addition, his harmonic language, though as simple as Gastoldi's, proves more direct and effective. The balletto is improved in its English guise. *—Timothy Dickey*

Recommended:

- **Of Kindly Lust & Love's Inspiring** / Minter (cond.), V-I Ens., Folger Consort / 1993 / Bard 9308
- **All at Once Well Met: English Madrigals** / King's Singers / 1987 / EMI 49265
- **Joyne Hands** / Musicians of Swanne Alley / Virgin 59032

Mormon Tabernacle Choir

f. 1847, Salt Lake City, UT
Ensemble
Perhaps America's best-known and longest-established large choral group, the Mormon Tabernacle Choir is known for full sound and fervent expression in its stirring renditions of classical standards and evergreen Americana.

Under the leadership of Brigham Young, 148 members of the Mormon Church (Church of Jesus Christ of Latter-day Saints, or LDS Church), seeking a place to pursue their unique religious beliefs without interference, found the Salt Lake basin and chose it as their site. One of the expressions of faith that had sustained them on their trip was their singing, and almost immediately after settling, they formed a choral group. The choir gave its debut performance on August 22, 1847, only 29 days after the Mormons' arrival in Utah.

Within two years John Parry had been named the choir's first conductor, and the group has had an uninterrupted existence since then. It currently numbers around 330 members, all unpaid. The choir sings in and takes its name from the Mormon Tabernacle in Temple Square, Salt Lake City. The Tabernacle is the second building of that name, which designates a public meeting hall for the church. Thus it is distinct from the Temple, which is a place sacred to Mormons and open only to those who live by the precepts of the LDS church. The Tabernacle is a large, oval-shaped building with a unique domed roof. This unique roof is made of plaster and steamed, curved wooden planks lashed together with rawhide and wooden pegs. It was designed with clear acoustics in mind, so that a 6,500-member audience could hear speaking and music without difficulty in the days before electronic amplification. The building's tour staff proudly shows off its acoustics by means of such demonstrations as dropping pins and tearing newspapers.

When the present building opened on October 6, 1867, the (Mormon Tabernacle Choir, by then at 150 voices the largest in the United States, gave a performance. It was accompanied by a fine 700-pipe organ, since rebuilt and enlarged and now boasting 11,623 pipes. The choir made its first official recording on September 1, 1910, for the Columbia label; of the at least 130 it has made since then, among the most celebrated is a 1959 recording of "The Battle Hymn of the Republic" with the Philadelphia Orchestra, which earned a Grammy Award.

Today the choir performs weekly at 9:30 a.m. on Sundays, and these performances are broadcast on a radio program entitled "Music and the Spoken Word." Broadcast continually since July 15, 1929, the program is the longest uninterrupted network run in American radio history. Both the choir's Sunday morning concerts and its Thursday evening rehearsals are open to the public, as are regular organ recitals.

The Tabernacle has historically been the site of LDS church conferences, but has yielded that function to a facility north of Temple Square. The Tabernacle remains as a concert hall and place for special church meetings. *—Joseph Stevenson*

Recommended:

- ○ **A Mormon Tabernacle Choir Christmas** / Jessop (cond.), Longhurst, Breault, Orchestra at Temple Square, Mormon Tabernacle Choir / 2001 / Telarc 60552
- ○ **Super Hits Vol. 1** / Ormandy (cond.), Condie, Schreiner, Asper, Philadelphia Orch., Mormon Tabernacle Choir / 2000 / Sony 89275
- ○ **Joy To The World** / Ormandy, Ottley, Condie (conds.), Schreiner, Columbia SO, Mormon Tabernacle Choir / 2002 / Legacy 87769
- ○ **Spirit of America** / Jessop (cond.), Longhurst, Christiansen, Elliott, Mormon Tabernacle Choir / 2003 / Mormon Tabernacle 0302

Davitt Moroney

b. Dec. 23, 1950, Leicester, England
Harpsichordist
Davitt Moroney is one of today's top specialists in older keyboard instruments, one who has delved deeply into the music and aesthetics of French and English harpsichord music. He has perhaps the most scholarly orientation among leading early music performers, but his performances are accessible to any listener. Born in Britain of Irish-Italian ancestry, he studied in England, France, and the United States, coming to early music through scholarly study. His Ph.D., granted at the University of California in 1980, dealt with the choral music of Tallis and Byrd. Through the 1970s, however, he studied organ (with the Austrian player Susi Jeans) and harpsichord (with the Canadian Kenneth Gilbert, and after finishing his degree he embarked on a career as a recitalist, with Paris as his home base.

Moroney has released over 50 compact discs of keyboard music of the sixteenth through eighteenth centuries, as a soloist, chamber player, and participant in concertos, winning several Gramophone Awards and France's Grand Prix du Disque de l'Académie Charles Cros. His most ambitions project, which took 15 years of planning, research, and rehearsal, is a complete survey of the keyboard music of the great Elizabethan-era English composer William Byrd. A seven-disc set (for the price of five), on the Hyperion label, it was the first album of its kind. Meticulously researched, it includes a 45,000-word program book written by Moroney himself. The recording uses the most appropriate instruments available, including two different harpsichords, clavichord, chamber organ, the Ahrend organ of the Church-Museum des Augustins, Toulouse, and a muselar virginal especially built for the recording. Many of the recordings were made in the actual locations where Byrd himself had played his music, including Lincoln Cathedral, Ingatestone Hall in Essex, and L'Abbaye Royale de Fontevraid, France.

Despite all the research and intellectual effort involved, and the strict authenticity for which he strives, Moroney's performances are vivid and expressive, delighting contemporary audiences. One way he is known for putting his insights across to audiences is to address them directly. In the year 2000, Moroney's biography *Bach: An Extraordinary Life* appeared, and his critical edition of Bach's *Art of the Fugue* (one of over a dozen he has edited) included a new completion of that work's massive unfinished closing fugue. Since 2001 he has been professor of music and university organist at the University of California, Berkeley. *—Joseph Stevenson*

Recommended:

- ○ **Bach: Die Kunst der Fuge** / Moroney / HM 1951169/70
- ○ **Couperin: Complete Organ Works** / Moroney / Sacem 316001
- ○ **Les Idées Heureuses** / Moroney / Harmonia Mundi 1901275
- ○ **Couperin: Livre de Tablature de Clavescin** / Moroney / 1999 / Hyperion 67164
- ○ **Bach: Die Kunst der Fuge** / Moroney / Harmonia Mundi 2901169/70
- ○ **Byrd: Keyboard Music** / Moroney / Hyperion 66558

James Morris

b. Jan. 10, 1947, Baltimore, MD
Bass
Morris has become the most noted Wotan of the turn of the century, known for his acting as well as a musical approach that emphasizes the legato, even lyrical parts of the role. His voice has a strong upper extension that allows him to tackle such baritone roles and Scarpia in Puccini's *Tosca* and Mozart's *Don Giovanni* to critical acclaim.

Appropriately enough, his two main teachers were a baritone and a bass. Morris, a native of Baltimore, first studied with Forrest Barrett, and then won the first voice scholarship that the University of Maryland offered. However, at the advice of his mentor (and distant in-law), Rosa Ponselle, who recognized his potential but did not think that she herself would be the best teacher for him, he instead enrolled at the Peabody Conservatory, and continued his studies with Frank Valentino there. After some time there, he continued his studies at the Philadelphia Academy of Vocal Arts with Nicola Moscona.

He first performed on stage with the Baltimore Civic Opera Company, and advanced in 1967 to the Baltimore Opera, making his debut there as Crespel in Offenbach's *The Tales of Hoffmann.* In 1970, he had his first Metropolitan Opera audition, though he turned down the subsequent offer to join their Opera Studio. Moscona, who himself had had a long Met career, persuaded the management to re-audition Morris for the regular company, and this time he was offered a contract for 1971, and he made his debut as the King in Verdi's *Aida.* He made his Glyndebourne Festival debut as Banquo in Verdi's *Macbeth.*

In 1976, again at the Baltimore Opera, he created the role of King Alfonso in Pasatieri's *Ines de Castro.* He began to study Wagnerian roles, first Wotan in *Die Walküre* and the Dutchman, and made his Vienna State Opera debut as Wotan in 1984. In 1985, he took on the role of Wotan for the entire *Ring* cycle in San Francisco, to great acclaim, and followed that success in many other productions worldwide.

He recorded the complete *Ring* cycle with James Levine on DG (445 354), and an aria recital disc on EMI (49287) gives selections from Verdi as well as two selections from *The Flying Dutchman* and *Die Walküre.* *—Ann Feeney*

Recommended:

- ○ **Wagner: Der fliegende Holländer** / Levine (cond.), Morris, Heppner, Voigt, Rooterings, Metropolitan Opera Orch. / 1997 / Sony 66342
- ○ **Wagner: Das Rheingold** / Levine (cond.), Morris, Ludwig, Jerusalem, Moll, Metropolitan Opera Orch. / 1989 / DG 445295

Ignaz Moscheles

b. May 23, 1794, Prague, Bohemia (Czech Rep.), **d.** Mar. 10, 1870, Leipzig, Germany
Composer: Keyboard, Concerto
A German pianist and composer of Czech birth, Moscheles received a solid technical education on the piano at Prague Conservatory. In 1808 he moved to Vienna to be near Beethoven, where he studied with Salieri and Albrechtsberger. A commission to prepare a piano reduction of Beethoven's *Fidelio* in 1814 secured his status as one of Vienna's most popular virtuoso pianists, a fame that brought him praise from composers he had studied, such as Clementi and J.B. Cramer. From 1825 to 1846 Moscheles taught piano at the Royal Academy of Music in London and played duets with Chopin and Mendelssohn. In 1846 he became principal professor of

piano at the Leipzig Conservatory. Known as one of the last great musicians of the classical school, Moscheles was a clear, precise technician on the keyboard. Although he admired Chopin and Liszt for their creativity and virtuosity, Moscheles found their improvisations to be showy and too decorative. His own were varied and full of atmosphere. Most of his own compositions were piano music, and his sonatas were the best of these. He also composed a number of concertos, and later in life turned to song writing. His work can be characterized by restraint and classical balance. *—Lynn Vought*

KEYBOARD

Characteristic Studies, Op. 95 (1836–1837)

Ignaz Moscheles composed well-known sets of etudes, including the *24 Etudes*, Op. 70, intended for advanced students, and the *12 Characteristic Studies*, Op. 95, for the higher development of execution and bravura, which is designed for a more intermediate level of skill. This latter set was composed in 1837 when Moscheles was still living and teaching in London. Despite that, Moscheles' catalog of opus numbers runs to 141, and the *12 Characteristic Studies*, Op. 95, is considered a late work since, by the time Moscheles departed London for Leipzig in 1845, he had practically stopped composing. The 12 pieces in Moscheles' *Characteristic Studies*, Op. 95, bear the following titles: "Der Zorn" (Wrath), "Versöhnung" (Reconciliation), "Der Widersprach" (Contradiction), "Juno," "Ein Kindermärchen" (A Nursery Tale), "Bacchanale," "Zärtlichkeit" (Affection, also known as "Tenderesse"), "Alla Napolitana," "Die Mondnacht am Lee Gestade" (Moonlight on the Seashore), "Terpsichore," "Der Traum" (A Dream), and "Die Angst" (Terror). Although the set as a whole still has currency among pianists as teaching material, the most familiar of the selections are "Der Widersprach" and "Zärtlichkeit." As etudes, the individual pieces in the set do not necessarily address themselves to specific points of keyboard technique and are equally useful in the context of both study and performance. Comparing the more formal set of *Etudes*, Op. 70, with the new Op. 95 set in a published foreword to the first edition of the latter, Robert Schumann wrote "These new etudes are different from the other ones; 15 years makes a difference. The style is more compact, the harmony more combined, (and) selective thought is the master here." Although Schumann could hardly have seen it coming from the vantage point of 1837, general wisdom dictates that the *Etudes*, Op. 95, represent the finest offering in Moscheles' large catalog of solo piano works to be found outside of his five piano sonatas. *—Uncle Dave Lewis*

Recommended:

○ **Romantic Etudes for Piano** / Ponti / 1996 / Vox 5151

CONCERTO

Piano Concerto No. 2 in E flat major, Op. 56 (1825)

Among the great Romantic piano virtuosos, Moscheles was known for his elegant reticence. In an age of flamboyant virtuosos, Moscheles, whose mastery of the keyboard was second to none, eschewed self-centered displays of virtuosity for its own sake, instead cultivating technical precision, clear phrasing, and a characteristic lightness of touch. These qualities are evident in his music, as well, for Moscheles, like Mendelssohn, introduced a spirit of Classical form into the Romantic idiom. Composed in the 1820s, the *Piano Concerto No. 2 in E flat major* is far more than a typical work by a Romantic composer. In fact, this is a work of remarkable originality. For example, as Nicholas Temperley observed in his liner notes for a Hyperion recording of Moscheles' music for piano and orchestra, the composer's idea to open the first movement with the tympani predates Beethoven's enormously effective tympani statement introducing the Scherzo of the *Symphony No. 9*. Indeed, the listener discerns a certain Beethovenian monumentality in the first movement, with its assertive, clearly stated introduction presenting the principal themes, one somewhat martial, the other discreetly lyrical. Working within a Classical formal framework, Moscheles nevertheless allows the piano to sing, presenting his musical ideas in the ornate, yet never overbearing garb of Romantic virtuosity. Opening with a deceptively simple statement, the second movement conjures up an atmosphere of exquisitely serene lyricism, the orchestra elegantly complementing the piano's richly expressive narrative. There is a certain fluidity in this movement, in which themes and ideas seamlessly blend to suggest a unique feeling of pensive repose. This tranquil atmosphere is interrupted, but not harshly, by the tympani, which Moscheles again uses to signal the start of a new movement. In the third movement, in which Moscheles ingeniously transforms a polonaise into a larger, more complex musical statement, the brilliant dialogue between piano and orchestra introduces a new spirit of dramatic exuberance. Ending in a triumphant burst of virtuosity, the final movement nevertheless remains faithful to a spirit of elegance and expressive balance. Not only is the music intrinsically interesting and engaging, but it reveals, in a charmingly tasteful manner, the immense expressive potential of the piano. *—Zoran Minderovic*

Recommended:

○ **Moscheles: Concertos 2 & 3; Anticipations of Scotland** / Shelley (cond. & piano), Tasmanian SO / 2002 / Hyperion 67276

Piano Concerto No. 3 in G minor, Op. 60 (1820)

Robert Schumann held the third of Moscheles' eight piano concertos in particularly high esteem, writing in 1836 that it was one of two works "through which alone he has secured for himself a place in the first row of contemporary piano composers." As a pianist, Moscheles had a crisp, precise, and brilliant approach to playing that echoes through his keyboard writing in this concerto. The music is beholden to Classical models and Beethoven, but its Romantic colorings provides a direct bridge to Mendelssohn. The Allegro moderato begins with a theme that, while avoiding theatrics, conveys worry and distress. The piano enters with domineering chords and offers its own, more virile approach to the theme as if reprimanding the wimpy orchestra. But then it launches into a far more ornate treatment of the music and introduces a new, music-box subject that initially wouldn't be out of place in a late Mozart concerto. Almost immediately, though, Moscheles veers off into showy figures and the soloist spends most of the movement's development section buzzing through scales and storming through passagework, while the orchestra provides only the most essential support. The piano's restatement of the themes in the recapitulation is, again, ornate and occasionally nervous, but essentially assertive. (Yet Moscheles carefully avoids thundering through the bass range, which was puny on the instruments of his time.) The composer provides only a brief cadenza; perhaps he improvised something more elaborate in his own performances. In the Adagio, the piano lays out a noble, thickly chordal theme and immediately thins the texture by reverting to the ornate filigree and scalar passages that characterized the first movement. At the movement's climax, the piano plays recitative material over orchestral tremolos, exactly as in the slow movement of the F minor concerto of Chopin, a composer whose music Moscheles denigrated as excessively feminine. This leads without a break into the Allegro agitato, which is indeed lively but less "agitato" than the first movement. Hummable tunes initially propel this suddenly good-natured music, although the piano soon dives into its characteristic, un-hummable glittering passagework. A melodramatic passage finally earns the movement its agitato label, but this soon makes way for a slow, lyrical section in D major. The movement's main theme then returns in the major, scampering carelessly toward what turns out to be a harrowing, prestissimo finale with the pianist playing the principal theme in octaves in an ending calculated by the pianist/composer to bring the house down. *—James Reel*

Recommended:

○ **Moscheles: Concertos 2 & 3; Anticipations of Scotland** / Shelley (cond. & piano), Tasmanian SO / 2002 / Hyperion 67276

Moscow State Symphony Orchestra

f. 1943, Moscow, U.S.S.R.

Ensemble

The Moscow State Symphony Orchestra was founded in 1943 by Leonid Steinberg, then conductor of the Bolshoi Theatre. Steinberg was succeeded by Moscow Conservatory professor Leo Ginzburg, under whom the orchestra became one of the best ensembles of the Soviet Union. He kept close ties with Shostakovich, Prokofiev, and other composers, premiering many of their works. Veronika Dudarova followed Ginzburg and served as music director for 20 years. Throughout its history, the orchestra concentrated on presenting the works of Russian masters. With the 1990 appointment of Pavel Kogan as music director, that changed. He has expanded the orchestra's repertoire to include works by German, Austrian, French, and American composers, and more contemporary Russian works. Kogan and the orchestra presented a full cycle of Mahler's symphonies in 1996. David Oistrakh, Mstislav Rostropovich, Janos Starker, Vadim Repin, Maxim Vengerov, Shlomo Mintz, Emil Gilels, Leonid Kogan, Irina Arkhipova, and Victor Tretyakov are just some of the many soloists the orchestra has hosted, and Kiril Kondrashin, Gennady Rozhdestvensky, Evgeny Svetlanov, and Valery Gergiev are some of its guest conductors. In addition to its regular appearances at music festivals in Russia and Europe, under Kogan the orchestra has toured around the world, and been recorded on video by RCA. At home in Moscow, it consistently sells out its concerts. *—AMG*

Recommended:

○ **Glazunov: Symphonies 5 & 8** / Anissimov (cond.), Moscow State SO / 2000 / Naxos 553660

○ **Best of Glazunov** / Golovschin, Anissimov (conds.), Kaler, Moscow State SO, Polish RSO / 2000 / Naxos 556687

Alexander Vasil'yevich Mosolov

b. Jul. 29, 1900, Kiev, Ukraine, **d.** Jul. 12, 1973, Moscow, Russia

Composer: Orchestral

Alexander Mosolov is considered the prime representative of 1920s Russian Futurism. His music from before 1930 is mechanistic, highly dramatic, anti-sentimental and demonstrates no concern for popular appeal. Mosolov emphasizes motor rhythms and ostinati, and his futurist pieces are written at an extremely high level of dissonance. Although Mosolov was forced to abandon this idiom with the rise of Stalin, his futurist compositions garnered a lot of attention, had a definite impact on composers such as Shostakovich, and speak effectively to later trends—in this sense they were truly "futuristic."

Mosolov was the son of an opera singer; he began piano studies with her at age three. His mother's second marriage brought Mosolov into contact with modernist painter Mikhail Leblan, who introduced him to international currents within the art world. Mosolov volunteered in the Red Army during the October Revolution, and in 1921 was discharged due to injuries. Mosolov enrolled in the Moscow Conservatoire, studying composition with Nikolai Myaskovsky and Reinhold Glière. While neither of them subscribed to the concept of industrial modernism Mosolov was already idealizing, both agreed that his talent was unmistakable, and offered their support to him for decades afterward.

Mosolov's first works were launched at an Association of Contemporary Music concert held in Moscow in September 1924. The immediate critical response to Mosolov's music was strongly negative, Mosolov being attacked over the "unsuitability" of his artistic goals and his aloof attitude towards public taste. Mosolov answered these charges with the ballet, *Stal* (Steel), first given in December 1927. The first section of the ballet (*Zavod* [The Iron Foundry]) was a monumental success both in Russia and throughout the world. While the piece is dissonant in the extreme, Mosolov coordinates the mechanistic rhythms into specific orchestral groups that work together like cogs in a well-oiled machine. The dramatic intensity of *Zavod* has kept it in use as cinematic stock library music long after it was forgotten as a concert work.

Mosolov's *String Quartet No. 1* was heard at the *ISCM Festival* in Frankfurt in 1927, earning him a contract with Universal Edition. Mosolov's most remarkable surviving composition, *Piano Concerto No. 1*, was first heard in Leningrad (St. Petersburg) in February 1928, with Mosolov himself as soloist. Other extant works from this period include *Four Newspaper Advertisements*, *Three Children's Songs*, and a wide miscellany of piano and chamber music.

With the piano pieces *Turkmenistan Nights* (1928) Mosolov began to work more extensively with ethnic folk forms. His interest in this realm would prove convenient, as Mosolov was already under scrutiny by the Soviet government, which regarded his music as of no use to the proletariat and too closely tied to Western modernism. Mosolov took it upon himself to make an exhaustive survey of folk songs in Kyrgyz, Turkmenistan, Stavropol, and other remote regions of the Soviet domain. His *Second Piano Concerto* (1932) combines these folk elements with a mild remainder of earlier stylistic gestures. This proved not enough to keep Mosolov out of trouble, and in 1938 he was arrested by the NKVD and sent to a forced labor camp. The intervention of Myaskovsky and Glière saw to it that Mosolov only served nine months of an eight-year sentence.

Afterward, Mosolov continued to compose, albeit largely in the idiom approved by the Soviet State. Mosolov's work list shows that he was one of the most prolific composers of the twentieth century, but the vast majority of his works are believed lost or otherwise unaccounted for. Fortunately, as Mosolov's value as a composer is better understood, once suppressed manuscripts of his work are coming to light. *—Uncle Dave Lewis*

ORCHESTRAL

Iron Foundry (Zavod), orchestral episode, Op. 19 (1926–1928)

This short, powerful piece from the ballet *Stal* (Steel) of 1928 is an exacting portrait of heavy industry against an emotional background of noble, socialist idealism. It is also an early example of music made almost solely from the combining of patterns (eschewing traditional melody, harmony, and counterpoint): triplet figures in the lower strings and trumpets over a strident four-beat bass suggest the turning of flywheels and other mechanisms; gradually added to this are high sliding figures like the sliding of steel against steel, loud metal-sheet crashes, orchestra anvil, and high, single-beat stabs. A noble theme of primary intervals stated in the French horns emerges from this mix. Suddenly, all the machines shut down and a new accumulation of patterns starts in the high winds accompanied by military rolls on the snare drum. The theme is then restated in the low brass, followed by an unremitting, driving, machine-like coda. Works like this one, intended as a glorification of Soviet industrialization, were later criticized as "naturalistic" and the Association for Contemporary Music, originally set up to encourage experimentation and anti-bourgeois music, was dissolved in 1934. Most of the composers, including Mosolov, were unfortunately compelled to adopt more conservative, popularistic styles. *—"Blue Gene" Tyranny*

Recommended:

○ **The Caviar of Russian Music** / Gorenstein (cond.), Russian SO / 1996 / Saison Russe 288149

Moritz Moszkowski

b. Aug. 23, 1854, Breslau, Germany, **d.** Mar. 4, 1925, Paris, France

Composer: Keyboard, Concerto

The Jewish pianist Moritz Moszkowski was German-born, but always claimed Polish nationality. A child prodigy, Moszkowski entered the Dresden conservatory at age 11, and from there moved on to Berlin where he studied piano with Eduard Frank and Theodor Kullak and composition with Friedrich Kiel. Kullak was so impressed by Moszkowski that he made the latter an instructor at the *Neue Akademie der Tonkunst*; Moszkowski was then only 17 years of age, and he remained in this position until 1896. In 1873, Moszkowski made his debut appearance in Berlin and swiftly rose through ranks to recognition as one of the top piano virtuosi in Europe. In 1875, Moszkowski premiered his *First Piano Concerto*; soon after the premiere, Franz Liszt joined performed a two-piano version with him.

By the mid-1880s, Moszkowski was suffering from nerves and began to curtail his recital activity in favor of composing, conducting and teaching. His many published compositions proved very popular in the era of salon pianism, and netted the composer a handsome income. These included the *Serenata* Op. 15/1, *Concert Studies* Op. 24, *Caprice Espagnol* Op. 37, *Etincelles* Op. 36/6 and *Guitarre* Op. 45/2. Moszkowski's music for piano duet was especially popular, in particular the Spanish Dances Opp. 12, 21, and 65. Early in his career Moszkowski had some success with orchestral music as well, but these pieces remained largely unpublished and most are now lost.

Among Moszkowski's honors were membership in the Berlin Academy of Art, and an honorary lifetime membership in the Philharmonic Society in Britain, where he often appeared as conductor. Upon leaving the Neue Akademie der Tonkunst, Moszkowski resettled in Paris with his wife, the sister of the composer Cecile Chaminade. In 1910 Moszkowski's wife left him for his best friend, taking their daughter with her; he never truly recovered from this personal tragedy.

In the early years of the twentieth century Moszkowski proved unable to adapt to changing musical styles, and sales of his works quickly declined. Having lost his considerable fortune during the tumult of the First World War, Moszkowski was living in poverty by the early 1920s. On December 21, 1921 a group of concerned colleagues arranged a benefit concert at Carnegie Hall on his behalf; among the 14 pianists who played the event were Percy Grainger, Harold Bauer, Wilhelm Backhaus, Leo Ornstein, and Ignaz Freidman. The conductor of this "monster concert" was Walter Damrosch, who remembered that this event as the most difficult assignment of his career. Nonetheless, the concert generated $10,000; however Moszkowski was unable to access this windfall of cash until mere weeks before his death in Paris at age 70. Despite living up to the very eve of electrical recording, Moszkowski is not known to have left behind any records or piano rolls of his own playing. *—Uncle Dave Lewis*

KEYBOARD

Works for Piano (1880–1920)

Sometimes a great virtuoso is as much illusionist as anything else. This is not to say that any world-touring performing musician can make do with an underdeveloped technique, only that a top-caliber performer has the valuable ability to make a given piece of music seem more or less difficult than it actually is. Back in Polish-German pianist Moritz Moszkowski's day, when most virtuosi were still composing music for themselves to play, this knack translated into a capacity to write pieces that drew the most from the instrument—the most excitement, the most grace, the most rapture, the most raw impressiveness—at a minimum of physical cost to the performer. Moszkowski had this ability in spades. His many fine salon piano pieces are all perfectly shaped for the human hand; they are comfortable, relatively easy (by comparison with other piano music from the last quarter of the nineteenth century), and, at times, abundantly charming.

Moszkowski was most famous during his lifetime for two books of *Spanish Dances*, Op. 12 (originally for piano four-hands, later adapted for solo piano). These mock-Spanish trinkets are built from supple tunes and rich, but not complex, harmonies; and Moszkowski finds plenty of room for a few musical winks here and there—he always had a good sense of humor. It is nearly impossible to dislike a piece like "Guitarre," which is probably the most cherished of the *Spanish Dance* lot.

Moszkowski's three *Concert Studies*, Op. 24 were, if maybe never a staple of the student diet, certainly well-used by teachers during the early twentieth century. Here, as is wholly appropriate for the genre, the composer lets loose a little bit and makes heavy demands on the player's mechanism. Miscellaneous light music items, including a *Barcarolle*, Op. 27, and a light-footed *Humoresque*, were often featured in recitals by Rachmaninov and Josef Hofmann (the latter of whom studied with Moszkowski once upon a time). There are also a handful of chamber pieces for either violin or cello and piano, though none is even occasionally put on concert programs today.

The more weighty music of Moritz Moszkowski met with considerably less success than his sweetmeat salon stuff, but it is not without merit. In this category are two solo concertos. One is a completely forgotten violin concerto; the other is the *Piano Concerto in E major*, Op. 59, a sparkling representative of the high-Romantic virtuoso concerto class that deserves to be better known and has been brought back to light through the power of the compact disc. *—Blair Johnston*

Recommended:

- ○ **Piano Music by Moritz Moszkowski Vol. 1** / Tanyel / 2002 / Hyperion 55141
- ○ **Piano Music by Moritz Moszkowski** / Tanyel / 2003 / HM 55143
- ○ **Moszkowski: Violin Concerto; etc.** / Brabbins (cond.), Thomas, Little, BBC Scottish SO / Hyperion 67389

Etudes

Moszkowski made his initial reputation as a traveling piano virtuoso, one of several late nineteenth century keyboard showmen following in the footsteps of Liszt. A nervous disorder began to restrict his ability to perform in the 1880s, whereupon he threw himself more fully into composing. Although he was no longer writing pieces for his own use, many of his works—aside from the salon items designed for household amusement—were uncompromisingly difficult. Most notable among these are several sets of etudes, or studies. Unlike the ubiquitous studies of Hanon, Moszkowski's were designed for public performance, as were those of Chopin, as well as Schumann's *Symphonic Études* and Liszt's *Transcendental Études*. Harmonically, Moszkowski's style was strongly influenced by those first two composers, while from Liszt he developed a taste for unrestrained showmanship, displayed to best effect in his various studies. Moszkowski's principal sets of studies are the *Three Concert Études*, Op. 24; the two published as Op. 48; a dozen gathered as Op. 92; and, above all, the *15 Études de Virtuosité* (Virtuosic Etudes), Op. 72, published in 1903. Although Moszkowski intended these for concert use, he was not always able to make them sound consistently more than knuckle-busting technical exercises, particularly in scale passages and unison playing. The phrases tend to be short and repetitive, obsessing on a particular challenge. Arpeggios, thirds, and sixths whip by with locomotive force and although Moszkowski couldn't consistently muster the melodic interest found in similar works by Chopin, he always generated music of tremendous excitement. All of the Op. 72 etudes, for example, are quite fast and loud, littered with markings like Allegro energico and Vivo e con fuoco, and often building to triple-forte climaxes. This leads some pianists to overlook the music's more subtle passages, few as they are, giving short shrift to the measures marked espressivo or cantabile. Still, these are works of power, not poetry, meant to showcase the performer's fearless technique. In this respect, they are tremendously successful. *—James Reel*

Recommended:

- ○ **Moszkowski: Etudes, Opp. 72 & 92** / Raes / Solstice SO 102

CONCERTO

Piano Concerto in E major, Op. 59 (1898)

Moszkowski primarily wrote for the piano, but did compose an opera, violin concerto, and other works for orchestra. This piano concerto, Op. 59, may well be his finest large score and its general neglect is hard to explain. It had once achieved a certain level of popularity in European concert halls, even if it did not quite move into the standard repertory. In the post-World War I era, however, it gradually faded. Cast in four movements, it is a fairly lengthy work, lasting 35 to 40 minutes in most performances. The first movement is marked Moderato and has a somewhat Schumann-esque character. It exudes great passion in places, with big powerful chords to punctuate the mood; there are also moments of lovely repose. The stormy development section contains much interesting and exciting music and the coda is particularly well-crafted, too. Thematically, this opening panel is also quite appealing. The second movement Andante features a light, attractive march and the ensuing Scherzo, marked Vivace, is busy in its Lisztian menace and glitter. The Allegro deciso finale offers a joyous melody and cheerful mood throughout. The writing for both the piano and orchestra is skillfully crafted in this concerto and Moszkowski exhibits a fine sense for contrast and balance. In the end, this mostly light work must be assessed as one of the finer efforts in the piano concerto genre from one of the last of the Romantics, a conservative who knew his tradition well. *—Robert Cummings*

Recommended:

- ○ **Moszkowski: Concerto for piano in E; Paderewski: Concerto for piano in Am** / Maksymiuk (cond.), Lane, BBC Scottish SO / 1991 / Hyperion 66452

Jean-Joseph Mouret

b. Apr. 11, 1682, Avignon, France, **d.** Dec. 22, 1738, Charenton, France

Composer: Orchestral

Jean-Joseph Mouret had a career including vast popularity and a sudden fall from success. His father was a silk merchant and avid amateur violinist who saw to it that his son received complete instruction in music. Details of this education are unknown, but musical historians consider it likely that it occurred in the choir school of Notre Dame des Doms, an important regional church.

Mouret's family's wealth, his charm, and his lovely singing voice made him welcome in the best company. By 1707, he was in Paris, where he was appointed music master for the Marshall of Noailles. By 1709, he had the position of *surintendent de la musique* at the court of Sceaux. There, from 1714 through 1715, the Duchess of Maine was the hostess of the renowned *Grandes Nuits*, for which Mouret wrote much of the music. In 1714 to 1718, he was the orchestra director of the Paris Opéra. In an age when elevated Greek tragedy, pastoral romance, and histories based on figures of antiquity were *de rigeur*, Mouret was bold enough to introduce comedy into his operas.

Mouret's first opera, *Le fêtes ou le triomphe de Thalia*, told of the humiliating rout by Thalia, the Muse of Comedy, over her sister, Melpomene, the Muse of Tragedy. The main body of the story is not set in some vague legendary scene, but involves clearly contemporary figures, such as a group of "coquettish widows" all dressed in recognizably French costumes. Mouret and his librettist, La Font, daringly placed this production on the august stage of the Paris Opéra, a virtual shrine to tragedy. This resulted in a scandal and La Font honorably took the blame for the sacrilege and in a new prologue said all the success of the work was due to the music and dance. Mouret went on to write *Le mariage de Ragonde* (1714), a true lyric comedy anticipating by 30 years Rameau's *Platée*, which is often considered the origin of French musical comedy.

Mouret also wrote standard tragedies and heroic ballets, but was notably less successful with them than in his more lighthearted works, which also included a series of divertissements for Paris' *French Theater* (beginning in 1716) and *the New Italian Theater*, where Mouret became director in 1717; he also wrote motets and cantatas.

In 1718, he was given a royal privilege to publish music and in 1720 was appointed an *ordinaire du Roy*, as singer in the King's chamber. He was music director of the Concert Spirituel from 1728 to 1734. This appointment marked the beginning of the end of his great success, for the Concert Spirituel had financial and legal problems that affected him personally. Then in 1734, the troubled institution was taken over by the Académie Royale de Musique, which sacked Mouret. In 1736, the Duke of Maine died and Mouret lost his position at Sceaux. In 1737, the Italian Theater had a change of policy that resulted in Mouret losing that job as well. Within four years, he had lost all sources of income and was essentially maintained as a charity case by the Prince of Carignan, who annually gave him a pension.

It is intriguing to note that George Frideric Handel went through periods of such reverses but was able to find a way to have a comeback. Mouret was not as fortunate or resilient; his spirit was progressively broken by all of these career misfortunes and in 1737, he began to go mad. Just after his 50th birthday, he was placed in the care of the Fathers of Charity at Carenton and died in that institution eight months later. *—Joseph Stevenson*

ORCHESTRAL

Premiere Suite of Symphonies for brass, strings & timpani (1729)

Mouret spent much of his professional career in courtly circles, writing music for royal events while also composing for the Opéra de Paris and Paris' Italian theater. His two *Suites of Symphonies* were composed in 1729, while he was director of the Concert Spirituel. The first suite has also been called "Sinfonie de Fanfares" because it consists of four fanfare movements. It (and, indeed, Mouret's entire output) is pretty much known today only for its opening Rondeau (aka the *Masterpiece Theatre* theme). Mouret wrote the suites to make better use of a full range of instruments. This first suite is scored for trumpets, violins, oboes, bassoons, tympani, and continuo. It was dedicated to the Prince of Dombes, Louis Auguste de Bourbon, who had fought against the Turks in 1717, specifically to recognize his valor in battle. The Rondeau is followed by *Gracieusement sans lenteur*, Allegro, and Guay. The Rondeau is justifiably well-known, with its distinctive theme and harmony and celebratory demeanor. The "Gracieusement" is also a rondo, beginning as a regal slow march, stated by just the strings and woodwind before the brass and tympani come in. This pattern is repeated throughout the movement, interspersed with brief episodes of contrasting material for the strings and continuo. The Allegro is more dance-like in 2/4 meter, opening with the full ensemble, before the strings and occasionally the trumpets also begin developing the theme. The final Guay is a courtly Sicilienne, built much in the same fashion as the second movement, with each statement made first by the strings and woodwinds, then the full ensemble. *—Patsy Morita*

Recommended:

- ○ **Greatest Hits: Trumpet** / various / 1994 / Sony 66702
- ○ **Mobil Masterpiece Theater** / various / 1996 / Delos 3218

Marcel Moyse

b. May 17, 1889, Saint Amour, France, **d.** Nov. 1, 1984, Brattleboro, VT

Flutist

Marcel Moyse was one of the most influential flutists of the twentieth century, first in France and later in the United States. He entered the Paris Conservatory in 1905, where he studied with Hennebains, Gaubet, and Taffanel. He was awarded the premier prix in 1906. He developed a uniquely lyrical style, imitating the vibrato and phrasing of contemporary instrumentalists (such as Casals, Thibaud, and Kreisler) and singers (such as Caruso). He played principal flute at the Opéra-Comique from 1913 to 1938, and frequently performed as a soloist in concert and in some of the earliest recordings of the standard flute repertoire. Before World War I, Moyse took part in several significant world premieres, including Ravel's *Daphnis et Chloé* (1912) and Stravinsky's *Petrushka* and *Rite of Spring* (1913). In 1913, he toured the United States with the great Australian soprano Nellie Melba. While in Europe, he played under the batons of conductors such as Prokofiev, Stravinsky, Strauss, Straram, Koussevitzky, and Toscanini. Ibert dedicated his flute concerto to Moyse, who premiered it in 1934. Also in 1934, Moyse founded the Moyse Trio with his son Louis as pianist and daughter-in-law Blanche Honegger as violinist. Moyse taught at both the Paris Conservatory from 1932 until 1940 and at the Geneva Conservatory until 1949, when he emigrated (via Argentina) to North America. There he became one of the founders of the Marlboro Music Festival, where he taught from 1949 to 1966. From 1961 until his death, he gave yearly master classes for flutists and woodwind players in Brattleboro, VT (where he had set up his residence), as well as in Switzerland and England. Moyse's experience playing in the Paris opera orchestras influenced his teaching; in order to develop tonal flexibility, he encouraged his students to practice nineteenth century operatic arias on the flute. Moyse published many pedagogical works that are still widely used. Some of his most illustrious students include James Galway, Paula Robison, Michel Debost, Trevor Wye, William Bennett, Carol Wincenc, Bernard Goldberg, Robert Aitken, and Julia Bogorad. Moyse won several Grand Prix du Disques and was awarded the French Legion of Honor. *—Robert Adelson*

Recommended:

○ **Marcel Moÿse plays Mozart Flute Concertos** / Coppola, Bigot (conds.), Moyse, Laskine / Pearl 9118

Leopold Mozart

b. Nov. 14, 1719, Augsburg, Germany, **d.** May 28, 1787, Salzburg, Austria
Composer: Concerto

Johan Georg Leopold Mozart was born in Augsburg, Austria, on November 14, 1719, son of a bookbinder. On his father's death in 1736, he was sent to Salzburg to study for the priesthood. When he ended these studies, he found a job as a valet and musician in a noble family. He worked himself up through the ranks and in 1757 became court composer to the Prince-Archbishop of Salzburg. In 1747 he married Anna Maria Pertl. They had seven children, but only two survived. Maria Anna Wallburga Ignatia ("Nannerl") and the great Wolfgang Amadé Mozart. For the rest of his life he held his Salzburg position, educated these children, and directed the career of his son until Wolfgang's majority.

Leopold was a skilled composer of considerable imagination, good enough that some of his own work was confused with that of his son. Most of this music was written in the earlier part of his career; his composition trailed off as he devoted more of his attention to the development (and exploitation) of Wolfgang's talents. Another important contribution to music was his exceptionally fine treatise on violin playing, published in 1756. It details many things about musical expression and ornamentation that have proven invaluable to scholars investigating authentic performance practice. *—Joseph Stevenson*

CONCERTO

Trumpet Concerto in D major (Aug., 1762)

This concerto is one of Leopold Mozart's very few creations—aside from his son—keeping his name alive more than two centuries after his death. Wolfgang was only six years old and not yet a threat to his father's reputation as a composer when Leopold produced this work in an unusual two-movement format. The opening Adagio, complete with harpsichord continuo, provides a stately, graceful introduction for string orchestra and horns, ending in a sighing cadence typical of Austro-Germanic music of the period, especially among composers of the Mannheim school. The trumpet takes up the theme, ornamenting it with trills and venturing high into its range—a brilliant, clarion display despite the measured tempo. Sonata-allegro form had not yet settled into place by 1762, so the development section is little more than a light variation on the theme. Things grow much livelier with the arrival of the Allegro moderato, whose cheerful main theme begins with a passage that may strike American listeners as a Handelian treatment of "The Farmer in the Dell." The theme breaks into a series of trumpet calls, all of which is repeated with some variation and is wrapped up within three minutes. *—James Reel*

Recommended:

○ **Classical Trumpet Concertos** / King (cond.), Steele-Perkins, King's Consort / 2001 / Hyperion 67266

○ **Virtuoso Trumpet** / Ling (cond.), Smedvig, Scottish CO / 1993 / Telarc 80227

Wolfgang Amadeus Mozart

b. Jan. 27, 1756, Salzburg, Austria, **d.** Dec. 5, 1791, Vienna, Austria
Composer: Opera, Symphonic, Concerto, Choral, Keyboard, Orchestral, Chamber Music, Vocal

The incomparable and inimitable Mozart, who signed himself W.A. or Wolfgang Amadé (never "Amadeus" except in jest after 1773), was the lone surviving son of a proud, shrewd, exploitative father. Leopold toured the boy and his sister, Nannerl, as prodigies between 1762 and 1773, from London to Italy via Germany, France, England, the Netherlands, Switzerland, and, of course, Vienna, the Hapsburg capital. Mozart, although frequently and seriously ill, including with typhus and smallpox, spent less than four years at home in Salzburg before 1773. The arrival of a haughty, stingy new archbishop in 1771 curtailed father-son travel time (Nannerl was dropped from the act in 1766). Grudgingly, Leopold sent his wife in 1777 to chaperone an ill-fated trip to Paris (where she died). En route, Mozart fell in love at Mannheim with Aloisia Weber, whose sister Constanze he happily married in 1783, without papa's approval.

Mozart's reprieve from provincial Salzburg came from the Elector of Bavaria: a commission to compose the opera *Idomeneo* for Munich's 1781 Carnival season. From there, the archbishop summoned Mozart to Vienna for the coronation of Joseph II, Maria Theresa's successor, where he dismissed his exasperating employee. From 1782 on, Mozart was his own man (although perpetually nagged by papa, whose funeral in 1787 Mozart boycotted). Vienna emancipated him from a stultifying routine, although before age 20 he had written nine operas, five violin concertos, at least 30 symphonies, a sheaf of divertimentos and serenades, a ream of liturgical pieces, six sonatas, and six concertos for klavier. Several startlingly individual works were not the result of Leopold's tutelage, his son's first and strictest teacher, but came after instruction by Johann Christian, the "London Bach," in 1764–65; Padre Martini in Italy after 1769; and frequent advice from Michael Haydn, Franz Josef's younger brother, appointed musical director at Salzburg in 1762 and indubitably influential after 1771.

Although Mozart achieved celebrity in Vienna early on, Emperor Joseph II never formally employed him despite a high regard for Mozart's genius. Mozart began presenting solo concerts with orchestra, which produced a trove of sublime klavier concertos between 1782 and 1786 with *Nos. 12* to *25*. Only two more followed before his death five years later. After the successful singspiel *Die Entführung aus dem Serail* (The Abduction from the Harem) in 1782, he wrote just two operatic fragments and the single-act *Der Schauspieldirektor* before five final and uniquely brilliant operas. *La nozze di Figaro* offended many aristocratic sponsors, as the Emperor intended when he suggested the subject to librettist Lorenzo da Ponte (although Beaumarchais' original play was banned in Vienna). Prague, however, loved *Figaro* and immediately commissioned *Don Giovanni*. In 1784, Mozart joined the Freemasons, whose ideas would infuse many of his works. The Ottoman War of 1788–90 shuttered Vienna's theaters for two years: ergo, the belated creation of *Così fan tutte*, which Joseph's sudden death suspended after just five performances. When Constanze became chronically ill (six pregnancies in as many years), the family coffers that had been well-filled since 1783 emptied quickly as Mozart had no sense of money management whatsoever. In 1791, however, the *Die Zauberflöte* commission materialized and prospered greatly, followed by a Prague commission for *Tito* to celebrate the coronation of Leopold II (the son whom Maria Theresa had advised, when he was still King of Lombardy, not to engage Mozart as court composer because she considered his father vulgar and greedy). All debts were repaid before Mozart's untimely death, except 1,000 kroner owed a fellow mason, which Constanze settled posthumously. In his last year, Mozart earned the equivalent of 80,000 U.S. dollars, including his fee for the unfinished *Requiem*, completed by a pupil. *—Roger Dettmer*

OPERA

La Clemenza di Tito, K. 621 (1791)

In August 1791, Mozart was commissioned to compose an opera celebrating the coronation of Emperor Leopold II as King of Bohemia at Prague. The coronation was to take place in early September, leaving Mozart with little time to complete the work. Under pressure, Mozart finished the opera in just 18 days, completing some parts in the carriage on the way to the Prague premiere.

The opera, *La Clemenza di Tito*, is a setting of an old libretto by Metastasio, reworked by Caterino Mazzola to reflect the sensibilities of the day. It tells the story of the betrayal of the Roman Emperor Titus and his willingness to pardon those who conspire against him—even Sesto, who attempts to assassinate him. *La Clemenza* is an opera seria or serious opera, as opposed to opera buffa or comic opera; Mozart, however, adds some opera buffa elements to *La Clemenza*, including a number of ensemble finales. Ultimately, the opera is a rather austere Mozartean creation, with its relatively simple melodies, spare orchestral writing, and short numbers. The opera lacks arias in many of the conventional places, giving full-length arias only to the two principal characters. The aria texts themselves are less florid and more forthright than in Metastasio's original. Perhaps Mozart was not terribly inspired by the libretto or by the occasion; his talent was fired by the human dramas of the da Ponte libretti, not by Metastasio's stock characters. However, in the moments when the dramatic situation did catch his imagination, the music and drama are all that one expects from the mature Mozart.

La Clemenza di Tito was composed in Mozart's final year; he died in the winter of 1791. The opera was not successful at its premiere after the coronation banquet.

In fact, it was regarded by many as a complete flop. The opera grew in popularity after 1800, however, and was performed repeatedly in Prague in the early nineteenth century. *La Clemenza* is perhaps somewhat infamous as the opera whose commission interrupted Mozart's work on *The Magic Flute* and the *Requiem*. *—AMG*

Synopsis:

Act One. The story is set in Rome, around 80 A.D. The first scene takes place in the quarters of Vittelia, the daughter of the deposed Roman emperor Vittelius. Vittelia is jealous of Berenice, the Jewish queen for whom Emperor Titus has declared his love. She soon decides that Titus must be punished for toppling her father and thus conceives an assassination plot against him. She cajoles Sextus, who is both enamored of her and a close friend of Titus, into carrying out her scheme. For political reasons, Titus abruptly ends his relationship with Berenice, and Vittellia then decides to abandon the assassination plot. Annius, friend of Sextus, asks the latter to grant him permission to marry his sister, Servilia. Sextus happily accedes to his request.

At the Roman Senate, Titus is praised for his leadership by Publius and Annius. In a private conversation with Sextus and Annius, Titus tells them he must officially renounce Berenice by marrying a Roman woman. He then chooses Sextus' sister, Servilia. Annius, obviously dismayed at the choice, nevertheless praises the emperor's decision, then later sadly informs Servilia of the news.

In a garden in the Palatine Imperial Palace, Servilia informs Titus that she loves Annius, and in line with the Emperor's previously stated views of compassion and forgiveness (which extend even to his enemies), he declares her free to marry him. Vittelia, aware only that Titus has chosen Servilia, decides to go through with the assassination plot and orders Sextus to bring it off.

Publius and Annius inform Vittelia that she has been chosen by Titus to be his consort. She cannot contain her shock at the news, but her reaction is misinterpreted as an outpouring of joy. She now fears it is too late to abort the assassination plans.

Outside the Capitol building, which he has set afire, Sextus laments his treachery. Then Publius arrives, worried over the welfare of Titus. Vittelia searches frantically for Sextus, who reappears and is about to confess his part in the conspiracy. But Vittelia stops him.

Act Two. Annius informs Sextus that Titus has survived, but Sextus breaks down and confesses his guilt without implicating Vittelia. Annius advises him to admit his guilt to Titus and beg his mercy. Vittelia later informs him of his impending arrest, and before he can take flight, Publius arrives with guards and apprehends him. Vittelia fears he will betray her but also appreciates his blind devotion to her.

In a public hall, Titus hears that one of the lead conspirators, Lentulus, has implicated Sextus. He doubts the latter's guilt, but Publius presents his confession and word of his conviction by the Roman Senate. Annius begs him to be merciful, and Titus becomes hesitant over his punishment for Sextus. Sextus is summoned and led in, terrified but determined not to implicate Vittelia. Titus speaks kindly to him and then signs his death warrant, but immediately tears it up, withholding a final decision.

Vittelia is convinced that Sextus has revealed her role in the plot. Annius and Servilia beg her to intercede on his behalf in her new role as Empress-designate. Vittelia now realizes she could not have been chosen by Titus as his empress if Sextus had betrayed her. She decides she must forgo the throne and accept death to save Sextus.

Outside a temple, Titus speaks harshly of Sextus, but before he pronounces his judgment, Vittelia appears and asserts she is the sole guilty party in the plot. Titus is perplexed, but having intended to pardon Sextus anyway, he forgives both. *—Robert Cummings*

Recommended:

- ○ **Mozart: La Clemenza di Tito** / Harnoncourt (cond.), Popp, Langridge, Murray, Ziesak, Zurich Opera Orch. / Teldec 90857
- ○ **Mozart: La Clemenza di Tito** / Hogwood (cond.), Bartoli, Heilmann, Jones, Montague, Academy of Ancient Music / 1995 / L'Oiseau-Lyre 444131

Così fan tutte, K. 588 (1790)

Così fan tutte (All women act that way) is the last of Mozart's three "da Ponte" operas—those composed to libretti by Lorenzo da Ponte (the other two are *Le nozze di Figaro* and *Don Giovanni*). Long neglected and misunderstood, *Così* emerged from obscurity in the twentieth century and has come to be regarded as among the composer's finest, if also most problematic, works.

It has been assumed that the opera was commissioned by Emperor Joseph II, probably sometime during the summer of 1789. Coming as it did during a fallow period in Mozart's output, the work was a financial boon to him and allowed for the repayment of some debt. Little is known about the creation of the work, but the first rehearsal took place in Mozart's apartment on January 21, 1790, and the first performance was at the Burgtheater in Vienna five days later. This initial run was extremely brief, due to Joseph II's death after only five performances had been mounted; the closing of the Viennese theaters prevented any further performances until June.

Da Ponte's libretto is presumed to be an original work, but its numerous literary precedents included episodes in Ovid's *Metamorphosis* as well as da Ponte's own libretto for Martin y Soler's *L'abore di Diana*; the latter was written coincidentally with *Così*. Suggestions that the plot was based on actual events within Viennese society have not been substantiated. Two friends, Ferrando and Guglielmo, wager with Don Alfonso that their lovers, Fiordiligi and Dorabella, will remain constant in their absence. To prove the point, they depart under false pretenses and return as "Albanians" who try to woo the women away.

The libretto has long been considered flimsy, misogynistic, immoral, and dramatically unresolvable. However, any judgement of the opera as a whole must take account of Mozart's exceedingly fine and deeply interesting score. Through music, Fiordiligi transcends her role as the victim of cruel manipulation, revealing a complex personality that is sincere, capable of growth, and inarguably sympathetic. In contrast, Guglielmo never progresses beyond concern for his own ego and interests; his music, fittingly, remains within the stock traditions of opera buffa. Each of the six characters receives an equally insightful portrait, and the ambigous nature of the ending (who actually loves whom?), while vexing to directors and audiences, can be seen as appropriate, given the emotional issues aired during the drama.

The marriage of Mozart's score and da Ponte's libretto represents the apotheosis of the opera buffa genre (making its setting in Naples—the birthplace of the genre—all the more appropriate) and embodies the best of the Classical era. Moments that, at first glance, seem transparent, formulaic, and impersonal become instead clarifying, organic, and genuinely inspired.

There is an unusually large number of vocal ensembles in the score, far more than are found in either *Don Giovanni* or *Figaro*. All of these highlight Mozart's unique fusion of symphonic techniques with lyrical expression. The best-known ensemble is undoubtedly the trio "Soave sia il vento," sung by Fiordiligi, Dorabella, and Don Alfonso, in which farce, grief, and the musical depiction of gentle waves are seamlessly combined to form one of opera's brightest gems. The finales of both acts are typically Mozartean in their complexity, ambition, and symphonic logic, and, especially in the case of the Act One finale, they are arguably finer than those composed for any other of his operas. The combination of logical, restrained structure and lyrical outpouring in these finales encapsulates Mozart's unique operatic voice. *—Allen Schrott*

Synopsis:

Act One. The setting is Naples in the 1700s. Act One opens in a coffeehouse where Ferrando and Guglielmo insist to a cynical Alfonso that their fiancées are incapable of infidelity ("La mia Dorabella"). At his skepticism they demand a duel, but Alfonso instead suggests a bet. If they obey his orders for 24 hours, he can show that the women are fickle. Ferrando and Guglielmo are already planning what they'll do with their winnings ("Una bella serenata"). In their garden, the sisters lovingly contemplate portraits of their men ("Ah, guarda, sorella"). Don Alfonso enters, and in feigned agitation ("Vorrei dir, e cor non ho") says the men have been called to join their regiments to go to battle. The men follow, and the couples bid emotional farewells ("Sento, oddio, che questo piede"). The women swear they will die if their lovers are killed, and the men try to comfort them ("Al fato dan legge"). A military procession passes outside ("Bella vita militar"). The men promise to write, Alfonso snickers to himself, and the women plead for the men to be faithful ("Di scrivermi ogni giorno"). When the men embark, Alfonso and the sisters wish them bon voyage ("Soave sia il vento"). Despina, as she prepares the sisters' morning chocolate, grumbles about her life as a maid and samples the drink. Dorabella and Fiordiligi enter in full melodrama mode, and Dorabella exclaims that only death can heal her pain ("Smanie implacabili"). Despina suggests they take advantage of the men's absence to enjoy some variety in their love lives, since the men are hardly likely to be faithful ("In uomini, in soldati"), but the sisters leave in indignation. Alfonso enters and bribes Despina to help him encourage the sisters to accept two new suitors. The men, disguised as Albanians, enter, and Alfonso introduces them ("Alla bella Despinetta"). As the sisters enter, Alfonso hides, and the men throw themselves at their feet, to the ladies' extreme indignation. Alfonso enters and pretends to recognize them as old friends. The men continue their passionate courtship, and Fiordiligi says she is as constant as a rock amid storms ("Come scoglio"). Guglielmo pleads his cause ("Non siate ritrosi"; sometimes the alternate "Rivolgete a lui lo sguardo" is sung instead), and the women leave. Ferrando and Guglielmo are convinced they've won, Alfonso less so. He sends them outside to wait; Ferrando takes missing dinner philosophically, for love is more nourishing than food ("Un aura amorosa"). Despina assures him that she'll convince the women to see sense, and he assures her of a reward. In the garden, the women lament ("Ah, che tutta in un momento"). The men rush in, pretending not to see them, and despite Alfonso's protests drink "arsenic" and collapse at their feet ("Si mora"). Despina and Alfonso go for help, and the women cautiously draw closer and express their pity. Despina, disguised as a doctor, returns with Alfonso, and she draws a magnet across their bodies, citing Mesmer (a modern equivalent might be using crystals). The men pretend to revive, and they first mistake the women for goddesses ("Dove son"), asking for kisses to complete the cure. The women refuse, but so furiously that the plotters suspect this is a sign of hidden passion.

Act Two. Despina again advises the sisters to accept their suitors, who are handsome, brave, and rich. The women finally ask what they should do. Exasperated, Despina says a girl of 15 should know how to handle men ("Una donna a quindici anni"). Alone, the sisters discuss the situation, and Dorabella decides to take the dark-haired one ("Prendero quel brunettino"), Fiordiligi, the blonde (thus switching). In the garden, Ferrando and Guglielmo sing along with musicians ("Secondate, aurette amiche"). Despina and Alfonso convince the newly arranged couples to overcome their shyness ("La mano a me date"). As they stroll about, Guglielmo gives Dorabella a heart-shaped pendant, which she eventually accepts ("Il core vi dono"). She allows him to take away her locket with a portrait of Ferrando. Fiordiligi is far more difficult to convince, despite Ferrando's persistence ("Ah, lo veggio"). He leaves, and she is tormented by the thought of being unfaithful ("Per pietà, ben mio"). The two men compare notes; Guglielmo is delighted at the news of Fiordiligi's resistance, but Ferrando is furious at Dorabella's capitulation. Guglielmo says that women are adorable but faithless ("Donne mie, le fate a tanti"). Ferrando admits that he still loves Dorabella ("Tradito, schernito"). Alfonso enters and insists that the test isn't over yet. Fiordiligi confides her conflict to Despina and Dorabella, and Dorabella tries to convince her to do what love tells her ("È amore in ladroncello"). Alone, Fiordiligi decides to disguise herself as a man and go join Guglielmo ("Fra gli amplessi"), but when Ferrando enters and pleads with her, she finally gives in, much to the eavesdropping Guglielmo's fury. The men are now both desolate, but Alfonso advises them to take comfort in marrying them since underneath they still love the women, who aren't to blame for their essential nature ("Tutti accusan le donne"). He makes them repeat after him, "Così fan tutte." Despina comes in saying that the women have agreed to marry them and goes to find a notary. In the hall, Despina oversees preparations ("Fate presto, o cari amici"). The chorus sings in celebration ("Benedetti i doppi conjugi"), and Despina enters, disguised as the notary. Just as they are ready to sign, the soldiers are heard returning. The men rush off, to return as themselves ("Sani e salvi"). Despina pretends to drop the marriage contracts, which the men then pick up. The sisters confess and the men reveal the plot, to the amazement of all three women. However, they decide that a rational and optimistic approach to life is best, and the opera ends in relative contentment ("Fortunato l'uom che prende"). *—Ann Feeney*

Recommended:

- **Mozart: Così fan tutte** / Gardiner (cond.), Roocroft, Mannion, Gilfry, Trost, Feller, James / Archiv 437829
- **Mozart: Così fan tutte** / Böhm (cond.), Schwarzkopf, Ludwig, Kraus, Taddei, Berry / 2000 / Angel 67379
- **Mozart: Così fan tutte** / Solti (cond.), Lorengar, Berganza, Davies, Krause, Bacquier / 2003 / Decca 000064312
- **Mozart: Così fan tutte** / Jacobs (cond.), Gens, Fink, Spagnoli, Gura, Boone, Oddone / HM 2901663/65

Don Giovanni, K. 527 (1787)

While in Prague from January–February 1787, attending and conducting performances of his most recently completed opera *Le nozze di Figaro* and concerts of several of his instrumental works, Mozart received a commission from Prague impresario Pasquale Bondini for a new opera, which was to be produced in Prague during October 1787. Mozart returned to Vienna and asked Lorenzo Da Ponte, the librettist for *Figaro*, for another opera libretto. *Don Giovanni* became the second of three opere buffe Mozart would compose to a libretto by Da Ponte, the third of which, *Così fan tutte*, Mozart would complete in early 1790. Da Ponte's libretto shows the influence of Bertati's libretto for Gazzaniga's opera *Convitato di pietra*. The premiere of *Don Giovanni* took place to great public and critical acclaim in Prague on October 29, 1787. The Prague reception of *Don Giovanni* was more positive than that of the opera's first Vienna performances in 1788, for which reviews suggested mild dissatisfaction with the work's extended length and unnecessary plot elaborations.

Mozart creates levels of dramatic expression through recitativo secco, recitative accompagnato, and aria styles. Through recitativo secco, Mozart reveals large amounts of plot information with utmost musical economy. Recitativo accompagnato is reserved for moments of great emotion, in which the accompanying orchestra virtually assumes a dramatic role. In Act II, scene 10(d), the orchestra virtually speaks for the conflicted Donna Elvira, emphatic dotted rhythms in the orchestra conveying her rage and slurred couplets giving musical voice to her sighs. The dramatically stagnant da capo aria that was the mainstay of the operas of George Friedrich Handel is virtually absent from *Don Giovanni*. Leporello's so-called "catalog aria" ("Madamina, il catalogo è questo") in Act One, Scene Five, for example, suggests both through-composed and bi-partite formal elements. Some arias in *Don Giovanni*, however, such as Don Ottavio's Act One, Scene Fourteen aria ("Dalla sue pace"), contain traces of the ternary form idea of returning to beginning material after a section of contrasting music. Donna Elvira's aria in Act Two, Scene Ten (d) ("Mi tradì quell'alma ingrata") juxtaposes ternary and rondo form ideas, reinforcing through musical form Donna Elvira's returning to the same position of pity and longing for Don Giovanni. In keeping with the function of the opera overture to introduce the opera's important themes, the music that begins the overture, marked by alternations between the D minor tonic and its dominant, returns in the Commendatore's scene in Act Two, Scene Fifteen. The drama of this scene is set in relief by the light use popular music in the preceding party scene, where the on-stage musicians play melodies from arias by Martín y Soler, Sarti, and even Mozart's own *Le nozze di Figaro* during Don Giovanni's party. Don Giovanni's canzonetta ("Deh, vieni alla fenestra, o mio tesoro") in Act Two, Scene Three, an airy strophic song scored for pizzicato strings and mandolin, is a similarly witty musical juxtaposition of planes of realism. *—Jennifer Hambrick*

Synopsis:

Act One. The opera is set in Seville, Spain, in the 1600s. Outside the Commendatore's house, Leporello grumbles ("Notte e giorno faticar") that he'd rather be a nobleman than a servant, keeping watch while his master is inside with a woman. He hides as he hears voices, and Don Giovanni, masked, runs in, followed Donna Anna, who calls for help against the seducer. The Commendatore appears; as Anna runs off he challenges Giovanni, who first refuses to fight such an old man, but then agrees. He kills the Commendatore, and Leporello and Giovanni escape. Anna returns with Don Ottavio; finding him dead, she is beside herself with grief. They swear revenge.

Later that morning, Leporello receives permission to speak freely. But when he accuses Giovanni of leading a wicked life, Giovanni threatens to kill him, and Leporello backs down. Giovanni is pursuing a woman but is distracted by the sight of another entering, swearing revenge on the man who betrayed her ("Ah, chi mi dice mai"). He approaches, intending to "console" her, but she angrily recognizes him as the betrayer. He tells her that Leporello will explain why he left her, and takes off. Leporello explains his master's true nature by showing her the ever-growing list of Giovanni's conquests ("Madamina, il catalogo è questo"). Near Giovanni's house, Zerlina, Masetto, and other peasants are celebrating the impending wedding ("Giovinette, che fate all'amore"). Giovanni enters, and, noticing Zerlina, feigns friendship and orders Leporello to take the entire party, except for Zerlina, to his castle to show them the sights. Masetto is forced to agree, though he accuses Zerlina of ruining him ("Ho capito, signor, sì!"). Giovanni courts the indecisive Zerlina, who eventually gives in ("Là ci darem la mano." Elvira enters as they are about to leave and denounces Giovanni ("Ah, fuggi il traditor"), disillusioning Zerlina, who leaves with her. Ottavio and Anna enter, and Giovanni promises to help avenge her father. When Elvira enters, she once again begins accusing him of all kinds of treachery, leaving Anna and Ottavio unsure whether to believe their old friend or this convincing woman. When Giovanni, telling them Elvira is insane, leads her off, Anna recognizes his voice and demands that Ottavio avenge her ("Or sai chi l'onore"). He resolves to determine the truth and restore her peace of mind ("Dalla sua pace"). Leporello and Giovanni return, and Giovanni orders a magnificent party that evening, during which he hopes to expand his list ("Finch'an dal vino").

Outside his house, Zerlina convinces a suspicious Masetto that she is faithful ("Batti, batti, o bel Masetto"), but Giovanni finds them and brings them back inside. Ottavio, Elvira, and Anna enter, masked, and when Leporello invites them in, they pray for Heaven's protection ("Protegga il giusto ciel"). During the festivities, Giovanni attempts to force Zerlina into another room, and when she screams, Anna, Ottavio, and Elvira denounce Giovanni, though he first blames Leporello, threatening to kill him, and then escapes.

Act Two. The act opens with Leporello insisting that he will quit, but a bribe persuades him to stay. He tries to convince Giovanni to give up women, but Giovanni explains that to be faithful to one is to be cruel to all the rest. He then orders Leporello to change clothes with him so that he can seduce Elvira's maid. Elvira herself appears on the balcony, wishing she could stop loving Giovanni ("Ah, taci, ingiusto core"). Giovanni makes Leporello act his part as he calls to Elvira, feigning deep repentance and threatening suicide unless she comes to him. She finally agrees, and when she and Leporello (who she thinks is Giovanni) have left, Giovanni serenades the maid ("Deh, vieni alla finestra"). Masetto and a group of peasants come in, intent on revenge. Giovanni (who they think is Leporello) tells them how to search for Giovanni ("Metà di vio quà vadano") and orders Masetto to stay with him. He gets Masetto to show him his weapons, and then beats him with them for his presumption. Zerlina hears Masetto's groans and consoles him with the thought that her love will soothe all his injuries ("Vedrai, carino").

Outside Anna's home, Leporello is trying to lose Elvira, who is afraid ("Sola, sola in buio loco"). Ottavio and Anna enter, followed by Zerlina and Masetto, and when they see Leporello, Elvira tries to protect him. However, he reveals himself as the servant, not the master, begs for mercy, and escapes. Ottavio is now convinced of Giovanni's guilt, and he tells the others to console Anna while he goes to prepare revenge ("Il mio tesoro intanto"). Elvira, left alone, is torn between her anger and the love she still feels ("Mi tradi quell'alma ingrata"). In a graveyard, Giovanni and Leporello meet and exchange clothes again; Giovanni laughs about his latest attempted conquest, a girl who seems to have been smitten with Leporello. The statue of the Commendatore tells him his laughter will end before dawn. Leporello is terrified, Giovanni intrigued, and he forces Leporello to invite the statue to dinner. Leporello is frozen with fear when the statue nods.

In Anna's house, Ottavio suggests that they marry the next day, and she puts him off although she assures him she loves him ("Non mi dir"). Giovanni is enjoying a lavish supper and teasing Leporello. Elvira bursts in, begging him to repent, to save himself. Giovanni laughs at her. When she runs off, she screams in terror, and Giovanni sends Leporello to find out what the matter is. Leporello comes back, stammering that the statue is there. The statue arrives and orders Giovanni to repent ("Don Giovanni, a cenar teco"). Even when the statue seizes his hand in an icy grip, he refuses. He is cast down to Hell. The others come in, and Leporello tells them of his master's fate. They rejoice in his just punishment ("Or che tutti"). *—Ann Feeney*

Recommended:

- ○ **Mozart: Don Giovanni** / Krips (cond.), Siepi, Della Casa, Corena, Dermota, Berry, Danco / 2000 / Decca 466389
- ○ **Mozart: Don Giovanni** / Gardiner (cond.), Gilfry, D'Arcangelo, Orgonasova, Margiono, James, Prégardien, Clarkson, Silvestrelli / Archiv 445870
- ○ **Mozart: Don Giovanni** / Giulini (cond.), Wachter, Sutherland, Schwarzkopf, Taddei, Frick, Cappuccilli / 2002 / EMI 67873
- ○ **Mozart: Don Giovanni** / Abbado (cond.), Keenlyside, Terfel, Salminen, Heilmann, Isokoski, Pace, D'Arcangelo / 1998 / DG 457601

Die Entführung aus dem Serail (The Abduction from the Seraglio), K. 384 (1782)

Die Entführung aus dem Serail (The Abduction from the Seraglio) was Mozart's first important success. The singspiel (featuring spoken dialogue rather than sung recitatives) was both a wonderful achievement in itself and a gesture to Vienna's infatuation with "Turkish" music. Premiered during the composer's first full year in Vienna (July 1782), it holds a treasure trove of superb arias and ensembles. Requiring virtuoso singing from two of its principals and sustained lyric vocalism from the rest, it is both a charming entertainment and an example of Mozart's finest and most inventive writing.

Aside from the Turkish aspects, Mozart's orchestra here offers a more subtle and sophisticated complement of instruments than found in his earlier operas. Especially noteworthy are the woodwind combinations. Mozart wrote for clarinets in C (seldom used today) and basset horns at the lower end of the tonal spectrum. Horns, too, were varied. Performing decisions must be reached in several instances as to the octave in which the instruments are to be played; Mozart did not specify them. The "Turkish" element had evolved from earlier times to something slightly more specific. The large drum (Tambura Turca'), the cymbals, the piccolo, and the triangle had come from military bands and were employed by Mozart and Haydn (as conductor Nikolaus Harnoncourt has noted) to represent aggressive behavior. Earlier, these instruments had been used primarily for exotic coloration. Here, they signified overt conflict.

The libretto, by Johann Gottlieb Stephanie (who later provided him with the libretto for *Der Schauspieldirektor*), features another popular topic in later eighteenth century drama—the rescue of an abducted heroine. In this instance, she is a lady of noble Spanish birth who has been captured by Barbary pirates and sold into the captivity of the Pasha Selim, who has fallen in love with her. In the end, she is rescued by her beloved, Belmonte, with the assistance of his servant, Pedrillo.

Mozart composed with certain singers already in mind. For Konstanze, he had in mind Katherina Cavalieri, who was a dramatic singer with facility well above top C. The celebrated Ludwig Fischer was selected for Pasha Selim's overseer, Osmin, whose music descends to low D and demands agility rare for a bass as well as a trill, rarer still. Osmin has three major arias, two of them coming at the very beginning of Act One, while the third, "O, Wie will ich Triumphieren," is a centerpiece of the final act. Belmonte requires a fluent tenor of suppleness and suavity. Both Blonde and Pedrillo, too, have arias testing legato and requiring focused tone.

The exotic setting, a Turkish seraglio, was no impediment to the work's popularity. Vivid costumes and foreign stage sets made an immediate impression, and have continued to do so long as producers and directors do not attempt to make *Die Entführung* "relevant."

Die Entführung aus dem Serail is another of those works whose fate depends upon the availability of singers who can manage their difficult roles. Konstanzes are always in short supply. Coloraturas with the desired vocal weight are few in number—and often on call for roles in serious rather than comic works. Osmin is often assigned to artists accomplished in comedy but considerably short on the vocal end. *—Erik Eriksson*

Synopsis:

Act One. The act takes place outside Selim's palace in Turkey. Belmonte approaches cautiously, singing of his hopes of finding his lost beloved, Konstanze ("Hier soll ich dich denn sehen"). Osmin enters and picks figs while singing about the untrustworthiness of women ("Wer ein Liebchen"). Belmonte asks him about the palace and its inhabitants and gets terse answers, but when he asks if Osmin knows Pedrillo, he chases Belmonte away for mentioning that thorn in his side. Pedrillo himself enters, and Osmin sings of his disgust ("Solche hergelauf'ne Laffen") and goes off. Belmonte returns, and Pedrillo tells him that the three of them were captured at sea and are now Selim's prisoners. He is now Selim's gardener, Blonde is Osmin's maid, and Selim is in love with Konstanze. Belmonte tells him that he has a ship waiting in the harbor to rescue them, and Pedrillo suggests that Belmonte can gain entry by pretending to be an architect; architecture is one of Selim's favorite hobbies. Belmonte is torn between hope and fear ("O wie ängstlich, o wie feurig"). Selim arrives with Konstanze, and his Janissaries sing his praises. He asks Konstanze why she is still so unhappy, and she answers that she has been parted from the man she loves ("Ach, ich liebte"). Selim is displeased but privately admits he admires her the more for it. Pedrillo introduces Belmonte, and Selim welcomes him, much to Osmin's indignation, and they enter despite his attempting to block the door ("Marsch, marsch, marsch!").

Act Two. The setting is the palace garden. Osmin orders Blonde to love him, and she refuses, telling him a man courts a woman rather than ordering her ("Durch Zärtlichkeit und Schmiecheln"); when he does not change his tactics, she reminds him she is a free Englishwoman who knows how to defends herself ("Ich gehe, doch rate ich dir"). Konstanze returns, still mourning her lost love ("Traurigkeit ward mir zum Lose"), and when Selim tells her his patience is at an end and threatens her with torture, she defies him, saying that nothing will break her spirit ("Marten aller Arten") and that she would welcome death. He leaves, and Pedrillo tells Blonde that Belmonte is in the palace and will rescue them. She expresses her delight ("Welche Wonne, welche Lust!"), and Pedrillo commands himself to be brave ("Frisch zum Kampfe"). When Osmin returns, he persaudes him to drop his scruples about drinking and share a glass of wine. They eventually join in a drinking song celebrating wine and women ("Vivat Bacchus"), at the end of which Osmin is insensible. Pedrillo drags him off. Belmonte anticipates the joyous reunion ("Wenn der Freude"), and the two couples rush into one another's arms ("Ach, Belmonte! Ach, mein Leben!"). The men briefly stop to question whether the women have been faithful; Konstanze assures Belmonte with her tears, and Blonde convinces Pedrillo by smacking him soundly, but eventually forgives him.

Act Three. In the garden at midnight, Pedrillo and one of Belmonte's sailors bring in ladders. Pedrillo advises Belmonte to sing, to make their presence plausible to the guards who are closing the palace, and he sings of the power of love ("Ich baue ganz auf deine Stärke"). Pedrillo in turn sings about a maiden rescued from her Moorish captors ("In Mohrenland gefangen"). When the coast is clear, the women come down the ladders, but they are discovered. Osmin gloats over their impending fates ("Ha, wie will ich triumphieren"). They are brought inside the palace, and Konstanze begs for mercy for Belmonte. Belmonte, instead, tells Selim that he is from the wealthy Lostados family, who will be glad to ransom them. Selim informs him that Belmonte's father is his bitterest enemy and had him exiled; now that he has Belmonte in his hands, he will act as his enemy would. Selim leaves. Belmonte and Konstanze resign themselves to death ("Welch ein Geschick!"), but when Selim returns, he informs them that rather than descend to his enemy's level, he will offer them clemency so that they can return and inform Belmonte's father of his mercy. Blonde and Pedrillo, too, are set free, despite Osmin's protests, and the opera ends in a chorus of praise, "Bassa Selim lebe lange." *—Ann Feeney*

Recommended:

- ○ **Mozart: Die Entführung aus dem Serail** / Christie (cond.), Schäfer, Petibon, Bostridge, Paton, Ewing, Löw / 1999 / Teldec 25490
- ○ **Mozart: Die Entführung aus dem Serail** / Fricsay (cond.), Stader, Hafliger, Streich, Vantin, Greindl / DG 457730
- ○ **Mozart: Die Entführung aus dem Serail** / Solti (cond.), Gruberova, Battle, Talvela, Winbergh, Zednik, Quadflieg / 1987 / London 417402

Idomeneo, rè di Creta, K. 366 (1781)

Idomeneo, Mozart's first great opera, was the result of a commission from the Elector Karl Theodor of Bavaria. In 1778, the Elector had moved his court to Munich from Mannheim, where Mozart stayed nearly six months during his journey to Paris. By the time he commenced work on the opera in October 1780, Mozart, not yet 25, already had nine operas to his credit.

The libretto chosen was not new, having already been set by the French composer André Campra nearly 60 years earlier; for Mozart's purposes it was revised by Gianbattista Varesco, a Salzburg chaplain. Set on the island of Crete, it recounts the legend of the return of the Cretan king, Idomeneo, to his homeland at the end of the Trojan War. Beset by a storm, Idomeneo promises Neptune a human sacrifice if he and his crew are saved. That the potential sacrifice turns out to be the king's own son, Idamante, becomes the central conflict of the drama.

Idomeneo is often incorrectly termed an opera seria, a static, outmoded form which by Mozart's time had undergone considerable transformation at the hands of Jommelli and others. Although it retains certain elements of the style (da capo arias, for example) *Idomeneo*'s extensive use of the chorus, flexibility, and strong sense of action betrays a strong sense of the libretto's French origins; this observation is underlined by the inclusion of tableaux of the kind that appear in the operas of Rameau and Gluck. The opera concludes with an extensive ballet, an essential component of all French opera, but then only recently introduced to Italian opera by reformers such as Traetta.

One of the great glories of the work is the orchestration. Mozart obviously relished writing for the large and outstanding orchestra attached to the Elector's court, many of whose members had formerly belonged to the Mannheim orchestra, the finest in Europe. The score he produced includes pairs of flutes, oboes, clarinets, and bassoons along with four horns, two trumpets, three trombones, and strings; it is the richest of all his operatic scores, and it drew contemporary criticism for being "too much filled up with accompaniments."

Dramatically, too, *Idomeneo* shows a marked advance on the traditional opere serie Mozart had composed in Italy less than a decade before. That he had now become a complete man of the theater is shown in a remarkable correspondence with Varesco, who remained in Salzburg after Mozart had gone to Munich to work with the singers. The letters show Mozart not only tailoring the arias to the needs of his singers, as was customary, but also acutely aware of what would and would not work dramatically.

Idomeneo was given its first performance at the Residenz Theater on January 29, 1781; the spectacular staging was particularly praised in the sole contemporary account that was preserved. The opera was not taken up elsewhere, doubtless in part due the demanding orchestral writing, but also because its mixture of Italian and French styles was confusing to contemporary expectations. Mozart did adapt and revive the opera in Vienna in 1786, but *Idomeneo* has had to wait until the twentieth century to be fully accepted into the repertory. *—Brian Robins*

Synopsis:

Act One. The opera is set at the end of the Trojan War as the triumphant Greeks return home. The ship of the Cretan king Idomeneo is destroyed in a storm as it approaches the shore, and the king has made a bargain with Neptune, the sea god: if he is allowed to live, he will sacrifice the first person he meets on land. In a dungeon in the royal palace, Ilia, daughter of the defeated King Priam of Troy, is held prisoner. She is in love with Idamante, Idomeneo's son, but she is afraid that his heart belongs to another, Elettra ("Padre, germani, addio!"). Idamante sets Ilia free and tells her that he loves her ("Non ho colpa"). She does not let on how she feels. At this point comes a mistaken report that Idomeneo has died in the storm. Elettra despairs of her future when she observes the interaction between Ilia and Idamante ("Tutte nel cor vi sento").

Idomeneo struggles to safety on the shore ("Eccoci salvi alfin... Vedrommi intorno"). He encounters Idamante, but in the raging storm father and son do not recognize each other. Idomeneo prepares to carry out the sacrifice specified by his bargain with Neptune, but gradually he realizes who the stranger is. To Idamante's dismay, he runs off ("Il padre adorato").

Act Two. At the palace Idomeneo explains his situation to his confidant Arbace, who suggests that Idomeneo send Idamante and Elettra away to her homeland of Argos. With Idamante out of danger, they can then propitiate Neptune in some other way. Ilia worries about whether Idomeneo agrees with his son's decision to release her from prison ("Se il padre perdei"). Idomeneo reassures her, but now he begins to realize that Idamante and Ilia are in love. He fears that the love affair will only anger Neptune, and that he has only made things worse by agreeing to the release of Ilia along with other Trojan prisoners. Now, he says, there are three souls on the chopping block: Idamante, Ilia, and himself ("Qual mi conturba i sensi... Fuor del mar").

Elettra prepares to leave Crete with Idamante, telling herself that once they put some distance between themselves and Ilia she will gain Idamante's love ("Idol mio, se ritroso"). But another big storm begins to blow before they can take to the water ("Pria di partir, o Dio"). A fearsome monster appears in the furious waters, and the populace fears the displeasure of Neptune. Idomeneo accepts the blame in general terms but keeps silent about his bargain and its aftermath, but still does not tell of his shocking vow ("Eccoti in me, barbaro Nume").

Act Three. At the palace Idamante sets off to fight the monster and tells Ilia goodbye. Fearing that he will be killed, Ilia tells him that she loves him ("S'io non moro a questi accenti"). After this duet, Elettra and Idomeneo enter. The king reiterates his command that Idamante leave but still does not explain his seeming heartlessness as a classic Mozartean ensemble of at-odds aims and emotions ensues ("Andrò ramingo e solo").

Arbace enters and says that the Cretan people are in rebellion and demand that Idomeneo meet with their High Priest. The priest tells the king that the sea monster has attacked the island; many people have been killed, and there is blood running in the streets ("Volgi intorno lo sguardo"). Finally Idomeneo reveals the reason for the trials the Cretans are experiencing. When they hear Idamante must be sacrified, the Cretans are horrified ("O voto tremendo").

Their dismay increases as the time of the sacrifice approaches ("Accogli, o re del mar"), for news comes that Idamante has vanquished the monster. Idamante finally figures out what has been happening and realizes that his father has tried to spare him from the sacrifice that is being readied. He says that he will agree to be sacrificed ("Padre, mio caro padre—O figlio! o caro figlio!"). But now Ilia intervenes and says that she will be the one to take the fatal stroke of Idomeneo's sword ("Ferma, o sire, che fai?").

A rushing sound is heard all around, and the voice of the god's oracle proclaims that love is victorious ("Ha vinto Amor"). Idomeneo must relinquish his kingship and install Idamante as the new ruler, with Ilia as queen. There is general happiness on the part of all except Elettra, who sings a fiery aria of rage ("O smania! o furie!... D'Oreste, d'Aiace"). The opera ends as Idomeneo addresses the Cretan people to seal the deal ("Popoli, a voi l'ultima legge"). There is singing and dancing as Idamante is elevated to the throne. *—James Manheim*

Recommended:

○ **Mozart: Idomeneo** / Mackerras (cond.), Smith, Bostridge, Johnson, Milne, Scottish CO / 2002 / EMI 57260

Le nozze di Figaro (The Marriage of Figaro), K. 492 (1786)

Lorenzo da Ponte wrote the libretto for Mozart's *Figaro* after falling out with Antonio Salieri, who, as imperial court composer, had obtained the position of court poet for da Ponte. At the time of the opera's composition and first performances, there was a climate of antagonism among factions of Italian musicians and poets living in Vienna, among whom was counted Salieri. Although the efforts of the anti-Mozart Italian clique did not succeed in having Mozart's *Figaro* banned from the stage, the opera did receive fewer than ten performances in Vienna immediately after its première at the Burgtheater on May 1, 1786. *Figaro* would have tremendous success in Prague, however, before spreading to other parts of Europe and becoming a classic of the opera buffa repertory. So began the fortuitous Mozart/da Ponte relationship, from which would come two further masterworks, *Don Giovanni* (1787) and *Così fan tutte* (1789–90).

Mozart admired Pierre Auguste Caron de Beaumarchais' politically radical play *Le mariage de Figaro* (1781), the second play in what would become a trilogy based on the autobiographical character Figaro. Beaumarchais' *Le barbier de Séville* had been performed in 1775 and the third play of the trilogy, *La mère coupable*, would be premièred in 1793. In his Figaro plays, Beaumarchais, who himself was a participant in the Revolution, working towards anti-aristocratic revolutionary ideas, sharply spoofs pre-Revolution French society.

Mozart's music for *Figaro* consists of conventional dry and accompanied recitative, aria, and ensemble pieces. The overture, despite having no development section, is essentially in sonata form. Mozart musically conveys the range of Figaro's perturbation in his Act One cavatina, "Se vuol ballare," by whimsically changing the character of his music to correspond with Figaro's machinations. Mozart also imbues Figaro's rondo-form aria, "Non più andrai, farfallone amoroso," with colorful musical depictions of Cherubino's forthcoming military service through dotted rhythms and trumpet arpeggio fanfares. The Countess' cavatina, "Porgi amor," conveys the character's elevated social status through its graceful melodic language. The duet ("Aprite, presto, aprite") between Susanna and Cherubino in Act Two bristles expectantly with its moto perpetuo string writing and nervous, patter vocal declamation. In the Count's and Susanna's Act Three duet ("Crudel! Perchè finora"), the minor mode conveys the Count's initial grief and a shift to major mode, after Susanna agrees to come to the garden, confirms a sense of momentary resolution. Later, in the Count's accompanied recitative ("Hai già vinta la causa!"), the orchestra adds an extra emphasis to his verbal expression of anger and agitation through impetuous dotted rhythms and string tremolos. Through furiously rapid-scale passages and trills, the orchestra maintains this angry intensity in the Count's vengeance aria ("Vedrò mentr'io sospiro"). Barbaina's Act Four cavatina, "L'ho perduta... me meschina!" introduces a minor mode melody of classic Mozartean pathos. The finale of Act Four brings the principal characters to beg the Count's forgiveness and the music swells from a pious hymn-like ensemble to a triumphant fanfare-laden exultation. *—Jennifer Hambrick*

Synopsis:

Act One. The setting is Spain in the eighteenth century. Figaro measures a room for the new bed he will share with his bride, and Susanna tries on her wedding hat. She persuades him to stop and admire it ("Cinque... dieci..."). When he says the Count has given them the room, she retorts that it's because the Count wants her, not Figaro, convenient. She leaves, and Figaro declares that if the Count wants to dance ("Se vuol ballare"), Figaro will call the tune. He leaves, and Bartolo and Marcellina enter. Bartolo is helping Marcellina sue Figaro to repay a loan or marry her ("La vendetta"). Bartolo leaves, and when Susanna returns, she and Marcellina trade insults in the guise of compliments, ending when Marcellina is bested and storms off. Cherubino enters, distraught; the Count has caught him with Barbarina and dismissed him. Susanna teases Cherubino about his crush on the Countess, and he describes how the mere thought of love enraptures him ("Non so più"). The Count enters. Cherubino hides behind the chair and thus overhears the Count making advances to Susanna. Basilio comes in, and the Count himself hides behind the chair while Cherubino darts around and hides *in* it; Susanna covers him with a dress. Basilio promotes the Count's cause with Susanna and then gossips about Cherubino, suggesting that he is in love with the Countess. The Count emerges in a fury and finds Cherubino yet again. Figaro leads a group of village maidens in, and they sing in praise of the Count's abolition of the *droit du seigneur,* the right of the lord to have his way with his female servants ("Giovani liete"). Saying that proper festivities will require more time, the Count delays the marriage of Figaro and Susanna and also assigns Cherubino to a place in his regiment. The Count leaves, and Figaro mercilessly teases Cherubino about the glorious but far less luxurious life of a soldier ("Non più andrai").

Act Two. The Countess sighs over the Count's infidelities ("Porgi, amor"). Susanna enters and explains the Count's plans for herself, and Figaro comes in. He has sent an anonymous letter to the Count saying the Countess is meeting a lover, and he tells Susanna to agree to meet the Count but to send Cherubino, dressed as a girl, in her place. The Countess will catch the Count and teach him a lesson. Figaro leaves, and Cherubino enters. He sings another song for them, asking them to explain what love is ("Voi che sapete"). They start to dress him as a girl, finding the unsealed army commission ("Venite... inginocchiatevi"). Susanna leaves, and the Count, who has received the letter, pounds on the door. The Countess hides Cherubino in the closet and then admits the Count, who becomes enraged when he hears someone. The Countess says it is Susanna, but she refuses to open the door. He makes her leave with him while he gets tools to break in. Susanna has overheard, and Cherubino quickly jumps out the window. When the Count and Countess return, he is dumbfounded and is forced to ask for her forgiveness. Figaro returns, followed a moment later by Antonio, who complains that someone jumped from the window and broke his flowerpots. The Count's suspicions revive, but Figaro says he had come to get Cherubino's commission sealed, but jumped in fear at hearing the Count raging. Marcellina and Bartolo make their case, and the Count gladly rules that Figaro must pay or marry Marcellina.

Act Three. As the act opens, the Count is utterly confused. Susanna comes to agree to meet him that night ("Crudel! perchè finora"). She leaves, telling Figaro in passing that they have won, and the Count, overhearing, rages that a mere servant won't enjoy what he himself cannot have ("Hai gia vinta... Vedrò, mentr'io sospiro"). When Marcellina and Bartolo appear, Figaro tells them he can't marry Marcellina without his parent's permission, and since he is a foundling, well... Marcellina is revealed as his mother and Bartolo as his father, and the family embraces. Susanna returns to find Figaro embracing Marcellina. At first she slaps him, but then the situation is explained. The Count goes off in a huff, and the four arrange for a double wedding. Barbarina tells Cherubino to dress like a girl so he can return. The Countess again laments the loss of the Count's love ("Dove sono"). Antonio tells the Count that Cherubino is somewhere around; he has found his clothes. Susanna and the Countess compose a letter for Susanna to give to the Count, arranging the meeting ("Su l'aria"); they seal it with a pin, asking the Count to return it. Peasant girls, including Cherubino in disguise, bring the Countess flowers ("Ricevete, o padroncina"), and the Count and Antonio return, Antonio revealing Cherubino's disguise. Barbarina rescues the situation by reminding the Count that he once promised to give her anything she wanted. She asks to marry Cherubino, promising to love the Count as she does her kitten. During the wedding dance, Susanna passes the letter to the Count, while Figaro notices but thinks it is from some other woman.

Act Four. Barbarina looks for the pin, which the Count has sent her to find ("L'ho perduta, me meschina"). Figaro discovers that Susanna sent the note, and Marcellina tries to calm him. But he runs off. Marcellina wonders why, of all animals, only the human male is cruel to the female ("Il carpo e la capretta"). Figaro bemoans woman's infidelity ("Aprite un po'"). Susanna and the Countess enter, wearing one another's clothes; Susanna sees Figaro watching and decides to punish him for his jealousy by singing a love song ("Guinse alfin... Deh, vieni, non tardar"). In the various confused scenes that follow, the Count is caught making love to his own wife, whom he thinks is Susanna; when the deception is revealed, he begs his wife's forgiveness ("Contessa, perdona"). She agrees, and the opera ends with all the couples united. *—Ann Feeney*

Recommended:

- ○ **Mozart: Le Nozze di Figaro** / Gardiner (cond.), Terfel, Hagley, Martinpelto, Gilfry, Stephen / Archiv 439871
- ○ **Mozart: Le Nozze di Figaro** / Solti (cond.), Te Kanawa, Popp, Von Stade, Ramey, Allen, Moll / 1983 / Decca 410150
- ○ **Mozart: Le Nozze di Figaro** / Kleiber (cond.), della Casa, Siepi, Danco, Poell, Corena / 1999 / Decca 466369
- ○ **Mozart: Le Nozze di Figaro** / Giulini (cond.), Taddei, Schwarzkopf, Moffo, Cossotto, Wachter / 1989 / EMI 63266

Il rè pastore, K. 208 (1775)

In the spring of 1775, the 19-year-old Mozart was commissioned by his employer, the Archbishop of Salzburg, to write an opera to celebrate the visit to Salzburg of the Archduke Maximillian Franz, the youngest son of the empress Maria Theresa. The libretto chosen was *Il rè pastore* (The Shepherd King) by Pietro Metastasio, the most famous of all opera seria librettists. More than a quarter of a century old, it had already been set at least 14 times by other composers before being adapted for Mozart by the Archbishop's chaplain Gianbattista Varesco, later the librettist of Mozart's greatest serious opera, *Idomeneo.* The plot, based on Tasso's *Aminta* (1581), is set in the time of Alexander the Great. Having liberated Sidon from the tyrannical Stratone, Alessandro wishes to place Aminta, the rightful heir, on the throne. The latter has been living as a shepherd, happy in his love for the nymph Elisa. Alessandro's well-intentioned plan leads to a variety of misunderstandings before being happily resolved as Aminta takes the throne with Elisa as his consort. The stiff, old-fashioned plot, with its exploration of the popular Enlightenment topic of the contrast between noble duty and the innocence of pastoral life, allowed the young Mozart little opportunity for dramatic development. The opera does, however, include some fine arias, of which Aminta's "L'amero" has gained sufficient popularity to lead an independent life. *Il rè pastore* was first performed at the Archbishop's palace on April 23, 1775. Little is known of the first performance; the work waas variously and confusingly described in contemporary accounts as a "serenata" or "cantata." The latter designation in particular suggests that the work may even have been given a concert rather than a staged performance. *—Brian Robins*

Synopsis:

Act One. The opera is set in the time of Alexander the Great, in southeastern Europe in the fourth century B.C.E. The first act takes place in a meadow near the city of Sidon as Aminta, who is in reality the legitimate king of Sidon, is herding sheep. His girlfriend Elisa tells him she has heard that the Macedonian king Alessandro will soon discover the true king of Sidon and will install him on the throne. Caring little for political intrigue, Aminta gives thanks to the gods for his simple shepherd's life and for Elisa's love. But King Alessandro and his associate Agenore enter. Agenore, who knows that Aminta is the real king of Sidon, introduces him to Alessandro, who is pleased with his sincerity. As he leaves, Alessandro remarks to Agenore that Aminta will make a good king of Sidon.

Tamiri, a woman in love with Agenore and maltreated by Alessandro, enters. Agenore asks her to go away with him, but Tamiri says that she can't; Alessandro has destroyed her reputation. Elisa enters with good news for Aminta: her father has agreed to their marriage. But Agenore startles the couple by revealing that Aminta is in reality Abdolonymus, King of Sidon. Aminta is fearful of his new responsibilities, but Elisa tells him it is his duty to rule; he should only remain true to her, for she is the one who adores him.

Act Two. In the Macedonian camp, Elisa looks for Aminta. Agenore tells her she must leave, but Aminta sees her. Agenore tells him his primary duty is to Alessandro, and Aminta observes that he had more freedom when he was only a simple shepherd. Alessandro is planning to leave Sidon, and he announces that Tamiri, the daughter of one of his rival princes, will be given to Aminta in marriage in order to cement the region's political situation. He sends the shocked Agenore to find Tamiri, but Agenore instead runs into Aminta, en route to meet with Alessandro. Agenore tells Aminta to love the person he was destined for, and Aminta, knowing nothing of what has happened, says that certainly he will.

Agenore next encounters Elisa, who has heard about Alessandro's edict and wants to know whether the rumors are true. Agenore says that they are, but Elisa reserves judgment. Then Agenore finally finds Tamiri, who has also heard the news and is angry that she didn't hear it from Agenore personally. The suffering Agenore stammers in reply, and Tamiri sarcastically invites him to the wedding. He sadly accepts.

Alessandro is anxious to get the ceremony underway, but he runs into strong resistance from all involved. Tamiri enters and beseeches him to relent. The feisty Elisa tells him that he has stolen her happiness away. Finally Aminta informs Alessandro that he must give up his kingship if keeping it would mean the loss of Elisa.

All these pleas move the heart of the fundamentally just Alessandro, an Enlightenment ruler in ancient clothing. He announces that he will not block the future happiness of the two couples: Elisa will be elevated to Queen of Sidon, and Agenore and Tamiri not only may marry but also will be installed as monarchs of a different part of the kingdom. All sing the praises of Alessandro and of the power of love. *—James Manheim*

Recommended:

- ○ **Mozart: Il rè pastore** / Marriner (cond.), Constable, McNair, Hadley, Vermillion, Academy of St. Martin-in-the-Fields / 1991 / Philips 422535
- ○ **Mozart: Il rè pastore** / Harnoncourt (cond.), Murray, Mei, Nielsen, Sacca, Vienna Concentus Musicus / 1996 / Teldec 98419

Der Schauspieldirektor, K. 486 (1786)

In February 1785, Emperor Joseph II of Austria had given a lunch party, called "Spring Festival on a Winter's Day," in the long orangery of Schönbrunn Castle—the only hall that could be satisfactorily heated during the winter months. Having been pleased with the result, the Emperor wished to repeat the event in January 1786 in honor of his sister, the Archduchess Christine Marie, and her husband, Duke Albrecht Kasimir of Sachsen-Teschen. For entertainment, Joseph commissioned two musical parodies, one Italian, and one German. The Italian piece, *Prima la musica, e poi le parole*, was assigned to his court composer, Antonio Salieri, and the German *Der Schauspieldirektor* (The Impresario) went to Mozart.

While imperial orders for such a work may have come as an unwelcome interruption to Mozart (who was hard at work on *Le Nozze di Figaro* and his *Piano Concerto, K. 482 in E Flat*), he can hardly have failed to have gained a certain wry satisfaction from the libretto, furnished him by his friend Johann Gottleib Stephanie—for it concerned the tribulations of an impresario trying to mount a performance of an opera. Cast in one short act, the opera has just four numbers: one aria for each of the two sopranos (who quarrel relentlessly over which of them is the better), a trio in which the impresario (tenor) attempts to placate them, and a finale which points up the moral responsibility of all artists to devote themselves to their craft, and not to fame. The soprano arias, in particular, are vocal showpieces as well as effective comic moments. Mozart prefaced this short divertissement with an unexpectedly well-developed overture.

Both operas were duly performed in the orangery on February 7, and the event was fully reported in the Viennese press. One publication suggested that Mozart's "German piece infinitely surpassed the Italian one (Salieri's) in intrinsic value". Unfortunately for Mozart, such assessments were not reflected in his fee, which court records show to have been half the amount paid to Salieri (though, in fairness, the work commissioned from Salieri was more substantial). Later in February, three further performances of both works were given at the Kärntnertor-Theatre. Despite its brevity and occasional character, *Der Schauspieldirektor* has remained popular, and modern productions often update its satirical humor to contain contemporary references. *—Brian Robins*

Synopsis:

This work, essentially a brief singspiel, features seven spoken roles as well as several prominent singing parts. Frank, an impresario, and Buff, a comic singer, are in the midst of creating a theatrical troupe, consisting of actors and singers, for productions in Salzburg. Frank begins auditioning actors, and in the course of the endeavor encounters little trouble from the performers in filling the needed positions.

But when he begins auditioning for a soprano, turmoil (and much hilarity) ensues. First to perform is Madame Herz, who sings a "pathetic" aria. Mademoiselle Silberklang follows with a graceful rondo. Both women are quite good, but only one, of course, is needed by the company. Aware of this harsh reality, the two begin arguing over who should be selected in a brilliant trio, in which they are joined by Vogelsang, the troupe's tenor. In the end, both sopranos are hired for handsome sums and offered star treatment. *—Robert Cummings*

Recommended:

○ **Mozart: Zaide; Der Schauspieldirektor** / Davis (cond.), Cotrubas, Johnson, Grant, Adamberger, London SO / 1991 / Philips 422536

○ **Mozart: The Impresario; Mozart's Circle: The Beneficent Dervish** / Pearlman (cond.), Aler, Ewing, Deas, Baker, Boston Baroque / 2002 / Telarc 80573

Die Zauberflöte (The Magic Flute), K. 620 (1791)

Despite its whimsical libretto and obviously emblematic characters, Mozart's singspiel *The Magic Flute* is regarded as one of the greatest operas of the entire repertoire. In fact, as music historian Philip Downs has noted, many hold that *The Magic Flute* is among the greatest human documents, worthy to stand beside Bach's *St. Matthew's Passion*. In this story about good and evil, Sarastro, the high priest of an enlightened brotherhood, abducts Pamina, whose mother is the evil Queen of the NIght. The Queen sends Prince Tamino to save Pamina. Tamino not only falls in love with Pamina, but also accepts Sarastro as the incarnation of truth and goodness. Tamino's counterpart is Papageno, the Queen's bird catcher, whose earthiness counterbalances Tamino's idealism. Predictably, love and goodness triumph, Sarastro overcomes the Queen of the Night, Tamino and Pamina are united after many trials, and Papageno finds Papagena, a female version of himself. The possible sources of Emanuel Schikaneder's libretto include Jakob August Libeskind's story "Lulu or the Magic Flute," published in Wieland's *Dschinnistan*, a collection of fairy tales.

The Magic Flute was written in 1791, the year of Mozart's death. Although overwhelmed by many adversities, Mozart found great joy in working on an opera for Schikaneder's Theater auf der Wieden, in the suburbs of Vienna, which catered to unsophisticated audiences. *The Magic Flute* has been called a Masonic opera: both librettist and composer were Masons, and the opera abounds with Masonic symbolism, culminating in the triumph over light over darkness. Although the Masonic flavor of *The Magic Flute* is undeniable, what makes it a great work of art is Mozart's unique ability to translate his humanistic ideals into music of extraordinary beauty and evocativeness. The fundamental theme of this opera is love, a theme to which Mozart fully dedicates his entire genius. To the listener, Mozart's ode to love brings eighteenth century opera in its full splendor. Not only is the music, which includes sparkling arias, charming buffo scenes, and ensembles of transcendent beauty, enchanting and invigorating, but it also effectively coalesces with the story to create a powerful, convincing work of art. *—AMG*

Synopsis:

Act One. Tamino is pursued by a serpent. He falls unconscious, and three Ladies emerge and kill it. They leave to tell the Queen, none of them agreeing to leave the others alone with him. Tamino recovers, but hides as Papageno, all dressed in feathers, swaggers in ("Der Vogelfanger bin ich ja"), introducing himself as the birdcatcher who wants to catch a wife. Tamino emerges and Papageno takes credit for killing the serpent. The Ladies return and give Papageno water instead of wine and padlock his lips to punish his lying. The Ladies give Tamino Pamina's portrait, and he immediately falls in love ("Dies Bildnis ist bezaubernd schon"). They tell him an evil magician kidnapped her, and the Queen appears and plaintively asks him to rescue Pamina ("O zittre nicht"). She disappears and the Ladies take the lock off the gesticulating, whimpering Papageno, who promises never to lie again ("Hm! hm! hm! hm!").They give Tamino a magic flute and Papageno magic bells, and tell them that three young boys will guide them. In Sarastro's castle, the slaves exult that Pamina has escaped and Monastatos will pay with his life. However, Monastatos has found her and drags her in, and she faints. Papageno timidly enters, and he and Monastatos panic at the sight of one another. Monastatos rushes off, and Papageno tells Pamina that Tamino will rescue her. They agree that love is good ("Bei Mannern, weiche Liebe fuhlen"). Outside three temples, the boys advise Tamino to be manly. The Temples of Reason and Nature turn him away, but at the Temple of Wisdom, the priest says women have deceived him, and that Sarastro is good, not evil. Voices tell him that Pamina is alive, and he thankfully plays his flute ("Wie stark ist"), entrancing the wild animals. As Papageno and Pamina run to find him, Monastatos stops them. Papageno plays the bells, which send him and his men off, dancing. Sarastro and his entourage arrive and Pamina confesses that she ran away, to avoid Monastatos' attentions and to find her mother. He tells her she must be guided by a man, not a woman, and Monastatos brings in Tamino. Sarastro orders that Monastatos be beaten and Papageno and Tamino be taken into the temple for testing.

Act Two. Sarastro asks the priests of Isis and Osiris to accept Tamino as a potential initiate, and they agree. Tamino and Papageno are alone in the temple's forecourt, Papageno already frightened. The Speaker asks Tamino if he is ready to face death to achieve virtue, and Tamino readily agrees. Papageno declines until a priest tells him that Sarastro has a wife for him, his very own female counterpart. The Speaker and the Second Priest solemnly warn them against trusting women ("Bewhret euch"), ordering both of them not to talk, as the first test. After the priests leave, the Ladies burst in, telling them that Sarastro will kill them. Papageno starts to ask questions, despite Tamino's warnings, but sudden thunder sends the Ladies away. The Speaker returns and leads Tamino away, congratulating him for his success, and the first priest leads Papageno away. In a garden, Monastatos finds Pamina asleep and tries to steal a kiss, ("Alles fuhlt der Liebe Freuden"). The Queen appears in a peal of thunder and orders him away. Pamina falls into her arms, but the Queen tells her that she is powerless to protect her, and orders Pamina to kill Sarastro. When Pamina protests, the Queen declares that should Pamina disobey, she will renounce her ("Die Holle Rache"). She disappears, and Monastatos, who has been hiding, demands Pamina's love in order to save her and her mother. Sarastro appears and drives him away, and when Pamina asks Sarastro not to hurt her mother, he says that in their sacred halls, vengeance has no place ("In diesen heil'gen Hallen"). The priests tell Tamino and Papageno to prepare for the second test. An old woman comes in and Papageno begins flirting. She tells him she is Papagena, his sweetheart, and leaves. The three boys bring in a banquet, and Tamino plays his flute while Papageno stuffs himself. Pamina comes in, but Tamino remains silent. Not understanding, she longs for death ("Ach ich fuhl's"). Papageno is reluctant to leave at the summons, but the appearance of the temple lions convinces him. The priests praise Tamino's bravery and he and Pamina are joyously reunited. A priest tells Papageno he will never be initiated, which doesn't disturb Papageno in the least. What he wants is a girlfriend or wife ("Ein Madchen oder Weibchen"), and he plays his bells. The old woman appears and tells him he must marry her or remain there forever, with only bread and water to live on. He reluctantly agrees, and she changes into the young and lovely (and feathered) Papagena, though she is forced to leave until he is worthy. The three boys watch as Pamina enters, desperate and suicidal, thinking Tamino no longer loves her, but they assure her he loves her and they will be united. Tamino faces tests of fire and water, and Pamina insists on accompanying him. He plays his flute and they pass through safely. Papageno, without his Papagena, is about to hang himself, but the boys tell him to play his bells. Papagena promptly appears, and they plan their future, with plenty of little Papagenos and Papagenas on the way ("Pa-pa-pa-pa-pa-pa-Papagena!"). Monastatos, to whom the Queen has promised Pamina, the Queen, and the Ladies attempt to enter the temple to destroy it, but the ground swallows them up. Inside the temple, Sarastro and the priests celebrate Tamino's and Pamina's victory and the triumph of the sun over night. *—Ann Feeney*

Recommended:

○ **Mozart: Die Zauberflöte** / Solti (cond.), Heilmann, Ziesak, Kraus, Jo, Moll / 1991 / London 433210

○ **Mozart: Die Zauberflöte** / Böhm (cond.), Wunderlich, Lear, Fischer-Dieskau, Peters, Crass / DG 449749

○ **Mozart: Die Zauberflöte** / Klemperer (cond.), Gedda, Janowitz, Berry, Schwarzkopf, Popp, Ludwig, Frick, Crass / 2000 / Angel 67385B

○ **Mozart: Die Zauberflöte** / Marriner (cond.), Te Kanawa, Studer, Araiza, Ramey, Bär, Lind, Van Dam / 1990 / Philips 426276

SYMPHONIC

Symphonies Nos. 1–24 (1765–1773)

Mozart composed his first symphonies (E flat major, K. 16; D major, K. 19; and F major, K. Anh. 223/19a) while in London, in 1764–65. In December 1765 he wrote one in B flat major, K. 22, and another in G major, K. Anh. 221/45a, in March 1766, while in The Hague. All are in three movements, and the London examples are very much in the style of J.C. Bach and Carl Friedrich Abel. The Allegro first movements are in rounded binary form and 4/4 meter, the slow movements are in 3/4 meter and in either the subdominant or relative minor, and the finales are in 3/8 meter. Although filled with cliché, K. 16 does feature some melodic invention in the second theme of the Allegro. K. 19 and K. 22 are more mature, with more assured orchestration and imitative passages.

The seven symphonies Mozart composed in 1767–68 are in the Viennese style, with four movements, the third of which is a minuet and trio. Mozart obtained some key contrast in the minuet and trio movements, setting the minuets in the tonic and the trios in various related keys. In the opening movement of K. 48 we find his first substantial development section and full recapitulation; Mozart was beginning to move away from the binary forms favored by J.C. Bach.

During Mozart's first journey to Italy (December 1769–March 1771), he composed five known symphonies (K. 81, 97, 95, 84 and 74). Two (K. 81 and 84) are in four movements, the rest in three. Aspects of Italian style are clear in their light texture, lively string figurations and expositions without repeats (this being a feature of the Italian opera overture). All but one have complete recapitulations, but with little or no development. Most notable is Mozart's use of G minor for the alla turca episode in the G major symphony, K. 74.

Between March 1771 and August 1771, Mozart composed another 12 symphonies, in Salzburg and during a journey to Italy. With these works we find Mozart moving to a new level of maturity. Most are in four movements, and nearly all the first movements are in sonata form with full recapitulations. Mozart's ability to expand and develop an idea grows in these works, such as the Allegro of K. 114, in which the opening, cantabile melody is altered into the material that begins to lead away from the tonic. Mozart creates large-scale instability in the Allegro maestoso of K. 128, with its two-beat pattern in the theme at the beginning of a triple meter movement. The harmonic instability of the exposition is greater than that of the development and is one of Mozart's earliest attempts at Sturm und Drang. In K. 133, Mozart writes a type of "mirror-image" recapitulation in which the beginning of the movement appears last. In the opening of the Symphony in A, K. 134, we hear a rising and falling melody that progresses in a manner that betrays Mozart's intense study of Haydn's works. The tune consists of rhythmically aggressive arpeggios separated by sighing melodic material. These fragments, sometimes inverted, make up the entire first theme as well as the transitional material and their combination into a melodic unit represents a greater understanding of thematic construction than we find in Mozart's earlier works. *—John Palmer*

Recommended:

○ **Mozart: Early Symphonies** / Kehr (cond.), Mainz CO / 1992 / Vox 5070

○ **Mozart: Symphonies Vol. 1** / Linden (cond.), Amsterdam Mozart-Ens. / Brilliant 99730

Symphony No. 25 in G minor, K. 183 (1773)

Mozart and his father Leopold returned from the third of their Italian journeys in May 1773, having witnessed the success of his new opera seria *Lucia Silla*, K. 135 in Milan the previous December. In July, father and son once again set out for Vienna, possibly in the hopes of obtaining a post for Mozart, but although they were received by the Empress Maria Theresa on August 5, nothing is known of the details of the audience. By the end of September the Mozarts were back in Salzburg. Early the following month two new symphonies appeared, *No 24 in B flat*, K. 182, dated October 3, and the present work, which bears the date October 5. Both dates on the autograph manuscript were later crossed out. It seems probable that one or both symphonies were at least started in Vienna, since it is hardly likely that even Mozart would have suddenly produced two symphonies within a week of returning home.

The use of minor keys in symphonies was rare in the eighteenth century. (Mozart composed only one other, the *Symphony No.40 in G minor*, K. 550, and the use here of a key later identified with some of Mozart's most troubled and agitated music (the *Symphony No. 40*, the *Piano Quartet*, K. 478, and the *String Quintet*, K. 516) has excited much comment. In fact, rather than being viewed as a forerunner of Romanticism, K. 183 is more satisfactorily regarded as being part of a sudden wave of minor-key symphonies which appeared in the late 1760s and early 1770s. Among others, Vanhal, Ordonez, and Joseph Haydn produced during this period a number of minor-key works characterized by stormy drama and restlessness of spirit, attributes which have led some to refer to them as "Sturm und Drang" (storm and stress) pieces. (The name comes from that of a literary movement which was so called slightly later.) In particular, attention has been drawn to the relationship of K. 183 to Haydn's *Symphony No. 39 in G minor* (late 1760s), with which it shares not only its key but also an orchestration that unusually includes four horns in addition to pairs of oboes and bassoons, and strings. Mozart's opening Allegro con brio and closing Allegro betray characteristics typical of the Sturm und Drang style—nervous drama articulated by considerable use of tremolando and restless, angular melodies. Between these two large-scale sonata-form movements come an Andante in E flat which gives vent to more introverted passions, and a terse and stern Minuet which strays far from the courtly origins of the dance; its Trio section in G major is scored for wind instruments alone. *—Brian Robins*

Recommended:

○ **Mozart: Symphonies 25, 28, 29 & 35** / Walter (cond.), Columbia SO / 1995 / Sony 64473

○ **Mozart: Symphony 25, 26, 27, 29 & 32** / Marriner (cond.), Academy of St. Martin-in-the-Fields / 1991 / Decca 430268

○ **Mozart: Symphony 25, 29, 38 & 40; Serenata Notturna** / Britten (cond.), English CO / 1995 / London 444323

○ **Mozart: Symphony 25 & 29** / Hogwood (cond.), Academy of Ancient Music / 1985 / L'oiseau-Lyre 414631

Symphony No. 29 in A major, K. 201 (1774)

After the burst of symphonic writing during 1772 and 1773, each of which produced seven new symphonies, Mozart's activity in the field diminished. Over the next two years only three new works appeared, of which K. 201 is the most remarkable. It is dated April 6, 1774—a period of Mozart's life singularly lacking in documentary detail. Until December, when he went to Munich to supervise the forthcoming premiere of his opera buffa *La finta giardiniera*, the entire year was spent in Salzburg; there are thus no family letters from this period. Mozart was now finally salaried as joint concertmaster (with Michael Haydn, brother of the more famous Joseph) at the Salzburg court, for which he composed a number of sacred works in addition to two large-scale occasional serenades (one of which, K. 204 in D, was later reduced to four movements to serve as a symphony). Notwithstanding its major key, *Symphony No. 29* has many of the same serious and intense qualities as its immediate chronological predecessor, the *Symphony No. 25 in G minor*, K. 183, composed the previous fall.

The opening Allegro is unusual among Mozart's symphonies for its inclusion of a quiet introduction; the forward drive of the main part of the movement is maintained by repeated note and tremolando figurations. Both the Andante and the Minuet which succeed it are characterized by the use of dotted-rhythms which give the muted strings of the former a mood of dignified eloquence, and the Minuet rare energy. The final Allegro con spirito includes hunting-horn calls. Mozart's biographer Alfred Einstein described this finale as "the richest and most dramatic Mozart had written up to this time." One might indeed go further and suggest that K. 201 is overall the finest symphony Mozart had yet composed. He obviously thought sufficiently highly of the work to continue using it in Vienna; it was one of four symphonies he requested his father Leopold to send to him after settling in the city (letter of January 4, 1783). *—Brian Robins*

Recommended:

○ **Mozart: Symphony 25, 29, 38 & 40; Serenata Notturna** / Britten (cond.), English CO / 1995 / London 444323

○ **Mozart: Symphonies 25, 28, 29 & 35** / Walter (cond.), Columbia SO / 1995 / Sony 64473

○ **Mozart: Symphony 25, 26, 27, 29 & 32** / Marriner (cond.), Academy of St. Martin-in-the-Fields / 1991 / Decca 430268

○ **Mozart: Symphonies; Clarinet Concerto** / Bernstein (cond.), Vienna PO / DG 429221

○ **Mozart: Symphonies 25, 26 & 29** / Pinnock (cone.), English Concert / Archiv 431679

○ **Mozart: Symphonies Vol. 4** / Hogwood (cond.), Academy of Ancient Music / 1987 / L'Oiseau-Lyre 417841

Symphony No. 30 in D major, K. 202 (1774)

This festive *Symphony No. 30* of Mozart was written for an unknown occasion in Salzburg. Mozart symphonies in C, D, or E flat often were, for technical reasons, the only ones that might include trumpets. Accordingly, this symphony is written for an orchestra of pairs of oboes and horns, two trumpets, kettledrums, strings, and a continuo of bassoon and harpsichord.

While the previous symphony attained a noble serenity and the one before that (commonly designated "No. 25") was the first truly tragic Mozart symphony, this one seems more interested in lightness and good times. This caused Romantic-era commentators to view it as a step backwards in that it was a less "serious" work. In the variety of its musical ideas and the cleverness of their treatment, it actually is the equal to the other two. How important "seriousness" is as a determinative musical quality is left to the listener.

The work is unified by the fact that both the first and last movements begin with a melody tracing the D major chord downward: D, A, F sharp, D. In the first movement, this is preceded by some introductory chords and figurations, including one that includes a simple little trill. In the course of the exposition, this trill grows and grows in importance until the whole orchestra is dominated by its buzzing.

The second movement is in a small-scale sonata form. It is scored for strings alone. It is rich in cantabile melodies, and exhibits the composer's care to keep all four voices interesting. Thus, it is very rich listening. The minuet movement is one of the more dance-like among those of Mozart's more mature symphonies.

The final movement, again in a full sonata-allegro form, nicely contrasts a quick-march opening figure in dotted rhythms with a contrasting lyrical idea. The development section is in a rather serious vein, but the coda of the movement stops short in a musical joke. *—Joseph Stevenson*

Recommended:

- ○ **Symphonies 21–41** / Marriner (cond.), Academy of St. Martin-in-the-Fields / 1990 / Philips 422502
- ○ **Mozart: Symphonies 24, 26, 27 & 30** / Mackerras (cond.), Prague CO / 1989 / Telarc 80186
- ○ **Mozart: Symphonies 26–34** / Kehr (cond.), Mainz CO / 1992 / Vox 5072
- ○ **Mozart: Symphonies Vol. 4** / Hogwood (cond.), Academy of Ancient Music / 1987 / L'Oiseau-Lyre 417841

Symphony No. 31 in D major ("Paris"), K. 297 (1778)

After nearly four years during which time he wrote no symphonies (although still producing opera overtures and works which were extracted from orchestral serenades), Mozart composed this work for performance in Paris. He and his mother were in the city when Mozart received the commission from Joseph Legros, director of the Concerts. Despite a dismal rehearsal, the performance went well and the symphony was well received by the audience. Mozart had taken pains to write it in a style that would appeal to the French. It is written for the largest orchestra Mozart had used until then in a symphony: pairs of flutes, oboes, clarinets, bassoons, horns, trumpets, and kettledrums, and the usual strings. This marks the first time that Mozart used clarinets in a symphony. The symphony begins with the bold (and popular) gesture called the "coup d'archet," quick separated string chords. The second theme is lighter in mood. The development section mainly concerns itself with the first subject. The two themes of the second movement are solemn and high-minded, although there are variations that introduce a lighter mood. Mozart originally marked the movement Andantino, but it came to be called "Andante," which also is the marking for an alternate slow movement Mozart wrote at about the same time. The final movement begins quietly with a syncopated theme. The bassoons and strings have a contrasting theme. There is a lengthy working out of some of these ideas in the transition to the second subject, which when it comes is a fugato for strings. This idea is also the main basis of the development. The symphony ends with a restatement of the vivacious opening subject. When Mozart wrote his father concerning the success of the "Paris" Symphony, he mentioned that he had composed a second slow movement for the symphony. There has been some question as to which version was first played in Paris. The version published in Paris (believed to be the second version) has a time signature of 3/4; the version found in German autographs is in 6/8, with a graceful, cantilena theme. *—Joseph Stevenson*

Recommended:

- ○ **Mozart: Symphonies & Funeral Music** / Abbado (cond.), Berlin PO / 1994 / Sony 48385
- ○ **Mozart: Symphonies 31, 36 & 39** / Marriner (cond.), Academy of St. Martin-in-the-Fields / Philips 446223
- ○ **Mozart: Symphonies 40 & 31** / Schröder (cond.), Academy of Ancient Music / 1983 / L'Oiseau-Lyre 410197

Symphony No. 32 in G major, K. 318 (1779)

This short symphony was the first Mozart wrote after his return to Salzburg after his disastrous trip to Paris, during which his mother died and his only major output was the *Symphony No. 31 "Paris".* Because the *Symphony No. 32* is in the form of an opera or operetta overture, some commentators have concluded that it was written as the "sinfonia," or overture for one of the stage pieces that Mozart was working on during 1779, such as *Thamos, King of Egypt,* K. 345/336a or *Zaide,* K. 334/336b. Ludwig Ritter von Köchel, editor of the *Thematic Catalogue of Mozart's Work* (1862) appended the subtitle ("Ouverture"). But Köchel was probably reflecting nineteenth century views, which considered overtures a separate type of composition from a symphony, whereas in Mozart's time there was little distinction between the two. Some commentators conclude that of *Zaide* and *Thamos,* one was too early and the other too late for this composition to be connected to it. The symphony is for strings, pairs of flutes, oboes, and bassoons, four horns, two trumpets, and kettledrums. It is Mozart's only symphony in G that calls for trumpets. It does not have a continuo part: the bassoons, cellos, and at times the double basses have independent parts. The first movement is in sonata-allegro form, but it stops short with a full-orchestra pause just where the main material should come in for a recapitulation. At that point the Andante starts, in a rondo form of ABA'CA"B'. (The apostrophes indicate that the recurring sections are varied.) This, too, does not come to a conclusion; note that a final repeat of the "A" material is missing. Now Mozart returns to the opening tempo and finally opens the recapitulation, but actually begins six measures before the return of the second subject. Having gotten through the foreshortened recapitulation, the symphony would naturally end with a coda; the surprise here is that the coda is the opening subject that was "missing" from the recapitulation. The symphony is quite brief, being in a compact, continuous style, but it is very inventive in form and highly attractive in its ideas. *—Joseph Stevenson*

Recommended:

- ○ **Mozart: Symphony 25, 26, 27, 29 & 32** / Marriner (cond.), Academy of St. Martin-in-the-Fields / 1991 / Decca 430268
- ○ **Mozart: Symphonies Vol. 5** / Hogwood (cond.), Academy of Ancient Music / 1987 / L'Oiseau-Lyre 421104

Symphony No. 33 in B flat major, K. 319 (1779)

According to the date inscribed on Mozart's manuscript of the *Symphony No. 33 in B flat major,* K. 319, the works was completed on July 9, 1779, in Salzburg. It was the second symphony Mozart composed after returning to Salzburg from his lengthy, fateful trip to Mannheim and Paris.

Scored for paired oboes, bassoons, horns, and strings featuring a divided viola part, the symphony was originally in three movements; the Minuet and Trio was added for performances in Vienna. Artaria published the four-movement version in Vienna in 1785, as Op. 7, No. 2, along with the *Symphony in D major,* K. 385 ("Haffner"). Throughout the *Symphony in B flat major,* the writing is of a "chamber-music" nature in its detail and procedures. This is probably why Mozart chose this particular work when Sebastian Winter, the Mozart family's former servant, requested in 1786 a work from the composer that would be suitable for Prince Fürstenberg's small orchestra in Donaueschingen.

Each of the original three movements of K. 319 has a development section that begins with new material that, in each case, is thematically related to the material at the equivalent spot in the other movements. Overall, Mozart's handling of the woodwinds and orchestration in general is as advanced as we find in his later symphonies.

The opening Allegro assai, in sonata form, is set in an unusual triple meter. Its quiet, hesitant opening, with sudden, forte outbursts, suggests a youthful playfulness. Strikingly jolly in mood, the movement does not have a repeated exposition and the development section is relatively brief. A rising and falling four-note motive, not a part of the exposition, figures prominently in the development and looks forward to the finale of the *"Jupiter" symphony* of 1788.

The E flat major Andante moderato closes with a "mirror image" recapitulation, in which the secondary theme appears first and is resolved to the tonic before the appearance of the primary theme. This device, used often by the very Mannheim composers Mozart had recently visited, is not so much an innovation as it is a nod to earlier binary movements in which the principle theme does not appear at all. The delayed return of the primary theme sounds very much like a coda and the "rounding" effect is pure, high-Classical rhetoric.

In 1782, Mozart added a Minuet and Trio to the symphony, placing it in third position. The generally dark mood is an unusual trait of this B flat major movement. The Trio tune slightly resembles the second theme of the first movement and does nothing to lighten the atmosphere.

Cheerful energy supplants the ominous Minuet at the opening of the Finale, marked Allegro assai. Passages that remind us of Mozart's later operas appear at numerous places in this sonata-form movement, filled with abundant energy and endless musicality. *—John Palmer*

Recommended:

- ○ **Mozart: Symphony 33; Sinfonia Concertante; Serenade 6** / Böhm (cond.), Vienna PO / 1992 / Orfeo 301921
- ○ **Mozart: Symphony 33; Posthorn Serenade** / Brown, Academy of St. Martin-in-the-Fields / 1997 / Haenssler 98129
- ○ **Mozart: Symphonies Vol. 5** / Hogwood (cond.) Academy of Ancient Music / 1987 / L'Oiseau-Lyre 421104

Symphony No. 34 in C major, K. 338 (1780)

Mozart's *Symphony No. 34 in C major, K. 338,* is one of the composer's more assured and consistent works from his last years in Salzburg. Arguably the most original of Mozart's symphonies to that point, it looks forward to his later, more mature efforts in the genre.

One unusual characteristic of the Allegro vivace first movement is that there is no real melody for nearly 40 measures. Instead, Mozart bombards the listener with rising arpeggios and repeated notes in a march-like rhythm. As in K. 319 and the earlier *Symphony No. 31 in D major*, K. 297, the movement lacks the customary repeat of the exposition, instead moving directly into the development. The development does not concern itself with themes from the exposition, but presents new material in the striking key of A flat major, creating a powerful, intense harmonic relationship with the dominant just before the recapitulation. The recapitulation is presented as a "mirror image" of the exposition, beginning with the resolution of the secondary material and closing with the main theme.

Mozart added the bassoon part of the second movement, Andante di molto, in 1786; it had originally been written for strings only. This movement is characterized throughout by a sense of repose, initiated by the key of F major and its relaxed relationship to the C major of the Allegro. Mozart's quest for symmetry is clear in the contrast between the melodic shapes of the first theme, a rising, turning idea with minute pauses, and the second, a continuous, generally descending melody. A brief development passage, really just a transition, connects the exposition to the recapitulation.

The third movement, a Minuet and Trio in C major, presents something of a problem. Mozart had previously added a minuet to the *Symphony No. 33 in B flat major*, K. 319 (1779) for a performance at the Vienna Auergarten in 1782. Noted Mozart scholar Alfred Einstein believes that the composer did the same for K. 338, and that a stray *Minuet in C major*, K. 409 dating from May 1782 was meant to be inserted between the symphony's slow movement and finale. Einstein points to the fact that the autograph of the symphony contains the first few measures of a minuet in C major, later crossed out. However, this minuet was to be in second position and is nothing like K. 409; furthermore, K. 409 includes flutes, which are not present in the other movements of the symphony. Einstein suggests, without concrete evidence, that Mozart added flutes to the remaining movements, but neither flutes nor a minuet appear in the revised orchestral parts Mozart sent to Prince Fürstenberg in Donaueschingen in the summer of 1786. The controversial Minuet has a sturdy, assertive character that seems a little out of place in this work. After the first section closes on the dominant, the second half follows a traditional path and is rounded by a full return of the earlier material. A solo oboe takes the lead in the first part of the Trio, while the flutes are prominent in the second.

The finale is permeated by the language of Italian opera buffa in the context of a symphonic argument. As in the first movement, the main thematic material is unmelodic, unfolding as a series of ideas rather than real tunes, in the tonic and dominant. The movement's energy, fueled by its propulsive 6/8 meter, continues unabated from the downbeat to the end. *—John Palmer*

Recommended:

- ○ **Mozart: Symphonies 31, 33 & 34** / Mackerras (cond.), Prague CO / 1989 / Telarc 80190
- ○ **Mozart: Symphonies 21–41** / Marriner (cond.), Academy of St. Martin-in-the-Fields / 1990 / Philips 422502

Symphony No. 35 in D major ("Haffner"), K. 385 (1782)

By mid-1782 Mozart had been a Vienna resident for more than a year, beginning to prosper from the success of his new singspiel, *The Abduction from the Seraglio*. Yet Leopold Mozart refused to bless his marriage proposal to Constanze Weber, and thought nothing of disrupting his son's professional life. In the midst of preparations for the first all-Mozart concert in Joseph II's imperial capital, Papa insisted that Wolfgang compose a new work for the ennoblement of Salzburg's mayor, Sigmund Haffner. In other words, a gratis job, unrelated to Wolfgang's new career and income. The wonder is that Mozart obliged posthaste, despite being harried. Between July 20 and August 5 he wrote the new D major serenade-symphony in six movements (not to be confused, however, with an earlier Haffner *Serenade*, K. 250). During the same fortnight he also made a wind-band arrangement of music from *The Abduction* ("If I don't do this, someone else will beat me to it and take my profit"), composed the noble *C minor Serenade for winds* (K. 388/384a), and married Constanze without Leopold's permission.

Six months later, needing a new symphony for further concerts in the Burgtheater, Mozart remembered that Leopold had pestered him for a piece and asked for its return. Papa of course took his mean-spirited time, but finally did send it. Upon receipt Wolfgang wrote that "the music has positively amazed me, for I had forgotten every single note it!" He dropped one of the *Serenade*'s two minuets (subsequently lost) and a concluding march, then added a pair each of flutes and clarinets in movements 1 and 4, and offered K. 385 as a new piece. He conducted the first performance in Vienna's Royal Burgtheater on March 23, 1783. To Papa he wrote that "the theater could not have been more crowded... every box was full. But what pleased me most of all was that His Majesty the Emperor was present and, goodness!—how delighted he was and how he applauded me!"

Celebratory pomp suffuses the concisely argued, monothematic sonata-form, Allegro con spirito movement without exposition-repeat. Everything relates to the main theme with its two-octave leaps, dum-dum-da-dum-dum rhythm, skirling trills and racing scales.

A sinuous song and trio with translucent textures and operatic ornamentation for the violins makes the G major Andante the longest movement if all repeats are played. The trio silences flutes, clarinets, and trumpets, yet begins with marvelously sonorous wind chords. Low strings carry the melody until violins take over with more trills, birdcalls, and galant-period embellishments, after which the song repeats.

The Menuetto movement—not four minutes long even with repeats—is emphatically rhythmic, and countrified rather than courtly in the song sections. Contrastingly, the trio is played legato throughout.

The final Presto is sonata form again, even more concise than in the first movement. Although Mozart wanted it played "as fast as possible," he still meant slower than the capability of most twentieth century instruments. *—Roger Dettmer*

Recommended:

- ○ **Mozart: Symphonies 35, 40 & 41** / Szell (cond.), Cleveland Orch. / 1990 / Sony 46333
- ○ **Mozart: Symphonies 35–41** / Böhm (cond.), Berlin PO / DG 447416
- ○ **Mozart: Symphonies 25, 28, 29 & 35** / Walter (cond.), New York PO / 1995 / Sony 64473
- ○ **Mozart Symphonies 29, 35 & 41** / Marriner (cond.), Academy of St. Martin-in-the-Fields / 1995 / Philips 446225
- ○ **Mozart: Symphonies, Vol. 5** / Hogwood (cond.), Academy of Ancient Music / 1987 / L'Oiseau-Lyre 421104

Symphony No. 36 in C major ("Linz"), K. 425 (1783)

Mozart's marriage to Constanze Weber in Vienna on August 4, 1782, left relations with his father strained. After stalling for nearly a year, Mozart and his new wife made the journey to Salzburg in order to effect introductions in July 1783, remaining until October 27. Their journey back to Vienna was broken in Linz, where they stayed three weeks during which Mozart gave a concert in the Ballhaus. The genesis of the symphony he composed for the occasion, and which has since born the name of the city for which it was composed, is explained in a letter written by Mozart to his father on October 31. After giving details of the journey and the hospitable reception accorded to him and his wife by their hosts, the Thun family, Mozart continues: "On Tuesday, November 4th, I an giving a concert in the theatre here and, as I have not a single symphony with me, I am writing a new one at breakneck speed, which must be finished by that time." No details of the remaining program are extant, but it probably followed the format of the Mozart's concerts in Vienna—one or two piano concertos, arias, and the solo keyboard improvisations for which he was famed. After the Mozarts returned to Vienna, the *"Linz" Symphony* was again performed at Mozart's concert at the Burgtheater on April 1, 1784.

The symphony is scored for strings, timpani, and pairs of oboes, bassoons, horns, and trumpets. Cast in the usual four movements, K. 425 is the first of a trio of symphonies (the others are the *"Prague" Symphony* No. 38 in D, K. 504, and the *Symphony No. 39* in E flat, K. 543) in which the main allegro (here marked Allegro spiritoso) is prefaced by a slow Adagio introduction, to which may be added the Adagio maestoso Mozart added to a *Symphony in G* by Michael Haydn (P16) when he was in need of new works during the height of his Viennese concert promotion activities. (The work was long accepted within the canon of Mozart's works as his *Symphony No. 37 in G*, K. 444). Also unusual is the introduction of trumpets and drums in the Andante, a rare incursion in slow movements in symphonies of this period. The brilliant Presto finale is a close relative of that of the *"Haffner" Symphony* of the previous year, with the additional interest of contrapuntal passages to contrast with the prevailing homophonic texture. The symphony as a whole is Mozart's most successful essay in the form so far, showing little sign of the haste with which it was written. *—Brian Robins*

Recommended:

- ○ **Mozart: 6 Symphonies** / Walter (cond.), Columbia SO / 1991 / Sony 46511
- ○ **Mozart: Symphonies 35–41** / Böhm (cond.), Berlin PO / DG 447416
- ○ **Mozart: Piano Concerto 15; Symphony 36** / Bernstein (cond.), Vienna PO / 2000 / Decca 467123
- ○ **Mozart: Symphonies, Vol. 5** / Hogwood (cond.), Academy of Ancient Music / 1987 / L'Oiseau-Lyre 421104
- ○ **Mozart: The Last 5 Symphonies** / Marriner (cond.), Academy of St. Martin-in-the-Fields / 1993 / Philips 438332

Symphony No. 38 in D major ("Prague"), K. 504 (1786)

On May 1, 1786, Mozart's new opera *Le nozze di Figaro* received its first performance at the Burgtheater in Vienna. Enthusiastically received by connoisseurs, the long and complex opera puzzled many of the general public and it received only eight performances. Early in December, *Figaro* was staged at the National Theater (today known as the Tyl Theater) in Prague, where it became such a triumphant success that Mozart was induced to visit the Bohemian capital to see the production for himself. When he and his wife Constanze arrived on January 11, 1787, he had with him a new symphony which had been completed early in December (it was entered in Mozart's thematic catalog on December 6). The symphony was included in the concert Mozart gave eight days later, resulting in the first performance of a work which would subsequently become irrevocably associated with the city in which the composer witnessed his greatest triumph in later years. A decade after the concert, the Prague schoolmaster Franz Niemetschek (who educated Mozart's son Carl after the composer's death in 1791) testified to the symphony's enduring popularity: "The symphonies he composed for this occasion are real masterpieces of instrumental composition.... This applied particularly to the grand Symphony in D, which is always a favorite in Prague, although it has no doubt been heard a hundred times."

Such connections have led to the general assumption by Mozart's biographers that the "Prague" symphony was composed for his visit there, but this cannot be the case—Mozart composed the work before he received the invitation to visit the city. Indeed, a letter of his father's (November 17, 1786) clearly shows that at the time of composition Mozart was planning a visit to England, a visit which never took place becase Leopold refused to look after the composer's two young children. It therefore seems perfectly reasonable to suggest that the work was composed with Mozart's projected London visit in mind—what we know as the "Prague" symphony might have become Mozart's "London" symphony had his plans come to fruition. An unusual feature of the symphony is that it is in only three movements; it is the only major symphonic work from the Classical period to lack the usual minuet and trio or scherzo movement. But there is nothing small-scale about the work; it amply justifies Niemetschek's epithet "grand." The opening movement, a broad, imposing Adagio introduction followed by a hugely powerful Allegro, is one of the most impressive of all Classical symphonic movements, with dramatic qualities that foreshadow *Don Giovanni* and a mastery of counterpoint hitherto restricted to Mozart's chamber works. The central Andante utterly transcends the easygoing implication of such a heading; it is a movement of profound, songful depth and contrapuntal skill. The final Presto also shares some of the demonic power of *Don Giovanni*, the opera Mozart would shortly compose for Prague, while at the same time inhabiting a world in which, for all the bright major-mode music, tragedy never seems too far away. *—Brian Robins*

Recommended:

- ○ **Mozart: 6 Symphonies** / Walter (cond.), Columbia SO / 1991 / Sony 46511
- ○ **Mozart: Symphonies 35–41** / Böhm (cond.), Berlin PO / DG 447416
- ○ **Mozart: Symphonies 38–41** / Norrington (cond.), London Classical Players / 2002 / Virgin 562010
- ○ **Mozart: The Last 5 Symphonies** / Marriner (cond.), Academy of St. Martin-in-the-Fields / 1993 / Philips 438332
- ○ **Mozart: Symphonies, Vol. 6** / Schröder (cond.), Academy of Ancient Music / 1988 / L'Oiseau-Lyre 421085

Symphony No. 39 in E flat major, K. 543 (1788)

No group of Mozart's works has been the subject of more discussion than his final three symphonies, Nos. 39 in E flat, No. 40 in G minor, and the *"Jupiter," No. 41*, in C. They were apparently composed within the remarkably short space of about two months during the summer of 1788, and the composer's motivation for writing them has since been vigorously debated. In common with his contemporaries, Mozart composed nearly exclusively for practical purposes, yet none has been positively identified in this instance. Still, the least plausible explanation advanced is that Mozart composed his great final symphonic trilogy as a result of some personal "inner need," the attractive romanticism of the theory being compounded by the assertion that he did not live to hear these three pinnacles of the symphonic repertoire performed. Such a theory runs counter to all we know about Mozart's working practices. In particular, he would not have had the time for such indulgence during the period concerned, a summer during which his surviving correspondence is predominantly concerned with increasingly desperate begging letters to his benefactor and fellow Freemason Michael Puchberg. More practically, it has been suggested that Mozart intended to mount a series of subscription concerts for the fall or Advent season. It was thought that these concerts never took place, but recently the scholar H.C. Robbins Landon has persuasively argued that these concerts were in fact held, with the three last symphonies as the principal new works performed at them. It also appears highly likely that Mozart took the new works on the tour of Germany he undertook the following year.

In the three symphonies of 1788 (to which must be added in this regard the *"Prague" Symphony* of 1786) we find the culmination of Mozart's assimilation of the contrapuntal style of Bach and Handel he had first begun to study during the early 1780s. It was this synthesis of "learned" style with the clean clarity of classicism that caused so much trouble for Mozart's contemporaries, to whom his late style became increasingly "difficult." Each of the symphonies occupies a very specific world of its own. The E flat Symphony, entered by Mozart into his thematic catalog on June 26, 1786, is often characterized as being "warm and autumnal" (Robbins Landon), a description that (as so often with Mozart) tells only part of the story; it fails to bring to attention the symphony's tensile strength and a dramatic quality that does not preclude moments of pathos more readily associated with the G minor symphony. There are four movements. The opening Allegro is prefaced (as it had been in both the "Prague" and "Linz" symphonies, its immediate numerical predecessors) by a powerful slow Adagio introduction. The following Andante has a secondary theme which is much stormier (and also subjected to considerable development) than might be expected in a "slow" movement, while the succeeding Minuet has an elegant gait set off by a rustic central trio. The final Allegro is a dazzling display of good humor and contrapuntal wizardry, its complexity skillfully masked in one of those movements in which the composer conceals his art. The symphony is scored for flute, pairs of clarinets, bassoons, horns, trumpets, timpani, and strings. *—Brian Robins*

Recommended:

- ○ **Mozart: Symphonies 35–41** / Böhm (cond.), Berlin PO / DG 447416
- ○ **Mozart: Symphonies 29, 39–41** / Fricsay (cond.), VSO / 1992 / DG 437386
- ○ **Mozart: Symphonies 31, 36 & 39** / Marriner (cond.), Academy of St. Martin-in-the-Fields / Philips 446223
- ○ **Mozart: Symphonies 39 & 40; Exsultate, Jubilate** / Szell (cond.), Cleveland Orch. / 2000 / Sony 89340
- ○ **Mozart: Symphonies 39, 40 & 41** / Walter (cond.), New York PO / 1995 / Sony 64477
- ○ **Mozart: Symphonies, Vol. 6** / Schröder (cond.), Academy of Ancient Music / 1988 / L'Oiseau-Lyre 421085

Symphony No. 40 in G minor, K. 550 (1788)

Mozart composed his final three symphonies during the summer of 1788. His entries in the thematic catalog he maintained suggest that all were written during the space of about two months. Much critical discussion has been devoted to the reasons for their composition, for it appeared that Mozart had no specific occasion in mind for their performance. The romantic notion that he composed them without practical purpose is now widely disregarded as being out of character with Mozart's known compositional procedures, and the scholar H. C. Robbins Landon has recently advanced convincing arguments to suggest that they were in fact written for a series of concerts he gave in the fall or Advent season of 1788. Robbins Landon's argument is largely based on an undated letter written by Mozart to his principal benefactor, his fellow Freemason Michael Puchberg. In this letter he refers to his concerts which will begin "next week," concerts which scholars formerly believed never to have taken place. Evidence also supports the idea (advanced by Neal Zaslaw) that Mozart took the three symphonies on the tour he made to Germany the following year, which would further undermine the long-held notion that the composer never heard three of the greatest works in the symphonic literature performed.

One aspect of the symphonies upon which commentators reach universal agreement is their extraordinary diversity of character; each has unique qualities which together utterly explode the myth that the extreme agitation and pathos of the G minor Symphony reflected the abject circumstances in which Mozart found himself at this period. The begging letters addressed to Puchberg during these months are indeed pitiful documents that might be cited as evidence of Mozart's state of mind at the time he was composing the G minor symphony. But they will hardly do for the mellow warmth, strength and humor of E flat symphony or the elevated grandeur of the *"Jupiter" Symphony*. Neither should it be forgotten that the tragic qualities so often associated with the symphony today have not always been apparent to all. To Robert Schumann the symphony was a work of "Grecian lightness and grace," while for a later writer, Alfred Einstein, there are passages that "plunge to the abyss of the soul."

Such ambiguity is perhaps apt for one of the greatest works of a composer whose music so frequently defies adequate description. The symphony is cast in the usual four movements; the opening Molto allegro immediately announces something unusual by starting not with characteristic loud "call to attention," but with quietly spoken agitation. The uneasy passion of the main theme leads to conclusions that seem to protest rather than find any consolation. The movement's dominant feeling is urgency: upbeat after upbeat after upbeat occurs. Amid great instability and a questioning aura, we experience a peek into *Don Giovanni*'s abyss. In the finale, the horns intrude with wild swatches of color. There is even an eerie twelve-note insertion after the double bar in the Allegro assai section.

There are two versions of the G minor symphony. The first is modestly scored for flute and pairs of oboes, horns, and strings, but at some point shortly after composition Mozart added parts for two clarinets, slightly altering the oboe parts to accommodate them. Such second thoughts surely also add credibility to the idea that Mozart led performances of the work—he would hardly have bothered with such refinements if the symphony was not being used for practical purposes. *—Brian Robins*

Recommended:

- ○ **Mozart: Symphonies 39, 40 & 41** / Walter (cond.), New York PO / 1995 / Sony 64477
- ○ **Mozart: Symphonies 40 & 41** / Levine (cond.), Vienna PO / 1990 / DG 429731

○ **Mozart: Symphonies 40 & 41** / Pinnock (cond.), English Concert / 2003 / Archiv 000041302
○ **Mozart: Symphonies 35, 40 & 41** / Szell (cond.), Cleveland Orch. / 2002 / Sony 89834
○ **Mozart: Symphonies 40 & 31** / Schröder (cond.), Academy of Ancient Music / 1983 / L'Oiseau-Lyre 410197
○ **Mozart: Symphonies 35–41** / Böhm (cond.), Berlin PO / DG 447416

Symphony No. 41 in C major ("Jupiter"), K. 551 (1788)

The near-quarter century that separates Mozart's first symphony and his last—the *Symphony No. 41 in C major* (1788)—was marked by the composer's recurrent, if not ongoing, interest in the possibilities inherent in this form. Upon examination of the chronology of Mozart's works, one finds that the composition of his symphonies tends to occur in irregularly spaced groups, of as many as nine or ten examples in a row, rather than regularly or singly. What this might suggest, aside from any financially based motivation, is that he employed these various periods specifically for the working out of the problems and challenges of the symphonic form. In surveying these works, one finds that the prominent benchmarks increase almost geometrically as time progresses, so that by the production of the *"Jupiter" Symphony* two years before his death—as part of a group of three composed within the space of less than three months—the full extent of the evolution which has taken place is striking indeed.

The *Symphony No. 41* aptly embodies what is now identified as a paradigm of Classical symphonic form: four movements, the first and last in a quick tempo, the second slower, the third a minuet with trio. Unencumbered by norms suggested by any model, however, Mozart's deft imagination distinguishes this work from others in a similar cast. The first movement is characterized in part by the dramatic and effective employment of unexpected pauses in the rhythmic flow through the use of rests, a trait shared with and perhaps influenced by the symphonies of Haydn. After an initial regularity, irregular and changing phrase lengths contribute as well to the dramatic impetus. The serene F major quietude of the second movement's opening is soon disrupted, posed against more restless, rhythmically insistent minor-key episodes. This calm/dark conflict continues throughout, the initial spirit eventually prevailing. The falling chromatic theme and flowing, even accompaniment of the Minuet set a graceful tone for the third movement. The companion Trio provides an earthier, more overtly dancelike mood, which is, however, interrupted by a suddenly more serious tutti outburst. The final movement is exceptional for the richness of its contrapuntal language, a somewhat unexpected—and, some of Mozart's contemporaries would venture, unfashionable—attribute in a symphonic work of the time. The four-note motive that begins the movement is put through its paces in a number of guises, most prominently as the beginning of a recurrent canon and fugue subject which occurs both as originally presented and in inversion. The effect is one not of academicism but of great tension and dramatic impulse which, borne bristling and in search of resolution, finds its resting place only in the final bars.—*Michael Rodman*

Recommended:
○ **Mozart: Symphonies 35–41** / Böhm (cond.), Berlin PO / DG 447416
○ **Mozart: Symphonies 35, 40 & 41** / Szell (cond.), Cleveland Orch. / 2002 / Sony 89834
○ **Mozart: Symphonies 29, 35, 41** / Marriner (cond.), Academy of St. Martin-in-the-Fields / 1995 / Philips 446225
○ **Mozart: Symphonies 39, 40 & 41** / Walter (cond.), New York PO / 1995 / Sony 64477
○ **Mozart: Symphonies, Vol. 6** / Schröder (cond.), Academy of Ancient Music / 1988 / L'Oiseau-Lyre 421085

CONCERTO

Bassoon Concerto in B flat major, K. 191 (1774)

With the exception of a spurious work now attributed to François Devienne (K.Anh. 230a), the piece at hand is the only extant work Mozart wrote for solo bassoon. It is possible that he composed others; he is reputed to have composed three further bassoon concertos and a bassoon sonata for Thaddäus Baron von Dürnitz, the recipient of the *Piano Sonata in D*, K. 284. But none has been accounted for. The B flat concerto was completed in Salzburg in June 1774. That year the teenage Mozart was afforded the rare luxury of remaining at home, at least until he and his father traveled to Munich in December to supervise the first performances of his opera buffa, *La finta giardiniera*. The concerto, composed for an unknown recipient, is cast in the usual three movements, and its sunny, bubbling lyricism perhaps shows the influence of Italian opera. The thoroughly idiomatic writing for the solo instrument exploits both its lyrical qualities (especially in the central movement, unusually marked Andante ma adagio) and its playful ones, making one regret the possible loss of other concertos. The most notable feature of the work is the theme of the slow movement, which bears a close resemblance to the famous aria "Porgi amor" from *The Marriage of Figaro*. The first movement goes by the book, with an orchestral exposition that introduces two themes. Despite its youthful origin, which does show up in the concerto's lack of depth, this is a centerpiece of the bassoon's limited concerto repertoire. It is the among the first concertos that Mozart composed. —*Brian Robins*

Recommended:
○ **Chicago Principal: First Chair Soloists Play Famous Concertos** / Abbado (cond.), Elliot, Chicago SO / 2003 / DG 000002502
○ **Mozart: Clarinet Concerto; Sonata in B flat; Bassoon Concerto** / Marriner (cond.), Leister, Orton, Thunemann, Academy of St. Martin-in-the-Fields / 1989 / Philips 422390
○ **Mozart: The Wind Concertos** / Hogwood (cond.), Kelly, Beznosiuk, Bond, Academy of Ancient Music / 1998 / Decca 460027

Clarinet Concerto in A major, K. 622 (1791)

Of the works which Mozart composed for the outstanding Viennese clarinetist Anton Stadler (1753–1812), the *Clarinet Quintet in A, K581*, written in 1789, and the present *Concerto in A*, completed less than two months before the composer's death in 1791, are the crowning achievements. Work on the Concerto was started in 1789. Mozart originally intended the work to be for basset horn, but revised it for clarinet. However, the version widely known today differs from the work Mozart produced for Stadler, since the original version was written for an instrument with an extended bass compass that allowed Stadler to demonstrate his famed ability to play low notes. The transcription for standard clarinet (published ten years after Mozart's death) therefore requires an octave transcription of the notes that cannot be produced on it, which changes the color of the work. The first performance was given by Stadler on 16 October 1791, not in Vienna, but at his benefit concert in the Prague Theatre. It therefore seems certain that the composer never heard the composition that has become one of his best known. Cast in the usual three movements, the gentle, nostalgic lyricism of much of the *Clarinet Concerto* has drawn such epithets as "valedictory" and "autumnal," an assessment that downplays the extraordinary vigor and verve of this inspired work. —*Brian Robins*

Recommended:
○ **Mozart: Clarinet Concerto; Sonata in B flat; Bassoon Concerto** / Marriner (cond.), Leister, Orton, Thunemann, Academy of St. Martin-in-the-Fields / 1989 / Philips 422390
○ **Mozart: Flute Concerto 1; Clarinet Concerto; Concerto for Flute & Harp** / Abbado (cond.), Meyer, Berlin PO / 2001 / EMI 57128

Concerto for flute, harp & orchestra in C major, K. 299 (1778)

At the end of March 1778, Mozart and his mother, Maria Anna, finally arrived in Paris after a prolonged stay in Mannheim (where Mozart had fallen in love with Aloysia Weber). On April 5 Maria Anna reported to Leopold (who had to remain in Salzburg) that Wolfgang had received a commission from the flute-playing Duke of Guines and his harpist daughter, who was taking music lessons from the composer. The commission, for a concerto for flute and harp, could hardly have inspired the young composer, who professed a dislike for both solo instruments and generally despised French musical taste, but he delivered the concerto dutifully. The combination of flute and harp, moreover, is a difficult one; "as a duo," notes writer Ethan Mordden, "they sound like a nymph going bonkers in a plashing spring." In spite of all this, however, the work is often played and is a perennial crowd-pleaser. Orchestras have few other opportunties to put their harpists on display in a concerto. Like almost everything else that happened on his trip with his mother to Paris, this concerto caused Mozart trouble; the Duke failed to pay the composer for it.

In its small forces (the orchestra has only two oboes, two horns, and the standard string ensemble) it is suited for the salon. In line with the standard concerto form, the two soloists wait for the orchestra to present the opening material of the first movement, then take it up in unison. The movement as a whole is most charming in the dialogue-like writing for the flute and harp and in its overflowing lyricism. The second movement is accompanied only by the string section (the violas are divided into two parts for a richer sound). It is warm, uncomplicated, and somewhat florid. The finale is a lively rondo with a veritable parade of attractive tunes. The concerto as a whole, notwithstanding its background, stands as one of the most pleasant mementos of Mozart's Paris sojourn, which would continue to reverberate stylistically through the rest of his output. —*Joseph Stevenson*

Recommended:
○ **Mozart: Flute Concertos; Concerto for Flute & Harp** / Marriner (cond.), Galway, Robles, Academy of St. Martin-in-the-Fields / 1997 / BMG 68256
○ **Mozart: Wind Concertos** / Marriner (cond.), Graf, Grafenauer, Academy of St. Martin-in-the-Fields / 1991 / Philips 422509
○ **Mozart: Concerto for Flute & Harp; Clarinet Concerto** / Paillard (cond.), Rampal, Laskine, Jean-Francois Paillard CO / 1993 / Erato 45978

Horn Concerto No. 1 in D major, K. 412 (1782)

Alan Tyson has demonstrated that Mozart's *Horn Concerto No. 1* in D major, K. 412/514 (K. 386b), long thought to have been composed in 1782, dates from 1791—the year of the composer's death. The second movement is left incomplete in the autograph; in fact, the concerto was completed by Mozart's student Franz Xaver

Süssmayer (1766–1803), who also finished Mozart's *Requiem*. Süssmayer took great liberties with the piece, inserting into the rondo finale a segment based on the Gregorian chant for the Lamentations of Jeremiah. This particular melody forms part of the music used during Holy Week in the Catholic Church, in light of which the inscription on the completed manuscript, "April 6, 1792," makes sense—that date was the Catholic feast of Good Friday in 1792.

The inspiration for Mozart's horn concertos came from virtuoso hornist Joseph Leutgeb (1732–1811), whom the Mozarts knew in Salzburg. In 1777, he moved to Vienna and took over a cheesemonger's shop, borrowing money from Leopold Mozart. Leutgeb seems to have indulged the younger Mozart's base sense of humor: on the solo part of the *Horn Concerto No. 1* in D major Mozart inscribed a text that matched the melody, parts of which read: "For you , Mr. Donkey," and "For you—beast—what a dissonance—Oh!—Woe is me!!" Scattered among the remarks are references to a certain male body part.

In two movements, each an Allegro in D major, the *Concerto for Horn in D major*, K. 412, is scored for solo horn in D, strings, two oboes, and two bassoons. The first movement features a typical structure for the first movement of a concerto—a combination of ritornello and sonata form in which the opening orchestra exposition introduces material but does not change keys. The soloist enters, beginning with the first tune played by the orchestra, but continues on a different track toward a modulation to the dominant. Throughout, the writing for the horn is masterfully idiomatic, taking full advantage of the instrument's ability to produce easily leaps of a fourth and fifth as well as arpeggios. Undoubtedly, Leutgeb's excellent technique prompted Mozart's writing of extended florid passages.

The rousing 6/8-meter finale, a rondo in D major, recalls the horn's association with the hunt. Opening once again with the orchestra, the movement features a leaping main theme built of falling triads. The horn quickly takes up the tune before the movement spins off into the first episode. Marked by a youthful ebullience, the finale proceeds with alternations of new ideas with nearly literal returns of the rondo theme. Passages that stray significantly from the key of D major attest to Leutgeb's ear and technical facility. *—John Palmer*

Recommended:

- ○ **Mozart: Horn Concertos** / Marriner (cond.), Tuckwell, Academy of St. Martin-in-the-Fields / 2001 / EMI 74967
- ○ **Mozart: Horn Concertos** / Karajan (cond.), Brain, Philharmonia / 1998 / EMI 66950
- ○ **Mozart: Horn Concertos** / Marriner (cond.), Civil, Academy of St. Martin-in-the-Fields Chamber Ens. / 2001 / Philips 464717

Horn Concerto No. 2 in E flat major, K. 417 (1783)

Mozart completed this work in 1783 for the hornist Joseph Leutgeb; the accompaniment is scored for pairs of oboes and horns, plus strings. Leutgeb, 24 years older than Mozart and a horn player in the court orchestra at Salzburg, had known the composer since childhood. He moved to Vienna in 1777, four years before Wolfgang, to become a cheesemonger (with money from Leopold Mozart, who was normally tightfisted). Leutgeb's virtuosity, acclaimed by Parisians as well as the Viennese, was obviously still intact when Mozart wrote a concert Rondo for him (K. 371), then a quintet with strings (K. 407/386c) and the first two of four misnumbered concertos, all in E flat for the valveless hand horn. If, by 1787, aging had begun to impair his technique, Leutgeb remained a superb legato player.

K. 417, despite its published number, was the first concerto and bore this autograph: "Wolfgang Amadè Mozart takes pity on Leutgeb, ass, ox, and simpleton, at Vienna on May 27, 1783." He would write even more insultingly later on, yet plainly cared very much for this lifelong friend who survived him by a decade.

The music is a treasurehouse of melody, with an expansive opening movement in common time but no tempo marking (Allegro maestoso was a publisher's, or editor's, educated guess). Following an abbreviated first exposition, the soloist enters with a new theme; later on, the development shifts to a minor key. The succeeding Andante, in the dominant key of B flat, has basic song structure with a middle-section melody of rare beauty for the soloist. A concluding, hunt-inspired Rondo in 6/8 time set the pattern for the rest of Mozart's Leutgeb concertos: irrepressibly jolly as well as comic—by intention, of course—this one with an accelerated coda that leaves the hounds to catch up. *—Roger Dettmer*

Recommended:

- ○ **Mozart: Wind Concertos** / Süsskind (cond.), Brain, London PO / 1997 / Avid 605
- ○ **Mozart: Horn Concertos** / Karajan (cond.), Brain, Philharmonia / 1998 / EMI 66950
- ○ **Mozart: Horn Concertos 2 & 3** / Purvis, Orpheus CO / 1988 / DG 423623
- ○ **Mozart: Horn Concertos** / Marriner (cond.), Tuckwell, Academy of St. Martin-in-the-Fields / 2001 / EMI 74967

Horn Concerto No. 3 in E flat major, K. 447 (1783)

The concerto K. 447 is the third of the four horn concertos composed by Mozart between 1783 and 1791 for the French horn player Joseph Leutgeb (1732–1811), a friend whom Mozart knew for most of his life. In 1777 Leutgeb moved from Salzburg (where he was member of the court orchestra) to Vienna, where he opened a cheese shop (with the help of a loan from Mozart's father Leopold) in addition to continuing his musical career. The jocular, at times insulting comments that litter the autograph parts of the horn concertos bear witness to the close nature of the friendship between Mozart and Leutgeb. More important, they are also a testament to the artistry of the latter; the solo parts contain many passages that present a considerable challenge to players on the natural (valveless) horn. Among these was the use of so-called "stopped notes," a technique that involved the player's inserting his right hand into the bell to enable him to play notes otherwise unavailable on the horns of the day. Mozart's horn concertos all include such stopped notes, in addition to bass notes obtained by the technique known as "overblowing," another skill developed by Leutgeb. The concerto was originally given a dating of 1783 by Köchel, but more recent research has established that K. 447 probably belongs to 1787—although that leaves open the question as to why Mozart did not enter the work into the thematic catalog he started in 1784. As with all the concertos with the exception of "No. 1," K. 412 (the last in order of composition), K. 447 is in the usual three-movement concerto form, with an Allegro followed by a slow movement marked Romance and a concluding Allegro in rondo form with plenty of hunting-horn atmosphere. The concerto is scored for two clarinets, two bassoons, and the usual complement of strings. *—Brian Robins*

Recommended:

- ○ **Mozart: Horn Concertos** / Marriner (cond.), Tuckwell, Academy of St. Martin-in-the-Fields / 2001 / EMI 74967
- ○ **Mozart: Horn Concertos** / Karajan (cond.), Brain, Philharmonia / 1998 / EMI 66950
- ○ **Mozart: Horn Concertos** / Mackerras (cond.), Ruske, Scottish CO / 1994 / Telarc 80367

Horn Concerto No. 4 in E flat major, K. 495 (1786)

The only one of Mozart's four concertos to be included in his thematic catalog, K. 495 was entered on June 26, 1786, a few weeks after the first performances of *Le nozze di Figaro*. Such a date makes it, by currently prevailing chronology, the second in order of composition. Like the other three horn concertos, it was composed for his old friend Joseph Leutgeb (1732–1811), who had moved to Vienna from Salzburg (where he was member of the court orchestra) in 1777, four years before Mozart. Mozart described the concerto in his entry as being composed for Waldhorn (literally "woods or forest horn"), an alternative name for the French horn that reminds us of the instrument's associations with hunting. The partially incomplete score is notated in four different colors of ink, an idea that has generally been supposed to be another of the jokes Mozart made at the expense of Leutgeb. More recently it has been suggested (in the notes accompanying the New Mozart Edition) that the use of varying colors serves the purpose of coded instructions denoting refinements of dynamics and nuance. In common with all four concertos, the solo part contains many passages that present a considerable challenge to players on the natural (valveless) horn. Among these was the use of so-called "stopped notes," a procedure that involved the player inserting his right hand into the bell to enable him to play notes otherwise unavailable on the horns of the day. Mozart's horn concertos all include such stopped notes, in addition to bass notes obtained by the technique known as "overblowing," another skill developed by Leutgeb. Like K. 417, the first of the Leutgeb concertos (and to which it bears a certain resemblance), K. 495 is scored for two horns, two oboes, and strings, and cast in three movements: Allegro maestoso, Romance, and Rondo. *—Brian Robins*

Recommended:

- ○ **Mozart: Wind Concertos** / Sargent (cond.), Brain, Halle Orch. / 1997 / Avid 605
- ○ **Mozart: Horn Concertos** / Karajan (cond.), Brain, Philharmonia / 1998 / EMI 66950
- ○ **Mozart: Horn Concertos** / McGegan (cond.), Greer, Philharmonia Baroque Orch. / 2001 / Classical Express 3957012
- ○ **Mozart: Horn Concertos** / Marriner (cond.), Tuckwell, Academy of St. Martin-in-the-Fields / 2001 / EMI 74967

Oboe Concerto in C major, K. 314 (1777)

Most of Mozart's concertos for wind instruments are for the horn and were composed in Vienna. There are several earlier works for other instruments; among these are two for oboe and orchestra. Mozart composed the *Oboe Concerto in C major*, K. 314, for Giuseppe Ferlendis, oboist in the orchestra of the Archbishop of Salzburg, sometime between the beginning of Ferlendis' service at the Salzburg court, on April 1, 1777, and Mozart's departure for Mannheim on September 22, 1777.

The *Oboe Concerto in C major* is scored for solo oboe with an orchestra of two oboes, two horns, and strings. The orchestration is light and transparent, highlighting the soloist and giving the numerous recurrent rhythmic figures more presence, especially a falling passage in the orchestra that first introduces the solo oboe. Mozart's central slow movement is elegiac, with the oboe placed throughout in its most liquid range. Mozart once wrote that he disliked writing such pieces, but the elegance of this movement makes this difficult to believe. The ebullient, Haydnesque finale is a rondo in a quick 2/4 time, with a theme that is bouncy and jagged. Most notable is the beginning of the central episode in which a tune based on the rondo theme is developed in three-part counterpoint. It is one of those moments of brilliance that bubble forth even from Mozart's more workaday pieces.

During the period Mozart was in Mannheim, he transcribed the concerto for flute to fulfill a commission from a Dutch amateur, Ferdinand Dejean (*Flute Concerto No. 2 in D*, K. 314 [K. 285d]). It is this version that was known until the original parts of the oboe concerto were discovered in Salzburg in 1920. *—John Palmer*

Recommended:

- ○ **Mozart: Horn Concertos, Oboe Concerto** / Marriner (cond.), Black, Academy of St. Martin-in-the-Fields Chamber Ens. / 2001 / Philips 464717
- ○ **Indermuhle Plays Mozart** / Hager (cond.), Indermühle, English CO / 1989 / Novalis 150043

Piano Concertos Nos. 1–8 (1767–1776)

Mozart's first eight keyboard concertos demonstrate that genius does not grace every item in the Köchel catalog. They are competent, precocious works, particularly impressive coming from a composer who started writing these at age 11. But they are more important as evidence of Mozart's evolution from a child imitating the conventions of the day to a unique talent who would ultimately write concertos of a sparkle and drama unequalled in his lifetime.

The first four concertos, composed in Salzburg in 1767, are simply arrangements of other composers' keyboard sonata movements. Most likely they were exercises in orchestral writing imposed by his father Leopold Mozart. The orchestration is already confident, if unexceptional, and the people truly responsible for the works' modest musical interest are the source composers: C.P.E. Bach, and the now obscure Johann Gottfried Eckard, Johann Schobert, Hermann Friedrich Raupach, and Leontzi Honauer. One of the touches for which young Wolfgang was responsible is the prominent use of the horn in the second concerto, in B flat. Also notable is the slow movement of the fourth concerto, a minor mode movement in a major-key concerto—some of Mozart's finest work would come in the minor mode movements of his mature concertos.

With the *Concerto in D major No. 5*, composed in 1773, we arrive at Mozart's first wholly original keyboard concerto. It's a flashy work designed to show off Mozart's skill as a pianist rather than as a composer. Around 1783, Mozart composed a new finale for the concerto, a rondo that is now given the separate Köchel number of 382. Five violin concertos separate Mozart's fifth keyboard concerto from his sixth, written in early 1776. Oddly, though, this modest work sounds as if it could date from well before the fifth, let alone the fully mature and brilliant *Violin Concerto No. 5*. Probably written for some now unknown aristocratic Salzburg amateur, the sixth is notable only for its expressive Andante. It's certain that Mozart had an aristocratic amateur in mind for his seventh concerto: it's inscribed to the Countess Lodron and her daughters. Yes, this is a work for *three* pianos and orchestra, although Mozart also prepared a two-piano version (possibly for him to play with his own sister). In the original, each solo part is graded in difficulty according to the player's ability; thus, the first and second parts are moderately challenging (certainly more so than in the sixth concerto), while the third part is quite simple. Most effective here are the first movement's counterpoint and the extended Adagio. Yet another countess, Antonia Lützow, was the beneficiary of Mozart's eighth concerto—his third from 1776 and that's only into April. Again, the solo work is not highly demanding, but it does require agility (Mozart wrote three sets of cadenzas of varying difficulty, accommodating the abilities of performers from student level to professional.) The most remarkable aspect of this work is the rich woodwind scoring, another hint of the glories in the concertos soon to come. *—James Reel*

Recommended:

- ○ **Mozart: Keyboard Concertos 1–4** / Hogwood (cond.), Levin, Academy of Ancient Music / Decca 466131
- ○ **Mozart: Complete Piano Concertos** / Barenboim (cond. & piano), English CO / 1998 / EMI 72930

Concerto for 3 pianos & orchestra in F major ("Lodron" / "Concerto No. 7"), K. 242 (1776)

As he often did, Mozart composed this unusually scored concerto for specific performers. In this case—according to an ascription in his own handwriting on a special presentation copy—for "Her Excellency, Her Ladyship, the Countess Lodron ... and her daughters, their Ladyships the Countesses Aloysia and Giuseppa." And, as he frequently did on such occasions, each part was geared to the performer who would play it, with the degree of difficulty adjusted for differences in skill and experience. In this case, two of the solo parts are moderately difficult, while the third, for the younger of the two daughters, is more modest in its demands. Some confusion surrounds this concerto, since a version for two soloists also exists and is supposed to have been intended for performance by Mozart and his sister. Given the modest contribution of the third piano part, the work loses little in the transfer to just two soloists, and is frequently performed and recorded that way. That the solo parts do not require virtuoso performers in no way renders the work simple or unimaginative; maybe Mozart of all composers could best accommodate modest performing talent with brilliant composition.

The first movement opens with a typical barking opening and soon the combined presence of three soloists produces rich counterpoint. Midway through the movement, a cadenza combining all three is superbly effective and noticeably out of reach of any single performer. The second movement, an eight-minute adagio, is lyrical and melodic. A minuet-like rondo concludes the work, allowing each soloist considerable individual attention, but assigning most of the burden of building to a dramatic finale to the orchestra. Though barely out of his teens, Mozart here crafted a full-blown, mature concerto. *—Michael Morrison*

Recommended:

- ○ **Mozart: Piano Concertos** / Bychkov (cond.), Labèques, Berlin PO / 1990 / Philips 422507
- ○ **Mozart: Concertos for 2 & 3 Pianos** / Perahia, Lupu, English CO / 1991 / Sony 44915

Piano Concerto No. 9 in E flat major ("Jeunehomme" / "Jenamy"), K. 271 (1777)

When Mozart first started composing keyboard concertos in 1767, the form was still in its early stages of development. Sufficiently confident to embark on the composition of symphonies as a child, his earliest attempts at the concerto show him feeling his way, producing pastiche works that involved adding orchestral accompaniments to solo keyboard sonatas by other composers, most notably those of one of the principal influences on his early style, Johann Christian Bach (three Concertos, K. 107). Mozart's first wholly original concerto (No. 5 in D, K. 175) did not appear until December 1773, by which time he had already composed more than 30 symphonies. With the *Concerto in E flat*, K. 271, we arrive not only at the first of Mozart's mature piano concertos, but the maturity of the form itself—one that the composer would dominate until the appearance of Beethoven.

Composed in Salzburg in January 1777, the month in which the composer celebrated his 21st birthday, the ninth concerto represents a considerable expansion both in scale and ambition over his earlier concertos. It was written for a young French keyboard player, Mlle. Jeunehomme, who visited Salzburg during the winter of 1776–77. Nothing is known about her or her abilities as a performer, but the concerto she inspired suggests they must have been considerable.

Cast in the usual three-movement form (*Allegro*; *Andantino*; *Rondeau: Presto*), the work has unusual qualities that are immediately apparent in the opening bars. Instead of the expected extended orchestral introduction, the piano immediately replies to the orchestra's opening motif—a device Mozart never again employed. The entire concerto is planned on a grand scale, obviously remaining a favorite with its composer, who took it with him on his tour to Mannheim and Paris in 1777–78 and scheduled it several times in his Viennese concerts during the 1780s. The orchestral scoring is for pairs of horns and oboes plus the usual complement of strings. *—Brian Robins*

Recommended:

- ○ **Mozart: Piano Concertos** / Rosbaud (cond.), Gieseking, Berlin State Opera Orch. / 2003 / Andante 1120
- ○ **Mozart: Piano Concertos 9 & 21** / Perahia, English CO / 1993 / Sony 34562
- ○ **Mozart: Piano Concertos 11 & 9** / Gardiner, Bilson, English Baroque Soloists / Archiv 410905

Concerto for 2 pianos & orchestra in E flat major ("Concerto No. 10"), K. 365 (1779)

Mozart's musically gifted sister, Nannerl, figured prominently in several of his compositions. Some accounts insist she was at least as gifted a keyboard performer as her younger brother, and as early as 1764, when Wolfgang was eight and Nannerl was 13, they toured and performed together at either one or two keyboard instruments. Thus, several years later, the idea of a concerto for two pianos likely came naturally to Wolfgang. No specific circumstances of this work's creation have been unearthed, however.

In 1779, the young composer had thrashed his way through the shoals and pitfalls of adolescence and endured his first heartbreak. After an extended tour of Europe, he reluctantly accepted the forgiveness and employ of the Archbishop of Salzburg and although the man was a Philistine when it came to music, Wolfgang set about trying to please him. With both the French and Italian styles still fresh in his mind, he set down two fine works in the double concerto format. The second of these was the *Sinfonia Concertante for Violin and Viola in E flat*, K. 364 and the first was the present piece. While there is some evidence that fragments of the work were set down as early as 1775, the piece is generally considered to have been finally assembled and finished in early 1779.

In three movements, and relatively long at 25 minutes, the work is challenging for both soloists. The parts are also equally assigned so that there is not a first solo and a second solo. Passages intermingle, and the piece in general is a tour de force for performers and listeners alike. The first movement, a ten-minute Allegro, opens with a lengthy orchestral introduction containing an ambitious theme. Both pianos finally enter together, and after briefly alternating introductory phrases, join together in the first theme. A second theme is more ominous, and sounds as if it could be the basis for early silent film dramatic accompaniment. The orchestra puts a stop to this with a repeat of the brusque opening; after a gentle recapitulation, the movement ends in a tripping double cadenza and coda.

The second movement, an eight-minute Andante, begins as a stately Minuet in the orchestra. When the theme appears in the pianos, it is divided into two solo passages. The two soon seem to flow together, and passages alternate between soloists and orchestra, nicely leading and accompanying each other. The movement also offers one of the mature Mozart's first uses of surprise dissonance, as unexpected notes appear in exposed piano passages. The movement ends abruptly. The finale is a marvelous rondo. Although it is appropriately scored for the instruments and orchestra of his day, the size and power of it make one wonder what Mozart might have crafted with modern concert grand pianos at his disposal.

The genius of the work lies in its seamlessness. Even the casual listener will discern that there are too many notes to be played by a single instrument, yet without visual reinforcement it is essentially impossible for the hearer to separate the solo parts. Mozart created here a large work for four perfectly coordinated hands and two full-size keyboards. It is significant in his output as standing among the first works of his maturity following his return to Salzburg and the death of his mother. *—Michael Morrison*

Recommended:

- ○ **Mozart: Piano Concerto 27; Concerto for 2 Pianos** / Böhm (cond.), Gilels, Vienna PO / 1998 / DG 459035
- ○ **Double Piano Concertos** / Marriner (cond.), Pekinel Duo, London PO / 1999 / Chandos 9711
- ○ **Mozart: Concerto for 2 Pianos; Sonata for 2 Pianos, K448** / Previn (cond.), Larrocha, Orch. of St. Luke's / 1995 / RCA 902668044

Piano Concerto No. 11 in F major, K. 413 (1783)

For his subscription concerts in Vienna, a primary source of income, Mozart generally composed piano concertos, enabling him to showcase his exceptional facility at the keyboard. Between 1782 and 1786, the years in which he gave the most concerts, Mozart wrote 15 concertos, nearly all for his own use.

Scored for an orchestra of paired oboes, bassoons, and horns, with strings, the *Piano Concerto in F major,* K. 413, was composed sometime in 1782–83 and printed in 1785 by Artaria Vienna as Op. 4, No. 2. The F major concerto forms part of a set of three, the other two being in A major, K. 414, and C major, K. 415. Just how quickly Mozart could compose is made evident by the history of these concertos. In a letter of December 28, 1782, to his father, Mozart describes the three projected works and notes that only one is finished. On January 15, 1783, the *Wiener Zeitung* advertised the concertos, with optional wind parts, available in manuscript.

To his father, Mozart described these three concertos as "a happy medium between what is too easy and too difficult; they are very brilliant, pleasing to the ear, and natural, without being vapid." Of the three concertos, the F major is generally considered the most conservative. Like Mozart's other works in the genre, there are three movements in a fast-slow-fast format, the first of which is cast in the typical form for concerto first movements, a combination of ritornello and sonata form. After the Allegro opens with firm, repeated chords, the orchestra goes on to state the principal themes of the movement, without modulating. When the soloist enters, it is not immediately with the first theme, but with a new idea, after which we hear the principal themes, developed and extended, including the modulation that is usually reserved for the soloist. Throughout the large central section both the orchestra and soloist develop the themes from the exposition and occasionally spin out new ideas. Mozart did realize a cadenza for the movement, and this is what is usually heard on recordings.

Mozart set the middle movement, marked Larghetto, in B flat major, a key that, when following a movement in F major, creates a sense of relaxation. The blithe theme is harmonized in such a way that its joy is infused with a hint of melancholy.

The Finale is a minuet-rondo, an outdated form by the early 1780s. As in the first movement, the rondo theme is announced first by the orchestra. The theme takes on the shape of a minuet in that it is in two repeated parts, the second of which begins with new material before being rounded off by a return of the first part. This memorable movement was clearly meant to entertain concertgoers and give them something to hum on the way home. *—John Palmer*

Recommended:

- ○ **Mozart: Piano Concertos 22 & 11** / Antal (cond.), Jando, Hungaricus Concentus / 1991 / Naxos 550206
- ○ **Mozart: Piano Concertos 9 & 11** / Gardiner (cond.), Bilson, EBS / Archiv 410905

Piano Concerto No. 12 in A major, K. 414 (1782)

The undated *A major Piano Concerto* of late 1782 was the first of 15 that Mozart composed, mainly for his own use, before the end of 1786. Infused throughout with his special genius, these concertos became (and remain) unparalleled in Western music as a body of work, all the more astounding given the chronologically brief span in which he created them.

In the late spring of 1781, Mozart succeeded in breaking free from Hieronymous Colloredo—the haughty and parsimonious prince-archbishop of Salzburg, in whose service he felt stultified—determined to make his fortune in Vienna. If his income over the next decade did not regularly reflect the quality or quantity of music that Mozart produced, he did become famous. For four years the fickle Hapsburg capital proclaimed him its favorite pianist until, in 1786, *The Marriage of Figaro* triggered his fall from grace.

The patronage of his Empire's aristocracy supported Mozart after 1782 as a concert artist, publisher, piano teacher, and soloist at their soirées. When the anti-aristocratic *Figaro* seemed to bite this feeding hand, it was withdrawn—a situation grimly worsened by the Ottoman armies' 1788 attack on the southeastern flank of the Hapsburg' Holy Roman Empire. Music lost its priority in Vienna, then fell largely silent when Joseph II died in 1790, of a disease contracted in the field.

Early in the decade, Mozart had written the *Concerto No. 12* along with *Nos. 11* and *13*, completing them in that order for his debut concerts of 1783 (during Lent, when theaters and the opera went dark by decree until Easter). He described their character in a letter to his father dated December 28, 1782, as "... a happy medium between what is too easy and too difficult; they are very brilliant to the ear, and natural, without being vapid. There are passages here and there from which connoisseurs alone can derive satisfaction; but these passages are written in such a way that the less discriminating cannot fail to be pleased, though without knowing why."

He could have remarked, too, on their thematic abundance—there are no fewer than six major subjects in the first movement alone of *No. 12*, two of which are new in the development section. Charles Rosen has pointed out in *The Classical Style* that here, as well as in later concertos, "Mozart uses melodies at once so complex and so complete that they do not bear the weight of [further] development." Because he hoped to sell the three concertos for home performance with string quartet, he scored *No. 12* lightly—the orchestra consists of just two oboes, two horns, and strings. The middle movement is a solemn, sonata-structured Andante in D major with a minor-key development. Its main subject is taken from an overture by Johann Christian Bach, Mozart's childhood friend and teacher, who had died on January 1, 1782—"a sad day for the world of music," wrote the boy-prodigy, now grown to manhood. The final movement is an Allegretto rondo, no less genial for being gentle, with a refrain in 2/4 time built on three motifs and contrapuntal complexities that are submerged in a delightfully light exterior in the way that only Mozart could. Here as elsewhere in the *A major Concerto,* cadenzas are by the composer; the soloist may choose from among several. *—Roger Dettmer*

Recommended:

- ○ **Rudolf Serkin** / Abbado (cond.), Serkin, London SO / 1999 / Philips 456964
- ○ **Mozart: Piano Concertos in A major, K414 & 488** / Rolla (cond.), Kocsis, Franz Liszt CO / Hungaroton 12472
- ○ **Mozart: Piano Concertos 12 & 14** / Gardiner (cond.), Bilson, EBS / Archiv 413463

Piano Concerto No. 13 in C major, K. 415 (1783)

During Mozart's first few years in Vienna, one of his primary sources of income was the subscription concert. For such concerts, he generally composed piano concertos, enabling him to showcase his exceptional facility at the keyboard. Between 1782 and 1786, the years in which he gave the most concerts, Mozart wrote 15 concertos for piano and orchestra, nearly all for his own use, which have come to represent the Classical ideal of the genre.

Mozart evidently composed his first Vienna concertos, K. 413–415, very quickly. In a letter of December 28, 1782 to his father, Mozart mentioned the three projected works and noted that only one was finished. On January 15, 1783 the *Wiener Zeitung* advertised the concertos, with optional wind parts, available in manuscript. To his father, Mozart described these three concertos as "a happy medium between what is too easy and too difficult; they are very brilliant, pleasing to the ear, and natural, without being vapid."

Scored for piano, strings, and two each of oboe, bassoon, horn, trumpet, and timpani, the Concerto in C major was begun very late in 1782 and completed early the next year. It was printed in 1785 by Artaria in Vienna as Op. 4, No. 3. (The Concertos, K. 414 and K. 413, were published as Op. 4, Nos. 1 and 2, respectively.) Although the material of the C major concerto is conventional, Mozart's formal treatment of it is often bold.

Military rhythms dominate the opening measures of the first movement, which begins with the traditional orchestral exposition. For the soloist, Mozart reserves new material, intermingling it with the opening theme, which remains the property of the orchestra. The central, developmental ritornello opens with the first theme, a procedure Mozart used in none of his other piano concertos. Throughout this large central span, the piano part maintains a high level of virtuosity against a background of orchestral interjections. Most of the cadenzas heard on recordings are those realized and written down by Mozart himself.

Mozart had planned an Adagio in C minor as the middle movement, but opted instead for the F major Andante. However, passages from the abandoned C minor movement survive in the Adagio sections of the Finale. The orchestra introduces the Andante, pausing on the dominant before the soloist enters, restating the opening material. Lacking trumpets, the movement takes on a warmer, more subtle sound than its neighbors.

The Finale is a sonata-rondo with a double exposition, the first of which remains in C major—a typical trait of concerto first movements, but unusual in finales. Between the two expositions, there is the Adagio segment in C minor. This passage once again interrupts the progress of the movement during the recapitulation, just before the last presentation of the main theme in the piano part. The resulting pattern creates a ternary rondo format—ABACABA—while the modulations and development of material are characteristic sonata-form procedures. Mozart alters his rondo section (A) with each appearance, either developing one of its three themes or replacing one or more of them with a new idea. *—John Palmer*

Recommended:

- ○ **Mozart: Piano Concertos 13 & 15** / Giulini (cond.), Michelangeli, Rome Italian Radio Orch. / Hommage 7001850
- ○ **Mozart: Piano Concertos 13 & 15** / Gardiner (cond.), Bilson, EBS / Archiv 413464

Piano Concerto No. 14 in E flat major, K. 449 (1784)

The leap in artistic growth between Mozart's piano concertos of 1782 (K. 413–415) and the series composed in 1784 (K. 449–451, 453, 456, 459) is one of the greatest in the composer's brief career. The *Piano Concerto No. 14 in E flat major,* K. 449, is generally regarded as *Mozart*'s first mature work in the genre.

By 1784, Mozart was the star keyboard performer in Vienna. Mozart dated his manuscript of the E flat major concerto February 9, 1784. The concerto was composed for Mozart's student Barbara Ployer, whose father was an agent in Vienna for the Salzburg court. In April, Mozart would prepare another concerto for her, that in G major, K. 453.

The concerto, K. 449, is scored for piano, strings, and paired oboes and horns, although it may be played with only string accompaniment. Ms. Ployer must have been an excellent student, for the keyboard part is not easy. The structure of the work, too, is advanced and a great diversity of melodic material in the first movement requires a much larger form than in the earlier concertos. Possibly in reference to the finale and the opening of the first movement, Mozart described K. 449 to his father as "a concerto of a peculiar kind."

One great difference between K. 449 and Mozart's earlier concertos is that the first ritornello of the opening movement modulates to the dominant, an event usually reserved for the solo exposition. The opening themes and orchestration of the movement bring to mind the dramatic writing in the composer's operas with their sudden changes in mood and affective use of the minor mode. Throughout the Allegro the soloist seems more an integral part of the proceedings than the star supported by an orchestral backup. Nevertheless, the importance of the piano part is indisputable in this brief, tightly argued movement. Mozart realized one cadenza for use by Ms. Ployer.

Elegance and delicacy characterize the Andantino second movement. A perfect foil to the dramatic power of the Allegro, the Andantino's only tension stems from being set in the dominant, B flat major. Its main material consists of two successive passages, first played by the orchestra and then decorated by the soloist. The result is a movement with a through-composed feel whose wide, pathetic descending leaps look forward to the slow movements of Schumann.

The Allegro ma non troppo finale is a highly idiosyncratic structure that is like a sonata-rondo, but the contrasting material is based on variations of the first theme, creating a monothematic movement. Its overall texture is the result of Mozart's combination of contrapuntal ingenuity with opera buffa style melodies and accompaniment. The leaping, jagged principal theme makes each of its appearances in a different guise, occasionally spreading its material between different instruments. The eighth note triplets in the middle of the movement make the 6/8-meter coda less obtrusive than it might be in this seamlessly composed essay. *—John Palmer*

Recommended:

- ○ **Maria João Pires** / Abbado (cond.), Pires, Vienna PO / 1999 / Philips 456928
- ○ **Mozart: Piano Concertos 5, 14 & 16** / Hogwood (cond.), Levin, Academy of Ancient Music / 1999 / Archiv 458285
- ○ **Mozart: Piano Concertos 12 & 14** / Gardiner (cond.), Bilson, EBS / Archiv 413463

Piano Concerto No. 15 in B flat major, K. 450 (1784)

The leap in artistic growth between Mozart's piano concertos of 1782 (K. 413–5) and the series composed in 1784 (K. 449–451, 453, 456, 459) was one of the greatest in the composer's brief career. Thus the *Piano Concerto No. 14 in E flat major,* K. 449, is sometimes regarded as Mozart's first mature work in the genre. Five weeks after the composition of K. 449 Mozart completed a strikingly different work in the *Concerto in B flat major,* K. 450. Mozart's entry for the piece in his "List of All My Works" is dated March 15, 1784. The *Piano Concerto in D major,* K. 451, would follow only seven days later. Mozart composed both these works for his own use in public concerts, describing them to his father as "concertos to make you sweat." Not surprisingly, then, the part for the soloist is far more virtuosic than in K. 449, which was composed for one of Mozart's students. Furthermore, the writing for the wind instruments, in K. 450 in particular, is more involved and advanced than in any of Mozart's earlier piano concertos. Scored for piano, strings, paired oboes, bassoons, and horns, with a single flute in the finale, K. 450 features a woodwind section more deeply integrated into the total texture than in K. 449.

Opening with a tune reminiscent of Mozart's Salzburg-era serenades, the Allegro throughout is marked by unusual orchestration. Once the piano part begins, the soloist dominates the movement, with the orchestra occasionally reduced to providing only punctuation. Indeed, the soloist's initial lengthy passage contains no references to the opening ritornello. It would be wrong to call the central solo span a development section, for absolutely no development occurs in this continuous wash of flashy, bravura piano figurations. There is, however, a "recapitulation" containing themes omitted by the piano during its first episode and the central section.

In 3/8 time, the E flat major Andante consists of a theme with two variations and a coda. The two-part theme modulates to the dominant (B flat major) at the midpoint. Mozart's variations are decorative; no fundamental changes occur in the melodies.

B flat major is generally considered one of Mozart's "happy" keys, and the Allegro finale does nothing to alter this conception. A rondo in 6/8 time, the movement is filled with flashy piano passages and hand crossings. Mozart varies the returns of the rondo section, altering the order of the melodies and extending them, and thus making it seem as though we are hearing a chain of variations. As in the first movement, the piano part is technically difficult, designed to highlight the performer: Mozart. *—John Palmer*

Recommended:

- ○ **Mozart: Piano Concertos 15, 21 & 23** / Marriner (cond.), Brendel, Academy of St. Martin-in-the-Fields / 2001 / Philips 464719
- ○ **Mozart: Piano Concertos 15 & 26** / Hogwood (cond.), Levin, Academy of Ancient Music / 1997 / L'Oiseau-Lyre 455814
- ○ **Mozart: Piano Concertos 13 & 15** / Gardiner (cond.), Bilson, EBS / Archiv 413464

Piano Concerto No. 16 in D major, K. 451 (1784)

Contemporary records show that Mozart gave no fewer than 22 public performances between February 26 and April 3, 1784. In this period, it should come as no surprise to discover that he chose to return to a grand and brilliant format in the composition of his *Piano Concerto No. 16 in D major,* K. 451. As with its nearest predecessor in the same key of D major, *Concerto No. 5,* K. 175, the concerto includes parts in its orchestration for trumpets and drums, always emblematic of a pronounced celebratory and public style in Mozart concertos. (An even earlier *D major Concerto,* listed as K. 40, the third of Mozart's 27 piano concertos, was in fact an arrangement of sonata movements by Honauer, Eckard, and in the finale, C.P.E. Bach.) *No. 16* is, however, an altogether deeper work, both more passionate and vital in character, more structurally masterful, and with a slow movement of remarkable intellectual substance.

The first movement (Allegro) opens with a typically Mozartean marchlike figure, evoking a rhythmic formula virtually identical to that which opened *Concerto No. 13 in C,* K. 415. Mozart was to employ the same solution again in a number of his subsequent piano concertos, notably *Nos. 18 in B flat,* K. 456, and *19 in F,* K. 459. Mozart's solitary *Piano Concerto in G,* K. 453, differs only slightly in that it features a trill on the second note, though the generally purposeful demeanor of its opening is the same. The most arresting characteristic of the *D major Concerto,* K. 451, is its near-symphonic robustness and ambitious sense of scale throughout each of its three movements, and in this work, Mozart undoubtedly achieved a significant advance in unifying both symphonic and concerto genres in a new, all-embracing creative unity. Indeed, it may well be reasonable to suggest that the "modern" Classical piano concerto was born on March 22, 1784, the completion date which appears at the head of the manuscript. Although Mozart probably played the work himself soon afterwards, the copy he later sent to his sister contained one passage of the Andante in fragmentary form. He, therefore, sent her a substitute passage in richer harmonies, although on many occasions, Mozart's copies of concertos he played himself seem to have been at best sketchy, including just the bare outlines of themes upon which he would extemporize in performance. Listeners new to the work will find the bracing final rondo (marked Allegro di molto) especially powerful and dramatic, offering an affirmative summary of one of Mozart's most innovative middle-period piano concertos. *—Michael Jameson*

Recommended:

- ○ **Mozart: Piano Concertos 14–16** / Barenboim (cond. & piano), Berlin PO / 1998 / Teldec 16827
- ○ **Mozart: Piano Concertos 5, 14 & 16** / Hogwood (cond.), Levin, Academy of Ancient Music / 1999 / Decca 458285

○ **Rudolf Serkin** / Abbado (cond.), R. Serkin, CO of Europe / 1999 / Philips 456964

Piano Concerto No. 17 in G major, K. 453 (1784)

After Mozart settled in Vienna in 1781 he became for all intents and purposes (even if not wholly intentionally) a freelancer, almost entirely dependent on teaching and his skill as a keyboard player for his income. The G Major concerto is one of the few not originally composed for Mozart himself to play (although he would undoubtedly have used it subsequently); it was intended for one of his pupils, Barbara von Ployer, for whom he also wrote the *Piano Concerto No.14 in E flat,* K. 449, and who apparently paid him well. In a letter dated April 10, 1784, Mozart told his father Leopold that he had finished the concerto that day. Two days later it became one of the first works to be entered in his new thematic catalog. Barbara's father Gottfried Ignaz von Ployer, a Viennese agent of the Salzburg court, hired an orchestra for the first performance, which took place at his summer residence in the Viennese suburb of Döbling on June 13. In the audience was the Italian opera composer Paisiello, to whom Mozart wanted to show off his pupil. In addition to the concerto, Mozart and von Ployer also played the demanding *Sonata for Two Pianos,* K. 448.

The orchestral accompaniment is scored for flute, strings, and pairs of oboes, bassoons, and horns, and the concerto is cast in the usual three movements, with an opening Allegro followed by an Andante and an Allegretto. The last movement with its bourée-like theme has become noted for a charming incident in which Mozart taught the melody to his pet starling, although it apparently persisted in always getting one note wrong.

The G Major concerto was one of the few Mozart piano concertos published during his lifetime—by Bössler of Speyer. The event that produced a rare contemporary review of his music. While praising the elegance of the Andante and "exceptionally beautiful modulations" of the Allegretto, the writer also noted the difficulties of that movement. The caveat presaged the decline of Mozart's popularity among his Viennese public, which increasingly found his music too dense and difficult to understand. Indeed its structure has provided theorists with two centuries' worth of problems to chew on, containing as it does elements of sonata, rondo, and variation forms. The opening movement is dense with sheer melody, introducing half a dozen tunes before the piano even makes its entrance and giving each its part to play in the ensuing dialogue. *—Brian Robins*

Recommended:

○ **Mozart: Piano Concertos 17 & 21** / Abbado (cond.), Pires, CO of Europe / 1995 / DG 439941

○ **Mozart: Piano Concertos, K453, 466** / Hogwood, Levin, Academy of Ancient Music / 1997 / L'Oiseau-Lyre 455607

○ **Mozart: Piano Concertos 6, 17 & 21** / Anda (cond. & piano), Camerata Academica des Salzburger Mozarteum / 1995 / DG 447436

Piano Concerto No. 18 in B flat major, K. 456 (1784)

Neglected as Mozart's "other" B flat concerto (the more famous being his last, K. 595), K. 456 rests just at the cusp of Mozart's greatest, most individual piano concertos. The interplay of piano and orchestra is assured, and the music occasionally drifts into minor mode realms hinting at the poignance to come in some of the later works. What holds this concerto back from Mozart's absolute first rank is the frilly nature of much of the piano writing; it's more entertaining than expressive. Mozart apparently composed this *Concerto in B flat*—the fifth of six concerti he wrote in 1784—not for himself but for a 25-year-old blind pianist Maria Theresia Paradis. Blind or not, Paradis was famous as a virtuosa, and Mozart would later play the concerto in public himself.

The orchestra creeps into the opening Allegro vivace with an almost tentative march figure that builds in busyness and loudness, only to give way to a vague, questioning passage in the woodwinds that is soon replaced by more chattering yet pastoral material, the strings eventually returning with music distantly related to a hunting call. The material Mozart has set out is fragmentary and harmonically unsettled, but the effect is hardly disturbing; it calls to mind the little surprises one encounters throughout a day in the countryside. The piano arrives to launch a recap of the themes, presenting, with orchestral backing, a more ornate version of several of the motifs. The keyboard often works in dialogue with the woodwinds, a trait of all Mozart's later concertos. The piano skips into the development section with a tripping, lighthearted version of the little march, and proceeds through the other themes with trills and filigree. A solo cadenza interrupts the loose recapitulation just before the brief coda.

The slow movement, Andante un poco sostenuto, again foreshadows the minor key miracles of the concertos to come. It's a series of variations on a bittersweet theme presented by the orchestra and immediately ornamented by the piano. The melody becomes rather hazy in the pianist's hands, but intervening orchestral statements redefine it in treatments that become increasingly tragic and dramatic. The piano returns to relieve much of the tension, leading into a sequence of gentler, more pastoral and intermittently sunny variations. A caressing darkness descends, though, upon the movement's final passages.

The Allegro vivace is a rondo taking off from a joyful, repeated-note theme. Mozart's piano writing here veers from music-box ornate to flashily virtuosic (by the standards of the 1780s) with much rapid passagework. Mozart aims for great contrast of tempos, although the mood always remains bright, with notes cascading through the dexterous cadenza just before the end. *—James Reel*

Recommended:

○ **Mozart: Piano Concertos 18 & 20** / Goode, Orpheus CO / Nonesuch 79439

○ **Mozart: Piano Concertos 18 & 19** / Bilson, Gardiner (cond.) / Archiv 415111

○ **Leif Ove Andsnes: Mozart** / Andsnes, Norwegian CO / 2004 / EMI 57803

Piano Concerto No. 19 in F major, K. 459 (1784)

Like the majority of the piano concertos Mozart composed in Vienna, the *F Major concerto, No. 19,* was written for his own use, possibly at an Advent concert in December 1784. The extant autograph score gives no date of composition, but Mozart entered the concerto in his thematic catalog on 11 December of that year. He would also likely have included it along with another new concerto, K. 466 in D Minor, in a series of six Lenten subscription concerts he gave in the Mehlgrabe in Vienna the following February. 1784 was in fact something of a "year of the piano" for Mozart, for it witnessed the composition of no fewer than six piano concertos, in addition to the great *Quintet in E flat for piano, oboe, clarinet, horn and bassoon,* K. 452. At this point Mozart's repute as a pianist was at its height, with writers falling over themselves to outdo each other's panegyrics. An example comes in this account from April 1784: "His concerto on the pianoforte, how excellent that was! And his improvisations, what a wealth of ideas! what variety!.... One is washed away unresistingly on the stream of his emotions."

Mozart's catalog entry for the *F Major Concerto* includes timpani and trumpets in the scoring, although such parts have never been found, and they are not normally included in the composer's music written in that key. They would, however, not be out of place in the festive, martial opening Allegro of this work sometimes referred to as Mozart's second "Coronation" concerto (the other being the *Concerto No. 26 in D,* K. 537, the work usually known by the "Coronation" nickname), since he chose to perform it in 1790 at a concert marking the coronation festivities of the Emperor Leopold II in Frankfurt. In modern times the concerto has unjustifiably been something of a Cinderella work among Mozart's mature piano concertos, yet it as every bit as fine as the better-known works that surround it, with wind writing that is particularly felicitous even by Mozartean standards.

Although the mood of this concerto is sunny and its weight light, there is an aspect to the first movement which is worthy of close attention: Mozart builds a convicing sonata form out of two themes of similar mood, both of them exceptionally lyrical, and he sustains their basic moods in a masterful development. The middle movement is not especially slow, being marked "Allegretto." It is based on two themes, one of them an expressive opening melody. The finale is a very lively movement, with wonderful contrapuntal writing hidden by the overall jocularity. This is already an exceptionally fine concerto, showing great advances in the use of winds, and pointing the way towards even greater achievements to come. *—Brian Robins*

Recommended:

○ **Mozart: Piano Concertos 19 & 27; Sonata K280** / Fricsay (cond.), Haskil, Berlin PO / 1996 / DG 449722

○ **Mozart: Piano Concertos 19 & 27** / Goode, Orpheus CO / Nonesuch 79608

○ **Mozart: Piano Concertos 18 & 19** / Gardiner (cond.), Bilson, EBS / Archiv 415111

○ **Mozart: Piano Concertos 18 & 19** / Staier (cond. & piano), Concerto Cologne / 2000 / Teldec 80676

Piano Concerto No. 20 in D minor, K. 466 (1785)

Mozart completed this work on February 10, 1785, and played the first performance the next evening in Vienna. Scoring adds a flute and two trumpets to winds, horns, timpani, and strings.

On February 11, 1785, Leopold Mozart arrived in Vienna after a wintry, bone-rattling, coach journey from Salzburg—his first visit to the capital in 12 years and his last. On the same night he attended an Akademie by his celebrated son, who had just turned 29 and was at the peak of his popularity in ever-fickle Vienna. Leopold wrote to daughter Nannerl that, in the Casino on the Mehlgrube, he beheld "a vast concourse of people of rank.... The concert was incomparable, the orchestra excellent." After two arias by a singer from the Italian opera, there "came a new, superb piano concerto by Wolfgang, which the copyist was still writing when we arrived, and the rondo of which your brother hadn't time to play because he had to revise copies [of the orchestral parts]." This was the trailblazing *D minor Concerto* that survived the neglect of so much of Mozart's music during the nineteenth century. Beethoven, both smitten and influenced, played it publicly, with his own cadenzas in the first and last movements, where Mozart had improvised. No reports have survived of the audience's acceptance, but had they been hostile or even cool, surely Leopold would have reported this to Nannerl. His son's marriage without paternal permission in 1782 to Constanze Weber still rankled; so did their newfound independence. However, Papa's immediate and unreserved acceptance of Wolfgang's departures from tradition in the new concerto—beginning immediately with an agitated, subtly changing bass line beneath the throbbing syncopation of violins and violas —revealed a flexibility otherwise missing in his personal character. One can almost admire the manipulative Leopold for that.

In the first movement, Allegro (D minor, common time), Mozart's themes are motivic rather than conventionally melodic; more than two centuries later it remains a miracle that the soloist never plays exactly what the orchestra sets forth in the exposition, despite a rock-solid sonata structure throughout. When the piano finally enters in measure 77, it does so as an alien in a threateningly troubled land. Nor does the soloist take complete charge until the coda of the finale where, half-an-hour later, he coaxes the music into D major.

The second movement is a Romanza (B flat major, common time). Not to underrate Mozart's incomparable genius in music before this, nothing had equaled the unity of expression achieved in 1785 and after. Beyond integrating the outer movements, he made the slow movement part and parcel of the whole. This Romanza without tempo marking (but clearly Andante) is a rondo in ABACA form that plunges dramatically into G minor before the end couplet—a significant harmonic departure not just here but in the concerto's overall context.

Mozart returns to D minor in the third movement (Allegro assai; alla breve). Until the coda, we hear one of Mozart's rare rondos in a minor key. More precisely, it is an extended sonata-rondo (ABACDA, plus coda), since C is a development, with the reprise in section D. The development again as before in the second movement seeks out G minor—the darkest key in Mozart's harmonic lexicon—before D major is finally allowed to break through, albeit a whitish and wintry sun. *—Roger Dettmer*

Recommended:

- ○ **Mozart: Piano Concertos 20 & 23** / Marriner (cond.), Moravec, Academy of St. Martin-in-the-Fields / Haenssler 98142
- ○ **Mozart: Piano Concertos 20, 23, 24, 26 & 27** / Britten (cond.), Curzon, English CO / 2001 / Decca 468491
- ○ **Mozart: Great Piano Concertos** / Ashkenazy (cond. & piano), Philharmonia / 1997 / London 452958

Piano Concerto No. 21 in C major ("Elvira Madigan") K. 467 (1785)

In keeping with the *Piano Concerto in D Minor*, K. 466, the *C Major Concerto* was composed for the series of Lenten subscription concerts given by Mozart in 1765. This was an extraordinarily busy and successful period of Mozart's life, as we can gauge from a series of letters sent by his father Leopold to Mozart's sister Nannerl, now married and living with her husband in St. Gilgen. "Every day there are concerts; and the whole time is given up to teaching, music, composing and so forth ... It is impossible for me to describe the rush and the bustle." Leopold had arrived on February 11, the day of the first of the concerts and the occasion of the premiere of the *D Minor Concerto*. Mozart first played the newly completed K. 467 not at one of his subscription concerts (although he must surely have included it in one of the last of those as well), but at his benefit concert at the National Court Theater on March 10, the day after it was entered into his thematic catalog. A handbill for the concert announced that it would include "a new, just finished Forte piano Concerto," in addition to Mozart playing improvisations (for which he was particularly famed) employing "an especially large Forte piano pedal."

The *C Major Concerto* gives absolutely no sign of being composed in an atmosphere of "rush and bustle"; neither could the contrast with the stormy drama of its immediate predecessor be greater. The first movement, an expansive Allegro of Olympian grandeur and design is followed by an Andante of sublime beauty made famous in more recent times by its use in the film *Elvira Madigan*. This movement, with its few notes and bare outline, is incidentally a classic example of the manner in which Mozart frequently left himself room to improvise within the context of his own concertos, a technique lately reintroduced by performers such as Malcolm Bilson and Robert Levin. The final movement is an Allegro vivace assai, its evocation of the world of opera buffo typical of many of Mozart's finales, both in concerto and symphony. Like the *D Minor Concerto*, K. 467 is scored for a large orchestra: flute, pairs of oboes, bassoons, horns and trumpets, timpani and strings. *—Brian Robins*

Recommended:

- ○ **Mozart: Piano Concertos 21 & 24** / Szell (cond.), Casadesus, Cleveland Orch. / 1983 / CBS 38523
- ○ **Mozart: Piano Concertos 20 & 21** / Abbado (cond.), Gulda, Vienna PO / 2003 / DG 000055102
- ○ **Mozart: Piano Concertos 6, 17 & 21** / Anda (cond. & piano), Camerata Academica des Salzburger Mozarteum / 1995 / DG 447436
- ○ **Mozart: Piano Concertos 20 & 21** / Gardiner (cond.), Bilson, EBS / 1987 / Archiv 419609

Piano Concerto No. 22 in E flat major, K. 482 (1785)

Doubtless recalling the great success of the six subscription concerts Mozart had promoted during the Lenten season of 1785, he decided to mount another series of three concerts during the Advent season at the end of the year. According to a letter from Mozart's father Leopold to his daughter Nannerl, Mozart had told him that he mounted the new series "without much preparation." Nevertheless the subscription amounted to 120, a respectable number and only 30 short of that he had attracted to his Lenten series. For this series, as was his habit, Mozart composed a new piano concerto, the present work in E flat, which he entered in his catalog on December 16. It has been conjectured that the first performance was not in fact given at Mozart's own concert, but on the occasion of the second of two performances of Dittersdorf's oratorio *Esther*, when it would have been played between the acts. These concerts were given on December 22 and 23 by the Society of Musicians at the annual benefit concerts for their widows and orphans, the bill announcing the second concert advertising that Mozart would play "a new Concerto of his own composition." The report of the two concerts in the *Wiener Zeitung* decided that it could forbear to mention the favorable reception the concerto received, "since our praise is superfluous in view of the deserved fame of this master."

The date at which Mozart first played K. 482 at his own subscription concert is not known, but it obviously repeated (if that was indeed the order of events) the success it had achieved at the charity concert. Mozart was able to report to Leopold that the central Andante had to be repeated—"a rather unusual occurrence," Leopold told Nannerl. As has been noted, the E flat Concerto is notable for its strong echoes of *Le nozze di Figaro*, on which Mozart was working at the time he composed the concerto. This applies particularly to the complex Rondo finale, with its delicious minuetto interpolation. The work is also notable for being the first instance on which Mozart had included clarinets in the scoring of one his concertos, which also calls for a flute, pairs of bassoons, horns and trumpets, timpani, and strings. The spacious opening movement is an *Allegro*. The concerto was published by the Viennese house of Johann Traeg in August 1789. *—Brian Robins*

Recommended:

- ○ **Beethoven: Concerto 3; Mozart: Concerto 22** / Muti (cond.), Richter, Philharmonia / 1993 / EMI 64750
- ○ **Mozart: Piano Concertos 20 & 22** / Mackerras (cond.), O'Conor, Scottish CO / 1993 / Telarc 80308
- ○ **Mozart: Piano Concertos 22 & 23** / Gardiner (cond.), Bilson, EBS / 1988 / Archiv 423595
- ○ **Mozart: Piano Concertos 22 & 23** / Hogwood (cond.), Levin, Academy of Ancient Music / 1998 / L'Oiseau-Lyre 452052

Piano Concerto No. 23 in A major, K. 488 (1786)

Mozart completed this work on March 2, 1786, and most likely played the first performance a few days later in Vienna. For the coronation, in 1781, of Austrian Emperor Joseph II and attendant celebrations, Prince-Archbishop Hieronymous Colloredo of Salzburg moved his entire court to Vienna. He summoned his most famous musical employee, the younger Mozart, who'd been savoring the success of *Idomeneo* in Munich, an opera specially commissioned by the Elector of Bavaria. The reluctant Wolfgang Amadé, by then thoroughly detesting his pfennig-pinching employer, arrived in the Hapsburg capital on March 16. By June 8, he had managed to get dismissed from Colloredo's service (with a boot in the backside), leaving him free to conquer Vienna, which he did with the new Emperor's erratic help. For the next four years, he reigned as Vienna's favorite composer of instrumental music. While he rode the crest, his music was both anticipated and appreciated. In response to public demand between 1782 and 1786, he wrote 14 glorious piano concertos—Nos. 11 through 24—most of them for his own use. *No. 23* was intended for the Lenten series of 1786, along with *Nos. 22* and *24*, the last ones before *Figaro*. While the dates of these concerts have been lost, we know that the A major was an immediate success, and has remained popular ever since, as much for wistfulness as for melodies verging on sublimity. In the company of a flute, two bassoons, two horns, and strings, a pair of clarinets lend the music a moody character.

The Allegro first movement, with double exposition, goes by the rules of structure for the most part, although there is an incursion of drama in the development section (Cuthbert Girdlestone wrote that "Mozart's daimon... suddenly surges up from the depth") plus a through-written cadenza, rare in his mature concertos.

Rather than an Andante, the slow movement is the only Adagio in all of Mozart's concertos, with melancholy taking center stage that heretofore had hovered in the wings. Startlingly and somberly the key is F sharp minor (A major's harmonic alter-ego), not really leavened by a sweet subject in A major for flute and clarinet that forms the middle part of an ABA structure, despite elements of sonata form.

After two introverted movements, the second one confined to a sickroom, the rondo-finale rallies ebulliently—an Allegro assai among the most buoyant in Mozart's concerto canon, with key-changes and even high comedy that find the patient recovered and happy, as are all of us are who have been worried till now about his health. *—Roger Dettmer*

Recommended:

- ○ **Mozart: Piano Concertos 20 & 23** / Giulini (cond.), Michelangeli, Rome Italian Radio Orch. / Hommage 7001850

- ○ **Mozart: Concerto 23; Beethoven: Concerto 5** / Böhm (cond.), Pollini, Vienna PO / 2001 / DG 471351
- ○ **Mozart: Piano Concertos 20 & 23** / Marriner (cond.), Moravec, Academy of St. Martin-in-the-Fields / Haenssler 98142
- ○ **Mozart: Piano Concertos 23 & 26** / Harnoncourt (cond.), Gulda, Concertgebouw / 2001 / Apex 89091
- ○ **Mozart: Piano Concertos 22 & 23** / Hogwood, Levin, Academy of Ancient Music / 1998 / L'Oiseau-Lyre 452052

Piano Concerto No. 24 in C minor, K. 491 (1786)

During the early part of 1786 Mozart was busily engaged in the process of completing his opera *Le nozze di Figaro*, which received its premiere at the National Court Theater in Vienna on May 1. Lack of documentation for the winter and spring months of that year means that we do not know if he repeated the series of Lenten subscription concerts he had mounted the two previous years, but they did witness the completion of two new piano concertos, a genre that from 1784 to 1786 can normally be related to such concert series. One of these, *No. 23 in A*, K. 488, is a work now known to have been started two years earlier, but the magnificent concerto under consideration was an entirely new work. It was entered into his thematic catalog on March 24, and is believed to have been premiered at Mozart's benefit concert at the Burgtheater on April 7, the last concert he would give there.

The popularity Mozart had enjoyed with the Viennese public as a performer would henceforth start to decline, the *C minor Concerto* the penultimate of the great series of piano concertos composed for his concerts between 1784 and 1786. One of only two concertos composed by Mozart in a minor key, it is a work that reflects the increasing density and complexity of Mozart's music, the development of a style that already perplexed many of his contemporaries. What, for example, must they have made of the stormy, Beethovenian drama of the opening Allegro, or the chromatic intensity that pervades the concerto?

The autograph score, housed in the British Library, also shows thoroughly uncharacteristic signs of struggle, particularly in the final movement where Mozart attempted several versions of the third variation without ever attaining a resolution. The very full orchestration, the largest forces Mozart ever wrote for in a concerto, is commensurate with the size and power of the work—flute, two oboes, two clarinets, two bassoons, two horns, two trumpets, timpani, and strings. *—Brian Robins*

Recommended:

- ○ **Mozart: Piano Concertos 8, 23 & 24** / Leitner (cond.), Kempff, Bamberg Symphony / 1999 / DG 457759
- ○ **Mozart: Piano Concertos 24 & 25** / Marriner (cond.), Moravec, Academy of St. Martin-in-the-Fields / 1996 / Haenssler 98955
- ○ **Mozart: Piano Concertos 20, 23, 24, 26 & 27** / Kertész (cond.), Curzon, London SO / 2001 / Decca 468491

Piano Concerto No. 25 in C major, K. 503 (1786)

Mozart completed this work on December 4, 1786, and very likely premiered it the following night in Johann Trattner's *Viennese Casino*. It is scored for single flute, two each of oboes, bassoons, horns, and trumpets, strings, and solo keyboard, of course.

This last of Mozart's four C major piano concertos is a work of immense structural integrity (rather than cultivated thematic charm), employing alternations between parallel major and minor keys throughout. It is furthermore a work whose three movements use sonata-form: pristinely so in the first; without a development section in the second, and as part of a seven-part rondo format in the last (i.e., the development of materials introduced during the first refrain in couplets B and C). *Concerto No. 25* and the *Prague Symphony* (D major, K. 504) were composed conjunctively—Mozart wrote December 4 and 6, 1786, as their completion dates in his Verzeichnis—for a series of four Advent Akademien in the *Casino* of his friend Johann Trattner. Evidence suggests that he repeated the concerto on several subsequent occasions, and that Beethoven chose it in 1795 for one of his first Viennese appearances as soloist.

"Magisterial" befits the main thrust of the opening Allegro maestoso, the longest movement in Mozart's orchestral canon: 432 measures without cadenza (which surely would have extended it). The outset of his double exposition is built on a C major triad, although subsequent materials and their treatment contain passages of expressive intimacy, not to be confused with softness or effeminacy. As if by Schubert, the music slips in and out of minor keys (always the opposite of prevailing major keys). The music recalls pensive moments from *Figaro* when it is not being assertively symphonic—as if Mozart were getting ready for the *"Jupiter" Symphony* of 1788.

For the middle movement, a generic Andante tempo marking belies the depth and variety of fantasy in this F major sonatina in triple time. Again, the orchestra plays an exposition with two theme groups before the piano enters, a highly decorated part that doesn't need further embroidery. The prevailing mood is pensive without solemnity; Mozart was too professional by this time to be caught out.

While the manuscript had no tempo marking for the final C major sonata-rondo in 6/8 time, Allegretto has been the consensus ever since Mozart's widow published K. 503 in 1789 (her only venture into business and a failure). The refrain-theme begins with eight measures of gavotte from the ballet music in *Idomeneo*—the opera seria Mozart composed six years earlier, at Munich. Although Erik Smith considers this movement "festive," Cuthbert Girdlestone ranks it among the "most serious-minded rondos, [having] nothing of the merry tone of the usual rondo." The first theme is "tinted with melancholy, serious, almost brooding...full of a languishing grace unexpected in a concerto finale." Major-minor mood swings carry over from the first movement until, in couplet-B, "intensity reaches passion." It is "an epiphany" for Michael Steinberg when "the piano, accompanied by cellos and basses alone, a sound that occurs nowhere else in Mozart, [leads to] music whose richness of texture, poignancy and passion astonish us." However, sunlight pours illuminates the final refrain. *—Roger Dettmer*

Recommended:

- ○ **Serkin: The Legenday Recordings** / Szell (cond.), R. Serkin / 1991 / Sony 47269
- ○ **Mozart: Piano Concertos 24 & 25** / Marriner (cond.), Moravec, Academy of St. Martin-in-the-Fields / 1996 / Haenssler 98955
- ○ **Mozart: Piano Concertos 5 & 25** / Perahia (cond. & piano), English CO / 1982 / CBS 37267

Piano Concerto No. 26 in D major ("Coronation") K. 537 (1788)

The series of piano concertos Mozart composed between 1784 and 1786—12 in all—is directly linked to his success as a concert pianist during those years. Actively promoting concert series during the seasons of Advent and Lent, he needed a constant supply of new concertos to play to his public. With the waning of his popularity in Vienna, such works were no longer required. The last five years of his life witnessed the composition of only two further piano concertos, the present work and the *Piano Concerto No. 27 in B flat*, K. 595, completed in January, 1791.

Paper dating of the manuscript paper on which the D major Concerto was commenced suggests that it was started as early as the spring as 1787, shortly after Mozart had returned from Prague, where he had witnessed the triumphant success of his opera *Le nozze di Figaro*. At this time he might still have had plans for a new concerto for the Lenten season of that year, but significantly the work was not completed until February 1788, when Mozart entered it into his thematic catalog on the 24th of that month.

No opportunity for performance is known at that time, and although Mozart claimed in one of many letters begging money from his fellow Freemason Michael Puchburg (June, 1788) that he was mounting a new subscriptions series that month, no concerts appear to have taken place. It thus seems likely the D major Concerto waited for its first performance until April 14, 1789, when Mozart played it in Dresden during the course of a three-month tour of Germany. The following year Mozart was again back in Germany, visiting Frankfurt on the occasion of the coronation of Leopold II as Holy Roman Emperor. On October 15 he gave a concert as part of the festivities, a performance that earned the work the popular name by which it is known today.

Although the concerto is known today in a fully-scored version (flute, two oboes, two bassoons, two horns, two trumpets, timpani and strings) Mozart scholars believe the work was originally planned on a smaller scale, the wind and brass parts being added during the composition of the opening *Allegro*. Although this movement is brilliant and festive, the concerto lacks the density of thought of the great Viennese concertos; its *Larghetto* is amiable rather than profound, and the final *Allegretto* is playfully humorous. *—Brian Robins*

Recommended:

- ○ **Mozart: Piano Concertos 18 & 26** / Freeman (cond.), Han, Philharmonia / Brilliant 99720/9
- ○ **Mozart: Piano Concertos 15 & 26** / Hogwood (cond.), Levin, Academy of Ancient Music / 1997 / L'Oiseau-Lyre 455814
- ○ **Mozart: Piano Concertos 20, 23, 24, 26 & 27** / Kertész (cond.), Curzon, London SO / 2001 / Decca 468491
- ○ **Mozart: Piano Concertos 22 & 26** / Gardiner (cond.), Bilson, EBS / Archiv 447283

Piano Concerto No. 27 in B flat major, K. 595 (1791)

Mozart's final piano concerto was entered into his thematic catalog on January 5, 1791, the year of his death. However, it appears that, like its immediate predesessor (No. 26 in D, "Coronation"), the concerto was started some time earlier, possibly in 1788. Mozart himself gave the first performance two months after the concerto's completion at a benefit concert for the clarintetist Josef Bähr, whom Mozart met in Paris. The concert took place in the great room situated above an inn owned by one Ignaz Jahn, close to where Mozart was living in the Himmelpfortgasse, and also featured arias sung by Aloysia Lange (Weber), Mozart's sister-in-law and first love. The "grand musical concert" (*Wiener Zeitung*, March 12, 1791), proved to be Mozart's final appearance on the concert platform. The report went to record that "everyone admired his art, in composition as well as in performance," an ironic statement from the press of a city that by this time had long tired of Mozart as a performer. Only a few weeks later the concerto was played by the Czech pianist Jan Witásek at a concert given by Mozart's soprano friend Josepha Duschek in his beloved Prague.

The concerto bears scant relationship to the bold, powerful works of 1784 to 1786, the golden years of the composer's career as a concert pianist. Scored with an orchestral accompaniment consisting of flute, two oboes, two bassoons, two horns, and strings, the concerto inhabits a world of glowing, muted colors. Its mood is frequently described as autumnal or valedictory. That impression may be slanted by hindsight, but such impressions are enhanced by Mozart's choice of theme for the rondo finale: he uses the melody of a little song called "Sehnsucht nach dem Frühling" (Longing for Spring), one of three he had composed for a children's songbook, and which was entered into his catalog immediately after the concerto. (It was catalogued later as K. 596.) The opening Allegro and middle Larghetto are likewise restrained, with a sinuous weaving of the solo part into the texture rather than the virtuosic frills of the preceding D major concerto. Although it has little of the harmonic boldness found in some of Mozart's other late works, the concerto seems to look forward to Romantic lyricism in the way it finds beauty in melancholy. In certain passages the meditative breadth of Beethoven's Concerto No. 4 in G seems not far away. *—Brian Robins*

Recommended:

- ○ **Mozart: Piano Concertos 25 & 27** / Ashkenazy, London Philharmonia Orch. / Decca 467437
- ○ **Mozart: Piano Concertos 22 & 27** / Brendel, Mackerras (cond.), Scottish CO / 2001 / Philips 468367
- ○ **Great Pianists: Emil Gilels** / Gilels, Böhm (cond.), Vienna Philharmoniker / 1998 / Philips 456793
- ○ **Brahms: Piano Concerto 2; Mozart: Piano Concerto 27** / Backhaus, Böhm (cond.), Vienna PO / 1999 / Decca 466380

Sinfonia concertante for oboe, clarinet, horn, bassoon & orchestra in E flat major, K. 297b (1778)

Mozart's coming-of-age journey to Paris in 1777–79—albeit with his mother as chaperone—was not only circuitous but leisurely. When mother and son finally did reach Paris on March 23, 1778, he found the city that had hailed him as a prodigy 15 years earlier was now unhospitable—indeed, inimical. He was able, however, to contact a quartet of visiting wind players from Mannheim, and on May 1 wrote to his "très cher Pére" that they asked him for a new piece to be performed at the Concert Spirituel in the Loge Olympique, Paris' most distinguished orchestral series. He claimed to have finished a "sinfonie [sic] concertante in the current popular style" for solo flute, oboe, bassoon, and horn, with an orchestra of two oboes, two horns, and strings. But the work, supposedly given to the Loge's impresario for copying, was set aside by the latter and subsequently lost. Mozart considered this to be another Parisian plot against him and in a later letter to Salzburg assured Papa Leopold that he could recreate the music from memory. But no manuscript has survived. Nevertheless, this composition turned up nearly a century later, in a hand not the composer's, with solo clarinet rather than flute. It became "K. Anhang 9/K. 297b" in the second edition (1905) of Ludwig Ritter von Köchel's storied Verzeichnis, originally published in 1862, and "K. Anhang C14.01" in the third version, edited by Alfred Einstein in 1937.

While Georges de Saint-Foix in 1932 and J.W. Turner in 1938 accepted it as authentic, *The New Grove Mozart* in 1982 concluded that "its credentials are dubious, and any music by Mozart that it may contain can only be in corrupt form." Even more recently, Robert Levin has written in the *Mozart-Jahrbuch 1984/1985* that the orchestral part is authentic but the solo sections "adapted." Corrupt or not, the best pages are surely too beautiful to be spurious: the work overall has a recollective, even autumnal character found nowhere else found until the sublime *B flat wind Serenade* of 1781 (K. 361/370a).

All three movements are rooted in E flat major, a key shared by the *"Jeunehomme" Piano Concerto* (No. 9; K. 271) and the later *Sinfonia concertante for violin and viola* (K. 364/320d). The opening Allegro has three (rather than two) expositions of the principal and secondary subjects, first by the orchestra's strings, then twice by the solo quartet. Development and reprise ensue, with a through-composed cadenza before the coda. Though the nineteenth century source copy marked the middle movement Adagio, an Andante tempo is likelier, continuing in a vein of almost reflective lyricism with gentle exchanges of thematic material. Like the first movement, this one is in common time (4/4). The finale, Andante con variazioni, is in 2/4 until, after the last variation, six Adagio bars in common time lead to an Allegro coda in 6/8. There are ten variations altogether, each one 15 or 16 bars long, with identical, basically decorative orchestral ritornelli separating them. *—Roger Dettmer*

Recommended:

- ○ **Mozart: Quintet in E flat; Sinfonia concertante; Beethoven: Quintet in E flat** / Brain, Sutcliffe, Walton, James / 1996 / Testament 1091
- ○ **Mozart: Complete Wind Concertos** / Orpheus CO / 2002 / DG 469362

Sinfonia concertante for violin, viola & orchestra in E flat major, K. 364 (1779)

The magnificent *Sinfonia concertante for violin, viola, and orchestra in E flat major*, K. 364, is Mozart's only surviving complete work of this type, a genre that incorporates elements of both the symphony and concerto. Generally scored for two or more solo instruments and orchestra, the sinfonia concertante was particularly popular in Paris in the eighteenth century. It was there, in fact, that Mozart composed such a work in 1778 for four outstanding wind soloists from the Mannheim orchestra who were also then in the French capital; that work, however, is now known only in a spurious nineteenthth century edition.

During this period Mozart also began two other works in the sinfonia concertante genre, one for violin and piano in D major (1778), and another for violin, viola and cello in A major, K. 320e (ca. 1779–80), neither of which progressed beyond the first 130 or so measures before the composer set it aside. The present work may be a replacement for the aborted D major work. It was composed in Salzburg during the summer or fall of 1779, about the same time as that work. In both works, Mozart calls for a higher tuning than is usual for the viola; his purpose in so doing was undoubtedly to give the instrument a brighter sound to avoid being overshadowed by its more penetrating violin companion.

The soloists for whom the *Sinfonia concertante* was composed are not known, but they may have been Antonio Brunetti, the leader of the Salzburg court orchestra, and the violinist Joseph Hafender. The work is in three movements: Allegro maestoso, Andante and Rondo. The orchestra includes two oboes, two horns, an optional pair of bassoons, and strings. The work is notable for its warm expansiveness; the Andante is particularly delectable with its ravishing dialogue between the two soloists. The scoring is unusually full and rich; Mozart's frequent divisi writing for the violas produces textures that presage the sumptuous writing in *Idomeneo, ré di Creta* (1781), the opera seria composed for Munich less than a year later. *—Brian Robins*

Recommended:

- ○ **Mozart: Violin Concertos, etc.** / Davis (cond.), Grumiaux, Pelliccia, London SO / 1993 / Philips 438323
- ○ **Mozart: Sinfonia Concertante** / Mehta (cond.), Perlman, Zukerman, Israel PO / DG 415486

Violin Concerto No. 2 in D major, K. 211 (1775)

Between April 14 and December 20, 1775, Mozart composed five violin concertos. In style, they are related to his serenades from the same period. Aside from two concertos incorporated into serenades, these represent Mozart's only authentic concertos for violin and orchestra. At the time, the 19-year-old Mozart was concertmaster of the Archbishop's court orchestra in Salzburg. Thus, he may have composed the concertos for his own use as a soloist. The pieces show a gradual increase in Mozart's mastery of the genre.

The second of the concertos (D major, completed on June 14, 1775), recalls the style of the late-Baroque, resembling works by Tartini; it strikes an awkward balance between bravura flourishes and thematic presentation and development for the soloist. Each movement boasts an abundance of melodies, one after another. In general, the concerto lacks the dramatic force we hear in Mozart's piano concertos.

The opening tutti, or ritornello, of the Allegro moderato juxtaposes sections of vivacious texture with unison passages. The main theme, first played by the entire orchestra then by the soloist, jaggedly outlines the tonic triad. Mozart's secondary theme resembles Tyrolean folk music and yodeling. Hints of this new theme appear first in the orchestra before the solo violin takes over almost imperceptibly. Mozart exercises a great deal of license in the returning statements of the ritornello, varying them in several ways.

In G major, the Andante second movement is a sonata-form structure without development. Its melodic material is reminiscent of some of Mozart's arias composed at this time, particularly "L'amerò sarò costante" from *Il Rè pastore.*

In contrast to the opening Allegro, the closing Rondeau, marked Allegro, is light and jocular. The principal theme is minuet-like both in its 3/4 meter and pattern of repetition; all of the episodes also sound like dances. Blithe, entertaining movements are not unusual conclusions to concertos of the period, but the seriousness and ingenuity of the first movement make this Rondeau seem especially unambitious. *—John Palmer*

Recommended:

- ○ **Mozart: Violin Concertos** / Davis (cond.), Grumiaux, London SO / 2001 / Philips 464722
- ○ **Mozart: Violin Concertos** / Hogwood (cond.), Standage, Academy of Ancient Music / 1997 / Decca 455721

Violin Concerto No. 3 in G major, K. 216 (1775)

Mozart's five authentic violin concertos are traditionally attributed to the year 1775, but recently there has been some speculation that the first and possibly the second are in fact products from a few years earlier. If this is indeed the case, the distinctly greater sophistication of the *Violin Concerto No. 3 in G major*, K. 216 as compared to its immediate predecessors ceases to be the great mystery that it has for so long been. Even a composer given to as rapid spurts of artistic growth as Mozart would have been hard-pressed to travel such a great distance in the span of only a few months.

This is arguably Mozart's most popular violin concerto; it has neither the boisterous enthusiasm of *No. 4 in D* nor the electric virtuosity of *No. 5 in A*—it is a far more intimate work than either of those—but the sweetness and ingratiating simplicity of its melodies are surpassed by virtually nothing Mozart ever wrote. Furthermore, it is here that for perhaps the first time Mozart is completely successful in his effort to fill the outlines of the three-movement Classical chamber concerto with the kind of clever, colorful, and continually changing dramatic course that makes Mozart's operas the glorious events that they are.

So, when the orchestra decides in the middle of the Allegro first movement to interrupt the happy, charming discussion and shove the violinist, willing or not, into the role of unhappy protagonist for a while we can feel safe chalking it up to Italian opera: a pair of sobbing outbursts grow into a vehement series of sixteenth notes; a little later on, at one of the concerto's most spectacular moments, the sobbing outburst becomes nearly heroic, and, satisfied at having achieved concord from discord, launches the recapitulation.

During the celebrated Adagio, Mozart asks the two oboists to cast their instruments aside and play flutes instead. Each of the finales of Mozart's last three violin concertos is interrupted mid-course by an episode that contrasts with the main music far more than one normally finds in a rondo (the movements are examples of the so-called French Rondo, or Rondeau, then just entering its heyday). In the *Concerto No. 3*, that episode is a delightfully impish Allegretto whose folk-like tune is so full of joie de vivre that the violinist cannot but explode into effervescent triplet arpeggios. Another sign of Mozart's growing mastery is found at the very end of the concerto, as the traditional bombastic conclusion is thrown out in favor of lighthearted little cadence for just oboes and horns. *—Blair Johnston*

Recommended:

- ○ **Mozart: Violin Concertos** / Davis (cond.), Grumiaux, London SO / 2001 / Philips 464722
- ○ **Mozart: Violin Concertos 1, 3 & 4** / Mullova (cond. & violin), Orch of the Age of Enlightenment / 2002 / Philips 470292
- ○ **Mozart: Violin Concertos** / Huggett (cond. & violin), Orch of the Age of Enlightenment / 1999 / Virgin 6157620

Violin Concerto No. 4 in D major, K. 218 (1775)

Wolfgang Amadeus Mozart was still a teenager in the service of the Salzburg court when, in 1775, he composed his *Violin Concerto No. 4 in D major*, K. 218. Mozart was a violinist of reasonable skill, and each of his five violin concertos seems to have been originally composed for his own use; but when Mozart relinquished his position with the court orchestra and was replaced by an altogether more skilled violinist named Antonio Brunetti (who was interested in playing Mozart's concertos), he took the concertos and put them back on the assembly line, revising and updating the violin writing. It would be very interesting to know whether or not the finalized, difficult, and brilliantly-figured score of the *Violin Concerto No. 4* lay within the grasp of Mozart the violinist, or if it was on account of Brunetti's greater mastery that Mozart made his last two violin concertos so technically demanding. Whatever the case may be, the fourth Mozart violin concerto remains the most immediately scintillating of the five—when asked to bring a Mozart concerto to the audition room, this is the one that is selected most often by aspiring violinists.

It is not happenstance that D major is the key most often selected by composers in which to cast their violin concertos (two of Mozart's are in that key), for it is in D major that the instrument, because of the tuning of its strings, vibrates most freely and rings longest. Mozart exploits this tonally-concocted capacity many times as the *Concerto No. 4* moves along, from the resounding unisons and octaves of the orchestra opening to the shining entrance of the soloist on that same material (two octaves higher) to the rich arpeggios that later on lead the way into the recapitulation of the opening.

The Andante cantabile slow movement has not the fame of either the slow movement of the *Concerto No. 3 in G* or that of the *Concerto No. 5 in A*, but there is no shame in being a lesser-known gem. The main music of the Andante grazioso finale cannot decide between a light 2/4 and a more energized 6/8. But this is not the only such argument of tempo and meter in the movement: Mozart has returned to the kind of French Rondo finale that he used in the previous violin concerto, this time incorporating a rolling gigue and a folkish gavotte in the middle portion (all rondos are defined by alternation of a refrain theme with somewhat different material, but in a French Rondo the music stops altogether and suddenly, and sometimes very humorously, shoots off in an entirely new direction for a while). *—Blair Johnston*

Recommended:

- ○ **Mozart: Violin Concertos** / Davis (cond.), Grumiaux, London SO / 2001 / Philips 464722
- ○ **Mozart: Violin Concertos Nos. 4 & 5** / Sitkovetsky (cond. & violin), English CO / 1986 / Novalis 150007
- ○ **Mozart: Violin Concertos** / Huggett (cond. & violin), Orch. of the Age of Enlightenment / 1999 / Virgin 6157620
- ○ **Mozart: Violin Concertos** / Hogwood (cond.), Standage, Academy of Ancient Music / 1997 / Decca 455721

Violin Concerto No. 5 in A major ("Turkish") K. 219 (1775)

Each of Wolfgang Amadeus Mozart's successive violin concertos is longer and more epic than the one that preceded it, and by the time he reached the last of the authentic ones, the *Violin Concerto No. 5 in A major*, K. 219 (the *"Turkish" Concerto*), Mozart had managed to create something very nearly in line with the instrumental concerto of the next century. Though the piece itself is clearly within the Classical chamber concerto tradition, its scale (better than 25 minutes, usually) and the degree of its technical demands mark the work as something new for the violin. Many pieces with equal or greater raw physical demands had already been composed by the time of the *Concerto No. 5*, but none of them has survived the test of time, and certainly none is as formidable a piece of music—it is not without reason that this is the only one of the five to regularly receive as much attention from musicologists and historians as do the crown jewels of Mozart's piano concerto catalog. A war-horse of the student repertory and a staple of the professional's diet, this may well be the most frequently-played violin concerto ever written.

The dramatic scope of the *Concerto No. 5* is truly impressive: it is very nearly an opera in concerto guise, with the soloist as protagonist. Mozart no longer asks the soloist to be content merely to slip into the first movement after the orchestra has made the requisite exposition of the main material, but instead actually stops the Allegro aperto movement altogether at the point of the solo violin entry and provides a wonderfully rich six-measure Adagio. The Allegro aperto almost immediately begins anew, but the fact that the solo violin had the power to halt the entire ensemble at so unlikely a juncture remains fresh in the mind throughout the rest of the concerto—and it is worth noting that even as that Allegro aperto opening music takes off again, the violinist supplies a completely new melody, a high-flying, electrifying one, to go along with it.

The Adagio is a superb movement, longer by a considerable span than the slow movements of the previous four concertos. The melody tumbles along sublimely, and in the central portion we are treated to one of the most astoundingly beautiful passages ever conceived.

Mozart turns again to the French Rondo finale that he used in the third and fourth violin concertos for his third movement (Tempo di menuetto). In a French Rondo, the basic movement is interrupted in mid-stride by a section that contrasts with it in every way, and it is from this contrasting section—a wild, frenzied Allegro—that the *"Turkish" Concerto* gets its nickname. *—Blair Johnston*

Recommended:

- ○ **Mozart: Violin Concertos** / Davis (cond.), Grumiaux, London SO / 2001 / Philips 464722
- ○ **Mozart: Violin Concertos** / Huggett (cond. & violin), Orch. of the Age of Enlightenment / 1999 / Virgin 6157620
- ○ **Mozart: Violin Concertos** / Hogwood (cond.), Standage, Academy of Ancient Music / 1997 / Decca 455721

CHORAL

Ave verum Corpus, motet, K. 618 (1791)

Wolfgang Amadeus Mozart (1756–1791) composed his final motet *Ave Verum Corpus in D major*, K. 618, in the spring of June 1791 for a schoolmaster in Baden near Vienna. It was his first sacred work since the unfinished *Mass in C minor* of 1781. Setting the four-line Catholic communion hymn for four-part chorus, strings, and organ in a simple yet sublime 46 bars, Mozart's *Ave Verum Corpus* was also his last completed sacred work as he did not live long enough to complete his *Requiem*. But with its severe serenity, the motet is transcendentally glorious, and in its final line, "Be for us a foretaste of the trial of death," the work achieves the sense of the eternal and the infinite that the *Requiem* never attains. *—James Leonard*

Recommended:

- ○ **Complete Sacred Works** / Harnoncourt, Vienna Concentus Musicus, Arnold Schoenberg Choir / 1998 / Teldec 21885
- ○ **Mozart: Litanies, Vespers, Etc.** / Davis (cond.), Constable, London SO & Chorus / 1991 / Philips 422520
- ○ **Mozart: Mass in C minor; Ave Verum Corpus** / Marriner (cond.), Te Kanawa, Otter, Johnson, Lloyd, Academy of St. Martin-in-the-Fields / 1994 / Philips 438999

Mass No. 15 in C major ("Coronation"), K. 317 (1779)

Mozart composed this *C major Mass*, K. 317, the finest of his 16 complete masses, for services in St. Peter's Cathedral at Salzburg on March 23, 1779, shortly after his return from the ill-starred journey to Mannheim and Paris. Thereafter, he wrote only the 1780 *Missa solemnis in C*, K. 337, and in Vienna those two colossal torsos, the "Great" but incomplete *C minor Mass* of 1783 (K. 427/417a), and the unfinished *Requiem* (K. 626).

When Hieronymous Colloredo became Prince-Archbishop of Salzburg in 1772, he decreed that masses—music and all—not last more than 45 minutes. This accounts for Mozart's designation of eight as Missa brevis or short mass. Two more are formally entitled Missa solemnis (solemn mass; K. 61a, and K. 337), and a third one Missa longa (long mass; K. 246a). The rest, all in C major culminating in K. 317, were called simply Missa, though several would acquire subtitles—including *"Coronation."* For more than a century, it was supposed that K. 317 celebrated the local investiture of a statue of the Virgin. Not so, according to more recent scholarly consensus: it was assigned that sobriquet in Hapsburg court circles after Antonio Salieri conducted a performance at the Prague coronation of Leopold II in August 1791, less than four months before Mozart's death.

Like the other C major/minor masses in Mozart's Salzburg portfolio, this one is scored for trumpets, plus two oboes and horns, three trombones, timpani, continuo, organ, and two violins. The use of musical structure is notable beyond the Kyrie's traditional ABA form. The Gloria is likewise ternary, while the Credo is a rondo, with a hushed, harmonically venturesome, heart-stopping "Et incarnatus est" at its center. Even more striking are thematic recurrences throughout; for example, Kyrie music in the concluding "Dona nobis pacem," and the Credo's "leap of faith" subject in subsequent movements. Just as striking is the soprano's "Agnus Dei... miserere nobis" aria, which anticipates the Countess Almaviva's despairing "Dove sono" in *The Marriage of Figaro* by seven years.

The Kyrie, Gloria, Credo, and Sanctus all begin with C major choral proclamations, accompanied by timpani and trombones. The four solo voices don't come prominently to the fore until "benedicamus te, adoramus te" in the Gloria. Mozart gives them the "Dominus Deus... Filius Patris" stanza before the chorus sings a solemn, minor-key "Qui tollis peccata mundi... Qui sedes." The Gloria "Amen" features soloists until a final choral interjection.

Hearing a jubilant "Et resurrexit" after the murmured pieties of "Et incarnatus" and "Crucifixus" in the Credo, one realizes that Mass music of this sustained expressivity would not be repeated until Haydn's last six masterpieces of 1796–1802, although Mozart's comparable mastery of counterpoint remained shackled until he finally freed himself from Prince-Archbishop Colloredo's prescriptions.

The Sanctus in K. 317 is more solemn than jubilant; likewise the Hostias, although it moves at a quickened tempo. Surely Beethoven knew this Mass; his Benedictus in the *Missa solemnis* of 1823 begins with a consolatory violin solo, as Mozart's does here. Wind writing throughout anticipates the great Viennese piano concertos between 1782 and 1791. On the threshold of permanent liberation from Salzburg without yet knowing it—indeed, while feeling early on in 1779 that he'd been remanded to servitude in a provincial purgatory—the incomparable Mozart came of age musically. *—Roger Dettmer*

Recommended:

- ○ **Mozart: Coronation Mass; Exsultate, Jubilate; Vesperae Solennes** / Pinnock (cond.), Bonney, MacDougall, Wyn-Rogers, Gadd, English Concert / 1994 / Archiv 445353
- ○ **Mozart: 5 Masses** / Cleobury (cond.), King's College Choir, English CO / 1997 / London 455032
- ○ **Mozart: Cornoation Mass; Vesperae Solennes de Confessore** / Hogwood (cond.), Academy of Ancient Music / 1993 / L'Oiseau-Lyre 436585

Mass No. 16 in C major ("Missa solemnis"), K. 337 (1780)

Composed in Salzburg in March 1780, the *Missa Solemnis in C*, K. 337, is not only the last mass Mozart composed in Salzburg, but also his last completed mass setting. Within a year he would have settled in Vienna, having lost his position with Archbishop Hieronymous Colloredo following their famous and acrimonious row. In Vienna there was no call for Mozart to compose church music; both masses begun after he moved there, the *Mass in C minor*, K. 427, and the *Requiem in D minor*, K. 626, were left incomplete. In marked contrast to the brilliant and popular *"Coronation" Mass*, K. 317, composed a year earlier, this *Mass in C* is a more personal work, suggesting perhaps that Mozart wanted to demonstrate that he could break from the prevailing orthodoxy of Salzburg church music. Although designated as a Missa solemnis (Solemn Mass) and including the trombones as usual in such works, it is in fact closer in length (if not spirit) to a Missa brevis (Short Mass), the six movements of the Ordinary lasting barely 20 minutes in all. Nevertheless there is less of a feeling of hurry than in some of the earlier Salzburg masses. Among a number of memorable moments one might cite the sublime opening Kyrie, the remarkable and unusual treatment of the Benedictus as a fugue, and the lyrical beauty of the soprano solo in the Agnus Dei. The vocal disposition consists of the usual soprano, alto, tenor, and bass soloists and chorus, while the orchestration includes trumpets and timpani in addition to pairs of bassoons and oboes, and strings without violas—the last in accordance with normal Salzburg practice. *—Brian Robins*

Recommended:

- ○ **Mozart: Missae; Requiem** / Kegel (cond.), Shirai, Baldin, Polster, Winkler, Leipzig RSO / 1991 / Philips 422519
- ○ **Mozart: 5 Masses** / Cleobury (cond.), King's College Choir, English CO / 1997 / London 455032
- ○ **Mozart: Coronation Mass; Missa Solemnis** / P. Neumann (cond.), Kwella, Prégardien, Selig, Groenewold, Cologne Chamber Chorus, Collegium Cartusianum / 1995 / Virgin 61244

Mass No. 17 in C minor ("Great Mass"), K. 427 (1783)

After Mozart married Constanze Weber on August 4, 1782, he pledged to compose a mass in her honor to be performed in Salzburg when the newlyweds visited Mozart's father. (According to Constanze, the mass was composed in thanks for her safe recovery from the birth of their first child.) When Mozart wrote to his father in January 1783, he noted that the *Mass in C minor* was half finished, but when he arrived in Salzburg in late July, it was still incomplete and would remain so at Mozart's death. In fact, Mozart finished almost none of the pieces he wrote for his wife (she particularly liked fugues and canons). Because of reforms handed down from Emperor Joseph II, there was little chance of having a large sacred piece performed in Vienna, so there was no professional motivation for Mozart to complete the piece. Also, Mozart was very busy trying to secure commissions and a court appointment.

Mozart and Constanze stayed in Salzburg for several months, during which time their new baby, left behind in Vienna, died. On October 26, 1783, the Kyrie and Gloria of the *C minor Mass* received their first performance in St. Peter's Church, with Constanze singing the soprano solos. (St. Peter's was not under the jurisdiction of the Archbishop of Salzburg, who by this time despised the younger Mozart.) References to a "finished mass" suggest Mozart may have filled in the Credo, Sanctus, and Agnus Dei with sections from his earlier masses. In Mozart's autograph manuscript of the *Mass in C minor* we find only the Kyrie, Gloria, the Credo through the "Et incarnatus est," and drafts of the Sanctus and Benedictus. Mozart musically reflects the ternary division of the Kyrie and divides the Gloria into its traditional seven parts.

Composition on the *Mass in C minor* took place in the midst of Mozart's introduction, through Baron Gottfried van Swieten, to late Baroque vocal composition, particularly the works of J.S. Bach and Handel. This influence is clear in the large, stately choruses, some in eight parts. In the "Qui tollis" movement we hear a recurring bass line that descends through a fourth in Baroque fashion. Both the duet, "Domine Deus," and the "Quoniam" trio have a Handelian flavor, not least in their light, somewhat continuo-like scoring. Handel's presence is most clear in the quotation of a rhythmic idea from *Messiah*, with which Mozart sets the words "in excelsis." Much of the work, however, is firmly rooted in the Austrian Church-music style, and for many of the fugues in the *C minor Mass* there are Austrian precedents. Mozart used parts of the Kyrie and Gloria for an oratorio (with a libretto by Lorenzo Da Ponte?), *Davidde penitente*, K. 469, in 1785. *—John Palmer*

Recommended:

- ○ **Mozart: Missae; Requiem** / Gardiner (cond.), McNair, Montague, Johnson, Beznosiuk, English Baroque Soloists / 1991 / Philips 422519
- ○ **Mozart: Mass In C Minor** / Abbado (cond.), Auger, Bonney, Blochwitz, Holl, Berlin PO / 1991 / Sony 46671
- ○ **Mozart: Mass In C Minor** / Karajan (cond.), Hendricks, Luxon, Schreier, Bell, Berlin PO / 1982 / DG 439012

Requiem, K. 626 (1791)

E.T.A. Hoffmann once wrote that "[Mozart's] *Requiem* is the sublimest achievement that the modern period has contributed to the church." Mozart's deathbed composition held a high appeal for the nineteenth century; in the supposedly more rational twentieth, it ascended to truly iconic status. It did so despite fundamental mysteries of its composition and even its authenticity, mysteries still unsolved in the twenty-first century. Something in the music's *gravitas* and subtlety touches each successive generation.

A tangled skein of myths and fairy tales imagine the deathbed genius collapsing upon his manuscript (myths powerfully reinforced by the 1984 film *Amadeus*), but many facts about the piece are clear. The Countess von Walsegg passed away in February 1791. The Count commissioned a requiem mass from Mozart via a clerk (the "Grey Messenger" of *Requiem*-mythology). Mozart accepted the job for his unknown patron, having desired to compose some "higher form of church music" (his *Ave verum corpus* reflects the same wish). After working on the *Requiem* through October and Novmeber, however, Mozart fell ill and died without completing it. Mozart's widow, needing money, arranged for his friends and pupils to complete the other movements. The Count eventually received a complete *Requiem*, which he tried to pass off as his own composition; the bulk of this copy derives from the hand of Franz Süssmayr. Scholars have diligently attempted to distinguish Mozart's work from Süssmayr's mishandling of his intentions.

Mozart's *Requiem* contains five sections, each capped by a fugue: Requiem/Kyrie, Sequence ("Dies Irae"), Offertory, Sanctus, and Agnus Dei. Throughout, choral writing drives Mozart's music; even the four soloists rarely sing alone. The darkly colored orchestra supports the choir with often vivid motives. This pictorial aspect is most evident in the Sequence: "Tuba mirum" (solo trombone), "Rex tremendae" (regal dotted-rhythms), "Confutatis" (fiery accompaniment), and "Lachrymosa" (sighing strings). Not only do individual movements display an extraordinary level of motivic unity, Mozart carefully creates motivic relationships across the entire *Requiem.* The very first melody sung by the basses ("Requiem aeternam"), for instance, is repeated at the very end and also echoes throughout the work; the opening melody of "Dies irae" translates into major mode to open the "Sanctus." Mozart is never afraid, however, of acknowledging his debt to earlier traditions of church music. His fugues deliberately reference Bach, and in the first movement alone he quotes from Michael Haydn's *Requiem,* Handel's funeral anthem for Queen Caroline, *Messiah,* and the Gregorian chant known as the "Pilgrim's Tone." *—Timothy Dickey*

Recommended:

- ○ **Mozart: Requiem** / Böhm (cond.), Mathis, Hamari, Ochman, Ridderbusch, Haselbock, Vienna PO / 1983 / DG 413553
- ○ **Mozart: Requiem** / Marriner (cond.), Cotrubas, Tear, Shirley-Quirk, Watt, Academy of St. Martin-in-the-Fields / 1987 / Decca 417746
- ○ **Mozart: Requiem; Maurerische Trauermusik** / Savall (cond.), Figueras, Turk, Schreckenberger, Schubert, Capella Reial de Catalunya, Le Concert des Nations / 1992 / Astree 8759
- ○ **Mozart: Requiem; Ave Verum Corpus** / Christie (cond.), Prégardien, Stutzmann, Berg, Panzarella, Les Arts Florissants Orch. & Chorus / Erato 10697

Vesperae solennes de confessore, K. 339 (1780)

Famed for the beauty of its solo soprano aria *Laudate Dominum* (Psalm 116), the *Vesperae solennes de confessore* is the second of two settings of the early evening Vespers service composed by Mozart for liturgical use in Salzburg Cathedral. Both date from shortly after the composer returned from the abortive trip to Paris which witnessed the death of his mother, a period which also saw the composition of two important masses, *"Coronation" Mass,* K. 317, and the *Mass in C,* K. 337. The first, the *Vesperae solennes de Dominica in C,* K. 321 dates from 1779, the present work from 1780. Like its predecessor, K. 339 follows the standard Catholic liturgy in including the Magnificat and the five psalms utilized in the Vespers service. In addition to the concluding *Laudate Dominum* they are as follows: Dixit Dominus (Ps. 109), Confitebur tibi (Ps. 110), Beatus vir (Ps. 111), and Laudate pueri (Ps. 112). In liturgical context, the Magnificat and each of the psalms were prefaced and followed by a plainsong antiphon. The two settings are identically scored for soprano, alto, tenor, and bass soloists and chorus, with an orchestration including bassoon, two trumpets, three trombones, strings, and organ. The addition "de confessore" (not Mozart's own) suggests that the work may have been employed for a saint's day, although no specific connection has been established. "Solennes," incidentally, simply indicates that the work has orchestral accompaniment. As in the earlier setting, Mozart composed some of his boldest Salzburg church music in the first three psalms, while Laudate pueri, like the parallel movement in K. 321, is an exercise in strict, old-fashioned counterpoint, a movement in total contrast to the tranquil radiant beauty of *Laudate Dominum.* Here Mozart does vary from K. 321 in allowing the choir to steal in quietly halfway through. More than in the Salzburg masses, the two Vespers settings reveal a personal side of Mozart's approach to sacred music. To Alfred Einstein, "anyone who does not know such settings does not know Mozart." Two years after Mozart settled in Vienna in 1781, he wrote to ask his father to send the two Vespers settings to him in order that he could perform them to Baron van Swieten, the eccentric nobleman who had introduced him to the works of Bach and Handel. *—Brian Robins*

Recommended:

- ○ **Mozart: Coronation Mass; Exsultate, Jubilate; Vesperae Solennes** / Pinnock (cond.), Bonney, MacDougall, Wyn-Rogers, Gadd, English Concert / 1994 / Archiv 445353
- ○ **Mozart: Litanies, Vespers, Etc.** / Davis (cond.), Te Kanawa, Constable, Howell, Davies, Bainbridge, London SO / 1991 / Philips 422520
- ○ **Mozart: Mass In C; Vesperae Solennes** / Hogwood (cond.), Kirkby, Robbin, Ainsley, George, Academy of Ancient Music / 1993 / L'Oiseau-Lyre 436585

KEYBOARD

Adagio for piano in B minor, K. 540 (1788)

Mozart entered the *Adagio for piano in B minor,* K. 540, into his "List of All My Works" on March 19, 1788. It was composed between the Prague and Vienna premieres of *Don Giovanni.*

Mozart rarely used the key of B minor; his only other movement in this key is the *Adagio from the Quartet for flute, violin, viola, and cello,* K. 285, composed eleven years earlier. The key must have held special significance, for next to the entry in his personal catalogue Mozart wrote, "H moll" (B minor), the only time he ever listed the key of a work. Throughout this short piece, Mozart creates a tense, emotional atmosphere through the poignant use of suspensions and diminished sevenths.

Mozart's sense of symmetry and balance is everywhere evident in this highly dramatic but eerie and weary work. In sonata form, the piece opens by outlining a B minor triad; the rhythmically diverse theme continues through several dynamic changes. After an unexpected stop on the dominant, the theme begins again, but in the left hand, initiating the transition to D major (the relative major, a third above the tonic). The transition is brief, and the second theme consists of an ascending arpeggio, played forte, deep in the lower register of the piano, immediately balanced by a rising half step in the treble, played piano, after crossing the hands. Balance is again an issue in the development section, which starts with the main theme on G major (a third *below* the tonic), followed by the second theme, but inverted. Here, a descending arpeggio in the treble is answered by a rising half step in the bass. The recapitulation proceeds as we might expect, without the transitional passage. After a repeat of the entire development/recapitulation complex, a brief coda built of new material closes the piece in B major.

Mozart's Adagio has inspired numerous writers to wax poetic about musical meaning. Representative is Wilhelm Mohr, who in 1962 wrote, "Everyone who knows and loves the work agrees that in it the spirit of music has taken on form and sonority in one sublimely significant moment. One may try to get at it with analyses, but, however thoughtful they may be one realizes at the end of all effort that the true mystery begins only after them." *—John Palmer*

Recommended:

- ○ **Maurizio Pollini Plays Mozart** / Pollini / Exclusive 16
- ○ **Mozart: Piano Sonatas** / Brendel / 2001 / Philips 468048
- ○ **Mozart - Horowitz** / Horowitz / 1989 / DG 445517

Fantasia for piano in C minor, K. 475 (1785)

Mozart entered the Fantasia in C minor, K. 475 into his "List of All My Works" on May 20, 1785. In the same year, the piece was published in Vienna together with the *Piano Sonata in C minor* under the collective designation "Op. 11." In this version, the Fantasia serves as an introduction to the sonata, its improvisatory character placing the structural weight upon the sonata itself.

The Fantasia is one of very few works Mozart composed in C minor during his years in Vienna. Because of the formal freedom traditionally associated with such pieces, the composer was able to produce in the Fantasia a notably expressive example of keyboard music; in contrast to the prescriptions of traditional forms, the Fantasia instead draws upon Mozart's intuition and supreme sensitivity as a composer and pianist.

The opening theme makes it clear that this is no unfolding sonata form: although the melodic material is symmetrical, the harmony avoids the relationships common to the first themes of sonata movements. The unusual changes in harmony blur the primacy of the tonic and wander in such a way that later resolution seems impossible. The dominant does arrive during a passage of repeated, right-hand chords, but this has little effect since the tonic was never firmly established. This material returns at the end, but the result is symmetry rather than resolution.

The Fantasia unfolds through four tempi—Adagio, Allegro, Andantino, and Più Allegro—which help to delineate is sections. Each change of tempo signals the introduction of new material. The Adagio departs from C minor immediately and ventures as far away as B minor over repeated figures in the left hand. The Allegro begins with a wobbling idea in the right hand that focuses on D major, eventually giving way to an area of continuous modulation. For the most part, the ensuing Andantino is so stable that it could almost be performed alone, but it, too, gives way to further modulation and the continuous C minor of the Più Allegro, which emphasizes rapid, expressive figuration. *—John Palmer*

Recommended:

- ○ **Richter Plays Mozart & Beethoven** / Richter / 1992 / Classics Live 422
- ○ **Ivan Moravec Plays Mozart** / Moravec / 2001 / Supraphon 3581
- ○ **Mozart: Piano Sonatas; Fantasia In C** / Uchida / Philips 412617

Piano Sonata in F major, K. 533/494 (1788)

Mozart entered the Piano Sonata in F major, K. 533, into his "List of All my Works" on January 8, 1788. It was published in Vienna in 1788 with a revision of the *Rondo,* K. 494, as a finale. Mozart had completed the *Rondo* on June 10, 1786, and had it published in London and Speyer in 1788, separately from the *Sonata.* To the *Rondo* Mozart added a cadenza to make the movement more substantial and, therefore, a better fit with the Allegro and Andante. At this time Mozart composed relatively little music as he was preoccupied with the arrangement of a Vienna performance of *Don Giovanni,* for which he wrote a few new numbers.

Considered Mozart's most contrapuntal keyboard work, the Allegro has a very sparse texture and Mozart's use of dissonance is freer than in many of his other pieces. Occasionally, Mozart seems to be writing chamber music for one instrument. He exchanges material between the hands, creating a "dialogue" much as we might find in a string quartet. We hear the first example of this only a few measures into the movement at the repeat of the first theme, which occurs in the left hand instead of the right. The movement boasts one of Mozart's longest expositions in a work for solo piano, with numerous ideas in each of the two key areas. The development section presents a fascinating combination of material. In its first few measures, Mozart brings together the first two measures and the last four measures of the exposition while maintaining independence between the two motives. He uses a similar procedure during the recapitulation of one of the secondary themes, where the tune is combined contrapuntally with the opening of the first theme.

The chromatic slow movement is reminiscent of C.P.E. Bach in its ornamentation, and florid melodies, rather than those constructed of short motives, are the order of the day. What has been called Mozart's process of "increasing animation" appears throughout this movement, in which the composer gradually quickens rhythms and stretches phrases. The most fascinating passage of the Andante occurs almost exactly halfway through the movement, at the end of the development section. Persistent chromatic alterations produce strident dissonance as daring as any found in Mozart's music. The sequential nature of the material makes the passage sound even more relentless in its passage through distant harmonies on the way to a strong arrival on the tonic and the beginning of the recapitulation.

Mozart unites the Rondo finale with the preceding movement by incorporating a motive from the closing area of the Andante into the first episode. The high point of the finale is a central episode on F minor, which is really a variant of the Rondo theme. The cadenza near the end begins after an extended dominant pedal and continues to remain unstable until a strong cadence on the tonic that initiates the final reprise of the Rondo theme, although in an abbreviated form. *—John Palmer*

Recommended:

○ **Mozart: Piano Sonatas** / Brendel / 2003 / Philips 473689

○ **Mozart: Sonata in C; Rondo in A; Sonata in F** / Uchida / Philips 412122

Piano Sonata No. 8 in A minor, K. 310 (1778)

Mozart's famous *Piano Sonata No. 8 in A minor* (K. 310 or K. 300d, depending on whose reckoning you go by) was composed in Paris in 1778 and published there a few years later as Op. 4/3. In this work, written at age 22 or so, Mozart at last tries his hand at a sonata in the minor mode. The *Piano Sonata No. 8* is, in fact, one of just three minor mode instrumental sonatas ever composed by the man: of the 22 piano sonatas (that includes four lost early ones), just two are not in the major mode, and this is the earlier of them (the other is K. 457 in C minor); and of the 30-some sonatas for keyboard and violin, only No. 21 in E minor (K. 300c, composed, like the *Piano Sonata No. 8*, in 1778) represents its side of the modal spectrum. One gets the feeling, listening to the *Sonata in A minor*, that Mozart had been stocking up on minor mode drama for some time when he wrote it. Its stormy music is a far cry from the happy-hearted, light-footed sonata fare composed up to that point.

The first of the sonata's three movements is an Allegro maestoso, whose heavy, dotted principal theme is pounded out to a stomping chordal left-hand accompaniment—the rhythm and the texture are heavy from the get-go, and only after some time does Mozart fall into the more familiar streamlined, Alberti bass style of piano writing. The second theme, in the expected key of C major, is by contrast all grace—the running sixteenth notes of its melody should be played as though tickling the keys. For a middle movement, Mozart concocted a lovely Andante cantabile in F major. The Presto finale bounds forth in 2/4 meter, its tune driven by an accompaniment whose one-bar pattern begins on the offbeat. *—Blair Johnston*

Recommended:

○ **Mozart: Piano Sonatas** / Brendel / 2003 / Philips 473689

○ **Mozart: 3 Piano Sonatas; Schubert: Impromptu 1** / Pires / 1998 / DG 459055

○ **Dinu Lipatti** / Lipatti / 1999 / EMI 6700321

Piano Sonata No. 9 in D major, K. 311 (1777)

Mozart's Piano Sonata in D major, K. 311, was composed in Mannheim in November 1777, while he and his mother were on a lengthy trip that would take them to Paris the next spring. Aspects of the mannered Mannheim style are evident in this sonata, particularly in its sharp dynamic contrasts. Mozart composed another piano sonata while in Mannheim, that in C major, K. 309, possibly for performances in Paris.

In these sonatas we find Mozart's powers of expression growing, assimilating not only characteristics of works by Mannheim composers, but many of the ideas of Haydn, especially in respect to his use of sonata form in both first and second movements of a multi-movement instrumental work. Also, some of Mozart's writing for the keyboard is in an orchestral style, removed from the typical keyboard technique of the day. The sonata was published in Paris by Heina in 1782 as Op. 4, No. 2.

The Piano Sonata in D major is in three movements: Allegro, Andante con espressione, and a Rondeau: Allegro. The Allegro opens with a theme that is orchestral in conception, with a flourish in the right hand over chords in the left. After a modulation to the dominant, A major, there is a secondary theme that sounds much more like a keyboard solo with its Alberti bass figures and scalar melody. Mozart slowly increases the rhythmic intensity of the development section until a sudden stop near the middle, where piano and forte dynamics alternate unpredictably. The order of events in the recapitulation is unusual. The second theme, now in the tonic, is followed by two ideas from the closing area, then the first theme, and finally a brief coda of entirely new material followed by the third closing idea. Such a "mirror image" recapitulation also occurs in Mozart's *Violin Sonata in D major*, K. 306, and his *Symphony in C major*, K. 338.

Mozart sets the G major Andante in what is often referred to as "rondo-slow-movement form," a variant of slow-movement sonata form (sonata form without a development section) in which the contrasting material (section B) is recapitulated on the tonic and followed by a return of section A. Sudden and wide dynamic contrasts are also a part of the Andante, which features an elegant opening theme fit for a vocal composition.

The closing Rondeau is filled with youthful energy and surprises. The first return of the rondo theme features a transposition of its second half to G major, which then introduces the second episode. The close of this episode is a cadenza passage with three different tempos that leads, concerto-like, into the return of the rondo theme and the close of the movement. *—John Palmer*

Recommended:

○ **Mozart: Piano Sonatas** / Brendel / 2003 / Philips 473689

○ **Mozart: Sonatas & Allegros** / Badura-Skoda / Astrée 8682

○ **Mozart: Piano Sonatas** / Larrocha / 1992 / RCA 60454

Piano Sonata No. 10 in C major, K. 330 (1783)

Just as the first piano sonatas composed by Mozart during the early months of 1775 were clearly intended as group, so K. 330 is the first of a trio of works that forms another unified set; the composer numbered this work and its companions (K. 331 in A, and K. 332 in F) as 1, 2, and 3. All three were composed in 1783, with most authorities dating them to the summer of that year during the course of the visit Mozart made to Salzburg with his new wife Constanze. There must, however, be a question mark over Salzburg as their place of composition. In a letter to his father dated June 9/12, 1784, Mozart mentions these works as being the "sonatas he once sent to his sister," a course of action which would have been unnecessary if they were composed in Salzburg, where Nannerl was still living with her father prior to her own marriage in 1784. After Mozart settled in Vienna as a freelancer in 1781, one of his prime sources of income was teaching the piano to mainly aristocratic pupils. Like its two companions, the C major Sonata was almost certainly composed with such pupils in mind. Mozart also saw the potential for wider circulation of these three contrasted works, having them published in 1784 by the Viennese publisher Artaria, whose advertisement for them appeared in the August of that year. The Sonata in C has the usual three movements, the opening Allegro moderato being followed by an Andante cantabile in which Mozart's lyrical vocal style of writing predominates. The closing Allegretto is a sonata form movement in concerto style, with contrasting full (tutti) sections and solos. *—Brian Robins*

Recommended:

○ **Mozart: Piano Sonatas K330, 331 & 570; Rondo K511** / Brendel / 2000 / Philips 462903

○ **Mozart: Piano Sonatas K310 & 331** / Badura-Skoda / 2001 / Astrée 8867

○ **Mozart: Piano Sonatas KV28, 330 & 333; Rondo, KV485; Adagio, KV540** / Horowitz / 1989 / DG 445517

Piano Sonata No. 11 in A major ("Alla Turca") K. 331 (1783)

The Sonata in A is the second of three sonatas now established as likely to have been composed during 1783, perhaps during the period Mozart and his wife Constanze spent in Salzburg in the summer months of that year. This was the occasion on which the composer introduced his new bride to his father Leopold. Mozart clearly intended this trio to form a group, numbering them from one to three. They were almost certainly composed with his Viennese pupils in mind, teaching forming one of Mozart's principal sources of income during his early years in the Austrian capital. The present sonata has gained particular fame for its last movement, the "Rondo alla turca." That movement took its inspiration from the popularity of quasi-Turkish music in Vienna, a fashionable form already exploited by Mozart in his German singspiel, *Die Entführung aus dem Serail* (The Abduction form the Harem) of the previous year. The Rondo includes a march-like B section in a major key with rolled block chords that evoked the drums of the Turkish Janissary bands, ancestors of the modern marching band. Some commentators have also heard echoes of the opera in the opening movement, which, uniquely among Mozart's sonatas, is a set of variations. Its lilting theme one of the composer's most memorable inventions. The central movement is a Minuetto in the tonic key of A, with a central trio section in D, making the sonata also unique in Mozart's output in that none of the three movements is in sonata form. Along with its two companions, the A major Sonata was published in Vienna by Artaria in 1784, rapidly attaining a popularity that has persisted until the present day. As with so many of Mozart's works, it offers much for both *Kenner* and *Liebhaber,* connoisseurs and mere lovers. Its Turkish element places it among the first pieces of music in the European tradition to show any kind of non-Western influence. Beyond that, it offers a greater-than-usual complement of unforgettable Mozartian melodies. *—Brian Robins*

Recommended:

○ **Mozart: Piano Sonatas, K330, 331 & 570; Rondo, K511** / Brendel / 2000 / Philips 462903

○ **Mozart: Piano Sonatas K310 & 331** / Badura-Skoda / 2001 / Astrée 8867

○ **Mozart: Piano Sonatas K310, 331 & 533/494** / Perahia / 1992 / Sony 48233

Piano Sonata No. 12 in F major, K. 332 (1783)

The composer's original autograph manuscript lists the F Major Sonata as "No. 3" of a group that also includes the Sonatas in C, K. 330 and A, K. 331. They were issued in this ordering by the Viennese publisher Artaria in 1784, the year following the composition of all three sonatas. Most authorities now suggest that they may have been composed in Salzburg during the summer visit Mozart made to introduce his new wife Constanze to his father Leopold and sister Nannerl. This, however, seems questionable in the light of the letter to his father of June 9/12, 1784, in which he mentions having sent the three sonatas to Nannerl, hardly necessary had she been around when they were composed.

The group were undoubtedly composed for the use of Mozart's pupils in Vienna, and he no doubt published them with a view to widening their circulation in addition to cashing in on his own growing reputation as a pianist. Traditionally the Sonata in F has lagged behind its two companions in popularity, but, according to the Mozart authority László Somfai, has been revealed by the revival of the fortepiano to be a work of kaleidoscopic brilliance not apparent when the work is played on a modern piano. The differences, believes Somfai, are particularly evident in the opening Allegro. An interesting feature of the Adagio is the ornamentation added to the Artaria printed edition, which was overseen by Mozart himself—therefore providing valuable clues as to how the composer expected his slower movements to be embellished in performance. The final Allegro assai juxtaposes sections of brilliant passagework with a more cantabile style. *—Brian Robins*

Recommended:

- ○ **Mozart: Piano Sonatas** / Brendel / 2001 / Philips 468048
- ○ **Mozart: Piano Sonatas, K332, 333, 457 & 475** / Badura-Skoda / 2001 / Astree 8868
- ○ **Mozart: Piano Sonatas Vol. 2** / Klien / 1991 / Vox 5046

Piano Sonata No. 13 in B flat major, K. 333 (1783)

One of Mozart's longest and most demanding piano sonatas, this superb work was almost certainly designed as a concert vehicle for the composer himself, rather than being intended as teaching material. Like its immediate predecessors (K. 330–332), the B flat sonata was originally believed to have been composed some years earlier than its present dating of 1783. Modern paper analysis has placed its probable composition in Linz, where Mozart and his wife Constanze stayed for three weeks in November on their return journey from Salzburg to Vienna. In a letter to his father dated October 31, Mozart told Leopold that because he would be giving a concert in the theater in Linz on November 4, he was having to write a new symphony "at breakneck speed," not having any of his other symphonies with him. The result was the *Symphony No. 36* in C, K. 425 ("Linz"), It would seem plausible that he wrote the sonata for the same concert. In July, 1784, the sonata was published in Vienna along with the *Sonata in D*, K. 284 and the *Sonata for Piano and Violin*, K. 454. The sonata is written in a concerto style, with an opening Allegro that alternates "solo" and "full" passages, bravura passage work with delicate filigree, and a final Rondo that includes a cadenza. The central Andante cantabile in E flat is clearly influenced by Mozart's experience as an opera composer; its melodies may justifiably be compared with those of a love duet. *—Brian Robins*

Recommended:

- ○ **Mozart: 3 Piano Sonatas; Schubert: Impromptu 1** / Pires / 1998 / DG 459055
- ○ **Mozart: Piano Sonatas** / Brendel / 2001 / Philips 468048
- ○ **Mozart: Sonatas & Fantasia** / Badura-Skoda / Astrée 8684
- ○ **Mozart: Concerto 23; Sonata 13** / Giulini (cond.), Horowitz, La Scala Theater Orch. / DG 423287

Piano Sonata No. 14 in C minor, K. 457 (1784)

Composed in Vienna in the fall of 1784, the C minor sonata was entered in the thematic catalog Mozart started earlier that year on October 14. For Mozart, 1784 was a year of intense compositional activity for the piano, the eight preceding entries in the catalog all indicating piano works. Six months later, Mozart composed a *Fantasia in C Minor*, K. 475, that has become irrevocably associated with the sonata and invariably precedes it in performance, forming an expansive prelude. It was the composer himself who originally linked the two works, which were published together by the Viennese publisher Artaria under the title "Fantasie et Sonate Pour le Forte-Piano" late in 1785. Although unusual, such a coupling of a work in free, improvisatory style with the stricter form of a sonata was not unparalleled, particularly in the works of Carl Philipp Emanuel Bach—with whose music Mozart was well acquainted. The title page of the first publication bears a dedication to Therese von Trattner, who was a pupil of Mozart's and the wife of Johann von Trattner, a printer and publisher who was also Mozart's landlord at the time the works were composed. As usual with Mozart's relatively few minor-mode works, the C minor sonata is a highly personal work. But here the mood is not one of storminess or tragedy, as in his G minor works, but of high drama in the operatic sense. The mood of noble suffering in the central E flat Adagio has, for example, been viewed by at least one commentator as music that appears to be a direct precursor of that Mozart was to write for the Countess in *Le nozze di Figaro*, while the final Allegro assai is a movement in intense dramatic agitation that looks forward to the Romantics, most immediately to the "Pathétique" sonata of Beethoven. *—Brian Robins*

Recommended:

- ○ **Mozart: Piano Sonatas** / Brendel / 2001 / Philips 468048
- ○ **Ivan Moravec Plays Mozart** / Moravec / 2001 / Supraphon 3581
- ○ **Mozart: Sonatas & Fantasia** / Badura-Skoda / Astrée 8684
- ○ **Walter Gieseking 2** / Gieseking / 1999 / Philips 456790

Piano Sonata No. 15 in C major ("Sonata semplice") K. 545 (1788)

Universally known as the *"Sonata facile (or semplice),"* the relative ease of K. 545 has ensured that it has become the most of famous of all Mozart's piano sonatas, a work that scarcely a student of the instrument fails to learn at some point in his or her career. The entry in Mozart's own thematic catalog, dated June 26, 1788, adds that the sonata was intended "for beginners." Yet despite its fame today, the circumstances of its composition are not known, the original manuscript is lost, and the sonata was not published in Mozart's lifetime, the first edition appearing in 1805 from the press of the composer and publisher Johann André of Offenbach.

There are three short movements: an Allegro, often quoted as a paradigm of the ambiguity of Classical "simplicity," a charming central Andante, and a tiny finale in Rondo form. It is remarkable to note that this unpretentious little work must have been composed at the same time as the great last trilogy of symphonies; indeed it was added by Mozart to his catalog of works on the same day as the first of those magnificent works, the great *Symphony No. 39 in E flat*, K. 543, one of his grandest conceptions. *—Brian Robins*

Recommended:

- ○ **Mozart: 3 Piano Sonatas; Schubert: Impromptu 1** / Pires / 1998 / DG 459055
- ○ **Mozart: Piano Sonatas K533/494, 545, 570 & 576** / Badura-Skoda / 2001 / Astree 8869
- ○ **András Schiff** / Schiff / 1999 / Philips 456925

Piano Sonata No. 16 in B flat major, K. 570 (1789)

Mozart's penultimate piano sonata dates from 1789, a barren year for composition by his prolific standards, the only other major works produced being the final *Piano Sonata in D major*, K. 576, the first of the "Prussian" string quartets (in D major, K. 575), and the *Clarinet Quintet in A major*, K. 581. It was also the year of the composer's speculative journey to Berlin, Leipzig, and Dresden, a tour that failed to alleviate Mozart's by then desperate financial straits. Prior to setting off for Germany in the spring, he composed the B flat Sonata, entering it into his thematic catalog during February. His entry for it specifies the work as being a sonata *auf Klavier allein* (for piano alone), but curiously the sonata was long known in a version for violin and piano. This originated with the first published version, which appeared in Vienna in 1796 with a violin part so lacking in invention that it can be considered spurious with near certainty. It seems likely that, like its immediate predecessor, the so-called "facile" *Sonata in C major*, K. 545, the sonata was composed for didactic purposes. The opening Allegro is quite light in character; although on an altogether more modest scale than the sonatas composed earlier in the decade, it is masterful in the way it wrings various structural and contrapuntal implications from its deceptively bare opening. E flat Adagio is a rondo with two episodes that sets out to beguile rather than convey profundity. The final Allegretto bubbles with humor and surprise effects; it is one of the many finales in which Mozart evokes the world of opera buffa. Musicologist Alfred Einstein called the work "perhaps the most completely rounded of... all [the Mozart piano sonatas], the ideal of his piano sonata." *—Brian Robins*

Recommended:

- ○ **Mozart: Piano Sonatas K330, 331 & 570; Rondo K511** / Brendel / 2000 / Philips 462903
- ○ **Ivan Moravec Plays Mozart** / Moravec / 2001 / Supraphon 3581
- ○ **Mozart: Piano Sonatas, K533/494, 545, 570 & 576** / Badura-Skoda / 2001 / Astree 8869
- ○ **Mozart: Piano Sonatas Vol. 4** / Katin / Olympia 233

Piano Sonata No. 17 in D major ("Trumpet", "Hunt"), K. 576 (1789)

Pity the pianist who relies on Mozart's designation of K. 576 as a "leichte Klaviersonate"—an easy piano sonata. The work was written in 1789, shortly after the composer's return from a largely unsuccessful concert tour of Potsdam, Leipzig, and finally, Berlin, where the sonata may have been aimed at a princess at the Prussian court. Little came of Mozart's journey in the way of fresh commissions, and small wonder: some have suggested that this D major sonata is actually the *most* difficult of the composer's 18 in technical terms. The technical problems come not in the sprightly thematic material, but in its thoroughly contrapuntal treatment, perhaps inspired by Mozart's visit to Leipzig and his reacquaintance with the dormant but still enormously influential masterpieces of J.S. Bach. The sonata has three movements in the usual fast-slow-fast configuration. The first movement, an

Allegro in a jaunty 6/8 time, abounds with imitative entrances that, taken individually, might have come from Bach inventions, but they resolve themselves into chordally accompanied scale material; the music never loses its graceful, Classical flow. This sonata, owing to its horn-call opening, has sometimes been given the nicknames of "Trumpet" or "Hunt," and the work's basic intellectual attraction is established at the outset when this stereotypical figure is unexpectedly subjected to imitation. The second subject area of the exposition is extracted from the opening material in a way Haydn would have been proud of, and the development section is an especially dense contrapuntal essay. The Adagio middle movement, in A major, is a limpid melody gently darkened by chromatic runs, and the Allegretto finale, nearly as contrapuntal as the first movement, sandwiches forte, chromatic, and virtuosic treatments of its main material between the seemingly meek statements of that material that mark off the movement's basic divisions. This was Mozart's last piano sonata, and it perennially appeals both to pianists seeking a Mozartean challenge and to those interested in the point of counterpoint in Mozart's late works. *—James Manheim*

Recommended:

- ○ **Mozart: Complete Sonatas for Piano Vol. 5** / Pires / 1990 / Denon 8075
- ○ **Mozart: Piano Sonatas, K533/494, 545, 570 & 576** / Badura-Skoda / 2001 / Astree 8869
- ○ **Favourite Mozart** / Ashkenazy (cond. & piano), London PO / 1992 / London 436383

6 Preludes and fugues (after J.S. and W.F. Bach) for violin, viola & bass (K. 404a) (1782)

"I go every Sunday at 12 to the Baron van Swieten, where nothing is played but Handel and Bach." Thus wrote Mozart in a letter to his father Leopold dated April 10, 1782. Van Swieten was a Viennese noblemen whom Mozart appears to have initially encountered at about the same time as he settled in Vienna the previous year. The exclusivity of the Baron's taste would have been considered highly unusual, not to say eccentric, during a period that concentrated almost entirely on the music of the day rather than the revival of old music. Nevertheless, the music Mozart encountered at those Sunday morning meetings was to have profound and far-reaching effects on the development of his own compositional style, a deepening of contrapuntal complexity most immediately apparent in the six great string quartets dedicated to Haydn. We know from Mozart himself that the usually fecund composer experienced much trouble with these works; the assimilation of Bach's contrapuntal techniques into his own personal style did not come easily to him. The present set of six works may therefore be viewed as a stepping stone in Mozart's own learning process. Scored for a string trio of violin, viola and cello, each consists of a transcription of a fugue. Five of the fugues are by J.S. Bach, the sixth being the work of his eldest son Wilhelm Friedemann. Each is prefaced by a prelude; some of these are by Mozart and some are again transcriptions from Bach. The full details: No. 1 in D minor, Prelude (Mozart) and Fugue (J.S. Bach, BWV 853); No. 2 in G minor, Prelude (Mozart) and Fugue (J.S. Bach, BWV 883); No. 3 in F major, Prelude (Mozart) and Fugue (J.S. Bach, BWV 882); No. 4 in F major, Prelude (J.S. Bach, BWV 527/ii) and Fugue (J.S. Bach, BWV 1080); No. 5 in E flat major, Prelude and Fugue (J. S. Bach, BWV 526/ii and iii); No. 6 in F minor, Prelude (Mozart) and Fugue (W.F. Bach, Fugue No. 8). *—Brian Robins*

Recommended:

- ○ **Mozart: Complete String Trios & Duos** / Grumiaux Trio / 1996 / Philips 454023

Sonata for 2 pianos in D major, K. 448 (1781)

Mozart reserved the key of D major for happy compositions usually calling for a degree of virtuosity, as may be easily heard in his *Sonata for two pianos*. This is a work in the galant style, light, brilliant, yet refined. Mozart wrote it for a performance he would give with Josephine von Aurnhammer, who also appeared with him in his *Concerto for two pianos and orchestra*. This two-piano sonata is clearly meant for public use, rather than as a teaching tool like his pieces for four hands at a single keyboard.

The opening Allegro con spirito begins with a trilling fanfare, then immediately launches into a quick, bubbling theme, followed by a somewhat more chordal, low-key, second subject adorned with witty grace notes; a third section returns to the spirit and technique of the first part, but without quite quoting the earlier material until the very end. These are the building blocks of the sonata-form movement, which, after an exposition repeat, launches the development section with a descending version of the opening fanfare, sounding like the subject of a fugue. Mozart never really embarks on counterpoint, though, and after a very few bars he moves impatiently to the recapitulation.

The Andante begins with a seemingly simple yet highly adorned melody and flowing accompaniment that might serve nicely as an aria or duet in *The Magic Flute* or *Così fan tutte*. The theme of the middle section in this ABA movement is more spare, almost a lullaby. A quiet, tinkling delicacy pervades most of this movement, particularly upon the return of the A section, after a transition that is almost substantial enough to serve as yet another section.

Finally, the Molto allegro movement leaps off the page with a spirited tune that might be called "galloping" if it weren't so elegant. This is the recurring theme that binds together a rondo featuring an assortment of highly contrasting melodies, one of which—heard early on and returning at the end—includes a Turkish-style cadence that calls to mind Mozart's famous *Rondo alla turca*.

As an aside, this sonata was the one used in the scientific study that tested the theory of the "Mozart Effect," suggesting that Classical music increases brain activity more positively than other kinds of music. *—James Reel*

Recommended:

- ○ **Music for 2 Pianos** / Schiff, Serkin / 1999 / ECM 465062
- ○ **Mozart & Schubert: Music for Piano 4 Hands** / Perahia, Lupu / 1992 / Sony 39511
- ○ **Piano Duets** / Kocsis, Ranki / Hungaroton 11646

Sonata for piano, 4 hands in B flat major, K. 358 (1774)

Wolfgang Amadeus Mozart composed his *Sonata for piano duet in B flat major*, K. 358, in Salzburg some time in 1773 or 1774 for his sister Nanerl and himself to perform in Paris and Vienna. A three-movement work, the first two without tempo markings, but self-evidently an Allegro and an Adagio, and a finale marked Molto presto, Mozart's *Sonata in B flat* is full of virtuoso fingerwork and lightly lyrical melodies, and its finale is especially brilliant. The work was published in 1783, and it remains a repertoire item for piano duet teams both professional and amateur. *—James Leonard*

Recommended:

- ○ **Mozart: Music for 2 Pianos & Piano Duets** / Haebler, Hoffmann / 1996 / Philips 454026
- ○ **Mozart: Complete Works For Piano, 4 Hands Vol. 1** / Balsam, Raps / 1993 / Arabesque 6635
- ○ **Mozart: Sonata for Piano Duets** / Kocsis, Ranki / Hungaroton 11794

Sonata for piano, 4 hands in C major, K. 521 (1787)

The *Sonata in C* is Mozart's final essay in a form he had made very much made his own. His earliest duet sonata, K. 19d in C major, dates from 1765 and is the only survivor of several probably composed during his childhood years for him and his sister Nannerl to play during the tours they were taken on by their father Leopold. It dates from 1787, being entered by Mozart in his thematic catalog on May 29 of that year. The same day he sent a copy of it to his friend Baron Gottfried von Jacquin with a covering letter requesting that he should give it to his sister Franziska, a pupil for whom he had composed the piano part in the *Trio for Clarinet, Viola and Piano in E flat major*, K. 498. Mozart asks Jacquin to give his sister the sonata "with my compliments and tell her to tackle it at once, for it is rather difficult." Mozart subsequently dedicated the sonata to two sisters, Babette and Marianne (Nanette) Nortrop, the daughters of a wealthy Viennese merchant and possibly also pupils. Uniquely among his duet sonatas, the autograph manuscript specifically designates cembalo primo and cembalo secondo (first and second piano), leading Mozart's biographer Einstein to conjecture that the sonata would gain from being played on two pianos. Both the opening and closing movements are of exceptional brilliance, lending weight to Mozart's assertion that the sonata is "rather difficult." As with its immediate predecessor, the F major Sonata, K. 497, both parts are equally demanding, with little of the concertante character evident in the earlier duet sonatas. The work may have been published in Paris in late in 1789 and was also included in a series of keyboard works by various composers issued by the Viennese publisher Hoffmeister between 1785 and 1787. *—Brian Robins*

Recommended:

- ○ **Mozart: Piano Duets, Vol. 1** / Jandó, Kollar / 2000 / Naxos 553518
- ○ **Mozart: Piano Sonatas, K488, 501, 521 & 381** / Argerich, Rabinovitch / 1994 / Teldec 91378
- ○ **Mozart: Sonata for Piano Duets** / Kocsis, Ranki / Hungaroton 11794

Sonata for piano, 4 hands in D major, K. 381 (1772)

Although it is undated, the *Sonata in D major for four hands at one piano* was composed at some time during the middle of 1772, the year in which Mozart later returned to Italy with his father Leopold to supervise the opening of his new opera *Lucio Silla*, K. 135. Like two other early four-hand sonatas, K. 19d, composed in London in 1765, and K. 358 in B flat, which dates from 1773 or 1774, it was written for Mozart and his sister Nannerl to play. In her youth, she was considered as accomplished a performer as her brother and there is a famous portrait that shows the two seated at the same piano. Brother and sister are recorded as having played the work at arch-episcopal court in Salzburg on September 3, 1780, an event that also included them playing either the *Concerto in E flat for two pianos*, K. 365, or the two-piano version of K. 242, originally designed as a concerto for three pianos. According to Mozart's biographer Alfred Einstein, the three-movement work is best described as a reduction of an Italian symphony where the distinctive writing for strings and winds and of solos and tuttis is clearly laid out. *—Brian Robins*

Recommended:

- ○ **Mozart: Piano Duets Vol. 1** / Jandó, Kollar / 2000 / Naxos 553518
- ○ **Mozart: Music for 2 Pianos & Piano Duets** / Haebler, Hoffmann / 1996 / Philips 454026
- ○ **Mozart: Sonata for Piano Duets** / Kocsis, Ranki / Hungaroton 11794

Sonata for piano, 4 hands in F major, K. 497 (1786)

Wolfgang Amadeus Mozart entered his *Sonata for piano duet in F major,* K. 497, into his personal catalog of works on August 1, 1786, 12 years after he had composed his last sonata for piano duet. Prior to 1786, he had composed three sonatas for piano duet for himself and his sister. But after he left Salzburg for Vienna, Mozart no longer had his sister at hand, and his production of duet sonatas abruptly stopped. Indeed, he was to write only one more sonata in 1787 for piano duet before he stopped writing piano duets altogether. The four-movement *Sonata in F major* is in the form of a church sonata opening with an Adagio followed by an Allegro di molto, an Andante, and an unmarked closing movement that is self-evidently an Allegro. Although the virtuoso technique and witty dialogue of the players is as elegant as earlier, the tender charm of his youthful music is replaced by a more self-consciously bright and brilliant elegance of his mature music. *—James Leonard*

Recommended:

- ○ **Mozart: Music for 2 Pianos & Piano Duets** / Haebler, Hoffmann / 1996 / Philips 454026
- ○ **Mozart: Sonata for Piano Duets** / Kocsis, Ranki / Hungaroton 11794

Variations for piano (1765–1791)

Throughout his life, Mozart composed variations on diverse themes. Aside from variation movements in piano sonatas, there exist fifteen sets for solo keyboard. Another set of variations, *K. 547b in F major,* was incorporated into the violin sonata in F major, K. 547.

In the first two surviving sets of variations, K. 24 and 25, both on Dutch songs, Mozart places fewer technical demands on the player than he does in the violin sonatas of the same time. Some of the traits we find in his later sets already appear, such as an Adagio variation near the end of each set; however, unlike the later sets, these very early ones preserve the same meter throughout.

Surprisingly, Mozart wrote out very few variations during his youth. Only two are known from his "teenage" years in Salzburg. The first of these is a set of six in G major on Salieri's *Mio caro adone,* written in Vienna in the fall of 1773. Another set (K. 179), on a minuet by Johann Fischer, followed in the summer of 1774, after Mozart had returned to Salzburg. With K. 180, Mozart establishes the pattern of his later variations, in which the penultimate variation is an Adagio and the final variation changes meter. In K. 179, there is an Adagio, but no meter change. Neither set contains a minor-mode variation, and both are of the decorative variety, with little or nor harmonic adventurousness or fundamental alteration of the theme.

Mozart composed the twelve variations on A.L. Baudron's melody for Beaumarchais' "Je suis Lindor" (from *Barbier de Seville*) in E flat major, K. 354/299a, while in Paris in early 1778. This was printed in Paris in 1778, along with the Variations, K. 179 and 180. A set of nine variations in C major, on N. Dezède's *Julie,* was also composed in Paris, in the late summer of 1778. The textural polyphony we find in these variations is derived from the keyboard style of Johann Schobert (c.1735–67), who lived in Paris after about 1760.

The variations Mozart composed in 1781–82, just after relocating permanently to Vienna, are among his best known. In K. 265, on *Ah vous dirai-je, Maman* (long believed to have originated in Paris in 1778), the degree of virtuosity rises to a new level. Referred to as "La belle françoise," Mozart's *Variations in E flat major,* K. 353/300f, are based on the French song, "Adieu donc, dame françoise." Many of the "typical" traits of Mozart's variations appear here, including variations that become progressively difficult, a variation in the minor mode, an Adagio tempo for the penultimate variation and a change in meter in the last. The eight variations on Grétry's *Dieu d'amour,* K. 352/300f, written for one of Mozart's students, are not as difficult as they sound.

In 1783–84, Mozart completed three more sets of variations, K. 398/416e, 460/454a and 455. Of these, the *Ten Variations in G major,* on Gluck's "Unser dummer Pöbel Meint," K. 455, are considered his finest. Mozart shows his mastery of melodic, harmonic and contrapuntal elements in this essay on Gluck's simple tune. The Variations in B flat, K. 500, of 1786 are based on an original Allegretto. Mozart's nine *Variations on a Minuet* by Jean Pierre Duport, the director of chamber music at the Prussian court, were written in April 1789 to earn a position at the court. The last set of *Variations,* K. 613, is on a tune by either B. Schack or F. Gerl written for Emanuel Schikaneder's play, *Der dumme Gärtner. —John Palmer*

Recommended:

- ○ **Mozart: Piano Variations Vol. 2** / Nicolosi / 1993 / Naxos 550612
- ○ **Colin Tilney Plays Mozart** / Tilney / 2000 / Doremi 71137

Variations on "Ah, vous dirai-je maman," for piano in C major, K. 265 (1778)

Variation form was one Mozart frequently employed in the solo piano extemporizations for which his concerts were famed (cf. K. 398 and K. 455). The present set is probably Mozart's best known set of variations, the French song on which they are based being familiar in the English-speaking world as the nursery tunes "Twinkle, Twinkle, Little Star" or "Baa-Baa Black Sheep." Traditionally assigned to the disastrous summer of 1778 during which Mozart's mother fell ill and died in Paris during their sojourn in the French capital, the work according to recent research was probably composed in Vienna in either 1781 or 1782. The variations are a perfect example of Mozart's oft-demonstrated ability to build a substantial work from the simplest (and, in this instance, deliberately childish) materials. Particularly noteworthy is the chromatic writing in Variation 8 and the near-tragic tone of the minor mode Variation 9. The work was one of three sets of variations (the others are K. 398 in F and K. 455 in G) published in Vienna by Torricella in 1785. *—Brian Robins*

Recommended:

- ○ **Variations, Rondo, Adagios & Andante** / Schiff / 1988 / London 421369
- ○ **Mozart: Pièces pour le pianoforte** / Badura-Skoda / 2001 / Astrée 8864
- ○ **Mozart: Piano Sonatas 11 & 14; Fantasia, K475; Variations, K265** / Jandó / 1989 / Naxos 550258

ORCHESTRAL

Divertimenti, Serenades, and Cassations (1766–1787)

The divertimento, serenade, cassation, nocturne (or notturno), and finalmusik were the light entertainment music of Mozart's day, and he applied these terms rather indiscriminately. These works in Mozart's output tend to share certain characteristics, including a wealth of material distributed among an opening march, two slow movements and two minuets, often joined with another fast movement or two in sonata form.

Mozart's youthful Cassations of 1769 fit this formal pattern. The first, K. 100/62a, is in eight movements (including the *March,* K. 62) and is scored for two each of oboes or flutes, horns, and trumpets with strings. The others are in seven movements and lack trumpets. Each is introduced by a march, contains at least two minuets and closes with an ebullient finale. The most interesting of the three is K. 99. Some scholars believe that its March theme is by Telemann. The Allegro molto is Handelian in style, while the Andante is entirely for muted strings, as is typical of many of Mozart's serenades. The first of the two Minuets is composed in a courtly style with three distinct beats per measure, but the second "swings" a little with a one-beat-per-measure feel. The intervening Andante, without horns, is reminiscent of J. S. Bach. Mozart's Finale is in two parts, each contrasting an Allegro section with a quiet Siciliana before the opening March returns to close the piece.

The three Divertimenti (not Mozart's designation) of early 1772 do not fit the mold of these earlier works. The one in D major, K. 136, is representative in its three movements (Allegro, Andante, Presto) and scoring for string quartet with double bass. The virtuosity of the Allegro and fugal development section in the Presto show the influence of Michael Haydn, while the cantabile writing in the G major Andante betrays the influence of Italian music. The thematic ties between first and last movements are among the clearest in any of Mozart's works.

Between January 1776 and June 1777, Mozart composed six occasional works containing between six and eight movements. Two of these, K. 287 and K. 247, are for two violins, viola, bass (not cello) and two horns, and the writing is soloistic rather than orchestral. Most curious is the Notturno K. 286/269a, in which four separate groups, each consisting of two horns and strings, create echo effects; K. 250/248b is the most symphonic of Mozart's occasional pieces, even incorporating a miniature violin concerto.

Mozart's wind Serenades of 1781–84 (K. 361/370a, 375 and 388/384a) are among his greatest works, and in many ways transcend their genre. It is difficult to imagine the shrill gloom of K. 388 serving in the traditional role of the serenade. The B flat serenade, K. 361/370a, is an especially popular masterpiece of refined sonority. Two basset horns add a liquid timbre to an ensemble of paired oboes, clarinets, bassoons, four horns, and double bass. Mozart mixes the colors of the ensemble differently in each of the seven movements, and melodies are abundant; each of the two Minuets features two Trios.

Mozart's last two Serenades, *Ein musikalischer Spass,* K. 522, and *Eine kleine Nachtmusik,* K. 525, date from the summer of 1787. The former is a unique satire on the hapless small-town composers of Mozart's day. *Eine kleine Nachtmusik* (A Little Night Music), however, is perhaps the apotheosis of Mozart's occasional music. It is scored essentially for string quartet with double bass, and it has four movements beginning with a concise sonata form, but stylistically it is miles away from the introspection and adventurous experimentation that characterize Mozart's quartets. The style is familiar and light, entertainment music raised to perfection. *—John Palmer*

Recommended:

- ○ **Mozart: Serenades & Divertimenti** / various / Brilliant 99733
- ○ **Mozart: Eine Kleine Nachtmusik** / various / 1995 / Naxos 553225
- ○ **Mozart: Serenades & Divertimenti** / Frigyes (cond.), Franz Liszt CO / Capriccio 51030

Divertimento for 2 horns & strings in F major ("Ein musikalischer Spass" / "A Musical Joke"), K. 522 (1787)

During the summer of 1787, Mozart entered two works of the divertimento type (light, multi-movement works for a small assortment of instruments) in his catalog. Neither was given the divertimento title, and it would be difficult to imagine a greater contrast between the two works concerned: *Ein musikalischer Spass* (A Musical Joke) and *Eine kleine Nachtmusik*, K. 525 (A Little Night Music). Whereas the latter is probably the most popular of all Mozart's works and a perfect example of entertainment music at its most refined, K. 522 is a satire on inept composers and performers, a deliberately clumsy work. Mozart's sense of humor is well documented; its more childish aspects were highlighted in the now famous Peter Shaffer play (and later film), *Amadeus*. Yet his "musical joke," despite some obvious moments of sheer farce, goes beyond mere horseplay; it contains subtler forms of stylistic satire as well. Some of the jokes are technical "in-jokes" that only those aware of the work of Mozart's more mediocre contemporaries would appreciate. Indeed the work may have at least in part have served Mozart as a sort of personal revenge upon poor composers with whom he constantly found himself in competition. The fugue in the final Presto, for instance, has been shown to be based on an exercise by Mozart's English pupil Thomas Attwood.

Research has shown that Mozart worked on the idea of *Ein musikalischer Spass* for some two years, the opening Allegro having been started before the end of 1785. There are four movements in all, with the outer sections already mentioned framing a Menuetto and an Adagio cantabile. The work is scored for two horns, two violins, viola and bass; the string parts are intended for single instruments. *—Brian Robins*

Recommended:

- ○ **Mozart: Sextet: Eine kleine Nachtmusik; Divertimento K136** / ASMF Chamber Ens. / Philips 412269
- ○ **Mozart: Chamber Music** / Kodaly Quartet / 1991 / Naxos 550437

German Dances, Marches, and Minuets for Orchestra (1767–1791)

Mozart's enormous quantity of entertainment music is often overlooked by music historians. By the end of his short life, he had composed dozens of contredances, German dances, and over a hundred minuets. Minuets were danced at court, generally by one couple at a time. The German dance, or Deutsche, is derived from the Ländler, a triple-meter country dance. The contredance is a group dance with set figures.

Mozart's earliest and latest known marches, K. 41c and K. 544, are lost. The ten composed between 1769 and 1780 are linked with other occasional music—serenades, cassations and divertimenti. From 1782, there are three marches, K. 488, Nos. 1–3, that are evidently independent works. The best known of Mozart's marches are the two in D major, K. 335 and 320a, that are coupled with the *"Posthorn" Serenade in D major*, K. 320, composed in August 1779 as university *Finalmusik*. At these ceremonies, it was traditional for the musicians to march to the site where they would play the Serenade written for the occasion. At the close of the ceremony, the musicians marched off, usually playing the same music to which they had entered. For the Salzburg University closing ceremonies of August 3, 1779, however, Mozart composed two different marches, one for the entrance of the players and the other for their exit. These marches for actual marching are scored without timpani.

Most of Mozart's minuets and contredances from the Salzburg era were composed between 1769 and 1777. These were written for Carnival, the season of feasting preceding Lent. In most of the early dances (K. 61g, 103/61d, 104/61e, 122/73t, 123/73g, 164/130a, 61h and 103/61d) Mozart gives the essential material to the strings, leaving the winds to add color. The young composer exercised greater rhythmic freedom in his first such compositions (K. 65a/61b) than he would in his mature, Viennese dances. Among these early works, the Contredance in B flat major, composed in Bologna in 1770, stands out. Only a minute in length, the piece features exceptional melodic clarity and a Handelian sense of the uses of texture.

Between 1782 and 1784, Mozart wrote six contredances and eight minuets, mostly in sets. (Some scholars argue that the *Overture and Three Contredances*, K. 106/588a, also belong to this period.) One of the minuets, the *Minuet in C major*, K. 409/383f, was probably intended for the *Symphony in C major*, K. 338. In the five minuets of K. 461/448a, we hear the wind instruments developing a measure of independence, especially the bassoon, which does not always follow the string bass.

After his appointment as Court Chamber Music Composer in December 1787, Mozart's output of dance music increased. He composed ten sets of German dances, mostly for balls held in the famous Redoutensaal of the Vienna Hofburg. Restrictions allowed for little structural creativity, but Mozart found some room for expression in orchestration and melodic shapes, even including a hurdy-gurdy in No. 3 of K. 602. Nearly all of the dances are in major keys and are in triple meter with two repeated phrases of eight measures in length, usually with a da capo instruction. Orchestration varies from dance to dance, but almost all include two violins and a contrabass with paired flutes, oboes, horns and bassoons. Clarinets, trumpets, timpani, posthorns, and even sleigh bells appear in many of the dances. Mozart's work for the court in Vienna and its attendant salary once prompted him to lament that "I am paid too much for what I do and too little for what I could do." *—John Palmer*

Recommended:

- ○ **Mozart: Dances & Marches** / Boskovsky (cond.), Vienna Mozart Ens. / 1990 / Philips 422506
- ○ **Mozart: Dances & Marches** / Graf (cond.), Salzburg Mozart Orch. / Capriccio 51024

Maurerische Trauermusik (Masonic Funeral Music), in C minor, K. 477 (1785)

Wolfgang Mozart joined the order of the freemasons at the lodge "Zur Wohltätigkeit" (Benefaction) in Vienna on December 14, 1784. Mozart and freemasonry seemed an ideal match, and in a little over a year he would achieve the status of "master mason." A small number of works among Mozart's late output was intended directly for use in Masonic lodges, and two major non-Masonic works, the opera *Die Zauberflöte* (*The Magic Flute*, K. 620) and the *Requiem* K. 626, share strong Masonic connections. The best known of Mozart's Masonic compositions is the *Maurerische Trauermusik*, K. 477 (479a) scored originally for two violins, two violas, clarinet, basset horn, two oboes, two horns, and bass. Mozart later added parts for two additional basset horns and bassoon, resulting in an instrumentation absolutely unique in Mozart's vast output.

According to Mozart's handwritten inventory of his music, the *Masonic Funeral Music* was written "on the death of brothers Mecklenburg and Esterházy" in November 1785. Duke Georg August of Mecklenburg-Strelitz and Count Franz Esterházy von Galántha were both members of the Viennese aristocracy, the former a major-general in the Army and the latter Hungarian Court Chancellor. Their combined memorial service was given at the Lodge of Sorrows on November 17, 1785. Research undertaken in the 1980s suggests that an early version of the *Maurerische Trauermusik* was played at the induction of a new Mason at the lodge "Zur wahren Eintracht" on August 12, 1785. Also, the instrumental incarnation that we now know did not make its bow until the occasion of a concert performance given December 9, 1785.

The music, marked Adagio, is dark and serious in the manner of Mozart's *Requiem*, K. 626. He makes use of the plainchant Tonus peregrinus, which appears at first in the clarinet part. This tone is used in connection with the Lamentation chants sung on Good Friday and the "miserere" section of the requiem mass. In the *Maurerische Trauermusik*, the tone is used to hold together what is for Mozart an unusually thin texture. The strings and winds alternate in antiphonal groups, finally settling on a C major chord, which suggests a transcendent spirituality rather than a pleasing conclusion to a musical piece cast in a predominantly minor mood. This may well reflect sentiments expressed by Mozart in his letters of the time, such as "Death, if we think about it soberly, is the true and ultimate purpose of our life. (The) image (of Death) holds nothing terrifying for me anymore; instead it holds much that is soothing and consoling!" *—Uncle Dave Lewis*

Recommended:

- ○ **Mozart: Symphonies & Funeral Music** / Abbado (cond.), Berlin PO / 1994 / Sony 48385
- ○ **Mozart: Opera Overtures; Haydn: Symphony 96** / Walter (cond.), Columbia SO / 1996 / Sony 64486

Serenade No. 13 for strings in G major ("Eine kleine Nachtmusik"), K. 525 (1787)

The Serenade in G major (1787), the most enduringly popular of all of Mozart's works, was written during the a period when the composer was also hard at work on his opera *Don Giovanni*. The title "Eine kleine Nachtmusik" (A Little Night Music) is Mozart's own; "Nachtmusik" was actually a common designation for serenades of this type. While Mozart composed several such works during his years in Salzburg, the Serenade in G is unique to the period of his residence in Vienna (1781–91). The work differs from Mozart's earlier serenades in its comparatively lean scoring: two violins, viola, cello, and double bass. Mozart's entry for this work in his catalogue shows that the work originally had five movements; the original second movement, a minuet, was later removed.

The specific occasion for which the Serenade was written is not known, but some have suggested that the work's grace, elegance, and perfection of form were intended as an antidote to the deliberate banality and clumsiness of the composer's *Ein musikalischer Spass* (A musical joke), K. 522, composed some six weeks earlier. However, this seems to run counter to the character of a composer quite capable of unapologetically coarse musical humor (as in some of his vocal canons, for example). The musicologist Alfred Einstein, also makes the questionable assertion that Mozart wrote the Serenade to fulfill a personal inner need—if true, certainly atypical for a composer who rarely produced music without some external motivation or purpose, whether financial or otherwise.

The extant movements of the Serenade are as follows: Allegro; Romance (Andante); Menuetto (Allegretto); and Rondo (Allegro). *—Brian Robins*

Recommended:

- ○ **Mozart: Serenades** / Böhm (cond.), Vienna PO / DG 453076
- ○ **Mozart: Night Music** / Manze (cond.), English Concert / 2003 / HM 907280
- ○ **Mozart: The Great Serenades** / Marriner (cond.), Academy of St. Martin-in-the-Fields / 1999 / Philips 464022

CHAMBER MUSIC

Adagio and Fugue for string quartet in C minor, K. 546 (1788)

The fugue of this pair was originally composed for keyboard duet (K. 426) in 1783, a period during which Mozart was greatly interested in studying and learning from the contrapuntal techniques of Bach and Handel. In 1788, Mozart arranged this austere fugue for string orchestra, prefacing it with what he termed in his thematic catalog "a brief Adagio" whose profundity of utterance belies its comparative brevity. In its two-part structure, the work belongs to the tradition of Viennese church sonatas found in the works of such composers as Fux and Tuma. Quite why Mozart returned to his earlier fugue is not clear, and no practical purpose for the new work is known. It is, however, perhaps worth recalling that the summer of 1788 witnessed the composition of the three great final symphonies, *No. 39 in E flat*, K. 543, *No. 40 in G minor*, K. 550, and *No. 41 in C, "Jupiter,"* K. 551 (K. 546 was entered in Mozart's catalog on June 22, the same day as the E flat symphony). Perhaps it would not be too far-fetched to link the orchestration of the fugue with the composition of the greatest of all Mozart's contrapuntal essays, the Finale of the *"Jupiter" Symphony*. *—Brian Robins*

Recommended:

- ○ **Schubert: Quartet 15; Mozart: Adagio & Fugue In C** / Ma, Kashkashian, Kremer, Phillips / 1987 / CBS 42134
- ○ **Mozart: Complete Quintets Vol. 2** / Quartetto Italiano / 1997 / Philips 456058
- ○ **Mozart: Piano Concertos; Adagio & Fugue** / Davies (cond.), Stuttgart CO / 1999 / ECM 462651

Clarinet Quintet in A major ("Stadler"), K. 581 (1789)

The years 1789 and 1790 were the most difficult of Mozart's career; during this period his financial difficulties escalated, and his popularity as a performer waned with the fickle Viennese public. Not surprisingly given such circumstances, these years witnessed a dramatic decline in the number of works Mozart produced. However at some point late in the summer of 1789 Mozart received a commission for a new opera from the Emperor Joseph II. By the time he began composing the opera in question, *Così fan tutte*, he must also have been at work on what would become one of his most popular chamber works, the *Clarinet Quintet in A*. Not only does the quintet predominantly bask in that same golden warmth and mellowness that characterizes much of *Così*, but a sketch for its finale became "Ah lo veggio," one of Ferrando's arias from Act Two of the opera. The Quintet was completed by the end of September 1789—perhaps the 29th, as indicated in Mozart's thematic catalog.

It was composed for the outstanding clarinetist Anton Stadler (1753–1812), a member of the court orchestra in Vienna and a friend of Mozart's from the time the latter first settled in Vienna in 1781. Mozart had already composed a number of chamber works for Stadler and his brother Mathias, some of which were actually for basset horn. In addition this playing the lower pitched instrument, Anton Stadler was noted for his ability to exploit the low register of the standard clarinet; to enable his exploration of this so-called *chalumeau* range he devised an additional extension for the instrument. It was for this modified instrument that Mozart composed both the *Clarinet Quintet* and the famous *Clarinet Concerto in A*, K. 622—one of his last works. Although playing the work on a modern clarinet requires less transposition of low notes than is the case with the Concerto, the work is still best heard on an instrument that allows the original pitch to be heard; several recordings have been made on clarinets that reconstruct Stadler's instrument.

The quintet is scored for clarinet, two violins, viola, and cello, and is cast in four movements. The opening *Allegro*, a discourse between all five instruments, is tinged with sadness; the exquisitely lovely *Larghetto* that follows brings the clarinet more into the limelight, its rapturous lines supported throughout by muted strings. The *Minuetto* is particularly notable for the first of its two trios. The final movement is a set of variations based on one of those innocent, almost childish-sounding themes Mozart so often employed in his finales. But, as is also typical of Mozart, the manner in which the composer develops a wide variety of moods and musical textures rings enormous richness from the material, and allows the clarinetist to display great virtuosity. *—Brian Robins*

Recommended:

- ○ **David Oistrakh Collection Vol. 2** / Oistrakh, Knushevitsky, Terian, Bondarenko, Sorokin / 1997 / Doremi 7702
- ○ **Mozart: The Complete Quintets Vol. 2** / Brymer, etc. / 1997 / Philips 456058
- ○ **Mozart: Clarinet & Horn Quintets** / Meyer, Hobarth, Matzka, Leopold, Riebl / 2001 / EMI 567648
- ○ **Mozart: Quintet in A; Trio in E flat** / Meyer, Quatuor Mosaiques / 1993 / Astrée 8736
- ○ **Mozart: Clarinet Quintets** / Hacker, Salomon SQ / Amon Ra 17

Divertimento for violin, viola & cello in E flat major, K. 563 (1788)

Among the greatest works ever penned for the "difficult" combination of violin, viola, and cello, Mozart's sublime and masterful *Divertimento for strings trio in E flat major*, K. 563, dates from the miraculous summer months of 1788. Although plagued by debts (K. 563 is dedicated to Mozart's fellow freemason Michael Puchberg, who advanced a number of loans to the composer) and anxieties, and saddened by the premature death of his young daughter Theresia on June 29, Mozart produced a string of astounding works during this period, regardless of the adversity of his personal circumstances.

Although string trios were also written by Boccherini and the Haydn brothers, (and later by Schubert, Beethoven Reger, Dohnányi, and others) the genre almost invariably proves troublesome. The absence of a second violin requires that the harmonic texture be reinforced by viola and cello, placing demands upon the players who are often required to exploit extreme registers. Meanwhile, the violin parts are of virtuoso difficulty, and hence the string trio genre was not widely accepted by a musical public which had shown an insatiable appetite for Joseph Haydn's string quartets.

Mozart's *Divertimento*, K. 563, comprises six movements, the first of which, an Allegro in common time and regular sonata form, opens with a unison tonic descending arpeggio. The lyrical, soaring second subject theme is debated by violin and cello playing a sixth apart, but the labyrinthine fugal exchanges of the development section attain a depth and sonority that seems hardly credible given that just three players are involved. The A flat Adagio has a noble seriousness which echoes the slow movement of Mozart's *Symphony No. 39*, written earlier that summer. The roots of divertimento style in the popular entertainment music of Mozart's day are re-created in each of the two minuets, the second of which is remarkable for its two trios, in the form of an Austrian Ländler. These enfold a magnificent movement in variation form, an Andante in B flat, built upon a charming folklike melody. By the time the final variation (a chorale theme played by the viola in half notes against a brilliant counterpoint between violin and cello, both playing running passages) is reached, the original theme is hardly discernible, although it returns in unmistakable form at the close of the movement. Mozart's K. 563 *Divertimento* ends with a brilliant Rondo in opera buffa style, which again places bravura demands upon each of the three players with its complex instrumental dialogue. *—Michael Jameson*

Recommended:

- ○ **Mozart: Divertimento in E; etc.** / Ma, Kashkashian, Kremer / 1992 / Sony 39561
- ○ **Mozart: Complete String Trios & Duos** / Grumiaux Trio / 1996 / Philips 454023

Flute Quartets (4) for flute, violin, viola & cello (1777–1787)

Mozart once wrote to his father that he hated the flute; nevertheless, he wrote numerous works for the instrument, including four concertos or concerto movements and a sinfonia concertante, all composed in 1778–80, while Mozart was in Paris. Also, there are four flute quartets (for flute, violin, viola, and cello), the first two of which (in *D major*, K. 285, and in G major, 285a) were composed in Mannheim in late 1777 and early 1778; the third and fourth (in C major, K. Anh. 171/285b, and in A major, 298), were composed in Vienna in 1781–82 and 1786–87, respectively. The professionalism and sensitivity with which Mozart crafted these works belie any dislike he may have had for the instrument.

According to Mozart, Ferdinand Dejean, a surgeon with the Dutch East India Co. whom Mozart had met in Mannheim, commissioned three flute quartets from the composer. Only two exist from this period (K. 285 and 285a). Most likely, Mozart never finished the third, for the two completed works were composed very slowly and the composer's fee was not fully paid. While in Mannheim, he also wrote two flute concertos, 313/285c and 313/285d, probably also commissioned by Dejean.

Mozart dated the manuscript of the first of these flute quartets, that in *D major*, K. 285, December 25, 1777. Throughout, the writing is "concertante," with the string parts subordinate to the flute. Of greatest interest in the first movement are the long segments in the tonic and dominant minor in the midst of the development section and a theme that looks forward to the *String Quintet in G minor*, K. 516. The second movement, marked Adagio, is set in the relative minor (B minor); only 35 measures in length, it is touching, with delicate scoring for all of the instruments. Mozart varies the returns of the main theme in the concluding D major Rondo. The intimacy of the writing and greater participation of the strings brings the sound closer to that of Mozart's other chamber works.

The Quartet in G major, K. 285a, is in only two movements and of little interest. Here, it seems, Mozart is indeed bored with the idiom, creating music that, while melodious, is very conventional and predictable, with the flute taking the primary role.

Also less significant is the *Quartet in C major,* K. Anh, 171/285c, the second movement of which is an arrangement, probably not by Mozart, of the sixth movement (a theme and variations) from Mozart's *Serenade for Winds,* K. 361/370a.

For years, it was thought that the Flute *Quartet in A major,* K. 298, dated from the period of the first three quartets, 1777–78. That the manuscript was once in the possession of Baron von Jacquin suggests otherwise, and handwriting analysis points to late 1786 as the period of composition. Mozart composed the piece for a circle of Viennese friends who often met at the home of the Jacquin family.

Written as a kind of music a joke, the *Quartet in A major,* K. 298, features a contemporary popular tune in each movement. The first of these is from a song by F.A. Hoffmeister, the next is a traditional French folk song, and the third is from Paisiello's aria, "La gare generose." (Because Paisiello's melody was not known in Vienna before the fall of 1786, Mozart could not have composed the piece—certainly not the finale—until later that year.) A sort of conversation takes place in the Finale, as the flute and strings take turns with the main theme. *—John Palmer*

Recommended:

- ○ **Mozart: Complete Music for Flute** / Grauwels, Labadie (conds.), Brussels Virtuosi, Les Violons du Roy / Hyperion 44011

Oboe Quartet in F major, K. 370 (1781)

Mozart spent the winter of 1780–81 in Munich, putting the finishing touches on *Idomeneo* in preparation for the opera's premiere, in the Hoftheater on January 29, 1781. While there he met Friedrich Ramm, who was by all accounts an extraordinary oboist; for him Mozart composed the *Quartet for oboe, violin, viola & cello in F major, K. 370/368b,* giving the oboe the greatest possible level of prominence.

The importance of the oboe part in the quartet does not, however, mean that the string parts are negligible. On the contrary, Mozart gives them a greater role in the dialectic of the piece than he does in the Flute Quartets, making the *Oboe Quartet* rank among his best-integrated chamber compositions.

Ramm's artistry must have been exceptional, judging by the Quartet's opening Allegro. Not surprisingly, the oboe is charged with most of the thematic presentation, although the violin and viola share in the musical argument throughout this sonata-form movement.

The Adagio slow movement illustrates the wide range of expression we find in the Quartet. It is set in D minor (the relative minor), a key in which Mozart wrote some of his most expressive music, and which in his operatic arias is generally associated with vengeance. The depth of feeling in this movement is more profound than in the Adagio of the *Flute Quartet,* K. 285, also in the relative minor.

The work closes with a spirited Rondo, in which contrasting episodes see the trading of musical material between instruments. The most notable feature of the movement is an unusual, thirteen-measure polymetric segment in which the oboe plays in 4/4 meter while the strings continue in 6/8, not noticing that one of their number has gone astray. Otherwise, the movement is bright and cheerful in mood. *—John Palmer*

Recommended:

- ○ **Quintets, Quartets, Movements & Fragments** / ASMF / 1991 / Philips 422510
- ○ **Mozart: Flute Quartets** / Nash Ens. / 1998 / Virgin 61448

Piano Quartet No. 1 in G minor, K. 478 (1785)

Mozart composed two quartets for piano, violin, viola, and cello. The present work is the earlier, being entered by the composer into his thematic catalog on October 16, 1785. The form was relatively unusual in Mozart's time, and what models there were tended to treat the strings as accompaniment to the keyboard rather than as equal partners. It appears that Mozart's work has its genesis in a commission from the Viennese publisher Franz Anton Hoffmeister for three such works, the remaining two being canceled by Hoffmeister when he saw the G Minor work and recognized that it would be far too difficult for amateurs, the usual market for keyboard-based chamber music. Such qualities seem to have been widely recognized. A well-known passage published in a Weimar magazine (almost certainly referring to the G Minor Quartet) comments that even when well-played, the work seems "able and intended to delight only connoisseurs of music," before going on to express the opinion that it "can in truth hardly bear listening to when it falls into mediocre amateurish hands."

Cast in Mozart's most dramatic key, the work (like its companion, the *Piano Quartet in E flat,* K. 493) certainly goes far beyond the conventional domestic character of similar chamber works, its dark, romantic sonorities enhanced by a true chamber music equality of part-writing that emphasizes the lower strings. The writing for piano skillfully juxtaposes passages of concerto-like virtuosity with others in which the instrument fades and blends into the texture of the strings, a feature achieved far more effectively in performance with the use of a piano of Mozart's time than with a modern concert grand. There are three movements, the first a powerful Allegro that contrasts stormy drama with more lyrical introspection. This unsettled mood carries through into the central Andante, while even the final movement, a rondo, fails to bring the lighthearted relief generally expected from such movements. *—Brian Robins*

Recommended:

- ○ **Rubinstein Collection Vol. 75** / Rubinstein, Tree, Soyer, Dalley / 1999 / RCA 63075
- ○ **Mozart: Piano Quintets, Quartets, Trios, etc.** / Giuranna, Beaux Arts Trio / 1991 / Philips 422514
- ○ **Mozart: Piano Quartets** / Ma, Ax, Stern, Laredo / 2001 / Sony 89794

Piano Quartet No. 2 in E flat major, K. 493 (1786)

Mozart composed two piano quartets, a relatively rare genre during the Viennese Classical era. The E flat Quartet is the second, a work entered in the composer's thematic catalog on June 3, 1786. According to Mozart's earliest biographer Georg Nissen, he entered into an agreement with the Viennese publisher Hoffmeister for three piano quartets. Hoffmeister published the first, the *Piano Quartet in G minor,* K. 478, in either late 1785 or early 1786. A work of considerable complexity, K. 478 failed to appeal to the large amateur market at which such chamber music was generally directed. Poor sales resulted in Hoffmeister's abandoning the project, paying Mozart for the work he had published on condition that the second and third works not be composed. Why Mozart, who rarely composed without a purpose in mind, wrote a second work is not clear. Like the earlier work, it makes few concessions to the domestic amateur market, and the most likely explanation is that he composed it for use in his own concerts. It was probably the quartet played by Mozart in Prague early in 1787, the occasion on which the composer witnessed the triumphant success of *Le nozze di Figaro* in the Bohemian capital. Later that year, it was published in Vienna by Artaria as Op. 13, and the quartet also became one of Mozart's first works to be published in England when it appeared within a few months of its first appearance in Artaria's catalog. Like its companion, the E flat Quartet skillfully juxtaposes concerto-like writing for the piano with more integrated chamber textures. The overall mood of mellowness contrasts strongly with the dark drama of the G minor quartet. There are three movements, with a sonata-form Allegro followed by a Larghetto featuring a rapt dialogue between piano and strings. Exchange of material between piano and strings is also a feature of the high-spirited Allegretto that concludes the work. Both this work and the G minor quartet are among the peaks of Mozart's chamber music; they are works that far transcend the few models Mozart had available—works that in any case relied too much on a texture in which the strings merely accompanied the piano. *—Brian Robins*

Recommended:

- ○ **Mozart: Piano Quartets** / C. Zimmermann, FP. Zimmermann, Zacharias, Wick / 2003 / EMI 75874
- ○ **Mozart: Piano Quintets, Quartets, Trios, etc.** / Giuranna, Beaux Arts Trio / 1991 / Philips 422514
- ○ **Mozart: Piano Concerto 12; Piano Quartet 2** / Brendel, Alban Berg Quartet / 2000 / EMI 56962

Piano Trios (1786–1791)

Mozart's first piano trio emerges straight from the conventional mode of the day: a piano-centered composition with minimal work for the cello and little more than ornamental use of the violin. Composed in 1776, this B flat trio, K. 254, originally was designated a divertimento, implying a light piece for household use. The structure is typical of Mozart's later trios: three movements, the first in sonata form with two clear subjects sent through a full development, although in this case they are elaborated with more charm than rigor. The slow second movement is the spiritual heart of the work, bringing the violin into its own for a while. The finale, typically, is a rondo, here in minuet tempo.

Mozart did not return to the piano trio genre until 1786 when he wrote one in G major, K. 496, and one in B flat, K. 502. He turned out the final three in 1788: K. 542 in B flat, K. 548 in C major, and K. 564 in G major. As a group, they are far more sophisticated than Mozart's initial effort, providing a more prominent place for the violin and an increasingly key, though never substantial, role for the cello. Yet as before, the slow movements carry the greatest weight in terms both of length and profundity. They are also not terribly difficult to play, the piano part as always being the most elaborate; Mozart intended these to be income-generating pieces for amateur use and he gauged his audience perfectly, the scores selling well for the next two decades. Although the final two trios are perfectly adept and fully entertaining, they, like the composer's final three piano concertos, find Mozart at what was by his adult standards a lower level of inspiration. The second and particularly the third and fourth trios are the real masterpieces in this unassuming series. K. 496 gives the violin some meaty antiphonal material to work with in the first movement and the finale is a set of particularly ingratiating variations. K. 502 and K. 542, the best of the lot, are piano concertos in miniature—not to say that the keyboard plays an unduly prominent role, for the strings are really coming into their own here. But they share the sophistication of Mozart's finest piano concertos, with richly ornamented, heartfelt slow movements and buoyant, emotionally complex outer movements with dramatic modulations and a disquieting use of chromaticism. They strike a masterly balance between intellectual rigor and emotional appeal. *—James Reel*

Recommended:

○ **Mozart: 6 Piano Trios** / London Fortepiano Trio / 1991 / Hyperion 44021

Quintet for piano, oboe, clarinet, horn & bassoon in E flat major, K. 452 (1784)

By 1784, Mozart's career and indeed his life were in full bloom and he was as happy and wealthy as he would ever be. His next successful opera—*Figaro*—and his next great symphony—the *38th*—were still at least two years off and he had turned instead in this period to the piano concerto. In 1784 alone he wrote six of these and in 1785 three more. His four horn concertos were also products of this period. In the midst of all this large scale writing he crafted this quintet and upon performing in it himself on April Fool's Day, he pronounced it "the best thing I have so far written in my life" in a letter to Leopold. In three movements and lasting only 25 minutes, it would seem an unlikely candidate for such an appellation. An unexpected but powerful vote of confidence for it came in during 1797 when another well known resident of Vienna produced a similar work which aped it in key signature, instrumentation, and general design. The younger man was Beethoven and his quintet, Op. 16, is high tribute indeed. In some respects, Mozart's quintet reflects his ongoing preoccupation with the piano concerto as the piano's role in the piece is at times disproportionate. It is also unabashedly a chamber work, Mozart having at last washed his hands of writing dinner music for the archbishop. Opening with an extended largo, the first movement in particular is concerto-like with the piano either in charge or very near the surface virtually throughout. The writing is open and insistent rather than forceful, and charm prevails. The second movement is a gentle and lightly textured larghetto in which the wind instruments at last emerge with passages of their own and the balance of the piece is here more chamberlike. The five-minute allegretto finale once again appears to be a sort of miniature piano concerto although cadenza-like passages for the various wind instruments appear at several points. The work ends with a flourish from the piano and tonic chords in the winds—a concerto-like ending. The piece is superbly crafted and effective, but one would wonder at Mozart's exuberance in describing it as "the best thing I have so far written." *—Michael Morrison*

Recommended:

○ **Mozart: Piano Quintets, Quartets, Trios, etc.** / Brendel, Holliger, Brunner, Baumann, Thunemann / 1991 / Philips 422514

○ **Mozart & Beethoven: Quintets** / Barenboim, Schellenberger, Clevenger, Combs, Damiano / Erato 96359

Serenade No. 10 for winds in B flat major ("Gran Partita"), K. 361 (1781)

Music for wind ensemble played an important role in Mozart's Austria. Known as *Harmoniemusik*, such ensembles were based on a nucleus of a pair of bassoons to provide the bass, and two horns. Upper parts were provided by one or more pairs of treble winds, most frequently oboes and clarinets. Dispositions of this kind not only formed the basis of military bands, but also the *Hausmusik* of the lesser nobility, for whom wind ensembles were not only cheaper than employing a full orchestra, but also had the advantage of being suitable for both outdoor and indoor performance. Mozart himself introduces one function of *Harmoniemusik* in the supper scene of *Don Giovanni*, where the Don is seen enjoying his supper to the accompaniment of some of the popular operatic tunes of the day played by his own wind ensemble.

During his earlier years in Salzburg, Mozart composed eight wind divertimentos, works almost certainly designed for outdoor use, and primarily intended to fall pleasingly on the ear as little more than background music. Mozart being Mozart, many movements, of course, transcend such modest pretensions. Nevertheless, the three great wind serenades Mozart composed after settling in Vienna in 1781 elevate the form to unprecedented heights. While only one, the *Serenade in C Minor*, K. 388, can be dated with any degree of certainty, it appears that all three were composed during the composer's first two years in Vienna. The first and most obvious difference between the Serenade in B flat and its Salzburg predecessors is the huge expansion in scale, both in terms of instrumentation and length. Instead of six (or eight) instruments, K. 361 is scored for no less than thirteen—pairs of oboes, clarinets, basset horns (lower pitched members of the clarinet family), horns in F and B flat, and bassoons, with the bottom line strengthened by a string double bass. The presence of a double bass suggests that the work was intended for indoor rather than outdoor performance; this notion is augmented by the first recorded performance, which took place at a benefit concert given on March 23, 1784 at the Burgtheater in Vienna. The concert was to benefit Mozart's friend Anton Stadler, a brilliant clarinetist and basset horn player for whom he later composed both the *Clarinet Quintet in A major*, K. 581 and *Concerto in A major*, K. 622. A member of the audience who heard the performance recorded the effect it made on him: "... glorious and sublime! It consisted of thirteen instruments... At each instrument sat a master—oh, what an effect it made—glorious and grand, excellent and sublime." One curious aspect of the report by this enthusiastic auditor is that he mentions the work as being in four movements, whereas K. 361 has no less than seven: Largo—Molto allegro; Menuetto; Adagio; Menuetto (Allegretto); Romance; Theme and Variations; Finale (Molto allegro). This leads to the conclusion that Stadler's "first" performance only included part of the work, a procedure frequently followed in early published editions. Whatever the somewhat mysterious background to this unique work, modern listeners will surely echo those sentiments penned over 200 years ago—glorious, grand, excellent, and sublime are indeed just epithets. *—Brian Robins*

Recommended:

○ **Furtwängler Conducts Mozart** / Furtwängler (cond.), Vienna PO / Music & Arts 1097

○ **Mozart: Serenades & Divertimenti for Winds** / Marriner (cond.), Academy of St. Martin-in-the-Fields / 1990 / Philips 422505

○ **Mozart: Serenade for 13 Winds** / Mackerras (cond.), Orch. of St. Luke's / 1994 / Telarc 80359

Serenade No. 11 for winds in E flat major, K. 375 (1782)

In April 1782, the Austrian Emperor founded his own wind band or *Harmoniemusik*—a type of ensemble popular throughout the Austrian empire, particularly in Bohemia, but not hitherto especially cultivated in Vienna. Having recently settled in the capital, and already having considerable experience at composing such pieces (wind ensembles played an important part in the musical life of Salzburg), Mozart took special note of the new imperial ensemble. In September or October 1781, Mozart set to work on a new piece, ostensibly (as he told his father Leopold in a letter) for the sister-in-law of the court painter Joseph Heckel. It was scored for the usual sextet of instruments, two each of a treble instrument (in this instance clarinets), horns, and bassoons. By mid-October, the *Serenade in E flat* was completed, and on the 15th given its first performance at Heckel's home. On October 31, it was played again—as a nocturnal serenade to the composer himself on the occasion of his name-day.

The letter mentioned above (dated November 3) goes on to reveal Mozart's true reason for composing the serenade: "the chief reason why I composed it was in order to let Herr von Strack, who goes there [Heckel's house] every day, hear something of mine." Johann Kilian Strack was none other than valet and musical confidant to the Emperor, for which reason Mozart apparently expended much effort in cultivating him during the following year. It was all to no avail, for the influential Strack would prove no friend of Mozart.

Perhaps in order to distinguish his band from that of the many members of the aristocracy who employed wind ensembles, Joseph decided that his band should consist of not six, but eight players. In a letter written to Leopold on July 27, Mozart mentions that he has had to write a *Nacht musique* (a term often used for serenades) in a hurry. Formerly this was believed to be the *Serenade in C minor*, K. 388, which dates from much the same period, but most scholars now believe it was the revision of the E flat Serenade that Mozart was so hastily working on in order to turn it into an octet suitable for the Emperor's new ensemble. To do so, he added parts for two oboes, making revisions to the other parts where necessary; it is this octet version that is normally heard today. There are five movements; an opening Allegro maestoso is followed by a Minuetto. At the heart of the serenade lies an Adagio that fully justifies the term "night music," its warm Romantic murmuring conjures images of an enchanted nocturnal scene. A second Minuet follows before the work concludes with a final Allegro. The extraordinarily felicitous writing throughout the work speaks of a mastery of wind writing shortly to be translated with such memorable effect to the great series of piano concertos composed between 1782 and 1786. *—Brian Robins*

Recommended:

○ **Mozart: Serenades & Divertimenti for Winds** / Holliger, Brunner, Baumann, Vlatkovic, etc. / 1990 / Philips 422505

○ **Mozart: Serenades, K375 & 388; 2 Overtures** / English Concert Winds / 2002 / Hyperion 55092

Serenade No. 12 for winds in C minor ("Nacht Musique"), K. 388 (1782)

As was also the case with his contemporaries, Mozart composed relatively little music in minor keys. When he did so it was almost always with specific purpose, and in forms that we would today consider "serious"—the string quartet, the symphony and concerto. How then are we to account for a serenade (Mozart's own rubric for K. 388, unlike the *Wind Serenade in E flat*, K. 375, which he left untitled) in the minor mode composed for wind instruments? After all, the serenade was traditionally a work for light, relaxed entertainment on ceremonial or civic occasions. Those composed for wind band, or *Harmoniemusik*, in particular were associated with outdoor entertainment—pieces to be casually overheard rather than listened to intently. Yet there is every evidence that after he settled in Vienna in 1781, Mozart took the genre seriously; all three wind serenades he composed during 1781 and 1782 are major works that far transcend the normal modest ambitions of such works.

The composer himself told his father Leopold in a letter that he had taken particular care over the *E flat Serenade*, although this may be because he was hoping to impress the Emperor Joseph II, who in the spring of 1782 had formed his own *Harmoniemusik* consisting of eight, rather than the usual six, performers. We know a fair amount about the genesis of that work and its revision from sextet to octet; virtually nothing, however, is known about Mozart's motivation to compose of the C minor Serenade other than the fact that it dates from much the same period as K. 375, July 1782—the date on Mozart's own autograph manuscript. Was it perhaps also designed in the hope of making an impression on the new Emperor (Joseph had been on the throne only two years)?

Whatever the reason, this radical work—with its stormy, explosive opening Allegro, and "learned" canonic Minuet, and its contrapuntal complexity—was totally out of keeping with then-current expectations for the genre, and one can only guess at the composer's reasons. Mozart never mentioned the work in his correspondence, and no documentary evidence relating to it has yet emerged. Like the revised version of K. 375, it is scored for the octet forces of Joseph's *Harmoniemusik*—pairs of oboes, clarinets, horns and bassoons.

That Mozart himself was obviously aware of the serenade's unusual and atypical character (and perhaps quality) may be gauged by the fact that several years later, probably in 1788, he arranged it for a very different genre, transforming it into the *String Quintet in C minor,* K. 406 (K. 516b). *—Brian Robins*

Recommended:

- **Mozart: Serenades & Divertimenti for Winds** / Holliger, Brunner, Baumann, Vlatkovic, etc. / 1990 / Philips 422505
- **Mozart: Serenades** / Herreweghe (cond.), Champs Elysées Orch. / HM 901570

String Quartet No. 14 in G major ("Spring"), K. 387 (1782)

Completed on the last day of 1782, this work would serve as the first of a set of six string quartets Mozart would dedicate to Haydn. Over nine years separate the first of this group from its predecessor among the quartets, K. 173 in D minor, composed in 1773. The string quartet was, at this time, a relatively new medium still in the process of development. From the genre's beginnings in works that were little more than divertimenti, one man above all others was bringing the string quartet toward the point where it would ultimately be recognized as the most challenging of all forms of composition. That man was Joseph Haydn. A direct impetus for Mozart's return to quartet writing seems to have come from Haydn, who in 1781 published a new set of six as his Op. 33. Mozart almost certainly first met Haydn shortly after settling in Vienna in 1781, and the two men soon established a friendship based on mutual admiration. As is known from a famous anecdote recorded by Irish tenor Michael Kelly, they also played quartets together with two other notable Viennese composers, Johann Vanhal and Karl Ditters von Dittersdorf. The inspiration provided by Haydn is clearly apparent in the quartets Mozart composed in the wake of these encounters. It is therefore hardly surprising that on completing six quartets of his own (K. 387, K. 421, K. 428, K. 458, K. 464, and K. 465) Mozart's publication would bear a famous dedicatory preface to Haydn that has led to them becoming somewhat confusingly known as Mozart's "Haydn" quartets. In the course of Mozart's touching tribute to the older master, he refers to the "long and laborious endeavor" that had gone into them, a unique admission from a man who normally composed with extraordinary facility, and a pointed reminder of the extreme challenge posed by this most pure of musical forms. Cast in four movements, this G major effort may divulge a few characteristics of the older master's style, but would in the end influence Haydn in his subsequent quartets as well. The opening movement, marked Allegro vivace assai, features fairly intricate instrumental writing: thematic lines are often started by one instrument and completed by another. It also contains a complex, substantial development section; yet the music is quite easy for the listener to grasp. The main theme is graceful and light, lengthy in its winding, sunny pathway. For all its seeming lightness, however, the music has considerable expressive depth, even if the alternate theme is carefree and largely devoid of deeper significance. The development section begins in a somewhat ponderous manner, the music at first appearing a bit hesitant before taking on an animated, more serious character. A delightful reprise closes out this joyful and masterful movement. The ensuing Minuet is elegant and light, but can jolt the listener with its sudden changes in dynamics in both the main theme and second subject. The Trio is deftly imagined in its mixture of gruff playfulness and gentle mystery. The Andante cantabile third movement sings its music in an exalted way, the main theme presented in a sort of complex unraveling of its wares, with many highs accompanied by deep lows from the cello. The whole movement conveys a serene, almost celestial quality, at times sounding mysterious, at others rapturous. The finale, marked Molto Allegro, presents a lively, joyous main theme, which Mozart treats contrapuntally for much of the movement, again with instrumental writing divulging much complexity. The alternate theme is just as lively, but more playful, not exhibiting the vigor and glorious manner of the main material. The music effervesces with energy and color throughout the finale, crowning this half-hour quartet with a blissful close. *—Robert Cummings*

Recommended:

- **Mozart: Les quatuors dedié à Haydn** / Mosaiques Quartet / 2001 / Astrée Naïve 8843
- **Mozart: String Quartets KV387 & 421** / Emerson SQ / DG 439861

String Quartet No. 15 in D minor, K. 421 (1783)

The second quartet in the famous series of six dedicated to Haydn—and the only mature Mozart string quartet in a minor key—commands our attention at the outset (Allegro) with the drop of an octave from the first violin that ushers in its plaintive main subject. The contrasting second subject is a songful melody over a throbbing background. Mozart shows how much he learned from Haydn (and Bach) in the development, which features a good deal of contrapuntal passagework. Throughout this movement, harmonies are stretched out before being resolved, increasing the emotional tension. The nocturnal slow movement (Andante), in ABA song form and triple meter, is remarkable for the recurring rising three-note figure in the accompaniment, particularly from the cello, that expands the lovely main melody. In the middle section, this is transmuted into a series of little dissonant stabs of pain. The stately minuet (allegretto) is both elegant and deeply, gravely serious; the middle section, with its dancing first violin over a pizzicato accompaniment, provides the greatest possible contrast. The finale (Allegro ma non troppo) is a set of variations on a theme in a 6/8 siciliano rhythm. The prevailing mood is bittersweet, the harmonies rich, the invention consistently fine. A violin figure that appeared at the start of the movement, resembling the call of a cricket, returns to dominate the coda as the music rises in emotional pitch and then sinks into resigned peace. *—Sol Louis Siegel*

Recommended:

- **Mozart: Les quatuors dedié à Haydn** / Mosaiques Quartet / 2001 / Astrée Naïve 8843
- **Mozart: String Quartets 14 &15** / Alban Berg Quartet / 1989 / EMI 49220

String Quartet No. 16 in E flat, K. 428 (1783)

Of Mozart's six quartets dedicated to Haydn, this is one of the most genial and, in some respects, most Haydn-esque in its delight in unexpected shifts of harmony. Mozart worked on this quartet over the course of two months in summer 1783; perhaps he had this piece in mind when in his dedication he described the group as "the fruit of a long and laborious effort"—it seems he knocked each of the others off in as little as a single day. It is believed that this may have been one of the pieces performed at a quartet party the following year in which the players were violinists Haydn and Dittersdorf, violist Mozart, and cellist Vanhal.

The opening Allegro ma non troppo movement initially seems to ease itself in, Haydn style, with a slow introduction, but this turns out to be merely a somewhat broad, harmonically teasing short statement that rambles straight into the cheerful first subject. Playfulness suffuses the themes, with little phrases tossed imitatively among the instruments and a clucking motif holding the material together. Skies darken somewhat in the brief development section, perhaps a mild allusion to Haydn's dramatic *Sturm und Drang* period, but good cheer returns with the recapitulation, which subtly varies the material rather than merely repeating it.

The Andante con moto is more serious, with most of the instruments playing a noble progression of chords while one member, often the cello, winds a dignified melody through the harmonic foundation. Oddly, that initial melody devolves into a routine bass line of triplets while the chords resolve into more of a melody. The movement is in what was at the time considered the "Romantic" key of A flat major, but a moment of harmonic uncertainty causes the melody to lose its bearings after its first statement, leaving a skeletal variation on the theme before the first section is repeated. This time the theme overcomes the episode of harmonic instability after nothing more than a brief pause for the players to find their way back home.

The minuet begins with either a gentle sneeze or a donkey bray, depending on the performers' forcefulness, surely a Haydn-esque effect. It then proceeds in a fairly stately fashion, except for braying interruptions and humorously hesitant episodes, as if the players were tiptoeing through an especially tricky patch of music. The trio section, coming before a repeat of all of this, noodles a troubled little tune over a bass drone.

The finale, Allegro vivace, alternates a teasingly hesitant series of chords with boisterous passage work—an effect of "on your mark, go!" The energetic second subject refuses to trip over its offbeat chords. The first theme returns, then gives way to a melodramatic episode culminating in a passage that overlaps material drawn from both the chords and the passage work from the beginning. The music reappears in its original form, prepares to scamper away quietly, but ultimately makes a grander exit with four loud, affirmative chords. *—James Reel*

Recommended:

- **Mozart: Les quatuors dedié à Haydn** / Mosaiques Quartet / 2001 / Astrée Naïve 8844
- **Mozart: String Quartets KV428 & 464** / Leipzig SQ / 2003 / MDG 3071160

String Quartet No. 17 in B flat major ("Hunt"), K. 458 (1784)

Nicknamed the "Hunt" because of the hunting-call motif that opens the work, the B flat quartet is the fourth of six string quartets composed by Mozart between 1782 and 1785. Over nine years separate the first of this group, K. 387 in G, from its predecessor among the quartets, K. 173 in D minor, composed in 1773. Various factors may account for this long gap. On a practical level, Mozart had been much occupied with long journeys to Italy, Germany, and France. But the string quartet was also, at this time, a relatively new medium still in the process of development. From the genre's beginnings in works that were little more than divertimenti, one man above all others was bringing the string quartet toward the point where it would ultimately be recognized as the most challenging of all forms of composition. That man was Joseph Haydn, whose long effort would be fully acknowledged by Mozart. Indeed, a direct impetus for Mozart's return to quartet writing seems to have come from Haydn, who in 1781 published a new set of six as his Op. 33. Mozart almost certainly first met Haydn shortly after settling in Vienna in 1781, and the two men soon established a friendship based on mutual admiration. As is known from a famous anecdote recorded by Irish tenor Michael Kelly, they also played quartets together with two other notable Viennese composers, Johann Vanhal and Karl Ditters von Dittersdorf. The inspiration provided by Haydn is clearly apparent in the quartets Mozart composed in the wake of these encounters. It is therefore hardly surprising that on completing six quartets of his own (K. 387, K. 421, K. 428, K. 458, K. 464, and K. 465) Mozart's publication would bear a famous dedicatory preface to Haydn that has led to them becoming somewhat confusingly known as Mozart's "Haydn" quartets. In the course of Mozart's touching tribute to the older master, he refers to the "long and laborious endeavor" that had gone into them, a unique admission from a man who normally composed with extraordinary facility, and a pointed reminder of the extreme challenge posed by this most pure of musical forms.

The B flat quartet was entered in Mozart's own thematic catalog on November 9, 1784, although he probably started work on it some 18 months earlier. Like all its companions, it is cast in four movements. The jaunty opening of the Allegro vivace assai with its hunting call prefaces a movement whose ease seems at odds with compositional problems, yet sketches show that it took the composer several attempts to satisfy himself. As in the case of all but two of the six quartets, the Menuetto is placed second, a brief movement not without its moments of gentle humor. The Adagio that follows is dominated by a long, decorated theme in the first violin and a quietly eloquent dialogue between violin and cello. The final Allegro assai returns to the opening movement's mood of good-humored ease. *—Brian Robins*

Recommended:

- ○ **Mozart: Les quatuors dedié à Haydn** / Mosaiques Quartet / 2001 / Astrée Naïve 8844
- ○ **Mozart: The 6 'Haydn' String Quartets** / Salomon SQ / 1991 / Hyperion 44001

String Quartet No. 18 in A major, K. 464 (1785)

The penultimate of a group of six quartets composed between 1782 and 1785, the *A major String Quartet* (for two violins, viola and cello) was entered in Mozart's thematic catalog on January 10, 1785, just four days before the final work, the *Quartet in C*, K. 465. In a letter to his daughter Nannerl dated February 16th, Leopold, the composer's father, remarks on the "very fine quarters" Mozart now occupies, continuing with an account of the success of his son's latest series of subscription concerts. "On Saturday evening," continues Leopold, "Herr Josef Haydn... came to see us and the new quartets were performed, or rather the three new ones which Wolfgang has added to the other three which we have already. The new ones are somewhat easier, but at the same time excellent compositions. Haydn said to me 'Before God and as an honest man I tell you that your son is the greatest composer known to me either in person or by name. He has taste and, what is more, the most profound knowledge of composition.'"

Behind this famous anecdote lies a friendship founded on mutual respect and admiration, on Mozart's part engendered to no small degree by recognition of the unique role played by his older colleague in the development of the string quartet. Haydn's own set of six *String Quartets*, Op. 33 is widely recognized as inspiring Mozart's interest in the medium. The two had first met shortly after Mozart settled in Vienna in 1781, the same year Op. 33 first appeared in print. Mozart doubtless had early practical experience of playing the older man's influential works with their composer—the two composers are known to have played quartets together. It is, therefore, not surprising that when Mozart came to have his six quartets published in Vienna by Artaria later in 1785 they bore a famous dedication entrusting them to the protection of his "dear friend Haydn."

The dedication also makes reference to the "long and laborious endeavor" the quartets had cost Mozart, a highly significant admission from one of the most fluently equipped of all composers. Despite Leopold's suggestion that the last three quartets (K. 458, K. 464, and K. 465) are "somewhat easier," the signs are that K. 464 caused Mozart more trouble than any of the other quartets. The autograph manuscript shows that the construction of the Andante's set of variations underwent changes, and there are also uncharacteristic alterations in the Minuet. A fragmentary Rondo (K. Anh. 72) is probably a discarded initial attempt at the final movement. There is, needless to say, scant evidence of these problems in the finished result, Beethoven's favorite among the "Haydn" set. The opening Allegro is a sonata-form movement of both grace and power, while the variations that form the Andante are richly varied. Both the Minuet and final Allegro non troppo are notable for their economy of thematic material, a trait characteristic of both Haydn and Beethoven. *—Brian Robins*

Recommended:

- ○ **Mozart: Les quatuors dedié à Haydn** / Mosaiques Quartet / 2001 / Astrée Naïve 8845
- ○ **Mozart: Complete String Quartets Vol. 1** / Eder Quartet / 1992 / Naxos 550540

String Quartet No. 19 in C major ("Dissonant"), K. 465 (1785)

The last of the six quartets Mozart dedicated to Haydn, K. 465 is officially in the sunny key of C major, but it owes its "Dissonant" nickname to its slow, tense introduction, full of unresolved harmonies over a throbbing cello line. Soon enough, this disorienting Adagio gives way to the first movement's bright, Allegro main matter. The first violin sings out the short-phrased principal theme, which the other instruments soon pick up in contrapuntal imitation. A second, more jittery melody and a third in triplets all become fodder for a brief development section, although it's the first theme, now with a minor cast, that dominates the proceedings until the recapitulation soothes the troubled quartet—the exposition returning, of course, without the baggage of the "dissonant" introduction.

The second movement, Andante cantabile, wraps itself in warm F major, with all four instruments exploring a variety of highly lyrical thematic passages. Third comes a witty, Haydn-esque *Minuet* (and one that would influence Beethoven), full of sudden dynamic contrasts and pitting various combinations of instruments against each other. The brief Trio section dips into C minor for an episode of agitated pathos. As it begins, the finale (Allegro) has every indication of being a conventional if quick rondo, but the music continually veers into unexpected harmonic territory, skidding into the minor and fragmenting the themes; this is perhaps a sonata-allegro movement, with the development section split among the episodes of a rondo. Performers may play this as either comedy or drama, but the music is really a bold melding of the two. *—James Reel*

Recommended:

- ○ **Mozart: Les quatuors dedié à Haydn** / Mosaiques Quartet / 2001 / Astrée Naïve 8845
- ○ **Hunt & Dissonance Quartets** / Melos-Quartett Stuttgart / 1978 / DG 429818

String Quartet No. 20 in D major ("Hoffmeister"), K. 499 (1786)

Between 1782 and 1785, Mozart composed six string quartets, which were subsequently published late in 1785 with a dedication to Joseph Haydn. They represent the pinnacle of Mozart's contribution to the form, a group of works that not only solve the problems of this difficult medium, but which also represent his tribute to the pioneering quartets of his friend and colleague. Thereafter, Mozart would compose only four more string quartets, including this one, subsequently turning his attention to the string quintet.

This isolated D major Quartet (scored for the normal disposition of two violins, viola and cello) was entered in his own thematic catalogue on August 19, 1786, less than two months after the premiere of *Le nozze di Figaro*. It owes its nickname to the Viennese publisher Franz Anton Hoffmeister, who first issued the quartet in the same year it was composed. Nothing is known of the circumstances of its composition, although it has been suggested that it was commissioned by Hoffmeister, who was also a friend of Mozart's.

Shortly before the composer's death in December, 1791, the quartet was the subject of a review in the journal of the German Philharmonic Society. The reviewer, who was also considering the *Piano Quartet in E flat*, K. 493, notes that "Both these quartets are written with that fire of the imagination and that correctness, which long since won for Herr M. the reputation of one of the best composers in Germany. The first [the string quartet] consists of four, the second of only three movements, and even the Minuet in the former is composed with an ingenuity (being interwoven with canonic imitations) that one not infrequently finds wanting in other such compositions." It is the Minuet (the second movement) that has subsequently excited particular comment from Mozart's biographers, being described by H. C. Robbins Landon as "one of the most original in eighteenth century music" and by Alfred Einstein as "unique." While the quartet is generally recognized as being less complex than the six "Haydn" Quartets, it remains a work of great beauty, with an Adagio of great profundity, and a final Molto Allegro which treads the ambiguous line between tragedy and comedy that so often characterizes Mozart's later works. *—Brian Robins*

Recommended:

- ○ **Mozart: Quatuors K499 & 589** / Mosaiques Quartet / 2001 / Astrée Naïve 8834
- ○ **Mozart: String Quartets, K499 & 589** / Endellion SQ / 1990 / Virgin 259541

String Quartet No. 21 in D major ("Prussian 1"), K. 575 (1789)

In the spring of 1789, Mozart, in financial straits and desperately in need of new work, set off on a journey to Germany. After visiting Dresden and Leipzig, he arrived in Potsdam on April 25. The city was at the time the virtual capital of Prussia and the residence of the cello-playing King Frederick William II. The following day a memorandum requesting that "one Motzart" had requested an audience with the king to "lay before him" his talents was presented to Frederick William, who referred the request to his director of chamber music, Jean Pierre Duport. What resulted is unfortunately not recorded at the time, but according to later reports supplied by Mozart's widow Constanze the king offered Mozart a post worth 3,000 thaler a year. The composer is said to have expressed concerns about leaving his "good Emperor" (Joseph II) in Vienna. Whatever the truth of the story, Mozart returned to Vienna with some kind of a commission from Frederick William to compose six new string quartets.

By June the present D major Quartet had already been completed, but of the remaining quartets only two were composed, and then only after the lapse of a year. Various reasons have been advanced as an explanation as to why Mozart was so slow in producing the "Prussian" quartets, but one is that the composer had received money "upfront" from the Prussian king; in a money-begging letter to Puchberg he mentions having the quartets engraved at his own expense. The three "Prussian" quartets which were completed are notable for the prominence of their cello parts, obviously intended to please the cello-playing king. In the opening Allegretto of K. 575, for instance, it is the cello that is given the task of presenting the second theme, and all three quartets contain many passages in which the cello emerges either as soloist or in dialogue with one of the other instruments. The K. 575 quartet as a whole is notable for its understated, almost secretive mood. The Andante is a deceptively simple movement that showcases the cello as an agent independent of the other instruments, and the Menuetto (Allegretto) is distinguished by a brief eruption of passion at the start of its second half. The concluding Allegretto opens with a theme given to the cello high in its register before proceeding to run a more disturbed course than is apparent in the remainder of the work. As in other works from the last years of Mozart's life, there is a delightful incorporation of counterpoint into a texture of Classical ease, here in the form of an ornate canon. Scholars have also found fragments of an alternate finale in which Mozart seemed to indulge his puckish side. *—Brian Robins*

Recommended:

- ○ **Mozart: String Quartets KV575 & 590** / Mosaiques Quartet / 1999 / Astrée 8659
- ○ **Mozart: String Quartets** / Prague SQ / 2002 / Supraphon 3608

String Quartet No. 22 in B flat major ("Prussian 2"), K. 589 (1790)

Mozart's greatest contribution to the string quartet repertoire dates from 1782 and 1785, the period during which he composed the six quartets dedicated to his friend Joseph Haydn. Only four quartets follow them, the lone K. 499 in D major, composed in 1786 and known as the *"Hoffmeister" quartet*, and the three quartets known as the *"Prussian" quartets*.

The B flat Quartet, the second to be completed, was entered in Mozart's own thematic catalog in May 1790. Mozart had obviously returned to the quartets after the first performances of *Così* in January 1790, since the third, K. 590 in B flat followed a month later. With the notable exception of the great String Quintet in D, K. 593, the two quartets represent the only major works composed by Mozart during the whole of 1790, a year in which increasing financial worries resulted in the bleakest compositional year of his adult life. In the three completed quartets, Mozart concentrated on giving the cello-playing king a dominant role, often pushing the second violin and viola into the background to enable the cello to present thematic material or engage in dialogue with the first violin. The second quartet is in the customary four movements, an opening Allegro, followed by a relatively brief Larghetto, a Minuet of almost symphonic proportions and a finale marked Allegro assai. While the quartet (like its companions) fails to attain the elevated status of the six *"Haydn" quartets*, it is nevertheless a work of enigmatic beauty typical of Mozart's late works. *—Brian Robins*

Recommended:

- ○ **Mozart: Quatuors K499 & 589** / Mosaiques Quartet / 2001 / Astrée Naïve 8834
- ○ **Mozart: String Quartets, K499 & 589** / Salomon SQ / 2002 / Hyperion 55094

String Quartet No. 23 in F major ("Prussian 3"), K. 590 (1790)

Mozart's final string quartet was to have been the third of six the composer intended to dedicate to King Frederick William II of Prussia, the cello-playing monarch whom Boccherini served as exclusive chamber musician from 1787 until the death of the king ten years later. Shortly after entering the F major Quartet in his thematic catalog in June, 1790, Mozart told Puchberg in a further letter that he had been "obliged" to give away the quartets "for a mere song in order to have cash in hand to meet my present difficulties." Along with its two companions, K. 590 has been generally regarded by commentators as being less successful than the great set of six "Haydn" quartets composed between 1782 and 1785. Artaria's advertisement for the "Prussian" quartets describes them as "concertante quartets," thus paying due recognition to the prominence of their cello parts, which were obviously designed to give Frederick William significance. Yet if the structure is frequently looser than in the more tightly organized "Haydn" quartets, there is much compensation in the skillful manner in which Mozart allows the royal cello discourse with its colleagues, a refinement the composer confessed to finding "troublesome" in execution. The customary four movements are an opening Allegro moderato, an affecting, valedictory Andante, Menuetto, and Allegro finale. From the first movement this piece is filled with aural miracles. Dialogues scurry about and return slightly altered, like double entendres uttered in one of Mozart's operas. At the movement's end, the coda restates the development, gracefully winds down, and ends on a witty high note. Mozart never specified whether the second movement is an Allegretto or an Andante. Alfred Einstein said of it: "It seems to mingle the bliss and sorrow of a farewell to life. How beautiful life has been! How sad! How brief!" The Menuetto is charged with ornamental appoggiaturas and contrary phrases. The finale is packed with wondrous devices, such as unexpected silences and intricate counterpoint. Listen closely in the last bars and you'll even hear a bagpipe-like drone. *—AMG*

Recommended:

- ○ **Mozart: String Quartet KV575 & 590** / Mosaiques Quartet / 1999 / Astrée 8659
- ○ **Mozart: String Quartet 22 & 23** / Shanghai Quartet / 1996 / Delos 3192

String Quintet No. 1 in B flat major, K. 174 (1773)

This remarkable work was the first of Mozart's string quintets, a group of works completed only in his final years with the composition of the four great quintets of 1787 to 1791 (a fifth, K. 406 [516b], is an arrangement of the *Wind Serenade in C minor*, K. 388). At the time of its composition in 1773, the quintet for two violins, two violas, and cello was a little-explored genre, composers such as Boccherini preferring the alternative disposition of two cellos rather than two violas. It was originally composed in Salzburg in the spring of 1773 in the aftermath of the Mozarts' (Wolfgang and his father Leopold) return from their third and final visit to Italy. Its immediate inspiration appears to have been two string quintets by Michael Haydn, the younger brother of the famous Joseph Haydn. Michael Haydn, who held the post of Konzertmeister (concertmaster) at the court of the Archbishop of Salzburg from 1763, composed a number of string quintets which he styled "notturni," a designation generally applied during this period to works of a lighter, serenade-like character.

Although Mozart's quintet displays some signs of the direct influence of Haydn's works (a duet for violin and viola in the second of the four movements), it is a far more ambitious and experimental work, displaying signs of immaturity only in the limited scope of the writing for the second viola. The four movements are marked Allegro moderato, Adagio, Menuetto, and Allegro. The first has a quasi-symphonic feel to it, with a particularly strong development section, while the final movement provides an early example of the contrapuntal skills Mozart would hone so finely in later years. Only in the inner movements is there evidence of the notturno-like style, with suggestions of echo-effects implied in the Adagio, explicit in the trio section of the Menuetto.

In the December of the same year Mozart made revisions to the work, the most substantial of which involved a complete rewriting of the extensive and complex finale. These were apparently made after Mozart had heard Joseph Haydn's Opp. 17 and 20 string quartets during a visit to Vienna in July and August 1773. Mozart himself obviously thought highly enough of the quintet for it to be one of a selected group of works he took with him on the long journey to Mannheim and Paris four years; a letter to his father from Mannheim states that it was one of the works he had copied and left there before resuming the journey to Paris. *—Brian Robins*

Recommended:

- ○ **Mozart: Complete Quintets Vol. 1** / Grumiaux, Janzer, Czako, Lesueur, Gerecz / 1997 / Philips 456055
- ○ **Mozart: String Quintets K174 & 406** / Imai, Orlando Quartet / 1990 / Bis 433

String Quintet No. 2 in C minor, K. 406 (1787)

In 1788, Mozart set about transcribing for string quintet his *Serenade for Winds in C minor*, K. 388/384a, of 1782–83. Lost in translation are some of the subtle shades of contrast in timbre. Imbued with an intensity that belies its purpose of social entertainment, the *Serenade* features a driving intensity fueled by chromaticism and irregular phrase structures that make it a more personal work than most of Mozart's occasional pieces. Thus, Mozart's transference of the piece to the more "serious" chamber music idiom of the string quintet seems quite natural. Unlike the transcription of the *B flat major Serenade*, K. 361/370a, that of the *C minor Serenade* is generally ranked with the original string quintets.

A spirited Allegro opens the *Quintet* with a unison statement of the main theme. Sudden and drastic dynamic contrasts characterize the exposition. After a brief development, the recapitulation begins like the exposition, but the secondary themes are varied.

In E flat major, the Andante second movement juxtaposes passages in which all the instruments move equally with those in which the first violin is clearly the leader. Moments of technical display, however, appear in each part. A figure of three repeated notes unifies the monothematic structure.

The Menuetto in Canone returns to C minor. The Haydnesque canon referred to in the title occurs between the first violin and the cello and is strict through nearly the entire first part of the Menuetto. There are several canonic passages in the second half, one of them in three voices, but nothing lengthy until the return of the first theme at the end. The C major Trio al Rovescio (Trio in inversion) boasts a double canon in inversion. The second violin takes the lead and is followed by the first violin, inverting the same tune and beginning a fourth higher. The first viola then enters at a fourth below the second violin and the cello enters a fourth below the viola, the theme inverted. Almost immediately after the cello begins, the canons fall apart and the phrase closes on G major. The second half of the Trio follows a similar process, but with two different tunes, one the subject of an inverted canon between the violins and the other a canon in inversion between the first viola and cello.

In variation form, the closing Allegro contains a passage of great instrumental ingenuity that seems more suited to the string quintet format than that of a small wind band. Early on, Mozart abandons the details of the theme, preferring instead to refer to its shape and harmonic progression. One consistent element throughout the variations are the leaps of a fourth and third that open each half of the two-part theme. The variation that most nearly replicates the theme is the very last, closing the work in C major. *—John Palmer*

Recommended:

- ○ **Mozart: Complete String Quintets** / Grumiaux Trio, Lesueur, Gerecz / 2002 / Philips 470950

String Quintet No. 3 in C major, K. 515 (1787)

All five of Mozart's numbered string quintets are composed for a combination of two violins, two violas, and cello, an unusual disposition that varies from the more customary quintet that calls for viola and two cellos (the ensemble used, for example, by Boccherini and Schubert). Mozart's choice of two violas undoubtedly reflects his great love for the instrument, and its use profoundly affects the color and structure of all his string quintets.

The C major Quintet is the first of a pair completed in the spring of 1787. Why Mozart should have returned to the genre fourteen years after his previous effort, the *Quintet in B flat major,* K. 174, is unclear. Having recently explored the potential of the string quartet in the six works dedicated to Haydn and the "Hoffmeister" Quartet, K. 499 (1786), perhaps he felt the need to seek a new challenge in the chamber medium. Mozart entered the Quintet into his thematic catalog on April 19, 1787, shortly after returning to Vienna from Prague, where the triumphant reception of *Le nozze di Figaro* had resulted in a commission for a new opera. He likely worked on the Quintet while waiting to receive the libretto for *Don Giovanni* from his collaborator Lorenzo da Ponte.

There seems to be little doubt that Mozart planned the C major Quintet and its sucessor, the *Quintet in G minor,* K. 516 as a contrasting pair, in much the same manner as the Symphonies Nos. 40 and 41 (interestingly, also in G minor and C major, respectively). Indeed, in its elevated character, breadth, and scope, the C major Quintet inhabits a world very close to that of the *"Jupiter" Symphony.*

The opening Allegro of the Quintet is one of Mozart's boldest and most substantial conceptions, a truly noble movement that includes a development section of exceptional richness and diversity. The Minuet, more customarily the third movement in such works, follows; its nearly symphonic construction is far removed from a typical stylized dance. The Andante flows with a heart-easing tranquility that is hardly dissipated by the glowing harmonies of the finale, a movement of deceptive simplicity that was once characterized by Mozart's biographer Alfred Einstein as "godlike and childlike." *—Brian Robins*

Recommended:

- ○ **Mozart: Complete Quintets Vol. 1** / Grumiaux, Janzer, Czako, Lesueur, Gerecz / 1997 / Philips 456055
- ○ **Mozart: String Quintets, KV515 & 516** / Alban Berg SQ, Wolf / EMI 49085

String Quintet No. 4 in G minor, K. 516 (1787)

The *Quintet in G minor,* K. 516 is the second of two string quintets Mozart completed within a month's time during the spring of 1787. Prior to that year, he had contributed but a single example to the genre, nearly 15 years earlier: the *Quintet in B flat major,* K. 174. Mozart's choice of two violins, two violas, and cello for all of his string quintets is unusual in the Classical era; composers like Boccherini generally opted for the use of viola and two cellos. A precedent for Mozart's choice may be found in a number of light Austrian divertimento-type works, including a *Notturno* by Michael Haydn, active at the Salzburg court and well-known to Mozart and his family.

Mozart entered the G minor Quintet in his thematic catalog on May 16, 1787, on the heels of the *Quintet in C major,* K. 515. While there is no documentary evidence to explain why Mozart returned to the medium after so many years, there seems to be little doubt that K. 515 and K. 516 were composed as a contrasting pair in much the same manner as the Symphonies Nos. 40 and 41. Indeed, while the C major Quintet may be seen as directly analogous with the "Jupiter" (the *Symphony No. 41 in C major,* K. 551) in its breadth and elevated Olympian utterances, the G minor may be seen as counterpart to the *Symphony No. 40 in G minor,* K. 550. The use of minor modes was comparatively rare during the Classical era, and for Mozart, G minor was perhaps the most deeply personal of all keys, one in which he expressed not only powerful passions but also tragedy. The prevailing combination of melancholy and sometimes violent drama in the G minor Quintet is underlined by Mozart's extraordinarily skillful exploitation of the dark sonorities inherently possibly within this instrumentation.This is particularly evident, for instance, in the vivid contrast drawn between the prevalent somber coloring and passages that highlight the violin's topmost registers.

Efforts to escape to the major mode in the opening Allegro are resolutely denied by the prevailing darkness. As in the C major Quintet, the Menuetto is placed second in the work, though it does little to lift the mood. The Adagio non troppo is a lonely, despairing hymn. Though the finale finally turns to the parallel major key of G, it is not a "happy" major but one that occupies an ambiguous terrain, a characteristic common in Mozart's late works. A year after completing the C major and G minor Quintets, Mozart advertised them for sale, along with his string quintet arrangement of the *Serenade in C minor,* K. 388. *—Brian Robins*

Recommended:

- ○ **Mozart: The Complete Quintets Vol. 2** / Grumiaux, Janzer, Czako, Gerecz / 1997 / Philips 456058
- ○ **Mozart: String Quintets** / Salomon SQ, Whistler / 1996 / Hyperion 22005

String Quintet No. 5 in D major, K. 593 (1790)

Mozart's six string quintets span a period ranging from 1773 to 1791, the last year of his life. The earliest, K. 174 in B flat, was possibly modeled on a Notturno by Haydn's brother Michael, who was employed at the Salzburg court and well known to Mozart and his family. In his *Notturno,* Haydn employed the same instrumentation—two violins, two violas, and cello, that had been used for lighter divertimento-type works by such Austrian composers as Ignaz Holzbauer. Mozart adopted the same disposition in all his string quintets, elevating the form to a peak that had no contemporary, or indeed subsequent, parallel. By fairly common consent, Mozart's supreme examples of the genre are the two quintets he composed in close succession in 1787, those in C major, K. 515, and G minor, K. 516, works unchallenged as the twin peaks of the repertoire. The two quintets that followed in 1790 and 1791 (the present work, and K. 614 in E flat) are more controversial, commentators such as Hans Keller finding them full of "stylistic mystery" and "textural failures." Like K. 515 and K. 516, it seems likely they were designed as a pair, and when they were posthumously issued in 1793 by the Viennese publisher Artaria, an appended note states that they were composed for an unidentified "Hungarian music lover," who may have been Johann Tost, the leader of Haydn's violins at Esterházy. The *D major Quintet,* the first of the pair, was entered in Mozart's thematic catalog in December 1790, the year which also saw the composition of his last two string quartets, K. 589 in B flat, and K. 590 in F (the second and third of the so-called "Prussian quartets"). Much of the work was probably composed before Mozart undertook the tour he and his brother-in-law Josef Hofer made to Germany in the fall of 1790, a desperate trip made in the vain hope of alleviating his precarious financial state. The quintet is cast in the usual four movements, the first an unusual structure opening with a slow Larghetto section that returns after the main Allegro, giving the movement a cyclic form. The second movement is a highly expressive Adagio, the counterpoint at times, as Alfred Einstein pointed out, often reminiscent of the five-part madrigals of the sixteenth century. The succeeding Menuetto is rather Haydnesque, while the concluding Allegro is a rondo whose playful theme fails to mask the sense of underlying melancholy that pervades the whole work, a characteristic typical of Mozart's late works. *—Brian Robins*

Recommended:

- ○ **Mozart: The Complete Quintets Vol. 2** / Grumiaux, Janzer, Czako, Gerecz / 1997 / Philips 456058
- ○ **Mozart: Complete String Quintets Vol. 3** / Villa Musica Ens. / 2002 / MDG 3041106

String Quintet No. 6 in E flat major, K. 614 (1791)

The Quintet in E flat major (1791) is the last of Mozart's six numbered string quintets and the penultimate chamber work the composer entered into his thematic catalog before his death on December 5, 1791. It was almost certainly designed as one of a pair, a counterpart to the *Quintet in D major,* K. 593, completed the previous December. Undated sketches for quintet movements from Mozart's final years suggest that he may have planned even further works in the genre he had transformed from the divertimento-like character of earlier Austrian examples to works that take a place among the supreme achievements of the chamber repertoire. Like its predecessors, the *Quintet in E* flat is scored for two violins, two violas, and cello, a disposition that distinguishes it from Boccherini's string quintets and Schubert's great *String Quintet in C major* (which opt for two cellos and one viola). Mozart's employment of two violas not only reflected his own love for the instrument, but also allowed him to explore colors and textures quite different from those of the string quartet medium.

In the *Quintet in E flat* Mozart fully exploits the more extensive and varied palette afforded by this instrumental configuration. The opening Allegro di molto, for instance, starts with the violas playing unaccompanied, granting the instrument—normally embedded in the middle of the texture—unusual prominence. The texture of the Quintet is unusually open and clear for large stretches, leading some commentators to suggest that it represents Mozart's conscious reaction to the heavily wrought counterpoint of the great quintets of 1787 (K. 515 and 516). This hardly applies to the finale, however, which features a dazzling display of fugal virtuosity. The Andante second movement features a judicious mixture of true chamber writing and more soloistic elements, while the Menuetto pays a final tribute to the man from whom Mozart learned so much about composing chamber music, his friend Joseph Haydn. Both the E flat Quintet and its companion work were posthumously published in 1793 with a note stating that they had been composed for a "Hungarian Music Lover," whom it is conjectured may have been Johann Tost, the leader of Haydn's Esterházy orchestra. —*Brian Robins*

Recommended:

○ **Mozart: The Complete Quintets Vol. 2** / Grumiaux, Janzer, Czako, Gerecz / 1997 / Philips 456058

○ **Mozart: String Quintets K593 & 614** / Takacs SQ / Hungaroton 12881

Trio for clarinet, viola & piano in E flat major ("Kegelstatt"), K. 498 (1786)

Mozart's earliest work involving the clarinet, a *Divertimento in E flat for two clarinets and two horns*, K. 113, was composed in Milan during November 1771. It was to herald a number of exceptional masterpieces featuring the instrument, which culminated in the *Clarinet Concerto*, K. 622, Mozart's final instrumental work, and the *Clarinet Quintet*, K. 581.

Another outstanding creation involving the instrument was written under circumstances that, if popular tradition is to be believed, seem highly improbable. Nevertheless, it is widely held that Mozart composed the *Trio in E flat for clarinet, viola, and piano*, K. 498 while participating in a game of skittles; this would account for its nickname, the *"Kegelstatt" Trio* ("Kegelstatt" = "Skittle Alley"). The score is dated August 5, 1786, and the work is, by any reckoning, extremely dense and cerebral, and hardly the outcome of any frivolous diversion.

The Trio largely eschewes virtuosity in favor of exploiting the natural lyrical qualities of the clarinet and viola. The result is what has been aptly termed one of his most perfectly integrated compositions, with an interplay among the three instruments full of delightfully subtle touches. According to Mozart's friend and informal pupil Caroline von Pichler the trio was composed for Franziska von Jaquin, another pupil, and a member of a family who were close friends of the Mozarts. It is probable it was first performed by Franziska accompanied by Mozart, and the outstanding clarinetist Anton Stadler, for whom Mozart composed a number of works (including the above-mentioned *Clarinet Quintet in A*, K. 581 and *Concerto in A*, K. 621). In 1788, the trio was published in Vienna by Artaria with an optional violin part as an alternative to the clarinet.

Set in three movements, the *"Kegelstatt" Trio* opens with an Andante in the tonic key of E flat, featuring complex dialogue between these three unusual instrumental collaborators. As French musicologist Jean Gallois observes, "delicacy and intimacy are skillfully expressed in the questions and answers exchanged by the protagonists. The second motif, on the clarinet, is also similar to the first theme; there are no great conflicts, therefore. On the contrary, a dialogue is gradually built up, a series of confidences like those one shares with friends." The B flat Menuetto, which follows, is also built upon contrasts, though the main theme is announced in unequivocal terms at the outset. Interestingly, the main theme of the trio section also reappears at the close of the recapitulation. The work ends with a dazzling and exhilarating Rondeaux—the French term here substituted for the more customary "Rondo." The final movement is remarkable for its two intermezzo-like passages in which the piano comes to the fore. The work ends in sublime fashion, as the clarinet offers commentary on earlier ideas. —*AMG*

Recommended:

○ **Mozart: Piano Quintets, Quartets, Trios, etc.** / Kovacevich, Brymer, Ireland / 1991 / Philips 422514

○ **Ax, Stoltzman, Ma** / Ax, Ma, Stoltzman / 1995 / Sony 57499

Violin Sonatas (1762–1788)

Mozart composed his first sonatas for violin and piano during the first of his lengthy European tours. The first four, K. 6–9, were begun in Salzburg in 1762 and completed in Paris before 1764. Parts of the surviving manuscripts are in Leopold's hand, and they imitate the short keyboard pieces Leopold had written for his children. These were published as Opp. 1 and 2. Modeled on the sonatas of Schobert, they rely heavily on sequential repetition and Alberti bass figures. One notable event occurs in the recapitulation of *K. 9*, where the main theme appears first in the tonic minor before immediately shifting to major. This device, of Neapolitan origin, was considered *passé* at the time, but Mozart was, after all, only eight years old.

Six more violin and piano sonatas were composed in London in 1764 and published as Op. 3 the next year. These, featuring a cello *ad libitum*, are composed along the same lines as their predecessors. Six sonatas K. 26–31 were composed in February 1766 and published later that year as Op. 4. K. 26 is in three movements and the rest are in two. While Mozart's handling of form and general melodic invention is improved, the violin still doubles the piano part, with occasional imitative passages.

In 1778, Mozart again took up the violin sonata, composing over 20 in the ensuing decade, plus two sets of variations for violin and piano (K. 359/374a and 360/374b). Although the violin is generally of secondary importance in these works, the concertante elements of those composed in the first six months of 1778 are remarkable. In almost every movement, the violin, at some point, alternates material with the piano and occasionally takes the lead. The *Sonata in E minor*, K. 304, features a first movement in which the two instruments are closely intertwined, creating a piano part that makes little sense without the violin. The Andante of K. 306 has an independent, aria-like melody for the violin.

Mozart composed his next five sonatas, K. 376–380, between early 1779 and the summer of 1781. These works show an increase in concertante writing for the violin, which mingles with the keyboard as a equal partner. Highlights from this group include the slow movement of K. 377, which is a set of variations in D minor, and the first movement of the K. 379, in G major, in which a majestic introduction leads to a G minor Allegro. The influence of Mozart's predecessors has waned; the style is entirely his own.

The last sonatas are among Mozart's greatest masterpieces. Violinist Regina Strinasacchi was the recipient of the *Sonata in B flat*, K. 454. Mozart blends concerto-like piano virtuosity with rhapsodic, intimate violin writing. The next sonata, K. 481, was completed on December 12, 1784 and compared to its predecessor, is cold and serious, with fascinating interplay between the instruments. The striking Adagio contains some of Mozart's most distant modulations, and the finale is an intense set of variations. Many consider K. 526 in A major, to be his best sonata. The equality of the instruments is reinforced by the frequent use of counterpoint and an ubiquitous melodic fluency. Mozart's last violin sonata, K. 547, in F major, was completed on July 10, 1788, the summer in which he composed his last three symphonies. —*John Palmer*

Recommended:

○ **Mozart: 16 Sonatas for Violin & Harpischord** / Verlet, Poulet / 1993 / Philips 438803

VOCAL

Arias for voice & orchestra (1765–1790)

Mozart composed dozens of concert arias, mostly for soprano, but also for alto, tenor, and bass. These arias, most of which are not associated with any of Mozart's operas, range from childhood studies to works presented to women with whom the composer was infatuated.

Mozart's earliest known concert aria is a setting of *Va, dal furor portata*, K. 21/19c, composed in London in 1765. The text is from Metastasio's *Enzi.* Although lacking in originality, this and several other Metastasio settings from the next year demonstrate Mozart's understanding of the standard procedures for arias as well as his ability to compose accompanied recitative. Two arias Mozart wrote in January to March 1770 in Milan are more impressive: *Misero me!—Misero pargoletto*, K. 77/73e, and *Fra cento affanni*, K. 88/73c, show an understanding of the bel canto style and are much more confidently orchestrated, including a trumpet in "Fra cento affanni." These two arias are among the samples Mozart presented to an assembly in Milan that was so impressed they offered him the commission for *Mitridate, rè di Ponto.*

Ah, lo previdi,—Ah, t'invola agl'occhi miei, K. 272, dates from August 1777. The recitative and aria were composed for Czech soprano Josepha Dušek on the occasion of her visit to Salzburg in August 1777. Sparse and restrained in comparison to earlier arias, "Ah, t'invola agl'occhi miei" is perhaps more effective than its predecessors in conveying the profundity of the text. Although it was not written for her, Mozart later gave the piece to Aloysia Weber, his future sister-in-law, with whom he was in love.

During Mozart's journey to Paris in 1777–78, he composed several more recitatives and arias. Among these are two for Aloysia Weber. The first of these is *Alcandro, Io confesso—Non só d'onde viene*, dated February 27, 1778 in Mannheim. In this work, Mozart emulates the style of J. C. Bach, possibly because Bach had set the text, which is by Metastasio. The mellow eloquence of the piece stems from both the fluid writing for the voice and Mozart's inclusion of clarinets in the orchestra. Mozart presented Aloysia with *Io non chiedo*, K. 316/300b, in January 1779 while in Munich. This aria is far more difficult than "Non sò d'onde viene," with high, coloratura passages.

In April 1781, Mozart composed a recitative and aria, *A questo seno—Or che il cielo*, for castrato Francesco Ceccarelli. In the aria's sustained passages, Mozart takes full advantage of the strength of the male castrato. Even after his marriage to Constanze Weber on August 4, 1782, Mozart continued to write arias for his now sister-in-law, Aloysia. On January 8, 1783, he completed *Mia speranza adorata*, K. 416, which is cast in rondo form, a trend in vocal composition at the time. The alternation of fast and slow sections in the piece would become a trait of many of Mozart's operatic arias.

While in Prague for the production of *Don Giovanni*, Mozart spent time with the family of Josepha Dušek, whose acquaintance he had made in Salzburg ten years earlier. On November 3, 1787 he completed a scene and aria for her, *Bella mia fiamma—Resta, o cara*, K. 528. The difficulty of this aria, from the opening note to the last, attests to Dušek's excellent technique, and she was pleased with the piece despite the arm-twisting she had to employ to get Mozart to write it down.

One of the more unusual treasures among Mozart's arias is *Per questa bella mano*, for bass voice and double-bass obbligato. It remains one of the most virtuosic works for the string bass, and captures the composer at his most good natured and melodic. *—John Palmer*

Recommended:

- ○ **Great Mozart Singers Vol. 4** / Paumgartner (cond.), Schreier, Van Dam, Koth, Mathis, Wurzburg Camerata Academica / 1995 / Orfeo 401
- ○ **Great Mozart Singers Vol. 5** / Auger, Popp, Moll, Fassbaender, Varady, etc. / 1995 / Orfeo 501
- ○ **Mozart: Arias, Vocal Ensembles, Canons** / Terfel, Popp, Schreier, Jansen, Mathis, Gruberova, etc. / 1991 / Philips 422523

Exsultate, jubilate, motet for soprano & orchestra, K. 165 (1773)

The motet *Exsultate, jubilate* was composed in Milan in January 1773 while Mozart and his father Leopold were on the last of their three visits to Italy. They had traveled to oversee the first performances of the young composer's *Lucio Silla*, K. 135, an opera seria commissioned by the ducal theater in Milan. The principal uomo (male soprano) for the premiere was Venanzio Rauzzini (1746–1810)—one of the most famous castrati of the day, as well as a keyboard player and composer, who later pursued a successful career as a teacher and impresario in Bath, England. It was for Rauzzini that Mozart composed this work. The approximate date of composition and the date of the first performance are established by a characteristically playful and childish postscript to a letter to his sister Nannerl, dated January 16, in which Mozart stated that he had composed a motet to be performed at church the following day. *Exsultate, jubilate* follows a formal pattern little changed from that of the early eighteenth century Italian motet: two da capo arias framing a brief recitative, followed by a brilliant "Alleluia." The formidable virtuosity of the opening Allegro and the concluding Alleluia are set off by the elegant, cantabile middle movement (Andante) "Tu virginum corona." The great contrast of mood and style required of the singer—who must negotiate both fast, florid passages and moments of great lyricism—is surely a testimony to Rauzzini's great skill and continues as a benchmark of technical and expressive achievement. One of the most confident and exuberant of Mozart's early works, the motet has justifiably remained one of his most popular works and a glittering showcase for generations of sopranos. The Alleluia section is, by far, the most familiar to listeners, and it is often excerpted for use as a concert aria. *—Brian Robins*

Recommended:

- ○ **Mozart: Litanies, Vespers, Etc.** / Davis (cond.), Te Kanawa, Constable, London SO / 1991 / Philips 422520
- ○ **Mozart: Coronation Mass; Exsultate, Jubilate; Vesperae Solennes** / Pinnock (cond.), Bonney, English Concert / 1994 / Archiv 445353
- ○ **Christine Schäfer: Mozart Arias & Strauss Songs** / Abbado (cond.), Pires, Schäfer, Johannsen, Berlin PO / DG 457582
- ○ **Mozart: Vesperae Solennes de Confessore; Kyrie in D; Ave Verum Corpus; Exsultate, Jubilate** / Davis (cond.), Te Kanawa, Constable, London SO / Philips 412873

Songs (1768–1791)

It is a testament to Mozart's prolific nature that his over 30 songs are a mere "blip" in the catalogue of his works—so minor a component that they are frequently ignored. More important than their number, however (after all, Henri Duparc achieved fame on the merit of a mere 16 songs), is the fact that Mozart's songs were composed before the great flowering of Romantic poetry and ideology that would bring Germanic song to its pinnacle in the nineteenth century. The remarkable confluence of music and poetry that appeared in the works of Franz Schubert, Robert Schumann, and Hugo Wolf made the diminutive lied a vessel for Romantic outpouring and a unique distillation of the nineteenth century spirit. However, the extent to which the Romantic lied was indebted to a long standing tradition of Germanic song, and specifically the songs of Mozart, Haydn, and Beethoven—the authors of the first true masterpieces of the genre—is frequently overlooked.

Though not extensive, Mozart's song output is extremely various, including songs in German, French and Italian. They illustrate the breadth of his talent for vocal composition, the cosmopolitan nature of his musical influences, and the degree to which his musical choices were shaped by poetry. Of his German songs, *Das Veilchen* (The Violet) is his best known and regarded. *Das Veilchen* is a setting of Wolfgang von Goethe, the most famous of German poets, and it shows Mozart's attentiveness to text. Subtle changes of inflection, modality, and vocal contour bring out the tragic irony of Goethe's ostensibly simple poem and create a psychological mini-drama, foreshadowing the direction lieder composition would take under the influence of a new generation of poets. Other fine German songs include *Abendempfindung* (Evening Reflections), *An Chloë* (To Chloe), and the comical *Warnung* (Warning), which warns parents to "lock away their young maidens."

Mozart's two Italian songs, not surprisingly, resemble operatic arias in their style and construction. *Ridente la calma* (Tranquility fills my soul) is reminiscent especially of the composer's arias for his serious operas, and *Un moto di gioja* (A surge of joy) was intended to replace Susanna's "Deh vieni, non tardar" from the fourth act of *The Marriage of Figaro.*

Oiseaux, si tous les ans (Birds, if every year...) and Dans un bois solitaire (in a lonely wood), Mozart's two French songs, were written during a stay in Mannheim, and they are remarkable mostly as examples of the composer's adaptability to language. Whether composing in Italian, German, or French, he managed to highlight the flow, stress, and cadence of the particular text without ever sacrificing his individual melodic gift. Although the French songs were very popular when written, they have since become better-known in German translation. *—Allen Schrott*

Recommended:

- ○ **Mozart: Lieder & Notturni** / Ameling, Baldwin, Cooymans, Vanderbilt, Ludemann, Netherlands Wind Ens. [members of] / 1991 / Philips 422524
- ○ **Mozart Songs** / Ainsley, Vignoles, Rodgers / 1998 / Hyperion 66989

MISCELLANEOUS

Works for Mechanical Organ (1790–1791)

In late 1790, Mozart received a commission that he found uninspiring. "It is the kind of composition I detest," he wrote to his wife Constanze on October 3, 1790; but he took the work in order to "slip a few ducats into the hand of my dear little wife." He was to compose for the mechanical organ, which he described as, "consist[ing] solely of little pipes, which sound too high-pitched and childish for my taste." Mozart completed three works for this instrument, the *Adagio und Allegro für ein Orgelwerk in einer Uhr*, K. 594; the *Orgelstücke für eine Uhr*, K. 608; and the *Andante für eine Walze in eine kleine Orgel*, K. 616. The titles suggest the composer did not know exactly what to call the dreaded instrument; however, Mozart's disdain for the mechanical organ did not prevent him from realizing masterful music for it.

The three pieces for mechanical organ were commissioned by Count Deym, who wished to use the music in his new wax museum consisting of monuments to notable, recently deceased persons. One of the instruments, a little larger in size than the average microwave oven, was to stand beside each exhibit and play music on the hour.

The *Adagio and Allegro in F minor*, K. 594 was composed in memory of Field Marshal Landon, a hero in the then-contemporary war between the Austrians and the Turks. Mozart began the composition in October 1790, while en route to Frankfurt, and completed it in Vienna in December. The piece, in F minor, is written out on four staves and is usually played by four hands on one piano or on the organ. It is a serious work with great contrapuntal detail. Because Mozart was working in an idiom with no established tradition, the formal characteristics are unusual. A sonata-form Allegro section in F major, featuring much four-part writing, is enclosed by an F minor Adagio. The profundity of the work is perfect for its solemn purpose.

K. 608 is a double fugue in F minor with a recurring introductory episode. The fugue is interrupted by an Andante in the relative major (A flat), after which the contrapuntal writing resumes at a faster pace, pushing to the conclusion. The work's technical brilliance belies any lack of inspiration on the part of the composer. Mozart entered the piece in his "List of All my Works" on March 3, 1791.

The work in F major, K. 616, is considered by some to be the weakest of the three pieces for Deym. Partially because of its major key, it does not achieve the level of seriousness of the other two, but it is an admirable piece in Mozart's "late" style, showing the seemingly effortless combination of simple and complicated passages. It was completed on or before May 4, 1791. *—John Palmer*

Recommended:

- ○ **Mozart & the Organ** / Lippincott / 1998 / Gothic 49051
- ○ **Mozart on the Organ** / Fagius / 1992 / Bis 606

Yevgeny Mravinsky

b. Jun. 4, 1906, St. Petersburg, Russia, **d.** Jan. 19, 1988, Leningrad, U.S.S.R.
Conductor

Like so many Russian musicians, Mravinsky seemed first headed toward a career in the sciences. He studied biology at St. Petersburg University, but had to quit in 1920 after his father's death. To support himself, he signed on with the Imperial Ballet as a rehearsal pianist. In 1923, he finally enrolled in the Leningrad Conservatory, where he studied composition with Vladimir Shcherbachov and conducting with Alexander Gauk and Nikolai Malko. He graduated in 1931, and left his Imperial Ballet job to become a musical assistant and ballet conductor at the Bolshoi Opera from 1931 to 1937, with a stint at the Kirov from 1934. Mravinsky gave up these posts in 1938, after winning first prize in the All-Union Conductors' Competition in Moscow, to become principal conductor of the Leningrad Philharmonic. He remained there until 1982, long ignoring many guest-conducting offers from abroad. Under Mravinsky's direction the Leningrad Philharmonic came to be regarded as one of the finest orchestras in the world, although the world had comparatively few opportunities to hear it aside from the rare tour (about 30 performances in 25 years, starting in 1956), some dim Soviet recordings, and a very few highly acclaimed records for such Western European companies as Deutsche Grammophon and, in the end, Erato. Mravinsky was made People's Artist of the U.S.S.R. in 1954, and in 1973, he received the order of Hero of Socialist Labor. But his more lasting international acclaim came for his performances of Mozart, Beethoven, Bruckner, Wagner, Sibelius, Bartók, Stravinsky, and anything Russian or Soviet. His reputation only rose upon his retirement from the Leningrad Philharmonic, particularly with the posthumous release in 1995 by Melodiya and BMG *Classics* of 20 CDs surveying Mravinsky's work from the 1940s into the 1980s.

Mravinsky's rehearsal manner was said to be autocratic and brutal, and the resulting performances were tightly clenched. Yet they were also technically precise, finely detailed, subtly colored, and highly dramatic—and this not always because he was in the habit of whipping fast finales into a frenzy. His readings had an intensity, concentration, and—despite the arduous rehearsal—spontaneity comparable to those of Wilhelm Furtwängler. In the West, Mravinsky was particularly noted as an interpreter of Shostakovich, whose Fifth, Sixth, Eighth, Ninth, and Tenth Symphonies he premiered, and of Tchaikovsky. His recordings of the Tchaikovsky's last three symphonies, made in 1960 for Deutsche Grammophon while the orchestra was on tour in London, are touchstones of the Russian repertory. *—James Reel*

Recommended:

- ○ **Tchaikovsky: Symphonies 4, 5 & 6** / Mravinsky (cond.), Leningrad PO / DG 419745
- ○ **Shostakovich: Symphonie 10** / Mravinsky (cond.), Leningrad PO / Erato 45753
- ○ **Shostakovich: Symphonie 5** / Mravinsky (cond.), Leningrad PO / Erato 45752
- ○ **Shostakovich: Violin Concertos** / Mackerras, Mravinsky (cond.), Oistrakh, Tomášek, Czech PO, Prague RSO / Praga 7250052

Georg Muffat

b. Jun. 1, 1653, Mégève, Savoy, France, **d.** Feb. 23, 1704, Passau, Bavaria, Germany

Composer: Keyboard

Georg Muffat is known primarily for several instrumental collections, among which are his *Florilegia* orchestral suites, comprised of two sets, dating from 1695 and 1698, respectively. They are unusual because, though written by a German composer, they are fashioned in the French style, featuring dance music divulging the influence of Muffat's teacher, Lully. Among Muffat's early works, the *Armonico tributo*, a collection of five sonatas for strings and basso continuo, is notable for its five-part string writing and mixture of French and Corellian influences. In the end, despite these influences, Muffat must be viewed as a generally original composer, who in his versatility and multi-faceted approach managed to unite the French, Italian and German styles in his music. Though he was primarily a composer of instrumental works, he also wrote operas, though none have survived.

Georg Muffat was baptized on June 1, 1653, and was thus probably born about a week before that date. He would consider himself German, though his parents were of Scottish origin and his birthplace, Megève, Savoy, is located in France. He showed unusual musical talent as a child, and at age ten traveled to Paris and began study with Lully. After six years of instruction with that master and others, he began studies at the Jesuit-run college in Sélestat, Alsace, in 1669.

Two years later, he was appointed organist at a church in Molsheim, through which the Strasbourg Cathedral functioned in exile. Muffat apparently was not wholly satisfied with his career up to this point, for by 1674 he would depart for Bavaria to study law. But the impending war in Alsace certainly had an influence on his decision to leave the region, if not to seek a change of career.

By 1678, he had secured a position in Salzburg in the service of Archbishop Gandolf, Count of Kuenberg. Here he served as organist and player in the chamber ensemble. Muffat took leave of his post in about 1681 for an extended stay in Italy, where he would study with Pasquini and come under the influence of Corelli. Muffat's aforementioned *Armonico tributo* dates to this period. The composer returned to Salzburg in the fall of 1682. He was apparently satisfied with conditions there, but after the death of the archbishop in 1687, he gradually became disenchanted with his post.

Muffat had earned the patronage of Emperor Leopold I of Vienna by 1677, and seems to have reestablished ties with him following his Salzburg departure, for he appeared at the Augsburg coronation of the Emperor's son as Roman king in 1690. Moreover, Muffat dedicated his solo organ composition, *Apparatus musico-organisticus*, to Emperor Leopold and presented him with a copy. In 1690 Muffat's son, Gottlieb (d. 1770), was born. He would go on to become a composer of significance himself, though his chosen field of composition was limited primarily to the keyboard genre.

Later on in 1690, Muffat secured a post as Kapellmeister at the Passau Court of Bishop Johann Philipp. In 1695, the composer produced the first of his important Florilegia orchestral suites, the *Suavioris harmoniae instrumentalis hyporchematicae florilegium primum*, which was comprised of seven suites. Three years later he produced the second set, *Florilegium secundum*, which consisted of eight suites for orchestra. Among his last important works was the 1701 collection of 12 concerti grossi, entitled *Ausserlesene Instrumental-Music*. Muffat stayed on in his post at Passau until his death. *—Robert Cummings*

Overview of Works (1677–1700)

Although born in the Savoy region of France, Georg Muffat (1653–1704) always considered himself a German. He may also have had Scottish ancestry. This pan-European background also extended to his career, which included musical study in Paris with Jean-Baptiste Lully, law studies in Ingolstadt, Bavaria, and a peripatetic existence that took him to Vienna, Rome, Augsburg, Salzburg (where he held posts as organist and chamber composer to the archbishop of Salzburg under Heinrich Biber), and Passau, where he became Kapellmeister to the archbishop.

Muffat was one of the most highly educated musicians of his day, and his importance as a composer stems from the eclectic influences he assimilated on his travels. He introduced elements of Italian and French elements into his instrumental works, while not forsaking more Germanic traits. The influence of Lully is apparent in Muffat's richly textured five-part string scoring, and the delicacy of his dance movements. In Italy Muffat came into contact with the influential Arcangelo Corelli and other progenitors of the brilliant Italian concerto style. This Italian influence is apparent in Muffat's first publication, *Tributo Armonico*, which he issued in Salzburg shortly after his return from Italy in 1682. Described by their composer as "chamber works for few or many instruments" (very practical!), the publication consists of six string sonatas, each of which opens with a harmonically rich "sonata" in the Corellian style succeeded by a mixture of stylized dances and other miscellaneous movements; the final *G major Sonata* is a more serious work in sonata da chiesa style that includes a fuga and concluding passacaglia.

In 1690 Muffat published *Apparatus musico-organisticus*, a collection of extended organ toccatas dedicated to the Habsburg Emperor Leopold I that overtly set out to juxtapose French and Italian idioms. Two collections of instrumental suites in the French style entitled respectively *Florilegium primum* and *Florilegium secundum* appeared in 1695 and 1698. The synthesis of styles is most completely effected in Muffat's final major publication *Ausserlesene Instrumental-Music*, which includes the sonatas of *Tributo Armonico* rewritten as concerti grossi with the addition of six new concertos. As can be heard in the broad opening Grave and following dance-like Allegro of the newly-composed *Concerto No. 1*, the conjunction of Corellian seriousness and Lullian pomp and elegance is now fully effected in the music of a composer who, in the words of Arthur Hutchings (*The Baroque Concerto*) "seems to have been incapable of slovenly or even mediocre work." In addition to his musical compositions Muffat also wrote a number of treatises that are important source material for students of performance practice. *—Brian Robins*

Recommended:

- ○ **Muffat: 12 Concerti Grossi** / Nemeth (cond.), Capella Savaria / 1996 / Hungaroton 31666/67
- ○ **Muffat: Armonico Tributo** / Holman, Goodman (conds.), Parley of Instruments / 1982 / Hyperion 66032

KEYBOARD

Apparatus Musico-Organisticus, for organ (1690)

Georg Muffat's *Apparatus Musico-Organisticus* (which is curiously described on the title page of the original 1690 Salzburg publication as "Liber Primus"; there was, however, apparently never a "Liber Secundus") represents the wealth of organ experience that this remarkable composer, who is by and large famous more for his ensemble music, acquired serving as organist for the Archbishop of Salzburg and later as Court Organist in Passau. Muffat was himself of diverse heritage—German and French, all the while working very near Italy—and like so many of the best composers of his day he sought ways to combine the various musical traditions of Europe into a single language; thus, throughout the *Apparatus Musico-Organisticus*, we find the rich German organ style riding side-by-side with elements drawn from Italian chamber music and elegant French court music.

A series of 12 toccatas makes up the bulk of the *Apparatus Musico-Organisticus*; four additional pieces are added after these 12 to round the volume out. The toccatas are all multi-sectioned, and each might contain any or all of the following, some more than once: a dramatic, virtuosic adagio or allegro episode filled with runs and purely organistic figurations, a miniature sonata da chiesa movement (sometimes strictly conceived for two "soloists" and continuo), something in the manner of a fugue, melodic arioso, homophonic pseudo-chorale, and perhaps even a passage of dance music. The toccatas generally grow longer and more involved as the volume progresses, and they are set up in the order of the Church modes.

After the dozen toccatas, at the end of which Muffat writes "Finis," implying that what comes afterwards might well be a publication afterthought of sorts, there is a Ciacona based on a four-bar, descending bass line, and then a Passacaglia built from an eight-bar ascending bass line. Lastly, the *Apparatus Musico-Organisticus* includes a binary-form organ aria headed by the words "Nova Cyclopedeias Harmonica," and a set of eight variations on a full theme (not just a simple bass progression, as in a chaconne or passacaglia) described as "Ad malleorum, Ictus Allusio." —*Blair Johnston*

Recommended:

- ○ **Muffat: Apparatus Musico-Organisticus** / Tuma / Panton 1016

Charles Münch

b. Sep. 26, 1891, Strasbourg, France, **d.** Nov. 6, 1968, Richmond, VA
Conductor

A genial conductor with a particular gift for French music, Charles Münch extended the Boston Symphony's glory years (begun under the baton of Serge Koussevitzky) into the early 1960s. Munch was born in the province of Alsace-Lorraine, which at the time (1891) was controlled by Germany and has long hovered between two cultural worlds. Munch himself benefited from both French and German musical training, and his first important musical posts were in Germany. Yet he came to be regarded as the quintessential French conductor, and his recordings of French repertory with the Boston Symphony remain standards by which others are judged. Münch studied violin at the Strasbourg Conservatory, where his father was a professor, and, from 1912, in Paris with Lucien Capet. As an Alsatian, he was conscripted into the German army at the outbreak of World War I. Gassed and wounded as an artillery sergeant, he nevertheless survived the war through sheer resiliency. In 1919, upon returning to Alsace-Lorraine (now back in French hands), he took French citizenship, and a violin professorship in Strasbourg. Nevertheless, his professional interests soon sent him to Germany; he studied violin with Carl Flesch in Berlin, then moved to Leipzig to take a violin professorship at the conservatory there, and then became concertmaster of the Leipzig Gewandhaus Orchestra from 1926 to 1933, during Furtwängler's tenure.

But it was back in Paris, in 1933, where Münch made his successful conducting debut in a self-financed concert with the Straram Orchestra. He conducted the Paris Orchestre de la Société Philharmonique (1935–38) and in 1937 was named director of the Société des Concerts du Conservatoire de Paris, a post he held through World War II. Münch introduced many new works, including, in 1945, Messiaen's *L'Ascension*; he quickly became known as a conductor attentive to music's larger formal structures, as well as details of color and sonority. Despite his allegiances 25 years before, Münch refused to collaborate with the Nazis, and indeed supported the French resistance; he was awarded the Légion d'honneur in 1945.

Münch's career quickly accelerated after the war. In 1946, he made his debut with the Boston Symphony (and several other American orchestras) as a guest conductor, and he toured America with the French National Radio Orchestra in 1948. The following year, he was appointed music director of the Boston Symphony, which he took on an unprecedented tour of the Soviet Union in 1956. Münch retired from the BSO in 1962 but continued to guest conduct, and helped Serge Baudo launch the Orchestre de Paris in 1967. On tour in America with that orchestra, he died the following year.

Münch was easygoing in rehearsal, reluctant to drill the spontaneity out of an orchestra. He was particularly noted as an elegant, colorful interpreter of French music of the nineteenth and twentieth centuries; his recordings of that material with the Boston Symphony for RCA are still regarded as classics of their kind. He was a strong advocate for the Franco-Swiss composers of his own generation, especially Roussel, Milhaud, and Honegger. But he also had a good touch with the conservative contemporary music of other lands, as may be heard in his few but important recordings of Martinů, Piston, and Barber. Indeed, during his Boston years Munch's commitment to American music was almost as strong as his allegiance to new French works.—*James Reel*

Recommended:

- ○ **Berlioz: Symphonie Fantastique; Roméo Et Juliette** / Münch (cond.), BSO / 1993 / RCA 902668979
- ○ **Brahms: Symphony; Honegger: Symphony 3** / Münch (cond.), BSO / Multisonic 310025
- ○ **Franck: Symphony** / Münch (cond.), BSO / 2002 / JVC 18
- ○ **Berlioz: Overtures; Saint-Saëns: Omphale's Spinning Wheel** / Münch (cond.), BSO / 1993 / BMG 61400

David Munrow

b. Aug. 12, 1942, Birmingham, England, **d.** May 15, 1976, Chesham Bois, England
Conductor, Recorder Player

David John Munrow, in his brief career, was one of the most exciting and influential leaders of the British early music movement. After he completed his school education, he taught for a year in South America. He returned to England to attend Pembroke College, Cambridge, where he read for a degree in English from 1961 to 1964. He was an avid and talented flute player and while at Cambridge founded an organization to play early music. After he graduated, he studied seventeenth century music at Birmingham University. It was his exposure to South American indigenous music, with its strong use of wooden instruments of the flute family, that stimulated his interest in such instruments, including the recorder.

At that time, interest in England in early music was growing. Munrow found himself in great demand as a recorder player. In 1967, he founded the Early Music Consort of London, with counter tenor James Bowman, violist Oliver Brookes, lutenist James Tyler, and harpsichordist Christopher Hogwood. They gave their first performance at Louvain the same year, making a London debut in 1968. Also in 1967, he became a lecturer in early music at Leicester University. Munrow's consort shook up the regular concert world and the growing early music establishment with its performing style. Their approach was entertaining, attractive, and exuberant, even brash, without traducing the boundaries of what was known to be authentic. Suddenly, "authentic" performances were no longer scholarly affairs of main interest to academics, but popular concert events eagerly attended by the general classical music audience.

The Consort appeared on television and in an intriguing development, the group also kept an interest in contemporary music. Therefore, several living composers wrote new music—often in the most advanced musical style—for these old-style instruments. These included Peter Dickinson (*Translations*, 1971), Elisabeth Lutyens (*The Tears of Night*, 1972), and Peter Maxwell Davies, who used the group as the on-stage band during his opera *Taverner* (1972), which is about a medieval English composer.

In 1969, Munrow became a teacher of the recorder at London's Royal Academy of Music. In 1971, he started making lecture appearances on BBC radio. His show, "Pied Piper," was aimed at young listeners and had a listenership among all ages. For reasons that remain obscure, he took his own life in 1976. Had he not, he surely would have been recognized as one of the most influential musicians of the last half of the twentieth century. —*Joseph Stevenson*

Recommended:

- ○ **Two Renaissance Dance Bands; Monteverdi's Contemporaries** / Munrow (cond.), London Early Music Consort, Morley Consort / 1996 / Testament 1080
- ○ **Music of the Gothic Era** / Munrow (cond.), London Early Music Consort / Archiv 471731
- ○ **Early Music Festival** / Munrow (cond.), London Early Music Consort / 1998 / London 452967
- ○ **Music Of The Crusades** / Munrow (cond.), London Early Music Consort / 1991 / Decca 430264
- ○ **Praetorius: Terpsichore; Motets** / Munrow (cond.), London Early Music Consort / 1996 / Virgin 61289

Heidi Grant Murphy

b. 1962, Bellingham, WA
Soprano

Heidi Grant Murphy distinguished herself as a strong and promising new American singer in the early 1990s. She began studying voice at Western Washington University, and continued at the Indiana University School of Music in Bloomington, IN, as a graduate student. While pursuing those studies, she entered the Metropolitan Opera National Council Auditions. When she was named a winner, she left Bloomington to enter the Metropolitan Opera's Young Artist Development Program. She made her Metropolitan Opera debut in 1989 in Richard Strauss' *Die Frau ohne Schatten*. Since then, she has appeared on the Met stage as Sophie in Strauss' *Der Rosenkavalier*, Nanetta in Verdi's *Falstaff*, Ilia in Mozart's *Idomeneo*, Pamina in his *Magic Flute*, Susanna in his *Marriage of Figaro*, and Sister Constance in Poulenc's *Dialogues of the Carmelites*. She frequently sings at the Salzburg Festival.

Besides the Met, she has appeared with the Frankfurt Opera, Netherlands Opera, Santa Fe Opera, with Theatre Royale de la Monnaie, and with major American symphony orchestras. She sang the soprano role in the world premiere of David Del Tredici's *The Spider and the Fly* with Kurt Masur and the New York Philharmonic and in Saariaho's *Chateau de l'ame* with Kent Nagano and the Hallé Orchestra. She is a frequent recitalist and recording artist. She appeared on recordings on several labels, including Deutsche Grammophon (*Marriage of Figaro*, *Parsifal*) and on Telarc (Mahler's *Symphony No. 8* and Haydn's *The Creation*.) She became an exclusive recording artist for Arabesque Records, recording a recital disc (with her husband, Metropolitan Opera conductor Kevin Murphy) and a pair of Bach wedding cantatas. —*Joseph Stevenson*

Recommended:

- ○ **Bach Wedding Cantatas** / Murphy, St. Luke's Chamber Ens. / 1997 / Arabesque 6690
- ○ **Times Like This** / Murphy, Gilbert, Hammann, Shames, Rostron, Clark, DiPippo, James, James, Okura, Rostad / 2003 / Koch 7569

○ **Taverner: To a Child Dancing in the Wind; Birtwistle: Entr'actes & Sappho Fragments** / Hostetter (cond.), Murphy, Baker, Ferrillo, Aureole Trio / 2001 / Koch 7486

Ann Murray

b. Aug. 27, 1949, Dublin, Ireland
Mezzo-Soprano
Ann Murray is one of the leading mezzo-sopranos on the international scene. She is not related to the famous Canadian popular music singer with a similar name. The Irish-born singer was educated at the Royal Manchester College of Music, where she studied with Frederic Cox. She bases her career in London, where she sings regularly at the English National Opera and the Royal Opera House, Covent Garden. With the former she has sung Charlotte, Rosina, Beatrice, Xerxes, and Ariodante. At the Royal Opera House she has sung Cherubino, Dorabella, Rosina, Oktavian, and Donna Elvira and has been given roles in the openings of new productions of Ravel's *L'Enfant et les Sortilèges*; Strauss' *Ariadne auf Naxos*; Mozart's *Idomeneo*, *Mitridate Rè de Ponto*, and *Così fan tutte*; Rossini's *Moses in Egypt*; Wagner's *Götterdämmerung*; and Handel's *Alcina* and *Giulio Cesare*.

Other opera houses where she has appeared are the major houses of Hamburg, Dresden, Berlin, Zürich, and Cologne, La Monnaie of Brussels, the Opéra de Paris, the Metropolitan Opera of New York, and the Chicago Lyric Opera. At La Scala in Milan, she has sung Donna Elvira, Sextus, Dorabella, and Cherubino under the baton of Riccardo Muti.

At the end of the century, she was invited to make frequent appearances at the Vienna State Opera, the Bavarian State Opera, and the Salzburg Festival. In one or more of these houses, in addition to several of the roles already mentioned, she was to sing Oktavian (Strauss' *Der Rosenkavalier*), Nicklaus in Offenbach's *Les Contes d'Hoffmann*, and the title role of *La Cenerentola* under such conductors as Maazel, Muti, Levine, Chailly, and Cambreling. She also planned to sing *Maria Stuarda* for the English National Opera and *Alceste* for the Netherlands Opera.

She has sung in orchestral concerts with many major orchestras, including the Orchestre de Paris under Rafael Kubelik, the Philadelphia Orchestra under Wolfgang Sawallisch, the Berlin Philharmonic Orchestra under Muti, and the Chicago Symphony Orchestra under Solti. Her concert appearances also include all the major symphony orchestras of the British Isles under many leading conductors, including both the first nights and the last nights of the BBC Promenade Concerts.

She is also an esteemed solo recitalist. She is a founding member of Graham Johnson's organization The Songmakers' Almanac. She has sung at the Aldeburgh, Edinburgh, and Munich Festivals, as well as giving recitals in Paris, Brussels, Geneva, Dresden, Zürich, Frankfurt, Madrid, London, Dublin, and Vienna (both the Konzerthaus and the Musikverein).

She has recorded for Hyperion and other labels in a wide variety of music from her concert and recital repertoire as well as several operas. These include Dido in Purcell's *Dido and Aeneas* under Harnoncourt, Dorabella under Levine, Cherubino under Muti, Despina under Rattle, Hansel under Colin Davis, Sextus under Harnoncourt, and Donna Elvira under Solti. Her recital recordings include songs of Bizet and Gounod, as well as entries in Graham Johnson's complete Schubert series. *—Joseph Stevenson*

Recommended:

○ **The Last Rose of Summer: Best Loved Songs of Ireland** / Murray, Johnson / Hyperion 66627

○ **Songs by Bizet** / Murray, Johnson / 1998 / Hyperion 66976

○ **Great Handel Arias** / Mackerras (cond.), Murray, Wallfisch, Beznosiuk, Clark, Orch. of the Age of Enlightenment / Forlane 16738

Michael Murray

b. Mar. 19, 1943, Kokomo, IN
Organist
American organist Michael Murray is best recognized for his many strong-selling recordings on the Telarc label. Murray attended Butler University and Oberlin College, where he studied with Haskell Thomson, and he also studied with Marcel Dupré between 1961 and 1965. He made his performance debut in a series of 12 recitals in Cleveland during the 1968–69 season, playing all of Bach's organ works. His European debut was at the Galtus and Garmer van Hagerbeer organ, built in 1642, at Leiden University in the Netherlands in 1972. That was also the year that he performed all the organ works of César Franck and made his first recording for what would become the Telarc label. Since then, he has performed on organs throughout the U.S. and Europe, dedicating and re-dedicating many instruments. Murray has been soloist with the Chicago Symphony, the Philadelphia Orchestra, the San Francisco Symphony, and the Atlanta Symphony, to name just a few of his guest appearances. He has played the organs of St. Bavo's in Haarlem, St. Ouen in Rouen, Grace Cathedral in San Francisco, Salisbury Cathedral, and the Royal Albert Hall for some of his recordings. To celebrate 30 years with Telarc, Murray recorded a recital of Dupré, Franck, and Widor on the same organ the composers played, that of St. Sulpice in Paris. His playing is noted for its stunning but natural technique and his musical intuition. Murray has also distinguished himself as a scholar and author. In addition to hosting radio interviews with fellow musicians and authors, and writing numerous articles for *Diapason* and *The American Organist*, he has published three books. His first, *Marcel Dupré: The Work of a Master Organist*, from 1985, was the first major publication about the composer's life and work. He followed this up with one about Albert Schweitzer's musical life and the 1998 *French Masters of the Organ*. Murray has been on the staff of St. Mark's Episcopal Church in Columbus, OH, since 1994 and serves on the advisory board to the Schweitzer Institute for the Humanities. In 2000, he received an honorary doctorate from Ohio State University. *—Patsy Morita*

Recommended:

○ **Dupré, Franck, Widor** / Murray / 2002 / Telarc 80516

○ **Bach: Toccata & Fugue in D minor, etc.** / Murray / 1983 / Telarc 80088

○ **Saint-Saëns: Symphony 3; Phaéton** / Badea (cond.), Murray, Royal PO / 1991 / Telarc 80274

Thea Musgrave

b. May 27, 1928, Barnton, Midlothian, Scotland
Composer
Thea Musgrave (b. 1928) is a contemporary composer, conductor, and lecturer. She studied at the University of Edinburgh and later at the Paris Conservatory with Nadia Boulanger. She also studied composition with Aaron Copland. Her music was initially recognized in Scotland, and it was from there that she received her earliest commissions. Among these are *A Suite o' Bairnsongs*, *A Tale for Thieves*, and *The Abbott of Drimrock*. She has composed in many genres, but showed an early aptitude for dramatic mediums. The ballet *A Tale for Thieves* and the chamber opera *The Abbot of Drimrock* (1955), were both written on commissions from the Scottish BBC. Her early works also possess a lyrical, picturesque charm within a largely diatonic idiom, and no evidence of avant-garde explorations. However, around 1955 Musgrave began experimenting with denser chromaticism and abstract forms. In the 1960s she also embraced serialism, which infused her work with a newfound liveliness and energy. A confident, original personality emerged in her later work, which loses nothing of the lyricism and plasticity of her earlier works.

The Decision was Musgrave's major work of the 1960's, produced for the first time by the New Opera Company in 1967. A full scale opera, it deals with the grim realities of a mining accident, and confronts a variety of moral questions. It is illustrative of the changes that her compositional style was undergoing at the time, for it is imbued with a distinctive energy. Much of the immediate work that followed was derived from this stylistic transformation. Her concertos also reflect a heightened dramatic sense. They contain asynchronous passages and borrowings in the manner of Charles Ives, a composer whom Musgrave studied and emulated. Musgrave's concertos are complex, dramatic happenings in which the soloist affects different groups of instrumentalists throughout the orchestra. In her Clarinet Concerto, commissioned by the Royal Philharmonic Society, the soloist walks about the stage while interacting with different groups of instrumentalists in the orchestra. In her French horn concerto, the soloist "activates" a group, and then conducts them. The soloists in her concertos initiate interactions among various groups in an abstract dramatic medium in which the orchestra divides and recombines, and eventually unites as a tutti ensemble.

Thea Musgrave's later work has centered on the operatic. Her first major opera of this period is *The Voice of Ariadne*, a sophisticated tale about being haunted. *Mary Queen of Scots* (1977) was the first opera for which Musgrave wrote her own libretto. She has continued this practice in works such as *A Christmas Carol* and *Harriet, The Woman called Moses*.

Musgrave's compositions have been performed by most of the major symphony orchestras, and she has often conducted her works as well. She has won many awards, including the Koussevitsky award in 1973. *The Voice of Ariadne* was performed by the New York City Opera Company, and her Clarinet Concerto by the New York Philharmonic. She has lectured at major universities both in the United States and abroad, and in 1987 was made a distinguished professor at the City University of New York.*—Rita Laurance*

Overview of Works

Musgrave, while not well-known outside of classical music circles, is one of the most successful instrumental and opera composers of the last half of the twentieth and early twenty-first centuries, as well as a noted conductor. While Nadia Boulanger, her teacher for four years (1950 to 1954), was a major influence in her musical development, her work draws from a wide variety of sources and inspirations. A dominant theme has been music drama, whether on the stage or in the concert hall. She once commented that she has felt a challenge to explore "dramatic-abstract musical forms . . . a kind of extension of the concerto principle." Within this experimentation, however, her work has remained accessible rather than academic. Like other contemporary composers, she has experimented with the physical traditions of concert performance. For example, in her *Clarinet Concerto*, the soloist performs from different sections of the orchestra, not only providing different musical subtleties and actually conducting smaller concertantes, but making the soloist a plastic rather than a static figure. She also experimented with other traditions, including writing *Space Play* for an ensemble without a conductor, in which the physical placement of the players (one woodwind at each corner of the stage, strings forming a circle around the horn in the center) again plays an important part. Electronics have also figured strongly in her music by enhancing dramatic effects. In her radio opera *An Occurrence at Owl Creek Bridge*, she included an audio tape background and a narrator (who is finally revealed as the protagonist's wife, a dramatic touch that, while it detracts from Bierce's detached tone, does add another level of immediacy to the work). Similarly, *Narcissus* uses a solo flutist to portray Narcissus and a digital delay system to portray the reflection that enraptures him. In common with many other contemporary composers, she has also incorporated global influences into her works, such as her *Journey Through a Japanese Landscape*, written for marimba and winds, based on a series of haiku. Her operas are almost exclusively to her own librettos, though drawn from history, such as *Mary, Queen of Scots*; *Harriet, the Woman Called Moses*; and *Simón Bolívar*, or literary sources, such as *A Christmas Carol* and *Occurrence*. (Some of her early works, including the children's opera *Marko the Miser*, were written to others' libretti.) She is keenly aware of the archetypical aspects of these figures, declaring that "Harriet is every woman who dared to defy injustice and tyranny; she is Joan of Arc, she is Susan B. Anthony, she is Anne Frank, she is Mother Teresa," so it is no surprise that classical mythology has been another fertile source, inspiring *Niobe* (another instrumental work that uses audio recording to great dramatic effect), *Lamenting With Ariadne*, and her *Orfeo* pieces, which draw from and experiment with Gluck in an electronic (and later ensemble) setting. *—Ann Feeney*

Recommended:

- ○ **The Fall of Narcissus** / Samek, Varcoe, Masters, Page, Robinson, Sharp / 2002 / Clarinet Classics 39
- ○ **Pierrot Dreaming** / Samek, Page, Byam-Grounds, Sharp / 2002 / Clarinet Classics 38
- ○ **Musgrave: Clarinet Concerto; The Seasons; Autumn Sonata** / Soames, Musgrave (cond.), Nicholson, BBC Scottish SO / 2001 / Clarinet Classics 35
- ○ **Musgrave: Helios; Momento Vitae; etc.** / Kraemer, Steen (conds.), Daniel, Scottish CO, BBCSO / Ancora+ 74

Musica Antiqua Köln

f. 1973, Cologne, Germany

Ensemble

Reinhard Goebel founded Musica Antiqua Köln in 1973. The ensemble devoted itself to playing Baroque music on period instruments, with a particular penchant for playing neglected or overlooked repertoire. Many of their best albums have sold well without featuring music by well-known composers. These releases also appear to have boosted the (posthumous) careers of composers such as Heinichen, with their concerti album from 1993, and the Veracini Overture album from 1994. Goebel has not only shown courage in programming unconventional repertoire, but has also been known to take risks in his approach to relatively well-known works. For instance, his ensemble plays the last movement of Bach's third *Brandenburg concerto* at a then unrivaled, break-neck tempo. Furthermore, Goebel had sound musicological evidence that the piece should be played that way.

The original core ensemble included Reinhard Goebel and Hajo Bass on violin, with Eva Bartos on viola da gamba. However, the constituency of the ensemble has changed over the years, with only Reinhard Goebel remaining constant. Eva Bartos only appears on Musica Antiqua Köln recordings until 1977, and was replaced by Jonathan Cable and Charles Medlam. By 1980, Jap ter Linden appears most frequently as either cellist or gambist, and by the mid-1980s, he is replaced again by Phoebe Carrai. Goebel's partners on violin have included Hajo Bass, Manfredo Kremer, and Florian Deuter among others. Many players who have left the ensemble have enjoyed spectacular careers afterward, including the harpsichordists Andreas Staier, Robert Hill, the violinists Hajo Bass and Manfredo Kremer, as well as Charles Medlam, and Jap ter Linden playing bowed bass instruments, and Wilbert Hazelzet playing flute.

In 1990, Goebel developed tendinitis and was forced to abandon his solo playing career. The last album in which he played as a soloist was his 1990 recording of the *Rosenkranz* sonatas by Heinrich Biber. After 1990, he continued to direct the ensemble, and eventually returned in a limited capacity by playing his violin left handed. The ensemble continues to tour and record very actively, but their best work came from the period before Goebel injured himself. *—Andrus Madsen*

Recommended:

- ○ **Sonatas of Dresden** / Goebel (cond.), Cologne Musica Antiqua / 2001 / Challenge 72032
- ○ **Telemann: String Concertos** / Goebel (cond.), Cologne Musica Antiqua / Archiv 463074
- ○ **Cantatas by Members of the Bach Family** / Goebel (cond.), Elliott, Varcoe, Schopper, Cordier, Cologne Musica Antiqua, Rheinische Kantorei / Archiv 000129602
- ○ **Telemann: Watermusic** / Goebel (cond.), Cologne Musica Antiqua / Archiv 413788
- ○ **Bach: Brandenburg Concertos; Orchestral Suites; Chamber Music** / Goebel (cond.), Cologne Musica Antiqua / Archiv 471656
- ○ **Biber: Missa Salisburgensis** / McCreesh, Goebel (conds.), Cologne Musica Antiqua, Gabrieli Consort & Players / 1998 / Archiv 457611

I Musici

f. Mar., 1952, Rome, Italy

Ensemble

After hearing I Musici perform, Arturo Toscanini remarked, "Twelve individual instrumental masters, and together the finest chamber orchestra in the world." This Italian ensemble has long attracted international attention for their emphasis on brilliance, strength of attack, and high level of discipline, beginning with their first performances of seventeenth and eighteenth century Italian music. The group was formed in March 1952 by 12 students at the Accademia di Santa Cecilia, Rome, who developed a common interest in pre-Classical music during conservatory meetings. Upon origination the ensemble was composed of six violins, two violas, two cellos, a double bass, and a harpsichord; there were three women and nine men. Nearly all of the original violinists were pupils of the same Accademia teacher, Remy Principe. The name "I Musici," literally "The Musicians," was chosen by the performers to reflect their enthusiasm for the spirit of the music of an epoch in which "professionalism" had not yet assumed its present pervasive significance. They came together with the single purpose of expressing their deep love for music, and the purity of their intention is heard at performances and on recordings.

Making their debut performance at the Accademia in 1952, I Musici began to achieve international fame the following year. Their career developed rapidly, beginning with concert tours throughout Europe. They then toured Central, North and South America, South Africa, Japan, and Australia. They have also played at many music festivals, including those of Salzburg, Holland, Graz, Menton, Venice, York, Copenhagen, Aix-en-Provence, and Edinburgh. Early in their career, they primarily played the music of Italian Baroque composers such as Albinoni, Bononcini, Corelli, Locatelli, Alessandro Scarlatti, Torelli, and Vivaldi, later taking on the non-Baroque works of Bach, Barber, Bartók, Britten, Handel, Hindemith, Martin, and Respighi. One of the most characteristic (and widely influential) features of the ensemble is its lack of a conductor during performance. Felix Ayo, leader of the group between 1952–68, has said that "to perform without a conductor is normal, I think. It is in the true tradition of the élite music of the Italian Baroque. One finds a conductor only later, after Vivaldi and Corelli. Before, with the concerto grosso and the concerto da camera, there was only the first violin giving the start and tempo with some head movements. And that was all." Among I Musici, Ayo said, music making is a democratic experience. "During rehearsals, the music is discussed by everyone. Everyone's opinion has the same value. It is by mutual agreement that we finally decide how certain details should be handled." The group does have a leader, however; the post has changed hands over the years between Ayo, Roberto Michelucci (1968–72); conductor, music director, and virtuoso violinist Salvatore Accardo (1972–77); Boccherini Quintet and Carmirelli Quartet founder Pina Carmirelli (1977–86); and Federico Agostini.

I Musici over the years has constantly built upon its strengths, and the group members to apply the same dedication to their artistry as they did upon formation. Their performances can be heard on over 45 recordings, almost all under the Philips label, at times with flute and harp. *—Meredith Gailey*

Recommended:

- ○ **Vivaldi: The 4 Seasons, etc.** / I Musici / Philips 000122302
- ○ **Albinoni: Adagio; Pachelbel: Cannon & Gigue, etc.** / I Musici / 1992 / Philips 434787
- ○ **Bach: Brandenburg Concertos** / Holliger, Andre, Brueggen, I Musici / 1993 / Philips 438317

Les Musiciens du Louvre

f. 1984, Grenoble, France

Ensemble

Les Musiciens du Louvre-Grenoble was created by Marc Minkowski, its conductor, in 1984, and since that time the group has been ranked among the leading interpreters of Baroque music in Europe. The repertoire of Les Musiciens du Louvre clearly reflects Minkowski's tastes: he has championed music by Marais, Mouret, Charpentier, Lully, and Rameau, and is determined to revive interest in Handel's lesser-known operas. Playing period instruments and informed by extensive research, Les Musiciens du Louvre is one of a number of ensembles attempting to recreate Baroque-era music as they believe it was heard by the composers' contemporaries. Occasionally, the group performs works from other periods.

In 1984, Minkowski won First Prize at the first International Early Music Competition in Bruges. Encouraged by this success, he founded that same year the period-instrument ensemble Les Musiciens du Louvre. Recognition came quickly and soon they were asked participate in high-profile events. In 1992, they inaugurated the Baroque Festival in Versailles with a revival of Gluck's *Armide*, and in 1993 they participated in the official reopening of the Lyon Opera, performing *Phaéton*, by Lully.

Their wide discography with Erato/Warner includes works such as *Teseo* by Handel, *Les Amour de Ragonde* by Mouret, the *symphonie nouvelle*, *Les éléments*, by Jean-Féry Rebel (1666–1747), Handel's *Concerti Grossi*, Op. 3, and *Phaeton*, by Lully. In 1993, they were awarded the coveted Gramophone Award, "Best Baroque Vocal Recording," for their rendering of Alessandro Stradella's *San Giovanni Battista*. In 1995, they performed Purcell's *Dido and Aeneas* at the Toronto Opera, the Houston Opera, the BBC Proms, and the Opéra Royal in Versailles.

In 1990, the French Académie du Disque Lyrique awarded Marc Minkowski the *Orphée d'or* for "Best Young Conductor." Minkowski still finds time to work with other ensembles, including the Welsh National Orchestra, the Salzburg Mozarteum Orchestra, the Monte-Carlo Opera and the Deutsche Oper in Berlin.

Since 1994, Les Musiciens du Louvre have recorded exclusively for Archiv Produktion–Deutsche Grammophon; their first release on that label was *Hippolyte et Aricie*, Rameau's first lyric tragedy. They also recorded Handel's very early *Oratorio per la Resurrezione di Nostro Signor Gesù Cristo*, of 1708, *Anacréon* by Rameau and *Acis et Galatée* by Lully.

Les Musiciens du Louvre established their permanent residence in Grenoble in 1996, joining forces with the Orchestre de Chambre de Grenoble. During the following seasons, they performed and recorded Gluck's *Armide*, Handel's *Ariodante*, Charpentier's *Te Deum*, Rameau's *Dardanus* and Handel's "Roman" motets. The original soundtrack of *Le Messie*, a film by William Klein, was released in 2000.

In 1998/1999, they recorded *Iphigénie en Tauride* by Gluck, performed Rameau's difficult *Platée* at the Opéra national de Paris and at the *Salzburger Pfingstfestspiele*. They also presented their interpretation of Monteverdi's *L'incoronazione di Poppea* at the Festival international d'Aix-en-Provence. The ensemble's tour that year took them to Ambronay, Lyon, Poissy, Caen, Utrecht, Amsterdam, Halle, Madrid, and Santiago di Compostela. In 1999/2000, they toured throughout Europe with Magdalena Kozená performing Handel's "Italian" cantatas and *Hercules*, with Anne Sofie von Otter, as well as J.S. Bach's *Orchestra Suites*. They also presented a revival of *L'incoronazione di Poppea* at the Festival international d'Aix-en-Provence and the Wiener Festwochen.

The 2000/2001 season features productions of Offenbach's *La Belle Hélène* at the *Théâtre du Châtelet* in Paris, Handel's *Ariodante* at the Opéra national de Paris with Anne Sofie von Otter, as well as a revival of *Platée* in Geneva, Montpellier, Metz, Grenoble and Bordeaux. *—John Palmer*

Recommended:

- ○ **Mondonville: 6 Sonates** / Minkowski (cond.), Les Musiciens de Louvre / Archiv 000129802
- ○ **Handel: Italian Cantatas** / Minkowski (cond.), Kožená, Les Musiciens de Louvre / Archiv 469065
- ○ **Rameau: Les Surprises de l'Amour, suite** / Minkowski (cond.), Les Musiciens de Louvre / Erato 45004

Modest Mussorgsky

b. Mar. 21, 1839, Karevo, Pskov, Russia, **d.** Mar. 28, 1881, St. Petersburg, Russia
Composer: Orchestral, Vocal, Keyboard, Opera

His musical education was erratic, he toiled as a civil servant and wrote music only part-time, influenced few if any of his contemporaries, died early from alcoholism, and left a small body of work. Yet Modest Mussorgsky was a towering figure in nineteenth century Russian music. His works exhibit a daring, raw individuality, a unique sound that well-meaning associates tried to conventionalize and smooth over. He is best known for *Night on Bald Mountain* (bowdlerized by Rimsky-Korsakov), *Pictures at an Exhibition* (a difficult piano suite orchestrated by Ravel), and the dark, declamatory opera *Boris Godunov* (polished by Rimsky-Korsakov)—bastardized works all, yet each one full of arresting harmonies, disturbing colors, and grim celebrations of Russian nationalism.

Mussorgsky died in poverty, but he was born to a wealthy landowning family. Under his mother's tutelage, he developed a facility at the piano, but entered a cadet school in preparation for a military career. He joined a choir and discovered Russian church music, which would profoundly influence his later work.

Upon graduation in 1856, Mussorgsky entered the Russian Imperial Guard. That year he started to socialize with the composers Dargomizhsky and Cui, and through them Balakirev, with whom he began composition lessons. During this period he wrote small piano pieces and songs, and after an emotional crisis in 1858 resigned his commission with the intention of composing full-time. He began to go his own way as a composer in 1861, but was preoccupied helping to manage his family's estate. The decline in his family's fortunes led him to accept low-level civil service positions. He joined a commune with other intellectuals and became a proponent of musical Realism, applying the style to his songs. He had difficulty finishing works in larger formats, but his music circulated widely enough that by the late 1860s he was cast with Balakirev, Cui, Rimsky-Korsakov, and Borodin as part of Russia's "Mighty Handful."

Mussorgsky toiled many years at his masterpiece, *Boris Godunov*, which reflected in music the inflections of Russian speech and met with great success in 1874. That year he also produced his innovative piano suite *Pictures at an Exhibition*. Yet his heavy drinking led to his dismissal from government service in 1880. Friends offered some financial help and Mussorgsky occasionally accompanied singers at the piano, but his finances and mental state quickly deteriorated. He died in 1881, leaving it to posterity to sort through and complete his unfinished works of unruly genius. *—James Reel*

ORCHESTRAL

Night on Bald Mountain (Noch' na Lïsoy gore), symphonic poem (1886)

In a July 5, 1867 letter to Nikolay Rimsky-Korsakov, Modest Mussorgsky wrote "(I have) finished *St. John's Night on Bald Mountain*, a musical picture with the following program: (1) assembly of the witches, their chatter and gossip; (2) cortege of Satan; (3) unholy gratification of Satan; and (4) witches' sabbath." Mussorgsky proclaims "in form and character my composition is Russian and original. Its tone is hot and chaotic.... *St. John's Night* is something new and is bound to produce a satisfactory impression...."

The impression was not so satisfactory for Mily Balakirev, who rejected the work in 1869 from consideration for a Free School concert. Balakirev sent the manuscript back to Mussorgsky bearing handwritten marks such as the comment "Rubbish!" in the margins. Later, under the spell of Liszt's *Totentanz*, Mussorgsky considered refashioning the movement as a piano/orchestral work, but nothing came of this plan.

In May 1877, Mussorgsky drew up the scenario of his comic opera *Sorochintsy Fair*, proposing an extensive revision of the *St. John's Night* music as an Intermezzo opening the third act. Mussorgsky completed this part of the opera in 1880, retaining music from (1) and (3) of the original work, and adding new material. Identified as "Dream of the Young Peasant Lad," this also had a new program: as a boy dreams on a hill, he is threatened by inhuman voices and finds himself mocked in the realm of shadows. The voices warn of the Devil and the "Black God" Chernobog; as the shadows fade, both appear. Chernobog is glorified, a Black Mass is sung, and a Witches' Sabbath breaks out. As a church bell intones, Chernobog disappears and the demons writhe in agony. A church choir sings, the demons fade away, awakening the boy. Mussorgsky was never to complete *Sorochintsy Fair*.

In 1867 letter quoted above, Mussorgsky wrote Rimsky-Korsakov "I should like us to examine the orchestration together (...) we might clear up many things." Rimsky-Korsakov fulfilled his end of the bargain in 1886, five years after Mussorgsky's death, in producing *Night on Bald Mountain* (also "Night on the Bare Mountain"). This was the "Lad's Dream" music, minus its choral parts and with its abrupt, dramatic effectual "stings" removed. The first half of the second section was removed, and Rimsky-Korsakov dropped most of the major-key material save a brief fanfare figure. The whole work was subjected to a streamlining of orchestration and meter, and divided into symmetrical sections. Rimsky-Korsakov has often been accused of "composing" the "Matins Bell" section that concludes *Bald Mountain*, but in truth the music is all Mussorgsky's save the final flute trio at the very end. The Rimsky-Korsakov edition was an immediate worldwide success from the day it was launched and helped to establish Mussorgsky's name. It remains the most popular version of Mussorgsky's famous piece, although the original versions are available in modern editions and are revived to acclaim as well. Some conductors, such as Claudio Abbado and Esa-Pekka Salonen, have made personal specialties of the 1867 version. *—Uncle Dave Lewis*

Recommended:

- ○ **Mussorgsky: Pictures at an Exhibition; etc.** / Reiner (cond.), Chicago SO / 1994 / RCA Victor 61958
- ○ **Dukas: Sorcerer's Apprentice; Mussorgsky: Night on Bald Mountain** / Ormandy (cond.), Philadelphia Orch. / 2002 / Sony 89833

Pictures at an Exhibition (Kartinki s vïstavski) (1874)

Mussorgsky composed this music in June 1874. One of Mussorgsky's few unalienated friends was the St. Petersburg artist, architect and stage designer Viktor Hartmann (1834–73), who lived even fewer years than the composer's 42. Vladimir Stasov, librarian and critic, arranged a memorial retrospective of some 400 Hartmann drawings and watercolors. Deeply moved, Mussorgsky wrote a piano suite, one of the few works he actually completed, apart from a trove of songs. Rimsky-Korsakov edited it for publication in 1886, albeit less radically than his gutted versions of *Boris Godunov*, *Khovanshchina*, and *A Night on Bare Mountain*. By 1891, one Mikhail Tushmalov had already orchestrated seven of the ten *Pictures*. In the century since, there have been more than a dozen other versions, but none that challenge the finesse, subtlety, and cumulative impact of Maurice Ravel's (1875–1937), made for Sergey Koussevitzky, who led not only the world and American premieres (the latter with his Boston Symphony in 1926), but the first recording in 1930. Ravel's 1922 orchestration was premiered by Koussevitzky in Paris on October 19, 1923. Ravel was a logical choice, beyond his cachet as France's foremost living composer (a celebrity that cost Koussevitzky 10,000 francs). For the 1913 Paris production of *Khovanshchina*, Sergey Diaghilev commissioned him and Stravinsky to score what Rimsky-Korsakov had omitted from his "official version" of 1883.

Scoring for *Pictures* includes triple winds, alto saxophone, two harps, and lots of percussion. Ravel left out only one of the "Promenades" that Stasov called Mussorgsky's self-portraits, which have alternating measures of 5/4 and 6/4 time. The first one, Allegro giusto nel modo russico in B flat, is played by the solo trumpet. "Gnomus" comes next at a lively tempo—a nutcracker drawn in the shape of a gnome—followed by a contemplative "Promenade" that sets up "The Old Castle," drawn during Hartmann's student years in Italy. Its sad song in G sharp minor is played by the alto saxophone.

A more heavily scored "Promenade" introduces "Tuileries," the famous Parisian garden, with winds reproducing the "dispute of children after play" in B major. "Bydlo" with solo tuba follows lumberingly in duple meter—Hartmann's sketch of a Polish ox-cart on large wooden wheels. Following a "tranquil" "Promenade" for winds and low-strings, "Ballet of the Chicks in Their Shells" is a "scherzino" in F major, illustrating children's' costumes from which legs protrude.

"Samuel Goldenberg and Schmuyle" was Stasov's euphemistic title for a pair of drawings Hartmann called "Two Polish Jews, one rich, one poor." While Goldenberg pontificates weightily, the solo trumpet natters obsequiously in triplets. The ensuing "Marketplace at Limoges" is another scherzino, where marketing women gossip and quarrel.

Without pause, solemn brass chords transport us to "Catacombs" beneath Paris, where Hartmann sketched himself and two companions. The scene continues with "Cum mortuis in lingua morta": "skulls begin to glow dimly from within." Another "Promenade," in effect a "Requiescat," leads to "The Hut on Fowl's Legs," a clock shaped as the witch Baba Yaga's hut, from which she flies astride a mortar, used to mash human bones into paste. "The Great Gate of Kiev" concludes without a break—a contest design commemorating Tsar Aleksandr's escape from assassins. On one side is a bell tower, and in the middle a cupola shaped like an old Bogatir helmet. Processional music in E flat includes a grandiose expansion of the "Promenade" theme, leading to an awesome climax punctuated by bass drum, tubular bells, and tam-tam. *—Roger Dettmer*

Recommended:

- ○ **Mussorgsky: Pictures at an Exhibition** / Gergiev (cond.), Vienna PO / 2002 / Philips 468526
- ○ **Mussorgsky: Pictures at an Exhibition; Kodaly: Háry János Suite** / Szell (cond.), Cleveland Orch. / 1992 / Sony 48162
- ○ **Mussorgsky: Pictures at an Exhibiton; Stravinsky: Rite of Spring** / Muti (cond.), Philadelphia Orch. / 2001 / EMI 74742

St. John's Night on the Bare Mountain (Ivanova noch' na Lisoy gore), symphonic poem (1867)

Like nearly every piece Mussorgsky wrote, the compositional history of *Night on Bald Mountain* is convoluted to the point of near total confusion.

The work was first mentioned by the 19-year-old Mussorgsky on Christmas Day 1858 when he and his brother and a few other friends including Mussorgsky's composition teacher Mily Balakirev, proposed a three-act opera on the subject of Gogol's *St. John's Eve*. A year and a half later, Mussorgsky writes to Balakirev to tell him that he has been commissioned "to set to music of whole of act of [Baron] Mengden's drama *The Witch* depicting a witches' Sabbath on *St. John's Night*." There is not, however, any trace of either a commission nor a drama by Mengden called *The Witch*. Six years later, Mussorgsky mentions the piece again, this time as an orchestra tone-poem, in a letter dated April 20, 1866, to Balakirev: "I have started outlining the witches. Got into trouble. Satan's journey does not please me yet."

After completing the original version of the work on June 23, 1867, now called *St. John's Night*, that is, midsummer night, the night of the witches' Sabbath, Mussorgsky wrote the following description of the work to Rimsky-Korsakov, his friend and fellow composition student with Balakirev:

"All your favorite bits came off splendidly in the scoring. In the Black mass there is a bit in B minor (the witches glorifying Satan), thoroughly foul and barbarous.... The form is rather original.... The whole thing is fiery, brisk, close-knit without German transactions. In my opinion *St. John's Night* is something new, and ought to produce a satisfactory impression on any thinking musician."

Mussorgsky also wrote a description of the work to his friend Professor Nikolsky:

"My *St. John's Night on the Bald Mountain* (A far better title than *The Witches*) is, in form and character, Russian and original;... I wrote it very quickly[!], straightaway in full score without preliminary rough drafts, in twelve days. It seethed within me, and I worked day and night, hardly knowing what was happening within me. And now I see in my sinful prank an independent Russian product, free from German profundity and routine, and, like my *Savishna* (the song *O Darling Savishna!*), grown on our country's soil and nurtured on Russian bread.

At the head of my score I've put its contents: 1. Assembly of the witches, their talk and gossip; 2. Satan's journey; 3. Obscene praises of Satan [titled in the score Black mass]; and 4. Sabbath.... The form and character of composition are both Russian and original."

The original *St. John's Night* is indeed wholly Russian and highly original. Compared with Rimsky's tepid reorchestration and turgid recomposition, it is an infinitely more characteristic and effective work. *—James Leonard*

Recommended:

- ○ **Moussorgsky: Pictures at an Exhibition, etc.** / Gergiev (cond.), Vienna PO / 2002 / Philips 468526
- ○ **Claudio Abbado Conducts Mussorgsky** / Abbado (cond.), London SO / 1981 / RCA 61354
- ○ **Modest Mussorgsky** / Maazel (cond.), Berlin PO / DG 469169

VOCAL

Gopak (Hopak), song (1866)

Modest Mussorgsky completed his song, *Hopak* (also known as *Gopak*) on August 31, 1866. The lyrics are based on a text entitled "The Haidamaks" by Taras Schevchenko, originally in Ukrainian; Mussorgsky used a translation into Russian by Lvov Mey. Three days later Mussorgsky composed the song *Lovely Savishna*, and dedicated *Hopak* to Nikolay Rimsky-Korsakov and *Savishna* to Cesar Cui. Both songs were heard in the St. Petersburg-based salons of the "mighty handful" held in the fall of 1866, and both were published in early 1867, although *Savishna* was banned by the Russian censor.

These songs were Mussorgsky's earliest acknowledged efforts in the realist style he was espousing at the time—a warts-and-all exploration of the Russian soul as seen through its folk culture. In *Hopak*, the narrator is an aged male lute player who sings a woman's song; some writers have suggested that the singer is perhaps an old man dressed up as a woman. "She" opens with a nursery-rhyme-like phrase that is chanted over a pulsating dance rhythm. The pace slows down at the words "vyso chok da chok," and then the singer describes the ironies of marriage in short, declamatory phrases, ending with the exclamation "vot tak" ("that's what!"). After the singer demands that her husband "give up your evil ways and rock that cradle," Mussorgsky adds an interesting and rather dissonant "rocking" accompaniment figure. The singer launches into a sad, nostalgic section that recalls distant memories of the romance and fun she had known in youth. With the repeated syllable "hoy, hoy, hoy, hoy," the song returns to the nursery-rhyme pattern and dancing music of the opening briefly before concluding.

Nikolay Rimsky-Korsakov later recast *Hopak* as a solo song with orchestra. The 1866 song *Hopak* is not to be confused with the famous instrumental *Gopak*, written in 1874 to conclude the first act of Mussorgsky's unfinished opera *Sorochintsy Fair*; this latter "Hopak" was itself later arranged by Lyadov and Rachmaninov. *—Uncle Dave Lewis*

Recommended:

- ○ **Mussorgsky: The Nursery: Sunless; Songs & Dances of Death** / Tzipine (cond.), Christoff, L'Orch. National de la Radiodiffusion Francaise / 2003 / EMI 67997
- ○ **Mussorgsky Songs Vol. 4** / Leiferkus, Skigin / 1997 / Conifer 51274

Mephistopheles' Song of the Flea (1879)

Dating from August-September 1879, Modest Mussorgsky's setting of *Mephistopheles' Song of the Flea* is one of the last-preserved of his compositions. On July 21, 1879, Mussorgsky embarked as accompanist on a hardscrabble tour of southern Russia with aging diva Daria Leonova. Through the end of October, Mussorgsky and Leonova appeared in cities such as Poltava, Odessa, Sevastopol, Yalta, and Tver. While the tour proved ultimately a financial disappointment, Mussorgsky and Leonova reached many audiences that were totally unaware of Russian Nationalist style. The tour also allowed Mussorgsky, who'd operated in a limited geographic range all his life; to see parts of Russia he'd only dreamed of or heard about.

It was during this tour that *Mephistopheles' Song of the Flea* was written by Mussorgsky and first sung by Leonova. It was paired with a newly composed piano piece of Mussorgsky's entitled *Storm on the Black Sea* that is not now extant. Upon the conclusion of the tour, Leonova and Mussorgsky performed in the St. Petersburg salons of the Balakirev circle. *Mephistopheles' Song of the Flea* was an immediate sensation, according to Victor Belayev; "(it) brought an uproar of applause from the audience. Here Mussorgsky's skill in picturesque accompaniment was vividly demonstrated, and at times one could almost hear the flea jump. The audience became so enthusiastic that they all crowded up to the platform...."

Mussorgsky drew his text from scene five of Johann Wolfgang von Goethe's verse play Faust, Part One. Mussorgsky utilized a Russian translation by A. N. Strugovshchikov; the proper title of this song being *Mephistopheles' Song in Auerbach's Tavern* (or Cellar). In the scene, Satan sings a lusty song about a king who lavishes extravagant attention towards a flea in his court. The king calls upon the royal tailor to fashion a velvet caftan and satin gown for the flea, and names the flea to his circle of advisors. Along with the flea comes his "train (of) henchmen," namely "all fleas that are." The ladies of the court have "not a minute's peace" and life at the king's court is ruined.

There is no autograph source for this song in Mussorgsky's hand; this was lost in the chaos that ensued regarding his manuscripts in the months after his death. Fortunately, Mussorgsky's friend and benefactor Vladimir Stasov had the foresight to make his own copy of this music before the original vanished forever.

From Stasov's copy the song was printed shortly after Mussorgsky died, and several orchestrations of the piano part have been prepared, including one by composer Igor Stravinsky made about 1913. *Mephistopheles' Song of the Flea* was most closely associated with the Russian bass-baritone Feodor Chaliapin, who made two recordings of it and included it in recitals given worldwide. Through Chaliapin, *Mephistopheles' Song of the Flea* has become the best known solo song among the 65 written by Mussorgsky. *—Uncle Dave Lewis*

Recommended:

- ○ **Mussorgsky: The Nursery: Sunless; Songs & Dances of Death** / Tzipine (cond.), Christoff, L'Orch. National de la Radiodiffusion Francaise / 2003 / EMI 67997
- ○ **The Chaliapin Edition Vol. 4** / Pitt (cond.), Chaliapin / 2002 / Arbiter 132

The Nursery (Detskaya), song cycle (1868–1872)

This is an immensely sophisticated and masterful song cycle. Mussorgsky was one of the first composers to fashion music from speech patterns, and in least one of the songs in this collection, "The Nanny," that technique is in evidence. He first began to develop this method with the songs "Darling Savishna," "You Drunken Sot," and "The Seminarist," all from 1866. But what Mussorgsky was striving for in "The Nanny" goes beyond mere reproduction of speech sounds: he attempts to express musically the feelings and ideas of the child.

The composer used his own texts in this cycle and the subject matter, of course, deals with the world of children, as the titles of the seven songs suggest: 1) "With Nanny," 2) "In the Corner," 3) "The Beetle," 4) "With the Doll," 5) "At Bedtime," 6) "Riding on a Hobby-Horse," and 7) "Matros the Cat" (also translated as "Sailor the Cat"). Yet, the music is not for children; it is formally, thematically, and harmonically as advanced as almost anything in its genre from that era. In certain ways, these songs are a vocal parallel to Schumann's keyboard collection *Kinderszenen* (Scenes of Childhood) (1838), which also represents an adult view of a children's world. But Mussorgsky's effort here was even more innovative and radical in its time than Schumann's work.

As suggested above, the first song in the cycle, "The Nanny," is the most iconoclastic. It was written just before Mussorgsky embarked on his operatic masterpiece *Boris Godunov*. In "The Nanny," the composer shatters all convention in the realm of song as he depicts an anxious, talkative child in music that pays little heed to thematic, harmonic, and rhythmic traditions. He makes the listener feel the text in vivid, lifelike sounds. In one passage the nervous child intones: "Nanny dear! Surely the reason the bogeyman ate the children is because they were bad to their old nanny, and they didn't listen to their daddy and mommy. . . ." The music is powerful and touching throughout, the words realistic and innocent, the effect astonishing. All this Mussorgsky achieves, and yet the song is the shortest in the collection, typically taking less than two minutes in a performance.

While most of the other items in the set are nearly as effective, they are not quite as uncompromising and are more lyrically inclined. No. 4, "With the Doll," is an attractive lullaby, but with the child acting the role of the Nanny to the "Dolly." The fifth, "At Bedtime," is a prayer of sorts, with the child delightfully rattling off names of aunts and uncles for God to watch over. While humor is sprinkled throughout most of the songs, two in particular that divulge this trait are No. 2, "In the Corner," in which the child pleads innocent to accusations of mischief to his Nanny, then gradually turns bold with her diminishing anger, and No. 6, "Riding on a Hobby-Horse," in which the child animatedly pretends to be riding a toy horse. Nos. 3 ("The Beetle") and 7 ("Matros the Cat") divulge an agitation in the music to accompany the child's adventures with an insect and a pet cat, respectively.

Though less known than Mussorgsky's operas and not often performed in the West due to the language barrier, this must be regarded as among the most important song cycles from the later nineteenth century. *—Robert Cummings*

Recommended:

- ○ **Mussorgsky: The Nursery: Sunless; Songs & Dances of Death** / Christoff, Labinsky / 2003 / EMI 67997
- ○ **Mussorgsky: Song Cycles** / Demidenko, Safiulin / 1995 / Hyperion 66775

Songs & Dances of Death (Pesni y plyaski smerti), song cycle (1875–1877)

Mussorgsky's last cycle *Songs and Dances of Death* was composed in 1877. The texts were by the amateur poet and dramatist Count Arseny Golenishchev-Kutuzov (1848–1913). The first setting, "Cradle Song," portrays a fearful mother's vigil over her dying child. Her dialogue with Death is poignant, but realized with utmost simplicity. We hear Death's insidious refrain "Hush-a-by, hush-a-by" four times, while the piano suggests the rocking of the cradle. Finally, Death announces "Calm your fear and despair! See, through the window peeps the pale morrow." False reassurance conceals his real intention—Death's lullaby calls the child unto himself, with the words "See, there he slumbers . . . my song stilled his pain."

The next song "Serenade" describes a sickly young woman before whom Death appears as a gallant suitor. As the critic Montagu-Nathan writes, "This sinister cavalier prosecutes a brief and horrible courtship . . . Flattering utterances are but a veil that will not long obscure the end." When at the close the melody fades into silence, Death casts aside his disguise with a triumphant cry of "Be still . . . you are mine!"

In No. 3, "Trepak," the accompaniment derives from the ancient Dies irae plainchant, heard in Liszt's *Totentanz* and the *Symphonie Fantastique* of Berlioz, both of which Mussorgsky had heard in St. Petersburg. The accompaniment becomes the theme of the nationalistic "Trepak" danced by Death himself. In a snow-gripped forest, Death meets a drunken peasant, to whom he sings "a song fair and pleasant" before bidding him rest until daybreak.

The last song "The Field-Marshal" was probably inspired by Glinka's setting *Midnight Review*. Written two years after the others, Death is portrayed here as a ghostly commander, now proud in victory, riding through scenes of death and devastation on the battlefield. He summons his loyal victims to form up in parade and pass before him in ghostly review. Death's inexorable march theme quotes the Polish patriotic song "Z dymen pozarow." The original version included a remarkable chord cluster four measures from the close, which does not appear in Rimsky-Korsakov's edition, issued after Mussorgsky's own death in 1881. *—Michael Jameson*

Recommended:

- ○ **Mussorgsky Songs** / Leiferkus, Skigin / 1995 / Conifer 51229
- ○ **Mussorgsky: Complete Songs** / Tzipine (cond.), Christoff, L'Orch. National de la Radiodiffusion Francaise / EMI 63025
- ○ **Songs & Dances of Death** / Gergiev (cond.), Hvorostovsky, Kirov Orch. / 1994 / Philips 438872

Sunless (Bez solntsa), song cycle (1874)

Modest Mussorgsky composed the song cycle *Bez solntsa* (*Sunless*, or, more literally, "Without Sun") on six poems written by his close friend, the poet Arseni Golenishchev-Kutuzov (1848–1913). While the cycle was completed in November 1874, at least one song, "Ennui," was ready by June 2, a date that falls amid the composition of *Pictures at an Exhibition*. This was a time of major ups and downs for Mussorgsky; in January 1874 the premiere of the opera *Boris Godunov* had been given to the acclaim of the Russian public and, to Mussorgsky's dismay, utter rejection by music critics. Several sources make the claim that Mussorgsky spent this period mostly drunk and miserable, but he was also extraordinarily productive in 1874.

The overall mood of *Sunless* is bleak. Speech-like melody is generously applied in more or less literal realizations of Golenishchev-Kutuzov's texts, which deal primarily with insomnia, loneliness, and boredom. In the first three songs, "V chetyryokh stenakh" (Within Four Walls), "Menya ty v tolpe ne uznala" (You Did Not Recognize Me in the Crowd), and "Okonchen prazdny, shummy den" (The Idle, Noisy Day Has Ended), Mussorgsky uses the accompaniment very sparingly, limiting it mostly to single chords and octaves, including some fierce dissonances in "Within Four Walls." Midway in "The Idle, Noisy Day Has Ended," Mussorgsky introduces an accompaniment figure of falling sixths that is vaguely modal; this motive inspired Claude Debussy to borrow it for "Nuages," the first of his three orchestral *Nocturnes*. In "Skuchay" (Ennui) Mussorgsky allows himself a little chromatic phrase that hearkens back to the salon, albeit one that is stood on its head. In the final two settings, "Elegiya" (Elegy) and "Nad rekoy" (On the River), Mussorgsky produces accompaniment that is more in line with what we would expect from a member of the "Mighty Handful," although this too is modal in character and lightly applied. "On the River" makes use of an insistent half step that recalls the music written for Prince Golitsin's journey in Mussorgsky's opera *Khovantschna*.

In the context of the 1870s, Mussorgsky's *Sunless* cycle sounds like something that was beamed in from outer space, as there is hardly anything in it that bears witness to that era. Curiously, in spite of the achievement made here, Mussorgsky and his circle seem to have had an uncharacteristically modest appraisal of the quality of *Sunless*. Mussorgsky's only relevant comment records that the cycle "turned out pretty well." Mussorgsky's patron Vladimir Stasov felt that "Ennui" was "not a first-rate song, but all the same it is one of Mussorgsky's good songs." Composer Alexander Borodin wrote that "[the songs] all remind one of *Boris*, or are the fruit of a purely intellectual invention, and produce a very unsatisfactory impression." Something of Mussorgsky's intentions may be gleaned from a remark that he made to Golenishchev-Kutuzov; "here is nothing more than feeling." In a purely psychological sense, *Sunless* is an absolute rendering of the mental state associated with advanced depression and its symptomatic effects. *—Uncle Dave Lewis*

Recommended:

- ○ **Mussorgsky: The Nursery: Sunless; Songs & Dances of Death** / Christoff, Labinsky / 2003 / EMI 67997
- ○ **Mussorgsky Songs Vol. 2** / Leiferkus, Skigin / 1995 / Conifer 51248
- ○ **Mussorgsky: Without the Sun** / Svetlanov, Gerasimova, State SO of Russia / 1996 / RCA 68406

KEYBOARD

Works for Piano (1852–1880)

Modest Mussorgsky's major piano work is *Pictures at an Exhibition* (1874), a suite of ten musical "pictures" separated by five "promenades" depicting the composer viewing the paintings at a memorial show for Mussorgsky's friend, painter and architect Victor Hartmann (1842–73). Mussorgsky uses a 5/4 time signature for the promenades, frequently harmonizes with bare octaves only, and the "Gnomus," "Ballet of the Unhatched Chicks," and "Baba Yaga" movements make use of a tritone/chromatic harmony that is uniquely Mussorgsky's. Certain aspects of the "Tuileries," "Catacombae," and "Great Gate of Kiev" movements look forward to emerging trends in French music that appeared later in the nineteenth century. *Pictures at an Exhibition* was little-known before the advent of Maurice Ravel's 1922 orchestration, but since then the original piano work has become standard fare at recitals and competitions. Much less known are a small number of occasional compositions belonging to Mussorgsky's catalog. Reviewing a number of sources, it appears that 16 or 17 pieces exist independently from the *Pictures*, with several scores having been lost, or perhaps never written down. At least six of the pieces belong to the general category of "childhood memories"; *Nanny and I* and *First Punishment* (both 1865) are so designated within a cycle, *Souvenirs d'enfance*. A work sometimes designated as *Souvenir d'enfance No. 3* is a much earlier piece (1857) bearing this same title. Of these, *First Punishment* is the most impressive, scored as a virtuoso work stated in rapid octaves and abrupt, dissonant chords, representing its ominous program "Nanny shuts me up in a dark room." This group is rounded out by *Jeux d'enfants* (Hide and Seek, in two versions [1859] and [1860]), *La capricieuse* (Mischievous Girl [1865]) and *La couturiére* (The Seamstress [1870–72]). A single work, *Porte-Enseigne Polka* (Ensign Polka [1852]) is Mussorgsky juvenilia, written when he was 13. This lively yet insubstantial piece of pop music was published through the influence of a well-meaning relative, but only served as a source of embarrassment for the composer in later years. Among other early surviving pieces, the *Intermezzo in modo Classico* (1861) is a peasant scene orchestrated by Mussorgsky in 1867, and there is a *Scherzo in C sharp minor* (1858). Another group of piano pieces falls into a "salon" category, comprising four works. Of *Impromptu Passioné* (1859), *Reverie* (1865), *Meditation* (1880), and *Une larme* (A Tear [1880]), the *Impromptu* is best known, but *Une larme* is the most interesting. Two more works relate directly to Mussorgsky's impressions while touring the Crimea with singer Daria Leonova in 1879: *Bayadariki* (Canoes) and *Gorzuf at Ayu-Dagh* (both 1879–80). Of these two, *Gorzuf at Ayu-Dagh* has fascinating outer sections reminiscent of the language of *Pictures*, as Mussorgsky states in octave a theme which combines chromatic and whole-tone scales. A third work in this group, *Storm on the Black Sea*, is not extant. Another work, *In the Village* (1880), appears in the same publication as the Crimea pieces, but is apparently unrelated. *—Uncle Dave Lewis*

Recommended:

- ○ **Mussorgsky: Complete Piano Works Vol. 1** / Kavtaradze / 2000 / Danacord 551
- ○ **Moussorgsky: L'Oeuvre Complète pour piano** / Carbonel / 2003 / Skarbo 1037

Pictures at an Exhibition (Kartinki s vïstavski) (1874)

Victor Hartmann, a Russian painter and architect, was one of Mussorgsky's close friends. When Hartmann died in St. Petersburg in 1873 at the age of 41, the composer was crushed. He wrote to the art critic Vladimir Stasov, paraphrasing Shakespeare: "Why should a dog, a horse, a rat have life, and the Hartmanns perish?" In January 1874, the Russian Academy of Arts organized an exhibition of Hartmann's work. Mussorgsky attended the show, where he saw the varied images that became the basis for *Pictures of an Exhibition*. On June 2, Mussorgsky began work on *Pictures*, a musical impression of ten of Hartmann's paintings (plus five "promenades") for piano, and finished the work later in the same month.

Pictures of an Exhibition opens with a "Promenade" in 5/4 that serves as a unifying device throughout; it is a portrayal of the composer himself walking from one painting to the next. The first picture is "Gnomus," inspired by a design for a toy nutcracker that Hartmann drew in 1869. Another promenade is followed by "The Old Castle," a mysterious, lonely evocation built on pedal tones. "Tuileries" is inspired by a watercolor of children at play in the garden of the Tuileries. This bright and impressionistic piece is followed by the heavy tread of "Bydlo" (a Polish oxcart). Mussorgsky's setting of "Ballet of the Unhatched Chicks" is a wildly imaginative scherzo. A stern melody in a Jewish-music-derived scale opens "Samuel Goldberg and Schmuyle," in which a wealthy Jew is portrayed by an insistent repeating figure in the treble, a poor Jew in the bass. The rapid patter of haggling housewives characterizes "The Market Place in Limoges." In another sudden change in mood, "Catacombs," which pictures Hartmann himself touring a vast catacomb of skulls, is rendered in naked chord progressions. "The Hut on Fowl's Legs (Baba-Yaga)" was inspired by Hartmann's design for a fourteenth century-style clock in the shape of a witch's hat. Mussorgsky transforms it into a miniature tone poem about Baba Yaga, the legendary Russian witch who devoured the souls of children. After a grand flourish, the work ends with "The Great Gate of Kiev," inspired by a never-implemented design Hartmann submitted to an architecture competition. *Pictures of an Exhibition* comes to a close with rich, booming chords which evoke bells.

Although Mussorgsky is known to have played *Pictures of an Exhibition* in recital, the work did not appear in print until 1886, five years after the composer's death. It remained relatively little known until Ravel made a colorful orchestration of it in 1922, and in this form it has enjoyed even greater popularity than the original. *—Uncle Dave Lewis*

Recommended:

- ○ **The Sofia Recital, 1958** / Richter / 2001 / Philips 464734
- ○ **Mussorgsky: Pictures at an Exhibition; Ravel: Vales Nobles & Sentimentales** / Pogorelich / 1997 / DG 437667
- ○ **Noriko Ogawa Plays Mussorgsky** / Ogawa / 1997 / Bis 905

OPERA

Boris Godunov (Rimsky-Korsakov edition) (1896–1908)

Nikolay Rimsky-Korsakov's contact with Modest Mussorgsky's opera *Boris Godunov* came quite literally as it was written. Rimsky-Korsakov and Mussorgsky had shared the same worktable as both *Boris* and Rimsky-Korsakov's opera *The Maid of Pskov* were composed. After Mussorgsky's death in 1881, and long after *Boris Godunov* had been a success at the Mariinsky Theater, Rimsky-Korsakov undertook a general review of the quality of Mussorgsky's work in regard to its orchestration. Rimsky-Korsakov's assessment of Mussorgsky's orchestral ability was not particularly favorable; in letters Rimsky-Korsakov writes of Mussorgsky's "unbelievably bad voice leading," his propensity toward thick textures, uneven rhythmic patterns, and, by Rimsky-Korsakov's own standards, questionable harmonic practices.

In terms of refashioning the music of *Boris Godunov*, Rimsky-Korsakov initially limited himself to an arrangement made in 1886 of the Act One Prelude and Act Three Polonaise, neatly dovetailed together as a sort of overture. In 1891, Rimsky-Korsakov re-scored the Coronation Scene, and six years later his first edition of *Boris Godunov* was staged. Rimsky-Korsakov had, by this time, made deep cuts in the score and had switched the running order of the last two scenes. Rimsky-Korsakov proclaimed "For the present, there is need of an edition for performances, for practical artistic purposes, for making Mussorgsky's colossal talent known, and not for the mere studying of his personality and artistic sins." Rimsky-Korsakov clearly viewed *Boris Godunov* as being non-performable in its original state, despite that the opera had already been given 22 times from Mussorgsky's own score.

Rimsky-Korsakov returned to *Boris* in 1906 at the request of Sergei Diaghilev, who was looking for a version to use in Paris with the Bolshoi Opera and its formidable Russian bass, Feodor Chaliapin. In this instance, Rimsky-Korsakov restored some of the cuts, but elected to rewrite some of the music himself. This became the version the whole world came to know, and was the performance standard even in Russia until the 1970s. It is certainly an impressive piece of work, fitted with a gorgeous, sweeping orchestration and generous melody for the singers. But it is far different from Mussorgsky's original conception, with its speech-like vocal lines and its disdain for accepted notions of scoring and dramaturgy.

"If for some reason in the future my *Boris Godunov* should be determined as inferior to the original, then by all means, I invite you to discard it" Rimsky-Korsakov once stated, perhaps a bit facetiously. Rimsky-Korsakov would doubtless express surprise to know that it has been indeed "discarded" in Russia, toppled like statues of Lenin after the collapse of the Soviet Union. Post-Soviet audiences seem to prefer the short, 1869 version best of the three *Boris Godunovs*. However, Rimsky-Korsakov's conception of the opera maintains a stronghold in the West, and perhaps this is appropriate, as Gerald Abraham stated in 1945, "both (Rimsky-Korsakov and Mussorgsky versions of *Boris*) are masterpieces." *—Uncle Dave Lewis*

Synopsis:

Prologue. The story is set in Russia and Poland from 1598 to 1605. In the courtyard of the Novodevichy Monastery, the Boyars, led by Prince Shuisky, have instigated a demonstration in support of Boris Godunov's ascension to the throne. However, Andrei Tchelkalov, Duma Secretary, announces Godunov will not accept the crown. In the second scene, Godunov relents and a grand coronation is held.

Act One. Five years later, the elderly monk Pimen, in his Chudov Monastery cell, is finishing his history of Russia. The novice monk Grigory learns from Pimen how Godunov ordered the assassination of Dmitri, brother of (the preceding) Tsar Fyodor, and rightful heir to the throne. Alone, Grigory expresses revulsion at Godunov's crime and determines to leave the monastic life.

At an inn near the Lithuanian border, Grigory, in disguise and on the lam from police for fleeing the monastery, converses with two inebriated monks, Varlaam and Missail. Grigory, intent on exposing Godunov, has decided he will flee to Lithuania and claim to be Dmitri so as to depose Godunov. An illiterate policeman enters with a warrant for Grigory, but when Grigory deceives him into believing the warrant pertains to Varlaam, he is able to escape.

Act Two. After his daughter Xenia is consoled by her nurse over her betrothed's death, Godunov tells his son Fyodor he will be his father's successor. Prince Shuisky, whom Godunov despises, soon arrives with news that a pretender to the throne, claiming to be Dmitri, has surfaced in Poland and garnered the support of both the Pope and Polish aristocracy. Godunov informs Shuisky that he will forgive his past intrigues if he can honestly assure him that Dmitri was assassinated. Shuisky pledges that he was. After the Prince departs, Godunov is horror-stricken by a vision of Dmitri.

Act Three. In her apartments, the Polish Princess Marina Mnishek plots ascension to the Russian throne via marriage to the pretender Dmitri. The Jesuit Rangoni enters and prevails upon her to carry out her most important duty: once in power, she must convert the wayward Russians to Roman Catholicism.

In the gardens outside, Rangoni reassures Dmitri of Mnishek's love for him. Later, Dmitri and Mnishek proclaim their mutual love, but only after the latter has forced Dmitri to declare his intentions to become Tsar.

Act Four. (In both his versions, Rimsky-Korsakov reversed the order of the final act's two scenes from Mussorgsky's original, as follows. Rimsky-Korsakov's first *Boris Godunov* contained substantial cuts, which were restored in the second version.)

The peasants taunt the boyar Khruschov, asking him if he enjoys the kind of mistreatment the poor have endured under Godunov. Varlaam and Missail soon appear to rally the crowd in support of Dmitri and to bring death to Godunov. Two Jesuit priests are captured and held for hanging. Dmitri appears with his army and gains the support of the crowd in his drive on Moscow.

At the Kremlin, the Duma meets to discuss strategies to deal with the invasion and how to punish Dmitri. Prince Shuisky interrupts the proceedings with a harrowing account of the now-deranged Godunov, who is overcome with visions of the deceased Dmitri. Godunov enters declaring Shuisky should be executed for such untruths, but the latter convinces Godunov to meet with Pimen. Pimen assures Godunov that Dmitri is dead, but the news merely causes Godunov to descend to greater despair. Aware he is dying, Godunov sends for his son, and when they are alone, he tells him the throne belongs to him. Godunov bids farewell and dies. *—Robert Cummings*

Recommended:

- ○ **Mussorgsky: Boris Godunov** / Gergiev (cond.), Borodina, Pluzhnikov, Gassiev, Laptev, Kirov Opera & Orch. / 1998 / Philips 462230
- ○ **Mussorgsky: Boris Godunov** / Melik-Pashaev (cond.), London, Arkhipova, Ktitorov, Ivanov, Bolshoi Theatre Orch. / 2002 / Sony 52571
- ○ **Mussorgsky: Boris Godunov** / Cluytens (cond.), Christoff, Lear, Mars, Lanigan, Orch. de la Société des Concerts du Conservatoire / 2002 / EMI 67881

Khovanshchina (1872–1880)

Khovanshchina (The Khovansky Affair) was Modest Mussorgsky's final opera, left unfinished at the time of this death in March of 1881. Inconsistencies among the variety of completed editions makes pinning down its essential nature difficult. Ironically, this dramatic and musical malleability is perhaps what best suits *Khovanshchina* to its subject matter, namely the ascension of Tsar Peter I ("The Great"). Depending on one's perspective, the changes he wrought were either the most beneficial or most tragic in Russia's history, and, depending on which version of *Khovanshchina* one encounters in performance, one either leaves with a sense of emerging optimism or a sense of desperate resignation.

Khovanshchina takes its name from the two Khovansky princes, Ivan and Andrey, whose *Strel'tsï* musketeers rose up against the new Tsar in 1689. However, the adoption of their family name for the work's title is potentially misleading; while the drama is related through the eyes of the three principle groups that opposed Peter's reign (the Khovanskys, the schismatics ["Old Believers"], and the family of Peter's older brother), the Tsar himself and his historical legacy are clearly the focus of the opera. Had censorship not explicitly proscribed the depiction of Russian royalty on stage, *Khovanshchina* would have taken a very different shape, and most likely a different name.

Vladimir Vasil'yevich Stasov compiled the libretto from various historical documents, and the resulting text remains truthful, in the broad sense, to history. However, there is no attempt to recreate the specific events therein; rather, the various figures and events are used as raw material for the invention of appropriately operatic scenes. The most conspicuous liberty was the character of Marfa, who is a member of the schismatic sect, the lover of Andrey Khovansky, and a fortune teller with influence over Ivan's chief agent, Prince Golitsïn. Completely a work of fiction, she is the only character in the opera who has ties to all three factions, and as such she takes on a unique dramatic importance. Stasov most likely invented her to compensate for his inability to depict the Tsar himself—the work's only true common thread—on stage.

Mussorgsky conceived of *Khovanshchina* in six scenes, the last two of which only survive as sketches; they form matched pairs, so that each of the three opposition factions receives two—one in which they are seen plotting against Peter, and one in which they meet their demise. For its 1886 premiere, Rimsky-Korsakov completed and orchestrated the work, and cast it into the five-act form that has become standard; this edition was subsequently used for its 1911 revival and Maurice Ravel and Igor Stravinsky's own 1913 revision. In his completion, Rimsky-Korsakov recycled some of the more uplifting passages from the orchestral prelude for use in the final scene, in which the "Old Believers"—those who advocated the return to a church-based government—leave to commit ritual suicide in protest of Peter's ascension. By doing this, Rimsky-Korsakov gave the ending a philosophical "shot in the arm" by suggesting that, despite the upheaval that accompanied Peter's reign, the resulting "modern era" of Russian society was worth the price. There is evidence from Mussorgsky's correspondence that he never intended this, but rather wanted the disenfranchised believers' sacrifice to speak to a greater sense of national loss. In 1952, Dmitri Shostakovich fashioned an entirely new version of the score for use in a film version. This new score was published in 1963, and has been used for a number of modern performances; it is arguably more representative of Mussorgsky's dramatic intentions. *—Allen Schrott*

Synopsis:

Act One. As the opera begins, Russia has been shaken up in the wake of Peter the Great's headlong effort to Westernize the entire country. One of the most tragic results is the plight of the "Old Believers," since religious reforms are part of Peter's agenda. Prince Ivan Khovansky supports the Old Believers, whose ranks include Dositheus, their leader, and Marfa, a mystic. The clannish Streltsy serve as Ivan Khovansky's bodyguard. Ivan's main political opponent is the Boyar Shaklovity.

After a lovely Prelude, morning activity begins in Red Square, where members of the Streltsy talk about a clash that occurred the previous night. Shaklovity has a scribe write a forged letter to implicate Ivan Khovansky in a plot against the throne. Ivan himself appears and addresses his followers with a speech that opposes the Tsar's policies. A German girl, Emma, later appears as she is trying to escape the unwelcome advances of Ivan's son, Andrei. She is protected by Marfa, who had previously been seduced by Andrei. When Andrei appears, Marfa enters a trance and prophecies a sad fate for him. Ivan reappears and has Emma arrested, and father and son quarrel bitterly over her.

Act Two. This act also contains a prophecy, but now it is Galitsyn who receives a dire warning from Marfa. Despite his Western education, Galitsyn remains superstitious and summons her. Her prediction of poverty and sorrow enrages him, and he orders her drowned.

Act Three. Marfa, who has escaped, recalls her love for Andrei. Shaklovity appears in the now-deserted street and prays for the future of his troubled country. The Streltsy return, but are soon greeted by the unwelcome news that the planned revolt by Tsar Peter's guard has failed: The Tsar has returned to Moscow with his bodyguards and foreign mercenary troops and has won the struggle against the forces of Old Russia.

Act Four. Ivan is trying to divert the followers with a banquet. Shakovity appears to summon Ivan before the council. Upon leaving his house, Ivan is stabbed to death. In the second scene, the people lament as Galitsyn is sent off into exile, fulfilling Marfa's prophecy. In Scene Three news comes that the mercenaries have been ordered to surround the Old Believers to their church and execute them. Dositheus decides that they should protest by an act of self-immolation and charges Marfa to bring Prince Andrei with them. When Andrei learns that Emma has safely married her beloved, he curses Marfa as a witch and sends orders for the Streltsy to put her to death. However, the Streltsy are already in custody and marching to the execution site. At the last moment, though, word arrives of the Tsar's clemency, and they are pardoned.

Act Five. The act portrays the self-sacrifice of the Old Believers, who have built a funeral pyre for themselves, for their faith. Dositheus bids them be steadfast in their beliefs. Moved by their faith and Marfa's devotion, Prince Andrei also mounts the pyre, which is set ablaze, to the horror of the approaching troops. The Old Believers continue their chanting until overcome by the flames. An era has passed, and a new day in Russia dawns to pealing trumpets. *—Joseph Stevenson*

Recommended:

- ○ **Mussorgsky: Kovanschina** / Gergiev (cond.), Borodina, Gassiev, Galusin, Minjelkiev, Tselovalnik, Kirov Opera & Orch. / 1992 / Philips 432147
- ○ **Mussorgsky: Kovanschina** / Abbado (cond.), Hossfeld, Zednik, Haugland, Lipovsek, Vienna State Opera Orch. / DG 429758

Sorochintsï Fair (Sorochinskaya yarmarka) (1874–1880)

Mussorgsky's comic opera *The Fair at Sorochinsky* has as confusing a compositional history as its sister opera, the historical tragedy *Khovanshchina.* And, like *Khovanshchina, The Fair at Sorochinsky* remained incomplete at his death.

Mussorgsky first mentioned *The Fair* in a letter to Lubov Karmalina in the summer of 1874: "In the air sounds the command 'draw in the reins' and *Khovanshchina* will appear (if it is destined to) later, and before it a comic opera, *The Fair at Sorochinsky,* after *Gogol,* will be done." Mussorgsky recognized that his aesthetic of "truth in art" would require that he learn how to compose not only an opera using Ukrainian folk tune (*Sorochinsky* is located in what Russians called "Little Russia," which is now called the Ukraine), but also how to compose music to fit the speech patterns of Ukrainians. Nevertheless, he thought that composing a comic opera would be an appropriate way to relax and stretch between work on two tragic operas: "In a word, my work is well in hand."

As was usual for Mussorgsky's working methods, he did not write the libretto out, but rather outlined the plot and wrote the words as he went along. He also choose not to start with the first of the three projected acts, but rather to start in the central act. While working on *The Fair*, he decided to return to *Khovanshchina* and then back to *The Fair* and so on until the winter of 1881. When he died in March 1881, Mussorgsky left *The Fair* for the most part unfinished: much of the first act was complete in piano-vocal score, most of the second act was complete in piano-vocal score with the intermezzo of a choral version of *St. John's Night on Bald Mountain* completed in full score, but most of the third act was only roughed out or simply left as a few themes based on Ukrainian folk songs. Various composers have over time attempted to complete *The Fair*, among them Lyadov, Cui, and Tcherepnin. The most accepted version is Vissarion Shebalin (1931).

The Fair at Sorochinsky is an extension of the comic songs of the late 1860s (*O Darling Savishna!*) and the completed first act of *The Marriage*. The melodies are based in Ukrainian folk tunes and are crafted into a style which might be called heightened recitative which at times becomes lyrical. It is a peasant opera and Mussorgsky's humor is sometimes crude and often broad, but it is always appropriately mirrored in the music. While it is difficult to judge from Shebalin's completion the opera what it would have been if it had it been completed by Mussorgsky, Shebalin's version does hold together as a stage work. One would like to believe that Mussorgsky, had he not been in the final years of his slow death from alcoholism, might have been able to create a wholly successful and wholly characteristic type of Russian comic opera. *—James Leonard*

Synopsis:

Act One. The story is set in the nineteenth century, in Velikiye Sorochintsi, Ukraine, a village near Poltava. Cherevik arrives at the fair with his daughter Parassia. The young Gritzko and his friends are also present to observe the bustle and variety of the vendors and their goods. The lively crowd soon focuses on an old gypsy, who cautions onlookers that a devil, in search of his red jacket, has cursed the grounds. Cherevik becomes displeased that Gritzko has started courting his daughter, but when he learns the young man is an old friend's son, he grants him permission to marry her. After an inebriated Cherevik leaves a tavern that evening, his wife Khivria (step-mother to Parassia) encounters him and chides him. She insists that he refuse permission for Parassia's marriage to Gritzko, who overhears their conversation.

Gritzko becomes disheartened at her words, but when the old gypsy offers to fix things in exchange for lower oxen prices, he happily accepts the proposal.

Act Two. At the home of Cherevik's friend Kum, where they are living, Cherevik and Khivria have an argument and the former departs. Khivria had instigated the quarrel in hopes of driving Cherevik off, because she is planning a rendezvous there with her lover, Afanasy Ivanovich, son of the local priest. The young man soon arrives, and the two begin an amorous encounter, but Cherevik, Kum, and others barge in, and Afanasy Ivanovich barely manages to hide in time. Cherevik explains that the red jacket has been seen, and also the devil himself, carrying a pig's snout. They all drink to bolster their courage and then Kum recounts the story of the red jacket.

When he is finished a pig's snout is hurled into the house through an open window. All are startled, including Afanasy Ivanovich, who comes out of hiding thereby betraying his affair with Khivria.

Act Three. As Cherevik and Kum scramble, the old gypsy, accompanied by several young peasants, enters to accuse Cherevik of stealing. Gritzko appears and proposes that the charges against Cherevik and his friend be dropped, provided he is allowed to marry Parassia. Cherevik agrees and all depart except the triumphant Gritzko, who sits down beneath a tree and falls asleep. His mind conjures a fantastic demonic dream, featuring Chernobog, the devil, conducting a Witches' Sabbath.

The next morning Cherevik joins his daughter for a moment of merriment to celebrate her forthcoming marriage to Gritzko. Soon Kum and Gritzko appear and Cherevik offers his blessing to Parassia's forthcoming marriage. Khivria attempts to disrupt the proceedings, but the old gypsy drags her off and the story ends happily. (Because Mussorgsky left the opera incomplete, several completed versions appeared, including ones by Tcherepnin, Lamm, and Sakhnovsky. Some events in them, especially in the last act, appear in different order or are eliminated altogether.) *—Robert Cummings*

Riccardo Muti

b. Jul. 28, 1941, Naples, Italy

Conductor

One of the best-known conductors of recent times, Riccardo Muti is revered for charismatic, brilliant renderings of both concert and operatic repertoire. His father was a physician with a natural vocal talent who supported Riccardo's interest in music by giving him his initial piano and voice lessons. Muti then undertook formal musical studies at the Conservatorio di Musica San Pietro a Majella in Naples, where he earned a diploma in piano; his teachers there included Nino Rota, the well-known composer of film and concert music. Muti's education continued with studies in composition and conduction at the Verdi Conservatory in Milan, and a conducting seminar with Franco Ferrara in Venice.

Muti first came to widespread public attention as the winner of the prestigious Guido Cantelli Conducting Prize in 1967. Soon after that, he made his official debut, conducting the Italian Radio and Television Orchestra. He quickly became a sought-after guest conductor, and his successes in that capacity led to his first full-time appointment in 1970, as principal conductor of the Maggio Musicale of Florence.

All the while, Muti maintained a busy schedule of high-profile engagements, including annual appearances at the Salzburg Festival (beginning in 1971), and with the Berlin Philharmonic (1972). That year, he became principal conductor of the London Philharmonic (succeeding Otto Klemperer) and made his first appearance in the United States with the Philadelphia Orchestra. With the retirement of Eugene Ormandy in 1980, Muti becamee the Philadelphia Orchestra's music director. That proved to be the most illustrious and fruitful of Muti's professional associations, extending beyond his resignation in 1990 to a post as laureate conductor. Some have observed that Muti pushed the fabled "Philadelphia sound" toward increased brightness and incisiveness while preserving the ensemble's singular luster.

Before taking the helm of the Philadelphia Orchestra, Muti continued his journey toward international stardom in posts with the New Philharmonia Orchestra, and the Vienna State Opera. During his tenure in Philadelphia, In 1986 Muti also assumed the music directorship of La Scala, eventually becoming one of the few conductors to succeed equally in operatic and concert realms. His 1974 recordign of *Aida* with Plácido Domingo and Montserrat Caballé is a classic of the operatic genre. Muti has proven himself particularly versatile in operatic repertoire, excelling in interpretations of Mozart, the Italian Romantics, Wagner, and the masterpieces of the twentieth century. Of a 2003 live CD release of a La Scala production of *Tosca* that Muti conducted, *Opera News* noted that the maestro "keeps things moving along with his usual admirable fidelity." *—AMG*

Recommended:

- ○ **Cherubini: Messes pour les ceremonies royales** / Muti (cond.), Ambrosian Singers, Philharmonia, London PO / 2003 / EMI 585258
- ○ **Mussorgsky: Pictures; Stravinsky: Rite of Spring** / Muti (cond.), Philadelphia Orch. / 2001 / EMI 74742
- ○ **Busoni, Casella, Martucci** / Muti (cond.), La Scala Theater Orch. / 1993 / Sony 53280

Anne-Sophie Mutter

b. Jun. 29, 1963, Rheinfeldin, Germany

Violinist

One of the most charismatic and best-loved violinists of modern times, Germany's Anne-Sophie Mutter began her studies on the piano at the age of five. She shortly added violin lessons with Erna Hornigberger. In 1970 and again in 1974, she won first place in the Jugend Musiziert contest for young musicians. Herbert von Karajan heard her play at the age of 13 and paved the way for her international career. This began in 1977 with appearances at the Salzburg Festival and with her English debut under Daniel Barenboim. The next year, 1978, she made her debut with the Berlin Philharmonic and released her first recording, of the Mozart Third and Fifth Concertos. In 1980, she debuted in America under Zubin Mehta, then made her first Carnegie Hall recital appearance in 1988. In spite of a difficult personal life (she lost her husband in 1995, leaving her with two small children to care for), Mutter has accelerated an already successful career to the level of super-stardom. She is currently one of the most sought after violinists and her recordings are always eagerly awaited best sellers.

Mutter is best known for her rich tone and her impassioned and exciting performances of the classic violin repertory, but she has also been instrumental in commissioning and performing new works for the violin. Among the composers she has worked with are Wolfgang Rihm, Sebastian Currier, Norbert Moret, Witold Lutosławski, and Krzysztof Penderecki. Both before and after Mutter's marriage to septuagenarian conductor André Previn in 2002, the pair performed and recorded together frequently. *—Steven Coburn*

Recommended:

- ○ **Brahms: Violin Sonatas** / Mutter, Weissenberg / 2001 / EMI 74725
- ○ **Anne-Sophie Mutter: The Berlin Recital** / Mutter, Orkis / 1996 / DG 445826
- ○ **Tchaikovsky: Violin Concerto** / Karajan (cond.), Mutter, Vienna PO / DG 419241
- ○ **Sibelius: Violinkonzert; Serenaden; Humoreske** / Previn (cond.), Mutter, Dresden Staatskapelle / DG 447895
- ○ **Carmen-Fantasie** / Levine (cond.), Mutter, Vienna PO / DG 437544
- ○ **Mutter Modern** / Mutter, etc. / DG 445487
- ○ **Great Violin Concertos** / Karajan (cond.), Mutter, Berlin PO / DG 415565

Claudia Muzio

b. Feb. 7, 1889, Pavia, Italy, **d.** May 24, 1936, Rome, Italy
Soprano

Opera, like any other art form, has its cult figures, typically singers who died young and enacted tragedies, on stage or (sometimes "and") in their own lives. While Maria Callas is probably the best known of these, Claudia Muzio has her own legion of devotees. Like Callas, her voice had a certain veiled tone, one making it near-perfect for tragic heroines; she was an excellent actress and a beautiful woman, and also had some major vocal troubles towards the end of her career, though was still able to thrill audiences by her vocal and physical communication. (There was something of a personal connection as well—Aristotle Onassis had been Muzio's lover earlier in his life, Callas' much later.) Muzio's vocal acting was poignantly subtle, based on colors and shading of her tone, rather than the harsh-toned, uncontrolled shrieks or melodramatic gulping sobs that too often passed (and still do) for dramatic high notes or powerful involvement, and she was known as "the Duse of song," after Eleonora Duse, an actress famed for her intensity. During most of her life she was more or less a recluse, and avoided society.

She came from a background that combined music and drama; her father was an operatic stage director at both the Met and Covent Garden, and her mother an opera house chorister. She studied at an early age with Annetta Casaloni, the mezzo-soprano who created the role of Maddalena in Verdi's *Rigoletto*, in Turin, and made her own operatic debut as Massenet's Manon in Arezzo in 1910; in 1911, she made her first recordings, an aria from *La bohème* and part of *La traviata*. Her La Scala debut was as Desdemona in 1913. This was so successful that a member of the Paris Opera management immediately offered her the same part for the next season, and a representative of the Covent Garden management heard her in rehearsals, and immediately offered her the role of Manon for the next year. However, while she sang several roles during just ten weeks there, that was the only season she sang at Covent Garden; much of the remainder of her career was in Italy and North and South America, especially at the Teatro Colon, where she was known as "La unica."

Her Met debut was as Tosca, in 1916, singing with Enrico Caruso and Antonio Scotti, and she appeared in each season there for the next six years, singing a total of 15 roles and 152 performances, including, in 1918, the role of Georgetta in the world premiere of Puccini's *Il tabarro*. Her Chicago debut was in 1922 as Aida, and she remained there for nine seasons, singing a combination of contemporary (such as Fevrier's Monna Vanna and Ginevra in Giordano's *La cena delle beffe*), and nineteenth century works. She died in Rome, probably from either a rheumatic heart condition or Bright's Disease, though to this day, rumors of suicide persist, as her love life was never a happy one and the stock market crash had affected her finances deeply.

Among the relatively few recordings that she left, her "Del mio amato bene," by Donaudy (available on both EMI and Nimbus recital discs; the listener's choice can be dictated by preference of transferring methods), is an enduring classic, simple, without histrionics, and yet haunting. *—Ann Feeney*

Recommended:

- ○ **Complete Pathé Recordings** / Muzio, Spalding, Howard / 1994 / Romophone 81010
- ○ **Muzio** / Molajoli (cond.), Refice (cond.), Merli / 1990 / Nimbus 7814

Nikolay Myaskovsky

b. Aug. 20, 1881, Novogeorgievsk, Poland, **d.** Aug. 8, 1950, Moscow, Russia
Composer: Concerto

The son of an army engineer who eventually attained the rank of general in the Russian army, composer Nikolay Myaskovsky was expected to follow in his father's footsteps. However, after his mother's death in 1890, Myaskovsky was brought up by his aunt, a former singer, who encouraged his musical interests; his first compositions—piano pieces much influenced by Chopin—date from that time.

In 1903, Myaskovsky took a course in harmony from Reinhold Glière, which helped him decide on a music career. He continued his studies with Nikolay Rimsky-Korsakov and Anatoly Liadov at the St. Petersburg Conservatory (1906–11); his *Symphony No. 1* (1908) won him a scholarship that allowed him to complete his education. Myaskovsky then spent some time as a private teacher and music journalist. During World War I, he served on the front for three years, then worked on military fortifications. Some of those experiences are reflected in his *Symphonies Nos. 4 and 5*, both of which were partially sketched on the front.

In 1921, Myaskovsky became a professor of composition at the Moscow Conservatory, a position he held until his death. He also was appointed assistant director of the music department of the People's Commissariat (1921–22) and editor at the Music Publishing House (1922–31). In later years, he would become a consultant for music broadcasts for the All-Union Radio Committee, and would hold an important position in the Union of Soviet Composers. With his *Symphony No. 6* (1921–23) nationalistic themes entered his music; the Symphony's fourth movement is an evocation of the Russian Revolution. His *Symphony No. 12* (1931–32), written in commemoration of the 50th anniversary of the Revolution, was his first explicitly Soviet work, with its portrait of the past, present, and future of a Russian village.

In 1940, Myaskovsky received an honorary Doctor of Arts degree from the Moscow Conservatory. His *Symphony No. 21* of that year, written for the 50th anniversary of the Chicago Symphony, earned for the composer the first of his three Stalin Prizes and remains perhaps his best-known work. During World War II he was relocated to the Caucasus, later to Tbilisi and Kirghizia. The hardships he experienced didn't prevent him from composing, and he completed two symphonies, a *Cello Concerto*, and other works during those years.

Despite the prominent place he held in Russian musical society and the title of People's Artist he received in 1946, Myaskovsky was one of the composers—along with Sergei Prokofiev, Dmitri Shostakovich, Aram Khachaturian, and others—denounced in 1948 by the Central Committee of the Communist Party for formalism, modernism, and ignoring the needs of the Soviet people and society. He wasn't criticized as harshly as the others, but the frequently pessimistic tone of his music was noted, and he was accused, through his teaching, of injecting "inharmonious music into the Soviet educational system." Myaskovsky was quite ill by this time, but was able to reply in part to the charges made against him with his *Symphony No. 27* (1949–50), which was premiered four months after his death and won him his third, posthumous, Stalin Prize.

Myaskovsky wrote 27 symphonies, 13 string quartets, nine piano sonatas, and a host of other works. Among his many students at the Moscow Conservatory were Aram Khachaturian and Dmitri Kabalevsky; his generosity as a teacher earned for him the nickname "the musical conscience of Moscow." On his death, just eighteen months after his denunciation, he was lauded by the Soviet Council of Ministers as an "outstanding Soviet musical worker and people's artist." *—Chris Morrison*

Overview of Works (1901–1948)

It is probably safe to say that, with the sole exception of the ceaselessly prolific Alan Hovhaness, no twentieth century composer's symphonic output begins to approach that of Nikolay Myaskovsky. Twenty-seven is the final count of his symphonies, and though he also authored large bodies of chamber, solo, and vocal music, it was, and is always, the symphonies that come to mind with the mention of his name. During Myaskovsky's lifetime he was widely considered the finest Soviet symphonist, and in spite of the fact that his fame dwindled rapidly after his death, there are some today who still consider him to be a rung or two above Soviet symphonist poster-boy Dmitri Shostakovich.

Myaskovsky came late to music, and during the first decade of the new century he was still very much feeling his way along, taking lessons and eventually enrolling at the St. Petersburg Conservatory as a pupil of Rimsky-Korsakov in 1906. While Myaskovsky's mastery of orchestration never reached the Rimsky-Korsakov standard, we can hear in Myaskovsky's mature music a very Russian seriousness and refinement, something near and dear to Rimsky-Korsakov's own heart. Still, during these early years Myaskovsky was trying to write very complicated music, progressive stuff quite unlike the music of his maturity. Myaskovsky's *Symphony No. 1 in C minor*, Op. 3, dates from 1908 and is predated only by two song cycles: *Reflections* (1907) and *From Youthful Years* (1903–06), Op. 1 and Op. 2, respectively. After World War I, his style began to change. Myaskovsky's experiences at the front had, naturally, not been pleasant ones, and he poured them into the *Symphonies Nos. 4, 5,* and to a certain degree *6* (collectively, 1917–23). The Communist Party heard a musical voice that seemed ideally suited to carry their banner in Myaskovsky's straightforward, passionate, but direct, devoid of empty rhetoric orchestral essays. This didn't completely deter Myaskovsky from experimenting—some of the 1920s pieces (which include *Symphonies Nos. 6–10*) contain startling moments—but, over time, a plainer Myaskovsky style took over: diatonic, square and strong, but melodically and thematically flexible all the same.

Myaskovsky loved the traditional, "pure" symphony, and when he allowed himself to compose such a symphony, unfettered by explicit or implicit programs or other extra-musical associations, he was usually quite successful. The *Symphony No. 21 in F sharp minor*, Op. 51, of 1940, which earned for its composer the first of three Stalin Prizes, is among the best such efforts; it is in some ways rivaled in quality only by the 27th and last symphony, Op. 85, in C minor (poignantly enough, the key of the *First Symphony*) of 1949–50.

Nikolay Myaskovsky's list of works also includes 13 string quartets, composed 1929–49 (wisely, he attempted string quartet composition only after maturing as a composer) and nine piano sonatas that span the entirety of his creative career, but have been all but forgotten in the wake of his friend Prokofiev's far greater efforts in the genre. *—Blair Johnston*

Recommended:

- ○ **Myaskovsky: Symphony 12; Silence** / Stankovsky (cond.), Czecho-Slovak RSO / 1991 / Marco Polo 223302
- ○ **Myaskovsky: Symphonies 5 & 11** / Dudarova, Ivanov (conds.), Moscow SO, USSR RSO / Olympia 133

- ○ **Myaskovsky: Symphony 17** / Svetlanov (cond.), State SO or Russia / 1991 / Melodiya 472
- ○ **Myaskovsky: Symphony 6** / Järvi (cond.), Goteborgs SO / 2002 / Universal 471655
- ○ **Myaskovsky: Symphonies 24 & 25** / Yablonsky (cond.), Moscow Phil. SO / 2003 / Naxos 8555376
- ○ **Myaskovsky: Complete Piano Sonatas** / McLachlan / Olympia 704
- ○ **Myaskovsky: String Quartets 2, 6 & 10** / Taneyev Quartet / 1996 / Russian Disc 11031

CONCERTO

Cello Concerto in C minor, Op. 66 (1944–1945)

Myaskovsky's only cello concerto was written over the last three months of 1944 and dedicated to cellist Svyatoslav Knushevitsky. Despite being denounced, in 1948, along with fellow composers Prokofiev, Khachaturian, and Shostakovich, among others, for their "formalism" and "cosmopolitanism" over the previous decade and earlier, Myaskovsky was viewed quite favorably by the Soviet government and, as was the case with his *Symphony No. 21* (1940), his *Cello Concerto* won the Stalin Prize. The concerto, one of Myaskovsky's most gentle and lovely works, happens to share the same orchestral complement as the *Piano Concerto No. 1* by Johannes Brahms—pairs of woodwinds, four horns, two trumpets, timpani, and strings—but has little of the dynamism and sense of titanic struggle of Brahms' concerto. If Myaskovsky is reflecting any of his own feelings about World War II in the cello concerto, they are feelings of sadness and eventual consolation, rather than of anger. The concerto is in two fairly lengthy movements, totaling just over half an hour. It begins with a restrained Lento, ma non troppo. The mournful opening melody, darkly colored by strings and bassoon, leads into the cello's entry. The flute and oboe gradually bring some lighter colors into the mix. Rather than stressing virtuosity, this opening movement employs the cello primarily as a melodic voice. What little display the soloist is allowed comes in the short cadenza toward the end of the movement. The second movement, Allegro vivace, starts with a tarantella-like theme, to which the cello adds a second, folk song-like melody. These and other ideas are woven together and varied over the course of the movement's 20 minutes. After a cadenza for the soloist, a fanfare leads into a passionate restatement of the first movement's opening theme. The mournful tone of that opening movement returns for a time, but the work ends on a more peaceful note, resolving into a gentle C major. —*Chris Morrison*

Recommended:

- ○ **The Russian Years** / Svetlanov (cond.), Rostropovich, USSR SO / 1997 / EMI 72016
- ○ **Prokofiev: Sinfonia Concertante; Miaskovsky: Cello Concerto** / P. Järvi (cond.), Moerk, Birmingham SO / 1998 / Virgin 45282

N

Kent Nagano

b. Nov. 22, 1951, Morro Bay, CA
Conductor
Given the impact of his career upon music, it seems incredible that Kent Nagano almost became a lawyer. Despite thorough musical training beginning at age six and obvious talent, Nagano simultaneously worked toward degrees at the University of California, Santa Cruz, in sociology and music in 1974 before moving on to San Francisco State University in 1976 to study law. There, composition courses with Grosvenor Cooper and Roger Nixon turned him toward music, and an encounter with Laszlo Varga—former first cellist of the New York Philharmonic under Walter, Mitropoulos, and Bernstein—prompted him toward conducting. Though he no longer composes, Nagano has said, "While I seemed to be quite able from the point of view of craftsmanship, I was not very good at the creative aspects! However, having the skills of composition only increases the admiration that one can have for the exceptionally talented who have composed great works." His apprenticeship was spent under Sarah Caldwell at the Opera Company of Boston from 1977 to 1979, where he eventually became assistant conductor. In 1978 he was named music director of the Berkeley Symphony Orchestra, a post he has continuously held. It was with the Berkeley Symphony in 1982 where he led the first American performance of Pfitzner's opera *Palestrina*. As assistant conductor of the Boston Symphony Orchestra, he stood in, without rehearsal, to conduct Mahler's *Symphony No. 9* in 1984. An adventurous spirit and a major interpretive grasp were clearly at work. These traits were confirmed when Olivier Messiaen tapped Nagano to assist Seiji Ozawa in preparing the world premiere of his sprawling, luminous opera *Saint Françoise d'Assisse* in 1984, a work Nagano later recorded. His years as musical director of the Opéra National de Lyon (1988–98) were marked by a number of distinguished premieres (including Peter Eötvös' opera *Three Sisters*, which he commissioned) and recordings, among the latter, Debussy's abandoned opera *Rodrigue et Chimène*, John Adams' *Death of Klinghoffer*, Busoni's comic opera double bill of *Arlecchino* and *Turandot*, and his testament, the unfinished *Doktor Faust* (with alternate completions by Philipp Jarnach and Antony Beaumont). As music director of the Hallé Orchestra from 1991–2000, he recorded John Adams' *El Niño* and the four-act version of Britten's *Billy Budd*. Nagano is a frequent guest conductor with the world's greatest orchestras, including the Vienna Philharmonic, Berlin Philharmonic, Dresden Staatskapelle, and the Russian National Orchestra. He was named music advisor to the Orchestre Symphonique de Montréal for 2004–05. *—Adrian Corleonis*

Recommended:

- ○ **Messiaen: Turangalîla-Symphonie** / Nagano (cond.), Aimard, Berlin PO / 2001 / Teldec 82043
- ○ **Poulence: Dialogues des Carmélites** / Nagano (cond.), Van Dam, Dubosc, Yakar, Sénéchal, Lyon National Opera Orch. / 1992 / Virgin 59227
- ○ **Busoni: Doktor Faust** / Nagano (cond.), Fischer-Dieskau, Henschel, Hollop, Begley, Lyon National Opera Orch. / 1999 / Erato 25501
- ○ **Varese Vol. 1** / Nagano (cond.), Bryn-Julson, National Orch. of France / Erato 92137
- ○ **Floyd: Susannah** / Nagano (cond.), Studer, Ramey, Hadley, Lyon National Opera Orch. / 1994 / Virgin 45039

Conlon Nancarrow

b. Oct. 27, 1912, Texarkana, AR, **d.** Aug. 10, 1997, Mexico City, Mexico
Composer: Keyboard
Conlon Nancarrow was an iconoclastic American composer who wrote in an utterly new way using new instrumental resources. While isolated from the main currents of music, he was virtually ignored by the public and his colleagues until the 1970s. In the 1980s composer György Ligeti said Nancarrow was writing "the best music by any living composer." In his early years Nancarrow played jazz trumpet and enrolled in the Cincinnati College-Conservatory of Music in 1929. He later relocated to Boston for private study with Nicolas Slonimsky, Walter Piston, and Roger Sessions. Nancarrow cites his study of counterpoint with Sessions as his most important formal training. He also studied Indian and African music with Henry Cowell in New York. At the outbreak of the Spanish Civil War in 1937, Nancarrow joined the Lincoln Brigade, an organization of Americans fighting for the Loyalists against General Franco. Upon his return to the United States in 1939, the State Department confiscated his passport for "communist associations." Outraged and fearing persecution, he went to Mexico City, not returning to the States for the next 40 years. He took Mexican citizenship in 1956.

Nancarrow is primarily known for his 50 studies for player piano, which combine a quasi-improvisatory likening to jazz pianists Art Tatum and Earl Hines, with dazzling rhythmic complexity rendered at tempos that exceed the capabilities of human performers. Nancarrow adopted the player piano as his instrument of choice because of its ability to exactingly reproduce his complex rhythmic layers—sometimes up to 12 layers simultaneously—and because of his relative isolation from performers while in Mexico. Nancarrow obtained a player piano in the 1940s and began laboriously hand-punching each note onto a piano roll, ultimately producing completed compositions.

Although in 1969 Columbia released an LP of several of his etudes, Nancarrow took no effort to promote his work until he was 59 years old. Motivated by a desire to show his teenaged son that he hadn't wasted his life, he visited the United States in 1981 to participate in the New American Music Festival in San Francisco. In 1982 he was composer in residence at the Cabrillo Festival, and subsequently toured in Europe. In 1982 he won a MacArthur Award (the so-called "genius grant").

Interest in his music increased in the 1980s. Some musicians began to transcribe the piano rolls into conventional musical notation. Guided by the rolls in grasping the rhythmic complexity, pianists Robert MacGregor, Joanna MacGregor, and Ursula Oppens began to perform some of the etudes. The dry wit and frequent warmth of the music comes through in live performance as they never have on a mechanical piano. Some of the more complex works have been arranged for two pianos or chamber ensembles by Yvar Mikhashoff, and played by such groups as the Arditti Ensemble and Ensemble Moderne.

Nancarrow's piano rolls and the player pianos were bought by the wealthy conductor and music collector Paul Sacher. Thus they have remained intact and archived together in the Sacher Foundation's extensive and well-protected archive of original musical documents. *—Joseph Stevenson*

KEYBOARD

Studies for Player Piano (ca. 1948–1992)
Secluded in a quiet surburban district of Mexico City, Conlon Nancarrow spent decades composing these incomparable pieces, punching the player piano rolls himself. These *Studies*, of unparalleled rhythmic complexity and fascinating energy, were begun in 1949. A jazz trumpeter in the 1930s, the composer also studied world music in great detail, giving special attention to the musics of Africa and India. The consideration given to all those musical structures shows up in the *Studies*, not in stylistic imitation, but in rethinking shared musical "problems" and coming up with his own solution.

One of the best-known is the delightful five-movement *"Boogie Woogie Suite," Study No. 3*. *No. 3a* is based on traditional boogie and jazz (like *Studies Nos. 1–10*), but is manically sped-up and eventually attains eight superimposed layers of activity. In the casual and polytonal *3b*, the bass is a constant chromatically-altered cycle, the treble staying in one key. Eventually the right-hand key moves to a more complex rhythmic relationship to the bass, and several internal layers in their own tempi are added before the boogie gently drifts off. *No. 3c* has extended canonic passages that are sometimes in a steady kind of stride piano style, but also has voices that lurch forward at times. The main melody is more of a bebop form than a boogie improv. *No. 3d* is more of an earthy blues which becomes abstracted into chromatic gestures, and frequently recalls honky-tonk style. The last piece, *No. 3e*, is even speedier than *No. 3a* which it recalls. Here the gestures truly become transmuted into sounds, streak lightning and roaring storms.

Study No. 20 is a more "pure music" piece (like *Nos. 21–27*), a three-voice canon on aperiodic rhythmic patterns. Each pattern is given a certain restricted set of pitches, which are first introduced in a staggered, gentle manner, then later played in octaves over the full range of the piano resulting in a dramatic, impassioned angularity.

Study No. 41 is in three parts, the last of which, *No. 41c*, consists of two piano rolls played on two player pianos. Constructed in irrational tempo ratios, *41a* and

41b introduce layered combinations of bebop lines at many tempi and pitch registers, fast glissandi, and rhythmic punctuations. These develop into extremely dense textures with the glissandi taking on the aspect of hurricanes and twisters and the melodies becoming shattering crystalline structures. In *41c*, *41b* is introduced slightly after *41a* begins. The cumulative effect is overwhelming and completely new.

In *Study No. 37*, pitch ratios of a just-tempered scale are turned into rhythmic ratios; in *Study No. 21 "Canon X"* rational tempo ratios between voices constantly shift; in *Study No. 33*, shifting between irrational (in this case, quarter note = the square root of 2 times 140 MM) and rational (quarter note = 280 MM) tempi occur five times in the piece. All of Nancarrow's innovations and "experiments" make for wonderful listening. *—"Blue Gene" Tyranny*

Recommended:

○ **Nancarrow: Studies for Player Piano** / player piano / 1999 / Wergo 66907

National Philharmonic Orchestra

f. 1972, London, England
Ensemble

Like the RCA Victor and Columbia Symphony Orchestras stateside, the National Philharmonic Orchestra (sometimes "of London," sometime not) was a *nom du disque*. It grew out of the eponymous RCA Orchestra based in London that producer-arranger-conductor Charles Gerhardt (1928–99) assembled after 1960. After several years at American RCA as an engineer and editor, Gerhardt had been sent to England by George Marek, then the director of Red Seal artists and repertoire, to produce recordings for the Readers Digest label, an RCA ally at the time (as was Decca/London). For these recordings, Gerhardt engaged Kenneth Wilkerson as his recording engineer, and the late Sir Thomas Beecham's Royal Philharmonic. His conductors in the early 1960s included Fritz Reiner, René Leibowitz, Sir John Barbirolli, Jascha Horenstein, Massimo Freccia, and on occasions Gerhardt himself (whom Toscanini had admired and encouraged in his last years).

For projects of lighter music, however, Gerhardt assembled freelance musicians along with players from various London orchestras—always a plenitude in the U.K. capital, where stringent U.S. union restrictions did not apply and salaries were cheaper, with fewer permanent jobs available nationwide. Early on he called these recording orchestras the London Promenade (basically London Philharmonic personnel) or the RCASO. In addition to concert, concerto, and bon-bon repertoire, Gerhardt arranged and conducted ten stereo LPs of film music for the Digest that were released in two volumes. Their quality so impressed Marek's successor, R. Peter Munves, that he commissioned Gerhardt to make an LP of *The Classic Film Scores of Erich Wolfgang Korngold* for RCA's own Red Seal label. Throughout what became a series of 15 *Classic Film Scores*, Gerhardt's producer was the late George Korngold, son of the composer, to whom concertmaster Sidney Sax had introduced him.

Enter the ad hoc National Philharmonic, contracted for at least a decade by Sax. Under Gerhardt's direction they played his arrangements of motion picture music by Max Steiner (numerically the all-time champ), Bernard Herrmann, Franz Waxman, Miklos Rozsa, Dmitri Tiomkin, John Williams (all three *Stars Wars* scores), Alfred Newman, Victor Young, John Barry, Leonard Rosenman, and of course Korngold.

Subsequently Chesky Records leased some of the earlier Readers Digest material for a superbly remastered and custom-pressed series of discs, on one of which the name National Philharmonic first appeared, dated 1967. The actual year of origin, however, seems to have been 1972, starting with the RCA Korngold collection. That trailblazing film series was completed by 1985, although Gerhardt himself recorded a Wagner collection with the NPO for Chesky as late as 1995.

The National Philharmonic, however, ceased to be RCA's or the producer's personal orchestra when Gerhardt replaced Sax as concertmaster, feeling that his playing had deteriorated beyond repair. Thus, Richard Bonynge conducted the NPO extensively for Decca/London recordings of opera and ballet; so did Riccardo Chailly, Bernard Herrmann, Nicola Rescigno, Gianandrea Gavazzeni, even Sir Georg Solti. James Levine led operas and recital discs for RCA and Sony. Also for Sony, Leopold Stokowski led the NPO in final-period recordings till the day before his death in 1977, at the age of 95.

After his farewell Wagner CD, Gerhardt retired to California, where he died four years later. From the available evidence, his informal NPO also gave up the ghost after 25 years, when the classical market went soft worldwide in the later 1990s, and London players with permanent posts clung to them like becalmed sailors, waiting for a breeze to rescue them from irrelevance as a professional breed. *—Roger Dettmer*

Recommended:

○ **Tchaikovsky: The 3 Ballets** / Bonynge (cond.), National PO / 1999 / Decca 460411

○ **Evelyn Glennie: Rhythm Song** / Wordsworth (cond.), Russell (cond.), Glennie, National PO / 1990 / BMG 60242

○ **Rossini: Overtures** / Chailly (cond.), National PO / 1995 / London 443850

National Symphony Orchestra

f. Nov. 2, 1931, Washington, DC
Ensemble

Although the National Symphony Orchestra gave its first official concert on November 2, 1931, its roots actually date to the previous year, when about 80 musicians assembled for a series of three concerts, the first of which took place on January 1, 1930. The conductor was Rudolph Schueller; Hans Kindler, however, led the two succeeding concerts and was subsequently named music director of the N.S.O. by a newly formed board of directors. The ensemble played in Constitution Hall, its home for exactly the next four decades. Kindler was a cellist, but showed talent on the podium and innovation in his programming, which tended to be conservative but inclusive of many works by American composers. He also demonstrated a keen sense for orchestra building, as the ensemble improved steadily during his nearly two-decade tenure. The N.S.O. performed for the inauguration of newly elected President Franklin Delano Roosevelt in 1932 and thereafter played for all subsequent inaugurations until the installation of the 1972 second Nixon administration, which chose the Philadelphia Orchestra. Financial difficulties plagued the organization by the late 1930s, owing in part to the national Depression. Yet the N.S.O. rarely seemed completely free of fiscal problems in the twentieth century, even in good times.

In 1941, Kindler and the N.S.O. made their first recording, for RCA, of a toccata generally attributed to Girolamo Frescobaldi, in a colorful transcription by the conductor. American Howard Mitchell succeeded Kindler as music director in 1949 and would also have a long tenure, serving until 1969. Mitchell's reign, however, was plagued by controversy regarding his interpretive and technical skills on the podium, as well as by continued financial woes and discontent among orchestra members, which resulted in strikes in the early 1960s. Nevertheless, he managed to attract major artists, such as pianists Emil Gilels, Van Cliburn, and Byron Janis, all three during this very troubling period in his second decade. Mitchell also increased the size of the ensemble and number of concerts and he frequently conducted works by American composers. He had a number of successful tours with the N.S.O., too, including the 1959 19-country excursion through South America and the 1967 European tour. Mitchell stepped down in 1969 and the N.S.O. spent a year under guest conductors. Antal Dorati was named music director in 1970 and the following year, the orchestra's home was relocated to the Kennedy Center for the Performing Arts. Dorati's programming was more mainstream, but because he was a composer himself, he also included a fair number of contemporary works. He made a few notable recordings with the N.S.O., particularly one of his piano concertos that featured his piano-playing wife, Ilse von Alpenheim, as soloist. Many musicologists believe the orchestra improved to front-rank status under Dorati. Mstislav Rostropovich succeeded Dorati in 1977 and ushered in an era in which the orchestra attracted many first-rate artists such as Martha Argerich (who made a highly praised recording of the Schumann piano concerto with Rostropovich and the N.S.O.), Isaac Stern, and many others. Moreover, there were numerous successful tours and award-winning recordings. Yet critics were not always kind to Rostropovich, some finding him erratic both in concert and on recordings. Still, his tenure was hugely successful, even if it was also often hampered by financial difficulties.

Rostropovich was succeeded in 1994 by Leonard Slatkin, who had been music director of the St. Louis Symphony Orchestra. Slatkin also made successful tours and recordings, including a critically acclaimed CD of Prokofiev's *Symphony No. 6*. Slatkin remained music director of the 100-member N.S.O. into the 2002–03 season. *—Robert Cummings*

Recommended:

○ **Prokofiev: Romeo & Juliet** / Mogrelia (cond.), National SO / 1995 / Naxos 553184

○ **Anything Goes** / Edwards (cond.), Gold, Murphy, Fardell, Griffiths, National SO / 2003 / Jay 1374

○ **Barber: Vanessa** / Rose (cond.), Savchuk, Matthews, Dry, Conrad, National SO / 2003 / Naxos 8669140–41

○ **Ives: Emerson Concerto; Symphony 1** / Sinclair (cond.), Feinberg, National SO / 2003 / Naxos 8559175

André Navarra

b. Oct. 13, 1911, Biarritz, France, **d.** Jul. 31, 1988, Siena, Italy
Cellist

Cellist André-Nicolas Navarra's family was musical. They took the sensible step of preparing him for music before they gave him an instrument, teaching him the scales and solfège by the age of seven. Once he showed a musical ear and willingness to work, they quickly started him on cello. He entered the Toulouse Conservatoire at the age of nine and graduated at 13 with first prize in cello. He was referred to the Paris Conservatoire where he studied cello with Jules Leopold-Loeb and chamber music with Tournemire, winning first prize there at the age of 15. Very unusually among first-rate soloists, he stopped taking lessons at that point; he worked out his own course of study and practiced at it. He studied violin method books, particularly the Flesch and Sevcik methods, because the student literature for cello was not as abundant.

During this time of self-teaching, he remained in Paris. The city was salutary for a developing young musician. He had contact with and observed the playing of Emanuel Feuermann and also pianist Alfred Cortot and violinist Jacques Thibaud. He also became friends with composers Jacques Ibert, Florent Schmitt, and Arthur Honegger. Later, he was advised as to artistic matters by the great cellist Pablo Casals.

He started to play professionally when he was 18, becoming a member of the Krettly String Quartet, which he played with for seven years. He also helped form an ensemble called the B.B.N. Trio with pianist G. Benvenuti and violinist René Benedetti. His solo debut was in 1931, playing the Lalo *Concerto* with the Colonne Orchestra in Paris in 1931. He joined the Paris Opéra Orchestra in 1933.

During these young years, he was exceptionally athletic. His favorite sport was swimming, but he also enjoyed boxing. For years afterward, he had a strong and stocky physique. Not surprisingly, he regarded his shape as ideal for a cellist, allowing one to dominate the large instrument.

He slowly continued to establish his career during the 1930s, which received a major boost in 1937 when he won first prize at the Vienna International Competition. However, his career was cut short by the outbreak of World War II in 1939, when he joined the infantry. He did not return to the cello until the war ended in 1945.

After a period of practice to regain his physical skills, he reestablished his career. In 1949, he was appointed professor of cello at the Paris Conservatoire. Meanwhile, he toured extensively in the U.S., Asia, and the Soviet Union, as well as Europe, and made a great recording of the Elgar *Cello concerto* with John Barbirolli conducting. Several composers wrote works for him, including Tomassi and Jolivet, whose cello concertos he premiered. He was particularly known for his splendid bowing technique, which he attributed to his studies of Sevcik and Flesch. His legato playing could be ravishing.

For many years, he taught summer courses at the Accademia Cigiana in Siena, Italy, and autumn master classes at St. Jean-de-Luz. As a teacher, he could be tough, but generally he had a friendly, upbeat temperament and a sympathetic understanding of his pupils' problems. About the only sin that commonly aroused his anger was when a student's attention wandered from total focus on the instruction. Alexander Baillie, a British cellist who studied with Navarra, said his teacher was one of the few who had developed and taught a comprehensive and successful school of cello playing. As such, he became one of the most influential of European cellists. *—Joseph Stevenson*

Recommended:

○ **Schumann, Bloch, Respighi** / Ancerl (cond.), Navarra, Czech PO / Supraphon 1940

○ **Saint-Saëns, Fauré, Chopin** / Navarra, Kisselhoff & D'Arco / 1988 / Calliope 9854

○ **Bach: Suites for Cello** / Navarra / 1987 / Calliope 3641/2

Ernesto Nazareth

b. Mar. 20, 1863, Rio de Janeiro, Brazil, **d.** Feb. 2, 1934, Rio de Janeiro, Brazil
Composer: Keyboard

Ernesto Júlio Nazareth was the most popular composer of Brazilian national music. He had a profound influence on the course of future Brazilian music, both popular and classical. Fellow countryman Heitor Villa-Lobos called him "the truest incarnation of the Brazilian musical soul."

He was born into a modest family in the Morro do Nheco (later Cidade Nova) district of Rio. His father, Vasco Lourenço da Silva Nazareth, was a customs official. His mother, Dona Carolina, was a pianist and gave the boy his first music lessons. She died when he was ten years old, and his father continued his education, arranging for further piano lessons from Eduardo Madiera and Lucien Lambert. They taught him good piano technique and familiarized young Ernesto with European music. He was particularly pleased with the shorter, fanciful pieces of Fryderyk Chopin. It is likely that he was also influenced by the American composer Louis Moreau Gottschalk (1829–69), who died in Rio and was one of the first to mix European and Brazilian musical elements.

At the age of 14, Ernesto wrote his first composition, the polka *Você bem sabe*, which was published the same year. He continued to write popular short pieces, and joined several musicians in giving a concert when he was 17 at the Club Rossini in São Cristóvão. That same year, Nazareth joined a band of chorinhos, performers of the urban variety of folk music he loved. The strolling serenaders used guitar, mandolin, flute, clarinet, and the small Portuguese guitar called the cavaquinho and had evolved the nostalgic song form called choro.

Nazareth was one of the first to blend polka and maxixe with the habanera, resulting in a new dance rhythm that Nazareth called the "Brazilian tango." It is not closely related to the more sultry Argentine tango, but is faster and more joyful. In similar fashion Nazareth added Brazilian elements to European forms, creating what he called the "Brazilian march," "Brazilian polka," "Brazilian waltz" and "Brazilian fado."

He married, and, to support his growing family (he had four children), sold the full rights to what would be one of his most popular compositions, the tango *Brejeiro*. He was employed by the music publisher Casa Carlos Gomes to demonstrate new publications. When silent films came along, he was one of a few musicians to provide concerts before the films were shown, on the piano and with the theater orchestras, in one of which Villa-Lobos was a cellist. He eventually came to be one of the most popular movie theater musicians, drawing crowds that came to hear him at least as much as to see the film. Another of his popular works, *Odeon*, is named after the most famous of these theaters.

In 1918, his daughter Maria de Lourdes died during the worldwide Spanish influenza epidemic. He began showing signs of depression, which worsened after his wife died in 1929. Despite these tragedies, he had attained national fame, and attracted large audiences in one of Brazil's largest cities, São Paulo, where his admirers presented him with a new piano. When the new radio station, Radio Sociedade, went on their air in 1930, it chose his music for its first presentation.

Then he was struck by deafness in his right ear, deepening his depression. He began to exhibit irrational behavior, and was ultimately hospitalized in the Colônia Juliano Moreira in Jacarepaguá, a forested part of Rio. On February 1, 1934, he went for a stroll. Some speculate he was attempting to escape the hospital, but, nonetheless, he got lost in the woods and was found dead three days later. *—Joseph Stevenson*

KEYBOARD

Tangos, Dances, and Other Works for Piano (ca. 1875–1932)

The tango is not native to Brazil, but there are many Brazilians who consider it theirs as much or more than any other country's (and also many who even believe that it is a native folk tradition). The light but suave piano dance music of turn-of-the-twentieth century Brazilian pianist-composer Ernesto Nazareth is at least in part responsible for this. In fact, Nazareth made sure to call most of his piano tangos "tangos brasileiros" to make clear that these were tangos not in the reigning Argentine manner, but in a fresh, newly emerging Brazilian manner.

In all, Nazareth composed more than 100 tangos brasileiros, each of which has its own proper name (like *Nove de Julho* or *Cutuba*). They are stylish and, by comparison with European piano music of the day, not too hard to play (Nazareth has something in common with Scott Joplin, who was active around the same time and who wrote at least one tango of his own), and they are built around a variety of repeating left-hand rhythm patterns, not just the stereotypical "tango rhythm" that we hear so often at the movies. Some of these pieces, including a well-known one called *Sarambeque*, perhaps should not even really be put into the tango category (*Sarambeque*, for instance, is really a modified version of a tribal African dance basically unrelated to the tango), but Nazareth put them there, and there is no need to second-guess him. Nearly all of his tangos are just two or three pages long.

Nazareth did not compose only tangos, however. His first published piece is a polka titled *Você bem sabe* that he wrote when he was just 14 years old, and throughout his long career (the 1880s through the 1930s) he would occasionally dash off a polka or a waltz (or rather, valse) or some other type of pseudo-popular short piece, creating over the span of a half-decade a catalog of charming Brazilian miniatures numbering in the hundreds. *—Blair Johnston*

Recommended:

○ **Nazareth: Brazilian Ragtime** / Almeida / 1998 / Klavier 77026

○ **Nazareth: Piano Works** / Lima / Pro Arte 144

Marc Neikrug

b. Sep. 24, 1946, New York, NY
Pianist

It is not a simple thing for a musician, however versatile, to build and maintain two careers—as both performer and composer, performer and conductor, or otherwise. Precious few can divide their energies without seeming like a gifted player with vain aspirations to compose/conduct, or the reverse—a well-known composer using fame in that arena to gain entrance to the concert platform. Marc Neikrug, an American musical jack-of-all-trades, is one of those successful few. As a pianist, his tours with violinist Pinchas Zukerman have since 1975 been highlights of each year's concert season, and recordings made by the duo have long since run into double digits. His work as a composer is perhaps not as plentiful as that of some other composers in his generation, but he is no pretender to the craft.

Born in 1946, Marc Neikrug is the son of the remarkable concert cellist and pedagogue George Neikrug. From 1964 to 1968 he studied at the University of Detmold, and in 1971 he received a M.M. from SUNY Stony Brook; he also studied with Gunther Schuller at Tanglewood. He was the composer-in-residence at Rudolf Serkin's Marlboro Festival in 1972, and during the early 1980s served as new music consultant for the St. Paul Chamber Orchestra (helping it earn a series of ASCAP awards for adventuresome programming)—the latter proving to be a valuable administrative experience when, many years later (1998), he accepted the Artistic Directorship of the Santa Fe Chamber Music Festival.

Neikrug commands a sturdy and clean keyboard technique, which he uses to provide audiences with objective, unaffected interpretations of the literature (he is in this regard perfectly suited to play alongside the objective, unaffected Zukerman). He has covered much ground as a composer, having written "traditional" tonal works and also works more obviously modern, clinically dissonant and atonal. His *Piano Concerto* (1966), whose solo part he himself played at the premiere, is the earliest large-scale work that he allowed to survive; one year later he composed a *Sonata for solo cello* for his father that has since become a cult favorite of some cellists. His theater-piece *Through Roses* (1980), for singer and eight instrumentalists, has been widely praised, as has the opera *Los Alamos* (1988), a compelling anti-nuclear statement. *—Blair Johnston*

Recommended:

- ○ **Franck & Saint-Saëns: Violin Sonatas** / Zukerman, Neikrug / Philips 416157
- ○ **Mozart: Sonatas for Piano & Violin** / Zukerman, Neikrug / 1991 / RCA 60447

Netherlands Chamber Choir

f. 1937, Hilversum, Netherlands

Ensemble

The Netherlands Chamber Choir was founded as the chorus Pro Musica in 1937 by Felix de Nobel for a series of radio broadcasts of Bach cantatas. The following year, de Nobel changed the ensemble's name to the Netherlands Chamber Choir. The early days of the choir featured a host of famous Dutch singers just beginning their careers, including Theo Baylé, Corry Bijster, Greet Koeman, Roos Boelsma, Annie Hermes, and Guus Hoekman. Over the course of the next decade, de Nobel struggled to develop an identity for the choir, which was becoming known as simply a stepping stone for singers on their way to operatic careers. Just after World War II, the choir found sponsorship by the Netherlands Transitional Radio Authority, but soon thereafter, it established itself as an independent organization. The group soon developed a large a cappella repertoire of music from the early medieval period to the present. A series of international tours followed, solidifying its position as leaders in the field. The Netherlands Chamber Choir has performed numerous premieres, including works by Francis Poulenc, Frank Martin, Hendrik Andriessen, Henk Badings, Lex van Delden, and Rudolf Escher. In 1953, the government of the Netherlands instituted an annual subsidy that allowed the choir to remain financially sound and to attract leading singers who could make a career in the ensemble. The next decade saw frequent collaborations with Carlo Maria Giulini in opera productions at the Holland Festival and on tour. As the choir personnel aged, they became the target of critics who felt that they were unable to match developments in younger ensembles that specialized in a period approach to early music. In 1972, Felix de Nobel resigned his leadership. After a brief period of stagnation, the choir re-emerged in the 1980s as a more youthful ensemble of 26 singers without a single conductor. Instead, the group collaborated with various conductors from the thriving early music movement, including Gustav Leonhardt, Nikolaus Harnoncourt, Ton Koopman, Jos van Immerseel, Paul Van Nevel, Christopher Hogwood, Roger Norrington, Andrew Parrott, Peter Philips, and William Christie. In 1987, Uwe Gronostay was appointed chief conductor and artistic director, leading the choir in critically acclaimed performances of late nineteenth century works. Gronostay left in 1997 and was succeeded by the team of artistic director Ivar Munk and chief conductor Tõnu Kaljuste. Under Munk and Kaljuste, the choir has expanded its repertoire of contemporary music. Each season, the choir offers its own a cappella concert series in ten cities across the Netherlands. It has performed with the Royal Concertgebouw Orchestra, the Budapest Festival Orchestra, and the Orchestra of the Eighteenth Century. In 2002, Stephen Layton became chief conductor.

During the 1990s, the group was found on a number of award-winning recordings, including *Vox Neerlandica I* and *Vox Neerlandica II*, surveying the entire history of Dutch vocal music, and those featuring choral works of Poulenc, Hindemith, and Janáček. *—Robert Adelson*

Recommended:

- ○ **Escher: Choral Works** / Spanjaard (cond.), Netherlands Chamber Choir / N.M. Classics 92057
- ○ **Sweelinck: Choral Works Vol. 3** / Nevel (cond.), Netherlands Chamber Choir / N.M. Classics 92015

Netherlands Wind Ensemble

f. 1959, Amsterdam, Netherlands

Ensemble

The Netherlands Wind Ensemble was founded in 1959 by students at the Amsterdam Conservatory and was initially directed by Thom de Klerk, principal bassoonist of the Concertgebouw Orchestra. After de Klerk's death in 1966, conductor Edo de Waart (himself a former principal oboist in the Concertgebouw Orchestra) became music director and helped establish it as an internationally recognized ensemble through tours and recordings. Although the core repertoire was music for woodwind octet (pairs of oboes, clarinets, bassoons, and horns), the ensemble regularly expanded to larger dimensions. In 1988, the ensemble reorganized with younger musicians from various Dutch orchestras replacing many long-standing members. The ensemble has cultivated a large and diverse audience through unconventional programming and juxtaposing works of Mozart and Strauss with new music (often commissioned from Dutch composers). Since 1972, the ensemble has presented a popular annual New Year concert in the Concertgebouw, which has been televised since 1995. *—Robert Adelson*

Recommended:

- ○ **Greatest Hits** / Waart (cond.), Netherlands Wind Ensemble / 2003 / Philips 472678
- ○ **Adams & Lang; Works for Wind Ensemble** / Mosko (cond.), Netherlands Wind Ensemble / 1995 / Chandos 9363
- ○ **Bernstein & Gershwin** / Dufallo (cond.), Netherlands Wind Ensemble, Lortie, DeBoer / 1993 / Chandos 9210
- ○ **Cornelis de Bondt** / Netherlands Wind Ensemble, etc. / 1998 / Donemus 70/71

Václav Neumann

b. Oct. 29, 1920, Prague, Czechoslovakia, **d.** Sep. 2, 1995, Vienna, Austria

Conductor

The career of Czech conductor Václav Neumann was closely tied to the Czech Philharmonic Orchestra, for which he served as chief conductor during three separate tenures, totaling 25 years, starting in 1948 and ending in 1993. He also garnered other important podium assignments, including chief conductor of the Gewandhausorchester Leipzig and musical general-director of the Leipzig Opera.

As a child Václav Neumann showed musical talent early on and by his mid-teens could play the violin with considerable proficiency, if not seasoned mastery. He entered the Prague Conservatory in 1940, where he spent the war years receiving instruction on the violin from Josef Micka. Liked many violinists Neumann also developed impressive skills on the viola during this period. In addition, he studied conducting at the conservatory with Pavel Dedecek and Metod Dolezil. In 1945, Neumann helped found the Smetana Quartet, a group for which he played viola. He also played that instrument as one of the members of the Czech Philharmonic Orchestra in the early postwar years. In 1948, he accepted the appointment of conductor of the CPO, but his selection seemed a stopgap one in light of the political instabilities and other difficulties afflicting Prague during this period. Once the services of veteran Czech conductor Karel Ancerl were obtained in 1950, the 33-year-old Neumann had to step down. He took on the post as chief conductor at the Karlovy Vary State Philharmonic Orchestra that same year. He served but three years there, then accepted the music directorship of the Brno Symphony Orchestra in 1954, where he remained for just two seasons. In 1956, he began a lengthy association with the Berlin Comic Opera, where he was a conductor for eight seasons—two as the company's chief conductor. He stepped down in 1964 and that year accepted the post of chief conductor of the Gewandhausorchester Leipzig. Neumann's first important recordings came during his tenure with Leipzig and included an impressive performance of the Mahler *Symphony No. 5*, released on Vanguard Records. Because of the invading Soviet troops who had arrived in Prague, Ancerl departed his CPO conducting post in 1968, eventually to serve as music director of the Toronto Symphony Orchestra (1970–73). Ironically, Neumann replaced him, assuming the chief conductor's duties that year. Under his guidance, the CPO, already a world-class orchestra, grew in both ability and prestige. He made numerous successful tours abroad, as well as a number of critically acclaimed recordings over the next two decades, including complete cycles of the symphonies of Mahler and Martinů. From 1970–73, Neumann concurrently served as the musical general director of the Stuttgart Staatsoper. Here and in his earlier opera position in Berlin, Neumann developed a broad repertory that encompassed Janáček (*The Cunning Little Vixen* was an especial success in Berlin), Mozart (*Don Giovanni*, *Le nozze di Figaro*), Wagner (*Tristan und Isolde*), and Shostakovich (*Katerina Ismailova*). Although his symphonic output on records was large, he turned out relatively few operatic efforts on disc. Among them was the Janáček pair *The Cunning Little Vixen* and *From the House of the Dead*. In 1989, Neumann led protests against the now-weakened Czech Communist government, which helped hasten its collapse later that year. He stepped down as chief conductor of the CPO in 1990, but because of wrangling among orchestra members and other complexities regarding a successor, he returned for one more season in 1992–93. *—Robert Cummings*

Recommended:

- ○ **Dvořák & Smetana** / Neumann (cond.), Czech PO / Supraphon 112249
- ○ **Janáček: The Cunning Little Vixen** / Neumann (cond.), Hajossyova, Beňačková, Novák, Prusa, Czech PO / Supraphon 103471
- ○ **Mahler: Symphony 5** / Neumann (cond.), Czech PO / Supraphon 111976

- ○ **Suk: Ripening** / Neumann (cond., Czech PO & Chorus / Supraphon 33C37-7955
- ○ **Vanhal: Stabat Mater; Symphony** / Neumann (cond.), Beňačková, Prague CO / 1994 / Orfeo 324941
- ○ **Dvořák: Rusalka** / Neumann (cond.), Beňačková, Novák, Ochman, Soukupova, Czech PO & Chorus / Supraphon 3641

Paul van Nevel

b. 1946, Hasselt, Belgium
Conductor
An acclaimed conductor and scholar researching and performing Renaissance and Medieval music, Paul van Nevel is particularly known as the founder and conductor of the vocal group the Huelgas Ensemble. Van Nevel's passionate interest in Medieval and Renaissance music reflects his belief that modern culture, being fundamentally visual, neglects a fundamental aspect of its history. According to Van Nevel, most people who are familiar with the art works of Bosch, Van Eyck, and Memling, know nothing about the music these great artists listened to. Van Nevel named his group after Las Huelgas Codex, an important source of knowledge about thirteenth century music. This codex was produced at the Cistercian convent near Burgos, Spain, the Monasterio de Santa Maria la Real de Las Huelgas. Van Nevel spends much of his time researching and transcribing early music, and many of his transcriptions have been published by Bärenreiter. Among his scholarly publications are a monograph on Johannes Ciconia, an essay on Nicolas Gombert and Flemish polyphony, and a study of the Franco-Flemish style of Northern France during the Renaissance. In addition to leading the Huelgas Ensemble, Van Nevel has appeared as guest conductor with many groups, including the Nederlandse Bach Vereniging, the Collegium Vocale Gent, and the Nederlands Kamerkoor. A lecturer at the Sweelinck School of Music in Amsterdam, he teaches prospective choir masters the principles of notation, transcription, and interpretation of early music. The recording projects conceived for the Huelgas Ensemble are often associated with a particular time and place. One example is *La Pellegrina*, which features music which may have been used as entertainment at the 1598 wedding of the Grand Duke Ferdinando de Medici and Christine of Lorraine. Van Nevel has been instrumental in bringing to the public the music of many Medieval and Renaissance masters, including Agricola and Mattheus Pipelare. Under his leadership, the Huelgas Ensemble received numerous recording prizes, including the Edison Award, the First Prize of the CD Compact Records Awards of 1991, the Diapason d'Or (twice), the de Caecilia Award, the Snepvangers Award of the Belgian Music Press, the German ECHO Prize, the Cannes Classical Award, and the French Prix in Honorem from the Académie Charles Cros. *—AMG*

Recommended:

- ○ **Ciconia: Complete Works** / Nevel (cond.), Huelgas Ensemble / 1997 / Pavane 7345
- ○ **Pipelare: Mass, Chansons, Motets** / Nevel (cond.), Huelgas Ensemble / 1996 / Sony 68258
- ○ **Lassus: Lagrime Di San Pietro** / Nevel (cond.), Huelgas Ensemble / 1993 / Sony 53373
- ○ **Festa: Magnificat; Mass Parts; Motets; Madrigals** / Nevel (cond.), Huelgas Ensemble / 1994 / Sony 53116
- ○ **Padovano: Mass for 24 Parts** / Nevel (cond.), Huelgas Ensemble / HM 901727

New Philharmonia Orchestra

f. 1964, London, England, **db.** 1977, London, England
Ensemble
The New Philharmonia Orchestra had an unusual history, as one might suspect from the 13-year span listed in the headnote. Yet, these vital dates are quite misleading: the orchestra did not actually come into being in 1964 as a new ensemble and then disband in 1977, never to be heard from again. The orchestra was originally founded by Walter Legge in 1945, but under the name Philharmonia Orchestra. Legge was an executive with EMI Records and controlled the ensemble in its first two decades. When he realized in 1964 he would likely be unable to run the orchestra as he desired, owing to a reduced recording schedule and other circumstances beyond his reach, he suggested disbandment. In response, members of the Philharmonia re-formed the orchestra that year, adopted the name New Philharmonia Orchestra, and decided to retain their conductor, the renowned 79-year-old Otto Klemperer. In effect, the ensemble remained the same world-class group it had been in the late 1950s and early 1960s, but without the guidance and control of Legge. A trust fund was established to aid the NPO and the London Orchestral Concert Board offered financial support for concerts at home. The New Philharmonia also began recording with labels other than EMI and thus, drawing from these various sources of income, garnered sufficient monies not only to meet expenses but fund a tour of South America in 1965. In general, the ensemble retained its high ranking throughout the 1960s as being what many considered the finest orchestra in the United Kingdom. In 1971, Klemperer retired and the young American conductor Lorin Maazel was named his successor. Maazel's more energetic style and greater intensity did not fit in well with the sensibilities of orchestra members and as a result, performance standards declined. Riccardo Muti succeeded him in 1973 and quickly became a popular figure with both audience and critics alike. He expanded the repertory and drew more consistent playing from the ensemble. In 1977, the orchestra decided to revert to its founding name, the Philharmonia, or Philharmonia Orchestra. During its 13 years, the NPO made many memorable recordings, including Klemperer's accounts of Mozart's *Symphony No. 29* and *Così fan tutte* overture, Maazel's *A German Requiem* by Brahms, and Muti's rendition of Verdi's *Macbeth*. *—Robert Cummings*

Recommended:

- ○ **Mussorgsky: Pictures; Khovanshchina Prelude** / Mackerras (cond.), New Philharmonia / 2004 / Artemis 1504
- ○ **Orff: Carmina Burana; Stravinsky: Fireworks; Circus Polka** / Frühbeck de Burgos (cond.), Popp, Unger, Noble, Wolansky, New Philharmonia / 2001 / EMI 74747
- ○ **Respighi: Roman Festivals; Fountains of Rome** / Kempe (cond.), New Philharmonia, Royal PO / 1988 / Chesky 18

New York Philharmonic

f. Apr. 2, 1842, New York, NY
Ensemble
The New York Philharmonic, an indisputable giant among the world's orchestras, is the oldest symphony organization in the United States.

Though amateur orchestras had cropped up in New York in the eighteenth century, none proved durable. On April 2, 1842, however, Ureli Corelli Hill called the first organizational meeting of the Philharmonic Symphony Society of New York, planting the seeds of the New York Philharmonic. The organization was a cooperative, to which the players paid dues and then shared profits. The Philharmonic Society commenced its inaugural season on December 7, 1842, with fifty players and a first-year schedule of four concerts.

By 1867, the size of the orchestra had grown to 100 players, and in that year the ensemble moved to the Academy of Music. By the late nineteenth century, the Philharmonic Society was only one among a number of orchestras in New York. In 1867, Theodore Thomas founded his own orchestra, which remained in existence until 1891. In 1878 Leopold Damrosch established the New York Symphony, which was the favorite among upper-crust New Yorkers, and which was chosen to open Carnegie Hall in 1891. The Philharmonic Society also faced competition from the Boston Symphony, which from 1887 gave regular New York concerts (and still does).

In 1909 the Philharmonic was reconstituted, at last becoming a full-time professional organization; the players were now employees. Under this new arrangement, renowned German composer/conductor Gustav Mahler became the new ensemble's first music director, a post he held until 1911. In 1921 the orchestra combined forces with the still-wet-behind-the-ears New/National Symphony Orchestra, marking the beginning of a series of "takeovers" that continually strengthened the group's performing forces. In 1927, the Philharmonic merged with Damrosch's New York Symphony Society (now conducted by the founder's son, Walter Damrosch). The new organization emerged as the Philharmonic-Symphony Society Orchestra of New York and is today known as the New York Philharmonic.

In 1922, the Philharmonic became the first major orchestra to broadcast live on the radio; today it is the only American orchestra with a regular live national radio network. The ensemble has recorded extensively, and its roster of recording-era conductors and music directors is indeed stellar: among others, Arturo Toscanini, Bruno Walter, Leopold Stokowski, Dimitri Mitropoulos, Pierre Boulez, and Zubin Mehta shepherded the orchestra to ever greater heights. The most spectacular of the Philharmonic's music directors was Leonard Bernstein, who led the group from 1958 to 1969 and maintained a lifetime relationship with the orchestra after his tenure. Bernstein's televised *Young People's Concerts* and hundreds of recordings with the orchestra did more to establish the Philharmonic's worldwide "brand identification" than any public relations firm could have achieved. Bernstein also oversaw the orchestra's change of homes from Carnegie Hall to Philharmonic Hall (now Avery Fisher Hall). The Philharmonic's music director from 1991 to 2002, Kurt Masur, restored the orchestra to the highest technical level and specialized in the classic European repertory, while occasionally presenting the new and unusual. In the 2002–2003 season, Lorin Maazel became music director. He was in the later stages of his career, and jockeying for the chance to succeed him in this choicest of all American plum posts began soon after he was named. *—Joseph Stevenson*

Recommended:

- ○ **Concertos From The New World** / Masur, Ozawa (conds.), Ma, Perlman, New York PO, BSO / 2004 / Sony 93072
- ○ **Copland Album** / Bernstein (cond.), New York PO / 2003 / Sony 87327

- ○ **Music of Our Time** / Bernstein (cond.), Jacobs, New York PO / 1999 / Sony 61845
- ○ **Latin American Fiesta** / Bernstein (cond.), Davrath, Stern, New York PO / 1998 / Sony 60571
- ○ **Stravinsky: Composer & Performer Vol. 3** / Bernstein, Stravinsky (conds.), Bloom, Vacchiano, Herman, Garfield, New York PO, RCA Victor SO / 2003 / Andante 1140
- ○ **Bernstein Live** / Bernstein (cond.), Ashkenazy, Janis, Du Pré, Farrell, Thomas, New York PO / 2000 / Special Editions NYP 2014

Anthony Newman

b. May 12, 1941, Los Angeles, CA
Organist, Harpsichordist

While Anthony Newman has worn many hats on the musical stage, he is best known as an organist, especially for his interpretations of the works of Bach. In recent years, he has attracted considerable attention as a fortepianist; his 1989 recording of the Beethoven *Third Piano Concerto* received a Recording of the Year award from *Stereo Review*. He has concertized widely, often performing his own works, and has recorded for many labels, with about 140 total releases by the end of the twentieth century.

Newman demonstrated remarkable musical talent in his childhood, and as a teen studied piano in Paris with Alfred Cortot and composition with Nadia Boulanger. He also took instruction on organ from Pierre Cochereau. Upon completion of his studies in France he received a Diplôme Supérieur from the École Normale de Musique, which carried special recognition from Cortot. Newman returned to the United States in the late 1950s and enrolled at the Mannes College of Music, where he earned a bachelor's degree in 1962.

Up to this point, Newman's musical education had largely been centered upon the keyboard, but in the early 1960s he began to focus more on composition, taking up studies with Leon Kirchner and Luciano Berio at Harvard University. But he also continued his efforts in the keyboard realm, working with pianist Edith Oppens. In 1963 he graduated from Harvard with a master's degree, and shortly afterward enrolled at Boston University for further study. After receiving his doctorate (1966) from that institution, he gave his first major concert when he appeared at Carnegie Hall with a pedal harpsichord recital. Newman joined the faculty at the Juilliard School of Music in New York in 1968. He also turned his attention to conducting, at first serving as an assistant to Noah Greenburg, director of the New York Pro Musica choral ensemble, and then founding his own period-instrument group, the Brandenburg Collegium.

In 1973, Newman left Juilliard and two years later joined the faculty at the State University of New York at Purchase. He taught master classes at the Indiana University School of Music from 1978 to 1981. During these years he remained active as a soloist and conductor—and as a composer. On October 26, 1979, his *Violin Concerto* was premiered in Indianapolis. In the 1980s, Newman made numerous appearances on the concert and recital stages and turned out a spate of recordings as his multiplicity of talents won him wide public recognition. Two major compositions appeared toward the latter part of the decade, his 1987 *Symphony for Strings and Percussion* and his *Sinfonia: On Fallen Heroes* (1988).

By the 1990s, Newman was easily among the best-known organists in the world, and his efforts on the fortepiano and harpsichord were garnering accolades as well. He appeared as soloist in his *Organ Concerto* with the New Jersey Symphony in the work's February 1994 premiere. Newman has recorded for numerous record labels over the years, including Sony, Infinity Digital, Albany, Vox, Helicon, and Newport Classic. He has guest conducted many important ensembles, typically showing a preference for the chamber-sized groups such as the Mostly Mozart Festival Orchestra, the Scottish Chamber Orchestra, and the Los Angeles Chamber Orchestra. He remains active as a composer in many genres, including vocal, piano, and chamber music. He is currently music director at St. Matthew's Church in Bedford, New York. Newman is also the founder of Hands On Outreach, a White Plains (N.Y.) organization that helps the poor. *—Robert Cummings*

Recommended:

- ○ **Bach: Toccatas; Chromatic Fantasy** / Newman / 1997 / Vox 7520
- ○ **Anthony Newman's Keyboard Companion** / Newman / Newport 60026
- ○ **Bach: Great Works for Organ** / Newman / 2000 / Kleos 5107
- ○ **Beethoven: Concertos 2 & 4** / Simon (cond.), Newman, NY Philomusica / 1988 / Newport 60081

Otto Nicolai

b. Jun. 9, 1810, Königsberg, Germany, **d.** May 11, 1849, Berlin, Germany
Composer: Opera

Otto Nicolai has come to be viewed by many as a one-work composer. The work that comes to mind, his opera, *Die lustigen Weiber von Windsor* (The Merry Wives of Windsor), is rightly regarded as his greatest. Yet others among his works are worth hearing, and he surely would have produced more had his life not ended so prematurely. Nicolai was artistically bound by a certain perfectionism and caution that hampered his productivity. He was offered the libretto to *Nabucco*, for instance, and turned it down, instead choosing the now-unknown *Il proscritto*; Verdi set *Nabucco* to music and scored his first great triumph. His self-critical views are well-documented in his various essays on aesthetics and in his diary entries. Nicolai is also remembered for his high performance standards and for having founded the Vienna Philharmonic Orchestra.

Nicolai was born in Königsberg (now Kaliningrad), and was raised by his father, a composer of lesser rank. The boy began showing talent early on, but became resentful of his father's attempts to benefit from making him a child prodigy. Young Nicolai made repeated failed attempts to run away from home in his teenage years. At 16, however, he lit out on his own as a traveling pianist and, after many difficulties, made his way to Berlin. There he took singing lessons at the Zum Grauen Kloster school and studied music with Goethe's favorite, Zelter.

In 1830, following two years further study at the Royal Institute for Church Music, he began teaching music and singing in concerts, but still struggled in poverty. He had already published his earliest compositions, including his Op. 4 choral work, *Preussens Stimme* and the *Six Lieder*, Op. 6. The following year he led a performance of his *Symphony in C* in Leipzig. Other works appeared as well, and his first concert in Berlin was a success. More stability came in 1833 when he accepted a post as organist at the Prussian embassy in Rome.

He became enamored of Italian culture and spoke of its great influence on him, not only in the realm of music but also in literature and painting. After returning to Vienna to serve as Kapellmeister at the Hoftheater for a year, he returned to Italy in 1838 and began working on his first operas. *Enrico II*, originally entitled *Rosmonda d'Inghilterra* (1839), and *Il templario* (1840) were successes at their premieres, though his subsequent Italian operas, much influenced by Bellini, received lukewarm receptions.

Nicolai returned to Vienna in 1841 and became conductor at the Hofoper, initiating instrumental concerts and thus founding what became the Vienna Philharmonic. For several years he had been interested in the musical masterworks of the past, stretching all the way back to Palestrina, and he deserves some of the credit for the formation of classical music's enduring canon. German arrangements of his some of his early operas, such as *Il proscritto*, met with success in the mid-1840s. When he was unable to interest the *Hofoper* in producing his yet-unfinished *The Merry Wives of Windsor*, he resigned. After a lengthy period of illness, Nicolai traveled to Berlin in 1848 to accept a post as Kapellmeister at the Berlin Opera. That year he completed *Merry Wives*; it was premiered with success and has held the stage ever since as one of German opera's few comic gems. His success was short-lived, however—he died on May 11, 1849, after suffering a stroke. *—Robert Cummings*

OPERA

Die lustigen Weiber von Windsor (The Merry Wives of Windsor) (1849)

Nicolai's Sir John Falstaff first appeared on the operatic stage two and a half centuries after his domination of Shakespeare's play *The Merry Wives of Windsor*. The Bard's introduction of the rotund knight had come in *Henry IV, Part 1*, where he played a short but memorable role. Still, it was his central role in Shakespeare's sole domestic comedy that made him a figure of legend. So potent a character and so finely drawn was he that many composers sought to work him into sung drama. Antonio Salieri set him in his *Falstaff* in 1799, enjoying 24 performances at Vienna's Kämtnertor-Theater as his reward. That opera shares with the operas of Nicolai and Verdi the distinction of having a viable life after its premiere; composers not so fortunate include Papavoine, Ritter, Ditters von Dittersdorf, Mercadante, Balfe, Thomas, and Adam. In the twentieth century, Ralph Vaughan Williams composed *Sir John in Love*, an opera with some merit, though nothing like the mercurial work of genius Verdi achieved.

As with Verdi's *Falstaff*, Nicolai's opera offers its cast members more opportunities for ensemble playing than arias for vocal display. The most frequently heard aria from *Die lustigen Weiber von Windsor*, both on recordings and in concert, is Falstaff's "Als Büblein Klein an die Mutter Brust," a rollicking tavern song and a chance at the beginning of Act II for the protagonist to demonstrate the lowest register of his bass voice. (Verdi wrote his hero's music in the baritone register, although a bass-baritone with a good top register can manage it as well.) There is in Nicolai's work, no Dame Quickly, whose "Reverenzas" in Verdi's *Falstaff* make for a quite unforgettable character. Nicolai's music is solid and often vivid, but not to be compared with the quicksilver fleetness and fecundity that informs Verdi's final stage work.

While Verdi had for a librettist Arrigo Boito, one of Italy's finest writers and a constant encouragement to the aged composer, Nicolai had someone of a considerably lesser order, Hermann Salomon Mosenthal. The result was a libretto (based closely on Shakespeare) of sturdy competence rather than the miraculous text Boito provided Verdi, but it sufficed for Nicolai's needs. The composer himself wrote of his deliberate and enthusiastic approach to composing the music. He began it in December 1845 and completed the work in 1848. The premiere took place at the Königlichen Opernhaus in Berlin on March 9, 1849.

If Nicolai was unable to match the blinding brilliance of Verdi's achievement (still some years to come), he nonetheless created a comic opera that still holds the stage in German-speaking countries and is occasionally mounted elsewhere when a bass of exceptional personality, histrionic ability, and vocal strength is available. *—Erik Eriksson*

Synopsis:

Act One. Frau Fluth (Mrs. Ford) and Frau Reich (Mrs. Page) have each received love notes—identical ones—from Sir John Falstaff, a ponderous, seedy-looking knight whose attentions are unwelcome. As they prepare to give him his comeuppance, a disturbance is heard in the street below as the three suitors of Anna Reich (Anne Page) scuffle. Junker Spärlich (Slender), Dr. Cajus (a French doctor of questionable repute who wishes to eliminate his rivals by killing them), and Fenton (an earnest young man loved by Anna but discounted by her parents as too poor) are the threesome vying for Anna's hand.

Frau Fluth invites Sir John to a tryst and sends, at the same time, an anonymous letter to her jealousy-prone husband, planning to teach him a lesson as well. Sir John arrives at the designated hour and begins to lavish his clumsy attentions upon the lady. Suddenly, Frau Reich arrives to warn them that Herr Fluth, who has been warned of his wife's rendezvous, is advancing on the house with several neighbors. Fearful, Sir John permits himself to be hidden in a laundry basket. Fluth enters in a rage and searches the house thoroughly. As he does, servants remove the basket and dump the contents into the Thames River. Finding nothing, Fluth is obliged to seek forgiveness as his wife feigns great offense at his actions. Believing their punishment to be insufficient, the women invite Sir John for another visit the following day.

Act Two. Sir John has taken a room at the Garter Inn. The new letter from Frau Fluth helps assuage his discomfort. Meanwhile, Herr Fluth still questions what happened and, introducing himself as Herr Bach (Mister Brook), meets the knight at the Inn. After rounds of champagne and gifts of money, Sir John tells him what happened the previous day and advises that he has a return engagement.

In the Reich garden, Spärlich and Dr. Cajus await Anna, but hide at the approach of Fenton. When Anna tells the young man that she loves him alone, the two suitors are much upset. Fluth, too, is angry when another search fails to yield evidence. His arrival, however, prompted the two women to disguise Sir John as an old woman he particularly despises. Raging, he removes the old lady forthwith from his home.

Act Three. When Frau Fluth and Frau Reich at last inform their husbands of their machinations, Fluth begs his wife's forgiveness and both husbands determine that the fat knight will be publicly ridiculed. They will mount a masquerade in a forest near Windsor and show Sir John as the buffoon he is. At the same time, Herr and Frau Reich each plot to marry off Anna to the suitor of choice. Frau Reich favors Dr. Cajus and arranges that Anna will wear a robe of red in order that the doctor may take her away in the melee to follow. Herr Reich, on the other hand, proposes that Anna wear Green and be taken off by Spärlich. Anna, though, sends Cajus the green robe and Spärlich the red one.

At the midnight hour, Sir John arrives disguised as Herne the Hunter, expecting redress of the double dose of humiliation he has experienced. Frau Fluth and Frau Reich enter the glen, feigning readiness to succumb to his lovemaking. Suddenly, however, an onslaught of spirits and goblins prompt them to fly from the scene as poor Falstaff is left, frightened and baffled. Anna, in the guise of Titania, and Fenton, dressed as Oberon, leave together for the forest chapel. At this point, the forest becomes a tempest of activity and Sir John the focus of attention as he is pinched, poked and thrown about. Chagrined, he realizes that the entire town now knows about his foolish attempts to seduce the two ladies and that he is the object of their ridicule. But, he is not alone in defeat. Junker Spärlich and Dr. Cajus have mistaken each other for the lovely Anna—and neither has won her favor. At this, Herr Reich anxiously wonders where his daughter may have gone. Anna and Fenton then appear from the chapel, having just been betrothed. Herr Reich and his wife yield and give their blessings to the young people. After being invited to the wedding, Sir John's cries of "O Weh!" change to "Danke!" and the ladies address the assembled townsfolk in triumph.*—Erik Eriksson*

Recommended:

- ○ **Nicolai: Die lustigen Weiber von Windsor** / Rother (cond.), Hann, Strienz, Ludwig, Beilke, Berlin RSO / 2002 / Aura Music 1118

Aurèle Nicolet

b. Jan. 22, 1926, Neuchâtel

Flutist

Aurele Nicolet is a Swiss flutist whose recordings of Bach and Mozart have received considerable critical acclaim. A remarkable stylist, Nicolet has been praised for meticulously nuanced and elegant playing. Having established himself as a preeminent performer of Bach and Mozart, Nicolet dedicated himself to contemporary music, playing works that prominent composers—including Klaus Huber, Toru Takemitsu, György Ligeti, Edison Denisov, and Heinz Holliger—had dedicated to him. Nicolet first studied with Willy Burckhard and Andre Jonet in Zurich, later moving to Paris, where his teachers were Yvonne Drappier and Marcel Moyse. During his studies at the Paris Conservatory, Nicolet thoroughly mastered the French style of flute playing, graduating in 1947 with a *premier prix*. The following year, Nicolet won first prize in the Geneva Competition. First flutist for the the Winterhur Symphony from 1948 to 1950, he was hired by Wilhelm Furtwängler to play first flute in the Berlin Philharmonic Orchestra. This engagement lasted until 1959. Furthermore, between 1952 and 1965, Nicolet taught at Hochschule für Musik in Berlin. In 1965, he went to Freiburg, where he taught master classes until 1981. Nicolet has also pursued a distinguished international career as a concert artist. *—Zoran Minderovic*

Recommended:

- ○ **Vivaldi: Flute Concertos Op10** / Faerber (cond.), Jaccottet, A. Nicolet, Wurttemberg CO / 1993 / Classical Creations 820501
- ○ **C.P.E. Bach: Flute Concertos; Oboe Concertos; Harp Solo** / Leppard, Zinman (conds.), A. Nicolet, Holliger, Jucker, English CO, Netherlands CO / 1994 / Philips 442592
- ○ **Mozart: The Works for Flute** / Marriner, Zinman, Davis (conds.), Grumiaux, Bennett, A. Nicolet, Ellis, Concertgebouw , London SO, Academy of St. Martin-in-the-Fields / 1994 / Philips 442299
- ○ **Aurèle & Christiane Nicolet** / A. Nicolet, C. Nicolet, Wyttenbach / Camerata 25CM302

Carl Nielsen

b. Jun. 9, 1865, Sortelung, Denmark, **d.** Oct. 3, 1931, Copenhagen, Denmark

Composer: Symphonic, Vocal, Orchestral, Chamber Music, Keyboard, Concerto, Opera

Although Finland's extraordinary Jean Sibelius may be foremost among Nordic composers, his contemporary, Carl Nielsen—best known for six highly original symphonies and simple popular songs—holds an honored place as Denmark's foremost post-Romantic musical ambassador, and has found considerable acclaim amongst musicians and audiences alike.

A painter by profession, Nielsen's father spent as much or more energy on his secondary activities as a violinist, and it was in this way that young Carl received his first musical instruction. At 14 Carl auditioned for a position with a military wind ensemble at Odense (he was hired as a bugler, despite his lack of formal training on the instrument). During a visit to Copenhagen in 1883, Nielsen was introduced to composer Niels W. Gade, who suggested that the young musician enroll at the Conservatory for serious studies. During Nielsen's three years at the Conservatory (1884–86) his primary subjects were violin and theory, and at no time did he actually receive formal instruction in composition. Nevertheless, in 1888 his *Suite for Strings*, Op. 1 received a successful debut in Copenhagen.

In 1889 Nielsen was hired as a violinist at the Royal Theatre in Copenhagen, a position he retained until 1905 (though in 1891 he journeyed to Paris, where he met and married Danish sculptress Anne Marie Brodersen). During the 1890s Nielsen composed prolifically, and much of his output was put into print. By 1903 he had signed a contract with the Wilhelm Hansen publishing firm in Copenhagen, effectively ending his tenure with the Royal Theatre (though he would not officially resign for two more years). His career as a conductor began in 1908 when he accepted a staff position with the Royal Theatre Orchestra. From 1916 until his death in 1931 (of heart disease), he taught at the Royal Danish Conservatory.

Nielsen's music is highly individual in both content and construction, although only the symphonies and the three concertos (violin, flute, and clarinet) have earned places in the repertory outside Denmark (where many of his choral pieces have become part of the national heritage). Each of the three concertos is a worthy contribution to its instrument's literature, though perhaps the *Clarinet Concerto* deserves the most attention. While starting out from the perspective of Classical form and harmony, his music later developed into an "extended" tonal and even atonal language, born of his highly expressive melodic style.

Like his colleague Sibelius, Nielsen poured his finest material into the symphonic mold. From the early *First Symphony* of 1892 (which is one of the first such works to begin and end in different keys), to the famous *Fourth Symphony* ("The Inextinguishable," a reference to the enduring power of both life and music), each is a noble testament to a remarkable man's view of the world around him. *—Blair Johnston*

SYMPHONIC

Symphony No. 1 in G minor, Op. 7 (1891–1892)

Audiences at the March 14, 1894, premiere in Copenhagen of this symphony by a new young Danish composer were charmed to see a handsome and shy young man rise from his desk among the second violins and step forward to take the composer's bows. The audience, which included the King and Queen and other members of the royal family, was enthusiastic and called him back for three bows. The most influential critic of the day, Charles Kjerulf, was not as happy: He called the symphony "unsettled and violent in its harmonies and modulations." It was not really appreciated until it was played in Berlin in 1896, where it was great admiration and praise.

Kjerulf was correct in identifying the most distinguished and historically important aspect of the symphony (although posterity disagrees with his judgment about them). In this highly organized, amazingly logical work Nielsen was treating harmony and tonality—and the modulations between keys—in an original way. He was consciously seeking to avoid the Wagnerian path of extended chromatic harmony, which confused the tonal center of the music. Instead of weakening tonality (the notion that ultimately led to atonality), Nielsen found a way to apply tonality. The older way was to establish that a piece was "in" a key, a basic tonality stated at the beginning and which rules the whole musical structure. Beginning with this first symphony, Nielsen treated a particular key as the goal of the piece, but usually withheld this key until the end. Thus, this symphony starts firmly in C major. Nielsen is also freed from the need to resolve the tensions set up by the progressions of his chords through the various tonal areas of the work, allowing a symphony-long structure of tension and partial release.

The first movement is marked to be played "proudly" and can be taken as a self-portrait in music. The slow movement is a deeply moving piece that gives the impression of being a nature portrait. However, it is not slow and pastoral, but contains some sense of urgency. The third movement is more complex than the usual scherzo, and has interesting different rhythms under the overall 6/4 time signature. The fourth movement again begins in C major; with a powerful, athletic flow it reaches a deeply satisfying conclusion in which G minor is finally achieved.

The symphony was highly successful and was published nearly at once. But it also stirred jealousy among Nielsen's contemporaries, resentful that a "mere second violinist" had suddenly emerged as a major voice among young European composers. *—Joseph Stevenson*

Recommended:

- ○ **Nielsen: Symphonies 1 & 6** / Vanska (cond.), BBC Scottish SO / 2000 / Bis 1079
- ○ **Nielsen: Symphonies 1–6** / Berglund (cond.), Royal Danish Orch. / 1994 / RCA 20290
- ○ **Neilsen: Symphonies 1 & 6** / Leaper (cond.), National SO / 1995 / Naxos 550826

Symphony No. 2 ("De fire temperamenter" / "The Four Temperaments"), Op. 16 (1901–1902)

Nielsen's *Symphony No. 2*, Op. 16 (1901–02) was inspired by a depiction of the four temperaments or "humours"—long used to describe one's personality and physical characteristics—on the wall of a village inn on the Danish island of Sjaeland. The composer fashioned a symphony based on the temperaments, cautioning that his treatment of them was not intended to be programmatic; instead, these four states merely provide an outline of the moods in the work. Nielsen described the musical depictions in the symphony's four movements thus: "... [T]he impetuous (Allegro collerico), the indolent (Allegro flemmatico), the melancholy (Andante malincolico) and the cheerful (Allegro sanguino). But the impetuous man can have his milder moments, the melancholy man his impetuous or brighter ones, and the boisterous, cheerful man can become a little contemplative, even quite serious—but only for a little while. The lazy, indolent man, on the other hand, only emerges from his phlegmatic state with the greatest of difficulty, so this movement is both brief (he can't be bothered) and uniform in its progress."

In addition to displaying the composer's masterful talent for sonic portraiture, the symphony also demonstrates one of Nielsen's highly individual techniques, which he called "progressive tonality": a series of adventurous modulations that bypass the formal key relationships characteristic of most Classical and Romantic symphonies. Nevertheless, the influence of Brahms is clearly in evidence, especially in the third movement. After a few early performance, the symphony was not often heard until the 1960s, when Nielsen's genius began to receive wider recognition. *—AMG*

Recommended:

- ○ **Nielsen: Symphony 2; etc.** / Salonen, Swedish RSO / 1989 / CBS 44934
- ○ **Nielsen: Symphonies 1–6** / Berglund (cond.), Royal Danish Orch. / 1994 / RCA 20290
- ○ **Nielsen: Symphonies 2 & 5** / Vanska (cond.), BBC Scottish SO / 2003 / BIS 1289
- ○ **Nielsen: Symphonies 1–3, etc.** / Blomstedt (cond.), San Francisco Symphony / 1999 / Decca 460985

Symphony No. 3 ("Sinfonia espansiva"), Op. 27 (1910–1911)

Carl Nielsen wished to demonstrate in his third symphony his conviction that music is driven by internal forces that seek to transcend their confines. The work begins with an energetic waltz of enormous scale. The melodic-rhythmic progression of this melody drives itself forward irresistibly, indeed expansively (the movement is marked Allegro espansiva), introducing several variations to which Nielsen returns throughout the symphony. As the opening theme is transformed and reinvented; one is reminded of Nielsen's fondness for Brahms' use of symphonic form, particularly his "developing variations" principle. The original theme serves as a "seed" that leads to new variations, which in turn give rise to new motifs. The movement ends merrily, almost flippantly, on an unexpected chord.

Nielsen wished to incorporate into the second movement, Andante pastorale, the sights and sounds of his rural childhood on the island of Funen (Fyn) in Denmark. The movement begins idyllically, with horn and strings sighing long, low tones, bringing to mind the shapeless sound of wind in the trees. A increasingly mournful mood creeps slowly into Arkady, while the opening melody is hinted at again in a heavier, more threatening manner. This is resolved by the soothing, wordless entrance of two human voices, baritone and soprano soloists who vocalize on the simple "Ah" vowel. Their contribution expands the tonal color of the orchestral palette. The movement ends with the orchestra and vocalists echoing each other as though in contented communication. Nielsen once expressed a desire to "imagine a music that would be similar to impressionistic painting, where the contours wash out in an atmospheric haze." This movement does just that, creating a rich and ethereal effect.

The third movement, marked Allegretto un poco, opens with a hushed brass fanfare, and proceeds into a flurry of restless energy in the oboe. This restlessness spreads throughout the orchestra, growing in urgency and volume as the movement progresses. As urgency settles slowly into calmness, punctuated only by occasional hushed alarms from individual instruments (violin, clarinet, flute), the oboe speaks again, this time reassuringly, bringing the movement to a peaceful close. The finale, Allegro, begins with a stately march theme. This expansive melody, in which the entire orchestra is involved, sums up the development of the entire work with a grandiose intensification reminiscent of Mahler. The loose ends, both emotional and musical, left by the first two movements are resolved in an exuberant closing.

The symphony proved to be Nielsen's international breakthrough. After its enthusiastic reception in Denmark, Nielsen conducted a performance at the Concertgebouw in Amsterdam, where the symphony was given high praise, launching a series of successful performances throughout Europe. It remains one of Nielsen's most often-performed works. *—Margaret Godfrey*

Recommended:

- ○ **Nielsen: Symphonies 3 & 5** / Bernstein (cond.), Moller, Guldbaek, Royal Danish Orch. / 1993 / Sony 47598
- ○ **Nielsen: Symphonies 3 & 4** / Vanska (cond.), Komsi, BBC Scottish SO / 2002 / Bis 1209
- ○ **Nielsen: Symphonies 3 & 6** / Saraste (cond.), Kortekangas, Kaappola, Finnish RSO / Finlandia 29714
- ○ **Nielsen: Symphonies 3 & 4** / Berglund (cond.), Royal Danish Orch. / 1994 / RCA 20292

Symphony No. 4 ("Det uudslukkelige" / "Inextinguishable"), Op. 29 (1914–1916)

Nielsen began writing this work (*Det uudslukkelige* in Danish) during the summer of 1915, and completed it two weeks before the first performance, which he conducted in Copenhagen on February 1, 1916. In addition to triple winds and full brass, Nielsen specified two sets of timpani, as far apart as possible on the stage. While *Symphony No. 3*, the *Espansiva* of 1910–11, proclaimed his indubitable maturity, the *Fourth* (which he started planning in 1914) became Nielsen's equivalent of Beethoven's *Eroica*, just as the *Fifth* would be his counterpart of Beethoven's *Fifth*. Years before, he had written, "It is a fact that he who brandishes the hardest fist will be remembered the longest." Certainly the proximity and brutality of World War I influenced the conflicts in his *Fourth Symphony*, although the *Fifth* of 1921–22 expressed his real horror. In the score of *The Inextinguishable* Nielsen wrote, "Under this title the composer has endeavored to indicate in one word what music alone is capable of expressing to the full: the elemental Will of Life. Music is Life, and like it is inextinguishable. The title... might therefore seem superfluous; the composer, however, has employed the word to underline the strictly musical character of his subject. It is not a program, but only a suggestion about the right approach to the music."

Taking a cue from Mendelssohn's *Scottish* and Schumann's *D minor* symphonies, he wrote all four movements of *The Inextinguishable* to be played without pause, beginning with a violent struggle between the keys of C major and D minor. More even than Franck's *D minor Symphony*, however, Nielsen's *Fourth* is a "motto" symphony based on the E major second theme of his opening Allegro. This is introduced in "sweet-sounding" thirds by a pair of clarinets, replaced by flutes, horns, and strings before the strident main theme returns to do battle—not only in the development but during the recapitulation—a contest won by the motto in the coda, although not decisively enough to forestall a later, even more vehement challenge in the finale. Without pause, the folk-colored Poco allegretto in G replaces a scherzo, piquant writing for winds that remembers *Serenata invano* of 1914 as much as it anticipates the *Quintet* of 1922 and the flute and clarinet concertos. Its principal subject derives from the motto theme, but Nielsen puts this on hold in the ensuing Poco adagio quasi andante, whose searing, starkly scored main theme is developed in two-part counterpoint, derived from old Netherlands polyphony according to one Nielsen scholar. A nervous, stuttering new theme increases the tension. While the movement climaxes in E major, this crumbles in the struggle between themes. Suddenly, the strings begin a wild race that plunges into a terminal Allegro whose swaggering main theme in E major declares itself, only to be challenged by two sets of timpani that duel brutally for control until E major can finally assert itself and hold. Triumphant, the motto theme invites both timpanists to punctuate the "inextinguishable" victory. *—Roger Dettmer*

Recommended:

- ○ **Nielsen: Symphonies 4 & 5** / Saraste (cond.), Finnish RSO / 1998 / Finlandia 21439
- ○ **Nielsen: Symphonies 3 & 4** / Vanska (cond.), BBC Scottish SO / 2002 / Bis 1209
- ○ **Nielsen: Symphonies 1–6** / Berglund (cond.), Royal Danish Orch. / 1994 / RCA 20290

Symphony No. 5, Op. 50 (1921–1922)

Nielsen began working on his *Symphony No. 5* shortly after World War I. He was deeply affected by that terrible conflict, and the intensity of the *Fifth* may reflect the composer's feelings about war. At any rate, the work represents a significant shift in the composer's attitude and philosophy; many of his postwar pieces reveal an increasingly strident, polyphonic, and dramatic style, much in contrast to those of the pre-war era. Notably warlike is the dramatic content of the *Fifth*; conflicting moods and aesthetics are played out throughout: the consonant versus the dissonant, contrapuntal versus harmonic, constructive versus destructive. The work also represents a complete break from Classical form in favor of a two-movement structure; according to biographer Robert Simpson, the first movement contains "the crux of the conflict itself," while the second part is "a finale that would rise out of the ashes in a great fount of regenerative energy. Even this finale is not to be free of difficulties, but it is to prove irresistible in the end."

The first part of the symphony is divided into two contrasting sections: a Tempo giusto in common time and an Adagio non troppo in 3/4 time. A viola tremolo opens the work, a hypnotic perpetual motion figure that several brief melodies try to overrun. As other destructive forces encroach—a flurry of notes here, an obsessive snare drum rhythm there—the music reaches a chaotic peak and an Adagio section abruptly brings in constructive forces. Soon, however, the destructive element intrudes, and a veritable battle breaks out with the snare drum rhythm symbolizing the darker side of the conflict. The lyrical Adagio wins out, and the movement fades away with a peaceful clarinet melody, though still accompanied by the distant snare drum figure. An uneasy peace has been won as the second movement gets underway. The movement is divided into four main sections: the brisk opening Allegro subject surges along over an ostinato fourth motif in the bass, which leads into a scherzo-like Presto in the form of a fugue. Soon, destructive forces symbolized by the clarinet and tympani diminish the stability of this passage, and the more the music tries to continue in the face of these obstacles, the more frantic it becomes before an Andante passage finally introduces a second fugue. The subject is developed in a sonorous, polyphonic string texture before leading into a triumphant Allegro section that concludes the work on a note of exaltation and synthesis. "With the *Fifth*," Nielsen scholar Povl Hamburger asserted, "Nielsen reached the absolute summit of his creative power, not only in his symphonic, but in his instrumental music altogether. Nothing that was added afterwards equals it in greatness of mind, vision, and imagination." *—Brian Wise*

Recommended:

- ○ **Nielsen: Symphonies 4 & 5** / Saraste (cond.), Finnish RSO / 1998 / Finlandia 21439
- ○ **Nielsen: Symphonies 2 & 5** / Vanska (cond.), Corbett, Ghiro, BBC Scottish SO / 2003 / BIS 1289
- ○ **Nielsen: Symphonies 1–6** / Berglund (cond.), Royal Danish Orch. / 1994 / RCA 20290
- ○ **Carl Nielsen Collection Vol. I** / Tuxen (cond.), Danish RSO / 1994 / Danacord 351353
- ○ **Nielsen: Symphonies 4 & 5** / Schoenwandt (cond.), Thomsen, Nybye, Danish RSO / 2000 / Dacapo 224156

Symphony No. 6 ("Sinfonia semplice") (1924–1925)

Nielsen originally planned to call his *Sixth Symphony Sinfonia semplice* (Simple Symphony). When he began working on it in August 1924, he expressed the desire to make it "completely idyllic" and "different from the others, gliding more amiably." Sixteen months passed before he finished the symphony, and during that time it underwent a complete transformation from its original intent, one that caused Nielsen to change the title before publication. Of the six symphonies, this last is the most emotionally ambiguous, full of quizzical humor and grim irony.

Instead of actively seeking the tonic key, this work insistently attempts to escape its clutches. When the final resolution arrives, there is a sense of having accepted the inevitable with resigned humor. The first movement, marked Tempo giusto, begins with four gentle notes from the glockenspiel. The violins enter serenely, in G major. Almost immediately, however, the idyll is broken by the introduction of clarinet and bassoon, which interject first an alien B flat, then E flat, D flat and A flat, in a rapid, unsettling succession. Though the violins attempt to restore their original serenity, they do so in F sharp major, as though reaching for, and almost touching their initial serenity, ultimately unable to recapture it. The effect is a combination of beauty and melancholy. This, too, is shortlived, interrupted suddenly by calamity: a crash of drums, a panicked fanfare, then frantic strings and woodwinds in the key of B flat—the key that had originally disrupted the violins' brief playfulness. Dissonance, punctuated by the alarm of the glockenspiel, leads to dreary lament; and after another frantic interlude the violins again hint at their opening melody.

Nielsen spoke of the necessity to actively awaken each instrument, urging each to life. Of the second movement, "Humoreske," barely four minutes long, Nielsen said, "I have in my new symphony a piece for small percussion instruments—triangle, glockenspiel, and side drum—that quarrel, each sticking to his own tastes and inclinations. Times are changing. Where is music going? What is permanent? We don't know! This idea is found in my little Humoreske." After an almost rude polyphony in which several mismatched instruments convene, two bassoons are overwhelmed by a disdainful trombone. The music then succumbs to quiet confusion, as though humbled.

The almost equally brief third movement, marked Adagio and entitled "Proposta seria" (Serious Proposition), begins with stark, longing lamentation from the strings. Keys—A flat, D flat—are hinted at and drawn away from, the resultant contrasts merging eventually and softly into a gentle, melancholy close.

A brief flurry starts off the fourth movement, "Tema con variazione," after which the flute and clarinet join on a long, anticipatory note. With the stage thus set, a theme is gravely presented on bassoon, and a series of variations on this theme follows. Among these is a startling and short-lived waltz variation in the strings. While variations and keys by turns overwhelm one another, there are moments of sardonic humor as well as bitter conflict. As the snare drum barks from within a climactic rushing of frantic strings, quite suddenly the conflict ends in a resigned but unmistakably humorous final cadence, firmly rooted in B flat major. *—Margaret Godfrey*

Recommended:

- ○ **Nielsen: Symphonies 3 & 6** / Saraste (cond.), Finnish RSO / Finlandia 29714
- ○ **Nielsen: Symphonies 1 & 6** / Vanska (cond.), BBC Scottish SO / 2000 / Bis 1079

VOCAL

Songs (ca. 1883–1931)

Aside from his symphonies, Carl Nielsen is best known for his mastery of Danish song. In his day, they earned him popularity with both cognoscenti and popular audiences, and over the years these songs have integrated themselves into the Danish singing tradition; largely because of his efforts, Denmark is one of the few western countries with a flourishing, modern-day folk music tradition. This phenomenon is only enhanced by the fact that Denmark is a largely rural country, and singing has always been an important social activity in small towns and the countryside.

Nielsen's songs rang from strophic settings of simple poetry to exquisitely crafted art songs. He had a deep understanding of not only Danish folk traditions, but Gregorian chant and fifteenth and sixteenth century vocal polyphony, which naturally enriched his own musical language. That said, he was always a firm believer in the simplicity of the tune and a faithful interpretation of the text.

Nielsen's earliest songs are fashioned mostly in the Danish lied tradition of Heise and Lange-Müller. The most successful of these include the *Five Songs*, Op. 4 (1891) and the *Viser og vers*, Op. 6 (1891), both with texts by Jacobsen; and the *Six Songs*, Op. 10 (1894), with texts by Holstein. A few years later, the songs *"Du danske mand"* (1906) and *"Jens Vejmand"* (1907) brought Nielsen even greater recognition, and led to increasingly frequent requests for stage music and occasional cantatas. Because of this, many of his songs were only published singly or in composite works (as the musical accompaniment to plays or in cantatas) rather than as part of large collections.

The simple popular Danish song was central to Nielsen's output from the period of 1914 onwards. As he became deeply involved in popular musical education as a lecturer and composer, there was a civic nature to his activities. In early 1914, for instance, he composed some 50 hymn tunes, both to meet a particular request and to contribute to the larger improvement in the quality of religious singing.

His most important achievement in the song genre came in 1915 when his friend, the composer Thomas Laub (1852–1927), suggested the two collaborate to help reform popular Danish song. As a result, they jointly composed two collections of 20 Danish songs (1915 and 1917) and Nielsen's subsequent collections included *Two Popular Melodies* (1917–21) and *Ten Little Danish Songs* (1923–24). These signified a turning point in the history of Danish song, as the romance and lieder traits disappeared in favor of a more accessible (typically strophic) style. With the publication of *Folkehøjskolens melodibog* (1922) Nielsen secured this renewal of Danish song for further generations, and younger composers came to adopt the ideals of Laub and Nielsen. *—Brian Wise*

Recommended:

○ **Nielsen: Songs** / Dam-Jensen, Lassen, Staerk / 2002 / Dacapo 8224218

○ **Complete Aksel Schiøtz Recordings Vol. 10: Carl Nielsen** / Schiøtz, various / 1998 / Danacord 460

Hymns and Sacred Songs, song collection (1913–1914)

Like Bach, Mozart, and Beethoven, Danish composer Carl Nielsen was as capable of writing music for the most sophisticated and the least sophisticated listeners, for public and private audiences, and for secular and sacred purposes. His piano music, for example, is very sophisticated; his symphonies are great public works; his cantata *Hymnus amoris* is intensely secular. But Nielsen could also compose simple songs that are still sung in Danish homes and simple hymns that are still sung in Danish churches. His set of *14 Hymns and Sacred Songs* for solo voice and piano or solo voice and organ were composed in 1919 for just such a purpose. For the most part setting texts by Danish spiritualist Bishop Grundtvig, Nielsen's hymns are easy to sing, easy to play, and easy to hear. Yet this does not mean Nielsen's hymns do not touch the infinite. After studying Lutheran hymns and chorales, Nielsen realized that spiritual greatness is not dependent on intellectual profundity, but on benevolence and compassion. While Nielsen conclusively demonstrated in his contemporary *Symphony No. 5* that he could be as intellectually profound and as compositionally sophisticated as any European composer, his *Hymns and Sacred Songs* prove that at heart, he was a plain man whose spirituality was, like Beethoven's, something between him and his God. *—James Leonard*

Recommended:

○ **Nielsen: Preludes; Hymns & Spiritual Songs** / Bertelsen, Stengaard / 1993 / Rondo Grammofon 8335

ORCHESTRAL

Aladdin, incidental music, Op. 34 (1918–1919)

Carl Nielsen was a modest, unpretentious man with no inclination to behave like the "great composer" he undoubtedly was. Despite his enormous influence on twentieth century music he regarded himself primarily as a musical craftsman, and was always ready to turn his hand to comparatively minor tasks.

One such was to write some music for a new production of the drama *Aladdin, or The Miraculous Lamp* by the Danish poet Adam Oehlenschlager (1779–1850), at the Royal Theater, Copenhagen. It can safely be assumed that this was more a pantomime than a serious play but, though time was short, Nielsen entered fully into the spirit of the venture and produced a work full of imagination, melodic beauty, and color.

At the first performance, the size of the orchestra had been reduced, cuts were made in the music and the overall effect ruined. Some years later Nielsen re-scored the work as an orchestral suite, and conducted the first full performance. Thereafter *Aladdin* become popular with Danish audiences, and is still frequently played. The fairy-tale atmosphere of the original remains as fresh and attractive as Grieg's equally-celebrated incidental music for Ibsen's *Peer Gynt* and, though movements such as "Aladdin's Dream," "Dance of the Morning Fog," and "Negro Dance" give little hint of the huge, complex canvases that Nielsen covers in his symphonies and other major works, the suite has a respectable place among musical scores that have long outlived their partners.

It might also be added that while the public at large might easily have found much of Nielsen's music too abstract and "experimental," this is but one of several examples of his willingness to put his skills to less challenging uses in light, entertaining pieces which nevertheless bear the unmistakable stamp of originality. *—Roy Brewer*

Recommended:

○ **Nielsen: Aladdin Suite; Symphony 2; Pan og Syrinx** / Salonen (cond.), Swedish RSO / 1989 / CBS 44934

○ **Nielsen: Aladdin Suite; Symphony 2** / Chung (cond.), Gothenburg SO / 1983 / Bis 247

Helios, concert overture, Op. 17 (1903)

The Nielsens had some good fortune in 1903. The composer's wife, Marie Carl-Nielsen, was a noted sculptor and had received the Ancker Scholarship. This carried with it a period of residence in Greece to study classical art. Meanwhile, the composer had earned money with his opera *Saul and David* and also received a permanent annual contract with the publishing firm of Hansen. Both feeling secure, they decided to go to Greece together. The artistic couple were treated as visiting celebrities. The Athens Conservatory provided Nielsen with a room with a view of the Acropolis, complete with piano. He was able to hike in the mountains, tour the galleries, and in general enjoy his popularity with the people and the warmth of the sunny Mediterranean climate. His visit included a trip to Constantinople and a dinner with King George I of Greece (who was Danish-born).

In general he sloughed off and wrote virtually nothing the entire year of 1903; this overture is the only substantial exception. Nielsen provided a simple program for the overture, the name of which is the Greek for "sun": "Silence and darkness/The sun rises with a joyous song of praise/It wanders on its golden way/And sinks quietly into the sea." The music is not physically descriptive; it is more about the feelings the sun arouses: exhilaration, veneration, and joy. It is a rich and glorious orchestral movement. *—Joseph Stevenson*

Recommended:

○ **Nielsen: Concertos & Orchestral Works Vol. 2** / Tuxen (cond.), Danish RSO / 1995 / Danacord 354356

○ **Thomas Jensen Conducts Nielsen** / Jensen (cond.), Danish RSO / 1995 / Dutton 2502

○ **Nielsen: Symphony 4; Helios Overture** / Salonen (cond.), Swedish RSO / 1986 / CBS 42093

Little Suite, for string orchestra in A minor, Op. 1 (1888; revised 1889)

When this work was premiered in 1888, the program notes that accompanied Carl Nielsen's *Little Suite for Strings in A minor* curiously identified the composer as "Mr. Carl Nielsen, whom nobody knows." While this was to be generally true of the musical world outside of Scandinavia for a half century, the designation would soon lose its accuracy in Denmark. While this work shows the fledgling composer paying homage to central European standards of form, Nielsen's own innovative musical language is already in evidence. In three movements (Prelude, Intermezzo, and Finale), the elegiac opening theme will actually fill a cyclic function, a device to which Nielsen would return to wholeheartedly a quarter century later in the *Symphony No. 4*. Against a solemnly treading ostinato, the music unfolds in the manner of the *Adagio for Strings* popularly thought to be by Albinoni. The second movement gives a premonitory hint of the composer's love of triple time: it is an engaging waltz peppered with the occasional flat seventh grace notes that would later become so characteristic. The comparatively expansive third movement opens again solemnly with the elegy theme but soon breaks loose into an animated sonata form. The inventiveness of Nielsen's mind can be seen in the development, where a fragment of the opening theme is worked over and then reappears as an ostinato with the main theme in the recapitulation. The fragment's emergence in the bass line in the coda further enhances the movement's integral unity and rounds the work off nicely, giving an intimation of the important symphonist to come. *— Wayne Gerard Reisig*

Recommended:

○ **Nielsen: Symphonies 4–6** / Schirmer (cond.), Danish RSO / 1999 / Decca 460988

○ **Grieg; Nielsen; Britten** / Brown (cond.), Norwegian CO / 2003 / Virgin 562179

CHAMBER MUSIC

Serenata in vano, for clarinet, bassoon, horn, cello & double-bass (1914)

Around the time that Nielsen was starting work on his *Symphony No. 4*, he was asked to write a short piece for several musicians from Det Kongelige Kapel, the orchestra of the Royal Theatre in Copenhagen (where he acted as a conductor). They were about to go on a tour playing Beethoven's *Septet*, and Nielsen used that work's scoring as a starting point in creating the *Serenata in vano* (Serenade in vain), completed in just a couple of days in May, 1914, and given its first performance on April 13, 1915.

This programmatic composition depicts a group of musicians sent to serenade someone's lover. Over a rustic accompaniment from the lower instruments, the clarinet and bassoon sing what Nielsen described as "a somewhat chivalrous and showy" melody in the hopes of enticing the woman out onto the balcony. The song becomes increasingly energetic, but still she does not appear. The musicians move on to a sweeter, more mellow song, but this doesn't work either. So, after a brief pause, the musicians decide that their performance has been "in vain" and head home, playing a distinctly tongue-in-cheek march to amuse themselves on their travels through the countryside. *—Chris Morrison*

Recommended:

○ **Nielsen: Wind Chamber Music** / Bergen Wind Quintet / 1988 / Bis 428

○ **Walton: Facade; etc.** / Chicago Pro Musica / 1985 / Reference Recordings 16

String Quartet in F major ("Piacevolezza"), Op. 44 (prev. Op. 19) (1906; revised 1919)

Nielsen's *F major String Quartet* of 1906 is the most perfectly wrought and original of his essays in that genre. Originally numbered Opus 19, it underwent extensive revision and reemerged as Opus 44, being published as such in 1923. Working in a medium in which he was almost as comfortable as that of the symphony, Nielsen drew on his own experience as a string player as well as his individualism in approaching the traditional to crown his series in that form.

Nielsen's penchant for unusual but very apt tempo indications is illustrated in the original one for the first movement, Allegro piacevolo ed indolente. Although he subsequently replaced this with the more conventional designation Allegro tanta e comodo, a feeling of contented indolence pervades, spiritually akin to the second movement of the *Second Symphony.* Despite this overall mood, a constant spring waterlike flow is maintained throughout. The following slow movement in C is chorale-like and weaves in and out of the relative A minor. That key pervades the following movement, Allegro moderato ed innocente; it is in the easy wry canter which Nielsen favored over the true, boisterous scherzo for his humorous movements, saving energy for the outer ones. This is true in the case of the ensuing finale, which returns to the classical ideal of a light and festive conclusion rather that an apotheosis. In it the winsome spirit of *Maskarade,* the composer's 1906 opera, abounds; this is particularly felt in the good-natured second theme. Throughout the four movements, Nielsen's understanding of string writing, already impressive in his works from the late 1880s, reaches perfection here in his achieving the maximum color and expressiveness from limited resources. *—Wayne Gerard Reisig*

Recommended:

- ○ **Nielsen: 4 String Quartets** / Kontra Quartet / 1990 / Bis 503/504
- ○ **Nielsen: String Quartets Vol. 1** / Oslo SQ / 1999 / Naxos 553907

Wind Quintet, Op. 43 (1922)

Since its composition in 1922, Carl Nielsen's *Wind Quintet in A major,* Op. 43, has become one of the most beloved pieces in the woodwind repertoire. Nielsen's *Quintet* is particularly ingratiating not only for its expressive accessibility, but for its conversational quality. In a medium characterized by the interactivity of contrasting timbres, Nielsen's Op. 43 excels for its ability to convey a distinct and vivid character in each of its voices while maintaining an overall sense of expressive cohesion. In this regard compositional virtuosity was no doubt enhanced by personal acquaintance: Nielsen knew each of the original performers of the piece personally, and colored their respective parts with his perceptions of their personalities, musical and otherwise.

The *Wind Quintet,* Op. 43, is cast in three movements, beginning with a pastoral scene marked Allegro ben moderato. The solo bassoon is the first to present the main theme, with its downward arpeggio, scalar ascent, and descending sequence. Much of the rest of the movement's melodic developments and accompanimental gestures can be traced back to this opening line, lending the various episodes and contrasting textures a strong sense of continuity. The second movement, a graceful Menuet, features a pair of duets, first between the clarinet and bassoon, then the flute and oboe (with occasional subtle underpinnings from the horn); these complement the instrumental density of the contrapuntal Trio. The final movement begins with a somber "Praeludium," but then strikes a brighter note with a hymn-like theme followed by 11 variations of ever-changing texture and character—including a nimbly scurrying flute solo, a clownishly mysterioso duet between the clarinet and bassoon, and pensive solo soliloquies by the bassoon, English horn, and French horn. The work's conclusion, which returns to the chorale-style hymn theme, employs a subtle bit of extended technique: to underpin the last cadence with an added sense of resolution, Nielsen instructs the bassoonist to lengthen the instrument by adding an attachment to the bell, in order to drop down to a low, sonorous A on the final chord. *—Jeremy Grimshaw*

Recommended:

- ○ **Nielsen: Wind Chamber Music** / Bergen Wind Quintet / 1988 / Bis 428
- ○ **Barber: Summer Music; Nielsen: Woodwind Quintet: Hindemith: Octet for Winds & Strings** / Robison, Combs, Turner, Winstead, Solis / 1990 / Sony 46250

KEYBOARD

Commotio, for organ, Op. 58 (1930–1931)

Commotio, Carl Nielsen's last composition, was also his first major composition for the organ. He had written the *29 Preludes* in 1929 to get the feel of the instrument, but the *Preludes* themselves were brief pieces, more character studies than fully worked out compositions. *Commotio,* however, is a nearly half-hour long work that uses all the devices of counterpoint and all the compositional techniques Nielsen had worked out over a lifetime to create what most critics have called the greatest Danish organ work since Buxtehude. As Nielsen wrote to a friend about *Commotio,* "The work is an attempt to revive the only true and vital style for the organ, polyphonic music, which is especially suited for this instrument, so long misleadingly considered as a kind of an orchestra." The work is in four movements played attaca: free introductory Adagio, first fugue, a slow interlude, and a second and final fugue ending in a massive stretto. Like so many of Nielsen's mature works, the *Commotio* begins in one key and closes in another, in this case G minor modulating to C major. Nielsen died before the work was performed, and it was posthumously premiered in October 1931. *—James Leonard*

Recommended:

- ○ **Nielsen: Complete Organ Music** / Westenholz / 1997 / Bis 131
- ○ **Nielsen's Commotio & Other Danish Organ Works** / Bowyer / 1996 / Nimbus 5468

CONCERTO

Clarinet Concerto, Op. 57 (1928)

Although born the same year as Sibelius, Carl Nielsen was starting to forge new paths at the same time that the great Finn decided to call it a day and enjoy a long retirement. This makes the Dane's death at 66 seem all the more premature when one looks at the *Fifth* and *Sixth Symphonies, Commotio* for organ, and the *Flute* and *Clarinet Concertos.* There could hardly be any further proof needed that Nielsen was a composer of the twentieth century despite his chronological grouping with the Post-Romantics. The last-mentioned work (1928) in particular is an uncompromising yet rewarding work to know, the fruit of a mind that remained inquisitive and daring to the end. Always seeming to display an uncanny understanding of each medium in which he worked, here too Nielsen seems to crawl inside of the instrument and stretch its capabilities; one soloist commented on the present work that the composer must have played the clarinet because of his tendency to find its most difficult notes. This challenge, as well as the frequently improvisatory quality of the soloist's part, indicate why such musicians as the late Benny Goodman "crossed lines" to tackle this concerto.

The work is in one movement, although musicologists generally discern four linked ones. The twisting yet leisurely opening theme in F is stated in the cellos and basses and is soon picked up and embellished by the soloist. In line with Nielsen's customary love of key combat, the orchestra seems to resent the clarinet's intrusion and tries to reinstate the theme in the proximate-yet-distant key of E. A more lyrical second theme emerges in the dominant key of C but the snare drum soon disrupts this, recalling that effective use of the percussion instrument in the *Fifth Symphony.* An incisive cadenza by the soloist precedes the recapitulation in which the key conflict continues. This is followed by what would pass for a slow movement, brooding and dominated by the horn (it is interesting to note that Nielsen gives important "supporting roles" to other instruments, even in a concerto). Presently the snare drum instigates a turbulent passage as the clarinet seems to inveigh against it in its highest register. This subsides to adagio again but shortly leads to a scherzo-like passage in 3/8 time which alternates a rapid chromatic perpetuum mobile with a slower but highly syncopated second subject. The latter is then taken up by the clarinet who "improvises" wildly upon it, interacting with the rest of the orchestra. This extended and active dialog subsides and changes to duple time; a long unwinding melody in the bassoon, which is transformed into a cadenza by the soloist, marks a transition to the finale. The snare-drum announces a "ten-hut!" as it were, and the clarinet intones a lively yet angular theme which is in turn picked up by the various strings. A more relaxed second subject follows, this in turn followed by a remembrance of the scherzo's second theme; the clarinet takes this up and another dialog between the soloist and orchestra develops. Presently the soloist branches off to make this an accompaniment to the restatement of the finale's main theme, now stated by the violins. This passage reaches a powerful climax with the clarinet sounding its highest notes. A subsiding pianissimo leads to the coda. The soloist makes a passing reference to the adagio; then the strings sensitively transform the finale's main theme. The soloist intones a few wistful, nebulous notes as the work seems to lightly touch down to its conclusion. *—Wayne Gerard Reisig*

Recommended:

- ○ **Nielsen: Complete Concertos** / Schoenwandt (cond.), Thomsen, Danish RSO / 1990 / Chandos 8894
- ○ **Nielsen: Concertos** / Blomstedt (cond.), Stevensson, Danish RSO / 1997 / EMI 69758

Flute Concerto (1926)

Nielsen was never much interested in writing a concerto on a heroic scale, saving his weightier material for his symphonies. As a result, each of his three concertos—for violin, flute and clarinet—are more or less intimate in character. If the *Violin Concerto* (1911) reflects an essentially traditional stylistic and harmonic outlook, the succeeding *Flute Concerto* mirrors the more modernistic currents of the 1920s.

This late work contains few real formal innovations; however, it is characterized by a conspicuous lack of tonal stability. Indeed, the first movement, marked Allegro moderato, seems to spend all of its time searching for a key center, beginning with a discordant sixteenth note theme in the violins. At first, D minor seems to be favored, but assertive themes in E flat minor and F major ensue, only to be followed by a dissonant, quasi-developmental section. Here, Nielsen interjects a coarse solo trombone part in an attempt to disrupt the demure proceedings. Eventually a new idea floats out radiantly on the solo flute, a simple cantabile melody in E major. This is quickly disturbed, however, and when the flute tries to reach it again in a cadenza, the orchestra contradicts it with a recapitulation of the opening themes. A brief second cadenza leads to a coda in the calming yet still uncertain key in G flat major.

While G flat is the relative of the initial E flat minor, it sounds unconvincing, as D minor and F major have been so much in evidence throughout the first movement. Thus, a second movement is needed. The movement begins with a charming melody in G major and proceeds with a rondo-like alternation between a 2/4 Allegretto section and a 3/4 Adagio section, leading to a culminating 6/8 Tempo di marcia, which is essentially a dance-like variation on the opening G major melody. Yet it is E major to which the movement really gravitates, and in a brilliant stroke, Nielsen brings back the bass trombone to provide the final tonal impetus, with a series of burlesque glissandi.

The *Flute Concerto* was composed for and premiered by the flautist Gilbert Jespersen. *—Brian Wise*

Recommended:

- ○ **Nielsen: Complete Concertos** / Schoenwandt (cond.), Christiansen, Danish RSO / 1990 / Chandos 8894
- ○ **Flötenkonzerte** / Francis (cond.), Faust, Cologne Radio Orch. / Capriccio 10495

Violin Concerto, Op. 33 (1911)

During the summer of 1911, Carl Nielsen was riding high on a major international success: his third symphony, whose premiere performance he had conducted that February in Copenhagen. Two months later, he was invited to present the work in Amsterdam with the Concertgebouw Orchestra, and it met with great approval once again. Nielsen was delighted with this long-awaited critical acclaim outside his native Denmark. He was equally delighted when, shortly after the Amsterdam performance, an invitation arrived from Nina Grieg, suggesting that he spend part of the summer at the Grieg home in Norway.

Grieg did much of his work in a small lakeside hut, and it was in this hut over the course of the summer that Nielsen began work on his first instrumental concerto, the *Violin Concerto,* Op. 33. The piece was written for Peder Møller, a Danish violinist and leader of the Royal Danish Orchestra. Writing in the concerto format for the first time was an interesting task for Nielsen, who was a trained violinist himself. He said of writing it: "It has to be good music and yet always show regard for the development of the solo instrument, putting it in the best possible light. The piece must have substance and be popular and showy without being superficial. These conflicting elements must and shall meet and form a higher unity."

This work, like Nielsen's earlier works, were informed by a Classicist aesthetic, one that avoided aspects of late Romanticism. The Neo-Classical structure of the unashamedly melody-oriented violin concerto gives it a simplicity and delicacy of texture as well as an air of (as composer Robert Simpson has called it) "spaciousness." In the mid- to late 1910s, only a few years after this work was written, Nielsen began increasingly to orient himself more toward new developments in European music. One need only listen to this work in juxtaposition with his far more modernist 1933 flute concerto in order to witness this change of direction.

The work was completed in December of 1911, and Nielsen conducted the Royal Danish Orchestra in the premiere performance two months later, with Møller as the soloist. It met with relative success among most of the Danish critics, and Nielsen and Møller gave the concerto considerable international exposure by way of taking it "on tour" to several major cities, among them Stockholm, Oslo, Paris, and Berlin.

Nielsen himself was pleased with his first concerto, describing the task of its composition as "essentially difficult and therefore a lot of fun."

Compared with the moody and tempestuous third symphony, the concerto is full of easygoing melody. The overall plan is unusual: there are three movements, but the work falls naturally into two slow movements, each followed by quick ones, producing a pattern rather like the two sides of a coin. The opening "Praeludium" is spacious and calm; it is followed by a jaunty tune for full orchestra. The violin is allowed to play tricks with this tune, and a brilliant cadenza comes before the development section. Though the concerto starts in G major, it moves gradually into D major. This feature is tied generally to Nielsen's style of composition, in which ideas tend to evolve though modulations and passing references rather than strong thematic development. The second-movement Adagio is a long, slow prelude to the final Scherzo, a rondo that gradually strips the music of its virtuosity and (as Nielsen himself said) "renounces everything that might dazzle or impress." Nevertheless it is full of good humor. The work requires repeated listening to reveal its depths and subtlties—a pleasant task, for the work's outlines are clear and enticing. *—Margaret Godfrey*

Recommended:

- ○ **Sibelius & Nielsen: Violin Concertos** / Salonen (cond.), Lin, Swedish RSO / 1988 / CBS 44548
- ○ **Sibelius & Nielsen: Violin Concertos** / Barenboim (cond.), Vengerov, Chicago SO / 1996 / Teldec 13161

OPERA

Maskarade (Masquerade) (1904–1906)

This brilliant comic opera was written in a remarkably short period of time. Nielsen, Denmark's leading composer, had been mulling over the project for a few months while he was fighting a battle over whether he would remain as a deputy conductor of the Royal Theater or revert to being nothing more than a back-desk second violinist. When he came out on the losing end, he resigned from the theater. He was ordered to bed with a heart condition. When he was able to work again, an "undercurrent" of creativity (as he described it) took over, and he wrote one of the most sparkling and delightful of all comic operas.

The original story comes from the play *Mascarade* by the revered Danish playwright Ludvig Holberg; Nielsen asked Vilhelm Anderson (an expert on Holberg) to make it into a suitable libretto. Holberg was so revered, in fact, that when word got around that Nielsen was adapting his sacrosanct words, a literary furor erupted. The opera had to be completed and submitted by a certain deadline to be considered for performance. Nielsen and Anderson took a gamble and submitted it unfinished, writing in a few perfunctory closing chords. The work was accepted for performance and the score returned for preparation—or, in Nielsen's case, completion. Nielsen managed to finish the opera, and then, with six weeks left before the premiere, he began work on the overture, completing it only eight days before opening night. The concert version of the overture has become one of the most popular of Nielsen's compositions.

The opera is a delightful satire on social conventions. The music was unreservedly praised and became a popular hit; the only substantial criticism concerned Anderson's treatment of Holberg's text. It has remained the most popular of all native operas in Denmark. Probably due to the unfamiliarity of Danish it was slow to catch on abroad: the first foreign production was in Sweden in 1930. It did not reach the United States until 1972, and Britain's first professional performance was only in 1990. By that time, the work was well on its way to becoming an international repertory item. The language really isn't much of an obstacle, for the work's high spirits and positively Mozartean language come through even to those who don't understand a word of the original. *—Joseph Stevenson*

Synopsis:

Act One. The story is set in Copenhagen, Denmark, in the spring of 1723. In his father's house, Leander sleeps late in the morning because he attended a masquerade party the previous night, where he met a beguiling young woman of unknown identity. He dreams about her now and plans to attend the masquerade again that night. But his rapidly growing love for her faces one huge obstacle: Jeronimus, his father, has agreed to an arranged marriage for Leander with Mr. Leonard's daughter Leonora, whom the young man has never even met. When Leander awakens he learns from his servant, Henrik, that there is a harsh penalty for breach of such marriage contracts. Leander's mother Magdelone enters and exhibits a strong interest in attending the masquerade herself.

Jeronimus learns from Henrik that Leander is in love with the mysterious woman he met at the masquerade. Mr. Leonard enters and divulges news that his daughter is unwilling to fulfill the contract. Both he and Jeronimus decide they must fashion a scheme to avoid any scandal that might result from the situation. Jeronimus appeals to Leander but fails to persuade him to agree to marriage with Leonora.

Act Two. Jeronimus has ordered his dim-witted servant Arv to stop anyone from leaving the house that night. Henrik, disguises himself as a ghost and induces Arv to confess his domestic misdeeds, such as stealing wine and flour. Arv soon realizes he has been fooled, and must now allow Leander and Henrik to sneak off to the masquerade. Others arrive at the masquerade, including Mr. Leonard and Leonora and her maid Pernille. As one suspects, it is Leonora whom Leander had met at the masquerade and fallen in love with. Jeronimus discovers that Leander and Henrik are missing from the house and presumes they have gone to the masquerade. He dresses up as Bacchus and Arv as Cupid, and the pair then depart for the masquerade.

Act Three. Amid the joyous festivities of the masquerade, Leander romances Leonora, the two eventually divulging their names to each other, and Henrik woos Pernille. Magdelone pretends to be unmarried in her flirtations with Mr. Leonard, but keeps her mask on to protect her identity. Jeronimus momentarily disrupts the romantic activities of Leander and Leonora, unaware of who the loving couple is.

Henrik discovers Jeronimus' identity and enlists the aid of a professor and his students to get him drunk. During a dance, Jeronimus flirts with a young girl and makes himself appear a foolish old man. The unmasking hour arrives: Magdelone and Mr. Leonard are surprised when they recognize each other, and it is revealed that Leander and Leonora, partners in the arranged marriage, fell in love by chance at the masquerade. Jeronimus at first is too inebriated to grasp the significance of the revelation, but soon realizes the happy conclusion in store for all parties. *—Robert Cummings*

Recommended:

- ○ **Nielsen: Maskarade** / Schirmer (cond.), Skovhus, Haugland, Rorholm, Bonde-Hansen, Danish National RSO / 1998 / Decca 460227

Birgit Nilsson

b. May 17, 1918, Västra Karups, Sweden

Soprano

The vocal talents of Birgit Nilsson were first recognized when began to sing in her church choir. She studied voice with Ragnar Blennow in Bastad and later at the

Royal Music Academy Stockholm with Joseph Hislop and Arne Sunnegard. She made her opera debut at Stockholm where her first important role was Agatha in *Der Freischütz*, and in 1947 she sang Lady Macbeth in Verdi's *Macbeth* there. Her first important international appearance came in 1951 as Elettra in Mozart's *Idomeneo* at the Glyndebourne Festival. In 1952, she sang Donna Anna in *Don Giovanni* at Florence. Her first important appearances in Wagner operas came in 1953 at Stockholm where she sang Elisabeth in *Tannhäuser* and Isolde for the first time. This marked the start of the most important Wagnerian career of the second half of the twentieth century. The following year she made her Bayrueth debut as Elsa in *Lohengrin* and in the same season sang Ortlinde in *Die Walküre*. She later appeared there as Isolde and as Brunnhilde. It was in Munich during the 1954–55 season that she first sang Brunnhilde in Wagner's *Das Ring der Nebelungen* and during the same season she sang her first Salome. In 1957, she sang the complete Ring cycle in London. At the Vienna State Opera she was heard as Elsa, Sieglinde, Elisabeth, Aida, and Sent. In 1957 she sang Leonore in Beethoven's *Fidelio* and the following season sang her first *Turandot*. She was also highly regarded for her interpretations of *Elektra* and the Barak's Wife in *Die Frau ohne Schatten*. Her other important Italian roles were Tosca, Amelia in *Un ballo in maschera* and Aida. She sang at all of the major opera centers of the world including Tokyo, Paris, Buenos Aires, Chicago, San Francisco, and Hamburg. Also she sang *Turandot* in Moscow with the Teatro alla Scala. At the age of 62, a performance of Strauss' *Elektra* was videotaped at the Metropolitan Opera House and broadcast around the world.

Because of her full schedule of opera performances, Nilsson did not sing in many concerts or recitals although early in her career she did sing the *Ninth Symphony* of Beethoven on several occasions including one at Bayreuth. She did give some recitals including tours of Australia and Japan as well the major music centers of Europe and North America. Her recital programs concentrated on the German and Scandinavian songs, including some rarely heard pieces by Stenhammar. She often sang "I Could Have Danced All Night" as an encore.

The voice of Birgit Nilsson was like a laser beam that cut through the orchestra, unlike the voice of Kirsten Flagstad or Jessye Norman which are like a wall of sound. It was a large voice with such brilliance that at times it gave the sensation of being sharp of the intended pitch. She was a congenial colleague except for her long standing difficulties with Franco Corelli regarding the length of the high Cs in Puccini's *Turandot* and with Herbert von Karjan. Happily all of her important roles have been preserved on recordings. As long as the operas of Wagner are performed, the voice of Birgit Nilsson will be remembered, and no one has sung Puccini's *Turandot* with more brilliance or security. Her autobiography, *Mina minnesbilder*, was published in 1977 at Stockholm. *—Richard LeSueur*

Recommended:

- ○ **Birgit Nilsson** / Nilsson, etc. / 2001 / Decca 467912
- ○ **Birgit Nilsson: Opera Arias** / Ludwig, Wallberg (conds.), Nilsson, London PO / 2000 / Testament 1200
- ○ **Wagner: Tristan und Isolde** / Solti (cond.), Nilsson, Krause, Kmentt, Resnik, Vienna PO / 2002 / Decca 470814
- ○ **Puccini: Turandot** / Leinsdorf (cond.), Nilsson, Tebaldi, Bjoerling, Tozzi, Rome Opera House Orch / 1996 / RCA 62687

Takako Nishizaki

b. Apr. 14, 1944, Aichi Prefecture, Japan
Violinist

Violinist Takako Nishizaki is perhaps the most frequently recorded concert violinist of the digital era. She was also the first violinist to learn by way of the Suzuki method; her father, Shinji Nishizaki, worked with Shinichi Suzuki in developing the method, and Takako Nishizaki took instruction from both teachers. She made her debut at the age of 9, and further studied with Broadus Erle, starting in Japan and later at Yale University. Nishizaki finished her violin studies at Juilliard under Joseph Fuchs and in 1967 won second prize in the Leventritt International competition behind Pinchas Zukerman.

One would surmise that with her talent and beauty that American record companies would be getting in each other's way to obtain Nishizaki's recording contract. But they weren't, and by 1974 Nishizaki settled in Hong Kong, where she established a career as the preeminent violin virtuoso on the Chinese concert circuit. This was no small feat, as in China they take the violin seriously and its literature is central to the entire establishment of Chinese classical music. Along the way Nishizaki met and married German businessman Klaus Heymann, founder of HNH International, the corporate parent to the popular classical label Naxos. Heymann sponsored Nishizaki in an extensive series of recordings of Chinese classical music on his Marco Polo label. Some of these recordings sold into the millions of copies in China, providing the nest egg that launched the Naxos label in the late 1980s.

With Naxos, Nishizaki has recorded much of the standard Western violin literature, as well, but has made a special mission of recording key violin literature that is known in concert and in the classroom, but seldom represented on records. The most celebrated example of this tendency is her recordings of the concertos of Chevalier de St-Georges, but it also includes her interpretations of Charles August de Bériot, Louis Spohr, and Joseph Joachim. All of Nishizaki's recordings are notable for her generous, singing tone; flexible rhythmic sensibility; her sense of architectural symmetry in regard to whole movements; her ability to excite; and the sheer beauty of Nishizaki's sound. *—Uncle Dave Lewis*

Recommended:

- ○ **Violin Miniatures** / Nishizaki, Jando / 1989 / Naxos 550306
- ○ **The Butterfly Lovers** / Chengwu (cond.), Nishizaki, Shanghai Conservatory SO / 1998 / Naxos 554334
- ○ **Boulogne: Violin Concertos** / Müller-Brühl (cond.), Nishizaki, Cologne CO / 2001 / Naxos 555040
- ○ **Popular Chinese Violin Pieces** / Nishizaki, Siufan, Koo Kwok Kuen / 1994 / Marco Polo 223910

Marni Nixon

b. Feb. 22, 1930, Altadena, CA
Soprano

Soprano Marni Nixon developed a highly successful career dubbing the singing for famous actresses in movie musicals from the late 1950s and early 1960s. She has also sung opera, appeared as soloist in orchestral concerts and taken roles in Broadway and off-Broadway musical productions.

Marni McEathron Nixon came from a family of minor show business performers. She began study of the violin at age four, later sang with her sisters in local productions, and had a few bit roles in movies. She eventually abandoned the violin and began vocal studies with Carl Ebert, Boris Goldovsky, and Sarah Caldwell. Nixon retained an interest in film work and often appeared as an extra in films of the late 1940s. Her vocal talents were soon recognized and her first significant breakthrough occurred when she sang the voices of angels in the 1948 film classic *Joan of Arc*, which starred Ingrid Bergman. Her first dubbing assignment came the following year, with the release of the 1949 film *The Secret Garden*, wherein she sang for actress Margaret O'Brien. In 1950, Nixon married composer Ernest Gold; their union would produce three children. She and Gold collaborated in recordings of some of his songs, a reissue of which appeared in the early 1990s. The couple divorced in 1969. Nixon's first major assignment came in the 1956 film version of the Rogers and Hammerstein classic *The King and I*, for which she dubbed the singing of Deborah Kerr. *An Affair to Remember* (1957) followed, wherein she once again sang for Kerr. Nixon's next success came with her behind-the-scenes vocals for Natalie Wood in the 1961 film version of Leonard Bernstein's *West Side Story*. Lerner and Loewe's *My Fair Lady* (1964) was her next major project, wherein she dubbed for Audrey Hepburn's Eliza Doolittle. According to Nixon, the key to a successful dub was "They have to share themselves with you. Once they realize you're like a sponge and aren't going to take over their performance, it's fine." In other words, she would try to adapt herself to the actress' characterization as well as singing style.

When the big musical film productions began fading in the mid-1960s, Nixon's dubbing career quickly withered. From 1969 to 1971, she taught at the California Institute of Arts. In the 1970s, she moved to Seattle and joined the Seattle Opera Company. She also hosted a children's television program there called *Boomerang*, which garnered four Emmy awards. In 1980, Nixon became a faculty member at the Santa Barbara Music Academy of the West. In 1983, she married Albert Block. Nixon has continued to sing in operas and musicals, and in orchestral concerts as well. She has appeared with many major American orchestras, including the Cleveland Orchestra and the New York Philharmonic, as well as ensembles abroad, such as the Israel Philharmonic. She has sung classical repertory ranging from Mozart to Webern and Stravinsky. In May, 2001, she took on the role of Heidi Schiller in the Broadway production of *Sondheim's Follies*, and in 2002 was touring with her one-woman show *Marni Nixon: The Voice of Hollywood*. *—Robert Cummings*

Recommended:

- ○ **West Side Story** / Green (cond.), Robbins, Wise, Nixon, Wand, Orch. / 2004 / Columbia 89226
- ○ **Marni Nixon Sings Classic Kern** / Nixon, etc. / Reference 28

Luigi Nono

b. Jan. 29, 1924, Venice, Italy, **d.** May 8, 1990, Venice, Italy
Composer: Avant-garde, Chamber Music, Choral

Luigi Nono achieved prominence after World War II as an uncompromising modernist seeking to revolutionize music in Europe. Along with fellow Italians Luciano Berio and Bruno Maderna, Nono attended the influential Darmstadt Summer Courses and became associated with other young modernists such as Pierre Boulez and Karlheinz Stockhausen. In many ways, Nono was the most radical of them all, choosing to combine a keen political engagement with a musical orientation that mixes austere beauty with fierce intensity.

Nono grew up in Venice as part of a reasonably well-to-do family. He studied composition with Gian Francesco Malipiero as an auditor but he graduated with a law degree. While he never practiced, his political interests were likely sharpened during that period. In 1946, just out of university, Nono met two important figures: Luigi Dallapiccolo, the first Italian to compose 12-tone music, and Maderna, the innovative composer and conductor who became his friend and mentor. In 1948, the two young musicians attended a conducting course with Hermann Scherchen, whose discipline and questing spirit were ennervating. Around this time, Nono was introduced to the writing of Federico García Lorca, whose poetry he would set on a number of occasions, and whose political engagement would ignite his interest. He joined the Italian Communist Party in 1952.

In 1950, Nono attended the summer course in Darmstadt, where his first orchestral composition, *Variazioni canoniche sulla serie dell'op. 41 di Arnold Schoenberg*, was premiered. He returned every year until 1960, meeting several influential personalities, giving lectures, and having several works premiered. His interest in electronic music developed in 1952, through lectures and demonstrations given by Werner Meyer-Eppler in Bonn. His most important composition during this period is probably *Il Canto Sospeso* (1956), for soloists, choir, and orchestra. One innovation was his fracturing of the text to distribute the syllables across the subdivided voices.

During a trip in 1954 to attend the premiere of Arnold Schoenberg's unfinished opera, *Moses und Aron*, Nono met the composer's daughter, Nuria. They married the following year. The first professional association Nono developed was with the Studio di Fonologia in Milan. Directed by Berio and Maderna, Nono carried on working there after the others had left, producing a whole series of pieces, both prerecorded and mixed (instruments/voices and tape), into the 1970s.

Nono's first stage work, *Intolleranza 1960*, was presented at the 1961 Venice Biennale. Collage-like, with a large collection of political texts, this "azione scenica" provoked a great deal of controversy. But Nono was unrelenting in his commitment to combining radical texts with revolutionary music. In 1964, he put his beliefs to the test by beginning a series of lecture-concerts in factories and other locales all over Italy. By far, the majority of Nono's compositions use voice, the "message" being of critical importance. A second stage-work, again with a mix of radical texts, *Al Gran Sole Carico d'Amore*, was presented in Milan in 1975, though it began as a collaboration at the Taganka Theater in Moscow. His last large-scale operatic work, *Prometeo*, was premiered in 1984, in Venice.

In the 1980s, Nono began a fruitful collaboration with the Experimentalstudio der Heinrich Strobel-Stiftung in Freiburg, developing elaborate schemes for transforming the sounds of live instruments. Outstanding pieces include *Omaggio a György Kurtág* (1983) and *A Pierre: Dell'azzurro silenzio, inquietum* (1985). At the same time, his style began to change, a shift attributed in part to the influence of Giacinto Scelsi, a mystic Italian composer. A number of Nono's late pieces explore variations on an individual pitch, such as *No Hay Caminos, Hay Que Caminar... Andrej Tarkowskij* (1987), for seven spatially separated orchestral groups. *—Jim Harley*

Overview of Works (1950–1989)

Luigi Nono was one of the most political and overtly intellectual composers of his era, as strongly influenced by the avant-garde in social thinking and approach to the theater and arts as by his musical mentors, who included Gian Francesco Malipiero (whom he later considered too conservative), Schoenberg, and Bruno Maderna. Aside from his teachers, Webern was another strong influence. Extramusical influences included such theatrical innovators as Vsevolod Meyerhold, Josef Svoboeda, Angelo Maria Ripellino, and Piscator, whose ideas on theater as political expression, theater in the round, and new approaches to the roles of plot and actors are all apparent in Nono's stage works. He was also a pioneer in the use of electronic music, which remained a major part of his output until his death. Later in life, his music showed remnants of Malipiero's influence in the way he incorporated classical mythological imagery and the spoken word in his *Prometeo: Tragedia dell'ascolto.* Musically, however, his works veer between modernism and lyricism. His early works, in particular, are largely based in 12-tone serialism and heavy emphasis on unconventional percussion, but even they often take on an almost Romantic melodic aspect, particularly in his smaller scale works such as his chamber music and Liebeslied. While Nono politically rejected the conventions of bourgeois art, he also recognized that music with a solely intellectual appeal is, of necessity, open only to a few, and that was distasteful to his socialist convictions. However, he was deeply interested in the science of music, ultimately considering music the application of formulas as can be seen in his intricately crafted 1956 composition for soloists, chorus, and orchestra, *Il Canto Sospeso*, or his *Varianti for Orchestra*, written the next year and in which he utilized a combination of tonalism and mirror composition. His earlier works, when socialism and communism were still politically spreading, display his "call to the barricades" enthusiasm and belief in a realizable socialist utopia, though his later music reflects a more pessimistic approach as it became increasingly clear that socialism was becoming less politically relevant worldwide. His 1960 opera *Intolleranza* is perhaps his best-known work, written during his more optimistic period. During World War II, he had been a member of the Italian Resistance and remained a committed anti-fascist, and the premiere was disrupted by fascist demonstrations, including stink bombs. He also wrote scores for two films, Leobardo Lopez's 1966 *El Jinete de cubo* and Humberto Solas' 1985 *Un hombre de exito*. *—Ann Feeney*

Recommended:

- ○ **Nono: Composizione per orchestra 1; Der rote mantel** / Hirsch, Gottschick, Luz, RIAS-Kammerchor, Berlin German SO / 2004 / Wergo 6667
- ○ **Nono: La lontanaza; Hay que caminar** / Kremer, Grindenko / DG 000140902
- ○ **Luigi Nono** / Bertola, Gottwald (conds.), Woytowicz, Henius, Miller / 1992 / Wergo 286038-2
- ○ **Nono 3** / Richard (cond.), Otto, Rasker, Recherche Ens. / 1995 / Disques Montaigne 782047
- ○ **Nono: La Lontananza Nostalgica Utopica Futura** / Arditti SQ / 2000 / Disques Montaigne 782133
- ○ **Luigi Nono** / Gielen (cond.), Baden South West RSO / 2000 / Disques Montaigne 782132

AVANT-GARDE

A Pierre. Dell' azzuro silenzio, inquietum (1985)

A Pierre, for bass flute, bass clarinet, and live electronics, which produce a swarm of harmonic resonances like the sound of many choral groups—which Nono indicates "a piú cori" in his title, but which is in fact not for voices—was written in 1985 and is dedicated to Pierre Boulez on his 60th birthday. In 1955, Nono had dedicated another work to Boulez "for his humanity," but withdrew it later for political and other reasons. It is difficult to tell if *A Pierre* represents Nono's idea of Boulez's music, as it suggests a more soothing, less angular, and hard-edged pointillistic composer. In any case, the sounds of the piece are very gentle: breath tones deep in reverberation, non-corporeal harmonics, deep and enveloping bass line waves, lovely transparent chordally tuned—electronic resonances, clarinet bleeps, and overblowings like whale and dolphin songs underwater (is the "blue silence" sky or sea, or an imagined heaven?)—the texture is surprisingly like the music of several American West Coast composers. This was a completely new poetic direction for Nono and is very compelling. *—"Blue Gene" Tyranny*

Recommended:

- ○ **Nono: A Pierre; Quando stanno morendo; Post-Prae-ludium** / various / Musica d'Oggi 1003

Como una ola de fuerza y luz, for soprano, piano, orchestra & tape (1971–1972)

Nono's title *Como una ola de fuerza y luz* might be rendered into English as "Like a wave of strength and light." The piece was completed in 1972 and is scored for piano, soprano, orchestra, and tape. Like so many piano compositions of the twentieth century, its existence owes much to pianist Maurizio Pollini, who has worked hard to ensure that the piano repertory does not become a mere museum.

Pollini met Nono in September 1966, and the pianist suggested to Nono that he write for the piano, even though (like so many late twentieth century composers) Nono had shown almost no interest in the instrument.

Nono had created the work specifically for Pollini and conductor Claudio Abbado, but without the soprano part. In September 1971, Nono had received news that his young friend Luciano Cruz had suddenly died. Cruz was leader of the Movement of the Revolutionary Left in Chile. His death inspired Nono to introduce a solo soprano part, setting the text of a poem by Julio Huasi and changing the work into a sort of memorial for his friend. Pollini and Abbado premiered the work at La Scala on June 28, 1972.

Throughout much of the work there is an interplay between the live performers and the tape, which contains a recording of Pollini's piano playing and women's voices. Loudspeakers are specifically placed in the hall to create an effect that Nono described as "resembling the opening and closing of a space upon itself, like the extending and receding of a life—a programmatic metaphor meant to be understood freely."

The piece is in four sections, full of Nono's usual contrasts of violence, tenderness, unbearable loudness, and total silences. *—Gerald Brennan*

Recommended:

- ○ **Nono: Como una ola; Epitaffio 1 & 3** / Kegel (cond.), Reinhardt-Kiss, Leipzig RSO / 1994 / Berlin Classics 0021412

CHAMBER MUSIC

Fragmente-Stille, an Diotima, for string quartet (1979–1980)

This composition seeks to "externalize as fully as possible that which has been internalized... that is what matters today" (Nono). The music is guided by lines from Holderlin's famous poem (Diotima was Socrates' teacher, and is associated with the concept "Time"), which are present only as unspoken meditations and guideposts written into the score in 52 places. Nono addresses the fundamental questions "Where am I, and who am I?" by examining, fragmenting, and modulating old music and memories from the distant past as producers of both pain and hope. Written for the 1980 Beethoven Festival in Bonn, Nono uses Beethoven's piano sonata instruction *mit innigster Empfindung* (roughly, "with innermost searching of the heart") to imply a readiness to break out of the habitual "into the open air." Toward its finale, this quartet manages to produce the sensation, appearing as an instruction in several of John Cage's works, "Play until you feel the presence of silence." This is a beautiful as well as a mentally rewarding experience. *—"Blue Gene" Tyranny*

Recommended:

○ **Nono: Fragmente; Hay que caminar** / Arditti SQ / 2003 / Montaigne Naive 782172

CHORAL

Il canto sospeso, cantata (1955–1956)

The music of Luigi Nono was known only to a few connoisseurs in the early 1950s, even though he was championed by a few powerful people, especially conductor Hermann Scherchen who had played Nono's music in Switzerland. Nono finally came to international attention in 1956 with the premiere of the song cycle *Il canto sospeso* (The Song Suspended) in Cologne, and the piece is still probably Nono's most acclaimed work.

Scored for soprano, contralto, tenor, mixed chorus, and orchestra, it consists of excerpts from the last letters of those condemned to death because they were members of the European Resistance movement. Nono's idea was to musicalize the texts by breaking the language up into syllables, thus making its musical content ready for the style of composition he was to apply. Nono didn't care much about making the text intelligible to the listener, an oddity considering the polemic nature of Nono's work. When he was criticized for this, he explained (according to Joachim Noller) that "the meaning of the texts was transferred to other, musical, means of expression. Whereas in certain forms of political aesthetics, music is degraded, as it were, to a mere handmaid of the text, with the spoken language as the standard by which all communication is judged, Nono prefers to set greater store by the variety and autonomy of musical expression."

Il canto sospeso is a serial piece, of the pointillistic variety, based on a clever 12-note row:

A rising to B flat (minor 2nd), down to A flat (major 2nd), up to B (augmented 2nd), down to G (major 3rd), up to C (perfect 4th), down to F sharp (diminished 5th), up to C sharp (perfect 5th), down to F (augmented 5th), up to D (major 6th), down to E (minor 7th), up to E flat (augmented 7th)—thus incorporating all tones and all intervals.

Like much of the cutting-edge music of the time, mathematics governs every detail of this composition including pitch, duration, loudness, attack, and timbre. Notwithstanding its strictly written 12-tone format, *Il canto sospeso* is imbued with a passion and lyricism that only the best composers working in this technique can conjure. *—Gerald Brennan*

Recommended:

○ **Nono: Il canto sospeso; Mahler: Kindertotenlieder** / Abbado (cond.), Bonney, Otto, Torzewski, Berlin PO / 1993 / Sony 53360

Marielle Nordmann

b. Jan. 24, 1941, Montpellier, France

Harpist

A 1958 graduate of Lily Laskine's harp class at the Paris Conservatory, Marielle Nordmann is the primary modern inheritor of that great French harpist's legacy. Like her mentor, she has shown a devotion to the harp in all its potentialities, from crossover and popular music to unknown classical compositions unearthed through musicological investigation. Nordmann was born in Montpellier in 1941 and enrolled early at the Conservatory. After her formal studies with Laskine were finished, the two performed and recorded together for some years. Nordmann carried forward Laskine's musical partnership with flutist Jean-Pierre Rampal, and that led her into recording work with Rampal's classical-jazz crossover collaborator, Claude Bolling. She recorded an album of harp-and-pan flute duets, *Harpe et Flûte de Pan*, with Simion Stanciu Syrinx in 1994, and she released a multimedia disc, *La harpe apprivoisé* (The Harp Tamed). On the other hand, Nordmann performs and has recorded much of the standard classical repertory of harp music, and she has championed the work of the little-known French Romantic composer Elias Parish Alvars. Her 1993 disc *Romantic Harp Concertos* includes harp concertos by Alvars and Boieldieu along with a transcription of a Viotti violin concerto. Nordmann has primarily been associated with the Erato label. The numerous honors that have flowed her way in France include designation as a Chevalier of the Legion of Honor in 1998. She has been active in recent years as the director of the Concours Lily Laskine festival and as professor at the Conservatoire Supérieure in Paris, where she also teaches a class for 9 to 12-year-olds. *—James Manheim*

Recommended:

○ **Romantic Harp Concertos** / Rampal (cond.), Nordmann, Franz Liszt CO / 1995 / Sony 58919

○ **Rautavaara: Harp Concerto; Symphony 8** / Segerstam (cond.), Nordmann, Helsinki PO / Ondine 978

○ **Harp Concertos** / Kantorow, Guschlbauer (conds.), Nordmann, Duchable, Strasbourg PO, Auvergne Orch. / 2003 / Virgin 562218

Per Nørgård

b. Jul. 13, 1932, Gentofte, Denmark

Composer: Symphonic

Per Nørgård (pronounced "Pair Ner-gore") has emerged as perhaps the most important Danish composer since Nielsen. His music has paralleled and contributed to avant-garde developments in European music since the 1950s, evolving from a Nordic Romanticism derived from Vagn Holmboe and Jean Sibelius, through a short period in the later 1950s when he used collage and other then-fashionable techniques, into a period in the 1960s and 1970s during which Nørgård invented the forward-looking "infinity row." He became a professor of music at the Royal Academy of Music in Aarhus in 1965, and has been influential as a teacher; through the work of his students (Hans Abrahamsen is perhaps the most famous), Nørgård inspired the Danish "New Simplicity" movement in the 1960s. Since the late 1970s, Nørgård has been inspired by the writings and drawings of the troubled Swiss artist Adolf Wölfli (d. 1930). Nørgård is extremely prolific and has written in every genre, from the major classical forms to amateur choral music.

Nørgård studied theory, music history, and composition at the Royal Danish Conservatory from 1952 to 1955, and continued his composition studies in Paris with Nadia Boulanger in 1956 and 1957. His early music shows the strong influence of the Finnish composer Jean Sibelius, and especially of Sibelius' characteristic working-out of motives. The *Symphony No. 1* and *Constellations* are highlights of this period. After brief experiments with collage in the later 1950s, Nørgård in 1960 developed the infinity row, a way of generating a constantly expanding melody from an initial two-note motive. Infinity row melodies are self-similar (for example, the second, third, and fourth pitches return as the fifth, ninth, and thirteenth pitches), and Nørgård uses self-similarity to create a hierarchical structure: a piece may be divided into four large sections of 1024 notes each, then into sections of 256 notes, and so on. Nørgård's early pieces using the infinity row (such as *Voyage Through the Golden Screen* are essentially orchestrations of an infinity row melody. However, in later pieces, Nørgård extended the technique to generate harmony as well.

Nørgård abruptly changed direction in the late 1970s under the influence of the writings, paintings, and musical ideas of Wölfli, who spent the last 35 years of his life in a Swiss asylum. One of the first results was the *Symphony No. 4: Indischer Roosengaarten und Chineesischer Hexensee* ("Indian Rose-Garden and Chinese Witch-Sea"—Wölfli was fond of doubling vowels). Though Nørgård continued to use the infinity row, his obsession with Wölfli has to some extent colored all his works since 1980. The Wölfli music, in contrast to the slowly changing textures of Nørgård's earlier infinity row music, is marked, in the terms Nørgård has used to describe Wölfli's art, by abrupt shifts "between idyll and catastrophe."

In the 1990s, Nørgård explored the idea of interference (the pattern that results when two or more regular patterns are played together or otherwise combined) through the use of thickly layered rhythmic and melodic patterns. This period has also been marked by the writing of many concertos, from works for each of the main stringed instruments to the *Concerto in Due Tempi* (1996) for piano and orchestra, and *Bach to the Future* (1997) for percussion and orchestra. In 1996, the premiere of *Nuit des hommes*, an hour-long "opera(torium)" based on poems by Apollinaire, marked an attempt to create a new kind of opera, without dramatic tension. The work exemplified the two forces which have driven Nørgård's music: a use of very eclectic sources (from Babylonian myth in the ritualistic opera *Gilgamesh* (1972) to the Beatles, in *Doing* (1968)), and a need for constant self-reinvention. *—David McCarthy*

Overview of Works (1950)

Norwegian composer Per Nørgård is best-known for a type of serial composition he developed called the "infinite series," a series of ordered pitches that supposedly expands to infinity. But Nørgård's music is much more than merely yet another personalization of Schoenberg's technique. Like nearly all Scandinavian composers of the 1930s and 1940s, Nørgård started his compositional career writing in the heroic style of Sibelius modified by the symphonic style of his teacher Holmboe. But his later trips, first to Paris to study under Nadia Boulanger and then to various meetings of the ISCM (International Society for Contemporary Music), broadened Nørgård's style to include the clarity of neo-Classicism and the serialism of Schoenberg. In works like *Triptychon* (1957) and *Konstellationer* (1958), Nørgård fused Scandinavian symphonism with continental neo-Classicism, while works like *Fragment VI* (1959–61) for orchestral groups and *Inscape* (1969) for string quartet revealed his fascination with serialism. In his opera *Labyrinten* (1963), Nørgård made use of quarter-tone modes, and in *The Young Man Shall Marry* (1964) he experimented with collage techniques. All these experiments became subsumed in his "infinite series" and his search for "conscious spirituality," ideas that permeated his later works like his *Second* and *Third* symphonies. In these works, Nørgård's harmonic and formal concepts became fused with a dramatic form of Scandinavian symphonism that is more concerned with achieving aesthetic and spiritual enlightenment than exploring new sounds and structures for their own sake. *—James Leonard*

Recommended:

- ○ **Nørgård: Symphony 6; Terrains Vagues** / Dausgaard (cond.), Danish National SO / 2002 / Chandos 9904
- ○ **Nørgård: Borderlines; Dream Play; Voyage into the Golden Screen** / Bellincampi (cond.), Hirsch, Copenhagen PO / 2003 / Dacapo 8226014
- ○ **Nørgard: Symphonies 4 & 5** / Segerstam (cond.), Veng, Danish RSO / 1997 / Chandos 9533
- ○ **Nørgård: Frostsalme** / Parkman (cond.), Hansen, Rummel, Hansen, Hjor, Athelas Sinfonietta / 2002 / Chandos 10008

SYMPHONIC

Symphony No. 3 (1972–1975)

Two developments in Nørgård's style gave rise to his *Third Symphony*: one was his adoption in the 1960s of a style of writing often called "orchestral polyphony," in which many voices of orchestral sound create a shimmering effect reminiscent of late Medieval and Renaissance vocal polyphony. Another was Nørgård's development of what he called the "infinite row," in which a single interval creates a series of new intervals, lining up pitches in a potentially endless stream. The row fits into itself like a set of Russian dolls. It can be written as a pattern spiraling outward, and as is the case with fractals, each new note can generate repeated patterns of the original.

The score was commissioned by Radio Denmark, which permitted him, during composition, to try out his orchestral effects using its house ensemble. The resulting symphony is long, comprising two movements of 20 minutes and a half hour, respectively. The first movement creates itself in stages: first the harmony by itself, then melody, then rhythm. The second movement is more complex, and opens up the first movement's contemplation of the complexities of nature on earth to a sense of cosmic space. Through a masterly manipulation of the "infinite row," Nørgård "discovers" the tune of a Schubert song within the texture. Toward the end a chorus is added, with a hymn praising the Virgin, and then Rilke's sonnet to Orpheus, "Singe die Grten, mein Herz, die du nicht kennst." *—Joseph Stevenson*

Recommended:

- ○ **Nørgård: Symphony 3; Piano Concerto** / Segerstam (cond.), Danish RSO / 1996 / Chandos 9491
- ○ **Nørgård: Symphony 3; Piano Concerto** / Veto (cond.), Danish RSO / Dacapo 8901

Jessye Norman

b. Sep. 15, 1945, Augusta, GA
Soprano

A prominent American soprano, Jessye Norman was the daughter of a schoolteacher and an insurance broker. She started singing spirituals at the age of four at Mount Calvary Baptist Church; one Saturday while doing her chores she heard an opera for the first time, broadcast on the radio. She became an instant opera fan and started listening to recordings of Marian Anderson and Leontyne Price. Nat "King" Cole was also a major inspiration for her.

When she was 16, she started studying at Howard University in Washington, where her voice teacher was Carolyn Grant. She sang in the university chorus and had a job as soloist the Lincoln Temple United Church of Christ. In 1965 she won the National Society of Arts and Letters singing competition. She continued her studies at Peabody Conservatory of Music in Baltimore, and at the University of Michigan in Ann Arbor, where her most important studies were with Elizabeth Mannion and Pierre Bernac.

In 1968 she won the Munich Competition, leading to her operatic debut as Elisabeth in Wagner's *Tannhäuser* in Berlin. A major European operatic career quickly developed: she appeared as Meyerbeer's *L'Africaine* at Maggio Musicale in Florence in 1971, Verdi's *Aïda* at La Scala in Milan in 1972, and as Cassandra in Berlioz's *Les Troyens* at London's Covent Garden the same year. These roles are all princesses and bespeak a major part of her stage persona, a commanding and noble bearing, partly due to her uncommon height and size. But this is even more a function of her unique, rich, and powerful voice. She has an uncommonly wide range, encompassing all female voice registers from contralto to high dramatic soprano.

As her operatic career developed, she also made important recital debuts, including London and New York in 1973. She made an extensive North American concert debut in 1976 and 1977, but did not appear in opera in the United States until 1982. This was with the Opera Company of Philadelphia, in a double bill as Dido in Purcell's *Dido and Aeneas* and Queen Jocasta in Stravinsky's *Oedipus Rex*. Her Metropolitan Opera debut was as Cassandra in 1983, the opening night of the Met's centennial season.

Her interpretation of Strauss's *Four Last Songs* is legendary. Its slowness is controversial, but the tonal qualities of her voice are ideal for these final works of the great Romantic German lieder tradition. She also sings the *Gurrelieder* of Arnold Schoenberg, and the same composer's *Erwartung*. She sang that opera on a memorable double bill at the Met with Bartók's *Bluebeard's Castle*, which was broadcast nationally. She has also appeared on live broadcasts of season-opening concerts of the New York Philharmonic.

In addition to the direct and emotionally expressive qualities of her singing, her performances also impress through formidable intellectual understanding of the music and its style, as well as first-rate musicianship. She studies the languages of the music she sings, and has been acclaimed in her singing of Mussorgsky songs in the original Russian, in the German Romantic lieder repertoire, and in French music from Berlioz to contemporary composers. *—Joseph Stevenson*

Recommended:

- ○ **Brava, Jessye!** / Norman, etc. / 1996 / Philips 454693
- ○ **Spirituals** / Patterson (cond.), Norman, Baldwin, Ambrosian Singers / Philips 416462
- ○ **Berg** / Boulez (cond.), Norman, Schein, London SO / 1995 / Sony 66826
- ○ **Very Best of Jessye Norman** / Norman, etc. / 2003 / EMI 75912

Roger Norrington

b. Mar. 16, 1934, Oxford, England
Conductor

Roger Norrington is representative of a modern school of international "journeyman" conductors. A versatile, sometimes controversial, figure, he has concentrated on exploring—many would say revitalizing—the Classical and Romantic repertory in accordance with historical precedents, and through close attention to the notation, expressive markings and period instruments. The care Norrington gives to such details highlights the many contrasts between his interpretations of such familiar works as the Beethoven symphonies, and the ways in which they are normally performed by modern symphony orchestras.

After studying at Cambridge University and the Royal College of Music, London, Norrington was a professional singer for ten years. He founded choirs specializing in the music of Schütz and Monteverdi and led the Schütz Choir of London from 1962–82. His conducting career has continued with a succession of high profile engagements: musical director and principal conductor of Kent Opera, one of Britain's leading provincial opera companies (1969–84); the Bournemouth Sinfonietta (1985–89); the London Baroque and London Classical Players (1978–98); music director of St. Luke's, New York (1990–94); conductor of Camerata Academica, Salzburg (1997); and Stuttgart Radio Symphony Orchestra (1998). He has also been a guest conductor of many British and American orchestras.

Norrington is remarkably consistent in his approach to performance practices, placing particular emphasis on details such as the size and layout of the orchestra, and the differences in sound quality and playing techniques that have taken place since the works were written. Practically all the instruments in a modern symphony orchestra have changed in important ways and, therefore, in sound from those that were available before the twentieth century. The effect of this attention to orchestral color is noticeable, as are the generally faster tempi of Norrington's interpretations and other factors that reveal new and unexpected aspects of familiar works. For example, he accepts Beethoven's own metronome markings, which are frequently ignored by others.

Predictably, he has been criticized for neglecting what many regard as more important traditions of orchestral playing but, as he has said, "No tradition is stronger than the latest tradition." Nor is he willfully idiosyncratic; his approach is based on detailed analysis, though he does not claim "authenticity" and asserts "there is no such thing as a definitive performance."

In an introduction to his performances of all Beethoven's nine symphonies with the London Classical Players for BBC Television in 1989—one which differs in almost every respect from Klemperer's Beethoven cycle of 1972 for instance—he spoke of the need to "reconsider every single aspect" of these works in the light of the composer's intentions. He has recorded a strikingly original performance of Haydn's oratorio *The Seasons*, and extended his task of "restoration" into late nineteenth century and even twentieth century works.

Norrington's interpretations have a persuasive freshness, clarity and vitality, and his approach to the Baroque and Classical orchestral repertory has had a considerable influence on both professional musicians and attentive audiences. He received a knighthood in 1997 and is an Honorary Fellow of the Royal Academy of Music and Royal College of Music. *—Roy Brewer*

Recommended:

- ○ **Berlioz: Symphonie Fantastique** / Norrington, LCP / 1997 / Virgin 61379
- ○ **Mozart: Don Giovanni; Die Zauberflöte** / Norrington (cond.), Upshaw, Schmidt, Dawson, Tubb, LCP / 2003 / Virgin 562267
- ○ **Beethoven: Symphonies 7 & 8** / Norrington (cond.), Stuttgart RSO / 2002 / Haenssler 93087

- **Purcell: The Fairy Queen** / Norrington (cond.), Wistreich, Hunt, Crook, Padmore, LCP / 2002 / Virgin 61955
- **Beethoven: Symphony 9** / Norrington (cond.), Kenny, Walker, Salomaa, Power, LCP / 1987 / EMI 100467

Nigel North

b. Jun. 5, 1954, London, England

Lutenist

English lutenist Nigel North picked up the lute in the late 1960s while studying guitar at the Guildhall School of Music. At the time, this was viewed as "slacking" to some extent, as the lute was then largely regarded as a historical curiosity rather than a pursuit that was liable to earn one a teaching position. But North found his voice in the lute and stuck with it, and managed to land a position as lute player within the Early Music Consort of London during the last part of its existence under David Munrow. North also backed up legendary countertenor Alfred Deller in some of his final recordings. As the period performance movement began to take off in the wake of Munrow's death, North was able to find work playing continuo parts in ensembles such as Academy of Ancient Music, English Concert, and le Grande Ecurie. In 1975 the Guildhall School of Music appointed North to the position of lute instructor, even though he was still a student at the time. He held on to this position for 21 years.

North's career as a solo artist on recordings began in 1978 with a L'Oiseau Lyre disc of music by Robert de Visée. Since then he has recorded most frequently (and arguably, best) with Linn Records in the U.K., but North has also appeared as a soloist on discs released by the Saydisc and Arcana labels. In 1988 North cofounded the ensemble Romanesca with violinist Andrew Manze and continuo keyboardist Toll. Together they recorded some of the finest discs of violin-led Baroque chamber music ever for Harmonia Mundi, including multi-award winning sets of works by Heinrich Ignaz Franz von Biber, Antonio Vivaldi, and Johann Rosenmüller. Unfortunately, when Manze accepted directorship of the Academy of Ancient Music in 1998, Romanesca's activity came to a close, and with the death of John Toll in 2001, their recorded output appears finite. North left the Guildhall School in 1996 and spent three years teaching at the Hochschule der Künst in Berlin. Since 1999, North has taught at Indiana University in Bloomington as a professor within the Early Music Institute there. *—Uncle Dave Lewis*

Recommended:

- **Nigel North - Baroque Lute** / North / 1991 / Linn 006
- **Locke: Consort of 4 Parts** / Nicholson, North, Fretwork / 1996 / Veritas 45142
- **Bach on the Lute, Vol. 1** / North / 1996 / Linn 5013

Guiomar Novaës

b. Feb. 28, 1895, Sao João da Boa Vista, Brazil, **d.** Mar. 7, 1979, São Paulo, Brazil

Pianist

Guiomar Novaës (No*vah*es) and Claudio Arrau were the most celebrated pianists born in South America immediately before and after 1900—she in Brazil in 1895 (not 1896, as some biographies continue to list), he in Chile, in 1903. They were first to win international acclaim since Venezuelan-born Teresa Carreño (1853–1917), who had studied with Gottschalk. In São Paulo, where the family had moved from a provincial village soon after her birth, she revealed precocity at age four, and began studying at age seven with Luigi Chiafarelli, a Busoni pupil. He helped her developed the basics of tonal nuance, legato, and pedaling that won her a grant from the Brazilian government to study in Paris. At the Conservatoire in 1909 she placed first among 388 candidates for admission (some sources say 398). The jurors were Fauré, Moritz Moszkowski, and Debussy, who wrote to his friend and amanuensis André Caplet that "the most artistic...was a young Brazilian girl of 13. She's not beautiful, but her eyes are 'drunk with music' and she has the ability to cut herself off from her surroundings, which is the rare but characteristic mark of the artist." She was assigned to the class of Isidor Philipp (1863–1958), formerly a pupil of Saint-Saëns, and graduated two years later with a First Prize. Novaës made her formal debut that same year with the Châtelet Orchestra conducted by Gabriel Pierné, then toured throughout Western Europe until the outbreak of World War I. Hardly had she returned to São Paulo when an invitation came from the U.S. She made her North American debut in Aeolian Hall, New York City, on November 11, 1915, and returned often during the next 57 years. Novaës played her U.S. farewell at Hunter College in 1972. To the end, her tone remained mellifluous, her touch varied, her pedaling a wonder, and her legato special, even after sheer strength had ebbed.

In 1922, she married the Brazilian architect and composer Octavio Pinto (1890–1950), who had also studied with Philipp. For their two children he composed *Scenas Infantis*, which Novaës played regularly as a recital encore. For the same Pinto children, Villa-Lobos wrote the suite *Prole do bebê*. Novaës appeared with every major U.S. orchestra as well as abroad. In England, Queen Elizabeth invited her to play the opening recital in the new London hall bearing her name on April 30, 1967—a program that featured Novaës' beloved Mozart and Chopin, Beethoven, and Debussy.

Her recorded repertoire was astonishing, starting with the Victor Company in 1919 through 1927, Duo-Art piano rolls in the 1920s, then Columbia (now Sony) until 1948. In Vienna and Bamberg after World War II, she recorded 11 concertos for Vox (two each of the Beethoven *Fourth* and the Schumann A minor, first with Klemperer, then with Hans Swarowsky). They ranged from Mozart to Falla's *Nights in the Gardens of Spain*, plus dozens of solo works including the complete waltzes, études, nocturnes, and préludes of Chopin, several of Schumann's major solo works, *Book I* of Debussy's *Préludes*, five Beethoven sonatas, and her husband's *Scenas Infantis*.

She also recorded Liszt, Chopin and Debussy for London; Chopin and Beethoven (Op. 111 for the first time) on Vanguard, and several Brazilian composers on Fermata. International Piano Archives issued a live recording of Gottschalk's *Grand Fantasy on the Brazilian National Anthem* from a Hunter College concert in 1970, one year after Vox/Turnabout released the same music from a Pan-American Union concert marking the centennial of Gottschalk's death.

Novaës died in her native Brazil at age 84, just seven years after her retirement. *—Roger Dettmer*

Recommended:

- **The Romantic Novaes** / Swarowsky, Perlea (conds.), Novaës, Vienna SO, Bamberg SO / 1993 / Vox 5513
- **Guiomar Novaës Plays Chopin** / Novaës / 1993 / Vox 3501

Vítězslav Novák

b. Dec. 5, 1870, Kamenice nad Lipou, Bohemia, **d.** Jul. 18, 1949, Skutec, Czechoslovakia

Composer

An eminent Czech composer, Vítězslav Novák is known for his evocative music in which innovative harmonies and memorable tone colors are used to express a wide range of emotions, including inner turmoil, diffuse melancholy, and nostalgia, as well as a mystical recognition of the awesome power of nature. Like many of his compatriots, Novák incorporated elements of Czech folk music into his work; however, the folk motifs are highly stylized, constituting a significant but not dominant strand in the rich texture of his music.

Novák's musical talent was discovered early by a sympathetic teacher who developed the youth's skills in piano and composition. In 1889, Novák obtained a scholarship to study law at Charles University in Prague, and he also enrolled at the Prague Conservatory. At the Conservatory, Novák studied piano with Josef Jiránek, counterpoint with Karel Stecker, and harmony with Karel Knittl. Of all of his teachers. Knittl was the least sympathetic; in fact, Knittl was so perturbed by Novák's inventive approach to harmony that he savagely criticized his student, effectively undermining his self-confidence as a composer. Fortunately, Stecker showed more intelligence and actually recommended Novák for Dvořák's master class in 1891. Novák and Dvořák may have disagreed about compositional technique, but Dvořák was known for his respect for every student's artistic individuality. Novák's early work was composed in the Romantic idiom, and he attracted the attention of Brahms, who recommended the young Czech composer to his publisher, Simrock. In 1896, during a visit to northern and eastern Moravia, Novák discovered the region's unusual and somewhat exotic folk music; while folk music never influenced Novák's work directly, this encounter prompted him to expand his musical language and transcend the idiom of Romanticism. The effect is evident in his remarkable *Quintet for piano & strings*, composed in 1896, in which Novák successfully blends elements of his early style with a natural melodic spontaneity inspired by folk music. In his popular symphonic poems, *V Tatràch* (*In the Tatra Mountains*), composed in 1902, and the *Slovak Suite*, written the following year, Novák created powerful musical representations of natural beauty. In fact, *In the Tatra Mountains*, which captures the many facets of the majestic landscape of the Tatras, has been favorably compared to the *Alpine Symphony* by Richard Strauss. Detailed in its description of the many splendors of nature, Novák's music also develops a few fundamental, archetypal images, such as the moonlit night and water. A quiet pond in the *South Bohemian Suite*, a mountain stream in the monumental tone poem for piano, *Pan* (1910), water becomes an overwhelming and boundless force in the *Storm*, a dramatic cantata also completed in 1910. Having succeeded Dvořák as professor of composition at the Prague Conservatory in 1908, Novák dedicated his energies to teaching. In 1919, when his popularity as a composer seemed to be waning, he started a master class at the Conservatory, attracting many promising composers, including Alois Hába. While Novák's works composed in the 1920s, including operas and ballets, were regarded as less-successful than his earlier compositions, the symphonic works written toward the end of his life are mature, thoughtful creations. These compositions include the *South Bohemian Suite* (1937), *De Profundis* (1941), and *May Symphony* (1943). The two last works expressed the composer's thoughts about the destiny of his country in the midst of World War II. As scholars have noted, while Novák's style is fundamentally melodic, he is also a master of harmonic development and contrapuntal construction. His compositional skill is exemplified by his extraordinary ability to create a towering structure, such as *Pan*, on the basis of a brief motif. *—Zoran Minderovic*

Overview of Works (1891–1949)

Czech composer Vítězslav Novák's life and works fall into four clearly defined periods. In his youth and young manhood (1870–1900), he was extremely poor, painfully shy, and completely lacking in self-confidence. In the first works of his maturity (1900–10), he was romantic and emotional with an egoism that bordered on arrogance. In his middle years (1910–30), he was humbled by the decline in popularity of his music and exhausted by his work as a professor of composition at the Prague Conservatory. In his final years (1930–49), he was proudly and self-consciously a Czech composer who wrote a series of works on Czech subjects. His first period has few compositions of conspicuous worth or much individuality: a *Sonata for violin in D minor* (1891) and a *Serenade for orchestra* (1894–95) are the best of works of this period. But with his discovery of both Moravian and Slovakian folk music, and, just as importantly, the beginning of his intense love of nature, Novák blossomed as a composer. In the works of this period—the massive symphonic poems *In the Tatra Mountains* (1902) and *Eternal Longing* (1903–05) and the concert overture *Lady Godiva* (1907)—Novák created his own passionately monumental *fin de siècle* orchestral style with soaring, surging melodies, powerful chromatic harmonies, and forms that grew out of small melodic cells or motifs. However, these characteristics seemed to wane as Novák's popularity declined and the operas of the 1910–1930 period were sarcastically comedic and at times even bitterly satiric. The plot of *Grandfather's Legacy* (1922–25), for example, concerns a young violinist and his disillusioning experiences with impresarios, concert audiences, and a career in music. But with the rise of fascism in the 1930s and the threat to the new Czechoslovakian nation, Novák became more acutely aware of his identity as a Czech composer. Several of his most popular works—the *South Bohemian Suite* (1936–37), the *St. Wenceslas Triptych* (1941), and the vocal/orchestral *May Symphony* (1943)—date from this period. The agonizing and cathartic *De Profundis* (1941) for large orchestra plus organ— written at the height of the Nazi occupation—is Novák's magnum opus. The supreme compositional skill demonstrates by its structure, and the spiritual and emotional depths of its emotional content give *De Profundis* a place as one of the greatest works of twentieth century Czech music. *—James Leonard*

Recommended:

- ○ **Novák: Piano Quintet; Songs; etc.** / Kožená, Kvapil, Kocian Quartet / 1998 / ASV 998
- ○ **Novák: Piano Works** / Rauch / 2003 / Supraphon 3744
- ○ **Novák: Nikotina; Toman & the Wood Nymph** / Jilek (cond.), Brno Madrigal Singers, Czech State PO / Supraphon 3050
- ○ **Novák: In The Tatra Mountains; Eternal Longing; Slovak Suite** / Pesek (cond.), Royal Liverpool PO / 1997 / Virgin 45251
- ○ **Novák: String Quartet; Piano Quintet** / Skovajsa, Kubin Quartet / 1994 / Centaur 2191
- ○ **Novák: Orchestral Works** / Pfund (cond.), Bergische Symphoniker / 2003 / MDG 6011159

O

John O'Conor

b. Jan. 18, 1947, Dublin, Ireland
Pianist
John O'Conor is sometimes called a "Poet of Piano" for his ability to play with particularly expressive phrasing, depth of tone color, and a technique that can make piano playing look like a lark. His specialties are Classical and Romantic music, and he is best known for his recordings of Beethoven's complete piano sonatas and the works of fellow Irishman John Field.

When O'Conor first told his parents he wanted to be a professional musician, giving up his love of rugby, he got the usual response of laughter followed by concern that he couldn't earn a real living. (This was the same response he had to his son Hugh's announcement that he wanted to be an actor.) O'Conor's studies began at Dublin's College of Music with J.J. O'Reilly, and, after he received a scholarship from the Austrian government, continued in Vienna under Dieter Weber. He studied Beethoven's music with Wilhelm Kempff, which in 1997 led to leading the annual Beethoven seminar at Kempff's villa in Positano, Italy. He was awarded first prize in Vienna's 1973 International Beethoven Piano Competition by unanimous vote and the Bösendorfer Piano Prize in 1975.

It was his first release in the series of complete sonatas of Beethoven for Telarc that brought O'Conor to the attention of the world in 1986, completing the cycle in 1994. As an exclusive Telarc artist, he alone has done more to revive interest in the life and works of John Field than anyone else. His initial Field recording of 15 of the *Nocturnes* spent several weeks on the *Billboard* charts.

O'Conor has an active travel schedule, going around the world to perform recitals and orchestra concerts, frequently combining these with master classes and seminars. He coaches piano chamber music, as well as the solo and concerto repertoire, and serves on the juries of several international piano competitions. He is director of the Royal Academy of Music in Dublin and founder and chairman of the Dublin International Piano Competition. O'Conor's interest in young musicians has led to his receiving an honorary doctorate from the University of Dublin and being decorated by the French, Austrian, Italian, and Polish governments. *—Patsy Morita*

Recommended:

- ○ **Field: 15 Nocturnes** / O'Conor / 1990 / Telarc 80199
- ○ **Schubert: Impromptus & Waltzes** / O'Conor / 1993 / Telarc 80337
- ○ **Piano Classics** / O'Conor / 1992 / Telarc 80313

Paul O'Dette

b. Feb. 2, 1954, Pittsburgh, PA
Lutenist
Few instrumentalists establish themselves with such firm authority as Paul O'Dette has on the lute. In fact, one writer described him as "the clearest case of genius ever to touch his instrument." In fact, O'Dette helped define the technical and stylistic standards to which twenty-first century performers of early music aspire. In doing so, he helped infuse the performance practice movement with a perfect combination of historical awareness, idiomatic accuracy, and ambitious self-expression. "I remember when I first started playing the lute," O'Dette once recalled, "the common perception of Renaissance music was that it was kind of pre-expression—that people didn't use dynamics, they didn't use tone colors.... [But] the more we've learned, we've realized that in fact all of these expressive devices were being used throughout the sixteenth century." O'Dette deserves much of the credit for bringing this aspect of early music to the fore of performance practice.

O'Dette's musical career can be traced at least back to high school, during which time he played electric guitar in a rock band. Frustrated with the lack of pedagogical consensus within the rock guitar world, and seeking a higher level of technical rigor and discipline, O'Dette took a friend's advice and sought out instruction from a classical guitar teacher in order to improve his rock playing. His first assignment under his new teacher was to learn some Renaissance lute pieces arranged for guitar. He was immediately transfixed by the sonorities of the Renaissance, and sought out recordings of the music on authentic instruments. Also, as luck would have it, his teacher had a kit-made lute that he had never learned to play, which he sold to his student. Over the next few decades, O'Dette's collection expanded to include over 20 instruments, including a lute, an archlute, a chittarone, and a Baroque guitar.

The expansion of his collection paralleled the development of his career as the world's foremost lutenist. In 1976, O'Dette became Director of Early Music at the Eastman School of Music. He was only 21, and still an undergraduate—but had already established a reputation that would eventually enable him to study with such influential figures as Thomas Binkley, guitarist Christopher Parkening, Michael Lorimer, and Eugen Dombois. Over the next 25 years, he would also appear on over 100 recordings, both as a featured performer, as well as with such prestigious company as Nigel Rogers, Christopher Hogwood, Jordi Savall, Trevor Pinnock, and Gustav Leonhardt. Among his accolades are several nominations for "Record of the Year" for his highly-respected 1995 recording of John Dowland's complete works for lute; the next year his CD of Purcell songs, a collaboration with Sylvia McNair, won a Grammy.

Perhaps O'Dette's style can be described as deeply *human.* Crucial to his sound is his awareness of the ethnic and dance topics that figure into the music. The dance gestures that correspond— albeit sometimes in only a stylized way—to the musical figures, find expression in the contour and phrasing of O'Dette's lines. He makes another enlightening comparison as well, one based on writings contemporaneous to the music: "All of the sixteenth century sources say that the best instrumentalists are those who can make you believe you are listening to words—that the best instrumental playing strives to imitate the voice in every way possible." This appealing (and historically informed) philosophy of performance and O'Dette's impeccable technique, have made his performance of early music a creative, rather than a curatorial, endeavor. *—Jeremy Grimshaw*

Recommended:

- ○ **Ancient Airs & Dances** / O'Dette, Covey-Crump / Hyperion 66228
- ○ **Baroque Lute Music Vol. 1** / O'Dette / 2001 / Classical Express 3957020
- ○ **Dowland: Lute Works Vol. 1** / O'Dette / 1995 / HM 907160
- ○ **Vivaldi: Music for Lute & Mandolin** / O'Dette, Parley of Instruments / 1987 / Hyperion 66160

Jacob Obrecht

b. 1450, Bergen-op-Zoom [?], Netherlands, **d.** 1505, Ferrara, Italy
Composer: Choral
In 1480, the Neapolitan theorist Johannes Tinctoris listed Jacob Obrecht (1450–1505) among the contemporary composers who had elevated the practice of music virtually to artistic perfection. In Obrecht's lifetime, the transmission of his music carried his fame across Europe: when the composer was only thirty, and before he had even set foot in Italy, two of his masses were in the repertoire of the Pope's Sistine Chapel choir. In 1487, the powerful Duke Ercole I of Ferrara mounted a strong campaign to recruit Obrecht into his personal service. By all contemporary accounts, Obrecht's compositional skill was known throughout Europe. After his premature death, however, and into our own time, he has remained in the shadow of his famous contemporary Josquin Desprez. Despite the lower trajectory both of Obrecht's career as a singer, and in posthumous publication, he deserves equal consideration as a founding father of the High Renaissance.

Obrecht was born in 1450, the son of a professional trumpeter for the city of Ghent. His early education at a choir school, followed by priestly ordination and the completion, by 1480, of the Master of Arts degree, placed him on an ecclesiastical career track. His first appointment (in 1480) was Choirmaster for the Guild of Our Lady at Bergen op Zoom, followed in 1484 by an election as succentor for the influential Cathedral of Cambrai. But Obrecht returned under a cloud to the Netherlands, hired by the church of St. Donatian's in Bruges while still technically working for Cambrai. His career became a rotating cycle of employments (and some firings) in Flemish churches of Bruges (1485–91; 1498–1500), Antwerp (1492–98; 1501–03), and Bergen op Zoom (1497–98). Though his music was being performed across the breadth of the Continent, it may be that Obrecht himself had a truly poor singing voice as well as a habit of neglecting his administrative and teaching duties, which together comprised the actual responsibilities of professional musicians in the church. Owing to Obrecht's compositional prowess, however, the Duke of

Ferrara finally gave him more lucrative employment in Italy, in 1504; unfortunately, the composer died of the plague there less than a year later.

The centerpiece of Obrecht's compositional output is a series of 30 settings of the Mass Ordinary, written under a number of different structural plans. From the early influence of the fluid music of Busnois and Ockeghem, he strives for a strongly moderated and rationally organized musical process. The facility and clarity of his contrapuntal writing is often highlighted by parallel-tenth motion in the outer voices; the careful elegance of his musical phrases by motivic repetition, and carefully-prepared cadences. In this sense, he crafts his musical architectures in a highly tonal idiom, based on the audible progress of vertical harmonies. Obrecht can be fond of "Medieval" and hyper-rationalist constructions, such as music based upon complex frameworks of multiple and simultaneously sounding cantus firmus melodies; at the same time, many of his motets demonstrate a "progressive" concern for the rhetorical emphases in text. *—Timothy Dickey*

Overview of Works

At the time of Jacob Obrecht's untimely death from the plague in 1505, his reputation was already being eclipsed by that of Josquin Desprez; commentary from the sixteenth century onward would consistently devalue the contributions of Obrecht—the "uncompromising rationalist" and favorite composer of Erasmus—as weighed against those of Josquin—the French superstar, favorite of Martin Luther. But the evidence of his own time presents Obrecht as the musical darling of his generation; his masses in particular circulated in the courts of Italy years before the man himself set foot on the peninsula. His music displays less of the declamatory and rhetorical text-driven style, which the influence of Italian humanism elevated to the international forefront of the art, relying instead on the scholastic rationalism of the late Middle Ages. His stylistic hallmarks are facility—assisted by frequent melodic parallelism in the outer voices and by sequential outworking of melodic cells—and an architectural rationalism, seen in highly creative manipulations of cantus-firmus technique and hints of cabalistic numerology. Both may be sublimated to the "tonal" power of elegant and carefully-prepared cadences to control the unfolding of a musical passage.

Thirty surviving masses form the cornerstone of Obrecht's fame, both in his own day and in our own. All apply some form of architectural patterning based upon a preexistent cantus firmus melody: paraphrase, rhythmic and mensural transformation, canons of many types, and—his unique contribution to compositional practice—segmentation of the melody for different movements of the cycle. Early works, such as the *Missa Petrus apostolus* and *Missa Sicut spina rosam*, consciously emulate the musical styles of older composers, but Obrecht quickly adopted his own mature style. The famous *Missa Fortuna desperata* (which apparently influenced Josquin's own mass of this title) and the *Missa Malheur me bat* exemplify the consummate sonic organization of his maturity.

Of a different sound-world entirely is the "Sphinx among his masses," the *Missa Maria zart*; its hour-long wash of undulating polyphony presents a kaleidoscopic tapestry of sound in the inexhaustible "spinning-out" of its simple devotional melody in all voices. The *Missa Sub tuum presidium* exemplifies, for many, Obrecht's constructivist tendencies: the opening three-voiced texture grows by one voice in each successive movement of the mass, and new cantus firmi are also added. Thus, by the end of the Agnus Dei, seven voices are singing, with four simultaneous plainchant quotations. The *Missa Plurimorum carminum I* employs a potpourri of no less than 20 secular tunes in its structure.

Quite a few of the nearly 30 surviving motets follow the constructivist tendencies of the masses. The polytextual *Factor orbis*, which has been elegantly termed a "Christmas sermon," deploys a collage of some 20 Advent liturgical excerpts among its five voices, each "commenting" upon the central cantus firmus in a fashion analogous to Medieval "glossing."

A simple Italian devotional Lauda, and a more Italianate clarity of texture apparently inform the motet *Beata es, Maria*. *Laudes Christi* and *Quis numerare queant* have been cited to exemplify a more forward-looking imitative style and rhetorical concern for textual nuance; the three-voiced song-motet *Si sumpsero* uses imitation in "modern" fashion as the primary organizational device. Obrecht's numerous secular works comprise both French chansons and robust, folk-like Dutch songs. *—Timothy Dickey*

Recommended:

- ○ **Obrecht: Missa Caput; Salve Regina** / Summerly (cond.), Oxford Camerata / 1997 / Naxos 553210
- ○ **Obrecht: Missa Sub Tuum Praesidium; Benedictus in laude; Salve Regina** / Wickham (dir.), Clerks' Group / 2003 / Gaudeamus 341
- ○ **Obrecht: Missa de Sancto Donatiano; Missa Sicut Spina Rosam** / Bali (cond.), ANS Chorus / Hungaroton 32192

CHORAL

Missa Fortuna desperata (ca. 1490)

An unassuming little three-voiced piece entitled *"Fortuna Desperata"* began appearing in music manuscripts towards the end of the fifteenth century; its simple yet jaunty counterpoint quickly became tremendously popular, being rearranged at least six times with up to three added voices, serving as the foundation for a number of keyboard and lute intabulations, and donating its second voice for the cantus firmus of several masses. The tune's origin remains unknown. Although an early source credits Antoine Busnois with the composition, Busnois is not known to have ever set an Italian text directly. It appears to be part of the (loose) vernacular genre of the frottola; its half-serious text has been roughly translated as "Desperate Fortune, unfair and cursed, who has denigrated the good name, of that chosen woman." At any rate, it proved fertile ground for adaptation to the cyclic mass, including settings by the eminent Josquin Desprez, and the "Orphic" Jacob Obrecht. Obrecht's mass on "Fortuna" seems to have been the first, with Josquin later paying homage to (and competing with) the Flemish master's. Its composition may even date from Obrecht's first Italian visit, to Ferrara, in 1487–88.

For Obrecht, "Fortuna" offered both a cantus firmus melody useful for the structural planning of his mass on the large scale and also a tune with clear potential for local harmonic organization. The Mass thus neatly embodies the two central musical concerns of his mature style. Taking the tenor voice of the frottola as his structural voice, Obrecht apportions it to each of the five movements of the Mass Ordinary. All four voices get the cantus firmus at least once (tenor in Kyrie I; alto in Kyrie II; superius in Sanctus; bassus in Osanna, etc.). But the most fascinating manipulation comes in the Gloria and Credo, the cantus firmus of both being marked with the a canon stating, "In medio consistit virtus" ("Virtue lies in moderation," or more literally, "Virtue stands in the middle"). The resolution of this canon requires the singer to begin with the single pitch F, which "stands in the middle" of the line, and then read the music from the middle backwards to the beginning; after this, the lonely note in the middle is repeated, and the second half sung to the end. The Credo, a movement of exactly equal length, reverses the process: lonely note, second half end to middle, lonely note, first half beginning to middle. This convoluted plan wittily suggests the unpredictable movement of Fortune's Wheel. (Note that in Josquin's *Mass*, the rhetorical coup comes in the Agnus Dei, when the bass sings Fortune's melody in inversion, literally upside down.) Obrecht also demonstrates in this Mass palpable control over local harmonic direction and cadences, one of the hallmarks of his mature style. One need listen no further than the opening of Kyrie I to see the well-paced progression of cadences, which build momentum until the final voice enters, culminating the snatches of the "Fortuna" melody in the cantus firmus statement. As early as the Mass might be, it already shows the composer's full compositional assurance. *—Timothy Dickey*

Missa L'homme armé (ca. 1480s)

A simple popular tune, "L'homme armé", or "The Armed Man," which seems to refer obliquely to a crusade planned by Charles the Bold, Duke of Burgundy, sparked an extremely rich tradition of mass compositions in the late fifteenth and early sixteenth centuries. Antoine Busnois may have written the tune and probably composed the first cyclic mass based upon it, in flattery of Charles the Bold, his patron. During the last decades of the century, Ockeghem, Dufay, Obrecht, and Josquin (who wrote two "L'homme armé" masses) each wrote masses on the same tune, apparently in each composition paying polite homage to the elder composers, as well as practicing a bit of compositional one-upmanship.

Obrecht not only takes the same chanson tune as the preexistent cantus firmus for the tenor voice of his mass, but quotes directly the specific elaboration found in Busnois' mass, down to the exact number of measures of rest between cantus firmus statements. However, he transforms it at the same time: whereas Busnois set the tune in G Dorian and D Aeolian modes, Obrecht uses the more somber E Phrygian; this choice also sets a new challenge for the composer, since the overall mode (harmonic structure) of Obrecht's mass is different from that of the structural tenor voice. His homage to Busnois is further tempered by a planned display of compositional prowess in the final Agnus Dei. Busnois constructs the climax of his mass setting by quoting the *L'homme Armé* tune in inversion at the end of the fifth movement; Obrecht goes further and uses retrograde inversion. The musical style of the other voices in this setting displays many features of Obrecht's mature writing: somewhat angular melodies, frequently formed from smaller melodic cells and sequences; parallel motion between the two outer voices; and a considerable level of rhythmic complexity in individual lines, which are often driven by syncopations and dotted rhythms. Hear, for instance, the rhythmic interplay between pairs of voices towards the end of the first section of the Sanctus movement. This rhythmic complexity often ornaments and supplements his final sectional cadences. In marked contrast to such writing, several times, at the outset of a movement (Gloria, Credo, Sanctus, Pleni sunt coeli), while the structural voice is waiting to enter, another voice will sing the *L'homme armé* tune in long notes, as if deceptively prefiguring the cantus firmus. *—Timothy Dickey*

Recommended:

- ○ **Ockeghem & Obrecht: Missae L'Homme Armé** / Gruss (dir.), Capella Fidicinia / 1997 / Querstand 9609

Missa Malheur me bat (before 1497)

In the mature masses of Jacob Obrecht, the perceptive listener can discern a scintillating tension between consciously archaic compositional techniques and progressive concern for the audible organization of musical process. The heyday of the isorhythmic motet (in which a melody in a single structural voice, subjected to rhythmic augmentation and diminution over the sections of the piece, provided the intellectual framework for composition) had passed earlier in the fifteenth century, and by the 1480s the musical climate was moving towards greater use of (audible) imitation and stronger tonal control over harmonic language. But in works such as the *Missa Malheur me bat*, Obrecht demonstrates his skill by crafting music of consummate sonic organization, while organizing the movements through transformations of an antique cantus firmus. The cantus firmus itself, which Obrecht takes from a popular chanson melody (attributed to Ockeghem, but more likely by the lesser-known Fleming Maelcourt), appears in the top voice throughout the Mass, unlike the more common placement in the tenor. It is also subjected to a technique of segmentation, Obrecht's unique contribution to cantus firmus composition. Whereas common practice at the time for unifying all five movements of a Mass setting around the same cantus firmus uses parallel compositional plans in each movement, Obrecht divides this chanson melody into a series of sections, each of which appears sequentially as a new cantus firmus for each section of the Mass. The entire melody appears in the final Agnus Dei, as a summation. So instead of conceiving the Mass as a series of five discrete pieces of music, Obrecht's large-scale plan views the entire cantus firmus spread out over the movements as one extended process. The composer's control over musical material may also be heard in local excerpts as well. Tidbits of the cantus firmus melody impregnate other voices; when the upper voice is not sounding, this serves to prepare for its entry. Shifts in vocal scoring and texture, as well as cadences and harmonic progressions, sound much more confident and directional than was the case in the music composed a few decades earlier. Indeed, Obrecht's control over the harmonic organization of his bass line proves so tight that he crafts that voice in Agnus Dei III almost entirely on two pitches: the modally significant A and E. The presence of this Mass (along with a setting on the same cantus firmus by Josquin Desprez) in a special presentation manuscript for Duke Ercole of Ferrara has led some scholars to suggest it was written during Obrecht's sojourn in the Ferrarese court, in 1487–88. Musicologist Rob Wegman, however, argues persuasively for a slightly later date considering the excellence of this work's mature style. *—Timothy Dickey*

Recommended:

○ **Obrecht: Missa Malheur me bat** / Wickham (dir.), Clerks' Group / 1998 / ASV 171

Missa Maria Zart (ca. 1503–1504)

"Elusive and mysterious," "special sound world," "the Sphinx among Obrecht's masses"—these are the phrases scholars try to attach to the *Missa Maria zart*, which indeed stands alone among the works of Jacob Obrecht. Taking over an hour to perform, this piece weighs in as the longest mass setting of the Renaissance, and must be heard in its entirety for the complete experience—an oceanic wash of undulating polyphony which no written words could encompass.

This Mass takes as its cantus firmus a Tyrolian song of Marian devotion, apparently dating from around 1500. Instead of placing complete statements of the preexistent melody in each movement, Obrecht uses his characteristic segmentation technique upon it, dividing the melody into twelve pieces, which are apportioned sequentially across the entire Mass. When segments are repeated, they are subject to a vast array of mensural transformations; at times the augmentation stretches to as much as twelve times the original note values! In the Agnus Dei, the entire melody is finally heard complete, as a summation or recapitulation: in the Bass in Agnus I, migrating among the three voices of Agnus II, and magnificently in the upper voice in Agnus III. This technique, common to several of his mature mass settings, yields a sense of large-scale process to the entirety of the five movements.

But such an account of the structure gives no concept of the kaleidescopic tapestry of sound resulting from the inexhaustible spinning-out of the voices. Long sections of musical text derive from antiphonal interplay of fragmentary motives, or manipluations which vary the rhythmic transformation within a melodic statement; the list of surface devices saturating the musical fabric with the melody could go on and on.

The musical impregnation also goes beneath the surface. For instance, clever scholarship has discovered hidden structure to the apparently "free" trio setting the text "et incarnatus est": the Bass voice, if all notes except the semibreves (half notes) are removed, contains the first half of "Maria zart," and the upper voice the second half in like manner. One scholar has even gone to great lengths to uncover a deep numerological subtext to the Mass.

Some of this speculation is driven by the piece's unique length and depth of sonic discourse. No liturgical occasion comes easily to mind which would require such music to be written in the fifteenth century. Perhaps, then, a more personal explanation could be sought. Obrecht, though aging, could not have predicted his immanent death of the plague. Nonetheless, one can readily imagine a musical testament by a composer at the height of his powers, set to an affective devotional song, which concludes, "Am lezten End, bitt, dich nit wend von mir in meinem Sterben" (At the final end, pray, turn not from me in my death). *—Timothy Dickey*

Recommended:

○ **Obrecht: Missa Maria Zart** / Phillips (cond.), Tallis Scholars / 2001 / Gimell 32

Johannes Ockeghem

b. ca. 1410, St.-Ghislain, Hainaut, Belgium, **d.** Feb. 6, 1497, Tours, France [?]
Composer: Choral

The birth of one of the most renowned singers and composers of the entire fifteenth century remains unfortunately shrouded in mystery. Though later poetic and archival sources confirm Johannes Ockeghem's birthplace, in the French-speaking province of Hainaut (modern-day Belgium, but at that time a part of the Duchy of Burgundy), only broad guesses may be advanced for his birthdate. A well-known poem laments his death "before reaching one hundred years," and a manuscript illustration of the French Royal chapel pictures one prominent aged figure with wrinkled skin and thick glasses. However, a visiting Italian as late as 1477 described Ockeghem as yet beautiful and utterly dignified in manner. Whatever his age, by the 1440s and 1450s, Jean de Okeghem (as many contemporary French documents call him) was well on the way to a musical career of international renown. He can reliably be documented in service as a singer at the Church of Our Lady in Antwerp at least from June 1443 till June 1444 and in the private chapel of the French Duke of Bourbon at Moulins from 1446 to 1448. In 1450, he began serving the Kings of France directly, and would remain to his death the jewel in the crown of the French Royal Chapel.

Ockeghem served three successive Kings over nearly 50 years: Charles VII (until the monarch's death in 1461, for which the *Requiem* may have been composed), Louis XI (1461–83), and Charles VIII. As early as 1454, court registers record Ockeghem giving a songbook to the King personally; these refer to him as *premier chapellain*. Along with this prestigious title, Charles VII named Ockeghem to the powerful and lucrative post of Treasurer of the Abbey of St. Martin in Tours, the wealthy monastery of which the King was himself titular Abbot. Then, in 1464, Louis XI elevated him to be called *Maistre de la chapelle de chant du roy;* the distinguished singer and composer would hold all three titles until his death. In addition, he held benefice incomes such as a canonicate at Notre Dame in Paris (later exchanged for one at St. Benoit, Paris). He appears not to have traveled much, though in 1464 he visited Guillaume Dufay in Cambrai, and in 1470 journeyed to Spain. His will in 1484 endowed the chapter of St. Martin with his goods and income; this may have been in response to an illness. His death, however, (apparently in retirement) did not occur until 1497.

Ockeghem enjoyed a stellar reputation among contemporary musicians as well as his employers. He apparently knew Gilles Binchois, composer to the Burgundian Court, for whom he composed the lament *Mort, tu as navré* in 1460. In turn, Antoine Busnois, singer of the count of Charolais (soon to be Duke of Burgundy) honored Ockeghem with the motet *In hydraulis* in 1465–67. Johannes Tinctoris, theorist and composer, called Ockeghem the first among all the most excellent composers of his time, and even Duke Galeazzo Maria Sforza of far-off Milan sought his assistance in the recruitment of singers. Upon Ockeghem's death, laments were composed by some of the greatest figures of his age, including poets (Guillaume Crétin and Jean Molinet), composer (Josquin Desprez), and thinker (Erasmus of Rotterdam). *—Timothy Dickey*

Overview of Works (ca. 1450–1490)

An Italian writing in 1567 credits Johannes Ockeghem with the "rediscovery" of music, much as Donatello "rediscovered" the art of sculpture. The reputation of this distinguished singer and composer, *Premier chapellain* and later Master of the French Royal Chapel, was in fact stellar among his contemporaries. However, from a historical perspective, the existence of certain esoteric "puzzle" pieces among his surviving works has tended to unfairly brand Ockeghem as a pedantic "intellectual" composer; the sometimes otherworldly ethos of his rhythmic constructions lend an air of stereotypical Mysticism (heightened by his apparent connections to the writings of Gerson). These two opposite caricatures may mingle in a more careful twenty-first century reassessment of the man who was certainly one of the most facile and innovative composers of his time. General attributes of his style—the sweeping melodic character, the often baffling rhythmic complexity, the potent cadential drives, and the daring approach to the basic systems of mode and mensuration—can only superficially gloss the remarkable individuality of his pieces.

The acknowledged centerpiece of his surviving works are the 14 masses, centrally influential to the development of the cyclic mass genre. Once again, general traits such as a new homogeneity of all voices and exploitation of an expanded vocal palette pale in comparison to the pieces' individuality. Most of the masses follow the English invention of a single unifying cantus firmus melody, but many treat this preexistent melody in remarkable ways. The *Caput Mass* places the melody improbably in the lowest voice; the *Missa Ecce ancilla* recomposes the familiar plainchant and infuses it into other voices; two incomplete mass settings on Ockeghem's own chansons (*Ma maistresse* and *Fors seulement*) borrow musical material from all voices of their respective models. The *Missa Au travail suis* treats the model loosely to the point of ignorance; the *Missa Mi-mi* and *Quinti toni* seem willfully to hide their models. Two masses were possibly written as personal compositional challenges, and transmitted as intellectual tours-de-force: the *Missa Cuiusvis toni*, whose notes may be sung in a variety of modal configurations, and the *Missa Prolationum*, a series of mensuration canons which completely exploit the current rhythmic system. Ockeghem also contributed the first surviving polyphonic setting of the requiem mass.

Ockeghem's Motets, though few, demonstrate nearly the same facility and individuality as the masses. The central Marian texts predominate, including *Ave Maria*, *Alma redemptoris mater*, and *Salve regina* (one setting with the cantus firmus in the Bass voice, as the *Missa Caput*). The valedictory *Intemerata Dei mater*, setting an original Marian text either by Gerson or Ockeghem himself, uses the same affectively low five-voiced scoring as the masses *Fors seulement* and *Sine nomine*, further personalized by quotations from several other Ockeghem works. Also related to the Motet genre are two unique works: the devastatingly esoteric canon *Ut heremita solus*, and the Motet-chanson memorializing the death of Binchois, *Mort, tu as navré*.

Roughly 20 Chansons from Ockeghem's pen survive. Most are for three voices, in the treble-dominated style of the earlier fifteenth century; in general these secular works are more conservative and traditional in outlook. The stamp of the composer's individuality, however, remains present, especially in rhythmic conception, and in frequent melodic enhancement of the "subsidiary" voices (as in *D'un aultre amer*, or the canonic *Prenez sur moi*). Ockeghem's chanson compositions quite frequently became the subject of emulation, rearrangement, and extensive traditions of adaptation, as in the prolific tradition which he himself began on his Rondeau *Fors seulement l'actente*. *—Timothy Dickey*

Recommended:

- ○ **Ockeghem: Masses** / Wickham (cond.), Clerks' Group / 2000 / ASV/Living Era 215
- ○ **Ockeghem: Requiem** / Peres (cond.), Organum Ens. / 1993 / HM 901441
- ○ **Cathedral Sounds: Johannes Ockeghem** / Clemencic (dir.), Clemencic Consort / 1998 / Arte Nova 56351

CHORAL

Missa cuiusvis toni

A well-known image from a sixteenth century illuminated manuscript presents the Royal Chapel of France at worship; a crabbed old figure to the right, gazing intensely through thick spectacles, is usually considered a (posthumous) portrait of *Maistre* Johannes Ockeghem. His reputation in the century following his death, based largely upon four works—a (now lost) 36-voiced canonic motet, the canonic chanson *Prenez sur moi*, the *Prolation Mass*, and the *Missa cuisvis toni*—was that of a crafty intellectual, a composer of nearly superhuman abilities and mystical insight. Alhough a spate of fresh scholarship and vibrant performances of his music in the 1980s and 1990s has illuminated further elements of his compositions, the image of "Ockeghem-as-puzzle-master" remains. Certain works, the *Missa cuisvis toni* (Mass to be sung on whatever tone you like) chiefly among them, certainly show a musical thinker whose compositions stretch his inherited musical system to its utmost boundaries.

The *Missa cuiusvis toni* is designed to be sung in several different modes. Its score (preserved in two fine manuscripts in the Vatican Library, as well as numerous sixteenth century prints and theoretical tracts) does not use clefs or key signatures, but rather a single curious sign at the beginning of each voice part. The singers of the day would have been trained to read music with solmization syllables (like the modern Kodály solfège), such that the particular syllable, and *not* a fixed staff system, would indicate to them at what interval the following note should be sung. If singing the syllable "mi" to a note, for instance, the note above would be sung as "fa," and thus a half-step above; but if the same note had been sung as "fa," the following note is "sol", and a whole step above. In the *Missa cuisvis toni*, the singers decide beforehand which syllable to assign to the pitch of the curlicue sign at the beginning of their staff; by selecting a different syllable, the ensemble may position Ockeghem's melody on a different part of the musical scale, and thus create a mass in a completely different sonic universe.

The famous, but sometimes unreliable, theorist Glareanus wrote in 1547 that this mass (and the chanson *Prenez sur moi*) might be considered *Catholica*—universal pieces of music. This statement has led to some deep misunderstandings of the *Missa cuisvis toni*. Although Glareanus first claimed the mass could be sung "in any mode," and he himself believed the musical system contained 12, closer analysis of this mass shows that it is unlikely to involve more than three (or possibly four) modal renditions. The smoothest incarnation of Ockeghem's work occurs when the singers choose to sing the final pitch as "mi," thus placing the mass in the somber harmonic richness of the Phrygian mode; since the twentieth century, this has been the mode selected for most performances. The other main possibilities use the final syllables "re" (for the Dorian mode) and "ut" (for the Mixolydian mode). These distinctions may seem utterly esoteric, and certainly one of the most useful contexts for the mass in Ockeghem's time was the didactic—teaching choirboys a hard lesson about sight-reading by solmization! However, even as a change of mode in later Western music (from major to minor key) signals a change of emotional effect, the modes in fifteenth century music were considered to be imbued with cosmic potentiality. A mass that could shift modes at will could be appropriate to different spiritual and emotional contexts at the drop of a syllable. *—Timothy Dickey*

Recommended:

- ○ **Ockeghem: Missa Cuiusvis Toni; Missa Quinti Toni** / Wickham (dir.), Clerks' Group / 1999 / ASV 189

Missa "De plus en plus" (ca. 1470–1480)

Though he spent the last 40 years of his life serving the French Royal Chapel, Johannes Ockeghem apparently began his musical career in Antwerp in the 1440s. He forged a professional relationship during these years with the famous elder composer Gilles de Bins (*dit* Binchois), who was serving the Court of the Dukes of Burgundy—possibly even studying music under his tutelage. Near the occasion of Binchois' death in 1460, Ockeghem composed a moving Déploration (lament) for his colleague—*Mort, tu as navré*—and quite possibly at the same time composed a cyclic cantus firmus mass based on the tenor voice to Binchois' rondeaux *De plus en plus*. Taken together, the Déploration and the Mass present a touching and powerful act of homage.

Ockeghem seems to have known several different versions of Binchois' chanson, as the various movements of his Mass preserve slightly different readings of the tune. However, on the surface, the form of the Mass appears straightforward: the Tenor voice of the chanson model is used as the structural foundation of each mass movement, being sung in the Mass' Tenor voice at least once, with no transpositions. The opening four notes of the model always appear in audible long-notes, calling attention to the beginning of the cantus firmus, and strongly identifying the tune. However, Ockeghem does manipulate the cantus firmus in several interesting ways. First, he subverts the odd harmonic implications of Binchois' model to a more uniform Mixolydian mode for his Mass. Partly, this is accomplished by his own contrapuntal setting in the other voices, and partly by the appending of a cantus firmus "tag" to four movements; this tag not only repeats the characteristic first phrase, but more importantly cadences on the correct tone. It is also the case that he never gives the chanson tune the same way twice—the treatment rather forms a spectrum from broad and consistent embellishment (in the Kyrie) to nearly strict quotation (in Sanctus and Agnus Dei III).

Unfortunately, no copies of the Mass survive which are early enough to securely date it. Instead, versions exist in one Italian manuscript from the 1470s or 1480s, and in the lavish Ockeghem "retrospective" anthology from around 1500, the *Chigi Codex*. Stylistically, it shares some features with the composer's earlier mass music such as the *Missa Caput* and *Missa l'Homme armé*, as well as with the English music (such as the anonymous English *Missa Caput*, falsely attributed to Dufay) which achieved popularity on the Continent in the 1440s. The level of rhythmic density in the Mass is similar to the composer's earlier masses. But the freedom of cantus firmus elaboration and the palpable climax carefully constructed in the Agnus Dei III are forward-looking features. *—Timothy Dickey*

Recommended:

- ○ **Ockeghem: Missa de plus en plus; 5 Motets** / Wickham (dir.), Clerks' Group / 1996 / ASV 153
- ○ **Ockeghem: Au travail suis; De plus en plus** / Phillips (dir.), Tallis Scholars / 2001 / Gimell 35

Missa "Fors seulement"

The five-voiced *Missa "Fors seulement"* by Johannes Ockeghem has often been called the first parody mass. Musicologist Fabrice Fitch points out this is somewhat misleading: while the term parody (or imitation) mass usually refers to later techniques wherein a mass setting borrows entire patches of the polyphonic fabric of a model composition, the *Missa "Fors seulement"* borrows from different voices of its model only for nonsimultaneous use. This technicality aside, this mass shows a composer who has built on certain experiments with cantus firmus treatment from his own *Missa "Ma maistresse,"* and treats the borrowed melodies from his model (Ockeghem's own Rondeau cinquain *Fors seulement l'attente*) with even greater freedom, facility, and saturation into the mass. Only one copy of the mass survives, in a posthumous manuscript, but its perceived advances in compositional technique—both in cantus firmus treatment and in greater use of imitation—have prompted most commentators to date it later in Ockeghem's life, presumably at some point during his magnificent career as *premier chapellain*, then later Master of the French Royal Chapel.

Three works for five voices appear in the so-called *Chigi Codex*, a retrospective and honorific anthology copied in the late fifteenth century—the motet *Intemerata Dei mater*, the *Missa sine nomine*, and the *Missa "Fors seulement."* All three share similarly extreme low ranges in the vocal parts, and may have been composed together at a time when the Royal Chapel enjoyed the services of a basso profundo (who may even have been Ockeghem himself). Of the *Missa "Fors seulement"* only three movements survive, the Kyrie, Gloria, and Credo. The fact that the scribe of this manuscript left blank pages after the Credo suggests the mass is incomplete as preserved in *Chigi.* The Credo deploys voices in a somewhat higher range than the first two movements; scholars have suggested a possible transposition of the movement, a change of the ensemble, or the outside chance that the Credo belongs to a different mass setting.

Ockeghem constructs the Kyrie and Credo *super* "Fors seullement" (as the manuscript indicates) under fairly obvious principles of cantus firmus organization. The Kyrie borrows the uppermost voice from the chanson model, with quotations from and allusions to the middle voice, as well. The first half of the Credo is organized around tenor statements of this same upper voice, the second half concluding with sequential quotations from the chanson's middle voice. Phrases containing cantus firmus material may be interspersed with passages that allude to different parts of the chanson; contrasting vocal textures often accomplish the phrasal articulation. Although the presentation of the cantus firmus in the Gloria more often wanders from voice to voice, its fidelity to the quoted melodies seems higher. In both the Gloria and Credo, the movements open with triple-time, though the quotations still may use the duple-time of the model. Throughout, the counterpoint tends toward density, coupled with a richness of harmonic fluctuation, especially between harmonies based on the pitch E (requiring B natural), and those based on F (implying B flat). The conclusion of the Gloria provides a potent example: in one passage, the two tenor voices resolutely alternate phrases at the melodic distance of a second. Emotionally, the work yields a sonic world that is rich, powerful, and even brooding. *—Timothy Dickey*

Recommended:

- ○ **Ockeghem: Requiem; Missa "Fors seulement, Ockeghem: Fors seulement l'attente** / Clerks' Group / 1997 / ASV 168
- ○ **Ockeghem: Missa "Fors seulement"; Missa "De plus en plus"** / Moll (dir.), Schola Discantus / 1997 / Lyrichord 8029

Missa "Mi-mi" (Missa quarti toni) (ca. 1450–1480)

From its composition in the fifteenth century until 1985, a reasonably well-documented mass by Johannes Ockeghem was known only by the mysterious title *Missa MyMy [Mi-Mi]* Three manuscripts in the Vatican Library, copied between around 1480 and 1503, preserve copies of the Mass, and a copying record from the church of St. Donatian in Bruges from 1475–76 may refer to the same piece. Jacob Obrecht knew the Mass, quoting from it in his own *Missa Sicut spina rosam* and *Missa de Sancto Martino.* Two other, slightly later *"Mi-Mi" Mass* settings, by Mattheus Pipelare and Marbrianus de Orto, use a similar motif for organizational purposes; their tune comes from a popular song, *"Petite camusette,"* and bears no other apparent relation to Ockeghem's Mass. And so the question stood—where does the tenor voice designation "Mi-Mi" come from? An obvious "head motif" links the major movements of Ockeghem's Mass—a bass descent from the pitch E to low A; in the contemporary system of theory and singing practice, both pitches would be sung on the syllable "Mi." Furthermore, many of the movements begin with an upper voice repeating two pitches E, again requiring solmization of "Mi-Mi." This partial explanation of the enigmatic title failed to completely satisfy the natural curiosity about the Mass' origins, until musicologist Haruyo Miyazaki published in 1985 his discovery of the lost model for "Mi-Mi"—Ockeghem's own chanson, *Presque trainsi.*

Presque trainsi, a Bergerette in three voices, dates from around 1460, and contains, in its tenor voice (here the lowest) the head motif for the Missa "Mi-Mi," e-A-e-f-e. The upper voice beginning the second part of the chanson yields another common melodic motif from the Mass, e-a-g-a-b-c. A number of fleeting, but convincing, allusions to other fragments of chanson music lie scattered around the Mass, and several movements conclude with a tenor line quite similar to the tenor at the chanson's close. However, as became Ockeghem's later ethos, these references are used more as markers and echoes than for any structural foundation (see the *Missa Au travail suis* and *Missa Quinti toni*). The apparent irrationality of Ockeghem's practice has led generations of analysts to retreat behind the term "mystical" to describe it. Most of the Mass is in fact "free-composed," but not random. Close analysis of the music demonstrates an elusive but well-crafted level of motivic and rhythmic organization between voices, often involving subtle imitation in the background. Fascinatingly, Gayle Kirkwood traces "Mi-Mi" as a title directly to an esoteric strain of mystical allegory which Ockeghem almost certainly should have known. In the writings of Jean Charlier de Gerson, chancellor of the University of Paris, each note of the musical scale could be allegorically associated with a particular human emotion, and then to an attribute of God. While singing the note, the literal sound of the voice may be transformed into spiritual reflection, thereby becoming the music of one's soul. In this formulation, "Mi" is the syllable of compassion, of God's mercy, and of Christ Himself, since it contains Jesus' initial, which (in Greek and Latin) is "I." Thus a piece of music whose basis is a double "Mi" becomes a spiritual exercise of a doubly profound nature. *—Timothy Dickey*

Recommended:

- ○ **Ockeghem: Missa Mi-mi** / Wickham (dir.), Clerks' Group / 1994 / ASV 139
- ○ **Ockeghem: Requiem; Missa Mi-mi** / Hillier (dir.), Hilliard Ens. / 1995 / Veritas 61219

Missa prolationum (ca. 1450–1480)

Ockeghem's *Missa prolationum* may be the greatest exercise in contrapuntal virtuosity anywhere in the European Renaissance. Strict rhythmic transformation of a notated melody had existed within the tradition of the isorhythmic motet, wherein subsequent sections of the piece would apply such transformations to the tenor's fixed melody by means of new time signatures. Ockeghem's colleague in the 1440s at Our Lady's of Antwerp, Petrus de Domarto, apparently was the first to apply mensural rhythmic transformation to the various movements of a Mass Ordinary cycle, in his *Missa Spiritus alme.* Guillaume Dufay posed himself the challenge of a "mensuration canon"—two voices singing the same melody in different time signatures—in an early motet, *Inclita stella maris,* and a late chanson, *Les doleurs.* But it was left to the supreme craftsman, Ockeghem, to raise the compositional stakes and challenge himself to write an entire mass based on a series of such canons: in short, to exploit the system of mensural notation as never before (and not since). The musical feature which makes a mensuration canon possible is the fact that in the fifteenth century's system of notation, the same note symbol could take a different rhythmic value under different mensurations (or time signatures). This means that in addition to the more standard type of canon, where subsequent voices sing the same melody at a later time or a different pitch level, the same melody may be sung in counterpoint to itself in two different simultaneous time signatures. All of the movements of Ockeghem's Mass are examples of this most difficult type of canon. Moreover, all of the movements are double canons: two notated voices are each subjected to different mensuration canons to produce four vocal parts. As if this weren't enough of a challenge, Ockeghem sets each canon at a different musical interval: Kyrie at the unison, Christe at a whole step, Kyrie II at a third, Gloria at a fourth, etc., to Osanna at the octave. The Agnus Dei movements return to canonic intervals of the fourth and fifth. The *Prolation Mass* is not merely an intellectual curiosity, however. Music theorists from shortly after Ockeghem's death until the twentieth century have extolled the concept and contrapuntal workmanship of the Mass; the later twentieth century has even seen in Ockeghem a kinship with the hyper-intellectual esotericism of "Contemporary-classical" music written by academic composers. However, the elegance of Ockeghem's Mass is not restricted to the conceptual world of notation and thought; it presents a sonic experience fully commensurate with the harmonies and melodies expected by his contemporary listeners. The openings of movements often seem rhythmically unmoored, as different voices sing long notes of various lengths, but the true test of his skill is the aural facility of his melodic weavings and his cadences; he even successfully slips an expressive accidental into the canonic complex at Crucifixus. A harmonically warmer Sanctus cannot be found in his work, and the octave canon in Osanna provides for a powerful conclusion. Even as natural laws of staggering complexity may govern in secret the processes of a budding rose, a terribly difficult, but hidden, level of craftsmanship yields the sweetness of Ockeghem's music. *—Timothy Dickey*

Recommended:

- ○ **Ockeghem: Missa Prolationum: 5 Motets** / Wickham (dir.), Clerks' Group / 1995 / ASV 143
- ○ **Ockegham: Requiem; Missa Prolationum; Intemerata Dei Mater** / Holten (cond.), Musica Ficta / 1997 / Naxos 8554260

Jacques Offenbach

b. Jun. 20, 1819, Cologne, Germany, **d.** Oct. 5, 1880, Paris, France
Composer: Opera, Ballet

Jacques Offenbach is best known for his opera *Les contes d'Hoffman* (Tales of Hoffmann) and for a work he did not compose, *Gaîté parisienne,* which used his themes as assembled and arranged by Manuel Rosenthal. Offenbach was one of those populist figures whose tuneful and exhilarating music could, at its best, elevate his art to classic status. His chief importance was in the development of the operetta as a bona fide genre on the world's stages. In this endeavor he would exert influence to varying degrees over Johann Strauss II, Lehár, Sullivan, and many others.

Offenbach was born Jacob Offenbach in Cologne on June 20, 1819. His first lessons were on violin. At age nine his focus turned to the cello, possibly to become the third member of a family trio: his brother Julius was already proficient on the violin, and his sister Isabella was a good pianist. Together, the three played local engagements for small sums of money. Offenbach's teachers included Joseph Alexander and Bernhard Breuer.

In 1833, Offenbach's father took him to Paris, where he was enrolled at the Conservatory. It was during his early years there that he adopted the French version of his name, "Jacques." After leaving the Conservatory about a year later, Offenbach took further lessons on the cello from Louis Norblin, but, more importantly, studied composition with Halévy. He supported himself during this period by playing in the Opéra-Comique orchestra. By 1838, when he left his orchestral post, he had become one of the finest cellists in Europe and began performing with Flotow, who played the piano. Although he had been composing small pieces since his childhood, Offenbach began writing larger works now, like the score for the comedy, *Pascal et Chambord,* premiered in 1839.

Over the next several years, Offenbach met and performed with Anton Rubinstein and Franz Liszt, and he traveled to London in 1844 to give concerts with Mendelssohn and Joachim. That same year he married Herminie d'Alcain, following his conversion from Judaism to Catholicism. Clearly, Offenbach could have chosen to remain primarily a performing artist, but in 1847 he began composing operettas, his first being *L'alcove*. He was appointed conductor at the Théâtre Français in 1850, and by 1855, when he resigned that conducting post for another, began attaining regular performances of his works at important theaters like the Bouffes-Parisiens, at Salle Marigny.

Orphée aux enfers (Orpheus in the underworld) was a great success in 1858 and paved the way for his subsequent larger operettas. He had a string of hits in the mid-1860s: *La belle Hélène* (1864), *Barbe-bleue* (1866), *La vie parisienne* (1866), and *La Périchole* (1868). While his later works also achieved success, they did not generate the level of excitement attained by these.

In 1874, Offenbach, now director of the Théâtre de la Gaité, mounted new versions of some of his earlier successful operettas, like *La Périchole*, but failed to turn profits. Eventually he went into bankruptcy. A concert tour to the United States in 1876 and new productions of his works in London a few years later helped give him financial solvency. Offenbach continued composing up to his last days. He was working on his opera, the aforementioned *Les contes d'Hoffman*, when he died on October 5, 1880. The work, existing in piano score only, was orchestrated by Guiraud, who also made a few additions. *—Robert Cummings*

Overview of Works (1839–1880)

Comic opera, as a distinct genre, was a late arrival on the European musical scene. Masques, musical plays, and theatrical entertainments had long existed, but up to the nineteenth century, opera was generally considered superior to any form of popular culture. Jacques Offenbach led the way to freeing opera from the social and intellectual snobbery that had kept it virtually beyond the reach of a wider public. His American tours in 1871 prepared the way for the American musical. With the possible exception of Johann Strauss, Offenbach did more to revitalize musical theater than any composer of his day.

The skill with which Offenbach infused opera with the spirit and pace of cabaret and burlesque established him as a favorite with Parisian audiences. The blend of fantasy and drama in his last, and finest, opera *Les contes d'Hoffman* was preceded by a series of successes, including *La Belle Hélène, Orphée aux enfers, Barbe-Bleue, La vie Parisienne, La Grande Duchesse de Gérolstein* and *La Périchole*. In these the standard ingredients of light opera—romance, knockabout comedy, and exotic settings—are spiced with satirical, witty, and even cynical versions of conventional operatic plots that neatly avoid the timeworn conventions of most nineteenth century operetta. In this his chief librettist, Ludovic Halévy, ably abetted him. Some of the themes would not be out of place in "grand" opera, but in Offenbach's music are given a fresh lick of paint, with gay, tuneful, exhilarating melodies and lively staging, for example in *Orphée aux enfers*, a hilarious take-off of the Orpheus legend, with its famous Can-Can. Indeed, Offenbach makes an art form of frivolity, and only in *The Tales of Hoffman*, his single attempt at a large-scale serious work (in effect it comprises five interlinked one-act operas), do we find a latent dramatic talent.

Offenbach was a man of the theater and it is not surprising that, in addition to his more familiar output, he also wrote some 80 other stage works including five ballets, vaudevilles, and incidental music for plays. Nevertheless he found time to write songs, chamber music, and some pieces for solo violin and cello, though all are now rarely heard.*—Roy Brewer*

Recommended:

- ○ **Offenbach: Music from the Operettas** / Swierczewski (cond.), Rocha, Lisbon Gulbenkian Foundation Orch. / 1991 / Nimbus 5303
- ○ **Offenbach: Arias & Overtures** / Almeida (cond.), Von Stade, Scottish CO / 1995 / RCA 68116
- ○ **Offenbach: Overtures** / Karajan (cond.), Berlin PO / DG 400044
- ○ **Offenbach: Schüler polka; Souvenir d'Aix-les-Bains; etc.** / Harnoy, etc. / Vox 9011
- ○ **Offenbach: Suites pour deux violoncelles** / Pidoux, Peclard / 1980 / HM 1901043
- ○ **Vive Offenbach!** / Rosenthal (cond.), Mesplé, Quillevere, Hamel, Burles, Monte Carlo PO / EMI 774088
- ○ **Anne Sofie von Otter Sings Offenbach** / Minkowski (cond.), Otter, Musiciens du Louvre / DG 471501
- ○ **Offenbach Festival Vol. I** / various / 2001 / Capriccio 49305

OPERA

La belle Hélène (1864)

While some of the music from Offenbach's *La belle Hélène* was poached for inclusion in *Gaîté Parisienne*, it is best heard in the context of this amusing and tuneful opéra-bouffe. The giddy heroine—beautiful, but light of intellect—proved the perfect subject for a work that poked fun at many of the conventions of the past and present. Offenbach was fortunate in securing as leading lady the beautiful and celebrated music theatre star, Hortense Schneider, for a collaboration that brought heightened acclaim to them both. With librettists Ludovic Halévy and Henri Meilhac, Offenbach created a perfect vehicle for the Schneider and provided tenor José Dupuis the sparkling role of Pâris. Thus, at the Variétiés on December 17, 1864, the two singers and the composer all enjoyed a triumph. Their collaboration continued in *Barbe-Bleu* (1866), *La Grande-Duchess de Gérolstein* (1867) and *La Périchole* (1868).

La belle Hélène was, if not a watershed for Offenbach, at least a defining moment. He had already known considerable success with the public and had gained genuine, if grudging, recognition from other composers for his talent. Here, however, he raised the genre to a different level. His earlier two-act comic works were delightful, but restrictive; *La belle Hélène* afforded him more room to stretch, to create arias, duets and ensembles which had a satisfying completeness about them.

With deft and deceptive ease, Offenbach shifts in the Introduction from the animated "March of the Kings" to a light, off-handed waltz (Paris's theme, here voiced by a solo oboe), thence to a vigorous "Galop." Pâris's bounding waltz, "Au mond Ida" has achieved popularity aside from stage performance, sung in concert and recital by lyric tenors of flexibility and elegance. When Hélène cannot resist receiving Pâris, she protests in "Dismoi, Vénus," a breath-stopping aria melding beauty and parody (Berlioz seems to be the reference here).

Offenbach sustains his invention to provide a final act full of manic attractions, from a Handelian entr'acte" to the "Trio patriotique" sung by Ménélas, Agamemnon, and Calchas, all of that trumped by the whooping "Tyrolienne" led by Pâris. That Offenbach could imitate the styles of others in so winning a fashion speaks to an inimitable and treasurable gift. *—Erik Eriksson*

Synopsis:

Act One. The Feast of Adonis should bring gaiety to Sparta, but Calchas, a rather shady soothsayer attached to the Temple of Jupiter, complains of the meager offerings, while the women of Troy sigh at the general lack of earthly passion. Queen Hélène, too, is disgruntled; she's married to the feeble King Ménélas. Making matters worse, Calchas passes to Hélène a rumor of a certain beauty contest on Mount Ida; in the end, Venus, the goddess of love, has promised a worthy and handsome fellow named Paris the hand of the world's most beautiful woman. Hélène is well aware that she is the world's most beautiful woman, but little does she know that Paris has arrived in Troy disguised as a shepherd, bearing a letter from Venus instructing Calchas to bring Paris and Hélène together. Paris enters a contest for composing verse (the fanfares include a brassy quotation from Wagner's *Tannhäuser*, which Ménélas announces as "German music I commissioned for the ceremony"). Paris wins with his clever wordplay, whereupon he reveals that he is no shepherd, but the Prince of Troy. Hélène is immediately taken by Paris, so to speak, and Calchas contrives an oracular pronouncement that conveniently sends Ménélas off to Crete for a month, so the would-be lovers will have some time together.

Act Two. Four weeks later, while the Kings of Greece who participated in the verse contest are still hanging around playing snakes and ladders, Hélène has been keeping her distance from Paris, though she is sorely tempted to stray. She tells Calchas that it would be best if she got to know Paris a little better, if only "in a dream." Calchas obligingly arranges a "dream" for her, in which Paris, disguised now as a slave, sneaks into her boudoir. Just in the nick of time, Ménélas breezes in from Crete and discovers his wife in bed with Paris. While Hélène scolds Ménélas for returning without warning, Paris slips away, thus avoiding a scandal.

Act Three. The Spartan court—the Kings of Greece who are still loitering around Hélène—is basking at the seaside resort of Nauplia, and Hélène is still trying to convince Ménélas that catching her in *flagrante delicto* was only a dream. Now a priest arrives, proclaiming that Hélène must travel to Chytherea to atone for her indiscretion, or at least for the gods' displeasure at her relative virtue. Despite Ménélas' objections, Hélène sets off with the priest, who reveals himself to be Paris. Although the people of Sparta seem to find nothing wrong in this and urge the couple on, the Kings of Greece, aghast at Paris' duplicity, declare war on Troy. *—James Reel*

Recommended:

- ○ **Offenbach: La Belle Hélène** / Minkowski (cond.), Lott, Sénéchal, LeRoux, Naouri; Musiciens du Louvre / 2001 / Virgin 45477

Les contes d'Hoffmann

Offenbach laid the foundations of a new musical genre with a series of tuneful operettas full of wit and Parisian joie de vivre, but by 1870 the fashion for comic opera had waned, and during a visit to America he conceived the idea of a large-scale opera that was to be his masterpiece. By 1878, he had completed all three acts of *Les Contes d'Hoffmannn* in piano score and orchestrated the *Prologue*. He did not live to see it staged and his friend, the composer Ernest Guiraud, completed the work, doing his best to adhere to Offenbach's clearly expressed wishes.

The opera opens in a Nuremburg tavern, to which the scene returns at various points as Hoffmann, with his companion Nicklausse and his poetic muse, tells of a series of amorous adventures with, in turn, a mechanical doll, a Venetian courtesan, and a young opera singer. The scheme works sufficiently well to avoid discontinuity, though it could easily be regarded as a linked set of one-act operas with related themes—deception, betrayal, and death. Lively stage action and Offenbach's talent for writing good tunes generally avoid such somber implications and there are moments of humor as well as pathos.

The following is a brief outline of what, on stage, turns out to be a series of fantastic, somewhat complicated adventures. The *Prologue*, with its student songs and noisy hilarity, is followed by a lively ballad (clearly a favorite with the students) of the knock-kneed dwarf Kleinsack.

Hoffmann's first story concerns the poet's infatuation with Olympia, "daughter" of her inventor Spalanzani, but since she happens to be a dancing automaton (and Hoffmann is a bit thick) this amour has no future. After various complications Olympia is destroyed by her creator and Hoffmann is back on the beer. The music is charming and excellent use is made of the comedic possibilities of Olympia's impresario.

Act two, the episode with the courtesan Giulietta, is set in Venice and graced by one of Offenbach's most celebrated and sensuous melodies, the *Barcarolle*. This liaison is, however, similarly ill-fated and culminates in a duel in which Hoffmann kills his rival for Giulietta's affections. After an intermezzo based on the *Barcarolle*, the story returns to the Tavern.

The third act concerns Antonia, an opera singer mourning her dead mother. Due to an illness, Antonia has been warned by her guardian not to sing but, under the malign influence of Dr. Miracle, Hoffmann's evil genius, she is tricked into a long, strenuous, and exceptionally brilliant duet with the poet. She collapses and dies.

A thread of philosophical melancholy runs through Hoffmann's tales, strongly suggesting that Offenbach was a dispirited and disappointed man, who no longer wished to be known only as a purveyor of musical soufflés. The work is often produced in differing versions, with cuts that do little for its musical or dramatic impact. —*Roy Brewer*

Synopsis:

Prologue. In Luther's tavern, the Muse, accompanied by the spirits of drink, emerges from a barrel and declares her intention to use drink to make Hoffmann forget Stella, the opera singer performing that night, and return to her. Lindorf enters and bribes Stella's servant to give him the note she had sent to Hoffmann, asking for a rendezvous and giving him her key. He intends to keep the appointment himself, declaring that though he is old, his diabolic aspect will give him victory: "Dans les roles." Students enter and sing a rowdy drinking song. Nicklausse brings in Hoffmann, who is moody, and to cheer him up the students ask him to sing. He responds with the song of the deformed Kleinzach: "Une fois a la cour." He notices Lindorf and the two spar verbally. Hoffmann goes on to describe the loves of three students as a virtuoso, an empty doll, and a brazen courtesan. When one responds angrily that his love must be a real treasure then, he starts to tell the story of his own three loves.

Act One. At Spalanzani's home, Spalanzani is overseeing the dressing of Olympia, a life-size automaton, for a party. Hoffmann enters as one of his students, and, when alone for a moment, sings of his adoration for her, thinking she is human: "Allons! Courage et confiance." Nicklausse follows him and teases him with a song about a doll, "Une poupee," but Hoffmann doesn't understand. Coppelius enters, with a bag of spectacles and eyes: "J'ai des yeux." He gives Hoffmann a pair of spectacles to try on. These make Olympia appear even more beautiful and alive. Spalanzani returns and dismisses Hoffmann and Nicklausse, after which he and Coppelius fight over the ownership of Olympia, since Coppelius provided her eyes. Spalanzani gives him a letter of credit to a bankrupt concern. He leaves, and the guests pour in. Olympia is asked to entertain them with a song, "Les oiseaux dans la charmille," the servant covertly winding her up when she slows. When the guests go in to supper, Hoffmann remains behind with her and passionately declares his love. Pressing her hand makes her leave, and he is about to follow when Nicklausse enters and again tries to explain the nature of his beloved, but Hoffmann is deaf to his assertions. Coppelius enters, having found that the letter is worthless, and announces his intention for revenge. Hoffmann and Olympia dance, but something goes wrong and she all but tosses him around the room. She is taken out, but a crash is heard. Coppelius emerges declaring he has smashed her, and Hoffmann is about as crushed as she is.

[In the traditional order, Act Two is Giulietta's, Act Three is Antonia's, but this is often reversed.]

Act Two. The act opens in the courtesan Giulietta's sumptuous Venetian palace. She and Nicklausse sing a sensual barcarolle, "Belle nuit." Hoffmann responds with the much more cynical "Amis! L'amour tendre" song, saying that everything but physical pleasure is a lie. Schlemil, Giulietta's current lover, is displeased, and Nicklausse warns Hoffmann against loving Giulietta, though Hoffmann is convinced he is not smitten. Everyone leaves and Dappertutto enters, singing of his dark powers in either "Scintille, diamant" or "Noir chasseur." Giulietta enters and he gives her a diamond as advance payment for giving him Hoffmann's reflection as she has already given him Schlemil's shadow. Hoffmann comes in, ready to leave, but it's a moment's work for Giulietta to seduce him, to his ecstasy—"O Dieu de quelle ivresse"—and takes his shadow in a magic mirror. She tells him Schlemil has her key. The guests re-enter, an angry Schlemil among them. Hoffmann now realizes that he has lost his shadow and that Giulietta is a hellish creature, but he still adores her, as he declares in the famous septet "Helas, mon coeur." Schlemil challenges him and is killed in their duel. Hoffmann realizes, though, that Giulietta has left with another admirer.

Act Three. In Munich, Antonia sings a sad song about a turtledove—"Elle a fui"—thinking of Hoffmann. Her father, Crespel, forbids her to sing, as it is dangerous to her. He leaves and Frantz, the servant, complains about how unappreciated his various talents are, though his techniques need work: "Jour et nuit." Hoffmann enters and is joyously reunited with Antonia: "J'ai le bonheur." She tells him that her father has forbidden her to sing, but she insists on doing so ("C'est une chanson"), even though the effort clearly exhausts her. When her father, who disapproves of their love, is heard returning, she leaves and Hoffmann hides. Dr. Miracle enters and Crespel angrily denounces him as his wife's murderer. However, he promises to cure Antonia's illness and conducts a bizarre examination in which he appears to be talking to her and feeling her pulse. He offers a frightened Crespel medications for her condition and departs. When Crespel follows, Hoffmann realizes that singing could be fatal and convinces Antonia to promise not to sing again. When he leaves, Miracle appears again and tells her she is renouncing all her dreams for the sake of a fickle man; when she hesitates, she conjures the image of her mother, a famous singer, from a portrait. The image and Miracle order her to sing ("Cher enfant"), and at the end of the trio, she collapses, dying. Crespel rushes in, followed by Hoffmann, and Miracle himself reappears to declare her dead.

Epilogue. Back at the tavern, the performance is over, and Stella, piqued by Hoffmann's non-appearance, comes looking for him. She finds him instead dead drunk, and leaves with Lindorf. —*Ann Feeney*

Recommended:

○ **Offenbach: Les Contes d'Hoffmann** / Tate (cond.), Otter, Ramey, Norman, Araiza, Studer, Lind, Staatskapelle Dresden / 1991 / Philips 422374

○ **Offenbach: Les Contes d'Hoffmann** / Rudel (cond.), Sills, Lloyd, Burrows, Treigle, London SO / 2002 / DG 471247

○ **Offenbach: Les Contes d'Hoffmann** / Cluytens (cond.), Schwarzkopf, Los Angeles, Gedda, Benoit, Societe des Concerts du Conservatoire / 2003 / EMI 67983

○ **Offenbach: Les Contes d'Hoffmann** / Nagano (cond.), Jo, Van Dam, Dessay, Dubosc, Alagna, Lyon National Opera Orch. / 1997 / Erato 063017355

Orphée aux enfers (Orpheus in the Underworld) (ca. 1858–1874)

Offenbach's theater license, granted in 1855, limited his stage works to one act and three performers. Three years later, authorities lifted these restrictions, enabling Offenbach to forge his most enduring creations, the first of which was *Orphée aux enfers*. It is one of numerous of Offenbach's works that are satires of familiar tales.

Ludovic Halévy (1799–1862) drafted a libretto on the *Orpheus* legend early in 1858, but its size placed it outside the limits set up by Offenbach's license. When the restrictions were lifted, Offenbach prompted Halévy and Hector Crémieux (1828–92) to complete the libretto. *Orphée aux enfers* was Offenbach's first two-act work and would become the archetypical French operetta. Orphée and Euridyce were the first operetta hero and heroine and the chorus became in integral part of the action and music. The reception of the first performance on October 21, 1858, at the *Théâtre des Bouffes-Parisiens*, was mediocre, although a few critics were genuinely impressed with the new work. Dissatisfied, Offenbach began to make cuts to the score, but this failed to bring people to the theater in great numbers. Vital publicity came about in early 1859 when a critic, Jules Janin, wrote desparagingly of *Orphée aux enfers*, calling it a "profanation of holy and glorious antiquity." Offenbach, in a public reply, noted that one of Pluto's numbers was derived from Janin's writings, a revelation that piqued the interest of the Parisian public and made the show a hit. After 228 performances *Orphée aux enfers* was withdrawn, not due to lack of ticket sales, but merely to give the performers a rest. The piece returned to the stage a few weeks later. For the Vienna production of 1860 Carl Binder provided an overture, which has become the standard, and famous, overture.

Halévy and Crémieux and Offenbach's thinly veiled caricatures of contemporary political and cultural figures and ideals fueled the success of *Orphée aux enfers*. The lustful Jupiter was easily interpreted as the womanizing Emperor Napoleon III; Orphée as a restless, bored bourgeois; and Eurydice's song to Bacchus and the wild cancans parallel the middle and upper classes' hedonistic predilections. Of course, Offenbach's music was ultimately responsible of the poplarity of *Orphée*. The composer parodies contemporary sentimental ballads in Orphée's violin solo and borrows Gluck's "Che farò" (from *Orfeo ed Euridice*) and the *Marseillaise*. Amusing incongruities, such as having the gods dance a cancan, pepper the score. Offenbach parodies elements of grand opera in the silly, bawdy *duo de la Mouche* (Fly duet) in Act Two. The finales are the high points of the operetta and feature increasing speed and intensity that lead to a climax. For example, the first act begins very quietly with Orphée and Eurydice alone, but ends in a very fast tempo with all the gods performing a galop and leaving the stage. —*John Palmer*

Synopsis:

Act One, Scene One. An open field between the houses of Orphée and Aristée. For quite some time, the married couple Orphée and Eurydice have lived together. Eurydice feels both annoyed and neglected because of Orphée's furious music making. Orphée feels offended at the minimal attention Eurydice gives to his artistic genius and her lack of appreciation of his job as music teacher and director at the Orpheon in Thebes. Moreover, they both have unconcealed, extramarital erotic inclinations. Orphée is supposedly attracted to the nymph, Chloe, and Eurydice is apparently drawn to her new neighbor, the quiet shepherd and bee handler, Aristée. She has no idea that Aristée is actually the god Pluto, who wants to bring her with him into the Underworld. Aristée suggests to Orphée a plan that will get Orphée what he wants and not jeopardize his reputation in the eyes of Public Opinion. Orphée warns Eurydice about a certain something he has concealed in a cornfield for her lover. Eurydice brings this warning to Aristée, who doesn't seem at all apprehensive. Eurydice, however, is drawn to the field to have a look. There, amidst thunder and lightning, Aristée transforms into Pluto. At the sight of this, Eurydice must die and the transfixed Orphée must deliver the news of her death. Pluto then takes Eurydice with him into the Underworld. Happily, Orphée conveys the news of Eurydice's demise and wants to find Chloe as soon as possible. Upset over all the frivolity, Public Opinion (fulfilling the function of the chorus in a Greek tragedy) demands that Orphée stop. They insist he ascend Mount Olympus to confer with the gods and reclaim his wife. At first, Orphée refuses, but the threat that the whole world will learn he set the deadly trap for Eurydice makes him submit to their wishes.

Act One, Scene Two. On Mount Olympus the gods awaken from a deep sleep and lie about like lazy people. They speak rebelliously against Jupiter's bland, sterile management of heavenly affairs, and they are particularly upset at being reduced to eating tasteless nectar and ambrosia whenever the chef is away on some out-of-town adventure. Jupiter's jealous wife, Juno, suspects that Jupiter has abducted Eurydice. Jupiter is pleased when the messenger Mercury appears and brings the news that Pluto has stolen Eurydice. Summoned to Olympus, Pluto denies everything. Orphée, accompanied by Public Opinion, shows up and, against his will, asks that his wife be returned to him. A general revolt among the gods breaks out and they all complain about Pluto. Jupiter declares that Pluto must return Eurydice and takes his entire retinue down to the Underworld with him. Ostensibly, Jupiter undertakes the task to help Orphée, but he really wants Eurydice for himself.

Act Two, Scene One. The Underworld, in Pluto's bedroom. Pluto has concealed Eurydice in his room. On Pluto's orders, John Styx, once Prince of Arcadia on the Earth's surface, watches over Eurydice. Styx laments the passing of his princely existence as he tells of his life. These stories bore the sullen Eurydice as much as her former life walking around on earth. She ponders Orphée and his culpability in what has happened to her, and wonders at her recent fantastic ride to the Underworld. As the Olympic Commission searches in vain for the captive, Eurydice discovers in the keyhole a card from one "Baron Jupiter." This changes into a mysterious insect, a fly with golden wings. Through a tremendous effort she captures the fly, who then explains that he is Jupiter in another form, promising that during the upcoming meal and celebration, which will distract Pluto, he will help her escape and return home.

Act Two, Scene Two. In the Underworld, near the river Styx, everyone dances and becomes drunk during the party Pluto gives for his visitors from Olympus. More spirited than ever, Jupiter gains the approval of the other guests by dancing a minuet, which then breaks out into an energetic cancan. However, the human world, through Public Opinion, makes its presence known. Orphée must demand from Jupiter his Eurydice, and Jupiter must give her up. There is one condition: Eurydice must follow Orphée along the path to the ferry across the river Styx, but Orphée cannot look at her or he will lose her forever. As the two are on their way to the boat, Jupiter, who notices that Orphée is not at all interested in looking at his wife, creates a flash of electricity, causing Orphée to look back and lose Eurydice. Orphée and Public Opinion step into the boat to cross the river. Jupiter decides that Eurydice will enter the service of Bacchus—neither Jupiter not Pluto will have her. Eurydice is overjoyed, because nothing interesting has started with anyone she has known, god or human. All dance a wild cancan. *—John Palmer*

Recommended:

- ○ **Offenbach: Orphée aux enfers** / Minkowski (cond.), Dessay, Fouchecourt, Podles, Gens, Lyon National Opera Orch. / 1998 / EMI 56725
- ○ **Offenbach: Orphée aux Enfers** / Plasson (cond.), Tortelier, Mesplé, Sénéchal, Berbie, Toulouse Orch. / EMI 749647

La Péricbole (ca. 1868–1874)

Jacques Offenbach, a German transplant to his beloved city of Paris, was responsible for the creation and popularization of the French operetta. After his famous and highly successful *Orphee d'Enfers*, comic operas and parodies of established composers of grand opera became the vogue. Only later in his career did Offenbach turn to composing works that were independent of parody and satiric wit. With *La Périchole*, he strikes a sentimental and lighthearted tone, creating a love story with delightful characterizations and comic dilemmas. His librettists were Henri Meilhac and Ludovic Halévy, who also collaborated with Offenbach on several other successful operettas. They based their *livret* on Prosper Merimée's comic play *La Carrousse de Saint-Sacrement*. The premiere of *La Perichole* at the Theatre des Varietes on October 16, 1868, was greeted with acclaim.

The opera takes place in eighteenth century Lima, Peru. Offenbach takes advantage of the foreign setting and spices up his score with Spanish dance forms such as fandangos, boleros, and seguidillas. The central character is *La Perichole*, an impoverished street singer. Throughout the opera, she is given prominence through the beauty and sophistication of her songs. The Letter Song from Act One is the most famous and well known of all the arias given to her. It is a tragic love song in which the heroine bids her dear Piquillo adieu. The poignant lyrical melody to the Letter Song is first introduced in the sprightly overture to the opera, and then restated after La Périchole sings her aria, reinforcing the mood and content of the dramatic moment. The remaining portion of Act One shows off Offenbach's incredible comic talents, as he stages a wedding for the inebriated lovers. La Perichole is again given center stage with a rollicking drinking song whose melody careens about along with the tipsy bride. The delicate orchestrations follow the weaving of the phrases and the spinning of the ceiling exactly. The bridegroom is completely smashed, and the wedding celebration is filled with broad humor and lively music.

La Périchole is one of Offenbach's best scores; it contains an abundance of fine melodies, lively action and wit, inventive harmonies and orchestral writing, and effective theatrics. It has earned a place among comic opera aficionados, and has been revived from time to time throughout the twentieth and twenty-first centuries. It is always well received by audiences, and will remain an important work in the operetta repertoire. *—Rita Laurance*

Synopsis:

Act One. In eighteenth century Lima, Peru, on the name-day of the Viceroy Don Andres de Ribeira, people are gathered to celebrate. The governor of Lima has ordered everyone to rejoice, and has purchased drinks at the government's expense. Now he comes through the crowd disguised as a vegetable peddler because he wishes to make sure that his orders are being followed, and that everyone is happy. The Count de Panatellas is disguised as a peddler of buttered rolls, and even the Viceroy has decided to come to the party incognito. But the people recognize him and applaud his disguise. What a dull life a monarch would lead, they say, if he weren't allowed to go among his people incognito!

Two impoverished itinerant street singers bustle through the crowd. It is La Périchole and Piquillo. They hope to earn a little extra money for the day, and maybe get some supper, by singing. They sing a love ballad, but the crowd ignores them. They try again, but are interrupted by some showmen with performing dogs, and the audience leaves them starving and penniless. Piquillo wanders off, and Perichole attracts the attention of the Viceroy, who offers her a position as a lady-in-waiting at court. She is very hungry, so she agrees, but first writes a farewell letter to Piquillo. It is very sad indeed. She tells him that she loves him dearly, but that she can't bear her life any longer.

The Viceroy tells Panatellas to find a suitable husband for La Périchole, for all ladies-in-waiting must be married. Panatellas finds Piquillo in the throes of despair and, after plying him with drink, convinces him to get married to an anonymous lady. The two notaries arrive completely drunk, and preparations are made for a quick wedding. La Périchole has also had too much to drink, and Piquillo is so plastered that he doesn't even recognize Périchole, although she recognizes him. The two promise to be unfaithful to one another, and to make each other perfectly miserable.

Act Two. At the Viceroy's palace, the Marquis of Tarapote has fainted from the shock of learning that the new court favorite is a common street singer! Piquillo enters, and all sing the praises of his wife, but slyly mock him for being the husband of the king's mistress. Piquillo asks for an explanation, for he has little memory of the previous evening. When he understands the situation, he requests permission to leave. Don Pedro and Panatellas agree, but tell him that he must present his wife to the king in a formal ceremony first. What is his shock and surprise when his own Perichole is brought to him as his wife and as the king's mistress! He tries to demand an explanation from La Périchole and finds himself in the center of a scene. He becomes angry, and tells King Don Andres that his new mistress is the falsest woman alive. He insults the king and throws Perichole at the foot of the throne! Don Andres has Piquillo seized and thrown into the dungeon for uncooperative husbands.

Act Three. An old man enters the dungeon cell through a trapdoor. He is attempting to escape after having been incarcerated for 12 years. He hides as Don Pedro and Panatellas enter with the angry Piquillo. Piquillo goes to sleep on a bed of straw, and La Périchole is let into the cell by a jailer. She kicks him to wake him up, then tells him how much she loves him. She tells him that they can bribe the jailer with all the jewels that the Viceroy has given her. But when they call for the jailer, it is King Don Andres in disguise, and he looks angry. When Perichole offers him her diamonds if he will help them escape, he has them both chained to posts. After he has gone, the old prisoner comes in and frees them. Piquillo pretends to be chained, the old man hides, and Périchole calls for the Viceroy, knowing that he will come to her. When he comes, the three pounce on him and grab his keys.

In the final scene, the entire town has turned out and is looking for the three escaped prisoners. Finally Piquillo and La Périchole present themselves, dressed again as street singers. They sing a ballad to Don Andres entitled Ballad of the Lovers, and are pardoned. *—Rita Laurance*

Recommended:

- ○ **Offenbach: La Périchole** / Lombard (cond.), Crespin, Bastin, Vanzo, Friedmann, Strasbourg PO / Erato 45686
- ○ **Offenbach: La Périchole** / Markevitch (cond.), Benoit, Linval, Amade, Noguera, Lamoureux Concert Assoc. Orch. / 2001 / EMI 574088

La Vie Parisienne (ca. 1866–1873)

Offenbach based his *La Vie Parisienne* on a one-act play of 1864, *Le Photographe*, by Henri Meilhac and Ludovic Halévy. Offenbach was so pleased with the play's cast that he wanted the same people for *La Vie Parisienne*, even if they could not sing: "If they are funny it's good enough for me." Although the entire company despised the book and music, *La Vie Parisienne* was a sensation. Of the first performance, in the Palais-Royal on October 31, 1866, one reviewer noted that the audience behaved as if "the whole house had been taking hashish." It was even more successful than Offenbach's *Barbe-Bleue*, staged earlier the same year. Timing could not have been better for *La Vie Parisienne*, for international visitors to the Paris exhibition of 1867 were intrigued by the plot, which revolves around tourists visiting the city. In the first act, a Swedish baron and baroness and a wealthy Brazilian become entangled in a web woven by two desperately amorous men-about-town at a railway station. The next four acts include all the elements necessary for a successful operetta: servants posing as members of the upper class, hidden identities, thwarted liaisons, hedonism and the consumption of alcoholic beverages. *La Vie Parisienne* was Offenbach's first successful venture into operetta with a contemporary setting, topical subjects and characters in modern dress. Similarities to Johann Strauss' *Die Fledermaus* (1874) abound, particularly in the acts featuring parties. *La Vie Parisienne* is a happy, comical work in praise of Paris, but it is not without its reservations. As the Gondremarcks are shuttled about and deceived, they begin to realize that Paris is not as fascinating as they had been led to believe by their imaginations. It is, however, fascinating enough, and does have new things to offer them, namely love, dancing, and drinking.

Offenbach's score reinforces the light-hearted atmosphere drawn by Meilhac and Halévy. The cheerful msuic contains only one hint of sentimentality: Metella's rondeaux. Possibly the most playful number appears in the third act with "Votre habit a craqué dans le dos" (Your coat is split down the back), Gondremarck's response to his sight of the phony Admiral's backside at the party. This leads to a finale featuring drunken revelry both on stage and in the orchestra that closes with a cancan. Other highlights include the chorus of railroad travelers at the beginning of the first act (No. 1), which smacks of the salon-style song, and Gondremarck's "Moi, je voudrais voir les théâtres" (No. 4), in which he looks forward to seeing all the wonders Paris has to offer. These numbers contrast greatly with Metella's later waltz-nocturne (No. 24). There are polka rhythms in Gabrielle's "Au-tre-fois plus d'un a-mant" (No. 7) and a bit later, the evocation of a hurdy-gurdy during the reading of Baron Frascata's letter (No. 9). In No. 18, "Tout tour-ne, tour-ne, tour-ne" Offenbach's swirling rhythms accompany a dance and song proclaiming the collective drinking of champagne, musically depicting the sweet and grotesque aspects of life in Paris. *—John Palmer*

Synopsis:

Act One. In the midst of the hustle and bustle at the station, Gare de l'Ouest, are two elegant gentlemen, Gardefeu and Bobinet, who intentionally overlook one another. The two men about town were once friends, but are now jealous of one another because of an all-too-loose grisette. Unbeknownst to them, they are both waiting to greet the same woman, the coquettish Metella, who is already there, on the arm of a third gentleman. Gardefeu and Bobinet's rage over Metella causes them to reconcile, whereupon they agree that from this point on they will associate only with finer society. Gardefeu immediately smells an opportunity. His former servant, Joseph, now a guide at the Grand Hotel, will pick up the elderly Swedish Baron Gondremarck with his wife, the Baroness Christine, at the train station and show them the sights in Paris. For a juicy fee, Joseph is glad to offer his services. Gardefeu promises the Swedes that, under his care, they will taste the best cultural and other delights of the city. Also hurrying off the train is the Brazilian millionaire Matadores, who sails across the ocean annually to squander his money recklessly in the Paris nightlife.

Act Two. A salon in Gardefeu's house. Joseph, an extraordinarily friendly guide, has convinced the naïve Swedish couple that Gardefeu's home is an up-scale branch of the Grand Hotel. To enable him to get closer to the beautiful Baroness Christine, Gardefeu recommends they take separate rooms. This is fine with the Baron, as he and his wife will be going their separate ways in Paris. Specifically, he has a letter of introduction to a certain Metella. The author of the letter, Metella's former lover Frascata, writes that Metella will introduce the inexperienced Gondremarck to Paris, but only to make jealous reproaches to Gardefeu: he has given her room, of all things, to a stranger. At the moment she has no interest in the awkwardly amorous Swede. However, Gardefeu can console him with a fancy menu at a table in his "hotel." Quickly, Gardefeu assembles his "high-society guests," among them the glove-maker Gabrielle as the sad widow of a colonel and the cobbler Frick as a major. All of them have fun celebrating the finest things in Paris. At least the Baron is excited, thinking that this feast is but a taste of the social "delicatessen" of tomorrow evening. Gardefeu has obtained for him an invitation to the house of an admiral. The Baron is to come alone, without his wife. The Baron's anticipation is just a great as that of Gardefeu's, who looks forward to spending an evening with the Baroness Christine.

Act Three. The next evening, in the large salon of Madame de Quimper's house. Madame de Quimper is away. As a result, her nephew, Bobinet, can oblige his friend Gardefeu by having the party for the "Admiral" at the house. Bobinet will play the part of the Admiral wearing a splendid, but too small, uniform. Likewise, the assembled servants of the household are pompously clothed in a effort to make Gondremarck feel almost at home in the big world. Above all, the presumptive wife of the master of the house, the maid Pauline, captivates him. The rest of the party-goers furnish a dazzling display of what Gondremarck believes is the aristocratic way of life. More than once the large grin from the rear of the Admiral's bursting uniform causes Gondremarck some consternation. But he is already filled with the swirling atmosphere.

Act Four. In Gardefeu's salon, the same evening. The Baroness Christine has just returned from the opera. The fake guide has done everything as best he could to make sure she made it to the house undisturbed. Nevertheless, unexpected guests arrive: Madame de Quimper and her niece, who wish to visit their friend Christine. They are here because the elderly, bad-tempered Quimper came home early from her trip and walked into an orgy in her own house. Gardefeu is having little luck with the Baroness, an anonymous note from the jealous Metella revealed the entire hotel scam to her. Now the resolute Quimper takes the initiative. Gardefeu, who believes the last of the visitors has left, approaches Christine's bedroom. Suddenly in front of him stands a militant old woman armed with tongs. At that moment the intoxicated Gondremarck arrives and staggers into his wife's room, also believing he has seen a ghost.

Act Five. Midnight in the salon of a luxurious restaurant. The wealthy Brazilian who arrived at the Gare de l'Ouest just after the Gondremarcks has not yet spent all of his money. Arm-in-arm with the glove-maker Gabrielle, he is giving a private masked ball, which the other guests immediately join. Next, the infuriated Gondremarck appears, now aware of all the tricks that have been played on him. He hopes to find comfort with Metella. But she also plays a trick on him in which she sends him three different masked women. His interest had barely been aroused when the first lifted her mask to reveal the horrid Quimper. Now, once and for all, he wants to take his revenge on Gardefeu, who has deceived him many times. He looks for him, finds him and challenges him to a duel, on the spot. Gardefeu halfheartedly accepts. Bobinet intervenes and interrogates the two aggressors, asking them what it is they really have to complain about, and whether or not all the pranks have not been at least somewhat amusing. Gondremarck, when he thinks about all that has happened, can hardly contest Bobinet's assertion. And his wife, one of the three masked women, is the best thing he has, without taking offense at the situation. He then sings in praise of the pleasure he experienced while incurring the wounds to his soul. All sing of Parisian life. *—John Palmer*

Recommended:

- ○ **Offenbach: La vie parisienne** / Plasson (cond.), Crespin, Benoit, Mesplé, Sénéchal, Toulouse Orch. / EMI 747154

BALLET

Gaîté Parisienne

Jacques Offenbach died in 1880, yet it is his name that is attached to this ballet that first appeared in 1938. While the tunes in *Gaîté Parisienne* are his, much of the orchestration, as well as the arrangement of the numbers, was done by Manuel Rosenthal. The idea for the ballet was conceived by the talented trio of choreographer Leonid Massine, the well-known impresario Sol Hurok, and René Blum, director of the Ballet Russes de Monte Carlo, who together engaged the services of Rosenthal after they had selected the Offenbach tunes for him to use. The scenario they contrived was taken from Offenbach's operetta *La Vie Parisienne*.

The story concerns the seedy patrons of a Paris bistro called Tortoni's Restaurant, an actual business establishment. There are many amorous adventures in the ballet, with the story centering on two men: a baron who chases after a young woman selling gloves, and a Peruvian who pursues a relationship with a flower girl. It is all quite mischievous fun, colorfully packaged and brilliantly suited by the

Offenbach/Rosenthal score. The premiere on April 5, 1938, at the Théâtre de Monte Carlo, was a great success and the music has been in the standard repertory ever since, often presented in "pops" concerts.

Much of the music in *Gaîté Parisienne*, of course, was already familiar when it was first presented, which may have aided its success. The popular "Can-Can," for example, is taken from Offenbach's operetta, *Orpheus in the Underworld* (1858; rev. 1874). The familiar Barcarolle, which closes the ballet, comes from the *Tales of Hoffman* (1881), his last operetta.

There is much other attractive music in *Gaîté Parisienne*, all of it in a light vein. There are two colorful polkas, five waltzes, a Ländler, and many other dances, most frothy and joyous, all quite tuneful and direct. In sum, this is unpretentious, well-crafted music, and while it will not appeal to those exclusively interested in serious listening, it is undeniably masterful within its genre. It should be noted that not all the music in the score is from Offenbach: Rosenthal himself wrote No. 14, "The Duel." He was a young composer of modest success when he took on the project, and would later become better known as a conductor, for a time leading the French National Radio Orchestra and later the Seattle Symphony Orchestra. Rosenthal himself recorded this score twice. *—Robert Cummings*

Recommended:

- ○ **Offenbach: Gaîté Parisienne, Rosenthal: Offenbachiana** / Rosenthal (cond.), Monte Carlo PO / 1999 / Naxos 554005

John Ogdon

b. Jan. 27, 1937, Manchester, England, **d.** Aug. 1, 1989, London, England
Pianist

John Ogdon's life and career might be summed up as prodigious. A player of great strength and protean technique, Ogdon was unafraid, and in fact preferred, to tackle the biggest scores, including Busoni's mammoth *Piano Concerto*, Beethoven's *"Hammerklavier" Sonata*, the *Concerto for Solo Piano* (from the Op. 39 Etudes) of Charles-Valentin Alkan, and the four-hour *Opus Clavicembalisticum* by Kaikhosru Sorabji, which he first played in private recital at the age of 22. His repertoire was also massive: more than 80 composers were represented, with literally hundreds of scores, many of them committed to his unparalleled memory and more than 260 of them preserved in recordings. Ogdon also was a composer of nearly 200 works in many forms, a symphony and piano concerto among them, and he taught and wrote extensively on music. Even his size was impressive. Tall and with a tendency toward obesity, Ogdon brought power and strength to his performances, with critics often resorting to words like "thunderous" in their assessments.

Yet John Ogdon was always sensitive to the demands of musical architecture. An affable and approachable artist among his more aloof colleagues, Ogdon's primary concern was to communicate music's essence through clear delineation of its form. He also was capable of sensitive intimacy with his repertoire. When he was at the height of his powers, it was Ogdon's concentration and unrelenting but plastic control that impressed audiences.

Born in Manchester in 1937, Ogdon early on showed such talent that he was taken on by such renowned teachers as Iso Elinson, Egon Petri, and Ilona Kabos. Following an acclaimed series of concerts in the north of England, Ogdon made his sensational London debut at the age of 21, playing Busoni's rarely-heard *Piano Concerto* under the baton of Sir Henry Wood. Two important prizes in the early 1960s established his international reputation: the Budapest Liszt Prize in 1961 and First Prize in the 1962 Moscow Tchaikovsky Competition—the latter shared with another rapidly emerging artist, the young Vladimir Ashkenazy.

A hectic career followed, in which Ogdon played acclaimed concerts and recitals around the world, recorded extensively, and wrote a number of well-received treatises, including *Sorabji and Melville* (1960), *Liszt's Later Piano Music* (1970) and *The Romantic Tradition* (1972). He also began studying composition with Richard Hall, Thomas Pittfield, and George Lloyd. Ogdon married pianist Brenda Lucas in 1960, and the two often appeared in recital together.

In 1973, Ogdon suffered a breakdown which, given the pace of his career, might not have been unexpected, but a more serious cause was at the heart of it. Like his father before him, Ogdon was diagnosed with schizophrenia and hospitalized for several years at the Maudley Hospital in London, where he was nevertheless reported to maintain a practice schedule of three hours a day on the hospital's Steinway. In 1980, he made a comeback in the concert hall, but critics found that his technique had suffered from the years of institutionalization and the medication he took to maintain his inner balance. Still, there were moments of great inspiration when the brilliance of his conceptions overshadowed any diminution of his keyboard powers, and his 1988 recording of Sorabji's *Opus Clavicembalisticum* (Altarus CD 9075, four discs) is an astonishing achievement. Between 1975 and 1980, Ogdon taught at Indiana University. His death in London from pneumonia at age 52 prematurely ended a dramatic career. *—Mark Satola*

Recommended:

- ○ **Ogdon Plays Rachmaninov** / Ogdon / 2003 / Testament 1295
- ○ **Skryabin: Piano Music** / Ogdon / 1998 / Angel 72652
- ○ **Sorabji: Opus Clavicembalisticum** / Ogdon / 1991 / Altarus 9075
- ○ **In Memoriam of John Ogdon** / Ogdon / 1994 / Altarus 9063
- ○ **John Ogdon** / Ogdon, etc. / 1998 / Philips 456913

Garrick Ohlsson

b. Apr. 3, 1948, Bronxville, NY
Pianist

An imposing physical presence at six feet four inches tall, with a reach of an octave and a fifth, Garrick Ohlsson is a pianist with a flawless technique, strong grasp of form, and a clean, non-romanticized style of performing. He began piano studies when he was eight years old, attending the Westchester Conservatory of Music. After he saw Rubinstein in concert, he told interviewer Michael Steinberg, his choice of career was set. "I was blasted into orbit. And that's when I said in my mind... when other little boys say, 'I want to be a fireman,' that's what I want to do." He entered the preparatory course of the Juilliard School when he was 13, where he studied with Sascha Gorodnitzki; remaining at Juilliard for his Bachelor's of Music (earned in 1971), he studied with Rosina Lhévinne. Private studies with Olga Barabini, Irma Wolpe, and Claudio Arrau rounded out Ohlsson's education.

In 1966 he won the Busoni Competition in Italy, and in 1968, the Montreal Piano Competition, but it was his 1970 victory in the Chopin Competition in Warsaw that launched his career. He was the first American winner, and his victory gained some of the same kind of attention as had Van Cliburn's Tchaikovsky Competition triumph a little over a decade earlier. A Warsaw critic called Ohlsson a "bear-butterfly" of a pianist, and the young pianist had a distinctive image to go with his credentials.

Ohlsson has maintained a strong association with the music of Chopin, and has played the Polish master's complete piano works several times in recital and on recordings. His Chopin interpretations favor intense emotionalism over a languid, swooning salon style. Ohlsson is by no means exclusively a player of Chopin however; his repertory extends from Haydn to twentieth century masters and includes more than 80 works for piano and orchestra. He tours and appears as a guest soloist with orchestras around the world and has made over a dozen tours to Poland alone, where he continues to be particularly esteemed for his Chopin playing. He is also an avid chamber performer and has collaborated with the Cleveland, Tokyo and Tákacs quartets. With violinist Jorja Fleezanis and cellist Michael Grebanier he founded the FOG Trio, based in San Francisco. During the 2002–2003 season, Ohlsson appeared as part of the Lincoln Center Great Performers series in New York, performing works by Busoni. A pianist completely consumed with musical life, Ohlsson has, when asked by an interviewer, been unable to remember what kind of car he drives. *—AMG*

Recommended:

- ○ **Chopin: Piano Works Vol. 3** / Ohlsson / 1991 / Arabesque 6630
- ○ **Busoni: Piano Concerto** / Dohnányi (cond.), Ohlsson, Page, Cleveland Orch. / 1989 / Telarc 80207
- ○ **Beethoven Sonatas: Pathetique; Moonlight; Waldstein** / Ohlsson / 1996 / Arabesque 6677
- ○ **Ewa Podles & Garrick Ohlsson** / Podles, Ohlsson / 2003 / Dux 405

David Oistrakh

b. Sep. 30, 1908, Odessa. Russia, **d.** Oct. 24, 1974, Amsterdam, Netherlands
Violinist

David Oistrakh is considered the premiere violinist of the mid-twentieth century Soviet Union. His recorded legacy includes nearly the entire standard violin repertory up to and including Prokofiev and Bartók. Oistrakh's violin studies began in 1913 with the famed teacher Pyotr Stolyarsky. Later he officially joined Stolyarsky's class at the Odessa Conservatory, graduating in 1926 by playing Prokofiev's *First Violin Concerto*. Performances of the Glazunov *Concerto* in Odessa and Kiev in 1927, and a 1928 debut in Leningrad (Tchaikovsky *Concerto*) gave Oistrakh the confidence to move to Moscow. He made his premiere there in early 1929, but the event went largely unnoticed. In 1934, however, after several years of patiently refining his craft, Oistrakh was invited to join the Moscow Conservatory, eventually rising to the rank of full professor in 1939.

Meanwhile, Oistrakh was gaining success on the competition circuit, winning the All-Ukrainian contest in 1930, and the All-Soviet competition three years later. In 1935 he took second prize at the Wieniawski competition. In 1937 the Soviet government sent the now veteran violinist to Brussels to compete in the International Ysaÿe Competition, where he took home first prize.

With his victory in Brussels, Soviet composers began to take notice of their young compatriot, enabling Oistrakh to work closely with Miaskovsky and Khachaturian on their concertos in 1939 and 1940, respectively. In addition, his close friendship with Shostakovich led the composer to write two concertos for the instrument (the first of which Oistrakh played at his, and its, triumphant American premiere in 1955). During the 1940s Oistrakh's active performing schedule took him across the Soviet Union but his international career had to wait until the 1950s, when the political climate had cooled enough for Soviet artists to be welcomed in the capitals of the West.

The remaining decades of Oistrakh's life were devoted to maintaining the highest possible standards of excellence throughout an exhausting touring schedule (he returned to the U.S. six times in the 1960s), and he began a small but successful sideline career as an orchestral conductor. His death came suddenly in Amsterdam in 1974, during a cycle of Brahms concerts in which he both played and conducted. Oistrakh's unexpected death left a void in the Soviet musical world which was never really filled.

Throughout his career David Oistrakh was known for his honest, warm personality; he developed close friendships with many of the leading musicians of the day. His violin technique was virtually flawless, though he never allowed purely physical matters to dominate his musical performances. He always demanded of himself (and his students) that musical proficiency, intelligence, and emotion be in balance, regardless of the particular style. Oistrakh felt that a violinist's essence was communicated through clever and subtle use of the bow, and not through overly expressive use of vibrato. To this end he developed a remarkably relaxed, flexible right arm technique, capable of producing the most delicate expressive nuances, but equally capable of generating great volume and projection.

As a teacher, David Oistrakh maintained that a teacher should do no more than necessary to help guide the student towards his or her own solutions to technical and interpretive difficulties. He rarely played during lessons, fearing that he might distract the student from developing a more individual approach, and even encouraged his students to challenge his interpretations. Perhaps the best evidence of the Oistrakh's gift for teaching is that he felt that he gained as much from the teaching experience as his students did. *—Blair Johnston*

Recommended:

- ○ **Concerto by Brahms & Tchaikovsky** / Sargent, del Mar (conds.), Oistrakh, London PO, Royal PO / 2002 / BBC 4102
- ○ **Beethoven: Sonatas for Piano & Violin** / Oistrakh, Oborin / 2001 / Philips 468406
- ○ **Sonatas & Concertos** / Rozhdestvensky, Khachaturian (conds.), Oistrakh, Richter, Moscow Radio Orch., Monaco RSO / 1994 / Vox 5120
- ○ **Concertos by Glazunov & Kabelevsky** / Kondrashin, Kabalevsky (conds.), Oistrakh, State SO of Russia / 1952 / Omega 1025
- ○ **David Oistrakh: The Essential** / Rozhdestvensky, Kondrashin, Mravinsky (conds.), Oistrakh, Leningrad PO, Moscow Phil. Symphony / 2000 / RCA 72914
- ○ **David Oistrach** / Goossens, Konwitschny, Malcolm, Oistrakh, Fischer, Royal PO, VSO, Dresden Staatskapelle / 1962 / DG 447427
- ○ **The Oistrakh Collection** / Oistrakh, etc. / 2002 / Classica d'Oro 9006

Kurt Ollmann

b. Jan. 9, 1957, Racine, WI
Baritone

Lyric baritone Kurt Ollmann benefited greatly from an artistic association with Leonard Bernstein. After thorough schooling and a fruitful beginning with Milwaukee's adventuresome Skylight Opera, he appeared in several prestigious world venues before being given a place among Bernstein's favored singers. Clear enunciation that could sound either international or comfortably American afforded him immediate access to both operatic and musical comedy roles and even more so for those works, such as Bernstein's *Candide* and *West Side Story*, that hover somewhere in between.

With a pliant voice of attractive quality, Ollmann made the most of studying with Marlena Malas and Yolanda Marculescu, but undoubtedly found in French baritone Gérard Souzay a true vocal and interpretive model. With an instrument similar in weight and flexibility to Souzay's and with something of his teacher's wide-ranging interest in recital and concert repertory, Ollmann artistically developed along similar lines. He was a member of the Skylight Opera in Milwaukee from 1979 to 1982, just as the company was making itself known for its small-scale but creative productions. Dramatic viability counted there as much as vocal accomplishment and Ollmann's tall, lithe frame afforded him an effective stage presence. Appearances followed in several American venues such as the Opera Theatre of St. Louis, Santa Fe, the Seattle Opera Company, and the growing company in Washington, D.C. He was also welcomed in Brussels and at La Scala, where he was heard as Pelléas in 1986 with Claudio Abbado conducting. His Mélisande in that production was Frederica von Stade. The same year, he took part in the first Vienna performance of Bernstein's *A Quiet Place*. Ollmann thereafter often worked with Bernstein, recording several of his stage works and appearing as the soloist in the orchestral work written by Bernstein for the reopening of Carnegie Hall. His Don Giovanni in Peter Sellers' 1987 production for New York's *Summerfare* seemed an interesting dramatic sidebar. With a voice that was from the beginning highly phonogenic, Ollmann recorded often. Bernstein's mentoring resulted in the singer's recording both *West Side Story* and *Candide* with him. The musical, an updated version of the *Romeo and Juliet* story, revealed Ollmann's comfort with English that had to be precise, but not formal. When Bernstein got around to recording what he regarded as the definitive version of his oft-revised *Candide*, Ollmann participated in both the live performance schedule in the flu-wracked London of December 1989, and the recording that followed. As Maximilian and the Captain, Ollmann fit deftly into an all-star cast including June Anderson, Jerry Hadley, Nicolai Gedda, and Christa Ludwig. Even after Bernstein's death in 1990, Ollmann continued to be identified with his work; he was featured in a 1992 recording of *On the Town* with Michael Tilson Thomas. Ollmann's Mercutio is preserved on disc in a recording of Gounod's *Roméo et Juliette* conducted by Leonard Slatkin. Several recordings attest to the baritone's advocacy of the song literature. Songs by Paul Bowles figure in two discs and Ollmann's participation in the AIDS Quilt Songbook project is memorable.

As Ollmann entered his mid-forties, his voice darkened and he seemed to be losing some of his former ease. His Jesus in a Milwaukee Symphony Orchestra performance of Bach's *St. Matthew Passion* in the spring 2002, however, was firmly and eloquently sung. *—Erik Eriksson*

Recommended:

- ○ **Gounod: Roméo Et Juliette** / Slatkin (cond.), Domingo, Graham, Ollmann, Swenson, Munich Radio Orch. / 1996 / RCA 68440
- ○ **Debussy: Pelléas et Mélisande** / Abbado (cond.), Von Stade, Ghiaurov, Ollmann, Giacomotti, La Scala Theater Orch. & Chorus / 1999 / Opera d'Oro 1195

Ursula Oppens

b. Feb. 2, 1944, New York, NY
Pianist

Ursula Oppens is an American concert pianist who has dedicated most of her career to performing and helping advance the cause of contemporary keyboard literature. Oppens initially studied piano with her mother and later took lessons with Guido Agosti, Leonard Shure, and Rosina Lhevinne. After earning her master's degree from the Juilliard School of Music, Oppens made her New York debut in 1969 and went on to take first prize at the Busoni International Piano Competition that same year. In 1971 Oppens co-founded the contemporary music ensemble Speculum Musicae, which still exists 30 years on, although she is no longer a member. Oppens has also performed with the Chamber Music Society of Lincoln Center.

In recent years Oppens has been serving as the John Evans Professor of Music Performance Studies at Northwestern University. Nonetheless, Oppens maintains a busy performance schedule that ranges worldwide and has racked up an equally long track record in the recording studio, recording for Nonesuch, Albany, Innova, Music and Arts, New World, Bridge, CRI, and many others. One area of endeavor in which Oppens has truly made her mark is in commissioning original works from contemporary composers. Among the composers who have written music especially for Oppens are Charles Wuorinen, Elliott Carter, Conlon Nancarrow, John Harbison, György Ligeti, and Witold Lutosławski. Her recordings *American Piano Music of Our Time* and of Frederic Rzewski's *The People United Shall Never Be Defeated* have both been nominated for Grammy Awards. She also played and recorded in a piano duet with the late pianist Paul Jacobs that is fondly remembered by many fans of contemporary music. *—Uncle Dave Lewis*

Recommended:

- ○ **Rzewski: The People United Will Never Be Defeated!** / Oppens / 1993 / Vanguard 8056
- ○ **Carter: Piano Concerto; Variations** / Gielen (cond.), Oppens, Cincinnati SO / 1986 / New World 80347
- ○ **Rzewski: Night Crossing** / Oppens, Rzewski (pianos) / Music & Arts 988
- ○ **American Piano Music of Our Time** / Oppens / Music & Arts 604

Orchestra of St. Luke's

f. 1979, New York, NY
Ensemble

One of the best-known chamber orchestras in America, the Orchestra of St. Luke's was organized in the summer of 1979 to perform at the Caramoor International Music Festival in Katonah, New York. The Orchestra grew out of the St. Luke's Chamber Ensemble, which was formed in 1974 to play concerts at the Church of St. Luke's in the Fields in New York's Greenwich Village. Sir Roger Norrington served as the Orchestra's first music director (1990–94); he was succeeded by Sir Charles Mackerras (1994–present).

The Orchestra performs an annual subscription series at Carnegie Hall, and is much involved in Carnegie Hall's family concerts and educational programs. It has toured extensively in the United States, Canada, Europe and Japan, and takes part in regular out-of-town residencies. The Orchestra has commissioned many compositions (and a few dance pieces), and has premiered over 100 new works by the likes of John Adams, Joan Tower, Anthony Davis, André Previn, and Nicholas Maw. The

Orchestra also gained some notoriety by taking part in the rock group Metallica's orchestral tour in 1999.

The Orchestra of St. Luke's has made over seventy recordings for a variety of labels. Two of its recordings on the Nonesuch label have received Grammy Awards: John Adams' *Nixon in China*, and Samuel Barber's *Knoxville: Summer of 1915* (with soprano Dawn Upshaw). *—Chris Morrison*

Recommended:

- ○ **Haydn: Symphonies 31 & 45** / Mackerras (cond.), Orch. of St. Luke's / 1989 / Telarc 80156
- ○ **Adams: Nixon in China (Highlights)** / Adams, de Waart (conds.), Sylvan, Friedman, Maddalena, Opatz, Orch. of St. Luke's / 1999 / Nonesuch 79453
- ○ **Adams: The Wound-Dresser, etc.** / Adams, de Waart (conds.), Upshaw, Sylvan, Crossley, Gekker, Orch. of St. Luke's, San Francisco SO / 1999 / Nonesuch 79453
- ○ **Adams: Violin Concerto; Shaker Loops** / Nagano, Adams (conds.), Kremer, London SO, Orch. of St. Luke's / 1996 / Nonesuch 79360
- ○ **Barber: Knoxville: Summer of 1915** / Zinman (cond.), Upshaw, Orch. of St. Luke's / 1989 / Nonesuch 79187
- ○ **Sumi Jo Live at Carnegie Hall** / Bonynge (cond.), Jo, Mann, Orch. of St. Luke's / 1997 / Samsung 019

Orchestra of the Age of Enlightenment

f. 1986, London, England

Ensemble

In the late 1970s and early 1980s the "original instruments" (or "authentic instruments") groups began to be appear. They ordinarily associated with particular individual conductors, usually the musician who formed each in the first place, and were not full-time organizations. Typically they gathered for a limited number of concerts and recordings a year, and their membership was variable. Half the people playing on one day's studio session as the London Classical Players might have been on stage the week before as part of the Academy of Ancient Music.

In 1986, a group of the best of these freelance players sought increased security and the artistic benefits of performing regularly as a permanent orchestra, and formed the Orchestra of the Age of Enlightenment. As most London orchestras, they organized themselves into a self-governing co-operative owned by its musicians. As a matter of policy, they decided against appointing anyone as its music director or permanent conductor. This meant they had to shine from the outset to attract the best interpreters to lead their performances.

That they did. They immediately made a mark in the central Baroque- and Classical-era repertory of composers like Purcell, Vivaldi, the Bachs, the Haydn brothers, and the Mozarts under such leaders in the period instrument field as Frans Brueggen, Ton Koopman, Gustav Leonhardt, Sigiswald Kuijken, and Charles Mackerras. An early success was when they served as the orchestra for a production of Mozart's *Idomeneo* with Simon Rattle in 1987.

In 1989, they were invited to perform in a major series of Haydn concerts, making their debut at the Glyndebourne Festival Opera, with which it has often performed since. In 1991, the anniversary year of Mozart's death, the OAE performed at the Salzburg Festival and in the "Mozart Now" series at London's South Bank Centre.

Being without a permanent conductor, the OAE held itself out as available to perform with conductors who are not part of the Baroque and Classical specialist crowd, such as Paavo Järvi, Sir Simon Rattle, Ivan Fischer, Andrew Davis, Heinrich Schiff, and Mark Elder. Most of the OAE's members can be considered scholar-specialists on the history of their own instrument and have mastered all the successive technical variants thereof that occurred over the years. Thus, the OAE often performs music of such composers of Rossini, Mendelssohn, Brahms, Wagner, and even Tchaikovsky and Mahler on instruments appropriate to these masters' own periods.

In 1992, Brueggen and Rattle agreed to be named the OAE's principal guest conductors, and have performed often with it since. Its regular venues are London's Royal Festival Hall (where it is an Associate Ensemble) and St. George's Bristol, where it is the Resident Ensemble. As of 2002, its long association with Glyndebourne is formalized as it officially is that venue's "Associate Orchestra."

The orchestra has toured widely, including 17 countries in Europe alone, as well as major venues in most other parts of the world and has recorded over 50 CD releases. *—Joseph Stevenson*

Recommended:

- ○ **Haydn: Paris Symphonies** / Kuijken (cond.), Age of Enlightenment / 1999 / Angel 61659
- ○ **Haydn: Violin Concertos in G & C; Sinfonia Concertante** / Wallfisch (violin), Age of Enlightenment / 1996 / Virgin 61301
- ○ **Schubert: Mass in A Flat Major; Deutsche Messe** / Weil (cond.), van der Kamp, Hartmann, Hering, Preyer, Age of Enlightenment / 1994 / Sony 53984
- ○ **Handel: Organ Concertos Op4** / Asperen (organ and cond.), Age of Enlightenment / 1996 / Virgin Veritas 545174
- ○ **Rameau: Les Paladins** / Leonhardt (cond.), Age of Enlightenment / 1992 / Philips 432968
- ○ **C.P.E. Bach: Resurrection and Ascension of Jesus** / Herreweghe (cond.), Harvey, Martinpelto, Pregardien, Age of Enlightenment / 1992 / Virgin 59069

L'Orchestre de la Suisse Romande

f. 1918, Geneva, Switzerland

Ensemble

Established at the end of a devastating war that had enveloped nearly all of Europe except for Switzerland, L'Orchestre de la Suisse Romande was named for the French-speaking portion of the small nation. Through the tenacity and devotion of its founder, conductor Ernest Ansermet, it became a regional, then national institution and grew despite problems resulting from the global economic instability between the World Wars. Ansermet's gifts for diplomacy were called into play both in maintaining an important advocacy for the best new music and for facing down disputes between partisans of Geneva, where the orchestra made its home, and Lausanne. Although Lausanne had a respectable orchestra, Geneva (where Ansermet had become a conductor in 1915) could boast only an ensemble that primarily accompanied performances at the opera house and performed only the occasional symphonic program. Once the determination to establish L'Orchestre de la Suisse Romande was made, Ansermet began recruiting his players. While some musicians were drawn from the existing Geneva ensemble, the 34-year-old conductor sought his string players from Italy, his horn players from Vienna, and his woodwind players from Paris. With a complement of 62 on stage at Geneva's Victoria Hall, L'Orchestre de la Suisse Romande made its debut on November 30, 1918, performing an ambitious program of Handel, Mozart, Benner, Jaques-Dalcroze, and—for the program's second half—Rimsky-Korsakov's *Scheherazade*. The following week, Ansermet and the orchestra presented an entire program of music by Debussy, who had died the previous March. Thus was initiated a direction that would mark the orchestra's path throughout its 50 years under its founding maestro. As Ansermet established himself as an outstanding interpreter of Bartók, Britten, Debussy, de Falla, Hindemith, Honegger, Martin, Martinů, Ravel, Roussel, and Stravinsky, so followed his orchestra. Although certain forces strove to move the emphasis away from contemporary music and closer to the Classical/Romantic repertory identified with Europe's other major orchestras, Ansermet continued to champion the works of his own time and to shape his players to be strong advocates for that repertory. And, to end the bickering that threatened to break apart symphonic life in the French-speaking cities and cantons, Ansermet devised a plan wherein those municipalities that enjoyed live performances by the O.S.R. would support the orchestra through the Associations of Friends of L'Orchestre de la Suisse Romande, divisions of which were begun in both Geneva and Lausanne. The public was encouraged to join, along with radio and business sponsors. The O.S.R. has performed numerous premieres by Swiss composers and, as the opera orchestra for the Geneva Grand Theatre, has introduced several important stage works, including operas by Martin (*Monsieur de Pourceaugnac*), Milhaud (*La mère coupable*), and Liebermann (*La forêt*). For the orchestra's Golden Jubilee in 1968, Ansermet once again led Rimsky-Korsakov's *Scheherazade*. At Ansermet's invitation, Paul Kletzki had been asked to assume responsibility for the orchestra beginning in 1967 and he remained as chief conductor until 1970. At that time, German conductor Wolfgang Sawallisch became artistic director and established himself a favorite with the public, albeit in a repertory centered around German/Austrian composers. From 1980 to 1985, Horst Stein continued the ongoing embrace of the Central European Classical and Romantic repertory, winning particular approval for his work in the Grand Theatre. Armin Jordan (1985–97) and Fabio Luisi followed, both balancing repertoires and theater and symphonic interests. Pinchas Steinberg was designated the O.S.R.'s artistic director in September 2002. *—Erik Eriksson*

Recommended:

- ○ **Debussy: La Mer; Nocturnes** / Ansermet (cond.), Suisse Romande / 1984 / London 414040
- ○ **Martin Album** / Ansermet, Munchinger (conds.), Schneiderhan, Hafliger, Stampfli, Hoffgen, Mollet, Buckel, Suisse Romande, Stuttgart CO / 1996 / London 448264
- ○ **Stravinsky Ballets** / Ansermet (cond.), Suisse Romande, Geneva Motet Choir / 1994 / London 443467
- ○ **Tchaikovsky: Swan Lake; Prokofiev: Romeo & Juliet, Suite** / Ansermet (cond.), Suisse Romande / 1994 / London 440630

Orchestre Revolutionnaire et Romantique

f. 1990

Ensemble

The Orchestre Revolutionnaire et Romantique, despite its Gallic moniker, was founded in England in 1990 by noted conductor John Eliot Gardiner. The organization was the next logical step in the evolution of the period-performance movement, its purpose to present the music of the Romantic era (broadly, from Beethoven to the early twentieth century with emphasis on the early Romantics) as authentically as possible. It is a sobering thought that orchestral music from the first half of the nineteenth century was heard on crooked horns, woodwinds with minimal keys, and now-extinct instruments such as the ophiclide, to say nothing of interpretive idiosyncrasies of the era. That said, even the best and most sincere recordings of Karajan or Solti of the Beethoven symphonies were bound to sound quite different from what audiences of 1820 heard. Gardiner's mission was to treat the music of Beethoven, Weber, and Berlioz with the same scholarly respect accorded to early, Renaissance, Baroque, and Classical period works as an alternative, rather than replacement, to the best modern treatments of the same.

The O.R.R. under Gardiner has released some musicologically significant recordings. The 1991 Antwerp discovery of a surviving score of Berlioz's *Messe Solennelle*, a work dismantled by the self-critical composer and used as "lumber" for future works, led to the 1994 premiere recording of the mass, revealing an energy and even joyfulness in the score. The Gardiner/O.R.R. 1997 recording of *Leonore* revealed to the musical public Beethoven's early attempt at the opera that would one day become *Fidelio*. Typical of the re-creative readings of the Orchestre are acclaimed sets of the Beethoven symphonies, Schumann's orchestral works, and Berlioz' *Symphonie fantastique*, the latter in which not only instrumentation and interpretation followed ca. 1830 practice, but was also recorded in the Ancien Conservatoire of Paris where Berlioz conducted his work, in order to obtain acoustic fidelity as well. The O.R.R.'s traversal of the large-scale music of Romantic era has extended to early Brahms and Verdi. It may be imagined that investigation by Gardiner and his ensemble in performance practices such as the use of elastic tempi and string portamento will yield rediscoveries of the late Romantic works by Brahms, Bruckner, Tchaikovsky, and others. *—Wayne Reisig*

Recommended:

- ○ **Beethoven: Nine Symphonies** / Gardiner (cond.), Otter, Orgonasova, Johnson, Cachemaille, Monteverdi Choir, Orch. Revolutionnaire et Romantique / 1994 / Archiv 439900
- ○ **Beethoven: Piano Concertos 1 & 2** / Gardiner (cond.), Levin, Orch. Revolutionnaire et Romantique / Archiv 453438
- ○ **Schumann: Symphonies 1 & 4; Konzertstück for 4 horns** / Gardiner (cond.), Dent, Edwards, Maskell, Montgomery, Orch. Revolutionnaire et Romantique / Archiv 000130002
- ○ **Berlioz: Symphonie fantastique** / Gardiner (cond.), Orch. Revolutionnaire et Romantique / 1993 / Philips 434402

Carl Orff

b. Jul. 10, 1895, Munich, Germany, **d.** Mar. 29, 1982, Munich, Germany
Composer: Choral

Although his fame rests on the success of a single work, the famous and frequently commercially mutilated *Carmina Burana*, Carl Orff was in fact a multi-faceted musician and prolific composer who wrote in many styles before developing the primal, driving language which informs his most famous work. In addition to his fame as the creator of *Carmina burana*, Orff enjoyed international renown as the world's preeminent authority on children's music education, his life's work in that area represented by *Musik für Kinder*, five eclectic collections of music to be performed by children, eventually developing into a more extensive series known as Orff *Schulwerk*.

Born in 1895 to an old Bavarian family, Orff studied piano and cello while still a young boy. He later studied at the Munich Academy of Music, graduating in 1914. The music that he composed during this period shows the influence of several composers, including Debussy and Richard Strauss. In 1914, Orff was appointed Kapellmeister at the Munich Kammerspiele, where he remained until joining the military in 1917. Discharged from service the following year, Orff continued to work as a conductor, accepting further positions in Mannheim and Darmstadt during the 1918–19 seasons. Returning to Munich in 1919, Orff studied composition privately with Heinrich Kaminski while supporting himself as a teacher. In 1924, he founded the Güntherschule for music and dance with Dorothee Günther, dedicating himself to making musical performance accessible to children. Under his guidance, an entire orchestra of special "Orff instruments" was designed, enabling children to play music without formal training. The following year, Orff made three stage adaptations of works by Monteverdi. Continuing his work in the area of Baroque music, Orff became conductor of the Munich Bach society in 1930, a position he held until 1933. The experience of performing Baroque music, particularly sacred works for the stage, convinced Orff that an effective musical performance must fuse music, words and movement, a goal no doubt partly inspired by his work with the Güntherschule. Orff embodied his conception of music in the fabulously successful *Carmina Burana* (1937), which in many ways defined him as a composer. Based on an important collection of Latin and German Goliard poems found in the monastery of Benediktbeuren, this work exemplifies Orff's search for an idiom that would reveal the elemental power of music, allowing the listener to experience music as a overwhelming, primitive force. Goliard poetry, which not only celebrates love and wine, but also pokes fun at the clergy, perfectly suited Orff's desire to create a musical work appealing to a fundamental musicality that, as he believed, every human being possesses. Eschewing melodic development and harmonic complexity, and articulating his musical ideas through basic sonorities and easily discernible rhythmic patterns, Orff created an idiom which many found irresistible. The perceived "primitivism" of *Carmina burana* notwithstanding, Orff believed that the profound appeal of music is not merely physical. This belief is reflected by many other works, including musical dramas based on Greek tragedies, namely, *Antigonae* (1949), *Oedipus der Tyrann* (1959), and *Prometheus* (1966). These works, as well as some compositions on Christian themes, followed the composer's established dramatic and compositional techniques, but failed to repeat the tremendous success of *Carmina burana*. His last work, *De temporum fine comoedia* (A Comedy About the End of Time) premiered at the 1973 Salzburg Festival. Nine years later, Carl Orff died in Munich, where he had spent his entire life. *—AMG*

CHORAL

Carmina Burana, scenic cantata (1935–1936)

Already 38 when he began composing *Carmina Burana—Songs from Benediktbeuern*—Orff was nearly 42 when it finally was produced. Despite the cotitle "Secular Songs," he designed the work as a theater piece, a "scenic cantata" to be danced as well as sung and played. In addition to soprano, tenor, and baritone soloists, large, small, and boys' choruses, *Carmina Burana* is scored for triple winds and brass, five timpani, percussion for six players, celesta, two pianos, and strings. Bertil Wetzelsberger conducted the premiere on June 8, 1937, at Frankfurt am Main.

The texts were written mostly by goliards, itinerant scholars, and lapsed clerics during the Middle Ages—medieval hippies, as it were, with skinheads mixed in. Preserved in a thirteenth century manuscript, these were discovered at a Bavarian monastery near the Passion Play town of Oberammergau in 1803 (Burana is a Latin neologism for Beuern, later Bayern: Bavaria in English). Written in low Latin, old German, and medieval French, most of the texts—variously bawdy, sensuous, comic, mock-tragic, but usually erotic—mock government and the church.

Carmina Burana is comprised of 26 sections in mostly major keys. A two-song choral Prolog, "Fortuna imperatrix mundi" (Fortune, Empress of the World), is about the ever-turning Wheel of Fortune that lifts man up only to cast him down. The next 22 sections are divided into three unequal parts.

First comes "Primo vere" (In springtime), nine frolicsome numbers that begin with small choir, then baritone solo, then full chorus. The concluding six are subtitled "Uf dem Anger" (On the lawn), commencing with a dance for orchestra; then a languorous waltz in for large and small choruses; another amatory adventure for both choruses to the accompaniment of sleigh bells and plucked violas; an ABA round dance that becomes Allegro molto midway, and finally a brief Allegro introduced by brass fanfares.

Next the music moves indoors—"In taberna" (In the tavern)—for a quartet of secular songs in praise of gluttony and drunkenness. A besotted goliard enumerates his amatory history, followed by a swan bewailing its mortality (in the person of a high tenor) while roasting on a spit. A tipsy abbot comes forward next, leading to a seditious melee for tipsy male choristers.

The concluding third is "Cour d'amours" (The court of love), whose ten parts tend to brevity; yet even when the music seems chaste, texts or subtexts are sexual, beginning with boys' chorus and a lovelorn soprano. After them, the solo baritone voices a courtier's despair. The soprano follows with "Stetit puella," about a pretty girl in a red tunic. The baritone sings a tale of planned seduction with choral punctuation, setting up the comedic encounter of male choristers and a maiden, a cappella. A lovestruck double chorus follows with piano/percussion accompaniment. The soprano's "In trutina" is torn between love and modesty, only to be overwhelmed by an erotic concatenation of everyone (excepting roasted solo tenor), pierced by the soprano's stratospheric "Dulcissime" (most sweet one, I give my all to you). The culmination of "Cour d'amours" is "Banziflor et Helena," another paean to Venus triumphant over virtue. Finally there's the repetition of "Fortuna, imperatrix mundi." *—Roger Dettmer*

Recommended:

- ○ **Orff: Carmina Burana** / Jochum (cond.), Fischer-Dieskau, Janowitz, Stolze, Chorus & Orch. of the German Opera, Berlin / 1995 / DG 447437
- ○ **Orff: Carmina Burana** / Plasson (cond.), Hampson, Dessay, Lesne, Stewart, Toulouse Orch. / 1996 / EMI 555392
- ○ **Orff: Carmina Burana** / Runnicles (cond.), MacKenzie, Hong, Olsen, Patriarco, Atlanta SO & Chorus / 2002 / Telarc 80575

Catulli Carmina, scenic cantata (1930–1943)

Catulli Carmina is the second of a three large-scale works for voices and instruments written between 1936 and 1953, the first being *Carmina Burana* and followed by *Trionfo di Afrodite*. It was Orff's intention that all three would be performed consecutively and would be presented with a certain amount of staged action. (*Carmina Burana* had considerable success and is now the one most likely to be heard.)

Written for choir, soloists, percussion group, and four pianos, it comprises settings of 11 poems by Catullus, a Roman poet of the first century BC. The poems, written in Latin, are short, some only a few lines long, and addressed to a married woman called Clodia, whom the poet calls Lesbia. Audiences might well find the poems' literal meanings as impenetrable as those of *Carmina Burana*, even with a suitable translation, but each displays considerable invention and panache. Though the cycle of poems are not narrative in character, Orff links them in a loose sequence to tell a story of love and loss, much as Schumann did for his settings of Heine's poems in the song cycle *Dichterliebe*. There, however, the resemblance ends.

Orff is not in the least concerned with classical authenticity. His pulsing rhythms are uncompromisingly modern—in places even jazzy—and far from what would be expected by a Latin scholar for declaiming poetry. Orff was particularly interested in the dramatic possibilities of percussion instruments, and throughout *Catulli* he uses them, with the pianos, to great effect. The singers are occasionally called upon to use what is called Sprechstimme, a kind of vocal enunciation somewhere between speech and song.

In strictly musical terms *Catulli* may now sound less original and challenging than it did when first performed, and though the trilogy as a whole calls out for the choreography it no longer gets, it has something in common with the spirited iconoclasm of certain popular musicals of the 1960s. *—Roy Brewer*

Recommended:

- **Orff: Catulli Carmina; Egk: La Tentation de Saint Antoine** / Jochum (cond.), Augér, Ochman, Chor der Deutschen Oper / DG 449097
- **Orff: Trionfi** / Schäfer (cond.), Dewald, Griffith, Ickstadt, Kramer, Flemish Conservatory Choir, Frankfurt Kantorei / 1995 / Wergo 6275

Trionfo di Afrodite, scenic concert (1949–1951)

This is the third part of "Trionfi," a trilogy of choral and vocal works celebrating love, also including the very popular *Carmina Burana* and *Catulli Carmina*. Like the first, it is for full orchestra in addition to the chorus and solo voices. This one celebrates the purity and passion of conjugal love, depicting a wedding ceremony before Aphrodite and extolling the estate of matrimony. Unlike the dalliance and revelry of *Carmina Burana* or the rather cynical disapproving description of carnal love which is the burden of *Catulli Carmina*, this composition is more high toned than the others, with a more flexible and more extended use of harmonies. Even so, the main emphasis is still on melody, rhythm, and orchestral color, all intended to serve the words of the texts (which come from Catullus, Sappho, and Euripides). The pounding rhythms and simple melodies which predominate are contrasted with florid, decorated lyrical phrases for the bride and bridegroom. *—Joseph Stevenson*

Synopsis:

Though some have called *Trionfo di Afrodite* [Triumph of Aphrodite] an opera, the work's seven scenes here do not present a story, but are each settings of text by Catullus, Sappho, and Euripides about nuptial traditions and activities.

Scene One. Canto Amebeo di Vergini. A group of young people, awaiting the appearance of the bride and groom, sing a song based on a poem by Catullus that glorifies the evening star.

Scene Two. Corteo Nuziale ed Arrivo Della Sposa e Dello Sposo. A poem here, by Sappho, comprises this short section, which joyously anticipates the arrival of the wedding couple.

Scene Three. Sposa e Sposo. A second Sappho setting of text follows, this one depicting the couple passionately declaring their love for each other.

Scene Four. Invocazione Dell'imeneo. Another song or hymn of praise, again from Catullus, is given, this one relating to the god of marriage, Hymenaios.

Scene Five. Ludi e Canti Nuziali Davanti al Talamo—La Sposa. This scene, drawn on a text by Catullus, deals with games played and songs sung outside the bride's chamber. It is the work's longest scene and is has three sections, the first calling on the timid bride to come to the wedding chamber. In the succeeding section she is taken into the chamber, while the groom is mocked; and the final chapter depicts the groom's entrance into the chamber, after which the couple receives encouragement to make the most of their youthful spirit.

Scene Six. Canto di Novelli Sposi dal Talamo. The couple declare their lover for each other in this setting of a poem by Sappho.

Scene Seven. Apparizione de Afrodite. The final scene, on a text by Euripides, provides a depiction of Aphrodite descending and blessing the marriage of the two lovers. *—Robert Cummings*

Recommended:

- **Orff: Trionfi** / Jochum (cond.), Kupper, Lindermeier, Holm, Delorko, Bavarian RSO / 2002 / DG 474131
- **Orff: Carmina Burana; Catulli Carmina; Trionfo di Afrodite** / Smetacek (cond.), Berman, Zidek, Bohacova, Lindauer, Tattermuschova; Prague SO / Supraphon 0321
- **Orff: Trionfi** / Tang (cond.), Schafer, Rarichs, Ickstadt, Kabitz, Frankfurt Kantorei / 1995 / Wergo 6275

MISCELLANEOUS

Orff-Schulwerk: Music for Children (5 volumes)

Over five decades, composer Carl Orff and colleague Gunild Keetman established a compendium of short didactic pieces that introduce basic musical concepts to very young children. Most of these involve simple rhythm instruments, such as clapping hands, but more often xylophones, glockenspiels, triangles, drums, and bells. The recorder is introduced early on and several of the more advanced pieces involve violin and cello, and there are also many items for speaker or singer and unaccompanied choir. The series begins with simple rhymes, rhythmic exercises, and pentatonic scales, and concludes with more complex material, including fairy tales, Goethe excerpts, and use of seven-note scales. Because much of the Orff method emphasizes improvisation, performances and recordings of the music vary greatly in instrumentation and structural details. The most famous piece is called "Gassenhauer," or "Street Song." It's actually a Keetman arrangement of a 1536 song by Hans Neusidler, beginning with a simple rhythmic foundation onto which is gradually layered other straightforward percussion lines, in a way that creates what sounds like a complex, vibrant crescendo.

The project began in the 1920s when Orff became interested in renewing music through its partnership with movement—not only in such concert works as *Carmina Burana*, but in educational pieces as well. Orff was influenced by Curt Sachs, the director of Berlin's State Collection of Musical Instruments, who emphasized rhythm as the foundation of musical and bodily expression. The project fell into place in 1924 when Orff began teaching music courses at Dorothee Günther's new school of modern dance and movement in Munich. Orff initially focused on the use of hand clapping, foot stomping, and finger snapping along with homemade rattles and some hand drums and tambourines. Piano exercises shortly entered the curriculum, emphasizing improvisation using pentatonic scales. Keetman joined the school in 1926 and was soon writing pieces centering on the xylophone and recorder, as well as conducting the school's dance orchestra. Piano builder Karl Maendler began designing simple mallet instruments especially for the music program and these Schulwerk instruments are now employed with the Orff method around the world.

The music-and-movement exercises were first published in 1930 under the title *Orff-Schulwerk: Elementare Musikübung*. These "elementary music works" were scheduled to be introduced into Berlin's elementary school curriculum, but the Nazi takeover and ensuing war destabilized the system and the Günther school itself was closed in 1944. After the war, Bavarian Radio's director of educational programming cajoled Orff and Keetman into producing a series of radio programs featuring music children could play along with at home. At this point—1948—the composers turned their attention to children's songs and rhymes, drawing material from Franz Magnus Böhme's 1897 collection of 6,000 German children's songs. Largely as a result of these programs, a new, five-volume edition came out in 1950, now called *Orff-Schulwerk: Musik für Kinder*. This became the basis of the Orff program, although pieces would continue to be added for nearly 30 more years. *—James Reel*

Recommended:

- **Orff-Schulwerk: Complete Edition** / various / RCA 68031
- **Orff: Schulwerk Vol. 2 - Musik für Kinder** / various / 1995 / Celestial Harmonies 13105
- **Orff: Piano Music Vol. 3** / Hiller, Lahusen / Celestial Harmonies 13106
- **Orff-Schulwerk, Musica Poetica Vol. 1** / Orff, Widmann, Zahnhausen, Koppelstetter, Lehrmann, Karl Peinkofer Percussion Ens. / 1995 / Celestial Harmonies 13104

Lambert Orkis

b. Apr. 20, 1946, Philadelphia, PA

Pianist

Lambert Orkis is one of the most respected American pianists, particularly in the fields of chamber music and accompaniment, and as a proponent of modern piano music.

He studied with Eleanor Sokoloff at the Curtis Institute of Music in Philadelphia. After obtaining his degree there, he went on to obtain a Master's degree from the Esther Boyer College of Music of Temple University (also in Philadelphia), where his teacher was Maryan Filar. He joined the Philadelphia Chamber Soloists, the Penn Contemporary Players of the University of Pennsylvania, and the Twentieth Century Consort in Washington, D.C. Another early musical association was with the Temple University Music Festival and Institute, and he has maintained a recital partnership since those days of the early 1970s with cellist Barbara Haffner, a fellow member of the Philadelphia Chamber Soloists. He has been a member of piano faculty of the Boyer College of Temple University since 1968. As a teacher he stresses the teaching of modern repertory to his students and concentrates on chamber music performance.

Early in his career, Orkis was the chosen accompanist of legendary American soprano Eleanor Steber when that former star made her successful comeback concert and established a second career. Since Steber was especially interested in American art song and opera, he found himself developing a major interest in new American music, which led to his commissioning many new works from major composers. A very partial list of such compositions includes Richard Wernick's *Piano Concerto*, George Crumb's *A Little Suite for Christmas*, and works by James Primosch and Maurice Wright.

In the late 1970s he served as pianist in a master class conducted by members of the National Symphony Orchestra of Washington, D.C., of which famed cellist-conductor Mstislav Rostropovich was then music director. Rostropovich was so taken with Orkis' playing that he invited the pianist to become his recital pianist and created the position of principal keyboard player of the orchestra for him. In the latter capacity Orkis plays piano, celesta, harpsichord, and synthesizer. He found that there was a difference between playing as part of the general lush orchestral sonority and of playing as a concerto soloist in front of an orchestra. Calling it a "thrilling experience," he says he is challenged by the different skills such a position requires when compared to solo or chamber music work and says it "...helps me maintain razor-sharp listening and flexible reaction abilities." He retained that position when Leonard Slatkin succeeded Rostropovich as music director.

As Rostropovich's partner, Orkis played in the U.S. and Asia, including performances before Presidents Reagan, George Bush, and Clinton, King Hussein of Jordan, Emperor Akahito of Japan, and President Gandhi of India. In 1988, Orkis also formed a performance partnership with violinist Anne-Sophie Mutter, which he calls "a pinnacle of my professional life and a continual source of artistic fulfillment." With her he has also performed before major world leaders, including the presidents of France and Germany, the Queen of Spain, and the King and Queen of Sweden. In 1998, the two gave 85 performances, playing all ten Beethoven violin sonatas exclusively, then recorded the cycle in live concerts in Wiesbaden, Germany. This Deutsche Grammophon recording won the NPR Performance Today Critics' Choice Award.

He is also a member of the Castle Trio, a major chamber group associated with the Smithsonian Institution in Washington, playing on instruments from the Smithsonian collection that are appropriate to the era of the music and has recorded on fortepianos. *—Joseph Stevenson*

Recommended:

○ **Lambert Orkis: Piano** / Orkis, Primosch / 2003 / Innova 605
○ **Anne-Sophie Mutter: The Berlin Recital** / Mutter, Orkis / 1996 / DG 445826
○ **Selected Piano Music of Gottschalk** / Orkis / Smithsonian 33ND
○ **Orkis plays Crumb, Wernick** / Orkis / Bridge 9003
○ **Beethoven: Violin Sonatas** / Mutter, Orkis / 1998 / DG 457619
○ **Schubert: Impromptus** / Orkis / Virgin 59600

Eugene Ormandy

b. Nov. 18, 1899, Budapest, Hungary, **d.** Mar. 12, 1985, Philadelphia, PA
Conductor

Longtime Philadelphia Orchestra conductor Eugene Ormandy developed what came to be known as the "Philadelphia Sound." (He groused that it should be called the "Ormandy Sound," even though its fundamentals had already been established during Leopold Stokowski's long tenure with the Philadelphia Orchestra.) Largely as an effort to overcome the dry acoustics of the orchestra's home, the Academy of Music, Ormandy emphasized lush string sonorities and, often, legato phrasing and rounded tone. He was lauded even by his own musicians for his ability to conduct everything from memory, even complex contemporary scores. Still, aside from the voluptuous tone, Ormandy's interpretations rarely bore an individual stamp. They were, however, highly polished, intelligently balanced, and well paced, always serving the scores honorably, and often with a dash of controlled excitement.

Ormandy initially studied violin with his father, and entered Budapest's Royal Academy of Music at age five, falling under the tutelage of Jenö Hubay at nine. He received a teacher's certificate at 17, and served as concertmaster of the Blüthner Orchestra in Germany, also giving recitals and performing as a concerto soloist.

He moved to the United States in 1921 (taking citizenship in 1927), lured by the promise of a lucrative concert tour. That tour fell through, though, and Ormandy was forced to make ends meet by taking a back-desk job with the Capitol Theater Orchestra in New York City, accompanying silent films. Ormandy soon advanced to the position of concertmaster, and made his conducting debut there in September 1924 when the regular conductor fell ill. By 1926 he was named the orchestra's associate music director, and made extra money conducting light classics on the radio. Important debuts soon followed: he conducted the New York Philharmonic at Lewisohn Stadium in 1929, and the following year became guest conductor of the Robin Hood Dell Orchestra in Philadelphia. On Oct. 30, 1931, came his first performance with the Philadelphia Orchestra.

The following year he was engaged as music director of the Minneapolis Symphony, with which he made several recordings, but he didn't remain long in the Midwest. In 1936 the Philadelphia Orchestra called him back as associate conductor, to share baton duties with Leopold Stokowski, who was being eased out. Ormandy became the orchestra's music director in the autumn of 1938, and held that position for 42 years, until his retirement at the end of the 1979–80 season (whereupon he was named Conductor Laureate). He led the Philadelphia Orchestra on several national and international tours, including, in 1973, the first appearance of an American symphony orchestra in the People's Republic of China. Ormandy was knighted in 1976—Queen Elizabeth II's way of observing the American bicentennial.

Ormandy was always a proficient, well-prepared conductor, but he was most comfortable in Romantic and post-Romantic music; especially noteworthy were his performances and recordings of Richard Strauss and Sergei Rachmaninov. He established an especially close professional relationship with the latter in the 1930s, and premiered his *Symphonic Dances*. Ormandy also led the first performances of many works by American composers, and gave the U.S. premieres of several Shostakovich symphonies, among other works. In 1948 he led the Philadelphia Orchestra in the first symphony concert broadcast on American TV, beating Arturo Toscanini and the NBC Symphony by 90 minutes. Ormandy and the orchestra recorded extensively for Columbia and RCA, especially during the stereo LP era; their discography ranged from the first recording of Shostakovich's thorny *Symphony No. 4* to "easy listening" treatments of recent movie music, harking back to his nights in the Capitol Orchestra. *—James Reel*

Recommended:

○ **Orff: Carmina Burana** / Ormandy (cond.), Walter, Blegen, Harsanyi, Petrak, Philadelphia Orch. / 2004 / Sony 93081
○ **Saint-Saëns: Organ Symphony** / Ormandy (cond.), Fox, Philadelphia Orch. / 1985 / RCA 66134
○ **J. Strauss: Waltzes and Polkas** / Ormandy (cond.), Philadelphia Orch. / 2003 / Sony 87281
○ **Sibelius: Legends** / Ormandy (cond.), Philadelphia Orch. / 1986 / EMI 47612
○ **Saint-Saëns: Symphony 3** / Ormandy (cond.), Murray, Philadelphia Orch. / 1980 / Telarc 80051
○ **Beethoven: Symphonies 5–8** / Ormandy (cond.), Philadelphia Orch. / Sony 63266
○ **Ormandy: Maestro Brillante** / Ormandy (cond.), Arrau, Piatigorsky, Casadesus, Philadelphia Orch. / 2000 / History 205236
○ **Fantastic Philadelphians** / Ormandy (cond.), Philadelphia Orch. / 1999 / RCA 63313

Krysia Osostowicz

b. 1960, London, England
Violinist

Polish-English violinist Krysia Osostowicz is a noted soloist and chamber musician. After studies at the Yehudi Menhuin School and Cambridge University, she went to Salzburg to train with Sándor Végh. She has performed as a recitalist and a concerto soloist throughout Europe. She was a member of the piano quartet Domus, which attracted attention when it toured with a large geodesic dome it used for its own portable concert hall. In 1995, she became founder and first violinist of the Dante Quartet. Osostowicz has collaborated with artists such as Radu Lupu, Steven Isserlis, Ernst Kovacic, Michael Collins, Levon Chilingirian, and Christoph Richter. Osostowicz has made over 20 recordings of solo and chamber music repertoire. Her Fauré recording (with pianist Susan Tomes) was awarded a Deutsche Schallplattenpreis. *—Robert Adelson*

Recommended:

○ **Brahms: Violin Sonatas** / Osostowicz, Tomes / 2001 / Hyperion 55087
○ **Fauré: Violin Sonatas** / Osostowicz, Tomes / 1999 / Hyperion 55030
○ **Bartok: Sonata for unaccompanied violin; Rhapsodies; etc.** / Osostowicz, Tomes, Collins / 1993 / Hyperion 66415

Oswald von Wolkenstein

b. ca. 1377, Schöneck in Pustertal, Germany, **d.** Aug. 2, 1445, Merano, Italy
Composer: Vocal

Oswald von Wolkenstein was a German composer whose music bridged the Medieval and Renaissance eras; the last of the poet-musician knights whose monophonic music explored the ideal of courtly love, he also wrote polyphonic music in more contemporary forms. As noble "von" indicates, Oswald was from a knightly family of the Villanders line. The surname "von Wolkenstein" comes from the name of their property of Wolkenstein in Groednertal, South Tyrol (a mountainous Austrian province that was taken by Italy in World War II). As he was of high birth, there is some information available about his life; key events were written in family archives. Still, as is the norm with composers of the day, there are numerous gaps that can be filled in only imperfectly by extrapolation from his works. Oswald was a second son, which put him at a disadvantage, but also gave him freedom to pursue an adventurous life, and to enter the political sphere. He spent his youth as a page in service, which took him to various countries and gave him fluency in several languages. He became a diplomat for the league of Tyrolean nobles and for Emperor Sigismund and took part in several German councils.

His seat was Hauenstein castle near Bolzano, but in 1407 he inherited only part of Hauenstein itself, and spent the rest of his life in a property dispute with the other tenant, the family of Martin Jaeger. As a result of this dispute, and also because of political intrigues, he was imprisoned several times. Nevertheless, he fell in love with Anna Hausmann, the daughter of one of his adversaries in this dispute. He wrote several love poems to her, continuing even after his marriage to Margarete von Schwangau in 1417. He also wrote poems addressed to a "Barbara," but fortunately did not neglect to write love poetry addressed to his wife.

Oswald himself preserved a quantity of his own in two manuscripts designated "A" and "B." There is also a manuscript "C" that contains text but no music, and a few other sources. His songs are typically in AABB form, with arched, flowing melodic lines. There are some exceptions, such as *Es komen neue mer gerant*, which is a description of a military raid in northern Italy and is written in an almost parlando style, scoffing at the losers.

Oswald's poetry often drew on events he himself experienced or witnessed. The unusual fit between text and musical line in his music inspired a description of him as the "creator of the individual lied," which is ahistorical. Nor was he, as has sometimes been said, a Meistersinger, the German counterpart to the French troubador or trouvère. His music includes not only monophonic songs but also polyphony in three or four parts. Towards the end of his life he composed religious music in simple textures. *—Joseph Stevenson*

VOCAL

Overview of Works (ca. 1415–1441)

An Austrian minnesinger, Oswald von Wolkenstein (ca. 1376–1445) was born in the Tyrol to a noble family well established in that area. Oswald lived a tumultuous life with travels and adventures sufficient for several lifetimes. He was touring as early as age ten and boasted of having covered most of the European continent as well as parts of Africa and Asia. He apparently had at least some facility in as many as ten languages.

In the company of King Sigismund, he visited Venice in 1412–1413 and was shortly thereafter brought into full service by the King, who seemingly sought to establish through Oswald an alliance with the Tyrolean nobles in his opposition to Duke Friedrich. In 1417 Oswald married Margarete von Schwangau, a union that resulted in seven children.

Oswald became involved in a lifelong dispute over the inheritance of the family's Hauenstein Castle and was imprisoned several times. Duke Friedrich assumed responsibility for Oswald's conduct. This eventually necessitated Oswald's pledging allegiance to the Duke and refraining from any political activity on his own behalf. Although he undertook a few more junkets following the settlement, he seems to have remained in the Tyrol after 1434.

Two large-format collections on parchment survive from Oswald's lifetime, songs with notation included. Both of these feature a portrait of the composer on the front-piece, that on the second collection said to be by the painter Pisanello or a member of his school. A 1425 collection contains 43 songs. Some 65 poems appear to have been appended around 1436 and 1441. The second manuscript held 72 songs and 58 melodies by 1432, the date included on the listing of contents. More songs were added over time through 1438. A third collection, this one on paper, was produced by a single scholar sometime within the decade after Oswald's death. This one contains poems but no melodies.

A total of 131 songs is substantial for an artist of Oswald's time. While 57 consist of a single melody, the rest are polyphonic and the troubadour's choice follows a certain discipline. Single melodies are utilized for storytelling and introspective texts, while love songs and humorous poems are given polyphonic settings. Of Oswald's single melodies, only 11 were used more than once, although two of them were employed seven times each.

While he seems to have taken the French chanson as a model for his polyphonic settings, the melodies of his monophonic songs offer little similarity to any others of his time. Here, he seems to have expressed himself with considerable originality, advancing from the quasi-recitative style of his predecessors. *—Erik Eriksson*

Recommended:

○ **Knightly Passions** / Pickett (dir.), George, Bott, Agnew, New London Consort / 1996 / L'Oiseau-Lyre 444173

○ **Wolkenstein: Songs** / Sequentia Ens. for Medieval Music / 1993 / DHM 77302

Anne Sofie von Otter

b. May 9, 1955, Stockholm, Sweden

Mezzo-Soprano

Anne Sofie von Otter is a leading mezzo-soprano known for her versatility in operatic roles, her interesting recital choices, and her willingness to take vocal risks. Her father was a Swedish diplomat whose career took the family to Bonn, London, and back to Stockholm while Anne Sofie was growing up. As a result, she gained fluency in languages. She studied music at the Guildhall School of Music and Drama in London. Her main voice teacher was Vera Rozsa, while Erik Werba and Geoffrey Parsons coached her in lieder interpretation.

She gained a contract with the Basle Opera in 1983 and remained with that company until 1985, debuting as Alcina in Franz Joseph Haydn's *Orlando Paladino*. She also took several male roles written for female mezzo-sopranos (which are known in operatic circles as "trousers" parts), including Cherubino in Mozart's *Marriage of Figaro*, Hänsel in Humperdinck's *Hänsel und Gretel*, and Orpheus in Gluck's *Orfée et Eurydice*.

In 1984 she debuted at the Aix-en-Provence Festival as Ramiro in Mozart's *La Finta Giardiniera*. Others of her trouser parts include Octavian in Strauss' *Rosenkavalier*, the Composer in Strauss' *Ariadne auf Naxos*, and the title role of Rossini's *Tancredi*, among others. A tall, statuesque woman, she is at home in numerous opera serie of the eighteenth century, in which alto voices routinely played the heroes.

Another reason for the high proportion of Baroque- and Classical-era operas in her repertory is an important working relationship with conductor John Eliot Gardiner, a British conductor who began as a Baroque specialist. She first auditioned for him in 1985, but failed to make an impression then. It was only with a subsequent chance for him to hear her that he began working with her. She has joined him in recordings of Beethoven's *Ninth Symphony*; Mozart's *Clemenza di Tito*, *Idomeneo* and *Requiem*; Monteverdi's *Favola d'Orfeo* and *L'Incoronazione di Poppea*; Handel's *Agrippina* and *Jephtha*; Gluck's *Orfée et Eurydice*; and Bach's *Christmas Oratorio* and *St. Matthew Passion*. He also conducted von Otter's recording of Weill's *Seven Deadly Sins* and selected theater songs.

Her other major artistic partner is the Swedish pianist Bengt Forsberg, her recital partner. Forsberg is a leading scholar in the field of song literature, so von Otter relies on him to suggest songs and organize the programs of her recitals. With him, she has tended to specialize in lieder from the periods around the beginning and end of the romantic period, including well received recordings of songs by Schubert, Schumann, Brahms, Zemlinsky, Korngold, and Mahler as well as the late Romantic Nordic composers Alfvén, Rangstrom, Stenhammer, and Sibelius.

She is a believer in singing songs in the keys the composers' originally specified. When she came to record Kurt Weill's *Seven Deadly Sins* she used the original version for high soprano, a range she possesses, rather than the once-traditional mezzo-soprano version made for Lotte Lenya late in that singer's career. von Otter also recorded Alban Berg's *Seven Early Songs*, also music that is a strain for many high sopranos. In addition, she is not averse to stretching her voice for dramatic effect. "I believe in shock effects," she once said in an interview.

However, past the age of 40 she has some particularly bad experiences as a result of these two tendencies and, she admits, hurt her voice. As a result, she has decided to be "sensible" and transpose down.

She has sung at Covent Garden, La Scala, Berlin, Munich, Rome, and other major opera houses. She is married to a stage designer and lives in Stockholm with him and their two children. *—Joseph Stevenson*

Recommended:

○ **Grieg: Lieder** / Otter, Forsberg / 1992 / DG 437521

○ **La Bonne Chanson: French Chamber Songs** / Otter, Forsberg / 1996 / DG 447752

○ **Handel: Hercules** / Minkowski (cond.), Otter, Daniels, Dawson, Croft, Musicians of the Louvre / 2002 / Archiv 469532

○ **Speak Low: Songs By Kurt Weill** / Gardiner (cond.), Otter, Forsberg, Martin, Biebrach, Hannover North German Radio Orch. / 1994 / DG 439894

○ **Schumann Songs** / Otter, Forsberg / DG 445881

Seiji Ozawa

b. Sep. 1, 1935, Fenytien (Shenyang), China

Conductor

Seiji Ozawa, born of Japanese parents in Manchuria, began music lessons at the age of seven. At 16 he entered the Toho School of Music in Tokyo, intending to pursue a career as a professional pianist. He abandoned that plan after breaking both of his index fingers in a rugby game. It was then that he turned to conducting and composition. While still a student Ozawa gained podium experience with professional ensembles, including the NHK Symphony Orchestra and the Japan Philharmonic. He graduated in 1959 with first prizes in conducting and composition and traveled to Europe to pursue further studies. There, Ozawa supported himself as a traveling salesman of Japanese motor scooters. In the course of his work he saw a notice for an international conducting competition, entered it, and won. So impressed was one of the judges—longtime Boston Symphony conductor Charles Münch—that he arranged for Ozawa to study at the Berkshire Music Center at Tanglewood in the summer of 1960. Ozawa won the Koussevitzky Award as well as a scholarship to work with Herbert von Karajan and the Berlin Philharmonic. During a visit to Berlin, Leonard Bernstein hired him as an assistant conductor of the New York Philharmonic. Ozawa made his debut with the orchestra in Carnegie Hall on April 14, 1961, and traveled with the ensemble on tour (including appearances in Japan). From 1964 to 1968 Ozawa served as music director of the Ravinia Festival. His career burgeoned as he became noted for his brilliant performances, penetrating musical insight, and total command of the most complex scores. He enjoyed multiple successes as music director of the Toronto Symphony Orchestra (1965–69), including a career-making recording of Messiaen's *Turangalila Symphony* and Takemitsu's *November Steps*. In 1968 he became music advisor to the Japan Philharmonic Orchestra. In the following year he made his operatic debut at the Salzburg Festival and became principal guest conductor of the Chicago Symphony Orchestra. In 1970 he became the music director of the San Francisco Symphony, and in that post proved himself a particular advocate of new music.

At the same time, Ozawa developed ever-closer ties to Boston. He became the co-artistic adviser of the Tanglewood Music Center in 1970, and in 1972 was named music advisor of the Boston Symphony Orchestra. 1973 brought him the music directorship of the BSO as well the sole artistic directorship of Tanglewood. His tenure in Boston, which reached into the twenty-first century, was one of the longest in the history of any American orchestra.

Ozawa's career-long dedication to new music is evident from his role in the commissioning and/or premiering of works like Ligeti's *San Francisco Polyphony* (1975), Messiaen's opera *Saint François d'Assise* (1983), Davies' *Symphony No. 2* (1981), and Harbison's *Symphony No. 1* (1983). He assumed the post of music director of the Vienna State Opera in 2002. —*AMG*

Recommended:

○ **Messiaen: Turangalîla Symphony** / Ozawa (cond.), Loriod, Toronto SO / 2004 / RCA 59418

○ **Russo: Street Music; 3 Pieces; Gershwin: American in Paris** / Ozawa (cond.), Canin, Siegel, San Francisco SO, Siegel-Schwall Band / 2002 / DG 463665

○ **Tchaikovsky: The Nutcracker** / Ozawa (cond.), BSO / DG 435619

○ **Prokofiev: Romeo & Juliet** / Ozawa (cond.), BSO / 1987 / DG 423268

Johann Pachelbel

b. Sep. 1, 1653, Nuremberg, Germany, **d.** Mar. 9, 1706, Nuremberg, Germany
Composer: Chamber Music, Keyboard

Johann Pachelbel is unfairly viewed as a one-work composer, that work being the popular *Canon in D major*, for three violins and continuo. He was an important figure from the Baroque period who is now seen as central in the development of both keyboard music and Protestant church music. Some have summarized his primary contribution as the uniting of Catholic Gregorian chant elements with the Northern German organ style, a style that reflected the influence of the Protestant chorale. A Lutheran, he spent several years in Vienna where he was exposed to music by Frohberger and Frescobaldi, which influenced his work with the chorale-prelude. His music in this genre would in turn influence the compositions of Johann Sebastian Bach, among others. It should be noted that many of Pachelbel's works are difficult to date, thus rendering judgments about his stylistic evolution questionable in many cases. Pachelbel was also a gifted organist and harpsichordist.

Pachelbel was born in August of 1653. He showed musical talent early on and began studies first with Heinrich Schwemmer and later with George Kaspar Wecker, the latter instructing in composition and on organ. Pachelbel received his general education at St. Lorenz high school, and in 1669 he enrolled at the university in Altdorf. Pachelbel did not come from a wealthy family and earned meager sums serving as organist at the Lorenzkirche. He thus could not garner enough money to keep up with the tuition costs at the university and had to leave after about a year.

After a brief period of private study following his departure, Pachelbel traveled to Vienna and obtained an assistant organist post at St. Stephen's Cathedral in 1673. Four years later he took a position as court organist in Eisenach, where Bach would be born in 1685. He would become a close friend of the Bach family and teach both Johann Sebastian and Johann Christoph. Pachelbel left after a year at Eisenach however, and became organist at the Predigerkirche in Erfurt, in 1678.

The composer married Barbara Gabler in 1681, and by 1683 he was a father. In September of that year however, tragedy struck as a plague swept through Erfurt, taking his wife and infant son. Four sets of chorale variations appeared around this time under the title of *Musicalische Sterbens-Gedancken* (Musical Thoughts of Death). During this period his organ chorales would become his most important works.

In August 1684, Pachelbel married Judith Drommer. One of their seven children would be the composer, organist and harpsichordist Wilhelm Hieronymus Pachelberg, born 1686. In 1690 Pachelbel took a post as Court organist at Stuttgart and appeared quite satisfied, but left after two years due to an impending invasion by French forces. He served next as municipal organist at Gotha, from the fall of 1692 until April 1695. He returned to Nuremberg around the latter time, eventually to become organist at St. Sebalduskirche (summer, 1695). He would serve for nearly 11 years in this post, producing his most famous vocal scores, as well as his great Magnificat fugues. In 1699 he produced his important collection of six arias, *Hexachordum Apollinis*, for organ or harpsichord. Pachelbel was buried in Nuremberg on March 9, 1706, and apparently had died on March 3. *—Robert Cummings*

Overview of Works (ca. 1679–1705)

Johann Pachelbel (1653-1706) is often seen as a one-work composer, owing to the widespread popularity of his *Canon in D*. However, he wrote many other works in a variety of genres, particularly organ music—both sacred and secular—keyboard compositions, concertos, masses, motets, and sacred vocal music. An organist at Lutheran churches, Pachelbel is credited with forging a new style from Gregorian Chant, Italian-Viennese Catholic music, and the Northern German organ tradition.

Many of Pachelbel's compositions cannot be accurately dated, thereby rendering analysis of his stylistic evolution a difficult task. The well-known *Canon in D* is actually atypical of the composer, since he wrote only a small amount of chamber music. The only other surviving works are the *Partie in G major* for strings and continuo and the six suites comprising his *Musicalische Ergötzung* for two violins and continuo.

Among Pachelbel's greatest contributions was his organ music. Here, his 95 Magnificat fugues and numerous organ chorales stand as his greatest instrumental accomplishments in the liturgical realm. He also wrote a significant amount of secular organ compositions, including toccatas, fugues, chaconnes (ciaccona), fantasias, ricercares, and other works. The G minor *Fantasia* is significant, along with the ricercares in C minor and F sharp minor, and the chaconnes in F minor and D minor. These latter two, along with the other four chaconnes, deftly explore the variation form.

One might describe the keyboard style of Pachelbel in general terms as sounding somewhat like Bach, but with less counterpoint. Bach is more animated and busier, while Pachelbel weaves fewer musical lines. His vocal music is also important and in many ways even superior to his keyboard works.

The 13 Magnificat settings used for Vespers have often been suggested as his greatest achievement. Most were written for four or five voices and chamber ensemble, and virtually all show the composer at his most masterful. It was here that he mixed elements from the Viennese and Italian Catholic traditions with the Northern German organ style, itself largely drawn from Protestant chorales, to forge a new Protestant church music style. Pachelbel's sacred concertos are also important efforts in this genre and include *"Gott sei uns gnädig"* and *"Lobet den Herrn in seinem Heiligtum,"* both scored for five voices and large ensembles.

Pachelbel's 11 motets are also inspired creations, ten of which call for two four-part choruses. *"Gott ist unser Zuversicht"* and *"Nun danket alle Gott"* are two examples of his exceptional art in this fairly restrictive form. The composer's arias comprise another form in which he scored a number of successes. In sum, Pachelbel's artistic worth rests on much more than just the *Canon in D*. *—Robert Cummings*

Recommended:

- ○ **Pachelbel: Organ Works Vol. 1** / Bouchard / Dorian 93173
- ○ **Pachelbel: Keyboard Suites** / Payne / 1995 / Bis 809
- ○ **Pachelbel: Easter Cantatas** / Wilson (cond.), Backes, Mauch, La Capella Ducale, Musica Fiata / CPO 999916
- ○ **Pachelbel: Arias & Duets** / Malina (dir.), Zadori, Nemeth, Kallay, Kovach, Affetti Musicali / Hungaroton Classics 31736
- ○ **Pachelbel Motetten** / Jacob (cond.), Capella Sebaldina / 1994 / Entree 50
- ○ **Pachelbel: Complete Organ Works Vol. 1** / Payne / 1996 / Centaur 2304

CHAMBER MUSIC

Canon and Gigue for 3 violins & continuo in D major (ca. 1700)

Johann Pachelbel was a well-known musician in his day. He composed a multitude of works for the organ (his native instrument), along with motets, sacred concertos, keyboard suites, and pieces in a variety of other genres. Of all these hundreds of compositions, however, far and away his best-known work is the *Canon in D major*, known colloquially as Pachelbel's *Canon*. This short piece has become a mainstay of chamber orchestras and other musicians and ensembles throughout the world. It has been arranged for almost any instrument or combination of instruments one might imagine, from synthesizer to brass quintet, and has been adapted for musical styles from jazz to new age.

A canon is simply an imitative piece in which one instrument plays a melody, and part way into it another instrument joins in with the same tune, followed by one or more further instruments. In the case of Pachelbel's work, a two bar ostinato (or repeating melodic phrase) in the bass becomes the foundation for a set of 28 variations, in which three violins interact in canon with one another. Baroque convention would have this work performed in a moderate-to-fast tempo; however, the work is most often heard played slowly. Played thus, the *Canon* becomes a quite beautiful and meditative work. Only occasionally is the *Canon* played in tandem with the lively *Gigue* that Pachelbel intended to follow it. *—Chris Morrison*

Recommended:

- ○ **Mozart: Eine Kleine Nachtmusik, etc.** / Marriner (cond.), Academy of St. Martin-in-the-Fields / Philips 416386
- ○ **Pachelbel: Canon & Gigue; Chamber Works** / London Baroque / HM 901539
- ○ **Pachelbel Canon & Other Baroque Favorites** / Stratta (cond.), Baroque CO / 1988 / RCA 7821

KEYBOARD

Chaconne for organ in F minor (before Apr., 1706)

Although the German composer Johann Pachelbel is best known—indeed, only known—for his *Canon in D major*, he was best known during his lifetime as an organist and a composer of organ music. Many critics still consider him to be the finest composer of German organ music before Bach. Most of Pachelbel's organ music was unpublished in his lifetime, but rather circulated in handwritten copies. This makes dating his works difficult and in some cases, impossible. The *Chaconne in F minor* is one of the longest and most involved single-movement works. The chaconne theme is a four-bar chromatically descending bass line, repeated twice, and all succeeding iterations of the theme are similarly paired. For the purposes of analysis, the 4/4 iterations of the chaconne theme may be considered as paired units, thereby yielding 22 iterations. The mood is different from that of the *Canon*; there were several variation-like Baroque forms, based on repetitions of a single theme or bass line, and each had its own flavor. Yet the work should certainly be of interest to that fraction of the millions of *Canon* listeners curious about the rest of this composer's output. *—James Leonard*

Recommended:

○ **Piet Kee at Weingarten** / Kee / 1991 / Chandos 0520

Ignace Jan Paderewski

b. Nov. 18, 1860, Kurylowka, Poland, **d.** Jun. 29, 1941, New York, NY

Pianist

Paderewski's career had a Faustian cast. His demonically driven determination to become a concert pianist, his magical audience rapport, his rapture-rife music, his political career as Poland's first prime minister, and his subsequent efforts to rescue Poland from political quagmire wear a legendary aura more often encountered in poetry. Born to a well-off, cultivated family, young Paderewski received piano lessons from an early age, entering the Warsaw Music Institute before he was 12 to study piano, harmony, and counterpoint. Upon graduation in 1878 the Institute engaged him as a piano teacher. By 1880 he was married and a year later found himself a widower and father of a son. Forsaking the musical backwater of Warsaw for cosmopolitan Berlin, Paderewski pursued composition studies between 1881 and 1883 while moving in the social orbit of the greatest musicians of the day: a young Richard Strauss, for instance, and the lionized Anton Rubinstein. Moszkowski was influential in having Paderewski's early piano pieces published. Feeling the need for further piano study, Paderewski applied in 1884 to the great Polish pianist and pedagogue Theodor Leschetizky who, upon hearing him, cried "Too late, too late!" Despite talent, Paderewski did not possess a fluent *mécanique*—during three intensive years with Leschetizky, he transformed mediocre ability into a world-class technique. But well before his Vienna debut in 1888, the beginning of his career, Paderewski possessed the hypnotic, leonine, compelling presence that informed his playing and brought him world fame. This began with appearances in London and New York in 1890 and over 100 concerts in the U.S. and Canada immediately following—a grueling schedule that was annually repeated. Other tours took him to South America, Australia, New Zealand, and South Africa, as well as the greater and lesser cities of Europe. From the late 1880s into the new century, major compositions fell from his pen—the celebrated *Minuet in G*, Op. 14/1 (1887), a *Piano Concerto* (1888), the opera *Manru* (1892–1901), a *Piano Sonata* (1903), and a *Symphony* (1903–09). Box office success was translated into good works, sponsorship of competitions, and in 1915, the Polish Victims Relief Fund. In 1919 he was chosen independent Poland's first Prime Minister, in which capacity he signed the Versailles treaty. He resumed his concert career in 1922, touring into old age and frailty to raise funds for the Polish cause in the wake of the Nazi invasion in 1939. Dying in New York in 1941, he was given a hero's burial in Arlington National Cemetery. *—Adrian Corleonis*

Recommended:

○ **Art of Paderewski Vol. I** / Paderewski / Pearl 9499

○ **Ignacy Jan Paderewski** / Paderewski / 1999 / Philips 456919

Niccolò Paganini

b. Oct. 27, 1782, Genoa, Italy, **d.** May 27, 1840, Nice, France

Composer: Chamber Music, Concerto

The remarkable international career of Niccolò Paganini—regarded in legend as the greatest virtuoso violinist ever—did not begin until relatively late in life. Born in Genoa in 1782, Paganini received his first musical instruction from his father, a devoted amateur musician. Niccolò's rapid progress on the violin, however, was such that his father (who was in fact a mandolinist, and thus little suited to train his precocious son) was soon compelled to send his son to Giacomo Costa, *maestro di capella* of the Cathedral at San Lorenzo, for further study. Although he quickly gained some local fame and even embarked on a minor tour of Italy in 1797, it would be many years before Paganini consented to perform outside his native land.

Paganini began composing seriously after his initial tour of Italy in 1797. He performed little during the initial years of the nineteenth century, preferring instead to devote his time to composition and romance (happily combining the two when he met a Florentine noblewoman, to this day anonymous, with a passion for the guitar). In 1805 he resumed his active musical career, accepting the directorship of the orchestra at Lucca, and in 1813 he embarked on a series of concert tours throughout the Italian peninsula.

In 1825, after nearly 30 years of intensive practice and self-scrutiny, Paganini felt he had developed his skills sufficiently to put them on display for all of Europe, and he left Italy for an extensive European tour (Vienna debut 1828, Paris 1831, London 1831). His astounding technical prowess amazed audiences of the day, and many fanciful legends arose to explain his remarkable abilities (one of the more popular held that he was in league with demonic powers, a legend rather supported by his gaunt, pale features). He died in 1840 from cancer of the larynx, having all but ended his concert career in 1834.

Paganini's impact on nineteenth century music cannot be overestimated: he set an entirely new standard of technical virtuosity; he was among the first musicians to champion the music of Berlioz (having commissioned, but never performed, *Harold in Italy*); and the inspirational effect that his works would have on the young Franz Liszt—who set out to duplicate Paganini's achievements on the piano—would alter both the course of music and the life of the young Liszt forever. Paganini's own compositions, including an unidentified number of violin concertos (some six are extant) and numerous chamber works, have more or less been abandoned. The concertos are written in the Italian operatic style of the day, oscillating between lyric charm and ferocious technical display, and are the only works of his which remain in the repertory (though many of the shorter works, by comparison, are gems and deserve to be played more). *—Blair Johnston*

CHAMBER MUSIC

Cantabile, for violin & piano in D major (1823)

Precious little of Niccolò Paganini's immense compositional output made it into print during his lifetime, a situation resulting less from neglect than from the virtuoso composer's own hesitation at revealing the technical tricks and tools by which he had made his name famous throughout Europe. A few pieces were published about ten years after his death, but it was not until the second decade of the twentieth century that his home city of Genoa finally allowed its enormous collection of original Paganini manuscripts to be sorted and eventually published.

The well-known *Cantabile in D major*, like a great deal of the music found in the Genoa collection, seems to have been composed not for public use but rather for the private enjoyment of Paganini and his circle. Here we find the composer's virtuoso fireworks tamed, his bag of tricks closed. Far removed from the pyrotechnic *Caprices*, the *Cantabile* is instead a gorgeous Italian vocalise. In a rare instance among his chamber works, Paganini passes over his favorite accompanimental instrument, the guitar (upon which he was also a virtuoso), in favor of the piano.

The *Cantabile* is a perfect example of three-part song form. In the opening bars of the violin melody, which begins without accompaniment, Paganini immediately betrays his indebtedness to two somewhat related influences: Italian opera and the decorative arabesque style of instrumental writing characteristic of the piano music of Chopin. A second section, in A major, follows in much the same manner as the first, climaxing in a three-measure cadential pattern whose elegant but fevered ornamentation spans nearly the entire range of the violin. As the music of the opening is reprised in the third and final section, Paganini allows the melody to unfold an octave lower than before. A wild virtuosic flourish—the only one of its kind in the piece—dissolves into the tender coda, which eventually sums up the work in two gentle pizzicati. *—Blair Johnston*

Recommended:

○ **Paganini: Works for Violin & Guitar** / Shaham, Sollscher / DG 437837

24 Caprices for solo violin, Op. 1 (ca. 1817)

It is perhaps sadly ironic that the works directly inspired by the last of Niccolò Paganini's prodigiously difficult *24 Caprices* for solo violin (ca. 1817) have overshadowed their source and indeed, the whole of this hugely influential set of technical exercises. But unquestionably, it is the demonic theme of *Caprice No. 24*, which provided the impetus for composers as diverse as Brahms, Rachmaninov, Lutosławski, and Lloyd-Webber to use the theme as the basis for their own variation works, which has become Paganini's musical epitaph. This sinister, angular theme conjures up in our minds the gaunt, white face of the violinist whom many thought was in league with Lucifer himself more palpably than any other!

Paganini's music has often been slighted for its lack of profundity; he was, after all, a superstar violinist first and a composer second. Among violinists, however, mastery of the *Caprices*, Op. 1, represents the summit of technical attainment, and beside the solo violin works of Bach, and perhaps the much later solo sonatas by Ysaÿe, this set stands as one of the greatest volumes of music ever devised for a solo string instrument.

The *Caprices* were published by Ricordi in 1820, and while their musical content reflected Paganini's astounding technical brilliance, they also served another groundbreaking function. Although primarily intended as technical exercises "A gli Artisti" (dedicated "To the Artists"), the caprices are so wide-ranging in their scope that they actually transcend all expected pedagogic constraints, and thus stand out impressively as bravura miniatures endowed with genuine musical as well as instructional value. In this regard, the series inspired a new interest in compositions which were at once formidably challenging, but also musically rewarding to both players and listeners alike. One of the earliest composers to recognize and emulate this was Chopin, whose Études for piano were directly inspired by the violin caprices. Other composers, notably Berlioz (who composed his symphony *Harold in Italy* to display Paganini's skills on the viola), Schumann, and especially Franz Liszt, were deeply impressed.

The *24 Caprices* for solo violin encompass every imaginable aspect of violin technique, and in many cases, for example in their use of complex multiple stopping, fast passagework, and imaginative bowing permutations, very few, if indeed any other violinist contemporary with Paganini himself could have actually played them! Some of the more spectacular violin pyrotechnics include the combination of bowing and pizzicato (plucking), a full exploration of the use of harmonics, double-stopped trills, and recourse to widely spaced chords based on Paganini's remarkable ability to stretch vast distances across the fingerboard. *—Michael Jameson*

Recommended:

- ○ **Paganini: 24 Caprices** / Accardo / DG 429714
- ○ **Paganini: 24 Caprices** / Rabin / 2003 / EMI 67998
- ○ **Paganini: Concertos 1 & 2; Capricci, Op1** / Markov / 1999 / Erato 27001

Duetto amoroso, for violin & guitar in C major (ca. 1807)

Paganini was one of the few important nineteenth century composers who wrote for the guitar, though he always paired it in his scores with the violin or other string instruments. He wrote two sets of six sonatas for violin and guitar (Opp. 2 & 3; 1805), for example, and several sets of quartets for violin, viola, cello, and guitar, one of which (1818–20) contained 15 works. That said, the guitar is not usually given a primary role in these compositions and certainly not in this charming duet. The music in the Duetto amoroso represents a dialogue between two lovers, but with the violin portraying both the male and female protagonists. The work begins in a chipper mood with a violin theme that is jaunty and full of optimism, the guitar playing mostly patterns of repeating rhythmic figures in accompaniment. A second theme follows that has a more romantic, more passionate quality in its yearning manner. Thereafter, the music becomes somewhat episodic, as it stops after each pair of exchanges between the lovers and then starts up again. The writing for the violin is brilliant and colorful, while that for the guitar remains strictly subordinate in providing only harmonic and rhythmic support. In the end, there is much variety here, but also a fantasy-like character that gives the music a seemingly less-tidy structure. *—Robert Cummings*

Recommended:

- ○ **Paganini: Music for Violin & Guitar Vol. 2** / Wynberg, St. John / 1994 / Naxos 550759

Grand Sonata, for guitar & violin in A major, Op. 35 (1805–1808)

While most of the works that Niccolò Paganini wrote for violin and guitar (including the 30 sonatas published during his lifetime as Op. 2, Op. 3, and the *Centone di sonate*) are brief, charming compositions in just two or perhaps three short movements, he did compose a pair of bulkier, more imposing vehicles for that instrumental duo. The *Grand Sonata for guitar and violin in A major,* MS 3 (posthumously printed as Op. 35) that Paganini penned around 1804 is one of those two weighty pieces (the *Sonata Concertata,* MS 2 is the other), and it pays to note that Paganini quite carefully and explicitly described these two works as being for "guitar and violin" rather than for "violin and guitar," as the rest of his sundry violin/guitar sonatas are marked (similarly, Beethoven and Brahms actually considered their substantial violin/piano sonatas to be works for "piano and violin"). Far from being a subordinate accompanist, the guitarist in the *Grand Sonata* is raised even past an equal level with the violin. To a large extent it is the sound of plucked strings and not bowed ones that drives and dominates the piece.

The *Grand Sonata* is in three movements (Allegro risoluto; Romance, Largo amorosamente; and Andantino variato) and fills about a quarter of an hour. Allegro risoluto is a real sonata-allegro opening movement, with two carefully balanced themes, a development, and a recapitulation, all in the positions one would anticipate. Paganini moves to the parallel minor for the following Romance; the traditional tables are truly turned on the violinist here, as he/she is asked to accompany the guitarist's sumptuously melancholic tune by plucking the strings of the violin! Although the movement is a slow one, the guitarist gets plenty of chances to provide impressive embellishments and indulge in some brief cadenzas. The scherzando third movement is intentionally cute; the light chromaticism at the start of the guitarist's melody and the slowly bouncing pizzicati of the violin are really quite disarming, and the subsequent variation making is as playful as variation making gets. *—Blair Johnston*

Recommended:

- ○ **Duets for Violin & Guitar** / Huggett, Savino / 2001 / Classical Express 3957116

Guitar Sonatas (ca. 1800–1825)

Although the individual pieces tend to be on the short side, Niccolò Paganini's music for guitar solo, as a whole, forms a surprisingly large part of his total output as a composer. If we add his music for guitar and violin and for guitar quartet—violin, viola, cello, and guitar—it becomes clear that he, the grandest of all nineteenth century violin virtuosi, wrote as much music involving guitar as he did music involving violin. The 43 *Ghiribizzi,* or "Whims," are probably the most played of Paganini's solo guitar works; but the 37 *Sonatas for guitar solo,* MS 84, of around 1810 are not far behind the *Ghiribizzi* in attractiveness.

The 37 *Sonatas* are not full-scale instrumental sonatas as we normally understand the term; they might better be described as miniature sonatas, or even miniature dance sonatas, since nearly all of the movements are dance forms of one variety or another. Two movements are the norm for the MS 84 *Sonatas,* though several have just one, and two (Nos. 23 and 31) have three; an entire sonata lasts just a few minutes and fills two or, at most, three pages of printed score. Each of the sonatas begins with a charming Minuetto; then usually comes a Waltz or an Allegretto/Andantino. In the two three-movement sonatas the extra movements are in one case an additional Allegretto and in the other a "Rondonicino" (a diminutive, and one might say underdeveloped, kind of rondo that appears once or twice elsewhere in the volume as a substitute for the Allegretto movement). Paganini's solo guitar music is often described as technically undemanding or even simple, but within this 37-piece volume are many movements that demand full virtuoso command of the instrument (the last few *Sonatas,* Nos. 34–37, each in a single Minuetto movement, are particularly flashy), and which in style are very much in keeping with the manner of Paganini's famous *24 Caprices for Solo Violin. —Blair Johnston*

Recommended:

- ○ **Paganini: Guitar Music Vol. 1** / Zigante / 2002 / Arts 47192
- ○ **Paganini: Guitar Music Vol. 2** / Zigante / 1994 / Arts 47193
- ○ **Paganini: Sonate & Ghirbizzi for Guitar** / Steidl / 2001 / Frame 135

Molto perpetuo, for violin & guitar in C major, Op. 11 (1835)

The degree to which Niccolò Paganini's skills on the violin boggled the minds of early to mid-nineteenth century audiences can hardly be appreciated today, when all of his much-guarded technical secrets have long since been revealed and the world's concert violinists are expected to duplicate his finesse—if perhaps not his profound expression—on a daily basis. It helps to remember that it was not for several generations after his death that European violinists were willing to make a go at playing much of his music.

The history of Paganini's now-famous *Allegro vivace a movimento perpetuo* (usually simply called "Moto Perpetuo") in C Major, Op. 11 for violin and orchestra, bears witness to this lengthy absorption. Originally composed during April of 1835, the *Moto Perpetuo* remained unpublished at the time of Paganini's death in 1840, and was among those pieces of his first put to print in 1851 by publishers in both Paris and Mainz. Aside from the occasional odd performance or two, however, the piece did not really enter the standard repertory until 1932, when Fritz Kreisler made and published a new transcription of the work for violin and piano; other violinists were quick to follow Kreisler's lead, and by mid-century, the piece had become a staple of virtually every virtuoso's encore list.

The *Moto Perpetuo in C* (there is another, posthumous, in A) is four minutes of sheer physical delight for the worthy performer, five or six minutes of absolute terror for the underdeveloped. The machine-gun 16th notes never once stop through 187 measures of music—measures 188 and 189, mercifully, are simple cadential chords! A basic sonata principle governs the music, though the usual idea of contrasting themes is omitted. Those who label Paganini as a thoughtless notespinner would do well to take a look at the apparently ordinary, but in fact ingeniously devised, way that he brings about the reprise of the opening passage in the *Moto Perpetuo.*

At a tempo that does service to Paganini's intentions, the piece is among the most fiendish the composer penned (it is perhaps not so difficult as the perpetual motion of the Caprice No. 5, but it is far longer), and anyone wishing to tackle the work at such a tempo would do well to familiarize himself with famed violinist Henryk Wieniawski's personal motto: "Il faut risquer" (I must risk it). Of course, Wieniawski never had to play the piece. *—Blair Johnston*

Recommended:

- ○ **My Favourite Kreisler** / Perlman, Sanders / EMI 47467

Sonata concertata, for guitar & violin in A major, Op. 61 (1804)

Listening to Paganini's lovely *Sonata concertata,* it is hard to believe it is by the same composer who is responsible for the dazzlingly brilliant *24 Caprices* and the dramatic *Violin Concerto No. 2.* With the opening Allegro spiritoso, which serves as the first movement of this loosely structured sonata, the work hearkens to the Classical style of Mozart or Haydn, where the balance between instruments leads to a unified musical expression, glorious but simple. Indeed, this entire piece may be described as dialogic, since a lilting call-and-response theme between the guitar and violin provides the structural basis. The second movement, Adagio, contains some simple but rewarding interplay between the two instruments; at certain moments, the guitar achieves an almost improvisatory freedom of expression, dragging the more relaxed violin along with it. This paves the way for the truly danceable final movement, Rondo, in which the violin takes on a more brilliant mode of expression than before. In sum, the work represents Paganini's most intimate, relaxed, and almost playful compositional mode. —*Edward Moore*

Recommended:

○ **Paganini: Music for Violin & Guitar Vol. I** / Wynberg, St. John / 1994 / Naxos 550690

CONCERTO

Introduction and Variations on "Dal tuo stellato soglio" from Rossini's "Mosè," for violin & orchestra (ca. 1819)

According to legend, Paganini was giving a recital when one string after another broke, first the E, then the A, and finally the D, leaving him only with the lowest, the G string. Refusing to give up—or pause to restring his instrument—Paganini is said to have improvised on his one remaining string. This is, in all likelihood, just a fanciful tale, but the fact remains that Paganini did write his *Moses Fantasy* solely for the G string, offering tremendous difficulties that strike fear into the hearts of violinists and ensure that the music is rarely played. At any rate, restriction to the G string gives even the high notes a dark coloring that can lead unwary listeners to believe they're hearing music for the viola. After a negligible introduction that performers feel free to cut, Paganini tenderly lays out a theme lifted from Rossini's opera *Mosè*; the music is flowing, lyrical yet minor key, typical of bel canto opera (a genre that gave Paganini much of his inspiration, particularly in slow movements). This occupies about one-third of the score, whereupon soloists must gird themselves for a few witty but bedeviling variations. The first is jaunty, with flirtatious repetitions of tiny phrases. Next comes a variation relying on flying passagework, the second section faster than the first. The next variation is a hyperactive little dance that requires notes as high as can be played on the G string, followed by a more galloping version of the same treatment. —*James Reel*

Recommended:

○ **Tutta bravura** / Repin / 1998 / Erato 25487

Violin Concerto No. 1 in E flat major, Op. 6 (1815–1816)

Paganini's *Concerto for Violin and Orchestra No. 1* is a virtuosic tour de force and reveals not only Paganini's incredible technical ability, but also his melodic sensitivity and skillful exploitation of dramatic structure. Like many of his other works, this concerto takes inspiration from the musical language of Gioachino Rossini's operas, which were extremely popular at the time. Paganini originally composed the *Concerto No. 1* in the unusual key of E flat major, in order to achieve a more brilliant tone for the violin. However, since modern concert pitches are much higher than was the norm in Paganini's era, the standard modern version of the piece is transposed to the key of D major, which also makes the very thin E string of the violin less susceptible to breakage (Paganini often broke several strings during a single concert performance). By modern standards the technical demands of the concerto are only moderate, but in Paganini's time they were considered tremendous, and many contemporaries branded the piece "unplayable." This, of course, served as valuable publicity that helped Paganini become the most popular soloist of his day. The work is indeed a catalog of such flashy techniques as extended arpeggios, left-hand pizzicati, rapid runs in thirds, fifths, and even harmonics. The work is more than a mere virtuoso showpiece, however. Paganini's concerto is filled with elegant melodic themes, and there are moments of striking beauty. One legend holds that Paganini composed the main theme of the second movement on a one-string violin while languishing in prison under suspicion of a murder he did not commit. Such legends grow up naturally around the dynamic (and, some said, demonic) Paganini, but they also reflect the appeal and mystique of his music. Paganini's aura of mystery was amplified by his refusal to allow his works to be published during his lifetime, making it impossible for his rivals to study and master his techniques. The *Concerto No. 1* was published only after his death, and it soon became a fixture in the repertoire of lesser virtuosos who were as adept, more or less, in the technical department, but not nearly as musically compeling as Paganini. Fortunately, many great twentieth century soloists have concentrated on the musicality of the piece as much as the virtuosity. —*Edward Moore*

Recommended:

○ **Paganini: Concerto 1; Saint-Saëns: Concerto 3** / Sinopoli (cond.), Shaham, New York PO / DG 29786

○ **Paganini: Violonkonzerte 1 & 2** / Dutoit (cond.), Accardo, London PO / DG 415378

Violin Concerto No. 2 in B minor ("La campanella"), Op. 7 (1826)

Paganini composed his second violin concerto about eight years after the first, when his fame as a virtuoso soloist had been fully established. It is perhaps for this reason that the *Concerto for Violin and Orchestra No. 2, in B minor,* Opus 7—subtitled "La Campanella" ("The Bell," after the persistent use of a triangle in the famous theme of the final movement)—focuses more on pure melodic content and thematic development than virtuoso flourish. Indeed, in this piece, perhaps more than any other, we see Paganini's virtues as a composer shining forth. Of course there are technical displays, but the focus is on the unity of the concerto and its effect as a dramatic, indeed operatic, piece of music. Paganini had an immense fondness for Italian opera, especially the music of Rossini (who in turn rejoiced that Paganini had not become an opera composer). Rossini's influence is especially marked in the opening movement of the *Concerto No. 2,* which bears a remarkable resemblance to the overture to Rossini's *Barber of Seville.* However, the rondo theme of the final movement is its most interesting feature. This brilliant theme has a marked gypsy feel, and is a fine example of pure virtuosity harnessed to the service of a grand musical idea. The theme was used by pianist-composer Franz Liszt in his influential *Études d'exécution transcendante d'après Paganini.* The overall structure of the *Concerto for Violin and Orchestra No. 2* is very precise, with each theme either presaging or echoing another, and echoes of the work resound in many later concertos of the Romantic era. —*Edward Moore*

Recommended:

○ **Paganini: Concertos 1 & 2; Capricci, Op1** / Viotti (cond.), Markov, Saarbrucken RSO / 1999 / Erato 27001

○ **Paganini: Violin Concertos** / Dutoit (cond.), Accardo, London PO / DG 437210

Violin Concerto No. 3 in E major (1826)

Composed in Naples in 1826, Niccolò Paganini's *Concerto No. 3 in E major for violin and orchestra* (MS 50) is not one of the man's more frequently played concertos; *No. 1* is, of course, the best known, and *No. 2* and *No. 4* are more or less tied for second place. But there are many people, including such luminary violinists as Henryk Szeryng, who felt and feel that *No. 3* is the most impressive of the set, both from a composition point of view and, as always with Paganini's violin music, from a technical show-off point of view. It is also usually the longest of the set, lasting better than half an hour in performance.

Only a few of Paganini's concertos survive intact. He was a tight-fisted man when it came to distributing copies of his pieces, and eagerly snatched the orchestral parts back up as soon as a performance of one of his concertos was finished. Thus, the orchestral parts and scores for several of the concertos are missing, and must be reconstructed if a performance is wished. Not so with the *Concerto No. 3,* whose autographed manuscript solo parts and orchestral score are intact and carefully preserved in a Roman library.

The concerto is in the usual three-movement format, and, as always in Paganini's concertos, Classical concerto form and turn-of-the century Italian opera style meet head-on. The first movement, "Introduzione" (Andante—Allegro marziale), begins playfully, with a series of pizzicato chirps from the orchestral strings; the winds and percussion, however, beg to differ, and, after a brief exuberant outburst, a stately, wholly operatic tune (complete with rhythmic blasts from the cymbal) is presented. Silken melody and jaw-dropping pyrotechnics take turns after the violinist enters. And, just as happens in the famous *Concerto No. 1,* there are episodes dedicated entirely to the playing of difficult parallel thirds.

The second movement is an Adagio that Paganini describes as Cantabile spianato, while the finale is a happy Polacca (in the polonaise's standard triple meter) that, at better than ten minutes, is quite a bit more bulky than most of Paganini's finales. Paganini gave the world premiere of this concerto in Vienna on July 24, 1828. —*Blair Johnston*

Recommended:

○ **Paganini: Concertos 3 & 4** / Dutoit (cond.), Accardo, London PO / 1988 / DG 423370

Violin Concerto No. 4 in D minor (ca. 1829–1830)

Niccolò Paganini composed his *Violin Concerto No. 4 in D minor* between the autumn of 1829 and the winter of 1830. He had already made his triumphant Viennese debut in 1828 using his astoundingly difficult first three *Violin Concertos* to demonstrate his unequaled virtuosity. But feeling a need for new repertoire while touring Germany, Paganini wrote his *Fourth* between performances, and although he wrote to his publisher that he intended to "deflower" the work in Paris, he actually performed it several times in Germany. In his review of the work, Ludwig Spohr wrote "in his composition and his style there is a strange mixture of consummate genius, childishness, and lack of taste that alternately charms and repels." Writing of the Parisian premiere, critic Castil-Blaze said that the work had a "most original form" and had "several highly picturesque effects." Cast in the standard three-movement form, Paganini's *Concerto No. 4* opens with a stormy Allegro maestoso in D minor followed by a highly emotional Adagio flebile con sentimento in F sharp minor and closes with a racing *Rondo galante in D minor* with a novel obbligato triangle that no doubt elicited Castil-Blaze's comment on "picturesque effects." —*James Leonard*

Recommended:

- ○ **Paganini: Violin Concertos** / Dutoit (cond.), Accardo, London PO / DG 437210
- ○ **Best of Paganini** / Bellugi (cond.), Grumiaux, Monte Carlo National Opera Orch. / 1999 / Philips 462865

Christopher Page

b. Apr. 8, 1952, London, England
Conductor

A philologist by training, a musicologist by proven merit, and a performer by deep instinct, Christopher Page integrates the various aspects of his professional life as a humanist in the best sense of the word. He once welcomed a reviewer's comment that described his book as "Social history illuminated by its interest in music as an essential part of human experience." Page's career in scholarly teaching and publication freely informs his life as a performer of medieval musics and vice versa; both contribute to his vibrant analyses of medieval thought, especially that concerning music and the experience of music in human society. Page's academic credentials include a bachelor's degree in English from Oxford University (1974) and a PhD. from the University of York (1981). While completing his dissertation on Anglo-Saxon verse forms, he began publishing articles on the history of musical instruments as seen in medieval texts and illuminations, as well as papers on performance practice. New College, Oxford, appointed him lecturer in Old and Middle English (1980–85), followed by the University of Cambridge in 1985. In 1997, Cambridge named him Reader in Medieval Literature and Music; he also served as a Fellow of Sidney Sussex College. In 1991, he was awarded the Dent Medal of the Royal Musical Association for outstanding services to musicology. Among his publications, three books have held particular interest to musicians. *Voices and Instruments in the Middle Ages* (1986) argues that a medieval lyric's genre directly relates to the use and type of instrumental accompaniment; *The Owl and the Nightingale* (1989) traces social changes regarding music and musicians in the newly "invented" state of medieval France, and *Discarding Images* (1993) explores the diversity of twelfth to fifteenth century life in the face of a "cultural myth of the Middle Ages" as monolithic unity, perpetuated (according to Page) in part by art historians and musicologists. Page's ensemble the Gothic Voices has brought medieval European culture even closer to the present through a score of recording projects and a vigorous touring schedule. The recordings (supported by Page's own extensive program notes) include two critically acclaimed series on varieties of medieval French and English musics and span the gamut from the sequences of Hildegard of Bingen, music for the coronation of Richard the Lionhearted, and troubador/touvère repertories to masses of Pierre de la Rue from the turn of the sixteenth century. The group's first recording (*A Feather on the Breath of God*) earned Page the first of three Grammys for early music performance. He has contributed his own skills as a lutenist and harpist on several recordings, but has also used compelling all-vocal performances as a laboratory for his scholarly hypotheses on the absence of instruments in the performance of certain types of medieval polyphony. *—Timothy Dickey*

Recommended:

- ○ **The Medieval Romantics** / Page (cond.), Gothic Voices / 1991 / Hyperion 66463
- ○ **The Marriage of Heaven and Hell** / Page (cond.), Gothic Voices / 1990 / Hyperion 66423
- ○ **The Spirits of England and France Vol. 1** / Page (cond.), Gothic Voices / 1994 / Hyperion 66739
- ○ **Hildegard: A Feather on the Breath of God** / Page (cond.), Kirkby, Parrott, Philpot, Evera, Gothic Voices / 2003 / Hyperion 21039
- ○ **de la Rue: 2 Masses** / Page (cond.), Gothic Voices / 1998 / Hyperion 67010

Jean-François Paillard

b. Apr. 12, 1928, Vitry-le-François, France
Conductor

Conductor and musicologist Jean-François Paillard was one of the most visible French exponents of Baroque music from the 1960s onward. Paillard earned a degree in mathematics from the Sorbonne, but he turned to music soon after. He attended the Paris Conservatory as a musicology student, where he won first prize in music history; he later studied conducting at the Salzburg Mozarteum with Igor Markevitch. He formed the Ensemble Jean-Marie Leclair in 1952, which was renamed the Jean-François Paillard Chamber Orchestra the following year. Comprised of a dozen string players and a harpsichord, the group paralleled such small-scale English ensembles as the Boyd Neel Orchestra in performing Baroque-era works—especially those from France—as well as contemporary works for string orchestra. As the public's interest in Baroque music rose, the orchestra's popularity grew and was aided by a series of international tours covering dozens of countries. The group's recordings on Erato—which included the standard Baroque repertory such as Bach's *Brandenburg Concertos* and the *Orchestral Suites*, as well as pieces by Couperin and Rameau—were initially easier to find in Europe. But when RCA Victor picked up the Erato catalog for U.S. distribution in the 1970s, Paillard's records were snapped up by American listeners. Lightning struck for Paillard late in the decade with his recording of the *Canon in D* by Johann Pachelbel. Paillard's ran nearly twice as long as most rival recordings, by virtue of its uniquely slow tempo and its finely delineated parts for the strings, both bowed and pizzicato. Paillard further benefited when Victor issued it on a full-priced LP and paired it with Fasch's *Trumpet Concerto* and grouped with various RCA artists on a budget-priced compilation LP called *Go for Baroque*. Sales of *Go for Baroque* moved faster than Beatles' albums were sold. Paillard's performances and recordings have also included works by Roussel and Debussy. He has worked with such celebrated soloists as Maurice André and Jean-Pierre Rampal. Paillard has won numerous *Grand Prix du Disque* awards in France and *Prix Edison* awards in Holland and his release of Rameau's *Les Indes galantes* remains a highly regarded recording. Later in his career, Paillard turned more to guest conducting orchestras around the world and his avid interest in the sciences. *—Bruce Eder*

Recommended:

- ○ **Pachelbel: Canon, etc.** / Paillard (cond.), Andre, Chambon, Pierlot, Jean-François Paillard CO / Erato 98475
- ○ **Handel: Water Music; Fireworks** / Paillard (cond.), Jean-François Paillard CO / 2002 / Apex 48685

John Knowles Paine

b. Jan. 9, 1839, Portland, ME, **d.** Apr. 25, 1906, Cambridge, MA
Composer

Until the appearance of composer Johns Knowles Paine during the latter half of the nineteenth century, American musical culture was a pale reflection of its European counterpart. Although it would be decades before Paine's legacy would bear real fruit—during the explosion of U.S. compositional activity during the first two or three decades of the twentieth century—his importance as the first professor of music at an American institution of higher learning (Harvard University), and the subsequent dissemination of his ideas by three generations of students, have earned him a special place in the history of American music.

Paine was born in Maine during February of 1839. His childhood training, received through a German-born musician named Herman Kotschmar, was thorough; by the time Paine departed for Europe in 1858 he was a skilled pianist, organist and composer. Studies at the Berlin Hochschule für Musik (mainly with organist Karl-August Haupt) made a lasting impression on the composer, whose work would bear the mark of healthy German Romanticism until the end of his days. Paine returned to the United States in 1861, made a new home in Boston, and by 1863 had won, largely on the merit of his many appearances as an organist and his countless public lectures on musical form and history, a position on the faculty of Harvard University.

Paine's accomplishments as an administrator and teacher are important indeed. In addition to his work at Harvard—where he almost single-handedly organized a department of music which would prove to be the model of every later American University—Paine also played an important role during the formation of the Boston Symphony Orchestra. His many notable students include composer Arthur Foote and musicologist/critic Olin Downes.

Paine's virtues as a composer are less unimpeachable, particularly in the later years when poor health robbed him of some of his creative faculty. At his best, as in the *Mass in D* from 1866–67, and, to a somewhat lesser degree, in the *First Symphony* of 1875, Paine's language is clear and natural, owing much to the German classics he studied with Kotschmar and at the Hochschule in Berlin. Paine, however, did not move with great ease or fluidity into the more chromatic style of composition that emerged during the later years of the century, and when he began to stretch his tonal and expressive language—in an effort to remain more "current"—his music suffered noticeably (as in the programmatic *Second Symphony* of 1880). Within a few years of Paine's death his music had all but disappeared from the concert hall, though the general resurgence of interest in early American composers during the later years of the twentieth century provided Paine with a welcome (albeit temporary) respite from his place in musical limbo.*—Blair Johnston*

Overview of Works

John Knowles Paine represented the first big step away from provinciality in the evolution of American music. Lengthy studies in Germany, as well as extensive performing as organist and pianist in Germany and England during vacations, were to form the character of Paine's own music as well as his inclination as an educator at Harvard and other New England schools. Paine's achievement was a move toward "validity" for American music. Paine's music embraces the German conservative school of Mendelssohn and Schumann, rather than the "music of the future" of Wagner and Liszt, although later he would test the chromatic waters in his own works, despite his arguments against the latter in his own writings, which stopped short of polemics. Thus, one may divide Paine's output into two distinct periods. The first, which began in his student years, includes numerous piano works, the *Symphony No. 1*, the *Mass in D*, the oratorio *St. Peter*, the *Centennial Hymn* (text by Whittier), and the cantata *Realm of Fancy* (text by Keats). The choral works especially show the influence of the then seemingly omnipresent Mendelssohn. The symphony looks toward Schumann's as its model, but some changes may be perceived in *Symphony No. 2*. In it, mature Wagnerian harmony is cautiously injected and coupled with cyclic procedure. This influence continues in such second period works as the incidental music to Sophocles' *Oedipus Tyrannus* (which also reflects Liszt's processes transformation) and the late opera *Azara*, with a libretto by the composer based on medieval legend. Yet throughout his entire output, there is never a loss of firm tonal grip. Experimentation with newer trends is applied rather than injected. For Paine, the designation of "classicist" is most accurate. Unfortunately, this is accompanied by a certain earnestness that borders on dryness, as well as an aversion to anything humorous or evocative of his native land. One amusing exception is worth noting: a fugue on "Over the fence is out," the familiar little two-measure musical theme that so often capped a comedy sketch in vaudeville. In his own time, Paine achieved national recognition, respect, and success by achieving the standards that were the international norm. A younger generation of men, such as Chadwick, Parker, and Foote, would follow his lead. While a break, even upheaval, from the mainstream lay in the future with Ives and later the Boulanger-trained school of American composers, it was the mastery of the traditional that was necessary to give rise to breaking with the same. As such, John Knowles Paine provided a necessary link as well as providing well-crafted and sincerely felt works that deserve to be better known. *—Wayne Reisig*

Recommended:

- ○ **Paine: Mass in D** / Schuller (cond.), Cole, Cheek, Balthrop, Blackett, St. Louis SO & Chorus / 1979 / New World 80262
- ○ **Paine: Symphony 2** / Mehta (cond.), New York PO / 1987 / New World 80350
- ○ **Paine: Overture to Shakespeare's "As You Like It"; Symphony 1** / Mehta (cond.), New York PO / 1989 / New World 80374
- ○ **Paine: Selected Piano Works** / Oldham / 1993 / New World 80424
- ○ **Paine: Chamber Music** / Silverstein, Eskin, Eskin / Northeastern 219
- ○ **Paine: Organ Music** / Somerville / 1999 / Raven 460

Giovanni Paisiello

b. May 9, 1740, Roccaforzata, Italy, **d.** Jun. 5, 1816, Naples, Italy
Composer: Opera, Concerto

As the eighteenth century operatic scene that surrounded and influenced Mozart emerged into clearer view, Giovanni Paisiello was recognized as one of its most significant shapers. He began composing opera as soon as he left the Conservatory of San Onofrio in Naples in 1763. In Naples he soon became established as a popular local composer. He was noted for simplifying operatic style in the interests of getting more quickly to the plot and keeping it moving. His librettist Giambattista Lorenzi crafted fast-moving, usually humorous plots as well as larger, dramatic operas.

His tendency towards concision was strengthened when he accepted employment in the court of Catherine the Great of Russia in 1776. She demanded that productions in her theater last no more than an hour and a half. He strove to make his melodies more appealing, his orchestration more colorful, and make the music help illustrate the plot. Young Mozart studied Paisiello, greatly benefiting his own style. In 1781 Paisiello wrote an intermezzo-opera, *La serva padrona* (The Serving-wench Mistress), and, in 1782 the *Il barbiere di Siviglia* (The Barber of Seville). Mozart quickly wrote a sequel to it, *Le nozze di Figaro.*

Paisiello, who had been secretly prospecting for a job in Naples, left Russia on leave (pocketing a year's advance pay), and took up his new post as court theater composer to King Ferdinand IV of Naples. He never returned to Russia. King Ferdinand granted him liberal and generous employment terms. In 1799, Ferdinand was overthrown and fled with his court to Sicily. Paisiello stayed behind and received the post of the rebel Republic's "National Music Master." The King raised an army and retook Naples five months later. Paisiello was fired, even though he insisted that he had not asked for nor wanted the appointment. He was reinstated in 1801. Then Paisiello learned that Napoleon admired his music. In 1802 he left for Paris to take a job with Napoleon, somehow persuading Ferdinand to keep his salary going. In 1804 Napoleon permitted Paisiello to return to Naples. After some wrangling, Paisiello got a French pension for his two years of work. In 1806 Joseph Bonaparte ousted Ferdinand and became king of Naples. Paisiello got most of the top musical jobs King Joseph gave out.

In 1815, when he was 75, Paisiello's sun set. As all of Napoleon's little kingdoms collapsed, the resilient Ferdinand returned to his throne, and Paisiello was kicked out of all his jobs except for a chapel position. The Napoleonic pension was repudiated by the restored French monarchy; and in that year Rossini's new version of *Il barbiere di Siviglia* swept Paisiello's off the boards, beginning a long period when the older composer was entirely ignored and nearly forgotten. Paisiello's *Barber* barely hung on by dint of sporadic revivals. When it was recorded in the 1960s, listeners recognized its true merit. It has regained a limited place in the repertory, along with *Serva padrona*, *L'Inganno felice*, and a few other Paisiello works. *—Joseph Stevenson*

Overview of Works (1762–1813)

Born in a small town near Taranto, Giovanni Paisiello (1740–1816) received his musical education at the Conservatorio di S. Onofrio in Naples, where according to his autobiographical sketch he composed his first opera, a short comic intermezzo, while still a student. Subsequently Paisiello went on to become one of the most famous and influential opera composers in Europe, his prestige leading to an invitation from the Empress Catherine II to become her maestro di cappella in St. Petersburg (in 1776) with the substantial salary of 3,000 rubles (it was later increased to 4,000). At the end of 1783 Paisiello returned to Italy, ostensibly on leave from the Russian court. However, an offer in Naples (always his first choice of home) resulted in him leaving the service of Catherine to spend the remainder of his life there.

Although Paisiello composed a number of orchestral and chamber works, and a substantial body of sacred music in the florid Neapolitan style of the day, his fame rests almost entirely on his operas, which number around 80. His particular strength was comic opera (opera buffa), to which his easy melodic style was especially suited. Many of his graceful arias became exceptionally popular. No small part of his success in Naples was due to his collaboration with the librettist Giambattista Lorenzi, whose well-crafted, witty books provided Paisiello with ideal vehicles with which to express a rich vein of comedy in music of wit and elegant charm that is sometimes touched by the gently melancholic sentimental streak that was such an essential ingredient of comic operas of the period. The operas of his Russian period display the composer writing in a more concentrated style, with more emphasis on orchestration, traits that he tended to turn his back on once back in Italy. Paisiello's comic operas reached their height of success with his *Il barbiere di Siviglia*, first performed in St. Petersburg in 1782, and subsequently throughout Europe, and *Nina, o sia La pazza per amore* (*Nina*, or the love-distressed maid) of 1789, possibly the most popular of all his operas. The first was based on the first of the famous trilogy of plays by the French playwright Pierre-Augustin Beaumarchais, a cycle that four years later became the inspiration for Mozart's *Le nozze di Figaro* and in 1816 Rossini's version of *Il barbiere*, which finally eclipsed the setting by Paisiello. *Nina* also has a French source: the story of a much-loved heroine who loses her mind when she believes her lover to have been killed in a duel is typical of sentimental comic opera, its melodies suffused with a memorable, gentle warmth. Paisiello's serious operas have tended to be dismissed as lacking in depth, but he was a great admirer of Pietro Metastasio, the great librettist of opera seria and later in his career set a number of his books, including such oft-set texts as *Olimpiade* (Naples, 1786), and *Didone abbandonata* (Naples, 1794). *—Brian Robins*

Recommended:

- ○ **Paisiello: Overtures & Symphonies** / Mazzola (cond.), Swiss-Italian Radio Orch. / 2001 / Dynamic 376
- ○ **Paisiello: Divertimentos** / Mezzena, etc. / Dynamic 12

OPERA

Il Barbiere di Siviglia (1872)

Among the most successful operas of its day, Paisiello's *Il barbiere di Siviglia* (The Barber of Seville) was subsequently eclipsed by Rossini's work of the same name. Yet even by 1816, the year Rossini's evergreen comedy appeared and of Paisiello's death, the latter's opera was still so popular that some attacked Rossini for turning to the same story. *Il Barbiere* was written during Paisiello's tenure as maestro di cappella for Empress Catherine II in St. Petersburg, and received its first performance at the Hermitage on September 15, 1776 (although by that time, Paisiello had already left the court to assume a new position in Naples). The libretto for *Il Barbiere* was most likely written by Giuseppe Petrosellini, and the work is dedicated to Catherine.

The opera is based on the first installment of French playwright Pierre-Augustin Beaumarchais' famous trilogy that also includes *Le mariage de Figaro* (memorably set by Mozart as *Le nozze di Figaro* four years after Paisiello's *Barber*). Although Beaumarchais' *Figaro* was considered subversive (performances were banned in Mozart's Vienna), the doings of the wily barber Figaro and his aristocratic patron Count Almaviva are less contentious in the opening of the cycle. Indeed, according to the composer's dedication the idea of setting the famous play came from the Empress herself. *Il barbiere di Siviglia* is cast in four acts, in the course of which Figaro assists a disguised Almaviva in marrying Rosina, the ward of Dr. Bartolo, who himself has designs on the girl. The story is told with the customary alternation of rapid, witty recitative punctuated with arias and ensembles; these reveal Paisiello to have been a master of the theater and the possessor of considerable melodic gifts. The work's only real weakness is the thinly conceived orchestration, which pales next to the brilliant effects in Rossini's setting. Nonetheless, by the standards of the day, *Il barbiere di Siviglia* is an excellent example of opera buffa; its contemporary success is marked by its rapid transference to such European opera centers as Naples, Venice, Vienna (where it received nearly 100 performances between 1783 and 1804), and London. *—Brian Robins*

Synopsis:

Act One. This *Barber of Seville* adaptation is set in eighteenth century Seville, Spain. Count Almaviva, using the name of Lindoro, desperately wants a rendezvous with the beautiful Rosina, an orphan raised under the guardianship of Dr. Bartolo, at whose residence she lives and studies. In the street outside the Bartolo house at night, Lindoro stands anxiously awaiting Rosina's appearance at a bedroom window above. He has a chance encounter with Figaro first, a barber and his former servant, now in the employ of Bartolo. Rosina comes to the window, and when Bartolo begins to pull her away, she drops a letter. The jealous Bartolo, who has arranged a secret wedding on the following day with Rosina—without informing her—hurries after it, while Rosina signals Lindoro to fetch it. When Figaro learns of Lindoro's romantic intentions, he offers to help him by disguising his former employer as a drunken soldier.

Act Two. Inside the Bartolo house, Figaro slips a sleeping potion to one servant and a sneezing potion to another. He then goes to Rosina's room to do Lindoro's romantic bidding. But he must hide when he recognizes the voice outside as that of Bartolo, who attempts to learn from his two drugged servants—to no avail—who may have entered the house while he was outside looking for the dropped letter. Don Basilio, Rosina's music teacher, enters now to warn Bartolo that Almaviva is in town, and he suggests that he must smear his rival's character.

Having overheard Bartolo's intrigues, Figaro apprises Rosina of them, including his plans to marry her. Almaviva arrives posing as a tipsy soldier, but reveals his identity as Lindoro to Rosina and hands her a letter. He also gives Bartolo a document, asking that soldiers be afforded lodging for the night. Rosina surreptitiously hands Almaviva a letter wrapped in a handkerchief, and Bartolo gradually becomes suspicious of the masquerade. Rosina is becoming overwrought under the circumstances, wishing to be free of Bartolo's overprotective antics.

Act Three. Almaviva adopts a new disguise, posing as Alonso, a student of Basilio, paying a visit to give Rosina a music lesson, since his master is too ill to teach her. The ruse succeeds and Almaviva tells Rosina in her room he will return for her in the evening and enter via the bedroom window, having obtained a purloined key to it from Figaro. Basilio arrives, and his presence threatens to spoil the elopement plans. However, everyone tells him he is sick; bewildered by their claims, he departs, half-believing he is ill. Figaro then gives Bartolo a shave to take the escape-plotting Almaviva and Rosina out of his view.

Act Four. As Rosina waits at her window for the arrival of Almaviva, Bartolo seizes her and displays a letter proving that Alonso was a fraud, sent by Almaviva. Rosina falls under the misapprehension that Lindoro was deceitful to her and thus consents to marry Bartolo. But Almaviva soon arrives via the window and divulges his identity to her. The two embrace lovingly, but when they attempt to escape via the ladder used by Almaviva, Figaro informs them it has been taken away. With no other way out, the resourceful Almaviva bribes a notary to wed them quickly before the return of Bartolo. They are married and the opera ends happily. *—Robert Cummings*

Recommended:

- ○ **Paisiello: Il Barbiere di Siviglia** / Carella (cond.), Spagnoli, Orlandi, Consolini, Siragusa / 2002 / Dynamic 417/1-2

CONCERTO

Keyboard Concertos (ca. 1781–1788)

Paisiello produced eight keyboard concertos of modest dimensions, most of them ranging from 10 to 20 minutes. The first two, explicitly for harpsichord, were composed in Russia in the 1780s. Paisiello wrote the other six, he said, "expressly for the Infante Princess of Parma, afterwards Queen of Spain," specifying that the fortepiano could optionally be employed instead of harpsichord.

Paisiello penned his two Russian concertos before 1784 for specific pupils; the first, in C major, was for a lady-in-waiting to the empress known as Signora de Sinnavine, while the second, in F major, was for Grand Duchess Maria Feodorovna, wife of the heir apparent to the Russian throne. She was not a particularly advanced harpsichordist, as may be deduced from her concerto's rather simple solo part. Nevertheless, these two early concertos are among Paisiello's most substantial works in the form.

Concerto No. 1 in C major, like all Paisiello's concertos, follows the period's conventional fast-slow-fast, three-movement pattern. It uses formulaic structures but favors irregular phrase lengths and resists repeating material exactly the same way. Scales, arpeggios, and broken chords constitute the paltry technical challenges in the solo part. Similarly, the keyboard part of the *Concerto No. 2 in F major* demands little more than the ability to play scales and broken octaves, and is written in short phrases answered by the orchestra, thus not taxing the soloist's endurance.

These works and their successors all cast the first movements in rudimentary sonata-allegro form, with the development sections overshadowed by the expositions and recapitulations. Paisiello always made a provision for a cadenza, but wrote only the cadenza for the F major concerto. Slow movements may be in binary, tripartite, or rondo form, but all display Paisiello's lyricism to best advantage and are the works' primary points of interest today. The finales are usually rondos, but are sometimes sonata movements.

Paisiello probably wrote the last six concertos between 1784 and 1788, but evidently not for the princess herself to play; here, the solo parts would have been far too difficult for her. Not only is the keyboard work more demanding than in the Russian concertos, calling for more sustained passagework and greater digital dexterity, but Paisiello makes more colorful use of the small orchestra and is more willing to try chromatic harmonies. Also, the melodies here tend to be more memorable than anything in the earlier pair, except for the main tune of the first concerto's rondo. *—James Reel*

Recommended:

- ○ **Paisello: Complete Piano Concertos** / Gonley (cond.), Monetti, English CO / 1996 / ASV 229

Giovanni Pierluigi da Palestrina

b. ca. 1525, Palestrina [?], Italy, **d.** Feb. 2, 1594, Rome, Italy

Composer: Choral

It can be difficult to separate myth from reality in the life of Giovanni Pierluigi da Palestrina. He was one of the most highly acclaimed musicians of the sixteenth century, but was not the "Savior of Church Music." He did write a tremendous number of musical works, refining the very musical style of his time. He did not single-handedly transmit The Way to Write Spiritual Music, but apparently he was a diligent and reasonably pious family man, hard-nosed in his business dealings and savvy in manipulating professional contacts. He was not a priest, though he once considered Holy Orders after losing a wife and two sons to the plague. The balance and elegant moderation of his music may derive more from conservative melodic and harmonic style than from divine mediation. But centuries after his death, Palestrina's music is still actively serving devotional needs across the world, and echoes of his first biographer's awe still cling to his name. Palestrina's life is generally well documented: he spent all of his career around Rome, working in churches with good archival records. His exact birth date remains unknown, but his age at death is given in a famous eulogy. Whether he was born in Rome or in the provincial town of Palestrina, "Gianetto" received his first musical training in Rome as choir boy at Santa Maria Maggiore by 1537. In 1544, he accepted a post as organist for the Cathedral of Palestrina. While there, he married Lucrezia Gori and met the future Pope Julius III (whom Palestrina honored with the dedication of his *First Book of Masses*). He returned to Rome in 1551, serving as Master of the Boys for the Vatican's Capella Giulia and then, at Pope Julius' instigation, singing in the Sistine Chapel. Fired by a later Pope because of his marital status, he quickly became choirmaster for Saint John Lateran (a job previously held by Lasso). The 1560s were a time of great professional development for Palestrina: He served the basilica of Santa Maria Maggiore, the Seminario Romano and the wealthy Cardinal Ippolito d'Este, published four more books of music, and turned down an offer to become chapelmaster for the Holy Roman Emperor. His last professional appointment was a long tenure (1571–94) as master of the Capella Giulia in St. Peter's. In addition, he performed freelance work for at least 12 other Roman churches and institutions, managed his second wife's fur business, and invested in Roman real estate. Palestrina marketed his immense compositional output in nearly 30 published collections during his lifetime; many more of his roughly 700 works survive in manuscripts. He is best known for the 104 masses, though he composed in every other liturgical genre of his day, as well as nearly 100 madrigals. The polished reserve of his style helped fuel the myth first published in 1607 that his *Pope Marcellus Mass* was written to save polyphony from banishment in the church; the German theorist Fux enthroned his style for centuries to come in his 1725 *Gradus ad parnassum*. *—Timothy Dickey*

Overview of Works (1550–1594)

Giovanni Pierluigi da Palestrina was the most important composer of sacred music in the sixteenth century, and the Roman Church regards him as the greatest composer of liturgical music in its history. To say that Palestrina's output was prolific is an understatement—it is immense.

However, considering the size of Palestrina's output (within a limited range of forms), surprisingly little of it is familiar. He is best known for just a few works—the *Missa Papae Marcelli* and *Missa Assumpta est Maria*, his setting of Psalm 136 (*Super flumina Babylonis*), the motet *Tu es Petrus*, 29 motets belonging to a cycle after the Song of Songs, and his Lamentation cycles. But for all their fame, these few works cannot eclipse the rest of the composer's work in its quality; Palestrina's output shows very little variance in this respect, although it does go through subtle changes in style and approach.

Palestrina's largest, and most deservedly famous body of work is his 104 masses, the majority of which were published in 13 volumes issued between 1554 and 1601 (a few more are extant in manuscript sources). Of those published, more than half first appeared in the years following Palestrina's death. Conversely, Palestrina's motets, more than 300 in number and all sacred, appeared mainly during his lifetime. These were published in seven volumes between 1563 and 1595; the volume containing the "Song of Songs" cycle appeared in 1584. Related to the motet cycle are 72 hymn-settings, most appearing in a single volume in 1589. Two volumes of litanies published in 1593 have been lost, however 11 such settings have been found in other publications and in manuscripts. His Lamentations, encompassing four or five complete settings of the text, appeared in 1588. Likewise Palestrina's 35 Magnificat settings, appearing in 1591, include three to five settings of the Magnificat for each "Tone" (psalm tones with formulae for chanting that were later conflated with the modes for polyphonic usage). Palestrina's offertories, 68 in number, mostly debuted in a volume published in 1593, rounding out Palestrina's work in exclusively sacred genres.

Two sets of instrumental pieces attributed to Palestrina are doubtful, so for Palestrina's secular music we must turn to his madrigals; like the masses they number 104. These appeared in four dedicated volumes between 1555 and 1594, and were scattered throughout other editions of the era, none appearing past 1596. Palestrina's first book of madrigals was considered a source of embarrassment for the composer, and it seems to have disappeared without a trace. Most hold that they are inferior to the efforts of Lassus and others working within this field of endeavor in the late Renaissance. Nonetheless, a minority view holds that Palestrina's secular madrigals are stylistically secure within their own idiom and deserve revival. Palestrina augmented his secular madrigals with 49 sacred works within the genre, including his famous setting of *Vergine bella*. *—Uncle Dave Lewis*

Recommended:

- ○ **Renaissance Masterpieces** / Higginbottom (cond.), New College Choir Oxford / Brilliant 99937/4
- ○ **Palestrina: Lamentation of Jeremiah the Prophet** / Turner (cond.), Pro Cantione Antiqua / Brilliant 971124
- ○ **Palestrina: Offertoria** / Marlow (dir.), Trinity College Choir / 2001 / Gmn.com 115

CHORAL

Canticis canticorum (Motets Book IV) (1584)

We can usually only guess at what criteria Giovanni Pierluigi da Palestrina used when deciding which of his sacred Latin motets to include in the five or six various published volumes of motets that appeared during his lifetime and which to let sit on the shelf, so to speak (fewer than half of his 375 or so motets were printed during his lifetime). In the case of the *Motettorum liber quartus* (Motets, Book 4) published in Rome by Alessandro Gardano in 1584, however, there is no difficulty at all in finding the thread that binds the individual motets together as a single cycle of liturgical music and which makes their compilation immediately understandable: each of these 29 five-voice pieces is a setting of text from the *Canticum Canticorum*, or Song of Songs, that most unusual and apparently worldly book of the Old Testament.

The motets themselves are stunning examples of their breed, displaying the balance of line and refined symmetry of design so much a part of the composer's personal style while at the same time seeming quite a bit more energetic and outgoing in tone than one normally expects from this most "serious" of liturgical composers.

Palestrina himself describes the energetic, bustling quality of the Song of Songs motets in his dedication, explaining that the nature of the text involved demands such treatment. Each of the motets is set usually SATTB, but occasionally SSATB or AATTB. Generally speaking, the Song of Songs motets are more compact in both design and gesture than the typical Renaissance motet; one should listen for large, single-stroke musical designs (not divided into a Prima and a Secunda pars) whose counterpoint spins more or less continuously from start to finish and whose phrases only occasionally fail to overlap one another. Repetition of text is kept to a bare minimum by Renaissance standards.

The *Motettorum liber quartus* may or may not have been a bona fide gesture of repentance at having indulged in the world of secular madrigal; in either case, Palestrina certainly employs a recognizably madrigalian idiom in the book. Text-paintings abound, as at the start of motets Nos. 15, 16, and 18 (Surge propera; Surge amica mea; Surgam et circuibo), each of which begins with the word "arise" and whose opening imitation aptly reflects the fact. The rapidity with which Palestrina shifts expressive gears from phrase to phrase owes perhaps more to Palestrina's familiarity with, and enjoyment of, high secular art, as it does to any intrinsic quality of the *Canticum Canticorum*. *—Blair Johnston*

Recommended:

- ○ **Palestrina: Canticum canticorum** / Turner (dir.), Pro Cantione Antiqua / 1994 / Hyperion 66733
- ○ **Palestrina: Canticum canticorum; madrigals** / Hillier (dir.), Hilliard Ens. / 1994 / Virgin 61168

Missa Aeterna Christi munera, for 4 voices (1590)

This late mass presents Palestrina at the height of his creative powers. Scored for four voices, with the usual addition of an extra voice (in this case a second tenor) for the final movement, this brief, concise mass is characterized throughout by the simplicity and clarity of the vocal writing, as well as the fluency and charm of its melodic lines. The purity, delicacy, and balance of the part-writing have been likened to that of a string quartet.

Aeterna Christi munera is of the "paraphrase" type, meaning that a short phrase of plainsong (such as a hymn or an antiphon from the Catholic liturgy) provides the melodic basis on which the work is constructed. Motifs) are extracted from this melody and used as points of imitation throughout the mass. Moreover, the structure of the hymn verse (ABCA) is reflected in the structure of individual mass movements as well.

The shorter movements (Kyrie, Sanctus, Benedictus, Agnus Dei) use imitation, where a melodic fragment is repeated by all the voices in succession, to develop the motifs borrowed from the paraphrased hymn-tune into a complex, florid counterpoint. A simpler homophonic texture prevails in the longer movements (Gloria, Credo), as was typical of Palestrina's late works.

Palestrina also distances himself from his Franco-Flemish predecessors by his suave, flowing melodies, which contrast sharply with the more angular melodic contours favored by earlier composers. As well, the mass shows unending melodic inventiveness: themes are transformed and renewed from one movement to the next, providing the work with a sense of unity imbued with freshness. Palestrina makes good use of the sense of architectural balance acquired from the earlier composer Josquin, using repetition and reprise to structure the movements, for example, structuring the tripartite Kyrie with cadences in F, C, and F again.

The mass contains a few examples of the technique of word-painting. Particularly striking are his use of the low register to represent death at the words "Crucifixus" and "vivos et mortuos," while a dance-like triple rhythm animates the "Et spiritum"; more subtly, Palestrina expands the second motif of the hymn-tune into a very expressive melody which recurs with every allusion to the Saviour. *—Natalie Boisvert*

Recommended:

- ○ **Palestrina: Missa Aeterna Christi Munera; Missa L'Homme Arme** / Brown (dir.), Pro Cantione Antiqua / Brilliant 971148
- ○ **Palestrina: Missa Aeterna Christi Munera; motets** / O'Donnell (cond.), Westminster Cathedral Choir / 1986 / Hyperion 66490

Missa Brevis, for 4 voices (1570)

In a long and productive life serving the Catholic Church, Giovanni Pierluigi da Palestrina produced well over 100 settings of the mass Ordinary. They were fully published in six books during his lifetime, and a further six posthumous editions. His truly immense output of Catholic worship music includes highly polished examples of every type of mass composition known to his time. Sixteenth and seventeenth century musicians especially remembered Palestrina for his more than 50 contributions to the so-called "parody" mass genre; theorist Pietro Cerone in 1613 issued a set of "rules" for mass composition based on Palestrina's practice. Fewer of Palestrina's chant-based masses survive, with only six examples of "free" masses—those not composed with any known, preexistent model. Yet it is in the masses thus unfettered by preconceived melodies in which Palestrina's own musical fantasy may shine brightest. The four-voiced *Missa Brevis* from his *Third Book of Masses* (1570) provides an excellent example.

Palestrina's *Missa Brevis* is often compared to the *Missa Papae Marcelli*, his most famous free mass. In both pieces, the composer executed an elegantly coherent musical plan despite the absence of preexistent structure (both pieces also share music, strengthening the comparison). The five movements of the *Missa Brevis* are linked by a common mode—the rich sounds of F mode with B flat—and by repeated motives and musical gestures. The Kyrie begins with a sevenfold opening imitation, contrasts a new melody for the Christe, and then closes with a motive similar to the first; the bassus voice caps the movement with an extended, downward melodic sequence. In the Gloria movement, Palestrina introduces textural constrasts, carefully balancing chordal and imitative textures. The lengthy text passes quickly with much syllabic writing and "telescoping"; the only repetition comes at the end, once again with a bass sequence. The Credo features balanced alternations between duo, trio, and full four-voiced textures, with a striking chordal homophony at the heart: *Et incarnatus est*. Yet again a bass sequence marks the end. It is in the Sanctus that Palestrina quotes the same chant melody (from the *Gregorian Mass XV*) as in the *Missa Papae Marcelli*; the movement's opening also resembles the melismatic Sanctus of that mass. He rounds out the mass cycle with two Agnus Dei settings; the second canonically expands the vocal texture by adding a second superius voice. To finish on an aspirant note, the very last concluding sequence arrives in this canonic upper pair. *—Timothy Dickey*

Recommended:

- ○ **Giovanni Pierluigi da Palestrina** / Phillips (dir.), Tallis Scholars / Gimell 454890
- ○ **Palestrina: Missa Papae Marcelli; Missa Brevis** / Hill (cond.), Westminster Cathedral Choir / Hyperion 66266

Missa De Beata Virgine II, for 6 voices (1570)

One of the examples of Palestrina's ability to transform the melodies of plainsong into fresh and vital musical themes that entirely suit his own characteristic contrapuntal demands is the six-voice *Missa de beata Virgine*, published in his 1570 collection of masses titled *Missarum liber tertius*. The work is a paraphrase mass, taking chants from masses I, IX and XVII as laid out in the *Liber Usualis* collection of plainsong and weaving them into a newly composed polyphonic structure. The *Missa de beata Virgine* (which should not be confused with Palestrina's 1567 four-voice work by the same title), is so called because it employs liturgical melodies only used on the feast day of the same name.

The usual five major sections of the Mass Ordinary are all present. In the original version of the mass, Palestrina incorporated two Marian tropes—"Mariam gubernans" and "Mariam coronans"—into the text. The reform-minded Council of Trent, however, expunged both of these tropes from the official liturgy, and Palestrina, in a 1599 reissue, replaced the forbidden text with simple repetitions of the traditional mass texts around them.

The traditional Dorian-mode Kyrie chant for the Beata Virgine festival is in full six-voice imitation at the beginning of the movement. Four voices only are required for the following Christe. Palestrina cleverly combines the melodies of Kyrie I and Christe at the beginning of the second Kyrie: a three-layered contrapuntal structure built of two Christe motives and a single Kyrie motive is shifted about between the voices. Halfway through, a new fragment of plainchant sneaks in, undergoes imitative treatment, and then finds a home, in even, very chantlike whole notes, in the second tenor.

The Gloria is set, as per tradition, in two halves (divided at the text "Qui tollis peccata mundi"); during the second of these there is a brief but colorful change from binary to ternary rhythm. During the Credo, this same mechanism is employed to help convey the essence of the text "and rose again on the THIRD day"; the texture, appropriately, thins to three voices. The extensive Credo text is divided into three portions, each of which ends with a substantial cadence.

The Sanctus is divided into three (or, if you count the appended Benedictus, four) sections, alternating between six-and four-voice textures. Here the ancient cantus firmus technique is given new life, as the traditional Sanctus plainchant is given in whole and half notes (against an imitative background that sets the same basic intervalic material to much freer rhythmic values) by first the second tenor, then the first tenor (in the four-voice second section, beginning with the text "Plenisunt coeli"), and then the second tenor again as the six voices all cry "Hosanna in excelsis deo." During the Benedictus, the alto is given a chance to carry the cantus firmus. Having begun a cantus-firmus style, Palestrina is loathe to quit it, and during both the Agnus Dei I and Agnus Dei II the second tenor gives the traditional chant melody in long note-values. *—Blair Johnston*

Recommended:

- ○ **Palestrina: Missa Ave Maria; Missa Beata Virgine** / O'Donnell (cond.), Westminster Cathedral Choir / 1990 / Hyperion 66364

Missa Hodie Christus natus est, for 8 voices (1601)

Giovanni Pierluigi da Palestrina literally set the compositional standard for a generation of musicians. His over 100 surviving masses not only established a stylistic norm for "serious" church music (music "*alla Palestrina*"), but his techniques of parody or imitation would be emulated for generations. A famous Italian music theorist in 1613 wrote a manual for the composition of masses in imitation of a motet; he overtly derived his theory from the practice of Palestrina. This is not to imply, however, that Palestrina's "parody" masses are formulaic. In a piece such as his *Missa Hodie Christus natus est*, Palestrina willfully flaunts his own compositional principles to craft a singular and most effective cycle.

Palestrina modeled his *Missa Hodie Christus natus est*, or "Christmas Mass," on his own eight-voiced motet setting of the Christmas antiphon. In his motet, he opposes a high and a low choir in musical antiphony; each phrase of the motet passes from one to the other. Though brief, it also features distinctive melismas that cascade through each voice in a choir, and a joyous triple-meter section at the close. The composer retains these features in the parody mass, extending them to much grander proportions. It is in his extensions, and the departures from his usual practice, where Palestrina's mature genius shows in the mass.

A standard parody mass might begin each movement with the motive that also opens the model, and concludes each with music from its closing; musical motives from inside the motet judiciously appear throughout the internal moments. But Palestrina here is working with a much shorter model and must exercise greater creativity. Indeed, the first three movements open with music strongly reminiscent of the beginning of the motet *Hodie Christus natus est*. The most common textures throughout the mass, furthermore, are the same antiphonal alternations between the two choirs, often punctuated by the characteristic melismas. And most movements close with distinctive triple-meter music. But Palestrina boldly abandons the model's headmotive in both the Sanctus and Agnus Dei; these two both begin with similarly lush new imitative textures on a rising motive. He uses his freedom to manipulate internal textures, giving aurally striking arrivals on, for instance, the "One Holy and Catholic Church." Both this emphasis, and the generally crystalline clarity of the text-setting, suggest the deeply Catholic Palestrina was composing the *Missa Hodie Christus natus est after* the Council of Trent. *—Timothy Dickey*

Recommended:

- ○ **Palestrina & Lassus: Masses** / Summerly (cond.), Oxford Schola Cantorum / 1993 / Naxos 550836
- ○ **Christmas Mass in Rome** / McCreesh (cond.), Gabrieli Consort & Players / 1993 / Archiv 437833

Missa Papae Marcelli, for 6 voices (1567)

Arguably Palestrina's best-known work, this mass owes its formidable reputation to an oft-repeated legend, according to which Catholic authorities, overwhelmed by the spiritual beauty and dignity of this piece, reversed a proposed ban on the use of music during religious services. Without the *Missa Papae Marcelli*, the legend continues, sacred music would have ceased to exist after the sixteenth century. The true story is somewhat less dramatic. While a total ban on church music was never seriously considered, Catholic authorities were indeed concerned with the growing secularization and excessive complexity of liturgical music. In 1555, Pope Marcellus II (after whom the mass is named) addressed the Papal choir, urging musicians to strive for simplicity, clarity, and intelligibility in their compositions. Marcellus' recommendations became official policy with the pronouncements of the Council of Trent concerning music, in 1562 and 1563. There is no doubt that *Palestrina* heard and heeded Marcellus' recommendations. In fact, a Commision of Cardinals, which worked in 1564 and 1565 to enforce the Council's decisions regarding music, knew Palestrina's music. It is quite significant that one of the Commission's members was the powerful Cardinal Carlo Borromeo, archbishop of Milan, who had an exceptional understanding of Palestrina's work. The composer himself states explicitly, in the preface to the *Second Book of Masses* (published in 1567, which contains the *Missa Papae Marcelli*) that these masses are written in a "new style" to please "the most serious and religious-minded persons in high places." This "new" style, inaugurated with and most self-consciously evident in the *Missa Papae Marcelli*, originates, essentially, from the very source of Catholic music, plainchant. Palestrina eliminated from his sacred music practically all references to popular song, using instead motivic material extracted from plainchant melodies, and developing a style of vocal writing which owed much to the melodic structure of plainsong. The result was music of great unity, clarity, and beauty, based on the Church's time-honored monophonic repertoire. Nowhere in Palestrina's enormous output are Marcellus' musical ideals more obviously realized. The piece is singularly austere and dignified, darkly colored through an emphasis on low voices. The contrapuntal motion is slow and exquisitely controlled, the proportions architecturally conceived. The movements with longer texts (Gloria, Credo) are written homophonically, that is, moving all the voices together in stately chords. This novel technique, which effectively emphasized the words while providing a welcome contrast to the more contrapuntally active polyphonic movements, proved so effective that it became a standard feature of all his later masses. Despite its restrained style, the mass is not without remarkable highlights. Beautifully controlled dissonant clashes lend the Kyrie a touching poignancy, while the Christe and Sanctus foreshadow the suave melodic writing characteristic of later works. The lush, cascading "Amen" at the end of the Credo remains one of the most beautiful passages of sixteenth century polyphony. *—Natalie Boisvert*

Recommended:

- ○ **Allegri: Miserere** / Phillips (dir.), Tallis Scholars / 2001 / Gimell 339
- ○ **Palestrina: Missa Papae Marcelli; Stabat Mater; motets** / Turner (cond.), Pro Cantione Antiqua / 1992 / ASV 6086
- ○ **Palestrina: Missa Papae Marcelli; Allegri: Miserere** / Preston (cond.), Westminster Abbey Choir / Archiv 415517

Missa Sine nomine, for 6 voices (1590)

During the early 1590s, Giovanni Pierluigi da Palestrina (or, more likely, his publisher) added two further works to a collection of masses—his *Liber primus*—that had originally been published in 1554. The first of the two additional masses added in the 1591 edition is the well-known *Missa pro defunctis*, or *Requiem Mass*, while the second is a six-voice work that goes by the title *Missa sine nomine* (not to be confused with the composer's many four- and five-voice masses by the same name). The *Missa sine nomine* is a parody mass, each of its sections taking a preexisting polyphonic set of motives and themes as a starting point; the source of these underlying melodic fragments seems to be an anonymous motet titled *Cantabo Domine*. While it is possible that the mass had been in existence for some time before the 1591 publication, it seems far more likely that the work, like its companion the *Missa pro defunctis*, had only recently been composed. (The mass also appears in the 1591 reissue of the *Liber quintus*, originally published in 1590.)

The usual Kyrie, Gloria, Credo, Sanctus (with Benedictus), and Agnus Dei are present. As per tradition, the opening Kyrie is cast in three sections. The six voices enter in two groups of three, the bottom three setting up a three-layered, subtly imitative structure that the others will duplicate—this basic polyphonic cell, drawn from the *Cantabo Domine* motet, recurs throughout the movements. The texture is thinned to just four voices for the following Christe, while a brief try at homophony ushers in the second Kyrie eleison. Soon the rising filled-in fifth motive that appeared three times (more if we count rhythmic alterations) in the first Kyrie returns in full imitative regalia.

The first line of the Gloria text (and, for that matter, the Credo text) is not set to music, as the singers would normally be expected to chant it as a kind of introduction to the polyphony. The Gloria falls into two sections of nearly equal length. The same motivic layers that began the Kyrie are at work here and that the bass entry is again imitated by an upper voice.

These same two generative ideas are brought back to begin the lengthy, four-section Credo (laid out in 6, 4, 4, and 6 voices). The second section (beginning with the text "Crucifixus etiam pro nobis") makes striking use of the filled-in fifth that appeared to such good effect in the second Kyrie; the idea is again initiated by the bass.

A comparison of the opening gesture of the Sanctus to those of the previous three sections reveals just how flexibly Palestrina can deploy the same basic material. The appended Benedictus begins with a wonderfully drawn-out imitation of the upper neighbor-note idea.

Palestrina provides polyphony for the two traditional Agnus Deis, the first setting the text "Lamb of God, who takes away the sins of the world: have mercy upon us," the second replacing the final four words with the plea, "Grant us peace." *—Blair Johnston*

Recommended:

- ○ **Palestrina: Missa sine nomine; Missa L'homme armé; 3 Motets** / Vartolo (cond.), Bologna Capella Musicale di S. Petronio / 1996 / Naxos 553314

Missa Tu es Petrus, for 6 voices (1572)

Over half of Palestrina's masses are parodies of a musical model. Often the model is one of his own motets, as with the *Missa Tu es Petrus*, on a motet of the same name. His parody masses are placed among the best of his works, particularly those based on his own music. *Missa Tu es Petrus*, although underrecorded, has been enthusiastically written about. Palestrina was a highly economical composer whose constructive techniques were already based on repetition, recycling, and reuse, so it's not a shock that the technique of parody worked so well for him when applied to his own music. The qualities of Palestrina's music that are most impressive come through clearly in this Mass: unity, balance, a richness of surface detail, conceptual lucidity.

Palestrina's use of imitation isn't as clear-cut as his predecessors: he likes to simultaneously introduce and develop several points. But because his material is so straightforward and because the pace and manner of development are so lucid, it is much easier to follow him than it can be with other composers. A particular form of regularity he thankfully avoids is metrical regularity. Because his music is built from the inside, as it were, in the rhythmic units of the line rather than being driven by a metrical engine, it rarely falls into predictable metrical patterns. This also helps account for the tremendous effect it has, as the lack of the metric regularity makes the music feel like it comes from a yet more remote source. The music also resonates because of his careful harmonic planning. It is considered a modal, pretonal music, but that doesn't mean it won't submit to scrutiny within the tonal system. In fact, the V–I and the IV–V chordal motions that produce much of the sense of direction and structural meaning in tonal music emerge as key structural principles in Palestrina's music. Palestrina's style has virtually become a stand-in for sacred-sounding music, partly because his was the last generation of composers dedicated to a purely contrapuntal style. His own stylistic aim seems to have been to sum up and bring to a peak of refinement and clarity the accomplishments of those who came before him. *Missa Tu es Petrus* is one of those works where that aim is most perfectly achieved. *—Donato Mancini*

Recommended:

- ○ **Palestrina: 5 Masses** / Cleobury (dir.), King's College Choir / 1998 / Decca 458386

Missa Ut re mi fa sol la, for 6 voices (1570)

Also called the *Hexachord Mass*, this work for six voices (SSAATB) is named for the melody on which the composition is based. The hexachord was a six-note scale (ut re mi fa sol la), identical to the first six notes of the modern major scale, which functioned, much like the modern scales in tonal theory, as the theoretical and pedagogical foundation of sixteenth century music. That such a piece could be constructed from the most basic musical material testifies to the cleverness and ingenuity of its composer.

It has been suggested that Palestrina published this piece (in 1570) to silence his critics, who contended that he had adopted a new, simpler style because he was incapable of writing in the very popular but highly complex Franco-Flemish manner (in fact, Palestrina had simplified his compositional style in response to the Pope's criticism of excessively ornamented liturgical music). The contrapuntal wizardry of the *Hexachord Mass* rivals that of any Franco-Flemish masterpiece.

Ut re mi fa sol la is a cantus firmus mass. One voice intones the melody in long notes, like pedal-tones, around which a counterpoint is developed. The short movements (Kyrie, Sanctus, Agnus) follow the tradition most closely, with angular melodies and a thick texture constructed of short scale fragments playfully and artfully combined in varying note values. The Sanctus especially is a complex labyrinth of ascending and descending fragments, superimposed in ever-changing ways like pieces of a dazzling rhythmic puzzle.

Despite the heavy debt to Franco-Flemish contrapuntal techniques, Palestrina's individuality shines throughout the mass. The Gloria and Credo are primarily homophonic, in keeping with his new style, and the composer takes many liberties with the cantus firmus: rather than disposing it in long notes of equal value, as was the trend, Palestrina freely alters its note values to integrate it more fully into the overall texture of the piece. And, as always, Palestrina's unequaled mastery of vocal grouping comes through, buttressing the brilliance of the contrapuntal writing with a frequent emphasis on bright upper voices. *—Natalie Boisvert*

Recommended:

- ○ **Palestrina: Missa Ut, re, mi, fa, sol, la; etc.** / Jackson (cond.), Chorus of the Studio of Ancient Music, Montreal / Analekta 23120
- ○ **Palestrina: Missa Ut re mi fa sol la; Missa Hodie Christus; motets** / Loehrer (cond.) / 1999 / Nuova Era 1241

Paolo Pandolfo

Gambist, Viol Player

Paolo Pandolfo is one of Europe's leading exponents of the viola da gamba. In 1979, after studies at the Rome Conservatory, he co-founded (with Rinaldo Alessandrini and Enrico Gatti) la Stravaganza. In 1981, he moved to Basel, Switzerland, where he began collaborating with gambist Jordi Savall and his ensemble Hespèrion XX. In 1989, Pandolfo was named professor of viola da gamba at the Schola Cantorum Basiliensis, one of the leading centers for training early music performers. Since 1992, he has directed the viol consort Ensemble di viole Labyrinto, with which he has toured internationally. *—Robert Adelson*

Recommended:

- ○ **Bach: Sonates pour viole de gambe et clavecin** / Pandolfo, Alessandrini / HM 1955218
- ○ **Marais: Grand Ballet** / Pandolfo, Meyerson, Balestracci / 2002 / Glossa 920406
- ○ **Vivaldi: Concerti Per Archi** / Alessandrini, Naddeo, Biondi, Onofri, Pandolfo, Italiano Concerto / Tactus 67220101
- ○ **Marais: Le Labyrinthe & autre hitoires...** / Pandolfo, Meyerson, Estevan, Mulder, Fresno / 2000 / Glossa 920404

Rolando Panerai

b. Oct. 17, 1924, Campi Bisenzio, Italy

Baritone

Italian baritone Rolando Panerai has had one of the most durable of singing careers, mainly in supporting roles. His career lasted over half a century, beginning with his appearance at Naples in 1947 in Rossini's *Mosè*. He joined the roster at La Scala in 1951 after debuting in *Samson et Dalila*. He sang performances of the title role of *Falstaff* and the part of Dr. Dulcamara in *L'Elisir d'Amore* in 2001.

He studied in Florence with Frazzi and in Milan with Giulia Tess. In his debut year of 1947 he also sang Luna, Giorgio Germont, and Rossini's Count Almaviva. Another of his best-known roles is Ford in *Falstaff*, which was he debut role in the Salzburg Festival of 1957.

He frequently collaborated in performance and recording with conductor Herbert von Karajan, who brought out Panerai's best work. He sang in the Italian premiere of Hindemith's *Mathis der Maler* in 1957.

He recorded *Così fan tutte*, *Falstaff*, and *La Bohème* twice, and also appeared in recordings of *Cavalleria rusticana*, *I Puritani*, *Il Trovatore*, *Madama Butterfly*, *I Pagliacci*, *L'Elisir d'amore*, and *Lucia di Lamermoor*. *—Joseph Stevenson*

Recommended:

- ○ **Bellini: I Puritani** / Serafin (cond.), Callas, di Stefano, Panerai, Mercuriali, La Scala Theater Orch. / 2003 / EMI 85647
- ○ **Puccini: La Bohème** / Karajan (cond.), Freni, Pavarotti, Ghiaurov, Panerai, Berlin PO / 1987 / London 421049
- ○ **Verdi: La Traviata** / Ceccato (cond.), Gedda, Sills, Lloyd, Panerai, Royal PO / 1988 / EMI 69827

Gregorio Paniagua

b. Oct. 30, 1821, Tlalpujahua, Michoacan, Mexico, **d.** Nov. 2, 1882, Córdoba, Veracruz, Mexico

Conductor

Gregorio Paniagua was born in Madrid, where he studied cello at the Royal Conservatory with Don Ricardo Vivó. He later studied viola da gamba with August Wenzinger and conducting with Sergiu Celibidache. In addition to the viola da gamba, Paniagua performs on the vihuela, lute, and hurdy gurdy. In 1964, he founded the ensemble Atrium Musicae de Madrid, with which he has performed in Europe, America, Asia, and Australia. *—Robert Adelson*

Recommended:

- ○ **Musique de la Grèce Antique** / Paniagua (cond.), Madrid Atrium Musicae / HM 1951015
- ○ **Tarentule-Tarentelle** / Paniagua (cond.), Madrid Atrium Musicae / HM 190379
- ○ **La Spagna** / Paniagua (cond.), Madrid Atrium Musicae / 1980 / Bis 163
- ○ **La Folia** / Paniagua (cond.), Madrid Atrium Musicae / HM 901050

Paul Paray

b. May 24, 1886, Le Tréport, France, **d.** Oct. 10, 1979, Monte Carlo, Monaco
Conductor

In the 1950s, Mercury records established its musical reputation largely with two intense, exciting European conductors performing miracles in the American provinces: Antal Dorati in Minneapolis, and Paul Paray in Detroit. With the less potent Howard Hanson advocating American music in Rochester, Dorati took most of the Austro-German, Hungarian, and Russian repertory, with Paray treating the French literature as far more than leftovers. Paray's interpretations were generally faster and more sharply pointed than those of the period's two other great French conductors, Charles Münch and Pierre Monteux. His Mercury recordings are the high point of a long, distinguished career spent largely away from the world's most prominent podiums.

As a child, Paray studied with his father, a church musician, and at 17 he briefly served as a church organist in Rouen. France enjoyed a strong tradition of composer-organists, so perhaps it was inevitable that Paray entered the Paris Conservatory in 1904 as a composition student; in 1911, his cantata *Yanitza* earned him the Prix de Rome. Drafted during World War I, he was taken prisoner by the Germans and wrote a string quartet during his internment.

After the war, performing drew more of his attention than composing. He took a job conducting the orchestra of the Casino de Cauterets, and in 1920 made his Paris debut with the Lamoureux Orchestra as a last-minute substitution for André Caplet. Soon he became assistant conductor of the ensemble, and was named its principal conductor in 1923. In 1928 Paray took over the symphonic concert series in Monte Carlo; in 1932 he became conductor of the Concerts Colonne, a tenure he held until the Nazis temporarily disbanded the orchestra in 1940, and then again from 1944 to 1952. During the Second World War, he fled south and conducted in Monte Carlo and Marseilles.

Paray had made his U.S. debut in New York in 1939, and it would be in America that he achieved his greatest renown. In 1952 he was named music director of the Detroit Symphony Orchestra, where he remained until 1963. Though not one of the world's sleekest ensembles, the Detroit Symphony under Paray's hands became noted for its snap and fire, especially through the recordings it made for Mercury. These LPs focused largely on French music, although Paray acquitted himself admirably with other works, including a Schumann cycle. The recorded performances tended to be bracingly fast (especially the Saint-Saëns *"Organ" Symphony* and Franck *D minor Symphony*), yet Paray's phrasing was supple and witty, and the orchestra played with great precision, high energy, and light heart. For decades these 1950s recordings, particularly of Ravel and various light overtures, inspired great affection among collectors.

After his departure from Detroit and return to France, Paray continued to conduct sporadically. At the age of 91 he led a concert in Nice to celebrate Marc Chagall's 90th birthday, and at 92 he made his last American appearance, with the orchestra of the Curtis Institute of Music in Philadelphia.

Paray never solidly established himself as a composer, although he produced a number of substantial works before his Detroit appointment. These include two full symphonies (1935, 1940), sonatas for violin and cello, the ballet *Artémis troublée* (also performed as a symphonic poem under the title *Adonis troublé*), and a *Mass for the 500th Anniversary of the Death of Joan of Arc*, first performed in Rouen in 1931 and recorded in Detroit in 1956. His style was traditionally diatonic, and very much in the manner of the academically-oriented early twentieth century French composers, including D'Indy and his followers. *—James Reel*

Recommended:

- ○ **Paul Paray Conducts Dances of Death** / Paray (cond.), DSO / 1994 / Mercury 434336
- ○ **Paray & Saint-Saëns** / Paray (cond.), DSO / 1991 / Mercury 432719
- ○ **Suppé & Auber** / Paray (cond.), DSO / 1992 / Mercury 434309
- ○ **Chabrier & Roussel** / Paray (cond.), DSO / 1991 / Mercury 434303
- ○ **Ibert & Ravel** / Paray (cond.), DSO / 1990 / Mercury 432003

Christopher Parkening

b. Dec. 14, 1947, Los Angeles, CA
Guitarist

Christopher Parkening is one of the world's leading classical guitarists, with a particular interest in continuing the legacy of Andrés Segovia.

Parkening was inspired to play guitar by his cousin Jack Marshall, the former staff guitarist at MGM Studios. Marshall had two recommendations: learn classical technique in order to establish firm technical skills, and study the recordings of Segovia. Hearing Segovia's recordings convinced Parkening to continue within the classical tradition. Parkening began his studies with Pépe Romero, and at the age of 15 entered Segovia's master class at the University of California, Berkeley. He also studied musical interpretation with cellist Gregor Piatigorsky. His college education was at the University of Southern California. Since the school had no guitar faculty, Parkening studied cello, first with Gabor Rajto, then with Piatigorsky. At the end of his sophomore year the Music Department asked him to start teaching guitar, thus beginning the guitar studies program at USC. At the same time he began playing professionally, launching a rising career that would cause Segovia to proclaim that "Christopher Parkening is a great artist—he is one of the most brilliant guitarists in the world."

While harboring a disdain for traveling, Parkening played over 90 concerts a year with the primary purpose of early retirement in order to pursue his "real" passion: fly-fishing. In addition to his touring and teaching, he authored two volumes of *The Christopher Parkening Guitar Method*, as well as transcriptions of works by composers such as Debussy, Ravel, Bach, and Dowland. In accordance with his plan, in 1977 he bought a ranch in Montana and announced his retirement. Aside from a small amount of teaching at the University of Montana, he had nothing to do with music; he even quit regular practicing. After four years he found himself restless and unfulfilled. On a visit to California, a neighbor invited him to Grace Community Church where Rev. John MacArthur's sermon led Parkening to an intensive self-examination. Parkening realized that his discontent was due to the selfishness of his original goal, and the subsequent aimlessness of his life. He found the Biblical verse Corinthians 10:31: "Whatsoever ye do, do all to the glory of God" and recalled J.S. Bach's statement that "The aim and final reason of all music is none but the glory of God."

With Christianity as his inspiration he returned to playing, but now with the purpose of glorifying God. He sold his Montana ranch, despite warnings that it would be difficult to re-establish his career. Parkening has since performed around the world, including Carnegie Hall and the White House. His television appearances include the Grammy Awards, *The Tonight Show*, *The Today Show*, *Good Morning America*, and *20/20*. He has recorded over twenty albums, and earned two Grammy nominations in the category of Best Classical Recording. He continues to appear with all the major orchestras of the United States while maintaining an active recital career. Voted "Best Classical Guitarist" in a nationwide readers' poll of *Guitar Player Magazine* for many years, he was placed in their "Gallery of Greats" along with Andrés Segovia, John Williams, and Julian Bream. Parkening has received commendations honoring his dedication and artistry including an Honorary Doctorate of Music from Montana State University and the Outstanding Alumnus Award from the University of Southern California. Parkening was also given the acclaimed American Academy of Achievement Award for his excellence in music. He has also won the International Gold Cup Tarpon Tournament (the "Wimbledon" of fly-fishing). *—Joseph Stevenson*

Recommended:

- ○ **In The Spanish Style** / Parkening / EMI 47194
- ○ **Pleasures of Their Company** / Battle, Parkening / 1986 / Angel 47196
- ○ **Christopher Parkening Celebrates Segovia** / Parkening / 1998 / Angel 56730
- ○ **The Great Recordings** / Parkening / 1993 / EMI 54905

Parley of Instruments

f. 1979, London, England
Ensemble

In the crowded field of period instrument groups, the Parley of Instruments distinguishes itself by focusing on the repertoire for the early violin, from the Renaissance and early Baroque periods, and by applying its knowledge of this and seventeenth century vocal music to its performances of later Baroque and early Classical works. The ensemble was established in 1979 by Peter Holman, harpsichordist and organist, who remains the group's director. The other three performers who form the core of the ensemble are violinists Judy Tarling and Theresa Caudle and bass viol and cellist Mark Caudle. Depending on the program, as many as two dozen other performers are added to this core to form a full violin consort, giving it the flexibility to perform works by Praetorius, Lully, Biber, and Purcell, among others. It has even expanded to the size of a Classical period orchestra to make period instrument recordings of early nineteenth century English music. Catherine Bott, Michael Chance, Crispian Steele-Perkins, Elizabeth Wallfisch, and Paul O'Dette are just a few of the soloists who have appeared with the Parley. A recording of Cavalli's *Messa Concertata* with the vocal consort Seicento was the beginning of an examination of important seventeenth century pieces. The Parley's programs are concentrated on one aspect or type of music, for example, "Lachrimae and the Music It Inspired," "Couperin & Charpentier Motets," and "The Concerto in Georgian England." The programs are performed throughout England, in both concert and workshop forms and in BBC Radio broadcasts, and many of them have been recorded on the Hyperion label. The Parley combines its members' knowledge and skill to create a consistent performance style and to present early music for strings as it was first imagined. *—Patsy Morita*

Recommended:

- ○ **Consort Music by Peter Philips** / Holman (cond.), Parley of Instruments / 1988 / Hyperion 66240
- ○ **Biber: Sonatae Tam Aris, Quam Aulis Servientes** / Holman (cond.), Parley of Instruments / 2000 / Hyperion 55041
- ○ **Purcell: Ayres for the Theatre** / Holman (cond.), Parley of Instruments / 1999 / Hyperion 55010
- ○ **Locke: The Broken Consort** / Holman (cond.), Parley of Instruments / 1995 / Hyperion 66727
- ○ **Arne: Artaxerxes** / Goodman (cond.), Parley of Instruments / Hyperion 67051

Edward Parmentier

Harpsichordist

American harpsichordist Edward Parmentier obtained degrees in classical languages and literatures, humanities, and musicology at Harvard and Princeton, while studying harpsichord with Albert Fuller and Gustav Leonhardt. He has toured throughout the United States, Russia, Western Europe, Japan, and Korea playing both harpsichord and historic organs. His recordings include Bach's partitas, seventeenth century French harpsichord music, sonatas of Scarlatti, and music of the English virginalists. He is professor of harpsichord at the University of Michigan. *—Robert Adelson*

Recommended:

- ○ **Early Italian Harpsichord Music** / Parmentier / 2003 / Wildboar 8001
- ○ **Musick as Befitts a Quene 1650** / Parmentier / 1994 / Wildboar 9102
- ○ **Splendor of the Harpsichord** / Parmentier / 1997 / Wildboar 9606
- ○ **Bach: English Suites** / Parmentier / 2000 / Wildboar 9302

Andrew Parrott

b. Mar. 10, 1947, Walsall, England

Conductor

Andrew Parrott is an English conductor especially well known for his part in the early music movement, but also as a conductor of general repertory with an emphasis on modern music. At Oxford University he studied research methods into early music performance practices, specializing in the sixteenth and seventeenth centuries. He became a musical assistant to composer Sir Michael Tippett, himself one of the earliest British music figures of the twentieth century to develop a strong interest in Renaissance English music. Tippett was associated with the Bath Festivals and suggested that Parrott form a choir for Renaissance music performance at the 1973 festival. Following Tippett's suggestion, Parrott organized The Taverner Choir, named after John Taverner (ca. 1490–1545), a leading English composer of that era. The choir was a success, becoming an independent ensemble of its own. Subsequently, Parrott organized the Taverner Players and the Taverner Consort with the same musical emphasis. The Players or Consort often appear with the choir.

Parrott and the Taverner groups have built one of the leading reputations in Baroque and pre-Baroque music. They appeared at the 1977 Promenade Concerts in London in Monteverdi's *Vespers* and were the first to give a period instruments performance in London of Bach's *Mass in B minor.*

Parrott's career includes substantial work researching, writing, and lecturing on early music. His *The Essential Bach Choir* was published in 2000, and he was co-editor of the *New Oxford Book of Carols.* His activities also include a substantial amount of performing later repertory and has expanded to a sizeable involvement in opera. He has appeared with the Orchestra of the Age of Enlightenment, and has a close relationship with the Slovak Philharmonic and the Residentie Orchestra of The Hague. In 1989 he became artistic director of the Kent Opera and has conducted at La Scala, the Royal Swedish Opera at Drottningholm, and the Royal Opera House at Covent Garden, London. He is an active conductor of modern music, including works of Tippett, Tavener, Nono, Varèse, Britten, and Stravinsky, and premiered Judith Weir's *A Night at the Chinese Opera.* In 2000, he was named musical director and principal conductor of the London Mozart Players and in 2002 took on the same positions with the New York Collegium.

Before becoming an exclusive Sony Classics artist, Parrott recorded on the L'Oiseau-Lyre and Hyperion labels and on the EMI Reflexe and Virgin Veritas labels. *—Joseph Stevenson*

Recommended:

- ○ **Monteverdi: Vespro della Beata Vergine** / Parrott (cond.), Kirkby, Wistreich, Daniels, Cornwell, Taverner Consort, Choir & Players / 1992 / EMI 47078
- ○ **Tallis: Latin Church Music** / Parrott (cond.), Taverner Consort & Choir / 2003 / Virgin 562230
- ○ **Purcell: Hail! Bright Cecilia** / Parrott (cond.), Taverner Consort, Choir & Players / 1995 / Virgin 45160
- ○ **Gesualdo: Tenebrae Responses for Good Friday** / Parrott, Taverner Consort Choir / 2000 / Sony 62977
- ○ **Heart's Solace** / Parrott (cond.), Taverner Consort & Players / 1998 / Sony 60155

Sir Hubert Parry

b. Feb. 27, 1848, Bournemouth, England, **d.** Oct. 7, 1918, Knight's Croft, Rustington, England

Composer

The importance of Hubert Parry to the renaissance of English musical life is often underestimated, but like his equally great colleague in that endeavor, Sir Charles Villiers Stanford, Parry is more often found in music encyclopedias than on the programs of modern orchestras. His profound influence on generations of composers, exerted during his years as director of the Royal College of Music, qualifies him as a genuine paterfamilias to music in the British Isles.

Parry's family was distinguished. His father, Thomas Gambier Parry, was a director of the East India Company; Thomas' great-uncle was Lord Gambier, Admiral of the Fleet. Salt water was, as it were, in Parry's blood, and one of his lifelong favorite recreations was piloting his own seaworthy yacht.

Parry must have seemed unusually talented for a young man of his day. One summer while at Eton, Parry had to travel to Stuttgart in order to study composition with the English pedagogue Henry Hugo Pierson, who had left England for an artistic climate more congenial to his endeavors. While still at Eton, Parry earned the Oxford bachelor of music degree, subsequently entering Exeter College at Oxford. His marriage to Maude Herbert, sister of his school chum George Herbert, 13th Earl of Pembroke, forced him to seek nonmusical work with Lloyd's register in London while establishing himself as a composer, but it was while working in London that he met and allied himself with teacher and pianist Edward Dannreuther, who was a great influence on the young man, arranging for private performances of much of Parry's early chamber music, and introducing him to the music of Wagner by procuring for Parry tickets for the second ever performance at Bayreuth of the *Ring.* Dannreuther was the pianist at Parry's first public triumph, a performance of his *Piano Concerto in F sharp major* at the Crystal Palace in 1880.

Parry made his mark at the many choral society festivals throughout England, with 1880's *Scenes from Shelley's Prometheus Bound, Blest Pair of Sirens* (1887; to words of Milton), a setting of Milton's *L'allegro ed il penseroso* (1890), the oratorio *Job* (1892; considered by some to be his masterpiece of the 1890s), and the sublime *Invocation to Music,* with words by Robert Bridges (1895). In these works, Parry came up with a tangible English style, all the more noteworthy for its originality and wit.

Parry got in on the ground floor when it came to creating a viable musical education establishment for England, joining the staff of the Royal College of Music upon its opening in 1883. Eleven years later he succeeded Sir George Grove as the RCM's director. Parry also was Choragus at Oxford, beginning in 1883, and in 1900 took John Stainer's place as professor of music there. Parry wrote extensively and quite vigorously about music, in 1893's *The Art of Music, Style in Musical Art* (1911), and the unpublished *Instinct and Character.* He also wrote an excellent critical biography of J.S. Bach (1909), and was responsible for the third volume of the *Oxford History of Music,* Music of the Seventeenth Century.

Toward the end of his life, Parry was honored with knighthood and a baronetcy, as well as the genuine affection of the many composers who had benefited from his prescient and understanding way with helping his students find their own voices. In 1908, a breakdown of health forced Parry to retire from his administrative posts, but instead of causing a cessation creative activity, this crisis actually brought about what is frequently described as his "Indian summer," in which some of his very finest music was written. *—Mark Satola*

Overview of Works (1863–1915)

Sir Charles H.H. Parry, usually referred to as Hubert Parry, was central to the formation of the English school around the turn of the twentieth century. Yet, this post-Romantic composer is often remembered primarily as a teacher. Known by many music lovers only for his choral song *Jerusalem* (1916), Parry was versatile in his output, producing five symphonies (counting the *Symphonic Fantasia "1912"* as the fifth), a piano concerto, an opera, several oratorios and numerous choral works, church services in the Anglican liturgy and other sacred music, songs, chamber works, and piano and organ music.

If *Jerusalem* is Parry's most widely known work, not surprisingly the song genre has garnered the most attention for him. Another unison song, *England* (1916), has also achieved a measure of popularity. His vocal works in general began receiving attention in the latter half of the twentieth century, with the oratorio *Job* (1892) emerging as a major effort, perhaps a true masterpiece. A large work, conceived in four scenes for treble, tenor, baritone, and bass soloists, chorus, and orchestra, its many individual numbers feature brilliant vocal and choral writing, and a variety of expression. His *Blest Pair of Sirens,* for chorus and orchestra (1887), on texts by Milton, has also rightly received attention over the years.

Parry's cantata, *Scenes From Shelley's Prometheus Unbound,* for chorus and orchestra (1880), was his first choral effort and one of his most important early works, already showing his style nearing maturity, despite some obvious Wagnerian elements. His first sacred music efforts date back to an 1864 *Magnificat*, and include many anthems and hymns. It is an irony that Parry showed so much interest in this genre, since he rejected Christian teaching altogether.

His symphonies are all interesting works, with only the *Symphony No. 3 in C major "English"* (1889) receiving some currency in the decades following his death. In the 1990s, however, several recordings of the symphonies appeared, including an entire cycle of the five, resulting in renewed interest and reassessment. Still, solidly wrought though they are, one must stop short of calling them genuine masterpieces.

In the chamber music realm, Parry was quite active in the nineteenth century, but made few additions to his output thereafter. Three string quartets, three piano trios, a nonet (an experimental piece not performed in the composer's lifetime) and a quintet all come from his earlier years and failed to catch on. His *Sonata for Violin and Piano* (1899), however, has proven to have some appeal. Cast in three movements, with a fast-slow-fast pattern, this short work offers both excellent instrumental writing and thematic charm.

Parry's piano music comes largely from his early years and includes two sonatas (1877, 1878), which are an improvement on his Mendelssohn-flavored early efforts. Still, he failed to make a mark here. His organ music, however, largely coming near the end of his career, features some worthwhile compositions, including the second set of (7) *Chorale Preludes* (1916). *—Robert Cummings*

Recommended:

- ○ **I Was Glad** / Robinson (cond.), Judd, St. George Chapel Choir / 1988 / Hyperion 66273
- ○ **Parry: Complete Symphonies** / Bamert (cond.), London PO / 1992 / Chandos 9120
- ○ **Piano Music of Parry** / Jacobs / Priory 451
- ○ **Parry's English Lyrics** / Varcoe, Benson / Hyperion 67044
- ○ **Parry: Job - An Oratorio** / Bean (cond.), Birch, Davies, Coleman-Wright, Hitchcock, Spence, Royal PO / 1998 / Hyperion 67025
- ○ **Parry** / Bamert (cond.), London PO / 2000 / Chandos 6610
- ○ **The Wanderer** / Dobey / 1997 / Pro Organo 7059

Arvo Pärt

b. Sep. 11, 1935, Paide, Estonia

Composer: Choral, Orchestral, Chamber Music, Keyboard, Concerto

Arvo Pärt is one of the most important living composers of concert music. His first works, dating from the 1950s, showed the influence of Prokofiev and Shostakovich, as heard in his two Sonatinas for piano (1958). But as his musical studies under Heino Eller continued, he was drawn toward serial techniques and turned out a number of works in the 1960s in this vein. His First Symphony (1961), for instance, displays this method and is dedicated to Eller. By the end of that decade, Pärt had become disenchanted by the 12-tone technique and began writing music in varying styles. In 1976, however, Pärt started composing in what he called his tintinnabulation (or tintinnabuli) method, which involves the constant presence throughout the work of a lone unchanging triad. This new style resulted in music so radically different from that which had preceded it, that many observed that it seemed to have come from a different hand altogether.

Unlike most composers of major rank, Pärt did not show remarkable talent in his childhood or even in his early adolescence. His first serious study came in 1954 at the Tallinn Music Middle School, but less than a year later he temporarily abandoned it to fulfill military service, playing oboe and percussion in the army band.

In 1957, Pärt enrolled at the Tallinn Conservatory where he studied under Eller. He graduated in 1963, having worked throughout his student years and afterward as a recording engineer for Estonian Radio. He wrote several film scores and other works during this period, among them his two Sonatinas for piano, from 1958, and *Nekrolog*, a serial work for orchestra, from 1960. He also wrote a number of choral pieces at this time, among which was the ethereal a cappella effort, *Solfeggio* (1964). Pärt continued to compose music mainly in the serial vein throughout the 1960s, but received little recognition, since that method of composition was generally anathema throughout the Soviet Union. In the late 1960s and early 1970s Pärt studied the music of Renaissance era composers, particularly that of Machaut, Josquin Desprez, and Obrecht. His *Symphony No. 3* reflected these influences in its austere, Medieval sound world.

By the mid-1970s, Pärt was working on an altogether new style of composition. In 1976 he unveiled this method, the aforementioned tintinnabulation, with the piano work, *Für Alina*. A trio of more popular works followed in 1977, *Fratres*, for string quintet and wind quintet (later given additional arrangements by the composer), *Cantus In Memoriam Benjamin Britten* (revised 1980) and *Tabula Rasa*, for two violins, prepared piano, and string orchestra. Owing to the continued political oppression he found in Estonia, Pärt and his wife and two sons emigrated to the West in 1980, settling first in Vienna, then in West Berlin.

In the 1980s and 1990s, Pärt, a devout member of the Eastern Orthodox Church, wrote a number of large-scale choral religious works, including the *St. John Passion* (1982), *Magnificat* (1989), *The Beatitudes* (1990), and *Litany* (1994). He has declared a preference for vocal music in his later years, and continues, like the English composer John Tavener, also an adherent of the Eastern Orthodox religion, to write much religious music.

In 1995, Pärt was recognized for his many artistic achievements by being elected to the American Academy of Arts and Letters. He remains among the most popular serious composers of the late twentieth and early twenty-first centuries. *—Robert Cummings*

Overview of Works

The works of Arvo Pärt are often considered in company with those of other "mystical minimalists" such as John Tavener and Henryk Górecki, and he shares their emphasis on slowly developing harmonic fields, symmetrical harmonic and structural designs, and spiritual subject matter. His unique compositional method, however, gives all of his later works an easily discernible sound that sets him apart, whether scored for orchestra, string ensemble, or vocal forces. This signature "tintinnabula" style, as it is known, was arrived at only after considerable musical experimentation, and so his earlier output reflects a variety of compositional styles.

His earliest pieces demonstrate his training in the serialist method. His *Symphony No. 1 ("Polyphonic")* from 1964 threads densely woven melodic lines through a carefully constructed 12-tone system. Another orchestral work, *Perpetuum Mobile* (1963), likewise observes dodecaphonic practice, while articulating other tightly structured compositional schemes: virtually every compositional parameter, including harmony, rhythm, and dynamics, features replicating, fractally nested arc shapes. Other works from the 1960s adopted techniques of collage and pastiche. As suggested by the title, his chamber work *Collage on B-A-C-H* (1964) assembles all manner of styles and textures in a historically lively homage to the Baroque master. Pärt's *Concerto for Cello and Orchestra ("Pro et Contra")* uses stylistic allusion to highlight and comment upon the sense of confrontation often associated with the concerto genre.

Pärt eventually became dissatisfied with the methods at his disposal, and in the late 1960s and early 1970s underwent a period of deep reflection and extensive study. Much of his research during this time was devoted to sacred polyphonic vocal music from the Renaissance, which repertory would exercise considerable influence upon his later output. Finally in the late 1970s Pärt emerged from his extended musical retreat, prepared to demonstrate a new approach to tonality and dissonance, which he called the "tintinnabula" method. Taking its name from word describing the sound of a bell, this approach to composition combines stepwise moving melodic lines with omnipresent tonic chord tones, creating both a steady harmonic center and shimmering alternations of consonance and dissonance. A devout subscriber to the Orthodox faith, Pärt infused this compositional method with spiritual meaning, mapping dichotomies such as good/evil, spirit/matter, and sin/redemption onto the musical interaction of the consonant and dissonant tones. Likewise, from this period on the majority of his numerous works deal with sacred, scriptural, or otherwise spiritual topics. He continued to write for various instrumental configurations including organ (*Pari Intervallo*, 1976), string ensemble (*Fratres*, 1985; *Summa*, 1991), chamber orchestra (*Cantus in memoriam Benjamin Britten*, 1977), and strings with two violins and piano (*Tabula Rasa*, 1977). His new method placed particular emphasis on vocal music, however, and in fact included language as one of its parameters. In works such as *Missa Sillabica* (1977), *Miserere* (1989), and the *Berliner Messe* (1990), the lengths of words, phrases, or poetic lines directly affect the distances which the melodic lines are allowed to wander from certain gravitational "home" tones. His mature works are thus both carefully structured and very accessible. *—Jeremy Grimshaw*

Recommended:

- ○ **Pärt: Triodion** / Layton (cond.), James, Bowers-Broadbent, Thomas, Polyphony / 2003 / Hyperion 67375
- ○ **Pärt: Orient & Occident** / Kaljuste (cond.), Olsson, Swedish Radio Choir, Swedish RSO / 2002 / ECM 472080
- ○ **Pärt: Johannes-Passion** / Satomaa (cond.), Hynninen, Jussila, Talka, Candomino Choir / Finlandia 87182
- ○ **Pärt: Cello Concerto; Perpetuum Mobile; Symphonies 1–3** / Järvi (cond.), Forchert, Helmerson, Bamberg SO / 1989 / Bis 434
- ○ **Pärt: Miserere** / Davies (cond.), Leonard, Potter, Covey-Crump, Bowers-Broadbent, Favre, Hilliard Ens., Beethovenhalle Orch. / 1991 / ECM 847539
- ○ **Pärt: I am the True Vine** / Hillier (cond.), Bowers-Broadbent, Pro Arte Singers, Theatre of Voices / 1999 / HM 907242
- ○ **Pärt: Alina** / Spivakov, Bezrodny, Schwalke / ECM 449958
- ○ **Pärt: Kanon Pokajanen** / Kaljuste (cond.), Estonian Philharmonic Chamber Choir / 1998 / ECM 457834
- ○ **Pärt: Arbos** / Davies (cond.), Kremer, Dawson, James, Demenga, Bowers-Broadbent, Covey-Crump, Hilliard Ens. / 1987 / ECM 831959
- ○ **Pärt: Beatus** / Kaljuste (cond.), Bowers-Broadbent, Kogermann, Urb, Salumae, Saul, Estonian Phil. Chamber Choir / 1997 / Virgin 45276

CHORAL

Berliner Messe (1990–1991; revised 1997)

Estonian composer Arvo Pärt has always drawn attention (and occasionally criticism) for the heavily religious content of his works, and even a preliminary sampling of his *Berliner Messe* testifies to the depth of the composer's spiritual sensibilities. The very compositional techniques he uses here can be read as religious symbols, and the care with which he applies them enhances the profound reverence that the work conveys.

Composed for the 1990 "German Catholic Days" and premiered in an ecclesiastical context, the *Berliner Messe* is a liturgically complete work. The inclusion of two Alleluias and the sequence *"Veni Sancte Spiritus"* identifies it as a mass for Pentecost, though the added sections are optional in concert or church settings. Its original incarnation was for four SATB soloists and organ; after its premiere, the composer arranged it for strings and SATB choir.

To understand the inherent musical religiosity of the work—a spiritual element that exists independently of this composition's liturgical nature—one must first understand the Pärt's compositional method. After stylistic periods in which Pärt variously explored modern "Russian tonality" (à la Prokofiev and Shostakovich), serialism, and collage techniques, he suspended public composition for several years, during which time he applied himself—as did other minimalist composers, including Steve Reich—to the study of Medieval and Renaissance music (the influence of which can be found in the numerous Josquin-esque voice-pair textures that appear throughout the *Berlin Mass*). Pärt emerged from his sabbatical with an approach to composition that emphasized tonality in a new way: rather than using "functional" harmony to create tension with, and resistance to, a kind of tonic gravitational pull, he explored the sonic possibilities of an omnipresent tonic triad combined with diatonic contrapuntal dissonances. Adopting the name "Tintinnabuli" (after the complexly tonic sound of a bell), such pieces utilized paired lines: one voice—identified conveniently by Paul Hillier as the "M-voice"—undertook scalar passages, while the "T-voice," usually in homophony with the M, restricted itself to tonic chord tones beneath and above the melodic line. The effect is striking: an atmosphere of absolute harmonic stability filled with colorful and irregular dissonances.

This technique has poignant religious connotations. Pärt himself associates the M-voice with things mortal and carnal, like temptation, sin, and death. The triadic purity of the T-voice (for "Tintinnabula") has divine connotations, suggesting redemption, immortality, and godliness. The combination of these two voices suggests all sorts of corollaries—man's eternal spirit housed in the mortal tabernacle, or perhaps the paradox of Christ's essential humanity and divinity.

Certainly the text and context of the mass provides numerous interpretive possibilities. In the *Berliner Messe*, this symbolism is most striking in Pärt's setting of the Pentecostal sequence, *"Veni Sancte Spiritus."* The texture is extremely sheer—it consists entirely of duets (until the "Amens" at the end), and its translucence is enhanced by the very sparse participation of the T-voice within each of the duet passages. Moreover, the M-voice seems to mimic the ethereal sonority of the T-voice, eschewing its usual scalar figures in favor of nearly triadic motion by leap. Recalling the Biblical account of the Pentecost, the mortal voice seems to aspire the divine, as embodied by the T-voice. Such enlightenment seems to have been obtained: the Credo that follows brims with exuberance and energy. Recalling Pärt's *Summa* (another Credo setting) with its lilting, leaping eighth notes that jump out of the otherwise strictly homophonic texture, the tintinnabular technique used in the Credo the *Berliner Messe* is carefully controlled in order to allow for an unusual degree of lyricism. *—Jeremy Grimshaw*

Recommended:

- ○ **Pärt: Te Deum** / Kaljuste (cond.), Estonian Philharmonic Chamber Choir, Tallinn CO / 1993 / ECM 439162
- ○ **Pärt: I am the True Vine** / Hillier (dir.), Bowers-Broadbent, Theatre of Voices, Pro Arte Singers / 1999 / HM 907242

Magnificat (1989)

"And when they had seen it, they made known abroad the saying which was told them concerning this child. And all they that heard it wondered at those things which were told them by the shepherds. But Mary kept all these things, and pondered them in her heart." Luke 2:17–19 KJV. While countless modern composers have produced liturgically based produced works, their attitude towards the textual basis of their works usually seems an overwhelmingly detached one—a commentary on a musical (or cultural) tradition rather than an expression of faith. Arvo Pärt's personal convictions, however, make any reading of his works, particularly his sacred music, a very personal exploration of the composer's spirituality. Pärt's *Magnificat* (for SSATB choir with soprano soloist), though not considered among the composer's landmark works, nonetheless characterizes the composer's religious devotion, and places the listener within a startlingly sensitive musical environment. Perhaps the personal nature of the piece can be partly attributed to the personal nature of the text: Mary's prayer of gratitude at being chosen as the mother of Jesus. Pärt's setting, built upon his trademark "tintinnabular" technique, is at once breathlessly serene and taut with anticipation. The technique, which takes its name from a word describing the sound of a struck bell, combines voices homophonically in such a way that one voice outlines simple, scalar melodies, while the other leaps above and below the melodic line, always to notes within the tonic triad. The result is a kind of sonorous tonal reverberation that is always harmonically stable, but full of shimmering dissonances from the melodic voices. This texture lends itself well to the kind of contemplation and introspection suggested by the text. Pärt maps the music onto the text in such a way that melodic lines emphasize the rhythmic contours of speech and emphasized syllables receive the appropriate melodic and duration weight. Throughout this work, the texture alternates between two-voices and tutti. The paired-voice passages are strikingly crystalline; in every case, they consist of a single melodic part set against a meditatively repeated note, in the solo or first soprano part, on the fifth scale degree of F minor (C an octave above middle C). The tutti sections provide lush contrasts to the delicate voice-pair sections. In a few places, Pärt surprisingly strays from the strict diatonicism that predominates the piece by preceding unison "cadences" with colorful chromatic inflections. And though the F minor tonality is never doubted or challenged, at many places where one would expect a solid triadic repose—including the last chord of the piece—Pärt's melodic formula leaves non-chord tones glimmering dissonantly in the air. *—Jeremy Grimshaw*

Recommended:

- ○ **Pärt: Te Deum** / Kaljuste (cond.), Estonian Phil. Chamber Choir, Tallinn CO / 1993 / ECM 439162
- ○ **Lux Aeterna** / Hill (cond.), Winchester Cathedral Choir / 2002 / Virgin 562086

Seven Magnificat Antiphones (1988)

Arvo Pärt's early choral works—those in the so-called tintinnabular style—were composed almost exclusively to Latin texts. However, after his relocation to Germany the composer began to embrace the German language in his music, as evidenced by his *Seven Magnificat Antiphons* (composed in 1988, revised in 1991). The texts that make up this work would normally occur, individually, as antiphons to the Magnificat at Vespers on the seven evenings preceding Christmas Eve. Pärt, however, turned them into a single work in seven sections. These *Antiphons* should not be confused with Pärt's setting of the actual *Magnificat* text, which he composed in 1989.

These austere settings—like so much of Pärt's choral music evocative of the sacred music of the Middle Ages or Renaissance—are scored for mixed choir. Sometimes the musical content is so minimal as to evoke the quality of simple recitation. There is a dark quality in parts of the work, such as "O Adonai" or "O Spross aus Israels Wurzel." In "O Morgenstern," Pärt combines major and minor modes to evoke the Morning Star. The gradual crescendo of "O König aller Völkern" leads into the quiet opening of the concluding "O Immanuel," with its subtly dissonant chromatic shifts. *—Chris Morrison*

Recommended:

- ○ **Pärt: De Profundis** / Hillier (cond.), Theatre of Voices / 1996 / HM 907182
- ○ **Pärt: Beatus** / Kaljuste (cond.), Estonian Philharmonic Chamber Choir / 1997 / Virgin 45276

ORCHESTRAL

Cantus in Memory of Benjamin Britten, for string orchestra & bell (1977–1980)

Though the two never met, Arvo Pärt was profoundly saddened by the death of English composer Benjamin Britten in 1976. "I had just discovered Britten for myself," recalled Pärt. "Just before his death I began to appreciate the unusual purity of his music—I had had the impression of the same kind of purity in the ballads of Guillaume de Machaut." In his musical memorial to Britten, *Cantus in memoriam Benjamin Britten* (1977), Pärt demonstrates the kind of purity of concept to which he aspires in his own music.

The surface features of the work paint an almost macabre scene. A chime for dead tolls grimly, while the string lines consist of perpetually descending minor scales over elongated pedal tones. The overall shape seems to follow the procession to the cemetery and the lifeless body into the grave. However, a closer look at the processes at work in the *Cantus*, and a bit of insight into the philosophies behind those processes, reveal much deeper layers of spiritual meaning.

The work is constructed according to the principles of "tintinnabula," a style feature Pärt developed in the late 1970s after becoming disenchanted with his own experiments in functional tonality, serialism, collage, and polystylism. Taking its name from the word describing the sound of a pealing bell, this technique explores the possibilities of fleshing out a tonal center as a kind of omnipresent resonance rather than as a point of departure and return; in essence, Pärt removed the goal-directedness of functional harmony in order to explore the sheer sonority of the triad. To do so, he employed two kinds of musical line, which Paul Hillier, in his important 1997 study of the composer's music, identifies as M-lines and T-lines. M-lines are melodic lines that proceed in scalar or stepwise motion, usually within a diatonic scale and usually according to some kind of patterning system. T-lines, or tintinnabular lines, emphasize the sonority of the tonal center by confining themselves to chord tones. In the *Cantus*, the first and second violins, cellos, and basses are all employed divisi, with each section accommodating both a T- and an M-line. To these four pairs is added a single melodic line in the viola, the only one without a corresponding tintinnabular voice. This texture is maintained until the last section of the work, at which point the melodic voices gradually conform to the predominating chord tones.

Another process is also at work in the *Cantus*. The most prominent melodic contour is a simple descending A minor scale; this descending line, however, appears concurrently in various octaves and in various rhythmic values. The aural result is that each of the melodic voices in the five instrumental groups plays the line at a different but proportional rate of speed, so that the first violins are 16 times as fast as the basses. This kind of telescopic unity is cosmologically poignant, in the composer's aesthetic, and hints at a kind of multidimensional chronology that exists only in the hereafter.

Even deeper meanings can be found in the use of tintinnabular technique. Pärt proposes that the practice evokes all kinds of spiritual dualities. The melodic voice can be read to correspond with the mortal, the tintinnabular voice with the eternal—a dichotomy of body and spirit. Thus, before the final bell tolls, and as the M-voices melt into the triadic ether, the body doesn't just descend into the earth: the immortal spirit ascends into heaven. *—Jeremy Grimshaw*

Recommended:

○ **Pärt: Cantus; Fratres; etc.** / Kremer, Jarrett / ECM 21275

○ **Britten & Pärt** / Jarvi (cond.), Bergen PO / 1988 / Bis 420

Summa, for string orchestra (1990)

Actually, the date in the headnote is slightly misleading here: Pärt wrote the first version of this work in 1978, but scored it for four vocalists using the Credo from the mass for its text. Twelve years later, he arranged the piece for string orchestra, giving the work a quite different dimension while retaining its lively, Baroque-like spirit. While much of Pärt's post-serial output has an early music character—chant-like serenity, medieval rawness in some of his orchestral scoring, and simplicity of design and form—this piece exhibits not only a Baroque sound, but a joyous, almost nonchalant manner not frequently heard in the compositions of Pärt. The work opens with a moderately lively theme that repeats throughout the nearly four-minute duration in slightly different guises. The music is jaunty, yet more than vaguely exhibits that Pärtian serenity in its noble confidence, largely built on a lilting two-note idea that appears throughout the theme. There is also a sense of the music constantly ascending, as much of the writing is in the upper ranges of the strings or is rising from the lower ones. One characteristic of the piece typical of Pärt is its spiritual, mesmeric sense conveyed through much repetition of the material. Indeed, like the many versions of *Fratres*—a work scored for various chamber groups—it comes across with a hypnotic and somewhat mystical glow. *—Robert Cummings*

Recommended:

○ **Pärt: Fratres** / Werthen (cond.), I Fiamminghi / Telarc 80387

○ **Pärt: Summa** / Järvi (cond.), Estonian National SO / 2002 / Virgin 45501

○ **Pärt: Summa** / Kantorow (cond.), Tapiola Sinfonietta / 1996 / Bis 834

CHAMBER MUSIC

Fratres, for string quartet (1989)

There are seven versions of *Fratres* by Arvo Pärt, of which this string quartet rendition is chronologically the fifth. Originally, the composer scored the work for string quintet and wind quintet in 1977. Later versions included one for cello and piano (1980), one for eight cellos (1982), and one for solo violin (1992). All versions are similar, but hardly mere transcriptions of the original, some—like the cello/piano and solo violin rendition—sounding quite different from the others. Lengths of the versions vary from about eight to 12 minutes. Pärt, after an early tonal stage in the 1960s, began writing serial music. He soon abandoned it, however, after studying Gregorian chant and other medieval and Renaissance-era music, elements of which he used to forge a new style. The original *Fratres* (Brothers) was among his first successful works in this new mode.

In the string quartet version, the slow, mesmerizing theme—a mystical, medieval-sounding creation—is played softly, almost tentatively, as in the openings to the other renditions. String pizzicatos imitate percussive sonorities to punctuate ends of phrases here and a drone is heard throughout as the music gradually swells, conveying more passion and a greater sense of animation. But just when the music reaches its most voluminous levels, it begins to subside, imparting the effect of an approaching, then passing procession of singers or instrumentalists. *—Robert Cummings*

Recommended:

○ **Pärt: Fratres** / Werthen (cond.), I Fiamminghi / Telarc 80387

○ **Pärt: Fratres** / Benedek (cond.), Nagy, Domonkos, Schneider, Hajna, Hungarian State Opera Orch. / 1997 / Naxos 553750

KEYBOARD

Pari intervallo, for organ (1976)

Originally composed for four wind instruments, *Pari intervallo* was later arranged by the composer for organ (and later for recorder quartet), making it one of only a handful of works for organ within the composer's oeuvre. It was written in memory of a recently deceased friend and was one of seven works premiered in 1976 under the title *Tintinnabuli*. These pieces effectively and eponymously marked the beginning of a compositional style with connections to minimalism, but with a distinctive sonority entirely Pärt's. The title of *Pari intervallo* quite accurately describes the compositional process functioning in this and other "tintinnabular" works. It is characterized by a homophonic combination of two kinds of voices (to use Paul Hillier's helpful terminology): M- (melodic) lines and T- (tintinnabular) lines. M-lines usually move diatonically in a scalar or stepwise fashion, while T-lines emphasize a triadic sonority by leaping between chord tones. This effect is full of harmonic variety, but remains harmonically stable. In essence, Pärt's system insists on tonality, but divorces it from the idea of harmonic "function." The harmony isn't supposed to take the listener somewhere and then lead him/her back home; rather, it stays put while the listener explores it. *Pari intervallo* is comprised of two such pairs. Two M-voices are given in the outer voices, while the two inner voices undertake tintinnabular functions. Six phrases make up the work, each containing 12 measures. The melodic material in each phrase begins on a different note of the triad. The outer voices move in parallel motion, always separated by two octaves plus a third, except at the beginnings and endings of phrases, where they expand from and collapse to a double octave. The divergence and convergence of the M- and T- lines creates an interesting musical symbol, much of which Pärt himself suggests. According to the composer, the polarity of melodic and tintinnabular lines corresponds with spiritual dualities. Simply and reductively put, the M-line can be thought of as representing flesh, the Earth, and mortality, while the T-line suggests heaven, eternity, and spirit. As the two lines function independently but in rhythmic consonance, they effectively occupy the same space, like the body and spirit of a living being; as Pärt's wife suggested, "1+1=1." This idea is particularly poignant in considering the circumstances of mourning surrounding this piece—the transformation of a mortal soul into an immortal spirit. *—Jeremy Grimshaw*

Recommended:

○ **Pärt: Arbos** / Bowers-Broadbent / 1987 / ECM 831959

○ **Pärt: Music for Organ** / Bowyer / 2001 / Nimbus 5675

CONCERTO

Tabula rasa, concerto for 2 violins, prepared piano & string orchestra (1977)

Arvo Pärt composed *Tabula Rasa* in 1977, shortly after emerging from his self-imposed period of intense study and reflection to demonstrate what would become his characteristic musical technique: the so-called tintinnabuli method. The work is thus a prime example of the technique and demonstrates how, even in its early stages, Pärt's new and innovative musical language was connected indelibly with his sense of musical process and form. One not only hears the tintinnabula system working itself out in this piece, but also gets a clear sense of the aesthetic and spiritual underpinnings of the method and its implications for large-scale musical structure.

The work calls for two violin soloists supported by an ensemble of orchestral strings and an obbligato prepared piano. These three textural layers—soloists, prepared piano, and orchestra—assume distinct roles within the musical process at the heart of the piece. Stated simply, the tintinnabuli method as practiced by Pärt in this and numerous other works combines simple, usually stepwise diatonic melodies with ever-present interactions of tones from the tonic, or home, chord. There is thus both a strong sense of harmonic stability as well as a continually shifting surface of consonances and dissonances: as the melodic lines develop, the individual notes alternately concord and clash with the "tintinnabulating" tonic chord tones. In *Tabula Rasa*, the interaction of the two kinds of lines, as dispersed among the three textural layers, serves not only to provide the moment-to-moment interest of the piece, but to delineate the shape that the piece eventually comes to assume.

The work, which runs about half an hour in performance, is divided into two movements contrasting in their tempi and meter. The first movement, titled "Ludus," or "to play," is the more nimble of the two, and proceeds with delicate but consistent momentum. It begins with stark, loud A's in the violins, separated by four octaves and followed by a gaping, bar-long rest; these two gestures set the parameters of the rest of the movement. Over the course of several variations, which are separated by rests of decreasing length, the soloists move gradually, with arpeggiated figurations on the tonic chord, from the middle of their ranges outward to the extremes articulated in the first bar; at the same time, the orchestra slowly unveils an ever-expanding melodic line that gradually adds new hues to the harmonic color of the movement. The second movement, "Silentium," seems at first to deal much less with silence than the previous movement's conspicuously shrinking rests. In a slower tempo, a new key, and triple meter, this movement recasts much of the musical materials of the previous movement, and creates audible processes of ever-widening melodic arcs. The meaning of the movement's title becomes clear at the end: as the melody approaches its final tonic note it gradually grows quieter until, at what should be the piece's conclusion, the ensemble fades to silence and the final note is only implied. *—Jeremy Grimshaw*

Recommended:

○ **Pärt: Tabula Rasa** / Shaham, Anthony, Risberg / 1999 / DG 457647

○ **Pärt: Cantus; Fratres; etc.** / Kremer, Jarrett / ECM 21275

Harry Partch

b. Jun. 24, 1901, Oakland, CA, **d.** Sep. 3, 1974, San Diego, CA

Composer: Vocal, Chamber Music, Ballet, Opera

The child of former missionaries, composer Harry Partch grew up in a musical family, and at an early age taught himself to play the guitar, harmonium, clarinet, and other instruments. During his early school years in Arizona and New Mexico he had some rudimentary music lessons, which he found unexciting and conventional. He wrote a considerable amount of music as a youth, but set it all afire in a pot-bellied stove around 1930.

Partch's intensive studies in music history and intonation led him to reject conventional Western tunings and musical techniques. He devised a 43-note octave, and started adapting and building instruments to perform the new kind of music he was envisioning. Employment was hard to come by in those years, and Partch spent the Depression wandering the United States as a hobo, doing occasional odd jobs. Those experiences are reflected in his early works *Barstow—8 Hitchhiker Inscriptions from a Highway Railing at Barstow, California* (1941) and *U.S. Highball—A Musical Account of a Transcontinental Hobo Trip* (1943).

Over the next three-plus decades, Partch created dozens of new reed, string, and percussion instruments using a variety of materials including found objects like artillery shell casings, Pyrex jars, bottles, and old fuel tanks. Many of the works he wrote for this ensemble are ambitious theater pieces that incorporate dance, mime, costumes, and ritual: *Oedipus, The Bewitched* (A Dance Satire, 1955), *Revelation in the Courthouse Square*, and *Delusion of the Fury* (1969), perhaps his best-known work. Partch never held a formal teaching post, although he was employed as a researcher at various times at the Universities of Wisconsin, Illinois, and California. He supported himself through foundation grants, and the publication, performing, and recording of his works, working for much of that time out of an abandoned shipyard in Sausalito, California. The Gate 5 Ensemble (named after one of the gates at the shipyard) was created to perform his works, and Gate 5 Recordings made many of them available on record.

Partch's book *Genesis of a Music* (1949, revised 1974) details Partch's theories and methods, and describes many of his works in detail. The idiosyncratic list of influences Partch cites includes "Christian hymns, Chinese lullabyes, Yaqui Indian ritual, Congo puberty ritual, Cantonese music hall, and Okies in California vineyards, among others." Hints of all these, and many more besides, can be found in Partch's unique music. *—Chris Morrison*

VOCAL

Barstow, for two voices, surrogate kithara, chromelodeon, diamond marimba & boo (1941–1955)

Barstow is one of Harry Partch's earliest extant compositions and one of the most accessible and often performed. It originates from the years when he was, often as a hobo, riding the rails from one casual employment or temporary home to another. In late 1939, he went on a hitchhiking trip to take photos in the Southwestern deserts of California and Arizona. In the tough little Mojave Desert junction town of Barstow, California, in February 1941 while waiting for a lift, he noticed the following inscription on a highway railing:

It's January 26. I'm freezing.
Ed Fitzgerald. Age 19. Five feet, ten inches.
Black hair, brown eyes.
Going home to Boston, Massachusetts.
It's 4:00, and I'm hungry and broke.
I wish I was dead.
But today I am a man.

He was struck by this "unedited human expression" and jotted it down along with seven more that were legible.

By autumn Harry settled at an abandoned convict camp at Anderson Creek on the Big Sur coast, living in the old superintendent's office. While there, he built his first large string instrument, the kithara, from gigantic redwood railroad bridge supports. Early in 1941, he set the eight hitchhiker inscriptions, scarcely edited, for solo voice and adapted guitar, with the idea that he could perform them as a solo work. *Barstow* lasts about ten minutes, and in spare, natural language paints deft and telling portraits of the unknowns who left little fragments of their stories on that highway railing. There's Ed, quoted above. Then there's brown-eyed, brown-haired Marie from Las Vegas who leaves her address so she can be found. "Object: Matrimony," she says. "Dear Marie," answers a later hitchhiker, "a very good idea you have there. I too am on the lookout for a suitable mate. My description—." But "[n]o description follows, so he evidently got his ride." Each inscription is introduced by a little ritornello, then is quoted in a more or less spoken passage, then extended in more fanciful sung passages, more in the style of American folk music than classical vocalism.

In the end, *Barstow* is a touching and even inspiring portrait of Americans at the bottom of their luck, grittily carrying on and somehow sure of better days. Or at least that was the mood after revisions in 1943, 1954 (when he grouped *Barstow* with other hobo-era pieces collectively called *The Wayward*), and 1968. In each case, Partch added more of his growing number of hand-made instruments and more singers. The instrumentalists now sometimes make comments on the original inscriptions, and *Barstow* has become an illustration of how better times can take the painful edges away from old memories. The adapted guitar original version, however, is a tough, serious piece with a less optimistic tone. In 1941, Partch's hitchhiking days were just yesterday, and his "personal Great Depression" was to continue for a few more years of wandering. *—Joseph Stevenson*

Recommended:

○ **Just West Coast** / Schneider, Just Strings / 1993 / Bridge 9041

The Letter, for intoning voice, kithara, harmonic canon, surrogate kithara, diamond marimba & bass marimba (1943)

The three things most likely to be known by anyone who has heard of Harry Partch are that he wrote music in a strange 43-tone scale system, that he built a lot of musical instruments to his own design to play it, and that he spent some years as a hobo, mostly in the 1930s. He kept a notebook in those vagrant years, containing notations of "speech music": fragments he had heard, musical impressions, and even graffiti he had recorded. He worked these into a work called *Bitter Music*, which he considered a failure and destroyed (although a microfilm survived).

However, he did write some pieces based on similar material that he considered worthwhile. Among them is this humorous treatment of a letter he received in 1935 from a hobo pal named Pablo. In an oddly elliptical way, the text of the letter (as adapted and set by Partch) tells the story of how Pablo had a "swell time" in Cincinnati with a girl until her father found out, "and then the little lamb was led up to the altar" for a "shotgun wedding and I was the goat!"

In 1943, after receiving his first Guggenheim grant (ending his "personal Great Depression"), Partch wrote *Letter from Hobo Pablo*, scored for intoning voice with adapted guitar and kithara. Partch does not use his entire 43-tone scale in the work. As was his usual practice, he used the 43 available pitches as the source of a scale in just intonation that creates a melodic line linked tightly to the rise and fall of American speech.

He did not perform the work for some years, having grown worried about presenting too many of his "hobo works." In 1950, working in a rural setting in Gualala, California, he added additional instruments (mostly percussion) that appear only between the intoned lines of the letter. The work was recorded in this form in 1950 (now titled simply *"The Letter,"* with Partch doing the vocal part. In 1972, in preparing the film *The Dreamer that Remains*, Partch rescored *The Letter* again. In the 1950s, he grouped *The Letter* with other works with hobo-era words under the general title *The Wayward.*

Partch released a 1950 private recording of *The Letter* on his Gate Five Records in 1958. This recording was also included on the CRI release of Gate Five material, made in 1964 and entitled *From the Music of Harry Partch*. This was Partch's first "commercial" record release. *—Joseph Stevenson*

Recommended:

○ **The Composer-Performer 40th Anniversary** / Partch / 1994 / CRI 670

17 Lyrics by Li Po, for intoning voice & adapted viola (1930–1933; revised 1962)

Since 1928 Partch had experimented in adapting a viola to play gliding microtonal lines and harmonies, and by 1930 his success had given him sufficient confidence to turn his back upon traditional instruments and musical concepts and to embark upon a 40-year odyssey which would issue ultimately in a new and grandly substantiated aesthetic, an ensemble of some 30 unique instruments, and a body of work—including several large theater pieces—characterized by a piquantly potent, sophisticated primitivism. The initial impetus toward microtones came from an urge as old as Homeric minstrelsy (chanted, by the way, with pitch glides): the creation of a heightened speech "impressing the intangible beauty of tone into the vital power of the spoken word, without impairing either."

What was to become the *Seventeen Lyrics of Li Po* was begun in the fall of 1930 in New Orleans, where Partch had taken a stint as proofreader for the *Times-Picayune.* Turning to *The Works of Li Po the Chinese Poet Done into English Verse by Shigeyoshi Obata*—which had already prompted settings by Bliss and Lambert—Partch began his first extended essay in microtonally inflected bardic intonation with *The Long-Departed Lover* in December, adding three more settings by April, 1931. Partch called them "tone declamations." By September 1933, the number had grown to the canonical 17, though Partch continued to revise and renotate them as his ability to capture his aural imaginings became more refined. Recensions of the entire set were made over 1944–45 and again in 1962. Though he drew impetus from such things as Schoenberg's *Pierrot lunaire* (1912) or the Walton-Sitwell *Façade* (1921)—both mentioned in passing but approvingly in Partch's *Genesis of a Music*—his *Lyrics of Li Po* are distinguished by their rhythmic fluidity and mantic scrutiny which mimic and enlarge the gestures of speech into a hovering between speech and song. *The Intruder* plays off microtonal inflections against passages in the Dorian mode to amplify Li Po's already elusive poetry with great subtlety. By the summer of 1931, Partch was in San Francisco where he met and worked closely with soprano Rudolphine Radil, rehearsing the Li Po lyrics, performing them privately and at a concert for Henry Cowell's New Music Society on February 9, 1932. *—Adrian Corleonis*

Recommended:

○ **Historic Speech-Music Recordings** / Garvey, Schwartz (conds.), Hoiby, Thompson, Ludlow, Partch, Johnson, Burt, Mitchell, Olson, Gate Five Ens. of the World / 1995 / Innova 401

CHAMBER MUSIC

Two Studies on Ancient Greek Scales, for harmonic canon & bass marimba (1946–1950)

Harry Partch's deep commitment to the use of just intonation (where all the notes are expressed as integer ratios with each other) required him to invent numerous new instruments that could play up to 43 different notes of an octave.

These two short pieces are a result of the invention of the harmonic canon, which comprised 44 strings stretched across a flat table, like a large, furniture-sized zither. The strings are tuned in unison. Movable bridges create different pitches. They can be set up to create any kind of scale. The instrument was named "canon" in the sense that the placement of the bridges "laid down the law" of the scale used in a particular piece.

The two studies written for the instrument in 1946 employ two ancient scales. The first study is in a scale that seems to be found in virtually every culture, a pentatonic phrygian scale. Its use makes the first study sound oddly Eastern. It is a piece in moderate tempo, with an attractive melody.

The other scale is as strange as the first one is common. It is the ancient Greek enharmonic tetrachord scale, which has lowered second and sixth degrees far outside any common tuning and, hence, are microtones. When these notes appear in the study, they will sound sour (though oddly pure at the same time) with reference to the standard scale. Their expressive quality is something like "blues" notes.

The piece was originally written for solo performer on the harmonic canon. The right hand plucked strings tuned to the given scale, while the other strummed sets of strings tuned to produce chords. In 1950, Partch added his bass marimba to the music and added the *Two Studies* as the first two numbers in a suite called *Intrusions*.

The original score of the *Two Studies* was lost (though recordings survived). After Partch's death, guitarist John Schneider, having replicated Partch's original instrument the adapted guitar, adapted the work by adding a metal-stringed Celtic harp to the adapted guitar, with the lowest string of the guitar lowered to two octaves below middle C in order to play the bass marimba notes. *—Joseph Stevenson*

Recommended:

○ **Just West Coast** / Shulman, Schneider, Just Strings / 1993 / Bridge 9041

BALLET

The Bewitched (1955)

Harry Partch completed *The Bewitched* in 1955. The composer referred to it as a satyr play, ritual theatre, and "A Dance-Satire." It is in ten scenes and about 75 minutes in duration. It is exotic and bizarre, not resembling Western art in any knowable sense. This work appeals to the imagination of the listener as a work from a fictional past. The stage is dominated by instruments at different locations on stage and on risers of different heights. Among the instruments are those of the composer's own invention, as well as Western and Asian instruments, the majority of them being winds and percussion. The central figure of the concert is The Witch, who for the most part sits on a throne at the front of the stage, robed, and exposed to changing lights that often render her to a silhouette and always a powerful presence. She also conducts a mixed chorus, and none of the vocal work includes actual text, though the work has an extensive plot synopsis. The work's argument, provided by the composer, maintains that humanity is divided into those who prefer good music and those who prefer less-good music, and that both sorts of people are frequently forced to contend with the other musical preference. In the piece's prologue, musicians are on stage as though they had always been there, like the Egyptian phoenix that was the first living creature in the universe. They are eternal spirits of music, and it is also to be understood that they are on a university campus. The witch appears and complains (in nonsensical speak) that the world prefers background music, to her displeasure. Following the prologue are ten different scenes of deep strangeness, mingling academic life with figures from mythologies representing different cultures and periods in history. The scenes have strange names such as "A Lost Political Soul Finds Himself Among the Voteless Women of Paradise," and "A Court in its Own Contempt Rises to a Motherly Apotheosis."

None of the intensively detailed plots would be detectable in the score, making a recording of the music and a performance of the work different events entirely. As background to many different sorts of occasions, the soundtrack of *The Bewitched* is a wonderful find, not to be underestimated. It is wild in its exoticism and beautiful. There is no greater dramatic curve to be followed, and the listener is not missing anything vital if paying attention only periodically while the recording plays itself out. For other listeners, *The Bewitched* is a subtle set of variations of moods, featuring a unique nuance to each. It is a kind of religious music, unhappy with academia, sitting askew among the Western canon. *—John Keillor*

Synopsis:

Although there are no words to Harry Partch's full-length music drama, the participants do sing nonsense syllables. In ten scenes, framed by a Prologue and Epilogue, several groups of people—all of them "bewitched" (as everyone is) by the accidental circumstances that have shaped their habits and prejudices—are "unwitched" by the Witch and the Chorus of Lost Musicians.

Prologue. The Lost Musicians wander through the audience in a darkened hall. They carry no instruments and are dressed in topcoats, lighting their way to the stage where they discover the Partch instruments and individually begin to play them, creating a growing web of sound: the Lost Musicians Mix Magic. The Witch appears and unwitches the instrumentalists, permitting them to be singers as well as players. Now they unwitch others in the following scenes, as originally titled:

Scene One. Background for "The Transfiguration of American Undergrads in a Hong Kong Music Hall": the undergrads are under the spell of the stereotype of the "Mysterious East." The Witch slowly rises into view and stamps her feet, permanently transfiguring them. "The East no longer holds more mystery than it ought."

Scene Two. Background for "The Permutation of Exercises in Harmony and Counterpoint": attempts to dance are arrested by the music's insistence on "correct" eighteenth-century "common practice." When couples become unwitched, they find that they can dance the Dawn of Time, as if harmony rules will exist only in the dim future.

Scene Three. Background for "The Inspired Romancing of a Pathological Liar": a man automatically slips into an exaggerated version of male courtship posturing. The Witch saves him by breaking the woman from her expected role into equally exaggerated aggressiveness. The man flees from her up an endless flight of stairs.

Scene Four. Background for "The Alchemy of a Soul Tormented by Contemporary Music": the tormented soul is a Contemporary Serious Composer. He dances, striking tormented postures. He breaks free from contemporary torment when the witch gets him to take up slapstick comedy.

Scene Five. Background for "The Visions of a Defeated Basketball Team in the Shower Room": the god Hermes appears in a basketball uniform. He throws a team of women a basketball, sending them into a frenzy of activity, finally running offstage. Even the Lost Musicians don't know what this scene means.

Scene Six. Background for "The Euphoria on a Sausalito Stairway": a boy and a girl, in traditional ballet costumes, dance rigid and stylized dances until unwitched, their dances transformed into a pattern suggesting eternity.

Scene Seven. Background for "The Transmutation of Detectives on the Trail of a Culprit": both detectives hide their activities behind newspapers, then dance like chorus girls. The culprit has his own athletic dance. When unwitched, all three realize they need each other. They do a dance of cooperation.

Scene Eight. Background for "The Apotheosis of a Court in its Own Contempt": court opens to the drone of a Cahuilla Indian melody. Your-Honor wields his mallet as the questioning proceeds. When unwitched, the lawyers jump back, the judge jumps forward from his pedestal, and the witness (society itself) takes his place—and the mallet.

Scene Nine. Background for "A Political Soul Lost Among the Voteless Women of Paradise": houris "immobilized by pardisian hypnosis" stand motionless as if part of the set. The Lost Political Soul (a man) resembles Death, and dances in unison with a woman, his Transfiguration. The houris come to motion and dance in aggressive sexuality. "Unwitched, the Lost Political Soul finds himself contentedly at home among constituents who have never voted."

Scene Ten. Background for "The Demonic Descent of the Cognoscenti While Shouting over Cocktails": the orchestra of Lost Musicians does battle with the cognoscenti, who will not hear them and cannot move to their beat. The Witch concludes that the cognoscenti are "congenital recidivists" not worth the trouble of an unwitching and drives them out.

Epilogue. The Witch has had enough. "Later!" she says, and disappears. The Lost Musicians now wander individually offstage. They "get lost again ... [b]ut they know that they will never again be lost in the same way." *—Joseph Stevenson*

Recommended:

○ **The Harry Partch Collection Vol. 4** / Garvey (cond.), Schell, Lost Musicians Chorus / 1997 / CRI 754

OPERA

Revelation in the Courthouse Park (1959–1960)

This is one of the major music dramas by Harry Partch, the American pioneer of just intonation music. It is a powerful piece dramatically and musically, using the resources of Partch's collection of self-made microtonal instruments, including the bass instrument, the marimba eroica.

In 1955, Partch, intrigued by the hero-worship of the stars of the new rock & roll music (especially Elvis Presley), mentioned a plan for transplanting Euripides' *The Bacchae* into a contemporary American setting. Eventually, Partch alternated *The Bacchae*, set in ancient Thebes, with scenes in an American courthouse park, where Dion, the new popular music star, makes an appearance surrounded by his rapturous (mostly female) fans. The frenzied, half-nonsensical American segments provide a kind of relief from the searing tragedy of the King of Thebes, who, due to his lack of reverence for the newly-proclaimed god, Dionysus (or Bacchus), is mauled by the spellbound Theban women. The powerful stage spectacle is a telling of the classic tragedy, with running commentary on how the same phenomena noted by Euripides exist today. Partch's main target was the destructive nature of cultural conformism.

Partch, then associated with the University of Illinois, proposed his idea, called *Revel and Revelation*, to the University for the 1961 Festival of Contemporary Arts. He began seriously writing the text in June 1959 and the music in February 1960. Staging *Revelation* was an unusually smooth process. For the first time, Partch worked with a producer (Barnard Hewitt) and choreographer (Jean Cutler) who understood, and were in accord with, his ideas. The two sides to the drama were set on opposite sides of the stage, where Partch's often massively beautiful instruments and their players were on full display and gave the whole production a ritualistic quality. Partch, as always, had to teach the players how to play his instruments and how to read their parts, assisted by Danlee Mitchell and Jack McKenzie. The production was a success and largely well received.

While rehearsals were in progress, gymnastic coach Charles Pond saw a sequence from *Chorus III* of *Revelation* called *Tumble On*, using tumblers and a trampoline. He asked Partch to prepare the scene, "with added music," to be used in the upcoming NCAA Gymnastics Championship. This music was named *Rotate the Body in All Its Planes* and was premiered three days before the performance of the major work, on April 11, 1961.*—Joseph Stevenson*

Synopsis:

Partch's drama is divided into four sections called "Choruses" and four called "Scenes" that alternate, all followed by a coda. The Choruses are set in an unnamed contemporary American town (ca. 1960), where a visit is expected from the latest rock & roll "god" Dion. The Scenes are from Euripides' *The Bacchae*, about the deadly hysteria provoked by the new god in ancient Thebes, Dionysus (or Bacchus).

The "skeleton" of Euripides' drama (as Partch described his condensation of it) begins with two old men, Cadmus and the prophet Tiresias, discussing the arrival of the new god Dionysus. King Pentheus joins the conversation and denounces this dangerous cult. Pentheus has Dionysus arrested, personally interrogates him in insulting terms, and then has him jailed. Reacting to Dionysus' claim that he was born directly out of Zeus' thigh, a chorus sings, "Glory to the Male Womb" that Zeus must have possessed. A second confrontation occurs between the two after Dionysus has escaped.

Dionysus introduces a Herdsman to tell of what he has seen of the revels of Dionysus' all-female worshippers, including King Pentheus' mother, Agave. Rather than accepting this as a warning, Pentheus is now consumed with a desire to see these revels. Dionysus tells him that the only way is to dress as a woman.

Partch never shows the Dionysian revels or the death of Pentheus; these are only described. Instead, the contemporary "Choruses" are nearly all rituals and stand for them. In the first of these, Sonny confronts his mother. Her leadership of Dion's fan club embarrasses him. Dion arrives and sings a few songs (none of which, in Partch's score, are actually rock & roll).

The Second Chorus portrays Sonny's psychological state as related to the strong dominance his mother has over him. A fireworks display, further songs, and a gymnastics display represent the evening ritual. At end, the next morning finds the contemporary mother exhausted and disturbed, her irrationality caused by conforming to the hero-worship of the celebrity.

In Thebes, Agave regains her senses when she realizes that she and her followers have turned on an imposter during the night and torn him to shreds, only to discover that the victim was her son, King Pentheus. *—Joseph Stevenson*

Recommended:

- ○ **Partch: The Bewitched; Revelation in the Courthouse Park; etc.** / Garvey (cond.), Pierce / 1998 / Innova 405

Ian Partridge

b. Jun. 12, 1938, London, England

Tenor

One of England's most peripatetic and persuasive lyric tenors, Ian Partridge retained most of his vocal freshness into his sixties, cutting a wide swath through the repertory. Well schooled and long on musicianship, he is comfortable and exemplary in works from the Renaissance to modern times. His voice, though not large, has substance: a firm lower register and a fine-grained texture, it lent vocal authority to his performances. Although Partridge had earlier been disappointed by the relatively few opportunities for British artists to perform songs by German composers, he later went on to record many of them, preserving interpretations of warmth, wisdom, and vocal appeal. Almost exclusively a recitalist and oratorio singer, Partridge has enjoyed a low-key but enduring career and has won the respect and admiration of colleagues and audiences alike. Partridge began his advanced level musical studies at the Royal College of Music in 1956 before transferring to the Guildhall School of Music and Drama, where he trained under the bass Norman Walker and pursued conducting classes with Aylmer Buesst. His reputation grew rapidly following his solo debut in a 1958 performance of *Messiah* in Bexhill. Within a few years, he found himself one of his country's busiest tenors, valued for his reliability and interpretive suitability for several centuries' worth of music. From Monteverdi, Schütz, Handel, and Bach to Schoenberg, Weill, and Britten, Partridge was point-on in both his singing and interpretation. Benefiting from work with both Britten and Peter Pears (who instructed him in the art of singing through phrases), he further sharpened his already very precise diction, making it more flowing and conversational. With Pierre Boulez, Partridge recorded Schoenberg's *Die Jacobsleiter*, finding the French composer/conductor stimulating and pleasant to work with. Other projects Partridge has undertaken with Boulez include Schumann's *Der Rose Pilgerfahrt* and Stravinsky's *Le Rossignol*. In addition to performing the roles of the Evangelist in the Bach *Passions*, parts for which Partridge has long enjoyed a strong reputation, he recorded the Evangelist in Norwegian composer Trond Kverno's *St. Matthew Passion*, a work described by the tenor as "powerful," calling for unaccompanied singing over its hour and a half length in a contemporary adaptation of plainsong. Partridge's collaboration with actress Prunella Scales has resulted in more than 300 performances of a program entitled "An Evening with Queen Victoria," featuring songs written by Prince Albert. Partridge also portrayed St. Nicolas in a Thames Television production of Britten's score, winning the Prix Italia in its aftermath. Among the tenor's more than 150 recordings are Schubert's *Die Wintereisse* and *Die Schöne Müllerin* (the latter rated by *BBC Music Magazine* as a first choice); recordings of Schumann's *Liederkreis*, Op. 39, and *Dichterliebe*; Peter Warlock's haunting *Curlew River*, Ralph Vaughan Williams' equally affecting *On Wenlock Edge*; a complete edition of Handel's *Chandos Anthems*; Purcell's *The Fairy Queen*; and Iopas in the recording that grew from Colin Davis' Covent Garden production of Berlioz's *Les Troyens*, the occasion of Partridge's stage debut in 1969. As a professor at the Royal Academy of Music, Partridge has given master classes in song and early music from Aldeburgh to Ravinia to Versailles. The tenor received the CBE (knighted) in 1992 for his service to music. *—Erik Eriksson*

Recommended:

- ○ **Vaughan Williams: Popular Orchestral Works** / Partridge, Craxton, London Music Group / 1996 / EMI 65589
- ○ **Byrd Song** / Partridge, McGreevy, Phantasm / Simax 1191
- ○ **Handel: Chanos Anthems 1,2 & 3** / Christophers (cond.), Partridge, Dawson, George, Miller, Sixteen Orchestra & Choir / 1994 / Chandos 503
- ○ **Songs by Finzi and His Friends** / Partridge, Roberts, Benson / Hyperion 66015

Adelina Patti

b. Feb. 19, 1843, Madrid, Spain, **d.** Sep. 27, 1919, near Brecon, Wales

Soprano

Adelina Patti was the reigning diva of the latter half of the nineteenth century. A guaranteed audience draw from the very start, she burst onto the concert scene in her mid-teens and proceeded to dominate the vocal world for the duration of her career.

The daughter of two Italian opera singers, Patti was born while they were touring in Madrid on February 19, 1843. She studied voice with her half-brother, and was soon giving concert tours with the violinist Ole Bull, Louis Moreau Gottschalk, and others. At the age of 16 she sang the title role in Donizetti's *Lucia di Lammermoor* in New York City, and then toured the United States, capitalizing on her youth as an element of spectacle. In 1961, she made her debut at Covent Garden as Amina in *La Sonnambula*; London, and that theater specifically, would remain the center of her career.

Her voice was described as being very pure and with great flexibility. Because of this, she was best suited to playing vulnerable and ebullient young girls, and continued to do so even in the later stages of her career. As she matured she phased in a number of heavier roles, but she never stepped outside her natural vocal limits. The operas of Gounod, which she sang under his direction, were particular triumphs for Patti, and in 1876 she was the first to sing the role of *Aida* in London. An enormously successful 1879 tour of the United States helped cement her already considerable fame.

Patti's only real failure was an 1885 attempt at Bizet's *Carmen*—a role that has stumped many a famous singer. But the setback was inconsequential; she continued to appear with great success in Paris, Milan, Brussels, Monte Carlo, St. Petersburg, Moscow, Berlin, Vienna, Madrid, and Lisbon. In 1888, Patti sang for the first time in South America, receiving predictably warm receptions in Buenos Aires and Montevideo. In 1895, she gave a series of six "farewell" performances at Covent Garden; this was quite a misnomer, because while they did mark her last operatic performances in London, she continued to appear in numerous other cities, and gave a number of subsequent "farewell" tours. Her actual final public performance was not until 1914.

Patti made two series of recordings, first in 1905 and then again the following year. Although she was over 60 years old at the time, her voice still had a lovely purity and superb flexibility. They certainly do not represent her at the height of her abilities, but they give a clear sense of her extraordinary vocal gifts, and the care with which she nurtured them over the course of a long career.

Patti was married three times: first to the Marquis de Caux, then to the Italian tenor Nicolini, with whom she sang on many occasions, and finally (in 1899) to the Baron Cederstrom, with whom she finally settled down at her castle at Craig-y-Nos, Wales. *—Richard LeSueur*

Recommended:

○ **The Era of Adelina Patti** / Patti, etc. / 1993 / Nimbus 7840

○ **Adelina Patti** / Patti, etc. / Pearl 9312

Luciano Pavarotti

b. Oct. 12, 1935, Modena, Italy

Tenor

One of the most successful and admired opera singers of all time, Luciano Pavarotti was king among tenors from the late 1960s through the 1990s. His voice was noted for its exciting upper register, and tailor-made for the operas of Verdi, Bellini, Donizetti, and Puccini, and as it darkened slightly over the years, for the verismo composers as well. His vocal longevity, which kept him singing youthfully well into his sixties, and still beautifully after that, is a credit to his commanding technique and artistry, and remarkable considering his nearly 40 years of performing.

Pavarotti's father was a baker, and his mother worked in a cigar factory. As a boy, he sang alto in the cathedral choir, and when his voice changed he joined the Modena city choir. He had brief careers as a schoolteacher and an insurance agent; during that time, his major extracurricular activity was not music but soccer, and his play made him a local star. However, increased involvement in the choir (which took prizes in international competitions) led him to pursue vocal studies, and he eventually settled on singing as his aspiration.

Pavarotti studied voice with Arrigo Polo in Modena, then with Ettore Campogalliani in Mantua. His operatic debut was as Rodolfo in *La Bohème* in Reggio Emilia (April 19, 1961), and soon increasing success led to a debut in Amsterdam on January 18, 1963, as Edgardo in *Lucia di Lammermoor.* After singing the same role with Joan Sutherland in Miami in 1965, he was engaged to travel with her in the Sutherland Williamson International Grand Opera Company, touring Australia. In 1966 he appeared at Covent Garden as Tonio in *La fille du régiment*, where his seemingly effortless handling of the nine successive high Cs in the aria "Pour mon âme" sent his career into high orbit. He repeated the feat at the Metropolitan Opera in 1972, and for more than two decades after that he was a fixture on the operatic scene, appearing in nearly every major European and American house, and even China, where he performed Puccini's *La bohème* in the 1980s.

Pavarotti appeared in the first "Live from the Met" broadcast on the PBS network and has been the most consistent draw on that series for years. His outstanding catalogue of recordings on the London (Decca) record label preserves nearly every role he ever performed and will be hard to match for its quality and scope. His charity work has including AIDS benefit concerts and world hunger gala events, as well as his "Pavarotti and Friends" concerts to benefit children, especially in the former Yugoslav states. He also founded a quadrennial contest to identify talented young singers and boost their careers. And, as one of the "Three Tenors," he has brought operatic singing to a wider popular audience than previously might have been thought possible. In 2003 he released his first solo crossover CD, *Ti adoro*. *—AMG*

Recommended:

○ **Pavarotti: The Early Years** / Pavarotti, etc. / 1994 / BMG 62541

○ **Luciano Pavarotti** / Pavarotti, etc. / 2001 / Decca 467920

○ **Ti Adoro** / Pavarotti, etc. / 2003 / Decca 000109602

○ **Verdi: Rigoletto** / Bonynge (cond.), Pavarotti, Sutherland, Milnes, London SO / 1985 / London 414269

○ **Donizetti: La Fille Du Régiment** / Bonynge (cond.), Pavarotti, Sutherland, Sinclair, Garrett, Covent Garden Royal Opera House Orch. / 1986 / London 414520

○ **Puccini: La Bohème** / Karajan (cond.), Freni, Pavarotti, Ghiaurov, Panerai, Berlin PO / 1987 / London 421049

○ **Mascagni: Cavalleria Rusticana/Leoncavallo: Pagliacci** / Gavazzeni, Patane (conds.), Pavarotti, Freni, Cappuccilli, Varady, Nartional PO / 1988 / London 414590

○ **Pavarotti Edition** / Pavarotti, etc. / 2001 / Decca 470000

Joseph Payne

b. 1941, China

Organist, Harpsichordist

English harpsichordist, organist, and clavicembalist Joseph Payne is a scholarly, intelligent, and gifted artist who has amassed an impressively voluminous output of recordings on period keyboard instruments. While many players of pre-piano keyboards are happy to limit themselves to exploring a single composer or two's work in depth, Payne has recorded entire manuscript collections and has delved very deeply into the available repertoire that predates the Romantic era. In 1985 Payne enjoyed the privilege of being the first organist to record the then newly discovered Neumeister *Chorale Preludes* attributed to Johann Sebastian Bach. Since then Payne has recorded complete editions of the keyboard works of Johann Pachelbel, many more collections of Bach, and substantive collections such as the *Fitzwilliam Virginal Book*, the *Andreas Bach Manuscript*, the *Dublin Virginal Manuscript*, and the *Buxheimer Orgelbuch.* He has recorded the works of composers both famous and obscure, such as Couperin le Grand, Dulphy, Sebastiàn de Albero, Muffat, John Bull, William Byrd, and many others. Payne has recorded for Bis, Naxos, Centaur, Harmonia Mundi, Discover, Vox, Haenssler Classics, and more.

Payne was born to English missionaries near the border between Mongolia and mainland China. He studied primarily in Switzerland and the U.K. and among his teachers were Wanda Landowska and Fernando Valenti. Payne resettled in the Boston area in 1965, and for the next two decades concentrated on teaching and scholarship, much of it based at Yale University. The scholarship part of it continues, but since the breakthrough of the "Neumeister" recording, Payne maintains a busy annual concert schedule of about 60 dates a year, appearing in concert venues worldwide. Payne is also a frequent contributor to scholarly journals dealing with musicology and the disposition of historical keyboard instruments. *—Uncle Dave Lewis*

Recommended:

○ **Pachelbel: Keyboard Suites** / Payne / 1995 / Bis 809

○ **Albero: Harpsichord Sonatas** / Payne / 1993 / Bis 629

○ **Couperin: Pièces de Clavecin** / Payne / 1992 / Bis 559

○ **Duphly: Pièces de Clavecin** / Payne / 1999 / Centaur 2421

Martin Pearlman

b. May 21, 1945, Chicago, IL

Conductor

American conductor and harpsichordist Martin Pearlman studied harpsichord with both Ralph Kirkpatrick and Gustav Leonhardt, receiving degrees in music from Cornell and Yale Universities. In 1973, he founded the period instrument orchestra and chorus Banchetto Musicale, which he later renamed Boston Baroque. With this ensemble, Pearlman presented the Boston premiere of the surviving Monteverdi operas (including his own performing editions for *L'incoronazione di Poppea* and *Il ritorno d'Ulisse*), the American premiere of Rameau's *Zoroastre*, and the modern world premiere of the 1790 singspiel *The Philosopher's Stone* (with music by Mozart). His completion and orchestration of music from Mozart's *Lo sposo deluso* and his performing version of Purcell's *Comical History of Don Quixote* were both premiered by Boston Baroque. Pearlman directs the Department of Historical Performance Activities at Boston University, where Boston Baroque is an ensemble-in-residence. He has released several recordings on Telarc, three of which have been nominated for Grammy Awards (Handel's *Messiah*, Monteverdi's *Vespers* of 1610, and Bach's *Mass in B minor*). He has appeared as guest conductor with the Washington Opera, the National Arts Centre Orchestra of Ottawa, Utah Opera, Opera Columbus, Boston Lyric Opera, Minnesota Orchestra, San Antonio Symphony, Springfield Symphony, and the New World Symphony. *—Robert Adelson*

Recommended:

○ **Lost Music of Early America** / Pearlman (cond.), Sieden, Baker, Boston Baroque / 1998 / Telarc 80482

○ **Mozart: The Impresario; Mozart's Circle: The Beneficent Dervish** / Pearlman (cond.), Aler, Ewing, Deas, Baker, Boston Baroque / 2002 / Telarc 80573

○ **Mozart: Requiem** / Pearlman (cond.), Ziesak, Croft, Maultsby, Arnold, Boston Baroque / 1995 / Telarc 80410

○ **Handel: Messiah** / Pearlman (cond.), Robbin, Clift, Ledbetter, Fowler, Boston Baroque / 1992 / Telarc 80322

Peter Pears

b. Jun. 22, 1910, Farnham, England, **d.** Apr. 3, 1986, Aldeburgh, England
Tenor

Peter Pears, for many years, embodied British vocal music, both opera and song. Benjamin Britten wrote 14 operas and over 50 songs and song cycles for him, and he appeared in the premieres of many other major English works. He was one of the three founders of the Aldeburgh Festival, and he and Britten established the Britten-Pears School for Advanced Musical Studies, where he directed the various singing programs until his death.

Given these impressive credentials and influence, it is rather surprising that as a singer he had distinct limitations. While he was capable of excellent singing, his voice was not especially beautiful, with a rather reedy tone, and at times also with a pronounced wobble. However, his musical intelligence, elegant phrasing, and expressive use of text and the vocal line were to create his place in music history.

His first musical career plan was to be an organist, and he studied that at the Hertford College of Oxford, but he later enrolled at the Royal College of Music in London, where he remained from 1933 to 1935 as an "Operatic Exhibitioner." He then pursued studies with Elena Gerhardt and Dawson Freer. He began his professional singing career as a member of the BBC Singers in 1934, and it was through that group that he and Britten first met.

His first recital with Britten was in 1937 at Balliol, followed by a tour of the United States and Europe performing chamber music, including material written by Britten. When they returned, they performed his *Michelangelo Sonnets* at Wigmore Hall. His operatic debut was as Hoffmann in Offenbach's *The Tales of Hoffmann* at the Strand Theater in London in 1942; he joined the Sadler's Wells Opera Company in 1943, singing lyric tenor leads. Britten had begun to write the role of Peter Grimes for him, with funding from the Koussevitsky Foundation, and the opera had its world premiere in 1945 at the Sadler's Wells. Thereafter, while he still appeared in other composer's works, he and Britten were an established musical team, and the next decades saw the appearances of many more operas written for Pears. In 1946, he created the role of the Male Chorus in *The Rape of Lucretia*, the title role of *Albert Herring* in 1947, Captain Vere in *Billy Budd* in 1951, Essex in *Gloriana* in 1963, Peter Quint in *The Turn of the Screw* in 1954, Flute in *A Midsummer Night's Dream* in 1960, and Aschenbach in *Death in Venice* in 1973. He also created the role of Pandarus in Walton's *Troilus and Cressida*. In the song repertoire, he premiered Berkeley's *Stabat Mater*, Tippett's *A Child of Our Time* and *Boyhood's End*, as well as Britten's *Michelangelo Sonnets*, *Donne Sonnets*, and *Serenade for Tenor, Horn, and Orchestra*, to name just the most famous. He was a noted student of early music, frequently performing English lute songs in his recitals, and he and Britten published editions of several songs by Purcell.

While most strongly associated with English music and English venues, he was also a noted soloist at the Holland Festival and the Salzburg Festival.

Pears and Britten were necessarily discreet about the intimate nature of their relationship, but in music history, their lifelong partnership and love affair is one of the most productive and influential, perhaps surpassed only by that of Robert and Clara Schumann. They are buried next to one another in Aldeburgh. *—Ann Feeney*

Recommended:

- ○ **Britten: Turn of the Screw** / Britten (cond.), Pears, Vyvyan, Cross, Hemmings, Dyer, Mandikian / 1990 / London 425672
- ○ **Britten: The Performer** / Pears, Britten / 1999 / BBC 8006
- ○ **Britten: Serenade; Illuminations; Nocturne** / Britten (cond.), de Peyer, Pears, Ellis, Lord, English CO, London SO / 1986 / London 417153
- ○ **Britten: Peter Grimes** / Britten (cond.), Brannigan, Lanigan, Kelly, Nilsson, Covent Garden Royal Opera House Orch. / 1985 / London 414577
- ○ **Schubert: Winterreise** / Pears, Britten / 2000 / London 466382

Jan Peerce

b. Jun. 3, 1904, New York, NY, **d.** Oct. 15, 1984, New Rochelle, NY
Tenor

Jan Peerce was known as "Toscanini's tenor," with his clean, incisive singing, exceptional breath support, and immediately distinctive timbre (though some considered his vibrato overly rattling). Peerce did not always record well in the studio, his voice often becoming harsh with a microphone and his technique losing some of the nuances contemporary critics praised in his stage singing. However, many of his live performances are now out of copyright, so provide a more accurate overview of his singing and style. While Peerce is often compared to his brother-in-law Richard Tucker (Peerce married Tucker's sister, Sara)—both were born in New York, both were tenors, both studied to become cantors, and neither was a strong actor—the similarities were largely superficial. There was a good deal of animosity between the two of them, Peerce feeling his contributions towards Tucker's career were ignored, Tucker feeling Peerce was jealous of his own accomplishments, which he felt were the greater.

Peerce grew up in a musical family, where his mother opened the house to dinner guests and eventually boarders to pay for his violin lessons. He and four friends formed a band, Pinky Pearl and His Society Dance Band (Peerce was born Jacob Pincus Perelmutter and nicknamed "Pinky" at home), which became quite successful. Peerce soon discovered that when he sang, that got as much or more attention than their playing. He favorably impressed Samuel Rothafel, a major Broadway impresario, and sang first on the *Radio City Music Hall of the Air* and then on stage at the opening of the physical Radio City Music Hall in 1932. He rapidly became one of the most popular radio performers in both popular and cantorial music, and in 1936, first sang "The Bluebird of Happiness," which became his signature tune (and the title of his 1973 autobiography). Arturo Toscanini heard him in a broadcast of Act I of *Die Walküre* (Peerce's only foray into Wagner, though Toscanini himself suggested that he sing Siegmund on stage), and hired him to sing the tenor role in his broadcast of Beethoven's *Ninth*, with the legendary NBC Symphony Orchestra. He became Toscanini's tenor of choice, and began to study opera with Giuseppe Borgatti. He made his opera debut at the Philadelphia Opera as the Duke in *Rigoletto* in 1938, and sang Alfredo in *La Traviata* in San Francisco, where Lawrence Tibbett pushed him into taking an extra solo bow. 1941 was also the year of his Met debut as Alfredo in *La Traviata*, and he sang each season with that company until 1968. In the late 1940s, he had a vocal crisis, but studied with Robert Weede (with whom he had sung at the Music Hall), regaining his earlier vocal placement and projection. He made regular tours with the Bach Aria Group throughout the 1950s and early 1960s. In 1956, he toured in the then-Soviet Union, singing a service in the Great Synagogue in Moscow, an overwhelming emotional experience for him, and one that he repeated in 1963. In 1971, he made his Broadway debut as Tevye in *The Fiddler on the Roof*. He retired from performing in 1982. *—Ann Feeney*

Recommended:

- ○ **Verdi: Rigoletto** / Cellini (cond.), Warren, Peerce, Berger, Tajo, RCA Italiana Opera Orch. / 2000 / Myto 4050
- ○ **Lebendige Vergangenheit: Jan Peerce** / Peerce, etc. / Preiser 89562
- ○ **Bizet: Carmen** / Reiner (cond.), Merrill, Albanese, Peerce, Stevens, RCA Victor SO / 1964 / RCA 7981
- ○ **Jan Peerce Sings Hebrew Melodies** / Peerce, etc. / RCA 61687

Flor Peeters

b. Jul. 4, 1903, Tielen, Belgium, **d.** Jul. 4, 1986, Antwerp, Belgium
Composer

Flor Peeters was one of the most renowned organists and composers for organ of the twentieth century. He was also a great teacher and a respected researcher of older Flemish music. Peeters attended the Lemmens Institute in Mechelen where he studied organ with Depuydt. He won the highest award, the Lemmens-Tinel Prize and at the age of twenty and was appointed a professor at Lemmens. In addition, in 1923, he became assistant organist at the Cathedral of St. Rombout in Mechelen.

When Depuydt died in 1925, Peeters was appointed to succeed him as professor of organ. He also served as a professor of organ at Ghent Conservatory from 1931 to 1938 and professor of organ at the Tilburg Conservatory in the Netherlands from 1935 to 1948.

He began to write what would become a large catalog of organ music and sacred choral works. He was particularly masterful in his use of the variation forms. He became a close friend of Charles Tournemire (1870–1939), one of the great line of French organist-composers, from which he is said to have derived some of the style and technique of his improvisations. In his will, Tournemire bequeathed to Peeters the organ console that the great Belgian composer César Franck had used as organist of St. Clotilde.

Peeters had begun studying older music while he was still a student at Lemmens, where he took courses in Gregorian chant from van Nuffel. The influence of this ancient form of Roman Catholic Church chant is often found in his slower music and sometimes forms the basis of longer compositions, such as the *Toccata, Fugue, and Hymn on "Ave Maris Stella,"* Op. 28, which was dedicated to Tournemire. In 1943, he completed his *Practical Method for Accompanying Gregorian Chant*.

Germany attacked and occupied both Belgium and the Netherlands in 1940. Peeters refused to perform for the German occupiers. As a result, his passport was confiscated. Nevertheless, he was permitted to travel regularly across the border between Belgium and the Netherlands in order to continue his teaching at Tilburg, and, in the course of doing this, he carried secret messages between the authorities of the cathedrals of these two countries.

In addition to Gregorian chants, Peeters studied Renaissance music, particularly of the school of Flemish polyphony. This style was also absorbed into his music. Despite his friendship with Tournemire, and his role in carrying on the Franco-Belgian organ school that Tournemire represented, the styles of the two composers is not particularly close (aside from the incorporation of some of the keyboard technique of the older master in improvisatory passages). Instead, his style is closer to that of his younger French contemporary, Marcel Dupré (1886–1971). Peeters showed an interest in twentieth century tonal composition techniques such as polyrhythms and polytonality. One of his wartime works, the *Sinfonia*, Op. 48, seems clearly to express the suffering of the Belgians during the occupation in its stark, highly dissonant language. Other Peeters' compositions, by contrast, are often attractive and rhythmically bright, although almost always highly contrapuntal. Later in his life, his style became more neo-Classical and contemplative.

Peeters gave up his position in Tilburg in 1948, when he accepted the post of organ professor of Antwerp Conservatory. He became director of the Conservatory in 1952, at which time he resigned from his position at Lemmens. He was in much demand as a teacher and gave master classes in addition to concerts throughout the world, including several teaching visits to Boys' Town, Nebraska.

In 1971, King Boudoin elevated him to the Belgian peerage as Baron Peeters, only the third Belgian musician so honored. *—Joseph Stevenson*

Overview of Works (1923–1985)

Although Flor Peeters composed in a number of genres, including choral, chamber, vocal, and concerted works, his legacy lies in his nearly 500 works for the organ. As the longtime organist of St. Rombouts Cathedral in Mechelen, and professor of organ at the conservatories of Ghent, Tilburg, and Antwerp, he poured his lifelong musical energies into the grand instrument. His style was informed by studies of Renaissance polyphony and Gregorian chant, an interest in polytonality and polyrhythm, and by his contemporaries, including Marcel Dupré and Charles Tournemire; Peeters' contrapuntal music shows the inescapable legacy of Bach, whose music figured prominently on his recital programs. Peeters primarily worked within established forms for the instrument, including chorale preludes, variations, voluntaries, and preludes and fugues. Peeters' best-known compositions for the organ are his *Aria*, Op. 51a; *Toccata, Fugue and Hymn on "Ave Maris Stella,"* Op. 28; and his *Organ Concerto*, Op. 52. The concerto was composed during the liberation of Antwerp by British troops in 1944; it stands as one of his most extroverted and joyful compositions. Peeters was also a prolific composer of choral music, although few of these works have attained much success, with the possible exception of the *Missa Festiva*, Op. 62. As with his organ music, most of his choral music fits comfortably within standard genres, such as masses and motets, but there are more individual works as well; these include his *Entrata Festiva for unison voices with brass, tympani, and organ* and his *Wedding Song*, which, in an adaptation for solo voice and keyboard, has become a staple at wedding ceremonies. Peeters composed numerous works for the piano, including a set of *Ten Bagatelles*, Op. 88, two sonatinas, a toccata, and the *Steenhof Suite*. He also wrote a sonata for trumpet, a suite for four trombones, and an *Aria* for violin, cello, and piano, Op. 51/b. *—Allen Schrott*

Recommended:

- ○ **Peeters: Organ Concerto, etc.** / Hempfling (cond.), Wisskirchen, Meisner / Motette 40161
- ○ **3 Masses from Canterbury Cathedral** / Flood (dir.), Harris, Canterbury Cathedral Choir / York Ambisonic 127

Krzysztof Penderecki

b. Nov. 23, 1933, Debica, Poland

Composer: Orchestral, Symphonic, Chamber Music, Choral

One of the best known, most listened to, and most popular composers of the late twentieth and early twenty-first centuries, Krzysztof Penderecki has undergone a marked evolution in compositional style. After achieving fame with such astringent, often anguished, scores as his *Threnody for the Victims of Hiroshima* (1960) and *Passion According to St. Luke* (1965), both of which stretched tonal language, Penderecki followed a personal imperative in moving toward more tonal music. As early as 1980, his *Symphony No. 2* embraced pre-serialist notions of melody and harmony. This fertile exploration of traditional language has continued to yield rewarding works into the new millennium. Penderecki was given violin and piano lessons as a child. He studied art and literary history and philosophy at the local university while also attending the Kraków Conservatory. He privately studied composition before he entered the Kraków State Academy of Music in 1954. In 1959, three of his compositions, each submitted under pseudonyms, won first prizes in a competition sponsored by the Polish Composer's Union. Fame rapidly followed. Both his *Threnody* and *St. Luke Passion* received worldwide performances in numbers rare for contemporary works, especially those written with such demanding techniques: glissandi, tonal clusters, unpitched sounds, spoken interjections, aleatoric effects, and shouting. Commissions came in quick succession, a corollary career as a lecturer developed, and in 1972, Penderecki began to conduct his own works. The first of Penderecki's stage works, *The Devils of Loudon*, became a European sensation in 1969 with numerous performances and considerable discussion. A second opera, one of epic scale, was commissioned by the Chicago Lyric Opera. *Paradise Lost* (after Milton) was mounted in 1976 in an immensely expensive production seen in Chicago and Italy. *Die schwarze Maske* was premiered in 1986, followed in 1991 by the comic work *Ubu Rex*. Penderecki is among the most honored composers ever. He holds honorary memberships in many of the world's most prestigious conservatories, awards from numerous competitions, several honorary doctorates, and has been recognized with national orders from such nations as Germany, Austria, and his native Poland. Since his conducting debut, he has been a respected podium figure, leading both his own works and a variety of music by other composers representing several centuries. The North German Radio Symphony Orchestra, Hamburg engaged him as principal guest conductor. Though not extraordinarily prolific, Penderecki has amassed a sizeable catalog of orchestral works, chamber music, concertos, and choral works. *—Erik Eriksson*

ORCHESTRAL

The Dream of Jacob (1974)

Penderecki's *The Dream of Jacob* (aka *The Awakening of Jacob*) was composed for large orchestra in 1974, and lasts approximately seven and a half minutes. It was commissioned for the 25th anniversary of the accession of Prince Rainier III of Monaco. Like most of the composer's other work of the 1960s and 1970s (*De Natura Sonoris Nos. 1* and *2*, *Threnody to the Victims of Hiroshima*, *Fonogrammi*, *Dimensions of Time and Silence*, etc.), this piece is a giant soundscape employing tone clusters, unusual methods of playing instruments, some unusual instruments such as the musical saw, and, while producing strong emotional effects, avoiding melody, harmony, and development in the traditional sense. The title refers to Jacob's well-known dream in the desert of a ladder to heaven on which angels were ascending and descending: "Jacob woke from his sleep and said: Truly the Lord is in this place, and I did not know it," Genesis 28:16. *The Dream of Jacob* opens by creating a surreal dreamscape: low pitched brass chords pulse, a thin electronic-like sustain appears above that, and lower strings add to the drone. Shivering tremolos from the strings appear and disappear. Then great tone clusters in the strings and woodwinds sigh with the timbre of air raid sirens. This develops into larger glissandi interrupted several times with brass choir clusters with scattered punctuations among the solo instruments in the group. Everything slowly disappears except the upper strings which slide by themselves in clusters. This continues as an inverted high pedal point as on-rushing strings join in beneath, and again create a momentary, overwhelming wave. A gong interrupts this activity, everything becomes still again, like a lonely night in the desert, and we return to the opening airy sustain. The sound gradually dissipates. *—"Blue Gene" Tyranny*

Recommended:

- ○ **Penderecki: Polish Requiem; Dream of Jacob** / Penderecki (cond.), Stockholm PO / 1996 / Chandos 9459
- ○ **Penderecki: Anaklasis; Capriccio; Threnody; Dream of Jacob; etc.** / Penderecki (cond.), Katowice Polish Radio Orch. & Chorus / 1994 / EMI 65077

Threnody (for the Victims of Hiroshima), for 52 strings (1959–1961)

Threnody was completed in 1960, and remains one of Penderecki's best-known works. Composed at a time when serial technique dominated avant-garde music, *Threnody* is instead a deeply personal work, disturbing in its evocations of human misery and terror. Though it is dedicated to the victims of the atomic bomb dropped on Hiroshima at the end of the Second World War, Penderecki drew on his own experiences in Nazi-occupied Poland in composing this work. He noted that Nazi war crimes, especially "the great Apocalypse" of Auschwitz, have been in his "subconscious mind since the war." As a result, this work, like much of Penderecki's music, is emotionally powerful and in large part autobiographical, but at the same time expresses a universal mourning for the victims of war.

Threnody is scored for 52 strings, and features a number of spectacular instrumental effects—most significantly microtonal glissandi. *Threnody* is also a work of limited or "controlled" aleatoric elements: musical gestures are represented graphically on the score, but the performers are at times allowed some freedom in the realization of musical elements like pitch and duration. The work is divided roughly into three sections, with the outermost sections allowing the greatest freedom for the performers. At certain points in the score, performers may simply play their instruments' highest notes, or, when pitch is specified, performers may move from pitch to pitch by quarter tones.

Penderecki also demands unconventional bowing for effect, including bowing between the bridge and the tailpiece, and bowing the bridge or tailpiece. He also calls for striking the soundboard with the fingers. Instruments were divided into groups and assigned a particular range of pitches, within which they move by glissando. In terms of rhythm, *Threnody* is very nearly an arrhythmic piece, as there is no regular pulse to be found; instead, individual sections are measured by clock time, in minutes and seconds.

The result of Penderecki's controlled aleatoricism is a work of considerable expressive force—a musical representation of human suffering that, despite its considerable technical difficulties, strikes home with surprising sincerity. Each string section, as it ebbs and swells, engages in a kind of dialogue with other sections, and the effect of many instruments playing glissandi at once simulates, rather distressingly, the sound of human voices wailing in a swirling, hellish polyphony. It is a vivid evocation of the horrors of war, and also a good example of Penderecki's so-called "sensualist," Neo-Romantic style. *—Alexander Carpenter*

Recommended:

- **Penderecki: Anaklasis; Capriccio; Threnody; etc.** / Penderecki (cond.), Katowice Polish Radio Orch. & Chorus / 1994 / EMI 65077
- **Penderecki: Orchestral Works Vol. 1** / Wit (cond.), National Polish RSO / 2000 / Naxos 554491

SYMPHONIC

Symphonies (1972)

Krzysztof Penderecki didn't write his first symphony until he was 40 years old. It was his first large-scale orchestral work, and many, including himself, consider it a summation of his compostional style up to that point, but it also shows traces of his turning to more traditional forms that would become much more obvious and important in his other symphonies. The techniques and sonorities of his *Symphony No. 1* (1972–73) are similar to those used in the *Threnody* and other works, but the four continuous sections act somewhat as a sonata-allegro form based on sound, rather than a distinct melody. His next four symphonies are all in a neo-Romantic style and written with such an assured skill in that style that critics have said that Penderecki is no longer an innovative or interesting composer. The names of past symphonists Beethoven, Brahms, Mahler, and Shostakovich all come up in descriptions of Penderecki's symphonies. *Symphony No. 2*, from 1979–80, also known as the "Christmas Symphony" because it quotes *Silent Night*, has a fully notated score and full, dark orchestral sound, very much based on accessible melody with the occasional dissonances. The last two movements of his *Symphony No. 3* were written seven years before the first three movements. All recall much earlier musical periods and use very percussive techniques and intense counterpoint to convey nostalgia as well as tension and control. *Symphonies Nos. 4* (1989) and 5 (1992) return to a single movement form. *No. 4* also shows a return to some of Penderecki's earlier adventurousness and feels more open than the previous symphonies, but its emotional conflicts are not always resolved. The fifth symphony uses a Korean folksong as a melodic base and has a greater dynamism due to its strong contrasts of fast and slow sections and its more experimental textures. Penderecki's *Symphony No. 7*, the "Seven Gates of Jerusalem" (1996), is scored for 5 soloists, speaker, 3 choirs, and orchestra. Psalms and other Old Testament texts are sung in Latin for this oratorio-like work celebrating Jerusalem's 3,000th anniversary. It represents even further a reconciliation of his avant-garde earlier period with the neo-Romanticism, although the neo-Romanticism still prevails. *—Patsy Morita*

Recommended:

- **Penderecki: Orchestral Works Vol. 2** / Wit (cond.), National Polish RSO / 2000 / Naxos 554567
- **Penderecki: Orchestral Works Vol. 3** / Wit (cond.), National Polish RSO / 2000 / Naxos 554492
- **Penderecki: Orchestral Works Vol. 1** / Wit (cond.), National Polish RSO / 2000 / Naxos 554491
- **Penderecki: 7 Gates of Jerusalem** / Wit (cond.), National Polish RSO / 2000 / Wergo 6647-2

CHAMBER MUSIC

String Quartet No. 1 (1960)

Penderecki's *String Quartet No. 1* (1960) is a sonic study utilizing the entire range of traditional string techniques (arco, pizzicato, con sordino, sul ponticello, col legno, col legno battuta, senza vibrato) together with several developed by the composer: glissandi on trills, very rapid non-rhythmic tremolo, playing an indefinite highest possible pitch, playing between the bridge and tailpiece, playing on the tailpiece, striking strings with palm of hand, very slow vibrato with microtonal intervals, and others. The quartet was written quickly, within the span of a few days, and was premiered by the famous LaSalle Quartet in Cincinnati in May 1962.

Most of the score does not call for specific pitches, but rather for general pitch ranges. The work unfolds in measures of equal duration (one second each).

At the beginning, trills that begin on specific pitches "slide" in progressively wider glissandi. Percussive sounds, effected by hitting the strings with the wood of the bow, harsh pizzicatos, etc., are then played with dramatic abandon in quasi-random fashion. This gradually develops into a section of fast tremolos, followed by a brief pause. Long-held notes lead into tone clusters, marked by pizzicato glissandi. Quiet tones played near the bridge (sul ponticello) and harmonics are followed by a return of the percussive sounds. The work ends with high mysterious tones. *—"Blue Gene" Tyranny*

Recommended:

- **Penderecki: Music for Clarinet & String Quartet** / Tale SQ / 1994 / Bis 652
- **Ionisation: Music of Varèse, Penderecki, Ligeti** / Kohon SQ / 1995 / VoxBox 5142

CHORAL

Magnificat, for bass, 7 men's voices, boys' chorus, chorus & orchestra (1973–1974)

Krzysztof Penderecki's *Magnificat* from 1974 holds a distinctive position, both within the composer's oeuvre as well as within the arena of later twentieth century religious music. As a work by a religious composer on a liturgical text, it employs entirely new modes of expression in the act of musical devotion. The *Magnificat* expanded on and synthesized several of his most effective ideas, while at the same time smoothing over certain experimental edges. There is a stronger sense of continuity and cohesiveness than one finds in many of his earlier works, and some structural or stylistic principles familiar to earlier music traditions are used, such as the fugue and the passacaglia. Several of Penderecki's trademark techniques remain, however, with dramatic effect. Whereas some modern composers have rendered works in archaic and unfamiliar languages in order to occlude the semantic element of the text, Penderecki finds the Latin prose of the *Magnificat* full of expressive potential. "There is really nothing else that *means* so much" as the Latin liturgy, he insists (an idea manifested elsewhere as well, in the *Stabat Mater* from 1963, the *St. Luke Passion* in 1966, and the *Dies Irae* from 1967). Of course, the meaning he finds in the text is embedded in familiarity and tradition rather than directly conveyed, and his delivery of the text is often obscured by his innovative textures. At the conclusion of the first of the work's seven sections, for example, each of the chorus' ten parts proceeds through the syllables "salutari meo" at a different pace while rising slowly and smoothly in pitch; this takes place above pulsing percussion and thick bands of clustered string tones. The second movement engages in a more ordered but equally complex polyphony, with instruments and voices in an angular triple fugue held together by a steady triple meter. The fugal procedure becomes even more complex as segments of the individual lines are taken up and passed off by individual performers. Likewise, polyrhythmic complexes create elegant fans whose striking appearance on the page mimics the real-time aural phenomenon. The third movement resumes something of the second's triple meter polyphonies, but only after a haunting non-metered opening gesture in which each string player enters individually, in rapid succession, and on a different pitch within a huge wall of quarter-tonal, broadband noise. This is followed by the brief recitative of the fourth movement. The fifth movement is an uneasy, irregularly paced passacaglia that alternates orchestral episodes with choral text expositions, while the sixth omits the orchestra altogether and features the choir in 13 parts a cappella. The final movement, on "Gloria patri . . . ," is perhaps the most lucid, ultimately tethering the work's countless strands to a single, unison C on "Amen." *—Jeremy Grimshaw*

Recommended:

- **Penderecki: Orchestral & Choral Works** / Penderecki (cond.), Krakow Radio Chorus / 2001 / EMI 74852
- **Penderecki: Stabat Mater** / Kuivanen (cond.), Tapiola Chamber Choir / 1995 / Finlandia 98999

Polish Requiem (1980–1984; revised 1993)

As musicologists have noted, Penderecki is, above all else, these three things: a composer, a Polish patriot, and a Roman Catholic. In the *Polish Requiem*, these three aspects of Penderecki come together to produce a large-scale religious work for soloists, mixed choir, and orchestra. The work was composed over the course of nearly five years, and its many parts were composed in a number of different places in the world, as Penderecki undertook his conducting tours. The *Requiem* is certainly first and foremost a religious work, a mass for the dead in the Roman Catholic church service: the Agnus Dei was composed for the funeral of Penderecki's friend Cardinal Wyszynski, and the Recordare, Jesu pie was written for the beatification of Father Maximillian Kolbe. It should be noted, however, the Penderecki's *Requiem* also has a political side as well, revealing the composer as patriot: the Lacrimosa was written as a commission from Solidarity trade union leader Lech Walesa, and the Dies irae was composed to commemorate the Warsaw uprising against the Nazis in 1944.

Penderecki's *Requiem* omits several parts of the liturgical requiem, the Offertorium and Sanctus, replacing them with a Polish hymn and a finale taken from the psalms of David. In terms of its musical language, the *Requiem* represents Penderecki's mature style, a blending of modern sound and technique with a kind of post-Romantic sensibility. The work is pervasively polyphonic, the harmonic language chromatic. Moments of rich counterpoint are juxtaposed with noisy chord clusters and glissando effects. The Lacrimosa and Agnus Dei were originally composed as independent pieces, and were performed in the early 1980s before the entire *Requiem* was finished. These two sections of the *Requiem* are among its most profound, in particular the Lacrimosa, written in a decidedly tonal style and with a moving sorrowful character echoing the *Requiems* of Mozart and Verdi. The *Requiem* ends, like Verdi's, with a heartfelt Libera me, though Penderecki appends a finale which includes quotations from the sixth psalm of David and which brings back themes from earlier sections, including the Recordare and Lacrimosa.

The *Requiem* in its entirety was first performed in Stuttgart in September 1984. Guido Barth wrote, at the premiere, of the *Requiem*'s profound Polish Catholicism, and felt in it "at once the confrontation of present times with the submission of its people to their history." The *Polish Requiem* thus stands as Penderecki's monument to the Polish people, a musical accounting of their past and future sufferings. *—Alexander Carpenter*

Recommended:

○ **Penderecki: Polish Requiem; Dream of Jacob** / Penderecki (cond.), Royal Stockholm Phil. Chorus / 1996 / Chandos 9459

○ **Penderecki: Stabat Mater** / Kuivanen (cond.), Tapiola Chamber Choir / 1995 / Finlandia 98999

St. Luke Passion (1965–1966)

Penderecki wrote this monumental work just eight years after completing his formal composition studies. One of his first major works, it quickly earned Penderecki recognition as an important young composer. The full title of the work is "The Passion and Death of our Lord Jesus Christ according to St. Luke." It is scored for huge forces: solo soprano, baritone, bass, and speaker; three mixed choruses; a boys' choir; full orchestra without oboe or clarinet but including saxophones; full percussion including tympani, bass drums, tom-toms, rattles, bongos, bells, Chinese and Javanese gongs, vibraphone, harp, piano, organ, and harmonium. The text is a setting of St. Luke's account of the Passion, and also includes some psalms, Latin hymns, and other liturgical texts. Penderecki's *Passion* is part of the grand tradition of the Passion exemplified by J.S. Bach. Bach's *St. John* and *St. Matthew Passions* stand among the greatest pieces of religious music in the history of Western civilization, and Penderecki's *Passion* certainly bears the marks of Bach's influence.

The *St. Luke Passion*'s most obvious Bach-inspired features are its two-part structure and its alternation of narrated action with sung reflection. While musically there is little in Penderecki's *Passion* that directly draws on Bach's Baroque counterpoint, Penderecki does invoke at least the presence of the older composer through the use of the four note motive B-A-C-H ("b" is b flat and "h" is b natural in the German musical alphabet). There are, of course, also a number of significant differences between the Passions of Bach and the *St. Luke Passion*, especially in terms of language and scope: Penderecki's Passion is in Latin and is half as long as Bach's Passions, which set Luther's German and German Baroque religious poetry.

In Penderecki's *Passion* the narrative action is moved along by a speaker, who is set against an orchestral backdrop. Soloists sing the essential dramatic roles, Christ, Pilate, Peter, and the Maiden. The choirs are employed, typically, to represent crowds, but a large choral introduction and finale also serve to frame the work. Musically, the *St. Luke Passion* is a mélange of several different elements. Borrowings from Penderecki's own *Stabat Mater* of 1962 are audible, as are Gregorian chantlike fragments and manipulations of the B-A-C-H motive. Penderecki also employs 12-tone rows in the manner of Arnold Schoenberg and Anton Webern. There is no real sense of an overarching tonal harmonic system at work in the Passion, despite the occasional tonal moment. Instead, Penderecki selects individual notes as tonal centers, surrounding them with melodic fragments, chord clusters, and dense textures bordering on pure noise.

The *St. Luke Passion* is an important work in the history of music in the twentieth century, as it brings together and seemingly solves a number of stylistic problems, including the integration of tonal and non-tonal harmony and the blending of religious themes with modern soundscapes. *—Alexander Carpenter*

Recommended:

○ **Penderecki: Sacred Choral Works** / Kuivanen (cond.). Tapiola Chamber Choir / 2001 / Finlandia 88433

○ **Penderecki: Passio et mors Domini nostri Jesu Christi secundum Lucam** / Soustrot (cond.), WDR Rundfunkchor Koln / 2000 / MDG 3370981

Leonard Pennario

b. Jul. 9, 1924, Buffalo, NY

Pianist

Leonard Pennario was among the most popular American-born concert pianists of the twentieth century. Pennario's professional career began at the tender age of 12 when he filled in for an ailing soloist on the Grieg *Concerto in A minor* at a 1936 concert with the Dallas Symphony Orchestra. Freshly inducted into the U.S. Army, Pennario gave his Carnegie Hall debut in the uniform of an Army private, playing the Liszt *Piano Concerto No. 1* in November 1943. Pennario returned from his tour of duty to an eager reception in the concert world. At the time, a Minneapolis critic wrote "Pennario is endowed with temperament, interpretive imagination and the capacity to express it, above and beyond the flyingest ten fingers you ever saw. He made the concert one of the most exciting and exhilarating musical experiences in a long, long time." This sentiment would be repeated in city after city as Pennario dutifully traversed the concert circuit.

Where many young concert artists view resettling in New York as a necessity, Pennario stayed based in Los Angeles his entire career. Although he gave his first European tour in 1952, Pennario has concentrated his performances mostly within the continental U.S. and Hawaii. His choice of venue allowed him to build up long-standing relationships of value with other Los Angeles-based individuals and concerns, such as his friendship with composer Miklós Rózsa, who composed both a *Piano Concerto* and the outstanding *Piano Sonata* (1948) for him. Pennario also began an association with Hollywood-based Capitol Records, for whom he recorded for more than three decades. Among more than 60 albums made for Capitol is Pennario's recording of George Gershwin's *Rhapsody in Blue* with the Hollywood Bowl Orchestra under Felix Slatkin, one of the best-selling classical albums from the era of vinyl records.

When the classical division of Capitol went belly up in the early 1980s, it derailed Pennario's recording career, but it did not affect his standing in the concert world. In 1987 Pennario played a concert at Lincoln Center that was broadcast over PBS in observance of the 50th anniversary of Gershwin's death. Ultimately, by the 1990s, Pennario finally began to retreat from the concert stage, pursuing instead his other great ability—as a champion bridge player. Leonard Pennario was a great all-around pianist with an innate sense of musicianship—as one of his record producers put it "Pennario is one of those artists who just 'gets' the music." *—Uncle Dave Lewis*

Recommended:

○ **Leonard Pennario: Film Themes and Variations** / Pennario / 1993 / Cambria 1093

○ **Rachmaninov: Piano Concerto 3; Paganini Rhapsody** / Leinsdorf (cond.), Susskind (cond.), Pennario, London PO, Los Angeles PO / 2001 / Seraphim 74522

○ **Schuman: Kinderscenen, Op15/Papillons, Op2/Sonata No.1 In F** / Pennario / 1997 / Seraphim 69727

Murray Perahia

b. Apr. 19, 1947, New York, NY

Pianist

In a field in which each season heralds the arrival of new "talents" who are soon forgotten, pianist Murray Perahia has remained a reliable and immensely gifted presence on the international scene for more than three decades. Perahia began his music studies at the age of five with lessons from Jeanette Haien, who remained his teacher until he was well into his teens. In 1964 Perahia entered the Mannes College of Music in New York, where he studied composition and conducting; though both endeavors remained secondary to his career as a pianist, the latter proved particularly useful when, decades later, Perahia conducted and recorded a complete cycle of Mozart's piano concerti from the keyboard. Perahia pursued further piano studies with Artur Balsam and Mieczysław Horszowski. He also attended the Marlboro Festival in Vermont, which brought him into contact and collaboration with such artists as Rudolf Serkin, Pablo Casals, and the Budapest Quartet.

In 1968 Perahia made his Carnegie Hall debut to much acclaim, and his concert career blossomed in short order. He made headlines in 1972 by taking top honors at the prestigious Leeds Piano Competition, the first American to do so—and, no less, by unanimous decision. Perahia's success at Leeds led to his London recital debut at Queen Elizabeth Hall in 1973. Later that year he appeared at the Aldeburgh Festival, where he worked closely with the festival's founders, Benjamin Britten and Peter Pears. After Britten's declining health made it impossible for him to continue as Pears' accompanist, Perahia became one of Pears' frequent and favorite recital partners. In 1975 Perahia shared with cellist Lynn Harrell the first Avery Fisher Prize, intended to aid in the development of the most promising American musical careers. In 1981 he was appointed co-artistic director of the Aldeburgh Festival, a position he retained through 1989.

Perahia is often described as a "musician's musician," one who does not adopt a virtuoso persona but performs with a distinctive directness, without exaggerated or demonstrative gestures. His playing is clean and meticulous, his sound cool, transparent, sparkling, and exquisitely shaded. He is best known for his performances of Classical and early Romantic repertoire; from the late 1990s he developed an especial reputation as an interpreter of Bach. In 2000, his recording of Bach's *Goldberg Variations* was awarded two Grammy nominations for Best Classical Album and Best Instrumental Soloist.

Perahia's popularity has been sustained largely through his extensive catalogue of recordings. He signed an exclusive contract with CBS Masterworks in 1973 and has remained with that label through its corporate transformation into Sony Classics. His recordings have received numerous accolades, including multiple Grammies and Gramophone Awards for Instrumental Record of the Year. In addition to his Mozart concerto cycle, he has recorded all five Beethoven piano concerti with Bernard Haitink and the Concertgebouw Orchestra, as well as Schumann's complete works for piano and orchestra. *—AMG*

Recommended:

○ **Schumann: Davidsbündlertänze; Fantasiestücke** / Perahia / 1973 / CBS 32299

- ○ **The Art of Murray Perahia** / Perahia / Sony 48153
- ○ **Mozart: Concerto 26; Rondos** / Perahia, English CO / CBS 39224
- ○ **Perahia Plays & Conducts Mozart** / Perahia, English CO / 1978 / CBS 42243
- ○ **Mendelssohn: Concertos** / Marriner (cond.), Perahia, Academy of St. Martin-in-the-Fields / 1975 / Sony 42401
- ○ **Songs Without Words** / Perahia / 1999 / Sony 66511

Giovanni Pergolesi

b. Jan. 4, 1710, Jesi, Italy, **d.** Mar. 16, 1736, Pozzuoli, Italy
Composer: Vocal, Opera

Despite his tragically short life, Pergolesi left an impressive œuvre, including the intermezzo *La serva padrona*, one of the great examples of the Italian comic opera in the eighteenth century. A successful opera composer, Pergolesi was also a highly esteemed composer of church music, exemplified by his remarkable *Stabat Mater*.

Following musical studies in his native town, Pergolesi was sent to Naples in the early 1720s. He continued his studies at the Conservatorio dei Poveri di Gesu Cristo, where he also performed as a violinist, also making his debut as a composer. In 1731, Pergolesi received his first commission to compose an opera, which means that he had probably left the conservatory around that time. By early 1732, Pergolesi had composed two operas, which met with minimal success. That year, he became maestro di cappella to Prince Ferdinando Colona Stigliano, a prominent Neapolitan nobleman. Pergolesi's opera *Lo frate 'nnamorato* was performed, greeted with immense enthusiasm.

In 1733, Pergolesi was commissioned to write an opera for the celebration of the birthday of the Empress of Austria. Performed in 1733, this opera, *Il prigioner superbo*, contained a two-act intermezzo, *La serva padrona*, which eventually gained extraordinary popularity as a separate work. When Carlos de Bourbon entered Naples in 1734, reestablishing, with the support of Spanish troops, the Kingdom of Naples, Pergolesi was asked to write a mass. He composed his *Mass in F*, which was performed in Rome, eliciting considerable interest. Pergolesi was now maestro di cappella to another Neapolitan nobleman, the Duke Maddaloni.

The success of his *Mass* brought Pergolesi another commission: an opera, *L'Olimpiade*, for the 1735 Carnival season in Rome. The opera was a failure; fortunately, Pergolesi's last stage effort, *Il flaminio*, a comedy, was successfully produced in Naples. In 1736, Pergolesi, suffering from tuberculosis, moved to the Franciscan monastery in Pozzuoli. During his final year, he composed the *Stabat Mater*, which contemporaries lauded as a successful introduction of the new galant style into the traditional domain of church music.

Pergolesi's *Stabat Mater* was first published in London, in 1749, eventually becoming the most frequently printed musical composition in the eighteenth century. *La serva padrona*, based on a story about a witty servant girl who plots to marry her elderly master, enjoyed great success in Europe following Pergolesi's death. In 1752, a performance of this work in Paris sparked the famous *Querelle des Bouffons* (Quarrel of the Comedians), the dispute between the supporters of Italian opera and the patriotic traditionalists, who favored French opera. During this dispute, *La serva padrona* was upheld as representative of the Italian operatic genius. Eighteenth century critics, as well as ordinary listeners, admired the opera's brilliant characterization and masterful plot development. Admired in the eighteenth century, this concise stage work, which possesses a timeless charm, has been appreciated by generations of listeners. *—Zoran Minderovic*

Overview of Works (ca. 1730–1736)

Giovanni Battista Pergolesi (1710–36) took his name from Pergola, the town from which his family hailed. He studied in Naples under Vinci and Durante at Conservatorio dei Poveri, where he was a singer and later a violinist who led one of the string groups hired out by the conservatory in Naples and the surrounding area. In 1732 Pergolesi was appointed maestro di cappella to Prince Ferdinando Colonna Stigliano, and two years later maestro in the service of another Neapolitan nobleman, the Duke of Maddaloni. Throughout his life frail of health (he may have suffered a physical deformity as a result of tuberculosis), Pergolesi passed his final months at the Franciscan monastery of Puzzuoli, where he died at the age of 26.

At the time of his death, Pergolesi was virtually unknown outside Italy, where he had enjoyed only limited success. The unprecedented posthumous fame he achieved almost instantly following his death was in part almost certainly due to its premature nature, but may also be accounted for by the extraordinary success achieved throughout Europe by the two works for which Pergolesi remains best known, the intermezzo *La serva padrona*, and the *Stabat mater*. So great became the legend and commercial success surrounding the name Pergolesi that it was appended to many works by other composers. During his lifetime the composer's more limited reputation was built on his operas and sacred works. Of his eight surviving stage works, four are opera seria, two of which, *Adriano in Siria* (Naples, 1734), and *L'olimpiade* (Rome, 1735) have librettos by the most famous librettist of the eighteenth century, Pietro Metastasio. His earliest opera seria, *Salustia*, appeared in Naples when Pergolesi was only 22, and is a conservative work in the noble, high Baroque tradition. The later works in this form show greater signs of the more sentimental and gracious lyricism that is particularly associated with Neapolitan opera. However, it is Pergolesi's comic operas that were principally responsible for the spread of his fame, in particular the two short, two-act intermezzos, *La serva padrona* (Naples, 1733), and *Livietta e Tracolla* (Naples, 1734). Such pieces were originally performed between the acts of opera seria, but it was the troupes of players who traveled throughout Europe who were responsible for their widespread dissemination in the aftermath of the composer's death. In 1752, the arrival of *La serva padrona* in Paris sparked off the famous "Querelle des Bouffons." The huge success of Pergolesi's comic intermezzos led to extravagant claims, still prevalent today, that he was the progenitor of opera buffa, a distinction that more properly belongs to his teacher, Leonardo Vinci. The sacred works are dominated by two composed during his last illness, a *Salve regina* in C minor, and, most famously, the *Stabat mater*. Both are written in the affecting sentimental style, the latter being a bittersweet meditation for two soloists on the Virgin at the Cross, their plangent, gently dissonant interweavings creating an unforgettably poignant effect. *—Brian Robins*

Recommended:

- ○ **Pergolesi: Marian Vespers** / Higginbottom (cond.), Academy of Ancient Music, New College Choir Oxford / 2002 / Erato 46684
- ○ **Giovanni Battista Pergolesi** / Panni (dir.), Re, Dessi, Cesare, Omilian, Mazzaria, Chamber Opera Orch. of Rome / Bongiovanni 2078
- ○ **Pergolesi: Missa Romana; Magnificat; Salve Regina** / Pancik , Sieghart (conds.), Prague Chamber Choir, Stuttgart CO / 1994 / Orfeo 338941
- ○ **Pergolesi: Cantata da Camera** / Maestri (cond.), Banditelli, Rigacci / 2001 / Bis 2185

VOCAL

Stabat mater, in F major (1736)

Quis est homo? "Who is he that would not weep, to see the mother of Christ in such despair?" These words were first uttered in thirteenth century Italy in an affective and emotional Latin deovtional lyric; the obvious answer to its rhetorical question is that no true believer would not mourn with the Virgin over the dying Christ. The poem is the "Stabat mater," thought to be the work of the great Lauda-poet Jacopone da Todi. Its plangent strophes affect an emotional connection between the meditating believer and the mother of the Crucified, and first emerged from the intense strains of popular devotion following the Black Plague. In the eighteenth century, however, the text took on new life in popular devotional practice through the influence of one musical setting: the *Stabat mater dolorosa* of Giovanni Battista Pergolesi.

The Roman Catholic Church officially added the "Feast of the Seven Sorrows of the Virgin" to its calendar in 1727, but the "Stabat mater" text was already ensconsed in many local liturgies. According to Pergolesi's first biographer, a famous monastery in Naples comissioned a musical setting of the text from the great Alessandro Scarlatti in 1725. Soon thereafter, they sought a new setting from Pergolesi mandating that he had to compose for two high voices (sopranos or male castrati). He accepted the task, despite his then-current illness: the 25-year-old Pergolesi was already suffering from the tuberculosis that would claim his life. The legend goes that he composed in a devotional frenzy on his deathbed. Whether or not the story was true, Pergolesi's *Stabat mater* was quickly an international hit, drawing inevitable comparisons to Mozart's deathbed *Requiem*. This cantata was published more often than any other single piece of music in the entire eighteenth century.

Musically, Pergolesi sets the successive tercets of his poetic text to alternating duets and arias. From the very opening measures, he carefully sets a mournful affect. The violins (answered later by the vocal duet) open with a drawn-out chain of suspensions and a painfully extended pedal tone. Later movements similarly use overtly "sad" musical devices: the second duet features strong dissonant clashes for "O quam tristis et afflicta," and the third appears above a chromatically descending bass line. Surprisingly, however, Pergolesi also includes several arias that clothe the mournful text in much lighter musical raiment; he was, after all, the famed composer of light opera interludes (including *La serva padrona*). *—Timothy Dickey*

Recommended:

- ○ **Vivaldi: Gloria; Pergolesi: Stabat Mater** / Harnoncourt (cond.), Ortner, Lipovsek, Mei, Vienna Concentus Musicus / 1994 / Teldec 76989
- ○ **Pergolesi & Scarlatti: Stabat Mater** / Alessandrini (cond.), Mingardo, Bertagnolli, Concerto Italiano / 1998 / Opus 111 30160

OPERA

La serva padrona (1733)

One of the most successful comic stage works of the entire eighteenth century, Pergolesi's intermezzo *La serva padrona* was first produced in Naples at the San Bartolomeo theater on September 5, 1733. The function of such works was to serve as an entr'acte piece between the acts of a substantial opera seria—in this instance Pergolesi's own *Il prigioniero superbo*, a work subsequently eclipsed by the fame of the intermezzo.

In keeping with the characteristics of the genre, the plot and design of *La serva padrona* are extremely straightforward; there are only two short acts, and only three characters, one of whom is a mute male servant. The two singing parts are for a middle-aged man, Umberto, and his pert servant Serpina, both drawn from the traditions of commedia dell'arte. The plot concerns Serpina's tricking Umberto into marriage. Pergolesi's music clothes this inconsequential but naturalistic domestic drama in a rich vein of characterization and vitality; the simplicity of means employed would prove enormously influential in the development of comic opera. It is this feature that has led to the mistaken idea that Pergolesi was the founder of opera buffa—a distinction that more properly belongs to one of his teachers, Leonardo Vinci.

Notwithstanding, the great success achieved by *La serva padrona*, particularly after its composer's premature death at the age of only 26, unquestionably laid the foundations for the great comic operas of Mozart. In the archetypal characters of the intermezzo we find the progenitors of the more subtly drawn personages of Mozart's Count, and Susanna or Despina. The rapid Europe-wide dissemination of *La serva padrona* also hastened the reform of the stilted conventions of serious opera, whose stiff formalism lacked the color, verve, and flexibility of the lowbrow newcomer. When it reached Paris in 1752, performances sparked off the famous *Querelle des Bouffons*, a bitter pamphlet war fought between proponents of Italian opera buffa, and those who supported traditional French classical opera. Few works of such modest pretensions have achieved such great and lasting influence over the course of the development of music. *—Brian Robins*

Synopsis:

First Intermezzo. Following a sprightly overture, Uberto is seen dressing in preparation for venturing out. He complains vigorously that he has already waited three hours for his chocolate, but that no sign of it has yet appeared. His frustration is vented in a casually drawn aria, following which he aims his reproofs at his maid, Serpina. She, in turn, responds testily and decisively to Uberto before redirecting her attention to Vespone, a silent servant who quickly scurries off on his assigned tasks. Turning back to Uberto, Serpina informs him that it is now entirely too late for him to go out and proceeds to chastise him ("Stizzoso, mio Stizzoso"). By now vexed beyond endurance, Uberto summons Vespone and insists that he immediately undertake finding his master a wife. Serpina is quick to interject: "A wonderful idea—take me!" In the duet that brings the first intermezzo to a close, Uberto mutters his decision to be rid of Serpina entirely even while he admits the likelihood that he has already been overwhelmed by her domination. Serpina, all the while, rattles off a catalog of her qualifications.

Second Intermezzo. Serpina plots to cause Uberto to marry her, whether it be by means of outmaneuvering him, scaring him, or wheedling him. She enlists Vespone. Uberto is informed that she herself has found a mate; her intended is a soldier whose name is Captain Tempest. After describing his intemperate and uncompromising nature, she sings a pensive aria ("A Serpina penserete"), trusting that she will not be forgotten when she is no longer in the household. A sympathetic look from Uberto restores Serpina's minxlike demeanor and, as her master takes her hand, she has reason to believe that her approach is beginning to bear fruit. Thoroughly confused, Uberto questions whether he feels pity for Serpina, or might even be in love with her. His aria ("Son imbrogliato io già") perfectly mirrors his quandary in strains both comic and contemplative. Clear enough, however, is that Uberto is not quite the same man.

Meanwhile, Serpina returns to the chamber with a military man, her "Captain," who appears exceedingly edgy, not to say explosive. It is, of course, Vespone, who maintains his silence amidst his repertory of threatening gestures. Uberto recoils before the Captain's frightening appearance and aggressive deportment, looking anxiously from the stranger to Serpina and back again. Serpina informs him that the Captain insists that she be provided with a large dowry. Should she not be given that, the Captain will not accept her as a wife, but will demand that Uberto instead take her as his wife. With no such dowry forthcoming, Uberto finds himself engaged to his maid. This process completed, Vespone, still speaking not a word, removes his disguise. Uberto protests the deception, but to no avail. He has not only been outwitted, but also made to see that he is truly in love with Serpina. As the curtain falls, all is in readiness for the marriage that will make Serpina mistress of the household. *—Erik Eriksson*

Recommended:

○ **Pergolesi: Livietta e Tracollo; La Serva Padrona** / Kuijken (cond.), La Petite Bande / Accent 96123

Jacopo Peri

b. Aug. 20, 1561, Rome, Italy, **d.** Aug. 12, 1633, Florence, Italy

Composer: Opera

Jacopo Peri, to whom belongs the distinction of having composed the first opera, was born in Rome but grew up in Florence. A member of a noble family, Peri studied under Cristoforo Malvezzi of Lucca. From 1579 to 1606 he was an organist at the Badia in Florence, and in 1588, he entered the service of the court of the dominant Medici family as *maestro di cappella* first to Ferdinand I, Duke of Tuscany, and afterwards to his son, Cosimo II. In 1589 he performed to great acclaim in the giant musical production *La Pellegrina*, organized to commemorate Ferdinand's marriage to Christine of Lorraine.

Peri became associated with a group of humanists in Florence, headed by Giovanni de' Bardi, who were dedicated to attempting a revival of Greek tragedy as the Greeks themselves had experienced it. It was established knowledge that ancient performances had included long set pieces alternating with what might be termed duets and extended choral odes, all sung or declaimed in rhythms that varied according to the emotions being expressed. Dance and instrumental accompaniment were also involved. No music had survived from ancient Greece, however, so these Florentine intellectuals had to make their best guess as to how the music should sound.

The result of this experiment in reconstruction was *Dafne*, a pastoral drama by the poet Ottavio Rinuccini with music by Peri and Jacopo Corsi. Peri was responsible for the recitatives and some of the musical numbers. Now considered the first opera, *Dafne* was performed privately in 1597 at Corsi's home in Florence; as word of its novelty spread it received several more performances over the next few years.

In 1600, Peri was commissioned to write a second opera, again with Rinuccini, on the occasion of Maria de' Medici's marriage to Henry IV of France. Drawing on the ancient Greek legend of the miraculous powers of music, they produced *Euridice*; Peri himself probably sang the role of Orpheus in the first performance. This opera, by virtue of the more public circumstances of its creation, awakened wider interest in the new music. Opera came into its own as an art form over the next few decades.

Peri's compositional style emphasized monody and declamation, a break from the contrapuntal style of his predecessors, and an embrace of the style that would prove the foundation of modern music composition. In addition to *Dafne* and *Euridice*, Peri wrote recitatives for Rinuccini's *Arianna* in 1608 and also composed other operas, ballets, and madrigals. From the early 1600s, Peri was in the service of the Mantuan court, for which he wrote the opera *Adone* in 1620.

Peri died in Florence in 1633 and was buried in the church of Santa Maria Novella, where his gravestone, crediting him as opera's inventor, is still clearly visible in the nave. Most of his music, including the much of the score to *Dafne*, is now lost, but *Euridice* survives and is still occasionally performed. *—Roberta Klarreich*

OPERA

Euridice (1600)

Born either in Rome or Florence, Jacopo Peri (1561–1633), also known as Zazzerino, was one of the most important figures in the early development of opera. During the 1580s he became involved with a group of intellectuals meeting at the home of Count Bardi in Florence. Known as the Camerata, their discussions included ideas that would have a significant influence on the creation of opera. Primary among these was an attempt to recapture the precepts of Greek drama by employing a kind of rhetorical musical declamation in which music was subservient in importance to a clear exposition of the text. The result was the invention of recitative, the foundation stone, although not the only component, of the earliest operas. The principles of the Camerata are to be found in *Dafne* (1597–98), and *Euridice* (1600), the two earliest operas for which a complete music score survive. Both were composed in collaboration with other composers, a practice familiar from the lavish dramatic Florentine intermedii to which Peri had contributed, and which are a precursor of opera.

For *Euridice* Peri worked with the singer and composer Giulio Caccini, another major figure in the early development of opera, who provided several of *Euridice*'s songs and some choruses. Subsequently both men published their own versions with music totally of their own composition. The subject matter of *Euridice* was a topic frequently employed in music drama of the period—the power of music, in this instance the story of Orpheus, the paradigmatic musician poet. It is the power of song alone that enables Orpheus to overcome death by enchanting the underworld into releasing his wife *Euridice* from its grip. The story, set to a libretto by Ottavio Rinuccini, is one to which Monteverdi would return seven years later to create the first great opera, *Orfeo*.

Euridice builds on *Dafne* in the respect of demonstrating that a coherent dramatic story could be entirely set to music. The opera opens with a prologue that is followed by five scenes (including one set at the gates of Hell), each of which concludes with a homophonic dance chorus of the type found in the intermedii. In addition to music in recitative style (stile recitativo), there are set pieces, mostly strophic songs of the kind familiar from *Orfeo*. *Euridice* was first given at the Pitti Palace in Florence on October 6, 1600, on the occasion of the wedding celebrations of Maria de' Medici and Henry IV of France. The instrumental forces employed include a range of continuo instruments: harpsichord, chittarone, lute, and lyra, with the probable addition of a single melody instrument in the prologue and finale. *—Brian Robins*

Synopsis:

In 790 verses, not divided into scenes except by implication of the change of setting from Earth to Hades and back again, composer Jacopo Peri and librettist Ottavio

Rinuccini recount the famous story of Orpheus and Euridice as found in Ovid's "Metamorphoses," but tack on a happy ending. The opera was, after all, first presented as wedding entertainment.

After a brief prologue sung by the figure Tragedia, two choruses in alternation celebrate the wedding day of Euridice and the demigod Orpheus, known throughout ancient Greece as a beguiling singer. Orpheus' friend Arcetro joins the festivities, as the mood becomes increasingly lively. Euridice herself now puts in an appearance, but her nuptial aria is colored by foreboding and melancholy. The two choruses and a new character named Aminta try to outdo one another with praise for Euridice's beauty, and the wedding preparations turn into an interlude of dance and song.

Orfeo finally arrives, perhaps a bit unsure of the course of things and invoking Venus, the goddess of love. Orpheus and Arcetro engage in a brief but warm conversation, which is interrupted by Tirsi, who inaugurates a pastoral dance. Into this happy scene bursts the messenger Dafne; only under pressure from Orfeo does she relate in full what she has just witnessed: Euridice has been bitten by a snake and has died. Orfeo seems frozen by the news; Arcetro breaks down in an anguished monologue; Aminta and the choruses join in the lamentation.

Some time has apparently passed; Arcetro announces that Orfeo's mournful cries have drawn pity from the gods; he will be allowed to descend to Hades to plead with Pluto, the god of the underworld, for Euridice's return.

Guided by Venus, Orfeo ventures into the underworld; in his fairly well-known aria "Funeste piagge," he expresses horror at what he finds there. Horror turns into a prayer to the gods to show pity. His singing begins to have a slight effect on Pluto, who insists on the necessity of maintaining the "inexorable law" of death, yet Orfeo's song reminds Pluto of his own love for Proserpina. The latter now adds her own entreaty to Orfeo's. After more appeals from Orfeo, the onlooking Caronte also advocates for Euridice's release. Pluto finally relents, his generosity noted by a rather dark-hued chorus.

Orfeo and Euridice now make their way back to the surface; contrary to Ovid, who has Euridice swept back to Pluto's realm when Orfeo turns to look at her, the couple's ascent is uneventful. Topside, Arcetro and Aminta engage in a conversation marveling at the turn of events and the safe return of Orfeo's bride. Orfeo himself offers an arioso along these same lines, while Euridice expresses amazement to find herself back home in her original, lively form. On the subject of lively form, the choruses and a trio of shepherds then lead the way through a celebratory sequence of singing and dancing, the wedding concluding even more joyously than it would have before its tragic but temporary interruption. *—James Reel*

Recommended:

- ○ **Peri: Euridice** / Cetrangelo (cond.), La Compagnia dei Febi Armonici; Ensemble Albalonga / 1997 / Pavane 7372/3
- ○ **Peri: Euridice** / de Caro (cond.), Bertini, Foresti, Fagotto, Zanasi, Arpeggione Ens. / 1995 / Arts 47276

Itzhak Perlman

b. Aug. 31, 1945, Tel Aviv, Israel
Violinist

In the latter twentieth and early twenty-first centuries, Itzhak Perlman has been acclaimed as being among the leading violinists before the public, and, without doubt, has been the most visible of them in media venues, from recordings and radio broadcasts to television and film appearances. No other concert violinist and few other serious musicians have achieved the widespread exposure and popularity attained by Perlman.

Itzhak Perlman was born in Tel Aviv on August 31, 1945. At the age of four he was stricken with polio, which caused permanent paralysis of his legs, leaving him to rely on crutches and braces for the rest of his life. Despite his handicap, young Itzhak began showing talent on the violin, and his father Chaim, a barber, quickly recognized his son's unusual abilities and arranged for lessons for him at the Music Academy of Tel Aviv. Soon Itzhak began giving concerts and attracting attention throughout Israel. American television talent agent Ed Sullivan learned of Perlman's abilities and brought the 13-year-old to New York for a 1959 appearance on his *Caravan of Stars* show.

Perlman and his parents subsequently took up residency in New York City, where the young virtuoso continued to attract attention. He enrolled at the Juilliard School of Music, studying with Ivan Galamian and Dorothy DeLay. He made his official debut in 1963 at Carnegie Hall with a performance of the F sharp minor Wieniawski *Concerto* and went on to win the Leventritt Competition, one of whose prizes was an appearance with the New York Philharmonic, then led by Leonard Bernstein.

After these triumphs Perlman was taken on by impresario Sol Hurok and given a heavy schedule of concerts in the United States, Europe, Asia, and Israel over the coming years. He also began making recordings with RCA and would eventually sign contracts with EMI, Sony, Teldec, and others. Over the next three decades, his recordings would include the concertos of Beethoven, Brahms, Sibelius, Mendelssohn, Berg, the two by Prokofiev, Tchaikovsky's *Piano Trio*, Dvořák's *Sonatina*, Paganini's *Caprices*, and many others. In 1966, Perlman married Toby Friedlander. The couple would reside in the Upper West Side of Manhattan, where they would raise five children. Perlman had begun teaching as well, and in 1975 took a faculty post at Brooklyn College.

Perlman's fame grew rapidly in the 1970s and he began appearing regularly on television programs, like the children's show *Sesame Street*, *The Tonight Show*, *David Letterman*, and various specials on the PBS network. He also became a frequent performer at White House events, especially during the Reagan administration. In 1986, President Reagan awarded him a Medal of Liberty, an award recognizing the contributions of foreign-born Americans. By 1990 Perlman had performed with virtually every major orchestra in the world and with almost every important conductor. He also signed a new contract that year with EMI, the label for whom he has made the most recordings.

In 1994, Perlman hosted a program on the PBS network called the *Three Tenors, Encore!*, that featured the singing of Luciano Pavarotti, Plácido Domingo, and José Carreras. He also made a television special in 1995 for the PBS *Great Performances* series entitled *In the Fiddler's House*. Perlman has recently taken up conducting, his concerts including a Tanglewood Festival performance in 2000 with the Boston Symphony Orchestra that included critically successful readings of the Mozart *Symphony No. 29* and the Brahms *Symphony No. 4*.

In the twenty-first century, Perlman's career continues to yield him triumph after triumph, placing him among this age's top five or six musicians in the classical realm. *—Robert Cummings*

Recommended:

- ○ **Paganini: Caprices** / Perlman / 2000 / EMI 67257
- ○ **Bits And Pieces** / Perlman, Sanders / 1994 / EMI 54882
- ○ **Bach: Violin Concertos** / Barenboim (cond.), Perlman, Zukerman, English CO / 2001 / EMI 74720
- ○ **Dvořák: Violin Concerto, etc.** / Barenboim (cond.), Perlman, Sanders, London PO / 2003 / EMI 62595
- ○ **Elgar: Concerto; Chausson: Poème** / Barenboim, Mehta (conds.), Perlman, Chicago SO, New York PO / DG 445564
- ○ **Beethoven: Concerto** / Giulini (cond.), Perlman, Philharmonia / 1998 / EMI 66952
- ○ **Itzhak Perlman Collection** / Perlman, etc. / 1995 / EMI 83177

Pérotin

b. 1100s, France [?], **d.** 1200s, France [?]
Composer: Choral

At the end of the twelfth century, as the walls of the Cathedral of Notre Dame were slowly raised above the surrounding buildings of Paris, a school of composers associated with this Cathedral were in the process of fashioning a new type of musical structure to elevate the divine liturgy performed there. Surviving musical manuscripts from a number of European centers (Santiago de Compostella, St. Martial in Limoges, Winchester Cathedral) from the eleventh and twelfth centuries preserve early experiments in liturgical polyphony, adding to the prescribed plainchant sung in worship an extra ornamental voice for a more glorious service upon major feast days. But the center of Paris, home of an increasingly vigorous bourgeois class, and a renowned University, would host the revolutionary new music known as Notre Dame Organum.

Unfortunately, almost nothing is known of the two major composers of this school, Leonin and Pérotin. The barest of outlines survives in a thirteenth century document containing the notes of an anonymous English university student. He records that a Magister Leoninus, a great composer, produced an entire *Magnus liber organi* (Great Book of Organum) for use in celebrations of the liturgy; scholars believe this compilation took place between 1160 and 1180. The student (known as Anonymous IV) goes on to note that Magister Perotinus, an even better composer of "discant," revised the work of the earlier Master, adding to it many pieces of his own; presumably, this took place either in the 1180s and 1190s, or early in the following century. From the account of Anonymous IV, and from other contemporary historical records, specific music in surviving manuscripts is attributed to Pérotin the Great. For instance, an 1198 liturgical ordinance by the Bishop of Paris relating New Years' eve observances prohibits a popular ritual known as the Feast of Fools, and stipulates instead of these vulgar revels a solemn service including specific pieces of chant set in Organum.

Possibly these exact pieces by Pérotin—*Viderunt omnes* and *Sederunt principes*, for the liturgy of Christmas and St. Stephen (Dec. 26), respectively—represent the earliest music surviving in Europe set for four voices. A fragment of Gregorian chant, usually sung by a soloist, is in this style of Organum presented in a single voice, with very extended rhythmic values. Upon this tonal foundation Pérotin erects an interlocking series of upper voices, which vocalize melismatically upon the extended chant syllables. These upper voices adopt vigorous and sequential dance-rhythms made possible by a new theory of notation known as the rhythmic modes. In a complete performance, sections called Clausulae of this highly ornamented polyphony would alternate with passages of unison plainchant, and with shorter chordal sections in "discant" style. In this second style, also used to set Latin liturgical poetry, the voices move jointly according to the rhythmic patterns. Pérotin may have written or revised in excess of 150 discant-style liturgical pieces, most for two voices. *—Timothy Dickey*

CHORAL

Viderunt omnes, organum (ca. 1200)

The human eye beholding the interior of a Gothic cathedral perceives a deep harmony between a bewildering complexity of elements. Horizontal bands of architecture proceed upwards, each with their own internal rhythms: the ponderous steps of the great columns marching down the aisle, surmounted by a tripling of speed in the smaller rank of triforium gallery arches, in turn crowned by the radiance of the clerestory windows and often yet another celestial rank in the upper rose windows. Each builds upon its foundation in an architectural style that appears literally to strive upwards toward the transcendent Godhead. In much the same way, the music of the Notre Dame School of polyphony harmonizes a complex musical architecture to strive toward perfection in the act of divine worship.

Very little is known about the two leading composers of the Notre Dame School. An unnamed English student at the University of Paris (known to posterity only as Anonymous IV) wrote long after their deaths of the great masters Leoninus (Léonin) and Perotinus Magnus (Pérotin). Léonin apparently composed an entire book around the middle of the twelfth century, the *Magnus Liber Organi*, of polyphonic elaborations upon the Parisian liturgy, to which Pérotin later made revisions and additions. Two pieces of Pérotin's music Anonymous IV specifically mentions are *Viderunt omnes* and *Sederunt*, which may be identified in manuscript collections of Notre Dame polyphony as the first compositions for four voices anywhere in Europe. The foundation of *Viderunt omnes* is a plainchant that likely served the Parisian liturgy for Christmas Day. The text comes from verses of *Psalm 98* in the *Vulgate's Latin* (Ps. 98:3b-4a, 2), jubilantly singing of the moment when God's salvation is made known to all the Earth. (Incidentally, the text naturally seems to call for such a concord of many voices!) Following the responsory form of plainchant, *Viderunt omnes* consists of a solo incipit, a chanted conclusion, a short verset (also perhaps for solo), and a repeat of the opening section. Pérotin's setting preserves the form and retains the liturgically correct chant melody, but embellishes it by two "discant clausulae," sections of composed polyphony that substitute for the solo chants. For each clausula, the choir sings the notes of the chant melody, but each note is greatly extended. Above this abstracted chant is woven a web of three solo voices dancing about one another in long, metrical melismas on the chant syllables. The most astounding innovation of Notre Dame polyphony was the addition of rhythm to such ornamental voices: the upper voices sing dozens of notes above each step of the chant, regulated by the six modal rhythms. The rhythmic patterns possible (which may shift in each voice phrase to phrase) are each related to a poetic foot: long/short (trochaic), short/long (iambic), long/short/short (dactylic), short/short/long (anapestic), long/long (spondeic), and short/short (pyrrhic). Within the limitations of these rhythms, the voices move freely as if by elaborate improvisation. Often sequential melodic motifs are expounded, and in this piece Pérotin even uses canonic relationships between voices. But the power of the piece doesn't come from this intricacy, but rather from the deep sense of harmony. Each phrase begins with a "perfect" harmony of fifths and octaves; the music then progresses in a compelling filigree upon the chant tone, a lengthy marginal gloss. But each phrase returns irrevocably from dissonance to perfection of harmony. And the final moments of the music are given to the liturgically perfect plainchant alone, in unison singing as if to represent the unity of the Church itself. *—Timothy Dickey*

Recommended:

○ **Pérotin** / Hillier (cond.), Hilliard Ens. / ECM 837751

○ **Alleluia Nativitas** / Orlando Consort / 1992 / Metronome 1001

Vincent Persichetti

b. Jun. 6, 1915, Philadelphia, PA, **d.** Aug. 14, 1987, Philadelphia, PA

Composer: Band Music, Concerto

American composer Vincent Persichetti (1915–87) was, along with William Schuman and Walter Piston, one of the foremost representatives of what has become known, somewhat inappropriately, as the American academic school of composition. Born in Philadelphia during the First World War, Persichetti began studying music at the age of five, taking lessons in piano, organ, and, later, theory and composition. During the mid-1920s Persichetti began to find work as an accompanist and radio pianist, and by age 16 his skill at the organ had earned him a position at Arch Street Presbyterian Church, which he retained until the 1950s. Persichetti entered Combs College of Music, studying with composer Russel King Miller while still attending public school, and in 1935 he took a BM in composition from Combs. Persichetti was appointed Head of Music Theory at Combs immediately after graduating, and throughout the late 1930s combined these duties with studies in conducting with Fritz Reiner at the Curtis Institute, eventually earning a diploma in conducting, and in piano with Olga Samaroff at the Philadelphia Conservatory, taking both a MM and a MusD.

Persichetti accepted an invitation to take over as head of theory and composition at the Philadelphia Conservatory in 1941, and in 1947 he joined the composition faculty of the Juilliard School. To his already bursting résumé he added the distinction of becoming Editorial Director of the Elkan-Vogel publishing house in 1952. Awards and commendations were showered on Persichetti until his death in 1987. Three Guggenheim Fellowships, two grants from the National Endowment for the Arts, the Brandeis University Creative Award, the first ever Kennedy Center Friedham Award, and the Juilliard Publication award are just some of the more noteworthy such honors.

Persichetti was, by all accounts, a pianist of virtuoso caliber, and his 12 sonatas and three concertos are among the more important American works for the instrument, though there are relatively few performers who dare tackle the myriad technical and interpretive difficulties within this impressive body of work. His talent as a conductor is manifest in nine symphonies, and among his prolific chamber music output are four string quartets, a piano quintet, and 15 works called Serenade that employ 15 different instrumental combinations. Persichetti's compositional language was a panorama of twentieth century techniques; he moved between tonality, atonality, polytonality, and modality with fluency. In addition to his ceaseless activities as a composer and educator, Persichetti found the time to write an important textbook on modern compositional practice, *Twentieth Century Harmony: Creative Aspects and Practice*, and a 1954 biography of composer William Schuman.*—Blair Johnston*

Overview of Works (1929–1987)

A prominent fixture in music composition and pedagogy in the United States during the twentieth century, Vincent Persichetti was widely recognized as among the most well-rounded and broadly skilled composers of his time. His body of work reflects a comprehensive understanding of instrumental and orchestrational idioms, a thorough absorption of musical styles, and a keen sense of the performative aspects of music. The combination of these elements make his style rather difficult to pigeonhole since, as scholars have observed, Persichetti tended to take what had historically been ardent aesthetic positions and treat them instead as individual expressive possibilities within a multifaceted, eclectic, and ecumenical musical palette. He also conceived of music for a variety of skill levels, devoting a substantial portion of his creative energies to compositions for beginning or intermediate players.

Persichetti was a virtuoso pianist; it is no surprise, then, that special attention is paid to his numerous works for piano. These include character pieces, sonatinas, concertos, and sonatas for both two and four hands. He wrote several works for other keyboard instruments as well, including a series of harpsichord sonatas, a *Sonatina for Organ, Pedals Alone* (1940), and a stirring organ piece based on Psalm 130, *Shimah B'Koli* (1962).

Persichetti's output for other solo instruments and small chamber combinations is highlighted by two large collections, situated somewhere between Hindemith's solo sonatas and Berio's *Sequenzas*, which Persichetti titled *Serenades* and *Parables*, and which contain individual pieces for 15 and 25 different instruments or combinations, respectively. Other chamber pieces include a handful of chamber duos, a piano quintet, and four string quartets.

An accomplished conductor as well as performer, his intimate knowledge of orchestral sound is reflected in his large-scale works as well. These include nine symphonies, of which the *Fourth* (1951), *Fifth* (1953), and *Eighth* (1967) have enjoyed considerable acclaim. A number of other orchestral pieces have garnered attention as well, such as *Hollow Men for Trumpet and Strings* (1944) and the *Concerto for English Horn and Orchestra* (1977).

Among Persichetti's compositions most familiar to the general public are his works for wind ensemble, especially his *Divertimento* (1950), *Symphony for Band* (1963), and *A Lincoln Address* for band and narrator (1973).

Though not as widely known as his works for winds, Persichetti's compositions for solo voice and vocal ensemble are among his most ambitious and engaging. His most important work for solo voice is the extended song cycle *Harmonium*, on texts by Wallace Stevens. Persichetti's keen sense for poetic nuance, as well as his wide-ranging literary interests, are further demonstrated in his *Emily Dickinson Songs*, *Hilaire Belloc Songs*, *James Joyce Songs*, and *Robert Frost Songs*, all completed in 1957. His choral works include a number of cantatas, an a cappella *Mass*, and several substantial works for voices and instruments, including *Celebrations for Wind and Chorus* (1966), *The Pleiades* (1967), and the enormous choral-orchestral work *The Creation* (1969). *—Jeremy Grimshaw*

Recommended:

○ **Barber & Persichetti** / Malinova Sisters / 1995 / Koch 7213

○ **Persichetti: Symphony 5; Piano Concerto** / Muti, Dutoit (conds.), Taub, Philadelphia Orch. / 1990 / New World 80370

○ **Persichetti: 3 Choral Works** / Brooks (cond.), Barnes, Schultz, Philadelphia Mendelssohn Club / 1983 / New World 80316

○ **American Contrast** / DePreist (cond.), Oregon Symphony, Bassoon Brothers / 2003 / Delos 3291

BAND MUSIC

Works for Band (1950–1984)

Like so many other American composers of the mid-twentieth century, Vincent Persichetti composed a large body of music for symphonic and concert band. Although these pieces were never, and were never meant to be, as high-profile as Persichetti's nine symphonies, it may well be the case that today, many years after the composer's death, his band works are more frequently played than his once-upon-a-time better-known symphonic efforts, and the reason is simple: the band repertory is not nearly as large, nor is it as rich, as the orchestral repertory, and knowledgeable band directors are, as a result, quick to grab onto high-quality music for their groups. And, love or hate the style (call it neo-Classical meets neo-Romantic meets dissonant modernism), high-quality music is something of which Vincent Persichetti's works are chock-full.

The first item that might be considered a work for band is the *Serenade* for ten winds that Persichetti composed in 1929 (at the age of 14); but it is really better considered chamber music, and so we must leap ahead a couple of decades to find the earliest true Persichetti band piece. Previously scorned by serious composers, concert band music was, around the 1950s, becoming more and more attractive to composers, some of whom were looking for alternatives to the symphony orchestra, some of whom, on the other hand, received welcome commissions from the ever-growing and ever-present family of American bands. Starting with *Divertimento* for band (1950), Persichetti composed a dozen band works over the next two decades or so, often during these years ignoring the orchestral idiom altogether. This band music catalog includes: *Psalm* (1952), *Pageant* (1953), *Serenade No. 11* (1960), *Bagatelles* (1961), *Masquerade* (1965), *O Cool Is the Valley* (1971), and *Parable IX* (1972). Towards the end of his life Persichetti added one further band piece to the list, *O God Unseen* (1984), a chorale prelude setting that bears witness to Persichetti's growing interest in religious music in his final years—you might say that, musically speaking, he ended where, as a 15-year-old professional organist and choir-master in Philadelphia, he began. *—Blair Johnston*

Recommended:

○ **Persichetti: Divertimenti For Winds** / Amos (cond.), London SO Winds / 1994 / HM 907092

CONCERTO

The Hollow Men, for trumpet & string orchestra, Op. 25 (1944)

Vincent Persichetti, a most respected musician, is regarded as one of America's few successful symphonists. His best-known smaller work, *The Hollow Men*, is firmly rooted in American symphonic tradition. Originally scored for solo trumpet and string orchestra, the piece is an evocative response to the poems of T.S. Eliot. For the program notes at the 1946 premiere, the composer wrote the following: "The work parallels the mood of the T.S. Eliot poem of the same name. The music springs from the disillusioned subtleties of a poem that intensifies the sense of emptiness and hopelessness of mankind. This is quiet music, with an underlying tension that finds its only release in a crescendo that climaxes on a single note played by the double basses." This original version carries a special intensity in the string texture not found in a popular and often-recorded study version for trumpet and piano (or organ).

During this time that he wrote *The Hollow Men*, Persichetti was still in the process of developing his own style; his works of the period show the influence of Bartók, Hindemith, and others. Two years after he completed the work, Persichetti left an appointment as head of the theory and composition departments at the Philadelphia Conservatory for a teaching post at the Juilliard School, where he later became chairman of the composition department (1963). *—Meredith Gailey*

Recommended:

○ **Fantasy** / Russell (cond.), Hickman, Wilson, Naples PO / 1993 / D'Note 1002

La Petite Bande

f. 1972, Leuven, Belgium

Ensemble

The Belgian period instrument orchestra La Petite Bande takes its name and constitution from Lully's own orchestra at the court of Louis XIV. It was founded in 1972 by violinist and conductor Sigiswald Kuijken in order to record Lully's *Le bourgeois gentilhomme* with Gustav Leonhardt for Deutsche Harmonia Mundi. Although it had only been put together for a few recordings, it soon established a reputation as a leader in the performance of French Baroque music. La Petite Bande began giving regular concerts and appearing at festivals throughout the world. The orchestra's repertoire expanded to include music by Bach, Handel, Gluck, Haydn, and Mozart. La Petite Bande is subsidized by the Ministry of the Flemish Community of Belgium and by the Province of Vlaams-Brabant. Since 1997, La Petite Bande has been orchestra-in-residence in Leuven. *—Robert Adelson*

Recommended:

○ **Graun: Der Tod Jesu** / Kuijken (cond.), Genz, Schwabe, La Petite Bande, Ex Tempore / 2004 / Hyperion 67446

○ **Mozart: Davidde Penitente; Ave Verum Corpus** / Kuijken (cond.), Blochwitz, La Petite Bande, Nederlands Kamerkoor / 1988 / Deutsche Harmonia Mundi 7477402

○ **C.P.E. Bach: Die Auferstehung und Himmelfahrt Jesu** / Kuijken (cond.), Genz, Schwabe, Genz, La Petite Bande, Ex Tempore [chorus] / Hyperion 67364

○ **Bach: Motets** / Kuijken (cond.), La Petite Bande / Accent 9287

○ **Haydn: Symphonies 26, 52 & 53** / Kuijken (cond.), La Petite Bande / 1988 / Virgin 790743

Michala Petri

b. Jul. 7, 1958, Copenhagen, Denmark

Recorder Player

Petri began playing the recorder at the age of three and played for the Danish Radio by the time she was five. In 1969, she began studies with Ferdinand Conrad at the Hochschule für Musik und Theater in Hanover and debuted as a concerto soloist at the Tivoli Concert Hall. From that concert forward, Petri's career has skyrocketed, and she has become known as the preeminent recorder virtuoso of her generation. She records and concertizes regularly, working with such musicians as Heinz Holliger, Pinchas Zuckerman, James Galway, Salvatore Accardo, Maurice André, Keith Jarrett, Claudio Abbado, and Evelyn Glennie, among others, as well as with all the major early music ensembles and many of the major orchestras of Europe and America. Not surprisingly, her primary repertory is drawn from the Baroque and early Classical periods, including many transcriptions from other instruments. Petri also has been involved in much contemporary music, though, commissioning a substantial amount of new music for the recorder including a recent work for recorder, percussion, and orchestra by Piers Hellawell. Most recently she has even begun to record arrangements of nineteenth century composers, beginning with a Grieg CD done with the English Chamber Orchestra. *—Steven Coburn*

Recommended:

○ **The Ultimate Recorder Collection** / Petri, etc. / 1999 / RCA 59112

○ **Michala Petri Plays Bach & Telemann** / Kussmaul (cond.), Petri, Berlin Soloists / 1998 / RCA 57130

○ **Modern Recorder** / Petri, etc. / 1998 / RCA 7946

Gustaf Allan Pettersson

b. Sep. 19, 1911, Västra Rya, Sweden, **d.** Jun. 20, 1980, Stockholm, Sweden

Composer: Symphonic, Orchestral, Vocal

Gustaf Allan Pettersson was a symphonist of the twentieth century, specializing in giant, single-movement structures chronicling pain and despair. Like Mahler, he had an abusive alcoholic father. Pettersson's father was an atheist. His mother was a devoutly religious woman who sang Salvation Army hymns, often as a way to escape the atheistic proclamations of her husband. In his symphonies, as in Mahler's, the sudden emergence of folkish music breaks out as an antidote to tension. In Pettersson's case this often takes the form of broad, chorale harmonizations.

The family lived in a poor neighborhood of Stockholm. Allan had to sell Christmas cards on the street to get money for a violin. He taught himself how to play. He entered the Royal Conservatory of Music in 1930. Finally, he won the Jenny Lind Scholarship in 1930, using it to study viola in Paris with Maurice Vieux. He continued his education as a composer while holding down a job as violist in the Stockholm Concert Society Orchestra, and played in various radio ensembles. His composition teachers were Otto Ohlsson and Karl-Birger Blomdahl. During the 1940s he wrote his important large-scale cycle, *Barfotsånger* (Barefoot Songs). In another parallel with Mahler, he frequently used melodies from it in his symphonies. In 1943 he married Gudrun Gustafsson. In 1946 they moved into a small fifth floor apartment in the south side of Stockholm. It remained their home for 30 years, becoming Pettersson's prison.

In 1950 Pettersson committed himself to prepare for a career entirely devoted to composition. The orchestra gave him leave to study in Paris with Honegger, Milhaud, and Leibowitz. He rejected the neo-Classicism of the first, and the 12-tone proselytizing of the last-named of these. His long, difficult works failed to attract much enthusiasm at home, but he went through with his plans to resign from the orchestra in 1952. Soon, though, he began suffering joint pains that would later be diagnosed as rheumatoid arthritis. Somehow, Sweden's democratic welfare state failed to provide him with needed medical care, medications, or social support. Pettersson described himself as "a voice crying out, drowned in the noise of the times." For a decade and a half he was known as a composer only in narrow circles, though he received a few commissions. In 1963 a recording was made of one movement of one of his concerti for strings. In 1964 the government granted him a guaranteed income.

Then he scored his breakthrough with the *Symphony No. 7.* This one-movement work depicts a harsh inner struggle, relieved by a radiant Adagio section. Antal Dorati's premiere of it on October 10, 1968, was a triumph. It was the last concert Pettersson would attend. Soon, his debilitation made it impossible to descend the stairs. He was trapped in his apartment. Pettersson's only outside view was of a junkyard. He composed his music while a hostile neighbor blasted out rock & roll, often around the clock.

The *Seventh Symphony* led to international success. Pettersson received commissions for new works, and wrote a new symphony nearly every year. In 1976 the government moved him to a luxurious, ground-level apartment, and provided first-class medical care for him. He died while working on his *Seventeenth Symphony.* He left 15 extant symphonies and a formidable *Second Violin Concerto* in a single 50-minute movement. *—Joseph Stevenson*

SYMPHONIC

Symphonies (1950–1980)

Allan Pettersson was an important, but not mainstream composer, rare among his contemporaries for having developed a large and devoted following. He is also unusual in that, of his 17 symphonies, only the first and last are incomplete and remained unperformed through the end of the twentieth century. All the others received some attention, both in the concert hall and recording studio.

Pettersson's style is fairly broad, but has several characteristics that can be found in most of his symphonies: the music often seethes with tension, percussion sometimes seems to attack the strings or busily incites other instruments to violence, brass often play in their highest ranges at climactic moments, and the music generally seems to represent a series of conflicts and buildups, sometimes resolved, sometimes not. It should be noted that his orchestration became thicker from *Symphony No. 10* onward.

Pettersson's most popular symphony has been the *Seventh* (1966–67), probably his most approachable and lyrical. It seems quite at odds with the composer's image as an angry man wreaking much conflict and dissonance in his symphonies. In fact, that view, while having more than a grain of truth, is unfair. Clearly, it is supported by works like the *Tenth Symphony* (1972), written while the composer was recuperating from a life-threatening illness for nine months in a hospital. It is boisterous to the point that the music seems an unrelenting sonic rage, one section of the orchestra often blaring its notes out to trample others in a sort of survival-of-the-fittest contest.

Other Pettersson symphonies have their moments of conflict and rage as well, like the *Sixth* (1963–66). But here, the music turns sweetly sorrowful near the end, where the composer wrote one of his most touching orchestral passages, ever. The early Pettersson symphonies, *Nos. Two* (1952–53), *Three* (1954–55), and *Four* (1958–59), are generally austere, dramatic works that feature a variety of orchestral sonorities and expressions. His style in these works was still forming, though the music is quite effective and well crafted. The *Fifth* (1960–62) is a unique symphony because it sounds somewhat detached in its conflicts and emotions.

Symphonies Six through *Nine* (*Eight* [1968–69], *Nine* [1970]) often feature long stretches of unrelieved gloom or tragedy and sometimes make heavy use of ostinatos. *No. 11* is less frenzied and boisterous than its immediate predecessor, but is still powerful and contains several eruptions.

The *Twelfth* (1974), subtitled "The Dead in the Marketplace," is Pettersson's only choral symphony and delves into politics, though the composer insisted the work was more about man's inhumanity toward man. The text is from Pablo Neruda's *Canto general.* Pettersson's *Symphonies Nos. 13* (1976), *14* (1978), *15* (1978), and *16* (1979) are all worthwhile works, with the latter designated for saxophone and orchestra. Here, the music has a more diffuse manner, sounding almost improvisatory.

In sum, Pettersson is one of the more important modern symphonists and he may yet achieve front-rank status. *—Robert Cummings*

Recommended:

- ○ **Pettersson: Symphonies 3 & 4** / Francis (cond.), Saarbrucken Radio SO / 1994 / CPO 999223
- ○ **Pettersson: Symphonies 5 & 16** / Francis (cond.), Kelly, Saarbrucken Radio SO / CPO 999284
- ○ **Pettersson: Symphonies 7 & 11** / Segerstam (cond.), Lysell, Norrkoping SO / 1992 / Bis 580

ORCHESTRAL

Mesto, for string orchestra (1956–1957)

The *Mesto* (mournful, sad) for string orchestra is the enormous central movement of Swedish composer Allan Pettersson's *Concerto No. 3 for string orchestra* (1956–57). Although best known for his colossal series of symphonies, Pettersson demonstrated in the *Mesto* that even without the scale of a symphony and the resources of an orchestra, he could still create works of concentrated intensity and extreme pain. The pain is physical: Pettersson's writing is wholly idiomatic and takes advantage of the strings' ability to sound like human voices, in this case, anguished voices. The pain is intellectual: Pettersson's control of large structures sends towering waves of agonized strings smashing into each other with the force of breakers on the coast of Maine. The pain is emotional: Pettersson's themes are tormented, his harmonies are torturous, his rhythms are lugubrious, and the combination of all three is excruciating. The pain is spiritual: while Pettersson's harmonic language is the highly dissonant tonality of the late nineteenth century and his forms are based on the concerto grosso of the late seventeenth century, his music is steeped in the existential horror of the middle twentieth century. *—James Leonard*

Recommended:

- ○ **Pettersson: Concertos for String Orchestra** / Goritzki (cond.), Neuss German Chamber Academy / CPO 999225

VOCAL

24 Barefoot Songs (1943–1945)

Most assessments of Gustaf Allan Pettersson's music regard the *Concerto No. 1 for Violin and String Quartet* of 1949 as his first major work. Only in 1951 did he produce the first work (which remained incomplete) in his acclaimed sequence of symphonies. Through the 1940s Pettersson continued his musical education while making a living playing viola in the orchestra of the Stockholm Concert Society as well as various Swedish Radio ensembles. He was not left with much time to compose, and most of the music from this early portion of his career took the form of short songs. In fact, the only songs Pettersson ever wrote come from this early period—the *Six Songs* of 1935, and the cycle of 24 *Barfotasångerna* (*Barefoot Songs*), written between 1943 through 1945. The *Barefoot Songs* lay unperformed for quite some time. In October 1968 some of the songs were heard in a concert in Sweden, and the complete set had its premiere in a Swedish Radio broadcast in early December 1968.

The *Barefoot Songs* are comparatively simple in terms of structure, melody, and harmony, certainly so in comparison with Pettersson's complex later works. The composer himself wrote the texts, drawing extensively both on Swedish folklore and on the circumstances of his own difficult upbringing. The latter may also have been the source of the cycle's title; another possible source may be the final song of Franz Schubert's cycle *Winterreise,* "Der Leiermann"—that hurdy-gurdy man, it is said, stands "barefoot on the ice."

Certain themes predominate in the *Barefoot Songs*: a son's regard for his mother (in "Mother Is Poor" and "The Friend in Sunday Land"), death (in "Song of Lament" and "My Light Will Go Out," the melody of which later turns up in Pettersson's *Symphony No. 6* of 1963–66), and loneliness, particularly that of a child's world (in "The Little One Must Wait"). The songs contain some specific references to Pettersson's own life, one being the allusion to the composer's father's interest in astronomy in "The Star and the Bars." There are a couple of examples of tone painting, for instance the rustling of the wind in "The Maiden and the Fibbing Wind" and the hum of flies in "While the Flies Buzz." All in all, the *Barfotasångerna,* although a comparatively humble example of Pettersson's art, is a significant cycle that helped to pave the way for Pettersson's development into a composer of mammoth symphonic works. As was the case with Gustav Mahler and his song cycle *Des Knaben Wunderhorn,* Pettersson alluded to the melodies of the *Barefoot Songs* often in his later works. *—Chris Morrison*

Recommended:

- ○ **Pettersson: Complete Songs** / Groop, Garben / 1998 / CPO 999499

Hans Pfitzner

b. May 5, 1869, Moscow, Russia, **d.** May 22, 1949, Salzburg, Austria

Composer: Vocal, Opera, Symphonic, Concerto

Hans Pfitzner was one of the composers who carried the German Romantic tradition well into the twentieth century. Unlike those of his contemporaries Mahler and Richard Strauss, his reputation never seemed to extend beyond the borders of his homeland. Yet there is much that is individualistic and much to admire from his body of work—particularly in his best-known work, the opera *Palestrina.*

Born in Russia of German parents, Pfitzner moved with his family to Frankfurt when he was three. His musical talent manifested itself early on, and he received his first training from his parents. At 14 he entered the Hoch Conservatory, studying composition with Knorr and piano with Kwast. He then began his music career as a teacher, taking a position as a theater conductor in Mainz; the latter proved to be a strategic move, for although it was an unpaid position, it enabled him to have his first opera, *Der arme Heinrich,* performed. Paid positions now followed, culminating in a multiposition stay in Strasbourg; he became director of the conservatory there, as well as chief symphony and opera conductor. The security of a fixed income produced a creatively favorable environment; he composed prolifically in all forms, favoring opera.

The crown of Pfitzner's work is arguably his opera *Palestrina* (1915), based on the life of the Renaissance composer and quoting passages of that master's music.

Pfitzner may have seen himself in the opera's protagonist, as a man who, sticking to his principles, upholds musical tradition against the depredations of power. (The opera treats the legendary effort on Palestrina's part to compose a work beautiful and spiritual enough to foretall the banning of polyphony under consideration by the architects of the Counter Reformation.) Also noteworthy is Pfitzner's cantata *Von deutscher Seele* (Of the German Soul) of 1920. Both works are in the highly chromatic, richly sonorous tradition of post-Romanticism, and could never be mistaken for mere throwbacks to the nineteenth century. That Pfitzner could work in a less imposing idiom can be gathered from such works as the concise, melodic *Symphony in C* (1940).

But much of the non-German world's reluctance to hear Pfitzner's music may have been been the result of his politics. Always an ardent German patriot, he became enmeshed with the rise of the Third Reich. Yet he counted among his Jewish friends and supporters Mahler, Bruno Walter, and Otto Klemperer, and he was an admirer of Mendelssohn. In any event, as Pfitzner became more disillusioned with Nazism, he expressed disapproval and was thus relieved of his life membership at the Munich Academy of Music in 1934. This and various family tragedies took a toll on the composer's sanity. The wartime destruction of his Munich home left Pfitzner an aging, half-insane street person, but after the war a pension and residence were procured for the composer. He died in Salzburg, officially denazified and with his the ban on performances of his music lifted.

Although the Romantic revival of the 1960s did not do for Pfitzner what it did for many of his contemporaries, there is much of his output worth hearing. At his best, Pfitzner spoke with the eloquence and intensity of one who consciously lives during the close of a glorious era. *—Wayne Gerard Reisig*

VOCAL

Songs and Song Cycles (1884–1949)

There are 115 songs in Pfitzner's œuvre, beginning with the first of two efforts entitled *Ständchen* (1884) and endubg with his Op. 41 *Three Sonnets* (1931). All his songs feature piano accompaniment, though he did fashion orchestral versions of some. Of course, Pfitzner (1869–1949) also wrote other vocal works during this period, including six music dramas and his masterful opera, *Palestrina.*

Many of his earlier songs, as one might expect, show varying influences, like that of Weber. *Werners Lied* (1884), to cite an example, was inspired by Nessler's opera *Der Trompeter von Säckingen.* Despite whatever derivative elements one might discern here, however, many of Pfitzner's first efforts contain attractive music. The *Jugendlieder* date from the period 1884–87, but turned up unpublished in the United States in 1930. Pfitzner, apparently having initially suppressed them, allowed their publication without changes three years later. No. 4 in this set, *Nun, da so warm der Sonnenschein* (texts by Oscar von Redwitz), features a Romantic melody that impressed the composer enough to include it in his first musical drama, *Der arme Heinrich.*

Of his early compositions, almost all are songs: Opp. 2, 4, 5, 6, 7, 9, 10, and 11 are sets containing from three to seven songs, totaling 38 altogether. Probably among the more interesting of them is the song cycle comprising Op. 9 (1888–89). The folk songish "Der Gärtner" (No. 1), on texts by Joseph von Eichendorff, is probably his most popular effort from that group.

Without doubt it is the later songs of Pfitzner that have given him the reputation of one of the twentieth century's most distinguished song composers. But one of his most important efforts actually came in his middle years, the 1906 *An den Mond,* on texts by Goethe. It is one of his longest efforts and the only one to have an opus number assigned to it alone, in this case, Op. 18. Another fine song from this period is "In Danzig" (Joseph von Eichendorff), from the Op. 22 cycle of five songs (1907). It is Impressionistic in its mystery and dark atmosphere, and features a repeating motif of haunting character.

After completing his opera *Palestrina,* Pfitzner turned out his Op. 26 set of *Five Songs* in 1916. This group features a wide variety of moods, from the gentle "Gebet" (Friedrich Hebbel) to the joyous and rhythmic "Mailied" (Goethe). The Op. 29 *Four Songs*—"Abbitte," "Herbsthauch," "Willkomen und Abschied," and "Die still Nacht," on texts by four different poets—are all high-quality efforts, the first being especially compelling.

Pfitzner remained a conservative, though he ventured into new realms in his later works. The *Six Songs* of Op. 40 and the *Three Sonnets,* Op. 41, both from 1931, were Pfitzner's last efforts in the genre. While he remained a stylistic Romantic throughout his career, these songs show a simpler approach and brevity of expression. *—Robert Cummings*

Recommended:

- ○ **Pfitzner: Lieder: Complete Edition Vol. 1** / Schmidt, Jansen, Kaufmann, Prégardien, Sulzen, Gees / CPO 999228
- ○ **Pfitzner: Lieder: Complete Edition Vol. 2** / Schmidt, Jansen, Kaufmann, Prégardien, Sulzen, Gees / CPO 999364
- ○ **Pfitzner: Lieder: Complete Edition Vol. 3** / Schmidt, Jansen, Kaufmann, Prégardien, Vermillion / CPO 999461
- ○ **Pfitzner: Lieder: Complete Edition Vol. 4** / Schmidt, Jansen, Kaufmann, Vermillion, Prégardien / 1999 / CPO 999490

Alte Weisen, song cycle, Op. 33 (1923)

Hans Pfitzner set these eight songs in just one week, in the summer of 1923. Surprisingly though, he was not a prolific composer, and thus this Op. 33 set came relatively late in his career. The song cycle is one of Pfitzner's finest, and many musicologists believe it is the zenith of his lieder output and among the most important song cycles of the twentieth century. *Alte Weisen* (Old Tunes) is based on texts by Gottfried Keller, who had originally entitled his 1846 collection of 16 poems *Von Weibern: Alte Lieder* (Of Women: Old Songs). In 1883, he reduced their number to 12 and retitled the collection *Alte Weisen.*

Each item in Pfitzner's set depicts the character of a woman. "Mir glänzen die Augen" (My eyes glow as brightly), the first song, is short like most in the set. It is vibrant, but features humorous accompaniment that rather slashes at the music, as the text portrays a young woman complaining about her Hussar before sending him off. The second song, "Ich fürcht' nit Gespenster" (No fairies and witches), starts off with similar accompaniment, but the mood changes quickly, turning mysterious, then jumpy. In the end, it is all rather playful, with the poem relating the tale of a witch.

No. 3, "Du milchjunger Knabe" (Why do you gaze upon me), continues the generally bright mood, but showing much contrast with moments of seeming seriousness in the otherwise charming and cute song, as the woman sings rather haughtily about her young man. The next item, "Wandl' ich in dem Morgentau" (When in dewy fields at morn), is dreamy, the music matching the text which describes pastoral scenes and yearning for love. No. 5, "Singt mein Schatz wie ein Fink" (When my love sings like a finch), is capricious in mood and colorful, though the text tells of an unfortunate woman who has not found love. "Röschen biß den Apfel an" (Rosy, oh the careless girl!), is the shortest item, lasting under a minute. It is a humorous song with simple accompaniment, the music sounding rather detached. The text tells of a young girl breaking her tooth on a hard apple. The marchlike opening of the next song, "Tretet ein, hoher Krieger" (Enter in, lordly warrior), is bright and satiric, but the music's proud tread soon deteriorates. The woman speaks of her warrior respectfully, but gradually strips away his heroic qualities and finally advises him on feminine duties. The final song, the longest at nearly four minutes, "Wie glänzt der helle Mond" (How coldly shines the moon), is dark, the text telling of a woman who yearns for her lost beauty and believes she is in heaven.*—Robert Cummings*

Recommended:

- ○ **Pfitzner: Lieder** / Kaufmann, Sulzen / 1999 / CPO 999491
- ○ **Pfitzner: Songs** / Goetz, Schwarz / Ars 368301

OPERA

Palestrina (1911–1915)

The Counter-Reformation composer Giovanni Perluigi Palestrina and his most famous mass setting, the *Missa Papae Marcelli* (1567), became credited in legend with having saved polyphonic music in Europe from a ban proposed by Cardinal Borromeo and the Council of Trent. The actual circumstance was that the church sought to ensure that the words of the holy text of the mass would be audible to worshipers and not drowned in layers of complex polyphonic lines. After examining some examples of polyphonic writing, including some unidentified examples by Palestrina, the notables of the Council ultimately decided that no specific ban on the compositional style was needed.

Still, it was the legend that was important to German composer Hans Pfitzner, who probably did not doubt its veracity. Indeed, Pfitzner based his opera *Palestrina* (1911–15) on the romanticized version of the events, providing his own libretto. In Pfitzner's scenario, Palestrina complies with an edict from Cardinal Borromeo to ban all music in church except Gregorian chant and quits composition altogether. The spirits of nine great composers of the past appear to Palestrina in a vision and entreat him to continue. An angel then sings him the main theme of what was to become the Kyrie of the *Missa Papae Marcelli.* Palestrina feverishly composes a Gloria and collapses from exhaustion. His son and a pupil discover the music scattered about in sheets and gather it up, recognizing it as an inspired work. Act II portrays the debate in the Council of Trent. In Act III, Palestrina brings his new mass to the Pope, who is overcome with admiration, ends the Council's antimusic activities, and appoints Palestrina the director of his personal choir in the Sistine Chapel. The crowd cheers the composer, who is seen at the end of the opera seated at an organ, playing his music.

Palestrina is notable for its deeply spiritual tone, especially in the "vision" scene, the scenes in which Palestrina composes or performs, and the meeting of the composer and the Pope. Upon its appearance, the opera was wildly praised as sublime, nobly austere, and lofty. It remains very popular in the German-speaking world, though it has never caught on in opera houses elsewhere. The opera has found greater success on recordings and has enjoyed multiple performances thus. The preludes to the three acts are sometimes played in concert, either as a suite or individually. *—Joseph Stevenson*

Synopsis:

Act One. The story takes place in November and December 1563 in Rome and Trent. It is the afternoon in Palestrina's workroom in his Rome house. The composer's pupil Silla mulls over his upcoming trip to Florence as he performs a song. Ighino, Palestrina's son, enters and expresses concern over his father's prolonged melancholy mood. A few hours later, Palestrina enters with Cardinal Borromeo, who expresses sharp criticism of perceived cacophony in the song Silla is singing for Ighino. The composer reminds the two it is their bedtime and they depart. Palestrina shows tolerance for his pupil's progressive style in the song and suggests that new music may seem difficult at first to older generations.

The Cardinal does not challenge his assertion, but raises instead the subject of the ongoing Council of Trent and its forthcoming pronouncements on music, pronouncements that may proscribe all polyphonic composition in the sacred realm. He explains that Emperor Ferdinand I (ruler of the Holy Roman Empire) stands opposed to purists advocating a return to plainchant for sacred music. His influential opposition has, in fact, permitted Cardinal Borromeo to convince the Pope to allow consideration of the matter after the presentation of a new Mass illustrating the effectiveness of polyphonic writing. Borromeo asks Palestrina to compose the music for this grand and crucial demonstration before the Council members.

The composer cites his advancing age and other reasons for declining the offer and then goes on to anger the Cardinal, who storms out of his house. Alone, Palestrina is harassed by apparitions of composers from the past, including Josquin Desprez. They encourage him to take on Borromeo's challenge, but Palestrina is struck with fear and begins to pray. An angel appears in the background and sings a lovely motif—one that will open his famous *Missa Papae Marcelli.* The composer begins notating the music as he hears it. More angels join in, Palestrina writing notes down furiously, as if taking dictation, though he still does not see the performers who are the source of his inspiration. His late wife is even seen now among the singing angels. Ighino and Silla enter the next morning to find the composer sound asleep and the score of the Mass on his worktable.

Act Two. The final session of the Council of Trent is convening and intends to make its decision regarding polyphonic music in the Church. Palestrina has been imprisoned on orders from Cardinal Borromeo for refusing to write the Mass. The Cardinal is seen sitting uneasily among the many clergy and dignitaries attending the session, who include Cardinal Morone. The latter addresses the Council on behalf of Ferdinand I, but his words lead only to confusion and chaos, and the session ends with the polyphonic issue unresolved.

Act Three. At Palestrina's Rome residence, the composer talks with Ighino and singers from his choir. His Mass, the score of which was taken from his house during his imprisonment, is being performed before the Pope. Suddenly the papal singers enter, declaring Palestrina the savior of music. The Pope himself arrives to pay tribute to Palestrina, the man whose composition has decided the issue in favor of polyphonic music. Borromeo arrives to offer his apologies and to congratulate the composer. When Palestrina is left alone, he sits at his organ and sings in prayer. *—Robert Cummings*

Recommended:

- ○ **Palestrina** / Kempe (cond.), Heger, Wunderlich, Ludwig, Popp, Frick, Berry, Jurinac, Equiluz, Janowitz / Myto 92259
- ○ **Palestrina** / Kubelik (cond.), Fischer-Dieskau, Gedda, Fassbaender, Donath, Prey, Weikl / DG 427417

SYMPHONIC

Symphony in C major, Op. 46 (1940)

Pfitzner completed this work in 1940; it was premiered on October 11 of that year in Frankfurt.

Although lieder were his specialty for decades, he wrote three symphonies in the next-to-last period of his life, before he became disillusioned with the Nazi hierarchy which had classified him, alongside Richard Strauss, as a cultural treasure, and had encouraged him to concentrate on composing and guest conducting rather than teaching. The first symphony, in C sharp minor, was a 1932 transcription of his *String Quartet No. 2,* Op. 36. The second, composed in 1939, he called *Kleine Sinfonie.* The third one, in C, followed a year later with a dedication "To my Friends." To the end of his life, Pfitzner's harmonic vocabulary remained post-Wagnerian: diatonic in the case of the *C major Symphony,* which linked it to *Lohengrin* rather than later operas. Structurally, however, Schumann was his model: multiple movements within a single-movement frame, with a restatement at the end of the main theme.

Pfitzner begins Allegro moderato in common time. Over a cello ostinato of sextuplets, a solo horn announces the main theme, which trumpets and strings then take up. Three sub-themes of a more subdued nature follow, in the dominant key of G. Clarinets play the first one "very expressively." Oboes and flutes quietly introduce the second non-legato one. Oboes and clarinets combine "peacefully" for the third one. Both development and reprise are abbreviated before the tempo slows for the work's middle section, marked Sehr langsam = Adagio, in 3/4 time. The English horn gets to sing over a soft cushion of strings. Then all the winds play in canon until the English horn resumes, leading to the one surprise in this sinfonietta-size piece—a fortissimo attack, without warning, that launches the Presto finale in 6/8 time. A fugato section follows in Reger style until trumpets and trombones reintroduce the main theme of the first movement. With horns filling in harmony, winds and strings race up and down the scale until a triple-forte conclusion in tonic C major. *—Roger Dettmer*

Recommended:

- ○ **Furtwängler: Maestro Classico** / Furtwängler (cond.), Vienna PO / 2000 / History 20391
- ○ **Böhm: Maestro Decente** / Böhm (cond.), Dresden Staatskapelle / 2002 / Documents 220827-303
- ○ **Pfitzner: Complete Orchestral Works** / Albert (cond.), Bamberg SO / CPO 999249
- ○ **Late Romantics** / Tintner (cond.), Nova Scotia Symphony / 1997 / CBC 5167

CONCERTO

Piano Concerto in E flat major, Op. 31 (1922)

Hans Pfitzner composed his *Piano Concerto in E flat major,* Op. 31, while he was a teacher of composition at the Prussian Academy in Berlin. It is an excellent example of the composer's style, and a reminder that he was as esteemed a musician in Germany as was Richard Strauss before the Jewish Pfitzner's suppression by the Nazi government in 1934.

The *Piano Concerto* was first performed on March 16, 1923, in Dresden by pianist Walter Gieseking and conductor Fritz Busch. Gieseking so admired the piece that he retained it in his repertoire for many years, prompting Pfitzner's dedication of the *Five Piano Pieces,* Op. 47, to Gieseking in 1941.

Pfitzner's style, in general, is conservative in that it looks to the past for formal, melodic, and harmonic procedures. However, Pfitzner looks back to exclusively German sources, foregoing Italian or French developments. His nondemocratic political views during the Weimar years (1919-33) can be seen as manifest in his *Piano Concerto,* in which the hegemony of the piano is clear throughout most of the piece.

In four movements, the *Piano Concerto* begins with a fast movement in sonata form. The main theme, in E flat major, is marked, "Pomphaft, mit Kraft und Schwung" (pompous, with strength and vitality). For the secondary theme, Pfitzner slows the tempo and moves to the dominant minor (B flat minor), lending the contrasting theme an unusual expressiveness. Throughout the ensuing development section, the piano part continually attempts to impose its lyrical material on the adamant march theme of the orchestra.

The second movement, scherzo-like and cheerful, counters the seiousness of the first; the piano and orchestral parts intertwine rapidly, although the piano clearly comes out to be the "winner." The following slow movement, in contrast, is meditative and songlike in format, and the orchestra has almost as great a role in the presentation of thematic material as does the piano.

The beginning of the boisterous Finale is startling after the quiet third movement. Humorous and repetitive, the Finale features an extended fugal cadenza which stands in stark contrast to the purely homophonic writing in the rest of the movement, and, indeed, the whole concerto. *—John Palmer*

Recommended:

- ○ **Pfitzner: Piano Concerto, Op31** / Albert (cond.), Banfield, Munich PO / CPO 999045
- ○ **Pfitzner: Piano Concertos** / Gieseking, Hamburg State PO / Music & Arts 4925

Philadelphia Orchestra

f. 1900, Philadelphia, PA

Ensemble

The Philadelphia Orchestra has been called the Rolls Royce of orchestras. Its many partisans assert that it is, and has been for nearly a century, the finest orchestra in the world.

The Philadelphia Orchestra was founded in 1900. Fritz Scheel was appointed the ensemble's first music director and served until his 1907 death. In its earliest years, the orchestra could not boast the exalted reputation it would develop just two decades later, but it did manage to attract some notable figures, including Richard Strauss who guestconducted, and Artur Rubinstein who appeared as soloist in 1906. Scheel was succeeded by Carl Pohlig, a Mahler protégée. Under him, the orchestra remained a respectable, but hardly world-class, ensemble. Still, Rachmaninov and other major musicians appeared with the orchestra during his five-year tenure.

In 1912, the orchestra management appointed the young and then-obscure conductor, Leopold Stokowski, to be music director. By 1920, the orchestra had become widely recognized as the finest on American shores and among the greatest in the world. Stokowski had transformed a merely talented ensemble into a world-class orchestra in less than a decade. And his programming was boldly individual: he performed many new compositions, often ones requiring extravagant forces, such as the Mahler *Eighth Symphony*, which he introduced in 1916. He attracted the leading artists of the day and regularly conducted transcriptions of his own devising (often with the aid of Lucien Caillet) of works by Bach and others. More importantly, he led the Philadelphians in numerous recordings in the 1920s and 1930s for RCA, far outpacing most other conductors and orchestras of that period in this endeavor. Also under Stokowski, the orchestra became the first to have its own radio broadcast underwritten by commercial sponsors and to perform on a movie soundtrack, *The Big Broadcast of 1937*. Among Stokowski's innovations in the playing style of the orchestra was the introduction of "free bowing" for the string players, which resulted in a lusher, fuller sound. Many, however, asserted the thicker sonorities rendered a less appropriate sound to the more delicately-scored works from the Classical era.

In 1938, the management appointed a new music director, Eugene Ormandy, who had become assistant conductor in 1936. Stokowski still led performances and made recordings with the orchestra until 1940. Ormandy dispensed with Stokowski's "free bowing," and, many have claimed, fashioned an even greater collective virtuosity from his players. The leading musicians of the mid-twentieth century regularly played and recorded with the Philadelphians, including Rachmaninov (who died in 1943), Horowitz, Van Cliburn, Szigeti, and Oistrakh. Ormandy and the Philadelphia Orchestra continued to make recordings with RCA in the beginning of his tenure, but switched to Columbia in the 1940s. They would return to RCA, however, in 1968. For both labels they made recordings mainly from the standard repertory and its fringes, but paying particular attention to the works of Rachmaninov, Tchaikovsky, and Prokofiev. They also played and recorded a fair amount of American music, including works by Copland, Harris, Piston, and Gershwin.

By the early 1970s, the orchestra was said to be in decline by some critics and concertgoers. Ormandy selected his successor, Riccardo Muti, who became music director in 1980. Muti also made a large number of recordings during his ten years in Philadelphia, including a well-received cycle of Beethoven symphonies for EMI. Some view the Muti years negatively, but overall the orchestra maintained its generally high reputation.

Wolfgang Sawallisch was appointed music director in 1990 and serves in that capacity currently. Many have asserted that playing standards have risen under his direction, thus once again placing the orchestra among the top several in the world. —*Robert Cummings*

Recommended:

- ○ **Orff: Carmina Burana** / Ormandy (cond.), Walter, Presnell, Petrak, Harsanyi, Philadelphia Orch. / 2002 / Sony 87735
- ○ **Druckman: Brangle; Counterpoise; Viola Concerto** / Zinman, Sawallisch (conds.), Upshaw, Diaz, Philadelphia Orch. / 2001 / New World 80560
- ○ **Stokowski Conducts Wagner** / Stokowski (cond.), Tibbett, Traubel, Jagel, Davis, Philadelphia Orch. / 2003 / Andante 1130
- ○ **Sibelius: Legends** / Ormandy (cond.), Philadelphia Orch. / 1986 / EMI 47612
- ○ **Scriabin: Symphonies** / Muti (cond.), Flummerfelt, Toczyska, Myers, Philadelphia Orch., Westminster Choir / 2001 / EMI 567720
- ○ **Fantasia** / Stokowski (cond.), Philadelphia Orch. / Buena Vista 60007
- ○ **Saint-Saëns: Organ Symphony** / Ormandy (cond.), Fox, Philadelphia Orch. / 1985 / RCA Victor 66134

Philharmonia Orchestra of London

f. 1945, London, England
Ensemble

England's Philharmonia is a relative "youngster" among orchestras, having arisen out of the ashes of London's disrupted orchestral life in the wake of World War II. Within an astonishingly short time, it rose to a high level of quality with a deep, burnished tone similar to the best Austrian-German ensembles. Not surprisingly, its formative years were nurtured under the batons of Furtwängler, Karajan, and Klemperer. In 1945, EMI's Walter Legge realized a long-standing ambition to create a British recording orchestra chiefly for recording purposes that would rival the best Continental models. The Philharmonia was to be a flexible, democratic organization. With a rebuff to the offer from Sir Thomas Beecham to helm the impressive new ensemble, Legge set out to attract the best conductors and soloists on the international scene. Concerts were added, as well, and among the most outstanding events of the early years were a Beethoven cycle with pianist Artur Schnabel as soloist, a recording of Ravel's *Concerto in G major* with a young Leonard Bernstein as pianist, and concerts under the batons of composers Walton, Richard Strauss, and Hindemith. The basis for the Philharmonia's sonorous quality was undoubtedly laid by the procurement of Wilhelm Furtwängler and Herbert von Karajan. The great traditions of Berlin and Vienna were absorbed into the English ensemble. But with the death of Furtwängler in 1954, Karajan ascended to directorship of the Berlin Philharmonic and consequently minimized his ties with the Philharmonia. Legge then made the happy decision to approach Otto Klemperer, one of the last German conductors with nineteenth century roots, with a mutually happy result for both parties. The septuagenarian conductor's flagging career was rejuvenated and the orchestra continued to flourish. While some would cite Klemperer's performances as being idiosyncratic, his deliberate tempi legendary, all agreed to the integrity of the performance born of the artistic marriage. Concerts were sold out and scores of worthy recordings—particularly of Brahms, Bruckner, and Mahler—are found and revered on CD to this day. Meanwhile, in 1964, Legge, convinced that he could not maintain the Philharmonia as he wished, expressed his intent to disband the ensemble. The players, with the encouragement of Klemperer, immediately responded by re-forming and renaming as New Philharmonia Orchestra. They continued to flourish, a high point being an invitation from West Germany to perform at Bonn for the Beethoven Bicentennial. With Klemperer's passing in 1973, the orchestra was helmed by American Lorin Maazel and subsequently, Italian Riccardo Muti, who expanded upon the largely classic Austro-German repertoire to embrace a wider international and modern palette. In 1977, the "Philharmonia" reverted to its original name. In 1984, Giuseppe Sinopoli continued the tradition, along with numerous associate conductors. A noteworthy accomplishment was the first digital recording of the Beethoven symphonies under Kurt Sanderling in 1981. In 1997, Christoph von Dohnányi assumed chief conductorship, continuing the catholicity of repertoire of his predecessors. The Philharmonia has also thrived as a film orchestra, its credits including *Henry V*, *The Far Pavilions*, and *Nicholas and Alexandra*. The orchestra maintained residences in New York in 2002 and 2003. —*Wayne Reisig*

Recommended:

- ○ **Wagner: Tristan und Isolde** / Furtwängler (cond.), Flagstad, Fischer-Dieskau, Schock, Suthaus, Philharmonia / 2001 / EMI 85873
- ○ **Brahms: Symphonies** / Klemperer (cond.), Ludwig, Philharmonia / 2004 / EMI 62760
- ○ **Debussy: La Mer; Nocturnes; Ravel: Alborada del gracioso; Daphnis et Chloé Suite 2** / Giulini (cond.), Philharmonia / 2004 / EMI 62759
- ○ **Tchaikovsky: Symphony 6; Romeo & Juliet** / Cantelli (cond.), Philharmonia / 1989 / EMI 769785

Philip Jones Brass Ensemble

f. 1951, London, England
Ensemble

Although the Philip Jones Brass Ensemble actually formed in 1951, its first full-length concert did not take place until the 1962 Aldeburgh festival. Moreover, the group made its first recording only in 1970. It was the first such brass ensemble to perform in the world's major concert halls and to record with the preeminent labels. Philip Jones (born 1928), the ensemble's founder, was a virtuoso trumpet player whose first important position was with the Covent Garden orchestra, where he played from 1948 to 1951. About the time he resigned from there, Jones founded the ensemble bearing his name, which consisted of a quintet of players featuring two trumpets, a horn, trombone, and tuba. Later, it expanded to ten players for selected bigger concert dates in Europe and the U.S. Jones originally conceived the idea to form the group after hearing the Amsterdam Koper Quartet, an obscure ensemble of brass players whom he had heard in an Edinburgh concert. The players most closely associated with the Philip Jones Brass Ensemble during its 35-year existence were Elgar Howarth (trumpet), who was also a well-known composer and conductor; Ifor James (horn); John Iveson (trombone); John Fletcher (tuba); and of course, Jones. Other players over the years, generally those added when ten pieces were used, included the famed horn player Alan Civil, James Watson, John Wilbraham, Rod Franks, John Miller, Denis Wick, Dave Stewart, Chris Mowat, and Frank Lloyd. After founding the group in 1951, Jones freelanced over the next few years while his ensemble made infrequent appearances, advancing little toward establishing a reputation beyond the British Isles. Jones joined the Royal Philharmonic Orchestra for four seasons, beginning in 1956, then the Philharmonia in 1960 for an identical tenure. From 1962, the PJBE slowly built a reputation that evolved as their repertory grew, especially from pieces by Giovanni Gabrieli and Johann Pezel. Jones had shorter stints with other British orchestras in the 1960s: the London Philharmonic in 1964–65, the New Philharmonic Orchestra in 1965–67, and the BBC Symphony Orchestra from 1968 to 1972. By the time Jones had left the BBC, his ensemble had made its first recordings and was in demand not only in the U.K., but throughout Europe and the U.S. They began to draw important commissions too, including one from American composer Raymond Premru, who composed his *Divertimento* for them in 1976. But the PJBE also began playing other modern works, including ones by Richard Rodney Bennett, Hans Werner Henze, and Toru Takemitsu. The ensemble also began working with choral groups, in particular with the London Bach Choir. Much of the repertory of the PJBE were transcriptions of well-known classical works. Elgar Howarth made one of Mussorgsky's *Pictures at an Exhibition* in 1979, which the group then premiered and recorded.

Jones, who had allotted some of his time to teaching when he left the BBC Symphony Orchestra in 1972, retired from the ensemble in 1986, thereafter focusing his professional activities on teaching. Yet he might have continued the PJBE had a freak accident not hastened his decision to retire: he drove his automobile over his trumpet case. The group then disbanded, but re-formed under the name the London Brass. Without doubt, the PJBE was one of the most influential instrumental ensembles in terms of laying the groundwork for the establishment of similar highly successful groups, such as the Canadian Brass and the Empire Brass. *—Robert Cummings*

Recommended:

- ○ **Greatest Hits** / Philip Jones Brass Ens. / 2001 / Decca 467746
- ○ **Philip Jones Brass Ensemble** / Philip Jones Brass Ens. / Claves 500600
- ○ **Music from the Royal Court** / Philip Jones Brass Ens. / 2003 / Decca 000080702
- ○ **The 20th Century Album** / Philip Jones Brass Ens. / 2002 / Decca 470501

Peter Phillips

b. Oct. 15, 1953, Southampton, England

Conductor

Peter Phillips is one of Britain's foremost early music choral ensemble conductors and the founder and head of a leading independent record company, Gimell Records.

Phillips earned a scholarship to Oxford University in 1972 and specialized in Renaissance music, studying with Denis Arnold and David Wulstan. In 1973, Phillips brought together the choral scholars of the various chapels of Oxford and Cambridge Universities to sing sacred vocal Renaissance music. He named the group the Tallis Scholars in recognition of its members' achievement and to honor Thomas Tallis, one of the leading British Renaissance composers. In 1978, the group was organized as a permanent ensemble. At that point, they began regular concerts and tours, which have taken them through Europe, Australia, Asia, Israel, and North America.

Phillips has established himself as one of the foremost scholarly researchers in the field of sacred music before 1600. He is the contributor of a regular column on early music to *The Spectator*, and published a book *English Sacred Music 1549–1649* (the dates of the English Reformation and the foundation of the Puritan Commonwealth), an encyclopedic account of those dramatic years in English music. He has taken an interest in the other arts of the period and is working on a companion volume on the general cultural background of those years. Since 1995, Phillips has been publisher of *The Musical Times*.

In 1981, Phillips and Steve Smith founded an independent record label called Gimell (the name of a letter of the Hebrew alphabet), solely to record the Tallis Scholars. The label quickly won a strong international reputation for the quality of the Scholars' performances and production quality, particularly for a highly acclaimed CD featuring Tallis' *Spem in Alium*, a masterpiece of polyphony in 40 voices.

In addition to performing nearly 100 concerts with the Tallis Scholars annually, Phillips also appears frequently on British radio and television programs on musical topics, such as Radio 3's *Music Weekly*, the BBC World Service, Kaleidoscope, and Today (both on Radio 4), and on American, Canadian, and European stations. The *South Bank Show* did a major documentary on the Tallis Scholars, showing how Phillips researched the music and prepared the performances, as well as taking the viewer on a Phillips-led overview of the Renaissance period in sacred vocal music. Phillips has conducted the Tallis Scholars at the BBC Promenade Concerts, the Aldeburgh Festival, the Bath Festival, and the Cheltenham Festival. In 1994, they were invited to sing two concerts in the Basilica of Santa Maria Maggiore in Rome to celebrate the 400th anniversary of the death of Palestrina, which were recorded and released on Gimell.*—Joseph Stevenson*

Recommended:

- ○ **Byrd: Masses** / Philips (cond.), Tallis Scholars / 1993 / Gimell 454945
- ○ **Allegri: Miserere** / Philips (cond.), Tallis Scholars / 2001 / Gimell 339
- ○ **Ockeghem: Au travail suis; De plus en plus** / Philips (cond.), Tallis Scholars / 2001 / Gimell 35
- ○ **Tallis: Spem in Alium** / Philips (cond.), Tallis Scholars / 2001 / Gimell 6
- ○ **Obrecht: Missa Maria Zart** / Philips (cond.), Tallis Scholars / 2001 / Gimell 32
- ○ **Tavener: Ikon of Light; Funeral Ikos; The Lamb** / Philips (cond.), Chilingirian Quartet, Tallis Scholars / 2001 / Gimell 5

Gregor Piatigorsky

b. Apr. 17, 1903, Ekaterinoslav, Russia, **d.** Aug. 6, 1976, Los Angeles, CA

Cellist

Gregor Piatigorsky began playing the cello at the age of seven and was admitted to the Moscow Conservatory at nine, studying there with Alfred von Glehn. In 1919, he joined the Lenin Quartet and was appointed principal cellist of the Bol'shoy Theater Orchestra. In 1921, Piatigorsky left the Soviet Union, going to Leipzig by way of Warsaw, and studied for a time with Julius Klengel. Furtwängler appointed him principal cellist of the Berlin Philharmonic in 1924 where he came into contact with the leading German musicians of the time, including Schnabel and Flesch, with whom he formed a trio. In 1928, Piatigorsky left Berlin to concentrate on a solo career, which began triumphantly with his New York debut in 1929. Although Piatigorsky concertized regularly as a soloist, he continued his activity as a chamber musician. Starting in 1930, he formed a trio with Horowitz and Milstein, and later, in 1949 with Heifitz and Rubinstein. In 1961, Piatigorsky and Heifitz formed a chamber music series in Los Angeles, much of which was recorded, and remain among the treasures of chamber music performances.

For many years Piatigorsky directed the chamber music program at Tanglewood, helped found the Meadowmount School, succeed Emanuel Feuermann as professor of cello at the Curtis Institute, and in 1962 became a professor at the University of Southern California. His legacy as a teacher remains a powerful fixture in the world of cello playing; his famous students include Erling Blöndal Bengtsson, Mischa Maisky, and Nathaniel Rosen, among many others. Piatigorsky was known for his Romantic expressiveness and virtuosic flair, and was at his best in the big nineteenth and early twentieth century concerto repertory. He premiered works by Walton, Hindemith, and Castelnuovo-Tedesco, published a number of original works and arrangements for the cello, and collaborated with Stravinsky on his *Suite Italienne*. Widely revered and honored, Piatigorsky was one of the most important and influential musicians of his generation. *—Steven Coburn*

Recommended:

- ○ **Piatigorsky, Solomon & Rubinstein: Beethoven Cello Sonatas** / Piatigorsky, Rubinstein, Solomon / 1999 / Testament 2158
- ○ **Rubinstein Collection, Vol. 25** / Rubinstein, Heifetz, Piatigorsky / 1999 / RCA 63025
- ○ **Brahms, Double Concerto, etc.** / Piatigorsky, etc. / RCA 61485

Astor Piazzolla

b. Mar. 11, 1921, Mar del Plata, Argentina, **d.** Jul. 5, 1992, Buenos Aires, Argentina

Composer: Chamber Music

"For me," Astor Piazzolla once said, "tango was always for the ear rather than the feet." Piazzolla expanded upon one of the great popular dance traditions of the Western Hemisphere, constantly crossing and recrossing the line between popular and classical music.

A tango master not of the barrooms but of the concert hall, Astor Piazzolla was born in Mar del Plata, Argentina in 1921. His family moved to New York's Little Italy, and his musical education was shaped by American jazz and pop. But his father gave him a bandoneón, a large Argentine concertina, to keep the family's connection to Argentine culture alive, and he also studied classical music. In 1934, he recorded with the Argentine tango pioneer Carlos Gardel, who soon would be killed in a plane crash. Returning to Argentina, he played the bandoneón in a Buenos Aires tango orchestra from 1936 to 1944, but the world of classical music had made a deep impression on him. A chance meeting with the great pianist Artur Rubinstein brought him into contact with Alberto Ginastera, Argentina's leading composer, and that led to several years of classical study. Piazzolla's *Sinfonia Buenos Aires* gained international acclaim but was poorly received in the composer's home country.

In 1954, Piazzolla went to Paris for further classical studies with the most famous composition teacher of the time, Nadia Boulanger. However, the experience led him to reconnect with the tango; Boulanger, after hearing him play one of his tango pieces, told him to discard the rest of his compositions. Back in Argentina, Piazzolla created *nuevo tango* (new tango), which broke sharply with the genre's traditional sound, and once again antagonized tango's Argentine partisans (he was even beaten up on the street on one occasion). Abroad, however, Piazzolla's reputation began to spread. Often written for his Quinteto Tango Nuevo (formed in 1960), featuring violin, guitar, piano, bass, and bandoneón, Piazzolla's more than 750 tango compositions included complex harmonies drawn from the world of modern concert music. The 1968 stage work *Maria de Buenos Aires*, inspired by Gershwin's *Porgy and Bess*, finally won over tango traditionalists, and for the last two decades of his life Piazzolla was an Argentine hero. Internationally, his reputation with both popular and specialized audiences continued to grow; his compositions became part of the 1986 musical *Tango Argentina* and also attracted progressive musicians like the members of the Kronos Quartet, who recorded Piazzolla's *Five Tango Sensations* of 1989. He died in Buenos Aires on July 5, 1992.

Piazzolla reawakened interest in the tango, and the international exposure given his works touched off a series of tango films, stage productions, and recordings. The key to Piazzolla's popularity was that no matter how much he experimented with the musical materials of the tango, he never lost touch with its sensual yet despairing emotional essence. The popularity of Piazzolla's unique blend of tango, classical music, and jazz continued to grow after his death. Jazz musicians, such as guitarists Al di Meola and Charlie Byrd and the vibraphonist Gary Burton have used Piazzolla's music as a point of departure, and classical performers as well took to his music; at the end of the 1990s, recordings by the famed Latvian violinist Gidon Kremer showed that despite its association with the bandoneón, Piazzolla's music could be transferred to other instruments. At the turn of the century, Piazzolla's boundary-crossing music was continuing to gain listeners of all kinds. *—AMG*

CHAMBER MUSIC

Adiós Nonino, tango (1959)

Astor Piazzolla was the leader of the "Tango Nuevo" (New Tango) movement. His father was Vicente Piazzolla and his mother was Asunta Manetti Piazzolla, both of wholly Italian descent. His daughter, Diana, gave Astor's parents the traditional Italian names for Grandpa and Grandma—Nonino and Nonina.

One of Piazzolla's jobs was as music director to the dance team of Juan Carlos Copes and Maria Nieves, which included a trip to San Juan, Puerto Rico in October 1960, to appear in the Club Flamboyan. There, on the last night of the engagement, he received a telegram. Nonino had been injured in a fall from his bicycle and, due to complications, was in critical condition. When he called Argentina, his cousin informed him that Nonino had died just after noon that day. "It was the only time I ever saw [Astor] cry," remembered Copes. Once home, Piazzolla asked to be left alone for a while. The emotions now caught up with him. His wife, Dedé, heard only sighs for a while. Then the sound of her husband playing a bright little tune he had written some time earlier, called *Nonino.* Then a pause, and then, amid continued sighs and the sound of crying came a new tune, a soul-haunting melody. It was the composer's way of saying farewell to his father—*Adios, Nonino.* It became Piazzolla's most famous piece. "Perhaps I was surrounded by angels," he said 20 years later. "I was able to write the finest tune I have written. I don't know if I shall ever do better. I doubt it." He performed well over a thousand times, making 20 different arrangements of it.

His father's death impelled him to go back to Argentina to try his new tango there again with the lessons he had assimilated in America. Lacking the money for four fares for the family, he phoned his publisher in Paris, offering to renegotiate his contract for an advance, which he was granted. Gratefully, Piazzolla immediately sent the publisher *Adios, Nonino,* an act that benefited them both as it became what Piazzolla's biographers Maria Susana Azzi and Simon Collier called "the jewel in the crown of the Piazzolla list at Éditions Universelles."

For years, Piazzolla refused any efforts to set words to *Adios, Nonino,* but in the 1980s that talented singer Eladia Blásquez played him a tape in which she had sung lyrics she wrote for it: "Adiós Nonino... qué largo sin vos será el camino..." it began, "Farewell, Nonino... how long the road will be without you...." His eyes slightly misty, he nodded his assent. *—Joseph Stevenson*

Recommended:

- ○ **Piazzolla: Concerto for Bandonéon; etc.** / Pons (cond.), Mainetti, Orquesta da Camara Teatro Lliure / HM 901595
- ○ **Astor Piazzolla & His Tango Quintet** / Piazzolla Tango Quintet / 1992 / Ermitage 12007
- ○ **Piazzolla: Libertango** / Piazzolla (cond.), various / Trova 5053

Six Études tanguistiques, for solo flute (1987)

These six tango etudes are a highly original blending of the classical concert etude and Piazzolla's "new tango" music. They present the player with technical challenges pertaining to given aspect of flute playing, yet are effective concert works. Although the tango rhythm is never very far away in this set, much of the interest of the music lies in how Piazzolla finds new textures and playing techniques for the solo flute. Gidon Kremer effectively transferred these pieces to the violin on his *Tracing Astor* album, and there is also a well-known arrangement for saxophone, by Delangle. For no very good reason other than the solo instrumentation, these works are often likened to Bach's partitas and sonatas for solo violin. They were composed in 1987 and belong to a group of works from Piazzolla's later career in which he returned to "classical" specification of the musical moment while by no means abandoning his connection to the tango.

No. 1 Decidé (Decisively): This etude has a strong, underlying tango rhythm, though the triplet subdivision of the beat makes it a work in 12/8 rather than 4/4. This is a study in accentuation and in creating the illusion of two separate melodic lines. The notes that fall on the beat are accented to bring out a melody, while the remaining two notes of the beat are played more softly and less staccato, to make a florid accompaniment.

No 2 Anxieux et rubato (Anxiously and with rubato): This melodically based etude is the longest in the set at over seven minutes. The melody has a haunting quality; two phrases are played in a florid, flowing manner, then followed with a nervous descending scale figure, creating a mood like nervous laughter. As the direction "rubato" requires, the beat is flexible. A central section rises to a more assertive emotional level, but the music returns to the uncertain main theme.

No. 3 Molto marcato e energico (Very markedly and energetically): This etude takes up the texture and technique of the first etude but demands even more florid and difficult playing, with stronger dance rhythms. The central section has a more lyrical quality but preserves features of the first part, and the quick shifting of register creates the impression of a duet texture.

No. 4 Lento meditativo (Sadly meditative): Technical flourishes are all but abandoned here, in favor of one of Piazzolla's heartfelt legato melodies. The piece tests breath control and the ability to shape and communicate a line directly to the listener. The final, quieter repetition of the opening material is deeply touching.

In *No. 5 Sans indication* (Without tempo/expression marking), it seems that Piazzolla's next test is to let the artist decide how fast and of what character this music should be. It is the shortest of the etudes and contrasts florid runs with a bobbing staccato motive, ending with something of a musical question mark.

No. 6 Avec anxieté (With anxiety) is a fast counterpart to the second etude. Fast, constrained triplet figurations create the impression of being locked into a place or situation while the anxiety to escape escalates. The melody suddenly sounds liberated and calm. Then, once again, the melody seems to be trapped in its box, and the etude comes rapidly to a conclusion. *—Joseph Stevenson*

Recommended:

- ○ **Pizzolla: Histoire du Tango** / Daroux, Marquez / HM 911674

L'histoire du tango, tango cycle for flute & guitar (before 1985)

Astor Piazzolla was keenly aware of the changing style of the Argentine national dance over his lifetime. It was entirely natural that he should seek to remind his critics and fans alike of the fact that tango had begun in the process of musical evolution and altered its sound and mood through that same process.

Histoire du Tango is the vehicle by which he did so. It is not written for the standard tango band, but is a kind of abstraction of that sound into a classical suite, originally written for flute and guitar. (There is also a version for violin and guitar, as well as other arrangements, and the work's title is sometimes given in Spanish, *La Historia del Tango.*)

The music is a little over 20 minutes long and covers the evolution of the dance through the twentieth century. Tango evolved from an earlier popular dance called the milonga, which is itself evolved from the Cuban rhythm known as habanera. Tango was initially regarded as a low dance. Like North American jazz, it originated in bordellos, and so the first movement is entitled "Bordel 1900." The relatively genteel milonga is depicted here as having been jolted into a new form by a heavy injection of eroticism. The dotted habanera/milonga rhythm is exaggerated and in this form not accepted in polite society.

The second movement is called "Café 1930." By now, tango was the favorite dance of all classes in Argentina and was known as a daring dance around the world. Piazzolla is now writing directly from his memories of the type of tango played in cafés in Buenos Aires. This is a respectful depiction of the full-blown traditional tango.

The third movement, "Nightclub 1960" evokes the precise time when Piazzolla returned to Buenos Aires after his efforts to create Jazz Tango in the U.S. It now becomes clear that Piazzolla is dealing in the overall composition with his own place in the history of the music, as more sophisticated jazz elements enliven a music that had become standardized and complacent. This is a picture of the early version of Tango Nuevo.

The final movement is called "Concert d'aujourd'hui," a title that most literally translates as "Concert of Today" but which might also be called "Contemporary Concert." By the 1980s, Piazzolla was becoming an exciting voice in classical concert music. He shows himself here as having taken tango from its polite café form through its new nightclub dance form and making it into a new form for concert music. The harmonic vocabulary here is advanced and often startling, and it is music for listening more than dancing. *—Joseph Stevenson*

Recommended:

- ○ **Piazzolla for 2: Tangos for flute & guitar** / Sollscher, Gallois / DG 449185

Libertango, tango (1974)

Pressured by his European agent to write shorter, more "airplay-friendly" pieces, Piazzolla produced *Libertango* in 1974. This was during the period from 1971 to 1978 when he was working with a highly electric and eclectic nonet, Conjunto 9, which gave his work a more commercial, rock- and jazz-influenced sound. But when Piazzolla re-formed his mainly acoustic quintet in 1978, *Libertango* was one of the pieces that easily survived the transition back to Piazzolla's earlier, grittier, more intimate sound.

Although details varied from one performance and recording to another, *Libertango,* a "sort of song to liberty," begins with an extremely fast, busy piano solo with bass (acoustic and electric) support. Piazzolla's own bandoneón soon takes center stage for the remainder of the piece, which moves forward relentlessly. After a very brief respite three-quarters of the way through, the material returns even faster and more urgently. Too frantic to be either a successful song (although French vocalist Guy Marchand did record a best-selling version in 1975) or a practical dance (except for the most elite specialists), *Libertango* is one of Piazzolla's pure concert tangos: compact, dynamic, and unforgiving. *—James Reel*

Recommended:

○ **Play** / MacGregor, Piazzolla / 2001 / Sound Circus 15007

○ **Astor Piazzolla & His Tango Quintet** / Piazzolla Tango Quintet / 1992 / Ermitage 12007

○ **Piazzolla: Libertango** / Piazzolla (cond.), various / Trova 5053

Milonga del ángel, tango (1965)

For Alberto Rodriguez Muñoz's 1962 stage play *Tango del Angel*, in which an angel heals the spirits of the residents of a shabby Buenos Aires neighborhood, Piazzolla added two new pieces to an earlier tango that gave the play its name. This music reappeared in at least two different concert forms, but one of the unifying elements is the piece *Milonga del ángel*. A milonga is a sort of proto-tango, lighter and gentler than the more familiar form. This milonga is openly sentimental and begins with a lounge music feel with strummed bass chords; a simple, keening violin line; and a few tinkles from the piano. The bandoneón creeps in almost unnoticed, but takes control of the piece with a sad, nostalgic melody (at this point, one could easily imagine the piece being played in a jazz club). Just as the treatment of the melody becomes more complex and emotional, a secondary section arrives to allow some air around the music. It initially seems like a transition, but opens into a highly romantic and sensual violin solo. The bandoneón reclaims its place, offering its own variation on this melody, which is actually closely tied to the main theme, and musing on it with the violin and electric bass. A more intense passage leads to the coda, which strips the music down to a series of chords, much as the piece began. *—James Reel*

Recommended:

○ **Piazzolla: El Porteño** / Tanenbaum / 1994 / New Albion 065

○ **Astor Piazzolla & His Tango Quintet** / Piazzolla Tango Quintet / 1992 / Ermitage 12007

La Muerte del ángel, tango (1962)

This is the climactic piece Piazzolla provided for his incidental music to the 1962 Alberto Rodriguez Muñoz play *Tango del ángel*, in which an angel heals the spirits of the residents of a shabby Buenos Aires neighborhood, but is ultimately killed in that most Argentine of pastimes, a knife fight. *Death of the Angel* later found its way into at least two suites of Piazzolla's Angel-related music. Piazzolla performed and recorded the piece on many occasions, usually as a companion to *Milonga del ángel*, from the same source. This begins as a remarkable three-voice fugue, slicing out from a fast, jagged theme passed dissonantly among the instruments of the standard Piazzolla quintet (bandoneón, violin, piano, and acoustic and electric bass). The fugue pulls up short, though, for a central bandoneón-dominated section that is simultaneously sentimental and unsettled. The fugue theme then resumes, although it is no longer treated contrapuntally, and ends, appropriately, with slashing violin glissandi. *—James Reel*

Recommended:

○ **Death Of An Angel** / Volk / 1994 / Chiron 4853

○ **Astor Piazzolla & His Tango Quintet** / Piazzolla Tango Quintet / 1992 / Ermitage 12007

Five Pieces for guitar (1980)

Piazzolla's *Five Pieces for Guitar* were written around 1980 and were published by Edizioni Musicali Bèrben in Italy in 1981. They are the composer's only works for guitar solo. Even without much of a track record in the field (he did write several other works for ensembles that included a guitar), Piazzolla confidently proclaimed that these pieces would make his name well known among guitarists. He was right; the *Pieces* are staples of the Latin American guitar recital, and they have been recorded several times.

Though not virtuoso works, the pieces are nicely idiomatic to the guitar, containing overtone effects and passages in which the fingers strike or are trilled on the instrument's surface. They are mostly slow and quite harmonically involved; the only one with more than a hint of Piazzolla's usual tango rhythms is the third piece, and that one is a tango that is both minimal and edgy. Especially evocative is the first piece, in triple meter and cast in a ternary form. In the middle section, after a gradual and complicated shift to duple meter, a halting melody emerges, very vocal in nature, like the verse of a tortured ballad intoned by one of the classic Latin female vocalists, imprisoned in the cage of a repressive society. For that moment alone these pieces are worthy of wider familiarity, and there are several others equally as beautiful.

Periodic suggestions that versions other than the printed one exist are both unsubstantiated and pointless, for these works, even if somewhat more compositionally specified than the general run of Piazzolla's works, certainly permit variation in performance. The unique essence of Piazzolla's method is the grafting of popular ensemble performance techniques onto written compositions of a fairly rigorous sort. Piazzolla wrote out most of his own music but then treated it freely in performances with his quintet, and even though these pieces began their public existence as a publication in musical notation, there is no reason to think that their composer would not have approved of similar freedoms in this particular case. *—James Manheim*

Recommended:

○ **Piazzolla: Complete Music for Flute & Guitar** / Toepper, Galdo / 1999 / Naxos 554760

Verano porteño, tango (1965)

This is one of Astor Piazzolla's best-known *tango nuevo* (new tango) compositions. It derives from one of his most fertile and creative periods, during which he advanced the venerable Argentine dance/popular music form into new territory.

By the time he wrote this work, Piazzolla must have realized that he was in the position of the proverbial prophet without honor in his own country. He had returned to Buenos Aires in July 1960 after a disappointing attempt in the United States to create what he then called "tango-jazz." His spirit was, however, far from broken, but he was personally disappointed that just the type of revolution he was seeking in tango had been accepted in Brazil when that country's national dance, the samba, evolved into a new form called either jazz-samba or "bossa nova," ("new thing").

At home, however, Piazzolla's efforts ran into walls of controversy. He and a leading exponent of classic tango, the dancer Jorge Vidal (whose style Piazzolla detested and called "archaic"), actually came to blows in the studios of Argentina's Channel 7. Sometimes taxi drivers would refuse to transport him, accusing him of having "destroyed the tango." He enjoyed some success among certain segments of the public and was encouraged when RCA Victor, CBS, and Philips Records all issued LPs or 45 rpm EPs of his music. This raised interest abroad in Piazzolla's music. Argentine president Arturo Illia responded to requests to include Piazzolla on cultural exchanges by backing a tour to Brazil and the United States.

Before Piazzolla left on the trip, he had a commitment on the table: a set of four compositions for a play called *Melenita de Oro*, by Alberto Rodriguez Muñoz. One of the pieces was *Verano porteño*. The word "Porteño" is an adjectival nickname pertaining to Buenos Aires, so the title is an informal way to say "Buenos Aires Summer." Newspapers found the music "original and agreeable." Piazzolla over time wrote three other pieces with similar titles for spring, winter, and autumn, and later assembled the four into a suite called "Buenos Aires Seasons." As a sort of exotic modern counterpart to the *Four Seasons* violin concertos of Vivaldi, these have enjoyed particular popularity among Piazzolla's large corpus of tangos, even though they were not initially conceived as a set. Either separately or as part of this suite, the very pretty, lightly swaying tango *Verano porteño* became one of Piazzolla's most beloved works. Often heard in a version for guitar solo, it has also been arranged for the small instrumental combinations in which the composer's music is typically heard. *—Joseph Stevenson*

Recommended:

○ **Classic Williams** / Williams / 2000 / Sony 89141

○ **Vivaldi & Piazzolla: 8 Seasons** / Kremer, Kremerata Baltica / 2000 / Nonesuch 79568

Gabriel Pierné

b. Aug. 16, 1863, Metz, France, **d.** Jul. 17, 1937, Ploujean, France

Composer: Chamber Music

Gabriel Pierné has been called the most complete French musician of the late Romantic/early twentieth century era. In his own music Pierné blended a seriousness of purpose (acquired in part through his studies with Cesar Franck) with a lighter, more popular flavor reminiscent of Jules Massenet (with whom Pierné also studied); his dedication to the music of his contemporary French composers earned him a reputation as a conductor of deep integrity.

Pierné was born in 1863 in the town of Metz. He displayed great musical promise as a child, and by 1871 he had entered the Paris Conservatoire to study composition with Massenet and organ with Franck (Franck's organ class, however, often focusing more on composing than on playing). At age eleven Pierné earned a medal for his solfège skills, and he later went on to win top prizes in organ, composition, and piano, as well as (in 1882) the coveted Prix de Rome (for the cantata *Edith*).

In 1890 Pierné succeeded his teacher, Franck, as organist at St. Clotilde cathedral, a distinct honor for a young man of 27. In the late 1890s he abandoned his career as an organist and in 1903 made his debut as assistant conductor of the Concerts Colonne (of which he served as principal conductor from 1910 to 1934, devoting a great deal of rehearsal time to the preparation of new works). In addition to his activities on the podium, Pierné served on the administration of the Paris Conservatoire and composed for the ballet russes (three successful ballets produced between 1923 and 1934). In the years prior to his death in 1937 he was elected to the Académie des Beaux Arts and made a Chevalier of the Légion d'honneur.

Pierné's output as a composer, while by no means as vast as some of his Parisian colleagues (one thinks in particular of Saint-Saëns), includes entries in most of the standard genres; in typically French style, he avoided symphonic form in favor of orchestral poems and character pieces. While Pierné's large-scale works, such as the 1897 oratorio *L'an mil* and the opera *Vendée* from the same year, showcase a solid grasp of musical architecture, the smaller chamber works (sonatas for both violin and cello and a *String Quintet*, among other pieces), are more indicative of his exceptional facility. *—Blair Johnston*

Overview of Works (1879–1937)

Like his contemporaries, Chausson and Magnard, Pierné studied at the Paris Conservatoire with Massenet and Franck, both of whom struck very different chords in his musical personality—chords which would resonate for a lifetime. Massenet drew from him that vein of elegant fastidiousness and suave charm for which he is principally remembered, while Franck's example eventually opened the way both to a surprisingly intense personal utterance and religious affirmation on a grand scale.

Despite an active career as a teacher, organist, and conductor, Pierné was a prolific composer. Beginning in 1879 and continuing until century's end, an amazing spate of songs, chamber, and piano pieces, light orchestral works, incidental music, ballets, and operettas poured forth in bewildering profusion, most of them trifles skimming delicate surfaces with the lightest of touches. If not great music, it is well-made, often spurred by robust gaiety, and of engaging freshness; the *Fantaisie-ballet for Piano and Orchestra* (1885) and the *Piano Concerto* (1887) are imposing examples, their mock seriousness yielding to caressing lyricism. With the oratorio *L'An mil* in 1895—followed by *La Croisade des enfants* (1902), the exquisite "mystery," *Les Enfants à Bethléem* (1907), and *Saint François d'Assise* (1912)—Pierné's work became more substantial, ambitious, and deeply striking, without losing touch with lyric enchantment and a certain naïveté. The rapturous, winsome, passionate *Violin Sonata* (1900) confirms the trend with an aerial refinement owing to the example of Debussy. Incidental music to Pierre Loti's *Ramuntcho* (1908) mines this vein orchestrally and spices it with Basque themes; the two suites drawn from it are occasionally revived. The orchestral *Les Cathédrals* (1915) and the great chamber works of the war years and their aftermath—the *Piano Quintet* (1917), the ruminative, despairing *Cello Sonata* (1919), and the *Piano Trio* (1922)—seem efforts to retain composure and classical limpidity in the face of turbid emotions, in which they largely succeed but with a disquieting undertow. The tripartite orchestral suite, *Paysages franciscains* (1919), is, in its mystical evocations, to Pierné's work what *La Mer* is to Debussy's. With the ballet *Cydalise et le chèvre-pied* (composed 1919, premiered 1923), Pierné regains an unclouded serenity rippled with boisterous high spirits. The two suites drawn from it are, perhaps, his best known music. With its Versailles setting and Watteau evocation, it is the first in a series of nostalgic returns to a magical past which would include the operettas *Sophie Arnould* (1927) and *Fragonard* (1930), the *Divertissement sur un thème pastoral* (1931) and the waltz suite *Viennois* (1935)—both incorporated in the ballet *Images* (1935)—and such delightful chamber effusions as the *Sonata da camera* (1927) for flute, cello, and piano, and the *Voyages au pays du Tendres* for flute, violin, cello, and harp (1937). Nor did Pierné turn his back upon the jazz age, to which he gave a suavely, deftly deferential nod in the ballets *Impressions de music-hall* (1927) and *Giration* (1934). *—Adrian Corleonis*

Recommended:

- ○ **Pierné: Music for Piano** / Katahn / 1999 / Gasparo 302
- ○ **Pierné: Piano Concerto; Ramuntcho Suites** / Houtmann (cond.), Achatz, Lorraine Philharmonie / 1988 / Bis 381
- ○ **Pierné: Cydalise et le chèvre-pied** / Shallon (cond.), Luxembourg SO / 2000 / Timpani 1059
- ○ **Pierné: Complete Works for Piano & Orchestra** / Corp (cond.), Coombs, BBC Scottish SO / 2003 / Hyperion 67348
- ○ **Pierné: Flute Sonata; Piano Trio** / Banfalvi, Matuz, Vas, Szelecsenyi / 1989 / Marco Polo 223189
- ○ **Pierné: Piano Quintet; Violin Sonata** / Hubeau, Charlier, Quatour Viotti / Erato 45525

CHAMBER MUSIC

Canzonetta, for clarinet & piano, Op. 19 (1888)

Gabriel Pierné, French composer and successor to his teacher Cesar Franck as organist at Sainte-Clotilde Cathedral in Paris, was a master musical craftsman, and his skill is as apparent in ear candy such as the *Canzonetta for clarinet and piano,* Op. 19 (probably composed sometime during the final decade of the nineteenth century), as it is in his more weighty, "serious" organ and dramatic music. The *Canzonetta* is dedicated "to [his] friend Charles Turban."

The single-movement *Canzonetta* divides into several distinct but connected sections of music. The clarinet's wistful opening melody has hints of the siciliano in its dotted rhythms; it is followed by a new "scherzando" episode in C minor. Here the pianist is granted the body of thematic action while the clarinetist adds isolated arpeggios that are derived from the very first gesture the clarinetist played in the piece. The dotted rhythms of the opening are completely dissolved during a more syrupy section in A flat major (Più lento), but soon the players develop a hankering for those old siciliano rhythms and return to the opening music, this time with the tune in the piano. The close is magical if played well: the clarinetist makes a whispering run up the treble clef as the music drops from pianissimo to triple-piano, and then disappears into the very highest register of the instrument—E flat three lines above the staff (written F on a B flat clarinet)!—as the pianist provides a soft harmonic cushion. *—Blair Johnston*

Recommended:

- ○ **La Clarinette Française** / Johnson, Back / 1997 / ASV 621

Impromptu-Caprice, for harp in A flat major, Op. 9 (1885)

Although Pierné's *Impromptu-Caprice* was first published in 1887, a reliable edition of this now-standard harp solo did not appear until 1963. (Claims that it was performed with orchestra in 1901 almost certainly confuse this piece with Pierné's *Concertstück for Harp and Orchestra,* Op. 39, which was written that year.) After a trilling prelude that doubles as a miniature cadenza, the childlike main melody appears, floating on typical harp arpeggios and rounded out by a brief return of the introduction. The middle of this ABA-form piece is an exotic bolero in 3/8 time. The first section then returns, in a slightly varied and more flowing form, and the work concludes with impressive running octaves. *—James Reel*

Recommended:

- ○ **Harp Favourites** / Robles / 1993 / Decca 436293
- ○ **Harpe Passion** / Geliot / 2003 / EMI 585201

J. Samuel ("Sam") Pilafian

b. 1949, Miami, FL

Tubist

Tubist Samuel Pilafian is noted for having achieved a degree of fame on an instrument that usually fills an accompanimental role. Equally noteworthy, however, is the ease with which Pilafian moves between classical music and pop. A native of Miami, Pilafian started early on the tuba. He attended the National Music Camp in Interlochen, Michigan, becoming only the second tuba player in history to win the school's concerto competition. That propelled Pilafian to scholarships at Dartmouth College and the Tanglewood Music Center in Massachusetts. While he was studying in the latter program, he was selected by Leonard Bernstein to perform in the world premiere of Bernstein's *Mass,* which was simultaneously part of the opening ceremonies for Washington, D.C.'s John F. Kennedy Center for the Performing Arts.

With his performance of that thoroughly eclectic composition as a starting point, Pilafian developed dual careers. In the classical sphere, Pilafian is best known as a founding member of the Empire Brass Quintet. He has also performed and recorded with the Boston Symphony, the New York Philharmonic, the Orchestra of St. Luke's, and the Metropolitan Opera Orchestra. Pilafian has played recitals and made orchestral appearances in Canada, Spain, Sweden, Switzerland, Japan, Italy, Austria, Germany, and England. He served on the faculties of Boston University and the Boston University Tanglewood Institute, and was a consultant at the Royal Academy of Music in London before joining the faculty at Arizona State University, where he has taught since 1994. Pilafian has released 12 solo albums as a jazz performer and has recorded with the Duke Ellington Orchestra. With guitarist Frank Vignola, Pilafian formed the jazz duo Travelin' Light, which released three discs on the Telarc label. While many classical artists have ventured into jazz with notable success, few have diverged as far from their original training as has Pilafian. He recorded with the rock group Pink Floyd, and under the designation of the Pilafian Project he has recorded an experimental mix of tuba sounds that transcends genre categories. An example is the 1998 album *Meltdown,* which includes music by composers such as Bartók, Sidney Bechet, Ornette Coleman, Ravel, and Captain Beefheart. A past president of T.U.B.A. (the Tubists' Universal Brotherhood Association), Pilafian serves as chairman of that group's board of directors. *—James Manheim*

Recommended:

- ○ **Perception** / Russell (cond.), Pilafian, Morrison, Arizona State U. SO / 1998 / D'Note 1027
- ○ **Meltdown** / Pilafian, Zimmer / 1998 / Summit 227

Trevor Pinnock

b. Dec. 16, 1946, Canterbury, England

Conductor, Harpsichordist

A boy chorister at Canterbury Cathedral, Trevor Pinnock attended the Cathedral Choir School, and as a Foundation Scholar at the Royal College of Music he won a number of prizes for harpsichord and organ. Together with the flutist Stephen Preston and the cellist Anthony Pleeth, he made his performing debut with the Galliard Ensemble at the Royal Festival Hall in 1966 and his conducting debut at the English Bach Festival in 1973. Since 1973 he has been director of the English Concert, specializing in the performance of Baroque music on period instruments.

He has toured Europe, the U.S., Canada, Japan, and South America, and in 1988 conducted Handel's oratorio *Giulio Caesare* at the New York Metropolitan Opera. His recordings include Handel's *Messiah,* and the complete symphonies of Mozart.

As a harpsichord soloist, he has recorded the complete keyboard works of Rameau and many of J.S. Bach's major keyboard works.

Pinnock was advisor and principal conductor of the National Arts Center Orchestra in Ottowa, Canada, from 1991 to 1996, and in 1993 was made an honorary Doctor of Music at Ottowa University. In 1992 he received the civil honor of Commander of the British Empire for his services to music.

Pinnock is a member of an international group of musicians who, from the 1960s onwards, have worked to establish the artistic criteria of "historically informed" performance practices, using original editions and modern research facilities to recreate the techniques and performing styles is use when the music was written. His experience has been brought to bear on the training and development of instrumentalists and singers in the music of Vivaldi, Bach, Mozart and less well known composers whose works are now being assessed in the light of Baroque and early Classical performance conventions. *—Roy Brewer*

Recommended:

- ○ **Purcell** / Pinnock (cond.), English Concert & Choir / Archiv 474672
- ○ **Handel: Ode for St. Cecilia's Day** / Pinnock (cond.), English Concert & Choir / Archiv 000129902
- ○ **Bach: 6 Brandenburg Concertos; 4 Orchestral Suites** / Pinnock (cond.), English Concert / 1982 / Archiv 423492
- ○ **Rameau: Pièces de Clavecin en Concerts** / Pinnock, Podger, Manson / 2002 / Channel 19002
- ○ **Corelli: Concerti Grossi Op6** / Pinnock (cond.), Standage, Comberti, Linden, English Concert / 1998 / Archiv 459451
- ○ **Vivaldi: 7 Concerti** / Pinnock (cond.), English Concert / 1995 / Archiv 445839

Ezio Pinza

b. May 18, 1892, Rome, Italy, **d.** May 9, 1957, Stamford, CT
Bass

Ezio Pinza (né Fortunato Pinza) was one of the most popular and important basses of the twentieth century. Born in Rome in 1892, he originally wanted to make a career in sports, or perhaps engineering, but after discovering his voice he began studies at Ravenna and Bologna. He made his debut in the town of Spezia as Oroveso in Bellini's *Norma* in 1914, but his career was soon delayed by service in the Italian Army during World War I.

After the war, he sang at the Teatro Verdi in Florence in 1919 and then the Teatro Costanzi in Rome where he sang leading roles in *La Forza del Destino*, *La Gioconda*, *Il barbiere di Siviglia*, and *Aida*. He made his Teatro alla Scala debut in 1921 as Pogner in *Die Meistersinger*. This and other German roles in *Tristan und Isolde* and *Salome* were sung in Italian translations. He sang Tagellino in the premiere of Boito's *Nerone* in 1924. During this time, he also sang in Naples, Turin, and other Italian opera houses.

His Metropolitan Opera debut came in 1926 as Pontifex Maximus in Spontini's *La Vestale*. He sang there for the next 22 years, and was greatly admired for his interpretations of leading Verdi roles in *La Forza del Destino*, *Simon Boccanegra*, *Aida*, and *Rigoletto*. Even more important was his participation in the revivals of Mozart's *Don Giovanni* and *Le Nozze di Figaro*; his importance to the success of these productions cannot be overestimated, with his good looks having as much to do with his fame as his superb vocal abilities. Pinza was equally popular in several French operas including Gounod's *Faust*, Delibes' *Lakme*, and Bizet's *Carmen*. His Russian roles included King Didon in Rimsky-Korsakov's *Le Coq d'Or* (in French) and *Boris Godunov* (in Italian). Other important roles at the Metropolian Opera were Raimondo in *Lucia di Lammermoor*, Basilio in *Il Barbiere di Siviglia* and the Father in *Louise*.

Pinza also appeared regularly in Europe at Covent Garden, the Paris Opera, Salzburg Festival, Florence, and Vienna State Opera. He appeared every season at the Teatro Colon in Buenos Aires from 1925 until 1932. In the United States, he also sang in Chicago and San Francisco. Late in his career, he appeared with his daughter Claudia Pinza, who had a minor career singing leading soprano roles. After his retirement from the opera stage, he made a successful Broadway debut in *South Pacific* and later in *Fanny*. He also appeared in several motion pictures.

The voice of Ezio Pinza was a rich basso cantante. He had an easy elegance of phrasing, which is exhibited in nearly all of his recordings. He was at a disadvantage from some of his colleagues because he could not read music, but this meant that he was more willing to follow the concept of the conductor and, indeed, he was a favorite of Arturo Toscanini, Tullio Serafin, and Bruno Walter. He was able to sing the baritone role of Escamillo in *Carmen* as easily as most baritones. Although he had the lower notes of a bass, they did not have the presence usually associated with the true bass voice, which meant that his Sarastro (*The Magic Flute*) was not as effective as his Figaro or Don Giovanni. He willingly undertook smaller roles such as Ferrando in *Il Trovatore* and Colline in *La Bohème*. *—Richard LeSueur*

Recommended:

- ○ **Lebendige Vergangenheit: Ezio Pinza** / Bourdon (cond.), Setti (cond.), Pinza, Metropolitan Opera House Orch. & Chorus / Preiser 89050
- ○ **Golden Years of Ezio Pinza** / Pinza, Martinelli / Pearl 9306
- ○ **Verdi: Requiem Mass** / Serafin (cond.), Gigli, Caniglia, Stignani, Pinza, Rome Opera House Orch. / 2001 / Naxos 110159

Maria-João Pires

b. Jul. 23, 1944, Lisbon, Portugal
Pianist

Acclaimed as one of the greatest interpreters of Mozart, Portuguese pianist Maria-João Pires is an artist who combines exquisite stylistic refinement with a serious effort to plumb the intellectual complexities and spiritual depths of music. Refusing to conform to the traditional image of a concert virtuoso, Pires emphasizes the spiritual dimensions of music, always searching for hidden meanings which may elude the analytical performer. This remarkable reverence towards works of music, clearly manifested in her performances of Mozart, was made explicit by her remark that, as a performer, she acts as a channel for the composer's ideas. Interestingly, Pires views both the composer and the performer as conduits for a transcendent force. However, while approaching the work of music with immense awe, Pires is acutely aware of its formal structure, finding a certain transparency in the most intricate formal constructions. In her performances of Romantic masters, particularly Chopin and Schumann, Pires masterfully reconciles her passionate experience of the music with an admirable appreciation for the inner logic of the work she is interpreting. Reflecting her vast emotional range, her tone, as critics have observed, encompasses a dizzying variety of intensities, from an almost imperceptible lightness to an imposing monumentality, with a rich scale of intervening nuances. Another hallmark of her style is her uncanny ability to capture, and convey, the precise variety of inner movement which constitutes the being of a particular musical creation.

Pires started playing at the age of three, giving her first public performance two years later. Pires performed Mozart concertos when she was seven and received Portugal's major prize for musicians at nine. She studied with Campos Coelho and Francine Benoit at the Lisbon Conservatory, graduating at 16. Post-graduate studies took her to Germany, where she studied with Rösl Schmidt, in Munich, and with Karl Engel, in Hanover. In 1970, she won the Beethoven Bicentennial Competition in Brussels. Pires made her London debut in 1986, and she first played in New York three years later. She has performed with the major European and American orchestras, including the Berlin Philharmonic Orchestra, the Boston Symphony Orchestra, the London Philharmonic Orchestra, the Orchestre de Paris, and the Concertgebouw Orchestra. Often praised for her extraordinary renditions of Mozart's works, Pires has shown a remarkable affinity with several of the greatest composers, including Bach, Chopin, and Schubert. An enormously successful recording artist, Pires, who since 1989 records exclusively for Deutsche Grammophon, released several critically acclaimed discs, including a Bach disc, recordings of Chopin's *Nocturnes* and Schubert's *Impromptus*, and a recording of two Mozart concertos with Claudio Abbado. Her recording of Mozart's complete sonatas received the 1990 Grand Prix du Disque. Since 1989, Pires has been an enthusiastic performer of chamber music, touring Europe and the Far East with violinist Augustin Dumay. Forming a trio with Dumay and cellist Jian Wang, Pires toured the Far East in 1998, playing Beethoven's *Concerto for piano, violin, cello, and orchestra* in several European centers in 1999. In 2000, Pires decided to take several months off in order to concentrate on a variety of educational projects in Portugal. Several collections of her performances, including *Artist Portrait: Maria-João Pires*, appeared in the early 2000s. *—Zoran Minderovic*

Recommended:

- ○ **Beethoven: 4 Piano Sonatas** / Pires / 2001 / Erato 89225
- ○ **Schubert: Sonata 21; Impromptus** / Pires / 1986 / Erato 45250
- ○ **Mozart: 4 Piano Sonatas** / Pires / 1987 / Denon 8007
- ○ **Maria João Pires** / Abbado (cond.), Pires, Vienna PO / 1999 / Philips 456928
- ○ **Chopin: Nocturnes** / Pires / DG 447096
- ○ **Bach: Partita 1; English Suite 3; French Suite 2** / Pires / DG 447894

Walter Piston

b. Jan. 20, 1894, Rockland, ME, **d.** Nov. 12, 1976, Belmont, MA
Composer: Chamber Music, Symphonic, Concerto, Ballet

Walter Piston was a leading light among those mid-twentieth century American composers who opted to explore traditional musical forms and language. Although he was perhaps better known as a teacher and the author of a widely used book on harmony than as a composer, Piston's music displays superb craftsmanship within his selected neo-Classic-Romantic idiom.

Piston was born in Rockland, ME, of Italian lineage; the family name had been Pistone but his grandparents had Anglicized it by dropping the "e." His parents moved to Boston in 1904. In his teens, Piston's musical education commenced with piano and violin lessons. At that time, however, painting was his main interest, but he conceded the superiority of his future wife, Kathryn Nason, in that field and concentrated on music. With the entry of the United States into the First World War,

Piston hurriedly crammed the rudiments of saxophone technique and enlisted in the Navy as a band musician. In between rehearsals and performances, he familiarized himself with most of the other instruments in the band, learning to produce at least a few tunes on each one. This was an invaluable experience for one whose name would become linked to orchestral composition.

After the war, Piston entered Harvard and began to study music in earnest, graduating summa cum laude in 1924. From there he went to Paris on a Paine Fellowship to study with Paul Dukas and Nadia Boulanger. This was a heady time, for many of who would become America's most noted composers were under the wing of the latter: Copland, Harris, Thompson, and Barber, to name a few. Piston returned to the U.S. in 1926 and joined the faculty of Harvard, retiring in 1960.

In 1928 the Boston Symphony under Koussevitzky performed Piston's *Symphonic Piece.* Although it met with moderate success and acclaim, the composer chose not to publish it and followed it with his *Suite for Orchestra* which met with more acclaim, finding a champion in Stokowski, who performed the work with the Philadelphia Orchestra. In 1938 his ballet *The Incredible Flutist* was performed, and the suite from this was for a long time his most celebrated work. Meanwhile, Piston had commenced upon his series of eight symphonies with his *First* in 1937. With these the composer revealed his prowess in the field of large-scale absolute music, garnering a steady stream of prestigious awards and honors, among them the New York Music Critics Circle for the *Second Symphony* (1945), and the Pulitzer Prize for the *Third* (1948) and the *Seventh* (1959). In the last year of his life, Piston achieved what may have been his largest audience when a performance of the *Second Symphony* was televised on PBS's *Evening at Symphony.*

As a composer, Walter Piston remained an enlightened conservative. Taking the neo-Classic mode of expression and infusing it into larger Romantic forms with flawless craftsmanship, he was one of the great bearers of the symphonic tradition in the twentieth century. *—Wayne Gerard Reisig*

Overview of Works (1925–1976)

Composer Walter Piston was truly American in the best sense of the word. A New Englander (he was born in Maine and lived most of his life in Boston and Massachusetts), a son of the working-class (he worked for the Boston Elevated Train Company), an intellectual (he graduated from and later taught at Harvard), a self-made musician (he taught himself violin, piano, and saxophone), and a highly trained musician (like so many other American composers of the period, he studied in Paris under Nadia Boulanger), Piston's music is quintessentially American. With the wide open spaces of his harmonies in fourths, fifths, and octaves, the long-limbed arches of his melodies that start in seconds and thirds and grow into soaring cantilenas, with the motor-driven energy of his rhythms in syncopated compound time, with the amber and purple hues of his orchestra, Piston's music sounds as American as Copland's, Gershwin's, or Waller's. Piston's oeuvre falls into two categories: orchestral music and chamber music. Of the former, the series of eight symphonies (1937–65) and the ballet *The Incredible Flutist* (1938) are the best-known. Piston wrote the bulk of his music with the sound of the Boston Symphony in his mind's ear. That orchestra gave the premiere of 11 of Piston's orchestral works, and the rich yet clear sound of the orchestra can be heard in nearly all his scores. Of the latter, he composed five powerfully intellectual string quartets (1933–62), a pair of piano trios (1935 and 1966), and several other works including the lovely flute sonata (1930) and oboe suite (1931). Although Piston's name has become synonymous with academic composition because of his long tenure at Harvard and his many superb theory textbooks, his music is in fact as approachable as Copland or Barber's. *—James Leonard*

Recommended:

- ○ **Piston: Concertos** / Kuchar (cond.), Buswell, Ukrainian State SO / 1998 / Naxos 559003
- ○ **Piston: Chamber Music** / Kuchar, Glyde, Buswell, Munro, Kelly, Walsh / 2000 / Naxos 559071

CHAMBER MUSIC

Quintet for winds (1956)

Piston's only wind quintet is a straightforward and highly accessible neo-Classicist piece. The work was commissioned by the Elizabeth Sprague Coolidge Foundation of the Library of Congress and premiered there in early 1957 by the Boston Woodwind Quintet. Judging from the defiantly sketchy program note he provided, Piston seems mainly concerned here with sorting, blending, and balancing the five highly disparate woodwind voices. Structurally, the four-movement work is quite straightforward, following the same Mozart-Haydn models as most of his string quartets and symphonies do. The opening movement, Animato, begins with a perky, syncopated theme mainly carried by the flute with the other instruments following independent yet supportive lines. The horn introduces the more lyrical second subject, with the other instruments in turn having their say on it. Perkiness pervades the development section, with the second subject nearly forgotten until the recapitulation. A slow movement is generally the heart of any Piston work and this holds true for the Con tenerezza movement of this quintet. Over quiet, harmonically hazy chords, the oboe cries out a soft melody initially reminiscent—at least in its mood—of the countryside scene in Berlioz's *Symphonie fantastique.* The other instruments soon begin elaborating on this theme and guide it through several reserved metamorphoses. Although at one point the music does become slightly louder, Piston never produces a true climax either dynamically or emotionally. The tiny Scherzando twitters and trills like a small musical aviary, pausing for only a rudimentary midpoint trio section. Rather than the boisterous finale some might expect from Piston's other works, the fourth movement, marked Allegro comodo, establishes a pastoral mood even at its fairly quick clip. The tune meanders through some colorful variations, sometimes cheeky, sometimes slow and furtive (as in the long passage that threatens to become a B section in its own right). The movement ends suddenly, as if Piston had lost patience with the piece and decided to wrap it up with only a couple of unceremonious chords. *—James Reel*

Recommended:

- ○ **Another View** / Sierra Wind Quintet / 1992 / Cambria 1091

SYMPHONIC

Symphonies (1937–1965)

The eight symphonies of Walter Piston are one of the strongest series of symphonies written by a twentieth century American composer. Highly regarded in his day, Piston was often commissioned by major American orchestras: the *Second, Third,* and *Sixth* were written for the Boston Symphony and the *Seventh* for the Philadelphia Orchestra. Although his rhythms are sometimes regarded as being derived from Stravinsky's, his textures from Roussel, and his seriousness from Hindemith, the fact of the matter is that Piston's symphonies are quintessentially American in form and content. His opening themes are often dramatic and even pugnacious, his big melodies are often either sweetly sung folk tunes or grandly arching hymn tunes, his tonal harmonies have the same sense of vastness as Copland, his forms are based on European models but infused with American concision and cohesion, and his rhythms have more in common with the syncopations of American jazz than with Stravinsky's neo-Classicism. Although few of Piston's symphonies are available in recordings and they are infrequently programmed by orchestras, the powerful yet charming *Second,* the muscular and supple *Fourth,* and the magisterial *Sixth* seem to be the most immediately appealing of his works. *—James Leonard*

Recommended:

- ○ **Piston: Symphony 5, 7 & 8** / Mester, Whitney (conds.), Louisville Orch., / Albany 011
- ○ **Piston: Symphony 2 & 6; Sinfonietta** / Schwarz (cond.), Seattle SO, NY Chamber Symphony / 1990 / Delos 3074

CONCERTO

Concerto for Orchestra (1933)

Walter Piston premiered his *Concerto for Orchestra* with the Boston Symphony Orchestra in 1934. It quickly became a favorite of the orchestra's conductor, Sergey Koussevitzky, who often performed it with the orchestra. Perhaps it was unfortunate that it became so closely associated with Koussevitzky, for the work has remained neglected since his death. Many commentators in the 1930s and 1940s ranked it as one of Piston's boldest conceptions.

There is a clear model for the work in Hindemith's 1925 composition of the same title. While the Piston work is in his typical three-movement format, these three movements closely track Hindemith's outline. The first movement is in a ritornello form, like Hindemith's, and includes much work for the orchestra's soloists, including the string section leaders. Both composers used chromatic counterpoint as the main element of the texture.

The second movement (and again this applies to both works) is a scherzo with a perpetuum mobile in the strings. There is a major different in Piston's clear American musical accent. Piston commits a technical *tour de force* by playing his scherzo in retrograde. It's a very funny moment, since it sounds truly backwards.

The finale is a passacaglia. The ground bass is stated by solo tuba. It grows to a full-bodied statement on brass, then the woodwinds take over with an ethereal treatment. When the strings enter, it is in the form of a fugue on the passacaglia subject, which continues as a ground on double basses. Finally, the music breaks out into a gigue-fugue. With the addition of the brass chorale from near the opening, the concerto ends in a blazing climax. *—Joseph Stevenson*

Recommended:

- ○ **Piston: Symphony 6; Concerto for Orch.; etc.** / Strickland (cond.), Polish National Radio Orch. / CTD 88134

BALLET

The Incredible Flutist (1938)

Piston was so firmly associated with absolute music that it comes as a surprise to some that he occasionally ventured into a more pictorial style. The most notable of such efforts was his only ballet, *The Incredible Flutist.* While the ballet itself is not often performed, Piston's delightful, colorful, and humorous score has gained much popularity as a concert suite.

Piston wrote *The Incredible Flutist* for a concert on which conductor Arthur Fiedler and the Boston Pops shared the stage with dancer-choreographer Hans Wiener (better known as Jan Veen) and his company. The story of the ballet revolves around the arrival of a circus in a sleepy Southern town. The work begins as the town awakens from its afternoon siesta. An apprentice and the merchants' daughters go back to work; shoppers make their rounds of the stores; a busybody and a crank argue. Soon, an offstage march is heard, heralding the arrival of a circus band. The band, followed by the circus acts, marches onstage. Among the performers is the incredible flutist of the title, whose music charms everyone present (including the snake charmer!). His playing, in fact, so charms one of the merchant's daughters that the two of them meet that evening. Indeed, much of the cast gathers for romance, including a rich widow and a merchant. The widow faints when she is discovered kissing the merchant. The flutist, after leading a dance among the assembled folk, finally breaks the spell. The circus mysteriously marches away into the night.

The Boston Pops began a pair of traditions at the first performance, which are still observed. When the circus band marches in, the orchestra lets out cheers to depict the townspeople. More whimsically still, the winner of a barking contest among the orchestral personnel impersonates one or two dogs; on Leonard Slatkin's recording of the work, credit for this role is given to the conductor's own pets. *—Joseph Stevenson*

Recommended:

- ○ **Howard Hanson Conducts** / Hanson (cond.), Mariano, Eastman-Rochester Orch. / 1992 / Mercury 434307
- ○ **The Incredible Walter Piston** / Schwarz (cond.), Seattle SO / 1993 / Deklos 3126

Pol Plançon

b. Jun. 12, 1851, Fumay, Ardennes, France, **d.** Aug. 11, 1914, Paris, France
Bass

It's rare for a singer to be known as a superb vocal technician and a fine singing actor, as well as a proficient stylist. Plançon was all three of these, and while his recordings were made too early in the technology and too late in his career to give a fully accurate sense of his voice's timbre, they do capture his immense range (from top F, where most tenors have their passagio, to low D, a note at the bottom of the basso profondo range), tremendous agility, including a superb trill, and beautiful legato. A Romophone compilation shows him off in excellent vocal form, performing songs and arias.

He came from an educational line of technicians—one of his teachers was Gilbert Duprez (who revolutionized tenor singing with his famous high C in full voice rather than falsetto and also taught Emma Albani). He made his operatic debut as Saint-Bris in Meyerbeer's *Les Huguenots* at the Opera de Leon in 1877, and his Paris Opera debut as Gounod's Mephistopheles (the first of many performances of that role) in 1883. There he sang in many of Meyerbeer's operas, such as *L'Africaine* and *Le Prophète*, as well as other French roles and some Italian ones. He created the roles of Don Gormas in Massenet's *Le Cid* and King Francois I in Saint-Saëns' *Ascanio*. In 1891, he joined Covent Garden for 13 seasons, and appeared in the world premiere of Stanford's *Much Ado about Nothing* as Friar Francis. He made his Met debut in 1893, and in later seasons sang Mephistopheles, Pere Laurent in *Romeo et Juliette*, Escamillo, and Saint-Bris, from the French repertoire, and also German roles such as Sarastro in the Met premiere of *Die Zauberflöte* and King Heinrich in *Lohengrin*, and Italian roles such as Ramfis in *Aida*. He remained at the Met until 1908. *—Ann Feeney*

Recommended:

- ○ **Eames & Plançon** / Plançon, etc / 1994 / Nimbus 7860
- ○ **Pol Plançon** / Plançon, etc. / Pearl 9497

Michel Plasson

b. Oct. 2, 1933, Paris, France
Conductor

Michel Plasson is one of the most important French conductors from the later twentieth and early twenty-first centuries. He is well known for his interpretations of French opera, particularly those of Gounod and Massenet. He has also received praise for his work in the choral music of Duruflé and Fauré, and the orchestral works of Magnard, Ravel, and other French composers. He has not, however, limited himself to the French repertory, having conducted (and recorded) the Rachmaninov piano concertos with soloist Jean-Philippe Collard, the Brahms *Schicksalslied*, and works by Wagner and Verdi.

Plasson was born into a family of musicians. He showed unusual talent on piano as a child and took lessons from Lazare Lévy. He later enrolled at the Paris Conservatory, where he studied composition and percussion. In 1962, he received first prize in conducting at Besançon, then, at the suggestion of Charles Münch, traveled to the United States to study conducting for the next several years with Erich Leinsdorf, Pierre Monteux, and Leopold Stokowski.

Plasson's first major appointment came in 1966 when he was engaged to become musical director at Metz, a post he held for two years. In 1968, he accepted the dual conducting assignments of director of the orchestra and of the Théâtre du Capitole de Toulouse. In 1974, Plasson initiated a refurbishing effort on the Halle aux Grains, increasing its seating capacity to 3,000. Upon completion of the project in 1977, he moved his orchestral operations there, where they have remained ever since. *Fidelio* was the first important opera he conducted in the new hall. In 1979, he debuted at Covent Garden to critical acclaim and by the early 1980s had developed a concert schedule laden with so many guest appearances that in 1983 he had to resign his post as director of the Théâtre du Capitole de Toulouse, although he retained the orchestral directorship there. This move in no way signaled a reduced focus on opera by Plasson: in 1985, for example, he performed Puccini's *Turandot* to great acclaim and the following year, the Verdi *Requiem*, which he went on to record for EMI with his Toulouse ensemble and a quartet of soloists led by Julia Varady. In 1987, Plasson took on another conducting post, that of principal guest conductor of the Zurich Tonhalle Orchestra. Then in 1994, he accepted the position as music director of the Dresden Philharmonic Orchestra, which he concurrently held with his music directorship in Toulouse. All through the 1990s, his recording activity remained intense, especially in his Massenet series of operas. In 1999, he left the Dresden Philharmonic, but retained his long-held French post. In 2002, he was still music director of the Orchestre Capitole de Toulouse and continues making numerous guest conducting appearances with various European and American orchestras. He also regularly conducts at the world's most prominent opera houses, including the Met, the Chicago Lyric Opera, Covent Garden, and many others. By 2002, he had made about 50 recordings for EMI and a fair number for other labels as well. *—Robert Cummings*

Recommended:

- ○ **French Symphonic Poems** / Plasson (cond.), Toulouse Orchestra / 1996 / MHS 514461
- ○ **Offenbach: Orphée aux Enfers** / Plasson (cond.), Tortelier, Mesplé, Sénéchal, Berbie, Toulouse Orchestra / EMI 749647
- ○ **Gounod: Romeo and Juliette** / Plasson (cond.), Van Dam, Alagna, Gheorghiu, Henry, Toulouse Orchestra / 1998 / EMI 56123
- ○ **Delibes: Lakmé** / Plasson (cond.), Dessay, Van Dam, Leguerinel, Petibon, Toulouse Orchestra / 1998 / EMI 56569

Mikhail Pletnev

b. Apr. 14, 1957, Archangelsk, USSR
Pianist, Conductor

Mikhail Pletnev was born in Archangelsk, which is located in the north of Russia on the coast of the White Sea. By the time Pletnev began piano studies at age seven, with pianist Julia Shaskina, his family had moved to the central Russian City of Kazan in Tatarstan. Pletnev demonstrated promise and was enrolled at age 13 in Evgeny Timakin's piano preparatory class at the Moscow Central Music School. At 14, Pletnev earned the Grand Prix awarded by the International Jeunesses Musicales in Paris, and at 15 he transferred into master classes headed by Yakov Flier at the Moscow Conservatory. It was under Flier that Pletnev's talent really took wing, and after taking the gold medal at the All-Union Competition in 1977, Pletnev won the coveted gold at the Tchaikovsky Competition in 1978. "Having rehearsed for the Tchaikovsky Competition under (Flier's) guiding hand," Pletnev once remembered, "I effectively performed there in his name."

Having paid his dues in the tough Russian competition circuit, Pletnev was now free to tour, and appeared on the concert circuit to worldwide acclaim. Critics from London, to New York, and to Tokyo alike praised Pletnev's interpretations of Scarlatti, Liszt, Mozart, Haydn, Beethoven, Chopin, and other primarily mainstream piano composers. Some critics likened Pletnev's approach to that of Michelangeli or Horowitz. In particular, Pletnev is recognized by his affinity for Tchaikovsky, and the pianist has prepared his own transcriptions of Tchaikovsky's ballet *The Nutcracker*, as well as recasting his opera *Eugene Onegin* as a ballet.

As the Berlin Wall came down, Pletnev was in the process of founding and organizing the Russian National Orchestra in Moscow. Since that time Pletnev has appeared less often in public as a pianist; he took up the mantle of conductor of the RNO and held the post until 1999. The orchestra under Pletnev made several critically acclaimed recordings for Deutsche Grammophon, including an award-winning set of Tchaikovsky's six symphonies released in 1996. Pletnev also took the orchestra on a tour to the United States during the 1992–93 season. In addition to his world-class skills with the baton and at the keyboard, Pletnev is also a better-than-average amateur violinist, and finds the time to compose orchestral pieces and chamber music. *—Uncle Dave Lewis*

Recommended:

- ○ **Pletnev plays Schumann** / Pletnev / 2004 / DG 2055

○ **Haydn: Piano Concertos** / Neuss German Chamber PO, Pletnev / Virgin 45196

○ **Scarlatti: Sonatas** / Pletnev / 2001 / Virgin 61961

○ **Pletnev Live at Carnegie Hall** / Pletnev / DG 471157

○ **Stravinsky; Symphony in E flat; Firebird Suite** / Pletnev (cond.), Russian National Orch. / 1997 / DG 453434

Ignace Joseph Pleyel

b. Jun. 18, 1757, Ruppertsthal, Austria, **d.** Nov. 14, 1831, near Paris, France

Composer

Remembered mostly as Haydn's rival during his London journey of 1792, Ignaz Josef Pleyel was the 24th child (out of 38!) of an impoverished schoolteacher. He was admitted to the class of the composer Vanhal and came to the attention of a Hungarian nobleman who paid Pleyel's way to study and live with Franz Joseph Haydn at Eisenstadt. Pleyel made rapid progress, and he reported that he and Haydn enjoyed a close, friendly relationship. In 1776, Haydn placed Pleyel's marionette opera *Die Fee Urgele* (The Fairy Urgele) on the schedule for performance at Esterháza. It was also played at the Vienna Nationaltheater.

Pleyel probably worked briefly for the his noble patron, Count Ladislaus Erdödy, and in the early 1780s he traveled widely in Italy. He composed lira (hurdy-gurdy) pieces for King Ferdinand IV of Naples to play and wrote an opera, *Ifigenia in Aulide*, that was premiered at the Teatro San Carlo (Naples' major opera house) in 1785. Its success generated a further 18 performances. The previous year Pleyel had become the assistant to Franz Xaver Richter, Kapellmeister of Strasbourg Cathedral, and inherited the post when Richter died in 1789. He gave public concerts as well. During this period, Pleyel wrote accompaniments for Scottish songs and a set of piano trios. In general, the years 1785 to 1795 were his most productive period as a composer.

During the French Revolution, Pleyel moved to London, where he was invited to conduct the Professional Concerts from 1791 to 1792. This was the period when Haydn was also giving concerts in London, but the two composers personally ignored the rival publicity that their respective impresarios generated. As it turned out, there was room for both; while Haydn's concerts were better attended and got more attention, Pleyel's concerts were successes. The London tour did well enough, in fact, that in 1792 Pleyel bought the Château d'Itenwiller at St. Pierre, near Strasbourg. He immediately wrote a pro-Revolutionary hymn called *La revolution du 10 août 1792 ou Le tocsin allégorique* (The Revolution of August 10, 1792, or The Allegorical Alarm), which is certainly something of a potboiler (like Tchaikovsky's *1812 Overture* it calls for cannons in the score). No doubt he wrote it in part to cultivate the good graces of the revolutionary authorities, but there is no documentation for the often-told tale that he was arrested and released only after composing the hymn under guard.

In 1795 Pleyel also acquired a house in Paris, opened a piano factory, and founded a publishing house. This became one of the most important in Europe, publishing over 4,000 compositions during its nearly four decades of existence. Pleyel pioneered a system of mutual reissues between his own firm and other great publishers of the time, including Artaria, Breitkopf, and Simrock. He was also the first person to issue miniature scores for study. Among the composers Pleyel published were Beethoven, Haydn, Boccherini, Clementi, Méhul, and Rossini.

In 1805 (during a temporary peace between Napoleon and Austria) Pleyel returned to Vienna, was reunited with the aging Haydn, praised Beethoven's skill as an improviser, and arranged performances of his string quartets, which won favor with the Viennese. After his return to Paris, he gradually retired to a rural estate. In 1834 he retired and sold the assets of his still-successful firm. During his life, his tuneful music, often not too difficult for home music-making, was very popular.—*Joseph Stevenson*

Overview of Works (1778–1812)

An immensely popular Austrian composer, Ignace Joseph Pleyel (1757–1831) was his parents' 24th child, one whose musical gifts manifested themselves early. By about 1774, he was a student of Haydn. In the early 1780s he traveled to Italy where he was asked by the King of Naples, Ferdinand IV, to provide compositions for the hurdy-gurdy. In Italy, he found himself seduced by Italian opera and consorted with the most important composers and singers of the day. Pleyel received a call to Strasbourg in 1783 where he was appointed a deputy, later becoming first kapellmeister. After clearing himself of a false charge that he was an enemy of the Republic, Pleyel settled in Paris, where he became and important music merchant and publisher.

Pleyel was highly regarded by both Haydn and Mozart, particularly upon publication of his first set of string quartets. Increasingly, however, he poached ideas from his former teacher and recast his own works over and over in varying forms. Thus, some charming songs will be found to have their origins in one or more of his own symphonies or quartets. Piano trios were rewritten as flute quartets and one concerto was readily available for clarinet, cello, or flute.

Nonetheless, Pleyel wrote a vast number of works. To his credit are ten books of piano solos, 12 sonatas for violin and piano, seven books of quartets, five books of quintets, four books of trios, six flute quartets, eight books of string duets, five *symphonies concertantes* and 29 symphonies.

A first opera, *Die Fee Urgele*, was written in 1776 for the marionette theatre at Esterháza. While in living in Italy, Pleyel composed an opera, *Ifigenia in Aulide*, which had its premiere in Naples in 1785, more than a decade after Gluck's French-language work.

In the year 1791, Pleyel was invited to London to direct the Professional Concerts. Haydn was in the city during that same period, and the city was abuzz with the projected rivalry between master and student. But both enjoyed substantial successes artistically and financially. In fact, Pleyel managed well enough to purchase a chateau near Strasbourg. He set about composing his hymn *La revolution du 10 août (1792) ou Le Tocsin allégorique*, in praise of the French Revolution. This may be seen either as a heartfelt response to triumph of liberty, or as another example of the composer's opportunism. In 1795 Pleyel settled in Paris, where he established a music-publishing firm that issued, among other compositions, works by Beethoven, Clementi, Haydn and Méhul. Pleyel was also responsible for the introduction of the miniature study score. A successful music shop was part of this enterprise.

Pleyel's music, however, enthusiastically received during his own time, slowly but steadily faded in the years following his death. For a time, suitability for domestic performance kept many of his more intimate scores popular. —*Erik Eriksson*

Recommended:

○ **Pleyell: Piano trios** / Joachim Trio / Dynamic 2017

○ **Pleyel: Symphonies in C, G & D** / Bamert (cond.), London Mozart Players / 1997 / Chandos 9525

○ **Pleyel: Concertos** / Jensen, Lethiec, etc. / Talent 291036

○ **Pleyel: Music for fortepiano** / Fuller / Preiser 90583

○ **Pleyel: Octet & Trios** / Klocker (cond.), Classicum Consortium / CPO 999743

○ **Pleyel: Sonatas for violin, cello & piano** / Gobel-Trio Berlin / 1994 / Thorofon 2207

Paul Plishka

b. Aug. 28, 1941, Old Forge, PA

Bass

Paul Plishka is a notable American bass singer, known for a wide range of major and supporting roles. Both his parents were American-born children of Ukrainian immigrants. As a boy, he was interested in farming and football, but also took guitar lessons. His teacher insisted that he learn to sing while playing, so he would sing popular songs such as *Love is a Many-Splendored Thing*. When his father moved to a new job in Paterson, New Jersey, Paul, joined the school chorus. Soon, he was offered the part of Judd Fry in the school production of *Oklahoma!* He was spotted by Armen Boyajian, who was starting a local opera workshop. Paul joined Boyajian's Paterson Lyric Opera Theatre.

Plishka sang major roles—Raimondo in *Ludia di Lamermoor*, Guardiano in *La Forza del Destino*, and King Philip in *Don Carlos*—when he was only 21. Meanwhile, Boyajian taught him singing. Plishka was his first student, and Boyajian was Plishka's only teacher.

Plishka attended Montclair State College in New Jersey, where he met his future wife, Judy. At the age of 23, he won the Baltimore Opera Auditions, and then won a prize in the Metropolitan Opera Regional Auditions. This earned him a contract with the national touring company of the Met during what turned out to be its final year. After that, they offered him a contract to be a cover (understudy) singer in buffo parts. Plishka accepted the offer, becoming a member of the company in 1966 and debuting onstage as the Monk in *La Gioconda* in 1967, followed by "all these real ham, basso-buffo roles" (Plishka's description), parts such as the Sacristan in *Tosca* and Benoit in *La Bohème*.

As a member of the Met company, he earned a reputation as a "house singer," a term which, when the house is of the caliber of the Met, is respectable, but which also carries an implication that the singer somehow lacks some ingredient required for stardom. He was reliable; he did 118 performances in his second season, with Boyajian listening carefully to all of them and making needed corrections at any sign of strain from this heavy schedule. The roles were generally small ones, but each season Plishka got opportunities the next season to sing roles of increasing importance and depth, so he remained attached to the Met. The roles he was singing included King Marke in *Tristan*, Oroveso in *Norma*, and both Pimen and Varlaam in *Boris Godunov*. Eventually, he got to sing more important parts, like Leporello in *Don Giovanni* and King Philip.

After several years, he began appearing widely in other houses, taking major parts. He debuted as Mephistofeles in Berlioz's *Damnation de Faust* in Strasbourg in 1974, and began getting the more important bass parts. The Met, in turn, graduated him from Pimen and Varlaam to the part of Tsar Boris in 1983. His singing and physical acting (including a daring fall) electrified the audience.

He has sung in almost all the major bass parts in several leading opera theaters. In his 25th season with the Met, the house honored him by casting him in many of the major Verdi bass parts, including his first appearance as *Falstaff*.

Plishka is also a renowned concert singer, and has sung with many leading symphony orchestras and conductors. He remains with the Met, where he has sung over 1,000 performances, and frequently appears in other leading houses in the United States and Europe. He has been inducted into the Hall of Fame for Great American Opera Singers. *—Joseph Stevenson*

Recommended:

- ○ **Paul Plishka Sings Songs of Ukraine** / Plishka, etc. / Forlane 16645
- ○ **Verdi: Requiem & Operatic Choruses** / Shaw (cond.), Hadley, Plishka, Dunn, Curry, Atlanta SO / 1987 / Telarc 80152
- ○ **Paul Plishka, A Bordeaux** / Lombard (cond.), Plishka, Viala, Bordeaux Aquitaine National Orch. / 1990 / Forlane 16613
- ○ **Donizetti: Anna Bolena** / Rudel (cond.), Sills, Verrett, Plishka, Lloyd, Tear, London SO / 2000 / DG 465957

Ewa Podleś

b. Apr. 26, 1952, Warsaw, Poland

Contralto

Ewa Podleś is one of the world's leading contraltos, equally successful in the worlds of opera and concert music. Her voice possesses the rich, flexible, perhaps even masculine, quality that separates the true contralto from the mezzo-soprano, and which has invited comparison to the likes of Marilyn Horne, Kathleen Ferrier, and Marian Anderson. Her range, both musically and vocally, has made her succesful in a variety of genres and styles, including the operas of Rossini and Verdi, the songs of Chopin, and a broad selection of Russian repertoire.

The daughter of a successful Polish contralto, Podleś first attracted attention while still a student in her native Warsaw, where she was engaged by the local company to sing Rosina in Rossini's *Barber of Seville*. Her career developed quickly, and she began to make international appearances as early as 1982. The lighter quality that characterized her voice early on allowed for excellent performances of such roles as Rossini's *Cenerentola* and Bizet's *Carmen* as well as some lighter Russian roles. However, as her voice developed it took on a more characteristic dark quality that opened up a wider selection of parts, including Verdi's Eboli (*Don Carlos*) and Ulrica (*Un Ballo in maschera*). Her signature performance has for some time been the title role in Rossini's *Tancredi*. She also sings *La Donna del Lago* and *L'Italiana in Algeri*. She has a very effective recital program called "Rossini Arias for Contralto," which she has sung with the Moscow Chamber Orchestra in New York's Carnegie Hall.

Podleś' recordings have been well received, including a disc of Chopin songs with pianist Garrick Ohlsson, *Melodies Russes* (Grand Prix de L'Academie Française du Disque), and *Tancredi* (nominated for a Grammy). *—AMG*

Recommended:

- ○ **Rossini: Arias for Contralto** / Morandi (cond.), Podleś, Hungarian State Opera Orch. / 1996 / Naxos 553543
- ○ **Chopin: Songs** / Podleś, Ohlsson, Mann / 2000 / Arabesque 6746
- ○ **Russian Arias** / Orbelian (cond.), Podleś, Kontorovich, Russian PO / 2002 / Delos 3298
- ○ **Récital Ewa Podleś: Mélodies Russes** / Podleś, Johnson (piano) / Forlane 16683

Ivo Pogorelich

b. Oct. 20, 1958, Belgrade, Yugoslavia

Pianist

Ivo Pogorelich is one of the most provocative and unpredictable major pianists, known for dynamic and original interpretations. He started studying piano when he was seven. At the age of 12 he went to the Central Music School in Moscow where he studied with Timakin. He graduated to the Tchaikovsky Conservatory in Moscow. In 1976 he became a pupil of the famous teacher Aliza Keseradze, whom he married in 1980. She died at an early age in 1996.

Pogorelich won the Casagrande Competition in Terni, Italy, in 1978 and the Montreal International Competition in 1980. At the International Chopin Competition in Warsaw of 1980 controversy erupted when the jury voted to eliminate him after the third round; it touched off a firestorm, sparked by the public resignation of Argentine pianist Martha Argerich in protest. She proclaimed Pogorelich a "genius" and a group of Polish critics banded together to award Pogorelich a special prize. (The eventual winner was Dang Thai Son of Vietnam.)

Pogorelich made his Carnegie Hall debut in 1981, creating a sensation. He debuted in London the same year. Since then, he has pursued a notable international career as a recitalist and as soloist with the major symphony orchestras of the world. Pogorelich began recording for Deutsche Grammophon, becoming one of their exclusive artists in 1982. An early recording was an electrifying account of Prokofiev's *Sixth Piano Sonata*.

His playing is marked by exceptional strength and accuracy. He has a power and momentum in pieces requiring driving rhythmic interpretation that is rarely matched. His interpretations are often unorthodox; controversy continues to be a feature of his performances.

He has also sought to use his fame and earnings for humanitarian purposes and to assist young artists. In 1986 he established a foundation in Croatia to grant scholarships for young artists to study abroad. In 1994 he established a fund in Sarajevo to build a hospital and provide further medical support for that violence-torn city. Each year he plays some concerts for the benefit of UNESCO and for such charities at the Red Cross and for organizations fighting illnesses such as cancer and multiple sclerosis. UNESCO has named him an "ambassador of goodwill."

In 1989 he established an annual Ivo Pogorelich Festival. It invites promising young artists to perform in ensembles with mature, renowned artists. In 1993 he initiated the Ivo Pogorelich Piano Competition in California. *—Joseph Stevenson*

Recommended:

- ○ **Chopin: Sonata 2; Ravel: Gaspard de la Nuit** / Pogorelich / 1998 / DG 459045
- ○ **Scarlatti: Sonatas** / Pogorelich / DG 435855
- ○ **Mussorgsky: Pictures** / Pogorelich / 1997 / DG 437667
- ○ **Chopin: Scherzi** / Pogorelich / DG 439947
- ○ **Beethoven: Sonata 32; Schumann: Toccata; Symphonic Etudes** / Pogorelich / DG 410520

Maurizio Pollini

b. Jan. 5, 1942, Milan, Italy

Pianist

Perhaps more of an advocate for contemporary music than any other major pianist essentially rooted in traditional repertory, Maurizio Pollini was born in Milan, Italy. He learned quickly and was given piano lessons from Carlo Lonati from an early age, making his public debut at the age of nine. Enrolling in the Milan Conservatory, he studied with Carlo Vidusso. In 1957 he performed a recital of Chopin etudes in Milan that drew favorable attention from the national Italian press. He won a second prize in the Geneva Competition in 1958. Embarking on further studies with Arturo Benedetto Michelangeli, he won first prize in the Warsaw Chopin competition in 1960. At this point he began a highly successful and acclaimed international career as a piano virtuoso. He appeared in concert throughout Europe, performing concertos with top conductors, and also giving recitals. He found a particular affinity with his countryman, conductor Claudio Abbado; the two shared a similarly analytical approach in their interpretations. Many of Pollini's best concerto recordings and concert collaborations have been with Abbado. Pollini debuted in the United States at Carnegie Hall in New York on November 1, 1968. Since then his international and recording career has continued without pause.

He is a pianist with a clean, bright though weighty, and refined sound, with exceptional clarity. His repertoire is extraordinarily wide. He frequently performs Bach, Mozart, Beethoven, and the Romantics such as Schubert and Schumann, but also the early modernists such as Prokofiev and Bartók. In the 1974 centenary celebrations of Arnold Schoenberg's birth he played programs encompassing that composer's complete piano music in several major musical centers, and he later recorded the entire body of work. His repertoire also extends into the avant-garde; in 1972 he gave the world premiere of Luigi Nono's *Como una ola de fuerza y luz*, (Milan, 1972) and recorded the work. He is also an enthusiastic performer of Boulez's *Second Piano Sonata*, regarded by some as the most difficult of all piano sonatas. He has recorded extensively, committing to disc works by Schoenberg, Stravinsky, Chopin, Bach, Boulez, and many others.

Since the 1980s, Pollini has been widening his activities as a conductor. He frequently led concerts from the keyboard, and has conducted orchestra concerts from the podium as well as leading operas. In 1987 he received the Ehrenring prize of the Vienna Philharmonic Orchestra. His piano career has the individualism achieved by only a few great artists, continuing to focus on contemporary music and including concert series of his own design at such prestigious venues as the Salzburg Festival (in 1995 and 1999) and Carnegie Hall (in the 1999–2000 and 2000–2001 seasons). *—Joseph Stevenson*

Recommended:

- ○ **Chopin: Polonaises** / Pollini / 1976 / DG 457711
- ○ **Maurizio Pollini Edition** / Abbado, Sinopoli (conds.), Pollini, Berlin PO, Bavarian RSO / 2001 / DG 471362
- ○ **Schoenberg & Webern: Piano Works** / Abbado (cond.), Pollini, Berlin PO / 2001 / DG 471361
- ○ **Debussy: Études; Boulez: Sonata 2** / Pollini / 2001 / DG 471359
- ○ **Schumann: Concerto; Brahms: Concerto 1** / Abbado (cond.), Pollini, Berlin PO / 2001 / DG 471353
- ○ **The Art of Pollini** / Böhm, Abbado (conds.), Pollini, Vienna PO, Berlin PO / 2001 / DG 471000
- ○ **Late Beethoven Sonatas** / Pollini / DG 449740
- ○ **Maurizio Pollini** / Pollini / 1999 / Philips 456937

Manuel Ponce

b. Dec. 8, 1882, Fresnillo, Mexico, **d.** Apr. 24, 1948, Mexico City, Mexico
Composer: Chamber Music, Concerto, Vocal

Manuel Ponce was a Mexican pianist and composer whose style underwent a profound change in midlife; his works are clearly divisible into two types. The earlier style was derived primarily from the brilliant salon style of Moszkowski and Chaminade, and is represented by numerous light works for the piano and a huge quantity of sentimental songs. After studying with Dukas, Ponce developed a style that combined French Impressionism and Neo-Classical contrapuntal techniques. Most of his guitar music and the majority of his more serious and larger works were written in this style. In addition to the songs and early piano works, Ponce composed a piano concerto, several large symphonic works for orchestra, the *Concierto del sur* for guitar and orchestra, which was premiered by Segovia, some chamber music, two piano sonatas, and a large quantity of guitar music.

Born in 1882, Ponce had no important teachers during his childhood in Mexico. In 1895 he was made organist of Saint Diego, Aguascalientes, and in 1900 he went to Mexico City to study piano with Vicente Mañes. From 1901 until 1904 he supported himself as an organist, teacher and music critic back in Aguascalientes. Ponce left for Europe in 1904, giving his first recital abroad in St. Louis on the way. He stayed in Berlin, teaching and concertizing until his return to Mexico City in 1909 to succeed Castro as the piano instructor at the Mexico City Conservatory. During this time, his compositions became fairly popular in Latin countries, and his renown grew; he became conductor of the National Symphony Orchestra from 1917–19. In 1925, Ponce moved to Paris and edited a music periodical; it was during this period that he studied with Dukas and reformulated his compositional style. He returned to Mexico in 1933, and remained there until his death. Many of Ponce's earlier works have faded into obscurity, but some of his songs, particularly *Estrellita* (1914), became enormously popular, and are still occasionally performed. Although most of his guitar pieces have become part of the standard repertory, his major works are seldom performed outside of Mexico. *—Steven Coburn*

CHAMBER MUSIC

Sonata Romántica, for guitar (1929)

In the 1920s, Ponce wrote a pair of contrasting guitar sonatas for his friend Andrés Segovia. The first he dubbed *Sonata Clásica*, offering it as an homage to Classical-era guitar master Fernando Sor. The second he called *Sonata Romántica*, and the Romantic composer he had in mind was clear from the subtitle, which in English reads "Homage to Fr. Schubert, who loved the guitar." Although this music could not quite be mistaken for Schubert, it does employ several Schubertian touches. In the first movement, Allegro moderato, Ponce leads his two pleasing, elegant themes through the same high contrasts of mood and sudden jolts from major to minor and back that have led scholars to question Schubert's understanding of "proper" key relationships in sonata form. The Andante espressivo is more Ponce's own style, full of the tender (and, by 1929, old-fashioned) lyricism that had made his song *Estrellita* an international hit. Perhaps the spirit of Schubert does hover briefly in the hesitant, solemn chordal passages that dominate the movement's central portion. Schubert's influence is more strongly felt in the third movement, Allegro vivo—più lento espressivo. The first of those two tempo indications applies to a fast but bittersweet opening and closing section; the other covers the movement's second section, sentimental and, again, hesitant. The final movement, Allegro non troppo e serioso, is dour music with an implacable and sometimes desolate bass line. When the bass isn't forcing the music into a dark little march, the treble part becomes highly active; what initially hints at imitative counterpoint more often disintegrates into nervous tremolos. This is not highly dramatic music, but its sentiment and emotional range link it securely to the early Romanticism popular a century earlier. *—James Reel*

Recommended:

- ○ **Romantic Works for Guitar** / Kraft / 1992 / Chandos 9033
- ○ **Ana Vidovic Guitar Recital** / Vidovic / 2000 / Naxos 554563

Sonatina Méridional, for guitar in D major (1932)

Manuel Ponce was a Mexican composer, but struck up a friendship with the great guitarist Andrés Segovia during his studies in Europe. This friendship understandably encouraged Ponce to compose plenty of solo guitar music, some of it with Spanish inflections, as in his *Sonatina meridional* (Sonata of the South). The first movement of the *Sonatina meridional* is titled "Campo," or "countryside," and this countryside is redolent of Spain. The movement unfolds in sonata form, as a fast-plucking introduction yields to a melancholy first theme and a sunny, pastoral second theme. The exposition repeats before plunging into a development full of daring feats for the guitarist. While the development initially focuses on the second theme, the first theme keeps trying to break in before erupting in a series of emphatic chords leading into the recapitulation.

Although the somber second movement is titled "Copla" (Song), this is definitely a song for guitar, featuring expressive flourishes no human voice could ever manage. This despairing Andante lasts only a short while, leading into a rambunctious "Fiesta." This begins with unambiguously cheery music but unexpectedly becomes more equivocal, moving all the while at a frenetic Allegro con brio pace. After some virtuoso fireworks lead to a confrontation between two opposed chords, the guitar plays a few bold runs. and happiness reigns over the close of the work. Any friend of Segovia's could be expected to understand how to write for guitar, and Ponce's invention is attractive and winning. *—Andrew Lindemann Malone*

Recommended:

- ○ **Ponce: Guitar Sonatas** / Vieaux / 2001 / Azica 71212

CONCERTO

Concierto del sur, for guitar & orchestra (1941)

The *Concierto del sur* for guitar and orchestra is one of the pieces—there are many—that Mexican composer Manuel Ponce wrote for the legendary Spanish guitarist Andrés Segovia. Ponce finished the piece in autumn of 1941, just as the country to the north of Ponce's was amending the Neutrality Act of 1939 and, though they didn't know it at the time, about to be drawn into World War II by the surprise attack at Pearl harbor.

Ponce takes up the standard three-movement format for the *Concierto*. The orchestra manages to put together just four bars of its own at the start of the Allegro moderato first movement before the impatient soloist jumps in with a series of firm, rolled six-note chords, which together with quiet orchestral offbeats encompass a full seven of the 12 possible chromatic tones. Soon the soloist settles down to play around with the lean, spritely idea offered in those four opening orchestral bars. At the end of the movement there is an extended cadenza for the guitarist.

The second movement is an Andante that is more a gracefully florid intermezzo than a slow movement per se. The finale is a festive, dancing Allegro that returns to us via bouncing 3/8 time eighth notes, to the A major in which the first movement closed. *—Blair Johnston*

Recommended:

- ○ **The Great Guitar Concertos** / Williams, Previn (cond.) / 1989 / CBS 44791
- ○ **Rodrigo: Concierto de Aranjuez; Villa-Lobos: Concerto for guitar; Ponce: Concierto del sur** / Isbin, Serebrier (cond.), New York PO / 2004 / Warner Classics 60296

VOCAL

Estrellita, song (ca. 1913)

Sometimes a song can become so popular and be so frequently sung (and sung in such diverse musical environments) that eventually people start to take the song for folk music, and its author disappears into the shadow his or her work has created. The great Mexican composer Manuel Ponce's wonderful *Estrellita* was so much a part of Latin American popular culture during the first few decades of the twentieth century that even just a few years after its first appearance in print (1914) it had come to seem part of the folk tradition. But this delightful "Little Star" is entirely Ponce's own.

Estrellita, originally for voice and piano, but later arranged by various people for voice and orchestra as well as any number of solo instruments, is the second song of Ponce's *Dos Canciones Mexicanas*, first published in 1914 and composed in the few years immediately preceding. The female singer tells Estrellita, the little star, of the anguish of her burning love. Ponce sets the two stanzas of the song's text in a parallel fashion: the last three lines of both stanzas form a tender refrain in which the singer asks the little star to come down to earth to tell her whether or not her love might be requited, and Ponce sets them more or less identically, using a modified version of the melodic strain that begins the whole affair. The lush, rising opening tune spans a full octave and a half in a matter of just seven notes, with the largest leap occurring at just the moment when the text speaks of the "distant sky." Its even more impassioned restatement rises a whole tone higher, and it is this melodic material that burns so long and so bright in the memory of all who hear the song. The opening gesture of the second stanza differs somewhat in tone from the first, as the singer mulls her impending death from heartache in some broad triplets. Even here, however, the music is full of tenderness and, in sublime contradiction of the text, a kind of warm contentedness.

Interestingly enough, *Estrellita* has had a rich association with the violin, having been made into a sparkling gem of an encore by Jascha Heifetz. The arrangement, like most of Heifetz's, goes far beyond just adapting the voice part for violin, and might justly be called an improvement over the original on several counts. In 1943, Ponce himself adapted the song for use in the central movement of the *Violin Concerto* he composed for Henryk Szeryng. *—Blair Johnston*

Recommended:

- ○ **Latin American Classics Vol. 1** / Batiz (cond.), Mexico Festival Orch. / 1994 / Naxos 550838

Amilcare Ponchielli

b. Aug. 31, 1834, Paderno Fasolaro, Italy, **d.** Jan. 17, 1886, Milan, Italy
Composer: Opera

Amilcare Ponchielli was an important nineteenth century Italian composer, primarily of operas. He is best known for his 1876 *La Gioconda*, though he wrote other significant operas, as well as ballets, orchestral, chamber music, and various vocal works. He was a rare example of a meek, but immensely talented, artist, whose backward nature sabotaged his career in certain respects. He had a vivid imagination, an uncanny ability to express varied situations and emotions, and superior orchestrational skills. If he had a weakness in his artistic makeup, it was his inconsistency of inspiration. In the end, he must be ranked a truly gifted composer who might have achieved the front rank were it not for his humble and kind demeanor, and lack of personal ambition. Actually, only Verdi stood above him among Italian composers of the day, but considerably above him. Other works of significance in Ponchielli's oeuvre are *I promessi sposi*, his first opera, and *Marion Delorme*, his last. He was also an important teacher, his students included Puccini and Mascagni.

Ponchielli was born in Paderno Fasolaro (now Paderno Ponchielli), Italy, on August 31, 1834. His father was a good amateur organist who gave young Amilcare his first lessons. After showing remarkable advancement, he began study with an organist from a nearby village. At the age of nine, Ponchielli was taken into the Milan Conservatory, where he would remain, tuition free, for 11 years. There he began study with Arturo Angeleri on piano and Pietro Ray in music theory. At age ten, the precocious Ponchielli wrote a symphony in piano score.

In 1851, he began instruction in composition with Felice Frasi, and was already delving into opera. His first flirtation with it came when he collaborated with three other students in the 1851 effort, *Il sindaco babbeo*. After graduating from the Conservatory in 1854, Ponchielli took an organist position at a church in Cremona, not far from his native Paderno. The following year, he became assistant to the director of the Teatro Concordia. It was here that his first opera, the aforementioned *I promessi sposi*, was staged in 1856 with some success. Over the next 15 years, Ponchielli struggled to achieve a significant triumph, but his operas either failed (sometimes to even reach the stage) or had success only in provincial opera houses.

In 1864, he became conductor of the Cremona municipal band and started work on his ballet, *Grisetta* (1864-65). While it was a mild success, he wanted to focus his attention on opera. Eventually he returned to *I promessi sposi*, which scored a success in its revised version in Milan in 1872. Soon it was taken up by many other theaters in Italy, and in the meantime Ponchielli found an ally in the publishing world when Ricordi began issuing his music scores. In addition, his recently-composed ballet, *Le due gemelle*, was staged at La Scala in 1873 and scored a major success.

Ponchielli had now emerged as one of the leading composers in Italy. In 1874 he married soprano Teresina Brambilla. Together they had three children. Ponchielli's reputation was bolstered further in 1876 by his greatest triumph, *La gioconda*, with libretto by Arrigo Boito. The work would be taken up by opera houses all over Europe, as far away as St. Petersburg, where Ponchielli would attend performances in 1884. In 1880, following further successes, he was appointed head of composition at the Milan Conservatory and, in 1881, *maestro di cappella* at the Bergamo Cathedral. He died five years later, on January 17, 1886. *—Robert Cummings*

OPERA

La Gioconda (1876)

Premiered in 1876, Ponchielli's *La Gioconda* was already somewhat behind current fashion. A grand opera in the literal sense (six principal roles, chorus, ballet, and spectacle), it is large in scale and unwieldy in storyline. Still, it has maintained a place in the repertory of most major opera houses through the sheer force of its sweeping music and edge-of-the-seat drama; it remains Ponchielli's only repertory work.

Set to a libretto by Arrigo Boito (who used the pseudonym Tobia Gorrio), *La Gioconda* contains memorable arias for all six principals (dramatic soprano, dramatic mezzo, contralto, tenor, baritone, and bass), an extremely popular ballet (the *Dance of the Hours*), many striking pages for chorus, and a grandeur which even modern audiences find compelling. Many derogatory remarks have been directed toward Boito's often hackneyed libretto, while neglecting to note that it provides innumerable moments for vivid, if sometimes improbable, stage action.

Gioconda requires first-class soloists and is therefore expensive to cast well. The title role demands a dramatic soprano with a soaring top register, a powerful chest voice, and the ability to spin floating soft notes at the top of her range. Rosa Ponselle and Zinka Milanov, for example, both created a sensational effect with the pianissimo B flat at the end of Act One while having the strength and sweep to deliver an authoritative "Suicidio" in the fourth act. Enzo affords the tenor who can manage the difficult intervals of his aria "Cielo e mar!" a rewarding role, mixing clarion top notes with moments of dulcet intimacy. Barnaba is the prototypical sinister baritone, drawn along the vocal lines of Verdi's baritone characters. A large, rolling instrument with easy top notes is an absolute requirement and those who bring these qualities can make a sensational impression.

For all its magnificence, *La Gioconda* is very much a singers' opera and that, above all, is what has sustained it through the decades. Some other artists who have been attracted to the title role are Emmy Destinn, Gina Cigna, Maria Callas, and Renata Tebaldi. Laura has been sung by such stellar mezzos as Ebe Stignani, Bruna Castagna, Fedora Barbieri, and Giulietta Simionato. Famous Enzos have included Enrico Caruso, Beniamino Gigli, Giacomo Lauri-Volpi, and Carlo Bergonzi. Among the great Barnabas have been such distinguished baritones as Pasquale Amato, Antonio Scotti, Titta Ruffo, and Leonard Warren. *—Erik Eriksson*

Synopsis:

Act One. The setting is Venice, in the 1600s. In the plaza on Mardi Gras, the crowd is celebrating ("Feste! Pane!"). The spy Barnaba, dressed as a street singer, sneers ominously in true villainous fashion and avidly watches Gioconda and her blind mother Cieca enter ("Madre adorata"). Gioconda settles Cieca on the church steps and goes to find Enzo, but Barnaba tries to stop her, declaring his love. She runs away, and Barnaba decides to use Cieca to entrap her. He tells Zuane, who lost the gondola race, that Cieca bewitched his boat and incites the crowd to seize her as a witch. Enzo comes in and denounces them as cowards, then runs to get his sailors to rescue her. Alvise, an Inquisition official, and Laura, his wife, enter, and Laura persuades Alvise to release Cieca, saying a woman who carries a rosary cannot be a witch, and in gratitude, Cieca gives Laura her rosary ("Voce di donna"). As the crowd now declares Cieca blessed by heaven, Barnaba quietly tells Alvise he is on the track of a lion, and Enzo and Laura covertly eye one another. All leave but Enzo and Barnaba, and with sinister amiability, Barnaba greets Enzo by his true identity, "Enzo Grimaldo, Principe di Santafior," telling him he knows all about him. Enzo is a prince from Santafior, once engaged to Laura, and has risked his life by coming in disguise to Venice to find her. Though he has promised to marry Gioconda, he still loves Laura. Barnaba offers to bring Laura to Enzo's ship so they can run away together that night, and then reveals his motivation; he wants to break Gioconda by making Enzo unfaithful to her. Enzo doesn't want to hurt Gioconda, but still accepts Barnaba's offer. When he leaves, Barnaba has a denunciation written, which he stuffs into the lion's mouth, where such anonymous denunciations of treachery are left ("O monumento!") and revels in his power. Gioconda has overheard and is heartbroken.

Act Two. Sailors are singing on Enzo's ship. Barnaba approaches disguised as a fisherman and singing ("Pescator, affonda l'esca"). Enzo appears and orders the sailors to prepare to set sail tonight, then waits ecstatically for Laura ("Cielo e mar"). Barnaba brings her aboard and they fall into one another's arms, anticipating a happy future together ("Laggu fra le nebbie"). Enzo goes to prepare to embark and Laura prays at a small altar for Mary's blessing ("Stella del marinar"). Gioconda comes forward, cursing her, and they quarrel over who loves Enzo most ("L'amo come il fulgor del creato"). Gioconda is ready to stab her, but then sees Alvise approaching and announces that this is a better revenge. Laura pulls out the rosary Cieca gave her, and Gioconda, recognizing it, resolves instead to save the woman who saved her mother, and helps her escape. Enzo returns, and Gioconda triumphantly tells him that Laura fled to save herself, but she, who loves him more, stayed with him. When he sees Alvise and Venetian soldiers approaching, he burns the ship rather than let it be captured, and jumps into the sea, calling Laura's name.

Act Three. In the Ca d'oro, Alvise's palace, Alvise meditates on his revenge ("Si, morir ella de!") and prepares to poison Laura. He anticipates her dying during the festivities of that night's party. When she comes in, he first greets her with chilling courtesy and then shows her a bier and orders her to drink the poison. She pleads for her life but in vain. Alvise leaves her with the poison as gondoliers sing outside. She is about to drink, but Gioconda enters, gives her a sleeping drug instead, and leaves, taking the poison with her. Alvise returns and sees Laura, seemingly lifeless. In the ballroom, Alvise greets his guests in a courtly manner and invites them to watch a ballet (*The Dance of the Hours*). After it ends, Barnaba drags in Cieca, who says she was praying for the dead. Enzo, who has entered disguised, is horrified to hear that Laura is dead, and as Alvise gloats, reveals himself. The guests are horrified ("D'un vampiro fatal"). Cieca denounces Barnaba, who says he will punish her. Enzo is arrested and Gioconda offers her body to Barnaba if he will free Enzo. Alvise, further gloating, shows the guests Laura's corpse.

Act Four. Gioconda's home is the ruins of a mansion. Two of her friends bring in Laura's body, and she asks them to find her mother, who has disappeared. She is desperate and suicidal at having lost her mother and Enzo ("Suicido! In questi fieri momenti") and is even tempted to kill Laura. Enzo enters and Gioconda passionately says she wants to make him happy. Instead, he bids her goodbye, saying he wants to die at Laura's tomb. She tells him he will find it empty, and he thinks she has despoiled it and pulls a dagger to kill her. She is masochistically delighted, but Laura calls to him. He realizes what Gioconda has done, and they both thank her as she says she has arranged for their escape. She asks them to think of her occasionally, and they leave. She reaches for the poison, but remembers her mother and prays. Barnaba enters and watches her. She turns to leave, but he stops her, reminding her of her promise. She says she will keep it and pretending to want to seduce him, puts on her finery and sings to him, as he raptly watches. As he moves to embrace her, she says she indeed promised him her body, and stabs herself. He shouts that he drowned her mother for having insulted him, but realizes she cannot hear him. *—Ann Feeney*

Recommended:

- ○ **Ponchielli: La Gioconda** / Votto (cond.), Callas, Cappuccilli, Cossotto, Ercolani, La Scala Theater Orch. / 1997 / EMI 56291

Lily Pons

b. Apr. 12, 1898, Draguignan, France, **d.** Feb. 13, 1976, Dallas,TX
Soprano

Lily Pons (nee Alice-Josephine) began her musical studies at the piano and attended the Paris Conservatory. When Albert di Gorostiaga heard her sing, he persuaded her that singing was where her true talent lay and she began studying with him at the Conservatory. She made her debut in 1917 in a concert at Paris. She continued studying for ten more years, making her operatic debut in *Mulhouse* as Lakmé. Because of her youthful beauty, she lied about her age in all interviews saying that she was born in 1904. The ruse was not discovered until after her retirement. She appeared in many provincial French opera houses where she came to the attention of the Italian tenor Giovanni Zenatello and his wife Maria Gay. They assisted Pons in obtaining an audition with the Metropolitan Opera and in 1931 she made her debut as *Lucia di Lammermoor*, the role she was to be associated with throughout her career and which marked her farewell in 1962. The Metropolitan Opera became her home base, but she continued to appear at the Paris Opera, Royal Opera Covent Garden in London, Chicago Lyric Opera, San Francisco Opera, and Teatro Colon Buenos Aires. She concentrated her appearances on a few well chosen roles which fit her style and temperament perfectly. These roles were *Lucia di Lammermoor*, Gilda in *Rigoletto*, Rosina in *The Barber of Seville*, Lakmé and Marie in *La fille du regiment*. She also made occasional appearances in *Tales of Hoffmann*, *Mignon*, *La Sonnambula*, *Linda di Chamounix*, and *Le coq d'or*. In 1951, she sang two performances of Violetta in *La Traviata*, but this excursion into a more dramatic repertoire was never repeated.

Pons traveled for several months every year, giving recitals and concerts. She was always a welcome visitor for she embodied the essence of the prima donna. She was always made up perfectly and her gowns were created by the finest fashion designers. During World War II, she toured many of the battle theaters, often near the front lines, and even under those difficult conditions she insisted that she look her best in order to lift the spirits of the military personnel. Although her orchestral concerts usually concentrated on famous arias and coloratura showpieces, she did sing the premiere of the *Chanson de Ronsard* by Milhaud. In her recitals, she often sang songs of Fauré and Debussy as well as the entire Mad Scene from *Lucia di Lammermoor*. Pons also appeared in several of Hollywood films including *I Dream Too Much* and *That Girl from Paris*. Her last public performance was with the New York Philharmonic under the direction of Andre Kostelanetz in May, 1972.

The voice of Lily Pons was a very high, light coloratura soprano. Her ease in the extreme upper register and the weakness of her lower notes was the basis of her decision to sing the mad scene from *Lucia di Lammermoor* a whole step higher than the published score (the key of the original French edition). In her later years, she would have pitch problems, but the public rarely complained because she was so charming. She was a very small woman, about five feet tall and very slight, so she always appeared fragile, and yet she was always in total control of her life and career. She married the conductor Andre Kostelanetz in 1938, but the union dissolved in 1958. She was one of the most popular classical singers of her era. *—Richard LeSueur*

Recommended:

- ○ **Lily Pons Coloratura Assoluta** / Pons, etc. / 1998 / Sony 60655
- ○ **Lily Pons** / Pons, etc. / 1993 / RCA 61411
- ○ **The Odeon Recordings, 1928–1929** / Cloez (cond.), Pons, Mazzei, Grand Theatre Chorus & Orch. / 1995 / VAI Audio 1125
- ○ **Lily Pons** / Pons, Luca, Mazzei / Pearl 9415

Rosa Ponselle

b. Jan. 22, 1897, Meriden, CT, **d.** May 25, 1981, Green Spring Valley, MD
Soprano

The mother of American soprano Rosa Ponselle (born Ponzillo) was her first voice teacher; later she studied with Anna Ryan. As a teenager, she teamed with her sister Carmela to form a vaudeville act which included classical as well as popular songs. In 1918, she came to the attention of Giulio Gatti-Casazzi, the manager of the Metropolitan Opera Company and the great tenor Enrico Caruso. Together, they orchestrated her debut at the Metropolitan Opera on November 15, 1918, as Leonore in Verdi's *La forza del destino*. Her success that evening—having never been on an opera stage before—made her an instant star, and careful management of her career kept her continually active until her abrupt retirement in 1937 at the age of 40.

During her tenure at the Metropolitan Opera, she excelled in the heavier bel canto and Verdi roles. Only the second soprano to sing the role of *Norma* there, she also sang Giulia in *La vestale*, Rachel in *La Juive*, *Aida*, Elisabetta in *Don Carlo*, Gioconda and Selika in *L'africaine*. Late in her career, she added Violetta in *La Traviata* and *Carmen* to her repertoire. These two roles caused much controversy. Violetta is usually associated with much lighter voices, and her performance of "Sempre libera" was certainly not as clean as those of many of her rivals. Her interpretation of *Carmen* was criticized for being too vulgar by critics who said that she looked more like a vamp than a gypsy.

These criticisms are often held as the reason for her early retirement; however, an additional factor may have been her fear of the soprano high C. An audible vocal crack during a performance of *Aida* in the mid-1920s contributed to a lack of confidence in singing that note. She never sang *Aida* again in New York although she did sing it on tour. She had sections of *Norma* and *La Traviata* transposed down in order to avoid the high C.

She made only two trips to Europe to sing in opera. Though both trips were a great success, she preferred to stay in the comfort and congeniality of the Metropolitan Opera. Annually, she toured the United States and Canada in concert and recital programs.

After her retirement, she married and moved to Baltimore where she was a driving force with the Baltimore Opera. She rarely left her home, the Villa Pace, after 1950. However, at her home, she was a coach to many great singers and was a generous hostess to young artists.

Ponselle's voice was a rich dramatic soprano, with great natural beauty. The range and technique were excellent and the tone was even throughout the entire range. Her repertoire ranged from Mozart to Mascagni, but surprisingly she never sang any Puccini or Wagner on stage, although their arias did figure in her concerts and recordings. Ponselle left many fine recordings including a series recorded in her home in 1954. The best are selections from *Norma* and from *La Forza del Destino*. Her "Ernani, involami" is justly famous, as are the arias from Spontini's *La Vestale*. Private recordings of her Violetta and Carmen from Metropolitan Opera broadcasts have been issued and allow for a view of her art in the context of a complete performance. *—Richard LeSueur*

Recommended:

- ○ **In Opera And Song** / Ponselle, etc. / 1996 / Nimbus 1777
- ○ **Casta Diva** / Ponselle, etc. / Pearl 9210
- ○ **1939 Victor & 1954 "Villa Pace" Recordings** / Ponselle, Romani, Chicagov, Schmidt / 1996 / Romophone 81022
- ○ **Columbia Acoustic Recordings** / Ponselle, Stracciari, Hackett, Ponselle / Pearl 9964

Roland Pöntinen

b. 1963, Stockholm, Sweden
Pianist

Roland Pöntinen is one of Sweden's best-known pianists and is particularly in demand as an accompanist and chamber player.

He studied at the Adolf Fredrik Music School and the Royal Music Academy in Stockholm with Gunnar Hallhagen, then with Menahem Pressler, György Sebok, and Elizabeth Leonskaya at Indiana University in Bloomington, Indiana. He has a particular interest in lesser-known repertory, which he has played in concert halls and festivals in many cities in Europe and in North America, Australia, and New Zealand. Pöntinen frequently records on the BIS records label. *—Joseph Stevenson*

Recommended:

- ○ **Roland Pöntinen Plays Chopin** / Pöntinen / 1995 / Bis 673
- ○ **Satie** / Pöntinen / 1986 / Bis 317
- ○ **Russian Vituoso Piano Music** / Pöntinen / 1984 / Bis 276
- ○ **Legendary Encores** / Pöntinen / Bis 661

Lucia Popp

b. Nov. 12, 1939, Uhorska, Czechoslovakia, **d.** Nov. 16, 1993
Soprano

Lucia Popp was an accomplished coloratura soprano in the early years of her career, but later she moved with great success into the lyric repertoire and, still later, into the lighter Strauss and Wagner operas. She had the ideal voice and personality for Viennese operetta, and was one of the best Rosalindes (*Die Fledermaus*) and Hanna Glawaris (*The Merry Widow*) of her time. She was also a celebrated recitalist and lieder singer, where her singing benefited from her charming stage presence. Her untimely death in 1993 (the same year that saw the early deaths of Arleen Auger and Tatiana Troyanos) cut short a major career.

Popp initially entered the Bratislava Academy to study drama. Anna Hrusovska-Prosenkova, a voice teacher at the Academy, happened to hear her singing during a performance of Molière's *Le Bourgeois Gentilhomme*, and offered her voice lessons. She began her studies as a mezzo-soprano, but her voice quite suddenly developed a high upper register—so much so that her professional debut was as Mozart's Queen of the Night at the Bratislava Opera. That role was to remain a staple for many years of her early career.

Popp soon made debuts at the Theater an der Wien and the Vienna State Opera, where her first role was Barbarina in *Le Nozze di Figaro*. She had strong ties to the Vienna State Opera during her career, though she left their regular roster in 1967, and in 1979 she was named an Austrian *Kammersängerin*. She made her Covent Garden debut in 1966 as Oscar in *Un Ballo in Maschera*, and her *Met* debut in 1967 as the Queen of the Night.

During the 1970s, she left coloratura roles for lyric ones, particularly of Mozart, where she was an especially effective Pamina and Susanna, and in the 1980s she began to add even heavier roles, including Eva in *Die Meistersinger* and Strauss' *Arabella* (both in 1983) with similar success. *—Ann Feeney*

Recommended:

○ **The Very Best of Lucia Popp** / Popp, etc. / 2003 / EMI 85102

○ **Mozart: Le Nozze di Figaro** / Marriner (cond.), Constable, Hendricks, Popp, Van Dam, Academy of St. Martin-in-the-Fields / 2002 / Decca 470573

○ **J. Strauss: Die Fledermaus** / Kleiber (cond.), Popp, Prey, Varady, Kollo, Bavarian State Orch. / 1999 / DG 457765

○ **R. Strauss: Lieder** / Popp, Sawallisch / 1988 / EMI 49318

Nicola Porpora

b. Aug. 17, 1686, Naples, Italy, **d.** Mar. 3, 1768, Naples, Italy

Composer

Nicola Porpora is a mostly forgotten figure in composition today; however, he exerted considerable influence as a teacher in his day, and much of his own compositional output is of exceptional quality. He made his chief contribution in the vocal realm, having written many worthwhile secular and sacred operas, oratorios, serenatas, and cantatas. Porpora helped to enrich the melodic qualties of vocal music by drawing on greater technical resources—which he understood as well as any contemporary. His embellishing of the vocal melodic line, while not strictly his own development, helped shape the course of vocal music in opera and various other forms in the nineteenth and twentieth centuries. Among his important works are his operas *Arianna e Teseo* and *Faramondo*, and his serenata *Gli orti esperidi*. Porpora may be better known as a teacher of Franz Joseph Haydn, and of the singers Uberti, Farinelli, and Caffarelli, as well as of the poet and librettist Pietro Metastasio.

Porpora was born on August 17, 1686, in Naples. He showed talent early in his childhood, and at the age of ten was placed in the Conservatorio dei Poveri di Gesu Cristo. Not much is known about his teachers there, but upon his departure he was well-grounded in voice and composition. His first opera, *Agrippina*, came in 1708, though he took three years to produce his next significant work in any genre.

By 1711, Porpora had become maestro di cappella under the Prince of Hessen-Darmstadt at Naples, and two years later, following the departure of the Prince for Austria, the maestro di cappella for the Portuguese ambassador. Porpora was well connected then, even receiving a Viennese Court commission for his opera *Arianna e Teseo* (1714). Four years later he provided another opera, *Temistocle*, for that same court. Around this time, the composer was also coming to be regarded as one of the finest teachers of singing in Italy, his pupils including the castrato Caffarelli.

By the early 1720s, Porpora's reputation throughout Italy as a composer was growing as well, owing in great part to a string of successes in Rome. He settled in Venice in 1726 to teach at the Ospedale degli Incurabili. Perhaps sensing a decline in his art, he departed for London in 1733 at the invitation of some English patrons. He would write five operas in London, including *Arianna in Nasso* (1733), and other vocal works, like the serenata *La festa d'Imeneo*. He left England in 1736, having achieved many successes there.

The composer returned to Italy and held a series of posts over the next decade, perhaps divulging a certain restlessness, and perhaps insecurity. In Naples, he accepted the position as *maestro di cappella* at the Conservatorio di Santa Maria di Loreto in 1739; in Venice he was appointed similar posts in 1742 and 1743, none served concurrently. After unsuccessfully seeking yet another *maestro* appointment in Naples, he traveled to Dresden to serve as court kapellmeister and teacher to Maria Antonia, the Electoral Princess. He departed around the beginning of 1753 and traveled to Vienna, mainly as it turned out, to teach. His most prominent student there was the young Haydn. Owing to dwindling finances, Porpora returned to Naples in 1760 to serve as maestro di cappella again at the Conservatorio di Santa Maria, and later at the Conservatorio di Santo Onofrio. He resigned all posts the following year and lived in poverty until his death in 1768. *—Robert Cummings*

Overview of Works (ca. 1710–1760)

Born in 1686, the opera composer and renowned teacher Nicola Porpora was trained as a musician at the *Conservatorio dei Poveri di Gesù Christi* in his native Naples. It was also in Naples that his first operas were produced. During the second decade of the eighteenth century, his fame spread rapidly throughout Europe, his operas being produced in Naples, Rome, and Vienna. In 1726, Porpora became maestro di cappella of one of the famous *ospedali* in Venice, but when he failed to gain the coveted post of maestro of St. Mark's, he accepted an invitation from the Opera of the Nobility to come to London in opposition to Handel. Although Porpora produced some of his finest operas for London, the venture failed and he returned to Venice. During the next few years, he divided his time between Venice and Naples, but in 1747 went to Dresden, where he was appointed kapellmeister in succession to Hasse in 1748. Porpora's final years were passed in retirement in Vienna and Naples, where he died in 1768.

Today Porpora's principal claim to fame lies in his distinguished line of pupils, notable among them the composer Johann Hasse and the castrato Farinelli, the most famous singer of the age. However, for a period he was a much admired composer of operas and sacred music, although his popularity waned during the last 20 years of his life. The vast majority of his operas are opere serie, or serious operas, conforming to the strict rules laid down for the genre. The earliest was *Agrippina*, first given in Naples in 1708. During the succeeding years Porpora also composed serenatas, dramatic works on a more modest scale than full operas, among them *Angelica* (1720), the first music drama to employ a libretto by the famous poet Metastasio. His other works include *Arianna e Teseo* (1714) and *Temistocle* (1718). Porpora's commissions included operas for the *Hoftheater* of Charles VI in Vienna. During the 1720s and early 1730s Porpora's unrivalled understanding of the human voice tempted him into composing arias that exploited virtuoso technique while neglecting any true characterization. After arriving in England, where Porpora encountered the operas of his rival Handel, he adapted his style to a more flexible treatment of the standard da capo aria, attempted a greater depth of characterization, and introduced accompanied recitative, hitherto largely absent in his operas. After his return to Italy Porpora composed several comic operas, a form that was increasingly challenging the near-hegemony of serious opera. In addition to his operas Porpora composed a substantial body of sacred music for the institutions in which he worked, or with which had contacts. This corpus includes oratorios, masses, and motets. A much smaller part of Porpora's output was devoted to a few instrumental compositions. *—Brian Robins*

Recommended:

○ **Nicola Porpora** / Cosmi (cond.), Rigacci, Lazzara, Bonfatti, Theatre Orch. of Giglio di Lucca / Bongiovanni 2249

○ **Porpora: Arianna in Nasso** / Carraro (cond.), Fabbricini, Micco, Savona SO / Bongiovanni 2250/1

○ **Porpora: Cantate Vol. 1** / Anfuso, Alvini / Stilnovo 8810

○ **Porpora: Violin Sonatas** / Steck, Rieger / 2001 / MDG 6201034

Francis Poulenc

b. Jan. 7, 1899, Paris, France, **d.** Jan. 30, 1963, Paris, France

Composer: Vocal, Choral, Opera, Keyboard, Chamber Music, Concerto, Ballet

Francis Poulenc was the leading composer of Les Six, the French group devoted to turning music away from Impressionism, formality, and intellectualism. He wrote in a direct and tuneful manner, often juxtaposing the witty and ironic with the sentimental or melancholy. He heavily favored diatonic and modal textures over chromatic writing. His music also shows many elements of pandiatonicism, introduced around 1920 by Stravinsky, whose influence can be heard in some of Poulenc's compositions, such as the religious choral work, *Gloria*. Poulenc is regarded as one of the most important twentieth century composers of religious music, and in the realm of the French art song he is also a major voice of his time. Poulenc was also a pianist of considerable ability.

Poulenc was born into a wealthy family of pharmaceutical magnates. The agrochemical giant Rhone-Poulenc is the present-day corporation started by his forebears. His mother was a talented amateur pianist who began giving him piano lessons at age five. Later Poulenc studied with a niece of César Franck, and then with the eminent Spanish virtuoso Ricardo Viñes, for whom he would later write music.

At age 18, Poulenc wrote *Rapsodie Nègre* for baritone and chamber ensemble, which made him an overnight sensation in France. The young composer served in the military during the years 1918–21, during which time he composed the popular *Trois Mouvements Perpétuels* (1918).

By 1920, Les Six—Georges Auric, Arthur Honegger, Darius Milhaud, Germaine Tailleferre (the sextet's lone female representative), Louis Durey, and Francis Poulenc—had begun making its impression on the music world. In 1923, Poulenc wrote the ballet *Les Biches*, which Diaghilev staged the following year with great success, the public finding its mixture of lightness, gaiety, and occasional moments of sentimentality irresistible. Poulenc continued writing at a fairly prolific pace in the late 1920s and early 1930s, producing many piano compositions, songs and other works. In 1935, he rekindled his friendship with baritone Pierre Bernac, thus launching a productive and enduring professional relationship. He also returned to the Roman Catholic Church that year when close friend Pierre-Octave Ferroud was killed in an automobile accident. Thereafter he wrote many important works of a religious nature, the first of which were *Litanies à la Vierge Noire*, for soloists, chorus and organ, and *Mass in G* for mixed a cappella chorus, both from 1936.

During the war, Poulenc remained in German-occupied France, writing music of an antiwar or defiantly anti-Nazi bent, sometimes writing songs on texts by banned authors, such as Lorca. He also wrote a ballet *Les Animaux Modèles* (1940–41),

Sonata for violin and piano (1942–43; rev. 1949) dedicated to Lorca, and the masterful *Figure Humaine* (1943), a choral cantata which is a hymn to freedom.

In the postwar years, Poulenc turned out his *Sinfonietta* (1947) and *Piano Concerto* (1949), both not entirely successful. In the period 1953–56, Poulenc produced his most ambitious work, the opera *Dialogue of The Carmelites*, considered by many the greatest French opera of the twentieth century.

Poulenc finished his last opera in 1958, *La Voix Humaine*, a work whose lone character talks (sings) on the phone to her deserting lover for the work's 45-minute length. Notable also in this period is his *Gloria* (1959), a work shorn of sanctimony and rich in communicative simplicity and fervent religiosity. Poulenc's last major work was his *Sonata for Oboe and Piano* in 1962, dedicated to the memory of Prokofiev, whom he had befriended in the 1920s. Poulenc died suddenly of a heart attack. *—Robert Cummings*

VOCAL

Songs and Song Cycles (1917–1962)

Though he contributed to a wide variety of genres, Poulenc's songs are his most enduring legacy, and he is widely regarded as the successor to Debussy and Ravel in this genre. Poulenc composed over 150 songs for voice and piano, many of which are grouped into collections or song cycles. He wrote two different types of songs: mélodies and chansons. The former are serious art songs in the tradition of Fauré, Debussy, and Ravel; the latter, according to Poulenc, are more folklike, with a freer treatment of the text (more repetition, more cuts). Poulenc's songs are, in general, quite short, and many are through-composed. They are strikingly rich in emotion, but also careful and concise. The piano accompaniments tend to be important contributors to the texture and tone of each song; often complex and technically demanding, they are also always intimately tied to the expression of the text and the legato flow of the vocal melody.

Most of Poulenc's songs are composed in a tonal idiom, with frequent key changes. He often patched together melodic fragments in whatever key they first came to his mind; as a result, many songs feature fluid modulations as the vocal melodies shift from key to key. Metrically and rhythmically, the songs are structured to closely follow the natural rhythms of the French language. This is perhaps the most important aspect of Poulenc's song style: his approach to language was extremely rigorous, and he detected precisely the qualities of the poetic texts that he set. Poulenc was noted for spending a great deal of time analyzing and understanding the poems that he worked with; after choosing a poem he would, in his own words, "examine it from all angles." Among Poulenc's most important song cycles and collections are the *Chansons gaillardes*, the *Airs chantes*, the *Cinq Poems de Paul Éluard*, and the *Huit chansons polonaises*. *—Alexander Carpenter*

Recommended:

- ○ **Francis Poulenc: Mélodies** / (complete) / Baldwin, Ameling, Souzay, Gedda, Parker, Sénéchal / EMI 64087

Banalités, song cycle (1940)

During one of the darkest periods of the Second World War, Francis Poulenc turned again to the verses of Guillaume Apollinaire. This groundbreaking poet numbered Picasso and Braque among his friends, and coined the word "cubism." One of the most important poets in France in the early twentieth century, he helped shape the new direction of French literature, moving it away from the preciousness and indirect glances of symbolism toward a more robust, urbanized exploration of life, especially the life of Poulenc's beloved birthplace, Paris. Although Apollinaire died of wounds suffered in World War I, Poulenc had met him once or twice, and remembered the cadence of Apollinaire's speech until the end of his life. Poulenc's first group of songs, the cycle *Le Bestiare*, was set to texts by Apollinaire.

Poulenc later wrote that he had long planned to set "Sanglots" and "Fagnes de Wallonie." Then he reread "Hôtel" and "Voyage à Paris" in old literary journals he had saved since his teenage years and decided the time was right. The absolute silliness of the latter poem delighted him, and the appeal of a text like "Hôtel" is obvious. Poulenc handles these two songs deftly. Surely nothing could be more luxuriantly indolent than the setting of "Hôtel"; the last four chords evaporate into the air like a curl of tobacco smoke. "Voyage à Paris" is an example of Poulenc at his most carnivalesque, with its bawdy, clownish introduction and its vocal line that can only be called a tune even though it is not without chromatic quirkiness. The heaths of "Fagnes de Wallonie" are found in Belgium, on a high, windswept plateau. Poulenc's setting for this somewhat fierce text flies by, as he himself notes at the beginning, "extremely quickly, in a single bound." The protosurrealist scene at the Orkenise city gates where the handsome guards proudly knit elicits a setting Poulenc notes as "frank, in a folk-song style." Its skipping duplet articulation in the right hand of the piano is repeated in "Fagnes de Wallonie," while at the words, "Love intoxicates, carter," Poulenc doubles the vocal line in an inner part of the accompaniment just as he later does in "Sanglots." Such transient, almost hidden doublings are frequent elements of Poulenc's songs. "Sanglots" is arguably one of Poulenc's most moving vocal pieces. Following on the heels of the flamboyant finale of "Voyage à Paris," its beginning (marked "very calm") is clear and wistful. As the speaker recalls his heartbreak, as well as the joyous times that preceded it, the setting gradually grows in depth and intensity, exchanging a thinly "scored" accompaniment for one of great density and harmonic richness. Poulenc's profound love for the poetry of Apollinaire and others of his generation translated into a sophisticated and sensitive ability to set that poetry to music in ways that both honor and illuminate the texts. *—Virginia Sublett*

Recommended:

- ○ **French Songs** / Jones, Martineau / 1993 / Chandos 9147
- ○ **Poulenc: Mélodies** / Baldwin, Parker / EMI 64087
- ○ **Poulenc: Songs** / Piquemal, Lajarrige / 2000 / Naxos 553642

Le bestiaire (Cortège d'Orphée), song cycle (1919)

Though Francis Poulenc's favored poet seems to have been Paul Eluard (the author of about three dozen of Poulenc's song texts), the composer also frequented the writings of Apollinaire; in fact, Edward Lockspeiser, writing in 1940, observed an important parallel between Apollinaire's poetic style and that of Poulenc and his French musical predecessors: "[Apollinaire] reveals a remarkably pure lyrical strain, derived from the music inherent in words.... Yet mated with this entrancing simplicity is a rasping sarcasm, a cynical despondency which French artists have again and again used as an antidote to any semblance of too obvious sentimentality. We find this combination in the music of Poulenc itself, as in the music of Chabrier, Satie, and Ravel." Scholar and biographer Keith Daniel ventures further in comparing the two: "On a deeper, more personal level, Poulenc found a kindred spirit in Apollinaire, a spirit of deep tenderness and biting humor, a modern spirit rooted in tradition; in a word, Poulenc and Apollinaire shared a temperament of contradictions." Though Poulenc had read Apollinaire before, it was a live recitation by the poet in 1919 that inspired the composer to set his texts to music; the resulting song cycle, *Le Bestiaire*, stands as the first of several convergences between Apollinaire's poetry and Poulenc's music.

Though the cycle is most often heard today in its version for voice and piano, Poulenc's original scoring called for the singer to be accompanied by a flute, clarinet, bassoon, and string quartet. This perhaps explains the rather unpianistic nature of the accompaniment in the piano/vocal version. Elsewhere, Poulenc's approach to song seems to treat the singer's voice like the white froth discernable at the tip of a contiguous wave of sound; here, the piano must parse itself up to cover the roles of the various instruments. The result is a sonority that is occasionally unidiomatic, but sometimes endearingly so. One example can be found in the rhythmically dwindling bass and martial melody to which Don Pedro's fine quartet of camels saunters in "Le Dromadaire," which, when given over to the piano, seem to make the awkward and unwieldy beasts just a little more cartoonish. Likewise, the murky depths through which "L'Écrevisse" ("The Crayfish") wanders are somewhat overly evoked by the constant "tidal" shifts in mode and the unmoving bass drone.

This is not to say that Poulenc means to caricaturize Apollinaire's images. The musical exaggerations in "Le Dromadaire," for example, serve only to enhance and comment upon the air of odd ambition exhibited by the mysterious Don Pedro. In recalling his hearing the poet read his own poetry, Poulenc commented that "Apollinaire's voice is like that of his works, melancholy and joyful at the same time. This is why my Apollinaire songs must be sung without emphasizing the ludicrousness of certain phrases. *Le Bestiaire* is a most serious work."

Other songs in the cycle bear this out. The second, "La Chèvre du Thibet," compares a goat's soft coat to the golden fleece sought by Jason; this comparison is then rendered moot upon considering the tresses of the speaker's beloved. As the poem finds ultimate beauty in the simplest or smallest of ideas, so does the music draw comparison between grandeur and plainness: the globe-trotting adventurer Jason is reflected in the music by lush, flowery harmonies and figuration; the greater beauty, as embodied by the lover, is answered in the score by a simple, diatonic line. In passages such as this, Apollinaire and Poulenc demonstrate the complementarity of their styles, characterized by a mode of expression at once concise, precise, and profound.*—Jeremy Grimshaw*

Recommended:

- ○ **Poulenc: Mélodies** / Souzay, Baldwin / EMI 64087
- ○ **Poulenc: Bal masqué; Bestiaire; Sextet; Trio** / Friend (cond.), Allen, Nash Ens. / 1986 / CRD 3437

Chansons gaillardes, song cycle (1925–1926)

By 1926, when Heugel published the *Chansons gaillardes*, Poulenc was already the popular composer of the *Trois Mouvements perpétuels, for piano* and the hit ballet *Les Biches* and was in constant touch with everyone who was anyone in Paris—Stravinsky (whose influence he gratefully acknowledged) and Falla, Stokowski, and Koussevitzky, Diaghilev and Landowska, Cocteau and Max Jacob, to take names at random. But if his great lyrical gifts and smartalecky chic brought him eager acclaim, he was both avid and insecure regarding technique, his private studies with Koechlin having finished but two years previously. And if the *Chansons gaillardes*—ribald songs—do not yet share the exquisite balance and appositeness of his mature *mélodies*, especially those set to poems by Apollinaire and Eluard, they nevertheless partake imperishably of the insouciance and brilliant whirl of the pampered playboy-composer. In *The Diary of My Songs*, Poulenc remarked of the

Chansons gaillardes, "I am fond of this collection where I tried to show that outright obscenity can adapt itself to music... The texts were found in an anthology of songs of the seventeenth century (an old edition)." Wry comment on the fidelity of his mistress and frenzied panegyrics to wine and the pleasures of the bed—"'Couplets bachiques' and 'La belle jeunesse' must be performed *very fast*," Poulenc noted—alternate with an eerily serene prayer to the Fates and the elegant conceit of Sérénade. The airy Madrigal tells little Jeanneton that, while she's lovely as an angel and sweet as a lamb, a girl without breasts is like partridge served without orange. By postmodern standards, "L'Offrande" is the only truly obscene item in the collection—a virgin offers the god of love a candle to obtain a lover and he replies that, while she waits, she could always make use of her offering ("Servez-vous toujours de l'offrande"). The first performance of the *Chansons gaillardes* was given by baritone Pierre Bernac with Poulenc accompanying on May 2, 1926, in company with the premiere of the latter's *Trio for oboe, bassoon, and piano* (dedicated to Falla), and works by Auric at a concert so well attended that over 200 people had to be turned away. From 1934 until his retirement in 1960, Bernac was Poulenc's preferred interpreter, giving premieres and recording many of his songs with the composer, including two numbers from *Chansons gaillardes*. *—Adrian Corleonis*

Recommended:

○ **Poulenc: Mélodies** / Souzay, Baldwin / EMI 64087

Fiançailles pour rire, song cycle (1939)

Francis Poulenc did not approve of female singers performing songs that addressed women as love objects; in his book, *Diary of my Songs*, he noted a particular objection to hearing a woman sing Fauré's lines, "J'aime ton front, j'aime ta bouche, ô ma rebelle, ô ma farouche" (were the beloved a man, he would be "mon rebel"). Because of that slight squeamishness in his character, he made a point of finding and setting texts that he felt were "truly feminine." It caused him no difficulty to do so when the poet was his dear friend, Louise de Vilmorin. During the early years of World War II, she and her husband, a Hungarian count, were marooned in their castle behind enemy lines and no communication was possible with them. Poulenc wrote that he decided to compose this cycle so as to have an excuse to think of her.

The poetry is slight, modest, elegant: nostalgia and reflection, rather than action or immediacy, are the important themes throughout the otherwise unrelated poems. The overall emotional atmosphere is bittersweet, which Poulenc delicately underscores. Only two of the six songs ("Il vole" and "Fleurs") begin in major keys, and even then the mood is not robust or cheerful, but (in the former) anxious and (the latter) wistful. In addition, "Fleurs," the cycle's coda, ends with a minor cadence. These songs lack the brilliance and contrast of Poulenc's cycles written around the same time: *Tel jour, telle nuit* (December 1936–January 1937) on texts by Paul Éluard, and *Banalités* (1940), on texts by Guillaume Apollinaire. Nevertheless, they have charm, and display Poulenc's characteristic harmonic sophistication and melodic inventiveness. Of the six, "Dans l'herbe" is the most intense, building from the quiet futility of "I can do nothing more for him," to the anguished despair at "He was calling me." The strangest is number six, in which the alienated speaker describes herself as if she were in her own casket; not surprisingly, Poulenc's harmonic language here is highly chromatic, some of the melodies almost tortuously so. A virtuosic romp for both singer and pianist is "Il vole"; the text plays on the pun between "to steal" and "to flee" and the sparklingly contrapuntal accompaniment (tempo marking: relentlessly presto!) supports a wide-ranging vocal line which lifts off and trails away at last, like the flying, thieving lover it bemoans. *—Virginia Sublett*

Recommended:

○ **Poulenc: Mélodies** / Ameling, Baldwin / EMI 64087

Tel jour, telle nuit, song cycle (1936–1937)

Following a first reading of a new song cycle, "Plain-chant," which dissapointed the singer Pierre Bernac, Francis Poulenc took his own manuscript and cheerfully tossed it into the fireplace. To the horrified baritone he said only that by the time of their next recital, there would be a new and better cycle in its place. Over December 1936 and January 1937, he made good on his promise, composing the nine-song cycle *Tel jour, telle nuit* (As is the day, so is the night) to poems by the surrealist lyric poet Paul Éluard. The highly unified group of mysteriously serene melodies is one of the most acclaimed cycles in French art song.

Dedicated to Pablo Picasso by both poet and composer, "Bonne Journee" (A Good Day) begins the cycle with a calm sense of forward motion. Poulenc asked that it be sung "with very peaceful joy." "Une ruine coquille vide" (A Ruin an empty shell) continues in the same restrainedly tranquil mood, with the same tempo and meter; the slow lyrical melody with its elegiac piano accompaniment suggests a nocturne. The third song, "Le front comme un drapeau perdu" (Your face like a lost flag) is one of several songs that seem unable to be removed from their context in this cycle. Bernac, who premiered the cycle, described the song aptly when he said it "begins in violence and concludes with a strange appeasement."

Short and sinister in mood, "Une roulotte couverte entuiles" (A gypsy wagon roofed with tiles) paints a surreal melodramatic scene with carefully accented rhythm. "A toutes brides" (Riding full tilt) is a quick and spirited dance-like number leading into the introspective "Une herbe pauvre" (Scant grass). The sixth song captures an ephemeral moment with a distant, hushed melodic line that moves immutably in the same tempo as the first two songs of the cycle.

"Je n'ai envie que de t'aimer" (I long only to love you) is an earnestly cheerful love song, fast-moving but never agitated. Poulenc dedicated the eighth song, "Figure de force brûlante et farouche" (Figure of wild fiery force), to its first interpreter, Bernac. As in the third song, the song begins vehemently before resuming the slow calm characteristic of the cycle. Its strong climax is meant to contrast with the peaceful beginning of the incandescent love poem with which the cycle concludes, "Nous avons fait la nuit" (We have made night). Poulenc constructed the song to bear the musical and dramatic focus of the cycle, and the result has consistently been acknowledged as one of his finest songs. In the same tempo and meter as the opening songs, the hushed wonder of the melodic line crescendos to a carefully restrained, lyrical passion. Poulenc meant its piano coda to prolong the emotion of *Tel jour, telle nuit* for the audience, as in Schumann's *Dichterliebe*. The composer, summing up the unique mood of the cycle, noted the difficulty of making interpreters grasp that "calmness alone can give intensity to a love poem." *—Thomas Oram*

Recommended:

○ **Poulenc: Mélodies** / Gedda, Baldwin / EMI 64087

○ **Mélodies of Francis Poulenc** / Johnson, Lott, Murray, Jackson, Songmakers' Almanac / Hyperion 66147

CHORAL

Exultate Deo, motet (1941)

Though raised as a devout Catholic, throughout the first years of his adulthood Francis Poulenc had little interest in religion. It was upon hearing of the horrendous automobile accident that had killed his friend, the composer Pierre-Octave Ferroud, that Poulenc began to "ponder... on the fragility of the human frame" and seek a deeper spiritual life. The musical result of this religious awakening was a drastic shift towards sacred subjects. Poulenc's setting of Psalm 81, *Exultate Deo* ("Sing Aloud Unto God") reflects the point at which the composer's devotion to music crosses paths with his faith in God.

The psalm text is full of musical images: voices, trumpets, harps, and timbrels are all enlisted in the praise of God. Poulenc's setting is both reverent and vivid, and his characteristic harmonic tricks are used to dramatic ends. Though perhaps not always as strictly reverent as one might expect in a piece of church music, the listener must keep in mind that the harmonic twists and turns Poulenc employs are not (at least in this case) gags, but rather dramatic devices.

For the opening words the voice groups enter one at a time in imitation, on a rising scalar line. The antiquated construction is updated by the occasional introduction of colorful dissonances and striking harmonic twists. Once the entire ensemble had entered, the choir declaims the text in strict homophony. Repetitive emphasis is given to the words "iubilate Deo"; this text is further highlighted by what might be termed a harmonic crescendo—a series of quick modulations upward, finally apexing with a leaping ascent on "Jacob." The text then invokes the music of the psalm and the tabret, repeating the entreaty three times with increasing intensity and insistence. As the phrase "exultate Deo" reappears in the text, we hear the rising motive from the beginning, sung as if to start another imitative entrance; it takes a different turn at the end, however, leading to a hushed homophonic passage. Once again, the call for music grows louder as it is repeated. The next phrase, "Buccinate in neomenia tuba" ("Blow up the trumpet in the new moon"), is set to another harmonic crescendo; its intensity is enhanced by a new and unexpected chordal tangent that accompanies each appearance of the last word of the phrase, "tuba" (trumpet). A dramatic pause sets the stage for the final text phrase, "insigni die solemnitatis vestrae" ("in the time appointed, and on our solemn feast day"). The texture is suddenly a rich, drawn out chorale, expanded and thickened with added tones, and finally concluding on a broadly voiced chord with a shimmering sixth coloring the harmony. *—Jeremy Grimshaw*

Recommended:

○ **Poulenc: Mass in G; 4 Petites Prières; 4 Motets** / O'Donnell (cond.), Westminster Cathedral Choir / 1994 / Hyperion 66664

○ **Poulenc: Sacred Music** / Rutter (cond.), Cambridge Singers, City of London Sinfonia / 2002 / Collegium 506

Gloria, for soprano, chorus & orchestra (1959–1960)

"[The Laudamus Te] caused a scandal; I wonder why? I was simply thinking, in writing it, of the Gozzoli frescoes in which the angels stick out their tongues; I was thinking also of the serious Benedictines whom I saw playing soccer one day." This, Poulenc's own description of the second movement of his *Gloria* (for orchestra, chorus, and soloist), captures the essential nature of his approach to sacred music. An odd mixture of lightheartedness and spirituality—which, Poulenc argues through his music, are not mutually exclusive—has come to be one of the composer's trademarks; indeed, these seemingly opposing values can be represented by the triumphant trumpet fanfare that begins the *Gloria* and the peppy melody of the

"Laudamus Te"—the two themes are perhaps the most familiar in Poulenc's entire output. The style is a distinctive combination of Poulenc's devil-may-care attitude from the early years of Les Six and the profound religiosity that he encountered in mid-life.

Composed in 1959, the work is one of three sacred pieces from Poulenc's "mature" years (the others being the *Stabat Mater* from 1950 and *Sept répons des ténèbres* from 1962). It was commissioned by the Koussevitzky Foundation after one of Poulenc's trips to America, receiving its premiere in Boston in 1961.

In composing his *Gloria*, Poulenc divided the text into six sections. The first movement, marked maestoso, begins with three iterations of the heraldic theme—a stately, dotted fanfare concluding with a triplet flourish—in different orchestrational settings and with slightly different harmonic conclusions. The chorus enters above a bubbling orchestral texture, singing the text in lively declamatory syncopation. The second movement begins with a short, playful instrumental introduction, the chorus enters with the famous "Laudamus Te." The tune itself, marked Très vite et joyeux, isn't all that irreverent; its playfulness stems largely from the orchestration, which puts high and low registers alike on the offbeats. This gives the piece a delightfully awkward momentum—likely similar to that of a monk in full Benedictine garb footing the ball towards the goal.

The third movement contrasts with the previous two in its tranquillity and restraint. Marked Très lente et calme, it begins with a plaintive woodwind interlude. The soprano soloist then enters on a melody characterized by initial notes in the upper register that plunge dramatically into the lower range. The harmonies in the orchestra and chorus are striking, sometimes approaching a Debussyian wash of impressionistic color.

For the fourth movement, Poulenc once again returns to the Très vite et joyeux mood of the second movement, while the instrumental interludes vaguely resemble the opening brass fanfare. The fifth returns to more staid feel, with a slow tempo and dark orchestrational introduction that precedes a haunting soprano solo. Emerging from the upper atmosphere, the soloist counters the descending lines of the third movement with an angular melody that reaches impossibly upwards. The rising line resonates vividly with the corresponding portion of the text, which constitutes a humble and penitent prayer for mercy. The final movement begins with a bold a capella exclamation, followed by a return of the brass fanfare. The soloist returns for a rhapsodic solo underscored by impressionist harmonies, with special attention given to the lush major seventh chord. This harmony accommodates a final return of the brass fanfare, before the soloist brings the work to a serene conclusion. *—Jeremy Grimshaw*

Recommended:

- ○ **Poulenc: Gloria; Stabat Mater** / Ozawa (cond.), Battle, Boston SO, Tanglewood Festival Chorus / 1989 / DG 427304
- ○ **Poulenc: Sacred Music** / Rutter (cond.), Deam, Cambridge Singers, City of London Sinfonia / 2002 / Collegium 506

Litanies à la Vierge Noire, for women's chorus & organ (1936; revised 1947)

The *Litanies à la Vierge noire* signaled a new phase in Poulenc's career, one marked by religious choral works of a mysterious, ethereal, and often extremely moving nature. Not surprisingly, this trend directly stemmed from events in the composer's life. Raised Catholic, Poulenc did not practice the faith seriously until his close friend Pierre-Octave Ferroud was killed in an auto accident in 1936. Deeply anguished by this, Poulenc proceeded to embark on a pilgrimage to Notre Dame de Rocamadour, a church in the mountains of southwestern France. The church—which holds a statue of the Virgin carved in black stone—has been a pilgrimage site for some nine centuries, and while there, Poulenc experienced a reconversion to Catholicism. The *Litanies* were the product of that experience.

"The text is a plea to the Virgin Mary and the Holy Trinity for mercy and understanding," he wrote; he adapted the text from the recitations of one of his fellow pilgrims. Scored for three-part female chorus, the work features a modal, chantlike style that avoids conventional cadences. Particularly notable is the organ part—the liturgical instrument par excellence—which punctuates the choral discourse with numerous dramatic dissonances. Poulenc's interest in the instrument here paved the way for his *Organ Concerto* of 1937.

The sweet, poignant tone of *Litanies à la Vierge noire* stands in contrast to Poulenc's more famously irreverent, silly side. He once said his mother was something of a bon vivant while his father was very serious and reserved; the alternation between these characteristics would mark his own music from this point forward. *—Brian Wise*

Recommended:

- ○ **Poulenc: Mass in G; 4 Petites Prières; 4 Motets** / O'Donnell (cond.), Simcock, Westminster Cathedral Choir / 1994 / Hyperion 66664
- ○ **Fauré & Duruflé: Requiem** / Guest (cond.), Cleobury, St. John's College Choir / 1994 / London 436286

Mass in G major (1937)

In 1936, attempting to overcome his reputation for musical flippancy, Poulenc began studying Monteverdi's motets with Nadia Boulanger. Around the same time, his close friend Pierre-Octave Ferroud, a composer and critic, was killed in an auto accident. This triggered a personal crisis that led Poulenc back to the Catholicism of his youth. This confluence of spiritual and musical interests led directly to an a cappella mass for soprano solo and choir. The work, dedicated to Poulenc's father, is generally serene and confident and follows the usual sequence of Latin movements, although it omits the Credo. Poulenc's musical language here gives the impression of austerity, thanks to its firm, no-nonsense melodic writing, but the harmony is actually lush though occasionally mildly dissonant. The outer sections of the Kyrie are strongly rhythmic and affirmative, with a more meditative "Christe eleison" section at its center. The Gloria—not to be confused with Poulenc's full-scale, jubilant late work of that name for chorus and orchestra—changes melody, harmony, and inflection from phrase to phrase, with solo voices often emerging over a firm bass foundation. The brief Sanctus is light, loving, and cheerful, broadening out near the end for sonorous statements of "Osanna in excelsis." The Benedictus naturally emerges from those measured osannas; it is slow, patient, ethereal, and dominated by the highest voices. This time, the concluding homophonic "Osanna in excelsis" section resembles the stately, antiphonal brass chorales of the Italian Renaissance. The solo soprano introduces the concluding Agnus Dei. The chorus echoes the soloist's haunting melismas in unison octaves, breaking into harmony only upon the striking, hushed appearance of the words "Miserere nobis" ("have mercy on us"). The harmony now is Romantic, lush, and comforting, but soon the chorus is reduced to ethereal pedal tones as a cushion for the soprano's final, serene utterance of "Dona nobis pacem" ("give us peace"). *—James Reel*

Recommended:

- ○ **Poulenc: Mass in G; 4 Petites Prières; 4 Motets** / O'Donnell (cond.), Kennedy, Westminster Cathedral Choir / 1994 / Hyperion 66664
- ○ **Poulenc: Mass in G major; Motets** / Shaw (cond.), Carter, Robert Shaw Festival Singers / 1990 / Telarc 80236
- ○ **Poulenc: Mass in G major; Motets** / Creed (cond.), RIAS-Kammerchor / HM 901588

Quatre motets pour le temps de Noël (1951–1952)

The *Quatre Motets pour un temps de Noel* (1952) are representative of the "pious" Poulenc—the composer who left behind his wit, sarcasm and Les Six-inspired aesthetic to give sincere voice to his own Catholic faith; they were also some of Poulenc's favorite choral pieces. Written as counterparts to the earlier *Quatre Motets pour un temps de Penitence* (1939), which were quite solemn in tone, the Christmas motets are of a gentler nature, both musically and thematically. They are light in texture, and exude a sense of joyful serenity.

Poulenc began these short motets for four-part mixed chorus in November 1951, completing them the following May. Composition took place in Paris, at Provence, and at Poulenc's home, in Noizay. Poulenc was writing with a newfound confidence at the time: having felt himself to be in the creative doldrums, he had reawakened his senses with the 12-part *Stabat Mater* (also 1951), which he felt to be entirely satisfactory; the Christmas motets, while much smaller in scope and resources, exhibit the same sense of assurance. The *Quatre Motets pour un temps de Noel* also reflect Poulenc's love of religious paintings and architecture through subtle musical/visual imagery. The composer often studied religious art, and he kept a picture of a Romanesque cathedral bathed in sunlight on his mantelpiece.

The first motet, "O magnum mysterium" (O great mystery), announces the coming of the Baby Jesus, and praises the Virgin Mary; it superimposes a crystalline soprano melody over the hushed accompaniment of the lower three voices. "Quem vidistis pastores dicite" (Shepherds, tell whom you saw), the second motet, takes its text from the Christmas Matins service. As a "choros Angelorum" (chorus of angels), the soprano, alto, and tenor play off the bass voice extensively in this painstaking word-by-word setting. A fortissimo unison on the word "Dicite" (tell!) heightens the theatricality of the scene.

"Videntes stellam" (Seeing a Star), the third motet, also makes extensive use of the upper three voices alone to create an airy, suitably celestial texture. The textual entrance of the Magi and their gifts of gold and myrrh ushers in a more complex chromatic texture. The final motet, "Hodie, Christus natus est" (Today Christ is Born), is the most exuberant and florid; Poulenc's celebrated sense of humor is evident in the "kiss" given in the final chord. *—AMG*

Recommended:

- ○ **Poulenc: Mass in G major; Motets** / Shaw (cond.), Robert Shaw Festival Singers / 1990 / Telarc 80236
- ○ **Poulenc: Mass in G; 4 Petites Prières; 4 Motets** / O'Donnell (cond.), Westminster Cathedral Choir / 1994 / Hyperion 66664
- ○ **Poulenc: Figure Humaine** / Christophers (cond.), The Sixteen / 1993 / Virgin 59192

Quatre motets pour un temps de pénitence (1938–1939)

"While attending... the premiere of Milhaud's wonderful *Cantates de la paix and Deux cités*... the exact image of my Motets suddenly came to me... as vivid and as tragic as a painting by Mantegna." Completed in 1939, the *Quatre motets pour un temps de pénitence* are among Poulenc's most popular works. His setting of texts from the Holy Week offices demonstrates a balance of restraint and expression and a careful economy of texture that set it apart from much of his choral music. Poulenc uses his characteristic harmonic, melodic, and textural stylistic tools, but with an added measure of deliberation and dramatic control.

The dramatic trajectory traced by the text of the first motet, "Timor et tremor," is followed and enhanced by the music. The setting is at first quite staid, with a pensive homophonic texture dominating the landscape. The departure coincides with the end of a dramatic crescendo at the phrase "darkness engulfs me." More harmonic color is introduced in the next phrase, along with the first break from strict homophony. The supplicant text that follows is declaimed in a gentler tone, first with serenely static harmonies, then with reduced men's voices. The increasing desperation of the text finds resonance in the increasingly complex harmony.

Poulenc exercises a bit of poetic license in the second motet, creating a drastically different expressive shape. The first and last words in the text describe the loving care of the Lord: "...With a hedge I shielded you, the stones I have cleared from around you"; the middle of the text grows tense and accusatory: "How have you turned bitter, crucifying me while setting Barabbas free?" Poulenc brings the middle section back, harmonically altering the repeating music with painful dissonances and chromatic stress.

By carefully conserving his textural resources up to this point, Poulenc is free to devote them with greater dramatic effect to the text of "Tenebrae factae sunt." A wide variety of vocal ensemble colors are employed to depict this text more vividly. Divisi altos and basses declaim in octaves against long sustained incantations of the evocative opening words. A particularly poignant effect is achieved at the phrase "Deus meus, Deus meus, ut quid me dereliquisti?" ("My God, my God, oh why hast thou forsaken me?"), where the texture is reduced suddenly to altos and sopranos only. Later, a descending chromatic solo by the tenors reverently describes Jesus bowing his head before surrendering his spirit. This kind of focused, intense textual treatment continues throughout the rest of the motet.

If the third motet is the most emotionally vivid, the fourth, "Tristis est anima mea," is the most pictorial. The heretofore-conserved resource is figuration, which is employed here with precision. A wide variety of rhythmic and melodic gestures depict Jesus being taken in the Garden, while his disciples flee. Moreover, by putting this motet at the end of the cycle, Poulenc seems to be making the story not just a narrative one, but an allegorical one involving the listener as well. *—Jeremy Grimshaw*

Recommended:

○ **Poulenc: Mass in G major; Motets** / Shaw (cond.), Robert Shaw Festival Singers / 1990 / Telarc 80236

○ **Poulenc: Mass in G; 4 Petites Prières; 4 Motets** / O'Donnell (cond.), O'Dwyer, Westminster Cathedral Choir / 1994 / Hyperion 66664

Salve Regina (1941)

Francis Poulenc had little interest in religion until a terrible automobile accident took the life his friend, the composer Pierre-Octave Ferroud. The sudden loss of his friend caused Poulenc to "ponder... on the fragility of the human frame" and seek a deeper spiritual life. The musical result of this religious awakening was a drastic shift towards sacred subjects.

Salve Regina is one of two motets Poulenc composed in 1941and dedicated to his close friends, Georges and Hélène Salle. The text of the other motet, *Exultate Deo*, invokes the trumpet, tabret, harp, and lute to praise "God, our strength" with a "joyful noise"; the musical setting is likewise exclamatory and triumphant, alternating between strict imitation and assertive homophony. *Salve Regina* serves as a contrast to the vibrancy of its counterpart, with a text and tone that conveys reverence, penitence, hope, and a much quieter kind of jubilation.

The work begins in homophony, a texture that will predominate throughout the work. The harmonies are both rich and stark, creating a carefully shaped melodic contour that alternately rises, arcs, or descends across each phrase of the text. These smoothed shapes are first broken up by a dramatic leap upwards in the sopranos on the phrase "ad te clamamus" ("our cries to thee we raise"), a gesture and text that is repeated for emphasis. At the phrase "ad te suspiramus" ("to thee we raise our sighs") the texture and harmony suddenly grow darker. A subtle but effective nuance is created by the men's voices as they emerge with pictorial design from the lower range alone, to be joined by the upper voices in the middle of the phrase.

The chordal texture is further broken up for expressive effect at "eia ergo, advocata nostra, illos tuos misericordes oculos" ("Therefore, our advocate, [turn] your merciful eyes"). The men begin with a rising melody presented in lush parallel tenths, before being joined by the women on a plaintively leaping line. At the words "Et Iesum" ("And Jesus") the ensemble converges on unison and octaves, with a pensive, angular melody, before returning to solemn homophony. Here the harmony becomes transitory, sequencing its way into new places; the expressive effect is one of fallibility, insecurity, and entreaty. The harmonies become most colorful near the end, on the words "O clemens, O pia, O dulcis Virgo Maria" ("O merciful, O loving, O sweet Virgin Mary"), as bass ostinati gradually lose their footing and chromatic twists alter the harmonic trajectory. The final dissonance resolves into submissive parallel fifths, bringing the work to a solemn close. *—Jeremy Grimshaw*

Recommended:

○ **Poulenc: Mass in G; 4 Petites Prières; 4 Motets** / O'Donnell (cond.), Westminster Cathedral Choir / 1994 / Hyperion 66664

○ **Poulenc: Chansons françaises** / Christophers (cond.), The Sixteen / 1993 / Virgin 59311

Un soir de neige, chamber cantata for 6 voices (1944)

Francis Poulenc's solo vocal settings of poems of Paul Éluard have been widely celebrated, while his cantata *Figure humaine*, to Éluard texts, has been labeled his finest a cappella choral work. An exception to the fame bestowed upon their collaborations, however, has been the little-known six-voice chamber cantata *Un soir de neige* ("Night of Snow"). That the four brief movements were written over the span of three days during the dead of the French winter is perhaps not surprising, given Éluard's bleak, shadowy landscape. That the days were December 24–26, 1944, however, gives one pause. Even days after the Battle of the Bulge had effectively ended the German threat, and during a holiday that had particular significance to Poulenc following his rediscovery of his Catholic faith, he was peculiarly inspired by these poems whose journey brutally juxtaposes the beauty of nature with cold and death. In this sense the cycle resembles Schubert's *Winterreise*, and the musical settings in some sense are also a look back to earlier styles, with their relatively simple forms and occasional passage reminiscent of Renaissance polyphony. Yet in spite of these there can be no doubt that both text and music are creations of the mid-twentieth century.

"De grandes cuillers de neige" (Great drifts of snow) begins the work with a unison soprano melody line painting the wandering steps through the winter weather. Alto, tenor, and bass then comment on the orderliness of nature, but the entire chorus contrasts this with the incongruous presence of the wanderer, over a series of disparate chords that at the same time mark a return to the opening melody, a modified AABA form, characteristic of Poulenc and of this set. The second movement, "La bonne neige" (The lovely snow), also engages in text painting, as alto and tenor weave around a soprano drone like snow through the branches. Heavily chromaticism breaks off into the four upper voices intoning starkly "et c'est toujours/Le dernier vivant que menace/La masse absolue de la mort" (and [the wolf] is always/The last one living, menaced/by total, absolute death). The B section provides a welcome warm contrast over a bass pedal, but the return of the A section in part proves this to be fleeting.

"Bois meurtri" (Wounded woods) follows after a "long silence"; stark homophonic minor chords characterize it at the interval of the tritone. Its B section has a lovely, jagged line sung by the lower two voices which belies the text (about drowning). The final movement, "La nuit le froid la solitude" (Night of chill and isolation), stands out not only for its extended chromaticism, but also for its AAB form. The lack of a return seals the bleak mood of the composition.

Un soir de neige is scored for a mixed chorus of six parts, and could very well be performed by six solo voices. Though overlooked, it is a fine representation of Poulenc's mature choral style. *—Thomas Oram*

Recommended:

○ **Poulenc: Chansons françaises** / Christophers (cond.), The Sixteen / 1993 / Virgin 59311

○ **Poulenc: Secular Choral Music** / Wood (cond.), New London Chamber Choir / 1995 / Hyperion 66798

Stabat Mater, for soprano, chorus & orchestra (1950–1951)

Poulenc is remembered mainly as a gay boulevardier, but he also had a serious, deeply sincere religious side, expressed with austere beauty in his *Stabat Mater*. Poulenc wanted to write something in memory of a friend, painter Christian Bérard. Although he resisted writing a requiem, the slow movements of this work often call to mind the gentle *Requiem* of Gabriel Fauré, and structurally it adheres to the old motet patterns employed by Jean-Baptiste Lully. The *Stabat Mater* calls for mixed chorus, full orchestra, and soprano solo.

The opening "Stabat Mater dolorosa," grave and dignified and at about four minutes, is one of the work's longest movements. This is followed by the turbulent "Cujus animam gementem," then the quiet, initially a cappella "O quam tristis et afflicta," whose austerity is relieved by sensuous harp glissandi halfway through.

The tuneful "Quae moerebat et dolebat" has an agreeable, antique pastoral air, whereas "Quis est homo, qui non fleret" is highly dramatic, full of slamming brass chords in its first half and breaking into Stravinsky-like jaggedness in the second part. Complete contrast comes with the tender yet harmonically restless "Vidit suum dulcem natum," where the soprano first appears; the two halves of the *Stabat Mater* symmetrically hinge on this movement.

"Eja Mater, fons amoris" is more celebratory, despite a suggestion of tragedy at the mid and end points. "Fac ut ardeat cor meum" begins canonically for unaccompanied chorus, but soon the writing becomes more traditionally vertical (harmonic) rather than horizontal (polyphony was not one of Poulenc's major concerns). "Sancta mater, istud agas" begins as one of the score's darkest sections, and takes its inspiration partly from plainchant, but in the middle it rises to a peak of religious ardor.

"Fac ut portem Christi mortem" is a severe funeral march, and very distantly recalls the Berlioz *Symphonie funèbre et triomphale*; before long, though, the solo soprano returns, bringing with her a harmonic environment that is simultaneously rarefied and voluptuous. "Inflammatus et accensus" begins turbulently, withdraws into a hushed passage for chorus, then rises steadily through a passage that recalls the soprano solo in "Vidit suum dulcem natum." From that dramatic peak, the beginning of "Quando corpus moritur" drops to a whisper; this quiet writing alternates with outbursts at full volume, some involving the soprano. The music levels off and becomes more soothing, although it does rise to a fierce conclusion on the word "Amen." *—James Reel*

Recommended:

- ○ **Poulenc: Gloria; Stabat Mater** / Ozawa (cond.), Battle, Boston SO, Tanglewood Festival Chorus / 1989 / DG 427304
- ○ **Poulenc: Gloria; Stabat Mater** / Hickox (cond.), Dubosc, Westminster Singers, City of London Sinfonia / 1993 / Virgin 59286

OPERA

Dialogues des Carmélites (1953–1956)

It is curious that such an essentially lyric composer as Poulenc, who had first come before the public as a teenager near the end of World War I with the smartalecky *Rapsodie nègre*, should have waited until near the end of World War II to compose his first opera, *Les Mamelles de Tirésias*. The immediate success of *Tirésias*, premiered June 3, 1947, coupled with its resourcefulness in adapting his gift for the arrestingly ravishing melodic oddment to a large canvas, boosted Poulenc's confidence. But as the 1950s loomed, inspiration flagged. When, in March 1953, Guido Valcarenghi, director the Italian publishing firm Ricordi, suggested a commission for a ballet to be performed at La Scala, Poulenc replied "If only you could give me an opera libretto." Valcarenghi shot back with the suggestion of Georges Bernanos' *Dialogues des Carmélites*, with which Poulenc was already familiar. Originally a screenplay, *Dialogues*' brief scenes and series of psychological moments were in accord with Poulenc's manner, while its exploration of the vicissitudes of religious devotion struck a deep resonance with the composer of the *Mass in G* (1937) and the *Stabat Mater* (1950). Days later, finding a copy of *Dialogues* in a Roman bookstore, Poulenc took it to a café to discover that its lines began to sing themselves to him. Ricordi's commission was accepted, and by August Poulenc was intensely involved in its composition. By March 1954 he was well into the second act when the matter of rights, combined with a disturbing homosexual relationship, threatened to derail the project, prompting a physical and mental breakdown. With the legal question resolved, Poulenc returned to the composition at the beginning of 1955, completing the vocal score by August and orchestration in June 1956. The predominantly female cast, with its anxiety-ridden protagonist—the novice Blanche de la Force—and their spiritual struggles as the French Revolution overtakes and propels them to a martyrs' death, are realized with startling power by Poulenc's atmospheric evocations and caressing lyricism. As the composer confessed, "Blanche was me, and still is me"—the part was composed expressly for soprano Denise Duval. La Scala received a premiere January 26, 1957, sung in Italian, and conducted by Nino Sanzogno. Pierre Dervaux led the French premiere at the Opéra on June 21, 1957, with Duval (Blanche), Régine Crespin (Second Prioress), and Rita Gorr (Mére Marie)—all of whom participated in a classic recording of the work the following year. *—Adrian Corleonis*

Synopsis:

Act One. The action takes place during the French Revolution and its aftermath, 1789–94. In his home, the Marquis de la Force and his son the Chevalier worry about the Marquis' daughter Blanche, whose carriage is surrounded by a hostile crowd. Blanche, however, arrives unharmed, but announces she will enter the Carmelite order of nuns.

At the Carmelite convent several weeks later, Blanche is interviewed by the elderly Prioress and then accepted into the order. Blanche later meets the chipper young nun Sister Constance, who shocks her by calmly revealing a dark premonition: both she and Blanche will die on the same day, still in their youth.

In her cell the ailing Prioress is dying a protracted death, displaying both defiance and spiritual weakness. She tells the assistant Prioress, Mother Marie, that she must watch over Blanche. When, near the end of the scene, the Prioress attempts to speak to Blanche, she dies.

Act Two. In the chapel, Blanche keeps vigil alone over the body of the Prioress, but panics suddenly and flees. While taking flowers to the Prioress' grave, Sister Constance tells Blanche that a person's death may be for the benefit of others or that people may actually exchange each other's deaths. The Prioress' agonizing passing might therefore have allowed someone else an easy death.

In the convent's chapter room, the new Prioress, Madame Lidoine (Mother Marie of St. Augustine) warns of troubles ahead. Soon the Chevalier appears to see his sister. During his visit with her, he warns she may not be safe here because of her aristocratic background and accuses her of remaining in the convent because of her fears of the outside.

In the sacristy of the convent, the Father Confessor announces that the Mass he has just finished would be his last, as he is forced to go into hiding because of the political turmoil. Knocks at the door are heard and an angry throng pours in. Two Commissars proclaim banishment of the nuns from the convent.

Act Three. Sometime later, the nuns, with the Prioress absent, assemble in the chapel, now in ruins. Mother Marie proposes that they vow to accept martyrdom. A vote is taken, with a unanimous result needed to effect adoption. Blanche casts the only negative vote, but Sister Constance claims to be the dissenter and to have now changed her mind. Her ploy works, but in the confusion that soon grips the scene, Blanche escapes.

In the Marquis' library, Blanche, now working as a servant, has learned that her father has gone to the guillotine. While she cooks, Mother Marie enters and informs her that the Carmelite nuns have been arrested. She also tells her of a place where she will be safe and where they can later meet.

In the Conciergie prison, the Prioress consoles the nuns and promises that she too will follow the vow of martyrdom, even though she was not present for the vote. The jailer enters to inform the nuns that they have been sentenced to death. Sister Constance is certain that Blanche will return because of her premonition. When Mother Marie hears of the death sentences, she decides she must be with the others, but the Father Confessor dissuades her.

In the final scene, the Carmelites sing the *Salve Regina* as they are led to the guillotine, one by one. Sister Constance is about to die when she spots Blanche amid the spectators. Blanche begins singing and soon joins her sisters to fulfill the vow she eschewed. *—Robert Cummings*

Recommended:

- ○ **Poulence: Dialogues des Carmélites** / Nagano (cond.), Van Dam, Dubosc, Yakar, Senechal, Lyon Opera Orch. / 1992 / Virgin 59227

KEYBOARD

Works for Piano (1916–1959)

Poulenc, though a very talented pianist, is not remembered for his piano music. Poulenc always struggled with composing for piano solo, remarking that "it is the solo piano that somehow escapes me. With it I am the victim of false pretenses." Musicologists have suggested that because Poulenc's knew so much piano music and played piano so well, he could adroitly borrow from a variety of sources for his compositions; unfortunately, he often chose to borrow from bad music. The result is an oeuvre often bereft of personal style.

Poulenc composed 32 pieces for piano, solo and four-hands. They can be divided roughly into three periods: the first, from 1916–21, represents his early efforts and feature a liberal use of dissonance together with a spare, linear texture; the second period, from 1922–37, is the period of the virtuosic works; the third period, from 1940–59, marks a return to the simplicity of the early works. The works of the first period show the influence of contemporary French composers like Satie. This is especially evident in his *Sonata for Four Hands* of 1918, which also bears the influence of Stravinsky, with its clarity, dissonance, and rhythmic verve. Poulenc also composed one of his most famous piano works in 1918, his *Mouvements perpetuals*. These little pieces are decidedly French in character, recalling the blurred tonalities of Debussy, together with a Satiean indifference to harmonic movement and melodic development. At the end of Poulenc's first period he composed his five *Impromptus* (1920–21) and the *Promenades* (1921), both representing a departure from the simplicity of the preceding piano works. They are more dissonant, and reveal the burgeoning influence of Milhaud.

Poulenc's second period is marked by a turning away from contemporary French music toward the nineteenth century. Poulenc took Schumann and Chopin as his models, producing technically demanding, texturally dense, "serious" piano music, eschewing Satiean simplicity in favor of a more romantic esthetic. Several of the works from this period, such as *Napoli* of 1925 and the eight *Nocturnes* of 1929–38, exemplify this new style. The major work from this period is a set of 15 *Improvisations*, the first ten composed between 1932–34, the last five between 1941 and 1959. These short pieces are bright and inventive, suggesting both Chopin with their light, florid melodies and Debussy with their harmonic language.

Poulenc's second period was particularly productive, but his third period was not. He completed only eight piano works during this time, his style changing yet again, returning to the clarity and simplicity of his younger years. *Melancholie* of 1940 is a good example of Poulenc's simple yet charming late piano style, with its clear separation of left and right hands and its lyrical melodies. *L'Embarquement pour Cythere* of 1951, a sweetly nostalgic waltz for two pianos, also exemplifies Poulenc's return to a lighthearted approach. *—Alexander Carpenter*

Recommended:

- ○ **Poulenc: Complete Music for Piano** / Tanyel, Brown / 1987 / Chandos 8519
- ○ **Poulenc: Works for Piano** / Tacchino / 1988 / EMI 569671
- ○ **Poulenc: Piano Music Vol. 1** / Cazal / 1998 / Naxos 553929
- ○ **Poulenc: Piano Music Vol. 2** / Cazal / 1999 / Naxos 553930

Capriccio for 2 pianos (1952)

In the early 1950s, Francis Poulenc composed numerous pieces for Arthur Gold and Robert Fizdale, two American pianists affectionately referred to as "les boys." These included substantial works like the *Sonata for Two Pianos*, which Poulenc dedicated to the two men "as much with friendship as with admiration," along with several shorter works that also reflect this friendship. The *Capriccio d'après le bal masqué* was one of these; although it is dedicated to Samuel Barber, whose piano music Poulenc held in high esteem, it is hard to imagine it coming into being without the presence of "les boys." This Capriccio adapts the finale of *Le bal masqué*, Poulenc's cantata profana, to texts by Max Jacob, and remains essentially faithful to the original for baritone and chamber orchestra: carnival rhythms and playfulness in the opening, a collapse into a melancholy middle section, a return to the jerky rhythms, and eventually the music of the opening to close. However, Poulenc luxuriates in the expanded palette of the two pianos rather than slavishly imitating orchestral effects, justifying this piece's existence by presenting it as nothing more than a mere transcription. *—Andrew Lindemann Malone*

Recommended:

- ○ **Poulenc: Complete Works for 2 Pianos** / Pontinen, Derwinger / 1993 / Bis 593
- ○ **Poulenc: Complete Music for Piano** / Tanyel, Brown / 1987 / Chandos 8519

L'histoire de Babar, le petit éléphant, melodrama for narrator & piano (1940–1945)

One day during World War II, while Francis Poulenc was visiting some relatives in Bordeaux, his four-year-old niece expressed displeasure with what the composer was playing on the piano. With the certainty of youth, she removed Poulenc's hands from the keyboard and said "Oh, that is so ugly. Play this," placing one of Jean de Brunhoff's Babar books on the music stand. Poulenc improvised an accompaniment as he read the story. Word must have spread through the neighborhood, for the composer soon found himself surrounded by neighborhood children; their names, in fact, appear in the dedication to the work inspired by the occasion, *L'histoire de Babar, le petit éléphant.*

Poulenc's work is a melodrama which combines de Brunhoff's narrative with evocative musical interludes. The story follows the life of the anthropomorphic elephant Babar from his birth and youth in the jungle to to his life in Paris (where he learns to drive a car) to his marriage to Celeste, his childhood sweetheart. In lending a musical element to the story, Poulenc relies on a number of pictorial devices as well as the kind of stylized forms in which he excelled: a nocturne, a grand march, a lullaby, a waltz, a schottische. Composer Jean Françaix, whose style was greatly in sympathy with Poulenc's own, made an orchestration of the work that is as well known as the original version. Another version, for chamber orchestra, has been made by British composer David Matthews. *—AMG*

Recommended:

- ○ **Prokofiev: Peter & the Wolf, etc.** / Lanchbery (cond.), Melbourne SO / 1997 / Naxos 554170

Sonata for 2 pianos (1952–1953)

While extensive, Francis Poulenc's catalogue of music for the piano consists largely of miniatures and character pieces, both singly and in sets. Poulenc's *Sonata for Piano Duo* is one of the composer's most ambitious and substantial works for the instrument; as such, it has emerged as one of the standards of the two-piano repertoire.

Though Poulenc had written a *Sonata for Piano Duet* (that is, for two players at one instrument) in 1918, it wasn't until late in his career that he began to produce works for two pianos. He dedicated the *Sonata for Piano Duo*, completed in 1953, to the piano duo of Gold and Fizdale, who had long championed the composer's *Concerto for Two Pianos* (1932). While the Sonata is a serious and demanding work for audiences and performers alike, Poulenc's essential qualities as a composer are evident throughout; at no time does his musical language lapse into arcana.

The contrast between bustling movement and extraordinary calm is one of the hallmarks of the Sonata. The work contains a number of allusions to church bells—not the clangorous peals of Mussorgsky's *Pictures at an Exhibition*, but evocations of a gentler sort, more like the suggestion of a village church. The first movement, marked Prologue, is assertive and passionate, almost Schumannesque. The central section provides a moment of quiet contrast, while a tolling effect in the coda brings the movement to its end. The Allegro Molto is a scherzo characterized by jaunty, agitated themes. The Trio starts dramatically, ultimately receding into ethereal quiet. The Andante Lyrico opens with a chorale that summons forth the sound of a carillon; this simple beginning builds with an ever-increasing weight. The sprightly, playful Epilogue rounds out the work with the kind of exuberant finish that is characteristic of Poulenc's multimovement works. The mood darkens as the movement pushes forward to a tragic climax; the gravity is dissipated, however, with a spirited burst at the conclusion. *—Eric Goldberg*

Recommended:

- ○ **Poulenc: Complete Chamber Music Vol. 3** / Tharaud, Chaplin / 2000 / Naxos 553613
- ○ **Rhapsody** / Mack, Mack / Arizona University 3076

CHAMBER MUSIC

Cello Sonata (1948)

Woodwind pieces dominate Poulenc's chamber music oeuvre, but the *Cello Sonata*, like the somewhat earlier *Violin Sonata*, is a substantial work finding the composer at the height of his powers, and his tongue planted less firmly in his cheek.

Despite a rather rude initial outburst from the piano, the sonata-form first movement, Allegro (tempo di marcia), leavens its fragmentary fanfare-like motifs with lyrical, good-humored material for the cello. One important theme is especially broad, romantic, and bittersweet, although much of the development section is given over to playful treatments of the melodies, with staccato piano accompaniment to cello pizzicato.

The slow second movement, Cavatine, is one of Poulenc's most tenderly songful creations. After a long introduction, the cello takes up a mournful, nostalgic theme, and with the piano subjects it to several elaborations, some intense, some hesitant, ending with a lullaby for lost souls.

Unusually for Poulenc, an extra movement separates the slow section from the finale. This Ballabile—a word suggesting a dance-like nature—is a playful intermezzo offering a nod to the music hall in its outer sections. A trace of wistfulness colors the still cheerful middle portion.

The Finale begins with a stern cello recitative over sour piano chords, pausing for an eerie passage of harmonics. The movement's main matter scampers quickly through several episodes of short-breathed cello phrases and rippling piano passagework, with time out midway and again just before the end for more tender if occasionally dizzy music. The movement concludes with the recitative with which it began. *—James Reel*

Recommended:

- ○ **In The Shadow of World War II** / Kalish, Krosnick / 1996 / Arabesque 6682

Clarinet Sonata (1962)

The premiere of Francis Poulenc's *Sonata for Clarinet and Piano* took place on April 10, 1963, with Benny Goodman on clarinet and Leonard Bernstein at the piano. But what was originally to be the premiere of a piece *in memoriam*— the work bears the dedication "to the memory of Arthur Honegger—turned out to be an *in memoriam* performance; Poulenc had died suddenly of a heart attack in January of that year, just shy of his 63rd birthday. "His death is a disaster for music and for personal friendship," lamented Jean Cocteau; "Poulenc had inherited Ravel's mantle," commented Ned Rorem, "and today, in leaving us, he has taken with him the best of what remained in musical France." Perhaps some of those in attendance at the premiere of the *Sonata for Clarinet and Piano* heard a musical self-eulogy, a documentary looking backwards through Poulenc's musical career. The religious devotion of his maturity finds expression in the first two movements, while in the third Poulenc returns to the devil-may-care style of his youth. One reviewer called the Sonata a "swan song . . . as delightful as ever."

This sonata is one of three Poulenc wrote for solo woodwind and piano. The other are one for flute from 1956, and one for oboe from 1962; Poulenc meant to work on a bassoon sonata next, but never got around to composing it before his untimely death. Though an autonomous work, the *Sonata for Clarinet and Piano* holds several formal and thematic traits in common with other works in the group. The *Flute Sonata* shares with the clarinet/piano work a structure that features a more restrained attitude in the first two movements, followed by a more playful finale. Also, as scholar and biographer Keith Daniel observes, certain thematic materials appear in all three works. The 32nd note figure that opens the *Flute Sonata* appears with some alteration in the first movement of the *Oboe Sonata*, and in rough inversion during the second movement of the clarinet piece; likewise, a motive consisting of a dotted note filled out by two shorter notes appears in multiple places in all three sonatas. Finally, Daniel notes the overall similarity of mood in the second movements of the Flute and Clarinet Sonatas.

The first movement of the *Clarinet Sonata* bears the somewhat enigmatic subtitle "Allegro Tristamente"; accordingly, the piece is always in motion, but proceeds with a sense of trepidation. After a brief fortissimo introduction consisting of angry spurts of figuration in the clarinet punctuated by piano chords, the piano quiets to a murmur. The clarinet's lines are built of a self-perpetuating series of arcs that leave a shape but not a tune in our ears. At one point the clarinet seems stuck in a motivic rut, sadly leaping up and down between octave B tones over a shifting harmonic background. As the movement ends, the lingering memory is a fuzzy one of melancholy gestures and moods.

The second movement, "Romanza," is both clearer in its melodic makeup and more cathartic, perhaps, in its emotional expression. The clarinet melody is simple and somber throughout, but is elaborately embroidered in a few places, as if losing composure. Two particularly poignant examples are the 64th note runs near the beginning, and the trembling half-step figure that appears at the beginning and end. The third movement, "Allegro con fuoco," energetically combines various nimble, articulate, and rhapsodic themes, bookended by a delightfully clownish tune—a mixture of serious and silly that well represents Poulenc's oeuvre as a whole. *—Jeremy Grimshaw*

Recommended:

- ○ **Poulenc: Chamber Music** / Rogé, Bourgue / 1989 / London 421581
- ○ **Poulenc: Chamber Music** / Levine, Schellenberger, Turkovic, Leister, Schulz, Hogner / 1989 / DG 427639

Flute Sonata (1956–1957)

The French affection for the flute is brilliantly demonstrated in Francis Poulenc's virtuosic *Sonata for Flute and Piano* (1956). Each of the work's three movements is fluent and graceful in different ways. The first movement, Allegro malincolico, sounds sweetly sad rather than melancholy. The second movement is a dreamy cantilena for flute in an indeterminate key, while the third, a chirpy Presto giocoso, puts Romantic ideas to rest with a skittish tune full of relaxed good humor. The whole is typical of the suave yet piquant style of Poulenc's instrumental music, and the honors (and difficulties!) are shared by both flutist and pianist. *—Roy Brewer*

Recommended:

- ○ **Poulenc: Chamber Music** / Rogé, Bourgue, Portal, Cazalet, Wallez, Gallois / 1989 / London 421581
- ○ **Poulenc: Complete Chamber Music** / Davies, Brown / 1999 / Hyperion 67255/6

Oboe Sonata (1962)

Francis Poulenc dedicated his *Sonata for oboe and piano*, the last of this three wind sonatas, to the memory of Sergey Prokofiev; Poulenc composed it one year before his own death in 1962. Given the first movement's title "Elegie," it sounds remarkably peaceful. The oboe begins with a four-note phrase starting on its high D, from which both instruments derive and unspool a winding, lyrical theme; the piano brings in a rising theme just as lyrical, before a third theme, in a double-dotted, tripping rhythm, enters. This provokes an unexpectedly thunderous outburst before the pastoral material of the opening returns. The mercurial emotional turn of the first movement comes back in the second-movement Scherzo, albeit reversed. Here, an A section full of pointed, racing rhythms, contrasted briefly with smoother phrases, brakes at the behest of a few piano chords for a far slower B section with a rhapsodic theme introduced and mostly developed by the piano. The third movement, titled "Deploration" and marked Tres calme, is the most obviously funerary of the three. After a piano introduction, the oboe takes a lamenting, chorale-like theme over a stolid piano pulse. The pulse quickens and the tripping rhythm from the first movement makes a re-appearance, but the brief moments of solace in the music always feel unstable and fleeting, an impression confirmed by a bleak ending with distant, ghostly piano chords supporting inward lyrical imprecations from the oboe. The oboe's final sustained note, with dissonant splashes by the piano underneath, seems to hang in the air for long after its sound dies. *—Andrew Lindemann Malone*

Recommended:

- ○ **Expressive Oboe** / Thomas, Cole / 1994 / Musica Viva 1070

Sextet for wind quintet & piano in C major (1932–1939; revised 1939)

The *Sextet* has earned a place in Poulenc's canon as one of his most popular works, and in the right interpretive hands the work exudes French wit as well as a degree of emotional depth. Poulenc wrote the three-movement work in 1932, scoring it for flute, clarinet, oboe, bassoon, horn, and piano; he revised it in 1939. The piece offers a mix of elegant, deceptively simple motives, rhythmic vitality, and playful harmonic turns in a virtuosic framework.

In three movements—Allegro Vivace, Divertissement, and Finale—the sextet lasts just over 15 minutes in performance. The first movement opens with a fast, toccata-like statement that is obviously indebted to Stravinsky's neo-Classicism. The second movement, marked Andantino, begins with an oboe melody that is passed off to other instruments and developed before returning to the oboe at the conclusion. This symmetry is matched by a slow-fast-slow classical structure. The prestissimo Finale is a modified rondo in which rhythmic and lyrical sections are present in equal measure, with an intense conclusion. The *Sextet* was first performed in Paris in December of 1940. *—Brian Wise*

Recommended:

- ○ **Poulenc** / Rogé, Bourgue, Portal, Cazalet, Wallez, Gallois / 1996 / London 448270
- ○ **Poulenc: Chamber Music** / Levine, Schellenberger, Turkovic, Leister, Schulz, Hogner, Wien-Berlin Ens. / 1989 / DG 427639

Suite française (d'après Claude Gervaise), for winds, percussion & harpsichord (1935)

Commissioned to provide incidental music for *La Reine Margot*, a play by Edouard Bourdet about Margaret of Valois, wife of the future King Henry IV of France, Poulenc raided a collection of dances from the characters' period, the sixteenth century. His source was Claude Gervaise's *Livre de danceries*; his techniques in manipulating the music, however, were entirely his own. Poulenc employed a harpsichord for period color (a harp or piano may substitute, to lesser effect), but otherwise he used a contemporary wind ensemble (pairs of oboes, bassoons, and trumpets and three trombones), plus modest percussion. Poulenc doused the old tunes in his characteristically impertinent, sour harmonies, creating something that sounded both antique and modern.

The concert suite falls into six movements. The first, "Bransle de Bourgogne," has the sense of an intrada with its snappy snare drum rolls punctuating phrases traded among the woodwinds, brass, and sometimes even harpsichord. The "Pavane" begins and ends as a brass chorale, the middle section appropriated by woodwinds. The "Petite marche militaire" is, as its title suggests, short and bellicose, but the piece is so fast that it's more of a fanfare than a march. The fourth movement falls into two sections. "Complainte" arrives as a mournful oboe solo given a spidery response from the harpsichord, with the full woodwind complement soon taking control of the melody. This is followed by an unusually stately and dignified "Bransle de Champagne." Fifth comes a "Sicilienne," another stately piece in which brass phrases are answered by the harpsichord, and once by the woodwinds. The concluding "Carillon" is a perky theme, in some ways an extension of the opening "Bransle de Bourgogne," played in moderate tempo and shifted back and forth from brass to woodwinds to harpsichord, the three instrumental elements only rarely overlapping. *—James Reel*

Recommended:

- ○ **Platinum Poulenc** / Wick (cond.), London Wind Orch. / 2002 / ASV 8515

Trio for oboe, bassoon & piano (1926)

During the 1920s Poulenc conscioiusly began to pursue a neo-Classical ideal, fashioning many of his works in the molds of Stravinsky and late Debussy. In his *Trio for piano, oboe and bassoon*—the composer's first true chamber work—he imitated the French Baroque style, with its emphasis on clarity, balance, simplicity and a generous dose of humor. In a letter to the critic Claude Rostand, Poulenc admitted that "I love my Trio because it sounds clear and it is well balanced."

The *Trio*, which is cast in a traditional three-movement form (Presto, Andante, and Rondo), is imbued with elegant symmetries throughout. As Poulenc acknowledged, the first movement rather self-consciously emulates a Haydn Allegro, while the Rondo draws from the Scherzo of Saint-Saëns' *Piano Concerto No. 2.* Yet a sly sense of humor is never far beneath the surface. Early in the first movement, the oboe and bassoon play a mocking variation on the military bugle call "Taps," as angular piano chords provide a jazzy foundation that suggests Duke Ellington. Later in the movement the oboe offers some lyric phrases while the piano retorts with more splashy, descending chordal figures. The Andante is Mozartean in character, while the Rondo is brisk and whimsical. If the piano dominates the *Trio*, Poulenc's love of wind sonorities is still present throughout, and the bassoon and oboe never become mere accompanying instruments. *—Brian Wise*

Recommended:

- ○ **Saint-Saëns & Poulenc** / Requejo, Thunemann / 1991 / Claves 509020
- ○ **Poulenc: Chamber Music** / Rogé, Bourgue, Portal, Cazalet, Wallez, Gallois / 1989 / London 421581

Violin Sonata (1942–1943; revised 1949)

Francis Poulenc's *Sonata for violin and piano* was composed during 1942 and 1943 while his country was at war and its dedication is to the memory of a victim of a then-recent foreign conflict: Federico Garcia Lorca, the poet, who was slain during the Spanish Civil War. In these circumstances, even this most delightful of composers acquired a harder edge, as displayed immediately in the Allegro con fuoco first movement with a dark, jagged opening theme on the violin and percussive support on the piano. This theme, reminiscent of Poulenc's friend and model Igor Stravinsky, dominates the movement, providing the basis for both the quieter, melancholic passages, as well as further eruptions of rage. Emotions become more extreme as the movement goes on before it closes on an unexpected major chord. Tentative, repeated chords in the piano open the second movement, an "Intermezzo tres lent et calme"; the violin first enters with a pizzicato accompaniment reminiscent of guitar-plucking, then takes a short, pregnant lyrical phrase. Soon, these elements build up into a rapturous melodic interlude, with the violin's phrasing often recalling Spanish song in the work's only obvious reference to its dedicatee. After the lyrical rapture has risen and fallen, the piano enters with angular, unsettled chords that lead into an astringently harmonized violin melody; the movement ends on a weird, unresolved glissando, leading into a Presto tragico third movement that brings back the fire of the first. This soon yields to happier melodies, which the violin initially fights with furious fiddling but eventually joins. After the rush leads each instrument to an exposed solo, however, their energy seems spent, the tempo slows to Strictement le double plus lent, and the mood becomes funereal; an odd coda appears to end on an inappropriate smirk, but undercuts that with one last angry outburst. *—Andrew Lindemann Malone*

Recommended:

- ○ **French Violin Sonatas** / Devoyon, Kang / 1991 / Naxos 550276
- ○ **French Violin Sonatas** / Midori, McDonald / 2002 / Sony 89699

CONCERTO

Concert champêtre, for harpsichord & orchestra (1927–1928)

Having already established himself as a musical rebel by the age of 18, Poulenc paid no homage to the Germanic tradition still prevalent in French music in his early years but instead crafted clever, unique works which remind some listeners of a sort of French Prokofiev. A mere ten years later, Poulenc, in response to a personal suggestion from the great harpsichordist Wanda Landowska, began composing a rustic concerto for harpsichord and orchestra. It turned out not only was this his first true work in the concerto form, it was, except for his early ballet *Les Biches*, his first large-scale orchestral work. Because Landowska performed on a specially made, modern, and more powerful harpsichord, the work sets soloist against orchestra on a grand scale. In fact, the orchestra is a large one with full brass and percussion sections and it is only Poulenc's skillful scoring which preserves the textural balance. Also—because the piece was created with the great Landowska in mind—it is difficult in the extreme. The result of all this is a fiery three-movement work which sandwiches turns of Baroque-like ornamentalism in between twentieth century riffs to marvelous effect. The work is in fact a delightful study in contrasts. Passages in major and minor modes alternate and the delicate texture of the harpsichord splashes across great, slashing brass chords and amid the thunder of percussion. Even the setting and inspiration for the piece are somewhat contradictory: A self proclaimed city dweller, Poulenc's idea of a rustic setting included mostly the outskirts and near environs of Paris, and the military flourishes and fanfares in the outer movements seem to be an allusion to a French army camp situated near Landowska's forest retreat. The first movement, a sprawling Allegro molto, opens with tootling in the woodwinds and a fanfare in the horns. The harpsichord provides a plaintive introduction and then launches into a jaunty main theme. During the course of this, it fends off thunder from the tympani and more fanfares and even some marching from the brass. Eventually the solo instrument once again gently reasserts itself, restates a minor variant of the main theme, this time at half speed, and after enduring yet another fanfare from the horns, repeats the theme in its original form and ends the movement. The Andante begins simply enough with a soft major melody from the strings and after a transitional passage from the harpsichord, this melody appears twice more with the harpsichord soloist acting only as accompanist. The solo instrument opens the finale by itself with a brisk march and maintains control throughout, stepping aside only to allow punctuation from the percussion and a few more brass fanfares. After the recapitulation, the harpsichord turns to a quiet coda and ends the piece, not with a crash but more like one turning out the light and leaving the room. While not among Poulenc's most mature works, the concerto is top-drawer and satisfying in every respect. *—Michael Morrison*

Recommended:

- ○ **Poulenc: Organ Concerto; Concert Champêtre; Suite française** / Casadesus (cond.), Chojnacka, National Orch. de Lille / 1999 / Naxos 554241
- ○ **Poulenc** / Brown (cond.), Malcolm, Academy of St. Martin-in-the-Fields / 1996 / London 448270

Concerto for organ, strings & timpani in G minor (1938)

In reference to his nearly completed Concerto for organ, strings, and timpani (1938), Poulenc wrote that "This is not the happy-go-lucky Poulenc who wrote the *Concerto for two pianos*, but a Poulenc en route to the cloister—a fifteenth century Poulenc, if you like." Though not explicitly religious, the concerto follows a new development in the composer's style that led to the composition of numerous sacred works and several secular works distinct in their sense of gravity and deliberation.

The concerto was commissioned by and dedicated to Princess Edmond de Polgnac. In essaying his first work for organ, Poulenc sought counsel from masters living and dead. Maurice Duruflé, who was the solost in the earliest performances, advised the composer on matters of the instrument's registration. Poulenc also studied the organ music of Buxtehude and Bach, whose influence is reflected in the work's neo-Baroque figuration and ornamentation and in its occasional harmonic anachronisms.

The concerto is structured as a single continuous movement with the character of a fantasia. It begins with a dense chord in the organ, followed by a graceful unaccompanied melody in dotted rhythms. The slightly askew sonority of the next chord bumps the melody from its previously diatonic path. A duet follows between the organ, mysterious in its high range, and foreboding timpani. The opening material returns with a different "wrong" chord, followed by a lushly harmonized string melody underpinned by timpani. The intensity increases with a low faint rumble in the timpani and organ pedal, which is suddenly punctuated with percussive exclamations.

The long-building tension finds release in the subesquent Allegro section, in which the strings and organ alternately take the foreground with a nimble melody that makes its way through an ever-changing harmonic context. A new figure enters, characterized by of a series of repeated ascending tetrachords that outline a triumphant major seventh chord. The Andante section begins abruptly with a plaintive organ solo that eventually evokes a rich, lyrical response from the strings. This conversational passage is followed by a more somber mood, evoked by worrisome melodies and an unyielding pulse. Poulenc once again builds dramatic tension by thickening the harmonies, bringing the music to a peak with a series of stout, cathartic chords in the organ.

A dreamy string interlude provides a transition to a brief Allegro section. A rhapsodic melody floats atop lucid, soothing harmonic progressions borne upon a gentle pulse. The organ emerges with ever-thickening harmonies to usher in the next section, a fast passage with thematic roots in the first Allegro. The organ introduction returns, followed by a reverent viola solo accompanied by delicately plucked strings. As the orchestra fades, the organ ends the concerto with a final emphatic proclamation. *—Jeremy Grimshaw*

Recommended:

- ○ **Saint-Saëns: Symphony 3; Poulenc: Organ Concerto** / Martinon (cond.), Alain, O.R.T.F. / 2001 / Apex 89244
- ○ **Poulenc** / Brown (cond.), Malcolm, Academy of St. Martin-in-the-Fields / 1996 / London 448270

Concerto for 2 pianos & orchestra in D minor (1932)

Poulenc composed this music in 1932, and played the first performance with Jacques Fevrier on September 5 during the Fifth International Music Festival in Venice, with Désire Defauw conducting the La Scala Orchestra from Milan. It is scored for double winds and brass plus piccolo, English horn, tuba, assorted drums, and reduced strings.

While Poulenc was studying with Koechlin, Serge Diaghilev commissioned him to write *Les biches* (colloquially "The Girls") for his ballets russes. Produced in 1924, this made Poulenc famous. He solidified his reputation in 1928 with the delectable *Concert champêtre* for harpsichord. The saucy-sentimental *Two-Piano Concerto* followed in 1932, commissioned by the Princesse Edmond de Polignac (herself a composer, but more famous as a Parisian hostess and patron of the arts). Songs apart, the *Two-Piano Concerto* has proved to be the composer's hardiest work, clearly influenced by Ravel's *G major Concerto*, which was premiered at Paris in January 1932—especially its instrumentation and "blues" passages (in their very French way). Each of the three movements has a slow central section, part-bittersweet, part-sentimental, amounting to ABA form in the first and second, but a rondo-component in the finale.

The opening Allegro ma non troppo has a sonata-form exposition and recapitulation along with bits of once-popular chansons (like croutons in salad) that complement the composer's own jaunty first and second subjects. The slow, sighing central section replaces a development group before Poulenc returns to the boulevards and boites.

The Larghetto pays homage to Mozart throughout, at one point to the slow movement of the *C major Piano Concerto*, K. 467. Piano I leads in effect a musette, as if on a toy piano. The middle section becomes more impassioned, building to a sonorous climax before calm is restored.

Returning to the mood of the first movement, the Allegro molto finale begins with percussive flourishes before it takes off like an Alfa-Romeo in a Grand prix through the avenues and allées of day-and-night Paris, past marching bands and music halls. There is, however, an *interlude lyrique et romantique* when the Alfa stops for a bedroom tryst, where perfume and perspiration mix with the smoke from Gauloises, after which the race resumes, even more racily. *—Roger Dettmer*

Recommended:

- ○ **Lyubov Bruk & Mark Taimanov** / Katz (cond.), Bruk, Taimanov, Leningrad PO / 1998 / Philips 456736
- ○ **Poulenc** / Hickox (cond.), Queffelec, Pommier, City of London Sinfonia / 1996 / Virgin 45028

BALLET

Aubade, choreographic concerto for piano & 18 instruments (1929)

Poulenc's *Aubade* is a curious if charming blend of piano concerto, ballet, and chamber salon piece. The work's unconventional makeup and manageable scale were in some part determined by its origins: It was commissioned by Poulenc's friends (and noted patrons and salon hosts) Marie-Laure and Charles de Noailles. A concert version was premiered December 1, 1929 in the couple's townhouse, followed by a full stage version on January 21, 1930.

Aubade is segmented into eight movements: Toccata, Récitatif, Rondeau, Presto, Récitatif, Andante, Allegro féroce, and Conclusion (Adagio). Given its hybrid structure, it is less a strict piano concerto than a modern cousin to Rameau's opéra-ballets in the galant style. That said, Poulenc fashioned his musical materials with great care and sophistication, blending themes which borrow from such sources as Stravinsky's *Le Sacre du printemps* and *Petrushka*, as well as Mozart's keyboard works. Poulenc also incorporates two melodies from earlier minor piano works—a

Sérénade from *Trois pièces* (1928) and the *Première nocturne* (1929)—which serve to unify the various strands of *Aubade*. The music alternates between Stravinskian percussiveness and Mozartean lyricism, at the same time incorporating several brass fanfares, gracious eighteenth century rondos and moments of Lisztian grandiosity.

Poulenc described *Aubade* as "amphibious," implying that the role of protagonist is more or less shared between the onstage woman dancer and the pianist in the orchestra pit. The ballet is a series of tableaux said to be inspired by paintings from the École de Fontainebleau. At the work's center is Diana, the mythological huntress, who finds herself "burning with a love that consumes her purity." Awaking at dawn in the forest of Fontainebleau, she is dressed by her woman friends. Condemned to chastity and despondent over an impure love, she dances a variation, clasping to her breast a bow her friends had given her. Suddenly, she throws the bow away and darts into the woods.

The choreographer for the Paris production was George Balanchine, who ignored Poulenc's plot for the dance, introducing a handsome, muscular dancer to portray Actéon in a *pas de deux* with Diana. The composer complained that *Aubade* was to be exclusively "a woman's ballet," but Balanchine ultimately had his way. The ballet was designed by Jean-Michel Frank, who redid the interior of the Noailles' home with fanciful, stylized sets. *—Brian Wise*

Recommended:

○ **Poulenc: Aubade; Les Biches; etc.** / Dutoit (cond.), Roge, National Orch. of France / 1998 / London 452937

Michael Praetorius

b. ca. 1571, Creuzburg an der Werra, Germany, **d.** Feb. 15, 1621, Wolfenbüttel, Germany

Composer: Choral, Chamber Music

Michael Praetorius was not only one of the most versatile and prolific German composers of the early seventeenth century (only the remarkable, slightly younger Heinrich Schütz is of comparable importance) but also the author of *Syntagma musicum*, a historically significant theoretical treatise on music. The exact year of Praetorius' birth remains unknown; February 15, 1571, is the generally accepted date, selected on the basis of two contemporary sources which claim that Praetorius died on his 50th birthday. After schooling at the University of Frankfurt an der Oder and at the Lateinschule at Zerbst, Anhalt, during his teens, Praetorius was appointed organist of St. Marien Church in Frankfurt in 1587. Praetorius later wrote that he left the position after three years, and, while it remains unclear what his activities during the early 1590s might have been, by 1595 he reappears in the historical record as organist for Duke Heinrich Julius of Brunswick-Wolfenbüttel. After 1604, Praetorius combined his duties as organist with the more demanding position of kapellmeister at the court, often traveling with the duke and his court musicians. The following several years were a very productive time during which most of the composer's published collections of music appeared.

After Duke Heinrich Julius' death in 1613 Praetorius, though officially still attached to the new Duke at Wolfenbüttel, was invited to serve for two years at the court of Elector John Georg of Saxony, and he maintained a close relationship with the Saxony court even after the appointment ended. Indeed, from 1615 on, Praetorius spent more time away from Wolfenbüttel than he did attending to his duties as kapellmeister, and by 1620 Praetorius' frequent absence and poor health had caused so drastic a decline in the quality of music at Wolfenbüttel that he was dismissed from the position. He died just one year later, leaving his sizeable fortune to charity.

Praetorius' father and grandfather were both Lutheran theologians, and the composer inherited their deep religious sentiment, composing over 1,000 sacred compositions based on Protestant hymns and the Latin liturgy used in the Lutheran service. By comparison, only one small collection of secular compositions—a group of instrumental dances—survives. While such early works as *Megalynodia Sionia*, a collection of parody madrigals based on the music of Orlando di Lassus, among others, fail to display a real individuality of musical style. By the time of the *Polyhymnia caduceatrix* of 1619, Praetorius had embraced a remarkably forward-looking musical aesthetic in which the highly ornamented Italian vocal style of the times, and a dense scoring employing as many as 16 voices are all expressive possibilities at his disposal. Praetorius' *Syntagma musicum*, while never completed (the final section, intended to provide instruction in actual composition, remains missing), is one of the most important systematic compilations of early seventeenth century musical thinking. *—Blair Johnston*

Overview of Works (ca. 1595–1620)

Michael Praetorius is known for his huge output and for the variety of the many works it contained. He was also an organist and one of the most important music theorists of his time. Praetorius based many of his compositions on Lutheran hymns and Lutheran Latin liturgical music. Among his most important efforts are the nine-part (mostly) vocal collection, *Musae Sioniae* (1605–12) and the *Polyhymnia caduceatrix* (1619), whose music does not derive from Lutheran liturgical or hymnal sources. Though most of his compositions are in the sacred realm, his most well-known work today is his only surviving secular instrumental effort, *Terpsichore*, a set of arrangements of over 300 French dance melodies.

The first volume of the *Musae Sioniae* appeared in 1605, the next four in 1607, with the ensuing pair following in 1609, and the last two coming in the period 1610–12. It should be noted that in the seventh book Praetorius included four pieces for organ. The hymns in the first four books are scored mostly in eight parts (in two choirs), though there are some 12-part hymns in No. 2, and nine- and 12-part hymns in No. 3. The Fifth Book features two- to eight-part items, while Books 6–8 contain mostly homophonically-scored hymns and the last volume is comprised of two- and three-part pieces. The individual hymns here derive from various Lutheran and other religious sources. The carol *Es ist ein Ros' entsprungen* is by the far most familiar item in the nine-book collection. Its mellow beauty and sunny spirit impart an of air sweet reverence. *Vom Himmel kommt*, from the First Book, has also achieved a measure of popularity.

Praetorius' style is in the early-Baroque German tradition, featuring lively and deft polyphonic activity in the multi-part hymns, though nowhere nearly as developed or complex as in Bach's music of a century later.

Collections in Praetorius' output similar in content and musical style to the *Musae Sioniae* are *Urania* and *Kleine und Grosse Litaney*, both appearing in 1613. The composer's early vocal efforts, like the *Motectae et psalmi* and *Megalynodia Sionia*, dating to 1602, are collections also based on pre-existing material (the latter having Italian sources). The aforementioned *Polyhymnia caduceatrix*, scored for one to 21 voices and basso continuo, is rather experimental in its vocal writing.

In the instrumental realm it is, of course, *Terpsichore* that stands as Praetorius' lone but substantial contribution. Containing many galliards, courantes, gavottes, and other French dances, this collection has appeared in excerpts on numerous recordings using various Baroque-era instruments. *—Robert Cummings*

Recommended:

○ **Christmas Music by Michael Praetorius** / Hill (cond.), Parley of Instruments, Westminster Cathedral Choir / 1986 / Hyperion 66200

○ **Praetorius: Magnificat** / Nevel (cond.), Huelgas Ens. / 1992 / Sony 48039

○ **Praetorius: Terpsichore; Motets** / Munrow (cond.), London Early Music Consort / 1996 / Virgin 61289

CHORAL

Es ist ein Ros entsprungen (Lo, How A Rose E'er Blooming) (before 1609)

In spite of Martin Luther's desire to limit the role and worship of The Virgin Mary after the Reformation, a number of Marian Lieder, or hymns, continued to find their way into the Lutheran church, often with little or no alteration. The most famous of these was *Es ist ein Ros' entsprungen* (most popularly translated as "Lo, how a Rose e'er blooming"), which Michael Praetorius adapted and set in *Book VI* of his *Musae Sioniae*, from 1609.

Musae Sioniae (The Muses of Zion) was Praetorius' first published work, a massive undertaking of nine volumes incorporating more than 1,200 songs (composed between 1605 and 1610). *Book VI* consists of a cappella, four-voice settings of hymns and psalms, or cantionale, for feast days. *Es ist ein Ros' entsprungen*, for the Christmas season, was curiously only set this once; in general, it was Praetorius' tendency to set other melodies half a dozen times.

The tune and text were likely originally written between 10 and 30 years before Praetorius made his adaptation. His table of contents for the sixth volume does acknowledge the hymn tune's "Catholic" origin. The earliest version of the text dates from 1582 and contains 19 verses. Praetorius' setting (in F major) is, in contrast, a marvel of simplicity. Just two verses of this seven-line hymn are included, and the composer's four-part writing is restrained. The result is an AABA phrase structure: the A, a musical period with two lines of text each; the B, a phrase half the length.

The first half of each A phrase is serenely and strictly homophonic ("Es ist ein Ros' entsprungen"); the second phrase, due to an irregular stress in the soprano line, is full of bittersweet suspensions ("aus einer Wurzel zart"). The identical repeat yields to the brief contrast of the B phrase, in which the contrary motion of soprano and bass results in closely spaced voices cadencing on the dominant. The return of the A phrase restores the open voicings, but with different harmonies, especially the colorful cadence on D major on the word "winter." Practically hidden within a larger volume of a huge work, this tranquilly simple hymn has enjoyed almost constant popularity since its publication; even in a popular twentieth century setting of *Es ist ein Ros' entsprungen*, Hugo Distler pays homage to his Lutheran predecessor Praetorius. *—Thomas Oram*

Recommended:

○ **A Renaissance Christmas** / Cohen (cond.), Boston Camerata / Elektra 79134

○ **Sing We Christmas** / Jennings (cond.), Chanticleer / 1995 / Teldec 94563

In Dulci Jubilo, for chorus & ensemble (before 1619)

Michael Praetorius' *In dulci jubilo* is a gloriously expansive amalgam of sound and text. Composed near the end of Praetorius' life as part of his *Polyhymnia Caduceatrix et Panegyrica* (Polychoral Hymns of Peace and Festivals) of 1619, this setting of the well-known tune *In dulci jubilo* was actually his 11th, and most ornate. Praetorius sets the stanzas of this thirteenth century macaronic hymn (written in both Latin and German) utilizing a highly flexible ensemble of three to five choruses and brass ensemble, continuo (organ), and tympani.

Twelve, 16, or 20 voices are possible: one or two SATB choruses, an ATBB chorus, and a SATB chorus of soloists that may be doubled at the octave. A brass chorus adds to the available color palette. In this work, indeed, throughout the *Polyhymnia*, Praetorius made excellent use of his resources to create aural contrasts. Solo chorus phrases are answered by the power of the tutti forces, as at the opening of the piece. Various solo choruses pass the melody from one to another, making use of spatial effects, heard, for example, at the beginning of the second verse. Polyphony and homophony, voices and instruments, all vie for superiority in a vast collage of sound.

The three verses are all stated in the first half of the piece. After the dizzyingly fast presto opening with an introductory pedal tone in the continuo, the first verse develops comparatively simply, its extended cadence ("Alpha es et o," "You are alpha and omega") the only hint of the extension and repetition to come. The second verse, a leisurely lento, plays the various choruses against each other, returning to the fast tempo for the cadence. The third verse develops similarly, beginning slowly and quietly before accelerating. Yet like the first verse, the cadence is extended. The tempo returns to lento as the last line of the verse, "Eya waren wir da" (We will praise him there), circulates slowly between choruses.

The second half of the work (labeled as such by Praetorius himself) consists of a repeat of the third verse. Praetorius again uses the contrasts of tempo and ensemble, and other specific techniques from the first half: the pedal tone on "und die Schellen klingen" (and the bells ring). The final line ("Eya waren wir da") receives even more extensive treatment than the first time, as it passes not only between choruses, but groups of choruses. Then this homophonic treatment dissolves into a breathlessly polyphonic setting that alternately speeds (presto) and crawls (lento) along. Praetorius pulls everything back together for a great cadence, after which the first half may be repeated.

Praetorius' *In dulci jubilo* is remarkable for its composer's use of contrasting sound, virtuosic singing, and appropriate instrumental writing. As a polychoral work it compares well with anything by his contemporary Schütz or even the Gabrielis of Venice. —*Thomas Oram*

Recommended:

- ○ **A Rose of Swych Virtu** / Musica Antigua de Albuquerque / 1991 / Dorian 80104
- ○ **Ther is no Rose** / various / 1997 / Virgin 45286
- ○ **Praetorius: Christmas Motets; Chorale Concertos** / Raml (cond.), Hassler-Consort / MDG 6140660

CHAMBER MUSIC

Terpsichore Dances (1612)

Michael Praetorius is one of the major figures of German music during the early Baroque period. An organist and prolific composer of Lutheran church music, he was also an influential theorist whose major work in the field, *Syntagma musicum* (Treatise of Music) appeared in three parts between 1614 and 1618. In this work, Praetorius revealed his intention of publishing eight volumes of secular music to complement his huge sacred publication, the nine volume *Musae Sionae* (1607–1610), but he produced only one volume, *Terpsichore* (1612). This volume contains 312 short French and Italian instrumental and vocal dances in four, five, or six parts, with no specific instrumentation. Selections produced today therefore generally feature a wide number of the instruments of the period, including bowed strings of the violin and viol family, plucked string instruments, such as lutes and harp, wind instruments, including recorders, crumhorns, and sackbuts, and a variety of percussion instruments. Many of the pieces included are anonymous, although composers such as Vecchi and Certon are represented. In particular, Praetorius was much indebted to the music of Pierre-Francisque Caroubel, a French composer of Italian origin who was responsible for 78 of the five-part arrangements. Among the major dance forms included are courantes (162), voltes (48), bransles (21), gaillardes (23), and ballets (37), in addition to which smaller numbers of pavanes, canaries, and bourees make up the total. A remarkable work of musical scholarship, *Terpsichore* represents one of the major Baroque collections of French dances. —*Brian Robins*

Recommended:

- ○ **Ancient Dances And Ballets** / Mendoze (dir.), Musica Antiqua / 1994 / Disques Pierre Verany 730006
- ○ **Praetorius: Terpsichore; Motets** / Munrow (cond.), London Early Music Consort / 1996 / Virgin 61289

Prague Chamber Orchestra

f. 1951, Prague, Czechoslovakia

Ensemble

The Prague Chamber Orchestra is the premier chamber ensemble in the Czech Republic. As is traditional in chamber orchestras, the ensemble performs without a conductor, and is generally lead by the concertmaster. Considerably larger than most chamber orchestras, the Prague Chamber Orchestra employs 36 players. It presents a series of subscription concerts each year in the Dvořák Hall of the House of Artists, which is also the home of the Czech Philharmonic Orchestra. The ensemble tours widely at home and abroad, and participates in many music festivals such as the Prague Spring Festival and the Bratislava Music Festival. The orchestra's repertoire focuses on Classical-era works by Haydn, Mozart and Beethoven but also extends to some early Romantic pieces, and a substantial number of contemporary compositions. Most of its concerts include at least one work by a Czech composer. Many new works have been composed for or dedicated to the Prague Chamber Orchestra, and a number of these have had their premier performances with the ensemble. Known for its sweet and lyrical tonal quality, the Prague Chamber Orchestra is one of the most highly regarded chamber ensembles in Europe.

Established in 1951, the Prague Chamber Orchestra had its beginnings in the Czechoslovak Radio Symphony Orchestra when a chamber group was formed from the Symphony's members to record works that did not require the full orchestra. The ensemble's original repertoire was taken primarily from the Baroque and early Classical periods with an emphasis on the old Czech masters such as Jan Dusek, Johann Stamitz, Anton Reicha, and the masters of Citoliby. The orchestra made its first recording in the year it was founded, and has continued to record extensively throughout its history.

As the orchestra's popularity grew and its public concerts began to overshadow its recording and broadcasting duties, the ensemble gradually separated from its parent organization. In 1955, the group gained the sponsorship of the National Museum and was allowed to use the museum's archive of musical scores. By 1964, administration of the orchestra was placed in the hands of the government Ministry of Culture. The orchestra began its work with young artists and students when it came under the management of the Music Studio of the Czech Music Fund in 1967. Instructive concerts were introduced and many gifted young soloists and composers have had the opportunity to work with this eminent chamber orchestra since the early 1970s. An 11-member string ensemble under the leadership of concertmaster Oldrich Vlcek, was established from within the Prague Chamber Orchestra in 1976. The Virtuosi di Praga, as it is named, tours and performs separately from the full ensemble, and sometimes acts as a virtuoso ensemble when needed for concerto works.

Known for its sensitive interpretations of works by Czech composers from the Baroque to the Contemporary, the Prague Chamber Orchestra is truly worthy of its reputation as one of the finest chamber ensembles in Europe. —*Corie Stanton Root*

Recommended:

- ○ **Mozart: Haffner Serenade; Serenata Notturna** / Mackerras (cond.), Prague CO / 1988 / Telarc 80161
- ○ **Martinů: Serenades** / Vlcek (cond.), Prague CO / 2002 / Supraphon 3643
- ○ **Benda: Sinfonias 7–12** / Benda (cond.), Prague CO / 1995 / Naxos 553409
- ○ **Dvořák: Slavonic Dances** / Belohlavek (cond.), Prague CO / 1998 / Multisonic 310451
- ○ **Mozart: Symphonies 40 & 41** / Mackerras (cond.), Prague CO / 1986 / Telarc 80139
- ○ **Mozart: Symphonies 36 & 38** / Mackerras (cond.), Prague CO / 1987 / Telarc 80148

Christoph Prégardien

b. Jan. 18, 1956, Limburg, Germany

Tenor

Tenor Christoph Prégardien began his musical education at the Limburg Cathedral Choir School. He went on to study at the Frankfurt Musikhochschule with Martin Gründeler, and later with Carla Castellani in Milan, Karlheinz Jarius in Frankfurt, and Alois Treml in Stuttgart.

Prégardien has built up a major reputation as a concert artist, performing the oratorios and Passions of the Baroque, Classical, and Romantic periods. His repertoire also encompasses the works of seventeenth century composers Monteverdi, Schütz, and Purcell, and twentieth century composers Britten, Stravinsky, Killmayer, and Rihm. Among the conductors he has performed and recorded with are Brueggen, Gardiner, Harnoncourt, Herreweghe, Hogwood, Jacobs, Koopman, Kuijken, Leonhardt, and Rilling.

As an operatic tenor, he has given performances in many major venues, among them London, Amsterdam, Frankfurt, Montpellier, and Tokyo. His roles have included such characters as Monterverdi's Ulisse, Mozart's Tamino and Don Ottavio, and Rossini's Count Almaviva.

His special love is lieder, which he studied at the Frankfurt Musikhochschule in classes with Hartmut Höll. After the great success of his first lieder recordings he embarked on a major recording career. His outstanding achievements as lieder singer have been acknowledged by numerous awards, such as the Preis der deutschen Schallplattenkritik, Edison Award, Diapason D'or de l'année and the Cannes Classical Award, among others.

Prégardien and Andreas Staier have performed together internationally since 1991, and in 1997 they signed an exclusive contract with Teldec. Their début CD for the label, Schubert's *Winterreise*, won numerous awards including the Caecilia Prize, the Edison Award, a Diapason d'Or and a Choc du Monde de la Musique, as well as being chosen for the German Record Critics' Quarterly List. His other favorite piano partner is Michael Gees. Other releases by Prégardien have included a CD of songs by Beethoven and his contemporaries Nikolaus von Krufft and Franz Lachner, and Brahms' *Die schöne Magelone*. *—AMG*

Recommended:

- ○ **Schumann: Liederkreis; Kerner-lieder** / Prégardien, Gees / 2001 / RCA 73235
- ○ **Songs of Love and Death** / Pregardien, Hoppstock / Signum 9500
- ○ **Follow Goethe** / Pregardien, Gees / CPO 999685
- ○ **Loewe: Lieder & Balladen Vol. 9** / Pregardien, Garben / CPO 999417

Simon Preston

b. Aug. 4, 1938, Bournemouth, England
Organist, Conductor

Preston studied organ with C.H. Trevor at the Royal Academy of Music from 1956 to 1958. He later became an organ scholar at King's College Cambridge. His debut was at Festival Hall in 1962 in Janáček's *Glagolitic Mass*. From 1962–67, Preston was sub-organist at Westminster Abbey, then proceeded to initiate his solo concert career. At this same time he began building his reputation as a harpsichordist. In 1970, Preston was named organist and lecturer at Christ Church, Oxford, and since 1981 has been organist of Westminster Abbey.

Preston is known not only for his impeccable technique, but also for his imaginative use of color. This latter quality has made him a leading exponent of the music of Messiaen and Liszt. His repertory encompasses the entire literature from the Baroque on, and his recording of the Handel concertos is highly esteemed. *—Steven Coburn*

Recommended:

- ○ **Handel: Organ Concertos I** / Menuhin (cond.), Preston, Tilney, Aveling, Menuhin Festival Orch. / 1998 / EMI 72676
- ○ **Bach: Orgelbüchlein** / Preston / DG 431816
- ○ **Bach: Schübler Chorales; Passacaglia & Fugue** / Preston / 1992 / DG 435381
- ○ **Palestrina: Missa Papae Marcelli; Allegri: Miserere** / Preston (cond.), Westminster Abbey Choir / Archiv 415517

Georges Prêtre

b. Aug. 14, 1924, Waziers, France
Conductor

Georges Prêtre is one of the leading conductors of the last half of the twentieth century, especially known for operatic conducting and performances of French music.

He studied trumpet as a boy, graduating from the Douai Conservatory. Nazi occupation of Paris did not substantially interfere with the teaching activities of the famous Paris Conservatory, where Prêtre continued his musical studies. He took First Prize in trumpet in 1944 and studied harmony with Henri Challan and Maurice Duruflé. He began studying conducting with André Cluytens, Pierre Dervaux, and Richard Blareau. His conducting debut was in operetta, a fact that eluded biographers since he used the assumed name of Georges Dherain.

His official conducting debut was at the Marseilles Opera in 1946, in Lalo's *Le Roi d'Ys*. He spent a decade primarily in provincial French opera houses: Marseilles (1946–48), Lille (1948), Casablanca (1949–51) and Toulouse (1951–55).

He was appointed music director of the Opéra-Comique in Paris in 1956, debuting with Richard Strauss' *Capriccio* and conducting a wide variety of repertory there. He made his American conducting debut at the Chicago Lyric Opera in 1958. By 1960, he had become well-known and was selected by composer Francis Poulenc, who selected Prêtre to conduct the premiere of *Le voix humaine* (1959) and was highly esteemed for his performances of Poulenc's full length opera *Dialogues de Carmelites*. He also led the premiere of the *Sept répons des ténèbres* (1963).

In 1959, he joined the staff of the Paris Opéra, becoming music director in 1966. He debuted at the Royal Opera House, Covent Garden (1961), the Metropolitan Opera in New York (1965), and La Scala (1965). During this period he became a conductor often requested by opera super-star Maria Callas. He frequently returned to the Met and La Scala, especially known for his French repertory.

His concert conducting career also advanced during this period. Over the years he conducted most of the important orchestras of Europe and America, and in 1962 was appointed deputy director of the Royal Philharmonic Orchestra. In 1971, the Paris Opera's periodic political problems erupted into a huge backstage dispute that closed the Opéra for several months, during which Prêtre left the company.

Since that painful experience, Prêtre most frequently has worked outside of France. He became principal guest conductor of the Vienna Symphony Orchestra in 1986, holding that post through 1991, when he was named one of its honorary conductors for life. In 1995, he became artistic director and principal conductor of the Stuttgart Radio Symphony Orchestra. Among his world premieres are Symphony No. 4 by Marcel Landowski (1988) and *Concerto for 15 Soloists and Orchestra* by Françaix (1990).

In 1999, he conducted a major series of concerts in Paris in honor of the 100th Anniversary of Poulenc's birth. *—Joseph Stevenson*

Recommended:

- ○ **Massenet: Werther** / Prêtre (cond.), Los Angeles, Gedda, Benoit, Mesplé, Maitrise de l'O.R.T.F., Paris Orch. / 2003 / EMI 62630
- ○ **Poulenc: Gloria; Stabat Mater** / Prêtre (cond.), Hendricks, French Radio Choir, National Orch. of France / EMI 749851
- ○ **French Orchestral Favorites** / Prêtre (cond.), Pierlot, Boussinot, Gantiez, France, National Orch. of France / 1999 / Angel 73427
- ○ **Bizet: Pearl Fishers** / Prêtre (cond.), Cotrubas, Soyer, Vanzo, Sarabia, Orch. & Chorus of the Paris Opera / EMI 4721

André Previn

b. Apr. 6, 1929, Berlin, Germany
Conductor

Successful as pianist, composer, and especially as conductor, André Previn has frequently bridged the gap between popular and so-called "serious" music, and in doing so broadened the horizons of both.

His father was an accomplished pianist (though a lawyer by profession) and determined that his son would follow in his musical footsteps. The talented young André received instruction on the piano at the Berlin Hochschule, and also absorbed music in a less formal environment during the many private recitals given in the Previn home. In the mid-1930s the Jewish family fled to France where André continued as a scholarship student at the Paris Conservatoire. In 1939, the Previn family relocated to southern California.

Life was difficult for the family (all their possessions had been left behind in Europe, and Previn's father was qualified only in German law), and though barely ten years old, André supplemented the family income by accompanying films at movie houses and playing in jazz clubs. At 14 he started working at MGM (Charles Previn, André's great uncle, was head of music at Universal Studios), orchestrating and arranging film music, and slowly saved enough money to study composition with Castelnuovo-Tedesco. At 18 André was asked to compose his own full-length film score (*The Sun Comes Up*, 1949), which resulted in his first experience on the podium in front of a real orchestra—Previn quickly realized that his future lay in conducting, though he understood the gulf between film music and serious conducting to be a wide one indeed.

Previn, who had taken U.S. citizenship in 1943, serving in San Francisco during the Korean War, where he had the opportunity to study conducting with Pierre Monteux. Following discharge from the army, Previn left MGM, but continued to compose, conduct, and arrange film music throughout the 1950s. He also recorded and released a series of best-selling jazz albums (something he would continue to do sporadically throughout the decades).

In 1963, having won four Academy Awards in as many years, Previn found the courage to abandon Hollywood and pursue his dream of becoming a respected conductor. His professional debut occurred that same year with the Saint Louis Symphony Orchestra, and he spent the next several years traveling around the country conducting various little-known orchestras in an effort to gain exposure and develop his own skill on the podium. His first big break occurred in 1967 when he was asked to succeed Sir John Barbirolli as music director of the Houston Symphony. When offered the job of principal conductor for the London Symphony Orchestra in 1968, Previn left Houston. During his 11 years with the orchestra (1969–79) a series of BBC television productions—entitled *André Previn's Music Hour*—made the LSO (and Previn) a household name around the world. Other conducting appointments have included the Pittsburgh Symphony, from 1977 to 1985; the Royal Philharmonic Orchestra in the 1985 and 1986 seasons; and, from 1987 on, the Los Angeles Philharmonic Orchestra. In 1993 he was named conductor laureate of the London Symphony Orchestra, and he continues to make frequent appearances around the globe as a guest conductor.

Previn readily admits that he is not driven to compose, but only does so on occasion, and then only on specific request. Nevertheless he has composed a generous quantity of concert music, including a piano concerto for Vladimir Ashkenazy and cello sonata at the request of Yo-Yo Ma. His musical play, *Every Good Boy Deserves Favour*, was produced in London in 1978. The year 1998 saw the release of his full-length opera, *A Streetcar Named Desire*. *—Blair Johnston*

Recommended:

- ○ **Korngold: Sea Hawk & Other Film Music** / Previn (cond.), London SO / DG 471347

- ○ **Prokofiev: Romeo & Juliet** / Previn (cond.), London SO / 1995 / EMI 68607
- ○ **Gershwin Album** / Previn (cond.), London SO / 1998 / EMI 66943
- ○ **Vaughan Williams: Symphony 2; Lark Ascending** / Previn (cond.), Griffiths, Royal PO / 1987 / Telarc 80138
- ○ **Vaughan Williams: Symphonies** / Previn (cond.), Bennett, Halstead, Georgiadis, Harper, London SO & Chorus / 2003 / RCA 55708
- ○ **Prokofiev: Cinderella; Symphony 1** / Previn (cond.), London SO / 1995 / EMI 68604

Hermann Prey

b. Jul. 11, 1929, Berlin, Germany, **d.** Jul. 23, 1998, Krailling vor München, Germany

Baritone

Growing up during the regime of the the National Socialist Party, Hermann Prey was scheduled to be drafted at the age of 15 when the end of World War II brought peace and a chance for him to study voice with Gunther Baum and Jaro Prohaska at the Hochschule fur Musik in Berlin. He sang his first lieder recital in 1952 and the following year he made his operatic debut as Monuccio in d'Albert's *Tiefland* at Wiesbaden. He was then engaged by the Hamburg State Opera (1953–60) where besides singing most of the standard baritone roles he was also highly acclaimed for his work in modern operas by Liebermann, Dallapiccola, and Henze. During the next several years, Prey sang at the Vienna State Opera, Deutsche Oper Berlin, and at Cologne. His Bayreuth debut came in 1956 as Wolfram in *Tannhäuser.* After 1959, Munich became his operatic home although he continued to sing at all of the important opera houses in the world including London, New York, Paris, Milan, Chicago, San Francisco, and Amsterdam. He was also a regular visitor to the festivals at Salzburg and Edinburgh. He was internationally recognized for his Mozart interpretations including Don Giovanni, Count Almaviva, Guglielmo, and Papageno, but achieved fame with his Figaro in *Barbiere di Siviglia,* the elder Germont in *La Traviata,* the Barber in *Die Schweigsame Frau* by Richard Strauss, Harlekin in *Ariadne auf Naxos* and Eisenstein in *Die Fledermaus* by Johann Strauss. He also sang in many contemporary operas including *Pallas Athene* by Krenek and *Prinz von Homburg* by Henze. Late in his career, he was a very successful Beckmesser in *Die Meistersinger.*

For all of his fame as an opera star, to many musicians, Hermann Prey is best remembered for his recitals. He gave his first American recital in 1956 and was a regular visitor until the end of his career. He was also a great favorite in Japan. He was especially well known for his interpretations of the songs of Schubert, but he was equally at home with the requirements of many other German and Austrian composers. He was less successful in the few times he moved outside of the German repertoire. On the concert stage, Prey was well known for his singing of the Bach *Passions* and more especially the Brahms *Deutsches Requiem.*

Many listeners compare Prey with Dietrich Fischer-Dieskau as a song interpreter, yet their approach to music making was quite different. Fischer-Dieskau gives each word and phrase an individual importance whereas Prey allowed the whole composition to unfold as an entity. Both approaches are valid and have their adherents. Hermann Prey's voice was a lyric baritone with great warmth and he had complete control of all dynamic variations. He was able to convey a sense of the comic elements of a song without losing the musical sense of the entire piece. He recorded a multivolume series for Philips to trace the history of German lieder from the Minnesingers to songs by Reutter and Blacher. In 1982, he began teaching at the Musikhochschule Hamburg in order to pass along what he learned about music interpretation. He was also one of the founders of a Schubert Festival in Austria. His son Florian has also made a career as a baritone singing some of the same roles for which his father was most famous. Hermann Prey will always be remembered for the fine musicianship and the beauty of his voice. *—Richard LeSueur*

Recommended:

- ○ **Hermann Prey** / Prey, etc. / 2000 / Decca 467901
- ○ **Loewe: Lieder & Balladen** / Prey, Endres / Capriccio 10759
- ○ **Mozart: Le Nozze Di Figaro** / Bohm (cond.), Fischer-Dieskau, Troyanos, Janowitz, Mathis, Prey, Berlin State Opera Orch. & Chorus / DG 449728
- ○ **Die Fledermaus** / Kleiber (cond.), Popp, Prey, Varady, Kollo, Weikl, Kusche, Bavarian State Orch. & Chorus / 1999 / DG 457765

Leontyne Price

b. Feb. 10, 1927, Laurel, MS

Soprano

The daughter of a carpenter and a midwife, African-American soprano Leontyne Price (née Mary Violet) studied piano and singing with the assistance of a local family that recognized her innate talents. After earning her degree from College of Education and Industrial Arts at Wilberforce, Ohio (where she studied with Catherine Van Buren), Price was awarded a scholarship to attend the Juilliard School of Music where she continued vocal training with Florence Page Kimball. Upon hearing her there, Virgil Thomson invited her to sing Saint Cecilia in the 1952 revival of his *Four Saints in Three Acts.* She then toured the United States and Europe as Bess in Gershwin's *Porgy and Bess* (1952–55); on this tour she met and married bass-baritone William Warfield who was singing the role of Porgy.

In October 1953, Price sang the premiere of Samuel Barber's *Hermit Songs* at the Library of Congress in Washington, D.C., and she gave her first New York recital in November 1954; in December of the same year she sang Barber's *Prayers of Kierkegaard* with the Boston Symphony Orchestra. Her appearances in *Tosca, Die Zauberflöte, Dialogues des Carmelites,* and *Don Giovanni* on television brought her to wide attention for both her outstanding singing, and for being the first African American leading soprano of note.

In the following seasons, she made her debuts at San Francisco, Chicago, Vienna, London, and Milan. This culminated in her first appearance at the Metropolitan Opera House as Leonore in *Il trovatore,* an evening that garnered a front page review in the *New York Times.* The Metropolitan would soon become her favored opera house; she sang most of her wide repertoire there, including *Aida, Tosca, Madama Butterfly,* Leonore in *La Forza del Destino, Ernani,* Amelia in *Un ballo in maschera,* Donna Anna (*Don Giovanni*), Pamina (*Die Zauberflöte*), Fiorgiligi (*Così*), Ariadne (*Ariadne auf Naxos*), and Tatiana in *Eugene Onegin.* She sang her last operatic performance there in 1985 as Aida.

Price was known as much for her concert and recital appearances as for those in opera. Besides performances of common repertory works, such as Beethoven's *Missa Solemnis* and the Verdi *Requiem,* she also undertook Honegger's rather obscure *Jeanne d'Arc* (with the New York Philharmonic) and Bruckner's *Te Deum* (at Salzburg). Her solo concerts often featured lesser-known arias and excerpts, including the "Awakening of Helen" from Strauss' *Egyptian Helen,* selections from Barber's *Anthony and Cleopatra* and *The Songs of the Rose of Sharon* by John La Montaine.

She gave annual recitals throughout North America and was also heard regularly in Europe, being a special favorite at the Salzburg Festival. Her recital repertoire was extensive, ranging from the songs of Poulenc, Hahn, and Marx, to traditional spirituals; her final encore was often "This little light of mine"—one of her mother's favorite pieces.

Leontyne Price's voice was a spinto soprano of great beauty. She had a wonderful feeling for the sweep of the long phrases of Verdi and her technique allowed her to encompass all of the difficulties of Donna Anna (*Don Giovanni*) and Elvira (*Ernani*). Her lower register had a quality often described as "dusky" which many listeners found quite sensual. Most of her important operatic roles were recorded by RCA, but only a small fraction of her recital repertoire found its way onto disc. Leontyne Price will always be remembered as one of the greatest Verdi sopranos of the twentieth century. *—Richard LeSueur*

Recommended:

- ○ **Leontyne Price** / Price, etc. / 2001 / Decca 467913
- ○ **Puccini: Madama Butterfly** / Leinsdorf (cond.), Price, Palma, Tucker, Elias, RCA Italiana Opera Chorus & Orch. / 1963 / BMG 68884
- ○ **Essential Leontyne Price** / Price, etc. / 1997 / BMG 68157
- ○ **Leontyne Price Sings Barber** / Schippers (cond.), Price, Barber, New Philharmonia / 1994 / BMG 61983
- ○ **Bizet: Carmen** / Karajan (cond.), Freni, Corelli, Price, Merrill, Vienna PO / 1998 / RCA 39495
- ○ **Verdi: Aida** / Leinsdorf (cond.), Alldis, Price, Domingo, Milnes, London SO / 1999 / RCA 39498

Margaret Price

b. Apr. 13, 1941, Blackwood, near Tredegar, England

Soprano

Soprano Margaret Price was one of the great international singers of the generation that came to the fore in the 1960s. She was classified as a lyric soprano, but also possessed a firm and brilliant coloratura.

Margaret Berenice Price began singing lessons when she was nine, in Wales. At the age of 15 she won the Charles Kennedy Scott scholarship to the Trinity School of Music in London, where she studied with Scott for four years.

After graduation, she joined the Ambrosian Singers. She refused to enter competitions. While she was singing with the Ambrosian, her father wrote letters to opera companies to introduce her.

She made her operatic debut as Cherubino in Mozart's *Marriage of Figaro* in 1962 with the Welsh National Opera. The next year, she was asked at the last minute to replace the indisposed Teresa Berganza in that same role. After that she formed an artistic partnership with James Lockhart, a conductor and pianist who became a vocal coach and accompanist and helped her in finding and judging repertory and formed a major recital team that was well known for its wide variety both as to language and style. She was particularly known for her interpretation of Schoenberg's *Das Buch der hängenden Gärten.*

In 1967, she joined the English National Opera Group where she debuted in Mozart's short divertimento *The Impresario,* as Tytania in Britten's *A Midsummer*

Night's Dream, and Galatea in *Acis and Galatea*. In the summer of 1968, she debuted at the Glyndebourne Festival Opera as Constanze in Mozart's *Die Entführung aus dem Serail*, which was widely acclaimed. Over the years, she has gone on to sing all of Mozart's major soprano roles at the major houses and festivals around the world. She debuted at San Francisco in 1969 as Pamina in *Die Zauberflöte*, and her debut in Chicago was as Fiordiligi in *Così fan tutte* in 1972.

She also chose Mozart's *Don Giovanni* for her German debut (1971 in Cologne). In 1973, she debuted at the Opéra de Paris, which she joined for that company's historic tour of the United States in 1976, where she sang Desdemona in Verdi's *Falstaff*. Typically for the time, the Metropolitan Opera was slow to secure her services. When she finally debuted there, in 1985, it was a triumphant portrayal of the same role. She says, by the way, that singing Mozart is all "sweat and labor" while Verdi, by comparison, is a "piece of cake."

Despite her successful operatic career, she says that her childhood love was art song and that she always wanted to sing lieder. Accordingly she sang in recital in all the world's major venues. A small sample of her recorded repertory includes songs of Franz Liszt with Cyprien Katsaris, songs of Richard Strauss with Wolfgang Sawallisch as pianist, and with Graham Johnson in songs of Schubert, Robert Schumann, Mendelssohn, and Brahms on the Hyperion label.

She has often appeared on radio and television (including a memorable portrayal of Tchaikovsky's Tatyana and Salud in Falla's *La Vida Breve*). He active concert life is represented on disc by recordings of Ravel's *Shéherazade* with Claudio Abbado, and Elgar's *The Kingdom* under Sir Adrian Boult.

Margaret Price was named a *Bayerischen Kammersängerin*, received a CBE in 1982, and in 1993 was knighted as Dame of the British Empire. —*Joseph Stevenson*

Recommended:

- ○ **Schubert: Lieder; Schumann: Frauenliebe und -leben** / Price, Lockhart / 2002 / EMI 575773
- ○ **Schubert: Complete Songs Vol. 15** / Price, Johnson (piano) / Hyperion 33015
- ○ **Berg: Lulu-Suite; Altenberg-Lieder; 3 Orchesterstücke** / Abbado (cond.), Price, London SO / 1997 / DG 449714
- ○ **Margaret Price sings Mozart** / Lockhart (cond.), Price, King, Black, Garcia, Heath, Adeney, Simons, English CO, London PO / 1994 / RCA 61635

William Primrose

b. Aug. 23, 1903, Glasgow, Scotland, **d.** May 1, 1982, Provo, UT
Violist

One of the most famous—and best—violists of the recording era, William Primrose was well schooled, diligent, highly musical, and accomplished in all areas of the repertory. His art was as direct and unassuming as his personality. Lacking application to his studies as a youth, he firmed up under the influence of one of history's most influential violinists; under that direction, he switched instruments and applied himself to viola, whose darker coloring had always appealed to him. Primrose had soon gained a reputation that placed him among the greatest violists of his day. Reared in a musical household, Primrose began violin lessons at four years of age. His father, who privately taught violin and was a member of the Scottish Orchestra, thought it better to place young William in the care of Camillo Ritter, an Austrian who had studied with Joseph Joachim. By the time he was 12, Primrose had made several modest appearances in his native Glasgow and had already absorbed much from listening to the Scottish Orchestra. Summers spent on the Isle of Man brought exposure to the art of singers such as Emmy Destinn and Enrico Caruso and many of the finest violinists of the day, from Mischa Elman to Eugene Ysaÿe. In 1919, the Primrose family moved to London to enroll William in the Guildhall School of Music, which had awarded the youth a scholarship. Despite his having been given a gold medal at graduation in 1924, Primrose later recalled that he had been anything but an exemplary student, skipping his theory and counterpoint lessons in favor of perusing a collection of concertos and hearing more great artists firsthand. Two years after graduation, Primrose found himself in some technical difficulty and was urged by Ivor Newton to study with the elderly Ysaÿe. Under the Belgian master, Primrose not only made his technique secure, but also resolved to devote himself to the viola. The move was made official when he joined the London String Quartet in March 1930. Touring brought exposure to international audiences as founder and leader Warwick Evan's intuitive musical understanding opened new vistas for Primrose. The quartet disbanded in 1935, and for the next two years, Primrose performed whenever and wherever possible, playing engagements from La Scala to Berlin. Primrose decided in 1937 to seek a position in the NBC Symphony being formed under Arturo Toscanini. Although not offered the principal chair, Primrose appeared as viola soloist on several occasions and in 1939 was invited by NBC to form the Primrose Quartet. In the years after his NBC orchestra tenure, Primrose performed as soloist throughout America and Europe, invariably under the leading conductors of the time. He was active in chamber music, performing with such celebrated ensembles as the Heifetz/Primrose/Feuermann Trio and the Schnabel/Szigeti/Primrose/Fournier Piano Quartet. His commission produced from Béla Bartók one of the great concertos for viola (completed by Tibor Serly after Bartók's death) and many other leading composers, such as Milhaud, Britten, and Rubbra, produced works specifically for the violist. After suffering a heart attack in 1953, Primrose concentrated on teaching, beginning at Indiana University (1965–72). At the time of his death, he was teaching at Brigham Young University. His memoirs, *Walk on the North Side*, published in 1978 afford an honest and amusing look at a great artist. Many first-rate examples of his elegant, shimmering work remain on disc. —*Erik Eriksson*

Recommended:

- ○ **William Primrose** / Primrose, Kitzinger, Cohen, Isaacs / Pearl 9453
- ○ **Berlioz: Harold en Italie** / Primrose, Henriot-Schweitzer / RCA 62582
- ○ **William Primrose** / Primrose, Kapell, Moore, Rupp, Harris, Sokoloff / Pearl 9253

Pro Cantione Antiqua

f. 1968, London, England
Ensemble

The 1960s were a period when pioneering singers followed the lead of instrumentalists to create ensembles devoted to researching and performing the long-forgotten treasure of Western music composed before the time of Bach and Handel, and it was in the middle of that decade that three British musicians and scholars founded Pro Cantione Antiqua. They were tenor James Griffett, countertenor Paul Esswood, and conductor Mark Brown, joined by conductor and musicologist Bruno Turner. The intent from the beginning was to make the group an ensemble of soloists, in the sense that they all had careers as professional solo singers. This blend of strength and beauty of each singer's tone and the individuality each member brings to his part is responsible for the special quality of the PCA. Its primary era of emphasis is the Renaissance era, the richest outpouring of polyphonic composition in history. Since polyphony is an interplay of truly independent lines, the individuality of the singers on each part enhances the performance and helps guide the listener through the complex part-writing. *Gramophone* magazine wrote of its recording of motets of Francisco de Peñalosa (ca. 1470–1528), "Careful listening will teach you much about the essence of early sixteenth century polyphony."

In addition to its Renaissance repertory, the PCA also sings considerable amounts of Medieval music and, as a number of early music groups have done, developed an interest in recent trends in contemporary music. PCA have commissioned works from composers including Sir Lennox Berkeley, Ian Parrott, Colin Mawby, and Ivan Moody, and regularly include other contemporary music on their programs.

The PCA has toured extensively through Europe, the Far East, and Latin America. It has made over 80 CD albums and won several major disc awards. Filmgoers have heard it singing an Arthur Sullivan partsong, "The Long Day Closes," as the title music of Terence Davies' 1992 film. The group has become particularly associated with the Monteverdi 1601 *Vespers* through performances with the early music groups the Orchestra and Choir of the Golden Age and His Majesty's Sagbutts and Cornettes.

As well as being pioneers for the appreciation of Portuguese, Polish, Croatian, and Jewish polyphony, Pro Cantione Antiqua has taken a particular interest in Iberian Renaissance music. In 1999 it participated in concerts in Madrid and Seville honoring the 400th anniversary of the death of Francisco Guerrero, and in 2000 creatively planned programs linking and contrasting the sixteenth century music of Spain, Portugal, and England.

The group is comprised of the following soloists, all, of them prominent in recital and opera: Paul Esswood, Robin Tyson, James Bowman, Timothy Penrose, and Robert Harre Jones (countertenors), James Griffett, Ian Partridge, Joseph Cornwell, and Andrew King (tenors), and Stephen Roberts, Michael George, Adrian Peacock, and David Beavan (basses/baritones). —*Joseph Stevenson*

Recommended:

- ○ **Lassus: Requiem; Magnificat** / Turner (cond.), Pro Cantione Antiqua / 2004 / Deutsche Harmonia Mundi 60153
- ○ **Palestrina: Masses** / Turner (cond.), Pro Cantione Antiqua / Brilliant 99711
- ○ **Palestrina: Lamentation of Jeremiah the Prophet** / Turner (cond.), Pro Cantione Antiqua / Brilliant 971124
- ○ **Palestrina: Canticum Canticorum Salomonis** / Turner (cond.), Pro Cantione Antiqua / 2002 / Hyperion 55095
- ○ **Palestrina: Missa Papae Marcelli, etc.** / Turner (cond.), Pro Cantione Antiqua / Brilliant 971155

Sergey Prokofiev

b. Apr. 23, 1891, Sontsovka, Russia, **d.** Mar. 5, 1953, Moscow, Russia
Composer: Symphonic, Ballet, Orchestral, Concerto, Keyboard, Film Music, Choral, Chamber Music, Opera

In breathing new life into the symphony, sonata, and concerto, Sergey Prokofiev emerged as one of the truly original musical voices of the twentieth century. Bridging the worlds of pre-revolutionary Russia and the Stalinist Soviet Union, Prokofiev enjoyed a successful worldwide career as composer and pianist. As in the case of most other Soviet-era composers, his creative life and his music came to suffer under the duress of official Party strictures. Still, despite the detrimental personal and professional effects of such outside influences, Prokofiev continued until the end of his career to produce music marked by a singular skill, inventiveness, and élan.

As an only child (his sisters had died in infancy), Prokofiev lived a comfortable, privileged life, which gave him a heightened sense of self-worth and an indifference to criticism, an attitude that would change as he matured. His mother taught him piano, and he began composing around the age of five. He eventually took piano, theory, and composition lessons from Reyngol'd Gliere, then enrolled at the St. Petersburg Conservatory when he was 13. He took theory with Lyadov, orchestration with Rimsky-Korsakov, and became lifelong friends with Nicolai Myaskovsky. After graduating, he began performing in St. Petersburg and in Moscow, then in Western Europe, all the while writing more and more music. Prokofiev's earliest renown, therefore, came as a result of both his formidable pianistic technique and the works he wrote to exploit it. He sprang onto the Russian musical scene with works like the *Sarcasms, Op. 17* (1912–14) and *Visions fugitives, Op. 22* (1915–17), and his first few piano sonatas. He also wrote orchestral works, concertos, and operas, and met with Diaghilev about producing ballets. The years immediately after the Revolution were spent in the U.S., where Prokofiev tried to follow Rachmaninov's lead and make his way as a pianist/composer. His commission for *The Love for Three Oranges* came from the Chicago Opera in 1919, but overall Prokofiev was disappointed by his American reception, and he returned to Europe in 1922. He married singer Lina Llubera in 1923, and the couple moved to Paris. He continued to compose on commission, meeting with mixed success from both critics and the public. He had maintained contact with the Soviet Union, even toured there in 1927. *The Love for Three Oranges* was part of the repertory there, and the government commissioned the music for the film *Lieutenant Kijé* and other pieces from him. In 1936, he decided to return to the Soviet Union with his wife and two sons. Most of his compositions from just after his return, including many for children, were written with the political atmosphere in mind. One work which wasn't, was the 1936 ballet *Romeo and Juliet*, which became an international success. He attempted another opera in 1939, *Semyon Kotko*, but was met with hostility from cultural ideologues. During World War II, Prokofiev and other artists were evacuated from Moscow. He spent the time in various places within the U.S.S.R. and produced propaganda music, but also violin sonatas, his "War Sonatas" for piano, the *String Quartet No. 2*, the opera *War and Peace*, and the ballet *Cinderella*. In 1948, with the resolution that criticized almost all Soviet composers, several of Prokofiev's works were banned from performance. His health declined and he became more insecure. The composer's last creative efforts were directed largely toward the production of "patriotic" and "national" works, typified by the cantata *Flourish, Mighty Homeland* (1947), and yet Prokofiev also continued to produce worthy if lesser-known works like the underrated ballet *The Stone Flower* (1943). In a rather bitter coincidence, Prokofiev died on March 5, 1953, the same day as Joseph Stalin. *—AMG*

SYMPHONIC

Symphony No. 1 in D major ("Classical"), Op. 25 (1916–1917)

Prokofiev's Symphony No. 1 (1916–17) represents the composer's earliest mature effort in a genre he returned to time and again for the remainder of his career. Though the symphony received a warm reception in Russia and abroad—and remains one of the composer's most frequently programmed works—Prokofiev's attitude toward it remained ambiguous, vacillating between dismissive and defensive.

The First Symphony is especially intriguing in light of the view of Prokofiev as a leading figure of the Russian avant-garde in the early decades of the twentieth century. The work's anachronistic "Classical" moniker seems particularly apt in respect to a number of its features. The symphony is in a familiar four-movement form, the two fast outer movements (Allegro and Vivace, respectively) bracketing a slow movement (Larghetto) and one inspired by a stylized dance (Gavotto); its textures are economical, its scoring appropriate to an orchestra of the late eighteenth or early nineteenth century; and it is of a decidely lighthearted, even humorous character, much in the spirit of the symphonies of Haydn. Indeed, it should be noted that the "Classical" subtitle was Prokofiev's own; scholar R.D. Darell has suggested that the composer may have chosen it partly to describe the work's character, partly because he hoped that the work would one day become a classic, and partly out of pure mischief directed at critics. (In regard to the last, Prokofiev wrote that he meant to "tease the geese.")

Though the symphony is at times sharply dissonant, it maintains a steadfastly tonal basis. Certainly, the "Classical" model is stretched in the work's harmonic language, which is marked by Prokofiev's characteristic ambiguous cadences and sudden shifts between tonal centers. Still, the work retains many of the trappings of Viennese Classicism, from the sonata-allegro form of the first movement, to the Mozartean gavotte and trio of the third, to the exuberant, witty finale. Despite the suggestion of its title, the "Classical" Symphony is not really neo-Classical along the lines of contemporaneous works by Stravinsky, but rather a work of elegant simplicity that evokes the spirit of high Viennese Classicism filtered through the more adventurous sensibilities of Prokofiev's own musical language. *—Alexander Carpenter*

Recommended:

- ○ **Prokofiev: Symphonies 1 & 5** / Bernstein (cond.), New York PO / 1993 / Sony 47602
- ○ **Prokofiev: Peter & the Wolf; March; Overture; Symphony 1** / Abbado (cond.), CO of Europe / 1990 / DG 429396
- ○ **Igor Markevich Conducts Prokofiev & Tchaikovsky** / Markevitch (cond.), Philharmonia / 1997 / Testament 1107

Symphony No. 5 in B flat major, Op. 100 (1944)

Prokofiev composed this music in 1944, and conducted its premiere in Moscow on January 13, 1945. Everyone everywhere assumed that it symbolized "world war agony and triumph"—in other words, his counterpart of Dmitry Shostakovich's 1941 *"Leningrad" Symphony*. It was the composer's *Sixth Symphony* of 1945–47, not his *Fifth*, that recollected the horrors of World War II. Those who insisted the *Fifth Symphony* was a mirror of wartime agonies didn't know that the scherzo movement was borrowed from *Cinderella*. Nor did Prokofiev help matters by issuing one of those "position papers" expected by Soviet officialdom: "I conceived [the *Fifth*] as a symphony of the greatness of the human spirit."

After the failure of his *Fourth Symphony* (a 1929 reworking of material from his then-recent ballet, *The Prodigal Son*), Prokofiev turned his back on the form. When finally he did return, his implicit model was Shostakovich's *Fifth* of 1937—four movements in concerto-grosso sequence: slow, fast, slow, fast. Otherwise, though, the music is pure Prokofiev both in substance and in style.

The inaugural Andante is a sonata-form movement that begins in 3/4 time with a fluid main theme played in octave unison by flutes and bassoon, with a tailpiece in triplets that later assumes a separate identity. A lot of working-over leads to a new tune in 4/4, introduced by flute and oboe. A jittery figure in the high and low strings acquires thematic status in the development that follows directly. Brass announce the reprise by playing the opening theme very dramatically. Rhetoric accumulates, culminating in a—why not?—"greatness of the human spirit" coda.

The Allegro marcato scherzo (in all but name) has a D minor, *Danse macabre*-ish song section, followed by a slightly faster, D major trio in waltz-time, borrowed from *Cinderella* without blinking (or acknowledgment).

The official slow movement is a passionately lyrical, ABA Adagio in F major that begins with a reminder of *Aleksandr Nyevsky* (1939), but continues in the mode of Prokofiev's *Romeo and Juliet* ballet. He changes keys frequently to intensify expression until the climax recalls Nyevsky's battle music.

A slow introduction (lightly scored, based on music from the first movement) sets up this Allegro giocoso finale in B flat major. The strings begin a rhythm in bar 23 that prepares for merriment with a sweet-sour sauce. The clarinet plays a syncopated main theme recalling the high-spirits in *Romeo and Juliet*, prior to the deaths of Mercutio and Tybalt; this returns throughout a rondo-like movement. Prokofiev's finale amounts to a retrospective of his stylistic direction following *Symphony No. 4*—including a return to the U.S.S.R. in 1933—and ends with a tour de force coda.

The first performance was a triumph, the climax of Prokofiev's Soviet years, followed shortly after by a physical tragedy from which he never fully recovered. Dizzied by undiagnosed hypertension, he fell downstairs (where remains moot), causing a massive concussion. *—Roger Dettmer*

Recommended:

- ○ **Prokofiev: Symphony 5; Romeo & Juliet: Suite 2** / Mravinski (cond.), Leningrad PO / 1995 / Leningrad Masters 1301
- ○ **Prokofiev: Symphonies 1 & 5** / Karajan (cond.), Berlin PO / 1988 / DG 423216
- ○ **Prokofiev: Symphonies 1 & 5, etc.** / Tilson Thomas (cond.), London SO / 1997 / Sony 63275

Symphony No. 6 in E flat minor, Op. 111 (1944–1947)

In 1945, Prokofiev had an accident, a fall caused by a heart attack, resulting in a brain concussion. He later suffered a stroke and would be plagued with ill health for the remaining eight years of his life. Prokofiev was no longer able to conduct, and composing became increasingly difficult. He did, however, manage to continue working until his death, and began working on the *Symphony No. 6* not long after the accident. The work was actually sketched out in the summer of 1945, but other projects demanded the composer's time, and the symphony was not orchestrated until two years later. The work shares an opus number with Beethoven's last piano sonata, and Prokofiev, profoundly influenced by Beethoven and specifically by the Op. 111 sonata, is said to have considered dedicating this symphony to Beethoven. The *Symphony No. 6*, though, owes more to Prokofiev's earlier symphonies than to Beethoven; it is especially close to the composer's own *Fifth Symphony*. The two works are almost identical in instrumentation, and are similar in texture and character.

The *Symphony No. 6* is a work in three movements, instead of the usual four. The form suggests the pre-Classical sinfonia, a work with two fast outer movements and a slow middle one. The symphony begins with an Allegro moderato movement in sonata-allegro form. For an opening movement however, it is a little grim, with nostalgic themes and a recurring funeral procession. Nonetheless, the lyricism that one associates with some of Prokofiev's music is still present. The second movement is a Largo, and the mood of the opening movement is maintained through dark timbres, solemn thematic material, and subdued dynamics. In the third movement, a quick Vivace, the work brightens considerably as Prokofiev uses dance rhythms and a march to invigorate the final themes. Themes from the opening movement return recontextualized in a coda as the work draws to its conclusion. The composer himself commented on the austerity of the first movement and on the similarities between the third movement of this work and the style of the *Symphony No. 5.*

In 1948, the Central Commission of the Communist Party condemned of most of the leading Soviet composers, accusing them of decadence. Prokofiev, however, was lucky: due to his ill health and to his lack of involvement in any official organizations, he suffered less than his colleagues. Though the *Symphony No. 6* was not among those singled out for condemnation in 1948, he was hardly in favor with the Party. Ten years later, however, Prokofiev was "posthumously vindicated," and his favorable evaluation restored. *—Alexander Carpenter*

Recommended:

- ○ **Prokofiev: Symphony 6; Stravinsky: Pétrouchka** / Mravinsky (cond.), Leningrad PO / 1993 / Multisonic 310189
- ○ **Prokofiev: Symphony 6; Waltzes** / Kuchar (cond.), National SO / 1995 / Naxos 553069

Symphony No. 7 in C sharp minor, Op. 131 (1951–1952)

Prokofiev had a serious heart attack in 1945 and suffered a fall at the same time; his health declined slowly for eight years. He was too weak to put up any objection to the 1948 Party edicts about how music should serve the Soviet State. This restrained and gentle 1952 symphony was composed in this situation, a year before his death. Many find its simplicity and lyricism deeply affecting. Others consider it a pale echo of Prokofiev's earlier muscular style.

The symphony is in the standard four movements, with a restrained first movement possessing a stately tempo and a lyrical opening theme of unusual melancholy and sense of resignation. The key of C sharp minor, which does not resound very brilliantly or richly from any standard orchestral instrument, seems to enforce the sense of life dimming. The scherzo second movement is much livelier, recasting Prokofiev's earlier, often grotesque, sense of humor into childish jokes. The third movement is also rather funny in effect, although it is a strained humor. The finale is more energetic, with lively woodwinds and tomfoolery, then a lyrical major transformation, considerably more optimistic in tone, of the symphony's opening theme. Whether the ending is a quicksilvery sparkling conclusion or a less brilliant winding down depends on which edition of the work is chosen by the conductor. *—Joseph Stevenson*

Recommended:

- ○ **Nicolai Malko** / Malko (cond.), Philharmonia / 2002 / EMI 75121
- ○ **Prokofiev: Symphonies 3 & 7** / Kuchar (cond.), National SO / 1995 / Naxos 553054
- ○ **Prokofiev: Symphony 7; Sinfonietta** / Järvi (cond.), Scottish National Orch. / 1986 / Chandos 8442

BALLET

Cinderella, Op. 87 (1940–1944)

Prokofiev was Tchaikovsky's greatest successor in the realm of narrative Russian ballet, evidenced by a body of works which have earned a permanent place in the international repertoire. The scenario of the composer's *Cinderella* is essentially faithful to the beloved tale by Charles Perrault.

Act One serves largely to introduce the characters. The heroine's father is a weak man who fails to protect his daughter from the wickedness of a stepmother and two stepsisters. Cinderella takes pity on an old beggar woman, who reveals herself as Cinderella's Fairy Godmother after all the others have departed for the Prince's ball.

The ball itself is the setting for Act Two, which is dominated by an exquisite, lusciously scored waltz. The Prince and Cinderella, in a classic instance of love at first sight, dance a rapturous pas de deux. The music for this concluding number of the act, when Cinderella realizes she must leave just as the clock strikes midnight, is remarkably powerful and threatening; snarling trombones and bass drum dominate the musical texture.

Act Three focuses on the Prince's search for the mysterious woman he has fallen in love with. To the accompaniment of an amusing recurring passage of "traveling" music, the Prince visits a number of foreign lands. In each he encounters a tempting beauty who dances for him. The next scene, "The Morning After the Ball," opens with all the characters in Cinderella's household discussing the events of the previous night. The Prince arrives in search of his love, and when Cinderella's identity is revealed, the Fairy Godmother magically transports the two lovers to an enchanted realm.

Composed over the span of four years, the score took Prokofiev an uncommonly long time to complete. Because of the German invasion of Russia in 1941, Prokofiev set aside the ballet to take on more patriotic themes, devoting his effort to the epic opera *War and Peace* (1941–43). He resumed work on *Cinderella* after an Allied victory over Germany seemed imminent, and it received a triumphant premiere on November 21, 1945. In the following year Prokofiev extracted three suites from the ballet which have become concert favorites; the third is notable for its incorporation of "The Three Oranges" from the composer's opera *The Love for Three Oranges* (1919). Other numbers from the ballet found their way into an independent *Waltz Suite* (1946) that also includes excerpts from *War and Peace* and the film score *Lermontov* (1941). *—Joseph Stevenson*

Synopsis:

Act One. The first scene takes place in the home of Cinderella's father. There, Cinderella's ugly sisters Khudyshka and Kubyshka (Skinny and Dumpy) quarrel and make life difficult for the forlorn and beautiful Cinderella. The Fairy Godmother, taking the appearance of a beggar woman, appears to Cinderella, her sisters, and father, but only Cinderella shows pity and helps her.

After taking a dancing lesson, Khudyshka and Kubyshka prepare for the ball, while Cinderella can only dream about attending. But the beggar woman reappears to her and unmasks her real identity as the Fairy Godmother. She waves her magic wand and Cinderella is suddenly standing in a magnificent garden, where she is provided with a beautiful gown and other adornments by the Spring, Summer, Autumn, and Winter Fairies. Cinderella is excited, but is warned that she must leave the ball before the clock strikes midnight, the time when the magic will end and the gown will transform back to the rags she usually wears.

Act Two. This act takes place at the ball, where Khudyshka and Kubyshka dance clumsily. The handsome Prince enters to much fanfare, and then Cinderella arrives. All in attendance are captivated by her beauty and innocence, but her sisters and stepmother do not recognize her. Alone with the Prince after the others have retreated to adjoining rooms, Cinderella dances with him and they fall in love. While they dance a waltz, she suddenly remembers the warning to depart before midnight. She flees in haste, losing one of her slippers. The Prince pursues her to no avail, but he finds the lost slipper.

Act Three. The Prince attempts to learn from the kingdom's cobblers which one of them had made the slipper. His efforts turn up nothing and he decides the charming girl must be from a foreign land. He goes in search of her, first to the South, then to the Far East, then nearer to his homeland, but can find her nowhere. Meanwhile, back home, Cinderella looks at the other slipper in her apron pocket and realizes the ballroom events were not a dream. Soon the Prince arrives with the slipper, and Khudyshka and Kubyshka both try it on, finding it much too small for their big feet. Cinderella helps her stepmother to try it on, and in the event loses the other slipper from her apron pocket. The Prince suddenly realizes he has found his princess and the two declare their mutual love. *—Robert Cummings*

Recommended:

- ○ **Glazunov: The Seasons; Prokofiev: Cinderella** / Ashkenazy (cond.), Cleveland Orch. / 1999 / Decca 455349
- ○ **Prokofiev: Cinderella; Symphony 1** / Previn (cond.), London SO / 1995 / EMI 68604
- ○ **Prokofiev: Cinderella; Summer Night** / Pletnev (cond.), Russian National Orch. / DG 445830

Romeo and Juliet, Op. 64 (1935–1936)

In the early- and mid-twentieth century, the three major Tchaikovsky ballets—*Swan Lake, The Sleeping Beauty* and *The Nutcracker*—were viewed as the three greatest full-length ballets. Not surprisingly, they were also more popular by wide margins than all other works in the genre. By the latter quarter of the century, however, Prokofiev's *Romeo and Juliet* had entered the trio's select company and remains exceedingly popular today. Some have even asserted it is the greatest of full-length ballets. Certainly, it is one of Prokofiev's supreme masterpieces and, via the three suites extracted from it, among his most often-played music.

His previous ballets had been shorter and more pungent, like *Chout*, Op. 21 (1915–20), and *Le Pas d'Acier*, Op. 41 (1925), which created a bit of a stir in Paris when it premiered. Both, along with *The Prodigal Son* (1929), were composed for Sergei Diaghilev's ballets russes. *Romeo and Juliet* was thus his first attempt at writing a full-length ballet, and while he would have further successes in the genre, most notably with *Cinderella*, no other stage work of his would quite approach it in popularity.

Prokofiev's *Romeo and Juliet*, based on Shakespeare's play, consists of four acts and ten scenes, within which are 52 separate dance numbers. The work opens with a six-note motif that appears throughout the ballet. This same theme, cut to four notes, opens the composer's *Symphony-Concerto for Cello and Orchestra*

(1950–52) and appears elsewhere in its first movement. There are many famous melodies in *Romeo and Juliet*, foremost among which is probably the marchlike theme that appears in No. 13, "Dance of the Knights." This music symbolizes the strife between the opposing families. A variant of it is played in the next number, "Juliet's Variation," where its character changes from the austere malevolence in No. 13 to innocence and playfulness.

Another important and immensely popular melody is the love theme of *Romeo and Juliet*. It is a soaring melody in an archlike pattern that exudes warmth and yearning, passion and grace. But there are many other memorable themes, including the joyous, rhythmic one in No. 12, "Masks," as well as the two in No. 22, "Folk Dance." Perhaps the most profound creation in the ballet, however, is the dark and tragic theme appearing in No. 51, "Juliet's Funeral," whose archlike pattern is similar to that of the love theme.

Prokofiev also quotes from his own *Classical Symphony* here (No. 18 "Gavotte"), using music from the third movement Gavotte. It is not for want of thematic material that he resorts to this reference, but to show irony: this post-Renaissance French dance is as much miscast here as the two teenage lovers who are caught up in an unforgiving adult world.

Romeo and Juliet lasts about two-and-one half hours in a typical performance. It was premiered in Brno, Czechoslovakia, in December 30, 1938. *—Robert Cummings*

Synopsis:

Act One. Romeo is strolling through the streets at dawn, and amid the marketplace bustle a skirmish breaks out between the ever-feuding families, his Montagues and the Capulets. The fighting is broken up by the arrival of the Prince, but the feeling of animosity between the two warring households remains. In the Capulet house, Juliet playfully prepares herself for that night's ball.

The uninvited Romeo, accompanied by his friends Mercutio and Benvolio, appears at the ball disguised in a mask. While Juliet dances with Paris—a young man selected by her parents for her—Romeo takes notice of her, and she of him. Juliet's cousin, Tybalt, recognizes Romeo through his mask and threatens to expel him violently. But Capulet intercedes and the ball soon ends. Juliet stands at her balcony later that night, obsessed with thoughts of Romeo, when suddenly he appears below. The two soon declare their love for each other.

Act Two. As a wedding procession passes by him on the streets, Romeo watches intently and dreams of his own wedding to Juliet. Juliet's nurse works her way through the crowd to Romeo and delivers a message to him. In it Juliet states that she accepts his proposal of marriage. The young couple are then wed in secret before Friar Laurence. The monk expresses his wish that their union will mark an end to the bitter feuding between the two families. Later, amid an atmosphere of much festivity in the streets, a fight breaks out between Tybalt and Mercutio. Their long sword duel ends with Tybalt stabbing Mercutio to death. Romeo then decides to avenge Mercutio's death and kills Tybalt. Benvolio leads Romeo away from the tragic scene, and the Prince declares that he is forthwith exiled for the slaying.

Act Three. Romeo, having secretly spent the night with Juliet as a romantic sendoff before beginning his exile, awakens in her bedroom and departs the Capulet household unnoticed. The Capulets bring Paris to Juliet once more in an attempt to interest her in marriage, but she rejects him. With Paris feeling insulted and her parents exasperated with her, Juliet flees and returns to the chapel where she and Romeo were married. She enlists the aid of Friar Laurence, who gives her a sleeping potion that will emulate death in her when she drinks it. Juliet's family, the Friar explains, will believe she is dead and place her in the family crypt. Meanwhile, Friar Laurence will send word to Romeo of the scheme and he will then come for her in the night and whisk her away to a new beginning in another town.

Later, Juliet decides to assuage her parents temporarily and consents to marry Paris. She then takes the potion and falls into a seeming death sleep. The next morning her body is found by the Capulets and taken to the crypt. Romeo hears of Juliet's death, Friar Laurence's message never having reached him. He goes to her tomb and becomes utterly devastated by the thought of life without his Juliet. He drinks poison and dies. Suddenly Juliet awakens and finds Romeo dead. She takes his dagger and plunges it into her chest and dies. *—Robert Cummings*

Recommended:

- ○ **Prokofiev: Romeo & Juliet** / Gergiev (cond.), Kirov Orch. / 2001 / Philips 464726
- ○ **Prokofiev: Romeo & Juliet** / Previn (cond.), London SO / 1995 / EMI 68607
- ○ **Prokofiev: Romeo & Juliet** / Maazel (cond.), Cleveland Orch. / 1998 / London 4529702
- ○ **Prokofiev: Romeo & Juliet** / Tilson Thomas (cond.), San Francisco SO / 1996 / RCA 68288

The Tale of the Stone Flower, Op. 118 (1948–1953)

Prokofiev's final ballet, *The Stone Flower*, was conceived at a time when the composer's health was in serious decline and his reputation with Soviet authorities in tatters. In January, 1948, the composer—along with such prominent Soviet colleagues as Shostakovich and Khachaturian—was summoned to appear at a meeting of the Central Committee of the Communist Party. The composers were attacked by Andrei Zhdanov and other party overlords for writing formalist and antidemocratic music. It was reported that Prokofiev sat defiantly with his back turned to the speaker as the charges were read. From this point, performances of his works in the Soviet Union were rare. Moreover, until his death in 1953, he not only had to be wary of every note he put to paper, but his precarious situation demanded that he also choose only inoffensive, politically safe subject matter for his stage works. Not surprisingly, then, Prokofiev selected a fairy-tale theme for his last ballet, setting it with appropriately light and colorful music.

The Stone Flower (1948–53) takes place in the Ural Mountains, where the stonecutter Danilo temporarily forsakes his betrothed, Katerina, to accompany the Mistress of Copper Mountain to her realm. There she shows him a legendary flower made of stone. Danilo becomes determined to carve one like it in malachite, a deep green marble-like mineral native to Russia. Meanwhile, Katarina is harassed by the story's villain, the drunken Severyan. The Mistress of Copper Mountain captures him and compels the ground to open and swallow him whole. Katarina searches for Danilo and finds him, but their reunion is spoiled when the Mistress becomes upset that he wants to leave the mountain paradise now that he has learned the secret of making the stone flower. In the end, however, Danilo gains the Mistress' respect through his love for and fidelity to Katarina, and the lovers depart to live happily ever after.

As suggested above, Prokofiev's score, one of the most approachable of his major works, is rather direct and uncomplicated. The work is rich with memorable tunes, most notably the one at the opening associated with the Mistress of Copper Mountain, which recurs throughout the ballet. Three successive dances present some of the most striking music in the score: No. 31 "Russian Dance," No. 32, "Gypsy Dance," and No. 33, "Severyan's Dance." In the end, *The Stone Flower* may not rank with Prokofiev's earlier ballet masterpieces, *Romeo and Juliet* (1935–36) and *Cinderella* (1940–44), but it is distinguished by a certain melodic and rhythmic charm; and while it blazes no new compositional trails, neither does it contain any obvious flaws.

Prokofiev extracted three orchestral works from the ballet in 1951: the *Wedding Suite*, Op. 126, *Gypsy Fantasy*, Op. 127, and *Ural Rhapsody*, Op. 128. The composer died shortly after completing revisions to a pas de deux in the ballet's final act. *—Robert Cummings*

Recommended:

- ○ **Prokofiev: The Tale Of The Stone Flower** / Rozhdestvensky (cond.). Bolshoi Theater Orch. / Russian Disc 11022
- ○ **Prokofiev: The Tale Of The Stone Flower** / Noseda (cond.), BBCPO / 2003 / Chandos 10058

ORCHESTRAL

Peter and the Wolf, Op. 67 (1936)

Prokofiev's *Peter and the Wolf*, for narrator and orchestra, was a commission from the Central Children's Theatre in 1936. The composer himself wrote the text, which tells the story of a young boy who manages to capture a vicious wolf. The piece is remarkable for many reasons, but perhaps most notably for its didactic scoring, designed by Prokofiev to introduce children to the sounds of orchestral instruments. The instrumentation is also important for the narration, since each character in the story is represented by a different instrument: the bird by a flute, the duck by an oboe, the grandfather by a bassoon, the cat by a clarinet, the wolf by three horns, and Peter by the strings. The entire work was composed in a single week (in piano score), and the orchestration was completed less than two weeks later.

Prokofiev's writing is intentionally direct and transparent, reflecting his desire to make the work enjoyable for children. His musical characterizations are broad and straightforward, from the delicate birdsong of the flute, to the thunderous kettledrums portraying the hunters' rifle shots.

The work is in three sections, loosely following a kind of sonata form. The opening section introduces the main characters, preparing the audience for the action to come. The middle section—the "development"—contains the most exciting action, beginning with the appearance of the wolf, his eating of the duck, and his eventual capture by young Peter. The final scene acts as a recapitulation, as the principal characters return for a final parade; here, Peter's opening theme returns transformed into a triumphant march.

Like most of Prokofiev's music, *Peter and the Wolf* features adroit thematic integration and development. Peter's theme, the dominant theme of the work, is stated at the beginning of the piece, and is then combined with other subordinate themes. This thematic blending is also closely tied to the dramatic action, underscoring developments in the story. Harmonically, the piece begins and ends in C major, but contains many sudden harmonic shifts, another important aspect of Prokofiev's style. Formally, though the piece does follow a loose sonata structure, it is by no means a case of textbook form; themes develop freely, harmonic direction is dictated largely by the action, and characterization assumes priority over any kind of academic musical construction.

Peter and the Wolf has long been a classic, loved by children for its vivid storytelling, and by adults for its gentle sense of humor and good-natured tunefulness. It was composed 22 years after a similar piece, *The Ugly Duckling* of 1914–15, which also features humorous musical sketches of animals. It also bears comparison with Benjamin Britten's *Young Person's Guide to the Orchestra*, which also seeks to acquaint children with the sounds of the symphony. *—Alexander Carpenter*

Recommended:

○ **Prokofiev: Peter & the Wolf; March; Overture; Symphony 1** / Abbado (cond.), Sting, CO of Europe / 1990 / DG 429396

○ **Peter & the Wolf** / Nagano (cond.), P. Stewart, Lyon Opera Orch. / Erato 97418

○ **Children's Classics** / Bernstein, New York Philharmonic / 1998 / Sony 60175

Scythian Suite, Op. 20 (1914–1915)

In the summer of 1914, Prokofiev, the then-emerging *enfant terrible* of Russian music, traveled to London to meet with the ballet impresario Sergei Diaghilev. Diaghilev commissioned the young composer to write a ballet with a prehistoric or fairy-tale scenario—hoping, perhaps, for the same kind of success he had recently enjoyed with the like-themed ballets of Stravinsky. Prokofiev returned to St. Petersburg and engaged the services of poet Sergei Gorodetzky in developing an effective story line.

The composer settled on a theme centered on a prehistoric tribe of barbarians, the Scythians, known to drink blood and engage in other similarly gruesome practices. The immediate musical result was *Ala and Lolli* (1914–15), which Prokofiev first presented to Diaghilev in the form of a nearly complete piano score. Diaghilev, however, rejected the work as too close in spirit to Stravinsky's *Rite of Spring*, fearing comparisons to the still-new *succès du scandale*. To placate Prokofiev, Diaghilev commissioned from the dejected composer a new ballet, *Chout* (1915). Before fulfulling that commission, though, Prokofiev turned his attention back to his orphaned ballet, distilling its most effective numbers into the *Scythian Suite*.

The suite is cast in four movements whose titles readily evoke the ballet's prehistoric themes: "The Adoration of Veles and Ala," "The Evil God and Dance of the Pagan Monster," "Night," and "The Glorious Departure of Lolli and the Sun's Procession." What is most immediately striking about the score is Prokofiev's brilliant orchestration. The music is the product of a 23 year old, yet it clearly demonstrates the unmistakable confidence, control, and imagination of a seasoned master. The vivid colors and instrumental effects are such that the work, despite its relative unfamiliarity, survives as one of the most brilliant orchestral essays of its era.

The first movement begins savagely, the discordant main theme calling to mind a titanic struggle between monstrous forces. The mood turns quiet but restless, and the sound darkens; here the writing for reeds and harp here is especially brilliant and atmospheric. The second movement is fast and brutal, the rhythms pounding and insistent, the themes menacing and ominous; this is the most unambiguously Russian music of the suite. The first half of "Night" is appropriately dark, the second half explosive and unsettling. "The Glorious Departure" begins with a rush of energy, then slows to a colorful march, followed by a menacing yet comical theme. The suite concludes with a brilliant depiction of the rising sun that smites Chuzbog.

The *Scythian Suite* was premiered under the composer's baton in St. Petersburg on January 29, 1916. *—Robert Cummings*

Recommended:

○ **Prokofiev: Alexander Nevsky; Skythische Suite; Leutnant Kije** / Abbado (cond.), Chicago SO / 1980 / DG 447419

○ **Dorati Conducts Prokofiev** / Dorati (cond.), London SO / 1991 / Mercury 432753

CONCERTO

Piano Concerto No. 1 in D flat major, Op. 10 (1911–1912)

Both his first and second piano concertos were composed while Prokofiev was a student at the St. Petersburg Conservatory. As a young composer, Prokofiev wrote mostly works for the piano, as he was a talented pianist. He was also known, however, as a rebel who liked to experiment with Modernist music in order to shock his conservative professors. The youthful Prokofiev was often criticized for his "decadence," but was also in the same breath praised for the obvious imagination and creativity of his works. His *Concerto No. 1* provides ample evidence of an early adroitness in composing for the piano and a desire to create provocative music.

The *First Concerto* was composed during 1911–12, and was dedicated to the dreaded Tcherepnin, with whom Prokofiev studied conducting. He was the "dreaded" Tcherepnin because his harsh criticisms of Prokofiev's conducting were destined to haunt him for years (Prokofiev often complained of feeling like Tcherepnin was at his back, watching him; Tcherepnin had only been so tough with Prokofiev because he recognized his great talent, and wanted to prevent him from developing a swelled head). Under Tcherepnin's influence, Prokofiev was exposed to the works of the great classical composers—Haydn, Mozart, and Beethoven—and it was probably Tcherepnin who was responsible for the classicism of Prokofiev's early works, in particular the first piano sonatas and concertos, and the *"Classical" First Symphony*.

The concerto received its premier in Moscow on August 7, 1912, with Prokofiev as the soloist. The reaction from audience and critics was resoundingly negative. The work was labeled "musical mud," the work of a madman. The ugliness and outcry at the premiere brought Prokofiev instant attention. Prokofiev would continue for years afterwards to be accused of decadence and modernism, which is ironic, since a strong thread of traditionalism runs through most of his works, particularly in terms of form and overall harmonic construction.

Prokofiev regarded this concerto as his first mature composition. It is a single-movement work in sonata-allegro form. As Prokofiev notes, there is an Andante inserted before the development, and the development is a Scherzo, with a final cadenza introducing the recapitulation. Although cast as a single movement, the inclusion of an Andante and Scherzo suggests that the work really has a broader symphonic dimension. The concerto contains much of Prokofiev's typical lyricism, especially in the Andante, but is at the same time a very sprightly work, from the dotted rhythms of the principal theme to the energetic cadenzas and rousing recapitulation. *—Alexander Carpenter*

Recommended:

○ **Rimsky-Korsakov: Piano Concerto; Glazunov: Piano Concerto 1; Prokofiev: Piano Concerto 1** / Kondrashin (cond.), Richter / 1995 / Melodiya 29468

○ **Bartok: Piano Concerto 3; Prokofiev: Piano Concerto 1 & 3** / Dutoit (cond.), Argerich, Montreal SO / 1998 / EMI 56654

○ **Prokofiev: Piano Concertos 1 & 3** / Abbado (cond.), Kissin, Berlin PO / 1994 / DG 439898

○ **Prokofiev: Piano Concertos 1, 3, & 5** / Mehta (cond.), Bronfman, Israel PO / 1993 / Sony 52483

○ **Prokofiev: Piano Concertos** / Previn (cond.), Ashkenazy, London SO / 1997 / London 452588

Piano Concerto No. 2 in G minor, Op. 16 (1912–1913; revised 1923)

There are in fact two versions of this concerto, the first written during the years 1912–13, the second written in 1923. During the Russian Civil War, the original manuscript score of the *Concerto* was destroyed in a fire in Prokofiev's St. Petersburg apartment; in 1923, he recreated the score from memory. According to the composer, the two versions of the work are very different; Prokofiev wrote to a friend that "I have so completely rewritten the *Second Concerto* that it might be considered the Fourth."

The original version of the *Second Concerto* was dedicated to the memory of a pianist and close friend of Prokofiev's, Maximilian Schmidt. Schmidt committed suicide in 1913, and left a note to Prokofiev that read, in part, "I am reporting the latest news to you. I have shot myself. Don't grieve overmuch. The reasons were not important." The *Concerto* is a challenging, virtuosic vehicle for pianistic display. It is a work of some excess, as Philip Ramey has noted, with perhaps the "longest, most demanding cadenza (post-Lisztian in its pyrotechnics) in the literature." It looks forward, according to Ramey, to the neo-primitivism of Prokofiev's works of 1915–18 (including the *Scythian Suite* and the cantata *Seven, They are Seven*), and probably, given the years of its genesis, owes something to Stravinsky as well. After being harshly criticized for the superficiality of his *First Concerto*, Prokofiev sought to create a work of greater substance and depth. The audience at the premiere was, as became usual for this composer, sharply divided between supporters who applauded and detractors who hissed. The Russian critics were vigorous in attacking this work: after the premiere, Prokofiev was vilified in the press as an uncivilized "futurist" who had created a "Babel of insane sounds." The work, typical of Prokofiev, is a forthright, uncompromising piece, with its bombast and "cacophony" tempered by the pervasive lyricism found in most of his music.

It is cast in four movements. The first movement, Andantino, utilizes sonata form, with two contrasting themes stated in the opening exposition. The development section consists entirely of the grand cadenza described above, and also spills over into the beginning of the recapitulation, where the opening theme is finally heard again. The second movement, Scherzo: Vivace, is very short, with a driving, mechanistic character. The third movement is slow, though it is called Intermezzo: Allegro moderato. There is a darkness and malevolence to this movement (another common trait of Prokofiev's music), and it may be the noisiest and least melodic movement of the whole work. The lyricism of the opening movement returns in the finale, an Allegro tempestoso. This lives up to its title with sharply contrasting themes, some widely spaced, angular melodies, pounding octave passages in the piano, and a second bravura cadenza. The work ends, after a sudden, unexpected false ending, with a brilliant tutti restatement of the opening theme. *—Alexander Carpenter*

Recommended:

○ **Prokofiev: Piano Concertos 2 & 3** / Lazarev (cond.), Demidenko, London PO / 1996 / Hyperion 66858

- ○ **Prokofiev: Piano Concertos** / Previn (cond.), Ashkenazy, London SO / 1997 / London 452588

Piano Concerto No. 3 in C major, Op. 26 (1917–1921)

For his third concerto for piano and orchestra, Prokofiev looked to the past for inspiration: this concerto incorporates material derived from sketches made between 1911 and 1918. The first movement contains two themes that were written in 1916, plus a chordal passage first sketched in 1911; the second movement contains a theme and variations that was written in 1913, while the final movement uses thematic material from a discarded string quartet begun in 1918. When he began composing this concerto during a holiday in Brittany, Prokofiev wrote, "I already had all the thematic material I needed except for the third theme of the finale and the subordinate theme of the first movement." The *Third Piano Concerto* is perhaps Prokofiev's best known essay in this genre, and approaches Tchaikovsky and Rachmaninov in popularity and frequency of performance. Its opus number places it just after the *"Classical" First Symphony* of 1917, and the concerto is, in its way, similar to the *First Symphony* is a number of ways: both works are lively, acerbic, with brilliant orchestration and a certain transparent texture. Both pieces are also clearly the work of a deft young composer of considerable technical skill; however, the two works differ greatly in regards to their reception. The *"Classical" Symphony* was reasonably well received in Russia, where it was performed only once before Prokofiev emigrated to the United States. Subsequent performances of the symphony in America were very successful. The *Third Concerto*, on the other hand, did not fare so well, and after a good premiere in Chicago (along with the opera *Love for Three Oranges*) in 1921, the work was roundly denounced in New York.

The concerto displays much of the "harmonic liveliness," in Nancy Siff's words, of the mid-period symphonies, with its sudden shifts from key to key and chromatic harmony. The sophistication and bravura generally associated with Prokofiev's music is ever present, as is the humor found in many of his orchestral works. The concerto is in a traditional three-movement concerto form (the only one of Prokofiev's five piano concertos to use the traditional form), beginning and ending with fast movements that flank a slow middle movement. Each movement is about the same length, and the thematic weight and interest is distributed evenly throughout the movements. The work begins with a vivacious opening movement, which includes a humorous march underlined by castanets, followed by the five variations of the second movement, and concludes with a grandiose display of colorful harmonies and virtuosic orchestration. The solo writing for the piano is also virtuosic, and at times quite percussive. *—Alexander Carpenter*

Recommended:

- ○ **Bartok: Piano Concerto 3; Prokofiev: Piano Concertos 1 & 3** / Dutoit (cond.), Argerich, Montreal SO / 1998 / EMI 56654
- ○ **William Kapell** / Dorati (cond.), Kapell, Dallas SO / 1999 / Philips 456853
- ○ **Sergey Prokofiev** / Abbado (cond.), Argerich, Berlin PO / 2000 / DG 469172
- ○ **Prokofiev: Piano Concertos 1 & 3** / Abbado (cond.), Kissin, Berlin PO / 1994 / DG 439898
- ○ **Prokofiev Plays Prokofiev** / Coppola (cond.), Prokofiev, London SO / 2001 / Naxos 110670

Piano Concerto No. 4 in B flat major (for the left hand), Op. 53 (1931)

Written for Austrian pianist Paul Wittgenstein, Prokofiev's *Fourth* remained the black sheep of his set of five piano concertos since it was the only one still unperformed at the composer's death in 1953. Wittgenstein, who lost his right arm to World War I combat, is better appreciated today for the works he commissioned, like the Ravel *Concerto for the left hand*, than for his keyboard artistry. He rejected Prokofiev's concerto and, curiously, the composer made no effort to introduce the work himself or offer it to another pianist or recast it for two hands.

The work has a unique structure: a short Rondo, marked Vivace, serves as the first movement, with a tamer condensed version of itself returning as the finale, a sort of built-in encore or jesting afterthought that Rondos are better suited at the end. In between are two larger movements, a Romantic Andante and a lively, dramatic Moderato.

The Vivace first movement features a rippling, somewhat angular main theme, whose driving manner brims with nervous energy and high spirits. There follows a second theme, relatively relaxed but still lively. The central section turns intense as both the piano and orchestra build toward seeming eruption, the climax yielding a queasy sense that catastrophe was averted. The themes reappear in reverse order and the movement ends with a brief coda. The Andante features a beautiful main theme whose Romantic warmth recalls the love music in the composer's popular ballet *Romeo and Juliet*. The alternate theme soars and is hardly less compelling in its beauty, especially as it dominates a central climactic episode where it is heard three times in succession. The ensuing movement begins ominously, with the brass presenting a dour melody, but soon the piano plays a bright theme over a lively rhythm. The dark theme returns quickly, however, now more spirited but still menacing. An ethereal theme is given briefly by the strings before the piano introduces a charming marchlike melody. A short cadenza leads to a climactic episode featuring the ethereal melody, after which the main theme returns to close out the movement. The brief but delightful finale features muted restatements of the first movement's main theme, then suddenly threatens to turn angry with rumblings in the piano's bass register before ending demurely on the ascent. *—Robert Cummings*

Recommended:

- ○ **Prokofiev: Piano Concertos 2 & 4** / Mehta (cond.), Bronfman, Israel PO / 1994 / Sony 58966
- ○ **Britten: Diversions; Ravel: Concerto for piano left hand; Prokofiev: Piano Concerto 4** / Ozawa (cond.), Fleisher, Boston SO / 1992 / Sony 47188

Piano Concerto No. 5 in G major, Op. 55 (1931–1932)

After the *Fourth Piano Concerto*, for the left hand, the *Fifth* is the least popular of the five piano concertos Prokofiev wrote. Yet the work offers much of great appeal and delivers a challenge to the finest virtuosos. The composer spoke of the *Fifth*'s abundance of melody, pointing out that each of its five movements contains four or more melodies. Those unfamiliar with the concerto might conclude from that statement that the work must be a large one; yet its duration is typically only 22 to 25 minutes.

The formal structure of the concerto is unusual and rather episodic, hardly clinging to a typical sonata-allegro scheme. If a tag can be put on the work, one to capture both its music and performance features, it would be "athletic," or perhaps "acrobatic." The first movement, marked Allegro con brio, offers a colorful, jumpy main theme, containing wide leaps for the piano and much difficult writing. A lyrical clarinet melody contrasts well with the main material and the movement eventually comes to a brilliant conclusion with a final backward leap on the piano. The second movement carries the marking Moderato ben accentuato, and while a bit less effervescent and driven, it is also lively in its march theme and contains glissandos and glissando-like elements that leap about and emphasize the grotesque and humorous nature of the main theme. Those coming to the concerto for the first time may find this colorful, rhythmic movement the most appealing of the five.

The third movement Toccata derives its main theme from the opening of the first, and serves almost as a belated development section to it. Its furious pace (Allegro con fuoco) and challenging writing for the orchestra, especially for the string section, give the piece a mood of brilliance and breathlessness typical of the composer's earlier *Toccata* and of other similar piano works. The Larghetto fourth movement is the deepest of the five and also the most lyrical. Its main theme is gentle and lovely. A tense middle section is brilliantly conceived, with crashing chords on the piano at the climax accompanying the eerie orchestral rendering of the profound theme. The finale, marked Vivo, contains a mixture of menace and humor, of otherworldliness and joy. Near the end of the exposition a variation on a theme from the third movement appears, and at the same racing tempo. After a dreamy, unearthly middle section, the mood brightens and the piece ends brilliantly.

Prokofiev was the soloist in the work's October 31, 1932, premiere in Berlin, led by Wilhelm Furtwängler and on the same program with Paul Hindemith as violist in Berlioz's *Harold in Italy*. While Prokofiev was only midway though his career, he wrote no more works for piano and orchestra after the tepidly-received *Fifth Concerto*. *—Robert Cummings*

Recommended:

- ○ **Prokofiev: Piano Concerto 5; Piano Sonata 8** / Rowicki (cond.), Richter, Warsaw National PO / DG 449744
- ○ **Sviatoslav Richter Archives Vol. 5** / Svetlanov (cond.), Richter, U.S.S.R. SO / 2000 / Doremi 7758
- ○ **Prokofiev: Piano Concertos 1, 3, & 5** / Mehta (cond.), Bronfman, Israel PO / 1993 / Sony 52483
- ○ **Prokofiev: The 5 Piano Concertos** / Masur (cond.), Beroff, Gewandhaus / 1992 / EMI 62542

Violin Concerto No. 1 in D major, Op. 19 (1916–1917)

Prokofiev began composing his *First Violin Concerto* in 1915. He was very fond of the opening theme, but was busy working on his opera, *The Gambler*. He regretted not having more time to work on the *Concerto*'s "pensive opening." When he got back to it, he intended to compose a "concertino" for violin and orchestra, but the piece grew into a three-movement concerto. As musicologist and Prokofiev scholar Israel Nestyev has noted, Prokofiev consulted Polish violinist Paul Kochanski while writing the violin part. Kochanski advised him on bow markings and other technical details, and was supposed to have been the soloist at the premiere, planned for November of 1917. The piano score of the work was completed in the summer of 1917, but because of the revolution in Russia, the *Concerto* did not receive its first performance until 1922, in Paris.

Instead of the usual fast-slow-fast concerto structure, Prokofiev's outer movements are slow, while the middle movement is a fast scherzo. The order of the *Concerto*'s movements is not the only unusual aspect of this violin concerto: the role of the solo violin is also atypical. While the violin dominates the piece, it is not set dramatically against the orchestra; instead, as Russian music critic I. Yampolsky wrote, the violin is "the first among equals," dominant but integrated into the orchestral texture.

The opening theme of the piece is simple and lyrical. The first movement is in sonata form, with the lyricism and simple sincerity of the first theme contrasted with a chromatic, angular second theme. The two themes are rigorously developed after the exposition, almost unrecognizably transformed. Prokofiev's love for the first theme is reinforced in the recapitulation, where only this theme is heard: the second theme and bridge material are eliminated. The second movement is typical Prokofiev, a virtuosic, "grotesque" Scherzo. It is cast in rondo form, and is full of numerous and sudden shifts of articulation and accent. It is, says Nestyev, music in which "images of sneering sarcasm and sinister forces predominate." In the final movement, Prokofiev returns to the calm, lyrical character of the opening movement, but with added harmonic color. This final movement is a work of ingenious thematic integration, realized in the large coda: the lyrical theme of the finale is played in the orchestra, against the "pensive," lyrical first theme from the opening movement, played by the solo violin.

While Prokofiev's *First Violin Concerto* is an important piece in the contemporary concerto repertoire, it was not well received earlier. Critics condemned the work for its nontraditional formal arrangement and treatment of the soloist and tutti. By this time in his career, Prokofiev was certainly growing accustomed to this kind of criticism of his innovations, particularly from Russian critics. The *Concerto* is a pivotal work, one which displays a maturation of the composer. If one compares the *First Violin Concerto* to Prokofiev's earlier piano concertos, it is easy to see that the former is decidedly more natural in its thematic unfolding, and formally less academic. *—Alexander Carpenter*

Recommended:

○ **David Oistrakh** / Temirkanov (cond.), Oistrakh / Praga 250041

○ **Prokofiev: Violin Concerto 1 & 2** / Rozhdestvensky (cond.), Perlman, BBCSO / EMI 47025

○ **Prokofiev & Shostakovich: Violin Concertos** / Rostropovich (cond.), Vengerov, London SO / 1994 / Teldec 92256

Violin Concerto No. 2 in G minor, Op. 63 (1935)

The multicolored strands of influence—personal and creative—that converged on composer Sergei Prokofiev lent to his musical career a strange richness and duality. Prokofiev's musical development evolved in the constant shadow of multiple and often paradoxical circumstances. Raised and trained in the culture of waning imperial Russia, he would nonetheless emerge as one of the brightest stars in the Soviet Union's world of stringent artistic doctrines. Though hailed early on as a "bad boy" modernist, simplicity, urged by Soviet strictures, became Prokofiev's ultimate goal. Still, he steadfastly continued to employ those aspects—novel and unexpected harmonic turns, melodic athleticism, and a prodigious handling of rhythm—which from the outset marked the uniqueness of his style.

The aspects of change and multiplicity in Prokofiev's music, both within individual works and in the larger scope of his evolving style, are in no place more in evidence than in the *Violin Concerto No. 2 in G minor, Op. 63* (1935). Indeed, the work took shape over the course of wide-ranging travels the composer undertook as part of his performing career. "Reflecting my nomadic concertizing existence," he wrote, "the Concerto was written in the most diverse countries: the main subject of the first movement was written in Paris, the first theme of the second movement—in Voronezh, the instrumentation was completed in Baku, and the premiere took place in December of 1935 in Madrid." Undertaken (probably unbeknownst to the composer) as his final commission from a non-Soviet source, the Concerto already exhibits a particular attention to a less complicated—though no less masterful—handling of musical materials.

The first movement, Allegro moderato, opens with a plaintive, five-beat motive in the solo violin which, even at this early stage, creates a sense of metric imbalance from having been placed into a 4/4 meter. It is spun into a full-fledged melody in G minor which pushes onward, eventually punctuated by episodes of abrupt changes in tonality, rhythmic impulse, and mood. The built-up energy and perfunctory close of the first movement is rapidly dissipated by the arrival of the second, Andante assai, which is characterized by a wistful and perhaps nostalgic, unpretentious and songlike theme in E flat major. The orchestra provides a gentle, harmonically unobtrusive accompaniment as the violin's theme is varied and developed—and later, gear shiftingly interrupted—in the course of the movement. The roles are reversed in the final bars as a thematic fragment and its pizzicato accompaniment, now provided by the solo violin, recapture the initial mood as they fade into quiet. The final movement, Allegro, ben marcato, emerges in triple-metered dance-like gestures, at times with the genteel reserve of a waltz, at others with a more rustic, uninhibited character. Episodes of grotesquerie and dark comedy spring forth and propel the movement forward toward its steely con brio, tumultuous close. *—Michael Rodman*

Recommended:

○ **Prokofiev: Violin Concerto 1 & 2** / Rozhdestvensky (cond.), Perlman, BBCSO / EMI 47025

○ **Shostakovich: Violin Concerto 1; Prokofiev: Violin Concerto 2** / Nagano (cond.), Repin, Halle Orch. / Erato 10696

KEYBOARD

Music for Children, 12 easy pieces, Op. 65 (1935)

Among the first pieces that Prokofiev wrote upon his return to the Soviet Union after years of being music's bad boy in Paris and America, *Music for Children* constitutes a significant change of pace for the composer. These dozen miniatures are explicitly educational—music to be played *by* children, rather than for them, much in the spirit of Bartók's own didactic collections, *For Children* and *Mikrokosmos*. Yet in producing this "accessible" music, Prokofiev was not writing down to his audience; formerly the master of dense, hard-hitting works, he was increasingly preoccupied with clarity, simplicity, and lyricism. With its necessary innocence, *Music for Children* suggests the direction Prokofiev would soon take in his concert works.

The suite begins with "Morning," a delicate little tune uttered tentatively in the middle register over quiet rumblings in the bass. A more extended melody unfolds slowly, before a return of the opening material. "Promenade," despite the Mussorgskyan connotations of the title, is a lighthearted skip at a fairly fast pace. "Fairy Tale" is slower and quieter, both its spare melody and nervous ostinato accompaniment written as a series of cleanly detached notes; indeed, much of this suite is decidedly nonlegato. "Tarantella" is an upbeat, but not intense, version of the familiar Italian dance, with rapid work for the left hand. "Regrets" (also translated as "Repentance") is the suite's longest movement, clocking in at about three minutes; it's a dirge of little thematic distinction, but full of atmosphere, written in a spare style reminiscent of the more somber works of Satie and Poulenc. "Waltz" begins with a rather salonish melody that takes some unexpected turns and harmonies. Contrast comes from a brief central section devoted to perky left-hand comments.

"Parade of the Grasshoppers" begins with a start-and-stop introduction, then eases into a more regular processional theme that still retains the appropriate bounce. The intro returns briefly at the end. "Rain and Rainbow," not surprisingly, is dominated by a long, wistful, descending melody rather like those that would later suffuse Prokofiev's ballet *Cinderella*. "Tag" is a light scherzo carried by chattering right-hand material with a more rudimentary left-hand accompaniment. "March" is militaristic only in the sense of children's parody, rather like the "Children's March" from Bizet's *Carmen*; the naughty little dissonances are more pronounced in this piano original than in Prokofiev's orchestration for the suite *Summer Day*. "Evening" offers brief treble phrases over a restless bass accompaniment; although there's no specific program attached to this movement, the gently flittering right-hand material might suggest fireflies, and the secondary section's quiet four-note ostinato implies frogs or nighttime insects in the brush. "Moonlit Meadows" is a poetically naïve musical scene, the primary interest being how Prokofiev passes thematic fragments up and down the keyboard; adult pianists such as György Sándor often take this movement at a much faster clip than most children could manage, sucking out its atmosphere and rendering it as pleasant, but generic, Prokofiev. *—James Reel*

Recommended:

○ **Gyorgy Sandor Plays Prokofiev** / Sandor / 1993 / Vox 5514

○ **Prolofiev: Piano Music Vol. 3** / Berman / 1991 / Chandos 8926

Piano Sonata No. 2 in D minor, Op. 14 (1912)

In this *Piano Sonata in D minor*, Prokofiev clearly broke from the influence of Rachmaninov and Scriabin, as exemplified in the *Sonata No. 1*, Op. 1, (1907; rev. 1909), and he thus laid the groundwork for his highly individual keyboard style. Cast in four movements, it is unified by shared thematic material in the outer panels and by other motivic and intervallic elements. The opening movement (Allegro ma non troppo) begins with a rapid descending theme that is heard twice, each time seeming to crash upon its conclusion. The ensuing theme is the dominant one, a lovely, lyrical, somewhat ethereal creation also of a mostly descending contour. The development features an exciting buildup, weaving the two themes and climaxing in a powerful statement of the second one. A reprise and brilliant coda close out this panel. The very brief succeeding Scherzo (Allegro marcato) is lively and spicy, motoric in its rhythmic drive, the kind of wild piano music with which Prokofiev became identified. The Andante third movement is lyrical but dark, with a theme that exudes tension in its constant roiling and harsh climaxes. It alternates with a gentle, descending melody whose mysterious manner brings calm following the two stormy appearances of the main theme. The finale (Vivace) features a playful opening theme and a more driven, almost jazzy alternate one. After the second theme from the first movement is recalled, there follow a brilliant reprise and coda. *—Robert Cummings*

Recommended:

○ **Prokofiev: Piano Sonatas Op14, 82, 103** / Richter / Praga 250015

○ **Prokofiev: Piano Sonatas 2, 7, 8** / Pletnev / 1998 / DG 457588

Piano Sonata No. 3 in A minor ("From Old Notebooks"), Op. 28 (1907; revised 1917)

Prokofiev completed both the *Third* and *Fourth Piano Sonatas* in 1917, though they owe much of their existence to sketches dating from ten years earlier. Both sonatas are subtitled "D'après de vieux cahiers" [From the Old Notebooks], and are reconstructions of compositions and sketches from 1907–08. Prokofiev's *First* and *Third Sonatas* are identical in structure; both are single movement works using sonata-allegro form. Both sonatas are also studies in contrast between the lyrical and what pianist Murray McLachlan calls Prokofiev's "Scherzando-motoric" style. The two works differ significantly in one important respect: the *Third Sonata* is a highly unified work, compared to the less mature, somewhat derivative *First Sonata*. In the *Third Sonata*, the themes are more original, and are developed in a more natural, less pedantic way than in the *First Sonata*, and thematic material is developed in the former all the way through the piece, whereas the latter sometimes substitutes figuration and sequential padding for development. This piece was surprisingly well received by critics (Prokofiev was no critic's darling, to be sure), who praised its unity and sincerity.

The *Third Sonata* is a short piece, but has been described by some commentators as one of Prokofiev's best piano compositions, by virtue of its passion and freshness. It is a definite departure from the *Second Sonata* of 1912, a light-hearted, witty virtuoso piece, profoundly humorous and volatile. By 1917, Prokofiev had moved beyond the humor and episodic structure of the *Second Sonata*, creating with his *Third Sonata* a work of great drama, symphonic in scope and character. The sophistication and maturity of this sonata are evident from the outset, as the two themes of the exposition—the angular first theme and the lyrical second theme—are clearly stated before dissolving into an energetic and powerful development section. Both themes are developed rigorously, and are transformed in character throughout this middle section of the piece, leading into the recapitulation. It is at this point that Prokofiev diverges significantly from standard sonata form, choosing to completely omit the first theme from the recapitulation; instead, the bridge passage from the exposition is heard, followed by an almost unrecognizably transformed version of the second theme. The piece ends with a coda, in which the second theme is finally heard in its original form.

After the *Third Sonata* would come a period of deep introspection for the composer, a period in which he would compose a number of extremely lyrical and introverted pieces, beginning with the *Fourth Piano Sonata*. *—Alexander Carpenter*

Recommended:

○ **Emil Gilels In Recital** / Gilels / Music & Arts 746

○ **Alexis Weissenberg** / Weissenberg / 1998 / Philips 456988

Piano Sonata No. 4 in C minor, Op. 29 (1908–1917)

Like the Third Piano Sonata Op. 28, Prokofiev's Fourth Piano Sonata was a revision of a work composed a decade earlier; both sonatas, in fact, are subtitled "D'apres de vieux cahiers" (From Old Notebooks). Completed in 1917, this sonata contains music taken directly from the composer's youthful Fifth Sonata (not to be confused with the mature Fifth Sonata, Op. 38) and from his Symphony in E minor, both written during his student days at the Moscow Conservatory in 1908.

Unlike the Third Sonata, which has an exciting, effusive character, this work is decidedly more restrained and introspective. Its austerity is more reminiscent of Schumann and Brahms than it is of the pyrotechnic pianism of Liszt or Rachmaninoff, whose influences can be clearly heard in other works by Prokofiev. Though the sonata was written when Russia was under the threat of the German advance in World War I and the October Revolution was imminent, it does not reflect the tension that must have filled the composer's life at this time, since its inspiration belongs, in a real sense, to the first decade of the century.

The work is cast in three movements: Allegro molto sostenuto, Andante assai, and Allegro con brio, ma non leggiere. The first and third movements are reworkings of the first movement and finale of the 1908 sonata, while the central Andante derives from the symphony mentioned above. Elements of Prokofiev's compositional idiom, including strongly diatonic melodies, polyphonic textures, and complex harmonic structures, are in evidence throughout. The first movement is in sonata-allegro form. Both of the primary themes are lyrical and colorful, and are treated polyphonically in the development. Like the first movement, the second contains two themes of contrasting character, and features broad, arched melodies over repeating thirds in the bass. In the final movement, some of the restraint of the previous movements is abandoned in favor of more exuberant musical statements, in what Boris Asafyev, a composer and associate of Prokofiev, described as "an outburst of long pent-up emotion." The finale is rhythmically vivacious and marked by accentuated dissonances and chromatic harmonies, and recalls, at least in spirit, the energy and clownishness of the Second Piano Sonata (1912).

If the Third Sonata is symphonic in structure and scope, then the Fourth is, as Sviatoslav Richter remarked, "intimately chamber in character, concealing riches which are not immediately obvious to the eye." If the intimate tone of this work perhaps makes it less immediately accessible than some of Prokofiev's more ebullient pieces, it nonetheless takes a place among his finest keyboard music, and is perhaps one of the most representative examples of the his simple and sincere lyrical style. *—Alexander Carpenter*

Recommended:

○ **Sviatoslav Richter Concert Performances & Broadcasts** / Richter / Music & Arts 775

○ **Prokofiev: Piano Sonatas** / Bronfman / 1994 / Sony 52484

Piano Sonata No. 5 in C major, Op. 38 (1923)

This is an initial and rarely heard version of a work that Prokofiev heavily revised and reissued in 1953 as his Op. 135 sonata. Although in the early 1920s Prokofiev was deeply involved in Western avant-garde trends and was becoming notorious for rough, aggressive orchestral scores, the early version of this sonata is a comparatively simple C major affair, in the charming manner of his earlier *Classical Symphony*. In the words of pianist Barbara Nissman, "The two versions can be viewed as stylistically different works from separate periods: Op. 38 is a Classical work; Op. 38/135 is a Romantic paraphrase of the Classical work."

The first movement, Allegro tranquillo, is in sonata-allegro form, with the first theme being a beguiling, almost childlike tune, and the second more urgent and dissonant (Prokofiev toned the dissonace down in the revision). The two themes are developed with the second subject at the forefront, then are separated out in a traditional recapitulation and a coda based primarily on the first theme.

The second movement, Andantino, again a bit more dissonant in this original version, takes an ABA format with the themes not really distinct from each other except for the first's reliance on quick, mocking arpeggios. The last movement, Un poco allegretto, takes up sonata form again. Both its themes are quite busy but not motoric; the first is an angular affair that juts out of an initial series of repeated notes, and the second is equally restless but smoother. *—James Reel*

Recommended:

○ **Arthur Loesser in Recital** / Loesser / 2001 / Marston 52036

○ **Prokofiev: Piano Sonatas Vol. 3** / Glemser / 2002 / Naxos 8555030

Piano Sonata No. 6 in A major ("War Sonata 1"), Op. 82 (1939–1940)

Prokofiev gave opus numbers to works as soon as he started them, which explains why the sixth, seventh, and eighth piano sonatas are listed successively. They were completed in different years through the World War II era and are collectively often called the "war sonatas," although technically this sonata was completed before Germany's invasion of 1941 brought the Soviet Union into the war. It was premiered by the composer, first privately, then on Radio Moscow, and finally in live concert by Sviatoslav Richter. Critics (and party officials) were puzzled and even outraged by what they saw as its brutality. It is in fact the largest, most emotionally powerful, and most "Romantic" of Prokofiev's sonatas. It starts with a unifying motto played with great force, a four-note descending pattern in thirds which outlines at once both the A major and minor chords. Thus uncertainty of mode and the cross relation between C natural and C sharp energize the entire work. The first movement is an explosive treatment of this idea, with the motive hurled back and forth in extreme registers of the piano, one of Prokofiev's most turbulent movements.

The second movement is a slowish scherzo with a theme that seemingly tries to capture the common Prokofiev mood of playful irony in the way it skips over the keys atop staccato accompanying chords. But despite the irony, it is far from carefree. The third movement is a sad waltz. The finale brings back the turbulence and the first movement and pounds to a violent statement of the main major/minor idea of the sonata. *—Joseph Stevenson*

Recommended:

○ **Richter Rediscovered** / Richter / 2001 / RCA 63844

○ **Chopin: Piano Sonata 2; Ravel: Gaspard de la Nuit** / Pogorelich / 1998 / DG 459045

○ **Prokofiev: Piano Sonatas** / Bronfman / 1994 / Sony 52484

Piano Sonata No. 7 in B flat major ("War Sonata 2" / "Stalingrad"), Op. 83 (1939–1942)

This is the middle panel in Prokofiev's grand trilogy of works called *War Sonatas*. It is the most popular of the three and, at about 16 or 17 minutes, the shortest as well. The first movement, marked Allegro inquieto, opens with a dark, menacing theme whose militaristic vehemence seizes the expressive reins at times with insistent bass chords that hammer out a crushing rhythm. The listener immediately senses a connection to war and struggle in this lively but conflicted opening. A lyrical second theme introduces gentler music, but does not break the dark mood. In the development section, a tense buildup constructed mainly on the first theme leads to a powerful climax, after which the music gradually becomes more tranquil, the second theme being reprised in a gloomy ethereality. A brief, rhythmic coda follows, its lively springiness seeming to sputter and stagger as it reaches the finish line.

The second movement is marked Andante caloroso and features a consoling main theme whose gently rocking lilt and overripe textures convey an almost decadent sense, as if its beauty is beginning to decay. Some listeners hear it as a kind of dark salonlike creation in its perfume-drenched melancholy and quasi-pop catchiness. The middle section turns intense and climaxes in a tolling-bell passage that eventually gives way to a reprise of the main theme.

The Precipitato finale is the most famous and dramatic movement of the three. Cast in an ABCBA structure, it opens with a driving main theme whose rhythmic jazzy elements convey a frenetic, fight-for-dear-life sense. The second theme maintains the perpetual-motion drive, but now the feeling of desperation takes on an insistent, if less harried manner, before yielding to the ensuing idea, which rises from the bass regions to turn almost subdued in the upper ranges. After the second theme reappears the main theme returns for a crashing, dissonant but ultimately triumphant conclusion in a blaze of dazzling virtuosic writing. *—Robert Cummings*

Recommended:

- ○ **The Glenn Gould Edition** / Gould / 1995 / Sony 52622
- ○ **Prokofiev: Piano Sonatas 7 & 8; Liszt: Mephisto Waltz** / Ashkenazy / 2001 / Decca 468497
- ○ **Live from the Concertgebouw, 1978 & 1979** / Argerich / 2000 / Angel 56975B
- ○ **Stravinsky, Prokofiev, Webern, Boulez** / Pollini / DG 447431

Piano Sonata No. 8 in B flat major ("War Sonata 3"), Op. 84 (1939–1944)

This is the third of the so-called trilogy of works dubbed the "War Sonatas." Its approximately five-year gestation was a period during which the exceedingly busy Prokofiev also wrote the *Piano Sonatas No. 6* and *No. 7*, the first version of his opera *War and Peace*, the ballet *Cinderella*, and other works. Cast in three movements, the *Eighth* is at once the gentlest and most tortured of the "War Sonatas." The outer panels are the longest in any Prokofiev sonata, with the first his largest by far. Marked Andante dolce—Allegro Moderato, it features two main themes, the first lyrical and mysterious in its wandering sense of melancholy and suppressed suffering, and the second conveying a feeling of desolation, its melody beginning quietly in the bass and concluding in a surreal mood in the upper register. The development section defies convention: rather than working toward greater complexity, the music develops backward, reducing its expressive character to its rudimentary and most violent aspects. A melancholy reprise closes out this profound movement. For the middle panel, also marked Andante dolce, Prokofiev uses a charming, bright theme from his abandoned orchestral score *Eugene Onegin*. This brief, playful minuet provides deft contrast to the more serious outer panels. The finale (Vivace) opens with a driving theme, but quickly turns heroic and majestic. The middle section builds to a weirdly powerful climax from seemingly insignificant rhythmic leftovers. The main material is reprised and the music ends ambivalently, with a rhythmic motif thrashing about before suddenly running short of energy. *—Robert Cummings*

Recommended:

- ○ **Prokofiev: Piano Concerto 5; Piano Sonata 8** / Richter / DG 449744
- ○ **Prokofiev: Piano Sonatas 7 & 8; Liszt: Mephisto Waltz** / Ashkenazy / 2001 / Decca 468497
- ○ **Prokofiev: Piano Sonatas 2, 7, 8** / Pletnev / 1998 / DG 457588
- ○ **Gyorgy Sandor Plays Prokofiev** / Sandor / 1993 / Vox 3500
- ○ **Prokofiev: Piano Sonatas 7 & 8** / Bronfman / 1988 / CBS 44680

Piano Sonata No. 9 in C major, Op. 103 (1947)

Completed near the end of his life, Prokofiev's *Ninth Piano Sonata* was his least successful, and remains his least known, work in this genre. It was also his last complete piano composition. Unlike the preceding *Sonatas Nos. 6–8*—the so-called "War sonatas," which are epic, emotionally intense works—the *Ninth Sonata* is a return to the intimacy of the *Fourth Sonata* of 1917. In general, the gentle lyricism and simplicity of Prokofiev's earlier works are in evidence in this piece, and familiar techniques, such as diatonicism, simple rhythms, and witty harmonic/cadential surprises are in abundance. The work is dedicated to pianist Sviatoslav Richter.

The *Ninth Sonata* has four movements: Allegretto, Allegro strepitoso, Andante tranquillo, and Allegro con brio, ma non troppo presto. Musicologist Israel Nestyev has remarked on the similarities between thematic material in the *Ninth Sonata* and some of Prokofiev's ballet music, including *Cinderella*, and especially *War and Peace*.

The opening movement, typically, is in sonata form and, in Nestyev's words, "is miniature in form, modestly developed, and devoid of dramatic conflicts." The second movement is a scherzo in which virtuosic figures appear. The third movement, like the first, is lyrical and melodic, with simple, songlike melodies. The finale is energetic and lighthearted, cast in sonata-rondo form, with more virtuosic running passages and challenging figurations; as in the *Fourth Sonata*, the finale includes material similar in character to the *Commedia del arte*-inspired clownishness of the *Second Sonata*. By the end of the finale, however, the gentle lyrical theme from the first movement returns, and the work concludes peacefully.

This last sonata exemplifies a number of stylistic traits of "late Prokofiev," most significantly the sophisticated harmonic language; however, these complex harmonies are juxtaposed with a disarmingly simple lyricism, resulting in what pianist Murray McLachlan has called a sonata of "contrasts and contradictions," a work "deeply felt and unified." The novelty with which Prokofiev achieves unity in this sonata is perhaps the work's most important feature: at the end of each of the first three movements, the opening theme of the following movement is heard. This thematic foreshadowing links the sonata's movements together, and this, along with the usual thematic/motivic integration, strongly unifies the work. Perhaps, after the bombast and intensity of the *War Sonatas*, simplicity and gentleness of the *Ninth Sonata* seemed somehow lacking, or a regression, and despite its many qualities, the work was not published until eight years after it was completed, and is rarely performed. *—Alexander Carpenter*

Recommended:

- ○ **Prokofiev: Piano Sonatas Opp14, 82 & 103** / Richter / Praga 250015
- ○ **Gyorgy Sandor Plays Prokofiev** / Sandor / 1993 / Vox 3500
- ○ **Prokofiev: Piano Sonatas 7–9** / Chiu / 1996 / HM 907199
- ○ **Prokofiev: Piano Sonatas** / Bronfman / 1996 / Sony 53273

Sarcasms, Op. 17 (1912–1914)

Sergei Prokofiev, a keyboard virtuoso of the first rank, always considered himself a composer first and a pianist second. He became greatly distressed when, early in his career, a photo he posed for with Stravinsky identified the pair as "Composer Stravinsky, Pianist Prokofiev." Still, he composed enthusiastically for the instrument, and he delighted in using his piano music, with its jarring dissonances, pungent harmonies, and brittle attacks, to shock audiences. Early in his career, his *Suggestion diabolique*, Op. 4/4 (1910–12) provided him with an avant-garde musical calling card, and his first two piano concerti helped to cement his reputation as Russia's *enfant terrible*.

The five pieces that constitute *Sarcasms* (1912–14) are the product of Prokofiev's most radical musical thinking up to that point. Contrary to what some musicologists have asserted, *Sarcasms* is not merely a collection of sonic shocks and musical pranks strung together in a group of truly "sarcastic" pieces. Indeed, Prokofiev shows his richly lyrical side in these pieces, especially in the first ("Tempestuoso") and third ("Allegro precipitato"). The fifth, "Precipitosissimo," is a depiction of laughter—not the laughter of sarcasm, but that in the face of tears.

The first piece opens stormily and features the sort of piano writing so recognizable as Prokofiev's most brittle and percussive vein; still, the second theme is extraordinarily lyrical. The second piece, "Allegro rubato," begins in a contemplative mood and features a rather nonchalant theme. "Allegro precipitato" features the most furious music of the five pieces; there is such an intense rush of energy at the outset that one expects a titanic explosion, yet the lyrical middle section tames the anxiety of the opening material. "Smanioso" ("Frenzied") seems almost improvisatory at first hearing; the mood is slippery as the music wanders nervously at the outset, moving toward subdued tension in the second half. The last of the *Sarcasms* is one of the most subtle in the set, occupying a sonic world of dark and hazy images, of gloom and anxiety. *—Robert Cummings*

Recommended:

- ○ **Gyorgy Sandor Plays Prokofiev** / Sandor / 1993 / Vox 5514
- ○ **Russian Piano School** / Ervy-Novitskaya / 1996 / Melodiya 332182

Tales of an Old Grandmother, Op. 31 (1918)

Tales of an Old Grandmother is sometimes regarded as children's music in the sense that it is a portrait of an old grandmother as would likely be seen through the eyes of a child. Prokofiev was well known for his children's music, of course, but this effort, written in New York during the first year of his self-imposed exile from Russia, is quite nostalgic in mood and a bit more complex than his other children's works. The set is made up of four untitled short pieces and lasts about ten minutes. Most are slow or moderately paced works and feature generally soft dynamics, each opening piano and closing pianissimo. The first piece, marked Moderato, features a playful theme whose lively but unhurried rhythms and numerous arpeggiated chords impart a quaint sense of nostalgia. The second work (Andantino) opens with a dreamy, lightly textured melody heard mostly in upper-register sonorities. In its somewhat mysterious character, it bears a resemblance to some of the more lyrical pieces in the composer's then-recent *Visions fugitives*. The third piece (Andante assai) is the sternest, calling to mind a grandmother who could be difficult. The mysterious, somewhat ethereal middle section contrasts with the darker marchlike theme in the outer sections, but itself eventually turns tense and almost angry. The last work in the set (Sostenuto) shares the nostalgic character of the first, with a lonely theme emerging from somber, marchlike chords and a second melody in the upper register that comes on like gradually heavier raindrops to etch out its gossamer theme. This is a fine set of piano works from a master of many musical genres. *—Robert Cummings*

Recommended:

- ○ **Gyorgy Sandor Plays Prokofiev** / Sandor / 1993 / Vox 5514
- ○ **Sofronitsky Plays Beethoven, Prokofiev, Liszt, Chopin** / Sofronitsky / Urania 4211

Toccata in C major, Op. 11 (1912)

Much of Sergei Prokofiev's compositional output in the early and mid-1910s consisted of stylistically bold keyboard compositions written for his own use as a pianist. The composer's *Toccata* (1912) belongs to this period, as do works like *Sarcasms* (1912–14) and the First (1911–12) and Second (1913) Piano Concerti. The advanced, aggressive musical language of these works led to Prokofiev's reputation as Russian music's *enfant terrible*, yet each demonstrates a mastery that clearly transcends mere bravura showiness.

The Toccata has a well-deserved reputation as a work of formidable difficulty. Unfortunately, while the piece has been popular over the years, attracting performances from pianists like Vladimir Horowitz and Martha Argerich, it has been looked upon in certain circles as a mere knuckle-buster, devoid of serious musical substance. True, the piece contains sonic effects, such as the bell-ringing sounds that climax the middle section, and the Toccata often appears as an encore, but this work is better-crafted than its Lisztian reputation might suggest.

The piece is built upon motoric rhythms in a *perpetuum mobile* framework that lets up only slightly in the middle section. The Toccata's two main themes are a part of the same energetic and somewhat sinister fabric, the anxiety in both auguring a forthcoming explosion in the music. After the themes are developed, there is a reprise, and the coda that ensues contains the promised explosion: the main theme is hammered out frenziedly in the upper register against motoric bass notes.

Because of the enormous popularity of the Toccata, it has become one of the most influential piano compositions of the century. Many composers have written their own versions of the Prokofiev Toccata and have employed its motor rhythms and driving energies in other piano works as well.

The work was first published in Russia in 1913, however it was not played publicly until three years later (by the composer, in St. Petersburg on December 10, 1916). *—Robert Cummings*

Recommended:

○ **Byron Janis** / Janis / 1994 / Mercury 434333

○ **Martha Argerich Debut Recital** / Argerich / DG 447430

Visions fugitives, Op. 22 (1915–1917)

While Prokofiev had written many provocative and often masterful piano compositions in his early career, this set of 20 pieces, along with the *Piano Sonata No. 2,* Op. 14 (1912), may have been his most important works in the solo realm until he produced his cycle of so-called "War Sonatas," Nos. 6 (1940), 7 (1942) and 8 (1944). Certainly the range of mood and the subtle gradations of color found in the *Visions Fugitives* show a deepening of expression in the young composer, not evident in his other piano music from the period with the exception of the *Piano Concerto No. 2,* Op. 16 (1913; rev. 1923) and the *Piano Sonata No. 2.*

This set of many very short piano sketches was composed at roughly the same time Schoenberg was struggling with tonality and tending to construct works of very short atonal units. Prokofiev's work, also constructed of short units, is far from atonal. But it does share some harmonic restlessness with the nearly contemporary works of Scriabin. This strange gem of piano writing, in many very tiny movements, evokes a half-dream in which one mood or impression is quickly replaced by a contrary or illogical leap out of the subconscious. It is one of Prokofiev's most striking and individual creations, unlike not only any other composer's piano music in tone and structure, but quite unlike much of Prokofiev's own music. It is certainy suited to listening with the lights dimmed and in a mood for free association. Incidentally, conductor Rudolf Barshai has arranged approximately the first two thirds of this set into an evocative orchestral version.

The title of the work, *Visions Fugitives*, is French for "Fleeting (or Fugitive) Visions." It derives from the words of Russian poet Konstantin Balmont: "In every fugitive vision I see worlds, full of the changing play of rainbow hues." Prokofiev thus fashioned an appropriate moniker for this assorted collection of short pieces, which in spirit—though not in style—are close to some of Schumann's piano compositions, like *Carnaval.*

Each of the 20 pieces bursts with musical ideas, and each conveys such vivid colors despite their generally short length—the entire collection lasts about 20 to 22 minutes in a typical performance. Only two or three of the pieces run over two minutes, with most of the others having a duration of around a minute. Several clock in at about a half minute.

Of those in this last group, No. 5, marked Molto giocoso, is perky and not a note too short or too long in its 25-second length. No. 7 (Pittoresco) is dreamy and serene, and sounds close to the hazy but slightly darker No. 20 (Lento Irrealmente). The tart dissonances that lead off No. 9 (Allegretto tranquillo) sound almost gentle, even cute, but never threatening. Threatening is how No. 14 (Feroce) begins, but its middle section features a subtle and arresting lyrical theme. The gloomy and mysterious No. 12 (Assai moderato) contrasts nicely with its predecessor, the buoyant and playful No. 11 (Con vivacita). The innocence and peacefulness of No. 1 is quite appealing, but probably the most popular and one of the finest of the 20 pieces here is No. 16 (Dolente), whose falling theme has an air of gloomy meditation about it.

This work was first published in Russia in 1917 and is today among Prokofiev's most popular piano works, though the pieces are often played in recitals only as excerpts. Performances of the whole collection are relatively rare. *—AMG*

Recommended:

○ **Sviatoslav Richter Archives Vol. 5** / Richter / 2000 / Doremi 7758

○ **Emil Gilels 2** / Gilels / 1999 / Philips 456796

FILM MUSIC

Lieutenant Kijé, film score and suite, Op. 60 (1933–1934)

Beginning in the 1930s, Prokofiev became one of the first composers of international repute to write music for films. His silver screen career began with the score to Alexander Feinzimmer's *Lieutenant Kijé* (1933), released in America under the title *The Czar Wants to Sleep.* Though the film is infrequently encountered today, Prokofiev's music has enjoyed tremendous popularity in its incarnation as a five-movement concert suite. Following *Kijé*, Prokofiev produced a number of film scores of great distinction, most notably those for *Alexander Nevsky* (1938) and *Ivan the Terrible* (1942–43). So highly regarded were his skills, in fact, that while researching film and sound techniques in Hollywood during 1937–38, he was offered a then-colossal $2,500 per week to become a full-time film composer. He rejected the offer and returned to the Soviet Union.

The music of *Lieutenant Kijé* is refreshingly satirical, a perfect counterpart to a story about a nonexistent soldier—"born" of a copyist's error—who is provided an identity, a heroic military background, and even a wife. Because the Czar himself is led to believe in Kijé's existence, his courtiers are afraid to tell him the truth. When the Czar desires to meet this great hero, it becomes clear that Kijé must be killed off. The Czar attends Kijé's funeral and, over an empty coffin, laments the loss of such a hero.

The first section of the suite, "The Birth of Kijé," begins with a mournful fanfare on cornets that is followed by comical "military" music on piccolo, flute, and snare drum. After a powerful martial outburst, Kijé's short and rather flaccid theme emerges on tenor saxophone and flute. The "Romance" features a darkly melancholy theme, played on the double bass, of decidedly Russian character. The middle section is more robust; throughout the entire movement, the orchestration remains engaging and colorful. "The Wedding of Kijé" presents the first of the work's two famous themes, a jovial tune on the cornet that serves as a colorful contrast to the pompous music that opens and closes the movement. The lively main theme of the "Troika," set against a glittering backdrop of sleigh bells, is contrasted by sardonic episodes in which brass instruments and pizzicato strings figure prominently. The final "Interment of Kijé" captures the story's ironic humor to splendid effect. Prokofiev begins this section with the same music that opened the suite, after which he presents Kijé's theme. This recap of the work's main material continues with the mournful theme from the "Romance," which carries on unabated when the cornet enters with the jovial wedding tune. These two themes—one in a slow tempo, the other fast; one melancholy, the other more cheerful—continue simultaneously, providing one of the most striking moments in the entire work. The "Interment" ends with the mournful cornet music that opened the suite. *—Robert Cummings*

Recommended:

○ **Prokofiev: Alexander Nevsky; Skythische Suite; Leutnant Kijé** / Abbado (cond.), Chicago SO / 1980 / DG 447419

○ **Hovhaness: Mysterious Mountain** / Reiner (cond.), Chicago SO / 1995 / RCA 902661957

CHORAL

Alexander Nevsky, cantata for mezzo-soprano, chorus & orchestra, Op. 78 (1938)

Prokofiev and the celebrated film director, Sergei Eisenstein (1898–1948), managed to survive the purges that decimated Russian intellectual life under Stalin. Together, they made two historically significant films: *Alexander Nevsky* in 1938, and *Ivan the Terrible*, Parts 1 and 2 (No. 3 never got beyond preproduction). Worsening relations between Nazi Germany and the U.S.S.R. decided Stalin to sponsor a film about Alexander Nevsky, a thirteenth century prince of Novgorod, who routed Swedish invaders in 1240 at the river Neva (hence his name) and two years later defeated a horde of Teutonic Knights at Lake Chud (aka Peipus), on what is today the Estonian border. Eisenstein offered to direct and persuaded Prokofiev to score the film. Ironically, because Stalin and Hitler signed a nonaggression treaty before *Nevsky* was ready for release, it was deep-sixed in the Soviet Union, although not elsewhere. Only after Hitler attacked the U.S.S.R. was the film repatriated as a propaganda tool, by which time Prokofiev had reworked sections of his soundtrack score into a "dramatic cantata" with texts by himself and V. Lugovskoy. Prokofiev conducted the Moscow premiere on May 17, 1939.

In "Russia under the Mongolian yoke," high and low registers of the orchestra accompanied Eisenstein's stark panoramas of bones, skulls, discarded weapons, wasted fields, and sacked villages in the wake of marauding tartars; music at once eerie, archaic and despairing.

The "Song about Alexander Nevsky" is an uncomplicated telling of Prince Alexander's defeat of invading Swedes "on the wide waters of the River Neva" in

1240, abetted by local peasants armed with axes and improvised weapons. A quicker middle section (Più mosso) effectively recreates the sounds of battle.

In "The Crusaders in Psko" swaggering, scornful Teuton invaders sing Latin words not easy to translate, perhaps because Prokofiev intended them to be onomatopoeic rather than narrative. An A minor middle section for legato strings, which are asked to play "expressively and sadly," hardens before the Crusaders quell a spirit of insurrection.

"Arise, Russian people" exhorts them to defend, in the populist style mastered by Prokofiev, plainly tuneful but nonetheless perfervid, with a new melody in the middle section that returns triumphantly in the fifth and seventh movements.

"The battle on the ice" is the longest of the movements and stunningly graphic without needing film to be effective. The Crusaders, shouting their Latin battle cry, ride wildly against *Nevsky*'s force, who sing "In our great native Russia no foe shall live...." The breakup of the ice is a terrifying sound, far surpassing a small studio orchestra and constricted mono sound on the original soundtrack.

In "The field of the dead" the mezzo-soprano soloist becomes a Russian girl, looking for the body of her lover slain in battle. She vows to kiss the eyelids of all who died, and to wed a "brave" survivor rather than a "handsome man."

A recapitulation of Russian themes celebrates "Alexander's entry into Pskov" and rejoices in Nevsky's victory, as appropriate in World War II and after as Stalin meant the film to be in 1937. *—Roger Dettmer*

Recommended:

- **Khachaturian: Violin Concerto, Prokofiev: Alexander Nevsky** / Reiner (cond.), Elias, Chicago SO & Chorus / 2000 / RCA 63708
- **Prokofiev: Alexander Nevsky; Skythische Suite; Leutnant Kije** / Abbado (cond.), London SO & Chorus / 1980 / DG 447419

CHAMBER MUSIC

Cello Sonata in C major, Op. 119 (1949)

It was a remarkable pair of Soviet musicians that gave the 1950 premiere of Sergey Prokofiev's *Sonata for cello and piano in C major*, Op. 119: pianist Sviatoslav Richter and cellist Mstislav Rostropovich. By 1949, when he composed the sonata, Prokofiev was in the last half-decade of his life; together, the *Sonata*, the *Seventh Symphony* (1951–52), and the *Sinfonia Concertante* for cello and orchestra (1952) make a remarkable final threesome of instrumental pieces.

Prokofiev was among those composers officially condemned for "formalism" in 1948, and it is both fascinating and stirring to witness how successfully Prokofiev managed, in these last works, to create a music that seems perhaps utterly conservative but which still pushes new expressive buttons in quiet ways that the *Pravda* officials would surely never have been astute enough to hear. The composer of the *Sonata for cello and piano* might seem a tame composer compared to, say, the composer of 1914's *Scythian Suite*; but he is really just a composer who has learned subtler, more patient, and, ultimately, clearer ways to fully speak his mind.

The sonata is in three movements: Andante grave, Moderato, and Allegro ma non troppo. True Classical sonata-allegro form meets stunning, voluptuous melody in the opening movement. A low, unpretentious cello solo raises the curtain; out of the piano's occasional comments grows a little tune whose steady chordal accompaniment is soon taken over by the cello's striking pizzicato chords. Prokofiev once said that he was no good at writing melodies. Looking at the music of his youth we might be forced to agree; but the G major second theme of the Andante grave proves beyond any doubt what can be learned through a lifetime of work—it is rich, full, and exceedingly flexible.

The Moderato is a bouncing, energetic movement that dances its way towards a sublimely smooth central episode. In the finale, Prokofiev makes little effort to hide the fact that he was steeped in the music of Rachmaninov and Tchaikovsky during his youth. He might as a young man have revolted against that heritage, but he never escaped it, and in the Allegro ma non troppo he matches deeply lyrical "Russian" tunefulness with an easy gracefulness worthy of Haydn, and then adds the kind of impish rhythms and (late in the piece) virtuosic fire that will always say "Prokofiev" to us. *—Blair Johnston*

Recommended:

- **The Russian Years** / Rostropovich / 1997 / EMI 72016
- **Prokofiev & Rachmaninov: Cello Sonatas** / Ma, Ax / 1991 / Sony 46486

Flute Sonata in D major, Op. 94 (1943)

It was at the prompting of famed violinist David Oistrakh that, in 1944, Sergey Prokofiev adapted his *Sonata for flute and piano in D major*, Op. 94, which he had composed one year earlier for violin and piano (the violin version is called Op. 94bis). Oistrakh had more in mind than just acquiring a new piece to play when he made the suggestion to his friend: he had legitimate concerns that it was an ultimately unsuccessful work in its original form. Prokofiev decided that he agreed, and had at it. The one version has never really replaced the other (Prokofiev never disowned the original flute version, and, even if he had, it's unlikely that the world's flutists would ever have given it up), but—perhaps only because there are so many more famous concert violinists than famous concert flutists—one is likely to hear Op. 94bis and find it on the shelves of record stores far more frequently than Op. 94.

The sonata has four movements: Moderato, Scherzo (marked Allegretto Scherzando in the flute version and Presto in the violin version), Andante, and Allegro con brio. The actual changes made in the adaptation for violin are minimal—the violin can play a few half steps lower than the flute, and the violin can play chords and double stops—but the natures of the two instruments are so different that a pianist playing the piece with first one and then the other would find that a completely different approach is needed. The flexible melody and generally thin scoring of the first movement are perfectly suited for the flute, and yet the music is so well-balanced for violin and piano that, even in the heavier middle portions Prokofiev makes almost no changes for the violin version. The trio comes across as a wonderfully fleeting, elfin wisp when played by flute; as a witty, barbed dialogue when played by violin and piano. The F major slow movement is given lovely, gentle chromatic tints. It is in the last movement that the sonata sounds most different in its two guises: the flute simply cannot produce the same robust, full tone in its low register that the violin can, and so the pianist is forced to hold back a great deal, and, as the entirety of the ending is rewritten in fortissimo double stops, the culmination of the sonata in its violin version is made via a happy, string-whacking bombast that the flute will never know. *—Blair Johnston*

Recommended:

- **60 Years, 60 Flute Masterpieces Vol. 7: 20th Century, Part 1** / Argerich, Galway / 1999 / RCA 63439
- **Souvenir D'un Lieu Cher** / Berlinsky, Gorakhovich / 1997 / Helicon 1015

Five Melodies for violin & piano, Op. 35bis (1925)

Prokofiev composed five "Songs without Words" for voice and piano (Op. 35) in 1920; five years later he arranged them for violin and piano as *Cinq Mélodies*, Op. 35a, in which form they are better known today. These pieces are subtle little gems. The first (Andante) is of unsettled tonality, which strengthens its emotional climax. The violin sings sweetly in the second (Lento, ma non troppo); the Poco più mosso middle section is more mysterious. No. 3 (Animato, ma non allegro) is a miniature rhapsody, with a Meno mosso middle section which requires the violin to tiptoe in its highest register. No. 4 (Allegro leggiero e scherzando) is a little melody with a vaguely Oriental flavor that is heard and is gone. No. 5 (Andante non troppo) actually has more of a scherzando feel; there is a Pochissimo più animato section that builds to a passionate climax before the main melody briefly reappears, almost as an afterthought. The pieces are dedicated to different musicians, Nos. 1, 3, and 4 to Paul Kochanski, No. 2 to Cecilia Hansen, and No. 5 to Joseph Szigeti. *—Sol Louis Siegel*

Recommended:

- **David Oistrakh in Prague** / Oistrakh, Bauer / Praga 256007
- **Sonatas & Dances for Violin** / Sitkovetsky, Gililov / 2001 / Angel 61887

Overture on Hebrew Themes, for clarinet, string quartet & piano, Op. 34 (1919)

Prokofiev only rarely used folk music or themes by other composers in his scores. Early in his career, in fact, he had decided as a matter of principle that he would employ only his own melodies and creative wares in his music. In 1919, when he was living in the United States, he was approached by clarinetist Simeon Bellison to write a chamber work on Hebrew themes. Bellison gave the composer a book containing some themes for possible use as source material. Prokofiev initially rejected the proposal, but several days later, after playing through and improvising upon some of the themes, he decided to write the work after all. Prokofiev sketched the *Overture on Hebrew Themes* in a single day and produced a finished score in less than two weeks' time.

The work is cast in a single movement featuring two main themes, the first lively and rhythmic, with a Middle Eastern flavor, the second slow and mournful and of a similar ethnic character. Prokofiev develops the themes, especially the first, in the middle section, and imparts much color and variety through Hebrew-flavored harmonies and lively rhythms. Despite the music's Yiddish flavoring, however, the composer's distinctive voice is prominent throughout. Prokofiev's adroit handling of the source material has led some listeners to assume that he himself was Jewish; he was, in fact, a lapsed member of the Russian Orthodox Church.

The chamber ensemble Zimro premiered the *Overture on Hebrew Themes* on January 20, 1920. The group used the proceeds from the concert—indeed, from most of their concert activities—to establish a music conservatory in Jerusalem. The work soon became quite popular, inducing a number of musicians to attempt orchestral transcriptions. Perhaps displeased with the adaptations he heard, Prokofiev made his own orchestration in 1934. It, too, became popular, but by the end of the twentieth century, the original chamber version had become by far the work's best-known and most often performed incarnation. *—Robert Cummings*

Recommended:

- **Prokofiev: Piano Concertos 2 & 4; Overture** / Mehta (cond.), Israel PO / 1994 / Sony 58966

Violin Sonata No. 1 in F minor, Op. 80 (1938–1946)

Cast in four movements of approximately equal length and lasting about a half-hour, this tormented *Sonata for violin and piano* must rank with Prokofiev's finest works in any genre. The Andante opening panel begins with an ominous theme in the bass on the piano, the death-rattle sounds of the violin soon entering overtop it. The mood remains tense as the violin struggles to steal center stage from the piano, finally doing so with a theme that cries out painfully. Eventually the music turns ethereal when the piano gently plays the opening theme in the upper register, while the violin delivers eerie, gossamer runs that slither about hauntingly. The movement ends softly but chillingly. A hard-driving Allegro brusco follows, its main theme slashing and harsh as the piano and violin exchange angry dissonances and crushing chords. An alternate theme imparts a sense of nobility and hope for a time, but cannot here or later dispel the sense of fear and frenzy brought on by the dominant main material. The third movement (Andante) opens with an ethereal, dreamy theme floating amid a sense of fantasy. An alternate theme, largely built on three notes that repeat obsessively, imparts a feeling of desolation, and the whole movement gradually turns darker, sounding bleak and fearful at the end. The finale, marked Allegrissimo—Andante assai, opens with a bustling theme that seems cheerful and almost playful, but its brightness soon appears threatened by dark undercurrents and, as tension accrues from stomping bass chords from the piano, it collapses. The ending of the first movement is recalled, and the music then turns bleaker and, finally, despairing. This exceedingly profound work will yield immeasurable rewards for patient listeners. *—Robert Cummings*

Recommended:

○ **Prokofiev: Melodies; Violin Sonata 1; etc.** / Oistrakh, Bauer / Praga 250041

○ **Prokofiev: Violin Sonatas; 5 Melodies** / Argerich, Kremer / DG 431803

○ **Prokofiev: Violin Sonatas; March; 5 Melodies** / Chiu, Amoyal / 1999 / HM 907237

Violin Sonata No. 2 in D major, Op. 94bis (1944)

Originally conceived as the *Sonata for flute and piano* (1943), this work immediately became more popular in its violin version. Even today it is still more commonly encountered in concert and on recordings than its sibling, not least because violinists outnumber flutists. Cast in four movements, this sonata transcription betrays little of its grim wartime origins, mixing Prokofiev's lyrical warmth with his playful mischief.

The first movement is marked Moderato and opens with a lovely melody on violin that seems to float lazily amid the clouds. The music springs to life in a jovial bridge passage leading to the alternate theme, also a lyrical, bright melody, but one that seems to hopscotch about. Both themes are repeated then developed, though in their working out they divulge relatively little transformation, but do show a more energetic sense. A reprise and lovely coda close out the movement.

The ensuing Scherzo, marked Presto, features that typical Prokofievian drive and mischievous abandon, the piano often seeming to propel the violin along. There are two themes in the outer sections, the first busy and impish, the second carefree and a bit less breathless. The brief trio is calmer and quite lovely in its subdued lyricism.

The Andante third movement features, in the outer sections, a lovely soaring theme on violin, which is just as beautiful when taken up by the piano. But it is the deliciously exotic middle section that seduces the ear: the violin's somewhat jazzy lilting theme receives a beguiling, almost Gershwinian response from the piano's upper register, forging a truly memorable melodic creation.

The finale, marked Allegro con brio, opens with a chipper melody whose festive character seems to turn to chuckles with the appearance of a bouncy second theme. An angular third melody soon appears, and there follows some imaginative development of the material and a reprise. The coda is ecstatic in its joy and wild abandon. *—Robert Cummings*

Recommended:

○ **David Oistrakh** / Oistrakh, Yampolsky / 1997 / Testament 1113

○ **Anne-Sophie Mutter: Recital 2000** / Mutter, Orkis / 2000 / DG 469503

OPERA

The Love for Three Oranges, Op. 33 (1919)

In 1917, with his opera *The Gambler* in rehearsals for a St. Petersburg production, Prokofiev, already recognized as one of the leading modernist composers in his country, was looking for a new subject for his next operatic effort. The composer found his inspiration in a magazine published by theatrical producer Vsevolod Meyerhold in 1914–16, called *The Love for Three Oranges*, after the comedy by Carlo Gozzi.

Following his arrival in Chicago in 1918, Prokofiev attempted to interest the Chicago Opera Company in a production of *The Gambler*, whose staging was canceled owing to the Bolshevik Revolution. The director, Cleofonte Campanini, turned him down, but did offer to do the new opera he suggested, *The Love for Three Oranges*. Prokofiev, a fast worker, completed the work in October that year, and it was premiered on December 30, 1921, in Chicago. Productions in New York (1922), Cologne (1925), Berlin (1926), and Leningrad (1926) followed, each helping to advance the cause of the composer, but meeting with little actual success. Yet, by the 1940s the music in the opera became widely known, mainly because of the often-played Suite adapted from it and use of its March as the theme of a popular radio show in America called "Your FBI in Peace and War." Throughout most of the twentieth century, *The Love for Three Oranges* opera had achieved more performances than any other Prokofiev opera.

The Love for Three Oranges begins with a prologue in which the supporters of tragedy, comedy, eccentricity and other forms of drama watch the story, not only commenting on it, but affecting the outcome of certain events. The story they watch centers on the hypochondriac Prince, who is cursed by the witch, Fata Morgana, to fall madly in love with three oranges and obsessively pursue them.

There is much humor and joy in Prokofiev's score. Some see the opera as a clever, updated Offenbach-like creation, full of slapstick and silliness. It is hard to dispute this view, though Prokofiev's occasional acid and handling of the story line perhaps place the work in a somewhat different arena, where farce and fun mix menace and mayhem in a sometimes cruel way. Just as the duck gets swallowed alive by the wolf in Prokofiev's children's classic, *Peter and the Wolf*, characters here can die or disappear as if quite dispensable: two of the three princesses who emerge from the oranges die immediately of thirst, the third being saved by the Eccentrics who intervene to give her water. However one interprets the opera, it is generally agreed that it is masterpiece of the twentieth century stage. *—Robert Cummings*

Synopsis:

Prologue. At the front of the stage the Highbrows and the Lowbrows vehemently argue over what kinds of plays are needed, tragedy or comedy. The dispute is joined by the Romantics, who want poetic plays; the Empty-heads, who want farces; and the Eccentrics, who want everyone off the stage so the opera can begin.

Act One. Scene One. In the palace, the despairing King is told by his physicians that the Prince's hypochondria is incurable. At Pantaloon's urging, they send Truffaldino to entertain the prince, then arrange with Leandro to organize lavish entertainments: laughter should cure the prince!

Scene Two. In darkness behind magical curtains, the good Magician Tchelio and sorceress Fata Morgana play a fateful card game. The Eccentrics provide commentary. Morgana wins: the Royal house is in danger.

Scene Three. In the palace Clarissa reminds Leandro that when the Prince dies, they will seize power. Leandro plans to kill him with hypochondria, but Clarissa thinks he should use quicker methods: bullet or poison. Smeraldina, sent by Morgana, is discovered spying. She assures the lovers that as long as Fata Morgana is at the party, the Prince will be unable to laugh and his condition will remain unimproved.

Act Two. Scene One. In the Prince's bedroom, Truffaldino, unable to entertain him with his dancing, discovers that the boy's been fed tragic meters and rhyme by Leandro. He urges the Prince to go to the party and be entertained, but only manages to rouse him from bed, in anger, by throwing all of his useless medicine bottles out the window.

Scene Two. The entertainments in the Courtyard have no effect on the Prince because Fata Morgana has slipped in, disguised as an old woman. Truffaldino tries to eject her, and the ensuing chase, to everyone's surprise, makes the Prince laugh uproariously. Incensed, Morgana reveals herself and curses the prince; "You are doomed to suffer love for three oranges!" She disappears, and the curse takes hold; he engages Truffaldino to accompany him to the castle of Creonte, the magician who possesses his beloved oranges. Farfarello, a demon, sends the adventurers flying off with a blast from his bellows. The king collapses in despair.

Act Three. Scene One. In the desert, the adventurers encounter Tchelio, who warns them of the terrible cook guarding the oranges; she wields a gigantic basting spoon that can kill. Truffaldino is wild with fear, while the prince thinks only of the oranges. Tchelio gives them a magic ribbon to distract the cook and sternly warns them to only open the oranges near water.

Scene Two. They arrive at Creonte's castle. Once in the kitchen, just as the cook is about to crack open Truffaldino's head, she notices the magic ribbon, becoming enchanted by it. Meanwhile, the prince steals the oranges. As she pores over the ribbon, the adventurers sneak away.

Scene Three. In the desert again, the Prince and Truffaldino are dragging the now gigantic oranges by a rope. The exhausted Prince has a nap. Incautiously, Truffaldino cuts open two of the oranges to get at the juice. Out of each steps a lovely princess, both of whom quickly die of thirst. Fearing the Prince's wrath, Truffaldino flees. When the Prince awakens, he cuts open the third orange, out of which steps the lovely Ninetta. He only manages to save her from drought when the Eccentrics bring out a bucket of water. Their love is sealed. The prince goes off to the palace to get some appropriate royal clothing for Ninetta. While she waits, Fata Morgana transforms her into a giant rat then replaces her with Smeraldina. The Prince returns with the King. Smeraldina swears it was to her the Prince made his marriage vows. The King drags the reluctant Prince back to the palace for the wedding.

Act Four. Scene One. The scene is the same as the card-playing scene of Act Two. Fata Morgana mocks Tchelio, who rages futilely until the Eccentrics approach, seize Morgana, and lock her in a tower, saying to him "Go, now you can save the royal line!"

Scene Two. When the wedding is set to begin, a giant rat is discovered on the Princess' throne. Tchelio appears in a flash and just succeeds in restoring Ninetta to human form before the guards slay her. Now all turn against Leandro, Clarissa, and Smeraldina, whom they intend to hang. When Fata Morgana suddenly frees herself, the villains all escape down a smoking hole in the ground. Cries rise up praising the King, the Prince, and Princess. *—Donato Mancini*

Recommended:

- ○ **Prokofiev: Love for Three Oranges** / Gergiev (cond.), Diadkova, Pluzhnikov, Kit, Akimov, Kirov Chorus & Orch. / 2001 / Philips 462913
- ○ **Prokofiev: Love for Three Oranges** / Nagano (cond.) Bacquier, Viala, Perraguin, Le Texier, Lyon Opera Chorus & Orch. / Virgin 59566

War and Peace, Op. 91 (1941–1943; revised 1946)

While Prokofiev spent 11 years on this opera, the bulk of his work (ten of 13 scenes) was actually written in eight months, between late summer 1941 and early spring 1942. This effort comprised the first version, but the composer later added what are now scenes 1, 2, and 10, and a choral epigraph, placed at the beginning of part 2, between scenes 7 and 8. In addition, political pressures from Soviet cultural authorities prevailed on him to further beef up the "War" half of the opera, and to enlarge the role of Field Marshal Kutuzov, who could be seen as a counterpart to Josef Stalin. Thus, the opera grew in size, but not necessarily in quality.

There have been many recordings of *War and Peace*—more than of any other Prokofiev opera—but few containing the same version of the score. The complete opera runs four hours or more, but all but a few recordings have reduced it by a half- to full-hour or more. Prokofiev intended performances to occur over two evenings.

To summarize the story of *War and Peace*, even from the libretto fashioned by Prokofiev and Mira Mendelson which merely portrayed key scenes from Tolstoy's enormous novel, is a nearly impossible task. Suffice it to say, that in Prokofiev's *War and Peace*, the action is divided into the "Peace" and "War" segments, with the latter being the larger half. The love story between Natasha Rostova and Andrei Bolkonsky is, of course, portrayed, as well as the actions of other key characters, such as Pierre Bezukhov, Anatol Kuragin, and Field Marshal Kutuzov.

There are many themes throughout the opera, as many as in Prokofiev's melody-rich *Romeo and Juliet* ballet (1935–36). Several were salvaged from his unused score for the 1936 *Eugene Onegin*, the most important of which is introduced at the beginning of the opening scene. It is associated with the love between Natasha and Andrei, and appears throughout the opera. While there are many other important melodies in first half of the opera, the most memorable ones come in the "War" section. Several of these are introduced in the choral epigraph, the most significant of which are the last two, a glorious theme—later blossoming into a grand chorus of victory-minded soldiers and volunteers at the end of scene 8—and a joyous, arch-shaped melody.

Without a doubt, the most memorable theme in the opera, however, is the one associated with victory, first sung by Kutuzov near the end of scene 10, when he agonizes over retreat. It is a warm and passionate melody that receives its most glorious incarnation at the opera's close, when it is taken up by the full chorus and orchestra. Despite the grandeur and beauty of this ending, the most touching moment and greatest vocal writing comes in scene 12, when the delirious Andrei is dying. Here the music for Andrei and Natasha brilliantly captures their desperation and love, their tragedy and sadness. *—Robert Cummings*

Synopsis:

First Tableau. It is nighttime, on the grounds of the Otradnoie estate owned by the Rostovs. Andrei Bolkonsky, a young prince staying as a guest, is at the open window of his room, meditating on the glories of spring. He hears the voices of Natasha Rostova and Sonia Rostova drifting down from the room above. Apparently the girls also feel excited and transported by this splendid evening. It dawns on Andrei that he has very strong feelings for Natasha.

Second Tableau. At a New Year's Eve ball in the home of a St. Petersburg dignitary, the guest roster includes Andrei and Natasha. When her friend Pierre sees how disappointed Natasha is that no one is dancing with her and sends Andrei to ask her to waltz. The two discover deep feelings for each other and are overjoyed at her father's invitation to Andrei to visit the following Sunday.

Third Tableau. In the city mansion of Andrei's father Prince Bolkonsky, there is a dispute over Andrei's betrothal to Natasha. Natasha arrives with her father, only to leave soon afterwards due to the contemptuous, condescending treatment she receives at the hands of old Bolkonsky and Andrei's sister. She also realizes that Andrei's year-long trip abroad is being taken only at the command of his father.

Fourth Tableau. At the home of Helena, wife of Pierre Bezukhov, Helena congratulates Natasha on her betrothal, but adds that her brother Anatole has fallen madly in love with her. The Count Rostov tries to get them out of there as quick as he can, but finds that neither Helena nor Natasha will allow it. Then Anatole arrives. He shamelessly swears a fanatical love for Natasha, boldly kisses her, then hands her an ultimatum in the form of a card that reads "My fate is in your hands: be loved by you or die." She is unwillingly swept away.

Fifth Tableau. Anatole is explaining to Dolokhov his dangerous and unlikely plan to elope abroad with Natasha. The help of the coachman Balaga, who is insanely devoted to Anatole, will be the keystone of the action. He says goodbye to his friends, including a young gypsy girl Matriosha, and they sledge off into the blizzard.

Sixth Tableau. At the home of Maria Akhrossimova, Natasha is awaiting Anatole, but a servant intercepts him and thwarts the elopement. The ensuing reprimands from Maria and revelations from Pierre of Anatole's previous marriage and his own love of her plunge Natasha into despair over her infidelity. She attempts suicide.

Seventh Tableau. At Pierre's home, he and Anatole violently quarrel over Natasha. Then he kicks the latter out, making him hand over Natasha's letters and promise never to speak of the affair again. News arrives that Napoleon's forces have ranged themselves along the borders of Russia.

Eighth Tableau. On the battlefield of Borondino, Andrei encounters Natasha's first fiancée, the strategist Denissov, who explains to him the battle plans. Pierre also arrives, eager to see a battle firsthand. Andrei is invited by some German generals to join their staff, but Andrei is loyal to his men. The battle begins.

Ninth Tableau. Napoleon is watching the battle from his command post, already imagining himself at Moscow with the keys to the city. Yet news comes that the French are losing badly. Reluctantly, he sends reinforcements.

Tenth Tableau. The Russian generals are conferring in the village of Fili, arguing over whether an offensive or defensive posture should be adopted. Marshal Kutuzov makes the decision to make a strategic retreat and temporarily give Moscow over to the enemy.

Eleventh Tableau. Napoleon in Moscow is beset by problems: the expected delegation has not arrived, arsonists are setting fire to the city, inmates of an insane asylum run amok. Pierre, who hungers for Napoleon's blood, narrowly escapes execution as an arsonist. Passing Moscovites vow revenge.

Twelfth Tableau. The wounded Andrei, in a village near Moscow and delirious with fever, has a vision of Natasha coming into the cottage he's in, dressed all in white. She begs forgiveness for her betrayal, but he has already forgiven her. Their vows of love are renewed, but Andrei soon slips away again toward his death.

Thirteenth Tableau. The French army is retreating along the road to Smolensk, while a pair of officers assess the extent of the defeat. Among the prisoners is Pierre, but he is freed when a detachment of Russian partisans attacks the convoy. Order is slowly being restored in Russia, all give gracious thanks for the victory. *—Donato Mancini*

Recommended:

- ○ **Prokofiev: War And Peace** / Rostropovich (cond.), Gedda, Stutzmann, Dubosc, Tumagian / 2002 / Warner Classics 49638
- ○ **Prokofiev: War And Peace** / Melik-Pashaev (cond.), Lisitsian, Vedernikov, Arkhipova, Eisen / 1996 / Melodiya 29650

Richard Proulx

b. 1937, St. Paul, MN

Conductor

Richard Proulx is one of the most successful American liturgical composers. His many and varied accomplishments as a composer, conductor, and organist have been acknowledged with a number of prestigious awards. These include a commission from the National Endowment for the Arts for a new opera (1989), an honorary doctorate from General Theological Seminary in New York (1994), and the Pax Christi Award from St. John's University College (1998). In 1994, the BENE award from *Modern Liturgy* magazine singled him out as "the most significant liturgical composer of the last 20 years." Proulx was raised to music from a young age, starting piano studies at the age of six. He partly attributes his later successes to the rigorous musical training he received in the Catholic school system of St. Paul, MN. After working for many years at the Church of the Holy Childhood in Seattle, his first major appointment was as the music director of St. Thomas Church in Medina/Seattle in 1970. At St. Thomas, he directed choirs and a chamber orchestra while also serving as organist at the Temple de Hirsh Sinai. In 1980, he rose to the prestigious position of organist and music director at the Cathedral of the Holy Name in Chicago. From his energetic devotion to renovating and improving the cathedral's music program, Proulx set an example at the Holy Name that positively influenced church music not only in the Chicago area, but throughout the U.S. He is credited with generally having raised the standards for liturgical music programs across the country. Besides his activities as an organist and conductor, Proulx has composed hundreds of works in sacred and secular genres, including a great deal of congregational music, song cycles, and two operas. He's known outside of church circles for such pieces as the Union Pacific Railroad theme song and for his various musical contributions to film and television. The action movie *The Devils Own* (1997) includes his organ arrangement of *Veni Creator.* Proulx has also served on the boards of liturgical music commissions and participated in choral festivals across North America and Western Europe. In 1994–95, he served a term as composer-in-residence at the Cathedral of the Madelaine in Salt Lake City. Since 1995, he has worked as a freelance composer and conductor. *—Donato Mancini*

Recommended:

- ○ **Proulx Conducts Proulx** / Proulx (cond.), Smelser, Folker, Flint, Freres, Cathedral Singers, Pro Musica Quintet / 1991 / GIA 260
- ○ **Rediscovered Masterpieces** / Proulx (cond.), Amend, McGonagle-French, Cathedral Singers & Chamber Orch. / 2001 / GIA 515

Arthur Pryor

b. Sep. 22, 1870, St. Louis, MO, **d.** Jun. 18, 1942, St. Louis, MO

Trombonist

Beyond doubt, Arthur Pryor was the foremost trombonist of his day and one of that instrument's most fervent advocates for all time. Although it is largely associated with the military band, the trombone's potential for poetry could be divined as early as Mozart's *Requiem* and Beethoven's *Symphony No. 5*; Berlioz waxed eloquent on the instrument's "noble" quality in his orchestration treatise. It remained only for Pryor to reveal in the instrument an eloquence to match that of violin or flute. In addition, he became one of the great bandsmen in the band's golden era and, incidentally, the composer of one of the best-known lighter tunes in music.

Early on, Pryor's musical education was nurtured by his father, a local bandmaster and music director. Grounded in myriad musical instruments, young Arthur was a boon to father, able to deputize for an absent player in the elder's band. Not until he was 15 did young Pryor turn to the slide trombone, when his father received one as payment for a debt. Within a few weeks, he had mastered the instrument. His prowess must have indeed been astonishing, for he went three years without applying oil to the slide, not aware of this facet of maintenance.

At 18, Pryor joined Allessandro Liberati's noted band, three years later returning to become conductor and pianist with the Stanley Opera Company in Denver. His sense of loyalty was so great that he declined an invitation from no less than Patrick S. Gilmore to perform as soloist with the latter's band. Here was an indication of how rapidly the young man's star had ascended in the brief Liberati stint. Arthur's loyalty was soon to be rewarded tenfold. In 1892, word of the young man's virtuosity had reached John Philip Sousa, who extended an invitation to audition for his newly forming civilian band. At rehearsals for the premiere concert, Pryor amazed all present, including the elder trombonists and Sousa himself, with the sounds he produced. Before long, Pryor's solos were one of the highlights of a Sousa concert. In 1895, Sousa appointed Pryor assistant conductor. In 1903, Pryor left Sousa to form his own ensemble and soon Pryor's band came to rival the best in an era when the wind band was omnipresent. Over the years, the band played at numerous World's Fairs, expositions, and other prestigious events, culminating in a performance before President Woodrow Wilson.

Pryor also composed more than 300 compositions. His best-known, even among those who have never heard of Pryor, is *The Whistler and His Dog.* Pryor also copiously recorded in the dawn of that industry's era, both as soloist and conductor. Indeed, a number of the Sousa band's early recordings were under Pryor's baton, Sousa showing distaste for the new medium. In later years, Pryor enjoyed a more leisurely pace, enjoying picnicking, fishing, dogs, and motor jaunts in convertibles. An easygoing, ready-to-laugh man, he continued practicing the trombone and composing until the end. *—Wayne Reisig*

Recommended:

- ○ **Arthur Pryor, Trombone Soloist Of The Sousa Band** / Pryor, Pryor Band, Pryor Orchestra, Sousa Band / Crystal 451

Giacomo Puccini

b. Dec. 23, 1858, Lucca, Italy, **d.** Nov. 29, 1924, Brussels, Belgium

Composer: Opera, Chamber Music

Giacomo Puccini was the most important composer of Italian opera after Verdi. He wrote in the verismo style, a counterpart to the movement of Realism in literature and a trend that favored subjects and characters from everyday life for opera. On his often commonplace settings Puccini lavished memorable melodies and lush orchestration. It was around the turn of the twentieth century that he reached his artistic zenith, composing in succession his three most popular and effective operas, *La Bohème*, *Tosca*, and *Madama Butterfly.*

Young Giacomo took organ lessons early on from his uncle, Fortunato Magi, and later from Carlo Angeloni. At ten, he sang in local church choirs and by age 14 was freelancing as an organist at religious services. His first compositions were for organ, often incorporating operatic and folk elements. By age 18, under the spell of Verdi's *Aida*, he decided he would study composition with a view to writing opera. At around this time, he composed his first large-scale work, a cantata, *Preludio Sinfonico*, for an 1877 competition. Other pieces came in the next few years, but none of significance.

In 1880, Puccini entered the Milan Conservatory, where he studied for three years under Ponchielli and Bazzini. While there, he wrote his first opera, *Le villi*, which he once more entered in a competition. Though he lost, Arrigo Boito and, more importantly, publisher Giulio Ricordi helped arrange a premiere in Milan on May 31, 1884. The work was enthusiastically received, and Puccini was on his way.

Around this time the composer met Elvira Gemignani, wife of a merchant in Lucca. They carried on an illicit affair, and she gave birth to his son in 1886. When her husband died in 1904, the two were married. Puccini's next opera, *Edgar*, was poorly received at its 1889 premiere. Subsequent revisions failed to rescue it from its encumbering libretto. His next effort, however, *Manon Lescaut*, was a sensational success at its 1893 Turin premiere. Subsequent performances in Italy and abroad bolstered the composer's growing reputation.

Puccini's next three operas confirmed his preeminence in Italian opera. *La Bohème* (1896), *Tosca* (1900), and *Madama Butterfly* (1904) were not immediately as successful as *Manon Lescaut*, but in time achieved greater acclaim. By the middle of the twentieth century, they had become—and remain today—his most often performed and recorded works.

Puccini suffered a creative dry spell for a time and was unable to finish another opera until the moderately successful *La fanciulla del West* (1910), which premiered in New York with Toscanini conducting and Caruso singing the role of Johnson. His sluggishness of inspiration owed much to charges by his wife he was having an affair with a servant girl, charges that drove the hapless, and as it turned out, innocent young girl to suicide in 1909.

In 1913, Puccini accepted a lucrative commission from Vienna interests, which resulted in *La rondine.* Received warmly at its 1917 Monte Carlo premiere, it faded under the judgment it was the least of his operatic efforts. Puccini followed this disappointment with his trilogy of one-act operas, *Il trittico*—comprised of *Il tabarro*, *Suor Angelica*, and *Gianni Schicchi*—all premiered at the Metropolitan Opera in New York in 1918. Only the latter work, a comedy, was well received.

While Puccini was working on his last opera, *Turandot*, he was diagnosed with throat cancer (1923). During radiation treatment in Brussels, he suffered a heart attack and died on November 29, 1924. *—Robert Cummings*

OPERA

La bohème (1896)

It was perhaps a common interest in the nineteenth century cultural fad of Bohemianism that led Giacomo Puccini and his contemporary Ruggiero Leoncavallo to decide to compose operas on the theme of Parisian starving artists. Whatever the initial catalysts, an 1893 meeting of the two composers, in which Puccini casually mentioned his *La bohème* project, induced the composers to publish in the Milanese press notices in which each laid a claim of priority to the subject. The validity of Puccini's claim is by no means certain. Nevertheless, although contemporary critics received Puccini's *La bohème* coolly after its premiere under Arturo Toscanini in Turin on February 1, 1896, it was a hit with the public, and has endured as a favorite in the operatic repertoire.

La bohème was the first libretto for Puccini on which Luigi Illica and Giuseppe Giacosa collaborated. By 1893, Puccini was considering composing an opera on Henri Murger's novel *Scènes de la vie de bohème.* Murger's work, originally published (1845–49) as a series of stories in a French journal, led an intermediary existence as a stage play before being transformed into a novel. Murger's novel enjoyed a favorable reception in Italy shortly after its initial publication and first translation into Italian in 1859.

Some of Puccini's loveliest lyrical moments grace *La bohème.* Rodolfo's first aria "Che gelida manina" in Act One, introduces a primarily conjunct melody of touching simplicity, conveying the innocence of pure love. This melody returns at the end of Act One, as Mimì and Rodolfo exit, and again, in Act Four as Mimì, on her deathbed, reminisces with Rodolfo on their first encounter. Puccini's debt to Wagner's leitmotivic procedure is also evident in his association of the music from Mimì's Act One aria "Mi chiamo Mimì," with Mimì herself, when it accompanies her later entrance in Act Three. This technique of associating music with characters incorporates timbral as well as thematic elements. The magical, sustained string instrumentation for the second inversion D major triad that announces Mimì's entrance in Act One is also the principal color in the orchestral accompaniment of her signature aria. Classic Puccinian orchestration and harmonic language mark the depiction of daybreak that opens Act Three. Here, flutes in parallel fifths peck out a modal melody, punctuated at phrase ends by subtle, sustained upper strings over tremolo cellos. A harp solo adds a delicate brilliance to the sparse orchestral palette and foreshadows the hazy timbre of the off-stage women's chorus. Puccini's expressive use of the orchestra is linked most intimately with the drama in Act Four. After Schaunard tells Marcello of Mimì's death, the orchestra drops out, leaving only a sustained A in the double bass to convey a sense of dramatic expectation and musical continuity. Even the soloists leave their songful world for one of spoken declamation until the orchestra explodes with C sharp minor triads in the brass, reflecting Rodolfo's realization of Mimì's death and accompanying his anguished cries. *—Jennifer Hambrick*

Synopsis:

Act One. It is Christmas Eve, and in the Bohemians' garret, Marcello and Rodolfo grumble about the cold. Rodolfo suggests burning the manuscript of his play. Colline comes in and joins them at the fire, and when it goes out, he and Marcello chase Rodolfo to punish him for such a fragile plot. Schaunard enters, with food, wine, and fuel, having played for an eccentric Englishman. Benoit comes for the overdue rent. Marcello shows him the money, but with wine and flattery, induces him to boast of amorous conquests, but when he mentions his wife, they feign indignation at a married man being so immoral, and toss him out, declaring the rent paid. They divide the money, but Rodolfo says he will stay a few minutes to finish a piece for a magazine. He hears a knock, and Mimì is outside, asking for a light for her candle. He invites her in, and sees her pallor and unsteadiness. She says she is just out of breath from the stairs, but faints. When she recovers, he offers her wine, which she accepts, but declines his invitation to stay longer. She returns after just a second, as she dropped her key. A draft extinguishes her candle, and he promptly extinguishes his own. They grope on the floor to find the key and Rodolfo pockets it. Their hands meet, and in his "Che gelida manina," he asks permission to warm her cold hand and introduce himself. He is a poet, poor in everything but dreams, though thieves have just stolen those. He is unconcerned because the thieves, two lovely eyes, have left hope behind. She talks about her quiet, solitary life as a seamstress ("Si, mi chiamano Mimì"), watching for the spring to come. Living at the top of the building, the first kiss of April is hers. His friends call from below, and he tells them to go on, and save two seats. Laughing, they go off. He rhapsodically tells her that in her he recognizes the dream he wishes always to dream ("O soave fanciulla"). They go out.

Act Two. In the crowded square outside Momus' is the restaurant where the Bohemians are meeting. Rodolfo enters with Mimì. He gallantly introduces her to his friends. Marcello is brooding over Musetta, who makes her appearance, accompanied by Alcindoro, her wealthy admirer. She is hungry for Marcello's attention and insists that she and Alcindoro sit near them. Finally, to Alcindoro's disgust, she sings a seductive waltz ("Quando men vo"), and Marcello cannot resist any longer. She sends Alcindoro to get her another pair of shoes, saying hers pinch. The Bohemians leave, and Alcindoro is stuck with the bill for their meal.

Act Three. The toll-gate guards admit street-sweepers and girls bringing in farm goods. Musetta's voice is heard from the nearby inn, singing. Mimì comes in and asks a cleaning lady to tell Marcello she is outside and needs to talk to him. She is coughing and clearly ill. She tells Marcello that Rodolfo's jealousy is making their life unbearable, and he says it's best that they part. They take things too seriously, unlike his lighthearted love with Musetta. Pretending to go, she hides to listen to his conversation with Rodolfo. Rodolfo comes out and at first complains about Mimì's flirtatious behavior. Marcello tells him it's clear he doesn't mean it, and Rodolfo admits he loves Mimì more than anything in the world, but all he can offer is poverty, which is killing her. She bursts into tears, revealing her presence. Marcello runs inside where he hears Musetta flirting. Mimì tells Rodolfo goodbye ("Donde lieta usci"). She has no hard feelings and asks him to pack her few possessions. Musetta and Marcello rush in, and while they trade insults and break up, Mimì and Rodolfo decide that spending winter alone is unbearable, and that they won't separate until spring.

Act Four. In the garret Marcello and Rodolfo are pretending to work, but brooding over their lost loves ("E un coupe") who have both found wealthy protectors. Schaunard and Colline return with a meager meal, which they pretend is a feast, and then clown around in a mock formal dance. Musetta bursts in, saying Mimì is outside and gravely ill. Rodolfo brings her in, and Musetta whispers to the others that she found Mimì, barely able to walk, but wanting to die in Rodolfo's arms. Mimì greets them, telling Marcello how kind Musetta is. Musetta gives Marcello her earrings to pawn to buy medicine, and herself goes to get a muff to warm Mimì's hands. Colline prepares to pawn his overcoat, bidding it farewell as a symbol of their earlier, carefree life ("Vecchia zimarra"). Left alone together, the lovers remember their meeting. He admits he pocketed the key, and she admits she guessed. The others return, one by one, as she falls asleep. Musetta prays as she warms the medicine. Rodolfo moves away to pull a curtain so the sun won't shine in Mimì's eyes, and Schaunard, followed by the others, sees that she is dead. Rodolfo turns, asks why they are looking at him like that, and as Marcello tells him to be brave, he rushes to the bed, crying Mimì's name. *—Ann Feeney*

Recommended:

○ **Puccini: La bohème** / Karajan (cond.), Freni, Pavarotti, Ghiaurov, Panerai / 1987 / London 421049

○ **Puccini: La bohème** / Beecham (cond.), Bjoerling, Los Angeles, Merrill, Tozzi / 2002 / Angel 67753

Edgar (1889; revised 1892)

Le Villi and *Edgar* are not only Puccini's first two operas, but also his two weakest. *Le Villi* is a strangely constructed work, called an "opera-ballet," so a case can be made that *Edgar*, completed in September 1887, is Puccini's first true work in the genre. Starting slowly is not always a bad thing. Pietro Mascagni wrote *Cavalleria Rusticana* early in his career and never came close to matching it in quality or popularity. Fortunately, for singers, lovers of singing, pop songwriters, record companies, opera companies, and even makers of movies and TV commercials, Puccini went on to write nine more operas, at least half of which must be counted among the most popular in the world.

Edgar is more than just a piece of juvenilia, however. Even when dramatic and musical hints of Verdi, Ponchielli, and Donizetti peek through, Puccini's distinct voice can be clearly discerned. Puccini had already collaborated with the librettist Ferdinando Fontana on *Le Villi*, and the publisher Ricordi believed in that work enough to commission another, more ambitious opera for presentation at La Scala. Fontana rewrote a play, "La Coupe et les Levres," which was conceived by its author, Alfred de Mussart, to be read aloud rather than staged; the tale is a romantic melodrama set in medieval Flanders.

The four-act version of the opera premiered at La Scala on April 21, 1889. Puccini reworked the score, and in 1891 he replaced the finale of Act Three with that for Act Four. Puccini continued to tinker with the piece until 1905, when he finally bowed to the inevitable and turned his full attention to the operas for which he is so well loved. After struggling to make *Edgar* a success, Puccini would never again allow himself to be saddled with such a weak drama. His tastes might run toward melodrama rather than great literature, but at least his characters were never again as ridiculous as those that populate the stage of *Edgar*.

For all their emotional button pushing, the one essential component of the success of Puccini's operas is the great aria. Unfortunately, *Edgar* does not have even one aria that has established a foothold in the concert or recording repertoire. There are many arresting musical moments scattered throughout the work, but most of the best ideas that Puccini had in *Edgar* are heard to better advantage in later works. The knowledgeable listener hearing this opera might easily find himself identifying similar passages from *Madama Butterfly, Turandot, La Bohème*, and most especially *Tosca*.

Neither the concert performance and recording by Eve Queler and the Opera Orchestra of New York, nor the mounting of the work by the New York City Opera and other adventurous companies, has led to its entry into the standard canon of Puccini's works. *Edgar* may be a culmination of all that Puccini had learned from the past. He would soon break new ground with *Manon Lescaut, Tosca*, and others, but *Edgar* will remain a work primarily of interest to the curious—who should find it quite rewarding. *—Eric Goldberg*

Synopsis:

Act One. In the square, Edgar is seated but asleep in front of the inn. Fidelia enters, singing of the first flowers of spring ("O fior del giorno") and calls to him, and they affectionately greet one another. She breaks off some almond blossoms and gives them to him ("Gia il mancorlo"). She leaves, and peasants are heard in the distance repeating her song as he goes to follow her. Tigrana enters and is ready to pursue him, but he returns, still contemplating the blossoms. She laughs mockingly, saying she can't believe a pastoral love would please him, and he tells her to leave. He sits outside his house, and as the organ sounds from the church, the villagers enter. Tigrana reminds Edgar of their earlier passion, of burning desire, vice, and gold, and he calls her a demon and runs into his house. She is about to leave, but Frank enters and angrily demands to know where she was last night, as he had expected her and she did not come. She tells him his love bores her, and when he exclaims in anguish, sardonically tells him that his mother never should have adopted her when wandering Moors abandoned her as a baby. He laments that they nurtured a viper in their bosoms, and she laughs and goes. Alone, he agonizes that his senses are enslaved by her ("Questo amor, vergogna mia"), and each time he resolves to flee her, he returns, while she laughs at his pain. As the villagers sing inside the church, asking for peace and love, instead of glory and gold, Tigrana mockingly stands outside the door singing a love song. They emerge, and when she mocks their demands that she stop singing, they threaten her. Edgar emerges and orders them to disperse. He then sets fire to his own home, forbidding any of them to stop him, and starts to leave with her, but Frank tries to stop him. He and Edgar are about to fight, but Gualtiero, entering with Fidelia, stops them. Edgar sheaths his sword and is ready to leave, but Frank insists upon fighting, and as the chorus and others exclaim in dismay, he is wounded.

Act Two. In a sumptuous palace, the chorus sings of pleasure. Edgar emerges and sings of the emptiness of the orgy he has just left and of the sensual life he leads ("Orgia, chimera dall'occhio"). He thinks longingly of Fidelia's love. Tigrana emerges and he berates her for bringing him back into a life of filth. She exclaims that he doesn't love her any more, and he orders her not to profane the word. She reminds him that without her he would be penniless and promises him voluptuous bliss, while he wonders if he will ever even be able to hope to be free of shame. An army passes by, and Edgar recognizes Frank at their head. He begs Frank for forgiveness and help, and Frank responds that the fight cured him of an unworthy love. Edgar asks to redeem himself by joining them and fighting for their country. Tigrana begs Frank not to take Edgar away and Edgar not to go, desperately saying she can't live without him. When he rejects her, she says he will be dead or be hers.

Act Three. Outside a fortress, altar boys and a chorus sing a requiem, as knights bring in a corpse dressed in Edgar's armor. Frank and a hooded monk accompany the procession. Fidelia and Gualtiero are among the watching crowd. At first, all pray for the repose of his soul, and Fidelia sobs Edgar's name to herself. Fidelia goes to the bier and sings of her sorrow and her desire to join him in death ("Addio, addio, mio dolce amor"). Frank begins a eulogy ("Del prode"), but the monk wanders among the crowd speaking disparagingly of Edgar's past, over Frank's protests. The crowd insists that the monk be allowed to continue, and he declares that Edgar, dying, asked him to reveal his sins and crimes. He asks if any are from Edgar's village and remember his burning his home, injuring Frank, and fleeing with Tigrana, and adds further condemnations, accusing him of being a murderous thief. The crowd is roused to tear his body from the bier to leave it for the animals rather than in a place of honor, but Fidelia defends him vehemently. He erred in some ways, but he was a good man who atoned with his valor ("D'ogni dolor"). She orders the soldiers to kneel in prayer, and all leave, except Frank and the monk. Tigrana enters and asks to pray beside his body. The monk, who of course is Edgar, is determined to show the emptiness of her feelings, and Frank agrees while she exclaims how much she loved him. They pay her elaborate compliments, asking her not to damage her eyes with tears or her knees with kneeling. She ignores them until they offer her one magnificent and expensive jewel after another to denounce Edgar. The monk declares that he loves her, and they have everyone called in, and Tigrana declares that Edgar was a traitor. When the crowd pulls apart the armor, they find it empty. Edgar contemptuously reveals himself, calling Tigrana a leper and the filth of the world, and declares his love for Fidelia, declaring that he has returned to life. Tigrana, furious, stabs Fidelia, and Edgar throws himself upon her body as the soldiers drag Tigrana away and the others kneel in prayer. *—Ann Feeney*

Recommended:

○ **Puccini: Edgar** / Queler (cond.), Scotto, Bergonzi, Sardinero, Killebrew, NY Opera Orch. / 1977 / CBS 34584

La fanciulla del West (The Girl of the Golden West) (1910)

Anyone familiar with the "Spaghetti Westerns" of the 1960s knows that the American west has held a particular fascination for film audiences in Italy—indeed throughout Europe. However, such memorable films such as *A Fistful of Dollars* and *The Good, the Bad, and the Ugly* were only the culmination of a European love affair with the folklore and adventure of the wild west that dates back to the end of the nineteenth century. With this in mind, then, it is easier to understand why, in 1907, Giacomo Puccini—the leading composer of Italian opera—would turn to the gold mining towns of California as inspiration for his most ambitious opera to date.

Puccini saw David Belasco's play *The Girl of the Golden West* while attending the premieres of *Manon Lescaut* and *Madama Butterfly* at the Metropolitan Opera. While he was not immediately sure of the work itself, he left New York with a lingering interest in western themes, and when his publisher, Tito Ricordi, engaged Carlo Zingarini to write a libretto based on Belasco's play, Puccini embraced the project with great enthusiasm. Composition would not begin, however, for a further nine months, as Puccini's time and energies were quickly consumed by a domestic tragedy involving the suicide of his maidservant, and a subsequent lawsuit against his wife, Elvira.

Work on the opera was finally completed in August of 1910.

Puccini's *Fanciulla* is the story of Minnie, a saloon owner in a mining town who falls in love with a notorious bandit; she places herself at risk to help him escape from an angry posse. The composer felt that the finished product was his finest work yet, integrating new tonal idioms and dramatic devices into his essentially lyrical style, while achieving a whole new level of concision. The organic, through-composed nature of the score makes excerpting arias and ensembles difficult; in fact, the bandit Ramerrez's third-act aria, "Ch'ella me creda liberto e lontano," is the only true set piece in the entire opera. However, there are other memorable tunes, not the least of which is the sentimental ballad, "Che faranno i vecchi miei là lontano," which appears early on in the first scene, and the tune of which recurs frequently as a unifying element.

The premiere, at the Metropolitan Opera in November, 1910, was notable for its inclusion of Enrico Caruso in the role of Ramerrez (a.k.a. Dick Johnson) and was by all accounts a triumph; but enthusiasm for *Fanciulla* quickly faded, and it has never firmly established itself in the repertory. *—AMG*

Synopsis:

Act One. In Minnie's saloon, The Polka, the miners are coming in after the day's work. Some gamble; others drink. They all ask about Minnie, who isn't there yet. Jake Wallace, a minstrel, comes in singing a song about homesickness, and Larkens breaks down. They pass the cap to get him enough money to go home. Sid is discovered cheating at cards, but Rance keeps them from lynching him, instead making him wear the card he had used. They agree that if he ever takes off this badge of disgrace, they can kill him. Ashby comes in and says he's on the trail of Ramerrez. Rance raises a toast to Minnie as the "future Mrs. Rance," and this provokes a fight, which Minnie breaks up when she enters. She chides them and they are immediately contrite, and some of them offer her little gifts and compliments. She begins their daily Bible lesson, a psalm about how repentance redeems even the worst sinner. Ashby gets a letter saying that Nina Micheltorena, Ramerrez's mistress, has double-crossed him. Minnie describes Nina's posing. A stranger sends in an order from outside, asking for whiskey and water. This gets a good laugh from everyone, including Minnie. Rance draws Minnie aside and tells her he is in love with her. She reminds him that he's married, and he says he'd divorce his wife for her. She tells him she prefers to be left in peace, and he responds by describing what was once his only love, gold, but now he'd give anything for just a kiss from her: "Minnie, dalla mia casa." She responds by telling him of how much her parents loved one another, "Laggu nel Soledad," and admits she does want to love. The stranger comes in, calling himself Dick Johnson, and he and Minnie recognize one another from an earlier meeting. Rance is resentful, but Minnie vouches for the stranger, and they dance. Ashby brings in one of Ramerrez's men, who tricks the men into taking a false trail. Minnie and "Johnson" stay behind. As they talk about their lives, they fall in love, and he does not take the opportunity to steal the gold she guards for the miners. She invites him to come to her cabin later to talk more, but tells him not to expect much, as she only had 30 dollars' worth of education. She bursts into tears, and he tells her not to cry, saying that she is a good, pure creature with the face of an angel. She repeats "with the face of an angel" to herself as he leaves.

Act Two. In Minnie's cabin, Minnie's housekeeper Wowkle sings a lullaby to her baby. Billy, the baby's father, comes in and tells her that Minnie says they ought to marry. She agrees. Minnie comes in and dresses in her finery. When Johnson arrives, he tries to kiss her, but when she avoids it, he says he's not sorry. She tells him of her happy life riding free in the summer and teaching miners during the winter: "Oh, se sapeste." She sends Wowkle away as their conversation becomes more amorous, and she and Johnson kiss. He suddenly declares that it's all an empty dream and that he had better leave; but snow has covered the path and he cannot depart, to Minnie's delight. They sing ecstatically of their love, she dreaming of being worthy of him, he of being purified by her. She gives him her bed for the night, over his protests, and says she will sleep in her bearskin. They hear miners outside and Johnson hides as they knock. When Minnie lets them in, they tell her they've learned from Nina that Johnson is none other than Ramerrez himself. Minnie demonstrates bitter amusement and they leave. Miserable and furious, she confronts her lover, and, while refusing to exculpate himself ("Or son sei mesi"), Johnson tells her that at first he had no idea that his father supported the family through banditry, but when his father died, he learned that the only way to continue to take care of his mother and younger siblings was to accept that bitter inheritance. When he met Minnie, he dreamt of a life of redemption, but it was in vain after all. He leaves, at her insistence, but when a shot is heard from outside, she runs out and brings him in, wounded. She hides him in the loft. Rance enters her cabin in pursuit of Ramerrez. He is willing to believe that he was mistaken, that he just shot at a shadow, and he seizes the moment to protest his love violently, grabbing her. When blood drips from the ceiling onto his hand, he realizes he was right after all. Minnie then offers to gamble with him. If she wins, he leaves her and Johnson in peace. If he wins, he gets to kill Johnson and have her. Minnie wins the first hand, Rance the second. For the third, her cards are worthless, so she cheats. Rance leaves and she bursts into hysterical laughter, embracing the unconscious Johnson.

Act Three. Nick and Rance gloomily talk about how they wish Johnson had never shown up. Ashby and the miners are chasing Johnson, and they finally catch him and bring him in to be hanged. The miners celebrate and Rance taunts him. Johnson asks one last favor ("Ch'ella mi creda"), that Minnie not be told about his death. Rance viciously hits him, to the miners' disapproval. Johnson is about to be hanged when Minnie herself rides in. At first she threatens to shoot Johnson and herself rather than let them kill him, but then reminds Rance of all she has done for them, and of the lesson she taught. She declares that Ramerrez died long ago, and that Johnson is a new, redeemed man. One by one, they agree, and Minnie and Johnson leave together to start a new life ("Addio, mia California"), leaving the miners desolate.*—Ann Feeney*

Recommended:

○ **Puccini: La Fanciulla del West** / Mehta (cond.), Domingo, Milnes, Lloyd, Howell, Royal Opera House Orch. / DG 419640

Gianni Schicchi (1918)

Gianni Schicchi is the third and final installment of *Il trittico*, Giacomo Puccini's trilogy of one-act operas. Though the trilogy itself is not often performed, *Schicchi* has remained a perennial favorite—well-loved for its lyrical concision and ensemble humor—and is often cited as a masterpiece of Italian comedy.

The story, which comes from an apparently true-to-life passage in Dante's *Inferno*, was adapted for the stage by the librettist Giovecchino Forzano. A wealthy miser has died, and the greedy members of his family are horrified to find that he has written all of them out of his will. In a scheme to steal back their inheritance, they enlist the help of the morally ambiguous title character, who then succeeds in bilking them out of the money. A side plot involves the young romance between Schicchi's daughter, Lauretta, and a member of the "grieving" (none of them cared a whit for the old man!) family, Rinuccio.

Puccini's score is notable for its use of recurring themes as organizational devices, and the skillful integration of many different characters' short utterances into larger lyrical structures. Lauretta's aria, "O, mio babbino caro" (Oh, my dearest papa), is among the most famous excerpts in all of opera, and certainly the most anticipated moment in any performance. Other memorable moments include the opening "weeping" scene, in which the exaggerated sobbing of the opportunistic relatives combines with clever orchestral underpinnings; and Schicchi's final-scene impersonation of the dead man, Buoso, during which he rewrites "his" will to suit his own liking. *—AMG*

Synopsis:

Gathered around his bed, Buoso Donati's relations are trying to outdo one another with their lamentations. However, when Betto mentions that there's gossip in Signa that Donati has left all his considerable wealth to a monastery, their attention rapidly changes focus, and soon they are tearing the house apart, looking for the will. Rinuccio is the first to find it, but holds it away from the others until they agree to let him marry Lauretta, Gianni Schicchi's daughter. In anticipation, he sends Gherardino, a little boy, to fetch Schicchi and Lauretta to come hear the good news.

Reading the will, they discover that the rumor was all too true, and promptly blow out the mourning candles they had lit. They bitterly imagine the monks living it up on Donati's money, and Zita wails that she never would have thought that she would truly cry at Donati's death. Rinuccio tells them that Schicchi might well help them get the inheritance after all, and Zita tells him she wants to hear no more about that poor peasant upstart or his daughter. Rinuccio bursts into a spirited defense of Schicchi's cleverness and of the contributions of the country folk who come to Florence to make it even more beautiful and splendid: "Avete torto!... Firenze e come un albero."

As he finishes, Schicchi and Lauretta arrive. Zita tells him she will never consent to Rinuccio marrying a dowerless nobody, and Schicchi sarcastically congratulates her for her principles, accusing her of both greed and snobbery. In a confused quartet, Rinuccio and Lauretta plead that they love one another, Zita insists she will not allow the marriage, and Schicchi tells Lauretta to have the pride and sense not to marry into such a grasping family. Rinuccio flatters Schicchi outrageously, saying that such a brilliant thinker must have a plan that can save them. He refuses to help such people, at least until Lauretta pleads with him herself in her famous "O mio babbino caro." Her tears and pleading wind him nicely around her little finger, and he gives in.

Reading the will, he at first doesn't see a solution to the lovers' despair. Getting an idea, he suddenly sends Lauretta out onto the balcony to feed the birds. He asks if anybody else knows that Donati has died, and, when they answer no, he orders them to hide the body. The doctor appears, and Schicchi hides behind the bed curtains. Imitating Donati's voice, he tells the doctor he is nearly asleep and asks him to return that evening. Congratulating himself on the fine training he received at the Bologna medical school, the doctor leaves.

Schicchi emerges and asks the relatives how the imitation was. When they tell him it was perfect, he bursts into a jubilant explanation of his plan: "Ah!... che zucconi!" He will dress in Donati's clothes and dictate a last will and testament to the notary as Donati. Rinuccio runs for the notary, and the remaining relatives promptly kiss his hands and garments, and embrace one another in their effusive joy, singing of their familial love. This love is put to the test when, after easily dividing the ready cash and lesser lands, they fiercely quarrel over the best bits of the estate: the Florence house, the mills at Signa, and the mule. There is a momentary despair when a requiem bell rings outside and they fear that somebody has learned of Donati's death, but they find it's for somebody else. Simone finally suggests that they leave the hard decisions to Schicchi's sense of honesty and justice.

While the women dress him in Donati's clothes, all the relatives whisper offers of various bribes that he will receive if he leaves them the choicest parts of the estate, and he agrees to each. Before the notary arrives, he warns the relatives of the penalty for forging a will: exile and amputation of a hand. He sings a mock farewell to Florence.

Rinuccio arrives with the notary and witnesses. Schicchi dictates a will, stipulating a modest funeral and a token gift to the monastery. The undisputed items are divided accordingly to plan, but to the relatives' growing horror and rage, "Donati" leaves the most coveted items to none other than his devoted friend Gianni Schicchi. He reminds the relatives of their own position by repeating, as if a dying man's farewell, the farewell he sang to Florence. The notary and witnesses leave and the relatives (except for Rinuccio, who has ignored all this and now slips out to join Lauretta) furiously turn on him, denouncing him as a thief. They drag out what plunder they can as he chases them out of the house, now *his* house.

Returning, he pulls aside the back curtain so the audience can see Rinuccio and Lauretta embracing and singing of their love. Taking off his cap, Schicchi turns directly to the audience and, gesturing to the young couple, asks if the money could possibly be put to any better use. Though Dante consigned him to the Inferno for this escapade, he asks that the audience, through applause, allow him to plead extenuating circumstances. *—Ann Feeney*

Recommended:

○ **Puccini: Gianni Schicchi** / Patane (cond.), Panerai, Donath, Seiffert, Federici, Munich Radio Orch. / 1988 / Eurodisc 7751

Madama Butterfly (1904)

Giacomo Puccini furthered his reputation as one of the leading figures in Italian opera of the late nineteenth and early twentieth centuries when he composed one of the world's most popular operas, *Madama Butterfly*, in 1904. It is on this work, along with *La bohème* and *Tosca*, that his fame rests. Influenced by Verdi, Wagner, Debussy, Lehár, and Stravinsky, he has been called a Massenet without the urbanity. His ability to master the verismo style, while blending in romanticism and exoticism, is most visible in the plot of *Madama Butterfly*, a tragic love story set in Japan. The work was written approximately 20 years after his first opera, *Le Villi*, gained the attention of the publisher Giulio Ricordi. From there Puccini worked with Toscanini, and was introduced, by Ricordi, to the talented librettists Giuseppe Giacosa and Luigi Illica, with whom he worked closely for several years. Together, they produced *Manon Lescaut*, *La bohème*, and *Tosca*, prior to completing *Madama Butterfly*.

The inspiration for the plot came from an American play by David Belasco, which captured the composer's immediate interest when he saw it in London. Based on the heartbreak of Madama Butterfly, a 15-year-old Japanese girl, who abandons her people and her religion in a marriage to Pinkerton, a United States Naval Lieutenant, and in a conversion to Christianity, the work undoubtedly had greater meaning to its American audiences following the occupation of U.S. troops in Asia, during the mid- and late twentieth century. In addition to its powerful story line, the solos contained in the opera achieved unprecedented fame. During a three-year wait for her husband's return from the U.S., Madame Butterfly sings what has probably become known as the most popular soprano aria ever written, "Un bel di vedremo" (One day he will come back). Anguished when her husband returns with another wife, Butterfly commits suicide, bringing the opera to a dramatic close.

The original version in two acts was first performed at *La Scala*, Milan, on February 17, 1904, where it was nearly hissed off the stage, in part because of the excessive length of the second act. Retreating to the country, Puccini recast the work, deleting a song from the first act and dividing the second act into two. The revision was presented at Brescia on May 28, 1904, where it began its long and triumphant career. Shortly thereafter, it was performed in English in Washington, D.C., by Henry W. Savage Company at the Belasco Theatre, on October 15, 1906, and also at the Metropolitan Opera House and Covent Garden. *—Meredith Gailey*

Synopsis:

Act One. Goro shows Pinkerton the house he has just leased for 999 years, where he will house the wife he has agreed to marry for the same term. He notes that both deals can be broken at any time with a month's notice. Sharpless arrives and, in their conversation over drinks, Pinkerton explains his philosophy ("Dovunque al mondo"): to take pleasure wherever he finds it. He further declares that although he doesn't know whether it is love or a whim ("Amore o grillo"), he finds himself fascinated by Butterfly, though he proposes a toast to the day he will be married for real, to an American woman. Sharpless tells him that Butterfly takes the marriage much more seriously; when she visited the consulate, her sincerity touched him. He warns Pinkerton to be careful: it would be wrong to break an utterly trusting heart. Pinkerton laughs these warnings off.

Butterfly and her relations arrive. She tells Sharpless and Pinkerton her age, 15, and her life's story. Her family was once rich, but now they are poor, and she had to become a geisha to support herself. She shows Pinkerton her few possessions, including a dagger, which arouses his curiousity. She says there are too many people around for her to explain, but Goro quietly tells him that the Mikado sent it to her father, who obeyed and used it to kill himself. Butterfly also tells Pinkerton that she has converted to his religion. In a lively ensemble, the relatives comment more or less favorably on Pinkerton's looks and their views of the marriage. The marriage contract is signed, but the following festivities are interrupted by the arrival of the Bonze, who tells them all that Butterfly has renounced her faith, and thus, her family. They renounce her in return, and Pinkerton drives them away. He consoles Butterfly, telling her not to cry. During their extended love duet, "Bimba, bimba," it is clear that he still considers her nothing more than a charming toy, but her feelings are much deeper. They go into the house together.

Act Two. The second act takes place three years later. Suzuki is praying to the gods for help, while Butterfly is convinced that Pinkerton will return, as she declares in the famous "Un bel di," as she imagines his return. Sharpless arrives with a letter containing news from Pinkerton. She greets him effusively, but before they can exchange more than a few words, Prince Yamadori arrives with Goro. Yamadori wants to marry Butterfly, but she refuses, saying she is a married woman. They remind her that according to Japanese law, Pinkerton's having left her is the equivalent of a divorce, but she responds that she is an American and such laws, which let a man leave a wife when he tires of her, do not apply to her. Yamadori leaves in frustration, followed by Goro. Sharpless starts to read the letter, but she reacts so joyfully at even the first few words that he cannot bear to finish reading the letter. He asks her what she would do if Pinkerton were never to come back, and, utterly bewildered at the thought, she says she would go back to her life as a geisha or, better, die rather than lead such a life again. He advises her to forget Pinkerton and marry the rich Yamadori. She finally understands that Pinkerton might have forgotten her, but shows Sharpless the child she bore after Pinkerton left. Now he is named Trouble, but when Pinkerton returns, she will change his name to Joy. Sharpless promises to tell Pinkerton of his son's existence and departs. Suzuki screams in rage at Goro, who has been saying that in America, a child without a father is considered an outcast. Butterfly seizes her father's dagger to threaten him and he runs away. The two women hear the sound of the cannon that announces the arrival of a ship. It is Pinkerton's ship, and Butterfly exults that her love has triumphed entirely. She and Suzuki, in the Flower Duet, strip the garden of flowers to adorn the house. Butterfly dresses in her wedding gown and the three of them wait for Pinkerton's arrival. A chorus hums softly.

The next morning, Butterfly has not slept, and when Suzuki wakes up, she persuades Butterfly to get some rest. Pinkerton and Sharpless arrive and, to Suzuki's despair, tell her that the woman with them is Pinkerton's wife, Kate. They have come to ask Butterfly to give Pinkerton and Kate the child, and ask Suzuki for her help to do what's best for the child: "Io so che alle sue pene." Pinkerton, realizing that Butterfly has waited for him, is overcome with remorse: "Addio, fiorito asil." Sharpless angrily reminds Pinkerton of his warnings and how they have come all too true. Pinkerton gives Sharpless money to give to Butterfly and rushes off, condemning himself as too cowardly to face her. Butterfly comes in and cannot understand why Pinkerton is not there, but Suzuki and Sharpless are downcast. She sees Kate and realizes what has happened. Kate asks for her forgiveness, whereupon Butterfly tells her there should be no woman on Earth happier than she and not to be saddened over her own plight. She agrees to give up the child if Pinkerton himself comes to fetch him. Kate and Sharpless leave. Butterfly tells Suzuki to go out to play in the garden with the child. Alone, she raises the dagger to her throat ("Con onore muore") and Suzuki pushes the child into the room. She bids him a loving farewell, "Tu, tu, tu," and blindfolds him. She cuts her throat and dies as Pinkerton rushes into the house, calling her name. *—Ann Feeney*

Recommended:

- ○ **Puccini: Madama Butterfly** / Santini (cond.), Bjoerling, Los Angeles, Sereni, dePalma, Rome Opera Orch. / 1990 / EMI 63634
- ○ **Puccini: Madama Butterfly** / Karajan (cond.), Freni, Pavarotti, Ludwig, Senechal, Vienna PO / 1987 / London 417577
- ○ **Puccini: Madama Butterfly** / Leinsdorf (cond.), Price, Palma, Tucker, Elias, Kerns, RCA Italiana Opera Orch. / 1963 / BMG 68884

Manon Lescaut (1893)

Manon Lescaut was premiered at the Teatro Regio, in Turin, Italy, on February 1, 1893. It was a sensation, immediately elevating Puccini to the front rank of Italian composers and making his name well-known throughout Europe. While he would have many other successes in his career—*Madama Butterfly* (in its revised version) and *Tosca*—he would never again experience this kind of overwhelming triumph.

The libretto, based on Antoine François Prévost's novel, is quite effective despite the participation of five hands in it, though not all in collaboration: Leoncavallo (who fashioned the first version), Marco Praga, Domenico Oliva, Luigi Illica, and Giuseppe Giacosa.

The story is set in late eighteenth century Paris, where the nobleman Des Grieux espies the beautiful Manon Lescaut, accompanied by her brother (Lescaut) and the treasurer-general, Geronte di Ravoir, who fancies himself her suitor. Des Grieux is captivated by her and learns from her she plans to join the convent. He convinces her to run off with him, but Geronte forges other plans and she eventually becomes his mistress, but not before living with and then leaving Des Grieux. Some time later, at Geronte's Paris residence, Manon confides in her brother that she is bored with Geronte and wishes to have Des Grieux back. Lescaut fetches the latter, and when Des Grieux and Manon attempt to run off, Geronte has her arrested as a thief and woman of loose morals. Authorities plan to deport her to a Louisiana prison. Des Grieux cannot bear to be without her, and following a failed attempt to free her, boards the ship bound for Louisiana. Later in America, Des Grieux flees with her after a duel with the nephew of the colony's Governor. On the run with Des Grieux, Manon becomes seriously ill and bids him a sad and dramatic farewell. He falls unconscious over her body.

Puccini's score is lushly orchestrated and features the usual quota of memorable tunes and imaginative vocal writing. Of the many popular numbers in the opera, the Act One "Cortese damigella" is among the more memorable, not least because of its soaring melody and deft writing for both Manon and Des Grieux. The ensuing "Donna non vidi Mai", in which Des Grieux declares his feelings for Manon, is one of Puccini's most beguiling arias, full of passion and yearning, instantly appealing even to the ear unaccustomed to operatic singing.

The Act Two aria, "In quelle trini morbide", sung by Manon who is now disenchanted by Geronte, is another gem. Later on in that act, when Des Grieux attempts to free Manon from Geronte, there is a passionate and intense love scene between the two lovers ("Tu, tu, amore? Tu?!"). "Sola perduta, abbandonata" is another attractive aria for Manon, that comes near the end of the opera. Here, she sings of her past life and her encumbering beauty. In sum, this is one of Puccini's finest operas. *—Robert Cummings*

Synopsis:

Act One. Edmondo and students sing cheerfully in the town square, and they jest with Des Grieux when he enters. He declares in response to their joking that love is a tragedy, or rather a farce, of which he knows nothing. He mock courts the girls present, asking which of them is his destiny: "Tra voi, belle." The coach arrives, and among the passengers are Lescaut, his sister Manon, whom he is taking to a convent, and Geronte, who has been much struck with Manon's charms, as is Des Grieux. He catches a brief word with her, asks for another meeting, and learns her name, inspiring him to sing a rhapsodic aria, "Donna non vidi mai," after she is gone. Edmondo and the students immediately tease him, and he goes off in something of a huff. Geronte and Lescaut talk obliquely about how Manon would doubtless be happier leading a life of luxury than one in a convent, and when Lescaut leaves, Geronte orders that a carriage be made available immediately for him and the young lady. Edmondo overhears and warns Des Grieux. Manon reappears and Des Grieux tells her of the plot. Their initial attraction warms to the point where they end up running away in Geronte's carriage. He is enraged, but Lescaut tells him that as it is evident that he has taken a "fatherly" interest in Manon, he might as well know that Manon will soon become quite bored with a life of poverty with a student.

Act Two. Manon is in her elegant bedroom in Geronte's house, surrounded by hairdressers and maids. Lescaut calls on her, congratulating her on her new lifestyle, but she is wistful for her life with Des Grieux: "In quelle trine morbide." Lescaut tells her that Des Grieux has been frantically searching for her, and he, Lescaut, has been teaching him how to gamble so that Des Grieux this time can provide her with money. She is ecstatic at the news. Musicians enter to perform a madrigal Geronte has written in Manon's honor. She gives Lescaut money to pay them, but he pockets it rather than "offend artists." He goes off, and Geronte and his cronies enter. They watch as a dancing master gives her a lesson, and then leave for a party. She asks them to wait for her while she puts the finishing touches on her appearance. Des Grieux enters, full of reproaches, but is soon won over by her pleas and protestations of love. They fall into one another's arms, just as Geronte returns. He ironically apologizes for the interruption and reproaches Manon for her ingratitude after all his love has given her. She picks up a mirror and tells him to look at himself, and then herself and Des Grieux. He leaves with elaborate courtesy, saying they will meet again quite soon. Des Grieux urges her to leave, but the thought of leaving all her luxuries gives her a pang. He realizes she has not really changed ("Ah, Manon, mi tradisce") and wonders where the blind infatuation that made him a gambler for her sake will take him next. Lescaut rushes in, reporting that Geronte has denounced Manon to the police as a prostitute. Instead of leaving immediately, as Des Grieux begs, she stops to gather her jewels, thus losing her opportunity to escape in time. She is arrested and Lescaut keeps Des Grieux from attacking the police so that he will be free to save Manon from deportation.

Act Three. At the port in Le Havre, Des Grieux and Lescaut are waiting for the men they have hired to help rescue Manon. Lescaut is confident as he heads off, but Des Grieux is troubled. He bribes the guard to let him speak to Manon, and tells her of the plan. She is grateful that he has not abandoned her in her disgrace. Shots are heard and Lescaut runs in, telling them the plan has failed and that Des Grieux must run to save his life. Des Grieux vows to save her, no matter what. The crowd watches, commenting on the various prostitutes as the roll call takes place. Manon and Des Grieux sadly say their goodbyes, while Lescaut circulates among the crowd, telling them that Manon and Des Grieux were married, but that a lustful old man had her kidnapped and then disposed of her by these means. When Manon is ordered onto the ship, Des Grieux clings to her desperately, threatening anyone to approach, and then begs to be allowed to accompany her, even if it's by doing the work of a cabin boy or even lower work: "No, pazzo son." The captain jokes that the young man clearly intends to populate the Americas and allows him aboard as a cabin boy.

Act Four. The final act is set in a "desert in Louisiana" (which could make sense if one considers the Louisiana territory). Since their departure from France, Manon and Des Grieux had been pretending to be married to keep Manon from being given to one of the settlers, the typical goal of deportation. Eventually, they had tried to marry for real. The governor's nephew had then claimed Manon, since she was unmarried after all, and Des Grieux had fought and apparently killed him, whereupon he and Manon were forced to flee. She is now dying of exhaustion and illness and collapses, to his despair: "Senti, senti, son io che piango." He goes to find water and help, and she gives in to desolation, thinking that he has left her: "Sola, perduta, abbandonata." He returns, alone and empty-handed, and she dies in his arms, saying that time will erase her sins, but her love will not die. *—Ann Feeney*

Recommended:

- ○ **Puccini: Manon Lescaut** / Levine (cond.), Freni, Pavarotti, Croft, Taddei, Vargas, Bartoli / 1993 / London 440200
- ○ **Puccini: Manon Lescaut** / Muti (cond.), Cura, Guleghina, Gallo / DG 463186

La Rondine (The Swallow) (1917)

La rondine has often been called a sequel to *La bohème*, but while they share similarities, the two works should be viewed as related mainly in spirit. Puccini composed it for Viennese producers who wanted an operetta, something the composer had declared he would never write. What he did produce, however, was a tuneful opera of lighter character, a *La traviata*—to draw on another comparison—without the tragic ending.

The libretto was fashioned by Giuseppe Adami from a German one by Alfred M. Willner and Heinz Reichert. Like *La bohème*, it is set in Paris, but circa 1855–60. Puccini's music shows allusions to other styles in a number of places in the score, here and there using waltz rhythms, and even, when Prunier makes reference to *Salome*, deftly quoting from that Richard Strauss opera. Also, the music that opens Act Three more than vaguely evokes Debussy. Still, the end product is pure Puccini, lush, melodious, and brilliantly but delicately scored.

La rondine does not contain as many famous numbers as are heard in such Puccini evergreens as *Madama Butterfly* and *Tosca*. But there are still a few familiar tunes, among which is Magda's Act One "Chi il bel sogno di Doretta," a beautiful soaring aria. *—Robert Cummings*

Synopsis:

Act One. The act opens in Rambaldo's house, where his mistress Magda is entertaining Rambaldo and her friends, including Prunier. Prunier declares with mock fear and solemnity that love is the latest fashion in Paris, and nobody can escape it. Lisette, to his apparent annoyance, declares that love is an utterly practical matter: "You want me? I want you. Done!" As evidence, he produces his latest verse, even though it is not yet finished, about a woman named Doretta who refuses a king's offer of riches. Magda, in her "Chi il bel sogno di Doretta," gives the story a truly romantic ending with Doretta entranced by the kisses of a student and avowing that riches are nothing compared with true happiness. The guests and Rambaldo comment admiringly, even though Rambaldo declares that his own romantic demon has been thoroughly conquered. He gives Magda a magnificent pearl necklace. She tells the story of an earlier romantic encounter from the days when she was a dreamy young girl: "Ore dolci e divine." She describes meeting a young man in a dancehall, but becoming afraid of her own emotions and fleeing. Lisette presently announces that a young man has been persistently coming by to see Rambaldo and has come back again. It is Ruggero Lastouc, the son of a friend of Rambaldo's, who is visiting Paris for the first time. He describes his excitement at the fascinating city: "Parigi." Prunier meanwhile tells fortunes and says that Magda's hand reveals that like a swallow ("la rondine") she will migrate toward the sun and love. The guests and Lisette debate where he should spend his first night. Prunier says that bed is the only sensible place, but Lisette fiercely defends the magic of the first night in Paris, and they agree that Bullier's is the best night spot. After Ruggero leaves, Rambaldo and the guests follow, but Prunier and Lisette creep back in. They, too, make plans to meet at Bullier's, and she raids Magda's wardrobe for the occasion. He melodramatically begs the Muses' pardon for loving her. Magda returns, dressed in very simple clothes, and goes out herself, semi-disguised.

Bullier's is crowded and bustling with activity. When Magda enters, students immediately court her, and she tells them she is expected by someone else, indicating Ruggero's table, where he is alone. They gallantly escort her over. He does not recognize her, and when she tells him she came over only to keep from being bothered, he asks her instead to dance. Prunier and Lisette arrive. He recognizes Magda, who promptly teases him gently about his companion, but he pretends to Lisette that there is only a chance resemblance between this woman and her employer. Ruggero and Magda return to their table and he orders drinks. When they arrive, she carelessly toasts "To your loves," and he takes mild offense, as he would love one woman and one woman alone for all his life. Prunier and Lisette join them. In the quartet "Bevo al tuo fresco sorriso," the two couples sing of their love. Rambaldo enters and Magda asks Prunier to get Ruggero away. He does so by asking Ruggero to help Lisette get away before her employer notices her presence. He urges Magda to leave, saying that he will speak to Rambaldo, but she refuses; she declares that she is too much in love to care about common sense and sends him away. Rambaldo gruffly asks her what this means, and is willing to dismiss the incident as a minor escapade, but Magda refuses to leave with him, declaring she has finally found her dream of love. She asks his forgiveness for hurting him, but her love is too strong. As he leaves, he coolly says that he hopes she will not regret her decision. Outside, a voice is heard singing of love's unreliability. Ruggero returns, and she dismisses her forebodings and embraces him passionately.

Act Two. Magda and Ruggero are blissfully enjoying their love, despite some pressing bills. He tells her that he has written to ask permission to marry. She is unable to hide her dismay, and, surprised, he asks if she thought he wouldn't do it. In his aria "Dimmi che vuoi seguirmi," he describes his home and relates how she will be part of his loving family, how eventually they will be joined by a child. He leaves to see if his letter has been answered. Alone, she is torn between breaking their love by confessing her past or continuing to deceive him. Prunier and Lisette appear, quarrelling. He had tried to make her an actress, but her debut was an ignominious failure. She wants her old job back, and Magda happily welcomes her. Prunier has a message for Magda from Rambaldo, that he will take her back any time she should choose. She and Prunier declare they want nothing more to do with one another, but still set a meeting for later that evening. Ruggero returns, excitedly bearing a letter from his mother, who welcomes the doubtlessly pure and virtuous girl that Ruggero has chosen, and sends her a kiss. Ruggero is about to deliver it, but Magda breaks down and tells him the truth. After a moment of astonishment, he declares that it doesn't matter, and when she protests that it does, he begs her not to leave him: "Ma come puoi lasciarmi." She is adamant that she is only saving him greater grief later. Telling him that he is to return to his serene, peaceful home, and she to her flight, she leaves.

(In the first version, Rambaldo visits to bring Magda money as a bribe to return to him. Ruggero receives an anonymous letter telling him of Magda's past, and their roles are reversed: she begs him not to leave, but he is is the one who is adamant and goes.) *—Ann Feeney*

Recommended:

- ○ **Puccini: La Rondine** / Maazel (cond.), Domingo, Te Kanawa, Finnie, Thomas, London SO / 1983 / CBS 37852
- ○ **Puccini: La Rondine** / Pappano (cond.), Alagna, Gheorghiu, Matteuzzi, Bacelli, London SO / 1997 / EMI 56338

Suor Angelica (1918)

Suor Angelica (1918) is the second installment in Puccini's triptych of one-act operas commonly known as *Il trittico*. The opera chronicles the fall, redemption, and final transfiguration of its central character, Sister Angelica, who has taken the veil in repentance for bearing a child out of wedlock. The libretto, by Giovacchino Forzano, was immediately appealing to the composer, whose sister Igenia was Mother Superior of the convent at Vicepelago. Though it contains some of Puccini's most adventurous writing—the musical language at times even flirts with polytonality—the work has not enjoyed popularity comparable to that of its companions, *Il Tabarro* and *Gianni Schicchi*, each of which has enjoyed an independent life in the repertory. However, Angelica's aria "Senza mamma" (Without your mother), one of the most poignant moments in any of Puccini's works, has remained a recital favorite, and the opera is still staged in productions of the entire *trittico*. *—AMG*

Synopsis:

In the convent, the Monitress is doling out gentle penances for minor infractions to convent rules, and then tells the sisters to amuse themselves. Suor Angelica hoes and waters flowers, other sisters watch the sunbeam that comes in at just the right angle three times a year and turns the fountain waters golden. Suor Genovieffa suggests watering the grave of one of the sisters, saying she is sure that the dead sister would like it, and Angelica says that only the living have any desires. The Monitress responds that in the convent, they should have no desires, and while some agree that they have none, others confess simple wishes. Angelica joins those who say they have none, but the other sisters know that isn't true and quietly tell her story to a new sister. Angelica was a rich princess, but seven years before, was made to enter the convent because she had had a child out of wedlock. Angelica seems resigned, but longs for news of her family. The Infirmary Sister comes in, saying another sister has been stung by wasps and asks Angelica to brew one of her herbal cures.

The convent's alms-collectors bring in the day's offerings and report that outside there is an elaborate carriage. Angelica prays that it is a visitor from her family, to the other sisters' sympathy. The Abbess tells her that it is indeed for her, but makes her calm herself before saying it is her aunt, the Princess.

When the Princess enters, she looks at Angelica coldly, and without a word of greeting, tells her to sign a paper dividing her parents' estate for her sister's wedding. Angelica exclaims in surprise and joy and asks who the groom is, but her aunt tells her that it is a man who has overlooked the disgrace that Angelica brought onto the previously untainted family honor. Angelica bursts out that her aunt is inexorable and is met with bitter reproaches. The Princess says that when she prays, she feels close to Angelica's mother, who weeps. She exhorts Angelica to atone for her sin. Angelica humbly asks for any word about her son, what he looks like, what color his eyes are. The Princess is silent for a moment, and Angelica warns that the Virgin Mary hears and judges her. The Princess says that he was taken ill two years ago and everything possible was done. Angelica asks if he is dead, and the Princess nods. Angelica collapses, and the Princess, after taking a step towards her, turns away to pray. The Prioress and Portress enter with pen and ink, and Angelica, without a word, drags herself to the table to sign. The Princess leaves, and Angelica is left alone. Kneeling, she laments that her child died without even knowing how much she loved him. She imagines him as an angel in Heaven and asks him to tell her when she will be allowed to die. She seems to enter a trance and tells the sisters, when they enter, that the Virgin's grace has descended upon her and she is happy. They go off to their cells. Angelica returns, and still as if in a trance, brews poison, singing as she does so that she has heard her son calling to her to come to Paradise. As she drinks the poison, the trance evaporates, and she is suddenly reminded that suicide is a mortal sin and begs the Virgin to save her, pleading for a sign of grace. She seems to hear angels singing to the Virgin, and the chapel door opens, the interior flooded with light. She sees Mary with her son, and as Angelica falls dying, the child walks towards her, while the angels continue to sing. *—Ann Feeney*

Recommended:

○ **Puccini: Suor Angelica** / Bonynge (cond.), Sutherland, Edwards, Howard, Ludwig, National PO / 1998 / London 458218

Il tabarro (The Cloak) (ca. 1916–1918)

Il Tabarro (The Cloak) was the first of three one-act operas composed for Puccini's *Il Trittico* (Triptych), the others being *Suor Angelica* (Sister Angelica) and *Gianni Schicchi.* Puccini commissioned the libretto from Guiseppe Adami after seeing Didier Gold's play, *La houppelande* (the cloak), in Paris, and reveling in its elements of *Grand Guignol* (a mixture of horror and melodrama). Puccini had originally requested that Giovacchino Forzano—who would eventually supply the libretti for the other two members of the composer's tryptych—adapt Gold's play, but both Forzano and Puccini's next choice, Ferdinando Martini, declined; in Adami, however, he found a willing collaborator. The resulting opera represents a new level of musico-dramatic unity for Puccini, and comes closer to the ideals of verismo than perhaps Leoncavallo or Mascagni ever did during the heyday of their style in the 1890s. Of the three *Trittico* operas, *Il Tabarro* has become the best-established in the repertory, although its comedic counterpart, *Gianni Schicchi,* has also enjoyed sustained popularity.

Set in Paris during the first years of the twentieth century, *Il Tabarro*'s tightly focused plot centers on Michele, the owner of a barge moored on the Seine; his much-younger wife, Giorgetta, who no longer enjoys their nomadic river life and has taken up with a man her own age; and her lover, Luigi, who wants to settle down in Paris to a more stable workman's life—hopefully with Giorgetta. As is typical of the grim verismo style, the outcome is unpleasant for all involved: Michele, who is already suspicious of his wife's behavior, unwittingly discovers Luigi arriving at the barge to meet Giorgetta; Michele strangles the young man and hides him under his cloak, only revealing the body when his horrified wife emerges to reconcile with him.

Puccini's score seems to grow almost seamlessly from the opening "Seine" music, the gently sway of which emerges as a unifying theme throughout the work. Unlike *Gianni Schicchi,* which lays claim to the evergreen "O mio babbino caro," and *Suor Angelica* which offers the heartrending "Senza mamma," *Il Tabarro* has no readily excerptable arias. However, because they are so rare, and so well integrated into the fluid orchestral texture, the few lyrical moments in this unforgiving drama have a greater impact in context. Among the most memorable moments are the impassioned duet between Giorgetta and Luigi as they dream of a better life in Paris, and Michele's jealous tirade on the deck of the barge when he realizes his wife's infidelity; his anger seems uncontainable, and the orchestra echoes this with near-boiling figurations. *—AMG*

Synopsis:

On the barge, Michele is smoking his pipe and looking at the sunset. Giorgetta suggests giving the stevedores some wine and, praising her for her thoughtfulness, Michele agrees. She pours it for them and when an organ grinder comes by, Luigi asks him to play. Giorgetta says she only likes dance music, and Tinca offers himself as an expert partner. However, when he steps on her feet, Luigi takes his place, and they dance languorously. Michele returns and, as the stevedores go back to work, she casually asks him about his plans for the men's future employment, talking mostly about Luigi. A song vendor sings about the story of Mimì, who died for love. Giorgetta asks Michele what is bothering him and he answers that it's nothing.

La Frugola comes looking for Talpa, carrying her sack of garbage pickings. She gives Giorgetta a rhinestone comb, and shows off her evening's real triumph, a heart of beef for her cat. She describes his contented life: better to be master of a hovel than servant in a palace, better to eat heart than tear one's own out for love. The stevedores emerge with the last of the load, and la Frugola chides Tinca for his drinking. He says that that's the way he keeps from thinking, and Luigi bitterly exclaims that he has the right idea ("Hai ben ragione"): the life of the poor is miserable, and every moment of joy is overshadowed by fear. Even those dim moments have to be fought for or stolen, so better to bow your head and bend under the burden. La Frugola talks of her dream of living in the country, but Giorgetta and Luigi reminisce about the friendly, bustling suburb where they both grew up.

La Frugola and Talpa go off, arm in arm, and Luigi and Giorgetta whisper briefly about their last night together. Michele returns and Luigi diffidently asks him if he may go with the barge to Rouen and disembark there. Michele tells him there's nothing there but misery, that he would do better to stay in Paris, and Luigi replies in that case, he'll stay. Michele leaves to put up the lights, and Giorgetta and Luigi tensely sing of the torment of being so close together, yet unable to meet in more than furtive, stolen moments, their words echoing Luigi's aria. They agree to meet that night; she will light a match as the signal for him to come on board. He leaves, and she muses on how difficult it is to be happy.

When Michele returns, he asks why she no longer loves him. She coolly assures him that she does, that he is good and honest. He tenderly reminds her of their earlier days, when she and their baby sat with him, all three wrapped in his cloak. She begs him not to remind her of the dead child. Now that their happiness is gone, he says his gray hairs seem to insult her youth. She again asks him to stop and says she is tired. Growing more passionate, he longs for her to return to him as she did before, when she loved him and ardently sought his kisses. She rebuffs him, saying they are both older and things are different, and that she is exhausted. When she leaves, he bitterly calls her a whore. In his great monologue, "Nulla! Silenzio," he looks into the cabin, where she hasn't undressed or gone to bed. He tries to guess who her lover might be, but rejects the possibility that it is one of the stevedores. After all, Tinca drinks, Talpa is too old, and Luigi had asked to leave. Burning with fury, he imagines seizing his rival by the throat, seeing him turn livid. He fiercely calls for the unknown lover to share his chains and fate with him as they go together into the darkest pit. Worn out, he automatically takes out his pipe and lights it. Luigi thinks this is Giorgetta's signal and comes aboard, furtively. Michele seizes him and, overpowering him despite Luigi's struggles, taunts him that he will indeed go to Rouen—as a swollen corpse in the river. Eventually, he offers to release him if Luigi will confess to his love. Choking, Luigi does so, and Michele, throttling him, makes him repeat it until he is dead. Giorgetta calls out from the cabin and Michele quickly hides the body under his cloak. Giorgetta comes out, telling him she is sorry for having been so cold. She asks if he doesn't want her under his cloak as before, and reminds him of something he had said before: that every human being wears a cloak that hides something, sometimes a joy, sometimes a sorrow. He interrupts, "And sometimes a crime. Come underneath my cloak!" He pulls aside the folds of cloth to show her the corpse and, grabbing her, forces her to the floor, pressing her face against Luigi's contorted, dead face. *—Ann Feeney*

Recommended:

○ **Puccini: Il Trittico** / Pappano (cond.), Gheorghiu, Alagna, Shicoff, Guleghina, London SO / 1999 / EMI 56587

○ **Puccini: Il Trittico** / Gardelli (cond.), Tebaldi, Merrill, Del Monaco, Palma, Maggio Musicale Fiorentino / 1990 / London 411665

Tosca (1900)

Giacomo Puccini (1858–1924) had composed four operas before officially taking up his pen with *Tosca* in 1895. After the poor reception of Puccini's first two operas, *Le villi* and *Edgar, Manon Lescaut* brought him considerable fame and financial success, and *La Bohème* was popularly (although not always critically) well received. In *Tosca,* Puccini explored the dark side of human emotion, a marked change from the late Romantic sentimentality of *La Bohème. Tosca* was premiered in 1900 at Rome's *Teatro Costanzi* to a temperate critical reception.

Luigi Illica and Giuseppe Giacosa based their libretto for *Tosca* on Victorien Sardou's play *La Tosca* (1887), which actress Sarah Bernhardt made famous in performances throughout Europe. Puccini first came into contact with Sardou's play in 1889. His delay in commencing the music for *Tosca* was largely the result of his flagging interest in the play, perhaps brought on by Sardou's admission of his dislike for Puccini's music. Puccini's publisher Giulio Ricordi eventually convinced the composer to complete *Tosca.*

Puccini creates coherence between story and music with themes that recur in association with characters and concepts. The opera begins as the orchestra states the low brass-laden three-chord motive outlining the sinister interval of a tritone (B flat major, A flat major, E major) that we come later in Act One to associate with the villainous confessor and executioner Scarpia. An expansive, major-mode theme, orchestrated for strings, is introduced in Act One as *Tosca*'s and Cavaradossi's love music, and returns in Act Two, when *Tosca* enters Scarpia's chamber and as Cavaradossi is led from the torture chamber to *Tosca,* and in Act Three, as pantomime music as Cavaradossi writes his farewell to *Tosca.* Although the continuous swaths of sound in Puccini's score avoid the sharp delineations between recitative and aria of earlier nineteenth century Italian operas, arias still function to uncover the emotions of the central characters in *Tosca.* Tosca utters her Act Two supplication *"Vissi d'arte"* in a soaring melodic idiom, reinforced by a rich harmonic language and orchestral palette. The cello melody that accompanied Tosca's first entrance and meeting with Cavaradossi in Act One, here accompanies Tosca's prayer, illustrating the extent to which love is Tosca's true religion. In Cavaradossi's Act Three aria, *"E lucevan le stelle",* the orchestra sings with him at key utterances in desperately empty octaves.

Puccini also upheld here the tradition of monumental end-of-act finales. The Act One finale ("Tre sbirri... una carrozza") is a cleverly crafted juxtaposition of diagetic and nondiagetic music in which the Latin chorus of working-class believers singing the Te Deum and the intermittent utterances of the godless Scarpia mesh musically on different planes of realistic perception. The Act Two finale, which grows out of Tosca's and Cavaradossi's duet, is a tragic rush as Sciaronne, Spoletta, and a chorus of soldiers chase Tosca to her death. The E minor tonality that accompanied Scarpia's death at Tosca's hands in Act Two, here accompanies her own demise, and binds Tosca and Scarpia beyond their earthly entanglement. *—Jennifer Hambrick*

Synopsis:

Act One. In the Church of Sant'Andrea della Valle, Angelotti, who has escaped from imprisonment for revolutionary activities, creeps in and searches for the key his sister has left. The Sacristan comes in, grumbling about Cavaradossi's dirty paintbrushes. Cavaradossi enters and begins work on his unfinished painting of Mary Magdalene and, in "Recondita armonia," muses on the strange harmony of two contrasting beauties: the blonde, blue-eyed unknown whom he has painted as she prayed and his beloved Tosca, with her dark hair and eyes. The Sacristan is shocked as such worldliness, even from an antimonarchist who reads Voltaire. He goes and Angelotti emerges from hiding. Cavaradossi offers any help he can give. They are interrupted by Tosca's voice from outside, calling to Mario. He hides Angelotti and gives him his lunch. When he lets Tosca in, she is suspicious at the delay and the sound of whispering she heard. He denies that he was with another woman and protests his love. She tells him to meet her that night, and then notices the portrait and is immediately suspicious again, especially when she recognizes the Marchesa Attavanti. He again reassures her, "Qual occhio al mondo," and she departs, but not before insisting that he give the portrait eyes like hers.

When she leaves, Angelotti tells how his sister, the Marchesa, enabled his escape. Cavaradossi offers Angelotti the use of his villa as a hideout, and describes a secret hiding place in the well. They hear the cannon that alerts the police of an escaped prisoner and they flee. A moment later, the Sacristan bursts in with news that Napoleon has been defeated. He and the choir boys celebrate loudly, but are interrupted by the arrival of Scarpia and his men. Scarpia questions the terrified Sacristan and suspects Cavaradossi of involvement. When Tosca returns, he hints that Cavaradossi was meeting a woman. She bursts into a jealous fury and then leaves in tears. He orders his men to follow her, and in the aria "Tre sbirri," while the Te Deum is being sung in the background, he gloats over his impending double victory, Mario's execution as a traitor and he himself possessing Tosca.

Act Two. In his apartments at the Farnese Palace, Scarpia sends a note to Tosca asking her to meet him. Alone, he sings of the joys of violent conquest rather than amorous consent: "Ha piu forte sapor." Spoletta enters and nervously tells Scarpia that they searched the villa but did not find Angelotti, but that they did arrest Cavaradossi. Cavaradossi is brought in and Scarpia questions him, first with elaborate courtesy, then with threats. Cavaradossi denies any knowledge of the escape or Angelotti's whereabouts. Tosca enters and Cavaradossi whispers to her not to say anything of what she has seen. He is taken away "to give his evidence." Scarpia remains with Tosca and asks her if the Marchesa was at the villa. She insists that Cavaradossi was alone and laughs that his repeated questions are futile. He darkly replies that they will soon see, and tells her that in the other room Cavaradossi is being tortured. To her helpless horror, she can hear Cavaradossi screaming, and alternates between pleading for the torture to stop and calling Scarpia a monster. Unable to bear it, she reveals Angelotti's hiding place in the well.

Cavaradossi is brought in, unconscious, just as Sciaronne runs in with the news that Napoleon has won. Cavaradossi bursts into a defiant paean to the victory: "Vittoria, vittoria!" Tosca begs him to be silent, and Scarpia orders him dragged away. Knowing his reputation, Tosca asks how much it will cost to bribe him. Laughing, he tells her the price he has in mind doesn't involve money ("Gia, mi dicon venal") and that he would much prefer to satisfy his lust for her. Desperate, she prays, asking God why a life devoted to art and love should be rewarded like this: "Vissi d'arte." Scarpia commands her to make her decision. Spoletta returns to say that the execution is ready and Tosca at last agrees to Scarpia's proposal. He orders that Cavaradossi be shot tomorrow in a mock execution, telling Spoletta meaningfully, "Like Palmieri." Spoletta indicates his understanding and leaves. Tosca demands that Scarpia give her a safe conduct as part of their bargain, so that she can leave the country with Cavaradossi. He agrees and, as he writes the document, she sees a knife on the table. When he seizes her, she plunges it into his chest. As he dies, she taunts him; but she puts a cross on his chest and candles beside his body before she leaves.

Act Three. At dawn in the Castel Sant'Angelo, a shepherd boy sings as the church bells ring. Cavaradossi is brought in. Alone with the jailer, he bribes him with his last possession, a ring, to let him write a farewell note to Tosca. As he writes, he is overwhelmed with the memory of their last night together, and exclaims he never loved life as much as now: "E lucevan le stelle." Tosca enters and shows him the signed document of safe conduct. He exclaims that it is Scarpia's first act of clemency, and responding, "And his last," she tells him of the bargain they had struck, and remembers his blood on her hands. He lovingly comforts her: "O dolci mani." She tells him of the mock execution, and urges him to fall down naturally, as though dead. The firing squad enters and she watches as he is shot, exclaiming that he is a fine actor. When they leave, she calls to him to get up, but he does not. Running over, she sees that the execution was real. Scarpia's death has been discovered, and his men rush in to arrest her. Crying, "O Scarpia, we meet before God," she leaps from the parapet to her death. *—Ann Feeney*

Recommended:

○ **Puccini: Tosca** / De Sabata (cond.), Callas, di Stefano, Gobbi / 1997 / EMI 56304

○ **Puccini: Tosca** / Karajan (cond.), Price, di Stefano, Taddei, Corena / 1997 / London 452620

○ **Puccini: Tosca** / Maazel (cond.), Nilsson, Corelli, Fischer-Dieskau / 1999 / London 460753

○ **Puccini: Tosca** / Levine (cond.), Domingo, Scotto, Bruson / 1997 / EMI 73155

Turandot (1926)

Puccini was nearing the completion of *Turandot*, when he died in rather short order following surgery for throat cancer. At the behest of Arturo Toscanini, Franco Alfano, a former student of Puccini, finished the opera—the final duet and last scene—using Puccini's sketches. *Turandot* was premiered on April 25, 1926, at Il Teatro alla Scala in Milan, in a performance led by Toscanini; strangely enough, the maestro did not then use Alfano's ending, instead ending the performance where Puccini's finished score left off.

Turandot's libretto was fashioned by Giuseppe Adami and Renato Simoni, based on Schiller's adaptation of a Carlo Gozzi drama. The story is set in Imperial China, Act One beginning near the walls of Beijing. A royal edict from Princess Turandot, daughter of the Emperor, is read: she will marry the first man of royal blood able to answer three riddles. Failure by the suitor will result in his death. Accompanied by his slave girl Liu, the old vanquished Tartar king, Timur, now blind, falls to the ground. Prince Calaf comes to his aid and recognizes him as his father, with whom he had lost contact. The crowd gathering outside cries for the head of the latest failed suitor, the Prince of Persia. Calaf becomes enraged at Turandot's cruelty in requiring the executions, but when he sees her, he becomes instantly enamored of her. Over the objections of Timur and Liu, Calaf seeks to answer the three riddles, which he does successfully. Turandot begs her father for release from the terms of the edict, but is refused. Calaf, however, offers to sacrifice his life if she can learn his name before dawn. Liu and Timur are brought to Turandot, but the latter commits suicide rather than divulge his name. Later Calaf, alone with Turandot, kisses her passionately and then trusts in her sudden change of heart by revealing his name. They later appear before the Emperor and Turandot discloses his name—Love.

Puccini's score features his usual quota of popular numbers and brilliant scoring. There are effective choruses, as well: "Muoia! Noi vogliamo il carnefice," sung when the crowd calls for the execution of the Prince of Persia, and in the dark and atmospheric "Arrota! Che la lama guizzi," sung by the executioner's assistants. But it is the individual numbers that are best known in this opera. Liu's "Signore Ascolta" is the slave girl's beautiful attempt to dissuade Calaf from seeking to be Turandot's suitor. His heartfelt response to her comes with his "Non pangiere, Liu."

The most famous aria in the opera, though, is *"Nessun dorma,"* sung by Calaf, confident Turandot will not learn his name. As for this composition's artistic worth, *Turandot* may well be Puccini's finest opera. *—Robert Cummings*

Synopsis:

Act One. In a public square outside the royal palace, a Mandarin reads the law that Turandot will marry whichever man of royal blood who can answer the three riddles she sets, but that if he should fail, he will be beheaded. The Prince of Persia, the latest unlucky suitor, will be executed at moonrise. As the crowd mills about in anticipation, a blind old man is knocked to the ground, and the girl with him pleads for help. A young man comes over and he recognizes the old man as his father, Timur. They greet one another joyously, each having thought the other dead. Timur tells his story, how he was wandering about helplessly after the battle that overthrew him, and Liu saved him and remained with him. Calaf asks why she made such a sacrifice, and she answers that he had smiled at her one day in the palace. The crowd enthusiastically watches the axe being sharpened, and compares its cold, deadly beauty with Turandot's. However, when they see the Prince, they are moved by his youth and unfrightened, dreamy expression, and they call to Turandot for mercy. She steps out and silently gestures for the execution to continue, and the crowd follows the procession offstage.

Calaf is bedazzled by her beauty and, despite Timur and Liu's pleas, vows to try to answer the riddles. Ping, Pang, and Pong appear and also try to dissuade him, using slightly earthier arguments. Offstage, the Prince of Persia cries out, "Turandot!" as the axe falls. Liu, weeping, begs Calaf to listen—"Signore, ascolta"—and tells him that she and his father will die without him. He tells her not to cry ("Non piangere, Liu") and asks her to remain with Timur should he be killed. The ghosts of Turandot's former suitors plaintively call out that they love her. Calaf fiercely declares that he alone loves her, and Ping, Pang, and Pong point out the latest prince's head, which has been placed on a spike for display. Calaf refuses to change his mind and beats the gong that announces another suitor's intentions.

Act Two. Ping, Pang, and Pong recall the other aspirants who ended up dead and dream of their peaceful homes, in contrast to this city of bloodletting. The sound of the ceremony arouses them from their reverie. In the courtyard, the crowd hails the Emperor. He regrets the bloodshed his oath has led to, and he himself pleads with Calaf to save his own life and the Emperor from further guilt. Calaf repeats his determination and Altoum gives in. Turandot appears and tells the crowd of the rape and murder of her ancestress: "In questa reggia." She will avenge that terrible death, and no man shall ever possess her. She warns Calaf away, telling him there are three riddles and one death. He responds that there are three riddles and one life. She asks them one by one, and he answers each. She is horrified and begs Altoum to release her. He responds that the oath is sacred, and she rounds on Calaf, saying he will have to take her by force. He declares he wants her burning with love, and offers her another riddle. If she can discover his name by dawn, he will agree to die. She nods her agreement, and Altoum hopes for him to win.

Act Three. In the gardens, Calaf is dreaming of his eventual victory (*"Nessun dorma"*) while guards declare Turandot's proclamation that nobody in the city may sleep until the stranger's name is known. Ping, Pang, and Pong appear, followed by a crowd. They beseech him to leave, terrified of how they will suffer from Turandot's rage, and offer him riches and other women, and declare that they follow him to other victories. He refuses, but the guards drag in Timur and Liu. Turandot appears and questions Timur, who groans as he is manhandled. Liu cries out that she alone knows the name, but that she will keep it as her dearest secret. As Liu is knocked about and threatened, Turandot asks her what gives her such strength, and Liu responds that it is love, her secret, hopeless, immense love. She defies the torture, but when the executioner appears, she says that she will speak. She declares that Turandot, though bound in ice, will be melted by great fire, and she, too, will love him: "Tu, che di gel." Seizing a dagger from a guard, she stabs herself. Timur is almost insane with grief and tries to awaken her. When told that she is dead, he shouts that her offended spirit will avenge itself, and then laments her death. The crowd is moved and carries her body away, asking her forgiveness.

Calaf is left with Turandot, and he upbraids her for her cruelty. She orders him not to touch her as she is no ordinary human, but the daughter of Heaven, and her spirit resides on high. He declares his passion. Frightened, she tells him that to touch her is sacrilege, but he replies that her kiss gives him eternity. As he does so, she finds herself responding, murmurs in fear, and begins to weep. She tells him these are her first tears. She had held all her other suitors in contempt, but she confesses she was afraid of him, and also afraid of the consequences of defeating him. She declares that his pride and certainty have conquered her heart, and now she is defeated. She begs him to leave and take the mystery of his identity with him. Instead, he himself tells her his name, and they leave. In the courtyard, the crowd assembles before the Emperor at dawn. Turandot informs him that she now knows the stranger's name: "Love." The crowd rejoices at the power of love. *—Ann Feeney*

Recommended:

○ **Puccini: Turandot** / Leinsdorf (cond.), Nilsson, Tebaldi, Bjoerling, Tozzi / 1996 / RCA 62687

○ **Puccini: Turandot** / Mehta (cond.), Sutherland, Pavarotti, Caballe, Ghiaurov, Krause / 1984 / London 414274

CHAMBER MUSIC

Crisantemi, elegy for string quartet (1890)

Giacomo Puccini himself acknowledged that his true talent lay "only in the theater," and so his non-operatic works are understandably few. But there are more of them than the average concertgoer might imagine. The string quartet was a medium for which Puccini had a certain undeniable affinity, and over the years he composed some five works or groups of pieces for it. All of these string quartet pieces have been virtually forgotten except for the elegy, *Crisantemi* ("Chrysanthemums"), that Puccini wrote in 1890—in a single night, he said—as a response to the death of the Duke of Savoy.

Crisantemi is a single, dark-hued, continuous movement. Puccini found his two liquid melodic ideas worthy enough to re-use in the last act of his opera, *Manon Lescaut*, of 1893. Almost never heard in its original string quartet guise, *Crisantemi* frequented the music stands of the world's orchestras in an arrangement for string orchestra throughout the twentieth century. *—Blair Johnston*

Recommended:

○ **Favourite Encores for String Quartet** / Delme SQ / 1999 / Hyperion 55002

Henry Purcell

b. 1659, London, England, **d.** Nov. 21, 1695, London, England

Composer: Opera, Vocal, Choral, Chamber Music, Keyboard

As England's greatest composer of the Baroque, Henry Purcell was dubbed the "Orpheus Britannicus" for his ability to combine pungent English counterpoint with expressive, flexible, and dramatic word settings. While he did write instrumental music, including the important viol fantasias, the vast majority of his output was in the vocal/choral realm. His only opera, *Dido and Aeneas*, divulged his sheer mastery in the handling of the work's vast expressive canvas, which included lively dance numbers, passionate arias and rollicking choruses. Purcell also wrote much incidental music for stage productions, including that for Dryden's *King Arthur*. His church music includes many anthems, devotional songs, and other sacred works, but few items for Anglican services.

Purcell was born in 1659 to Henry Purcell, master of choristers at Westminster Abbey, and his wife Elizabeth. When he was five, his father died, forcing his mother to resettle the family of six children into a more modest house and lifestyle. In about 1668, Purcell became a chorister in the Chapel Royal, studying under chorus master Henry Cooke. He also took keyboard lessons from Christopher Gibbons, son of the composer Orlando Gibbons, and it is likely that he studied with John Blow and Matthew Locke. In 1673, Purcell was appointed assistant to John Hingeston, the royal instrument keeper.

On September 10, 1677, Purcell was given the Court position of composer-in-ordinary for the violins. It is believed that many of his church works date from this time. Purcell, a great keyboard virtuoso by his late teens, received a second important post in 1679, this one succeeding Blow as organist at Westminster Abbey, a position he would retain all his life. That same year saw the publication of five of the young composer's songs in John Playford's *Choice Ayres and Songs to Sing to the Theorbo-lute or Bass-viol*. Around the same time, he began writing anthems with string accompaniment, completing over a dozen before 1685, and welcome songs. Purcell was appointed one of three organists at the Chapel Royal in the summer of 1682, his most prestigious post yet.

Purcell composed his first ode for St. Cecilia's Day in 1683. The following month, upon Hingeston's death, he was named royal instrument keeper while retaining his other posts. The composer remained quite prolific in the middle part of the decade, primarily producing music for royal occasions. In 1685 the new King, James II, introduced many changes at Court, one of which was to make Purcell the Court harpsichordist and Blow the Court composer. Near the end of 1687, Queen Mary's pregnancy was announced and Purcell was commissioned to compose an anthem for Psalm 128, *Blessed are they that fear the Lord*. Many other of his anthems appeared in 1688, as did one of his more famous ones for church use, *O sing unto the Lord*.

With the ascension of William and Mary to the throne on April 11, 1689, Purcell retained his post as royal instrument keeper, and he, along with Blow and Alexander Damazene, shared the duties of Court composers. With his royal duties reduced, he was able to pursue other opportunities, including teaching and writing for other organizations. One of Purcell's greatest successes came in 1689 with the production of *Dido and Aeneas*. He then collaborated with John Dryden on *King Arthur* in 1691, and also composed the music for *The Fairy-Queen* (1692), based on Shakespeare's *A Midsummer Night's Dream* both productions also scoring triumphs. In the final year of his life Purcell remained exceedingly busy, writing much for the stage, including *The Indian Queen*, left incomplete at his death on November 21, 1695. *—Robert Cummings*

OPERA

Incidental Music (1680–1695)

Incidental music for plays had an important place in the life of Restoration England (from 1660). Following the return of Charles II, the theater entered into a new and vigorous phase based almost entirely on drama, neither native nor Italian opera making much impact at this time. During the earlier part of his short life Purcell had little connection with the theater, the majority of his compositions comprised of sacred works, instrumental music, and the numerous odes composed to celebrate royal occasions, the New Year, or St. Cecilia's Day. As so often in earlier musical history, Purcell's sudden turn to composing incidental music for the theater was largely dictated not by his own predilections, but by external events. In 1688 the quasi-Catholic James II was ousted from the throne by the reliably Protestant William of Orange and his consort Mary. Under William and Mary royal patronage of music became increasingly diminished, particularly in the field of sacred music, where the brilliant orchestrally accompanied anthem gave way to a more sober style of church music. Purcell thus sought new ground, and that he chose was the theater.

From 1690, when he produced the incidental music for John Dryden's *Amphitrion*, until his death in 1695, Purcell produced incidental music for nearly 40 plays. In some instances his contribution amounted to no more than a single song; for others, such as William Congreve's famous play *The Double Dealer* (1693), Purcell composed up to nine or ten pieces, both orchestral music and songs. The orchestral music generally included an overture, usually in the French style developed by Lully, and a number of short dances and pieces termed airs. These had little dramatic function, serving the purpose of entr'acte pieces between scenes or the opening or closing of an act. For these reason they are frequently referred to as "curtain tunes" or "act tunes." Generally of light, even breezy nature they include some of Purcell's best known tunes, among which are the rondeau in hornpipe rhythm from Aphra Behn's *Abdelazer*, made famous by Benjamin Britten in his *Young Persons Guide to the Orchestra*, and the jig *Lullibulero*, which, although now known as a popular tune, originally comes from *The Gordian Knot Untied* of 1690. The songs appeared within the context of the play, although rarely serving any function other than to entertain whoever was on stage at the time. Some, like "Dear pretty youth" (from *The Tempest*) or "The cares of lovers" (from *Timon of Athens*) were included in Shakespeare's plays, which were often given in bowdlerized versions during the Restoration period. Others, including "Sweeter than roses," became Purcell's most enduringly popular songs, originating from long-forgotten plays, in this instance *Pausanius, the Betrayer of his Country* (1695). In sum, Purcell's incidental music represents a widely varied repertoire of often tiny pieces sharing one quality—the rich melodic vein that runs through all his music. *—Brian Robins*

Recommended:

○ **Purcell: Complete Ayres for the Theatre** / Goodman (cond.), Holman, Steele-Perkins, Keavy, Parley of Instruments / 1995 / Hyperion 67001

Dido and Aeneas, Z. 626 (1689)

Purcell's *Dido and Aeneas* was commissioned by and first performed at Josias Priest's School for Young Ladies in Chelsea. The libretto is by Nahum Tate, who extracted the story of Queen Dido and the sailor, Aeneas, from Virgil's *Aeneid*. Into Virgil's story Tate introduced some of the more popular elements of Baroque opera, including a sorceress, a hunt, and a storm. The first performance took place in 1689, probably in mid-May.

The story concerns Aeneas, who is shipwrecked at Carthage, where the Carthagenian Queen, Dido, falls in love with him. Aeneas returns her love, but knows he must leave eventually—it is his destiny to found Rome. After their final parting, Dido realizes she cannot live without him and looks forward to her death.

Dido and Aeneas is considered to be the only true opera that Purcell composed; its continuous music and purpose-written libretto set it apart from his other dramatic works, which are more properly considered semi-operas or, in the case of *Timon of Athens*, a masque. Although brief, *Dido and Aeneas* nevertheless embraces a wide range of emotional content, and achieves a dramatic lyricism that was then unprecedented in England.

Purcell deftly tailored the score to the performing forces available at Josias Priest's school. There are only four principal roles and the orchestra consists of just strings and continuo; together, the opera's three acts last only about one hour. However, *Dido* is not a work for amateurs: the vocal writing demands highly skilled singers, and the presence of male voices in the score (not least of which is Aeneas himself, a tenor) indicate that some professional performers were most likely imported for the first production. Dances in the piece, such as the "Dance of Triumph" for Dido's court and another for the witches, were most likely written at the suggestion of Priest, who was a dance instructor.

The French overture that opens the work is reminiscent of Lully, as is the homophonic chorus in minuet rhythm, "Fear no danger." More akin to the music of Purcell's English contemporaries are "Purse thy conquest, Love" and "Come away, fellow sailors" (which boasts a metrically irregular melody). Most interesting are the recitatives, which are in neither the quick, Italian recitativo secco style nor the more rhythmically regular French fashion. Instead, Purcell tailored his writing to the particular accents and cadence of the English language, creating an entirely new declamatory style.

Three of the arias in *Dido and Aeneas* are of the ground bass variety. The most famous of these, "When I am laid in Earth," is the last in the opera and is often referred to as "Dido's Lament." In the aria, we hear a chromatic bass line that descends through a fourth, then closing an octave below where it starts. This ground bass is repeated nine times, supporting a vocal line filled with expressive dissonance. The opera close with the chorus, "With drooping wings," in which descending minor scales suggest the text of the title. *—John Palmer*

Synopsis:

Act One. Aeneas and his men are the sole free survivors from Troy's fall to the Greeks. The gods have commanded him to rebuild in Greece a city that will become Rome and rule the world. On his way there, he was shipwrecked in Carthage, the city where Dido, also a refugee, has built her city and reigns as queen. He helped her defeat a neighboring king who had declared war when she refused to marry him, and the two of them fell in love.

In the palace, Belinda urges Dido to dismiss her worries ("Shake the cloud from off your brow"), but Dido responds by saying that she cannot admit the cause of her unrelenting sorrows. Belinda has no trouble guessing that her feelings for Aeneas are the cause, and she and Dido's attendants urge her to marry him, for in this way Carthage retains his protection and he and his Trojans can rebuild there. Dido muses that his valor and virtue, combined with the sufferings he has undergone, have completely won her heart: "Whence could so much virtue spring?" Her own misfortunes have made her compassionate toward others, but she fears she feels too deeply for him. Belinda and one of her women, combined with the chorus, assure her that Aeneas is as much in love as she: "Fear no danger to ensue." He arrives and declares his love, saying he will defy destiny for her. He then pleads that he is burning in the fire of passion as Troy burnt, "If not for mine, for Empire's sake"; and while the queen says nothing, Belinda notices that Dido is overcome. The chorus declares that love has triumphed: "To the hills and the vales."

Act Two. The Sorceress summons the witches—"Wayward sisters, you that fright"—and they appear. She tells them that their plan to ruin Dido is succeeding; by that night Dido will be deprived "of fame, of life, and love." Dido and Aeneas are out hunting that day, and she will send one of her elves, disguised as Mercury, the messenger of the gods, to tell Aeneas that he must desert Dido. The witches prepare a spell to summon a storm ("But ere we this perform") and as the furies dance, the spell is created.

In a grove, where Aeneas, Dido, Belinda, and their followers are resting, Belinda and the chorus sing of the successful hunt: "Thanks to these lonesome vales." One woman says that Diana, the goddess of the hunt, often comes to bathe in the fountain, saying, "Oft she visits this lone mountain," where she had Actaeon killed by his own hounds for having seen her bathe. Dido's attendants dance, and Aeneas shows off the head of the boar he killed, which he boasts is even larger than the one that killed Adonis, Venus' mortal lover. The storm begins and Dido and the other women leave, but the spirit sent by the Sorceress appears to Aeneas ("Tonight thou must forsake this land"), ordering him to obey the gods and leave to rebuild Troy. He sadly agrees, though distraught at the thought of leaving Dido, and declares death would be less painful: "Jove's commands shall be obeyed... But ah! what language can I try."

Act Three. The Trojans are preparing to set sail and one of them, echoed by the chorus, urges the others to console their lovers by pretending they will return: "Come away, fellow sailors, your anchors be weighing." They dance. The Sorceress and witches come and watch gleefully, declaring that Dido (whom they call Elissa, her other name) will die that day, and Carthage will later burn: "Destruction's our delight." (Carthage and Rome became mortal enemies, Rome eventually destroying it completely.) They dance as well. Inside the palace, Dido longs to die, and Belinda tries to comfort her. Aeneas enters and tries to assure her that he still loves her, but she now spurns him: "Thus on the fatal banks of Nile." He even declares that he will refuse to obey the gods and remain, but she refuses, telling him that now that he has decided just the once to leave her, she is as resolved as he. He leaves, and she feels death approaching: "Thy hand, Belinda... When I am laid in earth." She urges them to remember her but to forget her fate. Cupids come to mourn over her: "With drooping wings ye Cupids come." *—Ann Feeney*

Recommended:

○ **Purcell: Dido & Aeneas** / Barbirolli (cond.), Angeles, Glossop, Harper, Johnson, English CO / 1995 / EMI 65664

○ **Purcell: Dido & Aeneas** / Harnoncourt (cond.), Esswood, Murray, Yakar, Scharinger, Vienna Concentus Musicus / 1994 / Teldec 93686

○ **Purcell: Dido & Aeneas** / Christie (cond.), Gens, Berg, Brua, Marin-Degor, Les Arts Florissants / 1995 / Erato 98477

○ **Purcell: Dido & Aeneas** / Parrott (cond.), Kirkby, Nelson, Bonner, Thomas, Taverner Choir & Players / 1991 / Chandos 521

The Fairy Queen, semi-opera, Z. 629 (1689)

By 1692 the British masque or semi-opera had become the British answer to foreign operatic composition. The plot of Purcell's *Fairy Queen* is that of William Shakespeare's *A Midsummer Night's Dream*. Purcell wrote overtures, instrumental preludes, ritornellos, and musical numbers and choruses, to be performed during the play. The masques, or "Divertissements," were inserted at appropriate points in the dramatic action, and added to the spectacle of the theatrical presentation.

The instrumental First Musik and Second Musik were played to make the audience aware that the drama was about to commence. There is not much music to Act One except for the scene of the Drunken Poet. Fairies chase the poet about the stage to mischievous and spritely music, and the poet's music is as inebriated as he is.

Act Two is in fairyland, and the musical entertainment is of two parts. The first is an entertainment put on for Titania. Light dances for the fairies and songs such as "Sing while we trip it" and "Come ye youngsters of the sky" are performed by the sprites. Recorders imitate bird songs, and the fairy chorus sings light and lively music. Stock characters then lull her to sleep in an erotic set of songs. Their solos are peaceful and dreamy, with languorous melodies accompanied by muted strings that move from the upper registers of the orchestra to the lowest. The music is rich and dissonant, and the Followers of Night end the scene with a dance.

In Act Three Titania entertains her new love Nick Bottom with a masque. "If Love's a sweet passion" is a beautiful song about the pleasures and pains of love. "When I have often heard young maids complaining" is a rather defiant text by a seducee about the battle between the sexes. In the scene that follows, two characters named Corydon and Mopsa sing a rustic seduction duet, dressed in drag. It's full of broad, slapstick humor.

The music of Act Four centers around a masque in honor of Oberon's birthday. The scene opens with an exuberant and joyous symphony. Soprano, alto, tenor, and bass soloists depict spring, summer, fall, and winter respectively. The first three seasons are accompanied only by obbligato in very short, intimate pieces. But the longer winter is accompanied by chromatic and dissonant strings. The chorus hails Phoebus to end the masque.

Act Five has a masque put on by Oberon for Duke Theseus. This earthy masque of Juno celebrates love in all of its manifestations. During a symphony, Juno descends out of the sky in a chariot, then sings of happy love and a "plaint" about the loss of the loved one. Next, in a Chinese garden, a rousing song about free love and the natural world is sung, until a group of monkeys joins in, in a dance of bestiality. Hymen, the god of married love, complains cynically about broken vows but "They shall be happy as they are fair" is the conclusion of the poetic argument. The masque ends with a stately chaconne. *—Rita Laurance*

Synopsis:

Note: the plot of *The Fairy Queen* is nonsensical. The librettist, possibly actor Thomas Burton, simply excerpted his favorite bits from Shakespeare's *A Midsummer Night's*

Dream and added as much singing and dancing as possible, without concern for narrative coherence.

Act One. Enter Titania, Queen of the Fairies, with the Indian boy and attendant fairies. She gathers the fairies round, suggesting they leave the town and live idyllically "where crowds and noise were never known." Enter more fairies, bringing with them three drunken poets whom they begin to torment for sport, pinching and wrenching and prodding them for a confession of their sins. One of the poets finally steps forth to confess his uselessness as a poet, his drunkenness, and his poverty. Finally the fairies drive them away.

Act Two. The scene is a moonlit wood. Titania enters with her entourage. She quarrels with Oberon and afterwards transforms the scene into a fairyland of picturesque grottoes and flowering trees. The fairies dance in an attempt to soothe the distressed Titania, and she requests that they sing a lullaby. The allegorical figures of Night, Mystery, Secresie, and Sleep step forth to sing for Titania each in turn, until she falls asleep. Oberon approaches and squeezes the juices from a magic flower into her slumbering eyes.

Act Three. Enter Titania with her fairies and the ass-headed Bottom, with whom she has fallen in love. She uses her magic to make the scene change to a lush forest grove with a river, a bridge formed by a pair of dragons, and swimming swans. The Fauns, Dryades, and Naides arrive to dance and sing for all. Some savages interrupt the merrymaking with a raucous dance that scares the fairies away, causing the dragon bridge to vanish and the gracefully arching trees to right themselves. Enter Coridon and Mopsa. Coridon is trying to convince Mopsa to kiss him and she is patiently resisting, "till I kiss you for good and all." A Nymph arrives, singing of the battle of desire versus good sense, and proclaims her strategy of being as false and inconstant as men in order to have as much pleasure as they. The act concludes with the merry dance of the Haymakers.

Act Four. Titania and Bottom are asleep. A pair of couples, Hermia and Lysander and Helena and Demetrius, get embroiled in a terrible confusion, as in Shakespeare's play, until they both fall asleep as well. Titania and Bottom are awakened by Oberon, and he asks Titania for music to celebrate his birthday. Happy to meet his request, she changes the scene to the sumptuous Garden of Fountains at sunrise. The clouds part and Pheobus appears in his glorious chariot. Allegorical figures of each of the four seasons sing for Oberon, each in turn, starting with Spring.

Act Five. Theseus grants consent for the marriages of Hermia to Lysander. Demetrius is skeptical when told of the previous night's magical adventures, upon which the most spectacular of all the scenes begins to appear. Oberon summons Juno, who descends from the heavens in a peacock-drawn chariot, and a spectacular Chinese garden appears. A Chinese man enters and sings, followed by a Chinese woman, who also sings, followed by dancing monkeys. The fairies sing, and Hymen appears, lamenting the flameless torch he carries. The Chinese women instruct him how to light it—"Turn then thine eyes upon the glories there"—and all ends with a gigantic song and dance. *—Donato Mancini*

Recommended:

○ **Purcell: The Fairy Queen** / Harnoncourt (cond.), Bonney, McNair, Chance, Dale, Vienna Concentus Musicus / 1995 / Teldec 97684

○ **Purcell: The Fairy Queen** / Norrington (cond.), Wistreich, Hunt, Crook, Padmore, London Classical Players / 2002 / Virgin 61955

The Indian Queen, semi-opera, Z. 630 (1695)

The Indian Queen was originally a play written by Sir Robert Howard in collaboration with his brother-in-law Sir John Dryden, first performed in 1664. It wasn't until 1694 that Thomas Betterton, the impresario of United Company decided to turn it into a musical. *The Indian Queen* has much less music than Purcell's other operas, and it is thought that perhaps he wrote less music because all the actors and singers had walked out of the company prior to its first performance. Purcell composed 16 vocal numbers to the play, and 22 instrumental pieces.

The opening poem is about the imminent takeover of Mexico by the Spanish; a dialogue between an Indian boy and girl, it becomes a statement of protest to the coming war.

The masque of "Fame and Envy" makes up most of the music for Act Two. "Fame" begins by proclaiming the greatness of Zempoalla, saying her wonders cannot be matched. "Envy" rises up scornfully singing "What flatt'ring noise is this...?" In a jauntily evil piece, all the snakes of "Envy" hiss dramatically at "Fame," whose music is all innocence and lyricism. "Fame" eventually wins the argument and sends "the fiends of hell" back whence they came. In Act Three, music is introduced in an incantation scene. Queen Zempoalla's soothsayer Ismeron opens with the recitative "Ye twice ten hundred deities," and then has an extended solo while he calls forth the God of Dreams. On the words "Pants for breath," slight panting pauses occur in the solo line, as Ismeron tries to get his breath and move on. When he asks the God of Dreams to rise, the music slowly and gradually rises chromatically to a grand climax. Then it falls gently back on the words "lull thee in thy sleep." The God of Dreams eventually rises accompanied by an obbligato for solo oboe. Act Three also includes an overture and canzona in free fugato style, featuring a solo trumpet matched and in harmony with the violins. The work is expansive and brilliant and full of imitative invention. The spirits, to a rather sad melody over a moving bass, sing about how happy they are that they do not suffer from human passions. "I attempt from love's sickness to fly" is one of Purcell's most beautiful and famous arias, capturing the Queen's despair and longing.

The final scene to which Purcell added music is when Zempoalla is about to sacrifice all her prisoners to the gods. There are three numbers: a chorus for the crowd of people at the ritual sacrifice; a priest has a recitative, to which the chorus responds; and a solemn and sad procession follows. All lend importance to the dramatic content of the moment.

Henry Purcell died before he had a chance to finish the opera. There was another masque composed for the play by Daniel Purcell, celebrating the wedding of Orazia and Montezuma. It is very often omitted, as it isn't as musically fine as the rest of the opera. *—Rita Laurance*

Recommended:

○ **Purcell: Indian Queen** / Gardiner (cond.), Hill, Varcoe, Standage, Kraemer, English Baroque Soloists / Erato 96551

King Arthur, or The British Worthy, semi-opera, Z. 628 (1691)

King Arthur was originally based on a poem written by Sir John Dryden in celebration of the second half of King Charles II's reign. In commercial terms, it was Purcell's most successful work. Dryden's text is rich and beautiful, and Purcell's setting is lively and refined.

The topics chosen for the poetry and masques often included fairies, love, evil spirits, and heroism. The opening act of *King Arthur* includes gods, as the pagan Saxons make sacrifice, and heroics. "Come if you dare, the trumpets sound" is heroic military music sung by a heroic tenor, with drum rhythms as part of the melody. The vocal chorus imitates military drums in their rhythmic enunciations, and the trumpets blast victory music.

Act Two has two main musical episodes, the first of which is all about fairies. In a foggy mist of music the sprites sing a song that imitates the lightness of spirits flitting through the dusk. It is followed by "We brethren of the air," a peaceful exhaling phrase that gently breathes forth fairy dust. The second is a masque celebrating the bucolic life. The gentle pastoral "How blest are the shepherds" has an almost religious beauty to it. The bawdier side of country living is struck up in "Shepherds leave decoying" and "Come, shepherds, lead up a lively measure." The songs get quicker and wilder as the scene progresses, and are punctuated at the end with a lively hornpipe, Purcell's favorite dance.

The masque of Act Three is pure fantasy. The Frost Scene, as it is called, features Cupid descending in a vast machine accompanied in the orchestra by a French symphony. Cupid, a soprano, calls forth the Genius of Winter in a powerful recitative. The Genius rises slowly in an extremely extended melodic line, because he is frozen stiff, to cold trembling strings. The Genius is a rich bass voice accompanied by brilliant and icy chromatic harmonies, prefiguring Vivaldi's *Four Seasons.* Cupid and the Genius have a duet, and the Cold People all sing and dance of the wonders of love. This scene ends with a lively hornpipe also.

In Act Four, Purcell had the opportunity to write for two sopranos, which he loved to do. Two sirens, in a lyrical tour de force, accompanied only by continuo, invite Arthur skinny-dipping. Water nymphs and sirens also sing the passacaglia "How happy the lovers." The final masque of Britannia, has been much maligned as being dramatically incoherent and beside the point. However, it closes out the semi-opera wonderfully. As Britannia arises, a symphony composed in a florid Baroque style accompanies her. "Your hay is mow'd" is sung by Comus and three peasants. It is a comic, rustic romp. In stark contrast is the beautiful "Fairest Isle" sung by none other than Venus in an aria inspired and heavenly. A grand dance and chorus ends the act as the Britons and the Saxons unite as one people. *—Rita Laurance*

Synopsis:

Act One, Scene One. King Arthur has at last secured his entire kingdom against the Saxons. Their leader is Oswald, whose ambitions include Arthur's beloved, the blind Emmeline. For his decisive battle against Oswald's forces, Arthur is forced to part from Emmeline.

Scene Two (Sung). Oswald, his magician Osmond, and the spirit Grimbald gather in their place of worship to perform a victory ceremony. Grimbald brings in six Saxon victims, while priests and singers crowd around. They pray, and the six victims are led off-stage by priests. An off-stage battle can be heard, followed by a Briton song of triumph.

Act Two, Scene One. The spirit Philidel comes to warn Merlin that the Britons, in pursuit of the Saxons, are being led by Grimbald toward cliffs, where they will be tricked into falling to their deaths. Merlin commands him to protect the Britons.

(Sung) Grimbald enters, disguised as a shepherd, with Arthur and his forces following behind. When he's about to lead them off the cliff, Philidel and Merlin's spirits intervene. Grimbald disappears in a flash of light. Arthur gives thanks.

(Unsung) Emmeline and Matilda enter, discussing Arthur. Matilda encourages Emmeline to allow herself to be entertained by the present group of Kentish folk.

(Sung) The Kentish folk arrive, sing happy songs, and dance, enacting rituals of courtship. Oswald captures Emmeline and Matilda. The Britons prepare to rescue them.

Act Three, Scene One. The Britons are frightened by the magic the Saxons are using to protect themselves, but Arthur wants to rescue Emmeline and is prepared to do so alone. Merlin makes a promise to teleport him to her side and cure her blindness.

Scene Two. In a deep wood, Grimbald has captured Philidel, but the latter escapes and casts a spell over Grimbald. Merlin and Arthur enter. The wizard gives Philidel the potion that will cure Emmeline and leaves, planning to break Osmond's enchantment of the wood.

Emmeline and Matilda enter. Philidel sprinkles the potion over Emmeline's eyes, curing her. Philidel warns that the enemy is approaching. All exit but the two women. Osmond approaches and passionately woos Emmeline, declaring that he's jailed Oswald, his rival for her.

The Frost Scene (sung). To impress Emmeline, Osmond transforms the British climate into that of Iceland. Cupid arrives, singing awake the Cold Genius who lies beneath the snow. Cupid then uses his wand to reveal a prospect of ice and snow, whereupon dancers and singers merrily dance and sing, then depart. Osmond makes lustful advances upon Emmeline, from which she is saved only when the ensnared Grimbald cries out for rescue, distracting Osmond.

Act Four, Scene One. Learning that Merlin has broken his spells, Osmond makes plans to seduce Arthur with beautiful visions.

Scene Two. Arthur is left alone in a wood, Merlin having warned him against Osmond's illusions, only Philidel is there to watch over him.

(Sung) Instead of the expected dangers, Arthur finds a golden bridge across a silvery stream. As he approaches, a pair of sirens emerge from the water and entreat him to stay. Despite temptation, Arthur moves on. Nymphs and sylvans now emerge from behind trees, dancing, bedecked with branches, and singing of love.

Arthur dispels them all with a command. Drawing his sword, he strikes at the finest tree in the wood. A phantasm of Emmeline appears, with her arm wounded from the blow. As he lays down his weapon to take her hand, Philidel reveals that she is Grimbald in disguise. Arthur breaks the enchantment by chopping down the tree.

Act Five, Scene One. Osmond releases Oswald so they can fight Arthur together.

Scene Two. Oswald proposes single combat between himself and Arthur. Arthur disarms Oswald, but allows him to live. Meanwhile, Merlin overpowers Osmond and imprisons him. Arthur sends Oswald and his forces back to Saxony.

(Sung) Upon a wave of Merlin's wand, the scene changes to the stormy British Ocean. Aeolus is there in a cloud above. He sings, then ascends away and the sea grows calm. An island arises, with Britannia enthroned upon it. The fishermen at her feet come ashore and dance, followed by the arrival of Pan and Nereid. They also sing and Comus arrives with a group of peasants who sing of the joys of country life. As they dance, Venus descends, accompanied by the Masculine and Feminine aspects of love. Venus praises Britain, and the couple dialogue in song about the vicissitudes of love.

(Sung) The scene now opens upon the Order of the Garter. Honour enters, with various heroes in attendance, and the opera ends. *—Donato Mancini*

Recommended:

○ **Purcell: King Arthur** / Christie (cond.), Gens, Padmore, Piau, Bazola, Les Arts Florissants / Erato 98535

○ **Purcell: King Arthur** / Pinnock (cond.), Argenta, Finley, MacDougall, Gooding, English Concert / Archiv 435490

Prophetess, or The History of Dioclesian, semi-opera, Z. 627 (1690)

There were popular myths surrounding the life of Roman Emporer Diocletian (AD 284–305), and this opera is about two of those. The first concerns the prophecy leading up to Diocletian becoming Emperor. The second myth surrounded his abdication. The story of Diocletian was first turned into a play by Beaumont and Fletcher in 1622. It was revived several times until Thomas Betterton, impresario of the United Company, got hold of it and decided to turn it into a semi-opera in 1690. He altered the play and added operatic elements: elaborate machinery, costumes, effects, and staging. M. Priest supplied the dances, and H. Purcell the music.

Dioclesian was a major turning point in Henry Purcell's musical career. As a semi-opera, it was very well received by the British public. It was the first semi-opera to be published in full score, in 1691. Today it provides a good resource for his theater and his music. He included in the score an oboe quartet which is at times used to double the violins and at times stands alone. It includes a tenor oboe, a very rare instrument, and a bass line written for the bass violin.

The opera has two main musical episodes. The first act is an extended triumphal scene full of original and clever dances, instrumental pieces, choruses, solos, and duets. They vary in texture and form and are loosely connected. Purcell opens with a prelude and a bass solo. "Great Diocles the boar has killed" introduces the celebration. Then Purcell's large scale organization carries the listener through a victory celebration, a coronation scene, and a betrothal. In many of these pieces Purcell uses one rhythmic figure throughout. The variety is supplied through thematic variation, canonic entrances, and imitation. "Since the toils and hazards" features a tenor solo and chorus, followed by a symphony for two flutes and continuo. It's full of suspensions, imitative figures, and an extensive four-bar melisma on the word joy.

The second major musical episode is in Act Five, which consists of the "Masque of the Triumph of Love." It is often removed and performed alone. As a symphony is playing, three elaborate machines set the stage for the palatial scene. Many of the songs are about the pains and pleasures of love, pastoral contentment, and the delights of wine. There is a prelude for violins and oboes and Cupid begins the masque with "Call the Nymphs," a solo for Cupid and chorus. Purcell's writing in this masque is filled with invention and vitality. The variety of solos, choruses, duets, and dances is exciting, and the action doesn't cease from the beginning of the masque until its culmination in the choral number "Triumph victorious love." Full of trumpets and oboes again, it is a grand and spacious chaconne, in which the entire chorus breaks into dance. *—Rita Laurance*

Recommended:

○ **Purcell: Dioclesian; Timon of Athens** / Pinnock (cond.), Argenta, Monoyios, Agnew, Birchall, English Concert / Archiv 447071

○ **Purcell: Dioclesian; Masque from Timon of Athens** / Hickox (cond.), George, Bostridge, Ainsley, Padmore, Collegium Musicum 90 / 1995 / Chandos 569

VOCAL

Songs, Arias, and Catches (1678–1695)

Perhaps comparable to Schubert in his prolific creativity and in his effortless manipulation of the musical language he inherited, Purcell was the representative songwriter of his time and place. Schubert's songs, however, went on to inspire succeeding generations of composers, while Purcell's all but disappeared, pushed aside by the growing preference for technically dazzling vocal display and Italian opera. The twentieth century rediscovered Purcell's songs.

Many of them were composed as parts of theater pieces, integrated into the drama and effective in spite of the occasional mediocre text. Among these are "Music for a while," from *Oedipus*, Z. 583 (1692), and "Thrice happy lovers," from *The Fairy Queen*, Z. 629 (1692). The chromatic ground bass of the former creates a harmonically adventurous composition. An earlier ground-bass song, "O solitude, my sweetest choice," Z. 406, also shows Purcell's ability to make a colorful composition using a potentially monotonous device. Purcell composed two completely different settings of "If music be the food of love," the second of which became one of his most popular works.

Throughout his brief career, Purcell composed dance songs, many of which were published in Henry Playford's second volume of *Banquet of Musick* (1688). Among these, the gavotte "Sylvia, now your scorn give over," Z. 420, and the minuet "Ah! how pleasant 'tis to love," Z. 353, achieved such popularity that Purcell transcribed them for harpsichord and had them published in *The Second Part of Musick's Hand-maid* of 1689. "Love's power in my heart shall find no compliance," Z. 395, is an excellent example, with a fluid, dotted melody over simple harmonies and a trumpet-like fanfare setting the cheers "Tararara" and "Victoria!"

Declamatory songs were old-fashioned in Purcell's time, but he did write a few. They are in duple meter, with a grave character and vocal lines that freely follow the inflections of spoken English and occasionally illustrate the words musically. "More love or more disdain I crave," Z. 397, is an example, as is "From rosy bowers," from the third part of *The Comical History of Don Quixote*, Z. 578.

Catches, a type of round, were in fashion in Purcell's time, partly due to the success of John Hilton's 1652 anthology *Catch That Catch Can*. Phrases are longer than in other rounds, and the first voice usually completes a line before the second comes in. Purcell wrote about 60 of these; most concern wine and women, but many are about politics, current events and various human emotions. Many are sexually explicit, such as "Sir Walter enjoying his damsel," Z. 273, which describes the acts of Sir Walter Raleigh and a young lady in the forest.

Purcell's arias betray the influence of Italian vocal composition in their multi-sectional format. "Hail, bright Cecilia," No. 8 from the *Ode for St. Cecilia's Day*, Z. 328, is an example that resembles a da capo aria in its modulation away from the tonic for a central section, with a final return to the tonic and the opening music and words. Playford's *The Theater of Music* series contains a number of Purcell's multi-sectional songs. *—John Palmer*

Recommended:

○ **Purcell: Songs & Airs** / Argenta, Boothby, Nicholson, Toll / 2001 / Angel 61866

○ **Secular Solo Songs of Henry Purcell, Vol. 1** / King, Bonney, George, Caudle / 1994 / Hyperion 66710

CHORAL

Come ye sons of art away (Birthday ode for Queen Mary), for soloists, chorus & instruments, Z. 323 (1694)

In the time of Purcell, odes were composed by the Master of the Children of the Chapel Royal. Although Purcell was never appointed to head the Chapel Royal, he was a favorite composer of the king, so it fell to him to compose odes for the birthday of Queen Mary II in 1694. *Come, Ye Sons of Art, Away* was the final birthday ode Purcell composed for Queen Mary; by the end of 1695 both she and Purcell had passed away. It has seven movements, plus an opening symphony, which Purcell later rewrote and incorporated into his opera *The Indian Queen.* The overture has three movements. The refined and majestic Largo is followed by a fugal Canzona and a lush Adagio. The opening chorus is on the words "Come, Ye sons of Art," and serves as an introduction to the poetic text. "Sound the Trumpet" is a striking duet for two countertenors. The melody dances over a ground bass as the singers imitate the sound of trumpets. "Strike the Viol" is a haunting countertenor solo in three, with an instrumental ritornello. The solo features an obbligato for two flutes, and the ritornello has the flutes and violins answer one another. Each of these movements is a complete work in itself. Purcell changes the orchestration, the voice to which he gives the solo line, the form, and the mood of each. After the two countertenor pieces, he writes the bass solo with chorus "No day that such a blessing gave." It is a prayer that this day be a day of jubilee, and with the remaining portion of the composition, the prayer is heard. Jubilation and rejoicing are in every note. "Bid the Virtues" is a fanciful soprano solo with oboe obbligato, followed by a florid bass solo over a ground bass called "These are the Sacred Charms that Shield." A soprano and bass duet comprises the main body of the final movement, with a choral ritornello. This is Purcell at his happiest and most innocent. When the chorus enters to restate the final verse, it is accompanied by the entire ensemble of instruments, which emphasizes the joyful mood. *—Rita Laurance*

Recommended:

○ **Purcell: Birthday Odes for Queen Mary** / Munrow (cond.), London Early Music Consort / 1998 / Virgin 61333

Music for the Funeral of Queen Mary, Z. 860 (1695)

Queen Mary was one of England's most beloved monarchs, and her death from smallpox just after Christmas 1694 plunged the nation into genuine grief. The queen's body lay in state for public observation until her funeral in March. Henry Purcell thus had time to compose music especially for the ceremony, and he did write a brass canzona and the anthem *Thou know'st, Lord* for the burial, but otherwise he seems to have fallen back on earlier scores, including two funeral anthems. Precisely what was performed is a matter of argument; no autograph scores exist, and Purcell left no account of his own of the ceremony. Trumpets and drums are known to have participated in the event, but Purcell's funeral march and canzona for the occasion are for "flatt trumpets," which were similar to sackbuts or trombones, and no tympani part has been connected to the brass movements. (Tympani are often included in modern performances, especially since Thurston Dart made a reconstruction in the 1950s.)

The march is written for a quartet of flatt trumpets, which could play in a minor key, something Purcell uses to good effect to provide interest for his repetitive sequence of variants on a very simple four- or five-note phrase. Recordings may place this march at the beginning and/or the end of the work, and sometimes drop it into the middle, too. Somewhere in the middle also comes the brass canzona, a pulsing, polyphonic piece in two related and repeated sections.

The first of the choral selections, "Man that is born of a woman," holds some of Purcell's most deeply melancholy and expressive music. The composer brings particular tension to the phrase "hath but a short time to live," and the melody rises and falls in imitation of the words "he cometh up and is cast down like a flower." "In the midst of life we are in death" begins in the soprano section (almost certainly boys in the first performance) and spreads through the choir. The music is angular, chromatic, and, by the standards of the time, a dissonant cry of anguish.

"Thou know'st, Lord, the secrets of our hearts" is hushed and resigned, a fitting send-off to the departing spirit. Purcell's contrapuntal version of this anthem is quite complex; his more homophonic setting is far more serene and seems a more fitting conclusion to this music, which was performed again in November 1695 at Purcell's own funeral. *—James Reel*

Recommended:

○ **Music for Queen Mary** / Neary (cond.), Bostridge, Chance, Kirkby, Tubb, New London Consort / 1995 / Sony 66243

○ **Purcell: Odes for St. Cecilia's Day; Music for Queen Mary** / Parrott (cond.), Daniels, Ainsley, Thomas, Evera, Taverner Consort, Choir & Players / 1999 / Virgin 61582

Odes & Welcome Songs, Z. 320–344 (1680–1695)

Odes were composed for celebratory occasions, especially the birthdays of monarchs or the feast day of St. Cecilia, the patron saint of music. Purcell wrote Welcome Songs for the return of a monarch from some excursion, usually out to Windsor; he composed nine during the reigns of Charles II and James II, but none during William III's reign. The composer did, however, produce six birthday odes for Queen Mary in 1689–94.

Purcell's odes begin with an overture in the French style, with a stately opening section, a fugal central segment and a closing adagio that introduces the first vocal movement; alternating numbers for the chorus and soloists follow. The orchestras of these cantata-like works generally consist of strings, although three include parts for recorders, and *Swifter, Isis, Swifter flow,* of 1681 (Z. 336), is the first of Purcell's odes to include oboe. An excellent obbligato part for oboe also appears in the soprano solo, "Bid the virtues," from *Come, ye sons of art, away* (Z. 323; 1694), the last of Purcell's birthday odes for Queen Mary. Most of the odes written under William III have both oboes and trumpets, fitting the pomp and ceremony of their intended occasions.

Solo numbers are often set with a ground bass; among the best of these are "Welcome, more welcome does he come," in *From those serene and rapturous joys* (Z. 326; 1684), and "See how the glitt'ring ruler of the day," from *Arise, my muse* (Z. 320; 1690). The latter uses a minuet rhythm to illustrate the sun asking the planets to join in a dance. In the choruses Purcell does not hesitate to display his mastery of counterpoint.

Purcell's first welcome song, *Welcome, viceregent of the mighty king* (Z. 340; 1680) composed to order for King Charles II, shows the composer at the top of his form. Like many other such works, it is for two sopranos, alto, tenor, and bass with orchestra; the text, welcoming Charles II back to London after spending the summer at Windsor, is typically obsequious and flattering, exemplified by the lines, "When the summer in his glory, / Was delightful, warm and gay, / All was but a winter's storm / While our sovereign was away."

The last of Purcell's several Odes for St. Cecilia's Day, *Hail, bright Cecilia,* of 1692 (Z. 328) has one of the best ode texts Purcell set. Nicholas Brady's verses are filled with references to musical instruments and Purcell illustrated these references appropriately. For instance, for the lines, "Hark, each tree its silence breaks / The box and fir to talk begin," Purcell writes a passage featuring three recorders (wooden instruments). Also, "The fife and all the harmony of war" is colorfully accompanied by trumpets and timpani. Purcell's choruses, in six parts, are very intricate, the final one containing a strict canon.

The ode, *Welcome to all the pleasures,* (Z. 339) written in 1683 for St. Cecilia's Day festivities, is one of the few of Purcell's large works published in this lifetime. *—John Palmer*

Recommended:

○ **Complete Odes & Welcome Songs** / King (cond.), Chance, Daniels, George, Muller, King's Consort / 1992 / Hyperion 44031/8

Te Deum and Jubilate Deo, for soloists, chorus & instruments in D major, Z. 232 (1694)

That Henry Purcell was one of the greatest English composers was a fact affirmed in his lifetime. His position as the court composer for first James II, then William III, and finally Queen Mary enabled him to write music for the most important court functions with the best possible performers under the finest possible circumstances. His *Te Deum and Jubilate Deo* is one of his last works of church music and, indeed, one of his last works. Written for St. Cecilia's Day, November 22, 1694, and scored for soloist, mixed choir, and an orchestra of trumpets, drums, strings, and continuo, it is one of Purcell's grandest and most ornate works. Setting the Ambrosian hymn in English, Purcell conceived his *Te Deum and Jubilate Deo* as a sort of English celebratory cantata with arias, duets, and trios alternating with choruses and highly embellished instrumental passages. Although there are meditative and even melancholy sections of the work, its overall tone is joyous from its festive opening chorus to its serene and sublime closing *Jubilate Deo. —James Leonard*

Recommended:

○ **Purcell: Funeral Sentences** / Herreweghe (cond.), Kooy, Agnew, Bonner, Kendall, Collegium Vocale / HM 901462

CHAMBER MUSIC

Fantasias for viols (ca. 1680)

"A greater musical genius England never had," wrote a contemporary of Henry Purcell. Among the various genres which this versatile and prolific composer essayed during his short lifespan stands a remarkable series of Fantasias for viol consort—a *summa* of contrapuntal experiment comparable to J. S. Bach's *Art of the Fugue*; however, Purcell was only 20 or 21 years old when he wrote them. A number of these pieces survive with precise composition dates (from the tenth of June to the 31st of August 1680), each found in one of the three great autograph manuscript collections, British Library MS. Additional 30930.

The composer seems to have selected the old-fashioned Fancy, or Fantasia, as a medium in which to challenge himself contrapuntally; even Purcell in his capacity of Assistant Keeper of the King's instrument collection, would have known fewer opportunities to play in a viol consort than musicians a generation before. The "newfangled" violin was making headway in its popular appeal, and was greatly diminishing the fashionability of viol consort music, despite the musical conservatism of the Restoration Court. But Purcell set out to compose, and collect in manuscript, a large series of such pieces, grouped according to arrangement: three Fantasias for three voices (Z. 732–734), nine and the beginnings of a tenth in four parts (Z. 735–744; these are all dated), and one each in five, six and seven parts (Z. 745–747).

The last two of this collection exemplify a special English sub-genre, called the In Nomine. One voice of each quotes a long-note cantus firmus borrowed from a sixteenth century setting of the Mass by John Taverner. Purcell's contributions to a by then lengthy tradition of instrumental chamber music based on this tune are both fairly austere and monochromatic. Special scoring also appears in the single piece for five parts (Z. 745): its full title is "Fantasia Upon One Note," as one of the five voices sustains the pitch C throughout the entire composition, while the other four weave placid and beguiling harmonies about it.

Each of the other Fantasias proper unfolds (as do their nearest relations, the *Consort of Four Parts* by Matthew Locke, published in 1660) in two to five contrasting sections, most based upon imitation; among the technical feats present are a number of contrapuntal inversions, augmentations, and even motivic linkages between sections (as in the falling fourth motive which dominates Z. 739). The collected repertory of four-part Fantasias, gradually but clearly strives towards greater motivic compactness; the ninth (Z. 443, dated 31 August) culminates this tendency by its complete construction on two motives of but four notes each. And yet the affect of the music in performance transcends the merely pedantic, allowing for flights of virtuosity and moments of passionate and surprising chromaticism. Indeed, the venturesome harmonic content of the music dominates the surface details; the composer may present four or five different tonalities within the same measure, and travel briefly to keys his contemporaries would have found incomprehensibly distant. *—Timothy Dickey*

Recommended:

○ **Purcell: Fantasias for the Viols** / Savall (cond.), Hesperion XX / 1999 / Astree 9922

Sonata for trumpet, 2 violins, viola & continuo in D major, Z. 850 (1690–1695)

Purcell's *Sonata for Trumpet*, Z. 850, for trumpet, two violins, viola, and basso continuo, is one of two such works by Purcell, the other being absorbed into the overture to the masque, *Timon of Athens*. Neither of these, however, is as representative of Purcell's music for trumpet as are the obbligato trumpet parts in "Sound the Trumpet," from the *Birthday Ode for the Duke of Gloucester* (1695), and "Thus the gloomy world," from *The Fairy Queen*. For these and other works for trumpet, including the *Sonata*, Purcell almost certainly had in mind either John Shore or his uncle William Shore, the most renowned trumpet players in England at the time. Michael Tilmouth has suggested that the *Trumpet Sonata*, Z. 850, was the opening symphony for the *New Year Ode* for 1693, of which only the text exists. For many years after the discovery of the manuscript, there was doubt that the piece was by Purcell. Since then, scholars have become certain it is by Purcell and, on the basis of its harmonic content, believe it was composed very late, probably around 1694.

Purcell's understanding of the trumpet is clear in the fanfare-like main theme of the first movement. Graceful and ebullient, this Allegro opens with a bouncy, three-measure theme that is immediately echoed in the strings. A single motive from the theme propels the music forward until the dynamic drops to piano and the trumpet and strings exchange florid outbursts. Halfway through the movement Purcell emphasizes the dominant.

As in earlier examples of such works, the short, slow, middle movement is for the strings and continuo only and is essentially a succession of harmonies that provides a foundation for an improvised violin melody. Marked Adagio and in 4/4 time, the movement begins in B minor and closes on D major. Chromatic inflections create a circle of fifths progression from B minor through E major and on to D.

In the lilting finale, a repeated tone that is characteristic of music for the trumpet appears in the accompaniment as well. The movement is formally curious and inventive. At the beginning, instruments have staggered, imitative entries, first in the strings and lastly the trumpet, in the manner of a fugue. A passage of fragmentation follows, with a rhythmic motive stated by all the strings and continuo answered by falling triads in the trumpet. The fugal process begins again, but the theme is inverted. After another fragmentation episode the theme returns, in the trumpet and in its original form. A coda based on a string figure from earlier in the movement closes the piece. *—John Palmer*

Recommended:

○ **Trumpet Voluntary** / André / 1993 / Erato 92123

KEYBOARD

Eight Suites for harpsichord, Z. 660–669

Purcell's *Suites for Harpsichord* were dedicated to Princess Anne of Denmark by Purcell's widow, Frances, in *A Choice Collection of Lessons for the Harpsichord or Spinnet*, printed by Henry Playford in 1696. It was the first volume of English keyboard works by one composer. The brief pieces were assembled according to key into "suites." None of the suites in *A Choice Collection*, however, was described as such. The volume includes transcriptions of six of Purcell's instrumental works.

The suites are not grouped consistently: No. 3 lacks a Saraband, No. 6 a Corant, and the seventh a Prelude. (In England, a standard number or sequence of dance movements never developed.) Also, the last movements of Nos. 7 and 8 are transcriptions and the Corant and Saraband of the fifth suite appears in *The Second Part of Musick's Hand-maid*, published in 1689. Almands and Corants tend to have the thickest texture, which seem polyphonic because of the broken chords in the left hand. The Sarabands are simpler, some incorporating popular tunes.

The first of the eight, in G major (Z. 660) is the simplest of the set. Its individual movements, especially the improvisatory prelude, may have been composed as teaching pieces. The next two suites, in G minor (Z. 661) and G major (Z. 662), both of which begin with fluid, imitative Preludes in the Italian style, require greater technique. The fourth suite, in A minor (Z. 663) is only in three movements, lacking an Almand. In a recently discovered manuscript, the concluding Saraband is replaced by a jig.

In C major, the fifth suite (Z. 666) begins with a different Prelude in the 1689 publication and yet another Prelude in a surviving manuscript. Neither one of these bears any resemblance to that in the 1696 version, which is an Italianate, contrapuntal invention mostly in two parts, but becomes thicker in the noncontrapuntal closing measures. The three-movement suite in D major, Z. 667, ends with a Hornpipe. Purcell's example is traditional in its lively 3/2 meter, short motives and four-measure phrases.

No. 7, in D minor, Z. 668, concludes with a Hornpipe from Purcell's incidental music for *The Married Beau* (Z. 603, No. 3), composed in April 1694. The lengthy Almand that opens the D minor suite is the most impressive movement of the piece and perhaps of the whole set. Its rising and falling dotted figures in the right hand traverse several harmonies and include several striking cross-relations, particularly in the second half. In the first publication the Almand was subtitled "Bell-bar," possibly indicating a hamlet in Hertfordshire, where Purcell may have composed the piece in 1693–94.

The fourth and final movement of the eighth suite, in F major (Z. 669) is a Minuet from the incidental music for *The Double Dealer* (Z. 592, No. 3), which Purcell completed in October or November 1693. *—John Palmer*

Recommended:

○ **Purcell: Suites & Transcriptions for Harpsichord** / Charlston / 1997 / Naxos 553982

Q

Thomas Quasthoff

b. Nov. 9, 1959, Hildesheim, Germany
Bass

Thomas Quasthoff's mother was one of thousands who took the drug thalidomide to relieve morning sickness. As a result, Quasthoff grew to only about four feet tall and, in common with many of his fellow victims of the drug, has severely undeveloped arms, with his hands emerging almost directly from his shoulders. However, his voice and breathing apparatus developed normally—if a bass-baritone voice that is uncommonly magnificent can be considered "normal."

Germany was ill-prepared to cope with the thalidomide generation. When Quasthoff reached school age, he was assigned, according to government policy, to school programs designed for children with cerebral palsy. A lively, intelligent, and artistic child, Quasthoff clearly needed the stimulation of normal schooling, which a change in policy soon permitted. He was raised in a highly supportive environment, being treated in exactly the same way as his normal brother. The phrase he remembers being said most often to him when he was young was "Tommy, you can do that. Do it!" As a result he grew up with a sunny and optimistic outlook. Music was special to him. But when he tried to get a musical education, he found that the highly regarded conservatory to which he applied had a strict policy that all students had to learn to play piano, and turned him away on the grounds that this was impossible for him. "That was legally correct. I have to admit that," he says. "Morally—well, that raises a big question." (Years later, the same school asked him to join its staff as a voice instructor. He accepted.)

His parents procured private voice lessons for him with Charlotte Lehmann, a concert singer of Hannover. She taught him music and singing for seventeen years, and proved a superb voice teacher. The great baritone Dietrich Fischer-Dieskau says "It's clear to everyone who has heard Thomas Quasthoff that he has a wondrously beautiful voice and that he has had excellent previous training. . . ."

While studying, Quasthoff found a position as a radio announcer in Hannover, becoming highly popular. In 1988 he won first price in voice at the prestigious ARD music competition of Munich. This led to his beginning a concert and recital career that rapidly grew. Cautiously, Quasthoff retained his radio job for six more years. He finally adopted music as his full-time profession in 1996, the year he won the Shostakovich Prize in Moscow and the Hamada Trust/Scotsman Festival Prize, and in 1998 he won the Echo Prize. In 1996 he was appointed professor at the Detmold Music Academy, where he is one of the most popular voice teachers. He is also associated with the University of Oregon at Eugene, where he appears regularly in the Oregon Bach Festival.

He has performed with many leading orchestras and conductors. His repertory includes the great choral/vocal/orchestral works of Bach, Mozart, Beethoven, Berlioz, Brahms, Mahler, and Britten. He sings opera arias in his programs, and has sung operatic roles in recordings of Beethoven's *Fidelio,* Haydn's *L'Anima del Philosopho,* and Schumann's *Genoveva,* but not on stage, although an appearance in *Fidelio* (as Don Fernando) was set for 2003 and as Amfortas in *Parsifal* for 2004. He is frequently asked about singing *Rigoletto,* but considers his voice too youthful and low-lying.

He has recorded on the Hännsler, MDG, RCA, Teldec, Orfeo, and Philips labels, and since mid-1999 has been an exclusive artist on Deutsche Grammophon. *—Joseph Stevenson*

Recommended:

- ○ **A Portrait** / Quasthoff, etc. / 2001 / RCA 86952
- ○ **Schubert: Schwanengesang; Brahms: 4 Ernste Gesänge** / Quasthoff, Zeyen / 2001 / DG 471030
- ○ **Schubert: Goethe Lieder** / Quasthoff, Spencer / 1995 / RCA 61864
- ○ **Brahms & Liszt Lieder** / Quasthoff, Zeyen / 2000 / DG 463183

Quatuor Mosaïques

f. 1985, Vienna, Austria
Ensemble

Quatuor Mosaïques is among the leading original instrument or authentic performance string quartets.

Its members were all part of the Concentus Musicus Wien, the pioneer original instruments group associated with Nikolaus Harnoncourt. In 1983 Christoph Coin, the cellist and viola da gamba player of the Concentus Musicus, founded Ensemble Mosaïques, a smaller group, inviting a number of his colleagues from Concentus Musicus to join. In 1985, four members of Ensemble Mosaïques formed the Quatuor Mosaïques, one of the first string quartets devoted to use of period instruments and authentic performance practices.

Its members are Erich Hobarth, who plays a 1683 violin by Francesco Ruggieri of Cremona; Andrea Bischof, with an eighteenth century French violin; Anita Mitterer, who plays a viola made by Chrisopher Lüthi as a replica of an Amati instrument; and Coin, whose cello was made by Carlo Antonio Testore of Milan in 1758.

It is not particularly the age of a string instrument that makes it a "period instrument." Many string players have instruments that were made in the Baroque era that are classified as modern instruments. Rather, it is the way the instrument is set up. Instruments intended to be authentic to the Baroque and most of the Classical period have bridges that are shaped differently than the modern violin bridge, use gut strings (rather than today's wire or wire-wrapped strings), lack a chin rest, and are played with a convex rather than a concave bow. These differences give the Quatuor Mosaïques a very different sound from a modern string quartet. The instruments have a clearer though less penetrating sound, and the different style of bow softens the attack of a note. Since the string quartet was apparently not perceived until the mid-eighteenth century, the Quatuor Mosaïques repertory is virtually confined to the Classical period and part of the early Romantic era, but this is a rich field, including the many quartets of Mozart, Beethoven, Schubert, both Haydn brothers, Boccherini, and others.

Quatuor Mosaïques rapidly became well known for its informed and stylistically correct approach to this repertory, and for the accuracy and poetic nature of its performances. Soon it was invited to perform in major European festivals, including the Vienna Festival Week, the Salzburg Festival, Resonances, the Styrian Arts Festival, the Edinburgh Festival and the Aldeburgh Festivals in Great Britain, and others. It has performed in major European cities and has presented complete Beethoven quartet cycles in several venues.

It records for the Auvidis/Astrée and Auvidis/Valois labels and has received Gramophone Awards for its sets of the opus 20 and opus 33 quartets by Joseph Haydn, and the Diapason d'Or and Recording of the Year 1989 for its set of Haydn's opus 77 quartets and the opus 103 quartet. *—Joseph Stevenson*

Recommended:

- ○ **Mozart: String Quartets** / Mosaiques Quartet / 2003 / Naive 8889
- ○ **Haydn: String Quartets Op33** / Mosaiques Quartet / 2000 / Astrée 8801
- ○ **Boccherini: Quintetti Opp56 & 57** / Cohen, Mosaiques Quartet / 2002 / Naïve 3001
- ○ **Mendelssohn: Quatuors Opp12 & 13** / Mosaiques Quartet / 1998 / Astrée 8622
- ○ **Luigi Boccherini: 3 Quintetti** / Cohen, Mosaiques Quartet / 1992 / Astrée 8721
- ○ **Beethoven: Quatuors Op18/5 & 6** / Mosaiques Quartet / 1995 / Astrée 8541
- ○ **Haydn: String Quartets Op76** / Mosaiques Quartet / 2000 / Astrée 8665

Roger Quilter

b. Nov. 1, 1877, Brighton, England, **d.** Sep. 21, 1953, London, England
Composer: Vocal

English composer Roger Quilter remains known primarily for his distinguished art song output, although he also produced choral, instrumental, and stage works. He had to work hard at composition, for it never came naturally, but his output shows a composer with exceptional sensitivity and seemingly effortless grace. Indeed, he was a fan of light and graceful music, from Schubert to Maude Valérie White to Gershwin. Quilter never had to make a living, but he was a philanthropic artist, helping to found and administer the Musicians' Benevolent Fund, as well as privately aiding his colleagues. After a productive and benevolent artistic life, Quilter experienced a period of mental decline that ended with his death.

Quilter was educated at prestigious Eton College, later going abroad to Germany to study with Ivan Knorr at Frankfurt's Hoch Conservatory. All students in

Frankfurt in the 1890s, Percy Grainger, Cyril Scott, Norman O'Neill, Balfour Gardiner, and Quilter became known as the "Frankfurt Group." As a song composer, Quilter became well established in 1900 when Denham Price gave a performance of his *Songs of the Sea* at the Crystal Palace in London, and also when tenor Gervase Elwes premiered *To Julia* in 1905 and *Seven Elizabethan Lyrics* in 1908. On occasion Quilter would accompany his songs in public performance, and he did record many of them with close friend and colleague Mark Raphael.

His only attempt at opera, *Julia* (1936), was a failure, but several pieces from it were extracted and published as separate songs (e.g., *Love at the Inn*). His light orchestral music was more successful, including *A Children's Overture* (1919), written for the *Promenade Concerts* and conducted by Henry Wood. That work and Quilter's popular incidental music for the fairy play *Where the Rainbow Ends* (1911) were both inspired by Walter Crane's illustrated book of nursery rhymes, *Baby's Opera*. Still, it is his songs (more than 100 of them) upon which Quilter's reputation was based, and for which he will continued to be remembered quite fondly. *—Rachael Unite*

VOCAL

Songs and Song Cycles (1901–1953)

Roger Quilter (1877–1953) wrote numerous songs that hold a place in the repertoires of virtually every English recitalist as well as those of many other singers. Although trained at the Hoch Conservatory in Frankfurt, Quilter was never anything other than quintessentially English in temperament and perspective. He forged a style of pastoral composition for voice and piano that rose above the drawing room ballad, yet was free of the artifice that sometimes afflicted the serious lyric works of some contemporaries. Peter Warlock acknowledged his indebtedness to Quilter on several occasions.

Some of Quilter's songs and settings of traditional folk melodies have long since passed into popular iconography. "Drink to Me Only With Thine Eyes" and Tennyson's "Now Sleeps the Crimson Petal" are nearly unimaginable set to any other melody and/or harmonization. Quilter's setting of the anonymous Elizabethan lyric "Fair House of Joy" is likewise of an imperishable order. Quilter focused upon choosing only first-rate texts, and his taste in poetry proved to be quite discerning.

Quilter's reputation was made quickly. In 1901, the same year he graduated from Hoch Conservatory, Denham Price sang his *Four Songs of the Sea*. Soon, Quilter's songs were taken up by three of the most beloved concert singers of the day. Tenor John Coates, tenor Gervase Elwes (who premiered the cycle *To Julia*, to lyrics by Robert Herrick), and baritone Harry Plunket Greene used their frequent concert appearances to speed this new music to the public. Then other prominent singers soon began programming Quilter's songs.

While Quilter continued (despite fragile health) to compose until a half-decade before his death, many of his most memorable songs were written in the first quarter of the century. "Now Sleeps the Crimson Petal" was an early work, completed in 1904. "Love's Philosophy," to a text by Shelley, came the following year. In 1905 appeared the first of several sets of Shakespeare songs, this one consisting of "Come Away, Death," "O Mistress Mine," and "Blow, Blow, Thou Winter Wind." The six songs of *To Julia* were written in 1906, and *Seven Elizabethan Lyrics* came two years later. A setting of Ernest Dowson's *Songs of Sorrow* likewise was published in 1908. Three *Songs of the Sea* setting Quilter's own lyrics saw publication in 1911. Robert Louis Stevenson's poetry provided the basis for *Four Child Songs* in 1914. *Three Songs of William Blake* appeared in 1916, another *Five Shakespeare Songs* came in 1921, and *Five Jacobean Lyrics* were published in 1925. Amidst these cycles, or groupings, were many single songs, most of them worthy. Quilter's *Arnold Book of Old Songs* was published in 1947. *—Erik Eriksson*

Recommended:

- ○ **Songs by Roger Quilter** / Ainsley, Martineau / 1996 / Hyperion 66878

Now Sleeps the Crimson Petal, for voice & piano, Op. 3/2 (1904–1905)

"Now Sleeps the Crimson Petal," the second of *Three Songs*, Op. 3, did much to further the early reputation of the English composer Roger Quilter. The famed English tenor Gervase Elwes was so enamored of Quilter's setting of this Tennyson poem that he personally convinced the Boosey publishing house to print it. Elwes became one of the composer's most important champions, but this song actually predated any creative contact between the two—it was composed well before its publication date of 1904 and was actually first written when the composer was 20, in 1897.

Quilter's indication of tempo rubato was to become a frequent trait, as was his use of a modified strophic form. While "Now Sleeps the Crimson Petal" can be traced to the English tradition of the drawing-room ballad, it is Quilter's lush accompaniment that distinguishes it from its less urbane predecessors. Only during important melodic moments does the accompaniment reiterate the vocal melody; indeed, often the piano spins out charmingly brief melodic lines of its own. That Quilter was later to arrange the accompaniment for strings seems more than appropriate.

The vocal writing is perhaps best described as inevitable. Where Tennyson's lines peak and contract, so does the melodic line; where the poetic accents fall, so too do the rhythmic pulses. Quilter's use of rubato smoothes out his juxtaposition of three- and five-beat measures, and makes the chromatic harmonies more natural. Also characteristic of his later work is his avoidance of a perfect authentic cadence at the conclusion of the song. "Now Sleeps the Crimson Petal," indeed all of the Op. 3 songs, begins to bring into relief the talents a composer who would be reluctant to set contemporary poetry, as his restrained, always tonal style was best suited to the setting of earlier works. This fleetingly brief (27-measure) song shows that its composer was soon to become, if he was not already, a master of the craft of the art song. *—Thomas Oram*

Recommended:

- ○ **On the Idle Hill of Summer by Vaughan Williams, Butterworth, Quilter, Peel** / Allen, Parsons / 2001 / EMI 67428
- ○ **Bostridge: The English Songbook** / Bostridge, Drake / 1999 / Angel 56830B
- ○ **Maggie Teyte: A Vocal Portrait** / Moore, Teyte / 2002 / Naxos 6

Florence Quivar

b. Mar. 3, 1944, Philadelphia, PA

Mezzo-Soprano

Florence Quivar is one of the most prominent American mezzos of her generation and has appeared all over the world in concerts and recitals, winning consistent praise for her musicality and expressiveness. Though her oratorio performances are less frequent, she has enjoyed notable success in that field. And although she has been far less active in the world of staged opera, she has appeared at most of the major opera houses of the world, performing coloratura as well as dramatic mezzo-soprano roles, though most of her performances are in lyric mezzo roles. She has also been particularly active in championing new music, appearing in the world premieres of works by Anthony Davis (The Goddess of the Waters in his opera *Amistad* at the Lyric Opera of Chicago) in 1999 and William Bolcom (in his song cycle *From the Diary of Sally Hemmings* at the Library of Congress) in 2001. Her interest in music started early; her mother was a piano teacher who taught voice and who also formed the gospel group the Harmonic Choraliers. Quivar herself made her singing debut at the age of six in a church performance. She became fascinated when she saw *Madama Butterfly* when the Met company tour performed in Philadelphia, though practical matters made her plan to be an elementary school teacher and enrolled in a teachers' college. Realizing that her true love was really music after just one day of classes, she joined the Philadelphia Academy of Music. After graduating, she briefly enrolled in Juilliard, where she made her stage debut in 1975 as the witch Jezibaba and the Foreign Princess in Dvořák's *Rusalka*. Not feeling ready to establish herself in New York, she returned to Philadelphia, where she taught and sang recitals with the Franklin Concert Series. Inspired by master classes with Maureen Forrester, Quivar became deeply interested in lieder, as well as oratorio. Returning to New York, she won the Marian Anderson Award, and after drawing the attention of noted impresario Harold Shaw, she began to appear with orchestras all over the United States. She made her Met debut in 1977 as Marina in Mussorgsky's *Boris Godunov*, the house at which she has sung the most stage performances. *—Ann Feeney*

Recommended:

- ○ **Thomson: Four Saints in Three Acts** / Quivar, Childs, Thompkins, Stewart, Orch. of Our Time / 1982 / Nonesuch 79035
- ○ **Sessions: When Lilacs Last In The Dooryard Bloom'd** / Ozawa, Steinberg (conds.), Quivar, Cossa, Hinds, BSO / 1977 / New World 80296
- ○ **Mendelssohn: Elijah** / Shaw (cond.), Hampson, Bonney, Quivar, Hadley, Atlanta SO & Chorus / 1995 / Telarc 80389

R

Sergey Rachmaninov

b. Apr. 1, 1873, Semyonovo, Russia, **d.** Mar. 28, 1943, Beverly Hills, CA
Composer: Keyboard, Concerto, Vocal, Orchestral, Choral, Symphonic, Chamber Music, Opera
Pianist

Sergey Vasilyevich Rachmaninov, born in Semyonovo, Russia, on April 1, 1873, is today remembered as one of the most formidable pianists of all time and the last truly great composer in the Russian Romantic tradition. Rachmaninov came from a music-loving, land-owning family; young Sergey's mother fostered the boy's innate talent by giving him his first piano lessons. After a decline in the family fortunes, the Rachmaninovs moved to St. Petersburg, where Sergey studied with Vladimir Delyansky at the Conservatory. As his star continued to rise, Sergey went to the Moscow Conservatory, where he received a sound musical training: piano lessons from the strict disciplinarian Nikolay Zverev and Alexander Siloti (Rachmaninov's cousin), counterpoint with Taneyev, and harmony with Arensky. During his time at the Conservatory, Rachmaninov boarded with Zverev, whose weekly musical Sundays provided the young musician the valuable opportunity to make important contacts and to hear a wide variety of music.

As Rachmaninov's conservatory studies continued, his burgeoning talent came into full flower; he received the personal encouragement of Tchaikovsky, and, a year after earning a degree in piano, took the Conservatory's gold medal in composition for his opera *Aleko* (1892). Early setbacks in his compositional career—particularly, the dismal reception of his *Symphony No. 1* (1895)—led to an extended period of depression and self-doubt, which he overcame with the aid of hypnosis. With the resounding success of his *Piano Concerto No. 2* (1900–01), however, his lasting fame as a composer was assured. The first decade of the twentieth century proved a productive and happy one for Rachmaninov, who during that time produced such masterpieces as the *Symphony No. 2* (1907), the tone poem *Isle of the Dead* (1907), and the *Piano Concerto No. 3* (1909). On May 12, 1902, the composer married his cousin, Natalya Satina.

By the end of the decade, Rachmaninov had embarked on his first American tour, which cemented his fame and popularity in the United States. He continued to make his home in Russia but left permanently following the Revolution in 1917; he thereafter lived in Switzerland and the United States between extensive European and American tours. While his tours included conducting engagements (he was twice offered, and twice refused, leadership of the Boston Symphony Orchestra), it was his astounding pianistic abilities which won him his greatest glory. Rachmaninov was possessed of a keyboard technique marked by precision, clarity, and a singular legato sense. Indeed, the pianist's hands became the stuff of legend. He had an enormous span—he could, with his left hand, play the chord C-E flat-G-C-G—and his playing had a characteristic power, which pianists have described as "cosmic" and "overwhelming." He is, for example, credited with the uncanny ability to discern, and articulate profound, mysterious movements in a musical composition which usually remain undetected by the superficial perception of rhythmic structures.

Fortunately for posterity, Rachmaninov recorded much of his own music, including the four piano concerti and what is perhaps his most beloved work, the *Rhapsody on a Theme of Paganini* (1934). He became an American citizen a few weeks before his death in Beverly Hills, California, on March 28, 1943. *—Michael Rodman*

Recommended:

- ○ **Rachmaninov: Concertos 1 & 4** / Stokowski, Ormandy (cond.), Rachmaninov, Philadelphia Orchestra / 1999 / Naxos 110602
- ○ **Rachmaninov: Concertos 2 & 3** / Stokowski, Ormandy (cond.), Rachmaninov, Philadelphia Orchestra / 1999 / Naxos 8110601
- ○ **Chopin, Tchaikovsky, Bach, Debussy** / Rachmaninov / Pearl 9457
- ○ **Rachmaninov Plays Rachmaninov** / Rachmaninov / London 425964
- ○ **Rachmaninov: Isle of the Dead; Vocalise; Symphony 3** / Rachmaninov (cond.), Philadelphia Orch. / 1996 / BMG 62532
- ○ **Rachmaninoff Plays Chopin** / Rachmaninov / 1994 / BMG 62533

KEYBOARD

Etudes-Tableaux, Opp. 33, 39 (1911–1917)

When the Op. 33 *Etudes-Tableaux* were published in 1914, they contained six pieces, though Rachmaninov had originally written nine. During the three years between their completion and publication the composer had withdrawn Nos. 3, 4, and 5. The middle of these was revised and appeared as No. 6 in the Op. 39 set, and Nos. 3 and 5 were published posthumously.

The first etude from Op. 33, marked Allegro non troppo, is jaunty and rhythmic, bordering on jazz. The second, Allegro, features typical Rachmaninovian melancholy. Marked Grave, the next piece's somber and gloomy world eventually gives way to a beautiful theme. No. 4 (Moderato) is similar in mood and style to the first, although a bit less rhythmically inclined and more serious in mood in the latter half. The brief fifth piece (Non allegro) is mysterious and hesitant, playful and mostly delicate; a colorful and varied offering. So is the next item, marked Allegro con fuoco, probably the most brilliant and scintillating of the eight pieces, short though it also is. The next two etudes are serious affairs: No. 7 (Moderato) features one of those dark Russian themes, and No. 8, probably the most profound entry in the set, contains no actual melody and borders at times on atonality, yet it manages to sound very much like Rachmaninov. It should be noted that some recordings retain the older numbering of the Op. 33 etudes, thus eliminating No. 4 and ending with No. 9.

The later *Etudes-Tableaux* set is generally viewed as the better of the pair. The first etude sounds as if it is nervously in search of something, the Allegro agitato tempo quite adequately indicating the mood. The next, marked Lento assai, begins with an allusion to the composer's trademark theme, the Dies Irae, and this variant then dominates the whole piece; one of the more effectively atmospheric items in the set, even if it does seem overlong. No. 3 (Allegro molto) is bright and lively, though not completely free of the composer's tendency toward gloom: again the Dies Irae appears, though less recognizably. The next Allegro assai is similar, but its theme is more aristocratic and its colors brighter. The fifth etude, appropriately marked Appassionato, is probably the most famous in the set. The theme yearns and cries, and the middle section offers little change from the passionate emotions. The sixth, starts off ominously with ascending chromatic scales in the bass, followed by frantic semiquavers in the right hand that call to mind an innocent figure fleeing dark forces. The whole piece is colorful and attractive, even containing some humor. No. 7 (Lento) is, at around ten minutes, the longest etude in either collection. Slow and somber, it features a grim buildup beginning nearly halfway through that climaxes in tolling bell-like chords. The last two etudes are both marked Allegro moderato, with the former offering contrast to the last piece in its gentleness and brighter colors, and the latter a rousing brilliant display that is both joyous and playful. *—Robert Cummings*

Recommended:

- ○ **Rachmaninov: Etudes-Tableaux** / Biret / 1991 / Naxos 550347
- ○ **Rachmaninov: Etudes-Tableaux** / Shelley / 1988 / Hyperion 66091

Moments Musicaux, Op. 16 (1896)

In their seriousness and complexity, these imposing and difficult *Moments Musicaux* anticipate the later *Etudes-Tableaux*. They seem to be ordered in a way that makes for an effective complete performance. The first piece in the collection, in B flat minor, is a long composition, in four sections, the last being a varied reprise of the first. It opens with a beautiful and longing melody over triplet sixths in the left hand. This section, nearly a complete piece in itself, rises to a climax then gives way to an improvisatory and transitional passage that culminates in a cadenza. This is followed by a breathless and mostly quiet passage featuring the principal melody of the opening section now elaborated into rapid figuration. The entire piece is beautifully effective. The Moment musical No. 2, in E flat minor, can be described as an etude. A syncopated melody in octaves rises up out of rapid triplet figuration in both hands in a distinctively Rachmaninov style. The exciting climax in E flat major is prepared and developed brilliantly, then subsides to a quiet ending. The third piece opens with a noble and stately march, which is played twice: once simply, and once with an elaborated bass in staccato octaves. Rachmaninov makes effective use of the ninth chord throughout the work. Moment musical No. 4, in E minor, is another etude presenting a sustained rising melody set against rapid sextuplet figuration. A more lyrical central section retains the rapid figuration while presenting a new melody in descending thirds. The reprise of the original material is elaborated into an enormous climax that stretches the characteristic figuration over the entire keyboard, culminating in the sudden and fortissimo ending. The fifth composition, in D flat major, more of a *barcarolle* than the *Barcarolle,* Op. 10, is a gentle and lovely interlude: the only emotionally relaxed piece in the entire set. It seems likely that No. 6 was inspired by Chopin's *Etude No. 12,* Op. 25, known as the "Ocean Etude." Rachmaninov's figuration is more static, but the massive sweep and drive is the same. A powerful and surging melody is accompanied by rapid figuration in both hands. The massive central and ending climaxes are among the most sonorous pages ever written for the piano. *—Steven Coburn*

Recommended:

- ○ **Complete Piano Music of Rachmaninov** / Shelley / 1993 / Hyperion 44041/8
- ○ **Rachmaninoff: Early Piano Works** / Hobson / 1997 / Arabesque 6685

Morceaux de fantaisie, Op. 3 (1892; revised 1940)

These five pieces, not intended to be played as a group, represent a step forward toward Rachmaninov's mature style. Substantially more original than the *Nocturnes* or the early composition exercises, these all show an increasing confidence and stylistic command. With the exception of the brief Sérénade, they are all in three-part form (ABA) and are recognizably characteristic of Rachmaninov in style. The Elégie in E flat minor is an epic and tragic work, with sweeping melodies, an imposing climax, and a fine melancholic atmosphere. The justly famous Prélude in C sharp minor recalls the central section of the C minor Nocturne with its widely spaced chordal opening. The central section is in one of Rachmaninov's typical styles: a lyrical melody rises above a swirling accompaniment. It is highly effective, even if worn out by familiarity. Something like a Nocturne, the E major Mélodie is both lyrical and dramatic, rising to a powerful climax before the central cadenza. The ending is Chopin-esque and features another cadenza. Puckish and almost demonic, the Polichinelle, in F sharp minor, is a technical tour de force. It is the first of Rachmaninov's fast marchlike works that finally culminate in his *Symphonic Dances* of many years later. It is brilliantly effective. The final Sérénade, an unpretentious waltz with a Spanish inflection, is the smallest work of the collection and is a bit repetitious. *—Steven Coburn*

Recommended:

- ○ **Rachmaninov Plays Rachmaninov** / Rachmaninov / London 425964
- ○ **Rachmaninov: Preludes, Op23; Morceaux de Fantaisie** / Shelley / 1983 / Hyperion 66081

Morceaux de salon, Op. 10 (1893–1894; revised 1940)

Rachmaninov composed these seven *Salon pieces* beginning probably in the latter half of December 1893 and finished them by early February 1894. The style of them is varied, coming early enough in his career for some to sound immature or derivative in certain passages.

The first, Nocturne in A minor, is Tchaikovskyan in its themes and reminiscent of Chopin in its writing. It does feature Rachmaninov's trademark melancholy, however. The next piece, Valse in A, may be marginally superior, but still not of great interest. Here the influence of Chopin can also be heard, and while the music is pleasant and colorful enough, it is not particularly distinctive.

The third, Barcarolle in G minor, is probably the best known piece in the set. It features an attractive and typically melancholy, Russian melody, with nervous-sounding accompaniment that imparts a haunting atmosphere. Mélodie in E minor follows, and offers an appealing theme, with arpeggiated chordal accompaniment of some interest. No. 5, the Humoresque in G, is bright and features one of those stately Rachmaninovian themes. Overall, however, the music is not memorable, though the composer liked it and played it frequently. He made minor revisions to it in 1940.

The "Romance in F minor" that follows is sweet and attractive but overlong and not among the better entries here. The closing piece, Mazurka in D flat, is more appealing on just about every level. While it ultimately is not a great masterpiece, it is colorful and contains humor, not an ingredient one often finds in Rachmaninov. The music is not derivative, despite the fact that its form is taken from Chopin. There are many unexpected thematic and harmonic surprises throughout, and the bright mood and colors are most engaging. *—Robert Cummings*

Recommended:

- ○ **Rachmaninoff Plays Rachmaninoff** / Rachmaninov / RCA 7766
- ○ **Rachmaninov: Morceaux de salon; 3 Nocturnes; 4 Pieces** / Biret / 1999 / Naxos 553004

Piano Sonata No. 1 in D minor, Op. 28 (1907)

As the nineteenth century melted into the twentieth, Rachmaninov hit his stride as a composer with overtly derivative works from the 1890s yielding to the distilled and highly personal utterance of the *Preludes,* Op. 23, hand-in-hand with large ambitions and works laid out on an expansive scale, for instance, the sprawling *Symphony No. 2 in E minor,* completed in tandem with the *Piano Sonata No. 1.* Against a background of family illnesses, grueling performance engagements, and the 1905 uprising in Russia, Rachmaninov resigned his position as conductor at the Bolshoi in February 1906 and immediately left with his family for Italy, moving on to Dresden in the fall. There, he completed the orchestration of his *Symphony No. 2* and entertained ultimately abortive plans for operas based upon Flaubert's *Salammbô* (already attempted by Mussorgsky) and Maeterlinck's *Monna Vanna.* With the latter, he had composed the first act in vocal score when it became apparent that copyright restrictions would bar its European production. Something of this jaded late Romantic tumult informs the *Piano Sonata No. 1,* completed May 14, 1907. Geoffrey Norris, in his survey of Rachmaninov's music, noted "... although the original idea for it to be a programme sonata based on *Faust* was abandoned, it is tempting to link the three movements with Faust, Gretchen, and Mephistopheles." This had already been done in Liszt's *Eine Faust Symphonie,* while the critical consensus is that Liszt's single-movement *Piano Sonata* embodies a Faustian drama. Rachmaninov was attracted to the figure of the disconsolate magus, whether from Goethe's *Faust* or Lord Byron's spin-off *Manfred*—as a 13-year-old he transcribed Tchaikovsky's *Manfred Symphony* for piano duet and in 1890 sketched two movements of a *Manfred Symphony* of his own. The nervously ruminative gestures of the sonata's first movement, organized around a recurrent falling major fifth, accord well with the transformative aspirations of the sorcerer/philosopher. But the sultry second movement suggests less demure innocence than a siren or the vastness and mystery of a star-clad Russian night, laced with nostalgia, while nothing in the third movement is overtly Mephistophelean. A mood of impassioned questioning arises as material from the preceding movements returns in cyclical fashion to be tortured over a long stretch to a near climax, only to yield to further reminiscences before finally escalating to a towering apotheosis. Though lyrically alive, it requires an adept, highly concentrated pianist to keep its elaboration from diffuseness. *—Adrian Corleonis*

Recommended:

- ○ **The Complete Piano Music of Sergei Rachmaninov** / Shelley / 1993 / Hyperion 44041/8
- ○ **Rachmaninov: Variations, Op22; Piano Sonata, Op28** / Berezovsky / 1994 / Teldec 90890

Piano Sonata No. 2 in B flat minor, Op. 36 (1913; revised 1931)

Turning 40 in 1913, Rachmaninov began the year with respite from a grueling schedule of concerts in Moscow, where he was in demand as pianist and conductor. In December 1912, he left for holiday in Switzerland and moved on to Rome with the new year, where he began in earnest the composition of his great choral work *The Bells,* setting an adaptation of Poe's poem by symbolist poet Konstantin Balmont. Two of his daughters contracted typhoid there, forcing an abrupt removal to Berlin for a hospital stay, before the family returned to their country estate, Ivanovka, in southern Russia. Composition of the *Piano Sonata No. 2* occupied him from January into September of that year, concomitantly with orchestration of *The Bells.* To place the lush, late Romanticism of these works in perspective, one may recall that such foundation documents of Modernism as Schoenberg's *Three Pieces for piano,* Op. 11, had appeared in 1909, his *Pierrot lunaire* and Busoni's *Sonatina seconda* in 1912, while Stravinsky's *Sacre du printemps* received its premiere May 29, 1913. The *Sonata No. 2* demonstrates in abundance those qualities of Rachmaninov's art that make his music permanently appealing, hence valuable, and great. The Allegro agitato opening seizes one by the hair with an arpeggiated plunge to the bass, two sharply peremptory chords (announcing the crucial interval of a third), and a falling, wailing figure in the left hand beneath tremolando triplets in the right, giving way to great waves of kinetic *nervosité.* It is the entrance of a great actor. Where the *Sonata No. 1* indulged a luxuriant sprawl to play for over half-an-hour, the *Second* rushes past in about 20 tensely breathless minutes, its taut organization and formal elegance apt to be overlooked in its rhapsodic outpouring. Rachmaninov's 1931 revision—the version usually heard—cut 120 bars from the original, pared some of the virtuosic extravagances, and made for more transparent textures. The second movement, following without a break, works melancholy from nostalgic elegy to a fever before a slashing arpeggiated descent brings on the alternately anxious and towering finale—with its snatches of a parodied march—shot through with one of Rachmaninov's most compelling lyric inspirations confided first in single notes and valorized in the peroration in massive, surging chords before a final virtuoso wash of triumphant sonority. While its impeccable musical logic may be demonstrated, its impact—in the hands of great pianist—is compellingly visceral. *—Adrian Corleonis*

Recommended:

- ○ **Rachmaninov: Complete Piano Concertos; Rhapsody** / Ashkenazy / 2002 / Decca 473251
- ○ **Complete Piano Music of Sergei Rachmaninov** / Shelley / 1993 / Hyperion 44041/8
- ○ **John Ogdon Plays Rachmaninov** / Ogdon / 2002 / EMI 567938

Prelude No. 1 in C sharp minor ("The Bells of Moscow"), Op. 3/2 (1892)

While Rachmaninov's early compositions divulge the influence of Tchaikovsky, this *Prelude* in C sharp minor foreshadows his later style and is one of his most masterfully crafted compositions from his student years. It was written, in fact, shortly after he graduated from the Moscow Conservatory, and dedicated to one of his teachers there, Arensky. Chronologically it came first in the group of pieces Rachmaninov composed for a set he entitled *Morceaux de Fantasie.* He placed it second among three other works, then added a fourth. The others in the set are, Elegie (No. 1), Melodie (No. 3), Polichinelle (No. 4) and Serenade (No. 5).

The C sharp minor *Prelude* became popular immediately after Rachmaninov premiered it on October 8, 1892. He had to accommodate audiences at virtually every recital he gave thereafter by including it as an encore. Rachmaninov played it so often, in fact, that he grew tired of the piece.

The *Prelude* begins with ominous descending chords that lead to one of the composer's most melancholy and memorable themes. Its slow lilting character, conveyed in big gloomy chords, is reminiscent of tolling bells on a dark wintry night, an image which accounts for its nickname, "The Bells of Moscow." The theme offers no consolation in its dire gloom, but instead proceeds to proudly proclaim its beguiling pessimism. The middle section is restless and tense, not breaking the dark mood, but offering livelier and more driven music before returning to the chordal theme with doubled intensity.

In the end, despite damning judgments so often associated with short popular piano works, this piece must be considered one of the most perfect from Rachmaninov's early years and a masterpiece of the late nineteenth century keyboard literature. A typical performance of the *Prelude* lasts about four-and-a-half minutes. Today, it is rarely heard as part of the entire set of the *Morceaux de Fantasie* and is still programmed separately or as an encore. While it remains popular, it is performed far less than it was 50 or 100 years ago. Rachmaninov made an arrangement of it for two pianos in 1938. *—Robert Cummings*

Recommended:

- ○ **Für Elise: Romantic Piano Music** / Biret / 2001 / Naxos 550647
- ○ **Rachmaninov: 24 Preludes; Piano Sonata 2** / Ashkenazy / 1995 / London 443841

Preludes for Piano (1892–1910)

Aside from several youthful efforts lacking an opus number, Rachmaninov wrote 24 preludes for piano: the *C sharp Minor Prelude,* part of the Op. 3 *Morceaux de Fantasie* (1892); the *Ten Preludes,* Op. 23 (1903); and the *Thirteen Preludes* Op. 32 (1910).

The earliest of these is Rachmaninov's most popular solo piano composition. The *C sharp Minor Prelude,* with its gloomy yet stately and memorable Russian theme, became overplayed by the mid-twentieth century, and many pianists declined to include it in their repertories. Still, the popularity of the piece is undying, even if it hardly offers serious artistic challenge to some of the later preludes.

The better efforts from the Op. 23 set include the third, in D minor, marked Tempo di menuetto. This piece has a quiet majesty to its theme, a Russian, Bach-like creation that possesses both melancholy and playful elements. The ensuing prelude, in D major, is one of the more popular in the set. Its melody blossoms against a flowing, counter-thematic accompaniment, and the whole is reminiscent of Chopin nocturnes. The fifth prelude, the G minor (Alla marcia), is the most popular among the ten in the collection. The vigorous, marchlike opening theme is followed by a lovely melody that surely would not have been out of place in the slow movement of the composer's *Second Piano Concerto,* so Russian and lyrical is its character. The seventh, in C minor, seems based upon the faster music in the *Second Concerto* that comes right after the first movement's opening theme.

The pieces in the Op. 32 set are wider ranging in expression and length, despite their sharing of certain themes and their composition occurring in a 19-day period. The third, in E major (Allegro vivace), is cheerful and brilliant throughout, and features an ending in which the music winds down subtly (poco a poco diminuendo, as if tired and joyous from triumph. The G major fifth (Moderato), the most popular of the set, is lovely, with an angelic theme in the upper register, supported by arpeggios in the left hand. No. 7, in F (Moderato), subdued and wistful, is beautiful and subtle in coloration. The ensuing A minor prelude (Vivo) is also popular, and features both confidence and playfulness that simply effervesce. No. 10, in B minor (Lento), is ponderous and one of the less obviously appealing entries at first hearing. Nevertheless, it offers rewards in its atmospheric coloration and subtle thematic transformation. The climax comes with powerful chords in the base grandly playing the now-passionate theme. The following prelude, in B major (Allegretto), is one of the more attractive lighter pieces in the set. The hesitations in the theme add effectively to the reflective nature of the music. The twelfth, in G sharp minor (Allegro), is another popular prelude. It contains a haunting and profound melody, reminiscent of the Dies Irae theme. The mood is tense, the music yearning even in the final quiet bars. *—Robert Cummings*

Recommended:

- ○ **Rachmaninov: Preludes (Complete)** / Lympany / 1993 / Erato 91714

Suite for 2 pianos No. 1 in G minor ("Fantaisie-tableaux"), Op. 5 (1893)

Rachmaninov dedicated this large-scale work to Tchaikovsky, and rightfully so, as that composer's influence is quite apparent. At the time this work was composed, however, Rachmaninov was beginning to develop a personal style. This work, more so than the pieces of Opus 3, already exhibits certain distinctive features of the composer's mature style. For example, the swirling accompaniments, the lugubrious harmonies, the repeated sequences rising to climax and the powerful rhythmic drive are all present. The first movement, Barcarolle, based upon a single melody, is lyric and ornamented with increasingly complex figuration. Like most of his other Barcarolles, it does not sound like a typical barcarolle; more like a waltz, in fact. Nevertheless, it is a lovely and effective work. The next movement, *La Nuit, l'Amour* (Night, Love), begins slowly and quietly only to expand into a passionate and expressive poem. Following an impressive climax, the poetic impulse subsides, amid florid passagework, as the movement heads to its atmospheric conclusion. Next is *Les Larmes* (Tears), a mournful Largo. As usual, there is a central climax, in this case quite original in its use of a hypnotic ostinato pattern. The use of ostinato continues in *Pâques* (Easter). Here, in the shortest movement of the Suite, Rachmaninov invokes Russian Liturgical chant set against the repetitive pattern of church bells, to great cumulative effect. This is a strikingly original and powerful movement.*—Steven Coburn*

Recommended:

- ○ **Rachmaninov: Music for 2 Pianos** / Ashkenazy, Previn / 1995 / London 444845
- ○ **Rachamaninov: Suites; Symphonic Dances** / Argerich, Rabinovitch / 1992 / Teldec 74717

Suite for 2 pianos No. 2 in C major, Op. 17 (1900–1901)

Rachmaninov composed his second *Suite for two pianos,* Op. 17 at about the same time as his *Second Piano Concerto,* and it is stylistically similar. The work is full of lush, lyrical melodies, florid and complex passagework, and Rachmaninov's characteristic driving rhythm. Rachmaninov's total command and mastery of the pianistic idiom permeates the entire Suite. It is one of his most successful masterpieces, completely effective on every level. A chordal and energetic March opens the Suite. It is in a simple three-part form (\ABA) with a brief coda. In the following movement, a swirling and hypnotic waltz, the rhythmic impulse is complemented by rapid and complex figurations that create a breathless quality. The middle section is richly lyrical, yet retains the underlying rhythmic drive. The third movement is an Romance. This title, so often found in Rachmaninov's early works, is here utterly descriptive of the movement's emotional qualities. A romantically lush melody rises out of an arpeggiated accompaniment, passes through a longing central section in the minor key, and eventually rises to an ecstatic climax. Closing the Suite is a Tarantelle. Based on the characteristic Italian folk dance, this movement elevates the genre to nearly orchestral proportions. Driving rhythms and powerful climaxes are contrasted with interludes of delicate passagework that ultimately build to the effective and virtuosic coda.*—Steven Coburn*

Recommended:

- ○ **Rachmaninov: Music for 2 Pianos** / Ashkenazy, Previn / 1995 / London 444845
- ○ **Medtner & Rachmaninov: Music for 2 Pianos** / Demidenko, Alexeyev / 1994 / Hyperion 66654

Variations on a Theme of Corelli, Op. 42 (1931)

This was the last original solo piano work by Rachmaninov and the only one he composed outside Russia. It was written in 1931, the same year the composer boldly denounced the Soviet Union, referring to its leaders as "Communist grave-diggers." Stalin banned Rachmaninov's music as a result, but, recognizing its more appealing and generally less radical nature, rehabilitated it three years later. This work is among the several that were subsequently well received in Moscow.

The *Variations on a Theme of Corelli* was written in Rachmaninov's less Romantic, more detached style, already heard in his *Piano Concerto No. 4* (1926; rev. 1941) and the much earlier *Piano Sonata No. 2* (1913). But the *Corelli Variations* go a step further in their icy, emotional demeanor, for here Rachmaninov displays a cerebral temperament more so than in any other composition in his oeuvre.

The work is cast in three movements, Allegro and Scherzo, Adagio, and Finale. The outer panels are in D minor, and the inner one in D major. The "Corelli" theme is elegant and pristine, sounding quite unlike Rachmaninov's normal style. Thirteen variations follow to fill out the first movement. The first is lively and easily related to the opening theme, the next three are a little slower, with growing complexities. Variations five through seven are faster and inclined toward divulging rhythmic aspects of the theme, though the music remains generally delicate and lean, almost Classical-sounding.

Variations 8 through 13 form the last group in the first movement. The first here is marked Adagio misterioso and establishes a sort of musical haze from which even the livelier variations in this section do not completely break free. The ninth is among the most beguiling, its thematic thread and haunting harmonies imparting a sense of mystery and desolation. Some of the faster music in the succeeding variations is reminiscent of the writing in the *Rhapsody on a Theme of Paganini.*

There is a brief Intermezzo following variation 13 and a reprise of the original theme, but now in D major. The two second movement variations, 14 and 15, are slow and sound closest to Rachmaninov's more Romantic style.

The Finale consists of variations 16 through 20 and the coda. The first of these is colorful and lively, the second delicate and somewhat exotic, some of the harmonies tinged with a slightly eastern flavor. The last three variations are the most muscular of all, featuring big, brilliant chords and powerful fortes. In the coda, the mood subsides, its thematic morsels are reminiscent of the slower music in the first movement of the *Piano Concerto No. 4.*

Curiously, Rachmaninov stipulated in the score that variations 11, 12, and 19 could be omitted, even though their presence is hardly superfluous. After performing this work for several seasons, the composer abandoned it and never played it again. In the end, while this music sounds like Rachmaninov, it is clearly representative of his drier, less Romantic side. A typical performance of the work lasts about 18 to 20 minutes. *—Robert Cummings*

Recommended:

- ○ **Rachmaninov: Music for 2 Pianos** / Ashkenazy / 1995 / London 444845
- ○ **Rachmaninov: Piano Works** / Biret / 1991 / Naxos 550349

CONCERTO

Piano Concerto No. 1 in F sharp minor, Op. 1 (1890–1891; revised 1917)

Rachmaninov composed the *Piano Concerto No. 1,* his Opus 1, at the age of 18, while he was still a student at the Moscow Conservatory. In 1917, more than two decades and two piano concerti later, he revised the score thoroughly, shaping the work into the form in which it is known today. This revised, "authoritative" version of the work is a tightly organized distillation of youthful passion and ardor, with the added influence of the turmoil that would soon force the composer to leave his native Russia for good.

The Concerto opens with a portentious declaration from the horns and a cascade of piano chords that recall the pealing of the composer's beloved Russian bells. The main theme is lyric and melancholy, the second sprightly by contrast. The first movement's huge solo cadenza, propelled by powerful chords—highly suggestive, again, of bells—and fiery expression, is the real heart of the work. The Andante second movement provides respite before the Allegro vivace finale, which is marked by a wild main subject in shifting rhythms and a fleet, virtuosic second theme. Rapid-fire chordal passagework from the keyboard brings this most melodramatic of Rachmaninov's concerti to a thrilling conclusion. *—Sol Louis Siegel*

Recommended:

- ○ **Richter Edition** / Richter, Sanderling (cond.), U.S.S.R. Radio & TV SO / 1995 / Melodiya 29467
- ○ **Rachmaninov: Piano Concertos; Paganini Rhapsody** / Ashkenazy, Previn (cond.), London SO / 2002 / Decca 473251
- ○ **Rachmaninov: Piano Concertos 1–4; Rhapsody on a Theme of Paganini** / Wild, Horenstein (cond.), Royal PO / 2003 / Chandos 10078
- ○ **Rachmaninov: Piano Concertos 1 & 4** / Rachmaninov, Ormandy (cond.), Philadelphia Orch. / 1999 / Naxos 110602
- ○ **Rachmaninov: Piano Concertos; Paganini Rhapsody** / Litton (cond.), Hough, Dallas SO / Hyperion 67501/2

Piano Concerto No. 2 in C minor, Op. 18 (1900–1901)

Rachmaninov composed this work in 1900, and played the first complete performance on November 9, 1901, with Alexandre Siloti conducting the Moscow Philharmonic Society.

He suffered a shattering career crisis in the 1897 massacre of his *First Symphony* in St. Petersburg, by its first conductor, Glazunov, who was reportedly disablingly drunk—a fiasco the critics en masse, led by César Cui, laid at the composer's feet like an animal carcass. The audience—ever mindful that Rachmaninov had been expelled in 1885 from the local temple of musical instruction—listened stonily, glad for the failure of a young lion schooled elsewhere (in Moscow, he completed the Conservatory course in 1891, and graduated a year later with highest possible grades). Because of the failure of the *Symphony No. 1,* Rachmaninov began to drink immoderately. Believing himself unfit to compose, he tried concentrating on parallel courses as a concert soloist and opera conductor, but embroiled himself in a love affair that ended very badly. By the end of 1899, he was an alcoholic whose hands shook, imperiling his keyboard career. Between January and April of 1900, Sergey Vassilyevich saw Dr. Dahl, a Moscow specialist in "neuropsychotherapy," daily, and was urged under hypnosis to compose the new piano concerto that a London impresario was asking for. Trance therapy roused the composer from his lethargy; indeed, he worked with great facility on an excellent new concerto—the *Second, in C minor,* Op. 18—dedicated to Dr. Dahl in gratitude. Never again in the remaining four decades of his life was Rachmaninov immobilized by depression, despite several convulsive changes of fortune.

The opening, C minor, movement in sonata form was composed last; structurally it is the most conventional. Ten bars of unaccompanied keyboard chords lead directly to a palpitant principal theme for violins, violas, and clarinets—motivic rather than tuneful, despite a melismatic extension for cellos. An episode links this to the second theme, in E flat, one of Rachmaninov's most celebrated melodies, introduced by the piano. Following the development and a maestoso alla marcia reprise, there's a brilliant coda—but no solo cadenza, yet.

In the E major, Adagio sostenuto movement, after four bars of Tchaikovskian string chords, piano arpeggios introduce a two-part principal theme, played first by the solo flute, then by the solo clarinet. Piano and orchestra develop both parts before a Tchaikovsky-like theme for bassoons nudges the tempo a bit. Further development goes even quicker, culminating in a solo cadenza that's been teasingly postponed, after which the original material returns, soulfully.

The finale is an Allegro scherzando in C major. The strings play a rhythmic figure that builds to a staccato climax. The piano enters with a flourish, setting up the principal subject—again, as before in I, motivic rather than tuneful, but admirably constructed for developing. This is followed by another of Rachmaninov's signature melodies, lushly undulant, sung by the solo oboe and strings. (In the post-war 1940s, this was garnished with words and performed unrelentingly by big-band vandals as "Full Moon and Empty Arms"). A fugato brings back the principal subject, followed by a Maestoso statement of "The Tune." Accelerating fistfuls of piano chords set up a crowd-rousing conclusion. *—Roger Dettmer*

Recommended:

- ○ **Tchaikovsky: Concerto 1; Rachmaninoff: Concerto 2** / Cliburn, Reiner (cond.), Chicago SO / 1958 / RCA 0786355912
- ○ **Richter Edition** / Richter, Sanderling (cond.), Leningrad PO / 1995 / Melodiya 29467
- ○ **Rachmaninoff: Concerto ; 6 Etudes-Tableaux** / Kissin, Gergiev (cond.), London SO / 1993 / RCA 0786357982
- ○ **Rachmaninov: Complete Piano Concertos; Paganini Rhapsody** / Ashkenazy, Previn (cond.), London SO / 2002 / Decca 473251
- ○ **Rachmaninov: Piano Concertos 2 & 3** / Rachmaninov, Stokowski (cond.), Philadelphia Orch. / 1999 / Naxos 8110601
- ○ **Rachmaninov: The Piano Concertos; Paganini Rhapsody** / Hough, Litton (cond.), Dallas SO / Hyperion 67501/2

Piano Concerto No. 3 in D minor, Op. 30 (1909)

Rachmaninov premiered the *Third Concerto* in New York with the New York Symphony Orchestra, led by Walter Damrosch, on November 28, 1909. The following January he played it with the New York Philharmonic Orchestra, conducted by Gustav Mahler. For many decades, it was neglected by pianists and public alike, in favor of the more compact, more tuneful and structurally sounder *Second Concerto.* It is a deeper work, full of virtuosic hurdles and lengthy cadenzas. But it was undermined by cuts Rachmaninov was prevailed upon to make, which, in the short run, served to make it more programmable in concerts, but ultimately sabotaged its artistic value. Since the last quarter of the twentieth century, however, most performances of the concerto have been of the original version, which can run around 45 minutes. (Abridged renditions shaved as much as ten minutes off the score's total timing.)

The *Third Concerto*'s first movement, marked Allegro ma non tanto, opens with the piano delivering a lively but solemn theme of Russian character, which then immediately begins to sprout new ideas. A yearning bridge passage leads to a rhythmic theme that slows and quickly takes on another melodic guise, a beautiful and typically Rachmaninovian one in its soaring and ecstatic manner. The main theme returns and a powerful development section yields to a lengthy cadenza, whose opening pages offer alternative versions for the soloist—a lighter, more athletic beginning or a darker more chordal one. A restatement of the main theme and brief coda close this generally subdued and reflective movement.

The second movement Adagio is formally rather unique, with the main theme dominating most of the movement, and a brief scherzo-like section appearing near the end. The mood ranges from the melancholy of the main theme by the oboe to the ecstatic glory of its big restatements by piano and orchestra in the middle part of the movement. After the playful scherzo-ish music, the piano is given a brief but brilliant cadenza that leads directly into the colorful finale.

This movement, marked Alla breve, offers a typical Rachmaninov fast theme on the piano right off: it is related to the first movement's alternate theme and is rhythmically buoyant and catchy in its repeated notes. A rhythmic chordal passage harkens back to the rhythm heard at the concerto's outset, and a lovely theme, related to the first movement bridge passage, is presented, hinting at triumphant resolution. Following a dramatic, suspenseful buildup near the end the theme makes one final and absolutely triumphant appearance, after which the brilliant coda closes the work. The middle section of this movement recalls both main themes from the first movement and was once the most heavily cut section of the concerto.

Today, this concerto carries the nickname of "Rach 3," and is the most popular choice among piano competition candidates wanting to perform a virtuoso display piece. *—Robert Cummings*

Recommended:

- **Rachmaninov: Piano Concertos 2 & 3** / Rachmaninov, Ormandy (cond.), Philadelphia Orch. / 1999 / Naxos 8110601
- **Great Pianists: Vladimir Horowitz Vol. 3** / Horowitz, Reiner (cond.), RCA Victor SO / 1999 / Philips 456841
- **Rachmaninov: Complete Piano Concertos; Paganini Rhapsody** / Ashkenazy, Previn (cond.), London SO / 2002 / Decca 473251
- **Rachmaninoff: Piano Concerto 3; Suite 2 for 2 pianos** / Argerich, Chailly (cond.), Berlin Radio SO / 2001 / Philips 464732
- **Rachmaninov: The Piano Concertos; Paganini Rhapsody** / Hough, Litton (cond.), Dallas SO / Hyperion 67501/2

Piano Concerto No. 4 in G minor, Op. 40 (1926; revised 1941)

When Rachmaninov came to America in the wake of the Bolshevik Revolution, he had little beside his family and his talent. Confronted with the need to make money quickly, he eschewed composition and conducting and went on long concert tours as a pianist. It was not until 1926 that he felt secure enough to take a break and start writing again. His first post-exile work, the *Fourth Piano Concerto*, was premiered in 1927 with the composer as soloist and Leopold Stokowski conducting the Philadelphia Orchestra. Its public and critical reception was chilly at best. Though Rachmaninov later revised it and rewrote the third movement, the *Fourth Concerto* has never really gained a foothold in the repertory. It could be that the tone is cooler and more remote than we expect from Rachmaninov—this is, after all, the work of an exile picking up a lost thread—or that the structure in the outer movements is harder to grasp. Or maybe it's just that its melodies aren't as memorable. In the hands of an inspired virtuoso, however, the concerto will yield its melancholy secrets.

The opening Allegro vivace (Alla breve) gets off to a dramatic start with an ascending crescendo from the orchestra and a grand chordal theme from the soloist that searches for a while before finding its home key. This theme and a restless, lyric second subject are developed in rhapsodic manner, reaching a great, extended climax before the movement's abrupt close. The main theme of the wistful and nostalgic Largo is in fact memorable, restlessly restated in a series of different keys. It crashes directly in the Allegro vivace finale, which in its whirlwind virtuosity and rhythmic instability recalls the finale of the *First Concerto*, albeit through the prism of regretful hindsight. Near the end the climactic material of the first movement returns, ushering in a brilliant coda expressing a hard-won optimism. *—Sol Louis Siegel*

Recommended:

- **Ravel & Rachmaninov: Piano Concertos** / Michelangeli, Gracis (cond.), London Philharmonia Orch. / 2000 / Angel 67258
- **Rachmaninov: Piano Concertos 1 & 4** / Rachmaninov, Ormandy (cond.), Philadelphia Orch. / 1999 / Naxos 110602
- **Rachmaninov: The Piano Concertos; Paganini Rhapsody** / Hough, Litton (cond.), Dallas SO / Hyperion 67501/2

Rhapsody on a Theme of Paganini, for piano & orchestra in A minor, Op. 43 (1934)

The last of Paganini's *24 Caprices* for violin has been the subject of many sets of variations, including the composer's own set of 12, Brahms' brilliant *Paganini Variations* for piano, those by twentieth century composers Lutosławski, Blacher, Lloyd-Webber, and others. But the best-known off-shoot of this Caprice is Rachmaninov's *Rhapsody on a Theme of Paganini*, not least because one of its variations—the 18th—has become more famous than the Paganini tune it is based on.

The *Rhapsody* was one of Rachmaninov's last compositions; however, it has little in common with the handful of works from the composer's last two decades. The *Corelli Variations* (1931), for piano, and the *Piano Concerto No. 4* (1926; rev. 1941) display a colder, more modernistic Rachmaninov, while the *Rhapsody* harkens back to the passionate, post-Romantic world of the 1909 *Third Piano Concerto*. Also unusual is that, while the composer's output was paltry in his later years, this piece was finished in a mere month and a half, from July 3 to August 18, 1934.

With three discernible sections, the *Rhapsody on a Theme of Paganini* resembles the fast-slow-fast movement structure of a piano concerto. Variations 11 through 18 serve as the slow movement, with the preceding and following groups representing the outer movements.

The work opens with an introduction that contains elements of Paganini's melody. There follows the first variation which states the theme, largely in the strings, the piano playing just single notes from the melodic line. The piano takes over in the next variation and shares the spotlight with the orchestra in numbers three through five, all of which are lively and light in mood. With the sixth variation, the tempo slows but the piano remains playful. The seventh brings on a drastic change, introducing what has become a trademark of Rachmaninov's major compositions: the Dies Irae theme, from the Roman Catholic Mass for the Dead; it appears in the next three variations as well. Some have suggested that this allusion to the biblical "day of wrath," while a feature of many of the composer's works, was here also a nod to the nineteenth century legend that the transcendentally gifted Paganini had bargained his soul to the Devil in exchange for his talents.

The 11th variation, as mentioned above, is the beginning of what serves as a slow movement; here the music is ethereal and subdued, remaining so until the fiery 13th, which is then gives way to a pair of more brilliant variations. The lively 15th variation is followed by a markedly subdued 16th and 17th in order to prepare for the climactic 18th, which offers one of the composer's most memorable themes; Rachmaninov surely could have used it in another work without the least suspicion of its relationship to Paganini.

The final "movement" begins with the 19th variation, which is somewhat academic-sounding. The next variations offer more color, though darker elements begin creeping in again with No. 22, which builds up to its finish in a way not unlike the finales of the *Second Symphony* and *Third Piano Concerto*. The next variation recalls parts of the Paganini theme closely and leads to the dramatic conclusion—a powerful and ominous, if glitzy, restatement of the Dies Irae theme by the piano and orchestra.

A typical performance of the *Rhapsody* lasts about 25 minutes. Rachmaninov premiered it on November 7, 1934, in Baltimore, with Leopold Stokowski conducting. *—Robert Cummings*

Recommended:

- **Rachmaninoff: Concerto 2; Paganini Rhapsody** / Kapell, Reiner (cond.), Robin Hood Dell Orch. / 1998 / RCA Red Seal 902668992
- **Rachmaninoff: Piano Concerto 2; Paganini Rhapsody** / Ashkenazy, Previn (cond.), London SO / 2003 / Decca 000055202
- **Rachmaninov: Piano Concertos 1 & 4** / Rachmaninov, Stokowski (cond.), Philadelphia Orch. / 1999 / Naxos 110602
- **Rachmaninov: The Piano Concertos; Paganini Rhapsody** / Hough, Litton (cond.), Dallas SO / Hyperion 67501/2

VOCAL

Six Songs, Op. 8 (1893)

This was Rachmaninov's second collection of songs, which he composed just a year after the promising first. The Opus 8 set of six are all based on poems translated by Alexei Plesheyev, who died around the time Rachmaninov was setting these texts.

The first two songs are on poems by Heine. "Water Lily" tells of the moon and water lily falling in love and features delightful and carefree music. The second, "My child, your beauty is that of a flower," is subdued and attractive throughout its short duration. The sentimental text tells of the poet's desire to invoke divine providence for the beautiful child he so loves.

The fifth song, "Dream" is also from Heine. The poet speaks of his homeland and happy times from the past, then realizes his recollections are merely a dream. The melody is beautiful and exquisitely wrought, and the accompaniment restrained and subtle. Many believe this to be the finest song in the collection. The third and fourth items, are on texts by Shevchenko. "Brooding" is gloomy but beautiful, and is an effective enactment of the poem's theme of struggling futilely against fate. "I fell in love to my sorrow" features another lovely but sad melody, which in this instance expresses the laments of a young woman whose husband has been taken off to be a "lifelong soldier."

The final song is "Prayer," on Goethe texts. It may be the least attractive item in the set, owing to its melodic lack of distinction and overly dramatic character. The text deals with a young girl who asks forgiveness for rejecting the love of a worthy young man who later dies. *—Robert Cummings*

Recommended:

- **Rachmaninov: Complete Songs Vol. 1** / Leiferkus, Rodgers, Popescu, Naoumenko, Shelley / 1996 / Chandos 9405
- **Rachamninov: Songs** / (5 songs) / Rautio, Skigin / 1997 / Conifer 51276

12 Songs, Op. 14 (1894–1896)

All but the first of these dozen songs were composed in 1896, two years after the initial item, "I await you." By the time the composer completed the set, he was finding the vocal idiom more to his liking, though his style was still evolving in all genres. This was his third song collection and probably the best to date.

The aforementioned opening number, on texts by Maria Davidova, offers a yearning melody to express the feelings of an anxious woman awaiting her lover. The piano accompaniment is mostly gentle and sensitive, but in the closing moments becomes quite powerful, perhaps too much so, thereby disclosing the composer's still somewhat immature talents. "Small Island," written on Konstantin Balmont texts, comes next. The melody is tranquil and flowing, and the mood remains serene throughout to depict the scenes of nature in the text.

The third song is "How few the joys," which sets a poem by Afanasy Fet about the agonies of lost love. Not surprisingly, the music has a dark character. "I was with her" expresses the Alexei Koltsov text about mutual love and faithfulness with passionate, exciting vocal writing, underpinned by many colorful arpeggios from the piano accompaniment. "These Summer Nights," using texts by Daniil Rathaus, expresses restive feelings aroused by the mood of the summer night. The piano accompaniment deftly modulates to underscore the uncertainty of the emotions.

The next two songs are on texts by Tolstoy. The first, "You are so loved by all," offers both spoken and musical roles for the voice, with soft piano accompaniment. The mood is sad throughout, the Tolstoy texts dealing with grief. The second of the pair is "Do not believe me, friend," which expresses the feelings of reaffirmation of love for someone apparently neglected. The mood is cheerful and a bit carefree, and the accompaniment deftly shaped and brilliant at the close.

"Oh, do not grieve," a setting of Alexei Apukhtin words, enacts a woman's caring and consoling abilities with a touching melody, that is beautifully elegiac in character. The ensuing pair of songs are on texts by Nikolai Minsky. "She is as beautiful as midday" and "In my soul" share a certain exotic quality in their thematic material and writing, and both songs deal with hopeless feelings owing to failure in love. "Spring Torrents" is one of Rachmaninov's most popular songs, especially in Russia. Using texts from Feodor Tyutchev that herald the onset of spring, it features a buoyant, happy theme, supported by fleet and colorful passages from the piano. The last song here is "It is time," on texts by Semyon Nadson. This is a rousing and powerful piece to close out the set, with potent accompaniment and a text that is an entreaty to a prophet to aid the people in a desperate time. *—Robert Cummings*

Recommended:

○ **Rachmaninov: Complete Songs Vol. 1** / Leiferkus, Rodgers, Naoumenko, Popescu, Shelley / 1996 / Chandos 9405

○ **Rachmaninov: Songs** / (5 songs) / Larin, Bekova / 1997 / Chandos 9562

12 Songs, Op. 21 (1900–1902)

This was Rachmaninov's fourth collection of songs, and all but the first of them date from 1902. By this time he had begun to regain his confidence following the depression and loss of artistic sense that resulted from the catastrophic failure of his *First Symphony* in March 1897, which owed more to the possibly drunk Glazunov's poor conducting than to the young composer's fairly impressive composition.

The first song in the collection, "Fate," was written in 1900 and is by far the longest of the 12. Indeed, the others here are quite short, being of two- or three-minutes' duration, about the usual length of most of the composer's previous efforts in the genre. "Fate" was said to be inspired by Beethoven's *Fifth Symphony*, whose dominant motto has been linked to fate, though never positively. The texts of the song derive from Alexei Apukhtin and the music is rather ponderous and overly dramatic. The second item, "By a fresh grave," is a setting of a poem by Semyon Nadson, as is the ninth, "Melody." The former broods over sorrow and loneliness and the latter deals with the sounds of nature a man desires to hear at the moment of his death. The former is morose and dramatic, while the piano theme and vocal line in "Melody" flow beautifully.

"Twilight," a poem by Jean-Marie Guyot, is a delicate, lyrical creation about a pensive woman looking through a window at a darkening sky. "They replied," on Victor Hugo texts, offers vigorous piano accompaniment and a gentle vocal line to enact the text about men on the run seeking love. "Lilacs" is one of the better known songs here, not least because it is only one of two that the composer transcribed for piano. The text, from Ekaterina Beketova, deals with scenes of nature, and the music is bright and cheery, though tinged with a hint of sadness near the end.

"Fragment from A. Musset" is about the suffering of loneliness, and Rachmaninov's music on Musset's texts is dark and effective. "How peaceful" and the collection's last song, "How painful," are settings of poems by Glafira Galina. The former presents a stark contrast to the Musset song. The text speaks of the joy of being in solitude with nature and God, and the music is simple and vibrant, deftly evolving from the singer's initial phrase. "How painful" features a dark theme to express a text in which the poet wants to hasten the arrival of old age as a means to lessen grief.

"On the death of a Linnet," on texts of Vasily Zhukovsky about the death of a pet bird, features an attractive melody for the singer and a piano part with some interesting counterpoint. The tenth item, "Before the icon," on words of Arseny Golenischev-Kutuzov, is religious is both in text and music, Rachmaninov subtly capturing a contemplative and serene mood. "I am not a prophet," the penultimate offering, effectively continues the religious vein. It is based on texts by Alexander Kruglov. *—Robert Cummings*

Recommended:

○ **Rachmaninov: Complete Songs Vol. 2** / Leiferkus, Rodgers, Popescu, Naoumenko, Shelley / 1996 / Chandos 9451

○ **Rachmaninov: Songs** / Rautio, Skigin / 1997 / Conifer 51276

○ **Rachmaninov: Songs** / Larin, Bekova / 1997 / Chandos 9562

15 Songs, Op. 26 (1906)

This was the fifth of the seven song collections of Rachmaninov and the largest in number. Though he was only 33 at the time he wrote them, he was already a master in the vocal realm, having also worked on four operas by then.

"There are many sounds" (texts by Alexei Tolstoi), "All taken from me" (Fyodor Tyutchev), and "We shall rest" (Anton Chekhov, from *Uncle Vanya*) all deliver powerful music and words. The first is somber in mood, dealing with suppressed desires and feelings; the middle song is brief—dramatic at the outset and quite lyrical thereafter—dealing with the central character losing everything, including health, as punishment by God. The last of the three is a dark and effective setting of Chekhov's text.

The long fourth entry, "Two farewells" (Alexei Koltsov), requires a soprano and baritone to sing alternately, as a woman in dialogue with an inquisitive young man. The music is compelling, making this one of the strongest songs in the collection. In "Beloved, let us fly" (Arseny Golenischev-Kutuzov) a man implores his love to go with him to the country. The vocal line is calm and lyrical, the accompaniment restrained.

The sixth and eighth songs are on texts by Dmitri Merezhkovsky. "Christ is risen" and "For mercy I beg" are both powerful works. The former deals with Christ's return to earth and his repulsion at the evil he would observe, while the latter implores oncoming spring not to arouse feelings of pain and suffering. "To Children" (Alexei Kholmyakov) tells of children growing up and leaving home and the parent's resultant pain of loss. The music is simple, if serious, with a gentle, flowing vocal line.

The ninth and twelfth songs are on texts by Ivan Bunin. In "I am again alone," a young man aware his beloved is leaving him. The music is perhaps a bit overdramatic here and, therefore, less compelling. "Night is sorrowful" portrays the poet's hopeless longing for happiness via an attractively mournful melody and deft contrapuntal accompaniment. The tenth song, "At my window," is a Glafira Galina poem about a cherry tree that sings wordlessly of love near the poet's window. The melody and mirroring accompaniment are beautiful, making this among the best items in the set.

The eleventh song, "The fountain," (Tyutchev), describes a fountain whose waters rise to the heavens, and offers vivid imaging in the vocal writing, with a climactic octave leap, and arpeggios on piano to enact the surges of rising water. "Yesterday we met" (Yakov Polonsky) is a man's happenstance meeting with a former lover, and offers simple and direct but constantly changing music, featuring several effective pauses. "The Ring" (Koltsov) tells of a woman discarding her deceased beloved's ring. The music is less compelling here, the nervous accompaniment at the outset and close providing some interest, however.

The final song, "All things depart" (Daniil Rathaus) deals with man's mortality, and Rachmaninov's music has more than a vague religious tone and rises to a powerful climax. *—Robert Cummings*

Recommended:

○ **Rachmaninov: Complete Songs Vol. 2** / Leiferkus, Rodgers, Popescu, Naoumenko, Shelley / 1996 / Chandos 9451

○ **Rachmaninov: Songs** / (8 songs) / Larin, Bekova / 1997 / Chandos 9562

○ **Mélodies Russes** / (5 songs) / Christoff, Labinsky / EMI 674962

14 Songs, Op. 34 (1912)

The Op. 34 songs were the penultimate set of Rachmaninov's seven. The songs here are wide-ranging in both mood and text selections.

The first, "The Muse," the third, "Storm," and the fifth, "Arion" are all texts by Pushkin. The first tells of the Muse teaching a child how to play and compose music; the mood is contemplative at the outset but builds to a powerful climax. The next deals with a maiden on a cliff surrounded by a violent storm. Rachmaninov's music is furious and exciting, though the quiet and subtle conclusion matches the poet's view that the maiden's beauty is greater than the powers of nature. The third tells of the eponymous Greek poet's survival of a shipwreck, and the dramatic music convincingly portrays the struggle in the deep waters. The second and fourth songs, "In the soul of each of us" (Apollon Korinfsky) and "A passing breeze" (Konstantin Balmont), are both effective. The former deals with sorrow and emotional swings, the music appropriately dark, and the latter, a fantasy about the wind assessing the powers of night and day, offers mostly delicate music with relaxed harmonies.

The six and seventh items here, "The Raising of Lazarus" (Alexei Khomyakov) and "It cannot be" (Apollon Maykov) deal with religious subjects and the death of a daughter, respectively. The music for the former is not a success, but that for the Maykov text is grim, tense, and full of grief in its passionate outpourings.

The eighth and thirteenth songs are on texts by Yakov Polonsky. "Music," about the mesmerizing sounds of that art form, is given an appropriately ethereal mood. The thirteenth, "Dissonance," is not a follow-up to "Music," but deals with a woman's erotic fantasies. This is by far the longest song in the collection, and the composer's subtle writing throughout, with many key and tempo changes, place it among the best here.

The ninth and tenth songs are on texts by Feodor Tyutchev. "You knew him" tells of a poet's varying moods, with music that is dramatic and at times harsh, but effectively so. "This day I remember" is the poet's recollections of the day his beloved revealed her love for him. The music is rather direct and quite delicate throughout, Rachmaninov's favorite in the collection.

Texts for the next two songs come from Afanasy Fet. The eleventh, "The Peasant," offers praise to God with music that is powerful but somewhat tedious in its rigid, unchanging rhythm. "What happiness" is a love poem with music that deftly encompasses the text: the racing drive of the piano expresses the poet's excitement at being alone with his beloved, a brief relative calm is interrupted by a return to the fast tempo to portray the torments of love. The music builds to an intense, impassioned climax.

The fourteenth song, "Vocalise," is wordless with a mournful mood, featuring a richly Romantic melody which descends slowly, then soars high before heading downward once again. This became the most popular song in the collection. *—Robert Cummings*

Recommended:

- ○ **Rachmaninov: Complete Songs Vol. 3** / Leiferkus, Rodgers, Naoumenko, Popescu, Shelley / 1996 / Chandos 9477

Six Songs, Op. 38 (1916)

Until Sergey Rachmaninov left Russia after the Revolution in 1917, he was a prolific songwriter. Once in the West, Rachmaninov had to concentrate on piano playing to make a living. Aside from the *Three Russian Songs for Chorus* of 1926, these beautiful and romantic songs are the last of his total of 85. The *Six Poems*, Op. 38, show that when this unfortunate cessation happened, Rachmaninov was at the top of his form as a vocal composer. The songs achieve a unique synthesis of his powerful style of keyboard writing and sensitive, informed composition technique for voice. Moreover, Rachmaninov's taste in poetry was rapidly improving, thanks to the intervention of an idolizing fan. Marietta Shaginian, age 25 and a poetess, started writing to the composer in 1912, signing her letters simply "Re." Their correspondence became open and intense, two creative artists baring their creative souls. Soon, Shaginian felt able to criticize Rachmaninov's selection of poems to set as songs, telling the composer he relied too much on works of deceased poets and even then often used weaker ones. Shaginian introduced him to the works of the living poets of the Symbolist school of poetry. This was a movement particularly strong in France and Russia, and oddly influenced by American Edgar Allan Poe. Their poems tended to use objects as triggers for emotional reminiscence.

Rachmaninov responded by making his use of harmonies and tonality more subtle and colorful, adding a layer of chord-based symbolism. The first poem, *At night in my garden* (Noch'yu v sadu u menya), has delicate piano figures to suggest the warm, sad night of Alexander Blok's translation of a poem by the Armenian Avetik Isaakian. *To Her (K Ney)* has a text by Byely. Rich harmonies reminiscent of *Isle of the Dead* depict the poem's final realization that love is lost. *Daisies (Margaritki)* by Severyanin is one of the composer's best-known songs, with a sparkling pianistic accompaniment. The Pied-Piper is a possible title for Bryusov's poem *Krysolov*, which literally means "rat catcher." This has an infectious rhythm and crisp, staccato piano playing. There is an improvisatory quality to the fifth song, a setting of a poem by Sologub. Its title, *Son*, is probably best translated as "Sleep," although sometimes "Dream" is seen. It is soft-textured with a lulling, rippling accompaniment. Finally comes a poem called *Au!* by Konstantin Balmont. Sometimes called "The Quest," the Russian title is simply a cry of pain that bursts out in the last line when, again, one's love cannot be found. The outburst brings out Rachmaninov's powerful keyboard idiom, which asks a lot of the singer to match it on the concert platform. *—Joseph Stevenson*

Recommended:

- ○ **Rachmaninov: Complete Songs Vol. 3** / Rodgers, Shelley / 1996 / Chandos 9477
- ○ **Clearings in the Sky** / H. Grant Murphy, K. Murphy / 2001 / Arabesque 6754

Vocalise, song, Op. 34/14 (1912; revised 1915)

Rachmaninov's *Vocalise*, Op. 34/14 (1912), is one of the few members of an elite repertory niche: popular, non-avant-garde vocal works without text. In fact, having been arranged for orchestra, piano, various chamber ensembles, and solo string instruments, it is easily the most popular and recognizable of such works, matched perhaps only by the aria from Heitor Villa Lobos' *Bacchianas Brasileiras No. 5*.

The Opus 34 group contains some of the Rachmaninov's best-loved songs, each of which was tailored to the vocal personality of a particular singer with whom he was acquainted from the Bolshoi opera. The highly declamatory examples, such as "In the Soul of Each of Us," Op. 34/2, were dedicated to the great bass Feodor Chaliapin, whose ability to shape words into dramatic musical statements was legendary. The *Vocalise*, on the other hand, was dedicated to Antonina Nezhdanova, who can be presumed to have possessed a singularly pleasing and flexible voice, given the sustained, almost violin-like character of the piece.

Though originally written for voice and piano, the *Vocalise* is most often heard in its orchestrated version as a concert hall delicacy. In this setting, the rich, seamless nature of the strings compliment the soaring voice to great effect, and make for an altogether more sensual piece. *—AMG*

Recommended:

- ○ **Rachmaninoff: Vocalise** / (vocal, instrumental, and orchestral versions) / various artists / 2000 / RCA 63669
- ○ **Divine Sopranos** / McNair, Zinman (cond.), Baltimore SO / 1994 / Telarc 80407
- ○ **Rachmaninov: Symphony 3; Vocalise** / Stokowski (cond.), National PO / 1998 / EMI 66759

ORCHESTRAL

The Isle of the Dead, symphonic poem, Op. 29 (1909)

Described by Stravinsky as "six feet two inches of Russian gloom," Rachmaninov was attracted by the Dies irae theme, a melody used in the Roman Catholic Mass for the Dead, or Requiem Mass. He very frequently quoted or alluded to this theme in his compositions, including the *The Isle of the Dead*, regarded as the quintessential expression of the composer's melancholy. This work was inspired by the painting by Swiss artist Arnold Böcklin. Böcklin's haunting painting depicts an island, in front of which stands a barricade of stones. Further out from it, jutting high out of the sea, is a huge rock, within which are large chambers for the dead. A boat can be seen on the waters operated by a black-clad helmsman, whose white-robed passenger stands ghostlike. Rachmaninov's composition begins with rhythmic motif played by muted cellos and harp, suggesting the movement of the dark waters near the barricade surrounding the lifeless isle. A somber second theme, presented by French horn, reinforces the despondent mood. Soon there are hints of the Dies irae theme, after which the opening motif returns. The music then becomes restless and intense, the tempo increasing, orchestral colors appearing. A climax is reached and the material from the opening reappears, now fuller and agitated. Finally the music subsides, but afterwards there are more allusions to the Dies irae melody. A new theme appears, on strings and reeds, and rises to an impassioned climax, the music yearning, struggling, it seems, to offer some consolation or hoping to escape this strange world. A further climactic episode ensues, after which the fragment of the Dies irae once more dominates this grim musical landscape. Afterward the music fades, and the dark material of the opening returns. Just before the ending there comes a nearly full statement of the Dies irae melody. *—Robert Cummings*

Recommended:

- ○ **Rachmaninov: Symphonies** / Ashkenazy (cond.), / London 455798
- ○ **Rachmaninov: Symphony 1; The Isle Of The Dead** / Jansons (cond.), St. Petersburg PO / 1999 / EMI 56754
- ○ **Rachmaninov: Isle Of The Dead; Vocalise; Symphony 3** / Rachmaninov (cond.), Philadelphia Orch. / 1996 / BMG 62532
- ○ **The Reiner Sound** / Reiner (cond.), Chicago SO / 1993 / BMG 61250
- ○ **Rachmaninov: Symphonic Dances; Isle of the Dead** / Batiz (cond.), Royal PO / 1992 / Naxos 550583

The Rock, symphonic poem, Op. 7 (1893)

Rachmaninov graduated from the Moscow Conservatory in 1892 with the highest of honors, owing to the initial success of his opera *Aleko*, which served as his primary graduation exercise in composition. *The Rock* (or as it is also known, *The Crag*) was the first orchestral composition he completed following his student years.

Ostensibly, the inspiration of this composition was Chekhov's *Along the way*. But the composer indicated in the 1893 score that Lermontov's poem *The Rock* served that purpose. Because Rachmaninov acknowledged Chekhov as the inspiration in an 1898 inscription on a printed score, however, his work is generally believed to be the program source for *The Rock*.

The Chekhov work tells of two travelers, one a middle-aged man ("the giant rock") and the other an attractive young woman ("the golden cloud"), meeting on Christmas Eve in a roadside inn when they seek shelter from a blizzard. They develop feelings for each other, but the woman departs in a sleigh the next morning, with the man watching her in the distance as the snow covers him, making him appear like a "lonely white rock."

The work begins darkly and ponderously in the low strings, the young composer already displaying a fine sense for atmosphere. Quickly the mood brightens, the orchestration showing much color in the reeds and shimmering strings. A short, rather nondescript theme which vaguely evokes Borodin, is heard in the woodwinds, and then the tempo increases. After the material is repeated, the strings play the theme in an animated fashion, imparting more color and personality to it. The mood then turns hushed and mysterious. Eventually, the music intensifies and takes on a threatening character. This grim atmosphere soon leads to a powerful yearning passage on strings that ends with a gripping, dark climax of Tchaikovskian character. Thereafter the music remains in a gloomy, regretful haze.

The Rock was premiered March 20, 1894, in Moscow. While this piece is interesting and has many effective moments, it is not a major achievement and shows the composer's style still evolving. A typical performance of this work lasts about 15 minutes. *—Robert Cummings*

Recommended:

- ○ **Russian Moods** / Svetlanov (cond.) / 1997 / Melodiya 34167
- ○ **Rachmaninoff: Symphony 2; Fantasy for Orchestra** / Previn (cond.), London SO / 1991 / RCA 60791

Symphonic Dances, Op. 45 (1940)

Rachmaninov's trio of *Symphonic Dances* (1940) represents the composer's last completed work, and the only one he wrote wholly in the United States. The first of the three dances, marked Non allegro—Lento—Tempo I, begins with a vibrant three-note motif that makes its way through the orchestra, from woodwinds to strings to brass, repeating, descending, ascending, climaxing in a proclamation of the theme in the strings, accompanied by tambourine. The slow middle section unfolds with an expansive melody on alto saxophone, soon taken up with warmth and passion by the strings. After a return to the main material, the central theme is recalled briefly as the movement draws to a quiet close.

The Andante con moto recalls characteristics of both the second movement of the composer's *Piano Concerto No. 3* (1935) and Ravel's *La Valse* (1919–20). Commencing in a slow waltz rhythm, the music momentarily hesitates before resuming the initial mood with a subdued, suave, nocturnal theme. Toward the center of the movement the music again becomes hesitant, its direction seemingly uncertain. The waltz theme returns, now becoming anxious and restive as the tempo increases. The climax is follwed by a subdued ending.

The Lento assai finale begins hesitantly, unhurriedly, lurching ahead and then slowing. With the entrance of *Dies irae*—the plainchant requiem theme that Rachmaninov used so effectively in the *Rhapsody on a Theme of Paganini* (1934)—the tempo picks up and the music takes on a brilliance that is anything but gloomy or funereal. After a climactic episode the music slows, seemingly suspended in an ethereal state. Gradually, the mood becomes reflective, and the textures darken. *Dies Irae* returns amid even greater color and majesty, as if the composer were willingly and happily embracing a fate he knew was near. The music builds to a powerful and brilliant climax as the *Dies irae* theme is proudly stated again and again. In what seems to suggest an ominous close, the orchestra delivers crushing chords, punctuated by a thundering gong stroke whose fading strains appear to bring the work to an end. From this gesture, however, emerges a quotation from Rachmaninov's own *Vespers* (1915) that corresponds to the Resurrection of Christ.

While the composer worked on the orchestration of the *Symphonic Dances*, he also sketched out a version for two pianos that is generally a literal and faithful transcription. The work in its full orchestral clothing was premiered by Eugene Ormandy and the Philadelphia Orchestra on January 4, 1941. *—Robert Cummings*

Recommended:

○ **Rachmaninov: Music for 2 Pianos** / Ashkenazy, Previn / 1995 / London 444845

○ **Rachmaninov: Symphonic Dances** / Temirkanov (cond.), St. Petersburg PO / 1995 / BMG 62710

CHORAL

The Bells, choral symphony, Op. 35 (1913)

While it is true that Rachmaninov's choral symphony *The Bells* was ultimately based on the Edgar Allan Poe poem of the same name, its more direct inspiration was the Konstantin Balmont translation into Russian, which takes substantial liberties with the text. He eliminated Poe's repetitions, which are so central to his onomatopoetic devices, and he generally ignored his meter. Ironically, *The Bells* is often performed in English, using a translation of Balmont's translation!

The score for *The Bells* requires a tenor, soprano, baritone, chorus and large orchestra. The three soloists never sing together, nor do they even appear in the same movement. The four sections of the work represent four aspects of life: birth, marriage, terror, and death.

The first movement, marked Allegro ma non troppo, is subtitled *The Silver Sleigh Bells* and features a prominent tenor part. The mood is effervescent and joyous, the scoring colorful and the themes and harmonies richly post-Romantic, typical of the works of the composer's middle years. After a nearly two-minute introduction dominated by an irresistible three-note "giddy-up" theme, the tenor enters to intone the words "Listen, hear the silver bells." With the chorus serving mostly in an accompanimental role, the merriment continues for a short while, then gradually subsides, leading to a slow but brief middle section. The tempo picks back up and the music quickly rises to an ecstatic climax, with the brass and bells (celesta) playing a marchlike motif while chorus and orchestra gradually fade.

The Lento second movement is subtitled *The Mellow Wedding Bells*, and features a soprano soloist. Rachmaninov focuses on the more passionate and intimate aspects associated with weddings. There is one glorious, climactic outburst in the middle of the movement, but the music is otherwise relatively subdued in its unabashedly Romantic demeanor. Without doubt, this is the warmest and most beautiful of the four movements. For all its sanguine beauty, though, there is an allusion near the beginning here to the *Dies Irae* theme, that ubiquitous motif that crops up in the finale here and in almost every major orchestral composition of Rachmaninov.

The Presto third movement has been described as demonic. Subtitled *The Loud Alarum Bells* and representing terror, the music sounds threatening almost from the outset. It begins softly and slowly, but swiftly gathers momentum and mass. The chorus enters with singing that verges on shouting, and thereafter the mood remains unsettled and tense, dark and dissonant. The climax features an outburst on percussion and grim singing by the chorus. As the music seems to fade for a quiet ending, suddenly the tempo picks up and the chorus rises in a powerful crescendo and the movement ends abruptly.

The finale, marked Lento lugubre and subtitled *The Mournful Iron Bells*, certainly lives up to these descriptions. It is gloomy; the sound of the baritone is dark, and that of the chorus cold and dispiriting. At the end Rachmaninov conveys only grudging hope, when the music turns sad and warmly Romantic, as the baritone tells of the "quiet of the tomb."

Premiered on February 8, 1914, in Moscow, this was the composer's favorite work. *—Robert Cummings*

Recommended:

○ **Rachmaninov: The Symphonies** / Ashkenazy (cond.), / London 455798

○ **Prokofiev: Ivan the Terrible; Alexander Nevsky; Rachmaninov: The Bells** / Previn (cond.), London SO / 1999 / EMI 73353

○ **Rachmaninoff: The Bells; Taneyev: John of Damascus** / Pletnev (cond.), Russian National Orch. / 2001 / DG 471029

Liturgy of St John Chrysostom, Op. 31 (1910)

Though Rachmaninov the composer is best remembered for his concerti and other piano works, the *Symphony No. 2* (1906–07), the tone poem *Isle of the Dead* (1909), and numerous songs, he also produced a small but distinguished body of choral music. The "choral symphony" *The Bells* (1913) is probably the best-known example of this part of the composer's output, but Rachmaninov also produced a number of other important choral works during the same decade. The *Liturgy of St. John Chrysostom for chorus*, Op. 31 (1910) was composed during one of the composer's regular summers in Ivanovka, a retreat where he also composed the *Études-tableaux*, Op. 33 (1911) and the *Piano Sonata No. 2*, Op. 36 (1913). The namesake of The Liturgy of St. John Chrysostom (ca. 307–407) is one of the most revered saints in the Orthodox tradition. St. John (whose full name denotes "golden mouth") is held in particular esteem for his powers as an orator and theologian. He has been honored by composers on numerous occaions; the mass text that bears his name was set by, among other composers, Tchaikovsky (his Op. 41, composed in 1878). Rachmaninov's setting of St. John's Liturgy reflects the work's age-old origins in the Orthodox Church. In keeping with the *Liturgy*'s roots, Rachmaninov makes use of unaccompanied voices, which sing the traditional text in Slavonic. Early on, the Russian Orthodox Church rejected the "modernist spirit" of Rachmaninov's work, causing it to lapse into obscurity as the Russian Revolution approached. The *Liturgy*, lost for decades, was reconstructed in the 1980s from archival sources and part books located in a New York monastery. *—AMG*

Recommended:

○ **Rachmaninov: Liturgy of St. John Chrysostom** / Popsavov (cond.), Sofia Orthodox Choir / Capriccio 10519/20

○ **Rachmaninov: Vespers; Liturgy of St John Chrysostom** / Moscow Academy Choir / Saison Russe 288154

○ **Rachmaninov: Liturgy of St. John Chrysostom** / Best (cond.), Corydon Singers / 1994 / Hyperion 66703

Vespers (All-Night Vigil), for alto, tenor & chorus, Op. 37 (1915)

Sergey Rachmaninov famously recalled the night when he first played the score of his *All-Night Vigil* for a pair of the most prominent Russian musicians. Nikolai Danilin, who had agreed to conduct the work's premiere, lamented that the basses able to sing his impossibly profundo pitches were "as rare as asparagus at Christmas." Yet the composer replied, "I know the voices of my countrymen!" And he did know both the voices of his countrymen and their deep religious spirit (which not even the Revolution could eradicate). Rachmaninov premiered the *Vsenoshchnoye bdeniye* (*All-Night Vigil*, or *Vespers Mass*) in 1915, amid the privations of World War I. Russian basses were found to sing the parts, and Russians were hailing the *Vespers* as a masterpiece even before the performance began.

Though not personally close to the Russian Orthodox Church, Rachmaninov had been throughout his life deeply moved by its music. He evoked Russian church bells frequently in his music, had quoted Orthodox chants in his *Symphony No. 1*, and achieved large-scale success in an earlier setting of the *Liturgy of St. John Chrysostom*. His *Vespers* resembles the earlier work in flavor, but greatly expands its harmonic pallette. The 15 movements of the *Vespers* together form the core of a well-known Russian Orthodox monastic service; larger churches would also celebrate the Vigil on the night before greater feasts. Its series of texts (in traditional Church Slavonic) include several psalms and the Orthodox versions of the Magnificat, *Nunc dimittis*, and Greater and Lesser Doxologies. In fully nine of the movements, the composer adapts a rich variety of plainchant melodies: the most ancient "Znamenny" chants, simpler Russian "Greek" chants, and folklike Kiev chants.

On the scaffold of these chants the composer hangs a musical tapestry of Byzantine texture, sobriety, and power. Many of his eight-voiced choral textures remain in a flowing and chantlike homophony. His harmonic language is tonally grounded with frequent pedal points, but also rich modal and chromatic inflections. Antiphonal textures (Nos. 2, 8, 10) and liturgical refrains (Nos. 3, 9, 11, 12) evoke the incense-choked atmosperes of the church. At the same time, local text details can inspire him to exsquisite passages, such as the radiant harmonic shift before the first tenor solo (No. 4) and the clusters of angelic melismas at the climax of No. 7. The Orthodox *Nunc dimittis* (No. 5) closes with a slow bass descent to low B flat; it was Rachmaninov's favorite movement and the music he intended for his own funeral. *—Timothy Dickey*

Recommended:

- ○ **Evening Star** / Borodina (dir.), St. Petersburg Chamber Choir / 1994 / Philips 442344
- ○ **Rachmaninov: Vespers** / Cheenushenko (dir.), St. Petersburg Cappella / 1997 / Saison Russe 788050
- ○ **Rachmaninoff: Vespers** / Shaw (cond.), Robert Shaw Festival Singers / 1990 / Telarc 80172

SYMPHONIC

Symphony No. 1 in D minor, Op. 13 (1895)

The history of Rachmaninov's *Symphony No. 1* is almost as notable as the music itself. The 1897 premiere was a complete fiasco, poorly conducted by Glazunov and miserably received. "If there were a Conservatory in Hell," wrote César Cui, "Rachmaninov would certainly gain first prize for his symphony, so devilish are the discords he has dished up before us." Rachmaninov's reaction, beyond a nervous collapse, was to disown the work. However, the orchestral parts from that same premiere turned up after World War II, and the Symphony was revived as something of a historical curiosity.

Though far from the composer's best work—he was but 23, and in the earliest stages of his career, at the time of its composition—the Symphony is far from the unqualified failure suggested by its initial reception. It is, instead, a large, ambitious work that attempts to expand the bounds of the Russian symphony beyond the works of Tchaikovsky by incorporating music of the Russian Orthodox church.

The Symphony opens with a brief, introductory swirling motif that will signify Fate throughout the work. The first movement proper, Allegro ma non troppo, is an expression of storm and struggle, with climaxes that suggest the clangor of bells. Though dark and troubled, the Scherzo, marked Allegro animato, is colored with flashes of fantasy. The Larghetto is a poem in which love is overshadowed by the menace of the middle section. The "Fate" motive explodes at the beginning of the last movement, Allegro con fuoco, followed by a blazing fanfare that leads to another dramatic life-and-death struggle. At the end of the Symphony, the "Fate" figure hammers down again and again, obliterating all that has come before it. *—Sol Louis Siegel*

Recommended:

- ○ **Rachmaninov: Symphonies & Orchestral Music** / Previn (cond.), London SO / 1993 / EMI 64530
- ○ **Rachmaninov: Symphony 1** / Hughes (cond.), Scottish National Orch. / 2003 / BIS 1309
- ○ **Rachmaninov: Symphonies 1–3** / Ashkenazy (cond.), Concertgebouw / 1996 / London 448116

Symphony No. 2 in E minor, Op. 27 (1906–1907)

By 1906, the time when Rachmaninov began work of the *Second Symphony*, he had become not only a well-known pianist and conductor, but a composer of considerable renown. Ten years before, however, the abject failure of his *First Symphony* had robbed him of his confidence and plunged him into a dark depression. Unable to compose for the next three years, he finally sought the help of Dr. Nicolai Dahl at the behest of relatives. Dahl used the then-new technique of hypnotism, which rapidly restored the composer's confidence. Shortly after his therapeutic sessions with Dahl, Rachmaninov produced his popular *Second Piano Concerto*. It must have been with some trepidation, though, that he started work on the *Second Symphony*, memories of the fate of the First undoubtedly still lingering in his mind.

Indeed, after composing the first draft of this symphony in 1906–07, Rachmaninov declared his dissatisfaction with it; he would remark that it was not in his nature to compose symphonies. Nevertheless, he forced himself to rework the piece, and on February 8, 1908, he led the first performance in St. Petersburg. It was enthusiastically received, and by the end of the year, Rachmaninov was awarded the Glinka prize for his new work.

The Symphony opens with a brooding Largo introduction, drenched in mystery and ethereality; it features a motto theme that returns in various guises throughout the symphony. The agitated main theme (Allegro moderato) is followed by an alternate, more ecstatic melody, and then a rather stormy development section. The movement is quite long, especially when—as is now the practice—the exposition repeat is taken.

The second movement Scherzo offers a vigorous theme of seemingly brighter mood than that of most of the music in the opening panel. Yet, it is derived from the *Dies irae* theme, used in the Roman Catholic mass for the dead—a theme which Rachmaninov used in almost every major composition he wrote. There is a lovely alternate melody, which is related to the motto appearing in the Symphony's introduction.

The third movement (Adagio) opens a with a descending theme on strings, one of the composer's loveliest and most memorable creations. There follows an equally attractive melody on clarinet and another for violins and oboe. While to many this movement represents impassioned love music, to others it is profoundly meditative in its warm religiosity. No program was ever attached to the movement or to the symphony by the composer.

The Allegro vivace finale is happy and triumphant in its luminous main theme, and features a lushly orchestrated, beautiful alternate melody, similar in its ecstatic demeanor to several from the preceding movements. The coda brings on an all-conquering triumphant ending, resolving any lingering doubts spawned by the work's earlier darker elements.

A typical performance of the complete version of the *Second Symphony*, first movement repeat included, lasts about an hour. Many recordings up to the 1970s, and even a few years beyond, included cuts, eliminating as much as 20 minutes from the score. Rachmaninov himself had been convinced in the early 1930s to make cuts in the work, and in the end sanctioned nearly 20 in all. Most performances and recordings of the work today are faithful to Rachmaninov's original score. *—Robert Cummings*

Recommended:

- ○ **Rachmaninov: Symphony 2** / Previn (cond.), London SO / 1999 / EMI 66997
- ○ **Rachmaninov: Symphonies 1–3** / Ashkenazy (cond.), Concertgebouw / 1996 / London 448116

Symphony No. 3 in A minor, Op. 44 (1935–1936; revised 1938)

Rachmaninov composed his *Third Symphony* at his summer house on Lake Lucerne during the summers of 1935 and 1936, after the triumph of his *Rhapsody on a Theme of Paganini* had restored him to favor as a composer. After the symphony's 1937 premiere at the hands of Leopold Stokowski and the Philadelphia Orchestra (which Rachmaninov himself would conduct in the work's first recording two years later), the composer wrote, "It was played wonderfully. Both audience and critics responded sourly. Personally, I'm firmly convinced that this is a good work."

The first movement opens Lento as the saxophone introduces a motif that will take new forms throughout the work. Then the strings rise to usher in the main Allegro moderato in straightforward sonata form. A plaintive Russian folklike theme, introduced by oboes and bassoons, is juxtaposed with a great flowing melody in the strings. The development is so agitated that this melody seems even more sweetly nostalgic on its return in the recapitulation; the movement ends with the opening motif echoing unquietly in the lower strings. The second movement (Adagio ma non troppo—Allegro vivace) combines the usual slow movement and scherzo. A solo horn over the harp states the motif in a new form, which mutates into an aching, yearning theme introduced by the solo violin. This violin theme is developed at length, alternating legato strings and soulful passages for the solo instruments. The brisk, even angry middle section recalls Mussorgsky, or even Stravinsky, as much as Tchaikovsky; the Adagio theme on its return reaches a great climax before sinking into repose. The finale (Allegro) opens with a confident and energetic theme. This is alternated with episodes that are variously nostalgic, fantastic, or downright grotesque, with increasingly aggressive and acerbic harmonies—and yes, the *Dies Irae* turns up. But in the end the main theme emerges triumphantly, its forward momentum sweeping all before it. *—Sol Louis Siegel*

Recommended:

- ○ **Rachmaninov: Isle of The Dead; Vocalise; Symphony 3** / Rachmaninov (cond.), Philadelphia Orch. / 1996 / BMG 62532
- ○ **Rachmaninov: Symphony 3; Vocalise** / Stokowski (cond.), National PO / 1998 / EMI 66759
- ○ **Rachmaninov: Symphony 3; Symphonic Dances** / Pletnev (cond.), Russian National Orch. / DG 457598
- ○ **Rachmaninov: Symphonies 1–3** / Ashkenazy (cond.), Concertgebouw / 1996 / London 448116

CHAMBER MUSIC

Cello Sonata in G minor, Op. 19 (1901)

The common wisdom on Rachmaninov's *Sonata for Cello and Piano* is that it is really a piano sonata with cello accompaniment. While this assessment may be a slight exaggeration, it cannot be denied the piano is the dominant instrument in the work. The composer completed this sonata in November 1901, and gave the premiere in Moscow with cellist Anatoly Brandukov, on December 2 of that year, but apparently made several alterations over the next ten days, since he wrote the date of December 12, 1901, on the final page of the score.

The work is cast in four movements. The first is marked Lento—Allegro moderato—Moderato and is the longest of the four, especially when the exposition repeat is observed. It begins with a slow introduction in which the piano presents a six-note theme that at first appears insignificant, but in fact plays a key role throughout. The tempo picks up and the cello presents a passionate, beautiful theme.

A slower, somewhat more wistful melody follows, after which comes the stormy development section. The reprise ensues and the movement ends in typical Rachmaninovian fashion: the tempo speeds up as thematic morsels appear in a race to the finish, the piano crowning the coda with three resolute chords.

The second movement, marked Allegro scherzando, begins with piano writing reminiscent of the faster and more sinister passages in the *Rhapsody on a Theme of Paganini*. The cello presents a rhythmic idea in the opening moments of marginal interest. Two other themes are also presented, the latter of which is quite beautiful and recalls the mood of much of the slow music in the *Second* and *Third Piano Concertos*, especially in the piano writing.

The third movement is viewed by many as the strongest of the four. Marked Andante, it begins on the piano with a lovely theme of intimate and passionate character. After the cello enters, the material expands much the way the melody does in the second movement of the *Second Piano Concerto*. A powerful climax is reached, and the third movement ends softly.

The finale starts off with a robust theme on the cello that rather lacks the individual stamp of the composer. Still, the music is bright and vivacious and has strong appeal. There follows a second subject more in the Rachmaninovian vein, full of passion and beauty and seeming to soar to the heavens. The two themes reappear throughout, the composer deftly manipulating their interplay. In the beginning of the coda, the cello recalls the piano's opening (six-note) theme from the first movement, and then the work ends brilliantly. *—Robert Cummings*

Recommended:

- ○ **Schumann: Cello Concerto; Rachmaninov: Cello Sonata** / Rostropovich / 1998 / DG 459022
- ○ **Rachmaninov, & Miaskovsky: Cello Sonatas** / Moerk, Thibaudet / 1996 / Virgin 45119

Trio élégiaque, for piano & strings in G minor (1892)

In his youth, Rachmaninov wrote two piano trios one year apart, calling each *Trio élégiaque*. The second and far longer was written in memory of Tchaikovsky, begun the day he died and completed six weeks later. The first trio, though, is a concise, one-movement work not apparently meant to memorialize anyone in particular.

The G minor movement, marked Lento lugubre, begins with throbbing, almost electronic-sounding figures in the strings. Soon the piano comes in with the main theme, which is both deeply melancholy and deeply Slavic; it could have been lifted from Tchaikovsky's own trio of a year earlier. The strings take up the melody in separate, imitative lines over a flowing piano accompaniment, then recede as the piano plays a mysterious, hesitant figure that looks ahead to Rachmaninov's mature work, but before anything comes of this, the violin brings on a new, full, ardent theme back in the Tchaikovsky mode. Rachmaninov glides into a development of this material, splitting the melodies into often anguished fragments and repeating them at length, in the manner of Tchaikovsky (one accompanimental cello figure, in fact, comes directly from Tchaikovsky's *Manfred Symphony*). The recapitulation picks up at the point in the exposition where the strings took the melody, proceeds through a restatement of all the initial material, and ends with a funereal coda. *—James Reel*

Recommended:

- ○ **Rachmaninov: Trio Elegiaque** / Golub, Kaplan, Karr / 2000 / Arabesque 6739

Trio élégiaque, for piano & strings in D minor, Op. 9 (1893; revised 1907)

Sergei Rachmaninov wrote two piano trios, both of them essentially elegiac in character. The first was a doleful single-movement work in G minor written in four days in 1892. While it has the gloomy charm of youthful morbidity, its gloom seems facile and superficial compared to the profound emotions of the *Trio in D minor* that followed only a year later. Inspired by the shocking death of Tchaikovsky on October 23, 1893, Rachmaninov responded by beginning a work in his memory two days later. Laboring over it for six weeks, Rachmaninov composed a work in three huge and hugely despairing movements. Taking Tchaikovsky's own elegiac piano trio as a model, Rachmaninov's work consists of a large-scale sonata movement, an enormous central set of variations, and a resolutely defiant concluding fast movement. And like Tchaikovsky's *Trio*, Rachmaninov's features virtuoso writing for the piano, including a cadenza after the passionate climax of the opening movement. But despite its origins in the music of Tchaikovsky, Rachmaninov's *Trio* is wholly his own: the furiously mournful melodies, the fuliginously smoky textures, the weighty but virtuosic piano writing; all of these things are characteristic of no one but Rachmaninov. *—James Leonard*

Recommended:

- ○ **Rachmaninov: Trio Élégiaque 2** / Rostropovich, Serebrayakov, Vajman / 1995 / Leningrad Masters 1305
- ○ **Rachmaninov: String Quartets; Trio, Op 9** / Budapest Qt. / 1996 / Bridge 9063
- ○ **Rachmaninov: The "Elegiac" Piano Trios** / Borodin Trio / 1984 / Chandos 8341

OPERA

Aleko (1892)

Rachmaninov's *Aleko* was his first complete opera, written to satisfy graduation requirements at the Moscow Conservatory. As with many of his early works, it was composed in a relatively short period of time, the orchestration having been done in less than a month. The libretto was fashioned from Pushkin's poem *The Gypsies* by Vladimir Nemirovich-Danchenko, who cut the original text to about a third of its original size. For his score, Rachmaninov was awarded the Great Gold Medal in composition, becoming just the third composer at the conservatory to receive the honor.

The one-act opera divides into 13 sections, including an unusually large proportion of orchestral interludes ("Introduction," "Women's Dance," "Men's Dance," and "Intermezzo"). Although the text comes directly from Pushkin's narrative poem, its extreme truncation sacrifices a lot of the original's dramatic continuity, making the opera seem like a series of vignettes rather than a unified drama. Likewise, Rachmaninov's writing is not yet mature in style, representing a conglomeration of ideas gleaned from other Russian composers, such as Tchaikovsky, Borodin, and Glinka. However, the vocal writing is an impressive example of the young composer's emerging lyrical gifts, and he provided the score with enough unifying elements, such as recurring themes and leitmotives, to hold it together.

The story is that of the wandering nobleman, Aleko, who joins a troupe of gypsies and eventually murders his unfaithful young lover, Zemfira. This act of violence draws inevitable parallels to Mascagni's then-contemporary *Cavalleria Rusticana*, which played at the Bolshoi in 1891 while Rachmaninov was working on *Aleko*. The actual musical similarities between the two works are minimal, but Rachmaninov's use of an orchestral "Intermezzo" as a prelude to the murder suggests that he did indeed adopt Mascagni's work as a model in form, if not in style.

Recurring musical themes in the opera include a melancholy tune associated with the gypsies, and a restless leitmotiv that always accompanies the statement of Aleko's name. Other notable passages include the old gypsy's relating of his past wife's infidelity (foreshadowing Aleko's own circumstance), which is attractive and quite distinctly Russian in character, and the two dance sequences—the women's exotic and swirling, and the men's more rugged and muscular. The song Zemfira sings to her baby daughter is effective, as is the serenade of her young lover; the harp accompaniment adds to the emotional thrust of his music. *—AMG*

Synopsis:

In nineteenth century Russia, Aleko flees civilization and joins a band of gypsies. One night, after they have pitched their tents and prepared food, they begin celebrating the freedom of their iterant character. An old Gypsy begins recounting a true story. Many years before he had fallen in love with a beautiful woman, Mariula, who had a daughter named Zemfira. Mariula deserted the old Gypsy and her own daughter for a lover. Aleko now lives with Zemfira and they have a child. He is dismayed that the old Gypsy did not carry out some reprisal against Mariula. Zemfira challenges his vengeful reaction and declares that love must remain free, unbridled by possessive attitudes. She reveals that she herself has found a new lover, a young Gypsy.

A little while later she is seen exchanging an impassioned kiss with him before she withdraws to her quarters to tend to her child. Aleko follows her inside and is tormented by Zemfira, who speaks boldly of her exciting new lover. Aleko departs and ponders the abject failures in his life, both with regard to Zemfira and in his effort to find fulfillment away from civilization. At dawn Aleko enters Zemfira's tent and finds her with her lover. In a jealous rage he kills them. Aroused by the disturbance, the old Gypsy and the others gather together and banish Aleko from their group, but seek no further punishment. *—Robert Cummings*

Recommended:

- ○ **Rachmaninov: The 3 Operas** / Matorin, Borissova, Potchapski, Tarashchenko, Erasova, State Academy Russian Chorus / Saison Russe 388053
- ○ **Rachmaninov: Aleko** / Raichev (cond.), Ghiuselev, Petkov, Chirstova, Kourshoumov, Plovdiv PO / Capriccio 10782

Joachim Raff

b. May 27, 1822, Lachen, Switzerland, **d.** Jun. 24, 1882, Frankfurt am Main, Germany

Composer: Symphonic

One of several forgotten Romantic composers whose works found a performance renaissance near the twentieth century's end, Joachim Raff was the son of a German organist from Württemberg. The family had modest resources, and Raff's only formal education consisted of teacher-training studies at a Jesuit school. But he was determined on a musical career and taught himself the essentials of composition.

Raff eventually sent some of his piano music to Mendelssohn, who recommended them for publication. Encouraged, the young composer moved to Zurich, continuing to teach himself from treatises. In 1845 Liszt played a concert in Basle, and, in a journey reminiscent of Bach's supposed pilgrimage to hear Buxtehude a century and a half before, Raff walked all the way there to hear it. He met Liszt and showed him some of his music; the great virtuoso-composer took Raff back to

Germany and got him a job in a music shop in Cologne. However, Raff also became a critic, and his writings so antagonized certain local personalities that he was forced to leave the city. He settled in Stuttgart, where he formed a lifelong friendship with the conductor Hans von Bülow.

In 1846 he finally met Mendelssohn and made plans to study with him. However, Mendelssohn died in November of that year. Once again Liszt came to the rescue, finding a job for Raff in Hamburg as a representative of his publisher's firm, Schuberth. When Liszt gained a position as kapellmeister in Weimar, he hired Raff as an assistant. Like most composers, Liszt found the mundane part of the job, like making fair copies of the music to send to printers and extracting parts, to be tedious and uncreative, and he was happy to be able to delegate it to an employee; in addition, Raff orchestrated some of Liszt's early symphonic poems (some of which Liszt revised in later years when he was more skilled at orchestration).

In 1856 Raff gave up that position and moved to Wiesbaden to give piano lessons and compose. Raff had closely studied music of past eras, and as a result he saw his mission as one of reconciliation between the latest developments in music and the techniques of the past. Thus, many of his works combine Baroque counterpoint and Classical forms with his own generation's interest in program music. In 1877 Raff was appointed director of the Hoch Conservatory, and held the post until his death. He taught composition; among his pupils was the American, Edward MacDowell.

Raff's music was very highly regarded during his lifetime, a judgment that has not been seconded by history. Some commentators of the time ranked him with Wagner and Brahms. His music is well crafted, with brilliant orchestration and strong melodies; in fact, its entertaining qualities, it is now clear, damaged the music's durability by resembling too closely the salon music of the time. He was highly prolific, writing 11 symphonies (most of which have programs), and numerous other symphonic works and concertos. He wrote six operas, four of which have never been performed, and a huge amount of piano and chamber music. *—Joseph Stevenson*

SYMPHONIC

Symphonies (1859–1879)

Johannes Brahms once said that the only people who should have to listen to mid-nineteenth century German composer Joachim Raff's symphonies were his students, as torture for their unwise decision to take lessons from him. All things are relative, however, and now, a century and a half after Raff began writing symphonies, it must be said that of Europe's once-famous but now-forgotten composers, Raff was not by any means the least worthy. He was certainly one of Europe's most successful composers during the 1860s and 1870s, and also one of the most prolific. Of his more than 200 published works, 11 are full-blown symphonies, some of whose scores fill more than 300 pages. Of this gargantuan output, only a little *Cavatina* for violin and piano receives regular attention, as an encore piece, today. But a browse through the shelves of a well-stocked record store reveals that the late twentieth century interest in obscure hits of the past extended to Raff and some of his symphonies: *No. 5 in E major*, the *"Lenore" Symphony*, in particular is represented by a handful of decent (mostly German) recordings.

Raff's musical allegiance during his early career was more or less equally divided between the Mendelssohn/Schumann camp and the Liszt camp—Mendelssohn helped get some of his earliest music published and would have been among Raff's teachers had his death not prevented it, and Liszt took Raff on as one of his composition assistants, making copies and—a fact still not fully appreciated—orchestrating Liszt's music for him. (Raff was one of several musicians who orchestrated Liszt's tone poems in the years before Liszt felt sufficiently skilled to do it himself.) The services rendered for Liszt would, of course, prove immensely valuable to Raff when it came to composing his own orchestral works. Given this stylistically split background, it is not at all surprising that Raff in his symphonies usually mixes equal parts traditional symphonic structure and avant-garde programmatic music (of the tone-poem sort). Though the unintegrated eclecticism found in the symphonies was the trait that contributed most to the later decline in Raff's reputation, he did influence the composers who shaped the most important orchestral genre of the second half of the nineteenth century, the symphonic poem. Raff's own musical language and syntax are of the warm, middle-Romantic type, and, whatever else might be said about the symphonies, the orchestration is always skillful and often splendid.

Eleven Joachim Raff symphonies have come down to us; 12, however, is the number that he actually composed during his lifetime—the "missing" symphony is an early effort in E minor from 1854, either destroyed or lost. The last four symphonies, composed during a three-year period, make up a four-sided tone poem about the seasons, spring, summer, fall, and winter in order. The 11 are:

No. 1 in D major "An das Vaterland," Op. 140 (1861)
No. 2 in C major Op. 140 (1866)
No. 3 in F major "Im Walde," Op. 153 (1869)
No. 4 in G minor Op. 167 (1871)
No. 5 in E major "Lenore," Op. 177 (1872)
No. 6 in D minor Op. 189 (1873)
No. 7 in B flat major "In den Alpen," Op. 201 (1875)
No. 8 in A major "Frühlingsklänge," Op. 205 (1876)
No. 9 in E minor "Im Sommer," Op. 208 (1878)
No. 10 in F minor "Zur Herbstzeit," Op. 213 (1879)
No. 11 in A minor "Der Winter," Op. 214 (1876–79) *—Blair Johnston*

Recommended:

○ **Raff: Symphonies 3 & 4** / Milton Keynes City Orch., Wetton (cond.) / 1999 / Hyperion 55017

Konrad Ragossnig

b. 1932, Klagenfurt, Austria
Guitarist

Konrad Ragossnig has wide and varying musical interests, recording and publishing music for both guitar and lute. He studied in Vienna with Karl Scheit and won the Concours International de Guitar in Paris in 1961. He then began touring, performing with orchestras throughout Europe and with chamber ensembles such as the Barchet Quartet Stuttgart, Berner String Quartet, Lucerne Festival Strings, Kyndel String Quartet Stockholm, and the Prague String Quartet. He enjoys playing chamber works where the guitar has been neglected, such as in Schubert's *Die schöne Müllerin*, which he has performed with Peter Schreier at the Salzburg Festival. Other artists he has worked with include flutists Hans-Martin Linde, Aurèle Nicolet, and Peter-Lukas Graf; tenors Kurt Equiluz and Ian Partridge; cellist Marek Jerie; and his son, harpsichordist Thomas Ragossnig. Ragossnig is frequently found at music festivals in cities around the world, including Vienna, Ansbach, Berlin, Luxembourg, Paris, and Osaka. From 1964 until 1983 Ragossnig taught at Basel, and then took on a professorship in Vienna. He has also been a guest professor in Zürich and teaches master classes in conjunction with many of his performances in other countries. His repertoire ranges from Renaissance lute music to contemporary guitar music, and he has premiered works by two dozen composers, such as Hans Erich Apostel, Mario Castelnuovo-Tedesco, Friedrich Cerha, Hans Werner Henze, and Pierre Wissmer. In addition to teaching and performing, he has edited and had published over 70 scores of lute and guitar music, ranging from basic technique to arrangements of works such as Falla's *Suite Populaire Espagnole* (arranged for cello and guitar), and performing editions of works like Bach's *Fugue for Lute*, BWV 1000. His recordings are found on a number of labels and have won the Grand Prix du disque and Edison awards. His Archiv recording *Musik für Laute* was chosen as "Guitar and Lute Music Record of the Century" by the German magazine, *Fono Forum*. *—Patsy Morita*

Recommended:

○ **Schreier & Ragossnig perform Dowland, Schütz, von Einem & Schubert** / Ragossnig, Schreier (guitar) / Capriccio 10047

○ **Spanische Gitarre Musik** / Ragossnig / Claves 500806

○ **Dances from Spain & Latin America** / Ragossnig, Feybli (guitar) / 1992 / Christophorus 22

○ **Dances of the Renaissance** / Ulsamer, Neumeyer (conds.), Ragossnig, Ulsamer-Collegium, Terpsichore Collegium / 2000 / DG 469244

Jean-Philippe Rameau

b. Sep. 25, 1683, Dijon, France, **d.** Sep. 12, 1764, Paris, France
Composer: Keyboard, Chamber Music, Opera, Ballet

Jean-Philippe Rameau was one of the truly multifaceted musicians of his day. Acclaimed for his innovative and popular operas, he was also known as one of the greatest organists in France, and his theoretical writings continue to influence musical thinkers over two centuries later.

Although his father was a professional organist, Rameau was expected to pursue a career in the law. However, he was musically very precocious, teaching himself several instruments and the basics of harmony and composition. After spending more time on music than on his studies at the Jesuit College in Dijon (1693–97), Rameau was removed from school; only when he was 18 did his parents give in to his wishes for a musical career. He went to Italy for a few months, and spent some time playing violin in a travelling French opera troupe. Then he took organist posts in Clermont-Ferrand (1702–05), Paris (1705–08), Dijon (1709–14), Lyons (1714–15), and Clermont again (1715–22).

Rameau had begun composing for the harpsichord, publishing his first book of keyboard works in 1706 (subsequent volumes appeared in 1724, 1728, and 1741). He had also written a few motets and secular cantatas, and had started his first book, the *Traité de l'harmonie* (published 1722), which later made his reputation as an important theorist.

Hoping for greater fame as a composer, he moved to Paris in late 1722; there he took on some private students and composed numerous keyboard and short stage works. Eventually, he came to the attention of the financier and courtier Le Riche de la Pouplinière, who hired Rameau as conductor of his orchestra (a position he held for some 22 years) and allowed him and his family to live in his mansion.

Through La Pouplinière, Rameau also met many of the great writers of his day, including some who later became librettists for his operas.

Rameau produced his first opera, *Hippolyte et Aricie* (1733), at the age of 50. The work wasn't well received initially, but the opera *Castor et Pollux* (1737) was much more successful, and Rameau gradually became known as one of France's leading composers. For the rest of his life, he divided his time between composing and writing further theoretical works like *Nouveau système de musique théorique* (1726), *Dissertation sur les differents méthodes d'accompagnement pour le clavecin ou pour l'orgue* (1732), and *Démonstration du principe de l'harmonie* (1750). He felt his theoretical works were at least as important as his music, and defended his theories in extensive correspondences and debates with many of the leading musical thinkers in Europe.

In 1745, he was appointed composer of the King's chamber music. He continued writing operas, both tragic works like *Dardanus* (1739, rev. 1744) and comedies like *Platée* (1745) and *La Princesse de Navarre* (1745). These and his other operas and incidental music (he wrote about 30 stage works in all) were noteworthy for their expanded harmonic palate, their brilliant choruses and ballets, and the prominent role Rameau gave to the orchestra. But not everyone admired his music, and for years a bitter public rivalry existed between the Rameau partisans and the "Lullistes," who preferred the somewhat more conservative works of Jean-Baptiste Lully. Rameau also had to defend his musical style in the "War of the Buffoons" of 1752 against those who preferred the lighter Italian operas of composers like Giovanni Battista Pergolesi.

Four months before his death, Rameau was granted a patent of nobility by King Louis XV. He died just before his 81st birthday, and was buried at his parish church at St. Eustache. *—Chris Morrison*

KEYBOARD

Pièces de clavecin (1706–1727)

Rameau's *Pièces de clavecin* are equal to those of François Couperin in their importance to the history of literature for keyboard. Rameau completed 25 pieces in five suites, published in three books between 1706 and 1728. The suites are based on French dances, just as Couperin's are, and in the later suites also contain pieces of a descriptive nature. The final book, *Nouvelles suites de pièces de clavecin*, contains the kernels of the emerging sonata form. Rameau also meant to teach certain techniques with the pieces, such as hand-crossing. In more than one of the suites, he reused melodies from his stage works, such as *Les Indes galantes*. Overall, the character of the suites is more Baroque than Couperin's suites, featuring more complex textures; more regular, driving rhythms; and more pronounced accents. *—Patsy Morita*

Recommended:

- ○ **Bach, Rameau: Works for Harpsichord** / Fuller / 2002 / Reference 2105

Nouvelles suites de pièces de clavecin (1727)

Although principally known as a dramatic composer, Jean-Philippe Rameau also made a substantial contribution to the French keyboard repertoire, an important Baroque genre that reached its highest point in the harpsichord works of François Couperin. Like most of the output of the French clavecinistes, Rameau's harpsichord works were gathered into collections generally arranged in books according to key. There are three such major collections in the instance of Rameau; the *Premier livre de pièces de clavecin* (1706), the *Pièces de clavecin* (1724), and the present anthology, published around 1729. The *Nouvelles suites de pièces de clavecin* includes 15 pieces. Like all French keyboard works, they are notable for such characteristic devices as the broken chord (stile brisé) taken over by French keyboard composers from the influential school of early seventeenth century lutenists. Also highly characteristic are the lavishly decorated melodic lines, based on a code of ornamentation illustrated in didactic prefaces by composers such as d'Anglebert and Couperin. As in all three of Rameau's collections, the pieces are divided between the binary (two-part) dance movements of the Baroque suite and the character pieces unique to French instrumental music. The present collection is headed by three dance movements: an Allemande, a Courante, and a Sarabande (worthy of special mention as one of Rameau's noblest conceptions), and also includes a Gavotte et doubles (variations) and a pair of Minuets. The descriptive character or genre pieces sometimes have intriguing titles, the original meaning of which cannot always be determined. The *Nouvelles suites* includes ten such pieces, among them one of the composer's most famous keyboard works, *L'enharmonique*. It takes it name from the striking enharmonic modulation just after the start of the second half, reminding listeners that the composer was also an outstanding theorist whose *Traite d'harmonie* (Treatise on Harmony) was one of the most influential pedagogical publications of the eighteenth century. Another popular piece here is *La poule*, which graphically imitates the clucking of a hen in the most ingenious fashion. The contemporary vogue for the exotic is not ignored, either, as the inclusion of pieces entitled *Les sauvages* and *L'égyptienne* clearly illustrates. The first seven pieces of the anthology are grouped around A major and A minor, while the remainder are centered on G major and G minor. A number of Rameau's keyboard works were later orchestrated and reused in his operas, an example being the Sarabande, which later found its way into the third act of *Zaroastra* (1749). *—Brian Robins*

Recommended:

- ○ **The Masters of the French Harpsichord** / Christie / HM 2908060
- ○ **Harpsichord Works of Rameau** / Hashimoto / 2002 / Centaur 2579

Pièces de clavecin avec une méthode sur la mécanique des doigts (1724)

There is good reason to believe that Rameau did not assemble his two collections, respectively published in 1724 and 1728, over a long period. In 1723 he was still composing operas, but also found time for the harpsichord.

At first sight the ten movements of the E minor suite, the first in this earlier collection, are arranged as an eighteenth century French "Concert"—an Allemande, a Courante, two Gigues, two Rigaudons, a couple of "character" pieces, a Musette en rondeau, and a Tambourin. Girdlestone, Rameau's biographer, suggests that at least four movements—the two Rigadouns, Musette, and Tambourin—were derived from his opera-ballet *L'Endriague* (1723). (Rameau used the Musette and Tambourin yet again in 1739 in another opera-ballet, *Les fêtes d'Hébé*). All have an upbeat lilt, and even the courtly dances possess a hip-swaying, foot-tapping vivacity that takes them out of the salon and into the theater. "La Rappel des Oiseaux" and Rondeau "La Villageoise" are as fresh, intricate and colorful as petit-point needlework.

The second suite in the 1724 collection, the D major, could almost be called "themes from the classics" insofar as it replaces the traditional dance movements with illustratively titled movements. The mixture includes tunes derived from Rameau's theater works—"L'Entretien des Muses" from *Les fêtes d'Hébé*, "Les tendre plaints" and "Sarabande" from *Zoroastre*, "Les nais de Sologne" with doubles (variations) from *Dardanus*, and others, such as the popular *Les Indes Galantes*. The French rondeau is favored in five of the 12 movements. The effect is that of a finely proportioned, and by no means a random, group of divertissements. Rameau's raids on his own melodies are not particularly significant in the light of these sparkling keyboard transformations, though they were noticed by one contemporary critic who drew a caricature of the composer surrounded by harpsichord pieces marked "for use in new operas." *—Roy Brewer*

Recommended:

- ○ **Rameau: Harpsichord Pieces** / Yates / 2000 / Chandos 659
- ○ **L'Émergence instrumentale** / Christie / HM 2908001/11

CHAMBER MUSIC

Pièces de clavecin en concerts, for harpsichord, violin & viola da gamba (1741)

The "premier concert" from Jean-Phillippe Rameau's *Pièces de clavecin en concerts* was first published at Paris in 1741. It is the first in a series of five suites written for solo harpsichord with optional parts for violin or flute and violoncello or viol. Rameau was a prolific composer of opera and solo harpsichord music; however, these five suites represent his only contribution to the form of chamber music.

Contrary to the typical French suite of the period, which consist of six or seven movements, Rameau's "concerts" are short, consisting of only three to five pieces per suite. Rather than being titled in accordance with the names of dance steps, the *Pièces* are labeled with descriptive titles that are often rather obscure in their meaning. *Le Coulicam* is widely interpreted as meaning The Kubla Khan, or may be an anagram for something less delicate. It alternates drooping and leaping figures over a wide compass in the accompanying instruments, while the harpsichord keeps going on a continuous stream of notes. *La Livri* is the best known of the three pieces in the set; it was likely dedicated to the Count of Livri and features a falling progression that, though typically French and of the period, is not unlike similar gestures heard in popular music of the 1960s. The final movement, *La Vézinet*, likely refers to the Vézinet Wood once located about a mile from St. Germain de Paris; its lively rhythms and joyous spirit could indicate children at play.

The immediacy and charm of this short suite have led to its status as a favored filler item for classical music radio programs in the United States. Nonetheless, the "premier concert" of Rameau's *Pièces de clavecin en concerts* has long been known to lovers of chamber music as a standard recital work, and before the period instrument boom of the 1980s was often played in its alternate scoring of flute, cello, and keyboard. *—Uncle Dave Lewis*

Recommended:

- ○ **Rameau: Pièces de clavecin en concerts** / Rousset, Terakado, Uemura / HM 901418
- ○ **Rameau: Pièces de clavecin en concerts** / Bruggen, Leonhardt, S. & W. Kuijken / 1992 / Teldec 77618

OPERA

Castor et Pollux (1737)

Castor et Pollux was the brilliant success of the Paris Opera in 1754. Its success followed heated debate over the future of the French opera, debate which Rameau had initiated with his production of *Hippolyte et Aricie*. Although Rameau wrote in the traditional forms handed down by Lully, he was seen as too revolutionary and as a betrayer of French tastes. Rameau's operas are traditional tragédies-lyriques in the style of Lully. They contain a prologue and five acts, and a grand divertissement in each act. Rameau uses ballet, shimmering homophonic choruses, *dei ex machina*, and mythological and magical characters. But Rameau's harmonies are much more adventuresome than Lully's and show Italian influences. Rameau is an original and creative orchestrator; traces of Vivaldi can be heard in portions of *Castor et Pollux*, and his winds are given special prominence. His characters are deeply drawn and dramatically riveting. The emotions they feel are not godlike, but extremely human. After *Hippolyte et Aricie*, the Lullistes and the Ramistes began a heated debate over the merits of traditional French music, and the new style of Rameau. Jean-Jacques Rousseau joined the fray, and may have helped Rameau's cause, for he denigrated French music at the expense of Italian to such a degree that Rameau was begun to be seen as a champion of French tastes. When *Castor et Pollux* premiered, it was acclaimed a masterpiece by all.

Among Rameau's contributions to the genre of tragédies-lyriques were his inclusion of large orchestral numbers, and his treatment of the orchestra generally. In the orchestral accompaniments to his vocal music, he composes descriptive music, or music that greatly enhances the mood, ambience, and even the locale of the scene. In Act Five of *Castor et Pollux*, the wind whips up a storm, and the strings are heard playing furioso storm music that takes the form of Vivaldi-esque tremolandi. The chords in the wind instruments add to the stormy feel of the scene. As Jupiter descends and the storm abates, bassoons are heard piercing through the orchestra texture. Rameau is known to have written especially well for the bassoon, and to have expanded its range.

In keeping with French operatic tastes, Rameau writes no da capo arias in *Castor et Pollux*. Instead, the arias flow in and out of the dramatic recitative. There are several numbers that come close to the Italian conception of an aria. "Ariette," in Act Five, is in the da capo form, and written as part of a divertissement to be sung by one of the planets.

The libretto of *Castor et Pollux* was written by P.J. Gentil-Bernard, an author who enjoyed the distinction of being admired by Voltaire. He altered the original story slightly. In the original, Castor et Pollux are both the sons of Leda and Zeus, and are, therefore, both immortal. In Gentil-Bernard's version, Castor's father is a mortal, and only because of Castor's selfless love for his brother does Zeus make him immortal as well. In mythology, *Castor et Pollux* were made the morning and evening stars, and thus were a guide to sailors, as well as symbols of courage. *—Rita Laurance*

Synopsis:

Prologue. The story is set in ancient Sparta and in the Elysian Fields. Ruins and military encampments are seen, as Venus and Cupid are asked by Minerva to restore peace by putting Mars under the spell of love. Mars quickly acquiesces and peace reigns.

Act One. The scene opens at the burial grounds of the Spartan Kings. The citizens are mourning the death in battle of Castor, son of Tyndareus and Leda. Telaira, daughter of the Sun, is devastated at the loss of her lover. She confides her suffering in Phoebe, a Spartan Princess, who is in love with Pollux, the immortal brother of Castor. Pollux enters, accompanied by soldiers and athletes, who bring in the body of Lyncaeus, the one responsible for Castor's death. Their declarations of victory are tempered by memories of Castor. When he is alone with Telaira, Pollux asks her to accept him now as her lover in place of his deceased brother. She is startled, but sees this as an opportune moment, asking Pollux to petition Jupiter to bring Castor back to life.

Act Two. Pollux deliberates Telaira's appeal at the entrance of Jupiter's temple. Telaira arrives, and a short while later Jupiter appears. After initially refusing Pollux's request to restore Castor to life, he finally grants it, but with the costly proviso that Pollux trade places with Castor. He agrees, and remains steadfast in his decision even after Hebe, goddess of eternal youth, is summoned to sway him.

Act Three. Phoebe confronts Pollux at the entrance way to Hades and declares that if he goes forth into the underworld, she will follow him. She is further disheartened to learn of his love for Telaira. Pollux, Telaira, and Phoebe stand at the entranceway now as hellish demons appear. The first two drive them off, while the dispirited Phoebe exhorts them. Mercury soon appears, banishes the demons, and takes Pollux with him to Hades.

Act Four. Castor has known little peace in Elysium and misses his life as a mortal in Sparta. Soon Pollux appears and the brothers are overjoyed to see each other. But Castor is disturbed when he learns both of Pollux's love for Telaira and his brother's sacrifice to trade places with him. Castor is reluctant to return under those circumstances, but finally agrees to do so, but only for a day, after which he will reenter Hades and set Pollux free.

Act Five. Telaira and Castor are ecstatic at their reunion, while Phoebe is enraged. When Castor reveals his restoration is only for a day, Telaira is crushed and cannot persuade him to change his mind. Jupiter appears suddenly to announce, first, that Destiny is fully satisfied with the brothers now, and second, that Castor is empowered with immortality. Pollux arrives on the happy scene and repudiates feelings of love for Telaira, thus allowing the pair a happy reunion. But he also divulges the unfortunate fate of Phoebe, who is now in Hades. The ending is glorious, as the gods gather around Olympia's temple in the heavens, with the brothers assuming positions in the Zodiac and Telaira in the firmament. *—Robert Cummings*

Recommended:

- ○ **Rameau: Castor et Pollux** / Christie (cond.), Padmore, Gens, Crook, Piau, Schirrer, Les Arts Florissants / HM 901435
- ○ **Rameau: Castor et Pollux** / Frisch (cond.), Cantor, Goubioud, Correas, Vinson, Musique Des Lumieres / 1998 / Astree 8624

Dardanus (1739; revised 1744)

Jean-Philippe Rameau's *Dardanus* is typical of his works for the operatic stage: it contains innovative music of great inspiration and dramatic sensitivity, and it caused a public controversy at the time of its premiere. Rameau, who was a respected theorist and writer as well as a composer, employed harmonic devices, orchestrations, and a range of emotional expression that some listeners found grotesque, especially those who favored the works of his predecessor, Jean-Baptiste Lully. Lully's works were more typical of the period than were those of Rameau, especially in their relatively understated orchestrations and use of secco (dry) recitative—done with only keyboard accompaniment. For those who valued tradition over innovation, Rameau's work—full of dramatic instrumentation and accompanied recitatives (performed with orchestra)—was simply too adventuresome and, although Rameau's more forward-looking style would eventually win out, the conflict between the supporters of Rameau and Lully makes for one of opera history's more colorful chapters.

Based on Greek mythology, the libretto, by Charles-Antoine Leclerc de La Bruère, tells the story of Jupiter's son, *Dardanus*, and his war with The king of Phrygia. Bruère's libretto represents opera seria at both its most grand and its most absurd: the numerous processions, dream scenes and intrigues brought out the best in Rameau's dramatic writing, but the plot was so laden with supernatural events and interventions that it became a caricature of itself. For this reason, *Dardanus* was a less-than-spectacular success at its premiere (Paris Opéra, November, 1739), and underwent at least two extensive revisions, the first of which completely discarded the last three acts. Subsequent versions placed a greater emphasis on human relationships and simplified the plot—steps that were necessary for the sake of clarity and cohesion, but which also involved the removal of excellent music. Modern revivals of *Dardanus* have attempted to find an effective middle ground, keeping as much as possible of Rameau's colorful writing while trimming the plot into a coherent form—often with great success. *—AMG*

Synopsis:

Act One. Near the tombs of the Phyrgians who have been killed in the war with Dardanus, Iphise laments that she has fallen in love with Dardanus ("Cesse, cruel amour") and is unable to conquer her feelings. Even contemplating those he has killed makes him seem more glorious. Teucer comes in to tell her that Antenor has agreed to help them fight Dardanus and asks for her hand. She avoids either agreeing or refusing, and Antenor and Teucer swear revenge and pray for the gods' help. Their warriors enter, and pray for the protection of the gods of war, though some also comment that victory in love is still more pleasant than victory in war ("Mars, Belonne, guidez"). Iphise resolves to find Ismenor and ask for his help.

Act Two. In the wilderness Ismenor sings of his powers to see the secrets of the universe ("Tout l'avenir est present"). Dardanus enters, and Ismenor warns him that he is in a hostile land. Dardanus tells him he is in love with Iphise, and says he has heard she is coming to Ismenor, and he wants to at least see her. Ismenor responds that even if Iphise could bring herself to love him, Teucer would never agree to their marriage. Dardanus says if she returned his feelings, he would give up everything he has won in the battle and ask for her hand as a gesture of peace. Ismenor agrees to help and offers Dardanus magical assistance. He calls upon his mystical assistants, and they and he perform a spell that makes Dardanus appear to be Ismenor, and give Dardanus a magical wand to control the illusion. Ismenor warns him that if he lets go of the wand, he will be in grave danger, not only from earthly powers, but the anger of the underworld spirits who helped create the spell, as they resent a spell that helps love ("Nos cris ont penetre"). Antenor appears and consults Dardanus, in the guise of Ismenor, and Dardanus can barely restrain himself when Antenor speaks of his approaching wedding. He starts to predict the outcome of the battle, but Antenor stops him, he will learn by fighting, not magical means; what he wants to know is whether he has a rival for Iphise's love. Dardanus tries to find out whom Antenor suspects, but Iphise herself appears, asking him to help rid her of her love for a mortal enemy. She is reluctant even to name the man, but Dardanus makes her do so ("D'un penchant si fatal"). He fervently tells her that she should cherish this love, as it is fully returned, and finally drops the wand so she can see who he is. She is overwhelmed by conflicting emotions and flees. A crowd enters, recognizes him, and put him in chains.

Act Three. In Teucer's palace, Iphise is weeping that not only does she love Dardanus despite herself, but that he will be killed ("O jour affreux"). Antenor enters, convinced he must have a rival, but still deeply in love, and says they will be married that day. She protests saying that war is still causing havoc and it is no time to speak of love ("Les horreurs de la guerre"). He tells her that since Dardanus is their prisoner, there is nothing to fear, but if it would reassure her, he will immediately ask Teucer to have him killed. She says it would be a detestable crime, and he angrily tells her he sees that she is in love with Dardanus. He says he has lost all hope of happiness ("Le desespoir et la rage"), but at least when she belongs to him, she will be as unhappy as he. The chorus enters, singing joyously of how war is over and pleasure can return, but Teucer enters, warning them that Zeus, angry that his son has been put in chains, has made Neptune send a wild sea monster to ravage the land. Antenor offers to fight it.

Act Four. Dardanus laments his fate ("Lieux funestes"). Ismenor enters and says that Dardanus' act has made him lose his powers, but urges him to plead to Love to help. He does so ("Amour, Amour") and falls asleep, and Venus appears. She sings to the power of dreams to break his chains ("Venez, songes"). The chorus and a trio of dreams sing of the power of Love and urge him to continue sleeping. One of the dreams carries him to the shore where the monster is wreaking havoc. Antenor enters, saying that if he could choose for himself, he would let the monster devour him, as love is even more pitiless and fearsome. He fights it and is about to be killed, when Dardanus appears. Dardanus kills it, and Antenor asks who he is. When Dardanus refuses, Antenor gives him his sword in gratitude, saying he will grant him any wish he might ask. Dardanus demands that he give up Iphise. Antenor pleads to be killed instead, but Dardanus reminds him he is now bound by honor, not love.

Act Five. In Teucer's palace the chorus and Teucer celebrate the victory, which they think belongs solely to Antenor. Neptune, Teucer announces, has agreed that Iphise may marry the man who defeated the monster. Antenor bursts out in despair. Dardanus enters and tells Antenor to kill him, and hands him the sword. Antenor recognizes it and yields his claim to Dardanus. Venus appears and calls upon the pleasures to sing in celebration of Love's victory ("Plaisirs, chantez"), and the chorus, Dardanus, Iphise, and Teucer sing her praises. *—Ann Feeney*

Recommended:

○ **Rameau: Dardanus** / Minkowski (cond.), Ainsley, Gens, Kozena, Courtis, Les Musiciens Du Louvre / 2000 / Archiv 463476

Hippolyte et Aricie (1733)

Hippolyte was the first tragédie-lyrique composed by Jean-Philippe Rameau. He had already established himself as an innovative thinker in the field of music theory and harmony, and had published four books of harpsichord pieces. But at the age of 50, his dreams still had not come true. He wanted to compose operas, and he was to become as well known an innovator in the field of opera as he was in theory.

His librettist was the Abbe Pellegrin. Voltaire's work had recently been banned, and perhaps a clergyman was a wise choice for a librettist. But Pellegrin also gave Rameau a viable libretto on an ancient theme. The story of Hippolyte was well known to the French public, for it had been turned into a successful tragedy by the playwright Racine in very recent times. Racine had turned the story into a psychological study of jealousy and guilt, and Hippolyte's mother Phaedra was the central character in his plot. Rameau and Pellegrin were to make her counterpart, Theseus, one of the most memorable figures in all of operatic history. Theseus is a strong, vigorous, monumental hero, and the music Rameau gives him is likewise vital and heroic.

Rameau believed that all melody came from harmony. This greatly affected his writing, for his melodies are harmonically adventuresome, expressive, and plastic. He loved enharmonic modulations, as well as chromatic and diatonic modulations, and he was to try these on his unsuspecting French public. In the second act, Theseus descends into Hell to search for his lost friend, and is confronted by the Furies and the Fates. The second "Trio of Fates," in which they call forth Pluto's fury upon him, contains enharmonic modulations that the French musicians found too difficult to perform. The modulations happen rapidly, and pass through five keys in five measures. Rameau was forced to drop the passage because the orchestral players couldn't play it, but he made sure that it appeared in its original form when the score was published.

Hippolyte et Aricie is probably Rameau's most vigorous opera. It contains a great deal of action, a powerful hero, and many contrasts and extremes of emotion. The passions that tear apart Theseus and Phaedra and bring about their tragic downfall are nothing short of barbaric. There are five marches in the opera, and several choruses made up of active crowds. There are the fighting demons at the gates of Hell in the opening divertissement of Act Two, there is Pluto's court, as it tries Theseus, the groups of Furies and Fates who hound him, and the subjects of Theseus who rejoice jubilantly at his safe return. There are interventions by the gods Diana and Mercury, as well as invocations to Neptune on the part of the struggling Theseus. Hippolyte and Aricie provide a gentle contrast with all the mayhem, as does the *deus ex machina* of Diana which saves them. The extremes are reflected in the music, which, for the times, was filled with unusual dissonance and expressive powers. *—Rita Laurance*

Synopsis:

Prologue. The setting: ancient Sparta and various Greek mythological locales. In the forest of Erymanthus, Jupiter decides that Diana, goddess of chastity, must allow Cupid to have dominion over her forests for one day each year, in accordance with Destiny's decree. Diana accepts the pronouncement, but vows to defend Hippolytus and Aricia.

Act One. In the Temple of Diana, Aricia prepares to embrace a celibate life, following orders given by Theseus, who has usurped her father's throne in Athens. Aricia secretly loves his son, Hippolytus, who soon reveals his love for her. Phaedra, Theseus' wife and stepmother to Hippolytus, arrives to oversee the ceremony. When Aricia becomes hesitant to carry out the vows of chastity, Phaedra turns suspicious that she loves Hippolytus. She orders her guards to destroy the temple. The priestesses call on the gods to intercede; Diana descends to protect Aricia and Hippolytus.

Arcas, Theseus' attendant, reports that Theseus is apparently forever lost in Hades, having tried to rescue his friend, Peirithous, attempted kidnapper of Pluto's wife. Oenone, Phaedra's confidant, advises her that she, now a widow, is free to pursue Hippolytus.

Act Two. The Fury Tisiphone prevents Theseus from entering Hades to save Peirithous. In his court, Pluto announces that Theseus, as an accomplice of Peirithous, must also be punished. Theseus soon realizes he is doomed and petitions Neptune to intervene. Mercury descends and convinces Pluto to allow Neptune to save his son. Theseus is allowed to leave, but is warned by the Fates that, although he now departs hell, hell will plague him in his home.

Act Three. In her husband's palace, Phaedra plans to confess her love to Hippolytus. When he arrives she offers him the throne, but he declines it and expresses interest only in Aricia. In her sudden anger, Phaedra reveals that Aricia is a rival for his love. Hippolytus is shocked and Phaedra then realizes she has no chance with him. She asks him to stab her and he refuses. She then attempts to use his sword on herself, but he takes it from her.

Theseus enters and after demanding an explanation for the altercation, Oenone accuses Hippolytus of attempting to rape Phaedra. Theseus remembers the Fates' warning. A crowd of supporters interrupt the proceedings to celebrate Theseus' return. Theseus prays to Neptune, asking for vengeance against his son for his unspeakable act. As a sign his prayer has been heard, the sea rages.

Act Four. In a sacred wood of Diana, Hippolytus, committed to silence about the incident, laments his fate—he is to be banished. He asks Aricia to accompany him as his wife. The two then renew their love for each other, and soon a group of hunters arrives to give praise to Diana and to invite the young pair to join them in their sport. A monster, sent by Neptune, suddenly appears amid flames and smoke and makes Hippolytus disappear. Aricia faints; soon Phaedra arrives, guilt-stricken, and confesses the truth.

Act Five. The dying Phaedra has now confessed to Theseus, who is prevented from drowning himself in the sea by Neptune. The latter divulges that Hippolytus is alive, owing to the intercession of Diana. But Theseus must be punished for his rashness in the matter: he is denied ever seeing his son again. In her forest Aricia grieves over losing Hippolytus. Diana appears to announce a new king to rule over her dominion, then commands zephyrs to fetch Hippolytus. The two lovers are then reunited. *—Robert Cummings*

Recommended:

○ **Rameau: Hippolyte et Aricie** / Christie (cond.), Agnew, Hunt, Padmore, Berg, Les Arts Florissants / Erato 063015517

Les Paladins (1760)

Les Paladins was the last of Rameau's theatrical works to reach the stage, succeeded only by the unstaged *Les Boréades* of 1763. For it the 76-year-old composer returned to the three-act comédie-lyrique, a genre he had essayed only once previously in his *Platée* of 1745. It was first performed at the Paris Opéra on February 12, 1760. The libretto is written by an anonymous author, but attributed to Duplat de Monticourt, who padded out a story by La Fontaine, itself based on Ariosto's epic *Orlando Furioso.* The plot, described by Rameau's great biographer Girdlestone as "impossibly intricate," is set in medieval Venetia and includes all the ingredients of a chivalric tale: a knight-errant, a damsel in distress who is kept locked up in a castle by a wicked, if cowardly jailer, fairies and furies, magic transformations, and a fairy-tale castle in exotic Chinese style. Although the libretto includes its serious elements, all the characters are essentially comic, a feature which undoubtedly contributed, along with the poor quality of the libretto, to the work's failure at the time of its first performance. Audiences for French lyric theater were not accustomed to so much comedy mixed with seriousness, an issue that was currently being articulated in Paris by the famous conflict between the adherents of French opera and those favoring Italian comic opera. After only 15 performances, *Les Paladins* was dropped from the repertoire, not to reemerge until 200 years later, when it was revived at the 1967 Lyons Festival. It was then that the verve of the septuagenarian Rameau's astonishingly youthful score was recognized for the first time. Particularly striking is the orchestration, brilliant even by the composer's own exalted standards, especially in its thrilling use of the horns, which appear prominently in the overture and eight other numbers, and the highly original use of piccolos and bassoons in their higher register. For Girdlestone the return to life of "this unique little masterpiece" represented the single most sensational result of last century's Rameau revival. *—Brian Robins*

Recommended:

- ○ **Rameau: Les Paladins** / Leonhardt (cond.), Orch. of the Age of Enlightenment / 1992 / Philips 432968
- ○ **Rameau: Les Paladins** / Malgoire (cond.), Le Grande Ecurie et la Chambre du Roy / 1998 / Disques Pierre Verany 730094

Platée ou Junon jalouse (1745)

Rameau was either a brave musician or a fool; a work that might easily be interpreted as a mockery of its dedicatees could easily have been the undoing of its creator. *Platée* was composed for the wedding celebration of the French Dauphin and the Infanta of Spain, Maria Theresa, in 1745. Maria Theresa was almost universally recognized as unattractive; the primary character of *Platée*, who happens to be the bride in a mock wedding, is a vain, ugly marsh-nymph. Suprisingly, however, the possible comparison between the plot of the opera and the occasion for which it was composed drew little, if any, contemporary notice, and certainly no criticism; in fact, Rameau was shortly thereafter appointed "Composer in the King's Music Chamber."

In February 1749, *Platée* began a successful run of public performances at the Académie Royale de Musique. The Paris Opéra staged the work in 1750 with Bellot de Sauvot's revised libretto, and again 1754, after which only the Prologue appeared on concert programs. By 1773, *Platée* had disappeared from both stage and concert hall, not to be revived until the twentieth century.

Rameau fashioned the libretto himself (with the help of Le Valois d'Orville) from Jacque Autreau's epic poem, *Platée, or the Jealousy of Juno*. D'Orville's primary task was to augment the comic elements of the story. Described as a comédie-lyrique, *Platée* is an amalgam of varied styles and forms infused with an element of burlesque. Rameau and d'Orville determined that the comic characters would dress as babies and the serious ones as Greek philosophers. To increase the comic effect, the principal female character, *Platée*, was played by the leading countertenor of the time, Pierre Jelyotte. Onomatopoeic effects abound, most notably in *Platée*'s "dis done pourquoi? Quoi? Quoi?" from the fourth scene of Act One. Here, the repeated, single-syllable words deliberately evoke the croaking of frogs, as do the squawking oboes. Rameau illustrates *Platée*'s lively nature through verbal non sequiturs accompanied by shifts in rhythmic emphasis and rising arpeggios. Sound effects and their integration into the story also play a major role in producing a comic atmosphere. In the third scene of Act Two, Jupiter appears to *Platée* as a donkey, and she mistakes his braying—conveyed by the orchestra—as sighs of love. At this, however, Jupiter turns into in owl and flies off, chased by birds as the orchestra produces the sounds of various feathered animals.

Music, too, is subject to mockery in Act Three, Scene three, in which a test of *Platée*'s patience is set to a lengthy Chaconne; it draws on earlier musical elements of the opera, and includes passages with almost unbearably long soundings of a single chord. The score is filled with instructions to the orchestra regarding unusual techniques, including a representation of tears on the violin produced by sliding the finger on the fingerboard to produce quarter-tones.

Rameau's approach to musical content and structure is also adventurous; some sections go so far as to be seemingly formless, most peculiarly the "duet" in Act Three, Scene eight, which spins out without boundaries or landmarks. Rameau's overture, in a slow-fast format, is more than just a curtain raiser; it contains passages that appear in the opera. *Platée*'s aria "Je m'attendris," from the fourth scene of Act One, features numerous and unpredictable tempo changes and large, humorous leaps in the voice part. Throughout the work, the boundary between recitative and aria is constantly blurred. *—John Palmer*

Synopsis:

Prologue: In a Greek vineyard. Cupid, Momus (the god of ridicule), Thalia (the muse of comedy), and Thespis (the inventor of comedy) plan to teach both mortals and gods a moral lesson by re-creating the scene in which Jupiter rids his wife of her jealous feelings.

Act One. A marsh at the foot of Mount Cithaeron. Mercury descends to Mount Cithaeron to explain to King Cithaeron that the storm his people has just weathered (depicted by the orchestra in the prelude to the act) is the result of Jupiter's annoyance at Juno's behavior. In an attempt to cure Juno of her jealous tendencies, the king concocts a plan: Jupiter will feign interest in the ugly, but exceedingly vain marsh-nymph, Platée. Juno will be embarrassed when she realizes she has flown into a jealous rage for no reason. Platée enters and is sure that Cithaeron's indifference toward her is indicative of his attraction to her. She attempts to win him over, accompanied by frogs. When he does not respond she becomes offended ("Dis donc pourquoi!").

Mercury appears again and tells Platée that Jupiter is mesmerized by Platée's beauty and wants to marry her. Thunder and lightning herald the onset of a storm, the result, Mercury explains, of Juno's anger. Platée becomes defiant, noting that she and other marsh inhabitants will simply enjoy the rain ("Quittez, nymphes, quittez vos demeures profondes"). A divertissiment follows that features more frog noises before another storm segment in which the North Wind, Aquilons, blows the nymphs back into the marsh.

Act Two. Mercury tells Cithaeron that he has convinced Juno that Jupiter is in Athens with another lover. As Juno passes by in a cloud on her way to Athens, Mercury and Cithaeron await Jupiter. After Jupiter arrives in a cloud, Mercury and Cithaeron hide and Platée approaches ("A l'aspect de ce nuage"). Jupiter appears to Platée as a donkey, and she interprets his braying as sighs of love. He then appears as an owl, only to frighten away the nearby birds. Finally, after a burst of fire, he appears as himself, declaring his love for the scared and bewildered Platée. After the comical chorus ("Quelle est aima-a-a-able"), Folly enters with the "fous gais" (dressed as babies) and the "fous tristes" (dressed as Greek philosophers). In an Italian-style aria, Folly relates the story of Apollo and Daphne while playing a lyre she stole from Apollo ("Aux langueurs d'Apollon Daphné se refusa"). Two dances follow, after which Folly calls upon Hymen to bring together Jupiter and his "new Juno." When Platée hears herself referred to as such, she becomes very excited ("He bon, bon, bon!"), and so is the rest of the ensemble.

Act Three. Juno, very angry at not finding her husband, has returned from Athens and is told by Mercury to wait and watch the ceremony that is about to take place. As the chorus sings ("Chantons, célébrons en ce jour"), Platée enters wearing a thick veil and preceded by satyrs, dryads and nymphs. She rides a chariot pulled by frogs, with Mercury and Jupiter on either side of her. Platée then notices that Cupid and Hymen are not at the ceremony, to which Mercury replies that these to gods are rarely found together. Platée's impatience grows (to the accompaniment of a long chaconne) until Momus, dressed as Cupid, finally appears. Blindfolded and carrying a bow and a quiver of arrows, Momus explains that Cupid could not make it to the wedding and gives Platée Cupid's wedding gifts: sorrow, tears, and weeping. Platée rejects these gifts, embarrassing Momus, who is then mocked by Folly in her "Amour, lance tes traits, épuise ton carquois." After three of Momus' followers, dressed as Graces, dance, Jupiter begins reciting the marriage oath to Platée. Juno does not appear immediately, as Jupiter had anticipated, so he is forced to repeat "I swear" several times to avoid finishing the oath. Finally, Juno interrupts the proceedings and tears off Platée's veil. When Juno sees the marsh-nymph she realizes she has been fooled, and Platée rushes off. The gods ascend to the heavens, and Folly is left alone until the local people return with Platée and begin to mock her ("Chantons Platée, égayons-nous"). Platée then seizes Cithaeron around the throat and swears vengeance, but further mockery by the assembled crowd makes her flee into the swamp. Folly and the rest of the ensemble sing the praises of Juno and Jupiter. *—John Palmer*

Recommended:

- ○ **Rameau: Platée** / Minkowski (cond.), Laurens, Ragon, Smith, Deletre, Les Musiciens Du Louvre / 1990 / Erato 45028

Pygmalion, acte de ballet (1748)

Rameau's *Pygmalion* was labeled an *acte de ballet* in its own time; it was the composer's first work to bear that designation. The term denoted a one-act opera with the usual solo numbers, duets, and choruses, interspersed with dance episodes and generally somewhat more pageantlike than plot-driven. It was composed in 1748 to a libretto by Ballot de Savot, an associate of the all-powerful court arts patron La Pouplinière. The story of Pygmalion dates back to Greek and Roman mythology; the sculptor of the title forswears marriage, but then falls in love with his own perfect representation of a woman, beseeching Aphrodite (or Venus) to bring her to life. In Rameau's hands, the story is a sunny romantic comedy. With several famous passages, such as a group of repeated notes in the overture that evoked the sound of the sculptor's chisel, *Pygmalion* become one of Rameau's best-loved works. The opera was performed 30 times in 1748 and was revived to rapturous acclaim three years later. Most significantly, it inspired a musical retort from Jean-Jacques Rousseau, the philosopher and composer whose ideas were chipping away at the foundations of France's monarchical regime. Rousseau's *Pygmalion*, with its spoken dialogue, helped inspire the genre of melodrama and presented a darker view of the *Pygmalion* story and its attendant sexual politics. Thus Rameau's *Pygmalion* in a way has resonated, through Rousseau, George Bernard Shaw's play *Pygmalion*, and the musical *My Fair Lady*, down to our own time. Long forgotten, Rameau's work itself has been recorded several times in recent years, notably by Les Arts Florissants and its conductor, William Christie. *—James Manheim*

Recommended:

- ○ **Rameau: Pygmalion; Melée et Myrthis** / Christie (cond.), Les Arts Florissants / HM 7901381

BALLET

Anacréon (1754)

Anacreon, the Greek poet who sang of love and pleasures of wine, has exerted a strong influence on artists through the ages. He was the subject of two eponymous works by Rameau, both short acts de ballet in one act. The first was originally given at Fontainebleau on October 23, 1754, to a libretto by Cahusac, while the second appeared three years later, when it was added as an appendage to a revival of Rameau's comédie ballet *Les Surprises de l'Amour* given at the Paris Opéra on May 31, 1757. Despite the implications of the terminology, the acte de ballet included sung music in addition to dance; it is therefore akin to a one-act opera.

The earlier *Anacreon* is in fact notable for including fewer dances than are normally encountered in such works, and Rameau's biographer Cuthbert Girdlestone has drawn attention to the high quality of the airs and also the remarkable sequence that opens the work, a ritornello, or rondo-like structure.

The second, and better-known *Anacreon* has a libretto by Pierre-Joseph Bernard (who was also the librettist of Rameau's great tragédie en musique *Castor et Pollux* of 1737) which is constructed with satisfying symmetry. Both the opening and closing sections emphasize the central argument of the plot: Anacreon's assertions that love and drink are mutually compatible. The followers of Bacchus challenge such perceived profanities and a dramatic battle follows in which Anacreon and his cohorts give way to the pleasures of drink. Love now appears to upbraid Anacreon for deserting his lover, Lycoris. Ultimately compromise is reached, the opposed forces agreeing that love and drink can coexist.

While these charming scores may not be among Rameau's greatest works, both contain much enchanting music, the 1757 version quickly taking on a life of its own as an independent work. *—Brian Robins*

Recommended:

○ **Rameau: Anacréon** / Christie (cond.), Feldman, Visse, Schirrer, Mellon, Laplenie, Les Arts Florissants / HM 1901090

Les Indes galantes, opéra-ballet (1735; revised 1743)

Les Indes Galantes (The Gallant Indians) was Rameau's second theatrical work. Termed an opéra-ballet, it was essentially a dance spectacle with sung elements. (The form was descended from the earlier *ballet a entrées* of the French court.) There was more than one kind of opéra-ballet; the more dramatic works were termed *ballets heroïques*, and *Les Indes Galantes* was one of these. It was first given on August 23, 1735, to reviews that both praised and condemned it. Much of the music was quite adventuresome and elicited strong reactions from the Parisian public. The libretto was by Louis Fuzelier, a writer of comedies and a well-known author. The Prologue has a theme taken from mythology, and concerns the universality of Love. Each section or *entrée* is set in an exotic locale and contains a story of an amorous nature.

The exotic locations, while typical of the genre, here point vaguely toward Enlightenment-oriented human universals. Nevertheless, there is plenty of pure spectacle. *Le Turc Genereux* (The Generous Turk) contains a descriptive storm scene, a chorus of sailors, and a ballet by African slaves. The storm music is quite effective, and makes use of Vivaldi-like tremolos and scalar patterns, as well as dramatic key changes.

The Incas' Festival of the Sun is depicted in the second *entrée* in a grand spectacle full of choruses, symphonies, and airs. There is a long scene in which the sun is invoked by the priest Huascar, and the chorus "Brillant Soleil" (Brilliant Sun) is its climax. Although this scene was praised by Voltaire, many found it too new and unusual. The earthquake that follows is described in the orchestra by tremolos, rushing scales, and dissonant harmony, and was considered too difficult to perform. An unusual trio for Phani, Don Carlos, and Huascar is another highlight of this *entrée*; Huascar's voice argues in counterpoint with the two lovers, right before he is vanquished by the eruption of a volcano. The music of this entrée is very dissonant, emotionally sustained, and quite modern.

Les Indes Galantes contained only the first two *entrées* and the Prologue at its premiere. Afterwards, Rameau added *Les Fleurs*, which offers emotional release after so much drama. The dominant element in this *entrée* is the dance; there is no drama, only serene music. The final *Les Sauvages* (The Savages) was added at a much later date. Set in a North American forest, with Native American characters, after an initial amorous story, the main body of the *entrée* is built around the Ceremony of the Pipe of Peace. Much of the music for the ceremony was taken from harpsichord music Rameau had published in 1730, and the entree ends with a chaconne written for the opera *Samson*. *—Rita Laurance*

Synopsis:

Prologue. Hébé, goddess of pleasure, summons her followers to enjoy the pleasures of youth and love ("Vous, qui d'Hébé"), and a group of youths, representing Spain, France, Italy, and Poland enter and dance ("Entre des Quatre Nations"). This is interrupted by the arrival of Bellone, god of war ("La Gloire vous appelle"), summoning the men to the glory of war. Hébé and Amour, the god of love, respond indignantly, but to no avail. Since Europe is no longer friendly to love's pursuits, they will fly to the Indies (used to designate any exotic land) ("Traversez les plus vastes mers").

First scene, Le Turc Généreux (The Generous Turk)

Emile, a Frenchwoman, has been kidnapped and sold to the Pasha Osman, who urges her to accept him. She refuses, saying that she will be faithful to her fiance, Valere, and he leaves, angrily. Other captives come in, and Emile and Valere recognize one another. Osman has been watching and declares that he will punish them. However, he suddenly recognizes Valere. Osman had once been Valere's slave, but was freed, so Osman decides to return the deed by freeing Emile, though he admits that he envies their mutual bliss. He has his slaves bring them rich gifts, and the two lovers call for the winds to calm and carry them back home ("Volez, Zephyres"). The chorus dances and sees them off.

Second scene, Les Incas du Perou (The Incas of Peru)

Phani, an Inca princess, and Carlos, a conquistador, have fallen in love, and she has converted to Christianity for his sake. She warns him that the approaching festival of the sun is celebrated with bloodshed. He leaves, and she longs for their approaching marriage ("Viens, hymen"). Huascar, the Inca high priest who is in love with Phani, tells her that the sun god has selected him as her husband, and when she is reluctant, he declares that they must obey the god without any second thoughts ("Obeissons sans balancer"). The Incas enter for the ceremony and perform their sacred dances. Huascar leads a prayer ("Brillant soleil"). When there is an earthquake and the volcano erupts, Huascar declares that it is the sign of the sun's anger that Phani has not agreed to the selected marriage. She is distraught, but Carlos arrives and reveals that the disturbances have earthly rather than divine causes; some of Huascar's followers have been caught throwing rocks into the mouth of the volcano to force an eruption. Huascar's influence is broken, despite his fury, and the lovers are united ("Pour jamais, l'amour nous engage"). Huascar appeals to the volcano to punish him for his infidelity to his religion, and the volcano spews rocks that crush him.

Third scene, Les Fleurs, Fête persan (The Flowers, a Persian Festival)

In the gardens of the courtier Ali's palace, Tacmas, the prince, has disguised himself as a woman in order to find out whether one of Ali's slaves, Zaire, returns his affection. Ali does not recognize him, but is overjoyed when Tacmas tells him that the prince has no romantic interest in his own slave Fatime. Zaire enters, lamenting her sad fate ("Amour, Amour, quand du destin"), and Tacmas tries to discover whether she is in love with another. He shows her a portrait of himself, but she draws back in shock when he says that it is that of a man who loves her, and he misinterprets this as dismay. Fatime enters, disguised as a man, and confides that she is unhappy in love. Tacmas thinks he has found his rival and is ready to kill her, but she reveals her identity, and Zaire explains that her shock was that of joy, not horror. The two couples swear eternal love ("Tendre amour, que pour nous"), and the festival begins. As dancers portray flowers, Tacmas sings of the scent of the roses ("L'eclat des roses"), and Zaire and Fatime watch a butterfly flutter among the flowers ("Papillon inconstant"). The scene ends with the Ballet of the Flowers, showing a rose saved from the cold winds by a warm breeze.

Fourth scene, Les Sauvages (The Savages)

The French, Spanish, and Native Americans are ready to sign a peace treaty and smoke a peace pipe. Adario, a Native prince, is concerned about the attentions that both the Spanish and French leaders have been paying to the princess Zima, a worry that is entirely justified. The French commander Damon explains to Alvar that in his view, infidelity is by far the happiest course ("L'inconstance ne doit blesser"). Zima enters and explains that her people follow the dictates of nature, and thus lead innocent and happy lives ("Nous suivons sur nos bords"). Damon and the Spanish commander, Alvar, both take this as encouragement, and she goes on further to tell them that her people allow full freedom for their hearts to change their choices until marriage, but after that, they remain faithful. Alvar points out that Frenchmen are notorious for marital infidelity, and Damon retorts that the Spanish keep their wives locked up to assure their fidelity, but place no such guards upon themselves. Zima responds that Alvar loves too much and Damon not enough. Adario enters, and she tells him that they will enjoy a perfectly balanced love ("Sur nos bords l'amour vole"). A ballet follows, the Danse du Grand Calumet de la Paix, celebrating peace and living by nature's simple dictates. Zima calls for pleasure to reign ("Regnez, plaisirs et jeux"). *—Ann Feeney*

Recommended:

○ **Rameau: Les Indes Galantes** / Christie (cond.), Fouchecourt, Poulenard, Crook, Deletre, Les Arts Florissants / HM 901367/9

Les Surprises de l'amour (ca. 1757)

Having been added to, subtracted from, rearranged, and revised many times, this opera with dances is a kind of modular stage work consisting of a (sometimes omitted) prologue with two, three, or four "entrées." The first version was premiered at the Théâtre des Petits-Cabinets à Versailles on November 27, 1748, with a text (consequently often revised) by Pierre-Joseph Gentil-Bernard and consisting of the prologue "Le Retour d'Astrée" and two entrées "La lyre enchantée" and "Adonis." Two other entrées, "Les sibarites" and "Anacréon," were added around 1753.

Within each entrée, a wide variety of dances are interspersed between the various arias, duets, and trios, and choral pieces for muses, nymphs, and/or sylvains. There are minuets, gigues, passepieds, gavottes, sarabands, rondeaux, a ballet *général*, and a Loure pour Terpsichore.

The general style is elegant, mythological, and formal with exchanges such as the following between Urania and the student Linus in "La lyre enchantée":

Linus: "I listen to the birds that sing in the wood, I accompany their songs, imitate their patterns, and to understand their nature instruct my voice to speak their language."

Urania: "Let us take a glorious flight; contemplate the heavens, the earth and the waves with me, measure from the air the fertile quarry of the most brilliant of all the gods."

L'Amour (Cupid) and his fellows resolve in surprising ways the various conflicts which are the theme of each entrée: "Le retour d'Astrée" and "Les sibarites" concern the conflict between states of peace and aggression; "La lyre enchantée" concerns love and indifference; "Adonis" love and chastity; and "Anacréon" the conflict between lovers and wine drinkers, including a thrilling "Combat entre les Bacchantes, Lycoris et les Esclaves d'Anacréon" with wildly churning instrumentation.

"Anacréon" also includes many other splendid effects like the scene "Sommeil lent" (Slow Dream) for flute, two violins, and bass continuo (harpsichord, cello, and bass), which moves chromatically in mostly diminished and minor sixth chords, concluding with a "pluie" (rain) imitation with a sustained high flute note, pizzicato on the violins, and simple bass roots. This is immediately followed by a shocking "Orage" (Thunderstorm) with fast runs and arpeggios, and bass accents in the violas, bassoons, and continuo. Another "Anacréon" highlight is the beautifully written bass aria "Nouvelle Hébé, charmante Lycoris" with its instrumental imitation canon arising from the vocal part and surrounding the voice with glorious contrapuntal melisma and parallel harmonies in Mozartean thirds. —*"Blue Gene" Tyranny*

Recommended:

- ○ **Rameau: Les Surprises de l'Amour** / Minkowski (cond.), Les Musiciens Du Louvre / Erato 45004

Samuel Ramey

b. Mar. 28, 1942, Colby, KS

Bass

Basses are not typically the superstars of the operatic world, but Samuel Ramey is an exception to that rule. Though his voice does not have the sonority of a Nicolai Ghiaurov or a Boris Christoff, his instrument is remarkable for its easy flexibility—dealing effortlessly with long runs, ornaments, and leaps—and its brilliant intensity. His stage presence (particularly when portraying "devil" figures) is vivid and lively, aided by an attractive physique and a dancerlike grace. He and the various stage directors have tended to emphasize these aspects, giving rise to the comment that "Ramey's Mefistofele has everything one could desire, except possibly a shirt."

While he was attending Kansas State University, Ramey's interest in operatic music was awakened when a friend suggested that he audition for a summer program at Colorado's Central City Opera. He was accepted and got to sing in the chorus for two productions. Soon after, he began to study avidly, first at Wichita State University and later in New York with Armen Boyajian; he made his professional debut in 1973 as Zuniga in Bizet's *Carmen* at the New York City Opera. His Glyndebourne debut was in 1976 as Figaro in Mozart's *Le Nozze di Figaro.*

A 1980 performance of Rossini's *Semiramide* at Aix-en-Provence, opposite Monserrat Caballé and Marilyn Horne, made him an overnight sensation. For critics and audience alike, this new bass with the ideal power and agility was a welcome surprise. His La Scala debut came the next year as Mozart's Figaro, followed by his Covent Garden debut in 1982, in the same role. In 1984, he made his Metropolitan debut as Argante in *Rinaldo.* He has been a regular at the Pesaro Rossini Festival. Many Rossini bass roles had become "character parts" over the years—performed more in parlando than actually sung (partly for comedy, partly because of the extreme difficulty of the roles)—and Ramey determined to sing these as written. His instinctive gift for comedy without clownishness has served him well in these parts, as well as in his various diabolical roles, most of which contain a good deal of sardonic humor. He performs arias from his darker roles in his "Date with the Devil" concerts.

Later in his career, as his voice became darker and weightier, Ramey slowly began to drop the florid Rossini and Handel roles in favor of the heavier Verdi roles, such as King Philip in *Don Carlo,* Fiesco in *Simon Boccanegra,* and even Mussorgsky's *Boris Godunov.* He has also performed twentieth century repertoire widely, especially noted for his Reverend Olin Blitch in Floyd's *Susannah* and Nick Shadow in Stravinsky's *The Rake's Progress.*

Ramey is the most recorded bass in history, with dozens of recordings to his credit. These range from nearly all of his operatic roles to solo recordings of arias and song, and even some musical theater. He has appeared on the TV series *Live from Lincoln Center* and in TV and video recordings of many of his roles. —*Ann Feeney*

Recommended:

- ○ **Samuel Ramey** / Ramey, etc. / Decca 448251
- ○ **Floyd: Susannah** / Nagano (cond.), Brossmann, Erlo, Ramey, Hadley, Lyon National Opera Orch. / 1994 / Virgin 45039
- ○ **Rossini: L'Italiana in Algeri** / Scimone (cond.), Horne, Ramey, Battle, Palacio, I Solisti Veneti / Erato 45404
- ○ **Operatic Arias** / Delacote, Rauscher (conds.), Ramey, Weber, Greiner, Munich Radio Orch. / EMI 49582
- ○ **Boito: Mefistofele** / Patane (cond.), Ramey, Domingo, Marton, Takacs, Hungarian State SO / 1990 / Sony 44983

Jean-Pierre Rampal

b. Jan. 7, 1922, Marseilles, France, **d.** May 20, 2000, Paris, France

Flutist

Jean-Pierre Rampal was one of history's greatest flute players, and among the most recorded classical artists of all time. His father was the first flutist of the Marseilles Symphony Orchestra and was professor of flute at the Conservatory there. Although his father taught him to play the flute, he did not recommend a musical career for Jean-Pierre, who instead entered medical studies. He was in the third year of medical study when, in 1943, German occupying forces drafted Rampal for service in the military. He learned that he was, in fact, to be sent to Germany as forced labor. So he went absent without leave and joined the underground, traveling to Paris and assuming a new identity. In Paris, he decided to attend the National Conservatory as a flute student. Five months later he graduated with first prize. Paris was liberated a few months later, and Rampal was appointed first flutist with the Paris Vichy Opéra.

In 1950 Rampal embarked on a touring career. His favored accompanist was Robert Veyron-Lacroix, who could play both piano and harpsichord. Veyron-Lacroix's expertise helped Rampal deepen his performances of music of the eighteenth century—his favorite musical era—by drawing on contemporary performance practices. He eschewed the vibrato and the generally romantic sound of most flute playing, and in so doing he strongly influenced flutists of subsequent generations. In 1956 he joined the orchestra of the Paris Opéra, remaining there through 1962. During this period he appeared frequently on the radio in Paris, gaining great popularity. He taught at the Paris Conservatory and gave master classes around the world.

Rampal was devoted to chamber music, founding the French Wind Quintet (Quintette à Vent Française) in 1945 and the Ensemble Baroque de Paris in 1953. He appeared with every major orchestra, gave recitals worldwide, and recorded prolifically, covering all of the standard flute repertoire and many new and unknown pieces. Several of his recordings have won the Grand Prix du Disques.

Even beyond these endeavors his musical interests were quite diverse: he also appeared on recordings of English folksong, American ragtime, European jazz, and Japanese, Chinese, and Indian classical music. Some of his recording partners were Mstislav Rostropovich, Claude Bolling, Ravi Shankar, and Isaac Stern. Numerous composers wrote works for him, including Francis Poulenc, Pierre Boulez, André Jolivet, and Jean Françaix. His *Music, My Love: An Autobiography* was published in 1989. Rampal received various honors, including elevation to the ranks of Chevalier of the Légion d'Honneur (1996), Officier des Arts et Lettres (1971), Commandeur de l'Ordre National de Mérite. He also received the Prix du Président de la République, and the Prix du Académie Charles Cros. —*Joseph Stevenson*

Recommended:

- ○ **The Essential Jean-Pierre Rampal** / Scimone, Ristenpart (cond.), Rampal, Stern, Rose, Veyron-Lacroix, Jerusalem Music Centre CO, I Solisti Veneti / 2001 / Sony 89736
- ○ **Flute & Harp** / Rampal, Laskine, Pasquier / Erato 45837
- ○ **Japanese Melodies for Flute & Harp** / Rampal, Laskine (harp) / Denon 8115
- ○ **Bach: 3 Concertos for Flute; Sinfonia** / Munclinger, Rampal, Hala, Slama, Posta, Ars Rediviva of Prague / 1990 / CBS 46510
- ○ **Rampal: Encores** / Yamaoka (cond.), Rampal, Tokyo Concert Orch. / 1978 / CBS 34559
- ○ **The Best of Jean-Pierre Rampal** / Rampal, etc. / Erato 93242
- ○ **Romantic Flute Concertos** / Rampal, etc. / 1992 / Erato 45838

Sigurd Rascher

b. May 15, 1907, Elberfeld (Wuppertal), Germany, **d.** Feb. 25, 2001, Shushan, NY

Saxophonist

More than any other classical saxophonist before or since, Sigurd Rascher contributed to the legitimization of an instrument many composers and musicians disliked. With immense fluidity and lovely, rounded tone, Rascher mastered the instrument, giving heretofore-unimagined polish and variations in temperament from virginal to seductive. Works already written for the instrument emerged in new light while contemporary composers recognized fresh possibilities and devised new scores utilizing the alto saxophone.

Born in Germany to a Swedish father and an English mother, Rascher spent his early childhood in Switzerland. From 1921 to 1925, he attended secondary school in Stuttgart where he began his musical studies, concentrating on the clarinet. Financial problems forced Rascher to interrupt his schooling in 1927 and at that point, he switched instruments, taking up the alto saxophone thinking it would be easier to play and would offer him more performing opportunities. For three years, he played with jazz bands in Germany, Switzerland, and Holland in venues ranging from cafés to spas. Performing for 12 hours each day led to a breakdown in his health; after his recovery, Rascher returned to the Stuttgart Musikhochschule to complete his studies in 1930 and to take his examinations the following year. The graduate won first honors. For a year and a half, Rascher taught both music and woodcraft in primary schools, but soon determined that he would undertake a career as a concert saxophonist.

In view of the limited repertory for the instrument, Rascher began soliciting works from important composers. Among those who responded favorably were Eric Coates, Alexander Glazunov, Darius Milhaud, and Jacques Ibert. At his concert debut at the 1932 Hannover Music Festival, Rascher won acclaim for his even, silken tone; facile fingering; ability to manage long phrases in a single breath; and impressive mastery of the upper register (extended upward by an octave). After a concert appearance in Denmark, he was engaged for a special saxophone class. In 1934, he accepted an opportunity to become a faculty member at Malmö, Sweden. Over the next several years, Rascher's concert career expanded as he traveled to Italy, France, England, and Spain and in 1938, to Australia, New Zealand, and Tasmania under the sponsorship of the Australian Broadcasting Commission. In fall 1939, he came to the United States for his first American concert tour. On October 20, Boston Symphony Orchestra audiences heard two works that had become Rascher specialties, Debussy's *Rhapsody for Saxophone and Orchestra* and a work written for him by Ibert, the *Concertino for Saxophone and Orchestra*. On November 11, he presented the same program with the New York Philharmonic, once again to glowing reviews. With a growing reputation and a burgeoning list of compositions he could offer orchestras as concert fare, Rascher was as busy throughout the rest of his career as he chose to be. The list of works composed for him grew to nearly 150, while he was a guest soloist with no fewer than 250 symphonic ensembles worldwide.

Rascher settled in the United States and resumed his teaching; three of America's most distinguished schools benefited from his expert pedagogy: Juilliard, the Manhattan School of Music, and the Eastman School of Music in Rochester, NY. In 1969, Rascher formed the Rascher Saxophone Quartet and remained with the group until 1981. *—Erik Eriksson*

Recommended:

- ○ **Koch: Saxophone Concerto** / Westerberg (cond.), Rascher, Rohn, Hindart / 1991 / Phono Suecia 55

Simon Rattle

b. Jan. 19, 1955, Liverpool, England

Conductor

Sir Simon (Denis) Rattle became one of the world's leading conductors at an unusually early age. As a boy, Rattle studied percussion; at the age of 11, he appeared as a percussionist with the Royal Liverpool Philharmonic Orchestra. He joined the National Youth Orchestra, again as a percussionist, and began conducting when he was a teenager. At fifteen, he founded and conducted the Liverpool Sinfonia.

From 1971 to 1974, Rattle studied at the Royal Academy of Music in London. In his graduation year, still in his teens, he entered the John Player International Conductors' Competition and won first prize. He was soon appointed assistant conductor of the Bournemouth Symphony Orchestra, remaining with the orchestra until 1976.

In 1976 Rattle made his United States debut on tour with the London Schools Symphony Orchestra. His first American performance with a professional orchestra was a concert with the Los Angeles Philharmonic Orchestra in 1979. In 1981 that orchestra named him principal guest conductor, a post he retained until 1994.

Rattle made his first Glyndebourne Festival appearance in 1977, and retained his association with that insititution, lead productions of operas from the Classical period on. From 1977 to 1980, he was assistant conductor of the Royal Liverpool Philharmonic. During this time, he also appeared frequently with major American orchestras.

Rattle's longest-lasting association with an orchestra began when the City of Birmingham Symphony Orchestra named him its principal conductor and artistic adviser in 1980. With a change of title to music director in 1990, Rattle remained with the group until 1998. During their time together, both orchestra and the conductor attained remarkable artistic growth; they went on frequent wide-ranging tours, including visits to Europe, Scandinavia, the Far East, and North America. Even after giving up his directorship at the CBSO, Rattle continued to conduct the orchestra's ten-year Towards the Millennium festival of modern music. In 1992 Rattle became principal guest conductor of the Orchestra of the Age of Enlightenment; his appointments also include artistic adviser of the Birmingham Contemporary Music Group.

Rattle became a well-known television figure in Britain with an award-winning series, *Leaving Home*, the most extensive video production ever devoted to twentieth century orchestral music. He has made over 60 recordings, and today remains an exclusive EMI artist. Particularly honored are his recordings of Mahler's *Symphony No. 2* (three Gramophone Awards), Gershwin's *Porgy and Bess* (Gramophone, International Record Critics' , and Charles Cros Grand Prix Awards), and Szymanowski's *Stabat Mater* (Echo Award). His projects for the year 2000 included Szymanowski's opera *King Roger*, Bernstein's *Wonderful Town*, and Mahler's *Symphony No. 10*.

The conductor has frequently appeared at the Salzburg Festival, and made 55 appearances with the Berlin Philharmonic Orchestra before that ensemble announced in June 1999 that Rattle would become the orchestra's chief conductor and artistic adviser upon Claudio Abbado's retirement in 2002.

Rattle's other honors include Commander of the Order of the British Empire (1987) and a knighthood (1994). *—Joseph Stevenson*

Recommended:

- ○ **Janáček: Cunning Little Vixen** / Rattle (cond.), Allen, Tear, Montague, Howell, Royal Opera House Orch. Covent Garden / 2003 / Chandos 3101
- ○ **Holst: Planets; Britten: Sinfonia da Requiem** / Rattle (cond.), London PO, Birmingham SO / 2003 / EMI 75868
- ○ **Mahler: Symphony 5** / Rattle (cond.), Berlin PO / 2002 / EMI 57385
- ○ **Adams: Harmonielehre; The Chairman Dances; 2 Fanfares** / Rattle (cond.), Birmingham SO / 1994 / EMI 55051
- ○ **Gershwin: Porgy And Bess** / Rattle (cond.), Marshall, White, Clarey, Simpson, London PO / 1980 / EMI 56220
- ○ **In a Nutshell** / Rattle (cond.), Marshall, Elms, Wilson, Birmingham SO / 1997 / Angel 56412
- ○ **Schoenberg, Webern, Berg: Orchestral Works** / Rattle (cond.), Auger, Birmingham SO / 2003 / EMI 75880

Einojuhani Rautavaara

b. Oct. 9, 1928, Helsinki, Finland

Composer: Symphonic, Avant-garde, Opera

Einojuhani Rautavaara is the best-known composer in contemporary Finnish music. He began to study at the Sibelius Academy in Helsinki in the late1940s, but his professional career didn't begin until 1954 when his orchestral *A Requiem in Our Time* won a competition sponsored by Thor Johnson, then conductor of the Cincinnati Symphony Orchestra. That same year Rautavaara entered an advanced course in music composition with Aarre Merikanto and attracted the attention of Sibelius himself, who in 1955 recommended that Rautavaara be awarded a Tanglewood scholarship to study at the Julliard School for one year. In the United States Rautavaara studied with Aaron Copland and Roger Sessions, and once back in Europe, he completed his course of study in Switzerland with Wladimir Vogel and in Cologne with Rudolf Petzold.

Rautavaara, paraphrasing a statement usually made in reference to American politics, has said "If an artist is not a modernist when he is young, he has no heart. And if he is a modernist when he is old, he has no brain." Indeed, Rautavaara's style is rooted in modernism, and his earliest works are in a Nordic folk-derived idiom reminiscent of Bartók. Not surprisingly his approach shifted more strongly towards serialism after his experiences in Cologne. The political subject matter and often thorny 12-tone writing in Rautavaara's first opera, *Kaivos* (The Mine) led the Finnish National Opera to reject the work, but in a revised form *Kaivos* was aired on national Finnish television in 1963. This helped to establish Rautvoaara's reputation in his home country.

By 1970 Rautavaara began to lose interest in the rigorous requirements of serialism. With his next major work, the opera *Apollo contra Marsyas*, Rautavaara opted for a poly-stylistic approach, utilizing jazz and popular music in an ironic juxtaposition against light Viennese classical music. This breakthrough led to the development of Rautavaara's mature style, in which the music is subservient to the demands of his programmatic concepts, whether political, environmental, social or spiritual. While Rautavaara's prestige gained ground in Europe throughout the seventies and eighties, it was his Symphony No. 7 "Angel of Light" (1994) that established his international reputation. This appealing and meditative work came as a surprise to many who felt that contemporary composers had grown hopelessly out of touch with the emotional needs of the public.

Rautavaara is a prolific composer with a career spanning seven decades. So far he has created ten operas, of which *Thomas* (1982–1985), *Vincent* (1986–1987) and Aleksis Kivi (1995–1996) are the best known. He has also produced eight symphonies and many concertos including the popular *Cantus Arcticus; concerto for birds & orchestra* (1972) and the double bass concerto *Angel of Dusk* (1980). Rautavaara has also written reams of choral, chamber and vocal music and a small amount of electronic music. Through working directly from his emotions and not hewing to party line serialism, Einojuhani Rautavaara has emerged, in the autumn of his life, as one the major figures in contemporary music worldwide. *—AMG*

SYMPHONIC

Symphony No. 2 ("Sinfonia intima") (1957; revised 1984)

Finnish composer Einojuhani Rautavaara (born 1928) has exhibited an enormous curiosity regarding musical trends, often moving back and forth between tonal music and that which entirely braces serialism. After graduating from the University of Helsinki in 1952, he composed in a neo-Classical style that owed its primary character to Stravinsky and Bartók. Studies in New York, Tanglewood, and Europe broadened his perspectives, particularly his work with Aaron Copland and Roger Sessions.

In contrast to the tonal *First Symphony*, the *Second Symphony*, written just a year after the *First*, is firmly dissonant and does not trouble itself with the developmental concerns evidenced in most symphonic scores. If twentieth century Russian influences were felt in the *First Symphony*, the shadow of an expatriate Russian, Igor Stravinsky, may be found in the *Second*, particularly in the rhythmic motives of the second and fourth movements. This symphony is relatively short, running about 23 minutes.

The first movement, marked Quasi grave, opens with an imposing theme in the lower strings. The woodwinds enter briefly before relinquishing the stage to the lower strings once more. Primary among the harmonic building blocks are the tritone, a perfect fifth, and a minor ninth. The thematic tissue moves gropingly forward as horns enter and the timbre grows brighter and the pulsations more insistent. Solo winds appear and fade. A vibraphone adds its accents to the texture and sighing winds fall gently in glissandi here and there. While Stravinsky is in evidence, so also are the American composers from whom Rautavaara learned.

The second movement, Vivace, moves jaggedly in fragmented rhythms. Chords build and diminish and a flutter-tongued flute dances in and out.

The Largo third movement begins with a timpani roll and a solitary bass clarinet. Strings sound on a single note and gradually expand to a long-lined, wide-intervalled motive. More glissandi are heard amidst the winds and the section ends in ghostly fashion in the low winds.

The finale, a Presto, is begun with mallets assisting in voicing a jabbing rhythmic pattern carried then throughout the orchestra. The drumbeats come faster, interjections come from each section, and the movement bolts to an abrupt end.

In 1984, Rautavaara revised the score slightly, primarily to provide enrichment to its textures. *—Erik Eriksson*

Recommended:

- ○ **Rautavaara: Symphonies 1, 2 & 3** / Pommer (cond.), Leipzig RSO / Ondine 740

Symphony No. 3, Op. 20 (1959–1960)

Between the Romantic-sounding works Einojuhani Rautavaara composed early in his career and the overtly melodic works that helped bring him a worldwide audience in the 1970s and 1980s, there was a brief period in which he explored the possibilities of 12-tone composition. Rautavaara has referred to his *Symphony No. 3*, written over the years 1959–60, as a synthesis of the Romanticism of his *First Symphony* and the more angular modernism of his *Second*. The *Symphony No. 3* was given its first performance on April 10, 1962, in Helsinki, with Paavo Berglund conducting the Finnish Radio Symphony Orchestra.

Rautavaara actually uses 12-tone techniques in the *Symphony No. 3*, but they are seldom recognizable as such. Many commentators, in fact, have remarked on the Brucknerian quality of the work, responding not only to the composer's use of four Wagner tubas, but also to the long-limbed quality of the work's melodies and its many monumental, brass-drenched climaxes. An air of mystery, or expectation, marks the first and longest of the symphony's four movements, which opens with scalar patterns (somewhat resembling bird songs) in the woodwinds over quiet low string tremolos. More expansive themes in the strings dominate the middle of the movement. Then, after building to a noble, truly Bruckner-like climax, the scalar patterns return as a coda. The slow second movement is tense and dark, with fleeting consolation provided by some of the music for the horns and Wagner tubas. Lyrical ideas alternate with faster, more agitated material in the rustic scherzo third movement. In the finale, the lower strings set up a rhythm over which fanfare-like material from the brass gains momentum. There are some lighter moments, notably a curious bassoon theme that appears a couple of times. But for the most part the movement is forceful and serious-minded. A recollection of the tremolos and melodic fragments that opened the work provide its quiet ending. *—Chris Morrison*

Recommended:

- ○ **Rautavaara: Cantus Arcticus; Piano Concerto** / Lintu (cond.), Scottish National Orch. / 1998 / Naxos 554147
- ○ **Rautavaara: Symphonies 1, 2 & 3** / Pommer (cond.), Leipzig RSO / Ondine 740

Symphony No. 7 ("Angel of Light") (1994)

Born in 1928, Einojuhani Rautavaara established a reputation as Finland's leading composer of the late twentieth and early twenty-first centuries. His music identified a latent strand of the wider public consciousness worldwide, and of all his many works, his *Seventh Symphony, "Angel of Light,"* written in 1994, has perhaps aroused the widest response from audiences and critics alike. Many have commented that the work's beauty and spirituality of expression is a conduit for the cosmic and primal aspects of existence—attributes increasingly marginalized in a secularized and high-tech world.

Rautavaara has, in fact, become a respectable alternative for those who seek spiritual contentment but have found new age music unfulfilling. Other "angel" works of his, such as *Angels and Visitations* and *Angel of Dusk*, have also attracted wide attention. Commenting on his success, the composer writes, "it is probably down to the spirit of the times, the Zeitgeist. After all, angels are popular now. I felt self-conscious about putting angels in the titles of my works in the 1970s, when my colleagues were giving their works matter-of-fact titles such as *Structures for Strings*. Now, I feel self-conscious about the fact that angels have become popular in a banal sense with the New Age phenomenon." Rautavaara is a mystic who considers that his compositions already exist in "another reality." Nevertheless, Rautavaara's creative styles are firmly rooted in modernism and serialist techniques.

The *Seventh Symphony* is scored for a vast orchestra, though it is most often heard in small groups, so much so that massive tuttis, when reached, have a visionary, apocalyptic intensity. The work begins in a serene and contemplative fashion (tranquilo), but the influence of Sibelius (particularly his *Symphony No. 4*), one of Rautavaara's heroes, is often discernible throughout the score, though later stages are often suggestive of the equally mystical sound-world of U.S. composer Alan Hovhaness. This evocative and disembodied quality emanates from the unusual textural overlays of Rautavaara's orchestration, and is most palpably felt in the closing sequence, marked Pesante-cantabile. The notion of the angelic presence originated in a series of earlier works, and the composer explains them as "an archetype, one of mankind's oldest traditions and perennial companions." *—Michael Jameson*

Recommended:

- ○ **Rautavaara: Cantus Arcticus; Symphony 7; Flute Concerto** / Kuusisto (cond.), Lahti SO / 1999 / Bis 1038
- ○ **Rautavaara: Angel of Light** / Segerstam (cond.), Helsinki PO / Ondine 869
- ○ **Rautavaara: Symphony 7** / Koivula (cond.), Scottish National Orch. / 2003 / Naxos 8555814

AVANT-GARDE

Cantus Arcticus ("Concerto for Birds & Orchestra"), Op. 61 (1972)

In 1972, Einojuhani Rautavaara was commissioned by the University of Oulu, Finland, to write a piece for its first doctoral degree ceremony. Tradition would have him create a ceremonial festive cantata, but Rautavaara responded instead with the unusual *Cantus Arcticus*, often referred to as a *Concerto for Birds and Orchestra*, in which taped bird songs (some recorded in the vicinity of Oulu, others around the Arctic Circle and the marshlands of Liminka) interact with the orchestra.

The work is in three movements, each of which features a different set of bird songs. The first movement, titled "Suo" ("The Marsh"), opens with an impressionistic melody for two solo flutes, later joined by other woodwinds and by a recording of bog birds in springtime. A slow, rich, melody in the strings is superimposed over the winds and bird songs as the mood mellows, and the movement dies out with a reminiscence of the opening flute melody. The song of the shore lark, lowered by two octaves to turn it into what Rautavaara has called a "ghost bird," opens the second movement, "Melankolia" ("Melancholy"). A quiet melody in the strings enters tentatively and spins itself out, gaining in intensity as it goes. The movement ends as it began, with the shore lark. The final movement, "Joutsenet muuttavat" ("Swans Migrating"), opens with the chaotic sound of a large group of swans, combined with string tremolos and bird imitations in the woodwinds. This complex texture was described by Rautavaara thus:: "I imagined they [the swans] fly straight to the burning sun." As in the first movement, a slow, chorale-like melody in the strings emerges. The swan sounds increase in volume, and after a climactic cymbal crash and brass calls, the music and the swans' songs fade into the distance amid the gentle sounds of harp and percussion. *—Chris Morrison*

Recommended:

- ○ **Rautavaara: Cantus Arcticus; Symphony 7; Flute Concerto** / Vanska (cond.), Lahti SO / 1999 / Bis 1038
- ○ **Rautavaara: Symphonies 4 & 5; Cantus Arcticus** / Pommer (cond.), Leipzig RSO / Ondine 747

OPERA

Thomas (1982–1985)

Completing a tenth opera is an achievement for any composer, and Einojuhani Rautavaara reached this mark in the 1990s, when he was in his sixties. Of the operas he composed, which include *Apollo ja Marsyas* (1970), *Vincent* (1986–87), *Auringon talo* (1990), *Tietäjien lahja* (1993–95), *Aleksis Kivi* (1995–96), and *Thomas* (1982–85), the latter has become one of his best known. Written with the power of a sacred oratorio, the work focuses on the life of Bishop Tuomas, also known as Dominus Thomas episcopus Finlandiae, of the mid-thirteenth century. Thomas, a well-remembered historic Finnish figure, was probably the first person to have seen the potential to transform Finland and the Finns into a nation.

The project of composing the opera and its libretto was appointed to Rautavaara, in 1982, by baritone Jorma Hynninen, who was acting as the artistic director of the 1985 Joensuu Song Festival. As it had become clear that the Festival would be the main arena for celebrating the 150th anniversary of the Finnish national epic, the *Kalevala*, Hynninen chose to enhance the program with an opera. At the time Rautavaara accepted the project, he had finished working on *Angels and Visitations* (1978) and the double bass concerto *Angel of Dusk* (1980), which together with his *Fifth Symphony* of 1985 became known as his "angel trilogy." At this time he was creating orchestral works which contained dense waves of quickly repeated figures, multi-layered textures, and lyrical-nostalgic homophony in the upper register. Shortly before writing his "angel trilogy," Rautavaara was working on synthesizing modernism, traditional techniques, birdsong, aleatory counterpoint, jazz, and archaic liturgical chant in various combinations in his compositions. Two successful examples include *Marjatta matala neiti* (1975) and *Runo 42: Sammon ryöstö* (1974). In a way, both of the pieces prepared Rautavaara for his work on *Thomas*, as they were also based on the *Kalevala*. The dramatic scenario for *Thomas* developed simultaneously as the musical accompaniment was composed, while the libretto, at times, was written after the music was in place.

The plot of the opera *Thomas* is based on the goals of the main character, Thomas, to first overthrow the Eastern Pope in the infidel city of Novgorod, then to create an independent papal state in Finland, and eventually become the ruler. The outcome of the attack was a failure that resulted in the deaths of nearly all of the men on the crusading side. In the opera, Thomas' goals were not achieved prior to his condemnation, but ultimately, in the years which followed his death, the age-old *Kalevala* shamanist culture and the sprouting Christian culture merge and reshape Finnish identity and nationality. Rautavaara allowed the overlapping tonal systems of the opera, which include diatonic, dodecaphonic, free atonality, and synthetic-modal, to represent the fusion of the two cultures. Even though *Thomas* has not achieved worldwide recognition and fame, it occupies a significant place among Finland's nationalistic compositions and within Rautavaara's career. *—Meredith Gailey*

Recommended:

- ○ **Rautavaara: Thomas** / Haapasalo (cond.), Hynninen, Suhonen, Hietikko, Hirvonen, Joensuu City Orch. / Ondine 704

Maurice Ravel

b. Mar. 7, 1875, Ciboure, Basses-Pyrénées, France, **d.** Dec. 28, 1937, Paris, France
Composer: Orchestral, Ballet, Keyboard, Concerto, Chamber Music, Vocal, Opera

Young Maurice Ravel had to be bribed six sous an hour to practice the piano. This corruption paid off; Ravel grew up to become one of the leading composers of his generation, one of the two main figures (with Claude Debussy) in the musical Impressionist movement, and the producer of more than a dozen staples of the piano, chamber, and orchestral repertories.

Ravel enrolled at the Paris Conservatory in 1889 at age 14 and remained there until 1905, studying traditional form and technique. Initially Ravel was a renegade, but by the time he turned 40, he would refashion himself as an eighteenth century composer employing twentieth century harmony.

Despite his professional success, he nursed certain personal and public grudges for years. When the French government awarded him the Légion d'Honneur in 1919, Ravel rejected the decoration, still bitter that the state jurors had denied him the Prix de Rome three times in his conservatory days.

Aside from ongoing success and occasional mild artistic scandal, Ravel led an uneventful life. Although certainly not friendless, he never married and lived as a semirecluse at his forest retreat at Montfort-L'Amaury, near Paris. Sadly, Ravel ended up far more isolated than he could have wished. During the last five years of his life he suffered from aphasia, which made it impossible for him to compose, speak, or sign his name. He died at the end of 1937, at age 62, following unsuccessful surgery to relieve an obstructed vessel supplying blood to his brain.

Ravel's earliest surviving compositions were influenced by the music of César Franck and Gabriel Fauré, the most innovative composers at hand. *Jeux d'eau* was the first work to crystallize Ravel's style, full of pianistic innovations also harking back to the virtuosic music of Franz Liszt. Despite carrying the Lisztian tradition into the twentieth century, Ravel is best known for his works in the Impressionist style, including the lush ballet *Daphnis et Chloé*, the sinister *La Valse*, and the innocently childlike and bittersweet *Ma mere l'oye*. Ravel also dallied with Spanish, Gypsy, and Basque rhythms and melodies. The most famous examples of this sun-splashed style are the brilliantly scored *Rhapsodie espagnole* and the infamous *Boléro*. In the 1920s Ravel also developed an interest in jazz and blues. This became most obvious in his *Sonata for Violin and Cello*, *Sonata for Violin and Piano*, and the two jazz-influenced piano concertos of 1931. *—James Reel*

ORCHESTRAL

Alborada del Gracioso (1918)

In 1918, almost 14 years after originally composing the work, Maurice Ravel made an orchestral version of *Alborada del gracioso* (The Jester's Morning Serenade), the fourth of the pieces that make up *Miroirs* (1904–05). While the original piano version remains a recital favorite, the orchestral version has enjoyed even greater popularity as a concert-hall staple.

Ravel orchestrated a great many of his own piano works with great success—most famously, *Le tombeau de Couperin*, *Valses nobles et sentimentales*, *Menuet antique*, *Ma mère l'oye*, and *Tzigane*. In *Alborada del gracioso*, similarly, Ravel is in top form in translating his music from one medium to another. Most of the transcription is rather straightforward, with little in the way of actual recomposition, and the effective use of the percussion section is particularly striking.

The harp and pizzicato strings, which provide a spiky opening, are soon joined in more melodious fashion by members of the woodwind section. Energetic compound-meter rhythms and colorful glissandi in the woodwinds find splendid contrast in the stiller central section, which begins with a plaintive recitativo-like passage for solo bassoon. Ravel's few changes to the original score are subtle; most often, certain passages are elongated for maximal exploitation of coloristic possibilities, as in the woodwind flourishes that wrap around the final glissando. *—Blair Johnston*

Recommended:

- ○ **Ravel: Complete Orchestral Works** / Abbado (cond.), London SO / 2002 / DG 469354
- ○ **Ravel: Bolero; Rapsodie Espagnole** / Ormandy (cond.), Philadelphia Orch. / 1992 / Sony 48163

Bolero (1928)

Maurice Ravel's *Bolero* is easily its composer's most famous work. It is famous to historians and record books for ostensibly containing the longest-sustained single crescendo anywhere in the orchestral repertory; it is famous to collectors of anecdotes for having been humorously dubbed a "piece for orchestra without music" by Ravel; and it is famous to musicians and music lovers for being both the most repetitive 15 minutes of music they are likely to play/hear and also one of the most absolutely well-composed 15 such minutes. But, though Ravel would almost certainly have objected to this particular kind of fame, *Bolero* is most famous for having served as the background music for an erotic interlude in a major Hollywood motion picture (*10*, starring Bo Derek and Dudley Moore).

Bolero was commissioned by the dancer Ida Rubinstein in 1928; she specifically requested a work with Spanish character. Ravel's original intention was to orchestrate sections of Albéniz's *Iberia*, but he could not obtain the rights. Ravel wrote his miniature ballet as a technical exercise in composition, seeking to grow an entire orchestral work out of only a single melodic idea. It never occurred to him that it might become a popular work; but it did of course, and two years later Ravel crafted a version for two pianos so that he might continue to reap the harvest he had unwittingly sown. The premiere itself (at the Theatre of the Paris Opera with Rubinstein and her troupe, on November 22, 1928) was so enthusiastically received, that the audience shouted for the encore of the final scene.

Bolero is, on the surface, an astoundingly simple piece. An ostinato rhythm in the percussion begins at the beginning and maintains its steady pulse throughout; likewise an ostinato bass pattern. Atop this firm foundation is placed a theme in two halves that is made into what more-or-less amounts to a set of variations. Instruments are added, harmonies are filled-out, the music grows louder and more rambunctious, and, in a grand climax, C major is abandoned for E (if only for a brief time); here, for the very first time, we get the unsettling impression that it is perhaps not a happy piece after all, but a most disquieting commentary on aspects of life in the Roaring Twenties (Ravel himself was quite disturbed by how quickly high society took up *Bolero* as its own). C major is quickly reestablished, and pungent trombone glissandos lead the way to a hair-raising close. *—AMG*

Recommended:

- ○ **Ravel: Bolero** / Boulez (cond.), Berlin PO / DG 439859
- ○ **Ravel: Complete Orchestral Works** / Abbado (cond.), London SO / 2002 / DG 469354
- ○ **Ravel: The Orchestral Works** / Boulez (cond.), New York PO / 1990 / Sony 45842
- ○ **Ravel: Boléro** / Dutoit (cond.), Montreal SO / 1999 / Decca 460214
- ○ **Ravel: Bolero** / Haitink (cond.), Boston SO / 1998 / Philips 456589

Rhapsodie espagnole (1907)

Ravel composed this music in 1907, but didn't orchestrate it until just before the premiere on March 15, 1908, with Edouard Colonne conducting "his" orchestra at one of "his" Paris concerts. It is lavishly scored, with winds and brass mostly in threes and fours, and plenty of percussion. In fact if not in title, this kaleidoscope from Ravel's 33rd year is a symphonic suite in four related movements that derive—like the single-act comic opera, *L'Heure espagnole*, finished in 1909—from his

Basque mother's memories of Madrid, where she spent much of her childhood. During that time, the "Habanera" from Cuba—without a tilde over the "n," please—had enjoyed special but ephemeral popularity. Ravel's "Habanera" in the *Rapsodie* is a note-for-note orchestration of his early work for two pianos, composed in 1895, which he and Ricardo Viñes played.

The first performance was feebly conducted and restively heard by the audience in expensive seats on the main floor. In the upper gallery, however, Ravel's students and friends made a great noise, calling for an encore of the second movement ("Malagueña"), after which the young composer Florent Schmitt called out in a stentorian voice, "Just once more, for the gentlemen below who haven't been able to understand." Like most concert-hall outbursts in Paris, this one added to (rather than subtracted from) Ravel's reputation.

In the Prélude à la nuit (Très modéré (3/4, open key), two octaves apart, muted violins and violas play a descending four-note motif that repeats over and over, never louder than mezzo-forte throughout. A six-measure theme interrupts, in effect a cadenza for clarinets and later bassoons, before the music evanesces on a chord in the high strings. Ravel's own description was "voluptuously drowsy and ecstatic."

The Malagueña (Assez vif) begins in 3/4 with an open key, but later changes to 2/4 and B major. Originally a Spanish courting dance, this quick-moving evocation of Málaga is a long crescendo that begins very quietly with an ostinato motif in the bass, until a muted solo trumpet plays the main theme with tambourine accompaniment. The tempo slows for a new melody of Moorish cast, sung plaintively by the English horn, following which the opening motif from Movement 1 returns.

Ravel subtitled the Habanera in A major "Au pays parfumé que le soleil caresse" (In the fragrant land that the Sun caresses) both in his two-piano original of 1895 and 12 years later in this orchestral setting, with minor-second dissonances in the accompaniment and triplet-spiced themes.

The Feria, a high-spirited holiday scene, came several years after Debussy's "Fêtes" movement in *Trois Nocturnes*, but predated a similar fiesta finale in Debussy's *Ibéria*, the second *Image pour orchestre*. Ravel interrupts his celebration with a languorous interval, soft as suede, played by the English horn and solo clarinet, followed by the four-note motif from movement one, before the merriment resumes even more frenziedly and brilliantly. *—Roger Dettmer*

Recommended:

- ○ **Ravel: Boléro** / Dutoit (cond.), Montreal SO / 1999 / Decca 460214
- ○ **Ravel: Boléro** / Boulez (cond.), Berlin PO / DG 439859
- ○ **Debussy & Ravel** / Celibidache (cond.), Stuttgart SWR RSO / DG 453196

Shéhérazade, fairy overture (1898)

Ravel's early "fairy overture" *Shéhérazade* (1898) was long assumed to be lost for good; it was only in the mid-1970s, in fact, that the work came to light again and became available for study and performance. *Shéhérazade* is the earliest of Ravel's works for orchestra; while it by no means displays the mastery of the medium evident in works like *Daphnis and Chloé* (1909–12) and *Alborada del gracioso* (1918), the young Ravel is already clearly charting his compositional course. Ravel famously returned to the subject of *Shéhérazade* in the 1903 song cycle of the same name; despite the absence of obvious thematic or structural connections, it is not difficult to imagine that the overture served Ravel as a sort of study for the later work.

Shéhérazade takes shape as a sonata-allegro skeleton upon which Ravel overlays music of such remarkable flexibility that many contemporary audiences and critics found themselves lost within what is really a very clear formal design. Ravel treats the "oriental" subject matter in a manner consistent with other turn-of-the-century European works—that is, a sort of fanciful, evocative inauthenticity that relies upon features like arabesque melodies and whole-tone scales. Occasionally, and quite understandably, Ravel's work summons forth the sounds of Rimsky-Korsakov's earlier, better-known tone poem *Sheherazade* (1888).

A 24-measure Modèré introduction provides ample evidence of Ravel's early infatuation with constantly changing meter. With the arrival of the exposition, however, the meter snaps into 4/4 regularity, an active timpani helping to drive the exotic rhythms and chromatic melody forward. After an episodic development that makes thorough use of both the main melody and its many subsidiaries, Ravel forges a thrilling climax. During the recapitulation, both the main theme of the Allegro and that of the introduction are combined into a single utterance, and the initial introductory material is refashioned into an introspective coda.

Shéhérazade also exists in a version for piano, four hands, which may well predate the orchestral version, possibly serving as a kind of short score for the composer. *—Blair Johnston*

Recommended:

- ○ **Ravel: Complete Orchestral Works** / Abbado (cond.), London SO / 2002 / DG 469354
- ○ **Ravel: Orchestral Works** / Boulez (cond.), New York PO / 1990 / Sony 45842
- ○ **Ravel: Orchestral Music** / Tortelier (cond.), Ulster Orch. / 2000 / Chandos 7103

La valse, poème choréographique (1919–1920)

Ravel composed this music in 1919–20; Camille Chevillard led the premiere in Paris on December 12, 1920, with the Lamoureux Orchestra. Lavish scoring includes triple winds, two harps, five drums, and various metal percussion. Ravel planned as far back as 1906 to write *Wien* (the German for Vienna) as his tribute to Johann Strauss Jr.—"a kind of apotheosis of the Viennese waltz, mingled in my mind with the idea of destiny's fantastic whirl." What eventuated five years later, however, was *Valses nobles et sentimentales*, a keyboard suite inspired by Schubert's piano music that Ravel orchestrated diaphanously in 1912 for a ballet entitled *Adélaïde, ou la langage des fleurs*.

World War I shattered the composer's marzipan fantasy of the city that existed in his imagination. When in 1919 Serge Diaghilev requested a new work for his Paris-based ballets russes, *Wien* was reactivated—but this time as *La valse*, apocalyptic rather than prettily fanciful, with a brief program note in the score:

"Through rifts in swirling clouds, couples are glimpsed waltzing. As the clouds disperse little by little, one sees an immense hall peopled with a whirling crowd. The scene becomes progressively brighter. The light from chandeliers bursts forth at fortissimo (letter B in the score). An Imperial Court, around 1855."

One year later, with Marcelle Meyer at a second piano, Ravel played his four-hand reduction for Diaghilev and several guests, who included Stravinsky and Poulenc. At the end, as Poulenc wrote 40 years later in his autobiography, the impresario pronounced it "... a masterpiece ... but it is not a ballet.... It is the portrait of a ballet ... the painting of a ballet." To Poulenc's dismay, "Stravinsky said not a word! I was 22, and, you can imagine, absolutely flabbergasted. Ravel proceeded to give me a lesson in modesty that has lasted all my life: he picked up his music quietly and, without worrying what we all thought of it, calmly left the room." But never again did he shake Diaghilev's proffered hand, or speak to him.

Ravel published *La valse* as a "choreographic poem," which Bronislava Nijinska choreographed in 1928 for Ida Rubinstein's company. But it did not have the success of *Boléro* two nights later, which Rubinstein had commissioned and herself danced. Not until George Balanchine created *La valse* in 1951 for his New York City Ballet, using *Valses nobles et sentimentales* as a preface, was the music's dance potential finally, enthrallingly revealed. As a concert piece, however, it was an immediate and enduring triumph. *—Roger Dettmer*

Recommended:

- ○ **Ravel: Boléro** / Dutoit (cond.), Montreal SO / 1999 / Decca 460214
- ○ **Maurice Ravel** / Boulez (cond.), Berlin PO / 2000 / DG 469184
- ○ **Ravel: Orchestral Works** / Abbado (cond.), London SO / 1986 / DG 459439

BALLET

Daphnis et Chloé (1909–1912)

Many consider *Daphnis et Chloé*, a symphonie choréographique in three scenes to be Maurice Ravel's greatest work. The label may not really be a fair one; there were so many different Maurice Ravels throughout his life, each with a different set of musical goals, each exploring different musical worlds, that it is not right to assign the label of life masterpiece to the top work of any one of those periods, over the top works of all the others, just because it happens to be longer, more ambitious, and easier to access. But *Daphnis et Chloé* is certainly one of the most colorfully, intricately, and in a very immediate, almost physical sense, beautifully scored works ever written; if one were to assign preeminent status to any of Ravel's works solely on the basis of orchestration, this ballet would, without a doubt, be the one selected for the honor. There may be no more skillfully orchestrated work in all the twentieth century repertoire (Stravinsky's work included) and whole shelves of orchestration textbooks could be eliminated without loss by simply replacing them with an astute examination of this score.

Daphnis et Chloé was composed between 1909 and 1912, after a commission by Diaghilev and the ballets russes, and is a setting of a scenario adapted by Mikhail Fokine from the Greek work of the same name by Longus. It was premiered on June 8, 1912. The performance was not well prepared, and few people took note of Ravel's piece. Two orchestral suites derived from the score, however, did make a splash when Ravel brought them out just a short time after (especially the *Suite No. 2*, which is probably still Ravel's most often-played work).

Ravel was always far more interested in reproducing traditional musical forms and structures than he was in achieving the kind of sonic soundscapes that get rather callously lumped together as impressionist music; *Daphnis et Chloé* is, section-by-section, built along firmly classical lines (Ravel was extremely proud of the fact). Even the famous sunrise music at the opening of the third scene, with its scintillating 32nd notes strewn about the orchestra and bright chirrups from the flute and piccolo flute and ecstatic, rising melody, has nothing in it that might be called progressive or even especially innovative in a technical sense, though certainly nothing written before it sounds even remotely like it. This was the essence of Ravel's genius: the ability to take the old and make it somehow sound completely new and different. Whether *Daphnis et Chloé* is Ravel's greatest achievement may be an irrelevant question: from the very first call of the back-stage choir, distant and brought forth from an ancient world of shepherds and nymphs, to the rhythmic revelry of the final dance, it is proof on paper of Ravel's astounding capacity to fuse diverse elements into an astonishing new whole. *—Blair Johnston*

Synopsis:

Part One. The story is set in a mythological land. The action begins in a meadow in a wooded area held sacred by worshippers of the god Pan. Groups of young people assemble to pay homage at the altar of the Nymphs. The shepherd Daphnis and the maiden Chloe soon join them in their worship. A group of young women encircle Daphnis and begin dancing around him. Chloe becomes jealous at their wooing, but is herself now drawn into a dance with young men. The herdsman Dorcon dances with her, and when he tries to kiss her, he is thwarted by Daphnis. His action causes one of the youths to propose a contest between Daphnis and Dorcon: the two will perform a dance and the better one will receive a kiss from Chloe. Daphnis' graceful dance wins out over Dorcon's rather crude effort.

The ecstatic Daphnis receives his reward and is then left alone. Soon he is joined by Lyceion, who dances around him seductively before poking fun at him and running off. Cries of violence are heard as a group of girls flees from a band of pirates. Chloe is among the pursued and desperately seeks refuge at the altar of the Nymphs. She is carried away, however, and Daphnis, who had departed the meadow briefly in hopes of protecting her, returns to find a sandal she had lost in the abduction. He falls to the ground in abject despair, but the Nymphs soon appear around him and revive his spirit. They then call on the god Pan to come to the aid of Chloe.

Part Two. In the camp of the pirates Chloe is brought before the chief of the band, Bryaxis. He orders her to dance and she acquiesces for the moment, but then attempts to escape. She is seized, brought back and forced to resume her dance. Another escape attempt fails, and just when Bryaxis begins to carry her off in triumph, strange lights and flames appear, along with Satyrs. Suddenly the shadow of Pan can be seen and the pirates flee in horror.

Part Three. Back in the meadow, Daphnis sleeps at the altar of the Nymphs. It is dawn now and a group of shepherds arrives and awakens Daphnis, who immediately begins looking for Chloe. Soon she appears and the two embrace passionately. An old shepherd tells them that Pan saved Chloe in remembrance of Syrinx, the nymph whom the god had once deeply loved. In gratitude for Pan's intervention, Daphnis and Chloe do a mime of the story of Pan and Syrinx. Their dance ends with the two falling in each other's arms. Daphnis pledges his love to Chloe at the altar of the Nymphs, and the ballet ends with a joyful celebration. *—Robert Cummings*

Recommended:

- ○ **Ravel: Daphnis et Chloé** / Dutoit (cond.), Montreal SO / 1999 / Decca 458605
- ○ **Ravel: Daphnis et Chloé; La Valse** / Boulez (cond.), Berlin PO / DG 447057
- ○ **Ravel: Daphnis et Chloé** / Munch (cond.), Boston SO / 1993 / RCA 61846
- ○ **Ravel: Boléro; Daphnis & Chloé; Alborada del gracioso** / Abbado (cond.), London SO / DG 445519

Ma mère l'oye (1911–1912)

Maurice Ravel often remarked on the kinship he felt with children. When he met artist Cyprian Godebski in 1904, he also quickly befriended Godebski's two young children, Mimie and Jean, for whom he wrote a set of five simple pieces for piano, four hands, based on several of their favorite fairy tales, including some from Charles Perrault's collection of *Mother Goose* stories. The *Mother Goose Suite* proved to be too difficult for them to play, so the first public performance, in Paris on April 20, 1910, featured Jeanne Leleu and Geneviève Durony (themselves both under age ten).

Several months later, Ravel orchestrated the five pieces, and in 1911 he added another scene along with a prelude and interludes at the request of the impresario Jacques Rouché, who thought the music might work well as a ballet. The ballet, with a scenario by Ravel, was first performed in Paris on January 28, 1912.

A gentle fanfare opens the work and dominates the opening Prelude. A crescendo leads into the first tableau, "Spinning Wheel Dance and Scene," which depicts the spinning of an old woman working at her wheel. Princess Florine, the Sleeping Beauty, pricks her finger on the spindle and falls asleep. She sleepwalks, accompanied by two guards assigned her by a Good Fairy (the old woman transformed) in the second tableau, "Pavane of the Sleeping Beauty in the Woods." In "Conversations of Beauty and the Beast," Beauty accepts Beast's marriage proposal, and with a harp glissando and a triangle stroke Beast changes into a handsome prince.

Tom Thumb appears in the fourth tableau, "Hop o' My Thumb." The oboe plays Tom, who is wandering in the woods, dropping bread crumbs behind him to help him find his way out. But birds, heard in trills and harmonics in the violins and woodwinds, eat them up. A pentatonic tune heralds "Laideronnette, Princess of the Pagodas," in which a wicked witch has turned a princess into an Ugly Little Girl. The Girl meets a serpent, and they travel to the country of the Pagodas, tiny people with bodies made of jewels. Tuned percussion evokes the Oriental setting as the Pagodas play for the Girl on instruments made of nutshells. Ultimately the serpent is transformed into his original form as King of the Pagodas, the Girl becomes a princess again, and the two marry. In the concluding "The Fairy Garden," the Prince and Princess Charming are blessed and sent away by the Good Fairy to live happily ever after. The music begins quietly and prettily, builds in a long crescendo, and wedding bells are hinted at in the powerful climax. *—Chris Morrison*

Recommended:

- ○ **Ravel: Boléro** / Dutoit (cond.), Montreal SO / 1999 / Decca 460214
- ○ **Ravel: Boléro** / Boulez (cond.), Berlin PO / DG 439859
- ○ **Ravel: Complete Orchestral Works** / Abbado (cond.), London SO / 2002 / DG 469354

KEYBOARD

Gaspard de la nuit (1908)

Though competent at the piano, Ravel was no virtuoso; so, when he set out to compose a work for the instrument that would be, in his own words, "more difficult than [Balakirev's] *Islamey*," he drew heavily on the brilliant pianistic style of Franz Liszt to fulfill his ambition. The resulting three-part suite, *Gaspard de la nuit* (1908), forever changed the technical landscape of keyboard music. Perhaps pianist Alfred Cortot put it best when he called the work "one of the most extraordinary examples of instrumental ingenuity which the industry of composers has ever produced."

Gaspard de la nuit, subtitled "Three Poems after Aloysius Bertrand," takes as its inspiration Bertrand's same-titled 1842 collection of medieval tales, which the author claimed were whispered to him in the night by the devil, Gaspard. Each of the pieces in Ravel's suite is prefaced by one of the poems; no doubt the same macabre streak that led Ravel to spend many nights absorbed in the stories of Edgar Allen Poe is also responsible for the composer's powerful attraction to Bertrand's rather dark work. *Gaspard* was premiered in January 1909 by pianist Ricardo Viñes, who had introduced Ravel to Bertrand's work.

Each of the three pieces of the suite, "Ondine," "Le Gibet," and "Scarbo," presents not only an individual assortment of pianistic demands but also a unique musical language and narrative vision. In the first piece Ravel undertakes the portrayal of the water nymph Ondine's seduction of a mortal man. Shimmering C sharp major figuration soon becomes the background for a transparent melodic strand marked très doux et très expressif (very soft and expressive). The fluid background pauses only once during "Ondine"—for a brief pianissimo Très lent that precedes the final, quicksilver cadenza.

"Le Gibet" (The Gibbet) is a musical horror story of such textural density that Ravel notated nearly all of the piece on three staves. An extract from the preface of the corresponding poem provides some idea of the musical atmosphere: "It is the bell sounding from the walls of a city far away below the horizon, and the carcass of a dead man hanging from a gibbet, reddened by the setting sun." Ravel's "bells" are the slightly irregularly grouped B flats that sound continuously throughout the piece, around which the composer weaves music of total psychological suspense. The dynamic never exceeds piano, and Ravel demands that the performer play "without expression" for the last portion of the piece.

"Scarbo" is 19 pages of some of the most frightful digital difficulties ever devised. Scarbo himself is a somewhat malicious night-dwarf who comes, laughing, to horrify, and then disappears without a trace. Here Ravel places the greatest emphasis on his singular sense of rhythm; witness the perfectly placed pauses throughout. Rapid repeated notes, wild arpeggiations, and sudden shifts of texture and dynamics are among the hurdles pianists must overcome; a famous passage in parallel seconds seems to owe its existence to the composer's own peculiarly double-jointed thumb, and is therefore quite challenging for those without such a physical anomaly. After a tremendous triple-fortissimo climax, the music dissolves into impish pianissimo 32nd notes. *—Blair Johnston*

Recommended:

- ○ **Arturo Benedetti Michelangeli** / Michelangeli / 1999 / Philips 456901
- ○ **Ravel: Piano Works** / Roge / 1994 / Decca 440836
- ○ **Maurice Ravel** / Argerich / 2000 / DG 469184
- ○ **Ravel: L'Oeuvre pour Piano Seul** / Thibaudet / 1992 / London 433515

Jeux d'eau (1901)

During the first few years of the twentieth century Maurice Ravel's position as a student at the Paris Conservatoire was by no means a particularly comfortable one. His repeated failure to secure any of the school's academic prizes—including, on five different occasions, the coveted Prix de Rome—made it more and more difficult to remain an official student in Fauré's class, and he was eventually dismissed from the school in 1903. During these same years, however, Ravel completed several of his best-known works—works that were, even at that time, widely considered to be masterpieces. The *String Quartet* (1902–03) remains a repertory staple, as does the song cycle *Shéhérazade* (1903); in terms of sheer impact and immediate musical influence, though, perhaps the most striking work of all is the piano piece *Jeux d'eau* (1901).

Jeux d'eau, which translates as "Play of Water" or "Fountains," draws heavily on the technically brilliant pianistic style of Franz Liszt, one of Ravel's heroes; indeed, many think that Ravel's work is something of an homage to Liszt's similarly scintillating *Les jeux d'eau à la Villa d'Este* (1870). Still, *Jeux d'eau* is something almost totally new, incorporating a kind of pianism unlike any that had ever been dreamed of. With this work Ravel opened the gates for both his own later piano pieces (particularly *Miroirs* and *Gaspard de la nuit*) and those of other Parisian composers of the day. Debussy was particularly quick to capitalize on the innovations of his young colleague; during the first few years of the decade, as the two composers mutually influenced each other, there was in fact some confusion as to who, in fact, was the real creator of the new style.

Jeux d'eau is thoroughly saturated with the rich sonorities of major seventh chords—a feature found even in Ravel's earliest music, here taken to a new level. Added to this is the nearly bitonal juxtaposition of two harmonies (C major and F# major—a tritone removed!), which have been collectively dubbed the "Jeu d'eau chord." The ebb and flow of harmonic color is as near to a liquid state as music could ever achieve.

The atmosphere of great exuberance reflected in the quotation at the front of the score ("The river god laughs as the water tickles him"), combined with the continuous arpeggiations and chromatic flourishes, is positively electric in effect. The glistening texture never lets up, and with the approach of the final, pianissimo expanse in E major Ravel allows the pianist an opportunity to let loose with a dramatic, très rapide cadenza.

The kind of shimmering pianissimo textures that characterize so much of the composer's later music are already well developed in this work; his reluctance to rely on the same mock-archaic, highly sectional formal designs that hold his earlier piano pieces together indicates a growing appreciation of his own ability to successfully produce extended, self-defined textural essays. While there are clearly two recognizable themes in *Jeux d'eau*, they are by no means worked out in the Classical manner; to describe the piece as a sonata-allegro form, as indeed some have done, is out of the question. Even if the vague outlines of such a form can be excavated by musical archaeologists, the term has little meaning in regard to this most original of Ravel's keyboard works. *—Blair Johnston*

Recommended:

○ **Ravel: Piano Works** / Roge / 1994 / Decca 440836
○ **Maurice Ravel** / Argerich / 2000 / DG 469184
○ **Ravel: L'Oeuvre Pour Piano Seul** / Thibaudet / 1992 / London 433515
○ **Ravel: The Complete Solo Piano Music** / Hewitt / 2002 / Hyperion 67341/2

Menuet antique (1895)

The *Menuet antique* (1895), Ravel's earliest published work, is by no means one of the composer's best-known or most-accomplished efforts. Still, within these eight pages of music, one may clearly observe the distinctive and colorful blend of old (a stylized eighteenth century dance form and an archaic scale) and new (brightly chromatic harmonies) that would become a hallmark of the composer's singular musical language. As is the case with so many of his early works, Ravel later reworked the basic musical concept of the *Menuet antique* into a more mature effort, the piano suite *Le Tombeau de Couperin* (1914–17).

Ravel composed the *Menuet antique* while still a student at the Paris Conservatoire, and the work shows something of the same Chabrier influence that Ravel later heard and disliked in his own *Pavane pour une infante défunte* (1899). Indeed, some have seen the *Menuet antique* as something of a companion piece to Chabrier's *Menuet pompeaux* (1881), despite the lack of any evidence that Ravel himself viewed it as such.

The work is in a typical ABA minuet form, the densely-textured, minor-mode outer sections contrasted by much more transparent gestures in the major-mode middle section. Important features of the two outer sections, the second of which is absolutely identical to the first, include the pervasive use of accented major-seventh chords in a modified appoggiatura manner and a reliance on distinct sequential melodic gestures. A striking scale in octaves, rising from a piano to a fortissimo dynamic level (complete with marked sforzandi) over the span of just one measure, precedes the final utterance of the main theme. Dotted note gestures ride atop a steady eighth note pulse during the elfin central "Trio" section. Near the end of the section, Ravel cleverly fuses together the main melodies of both the A and B sections—Trio melody in the right hand, first-section melody in the left.

In 1929 Ravel made an orchestral version of the *Menuet antique*, suggesting that he, at least, considered it a work worth preserving. *—Blair Johnston*

Recommended:

○ **Ravel: Boléro** / Dutoit (cond.), Montreal SO / 1999 / Decca 460214
○ **Ravel: The Orchestral Works** / Boulez (cond.), New York PO / 1990 / Sony 45842
○ **Ravel: Complete Orchestral Works** / Abbado (cond.), London SO / 2002 / DG 469354
○ **Ravel: Piano Works** / Roge / 1994 / Decca 440836
○ **Ravel: Piano Works** / Queffelec / 1998 / Virgin 61489

Menuet sur le nom d'Haydn (1909)

Maurice Ravel composed his diminutive *Menuet sur la nom d'Haydn* (1909) as part of celebrations to mark the centenerary of the Austrian master's death. The *Menuet* is a movement of a larger work to which many other Parisian notables, including Debussy, Dukas, and D'Indy, made similar contributions. Ravel had been interested in archaic musical forms and styles since his early student days at the Conservatoire—his first published piece was the mock-Classical *Menuet antique* (1895)—and his parodistic skills were considerable, as evidenced in his good-natured imitations of Chabrier and Borodin (1913).

Still, when he sat down to compose his homage to Haydn, Ravel did not try to capture anything of the earlier composer's style beyond the vague superficial strokes. Instead, the *Menuet* is an agreeable mélange of old and new, a work somewhat Classical in gesture and form but distinctly Ravelian in harmony and narrative aesthetic.

The *Menuet* is reasonably short, spanning only 54 bars in the space of about a minute and a half. Part of the game Ravel plays is to employ Haydn's own name as a five-note motif. By interpreting H as the Germanic spelling of B natural, A and D as their respective pitches, and Y and N as D and G, respectively (according to a scheme that assigns the rest of the alphabet to pitches in revolving groups of seven), Ravel arrives at the musical formula HAYDN = B-A-D-D-G. Most of the occurrences of this subject are marked in the score, including several that use either inversion (i.e. turned upside down) and/or retrograde motion (backwards). The Minuet is a good deal more chromatic, and more reliant on typically Ravelian seventh and ninth chords, than anything Haydn would have written; at the same time, its basic dance flow is not at all contrary to the Classical style. Features such as dense, sliding parallel sonorities and characteristic, unexpected harmonic shifts bear the unmistakable stamp of Ravel's own musical language. *—Blair Johnston*

Recommended:

○ **Ravel: Piano Works** / Roge / 1994 / Decca 440836
○ **Ravel: L'Oeuvre pour Piano Seul** / Thibaudet / 1992 / London 433515
○ **Ravel: The Complete Solo Piano Music** / Hewitt / 2002 / Hyperion 67341/2
○ **Complete Piano Music of Ravel** / Casadesus / 1998 / Heritage 63316

Miroirs (1904–1905)

During the first decade of the twentieth century, Maurice Ravel was one of the leading figures in the most extensive expansion of the piano's technical and expressive means since the music of Liszt. If Ravel's *Jeux d'eau* (1901–02) is the first hint of the composer's foray into this remarkable, uncharted pianistic territory, then it is the suite *Miroirs* (1904–05) and *Gaspard de la nuit* (1908) in which the new style really crystallized. *Miroirs* is, as its title would seem to indicate, a group of "reflections" on various isolated glimpses of reality.

"Noctuelles" (Nocturnes or Night-Moths) is a piece of great rhythmic flexibility that incorporates extensive cross-rhythms and frequent meter changes. The extremely fluid opening is followed by a contrasting bit based on a syncopated pedal tone on F. Soon, the essence (if not the letter) of the opening is reprised, and the piece ends with a juxtaposition of the minor and major third scale degrees.

In "Oiseaux tristes" (Sad Birds) Ravel said that he was trying to evoke "birds lost in the torpor of a dark forest during the hottest summer hours." A syncopated triplet rhythm provides rather static support for the fragmentary birdcalls; some of the more energetic birds squawk forte, while the background never rises above a very quiet dynamic. A glistening cadenza paves the way for a final, somber musing on the opening repeated E flat gesture.

"Une barque sur l'océan" (A Boat on the Ocean) is based on a highly evocative, one-measure motivic cell that poses a gentle eighth note gesture in the right hand against rushing arpeggios in the left. The piece is both the longest and most difficult in the set, as the arpeggios soon take on far more imposing dimensions and the right hand is forced to join with the left in their execution. In the hands of a capable pianist, the texture positively shimmers.

"Alborada del gracioso" (Serenade, or Aubade, of the Jester) is in the composer's Spanish vein and has certainly become better known in the composer's popular orchestration. The piece is in three main sections; the rapid repeated notes and sweeping glissandi (in parallel fourths, no less) of the outer two sections require strong hands and supple wrists.

"La vallée des cloches" (The Valley of the Bells) is really a reincarnation, at least in spirit, of Ravel's early two-piano piece *Entre cloches* (1895). Bells sound all around, first as octave G sharps and then, in imitation of the complex overtone structure of actual bells, as increasingly complex sonorities. *—Blair Johnston*

Recommended:

○ **Sviatoslav Richter à Prague** / Richter / Praga 356020-34
○ **Ravel: Piano Works** / Roge / 1994 / Decca 440836
○ **Ravel: Boléro** / Dutoit (cond.), Montreal SO / 1999 / Decca 460214
○ **Ravel: Boléro** / Boulez (cond.), Berlin PO / DG 439859
○ **Reflections** / Chiu / HM 907166

Pavane pour une infante défunte (1899)

Ravel's *Pavane pour une infante défunte* (Pavane for a Dead Princess), composed in 1899, was the second of the composer's piano works to see publication. Despite Ravel's half-hearted efforts to later disown the piece—he felt it to be too clearly oriented around the musical language of Chabrier, an early hero of his—it is not at all difficult to understand why the *Pavane* instantly and irrevocably caught the attention of European concert-goers and why, along with *Boléro* (1928), it remains the composer's best-known music. It is a work of great but subtle charm, infused with the lightness of touch that emerged as one of Ravel's compositional hallmarks.

Ravel complained of the *Pavane*'s "quite poor form." Indeed, the work is perhaps excessively sectional; it basically unfolds in an ABACA scheme, with both the B and C sections containing two parallel but differing statements of the same theme. The key of G major seems an unlikely and unusually bright one for such a sober subject, yet it is just this harmonic context that makes the gently plaintive B and far more exuberant C sections so effective. Here is no adult weeping for a dead child, but in essence a gentle, nostalgic celebration of the sweet innocence of childhood on the tragic occasion of its loss. (The origin of the work's title is unclear; it has been suggested that Ravel simply liked the way it sounded.) The *Pavane* rides along upon a steady eighth note pulse, in keeping with the pavane's origins as a stately Renaissance dance, and is filled with stylized rhythmic gestures. The final iteration of the opening melody is much fuller than the previous two, and here Ravel allows himself to make a dramatic move from pianissimo to fortissimo over the course of the last few bars. *—Blair Johnston*

Recommended:

- ○ **Ravel: Boléro** / Dutoit (cond.), Montreal SO / 1999 / Decca 460214
- ○ **Ravel: Piano Works** / Roge / 1994 / Decca 440836
- ○ **Ravel: Orchestral Works** / Boulez (cond.), New York PO / 1990 / Sony 45842
- ○ **Ravel: Orchestral Works** / Abbado (cond.), London SO / 1986 / DG 459439
- ○ **Ravel: Orchestral Works** / Martinon (cond.), Paris Orch. / 1995 / EMI 68610

Sonatine for piano (1903–1905)

Ravel began composing what later became known as his *Sonatine* when the Anglo-French magazine *Weekly Critical Review* conducted a competition for the first movement of a piano sonata. He was at an advantage with a unique style that gave him the ability to take the traditional sonata form, which had come to a "dead end" during the second half of the nineteenth century, and bring life to it by avoiding pitfalls and clichés. When the magazine went bankrupt, Ravel added two more movements to his competition piece, and thus completed his *Sonatine*. Representative of his first formative period, the work is bright and clear, and only gently touches the listener's emotions. Using fluidity, light coloring, and the intervals of the fourth and fifth as unifying features, the work is written using primarily the three middle octaves of the piano. Ravel was known for his tightly written pieces and *Sonatine* was no exception; it easily reminds one of the refined *objets d'art* of the eighteenth century. The opening Modéré-doux et espressif—is written in strict sonata form, has a first theme around the tonality of F sharp minor, a second around D major and B minor, and a development section of intense excitement. The second movement—Mouvement de menuet—is an uncomplicated minuet in D flat, which flowers in its final measures. The work closes with virtuoso writing marked Animé. Moving nervously between 3/4 and 5/4, waves of music pour forward with a few horn calls in the left hand.

When on June 16, 1904, the first movement of the *Sonatine* was performed for its dedicatees Cipa and Ida Godebski (*Ma Mère l'oye* was dedicated to their children), it was very well received, and when the full work was given by Paule de Lestang on March 10, 1906, under the patronage of the Lyon Revue musicale, enthusiasm was so great that Durand put it into immediate publication. *—Meredith Gailey*

Recommended:

- ○ **Ravel: Complete Solo Piano Works, Vol. 1** / Crossley / 1983 / CRD 3383
- ○ **Ravel: L'Oeuvre pour Piano Seul** / Thibaudet / 1992 / London 433515
- ○ **Ivan Moravec Plays French Music** / Moravec / 2001 / Supraphon 3584

Le tombeau de Couperin (1914–1917)

In this extraordinary work, which is conceived as a Baroque suite, Ravel pays homage to the rich tradition of French Baroque music for the harpsichord, as exemplified by the works of François Couperin. It was certainly not Ravel's intention to imitate Couperin, or any other Baroque composer; instead, he included elements of Baroque style without altering his own unique style. While Ravel's pianism is unmistakably modern, his refined, meticulous approach to the keyboard clearly shows an affinity with the French Baroque masters. However, the word "tomb" in the title also had a deeper personal significance for Ravel, who dedicated each movement of the suite to a friend who died World War I. The manuscript is dated 1914–17, so it is difficult to determine if any significant portions of the work were written before the war. At any rate, Ravel intended the composition as a memorial to his friends; while there are moments of lightness and humor in this music, which prompted some to criticize the composer's supposedly irreverent attitude toward death, beneath the flashes of wit one hears profound melancholy tones in the returning soldier's tribute to his fallen comrades. Dedicated to Lieutenant Jacques Charlot, who worked for Ravel's publisher Durand, the Prélude is a veritable whirlpool of sound, the sensation of fluidity created by elegantly executed triplet figurations. A triplet figure also appears in the noble, marmoreal Fugue, dedicated to Lieutenant Jean Cruppi, whose mother had played an important role in the production of *L'Heure espagnole*. Deceptively simple, this movement is a demanding polyphonic construction which Ravel executes with his characteristically brilliant nonchalance. The Forlane, the French variant of an old Italian dance, bears a dedication to Lieutenant Gabriel Deluc, a friend from St-Jean-de-Luz, in Ravel's native Basque region. As Vladimir Jankélévitch remarked, this noble and melancholy movement is like a lullaby. However, there is something slightly jarring and manic in this lullaby, and the manic energy turns into a nervous—but infinitely charming—narrative, the Rigaudon. Dedicated to Ravel's St-Jean-de-Luz friends Pierre and Pascal Gaudin, two brothers who were killed by the same shell on their first day of combat, the Rigaudon is named after an ancient Provençal dance. This movement opens with a poignant figuration, which, recurring with the power of an irresistible fixation, defines the identity of the entire piece. Ravel dedicated the Menuet to Jean Dreyfus, step-brother of the composer and critic Roland-Manuel. Unfolding with the calm pace of an unassuming narrative, this movement, despite its apparently peaceful simplicity, unveils, if only for a moment, feelings of mournful foreboding. The final movement, Toccata is dedicated to Captain Joseph de Marliave, husband of Marguerite Long and devoted admirer of Fauré's music. In this movement, the half-hidden disquietude of the entire composition finally comes to the fore. While the percussive, obsessively recurring figurations may define this movement as a composition dominated by technical demands, there are, trapped in a carapace of busy, hammering gestures, enchanting moments of quiet lyricism. Marguerite Long gave the first performance of *Le Tombeau de Couperin* in 1919; that year, Ravel completed his brilliant orchestration of the Prelude, Forlane, Minuet, and Rigaudon, adding splendid orchestral color to these exquisite musical creations. *—Zoran Minderovic*

Recommended:

- ○ **Ravel: Piano Works** / Roge / 1994 / Decca 440836
- ○ **Ravel: L'Oeuvre pour Piano Seul** / Thibaudet / 1992 / London 433515
- ○ **Ravel: Complete Solo Piano Music** / Hewitt / 2002 / Hyperion 67341/2
- ○ **Kathryn Stott Plays Debussy & Ravel** / Stott / 1991 / Conifer 51755

Valses nobles et sentimentales (1911)

Maurice Ravel could be slightly obsessive in the way he allowed certain musical interests to reappear throughout his compositions. Two such interests were dance and the past, and in *Valses nobles et sentimentales* one can hear how Ravel was able to effectively fuse these two curiosities together. While *Le Tombeau de Couperin* was inspired by the eighteenth century, the *Valses* was oriented toward the nineteenth century. Written out of homage to Schubert's piano piece of the same name, the composer declared that the work's title, "indicates clearly enough my intention of composing a chain of waltzes following the example of Schubert. The virtuoso element that was the basis of *Gaspard de la nuit* is here replaced by a writing of greater clarity, which has the effect of sharpening the harmony as well as the outline of the music." Ravel achieved his goal of clarity, as the waltzes were written using intense precision, sophistication, and technical flawlessness.

Valses nobles et sentimentales contains eight waltzes presented in the following order: Modéré, Assez lent, Modéré, Assez animé, Presque lent, Assez vif, Moins vif, and the Epilogue. Originally written for solo piano, the waltzes stimulate but do not disturb, while displaying different aspects of Ravel's imagination including pride, tenderness, and sentiment. The work was dedicated to Louis Aubert and it was he who gave the first performance on May 9, 1911, at a concert held by the Société Musicale Indépendante, where Schubert's piece of the same name was also premiered. As a little game, the composers' names were withheld, leaving the audience to guess who had written each piece. Audience suggestions included Eric Satie, Zoltán Kodály, and even a correct answer from Debussy, whose ears could not be fooled by the identifiable quality he appreciated. Even though several of Ravel's friends confessed their dislike, others claimed to be strongly drawn to the piece. Tristan Klingsor commented that he was one among several who, "were immediately seduced by the music, and yet he had taken a lot of risks, at least for the period.... He had taken the use of unresolved dissonances to its furthest point. What we now find very piquant was extremely daring at the time. The first bars of the Valses seemed quite extraordinary. Then, since there was nothing there that was not well thought-out, the ear quickly grew to enjoy these pseudo-'wrong notes,' and a glance at the score revealed that they had a proper harmonic justification."

As with *Ma mère l'oye* Ravel allowed only himself to alter *Valses nobles et sentimentales* through orchestration. He adapted the waltzes for the ballet *Adélaïde ou Le langage des fleurs*, for a performance by the troupe of Natasha Trouhanova, and it was premiered as an orchestral work on April 22, 1912, at the Théâtre du Châtelet. Some say that the ironic overtones of the *Valses* foreshadow the superb choreographic poem *La Valse* while confirming to audiences that dissonance was indeed an essential element of his musical style. *—Meredith Gailey*

Recommended:

- ○ **Ravel: Boléro** / Dutoit (cond.), Montreal SO / 1999 / Decca 460214
- ○ **Ravel: Piano Works** / Roge / 1994 / Decca 440836
- ○ **Ravel: Piano Concertos** / Boulez (cond.), Cleveland Orch. / DG 449213
- ○ **Ravel: Complete Orchestral Works** / Abbado (cond.), London SO / 2002 / DG 469354
- ○ **Ravel** / Nagano (cond.), London SO / 1995 / Erato 98479

CONCERTO

Piano Concerto in D major (for the left hand) (1929–1931)

Between 1929 and 1931, Ravel, despite his failing health, worked feverishly, his imagination as powerful as ever. Among the works completed during this period are the two piano concertos: this extraordinary work and the scintillating *Piano Concerto in G major*. This concerto was commissioned by the prominent Austrian pianist Paul Wittgenstein, brother of the celebrated philosopher Ludwig Wittgenstein, who had lost his right arm due to a wound sustained in World War I. It is indeed a tragic irony that Ravel, who also served his country in World War I, and Wittgenstein were enemies in this terrible conflict. Nevertheless, Ravel, fascinated by the technical challenge of composing a concerto for the left hand, approached the project with immense interest and enthusiasm. In addition, Ravel admired Wittgenstein's determination to continue his career as a concert pianist. Piano works for the left hand were certainly not a novelty, as compositions by Scriabin, Alkan, and Liapunov attest, but Ravel wanted to create a unique work which would not merely demonstrate how a pianist can compensate for a physical handicap. He wished to compose a work which would stand out as a unique piano concerto. The outcome of Ravel's efforts is one of the great piano concertos of the twentieth century. However, the Concerto, completed in October or November of 1931, failed to please Wittgenstein, who only gradually developed an appreciation for Ravel's work. Furthermore, when the Austrian pianist premiered the work in Vienna, in 1932, he took certain liberties with the score, to the composer's extreme consternation. Despite Ravel's frustration, he conducted the orchestra in Wittgenstein's Paris premiere of the Concerto in 1933. Because Wittgenstein had sole rights on the work for six years, Ravel had to wait until 1937 to hear a performance (by Jacques Février), which satisfied him. The work, which is really in one movement, begins deep in the bass register, with the contrabassoon, along with the basses, presenting a subdued theme, which elicits a mournful response from the horns. The initial mournful mood is gradually, almost imperceptibly, transformed into an insistent, somewhat manic, musical idea. The piano enters with a simple statement, creating pentatonic resonances, which disappear, but remain in the background. As the initial somber atmosphere lifts, the piano gradually establishes a mood of exquisite lyricism, which pervades the middle section. Ravel's writing is so subtle and technically ingenious that the listener hears a gentle melody with a hypnotically diaphanous, but seemingly elaborate, accompaniment; it is easy to forget that one hand does all the playing. The energy behind the third section, in which the piano engages the orchestra, often mimicking particular instrumental sonorities, profoundly differs from the wave-like, fluid, ascending motion of the *Concerto in G major;* here, the energy is discontinuous, manifesting itself in obstinate, repetitive figurations and phrases which, if only for brief moments, conjure up the spirit of *Boléro*. At the same time, Ravel devotes truly marvelous pages to the piano, particularly in the cadenza-like part of the final section, in which the left hand leads an engaging and richly developed melody into a glowing orchestral finale. *—Zoran Minderovic*

Recommended:

- ○ **Ravel: Piano Concertos** / Abbado (cond.), Beroff, London SO / DG 423665
- ○ **Ravel: Piano Concertos** / Boulez (cond.), Zimerman, London SO / DG 449213
- ○ **Ravel: Piano Concertos; Pavane; Jeux d'eau; La valse** / Maazel (cond.), Collard, National Orch. of France / 2001 / EMI 74749

Piano Concerto in G major (1929–1931)

The piano was Ravel's favorite instrument, and of his two extraordinary concertos, the *Piano Concerto in G major* was, in his opinion, "more Ravelian." Indeed, the two works are profoundly different, but without being, as Vladimir Jankélévitch observed in his book about the composer, more (or less) Ravelian than the other. Nevertheless, Ravel's opinion should not be dismissed, for it reflects his personal predilection, and, as any listener can tell, the work literally overflows with exuberance, delight, and verve. The Concerto may have been conceived in 1928, the year Ravel received his honorary doctorate from the University of Oxford. While some commentators have found the source of this Concerto in Ravel's *Rhapsody on Basque themes Zazpiak bat*, a project which remained unfinished, Robert de Fragny remembered that the composer had remarked that the dazzling opening theme came to him during a train ride from Oxford to London in 1928. In 1929, despite failing health, Ravel talked about a world tour on which he would perform his Concerto. While the world tour never materialized, the composer's life was sufficiently hectic, as he received a commission to compose another piano concerto, the *Piano Concerto in D major (for the left hand)*.

Completed in November 1931, the Concerto was premiered in January 1932, in a legendary performance by Marguerite Long. The sensations that this work conjures up, right from the beginning, are brightness and boundless energy. Opening with a whiplash sound, the first movement, Allegramente, proceeds rapidly, from an initial burst of light, composed of a lively piccolo tune threading through crystalline, harplike piano figuration, to the incisive ending, traversing the many truly magical, even mysterious, moments of repose, when the piano indulges in dreamy, languid soliloquies. Delighting in the piano's expressive potential, Ravel fully employs the instrument's sonority, weaving, for example, a trill into a melody. The piano's rich and subtle discourse is magnificently matched by the orchestra, which, appearing in many guises, mimics and complements the piano, reinforcing the sensation of relentless energy by sharp, metallic, insistent statements by the trumpet. Ravel's splendid orchestration, which tempts the listener to experience this work as a brilliant, and almost self-sufficient, demonstration of sheer musical color, reflects the composer's interest in jazz, evidenced by trombone glissandi and similar effects. However, the jazz elements are profoundly Ravelian, which means that they hardly strike the listener as out of context. The remarkable second movement introduces an introspective, soulful atmosphere, seemingly quite remote from the bustle of the previous movement. A simply stated solo piano theme, of a disarming yet profoundly soulful simplicity, suggesting, perhaps, the image of a solitary promenade in the moonlight, yields to a timeless flute theme which expresses feelings of longing, sorrow, and subdued, yet clearly stated, passion. The final movement, as the piano wends its way through a series of shrieks and wails, executed by woodwind and brass instruments, affects the listener as a mounting wave of sound. A sudden, abrupt exclamation concludes the seductive cacophony of this climactic movement, and the listener experiences a desire to revisit the enchanted landscape of a musical work whose limpid formal structure contains a seemingly boundless world—without a trace of creative fatigue or ambivalence—of elegantly turned musical ideas. *—Zoran Minderovic*

Recommended:

- ○ **Ravel: Piano Concertos, Etc.** / Dutoit (cond.), Thibaudet, Montreal SO / 1996 / London 452448
- ○ **DG Centenary Collection, 1948–1957** / Schmidt-Isserstedt (cond.), Haas / DG 459067
- ○ **Ravel & Rachmaninov: Piano Concertos** / Gracis (cond.), Michelangeli, London PO / 2000 / Angel 67258
- ○ **Ravel: Piano Concertos** / Boulez (cond.), Zimerman, Cleveland Orch. / DG 449213
- ○ **Ravel: Gaspard; Piano Concerto in G, Prokofiev: Piano Concerto 3** / Abbado (cond.), Argerich, Berlin PO / 1975 / DG 447438

Tzigane, rhapsodie de concert for violin & piano (or orchestra) (1922–1924)

While a good part of Ravel's energies during the period 1920–25 were spent on the opera *L'Enfant et les sortilèges*, the composer did find time to produce a handful of smaller-scale works, most notably the *Sonata for violin and cello* (1920–22) and *Tzigane*, a virtuosic, gypsy-inflected vehicle for solo violin and piano. Though Ravel did not complete *Tzigane* until spring 1924, the idea of composing such a work came to him many years earlier, on the occasion of his introduction to the enormously gifted Hungarian violinist Jelly d'Aranyi. D'Aranyi had given a private London performance of the *Sonata for violin and cello* in the early 1920s, and after the concert had so impressed Ravel with her stock of gypsy tunes and bravura technique that he kept her playing until the sun rose the following day. By April 22, 1924 *Tzigane* was ready, and a few days later, it was premiered in London by d'Aranyi and pianist Henri Gil-Marchex. (True to form, Ravel continued to tinker with the piece for several weeks after the first performance.) During the summer of the same year Ravel made an orchestral version of the piano part; he also allowed for the substitution of the piano by a luthéal (a piano with a sound-modifying mechanism placed on its soundboard). Neither of these incarnations, however, entirely captures the nuances of the original.

Tzigane opens with an extended solo for the violin (Lento, quasi cadenza), buried in the middle of which is a theme characterized by a dotted-rhythm, falling-fifth figure which serves as the melodic meat for much of the work. The piano (or harp, in the orchestra version) enters with its own chromatic mini-cadenza as the soloist's fiery technical gestures and robust double stops subside into flickering double tremolos and a pair of unaccompanied trills that usher in the main body of the piece. The remainder of *Tzigane* is worked out in a clearly sectional manner. After a restatement of the falling-fifth idea by the violin, the piano produces its own little theme, a staccato tune that makes thorough use of the typically "gypsy" interval of an augmented second. Some time later, a bombastic Grandioso breaks in. After a brief pause, the violin resumes in 16th note perpetual motion, colored by such features as Paganini-like left-hand pizzicato. The musical line accelerates and decelerates time and again until it finally achieves unstoppable momentum. The work comes to an end with three incisive chords (marked pizzicato, but often played with the bow).—*Blair Johnston*

Recommended:

○ **Historic Philips Recordings, 1953–1962** / Fournet (cond.), Grumiaux, Lamoureux Concert Association Orch. / 2003 / Philips 000017902

○ **Carmen-Fantasie** / Levine (cond.), Mutter, Vienna PO / DG 437544

CHAMBER MUSIC

Berceuse sur le nom de Gabriel Fauré, for violin & piano (1922)

Ravel's simple, affecting lullaby *Berceuse sur le nom de Gabriel Fauré* was published in a special issue of the journal *La Revue Musicale* honoring the esteemed French composer in October 1922. The opening melody derives from the dedicatee's name (which Ravel "spells" musically as GABDBEE FAGDE) and is easily recognizable in subsequent appearances in both the violin and the piano.

The violin plays con sordino throughout the piece. The concluding parallel seconds call to mind "Jumbo's Lullaby" from Debussy's piano suite *Children's Corner* (1906–08). Fauré was flattered by Ravel's *hommage* and wrote in a letter to the composer: "I am thinking of your growth, dear friend . . . and I am happier than you can imagine about the solid position which you occupy and which you have acquired so brilliantly and so rapidly. It is a source of joy and pride for your old professor. . . ." —*Brian Wise*

Recommended:

○ **Un Coeur en Hiver** / Kantorow, Muller, Rouvier / 1974 / Erato 45920

○ **Ravel: Works for Violin & Piano** / Pasquier, Engerer / 1998 / HM 7901364

Introduction & Allegro for harp, flute, clarinet & string quartet (1905)

The Introduction and Allegro (1905) is one of the few pieces by Ravel that has remained more or less in the shadows—save in the minds of harpists—throughout the last century. While it is certainly not among the composer's most striking works, it is nevertheless a pleasant enough showpiece that looks forward to the raw sensuality of *Daphnis et Chloé* while hearkening back with great affection to the music of Chabrier and, especially, Franck. The full title of the work is *Introduction and Allegro for Harp, Accompanied by a Quartet of Strings, Flute, and Clarinet.* Although it is often conveniently designated a septet, it is really a kind of miniature (ten-minute) harp concerto, complete with virtuoso writing and an extended central cadenza for the instrument. Chamber performances of the work, in fact, are few and far between; it is far more frequently heard in the orchestra hall with a full complement of strings. The general simplicity of form and harmony have led some to conclude that the Introduction and Allegro might have originally been composed as a test piece for the Paris Conservatoire; certainly it did not stand out sufficiently in Ravel's own memory for him to include it in his list of works.

The brief Très lent introduction presents two themes, the first for the woodwinds in leaping parallel thirds, the second an inverted-arch-shaped gesture sung by the strings in octaves. Presently a shimmering texture of arpeggios and woodwind double-tonguing takes over, inviting the cello to explore another melody before the harp rejoins the lush musical fabric.

Twenty-six bars into the piece the Allegro commences. Now, as the harp makes an extended solo exploration of the melody presented earlier by the strings, a sonata form begins to take shape. A second, hemiola-ridden theme arrives in the woodwinds, accompanied pizzicato by the strings. The development of this material takes place in the usual fragmentary manner, building to an excited *fff* climax that breaks away abruptly as the harp assumes center stage with a cadenza. The recapitulation is quite straightforward, and the work ends without extensive fireworks or bombast of any kind.

The Introduction and Allegro was first performed in late February, 1907. —*Blair Johnston*

Recommended:

○ **Franck, Debussy, Ravel** / Melos Ens. of London, Chung, Lupu, Ellis / 1988 / London 421154

○ **The Hollywood String Quartet** / Hollywood SQ, Slatkin, Shure, Aller, Stockton, Robyn, Lurie / 1994 / Testament 1053

Piano Trio in A minor (1914)

The list of twentieth century piano trios may be short, but it contains several gems. One of the most precious is the brilliant specimen written by Maurice Ravel in 1914, shortly before he temporarily abandoned life as a musician to serve as a driver for the French army. The *Piano Trio in A minor* is a true sonata for three players, rich in the harmonic and textural innovations Ravel had accomplished in the prewar years, but ultimately, and very possibly more significantly (Ravel certainly felt so), composed around balanced, quintessentially Classical patterns.

The trio has four movements: Modéré, Pantoum (assez vif), Passacaille, and Final (animé). The first movement is a strikingly new variety of sonata-allegro form. The first theme, announced by the piano in pianissimo parallel chords at the very opening of the piece and then taken up by the strings in octaves, is like a shadowy recollection of something out of Basque folk music. Its unusual ostinato rhythm seems to echo in the mind's ear even after Ravel has moved on to the Plus lent qu'au début second theme—a second theme that is very unusually set in the same key as the first. (Ravel makes sense of this atypically tonic-saturated exposition by ending the movement not in the tonic but rather in the relative major, C.) A brief development makes way to a truncated recapitulation which in retrospect seems but a preface to an extended coda in which the ostinato's first idea lingers in the lowest bass of the piano until at last it becomes a faint, colorless drone that dies away into nothingness. This is a remarkable movement that deserves its reputation as a masterpiece.

The second movement is a playful scherzo that will likely sound the most typically French to most listeners. The Passacaille is of course a passacaglia, taking a slow, winding eight-measure pattern as the material to be repeated; the repetition is not strict, and soon a second thematic notion worms its way into the movement, helping to build a massive climax.

Ravel's love of shifting meters is put on display in the quick-paced Final, with contrasts between 5/4 / 7/4. Again sonata-allegro form shapes the course of the music, seeping through the cracks of what might at first seem to be a more freely composed exhibition of instrumental passion—and the closing bars, filled with shimmering, never-ending trills from the strings and a wild whoosh or two from the piano, are certainly passionate. —*Blair Johnston*

Recommended:

○ **Ravel & Debussy** / Ashkenazy, Harrell, Perlman / 1995 / London 444318

○ **Un Coeur en Hiver** / Kantorow, Muller, Rouvier / 1974 / Erato 45920

○ **Chamber Music of Debussy & Ravel** / Nash Ens. / 1997 / Virgin 61427

○ **Debussy, Fauré, Ravel: Piano Trios** / Florestan Trio / 1999 / Hyperion 67114

Sonata for violin & cello (1920–1922)

Maurice Ravel openly admired Debussy for his musical achievements, but refused to accept accusations of imitating his work. The desire for tonal and harmonic gradation is one of many similarities, which have been drawn between the work of the two men. Upon Debussy's death in 1918, Ravel became widely recognized as France's leading composer and was even offered the Légion d'Honneur in 1920, but being a man who considered popularity an offense, he publicly refused the decoration. Between 1920–24 he wrote works which gave homage to his predecessors including his *Sonata for Violin and Cello,* which he dedicated to Debussy's memory.

The work was a continuation of Ravel's interest in counterpoint, and he considered it a turning point, stating that in the piece "the music is stripped down to the bone. The allure of harmony is rejected and increasingly there is a return of emphasis on melody." The music was not only stripped of harmony, but Ravel stripped the traditional sonata down to merely two instruments. In doing so, difficulties arose as Ravel sought to solve the problem of balancing parts by eliminating them. This bold move was based upon Debussy's notion of "depouillement" (economy of means) and was of interest to Satie, Stravinsky, and the postwar generations of composers.

Ravel's *Sonata for Violin and Cello* was written following a period of physical and emotional recovery from the turbulence of the war, his own bout of dysentery, and the death of his mother. Similar to his *Piano Trio* and *String Quartet* Ravel employed a cyclical structure in his sonata. With a focus on coherent and reasoned development of form, the work contains four movements, which are marked in the following order: allegro, très vif (a scherzo), lent, and vif, avec entrain. The work is built upon two main themes, both of which are stated in the first 50 bars of the opening allegro movement. The first is an alternation of the minor and major triads and it is heard in its entirety in the second movement, a bit in the third, and in the middle of the fourth. The second theme is the succession of consecutive sevenths and is the more common of the two, appearing in the beginning of the second and third movements and in a climactic moment in the middle of the finale. The two methods Ravel used to continuously reintroduce the two themes throughout the work were an alternation of a single motif between the two instruments and a separation of parts to maintain clear counterpoint. In the third movement, the concepts of the first two themes combine when minor and major sevenths alternate as did the minor and major thirds of the first movement. This compositional decision reinforces the success of Ravel's achievement to accurately develop the work. The *Sonata for Violin and Cello* was a piece of thoughtful detail which superbly demonstrated the potential of Debussy's notion while helping Ravel to continue to stand out among his contemporaries. —*Meredith Gailey*

Recommended:

○ **French Music for Violin & Cello** / Turovsky, Turovsky / Chandos 8358

○ **Ravel: Works for Piano, Violin & Cello** / Kalichstein-Laredo-Robinson Trio / 2000 / Arabesque 6736

String Quartet in F major (1902–1903)

The similarities between Maurice Ravel's only work for string quartet, the *String Quartet in F major,* and Claude Debussy's only work for string quartet, the

String Quartet in G minor, Op. 10, can hardly be avoided or ignored. During the early years of his career, Ravel was frequently and sometimes vehemently criticized for having copied Debussy, and it was only later that musical society began to realize that, in the realm of piano music at least, it was equally possible that Debussy had imitated his younger colleague. With the *String Quartet in F,* composed in 1902 and 1903 and then revised up to 1910, however, Ravel seems more certain to have relied on Debussy's 1893 Op. 10; as emotionally, psychologically, and even structurally different as the two works are, one could never accuse them of having a language barrier. But, whereas Debussy's *Quartet* is the work of a headstrong progressive still on his way to developing a mature, personal style, Ravel's is the work of an already mature artist more concerned with craftsmanship and traditional structure than with innovation. Not surprisingly, given their relative places in their careers when the two composers wrote their string quartets, Ravel's is the more sound piece of music and Debussy's is the more groundbreaking. Incidentally, Debussy, by all accounts, adored Ravel's piece, and though it makes the cut by just a couple of years, it is probably the most oft-played string quartet of the twentieth century. Ravel dedicated it to his teacher, Gabriel Fauré.

Ravel's *String Quartet* is in four movements: *Moderato très doux, Assez vif-Très rythmé, Très lent,* and *Vif et agité.* The opening movement's pianissimo second theme is as hollow and melancholy as the first theme is warm and inviting. In the second movement, which serves as the *Quartet*'s scherzo, Ravel moves into the pizzicato world already explored by Debussy in the scherzo movement of his *String Quartet*; the central portion (one hesitates to call it a "trio section") calls for the players to put mutes on their instruments. Bits of music from earlier in the *Quartet* can be heard, wearing new clothes, in the slow movement; likewise in the finale, which plunges straight into a frantic 5/4 meter bombast at its start, lightens up in the middle, and then ends in a blaze of zeal. *—Blair Johnston*

Recommended:

- ○ **Debussy, Ravel, Stravinsky: String Quartets** / Alban Berg Quartet / 2001 / EMI 67551
- ○ **Debussy, Ravel, Webern: String Quartets** / Hagen Quartett / DG 437836
- ○ **Debussy, Ravel: Streichquartette** / Emerson SQ / DG 445509

Violin Sonata No. 1 (1897)

Ravel's so-called "posthumous" sonata, rather than having been penned from beyond the grave, is of course an early work not published until 1975, long after the composer's death. Not to be confused with Ravel's much better known G major sonata from 30 years later, which melds blues with neo-Classicism, this compact, one-movement sonata in A minor from 1897 adheres to the classic exposition-development-recapitulation-coda sequence. It shows the strong influence of Fauré and Franck, yet also uses a harmonic and melodic language Ravel would later make his own in his *Piano Trio* and *String Quartet.* The first theme, heard without introduction, is sinuous and dreamy; the second theme, brought in after a short piano solo, is smoother, broader, and at times vaguely Oriental, while still almost passing for Fauré. The coda, after a condensed recapitulation, is particularly chromatic, as if it were plucked from Franck's more famous violin sonata.

Throughout this work, Ravel constantly shifts meters and indulges in harmonic vagueness, helping place the sonata solidly in the French Impressionist style. Yet he also overly relies on triplets, allows his melody to descend frequently into repetition, and displays a competent but not entirely idiomatic knowledge of violin technique. Ravel obviously considered the work too flawed for publication, but it is nevertheless a beguiling piece that surely would have entered the standard repertory had Ravel tightened it up a few years after composing it. *—James Reel*

Recommended:

- ○ **Prague Spring Collection** / Oistrakh, Bauer / 1991 / Multisonic 310109
- ○ **Janáček, Debussy, Ravel, Nielsen: Violin Sonatas** / Tetzlaff, Andsnes / 1995 / Virgin 45122

Violin Sonata No. 2 (1923–1927)

Ravel's Sonata for violin and piano (1923–27) at once illustrates the composer's singular sense of instrumental color in its successful exaggeration of the differences between the violin and the piano. The Sonata's genesis was interrupted by several other compositions; their imprint is evident in the work's mixture of styles, from the blues idiom of the second movement to the perpetuum mobile finale.

Ravel felt that the violin and piano are essentially incompatible instruments, and he exploits something of this friction throughout the first movement. While a gentle lyricism pervades this Allegretto, it is frequently contrasted with sharp, angular themes and highly independent part-writing. An extended cantabile passage for the violin, superimposed over the first two themes, arrives near the end of the movement, which concludes with a three-voice fugato.

While the "Blues" movement predates Ravel's trip to the United States in 1928, the composer commented on it in the course of his visit: "To my mind, the 'blues' is one of your greatest musical assets, truly American despite earlier contributory influences from Africa and Spain. Musicians have asked me how I came to write 'blues' as the second movement of my recently completed sonata for violin and piano.... While I adopted this popular form of your music, I venture to say that nevertheless it is French music, Ravel's music, that I have written. Indeed, these popular forms are but the materials of construction, and the work of art appears only on mature conception where no detail has been left to chance."

Ravel's adoption of the blues idiom is characteristicallly stylized through the addition of bitonality and timbral enrichment, though elements from "pure" jazz, such as the use of the flatted seventh and syncopated rhythms, are also prevalent. The influence of jazz upon the composer would later be more fully manifested in his two piano concerti.

In the third movement, an Allegro perpetuum mobile, the brilliance of the violin writing is contrasted with the relative simplicity of the accompaniment. The musical discourse includes thematic references to the preceding two movements, and an abbreviated reprise of the finale's opening material is underpinned by a theme from "Blues."*—Brian Wise*

Recommended:

- ○ **David Oistrakh in Prague** / Oistrakh, Bauer / Praga 256007
- ○ **Transatlantic** / Kam, Presland / 2001 / Cypres 9615
- ○ **Ravel: Works for Violin & Piano** / Pasquier, Engerer / 1998 / HM 7901364

VOCAL

Chansons madécasses, song cycle for soprano, flute, cello & piano (1925–1926)

During the final phase of Maurice Ravel's career, he experienced hampered creativity and a confused emotional state—which in the years that followed evolved into a preoccupation with economy of means and ensemble combinations. For example, the *Chansons madécasses* (Madagascar Songs), with their unique chamber ensemble, was, as Ravel indicated, "a kind of quartet in which the voice plays the part of the main instrument." The vocal line is uncharacteristic of Ravel's detached and objective style; instead the song sensuously and frightfully declares its message. The texts, taken from the eighteenth century Creole poet Evariste-Desire de Parny, are a cry for liberation from colonialism, exploitation, and slavery as they occurred in Madagascar. "Nahandove" depicts the erotic seduction of a native woman, in which Ravel uses the cello in counterpoint to the flute and piano. "Aoua!" is the frightful warning of the deceiving and dangerous white men; it opens with shrieks of the song's title, made on descending minor thirds. The vocal line is supported by dissonant piano crunches, while a tam-tam effect is made by the resonances of the piano and low notes of the flute. "Aoua!" was probably the most discussed of the three songs. When it was sung by Jane Bathori in 1925, at a concert in the Paris *Salle Majestic,* it was well received, except by a few members of the audience, who found the song's message especially disturbing because fighting was occurring in Morocco. The song comes to a bitter ending where the singer again proclaims "mefiez-vous des blancs" ("Don't trust the whites"). "Il est doux," featuring exotic timbres, returns to the earlier sexual lure. The first complete performance of the three songs was in 1926. Elizabeth Sprague Coolidge, an American patroness of chamber music, made only one suggestion when she commissioned the songs, in regards to the instrumentation of the accompaniment; the choice of text reveals Ravel's interest in the exotic.

Ravel stated that he viewed the years shortly before and during which the *Chansons madécasses* were written as a turning point in his career. In that time he turned from harmonic techniques to "the spirit of melody." The composer revealed in a late interview that these three songs were his favorites. *—Meredith Gailey*

Recommended:

- ○ **Debussy & Ravel: Chamber Music** / Walker, Nash Ens. / 1997 / Virgin 61427
- ○ **Ravel: Mélodies** / Norman, Debost, Fontanarosa / 1984 / EMI 569299
- ○ **Ravel: Chansons madécasses; Two-Piano Pieces; Violin & Cello Sonata** / de Gaetani, Kalish, Dunkel, Anderson / 1978 / Nonesuch 71355

Deux mélodies hébraïques (1914)

Maurice Ravel's *Deux mélodies hébraïques* (Two Hebrew Songs), like so many songs by the man, exist in versions for voice and piano and for voice and orchestra, and when you can orchestrate as well as Ravel could, why not? The dates of the piano versions and of the later orchestral versions happen to coincide almost perfectly with the extreme boundaries of World War I: 1914 and 1919, respectively. (For whatever it's worth, Ravel got very little work done during the war years, and so this five-year gap between composition and orchestration might not have been entirely by his choosing.)

Both of the *Deux mélodies hébraïques* texts are biblical in origin, and Ravel provides both in two different languages—Aramaic and French in the case of the first song, and Yiddish and French in the case of the second.

No. 1, "Kaddisch," has on the surface a very un-Ravellian character. The singer bends and twists through a flashy, ethnically inflected (meaning, of course, Middle Eastern, in a manner sometimes seemingly authentic and sometimes less so), mock-improvised terrain to what is at first just sparse comment from the piano/orchestra. But, listening a little deeper, we realize that only Ravel would have fashioned those octave G naturals, and the sliding voice in between them, in just that way (and few indeed are the composers with courage enough to put the singer out there on a limb all alone for so much of the song!). As the song moves along and the piano begins a rich, harplike arpeggiated accompaniment, which prompts something a little more song-like from the singer; Ravel as we know him comes rather more to the surface of the music.

No. 2, "L'énigme éternelle" is, by comparison with the ever-changing, gust-and-blow rhythmic quality of the previous song, as stable and steady as it gets. A quietly repeating one-measure cell starts up in the accompaniment at the very beginning of the song and never lets up; but the way Ravel allows this little unit to shift around chromatically is masterful, and it never grows stale. The song, whose dynamic spends most of the time at pianissimo and never grows more robust than piano, is a wonderful example of the kind of tranquil but shimmering musical understatement of which Ravel was so admirably capable. *—Blair Johnston*

Recommended:

- ○ **Ravel: Mélodies** / Van Dam, Baldwin / 1984 / EMI 569299
- ○ **The Fabulous Victoria de los Angeles** / Los Angeles / 1993 / EMI 650612
- ○ **Chant d'amour** / Bartoli, Chung / 1996 / London 452667

Don Quichotte à Dulcinée, song cycle for voice & orchestra (1932–1933)

Since he was a native of Pays Basque, born of the Basses Pyrenées at Ciboure, it seems fitting that Maurice Ravel's last completed composition, *Don Quichotte à Dulcinée* (also known as *Trois chansons de Don Quichotte à Dulcinée*) (1932–33) should reflect his Spanish heritage. The work is alive with traditional Iberian music and also contains the most famous character in Iberian literature. The work was part of a competition of 1932 in which de Falla, Ravel, Milhaud, Marcel Delannoy, and Jacques Ibert took part, for the performance in George W. Pabst's film *Don Quixote* starring the Russian bass Feodor Chaliapin. Slightly occupied with a European tour of his *Piano Concerto in G* with Marguerite Long, Ravel's *Don Quichotte* was written slowly due to failing health that was complicated by a car accident, which occurred in the same year. Unable to deliver the work in time, Ravel's skills and composition were passed up for those of Ibert. Regardless of Pabst's rejection, Ravel's work had its first performance with conductor Paul Paray and baritone Martial Singher on December 1, 1934, and was recorded at that time.

The three songs of *Don Quichotte à Dulcinée*, poems by novelist Paul Morand, reflect the tenderly sincere and humorous moments of this well-known tale. The introductory quixotic song, "Chanson Romanesque," uses a pleasant vocal melody for Don Quixote's declaration of devotion to Dulcinea with a guitar-like accompaniment of the piano in a four-verse set of variations. "Chanson Epique" is the Knight's humble prayer, for blessings and protection, to the Virgin and the saints, in which the piano is used in the style of a church organ with rhythm derived from the Basque zortzico. Its austere chant, near the end of the song, concludes with a peaceful "Amen." The song cycle closes with "Chanson á boire," a robust jota in triple time, suitable for the lively exaggerations and embellishments written for the song's toast, "I drink to joy! Joy is the one aim for which I go straight... when I've drunk." Through this song Ravel bids an inadvertent adieu to music, from then on he suffered from ataxia and aphasia which kept him from coherently completing musical ideas such as the opéra-ballet *Morgiane* and the opéra-oratorio *Jeanne d'Arc*.

When Ravel provided the world with *Don Quichotte à Dulcinée* he furthered the possibility of his belief that "music must always be beautiful," by creating a composition that was charming, moving, and thoughtful. *—Meredith Gailey*

Recommended:

- ○ **José Van Dam: Martin; Ravel; Ibert; Poulenc** / Van Dam, Nagano (cond.), Lyon Opera Orch. / 1992 / Virgin 59236
- ○ **Ravel: Mélodies** / Van Dam, Baldwin / 1984 / EMI 569299
- ○ **Fauré, Ravel, Poulenc: Melodies** / Allen, Vignoles / 1994 / Virgin 545053

Histoires naturelles, song cycle (1906)

"I would wish," commented the poet Jules Renard, "[that my animal poems] be pleasing to the animals themselves. Were they able to read my miniature *Histoires naturelles*, I should wish that it would make them smile." Ravel perhaps had similar aims in composing his musical setting of five of Renard's poems, creating a cycle whose wit and charm has made it a favorite in the repertoire of twentieth century French song.

Ravel's cycle *Histoires naturelles* (1906) traces its inspiration to the same-titled 44-volume zoological treatise by French naturalist and mathematician Georges Louis Leclerc de Buffon (1707–88). Renard wrote a series of lighthearted poems based on Buffon's work and published them in 1895. They became quite popular and were no doubt familiar to those in attendance at the 1907 premiere of Ravel's cycle. The wry humor of the settings was not wholly appreciated at the first performance; one observer recalled that the audience interrupted the long pauses in the middle of "Grillon" (The Cricket) with derisive laughter, and read an ironic twist into the opening lines of "Martin-pêcheur" (The Kingfisher): "Ça n'a pas mordu, ce soir..." ("No luck this evening...").

Perhaps the audience rolled their eyes at Ravel's pictorialisms, which sometimes lend the songs an air of caricature. Still, in the spirit of Mussorgsky's *Pictures at an Exhibition* (which Ravel later orchestrated), some of these renderings, either in their affective or their literal representation, are delightfully accurate. Anyone familiar with the harsh, unmelodious song of the guinea hen will chuckle at the burbling beginning of "La Pintade"; likewise, the chirps that decorate "Le Grillon" are strikingly cricketish, but artfully and seamlessly blended into the musical texture.

However, Ravel's musical interpretation of Renard's texts goes much deeper than these surface felicities might suggest. Despite their subject matter, Ravel's and Renard's portraits tell deeply and profoundly human stories. Certainly, the grouchy, paranoid, and ever-confrontational guinea hen is a familiar social archetype, one meant to resonate cleverly and knowingly with the listener. Ravel's depiction follows Renard's, accompanying the unfriendly fowl with nervous vamps and answering her outbursts with broad pianistic flourishes; though a caricature, it does reserve a hint of sympathy for the miserable creature. The grandiose music to which the peacock struts has a kind of unresolved, pathetic buffoonery to it. Reading Renard's poem, one laughs at the proud bird; in Ravel's setting, one feels just a little sorry for the poor groom, waiting in ignorance and in vain for a bride that never arrives. The story of the swan is the most hopeful: Despite the graceful bird's unsuccessful attempts to capture the reflection of the clouds in the water, Renard in the end points out that, with each try, he pulls up a worm and gets as "fat as a goose." Ravel's music follows this epigrammatic turn with an optimistic change of tempo and a happy conclusion.

In setting Renard's poetry, Ravel renders it as a dramatic reading. Phrases are built around the semantic and dramatic contours of the poems, creating a fluid and breathable structure. Pauses, as if in thought, are not uncommon, and the action proceeds sporadically according to the alternating phases of rumination, observation, and action in the text. This makes the cycle a very singable one, and one in which the music enhances, rather than encumbers, the poetry. *—Jeremy Grimshaw*

Recommended:

- ○ **Ravel: Mélodies** / Bacquier, Baldwin / 1984 / EMI 569299
- ○ **Ravel: Melodies** / LeRoux, Roge / 2001 / Chant du Monde 2781131
- ○ **Hommage à Jane Bathori: The Inspiring Muse** / Upshaw / 1999 / Erato 27329
- ○ **Jane Bathori: Complete Solo Recordings** / Bathori / 1999 / Marston 51009

Cinq mélodies populaires grecques, song cycle (1904–1906)

It isn't hard to figure out why singers—and pianists, to be sure—love Maurice Ravel's *Cinq mélodies populaires grecques* (Five Greek Folksongs) as much as they do. The texts, which were translated from the Greek originals into French by Michel Dimitri Calvocoressi, are charmingly short and pithy, and the music to which Ravel has set them is, despite a vague Mediterranean flavor, pure Ravel—the kind of rich, modified-diatonic music that might to an uninitiated ear seem "impressionist" but really has an objectivity of line and a clarity, even thinness, of texture that marks it as something else altogether. The five songs were composed from 1904 to 1906; Ravel later orchestrated two of them, and the remaining three were orchestrated by another hand, making it possible to perform the entire cycle in the concert rather than the recital hall.

The *Cinq mélodies populaires grecques* are: 1. Chanson de la mariée (Song of the Bride), 2. Là-bas, vers église (Over by the Church), 3. Quel galant m'est comparable (Which Gallant Compares with Me), 4. Chanson des cueilleuses de lentisques (Song of the Lentisk Collectors), and 5. Tout Gai! (Be Gay!—these days often translated less literally).

In the first song, a man asks his bride-to-be to arise and enjoy the morning with him; he offers that the two might be married, so that their families might be as close as they are. The music is moderately paced and is in G minor, though more often than not Ravel leaves out the third and we hear only an open fifth. The piano makes a quiet, arpeggiated rustle as the singer calls up a melody that over the entire course of the song covers only the span of a minor sixth (from G up to E flat)—Ravel proves yet again that excess is not needed to create mood and inflection.

The texture of No. 2 is by comparison much stiller, but in the third song, a burst of machismo during which the singer boasts of his manliness by virtue of sword and pistol, we are treated to some rowdiness, both from the singer and from the accompaniment.

You might describe "Song of the Lentisk Collectors" as a cross between the steady, registrally-shifting chords of the second song and the flowing arpeggios of the first, though still that would but poorly describe the happenings of this gentle, Lydian mode-inflected number. A raucous outburst might be expected for the last song (it does bear the enthusiastic title "Tout Gai!" after all), but that's not really Ravel's way, and he keeps things plainly and firmly in check (the accompaniment, for instance, remains at the piano dynamic throughout), even as the singer happily explains how attractive the dancing legs are! Midway through the song the text dissolves into a good-natured "tra la la" that takes us to the end. *—Blair Johnston*

Recommended:

- ○ **Ravel: Mélodies** / Mesple, Baldwin / 1984 / EMI 569299
- ○ **Voyage à Paris** / Von Stade, Katz / 1995 / RCA 902662711

Trois poèmes de Stéphane Mallarmé, song cycle for voice & ensemble (1913)

In a 1927 interview, Maurice Ravel said of the symbolist poet Stéphane Mallarmé that he "exorcised our language, like the magician that he was. He has released the winged thoughts, the unconscious daydreams from their prison." Mallarmé had been an immense influence on a variety of artists, including Ravel, who had set his first Mallarmé poem, *Sainte*, in 1896 and returned to the poet's work in 1913 with the *Trois poèmes*. Around that time Ravel had heard Igor Stravinsky's *Trois poésies de la lyrique japonaise* (1912–13), and was particularly impressed by Stravinsky's arrangement, in which the singer was backed by an ensemble of piano, string quartet, two flutes, and two clarinets. Stravinsky, in turn, had been much influenced by Arnold Schoenberg's notorious *Pierrot lunaire* (1912), with its similar instrumentation. On completing his songs, which employed the same instrumental layout as Stravinsky's, Ravel envisioned what he called a "scandalous concert," featuring his songs along with Stravinsky's and Schoenberg's. That concert did take place, although with songs by Maurice Delage replacing the Schoenberg, under the auspices of the Société Musicale Indépendante on January 14, 1914. Soprano Jane Bathori, one of the best known French singers of her day, was featured, along with an ensemble conducted by Désiré-Emile Inghelbrecht.

The increasing angularity and dissonance of Ravel's *Trois poèmes* reflects the increasingly dissociative imagery of the three Mallarmé poems. The first song, "Soupir" (Sigh), is in two parts, the first slow and delicate (evoking the poet's "white fountains"), the second more spacious and evanescent. The vocal line becomes more a bit more jagged in "Placet futile" (Futile Petition), a gently melancholy love song. And with the third and final song, "Surgi de la croupe et du bond" (Risen from the Crupper and Leap), Ravel comes as close to the atonality of Arnold Schoenberg as he ever would. This setting of what Ravel once called "the strangest, if not the most hermetic" of Mallarmé's sonnets is still and mysterious, with a very spare accompaniment.

Coincidentally, at the very time that Ravel was composing his *Trois poèmes*, Claude Debussy was also setting three of Mallarmé's poems (both were perhaps inspired by a new complete edition of Mallarmé's poetry which had just been published). Not only that, but they had both chosen to set two of the same poems; Debussy called this a "phenomenon of autosuggestion worthy of communication to the Academy of Medicine." *—Chris Morrison*

Recommended:

○ **La Bonne Chanson** / Otter, Forsberg / 1996 / DG 447752

○ **Ravel: Mélodies** / Plasson, Lott / 1984 / EMI 569299

Vocalise-Étude en forme de Habanera, for voice & piano (1907)

French composers' fascination with Spain can be traced back to Lalo's *Symphonie espagnol* and Bizet's *Carmen*, both of which received their premieres in 1875. In the years that followed, Chabrier, Debussy, and Ravel would all compose a handful of works with a decidedly Spanish flavor. Ravel in particular was fond of the characteristically Spanish *habanera* rhythm, which occurs not only in this piece, but also in his *Rhapsodie espagnol* and the *Habanera* for piano. Ravel's *Vocalise-Etude en forme d'Habanera* may have been composed as a study in the contemporary style for students at the Paris Conservatoire, and indeed the piece's demanding vocal line—with its scales, trills, and staccato passages—and technically challenging piano accompaniment certainly suggest, along with the designation "etude," that this piece was composed in part to serve pedagogical aims. The *Vocalise-Etude* does appear, however, in a collection of vocalises assembled by A.L. Hettich, and it has been suggested that Ravel in fact wrote this piece specifically for Hettich's collection.

In the *Vocalise*, the insistent repetition of the *habanera* rhythm is set against the virtuosic runs and portamento effects in the voice part, showcasing Ravel's skill as a composer for the voice. The musical material for the *Vocalise* is thought to be derived from Ravel's opera *L'Heure espagnole*, which he was working on early in 1907. Though the work as a whole perhaps lacks substance, the *Vocalise* is a good example of Ravel's understanding of the musical potential of the voice, and it numbers among Ravel's other important works in the French-Spanish style. *—Alexander Carpenter*

Recommended:

○ **Ravel: Mélodies** / Berganza, Baldwin / 1984 / EMI 569299

○ **Live In Concert 1952–1960** / Los Angeles / 1993 / VAI Audio 1025

○ **Music For Flute & Harp** / Rampal, Nordmann / 1990 / Sony 44552

OPERA

L'enfant et les sortilèges, opera-ballet (1920–1925)

Although the finished product would not appear until 1925, Maurice Ravel had begun planning the opera (really a fantasie lyrique) *L'Enfant et les sortilèges* with librettist Sidonie-Gabrielle Colette (normally just credited as "Colette") as early as 1918. The partnership was neither particularly natural nor especially comfortable for either the composer or the writer, but, in the end they succeeded in producing an endearing and enduring theater-piece that many feel to be among Ravel's most thoroughly impressive works. Nearly half a decade was spent on the actual composition of the opera, and it was only when an inflexible premiere date was set that Ravel actually forced himself to wrap the work up; it was premiered at the Opéra de Monte Carlo on March 21, 1925, to warm, but not effusive, public and critical response.

It was no doubt Colette's ability to seamlessly and unpretentiously blend together innocence and suavity that first attracted Ravel to her work. While Ravel is known to have made some modifications to the text of *L'Enfant et les sortilèges*, the basic storyline—an insensitive young boy being taken to task by the very animals and objects he has mistreated, learning compassion and kindness along the way—was agreed upon at a very early stage. Ravel chose to dip his musical ladle into several pots as he composed the opera, and we find dramatic opera mixed together with operetta and even jazz (the foxtrot for the Teapot and the China Teacup). Ravel had the following to say of the basic musical design: "The preoccupation with melody that characterizes the work is accounted for by a storyline that it amused me to treat in the American operetta style. By dealing with a fantasy tale, Mme. Colette's libretto justified such a choice. Here, singing must come first; the orchestra, although capable of some virtuosity, remains firmly in the background."

And indeed, the opera is song and melody throughout. The fact that only a handful of the 20 or so solo roles are actual people, the rest being personifications of objects and animals (two cats, a chair, a clock, etc.), highlights the childlike, fairy-tale character of the opera. Melodiousness and precedence of voice over orchestra do not necessarily demand a "traditional" operatic approach, however, and only at a few isolated moments does Ravel allow anything even remotely resembling fiery Italian operatic writing into his score; the most extensive example is, quite understandably, the virtuosic solo aria of the Fire. Other highlights are the sensuous love-duet of the two cats and the gibberish-ridden song of the Teapot and China Teacup (an incoherent spattering of American and mock-Chinese idioms).

While the orchestra is certainly subordinate to the voices, the actual orchestration ranks right up there with the composer's other masterful instrumental blueprints. The ensemble is rather sizeable, and yet the music is scored with such skill that the orchestra creates the illusion of transparency while in fact never lacking in fullness or warmth. Ravel very clearly enjoyed the challenge of rendering such unusual effects as clocks ticking and cats meowing. Some of the opera's critics, however, have found the abundance of such musical superficialities to be both distracting and disconcerting; one writer has even described the opera as an excuse for "dazzling musical legerdemain," and, to be fair, in any but the most masterful performance, its juicy sentimentality rings a little bit false. No doubt most of this overt emotionalism is due to Ravel's deep affection for both his childhood and his mother, both of which play a huge role in the emotional content of *L'Enfant et les sortilèges*. *—Blair Johnston*

Synopsis:

Scene One. The story of The Child and The Spells takes place in an old Norman country house and its garden, within a fairy tale setting. The Child, aged about seven, sits bored with his homework before him. His mother encourages him to do his lessons, but he responds by sticking his tongue out at her. For this insolent act he is left alone, and told he will have a long wait before supper.

The Child pouts and takes out his frustration by smashing dinnerware, abusing his pet squirrel and tomcat, tearing off portions of wallpaper, and performing other destructive acts. Suddenly an armchair and Louis XV chair begin moving about, with other furniture soon following their lead. They all sing of the abuse they have suffered from the little brat in recent times, the grandfather clock and Chinese teacup in particular recounting their bad treatment.

Soon the fire emerges from the fireplace and begins to pursue the Child, and the shepherds and shepherdesses, which adorned the now-destroyed wallpaper, come to life. But through all this the Child remains defiant in his destruction, kicking his arithmetic book to the floor. Numbers jump out of it, however, led by a Little Old Man, who calls out a series of mathematical problems, albeit with arithmetic not quite accurate. After being drawn into a dance by the Little Old Man and his retinue, the Child becomes exhausted. The Tomcat emerges from beneath a chair, spits at the Child, then joins his mate, the white Cat, in a love duet.

Scene Two. The Child is transported into the garden along with the two cats. There, complaints about the Child from the garden's inhabitants abound: the Trees carp about the cuts made into their bark, and the Bat and Dragonfly lament the loss of their mates at the hands of the brat. The Squirrel then enters and pleads his case of abuse, too.

Soon the Child begins to grasp the sense of happiness the animals share and the resultant loneliness he feels being in their midst. He cries out "Mommie," alerting the animals to his vulnerability. They unite against the Child and attack him, but in the ensuing excitement to defeat their nemesis, the animals turn on their own. A little squirrel sustains an injury to its paw and in the aftermath of the conflict, the Child compassionately tends to its wound. The animals notice his act of kindness and suddenly change their feelings about him. They help him back inside the house, where he now confidently calls out "Mommie." *—Robert Cummings*

Recommended:

○ **Ravel: L'Enfant et les sortilèges; L'Heure espagnole** / Maazel (cond.), ORTF / DG 449769

○ **Ravel: L'Enfant et les sortilèges** / Bour (cond.), France National Radiodiffusion Orch. / 1994 / Testament 1044

L'heure espagnole (1907–1909)

Ravel's opera *L'heure espagnole*, completed in 1909, was his first work for the stage, and it richly exhibits the irony and refined humor that graced his *Histoires naturelles*. The vehicle for Ravel's sophisticated, convoluted humor is the quasi-parlando vocal line, a singing technique that combines elements of speech; not only is the effect a bit unreal, but the technique enables the composer to literally blend speech and music, often using purely musical effects to emphasize the narrative's comic point. Based on a play by Franc Nohain, *L'heure espagnole* is a parodic improvisation on the paradoxical and mysterious nature of time. Taking place in a watchmaker's shop, the story centers on his wife's grotesquely transparent ploys to get her husband out of the way so she can pursue a series of amorous trysts. In calling his opera The Spanish Hour, Ravel openly ridicules the perennial complaint of lovers whose time always seems to flow faster. Ravel only sees this hour as a framework to contain—if possible—a torrent of ridiculous events. Obviously, even time itself is ridiculous. The characters' names, too, are comical: the foolish watchmaker is called Torquemada (a grotesque reference to the cruel Torquemada of Spanish Inquisition "fame"). So, while Torquemada is away fixing clocks, his wife entertains her paramours. When Torquemada returns, the other characters hide in clocks or pretend to be customers. The burlesque climax of the opera is an amazing quintet of all of the characters poking fun at each other. In this work, Ravel indulges a fascination with mechanical devices that he inherited from his Swiss father, who was an engineer. *L'heure espagnole* opens with an introduction, a masterfully suggestive evocation of a hallucinatory world of ticking clocks and human-like automatons. Another fascination is Spain. Claiming Basque heritage, Ravel often turned to Spain for inspiration. But Ravel's Spain is an idealized, stylized realm, an imaginary world that only vaguely resembles the physical place. Thus, Ravel's Spanish, which sounds vaguely Hispanic, has no other source than Ravel's mind. And in this work, like in other Spanish compositions, Ravel revels in his prodigious talents as a colorist, using a variety of brass and percussion instruments to create the richly atmospheric background of the ridiculous and often frantic events. The opera concludes with a Habanera; true, the rhythms are Spanish, but the essence of this concluding dance, with its bright energy and vaguely modal melodic lines, brings the fantastic Spain of Ravel's imagination to brilliant life. *—Zoran Minderovic*

Synopsis:

The story is set in the shop of clockmaker Torquemada in eighteenth century Toledo, Spain. Torquemada sits at his workbench with conspicuous ticks from the clocks filling the room. The strapping muleteer Ramiro enters and presents Torquemada with a watch in need of repairs. He explains that it belonged to his uncle, a toreador, and protected him from the lethal thrust of a bull's horns one day in the ring.

Torquemada's wife Concepcion soon enters to remind her husband to carry out his weekly duties of winding up all the city's clocks. He asks Ramiro to wait until he returns, then departs, unaware that during the hour it usually takes him to carry out his municipal clock-winding chores, his wife regularly meets with lovers at the shop. To get rid of Ramiro, she asks him to carry a grandfather clock to her bedroom. He agrees to do so, and soon the young poet Gonzalve enters for his weekly tryst, temporarily immersed in thoughts of his poetry, though.

Ramiro returns sooner than Concepcion had anticipated. She tells him he moved the wrong clock and asks him to replace it with the correct one. He obliges, and while he fetches the "wrong" clock, Concepcion directs Gonzalve to climb into the large clock Ramiro will be carrying to her bedroom. Another of her lovers, the banker Don Inigo Gomez, enters. Soon Ramiro returns, and to allay any suspicions Don Inigo might develop about him, she explains that the muleteer is a mover. Ramiro picks up the clock housing Gonzalve and carries it up the steps, Concepcion following anxiously.

Don Inigo calculates that his only his hope of having a rendezvous with Concepcion is by climbing into one of the large clocks to await transport upstairs by the mover. Ramiro returns and soon Concepcion also comes back down, claiming now that the clock in her bedroom is broken. Ramiro leaves to fetch it and while he is gone, Concepcion, annoyed by Don Inigo's pathetic mimicry of a cuckoo, tells him to come out of the clock. But he has difficulty extricating himself and soon finds himself being carried upstairs by Ramiro. Meanwhile, Gonzalve, back down in the shop, refuses to step out of his clock.

Ramiro returns, now expressing his own affections for Concepcion. Soon she comes back down and sends him upstairs once more for the clock. Concepcion begins to have doubts about her lovers, and her libidinal muse soon turns to Ramiro, who, after returning with the clock housing Don Inigo, finds himself ascending the stairs at the behest of Concepcion, who follows closely behind.

Torquemada returns and opportunistically sells the two lovers the clocks they are hiding in. Gonzalve emerges from his clock, but the corpulent Don Inigo is stuck. Ramiro and Concepcion return and are finally able to extract Don Inigo. The five characters then sing the story's moral (from Boccaccio): "There is a time and place for the lover up to the task." *—Robert Cummings*

Recommended:

○ **Ravel: L'Enfant et les sortilèges; L'Heure espagnole,** / Maazel (cond.), ORTF / DG 449769

RCA Victor Symphony Orchestra

f. ca. 1936, Camden, NJ, **db.** ca. 1966

Ensemble

This eponymous orchestra had its roots in a salon ensemble created by Nat Shilkret, music director of the Victor Talking Machine Company between 1916 and 1935. Based in Camden, NJ, across the river from Philadelphia, Victor (which merged with RCA) was able to use players from Stokowski's orchestra on an ad hoc basis as late as 1940. By then it was called the "RCA Victor Orchestra"—not, however, to be confused with another ad hoc group, called simply the Victor Orchestra, in NYC for lighter music on the company's budget black and blue labels.

The merger with RCA, the Great Depression, union-czar's James Petrillo's ban on stateside recording in the early 1940s, and the Philadelphia Orchestra's defection in 1943 to Columbia Records (a CBS affiliate) changed the playing field. New alliances between overseas and U.S. labels complicated matters after World War II, exacerbated by Columbia's acquisition of the Metropolitan Opera, many of whose singers were already RCA artists. The "RCA Victor Symphony" suddenly became a major player, based chiefly but not solely in Manhattan, which boasted a vast reservoir of players.

The RCA SO wasn't, however, just an operatic project. Leonard Bernstein made his first records with it as a Victor artist (1944–50). Stravinsky, based in Hollywood, also conducted RCA SO records, both there and in Mexico City. Jascha Heifetz recorded several concertos with conductors William Steinberg and Izler Solomon. All of Robert Shaw's RCA recordings drew from the New York pool. However, the principal conductor of RCA's complete operas in a war with Columbia was Renato Cellini, until Fritz Reiner left Columbia for RCA in 1950.

Victor's NYC players came from the Philharmonic, the Met, the City Center and NBC Orchestras and radio staff musicians. When Reiner entered the picture, contractors of his choosing engaged the requisite number of players—thereby guaranteeing performance consistency—whether in Bach's *Brandenburg Concertos*, Strauss' tone poems, concerto accompaniments, or opera excerpts (with several of the Met's leading singers in then-current productions of *Die Fledermaus* and *Der Rosenkavalier*, plus a complete *Carmen*). But while Reiner may have been primus inter pares, others recorded with the RCA SO including Stokowski, Krips, Kondrashin, and Wallenstein. Los Angeles was the second center for eponymous recording orchestras—there were Columbia and MGM symphony orchestras as well as the one at RCA. The area had a pool of first-class studio players and Philharmonic personnel (who anchored most of Bruno Walter's last hurrahs, and whatever Stravinsky did not record in Toronto or New York).

Until the simultaneous advent of stereo and year-round contracts, major U.S. symphony orchestras played summer concerts. Thus, Everest could record the NY Phil as the Stadium SO; RCA could record Philadelphia as the Robin Hood Dell SO, and the LA Phil as the Hollywood Bowl SO. But those were aliases, not commercial eponyms.

However, when film production headed overseas in the 1960s to economize, so did RCA, whose U.S. Symphony Orchestra was replaced by an RCA Italiana Orchestra, off-season Rome Opera players recruited for operas by Verdi, Puccini, et al. In 1963, after Chicago, Reiner recorded Haydn symphonies in NYC with "his orchestra" (a Stokowski *nom du disque* dating back to the 1940s). Although U.S. record companies retained "name" orchestras to challenge a flood-tide of product from Europe, classical music sales dried up in the 1990s like the Serengeti. Bertelsmann, a German media conglomerate, bought RCA Red Seal Records but put its century-old backlog to the sword in 2001, so that the last published issue of *Schwann Artists* had no listing of the RCA Victor SO per se. *—Roger Dettmer*

Recommended:

○ **Leopold Stokowski—The Magician** / Stokowski (cond.), etc. / 1999 / RCA 70931

○ **Legendary RCA Recordings: Vladimir Horowitz** / Toscanini, Reiner (conds.), Horowitz, RCA Victor SSO, NBCSO / 2003 / RCA 56052

○ **Russian Orchestral Favorites** / Kondrashin (cond.), Shumsky, RCA Victor SO / 1999 / BMG 633022

Max Reger

b. Mar. 19, 1873, Brand, Germany, **d.** May 11, 1916, Leipzig, Germany

Composer: Keyboard, Chamber Music, Vocal, Orchestral, Concerto

Max Reger was an important composer whose artistic worth far surpasses his still generally meager representation on the concert stages and in recordings. In his teen years, he came under the disparate influences of Bach and Wagner, and eventually fused a style from these sources, adding his own unique and seemingly ubiquitous counterpoint, to fashion music that was both ahead of its time and inextricably bound to the past. His mature idiom melded Baroque structural ingredients with the opulent harmonic palette of the late Romantic period. His organ compositions include masterworks like the chorale fantasia *Ein feste Burg is unser Gott, Fantasia and Fugue in C minor*, and *Fantasia and Fugue on B-A-C-H.* His huge chamber music output, consisting of nine sonatas for violin and piano and many other works, is an important body of work.

Reger was born in Brand, Bavaria on March 19, 1873, and grew up in Weiden. He studied organ and violin with his father, and piano with his mother. At 11, he began studies with organist Adalbert Lindner. In 1888, Reger traveled to Bayreuth and heard performances of Wagner's *Parsifal* and *Die Meistersinger.* The experience had a lasting effect on him, the harmonies and sounds of the latter opera profoundly affecting his musical psyche. In 1890, he began studies in Wiesbaden with Hugo Riemann and soon produced his *Violin Sonata No. 1* (1890–91), Op. 1.

Reger developed a friendship with composers Eugen d'Albert and Ferruccio Busoni in the mid-1890s. During this time, he wrote several compositions for piano, including *Lose Blätter* (1894) and *Aus der Jugendzeit* (1895). After an unpleasant experience in the military that affected his physical and mental health, he returned to his parents' Weiden home to recuperate. During this period, he produced his Op. 27 chorale fantasia *Ein Feste Burg is Unser Gott*, and his Op. 29 *Fantasy & Fugue in C minor.* Reger also earned a reputation as a brilliant pianist at this time, playing many concerts of wide-ranging repertoire, including his own works.

In 1902 Reger married Elsa von Bercken. The *Sinfonietta in A* (1904–05) set off a most unwelcome stir for the composer, placing him at odds with the more conservative musical circles in Munich, where he had settled in 1901. By 1907 Reger had decided that the hostile climate in Munich was not worth enduring any longer, and accepted a professorship at Leipzig University. His many students there included Szell, von Hoesslin, Joseph Haas, Schoeck, Kvapil, and Weinberger. His Violin Concerto (1907–08) and the *Symphonic Prologue to a Tragedy* (1908) came during this period.

In 1911, Reger was appointed conductor of the Meiningen Court Orchestra by Duke George II. He continued appearing as a pianist and always found time to compose. In February, 1914, he suffered a breakdown from troubles in his Meiningen post and eventually resigned. By September of 1914, he had finished *Eight Sacred Songs* and the *Patriotic Overture* for orchestra. In March 1915, the composer and his family settled in Jena, where he completed his Sonata No. 9 for violin and piano, declaring it his greatest work in the genre, and the first in his so-called "Jena style." Other important works came during his "Jena" period, including the Op. 131 chamber works for various string instruments (Op. 131a, Op. 131b, Op. 131c, Op. 131d). His concert schedule took him to Holland in May, 1916, where he died of a heart attack. *—Robert Cummings*

KEYBOARD

Works for Organ (1892–1916)

As German composer Max Reger once wrote, "You'll probably be surprised by the 'turgidity' of my works. But I was always in earnest!" Although Reger was not writing specifically about his organ music, the term "turgidity" seems particularly apt when applied to his prodigious oeuvre for organ. And it was prodigious: in his total of 145 published works, only works for chamber ensembles (34) and piano (30) outnumber organ works (28) and the quantity and quality undoubtedly makes Reger the most important German organ composer after Bach. But as Reger himself realized, it is turgid albeit earnest stuff with four, five, or even six lines of simultaneous counterpoint creating an intensely dense texture. Although himself a Bavarian Catholic, Reger was by nature drawn to the chorales of Luther and the forms of Bach. Thus, his organ output is full of chorale preludes and chorale fantasies such as *Ein' Feste Burg ist unser Gott*, Op. 27 (1898); *Freu' dich Sehr, O meine Seele*, Op. 30 (1898); *Wachet Auf, Ruft uns die Stimme*, Op. 52 (1900); and *Halleluja! Gott zu Loben, Bleibe Meine Seelenfreud*, Op. 40 (1899). Yet these works, while conceived and executed in the contrapuntal grammar of Bach, are written in the highly chromatic language of Wagner and in the complex phrase structures of Brahms. The combination of all of these elements, plus Reger's intense intellectuality and his passionate emotionality, makes his organ music, like the rest of his oeuvre, extremely concentrated listening. But for those who can penetrate its complexities, Reger's organ music is as fully rewarding a listening experience as any of his other music. *—James Leonard*

Recommended:

- ○ **Maximum Reger** / Sykes / 1997 / Raven 430
- ○ **Reger: Organ Works Vol. 1** / B. Haas / 1998 / Naxos 553926
- ○ **Lionel Rogg Plays Reger** / Rogg / 1983 / Bis 242
- ○ **Reger: Organ Masterworks** / Hauk / 2000 / Guild 7192
- ○ **Max Reger: Complete Organ Works, Vol. 1** / R. Haas / 1991 / MDG 3150350

CHAMBER MUSIC

Clarinet Quintet in A major, Op. 146 (1915)

The very last of Max Reger's 146 opus-number work designations was assigned to the *Quintet for clarinet and strings in A major* of 1915. Reger continued working on a few pieces up to his death in May of the following year, but, excepting some short keyboard and organ works and an addendum to 1914's Op. 135, he would complete none of them, leaving the *Clarinet Quintet* to stand as his last statement. The *Quintet* helps us better appreciate the depth of Reger's contribution to the chamber literature—to understand that he was not just the last in a long line of great German organ composers. His many violin sonatas contain a quarter century's worth of development as a composer—really the whole span of his active career—and the last two string quartets (Opp. 109 and 121 of 1909 and 1911, respectively) are rarely heard gems of the repertory. And crowning the whole body of Reger's chamber music output is the *Clarinet Quintet*; many feel it to be among his very finest achievements.

A love of German musical tradition and all the finesse and subtlety that it demands from a composer informs the best of Reger's music, and Op. 146 is no exception. Classicism meets rich, sophisticated late Romantic chromaticism in ways one who has never run across Reger might well imagine to be impossible.

The first movement (Moderato ed amabile) is spacious and lyrical, with a broad first theme and a tranquil, stop-and-go second one that winds in and around the expected key of the dominant. The scherzo (Vivace) movement which follows, as per tradition, is the shortest of the four; the conflict of rhythm—"threes" in the strings and "twos" in the clarinet—is probably the movement's most becoming feature. The following Largo is a reflective, even introspective, essay in three parts. The final movement (Poco allegretto) is a theme and variations—one of Reger's hallmarks as a composer. Like his more famous examples, *The Variations and Fugue on a Theme of Mozart* for orchestra [or 2 pianos], Op. 132, and the *Variations and Fugue on a Theme of J. S. Bach for piano*, Op. 81, this final movement illuminates Reger's particular talent in the genre. *—Blair Johnston*

Recommended:

- ○ **Reger: String Quartet; Clarinet Quintet** / Leister, Vogler Quartet / 2000 / Nimbus 5644
- ○ **Reger: Chamber Music** / Fuchs, Berlin Philharmonia Quartet / 2001 / Naxos 554510

Clarinet Sonata No. 3 in B flat major, Op. 107 (1909)

This is the best known of the three clarinet sonatas written by Max Reger (1873–1916). Composed in 1909, it is one of the most important works in the clarinet solo repertory. Reger's style mixed strongly traditional formal procedures (dating back from Brahms all the way through Beethoven and Bach) with the harmonic language of Wagner and Richard Strauss. Though musicologist Carl Dahlhaus denigrated Reger as a "pedantic reactionary," Schoenberg admired him, and he falls clearly into the line of Brahmsian formal thinking that influenced the creator of the 12-tone row. His inclination toward absolute music, along with his successful career in the German university system, led him to compose generous quantities of chamber music, of which the present sonata is an excellent example. The work, at 31 minutes, is exceptionally long for a wind sonata; composers are usually more mindful of the fact that playing a wind instrument requires more endurance per unit of time than playing a string instrument.

True to the composer's usual practice, the forms of the work's four movements are entirely traditional (sonata-allegro, scherzo—although this scherzo has an unusually slow trio—a lyrical song form, and a sonata-rondo to close). The sonata is cyclic, unobtrusively quoting music from the scherzo in the slow movement and subjecting the same six-note motive to thematic transformations in both the opening and closing movements. In the finale, it generates a pastoral tune, a chorale, and a dance-like portion. The work ends by quoting both the slow movement and a codetta from the opening movement. *—Joseph Stevenson*

Recommended:

- ○ **Blackwood & Reger Clarinet Sonatas** / Blackwood, Yeh / 1995 / Cedille 22

VOCAL

Maria Wiegenlied (Mary's Lullaby: "Maria sitzt am Rosenhag"), Op. 76/52 (1912)

Max Reger composed his 60 *Schlichte Weisen* (*Simple Melodies*), Op. 76 (1904–12), largely in response to the accusation that his music was intentionally and needlessly complex. Most of these songs failed to impress and were soon forgotten, but one of them—the *Maria Wiegenlied*, Op. 76, No. 52—remains Reger's biggest commercial hit: more copies and arrangements of it were sold during the twentieth century than all of his other pieces combined.

The *Maria Wiegenlied* (Maria being Mary and a Wiegenlied being a lullaby) is a setting of a short text by Martin Boelitz. Reger's F major music sways gently in 6/8 time as Mary rocks Jesus' cradle. The birds sing; treetops sway in the warm breeze; the infant partakes of "holy slumber"—all set to a simple melody that moves only from piano down to triple piano (*p* to *ppp*). But this is still Reger, and simple for Reger might not mean simple for someone else. There are harmonic twists as the song moves along, and when the rocking opening melody returns after a short digression, Reger brilliantly casts it in imitation between piano and voice—sometimes on the beat, and sometimes at the half-bar in stretto.

The *Maria Wiegenlied* is dedicated, appropriately enough, to Princess Marie Elisabeth of Sachsen-Meiningen. *—Blair Johnston*

Recommended:

○ **Home for Christmas** / Otter, Sonstevold / DG 459685

○ **Erna Berger** / Berger / 2001 / Decca 467917

ORCHESTRAL

Suite in F major ("Im alten Stil"), Op. 93 (1916)

The *Suite for Orchestra*, Op. 93, by German composer Max Reger, is an orchestral arrangement from 1916 of his *Suite im alten Stil* for violin and piano from 1906. Like the original version, the orchestral suite consists of three movements: Präludium, Largo, and Fuge. Clearly based on Baroque forms and compositional methods with including allusions to Baroque works, including a near quotation in the Präludium from the opening movement of Bach's *Third Brandenburg Concerto*, Reger's *Suite* is nevertheless fully as modern in its harmonies as anything else Reger wrote. Indeed, the central Largo may well be the most beautiful and emotionally affecting slow movement he ever composed. Like so many of Reger's concluding fugues, the Fuge of the *Suite* tends to be overly ornate and intensely intellectual with a stretto which might prove bombastic to some listeners. *—James Leonard*

Recommended:

○ **Reger: Piano Concerto; Suite im alten Stil** / Segerstam (cond.), Norrkoping SO / 1994 / Bis 711

○ **Reger: Variations & Fugue; Concerto in the Old Style; Suite in the Old Style** / Neidlinger (cond.) / 1988 / Colosseum 340703

Variations and Fugue on a Theme of Beethoven, Op. 86 (1915)

Max Reger's *Variations on a theme by Beethoven* was originally written for two pianos, and received a successful premiere in that form on October 25, 1904, in Munich. Near the end of his life, however, Reger decided to revisit the work. Armed with knowledge he had gained from scoring his *Variations on a theme by Mozart* (a work with structure similar to the *Variations on a theme by Beethoven*, including a closing fugue which brings back the opening theme), he decided to orchestrate the *Beethoven Variations*. He dropped four variations from the original work, and resequenced the others. Reger never got to hear the orchestral version; it premiered at a memorial concert in Vienna, 12 years to the day after the premiere of the original two-piano version.

The work borrows its theme from Ludwig van Beethoven's last piano *Bagatelle* (Op. 119/11). Reger orchestrates it simply and sweetly, warm strings alternating with limpid winds. The variations partake of standard elaborations and key transformations, not groundbreaking, but nonetheless fluent and pleasing to the ear. Despite occasional dips into the minor mode, as in the brief, stormy fourth variation, the mood remains basically relaxed and tender throughout the variations. An Andante sostenuto (variation 5), with a broad tempo and high-Romantic orchestral swellings, forms the lyrical center of the work, reaching a passionate climax and descending from it with the utmost grace, including a lovely coda. The variations close with a good-natured Allegro pomposo that has an unexpectedly demure coda, leading into the massive fugue which closes the work.

This fugue is 103 bars long, far longer than any of the variations, and begins with a vivacious con grazioso idea stated quietly in the violins, which migrates to the rest of the strings and eventually the entire orchestra. Reger was a master of fugue, and his development of the theme is expertly controlled over the long span, while his orchestration remains lucid even in the densest parts of the counterpoint. The fugue reaches a climax with the simultaneous statement of the subject in the strings and a much-enlarged version of the original theme played in the brass. The effect is overwhelming. As a contemporary critic put it, the final fugue "rounds off [Reger's] colossal edifice in symphonic breadth and sonority like a massive iron portal." The *Beethoven Variations* is one of Reger's finest works, and it makes a good introduction to this neglected master's œuvre. *—Andrew Lindemann Malone*

Recommended:

○ **Scherchen conducts Reger** / Scherchen (cond.), Nordwestdeutsche Philharmonie / CPO 999143

○ **Reger: Variations & Fugue on a Theme of Beethoven; Bruckner: Symphony 8** / Jarvi (cond.) London PO / Chandos 8843

Variations and Fugue on a Theme of Mozart, Op. 132 (1914)

Max Reger's *Variations on a Theme of Mozart*, likely the composer's best-known work, was written at a time when atonality was nascent and Schoenberg's realization of the 12-tone method just a decade in the future. But Reger's sympathies lay resolutely without the avant-garde of his day. While possessed of a strong personality, Reger's musical language is clearly indebted to the music of 100—even 200—years earlier. Indeed, his aesthetic outlook is suggested by a number of works that take the music of Baroque and Classical masters as their point of departure; in addition to the present work, Reger produced variation sets on themes by Bach, Telemann, Hiller, and Beethoven. Perhaps the most distinctive hallmark of Reger's music is the melding of Bachian polyphony with a highly chromatic harmonic language, resulting in works marked sonic richness and elaborate counterpuntal interplay.

Reger's *Mozart Variations* were originally written for orchestra. As is the case with a number of his works, he made an arrangement for keyboard; that he calls for two pianos provides some hint of the work's complexity. The theme is the delicate air that opens Mozart's *Piano Sonata in A major*, K. 331; interestingly, Mozart himself used the theme as the basis for a variation movement, as opposed to a more conventional sonata-allegro. Reger's treatment is characterized by increasing abstraction and transformation. Each of the eight variations is more fantastic and distant from its source than the last, both harmonically and rhythmically; in the last dreamlike variation the theme is often unrecognizable within the thicket of Reger's invention. The work closes with an extended fugue whose connection to the source material is oblique indeed; as though coming into focus, however, Mozart's theme becomes plainly recognizable near the end, albeit now in a much grander guise. *—Michael Rodman*

Recommended:

○ **Scherchen conducts Reger** / Scherchen (cond.), Nordwestdeutsche Philharmonie / CPO 999143

○ **Beethoven: Missa Solemnis** / Bohm (cond.), Berlin PO / DG 449737

○ **Reger: Mozart-Variationen; Hindemith: Weber-Metamorphosen** / Davis (cond.), SO Bayerischen Rundfunks / 1990 / Philips 422347

CONCERTO

Piano Concerto in F minor, Op. 114 (1910)

On the one hand, Max Reger's 1910 *Piano Concerto in F minor*, Op. 114, is a perfectly traditional piece, even a Classical one, despite the date it bears. The orchestra employed by Reger for the work is just two horns larger than the one used by Beethoven in his celebrated *"Emperor" Concerto*, and the *Concerto*'s three movements are near-textbook examples of the venerable fast-slow-fast concerto movement models. However, even though Reger did sometimes love to compose pieces that replicate music from other eras (his solo string instrument suites, for example, take the Baroque idiom in stride and bring it "up to date" as little as possible), to regard this *Concerto* as an outmoded, easy-to-follow museum-piece would be foolhardy. Reger's serious concert music is terribly demanding both on performer and listener—every bit as challenging as, and in some cases more challenging (because the innovation is sometimes buried under a thick layer of tradition) than, the music being written by Arnold Schoenberg and Igor Stravinsky around the same time. Reger's *Piano Concerto*, like his *Violin Concerto* of a few yeas earlier, is not especially well-loved music; it is rarely performed, and one hand suffices to count the number of decent recordings that have been made of it. But few of Reger's pieces allow us to see so clearly into his peculiar musical mind—a mind tense, bent, and even fractured and yet, somehow, balanced by an overwhelming preservationist instinct.

The *Concerto* is scored for woodwinds in pairs, two trumpets, four horns (two more, as mentioned, than the Classical standard), timpani, strings, and, of course, pianoforte. In density and difficulty, the solo piano writing goes beyond that even of the two Johannes Brahms piano concertos, and yet, like the Brahms concertos, the style is not a demonstrative or a virtuoso one. There is simply an immense amount of information in each of the pianist's bars, and this, combined with the extent to which Reger plays around with severely chromatic counterpoint, has proven to be too much for many listeners (both at the time of the *Concerto*'s premiere and later).

For all its traditional features, the Allegro moderato first movement lacks one very standard item: a solo cadenza. In this movement, Reger's tendency to extremes comes to the surface—this is music that can move from a shattering *fff* or *ffff* climax down to a *ppp* whisper in just a bar or two; and there are many local climaxes, all adding up to 70 pages of hair-raising drama. The slow movement is marked Largo con gran espressione and shifts—softly, and at first ambiguously—from the F minor of the first movement up to F sharp. As Beethoven loved to do, Reger begins the Allegretto con spirito last movement with a phrase for the piano alone; but soon the orchestra joins, and the dance moves towards its rowdy F major conclusion. *—Blair Johnston*

Recommended:

○ **Reger: Piano Concerto; Suite im alten Stil** / Segerstam (cond.), Derwinger, Norrkoping SO / 1994 / Bis 711

Steve Reich

b. Oct. 3, 1936, New York, NY

Composer: Avant-garde, Vocal, Choral

Much though he may dislike the term, and however irrelevant it may be to his more recent music, Steve Reich will forever be identified with the musical style known as Minimalism. Over the years, Reich has embraced a wide variety of musical styles and interests, forging from them a unique synthesis.

Reich took piano lessons as a youngster, but his first big musical revelations came at 14, when he first encountered the music of Bach and Stravinsky. He also had his first exposure to bebop, and immediately started learning the drums and playing in a jazz band with friends. He continued to play jazz on weekends while studying at Cornell University, which he entered at age 16 and where he received a degree in philosophy, specializing in the work of Wittgenstein. After leaving Cornell in 1957, he moved to New York and entered the Juilliard School, where he studied with William Bergsma and Vincent Persichetti (and where he met fellow student Philip Glass for the first time). It was at Juilliard that Reich first heard 12-tone music; he got a further dose of it during graduate studies at Mills College in Oakland, working for three semesters with Luciano Berio and eventually earning his master's degree.

At about that time Reich met Terry Riley, who was in the process of writing and preparing for the first performance of his *In C*. Reich played in that premiere, and *In C*'s tonal approach and use of repeating patterns had a big influence on Reich's own music. Reich was by that time experimenting with tapes, creating loops of speech and layering them several times over, allowing the layers to move in and out of sync with one another. His early tape works *It's Gonna Rain* (1965) and *Come Out* (1966) led to similar experiments with live performers, the first of which was *Piano Phase for two pianos* (1967). Back in New York, Reich and Glass formed an ensemble to perform their music. It lasted from 1968 to 1971, and several of those players later formed Steve Reich and Musicians, which has toured the world many times over.

In 1970, Reich studied for several weeks at the University of Ghana. His encounter with Ghanaian music and dance inspired his ambitious work *Drumming* (1970). Encounters with Indonesian gamelan music in 1973–74 at Seattle and Berkeley were equally significant, and broadened Reich's rhythmic and timbral palette. His most significant composition of the time was *Music for 18 Musicians* (1974–76), a large and colorful work which brought Reich worldwide recognition.

In the mid-1970s, Reich started taking Torah classes with his future wife, video artist Beryl Korot. He also studied traditional Jewish cantillation, and incorporated those studies into his psalm settings, *Tehillim* (1981). Several chamber and orchestral works followed in the 1980s. For *Different Trains* (1988), Reich used a digital sampler to record speaking voices and derived the rhythmic and melodic ideas of the piece from those voices. Reich knew that *Different Trains* was going to lead to some kind of new documentary form incorporating both video and music. Collaborating with his wife for the first time, the two completed their theater work *The Cave* in 1993. They are continuing to explore the combination of music and video with *Three Tales*, the first of which, Hindenburg, was completed in 1998. *—Chris Morrison*

AVANT-GARDE

The Cave, multimedia theater work (1990–1993)

The Cave (1993) is an elaborate multimedia work, completed collaboratively by Steve Reich and his wife, filmmaker Beryl Korot. Drawing on characters from the biblical Old Testament, it seeks to answer five seemingly simple questions: Who is Abraham?; Who is Sarah?; Who is Hagar?; Who is Ishmael?; and Who is Isaac? Reich and Korot work to illuminate twentieth century perceptions of these biblical figures, and how traditional images and ideas are manifested in contemporary cultures. To do this, the collaborators interviewed artists, journalists, scholars, scientists, and others from three distinct geographic areas—West Jerusalem, East Jerusalem, and the United States—and pieced together the various videotaped responses to the above five questions. Drawing on Korot's work with multichannel video installations and Reich's experience with electro-acoustic composition, *The Cave* blends recorded interviews with live musical performance to create a type of musical theater that is both unprecedented and arrestingly clever.

While the videotaped interviews constitute a kind of libretto, and the work is organized into three acts (each devoted to a particular geographic location), *The Cave* lacks the narrative drama, staging, and bel canto style that would readily characterize it as an opera. Rather, the story of *The Cave*—precisely, the Cave of Machpelah, believed by Jews and Muslims to be the burial place of Abraham, Sarah, and their descendants—is told through the actual voices of the interviewees, whose responses range in tone from introspective to humorous. Reich's score, for voices, woodwinds, keyboards, percussion, and strings, derives melodic and rhythmic motifs and text from the recorded voices to highlight particular spoken phrases and to segue between speakers. Most novel, however, is Reich's translation of speech melodies and rhythms to an instrumental ensemble. Though *Different Trains* (1988) involves a similar technique, *The Cave* operates on a much larger scale by intertwining instrumental parts with a wide variety of recorded voices, drawing from a diverse textural palette and navigating serenely though numerous sudden modulations.

Reich and Korot allow the "answers" to their five questions to remain purposely ambiguous: the recorded responses are presented at face value and in a loose, general context that permits multiple viewpoints to emerge and celebrates subjectivity. While successfully grappling with such religious and political themes in any medium would be noteworthy, *The Cave*'s atypical format and imaginative scoring signal a particular spirit of innovation and suggest further directions for musical theater in the twenty-first century. *—D. J. Hoek*

Recommended:

○ **Reich: The Cave** / Hillier (cond.), Becker, Bush, Hartenberger, Niemann, Steve Reich Ens. / 1995 / Nonesuch 79327

Come Out, for tape (1966)

One of the seminal works of early minimalism, Steve Reich's *Come Out* from 1966 continued to explore the phasing techniques Reich had discovered in *It's Gonna Rain* from the previous year, and further examined the slippery relationship between the meaning of words as language and the emotional power of words as acoustical phenomena. It likewise utilized a prerecorded speech segment that carried its own considerable expressive weight: while *It's Gonna Rain* featured the charismatic sermon of a San Francisco street preacher, *Come Out* used as its sole musical material a segment of an interview with Daniel Hamm, a youth who had been taken into custody during the Harlem riots of 1964. As Hamm describes in the unaltered exposition at the beginning of Reich's piece, he and several other young men were detained at the Harlem 28th precinct and subjected to severe beatings at the hands of the police officers. Afterwards, the police took some of the boys to have their injuries treated, but only those that were bleeding visibly. As Hamm explains, in a hauntingly detached voice, "I had to like open the bruise up and let some of the bruise blood come out to show them." Reich then took the last five words of the excerpt and loops them, so that the words become ingrained in the listener's ears and the musical contours of the speech begin to emerge. Once the loop is established, Reich introduces his characteristic phasing technique. The tape loop is delivered over two channels, which begin in sync with each other, but very gradually fall out of phase. The effect is an intriguing continuum of sound-speech: at first, when the slower loop falls only slightly behind the faster one, the result is simply a reverb that gives the impression of a single voice in an echoing space. As the loops further separate, however, the reverberating voice distinguishes itself from the other, creating a kind of two-voice canon. Reich then continues the process by expanding the phasing texture into four-channel polyphony and finally, eight.

The criticism might be lodged that Reich takes advantage of the powerful expressivity inherent in Hamm's speech, redirecting its authentic, visceral expressivity through his own quasidocumentary art work and under his own name. To his credit, however, Reich harnessed the power of Hamm's testimony for benevolent purposes and to a laudable end. A benefit concert featuring *Come Out* was organized in order to raise money for the boys arrested in the riots to hire their own attorneys and mount a retrial. The effort was ultimately successful: at the retrial, Hamm and the others were acquitted. The work's topical urgency seems to relate to young audiences; in 1998, it underwent a provocative remix at the hands of DJ Ken Ishii for the Nonesuch collection *Reich Remixed*. *—Jeremy Grimshaw*

Recommended:

○ **Steve Reich: Works, 1965–1995** / Tilson Thomas (cond.), Double Edge / 1997 / Nonesuch 79451

VOCAL

Drumming, 2 female voices, piccolo & percussion (1971)

Following intensive study of West African music at the University of Ghana in 1970, Steve Reich returned to the United States with a heightened interest in polyrhythm and the desire to compose his first large-scale work. The resulting composition, *Drumming* (1971), requires more performers, employs greater variety in instrumentation, and—at ninety minutes in length—is longer than any of Reich's earlier works. This more expansive approach represents the culmination of Reich's experiments in phase shifting and positions *Drumming* as one of the first masterpieces of musical minimalism.

Although Reich's time in Ghana introduced him to the music and traditions of another culture, his studies there were most important in reinforcing his own predilection with repetition and slowly changing patterns. While the shifting polyrhythms of his compositions at the time seemed foreign to Western art music, Reich found similar manners of organization in African drumming, and this sense of musical heritage encouraged him to continue his experiments.

In *Drumming*, a single rhythmic pattern provides the source material for the entire composition. Although this sort of economy also characterizes most of his earlier pieces, Reich develops this cell not only through rhythmically shifting repetitions, but also through varying timbral combinations.

Each of the four parts that comprise *Drumming*—performed in sequence without pause—features a particular instrumental-vocal ensemble: Part One is written for bongos and male voice; Part Two is for marimbas and female voices; Part Three is for glockenspiels, piccolo, and whistling; and Part Four, the composition's apex, includes all the instrumental and vocal forces from the previous sections. These instrumental combinations would prove significant: the instrumentation for mallet percussion appears in a number of Reich's later works, and the textless vocalizations recur in *Music for Mallet Instruments, Voices, and Organ* (1973) and *Music for 18 Musicians* (1976), as well as in many works by fellow minimalist Philip Glass. By melding the crisp precision of percussion with the inherent lyricism of human voices (which are at times extended by whistling and the use of the piccolo), Reich creates smooth transitions between sections of contrasting orchestration while maintaining the timbral and textural interest that enhances *Drumming*'s fundamental rhythmic momentum. *—D. J. Hoek*

Recommended:

○ **Steve Reich: Works, 1965–1995** / Tilson Thomas (cond.), Becker, Velez, Hartenberger, Clayton / 1997 / Nonesuch 79451

Music for 18 Musicians, for 4 female voices & 16 instruments (1976)

Though *Music for 18 Musicians* includes repeated patterns, a steady tempo, and other such devices that characterize Reich's innovative works of the late 1960s and early 1970s, it is distinguished by an unprecedented harmonic variety and richness of sonority. In landmark compositions such as *Piano Phase* (1967) and *Drumming* (1971), Reich demonstrates a penchant for creating musical processes that are readily audible; in *Music for 18 Musicians*, organizational clarity is superseded by a more intuitive approach that takes aural appeal as its chief priority. This change in aesthetic begins a new phase in Reich's career and arguably marks the end of his reductive, minimalist period.

The harmonic structure for the entire work is introduced in the opening section: eleven lush, undulating chords, perhaps in imitation of electronic-studio trickery, successively fade in and out. These 11 harmonies define the formal layout of the entire composition: each of the following eleven sections is devoted to a particular chord. While Reich alludes to his earlier methods by limiting himself to only one chord within each section, the unfolding of musical material in *Music for 18 Musicians* does not adhere to a strict process; by abandoning the rigorous procedures of phase shifting, Reich leans toward free composition.

Although Reich's earlier *Six Pianos* (1973) and *Music for Mallet Instruments, Voices, and Organ* (1973) also show evidence of a less process-oriented style, neither of these works offers the harmonic variety of *Music for 18 Musicians*. Additionally, *Music for 18 Musicians* provides the first glimpse of Reich's skill and imagination as an orchestrator. In all sections, the composer explores unlikely sound combinations, from the urgent quirkiness of upper-register violin, piano, and xylophone to the dark resonance of bass clarinet, cello, and marimba, to the veiled presence of wordless voices. These colors and textures are juxtaposed and superimposed to create passages of near transparency as well as moments of grandeur; these foreshadow the larger, later orchestrations of *Music for a Large Ensemble* (1978), *The Desert Music* (1984), *The Four Sections* (1987), and *Three Movements* (1986). While in these other works Reich draws on more traditional, more considerable forces, *Music for 18 Musicians* occupies the border between stark experimentalism and orthodoxy; it thus stands not only as Reich's most important work, but also a milestone of the late twentieth century. *—D. J. Hoek*

Recommended:

○ **Reich: Music for 18 Musicians** / Becker, Velez, Tilles, Hartenberger, Clayton / 1978 / ECM 821417

Tehillim, for 3 sopranos, winds, strings, percussion & keyboards (1981)

The title *Tehillim* (1981), the Hebrew word for "psalms," succinctly connotes two key aspects of this composition and its importance: first, the word suggests the vocal-textual nature of the piece, particularly significant since none of Reich's previous compositions includes texts set in a conventional manner (though *It's Gonna Rain* (1965) and *Come Out* (1966) do make strikingly unconventional use of text); secondly, both the title and text of the composition evoke Jewish traditions, which from the mid-1970s became increasingly central to Reich's self-understanding. Though not aware of the richness and depth of his own ethnic and religious heritage until he was in his late thirties, Reich's intensive studies of the Torah, Hebrew, and scriptural cantillation gave him a larger historical framework from which to view his life and music. These features of *Tehillim*, combined with a free melodic approach unheard in Reich's previous endeavors, characterize an emerging style for the composer that is decreasingly systematic and increasingly personal.

Each of the four parts of *Tehillim*—respectively marked fast, fast, slow, fast—draws its text from a particular biblical psalm. While the Hebrew words carry extramusical associations for the composer, he also chose the language because it is no longer commonly spoken; like Stravinsky's use of Latin in the *Symphony of Psalms*, Reich's Hebrew texts are not bound by the strictures of linguistic accent and syllabism, therefore providing greater melodic and rhythmic options. Reich indeed exercises such liberties throughout *Tehillim*, balancing the solemnity of the texts with vocal lines that quickly shift in both mood and rhythm.

Tehillim's instrumentation includes woodwinds, keyboards, and strings, as well as four vocalists (two each of sopranos and mezzo-sopranos). True to form, Reich also draws on a battery of percussive resources, from familiar mallet instruments to exotic hand drums and maracas, imitating vocal canons with interlocking patterns. In addition to this instrumentation, composed after the model of his own performing ensemble, Reich also scored *Tehillim* in a version with full orchestral accompaniment, allowing orchestras to program this—his most accessible and immediately engaging work—in a traditional concert setting. *—D. J. Hoek*

Recommended:

○ **Reich: Tehillim** / Reich (cond.) / ECM 21215

○ **Reich: Tehillim; Movements** / Leeuw, Tilson Thomas (conds.), London SO, Schoenberg Ens. / 1994 / Nonesuch 79295

CHORAL

The Desert Music, for small chorus & large orchestra (1984)

Borrowing its title and text from a book of poetry by William Carlos Williams, Steve Reich's *The Desert Music* (1982–84) is not a pictorial work, but is, nonetheless an evocative one. *The Desert Music* addresses the idea of mankind's awareness of his own condition, a subject that appears in one way or another in each of the three included poems. From *Theocritus: Idyll/A version from the Greek*, Reich sets the words "Begin, my friend, for you cannot, you may be sure, take your song, which drives all things out of mind, with you to the other world." Part of the text from *The Orchestra* reads: "Is there a sound not addressed wholly to the ear? ... I am wide awake, the mind is listening." The connection between these phrases and the desert is indirect but sure; as Reich points out, it was in Sinai, not Jerusalem, that the children of Israel received revelation and guidance from God, and in the wilderness that Jesus confronted his temptations. And, referring indirectly to the deserts of Alamagordo, New Mexico, where the first A-bombs were detonated, Reich quotes again from *The Orchestra*: "Man has survived hitherto because he was too ignorant to know how to realize his wishes. Now that he can realize them, he must either change them or perish."

The Desert Music is characterized in part by a recurring element: harmonic progressions that unfold as rapidly repeated chords, without melodic or rhythmic adornment. The work's episodes of development and reflection are arranged into an arch form (ABCBA). The first and fifth movements share the same harmonic material, while the second and fourth—settings the same text—are both in a moderate tempo and use similar harmonic progressions. The central movement, the longest in the work, exhibits its own symmetrical form, beginning and ending with the same text. The middle portion, the work's focal point, sets a text from *The Orchestra* that sheds light upon the relationship between text and tone in *The Desert Music*: "It is a principle of music to repeat the theme. Repeat and repeat again, as the pace mounts. The theme is difficult but no more difficult than the facts to be resolved." *—Jeremy Grimshaw*

Recommended:

○ **Reich: The Desert Music** / Tilson Thomas (cond.), Brooklyn Philharmonic / 1985 / Nonesuch 79101

Antoine Reicha

b. Feb. 26, 1770, Prague, Bohemia (Czech Rep.), **d.** May 28, 1836, Paris, France

Composer

Antoine Reicha was a French composer and theorist whose career spanned the late eighteenth and early nineteenth centuries. While his music for woodwind quintet is well known, he was also an opera composer and the author of several important texts on music theory. In terms of his place historically, Reicha was not only a contemporary of Beethoven, but also the one-time teacher of Berlioz and Liszt.

Reicha's earliest training was with his uncle Josef Reicha, and he later studied music in Bonn and Hamburg. When he moved to Vienna in 1801, Reicha studied with Albrechtsberger and also made the acquaintance of the elderly Joseph Haydn and other important members of the musical community in that city. While in Vienna, Reicha composed a number of fugues for the keyboard and a large amount of chamber music. It was only when Reicha moved to Paris in 1808 that he worked on music of a larger scale. Here he attempted to establish himself as a composer of opera. Of his three surviving completed operas, though, only one achieved any degree of success. That opera, *Sappho*, was written in 1822.

Nevertheless, by that time Reicha had a reputation as an excellent teacher of composition, and in this capacity he was respected by most of the musicians of his day. His treatise on composition (*Cours de composition musicale* [1818]) became a standard text in the nineteenth century, and his *Traité de haute composition musicale* (1826) was one of the most important works of its kind in the nineteenth century. Reicha's *Art du compositeur dramatique* (1833) is a manual for composers of opera and is important for its insights into the approach to the form.

Reicha's musical style is relatively conservative and formal. His chamber music, for which he is best known, was written in the second decade of the nineteenth century. It sounds, however, more like eighteenth century music. Nevertheless, the works are strong melodically and quite competent in structure. *—James Zychowicz*

Overview of Works (1786–1825)

Antoine Reicha (1770–1836) was born the same year as Beethoven, and outlived him by nine. It is understandable that contemporaries of the iconic Beethoven would suffer by comparison, and Reicha was no exception. Today he is known chiefly for his chamber music, though he composed numerous symphonies, concertos, operas, piano, and choral works and much else. In general, Reicha's compositions divulge strong melodic skills, which often involve the use of folk material. He also displayed a deft sense for counterpoint and, not surprisingly, produced many fugues and fugal pieces.

If there is a Reicha revival afoot in the twenty-first century, it is still largely confined to his chamber works, not least because they comprise a substantial body of music. Reicha's wind quintets, perhaps his greatest chamber efforts, began to achieve greater currency in the late twentieth century. The six Op. 88 quintets (1811–17), scored for flute, oboe (or another flute), clarinet, bassoon, and horn, are among his most often-performed works. *Quintets* from the Opp. 91 (1817–19), 99 (1811–19) and 100 (?1820) sets, each containing six works and scored for the same combination of instruments, occasionally appear on concert programs and on records. The *24 Horn Trios*, Op. 82 (?1810–14), have managed to attract attention as well. Unfortunately, of the 23 string quartets, none have been recorded and only three are known to have been performed in the last century.

Reicha wrote perhaps 20 symphonies, though several are lost and many survive in fragmentary form. He did not have much success in the genre and none of his works here have achieved regular performance. Such a fate is hardly surprising since his symphonies were written concurrently with Beethoven's. Still, the *Symphony No. 3*, in F major (1808), and the *Symphony à petit orchestre* (date of composition unknown) have occasionally been performed and each has been recorded. The former effort shows Beethoven's influence in the orchestration and the latter divulges strains of Mozart, but both are worthwhile scores nevertheless.

Reicha's operas have suffered a similarly disappointing fate, though a few may yet emerge as substantial contributions to the repertory. *Cagliostro* (1810), *Natalie* (1816), and *Sapho* (1822) all had very limited success in their day, but each features fine vocal writing, and in the case of the latter work, quite skillful choral writing. Moreover, Reicha displayed a fine sense for dramatic flow.

Reicha's piano compositions have often been viewed as teaching tools first and as concert fare second. Yet, the *34 Etudes* of Op. 97 are quite inventive and attractive works, even if didactic in purpose. In the choral realm, Reicha produced a fairly substantial output of both sacred and secular works. His *Passion Oratorio* (date unknown), *Der neue Psalm* (1807) and *Te Deum* (1825) are especially strong works. *—Robert Cummings*

Recommended:

- ○ **Reicha: Wind Quintets** / Academia Wind Quintet / 1996 / Hyperion 22006
- ○ **Reicha: Chamber Music for Bassoon** / Hubner, Romhild, Nomos Quartett / CPO 999061
- ○ **Reicha: Quintets for Winds & String Quartet, Vol. 1** / Classicum Consortium / MDG 0501
- ○ **Rejcha: Requiem** / Matl (cond.), Dolezal, Barova, Vele, Tvrzsky, Dvořák CO / 1989 / Supraphon 110332
- ○ **Rijcha: Fugues for piano** / Langer / 2003 / Supraphon 3750
- ○ **Reicha: Sinfonia concertante; Symphony; Overture** / Gulke (cond.), Wuppertal SO / 1995 / MDG 3350661

Carl Reinecke

b. Jun. 23, 1824, Altona, Germany, **d.** Mar. 10, 1910, Leipzig, Germany
Composer: Chamber Music, Keyboard

Carl Heinrich Carsten Reinecke was the son of music teacher J.P. Rudolf Reinecke (1795–1883), who is known as the author of several important textbooks and works on music theory. Carl's father gave him a thorough musical education and training in playing piano.

At the age of 21, Reinecke started touring Northern Europe, as far east as Riga. He attracted favorable attention from Mendelssohn and Robert and Clara Schumann in Leipzig. In 1846, he was appointed court pianist at the Danish royal court of King Christian VIII in Copenhagen and served there into 1848. As such, he gave solo recitals and he also served as accompanist to the well-known violin virtuoso Heinrich Wilhelm Ernst (1814–65).

After his Copenhagen job, he traveled to Paris, where he taught. The great piano virtuoso Franz Liszt selected Reinecke to be piano teacher to his daughter, Cosima (future wife of Richard Wagner). Liszt described Reinecke's touch as "beautiful, gentle, legato, and lyrical."

In 1851, he joined the staff of the municipal music school in Cologne, which was being reorganized by Ferdinand Hiller (1814–65). There he taught piano and counterpoint and was also a recital partner of Hiller, who got him a position in Barmen as town musical director. He conducted several of the town's musical societies and improved the town's musical standards. Subsequently, he was hired as director of music at the University of Breslau and conductor of the Singakademie there.

In 1860, he became a faculty member at the Leipzig Conservatory. Even before he became director in 1897, he was a force for improving it. The teachers hired during his time were capable musicians and effective teachers and moreover, they generally shared Reinecke's conservative views about music. Among the prestigious pupils who studied there were Grieg, Svendsen, Sinding, Sullivan, and Weingartner. Reinecke considered it his mission to transmit the tradition of the Classical composers and even earlier composers such as Bach and even Palestrina. He and the Conservatory both got a reputation in some circles as reactionaries, but no one doubted the solid training it provided its students.

Along with his position at the Conservatory, Reinecke also was conductor of the Gewandhaus Orchestra, keeping that position until 1895 and raising this institution to a high artistic standard as well. In 1875, Reinecke also became a member of the Berlin Academy.

He retired from his teaching position in 1902, but continued composing until his death in 1910. A large proportion of his work (and that for which he is best remembered) is in the form of piano compositions, which are usually good examples of Romantic-era Hausmusik. His sound is warm, his melodies flowing, and sometimes majestic and harmonically, he did not stray much farther than the harmonic style of Robert Schumann. His orchestration is clear and colorful and in his operas, he was more apt to adopt some of the innovations of Richard Wagner. His piano etudes are charming enough that students find them rewarding to practice. *—Joseph Stevenson*

CHAMBER MUSIC

Flute Sonata in E major ("Undine"), Op. 167 (1885)

Carl Reinecke's *Sonata for flute and piano in E major*, Op. 167—subtitled "Undine" (a female water spirit)—is not programmatic music by any leap of the imagination; but there is something undeniably water-like about much of its music. When Reinecke composed the work around 1885, he had long been a fixture at the Leipzig Conservatory, where he continued in the vein of Felix Mendelssohn, espousing tradition. He seems to have acquired some of Mendelssohn's knack for capturing the essence and grace of natural phenomena without resorting to specific tone painting.

The sonata has four movements: 1. Allegro, 2. Intermezzo, 3. Andante tranquillo, 4. Finale (Allegro molto agitato ed appassionato, quasi Presto). The open fifths and light, up-and-down arpeggiation of the first movement's principal theme is perhaps the most waterlike element in the sonata. Reinecke seems very taken with this idea and spins it out at great length before allowing a much shorter secondary theme to enter. The B minor Intermezzo operates on the ternary principle: Allegretto vivace—Più lento, quasi Adagio—Tempo I. Light, staccato 16th notes fly all over the place throughout most of the opening music (Mendelssohn truly lives on here), though a subsidiary idea in G major is so forceful with its dotted rhythms that the flute is forced to drop out and leave the more percussive piano all alone. The central trio section is in B major. The slow third movement is cast in G major and lovingly molded out of a melody that stretches and reaches around from pitch to pitch, register to register, in the manner of elongated pick-up gestures. There is a contrasting central episode in B minor, Molto vivace. A broad, fiery tune in the flute part, matched by undulating arcs in the piano right hand and a deep bass line in long notes, drives the Finale forward towards its quiet Più lento, E major close.

Reinecke also made an arrangement of the sonata for violin or clarinet and piano. *—Blair Johnston*

Recommended:

- ○ **Franck: Violin Sonata; Reinecke: Flute Concerto; Sonata** / Racine, Meyer / 1997 / Novalis 150139

KEYBOARD

Works for Piano (ca. 1850–1910)

Carl Reinecke was a versatile composer who produced operas, vocal and choral works, orchestral and chamber music, and a fairly sizable output for piano, both in the solo and larger instrumental realms. Among his most important efforts are his four piano concertos whose high opus numbers indicate his prolific nature: the *Piano Concerto No. 1* (1879) is his Op. 72, while his last (1900) is Op. 254. (It should be noted that the first concerto, chronologically, was the E minor, which was written in 1873, but assigned Op. 120; it is now numbered as the *Second*.) Reinecke was stylistically conservative, taking Schumann and Mendelssohn as his models, though the influence of Brahms and even of Wagner can at times be noticed. The *First* and *Second* piano concertos are the most popular of the four. The *First*, in F sharp minor, is cast in three movements with vigorous outer panels framing a sentimental Adagio ma non troppo. The *Second* opens with a somewhat restless Allegro, while still maintaining Reinecke's typical pleasantness of expression, and follows with a playful Schumann-esque middle panel. The finale is also Schumann-esque in its bright muscularity and sometimes stormy character. The other two piano concertos, in C (1878) and B minor, are congenial, tuneful works of marginally less-inspired fabric.

Reinecke's most-popular chamber work involving piano is his *Sonata for Flute and Piano*, subtitled "Undine." Reinecke's three sonatas for cello and piano—the *First*, in A minor, dates to around 1855 and the last, in G, written in 1896—are neglected works that, in the case of the last two at least, deserve considerably more attention. After the Schumann-esque *First*, the *Second* (D major; 1869) and *Third* divulge greater individuality and mastery of form. There are other worthwhile chamber works for piano in Reinecke's output, including the *Three Sonatinas for Violin and Piano* (1873) and the *Two Serenades for Piano, Violin, and Cello* (1874).

Reinecke's output for solo piano contains some of his most popular works. Among them are the *Three Sonatinas*, Op. 47—in C major, D major, and B major—all dating to around 1854. They are very tuneful and fairly easy pieces, the second offering charming variations on Reinecke's children's song *Wer hat die schönsten Schäfchen?* (Who has the most beautiful lamb?). Reinecke also wrote sonatas and variation works for solo piano, though virtually all of them are neglected despite some worthwhile individual efforts among them. —*Robert Cummings*

Recommended:

- ○ **Reinecke: Piano Concertos 1 & 2** / Remoortel (cond.), Robbins, Monte Carlo Opera Orch. / 1989 / Genesis 102

Fritz Reiner

b. Dec. 19, 1888, Budapest, Hungary, **d.** Nov. 15, 1963, New York, NY
Conductor

Fritz Reiner was a legend among conductors. Universally admired for his music making, widely disliked for his aggressive and exacting temperament, and survived by a legacy of definitive recorded performances, he was largely responsible for the artistic ascendancy of the Chicago Symphony Orchestra, and exerted considerable influence on generations of musicians.

Born in Budapest in 1888, he studied piano with his mother and, at the age of 15, entered the Franz Liszt Academy—an institution that also boasts Bela Bartók, Zoltan Kodály, Ernst von Dohnányi, George Szell, Eugene Ormandy, Georg Solti and Antal Dorati as graduates. Reiner gained conducting experience at a number of regional opera houses before eventually returning to Budapest in 1911 to serve at the city's Volksoper, where his reputation as a conductor of special abilities finally emerged.

In 1914 Reiner accepted a position at the Dresden Court Opera, where he formed a fortuitous relationship with both the conductor Arthur Nikisch and the composer Richard Strauss; Reiner would eventually give the German premier of Strauss' *Die Frau ohne Schatten*, and would remain a devoted interpreter of the composer's works throughout his career. The economic chaos and emergent anti-Semitism that followed the First World War made Reiner anxious to leave Europe, and an invitation (in 1921) to become the music director of the Cincinnati Symphony Orchestra provided just the right opportunity. From that point onward, Reiner's career was firmly rooted in the United States, where he became a citizen in 1928.

After resigning his post at Cincinnati Reiner became a professor of conducting at the Curtis Institute of Music in Philadelphia, where his students included both the young Leonard Bernstein and Lukas Foss; Bernstein, in particular, credited Reiner with a great deal of influence in his development.

In 1938 he became the director of the Pittsburgh Symphony—one of several positions that established Reiner as a fine builder of orchestras, with a talent for steering ensembles toward new levels of quality and success. A number of Reiner's well-known recordings stem from his tenure there. Guest appearances during his Pittsburgh years include those at Covent Garden and the San Francisco Symphony. From Pittsburgh he moved to the Metropolitan opera, where he remained on the conductor roster until 1953; his advocacy of Strauss' operas was especially strong there, and his performances of *Salome* and *Elektra* number among the most memorable evenings in the Met's history.

1953 was a watershed year for Reiner, since it was then that he assumed the directorship of the Chicago Symphony Orchestra. This was to become his signature partnership, and the position that would establish his lasting legacy. His relationship with the orchestra was never a smooth one—he was known for hostility and impatience in rehearsal, and for firing musicians for mistakes in concerts—but he undeniably raised the ensemble from its status as a good American orchestra to that of one of the finest in the world. Unlike a number of other prominent conductors who excelled in narrow corners of the musical canon, Reiner maintained his excellent standards and clarifying precision throughout an especially broad repertory that crossed boundaries of nationality and style. He was as renowned for his performances of new works, such as Bartók's *Concerto for Orchestra*—a piece that Reiner himself commissioned from the dying composer—and Alan Hovhaness' *Mysterious Mountain* as he was for his Mahler, Strauss and Haydn. His tenure in Chicago also resulted in what was then an unprecedented volume of fine recordings, some of which still remain as favorites, despite the improved fidelity of modern competitors. Reiner resigned from Chicago in 1962 (after only nine seasons), and died the following year of heart failure.—*Allen Schrott*

Recommended:

- ○ **Strauss Waltzes** / Reiner (cond.), Chicago SO / 1983 / RCA 61336-2
- ○ **Bartok: Concerto for Orchestra, etc.** / Reiner (cond.), Chicago SO / 1993 / RCA 61504
- ○ **The Reiner Sound** / Reiner (cond.), Chicago SO / 2001 / JVC 215
- ○ **Respighi: Pines of Rome; Fountains of Rome** / Reiner (cond.), Chicago SO / 2000 / JVC 8

Ottorino Respighi

b. Jul. 9, 1879, Bologna, Italy, **d.** Apr. 18, 1936, Rome, Italy
Composer: Orchestral, Vocal, Chamber Music, Ballet

Mostly known for his richly descriptive symphonic poems *Fontane di Roma* (The Fountains of Rome) and *Pini di Roma* (*The Pines of Rome*), Respighi was a versatile composer who translated into music powerful visual experiences and feelings of deep attachment to cherished places. Respighi's symphonic works are praised primarily for their exquisite orchestration, but these compositions also possess a charm which transcends the merely picturesque. This charm is particularly evident in works inspired by Medieval and Renaissance music, such as Ancient Airs and Dances for orchestra.

Born in 1879, Respighi studied from 1891 to 1900 at the Liceo Musicale in Bologna. In 1900 and 1902, he traveled to Russia, where he played the viola in the Imperial Orchestra in St. Petersburg. During his two extended visits to Russia, Respighi studied with Rimsky-Korsakov, absorbing the Russian master's ideas regarding orchestral color. In 1903, Respighi turned to a career of a concert violinist; he also played chamber music, joining Bologna's Mugellini Quartet as a violist. During the early 1900s, Respighi started writing music, but his compositions (chamber and orchestral works) attracted little attention. In 1908–09, he was in Berlin, where he immersed himself in German musical culture. In 1913, Respighi settled in Rome, accepting a composition professorship at the Liceo (subsequently Conservatorio) di Santa Cecilia. Enchanted by Rome, Respighi found inspiration in the city's unique atmosphere and consequently formulated an original, personal musical language, exemplified by *Fontane di Roma* (Fountains of Rome), written in 1914–16.

Respighi's next project was a children's opera, *La bella dormente nel bosco* (Sleeping Beauty), finished in 1921, and regarded as his best stage work. After the *Fontane di Roma*, Respighi sought inspiration in early music, introducing Renaissance and Medieval themes into his compositions. In 1917, he composed the first set of his *Antiche arie e danze per liuto* (&Ancient Airs and Dances for Lute), for piano duet and strings. The second and third sets, for strings, were composed in 1923 and 1931, respectively. Sometimes regarded as adaptations, these compositions nevertheless exude a unique freshness and sincerity.

Works composed in the 1920s reflected both Respighi's fascination with early music and his desire to translate visual sensations into music. Thus, the *Concerto gregoriano for violin and orchestra*, composed in 1921, and *Quartetto dorico*, written in 1924, evoke the spirit of ancient music, while *The Pines of Rome* describes the splendor of the Roman landscape.

In 1924, Respighi was named director of the Conservatorio di Santa Cecilia, resigning, however, two years later, so he would have more time to compose. Nevertheless, this period included two American tours, in 1925–26 and 1932, as a conductor and pianist. He also accompanied singers, including his wife, Elsa Olivieri-Sangiacomo, who was also a composer. Works composed during this period include *Vetrate di chiesa* (Church Windows), for orchestra, written in 1925, and the *Trittico botticelliano (Three Botticelli Pictures)*, composed in 1927—a work inspired by three paintings by the great Renaissance artist Sandro Botticelli. Composed in 1928–30, Respighi's *Lauda per la Nativita del Signore*, for two pianos, wind ensembles, vocal soloists, and chorus, develops Renaissance motifs to create a charming, serene celebration of the spirit of Christmas. Elected to the Royal Academy of Italy in 1932, Respighi died in 1936. —*Zoran Minderovic*

ORCHESTRAL

Feste romane (Roman Festivals), symphonic poem (1928)

As angular, dissonant, and jazz-steeped breezes swept through the musical climate of Europe following World War I, Ottorino Respighi confidently braced himself against the whipping storm with a salvo of his own. He wrote in 1932:

"We take the stand against this art which cannot have and does not possess any human content and tends to be only a mechanical experiment and a cerebral conundrum. In the musical world today there reigns the biblical babel. For 20 years the most divese and disparate trends have been consolidated in an uninterrupted revolutionary chaos.... A logical connection must bind the past with the future, and the romanticism of yesterday must become the romanticism of tomorrow."

Respighi's steadfast sensibilities included most notably a particular sense of orchestral gigantism and real-as-life color, features abundantly on display in the *Feste Romane* (1928). This work, the last in the composer's trilogy of "Roman" tone poems (the previous two having celebrated the city's fountains and ancient sites) calls for, in addition to a standard configuration of instruments, a number of others intended to evoke those that might have been heard in earlier times: an organ, a mandolin, two tavolette (a sort of drum), and three buccine (a trumpetlike military instrument). The composer prefaced each movement with an elaborate written description to provide a sort of guided tour:

I. Circenses (The Circus Maximus). A threatening sky hangs of the Massimo Circus, but it is the people's holiday: "Ave Nero!" The iron doors are unlocked, the strains of a religious song and the howling of wild beasts float on the air. The crowd rises in agitation: unperturbed, the song of the martyrs develops, conquers, and is lost in the tumult.

II. Il Giubileo (The Jubilee). The pilgrims trail along the highway, praying. There finally appears from the summit of Monte Mario, to ardent eyes and gasping souls, the holy city: "Rome! Rome!" A hymn of praise bursts forth, the churches ring out their reply.

III. L'Ottobrata (The October Festival). The October festival in Roman Castelli covered with vines: hunting echoes, tinkling of bells, songs of love. Then in tender evenfall arises a romantic serenade.

IV. La Befana (The Epiphany). The night before Epiphany in the Piazza Navone: a characteristic rhythm of trumpets dominates the frantic clamor: above the swelling noise float, from time to time, rustic motives, saltarello cadenzas, the strains of a barrel-organ of a booth and the appeal of the proclaimer, the harsh song of the intoxicated and the lively stornello in which is expressed the popular feelings. "Lasstece pass! Semo Romani!"—"We are Romans! Let us pass!"—*Michael Rodman*

Recommended:

○ **Respighi: Feste romane; Pini di Roma; Impressione brasiliane** / Mata (cond.), Dallas SO / 1993 / Dorian 90182

Fontane di Roma (The Fountains of Rome), symphonic poem (1915–1916)

Ottorino Respighi explained that he composed his symphonic poem *Fontane di Roma* (The Fountains of Rome), "to reproduce by means of tone an expression of nature," and to impart a feeling for the "principal events of Roman life." Based upon the sentiments and visions suggested to him by four of Rome's fountains, he noted in the score that each movement was "contemplated at the hour in which their character is most in harmony with the surrounding landscape or in which their beauty appears most impressive to the observer." The poem is remembered as his most creative turning point, as it constituted his first great success as an orchestral composer and has become his best known work.

Respighi arrived in Rome in 1913, when it was becoming Italy's most vigorous center of orchestral concert-giving, thus providing stimulation for *Fontane di Roma*. Prior to his arrival there, he taught at the Bologna Liceo Musicale. While in Bologna, he associated with the *lega dei Cinque*, an anti-establishment pressure-group, whose members included Pizzetti, Malipiero, Bastianelli, and Renzo Bossi. Although he had studied violin as a child, during this time he was more active as a piano accompanist than as a string player. When he was denied a permanent post in Bologna, he applied elsewhere, gaining a position as professor of composition at the Liceo Musicale di S Cecilia, Rome. He flourished there as a teacher. His students included Elsa Olivieri, whom he married in 1919. Rome, in its positive stage of musical development, provided Respighi with the perfect opportunity to present *Fontane di Roma*, which, although not immediately accepted, eventually brought him enormous success, wealth, and reputation.

In Rome, where the water has been good since ancient times, fountains carrying public water are an attraction in nearly every square. The fountains about which Respighi wrote, as well as many others in the area, were actually created in the Baroque style in the seventeenth century by the sculptor Bernini. The first part of the poem is inspired by the "Fountain of Valle Giulia" and depicts its peaceful pastoral landscape, where cattle pass at dawn. Blasts of horns and trills from the orchestra conjure up the image of joyful tritons and water-nymphs mingling and splashing at the "Triton Fountain." The "Fountain of Trevi" at midday, with a solemn theme, assumes a triumphal character depicting Neptune's chariot passing across the water, drawn by seahorses, followed by tritons and sirens. Finally, birds sing and bells toll to close the day at the "Villa Medici Fountain."

The work had its first performance in Rome on March 11, 1917, and in the United States on February 13, 1919. Shortly thereafter, Respighi was appointed director of the now state-funded Conservatorio di S Cecilia. *Fontane di Roma* has become inseparably linked with two additional symphonic poems, *Pini di Roma* (1923–24) and *Feste romane* (1929), which were intentionally written as sequels. These works continue to have international success. —*Meredith Gailey*

Recommended:

○ **Respighi: Pini di Roma; Feste Romane; Fontane di Roma** / Dutoit (cond.), Montreal SO / 1983 / Decca 410145

○ **Respighi: Pini di Roma; Feste Romane; Fontane di Roma** / Sinopoli (cond.), New York PO / DG 437534

Impressione brasiliane (Brazilian Impressions) (1928)

Composer Ottorino Respighi made his first trip to Brazil in May 1927, in the company of his wife Elsa. Engaged to lead a concert series of his own music in Rio de Janeiro, Respighi struggled to bring to terms an orchestra largely schooled in opera and zarzuela accompaniment and thus unused to purely instrumental performance. To this end Respighi acquitted himself, and the concert series was a success. Before his return to Europe, Respighi announced to the Brazilian press that he'd been absorbing local music and custom during his stay and would return the following year with a five-part orchestral suite based on his experiences. Respighi did, in fact, return to Rio de Janeiro in June 1928, but more pressing matters had weighed upon him in the interim, and the promised five-movement suite was presented only as a three-movement work entitled *Brazilian Impressions*. It nonetheless was warmly received; the result being that Respighi subsequently dropped the plan to add the two additional movements.

"Tropical Night," the first movement, is a boldly colored and highly impressionistic piece which is paced very slowly and is decorated with light sprays of harp and distantly intoned Brazilian folk tunes. A bit more on edge is the second movement, "Butantan" (In a Snake Garden Near São Paulo) which is set in a snake farm visited by the Respighis that was maintained by the Butantan Reptile Institute. Thousands of snakes were being bred for the collection of medicinal venom; judging from the tense atmosphere of the piece, one may deduce that the composer was somewhat unnerved by this experience. Rattling tambourines and slithering clarinets (marked "strisciante") represent the massive pits of reptiles; towards the end a snaky "Dies Irae" may be heard in the strings, perhaps signifying a great need to take leave of this scene. The concluding "Canzone e danza" is based on folk dances heard at Carnival. Compared to the fireworks Respighi displays in conclusions such as that of *The Pines of Rome*, "Canzone e danza" is restrained, rather short and surprisingly low-key. *Brazilian Impressions* as a whole has something of a travelogue quality, suggesting that if Respighi did absorb Brazilian music and culture, he did not do so very deeply, or not at least with the all-embracing enthusiasm of French composer Darius Milhaud. However the *Brazilian Impressions* is highly attractive music of excellent quality, makes brilliant use of orchestral color and provides a pleasant, exotic diversion of about 20 minutes' duration. —*Uncle Dave Lewis*

Recommended:

○ **Respighi: Church Windows; Brazilian Impressions; Roman Festivals** / Lopez-Cobos (cond.), Cincinnati SO / 1994 / Telarc 80356

○ **Dorati Conducts Respighi** / Dorati (cond.), London SO / 1990 / Mercury 432007

Pini di Roma (The Pines of Rome), symphonic poem (1924)

Pines of Rome (*Pini di Roma*) is chronologically the second installment in Italian composer Ottorino Respighi's "Roman trilogy." It is a symphonic tone poem scored for a very large orchestra and cast in four movements, the musical content being representative of a literary plan. In *Pines of Rome*, Respighi succeeds spectacularly, producing a colorful and exciting montage of impressions that capture the imagination without wandering or becoming digressive.

"The Pines at the Villa Borghese" depicts a scene at a once-private resort, and Respighi's music captures the energy and irreverence of children at play, including a discordant trumpet "raspberry" towards the end. This is contrasted by an austere phrase of plainchant that begins "The Pines near the Catacombs." Meditative in mood, the movement leads to a climax built around an insistent, repeated figure stated in fifths in the strings. This leads seamlessly into the next section, "Pines of the Janiculum." Opening with a spray of color from the piano, the piece slowly evolves into a beautiful nocturne punctuated by the recorded sound of a nightingale's twittering, in one of the first instances where a recorded sound is specified for a concert score. This movement is successfully "impressionistic" without being particularly "French." "The Pines of the Appian Way" transforms from a slow, mysterious section into a loud, exciting march that evokes Ancient Rome, its gladiators, and its chivalry.

Italian music lovers in the early twentieth century more strongly resisted modern trends than those of greater Europe, as they were inclined toward opera and generally less enthusiastic about instrumental music. While Respighi was determined to lead Italian audiences, kicking and screaming if necessary, back to instrumental music, a field once dominated by Italian musicians, he was also keenly aware that it would not be an easy struggle. During the preparation of *Pines of Rome* for its 1924 premiere under conductor Bernardino Molinari, Respighi was quoted "Let them boo . . . what do I care?" And boo they did, at the raspberries in the "Villa Borghese," and at the sound of the recorded nightingale in the "Janiculum." But the triumphant march that concludes the work won the audience over, and the finale was greeted with an ovation.

Pines of Rome was soon played to great acclaim in the capitals of Europe, and even became a concert staple in the United States. Famous conductors such as Respighi's friend Toscanini, Koussevitzky, Fritz Reiner, Stokowski, and others, adopted *Pines* into their repertoires. The entire community of early Hollywood composers owes a huge debt of gratitude to Respighi for *Pines* and its scoring, which has been, time and again, acknowledged.

Nonetheless, many critics have condemned Respighi and *Pines* for being trashy, overblown, ultraconservative and even fascistic. Time has borne out that *Pines of Rome* is a work that's here to stay; audiences love it, and it's the sort of work that, with a little effort, can make a good conductor sound like a great one. —*Uncle Dave Lewis*

Recommended:

- ○ **Respighi: Pini di Roma; Feste Romane; Fontane di Roma** / Dutoit (cond.), Montreal SO / 1983 / Decca 410145
- ○ **Symphony of the Air** / Stokowski (cond.), / 1998 / Angel 66864
- ○ **Respighi: Symphonic Poems** / Batiz (cond.), Royal PO / 1991 / Naxos 550539

Trittico botticelliano (Three Botticelli Pictures) (1927)

Although Respighi is best known for his glittering, even garish, suites of tone poems for large orchestra, many feel that some of his best work may be found in his more restrained and modestly scaled efforts. One such example is the *Three Botticelli Pictures* (1927) for chamber orchestra, a three-movement suite based on famous paintings by the Renaissance master Botticelli. Despite the work's economical scoring, it is fully as colorful and beguiling as the fulsome and flashy *Pines of Rome* (1924) or *Fountains of Rome* (1916).

Commissioned by the Elizabeth Sprague Coolidge Foundation and premiered in Vienna in 1927, the *Pictures* demonstrate not only Respighi's ear for fresh and beautiful sonorities, but also his interest in the history of art in his native Italy. "La Primavera" (Spring) unfolds as a pastorale, with rustlings of nature, bird songs, and "antique" dance rhythms. "L'adorazione dei Magi" (Adoration of the Magi) evokes a mood of medieval devotion through its employment of old church modes and Gregorian chant-influenced melodies. The brilliant finale, "La nascita de Venere" (Birth of Venus), is an aural impression of the famous painting of the goddess borne upon a giant oyster shell. Skirling figures and bright sonorities suggest the play of waves, providing a backdrop for Venus' sensuous melody. —*Joseph Stevenson*

Recommended:

- ○ **Respighi: Orchestral Works** / Marriner (cond.), Academy of St. Martin-in-the-Fields / 1996 / EMI 69358
- ○ **Respighi: Ancient Airs & Dances** / Lopez-Cobos (cond.), Lausanne CO / 1992 / Telarc 80309

Gli uccelli (The Birds), suite (1928)

Respighi's affection for and knowledge of early music is amply demonstrated in his three suites of *Ancient Airs and Dances. Gli ucelli* (1928) represents another expedition into the past, in which Respighi transforms five characteristic keyboard pieces from the seventeenth and eighteenth centuries into a genial suite for orchestra.

The orchestration of early keyboard music is a risky undertaking: The bright, uninflected timbre of an instrument like the harpsichord cannot adequately be conveyed by orchestral sonorities. Wisely, Respighi makes no attempt to do so. Instead, he uses the borrowed material to exploit the innate strengths of the orchestra, relying on melodic ingenuity, sparkling instrumental color, and swift contrasts of volume and tempo for interest. While none of these five movements conveys the brittle brilliance of the original pieces, each is witty, playful, and unpretentious.

After a graceful Prelude based on a work by Bernardo Pasquini, the "uccelli" (birds) of the title make their appearances as follows: the dove (after Jacques de Gallot), the hen (after Jean-Phillippe Rameau), the nightingale (Anonymous, seventeenth century), and the cuckoo (after Pasquini). The Prelude's main theme returns in various guises throughout, and the work ends with a restatement of melodic fragments from earlier movements.—*Roy Brewer*

Recommended:

- ○ **Respighi: Pines of Rome; Fountains of Rome; The Birds** / Marriner (cond.), Academy of St. Martin-in-the-Fields / 2001 / Unesco 70722
- ○ **Respighi: The Birds; Boticelli Pictures; Il Tramonto** / Vasary (cond.), Bournemouth Sinfonietta / 1991 / Chandos 8913

VOCAL

La Sensitiva, for mezzo-soprano & orchestra (1915)

Composed in 1914–15, this cantata for soprano and orchestra is the second of the composer's three settings of Shelley poems, and among the most effective and beautiful depictions of nature in all of Western concert music. The first part (of three) dwells on the beauty of flowers—tulip, narcissi, rose, jessamine—in a spring garden; the music here suggests both ancient times and the sensuousness of the present moment with its flowing, exuberant swellings of impressionistic harmony, contrasted with single-note declamatory vocal lines that suddenly break away into beautiful melodies. At times we hear a nightingale in the garden, a "lontano" (distance) effect played by the flute. The second part introduces the woman who cares for the garden; this begins as a ballad, with voice and solo strings often forming duos, and becomes a somber, chordal funeral chant, with descending, shivering tremolos in the strings and winds. An orchestral interlude in G sharp minor introduces the third and final part of the cantata, in which the mimosa—the "sensitive plant" that gives the work its title—senses the onset of winter; the cold winds begin, illustrated by rushing orchestral effects, and they bring devastation to the garden. The fate of all life is paralleled in the inevitable change of season. —*"Blue Gene" Tyranny*

Recommended:

- ○ **Berlioz: Les nuits d'été; Respighi: La sensitiva** / Baker, Hickox, City of London Sinfonia / 1994 / Virgin 61118
- ○ **Respighi: La sensitiva; Nebbie; Aretusa; Deità silvane** / Finnie, Hickox (cond.), BBC PO / 1996 / Chandos 9453

Il tramonto (The Sunset), for voice & string quartet/string orchestra (1914)

Respighi set several of Percy Bysshe Shelley's poems, but only three were set for mezzo-soprano and orchestra: *Arethusa* in 1910, *Il tramonto* in 1914, and *La Sensitiva* between 1914 and 1915. Of the three, *Il tramonto* (The Sunset) was also written for voice and string quartet, and is heard in this version as often as in the chamber orchestral version. The smaller accompanimental forces give the piece a much more intimate feeling, beautifully suiting the nature of the poem. The strings open the work dramatically, then settle down to a calm lyricism. The singer describes the "One within whose subtle being... genius and death contended." The music swells as the poem tells of his love for a Lady. It then serenely describes the field they walk through, the nature around them, and the colors of the sunset with a repeated, rounded-contour figure similar to what is found in a Field or Chopin nocturne. Very quietly, with the strings almost still, the Youth wonders "Is it not strange... I never saw the sun?/We will walk here To-morrow; thou shall look on it with me." A brief interlude follows, and the nature figure returns before the music turns to hard chords as the Lady finds the Youth dead the next morning. The chords soften as the poem describes how she "died not, nor grew wild, but year by year lived on...." A lighter texture with moving musical lines underscores the poem's description of her life, with the lower strings sometimes moving in parallel lines to the voice. The Lady's final appeal for the same peace that the Youth found in death is uttered with a calm weariness before a violin solo concludes the piece in the major. The impression of the whole work is that of a romantic ballad or a tone poem in miniature, because the strings do not just provide a harmony to the voice's melody, but actually describe the text as well. The mezzo-soprano then fits in as essentially another instrument, reciting the poem in an arioso fashion. Respighi's wonderfully textured music not only convincingly evokes the scenes of the poem, but also expresses the sentiments of the two characters, revealing a more personal aspect of his talent. —*Patsy Morita*

Recommended:

- ○ **Respighi: String Quartets** / Otter, Brodsky Qt. / 2000 / Challenge 72008
- ○ **Schumann: Frauenliebe & Leben; Liederkreis; Respighi: Il Tramonto** / Jurinac, Barylli Qt. / 2002 / Westminster 471269

CHAMBER MUSIC

Violin Sonata in B minor (1917)

Respighi wrote in a wide-ranging style, or rather, styles, often within the same period of time. This sonata, for example, is contemporary with the composer's famous symphonic poem *Fountains of Rome* (1915–16) and with *Ancient Airs and Dances* (1917). Hearing these three works might induce the uninitiated listener to conclude they came from altogether different composers. The sonata is a challenging work that is probably the least popular of the three, though it is hardly neglected and turns up more than occasionally in the concert hall and on recordings. At one time, it enjoyed greater status, owing to the advocacy of Jascha Heifetz, who recorded it for RCA in 1950 with Emanuel Bay on piano. The sonata is cast in three movements, the first of which, marked Moderato—Agitato—Tempo I, is haunting in its passionate, quasinocturnal main theme given by the violin. Because Respighi was both a violinist and pianist, the writing for the two instruments is deftly wrought here and throughout the work in its exchanges and blending of sonorities. The middle panel is a lovely Andante espressivo that opens with an extended piano solo. The finale is a passacaglia marked Allegro moderato ma energico. It is a dramatic and powerful piece whose stormy main theme yields both profound and colorful music. The work generally lasts about 25 minutes in performance. —*Robert Cummings*

Recommended:

- ○ **Respighi: Original Compositions for Violin & Piano** / Turban, Nemirovitch-Dantchenko / 2002 / Claves 502109

BALLET

La boutique fantasque, after Rossini (1918)

After writing his opera *William Tell* in 1829, Rossini, while still a young man, decided to retire from full-time composition, though he continued to write piano pieces for his own amusement. The ballet music *La boutique fantasque* (The Fantastic Toy Shop), taken from some of these unpublished miniatures, could have no better advocate than Respighi, whose orchestral flair and Italianate bravura perfectly matched Rossini's lively tunes.

Like another nineteenth century ballet, *Coppélia* by Delibes, the ballet concerns a toy shop in which the toys come to life. A pair of can-can dancers who have been sold, respectively, to an American and a Russian family, decide to flee in order to avoid separation. Their owners return in fury, but are driven from the shop by the other toys. This pleasingly silly story is irrelevant to the music itself, which consists of an Overture followed by a set of dances—Tarantella, Mazurka, Can-Can, Galop, and Finale. But, thanks to the enduring popularity of the ballet (written for Diaghilev's ballets russes), Respighi's arrangement and deft orchestration have forstalled the almost certain extinction of this delightfully light and high-spirited music. A similar service to Rossini was later performed by Benjamin Britten in an equally sparkling version of the Tarantella. *—Roy Brewer*

Recommended:

- **Respighi: La boutique fantasque; Impressione brasiliane** / Dutoit (cond.), Montreal SO / 1999 / Decca 455983
- **Respighi: Transcriptions for Orchestra** / Lopez-Cobos (cond.), Cincinnati SO / 1996 / Telarc 80396

Elisabeth Rethberg

b. Sep. 22, 1894, Schwarzenberg, Germany, **d.** Jun. 6, 1976, Yorktown Heights, NY

Soprano

During the years between the world wars, Elisabeth Rethberg achieved international acclaim for her well-schooled spinto voice, deemed by Arturo Toscanini "the most beautiful in the world." Equal ease in both the German and Italian repertories made her invaluable to many opera houses during this time and her scrupulous musicianship and unfailingly lovely sound brought worshipful audiences to her feet. Despite a certain lack of dramatic impetus, her performances during the prime years ranked with the best.

Born Lisbeth Sättler, the soprano studied with Otto Watrin at the Dresden Conservatory and made her professional debut at the Dresden Opera in 1915. The role which introduced her was that of Arsena in Johann Strauss II's *Zigeunerbaron.* In her years at Dresden (up to 1922), Rethberg undertook a wide range of lyric-dramatic roles covering a spectrum from Susanna in *Le nozze di Figaro,* the Empress in Richard Strauss' *Die Frau ohne Schatten,* and Sophie in *Der Rosenkavalier* to Tosca. While this wide swath of styles and varying weights of roles suggested versatility, it may have meant that the house managers simply did not know quite what to do with their able young soprano. This uncertainty about a fach (vocal category) most suitable for her may have contributed to her early decline.

In 1922, she found herself at the Salzburg Festival where she continued her dizzying embrace of roles with widely differing demands. For that first season, she performed both the Countess in *Figaro* and the much higher-lying Konstanze in Mozart's *Die Entführung aus dem Serail* (Abduction from the Seraglio). In November 1922, Rethberg made her debut at the Metropolitan Opera in New York where her Aida brought glowing reviews and established her as a Met stalwart for 20 consecutive seasons. In New York, she concentrated on the spinto repertory, the area most congenial to her instrument. Other Italian roles there included Cio-Cio-San, Maddalena in *Andrea Chénier,* Amelia in Verdi's *Simon Boccanegra,* Desdemona, Leonora in *Il trovatore* and even Rautendelein in Respighi's *La campana sommersa* (The Sunken Bell), a rarity led in 1928 by conductor Tullio Serafin. Her German roles included Agathe in Weber's *Der Freischütz,* Sieglinde, Elsa, Elisabeth, Eva and an ill-advised *Siegfried* Brünnhilde late in her career.

In San Francisco, Rethberg appeared regularly from 1928 until 1940, her roles there including such relatively non-repertory operas as *The Bartered Bride* (Marenka) and Halévy's *La Juive* (Rachel). Rethberg was an occasional visitor to Chicago as well, offering appearances in such roles as Cio-Cio-San, Aida, Elsa, the *Trovatore* Leonora, and Amelia in *Ballo in maschera* from 1934 to 1941.

Meanwhile, Rethberg's engagements in Europe continued. She was chosen by Richard Strauss for the title role in the Dresden premiere of *Die Ägyptische Helena* in 1928 and in 1929 she made her debut at La Scala as Aida. In 1929, she sang in *La campana sommersa* in Rome and in 1930 she undertook the *Walküre* Brünnhilde (a role certainly too heavy for her) in Paris. Other Italian engagements paralleled her work in America and at Covent Garden where English audiences were delighted by her vocal art, if not her dramatic acuity. An appearance as the Marschallin produced reviews praising her exquisite singing but remarking on her inferiority to Lotte Lehmann as an actress.

By the early 1940s, Rethberg's voice had declined noticeably, her *Figaro* Countess making for an unmistakably labored close to her Metropolitan years. *—Erik Eriksson*

Recommended:

- **The Complete Brunswick Recordings (1924–29)** / Rethberg, etc. / 1994 / Romophone 81012
- **The Complete HMV, Parlophone and Victor Recordings (1927–34)** / Rethberg, etc. / 1995 / Romophone 81014
- **Lebendige Vergangenheit: Elisabeth Rethberg** / Rethberg, etc. / Preiser 89051

Silvestre Revueltas

b. Dec. 31, 1899, Santiago Papasquiaro, Mexico, **d.** Oct. 5, 1940, Mexico City, Mexico

Composer: Orchestral, Vocal, Film Music

Silvestre Revueltas' music—most of it written during the last decade of his short life—bursts with energy, instrumental color, and mocking humor. Revueltas began violin studies at age eight; the years 1913–16 found him in Mexico City studying composition and violin. From there Revueltas headed north to Texas to study at St. Edward College in Austin (1916–18) and then to the Chicago Musical College (1918–20). Revueltas returned to Mexico to give violin recitals in the capital and several states. But Chicago drew him back in 1922 for a four-year course of violin study. In the mid-1920s Revueltas made trips down to Mexico for several series of recitals of modern music; his piano accompanist was the young Carlos Chávez.

Ultimately, Chávez persuaded him to return to Mexico City to teach violin and chamber music at the National Conservatory and to serve as assistant conductor of Chávez's newly formed Orquesta Sinfónica de México, a position he held from 1929–35. During this time, Revueltas also became active in the cause of artists' and workers' rights.

Between 1931 and 1934, Revueltas wrote six "picture-postcard" pieces for orchestra, ten-minute tone poems usually inspired by Mexican scenes, although when asked what such compositions as *Ventanas* or *Caminos* were about, he would say only, "It all depends on the good or bad will of the listener."

After a rupture with Chávez, Revueltas quit the Orquesta Sinfónica de México and, in the spring of 1936, formed the rival and short-lived Orquesta Sinfónica Nacionál. The failure of that ensemble left him free to tour Spain in 1937. He traveled there in his capacity as secretary general of the League of Revolutionary Writers and Artists, supporting the cultural activities of the Loyalist government, directing various concerts and presenting some of his own music. Revueltas returned to Mexico the following year; he took up teaching again, and wrote a half-dozen scores for Mexican films. His first such effort, *Redes* (Nets), had come in 1935 for a social protest movie set in a poor fishing village. It became his most frequently played score, after the short, hypnotically brutal *Sensemayá* (1938). Revueltas was hard-living and self-destructive; although he officially succumbed to pneumonia at age 40, the long-term truth is that he drank himself to death. What survives is a decade's worth of arresting, concentrated works of differing character that shares a single, forceful voice. *—James Reel*

ORCHESTRAL

Homenaje a Federico García Lorca, for chamber orchestra (1936)

One might expect Silvestre Revueltas' *Homenaje a Federico Garcia Lorca* to be an impassioned lament for the murdered Spanish poet, but an homage is very different from a requiem. While Revueltas' work does contain its share of mournful cries, it juxtaposes mourning with raucous celebration. This mixture of high and low is characteristic of Revueltas, and the skill with which he mixes the two makes *Homenaje a Federico García Lorca* perhaps Revueltas' finest work for orchestra.

The work begins with a rippling, ambiguous chord on piano, followed by a trumpet's unaccompanied lament. The lament is cut off mid-phrase by an unexpected bump, after which the violins play a feverish accompaniment figure and a flute enters playing an infectious, carefree melody. Gradually, the rest of the orchestra joins in: the brass play bumptious, swaggering melodies, the strings whirl in accompaniment, the winds take turns with the melodic line and sometimes cut in on each other. It feels as though one has been plunged suddenly into a city festival, with happy chaos all around. This section pulls up unexpectedly, however, and the music of the opening returns. This time, instead of returning to the festival, Revueltas introduces a slow ostinato in the violins and piano to accompany the trumpet's continued solo laments. The trumpet assumes most of the melodic weight until a climactic section brings powerful dissonances in the brass and emphatic gong strokes. The trumpet music returns once again, but eventually fades away. After a long pause, with the trumpet's mournful tones still hanging in the air, there is another explosion of color in the orchestra. Led by the trumpet and piano, the orchestra transforms the earlier lamenting music into music with similar contours but a joyful tone, something reminiscent of a mariachi. Revueltas gradually whips the orchestra into a chaotic, brilliant climax, and the work ends with an emphatic coda. *Homenaje a Federico Garcia Lorca* is both one of Revueltas' most characteristic works and one of his best. *—Andrew Lindemann Malone*

Recommended:

- **Revueltas: Centennial Anthology** / Mata (cond.), New Philharmonia / 1999 / RCA 902663548
- **Music Of Silvestre Revueltas** / Salonen (cond.), Los Angeles PO New Music Group / 1999 / Sony 60676

Janitzio (1933–1936)

One of the most genial of Revueltas' short orchestral works, *Janitzio* (1933) takes its name from an island in Lake Patzcuaro in the Mexican state of Michoacán. Revueltas' composition is hardly a loving tribute to the island of the title; rather, the composer takes a gleeful poke at the tourists who had overrun the place. Revueltas wrote: "Lake Patzcuaro is filthy. Romantic travelers have dressed it up with postcard-style verses and music. Not to be outdone, I added my grain of sand. Posterity will undoubtedly reward me for this contribution to our tourist industry."

Loud and festive, but with an easy waltz-like swing, *Janitzio* evolves from a theme in 3/8, evoking a local melody as though played by an out-of-tune band. Typically, Revueltas frequently interrupts the flow with abrupt changes of instrumentation and character. The central section of the work's ABA structure allows the oboe and clarinet, then trumpet and horn, and finally strings to provide an unexpectedly tender respite; before long, however, the festive music of the opening returns in full force. *—James Reel*

Recommended:

○ **Musica Mexicana, Vol. 5** / Batiz (cond.), Mexico City PO / 1995 / ASV 894

○ **Danzón** / Wilson (cond.), Simon Bolivar SO of Venezuela / 1998 / Dorian 90254

La Noche de los Mayas, suite from the film score (1939)

More than just a suite from a film score, *La noche de los Mayas* (Mayan Night) hurls itself at an audience like a Mexican *Rite of Spring*. Extravagant sonorities, panoramic scene-painting, and driving rhythms abound in this half-hour work, derived from the soundtrack of a 1939 film of the same name. Comparisons to Stravinsky may not be entirely appropriate, though, for here Revueltas' textures tend to be less complex than was the norm for his own compositions or those of Stravinsky's early maturity. The music is based on fairly limited Indian-type melodies, although Revueltas seems not to be quoting any actual indigenous tunes. In the bulk of his catalog, Revueltas introduced primitivism into music that generally had to do with twentieth century contexts. Here, though, the primitivism is more organic; instead of employing his usual mock-mariachi nationalism, Revueltas takes his inspiration from pre-Columbian Mexico. The scene throughout is nighttime, when the protective sun has withdrawn and left the Mayans to contend with the lively denizens of the underworld.

The work is in four movements. The first, "La noche de los Mayas," establishes a ritualistic ambience by repeating short motifs obsessively. (Revueltas also used this technique in his greatest hit, *Sensemaya*.) The second, "La noche de Jaranas" (Night of Revelry), is highly typical of the composer's concise tone poems (especially the likes of *Alcancías*, *Caminos*, and *Janitzio*) with its exciting syncopations and irregular cross-rhythms. The battery of native percussion takes over for the climax, after which the fiesta fades into the dawn.

Contrast comes with the mostly contemplative third movement, "La noche de Yucatán." It's the most episodic section of the suite; this may have to do with the music's cinematic origins, but even in his concert works Revueltas made a virtue of short-attention-span forms. The movement begins with a simple drumbeat-accompanied melody; it would be at home in Carlos Chávez's *Sinfonía India*, which was also based on Indian motifs. But this immediately gives way to an impassioned, lyrical theme for strings. The long, slow melodies that wind through this movement suggest the romance of the jungle, but not without acknowledging the underlying menace of the supernatural forces at large. The stunning finale, "Noche de encantamiento" (Night of Incantation), is an orgy of elemental ritualism in theme-and-variations form. This piece is dominated by four percussion groups of mainly native instruments pounding out increasingly complex rhythms; it even features an obsessive repeated-note solo for the conch shell. *—James Reel*

Recommended:

○ **Musica Mexicana 2** / Batiz (cond.), Mexico City PO / 1993 / ASV 866

○ **Music Of Revueltas** / Salonen (cond.), Los Angeles PO New Music Group / 1999 / Sony 60676

○ **Revueltas: Orchestral Music** / Barrios (cond.), Aguascalientes SO / 2002 / Naxos 8555917

Sensemayá (1938)

Silvestre Revueltas' *Sensemayá* was written in 1937 for chamber orchestra; one year later, the composer transcribed it for a huge orchestra of 27 wind instruments, 14 percussion instruments, and strings. Either version packs a considerable wallop. The rhythms are laid out precisely and have considerable visceral impact, very much in a manner that recalls Igor Stravinsky's *The Rite of Spring*. However, Revueltas' masterful orchestration, and ability to evoke the ancient Maya civilization with decidedly modern music are uniquely his own. The work begins with a low note in the bassoon as the percussion plays the sinuous, syncopated rhythm that drives the work. Soon a solo horn enters playing the first of this work's two major themes, a muscular, ominous motif. Other horns join the first one to play the theme, growing louder and more emphatic, but rigorously yoked to the underlying rhythm. Eventually the horns blast as loudly as they can, with obsessive trills on the bassoon far underneath, and the violins enter with the slashing second theme. The horns eventually take up this new theme and bring it to a climax, after which the music returns to its opening texture. This recapitulation brings with it a mood of foreboding. The rhythm becomes even more obsessive, and the brass and violins cannot stop dueling with the two themes. Finally the music reaches a massive climax during which both themes are played, overlapping, sometimes in part and sometimes in whole, by woodwinds, brass and violins in what sounds like a musical riot. The coda feels like the final dropping of a knife. *Sensemayá* is a unique orchestral spectacle, something only Revueltas could have written, and in its way it is one of the most brutal works of its time. *—Andrew Lindemann Malone*

Recommended:

○ **Musica Mexicana, Vol. 5** / Batiz (cond.), Mexico City PO / 1995 / ASV 894

○ **Latin American Fiesta** / Bernstein (cond.), New York PO / 1998 / Sony 60571

VOCAL

Ranas (Frogs), for voice & instrumental ensemble (1932)

Generally, Silvestre Revueltas chose poems to set to music not on the basis of fame or reputation, but rather on consideration of the opportunities a poem offered for musical setting. Daniel Castañeda's *Ranas* (Frogs), with its references to music, distinct rhythms, and quirkily illustrated imagery, presents numerous possibilities to a witty arranger, and it became a delight for Revueltas. The setting begins with soggy, dark brass chords and a chirping piccolo, after which the rest of the instrumental ensemble adds phrases of its own. When the soprano comes in, she sounds almost as if she is trying to navigate this musical swamp by stepping carefully to the rhythm of the poem. Castañeda's references to various wind instruments are conveniently illustrated by the instruments themselves, and phrases like "the trapeze of space" and "reach the stars," which come at the ends of stanzas, let the soprano explore the upper registers. The only time the angular rhythms and dark color of the accompaniment shifts slightly is when the poem rhapsodizes about "sweet dissonance," which is illustrated appropriately. Revueltas' setting emphasizes the character of the poem in typically witty, incisive fashion. *—Andrew Lindemann Malone*

Recommended:

○ **Sensemayá** / Diemecke (cond.), Camerata de las Americas, Latino Americano Quartet / 1996 / Dorian 90244

FILM MUSIC

Redes (1935)

Until *La noche de los Mayas* gained popularity in the early 1990s, *Redes* ("Nets") was Revueltas's best-known extended work. It is a suite assembled by Revueltas and conductor Erich Kleiber from the composer's music for Paul Strand's 1935 social protest film about an impoverished fishing village. Scored for a rather small orchestra, *Redes* is one of the composer's most serious, perhaps even grimmest, efforts. Part One begins with "The Fishermen": a brass-heavy announcement of the strife faced by the people of this Veracruz village leads to a quieter depiction of the inhabitants. "The Child's Funeral" is a tender yet desolate lament introduced by the woodwinds and picked up by the violins. Following a lugubrious bass-and-cello passage that will form the basis of the finale, "Fishing Party" enlivens the proceedings with whirling music that is just a bit too desperate to be truly festive.

Part Two opens with a reminiscence of that ominous music for low strings; soon the full orchestra erupts with rough, jerking utterances; this is "The Fight." It's followed by a dirge that essentially reprises ideas from "The Child's Funeral." A trumpet picks up a distant, threatening call first heard near the work's beginning; this becomes the basis of the final section, "The Return of the Fishermen with their Dead Friend," a long, slow crescendo that begins in the depths of the strings and culminates in a stinging cry from the full orchestra, with the brass heard above all. *—James Reel*

Recommended:

○ **Musica Mexicana Vol. 4** / Batiz (cond.), Mexico City PO / 1994 / ASV 893

○ **Revuelta, Orbón, Ginastera** / Mata (cond.), LatinoAmericano Quartet / 1993 / Dorian 90178

Joseph Rheinberger

b. Mar. 17, 1839, Vaduz, Lichtenstein, **d.** Nov. 25, 1901, Munich, Germany

Composer: Keyboard, Concerto, Chamber Music

Joseph Rheinberger, influential German composer, organist, conductor, and teacher, was the son of the Prince of Liechtenstein's treasurer Johann Peter Rheinberger. His exceptional musical gifts astounded his first teacher, Sebastian Pohli, who instructed him from the age of five. As a child, Rheinberger progressed so rapidly that by the time he was just seven, he was already an organist in his hometown of Vaduz. By 1848, he had a complete mastery of harmony and had graduated to the piano and organ classes of Philipp Schmutzer, who introduced him to the works of J.S. Bach and the Viennese classicists. Rheinberger's father, who initially resisted his pursuing a musical career, finally submitted to persuasion from the composer Nagiller to permit the boy to study in Munich. He was allowed to settle there in 1851 and the city became his permanent home thereafter.

Rheinberger studied theory with J.H. Maier, organ with J.G. Herzog, and piano with J.E. Leonhard at the Munich Conservatory. By 1853, he was employed as organist at several city churches and supplementing his income offering private tuition. He dedicated every free moment to composition, and during the next few years wrote well over 100 apprentice works; none met with his approval, and they were never published. Rheinberger's four piano pieces, Op. 1, finally appeared in 1859, the same year he joined the staff of the conservatory to teach piano and music theory. In 1864, he also became the conductor of the Munich Oratorienverein, holding the post until 1877.

Rheinberger worked for a while as a coach at the court opera, witnessing Wagner's premiere of *Tristan und Isolde*. In 1867, he was appointed professor at the conservatory—a position he would hold until his death. During the same year, he married a former pupil, Franziska von Hoffnaass. Rheinberger was increasingly prone to poor health, but continued to work, almost without interruption. 1877 saw his appointment as hofkapellmeister and in 1894 he was ennobled, receiving the title of privy councillor.

Rheinberger died in 1901, shortly after his retirement. His grave in Munich was destroyed during World War II and his remains were transferred in 1950 to his birthplace. Hans von Bülow, a great conductor and tireless advocate of Rheinberger's music, called him "a truly ideal teacher of composition, unrivalled in the whole of Germany and beyond in skill, refinement, and devotion to his subject; in short, one of the worthiest musicians and human beings in the world." *—Michael Jameson*

Overview of Works (ca. 1853–1900)

Joseph Rheinberger composed a vast and varied output, but is largely known for his organ music, particularly his 20 sonatas. The greater portion of his compositions—chamber, orchestral, operatic—have thus been forgotten. Their almost complete neglect may in part be due to his ultra-conservative style, which took Bach, Mozart, and Beethoven as springboards to forge a Romantic style that stopped well short of the innovations of Wagner and Liszt. Rheinberger, in fact, was opposed to the latter pair's advancements and preferred instead the traditions of Mendelssohn and Brahms.

While much of his output may be unjustly overlooked, the organ sonatas are rightly considered his finest achievements. *No. 3*, *No. 4*, *No. 7*, *No. 8*, *No. 11*, and the last four are probably the most popular in the set. *No. 3*, in G, features a first movement marked Pastorale that fully matches that description in its largely serene and bucolic character. The middle panel offers serenity, too, but a more angelic than Earthly one. The heroic finale features some fine fugal writing that yields the work's best music. The *Fourth*, in A, is more widely performed, rivaling the popular *Eighth* as the most-recorded. It is far grander in conception than the *Third* and has a religious, almost Brucknerian character, though it certainly does not divulge such advanced, Wagner-tinged harmonies. The three-movement *Seventh*, in F minor, is relatively modest, but a finely crafted masterwork still, while the larger *No. 8*, both in its contrapuntal subtleties and leaner sonorities, is Bachian in spirit. The concluding Passacaglia is one of the composer's finest keyboard achievements. The four-movement *No. 11*, in D minor, features a lovely Adagio second movement and brilliant fugal finale. *No. 19*, in G, and *No. 20*, in F, are big works in both conception and length and while they may not indicate a continued growth on the part of the composer, they do not suggest declining powers either. Virtually all of the sonatas in the series are well-crafted and deserving of attention, as are the other 22 organ works in his oeuvre.

But what of Rheinberger's other compositions? His sacred output, consisting of 18 complete masses, four "Stabat Mater" settings, motets, and other works are of high quality, but rarely performed. The *Mass in E flat major* (Cantus Missae), Op. 109, and the *Mass in B major*, Op. 172, still garner some attention in live performances and in the recording studio. Some church choirs, especially Roman Catholic, still sing his works. Rheinberger also wrote a fair amount of secular music, including songs and five operas, but again, these receive little attention. He produced five symphonies, but only his *Second*, the F major (Florentine), survives and rarely appears in the concert hall or on recordings. Of his other compositions, the piano works—four-hand pieces, waltzes, rondos, fugues—may be the most unjustly neglected as they exhibit some of the same masterful keyboard writing found in the organ sonatas. *—Robert Cummings*

Recommended:

- ○ **Rheinberger: Cantus Missae** / Bernius (cond.), Stuttgart Chamber Choir / 1989 / Carus 83113
- ○ **Rheinberger: Suite, Op149, Sechs Stücke** / Haenchen (cond.), Ostertag, Juffinger, Sebestyen / Capriccio 337
- ○ **Josef Rheinberger** / Athinaos (cond.), St. Hedwig's Cathedral Chor / Signum 60
- ○ **Rheinberger: Motets, Masses & Hymns** / Patterson (cond.), Chalmers, Gloriae Dei Cantores / 1999 / Gloria Dei Cantores 108
- ○ **Rheinberger: Complete Chamber Music** / Gobel, Krug, Bronx Arts Ens., Sonare Quartett, Gobel-Trio Berlin / 1989 / Thorofon 2161
- ○ **Rheinberger: Sonatas, Opp47, 99 & 135** / Pompa-Baldi / 2003 / Centaur 2648

KEYBOARD

Organ Sonata No. 3 in G major, Op. 88 (1875)

Rheinberger's *Sonata No. 3* for organ is one of his more widely performed works, able to stand nearly with the more popular *Eighth* (1882) and *Fourth* (1876). It was conceived on a more modest scale than either of these later siblings and is much shorter too, lasting about 14 or 15 minutes. It also has a more youthful character, even though it was composed just a year before the grandiose *Fourth*. Not that it contains mostly light music: Rheinberger aims for a pastoral, serene sort of effect in the first two movements, but a grander one in the finale.

The opening panel, Pastorale, is lively but unhurried in its bucolic character. The main theme is happy and serene, and the whole movement conveys a carefree sense, a feeling of contentedness. The second movement, Intermezzo, at less than three minutes, is peaceful in its heavenly solemnity and upper-register sonorities. The finale is the most substantial movement, both in content and length, lasting about seven or eight minutes. It is a lively Fugue whose heroic main theme; brilliant keyboard writing; and glorious, powerful close elevate the music to masterpiece level. *—Robert Cummings*

Recommended:

- ○ **Rheinberger: Organ Sonatas** / Stevens / 1998 / Organ Historical Society 140

Organ Sonata No. 4 in A minor, Op. 98 (1876)

Joseph Rheinberger produced a huge output of works for organ, most notably his 20 sonatas. (He also wrote a significant body of piano, sacred, and vocal music, and composed five symphonies, five operas, three singspiels, and 12 string quartets.) The *Sonata No. 4* here is one of his most popular compositions, eclipsed perhaps only by the *Eighth* (1882). The *Fourth* is a bit smaller in scope than its later sibling, but just as appealing, both for its brilliant keyboard writing and for its noble, religious character. The work is cast in three movements, the opening panel (Tempo moderato) being the largest and most inspired. It begins in a somber mood, but soon turns ecstatic with a glorious theme of religious aspect played against a driving running figure. The whole movement, in fact, seems bathed in an aura of religious ecstasy. Much of the style recalls Bruckner, himself an organist whose symphonies many claim were filled with sonorities he imagined on the organ. The second movement Intermezzo is lighter and more lyrical in its gentler character, while the finale (Fuga cromatica) divulges the composer's deft contrapuntal skills. Lasting about 20 minutes, this sonata is a masterpiece in the organ repertory and ought to be even better known. *—Robert Cummings*

Recommended:

- ○ **Rheinberger: Works for Organ, Vol. 1** / Rubsam / 1999 / Naxos 554212

Organ Sonata No. 8 in E minor, Op. 132 (1882)

This is probably Rheinberger's most popular sonatas of the 20 he composed for organ. The *Fourth* has also achieved wide currency among organists and audiences alike and is compelling in its smaller scope and less-grandiose manner. The *Eighth* is cast in four movements: Praeludium, Intermezzo, Scherzoso, and Passacaglia. Lasting a bit under a half-hour, it is one of the composer's grandest organ works, though by no means his longest or most sonorously powerful.

If the *Fourth* divulged a somewhat Brucknerian character in its large washes of sound and sense of religious ecstasy, this sonata can be likened to the spirit, if not the style of Bach in its generally more scaled-down sonorities and contrapuntal writing. The first movement offers a sense of serenity in the mostly subdued character of its thematic material. The other three movements are played continuously, with the serenity of the second contrasted by the gruff and vigorous manner of the Scherzoso, and the concluding Passacaglia crowning the whole work with a sense of the profound, as it grows from quiet depths to ringing heights of triumph in some of the composer's finest thematic manipulations and transformations ever. In sum, this is not only one of Rheinberger's most successful organ sonatas, but one of his most worthy. *—Robert Cummings*

Recommended:

- ○ **Rheinberger: Complete Organ Works, Vol. 4** / Innig / 2001 / MDG 3170894

CONCERTO

Organ Concerto No. 1 in F major, Op. 137 (1884)

The first and better-known of Rheinberger's two organ concertos, though not derivative, reveals the strong influence of both Felix Mendelssohn (including his interest in Baroque music) and, mainly in structural details, César Franck. This concerto is by no means an overpowering display piece; the soloist is afforded few truly virtuosic passages in the company of a warm but modest ensemble of strings and three horns. With a Romantic organ on hand, Rheinberger apparently felt that most of the woodwind and brass colors were already accounted for. The first movement, Moderato, begins with three stately, ascending notes that will recur in later movements, sometimes as the foundation of completely new melodies. This, with Rheinberger's fondness for thematic metamorphosis instead of more conventional development and variation patterns, links the concerto to the cyclic practices of Franck. In sound, though, this first movement has more in common with

Mendelssohn, particularly the nobler passages of his second, third, and fifth symphonies. At any rate, these three notes are at first the basis of a chordal orchestral introduction, around which the soloist weaves a more elaborate melody that evolves without a break into a flowing second subject. There's also an important variant derived from the opening three notes, now played in descending order. Rheinberger develops this material within a standard sonata-allegro format.

The Andante begins with a hushed murmur from the organ, frankly the sort of tasteful background music one hears at funeral parlors. But the strings and horns arrive to provide a lusher setting, as well as an allusion to the three ascending notes from the concerto's very beginning. The organ introduces more animated material, its chromaticism now betraying a secret affinity for Franck's untethered approach to harmony. Eventually, there's even a repeated, sighing fall typical of that Belgian organ master. The three-note sequence from the first movement becomes more prominent in an episode just past the Andante's halfway point and these few themes continue to reappear in modestly different guises through the course of the free-form movement.

The bright finale, Con moto, begins with a measured, pompous bustle reminiscent of Handel. A broader, arclike theme takes over, alluding again to the recurring three-note motif (and looking ahead to the "transfiguration" theme in Richard Strauss' *Death and Transfiguration*, though without the Straussian melodrama). Again, the structure is a mere metamorphosis of the melodies. The work ends affirmatively, Rheinberger having accomplished the remarkable feat of writing a 25-minute organ concerto completely free of bombast. *—James Reel*

Recommended:

○ **Dupré: Symphony in G minor; Rheinberger: Organ Concerto 1** / Ling (cond.), Murray, Royal PO / 1986 / Telarc 80136

CHAMBER MUSIC

Horn Sonata in E flat major, Op. 178

This warm, lyrical sonata is typical of Rheinberger's compositional style: formally conservative, immaculately crafted, and possessed of a subdued good nature. Those looking for a shot of late nineteenth century moodiness or innovation should look elsewhere—Rheinberger never cared for the trends of Wagner and Liszt. But when taken on its own terms, Op. 178 makes a welcome addition to the relatively small repertory of sonatas for horn and piano. The E flat sonata is in three movements. The first is built on a syncopated theme that seems almost ungainly against the steady undulations in the piano; this relatively short motive serves as a unifying element throughout. The second movement has a touch of Chopinesque melancholy; the keyboard part's insistent rhythm and high-register figurations may remind some of the piano master's nocturnes. The work concludes with a cheerful Allegro, full of pianistic filigree and comical outbursts from the horn. *—Allen Schrott*

Recommended:

○ **Romantic Music for Horn & Piano** / Holtzel, Schnurr / 1999 / MDG 3240908

RIAS-Kammerchor

f. 1948, Berlin, Germany
Ensemble

Founded in 1948, the RIAS-Kammerchor (RIAS Chamber Choir) has played a crucial role in the revival of the musical life of the city of Berlin. Frequently heard in collaboration with the Berlin Radio Symphony and the Berlin Philharmonic Orchestra, the choir has been led by conductors Ferenc Friscay, Karl Böhm, Herbert von Karajan, Lorin Maazel, Claudio Abbado, James Levine, and Daniel Barenboïm. The choir has also made a specialty of performances of early music under the baton of such conductors as Nikolaus Harnoncourt, John Eliot Gardiner, Frans Brueggen, Roger Norrington, and René Jacobs. Under principal conductor Marcus Creed, the choir also independently performs as an a cappella chamber choir. *—Robert Adelson*

Recommended:

○ **Brahms: Lieder und Gesänger** / Creed (dir.), Klier, Langlamet, Jerierski, RIAS-Kammerchor / HM 901592

○ **Mendelssohn: Motets; Psaume 100; Missa breve** / Creed (cond.), RIAS-Kammerchor / HM 901704

○ **Poulenc: Motets; Messe** / Creed (cond.), RIAS-Kammerchor / HM 901588

Katia Ricciarelli

b. Jan. 18, 1946, Rovigo, Italy
Soprano

Katia Ricciarelli, in her prime, possessed a radiant lyric soprano voice with an individually sweet timbre, and a lovely stage presence that complemented her voice. However, like all too many singers, she became a textbook example of what happens when a voice is pushed beyond its limits. During her best years, she was one of the most touching Giuliettas (*I Capuleti e i Montecchi*), Desdemonas, and Anna Bolenas on the operatic stage, and had a special affinity for Rossini's music, enjoying great success in such roles as Bianca (*Bianca e Faliero*), Elena (*La donna del lago*), and Amenaide (*Tancredi*).

She came from a very poor family and after graduating from school, worked to afford the time and money to study at the Benedetto Marcello Conservatory in Venice, where she worked primarily with Iris Adami Corradetti, herself a noted lyric soprano. Upon graduation, she made her operatic debut as Mimì in Puccini's *La bohème*, in Mantua, Italy. Her appearance in Cherubini's *Anacreon* the next year in Siena created a small sensation, followed by a greater one when she won the Parma Verdi competition, followed in 1971 by her winning the Voce Verdiane competition. Largely on the strengths of these triumphs, in 1972, she debuted at the Lyric Opera of Chicago as Lucrezia in Verdi's *I due Foscari*, and at the Rome Opera as Verdi's Giovanna d'Arco. In 1974, she made her Covent Garden debut as Mimì. Her Met debut was also in *La bohème* in 1975, and her La Scala debut was in 1976 as Suor Angelica in Puccini's *Il trittico*.

Like many singers, her voice became larger as she matured, allowing her to take on such roles as Verdi's Desdemona and Luisa Miller. However, overencouraged by this, and also guided by Karajan, who often pitted essentially lyric voices against heavy roles, in the early 1980s, she began to sing roles that were considerably too dramatic, such as Tosca, Aida, and even Turandot (though only in the recording studio.) By the 1990s, while it had not lost all of its luster, her voice was no longer as limpid as it had been, both the top and middle were wobbly, and her pitch had become frequently imprecise. Some of the theaters where she had scored her major triumphs, such as La Scala, received her subsequent performances very badly.

Among her recordings, a collection of arias made in 1979 and 1980 (Ermitage) catches her still in fine voice, although some strain does show in the more dramatic roles. In complete operas, her recording of *La donna del lago* (Sony) is excellent. She also appeared as Desdemona in the 1986 film of *Otello*, directed by Franco Zeffirelli. *—Ann Feeney*

Recommended:

○ **Ricciarelli in Recital** / Amaducci (cond.), Ricciarelli, Lugano Radio Orch. / 1999 / Aura Classics 0159

○ **Rossini Arias** / Ferro (cond.), Ricciarelli, Orch. & Chorus of the Lyon Opera / 1991 / Virgin 91484

○ **Ricciarelli: Nuttata 'e sentimento** / Perulli (cond.), Ricciarelli / Kicco 01695

○ **Rossini: Biana e Falliero** / Renzetti (cond.), Ricciarelli, Horne, Merritt, Gavazzi, London Sinfonietta / Hommage 7001838

Karl Richter

b. Oct. 15, 1926, Plauen, Vogtland, Germany, **d.** Feb. 15, 1981, Munich, Germany
Conductor

Karl Richter was regarded as one of the great Bach conductors of the twentieth century, noted for solid regularity in rhythms and a serious approach to the music, though he was not given to following the changing pronouncements of musicologists concerning historical accuracy in performance.

He was brought up in the tradition of German Protestant religious music; his father was a minister in the central German regions near where Johann Sebastian Bach had lived. Richter learned piano and organ, and as he approached his twelfth birthday entered the Kreuzschule school in Dresden. After World War II, he entered the Leipzig Conservatory, where he studied with Rudolf Mauersberger, and also studied at the Leipzig Institute for Sacred Music, where he learned Bach interpretation from Karl Straube and Günther Ramin. Very soon he was appointed choirmaster of the Christuskirche in Leipzig at the age of 20, and in 1947 became the organist of the Thomanerkirche, both institutions with strong Bach traditions.

He left East Germany in 1950 to live in West Germany and settled in Munich, where he was organist of the Markuskirche and started teaching that same year at the Hochschule für Musik of Munich. He organized the Munich Bach Choir in 1951, and in 1953 added to it the Munich Bach Orchestra. His performances naturally centered on Bach and under Richter his musicians and singers became one of the most renowned organizations specializing in the music of the great German master and his era.

The formation of the Munich Bach Chorus and Orchestra reflected a growing international interest in music of the Baroque and, sparked by the advent of the LP record, the notion of integral series of composers' works. Deutsche Grammophon's Archiv label was the first of such historic specialty sublabels. Richter and his Bach Choir and Orchestra became a major pillar of that label and recorded numerous Bach choral works, gaining international recognition.

They toured frequently, and Richter also played and recorded often as an organist and harpsichordist. In 1968, Richter made one of his most dramatic guest conducting tours when he conducted the *St. John Passion* and the *B minor Mass* in both Moscow and Leningrad at a time when religious music of any sort was rarely heard in the Soviet Union.

Although his regularity of tempo (some called it inflexibility) placed him apart from the Romantic manner of performing Bach, Richter's performances otherwise retained the Romantic era's approach, stressing the solemnity of Bach's music and including dramatic large-scale dynamic contrasts. Newer research and the growing popularity of "original" or "period" instrument performances did not affect his interpretations, which used modern instruments. In some respects, younger interpreters who emerged in the 1970s considered him the representative of an approach against which they were reacting.

Later in his career, Richter enlarged his repertory to conduct Classical- and even Romantic-era works, but tended to remain known primarily as a Baroque specialist. He is best remembered for his mastery of Baroque choral/orchestral works of the largest scale, where his architectural approach to the music is most effective. His recordings of the Bach Passions, oratorios, *B minor Mass*, and *Magnificat*, as well as Handel oratorios such as the *Messiah*, are considered his most important contribution to the Baroque discography. *—Joseph Stevenson*

Recommended:

- ○ **Bach: Sacred Masterpieces** / Richter (cond.), Rothschuh, Fischer-Dieskau, Wunderlich, Ludwig, Munchener Bach-Orch. / 1985 / DG 463701
- ○ **Bach: Weihnachtsoratorium** / Richter (cond.), Wunderlich, Ludwig, Janowitz, Crass, Munchener Bach-Orch. / Archiv 427236
- ○ **Bach: Organ Recital** / Richter / 1997 / London 455291

Sviatoslav Richter

b. Mar. 20, 1915, Zhitomir, Russia, **d.** Aug. 1, 1997, Moscow, Russia
Pianist

Having learned the fundamentals of music from his father, Sviatoslav Teofilovich Richter taught himself the piano and had already given public concerts before entering the Moscow Conservatory in 1937. While still a student, Richter won first prize at the All-Union Contest of Performers of 1945. His playing earned him considerable renown, and by the time of his graduation in 1947 he had devoted fans. In 1949 he garnered the coveted Stalin Prize.

Richter gave the 1942 premiere of Sergei Prokofiev's *Piano Sonata No. 6*—the composer's first work in that form for years, and the first one he did not premiere himself. This resulted in wild acclaim for both performer and composer. Thereafter, Richter was a great proponent of Prokofiev's music, premiering also the *Seventh* and the *Ninth Sonatas*, the latter of which is dedicated to him.

Though word of Richter's excellence (and occasional poor-quality recordings) had spread outside of Russia, his foreign engagements were limited to Eastern Bloc countries (and, in one case, China) where Soviet officials felt there was reduced risk of defection. However, his 1958 performance of Prokofiev's *Fifth Piano Concerto* with the Philadelphia Orchestra (on tour in Leningrad) generated such excitement that he was finally permitted to tour the United States, further bolstering his reputation as a virtuoso. Engagements in all of world's musical centers followed. Richter was known as a pianist of transcendent abilities, particularly adept at highlighting the nuances of different styles. Though his interests focused primarily on music of Beethoven, and Prokofiev, he was also highly regarded for his Schubert, Schumann, Bach, Debussy, and Ravel; and in the early 1960s he made a memorable recording of Benjamin Britten's *Piano Concerto* with the composer conducting.

Richter did not favor studio recordings; therefore, most of his recordings are from live performances. Many of them, particularly those from Soviet concerts, suffer from indifferent sound quality and excessive audience noise, but his playing had an electric quality that transcended these handicaps.

The pianist earned a reputation for being difficult and aloof. He was notoriously apt to cancel performances on whims, or arrive late without explanation or apology. However, those who heard him were rarely disappointed. He preferred intimate concert settings over big auditoriums, and thus returned many times to the Aldeburgh and Spoleto Festivals. He was the centerpiece of the Fêtes Musicales, held annually beginning in 1964 at Grange de Meslay, near Tours.

Among his greatest recordings are his Schubert sonatas, Rachmaninov and Prokofiev concertos, Liszt concertos (these have the benefits of first-rate sound), and his Schumann. He has also served as a chamber musician and accompanist, playing piano duets with Britten, and accompanying Elisabeth Schwarzkopf and Dietrich Fischer-Dieskau, among others. *—AMG*

Recommended:

- ○ **Beethoven, Weber, Schubert, Chopin** / Sanderling (cond.), Richter, USSR Radio & TV SO / Urania 4219
- ○ **Sviatoslav Richter "Der Philosoph"** / Richter / 1997 / Philips 456549
- ○ **The Sofia Recital 1958** / Richter / 2001 / Philips 464734
- ○ **Schumann: Fantasy in C; Faschingsschwank aus Wien; Papillons** / Richter / 2002 / EMI 75233
- ○ **Sviatoslav Richter** / Richter / DG 457668
- ○ **Svjatoslav Richter in Prague** / Bakala (cond.), Richter, Czech State PO / 1993 / HM 254024
- ○ **Schumann & Grieg: Concertos** / Matacic (cond.), Richter, Monte Carlo National Opera Orch. / 2003 / EMI 67987
- ○ **Richter Rediscovered** / Richter / 2001 / RCA 63844
- ○ **Rachmaninoff: Concerto 2; Tchaikovsky: Concerto 1** / Karajan, Wislocki (conds.), Richter, VSO, Warsaw National Phil. / 1963 / DG 447420

Wallingford Riegger

b. Apr. 29, 1885, Albany, GA, **d.** Apr. 2, 1961, New York, NY
Composer

American composer Wallingford Riegger was a proponent of none of the major twentieth century "schools" of composition, and until the very end of his long career he received little more than cursory notice from the American musical establishment. Nevertheless, his 75 completed compositions have proved a source of enrichment to several generations of musicians who are drawn to Riegger's unique brand of modernism.

Riegger was born into a musically rich Georgia family in 1885, and was taught piano and violin from an early age. Riegger added the cello to his musical pursuits when the family decided to form a private string quartet in 1900. After a year at Cornell University (1904), Riegger enrolled at the newly formed Institute of Musical Arts in New York as a student of both cello and composition. After graduating from the Institute in 1907, Riegger traveled to Germany, where he took cello lessons from Robert Haussmann, and studied composition with Max Bruch and Edgar Stillman-Kelley. Riegger found employment as a cellist with the St. Paul Orchestra upon returning to the United States in 1910, but by 1914 he found himself back in Germany, working first as an opera conductor (Stadttheater of Würzburg) and then, during the 1916–17 season, as conductor of the Blüthner Orchestra in Berlin.

Riegger was lured back to the United States by the prospect of becoming professor of cello at Drake University in Iowa, a position which would offer him enough flexibility to pursue composition in a more serious way. His first published work, the *Piano Trio* Op.1 from (1920) was awarded the Paderewski Prize and gained Riegger some national attention, but during the next few years he began to question the long-term merits of his conservative musical style. From 1923 to 1926 he retired from active composition to sort out his own personal views on the future of music. By the late 1920s, Riegger had aligned himself with progressive composers Charles Ives, Henry Cowell, and Carl Ruggles, adopting a more dissonant but still fiercely independent, compositional language. This new language appears fully developed in the 1932 orchestra work *Dichotomy*. Unfortunately, this new musical direction failed to bring any recognition and financial reward. After he resigned from Drake University in 1922, Riegger was forced to work as an editor and musical arranger to make ends meet.

During the 1930s, an interest in modern dance led the composer to write almost exclusively for leaders in that field, including Martha Graham and José Limon. By 1941 Riegger had tired of his increasing isolation from other musicians and he recommitted himself to instrumental composition, this time with greater financial and popular success. The premiere of the *Symphony No.3* in 1948 provided him national exposure, and he remained in the front rank of American composers until his death in 1961. Later works employ 12-tone techniques in a very free manner. *—Blair Johnston*

Overview of Works (1902–1960)

Wallingford Riegger's music represents a curious blending of the severe academic criteria of the 12-tone era and rugged American individualism. As is typical, he began as a conservative, not out of philosophy but to gain the feel of working with the tools of his craft. This idiom ran concurrent with his salad years as a cellist in the St. Paul Orchestra, his later conducting positions in pre-Great War Germany, and subsequent teaching post on returning to America. Representative of this period was the *Piano Trio*, Op. 1, and *La belle dame sans merci* (after the Medieval legend), respectively garnering the Paderewski Prize in 1922 and the Coolidge Prize in 1924. Belated changes were in the air as the revolutions of the Second Viennese School a decade prior began to attract musical firebrands on both sides of the Atlantic. In 1923, Riegger took a sabbatical from composing for creative self-examination, in the process aligning himself with Charles Ives, Carl Ruggles, and Henry Cowell. The last mentioned was significant for having commenced in 1927 his journal *New Music* with works by Ruggles and Riegger. Meanwhile, Riegger had absorbed the 12-tone system into his musical vocabulary. Embraced would have been too strong a word, however, for Riegger always leavened the process with stretches of atonal, chromatic, and even diatonic music, hence a typically "American" approach and using instinct over textbook. To this period belong works that were given premieres by some of the century's most prestigious conductors: *Study in Sonority* for ten or more violins by Leopold Stokowski (1929), the orchestral *Rhapsody* by Erich Kleiber (1931), and Nicolas Slonimsky's Berlin performance of *Dichotomy* (1932). Like Ives, Riegger was destined to largely ply his craft amid "rumors" of his music. But something approaching popular recognition came during the great modern dance era of Copland-Graham. Such scores by Riegger as 1935's *New Dance* and the following year's *With My Red Fires* represented the more accessible aspect of his art. At the same time, Riegger was able to continue his more adventurous (which, after all, was by now becoming the academic norm) writing in his concert works. From 1938, he produced his two string quartets and three symphonies, the third of the latter of which was awarded the New York Music

Critics Circle Award in 1948. The work made its way across the Atlantic where it found a special advocate in conductor Hermann Scherchen, stalwart champion of serialism. The *Symphony No. 3* is perhaps the most representative of Riegger's pragmatic approach, featuring a highly chromatic second movement and a frankly tonal contrapuntal finale. In his last decade, Riegger's star rose as more frequent performances of his works coincided with awards and recognition. He is viewed, along with Ives, as one of the visionaries of twentieth century American music. *—Wayne Reisig*

Recommended:

○ **Wallingford Riegger** / Antonini, Barnett (conds.), Wingreen, American Brass Quintet, Oslo PO, Eastman-Rochester Orch. / 1990 / CRI 572

○ **Riegger: Music for Piano & Winds** / Kalish, NY Woodwind Quintet / 1996 / Bridge 9068

○ **Wallingford Riegger** / Whitney (cond.), Harth, Owen, Louisville Orch. / 2002 / First Edition 7

Wolfgang Rihm

b. Mar. 13, 1952, Karlsruhe, Germany

Composer: Vocal, Chamber Music

The prolific composer Wolfgang Rihm's music is unpredictable, with wide mood swings and shocking juxtapositions between harsh utter violence and gentle, lovely sounds.

He began composing at the age of 11. In 1968, he began studying at the State Hochschule für Musik in Karlsruhe where his composition teacher was Eugene Velte. He also attended a special course in Humanities on modern composition with composer Wolfgang Fortner and Humphrey Searle, one of the best-known British composers using Schoenberg's 12-tone system. In 1969, Rihm went to the German center of avant-garde music, Darmstadt, to attend a course in new music. He graduated from the conservatory in Karlsruhe in 1972. After that, he pursued further independent study with Karlheinz Stockhausen, then attended classes with composer Klaus Huber and musicology with Hans Heinrich Eggebrecht.

From 1973 to 1978, he was a member of the faculty of the Hochschule für Musik in Karlsruhe and, in 1978, was a lecturer at the Darmstadt Festival courses. He wrote two chamber operas, *Faust und Yorick* (1976) and *Jakob Lenz* (1977–78), which were given in Hamburg in 1979. He gained considerable recognition, including the Hamburg City Prize, the Berlin Arts Prize, the Darmstadt Kranichsteiner Music Prize, and Freiburg City Reinhold Schneider Prize, and the German Prix de Rome, which carried with it a residency at the Villa Massima of Rome.

In 1985 he was named professor of composition at Karlsruhe. He has continued to win awards and prizes, such as the 1986 Rolf Lieberman Prize for his opera *Hamlet-Machine* (1983–86), the 1997 Prince Pierre of Monaco Prize for Musical Composition, the Jacob Burckhardt Prize of the Johann Wolfgang von Goethe Foundation (1998), and an honorary doctorate from the Free University of Berlin.

He has gone on to write the operas *Oedipus* (1986–87); *Die Eroberung von Mexico* (1987–91); *Andere Schatten*, (1985) which is what he called a "musical scene"; and *Séraphim* (1994), designated "music theater without a text."

He tends to follow the 12-tone system as used by Anton Webern, Luigi Nono, the later composers William Killmayer and Helmuth Lachenmann, as well as being influenced by the music of Stockhausen and Morton Feldman. Most of his compositions are works for orchestra or for larger groups of instruments, although many of these works include vocal parts. The vocal-orchestral pieces include the *Third Symphony*, the *Konzertarie on a Telegram from King Ludwig II to Richard Wagner, O Notte, Hölderlin Fragments, Abgesangszene No. 1, Doppelgesang No. 1* and *Dies*. He wrote a series of seven works based on the writings of Antonin Artaud, *Tutuguri*, many of which feature leading parts for percussion. His chamber music, which includes several string quartets, also includes works with vocal parts and unusual combinations of instruments. One of the works for which he is best known internationally is his violin concerto, championed and recorded by Anne-Sophie Mutter. He has also written a small quantity of piano and organ music. *—Joseph Stevenson*

Overview of Works

Describing music is always a species of tragic action: tragic, because the best music demands a response, but also defeats any response—it beckons but resists, possesses, provokes, and then scatters. So to call German giant Wolfgang Rihm's music "difficult to describe" is also to identify it as particularly musical, exuberantly native to itself and wildly frustrating to the alien media of language. If we want to catch even its fleeting moments, we need guerilla tactics. So a myriad of minimethods then—"attempts" as Rihm might call them.

First, the autobiographical tack: Rihm is a hyper-articulate spokesperson for his own work, prone to the same logorrhea as anyone groping for ungraspables. Rihm knows at least what he wants: "I want to move and be moved. Everything about music is pathetic." Not of course pathetic as in "useless," but "pathetic" as in "overcome by and with expression." And thus, "Music must be full of emotion, and that emotion full of complexity." And that complexity always seeks the limits and margins: "In my music, there is always a search for extremes... the outburst: this is simply the one thing I have been seeking."

Next, an evocation: how does this music sound? For lack of clearer terms, extreme. Extremely fast, extremely slow; dangerously high and impossibly low; opaque or transparent, completely. The harmony? Paradoxical: a dissonant parade of consonances, a muddy jet of brilliant tones, a sparkling mire. But the gestures are the Molotovian foundation of this perilous music: they veer, careen, and collide with fabulous unruliness. Often Rihm's scores (and his working methods) radiate a startling disregard for "form." They don't deliberate, they "stream"—or, more often, dart and rush, with the full terror and exhilaration of a beast hunting or hunted. Death, as silence or immobility, is always on the heels of a Rihm piece, and so the sounds often emit a febrile, adrenaline stink of the living—extremely sensuous but also excruciating. A work often unfolds like an emergency, or an unrepressed necessity—shocking and irrefutable, a last confession.

But behind these fading articulations, which only clamor after the music's surface, there hides a knotty sphinx in Rihm's artistic personality. So many of his own declamations voice an obsession with freedom—freedom "to" (any techniques, any allusions, any systems) but also, perhaps more so, freedom "from" (all techniques, all allusions, all systems). One could call it a Romantic urge, though the music knows no refuge or repose; it might be Gnostic, if it weren't so outrageously fleshly. But one composite quality, wholly school-less and unsystematic, burns through Rihm's work: it is a search for Others, an uncompromising attempt to encounter the unknown. Hence a body of perpetually outsider works, autonomous by default, absurd by impulsive design. They remain unknown even to their author: "[my works] are individuals with a physiognomy of their own, they have a destiny, they come and go and come again. I really have nothing more to say to that." *—Seth Brodsky*

Recommended:

○ **Rihm: Orchestral Works & Chamber Music** / Gielen, Zender, Dmitriev (conds.), Wambach, Salter, Siebert, Fugiss, Leningrad PO, SWF Sinfonieorchester Baden-Baden / 2000 / Col Legno 20508

○ **Rihm: Jagden und Formen** / My (cond.), Ens. Modern / 2002 / DG 471558

○ **Rihm: St. Luke Passion** / Rilling (cond.), Schmidt, Banse, Vermillion, Kallisch, Pregardien, Stuttgart Bach Collegium / 2000 / Haenssler 98397

○ **Rihm: Lieder** / Pregardien, Mauser, Windmuller, Bauni, Blome / 1997 / Orfeo 434971

○ **Rihm: String Quartets 1, 8 & 5** / Arditti SQ / 2000 / Disques Montaigne 782134

○ **Wolfgang Rihm: Piano Works** / Mauser / 2000 / Kairos 12122

VOCAL

Hölderlin Fragments, song cycle (1976–1977)

"It is a burnt out or unborn song cycle. All extreme changes are an integral part of a destroyed or unformed language."—Wolfgang Rihm on his *Hölderlin- Fragmente*.

Not how, but where, exactly, does music lie in relation to the written word? A vague, idealistic question to be avoided at all costs—unless you have to write a song. Then the relative position of the two media hangs temptingly, terrifyingly over your head: will the music lie inside the word, or outside the word? Will music burrow and nestle deep within the poem's meaning, its "dark secret heart?" Or will music collect and bind itself into a web, or a matrix or a vase, holding the poem fast in its secure form? The history of song, from a medieval chanson through a Schubert lied to a Radiohead ballad, could therefore be this: the history of endless decisions as to exactly where music and word will stand in relation to each other.

In this history, Wolfgang Rihm's song cycles are a stick in the spokes, a splinter in the eye. The music often refuses to take a stand towards the poetry in the normal sense; instead Rihm's music often hides in paradoxical places: it lies both above and beneath the word, both inside and outside verse. Language and music pass in and out of each other as through air, each unreal and immanent at once, "burnt out or unborn... destroyed or unformed." And in this sense, Rihm's 1977 cycle *Hölderlin-Fragmente* may be his most archetypal essay in the genre, because of an extraordinary symbiosis: what Rihm's music does to Hölderlin's sublime poetic tatters, they themselves do to language. Hence the seventh of Rihm's nine "songs" remains utterly homeless, nomadic; it intercepts the musical dust of old lied-accompaniments, of single insistent tones and taut silences, without resting anywhere. And likewise, Hölderlin's verse itself remains impeccably disoriented. It diagnoses its own derelict freedom, and speaks on behalf of the music as well, "For nowhere does it stay./No sign/binds it./Not always a vessel to hold it."

In a certain sense, Rihm finds in Hölderlin's poetry an aesthetics of the fragment, as a notion and a body of works: these poems come from Hölderlin's early thirties (1801–06), just before he was hospitalized for insanity for the remaining near-40 years of his life. Born amidst an inextricable knot of sickness (schizophrenia) and alertness, these sharded verses narrate less than they glow: theirs is the magical, illusory continuity of the fragment, unconnected in body but emanating an uncanny glow which unaccountably binds it together—closing itself into openness. In setting these words, Rihm has admitted that they can't merely be "doubled in music," can't support the metaphor of reflection and imitation or the clichéd image of music as the secret "emotive" language beneath language. Instead, Rihm attempts the contradictory task of remaining true to Hölderlin's "spirit" of openness, an openness on the expressive limits, while refusing "the already established symbols of openness." *—Seth Brodsky*

Recommended:

○ **Brahms, Strauss, Reger, Rihm** / Abbado (cond.), Kosters, Berlin PO / 1994 / Sony 53975

CHAMBER MUSIC

Fremde Szenen I-III, for piano trio (1982–1984)

The first of Wolfgang Rihm's *Fremde Szenen* (Strange Scenes) for piano trio, begins—predictably enough—with a strange sound. It comes from the piano, a clean, blank interval spread wide like a horizon. Yawning over two octaves, pedal down, it would be an elegant intonation, but Rihm sets it down as *gellend* (shrill, crying). At once mechanical and vocal, the sound's resonance is caught by violin and cello, also playing molto vibrato. With strangulating urgency, the first strange scene takes flight but immediately the strings falter, scurrying in glassy harmonics. The piano slaps down another shrieking interval, the strings cry back, the music freezes again.

In the Freudian sense, this music is uncanny, at once deeply foreign and deeply familiar; it tantalizes and alienates ferociously, reverses course with the sharpest knives. What's most striking is Rihm's absolute refusal to relax this back-and-forth. Only once, towards the movement's end, does the music *go anywhere:* the piano bangs out a cluster in the highest range, the strings shred away; as they finally burst into hysterical operatic tones, the pianist slides effortlessly into an accompaniment pattern right out of the trios of Robert Schumann.. This isn't stolen, but faked, and as a self-punishment for this searing outburst of sustained action, the music chokes into quiet guttural scrambling; after some 15 bars, the texture becomes shallower, bates its breath, and suddenly springs into motion anew, only to be torn off on the brink.

Rihm's music is saturated with such a formal strategy: a fatal race, a frantic flight with clipped wings, a process of going nowhere desperately. What gives this itinerary such force in these pieces is the presence of Robert Schumann. Like an insidious guest, a splinter in the eye, the music of Schumann weaves its figures and its tenor into this stream-of-consciousness music. And for Rihm, few composers offer such fruitful haunting as Schumann; Rihm has written eloquently of Schumann, asking "What is different about Schumann's music? That something is different, different than usual we feel instinctively." Elsewhere, he writes of Schumann's later works, "The whole construction sways... [it is] music whose exertion is perceptible."

A structure, then, that does not contain fluidity, but is itself fluid, a form hunting its shape, making its writing audible for everyone to hear—these qualities become even more explicit in the extraordinary second movement, a 20-minute character piece to be played "fast and swaying." The music is stuffed with Schumannisms—rapturous lyricism, swirling arpeggios, tugging syncopations, and neo-Bach counterpoint—without quoting a note. Writes Rihm, "I have attempted... to invent my own personal portrait of Schumann and his musical 'handwriting.'" The effect is graphic, in both senses, jeopardy never leaves the sound-scene, and music rises persistently from its own burning embers.

The briefer last movement initially establishes a sincere funereal pathos, but again avalanches into pulverized lyrical outbursts and stuttering march patterns. Rihm describes the movement tersely: "Actually only notorious passages. Concentration and its loss." Exactly.*—Seth Brodsky*

Recommended:

○ **Rihm: Fremde Szenen** / Ravensburg Beethoven Trio / CPO 999119

Im Innersten ("String Quartet No. 3") (1976)

"Im Innersten" is the German subtitle of Wolfgang Rihm's *Third Quartet* (1976). It's a tricky phrase to translate into English; literally, it means "Into the innermost part," but the German carries a more subjective, corporeal tone, more like "Into the heart of hearts." Such a phrase immediately warps one back to the language of late-Romantic German music, and of its radical child Expressionism. In the world of Wagner's *Tristan und Isolde*, of Mahler's last symphonies, of the early string quartets of Schoenberg, Berg, and Webern-here lies a world of "hearts of hearts" and all their physiological counterparts; this is music of blood, of pulsing arteries, exposed nerves, sighs and gasps.

In his *Third Quartet*, one hears Rihm's conviction that "Art = Freedom" shouted out with an intensity, conviction, and virtuosity rare for most any 23-year-old. The result is a furious, unremitting work of will which seems to adhere to no principles, no rules or systems at all, only the proliferation of its own explosive, inexhaustible dynamism. It offers constant inconstancy at a manic pace, a continuum sewn entirely of shocks and threaded into six brief movements; each unfolds as its own independent fragment, loaded with its own insatiate urgency and torn off suddenly at its end. The representative first movement maintains itself only by devouring itself, pushing the instruments through quick, extreme crescendi into strangled pauses; any motives and figures which arise are instantaneously pulverized under the hysterical pressure of the expressive stream. The music moves paradoxically, always on the route to a trauma, and always coming from another trauma, yet thoroughly unable to actually tire itself into rest; every gesture carries a violent insistence, yet ultimately obliterates itself through that very violence.

Yet if Rihm's *Quartet* appears to resurrect the expressive utopia of the pre-World War I Schoenberg and his disciples, it is certainly not out of simple nostalgia. Rihm has no interest in worshipping idols, nor in "belonging" to traditions; "Tradition" for Rihm "is always MY TRADITION. I have to explore where I came from with myself...but it is much more interesting to discover *where I am going*." This unapologetic iconoclasm compels Rihm to put even expressionism itself (if such a thing ever really existed) on trial in the *Quartet*'s longer last movement. Here the idea of "immediate" or "direct" musical expression, the very thing that had so far generated the entire *Quartet*, is fatally overturned; everything is now frozen in mid-movement, separated and classified into Freudian psychoanalytic spaces. When this frame is finally shattered by an outpouring of confessional neo-Romantic lyricism, the whole work chokes on its own convictions; a sonic coffin lid descends in long silences, spasmodic chords and scratch-tones. It is an outrageous ending, not least because it still manages to shock after 25 minutes of shocks. *—Seth Brodsky*

Recommended:

○ **Rihm: String Quartets 1, 8 & 5** / Arditti SQ / 2000 / Disques Montaigne 782134

Music for Three Strings (1977)

Beethoven's late music occasionally presents little moments of sublime terror, of miniature oracle and epiphany: a familiar form abruptly falters, a chord or gesture rudely cracks in two, and the comfortable surface rips and expels an alien sound—something utterly strange, inexplicable, irreducible. It hangs in front of the ears with the tonnage of destiny, eked out in frightfully direct but indecipherable words. And then the outburst swallows its own chaos and wraithfully withdraws.

Wolfgang Rihm was savoring and submitting to such moments when he wrote his vast expressive juggernaut *Music for Three Strings* in 1977, at age 25. He clearly quotes certain cipherlike phrases from Beethoven's last string quartets, but a Beethovenian spirit haunts Rihm's work in more than isolated instance. In particular, he seems to perform an autopsy on the new expressive world opened up by Beethoven's last quartets, especially the obsession with expressive rupture, the notion that the moment of greatest expression is also the moment of tearing, of rip and rift in the musical fabric. Perhaps Rihm was thinking of the "Cavatina" from Beethoven's *Quartet* Op. 130: amidst the most tender song imaginable, the temperature drops; over a deep dirge in the other instruments, the first violin squirms through a sick, splintered line, as if catching some fatal knot in its throat. Beethoven famously marked the passage "beklemmt" (burdened).

Part of Rihm's project in *Music for Three Strings* (a string quartet minus one violin) is the attempt to take such Beethovenian outbursts, such windows into the exterior or interior world of anarchy, and amplify them into a totalizing condition, a whole world. What that "beklemmt" passage in Beethoven's quartet articulated for five measures, Rihm explodes into hundreds of bars; what Beethoven's music exposed in flashes and bursts, Rihm's music dilates into an hour-long landscape. The result is a shocking piece: all moments are torn off by other moments with greatest violence and dispatch, force derives from collision, velocity arises only through perpetual interruptions. Paradoxically, disjunction itself becomes the main method of binding this music together; the hearer experiences connection via total disconnection.

The result is an extraordinary type of free music, free not by disposition but through outrageously consistent struggle to break away from itself. Perhaps this is most exaggerated in the towering edifice's last movement (of seven total, like Beethoven's *Quartet*, Op. 131). Marked "energico," the music wheezes unstoppably in thick, dissonant chords, accelerating until it collapses, and picking itself up again. About midway through the movement, the music locks into an abominable C minor chord, sawed out maniacally. The closest thing to an actual climax in the whole work, it goes nowhere, remaining caged and foaming until brushed aside by an arduous new idea. But above the passage lies a little quote from Flaubert, a skeleton key to this work and to Rihm's general aesthetic: "The further I go, the more I find myself incapable of conveying the idea." *—Seth Brodsky*

Recommended:

○ **Rihm: Music For Three Strings** / Ostertag, Hock, Lemme, Ens. 13 / CPO 999050

Terry Riley

b. Jun. 24, 1935, Colfax, CA

Composer: Chamber Music, Keyboard

Terry Riley is an avant-garde composer who was present at the birth of the idea that became known as minimalism. Abandoning his original plans to become a concert pianist, Riley studied composition at San Francisco State College with Robert Erikson. In 1958, while supporting himself as a ragtime pianist at a local saloon, Riley attended graduate school at the University of California at Berkeley. It was at Berkeley that Riley met and felt a strong connection with fellow composition student (and, some would argue, the real father of Minimalism) La Monte Young. After graduating with an M.A. in composition in 1961, Riley moved to Europe, where he performed in officers' clubs.

In 1963 Riley composed the music for the play *The Gift*, written by Key Dewey, for the ORTF (French National Radio). Riley used the opportunity to utilize a new invention known as the time-lag accumulator. It consisted of two reel-to-reel tape recorders connected together to form a loop of layered echoes. According to Riley, *Music for the Gift* was "the forerunner of *In C*," utilizing repetition as an essential part of musical form. Riley's direct inspiration for *In C* occurred back in San Francisco while riding a bus to work at the Gold Street Saloon. Released in 1968 by Columbia Records, *In C* became a platform upon which the Minimalist movement was built.

At that point Riley was living in New York, collaborating occasionally with La Monte Young, and performing in Young's Theatre of Eternal Music. It was during this period that Riley stopped notating his compositions and focused more on improvisation. He also abandoned the use of his time-lag accumulator. Riley was able to experiment with his "self-interpretive improvisation" techniques on his 1969 album containing the works *Poppy Nogood and the Phantom Band* and *Rainbow in Curved Air*. During the 1970s, Terry Riley began to focus on Indian music, studying with singer Pandit Pran Nath. Traveling often to India and teaching Indian music at Mills College in Oakland, California, Riley found a new compositional angle for his music. Influenced by the raga, Riley began to create long, flowing melodic lines using raga-related scales in his improvisations. He also began to take interest in just intonation, an ancient form of tuning in which the intervals are mathematically pure, allowing for intervallic intricacies. Works from this period include *Persian Surgery Dervishes* (1971) and *Shri Camel* (1976).

In 1979 Riley received both a grant from the NEA and a Guggenheim Fellowship for his creative efforts. In the 1980s Riley returned to musical notation, composing several works for the Kronos String Quartet. Works such as *G-Song* and *Sunrise of the Planetary Dream Collector* (1981) call for string quartet, voice and synthesizer. The pieces draw very little upon the layering of structural motives as found in Riley's works of the 1960s, or the keyboard improvisations characteristic of the 1970s. Instead, Riley's string quartets are more lyrical and include influences of American jazz, Indian raga, and traditional Classical music—continuing, as well, in the Minimalist style. Yet no work of Riley's has had an impact equal to that of the groundbreaking *In C*. —*Kristen Grimshaw*

CHAMBER MUSIC

In C, for unspecified performers (1964)

After creating several graphically notated and pattern-based works for jazz ensembles in the late 1950s and early 1960s, Terry Riley developed a new type of pattern music strongly influenced by gamelan music and the classical traditions of India. *In C*, the composer's best-known work, is both the purest example of this phase of Riley's musical development and a landmark of the minimalist aesthetic.

The one-page score, which calls for any ensemble of pitched instruments, consists of 53 discrete, concentrated gestures—sometimes as small as a two-note motive—of varying lengths. The players enter independently, moving gradually through this progression of cells; each cell may (and should) be repeated indefinitely and independently of the other players. The result is that the interlocking of patterns, the evolution of texture, density, and sonority, and the work's duration are all unique to each performance. The work's main unifying element is a metronomic pulse on the pitch C, normally played in octaves in the highest register of a piano, which provides a fixed tempo and tonal center. Because of its inherent instrumental flexibility, *In C* has been performed in a countless variety of configurations, from conventional chamber groups to massed keyboards and percussion to an ensemble of Chinese instruments.

In C is significant for its deconstruction of the European classical tradition, accomplished partly through its harmonic and tonal stasis, partly through its lack of hierarchical development. Further, the work emphasizes the importance of the ensemble (group) over the virtuoso (individual), granting each player an autonomous though guided role in creating the work anew each time it is performed. —*AMG*

Recommended:

○ **Riley: In C** / Hassell, Dempster, Shostac, Singer, etc., State University Center of Creative & Performing Arts / 1968 / CBS 7178

○ **Riley: In C** / Harrington, Jeanrenaud, Dutt, Sherba, etc, / 1995 / New Albion 071

A Rainbow in Curved Air, for electric piano, dumbek & tambourines (1968)

After the first public performance of *In C*, the catalyst for the "minimalism" phenomenon, Riley increased his experimentation with electronic media. He found that feedback, tape delay systems and tape loops could be used to create, sustain and slowly transform conventional harmonies.

Riley first experimented with the combination of live and taped sounds in his *Poppy Nogood and the Phantom Band* (1967), in which he played the saxophone into tape recorders turning loops of tape; these were then replayed, allowing him to play a new line over the first one, creating layers of sound. Two years later, he transferred these ideas to a work for keyboard, *A Rainbow in Curved Air*, first heard on April 14, 1969, at the Electric Circus, a club in Manhattan's East Village.

A Rainbow in Curved Air has few genuine structural components. One of these is a rhythmic cycle that some have likened to the tala in Indian classical music. The returns of this rhythmic pattern, however, are usually obscured by the tremendous layering of sound. Also, Riley employs modal, rather than diatonic, scales as a starting point for his improvisation. Aside from these two elements, *A Rainbow in Curved Air* derives its "structure" from the process through which it takes shape.

Like Riley's *Poppy Nogood and the Phantom Band*, *A Rainbow in Curved Air* consists of pulsing, repeated "modules" of melody. Melodic segments played on an electric keyboard are recorded and then replayed endlessly while other "live" ideas are added and then recorded in turn. The layering continues, developing a dense web of sound, much like what we hear in *In C*, but with more of a jazz harmonic idiom and feel. As the improvisational ideas are altered electronically, the tape delay and tape loops produce endless canonic passages. Thus, the repetition creates a "timeless" experience while improvisation occasionally inserts something new. In this way, changing timbre becomes more structurally significant than motives and their manipulation, and the sound continuously washes over the listener.

Because of the combination of live and recorded (and then rerecorded) elements in *A Rainbow in Curved Air*, no two performances can ever be quite the same. The recording Riley made and released in 1969 is only one realization of the processes. This is precisely the effect sought by Riley, who prefers to compose during the act of playing. —*John Palmer*

Recommended:

○ **A Rainbow in Curved Air** / Riley / Columbia 477849

Salome Dances for Peace, for string quartet (1985–1987)

Terry Riley's *Salome Dances for Peace* is in five large sections, each of which (with the exception of the last) is further subdivided. The work came about at the suggestion of David Harrington of the Kronos Quartet, for whom Riley had already composed a string quartet in 1979. Riley at first intended the piece to be a ballet, but he eventually abandoned the dance component, deciding the music was sufficient to convey his imaginative plot.

Riley sketched a complex story line for his work: the main character is the legendary Salome, who asked for the head of John the Baptist in return for a striptease. In our time, however Salome has been chosen to regain peace for the earth because it has been stolen by evil entities. During the first large section of the piece, Salome is summoned by the Great Spirit, after which she learns discipline from sages and receives the gift of innocence, with which she is able to resist Wild Talker, who embodies sexual temptation. Half Wolf, a shaman, initiates her as a warrior. Like Orpheus, Salome and Half Wolf descend into the underworld and engage in battle, recapturing peace and redeeming the underworld itself. Salome then begins to tour the earth as a dancer, first visiting Tibet and then Mongolia. Once again, she is summoned and given a new task: she must seduce the world's two most powerful leaders and thereby secure world peace. This accomplished, Salome dances the "Good Medicine Dance," representing the return to old wisdom.

Of course, without foreknowledge of this "program," it is impossible to sense this story line while hearing the music. There are, however, representative musical gestures, such as the slithering tunes representing Salome that first appear after the opening trills of "The Summons." Wild Talker, too, is easily identifiable in the sleazy glissandi, which are most prominent in "Seduction of Bear Father" from the fourth movement, "The Ecstasy." Truly developmental procedures occur in the second movement, "Conquest of the War Demons," as motives clash while Salome fights to regain peace. Riley insists, however, that these motives are developed for purely musical reasons and not to convey anything extramusical.

Salome Dances for Peace is notable in part for its combination of various styles of music. We hear moments of jazz, blues, Indian classical music, Western classical music and patterns associated with the "minimalist" school. Riley once commented on this combination of idioms: "These styles all have their particular flavors and expressions but they can be united. Notes all work under certain universal laws; they observe laws just like everything else in the universe does." This aspect of Riley's music derives from both his eclectic interests and his compositional method, which he describes as making, "many, many minute sketches of ideas and filing them away, and at some point as I'm writing, one of these will be the right one for the time." —*John Palmer*

Recommended:

○ **Riley: Salome Dances for Peace** / Kronos Qt. / Elektra 79217

KEYBOARD

The Harp of New Albion (1986)

"New Albion" is the term explorer Sir Francis Drake gave to the area in and around San Francisco Bay. A myth that developed in that part of California after Drake's visit tells of a harp left behind by one of Drake's crew. One of the natives found the instrument, which was completely strange to him, and he and his people believed it to be sacred. They then mounted the harp on a headland next to the sea, where the wind set the strings in motion, creating wonderful, unpredictable sounds.

Riley's *The Harp of New Albion*, dedicated to La Monte Young, is for solo piano and, as for Young's *The Well-Tuned Piano*, the instrument is tuned using "just intonation." Just intonation is derived from acoustically pure intervals within the octave. Tuners create pure fifths and thirds when they wish to produce diatonic or chromatic scales. This results in a scale in which the half steps are of several sizes, making the modulations that are a salient feature of tonal music impossible. (Equal temperament solves this by making each half step the same.) The sound of a keyboard instrument tuned in just intonation can be unsettling to ears accustomed to equal temperament (which includes just about every Westerner). After a time, however, it is possible to adjust to its characteristics. Riley counts on this when performing *The Harp of New Albion*, which takes C sharp as its primary pitch.

In eleven movements, *The Harp of New Albion* begins with basic, notated motives, upon which the performer improvises. These motives may be combined and altered in a developmental fashion. Also, the performer is free to approach each of the movements in variable ways, creating numerous chances for spontaneous expression. Riley's ideas on development and improvisation in the context of *The Harp of New Albion* becomes clear in a recording of January 20, 1986, made in Padova. In the opening movement, "The New Albion Chorale—The Discovery," we hear an initial statement of a "dissonant" chord followed by a single bass note and many two-note melodic gestures played hesitantly between pregnant pauses. At the reprise of the "Chorale," many of the specific melodic gestures are unidentifiable, but the two-note concept returns, as does the hesitant rhythm. The "final reprise" of the "Chorale" is much more like the first movement, including the single bass note preceding the two-note falling gestures. Aside from this, there are no exact repetitions of material from the first movement, only great similarities. This should come as no surprise from a composer who prefers to compose during the act of playing. *—John Palmer*

Recommended:

- ○ **Keys Of Life** / Riley / Celestial Harmonies 13017

Helmuth Rilling

b. May 29, 1933, Stuttgart, Germany
Conductor

Over his career, Helmuth Rilling has become one of the most respected choral conductors in the world. Born in Stuttgart, Germany, Rilling grew up in a musical family; his father was an organist and choir conductor, while his mother played violin. He himself took up piano and organ as a child, showing a fine talent for each. He later studied at the Hochschule für Musik in his home city, becoming a distinguished Kantor in Kornwestheim and Stuttgart; he received his music diploma in 1954.

Rilling had already started down the path to a long and fruitful career when he founded the Gächinger Kantorei in December of 1953. Gachinger is a small town in southwest Germany, but Rilling's Kantorei were well enough supported by the locals that their reputation soon spread as leaders in the performance of unaccompanied choral repertoire. The Gächinger Kantorei's singers came, and still come, mostly from southwest Germany; the group's success is due both to the dedication of its members and the amazing pedagogical skills of its leader.

Eventually, Rilling founded the Stuttgart Bach-Collegium orchestra to accompany the Kantorei, and the synthesis was an immediate success. Rilling and his ensembles recorded all the major works of Bach: the *Passions of St. John* and *St. Matthew*, the *B Minor Mass*, and eventually the complete cantatas, a series which was finished in time for the 300th anniversary of Bach's birth in 1985. The Kantorei, under Rilling's direction, has also made extensive appearances with foreign orchestras, including one particularly memorable occasion in Israel in 1976. It was the first time German and Israeli musicians had performed together since World War II, and Rilling conducted the Kantorei in the Israeli national anthem as a further gesture of reconciliation.

Outreach through music was nothing new to Rilling; the Kantorei had undertaken a tour of East Germany almost immediately after its founding, and in general Rilling always tried to bridge the gap between East and West with music before the Iron Curtain lifted. He also conducted the premier performance of the *Requiem for Reconciliation*, which combined movements written for the occasion by composers from all the nations involved in World War II.

Even though his activites have been centered in Germany, Rilling's activities have taken him all over the world; he founded the Oregon Bach Festival in 1970, and he has instructed choral groups all over the world. Rilling gained prominence in an era when period practices were becoming dominant in Bach performance, yet Rilling has never used period instruments and has always used a good-sized choir for his performances. He feels that it is impossible to know exactly how Bach's music sounded in his time, not just to the musicians but to Bach's audience. While period practices have their place, Rilling feels, they should be used as a guide and not a doctrine. In performance, Rilling does not strive for a blend of choral tone, but a sound that is both controlled and full of character. Rilling's performances have become more and more deeply felt and subtle over the years. All of his performances are deeply felt, scrupulously detailed, and outstandingly sung. *—Andrew Lindemann Malone*

Recommended:

- ○ **Mendelssohn: Paulus** / Rilling (cond.), Schmidt, Banse, Danz, Schade, Czech PO / Brilliant 99953/3–4
- ○ **Liszt: Christus** / Rilling (cond.), Schmidt, Vermillion, Schade, Bonde-Hansen, Stuttgart RSO / Brilliant 99951
- ○ **M. Haydn: Mass & Requiem** / Rilling (cond.), Pertis, Frank, Nemeth, Verebits, Franz Liszt CO / Hungaroton 31022
- ○ **Bach: Magnificat** / Rilling (cond.), Auger, Quasthoff, Baldin, Schafer / 1995 / Haenssler 6006
- ○ **Rihm: St. Luke Passion** / Rilling (cond.), Schmidt, Banse, Vermillion, Kallisch, Stuttgart Bach Collegium / 2000 / Haenssler 98397

Nikolay Andreyevich Rimsky-Korsakov

b. Mar. 18, 1844, Tikhvin, Russia, **d.** Jun. 21, 1908, Lyubensk, Russia
Composer: Orchestral, Opera, Symphonic, Concerto

Mainly known for his symphonic works, especially the popular symphonic suite *Sheherazade*, as well as the *Capriccio Espagnol* and the *Russian Easter Festival Overture*, Rimsky-Korsakov left an oeuvre that also included operas, chamber works, and songs. Rimsky-Korsakov's music is accessible and engaging owing to his talent for tone-coloring and brilliant orchestration. Furthermore, his operas are masterful musical evocations of myths and legends.

Born in 1844, Rimsky-Korsakov studied the piano as a child but chose a naval career, entering the College of Naval Cadets in St. Petersburg in 1856. However, he continued with piano lessons; in fact, in 1859, Rimsky-Korsakov started working with the French pianist Theodore Canille, through whom he met Balakirev, an important mentor and friend.

In 1862, after graduating form the naval school, Rimsky-Korsakov was at sea for two and a half years, devoting his free time to composition. Upon Rimsky-Korsakov's return to St. Petersburg, in 1865, Balakirev conducted his friend's *First Symphony*, which was hailed as the first important symphonic work by a Russian composer.

Rimsky-Korsakov was appointed professor of composition and orchestration at the St. Petersburg Conservatory in 1871. The following year, he married Nadezhda Purgold, a pianist. In 1873, Rimsky-Korsakov left active duty, becoming inspector of navy orchestras, a job which he held until 1884.

During the 1870s, Rimsky-Korsakov composed, conducted, and collected Russian folk songs. In 1878, he started composing the opera *May Night*, after a story by Nikolai Gogol, his first stage work based on a story containing fantastic motifs. Following the production of *May Night*, in 1880, Rimsky-Korsakov began work on *Snow Maiden*, based on Nikolai Ostrovsky's poetic retelling of a Slavic myth, which was performed in 1882.

Saddened by Mussorgsky's death, in 1881, Rimsky-Korsakov devoted himself to editing his friend's unpublished manuscripts. A master orchestrator, Rimsky-Korsakov felt obliged to help colleagues whose manuscripts needed revision. Thus, in 1887, when Borodin died, Rimsky-Korsakov agreed to orchestrate and complete Borodin's opera *Prince Igor*.

Rimsky-Korsakov wrote the *Spanish Capriccio* in 1887, completing the *Russian Easter Overture* and *Sheherazade* the following year. Having composed these resplendent works, however, Rimsky-Korsakov went through a period of despondency; there were deaths in his family, and, in 1893, Tchaikovsky died.

In 1895, Rimsky-Korsakov's *Christmas Eve*, another opera after a Gogol story, was produced. The composer's subsequent works recreated the rich world of Russian myths and legends. *Sadko*, completed in 1896, conjured up a medieval Russian legend. In 1901, Rimsky-Korsakov blended the legend of Kitezh and the story of St. Fevroniya to create a complex Christian-pantheistic narrative. Completed in 1905, the year when the politically progressive composer was temporarily dismissed from this teaching post, *The Legend of the Invisible City of Kitezh and the Maiden*, was produced in 1907.

Rimsky-Korsakov's last opera, *The Golden Cockerel*, completed in 1907, was inspired by a politically subversive story by Alexander Pushkin. The production of this work was a struggle, because the subject matter aroused suspicions among government censors. The opera was finally produced, in 1909, the year following the composer's death, by a private opera company in Moscow. *—Zoran Minderovic*

ORCHESTRAL

Capriccio espagnol (Kaprichchio na ispankskiye temï), Op. 34 (1887)

Russian nationalists were adept at using folk materials and harmonies from their own country; it is perhaps not surprising then that they could work equally successfully with folk music from different lands. Nikolay Rimsky-Korsakov may have entertained that thought when he sat down with a book of songs by the Spanish composer Jose Inzenga y Castellanos, with the object of reworking them into an orchestral showpiece. The resulting *Capriccio espagnol* retains the original melodies, rhythms, and harmonization of Inzenga y Castellanos' songs; however, it is ultimately distinguished by the Russian master's sensitive and brilliant orchestral colors. After its premiere at the Russian Musical Society in 1887, the *Capriccio* entered the standard repertoire in Russia almost overnight and quickly became just as popular around the world.

The first movement "Alborada" ("morning serenade") immediately explodes with festive strings, whooping winds and florid percussion. This emphatic full orchestral texture contrasts with several individual solos, including seductive, pseudo-Gypsy melodic elaboration from a solo violin which closes the movement. The next movement presents four variations on a lovely sighing theme presented on the horns; the first variations is handled by the strings, the second by the French and English horns, and the last two by the full orchestra. The orchestration here is particularly skillful, especially in the witty French horn/English horn duet, accompanied by murmuring strings that fade in and out of the texture with extreme delicacy.

Next, the Alborada makes a reappearance, in a different key and with different orchestration that highlights the cheerful virtuoso escapades of the solo violin. After a brass fanfare, the violin takes a lead role in the fourth movement ("Scene and Gypsy Song") with a fiendishly difficult cadenza. The flute and clarinet each take their turn, providing extravagant flourishes, after which the harp plays shimmering, gossamer scales. Finally, the Gypsy Song itself enters, and the movement concludes with the song clothed in orchestral garb reminiscent of the opening Alborada.

A sensual, fiery Fandago follows, its rhythm emphasized by cutting strings and emphatic cymbals and castanets. The fandango moves through various sections of the orchestra until it has nowhere else to go, at which time the Alborada returns to close the work in superlatively high spirits. The *Capriccio espagnol* is one of the most famous orchestral showpieces ever and deservedly so. *—Andrew Lindemann Malone*

Recommended:

- ○ **Rimsky-Korsakov, Kabalevsky, Tchaikovsky, Khachaturian** / Kondrashin (cond.), Shumsky, RCA Victor SO / 1999 / BMG 633022
- ○ **Decca Legends: España** / Argenta (cond.), London SO / 1999 / Decca 466378

Christmas Eve (Noch' pered rozhdestvom), suite from the opera (1903)

Rimsky-Korsakov wrote his opera *Christmas Eve* during the period 1894–95, and it was premiered during the latter year. In 1903, he extracted this suite, which contains about a half-hour's worth of music from the opera. What is confusing to some listeners about the work is that it is often broken down in concert programs and on recordings into five, six, or as many as nine sections, with translations of the individual numbers that can vary widely. The lovely music in the "Introduction," first heard on the horn, sets the stage for the Romantic character of the score here. The lively and playful music from the "Games and Dances of the Stars" is charming, as is the "Round Dance," which reprises the theme from the opening. The "Czardas" is joyous and, as so often with Rimsky-Korsakov's works, brilliantly and colorfully orchestrated. The "Devil's Kolyada" is sinister, but ultimately its menace has an almost fairy tale-like lightness. The Polonaise is graceful and stately and the "Procession to Midnight Mass" is absolutely lovely and quite memorable, with the gently tolling bells deftly adding to the serene atmosphere at the quiet close. In the end, the music here is light and colorful, not as exotic as *Shéhérazade* or the *Capriccio espagnol*, but still with ethnic flavors and featuring Rimsky-Korsakov's usual brilliant scoring. *—Robert Cummings*

Recommended:

- ○ **Rimsky-Korsakov: Suites** / Jarvi (cond.), Scottish National Orch. / 1984 / Chandos 8327

Dubinushka (The Little Oak Stick), tone poem, Op. 62 (1906)

Rimsky-Korsakov's music fared well during the Soviet regime. Officials surely approved of his liberal use of Russian folk music, and it didn't hurt that Rimsky-Korsakov had sympathized with a student uprising in 1905. In fact, he was temporarily dismissed from the St. Petersburg Conservatory, and performances of his music were briefly banned. Later that year, on a visit to Moscow, Rimsky-Korsakov witnessed a demonstration along Tverskoi Boulevard and heard the marchers sing "Dubinushka" ("The Little Oak Stick"), an old folk tune. Inspired to make musical trouble, Rimsky-Korsakov went back to St. Petersburg and arranged the song for orchestra with optional chorus (usually omitted). Like Ravel's *Boléro, Dubinushka* is an exercise in orchestration rather than thematic development. The tune being simple, Rimsky-Korsakov repeats it—or, in the central section, important fragments of it—with various combinations of instruments. The first statement in full is brassy, with a string section response. Strings and woodwinds handle the quieter sections and of course, the full orchestra joins in the stirring finale. A similar effect with more varied thematic material may be heard in the "Procession of the Nobles" from Rimsky-Korsakov's opera *Mlada*. *—James Reel*

Recommended:

- ○ **Rimsky-Korsakov & Kalinnikov** / Jarvi (cond.), London SO / 1997 / Chandos 7093
- ○ **Stravinsky, Lyadov, Rimsky-Korsakyov** / Jarvi (cond.), London SO / 1989 / Chandos 8783

Mlada, suite from the opera (1903)

Nikolay Rimsky-Korsakov's opera *Mlada* is a Wagner-influenced epic teeming with national conflicts and battles in the spirit world; it draws on Russian myth, yet contains parallels to Goethe's *Faust* as well, making for a formidable challenge indeed for performer and listener. However, Rimsky-Korsakov was enough of a professional to prepare a short suite of catchy dances as he readied the opera for its premiere in 1892. A short introduction features an upward-spiraling melody, introduced in a delicate clarinet solo, that soon spreads to the rest of the orchestra. The three national dances which follow are, in the opera, performed for a vision of Cleopatra; they sound perfectly innocuous here, shorn of context. The "Redowa" is a stately but energetic Bohemian dance full of ebullient trills and strong rhythms. The "Lithuanian Dance" that follows is dark-colored and dashing, with the rhythm and melody traded quickly between sections of the orchestra. The "Indian Dance" allows Rimsky-Korsakov to indulge his genius for composing what the Russians thought of as "Oriental" melodies, sinuous yet cheery and played on felicitous combinations of woodwinds with snare drum underpinning. The final piece, the "Procession of the Nobles" that opens the second act of the opera, is by far the most famous; with its high-spirited brass fanfares and boisterous percussion, it comes extremely close to being a march in 3/4 time, and provides a rousing conclusion to a suite that doesn't exactly recall the opera from which it was drawn, but has its own charms. *—Andrew Lindemann Malone*

Recommended:

- ○ **Rimsky-Korsakov: Suites** / N. Jarvi (cond.), Scottish National Orch. / 1984 / Chandos 8327
- ○ **Rimsky-Korsakov: Suites** / Johanos (cond.), Czecho-Slovak RSO / 1991 / Naxos 550486

Night on Mount Triglav (Noch' na gore Triglov), tone poem (1899–1901)

The third act of Nikolai Rimsky-Korsakov's opera *Mlada* was performed a few times before the entire opera received its premiere. Rimsky-Korsakov wrote *Mlada* with the intention of using methods he had heard first in Richard Wagner's *Ring* cycle, particularly the leitmotivs and extravagant orchestration. In his memoirs, he reported that at the first concert of the third act "my orchestral contrivances hit the mark, and the succession of the fantastic coloring of the afterworld, of the flight of shadows and of Mlada's appearance, of the hellishly ominous appearance of Chernobog, of Cleopatra's Oriental bacchanal, and of day awakening with the birds produced a deep impression." Given this success, and the fact that after a promising premiere, *Mlada* faded fast in the esteem of both critics and the public, it seems natural that Rimsky-Korsakov would try to give the third act new life by making an orchestral arrangement of it. The result was *Night on Mount Triglav*, which debuted in 1901 at a charity concert for widows and orphans of artists and musicians in Moscow. Rimsky-Korsakov starts in a darkening dream with woodwinds entering sequentially and playing sustained notes at the extreme top of their ranges to contrast with a slow, tonally ambiguous churning in the strings. A dance for ghosts titled "Ronde fantastique," with a melody played on the flute that continually modulates from minor to major before restarting in the minor, also hints at the strangeness to come. Prince Yaromir follows Princess Mlada up the mountain, begging with a long, yearning cello melody to be allowed to come along with her into the spirit world. The mountain turns menacing with a short, sharp scene dominated by brass introducing the "Ronde infernale," a dance for the monsters that surround the demon Chernobog. This starts with a demonic trill in the strings that picks up speed and agitation until Chernobog himself enters, introduced from afar by menacing, widely spaced brass chords and a long, tense tympani crescendo. Chernobog hears the plea of Morena, goddess of the underworld, to use his magic to draw Yaromir's attentions to another, delivered with chirping woodwinds over low horns and double-bass chords that switch the mode from major to minor as they see fit—an effect both luminous and ominous. Kaschei the Deathless then conjures a vision of Cleopatra with an extravagant "Oriental" melody, filled with seductive accidentals and lavish sprays of notes and played on a panpipe, which Rimsky-Korsakov first heard in an Algerian band while writing *Mlada* in Paris. A crowing cock, represented by the oboe, wakes Yaromir up, and with heroic brass backing him, he resolves to make sense of this vivid, strange dream. *—Andrew Lindemann Malone*

Recommended:

- ○ **Rimsky-Korsakov: Night on Mount Triglav; Pan Voyevoda** / Rezucha (cond.), Slovak PO / Marco Polo 8220438

Russian Easter Festival Overture (Svetliy pazdnik), Op. 36 (1888)

In the summer of 1888, Rimsky-Korsakov completed the orchestration of the *Russian Easter Overture*, and he finished another of his major works, *Scheherezade*. The *Russian Easter Overture* was often regarded by the composer as "The Bright Holiday," which was a popular Russian name for Easter. The *Russian Easter Overture* is based on themes from the obikhod, which is a printed collection of the most important and most frequently used canticles of the Russian Orthodox Church. This volume represented the first music ever printed in Russia.

The overture begins with a long introduction of a very slow tempo. Rimsky-Korsakov wrote that this opening section of the piece was inspired by Isaiah's prophetic words concerning the future resurrection of the Messiah. The composer claims that the music of the section, which alternates themes from "Let God Arise" from the obikhod and the ecclesiastical theme of "An angel wailed," simply "appeared" to him. The voice of an archangel is represented by a dark trumpet solo.

The slow introduction leads into a transition which becomes the Allegro of the overture. While the introduction was solemn and mysterious, the Allegro is joyous, conveying a sense of excitement. Trumpet blasts, along with a sense of bell-tolling, push the idea of merriment to the fore. An image of a sexton quickly reading to the congregation is also present. Another obikhod theme, "Christ is arisen," is heard in this section, although it is greatly overshadowed by other sounds.

In the *Russian Easter Overture* Rimsky-Korsakov attempted to show the contrast between the ancient wonder of Isaiah's proclamation with the almost-Pagan celebration of Easter in modern times. The composer wanted the listener to recognize the parallels between their own actions and biblical tales of "pagan merry-making." He also believed that to make this connection, the listener would have needed to attend an Easter morning service in a cathedral with all types of people. In his childhood, the composer did experience this type of thing. Obviously, Rimsky-Korsakov believed that the religious services of his time were "a far cry from the philosophic and socialistic teaching of Christ." In the program for the first performance of the overture, Rimsky-Korsakov provided prose and Bible verses (two from Psalm 68 and six from the Gospel of Mark, chapter 16) to accompany the work, but he did not speak of his true intentions. He decided that it would be best to allow the "tones to speak for [him]." *—Chris Boyes*

Recommended:

- ○ **Rimsky-Korsakov: Antar; Russian Easter Festival** / Svetlanov (cond.), London PO / 1990 / Hyperion 66399
- ○ **Rimsky-Korsakov: Great Orchestral Works** / Zinman (cond.), Rotterdam PO / 1994 / Philips 442605
- ○ **Rimsky-Korsakov: Scheherazade** / Temirkanov (cond.), New York PO / RCA 61173
- ○ **Leopold Stokowski The Magician** / Stokowski (cond.), Chicago SO / 1999 / RCA 70931

Scheherazade, symphonic suite, Op. 35 (1888)

Nikolai Rimsky-Korsakov's works are distinguished by his colorful and imaginative orchestration, and *Scheherazade* is perhaps the finest example of them all (Claude Debussy, no slouch of an orchestrator himself, paid *Scheherazade* the highest compliment by using a passage from its second movement, virtually unaltered, in both *La mer* and *Daphnis et Chloe*). *Scheherazade's* gorgeous melodies and vast, impeccably employed palette of orchestral colors have made it Rimsky-Korsakov's most popular work.

Rimsky-Korsakov's headnote explains the scenario: "The Sultan Schahriar, persuaded of the falseness and faithlessness of women, has sworn to put to death each one of his wives after the first night. But the Sultana Scheherazade saved her life by interesting him in tales she told him during 1,001 nights. Pricked by curiosity, the Sultan put off his wife's execution from day to day, and at last gave up entirely his bloody plan." Four such lifesaving narratives, rendered in music, follow. In later years, Rimsky-Korsakov declared that *Scheherazade* should be regarded as a symphonic suite with an unspecified Oriental program. This makes sense in light of the fact that the music itself has very little narrative logic. However, some details of the program remain relevant.

The first movement, titled *The Sea and Sinbad's Ship*, opens with the growling chords that represent the Sultan, followed by the sinuous solo violin melody that depicts Scheherazade weaving her tales. Scheherazade recedes, and a swaying melody enters in barcarole time on the strings, swelling like the sea. Brass accents occasionally cause the sea to crash and storm, and sweetly scored interludes suggest island dalliances, but the movement ends with a quiet depiction of what must be calm seas and steady wind.

The Story of the Kalender Prince concerns a prince who disguises himself as a beggar and searches for wisdom. His melancholy theme first appears in solo woodwinds, then enters the strings and quickens as the Prince sets out on his journey. Rimsky-Korsakov suggested that "one might see a fight" when a martial variant of the Sultan's theme enters, surrounded by nervous string oscillations, while a later section with fluttering woodwinds and pizzicato string chords suggests "Sinbad's mighty bird, the Roc."

The third movement is called *The Prince and the Princess* and explores an unnamed Eastern palace; the Prince appears as a sensual, langorous string theme, the Princess as a relaxed arc of flute melody. Nevertheless, the beginning of the fourth movement finds the Sultan in an irascible mood, and Scheherazade tries to appease him by describing the restless energy of the festival at Baghdad. From there, the action moves out to the sea, where the weather has worsened. Brass cry out, winds sweep up and down, and the music grows to a massive climax topped by a frightening bitonal crash depicting the ship striking rocks and sinking. The storm subsides, and finally the themes of Scheherazade and the Sultan mingle, Scheherazade's violin playing its highest harmonics.*—Andrew Lindemann Malone*

Recommended:

- ○ **Rimsky-Korsakov: Sheherazade** / Gergiev (cond.), Levitin, Kirov Orch. / 2002 / Philips 470840
- ○ **Rimsky-Korsakov & Borodin: Symphonic Music** / Kondrashin (cond.), Krebbers, Concertgebouw / 2001 / Philips 464735
- ○ **Rimsky-Korsakov & Borodin** / Beecham (cond.), Staryk, Royal PO / 1999 / Angel 66998
- ○ **Rimsky-Korsakov: Sheherazade** / Bernstein (cond.), Corigliano, New York PO / 1998 / Sony 60737

OPERA

Le Coq d'Or (The Golden Cockerel / Zolotoy petushok) (1906–1907)

Le Coq d'Or (The Golden Cockerel) was the 15th and last opera of Nicolay Rimsky-Korsakov. Based on the faux fairytale by Alexander Pushkin (itself based on Washington Irving's *The Alhambra*) set as a libretto by Vladimir Belsky—the librettist of *Sadko, The Tale of Tsar Sultan,* and *The Legend of the Invisible City of Kitezh*—*Le Coq d'Or* is a not especially subtle attack on obdurate bureaucrats and dim-witted aristocrats disguised as a glittering *fin de siècle* spectacle. Coming as it did from the composer who had resigned his post as director of the St. Petersburg Conservatory in protest after the bloody 1905 Russian Revolution, *Le Coq d'Or* fooled no one and the work's premiere was delayed for months by the Imperial Censor. This delay was said to have hastened Rimsky-Korsakov's death on June 21, 1908, and the opera was finally premiered posthumously on October 7, 1909, in Zimin's Theater and not in the Imperial Theater. Set in three acts with a prologue and an epilogue, *Le Coq d'Or* is the story of simple-minded King Dodon, his two feeble-minded sons, his rude general, his untrustworthy advisors, and his Act One enemy, Act Two lover, and Act Three betrothed, the seductive Queen of Shemakha. Between the moralizing prologue and the mollifying epilogue, *Le Coq d'Or* tells the story of Dodon's stupidity, his sons' cupidity, his generals crudity, his advisors' imbecility, and Shemakha's erotic abilities. Not surprisingly, nearly everyone dies by the end, and, not surprisingly, Imperial Russia saw the opera as a mirror of its own faults. Rimsky-Korsakov's music is gloriously lyrical, grandly dramatic, grotesquely ironic, and beguilingly colored with all the resources of a master of the orchestra. The use of chromatic sonorities and whole-tone scales firmly places the work in the post-Romantic harmonic Europe of Debussy, Sibelius, and Strauss, while the use of pentatonic melodies and an unusual time signature firmly places the work in the late Silver Age Russia of Mussorgsky, Borodin, and even Balakirev. *—James Leonard*

Synopsis:

Prologue. The Astrologer announces ("Ya koldon") that this is just a fairy tale, but one with a valuable moral.

Act One. King Dodon is holding council in his palace. He complains that when he was young, he invaded neighboring countries, but now that he is old and less energetic, they are unfairly taking advantage of the fact by invading his ("Ya vas sdyes"). He demands advice; his son Guidon theorizes that their soldiers are stationed at the border, too close to the enemy. If they withdraw to the capital, then they can prepare while the enemy engages in border skirmishes. General Polkan is the only one who finds a flaw in this plan: what if the enemy takes advantage of the undefended borders to march directly on the capital? Dodon finds this nitpicking to verge on treason, but his son Aphron comes up with another suggestion, first stopping to explain that his brother is (as usual) wrong. He suggests that instead, they disband the army, luring the enemy into false confidence. Then, a month before the attack, the army will be called back for a surprise attack. Dodon is even more delighted with this plan, but Polkan again points out a problem. The enemy might not mention when they plan to attack. His objections are again dismissed. The discussion turns to the best way to predict the future. The Astrologer comes in, carrying a large bag. He says that he has the solution to Dodon's problem ("Slaven bood velikiy tsar"). Opening the bag, he shows the court the golden rooster, saying that it will keep an unceasing vigil and crow to warn the King of any approaching danger. Dodon offers him a reward, and the Astrologer says that he doesn't want wealth, but would rather have the King's promise of a favor to be granted later. He oversteps his bounds when he asks for the promise in writing, and Dodon snaps that his very whims are law. He dismisses them all and the rooster assures Dodon that all is calm and that he can rest peacefully. Dodon imagines the easy future he will have, without having to worry about any threats. As he lazes about, attended by his housekeeper Amalfa, he falls asleep. The rooster crows and a moment later, Polkan and the citizens crowd in, saying that the enemy is attacking. Dodon, waking up, tells the people to give their valuables to the war effort, and his sons to go to war, though they protest that later would be a better time. Dodon calls for his armor and a very docile horse. He is stuffed with some difficulty into the former and hoisted onto the latter. The people sing his praises and urge him not to get too close to the enemy.

Act Two. The two sons and their armies have been killed, and Dodon and Polkan enter. It is still dark, but Dodon sees his sons' bodies and laments for them ("Shto za strashniya"). Rising, he swears revenge. As the sun rises, they can see a beautiful tent, and Polkan orders the soldiers to fire on it. As they aim, the doors open, and the beautiful Queen of Chemakha emerges and sings the Hymn to the Sun ("Otvet mnye zorkoie"), asking the sun to tell her of her homeland's beauties. She greets Dodon and Polkan and coyly tells Dodon that she intends to conquer his kingdom through her charms, and that his sons died fighting over her. As they drink the wine she offers, she describes hearing a lover's voice during the night and wonders who it might have been. Dodon's infatuation is more to her taste than Polkan's sardonic comments, and she has Dodon dismiss him. To his stammering delight, she goes on to describe the beauties that he cannot see, as she is wearing clothing ("Sbrochu chopornya tkany"). She asks him to sing for her, and he makes a brave attempt ("Budu vek tibya lubit"). She returns to her seductions ("Da, doydesh do vostoka"), saying that she is lonely and unfulfilled without a man to be her lord and master. Dodon proposes himself for that role. She makes him dance for her, which he does, not noticing her derision. She accepts his offer, provided that he have Polkan punished, and Dodon offers to have him beheaded. As her slaves sing ironically of Dodon's glory, they leave.

Act Three. Outside Dodon's palace, the citizens are awaiting his return, many perturbed by the thought that the gathering storm is an evil omen. Amalfa announces that Dodon has conquered four kings (hearts, spades, diamonds, clubs) and rescued a princess, whom he is bringing back as his Queen. She orders them to celebrate. The Queen's bizarre retinue enters, followed by Dodon and the Queen. He is strangely uneasy and she looks about coldly. As the people shout Dodon's praises, the Astrologer enters. He demands the promised reward—the Queen. Dodon offers him treasures instead, but as the Astrologer insists that he keep his promise, Dodon finally angrily strikes him with his scepter, killing him. Thunder peals and the Queen laughs. Dodon tries to kiss her, but she pushes him away, telling him he is repulsive, and his own death is imminent. He gasps that she is joking. The rooster suddenly descends from the perch and strikes him on the head, killing him. As the stage goes dark, the Queen laughs wildly, and when it lightens again, she and the rooster are gone. The people wonder what will become of them without their King ("Umer tsar").

Epilogue. The Astrologer reminds the audience that this was not a tragedy; only he and the Queen were real, the rest of the characters just figures from a fairy tale. —*Ann Feeney*

Recommended:

○ **Rimsky- Korsakov: Le coq d'or** / Svetlanov (cond.), Nizinenko, Mishenkin, Redkin, Gaponova, Bolshoi Theater Orch. / 1991 / MCA 10391

Legend of the Invisible City of Kitezh (Skazaniye o nevidimom grade Kitezhe) (1903–1904)

The *Legend of the Invisible City of Kitezh and the Maiden Fevroniya* is frequently called Rimsky-Korsakov's operatic masterpiece; score and libretto combine to make the most emotionally engrossing of his works for the stage. Because of its mystical elements, some have compared it to Mozart's *The Magic Flute*, Wagner's *Parsifal*, and Messiaen's *St. Francis of Assisi*.

Vladimir Bielski, the librettist, worked closely with the composer on a number of other operas, including *Sadko* and *The Golden Cockerel*. For *Legend*, Bielski actually combined two medieval Russian legends into one the libretto: the folktale of the City of Kitezh, with its fascinating, yet gruesome clash between Russian and "oriental" cultures, and lore concerning St. Fevroniya. He bound the legends together by scripting a love affair between the maiden Fevroniya and the young prince who leads the army of Kitezh into battle against the invading Tartars. Both sources reach deeply into the mystic Russian imagination and powerfully combine Russian Orthodox Christianity, ecstatic mysticism, contemplative traditions, and pantheism. The latter had particular appeal to the composer, who vacillated between a rationalist agnosticism (veering towards atheism) and pagan nature worship. In Fevronias' universal love of man and nature, one can see a Christianizing of paganism. Her qualities are consonant with ethics espoused by a contemporary of the opera's author's, Tolstoy: pursuit of harmony between mankind and nature, aspiration to regain childhood purity, and nonviolent resistance to evil. Stylized use of Russian, forms of Church Slavonic, and phraseology from ancient and archaic ballads only add to the literary accomplishment of Bielski's libretto.

Musically the score more than matches the libretto. Not surprisingly for a Russian opera, the chorus plays a prominent role. As it is by Rimsky-Korsakov, one is also not surprised that the orchestra also plays an important part, and the orchestration is typically colorful. A factor that sets it apart from other contemporary Russian operas, even by this composer, is the exceptional balance between symphonic invention and vocal expression. Certain Wagnerian elements inform the score, especially the use of leitmotifs and the through-composed form (despite the occasional seemingly closed number). The composer's predilection for deriving many motifs from one theme (for example, the bells theme, from which are derived motifs associated with both the threat to and salvation of Kitezh) is on display here, along with what some commentators have termed "leit-tonalities"—a precise use of key to connote various dramatic ideas. Harmonically, the opera is more diatonic and simple than Rimsky-Korsakov's other operas of the period, but there is still sufficient use of his beloved artificial modes (though the whole-tone scale appears infrequently), particularly in connection with the Tartars.

The premiere, on February 7, 1907, at St. Petersburg's Mariinsky Theatre, was a great success. The forces needed to mount the opera were not only collectively sympathetic, but also sufficiently skilled and prepared. Libretto and score found an affinity with the audience. In fact, contemporary commentators saw the opera as a significant cultural event, even perceptively comparing it to the works of Tolstoy. —*Neil Cardew-Fanning*

Synopsis:

Act One. The story is set in the year 6751 (the date representing the number of years following the world's creation) in and around the cities of Lesser and Greater Kitezh. In the woods just outside Lesser Kitezh, Prince Vsevolod, injured by a bear on a hunting expedition, meets the maiden Fevroniya. They fall in love, and he claims her for his future bride. His hunting companions, from whom he had become separated, reappear and he goes off with them, promising Fevroniya he will find a bride for her woodsman brother. One of his hunting companions, Fyodor Poyarok, reveals to Fevroniya that Vsevolod is a Prince, the son of Prince Yuri Vsevolodovich of Greater Kitezh.

Act Two. In Lesser Kitezh's marketplace, the people assemble to celebrate the Prince's forthcoming marriage. Some wealthy citizens, unhappy with the Prince's choice of a commoner for a bride, bribe Grishka Kuter'ma, a local drunk, to ridicule Fevroniya when she passes by in the wedding procession. Grishka insults her on her arrival, but she urges tolerance toward him. The festivities end with a sudden attack by the Tartars, who capture Fevroniya and Grishka. The fearful latter aids the enemy in their quest to find and sack Greater Kitezh, while Fevroniya prays that the city be rendered invisible.

Act Three. In Greater Kitezh, blinded in battle by the Tartars, Fyodor Poyarok warns the citizenry of the enemy's advance, guided, he believes, by Fevroniya. Prince Yuri assembles a contingent, led by Vsevolod, to defend the city. Suddenly a mist enshrouds the city and church bells ring continuously—the city has become invisible. The Kitezh forces are defeated in the battle near Kerzhenets, however, and Prince Vsevolod is killed.

Grishka brings the Tartars to the banks of Lake Svetliy Yar, from where the city can normally be seen. Perceiving nothing but a golden mist, the Tartars believe they have been misled by Grishka. They tie him up and announce he will face execution the following day. After the Tartars begin dividing up their plunder, a fight over Fevroniya erupts between two of them, Burundai and Biediai, the latter dying in the action. After the Tartars are asleep Fevroniya unties Grishka, and he runs to the lake to drown himself—he cannot stand the tolling bells of Greater Kitezh, which serve to reinforce his guilt. But when he sees the reflection on the water of the rays coming from the invisible city, he flees, bringing Fevroniya with him.

In the Kerzhenets Forest that night, Grishka is still beset with guilt, which the compassionate Fevroniya cannot alleviate with her reassurances. He goes mad and runs off. When Fevroniya falls asleep, the woods surrounding her transform into a paradise, with lights illuminating the scenery from trees and magical birds singing. One of them, Alkonost, foretells of her death. The ghost of Vsevolod appears and another bird, Sirin, tells the lovers they will enjoy everlasting life together. Vsevolod leads Fevroniya to the invisible city.

The two enter Greater Kitezh, now a city of great visual splendor, with its slain inhabitants residing in complete happiness. The wedding ceremony of Vsevolod and Fevroniya resumes from where it had been interrupted by the Tartar invasion. Fevroniya pleads for saving the soul of Grishka, but learns he is not yet worthy. She offers encouragement to him in a message so he can later join her and the others in eternal happiness in the invisible city of Kitezh. —*Robert Cummings*

Recommended:

○ **Rimsky-Korsakov: Legend of the Invisible City of Kitezh** / Gergiev (cond.), Gorchakova, Diadkova, Gassiev, Boitsov, Kirov Chorus and Orch / 1999 / Philips 462225

Sadko (1895–1896)

Sadko, Rimsky-Korsakov's operatic masterpiece, opened at the Solodonikov Theater in Moskow on December 26, 1897. It is an opera in seven tableaux or scenes. Based on Russian *bilini* legends written about the life of a bard and hero who lived in twelfth century Novgorod, it combines the fantastical and imaginary world of Sea Kings, nymphs, and golden fish, with the daily life of Sadko and his fellow merchants of the sea. Rimsky-Korsakov uses many Russian folk tunes throughout the opera, and in several places he uses actual *bilini* formulae from the ancient songs to construct the melodies of his recitatives and arias. He wrote his own libretto with the help of several other Russian writers, including Stasov, Yastrebtsev, Shtrup, Findeyzen, and Vladimir Nikolayevich Bel'sky.

The composer began writing music based on the story of Sadko in 1867, with the composition of his tone poem *Episode from the legend of Sadko.* It quickly became a national favorite in Russia, and much of the music of the symphonic poem was used in the score to the opera. A central theme throughout the opera is the sea. Much of the music depicts the various moods of the sea, and gives the listener pictorial images of the open water. Recurring motifs, themes, and atmospheric orchestral writing bind the opera together and conjure up romantic images.

For the first half of the opera, Rimsky-Korsakov alternates scenes placed in the real world of Novgorod with scenes at Lake Ilmen, where the Sea King and his daughters dwell. The opening music of the opera comes directly from the symphonic poem, and depicts the movements of the waves through surging and pulsating movement and disturbing and mysterious harmonies. The vastness of the sea, its remoteness, and its offer of adventure are all realized in the highly atmospheric writing of the opening. We are then introduced to a crowd of Russian merchants in one of the many exciting crowd scenes that occur throughout the opera. Sadko enters and sings his opening number, accompanying himself on his *gusli,* which is a Russian relative of the dulcimer or psaltery. His music portrays him as both an Orpheic bard and an ambitious hero. It is an impassioned arioso solo that is met with hostility on the part of his mates. They ridicule him after he is gone in folk song based concerted writing. They sing and dance, and merrymaking closes the tableaux.

As Sadko reaches Lake Ilmen, orchestral writing again depicts the mood of the open water. It is still, calm and vast, and only as Sadko's song progresses does the sea begin to come to life. In the bottom of the orchestra, the currents and swellings of the waters are felt underneath the young bard's impassioned solo. His musicianship is rewarded with the love of the Sea King's daughter, who sings to him an extended aria filled with romantic love and desire. Both lyrical and passionate, her music is some of the most beautiful of the opera. It is contrasted by the lament in the following scene of Sadko's young wife, who fears that her husband no longer loves her. The vocal writing for this part is set lower, with the richer tones coloring the sadder mood of the music. Her music is also very beautiful, but now extremely human and broken hearted. The rest of the opera takes place over time, and the two contrasting worlds provide opportunity for adventure, spectacle, and miraculous happenings. *—Rita Laurance*

Synopsis:

Scene One. The opera takes place in Novgorod, in the early centuries of Christianity. The merchant-traders of the city are seated at a huge banquet where there is to be musical entertainment. First Nezhata, a gusli player from Kiev, strikes up a tune. He sings a traditional bilini, or legend set to song, about a snowmaiden, and another about a hero half human and half serpent. Other entertainers, called skomorokhi, provide comic entertainment. The merchants next want something in praise of their fair city, and another minstrel appears. It is the famous Sadko. But he rebukes them for their idle boasting, saying that if he were a powerful merchant, he would go forth in his ship and take his trade to far off lands. His feats of bravery would be known throughout the world! The merchants are incensed at his bravado, and a huge argument breaks out among them. After he is gone, the entire assembly joins in his ridicule. Wild revelry and merrymaking closes the scene.

Scene Two. The scene takes place on the shores of the magical Lake Ilmen. Sadko has come to the shores, filled with reflective melancholy. It is a clear night, and a crescent moon hangs in the sky. He sings a bitter plaint as he thinks on his sad fate; none listen to his songs, or hearken to his bilini legends. As he sings, a group of swans comes towards him and magically turn into maidens. They are the daughters of the Sea King, led by the Sea Princess Volkhova. Volkhova has been bewitched by his singing, and confesses her undying love for him. The other sea maidens surround him, and the Princess sits at his feet. She tells Sadko that she is destined to marry a mortal. Her sisters are the great rivers, and her father lives in an azure palace at the bottom of the ocean. At first, he replies that he cannot marry her, for he is already wed to a human woman, but in the end he acquiesces. As morning breaks, the sea Princess and her sisters return to their abode in the depths of the ocean.

Scene Three. At the home of Sadko, his wife Lyubava sits sadly dejected, for Sadko has been away all night. When she sees him returning, her spirits rise, but they quickly fall again when he is too distracted to notice her. He is thinking of the beautiful Volkhova, and the wonder of his newfound love. He tells Lyubava that there are golden fish at the bottom of Lake Ilmen, and that he means to make his fortune by harvesting them.

Scene Four. On the shores of Lake Ilmen, many ships are docked, and merchant wares from distant lands are displayed. Sadko enters and wagers his head that he can catch golden fish out of Lake Ilmen. The merchants and their attendants all expect it to be nothing but the venture of a crazy man, but they gather around him to watch. When he casts his net, Volkhova fills it with the magical fish. To everyone's amazement, Sadko is now a wealthy trader-merchant! He decides to set out on the travels about which he boasted at the opening of the opera. He begins buying up merchandise and fitting his ships for the voyage. He plans to leave Novgorod at sunset to go exploring unknown lands. As he departs, Lyubava laments.

Scene Five. Sadko's voyage is being hindered by the wrath of the Sea King, and he decides to offer himself up as a sacrifice so that his men may proceed without him. They have been sailing for 12 years, and are on their journey home. Sadko disappears down to the bottom of the ocean.

Scene Six. Sadko and Volkhova are finally married, in an elaborate wedding ceremony, with feasting and dancing. An apparition of a dead saint rebukes the Sea King for causing so much trouble. The ocean is a mass of turbulent waters, due to the riotous celebrations of the Sea King's court. The ghost commands the Sea King to release his daughter, so that she may go to the surface and become a great river like her sisters.

Secne Seven. As Sadko and the Princess reach the surface, they have a last love scene before she is transformed into the mighty river Volkhova. Sadko is reunited with his wife Lyubava, and all sing the praises of the city of Novgorod. *—Rita Laurance*

Recommended:

○ **Rimsky-Korsakov: Sadko** / Gergiev (cond.), Tarassova, Aleksashkin, Diadkova, Gassiev, Kirov Opera & Orch. / 1994 / Philips 442138

The Snow Maiden (Snegurochka) (1880–1895)

During the summer of 1880, Nikolay Rimsky-Korsakov spent his first season in the countryside of Russia, at Stelyovo. The composer had never before in his life been happier than he was at this time. Upon the first day that Rimsky-Korsakov settled in Stelyovo, he immediately began work on the composition of an opera based on the subject of *Snegurochka* (The Snow Maiden). Prior to this summer, he had gathered much of the musical material, such as themes and chord progressions, that were to be used in *The Snow Maiden.* Rimsky-Korsakov composed each scene of the opera for voices and piano at first. In only two and a half months, he managed to compose the entire opera. In his autobiography, the composer stated that "no previous composition had ever come to me with such ease and rapidity as *Snegurochka*." After returning home to St. Petersburg, Rimsky-Korsakov worked on orchestrating the opera, beginning in the winter, completing the task on April 7, 1881.

Once *The Snow Maiden* was finished, Rimsky-Korsakov felt that he had achieved a new compositional maturity. He believed that he had made considerable progress in the areas of recitative and orchestration, as well as vocal writing. An interesting aspect of *The Snow Maiden* is the presence of bird songs in the score. This definitely stems from Rimsky-Korsakov's newfound love for bird calls, which were discovered at Stelyovo. The composer also made extensive use of "leading motives" that represented certain aspects of the opera. Although very similar to Wagner's leitmotiv technique, Rimsky-Korsakov had only a limited knowledge of Wagner and his works at the time.

Rehearsals for *The Snow Maiden* began in December 1881, and the opera was premiered the following February. Although the production was a success with the audience, the musical critics were not too kind to the new work, claiming that the opera lacked dramaticism. They also criticized Rimsky-Korsakov for melodic lack of inventiveness due to his use of folk melodies. He did make slight use of folk tunes, but a far greater number of the opera's melodies were of his own creation. The critics acknowledged Rimsky-Korsakov's skill as a symphonist, but not as an operatic composer. Colleagues of the composer, such as Balakirev and Borodin, viewed the opera as a success. Mussorgsky was impressed by certain excerpts, but was largely indifferent concerning the opera. *—Chris Boyes*

Synopsis:

Prologue. Spring sings of the eternal cold in the land. She explains to the birds that she and King Frost have had a daughter, and the sun has become angry and therefore has given no warmth for the last 15 years. The birds dance and sing to warm themselves: "Sbiralis ptitsi." Frost sends in a burst of snow and follows himself, exuberantly exclaiming that he loves the cold he brings: "Po bogatim." She says that Snegurochka wants her freedom to live among humans, and he warns Spring that he has to go north, that the sun is determined to destroy Snegurochka and can do it if she is ever warmed by the fires of love. Frost calls her, and she is delighted at the thought of being free and sings of the wonderful songs she has heard a young singer, Lehl, perform. Her parents are afraid but she reassures them that she is not in love with him. Spring tells Snegurochka how to summon her and Frost tells the wood sprite to protect her if any man should ever pay unwelcome attentions to Snegurochka. The villagers come in, celebrating Carnival: "Ranim-rano kuri." Snegurochka hides at first, but then emerges and asks Bobil to take her in as his daughter. He and Bobilicka agree. When she calls goodbye to the forest, the villagers are amazed when the trees bow in response.

Act One. The act opens in Bobil's cottage. Lehl comes to sing for Snegurochka, "Zemlyanichka yagodka," but she is not overtly responsive and he runs out to entertain the livelier girls. Kupava runs in to tell Snegurochka that she has met a wonderful man, Misgir, a handsome and rich young merchant who has proposed to her. He comes in and, following tradition, gives the young men and women a "dowry" to make up for stealing their companion, in a lively ensemble. However, just a moment after declaring his love for Kupava, he notices Snegurochka and falls in love with her. When they all go out but he sees she is staying, Misgir insists on staying, too. Snegurochka tries to evade him but he heaps gifts in front of Bobil and Bobilicka and pleads his love. They make her order Lehl away, and she asks why he is weeping. He responds she will know the meaning of tears herself. Kupava brings the villagers back and they are outraged when he coolly explains he now loves Snegurochka instead of Kupava. When Kupava demands to know why, he tells her that she was too forward in accepting his attentions and responding. His final insult is that he assumed such an immodest woman might be faithless. She and the villagers are outraged and she vows to go to the Tsar for redress.

In the Tsar's palace, musicians entertain him with martial songs, but conclude that the peace his kingdom enjoys is better still. Bermate, one of his nobles, enters and obsequiously tells him his kingdom enjoys perfect bliss. The Tsar dismisses this and says that the sun has not warmed the kingdom for 15 years. He theorizes that if all the single people of the kingdom marry, surely the subsequent bridal hymns will please the sun into shining again. Kupava comes in and at first incoherently tells her story to the sympathetic Tsar: "Syerdtse to viznobiv." He has Misgir summoned, and Lehl and the others all come in as well. He orders Misgir to be banished. When Snegurochka appears, he recognizes that her coldness in rejecting love must be the cause of the sun's anger. The court ladies declare that Lehl would be the one who could win her heart, but Misgir proposes himself as a better candidate, and the Tsar agrees in the hopes of bringing the warmth of the sun back to his kingdom. He orders them all to gather for the weddings.

Act Three. In the forest, the villagers are dancing around Lehl and an increasingly interested Snegurochka, while Berendey and his court watch. He asks Lehl to sing and Lehl obliges ("Tuca so gromom"), with a song suggesting that should a girl be missing, seek her in the bushes. The Tsar says that one of the girls should reward Lehl with a kiss, but slighting the expectant Snegurochka, Lehl chooses and passionately kisses Kupava. All disperse, and Snegurochka returns, sadly. Misgir returns and ardently declares his love for her, pleading and offering her jewels. She runs away from him, and the Spirit of the Woods creates an illusion, blocking the path as he tries to chase her. Lehl and Kupava return and sing a passionate love duet: "Nasilu ya tebya." Snegurochka emerges and accuses Kupava of betraying her, but Lehl laughingly replies that Kupava actually knows how to love, and they leave together. As their voices are heard offstage, Snegurochka calls for help from Spring.

Act Four. In a valley, Snegurochka confides her wish for love to Spring, who adorns her daughter with flowers but warns her not to let the sun ever see her. Mizgir appears, and now it is she who declares her love. He responds in kind, but cannot understand her fear of the sun. When the Tsar, his court, and the villagers appear at sunrise, the Tsar blesses the couples. Snegurochka and Misgir declare their love and ask for his blessing, but as the sun begins to warm the valley, she melts away completely, whereupon Misgir throws himself into the lake. The Tsar cannot lament them since their deaths have brought an end to the coldness, and all sing in praise of the sun and its warmth, hoping for an abundant harvest at last. *—Ann Feeney*

Recommended:

○ **Rimsky-Korsakov: Snow Maiden** / Fedoseyev (cond.), Vedernikov, Arkhipova, Matorin, Arkhipov, Tchaikovsky SO / Relief 991049

The Tale of Tsar Saltan (Skazka o Tsare Saltane) (1900–1901)

During the winter of 1898, Nikolay Rimsky-Korsakov often visited with V.I. Byelsky, a librettist with whom he was familiar, for the purpose of developing subject matters, such as mythical legends or literary works, for possible operas. Only one of these proposed subjects was actually acted upon, Pushkin's *Tale of Tsar Saltan.* There were a few other ideas of merit developed during this time, but they were all set aside for another date in order that the librettist and composer could concentrate work on the opera that was to be *The Tale of Tsar Saltan* (1900).

Byelsky started on the libretto, which Rimsky-Korsakov thought was magnificent, in the spring of 1890. The librettist attempted to stay true to Pushkin's writing style as much as possible. As Byelsky would complete a scene of the opera, it would be handed to Rimsky-Korsakov, who subsequently began composing the music for the scene. The entire opera was constructed this way, piece by piece.

The composer described the manner in which he composed *The Tale of Tsar Saltan* as "instrumental-vocal." The story of the opera has elements of fantasy and realism. Rimsky-Korsakov composed in a pictorial, instrumental manner for the parts of the opera which were fantastic, while the realistic parts were written in an declamatory, vocal style. The opera begins with a scenic Prologue, in which the character of the Tsar Saltan is introduced. This dramatic prelude takes the place of the traditional orchestral overture to begin the opera. Also, each of the four acts was preceded by a rather lengthy orchestral prelude. At the beginning of each act, a short trumpet fanfare signaled the audience that the action of the opera was resuming. Rimsky-Korsakov considered the fanfare to be "a device quite original and suitable for a fairy-tale." The orchestral preludes heard before the beginning of Acts I, II, and IV were made into a concert suite by the composer titled *Little Pictures for the Tale of Tsar Saltan.—Chris Boyes*

Synopsis:

Prologue. In a cottage in the city of Tmutarakan, three sisters work in the company of their mother, the wicked Barbarikha. The youngest, the beautiful and kindly Militrissa, is treated like Cinderella by her two older siblings, Povarikha, the oldest, and Tkachikha. Each sister declares what her wishes would be if she were Tsaritsa (Queen). When Militrissa announces that she would only wish to bear a brave son for Tsar Saltan, the Tsar himself bursts in, having been eavesdropping outside. He declares that Militrissa will be his wife, and appoints Povarikha the royal cook and Tkachikha the royal weaver. The latter two are jealous, however, and scheme with Barbarikha against Militrissa.

Act One. In a room in the Tsar's palace, Tsaritsa Militrissa fretfully awaits her husband's return from war. She has already given birth to a son, Prince Guidon, and sent a message with news of the event to Tsar Saltan. But the Tsar receives a different message, one written by the scheming Barbarikha and her daughters: it informs him he is the father not of a princely son but of "a monster." A courier soon brings a message from the Tsar to his court, instructing that Militrissa and her offspring be placed in a barrel and set adrift at sea. The Tsaritsa is horrified, while her sisters and mother rejoice. The Tsar's orders are then carried out.

Act Two. It is many years later, and Militrissa lives with Prince Guidon, now grown, on the deserted and desolate Buyan Island. On a hunting expedition one day, Guidon encounters an enchanted swan and saves it from a diabolical hawk. The swan promises to protect him thereafter. The next morning, Guidon and Militrissa awaken to an astounding sight: they are surrounded by the magical city of Ledenets, which appeared on the island during the night. Its inhabitants, grateful that Guidon has thwarted a sorcerer in killing the hawk, choose him as their leader.

Act Three. Guidon yearns to meet his father. The swan empowers him to transform into a bumblebee and to fly to Tmutarakan. In his palace, Tsar Saltan fetes a group of boatmen, who tell him of the strange once-deserted Buyan Island, now home of the enchanted city of Ledenets, governed by Prince Guidon. Guidon is present, still in the form of a bumblebee. After Tsar Saltan learns of the magical animals and other wonders in the city, he decides to sail there. Barbarikha and Militrissa's sisters attempt to discourage him by promising greater marvels if he chooses to meet with an enchanted princess instead. They fail, however, and Guidon rewards their conniving by stinging them all.

Act Four. On his island, Guidon, back in human form, summons the enchanted swan so that he might be able to find the princess that Barbarikha and her daughters spoke of. The swan reveals herself to be the princess, in fact, and then transforms into a beautiful young woman with magical powers. The two immediately fall in love.

Tsar Saltan arrives on the island and is astonished to see his wife there. His amazement continues when he is greeted by the ruler of the enchanted city, Guidon, whom he learns is his son. In their disgrace, Barbarikha and her daughters are given mercy by the Tsar at the behest of Militrissa and Guidon, and the opera ends happily as all depart for Tmutarakan. *—Robert Cummings*

SYMPHONIC

Symphony No. 2 ("Antar"), Op. 9 (1868–1875; revised 1897)

Nikolay Rimsky-Korsakov had a work ethic which bordered on the obsessive, and when inspiration failed him, he would often busy himself by tidying up works from his youth. This habit accounts for the proliferation of versions of *Antar.* This work was composed between January and August 1868, and premiered in March of the next year. After a few alterations, it was published in 1880 as his *Second Symphony.* However, in the "new edition" of 1903, which was dated 1897, *Antar* was substantially revised and called a symphonic suite, with the words "Second Symphony" in a parenthetical subtitle. In 1913, a final version of *Antar* came out, called simply a "Symphonic Suite," as Rimsky-Korsakov had decided that *Antar* was "a poem, suite, fairy tale, story, anything you like, but not a symphony." The final version changes the key of the second movement and has more refined and detailed orchestration. However, the earlier version may best preserve the freshness of Rimsky-Korsakov's response to the myth of Antar, a great warrior from Arabian literature.

Rimsky-Korsakov's program opens with Antar wandering the ruins of the ancient desert city of Palmyra. Rimsky-Korsakov portrays the desert with grim, bare woodwind chords and elusive, chromatic fragments of melody sweeping over them. Antar's theme enters on the strings, in a lush, resigned harmonization, as he has come to the desert to renounce humanity. Suddenly, a beautiful gazelle appears, which Antar chases. A huge black bird swoops down on the gazelle, but Antar repels it with his lance. He then falls asleep, and in his dream he meets the Queen of Palmyra, Gul Nazar, who had taken the form of the gazelle that Antar saved. The Queen is represented by a lovely, winding wind theme. Gul Nazar promises Antar the three joys of life in exchange for his good deed; as Antar contemplates his newfound good fortune, he wakes up to the strains of the harp and the Gul Nazar theme, amid the ruins of Palmyra. So ends the first movement. The second and third movements are devoted to depicting the joys of revenge and power, respectively. Rimsky-Korsakov uses nervous tremolos in the strings and puts the Antar theme in defiant brass to suggest revenge, while the Antar theme is played sweetly on the strings and in fanfares by the brass to depict power. In the last movement, Antar is allowed to experience the ultimate joy, the love of Gul Nazar. He insists that she kill him when she feels his passion cooling; this she does, and Antar dies in her arms. This movement features some of Rimsky-Korsakov's finest orchestration, including transcendently poignant blends in the woodwinds which depict the two lovers as their passion swells and fades, ultimately ascending to heaven on a swirling harp and lying to rest with a few final chords. Anyone who enjoys *Scheherazade* should try *Antar* next, as this symphony is almost as inspired as that peak of Rimsky-Korsakov's symphonic oeuvre. *—Andrew Lindemann Malone*

Recommended:

- ○ **Rimsky-Korsakov: Great Orchestral Works** / Zinman (cond.), Rotterdam PO / 1994 / Philips 442605
- ○ **Tchaikovsky: Symphony 2; Rimsky-Korsakov: Symphony 2** / Maazel (cond.), Pittsburgh SO / 1986 / Telarc 80131

CONCERTO

Concerto (Concertstück) for clarinet & military band in E flat major (1878)

As inspector of the Russian Navy's bands during the 1870s, Rimsky-Korsakov was inspired to teach himself the rudiments of the brass and woodwind instruments. By his own account, he was an execrable player, but he did gain a sufficiently thorough understanding of the instruments to write three concertos for solo brass or woodwind and wind orchestra. He did it in part, he wrote, "to teach myself to handle a style of virtuosity till then unknown to me with solos, cadenzas, tuttis, etc." The last of these three works was the clarinet concerto. In rehearsal with the Kronstadt naval band, he decided the accompaniment was too heavy, so he withdrew the piece, and it was never performed in his lifetime. A tiny concerto at only about seven minutes long, the work nevertheless falls into the standard three movements, played without interruption. The Allegro moderato employs folk-like themes, but these sing out only in the dark-hued band accompaniment with the soloist's part twirling, spinning, and taking wide leaps no Russian folksinger would attempt. The Andante begins with a fragmentary cadenza based on the first movement's main theme, then proceeds with a lyrical tune over a gently oom-pah accompaniment; the movement would fit naturally into any ballet of the period. The finale, Allegro moderato, emerges from another, slightly more extended cadenza and revisits material from the first movement, now cast as a lilting waltz. *—James Reel*

Recommended:

- ○ **Dimitri Ashkenazy, Clarinet** / Mueller (cond.), D. Ashkenazy, Cincinnati PO / 1995 / Pan 510082
- ○ **Temple University Wind Symphony** / Chodoroff (cond.), Gigliotti, / 1997 / Albany 271

Concerto for trombone & military band in B flat major (1877)

As inspector of Russia's naval bands, Rimsky-Korsakov decided to learn as much as he could about wind instruments. By his own account, his attempts to play them were deafening, but he also composed small concertos for three key band instruments: trombone, oboe, and clarinet. The trombone concerto came first and is the most militaristic of the three. Yet there's also something of what Americans would recognize as the Sunday-afternoon bandstand about it, with its manner of expression derived in part from Italian opera arias. The first movement, Allegro vivace, contrasts a fast fanfare with a broad, lyrical motif that unfortunately does little more than repeat a short phrase several times, up or down a couple of steps. Rimsky-Korsakov dispatches this material, complete with recapitulation but no development, in little more than two minutes, moving along to the more extended Andante cantabile. Here the composer makes up for his lack of inspiration in the first movement's second subject with an ardent, singing line for the soloist, plus a rhapsodic cadenza. This leads straight into the final Allegro, which occupies nearly half the concerto's duration. This is a happy march handed back and forth from band to trombone. Still a two-step, the music sidles into a contrasting, low-key section but soon resumes its full marching stride. The trombone takes time for another cadenza and then is overtaken by the orchestra for a short march through the coda. *—James Reel*

Recommended:

- ○ **All the Lonely People** / Vanska (cond.), Lindberg, Tapiola Sinfonietta / 1993 / Bis 568
- ○ **Concerto** / John Foster Black Dyke Mills Band, Parkes (cond.) / 1993 / Chandos 4523

Piano Concerto in C sharp minor, Op. 30 (1882–1883)

"Among my own works, jotted down during this season [the early 1880s], must be set down the sketch of a *Piano concerto in C sharp minor* on a Russian theme, chosen not without [Mily] Balakirev's advice," writes Nikolay Rimsky-Korsakov in his memoirs. He continues with his characteristic engaging honesty, "In all ways this concerto proved a chip from Liszt's concertos. It must be said that it sounded beautiful and proved entirely satisfactory in the sense of piano technique and style; this greatly astonished Balakirev, who found my concerto to his liking. He had by no means expected that I, who was not a pianist, should know how to compose anything entirely pianistic." Rimsky-Korsakov leaves unsaid the thought that one could learn to compose pianistic music by studying Liszt, but it will occur to most listeners when hearing this piano concerto, which proceeds on the Lisztian one-movement, one-theme model. The theme the older Balakirev suggested for Rimsky-Korsakov's use is dark and dashing. Solo winds introduce it, and the piano answers, alternating between the coruscating runs, heavily ornamented lyrical passages and explosive chords expected in these works. The slow middle section expands on various gestures in the theme while rising to a grandiose fever pitch of emotion; Rimsky-Korsakov also borrows Liszt's use of solo instruments from the orchestra, with the piano acting as accompanist. A final Allegro con fuoco section, introduced by abrupt fanfares in the brass and chords tolling like bells in the piano, uses a slightly modified version of the original theme to drive the music quickly to a grand conclusion. *—Andrew Lindemann Malone*

Recommended:

- ○ **Rimsky-Korsakov: Piano Concerto; Glazunov: Piano Concerto No.1 / Prokofiev: Piano Concerto 1** / Kondrashin (cond.), Richter / 1995 / Melodiya 29468
- ○ **Rimsky-Korsakov: Piano Concerto; Tchaikovsky: Symphony 3** / Levine (cond.), Campbell, Royal PO / 1997 / Telarc 80454

Variations for oboe & military band in G minor (1878)

The second of three concertante works Rimsky-Korsakov wrote as director of Russia's Navy bands, this is billed not as a concerto (as are the compositions for trombone and clarinet), but simply as a set of variations. A short, ominous introduction lurching through the band's lower regions gives way to a hint of the main theme at the top of the ensemble, and the oboe quickly slips in to play Glinka's melody *Beautiful Maiden*, a lilting polonaise. Twelve very short variations ensue—the whole work can be played in less than nine minutes—with soloist and band taking nearly equal shares of the melodic work. Among the more striking variations are the fourth, in which the oboe plays recitative material over trills in the horns and flutes and a slightly sour waltz not long after that. Just before the end, the oboe takes a cadenza that is itself a sort of variation on the 12th variation. The band bursts in with a few peremptory measures and definitively halts the proceedings. *—James Reel*

Recommended:

- ○ **Russian Concert Band Music** / Rozhdestvensky (cond.), Nilsson, Stockholm Concert Band / 1996 / Chandos 9444

Robert Shaw Chorale

f. 1948, New York, NY, **db.** 1965

Ensemble

The Robert Shaw Chorale was one of the most renowned and probably the most popular American choral group from the mid-twentieth century. The R.S.C. gave many memorable concerts and made numerous recordings for the RCA label, beginning at the close of the 78 rpm age in 1948 and ending in the heart of the stereo LP era in 1965. Shaw and his Chorale made the first classical recording to sell over one million copies and they received numerous citations, including several Grammy awards. In fact, Shaw, with his Chorale and other choral groups, was awarded 14 Grammys during his career.

Robert Shaw (1916–99) had established a reputation as one of the finest American choral conductors in the 1930s and 1940s, and would later achieve considerable stature in the orchestral realm as well. Having greatly impressed Fred Waring as leader of the Pomona College Glee Club, Shaw was asked to serve as conductor of the Fred Waring Glee Club, a post he accepted in 1938. He left it in 1945, steeped in other assignments, including rehearsing the NBC Symphony Orchestra & Chorus for Toscanini. He would also head the Juilliard School of Music's choral department from 1946 to 1948.

Shaw formed the Robert Shaw Chorale in 1948 in New York City. It was the second major choral group he was then directing, the other being the Collegiate Chorale, an amateur ensemble of approximately 120 members that he founded in 1941 and conducted until 1954. The Robert Shaw Chorale consisted of about 40 professional singers, whose numbers often varied. The R.S.C.'s initial recordings were made in 1948 for RCA Victor, the first with Toscanini and the NBC Symphony Orchestra, in a performance of Brahms *Gesang der Parzen*, and the second, of highlights from Saint-Saëns' *Samson and Delilah*, with Stokowski and the NBC Symphony Orchestra. Numerous others would follow, including the 1950 recordings of the Mozart *Requiem* and Verdi operas *Rigoletto* and *Falstaff*, the latter with Toscanini. The R.S.C. also began doing lighter repertory, with recordings of Gershwin's *Porgy and Bess* in 1950 and two collections from 1951, *A Treasury of*

Easter Songs and *Joy to the World.* Later forays into more popular fare included the 1956 *My True Love Sings* and the 1958 *The Stephen Foster Songbook.* The group toured throughout the 1950s and 1960s, perhaps their grandest being the 36-city excursion through the United States in 1960 where the group, comprised of 33 singers, also took along 29 instrumentalists. Their performance of the Bach *Mass in B minor* at the Manhattan Center on that tour was among their more memorable concerts. The R.S.C. was perhaps at its height during the late 1950s and early 1960s, the group's popularity spilling over into many areas, allowing them to perform with some of the leading television personalities of the day. For example, their 1959 recordings entitled *The Lord's Prayer* and *Ave Maria* were done with the then-famous singer and television star Perry Como. After having achieved such popularity, it may seem difficult to comprehend why the group would disband in 1965, but Shaw moved onto other ventures, the most important of which was carrying out the duties of music director of the Atlanta Symphony Orchestra beginning in 1967. New recordings by the Robert Shaw Chorale continued to be issued well into 1967. Thereafter, reissues began to appear regularly, though they began tapering off in the 1990s. By 2002, about 40 recordings by the R.S.C. were widely available, mostly on the RCA label. *—Robert Cummings*

Recommended:

- ○ **Songs of Faith & Inspiration** / Shaw (cond.), Robert Shaw Chorale / RCA 63746
- ○ **Bach: B Minor Mass** / Shaw (cond.), Shumsky, Kopleff, Addison, Walker, Robert Shaw Chorale & Orch. / 1999 / BMG 635292
- ○ **Joy to the World** / Shaw (cond.), Robert Shaw Chorale / 2000 / Camden 21726

Paul Robeson

b. Apr. 9, 1898, Princeton, NJ, **d.** Jan. 23, 1976, Philadelphia, PA
Bass

Paul Robeson was one of the leading American black artists and social activists of his time. Though he was accomplished in many areas including acting and athletics, he was primarily a singer and had a penchant for taking up controversial stands on an array of political and civil rights issues. He became an outcast in his homeland by the late 1940s, but near the end of the twentieth century, over 20 years after his death, his artistry drew new appreciation and his reputation has been somewhat rehabilitated.

Paul Robeson's parents were Rev. William Drew Robeson and his wife Maria Louisa Robeson. The youngest of five children, Paul had a difficult childhood: when he was three, his father was driven out as pastor of the Witherspoon Street Presbyterian Church and became a common laborer for several years to support his family; his mother, a school teacher, was burned to death in a freak accident three years later.

The family moved to Westfield, NJ, when he was nine, and Paul was enrolled in an integrated school. At the age of 17 Robeson entered Rutgers University under a four-year scholarship. There he broke records in baseball, track, and football, winning 15 letters and being named an All-American in the latter sport, as well as becoming class valedictorian. He graduated from Columbia Law School in 1923. By this time he had married Eslanda Cordoza Goode and had long divulged superior talents in both singing and acting.

After confronting racism and prejudice in the law profession, Robeson turned to acting in 1924, playing the lead in Eugene O'Neill's play *All God's Chillun Got Wings* in New York. He sang in his first concert in Boston that same year, receiving many kudos for his rich baritone voice and deep interpretive sense. In the mid-1920s he began focusing more on his vocal talents, giving concerts throughout the U.S., singing mainly so-called Negro spirituals. 1928 London theater audiences saw his first performance of "Ol' Man River" in a production of *Show Boat.* By 1930 he had appeared in London, Vienna, Prague, and elsewhere in Europe singing both Negro spirituals and gypsy folk songs. He starred in his first talkie film, *The Emperor Jones,* in 1933.

In 1935, Robeson traveled to the Soviet Union, finding its socialist way of life much to his liking. He even pondered emigrating there. He became increasingly controversial in the late 1930s, returning to the Soviet Union, as well as traveling to Spain to support the anti-Franco forces. Robeson also continued giving concerts throughout Europe and elsewhere during this time.

Throughout the 1940s Robeson's leftist tendencies grew, and he eventually came under suspicion by the FBI for being a member of the Communist Party. In 1949, 85 of Robeson's scheduled concerts were canceled by booking agents fearful to be associated with the controversial artist. In 1950, he was banned from American television, and by then even prominent black leaders, such as Roy Wilkins and Walter White, considered him an outcast. Moreover, once-eager record labels and other entertainment industries now blacklisted him.

In 1958 an apparent third attempt on his life was made when his car went out of control, the result of someone tampering with the wheel assembly. Robeson's last concert tour was of New Zealand and Australia in 1960. He made trips to the Soviet Union that same year, and on a visit there in 1961, Robeson suffered a collapse and was hospitalized in Moscow and again in London. He was later diagnosed with Paget's disease and spent the remainder of his life in poor health. *—Robert Cummings*

Recommended:

- ○ **Songs of Free Men** / Balaban (cond.), Robeson, Columbia Concert Orch. / 1997 / Sony 63223
- ○ **The Essential Paul Robeson** / Robeson, etc. / 2000 / ASV 244
- ○ **Ballad for Americans & Great Songs of Faith, Love & Patriotism** / Robeson, etc. / Vanguard 117

Paula Robison

b. Jun. 8, 1941, Nashville, TN
Flutist

Sometimes known as "the first lady of the flute," Paula Robison has been an energetic and visible ambassador for her instrument as well as a gifted performer. She was born in Nashville but moved to California when she was young. Her first instrument was the piano, but she took up the flute at age 11 and eight years later entered the Juilliard School. While still at Juilliard she performed with the New York Philharmonic under Leonard Bernstein and made her New York recital debut. She graduated in 1963 and went on to study with the legendary Marcel Moyse at the Marlboro Festival in Vermont. After becoming the first American to win the top prize at Switzerland's Geneva International Competition in 1966, she performed in recital and with major orchestras in the U.S. and internationally. Her repertoire is broad, and her collaborators have ranged from Baroque-oriented groups like I Solisti Veneti to New York's Mostly Mozart Festival Orchestra to the New World Symphony, with whom she has often performed Berio's *Sequenza I.* She has also commissioned and premiered works by Leon Kirchner, Robert Beaser, Toru Takemitsu, and Oliver Knussen.

One of those rare performers with a gift for organizational leadership, Robison became a founding member of the Chamber Music Society of Lincoln Center in 1969 and held the title of artist-member there for 20 years. She and her husband, violist Scott Nickrenz, became co-artistic directors of chamber music at the Spoleto Festival of Two World in Spoleto, Italy, and Charleston, SC, in 1977 and later at the festival's Melbourne, Australia, branch. Achieving a degree of visibility uncommon among classical musicians, Robison has been profiled on CBS television's *Sunday Morning* and PBS' *Live from Lincoln Center.* She has been the subject of feature articles in such varied publications as *The New York Times, Esquire, People, Women Who Rock, Musical America* (where she was named "Musician of the Month"), and *Ovation.*

Active as a teacher at the New England Conservatory and other institutions in recent years, Robison has also undertaken several innovative recording projects in middle age. She has cultivated a strong interest in Brazilian music of all kinds, touring with Brazilian classical musicians, forming an ensemble called Brasileirinho that was devoted to the popular chôro dance genre, and, in the 2003–2004 season, performing her own transcriptions of Vivaldi's *Four Seasons* violin concertos for flute, strings, guitar, harpsichord organ, and Brazilian percussion. She is also the author of several books. *—James Manheim*

Recommended:

- ○ **Handel: Sonatas for Flute** / Robison, Cooper, Eddy / 2004 / Artemis 1494
- ○ **By the Old Pine Tree** / Robison, Sanders, Feeney, Feeney, Wiersma / 1996 / Arabesque 6679
- ○ **Mozart: Masterpieces for Flute** / Janigro (cond.), Robison, Isomura, Harada, Baker, Solisti di Zagreb / 2004 / Artemis 1271
- ○ **Brasileirinho: Chôros, Chôrinhos, Bossas & Bach** / Robison, etc. / Omega 3016

Marisa Robles

b. May 4, 1937, Madrid
Harpist

Marisa Robles studied harp as a child with Luisa Menarguez, made her debut at age nine, and went on to graduate from the Madrid Conservatory in 1953 at the age of 16. The next year, she made her concert debut in Madrid, performing with Jean-Pierre Rampal in Mozart's *Concerto for flute and harp,* K. 299. The work would become her signature piece; she recorded it four times with James Galway and has performed it in concert more than 1,000 times over the course of her career. Her time teaching at the Madrid Conservatory was brief: after joining the staff in 1958, she married and moved to England in 1959, eventually taking British citizenship. In England, Robles became known for television appearances, whereby she introduced harp music to new audiences. Between 1971 and 1993 she taught at the Royal College of Music, but also spent much time touring and performing around the world, including a 1988 trip to China. She has worked with such conductors as Zubin Mehta, Kurt Masur, Rafael Frühbeck de Burgos, Mstislav Rostropovich, and Yehudi Menuhin. She also frequently performed chamber music, especially with her second husband, flutist Christopher Hyde-Smith. Her amiable stage personality and her warm, clear playing endeared her not only to audiences, both live and television, but also to composers. Among those who dedicated harp concertos to her were Manuel Moreno-Buendia, who wrote a concerto for her in 1958 and a second one for harp, marimba, and strings for her in 1994; Joaquín Rodrigo (*Sones en la Giralda*, 1963); Malcolm Williamson; Jesús Guridi; and John Metcalf. She has also been the dedicatee of chamber works by William Mathias, Stephen Dodgson, Alun Hoddinott, and William Alwyn. Robles was artistic director for the first two Cardiff World Harp Festivals in 1991 and 1994. Around the same time, she appeared in the Emmy-winning television series *Concerto!* with Galway and Michael Tilson Thomas, again performing the Mozart. In addition to her recordings of Mozart, she has recorded the music of Debussy and Rodrigo, an album of popular harp solos, and music by Edwin Robertson based on C.S. Lewis' *Chronicles of Narnia* with both Hyde-Smith and her own harp ensemble. *—Patsy Morita*

Recommended:

- ○ **Harp Concertos** / Brown (cond.), Robles, Academy of St. Martin-in-the-Fields / 1990 / London 425723
- ○ **Harp Favourites** / Robles, etc. / 1993 / Decca 436293
- ○ **Serenade** / Galway, Robles, Yamashita / RCA 60033

George Rochberg

b. Jul. 5, 1918, Paterson, NJ, **d.** May 29, 2005, Philadelphia, PA

Composer: Chamber Music

Since the early 1970s George Rochberg has been one of the most controversial figures in American music. His struggle to escape the strictures of serial composition, which he had 20 years earlier hailed as the logical and unavoidable result of musical development, led him to reembrace traditional tonality and abandon the concepts of "originality" and "progress" which had defined modernism during the twentieth century. Born in 1918, Rochberg received a bachelor's degree from Montclair State Teacher's College and subsequently enrolled at the Mannes School of Music, where he worked with Georg Szell and Leopold Mannes himself. After serving in the military during World War II, Rochberg studied at the Curtis institute until 1947, when he received a Bachelor of Music degree. A year later he received a Master's degree from the University of Pennsylvania and returned to the Curtis Institute to teach. Impressed by the power of serial music during a 1950 stay at the American Academy in Rome, where he befriended 12-tone composer Luigi Dallapiccola. Rochberg then began to explore 12-tone procedures in his own music, eventually producing a string of expressive works in that language, including the *Second Symphony*, (1956), and the *Twelve Bagatelles* for solo piano, (1952). Also from the 1950s come a number of important theoretical treatises on aspects of 12-tone technique, specifically the ramifications of what is known in modern music theory as the hexachord.

By the early 1960s Rochberg was becoming increasingly frustrated with the limitations of strict serialism, and his last truly 12-tone work, a piano trio, was completed in 1963. Experimentation with quotation (i.e. the presentation of a snippet of older music within a newly-composed framework), as in the *Music for the Magic Theater*, left Rochberg dissatisfied. With the *Third String Quartet* of 1972, Rochberg publicly rejected the musical status quo, returning instead to a thoroughly tonal idiom, juxtaposed with bitter, often violent atonal music. The slow movement of the quartet is a set of variations composed in a style reminiscent of Beethoven, while the finale seeks to replicate Mahler. While the quartet was hailed by some as a masterpiece. and as the best hope for music in the future, others were less impressed, seeing instead a motley compilation of stylistic cliches which added up to something less than the sum of its parts. Masterful performances by the Concord String Quartet, for whom many of Rochberg's subsequent chamber works would be written, did a great deal to promote Rochberg's new musical aesthetic. Subsequent works, often cast in staggeringly large molds, such as the 50-minute, seven movement *Piano Quintet* of 1975, follow in much the same vein as the *Third Quartet*.

During his long career Rochberg served in a number of administrative and faculty positions. From 1951 to 1960 he worked for the Theodore Presser publishing house. He maintained a faculty position at the University of Pennsylvania from 1960 until the mid-1990s.*—Blair Johnston*

CHAMBER MUSIC

50 Caprice Variations for violin (1970)

Rochberg's *50 Caprice Variations* are variation studies on the theme from Paganini's *24th Caprice* for violin; fittingly, they are an hour-long test of skill and endurance that might have flabbergasted even the great 19th century master. They also show Rochberg turning away from the serialism of his early career and instead towards the tonal structures that would become his hallmark in the 1970s. There are some atonal variations to be found here, but the majority are firmly rooted in tonality, and some even feature borrowings from famous Romantic works, such as Beethoven's *Seventh Symphony*, Mahler's *Fifth Symphony*, and a Schubert waltz. Several variations also invoke older forms and styles, such as the can-can, the barcarolle and the scherzo. Realizing that the entire set is forbiddingly long for both performer and audience, Rochberg has sanctioned omitting the repeats in some of the longer etudes, or choosing only selections from the set. He also permits the performer to choose his own performing order. The *Caprice-Variations* have become recognized as one of the finest of the twentieth century's compositions for solo violin. They were premiered in New York by Zvi Zeitlin on February 6, 1975. *—Joseph Stevenson*

Recommended:

- ○ **George Rochberg** / Zeitlin / 1997 / Gasparo 1010
- ○ **Caoine** / Makarski / 1997 / ECM 449957

Music for the Magic Theater, for 15 instruments (1965–1969)

George Rochberg's 1965 *Music for the Magic Theatre* represents one of the composer's first departures in which he explored viable alternatives to the atonal and serial modes of expression of his formative years. Increasingly Rochberg felt an urge to say more than he could articulate within the techniques of the Second Viennese School. With the present work, along with the contemporary *Contra mortem et tempus*, Rochberg investigated the technique of assemblage or collage. Despite the suggestion of the title, the work was not conceived as incidental music; it draws its name from a phrase from Hermann Hesse's novel *Steppenwolf*, in which the "magic theatre" is an inner state evolved from many human possibilities, different in each person, and available to each of us. Rochberg's subjective application of this, in his own words, is "the whole world of musical possibilities from which I choose myself as a composer." The work was written at the commission of the Fromm Foundation for the University of Chicago's 75th anniversary and was premiered by that school's Contemporary Chamber Players under Ralph Shapey on January 24, 1967. A later orchestral version featured full strings and doubled horns.

Reaching back to the techniques of Charles Ives, Rochberg created a collage of borrowed materials that seeks to be more than pastiche. He assembled some very formidable "materials," among them Mozart's *Divertimento*, K. 287, Beethoven's Opus 130 *Quartet*, Mahler's *Ninth Symphony*, as well as Webern, Varèse, Stockhausen, Miles Davis, and Rochberg's own *Second Quartet* and *Piano Sonata-Fantasia*. These were all selected because they share a three-note descending pattern. Each of the three movements is designated as an "act" and in the first "present and past are all mixed up… it is difficult to… know where reality is…." After three horn swells, the sonorous quote from the adagio of Mahler's *Ninth* begins the pass-in-review of composers. Rochberg explores alternative possibilities of each allusion; the Mahler, for instance, originally a string chorale, is redone at one point by muted trumpets, its threnody transformed to Mahlerian irony. Act Two, in which the past haunts us with its nostalgic beauty," not surprisingly draws heavily from the sweet, period-saturated Mozart work, quoted almost verbatim in its entirety; this in fact seems to encompasses the bulk of the movement until the moderns emerge two-thirds of the way through, and the Mozart seems to pass through a filter of the modern age as it completes its progress. The existential Act Three draws mostly on the moderns, including Rochberg, and is largely subdued in nature. The quotations trail off into long-held tones, music of the spheres… or cosmic sighs? The work fades out to a detached yet serene finis. *—Wayne Reisig*

Recommended:

- ○ **Chamber Music of George Rochberg** / Radcliffe (cond.), New York Chamber Ens. / 1994 / New World 80462

Slow Fires of Autumn, for flute & harp ("Ukiyo-e II") (1978–1979)

Having been trained in the serialist methods inherited from Arnold Schoenberg and carried to new extremes of control by Webern, Boulez, and Babbitt, George Rochberg eventually sought to broaden his palette of compositional techniques and reconnect to an older sense of musical tradition (i.e., tonality) as well as to explore more intuitive, emotional, and subjective modes of expression.

Composed during 1978–79, *Slow Fires of Autumn* a duet for flute and harp, followed Rochberg's adoption of a "neo-tonal" or "neo-Romantic" musical language; within that broad category, the work represents the convergence of a number of influences and aesthetic concepts. Commissioned by the Naumburg Foundation on behalf of flutist Carol Wincenc (who appears on the remarkable CRI recording with harpist Nancy Allen), the piece immediately presents a combination of "Eastern" and "Western" sounds. The harp is heard first, but its unusual articulations and occasional pitch inflections hint at Oriental instruments; likewise, the dynamic contours and exaggerated attacks of the flute evoke for Western listeners something like the sound of the shakuhachi. In fact, Rochberg explicitly indicates the Orientalist leanings of the piece. Borrowing some of its musical materials from Rochberg's earlier work for harp, *Ukiyo-e*, *Slow Fires of Autumn* bears the earlier composition's title as its own subtitle. The word in Japanese refers to a style of painting that, according to Rochberg, sees the world "not as static, fixed forms of reality but as floating pictures of radiant qualities, which range from states of forlornness and emptiness to quiet or ecstatic joy." The piece even ends with a presentation of a Japanese folk tune, a plaintive lullaby rendered in F minor. The lullaby appears only in hints and snatches, before appearing only in the last few minutes before the conclusion as a tonally lucid and expressively focused culmination of the work. Previous to the folk tune's complete emergence, Rochberg engages in a number of episodes in which tonal orientation is ambiguous and gesture is direct. The work opens with dark, exaggerated textures in the harp and concise but graceful motions in the flute. The rhythm is initially quite free and the texture is spare (the cliché comparison to a Japanese rock garden is unavoidable, especially considering the idealized concepts of the East that Westerners still held in the 1970s). The fluidity of this opening material reflects the Rochberg's desire to contrast what he described as "the more strenuous world of Western traditions." The unpredictable ebb of the opening leads to a more active and uninhibited section in which both instruments execute more ambitious figurations and exaggerated gestures and textures. This moment eventually expends itself, winding down into the eventual presentation, in a relatively simple and unadorned fashion, of the Japanese lullaby. *—Jeremy Grimshaw*

Recommended:

○ **George Rochberg, Vol. 2** / Allen, Wincenc / 1997 / CRI 769

String Quartets (1952–1979)

If we mean to have any intelligent appreciation of them, George Rochberg's seven string quartets must be put into two groups: the two quartets (1952 and 1961) written before Rochberg's "Crisis" of the 1960s, and the five composed after it (1972–79). The former are the work of a hard-nosed American "academic" composer, the latter that of a man who has gone through a personal metamorphosis and reembraced the tonal idiom, happily burning many of the bridges to his own musical past in the process.

Rochberg's *Quartet No. 1* is a fairly straightforward piece, applying an atonal bite to a very traditional approach to rhythm: the meters of the movements seldom change once established, and, unlike a lot of serial music, the rhythms are generally simple—one can easily feel the beats. Nine years later, for his next quartet, Rochberg followed Schoenberg's example and added a soprano to the ensemble; in the process he explored a far more complex language than he did in the *Quartet No. 1*, especially with regard to rhythm and meter—things are much more disjunct now, much more demanding for listener and player.

Eleven years passed before Rochberg again plunged into quartet-writing; these were years of turmoil and probing, during which Rochberg questioned the whole apparatus—aesthetic and technical—of contemporary music. Many of the composer's works from the late 1960s touch upon an emerging new style, but the opening of the *Quartet No. 3* became the defining moment in Rochberg's post-Crisis music. The instruments shriek away in gruesomely dissonant parallel intervals, fortissimo—intentionally, violently ugly. But, to the great surprise of that unsuspecting audience at the 1973 premiere, the viola and cello soon slip in underneath the atonal blanket with thick chorale music in true, unadulterated B major. It is a moment frozen in time, and, if well played, of extraordinary power: with this single gesture, Rochberg redefined himself as a composer, becoming hero to some and villain to others. Rochberg's new pan-stylistic posture is made fully clear as the *Quartet No. 3* unfolds, first by the inclusion of a 15-minute set of variations in the style of Beethoven as the third movement, and then by the recurrent appearance of Mahler-like strains within the dissonant framework of the fifth and final movement.

Quartets Nos. 4 through *6* are known as the "*Concord Quartets*" after the remarkable ensemble by the same name, for whom they were written. In each of them, Rochberg tries out a different way of combining the tonal with the atonal, and we can observe him growing ever more comfortable composing traditional tonal music on a large scale. Though Rochberg remained an active composer for two decades after its composition, the *Quartet No. 7* of 1979 is his last work in the genre. As in the *String Quartet No. 2*, the four string players allow a singer to join them on stage—this time, a baritone. *—Blair Johnston*

Recommended:

○ **Rochberg: String Quartets 3–6** / Concord SQ / 1999 / New World 80551

To the Dark Wood, for woodwind quintet (1985)

The image of passing through the forest at night is a staple of pictorially oriented music since the Romantic period, a trope George Rochberg muses on in his work for wind quintet from 1985, *To the Dark Wood*. "The title of this work is metaphoric and is intended to indicate the nature of the music in the most general sense," the composer wrote in his preface to the piece. "There is no 'program' as such; but there is an expressive tone which pervades and characterizes the atmosphere, the world within which the music takes place: The world of nature and the old mythology which still haunts the mind of man." The work, then, seems not to be about woods, but rather about the long tradition of music about the woods. A wind ensemble, of course, is the obvious choice for a piece of music about the woods. Rochberg even adjusts the standard setup of the wind quintet to highlight the horn, whose own ancestry and sound is closely associated with huntsmen and hunting calls. In addition, according to the composer, the horn "best conveys not only the longing, sadness, and darkness I wanted to express, but also the nobility possible to these qualities." At the same time, the flute, clarinet, and oboe are sometimes given figurations in the style of bird calls. (And, rounding out the forest imagery, it shouldn't be forgotten that the fifth instrument, the bassoon, takes its name from the Italian fagotto, meaning a bundle of branches.) Beyond the symbolic and expressive associations of the instruments, the music itself evokes a kind of archetypal musical woodland. Certainly there are moments that recall—in mood, if not in melody—the eerie scene of Caspar and Max casting the magic bullets in the Wolf's Glen of Weber's *Der Freischütz*. Several passages borrow wholesale from the angular ostinati and delirious turns that accompany the sacrificial rites to the woodland deities of Stravinsky's *Le sacre du printemps*. The piece is structured as a set of juxtaposed tempi and textures designed to play off of the distinctive sounds of each instrument in the ensemble; many passages highlight single instruments in isolation, with intermittent and unobtrusive commentary from the tutti ensemble. Rochberg, while employing a variety of mutes, tone qualities, and articulations, attains a careful balance between idiomatic variety and continuity by intermittently aligning the instruments for strident chordal gestures or plaintive moments of harmonic repose in such a way that one is apt to forget that the ensemble consists of only five players. At the same time, these often sudden shifts of mood are unified by a cohesive, but subtle, thematic structure based on motifs introduced in the work's opening passages—most prominently, stodgy scalar descents and ascents in the bassoon, turning figures in upper winds, and, of course, the distant horn calls that begin and end the work. *—Jeremy Grimshaw*

Recommended:

○ **Westwood Wind Quintet** / 1993 / Crystal 752

Joaquín Rodrigo

b. Nov. 22, 1901, Sagunto, Valencia, Spain, **d.** Jul. 6, 1999, Madrid, Spain

Composer: Concerto, Chamber Music, Vocal

Joaquín Rodrigo is one of the most honored of twentieth century Spanish composers. Several of his compositions, in particular the *Concierto de Aranjuez* for guitar and orchestra, have attained worldwide fame.

Blind from the age of three due to diphtheria, Rodrigo had early musical studies under Francisco Antich in Valencia (1920–23) and Paul Dukas at the *École Normale de Musique* in Paris (1927–32). While in Paris, Rodrigo befriended many of the great composers of the time, and received particular encouragement from his fellow Spaniard Manuel de Falla. In 1933 he married the Turkish pianist Victoria Kamhi; they remained inseparable companions until her death in 1997.

After returning to Spain in 1934, Rodrigo quickly won, with some help from Falla, the Conde de Cartagena scholarship that allowed him to return to Paris to study musicology—with Maurice Emmanuel at the Paris Conservatoire and with André Pirro at the Sorbonne. Some of the most difficult years in Rodrigo's life were in the late 1930s during the Spanish Civil War: his scholarship was cancelled, and he and his wife lived in France and Germany, virtually penniless. They made a meager living giving Spanish and music lessons at the Institute for the Blind in Freiburg. But by 1939, they were able to return to Spain.

Rodrigo started composing in 1923, and won a National Prize in 1925 for his *Cinco Piezas Infantiles* for orchestra. (Due to his blindness, Rodrigo has always composed in Braille, and later painstakingly dictated the music to a copyist.) But his real breakthrough as a composer was with the *Concierto de Aranjuez* (1940, for guitar and orchestra), which was acclaimed from its first performance in Barcelona. Rodrigo was quickly recognized as one of Spain's great composers, and the awards and commissions started to roll in. In 1947, the Manuel de Falla Chair was created for him at the University of Madrid, where he taught music history for many years. He was much in demand as a pianist and lecturer, travelling to Europe, Central America, the U.S., Israel and Japan. Many of the world's great instrumentalists commissioned concertos of him, and he eventually wrote works for, among others, guitarist Andrés Segovia, flutist James Galway, harpist Nicanor Zabaleta, and cellist Julian Lloyd Webber.

In 1953, he was awarded the Cross of Alfonso X the Wise by the Spanish government, and as part of the celebration of his ninetieth birthday in 1991, Rodrigo was raised to the nobility by King Juan Carlos I with the title "Marqués de los jardines de Aranjuez." He was ultimately given Spain's highest international honor, the Prince of Asturias Prize for the Arts, in 1996. The government of France also recognized Rodrigo's importance, making him a Chevalier de la Légion d'Honneur in 1960 and promoting him to Commandeur des Arts et des Lettres in 1998. By the end of his life, he had also received six honorary doctorates from universities worldwide. Rodrigo died in 1999; he and his wife are both buried at the cemetery at Aranjuez. *—Chris Morrison*

CONCERTO

Concierto de Aranjuez, for guitar & orchestra (1939)

The *Concierto de Aranjuez* was Joaquín Rodrigo's first attempt in the concerto genre; it quickly became, and has subsequently remained, the most popular and recognizable of his works. Written for solo guitar and orchestra, it reveals the composer's great affinity for those two mediums, as well as his reverence for the long-standing traditions of Spanish Classical music. It was composed after Rodrigo's return to Madrid from France (he fled the turmoil of the Spanish Civil War) in 1939, and premiered there to great success in 1940.

Aside from its overt references to Spanish folk music and straightforward lyrical disposition, the *Concierto de Aranjuez* is notable for the way in which Rodrigo managed to wed the relatively small voice of the solo guitar to that of the full orchestra. His writing is extremely idiomatic for both guitar and orchestra, and one leaves a hearing of the work with the impression that writing for the two together is quite natural; the guitar never seems overmatched or out of its element. Rodrigo's orchestration is simple, clear, and yet interesting: at times he creates a dialog between soloist and ensemble, and at others he manages to turn them together into one giant guitar—an extremely imaginative and successful effect. Rodrigo also creates distinctive colors by combining the guitar with other solo instruments, such as the bassoon.

The opening movement (Allegro con Spirito) is primarily constructed from a single rhythmic motive, introduced at the outset by the solo guitar. This is later combined with a number of more lyrical themes, all of which are reminiscent of Spanish folk song. The mood turns melancholy in the second movement (Adagio), as the soloist accompanies a solo English horn with simple chords. The guitar eventually takes up this theme against an urgent orchestral background. As with the opening movement, the soloist introduces the main idea of the finale—a rather swaying and gentle melody; this theme becomes the basis for a long "conversation" involving many different solo instruments.*—Allen Schrott*

Recommended:

- ○ **Rodrigo: Concierto de Aranjuez; Fantasia para un Gentilhombre; Concierto Madrigal** / Marriner (cond.), Romero, Academy of St. Martin-in-the-Fields / 1992 / Philips 432828
- ○ **Rodrigo: Concierto de Aranjuez** / Foster (cond.), Isbin, Lausanne CO / 1991 / Virgin 59024
- ○ **The Great Guitar Concertos** / Fremaux (cond.), Williams / 1989 / CBS 44791
- ○ **Rodrigo & Villa-Lobos** / Gardiner (cond.), Bream, Munich Monteverdi Orch. / 1991 / BMG 6525

Concierto madrigal, for 2 guitars & orchestra (1966)

Rodrigo began this two-guitar concerto in 1966, intending it for the husband-and-wife duo of Alexandre Lagoya and Ida Presti. The 1970 premiere, however, fell to Pepe and Angel Romero, who recorded it several years later. More a suite than a traditional concerto, the *Concierto madrigal* falls into ten brief movements, many of them based on the anonymous Renaissance madrigal "Felices ojos mios" (Happy Eyes of Mine). The composer wrote that "the element that sustains [the work] is the variation. Each of the variations or episodes is indicated by the title, which gives a clue to its atmosphere or scenario, a delicate poetic sketching that imbues the whole score. At times, because of the origin of the theme, the episodes have a modal or archaic character; at other times, the melody that acts as a thread through the whole work is permeated by a much more popular feeling." All in all, the concerto is more akin to Rodrigo's similarly archaic *Fantasía para un gentilhombre* than to his more Romantic *Concierto de Aranjuez.*

The soloists gallop in during the opening "Fanfarre" (Allegro marziale), then the flute presents the madrigal theme over guitar accompaniment in the movement called Madrigal (Andante nostalgico). "Entrada" (Allegro vivace) transforms a fragment of the madrigal tune into a balletic duet. The ensuing Allegro vivace offers an antiphonal conversation between guitars, trumpet, and woodwinds based on the fifteenth century villancico "Pastorcito, tue que vienes, pastorcito, tu que vas" (Little shepherd, you who come, little shepherd, you who go). That tune is transformed into a fleet, urgent Andalusian dance in "Girardilla" (Presto); the movement's name is derived from a word for spin or pirouette.

The glittering "Pastoral" (Allegro), with suggestions of chiming bells, is interrupted by the fanfare from the first movement. Next, the "Fandango" traces that popular flamenco dance back to its more stately roots in the eighteenth century. The beautiful "Arieta" (Andante nostalgico) is by far the concerto's longest movement, with the madrigal theme now appearing in triple time over a hypnotic, descending accompaniment. The Zapateado (Allegro vivace) is a stomping Spanish dance pushing the soloists close to their limits of technique. The concluding "Caccia a la española" (Spanish hunt; Allegro vivace—Andante nostalgico) is a similar but less frenetic movement, still with piquant harmonies, and briefly quoting Rodrigo's *Concierto de Aranjuez* before bringing back madrigal theme at the end. *—James Reel*

Recommended:

- ○ **Rodrigo: Concierto de Aranjuez; Fantasia para un Gentilhombre; Concierto Madrigal** / Marriner (cond.), P. Romero, A. Romero, Academy of St. Martin-in-the-Fields / 1992 / Philips 432828
- ○ **Joaquín Rodrigo** / Navarro (cond.), Yepes, Monden, London PO / 2000 / DG 469190

Concierto para una fiesta, for guitar & orchestra (1982)

The "fiesta" from which Rodrigo's final guitar concerto takes its title was a coming out party for Texas debutantes Alden and Lauri McKay; their parents, William and Carol McKay, commissioned the concerto and had it premiered in 1983 by Pepe Romero and the Fort Worth Chamber Orchestra conducted by John Giordano. Despite the occasion of the commission and premiere, this is not a frivolous work, and from the soloist's standpoint it is one of the most difficult concertos in the repertory.

Bold, strummed guitar chords announce the first movement, Allegro deciso, after which the soloist takes on non-stop passagework while the woodwinds offer tart thematic fragments in A minor, which the strings interrupt with broader statements. A second, even more lyrical and nostalgic theme, almost Moorish, arrives in D minor. All the music carries a strong Spanish flavor; Rodrigo described it as Valencian. Rodrigo subjects these two themes to traditional classical development, with the guitar essentially providing a motoric accompaniment to the orchestra's more prominent thematic manipulations. Midway through the movement, though, the orchestra silences itself while the guitar undertakes a long, fully written out cadenza, which ultimately leads the orchestra into a recapitulation of the themes.

With its prominent use of English horn, the second movement, Andante calmo, invites comparison to the slow movement of Rodrigo's *Concierto de Aranjuez* of 43 years earlier. But instead of the serenity of the earlier work, Rodrigo here devises a movement of restlessness and quiet tension thanks to its rhythmic complexity. Two bars of 6/8 alternate with one of 5/8, with different groupings within each bar creating further metrical unpredictability. Again, the soloist is mainly assigned rhythmic, almost accompanimental material while the orchestra (predominantly woodwinds) provides the melodies. The guitar comes to the fore only in the written out cadenza, which increases the tension through intricate passagework before relaxing into a rhythmically simpler, ballad-like section.

The concluding Allegro moderato is an extroverted rondo, using an Andalusian sevillanas as its principal theme (and thereby evoking a bullfight more than a debutante's ball). Of the two secondary themes, the first is a piquant, strutting tune for woodwinds and brass; the second is a soaring melody for strings, recalling material from the first movement. *—James Reel*

Recommended:

- ○ **Rodrigo: Complete Concertos for Guitar & Harp** / Marriner (cond.), P. Romero, Academy of St. Martin-in-the-Fields / 199 / Philips 462296
- ○ **Rodrigo: Complete Orchestral Works, Vol. 5** / Valdes (cond.), Gallen, Asturias SO / 2003 / Naxos 8555842

Fantasía para un gentilhombre, for guitar & orchestra (1954)

In the *Fantasía para un gentilhombre* of 1954, written for and dedicated to Andrés Segovia, Joaquín Rodrigo turned for inspiration to a fellow Spaniard and one of the first great guitar virtuosi, Gaspar Sanz. Not much is known about Sanz. He was born somewhere around the middle of the seventeenth century and lived into the early eighteenth, and he wrote one of the earliest surviving guitar methods (published in 1674). He also composed a fair amount of guitar music that reflects the styles of song and dance popular in Spain at that time. Rodrigo borrowed several of Sanz's short pieces in crafting his *Fantasía* for guitar and orchestra. The result is a perennially charming work that evokes an antique world in a natural way, free of musty airs.

The opening movement is titled "Villano y Ricercare"; the Villano theme is heard in the violins at the very beginning of the work, and the Ricercare was completed by Rodrigo based on Sanz's sketches. The second movement, "Españoleta y Fanfare de la Caballería de Nápoles," is also in two parts. After a short woodwind introduction, the Españoleta theme, first heard in the strings, is subjected to several variations. The Fanfare makes use of string techniques like harmonics and col legno (using the wooden side of the bow); the title of the Fanfare reminds one that Spain governed Naples in Sanz's time. The guitar moves between solo and accompanist roles in the third movement "Danza de las Hachas," or "Hatchet Dance," and the *Fantasía* ends with a rousing "Canario," a folk dance in 6/8 time. *—Chris Morrison*

Recommended:

- ○ **Rodrigo: Concierto de Aranjuez; Fantasia para un Gentilhombre; Concierto Madrigal** / Marriner (cond.), P. Romero, Academy of St. Martin-in-the-Fields / 1992 / Philips 432828
- ○ **The Segovia Collection, Vol. 1** / Jorda (cond.), Segovia, Symphony of the Air / 2003 / DG 000066202
- ○ **Rodrigo: Concierto de Aranjuez; Walton: 5 Bagatelles** / Litton (cond.), Parkening, Royal PO / 1993 / EMI 54665
- ○ **The Great Guitar Concertos** / Fremaux (cond.), Williams / 1989 / CBS 44791

CHAMBER MUSIC

En los trigales, for guitar (Por los campos de España No. 1) (1938)

Rodrigo described this little piece as part of an "imaginary" suite touring the Spanish landscape. The composer managed neither to write music about every region nor to group what he did accomplish into a formal suite, although *Junto al Generalife* and *Bajando de la meseta* are also part of this family. *En los trigales* takes the listener to a wheat field in Castilla la Vieja. Rodrigo remarked that the people there have a taste for loud music, but this piece, no matter how fast and intricate its outer sections may be, lurks mainly at the low end of the dynamic scale. It begins with a quick figure immediately repeated more softly, as if a call and response between two field workers. This is more of a virile dance than a song, however, strongly accented with fast turns. The dance winds down and the music becomes more truly vocal, a very free recitative ornamented with an imitation of distant bell sounds in the instrument's high register, complete with harmonics. With fast runs up and down the scale, the dance music returns, but now the dance is heard from a greater remove and ends with a single, quietly ringing high note. *—James Reel*

Recommended:

○ **Spanish Guitar Music** / Yepes / 2003 / DG 474437

Invocación y danza, for guitar ("Homenaje a Manuel de Falla") (1962)

Rodrigo's tribute to Falla quotes passages from the earlier composer's scores, but is unmistakably the work of the later Spanish master. Yet it's not in the sunny, Spanish neo-Classical style of Rodrigo's popular guitar concertos; rather, it takes on the darker hues of much of his other, far less well-known work. It won the 1961 Coupe International de Guitare, a competition organized by the French broadcasting company. The "Invocation" section opens with a brief quote from Falla's *Le tombeau de Claude Debussy* (his only score originally for guitar, which itself quotes Debussy's *La soirée dans Grenade*). The music begins softly, with bell-like harmonics on the upper strings and a more resonant but hazily defined melody played on the bass string. The music becomes more animated and increasingly urgent, full of tremolos and obsessive repetitions of arpeggios and small phrases. Embedded in this at one point is the smallest hint of a rhythm from Falla's *El sombrero de tres picos*, although this is not developed. The "Dance" section offers quick relief from the tension of the first section, although it does not break into all-out exuberance. Marked Allegro moderato poco, it's a graceful, skipping dance with a hint of nostalgia (thanks to its B minor tonality). A second section revives the intensity of the "Invocation," returning to tremolo writing and arpeggios that elevate the needs of rhythm above those of melody. The more easygoing dance tune returns, but soon winds down into material reminiscent of the Invocation's opening passages, except that now the quote—barely recognizable—is from Falla's *El Amor brujo*. *—James Reel*

Recommended:

○ **Road to the Sun** / Isbin / 1990 / Virgin 59591

○ **Possession** / Afshar / 2002 / Archer 1919

Tres piezas españolas, for guitar (1954)

The first of Joaquín Rodrigo's *Tres piezas españolas* might strike the unfamiliar listener as just darned wrong. The guitarist—necessarily a virtuoso of high sophistication—goes to sweep the six shiny strings with polished thumbnail and produces a massive, and massively crunchy, six-note chord. What makes the sensual dissonance a cognitive dissonance as well is the chord's ringing origin? It is a big major chord, its rhetoric the big major-chord rhetoric of pompous Spanish pageant music, processions, and showy dancers. In injecting his famous wrong notes into not one but three all-string chords, Rodrigo makes two declarations: first, that he remains faithfully entrenched in national traditions (the title is "Fandango," the motives unmistakably Spanish in contour); and second, that he simultaneously remains Modernist in his perspective. Not perhaps a Schoenberg-modernist, but still donning the goggles of modernism, through which the confidence in the enduring reality of the old and everyday begins to dissolve or mutate, and in which traditional languages, for instance, break and reveal cracks or transform upon reflection into abstractions and absolute designs. From this perspective, Rodrigo is perhaps the mid-twentieth century's arch-modernist of the guitar. All of Rodrigo's creations for the instrument incorporate the archetypes of the Spanish guitar tradition in order to distort or reconceive them. This preservation of tradition may be conservative, but plenty of modernists were utterly dedicated to maintaining the traditions they reworked, under critique. One hears the inflections of this kind of critique in all three of Rodrigo's *Piezas españolas*. The outer movements, the aforementioned "Fandango" and the concluding "Zapateado," employ Spanish dance models with confident openness; but they also play with the expected gestures and harmonies so as to shift their guise from native to new soil. In this, they develop an effect brought to culmination in Rodrigo's guitar masterpiece from 1962, *Invocation and Dance*. The massive middle movement follows a common trope in artistic modernism, whereby a material of folkoric origin (in this case, Spanish elegy) is housed within a foreign, unfolkloric frame (in this case, the Baroque passacaglia). Here, a wrong-note harmony unfolds an expressive countenance whose gravity clearly derives from Bach's own ground-bass works. There is a strange, magical tension between folk gestures like the mid-movement eruption of flamenco-inspired rasgeado chords and the abstract, learned seriousness of the formal genre. But the wrong notes and distorting forms are perhaps not modernist in derivation; their skewed perspectives and crossed eyes look further back. Milder in estrangement effects than Picasso, Rodrigo seems to share with his roughly contemporary compatriot the Spanish awareness of rifts between pride and folly, stentorian majesty and the subversion of the jester. The location of these rifts, and of the poignant goofiness underlying the most serious postures, has been Iberian by right since Don Quixote chased windmills, dreamt of Dulcinea, and cluelessly wandered into the pages of his own book. *—Seth Brodsky*

Recommended:

○ **Rodrigo: Complete Guitar Works, Vol. 2** / Tennant / GHA 126044

VOCAL

Madrigales amatorios (1947; revised 1948)

These four wonderfully lyrical and peculiar love songs have both a neo-classical flavor in the style of their music and a surrealistic flavor in the handling and content of the texts.

"¿Con qué la lavaré?" has a touching Baroque-aria sound in F minor, with passing tones forming modern harmonies. The music could accompany a religious text, but is here a lament that asks with what substance the singer should wash his/her face. Shall it be "timidly... with cascades of lemon water" or "with grief and sadness"?

"Vos me matásteis" has the style of a Bach aria with an Italianate influence. The simple contrapuntal style is a perfect musical match for a text concerning someone enchanted with a young virgin girl on the banks of a river who has remarkable hair in which he feels tied up—"you have killed me," he says. Beautiful Dorian-mode harmonies begin the work. The text, which is only four lines long, is repeated in isolated phrases and reharmonized, taking on a surreal character as a result of this obsessiveness. For example, the words "vos me matásteis" soon are accompanied by descending fourths that alter its originally rich Baroque harmonies into a higher, dry, crystalline territory. The harmony becomes even more advanced with the description "riberas de un río" (on the shores of a river), where the text is accompanied by major seventh chords.

The charming "¿De dónde venís, amore?" is reminiscent of Mozart's *Ein musikalischer Spass*, and is in a jolly Allegro grazioso tempo. There is an ecstatic joy and a kind of teasing to the repetition of the text which continually inquires as to the direction a beloved one is going: "I see it is outside... and that's good to know," followed by "ah ah ah ah" on high staccatos over a major third. The melody itself has a lively Latin folk flavor accompanied by "wrong-note" tone clusters and tinkling motoric patterns.

"De los álamos vengo, madre" in a 2/4 Allegro has a sonatina-like piano introduction with rotating figures around a pedal point that eventually change into straightforward Spanish guitar rhythms. These underscore the text, which urges a mother to go to a stand of poplar trees. There is a steadily increasing Spanish-style melisma and skips of a perfect fourth in those passages that refer to the swaying of the trees in the wind. The text repeats and gradually adds more lines, eventually unfolding a complete image in which the mother is urged to go to see the popular trees in Seville, where the singer's beautiful girlfriend lives. The final exhortation is accompanied by light music box-like tinkling patterns in the high piano registers at a pianissimo dynamic, which leaves an aura of unreality hanging in the air at the conclusion of the whole set. *—"Blue Gene" Tyranny*

Recommended:

○ **The Fabulous Victoria De Los Angeles** / Los Angeles / 1993 / EMI 650612

○ **Debussy, Schubert, Granados, Rodrigo** / Caballe, Rossi / 1994 / Ornamenti 115

Pascal Rogé

b. Apr. 6, 1951, Paris, France

Pianist

It is perhaps not surprising that pianist Pascal Rogé—a third-generation French musician—has mastered the modern French piano repertoire. What is surprising is the actual breadth of his repertoire and the young age at which he excelled.

In 1962, at the age of 11, he was admitted to the Paris Conservatoire, having previously studied with his mother. By the age of fifteen, he had won first prize for both piano and chamber music. At eighteen, he performed solo recitals in both Paris and London. But his major breakthrough was the first prize in the Jacques Thibaud International Competition in 1971. Several European engagements followed, and in 1974 he made his first tour to the United States, returning nearly every season. He has also become a favorite in Australia and Japan, where he has made over twenty tours.

Rogé's particular strengths lie in his sensitive and personal interpretations of twentieth century French composers; he has made recordings of complete cycles of Ravel, Poulenc, and Satie, among others. His repertoire also includes d'Indy, Saint-Saëns, as well as the great German masters—Haydn, Mozart, Brahms, and Beethoven. His recordings have received numerous awards, including the Grand Prix du Disque and an Edison award for the Ravel concertos. His first volume of Poulenc won the 1988 Gramophone award for Best Instrumental Recording, and his collaboration with Chantal Juillet and Truls Mørk won the 1997 Gramophone award for Best Chamber Music recording.

He has taught at the Académie in Nice, but a busy international schedule has kept him from consistent teaching. More stylist than virtuosic, his solo pianism has been recognized for its decidedly French elegance, while his collaboration with orchestras has been noted for its faultless musicianship, and made him a favorite of conductors ranging from Charles Dutoit to Lorin Maazel to Kurt Masur. *—Thomas Oram*

Recommended:

- ○ **Ravel: Piano Works** / Rogé / 1994 / Decca 440836
- ○ **Debussy: Piano Works** / Rogé / 1994 / London 443021
- ○ **Poulenc: Piano Works** / Rogé / 2003 / Decca 475042
- ○ **Satie and the Four-Handed Piano** / Rogé, Collard, Juillet / 2000 / Decca 455401
- ○ **Saint-Saëns: Piano Concertos 1–5** / Dutoit (cond.), Rogé, Royal PO, London PO / 1995 / London 4438652

Lionel Rogg

b. Apr. 21, 1936, Geneva, Switzerland
Organist

Organist and composer Lionel Rogg was born in Geneva, Switzerland and educated at the Conservatory there, taking piano with Nikita Magaloff and organ with Pierre Segond. In 1961, Rogg gave the complete organ works of J.S. Bach in a series of ten recitals at Victoria Hall in Geneva. This established Rogg as one of the primary interpreters of Bach's organ music. His 1970 Angel recording of Bach's *The Art of Fugue* raised some controversy in critical circles as Rogg dared to complete the "Contrapunctus 28," which Bach had left unfinished. In spite of the controversy, the disc earned the Grand Prix du Disque from the Charles Cros Academy that year. Rogg has gone on to record the entire organ works of Bach three times over, his Harmonia Mundi set available on CD. Another complete set of Buxtehude's organ music took the Deutsche Schallplatten Prize in 1980. He has also recorded extensively on the harpsichord and clavicembalo. His recorded output is not exclusively limited to the Baroque period, as he has also recorded the organ music of Liszt, Brahms, and Reger, among others.

Rogg has taught and performed worldwide. In 1972, he was named professor of organ at the Geneva Conservatory, which awarded Rogg an honorary doctorate in 1989. In 1993, he dedicated the new organ installed in Victoria Hall, and since has acted as the organist in charge of this Van der Heuvel instrument.

As a composer, Rogg started out in the early 1950s writing in the serial style favored at that time. His activities as composer broke off as his career as an organist picked up, and Rogg resumed writing only in the 1980s. Casting off the doctrine of serialism in these later works, Rogg's music incorporates a broad number of stylistic elements, adding up to a result that defies distinct categorization. Rogg favors the term "free" in describing his music and these newer compositions have gained wide acceptance in Europe. In his attitude towards serialism, Rogg seems to have been a bit ahead of younger composers working within the post-modern era. Among his notable compositions are the piano duet *Face à Face*, the *Pièce for oboe and synthesizer*, the *Cantata Laudes organi*, and the organ work *Arcature*. A disc of Rogg playing his organ music was released on Wergo in August 2000. Rogg is married and has three children; his son, Olivier, is a jazz pianist. *—Uncle Dave Lewis*

Recommended:

- ○ **Rogg Plays Rogg** / Rogg / 1987 / Bis 346
- ○ **Portrait of a Free Composer** / Rogg, Larrieu, Friedli, Goy / Bis 546
- ○ **Bruckner: Symphony 8** / Rogg / 1997 / Bis 946
- ○ **Bach: Toccata & Fugue in D minor & other favorites** / Rogg / 1999 / EMI 73568

Johan Helmich Roman

b. Oct. 26, 1694, Stockholm, Sweden, **d.** Nov. 20, 1758, Haraldsmåla, Sweden
Composer

The "Father of Swedish Music," Johan Helmich Roman, was one of the most influential Swedish composers of his time, not only because of his numerous compositions, but also for his role in moving the music of the great composers from the royal court to public concerts in Stockholm. He was also influential in promoting the use of the Swedish language in sacred texts and in developing an indigenous tradition of vocal writing in secular and sacred music.

Roman spent a considerable part of his life and career in the courts of Sweden's royalty, from Charles XII to Adolph Fredrik and Lovisa Ulrica. Roman received an early education in music. His father served as a member of the court orchestra and at the age of seven, Roman performed as a violinist for the court. At the age of 16, he became a permanent member of the court orchestra. Roman is thought to have mastered many different instruments, but his primary interests were the violin and oboe.

Roman lived and worked in a time where music was in transition between Baroque and Classical styles. His music was influenced by the English and Italians, no doubt due to his contacts with Handel and Geminiani. However, there are also subtle flavors of French and German influence. He traveled abroad twice in his career; first to England from 1715 to 1721, and then an extensive tour of Europe from 1735 to 1737. During his European journey, Roman returned to England and then ventured on to Germany, Austria, France, and Italy. These travels allowed him to experience the music endemic to their region and to study with composers such as Pepusch.

During the reign of Charles XII, in 1721, Roman was appointed vice-kapellmeister of the royal chapel orchestra. On January 23, 1927, he achieved the position of Kapellmeister under the reign of Fredrik and Ulrica. It was under this new authority that he instigated the transition of musical performances from the nobles' courts to the bourgeoisie public. In addition to providing a larger audience for his own compositions, these concerts for the common people also served as vehicles with which to introduce foreign musical works.

There is little written record available today that details Roman's compositional career; much of what is written has relied on sources whose accuracy has been called into question. It appears to have begun in the mid-1720s. Roman's earliest known composition is the cantata *Festa musicale* (1725). During this period (1725–30), Roman produced a variety of cantatas, sonatas, and suites. In particular, he composed *12 Flute Sonatas* (1727), which was followed by *Golovin-musik* in 1728 and the *Suite 8*, circa 1730. The 1730s and 1740s were perhaps his most productive years. The suite in E major, a suite in D major, and his most famous orchestral suite, *Drottningholmsmusik*, were products of this period. Beyond this, it appears that Roman focused on sacred songs.

Roman survived two wives who bore him seven children between them. His first wife, whom he married in 1730, died four years later. He married his second wife in 1738, who died two years after she gave birth to their fourth child. In addition to the burden of raising a household of small children, Roman was afflicted with increasing deafness and later, increasingly poor health. These burdens made it more difficult to continue his duties in the capital, so in the mid-1740s he moved to the Baltic coast, where he translated theoretical works about music into Swedish. *—Bruce Lundgren*

Overview of Works (ca. 1720–1750)

Described as "the father of Swedish music," Roman not only composed and performed extensively for state and church festivities, but also was a tireless organizer of musical resources within his own country. Working at Sweden's royal court for much of his life, he assembled a first-rate orchestra and choir and led the musicians in performances both of his own works and of the finest international music of his time that he could assemble. He translated choral texts into Swedish and, in addition, produced translations of several treatises on music performance.

In his own music, Roman reflected the influences of his contemporaries, most obviously Handel. Only in his sacred works may one detect strains of native Swedish music; otherwise, Roman absorbed elements of the best music his time had to offer. In his lifetime, only two of his works found their way to publication. In 1727, his *Seven Sonatas for violin, viola da gamba and harpsichord* were issued and, in 1740, an *Assaggio for solo violin or viola* entered print. Several manuscripts were destroyed in an 1827 fire at the University of Åbo's library. Most, however, now reside within the libraries of the University of Uppsala and the Royal Academy of Music in Stockholm. Some are originals, others copies by as many as 200 various other hands.

Among the works composed by Roman are 21 symphonies, two church symphonies, six overtures, five suites, two concerti grossi, 82 motets, three cantatas, a *Svenska Messan* (1752), a substantial quantity of songs with continuo or orchestra, a dozen chamber sonatas, 17 trio sonatas, 20 or more solo sonatas for violin or viola, 12 harpsichord sonatas, a sonata for solo flute, 12 harpsichord suites, five violin concertos, a concerto for oboe d' amore and several more miscellaneous pieces. One of his most acclaimed suites, the *Drottningholmsmusiquen*, was written for the royal wedding in 1744. Despite the derivative aspects of his style, Roman was no traditionalist; he absorbed conservative and modern influences alike. The large number of symphonies in his output is notable for so early a date, and he was acquainted with the works of some of the composers who forged the galant style—Leo and Telemann, among others. *—Erik Eriksson*

Recommended:

- ○ **Roman: 12 Suites for Harpsichord** / Payne / 1994 / Bis 669
- ○ **Roman: Violin Concertos; Sinfonias** / Sparf, Orpheus CO / 1985 / Bis 284
- ○ **Roman: Sonatas & Assaggi** / Schroder, Sonnleitner / 1987 / Caprice 21344
- ○ **Roman: Drottingholms Musique; Concerto Grosso** / Bjorlin (cond.), Hucke, Capella Coloniensis / Capriccio 10624
- ○ **Roman: Songs** / Ryden, Sparf, Aberg, Gafvert, Nordenfelt, Ottesen / SCD 1066

Sigmund Romberg

b. Jul. 29, 1887, Nagykanizsa, Hungary, **d.** Nov. 9, 1951, Hartsdale, NY
Composer: Opera

Sigmund Romberg is best known for his operettas, among which were *Blossom Time* (1921), *The Student Prince* (1924), and *The Desert Song* (1926). He developed a style based on European Romantic operettas of the late nineteenth and early twentieth centuries, but eventually began writing in a more American style. With his 1945 *Up in Central Park* he had jettisoned European influences altogether in favor of the popular style of American musical comedy. He also wrote many songs for films and adapted his operettas to film. In addition, Romberg was a conductor of his own orchestra, playing mostly his own music.

Romberg was born in Nagykanizsa (Szeged), Hungary (then Austria-Hungary), on July 29, 1887. As a child, he showed musical ability early on and would develop talent as both a violinist and organist. Despite his musical proclivities, he studied engineering in his late teens in Vienna. But he also took instruction in composition there from Heuberger. Apparently his will to take on a profession in engineering was never very strong, and he decided on a career in music by his early twenties. After a stint in the Hungarian army, he traveled to the United States in 1909, believing the level of competition in music would be lower there and thus offer him greater opportunity.

After arriving on American shores, he found it necessary to take a job briefly in a pencil factory. But he soon obtained a position as a pianist in a café, and then became leader of an orchestra at a large and fashionable restaurant in New York. He was instrumental in developing the practice of playing dance music for the patrons of such establishments. In 1914, he was hired by Jacob Shubert to compose for musical shows. That same year he produced his first significant effort, *The Whirl of the World.* His first great success came in 1917, however, with the operetta *Maytime* (story and lyrics by R. J. Young and C. Wood).

In the 1920s, Romberg had a string of hits, beginning with *Blossom Time* in 1921, its story based on the life of Franz Schubert. Three years later, from the German operetta *Alt Heidelberg,* he fashioned *The Student Prince.* Romberg often used the music of other composers, as in the 1920 effort, *Poor Little Ritz Girl,* which used songs of Richard Rogers, and the 1928 *The New Moon,* that featured a melody partially derived from one by Tchaikovsky.

In 1929, Romberg began writing songs for motion pictures. A few years later he moved to Hollywood and began writing scores for film. He also was involved there in the motion picture adaptation of some of his operettas.

In 1942, Romberg formed his own orchestra and went on concert tour throughout the United States. With few breaks over the next decade, he continued to lead the ensemble until his death on November 9, 1951. In the first year of its tour, the orchestra performed a program of his music entitled *An Evening with Sigmund Romberg.* During the war years Romberg was not very productive as a composer, but in 1945 he wrote *Up in Central Park* (H. and Dorothy Fields), which he helped to adapt to film three years later.

A film was made about Romberg's life, entitled *Deep in my Heart.* It starred José Ferrer as Romberg, and was directed by Stanley Donen. The film features many of his most popular songs including "Lover Come Back to Me," "When I Grow Too Old to Dream," and "Stout-Hearted Men." *—Robert Cummings*

OPERA

The Desert Song (1926)

Desert Song is an exciting carryover from the theater productions of the roaring twenties. It is a three act musical play with an excellent libretto by Otto Harbach, Oscar Hammerstein II, and Frank Mandel. The production came at the peak of Romberg's career on Broadway, after the amazing success of *The Student Prince* and directly before the beautiful and popular musical *New Moon.* The show features a north African setting, the intrigue of a mysterious Arab chieftain who leads forays against the army in the deserts, and a romance which begins after the abduction of the main heroine. The show became an international success within the first few years of its existence, having lengthy runs not only on New York's Broadway and at London's Covent Garden, but in various theaters in Australia and France as well. *Desert Song* even became part of the repertoire of the New York City Opera.

The show began life entitled "Lady Fair," and opened first at Poli's Theater in Washington. When it went to Broadway, the producers changed its name to *Desert Song,* to capitalize on the exotic and strange locale of the play. The show's opening on Broadway took place at the Casino Theater in New York City on November 30, 1926. Opening night could have been a fiasco: a wooden ceiling beam fell, taking much of the scenery with it, and a donkey in the cast began braying loudly on stage. But the catchy music of Romberg and the excitement of the new play made for a successful evening despite the setbacks.

Several of the tunes, including "The Riff Song" and "One Alone," have since become standards in the popular song repertory. *Desert Song* was turned into a movie more than once; in 1929, 1943, and again in 1953 with Gordon Macrae and Kathryn Grayson. Nelson Eddy appeared as the mysterious "Red Shadow," the heroic Arab chieftain in the story, in a television version of the play. There have been many revivals of *Desert Song* since its inception, and it will remain an important part of American musical theatrical history in years to come. *—Rita Laurance*

Synopsis:

Act One. The show opens in the Riff Mountains of North Africa at the hideout of the Red Shadow and his gang. The are bold Morrocan raiders, trying to fight for their land against the French occupying forces. They are celebrating their camaraderie and the boldness of the chieftain, the Red Shadow. The French forces are seen approaching, and the men get ready to go and meet them in battle. The army Captain Paul Fontaine enters with two men, and they have a skirmish with some of the Arabs.

The Red Shadow is really the son of the French Governor of the region and in love with Margot Bonvalet. He disguises himself to lead his Arab friends against the forces of his father, but is known to the French soldiers and girls as Pierre. While Captain Paul reviews his troops back at the camp, Pierre sings Margot a love song and tries to woo her. She is unmoved, but the entire camp rejoices that he is in love. While she spurns him, the rest of the girls encourage him. And Bennie, a society columnist turned war corespondent, is in love with his secretary Susan. Plenty of dancing and singing surround both couples.

Pierre decides to get his friends to help him abduct Margot and carry her off by force, into the Riff mountains at his hideout. The two have a brief love scene when Pierre confronts her in his disguise as the Red Shadow. But Margot quickly calls for help and decides to marry Captain Paul instead. The girls all congratulate her and engage in a dance with the not too steady Captain, who seems to love all of the girls, especially the Arab girl Azuri. Pierre returns as himself and wishes Margot a lukewarm congratulations, while desperately trying to think of a way to get her to fall in love with him instead. The couple exits happily, with plans for a honeymoon in Paris.

Fires are seen on the hillside, and the entire French camp sounds the alarm. It is the band of the Red Shadow approaching! His forces enter and quickly subdue the French. He stands before Margot unarmed, and pleads with her to come along with him into the mountains, for the sake of romance and the beauty of the desert nights. By the time he carries her off, they are falling in love.

Act Two. Pierre has taken Margot and his men to hide in the harem of Ali Ben Ali. At first Margot misses Pierre and rejects The Red Shadow's advances. The harem girls all try to coach her in the art of falling in love, and gradually she finds herself succumbing. Bennie has also been taken captive and, finding himself surrounded by beautiful women all paying him lavish attention, doesn't know which way to turn. Love scenes for various members of the cast follow one after another in succession, until finally the overall exuberance is interrupted by the unexpected arrival of General Birabeau and his men. He has come to rescue Margot. When he enters the harem and confronts those assembled, the Red Shadow refuses to fight him, and tells Margot that she is free to leave. He is immediately disgraced in the eyes of his men, and loses his authority as their leader. He sadly says good-bye to each of his men, and Hassi takes over as the leader of the band of rebels. Then the infamous Red Shadow goes into hiding. There is now a price on his head, and if he is captured, he will be executed.

Back at the French camp, there are celebrations in honor of the bravery of General Birabeau, but Margot pines for the open desert skies and her lovely romance. The search for the Red Shadow continues until finally Azuri tells General Birabeau that the man he is seeking is none other than his own son. And Pierre returns to reveal his true identity to Margot. He shows her the costume of the Red Shadow and confesses that he led the raids against his father's forces. The two are reunited, and the show ends happily. *—Rita Laurance*

Recommended:

○ **The Desert Song; New Moon** / Grove (cond.), Evans, Hart, Knight, Vola / 2002 / Decca 018730

The New Moon (1928)

The New Moon was the last Broadway success of Sigmund Romberg before he moved on to the stages of Hollywood. It has the same romantic historical setting as Victor Herbert's *Naughty Marietta,* taking place in New Orleans on the eve of the French Revolution, and there are many other plot similarities. It features intrigue, disguises, a fugitive from justice, and an illicit romance. The original version was tried out at the Chestnut Street Opera House in Philadelphia. Romberg and his crew of writers, which included Oscar Hammerstein II (who wrote most of the song lyrics), Laurence Schwab, and Frank Mandel, worked to create a more effective piece. They added several new numbers, so that by the time of the second opening in Cleveland on August 27, 1928, the score was saturated with fine music and delightful songs. The highly romantic plot resulted in many new popular numbers, such as "Marianne" and "Lover, Come Back to Me." It was smash hit on Broadway, running for 509 performances, and traveled to international theaters as well. *The New Moon* was filmed twice. A 1930 version starring Lawrence Tibbett bore only a passing resemblance to the operetta's plot, but the 1940 film, entitled *New Moon* and starring Nelson Eddy and Jeanette MacDonald, was closer to the original.

By that time, a certain resistance to the suspension of disbelief operetta requires had set in among audiences and critics. Bosley Crowther of *The New York Times* mocked the plot. "With tears welling in our eyes, (sniff, sniff), we rather sadly suspect that this sort of sugar-coated musical fiction has seen its better days," he wrote in his review of the film, and other critics were similarly snarky. All were in agreement as to the high quality of Romberg's songs, however, and the plots of earlier Romberg operettas were no less preposterous. What has kept *The New Moon* from being as familiar as *Naughty Marietta* or *The Student Prince* is perhaps its chronological place at the end of operetta's reign over the musical stage. Other factors that discourage smaller theater companies from attempting productions of the show are its difficult vocal parts (Romberg resisted what he saw as a decline in the vocal abilities of musical stage performers) and its dated treatment of race relations. *—AMG*

Synopsis:

Act One. In the mansion of the wealthy New Orleans ship owner Monsieur Beaunoir, a seamstress is showing off a beautiful party gown of gossamer to some of the maids. Monsieur Beaunoir calls to one of them, named Julie, telling her to have everything in order for the arrival of their illustrious guest. It is a private detective from Paris, whom Monsieur Beaunoir wishes to hire to track down a fugitive from the French government. The detective is none other than the Vicomte Ribaud, the "secret eye" of the King of France. It is the eve of the French Revolution, and those with egalitarian sentiments are suspected and watched closely. Monsieur Beaunoir wishes to impress his royal guest with the lavishness of his hospitality. Monsieur Ribaud arrives accompanied by 12 courtiers, making a grand entrance. Monsieur Beaunoir asks him to spy on his bondservant Robert, in the hopes of discovering his true identity. Meanwhile, Robert is madly in love with Beaunoir's daughter Marianne. She has grown up on ships and is the darling of all the sailors. Duval, the Captain of the New Moon, also is in love with her, and while he tries to sing her a love song of his own composing, Robert interrupts repeatedly, awkwardly trying to interfere and get Marianne's attention.

The Vicomte Ribaud goes to the Chez Creole Tavern where he tries to gain information about Robert from Philippe. Dancing girls join in a song and chorus, and a bar fight breaks out. When Robert joins them, he rallies all those in the Tavern to join in defense of liberty and revolution.

The Beaunoirs' are having a cotillion at which Marianne plans to raffle off a kiss. Robert decides to go. He is now a runaway servant, and must disguise himself as a nobleman. Philippe worries that Robert may be caught and imprisoned. But Robert loves Marianne and longs to make a good impression on her. Dancing opens the evening's festivities. Then Robert wins the raffle with the help of Alexander, and he has just enough time alone with Marianne to declare his love for her. Vicomte Ribaud recognizes Robert as soon as he enters the room, and lays a trap for him. He will have his victory, too, he says to Beaunoir, before the evening is over. After Marianne and Robert have kissed, Ribaud enters and unmasks him. He declares before all present that it is Le Chevalier Robert Misson, wanted by King Louis XIV of France for treason, and that he is to be sent back to France to be tried and executed. Ribaud orders the sailors of the New Moon to take Robert all the way to France for his trial. Marianne pleads to be allowed to go along, for Robert now thinks that she helped with his capture.

Act Two. On the New Moon, the sailors are in preparation for the long voyage. None of them think that the trip is a good idea, and none of them feel any particular allegiance to the King of France. Robert is taken down to the brig, where Ribaud plans to cross examine him. Meanwhile, Marianne has come aboard and gives her maid a poem and a love letter to give to him.

A flag is spotted on the horizon, and all the sailors begin to watch with trepidation. It is Captain Ramsey's ship, a pirate known for marauding on the high seas. As the pirates begin bearing down on the New Moon, Captain Duval orders the prisoners released, so that they may join in the defense of the ship. But Robert immediately rallies the men to him and has Duval thrown in the brig. He seizes command of the New Moon and tells all to fight for their lives. But when the pirates board the ship, Robert discovers that they are led by his old friend Philippe, and have come to rescue him. Robert and Philippe have long dreamed of setting up a commune in a free land, full of people who believed in equality and liberty. Now they invite Marianne to join them. She is an aristocrat and at first thinks that they are just dreamers. But she is soon convinced that they will all be happy together. They sail off to form a republic, and Marianne and Robert agree to get married. After they are settled in their new home, news is brought of the beginning of the French Revolution. *—Rita Laurance*

Recommended:

- ○ **Music Of Sigmund Romberg** / Alexander (cond.), Kirsten, MacRae, Robinson, Wilkie, Roger Wagner Chorale & Orch. / 1987 / EMI 69052

The Student Prince (1924)

The Student Prince, a musical play with book and lyrics by Dorothy Donnelley and music by Sigmund Romberg, remains one of America's all-time musical theater classics. It was one of Romberg's greatest and most lasting successes, and came after a period of struggle with his producers, the Schubert brothers. He had to fight a legal battle with them in court over the content of the play; Romberg won and, ironically, the Schuberts enjoyed one of the biggest successes of their careers. The musical opened in New York City's Jolson Theater on December 2, 1924, and ran for six hundred and eight performances. After that, it toured extensively throughout the U.S., and even entered the international repertoire. MGM made a very popular film version of the musical in 1954, and New York City Opera began staging productions of it.

The writing of the book for the musical has quite an involved history of its own. The original version of *Old Heidelberg* was written by Wilhelm Meyer-Forster in 1901. It became well known internationally, and was especially popular in American theaters in its translation. It inspired several other theatrical version of the story, and even an Italian operetta. A version of *Old Heidelberg* in English by Rudolf Bleichmann was known to Dorothy Donnelly, and she based her musical play on this. The story is singular in the history of the early American theater, for it offers the audience no happy ending or fanfare conclusion; instead of dancing girls and light hearted comedy, it uses an all-male chorus of Heidelberg University students. Indeed, it is the type of story that might have been set by Lehár, given as a Viennese operetta. Romberg, a transplant to America from Hungary, had studied in Vienna, and he laced his score with polkas, marches, and operatic dance music. He filled the musical with memorable tunes, including both romantic ballads and vigorous set pieces. A poignant youthful romance, a university setting in Old Heidelberg, royalty and humbleness, all gave Romberg food for musical variety and inventiveness. "Golden Days," "Drinking Song," and "Serenade" are just of the few songs of enduring popularity from the show. *The Student Prince* is perhaps Romberg's finest masterpiece. *—Rita Laurance*

Recommended:

- ○ **Romberg: The Student Prince** / Engel (cond.), Kirsten, Rounseville, Dalton, Harvuot, Warner / 2002 / DRG 19018

Angel Romero

b. Aug. 17, 1946, Málaga, Spain

Guitarist

Of the guitarists of Spain's renowned Romero family, Angel Romero is noteworthy for the breadth of his musical activities. He has performed and recorded often with other family members, especially his brother Pepe, but his own career has taken an increasingly independent course.

The youngest of the the three performer sons of Celedonio Romero, Angel Romero was born in Málaga, Spain, in 1946. He gave his first professional performance at age six and was an international touring artist by the time he was in his mid-teens. The Romero family moved to California in 1957 to escape restrictions placed on them by the Franco dictatorship in Spain, and his first performance in the U.S. came when he was 16, at the Hollywood Bowl. Since then, Romero has been a familiar recitalist and soloist in all the major European and American capitals. He was especially close to the well-loved Spanish composer Joaquín Rodrigo and gave the premiere of that composer's *Rincones de España* in 1991. Romero studied conducting with Eugene Ormandy and in 1998 recorded a disc with the Academy of St. Martin-in-the-Fields as both guitarist and conductor. That recording was one of more than 20 Romero has released. Later on he has was affiliated with the Delos label. In 1986 Romero was given the Spanish Grand Cross of Civil Merit, and in 2000 he was honored with the Spanish equivalent of knighthood and began to use the name Sir Angel Romero.

In the 1980s and 1990s, Romero branched off in several new directions. With pianist George Shearing he recorded French composer Claude Bolling's *Concerto for guitar and jazz piano trio.* He was especially associated with film music, performing the whole score of the 1989 Robert Redford-directed epic *The Milagro Beanfield War* and composed scores for several other films, winning a Mexican Ariel award (similar to a U.S. Academy award) for his score for the film *Bienvendido* in 1995. He recorded crossover and flamenco material, which resulted in a new demand for his services among mid-sized U.S. orchestras that featured pops-oriented programming. *The New York Times* has said that Romero is "an artist of unfailing musicality. His playing is virtuosic but inevitably dignified." His is a secure place in the long line of Spanish guitarists issuing from the Segovia tradition, and he is an especially accessible representative of that tradition. *—James Manheim*

Recommended:

- ○ **Angel Romero: Spanish Guitar Virtuoso** / A. Romero / 2000 / Seraphim 74015
- ○ **Bella: The Incomparable Artistry of Angel Romero** / A. Romero / 2001 / Delos 3294
- ○ **Rodrigo & Vivaldi Concertos** / Lawrence (cond.), The Romeros, San Antonio SO / 1996 / Philips 434369
- ○ **Remembering the Future** / A. Romero / RCA 68268
- ○ **Vivaldi: Guitar Concertos** / Brown (cond.), The Romeros, Academy of St. Martin-in-the-Fields / Philips 412624

Pepe Romero

b. Mar. 8, 1944, Málaga, Spain

Guitarist

Pepe Romero has played the guitar for as long as he can remember, debuting at the age of seven. His father was the legendary guitarist Celedonio Romero and was his only teacher. Along with his father and brothers Celin and Angel, Romero formed the Romeros Quartet, and riding on the heels of Celedonio's celebrity in Spain, embarked on an international career that made them the most famous guitar ensemble in the world. From this secure base, Pepe Romero had little difficulty in establishing himself as one of the leading guitar virtuosos of his generation. With over 50 recordings to his credit and literally thousands of concerts, Romero's repertory spans the entire literature for the guitar. In addition, his stunning technique and exciting bravura have inspired many composers, including Joaquin Rodrigo, Federico Moreno Torroba, Lorenzo Palomo, and his father Celdonio Romero, to write major works for him. As a soloist, Romero has performed with nearly every major orchestra, and in virtually every major hall in Europe and the Americas. He is the pre-eminent Spanish guitar virtuoso, and one of the most popular concert artists on his instrument. *—Steven Coburn*

Recommended:

- ○ **Famous Spanish Guitar Music** / P. Romero / Philips 411033
- ○ **Noches de España: Romantic Guitar Classics** / P. Romero / 1994 / Philips 442150
- ○ **Rodrigo Concertos** / Marriner (cond.), P. Romero, Academy of St. Martin-in-the-Fields / 1994 / Philips 438016
- ○ **Boccherini: Guitar Quintets** / Brown (cond.), P. Romero, Academy of St. Martin-in-the-Fields / 1993 / Philips 438769
- ○ **Guitar Solos** / P. Romero / 1993 / Philips 434727

Anthony Rooley

b. Jun. 10, 1944, Leeds, England

Conductor, Lutenist

Anthony Rooley began his musical career as a classical guitarist, studying with Hector Quine at the Royal Academy of Music. By his own description, he felt "misfit" in this young performance program; he began teaching himself to play the lute, making his own transcriptions from the academy's library. While teaching at the RAM after graduation, Rooley formed the ensemble Consort of Musicke with James Tyler, lutenist and viol player. From its 1969 inception, the ensemble gave instrumental performances, often adding a single voice, of late Renaissance and early Baroque secular music. After a 1978 grant from the British Arts Council (and a new recording contract with Decca), Rooley and the Consort of Musicke began a long specialization in the madrigal repertory. His extensive discography highlights the music of lesser-known seventeenth century composers John Coprario, Sigismondo d'India, Henry Lawes, Biagio Marini, Barbara Strozzi, Giaches de Wert, John Ward. It often features integral recordings of complete published collections; his work may be found on l'Oiseau-Lyre, Harmonia Mundi, Hyperion, Virgin, and ASV, as well as his own label, Musica Oscura. Rooley's ensembles, freely alternating between all-vocal and accompanied orchestrations, have been credited with "bold elasticity of dynamics and phrasing," as well as an audible theatricality. In live performance, Rooley's musicians often intensify this with gesture and choreography. The dramatic renditions follow directly from his fascination with contemporary philosophy. Quoting Marsilio Ficino and other sixteenth century sources, Rooley seeks an "Orphic" performance of music that can bring the soul of the listener—through the medium of the senses—face to face with the Divine. *—Timothy Dickey*

Recommended:

- ○ **Monteverdi: Madrigals** / Rooley (cond.), Cornwell, Elliott, Kirkby, Tubb, Consort of Musicke / 1997 / L'Oiseau-Lyre 455718
- ○ **Classical Kirkby: Orpheus & Corinna** / Kirkby, Rooley / 2002 / BIS 1435
- ○ **Madrigals & Wedding Songs for Diana** / Rooley (cond.), Kirkby, Thomas, Consort of Musicke / Hyperion 66019
- ○ **Sitting by the Streams** / Rooley (cond.), Kirkby, Tubb, Cornwell, Wistreich, Consort of Musicke / 1993 / Hyperion 66135

Joseph Guy Ropartz

b. Jun. 15, 1864, Guingamp, France, **d.** Nov. 22, 1955, Lanloup, France

Composer

Joseph Guy Marie Ropartz was a Post-Romantic composer who adhered to his initial late Romantic style nearly until the end of his long life. Later in his life he changed his surname to "Guy-Ropartz."

As a child, he played bugle, horn, and double bass in a local orchestra, but his father desired him to prepare himself for life in a more secure profession. Therefore, he was given a Jesuit education, then studied law and literature, obtaining a degree from Rennes in 1885. Having thus satisfied his father's wishes that he prepare himself for profession, Ropartz then enrolled at the Paris Conservatoire. His early training in composition was with Theodore Dubois, then with Jules Massenet. He also wrote poetry at the time.

In 1886, Ropartz heard the composition *Le chant de la cloche* (*The Song of the Bell*) by Vincent d'Indy, a leading disciple of the Belgian-born composer César Franck. Highly impressed, Ropartz left the Conservatoire to study with Franck. He adopted elements of Franck's individual use of chromatic harmony and, even more important to Ropartz' music, Franck's use of cyclic forms.

The influence of d'Indy and Franck is evident in his first orchestral work, *La Cloche des morts* (*The Death Knell*). His next few works then began to show the literary, pictorial, and folk influence of Brittany, the northwest French region that was his native province, and were well received.

In 1894, he accepted an invitation to become the director of the Nancy Conservatory. Henceforth, he made his career outside Paris, the musical center of the country. Because of this, he remained less well known and continued composing in his habitual style, outside the mainstream of the historical development of twentieth century styles. At the time, he was the youngest conservatory director in France, but his directorship of the Nancy Conservatory was a brilliant success. It became one of the leading regional music training institutions in the country; the authoritative Groves Dictionary says he "brought about a musical renaissance in Nancy." Conducting and presenting serious and penetrating readings were among his talents.

After 25 years in Nancy, he accepted an invitation in 1919 to take a similar job in Strasbourg, in addition to taking the helm of the local symphony. Strasbourg, the capital of Alsace-Lorraine, had just been recovered from Germany, which had occupied it from the Franco-Prussian War in 1871 to the end of the First World War. Ropartz' task was to promote French music there, to bring the region and the conservatory back into French musical life. Again, he was highly successful. In 1929, at the age of 65, he retired from his positions and returned to his native Brittany.

He lived to be 91 and wrote about 200 works during this long life. His last large-scale work was his string quartet, composed in 1951. He wrote five symphonies, other orchestral music, chamber music, choral music, stage music, and an opera, *Le Pays* (*The Country*), premiered in Nancy in 1912 and later played in Paris. Most of his music kept to the rich harmonic language he learned from Franck. Despite this, his music was always well regarded for its logic, clarity, and lack of excessive material. The Swiss-French composer Arthur Honegger frequently praised Ropartz as a model of formal clarity. His style began to change during World War II. He adopted the neo-Classical style that had arisen in Paris in the period between the Wars, de-emphasizing Franckian chromaticism and striving for a new leanness of sound and more concise formal ideas.*—Joseph Stevenson*

Overview of Works (1887–1950)

The long-lived, prolific Ropartz left behind a catalog of some 165 opus numbers and close to 200 works, including six symphonies, seven symphonic poems (of which *La cloche des morts* and *La chasse du Prince Arthur* are occasionally heard), numerous choral works (including two masses and a requiem), chamber works (among which are six string quartets, two trios, three violin sonatas, two cello sonatas, and a quintet for flute, harp, and strings), *mélodies*, a dozen ambitious works or collections for piano, a trove of organ pieces, ballets, incidental music for plays, and his musical testament, the opera *Le pays*. Of these, but a random sampling have been revived and recorded and a just conspectus of Ropartz's oeuvre is not available, though enough has been heard to hazard some generalizations.

If Ropartz's art is more embracing than that of, say, Sévérac or Canteloube, he is, like them, a regional composer in that his works—though seldom explicitly reliant upon folk music—are informed by Breton folklore, Breton poets, the landscape, and above all, the seascape of his native Brittany. Composed in 1910, the very middle of Ropartz's life, *Le pays*, though set in Iceland, is the tale of a homesick Breton sailor. Roparts's advice to young musicians is a succinct statement of his own practice: "Begin by acquiring a solid musical training so that you are never restricted in the expression of your feeling, then, try to invent beautiful musical ideas which will give rise themselves to their own form and sonorous vestment." Though he lived through a number of musical "revolutions" that he avidly followed—Wagnerian, Impressionist, the Jazz Age, the many tributaries of Modernism—his own art is always firmly embedded in the late Romantic sound world he inherited as he entered maturity. And, having studied composition with Franck, his practice is harmonically adventurous, contrapuntally aware, and informed by architectural considerations that would take him beyond Franckist cyclical procedures later in his career. The habit of contrapuntal thinking keeps the fabric of his work lively, elaborate, and engaging, even when his gestures are predictable or his ideas slight. Ropartz is not a great melodist, but—as with his friend d'Indy —an omnicompetent technique can wring impressive results from slender material. At length, this can be taxing, as in his choral *Symphony No. 3* (1905), whose sheer gorgeousness outwears its welcome early on, or threading the austere seriousness of the string quartets. The monumentality, lush textures, and general earnestness of his nineteenth century outlook began to thin and simplify, allowing a vein of robust charm to emerge in works composed after the Great War, such as the ravishing *Prélude, Marine et Chanson* for flute, violin, viola, cello, and harp (1928). *—Adrian Corleonis*

Recommended:

- ○ **Ropartz: Organ Works** / Lecaudey / 1997 / Pavane 7393/4
- ○ **Ropartz: Masses & Motets** / Piquemal (cond.), Lebrun, Michel Piquemal Ens. Vocal / 2000 / Marco Polo 8225126
- ○ **Ropartz: Prélude, Marine et Chansons, etc.** / Haguenauer, Galperine, Tsan / 1999 / Timpani 1047

○ **Ropartz: Le Pays** / Ossonce (cond.), Ragon, Delunsch, Lallouette, Luxembourg SO / 2001 / Timpani 2065

○ **Ropartz: La Chasse du Prince Arthur; Cloches des morts; Soir sur les chaumes; etc.** / Krivine (cond.), Texier, Perrin, Luxembourg SO / 2003 / Timpani 1073

Cipriano de Rore

b. ca. 1515, Flanders (?), **d.** 1565, Parma, Italy

Composer: Vocal

He was known while still alive as il divino Cipriano. He directed two of the finest musical chapels in Italy. Aristocrats across Europe—the Emperor Charles V, the Count of Egmont, Duke Albrecht V of Bavaria—asked him to compose for them. His music not only provided one of the first single-composer madrigal prints ever, but it was also republished after his death for an astonishing 40 years. A generation of madrigal composers looked to him for inspiration, and no less a figure than Giulio Cesare Monteverdi named him as innovator of the secunda prattica, the foundation of the Baroque style. This was Cipriano de Rore, truly a musical legend in his own time.

Rore was born to a minor noble family in Flemish Ronse (Renaix). Very little information survives about his early education, musical or otherwise. By 1542, however, he had moved from the Low countries to Italy (specifically Brescia), seeking musical fame. He might have studied with Willaert at Venice's San Marco; he quickly became familiar with the man and his "circle." By the early 1540s, he was already composing heavily in both motets and madrigals; the dedications of several works indicate his ambition to serve some great Italian court. In 1546, he won the prestigious job of chapelmaster to Duke Ercole II d'Este of Ferrara. For decades Este Ferrara and nearby Mantua had maintained some of the finest musicians of the Renaissance; Rore's appointment secured him a highly visible position. He rose to the challenge, composing nearly half of all his extant music in the first decade of Ferrarese employment. Fully five books of his madrigals date from this period, including works in which his style shifted toward more radical and chromatic text-painting devices. This later Ferrarese style cemented Rore's European fame, as well as his influence upon a new generation.

In 1558, however, Rore seems to have attempted to resign from court life. He received permission to travel back to his hometown, though the town had been razed during a recent war. He lost his job in Ferrara upon the Duke's death, replaced it briefly with work for the smaller Farnese court of Parma, and finally took over the late Willaert's prestigious Venetian post of maestro di cappella for San Marco in 1563. Unfortunately, this employment failed for unknown reasons, and Rore returned to Parma in 1564. He died shortly thereafter, his reputation happily untarnished. *—Timothy Dickey*

VOCAL

Madrigals (ca. 1540–1565)

Cipriano de Rore is among the best known madrigal composers of the Renaissance era. A south Netherlandish composer, Rore was active in Italy and is an important figure in the development of the Italian madrigal. He composed over 100 madrigals, most of which were published in seven books bearing his name (though actually only two of the seven books are exclusively devoted to Rore's music, the rest are anthologies). Five of these books contain madrigals for five voices, and the remaining two books contain madrigals for four voices. The use of a five-voice texture represents just one of Rore's contributions to the evolution of the madrigal genre, as a four-voice texture had been the norm before him.

Rore's first collection of madrigals appeared in 1542, and they brought the composer almost immediate success and renown. This marked the beginning of what could be called the Rore legend: very little is known of Rore prior to 1542. He seems to have simply materialized as an already skilled, mature composer during this year. His early madrigals are in the Venetian style, are mostly settings of Petrarchan sonnets, and are decidedly polyphonic in texture. The continuous imitation in these madrigals reflect the influence of Rore's teacher, Adrian Willaert, but Rore's style is decidedly less harmonically and rhythmically conservative than Willaert's. The madrigals in the first book are interesting in that they are arranged in modal order. This is the first known instance of a composer ordering pieces of music in this manner.

After 1550, Rore's style changed significantly. He was no longer setting the poems of Petrarch, and his madrigals became less modal, less imitative, and more homophonic. Most importantly, Rore's text settings were becoming clearer, with a greater emphasis on text painting and expressing the mood of the poem. This was perhaps Rore's greatest contribution to the madrigal genre. His concern, especially in his late madrigals, with the expressive content of the poetic texts he was setting earned him a reputation as a master of rhetoric. Claudio Monteverdi, arguably the most significant composer of the late Renaissance, considered Rore the founder of the *Seconda pratica*, the musical practice that placed the importance of the words over the music. This practice allowed for the inclusion of previously unacceptable extreme chromaticism into vocal music, and it is a hallmark of Rore's late madrigal style, in which dissonance is used to emphasize the meaning of certain words in the poetic text. *—Alexander Carpenter*

Recommended:

○ **de Rore: Missa Praeter rerum seriem; motets** / Nevel (cond.), Huelgas Ens. / HM 901760

○ **de Rore: Le Vergine** / Hillier (cond.), Hilliard Ens. / HM 1901107

Ned Rorem

b. Oct. 23, 1923, Richmond, IN

Composer: Vocal, Chamber Music

"Anyone can be drunk, anyone can be in love, anyone can waste time and weep, but only I can pen my songs in the remaining years or minutes," wrote Ned Rorem. Known both as a writer and a composer, Rorem is intriguing as both a musical figure and as a personality. He is self-described as a profoundly diatonic composer and his music language betrays the influence of his French impressionist idols Debussy and Ravel. Rorem's harmonic palette is generally characterized by vertical extrapolations—through modality, polymodality, and chordal alterations—of an essentially tonal framework. Some works conduct innovative experiments in the song cycle form; *Poems of Love and Rain*, for example, sets eight different poems to music, then sets them again in reverse order to contrasting music. Many of his works juxtapose passages of harmonic and rhythmic complexity with moments of elegance and repose.

Rorem was the second of two children of Clarence Rufus Rorem, one of the founders of the Blue Cross, and Gladys Miller Rorem, a peace activist. The family soon moved to Chicago, where Rorem began studying piano and where he heard live such famous performers as Josef Hofmann, Sergey Rachmaninov, and the ballets russes. An early teacher exposed him to Debussy and the impressionists. Subsequent teachers taught him about American contemporary composers like Griffes and John Alden Carpenter, as well as the blues of Billie Holiday, and Rorem learned to notate the little tunes he had composed.

By the age of 16, Rorem had graduated from high school and already performed a concerto with the American Concerto Orchestra. He studied music theory with Leo Sowerby at the American Conservatory for a brief period before entering Northwestern University, where his time was largely spent absorbing a piano repertoire. In 1943, he accepted a scholarship from the Curtis Institute in Philadelphia, where he would study counterpoint with Rosario Scalero and musical-dramatic forms with Gian Carlo Menotti. After only a year there, Rorem moved to New York City, where he worked as Virgil Thomson's copyist in exchange for $20 a week plus composition lessons. Rorem also worked as rehearsal accompanist for Martha Graham and Eva Gauthier. Eventually Rorem entered Juilliard, where he completed bachelor's (1946) and master's (1948) degrees. He also studied with Aaron Copland during two summers at Tanglewood.

An award allowed Rorem to travel to France. What was intended to be a three-month visit ended up lasting 12 years. However, the first portion of his stay was largely spent in Morocco at the home of a friend, where he had the peace and quiet requisite for the 20 or so large-scale works he produced during this period. His work earned more honors, including the Lili Boulanger Award in 1950 and a Fulbright Fellowship the following year.

At this point, Rorem went on to Paris to study with Honegger. Through the influence of the Vicomtesse Marie-Laure de Noailles, he entered a social circle that included Jean Cocteau, Francis Poulenc, and Georges Auric. During this time, he also wrote several rather explicit diaries that were published a decade later to the shock and delight of many.

Rorem returned to New York in 1958 and during the next few decades held teaching positions at the University of Buffalo (1959–60), the University of Utah (1965–66), and the Curtis Institute (1980–86). He still remained more of a composer than pedagogue, and is widely revered as the modern master of the art song genre. He received a Pulitzer Prize in 1976 for *Air Music*, two Guggenheim Fellowships, and commissions from several major symphony orchestras. *—Jeremy Grimshaw*

VOCAL

Songs and Song Cycles

Though Ned Rorem's oeuvre covers the entire spectrum of ensembles and genres—from solo and chamber works to symphonies and other orchestral music to operas—he has long been recognized as America's foremost exponent of the art song. Rorem's lyrical, largely tonal musical language, greatly influenced by the French tradition of Debussy, Ravel, and Poulenc, seems to have lent itself particularly well to the production of vocal music. Though, unsurprisingly, Rorem's songs include settings of French texts, English is clearly the *lingua franca* of the composer's vocal imagination. The hundreds of examples in his catalogue bear testament not only to a remarkable fecundity, but also to an affinity for and sensitivity to the nuances of the English language equalled by few composers since Benjamin Britten. Rorem has demonstrated an especial attraction to the poetry of his own time as source material; among those whose work he has set most extensively are

Theodore Roethke and Paul Goodman; among earlier poets, Whitman and Tennyson figure especially prominently.

While the body of Rorem's vocal music is populated by a great many freestanding songs—including such outstanding examples as "I Am Rose" (Stein; 1955), "My Papa's Waltz" (Roethke; 1959), and "Now Sleeps the Crimson Petal" (Tennyson; 1963)—the composer's dozens of song cycles constitute his central contribution to the vocal literature. A number of Rorem's cycles are structured around the work of a particular poet; among these are *Four Dialogues* for soprano, tenor, and two pianos (O'Hara; 1953–54), *King Midas* (Moss; 1962), *Last Poems of Wallace Stevens* for soprano, cello, and piano (1971–72), and *The Auden Poems* for voice and piano trio (1989). Perhaps more interesting, though, are the thematic cycles which assemble the work of numerous poets around a central literary or philosophical idea. *Poems of Love and the Rain* (1962–63) thus employs the poetry of Windham, Auden, Moss, Dickinson, Roethke, Larson, Cummings, and Pitchford; in an intriguing experiment, Rorem sets each of the poems twice, arranging the pairs of different settings in a large arch form. Solar imagery takes center stage in *Sun* for voice and orchestra (Ikhnaton, Byron, Goodman, Blake, Morgan, Shakespeare, Whitman, and Roethke; 1966), while a feminine perspective infuses the texts of *Women's Voices* (Wylie, Rossetti, Bradstreet, Chudleigh, Pembroke, Coleridge, Rich, Dickinson, Boleyn, Ridge, and Mew; 1975–76). Rorem's pacifist bent, one of the most important facets of his personal credo, is clearly in evidence in *Poèms pour la paix* (Regnier, Ronsard, Magny, Daurat, Baif; 1953) and the Vietnam-era *War Scenes* (Whitman; 1969). *—AMG*

Recommended:

○ **Songs of Ned Rorem** / Bryn-Julson, Ciesinski, Curtin, Gramm, Wolff, Rorem / 1993 / CRI 657

○ **Rorem: War Scenes; Whitman Songs; Dialogues** / Gramm, Istomin / 1991 / Phoenix 116

○ **Songs of Ned Rorem** / Graham, Martineau, Oriol Ens. / 2000 / Erato 80222

Poems of Love and the Rain, song cycle for mezzo-soprano & piano (1962–1963)

"I had toyed with the notion of how it might be for a single composer to set on a poem several times, draining the words of their multiple implication," Ned Rorem explained. "If a poem were good, really good, wasn't there more than one way of musicalizing it?" Thus, in song cycle *Poems of Love and the Rain*, nine texts are presented, but all (except one) are presented within the context of two distinct (and sometimes contradictory) musical moods. First, the eight poems are each presented once, followed by a single "pivotal" iteration of the ninth (on Theodore Roethke's "Interlude"), after which each of the previous eight poems are set again in reverse order. This structural axis of symmetry thus corresponds with a semantic axis of contrast. The second and sixteenth songs, for example, both take as their text W.H. Auden's heartbreakingly mournful "Stop All the Clocks." The first time the song is heard, the singer, a mezzo-soprano, seems filled with anguish bordering on anger; a bold, chordal accompaniment underscores a forceful melodic line that forcefully moves across a broad range. When the singer returns to the text near the end of the cycle, however, the tone is one of resignation and disorientation with uneasy syncopations highlighting the blunt, rhymed-couplet structure of the poem. This kind of contrast appears throughout the work. The lonely lover in Roethke's "The Apparition" sings angular, anxious lines on the way out, with sudden changes of tessitura and terse responses from the piano; on the way back, though, a more woeful mood is set by the soft, steady chords in the piano while the melody is shadowed by the piano's bass line. In two cases, the symmetry is further disrupted by selective use of the text. In the first half of the cycle, Rorem sets only Part I of Jack Larson's "I Love You," and at the corresponding point in the second half of the cycle, sets only Part II of the poem. Likewise, Rorem takes two passes (No. 8 and No. 10 in the cycle) to complete the text of Kenneth Pitchford's searing "Song for Lying in Bed During a Night Rain." The moods set in such stark contrast by the cycle's symmetrical structure thus lend special significance to the first and last song, on an excerpt from Donald Windham's "The Rain." The setting is nearly the same both times: a kind of mysterious interlocking of a falling treble figure and a dissonant rising bass line. The notable difference is that the second setting is a half-step lower. "I wished for the singer to arrive on the stage one person," Rorem explains, "and to leave it another." *—Jeremy Grimshaw*

Recommended:

○ **Rorem: From an Unknown Past; Madrigals; Poems of Love & the Rain** / Wolff, Modern Madrigal Qt., Rorem / 1989 / Phoenix 108

Some Trees, song cycle for soprano, mezzo-soprano, bass-baritone & piano (1968)

"Community fun, amateur participation, has not been a major preoccupation of modern art," Ned Rorem observed in 1969 after composing his song cycle *Some Trees*. The work resulted not from a yearning for a musical manifestation of communal artistry, however, but by the participation of three different singers in a recital of Rorem's solo songs given at Town Hall in 1968. Knowing that soprano Phyllis Curtin, contralto Beverly Wolff, and baritone Donald Gramm would be together at hand, Rorem decided to augment the program with a song cycle for vocal trio (a scoring not frequently encountered in recital music of the late twentieth century). Rorem, whose career is marked by his enormous output of songs, chose for this work three texts by poet John Ashbery: "Some Trees," "Our Youth," and "The Grapevine." Although built of contrasting musical materials and evoking distinct moods, the three texts and Rorem's settings of them touch upon some of the very ideas about friendship, communication, and sociality that the composer associates with singing in a small ensemble. The first of the group, "Some Trees," is the boldest of the three songs, and its counterpoint is the densest. In a kind of busy, frictional musical language not unlike that found in the songs of Charles Ives, the trio declaims Ashbery's text in forceful chordal declamation. Its sentiments are joyous and thoughtful, though: "... You and I are suddenly what the trees try/To tell us we are/That their merely being there means something." Departures from homophonic declamation point up to crucial points in the text, one voice stopping on a word and sustaining its pitch, while another forges ahead to the subsequent thought in highlighted isolation. The piano leaps and dives as a kind of punctuation rather than accompaniment. The second song of the group assumes a more restrained mood and slower tempo, with sparse accompanimental gestures from the piano sometimes separated by long stretches of a cappella singing. When the piano does join the voices, it does so unobtrusively, sometimes outlining the vocal line in unison or contrasting it in simple polyphony. In contrast to the thick textures of the first song, here lines and phrases pass from one voice to the other in pensive succession, reflecting Ashbery's somewhat cryptic text on the passage of time and generations. The lack of resolution, both musical and philosophical, evoked by the song's last line is enhanced by Rorem's careful use of texture: The soprano alone sings the words "to die," holding the last note, after which the baritone enters with "so you live," sustaining his last word as well; the contralto completes the line with the words "and we know," ending the song with a resonant triad of pitches and words. The final song, *Our Youth*, is at once cryptic and nostalgic, utilizing sharp contrasts between lucid solos, intricate polyphonies, and calculated chordal convergences at crucial points in the text: "Our youth is dead/From the minute we discover it...." *—Jeremy Grimshaw*

Recommended:

○ **Songs of Ned Rorem** / Curtin, Gramm, Wolff, Rorem / 1993 / CRI 657

War Scenes, song cycle (1969)

The first page of Ned Rorem's *War Scenes* bears the dedication, "To those who died in Vietnam, both sides, during the composition: 20–30 June 1969." The ecumenical nature of that sentiment, and the frank, often gruesome, content of the poems combine to make *War Scenes* one of Rorem's most powerful musical statements, and a human, rather than political, indictment of war.

The texts for the five *War Scenes* are excerpted (by the composer) from Walt Whitman's *Specimen Days*, a poetic memoir of his time as a civil war nurse. The first and last are philosophical, reflecting on the nature of war and its ugliness, and serving as bookends for the other three songs. The three inner songs, in turn, relate more specific events, more or less as they occurred, without comment.

Rorem's response to the Whitman texts is unique in his output as a song composer; the settings are uncharacteristically austere, dissonant, and aggressive in tone. At the same time he reaches a new level of sympathy and expression. The centerpiece of the cycle, both musically and poetically, is the fourth song, "Inauguration Ball," in which the speaker (presumably Whitman) has left behind scenes of unimaginable brutality in order to attend a social function. As the speaker is overwhelmed by the perfumed air and gentility of the ball, Rorem envelopes his words in the most grotesque of waltzes; brutal and unrelenting, this exaggerated dance music embodies the great irony of the situation, and haunts the speaker, for whom such extremes of luxury and suffering are irreconcilable.

The vocal writing in *War Scenes* is jagged and rangy, making use of large intervals and extreme dynamics; the piano writing is rythmically complex and often highly percussive. As a listening experience, however, the songs are not so daunting. The dramatic effects are clear, and the texts are plainly communicative. The first performance was on October 19, 1969, by Gerard Souzay and pianist Dalton Baldwin, at Constitution Hall in Washington, D.C..*—Allen Schrott*

Recommended:

○ **Rorem: War Scenes; Whitman Songs; Dialogues** / Gramm, Istomin / 1991 / Phoenix 116

CHAMBER MUSIC

Chamber Music

Ned Rorem is not immediately thought of as a composer of instrumental chamber music; however, his chamber music has become more frequently performed and recorded in the 1990s and 2000s. Really, the only difference between his chamber music and vocal music is the instrumentation. He has said, "I conceive all music... vocally. Whatever my music is written for—tuba, tambourine, tubular bells—it is always the singer within me crying to get out." He frequently gives instrumental works or their movements graphic titles, just as he would a song. The chamber works are generally tonal, lyrical, clear, and frank, and often inspired by other artistic ideas, just as his other music is. In one of his earliest chamber works, *11 Studies for 11 Instruments*, even the percussionists have singing lines of melody. The *Scenes from Childhood* (1985) for oboe, horn, string quartet, and piano are pictures of places from his youth, while the *Book of Hours* (1975) for flute and harp is a series of contemplative and devotional pictures. Each of the ten movements of the *String Quartet No. 4* (1994) was inspired by a painting, and the movements are also linked both thematically and theatrically. The *Suite for Guitar* is a collection of mood paintings. The movements of *Bright Music*, from 1987, for flute, two violins, cello, and piano are each built from small fragments: a ritornello of four notes, a triad, an echo of Chopin. *The Unquestioned Answer*, composed for the same group in 2002, is a reaction to Ives' title *The Unanswered Question*. The somewhat unconventional instrumentation of his chamber music is usually due to the works being written for specific performers, but there are also many works for conventional chamber ensembles. Skimming the titles of these pieces immediately tells you something about the nature of each work: *After Reading Shakespeare, for cello*; *Picnic on the Marne*, a set of waltzes for saxophone and piano; *The End of Summer: Remembrance of Things Past for piano trio*; *United States* (*String Quartet No. 5*, 2001); and *Yesterday, Today, and Tomorrow for piano quartet*, premiered in 2004. *—Patsy Morita*

Recommended:

- ○ **Gotham Ensemble Plays Ned Rorem** / Gotham Ensemble / 2002 / Albany 520
- ○ **Rorem: Chamber Music with Flute** / Smith, Thomas, Pilot, Leisner, Lee / Etcetera 1184
- ○ **Day Music—Night Music** / Laredo, Laredo, Carlyss, Schein / 1991 / Phoenix 123

Aaron Rosand

b. Mar. 15, 1927, Hammond, IN
Violinist

Aaron Rosand is an arch-Romantic violinist, a beneficiary of two venerable European schools of violin technique as they were transplanted and grew in American music schools. A native of Hammond, IN, he was the child of a Polish father and a Russian mother. He made his debut at age 10 with the Chicago Symphony Orchestra, and his mature style was formed by two teachers, Leon Sametini of the Chicago College of Music and Efrem Zimbalist Sr. at Philadelphia's Curtis Institute. The former was a student of the great French virtuoso Eugène Ysaÿe, the latter of Leopold Auer, a Hungarian-born player who was the original dedicatee of Tchaikovsky's *Violin Concerto*. Maintaining a vigorous schedule of master classes in his later years, Rosand passed along those French and Russian traditions to a new generation of students, and he combined elements of his teachers' styles in his own playing. Pablo Casals, who knew Ysaÿe's playing firsthand, likened Rosand's work to that of the French master.

Appearing with major orchestras all over the U.S. and Europe for more than six decades, Rosand shone in High Romantic concerto repertoire and, with his full beard and dark good looks, seemed very much the exotic European genius despite his U.S. Midwestern origins. He has been perhaps best known for his large body of recordings on the budget-priced Vox label, where his interpretations of central concerto repertory were often deemed "best buys" by critics. Perhaps his most characteristic discs were those on which he ventured into lesser-known, late Romantic territory, well in advance of the current trend toward rediscovery of the music of that era. A late 1990s double-CD set offering concertos and shorter works by Ernst, Godard, Lehár, Joachim, Hubay, Enescu, Ysaÿe, and Wienawski was a good example.

Rosand did not slow down at all upon reaching senior citizen status, marking his 75th birthday with a Philadelphia performance of the Sibelius violin concerto and issuing a series of new recordings on the Audiofon label. By that time, the musical world was in the midst of a full-scale rediscovery of the Romantic aesthetic—but for Rosand, it had never really declined. *—James Manheim*

Recommended:

- ○ **My Legacy** / Rosand, Sung (piano) / 2002 / Artek 11
- ○ **Aaron Rosand Plays** / Reinhardt, Szoke (conds.), Rosand, Southwest German RSO / 1995 / Vox 5116
- ○ **Concertos: Arensky, Tchaikovsky, Mendelssohn** / Froment (cond.), Rosand, Luxembourg Radio Orch. / 1999 / Vox 7211
- ○ **Concertos: Beethoven & Brahms** / Inouye (cond.), Rosand, Monte Carlo PO / 1998 / Vox 7902

Leonard Rose

b. Jul. 27, 1918, Washington, DC, **d.** Nov. 16, 1984, White Plains, NY
Cellist

Cellist Leonard Joseph Rose was a member of a Russian family who had immigrated to the U.S. from Kiev. His father was an amateur cellist who gave him his first lessons on the instrument. Rose's formal studies began after the family had moved to Florida, at the Miami Conservatory with Walter Grossmann. After that, he moved to New York to study with Frank Miller, principal cellist of the NBC Symphony Orchestra, who was his cousin. At the age of 16, he won a scholarship to attend the Curtis Institute of Music in Philadelphia where his teacher was Felix Salmond. After two years of study, Rose became Salmond's assistant.

Rose is among those cellists whose career included a period of membership in an orchestra. Later, he would tell his students that this was the best way to gain experience. In Rose's case, he followed the path of his cousin by becoming a member of Toscanini's NBC Symphony Orchestra and by the age of 20 was principal cellist. After one season, he took a position with the Cleveland Orchestra, then conducted by Artur Rodzinski. In 1943, Rodzinski moved to New York, where he became the principal conductor of the New York Philharmonic. He brought Rose with him. Rose remained the leader of the orchestra's cellists through 1951. While with the Philharmonic, he made his debut playing the Lalo *Cello Concerto* in 1944. He also accepted a position teaching at the Juilliard School in 1947. Except for the years 1951 to 1962 when he taught at the Curtis Institute in Philadelphia, he was on the Juilliard faculty for the rest of his life.

Playing on a luscious-sounding Amati cello from 1662, Rose had a rich, flowing tone. His playing had a free, effortless sound, a free approach to rubato, and a resulting feeling of spontaneity. These were actually achieved by strenuous practice (four to five hours a day even on tour) and meticulous planning of all aspects of the performance. "I do not believe in receiving last-minute inspiration in public performance," he once said.

He developed a solid touring career, but he remained strongly devoted to teaching and developed into one of the most respected and successful cello teachers in America. Among his pupils were Yo-Yo Ma, Stephen Kates, and Lynn Harrell. Kates recalls that a student "generally speaking came out of a lesson feeling like a million dollars... he gave you confidence."

In his teaching, he favored positions and techniques that were natural. He disagreed with the school of thought that the cello bow could be held the way violinists held theirs, with the little finger on top of the bow. On the other hand, his approach to vibrato is directly taken from the technique of a violinist, Fritz Kreisler, in that the motion of the vibrato comes from the upper arm with the hand pivoting on the finger that is down on the string. He found the upper arm can move the most freely and allows vibrato of any width and speed.

Rose recorded for Columbia Records and among his great recordings are those of the Schumann *Concerto* with Bernstein accompanying and Bloch's *Schelomo* with Eugene Ormandy. He also formed a chamber trio, the Istomin-Stern-Rose-Trio, which made many fine recordings. *—Joseph Stevenson*

Recommended:

- ○ **The Memorial Edition** / Szell (cond.), Rose, Lincer, Machan, Owen, Corigliano, New York PO / Pearl 9273
- ○ **Schubert, Boccherini & Sammartini Sonatas** / Rose, Hambro (piano) / 2001 / Sony 89749
- ○ **Beethoven: Piano Trios** / Stern, Rose, Istomin / 1995 / Sony 64513

Charles Rosen

b. May 5, 1927, New York, NY
Pianist

Charles Rosen started young, with piano lessons at the age of four, then studied at the Juilliard School from ages seven to 11. For the next six years he was a pupil of Moriz Rosenthal (who in turn had been a pupil of Rafael Joseffy and Liszt). When Rosenthal died in 1946, Rosen continued studying with his widow, Hedwig Kanner-Rosenthal, for a total of eight years. He also studied music theory and composition with Karl Weigl, and at Princeton University majored in music history and romance languages. He received his B.A. summa cum laude in 1947; his M.A. in 1949, and his Ph.D. in 1951—the year he made his New York piano debut. In addition to concertizing, Rosen taught Modern Languages at M.I.T. (1953–55), returning to academe in 1971 as Professor of Music at SUNY in Stony Brook. In 1976–77 he served as Ernest Bloch Professor of Music at UC Berkeley; held the prestigious Charles Eliot Norton Chair at Harvard in 1980–81; was George Eastman Visiting Professor at Oxford in 1988, and from 1986 until his retirement in 1996, was Professor in the Committee on Social Thought and Music at the University of Chicago.

In three farewell concerts there on successive nights he played Elliott Carter's *Night Fantasies* (as a guest of the Contemporary Chamber Players); a solo program of Beethoven (Op. 110 *Sonata*), Schumann (the original manuscript version of *Fantasie in C*), and Chopin (one of whose pupils had been the first teacher of Rosen's own beloved teacher, Moriz Rosenthal); and finally the Brahms *First Piano Concerto* with the University of Chicago Symphony Orchestra. Three years later in London he broadcast "Rosen on Chopin," a series of programs on BBC Radio 3 commemorating the sesquicentennial of the composer's death.

Concurrently with concertizing, he recorded for Columbia/CBS Masterworks—Bach's *Art of the Fugue*, original editions of music by Schumann and Chopin, the Liszt *First Piano Concerto* (to the surprise of many unaware of his pedagogical heritage), Beethoven's last six sonatas (Opp. 90–111) and *"Diabelli" Variations*. He also recorded the complete solo piano music of Pierre Boulez, Stravinsky's *Movements for Piano and Orchestra* at the composer's request (with the composer conducting), and a CD of Elliott Carter's piano music: *Night Fantasies*, the *Piano Sonata*, and *90+* (composed in 1996). He also recorded Webern's Op. 7 *Violin Pieces* with the late Isaac Stern.

Pianism and pedagogy were not Rosen's only areas of concentration, however. In 1971 he published the provocative first edition of *The Classical Style*, later reprinted in five languages and revised in 1997 with an additional chapter. This was marketed with a CD of the author playing Beethoven's Opp. 106 and 110 sonatas. In 1995 he brought forth *The Romantic Generation*, which included a spirited and eloquent defense of Berlioz, and in 2000 published a selection of essays as *Critical Entertainments*. Among twentieth century artists he has been an intellectual of the first order—perhaps the most authentic of all—not excluding Alfred Brendel or Maurizio Pollini. If Rosen's piano tone has not always been ingratiating or his style unbending, at his best he illuminates the keyboard music of Western history's most "serious" composers—from Bach to Stravinsky, Carter and Boulez, by way of Haydn, Mozart, Beethoven, Schubert, Chopin, Schumann, Liszt, and Brahms. Nothing in his art has ever been trivial. As a performer, educator, and writer in one package, Charles Rosen is likely always to be recognized as unique. *—Roger Dettmer*

Recommended:

- ○ **Carter: The Complete Music for Piano** / Rosen / 1997 / Bridge 9090
- ○ **Beethoven: Late Piano Sonatas** / Rosen / 1994 / Sony 53531
- ○ **The Siena Pianoforte** / Rosen / 1995 / Boston Skyline 131

Nathaniel Rosen

b. Jun. 9, 1948, Altadena, CA
Cellist

Cellist Nathaniel Rosen began to study his instrument at age six with distinguished teacher Eleanore Schoenfeld. At 13 Rosen was heard by legendary cellist Gregor Piatigorsky during a local competition, and on the basis of this performance Piatigorsky agreed to take Rosen under his wing. At 17 Rosen first traveled to Moscow and was awarded a secondary prize in the 1966 Tchaikovsky Competition along with three other Americans. Afterward, Rosen entered Pasadena City College, and later attended the University of Southern California where from 1971–76 he served as Piatigorsky's teaching assistant. Rosen made his New York debut in 1970.

In the wake of Piatigorsky's death, Rosen entered a grueling round of competitions. This paid off initially, however, when he won the Naumberg Foundation Award in 1977. In 1978 Rosen returned to Moscow and won the gold medal in the Tchaikovsky Competition; being the first, and so far only, American cellist to win this prestigious prize. Rosen then took a job as principal cellist in the Pittsburgh Symphony under André Previn, and later would accept the same position with the Los Angeles Chamber Orchestra. Over time, Rosen moved more toward working as a soloist in recitals, in chamber music groups, and in teaching. Since 1980 Rosen has appeared in Europe, Asia, South America, and Africa in addition to giving regular concerts in North and Central Americas. Although Rosen's staple recital literature generally consists of short cello works, he has premiered several pieces by contemporary composers, as well, including William Kraft, Ezra Laderman, and Paul Schoenfeld.

While Rosen was a success on the concert circuit and remains in demand as a teacher, recording companies proved largely uninterested in his talents. In 1990 Rosen met John Marks, a Rhode Island-based lawyer who was also soon-to-be proprietor of the John Marks Records label. Marks helped connect Rosen with North Star Records, which issued Rosen's first disc, *Orientale* with pianist Doris Stevenson, which became a critical and commercial success. Since then, Rosen has recorded mostly with John Marks Records in a series of acclaimed audiophile recordings, with Rosen's *Suites for solo cello* of Johann Sebastian Bach being regarded by many as the best recorded version since Pablo Casals'. Rosen also performs often with his friend, violinist Arturo Delmoni, and has participated on the discs in the latter's series entitled *Rejoice: A String Quartet Christmas*. *—Uncle Dave Lewis*

Recommended:

- ○ **Rosen plays Brahms** / Rosen, Stevenson (piano) / JMR 5
- ○ **Reverie—Romantic Music for Quiet Times** / Rosen, Delmoni, Stevenson, Erickson / 1996 / JMR 10
- ○ **Romantic Music for Cello** / Rosen, Delmoni, Stevenson / North Star 0027

Nikolai Andreyevich Roslavets

b. Jan. 5, 1881, Dushatino, Ukraine, **d.** Aug. 23, 1944, Moscow, U.S.S.R.
Composer: Miscellaneous

Among Russian composers declared "non-persons" by the Soviet government, Nikolai Roslavets has enjoyed the most spectacular revival in terms of new recordings and concert programming.

Roslavets was born to a peasant family in the Ukraine, growing up in a community that was primarily illiterate. His boyhood talent for the violin paid off when he was accepted into the Russian Music Society in Kursk in a class for indigent pupils. Roslavets studied with Arkady M. Abaza, entering the Moscow Conservatory in 1901. He studied orchestration with Sergei Vasilenko, graduating from the Conservatory in 1912. At this early juncture his music still retained picaresque, popular elements, and this led to the creation of works such as the popular *Dance of the White Women* (1912). A piano prelude, *Largo* (1915), written as a memorial to Abaza, is one of Roslavets' finest creations.

Completely independently of the Second Vienna School, Roslavets developed his own form of non-dodecaphonic serial composition. Roslavets derived his series from "sintetakkord," synthetic chords inspired by the "Prometheus Chord" of Scriabin. These were large chords that also contained a note row, which was used to create harmonic fields of greatly varying character. Roslavets did not use the "sintetakkord" as a basis for creating melody. His organized music is structurally terse, succinct, and profoundly workmanlike; yet wildly colorful, otherworldly, and crystalline. In early pieces that utilize this technique, such as the *String Quartet No. 1* (1912), Roslavets alternates the organized material with tonal bridges and other points of reference. With the *Violin Sonata No. 1* (1913), Roslavets began to fashion whole works in this medium, but not to the total exclusion of other, more conventional pieces. By 1919, Roslavets reached the conclusion that his "sintetakkord" system is perfected, synthesizing its most characteristic gestures into the *Five Preludes* for piano (1919–21). Roslavets wrote a manual for use of the "sintetakkord" in 1927, which has since disappeared.

The watchful eye of the Soviet government was focused upon Roslavets beginning in 1924, as Roslavets suddenly undertook the composition of mass songs for the public taste in great numbers. These are reputedly awful works, dreary agit-prop texts winding through a soulless, banal, and repetitive folk melody setting. In a 1931 document, Roslavets officially repudiated his early work, deriding them as mere "experiments." He might not have bothered; the Soviet government continued to watch him closely anyway, as he moved through a soul draining progression of dull positions within the Soviet musical bureaucracy. He continued to compose Soviet Realist music until he suffered a stroke in 1939. Afterward, Roslavets lived on a military pension as the Soviets gradually erased his name from all encyclopedias and documents. When Roslavets died at age 63 he was buried without a headstone.

Many works of Roslavets are believed lost, but previously unknown manuscripts continue to turn up. Roslavets composed three symphonies, two violin concerti, and numerous symphonic poems. His chamber music is exceptionally fine, consisting of a chamber symphony, five string quartets, three piano trios, and assorted works for violin (five sonatas), viola (two sonatas) and cello (two sonatas). In his early phase, Roslavets also set songs by Russian "futurist" poets such as Elena Guro and Alexander Blok. Roslavets also left a considerable body of piano music, including five sonatas, although the scores of numbers 3 and 4 remain yet to be discovered. Roslavets' *Nocturne for harp, oboe, two violas and cello* (1913), written in a French impressionist manner, is immediately appealing. The "sintetakkord"-based works are less so, and are best appreciated by open-minded listeners; Roslavets' mature style can be tough going for the uninitiated. *—Uncle Dave Lewis*

Overview of Works (1907–1942)

Ukrainian composer Nikolai Roslavets is most often remembered as "the Russian Schoenberg." It is a wholly inaccurate label: not only was Roslavets not Russian, he was not a 12-tone composer in the style of Schoenberg. While he was a serial composer, his 12-tone technique was developed completely independently of Schoenberg and is completely unrelated to Schoenberg in its operations. But being mislabeled is the least of Roslavets' problems. In the artistic ferment of the *fin de siècle* Russian empire, Roslavets was the composer most influenced by the French Impressionists and his early cantata *Heaven and Hell* on texts by Byron (1912) sounds like Debussy or Chausson with a Russian accent. But Roslavets in several early songs—*Paysages trieste* (Verlaine) and *V i nosite lyubov* (Bolshakov)—quickly developed his own harmonic style based on what he called "synthetic chords," none of which were diatonic in function and applications. From this, Roslavets moved on to an independent approach to 12-tone composition in a series of piano pieces: *Three Etudes* (1914), *Two Pieces* (1915), and *Prelude 1915*. After the Revolution, Roslavets took his music and his career even further. He was, for a time, the head of the Association for Contemporary Music and the All-Russia Society for Contemporary Music. And his violin concerto (1925) and *Piano Sonata No. 5* (1925) are as harmonically advanced as anything being written in Europe. But the death of Lenin and the rise of Stalin, and with that, the rise of Association for Proletarian Music, these events effectively ended Roslavets' career and his music. He was reduced to writing Agit-prop songs (mass choral propaganda songs with simple tunes meant to excite workers) while his real music remained, for the most part, unpublished and unperformed. Roslavets died nearly forgotten, a victim of the triumph of Socialist Realism in Soviet art. *—James Leonard*

Recommended:

- ○ **Roslavets: Complete Music for Cello & Piano** / Ivashkin, Lazareva / 2001 / Chandos 9881
- ○ **Roslavets: Piano Music** / Hamelin / 1997 / Hyperion 66926

○ **Roslavets: In den Stunden des Neumonds; Violin Concerto 1** / Holliger, Grindenko, RSO Saarbrücken / Wergo 6207

○ **Roslavets: Works for Violin & Piano** / Lubotsky, Bochkovskaya / 1996 / Olympia 559

Scott Ross

b. Mar. 1, 1951, Pittsburgh, PA, **d.** Jun. 14, 1989, Assas, France

Harpsichordist

Scott Ross was an American harpsichordist who was both popular and renowned for his brilliant technique and insightful interpretations. He recorded the complete works of Scarlatti, Rameau, and Couperin, three composers, along with J.S. Bach, whose music he became identified with over his brief career. Ross was also a highly respected harpsichord teacher in Canada and France.

Ross's father died in 1956, about the time young Scott began showing strong interest in music. The following year, he began studies on organ and piano. In 1964, at age 13, he moved to France with his mother and brother (who together would later move back to the U.S.) and the next year enrolled at the Nice Conservatory, where he studied under Huguette Grémy-Chauliac (harpsichord) and René Saorgin (organ). He left in 1968, receiving first prize at his graduation recital. While his studies had included organ, the instrument he strongly favored in his early years in France, he began focusing on the harpsichord toward the later 1960s. He failed to win the international harpsichord competition in Bruges in 1969, but reentered two years later and was awarded first prize. That year, he finished studies at the Paris Conservatory, where he had been receiving instruction in harpsichord since 1969 from Robert Veyron-Lacroix. In 1970, Ross' mother committed suicide, dealing a harsh blow to the young artist. He rebounded from this "foul" time (as he would refer to this period in an interview in the French magazine *Diapason*) with his first recording, made in 1971 by the early music label Editions STIL. The album contained works by Bach and was appropriately entitled *Monsieur Bach*. Ross also took classes that year at the Royal Conservatory of Antwerp from Kenneth Gilbert. Two years later, he joined the faculty at the Laval University School of Music in Quebec, becoming assistant professor there in 1978. In 1975, Ross' recording of Rameau's *Pièces de Clavecin* was issued to generally positive notices and even received a grand prix du disque award the following year. His next major recording was the complete *Pièces de Clavecin* by Couperin, for which he again received high praise. In 1983, he requested a leave of absence from his teaching post in Quebec. The following year, he signed a five-year contract with the French label Erato. His first project for the company was the most ambitious of his career, the 555 sonatas of Domenico Scarlatti. He began the venture in June 1984 and finished it in September, 1985, a 15-month span during which he recorded two sonatas each day he entered the studio. The entire set was packaged on 34 compact discs. While Ross' reputation rests on many concert appearances and his other recordings, this massive effort was probably his greatest legacy. In 1986, several more recordings by Ross were issued containing works by Bach, Soler, and Forqueray. That same year, he resigned from Laval University. Ross' health began to seriously decline in 1988 with the first of several visits to Lapeyronie Hospital in Montpellier. He died in Assas, at the age of 38. *—Robert Cummings*

Recommended:

○ **Scarlatti: Best Sonatas** / Ross / Erato 45423

○ **The Art of Scott Ross** / Ross / 1993 / CBC 2006

○ **Scott Ross à l'Orgue** / Ross / Memoire Vive 262001

○ **Scarlatti: Complete Keyboard Works** / Ross, Huggett, Coin, Henry, Vallon / 1988 / Erato 45309

Gioachino Rossini

b. Feb. 29, 1792, Pesaro, Italy, **d.** Nov. 13, 1868, Paris, France

Composer: Opera, Orchestral, Vocal, Choral, Chamber Music, Concerto

Gioachino Rossini's parents were both working musicians. His father played the horn and taught at the prestigious Accademia Filharmonica in Bologna, and his mother, although not formally trained, was a soprano. Rossini was taught and encouraged at home until he eventually enrolled at the Liceo Musicale in Bologna. After graduation from that institution, the young musician was commissioned by the Venetian Teatro San Moise to compose *La cambiale di matrimonio*, a comedy in one act. In 1812, Rossini wrote *La pietra del paragone*, for La Scala theater in Milan and was already, at the tender age of 20, Italy's most prominent composer.

In 1815, Rossini accepted a contract to work for the theaters in Naples, where he would remain until 1822, composing prolifically in comfort. He composed 19 operas during this tenure, focusing his attention on opera seria and creating one of his most famous serious works, *Otello*, for the Teatro San Carlos. While he served in this capacity, Rossini met and courted Isabella Colbran, a local soprano whom he would eventually marry. Other cities, too, clamored for Rossini's works, and it was for Roman audiences that he composed the sparkling comedies *Il barbiere di Siviglia* (The Barber of Seville, 1816) and *La cenerentola* (Cinderella, 1817).

In 1822, Rossini left Naples and embarked on a European tour. The Italian musician was received enthusiastically to say the least, and enjoyed fame and acclaim everywhere. Even Beethoven, at the opposite stylistic pole in the musical scene of the day, praised him. The following year, Rossini was commissioned to write *Semiramide*, a serious opera, for La Fenice, a theater in Venice. This work was less successful in its own day than some of his previous efforts, but spawned several arias that remain part of any vocalist's songbook. In 1824, Rossini traveled, via London, to Paris where he would live for five years and serve as the music director at the Théâtre Italien from 1824 to 1826. The composer gained commissions from other opera houses in France, including the Paris Opéra. Rossini composed his final opera, *Guillaume Tell* (1829), before retiring from composition in that genre at the age of 37. Its overture is not only a concert favorite but an unmistakable reflection and continuation of Beethoven's heroic ideal. The catalog of work Rossini had written at the time of his retirement included 32 operas, two symphonies, numerous cantatas, and a handful of oratorios and chamber music pieces. After moving back to Italy, Rossini became a widower in 1845. His marriage to Isabella Colbran had not been particularly happy, and shortly after her death, the composer married Olympe Pelissier, a woman who had been his mistress.

In 1855, Rossini, along with his new bride, moved once again, this time settling in Passy, a suburb of Paris. He spent the remaining years of his life writing sacred music as well as delectable miniatures for both piano and voice (some of which he called "sins of my old age"). He was revered from the time he was a teenager until his death. Rossini was buried in Paris' Père Lachaise cemetery in proximity to the graves of Vincenzo Bellini, Luigi Cherubini, and Fryderyk Chopin. In 1887, Rossini's grave was transferred from Paris to Santa Croce, in Florence, in a ceremony attended by more than 6,000 admirers.

Rossini's chief legacy remains his extraordinary contribution to the operatic repertoire. His comedic masterpieces, including *L'Italiana in Algeri*, *La gazza ladra*, and perhaps his most famous work, *Il barbiere di Siviglia*, are regarded as cornerstones of the genre along with works by Wolfgang Amadeus Mozart and Giuseppe Verdi. *—David Brensilver*

OPERA

Armida (1817)

Rossini was taking something of a risk when he chose to write an opera about Armida, based on Torquato Tasso's *Gerusalemme Liberata*, a story of the Crusades. Armida had been one of the most popular subjects for Baroque opera, inspiring such composers as Gluck, Monteverdi, Handel, Haydn, and Jommelli, but the subject's popularity had declined during the Classical period, and was rarely touched upon in the Romantic era.

The opera revolves around the character of Armida, and the men who surround her are musically and dramatically fairly interchangeable. For one thing, the individual Crusaders are all tenors. Armida is the only female role in the opera and is given a wide range of musical and dramatic expression, from deliberate seductiveness to tender love to desolation at being abandoned to fury. As the opera opens, Armida comes to the camp of the Crusaders to ask for help, claiming that her throne has been stolen from her by her uncle. Her true intent is to sow dissent among the Crusaders and to seduce Rinaldo, with whom she has fallen in love. Various rivalries lead to her fleeing with Rinaldo to an enchanted island. However, Rinaldo's comrades follow them there, and persuade him that his duty is to the Crusade, not to Armida. She pleads with him to remain, or at least to allow her to go with him, but he still goes with the other Crusaders. Crushed, Armida hesitates between love and the thirst for revenge, and the opera ends with her fiery choice of revenge.

Armida's music reflects all the ranges of her emotions, and demands a singing actress of the highest caliber. The music for the individual Crusaders is fairly nondescript, except in the last act trio, when Rinaldo is persuaded that he has neglected his duty. This music is incredibly intricate and exposed, and very effective when well-sung. However, the opera remains very much Armida's. *—Ann Feeney*

Synopsis:

Act One. The story takes place around the beginning of the twelfth century in and around Jerusalem. The Christian Crusaders occupy Jerusalem while their Paladin Knights, under the leadership of Goffredo, are in the process of choosing a successor to Dudone, who died heroically in combat. But the proceedings are disrupted by the desperate pleas of the beautiful but diabolical Armida, who is accompanied by Idraote, usurper of the Damascus throne. Both hide their identity and claim to be in flight from Idraote. Armida asks for a contingent of soldiers to defeat him; in fact, she and Idraote are plotting the subjugation of Rinaldo and the Paladin Knights.

Eustazio proposes the selection of Rinaldo as the Knights' new leader, and he is then elected, but to the dismay of the jealous Gernando. Armida attempts to initiate her plans by seducing Rinaldo, and soon wins him over. He begins to depart with her, but Gernando provokes a duel with him and is killed. Rinaldo, repulsed by the killing, departs with Armida, who now has him entirely in her thrall.

Act Two. Astarotte and his army of Furies stake out a forest awaiting the arrival of Armida, who has summoned them. She arrives with Rinaldo in a chariot, which she transforms into beautiful flowers. She also magically changes the forest into a magnificent palace. (Most of this act is dominated by a ballet segment.)

Act Three. In an enchanted garden, the Paladin Knights Ubaldo and Carlo search for Rinaldo, intent on rescuing him from Armida's diabolical influence. They are aware the garden is an illusion, and foil attempts to seduce them by nymphs. The pair hide when Rinaldo and Armida appear, and when the latter departs they confront Rinaldo. Ubaldo presents him with his adamantine shield, which reflects Rinaldo's now craven image and awakens him to Armida's infernal grip on him. When Armida returns she realizes she has lost control of Rinaldo.

Later, outside her palace, Rinaldo struggles in his attempt to suppress the anguish he feels over losing Armida. She pleads to accompany him as his attendant, but he insists that she cannot come along. Armida becomes furious as Ubaldo and Carlo take him away. She determines to take revenge against Rinaldo, and then orders her palace destroyed by demons. She is then carried off by them. *—Robert Cummings*

Recommended:

- ○ **Rossini: Armida** / Gatti (cond.), Fleming, Francis, D'Arcangelo, Fowle, Bologna Teatro Comunale Orch. / 1994 / Sony 58968
- ○ **Rossini: Armida** / Scimone (cond.), Matteuzzi, Furlanetto, Ford, Merritt, I Solisti Veneti / 1999 / Arts 47327

Il barbière di Siviglia (The Barber of Seville) (1816)

This 1815 masterpiece is widely considered the greatest of comic operas. Even when operas of the bel canto period (Rossini's period of flourishing) were rarely performed, its frequent presence on operatic stages of the world was unabated. The first performance, in Rome in 1816 was a fiasco. The older opera composer Giovanni Paisiello had composed an opera on the same story, also called *The Barber of Seville*, in 1782. Rossini had misgivings about composing a new opera on the same text, so he first obtained Paisiello's gracious permission to go ahead, and originally called his new opera *Almaviva*. This did not prevent Paisiello's claque from sabotaging the premiere, a feat in which they were aided by underrehearsal, sloppy production, and stage effects which failed to work properly. Soon afterward, with some changes, the opera was presented again. Without Paisiello's fans creating an uproar, the performance was a success, and by the third performance it resulted in ovations and quickly went on to sweep the operatic world. (As for Paisiello's opera, it was soon eclipsed by Rossini's, but more recently it has regained some appreciation in the operatic world.)

The Barber of Seville is the first of a trilogy of plays by the French dramatist Beaumarchais. These plays, which tended to depict nobility as buffoons dependant on and manipulated by their wily servants, were considered subversive in the late 1700s. (*The Marriage of Figaro*, the second of the plays, was turned into an opera by Mozart in 1786. It is Rossini's opera, by the way, not Mozart's, which has the comic aria "Largo al factotum" containing the call: "Figaro, Figaro, Figaro.") Figaro is the barber of the title. The plot involves the efforts of the amorous young Count Almaviva to woo and win the lovely Rosina, in the process outwitting her ward, Dr. Bartolo, who fancies her for himself. There are textual difference among production of the opera. The primary decision is whether Rosina's part should be sung by a mezzo-soprano (as Rossini originally intended) or by a soprano, as it has commonly been done since 1826, apparently with Rossini's permission. An aria for Bartolo was lost, and has been replaced by one composed by a composer named Romani. And the "Lesson Scene" is also lost, so the soprano gets to choose music by another composer to use in its place. Some of the great popular numbers in the opera are Almaviva's serenade "Ecco ridente in cielo" and the more passionate "Se il mio nome." Rosina's"Una voce poco fa" is probably the most popular of all coloratura arias, while Bartolo gets his own aria, "La Calunnia" ("Calumny"), all about the evil power of slander. Incidentally, the famous overture to the opera, which is probably among the most frequently heard compositions of Rossini's in the concert hall, was not composed originally for this opera at all! Rossini was short of time, so he simply grabbed an overture he had written earlier. *—Joseph Stevenson*

Synopsis:

Act One. Outside Dr. Bartolo's house. Fiorello, a musician, is gathering his instrumentalists ("Piano, pianissimo"), instructing them to be quiet. Count Almaviva enters, and to their accompaniment, he sings to summon Bartolo's ward, Rosina ("Ecco ridente in cielo"). However, she does not appear, and he pays the musicians, who are so loud in their gratitude that he has to chase them away. The Count hides as he hears somebody arriving, and the barber Figaro makes his boisterous entrance, boasting of his accomplishments as the factotum of the entire city ("Largo al factotum"). The Count recognizes him and explains that he is in love with Rosina, and Figaro offers his help. Their conversation is interrupted when Rosina comes onto the balcony, carrying a letter. When the suspicious Bartolo questions her, she says it is an excerpt from the opera "The Futile Precaution" and pretends to drop it by accident. He hurries down to get it, but Almaviva has already retrieved it. Bartolo returns and grumbles that he will have the balcony walled up. Figaro reads the letter, which asks the unknown admirer his intentions and tells him that she is eager to escape her jealous guardian. They overhear Bartolo declaring his own plans to marry Rosina that night. Almaviva explains to Figaro that he wants to hide his rank from Rosina, so she will love him for himself, and at Figaro's urging, sings a song in which he introduces himself as the poor student Lindoro ("Se il mio nome") who can offer her only his love. She responds, expressing her strong interest, but Bartolo slams the window shut.

Almaviva asks Figaro for help, and at the mention of payment, his genius becomes truly inspired ("All'idea di quel metallo"). He tells Almaviva to dress as a drunken soldier, demanding billeting at Bartolo's; bóth anticipate future pleasures of love and money.

Inside the house, Rosina thinks about the handsome Lindoro who has captured her heart, ("Una voce poco fa... Io sono docile") and how she intends, despite her generally easygoing and obedient habits, to have her way in this. Figaro comes in, but before they have more than a moment to talk, Bartolo comes in and Figaro hides. Bartolo is grumbling and Rosina stalks off. Don Basilo, the music teacher, comes to warn Bartolo that Count Almaviva has been seen in the vicinity and suggests, since it seems that the Count is smitten, that he be driven out of town with a slander campaign ("La calumnia e un venticello"). Once they leave, Figaro calls to Rosina, and they resume their conversation. He tells her of Bartolo's plans, which she scoffs at, and then of the young man she might have noticed, his cousin Lindoro. After a few coy interchanges, he admits that Lindoro is madly in love with no other than Rosina, and she feigns surprise, though adding in an aside she knew it all along ("Dunque io son"). He urges her to write a letter to Lindoro, and after a moment of feigned reluctance, she produces one already completed, at which he realizes she could teach him a lesson or two. When Figaro leaves, Bartolo comes in, and despite her attempts to trick him, notices some of the paper is missing, and tells her he is not a man to be easily deceived ("A un dottor della mia sorte"). Almaviva appears, in disguise as a soldier and demanding billetting. He immediately tries to pick a fight with Bartolo, manages to get Rosina's letter, and makes such a ruckus that Bartolo calls the police. However, when Almaviva discreetly shows the captain his identity, the police immediately bow in respect, to general confusion.

Act Two. Bartolo is convinced the "soldier" was one of Almaviva's spies, and Almaviva himself appears, this time disguised as Don Alonso, a smarmy music teacher and a student of Basilio's ("Pace e gioia"). Bartolo is suspicious until Almaviva gives him Rosina's letter, suggesting that he show it to Rosina, saying one of Almaviva's mistresses was waving it about as a great joke. Rosina comes in for a music lesson and sings an aria from "The Futile Precaution" ("Contro un cor"). Almaviva quietly introduces himself as Lindoro. Bartolo himself offers an aria ("Quando mi sei"), but Figaro's entrance interrupts him. Figaro gets keys from Bartolo, in order to get the shaving basin. Basilio shows up unexpectedly, to general dismay, but Figaro convinces him he has all the symptoms of scarlet fever, and all tell him to go home and to bed ("Buona sera, mio signore"). As Figaro begins to shave Bartolo, the two lovers, out of hearing, plan to elope that night. Bartolo becomes suspicious again, eavesdrops, and chases Figaro and Almaviva out. Bartolo fumes and then sends for Basilio. The housekeeper, Berta, grumbles about the crazy household ("Il vecchiotto cerca moglie"). Basilio returns and confirms that he doesn't know anything about a Don Alonso. Bartolo sends him off to get a notary and calls to Rosina. Pretending to condole with her, he gives her the letter, telling her that it's clear Almaviva's intentions were dishonorable, and she is brokenhearted.

After a thunderstorm, the Count and Figaro return, but Rosina accuses them of deceiving her. However, when Almaviva reveals his real identity, she is overjoyed ("Ah! qual colpo"). Their delight is momentarily disrupted when Figaro notices the ladder is gone, but when Basilio returns with the notary, Almaviva offers him a bullet in the brain or a valuable ring, depending on whether he will witness the marriage contract. Bartolo returns with the police, but Almaviva explians that the contract is signed. Bartolo will let him keep Rosina's dowry ("Cessa di piu resistere"), is resigned, and the opera ends with general rejoicing ("Di si felice innesto"). *—Ann Feeney*

Recommended:

- ○ **Rossini: Il Barbiere di Siviglia** / Leinsdorf (cond.), Merrill, Valletti, Peters, Corena, Metropolitan Opera Orch. / 1996 / RCA 68552
- ○ **Rossini: Il Barbiere di Siviglia** / Patane (cond.), Bartoli, Matteuzzi, Pertusi, Banditelli, Bologna Teatro Comunale Orch., Bologna Teatro Comunale Orch. / 1989 / London 425520
- ○ **Rossini: Il Barbiere di Siviglia** / Lopez-Cobos (cond.), Ramey, Hagegård, Corbelli, Larmore, Lausanne CO / 1993 / Teldec 74885
- ○ **Rossini: Il Barbiere di Siviglia** / Abbado (cond.), Domingo, Battle, Raimondi, Sollscher, CO of Europe / DG 435763
- ○ **Rossini: Il Barbiere di Siviglia** / Gelmetti (cond.), Hampson, Ramey, Hadley, Mentzer, Toscana Orch. / 1993 / EMI 54863

La cenerentola (Cinderella) (1817)

This 1817 opera was a popular success when premiered and never entirely passed out of the operatic repertoire during the time when operas of Rossini's period were out of favor. Don't expect fairy godmothers and glass slippers. Perrault's famous fairy tale is stripped of all supernatural characters and events in this loose adaptation of it. According to librettist Jacopo Ferretti, this was done to please the Roman audience who disdained "children's tales." Cinderella here suffers indignities from her stepfather and two stepsisters, but still retains her kindness, charm, and interest in the latest fashions. The slipper is replaced by a bracelet (in order to comply with current moral standards and not show the ankle), by which the Prince recognizes Cinderella at the end of the opera.

Ferretti and Rossini spent just over one month working on the opera, beginning work December 23, 1816, with a premiere on January 27, 1817. It is consistently tuneful, lighthearted, and spirited. The overture represents another of those cases in which Rossini raided an earlier score (*La Gazetta*) as the last-minute source of an overture for the new opera. It fits this opera like a glove. Cinderella's part provides sopranos with two popular coloratura arias, "Una volta c'era un re" and "Ah prence, io cado ai vostri pie," more challenging than any music Rossini had composed previously. Cinderella's father has a great buffo aria, "Miei ramipoli" in which he complains of being awakened from sleep by noisy people. *—AMG*

Synopsis:

Act One. Inside Don Magnifico's shabby mansion, his daughters admire themselves, while Cenerentola tends the fire. She sings a plaintive ballad ("Una volta c'era un re") about a king who rejected pomp and beauty and married an innocent, good woman. The sisters mock her and order her to stop. A beggar, Alidoro, the Prince's tutor in disguise, knocks at the door, and the sisters order him away, but Cenerentola surreptitiously gives him bread and coffee. When they notice he is still there, they slap her, and he tries to stop them. Courtiers suddenly arrive to invite the daughters to the ball where Prince Ramiro will choose the most beautiful as his bride ("O figlie amabili"). The sisters become wildly excited, ordering Cenerentola to help them prepare ("Cenerentola, vien qua"), while she declares they are driving her crazy and laments that they will go enjoy themselves while she has to stay behind. Alidoro and the courtiers leave, and as the sisters prepare, Cenerentola calls them her "sisters," but they haughtily tell her never to call them that.

Don Magnifico appears, grumbling that they awakened him from a magnificent dream, which he describes (" Miei rampoli femminini"). A beautiful donkey sprouted wings and flew to the top of a bell tower, and the bells began to ring. He interprets it to mean that his two daughters are the wings who will elevate him to greatness through marriage; one of them will become a queen and also give him dozens of regal grandchildren. When they tell him of the ball, he becomes even more excited, and they all leave.

Ramiro enters, disguised as a servant, musing that Alidoro told him in this house he would find a virtuous and charming bride. Cenerentola comes in, balancing a pile of dishes, and seeing him, is startled and drops them all to the ground. The two are immediately attracted to one another ("Un soave non so che"), and he asks who she is. She tries to explain her situation, but becomes hopelessly confused. She leaves. Dandini, Ramiro's valet disguised as the prince, makes a grand entrance and compares his hunt for a bride to a bee among flowers ("Come un'ape"), then lavishes flattery on the sisters. Cenerentola returns and begs Magnifico to let her to to the ball ("Signor, una parola"), but he brusquely refuses, and even threatens to beat her when she continues to plead. Ramiro and Dandini stop him, and Magnifico tells them she is the lowliest of servants, of ignoble birth. Alidoro comes in with a birth register and asks about Magnifico's third daughter. Magnifico says she died, threatening Cenerentola again when she tries to speak up. Dandini and Ramiro again rescue her, and they all leave.

Alidoro and Cenerentola return, and calling her "daughter," he says everything will change for her, and she will go to the ball. He tells her that God has seen her suffering and virtue ("La del ciel nell'arcano"), and Alidoro watches her glow with joy.

In the palace, Dandini congratulates Magnifico on his drinking ability and flirts with the sisters. The chorus returns, celebrating Magnifico's prowess with wine and declaring he has been named keeper of the wine cellar. He pompously proclaims that nobody is to adulterate wine with water on pain of death ("Noi, Don Magnifico"). They all leave, and Ramiro and Dandini wonder why Alidoro would tell Ramiro to find a bride in one of those hideous sisters. The sisters return, and Dandini, saying he can't marry both, will give the other to his valet. The sisters loudly recoil at the thought of marrying a plebian, though hiding his amusement, he says he'd make a loving husband. The chorus comments on the arrival of a veiled lady, and Cenerentola appears, magnificently dressed. She takes her veil off, and Magnifico and his daughters are briefly confused by a resemblance to Cenerentola. Everyone wonders what is happening ("Mi par d'essere sognando").

Act Two. Magnifico tells the sisters he relies upon them to make his fortune as the king's father-in-law ("Sia qualunque della figlie"). He leaves, and Ramiro enters, musing that the unknown beauty at the ball resembles the woman he fell in love with at Magnifico's house. He hides as Dandini enters with Cenerentola. She refuses him, declaring herself in love with his servant. Ramiro emerges, and she avvows that she wants him, not rank or riches. However, she refuses to tell him her name. She gives him one of her bracelets, telling him to find her again, and if he still loves her when he knows more of her and her circumstances, then she will marry him. She leaves, and he vows to find her ("Si, ritrovarla io giuro"), then leaves. Magnifico rushes in, asking Dandini to choose. Dandini keeps him in suspense and then promises to reveal the great secret ("Un segreto d'importanza"). He finally reveals that he is a valet, not a prince, to Magnifico's consternation, which greatly amuses Dandini.

Back home, in her usual clothes, Cenerentola sings her ballad again, and the sisters and Magnifico enter, disgruntled by the turn of events. A storm rages outside, and Dandini comes in, with Ramiro, telling them the Prince's carriage overturned. Magnifico shouts for Cenerentola to bring a chair, and when she does so, Ramiro recognizes her, and they are reunited. The sisters turn on her for her presumption, but Ramiro castigates them, swearing he will marry her. She tries to embrace them, but they rebuff her. Everyone leaves but Alidoro, who reflects that virtue has won.

In the throne room, Cenerentola has been crowned, and Ramiro is ready to avenge her, but reflecting on how her life has changed, she embraces them ("Nacqui all'affanno...Non piu mesta") as they all praise her kindness. *—Ann Feeney*

Recommended:

- ○ **Rossini: La Cenerentola** / Chailly (cond.), Bartoli, Corbelli, Matteuzzi, Pertusi, Bologna Community Theater Orch. / 1993 / London 436902
- ○ **Rossini: La Cenerentola** / Rizzi (cond.), Corbelli, Larmore, Miles, Quilico, Fisher, Gimenez, Polverelli, Scarabelli, Covent Garden Opera Chorus / 1995 / Teldec 94553

Guillaume Tell (William Tell) (1829)

Guglielmo Tell, originally *Guillaume Tell* as Gioachino Rossini's second French opera, premiered on August 3, 1829, at the Paris Opéra. Although Rossini composed works in other genres after 1829, *Guglielmo Tell* was his last opera. As director of Paris' Théâtre Italien, Rossini led this organization to great heights; his goal was to compose French operas, the greatest of which came to be his *Le comte Ory* (1828) and *Guillaume Tell*. Personal illness, political troubles, and Meyerbeer's ascent in the world of French opera in the early 1830s possibly conspired to bring about Rossini's retirement as an opera composer. Etienne de Jouy, Hippolyte Louis-Florent Bis, and Armand Marrast collaborated on the libretto for Rossini's *Guglielmo Tell*, basing it on Friedrich von Schiller's play *Wilhelm Tell* (1804). Received well by the contemporary Parisian public and press, *Guglielmo Tell* remains today a popular work.

Although *Guglielmo Tell* was originally a French opera, it was translated into Italian in the early 1830s, making it accessible to Italian audiences. After the Italian premiere of *Guglielmo Tell* in Lucca in 1831, the Italian version was more frequently performed than the original French one.

A cello solo begins the overture to *Guglielmo Tell*, in a sectional arrangement typical of Rossini's overtures. Trumpet fanfares introduce the final section of the overture, which features a galloping tune, perhaps Rossini's most famous music, stated first by the violins, and adding sections of the orchestra in a crescendo to the end of the overture. After the overture a lilting chorus of villagers sets a pastoral scene with a gracefully simple instrumental tune supported by a perfect fifth drone in the horns. The 6/8 time, simple harp accompaniment, and modified strophic form and arrangement of the fisherman's song ("Il piccol legno ascendi o timida donzella") reinforces this opening pastoral image. The finale of Act I virtually enacts the plot's festivities, with a chorus of young people ("Cinto il crine di bei fiori"), a chorus of villagers ("Gloria, onore al giovinetto" and the chorus "Di destrezza il premio ottiene"), diagetic dance music, and pantomime music accompanying an archery competition. The chorus of villagers returns in a stormy minor mode supplication for Leuthold ("Nume pietoso, Dio di bontà!"). A lengthy, large ensemble passage for soloists and choruses closes the act. The extent to which Rossini relied on the chorus in *Guglielmo Tell* is evident in Act Two, which begins with a chorus of huntsmen ("Qual silvestre metro intorno"), accompanied by a bombastic orchestra featuring prominent horn motifs, and which is extended by choruses of men of the Swiss cantons, and also in Act Three, in which various groups of soldiers and Swiss people occupy a central position in triumphant choruses ("Gloria al poter supremo!"). Arnoldo's recitative and aria at the beginning of Act IV ("Non mi lasciare, o speme di vendetta" / "O muto asil del pianto") is a fine example of Rossini's treatment of this operatic convention, an expressive bel canto vocal idiom forming the basis for the ternary form aria. *—Jennifer Hambrick*

Synopsis:

Act One. The story is set in thirteenth century Switzerland. The opera opens with a triple-wedding celebration on the shores of Lake Lucerne, in the canton of Uri. Melchthal officiates at the ceremonies, which draw mixed feelings from William Tell, owing to the Austrian regime that has suppressed Swiss customs in the region. Tell and others in attendance actively resist Austrian rule. Melchthal's son Arnold has fallen in love with an Austrian Princess (Mathilde) and finds his allegiances in conflict.

After Tell's son Jemmy wins an archery competition, a Swiss herdsman, Leuthold, arrives and reveals he has just slain an Austrian soldier who was intent on raping his daughter. The Austrians are in hot pursuit of Leuthold now and he asks that someone ferry him away. Tell volunteers, and when he and Leuthold have departed, the Austrians, led by Rudolphe, arrive and begin interrogating the villagers. They remain loyal to Tell, but the frustrated Austrians take Melchthal as a hostage.

Act Two. In the Rutli mountains (which overlook Lake Lucerne), Mathilde sings of her love for Arnold, who soon joins her. He knows that to win her he must fight in the Austrian army outside of Switzerland and distinguish himself in battle. Tell and fellow insurgent Walter Furst are determined to convince Arnold to join their cause against the Austrians.

They are successful when they reveal to Arnold that the Austrians have murdered his father. Men from all three local cantons, Uri, Unterwalden, and Schwyz, gather now at the behest of Tell and swear allegiance to the anti-Austrian cause.

Act Three. At a chapel on the grounds of the Altdorf palace, Arnold meets with Mathilde and renounces his love for her and the pair acknowledge they must forever part.

Gessler, (Austrian) Governor of the Uri and Schwyz cantons, has organized festivities to celebrate Austrian rule and to honor him. Tell refuses to pay him homage and is soon discovered to be the party who aided in the escape of the fugitive Leuthold. He is arrested, as is his son Jemmy a short while later. Then Gessler arranges a torturous contest for Tell: he must prove his marksmanship with a bow and arrow by shooting an apple on Jemmy's head. Tell performs the feat, then boldly admits he was saving the second arrow for Gessler. Mathilde demands that Jemmy be released into her custody and he is set free. The defiant Tell, however, is taken off to prison.

Act Four. At the Melchthal household, Arnold decides he must now lead the uprising against the Austrians to avenge his father's murder. Villagers join him and he presents them arms stashed away by his father and Tell.

The final scene opens on a shore by Lake Lucerne, with Mathilde reuniting Jemmy with his mother Hedwige. Mathilde offers herself in exchange for Tell's release. Jemmy soon gives the signal to launch the revolt. Tell arrives on the shore, having braved a turbulent storm. He quickly tracks down Gessler and puts an arrow into his heart. Arnold extols his dead father and the storm soon ends as the sun brightens the sky. *—Robert Cummings*

Recommended:

- ○ **Rossini: Guglielmo Tell** / Chailly (cond.), Freni, Pavarotti, Ghiaurov, Milnes, National PO / London 417154
- ○ **Rossini: Guglielmo Tell** / Gardelli (cond.), Gedda, Caballe, Bacquier, Howell, Royal PO / 1995 / EMI 69951

L'italiana in Algeri (The Italian Girl in Algiers) (1813)

The year 1813 proved a productive one for Rossini, with four important works for four different theaters. *Il Signor Bruschino* was premiered in January at the Teatro San Moisè in Venice, *Tancredi* was produced at Venice's La Fenice in February, and *Aureliano in Palmira* was introduced at Milan's La Scala in December. In between came an opera that nearly didn't happen. Rossini's *La Pietra del Paragone* (1812) was announced for a revival, but the Teatro San Benedetto in Venice used Rossini's second act only, substituting a first act drawn from the work of another composer. It was not a success. Meanwhile, Carlo Coccia, who had accepted a commission to compose an opera for that theater, apparently ran into difficulty in completing his assignment. Rossini accepted the offer from the theater's impresario and wrote *L'Italiana in Algeri* in less than a month. Given the tight schedule, the composer turned to a libretto already in existence, one by Angelo Anelli, already set by Luigi Mosca.

Although Rossini was likely familiar with Mosca's opera, significant additions and changes were made to the libretto, quite possibly by Gaetano Rossi. The 21-year-old composer elected to go for broke with the effects of his ensemble writing. The impression made by the breathless piling up of rhythmic patterns using repeated consonants is often deliriously funny. The opera was premiered on May 22, 1813, to applause that, according to one critic, "thundered without pause."

L'Italiana was the first of several important Rossini comic operas to hold prominent roles for lower female voices. While voices were less rigidly categorized than they were to become in the twentieth century, Rossini clearly wrote for what we now call a coloratura mezzo-soprano. The deeper, fuller sound he had in mind lends a greater piquancy and strength to figures such as *L'Italiana*'s Isabella, Rosina in *Il Barbiere di Siviglia*, and Angelina in *La Cenerentola*.

The protagonist in *L'Italiana* is a determined Italian lady who travels to Algiers to search for her lover Lindoro, kidnapped and held as a slave by Mustafà, the Bey of Algiers. Isabella's wit and charm prove too much for Mustafà and his retinue, and she is able to escape with Lindoro at the end, leaving the Bey fuming until he realizes there is nothing to be done. The role of the Bey is a gift for that rare bass with agility, comic presence, and a gift for rapid patter.

L'Italiana, though often performed, existed in manuscript only until the Ricordi publishing house offered a printed score toward the end of the nineteenth century. Numerous errors and modifications had crept in by then, however, and a more accurate documentation of the composer's intentions was not made available to performing organizations until the critical edition was researched and prepared by the Rossini Foundation in the late twentieth century. *—Erik Eriksson*

Synopsis:

Act One. The opera begins in a room in the palace of Mustafà, the Bey of Algiers. The Bey's wife, Elvira is suffering from the indifference shown her by her husband, who wishes to get rid of her and take instead an Italian wife. In this endeavor, he enlists the aid of a pirate chieftain, Haly. The plan is that Elvira will marry a young Italian, Lindoro, kidnapped and now serving the Bey as a slave. Lindoro, however, still loves a young woman in Italy. On the coast, where an Italian ship is foundering, Haly and his followers seize the crew and passengers, among them Isabella, Lindoro's beloved, and her suitor, Taddeo, a man singularly lacking in courage. Haly informs Isabella that she will become part of the Bey's harem, but the she has other ideas. The Italian girl informs Haly that she is the niece of Taddeo, a ruse the poor man hesitantly undertakes.

In a richly arrayed hall, Isabella is brought before the Bey, who is at once smitten. First, Isabella manages to rescue Taddeo from being dispatched with a spear. When Elvira and Lindoro appear to say a farewell to the Bey, Isabella recognizes her beloved and inquires about the identity of the woman with him. Mustafà shares his plan. The quick-witted Isabella then puts an immediate stop to it by declaring that Elvira shall stay with the Bey while Lindoro shall be assigned to her as her slave. The Bey's protests are unavailing as he yields to the wishes of the lovely and persuasive Italian girl.

Act Two. Elvira, Zulma (her slave), Haly, and the court eunuchs are astounded by the change in the Bey from tyrannical overlord to a man existing entirely in the thrall of Isabella. After initial concerns about Lindoro's faithfulness, Isabella is assured of his love and arranges with him a plan for escape. Meanwhile, the Bey has sought Taddeo's support by making him his deputy. Fearing punishment, Taddeo agrees to the position and the task of pleading the Bey's lovesick desires to Isabella.

Isabella is seen next in her elaborately appointed suite, luxuriously dressed. The Bey, wishing to be alone with her, informs Taddeo that he is to take his leave along with Elvira and Zulma upon the Bey's sneezing. Isabella thinks otherwise, plying him with seductive gestures, then urging Elvira to join them. Isabella tells the Bey that he should return to his wife, whereupon the Bey realizes that he has been foiled. Despite his sneezing, Lindoro and Taddeo remain and Mustafà swears revenge.

Taddeo next collaborates with Lindoro in a plan to make their escape, convinced somehow that Isabella has finally chosen him, Taddeo, for a husband. The escape is also to lead to the release of all the Italian slaves. They set about convincing the Bey that, far from being the object of ridicule, he is about to be honored by Isabella who wishes to make him a "Pappataci," an honor that requires that he eat, drink, sleep—and remain silent. With the Bey now deliriously happy, Isabella initiates her plan. First, all the Italian slaves are entrusted to her in honor of the Bey's elevation to Pappataci. Then, she has liberal quantities of intoxicants passed out among the palace's Moors and eunuchs.

Mustafà comes before the Italian slaves who are themselves all dressed as Pappataci. They remove his royal robes and dress him in Pappataci garb. Isabella oversees the ceremony and engages in an amorous dialogue with Lindoro. Throughout all of this, the Bey is charmed and delighted. Suddenly, however, a ship comes into view, quickly mooring next to the palace. The Italian slaves scamper aboard. Taddeo now realizes that Isabella is truly in love with Lindoro. He reveals this to the Bey, who, as a good Pappataci, must remain silent. Once the ship sails off, however, Mustafà explodes in a rage, then turns for comfort to his much put upon wife, Elvira. She utters words of forgiveness, and the opera ends. *—Erik Eriksson*

Recommended:

- ○ **Rossini: L'Italiana in Algeri** / Scimone (cond.), Horne, Ramey, Battle, Palacio, I Solisti Veneti / Erato 45404
- ○ **Rossini: L'Italiana in Algeri** / Abbado (cond.), Corbelli, Raimondi, Baltsa, Dara, Vienna PO / DG 427331
- ○ **Rossini: L'Italiana in Algeri** / Lopez-Cobos (cond.), Larmore, Carrot, Lausanne CO / 1998 / Teldec 17130

Mosè in Egitto (1818; revised 1819)

Rossini dubbed his original version of *Mose in Egitto* a "tragico-sacred action"; the librettist, A.L. Tottola, combined the biblical narrative of the *Exodus* story with a typical love plot from a play called "L'Osiride" (Francesco Ringhieri, 1760). This peculiar combination of themes arose from Rossini's need to circumvent papal proscriptions against performances of secular opera during Lent; Tottola's creative fusion of sacred and secular elements made the resulting work a pseudo-oratorio. The dramatic themes from *Exodus* are treated as befits a sacred subject: choral numbers, large instrumental forces, depictions of plagues, miracles, prayers, and crowds of Egyptians and Israelites—all very Handelian in their grandeur. The part of Moses is monumental, set for the bass voice in authoritative declamation. The operatic elements, which include a love story between a Hebrew girl and the Egyptian Prince Osiris, are treated in an entirely secular manner. Within the context of the *Exodus* story, the death of Osiris is retributive; he has condemned Moses to death and the

Israelites must be avenged by their God; but within the love story the death of Osiris is tragic, mourned by Elcia in a tender cabaletta.

The premiere of *Mose in Egitto* took place on March 5, 1818, at the Teatro de San Carlo in Naples; it was extremely well received. The opening of the original version is particularly striking: the darkened stage is introduced by three ominous chords; the confused and distressed Egyptians lament the plague of darkness that has fallen over Egypt. As the Pharaoh relents and promises to allow Moses to lead the Israelites out of bondage, the chordal progression moves from minor to major, and light is restored. Haydn's *Creation* was one of Rossini's favorite works, and this scene was clearly inspired by Haydn's depiction of the creation of light and dark in that work. At the premiere, the opera was well received until the Red Sea crossing in the third act, during which the audience was reduced to helpless laughter at the clumsy machinery depicting the miracle. Rossini revived the opera the next year with changes to the third act; it was then that he added the famous prayer of Moses, "Dal tuo stellato soglio," or "From your starry throne."

Mose in Egitto enjoyed a second incarnation as a French opera, entitled *Moise et Pharaon*. This was by now traditional for the composer, who was in the habit of converting his Italian compositions for use in Paris. *Mose in Egitto* had already been a success on the Parisian stage both at the Theatre de l'Academie de Musique and at the Théâtre-Italien, where it was part of the standard repertory. In 1827, Rossini and two librettists, Luigi Balocchini and Etienne de Jouy, adapted the libretto, introducing a ballet in the third act, extending the work to five acts, and adding additional choral numbers. Although this French version loses some dramatic intensity, somewhat burdened under the weight of the additions, it is this version which is usually performed today. *—Rita Laurance*

Synopsis:

Act One. The stage is dark as a chorus of Egyptians is lamenting the curse of darkness which has fallen over their land. Pharaoh, Queen Amaltea, and Prince Osiris lament with their people. Pharaoh summons the prophet Moses, convinced that God is sending him a direct message, and Moses and Aaron arrive to negotiate the lifting of the curse over the Egyptians. When Pharaoh agrees to allow Moses to lead the Israelites out of bondage, the darkness miraculously turns to day, and happy rejoicing replaces the dark lamentations of the people. All are happy except Prince Osiris, who is secretly married to a Hebrew girl, and knows that she will go with the other Israelites when they leave. He doesn't want to lose his beloved Elcia, so he plots to turn the Egyptians against Pharaoh. He tells Mambre that the Egyptians will be worse off if the Israelites leave, and Mambre goes to convince the other Egyptians that Pharaoh is betraying their best interests. Elcia comes to bid her husband good-bye. Trumpets sound as the Israelites prepare to depart. However, Osiris' plan has succeeded, and Pharaoh must bow to the wish of the Egyptian people who are now rioting against the release of their slaves. To the objections of his wife, Pharaoh goes back on his word and refuses to allow Moses to leave.

The Israelites, meanwhile, are celebrating their imminent freedom. They sing a joyful hymn of praise to God for delivering them from the Egyptian monarch, and only Elcia is the least bit sad about leaving her home. However, Osiris interrupts their rejoicing. He enters to announce that Pharaoh, moved by the wishes of his own people, has gone back on his word and decreed that the Israelites must remain. Moses is outraged. He cries for vengeance against the intransigence of the Egyptian political leaders who stand in the way of God's will. Osiris scorns Moses and commands his soldiers to kill the prophet of the Hebrews, but just then, Pharaoh arrives and intervenes. Moses challenges Pharaoh to keep his word and allow the Jews to go free but Pharaoh, too, scorns him. Because of this, Moses raises his staff to the heavens, and hail and brimstone begin to rain down on the Egyptians. A scene of complete terror closes the act.

Act Two. At the palace, Pharaoh is overcome by fear at this latest plague and promises Aaron that the Israelites will be allowed to go free. Osiris enters, and Pharaoh tells him that he plans for him to marry the Princess of Armenia. He is completely unaware that his son has secretly been married to a Jewish girl. Osiris and he sing a divergent duet, each expressing their different emotions over the proposed union. Meanwhile Pharaoh's wife, sympathetic to the Hebrew cause, tells Moses and Aaron that she will try to get Pharaoh to keep his promise to them. She is tired of the plagues raining down on Egypt.

Osiris abducts Elcia and takes her to a cave, where he tries to convince her to remain with him. He does not want her to join the other Jews as they leave Egypt. The two lovers are discovered in their hiding place by Aaron and Amaltea. In the ensuing confusion, Aaron takes Elcia back to her people, and Amaltea restrains the objecting Osiris.

Pharaoh again refuses to let the Hebrews go free when he learns that the surrounding countries plan an attack if he does so. This time, the angry Moses threatens Pharaoh with the death of all the firstborn of the land, including the Pharaoh's own son. Pharaoh is completely beside himself with anger against the prophet, and has him taken prisoner. He decides that he will sentence Moses to death. The nobles of Egypt all arrive to witness the event. Pharaoh tells them that he has made his son, Osiris, a joint ruler with himself, and that Osiris will give the order for the execution. While Moses stands before the court in chains, Elcia tells them of her marriage to Osiris, but begs the Prince to remarry the Armenian princess. Osiris is implacable, however, and pronounces the death sentence on the prophet. As he does so, a lightening bolt shoots out of the sky and strikes him dead, before all of the assembled company. The Pharaoh grieves over the loss of his son, and Elcia also laments him.

Act Three. The Israelites are fleeing the land of Egypt via the shores of the Red Sea, but are blocked by the supposedly impassable body of water in their path. Moses leads them in a prayer to the Almighty ("Dal tuo stellato soglio"). Just as the angry Egyptians are heard approaching, Moses lifts his staff to the heavens, and their prayer is heard. The Red Sea parts and the Israelites are given safe passage across it. When the Egyptians attempt to follow the Israelites, they are drowned by the surging, angry waters that flow back over them. *—Rita Laurance*

Recommended:

○ **Rossini: Mosè** / Sawallisch (cond.), Raimondi, Araiza, Rootering, Vaness, Bavarian State Orch. / 1999 / Orfeo d'Or 514992

Semiramide (1823)

This opera, one of Rossini's most famous, is a dramatic work, from the unsettled rushing motif that opens the overture to the final tragedy in Nino's tomb. The first-act duet for Assur and Arsace is a hair-raising example of the duetto della sfida (literally, "duet of defiance"), with the bass and mezzo-soprano hurling runs, almost impossibly long lines, sudden jumps, and other demonstrations of vocal prowess at one another, pitting the voices of the antagonists against one another in a perfect reflection of the threats issuing from the characters. The melodiousness of Semiramide's deliciously amorous "Bel raggio lusinghier," and her subsequent tender duet with Arsace, provide an interlude that highlights the subsequent drama, culminating when Semiramide announces her intention to marry Arsace and give him the throne, and with the mysterious proclamations of Nino's ghost. Rossini here employs a large structure with two ensembles: the first consists largely of expressions of hushed horror, then there is a sweepingly melodic tutti passage, and finally come the loud, mostly ensemble expressions of bewilderment that bring down the curtain.

The second act uses the same structures, but in different ways, sometimes highlighting a direct contrast with the first act. The duetto della sfida is between Assur and Semiramide, and takes both soprano and bass to the extremes of their ranges. Here, however, the mood is more complex, as both remember their complicity in recent events. Assur threatens her not only in swift roulades, but in a menacing and yet melodic reminder, and her response is punctuated by harsh chords from the orchestra, before their voices weave together in the final passages preceding angry outbursts that end their scene. The central aria conveys Arsace's fiery reaction to the news that the murdered Nino is his father. It stands in sharp contrast to Semiramide's loving aria from the first act, and is punctuated by a martial male chorus rather than a sunny female one. The duet between Semiramide and Arsace is tense as well as tender, as he repulses instead of naively accepting her advances, and reveals his knowledge of the murder of his father, but then offers his forgiveness and compassion upon seeing her remorse and her maternal love. Assur, at least for the length of an aria, begs for forgiveness from the ghost of Nino for his murder, in relatively simple legato phrases rather than his earlier bombast, and the final chorus is an exuberant one of rejoicing, rather than confused dismay.

This work has had a spotted performance history, largely because of the casting demands. Each of the major roles demands two qualities rarely found in the same voice, and almost never together in a bass voice: power and incredible agility. During the latter half of the twentieth century—during the Rossini Renaissance, as it's sometimes been called—these casts have been available, boasting singers such as Sutherland, Horne, Caballe, and Ramey; listeners have luxuriated. *—Ann Feeney*

Synopsis:

Act One. The story takes place in Babylon, eighth century B.C. Outside the Temple of Baal, a crowd has assembled to await announcement by Semiramide, Queen of Babylon, of her choice for successor to King Nino, who, unknown to the public, was murdered by her and Prince Assur. The pair also attempted to kill her son Arsace 15 years earlier, and he is now commander of the Assyrian army. They are unaware that the popular Arsace is Semiramide's son. Assur waits inside the temple, with hopes he will ascend to the throne. He fears the high priest Oroe, however, who stands at the altar, for the secrets he may know. The Indian Prince Idreno also waits inside to receive the gods' countenancing of his love for Princess Azema.

As Semiramide arrives, the huge sacred flame on the altar glitters, but suddenly explodes before extinguishing. Arsace soon appears and presents a casket of belongings from King Nino (whom he does not know was his father) to high priest Oroe. The young commander, who is also in love with Princess Azema, confronts Assur, telling him he will not acknowledge him as King if he is chosen.

Semiramide happily greets Arsace in the Hanging Gardens of Babylon. She talks of Assur's untrustworthy character but erroneously concludes Arsace is in love with her, not Azema.

At the palace Semiramide at last proclaims the King—Arsace, who will also become her husband. Assur becomes enraged at the news, while Arsace is dismayed.

Later, as Idreno is about to marry Azema, the ghost of King Nino appears and announces that Arsace will indeed take the throne, but that atonement for past crimes must be made. Further, Arsace must make a sacrifice to the King's ashes.

Act Two. Semiramide and Assur quarrel in the palace, the former threatening to reveal the latter's misdeeds.

Oroe, about to lead Arsace to his father's tomb, informs him that he is the son of King Nino and Semiramide and that the King was slain by Semiramide and Assur. Arsace can accept the execution of Assur, but hopes for mercy for his mother.

In her private chambers Arsace tells Semiramide he is aware of her crimes. She is repentant and offers to give her life for her actions, but Arsace declares that he loves her as his mother.

By King Nino's tomb, Assur learns that Oroe has exposed his misdeeds. Determined to murder Arsace, he turns mad for a time, but gradually grows almost repentant for his crimes. Arsace enters King Nino's monument, followed by Semiramide and Assur. The latter attacks Arsace, who misdirects a fatal blow and strikes Semiramide, who dies as the people celebrate Arsace's ascension to the throne. *—Robert Cummings*

Recommended:

○ **Rossini: Semiramide** / Bonynge (cond.), Sutherland, Horne, Rouleau, Fyson, London SO / 1986 / Decca 425481

○ **Rossini: Semiramide** / Marin (cond.), Larmore, Rootering, Studer, Lopardo, London SO / DG 437797

Tancredi (1813)

Tancredi marks a turning point in Rossini's career, as well as in the evolution of nineteenth century opera. In it the essentially static and segmented forms of eighteenth century opera seria are infused with a more expansive, less structured lyricism, and the dramatic content is brought more into agreement with the romantic spirit of nineteenth century Europe. It is also the opera that clinched Rossini's already rising fame in his native Italy and abroad.

Tancredi is a melodrama in two acts to a libretto by Gaetano Rossi. The story, taken from Voltaire's play *Tancrède* (1760), is filled with sympathy for the ideals of the French revolution—a revolution which Rossini lived through (Rossini's own father had been a sympathizer with French Republican views and had been imprisoned for it). Patriotic ideals of liberty are espoused everywhere throughout the opera. *Tancredi* is the story of two young lovers, Tancredi and Amenaide, who struggle to realize their affections against a backdrop of political and family conflict, somewhat alà *Romeo and Juliet.* Although the music provides for plenty of vocal display, *Tancredi* has a strong dramatic purpose; it is a credible drama with vivid, vibrant characters, full of strong human emotions and motivations. Opera seria conventions are dispensed with in favor of a more supple drama with broader appeal.

Rossini composed two distinct version of *Tancredi.* The original version which premiered at the Teatro La Fenice in Venice, on February 6, 1813, was extremely well received by the public. This version, although filled with lyrical beauty and formal innovations, was not as revolutionary as its later version. Instead of the tragic ending written by Voltaire, Rossini and Rossi chose to alter the ending. They changed the plot so that Tancredi could live and marry the woman he loves. However, for the Ferrara revival one month later, Rossini reinstated Voltaire's original ending and supplied entirely new music. This version, now with a tragic arioso scena during which Tancredi dies of his wounds and Amenaide protests her innocence and love, proved a bit much for the Italian public, which was not prepared for such a formal and artistic innovation. In deference to taste, Rossini eventually returned to his original, more conventional ending.

Some of the highlights of *Tancredi* include two love duets for Amenaide and Tancredi and two solo scenes for each of the main protagonists. In Act Two, Amenaide has a prison scene, orchestrated with exquisite care and sensitivity. Here, the instrumental music is just as moving as the song in which Amenaide expresses her resolve to die rather than betray her love. In Tancredi's solo scene, he is given beautiful melodies and florid passagework as he expresses his resolve to win his battle against Solamir.

Semiramide can be seen as the direct descendent of the experimentations begun in *Tancredi.* Although the innovations in *Tancredi* were greatly expanded upon in *Semiramide,* the later work is missing the youthful vigor and ingenuity of its predecessor and it has not achieved the same lasting presence on operatic stages. *—AMG*

Synopsis:

The opera takes place in Syracuse, at the beginning of the ninth century. The families of the Orbazzani and the Argiri had been feuding for generations, but recently negotiated a truce. The powerful house of the Orbazzani was ruling Syracuse. During their time of ascendancy, Orbazzano had banished the wife and daughter of Argirio to the Byzantine court. There they made the acquaintance of a noble knight named Tancredi. With her mother's approval, Amenaide secretly became engaged to Tancredi, with whom she had fallen deeply in love. Now that the two feuding families agreed on peace, Amenaide has returned to Syracuse. There is general rejoicing as two families vow to fight together for the sake of their country against the forces of the Moors and any others who oppose them. Orbazzano warns them also against the knight Tancredi, who is well loved in Syracuse and very powerful. Orbazzano had him banished from Syracuse as a traitor against the state and seized all his lands for his own.

As a part of their peace agreement, Argirio decides to offer Orbazzano the hand of his daughter Amenaide in marriage. When Argirio brings up the wished-for betrothal, Amenaide procrastinates, begging her father to at least put the event off for another day. She has recently written a letter to Tancredi, urging him to return home, and begging him to liberate Syracuse with his knightly forces. Tancredi hasn't received her letter, but he and his knights have already returned. He sings of his passionate love for Amenaide and instructs his knights to hang their standard in the square and offer their aid in defense of the city. Argirio thinks that they have arrived to further the suit of the Moorish leader Solamir. Solamir was also in love with Amenaide and had asked for her hand in marriage when she was living at the Byzantine court. Argirio urges Amenaide to marry Orbazzano immediately, before the entire city is plunged into war. He wants her new husband to be able to come back to her victorious in battle. Her father also tells her that the senate has sentenced all enemies of the state to death, and she realizes that Tancredi is in grave danger. After her father leaves, Tancredi comes to Amenaide in private. In order that he might leave, she tells him that she doesn't love him. She urges him to think only of his own safety and to flee.

Preparations are made for the wedding of Amenaide to Orbazzano. Nobles, courtiers, and knights are all gathered to celebrate, and Tancredi joins in the celebrations. Orbazzano was a bitter enemy to Tancredi's father, and Tancredi wants revenge against him for stealing his love. He thinks that Amenaide is unfaithful, so in disguise joins Argirio in the battle against the Saracens. At the altar, Amenaide stops and begs her father to release her from her obligation to marry Orbazzano. She says to all present that she cannot wed someone whom she could never love. Her father and Orbazzano are both outraged, and Orbazzano decides to betray her. He produces the letter that she wrote to Tancredi. It does not have a named addressee on it, and all think that it was written to the leader of the Saracens in order to betray her country. In order to protect Tancredi, Amenaide refuses to defend herself, or to explain the circumstances of the letter. The entire populace calls for her punishment as a traitor to the state.

As Act Two opens, Orbazzano is demanding that Argirio sign a death warrant against his own daughter. Although he agonizes over it out of some semblance of fatherly love, he eventually signs the warrant. Amenaide, imprisoned and bound in chains, sings of her innocence and of her love for Tancredi. When she tells Orbazzano that she is innocent, he challenges anyone to champion her against her foes. The knight Tancredi accepts the challenge and also calls Orbazzano a cruel despot. Tancredi is convinced that Amenaide is guilty. However, in the ensuing combat with Orbazzano, he triumphs, and Orbazzano is slain.

Now the Syracusans have no military leader to fight with them against the Saracens. They ask Tancredi to lead their army but he refuses. Tancredi, however, does not know if Amenaide still loves him, and is filled with despondency and despair. He refuses to lead their army and instead prepares to depart Syracuse.

In the original opera, Tancredi joins the army of Syracuse, the Saracens are defeated, and he and Amenaide marry and live happily ever after. In the Ferrara version of the opera, Tancredi hopelessly wanders in the woods until he is challenged by some Saracen knights. In the ensuing battle he triumphs, but is mortally injured. As he lies dying of his wounds, Amenaide insists on her innocence and on her everlasting love for him. The two are reconciled only as Tancredi breathes his last breath. *—Rita Laurance*

Recommended:

○ **Rossini: Tancredi** / Abbado (cond.), Vargas, Kasarova, Mei, Paulsen, Munich Radio Orch. / 1996 / RCA 68349

○ **Rossini: Tancredi** / Zedda (cond.), Jo, Podles, Spagnoli, Baert, Brugense Collegium Instrumentale / 1995 / Naxos 660037

Il turco in Italia (The Turk in Italy) (1814)

Il Turco in Italia was commissioned by the famed La Scala in Milan for the autumn season of 1814. Although only 22 at the time of composition, Gioacchino Rossini was already esteemed as an operatic composer (having scored hits with several opere buffe as well as grander, more serious works such as *Tancredi*), and the success of his *L'italiana in Algeri* the year before spurred him to write a companion piece. Although the two cannot be considered sequels in the literal sense, the similarities are obvious: In *L'italiana,* amorous intrigues surround an Italian woman stranded in Algiers, while in *Il Turco,* a Turk arrives in Italy only to add himself to an existing love triangle (making a love quadrangle, perhaps?). Unfortunately for Rossini, the Milanese public was all too aware of these similarities and, although Rossini's score was every bit as fresh and inventive and his characterizations as well-drawn as those for *L'italiana,* they heartily disapproved. However, the quality of the score would eventually carry the day and, as Stendhal wrote in his biography of Rossini, the opera was revived just four years later to wild enthusiasm. Today *Il Turco in Italia* is considered a masterpiece of the buffo genre; it stands alongside *L'italiana in Algeri* and *Il Barbiere di Siviglia* as three of the composer's greatest.

The librettist for *Il Turco in Italia* was Felice Romani. A noteworthy feature of his book was the use of the fictitious poet, Prosdocimo—perhaps a whimsical blend of "prosa" (prose), "docente" (teacher), and "proscenio" (proscenium)—as both narrator and putative author of the story. Essentially a theatrical conceit personified, he is both detached from, and involved in, the story, and puts an amiable face on plot machinations that might otherwise seem weary. The inclusion of an exotic foreigner, on the other hand—in this case a caricature of a Turk—was a fairly stock device in opera buffa, allowing composers to add international spice to their scores. The combination of these things reveals the essence of what made Romani such a successful librettist: his writing provided an excellent foundation for the extremely formal and stylized musical concerns of early nineteenth century opera, while still maintaining its poetic integrity and dramatic interest.

The character of Fiorilla, whose affections form the center of the plot, is characterized superbly through witty, sparkling music; she shines forth more strongly than any of Rossini's buffa characters, including Rosina in *The Barber of Seville.* For the Turk himself, Rossini wrote some truly sensational virtuoso music; the part was initially sung by Filippo Galli, one of the finest bass voices in the history of opera, whose premiere performance is said to have brought down the house. The Act Two duet, in which the Turk tells Fiorilla's husband that he wishes to purchase her, if only to take her off the husband's hands, is also memorable. —*AMG*

Synopsis:

Act One. The opera opens on a hillside of Naples by the sea. Farmhouses and gypsy tents are scattered throughout the countryside. Groups of gypsies busy themselves with various activities. The gypsy fortuneteller Zaida bewails her broken heart. A poet enters. He is searching for a suitable subject for an operatic farce that he wants to write. He sees the band of gypsies and decides that they would make a vivid opening. Inspired, he decides to people his opera with their characters. He hopes that something that they do will help his libretto take direction. While drawing up his libretto, he adds his friends Fiorilla and her husband Don Geronio to the group. They make a colorful addition; she is capricious and flirtatious, and he a suspicious old lout. Don Geronio enters just at that moment. He is looking for someone to cure his crazy wife from what he this is a case of dementia. He also wants his fortune told by a gypsy woman, but is unhappy when he hears the news, for the fortuneteller thinks that his wife is unfaithful. The fortuneteller herself has had a rough time of it. She was in love with a Turkish Prince, but he rejected her when he thought that she had been unfaithful.

The group disbands and Fiorilla enters the scene. She hangs around idly out of boredom. A Turkish ship appears on the horizon. It eventually docks, and the Turkish Prince Selim disembarks. She flirts with him and teases him and he begins to find her attractive. Finally, they go off for a walk together. Don Geronio enters the scene completely beside himself. He announces to the company that he just saw his wife with... a Turk! He tells them that she is taking the Turk to their house for a coffee! Nonetheless, the poet is overjoyed when he learns about it, for now he feels that his play is as good as written. Gallant swains jilted, foolish husbands and crazy wives! However, Geronio and Fiorilla's jilted lover, Narciso, are somewhat offended at his glee. They threaten to write into the script the beating of a poet.

Back at the home of Fiorilla, the Turk has begun to make love to Fiorilla in earnest. He promises her riches, but she rebuffs him, saying that he probably has many wives, and sells them when he tires of them. Selim has almost convinced her to flee with him when Don Geronio arrives. The Prince is shocked to discover that Fiorilla has a husband. Fiorilla convinces Geronio that the Turk only wants to pay him homage. Then Narciso also arrives. Geronio complains to the poet that he is a foolish old husband, betrayed by his wife repeatedly. He wishes that she were a gentle, shy thing that he could control. He tells Fiorilla that she is bizarre and capricious, and they begin to argue. After arguing for a bit, Fiorilla decides that she must teach Don Geronio a lesson.

The poet, meanwhile, decides to influence the outcome of the story. It has come to his attention that Prince Selim is the Turk who was betrothed to the Gypsy fortuneteller Zaida. He arranges a meeting between the two, and they have a tender reunion. Fiorilla interrupts the two, however, and begins an argument that continues as Act One ends.

Act Two. Geronio and the poet are out having a drink at an inn. Prince Selim arrives and suggests to Don Geronio that he sell his wife to him. He, a prince, could pay a good price, and then the conniving woman would be off Don Geronio's hands. Geronio, however, is incensed at the idea, and the two fight. After Don Geronio has gone, Fiorilla arrives. She wants Prince Selim to choose between her and his old beloved, the gypsy fortuneteller Zaida. However, Zaida leaves in a huff, and Selim easily overcomes Fiorilla's resistance.

Fiorilla and Selim plan to come to a masked ball that evening masked so that only they will know their true identities. They plan to flee together before the ball is over, leaving Fiorilla's husband and lover far behind. However, the poet again intervenes, and tells Don Geronio their plans. He has Zaida come to the ball in the same costume as Fiorilla, and dresses Narciso up as a Turk. Selim mistakes Zaida for Fiorilla and proposes to her. She is overjoyed and of course accepts. He is perfectly happy at the outcome of the poet's machinations, and Fiorilla also is perfectly happy to go back to her husband. All apologize to one another, and Zaida and Selim leave on the Turk's ship. The poet announces the end of the play, and the chorus provides a moral for the ending: It is a small error that results in a more beautiful love.—*Rita Laurance*

Recommended:

○ **Rossini: La turco in Italia** / Chailly (cond.), Bartoli, Pertusi, Corbelli, Vargas, La Scala Theater Orch. / 1998 / London 458924

ORCHESTRAL

Overtures (1810–1829)

Nearly two centuries after all but a very few of Rossini's operas have fallen from the standard repertory, many of his opera overtures stand among the most popular concert pieces ever written. Well into the early nineteenth century, French and Italian audiences notoriously chattered through opera overtures, which they considered an inconsequential background noise preceding the evening's true entertainment, the singing. Consequently, most Italian and French composers—Cherubini being the major exception—invested little effort in their overtures. Rossini was not always diligent himself; he frequently recycled overtures from one opera to another. For example, that for *The Barber of Seville* was originally attached to *Aureliano in Palmira,* and *La cenerentola*'s first appeared at the head of *La gazzetta.* Yet Rossini lavished unusual invention on the overtures he did bother to write. Although for obvious reasons, almost none are thematically related to the operas themselves, the overtures abound in colorful instrumental touches, and most employ Rossini's signature effect: the long crescendo. Rossini's typical overture pattern is a stripped-down sonata form. There's generally a slow introduction followed by a first main theme played by the strings and a second featuring the winds. Rossini skips the usual development section and moves right along to a recapitulation of the themes, rounded out with a brilliant coda. Powerful rhythms drive the fast sections and the slow passages often center on lovely woodwind solos. Beginning around 1812 with *L'inganno felice,* the overture pivots around at least one of Rossini's trademark crescendos. This consists of a churning ostinato rhythm over which a tiny thematic fragment is obsessively played over and over. It begins with very few instruments, with more and more gradually joining in and it's a matter of thickening the texture as much as making the music louder. Rossini's early overtures require only a modest pit orchestra. There's a leanness and vivacity to the sound that makes the wind solos stand out and the use of a triangle becomes unusually prominent (to say nothing of the frequent cymbal crashes). Until the Fondazione Rossini issued clean critical editions of the scores in the 1980s, however, conductors had no choice but to use corrupt late nineteenth century editions that padded the orchestra with brass instruments and reassigned Rossini's intentionally shrill piccolo passages to the more agreeable flute. Even so, many of Rossini's most arresting effects survived the old editors' heavy hands. Among the highlights are the violinists icily playing sul ponticello, or close to the bridge, at the beginning of the crescendo in *L'italiana in Algeri* and striking their music stands with their bows in *Il signor Bruschino.* Most familiar are the martial drum rolls opening *La gazza ladra.* Rossini's most ubiquitous overture is his least characteristic. That for *Guillaume Tell,* his final opera, falls into four distinct sections, each painting a specific scene. Rossini lived well into the age of the programmatic tone poem and his *William Tell* overture suggests that, had he tried, he could have been a master of the genre. —*James Reel*

Recommended:

○ **Rossini: Overtures** / Orbelian (cond.), Moscow CO / 2000 / Chandos 9753

○ **Rossini: Overtures** / Chailly (cond.), National PO / 1995 / London 443850

○ **Arturo Toscanini Conducts Rossini Overtures** / Toscanini (cond.), BBC SO, NBC SO / 2000 / Aura Classics 0233

○ **Rossini: Overtures** / Dutoit (cond.), Montreal SO / Decca 467427

VOCAL

Duetto buffo di due gatti (Cat Duet), for 2 voices & piano (1816)

Many are the vocal recitals and opera galas that have ended with the *Cat Duet* as an encore. Though scored for two sopranos and piano, the work exists in orchestral versions and has been sung by male-female pairs and even as a tomcat duet. The text consists in its entirety of the single word "meow," and singers treat the melodies basically however they want to. The origins of this work are cloudy, but historians agree that it is not an authentic work by Rossini. It does, however, contain a good deal of Rossini's music, so the attribution is not completely off the mark. The *Cat Duet* contains elements of 1) the aria "Ah, come mai non senti," from the second act of Rossini's opera *Otello* (1816), 2) a nearby duet between the characters Otello and Iago, and 3) an earlier work in the same vein, the "Cat Cavatina" of Danish opera and song composer C.E.F. Weyse. The compiler was probably Robert Lucas Pearsall, a British composer better known for his output of hymns. In 1973, the Schott publishing house issued a facsimile of an 1825 edition of the *Cat Duet*, published by Ewer & Johanning and credited to Pearsall, but bearing the pseudonym G. Berthold. From Rossini's day down to ours, the piece has never lost its appeal for singers, concertgoers, and cat lovers; it often appears, of course, on compilations of classical music pertaining to felines. *—James Manheim*

Recommended:

○ **Tribute to Gerald Moore** / Moore, de los Angeles, Schwarzkopf, Fischer-Dieskau / 2003 / EMI 67994

La regata Veneziana, 3 songs in Venetian dialect (Péchés de vieillesse, book 1) (1857–1868)

In this short song cycle, set to a text in the Venetian dialect by Carlo Pepoli (who provided the texts for several other Rossini songs), a girl watches a Venice regatta (gondola race) and cheers on her lover. After retiring from opera composition, Rossini still composed, mostly sacred music and trifling pieces for his own amusement and for that of his guests at musical evenings. These songs and piano pieces were collected and published as *Les soirees musicales*.

In the first song, *Anzoleta avanti la regata* (Anzoleta before the regatta), Anzoleta excitedly encourages her lover, Momolo, to win and reminds him that she will be watching. The song begins with three repetitions of a recurrent rowing theme in the piano line, followed by a playfully lengthy pause before the piano takes up the main lilting theme that suggests the light glinting off the water and the voice enters with a lyrical, cajoling melody. The song ends with a brief series of trills as if Anzoleta is urging him by example to row even more quickly. The second, *Anzoleta co passa la regata* (Anzoleta during the regatta), begins with a fast, agitated piano theme that suggests both the rapid movements of the gondolas and Anzoleta's anxiety. The vocal lines are breathless and heavily repetitive, further enhancing the sense of excitement tinged with anxiety. The song ends with her final, excited exclamation as Momolo wins the race. The ending in the piano line is an unexpectedly subdued series of quiet chords, as if she is sitting down to catch her breath and reassure herself that he really did win. The third, *Anzoleta dopo la regata* (Anzoleta after the regatta), begins with a festive, dance-like theme in the piano introduction. The vocal line, over a light waltz theme in the piano, is one of Rossini's most seductive melodies as she urges him to take as many kisses as he wants in reward for his victory. This theme is briefly interrupted by more dramatic and insistent lines as she boasts that he's been named the winner and all Venice is talking about him, but it soon returns to the flirtatious waltz and, like the last song, the vocal line ends on a triumphant high note. The piano conclusion here, though, is full of flourishes and ends on a crashing forte major chord. *—Ann Feeney*

Recommended:

○ **Tatiana Troyanos in Recital** / Troyanos, Levine / 1999 / VAI Audio 1187

○ **Rossini Recital** / Bartoli, Spencer / 1991 / Decca 430518

Soirées musicales, song collection for voices & piano (ca. 1830–1835)

Gioachino Rossini lost no time in enjoying his self-imposed retirement in the wake of *William Tell*. By forty, he was already the avuncular, Falstavian figure presiding over parties well attended by fellow musicians, artists, writers and society elite. Yet, unlike the deafening silence of the oft-compared early retirement of Sibelius, the creative flame still burned, albeit at a low pilot, for the now-affluent Italian. Against this convivial backdrop, the *Soirees musicales* (Musical Evenings) came into being between 1830 and 1835.

This collection of a dozen songs is comprised of eight for solo voice and four duets, all with piano accompaniment. The texts are varied, but the bulk are provided by Count Carlo Pepoli, amateur man-of-letters and frequent guest at Rossini's. The first, "La Promessa," is in what has been described as the composer's "kittenish" mode, playful yet relaxed. This is followed by "Il Rimprovero," its languid spinning-wheel rhythm brought to a jolting close by a series of rapidly modulating chords, a favored device in the codas of the composer's overtures. "La Partenza," despite its bittersweet lyrics of farewell, is in the tempo of an old-fashioned minuet and is followed by the heartier excursion in triple time, "L'orgia." The following four form a suite of contrasting national dances: "L'invito," a Spanish bolero; "La Pastorella delle Alpi," a Tyrolean laendler; "La Gita in Gondola," a Venetian boat song; and the most famous of the set, the Neapolitan "La Danza," one of the most evocative pæans to the rising hormones of youth. Set against a swirling tarantella rhythm, the lyrics, including guitar onomatopoeia and exclamations of "Mama Mia!" rallies young lovers to a nocturnal dance. The following four duets for various vocal combinations includes "La Reganata veneziana"; its main theme is strikingly similar to one used by Von Suppe in his *Poet and Peasant* a decade later. The wandering chromatic melody of "La Pesca" may lead one to ponder the possible indebtedness of Berlioz to Rossini. "La Serentata" is in the same vein. The last of the works is the most striking, the darkly dramatic "I Marinai." No sunny Mediterranean view can be found in this brooding seascape, usually sung by tenor and baritone. The piano accompaniment seems to cry out for larger forces, unlike the technically uncomplicated others in the set. It is not surprising that this song caught the attention of young Richard Wagner, then a conductor in Riga, who made an orchestral transcription of "I Marinai" and performed it under his direction. *—Wayne Reisig*

Recommended:

○ **Rossini: Soirées musicales** / Corbelli, Walker, Gimenez / Nimbus 5132

CHORAL

Petite messe solennelle (1863; revised 1867)

Gioachino Rossini was 71 years old when he composed the *Petite messe solennelle* in 1863; this most celebrated of opera buffa composers had not issued a single new opera in over three decades, and it had been a full 51 years since his music was first head at La Scala. But Rossini's hand was not at all rusty, even though he spent the 1830s, 1840s, and 1850s in comparative retirement, dabbling only occasionally in this odd piece or that one. There are even those who consider this mass to be Rossini's most finely-crafted effort. Rossini composed the *Petite messe solennelle* for a private performance at the home of the Count Michel-Frédéric Pillet-Will and his wife Louise in Paris, and he scored it accordingly, using 12 solo and semi-solo singers, a pair of pianofortes and harmonium. A few years later Rossini orchestrated the work, not for any specific occasion but simply because he feared that if he didn't, someone else might, and that idea was as unacceptable to him as it has been to countless other composers over the generations.

The *Petite messe solennelle* is really not all that petite: it fills over 150 pages in its chamber version and covers all of the necessary Mass ordinary material at full length. The deployment of the soloists throughout the 16 musical numbers is varied: sometimes, as in No. 5 "Domine Deus" for tenor solo, No. 10 "Crucifixus" for soprano solo, and No. 15 "O salutaris hostia" for soprano again, a single soloist is left completely alone in an aria-like number; sometime the small chorus remains to back up a soloist; and yet other times the four soloists work together in the traditional vocal quartet fashion. Never, however, does the chorus get a number all to itself.

Rossini had a fine sense of humor (could he have written the operas he did without one?), and the manuscript to the score contains many wryly self-deprecating little written notes, including an apology to God for the shortcomings of this "poor little mass" and a note remarking that, unlike the 12 disciples, none of his 12 singers will "sing falsely"! But the mass is in no way meant to be a comedy; it is a serious piece, honestly and deeply felt in an innocent, straightforward way. If some of the passages sound as though they might have come from a light opera, well, Rossini's apology explains that that's just Rossini doing what Rossini did best, hoping that the God for whom he wrote the piece would give him the benefit of the doubt. The *Petite messe solennelle* joins Rossini's *Stabat mater* of some years earlier as a vital, yet all-but-unknown, piece of the nineteenth century European sacred music puzzle. *—Blair Johnston*

Recommended:

○ **Rossini: Petite Messe Solennelle** / Creed (cond.), Davislim, Muller-Brachmann, RIAS-Kammerchor / HM 901724

○ **Rossini: Petite Messe Solennelle** / Corboz (cond.), Sgrizzi, Fink, La Scola, Gasdia, Lausanne Ens. Vocal / Erato 45321

○ **Rossini: Petite Messe Solennelle** / Kuentz (cond.), Schlick, Langshaw, Perrier-Layec, Postec, P / 1999 / Disques Pierre Verany 730102

Stabat mater (1832; revised 1841)

Rossini's *Stabat Mater* was performed publicly in its final form in Paris on January 7, 1842. The first six sections of this ten-movement work had been composed earlier, on commission from Don Francesco de Varela, for an 1833 Good Friday performance in Madrid (with the last four movements written by Giuseppe Tadolini). The work was received enthusiastically in both of its incarnations and has remained a core piece of the choral repertory ever since.

Critics were initially less inclined to give their unqualified endorsement, however, citing its overtly operatic character. Nonetheless, one finds similar theatricality in other sacred music written by Italian composers (Verdi's *Requiem* is one of the most obvious) and whatever reservations one might cite are diminished by the sheer sweep and intensity of Rossini's music.

Scored for four soloists (two sopranos, tenor, and bass), chorus, and orchestra, the *Stabat Mater* features two movements for chorus and solo voices without accompaniment. Despite the near-decade separating the *Eia Mater fons amoris* (section five) and *Quando corpus morietur* (section nine), there is absolute consistency in style and inspiration.

The opening movement, *Stabat Mater dolorosa*, emerges out of the silence, first with orchestra, then orchestra joined by chorus, finally adding the soloists. Both solemnity and ardor are present. The second section, *Cujus animam gementem*, is a tenor aria of considerable difficulty, imposing on the singer a high D in its final moments. The springing naïveté of the vocal line and the metric simplicity of the accompaniment require that soloist and conductor approach the music with utmost dignity to avoid any sense of banality.

Section three is a duet for the two sopranos, *Quis est homo, qui non fleret*, often recalling duets the composer had written for his female protagonists in opera

(*Semiramide* and *Tancredi*, for example). *Pro peccatis suae gentis*, an aria for bass, alternates between a bold, striding motive and a more reflective, flowing one. Wide-ranging, this section, too, demands a seriousness of approach by the soloist if a descent into simple bravura is to be avoided. Section five, *Eia Mater*, finds the bass soloist alternating with the unaccompanied chorus in a moment of sublime reflection. The quartet, *Sancta Mater istud agas* (section six), presents the four soloists, each of whom restate and recast the primary musical theme with remarkable invention.

Section seven, *Fac, ut portem Christi mortem*, is a cavatina for the second soprano, technically demanding with its broad intervals in the vocal line. *Inflammatus et accensus* (section eight) burns with the flaming intensity of its text. The writing here is bold and forward-looking, as unyielding as was Verdi's in the *Libera me* section of his *Manzoni Requiem*. The first soprano makes two incendiary ascents to high C over the full-throated chorus.

The unaccompanied *Quando corpus morietur* and the *Amen* comprise sections nine and ten, the latter a magnificent example of polyphony and imperative finality.*—Erik Eriksson*

Recommended:

- ○ **Rossini: Stabat Mater** / Chung (cond.), Bartoli, Orgonasova, Gimenez, Scandiuzzi, Vienna PO / DG 449178
- ○ **Rossini: Stabat Mater** / Chailly (cond.), Pertusi, Sabbatini, Frittoli, Ganassi, Concertgebouw / 2003 / Decca 000018802
- ○ **Verdi: Messa da Requiem; Rossini: Stabat Mater** / Fricsay (cond.), Borg, Hafliger, Radev, Stader, RIAS SO / 1993 / DG 439684

CHAMBER MUSIC

Duo for cello & double bass in D major (1824)

Although Rossini wrote a number of offbeat works (which he put in a massive collection he called *Sins of Old Age*) in his later years, this oddity is not a part of it. The *Duo for cello and double bass*, in fact, came at the opposite end of his career when he was young and still turning out operas. This duo is a relatively easy work to play for double bass players, so much so that they often beef up the instrument's music to reflect the more virtuosic writing for the cello. The work is cast in three movements, with two lively Allegros framing a lovely Andante molto. The first movement begins with a lighthearted introduction in which the instruments seem to cackle mischievously after opening with dramatic trills. The music has an easygoing character here, especially in the jaunty manner of the main theme. The ensuing Andante offers a lovely, songful melody first presented on cello, then taken up by the double bass to wonderful musical effect. The finale opens with the double bass providing a rapid, tick-tock accompaniment to the cello's lengthy exposition of the merry, Italianate theme. But the double bass eventually takes up the tune and then the cello turns subordinate, supplying the same simple rhythmic support. The whole works brims with bright colors and optimism, and should appeal to fanciers of nineteenth century chamber music for strings. *—Robert Cummings*

Recommended:

- ○ **Rossini Pot-Pourri** / Giorgi, Gambini / Bongiovanni 2170

Six Sonate a quattro, for 2 violins, cello & bass (ca. 1804)

In the 1940s, composer Alfredo Casella discovered a set of six string sonatas written by Gioachino Rossini. The parts were discovered in the Library of Congress in Washington, D.C., and cleared up many unknown facts about the pieces. It was known that Rossini had composed instrumental chamber music early in life, but the only existing pieces were an out-of-print set of string quartets published by Schott in 1823. This set of quartets had been arranged anonymously into traditional string quartet instrumentation and also existed in a configuration for woodwinds. As it turns out, the original parts (on which the published parts were based) were actually written for the extremely unconventional string quartet form of two violins, a cello, and a double bass.

From Rossini's own handwriting, we know that the pieces were written in 1804 near Ravenna, Italy, when he was still quite young. If we are to believe his comments, which he added to the manuscripts much later in life, he says that he was only 12 years old when he composed these "horrendous" sonatas. He also states that he had no formal training in harmony and that he composed the complete set and performed them in three days. The pieces were written for his friend, Agostino Triossi, who was an accomplished amateur bassist. Triossi, Morini (Triossi's violinist cousin), Morini's cellist brother, and Rossini performed the pieces, apparently in a less-than-stellar fashion. Rossini says his playing (on the second violin part) was the worst of all.

Each of the sonatas follows a similar three-movement format (fast-slow-fast). The second movements contain many soloistic, lyrical passages that foreshadow the style of the composer's great operatic arias; the Andante from *Sonata No. 3* is especially striking for the somber quality of the melodic motive. The third movement of No. 3 is a lively theme with variations. The third movement of No. 6 is marked "Tempesta" and depicts music of a stormy nature, a musical predecessor to Rossini's "sturm" operatic style.

It is known that Rossini studied the quartets of Haydn and Mozart in his younger years, but the musical qualities of his string sonatas are not especially characteristic of these compositional influences. The voicing of harmonies is at times clumsy and problematic, no thanks to the strange instrumentation which doubles the lower strings and omits the viola. The pieces are, however, imaginative and lively, carrying Rossini's own stamp of originality. Each instrumental part contains numerous solo passages that require virtuosic skill from the performers—even the oft-neglected bass. The individual parts have a lot of melodic independence, and the pervading lyrical quality of these works suggests more of an Italianate influence than an Austrian one. The string sonatas are performed today not only in their original string quartet form, but also by chamber orchestras. *—Emily Stoops*

Recommended:

- ○ **Rossini: Complete String Sonatas** / I Musici / 1997 / Philips 456330
- ○ **Rossini: String Sonatas 1–6** / Marriner (cond.), Academy of St. Martin-in-the-Fields / 1995 / London 443838

CONCERTO

Variations for clarinet & orchestra (1809)

Rossini was barely 18 when he wrote this piece, originally for clarinet in C, but it is now almost always played on the conventional B flat instrument. It has almost nothing in common with his later opera overtures, aside from the presence of a slow introduction; it is, however, something of a coloratura aria for the clarinet. Following the introduction, its second half embellished by the soloist, there emerges a moderately paced but jaunty tune stated by the clarinet and then briefly recapped by the orchestra. Once this melody is in place, Rossini offers five variations. The first three are all animated, each adding to the density of the coloratura ornamentation. The fourth variation, in contrast, is slow and dips into the minor mode, yet Rossini retains a certain friskiness by having the strings play a pizzicato accompaniment. The fifth variation and coda abound in high spirits and a note-cluttered melodic line for the clarinet. The coda hints at, but does not quite achieve, the famous Rossini crescendo style yet to come. *—James Reel*

Recommended:

- ○ **A Night at the Opera** / Welser-Most (cond.), Meyer, Zurich Opera Orch. / 1996 / EMI 56137

MISCELLANEOUS

Péchés de vieillesse (Sins of Old Age), various piano, chamber, and vocal works (1857–1868)

Rossini shocked and disappointed the music world when he retired from opera at the age of 37 in 1829. Thereafter, his output was sporadic, but he did compose the *Stabat Mater* (1832–41); a host of other, mostly vocal compositions; and his famous group of over 150 works he called *Péchés de vieillesse* (Sins of Old Age). Comprised of piano pieces, songs, pieces for vocal and instrumental ensembles, and the *Petite messe solennelle*, they contain many worthwhile works, most of which have been overshadowed by the composer's many popular operas. Rossini never intended them for publication, though a few were issued in his lifetime. The compositions are in 13 volumes and most did not appear until the 1950s, another reason for their general neglect. Rossini divulged little advancement in his style in most of the works, and thus their expressive language is, on the whole, quite conservative. Not conservative is the character of many of the solo piano works: clever parodies abound among them. In the *Petite caprice in the style of Offenbach* (No. 6, Vol. 10), for instance, he parodies the music of Offenbach, who was then all the rage on European opera stages. Rossini deftly fashions a can-can here with an amusingly drunken gait. Parody takes other forms in this set too, as in the *Prélude prétentieux* (Pretentious prelude), wherein the composer lampoons not composers or prominent individuals, but stylistic clichés in contrapuntal keyboard writing. Rossini quotes from his own music in the *Marche et réminiscenes* (No. 7, Vol. 9). This piece features a funeral march that periodically yields to snatches from *Otello, The Barber of Seville*, and *William Tell* (the famous theme from the *Overture*). Some of the "Sins" works have humorous titles, such as the *Valse anti-dansante* (No. 7, Vol. 8) (Anti-dancing waltz), with witty music to match. Some also divulge the composer's willingness to poke fun at himself, as evidenced by the *Valse torturée* (No. 6, Vol. 6) (Tortured Waltz). There are also many gems among the vocal items in the set, but overall their character is a bit less striking. The *Chanson de Zora No. 5, Vol. 2* (Song of Zora), and the *Ballad élégie No. 11, Vol. 2* (L'orphéline du Tyrol), are attractive, but overly sentimental. *Le chanson du bébé* (The Baby's song), however, is another effective parody, this time a charming sendup of a popular nursery song of the day. Not contained in the 13 volumes is the last work under the "Sins" umbrella, and the most important, the aforementioned *Petite messe solennelle*. The composer scored it for vocal soloists, two pianos, and harmonium, but later fashioned an orchestral version, not to give the work another dimension, but out of fear a lesser talent would do so and botch the effort. More effective in its original scoring, this masterful work is quite dramatic and as its title suggest, solemn in mood. *—Robert Cummings*

Recommended:

- ○ **Rossini: Complete Piano Edition, Vol. 1** / Sollini / 2004 / Chandos 10190

Mstislav Rostropovich

b. Mar. 27, 1927, Baku, Azerbaijan

Cellist

Mstislav Rostropovich is one of the great cellists in all of history, and one of the leading conductors of his time, characterized by direct, affecting, and strongly emotional performances. His father, Leopold, was an acclaimed cellist and his mother was a professional pianist. In 1931, the family returned to Moscow, where Leopold taught at the Gnesin Institute. Taught by his father from the age of three, "Slava" gave his first recital at eight. He entered the Central Music School in 1939, remaining until 1941. In 1943 he entered the Moscow Conservatory. He studied cello with Semyon Kozolupov and composition with Vissarion Shebalin and Dmitri Shostakovich. He became a musical secretary to composer Sergei Prokofiev, and helped persuade the composer to rewrite his failed cello concerto in E minor as the *Symphony-Concerto for Cello and Orchestra*, Op. 125, one of the major masterpieces for the instrument.

Rostropovich won the International Competition for Cellists in Prague in 1950, and began to concertize throughout Russia. His first appearance in the West was in Florence in 1951. He married Galina Vishnevskaya, the star soprano of the Bol'shoi Opera. The couple found themselves at odds with the authorities for the first time, since she was then being amorously pursued by Soviet President Nikolai Bulganin, who canceled their long-planned 1956 tour of the West. But Bulganin was losing power to Party Secretary Khrushchev, and the tour was reinstated, allowing Rostropovich to debut in London at the Festival Hall in March and at Carnegie Hall in New York in April. He was immediately hailed as a great international star.

Returning to the U.S.S.R., Rostropovich found composers clamoring to write for him. The greatest of them, Shostakovich, wrote both his cello concertos for him. When the cellist brought the first concerto to the West for the first time, he premiered it on LP in a magnificent recording with Eugene Ormandy and the Philadelphia Orchestra, beginning a great discography of Western recordings. On the same tour, English composer Benjamin Britten attended the London premiere of the concerto, initiating another great musical friendship with Rostropovich that led to Britten writing five masterpieces for the cello (three solo suites, a sonata, and the *Cello Symphony*), and a song cycle for Galina.

In 1969, Rostropovich protested official mistreatment of the writer Alexander Solzhenitsyn in a letter that circulated in the West, embarrassing Soviet officials. Rostropovich and Vishnevskaya saw their scheduled concerts suddenly cancelled, and the soprano was expelled from the Bol'shoi roster. In 1974 the government granted their request to visit the West for two years, then exiled them by revoking their Soviet citizenship. Rostropovich became invisible at home, but a major star in the West. He bought the famous "Duport" Stradivarius. In September he made a London conducting debut with the New Philharmonic Orchestra and in March debuted with the National Symphony Orchestra of Washington, D.C. He was appointed its music director in 1977.

In 1990 Soviet President Gorbachev reversed the Rostropovich's expulsion, resulting in an emotional return documented in the film "Soldiers of Music." When Russian President Boris Yeltsin stood up to Soviet military power, Rostropovich rushed to stand beside him in the events that led to the collapse of Soviet power. Since then he has stepped down from leadership of the Washington orchestra, but appears as cellist and conductor around the world. He made his first recordings of Bach's six cello suites in 1996, the result of a lifetime of study. He has been a major force in inspiring new cello works from the great composers of his time. *—Joseph Stevenson*

Recommended:

- ○ **Britten: Cello Symphony; Cello Suite; Shostokovich: Concerto 1** / Rozhdestvensky, Britten (cond.), Rostropovich, Moscow PSO / 2004 / EMI 62828
- ○ **Dutilleux, Lutosławski: Cello Concertos** / Baudo, Lutosławski (cond.), Rostropovich, Paris Orch. / Angel 67868
- ○ **Slava 75: The Official 75th Birthday Edition** / Karajan, Giulini (conds.), Rostropovich, Oistrakh, Richter, BBPO, London PO, National SO, Paris Orchestra / 2002 / EMI 67807
- ○ **Rostropovich, Master Cellist** / Karajan, Rozhdestvensky, Ozawa (conds.), Rostropovich, Berlin PO, Leningrad PO, BSO / DG 471620
- ○ **Haydn: Cello Concertos** / Rostropovich (cond. & cello), Academy of St. Martin-in-the-Fields / 2000 / Angel 67263
- ○ **Great Works for Cello & Orchestra** / Rostropovich, etc. / 1993 / DG 437952
- ○ **The Russian Years** / Rostropovich, etc. / 1997 / EMI 72016

Helge Rosvaenge

b. Aug. 29, 1897, Copenhagen, Denmark, **d.** Jun. 19, 1972, Munich, Germany

Tenor

Helge Rosvaenge stood atop the heap of dramatic tenors in Central Europe for more than three decades. An unusual measure of vocal longevity sustained his popularity at several important venues (especially in Vienna) and lent his name a legendary aura even as his career remained an active one. With firmly concentrated lower and middle registers and a powerful, blossoming top, he was well-suited for a broad repertory from Mozart to Verdi to Strauss. While recordings of arias from Wagner's *Die Meistersinger* reveal an exemplary blend of thrust and lyricism, Rosvaenge wisely limited his stage appearances in this composer's works. Such caution almost certainly allowed him to maintain his voice in such remarkable order so far into his singing years.

Largely self-taught, Rosvaenge made his operatic debut in 1921 as Rodolfo at Neustrelitz, the invitation having been extended in the wake of a successful recital; appearances followed at Altenburg and Basle. Cologne engaged him from 1927 to 1930 and, beginning in 1930, he was a member at the Berlin Staatsoper. In Berlin, he was valued for his performances of the Italian repertory, surpassing his colleagues in the appropriate shaping of arias and ensembles in works by Verdi and Puccini. During this period, he also introduced himself to audiences in Munich and Vienna, quickly becoming a favorite in each house. He first appeared at the 1933 Salzburg Festival and remained there until the beginning of World War II in such varied roles as Tamino, Huon, and Florestan.

Rosvaenge ventured Parsifal at *Bayreuth* in 1934 and 1936 and made his debut at Covent Garden in a 1938 production of *Fidelio* conducted by Sir Thomas Beecham. With the Leonore of Rose Pauly and the Rocco of Ludwig Weber, Rosvaenge made a positive impression, bringing "authority and tenseness" to his performance. The Anschluss in Austria and outbreak of war the next year put a stop to further appearances.

Rosvaenge's Florestan was not his only collaboration with Beecham. He had been the conductor's choice (and that of producer Walter Legge) for a Berlin recording of *Die Zauberflöte* the preceding year. That his stentorian tenor was regarded by two such particular individuals as an exemplary fit for the lyric role of Tamino says much about the tenor's adaptability. Together with Tiana Lemnitz, Erna Berger, and Gerhard Hüsch, Rosvaenge was part of a recording project that was regarded from the outset as historic.

During World War II, Rosvaenge often sang for the Axis powers and found at war's end that his enthusiastic participation had caused considerable political problems. When he was finally cleared by the Allies, however, he actively resumed his career. He remained with the Vienna Staatsoper as an active member until 1958. His only American appearances were in recital. In his New York programs, sung when he was past his mid-sixties, he amazed audiences with the extraordinary power he could still summon and his clarion top register.

Rosvaenge recorded extensively: arias, longer excerpts from opera, occasional lighter works (he was notably successful in operetta), and lieder. In addition to his Tamino, his Bacchus in the 1935 Berlin recording of *Ariadne auf Naxos* with Viorica Ursuleac (opera only, not the prologue) set a standard not equaled since. The unwavering steadiness and heroic impact of his high range predestined him for Strauss' awkwardly written tenor protagonists. *—Erik Eriksson*

Recommended:

- ○ **Helge Roswaenge: The Dane with the High D** / Rosvaenge, etc. / 2002 / Dutton 9728
- ○ **The Decca Recordings of 1949** / Rosvaenge, Casa, Jungwirth, Zurich Tonhalle Orch. / 2000 / Preiser 90338
- ○ **Helge Rosvaenge in Concert 1959** / Lowlein (cond.), Rosvaenge, Stoll, Hungarian National PO / Preiser 90103
- ○ **Helge Roswaenge** / Rosvaenge, etc. / 1999 / Nimbus 7899

Nino Rota

b. Dec. 3, 1911, Milan, Italy, **d.** Apr. 10, 1979, Rome, Italy

Composer: Film Music

Like many fine concert music composers, such as Serge Prokofiev, Toru Takemitsu, and Bernard Herrmann, Rota created a unique film soundtrack style for which he became known worldwide.

Rota was born into a musical family: one of his grandfathers was the pianist-composer Giovanni Rinaldi (1840–95), and he studied the piano, on which he was to become known as a gifted improviser, with his mother. He also studied solfège and began to compose at the early age of eight. His oratorio *L'infanzia di S. Giovanni Battista* (The Infancy of Saint John the Baptist) for soloists, chorus, and orchestra was performed in Milan and Lille in 1923, when he was only 12.

Rota entered the Milan Conservatory in 1923 and wrote his (unperformed) first opera *Il principe porcaro* in 1925, basing his original libretto on Hans Christian Andersen's tale. About this time he established a lifelong friendship with Igor Stravinsky. He studied privately with Pizzetti and Casella, and received his diploma at the Accademia di S. Cecilia in Rome in 1930. In the U.S., he studied at the Curtis Institute in Philadelphia from 1931–32, and received an arts degree at Milan University (1937). During this time he composed several minor chamber works.

He became a teacher of harmony, solfège, and composition at the Taranto music school (1937–38) and the Bari Conservatory (1939–50) where he became director (in 1950).

Rota's first film score was for Renato Castellani's *Zazà* in 1944. He then went on to create music for many classic films by Luchino Visconti (*Rocco and his Brothers*), Franco Zeffirelli (*The Taming of the Shrew* and *Romeo and Juliet*), Mario Monicelli, H. Cass (*The Glass Mountain*), Francis Ford Coppola (*The Godfather*, which received an Oscar for best score), King Vidor (*War and Peace*), René Clément (*Plein soleil*), Edward Dmytrik, C. Borghesio, M. Soldati (*Le miserie del signor Travat*), L. Zampa (*Anni facili*), M. Monicelli (*La grande guerra*), S.F. Bondarchuk (*Waterloo*), and Eduardo de Filippo (*Napoli milionairia*). His 80 scores for Federico Fellini extended from *The White Sheik* (1952) to *The Orchestra Rehearsal* (1979). He also composed the music for many theater productions by Visconti, Zeffirelli, and de Filippo. These film scores have a distinctive "Rota" sound made from clear, directly expressive melodies and rhythms, unusual progressions of tonal chords, and often an earthy humor.

Of Rota's ten operas, the exciting *Il capello di paglia di Firenze* (1946) and the philosophical allegory *La visita meravigliosa* (1970, The Marvelous Visitation) were the most successful. Of his five choral works, the *Mysterium* (1962) and *La vita di Maria* (1970) are considered especially fine in compositional technique. He also composed five ballets, including *Amor di poeta* (1978) for Maurice Bejart, many chamber and piano works, several symphonies, and other orchestral works including the brilliant *Harp Concerto* (1948).

In February 1995, the Nino Rota Foundation was established at Fondazione Cini in Venice. *—"Blue Gene" Tyranny*

Overview of Works (1922–1979)

Nino Rota's music is likely more familiar to most listeners than his name; the creator of the score to the movie *The Godfather*, as well as music for numerous other films, Rota made a career as a preeminent film composer, even as much of his large body of concert works were undervalued by the musical establishment. Rota first rose to prominence in his native Italy in the 1930s with a string of successful chamber and orchestral works cast in a kind of late Romantic vein, with strong Russian, Eastern European, and French influences (conductor Gianandrea Gavazzeni called the young Rota the Italian Ravel). His *Symphonies No. 1* and *No. 2* appeared during this time, as well as several works for solo and chamber strings and his first opera, *Ariodante*. While continuing to compose concert works, Rota established himself as a prolific film composer in the 1940s, completing music for literally dozens of films while yet in his thirties. Many of his most important scores, however, date from the 1950s and 1960s, during which time he scored numerous films for the great director Federico Fellini, including *La Strada* (1954), *La Dolce Vita* (1960), *8 1/2* (1963), and *Satyricon* (1969), and many others. Rota also provided the music for Zeffirelli's film versions of Shakespeare's *Taming of the Shrew* (1967) and *Romeo and Juliet* (1968)—the love theme from which is particularly memorable—and was enlisted by Francis Ford Coppola to compose the scores for the first two films in *The Godfather* series. The sense of lyricism and dramatic engagement that made Rota's film scores so appealing to the world's most renowned directors made his concert works seem archaic and indulgent to the musical academia, whose progressivist obsessions in the 1950s and 1960s clearly favored serialism and experimentalism and eschewed overt accessibility. Nonetheless, Rota produced several notable works in between his numerous film projects (his incredibly busy schedule was aided by his practice of freely appropriating music from concert works for use in film scores and vice-versa). His dramatic voice lent itself particularly well to vocal works, as in the oratorio *Mysterium* (1962), as well as to the concerto genre, to which he contributed works for piano, harp, cello, trombone, bassoon, and horn. Rota composed numerous operas as well, including *Il cappello di paglia di Firenza* (1955), *Aladino e la lampada magica* (1965), *La visita meravigliosa* (1969), and *Napoli milionaria* (1977). *—Jeremy Grimshaw*

Recommended:

- ○ **Rota: Symphonies 1 & 2** / Ruud (cond.), Norrkoping SO / 1998 / Bis 970
- ○ **Rota: L'Oeuvre pour Piano Seul** / Laval / Valois 4698
- ○ **Rota: 2 Concerti per pianoforte** / Muti (cond.)Tomassi, La Scala Phil. / 1999 / Angel 56869
- ○ **Rota plays Nino Rota** / Rota / 1999 / IDIS 335
- ○ **Rota: Chamber Music** / Palumbo (dir.), Ens. Nino Rota / 2000 / Chandos 9832
- ○ **Rota: Cello Concertos 1 & 2** / Boico (cond.), Yablonsky, I Virtuosi Italiani / 2001 / Chandos 9892
- ○ **Essential Nino Rota Film Music** / various / 2003 / Silva Screen 1153
- ○ **Rota: Concertos** / Conti (cond.), Carlini, Corti, Prandina, I Virtuosi Italiani / 2002 / Chandos 9954
- ○ **Rota: Symphony 3; Concerto Festivo; Le Molière Imaginaire Suite** / Ruud, Koivula (conds.), Norrkoping SO / 1999 / BIS 1070

FILM MUSIC

Amarcord (1974)

One of Federico Fellini's most popular films is accompanied by one of Nino Rota's most popular themes: an unassuming little melody with a hint of nostalgia that suits the mood of the film perfectly. For *Amarcord*, Rota avoided the lush, full sound of an orchestral score with different themes for different characters. Here, the characters are united by community, so the bulk of the score for the film is made up of different instrumental arrangements of the one theme, sometimes taking on other moods, as well, from the swaggering "Gary Cooper" version on saxophones and strings, to the dreamy, muted dance band version of "Danzando nella Nebbia" (Dancing in the Mist). There are a few examples in the score of more original music, always scored for small ensembles or solo instrument, such as the accordion, as if played by musicians who live in the village. "La Fogaraccia" (Winter Fireworks) features the town band playing a bombastic march, "Le Manine di Primavera" (Feathers of Spring) is the solo accordion playing a quick-step dance, and "L'Emiro e le sue Odalische" (The Emir and his Odalisques) is similar to a circus band version of Khachaturian's *Sabre Dance*. Rota's ingenuity and the plasticity of his music makes the score as varied and memorable as the characters in the film's story. *—Patsy Morita*

Recommended:

- ○ **Amarcord** / Savina (cond.) / Cam 511317

The Godfather (1972)

Milan-born Nino Rota (1911–79) studied composition with Orefice and Pizzetti. He was encouraged by Arturo Toscanini to enroll at the Curtis Institute in Philadelphia, where he studied composition with Scalero and conducting with Fritz Reiner. His music uniquely blends his love for Italian popular song, American pop music and jazz, and operetta. He kept his music tonal and accessible and had success in concert works, popular and art songs, and opera. But he is best known for his film music. He formed one of the cinema's major director-composer partnerships, writing music for all the films of Federico Fellini up to Rota's death in 1979.

He had a major Hollywood soundtrack hit with the love theme from his score for Franco Zeffirelli's *Romeo and Juliet* and also was highly regarded for his score for Sergey Bondarchuk's epic film *War and Peace*. He was engaged by director Francis Ford Coppola to write the underscore for his film of Mario Puzo's best-selling and controversial novel *The Godfather*, about the reluctant rise of an Americanized younger son of a Sicilian-born crime boss to succeed his parent as the *padrone* of a crime family.

Coppola used music sparingly in his three-hour saga, and Rota's score switched effortlessly between Italian and American idioms. Rota used themes from prior scores (including the films *Fortunella*, *The Clowns*, and *Daniele Cortis*, and his oratorio *Mysterium*) in *The Godfather*. Meanwhile, the director's father, Carmine Coppola, wrote and recorded much of the "source music" in the film—music that the characters are supposed to be hearing, particularly in the opening wedding scene.

Rota was nominated for an Academy Award for Best Original Score, but the nomination was hastily withdrawn when Rota's use of earlier music was noticed. He and Carmine Coppola did win later for their joint composition of the score for *Godfather II*; Coppola composed all the music for *Godfather III*, incorporating some of Rota's main themes from the earlier films.

Some of these important themes include the lyrical but ominous trumpet theme that in *Godfather II* would be named the "Immigrant" theme. It opens all of the *Godfather* films. "Kay's Theme" is primarily used in *Godfather II*, and represents the troubled "American" wife of series protagonist Michael Corleone. The darkest theme of all in the series is Rota's "Michael's Theme," which appears in all three films. In all of them it presages his inability, in the first place, to stay clear of the "family business" and, ultimately his doomed dream of legitimizing the Corleones.

The two best-known themes in the movie are also Rota's: the sad waltz known as the "Love Theme from The Godfather" (first heard in its full form when Don Vito Corleone (Marlon Brando) dances with his daughter after her wedding; and the main theme, a yearning Italian popular-style song that, with words later added, has the incongruous title "Speak Softly, Love." *—Joseph Stevenson*

Recommended:

- ○ **The Godfather** / / 1972 / MCA MCAD-10231

Romeo and Juliet (1966)

Nino Rota's score for Franco Zeffirelli's 1968 version of Shakespeare's classic tragedy is an ideal complement to the story. Although the only part of the score that is actually remembered is the love theme, popularized as the song "A Time for Us," there are many more moments of beautiful, moving music. In addition to the love theme, there are separate ones for Romeo and Juliet; Romeo's is reflective, while Juliet's is more innocent. Those themes and the love theme are worked together throughout the score, the drama in the music increasing side-by-side with the drama in the film. Rota makes full use of the orchestra to underscore the pathos of the characters and as incidental music within the story. He divides the melodic duties between the strings and woodwinds, uses the bass for a splendid fanfare for the entrance of the Prince of Verona, and employs a guitar in imitation of the sixteenth century lute. A chorus is featured in the wedding scene, along with a boy soprano, and also in "The Likeness of Death," when Juliet takes the sleeping potion. Rota even creates fair imitations of pavanes, sarabandes, and a lively moresca for "The Feast at the House of Capulet." Although the original scores used by the studio musicians were lost, Mike Townend painstakingly reconstructed them by ear in the early 2000s in order to record the full work with a large orchestra. Rota's *Romeo and Juliet* is regarded as one of his best scores and deserves to be better known. —*Patsy Morita*

Recommended:

○ **Romeo & Juliet** / Rota (cond.) / 1998 / Silva Screen 200

La Strada (1954)

Italian composer Nino Rota enjoyed a collaborative career with world-famous film director Federico Fellini that lasted over two decades and included several of his best-known works. Among the scores Rota composed for Fellini is the music for the film *La Strada*, which was awarded an Oscar in 1954. The film depicts the tragic triangle of Zampano, a strong man in a circus; Gelsomina, an innocent but dim-witted country girl whom he buys into indentured servitude and seduces; and Il Matto, a tightrope walker who shows kindness to Gelsomina. By the time he penned the score for *La Strada*, Rota had a handful of operas under his belt, as well as a number of film scores (including music for Fellini's 1952 work *Lo Sceicco Bianco*) and thus had already established himself as a composer of dramatic music. So successful was the music for the film that later in 1966, he resurrected some of its more poignant moments as a ballet suite for La Scala that would continue to receive regular performances throughout the remainder of the twentieth century. Just as Fellini's films from the period tended toward a kind of neo-realism, Rota's approach to composition has a certain emotional pragmatism; that is, he doesn't unduly concern himself with formalistic complexities of technique or the psychological indulgence of expressionist exaggeration. At the same time, because Fellini's context places the music on the outskirts of the real by focusing on people whose livelihood depends on their ability to evoke the unreal (for Zampano, executing feats of unusual strength; for Il Matto, performing acts of uncommon danger), Rota is free to pursue a wide variety of musical emotions. In doing so, he draws on a wide range of styles. Because of the circus context, much of the music is designed as if happening as part of the visible action. The music for the circus performers and jugglers is light, energetic, and busy, with jazzy syncopated brass, galloping woodblocks, and gaudy oompahs from the drums and cymbals. Il Matto's solo violin music reflects his sympathetic nature in a rhapsodic, bittersweet fashion. When Zampano works into one of his fits of rage, however, his imposing stature, his grim personality, and the danger that he poses to the defenseless Gelsomina lead Rota to borrow almost verbatim from a violent passage of Stravinsky's *Rite of Spring* (where a young girl likewise finds her demise). Rota invokes more difficult musical vocabularies, but always in the service of dramatic tension; the murder scene is swathed in dissonance and unwieldy orchestration, while Gelsomina's consequent descent into insanity is accompanied by eerie string harmonics, faint brass echoes, and the surreal sounds of the celeste. Most effective, however, are Rota's memorable and unabashedly lyrical melodies, which sometimes formally function in a Leitmotiv fashion, but more directly convey and enhance the sheer emotion of the drama. —*Jeremy Grimshaw*

Christopher Rouse

b. Feb. 15, 1949, Baltimore, MD

Composer

Christopher Rouse is best known for his large body of concertos and symphonic works. He has been described as "the Stephen King of composition," since many of his works from the late 1980s and early 1990s dealt with issues of death, horror, tragedy, and mythology. Rouse's music is dramatic in an almost Mahlerian sense—a side effect of which seems to be that his music is the loudest and boldest of his time. One orchestra playing his music called in OSHA because orchestra members thought the volume level was too loud and, therefore, unsafe. That said, Rouse has written some of the most beautiful and touching music of any composer of the twentieth and twenty-first centuries. A *New York Times* article stated, "Rouse has written some of the most anguished, most memorable music around."

Rouse started out at as a rock & roll drummer. However, It was not long until his love for classical composing took over and he enrolled in the Oberlin Conservatory. Having received a degree in composition in 1971, he began his graduate work at Cornell University. In 1971 and 1972, Rouse won Student Composer Awards from BMI and in 1976, he received a fellowship from the National Endowment for the Arts. He received his doctor of musical arts degree from Cornell in 1977.

Accepted to the University of Michigan Society of Fellows, Rouse taught composition there from 1978 to 1981 and was the recipient of a Rockefeller Grant. When that position was over, he began teaching at the Eastman School of Music. In 1982, Rouse received a commission from the Boston Musica Viva. This signified the beginning of his professional career, and it was after this that he began to write his most important works.

Rouse, noticing at the time that many American composers were writing pieces that were entirely Adagio in nature, accepted a commission in 1984 from the Rochester Philharmonic. *Gorgon*, based on the mythological creatures, turned out to be a four-movement piece in which all of the movements are in a fast tempo. This prompted Rouse's reputation for being a fast and loud composer.

The year 1986 marked the completion of a three-movement work *Phantasmata* that was premiered by the Saint Louis Symphony with Leonard Slatkin conducting, and Rouse began a post as composer-in-residence with the Baltimore Symphony that lasted until 1989. The orchestra premiered his *Symphony No. 1* in 1988 which received a Kennedy Center Friedheim Award. On the coattails of this honor, Rouse wrote pieces for the Houston Symphony Orchestra, violinist Cho-Liang Lin, and the Aspen Festival Orchestra, and a *Trombone Concerto* for the New York Philharmonic, which was awarded the 1993 Pulitzer Prize in music. Having secured a reputation as one of the United States' most sought-after and respected composers, Rouse began the next phase of his career writing concertos for the most admired soloists in classical music, including cellist Yo-Yo Ma, flutist Carol Wincenc, percussionist Evelyn Glennie, soprano Dawn Upshaw, pianist Emanuel Ax, guitarist Sharon Isbin, and clarinetist Larry Combs with the Chicago Symphony Orchestra, and orchestral pieces for the likes of the St. Paul Chamber Orchestra, the Atlanta Symphony, the Dallas Symphony, and the Minnesota Orchestra, among others.

While maintaining his position at Eastman, Rouse began teaching composition at the Juilliard School in 1997 and became co-composer in residence at the Aspen Music Festival in 1999. —*DJ Sparr*

Overview of Works

Few contemporary composers have found as secure a place on modern orchestral programs as has Christopher Rouse. His music may be loosely grouped with the larger set of works of the late twentieth century that returned to tonal harmony and a Romantic musical ethos, but he often sets chromatic music against diatonic and unsettled nightmare passages against nostalgia. Rouse is not really neo-anything, and he is perhaps most notable as a composer who appeals both to popular audiences and to his academic peers. A composition professor at the Juilliard School and formerly at the Eastman School of Music and the University of Michigan, he has won both a Pulitzer Prize (for his *Trombone Concerto*, in 1993) and a Grammy award (for *Concert de Gaudí*, in 2002).

Rouse is primarily identified with orchestral music, although he has written music in various genres, including chamber and choral music; for much of the early 2000s he was occupied with the composition of a requiem mass inspired by the gigantic *Requiem* of Hector Berlioz. Berlioz has long been a fully acknowledged influence on Rouse, who also owed and expressed a debt to the classic rock music with which he grew up. The confluence of these streams resulted in fast, intense orchestral works such as *The Infernal Machine* (1981). Rouse's works often made extensive use of an expanded percussion section, and audiences drained by high-modernist calculation took enthusiastically to his visceral new music. Commissions flowed in, and orchestras began to record works such as the *Symphony No. 1* (1986), which won the Kennedy Center Friedheim Award.

That work featured tributes via quotation from Bruckner and Shostakovich, two more composers Rouse admired, and in general his music from the mid-1980s onward began to include elegiac or mystical elements that made an effective foil for his orchestral roller coaster rides. *Kabir Padavili* (1999), whose premiere featured top-rank soprano Dawn Upshaw, was a vocal work based on texts by the fifteenth century Indian mystic poet Kabir, who rejected both Hinduism and Islam. Upshaw was one of many soloists, vocal and instrumental, who premiered new Rouse works in the 1990s and 2000s; others included Yo-Yo Ma (the *Violoncello Concerto*, 1994), Cho-Liang Lin (the *Violin Concerto*, 1991), and Sharon Isbin (*Concert de Gaudí*, a guitar concerto). By 2004, Rouse was a composer whose major statements, such as the *Requiem*, were eagerly awaited by audiences and critics alike. —*James Manheim*

Recommended:

○ **Premiers** / Zinman (cond.), Ma, Philadelphia Orch. / 1996 / Sony 66299

○ **Rouse: Symphony 2; Flute Concerto; Phaethon** / Eschenbach (cond.), Wincenc, Houston SO / 1997 / Telarc 80452

○ **Rouse: Passion Wheels** / Alsop (cond.), Milarsky, Centanni, Gunji, Kolor, Concordia Orch. / 2000 / Koch International Classics 7468

○ **Rouse: Der gerettete Alberich; Rapture; Violin Concerto** / Segerstam (cond.), Glennie, Lin, Helsinki PO / Ondine 1016

○ **Rouse: Symphony 1; Phantasmata** / Zinman (cond.), Baltimore SO / 2004 / First Edition Music 26

○ **American Trombone Concertos, Vol. 2** / Lindberg, Petry, BBC National Orch. Wales / 1995 / Bis 788

○ **Sharon Isbin** / Tang (cond.), Isbin, Lisbon Gulbenkian Foundation Orch. / 2001 / Teldec 81830

Albert Roussel

b. Apr. 5, 1869, Tourcoing, France, **d.** Aug. 23, 1937, Royan, France

Composer: Chamber Music, Symphonic, Orchestral, Ballet

Though less well known than his contemporaries Ravel and Debussy, Albert Roussel is nevertheless regarded as one of the most important figures in early twentieth century French music. Roussel's music reflects his efforts to explore new possibilities of expression while remaining faithful to traditional musical ideas;

evident in his chamber music and works for the stage, this tension between traditionalism and experimentation is particularly successful in his symphonies.

Born into an affluent family, Roussel lost both his parents when he was very young, and was entrusted to the care of his grandfather at age seven; in 1880, the grandfather died, and a maternal aunt took over the responsibility of raising the boy. Although he was interested in music, Roussel decided to pursue a naval career; he graduated from the *Ecole Navale* in 1889, eventually serving in Indochina as an officer.

In 1894, however, Roussel resigned his commission, devoting himself completely to music. He went to Paris, where he studied with the composer and organist Eugene Gigout. Four years later, he began studies with Vincent d'Indy at the newly-founded *Schola Cantorum*. In 1902, although he had not yet completed his studies, Roussel became professor of counterpoint at the *Schola Cantorum*.

Having already composed several significant works (including his *Piano Trio* and the *First Symphony*), Roussel married Blanche Preisach in 1908; the following year, the two traveled to India, where he was exposed to the medieval Hindu legend of Queen Padmavati, who sacrificed her life for love. Fascinated by this story, Roussel decided to set it to music (his opera, *Padmâvatî*, 1923).

At the outbreak of World War I in 1914 Roussel applied for active duty, eventually obtaining an artillery commission; after the war, having retired to Perros-Guirec on the coast of Brittany, he focused on unfinished projects, which included the opera-ballet *Padmâvatî*. This work, which incorporates elements of traditional Indian music, marked a new period for Roussel, whose earlier compositions showed influences of Impressionism.

During the 1920s, Roussel struggled to balance an increasing structural complexity with emotional expressiveness in his works. His *Second Symphony*, completed in 1921, exemplifies this tension; in Roussel's subsequent works, the listener can also detect elements of neo-Classicism.

In 1922, Roussel settled in Vasterival, in the coast of Normandy. Despite increasingly frail health, he devoted much of his energy to composing; he completed the *Piano Concerto* in 1927. His increasing public esteem is evidenced by a festival entirely devoted to his works in Paris (1927) as well as a commission from the Boston Symphony Orchestra for that organization's 50th anniversary (*Third Symphony*, 1930); Roussel traveled to the United States for the performance.

Works composed toward the end of Roussel's life, such as the *String Quartet* (1931–32), the *Fourth Symphony* (1934), and the *String Trio* (1937), show his melodic idiom to be enriched by elements of chromaticism and polytonality. In these compositions, Roussel managed a successful synthesis of these new elements with the transparency of his earlier style. *—Zoran Minderovic*

CHAMBER MUSIC

Divertissement, for piano & wind quintet, Op. 6 (1906)

At the time he wrote his *Divertissement* (1906), Roussel was both a student at Vincent d'Indy's Schola Cantorum and a professor of counterpoint (in which capacity he taught, among others, Satie and Varèse). This ambiguous position is reflected in the early works—for example, the *Piano Trio* (1902) and the *First Violin Sonata* (1907–08)—in which Roussel's distinctive voice is almost smothered in the elaboration required by Schola-dictated cyclic procedures. The *Divertissement*, on the other hand, exhibits Roussel's emerging style to optimum, startling advantage. A rondo alternating a briskly heraldic theme with slower episodes of dreamy arabesque, the *Divertissement* is rhythmically alive in every bar. It is pithy without being complex or scholastic, harmonically fresh (with its prominent fourths) without system, robust but never knockabout, sensuous rather than sensual, and smart without suggesting the would-be-clever smart-alecking of Les Six, whose postwar brashness it seems to forecast. In effect, the *Divertissement* blows away the *fin de siècle* cobwebs of post-Romanticism, Symbolism, mysticism, Wagnerism, and the like as by a strong gust of fresh air. D'Indy's *Chansons et danses-divertissement* (1898) is often cited as an influence, though Albéric Magnard's great *Wind Quintet* (1894), a stronger work already rife with his notorious *brusquerie*, is a more likely model. But one might say with more justice that Roussel's *Divertissement* harks back to Rameau in its attractive vigor while looking ahead to such masterpieces as his own unique *Sérénade*, Op. 30 (1925) and *Trio*, Op. 40 (1929) in its engaging crispness. The *Divertissement*, about six to seven minutes in duration, was first performed by the Société Moderne des Instruments à Vent, (with E. Wagner playing the piano part) on April 10, 1906. *—Adrian Corleonis*

Recommended:

○ **Hexagon Plays Poulenc, Saint-Saëns, Roussel, Francaix** / Hexagon / 1997 / Bridge 9079

Impromptu for harp, Op. 21 (1919)

After World War I, Roussel began shifting from an Impressionist style into a harder, more dissonant manner, on his way to the motoric neo-Classicism by which he is best remembered. His *Impromptu for Harp* is a transitional piece, tightly structured, but still scented with Impressionist perfume. Roussel was no stranger to the harp—he had capitalized on its delicate effects in his ballet *Le Marchand de sable qui passe*—and so he generally avoided such harp clichés as broken chords, although he did indulge in the occasional glissando, at that time a novel effect. The piece, dedicated to and premiered by Lily Laskine, quickly became central to the harp repertory.

Its brief introduction builds from a three-note motif that evokes the Greek lyre (Roussel wrote the piece on the French Mediterranean coast); this gradually evolves into the hypnotic, tick-tock-rhythmed main theme of the Modéré animé section. Soon this pauses, replaced by a gentle, smoothly flowing Très calme passage. A repeated-note figure introduces a cadenza built largely of glissandi that dissolve back into the repeated-note sequence, which, it soon becomes clear, is a spinoff of the *Impromptu's* introductory motif. Next, Roussel develops and intertwines material from the earlier animated and calm sections, ultimately giving the flowing melody a stronger rhythmic underpinning before the piece dissolves into a placid treatment of the introductory motif. *—James Reel*

Recommended:

○ **Nostalgique** / Stockton / Crystal 171

○ **Harpe Passion** / Geliot / 2003 / EMI 585201

Joueurs de flûte, for flute & piano, Op. 27 (1924)

In Roussel's kinetically charged imagination, antiquity was frequently evoked with a propulsive yet sensuous vivacity that looms as one of the glories of Modernism. One thinks of the opera-ballet *Padmâvatî* (1914–18), spiriting up a Hindu legend of love, violence, and ritualistic sacrifice with compelling vividness, or the overwhelming blaze of melody and orchestral color in the ballet *Bacchus et Ariane* (1930). The turning point from such rhapsodically glowing works as the symphonic poems *Evocations* (1910–11) and *Pour une fête de printemps* (1920) to the concise integration of his neo-Classical last manner is marked, in part, by *La Naissance de la lyre* (1923–24), a play with music—based upon a discovered fragment of a satyr play by Euripides and appropriately inflected by Greek modes—which directly preceded the composition of *Joueurs de flûte* (1924). The latter's four movements depict four legendary flute players and are dedicated each to a famous flutist—"Pan" to Marcel Moyse (future founder of the Marlboro School of Music and teacher of James Galway and Paula Robison), "Tityre" to Gaston Blanquart, "Krishna" to Louis Fleury (dedicatee and first performer of Debussy's *Syrinx*, who gave *Joueurs de flûte* its premiere at a Concert de la Revue musicale, January 17, 1925), and "Monsieur de la Péjaudie" to Philippe Gaubert. Gaubert, pupil of Paul Taffanel and teacher of Moyse, was a highly respected musician—Busoni dedicated his *Divertimento for flute and orchestra* to him—who became professor of flute at the Paris Conservatoire, principal conductor of the Opéra de Paris and Orchestre de la Société des Concerts du Conservatoire, and who left classic recordings of the Franck *Symphony*, Fauré's *Ballade*, and the *Symphonie cevénole* of Roussel's teacher, d'Indy. Confirming his nod to the Franck school—at a time when his indebtedness to it had long been overwritten by a series of idiosyncratic masterpieces—Roussel dedicated the entire work to Franck pupil and composer J. Guy Ropartz, director of the Nancy Conservatoire. Playing around nine minutes together, these pieces capture Roussel's style in quintessence—spare lines and aphoristic utterance exotically colored. As the archetypal first flutist, Dorian arabesques in "Pan" slowly grow more animated, giving way to a moment of syncopated strut. "Tityrus," the rustic piper of Virgil's *Eclogues*, is represented by a briskly chirping dance. The sinuous sensuousness of "Krishna" looks back, with its Hindu scale, to the world of *Padmâvatî*, if not to aeons immemorial. And "Monsieur de la Péjaudie," the flutist of Henri de Régnier's novel *La Pécheresse*, appears with wryly blithesome diffidence. *—Adrian Corleonis*

Recommended:

○ **Flûte Panorama, Vol 1** / Ivaldi, Debost / 2001 / Skarbo 4955

○ **Piano & Flute** / Cardoso, Pinho / Cardoso & Pinho 803054

Ségovia, for guitar, Op. 29 (1925)

Guitarist Andrés Segovia received a miniature musical portrait of himself from Albert Roussel in the two-and-a-half-minute *Segovia*, Op. 29. It's a gentle, jovial piece, a blithe departure from Roussel's sterner manner of the period. The nearly identical outer sections employ a frankly Spanish melodic style, over an ostinato rhythm that sounds Iberian rather than motoric. Roussel here tempers his customary harshness by eschewing chordal writing, keeping everything bright and linear. The central section is both playful and superficially ominous, but obviously not ominous enough to challenge this composition's essentially sunny mood. *—James Reel*

Recommended:

○ **Art of Segovia** / Segovia / 2002 / DG 471697

○ **Julian Bream Ultimate Collection Vol 2** / Bream / 2000 / RCA 63713

Sérénade, for flute, violin, viola, cello & harp, Op. 30 (1925)

Composed between July and September 1925 at the prompting of flutist René le Roy, Roussel's pithily brief *Sérénade* heralds the series of acerbic, linear, corybantic masterpieces that would occupy him until his death—the *Suite in F* (1926), *Piano Concerto* (1927), *Psalm 80* (1928), the *Symphony No. 3* (1929–30), and the ballet *Bacchus et Ariane* (1930), to name but the greatest. Indeed, the *Sérénade* is something of a symphony in miniature, tripping its sonata-form tropes with elegant, aerial concision. Finally, it is the most brilliant, if not the most substantial, of several works for flute with which Roussel immeasurably enriched the literature for that instrument—the *Deux Poèmes de Ronsard for voice and flute* (1924), *Joueurs de Flûte for flute and piano* (1924), and the *Trio for flute, viola, and cello,* Op. 40 (1929).

Against a blithe, insouciantly coruscating background, the flute traverses an exposition with two themes, a development section, and a recapitulation within the space of about four minutes to make, with its adroit rhythmic shifts, an Allegro first movement of kaleidoscopic interest. The central mysterious Andante opens with a long-breathed melody for the flute over the plucked chords of a slow, sensual dance—reminiscent of the ballet sequences in *Padmâvatî*—sinuously answered by the cello and violin, which enter into an attenuated dialogue, rounded with an exquisite coda, suggesting an esoteric, erotic ritual. The final movement, Presto, synthesizes the visceral impact of the preceding in an animated opening dance, yielding to a sensuously sated interlude before the barbaric whirl resumes more wildly, with the flute calling through eerie string harmonics, only to vanish suddenly on a puckish cadence. The premiere was given by the Quintette Instrumental de Paris at the Salle Gaveau, Paris, on October 15, 1925. *—Adrian Corleonis*

Recommended:

- ○ **Academy of St. Martin-in-the-Fields Chamber Ens** / Kanga, . / 1997 / Chandos 8621

String Trio, Op. 58 (1937)

It is something of a paradox that as Roussel entered his last decade, the period of his most vigorous and intensely personal work, he was dogged by exhaustion and poor health. Pneumonia and jaundice over the winter of 1933–34 followed the composition of his opera bouffe, *Le Testament de la Tante Caroline* (1932–33), while his final two years—graced with such spirited masterpieces as the ballet, *Aeneas*, the boisterous *Rapsodie flamande*, and the zestful *Concertino* for cello and orchestra—were plagued by bouts of angina pectoris. He had just finished the wanly quirky Andante of a projected *Trio for oboe, clarinet, and bassoon* when he was struck down by a heart attack and died on August 23, 1937, leaving the *Trio for violin, viola, and cello,* composed over June and July 1937, as his last completed full work. The high spirits of his previous music seem muted, recalled in lassitude, and served on wry, so to speak. The first movement Allegro moderato manages a deftly contrapuntal—almost conversational—balance of the effusive and the pithy, while the Adagio is a prolonged meditation less sad than wistful, but accented with moments of stabbing poignance. The third movement Allegro con spirito is perhaps the most disturbing to the composer's admirers, as the bounding Rousselian corybantic mode comes only skippingly now, seemingly sketched, attenuated. The *Trio* was premiered by the Pasquier Trio at a memorial concert on April 4, 1938. *—Adrian Corleonis*

Recommended:

- ○ **Roussel: Complete Chamber Music** / Meer, Guittart, Hoog / 1998 / Olympia 706

SYMPHONIC

Symphony No. 3 in G minor, Op. 42 (1929–1930)

At every stage of his career, Roussel's best work is masterly finished, engaging, surefire. But for the connoisseur, tracing his stylistic evolution possesses a fascination of its own. If the opera-ballet *Padmâvatî* (1914–18) crowns his second manner, making explicit the preoccupation with instinct and annihilation ironically broached in the ballet *Le Festin de l'araignée* (1912), his *Symphony No. 2* (1919–20) encapsulates the period with formal yet disturbing point. The ironic detachment of *Le Festin* gives way to dark (and harmonically adventurous) foreboding, while the irrepressibly animated episodes are fraught with frenzied feverishness. But by the mid-1920s the skies had cleared, so to speak, and Roussel entered his final, neo-Classical, phase with the orchestral *Suite in F* (1926) whose three movements—two in Baroque dance forms—afford a foretaste of the *Symphony No. 3* in their effortless combination of energy and serenity. Commissioned by Koussevitzky, conductor of the Boston Symphony Orchestra, the *Suite* received its premiere by those forces January 21, 1927, continuing a Francophile tradition that had seen Henri Rabaud and Pierre Monteux as *chef d'orchestre*, and entertained Roussel's teacher and colleague, Vincent d'Indy, in 1905 and 1921.

To celebrate the B.S.O.'s 50th anniversary, Koussevitzky commissioned a number of works including Honegger's *Symphony No. 1*, Prokofiev's Fourth, Hindemith's *Concert Music*, Op. 50, Stravinsky's *Symphony of Psalms*, and Roussel's *Symphony No. 3*. The *Third* occupied Roussel from August 1929 through March 1930. Roussel and his wife were present for the Boston premiere, October 24, 1930, the composer remarking that Koussevitzky had conducted "with an extraordinary care and enthusiasm," and noting the day after, "As far as I can gauge after this hearing, it is the best thing I have done...." That, indeed, has been the consensus of critics and listeners alike—only the ballet *Bacchus et Ariane*, which followed it immediately, has rivaled it in popularity. From the sardonic strut of the opening, the *Third* is immediately arresting, while its tightly coiled argument—compact even for the form-conscious Roussel—compels by its melding of logic and vivacity, sophistication and primitivism. The second movement transcends counterpoint in a miracle of passionate, ostinato-driven polyphony, while the scherzo and final Allegro con spirito—elegant and rumbustious by turns—are wrought with colossal playfulness. Albert Wolff and the Concerts Lamoureux gave the Paris premiere on November 28, 1931, and made a classic recording of the work the following year. *—Adrian Corleonis*

Recommended:

- ○ **Roussel: Symphonies** / Dutoit (cond.), National Orch of France / 1998 / Teldec 21090
- ○ **Roussel: Symphonies 3 & 4; Bacchus et Ariane, Suite 2** / Munch (cond.), National Orch of France / 1998 / Valois 4832
- ○ **Roussel: Symphonies 3 & 4; Bacchus & Ariane, Suite 2; Sinfonietta** / Jarvi (cond.), Detroit SO / 1995 / Chandos 7007

Symphony No. 4 in A major, Op. 53 (1934)

Written by the sick and tired 65-year-old composer in a single three-and-a-half-month period in the fall of 1934, Albert Roussel's *Symphony No. 4* was nevertheless one of the most vigorous and optimistic symphonic works of the 1935 season. Written in the traditional four movements and in the conservative harmonic language of *la belle époque* expressed in the severe counterpoint of the Schola Cantorium, Roussel's *Fourth* is still an extremely powerful and affecting work imbued with sincerity, strength, nobility, and a very, very dry wit. After a radiantly glowering Lento introduction, the opening Allegro con brio in sonata form never varies its pulse as it builds to an abrupt coda. The Lento molto may be the most expressive music Roussel ever wrote, solemn but emotionally searing music of uncommon power and sincerity. The Allegro scherzando is a muscular jig with just the slightest trace of irony. The closing Allegro molto is also in sonata form, but a sonata form permeated by a concentrated wit and a joyful counterpoint culminating in a magnificent coda. *—James Leonard*

Recommended:

- ○ **Roussel: Symphonies 1–4** / Dutoit (cond.), National Orch. of France / 1998 / Teldec 21090
- ○ **Balakirev: Symphony 1; Roussel: Symphony 4** / Karajan (cond.), London PO / 1998 / EMI 66595

ORCHESTRAL

Bacchus et Ariane, suite from the ballet No. 2 (1930)

With the *Third Symphony* (1929–30), the ballet *Bacchus et Ariane*, composed between June and December 1930, is the radiant apogee of Roussel's oeuvre. Some other of his other scores may rival their piquant inspiration and motoric verve, but none approaches them for richness abruptly compact of poetry, élan, orchestral coruscation, grandeur, and sheer voltage. Conducted by the intuitively adept Philippe Gaubert, the premiere of *Bacchus et Ariane*, at the Paris Opéra on May 22, 1931, featured choreography by the young Serge Lifar, décor by Giorgio de Chirico, with Lifar and Spessivtseva in the title roles—that is, the makings of a major triumph. Unfortunately, in the critical carping over the staging, the power of the music was given short shrift and *Bacchus et Ariane* had but a short run. Fully aware of the worth of his achievement, Roussel wryly retitled the two acts of the ballet respectively *Bacchus et Ariane Suite No. 1* and *Suite No. 2*—the scores are identical—in which guise this sumptuous, glowing, rhythmically volatile music enjoys far greater currency as concert fare than it ever had as a ballet, which is puzzling, for it is so eminently danceable. From the opening propulsive bound, celebrating Theseus' slaying of the Minotaur, the listener is transported by a unique rhythmic vivacity of strongly accented, often enticingly irregular, and arrestingly shifting meters. For Roussel, the Dionysian is not (as it was for, say, Szymanowski) primarily intoxicating and erotic—Bacchus is a god of enchantments and compelling dynamism. And Ariane never fails to draw from him music of sinuous tenderness. Throughout, the score is rife with glowing melody and preternatural animation, couched in orchestral writing ranging from caressing sorcery to coruscating brilliance. The music rises to each moment—Ariane's *salto mortale*, Bacchus' kiss and spell, the procession of Bacchic worshippers, and so on—with richly compact, spellbinding invention. And it must be said that the final Bacchanale and coronation of Ariane ranks among the most powerfully whelming endings in French music of any genre. The *First Suite* was given its premiere on April 2, 1933, at the Salle Pleyel, with Charles Munch leading the Paris Symphony, and the *Second Suite* in the same venue with the same forces on February 2, 1934, led by Pierre Monteux. Of the two, the *Second Suite* has become the most popular for, while the first ends pianissimo, the second climaxes in a stupendously whelming Dionysian apotheosis. *—Adrian Corleonis*

Recommended:

- ○ **Roussel: Symphonies 3 & 4; Bacchus et Ariane, Suite 2** / Munch (cond.), National Orch. of France / 1998 / Valois 4832

Sinfonietta for strings, Op. 52 (1934)

In 1934, the year following completion of his three-act opéra-bouffe *Le Testament de la tante Caroline*, Roussel turned to the composition of two orchestral works, though a stretch of illness soon upset his timetable. Finally, in July, he wrote to a friend that "I have begun an Andante and Allegro for string orchestra that I promised to Jane Evard. It will be completed next week. You can see that I am making up for lost time!" By the end of August, not only was the *Sinfonietta*, Op. 52 finished, but Roussel had written a prefatory Allegro, longer than either succeeding movement (though the entire work lasts just over eight minutes).

The *Sinfonietta* begins much as the *Third Symphony* (1929–30) does: an insistent triple meter propels a jagged melodic line, while polytonal sonorities underneath keep the listener surprised and deliberately off balance. The second subject is lyrical, with wisps of a violin solo, but contrapuntal development takes precedence until the main theme returns, abbreviated but still untamed. The Andante commences chordally (recalling the slow movement of the Op. 30 *Sérénade*) before it dissolves into a legato subject with delicate counterpoint. The chords return, now modally embellished, before a segué into the duple-meter finale. The mood here is jauntier without trying to sound "youthful." Counterpoint—Roussel's abiding strength—enriches the mix when material from the subject repeats. The end is decisive, without pretentions of grandeur.

The *Sinfonietta* doesn't reveal its considerable riches in a single (much less a casual) hearing, but they are there and invite—and reward—careful listening. Four days after completing the *Sinfonietta*, Roussel began work on his Fourth (and final) Symphony, in which a continuity clearly can be heard. *—Roger Dettmer*

Recommended:

○ **French Orchestral Works** / P. Jarvi (cond.), Tapiola Sinfonietta / 1993 / Bis 630

Suite in F major, Op. 33 (1926)

Among Roussel's more curious works is a brief *Duo for bassoon and double bass* composed in 1925—a sardonic musical joke—as a gesture of congratulation to the conductor and patron of music, Sergey Koussevitzky, on becoming a chevalier of the *Légion d'honneur*. Before he took the baton, Koussevitzky had been an internationally known double bass virtuoso. He promptly returned the favor by commissioning an orchestral work from Roussel, thus providing the occasion for the composition of the *Suite in F*, which occupied him from January to September 1926. There can be no doubt that, even without the commission, something very like the *Suite in F* would have eventuated. Compact of rhythmic spring and bitonal piquancy, its deceptively simple three-movement design—two vigorous outer movements flanking a prolonged moment of the most movingly exquisite poetry—had already been forecast in the *Sérénade* for flute, string trio, and harp, Op. 30, of the year before. In these works, Roussel leaves behind the last vestiges of Romanticism, his brief flirtation with Impressionism, and the foreboding stylistic experiment embodied in the postwar *Symphony in B flat Major* (1919–21) to achieve his final, old-masterly manner. Titled Prélude, Sarabande, and Gigue, the suite's three movements seem to promise a faddishly Modern essay in neo-Classicism, after the manner of Stravinsky, Prokofiev, and their numerous followers. But Roussel's Classicism is of the eternally fashionable variety in its perfect cohesion of form, material, and intensely personal expression. Amid the stylistic melee of the 1920s, the *Suite in F* seems already to have answered the desideratum the Spanish philosopher, Ortega y Gasset, was to make in 1932: "In the hour of danger, life throws off all inessentials, all excrescences, all its adipose tissue, and tries to strip itself to pure nerve, pure muscle." The concentrated, rhythmically bounding, contrapuntally alive outer movements realize this athletic ideal with an ironic gaiety which Roussel's chronicler, Marc Pincherle, called "sportivité." The luminous Sarabande, on the other hand, tokens not merely repose but engagement—rising to an impassioned climax—with the enigma of life itself. The *Suite in F* was given its premiere in Boston, on January 21, 1927, with Koussevitzky conducting the Boston Symphony Orchestra. Its European premiere followed on May 21, 1927, at a *Koussevitzky à Paris* concert. *—Adrian Corleonis*

Recommended:

○ **Chabrier** / Paray (cond.), Detroit SO / 1991 / Mercury 434303

○ **Roussel: Bacchus et Ariane; Suite en fa** / Dutoit (cond.), Orch. de Paris / Erato 75348

BALLET

Le Festin de l'araignée, Op. 17 (1912–1913)

The first of Albert Roussel's three ballets, *Festin de l'araignée* (The Spider's Feast), was the culmination of his first period as a composer when, as he wrote, he was "slightly influenced by Debussy, but concerned above all with the solid architecture taught by Vincent d'Indy." His mentor at the Schola Cantorum, d'Indy, inculcated in Roussel an appreciation of muscular counterpoint and strong structures. But Roussel's appreciation of the sounds and colors of the later Debussy and the younger Ravel and of what one might call a catchy tune proved just as powerful as d'Indy's. As well as being full of strong structures, powerful counterpoint, and brilliant colors, *Festin de l'araignée* is full of catchy tunes. Roussel wrote it in 1912 to a libretto by Gilbert de Voisins about insect life in a country garden, and the ballet-pantomime in two parts was premiered in the Theatre des Arts on April 3, 1913. The principal characters are a butterfly; an ephemera; one pair each of ants, preying mantises, and dung beetles; and the spider of the title. Roussel sets this to music as clear as the summer sky and as evocative as a summer breeze. If the dances are more tuneful and more memorable than the pantomime's, the color and characterization of the orchestra are at their most brilliant in the pantomimes. If the music sounds distinctly conservative compared with Debussy's *Jeux* or Stravinsky's *La Sacre du printemps*, it is still superbly written, full of catchy tunes, and thoroughly danceable. If the music sounds distinctly silly compared with *La Sacre*'s fury, it does sound like a likely double-bill with Debussy's *La boîte à joujoux*. Roussel prepared a *fragmente symphoniques* from *Festin de l'araignée* that retains most of its ballets, but few of its pantomimes. *—James Leonard*

Recommended:

○ **Roussel: Orchestral Music** / Martinon (cond.), ORTFCO / 1998 / Teldec 24240

○ **Toscanini: Roussel; Roger-Ducasse, etc.** / Toscanini (cond.), NBCSO / 1999 / Urania 107

Christophe Rousset

b. Apr. 12, 1961, Avignon, France

Harpsichordist, Conductor

Christophe Rousset is one of the finest and most exciting harpsichordists, and as a conductor is a leader in the late twentieth century revival of French Baroque music.

After studying piano as a boy, he became deeply interested in the harpsichord at the age of 13. He studied with Huguette Dreyfus at the Schola Cantorum in Paris and, from 1980 to 1983, with Bob van Asperen at the Royal Conservatory of the Hague. He won a special certificate of distinction at the Schola Cantorum and, in 1983, the first prize at the International Harpsichord Competition in Bruges.

He began a professional career, in which he rose quickly in the ranks of the world's harpsichordists. He soon appeared at some of the most prestigious early music festivals, including those of Aix-en-Provence, Saintes, Veaune, Utrecht, La Roque d'Anthéron, and Les Printemps des Arts de Nantes.

He recorded for the Decca record label and its early music imprint L'Oiseau-Lyre. His recording of the *Piéces de Clavecin* of Rameau won the 1992 Gramophone Award for Best Baroque Non-Vocal Release and the Belgian Cecilia Prize.

During this time, as a specialist in Baroque harpsichord he often performed the harpsichord continuo parts in ensemble music. For the most part in the Baroque era, ensembles were led by the harpsichordist. Thus it was natural that Rousset's harpsichord appearances with such established authentic instrument ensembles as La Petite Bande, Musica Antique de Cologne, The Academy of Ancient Music, Il Seminario Musicale, and Les Arts Florisants led him to an interest in leading a Baroque ensemble.

In 1991, he founded such a group, which he named Les Talens Lyrics. This title, meaning "Lyrical Talents," is the name of a 1739 collection of compositions by Jean-Philippe Rameau. He and his group of young Baroque players adopted this name not only because it was snappy and imposed a certain requirement to live up to, but it also indicated their interest in reviving French Baroque music. Moreover, they intended to explore the connections between the distinct national styles of France and the other major European nations of the Baroque era (including England). In particular, Rousset and Les Talens explore the vital interchange of music that took place between France and the Kingdom of Naples. The group is flexible in size. It may amount to as little as five singers and players for a performance of court vocal works, or up to forty in playing opera and oratorio.

An important introduction of Les Talens came in 1993 at the Festival de Beaune, when they performed *Scipione* by Handel. The same year they presented *L'Incoronazione di Poppea* of Monteverdi at the Amsterdam Opera. They have also played ballets and operas of Cimarosa, Berutti, de Mondonville. They have recorded Henry Dumont's *Motets en Dialogue*, Jean-Marie Leclair's trios, Handel's *Scipione* and *Richard the First*, Jommelli's *Armida Abbandonnata*, ouvertures of Rameau, and the soundtrack for the movie *Farinelli*, which is about one of the leading castrato singers of the Baroque. The *Farinelli* soundtrack had extraordinary sales for an early music classical release, selling well over 600,000 copies worldwide.

Les Talens Lyriques is intended to track the Neapolitan-Parisian connection up to the time of the emergence of Rossini. In 2000, Rousset moved a step towards that by conducting Mozart's *Mitradate* at the Opéra National de Lyon. *—Joseph Stevenson*

Recommended:

○ **Rameau: 6 Concerts en sextuor** / Rousset, Les Talens Lyriques / 2004 / Decca 000184502

○ **W.F. Bach: Oeuvres pour clavecin** / Rousset / HM 1951305

○ **Froberger: Suites de clavecin & Toccatas** / Rousset / HM 1951372

○ **Rameau: Overtures** / Rousset, Les Talens Lyriques / 1997 / L'Oiseau-Lyre 455293

○ **Rameau: Pièces de clavecin en concerts** / Rousset, Terakado, Uemura / HM 901418

Royal Philharmonic Orchestra

f. 1813, London, England

Ensemble

The last orchestra nurtured by famed conductor Sir Thomas Beecham, the Royal Philharmonic Orchestra is one of five world-class orchestras based in London, a city where concert life in its modern form has roots three centuries deep. In 1813, a group of professional musicians founded the Philharmonic Society to organize regular concerts of orchestral music, and a century later. this Society was granted a royal charter by King George V, making it the Royal Philharmonic Society (RPS). Nevertheless, it took the independently wealthy Beecham to keep the group from collapsing during World War I.

In 1926, Beecham planned to form a permanent Royal Philharmonic Orchestra to serve the BBC and the RPS, but the BBC instead started its own BBC Symphony Orchestra. In 1932, Beecham founded the London Philharmonic Orchestra, financially backed by recording contracts and a contract to serve as the RPS's concert orchestra. Beecham left to take a position with the Seattle Symphony Orchestra when World War II broke out, and the LPO transformed itself into a self-governing organization.

Beecham returned to Britain in 1944 and formed a new orchestra, giving its first concert at the Davis Theatre in Croydon on September 15, 1946, just three weeks after Beecham started hiring musicians. Again, he placed the new orchestra under the RPS rubric, enabling it to take the Royal Philharmonic Orchestra name. In 1948, the RPO became the resident orchestra of the summer Glyndebourne Festival Opera, and in 1950 it became the first British orchestra to tour the United States since before World War I. Feeling his advancing age, Beecham engaged Rudolf Kempe as assistant conductor. When Beecham died in 1961, Kempe became principal conductor.

The orchestra's financial situation immediately worsened. Glyndebourne and the RPS itself declined to renew their contracts, and the RPO was excluded from the London Orchestral Concert Board's schedule of concerts in the new halls on the South Bank. The orchestra re-formed as a self-governing organization, but had to give its concerts in a movie house on the north side of London. Kempe received the titles of Artistic Director in 1964, and Conductor for Life in 1970.

Things took a turn for the better in 1966 when Queen Elizabeth II granted the orchestra its own Royal Charter, enabling it to continue calling itself the Royal Philharmonic Orchestra. After a difficult period following the death of Kempe, the orchestra appointed Antal Dorati, noted for building orchestral discipline and morale, as Conductor-in-Chief (1975–78). He has been followed by Walter Weller (1980–85), André Previn (Conductor-in Chief, 1985–87, and Principal Conductor, 1987–92), and Vladimir Ashkenazy (Music Director, 1987–94). Yuri Temirkanov became Principal Conductor in 1992 and remains as Emeritus Principal Conductor. Daniele Gatti, a young and exciting Italian conductor, became Music Director in 1996.

The orchestra is now firmly back in the center of London concert life. It plays its main series at the Royal Albert Hall with a few concerts also given at the Barbican Centre in the City of London. In addition, in an innovative move, it also established itself as the resident orchestra of the Royal Concert Hall in Nottingham, where it gives a series of ten concert programs a year.

The RPO has a 125-release contract with Tring International, the largest contract in history between one orchestra and a record company. It has a close association with Classic FM, the largest commercial radio company in Britain. It has formed two sub-ensembles. The Royal Philharmonic Concert Orchestra is essentially the RPO's "Pops" (or as the British say, "light classical") orchestra. Sharp Edge, a flexible ensemble of 10 to 30 musicians, plays innovative concerts of the newest music. *—Joseph Stevenson*

Recommended:

○ **The Royal Philharmonic Orchestra Play The Shows** / RPO / 2003 / Fabulous 236

○ **Queen's Rhapsody** / Weindorf (cond.), Oberreit, Paladino, Gebhard, Risavy, Royal PO / 2003 / Koch 8646

○ **Tchaikovsky: Fantasias after Shakespeare** / Leaper, Wit (conds.), Royal PO, Polish RSO / 1994 / Naxos 553017

○ **Bantock: Hebridean Symphony; Celtic Symphony; etc.** / Handley (cond.), Royal PO / 1991 / Hyperion 66450

Gennady Rozhdestvensky

b. May 4, 1931, Moscow, Russia

Conductor

Rozhdestvensky was the son of conductor Nikolai Anosov and soprano Natalya Rozhdestvenskaya. A pupil at the Gnesin School of Music and the Moscow Conservatory school for children, he entered the Conservatory in 1941 to study conducting with his father and piano with Lev Oborin. While still at the Conservatory, Rozhdestvensky conducted Tchaikovsky's *Nutcracker* at the Bolshoi Theater. Following his graduation in 1954, he was appointed assistant conductor at the Bolshoi and in 1956 made his first visit to England with the Bolshoi Ballet. In 1961, Rozhdestvensky was named artistic director of the Soviet Radio Symphony Orchestra, remaining there until 1974. Three years later, he became Bolshoi's youngest principal conductor, remaining at that post until 1970. During the Soviet era, Rozhdestvensky programmed music by contemporary foreign composers, most likely alienating the Soviet musical establishment; nevertheless, as chief conductor and director of the Moscow Radio Symphony Orchestra, he was allowed to lead performances of Stravinsky's *Rite of Spring*, Benjamin Britten's opera *A Midsummer Night's Dream*, as well as works by Poulenc, Hindemith, Orff, and other composers that were new to Soviet audiences. He also revived the symphonies of Sergey Prokofiev, who was regarded with suspicion in Russia, having lived in America from 1918 to 1936. Only the most eminent and respected Russian musicians were allowed extensive foreign tours, and Rozhdestvensky visited many European countries, the U.S., and Japan. He also appeared several times in Britain, mainly with the London Philharmonic Orchestra, and at Covent Garden. In 1971, he conducted the Leningrad Philharmonic Orchestra in three Promenade Concerts at London's Royal Albert Hall. The following year, Rozhdestvensky became music director of the Moscow Chamber Orchestra. Artistic director of the Stockholm Philharmonic Orchestra from 1974–77, he was principal conductor of the BBC Symphony Orchestra from 1978 to 1981. His next post was principal conductor of the Vienna Symphony Orchestra, where he stayed until 1983. In 1982, he founded, and became chief conductor of, the State Symphony Orchestra of the Ministry of Culture in Moscow. In 1987, Rozhdestvensky started teaching conducting at the Accademia Musicale Chigiana in Sienna. The Stockholm Philharmonic hired him as conductor in 1991, and three years later he was appointed chairman of the Bolshoi's artistic committee. Rozhdestvensky has maintained his reputation for adventurous programming in his many recordings and live performances. Known for his balanced and refined interpretations of Romantic and twentieth century music, he premiered numerous twentieth century works, including Denisov's *Symphony for Two String Orchestras and Percussion* (dedicated to Rozhdestvensky), Buzko's *White Nights*, Shchedrin's *Carmen Suite*, Prokofiev's opera *The Gambler*, Schnittke's *Symphony No. 2 "St. Florian"* and Gerhard's *Don Quixote*. An enthusiastic champion of contemporary composers, Rozhdestvensky has also performed works by Kancheli, Mirzoian, Organesian, and Skoryk. Rozhdestvensky's writings include *Techniques of Orchestral Direction* and *Reflections on Music*. He is married to Viktoria Postnikova, a pianist. *—Roy Brewer*

Recommended:

○ **Shostakovich: The Golden Age** / Rozhdestvensky (cond.), Stockholm PO / 1994 / Chandos 9251/2

○ **Enescu: Symphonies 1 & 3** / Rozhdestvensky (cond.), Shiran, Argiros, BBCPO / 1996 / Chandos 9507

○ **Vermeulen: Symphonies 2, 6 & 7** / Rozhdestvensky (cond.), Hague Residentie Orch. / 2002 / Chandos 9735

○ **Glazunov: King of the Jews** / Rozhdestvensky (cond.), Russian State SO / 1996 / Chandos 9467

○ **Shostakovich: The Bolt** / Rozhdestvensky (cond.), Stockholm PO / 1995 / Chandos 9343

○ **Shostakovich: Symphonies 1, 5, 6 & 9** / Rozhdestvensky (cond.), U.S.S.R. Ministry of Culture SO / 1997 / Melodiya 7432149611

○ **Shostakovich: Symphonies 14 & 15** / Rozhdestvensky (cond.), Maslennikov, Yakovenko, U.S.S.R. Ministry of Culture SO / 1998 / Melodiya 7432159057

Miklós Rózsa

b. Apr. 18, 1907, Budapest, Hungary, **d.** Jul. 27, 1995, Los Angeles, CA

Composer: Film Music, Orchestral, Chamber Music

Miklós Rózsa already had a promising career as a composer in the concert hall when he started writing movie scores in the mid-1930s. By the end of that decade, he was working on the most expensive movie being made in England, and by the end of the decade that followed, he was under contract to the biggest studio in Hollywood.

Born into a well-to-do family in Budapest, Rózsa had his musical sensibilities shaped by his contact with the Magyar peasants who lived around his father's summer estate. As a boy he could read music before he could read words, and proved a natural musician, taking up the violin at age six. His earliest influences as a student were Béla Bartók and Zoltán Kodály, who were regarded as dangerous radicals at the time. After studying at the Leipzig Conservatory, Rozsa embarked on a career as a composer and saw early success with his *Variations On a Hungarian Peasant Song* and his *Theme, Variations and Finale*—the latter entered the repertory of several major conductors, including Bruno Walter, in the mid-1930s, and Rózsa received encouragement in his career from none other than Richard Strauss. He began writing music for films at the inspiration and suggestion of his friend Arthur Honegger—Rózsa needed the income, and he liked the idea of writing music that would get performed and recorded quickly. Rozsa established himself as a film composer at London Films, the British studio founded by his fellow Hungarian Alexander Korda, and after impressing Korda with his work on thrillers like *Knight Without Armor* (1937), the producer chose Rózsa as the composer for his *Arabian Nights* fantasy film *The Thief of Baghdad* (1940). The latter proved too ambitious and expensive to finish in England once the war broke out, and the production was moved to Hollywood, and Rozsa with it. He spent the next eight years as a successful freelance composer, winning his first Oscar with his score for Alfred Hitchcock's *Spellbound* (1945), which broke new ground in movie music with its use of the electronic instrument the theremin (and also yielded a popular piece of light classical music with the *Spellbound Concerto*). He became known for his ability to score crime movies, particularly the category now known as film noir, psychologically oriented tales of personal and criminal disorder, including *The Killers* (1946) and *The Naked City* (1947). In 1948, after winning his second Oscar (for *A Double Life*), Rózsa joined MGM, then the biggest studio in Hollywood, where he earned a third Oscar (for *Ben-Hur* (1959)) and a brace of nominations; his music graced some of the biggest movies of the era, including epics like *Quo Vadis* (1949) and costume adventure yarns such as *Ivanhoe* (1952), and serious topical dramas like *The Red Danube* (1949). Rózsa continued writing for the concert hall, although as a post-Romantic composer whose work was rooted in tonality, he found himself out of favor with the critics as early as 1943, when his *Theme, Variations and Finale* was performed by the New York Philharmonic. That didn't stop the performances or prevent commissions from coming in; he wrote his *Violin Concerto* for Jascha Heifetz, and into the 1960s and 1970s was writing concertos for piano, cello, and viola that were performed and recorded by such soloists as Leonard Pennario and Janos Starker. Rózsa remained active into the 1980s, composing music for a new generation of filmmakers, including Alain Resnais. At the time of his death in 1995, his concert and film music were in the process of being rediscovered and newly recorded. *—Bruce Eder*

FILM MUSIC

Ben-Hur (1959)

No film won more Academy Awards than MGM's remake of *Ben-Hur.* A great contribution to its success was provided by the fine symphonic score by Miklós Rózsa, at the height of his powers. He had already developed a Roman/Christian style for an earlier film, *Quo Vadis,* which he used to fine effect here. The entire score, including various versions of the preludes and overtures as used in road show and standard releases, and some other alternate versions, contains over two hours of music. Rózsa's practice in preparing sound track albums was to make symphonically coherent movements from the soundtrack score, then conduct them specifically for record release, so for that reason also there are variant versions. The entirety is a treasure trove of marches, love music which often has a modal flavor suggesting Jewish or Middle Eastern music, music evoking Christ, and action music (notably the naval battle scene—the famous chariot race did not have music, being underscored only by crowd noises and beautifully controlled horses' hooves effects). From it conductors can make excellent selections of concert suites. Overall, the music translates very well as a classical music experience. *—Joseph Stevenson*

Recommended:

○ **Ben-Hur** / 1991 / Sony 47020

El Cid (1961)

Although the life story of the medieval Spanish hero Rodrigo Diaz (known as "El Cid" or "The lord" by the Moors) has been the subject of many classical compositions, there has only been one American film made about him, Robert Mann's film staring Charlton Heston and Sophia Loren, produced by Samuel Bronston. At the time, the undisputed king of music for period spectacles was Miklós Rózsa, who had written great scores for *Quo Vadis, Ben-Hur,* and *King of Kings.*

Although Rózsa went on to write 13 more film scores, he considered this one his last "major film score" and his last important film except for *Providence.* Director Mann had lived for years in Spain, and Bronston's production facility was in the Madrid area, so the picture was entirely shot there. This gave Rózsa an opportunity to spend the time needed to write the score in that country, where he soaked up the national atmosphere and music. In addition, he researched music of the Spanish Middle Ages with the help of Ramon Mendendez Pidal, particularly that found in the *Cantigas,* a collection of 250 melodies from the time of King Alfonso the Wise.

Rózsa's score is a rich, highly romantic piece in his usual twentieth century style, similar to the music of his fellow-countryman Zoltán Kodály. It is one of the finest film scores of the 1960s, and has been recorded in substantially complete form. *—Joseph Stevenson*

Recommended:

○ **El Cid** / Rozsa (cond.) / Sony 47704

ORCHESTRAL

The Vintner's Daughter, variations on a French song, Op. 23a (1953–1955)

Composed for piano in 1952, this work has had much greater circulation in its 1955 orchestral garb. It's a set of variations inspired by Swiss poet Juste Olivier's *La Fille du Vigneron,* telling of a vintner's daughter who dreams that three dashing Hungarian knights pay court to her. Rózsa employs a pastoral French folk song as his theme, gently introduced in the orchestral version by solo horn. Each of the following 12 variations is keyed to an individual stanza in Olivier's poem. The initial variations depict the girl as she falls asleep, describing her attractive face, neck, and hair as she slumbers in the sun. These first six variations evoke the sweetly astringent Impressionist style of Maurice Ravel. But in variation seven the knights ride into the daughter's dream to a quick, macho Hungarian march. Their attraction to her is described with faintly humorous yet warm music, until the arrival of variation 11. Here, in the poem, the third knight declares "My lady shall she be," and Rózsa's music broadens and swells with erotic passion. In the final variation, the girl slowly awakes and the horn restates the main theme, which now seems nostalgic and bittersweet in its gentle wash of orchestral color. *—James Reel*

Recommended:

○ **Rózsa: Symphony in 3 Movements; Vintner's Daughter** / Sedares (cond.), New Zealand SO / 1994 / Koch 7244

CHAMBER MUSIC

Concerto for string orchestra, Op. 17 (1943; revised 1957)

The first concert work Rózsa wrote upon emigrating to the United States, the fraught *Concerto for String Orchestra* may be heard as a lament for his disrupted Hungary. The melodies all carry what the composer called a "Hungarian accent," and this work could be mistaken for dour Kodály or unpercussive Bartók. Intense lyricism suffuses the concerto, but it is the lyricism of Hungary rather than Hollywood.

The tough-minded first movement—Moderato, ma risoluto ed energico—contrapuntally develops two brooding themes. These themes occasionally rise to vehemence within Rózsa's sonata-allegro structure, but avoid a really slashing intensity. The solo viola introduces the second movement—Lento con gran espressione—with a haunting, folklike melody. The feeling here is nostalgic, possibly elegiac, depending on the performance. The viola, this time accompanied by solo cello, also ushers in the second theme, which is much in the same mood and could be heard as a variation on the first motif. After a passionate climax, pitting the violins against the massed violas, cellos, and basses playing in octaves, the music recedes into a muted viola solo. The final movement—Allegro giusto—abounds with contrapuntal acrobatics. The main theme, syncopated and dance-like, is carried by the violins, and calls to mind parts of Bartók's *Divertimento for Strings.* The second theme, light-spirited if not exactly happy, is interrupted by a fugato episode that rumbles out of the lower strings, initially like a minuet for curmudgeonly elephants. This material builds gradually in texture and speed, and eventually even the first movement's main theme weaves its way into the finale's counterpoint.

The *Concerto for String Orchestra,* which is dedicated to the composer's wife, can accommodate a number of interpretations. It may validly be presented as a more serious counterpart to Bartók's spirited, highly accessible *Divertimento,* or it may take on a special urgency as a fierce musical essay on wartime Hungary. In any case, it speaks frankly and directly to a wide audience. *—James Reel*

Recommended:

○ **Rózsa: Violin Concerto; Concerto for Strings; Andante for Strings** / Sedares (cond.), Gruppman, New Zealand SO / 1997 / Koch International Classics 7379

Edmund Rubbra

b. Mar. 23, 1901, Northampton, England, **d.** Feb. 13, 1986, Gerard's Cross, England

Composer

Edmund Rubbra's emergence during the interwar period as one of England's most skillful symphonists, and the subsequent dissemination of his musical ideals through 40 years of teaching at major British institutions, have earned him a place of honor among twentieth century British musicians. Rubbra was born into an impoverished Northampton family in 1901. His mother gave him his first musical lessons at the age of eight, and, although Rubbra was forced to take a job as a railway clerk at age 14, his enthusiasm for music continued unabated. By 1917 he had discovered the music of Cyril Scott, and his subsequent recital of that composer's piano works impressed the composer enough that he invited Rubbra to study both piano and composition with him privately. After working with Scott for three years he attended Reading University on a musical scholarship for one year (1920–21), after which he entered the Royal College of Music to study composition with Gustav Holst and harmony/counterpoint with R. O. Morris.

Rubbra's career was somewhat uncertain after graduating from the Royal College in 1925, and he was forced to work in a number of capacities to make ends meet (teaching school, working as an accompanist on a part-time basis, and writing reviews of new music for the *Monthly Musical Record*). By the mid-1930s, however, Rubbra was beginning to make waves as a composer, and the premieres of his first three symphonies (between 1937 and 1939) were sufficient to thrust him into the front rank of contemporary British composers.

Rubbra found professional stability with an appointment as lecturer at Oxford in 1947 (for which purpose he made a thorough and insightful examination of both books of Bach's *Well-Tempered Clavier*), and in 1961 he was invited to join the composition faculty of the Guildhall School of Music, where he remained until the 1980s. His later years were marked by an increasing interest in Eastern spirituality, in conjunction with a devout Roman Catholicism. Rubbra died in 1986.

Although a major facet of British musical life during the second half of twentieth century, Rubbra's music has been sadly neglected by North American musicians. Rubbra developed his compositional voice slowly and with great care, absorbing the myriad influences of British composers, from Holst and Vaughan Williams to his childhood idol Cyril Scott, and eventually emerging with a musical language all his own. His later music shows a keen awareness of sixteenth century polyphony (especially that of Monteverdi). The eleven symphonies (the ninth, entitled *Sinfonia Sacra*, for soloists, chorus, and orchestra) are undoubtedly Rubbra's most significant contribution to the repertory. —*Blair Johnston*

Overview of Works (1920–1985)

The English composer Edmund Rubbra began as an epigone in the mold of John Ireland, Arnold Bax, and above all Cyril Scott; developed his compositional techniques while studying under Gustav Holst and, occasionally, Ralph Vaughan Williams; but quickly became his own man by amalgamating a wide variety of influences from Janáček to Indian music, from medieval polyphony to Taoism, into a distinctive personal style. Strongly rhythmic and superbly formed, Rubbra's music is intensely contrapuntal but his counterpoint is all essentially lyrical: every line of even his instrumental music could be sung. In his many accompanied and unaccompanied choral works, his four string quartets and other chamber works, but especially in his series of 11 symphonies Rubbra created a body of work at once highly individualistic and completely accessible. —*James Leonard*

Recommended:

- ○ **Rubbra: Complete Symphonies** / Hickox (cond.), Hatfield, Lester, Willey, Dawson, BBC National Orch. Wales / 2001 / Chandos 9944
- ○ **Rubbra: 9 Tenebrae Motets** / Robinson (dir.), St. John's College Choir / 2001 / Naxos 555255
- ○ **Rubbra: Mass in Honor of St. Teresa of Avila** / Voces Sacrae / 2000 / ASV/Living Era 1093
- ○ **Rubbra: Complete Solo Piano Music** / Dussek / 2001 / Dutton 7112
- ○ **Rubbra: Violin Sonatas** / Osostowicz, Dussek / 1999 / Dutton 7101

Anton Rubinstein

b. Nov. 28, 1829, Vikhvatinets, Russia, **d.** Nov. 20, 1894, Peterhof, Russia

Composer: Keyboard, Concerto, Opera

Anton Rubinstein was more controversial in his day as a composer and educator than he was as a pianist and conductor. Consensus in the nineteenth century ranked him with Liszt and von Bülow in the keyboard realm, and even if his works stirred debate, they were more widely performed than in the twentieth century, when his reputation as a composer went into decline. Rubinstein wrote in most genres, turning out hundreds of solo piano pieces, as well as several concertos for piano, violin and cello, various chamber compositions, operas, ballets, and choral and vocal works. His output in many ways parallels that of Tchaikovsky, and recent reexamination of Rubinstein's compositions augurs well for rehabilitation of many of them and a favorable reassessment of his standing. Among his more important works are his operas *The Demon* and *Nero*, his oratorios *Paradise Lost* and *Tower of Babel*, his *"Ocean" Symphony* and *Piano Concerto No. 4*.

When Rubinstein was five years old, the family moved from the village of his birth to Moscow, and by that time he was taking piano lessons from his mother. About two years later, he began study with Alexander Villoing and by the age of ten had given his first concerts. In 1840, Villoing took the youth on a successful three-year concert tour throughout Europe and England.

In 1844, young Anton, along with his sister Luba and brother Nikolai, both of whom also showed great musical talent, traveled to Berlin for advanced studies. Anton took instruction in composition from Siegfried Dehn until 1846, when his father, who had remained in Russia, died suddenly. After spending two years in near-poverty teaching in Vienna, Anton returned to Russia to join his mother and siblings.

Around 1850, Rubinstein's talents drew the attention, then the patronage, of Duchess Elena Pavlovna, sister-in-law of the Tsar. He lived in comfortable quarters at one of her palaces until 1854 and often performed for her and her guests, including the Tsar. During his years there, he composed many works, including the first three piano concertos, nearly fifty songs, and five operas, among them *Stenka Razin* and *Tom the Fool*.

In 1854, Rubinstein went on a highly successful European concert tour. Five years later, he and the duchess founded the Russian Musical Society, and, in 1862, the St. Petersburg Conservatory. Rubinstein was its director for the first five years and regularly led concerts sponsored by the Russian Musical Society. His views on a Russian nationalist style in both composition and performance led to conflicts with Balakirev and the Mighty Handful composers.

Rubinstein remained busy in composition throughout these years, though he wrote no opera between 1862 and 1869. In the period 1867–70, he made several successful concert tours of Europe and the United States. He composed what is probably his best-known opera, *The Demon*, in 1871, its premiere coming four years later. This so-called "fantastic opera" was a far cry from the 1869 sacred opera, with German texts, *Der Thurm zu Babel*, and other similar works, possibly written by Rubinstein as if to reinforce his Christian credentials—the Rubinstein family had converted to Christianity from Judaism some years before.

Until 1887, Rubinstein maintained a fairly active concert schedule, both as pianist and conductor. He took up the directorship of the St. Petersburg Conservatory once again, that year. From 1891 to 1894 he lived in Dresden and briefly taught Josef Hofmann. He returned to Russia in January, 1894, gravely ill with heart disease. Later that year he died in Peterhof, a summer retreat where Rubinstein owned a *dacha*. —*Robert Cummings*

KEYBOARD

Kamenniy-Ostrov (Rocky Island), 24 portraits, Op. 10 (1853–1854)

This collection of 24 pieces, or portraits, represents Rubinstein's largest effort for solo piano. The composer wrote it when he was in residence at one of the palaces of the Grand Duchess, Elena Pavlovna, sister-in-law of the Tsar. The palace, located at Kamenniy-Ostrov (Rocky Island)—hence, the name of this collection—was also occupied by a large number of the Duchess' attendants and members of court. These 24 pieces are actually portraits of them and show the influence of many other prominent composers of the day.

The first piece, marked Allegro moderato, begins with a Lisztian flourish, then moves on to present an attractive, sedate main theme and Romantic secondary one that both divulge the fingerprints of Chopin. The lively third portrait, marked Con moto, has an attractive lightness to its scamper in the outer sections, recalling both Liszt and Chopin. No. 7 is sweet and sounds reminiscent of Liszt's "Ricordanza" from his *Transcendental Etudes*. The 11th (Moderato) features a pair of attractive themes in the outer section, the first bright and lovely, the second Slavic and dark in character.

The 14th portrait, marked Moderato, is delightfully playful in its main material, but serious in the contrasting middle episode. The Mendelssohnian No. 17 effervesces in its cascades of notes until the elegant middle section slows the pace a bit. The main theme returns, shedding its lightness in favor of a more stately manner. The 19th, marked Agitato, has a Slavic flavor and somewhat agitated character, but turns more Lisztian as it proceeds, sounding sinister then sweet, finally ending in a generally subdued manner.

The best know portrait in the collection is No. 22, marked Andante. It features a memorable opening theme of ethereal quality, matching well the piece's nickname, "Angelic Dream." The alternate theme is Schumann-esque, and when the opening melody returns, it carries a more muscular cast. The final piece is marked Allegro con moto and provides an upbeat close to this massive set, which lasts about two hours when performed whole. —*Robert Cummings*

Recommended:

- ○ **Rubinstein: Kamenniy-Ostrov** / Banowetz / 1999 / Marco Polo 223846
- ○ **Rubinstein: Kamenniy-Ostrov Vol. 2** / Banowetz / 2000 / Naxos 223847
- ○ **Piano Classics, Vol. 3** / various / 1997 / Madacy 8097

Two Melodies, Op. 3 (1852)

When one encounters albums with titles such as "Romantic Piano Favorites" or "Best-Loved Piano Pieces," one often finds Rubinstein's *Melody in F*, the first of the two pieces comprising the composer's Op. 3. The second half of the set, the *Melody in B*, is rarely if ever encountered. The reasons for the disparity in the popularity of the two pieces become apparent after one hearing.

The *Melody in F*, marked Moderato, begins with a catchy sentimental theme that lingers in the mind long after the piece is ended. Rubinstein alternates this melody with variants of itself, thus allowing his thematic creation to permeate virtually the entire piece. The work blazes no new compositional trails; its wide popularity can be accounted for strictly by the sheer memorability of its melody. In its own day it was a salon bonbon with which young pianists around the globe tried to please their sweethearts or, perhaps, to woo new ones.

The second piece in the set, while it offers marginal appeal, lacks precisely what its companion possesses—a tune of the sort that the Germans call an "ear worm." It also features harmonies that do not blend into the musical fabric with the deftness that one hears in the *F major Melody*. While these pieces carry the opus number of 3, they actually were written later in the composer's career than that designation suggests, coming after the Op. 29 *Two Funeral Marches*. —*Robert Cummings*

Recommended:

- ○ **Rubinstein: Piano Music** / Howard / 1997 / Hyperion 22023

Waltz-Caprice, in E flat major (1870)

One of those delightful recital items that would have been known to anyone who went to piano concerts 100 years ago, but that the grim mask of Serious Classical Music nearly killed off, the Rubinstein *Waltz-Caprice* (or *Valse-Caprice*) of 1870 remains one of the better-known works of this Western-leaning Russian composer. Despite Rubinstein's overall indebtedness to Chopin, this eight-minute work does not have the flavor of Chopin's waltzes; it is a bigger, less lyrical piece that evokes Liszt to some degree. Harmonically straightforward until the action-packed finale, it consists mostly of a series of alternating waltz strains; the opening tonic-centered melody is limpid and innocent but contains a big leap to a solitary sforzando high note. That leap recurs and is amplified in later tonic strains. (This is the caprice part, one assumes.) The contrasting strains are more chromatic, with big chords and plenty for the left hand to do. At the end there's a spectacular shift to common time and some very flashy extended cadential passages that are guaranteed to please. The *Waltz-Caprice* is full of rumbling piano figurations that strongly suggest orchestral textures, and it is indeed known in a setting for orchestra. As the slow introduction leads into the opening theme, you can almost, when hearing the orchestral version, imagine that you're listening to a Strauss waltz—until you realize that if it really were Strauss there would be more happening rhythmically. *—James Manheim*

Recommended:

○ **Rare Piano Encores** / Howard / 1986 / Hyperion 66090

○ **Rubinstein Collection, Vol. 31** / Rubinstein / 1999 / RCA 63031

CONCERTO

Piano Concerto No. 4 in D minor, Op. 70 (1864)

Much of Rubinstein's output was quite popular in the late nineteenth and early twentieth centuries, even rivaling the appeal of Tchaikovsky's works. He preceded Tchaikovsky in the cosmopolitan (as opposed to nationalist) space in Russian music of his time, but infused that space with nowhere near Tchaikovsky's passion. His reputation faded by the middle of the twentieth century, but this D minor effort has remained his most enduring large composition and has hovered near the fringes of the standard repertory. Echoes of the work abound in Tchaikovsky's writing for piano.

The work's relative success is easy to understand; the piano writing is assured and colorful, actually quite dazzling in places, and this half-hour three-movement work offers strong thematic and harmonic appeal, as well as imaginative orchestration. The first movement, marked Moderato assai, features a stately but melancholy main theme of Russian character that is reworked in a lovely, flowing variation form. The powerful cadenza near the end of the movement is quite Lisztian, both in sound and in its technical demands.

The middle panel, marked Andante, features a beautiful, gentle theme in the outer sections that encloses a dramatic, restless central episode. The Allegro finale brims with energy and effervescence, its driving and colorful dance rhythms and rippling piano part yielding only briefly to relatively calmer music. Again the flavors are Russian, and now the mood is mostly joyous. The coda is brilliant, featuring breathtaking piano writing whose dramatic depth and virtuoso acrobatics combine for sonic thrills that never veer toward the bombastic but instead suggest the most satisfying encore before the fact. In sum, this is a fine composition, perhaps a major masterpiece. The composer arranged the concerto for two pianos in 1866. *—Robert Cummings*

Recommended:

○ **The Complete Josef Hoffmann, Vol. 2** / Reiner (cond.), Hofmann, Chicago SO / 1992 / VAI Audio 1020

○ **Raymond Lewenthal: The Concerto Recordings** / Carvalho (cond.), Lewenthal, London SO / 1999 / Elan 82284

OPERA

The Demon (Der Dämon) (1871)

The Demon was Anton Rubinstein's only successful opera. Its style and subject matter parallel those of Gounod's *Faust.* Composed in 1871, *The Demon* consists of a Prologue, three acts and an Apotheosis (Epilogue). The libretto is by Pavel A. Viskovatov, based on a scenario drafted by Rubinstein and Apollon Nidolayevich Maykov after the 1839 poem by Lermontov. The opera was first given in at the Mariinsky Theater in St. Petersburg on January 25, 1875. The vocal score was published in 1874, the full score in 1876.

Until 1860, Lermontov's poem about a fallen angel had been banned in Russia as blasphemous. Rubinstein's opera initially suffered a similar fate, delaying its premiere. After the ban was lifted, however, Lermontov's tale, with its supernatural scenes and exotic setting, became one of the most popular narratives in all of Russia. Viskovatov's libretto tells the story of The Demon, an angel cast out of heaven, and his love for the Princess Tamara, whom he sees as his only chance at redemption. The Demon kills Tamara's fiancé, Prince Sinodal, whose death sends Tamara to a convent to mourn. There, the Demon approaches Tamara and entreats her to be with him. When she acquiesces, she dies, but angels arrive to reclaim her soul and bring her to heaven, leaving the Demon to continue in his eternal suffering.

Rubinstein called *The Demon* a "fantastic" opera, but its style lies firmly in the realm of Russian lyric opera; Rubinstein was more concerned with the psychological representation of the principal characters, the Demon and Tamara, than with special effects. The composer draws the Mephistophelean Demon through passages of passionate music, culminating in his romance at the end of Act Two, "Ne plach', ditya'" (Do not weep, child). This remains the most popular number in the opera, and is often performed separately. Tamara's sincerity and compassion come through in her most important solo, the romance, "Noch' tepla, noch' tikha" (The night is warm, the night is still), which takes place in the monastery scene in the third act. Some of Tchaikovsky's passages for Tatyana in *Eugene Onegin* derive from Rubinstein's music for Tamara in *The Demon.*

Rubinstein and Viskovatov create an exotic atmosphere by using the typical Russian representation of Islamic culture, derived from Glinka's *Ruslan and Lyudmila.* Prince Sinodal and his caravan, appearing in the last scene of Act One, provide the vehicle for stereotypical Muslim imagery and the modal inflections associated with it.

Parts of *The Demon* feature what might be called a nationalist character. These moments of folkish music are more a reaction to the growing influence of Balakirev's circle of nationalist composers than any inclination on the part of the composer himself. Rubinstein's early operas on Russian nationalist subjects failed, leading the composer to write that Russian nationalist operas simply could not be made. By the 1870s, however, the wave of nationalist composition was too overpowering for even Rubinstein to resist. For example, in the first act of *The Demon* we hear the girls' chorus, "Khodim mï k Aragve svetloy" (We go the bright Aragva), which is based on a Georgian folk song. In spite of Rubinstein's efforts, however, the opera suffered criticism from nationalist composers and writers even as it gained public favor.

Most impressive is the third act of the opera, which takes place at the convent and is almost entirely made up of a nearly 30-minute-long seduction scene involving the Demon and Tamara.The scene is not a duet in the conventional sense, for the two never really sing together. Instead, Rubinstein construct a series of romances that alternate between the characters, creating an atmosphere of opposition appropriate for the drama. *—John Palmer*

Synopsis:

Prologue. Prince Gudal's castle in Georgia.

The Demon appears. The spirits of the three levels of the universe—hell, Earth, and heaven—come together and sing of the Demon. The Demon is disgusted with the Earth and at the same time he is bored, for humans offer no opposition or resistance to his powers and he gets no satisfaction from spreading evil. An Angel appears to the Demon and tells him he has a chance to reenter heaven if he gives in to love. The Demon, however, will have none of this. The Angel responds, "Your knowledge is negation, your love is hatred," telling the Demon to stay away from anything that is important to heaven. The Demon then tells the Angel that he welcomes such a challenge, adding that heaven must now be on its guard.

Act One. Evening on the banks of the river Aragva

Girls collect water from the river. Tamara, Prince Gudal's daughter, enters with her Nanny and joins the others. The Demon appears and notices Tamara, who hears him speak and becomes frightened. To calm her, the Nanny sings to Tamara about her fiancé, Prince Sinodal. Feeling better, Tamara intends to rejoin the others when she again hears the Demon's voice, this time telling her that he intends to enter into a new life with her as his "eternal companion." When Tamara finally sees the Demon, she is stunned. The Nanny notices a strange look on Tamara's face, and when she approaches the Demon vanishes. Tamara then relates to her Nanny how someone just sang wonderful songs to her. The Nanny has no idea who this "person" was and suggests they return to the castle. Tamara, mesmerized, reviews the Demon's song.

In the mountains, near a small chapel

Prince Sinodal's caravan approaches and his Old Servant commands the drivers to halt and prepare camp. The Prince arrives and sends a messenger ahead of the caravan to inform Tamara that he will be at the Gudal castle by noon the following day. The Prince imagines he is a falcon flying to meet Tamara, then is consoled by his Old Servant, who tells him he will soon reach his destination. The servants congratulate the Prince on his upcoming wedding, but the Old Servant scolds them for singing loudly, telling them that they are in an evil place, not fit for such behavior. He points out the nearby chapel, marking the spot where a saint was slain. He then suggests that the Prince go to the chapel and pray, for all who have done so have been protected from dangerous Muslims. The Prince says he will do so the next morning and, believing the image of Tamara will protect him, lies down for a night's sleep, dreaming of Tamara.

The Demon appears and reveals that it is he who has brought the Prince his dreams of Tamara and put him into a deep sleep. Quietly, Tartars sneak up on the lying men and attack them. The Prince is wounded by gunfire and brought back to his quarters by the Old Servant, who, after examining the injury, is convinced the Prince will not live another day. The Prince rises, determined to ride as quickly as possible to see his bride. The Demon reappears and the Prince, pronouncing Tamara's name, dies.

Act Two. A hall in Gudal's castle prepared for the arrival of Prince Sinodal

Wedding guests sing the praises of Prince Gudal. Sinodal's messenger arrives and informs everyone that the caravan should arrive by noon. Prince Gudal orders a toast to the bride and groom. The guests then hear cries from outside, and Prince Gudal and others leave to see what is wrong. When they return, they bring with them the body of Prince Sinodal, followed by the Old Servant. Tamara throws herself on Sinodal's body, begging him to come back to life. She eventually realizes that they can be united only through her death.

In her despair, Tamara hears the voice of the Demon telling her not to weep. She is confused because she is unsure of whose voice she has heard. Gudal has Sinodal's body removed. The Demon again speaks to Tamara, telling her that she should not concern herself with earthly things and that when night falls he will come to her. Just then Gudal returns, and Tamara rises and dreamily asks, "Where is he?" Gudal thinks she has lost touch with reality and Tamara asks to be allowed to join a convent, where she will be safe. Gudal reluctantly grants her wishes.

Act Three. The convent at night; Tamara's window is visible

The Old Servant sings of the power of prayer. He leaves and the Demon enters, watching Tamara's window, but afraid to enter the convent. An Angel appears and asks him why he is here. He tells the Angel that Tamara is his and he will take her, but the Angel reminds him to stay away from that which belongs to heaven. The Demon does not listen and enters the convent.

Inside Tamara's room

The Demon enters and the two stare at each other while the Old Servant continues his song about prayer. Tamara asks the Demon who he is and he tells her he is "the evil aspect of nature." Tamara is frightened as she tells the Demon to be quiet. The Demon then tells her that she is, for him, everything he wanted before he was barred from heaven; he asks for her understanding. Tamara feels compassion for the Demon and asks him to forswear evil, which he does. Tamara, exhausted, asks the Demon to leave her. Although she knows she could end all evil by giving in to the Demon, she cannot love him; she calls upon heaven for strength. Weakened, she declares her love for the Demon, but the Angel appears to rescue Tamara's soul and banish the Demon, who finds himself alone again.

Apotheosis. The Angels bear Tamara to heaven. *—John Palmer*

Recommended:

○ **Rubinstein: Der Dämon** / Fedoseyev (cond.), Levinsky, Silins, Meshcheriakova, Daniluk, VSO / 1998 / Koch 365432

○ **Rubinstein: Der Dämon** / Anissimov (cond.), Browner, Andrew, Lochak, Meshcheriakova, Wexford Festival Opera / 1995 / Marco Polo 223781

Artur Rubinstein

b. Jan. 28, 1887, Lodz, Poland, **d.** Dec. 20, 1982, Geneva, Switzerland

Pianist

Warm, lyrical, and aristocratic in his interpretations, Artur Rubinstein performed impressively into extremely old age, and he was a keyboard prodigy almost from the time he could climb onto a piano bench. He came from a mercantile rather than a musical family, but fixated on the piano as soon as he heard it. At age three he impressed Joseph Joachim, and by the age of seven he was playing Mozart, Schubert, and Mendelssohn at a charity concert in his hometown. In Warsaw, he had piano lessons with Alexander Róóycki; then in 1897 he was sent to Berlin to study piano with Heinrich Barth and theory with Robert Kahn and Max Bruch, all under Joachim's general supervision. In 1899 came his first notable concerto appearance in Potsdam. Soon thereafter, just barely a teenager, he began touring Germany and Poland.

After brief studies with Paderewski in Switzerland in 1903, Rubinstein moved to Paris, where he met Ravel, Dukas, and Jacques Thibaud, and played Saint-Saëns' *G minor Concerto* to the composer's approval. That work would remain a flashy Rubinstein vehicle for six decades, and it was the concerto he offered in his American debut with the Philadelphia Orchestra in New York's Carnegie Hall in 1906. His underprepared American tour was not especially well-received, though, so he withdrew to Europe for further study. Rubinstein became an adept and sensitive chamber musician and accompanist; his 1912 London debut was accompanying Pablo Casals, and during World War I he toured with Eugène Ysaÿe.

He gave several successful recitals in Spain during the 1916–17 season, and soon toured Latin America. Along the way he developed a great flair for Hispanic music; Heitor Villa-Lobos went so far as to dedicate to Rubinstein his *Rudepoema*, one of the toughest works in the repertory. Although Rubinstein would later be somewhat typecast as a Chopin authority, his readings of Falla, Granados, and Albéniz would always be equally idiomatic.

Rubinstein's international reputation grew quickly, although he was by his own account a sloppy technician. In the mid-1930s he withdrew again and drilled himself in technique. By 1937 he reemerged as a musician of great discipline, poise, and polish—qualities he would mostly retain until his farewell recital in London in 1976, at the age of 89. Rubinstein's temperament had sufficient fire for Beethoven but enough poetry for Chopin; his tempos and dynamics were always flexible, but never distorted. His 1960s recordings for RCA of nearly all Chopin's solo piano music have been considered basic to any record collection since their release, and his version of Falla's *Nights in the Gardens of Spain* is another classic, as are his various late collaborations with the Guarneri Quartet.

Rubinstein became a naturalized American citizen in 1946, but he maintained residences in California, New York, Paris, and Geneva; two of his children were born in the United States, one in Warsaw, and one in Buenos Aires. He had married Aniela Mlynarska in 1932, but womanizing remained integral to his reputation as an irrepressible *bon vivant.* He maintained that the slogan "wine, women, and song" as applied to him meant 80 percent women and only 20 percent wine and song.

Still, there was a serious side to his life. After World War II, he refused ever again to perform in Germany, in response to the Nazi extermination of his Polish family. Rubinstein became a strong supporter of Israel; in gratitude, an international piano competition in his name was instituted in Jerusalem in 1974. His honors included the Gold Medal of the Royal Philharmonic Society of London, the U.S. Medal of Freedom (1976), and membership in the French Legion of Honor. *—James Reel*

Recommended:

○ **Rubinstein Collection, Vol. 1** / Coates (cond.), Rubinstein, London SO / 1999 / RCA 63001

○ **Rubinstein Collection Highlights** / Leinsdorf, Golschmann (conds.), Rubinstein, Heifetz, Feuermann, etc. / RCA 63085

○ **Chopin Favorites** / Rubinstein / RCA 61717

○ **Rubinstein Collection, Vol. 82** / Rubinstein / 1999 / RCA 63082

Julius Rudel

b. Mar. 6, 1921, Vienna, Austria

Conductor

Julius Rudel is one of the best-known American conductors and musical administrators mainly associated with operatic performances. As a child, he was deeply attracted to music, regularly attended the Vienna Philharmonic concerts and saw some of the great conductors of the age, including Knappertsbusch, Furtwängler, and Walter. He began his formal musical studies at the Academy of Music in Vienna. At the time of the Nazi occupation of Austria, he left the country and completed his musical studies at Mannes School of Music in New York, graduating in 1943. He became a naturalized U.S. citizen in 1944.

After graduation, he was hired on the musical staff of the New York City Opera, where he helped prepare performances. His debut as a professional conductor was with the NYCO on November 25, 1944. He remained with the NYCO for 35 years, becoming its principal conductor and general director in 1957. Under his leadership, the company came to be respected as one of the leading opera companies of the United States. One of his most astute decisions was in engaging soprano Beverly Sills as its leading singer. Rudel already had an interest in opera written before the time of Mozart and in the then-neglected era of Italian bel canto opera. Operas of Handel, Donizetti, Bellini, and Rossini were frequently represented on the NYCO stage. Their style was also well-suited to the abilities of Sills and her frequent partner, mezzo-soprano Marilyn Horne, and made the New York City Opera's seasons more exciting than the standard fare offered by the rival Metropolitan Opera Company (which became the NYCO's neighbor at the Lincoln Center in the 1960s). A feature of his seasons was a strong support for American operas.

During his tenure at the NYCO, Rudel also often conducted in major opera centers in Vienna, Munich, Chicago, San Francisco, Paris, Rome, London, Hamburg, Berlin, and even the Met. He was also the first music director of the Kennedy Center in Washington and of the Wolf Trap Festival. He has been music director of *the* Cincinnati May Festival and the Caramoor Festival.

He left the City Opera in 1979 in order to have more time for symphonic conducting. He accepted a position as music director of the Buffalo Philharmonic and frequently conducts the Orchestra of St. Luke's in New York, with which he has recorded works of Weill, Schubert, and Mozart on the MusicMasters label. He also conducts the Montreal Symphony Orchestra, the Royal Scottish National Orchestra, and others. Meanwhile, he has continued as an opera conductor, appearing at the Met, Teatro Colón in Buenos Aires, the Bastille Opera, Lyric Opera of Chicago, the Royal Opera in Copenhagen, and the Deutsche Oper of Berlin.

He has made a number of successful opera recordings and has been nominated for Grammy Awards several times, winning once. In 1961, his home nation of Austria presented him a special award for his service to arts and sciences. He is also a Chevalier des Arts et Lettres in France, recipient of awards from Israel and Germany, and holder of several honorary doctorates. In 1996, New York City proclaimed his 75th birthday "Julius Rudel Day," which Rudel himself observed by conducting *Madame Butterfly* at the Met. *—Joseph Stevenson*

Recommended:

○ **Janáček: Concertino; Capriccio; Youth; Nursery Rhymes** / Rudel (cond.), Somer, Caramoor Festival Orch. / 1989 / Phoenix USA 109

○ **Boito: Mefistofele** / Rudel (cond.), Burgess, Domingo, Allen, Caballe, London SO / 1997 / EMI 66501

○ **Massenet: Manon** / Rudel (cond.), Souzay, Sills, Gedda, Bacquier, New Philharmonia / DG 000247002

○ **Handel: Julius Caesar** / Rudel (cond.), Sills, Forrester, Treigle, Malas, NYC Opera Orch. & Chorus / 1967 / RCA 6182

Titta Ruffo

b. Jun. 9, 1877, Pisa, Italy, **d.** Jul. 5, 1953, Florence, Italy

Baritone

Titta Ruffo (born Ruffo Cafiero Titta) was one of the top Italian baritones of the early twentieth century. He had a powerful, dark singing voice, yet his upper register had a ring usually characteristic of a tenor; these qualities embodied the full-blooded operatic baritone that has been in vogue ever since. His flowing hair earned him the nickname, "The Singing Lion."

Ruffo was brought up in a poor family headed by Orestes Titta, a factory worker who named the boy after his deceased hunting dog. Ruffo intended to apprentice himself to an ironworker, but his natural singing voice soon became evident and several patrons arranged for him to study in Rome. He studied briefly with Venceslao Persichini, but the pedagogue already had another promising baritone, Giuseppe di Luca, as a pupil and so sent Ruffo to other teachers.

Ruffo's progress was rapid, however, and he was soon singing important roles such as Verdi's *Rigoletto*, and Barnaba in *La Gioconda*, in provincial opera houses and in South America. In 1903, the Covent Garden opera house in London engaged him, and he debuted that year as Enrico in Donizetti's *Lucia di Lammermoor* and Figaro in Rossini's *Barber*.

Covent Garden also scheduled him to sing *Rigoletto*, but the famous Nelly Melba refused to appear with him, saying "he's too young to play my father." This was not a problem at La Scala, however, and he sang the role there several times during the 1903–04 season; this marked the start of his major European career. He returned to South America in 1908, now a major star, and was welcomed back there frequently over a 25-year period.

He was famous as a Verdi baritone, singing such roles as Don Carlo in *Ernani*, and Amonasro in *Aida*, in addition to Rigoletto. He was particularly effective in Ambroise Thomas' *Hamlet*. When he was booked to sing the role at Teatro San Carlo in Naples, Melba, there on her way to Australia, contacted the manager offering to sing Ophelia opposite Ruffo one evening. "Tell Melba she's too old to sing with me," Ruffo responded.

Ruffo's relationship with Enrico Caruso was better; the two were personal friends and sang in the same productions in Europe. But Caruso used his influence to keep Ruffo off the stage of the Metropolitan while the tenor starred there. Ruffo, therefore, did not appear in New York until 1922, becoming a favorite despite declining vocal powers.

Since Persichini had passed on him, Ruffo did not acquire as good a technique as he might have; his reliance on his raw natural gifts, and the resulting fatigue, probably shortened his career. At his prime, this was an exciting and vigorous color that strongly influenced Italian tastes in baritone singing.

By the mid-1930s Ruffo's enemies (and there were many, as he was a critic of Mussolini's fascist regime) were able to tag him "the dying lion." In 1936, Ruffo announced his retirement: "The lion is silent." Ruffo refused to teach, however: "I never knew how to sing," he answered. "That is why my voice went by the time I was 50. I have no right to capitalize on my former name and reputation and try to teach youngsters something I never knew how to do myself."

However, he did share the secrets of how he produced his remarkable range of tone colors in part of his autobiography, *La mia parabola* (My Parabola), published in 1937. Although he was practically unschooled, *My Parabola* is considered one of the best written, most entertaining, and most informative of operatic memoirs. *—Joseph Stevenson*

Recommended:

○ **Titta Ruffo Edition** / Ruffo, etc. / Preiser 89303

○ **Early Recordings, 1906/12** / Ruffo, etc. / Preiser 89220

○ **Prima Voce: Ruffo** / Ruffo, etc. / 1990 / Nimbus 7810

Carl Ruggles

b. Mar. 11, 1876, Marion, MA, **d.** Oct. 24, 1971, Bennington, VT

Composer

Carl Ruggles was born to a New England farming family and received his first musical instruction from his mother, who died when he was 14. Ruggles studied violin with Walter Spaulding and Felix Winternitz, theory with Josef Claus, and composition with Harvard educator John Knowles Paine. In 1899–1901 Ruggles published several songs for voice and piano, though only three titles survive; Ruggles had a lifelong habit of destroying older compositions. In 1907, Ruggles settled in Winona, MN, founding a symphony orchestra that yet exists. Ruggles piloted the Winona Symphony for its first ten seasons, and through it met and married the oratorio singer Charlotte Snell. Starting in 1912, Ruggles concentrated on an opera, *The Sunken Bell*. Despite acceptance of *The Sunken Bell* for performance at the Metropolitan Opera in New York, Ruggles never completed it, discarding the score around 1960. He neglected to dispose of a number of sketches relating to this work, and these reveal Ruggles arrived at his mature style during the years he devoted to its composition.

In 1919, Ruggles composed the song *Toys* as a fourth birthday present for his son Micah; this was the earliest work Ruggles allowed to stand as his own. In 1922, Ruggles joined the International Composers' Guild, founded by Edgard Varèse and Carlos Salzedo to promote the works of avant-garde composers in New York. On December 17, 1922, Ruggles' brass piece *Angels* was premiered at a Composer's Guild concert. Ruggles followed *Angels* with *Vox clamans in deserto*, a setting of seven poems for voice and chamber ensemble. Only three of the songs were heard in a concert of 1924, but the cycle failed to meet Ruggles' standard, and did not appear in print until 1974. *Portals* for string orchestra followed in 1926, *Men and Mountains*, a short, three-movement symphony including "Lilacs" for strings, was completed in 1927 and published in the first issue of Henry Cowell's periodical *New Music*. Also in the late 1920s Ruggles began to paint. Whereas Ruggles' musical reputation rests on only a dozen works, he created more than 300 paintings that were avidly purchased by museums and private individuals.

In 1932, Ruggles completed the orchestral piece *Sun-treader*, both his largest-scale work and his masterpiece. Ruggles' pieces were subject to years-long gestation periods, the final result produced through a painstaking process of trial and error. Ruggles' music is built out of "crooked" individual lines, frequent dissonances resulting from places where these lines intersect. Rhythmically his work is not complex, but in some respects is difficult to decipher, particularly in manuscripts, which involve sketches written on paper that is of every conceivable shape or size. Throughout his life, Ruggles would rely on the advice of musical friends to assist him with the knotty problems resulting from his style and method, including Varèse, Cowell, pianist John Kirkpatrick, and composer-musicologist Charles Seeger. Seeger first coined the phrase "dissonant counterpoint" in an attempt to describe Ruggles' approach.

In 1935–42 Ruggles enjoyed his only position as teacher at the University of Miami in Florida. From 1937–56 Ruggles concentrated his energies on the four *Evocations for John Kirkpatrick*, creating them in two distinct piano versions and an orchestration. The last completed work in his signature style is the orchestral *Organum* (1949). In 1957, Charlotte Ruggles died, and he paid tribute to her in his final piece, *Exaltation* (1958) a hymn setting for wordless chorus and organ based on "God Our Help in Ages Past." Ruggles took up residence in a nursing home in 1966, and died five years later at the age of 95. *—Uncle Dave Lewis*

Overview of Works (1889–1958)

There is nothing in the world like the music and career of American composer Carl Ruggles. The closest comparison might be the music and career of Charles Ives: both wrote music that owed very little to any other composer or any other time and place, and both were extremely independent past the point of belligerence. But although Ives and Ruggles strove for the transcendental, Ruggles music was craggier and gnarlier than that of Ives; for that matter, it was far gnarlier and craggier even than the music of Henry Cowell or Edgard Varèse. In terms of melody, harmony, rhythm, form, and orchestration, Ruggles was a true original. He was also extremely self-critical. He lived nearly a century and composed for most of it, but published only eight works, and nearly every one was revised and re-revised even after publication. Only three of his works exist in their original form: the early *Mood for violin & piano* (1918), the song *Toys* (1919) and the late *Exaltation* (1951) for unison chorus.

Men and Angels (1920), his first truly characteristic work, is typical of Ruggles' tendency to rework and revise. After it was published in 1920, Ruggles subsequently destroyed "Men," the original opening section; then rewrote *Angels*, the closing section, first for six trumpets and then for four trumpets and three trombones. He later rewrote "Men" as *Sun-Treader*, then inserted it back into *Men and Angels*, then withdrew it again and published it separately. All of this was not merely the compulsive activity of a composer who was rarely performed. It was all part of Ruggles' quest to capture the sublime in music of unprecedented ecstasy. His melodic language is extremely chromatic; his harmonic language is thoroughly atonal, his rhythms are complex; and his forms are nearly impenetrable and his orchestration is massive: all of it is intended to transcend mundane reality and achieve the infinite. In his smaller works, like *Portals for strings* (1925, rev. 1929, rev. 1941, rev 1952–53), his setting of *Browning* and Whitman *Vox clamans in deserto* for soprano and orchestra (1924, rev. 1936, rev. 1941), his *Evocations* (1935–43) for piano, or the final form of *Angels for brass*, Ruggles created a world of blissful serenity. But in his great orchestral work *Men and Mountains* (1924, rev. 1936, rev. 1941) or his masterpiece *Sun-Treader* (1926–31), Ruggles stormed the gates of heaven and won through to a spiritual rapture rarely equaled in all music. *—James Leonard*

Recommended:

- **Ives & Ruggles** / Dohnányi (cond.), Cleveland Orch. / 1995 / London 443776

Konrad Ruhland

b. Landau, Germany

Conductor

A student of the Greek-German medievalist Thrasybulos Georgiadis and the Renaissance music specialist Marie-Louise Göllner, musicologist and conductor Konrad Ruhland is a pioneering German figure in the field of early music performance, something of a Continental counterpart to Noah Greenberg in the U.S. or the similarly academically influenced David Munrow in Britain. He was born in Landau, Germany and obtained his earliest musical training as a chorister in the cathedral choir of Passau. He then studied history, medieval Latin, theology, and liturgical history, all of which he has applied to his performance practice research. In 1956, he founded the Capella Antiqua München, bringing together a group of young vocal students in Munich. This became one of the first ensembles to apply a historical approach to Renaissance and early Baroque music.

Many of the large number of albums he made contain choral music that had never been recorded before, and his interests as a performer ranged from the earliest music of the Christian era up to the seventeenth century. In line with Ruhland's academic interests, some of his recordings (such as *The Moosburg Gradual of 1360*) are devoted to specific manuscripts or settings. Though his style lacks the expression that later performers have brought to much of the music he unearthed, his music making is never pedantic or dull. His 1966 recording *Gregorian Chant* is considered a classic and has been reissued on CD by Sony Classical; Ruhland's notes offer a straightforward introduction to the music, free of the pop mysticism that has attended many chant releases. Through the 1960s and 1970s Ruhland led the group in recordings for a number of labels, including Telefunken, Seon, Christophorus, and Sony. After the Capella disbanded, he conducted recordings by the Niederaltaicher Scholaren. Still active as a choral conductor and educator in both Europe and the U.S., he is notable for his vast expertise on diverse repertories of music. *—AMG*

Recommended:

- **Te deum laudamus** / Ruhland (cond.), Munich Capella Antiqua, Netherlands Scholars / 1998 / Sony 60096
- **Carmina Burana** / Ruhland (cond.), Munich Capella Antiqua / 1992 / Christophorus 16
- **Gregorian Chant Sequences** / Ruhland (cond.), Munich Capella Antiqua / 1999 / Sony 61868

Shirley Rumsey

Lutenist

Shirley Rumsey studied lute and voice at the Royal College of Music, London. There she became interested in solo vocal music accompanied by lute and she soon developed a unique career in which she performs this repertoire. In addition to solo recitals, she frequently collaborates with lutenist Christopher Wilson with whom she co-directs the ensemble Kithara. Rumsey has performed extensively throughout Europe and Scandinavia, has taken part in numerous festivals, and made numerous recordings. *—Robert Adelson*

Recommended:

- **Music of the Spanish Renaissance** / Rumsey / 1993 / Naxos 550614
- **Music of the Italian Renaissance** / Rumsey / 1994 / Naxos 550615

John Rutter

b. Sep. 24, 1945, London, England

Composer: Choral

Conductor

John Rutter is one of England's best-known composers of the late twentieth century, as well as a widely respected choral conductor and music scholar and editor. While his choral works (including the *Te Deum*, *Magnificat*, and *Requiem*) are the most familiar, he has also written instrumental works, including a piano concerto, the *Suite Antique* for flute, harpsichord, and strings, and two children's operas.

Musically he could be characterized as a reactionary, as his works show very distinct influences from the past and show almost no signs of progressivism or even contemporary influences. He has a strong sense of the English musical traditions, and some of the more significant English musical influences on his work include Ralph Vaughn Williams, William Walton, and Benjamin Britten. Non-English influences include Fauré, Gregorian chant, and Bach, and his *Suite Antique* is a direct tribute to the *Brandenburg Concerto No. 5*, written for the same instruments and in the same style. However, his music's immediate accessibility, being both tuneful and expressive, and its wide general appeal have still earned him a place in the English musical tradition, though not the place of an innovator, and while he is most popular in England and the United States, his music is performed worldwide.

He began his musical career as a member of the Highgate School chorus, continued to study organ, and went on to Cambridge University, where he studied at Clare College. At the age of 30, in 1975, he returned to Clare, where he was director of music. In 1979, however, he left the position in order to give more attention to composing and to conducting, though he still contributed to the study of choral music, acting as an editor in the *Carols for Choirs* and *Oxford Choral Classics* series. He formed the Cambridge Singers in 1981, though once they were established as a leading chamber choir, he left off leadership of the group, again in order to concentrate on composing and conducting. In 1985, his *Requiem* had its first performance, followed in 1990 by his *Magnificat* and his 1993 *Psalmfest*. In 1996, he was awarded a Lambeth Doctorate of Music by the Archbishop of Canterbury, for his services to church music. In addition to all of these activities, he manages a CD label, Collegium Records, largely devoted to his own music. This was more or less by chance; he had no intention of doing so until an established label offered him a contract; the terms struck him as being so unsatisfactory that he decided to do it himself. *—Ann Feeney*

Recommended:

- **Poulenc: Sacred Music** / Rutter (cond.), Seers, Deam, Cambridge Singers, City of London Sinfonia / 2002 / Collegium 506
- **The John Rutter Collection** / Rutter (cond.), Orton, Ashton, Forbes, Cambridge Singers, City of London Sinfonia / 2002 / Decca 472622
- **Gloria: Sacred Music of John Rutter** / Rutter (cond.), Scott, Kettel, Poole, Cambridge Singers, Philip Jones Brass Ens., City of London Sinfonia / 1984 / Collegium 100
- **Rutter: Requiem & Magnificat** / Rutter (cond.), Ashton, Deam, Cambridge Singers, City of London Sinfonia / 1991 / Collegium 504
- **Portrait Of The Cambridge Singers** / Rutter (cond.), Cambridge Singers, City of London Sinfonia / Collegium 500

Overview of Works

John Rutter is one of the foremost figures in church music in the late twentieth and early twenty-first centuries, and his works solidly follow in the English sacred music traditions. While he is best known for his choral works, he has composed in nearly every genre, including settings of American folk songs, arrangements of classic carols and hymns, children's operas and school musicals, orchestral pieces, madrigals, and even jazz arrangements. Intensely prolific, he has become one of England's most popular classical composers, one whose works are staples in the liturgical and concert repertoire. His writing is consistently accessible and firmly rooted within the traditions of each genre, though written with contemporary audiences in mind. For example, for his arrangements of Shakespeare songs, Rutter used an almost jazzlike buoyancy and rhythmic accents, even though they also have elements of earlier lute and madrigal settings. His pieces are also typically written on a modest scale so as not to put them beyond the technical reach of amateur groups, although they provide enough demands and rewards to make them equally popular with professional ensembles. His gentle *Requiem* (1985) setting has much more in common with Fauré's or Duruflé's than Verdi's. He wrote most of his choral works for the Cambridge Singers, and in 1984, he formed a record label with the specific purpose of bringing more widespread popularity to choral music. *—Ann Feeney*

Recommended:

- **John Rutter Collection** / Rutter (cond.), Orton, Ashton, Forbes, Cambridge Singers, City of London Sinfonia / 2002 / Decca 472622
- **John Rutter: Distant Land** / Rutter (cond.), Birch, Williams, Wilson, Nicholson, Schaefer, Rostal, Royal PO / 2003 / Decca 000182102
- **Rutter: Gloria, & Other Sacred Music** / Layton (cond.), Lumsden, Polyphony, Wallace Collection, City of London Sinfonia / 2001 / Hyperion 67259

CHORAL

Requiem (1985)

Having recently prepared an edition of Fauré's *Requiem* restoring its small-scale scoring, John Rutter was naturally influenced by that tender, subtle, and comforting French work in writing his own *Requiem* in 1985. Many critics assailed Rutter's work for its old-fashioned tunefulness, its gentle harmonies, and its refusal to confront the darkness and violence of the twentieth century. Meanwhile, church and amateur choral societies, radio listeners, and CD buyers responded to the work with remarkable enthusiasm. Critical response has softened over the years, as it has become clear that Rutter was not cynically trying to write a commercial hit, but was employing his natural voice, a voice that resonates with many music lovers.

Rutter composed his *Requiem* in response to the death of a parent. He has explained, "The music is not a complete setting of the *Missa pro defunctis* as laid down in Catholic liturgy, but instead a meditation on themes of life and death using a personal compilation of texts. Like Fauré, I selected portions of the *Requiem Mass*, and like Britten, I wove other, English texts into them to form a counterpoint to the Latin.... The result is a concert work rather than a liturgical *Requiem*." Rutter creates a seven-movement arch. The first and last movements are prayers to God, drawn from the Latin format (Requiem aeternam and Lux aeterna, the latter including a passage in English from the Burial Sentences of the *Book of Common Prayer*). The second, "Out of the Deep," and sixth, "The Lord Is My Shepherd," are psalm settings (numbers 130 and 23, respectively); the former appropriately includes a double bass solo and the latter features the oboe, an instrument inextricably linked with English pastoralism. The third movement, Pie Jesu (from the standard *Requiem* sequence), and the fifth, Agnus Dei (the *Requiem* again, to which is appended a few words from the *Book of Common Prayer*), Rutter describes as "personal prayers to Christ." The central Sanctus, a standard mass text, is the briefest but most affirmative section, complete with celebratory bells. Short snatches of Gregorian chant find their way into the Agnus Dei and Lux aeterna, but the strongest influence here is surely Ralph Vaughan Williams, another composer well aware of the history of English hymnody and committed to imbuing his music with an identifiably English sound. Rutter's style, however, is more cinematic in its lush harmonies and occasionally syncopated melodies. The *Requiem* is available in two versions; in one, the chorus is accompanied by organ and six instruments, and in the other, by a small orchestra. *—James Reel*

Recommended:

- ○ **Rutter: Requiem** / Cleobury (cond.), King's College Choir, City of London Sinfonia / 1998 / EMI 56605
- ○ **Rutter: Requiem** / Brown (cond.), City of London Sinfonia, Cambridge Clare College Choir / 2003 / Naxos 8557130
- ○ **Rutter: Requiem** / Layton (cond.), Handy, Mannion, Knight, Nelson, Polyphony, Bournemouth Sinfonietta / 1997 / Hyperion 66947
- ○ **Rutter: Requiem & Magnificat** / Rutter (cond.), Ashton, Deam, Cambridge Singers, City of London Sinfonia / 1991 / Collegium 504

Leonie Rysanek

b. Nov. 14, 1929, Vienna, Austria, **d.** Mar. 7, 1998, Vienna, Austria

Soprano

While best known for her Wagner and Strauss, soprano Leonie Rysanek was also greatly admired in the dramatic Verdi roles, especially Lady Macbeth. She had a rich, full voice that could cut through heavy orchestration, but was also capable of fine piano singing. Her first career ambition was drama, and she was known for her formidable stage and vocal acting, though some critics commented unfavorably on her occasional disruptions of the vocal line and extramusical effects to emphasize a dramatic point. Modestly, she declined offers of the heaviest Strauss and Wagner such as Isolde and Brünnhilde, declaring that Birgit Nilsson's renditions were the ideal. (Compare that to the feuding of many divas and divos!) Vocally, her middle was a weak point through the early years of her career, though it strengthened with time.

She studied at the Vienna Conservatory with Alfred Jerger and Rudolf Grossman, and made her opera debut at the Innsbruck opera in 1949 as Agathe in Weber's *Der Freischütz*. Her feminine and yet powerfully-voiced Sieglinde at her Bayreuth Festival debut in 1951 brought her to world attention. She made her Covent Garden debut during a Vienna State Opera tour as Danae in Strauss' *Der Liebe der Danae* in 1953. Her United States debut was in San Francisco in 1956 as Senta in Wagner's *The Flying Dutchman*. Her Met debut was in 1959, replacing Maria Callas as Verdi's Lady Macbeth, though she was scheduled to appear later that season as Verdi's Aida. Though she had to win over a hostile audience, she became a Met favorite and for the rest of her career, was a regular there as well as in Vienna. In 1981, she starred in Götz Friedrich's film of *Elektra*, conducted by Karl Bohm and co-starring with Astrid Varnay. In the mid-1980s she began to sing mezzo roles, marking her 30th anniversary U.S. debut by appearing as the Kostelnicka in Janáček's *Jenufa* at San Francisco, and added such roles as Clytemnestra and Herodias to her repertoire. She retired as a singer in 1996 and became president of the Vienna Festival. *—Ann Feeney*

Recommended:

- ○ **Verdi: Otello** / Serafin (cond.), Vickers, Rysanek, Gobbi, Carlin, Rome Opera House Orch. / 1998 / RCA 63180
- ○ **Leonie Rysanek** / Rysanek, etc. / 2000 / Gala 100542
- ○ **Strauss: Salome** / Bohm (cond.), Rysanek, Equiluz, Kmentt, Zednik, Vienna State Opera / 1999 / RCA 69430
- ○ **Verdi: Macbeth** / Leinsdorf (cond.), Warren, Bergonzi, Rysanek, Marsh, Metropolitan Opera Orch. / 1959 / RCA 4516

Frederic Rzewski

b. Apr. 13, 1938, Westfield, MA

Composer: Keyboard

Frederic Rzewski is among the major figures of the American musical avant-garde to emerge in the 1960s, and he has been highly influential as a composer and performer. He was born in Westfield, Massachusetts, earned his B.A. in music at Harvard, and later received an M.F.A. from Princeton, where he had the privilege of studying with Roger Sessions and Milton Babbit. A Fulbright scholarship allowed him to travel to Florence in 1960 to study for a year with Luigi Dallapiccola. Since then, except for a five-year period in the 1970s, he has mainly lived in Europe. He first came to public attention as a performer of new piano music, having participated in the premieres of such monumental works as Stockhausen's *Klavierstück X* (1962). In 1966, he founded, with Alvin Curran and Richard Teitelbaum, the famous ensemble Musica Electronica Viva (MEV). MEV combined free improvisation with written music and electronics. These experimentations directly led to the creation of Rzewski's first important compositions, pieces such as *Les moutons de Panurge*, a so-called "process piece," which also combines elements of spontaneous improvisation with notated material and instructions. Rzewski's improv-classical hybrids are some of the most successful of the kind ever produced thanks to the fervent energy at the core of his music. During the 1970s, his music continued to develop along these lines, but as his socialist proclivities began to direct his artistic course, he developed new structures for instrumental music that used text elements and musical style as structuring features. *Attica*, which includes the recitation of a prison letter, and *The People United Will Never Be Defeated*, a virtuosic set of piano variations, are his most well-known works of the period. In 1977, he was made professor of composition at the Royal Conservatory of Liège, Belgium, and has continued to teach there since. During the 1980s, Rzewski produced a number of surprising twelve tone compositions that (happily) provided fresh ideas of what could be done with serial systems. The 1990s saw him revisiting, via scored music, some highly spontaneous approaches to composition that recall his inspired experiments of the late 1960s. Rzewski's music is among that which defines postwar American new music. He has consistently given the exuberant boyish pleasures of a composer like Copland within the rigorously experimental framework of a composer like Cage. Often unapologetically tonal and fun, Rzewski's music cuts right through the frequent churlishness of avant-garde music. *—Donato Mancini*

Overview of Works

Neither of the categories of "modern" nor "postmodern" seem to apply to the works of Frederic Rzewski with any consistency (his teachers, after all, included such varied musical voices as Walter Piston, Milton Babbitt, and Elliott Carter), and many of his pieces combine an ambitious penchant for the experimental with a keen sense of methodical development and structural rigor. He is at once a formalist and a revolutionary, and his works often embody bold ideas specifically about music, and more broadly, his strong socialist leanings.

A handful of important works for the electro-acoustic music ensemble Musica Elettronica Viva (which he co-founded) appeared during the late 1960s and early 1970s, including *Coming Together* (1972) and *Attica* (1972). This decade also found Rzewski composing a number of vocal works on highly political texts or setting texts in a highly politicized fashion. In *Jefferson* (1970), for example, Rzewski assumes a subversive stance by setting the first two paragraphs of the "Declaration of Independence," rendering the words in evenly paced, straightforward melodies that expand and contract according to a strict additive/subtractive procedure; the text unfolds above a minimalist ostinato in the piano that gradually multiplies into a dense, polyrhythmic web. Other works in this vein include *God to a Hungry Child*, with words from Langston Hughes, and *No Progress Without Struggle*, on a text by Frederick Douglass (both from 1974). Rzewski's ideological attitudes emerge in his instrumental works as well, such as the large-scale piano piece *The People United Will Never Be Defeated* (1975). This work demonstrates one of Rzewski's favored formal schemes: a theme and extended variations, a technique that prominently figures in such important later works as *Antigone-Legend* (1982), a substantial work for voice and piano on a text by Brecht. The formal regularity of the theme and variations structure is central to many of Rzewski's works, which often combine odd instrumental combinations and/or highly intertextual collage techniques with highly formalistic organizational and compositional methods.

A number of pieces utilize specialized 12-tone methods, including *Antigone-Legend* and the semi-theatrical chamber work *The Persians* (1985). Perhaps more striking, however, is his development in the mid-1980s of a system of formalized time blocks. *Spots*, a chamber work from 1986, comprises 13 one-minute pieces for any instrumentation, played in any order. The piano sonata from 1991 includes a dizzying hodgepodge of allusions, from a Bach invention, to the fifteenth century tune *L'homme armé*, to John Lennon's "Give Peace a Chance"; these are partitioned into set numbers of periods, the periods in each of the work's three movements having the exact same duration. Rzewski has also sought ways to expand the sonic palette of instrumental music: *De profundis* from 1991 calls on the solo pianist to speak and breathe loudly, while *Lost Melody* from 1989 combines the sound of a Klezmer band with steel drums. His most ambitious works include *The Road* (1998), a work for solo piano lasting nearly five hours, and *The Triumph of Death* (1997), an oratorio for voices and string quartet. *—Jeremy Grimshaw*

Recommended:

- ○ **Rzewski Plays Rzewski: Piano Works** / Rzewski / 2002 / Nonesuch 79623
- ○ **Rzewski: Jefferson; Antigone Legend** / Plantamura, Rzewski / 1987 / CRI 747
- ○ **Rzewski: Which Side Are You On?** / Moore / 2003 / Cantaloupe 21014

KEYBOARD

The People United Will Never Be Defeated (El pueblo unido jamás será vencido), 36 Variations on a Chilean Song, for piano (1975)

Few composers have integrated their political views with their compositional practice in as thorough a manner as Frederic Rzewski. In fact, much of his mature oeuvre is devoted to the idea of unifying political and musical language. Nowhere is this impulse more poignantly articulated than his hour-long set of piano variations from 1975, *The People United Will Never Be Defeated.*

The theme of the work is drawn from the popular Chilean revolutionary song "El Pueblo Unido Jamás Será Vencido," which was composed by Sergio Ortega and performed by the group Quilapayun just months before the 1973 coup led by Pinochet. Rzewski works out the song's textual message within the compositional structure of the piece, executing the musical metaphor with incredible rigor. The theme is subjected to 36 variations, which proceed in six sets of six; each set follows a similar structure of "stages," which the composer enumerates as "simple events," "rhythms," "melodies," "counterpoints," and "harmonies." The last variation of each set serves to combine elements from the previous five stages. The sets themselves are connected in the same way across a different axis: the first set is generally the simplest, the third the most lyrical, the fifth the most homophonic, even though within each of these sets the six stages apply on the level of the individual variations. The sixth set of variations, then, represents a busy intersection of structural trajectories, as each of its variations sums up the previous five variations at that position within each set—so, for example, the first variation in the sixth set combines elements from the first variations in all the previous sets, the third variation recalls all the other third variations, and so on. The final variation, then—the sixth of the sixth set—takes on exponential duties, as its recollections of the previous five variations, themselves recollective in nature, make up an elaborate reflection on the entire monumental work. At two points the piece is structurally disrupted but semantically enhanced as Rzewski weaves in quotations from two other tunes, the Italian revolutionary song "Bandiera Rosa" and Hanns Eisler's "Solidaritätslied." Despite its episodic and variational nature, the piece as a whole thus assumes a trajectory toward greater musical and semantic integration and unity, the wide diversity of sonorities and styles compositionally combining in a manner exactly analogous to the unity espoused Ortega's revolutionary song. *—Jeremy Grimshaw*

Recommended:

○ **Rzewski: The People United will Never be Defeated!** / Hamelin / 1999 / Hyperion 67077

S

Kaija Saariaho

b. Oct. 14, 1952, Helsinki, finland

Composer

Kaija Saariaho is not only among the most important Finnish composers of her time, but must be ranked as one of the leading composers of the late twentieth and early twenty first centuries. Born Kaija Anneli Laakkonen, she began studying visual arts at the University of Art and Design (then known as the University of Industrial Art). She married Markku Veikko Ilmari Saariaho in 1972, but the marriage was short lived, ending the following year. The composer, however, retained her married name.

In 1976, she began composition studies at the Sibelius Academy with Paavo Heininen. She obtained a degree in composition from the academy in 1980, but continued studies there for another year. Afterward, she enrolled at the Musikhochschule in Freiburg, Germany, to study with British composer Brian Ferneyhough and Germany's Klaus Huber. She was awarded a diploma there in 1983. By this time, Saariaho was already turning out some of her earliest works. The most noted efforts from this period include *Verblendungen for Orchestra and Tape* (1982–84) and the minimalist piece *Vers le blanc* (1982). This latter piece was composed with the use of a computer and software developed at the Paris-based IRCAM (L'Institut de Recherche et Coordination), where she had begun extensive studies in 1982 in computer techniques as they relate to musical composition. Saariaho had permanently relocated to Paris that same year. In 1984, she married Jean-Baptiste Barrière, also a composer, and their marriage produced two children, Alexandre (born 1989) and Aliisa (born 1995). In the mid-1980s, Saariaho's works began garnering much attention and she received many prestigious awards, such as the Kranichsteiner Prize in 1986, the Prix Italia in 1988, and the following year the Ars Electronica for her works *Stilleben* (1987–88) and *Io* (1986–87). She also attracted several impressive commissions, including one from the Lincoln Center, which resulted in the chamber work *Nymphéa* (1987), which was premiered by the Kronos Quartet. By the early 1990s, her music was beginning to appear with greater frequency on the concert stage and with some regularity on record labels. Saariaho had become one of the few composers to write in a modern, though not particularly dissonant, style who has achieved a good measure of popularity. Further commissions came to her, including an important one from the Finnish National Ballet, for which she produced *The Earth* (1991). Many of her compositions have been written specifically for major artists or groups, as with the violin work she produced for Gidon Kremer, entitled *Graal Théâtre* (1994), and the song cycle *Château de l'âme* (1996) for Dawn Upshaw. A 1993 trip to Japan led to a commission from Kunitachi College for which Saariaho composed a work for percussion and electronics, *Six Japanese Gardens* (1993–95). The composer spent a year at the Sibelius Academy teaching composition (1997–98), at a time when her stature could rival that of almost any other composer of the day. This preeminence is evidenced by the numerous major performances of her compositions, such as the 1999 Kurt Masur-led New York Philharmonic premiere of her choral work *Oltra mar*, and the Salzburg Festival premiere of her first *opera*, *L'amour de loin*, in August 2000, which featured Upshaw and conductor Kent Nagano. Saariaho also continues to collect prizes, including the German Kaske Prize and the Swedish Rolf Schock Prize, both in 2001. Many of her works have been made available on a variety of labels, including DG, BIS, Finlandia, and Ondine. *—Robert Cummings*

Overview of Works

When Kaija Saariaho's music first gained attention, she was composing in a style that mixed post-Webern serialist methods with electronics and computer processing. Eventually, she moved toward a more conventional manner of expression, scoring works for traditional ensembles like symphony orchestras while focusing less on electronics and more on melody. Saariaho even publicly criticized serial-related techniques for their strictures, particularly with regard to prohibiting use of tonal harmonies and melodies. While Saariaho's style is much more approachable from 1990 onward, it still contains discordant features and quite often conveys a static sense.

Among her first compositions to gain recognition were *Verblendungen* (1982–84), a work scored for small orchestra and tape, and *Vers le blanc*, a somewhat minimalist composition whose three-part harmony constantly evolves while the music itself remains largely static. Much of her work during these early years featured sonorities that slowly change, often almost imperceptibly. The first composition in which she employed computer processing was *Lichtbogen* (1985–86) for chamber ensemble and electronics. She had much success here and in the electronics realm in general. She received Ars Electronica awards in 1989 for her works *Stilleben* (1987–88) and *Io* (1986–87), which both divulged expansion of expressive means, but still exhibited no discernible rhythmic features. Saariaho broke with a tradition of her own when she turned out her first compositions for large orchestra in 1990, *Du cristal* and *A la fumée*, premiered separately in 1990 and 1991, respectively, despite the fact that she paired them to form a two-part work. While certain electronic processing is used in *A la fumée*, Saariaho continued to move closer to a more conservative idiom, which is most evident in her 1994 violin concerto *Graal Théâtre* specifically written for Gidon Kremer. Here she focused more on melody than in most previous compositions. Saariaho's vocal works from the 1990s also divulged a growing lyrical tendency, especially in *Château de l'âme* (1996), for soprano, chorus, and orchestra, commissioned by the Salzburg Festival. It was written for Dawn Upshaw, who recorded it for Sony Classical (2001), coupled with the Kremer performance of *Graal Théâtre*. But the composer did not abandon electronics in her music, as demonstrated by *Lohn*, her composition for soprano and electronics, also from 1996. Compositions from the late 1990s by Saariaho continued to divulge a more conventional manner of expression and included two of her most important efforts to date: the choral work *Oltra Mar*, premiered on November 11, 1999, by Kurt Masur and the New York Philharmonic Orchestra, and her first opera, *L'amour de loin*, first performed at the Salzburg Festival on August 15, 2000, in a performance led by Kent Nagano featuring soprano Dawn Upshaw. The opera is in six acts and is drawn from Amin Maalouf's *Le vida breve* (Love from afar), a tragic love story about a twelfth century troubadour. A flute concerto, *Aile du songe* was premiered in fall 2001 by flutist Camilla Hoitenga. *—Robert Cummings*

Recommended:

- ○ **Saariaho: Château de l'âme; Graal Théâtre; Amers** / Salonen (cond.), Upshaw, Kremer, Karttunen, BBC SO, Finnish Radio SO, Avanti CO / 2001 / Sony 60817
- ○ **Saariaho: From the Grammar of Dreams** / Lintu (cond.), Salomaa, Korhonen, Laivuori, Bister, Juutilainen, Komsi, Rantanen, Avanti! / Ondine 958
- ○ **Portrait of Kaija Saariaho** / Salonen (cond.), Almila (cond.), Hoitenga, Teikari, Finnish Radio SO / 1985 / Bis 307
- ○ **Saariaho: Graal théâtre: Solar; Lichtbogen** / Lintu (cond.), Storgaards, Liimatainen, Siirala, Avanti! / Ondine 997
- ○ **Saariaho: New Gates** / Wood (cond.), King, Wells, Champ d'Action / 2000 / Mode 91
- ○ **Saariaho: Private Gardens** / Upshaw, Karttunen, Hoitenga, Jodelet / Ondine 906
- ○ **Saariaho: Du Cristal; A la Fumée; Nymphea** / Salonen (cond.), Alanko, Karttunen, Los Angeles PO, Kronos Quartet / Ondine 804

Saint Paul Chamber Orchestra

f. 1959, St. Paul, MN

Ensemble

The Saint Paul Chamber Orchestra is the only full-time professional chamber orchestra in the United States and the country's most recorded such ensemble. It is located in St. Paul, Minnesota. Although Minneapolis had a long-established orchestra, the Minneapolis Symphony (now the Minnesota Orchestra), its "Twin City," Saint Paul, felt the need for an orchestral organization of its own. The Saint Paul Chamber Orchestra was founded in 1959. Its first concert, on November 18, 1959, was given by its music director, Leonard Sipe.

From the beginning the SPCO stated as it mission to play the classical and contemporary literature "that is not ordinarily played by large symphonies." Over the years, the orchestra has increased its season from four concerts to 150 in a 38-week season. It has won eight ASCAP awards for service in performing new works. It won the Grammy award in 1980 for its recording of the complete score of Aaron Copland's chamber ballet *Appalachian Spring*.

The SPCO's major conductors have been Dennis Russell Davies (1972–80), Pinchas Zukerman (1980–87), and Hugh Wolff (1992–2000). Under the diverse approaches of these three conductors the orchestra has consistently improved in quality and international acclaim. In 1980 Minnesota Public Radio launched its innovative radio series "St. Paul Sunday Morning," in which host Bill McLaughlin conducts informal conversations with musicians and the orchestra plays. The orchestra also broadcasts its concerts on a network of 100 radio stations, making it the most widely broadcast classical orchestra in the United States.

In 1987 the orchestra instituted an innovative program, appointing a three-member artistic commission (initially comprising Wolff, fellow-conductor Christopher Hogwood and composer John Adams) to advise it on repertory through 1992. In 1990 John Harbison replaced Adams as the composer on the commission.

In addition to Andreas Delfs, appointed in 2001 as music director, the conducting staff comprises principal guest conductor Christopher Hogwood, creative chair conductor Bobby McFerrin, and baroque series director Nicholas McGegan. Aaron Jay Kernis is the composer-in-residence. *—Joseph Stevenson*

Recommended:

- ○ **American Landscapes** / Wolff (cond.), Isbin, St. Paul CO / 2002 / Angel 67672B
- ○ **Barber & Meyer: Violin Concertos** / Hahn, Wolff (cond.), St. Paul CO / 2000 / Sony 89029
- ○ **Paper Music** / McFerrin (cond. & voice), Howard, James, St. Paul CO / 1995 / Sony 64600
- ○ **De Falla, Milhaud, Walton, Martin: Ballets** / Wolff (cond.), Larmore, St. Paul CO / 1994 / Teldec 90852

Saint Pierre de Solesmes Abbey Monks' Choir

f. 1833, Sarthe, France

Ensemble

The Saint Pierre de Solesmes Abbey Monks' Choir is one of the world's most renowned ensembles specializing in Gregorian chant, winning honors and recognition for its performances and its groundbreaking recordings. Ironically, the Benedictine monks' musical reputation comes as a by-product of their chosen form of prayer: Gregorian chant sung seven times each day. The Abbey of Saint Pierre de Solesmes was founded in 1833 by Dom Prosper Gueranger in Sarthe, France. A former priest, Gueranger's newer calling seemed to attract him to neglected structures worthy of salvage and restoration, for in addition to raising the Abbey on the ruins of an abandoned priory, he made it his life's work to revive the use of Gregorian chant in his monastery and also the editorial validity of Gregorian chant. This meant retrieving the scattered, disorganized remnants of that religious music legacy from across Europe and from centuries of neglect. Among the first of those now called early music researchers, Gueranger and his fellow monks drew together the various editions—which often had been handed down in corrupted form—into a coherent, scholarly, sound body of music. Their efforts formed the basis for the revival of the use of Gregorian chant in France during the late nineteenth century and resulted in the publication of chant books for use by the Congregation at Solesmes during the 1880s. Their efforts also resulted in the preservation of manuscripts and music that would otherwise have been lost to the ravages of two world wars in the twentieth century. In 1930, the British-based record label His Master's Voice (later part of EMI) recorded a large body of the monks' repertory, including *Ad te Domine* and *Alleluia Justus germinabit*, under the direction of Dom Joseph Gajard. The Monks' Choir next recorded a major body of work in 1958, again under Gajard's direction, including the *Feast of the Immaculate Conception* and *Good Friday Afternoon Services*, for Decca/London Records. During the 1960s, they made further recordings, but it was for their 1976 *Gregorian Chant* LP, recorded under the direction of Dom Jean Claire, that the group received a Grammy Award nomination. The Saint Pierre de Solesmes Abbey Monks' Choir remains a highly respected and widely recognized performing ensemble, with an international following among devotees of Gregorian chant and religious music in general, just as the Abbey occupies a unique place in religious music scholarship and study. *—Bruce Eder*

Recommended:

- ○ **The Complete 1930 French HMV Recordings** / Gajard, St. Pierre de Solesmes Abbe / Pearl 9152
- ○ **Gregorian Chant** / Gajard, St. Pierre de Solesmes Abbe / Gold Sound 757

Camille Saint-Saëns

b. Oct. 9, 1835, Paris, France, **d.** Dec. 16, 1921, Algiers, Algeria

Composer: Concerto, Symphonic, Orchestral, Opera, Chamber Music, Keyboard

Camille Saint-Saëns was something of an anomaly among French composers of the nineteenth century in that he wrote in virtually all genres, including opera, symphonies, concertos, songs, sacred and secular choral music, solo piano, and chamber music. He was generally not a pioneer, though he did help to revive some earlier and largely forgotten dance forms, like the bourée and gavotte. He was a conservative who wrote many popular scores scattered throughout the various genres: the *Piano Concerto No. 2*, *Symphony No. 3 ("Organ")*, the symphonic poem *Danse macabre*, the opera *Samson et Dalila*, and probably his most widely performed work, *The Carnival of The Animals*. While he remained a composer closely tied to tradition and traditional forms in his later years, he did develop a more arid style, less colorful and, in the end, less appealing. He was also a poet and playwright of some distinction.

Saint-Saëns was born in Paris on October 9, 1835. He was one of the most precocious musicians ever, beginning piano lessons with his aunt at two-and-a-half and composing his first work at three. At age seven he studied composition with Pierre Maleden. When he was ten, he gave a concert that included Beethoven's *Third Piano Concerto*, Mozart's *B flat Concerto*, K. 460, along with works by Bach, Handel, and Hummel. In his academic studies, he displayed the same genius, learning languages and advanced mathematics with ease and celerity. He would also develop keen, lifelong interests in geology and astronomy.

In 1848, he entered the Paris Conservatory and studied organ and composition, the latter with Halévy. By his early twenties, following the composition of two symphonies, he had won the admiration and support of Berlioz, Liszt, Gounod, Rossini, and other notable figures. From 1853 to 1876, he held church organist posts; he also taught at the École Niedermeyer (1861–65). He composed much throughout his early years, turning out the 1853 *Symphony in F ("Urbs Roma")*, a *Mass* (1855) and several concertos, including the popular second, for piano (1868).

In 1875, Saint-Saëns married the 19-year-old Marie Truffot, bringing on perhaps the saddest chapter in his life. The union produced two children who died within six weeks of each other, one from a four-story fall. The marriage ended in 1881. Oddly, this dark period in his life produced some of his most popular works, including *Danse macabre* (1875) and *Samson et Dalila* (1878). After the tragic events of his marriage, Saint-Saëns developed a fondness for Fauré and his family, acting as a second father to Fauré's children.

But he also remained very close to his mother, who had opposed his marriage. When she died in 1888, the composer fell into a deep depression, even contemplating suicide for a time. He did much travel in the years that followed and developed an interest in Algeria and Egypt, which eventually inspired him to write *Africa* (1891) and his *Piano Concerto No. 5, the "Egyptian"*. He also turned out works unrelated to exotic places, such as his popular and most enduring serious composition, the *Symphony No. 3*.

Curiously, after 1890, Saint-Saëns' music was regarded with some condescension in his homeland, while in England and the United States he was hailed as France's greatest living composer well into the twentieth century. Saint-Saëns experienced an especially triumphant concert tour when he visited the U.S. in 1915. In the last two decades of his life, he remained attached to his dogs and was largely a loner. He died in Algeria on December 16, 1921. *—Robert Cummings*

CONCERTO

Africa, fantaisie for piano & orchestra in G minor, Op. 89 (1891)

Among the many destinations of Saint-Saëns' travels, North Africa was clearly the composer's favorite. In 1890 Saint-Saëns traveled to Ceylon, then to Alexandria and Cairo. While in Egypt, he composed *Africa*, a fantasy for piano and orchestra based on genuine North African sources. Saint-Saëns collected much of the region's indigenous music, often transcribing themes on the spot. In this manner he absorbed both the materials and techniques of North African music, which he eventually employed in dozens of his own works.

Africa opens with a free, improvisatory passage based on music Saint-Saëns heard in the Algerian village of Beskra; other themes are drawn from various songs and dances of Egypt and Algeria. The piece is sectional, moving from rhapsodic slow passages to a fast 6/8 dance. The Arabic origin of most of the melodies is generally evidenced by the use of unusual, "exotic" scales; melodic augmented seconds emerge from the texture as a particularly pungent reminder of the work's African influence. Interestingly, Saint-Saëns makes only sparing use of the few extra percussion instruments he calls for. *Africa* is further notable as one of the very first concerted works to be recorded with its composer in the role of soloist; a 1904 recording, with Saint-Saëns at the piano, still survives. *—Joseph Stevenson*

Recommended:

- ○ **Saint-Saëns: Urbs Roma; Symphony 2; Africa** / Kantorow (cond.),Tapiola Sinfonietta / 1996 / Bis 790

Cello Concerto No. 1 in A minor, Op. 33 (1872)

The first performance of the *Cello Concerto* was given on January 19, 1873, at the Paris Conservatoire, then a bastion of conservatism that usually programmed only works by old or dead masters. The Conservatoire's acceptance of the concerto gives an idea of the esteem in which Saint-Saëns was held at the time.

Formally, the *Cello Concerto in A minor* is an extension of the technique Saint-Saëns used for the much earlier *Violin Concerto in A major* of 1859. There are no pauses between the three sections of the *Cello Concerto*, although these are clearly delineated and have different tempo markings. Some analysts have described the work as a single, sonata-form movement with a free recapitulation, while others have suggested the work is a three-movement structure with shared material between the first and last movements. What is most important is the element of contrast as a driving force in the piece, which was composed not long after Saint-Saëns conducted performances of Liszt's symphonic poems. Saint-Saëns now began composing such works himself, such as the *Danse macabre* of 1874. Much of the bombast found in Liszt's tone poems, however, is absent from those by Saint-Saëns, but the idea of thematic transformation is an important element.

Marked Allegro non troppo, the first movement begins with an aggressive melody built of triplets from the solo cello. The lyrical, meditative theme for the cello that follows is accompanied by the triplet figure in the orchestra. A new, Animato passage with double stops for the cello leads to an even faster tempo with yet another theme, this appearing in the orchestra and on F major. Just when it seems like this will be the new key, the opening triplet idea sounds again in the cello, but on D major, and development of the first and second themes ensues.

After a rest just long enough for the cellist to take a breath, the second section, Allegretto con moto, begins with the orchestra. This segment is a delicate minuet with a narrow-range and stately melody. When the cello enters, it first sounds alone before the orchestra begins the minuet again beneath the cello's countermelody. After the cello takes up the minuet tune, there is a cadenza for the soloist, which leads to fragments of the minuet theme in different harmonies, finally settling on B flat as the Allegro tempo returns.

The triplet theme from the first movement, now in the orchestra, opens the finale. Saint-Saëns varies this material to return to the tonic before a new idea, Un peu moins vite, sounds in the solo cello. Given forward impetus through syncopation, the rhythm is Sarabande-like until the cello takes off with a flurry of 16th notes that pushes the harmony away from A minor. Contrast is a salient feature of the rest of the piece, which behaves somewhat like a rondo. The opening triplet theme and the third theme of the first movement introduce the coda, which contains new material and closes the piece in A major. *—John Palmer*

Recommended:

○ **Dvořák & Saint-Saëns: Cello Concertos** / Giulini (cond.), Rostropovich, London PO / 2001 / Angel 67594

○ **Pierre Fornier, Violoncello** / Martinon (cond.), Fournier, Lamoureux Concert Association Orch. / 1999 / DG 457761

Cello Concerto No. 2 in D minor, Op. 119 (1902)

It seems odd that Camille Saint-Saëns' first cello concerto has become so much more popular than his second when the two share an unusual amount even for concerti written by the same composer. Both were composed at around the same time as a separate cello sonata (Op. 123, in this case). Both recall their first movements later in the work, leading to a structure Francois-Rene Tranchfort described, in commenting on the first concerto, as "enhanced sonata form." Both contain movements (a minuet in the first, a scherzo-like section in the second) that imply symphonic dimensions. And, unsurprisingly for Saint-Saëns, both make strenuous demands on the cellist's virtuosity. A striding theme in polonaise rhythm opens the concerto, with just a brief orchestral introduction before the cello dashes off with the melodic responsibilities. A tender theme, introduced and supported by the winds, makes an appearance before a heroic theme begins in the major and moves to the minor and then seems to close off the exposition. It's more complicated than that, however, as Saint-Saëns soon moves into a lush Andante sostenuto, with the cello again introducing the main theme, although there is one lovely moment when it circles the orchestra's rendition of the theme with seductive ornaments. Eventually, the cello needs only the barest orchestral interpolations to help it virtuosically close the movement. The second movement begins with a fiendishly difficult scherzo based on a restless theme and full of double stops and coruscating runs that remind the listener that Saint-Saëns actually had to notate the cello part for this concerto on two staves. The cadenza raises the bar even higher, literally, ending in a stratospheric register for the cello before the music suddenly returns to the heroic mood and rhythm from the first movement; new material is used to end the work on a triumphant note. This last section can be interpreted as a gesture at a sonata-form recapitulation after a very long development, or simply as a cyclic ending to a work whose themes often recall each other. Either way, it makes for intriguing listening. *—Andrew Lindemann Malone*

Recommended:

○ **Steven Isserlis Plays Saint-Saëns** / Eschenbach (cond.), Isserlis, NDRSO / 2001 / RCA 63518

○ **Saint-Saëns: The 2 Cello Concertos** / Kantorow (cond.), Thedeen, Tapiola Sinfonietta / 1998 / Bis 956

Introduction and Rondo Capriccioso, for violin & orchestra in A minor, Op. 28 (1863)

The *Introduction and Rondo capriccioso*, Op. 28 (1863), is one of Saint-Saëns' few genuine showpieces. It was composed for his friend, the virtuoso violinist Pablo de Sarasate (1844–1908), for whom he had already written the *Violin Concerto in A major*, Op. 28 (1859), and for whom he would eventually create the *Violin Concerto in B minor*, Op. 61 (1880). Whereas the Op. 28 *Violin Concerto* was written when the violinist was only 15 years of age, the *Introduction and Rondo capriccioso* is deliberately challenging—a testimony to the mature master's technique. Sarasate's frequent programming of the work did a great deal for its popularity in the years after its publication (1870); its appeal was wide enough, in fact, that both George Bizet and Claude Debussy made arrangements of it—the former for violin and piano, and the latter for piano, four hands.

As one would expect from the title, the *Introduction and Rondo capriccioso* begins with a slow section, marked Andante malinconico and characterized by a plaintive falling leap and rising arpeggio. Becoming gradually more animated, the introduction culminates in a scintillating minicadenza that leads into the Rondo proper (Allegro ma non troppo). When the violin enters, it states a theme that has a Spanish flavor, stemming from syncopation and chromatic inflections. The melody spins out into wild arpeggios and gigantic leaps before the orchestra begins a bridge to the contrasting theme, marked con morbidezza. This lyric melody is especially entrancing because it is in 2/4 time, played simultaneously with the continuing 6/8 time of the orchestra. The Rondo theme returns quietly in the solo violin before an orchestral outburst that is a reprise of the earlier bridge passage. The oboe takes the final statement of the rondo theme, which becomes fragmented and developed until the beginning of the brilliant coda, which is mainly a showcase for Sarasate's technical ability. *—John Palmer*

Recommended:

○ **Poème** / Litton (cond.), Bell, Royal PO / 1991 / London 433519

Morceau de concert, for violin & orchestra in G major, Op. 62 (1880)

Saint-Saëns began this ten-minute piece shortly after completing his *Violin Concerto No. 3* (published as Op. 61, suggesting a close sequence). The composer's exact intentions for the *Morceau de concert* are hazy; the piece stands perfectly well on its own, but it may be the beginning of an unfinished fourth concerto. It carries no tempo markings, which was unusual for Saint-Saëns and a suggestion that he released the piece before he was really done with it. Its dimensions are certainly substantial enough for a concerto's opening movement and its generic title further sets it apart from the composer's other single-movement works for violin and orchestra. In his concertos, sonatas, and shorter works, Saint-Saëns never made things easy for the violin; typically, this piece requires a high degree of virtuosity. A dramatic, cadenza-like figure for the violin launches the movement and hints at a gypsy interest that Saint-Saëns neglects to pursue. Shortly, this becomes a figure from which the entire concert piece is derived: a menacing, jagged seven-note motif immediately followed by long, fast runs fluttering up and down the staff. The soloist and orchestra toy with this material at some length and then Saint-Saëns transforms it into a softer, playful gesture coupled with a more lyrical phrase; this occupies the central third of the movement and includes a confident, theatrical climax. Saint-Saëns then recapitulates these related themes, awards the soloist a full cadenza based on the motif in its original incarnation, and hastens to the end with a short, loud coda. *—James Reel*

Recommended:

○ **Rare French Works for Violin & Orchestra** / Fischer (cond.), Graffin, Ulster Orch. / 2002 / Hyperion 67294

Piano Concerto No. 1 in D major, Op. 17 (1858)

Among Saint-Saëns' pieces written after Viennese Classical-era models are his piano concertos, the first few of which are some of the earliest works in the genre composed in France. Although it was written in 1858, his *Piano Concerto No. 1 in D major*, Op. 17, was not published until 1875. Through the 1860s Saint-Saëns performed the *First Piano Concerto* on numerous occasions and later, in 1920, wrote that the piece was inspired by the forest of Fontainebleau. Ten years separate this first concerto from the second, which may explain the adolescent abandon with which Saint-Saëns approaches the concerto, prompting his virtuoso technique to take center stage. With an unusual lack of sensitivity, Saint-Saëns supporter Emile Baumann described the first concerto as "youthful hyperbole; runs, arpeggios of exuberant proportions, an ambitious sortie into grandiose prolixity." Unfortunately, this tells us nothing of the composer's attempt to modify the Classical form of the concerto.

The Introduction to the first movement begins with a hunting call for horn that is taken up and completed by the piano. (Some have likened this theme to that of the Allegro vivace theme of Chopin's *F minor Concerto*.) Shortly thereafter we hear an idea that becomes the "motto" in this cyclically conceived concerto. This motto also marks off the sections of the first movement, acting as transitional material in a manner that shows Saint-Saëns working symphonic thinking into the concerto format. At times, especially in the middle of the movement, the piano is subservient to orchestra, the overall argument becoming an egalitarian conversation that is hinted at in the introduction when the piano finishes the horn theme.

Antagonism is at the heart of the second movement, in which the first theme, a descending phrase in the orchestra, is broken off several times by chords in the piano. Eventually, the piano wins and moves to a flashy cadenza, unusual for a slow movement. Ornamental trills at the close of the second movement are much more than decorative and serve a harmonic function, a concept pursued by Ravel in his *Jeux d'eau* of 1901.

In the lighthearted, sonata-form finale the horn calls and the motto theme of the introduction returns in the final measures. The secondary theme of the finale is, at first, very lyrical, but is transformed by the end to create a loud, crashing close. The alternation of chords between the piano and orchestra is the full realization of the implied equality between the forces found in the first movement. This process is also clear in the various presentations of the second theme, which in the first instance is performed in the piano with brief interruptions from the orchestra, but in the recapitulation the roles are reversed, with the orchestra stating the theme against piano outbursts. *—John Palmer*

Recommended:

○ **Saint-Saëns: Piano Concertos 1–5** / Dutoit (cond.), Rogé, London PO / 1995 / London 4438652

○ **Saint-Saëns: 5 Piano Concertos** / Baudo (cond.), Ciccolini, Paris Orch. / 1987 / EMI 569258

Piano Concerto No. 2 in G minor, Op. 22 (1868)

Saint-Saëns composed and first played this work in 1868. It is scored for pairs of winds, horns and trumpets, plus timpani and strings. During his long and prodigiously creative life—first as a child prodigy, then as a "Futurist," then as a conservative, and finally as a vituperating fossil—Saint-Saëns composed five piano concertos between the ages of 20 and 61. The *Second* (and enduringly most popular) was created hurriedly in the spring of 1868 after the Russian pianist/composer/conductor Anton Rubinstein asked him to arrange a Paris concert. Because the *Salle Pleyel* was solidly booked and therefore not available for three more weeks, Saint-Saëns proposed that he himself write a new piece for the occasion. On May 6, with Rubinstein conducting, he introduced the *Second Concerto*, although not with much success. There had not been time to practice it sufficiently, and a portion of the audience was put off by the work's stylistic swings ("from Bach to Offenbach" was pianist Sigismond Stojowski's bon mot of the month).

Gabriel Fauré, a pupil of Saint-Saëns at the time, remembered years later that he had shown his teacher a *Tantum ergo* setting. Saint-Saëns glanced at it hurriedly, then said, "Give this to me. I can make something of it!" What emerged was the main theme of the first movement (Andante sostenuto) of the new *G minor Piano Concerto*, following a solo improvisation in the manner of Bach to get things started. A gentler subtheme (the composer's own) has a Chopinesque flavor, especially in its keyboard embroidery in thirds.

Like Saint-Saëns' opening movement and finale, an Allegro scherzando in between is written in sonata form. The spirit is nonetheless elfin, in the Mendelssohn manner—much as the Frenchman's long-finished but not-yet-published *Second Symphony* had been —although the second theme in the second movement of the concerto anticipates the *Carnival des animaux*, still two decades down the road.

The finale is a Presto tarantella in 2/2 time, whose G minor tonality reminds us that Mendelssohn ended his *"Italian" Symphony* 35 years earlier with a minor-key tarantella. If Saint-Saëns' premiere audience was not immediately cordial—Parisians had become as exasperatingly superficial as the Viennese—Franz Liszt praised the *Second Concerto* without stint, saying that it pleased him "singularly." Not for the first time, nor for the last, was his praise prescient. Later on, of course, Parisian audiences let everyone believe they'd loved it from the start. *—Roger Dettmer*

Recommended:

○ **Saint-Saëns: Piano Concertos 1–5** / Dutoit (cond.), Rogé, Royal PO / 1995 / London 4438652

○ **Rubinstein Collection Vol. 53** / Wallenstein (cond.), Rubinstein, Symphony of the Air / 1999 / RCA 63055

Piano Concerto No. 4 in C minor, Op. 44 (1875)

Saint-Saëns' *Fourth Piano Concerto* was first performed October 31, 1875, at the opening of Edouard Colonne's "Artistic Association," a series of concerts dedicated to the memory of Georges Bizet. After a concert performance of the concerto in Antwerp the piece was praised as a combination of "the force of Liszt and the suavity Chopin."

In it, Saint-Saëns is engaging in an experiment with the Classical-era forms. There is only one full stop in the piece, dividing it into two movements. Each of these, however, is clearly divided into two parts, with further subdivisions in the second of the two movements. Thus, its form resembles that of his *Third Symphony*. Saint-Saëns maintains the traditional contrast between keys and fast and slow sections, but the order of events is experimental.

As in the *First Piano Concerto* there is no orchestral introduction, only an opening phrase played pizzicato in the strings that begins with an upward leap of a tritone (C natural to F sharp). And as in the *Second* and *Third Piano Concertos* there is no solo introduction: the piece begins with the orchestra and soloist alternating statements of the first phrase at different pitch levels. Segments in which this theme is transformed—intervals widened, rhythms altered—rotate with nearly literal restatements of the theme as the piano part becomes increasingly flashy. A loud C major chord in the orchestra and a brief ritard introduce the key of A flat major and a new section, marked Andante. Rapid, quiet arpeggios and scales for the soloist dominate this part, in which the rising tritone again appears. The virtuosity and weight of the piano part, including massive broken chords, increases relentlessly to the end of the movement.

Saint-Saëns approved of playing the two movements without pause, and this is generally how the piece is performed. The atmosphere of the second movement stands in stark contrast to the introspective tone of the first. A transformation of the main theme of the first movement becomes a Scherzo-like idea in triple meter that bounces along with unbounded energy. The closing theme of the movement is chorale-like and gives way to a close of almost Lisztian bravura, in C major.

The pitch F sharp is of great importance in every part of the concerto, functioning as a push toward the dominant in the first part of the first movement and as part of a path toward A flat major in the second half. In the second movement Saint-Saëns uses it first as a chromatic inflection and later to emphasize the dominant.

Some critics have suggested the lack of developmental procedures in Saint-Saëns' *Fourth Concerto* is a shortcoming or even a failing. It is difficult, however, to justify superimposing a Beethovenian concept of development on a work that is not constructed along such lines. The juxtaposition of, and interrelationships between, succeeding sections is formal device at work in this piece. *—John Palmer*

Recommended:

○ **Saint-Saëns: Piano Concertos 1–5** / Dutoit (cond.), Rogé, London PO / 1995 / London 4438652

○ **Saint-Saëns: Piano Concertos 2 & 4** / Loughran (cond.), Biret, London PO / 1989 / Naxos 550334

Piano Concerto No. 5 in F major ("Egyptian"), Op. 103 (1896)

Saint-Saëns composed his *Fifth Piano Concerto* while in Egypt in the winter of 1895–96. It was published in 1896 with a dedication to pianist Louis Diémer (1843–1919), who played the piece on several occasions. It is one of the composer's "exotic" works, in which he uses the minor mode with raised sixth and seventh degrees (often called the "melodic" minor). This is the earliest concerto by a French composer to incorporate such "exoticisms," effects that had hitherto been reserved for shorter works and suites. Saint-Saëns' *Africa*, Op. 89 (1891), and *Suite algérienne*, Op. 60 (1880), also employ modal inflections to produce local color.

In this grandiose work, Saint-Saëns' references to his time in Egypt include the imitation of croaking of frogs he heard in the Nile, a "Nubian love song," and the turning of a ship's propellers in the Finale. The composer wrote that the second part of the concerto, "in effect, takes us on a journey to the East and even, in the F sharp passage, to the Far East." These effects, plus the place of the concerto's origin, prompted the nickname, "Egyptian," which was not given by the composer. It is the most blatantly pictorial of Saint-Saëns' concertos.

At the first performance of the *Fifth Concerto*, critics hailed it as "a work of fantasy ornamented and colored like one of the prettiest buildings of the Alhambra. . . ." Both the composition of the *Fifth Concerto* and its positive reception were rejuvenating experiences for the composer, who had by this time been in the public eye for 60 years. To the orchestration of the earlier *Fourth Concerto* Saint-Saëns adds two horns, piccolo, and a gong, which slips in surreptitiously as the piano plays a modal, "oriental" passage.

The first movement seems at first to be in sonata form, but eventually reveals itself to be a much freer structure. Most impressive are the broken chords at the beginning, which rhythmically disguise a chorale.

The lightness and transparency of the second movement are often said to reflect the composer's happiness at being in the East. Fantasy-like in organization, the music takes an unpredictable path through transparent orchestration.

Saint-Saëns noted that the Finale describes "the joy of a sea crossing," which accounts for the imitation of propellers at the end. The first theme is similar to ragtime piano music in its lively, dancing rhythms. The secondary theme at first continues this ebullience, but later moves to a more lyrical, contrasting idea. Saint-Saëns evokes the "exotic" through unusual orchestration, particularly in the combination of horns and piano, which represents water through harplike rippling figures. While the strings reiterate a C sharp, the piano plays rapid figures which Saint-Saëns once said represented croaking frogs, while tremolos in the strings at the end of the movement refer to a similar effect in Egyptian singing. The piano part of the finale is so formidable that it was later used as an examination piece at the Paris Conservatoire. *—John Palmer*

Recommended:

○ **Chopin: Piano Concerto 2; Saint-Saëns: Piano Concerto 5; Franck: Les Djinns** / Kondrashin (cond.), Richter / 1995 / Melodiya 29466

○ **Saint-Saëns: Piano Concertos 1–5** / Previn (cond.), Collard, Royal PO / 1999 / Angel 73356

Romance for flute or violin & orchestra in D flat major, Op. 37 (1871)

One can hardly imagine a less likely memento of the Franco-Prussian War and its grisly aftermath than the sweetly yearning *Romance for flute and piano in D flat*. Inevitably, Saint-Saëns composed other pieces specifically alluding to those events—a cantata, *Chants de guerre*, for instance, recomposed as the orchestral *Marche héroïque* (1871)—but it is the *Romance* that has proven evergreen. News of the French defeat at Sedan reached Paris on September 3, 1870. With his fellow composers Bizet, Duparc, d'Indy, Fauré, Widor—to name the most prominent—Saint-Saëns joined the National Guard (Fourth Seine Battalion) and served during the Siege of Paris, which ended with an armistice on January 28, 1871, and the Germans' triumphal parade down the Champs Elysées on March 1. Toward the end of that bleak January, Saint-Saëns' close friend, the talented painter Henri Regnault, was killed by a stray German bullet. Redressing French humiliation—culturally, at least—Saint-Saëns and Conservatoire professor Romain Bussine met with Duparc at the latter's apartment February 25 to establish the Société Nationale de Musique, under the rubric "Ars Gallica," for the performance and promotion of French music. With the German withdrawal, a new revolutionary contingent within the French populace defied the Republican government and established the Paris Commune on March 18. Knowing that the antibourgeois Commune did not speak for him, Saint-Saëns decamped on the last train to leave Paris for the Channel. On a visit to London in 1880 he was to play before Queen Victoria, but in 1871 he arrived a penniless émigré. Meanwhile, before or during his flight he completed the *Romance in D flat*—the manuscript is dated March 25, 1871—lending a new facet to anecdotes of his famed facility. In May, as the Republic moved to crush the Commune, the Communards arrested and shot the Archbishop of Paris with Abbé Duguerry of the Madeleine, where Saint-Saëns was organist. By May 28 the Commune was over and Saint-Saëns returned to Paris in time for Duguerry's funeral. The Société Nationale gave its first concert in November, and the *Romance* received its première at an SNM concert in the Salle Pleyel with renowned flutist Paul Taffanel accompanied by Saint-Saëns on April 6, 1872. By 1878 the composer had scored the work for orchestra. In either version, the *Romance* has remained a repertoire staple, affording a winning epitome of Saint-Saëns' characteristic mixture of elegant melancholy with brilliance in easily graspable lied form, the caressing first and final strains enclosing a more animated elegy. *—Adrian Corleonis*

Recommended:

○ **Apéritif: A French Collection** / Kantorow (cond.), Bezaly, Tapiola Sinfonietta / 2002 / Bis 1359

Romance for horn or cello & orchestra in F major, Op. 36 (1874)

One finds in Saint-Saëns' *Romance* (1874) for horn and orchestra characteristics that have come to be considered typically French: elegant line and proportions scored with the utmost clarity. It is a highly compact example of Saint-Saëns' approach to composition.

Saint-Saëns composed the Romance in response to the need for original concert works for various neglected solo instruments, whose repertoires were then largely dependent on transcriptions. (He later wrote similar works for harp and flute.) The work is dedicated to the famous hornist Henri Garigue.

The *Romance's* moderato tempo and triple meter give it a waltz-like feel. The work's ternary form resembles a da capo aria, in that the final section is a near-literal return to the first. Considering the brevity of the piece, the main theme is rather long. It falls into two sections, both of which share the opening arching eighth note figure and a dotted idea, and, indeed, the entire rhythmic pattern. The more animated central section, marked by a wide dynamic range, develops fragments of the main theme, most notably the opening eighth note figure. Throughout the *Romance*, the orchestra is clearly subordinate to the horn, providing support for the melody. *—John Palmer*

Recommended:

○ **Treasures for Horn & Trumpet** / Neal (cond.), Hustis, Dallas CO / Crystal 512

Tarantella, for flute, clarinet & orchestra in A minor, Op. 6 (1857)

This is a relatively early work in Saint-Saëns' output, but it already shows the considerable skills of its creator. As many classical music enthusiasts know, the composer was a child prodigy and thus evolved his mature style rather quickly. This piece has all the sophistication of the work of a seasoned master, at least in its instrumental writing. Its music may not divulge the originality or thematic distinctiveness of many of Saint-Saëns' later works, but it has charm and a deft sense of humor. This *Tarantella* is catchy from its opening notes: zesty rhythms and menacing dance music combine to create an amusingly creepy atmosphere that augurs the mood and writing in such works as Dukas' *The Sorcerer's Apprentice*. The music is lively, not as fast, however, as that usually associated with tarantellas, which often have a frenzied character. Here, Saint-Saëns seems to want to underscore the myth about the origins of this Italian dance, which was thought to result from the bite of a tarantula spider or to serve as its cure. He makes the flute and clarinet slither and swirl and dance so menacingly, often in unison, and partners them with discreet and subtle orchestral writing. This is a fine piece now sometimes heard in an arrangement for flute, clarinet, and piano. *—Robert Cummings*

Recommended:

○ **Romantic Flute Concertos** / Vandernoot (cond.), Grauwels, Vanderborght, Belgian Radio & Television orch. / 2002 / Naxos 8555977

Violin Concerto No. 1 in A minor, Op. 20 (1859)

Camille Saint-Saëns' *Violin Concerto No. 1 in A major*, Op. 20, was often referred to by his contemporaries as a Konzertstück, the then-current term for a one-movement concerto, even though the composer wrote it as three distinct movements. It's easy to understand the confusion, though; the concerto is actually written in large-scale ternary form, with an Andante espressivo middle movement enclosed by an opening Allegro and what is called its reprise. However, that schematic layout doesn't quite capture Saint-Saëns' invention, which continually reuses, reorganizes, and recasts material over the concerto's quarter-hour span to create a dense, lively texture of ideas. Op. 20 must have proved a splendid concertante vehicle for Pablo de Sarasate, its dedicatee, who was only 15 at the time. The violin introduces the idea that will dominate the discourse; a few bold, choppy chords followed by a precipitous rise and descent. After the orchestra takes up the idea, the violins re-enters with a sinuous, suave derivative of the opening that it develops over shifting orchestral textures, before introducing another subject, in the minor mode. This subject, songful and hushed, contains a descent and rise which register as an opposition to the opposite movement in the opening subject. That opening subject returns to dominate the rest of the movement, which ends on more suave violin soloing that trills directly into the Andante. This Andante uses a reticent woodwind figure, derived from the opening subject's chords, to frame a leisurely violin melody that references both the opening subject and the minor subject of the previous movement. The third movement's title of "reprise" must be one of the bigger understatements in nineteenth century music; while the same material is developed, the development takes radically different turns, including a surprisingly peaceful moment in which the opening subject's chords, quiet and unadorned, move from section to section of the orchestra, pushed by sweet sustained notes on the violin. The interplay of subjects and derivatives thereof pushes the music onward with both wit and vigor throughout. *—Andrew Lindemann Malone*

Recommended:

○ **Saint-Saëns: Music for violin & orchestra** / Kantorow (cond. & violin), Tapiola Sinfonietta / 1987 / Bis 860

Violin Concerto No. 2 in C minor, Op. 58 (1858)

Nothing in Camille Saint-Saëns' correspondence or notes indicated why he composed his first violin concerto in 1858. The composer thought little enough of it to let it languish unpublished until 1879, although it was well received when Pierre Marsick took the solo role at its 1880 premiere. By this time Saint-Saëns' second violin concerto had been published, as No. 1, Op. 20, so this one became No. 2, Op. 58. Saint-Saëns may have regarded this concerto as an immature work, and it does hew closely to the style of Henri Vieuxtemps' *École liègoise*, especially when compared with the formal advances Saint-Saëns made just a year later in his second concerto. Nevertheless, Op. 58 is a witty, playful, and highly polished work. The solo violin, entering over a minimally intrusive accompaniment figure, introduces the first theme with spirited embellishment, establishing itself as a true virtuoso soloist before the orchestra is even allowed to play an unadorned version of the theme. A passing phrase in the violin's transition material from the first theme eventually provides the basis for the second theme; Saint-Saëns continues reusing and tweaking material throughout the fluent, if not especially adventuresome, development. An extensive cadenza ends dramatically as the orchestra re-enters gradually, beginning with the timpani, as the violin's music settles down. Three trombones, added for the A minor Andante, make the bare six-note motif that opens the movement sound even more bare, and the harp that accompanies the violin melody based on that motif contributes to a somewhat medieval atmosphere. A tempestuous middle section in the major yields to a free repeat of the first section in which the winds assume more prominence, both in solos and accompaniment, as the violin slithers in and out of the orchestra's chords. Saint-Saëns then takes a page from the man he thought was the true master of the concerto, Beethoven, with an extended, adventurous coda featuring a surprising modulation to A major. The rondo finale, following attacca, is based on what is admittedly a rather stale theme, but Saint-Saëns enlivens it with witty, detailed orchestration and continued virtuoso hijinks on the violin. *—Andrew Lindemann Malone*

Recommended:

○ **Saint-Saëns: La Muse et le poète; Violin Concerto 2; Spartacus Overture** / Kantorow, Tapiola Sinfonietta / 2001 / Bis 1060

Violin Concerto No. 3 in B minor, Op. 61 (1880)

Saint-Saëns composed a number of concertos, among them two for cello, five for piano, and three for violin. As he had the *Violin Concerto in A major*, Op. 28 (1859), and the *Introduction and Rondo capriccioso*, Op. 28 (1863), Saint-Saëns composed the *Violin Concerto No. 3 in B minor*, Op. 61, for the virtuoso violinist Pablo de Sarasate (1844–1908). Sarasate gave the first performance of the work at one of the composer's many Monday soirées in 1880, the year Saint-Saëns completed the piece.

As in all the pieces Saint-Saëns composed for Sarasate, the *Violin Concerto No. 3* frequently allows the soloist to display technical prowess; however, the piece requires refined musicality, as well. The *Third Concerto* stands out among Saint-Saëns' works in the genre because it reverts to a format with three clearly separated movements.

The concerto begins without an orchestral introduction; instead, only quietly rumbling chords that provide a harmonic background for the harsh violin theme can be heard. As the first movement progresses, it reveals itself as a very dramatic essay, contrasting passionate, effusive sections with more gentle passages. With a basic outline of sonata form, the movement features a first theme that conveys a sense of yearning and searching through numerous accents and an apparent lack of direction. After a few flashy flourishes from the soloist, the full orchestra powerfully re-states parts of the main theme, creating a transition to the contrasting, lyrical secondary theme. Fragmentation and thematic transformation propel the movement toward a rousing conclusion.

For the second movement, Saint-Saëns composed a barcarolle in which the violin and woodwinds exchange material. The key, B flat major, is striking in that it is a half step below that of the first movement. The melodies are Italianate in this 6/8 time movement, marked Andantino quasi Allegretto. Judging from Sarasate's own compositions, the second movement of Saint-Saëns' concerto is well suited to the violinist's elegant style. The excellent close features a violin line of harmonics that climbs to the stratosphere and seems to disappear.

Surprisingly, a slow introduction, which one might expect to open the first movement of a symphony or concerto, precedes the finale. Marked Molto moderato e maestoso, the introduction, with its coarse violin part alternating with busy orchestral passages, avoids the key of the movement, B minor. After reaching the dominant, the tempo shifts to Allegro non troppo and the movement begins. Throughout the finale, the orchestra is more involved in the musical argument than it is in the previous movements. The opening, leaping theme with triplets contrasts with a rising scale that is the secondary idea, and at the center of the movement can be heard an elegant, cantabile section in G major in which the orchestra takes a leading role. Occasionally the movement takes on a "gypsy" flavor before a return of the leaping theme leads to a change to B major, a brief, chorale-like passage for the orchestra and flashy conclusion in the new key. *—John Palmer*

Recommended:

- ○ **Paganini: Violin Concerto 1; Saint-Saëns: Violin Concerto 3** / Sinopoli (cond.), Shaham, New York PO / DG 429786

Wedding Cake, caprice-valse for piano & strings in A flat major, Op. 76 (1885)

Written as a nuptial tribute to pianist Caroline Montigny-Rémaury, Saint-Saëns' *Wedding Cake* (1885) for piano and strings is a slight but charming "caprice-valse" that's just a bit too big for the salon. The piano commences with a few sparkling cascades of notes that turn into a flighty waltz; the strings offer a more expansive, lilting tune, and the first third of this six-minute piece is simply an alternation of these two ideas. In the middle section, the piano misfires in starts and stops through several measures before it finally catches hold with brilliant passagework. The strings smooth things out; more explicitly waltz-like ideas return, and the piano now appropriates with gusto the strings' more developed theme from the first section. At the very end, the piano repeats its solo from the middle section; the piece ends not with fireworks, but with quietly tinkling utterances from the piano and a few almost offhanded pizzicati from the strings.*—James Reel*

Recommended:

- ○ **Saint-Saëns: Organ Symphony; Carnival of the Animals; etc.** / Batiz (cond.), Osorio, Royal PO / 1989 / ASV 665

SYMPHONIC

Symphony No. 2 in A minor, Op. 55 (1859)

During Saint-Saëns' long, prodigiously creative life as a child prodigy, then a "Futurist," then a conservative, and finally a vituperating fossil, he composed five symphonies, three of them before his 21st birthday. He suppressed the first one (in A major, circa 1850) and the third ("*Urbs Roma*," in F major, 1856), although both were performed early on; the middle one, dated 1853, he published as the *Symphony No. 1 in E flat major,* Op. 2. The chronological fourth, in A minor, followed in 1859, when he was only 23 but already principal organist in the Madeleine, Paris' très chic Church of St. Mary Magdalen. Although François Seghers led the first performance on January 17, 1862, in the Paris salon of *Pleyel-Wolff,* and the composer conducted it frequently thereafter, he did not publish the *Symphony No. 2* until 1878, which accounts for its midlife opus number. The last symphony, with organ—officially *Symphony No. 3 in C minor,* Op. 78—was written for London in 1886, and dedicated to his long-time champion, Franz Liszt.

It became a critical reflex to label all but the last of Saint-Saëns' symphonies as Schumann-influenced. The venturesome *Second,* however, fondly remembers Haydn and Mendelssohn. Scored for winds, horns, trumpets, timpani, and strings, it combines the former's structural surprises with misnomered Felix's orchestral finesse.

The first movement is an Allegro marcato (A minor, 6/4), later Allegro appassionato (D minor, 4/4). A brusque, arpeggiated introduction finally settles into a fugal exposition, inherently quasi-improvisatory but nonetheless structured to include development and reprise. The second-movement Adagio (E major) has a folk song flavor in its main theme, played by muted strings, then by the English horn. The tune, however, is original with Saint-Saëns, who reused it in the Allegretto slow movement of his 1872 *Cello Concerto.* The movement's brevity encouraged the premiere audience to demand a repetition. The Scherzo: Presto (A minor, 3/4) features a syncopated trio in A major, with pizzicato bass, that follows the bustling songlike main section, but that song never returns—as Haydnish a prank as the composer's fugal first movement. The Prestissimo Finale (A major, duple meter) is a fast-forward tarantella that evokes Mendelssohn without copying or kowtowing. Midway, Saint-Saëns reintroduces the folkish main theme of the Adagio, but otherwise his finale ends as it began, as fast as possible. *—Roger Dettmer*

Recommended:

- ○ **Saint-Saëns: Orchestral Music** / Prêtre (cond.), VSO / 1998 / Teldec 24236

Symphony No. 3 in C minor ("Organ"), Op. 78 (1886)

The London Philharmonic Society commissioned the Symphony No. 3 from Saint-Saëns, much as it had Beethoven's *Ninth Symphony.* Saint-Saëns directed the first performance in London on May 19, 1886. Although he lived until 1921, Saint-Saëns would not compose another symphony. He later explained: "With it I have given all I could give. What I did I could not achieve again." He had intended to dedicate the piece to Liszt, but the score was published after Liszt's death with the inscription, "Á la Memoire de Franz Liszt."

The *Symphony in C minor* shows Saint-Saëns' use of thematic transformation, also present in the overture *Spartacus* and the *Fourth Piano Concerto.* This technique Saint-Saëns observed in the symphonic poems of Liszt, as well as in Berlioz's *Symphonie fantastique.* Following their lead, Saint-Saëns takes his principal theme through transformations throughout his *Third Symphony.* To the typical forces of a large orchestra he added his and Liszt's primary instruments, the organ and piano. Saint-Saëns cast the symphony in two large sections, but each of these is in two clear parts, creating a traditional four-movement work.

After an Adagio introduction, the tempo shifts to Allegro moderato and the strings perform the main theme of the first movement, which incorporates the chant at the beginning of the Dies irae, a melody associated with both death and, in part because of the *Totentanz,* Liszt. The melody exhibits an AABB pattern, which is typical of the composer's works, and is the main idea, or "motto" theme, of the entire symphony. This restless theme is transformed and eventually gives way to a new, calmer idea. Afterward, these two themes appear simultaneously in the development section before a return brings more transformational episodes and prepares for the slow "movement," in D flat major.

Strings, supported by organ chords, perform the main theme of the second movement, Adagio, which is the best known section of the *Third Symphony.* Woodwinds take the peaceful theme and vary it until a new transformation of the "motto" theme injects contrasting, restless energy. A return of the Adagio theme rounds off the movement. Near the end we hear a brilliant mixture of woodwinds with reed stops on the organ.

An aggressive, brief theme opens the Scherzo, a transformation of the motto contained in the low string outburst that follows the first phrase. When the tempo changes to Presto, the piano enters with rapid, rising arpeggios and scales, played several times on different harmonies. The Scherzo material returns, and what seems like a reprise of the Presto section introduces a new theme, played by the lower instruments under busy figurations and anticipating the finale.

The finale opens with a powerful chord played on the organ. Yet another transformation of the "motto" theme appears; this time its ties with the Dies irae are very clear. A few quiet statements follow before the organ and orchestra join in a powerful presentation of the transformed theme. After a development section, the piece closes with all the available forces in C major. *—John Palmer*

Recommended:

- ○ **Saint-Saëns: Symphony 3; Debussy: La Mer; Ibert: Escales** / Münch (cond.), Zamkochian, Boston SO / 1959 / BMG 61500
- ○ **Saint-Saëns: Carnival of the Animals; Organ Symphony** / Ormandy (cond.), Biggs, Philadelphia Orch. / 2003 / Sony 87277
- ○ **Saint-Saëns: Danse macabre; Dukas: Sorcerer's Apprentice; etc.** / Ormandy (cond.), Fox, Philadelphia Orch. / 1994 / RCA 902662562

ORCHESTRAL

Danse macabre, symphonic poem in G minor, Op. 40 (1874)

Composed in 1874 and published in 1875, *Danse macabre* is the third of Saint-Saëns' four orchestral tone poems and is easily his most popular work in that medium. In his *Le carnaval des animaux* (The Carnival of the Animals), composed in 1886, Saint-Saëns parodies the *Danse macabre,* as well as works by other composers.

The title of *Danse macabre* is usually translated as Dance of Death, but Ghoulish Dance or Dance of Grim Humor might better communicate the character of the piece. Saint-Saëns did not originally write the *Danse macabre* as a work for orchestra. It was first a song for voice and piano that the composer later transcribed and modified for orchestra. A few lines from the song's text will aid in understanding the symphonic poem: "Death at midnight plays a dance-tune/Zig, zig, zig on his violin.... Through the gloom, white skeletons pass/Running and leaping in their shrouds.... The bones of the dancers are heard to crack." Once the cock crows, signaling the approach of morning, the fun ends. It is possible that this is the first instance of Death being portrayed as a violinist, an instrument generally associated with the devil.

After the orchestra strikes midnight, depicted by horns and pizzicato strings, the violin soloist plays as if he/she is tuning his/her instrument before a solo flute performs a bouncy melody, which is answered by the strings. The violin soloist then enters with a lilting waltz tune, played twice and answered first by a brief return of the flute theme, with added percussion, and then the entire orchestra with the waltz theme. The piece thus far has behaved like an exposition, presenting the principal material, while what follows consists of variations on that material. Xylophones playing the flute melody depict skeletons dancing just before a fugal presentation of the waltz begins. A new melody in the woodwinds is based on the *Dies irae*, a chant melody setting the text of the Judgment Day and often invoked by Romantic-era composers when the subject is death. Eventually, both the flute and waltz tune sound at once in the entire orchestra, just before the violin again begins "tuning." After a huge reprise of the combined melodies, a "cock crow" sounds in the oboe and rapid scales depict the scurrying off of the creatures of the night. *—John Palmer*

Recommended:

- ○ **Saint-Saëns: Symphony 3; Danse macabre; Poulenc: Organ Concerto** / Martinon (cond.), ORTF / Erato 55001
- ○ **Mephisto & Co.** / Oue (cond.), Fleezanis, Minnesota Orch. / 1998 / Reference 82
- ○ **Virtusos Organ Music** / Chorosinski / 1997 / MDG 3200818

Phaéton, symphonic poem in C major, Op. 39 (1873)

Phaéton was the son of Apollo; as a teenager he wanted to borrow the old man's chariot (which was the sun). Apollo allowed him to take the reins for one day. After a brief introduction (which we might imagine represents Phaéton yearning to drive) a galloping motive is introduced for the sun's day-horses. A warning figure sounds, but the galloping motive shows how little the boy heeds the advice of his parent. The rhythm is skittish—hinting at the difficulty in controlling the powerful sun-steeds. Soon a powerful melody on four horns shows that Phaéton is exulting over the thrill of controlling the horses and racing across the sky. But the mood reverses—in the myth he could not control the horses, who began to fly so low that the sun's heat scorched and parched the land. A stern chord with percussion represents Zeus, who hurls a thunderbolt at the sun, which causes the horses to return to their proper track but also makes Phaéton tumble in a fatal fall. At the end, Phaéton's exultant theme from the center of the piece reappears as a lament. As is the case with all of the tone poems Saint-Saëns wrote in the 1870s, Phaéton is concise, dramatic, skillfully drawn, and very entertaining pictorial music. It deserves to be heard in concert much more often. *—Joseph Stevenson*

Recommended:

- ○ **Saint-Saëns - Danse Macabre** / Dutoit (cond.), London PO / 1991 / London 425021
- ○ **Saint-Saëns: Symphony 3; Phaéton** / Badea (cond.), Murray, Royal PO / 1991 / Telarc 80274

Le Rouet d'Omphale, symphonic poem in A major, Op. 31 (1872)

Three of Saint-Saëns' four tone poems are inspired by Greek mythology and two have to do with the hero Hercules. The first of the series, *Le Rouet d'Omphale* (Omphale's Spinning Wheel), finds Hercules in temporary exile, dressed in women's clothes and working as a maid for the Lydian queen Omphale. The composer did not write a detailed musical narrative linked to the story; instead, this is more of an atmosphere piece, its inspiration derived from three quite different aesthetic experiences Saint-Saëns had in close succession: reading a Victor Hugo poem about Omphale, seeing a beautiful ebony spinning wheel in a friend's home, and admiring a sensuous painting of *Venus* in the studio of the painter Cabanel. "The basic idea of *Le Rouet d'Omphale*," the composer wrote, "is voluptuousness." Saint-Saëns provided a description of the tone poem: "The subject of this work is feminine seduction, the victorious struggle of weakness against strength. The spinning wheel is only a pretext, chosen solely from the point of view of the general style and movement of the piece. Hercules surprises Omphale spinning wool at her wheel and tries to win her by the story of his exploits. She laughs at this strength, having as her single weapon of defense her great beauty. Through the witchery of her charm, she vanquishes Hercules and compels him to spin at her feet." The music depicts the wheel with whirling string and woodwind figures and eventually, a melody and rhythm of jerky duplets, perhaps suggesting the spinner's use of a foot pedal. This music expands and fills out, but soon, though the spinning-wheel rhythm never relents, a new, sweeping, and ominous theme develops in relation to Hercules. This subsides, the music pauses, and then the oboe and other woodwinds introduce a light, mocking melody derived from Omphale's music. The spinning-wheel material returns, now in even more sparkling orchestration; aside from another sarcastic visit from the oboe, this music holds until the end. Each of these episodes follows a crescendo-decrescendo pattern and the tone poem as a whole can be heard as such, rising from quiet, hesitant string and flute notes, climaxing with the Hercules episode, and receding to a closing passage that is high, soft, and thinly scored—the final thread spun from Omphale's wheel. *—James Reel*

Recommended:

- ○ **Saint-Saëns - Danse macabre** / Dutoit (cond.), Philharmonia / 1991 / London 425021
- ○ **Saint-Saëns: Rouet d'Omphale; Phaéton; etc.** / Ozawa (cond.), Lefebvre, National Orch. of France / 1999 / Angel 73430

OPERA

Samson et Dalila, Op. 47 (1859–1877)

Even though Camille Saint-Saëns composed a dozen operas, his only work of this genre to have survived the stage is *Samson et Dalila* (1868–75). If not for his close and influential friendship with Liszt, the composition may never have been completed. Even though his chamber works and symphonies attracted considerable attention, more assured musical glory existed in the theater. This stimulated him enough to initiate efforts on what later became his best-known opera, *Samson et Dalila.*

Saint-Saëns first gained interest in the account of Samson and Delilah when he heard that Rameau's opera, based on Voltaire's libretto of the topic, had failed. Working with his librettist, Creole Ferdinand Lemaire, Saint-Saëns immediately began to work the subject into an oratorio. Under the influence of Lemaire, the composer changed directions and scored it as an opera, beginning with, for no apparent reason, the second act. Viewed as a sacrilegious transformation of biblical scripture, commercial theater managers avoided it as box-office poison. Upon hearing mention of the project, with his usual perspicacity Liszt saw the value of the work and, comfortably backed by the Grand Duke at Weimar, encouraged its completion and promised to have it performed. The outbreak of the Franco-Prussian war thwarted the timely completion of the project; thus, it required a total of eight years to finish. When a portion of the opera was heard on Good Friday 1875, in the Théâtre du Châtelet, the reaction was quite discouraging; nevertheless, it received a full premiere in 1877 at the Grand Ducal Theatre in Weimar, just as Liszt had assured. From there it had its French premiere at the Paris Opéra in 1892, where it was staged 500 times more prior to the composer's death, becoming comparable in success with *Faust* and *Rigoletto.*

Even though Saint-Saëns was considerably influenced by masters of the operas such as Wagner, Handel, Offenbach, Gounod, and Meyerbeer, none of his other operas came close to achieving the level of fame and prestige experienced by *Samson et Dalila*, perhaps due to the composer's lack of theatrical abilities. Attracted to the purity of music, he refused to recognize the emotional and sensual possibilities in his work. *Samson et Dalila*, which was actually more of a series of tableaux than an opera, had room to avoid these indulgences by nature of its biblical subject matter; however, his other works of this genre, in the eyes of critics, did not. The work is a synthesis of Wagnerian drama and French and Italian operatic forms, containing skillful structures and eloquent melodies. As one of the brightest jewels of French opera, the work is considered "a dream of antique purity and modern orchestral experimentation," which thoroughly demonstrates Saint-Saëns' compositional capabilities. *—Meredith Gailey*

Synopsis:

Act One, Scene One. In Gaza, Palestine, the Hebrews have assembled near the temple of Dagon in sorrowful prayer over their subservience to the Philistines. Samson speaks to the crowd in an attempt to renew their faith and enthusiasm to break the bonds of tyranny. His eloquence wins them over and calms their fear. They prepare to do battle again.

Scene Two. The Philistine Abimelech arrives with his soldiers and challenges Samson's brave words, unfavorably comparing the Hebrew god to the Philistine god Dagon. Enraged, Samson passionately calls on his people to rise up against their tormentors despite Abimelech's threats. The two men fight. Abimelech is killed and all the Philistines are driven off in confusion.

Scene Three. All the Hebrews have cleared away, and the high priest of Dagon, with guards and attendants, comes out of the temple, halting before the corpse of Abimelech. He urges his soldiers to pursue the Hebrews, but they find themselves paralyzed with fear.

Scene Four. A Philistine messenger now appears on the scene, bearing news that a Hebrew rebellion, led by Samson, has broken out. The priest vows a cruel revenge upon Samson's people, while his fellows urge they should abandon everything and flee into the mountains. The scene clears.

Scene Five. After sunrise, some aged Hebrews, followed by the victorious Hebrew warriors, appear with Samson. They are singing praises to their god in thanks for the victory he has brought them.

Scene Six. Delilah now comes out of the temple of Dagon, with attendant Philistine priestesses. She declares her love of Samson, inviting him to visit with her in Sorek valley, Palestine. Although the aged Hebrews warn Samson about her seductive charms, he cannot avoid her alluring gaze and becomes inflamed with passion when the priestesses do a voluptuous ritual dance.

Act Two, Scene One. At her house in Sorek, Delilah, heavily adorned, sits pensively as night falls, awaiting the arrival of Samson. She prays that the "poison" of love enter his heart and enslave him to her; this will be the Philistines' revenge.

Scene Two. The High Priest, Delilah's father, arrives. All this time he has believed that Delilah reciprocated Samson's love and is happy to learn that she despises the Hebrew warrior as much as her father does. She swears that Samson's remarkable restraint will be broken down this very night by Delilah's irresistible tears, and she will discover the secret of his power and rob him of it. The Priest leaves Delilah alone to await her victim.

Scene Three. Although tormented, Samson at last comes. Lightning faintly rumbles in the distance as Delilah throws herself upon him, and Samson's resistance dissolves. To fan the flames, she plays at not trusting the depth of his love, despite his almost hysterical declarations. Finally, as the storm now rages around them, he rushes into the house after her and Philistine soldiers follow; the trap is sprung.

Act Three, Scene One. Samson is chained to a millwheel and blinded in a Gaza prison with other Hebrews. He loudly laments the weakness of will that brought him down, while the others admonish him for selling them out for the mere favors of Delilah. Philistine soldiers enter and drag him away.

Scene Two. Inside the temple of Dagon, a crowd of Philistines gather, including Delilah, her maidens, and the High Priest. Their amorous celebrating continues through the dawn.

Scene Three. Samson is brought into their midst in chains, led by a child. The Philistines enrage him with their scorn and mockery. Samson prays silently and fervently as the Philistines enact various sacrificial and divinatory rituals. As they watch the brazier flames leaping higher, which they take as a good omen, the child leads Samson between the two supporting pillars, which he pulls down with a final burst of inspired strength, destroying the temple and killing everyone in it. *—Donato Mancini*

Recommended:

- ○ **Saint-Saëns: Samson & Dalila** / Davis (cond.), Cura, Ragon, Lloyd, Borodina, London SO / 1998 / Elektra 24756
- ○ **Saint-Saëns: Samson & Dalila** / Barenboim (cond.), Domingo, Bruson, Lloyd, Thau, Paris Orch. / DG 413297
- ○ **Saint-Saëns: Samson & Dalila** / Prêtre (cond.), Vickers, Blanc, Gorr, Corazza, Paris National Opera Theater Orch. / Angel 67602

CHAMBER MUSIC

Allegro appassionato, for cello & piano in B minor, Op. 43 (1875)

The first composition Saint-Saëns completed after marrying Marie Laurie Emilie Truffot on February 3, 1875, was the *Allegro appassionato in B minor for cello and piano or orchestra,* Op. 43. It was published soon after in 1875. Because of its lighthearted brevity and its appearance at roughly the same time as much larger works such as the *Piano Concerto No. 4,* Op. 44; the *Danse macabre,* Op. 40; and the *Piano Quartet in B flat major,* Op. 40, the *Allegro appassionato* almost seems like an afterthought. However, it remains one of the composer's most popular works, and the piece's showcasing of the cello makes it a favorite among performers.

Transparently scored and elegantly tuneful, the *Allegro appassionato*'s lively rhythms create a mood similar to that of the *Cello Concerto in A minor,* Op. 33. Undoubtedly, the piece's melodiousness and numerous repeats of minimal material are the reasons for its popular success.

Immediately after a few syncopated chords in the orchestra, the solo cello enters with a bouncy tune; the entire theme and then the second half are repeated, creating a melodic pattern heard in much of Saint-Saëns' music. The B section of the piece features a much more lyrical melody that opens with a large, aggressive leap in the cello. Section A returns but is abbreviated, giving way to the B material, this time in a new key. An extension of the B section tune leads back to a fiery repetition of section A that contains a reference to the aggressive leap of part B, while a spirited coda closes the piece with rapid triplets. Although only a few minutes in length, the *Allegro appassionato* makes an indelible impression. *—John Palmer*

Recommended:

- ○ **Saint-Saëns: Music for Cello** / Tilson Thomas, Isserlis, Devoyon, Grier / RCA 61678
- ○ **The Romantic Cello** / Lloyd Webber, Seow / 1978 / ASV 6014

Bassoon Sonata in G major, Op. 168 (1921)

In the last year of his life, at the age of 85, Camille Saint-Saëns was still active as a composer and conductor, traveling between Algiers and Paris. Besides a final piano album leaf, his last completed works were three sonatas, one each for oboe, clarinet, and bassoon. He sensed that he did not have much time left; he wrote to a friend, "I am using my last energies to add to the repertoire for these otherwise neglected instruments." He intended to write sonatas for another three wind instruments, but was never able to. Saint-Saëns began the pieces early in the year while in Algeria and completed them in April in Paris. He was not alone in wanting to write for these instruments. English composers, such as Holst and Bax, and other French composers, such as Honegger and Milhaud, were also starting to expand the literature for woodwind instruments around the same time. In fact, Saint-Saëns' sonatas have pastoral and humorous moments that are similar to those others' works, relying on simpler melodies and textures than are found even his earlier chamber works, yet retaining Classical forms for their structure. Although all three sonatas were published before Saint-Saëns' death, they were not premiered until later. The *Bassoon Sonata,* Op. 168, was dedicated to Saint-Saëns' friend, August Périer, a bassoon professor at the Paris Conservatoire. The opening Allegro moderato is liltingly charming as it drifts between major and minor, building to a not too dramatic climax in its development section. The second movement, Allegro scherzando, begins in minor mode, but it, too, changes frequently between major and minor during its lighthearted jaunt. The final movement is in two parts, Molto adagio and Allegro moderato. The Adagio, the longest section of the entire sonata at over five minutes, features a florid melody over a simple, essentially chordal accompaniment. It leads to the cadenza-like, minute-long final Allegro. *—Patsy Morita*

Recommended:

- ○ **Saint-Saëns & Poulenc** / Requejo, Thunemann / 1991 / Claves 509020
- ○ **Saint-Saëns: Chamber Music for Wind Instruments** / Villa Musica Ens. / 1991 / MDG 3040395

Carnival of the Animals, zoological fantasy for 2 pianos & ensemble (1886)

In 1885 Saint-Saëns wrote a witty, uncomplicated piece called *Wedding Cake* (1885), which to his chagrin became so popular that he gained a temporary reputation as a "light" composer. Because he wanted to be considered a composer of serious, substantial music, he suppressed *Carnival of the Animals* shortly after its premiere in the following year. However, this "zoological fantasy," one of the most successful examples of humourously themed music in the repertory, has become one of the composer's most popular works. *Carnival of the Animals,* cast as a suite of 14 short pieces, is scored for an ensemble comprising two pianos, two violins, viola, cello, double bass, flute, clarinet, and glockenspiel.

The work begins with a roar from the two pianos and low strings, an appropriate introduction to the "Royal March of the Lions." The crowing and pecking of strings effectively evokes the clamor of hens and roosters, while the depiction of tortoises takes the form of a sly musical joke: a drastically slowed-down version of the famous can-can from Offenbach's *Les contes d'Hoffmann* (1881). Saint-Saëns continues to parody his countrymen when he uses the "Waltz of the Sylphs" from Berlioz's *The Damnation of Faust* (1846) in depicting elephants. Graceful and rapid leaps on the keyboard naturally describe kangaroos. Liquid, rippling sounds on the piano and a magical, serene melody characterize one of the loveliest sections of the work, a sound portrait of an aquarium. Sliding string figures give voice to mules, whose braying is sharply contrasted with the deeply mysterious beauty of the clarinet in its imitation of a cuckoo. This single bird becomes an entire aviary aflutter with airy flute solos and rapid keyboard passagework. Saint-Saëns admits pianists themselves into the menagerie, good-naturedly mocking their hours of practice with a passage that unfolds as a ponderous keyboard exercise. "Fossils" pays homage to those creatures which have suffered extinction with the suggestion of rattling bones in the xylophone, including a quotation from the composer's own *Danse macabre* (1874). This is followed by the most famous movement, one so lovely that the composer permitted its publication as a solo work. "The Swan" has become a staple of every cellist's repertoire and a favorite accompaniment for dance works. The brisk finale includes a spirited, exuberant reprise of all of the animals' themes. *—Joseph Stevenson*

Recommended:

- ○ **Saint-Saëns: Carnival of the Animals; etc.** / Rozhdestvensky (cond.), Postnikova, Pierlot, Lauridon, Heisser / Erato 45772
- ○ **Saint-Saëns: Carnival of the Animals** / Dutoit (cond.), Rogé, Ortiz, Kampen, Bell, Pay, McGee, London Sinfonietta / 1986 / London 414460

Clarinet Sonata in E flat major, Op. 167 (1921)

Although he remained a very active composer throughout his very long life, even the biggest fan of Camille Saint-Saëns will admit (as Saint-Saëns himself sometimes admitted) that by the 1920s—nearly 70 years after his rise to fame—he was something of a dry well. Still, some of the pieces he composed during the last years of his life have real value; perhaps it is hard to take a work like the choral piece *Hail California* (1915) seriously, but the three woodwind sonatas of 1921, one of which is the *Sonata for clarinet and piano in E flat major,* Op. 167, are cherished by many performers.

Saint-Saëns' *Clarinet Sonata* has four movements, and thus might be said to reach back past the Romantic sonata tradition, with its normal three-movement vessel, to the Classical tradition that Saint-Saëns loved so dearly. The opening melodic strains of the Allegretto first movement float upon a sea of utterly calm eighth note waves in the piano (bobbing up and down in 12/8 meter); the composer is in no hurry to reveal the secrets of the movement, but there is still passion aplenty as we go along, even if the movement as a whole is not especially long.

A scherzo movement comes next, taking up A flat major, and then Saint-Saëns provides a Lento in the dark key of E flat minor; its steady half notes and, in time, quarter notes, are so persistent in their slow plodding that we almost feel anguish at their inability to break free from the dirge they create. Much happier, though, is the Molto Allegro fourth movement that follows it without pause. Here the clarinetist is given a chance to whirl and spin to some very florid virtuoso stuff, but at the end it is the quiet tone, and even in fact the very music, of the first movement that the composer uses to close. *—Blair Johnston*

Recommended:

○ **French Beasties & Swedish Beasts** / Pontinen, Frost / 1994 / Bis 693

Fantaisie for violin & harp in A major, Op. 124 (1907)

Saint-Saëns' *Fantaisie for Violin and Harp*, Op. 124, is representative of the general "thinning" of texture we find in the composer's output after the mid-1890s. His piano parts became lighter, and he even replaced the piano with the thin sound of the harp in several works, including the *Fantaisie*, Op. 95, for harp alone and the *Morceau de concert*, Op. 154, for harp and orchestra, in addition to the *Fantaisie*, Op. 124.

Saint-Saëns composed the *Fantaisie for Violin and Harp* while touring in the Mediterranean in February and March of 1907. After attending a performance of his *Le timbre d'argent* in Monte Carlo, the composer moved on to the Italian Riviera city of Bordighera to rest. There he composed the *Fantaisie for Violin and Harp*, published later the same year as his Op. 124. The work is dedicated to the sisters Marianne and Clara Eissler.

In four sections, the delicacy of the piece exemplifies Saint-Saëns' recently developed ideas on clarity. The first section shows a clear division of labor between the instruments as the violin plays a single melodic line over arpeggios and broken chords in the harp. Although rigorously organized, the section has an improvisatory feel. In the second section, the violin part is less melodious, with frequent, aggressive double-stops, while the harp accompaniment takes on a heavier pulse and pentatonic passages. A more equal exchange between the instruments marks the third section, in which the violin and harp at first follow one another. Later, the violin sounds low pitches, which the harp decorates in a fanciful manner, completely reversing the roles of the instruments in the first section and creating refreshing timbral contrast. In the fourth section, the harp returns to its accompanimental role, repeating groups of notes as the violin pursues invigorating lyrical outbursts. Saint-Saëns closes the piece with a return to the opening melody and its accompanimental texture. *—John Palmer*

Recommended:

○ **Music For Flute & Harp** / Rampal, Nordmann / 1990 / Sony 44552

Havanaise, for violin & orchestra in E major, Op. 83 (1887)

Saint-Saëns completed the *Havanaise* in E major for violin and orchestra, Op. 83, in 1887; however, the work's origins predate this by two years. In November 1885, the composer set out on a concert tour with the violinist, Raphael Diaz Albertini, playing throughout northern France before moving on to Germany. While in Brest on a cold night, Saint-Saëns built a fire in his hotel room, the popping sound of the burning wood sparking a melodic idea in his mind. Saint-Saëns originally wrote the piece for violin and piano, soon after orchestrating the piano accompaniment. The *Havanaise*, Op. 83, was published in 1888 in Paris with a dedication to Albertini.

A havanaise (habanera in Spanish) is a dance in 2/4 time that developed in Cuba from African rhythms. Saint-Saëns' Latin-sounding main theme consists of an eighth note triplet on the first beat of the measure and a duplet on the second, creating a Latin rhythm that appealed to Albertini, who had Cuban origins. The drooping melody is punctuated with fiery virtuosic passages and whenever it moves away from the havanaise rhythm and becomes reflective, a soft drum steps in to remind us of the opening dance. After a quick passage, we hear two more themes, these more Romantic in flavor than the main theme. Unlike the first theme, these are entirely the property of the soloist, and the orchestra is reduced to an accompanimental role while continuing to give us the havanaise rhythm. During the developmental, virtuosic passages, Saint-Saëns' inserts quick asides for the violin, as well as the smooth chromatic scales and trills, to suggest glances and caresses. A high, sustained harmonic on the solo violin closes the work. *—John Palmer*

Recommended:

○ **Heifetz Showpieces** / Steinberg (cond.), Heifetz, RCA Victor SO / 1994 / RCA 61753

Oboe Sonata in D major, Op. 166 (1921)

The last works of the great, French Romantic composer Camille Saint-Saëns are actually products of the twentieth century, but these sonatas, one each for oboe, clarinet, and bassoon, remain faithful to his Romantic sentiments and even reach back to the Classical era for their basic structure and simple musical lines. The *Sonata for oboe and piano*, Op. 166, was the first of the three to be completed over the course of a couple of months in early 1921. As soon as he was finished, Saint-Saëns wrote to his publisher in Paris that he wanted to have them "tested" before they were edited for publication. The *Oboe Sonata* was played by his friend Louis Bas, who seemed so pleased with the work that Saint-Saëns dedicated it to him. The structure and lines of the sonata are not unlike what other French and neo-Classical composers were using around the same period and, in fact, the *Oboe Sonata* also has almost a preternatural resemblance to the works of the English pastoralists (Saint-Saëns was living in Algeria when he wrote it). The sonata opens with a gentle Andantino, followed by the bipartite second movement, an ad libitum recitative leading into an Allegretto gigue. The final Molto allegro is almost dance-like with shades of the energy of Saint-Saëns' more youthful works. All in all, the sonata is a standard work in the oboe repertoire, giving the performer a gratifying match between technical challenges and melodic expression. *—Patsy Morita*

Recommended:

○ **Wayne Rapier Plays Oboe** / Rapier, Amlin / 1995 / Boston 1013

Piano Trio No. 1 in F major, Op. 18 (1863)

In the middle of the nineteenth century, French audiences were interested in hardly any music but opera. Only a few mavericks like Berlioz were devoting much effort to instrumental music, and so when the 28-year-old Saint-Saëns wrote his first piano trio in 1863, he could find no indigenous traditions to inspire him. So he seems to have modeled this work more or less on Mendelssohn's style, developing, nevertheless, a personal idiom characterized by melodic clarity and irresistible charm. This clarity, often perceived as transparence, and sometimes misinterpreted as superficiality, eventually became closely identified with the French style as it developed in the following decades.

The first movement, Allegro vivace, starts off with a short, dance-like theme played by the cello; the melody is then taken in turn by the violin and piano. A somewhat contrasting (but still light) legato second theme is subsequently introduced. Saint-Saëns generally lets the piano function as accompaniment while the strings handle the material of the greatest melodic interest, which, of course, does not mean that the keyboard part is easy. In fact, it's quite hectic and demanding compared to the more straightforward string parts. The composer works over his thematic material thoroughly, with the rhythm of the first melody providing most of the ideas for the development section. Throughout, the music retains a lively, optimistic character. The Andante begins with a mysterious, slightly sinister double-dotted melody that seems inspired by folk tunes Saint-Saëns may have encountered in the Pyrenees and the Auvergne. This theme evolves into a more smoothly undulating melody sung out at length by the strings with understated piano accompaniment. The original material returns, now even more mysterious than before, but eventually the cello takes over, presenting more animated material, which is appropriated for a concise piano solo before the movement closes with a repeat of its opening bars. The brief Scherzo is a playful exercise in syncopation, initially full of pizzicato effects in the strings and staccato writing for the piano. This syncopated episode then turns into a gently swinging and swooping tune with which the Scherzo's playful first subject alternates through the rest of the movement. The final Allegro opens with the violin and cello trading very brief phrases over a sparkling piano accompaniment. Further material, of some substance, is introduced, eventually transforming itself into a gentle, rocking motion up and down the scale. The movement progresses in this manner, the strings making fragmentary utterances that are held together by the extremely busy piano writing, which abruptly, but vaguely, conjures up the spirit of Saint-Saëns' beloved Beethoven. Although the trio's least melodically distinctive movement, it completes the work with steady, light-hearted grace. *—James Reel*

Recommended:

○ **French Piano Trios** / Golub Kaplan Carr Trio / 1994 / Arabesque 6643

Septet for piano, trumpet, string quartet & double bass in E flat major, Op. 65 (1881)

The unusual scoring (trumpet, piano, string quartet, double bass) of this septet may have limited its performances and recordings, but it's truly one of the most delightful chamber works of the nineteenth century. Saint-Saëns wrote it in 1881, for a Parisian music society called "La Trompette," and, given such a name, the composer could hardly have resisted working a trumpet into the piece. Inevitably, it becomes the dominant voice almost whenever it plays, but Saint-Saëns makes a valiant effort to keep the ensemble as balanced as possible. The septet takes the form of a Baroque suite, the composer paying homage especially to the colorful and elegant music of Rameau, whose collected works Saint-Saëns edited. Opening with an assertive chord for piano and strings, the first movement, Préambule, establishes an energetic and dynamic mood; the trumpet then emerges with a long, calming note, subsequently embarking on a mock-pompous processional theme accompanied by sharp chords and occasional piano flourishes. The last phrase of this march launches a little fugato section for everyone but the trumpet. The fugato eases into a smoother melody over a nervously pulsing accompaniment. The trumpet takes over this melody, then forces the full version of its march tune upon the group again. The movement ends in an atmosphere of Baroque pomp and ceremony, which is disturbed by the pianist's Lisztian cascades. Next comes a Minuet. With the trumpet leading the melody over a marcato accompaniment, this sounds more like a very quick march, but the strings offer a more sighing, Romantic second subject in which the trumpet participates as discreetly as possible. The movement's central trio section nicely melds the strings and trumpet into a single voice over a florid piano accompaniment for a flowing, sentimental waltz. Saint-Saëns calls the third movement Intermède. The strings and the trumpet, whose subdued, reticent expressiveness blends well with the strings, play a mysterious, long-breathed melody over a skulking, repeated-note piano accompaniment. That characteristic piano figure provides the basis for further melodic elaboration, after which the individual voices steal quietly into the shadows. The last movement, Gavotte et Finale, is a lively treatment of the eighteenth century dance, featuring considerable stretches of rapid up-front passagework for the piano over pizzicato figurations executed by the strings. The trumpet interjects some bugle calls that are imitated by the other instruments before the piano brings everyone back to the original material. Suddenly, the strings and piano plunge into a rapid, nervous fugato based on a little phrase from the first movement. The trumpet joins in, only to pull the ensemble into a headlong rush toward the final bar. *—James Reel*

Recommended:

○ **Le désir** / Tarr, various / 1994 / Christophorus 77168

○ **Saint-Saëns: Le Carnaval des Animaux; Septet; etc.** / Hobson, Sinfonia da Camera / 1989 / Arabesque 6570

Violin Sonata No. 1 in D minor, Op. 75 (1885)

The earlier of Saint-Saëns' two sonatas for violin and piano, in D minor, Op. 75, was written in 1885. Clearly modeled on the heroic Beethovenian ideal of sonata composition, the principal quality of this impressive work is, to quote William Livingstone, that it "embodies the Apollonian control and moderation that are highly prized in French arts."

Among several key attributes which the listener will readily associate with Beethoven's works in this genre is that the work is laid out on a vast, if not to say epic scale, having four substantial movements. The second, and equally tangible Beethovenian imprint concerns the power and urgency of the principal themes, especially those of the first and last movements, in which the element of heroic struggle is never deeply concealed, and indeed, made more vital by the choice of such a vehemently dramatic key. The work was dedicated to the great Belgian virtuoso and teacher Martin Marsick, with whom Saint-Saëns collaborated by playing the piano part himself at the first performance. The companion piece to this work, a *Second Sonata in E flat*, Op. 102, dates from 1896.

The huge opening movement (Allegro agitato), a taut, leonine construction built around Classical sonata-form lines, offers a gripping first subject heard at the very start, with no slow preamble. It conveys a sense of theatrical dialogue, powerfully underlined in complex exchanges between the two instruments. The second subject, somewhat more relaxed and lyrical, affords the required contrast, while the development section explores the potentiality of the two main subjects with great ingenuity. The slow movement (Adagio) is placed second, and again, the main melodies seem to draw heavily on the example of Beethoven, a composer whom Saint-Saëns greatly admired. The third movement (Allegretto moderato), is in fact a scherzo in all but name, and provides motifs of extreme clarity and translucence, perhaps reminiscent of Mendelssohn, while the brilliant finale (Allegro molto) places searching virtuoso demands on each of the players in more or less equal measure. *—Michael Jameson*

Recommended:

○ **French Violin Sonatas** / Midori, McDonald / 2002 / Sony 89699

KEYBOARD

Variations on a Theme of Beethoven, for 2 pianos, Op. 35 (1874)

This is the first and most substantial of a handful of original pieces that Saint-Saëns wrote for two pianos. The eight variations plus a fugue, presto, and coda are based on the Trio from the Menuetto third movement of Beethoven's *Piano Sonata No. 18 ("Hunt")*. It is a fairly strange choice for a theme; its short phrases consist of leaping chords followed by a brief, more melodic figure. On the other hand, it is perfect from a duo standpoint because the chords echo and are easily split between the two performers. Saint-Saëns' variations are comparable to Beethoven's own variation writing in their diversity of style and complete pianism. Saint-Saëns was able to use the two pianos to create almost orchestral sonorities, yet keep the music accessible to moderately skilled players. The variations move from an arpeggiated version of the theme to a filled out lyrical version, a partial inversion, pounding chords, and another arpeggiated version before heading into a funeral march. The march and the following section both feature exotic harmonies that give a more mysterious and Eastern flavor to the music. The fugue, presto, and coda are the meat of the work, requiring a certain amount of élan and a considerable amount of ensemble skill to be done well. Using an earlier master's work as inspiration, Saint-Saëns crafted a classic work for the piano duo repertoire. *—Patsy Morita*

Recommended:

○ **Saint-Saëns** / Onder Duo / 1998 / Pan 510106

○ **Piano Duos** / Uribe, Martina / 1997 / Helicon 1020

Nadja Salerno-Sonnenberg

b. Jan. 10, 1961, Rome, Italy

Violinist

Nadja Salerno-Sonnenberg remains one of the most popular and established concert violinists in an increasingly competitive international field. She has been referred to as the "bad girl of the violin" owing to her high-strung, sometimes abrasive personality and her former three-pack-a-day smoking habit. Asked once by an interviewer if she had a "gentle side," Salerno-Sonnenberg jokingly replied, "No, I'm a bitch all around." Nonetheless, she is a devotedly Romantic interpreter who infuses her performances with passion and technical mastery. Salerno-Sonnenberg often departs from the letter of the law in regard to the composer's written score in her interpretations, but she more than makes up for what is lost in her sincerity, originality, and intense expressiveness.

Salerno-Sonnenberg takes her name from that of her mother, Josephine Salerno (an Italian pianist), and that of her stepfather (her father left the family when she was three months old). In her native Rome, Salerno-Sonnenberg's natural talent for the violin was discovered early, and first nurtured there by Dr. Marianna Gabbi. At the age of eight, Salerno-Sonnenberg and her mother resettled in New Jersey so that Nadja could begin study at the Curtis Institute of Music in Philadelphia; during this time her mother made ends meet by teaching music in city schools. Salerno-Sonnenberg completed her education at the Julliard School with Dorothy DeLay.

In 1981, Salerno-Sonnenberg's professional career was launched by a win at the Naumberg Foundation award; this was further amplified by an Avery Fisher career grant in 1983 and several appearances on *The Tonight Show* with Johnny Carson. In 1988, Salerno-Sonnenberg began to record for EMI Classics, which promptly released several albums of standard repertoire featuring covers photographs of the violinist in sultry poses; avoiding the "success by marketing" stigma that often accompanies such packaging, she earned the Ovation Debut recording Artist of the Year for her artistry. In 1989, she published *Nadja: On My Way*, an autobiographical book on her career designed for children.

On Christmas Day, 1994, Salerno-Sonnenberg nearly took off the tip of her pinky finger with a knife while slicing vegetables; fortunately, an expert surgeon saved the sliced pinky, but this led to a long period of both personal and professional crisis. In 1997, Salerno-Sonnenberg made some positive changes; she moved from EMI to Nonesuch, whose Salerno-Sonnenberg releases are considerably more serious in tone and presentation, and she signed with management firm ICA (she had previously been with CAM.) January 1999 witnessed the Sundance Film Festival premiere of *Speaking In Strings*, a warts-and-all feature-length documentary on Salerno-Sonnenberg directed by her childhood friend Paola di Floria. The film was nominated for an Academy Award. That same year, Salerno-Sonnenberg was awarded the Avery Fisher Prize, and received an honorary Master of Musical Arts degree from New Mexico State University.

In August 2000, she premiered Mark O'Connor's *Double Violin Concerto* at the Cabrillo Music Festival with the composer and conductor Marin Alsop, and has recorded an acclaimed disc for Nonesuch of gypsy music with the Assad Brothers. Salerno-Sonnenberg has appeared as soloist with practically every major orchestra in the world, and is in high demand as a recitalist. While many of her recordings are outstanding, Salerno-Sonnenberg is best experienced in a concert setting, where her innate sense of drama and musical risk-taking are most vivid. *—Uncle Dave Lewis*

Recommended:

○ **Humoresque** / Litton (cond.), Salerno-Sonnenberg, Stifelman, Blazer, London SO / Nonesuch 79464

○ **Vivaldi: 4 Seasons** / Salerno-Sonnenberg, Feeney, Feeney, Lutzke, Wolinsky, Stern, St. Luke CO / 1990 / EMI 49767

○ **Speaking in Strings** / Tilson Thomas (cond.), Salerno-Sonnenberg, Harrell, Rivers, Kim / 1999 / EMI 56908

○ **It Ain't Necessarily So...** / Salerno-Sonnenberg, Rivers / 1992 / EMI 54576

Antonio Salieri

b. Aug. 18, 1750, Legnaga, Italy, **d.** May 7, 1825, Vienna, Austria

Composer: Opera, Orchestral

Antonio Salieri is still better known today for the renowned composers with whom he was associated than for his own many and varied compositions. While he cannot be ranked among the great masters himself, he has nevertheless come into view as an underrated and important composer deserving of closer attention. Salieri was the dominant figure in Parisian opera from the mid to late 1780s. *Tarare* (1787), generally considered his finest achievement in the genre, is a masterpiece. He also wrote significant instrumental, sacred, and vocal compositions, and shaped the Viennese musical world that would produce so many important composers for a century and a half. Salieri's illustrious students included Beethoven, Schubert, Liszt, Hummel, and Czerny. There is no evidence to support the durable legend that he poisoned Mozart and created intrigues against him. One of his students was Wolfgang A. Mozart Jr., whom he would probably not have selected for instruction had he harbored such malice toward his father.

Salieri was born in Legnago, Italy, in 1750. At an early age, he took his first lessons, on both violin and harpsichord, from his older brother, Francesco. Later on he studied violin with local organist Giuseppe Simoni. At 15, Salieri lived for a brief period in Padua with another brother, a monk, after his parents' deaths. But his already formidable musical talents had drawn notice, and a family friend, Giovanni Mocenigo, arranged for his continued musical education in Venice. Salieri studied for a year there with Giovanni Pescetti and Ferdinando Pacini.

Impressed by his talents, visiting Vienna Court composer Florian Leopold Gassman took him back to the Austrian capital in 1766, where he taught him composition and introduced him to the court of Joseph II. By 1768, Salieri had composed his first opera, *La vestale*, probably not a success and now lost. His first surviving opera, *Le donne letterate*, was good enough to have impressed his new friend Gluck. *Armida* followed in 1771 and achieved wide success, assuring Salieri recognition in the highest Viennese musical circles.

Salieri was appointed court composer upon the death of Gassman in 1774. In addition, he became conductor of the city's Italian opera company. He was now one of the most influential figures in European music, holding a position of eminence that Mozart and other talented composers of the day would never attain. Salieri went on to score triumphs in Milan (*L'Europa riconosciuta*; 1778) and in Venice (*La scuola de' gelosi*; 1778), while he was on leave from the Vienna court for two years. He surpassed these successes with his next operas, given in Paris. With the help of Gluck, *Les Danaïdes* (1784) was performed to enthusiastic audiences there, but was far overshadowed by the sensation of *Tarare* (1787). Salieri would never have a finer moment.

In 1788, Salieri became court music director, and he retained the post following the death of Joseph II in 1790. Over the next decade-and-a-half, he did not explore new directions in his operatic style, thus falling out of fashion even before the turn of the nineteenth century. Aware of his own conservatism, he wrote no operas after 1804. He served as court music director until March 1824, remaining active in the musical life of Vienna and teaching many students. He also continued writing sacred and instrumental music.

Salieri fathered eight children and by all accounts was a decent man. Near the end of his life, he was placed in an asylum owing to his deteriorating mental and physical states. He died in Vienna on May 7, 1826. *—Robert Cummings*

OPERA

Operas (1768–1804)

The name Antonio Salieri (1750–1825) is today inextricably associated with the play and film *Amadeus*, where he was depicted as a mediocre composer whose jealousy and machinations constantly thwarted the career of Mozart. Yet in truth the Italian was an accomplished composer who achieved great success in Italy, Paris, and Vienna, his operas being held in particularly high esteem at the Viennese court of the Emperor Joseph II. He was born in Legnano, near Vicenza, and received his early music training in Venice. At the age of 16, his talents were recognized by the Viennese composer Florian Gassmann, who took Salieri as his assistant to the imperial capital, where the young man also gained the friendship of Gluck and support of the emperor. Joseph's influence through his sister Marie Antoinette also allowed Salieri to compose for Versailles and the Paris Opéra. Salieri remained based in Vienna for the remainder of his long life (he died there in 1825), a powerful presence in the city and an accomplished teacher who numbered Beethoven and Schubert among his pupils.

Around 40 operas by Salieri are extant, a corpus encompassing serious and comic Italian pieces, German opera, and French tragédie lyrique. Dating from the early 1770s and influenced by Gassman, his earliest stage works mostly represent the opera buffa genre. In 1771, Salieri's first serious opera, *Armida*, was produced at the Burgtheater. In this work he followed the example of Gluck (who set the same story as a French opera six years later) in introducing such elements of tragédie lyrique as a dramatic role for the chorus and spectacular scenic effects. *Armida* also marked Salieri out as a skillful composer of accompanied recitative. During the 1770s, further comic operas followed along with another serious opera, *L'Europa riconosciuta*, commissioned by Milan in 1778. At the start of 1780s, Joseph II, anxious to establish native German opera in Vienna, commissioned *Der Rauchfangkehrer* from Salieri, a work that incorporates elements of opera buffa and German Singspiel. Successful from the time of its premiere in 1781, it was supplanted by the even greater popularity of Mozart's *Die Entführung aus dem Serail*. It was one of only two such works composed by Salieri during Joseph's short-lived ambitions for German opera. But Paris now also beckoned. In 1784, *Les Danaïdes*, Salieri's first tragédie lyrique, was produced at the Paris Opéra. A dark story of violence, *Les Danaïdes* is a Greek tragedy that established its composer as the inheritor of Gluck's mantle, combining nobility with melodic simplicity in the manner of the older master. Some of the powerful orchestral writing anticipates that of Mozart's *Don Giovanni*. Back in Vienna, Salieri became the first composer to work with Lorenzo da Ponte, who later gained immortality as the librettist of Mozart's greatest comic operas. Their most notable collaboration was the opera *Axur, re d'Ormus* (1788), a successful synthesis of the various styles in which Salieri had worked and thus the culmination of his operatic career. *—Brian Robins*

Recommended:

- ○ **Salieri: Axur, Re d'Ormus** / Clemencic (cond.), Martin, Rayam, Mei, Nova / 1990 / Nuova Era 7366
- ○ **The Salieri Album** / Bartoli, Fischer (cond.), Orch. of the Age of Enlightenment / 2003 / Decca 000109702

ORCHESTRAL

Variations on "La follia di spagna" (1815)

What makes Salieri's *Variations on "La follia di spagna"* noteworthy is that it is one of only very few sets of successful orchestral variations that was written before the late Romantic period, when the form became more popular after Brahms' 1873 *Haydn Variations*. Salieri's take on the famous Portuguese (not Spanish, as the title suggests) theme *La Folia* is fundamentally an exercise in orchestration. His score calls for strings, woodwinds, brass, harp, percussion, and tambourine, all featured at some point over the 26 variations. Salieri does not use any sophisticated variation techniques, such as inversion, nor does he alter the meter of the theme for much of the work or even the key until the very end. Instead he relies on rhythm and instrumentation to create the variations. The D minor theme is stated by the clarinets and bassoons in a stately manner, similar to the Sarabande in Handel's *Harpsichord Suite, Vol. 2, No. 3*, HWV 436. The variations, each lasting less than a minute, alternate between those for full orchestra and those for one to four soloists and accompaniment by either the full orchestra or just strings or winds. In the variations featuring the full orchestra—such as No. 5, the somewhat martial No. 8, No. 13 (foreshadowing Philip Glass with its constant arpeggios), and the gigue-like No. 24—he is able to achieve tonal colors worthy of Beethoven. Others that stand out are No. 4 for harp; No. 10, which features the percussion instruments; the Italian concerto grosso-like No. 11; No. 17, wherein the woodwinds pass the melody figure to each other from high to low, flute to bassoon, to tympani; and No. 18, which has two distant violins echoing the full orchestra. The final variation goes through all the soloists once more, for good measure, then into a full orchestral coda that makes its way to D major with the call of the horns and flourishes of the violin and harp. *—Patsy Morita*

Recommended:

- ○ **Salieri: Symphonies, Overtures** / Bamert (cond.), London Mozart Players / 2001 / Chandos 9877
- ○ **Salieri: The 2 Piano Concertos** / Spada (cond.), Philharmonia / 1996 / ASV 955

Aulis Sallinen

b. Apr. 9, 1935, Salmi, Finland

Composer: Opera, Symphonic, Chamber Music

Aulis Sallinen is one of the most prominent figures in Finnish music, and his music often focuses on figures from Finnish history. While his lyric writing shows a strong Sibelius influence, there is also a certain acerbic touch in both his subject matter and his music that is strongly reminiscent of Prokofiev, Shostakovich, and Weill. His opera *The Red Line*, in particular, has a sardonic, slightly bitter tone that strongly resembles Shostakovich's *Lady Macbeth of Mtsensk*. Like Weill, he also used jazz elements, as in the ironic song in *Kullervo* in which Kullervo learns that he has slept with his own sister.

He first studied the violin and then piano, and his interest in composing began when he started improvising jazz and themes and variations on the piano. At the Sibelius Academy in Helsinki, he studied composition under Aarre Merikanto and Joonas Kokkonen, and upon graduating, was the Administrator of the Finnish Radio Symphony, a position he held for nearly ten years. His first published composition was his 1962 *Mauermusik*, a tribute to a young German man who was killed while trying to cross the Berlin Wall. It is a powerful work with highly expressive writing, and brought him to international attention. Aside from its political content, it was hailed as an example of how contemporary classical music can be expressive and approachable. In 1963, he returned to the Academy as a professor, a post which he held for thirteen years.

His first operatic composition, *Ratsumies*, was written for the Savonlinna Opera Festival, and premiered in 1974. It was a major success, and many attributed the sudden spurt of major Finnish opera productions to its success, and that of Kokkonen's *Viimeiset kiusaukset.* This was followed by a commission for the Finnish National Opera, *Punainen viiva* (The red line), for which he wrote the libretto himself, and was premiered in 1978. It was also successful, and in 1981 he was named Professor of Arts for Life by the Finnish government. His next opera, *Kunningas lahtee Raskaan* (The King goes to France), was a joint commission from the Covent Garden, the BBC, and the Savonlinna Opera Festival, where it premiered in 1984. His fourth work, *Kullervo,* based on the legend that inspired Sibelius to one of his great nationalist works, was originally written for the Finnish National Opera, but since the opening of their new house was delayed, it was instead premiered in Los Angeles (1992).

In contrast to his operas, which are nearly all somber, even bleak, his instrumental and orchestral music has a strong spiritual element and is often even rhapsodic, as in his *Chamber Music II* or *Sunrise Serenade,* or even playful, as in the *Nocturnal Dances.* While his symphonies are generally more austere, particularly the Fifth and Sixth, they, too, show a strong lyrical element, reminiscent of *Sibelius.* As the title of the *Sunrise Serenade* suggests, he often finds the inspiration for these works in visual elements rather than dramatic or episodic ones. *—Ann Feeney*

OPERA

Ratsumies (The Horseman) (1973–1974)

The 1970s marked the rise of Finnish opera composing to international attention, and this opera (Sallinen's first), as well as *Viimeiset kiusaukets* (The Last Temptations) by Sallinen's teacher Joonas Kokkonen, and Aarre Merikanto's *Juha,* is one of the milestones of the decade. It was commissioned by Martti Talvela for the Savonlinna Opera Festival to commemorate the castle's 500th anniversary and was immediately hailed as a musical and dramatic success. The libretto is by Paavo Haavikko, arguably Finland's most prominent poet of the time, and combines symbolism and highly poetic, even literary, language with a stark, oppressive story, unfolding in a lurching, somewhat surreal manner that mixes folkish legend and rustic superstition with expressionist angst and disjunction. Sallinen's setting matches it with the music largely written in a highly lyrical style reminiscent not only of Sibelius, but at times of Puccini, and is accented by sardonic discords and bursts of percussion that hint at Shostakovich. He reused three of the four *Dream Songs,* which he wrote in 1972 to Haavikko texts, and they mesh easily with the rest of the writing in almost the same rhapsodic vein. (Sallinen has even been criticized for writing music that is too accessible, "fur hat" overly traditional, and folklike operas, but his response has typically been that nothing goes out of fashion faster than the radical.) Sallinen used several different methods to create a unified work, including repeated tonal and rhythmic motifs as well as recurrent melodies. Unlike his later works, he did not heavily rely on references to or borrowing from other styles; while there are quotations from church music and folksong, they are far more limited here. The work won the Nordic Council Music Prize in 1978. *—Ann Feeney*

Synopsis:

Act One. It is near Easter, and in the house of a wealthy merchant in Novgorod, Annti (the eponymous Horseman) and his wife Anna work as slaves. While Annti is out, the Merchant forces Anna to sleep with him. Annti comes looking for Anna just as the Merchant's wife arrives at the house; she suggests he take on the traditional role of the Bear, who visits at Easter looking for a maiden, dispensing prophetic wisdom, and dancing and singing. Encountering Annti disguised as the Bear, the Merchant becomes suspicious, but when his wife encourages him to kill both Anna and Annti, he tells the Bear to tie her up instead. Annti does so, but craftily tangles the Merchant in the same rope. They set fire to the house, leaving the Merchant and his wife trapped inside; as they flee, Annti is haunted by terrible visions.

Act Two. In a courtroom in Savonlinna, before the Judge stands a Woman accused of bearing a child out of wedlock and leaving it in the woods to die. She claims the child was the result of a rape by a dark, mysterious stranger who accosted her in the woods. Next before the judge is the Yeoman, who has come to claim ownership of a horse in the courtyard; he insists it is the horse he sent to war with a man who never returned. The judge, however, says the horse is his, purchased from a horseman. Anna appears in the court next, hoping to conceal her identity and claim the charitable benefits of legally recognized widowhood. Annti appears, disguised as an old man, to vouch for her. The people in the gallery seem to recognize him, though, while the previous woman thinks he is the rapist, the Yeoman sees him as the man who left to war with his horse, the Judge thinks he is the man who sold him the horse. Anna confesses to the scheme, and they are thrown into the dungeon. They escape, however, when the Judge comes to see the Woman and is overpowered by the prisoners.

Act Three. Anna, Annti, the Woman, and the Yeoman have taken residence at a hut in the forest of Sääminki with a mentally deranged thief named Matti. The Yeoman is organizing an uprising against the Court of Liistonsaari and has gathered a band of peasants together. They elect Annti as their leader, a role he accepts quite unwillingly. He devises a scheme in which the women will appear at the gates begging for entry, while the men approach underneath a camouflaged net, ready to attack. Unfortunately for them, the plan has been leaked, and the men are counterattacked and killed. In the final scene, Anna sings a lullaby for the dead Horseman, whose specter haunts her still. *—Jeremy Grimshaw*

Recommended:

○ **Sallinen: Horseman** / Söderblom (cond), Savonlinna Opera Festival Orch. / Finlandia 101

Punainen Viiva (The Red Line), Op. 46 (1978)

In the last half of the twentieth century, Finland's composers were among the most prolific sources of new operas. Much of this started in the late 1970s and early 1980s, with such works as *Ratsumies, Viimeiset kiusaukset* (The Last Temptations), and Sallinen's *Punainen viiva* (The Red Line). The novel by Ilmari Kianto is considered a national classic in Finland, and despite its relatively timely composition, almost from the moment of its premiere in 1978 at the Finnish National Opera, the opera achieved the same musical status. Sallinen wrote the libretto himself and it, too, has been hailed as a model for capturing the tone and thrust of a literary work while serving as a vehicle for a musical one. The story follows the plight of a destitute farmer who places his only remaining hopes for survival in the upcoming election, in which revolutionary forces promise relief to the poor and equality for all. The heated, but ultimately theoretical political debates taking place throughout the village find dark reflection in a much more immediate and practical concern: the bear who has been venturing out of the woods, threatening their livelihood and safety. Sallinen's first opera, *The Horseman,* had been a major success and *Red Line* cemented his place as a major new composer, both in Finland and on the international scene. In New York, for example, it was hailed in *The New York Times* as one of the best new operas to appear in many years. Despite the sharp-edged and ironic tragedy of the story, Sallinen's writing, though unmistakably modern, is almost without exception tonal and accessible. He skillfully used folk music, hymns, and even an almost plaintone chant, not just to portray the atmosphere of the village but to add a certain element of timelessness to the story, making it less about the specific events and more about the universality of hollow political promises, failure of institutions to help, and the plight of the powerless. While not a pastiche, the music varies strongly from scene to scene, changing from lyrical to stark to powerfully dramatic as the events of each situation dictate. *—Ann Feeney*

Synopsis:

Act One. In the rural woods of Northern Finland in 1907, Topi, a poor farmer, and his wife Riika, can barely scrape together subsistence for themselves and their children. The bear lurking in the nearby woods threatens what little livestock they own. When Topi boasts that he is going to kill the bear, however, Riika scoffs at his delusions. The argument that ensues ends as the wife sends her husband to fetch some grain; he discovers that they have none left, and collapses in despair. His troubles haunt his sleep as well: he dreams that his children have died, and that the priest offers to bury them all in one coffin for a reduced price. He awakes in terror, but remembers with relief that he has a hidden store of game that he can barter in the village. In his absence, a traveling salesman stops by, entertaining the children with odd riddles and speaking excitedly about the prospect of the upcoming election. Later, the village is alive with chatter about the election. The crowd seems swayed by the Agitator, who preached the virtues of social democracy.

Act Two. Topi and Riika have invited friends over to celebrate Twelfth Night, but politics dominate the conversation. The neighbor reads a socialist tract and speaks of the red line with which voters must mark the ballot. Topi confesses that he doesn't even know how to vote—does he mark the ballot with blood? He has never even used a pencil. As they speak, the dogs can be heard barking angrily; they have sensed the bear turning in his sleep. A few months later, Topi and Riika make their way through the boisterous crowds and political rallies to the polling station, where they cast their votes.

Later that spring, Riika is waiting anxiously—both for a hopeful word about the election, and, more urgently, for Topi to return from the logging camp with food. She waits in vain, though; grievously ill and starving, the children are dead by the time Topi returns. As he carries them off to be buried, he hears echoes of the priest's words from the dream: that it will be cheaper to put them in a single coffin. In the tragic epilogue, Topi goes out to kill the bear once and for all, but loses the fight. Riika finds him dead, the blood from his slit throat trickling in a red line across the snow. *—Jeremy Grimshaw*

SYMPHONIC

Symphony No. 4, Op. 49 (1979)

After the passing of Carl Nielsen and the early retirement of Jean Sibelius, there arose a Nordic (a more apt term than "Scandinavian" if one is to include Finland) symphonic school still active and thriving at the beginning of the twenty-first century. Among those quite willing to accept the traditional forms is Finland's Aulis Sallinen (born 1935). Initially a serialist, the composer soon chose to tread the turf of his illustrious countryman Sibelius and then to forge new trails. Sallinen admits that "I am old-fashioned inasmuch as I call a symphonic work a symphony... the symphonic concept is not dead." Exemplary is his *Fourth Symphony*, written to celebrate the 750th anniversary of the city of Turku in 1979.

The work is in three movements. The first commences with a bumptious cabaret tune in the brass; within a few measures it begins to alternate with a grim string threnody. There is an interplay of the two themes as they exchange moods, constantly changing their guises in varied and sparkling orchestral color. Then, at the point where one would expect a development, a third theme, very Nielsen-like in its infectious grace notes, emerges; its presence dominates the entire second half of the movement. Ratchet, xylophone, and other percussion instruments accompany the new theme as it becomes ever more insistent and finally brings the movement to a close. The overall humor and vivacity of the previous movement is dispelled by the middle "Dona nobis pacem" section, a reflection of the composer's world view. Again, Nielsen's presence is felt in the use of a recurrent solo snare drum to represent oppressive forces. Here, however, is no victory over adversity but, perhaps rather a stoic acknowledgement of what would seem an eternal state. The finale begins like a compact counterpart to that of Mahler's *Sixth* with its assemblage of glinting, colorful thematic fragments. These evolve into an animated perpetuum mobile that travels through the bulk of the movement, working up to an anguished climax and then subsiding to the overall mood that runs through to the work's end. The closing pages do not seem to depict despair but are imbued with brooding and mystery, those characteristics thought to be so salient in the Finnish national character. *—Wayne Reisig*

Recommended:

○ **Sallinen: Cello Concerto; Shadows; Symphony 4** / Kamu (cond.), Helsinki PO / Finlandia 346

CHAMBER MUSIC

String Quartet No. 4 ("Quiet Songs") (1971)

Although in the twenty-first century Finnish composer Aulis Sallinen is better known for his stage works, for example the opera *Punainen Viiva (The Red Line)*, he has also written five string quartets of outstanding quality. The most famous of these works is *String Quartet No. 3, "Some Aspects of Peltoniemi Hintrik's Funeral March"* (1969), but arguably the finest is the *String Quartet No. 4, "Quiet Songs"* (1971). It is scored in a single movement of around 12–15 minutes' duration, and, as per the subtitle, is quietly played throughout, with the dynamic level never indicated above mezzo piano. It is a work that is nonetheless pregnant with unresolved tension and a dramatic mood that succeeds in being deeply moving emotionally without being sentimental or sweet. It is stark and grainy like a black-and-white photograph and is somewhat reminiscent of the experience of driving a long distance in a light rainstorm at night.

Sallinen's *String Quartet No. 4, "Quiet Songs,"* is considerably ahead of its time in its forecasting of certain stylistic features one normally associates with post-minimalism, but that's not the only reason that it is a landmark work. In a musical world preoccupied with the chaos and debris of the avant-garde explosion of the 1960s, Aulis Sallinen stepped aside of such concerns and delivered a serious and personal work placed in a familiar, minor-key ambience and performed on conventional instruments. Yet *String Quartet No. 4, "Quiet Songs,"* was not backward-looking, nor did it assert a return to values from the past—it presents a fresh perspective on the string quartet and springs from a renewed understanding of Western Art Music vis-à-vis 1970. Much of the music that followed captured the imagination of the listening public in this vein, or something akin to it. *—Uncle Dave Lewis*

Recommended:

○ **Sallinen & Sibelius: String Quartets** / Fresk Quartet / 1991 / Bluebell 40

○ **Sallinen: String Quartets 1–5** / Jean Sibelius Quartet / Ondine 831

Esa-Pekka Salonen

b. Jun. 30, 1958, Helsinki, Finland

Conductor

Esa-Pekka Salonen emerged as one of the most exciting and fast-rising major conductors of the last two decades of the twentieth century. He entered the Sibelius Academy in Helsinki 1973, studying horn with Holgar Fransman. Having graduated in 1977, Salonen remained to take composition with Einojuhani Rautavaara and conducting with Jorma Panula. He also studied composition with Franco Donatoni in Siena, attended the summer course at Darmstadt, and, from 1980 to 1981, studied with Niccolò Castiglioni.

Salonen originally viewed composition as his main career. His first large-scale orchestral work was the *Concerto for saxophone & orchestra*, "...Auf den esten Blick und ohne zu wissen" (1980–81), based on Kafka's novel *The Trial*. His second orchestral work, *Giro*, dates from 1981.The following year, he composed *Floof* (revised in 1990), a bright work for soprano and ensemble based on texts by the Polish science-fiction writer Stanislaw Lem. This work won the UNESCO Rostrum Prize in 1992. During the 1980s, Salonen composed tape music and music with electronics and instruments combined. Works composed during this period include *Baalal*, a radiophonic piece, and *Yta* (Surface), a series of experimental compositions. Although Salonen's burgeoning conducting career somewhat slowed down his composition output, he continued developing as a composer. His 1996 orchestral piece, *L.A. Variations*, received its triumphant premiere at the Los Angeles Philharmonic in 1997. The following year, he wrote *Gambit*, an orchestral work dedicated to Magnus Lindberg. In 1999, he completed *Five Images after Sappho*, a song cycle for soprano and small ensemble. Salonen's music employs up-to-date compositional techniques within a central tonality.

Salonen started appearing as a horn soloist and guest conductor beginning in 1982. His conducting career took off in 1983, following his sensational London debut with the Philharmonia. Salonen made his American debut conducting the Los Angeles Philharmonic Orchestra in 1984. He received a record contract with CBS Masterworks (now Sony Classical), as well as the position of principal guest conductor of the Philharmonia (1985–94).

One of his early projects with Sony was a recording of Messiaen's *Turangalila* and Lutosławski's *Symphony No. 3*, the latter a world premiere recording that won a Gramophone Award for Best Contemporary Record in 1985. He took a second award in 1989 with the Sibelius and Nielsen violin concertos, featuring Cho-Liang Lin as soloist, and won further awards with the complete Stravinsky works for piano and orchestra, with Paul Crossley as soloist.

As a result of his highly successful performances with the L.A. Philharmonic at the Hollywood Bowl in 1989, Salonen was invited to become the orchestra's music director. He assumed that post in 1992, becoming the orchestra's youngest music director, and a successor to such luminaries as Zubin Mehta and Carlo Maria Giulini. Salonen has led the L.A. Philharmonic on major tours, also making a series of highly acclaimed recordings.

Salonen is known especially for his twentieth century music performances, though he is also praised for his interpretations of Haydn, Mahler, and Beethoven. In addition to established modern composers such as Bartók, Messiaen, Stravinsky, and Hindemith, he also frequently performs more recent masters such as Lutosławski, Ligeti, Lindberg, Saariaho, and Corigliano, whose concerto from the film *The Red Violin* he recorded with violinist Joshua Bell. *—Joseph Stevenson*

Recommended:

○ **Music of Magnus Lindberg** / Salonen (cond.), Karttunen, London PO / 2002 / Sony 89810

○ **Esa-Pekka Salonen: L.A. Variations** / Salonen (cond.), Upshaw, Karttunen, Los Angeles PO, London Sinfonietta / 2001 / Sony 89158

○ **Hermann: Film Scores** / Salonen (cond.), Los Angeles PO / 2000 / Sony 62700

○ **Music of Revueltas** / Salonen (cond.), Los Angeles PO, New Music Group / 1999 / Sony 60676

○ **Lutosławski: Symphonies 3 & 4** / Salonen (cond.), Shirley-Quirk, Los Angeles PO / 1994 / Sony 66280

○ **Sibelius: Kullervo** / Salonen (cond.), Rorholm, Hynninen, Los Angeles PO / 1993 / Sony 52563

○ **Adams: Naïve & Sentimental Music** / Salonen (cond.), Tanenbaum, Los Angeles PO / 2002 / Nonesuch 79636

○ **Saariaho: Château de l'âme; Graal Théâtre; Amers** / Salonen (cond.), Upshaw, Kremer, Karttunen, BBCSO, Finnish RSO, Avanti CO / 2001 / Sony 60817

Carlos Salzedo

b. Apr. 6, 1885, Arcachon, France, **d.** Aug. 17, 1961, Waterville, ME

Composer: Chamber Music

Carlos Salzédo was the foremost harpist of the first half of the twentieth century, and the single most significant composer for the instrument to date. His music is evocative of French Impressionism and technically demanding for the performer, and it breaks new ground in terms of the basic sound world of the harp.

While Salzédo was born in Arcachon, he studied in Bordeaux and, later, at the Paris Conservatoire, from which he graduated with an unprecedented two first prizes: one in harp and one in piano. He moved to New York in 1909, where he was part of the Metropolitan Opera Orchestra through 1913. He later performed with various chamber music ensembles, for which he also composed works, including the *Sonata for Harp and Piano* (1925) and his *Concerto No. 1 for Harp and Seven Winds* (1925–26). One of these ensembles was the flute-cello-harp Trio de Lutèce, with Georges Berrère and Paul Kéfer; another was the Salzédo Harp Ensemble. The Trio had traveled to Europe, combining a tour with Salzédo's honeymoon with his first wife, when World War I broke out. Salzédo briefly served in the French army, surprisingly as cook for his unit.

In 1921 Salzédo helped Edgard Varèse to establish the International Composer's Guild, and from 1921 to 1932 served as editor of the *Eolian Review*, which focused on new music. Salzédo helped to establish the harp department at the Curtis Institute for Music (Philadelphia) in 1924 and was responsible several years later for the Salzédo Harp Colony in Camden, ME. He would spend winters teaching in

Philadelphia and New York (at Juilliard), summers in Maine. The school in Maine was run by his protégée Alice Chalifoux after his death.

Salzédo's output is almost exclusively devoted to the harp, and as an exceptional performer, he knew well how to write for the instrument. In addition to his compositions, Salzédo contributed several pedagogical works to the harp literature, including his *Modern Study of the Harp* (1921, revised 1948) and the *Method for Harp* (1929). He left unfinished a second *Concerto for Harp*, which was completed in 1966 by the gifted American musician Richard Rodney Bennett. *—James Zychowicz*

Overview of Works (ca. 1913–1960)

When it came to promoting the general welfare of his own instrument—the concert harp—Carlos Salzedo seemed to be everywhere. Between his graduation from the Paris Conservatoire in 1901 and his death in rural Maine in 1961 he managed to completely overhaul the harp's status in modern music-making. In his hands, and through his own compositions, it became a real solo instrument, capable of expression beyond that previously thought possible; he designed a new model of harp, and he wrote treatises on various aspects of high-level harp technique. As happens to many virtuoso performers who write their own music, Salzedo was not generally considered a composer in his own right; but his catalog of works is a healthy one, full not only of solo harp vehicles but also a dozen and more chamber and concerted items.

Salzedo's most ambitious works are the symphonic tone poem *Terres enchantées* (The enchanted Isle, 1918) for orchestra and harp obbligato (first performed by the Chicago Symphony Orchestra with Salzedo playing the harp in 1919), and the two harp concertos—the first of which was written in 1926, and the second of which was still incomplete upon Salzedo's death. The famed English orchestrator and composer Richard Rodney Bennett completed the *Second Concerto*'s orchestration in 1966.

The works for solo harp are extremely varied in character and far too numerous to deal with individually here, but some representative examples include the 1937 suite *Panorama*, the early, lush *Trois Morceaux* of 1913, and the *Five Poetical Studies*. His textbook on playing technique, *Modern Study of Harp*, appeared in 1921.

Rather more fascinating are the many pieces that Salzedo composed for ensembles involving multiple harpists. He and his wife Marjorie Call performed for a time as a harp duo, and no doubt their repertoire included Salzedo's humorously titled *Four Preludes to the Afternoon of a Telephone* for harp duo (1921). *Pentacle* (1928) is another two-harp piece. The *Three Poems* of 1919 require the bizarre combination of soprano, six harps, and three wind players; even more harpists—seven to be exact—are required for *Bolmimerie*, also from 1919.

Salzedo's harp music is silken-textured in a recognizably French way (he was French by birth). There are occasional dissonances and unusual performance effects (for example, percussive parts played on his own special-model harp), but there can be no doubt that, for all his appreciation for and championship of new music, he was a man firmly rooted in the nineteenth century. *—Blair Johnston*

Recommended:

○ **Salzedo: Works for Solo Harp** / Giles / 1994 / Koch 312232

CHAMBER MUSIC

Scintillation, for harp (1936)

Salzedo wrote *Scintillation* in September 1936 after a trip to Mexico, where he was heavily influenced by the Spanish colors and rhythms he encountered in his wanderings.

In *Scintillation*, Salzedo develops established dance patterns, such as the sarabande in the opening leading to a rumba section. Then comes the "scintillating" portion of the piece—the composer works a consistent glissando that relies almost solely on pedal changes to vary the music, and sometimes three pedals at once are changed to achieve the effects he sought. This leads to a tango-like section and the piece ends with triumphant flourishes.

The work highlights techniques that Salzedo helped establish, such as using the fingernails for specific color applications and employing lots of harmonics. Salzedo wrote *Scintillation* as a showpiece vehicle for his own considerable and celebrated skills as a virtuoso, and it remains at the pinnacle of a harpist's career to master it. *—Gerald Brennan*

Recommended:

○ **Scintillation** / Kondonassis / 1993 / Telarc 80361

○ **Harp Showpieces** / Loman / 2000 / Naxos 554347

Giovanni Battista Sammartini

b. ca. 1700, Milan [?], Italy, **d.** Jan. 15, 1775, Milan, Italy

Composer: Symphonic, Chamber Music

Giovanni Sammartini, not to be confused with his brother Giuseppe Sammartini, also a composer, is widely regarded as "the father of the symphony." While he may not have invented the form, he was the first composer to master it and helped establish it as a separate entity from its direct ancestor, the opera overture. The spirit of Classicism is present in the earliest datable works of Sammartini, which represented a distinct break from Baroque traditions. Sammartini's influence on composers such as Christoph Willibald Gluck, Johann Christian Bach, and Luigi Boccherini has long been acknowledged, and even though Franz Josef Haydn disdained the shadow cast by Sammartini in reference to his own work, its presence is unmistakable. Giovanni Sammartini lived his entire life in Milan and was that city's most famous composer in the eighteenth century. By the time he was named maestro di cappella of the Congregazione SS Entierro in 1728, he was already "famous" as a composer of sacred music, most of which, unfortunately, is lost. He held the post at SS Entierro until ill health likely forced him to retire in 1773.

Sammartini's earliest-known symphonies date from around 1732 and the last from 1772; authentic Sammartini symphonies are 67 in number and are generally divided into three phases; early (18 symphonies, 1732–1739), middle (37 symphonies, 1740–1758), and late (12 symphonies, 1759–1772). An additional 75 symphonies attributed to Sammartini are either spurious or lost. One can trace the development of Classical style through this important cycle of works: the early symphonies reveal traces of Baroque influences, whereas the middle-period works dispense with these elements and add two horns to the ensemble. The late symphonies are longer, and yet more wind instruments are added to the texture, and the continuo is retired for good through his separation of the cello and bass parts. In addition to the symphonies, 31 concerti of Sammartini have been authenticated, and Sammartini deserves to be credited with helping foster the form of the classical symphony concertante. His orchestral music has a driving rhythmic profile and certain minor key works look forward to the Sturm und Drang style of the later classical era. Although it is said in some sources that he produced a four-movement symphony in the 1730s, it is clear that he favored three- and even two-movement symphonies throughout his life.

Sammartini also composed a wealth of chamber music, actually comprising the major part of his surviving output—he only composed three operas, and preferred to contribute an aria here and there to already existing works over composing whole operas. Sammartini's chamber music is of the highest quality and merits revival. *—Uncle Dave Lewis*

SYMPHONIC

Symphonies (ca. 1730–1750)

Although little-known today, the Milanese composer Giovanni Battista Sammartini (1700–75) was in his day a respected and influential composer who played a major role in the development of the symphony. To the Bohemian composer Myslivecek, who heard some of Sammartini's symphonies in Milan, he was indeed the true "father of the symphony," a man who, as he later suggested to Haydn, was the progenitor of the great Austrian's own symphonic style. Haydn's well-known response that Sammartini was "a scribbler" whose music he knew, but had never regarded highly was in some ways legitimate; his formative influences came from much further north—the symphonies of C.P.E. Bach. Yet there can be little doubt that Sammartini's earliest symphonies (probably composed in the early 1730s) predate those of the better-known Mannheim and Viennese schools. Later his works would come to have a profound influence on those of another of Bach's sons, Johann Christian (who was resident in Milan from 1757 to 1761), and by descent through him to the early symphonies of Mozart.

Thanks to the catalog prepared by Newell Jenkins and Bathia Churgin (the origin of their JC numbering), nearly 70 symphonies by Sammartini have been authenticated. The earlier symphonies are invariably scored for strings and continuo, and are cast in three movements with the single exception of a *Symphony in G* (JC 39), which adds a Minuetto to the expected Allegro finale. The absence of other examples has led commentators to suggest that this movement was added later by a copyist. Both this work and a brief *Symphony in D* (JC 14) display the hallmarks of Sammartini's style. The opening allegros announce themselves with a strong chordal "call to attention" before proceeding to present clear cut and contrasted themes; the periodic phrasing and dynamic contrasts mark a distinctive break from Baroque traditions. The thematic development that would come to play such an important role in the development of sonata form is present, although fairly rudimentary at this stage. The central slow movements are cast in an easy-going, warmly expressive cantabile style that owes much to the influence of Italian opera, while the lively finales are in triple time, and are also indebted to the stage, in this instance the bustling world of opera buffa. Later symphonies include wind instruments, for which Sammartini wrote with considerable facility. His writing is also notable for greatly enhancing the normally subservient role of the second violins, which frequently exchange thematic material with the first violins. Fresh, open, and melodically appealing, Sammartini's symphonies deserve greater attention than they have been accorded. *—Brian Robins*

Recommended:

○ **Sammartini: Symphonies & Overtures** / Gini (cond.), Bianchi, Orch. da Camera Milano Classica / 2002 / Dynamic 414

CHAMBER MUSIC

Cello Sonata in G major

A favorite among cellists, the work known as the Sammartini *Sonata for cello in G major* is definitely not by Sammartini. First of all, as Sammartini scholar Bathia Churgin asserted, the style is not Sammartini's. In fact, scholars attribute this piece to the French cellist and composer Martin Berteau (1709–71), one of the founders of the French cello tradition. According to Churgin, when this sonata first appeared, it was attributed to "Martino." Since Sammartini was also known as Martino, or Martini, Berteau's work became accepted as the Sammartini Sonata. In every way representative of the French virtuoso style, also exemplified by the by the elegantly and charming works by Jean-Baptiste Bréval, the *Sonata for cello in G major* opens with an expansive theme that, quickly moving from the middle to the higher register of the instrument, reveals the newly discovered sonic space of the instrument beyond the fourth position. Clearly exemplifying the new musical language, this movement features concise, well-defined thematic elements. Defined but not limited by a clear formal structure, the music moves briskly, even breathlessly, using several cadences as stepping stones toward higher levels of energy. In the second movement, the dominant atmosphere, in stark contrast to the previous movement, is languid, melancholy, and pensive. Moving to a lower, mellower register, the soloist is given the freedom to relax and explore the darker sonorities of the instrument. However, the somewhat dreamy feeling of timeless repose is sharply interrupted when the final movement literally forces the soloist to move forward, almost outpacing the accompanist. There is no repose in this movement. Like in the first movement, the themes are clearly defined, even somewhat schematic; but the music, almost suggesting a capriccio, relentlessly continues with extensive stretches in the higher register that finally lead, with increasing energy, to a brilliantly assertive conclusion. Like Bréval's works, the Sonata for cello in G major seamlessly balances the higher register with the fundamental sonority of the cello, elegantly demonstrating the natural sonic potential of the thumb position. *—Zoran Minderovic*

Recommended:

- ○ **Leonard Rose: Schubert, Boccherini & Sammartini Sonatas** / Rose, Hambro / 2001 / Sony 89749

San Francisco Symphony Orchestra

f. 1911, San Francisco, CA

Ensemble

San Francisco's population exploded during the 1849 Gold Rush. It quickly became the trading, entertainment, and arts center of the Far West, with a solid tradition of German-style choral societies and a symphony society. In 1906, civic leaders decided to establish a permanent orchestra; the San Francisco Symphony gave its first concert in December 1911, with the composer Henry Hadley at the podium. The 1915 Panama-Pacific Exposition allowed for appearances by guest orchestras, and local supporters soon realized that the San Francisco Symphony was not on a par with these groups. They then engaged Alfred Hertz, the conductor of German repertory at the Metropolitan Opera in New York, as the new music director. He stayed through 1929 and was succeeded by Basil Cameron and Isaay Dubrowen.

Much of the orchestra's history is connected to opera. Gaetano Merola founded the San Francisco Opera Company in 1923. In 1932 both organizations moved into the beautiful War Memorial Opera House. But in 1934 the orchestra's deficits, partly a result of the Great Depression, forced the Musical Association of San Francisco (the SFS's corporate identity) to declare bankruptcy and cancel its season. However, the opera was able to continue. In 1935 the citizens of San Francisco ratified an amendment to the city charter establishing municipal funding for the Symphony, with the stipulation that the orchestra would establish a series of municipal concerts. The orchestra organization, now known as the San Francisco Symphony Association, was reestablished in 1935. In the same year it hired Pierre Monteux as its conductor. In 1950 Arthur Fiedler began an annual series of summer Pops concerts (part of the municipal series). Monteux was succeeded by Enrique Jordá (1954), Josef Krips (19863), Seiji Ozawa (1970), and Edo de Waart (1977).

However, the orchestra suffered from its relationship with the Opera, which included sharing a venue and a substantial number of personnel. Traditionally, the Opera maintained an autumn season from September to December and in 1960 added a short Spring season, leaving the SFS only a short season from December to May. In 1973 plans began for a permanent symphony hall, culminating in the opening of Davies Symphony Hall in 1980 and the expansion of the SFS to a 52-week season. The Concerts Arts Orchestra of San Francisco was founded to provide accompaniment for opera and ballet. With the newly expanded season, the SFS inaugurated the "New and Unusual Music" series planned by its New Music Adviser, John Adams. Herbert Blomstedt's tenure (1984–94) lifted the orchestra to its highest standards, and yielded several excellent recordings. His successor, Michael Tilson Thomas, had to endure a long and potentially crippling strike in 1996. However, the labor issues were resolved, and the SFS has since maintained the high standards, fine recordings, and adventuresome programming that have become its tradition. *—Joseph Stevenson*

Recommended:

- ○ **Mahler: Symphony 1** / Tilson Thomas (cond.), San Francisco SO / San Francisco Symphony 0002
- ○ **Mahler: Symphony 3** / Tilson Thomas (cond.), George, DeYoung, San Francisco SO / 2002 / San Francisco Symphony 3
- ○ **Adams: Harmonium** / de Waart (cond.), George, San Francisco SO / 1984 / ECM 821465
- ○ **Pierre Monteux Conducts** / Monteux (cond.), San Francisco SO / Preiser 90563
- ○ **Hindemith: Orchestral Works** / Blomstedt (cond.), Suske, Funke, Walther, Freiberger, San Francisco SO, Gewandhaus / Decca 000201102
- ○ **Mahler: Symphony 4** / Tilson Thomas (cond.), Bennett, Giacobassi, Barantschik, McKee, San Francisco SO / San Francisco Symphony 4

Samuel Sanders

b. Jun. 27, 1937, New York. NY, **d.** Jul. 9, 1999, New York, NY

Pianist

Samuel Sanders is widely regarded as one of the most respected collaborative pianists of the twentieth century. He was born with a congenital heart condition that required him to undergo surgery at the age of nine. He studied at Hunter College and at the Juilliard School under Sergius Kagen and Irwin Freundlich. Sanders was famous for the loyalty of his collaborators. He accompanied violinist Itzhak Perlman from 1966 until 1999, during which time the duo recorded a dozen recordings, two of which were awarded Grammys. He also performed with Pinchas Zukerman, Jaime Laredo, Paula Robison, Robert White, Yo-Yo Ma, Joshua Bell, Mstislav Rostropovich, Hermann Baumann, Jacqueline Du Pré, Leonard Rose, Kyung-Wha Chung, Eugenia Zukerman, Jessye Norman, and Chilean cellist Andres Diaz, with whom he formed the Diaz-Sanders Duo. Sanders was the founder and artistic director of the Cape and Islands Chamber Music Festival in Cape Cod, MA. He performed with numerous string quartets, including the Lark, Colorado, Fine Arts, Borromeo, and Juilliard. He appeared with the Chamber Music Society of Lincoln Center and at major American festivals, including Lincoln Center's Mostly Mozart, Tanglewood, Marlboro, Ravinia, Saratoga, Spoleto (U.S. and Italy), and Wolf Trap. Sanders received an honorary award at the 1966 Tchaikovsky International Competition in Moscow and performed numerous times at the White House for five different presidents. He received honorary doctorates from Lehman College and the St. Louis Conservatory, and taught for more than three decades at the Juilliard School, where he helped found a degree program for collaborative pianists. *—Robert Adelson*

Recommended:

- ○ **Encores** / Perlman, Sanders / 2003 / EMI 62596
- ○ **The Kreisler Album** / Perlman, Sanders / 2003 / EMI Classics 62601
- ○ **Homage to Pablo De Sarasate** / Barton, Sanders / 1994 / Dorian 90183
- ○ **Mathé Plays Kreisler** / Mathé, Sanders / 1996 / Dorian 90231

György Sándor

b. Sep. 21, 1912, Budapest, Hungary

Pianist

György Sándor is an internationally respected pianist and piano teacher, especially known for his recordings of music of Bartók and Prokofiev. His cousin Arpád Sándor (1896–1972) was a noted pianist and music critic who toured widely as accompanist to such leading artists as Jascha Heifetz and Lily Pons. György studied at the Liszt Academy of Music in Budapest as a piano pupil of Béla Bartók and composition student of Zoltán Kodály. He made his concert debut in Budapest in 1930 and toured widely through Europe until 1939. In that year Sándor left for the United States. He became a naturalized citizen of that country in 1943.

In the competitive world of U.S. concert life at that time (when many great European artists escaped war-torn Europe), he began to reestablish his career. By the end of World War II he was positioned to begin a successful international touring career that took him to all the major musical centers of the West. In 1945 he played the first performance of Bartók's piano transcription of his orchestra work *Dance Suite* and in 1946 made the premiere the composer's posthumous masterpiece, the *Third Piano Concerto.* In 1956 he joined the faculty of Southern Methodist University in Dallas, TX, remaining there until 1961. In that year he moved to the University of Michigan, Ann Arbor, as director of graduate studies in piano. In those years he began making recordings, often for the Vox label. He produced noted *Vox Boxes* of the complete piano music of Bartók (wining the Grand Prix du Disque) and Prokofiev. For Vox's sister label Turnabout he produced the complete piano works of Kodály. Thirty years later he produced another recording of the complete Bartók for Sony Classical. In 1981 he published a book, *On Piano Playing: Motion, Sound, and Expression.* In 1982 he left Ann Arbor to join the piano faculty of the Juilliard School of Music in New York.

He tours widely and frequently is asked to serve as a juror in major international piano competitions. In addition, he has given master classes in institutions including the Paris Conservatory, Indiana University School of Music, the Jerusalem Music Center, the Assisi Festival, and the Mozarteum in Salzburg. His publications include bravura piano transcriptions of Dukas' *The Sorcerer's Apprentice*, Bach's *Chaconne and Fugue*, and selections of Bartók's *44 Violin Duos*. In 1982 he was presented with Hungary's highest award for artistic achievement. In the 1990s his activities in the recording studios increased, with recordings of Bartók's complete piano concertos joining his catalog of the Rachmaninov *Second*, and numerous works by Bach, Chopin, Schumann, Liszt, and the complete sets already noted.

Sándor cautions young pianists that the style of Bartók piano playing that arose in the decades after the master's death is inauthentic; that the composer wished a lyrical, elastic tempo with an emphasis on the melodic line. His later Bartók recordings are intended to exemplify the music as he learned it from Bartók himself. *—Joseph Stevenson*

Recommended:

○ **Bartok: Complete Solo Piano Music** / Sandor / 2003 / Vox 3610

○ **Sandor Plays Prokofiev Vol. 1** / Sandor / 1993 / Vox 3500

○ **Bartok: Piano Concertos** / Sandor / Sony 45835

Gaspar Sanz

b. Apr. 4, 1640, Calanda, Spain, **d.** 1710, Madrid, Spain

Composer: Chamber Music

It is generally accepted that composer Gaspar Sanz was born on April 4, 1640, in Calanda in the region of Aragon, Spain. As a young man, he received a bachelor of theology degree and subsequently took the vows of Holy Orders from the University of Salamanca. But the spirituality of music would become a second vocation for Sanz and he journeyed to Italy to study music with Cristofaro Caresana and Lelio Colista, as well as (speculatively) Orazio Benevoli and Pietro Andrea Ziani. Upon his return to Spain, he pursued literature, religion, and music in equal measure with, respectively, a translation of Bartoli (1678), a eulogy to Pope Innocent XI (1681), and his musical magnum opus in the three-volume *Instruccion de musica sobre la guitarra Espanola*. His musical prowess soon came to loom over his other achievements, becoming widely regarded as the foremost guitar theorist of his day as well as private instructor of guitar to Don Juan of Austria, the dedicatee of his *Instruccion*. A complete musician, Sanz was also organist to the viceroy of Napoles. He is believed to have died in Madrid in 1710.

By the time Sanz began his work, the guitar in its evolution had acquired a fifth course (string pair) and settled into the fourths-oriented tuning that led to the modern six-string guitar as is known today, the octave pairing of the lower strings surviving in the modern 12-string guitar. Sanz took advantage of these developments in the 90 pieces that comprise the three volumes of *Instruccion*. The result is of two-fold musical importance. First, the capabilities of the guitar, by this time achieving a status comparable to the lute as a serious instrument, were extended, moving away from the single-line melodic stretches punctuated by chords; although the said idiom may be found in the first volume, geared toward the novice, the subsequent volumes find writing for more active right-hand technique, independence of the thumb and fingers, and more varied and at times contrapuntal texture. All this is prefaced in the first volume by a tutorial, a manual for care of the instrument, and an essay on figured bass for the guitar. The music in the three volumes is written in tablature, although later arrangements for standard notation have since been made. The second great significance of the Sanz set is that it contains many examples of Spanish folk songs and dances, exposing these to the world at large. Some, like the *Zarabanda*, feature an alternation of meters that presage the flamenco guitar idiom. Also can be found are the more conventional forms of passacaglia, pavan, and galliard, as well as travel souvenirs such as a Neopolitan piece. Together, these reveal Gaspar Sanz to be a well-rounded and cosmopolitan musician for his time, as well as a prophet for an instrument that would one day rival the keyboard in popularity. *—Wayne Reisig*

CHAMBER MUSIC

Canarios (1674)

This lively, brief composition for solo guitar is one of 90 pieces of varying complexity to be found in the composer's masterpiece collection *Instrucción de música sobre la guitarra española y método de sus primeros rudimentos hasta tañerla con destreza* (Music instruction manual on the Spanish guitar and method on the first rudiments that concern playing with dexterity) that was published in three volumes between the years 1674 and 1697.

As indicated by the title, this piece is a dance from the Canary Islands (Islas Canarias), a Spanish possession off the southeast coast of Spain and nearer to the western Sahara desert in Africa. It flows along in a joyous triple meter with the melody in the upper voice at the beginning. Sprinkled throughout the tune are small turning embellishments, usually at the ends of phrases, that give the melody a certain elasticity and additional mirth while not actually ritarding the pulse. The first part of the melody gradually ascends by triplet patterns and the second half provides a symmetrical complement built of descending triplet patterns and grounding the dance from high steps to a kind of shuffling motion.

The recapitulation of the melody features imitation, questions, and answers between the upper and lower voices. There is a brief modulation into a close key, and then the tonic note is brilliantly trumpeted as a repeated treble octave (inverted pedal point) while arpeggios roll beneath. Again, a descending passage occurs as a balance and slight retreat from the ecstasy of the initial phrases. This last section is extended into more introspective gestures, and, with a bit of nostalgic reflection, the piece concludes calmly after slightly more than a minute's duration. *—"Blue Gene" Tyranny*

Recommended:

○ **Canto Mediterraneo** / Laurens, Sempe, Capriccio Stravagante / 2001 / Astrée 8870

○ **Spanish Guitar Music** / Williams / 2002 / Legacy 89837

Instrucción de Música sobre la Guitarra Española, Books 1–3 (1674–1697)

Among his varied accomplishments, Padre Gaspar Sanz (active in the seventeenth century) is chiefly remembered for his advocacy of and contribution to the literature of the guitar. This came at a time when that instrument was starting to ascend to a more prestigious position, similar to that held by the lute. Along with contemporary Robert DeVisée, Sanz inherited an instrument that had undergone significant physical change as well. The addition of a fifth course (string pair) greatly extended the guitar's sonorities, and it began its evolution from mere accompaniment to solo status.

Sanz's three-volume *Instrucción de Música sobre la Guitarra Española* is not only worthy for adding extensively to solo guitar literature but is also recognized as a source of contemporary Spanish dances and folk songs. In addition to such examples as "Españoletas," "Paradetas," and "Dance de la Hachas," one may also find applications to more cosmopolitan forms such as the Pavan, Galliard, and Passacaglia, and even an occasional "souvenir" such as "La Esfachata de Napoles." Largely these hundred-odd pages of short pieces show the guitar to be still in the shadow of the lute when it came to technique. Tablature in lieu of standard notation is used (although transcription to the latter has been common). Likewise showing the music's debt to the older style is the fact that melodic stretches are punctuated by chords, or else block chordal harmony accompanies each note of melody. However, some of the pieces, like the "Gallarda" in D, show an investigation of more pronounced contrapuntal procedure, which would come into fruition in the early nineteenth century with Sor and Giuliani. As such, the Sanz collection is a pivotal work for the performers and admirers of the guitar. *—Wayne Reisig*

Recommended:

○ **Spanish Guitar Music** / Williams / 1990 / Sony 46347

○ **Instrucción de Música sobre la Guitarra Española** / Fresno / MP Classics 11022

Pablo de Sarasate

b. Mar. 10, 1844, Pamplona, Spain, **d.** Sep. 20, 1908, Biarritz, France

Composer: Chamber Music, Concerto

Pablo de Sarasate was born Pablo Martin Melton Sarasate y Navascuez, the son of a local military bandmaster in the Spanish town of Pamplona, where each July brings the Fiesta de San Fermín and its notorious "running of the bulls." Sarasate demonstrated musical talent very early and began violin lessons at age five. Making his concert debut at eight, Sarasate went to Madrid to study with violinist Manuel Rodriguez Sáez. The boy proved a sensation at the court of Queen Isabel II.

When Sarasate was 12, he and his mother set out for Paris on a journey meant to advance his skills on the violin. But the mother expired of a heart attack on the train en route, and Sarasate himself was diagnosed with cholera. Upon recovery, Sarasate was sent on to Paris; finally he auditioned successfully for Jean-Delphin Alard, violin instructor at the Paris Conservatoire. After five years of study with Alard, Sarasate won the Conservatoire's annual first prize. Thus was launched one of the most exciting and enduring violin careers of the nineteenth century.

Beginning in 1859, Sarasate embarked on a world tour that ran, more or less continuously, for three decades. During a tour of the United States, American artist James McNeill Whistler painted a famous portrait of Sarasate entitled *Arrangements in Black*. His first appearance in Britain was received with indifference, but a return visit in 1874 yielded better results, and composer Alexander Mackenzie composed a violin concerto for Sarasate that was heard at the Birmingham Festival of 1885. He even became a star in Germany and Austria, where his easy virtuosity might have seemed out of step with German music's more cerebral mainstream. Several of the works written for Sarasate have become staples of violin repertoire, including Lalo's *Symphonie espagnole* and *F minor Concerto*, Saint-Saëns' *Introduction and Rondo Capriccioso* and his First and Third *Violin Concerti*, Bruch's *Second Violin Concerto* and the *Scottish Fantasy*.

Of Sarasate's 57 known compositions, many of which served him well in his own concerts, the majority have been forgotten; they were fashioned in a style that reached little beyond its own time. The *Zigeunerweisen*, Op. 20, remain an indispensable item in the violinist's repertory, however, and his splashy *Spanish Dances*, Opp. 21–23 and 26, still furnish enjoyable diversions in the course of many a violin recital. Sarasate's *Carmen Fantasy*, Op. 25 is likewise a violin standard, and suggests Sarasate's role in transmitting Spanish idioms to greater Europe. Sarasate was not a mainstream Romantic virtuoso in the mold of Joseph Joachim and did not play the Brahms concerto; he played with a lighter touch, and preferred lighter fare.

Sarasate made nine phonograph records in 1904, when he was 60. It is easy to hear from them what made Sarasate such an exciting performer; four decades as a touring concert artist had dimmed his powers very little. Though Sarasate had basically retired to a villa in the seacoast town ofBiarritz, France, by 1890, he continued keep his chops up, and performed at the Fiesta de San Fermín every year in his hometown of Pamplona. At his death from bronchitis in 1908 at age 64, Sarasate was in possession of two Stradivarius violins; one was bequeathed to the Paris Conservatoire, and the other the Conservatory of Madrid. The remainder of Sarasate's possessions was left to Pamplona, which has erected a museum in his memory. *—Uncle Dave Lewis*

CHAMBER MUSIC

Caprice basque, for violin & piano, Op. 24 (1881)

Although not actually a part of the series of *Spanish Dances* released by Pablo de Sarasate between 1878 and 1882, the *Caprice basque* for violin and piano, Op. 24, of 1881 falls very much in line, musically speaking (and chronologically speaking, for that matter), with those eight folk-dance oriented pieces. In the *Caprice basque* it is not just the shape and genre that are pulled from the Spanish (or in this case Basque) folk catalog, but also the very melodies themselves. The piece is in two halves, the first a Moderato in D minor that moves along atop a stern, peculiarly unsmooth rhythmic ostinato, the second a series of ever more daring and inventive virtuoso variations on an Allegro moderato tune in A minor. Intricate left-hand pizzicati and, at the very end, a high-flying arpeggio excursion up the violin's fingerboard provide plenty of fodder for the technically-minded, but the *Caprice basque* is better than a mere etude—it has, especially in the opening section, a great deal of charm and sophisticated earthiness. *—Blair Johnston*

Recommended:

○ **Virtuoso Violin** / Perlman, Sanders / 2001 / EMI 74765

Danzas españolas, for violin & piano, Opp. 21, 22, 23 & 26 (1878–1882)

Sarasate's first 19 published pieces (out of 54) are, for the most part, fairly routine fantasies on opera themes. The violinist/composer fully came into his own only with his Op. 20, the popular, heart-on-sleeve *Ziguenerweisen* drawn from gypsy music, and then proceeded to capitalize on his Spanish heritage with a long series of folk-inspired pieces. Most notable and durable among these are the *Eight Spanish Dances*, published in pairs and mostly composed in the late 1870s. Sarasate's standard operating procedure was to employ a traditional tune with very little initial embellishment; he would most often simply repeat it in different octaves, adding a few flourishes along the way, ending in the violin's highest range. As mentioned, he paired the dances, the first one usually slow and the second fast and invigorating, the conclusion in almost every case demonstrating that these are virtuoso showpieces for professionals, not quaint splashes of local color for home players. The Op. 21 set consists of a malagueña and a habanera. The former is dedicated to violinist Joseph Joachim; the latter employs a rhythm originally drawn from Cuba. In the Op. 22 set, the "Romanza Andaluza" is slowish and richly ornamented, evoking southern Spain, although it does not employ an actual folk tune. The ensuing "Jota Navarra" (the first of Sarasate's six jotas, including one for two violins) is much more vigorous. Op. 23 begins with a playera, another Andalusian piece, this one with mysterious Moorish overtones. Its companion, a zapateado, is a pounding, perpetual-motion piece, keeping the violin predominantly in its high register with splatters of pizzicato everywhere. The two dances of Op. 26 are merely given numbers; the first is a very free transcription of the song "La Partida" (Farewell) by Fermín María Alvarez linked to a popular song called "El Vito." The second is another habanera, this one more teasing than that in Op. 21. *—James Reel*

Recommended:

○ **Sarasate** / Csury, Simon / Classical Diamonds 4007

Zigeunerweisen, for violin & piano ("Gypsy Airs"), Op. 20 (1878)

By all accounts one of the greatest violinists who ever lived, Pablo Sarasate received dedications from some of the most famous composers of the nineteenth century. He was less known as a composer, even though he published 54 works with opus numbers and a number of others without. Among the most famous of these are the *Spanische Tänze*, Opp. 21, 22, 23, and 26 (1878–82); the *Fantasy on Carmen*, Op. 25 (ca. 1883); and, most importantly, the *Zigeunerweisen*, Op. 20, of 1878. These pieces are not only technically difficult, but contain Sarasate's most inspired moments, not to be found in many of his other works. Sarasate originally composed *Zigeunerweisen* for violin and piano, but later orchestrated the work; this is the form in which it is best known today.

From the opening of *Zigeunerweisen*, it is clear that Sarasate had composed the piece as a vehicle for his impeccable technique and "tone of unsurpassed sweetness and purity." The orchestra has the first word, but the soloist immediately takes over, performing the same melody introduced by the orchestra. All the "sweetness" and expression a performer has must find its way into this opening theme, a slow, arching figure with an accent on its highest note. It incorporates the chromatic inflections his audience associated with Hungarian Gypsy ("Zigeuner" in German) music. The orchestra pops in occasionally, separating the successive solo violin cadenzas and their harmonic minor scales and one particularly impressive spiccato flourish up to a note in the stratosphere. After a few of these alternations between orchestra and soloist, a new section begins, featuring a new, slow melody with a new set of virtuoso flourishes. Yet another theme, narrow in range, appears first in the orchestra and is then expanded by the solo violin. This theme, slowly rising and then falling in leaps, is the most plaintive yet. The sense Sarasate creates is one of a piece that is always beginning, never reaching its fundamental material. The fast and flashy coda shines its spotlight squarely on the soloist. *—John Palmer*

Recommended:

○ **Gypsy** / Rechtman, St. John / 1997 / Well-Tempered Productions 5185

CONCERTO

Carmen Fantasy, for violin & orchestra, Op. 25 (1883)

Georges Bizet's *Carmen* may well have been a failure at its premiere in 1875 (accounts of the opera's early reception differ only in the degree of animosity critics directed at the work, and none describes it as anything approaching successful), but by the early 1880s its fame was already such that the famous violinist Pablo de Sarasate felt justified in adding the opera to the list of famous ones—*Don Giovanni*, *Der Freischütz*, *La forza del destino*, among others—that he had already chosen to craft into concert fantasies for violin and orchestra or piano. The *Concert Fantasy on themes from Bizet's Carmen*, Op. 25, universally known as the *Carmen Fantasy*, is the only one of these operatic adaptations that still finds its way to the world's concert halls. Sarasate's appreciation of Bizet is total, and one cannot accuse him of defacing Bizet's remarkable music, Somehow, even in its most elaborately ornamented and virtuosically oriented passages, the *Carmen Fantasy* upholds the opera's dignity—something that can be said of few operatic fantasies indeed.

Sarasate's *Fantasy* is in four movements, with a prelude that in essence amounts to another movement. The prelude is an adaptation of the *Entr'acte* to Act Four of the opera (the "Aragonaise"), and the first movement adapts the famous Habanera sung by Carmen in Act I ("L'amour est un oiseau rebelle")—here, the little grace notes that Sarasate adds to the chromatic tune are perfect. The gentle second movement is expertly crafted to foil the active music all around it, while the F sharp/D major juxtaposition of the third movement shines every bit as brightly as does in its original guise (the Séguidilla aria of Act One). Sarasate makes a direct link between the third movement and the frenetic Bohemian Dance (from Act Two) that is the fourth. Here, raw virtuosity takes over, providing the violinist an athletic workout not at all unlike the one that Bizet's original version provides for the dancers and orchestra. *—Blair Johnston*

Recommended:

○ **Aaron Rosand Plays Sarasate** / Reinhardt (cond.), Rosand, Southwest German Radio Orch. / 1993 / Vox 8160

Erik Satie

b. May 17, 1866, Honfleur, France, **d.** Jul. 1, 1925, Paris, France

Composer: Keyboard, Ballet, Orchestral, Choral, Vocal, Musical Theater, Opera

Erik Satie was an important French composer from the generation of Debussy. Best remembered for several groups of piano pieces, including *Trois Gymnopédies* (1888), *Trois Sarabandes* (1887) and *Trois Gnossiennes* (1890), he was championed by Jean Cocteau and helped create the famous group of French composers, Les Six, which was fashioned after his artistic ideal of simplicity in the extreme. Some have viewed certain of his stylistic traits as components of Impressionism, but his harmonies and melodies have relatively little in common with the characteristics of that school. Much of his music has a subdued character, and its charm comes through in its directness and its lack of allegiance to any one aesthetic. Often his melodies are melancholy and hesitant, his moods exotic or humorous, and his compositions as a whole, or their several constituent episodes, short. He was a musical maverick who probably influenced Debussy and did influence Ravel, who freely acknowledged as much. After Satie's second period of study, he began turning more serious in his compositions, eventually producing his inspiring cantata, *Socrate*, considered by many his greatest work and clearly demonstrating a previously unexhibited agility. In his last decade he turned out several ballets, including *Parade* and *Relâche*, indicating his growing predilection for program and theater music. Satie was also a pianist of some ability.

As a child Erik Satie showed interest in music and began taking piano lessons from a local church organist, named Vinot. While he progressed during this period, he showed no unusual gifts. In 1879 he enrolled in the Paris Conservatory, where he studied under Descombe (piano) and Lavignac (*solfeggio*), but failed to meet minimum requirements and was expelled in 1882. Satie departed Paris on November 15, 1886, to join the infantry in Arras, but he found military life distasteful and intentionally courted illness to relieve himself of duty. That same year his first works were published: *Elégie*, *Trois Mélodies*, and *Chanson*.

The years following his military service formed a bohemian period in Satie's life, the most significant events of which would be the beginnings of his friendship with Debussy, his exposure to eastern music at the Paris World Exhibition, and his association with a number of philosophical and religious organizations (most notably the Rosicrucian Brotherhood).

In 1905 he decided to resume musical study, enrolling in the conservative and controversial Schola Cantorum, run by Vincent d'Indy. His music took on a more academic and rigorous quality, and also began to exhibit the dry wit that would become hallmarks of his style. Many of his compositions received odd titles, especially after 1910, such as *Dried up embryos* and *Three real flabby preludes (for a dog)*. Some of his works also featured odd instructions for the performer, not intended to be taken seriously, as in his 1893 piano work, *Vexations*, which carries the admonition in the score, "To play this motif 840 times in succession, it would be advisable to prepare oneself beforehand, in the deepest silence, by serious immobilities."

In 1925 Satie developed pleurisy and his fragile health worsened. He was taken to St. Joseph Hospital, where he lived on for several months. He received the last rites of the Catholic Church in his final days, and died on July 1, 1925. *—AMG*

KEYBOARD

Avant-dernières pensées (Next-to-last thoughts) (1915)

Avant-dernieres pensées (Next-to-Last Thoughts) consists of three pieces for solo piano, composed in just over a month in the late summer and early autumn of 1915. Each of the pieces is dedicated to a different person. The first, "Idylle," is dedicated to composer Claude Debussy. The second, "Aubade," is dedicated to composer and critic Paul Dukas. And the third piece, "Méditation," is dedicated to Satie's counterpoint teacher at Vincent d'Indy's Scuola Cantorum, the composer Albert Roussel. These pieces were likely premiered by Satie himself. These pieces have much in common with a group of more than a dozen works for solo piano written between 1912 and 1915, characterized by musicologist Eric Gilmore as the "Humoristic piano suites." *Avant-dernieres pensées*, like its contemporaries, is written with no bar lines and with no key signatures or time signatures. It is also one of a number of works comprising three smaller pieces—evidence, according to Gilmore, of Satie's "trinitarian obsession." Perhaps the most important feature of this work and the works preceding, however, is its texture. Gone are the relatively simple chordal textures of the solo piano works from the turn of the century and before; instead, this is a contrapuntal work, reflecting Satie's years of studies in counterpoint at the Scuola seven years earlier. Each of the three pieces is structured using an ostinato pattern against bitonal melodic phrases. In "Idylle," Satie uses an Alberti bass pattern as his ostinato; in "Aubade," the ostinato takes the form of two repeated chords, and in "Meditations," a triplet figure is repeated. Satie's score is as entertaining as the music itself, with breezy, abstract commentary included for the performer. The manuscript of the work was written in Satie's ebullient calligraphy. Like most of Satie's piano pieces, these are works of whimsy, and are an amalgam of "music, poetic fantasy, and calligraphy," in Gilmore's words. It is notable, however, that, unlike his other works from this period, *Avant-dernieres pensées* does not contain any musical quotations: Satie's melodies often included quotes from cabaret tunes, children's songs, or from other composers' works. *—Alexander Carpenter*

Recommended:

- ○ **Satie - Ciccolini** / Ciccolini / 2000 / Angel 67260
- ○ **Satie: Complete Solo Piano Music** / Thibaudet / 2003 / Decca 000023002
- ○ **After the Rain** / Rogé / 1995 / Decca 444958

Descriptions automatiques (1913)

Descriptions automatiques consists of three short pieces for piano: "Sur un vaisseau" ("On a Ship"), "Sur une lanterne" (On a Street Lamp), and "Sur un casque" (On a Helmet). This work is among the first of Satie's to make liberal use of folk songs, popular songs, and children's songs. Satie's borrowings are reminiscent of those of American composer Charles Ives, well-known for his use of folk, pop, and hymn tunes; however, Satie's use of borrowed tunes in this work does not approach the seriousness or complexity that characterizes Ives' treatments of similar tunes.

The first of the three *Descriptions*, "Sur un vaisseau," makes use of a children's song well-known in Satie's time: "Maman, les p' tits bateaux qui vont sur l'eau ontils des jambes?" ("Mama, do the little boats on the water have legs?"). The second *Description*, "Sur une lanterne," borrows a phrase from the revolutionary song "La Carmagnole" (a reference to the costumes, called "carmagnoles," of French revolutionaries). The final piece, "Sur un casque," has the piano playing martial rhythms and imitating bugle calls. Like many of Satie's piano pieces, "Sur une lanterne" also contains humorous instructions to the pianist, including directions to play "heavy as a sow" and "light as an egg." In the *Descriptions*, Satie juxtaposes borrowed, diatonic melodies with harmonies that are often dissonant, or at least tonally ambiguous—typical of Satie's style in his early "fantaisiste" period.

Although these little pieces stand on their own as charming examples of Satie the humorist, musicologists have rightly pointed out that Satie's works in this vein, like those of Ives, are self-limiting in terms of accessibility by the fact of their use of borrowed material. Street songs and children's rhymes that would have struck a chord and conveyed a multiplicity of meanings to a Parisian audience in 1913 say little to twenty-first century ears. *—Alexander Carpenter*

Recommended:

- ○ **Satie: Piano Works** / Entremont / 1992 / SBK 48283
- ○ **Satie: L'Oeuvre pour piano Vols. 1 & 2** / Ciccolini / 2001 / EMI 74534

Embryons desséchés (Dried-up embryos) (1913)

Erik Satie completed *Embryons desséchés* for solo piano in the summer of 1913. "Dried embryos" are not the subject matter of these evocative miniatures at all; the real focus is invertebrates, such as sea cucumbers, pictures of which Satie found in a school textbook. Stirred by these fantastic creatures, he produced three movements that are eminently typical of his style—alive with jokes and quirky lyricism, and evocative of the proto-Surrealism prevalent among Parisian bohemians at the time.

Embryons desséchés features a humorous preface—a practice he may have picked up from his fellow eccentric and sometime collaborator, Vincent Hyspa—that begins with the *Oxford English Dictionary*'s definition of "holothuria." This is then followed by the composer's explanation that some people call this creature a "sea cucumber," and that it purrs, spins threads, and dislikes sunlight. Satie was more-or-less describing himself in comedic terms: he hated the sun himself and spun threads of music.

The first movement of the *Embryons* ("d'Holothurie") makes use of a nineteenth century parlor song about love and the seafaring lifestyle, called "Mon rocher de Saint-Malo" (Luïsa Puget). Satie's chromatic and rhythmic alterations to the song make the movement an act of parody, and the manner in which the composer combines disparate musical elements makes for a movement that is both humorous and interesting. The final cadence from the parlor song is substituted with a melodic hook from a folk song that disparages the smoking of tobacco. How that is connected to feline sea cucumbers is cause for idle speculation.

The second movement, "d'Edriophthalma," concerns crustaceans. In the score Satie points out that shrimp, prawn, and other such animals with large eyes appear melancholic. In that spirit, the music parodies the funeral march from Chopin's *B flat Piano Sonata*, Op. 35. Satie rolls the chords and adjusts the melody enough to make it seem modal, Greek, and submarine. One could imagine Poseidon taking great pleasure in it, or a drunken fisherman. The composer jots down in the score that his shrimp are weeping. To make this more obscure, Satie refers to the second movement as a celebration of Schubert's mazurkas.

So, having made fun of a parlor song and a piece of well-known chamber music, Satie focuses his third movement on an operetta and a common hunting call. It begins with a written statement in the score about the work ethic of lobsters and crabs: they are tireless hunters. In this final movement the lobsters clamber towards some winged prey and the hunt is going rather badly. The hunting song sounds as well as an excerpt from Audran's *La Mascotte*: the part of the operetta where it is said "Don't worry so much. We'll catch 'em." The hunting signal is named "La Royale."

With so many musical references and allusions, one might think that *Embryons desséchés* amounts to little more than a pastiche; but this is not so. The charming suite has a spirit that is fully representative of Satie's brilliant imagination. Perhaps the most remarkable thing about the suite is that the passage of time has not diminished its comedic qualities; even though the quotes are no longer well known, the music is still engaging and communicative.*—John Keillor*

Recommended:

- ○ **Satie: Piano Works** / Rogé / 1984 / London 410220
- ○ **Satie - Ciccolini** / Ciccolini / 2000 / Angel 67260

Gnossiennes (1889–1897)

Erik Satie, a quirky, pioneering man, revealed his true nature in his six *Gnossiennes* for piano. The first three were written when he was in his early twenties and show his lighter, comical side, only slightly alluding to a period of deep mysticism which was to follow. The title of Satie's *Gnossiennes* has baffled interpreters. Some believe it is a reference to a gnostic doctrine, others see it as an insinuation to the ancient palace of Knossos (home of the Minotaur and of Ariadne) and the stately Cretan figures endlessly circling the dark pottery there. Whatever purpose the title serves, it is without a doubt that the Rumanian music at the Universal Exposition of Paris of 1889 greatly influenced the life of these works. The following year Satie was influenced even more when he encountered Joséphin Péladan and the sect of the Rose Croix.

The *Gnossiennes* stand out from Satie's other compositions in three fundamental ways: they are considered to be one of two priceless testimonies from his youth; they are the first compositions in modern musical history written in barless notation; and they are the first of his works to contain his famous witty instructions and indications. Neo-Classical in style, they are each made up of a single mutable rhythmic and harmonic idea that passes through a series of subtle changes. The unusual notations that Satie wrote (Debussy later followed this trend) appear at length throughout the entire work. In the first piece he instructs the player to perform "monotonously and whitely," "very shiningly," and "from afar." The pianist is also told to "ask insistently within yourself," "arm yourself with clairvoyance," "advice yourself carefully," and to "dig into the sound," while playing "with great kindness" and moving "step by step." They do contain repetitive modally-based melodies, which when paralleled with their chordal accompaniments, foreshadow Satie's interest in religious chant and monody that later developed into an obsession.

In 1968, three new *Gnossiennes* (4, 5, and 6), were published. They are thought to have been composed after the publication of the first group, which are by far the superior of the six and more popularly chosen for recording. The original *Gnossiennes* (1, 2, and 3), were orchestrated by Lachberry, the remaining three by Robert Caby. Bearing slight similarities to his *Gymnopédies* and *Sarabandes*, Satie's *Gnossiennes* concisely display his early abilities and his authentic character. *—Meredith Gailey*

Recommended:

○ **After the Rain** / Rogé / 1995 / Decca 444958

○ **The Magic of Satie** / Thibaudet / 2002 / Decca 470290

Trois Gymnopédies (1888)

Though much of Satie's music remains little known beyond the ranks of devoted connoisseurs, the three *Gymnopedies* (1888) for piano are instantly familiar. Indeed, Satie no doubt would have been amused by the range and absurdity of the contexts in which they have since been presented, from ballet scores to jazz-rock fusion arrangements to commercials for mundane consumer products. Debussy was very fond of these pieces—his orchestrations of the first and third likely exceed the popularity of the original version—and even Satie's critics grudgingly admired them. One of the composer's contemporaries famously remarked that these little pieces "seemed to have been written by a savage with taste."

The etymology of the title is important, and its significance is a source of some debate amongst scholars and critics. Though Satie insisted that the work was inspired by the writings of novelist Gustav Flaubert, "Gymnopedies" rather suggests Ancient Greece. Gymnopedia festivals, held in honor of warriors felled in battle, consisted of naked youths dancing and miming wrestling and boxing poses. As Satie scholar Eric Gillmor has noted, the composer had some knowledge of the Greek language and history by way of involuntary training in Greek as a boy. As with most of Satie's music, so steeped in satire and enigma, it is in the end difficult to make a connection between the *Gymnopedies* and their source of inspiration.

The *Gymnopedies* follow closely on the heels of the *Sarabandes* of 1887, which, Satie and his apologists insisted, marked a turning point in the history of French music. The *Sarabandes*, with their modal, plainchant-like melodies and static harmony comprised of unresolved chains of seventh chords, were a decidedly anti-Wagnerian statement in 1887, when the musical life of Paris was dominated by the German composer's works and admirers. As though a direct rebellion against the bombast of Wagnerian music drama, Satie composed the *Sarabandes*, described by the composer's friend Roland-Manuel as possessing "a sonorous magic of complete originality."

The same might be said of the *Gymnopedies*; they are certainly works of "sonorous magic" and share many of the musical traits of their predecessors. At the same time, they are somewhat more organic than the Sarabandes; the three pieces essentially explore a single idea, albeit each from a slightly altered perspective. This, according to Gillmor, betrays the influence of cubism on the work. Like the *Sarabandes*, only more so, the *Gymnopedies* "are one piece written three times—cast in the same mold as it were, but with the most subtle variations in phrasing, harmonic coloring, and balancing of part." The simple modal melodies are repeated with slight variations, while successions of seventh and ninth chords provide a gentle, colorful underpinning whose "sonorous magic" mitigates its dissonance. Each of the three pieces has a tonal center, in each case unstable, merely hinted at and encircled by the undulating harmonic shifts. Satie eschews melodic development in favor of repetition and juxtaposition of melodic elements, which, together with the static harmonic language, lend the work its characteristic dreamy quality. *—Alexander Carpenter*

Recommended:

○ **After the Rain** / Rogé / 1995 / Decca 444958

○ **Satie: Complete Solo Piano Music** / Thibaudet / 2003 / Decca 000023002

Heures séculaires et instantanées (Age-old and instantaneous hours) (1914)

Between about 1911 and 1917, Satie turned his attention from the sometimes dour music he'd written during his late studies of counterpoint at the Schola Cantorum and the repetitive, mystical style of his earlier Rosicrucian period, to quirky miniatures composed especially for pianist Ricardo Viñes, who introduced and promulgated many works by the likes of Ravel and Falla. Satie dedicated one such suite of three pieces, *Heures séculaires et instantanées*, to the imaginary figure Sir William Grant-Plumot, and laced the score with a surreal commentary he insisted should *not* be read aloud during performance. Whether the text has any direct bearing on the music is debatable, but it does reinforce the music's absurdist nature. The suite's first movement, "Obstacles venimeux" (Venemous Obstacles), begins with a limping, comically discordant figure that soon receives a more flowing treatment that is interrupted by quickly shifting march-like fragments. The limping version of the theme closes the piece. "Crépuscule matinal (de midi)," which translates as Morningtime Twilight (at Noon), begins with another fragmentary march that is constantly interrupted by a nattering motif and soon collapses in volleys of hiccups. "Affolements granitiques" (Granitic Panic) begins with an urgent little phrase repeated several times, which becomes the basis of several upward-rising gestures that abruptly end. *—James Reel*

Recommended:

○ **Satie: Complete Solo Piano Music** / Thibaudet / 2003 / Decca 000023002

○ **Satie: Piano Works Vol. 4** / Kormendi / 1994 / Naxos 550699

Trois Morceaux en forme de poire (3 pieces in the form of a pear), for piano, 4 hands (1903)

Satie is well known for his many eccentricities, both in his personal life (he could always be seen wearing one of his 12 gray velvet suits, all exactly identical) and in the titles he gave his compositions, like *Dried-up Embryos* and this one, *Three Pieces in the Form of a Pear.* But in this latter instance at least, the title is not just the by-product of his quirkiness or seeming whimsicality. He chose it to both satirize Impressionism and its chief proponent, Claude Debussy, who supposedly had once advised Satie to pay greater heed to form.

The work, lasting about 12 minutes, is divided into two movements, the first serving as a sort of prologue and the second consisting of seven (not three) pieces. The three pieces in the title refers to the three sections of the first movement, spelled out by Satie in the full title as the beginning (and extension), development, and reprise. It begins quietly and alludes to Impressionist sonorities before suddenly turning boisterous, then quite exotic in its colorful chirping sounds and other coloristic effects.

The spirited first piece of the second movement is playful and marchlike and may have influenced the early piano works of Prokofiev. The second piece is playful and mischievous in its leisurely pacing and humorously intrusive chords, while the third is jaunty, but at times rowdy in its infectious gaiety. The ensuing item is subdued and stately by contrast, while the short, lively fifth is quite attractive, if somewhat thematically repetitive. The sixth frames subdued and often exotic music with brief prankish episodes that feature sudden, loud chords. The last piece exudes several previously tasty flavors in its mixture of the exotic and carefree, of the marchlike and gently playful. *—Robert Cummings*

Recommended:

○ **Satie and the Four-Handed Piano** / Rogé, Collard / 2000 / Decca 455401

○ **Satie: Works for solo piano & piano 4 hands** / Queffelec, Collard / 2000 / Virgin 61846

Five Nocturnes (1919)

Erik Satie completed his five Nocturnes for solo piano between August and November 1919. They were his last piano works. These are oddly humorless works, but after the passing of Debussy in the previous year, Satie's mood remained less than light. His musical focus seemed more strained as well. While his *Nocturnes* are successful, beautiful pieces, alert listeners can hear the effort the composer put into them, which was not the case for his works from the 1890s. By the end of World War I, Satie's musical language had achieved a perfect union of almost-mechanical gesturing and French fluidity. Satie has included none of the qualities of Chopin or Field's nocturnes in his music, but the nocturnal effect is clearly there. There is something reductive about Satie's *Nocturnes* that gives them a specific value. One could say that they sound overheard rather than heard; there is no attempt to woo the listener, who is forced to listen closely to hear the striking, macabre pace of each movement that defines their unique qualities. What can be heard and appreciated by almost anyone in this music is an audible transformation of character of the composer that comes through in these works. Most mature people have seen those prone to humor come to an apex in their own thinking and develop a seriousness that cannot completely conceal their formerly humorous selves. This is what happened to Satie, and he became more interested in causing riots in theatrical venues than having attentive listeners in concert halls. His *Nocturnes* were his last pieces of pure music. They are a sort of swan song, featuring dedications to Marcelle Mayer, Valentine Hugo, and Jean Cocteau's mother.

At the end the war Satie had no money and was severely depressed. His own sort of stoicism was the sort that, when it gave way, permanent emotional damage was lurking underneath. Though a sudden change of fortune came his way, he did not fully recover. A young Belgian painter named Mesens somehow rejuvenated his spirits. Though Satie was more than a generation older, he seemed to enjoy the painter's company as if he were an old friend. From this rapport the composer found another burst of creative energy and wrote his *Nocturnes*. They are conventionally notated, using bar lines, which he eschewed in his earlier pieces. They demonstrate no joy, but have an eerie intimacy, saying goodbye not to music or to life but to something. Their sadness and focus combine for a quality that is not easily surmised in English, but they are among the underdiscovered masterpieces of the twentieth century. *—John Keillor*

Recommended:

- ○ **After the Rain** / Rogé / 1995 / Decca 444958
- ○ **Satie - Ciccolini** / Ciccolini / 2000 / Angel 67260

Passacaille (1906)

Erik Satie returned to school in 1905—at the not-so-tender age of 40. Enrolling at the Scuola Cantorum, an academic institution founded by renowned composer Vincent d'Indy, he studied theory and counterpoint in an effort to make up for what he felt were deficiencies in his technical knowledge of music. He was also likely seeking to abolish the tag of "amateur" often applied to him by critics. He graduated from the Scuola in 1908 with a diploma in counterpoint. The effects of his schooling on the compositions dating from the years during and immediately after his studies were enormous, and the *Passacaille* is just one of many works dating from this student period. While these student works are little known and are not among Satie's best, they nonetheless represent a period of stylistic growth and evolution. Despite its name, this piece is not a true passacaglia, which would use a repeated ground bass as a basis for melodic variation; instead it employs frequent repetition of its opening few bars as an organizing device. *—Alexander Carpenter*

Recommended:

- ○ **Satie: Complete Solo Piano Music** / Thibaudet / 2003 / Decca 000023002
- ○ **Satie: Piano Music** / Glazer / 1990 / VoxBox 5011

Pièces froides (Cold Pieces) (1897)

Satie completed his *Pièces froides for piano* in 1897. The work has two sets of three pieces, designated "Airs à faire fuir" (Tunes to Make You Run Away) and "Danses de travers" (Crooked Dances). The simplicity and charm of these pieces are reminiscent of Satie's early piano works, especially the *Gnossiennes* and *Gymnopédies* of the late 1880s: it shares with these pieces a tendency to present a single musical idea from a number of different perspectives. *Pièces froides*, with its 2x3 construction, also reflects Satie's interest in the number three, evident in many of his works for piano. The first set combines spare melodic lines, linear textures, and simple repeating left-hand figures. All together, the three pieces make up a perfectly symmetrical ternary form, with the first and third pieces having the same number of measures. The outer pieces feature symmetrical phrasing, gentle dissonances, and many motives, while the middle piece has asymmetrical phrasing and less motivic variety. There is a simple tonal plan to the music, essentially defining the tonic/dominant relationship; however, Satie also employs tonal chords in unexpected ways, and uses dissonance to undermine harmonic movement. The second set of pieces is in stark contrast to the previous set. They are formally looser and essentially based on a single idea, which is stated at the beginning of the first piece. Each piece in this set basically begins in the same way, though with the main musical idea—a narrow melodic line enmeshed with its arpeggiated accompaniment—slightly altered each time. The "Danse de travers" also differs from the "Airs à faire fuir" in that it features more harmonic movement, frequently shifting between remotely related key areas. *—Alexander Carpenter*

Recommended:

- ○ **After the Rain** / Rogé / 1995 / Decca 444958

Préludes flasques (pour un chien) [Flabby preludes (for a dog)] (1912)

The *Preludes flasques (pour un chien)*, or Flabby Preludes (For a Dog), were commissioned by the Demets publishing house in 1912. Satie completed them in July of that year, but they were rejected by Demets. In despair, Satie first planned to destroy them. Instead, he wrote a second set of preludes, the *Veritables preludes flasques (pour un chien)*, or "True Flabby Preludes (for a dog)," which he offered to Debussy's publisher, Durand. Like Demets, Durand was not pleased with these pieces and quickly returned them to Satie. It was not until the end of 1912 that Demets finally accepted the second set of preludes for publication.

This work consists of four pieces, each possessing an irreverent, esoteric, and decidedly characteristic title: "Voix d'interieur," "Idylle cynique," "Chanson canine," and "Avec camaraderie." The *Preludes flasques* strongly reflect Satie's post-Scuola Cantorum esthetic; in the years following his graduation from Vincent D'Indy's school, Satie produced a number of pieces that reflect a certain "academicism" with their precise contrapuntal textures. These *Preludes* are decidedly contrapuntal and austere, a sharp departure from the mostly chordal works that preceded the beginning of his studies at the Scuola Cantorum in 1905. Gone are the static harmonies and repetition of the *Gymnopedies* and *Gnossiennes*, written before the turn of the century; instead, the Preludes, along with the other piano pieces composed after 1912, are works of brevity and condensation. They are more or less tonal works, but Satie's tonality could be called expanded tonality, as there are moments when harmonic relationships are strained, dissonant, and occasionally bitonal. Unlike many of the humorous piano works written by Satie between 1912 and 1915, however, these preludes have barlines and time signatures. The Preludes also differ from Satie's other sets of piano pieces, as Alan Gillmor has noted, in that there are four pieces in the set rather than three: Satie, Gillmor writes, had a "trinitarian obsession, and most of his piano works consist of sets of three." *—Alexander Carpenter*

Recommended:

- ○ **Satie: Piano Works** / Rogé / 1984 / London 410220

Trois Sarabandes (1887; revised 1911)

The *Trois Sarabandes* for piano number among Satie's best known "trinitarian" piano works, including the *Trois Gymnopedies*, and the *Trois Gnossiennes*. In 1916 Satie's good friend Roland-Manuel described the Sarabandes thus: "these *Sarabandes* mark a date in the evolution of our music: here are three short pieces of an unprecedented harmonic technique, born of an entirely new aesthetic, which create a unique atmosphere, a sonorous magic of complete originality." Certainly this is true of much of Satie's early music, but especially the Sarabandes. These three pieces introduced a number of Satie techniques that would typify his early style, including the use of modes, and unresolved dissonances.

It has been suggested that the Sarabandes were directly influenced by Gustav Chabrier's opera *Le Roi malgre lui*, which Satie heard for the first time mere months before the appearance of the *Sarabandes*. Satie was no doubt taken by Chabrier's liberal use of seventh and ninth chords; however, as musicologist Alan Gillmor has noted, while Chabrier used these chords for color within an otherwise tonal context, Satie, in a sense, emancipated these chords, creating chains of "unresolved dissonances." Even though these pieces retain key signatures and nominal tonal centers, there is a sense of tonality being suspended as modal, plainchant-like melodies combined with evocative but non-functional diatonic harmonies.

Satie's music is often described as forward-looking, and indeed much of his music, some of the ballets in particular, clearly anticipate major movements in art and music, including Dadaism, Cubism, and Surrealism, by many years. In the case of the Sarabandes, one could perhaps extend this argument, and look forward 20 years to the music of Schoenberg, who insisted on the "emancipation of the dissonance" in the early years of the twentieth century. While Satie's Sarabandes are by no means atonal, in Gillmor's words, their music "comes very near to denying the constraining demands of the functional tonal system." *—Alexander Carpenter*

Recommended:

- ○ **Erik Satie** / de Leeuw / 1996 / Philips 446672

Sonatine bureaucratique (1916–1917)

While virtually all of Erik Satie's compositions brim with wit and vigor (except, perhaps, some of the *Gymnopedie* and *Gnossiennes*, which stretch out languorously), few works match the panache of his *Sonatine Bureaucratique* from 1917. With its articulate lines and only slightly skewed harmonies, the work exemplifies the character and musical language of Satie's young French devotees, the so-called Les Six. The odd familiarity of the music, though, lends it a slightly more acerbic tone: the entire piece is constructed as an almost blow-by-blow send-up of Clementi's ubiquitous *Sonatina in C major*, Op. 36/1. A staple of the middle-class parlor and the midgrade student repertoire, Clementi's *Sonatina* stands as a symbol of the bourgeois cultural airs of the "Bureaucrat" invoked in the title.

Like Clementi's original, Satie casts his *Sonatina* in three short movements. The first, marked Allegro, mimics the contours of its model quite closely, from the regal, repeated "dum-duhduh-dum dum" rhythm to the rising and falling runs that pass from hand to hand. Clementi's gestures, however, are caricaturized—in scales and sequences that overextend themselves, melodies that find themselves in a suddenly disjunct octave, and hiccups that disrupt cadential motions—and occasionally subverted outright, as in the opening line's upward, rather than downward orientation. Likewise, Satie's harmonic and melodic adjustments let a little of the air out of the original, replacing hornlike arpeggios with lackadaisical scales and tweaking the underlying harmonic progressions. The middle section of the movement takes particular liberties, veering off into an absurd modulation and recovering with in incongruously impressionistic shimmer. The middle movement, an Andante, borrows Clementi's slow triplet undercurrent, but connects the notes of Clementi's Spartan melody with scalar filigree. The final movement, marked Vivace, tames the boisterous triple meter and quick runs of the *Sonatina*, Op. 36, and gives it a Phrygian, almost Debussy-esque dreaminess, the foursquare phrases interrupted by coloristic chordal spells.

What the listener doesn't hear, but what lends the piece an added charm, is the set of quirky rubrics and narrations that Satie includes in the score, all of them given in witty, idiomatic, and idiosyncratic French. Various points in the music apparently correspond to the images of the bureaucrat happily walking to his office, sitting at his desk pondering his upward mobility, and even singing a Peruvian tune—while the neighbor is heard playing Clementi. *—Jeremy Grimshaw*

Recommended:

- ○ **Satie: Piano Works** / Rogé / 1984 / London 410220
- ○ **The Magic of Satie** / Thibaudet / 2002 / Decca 470290

Sports et divertissements (Sports and diversions) (1914)

Sports et divertissements is a collection of 21 pieces for piano. These pieces are miniatures, and they combine music, poetry, calligraphy, and art in a charming and intimate way. Each piece in this set is very short, none more than four lines long, and each is accompanied by a small poem, and by Satie's irreverent verbal commentary. When the work was first published, it appeared with in Satie's own hand, the music written in his idiomatic, calligraphic style, with red and black ink. It is also important to note that, along with the poetry, calligraphy, and commentary, each piece of music is accompanied by a tiny sketch.

With each piece, there is at least some connection between the music and the events or characters depicted in the accompanying poem. For example, in "Le Water-Chute," Satie depicts a waterfall with obvious descending scales; in "La Peche," the struggle between a fisherman and his would-be catch is depicted through the use of subtle ostinatos suggesting water, and short, skittish musical figures suggesting darting fish. The work as a whole offers perhaps the most in-depth access to Satie the composer; that is, every aspect of Satie's complex musical personality is represented here, as some of the pieces are witty, some pensive, some esoteric, some ironic, and some somber. For critics and musicologists alike, *Sports et divertissements* is generally regarded as one of Satie's best and most important works, for it represents, finally, the amalgamation of most of the stylistic idioms th composer had been developing in the years preceding this work. Alan Gillmor very elegantly has described Sports et divertissements as "the one work in which the variegated strands of Satie's artistic experience are unselfconsciously woven into a fragile tapestry of sight and sound—a precarious union of Satie the musician, the poet, and the calligrapher." *—Alexander Carpenter*

Recommended:

○ **Satie: Complete Solo Piano Music** / Thibaudet / 2003 / Decca 000023002

○ **Satie: Piano Works** / Legrand / 2002 / Apex 41380

BALLET

Parade (1916–1917; revised 1919)

Smarting from his failure to interest Stravinsky in a scenario strutting *King David* through a fairground setting—a *parade* of tableaux—Jean Cocteau, on furlough from driving ambulance at the front, heard Satie's *Trois Morceaux en forme de poire* performed by Ricardo Viñes at a Paris concert on April 18, 1916, and immediately recognized them as the ideal music for his project. Satie had other ideas—"Let's do something new, right? No joke." A tortured collaboration began, picking up Picasso in the summer for set, costumes, and (for Cocteau) an unwelcome hand in the scenario, and the interest of Diaghilev, who stimulated Satie's desultory inspiration with cash advances. In a piano duet version, the music was completed January 9, 1917, while the orchestration occupied Satie until May 8—ten days before the premiere. Playing under 15 minutes, *Parade* may be Satie's richest score—it is certainly his most finely wrought. Palindromic in form, beginning and end essay an eerie fugato complementing Picasso's red curtain, and depict a curtain drawn to reveal performers at leisure. Before the conclusion of the curtain music, the entrance and collapse of the Cubistically costumed Managers are heralded by an obstreperous cakewalk raising the curtain not only on the show, but on one of the great aesthetic preoccupations of the early twentieth century, namely, the interplay of antitheses called forth by art—interior and exterior, fantasy and reality, or (in Goethe's phrase) poetry and truth. The show proper begins with a Chinese conjuror, balanced, after the centerpiece, by Acrobats. The central, compactly elaborate act is the Little American Girl enacting (choreography by Massine) tropes from American films—typing, six-gun blazing, a Chaplin-esque shuffle, and so on. Irving Berlin's 1911 ragtime knock-off, *That Mysterious Rag*, is deliciously parodied, while *Parade* is suffused throughout with popular and music hall gestures alternating eldritch evocations with brisk vivacity. Satie is often credited with *Parade*'s extra-musical effects—sirens, foghorn, typewriter—though they were, in fact, included at Cocteau's insistence. As Satie wrote to Diaghilev, "I don't much like the 'noises' made by Jean, but there is nothing we can do here. We have before us an amiable maniac." The ballet's premiere on May 18, 1917, provoked hostilities. *—Adrian Corleonis*

Synopsis:

This ballet has no conventional story line and opens with a parade of various performers from a circus streaming across the stage. Each one displays features from his or her act to entice those in the crowd watching them to pay the admission fee and come inside for the full show. The circus company has two managers: a Parisian, depicted by a large caryatid of garish colors and construction; and an American, whose caryatid is part skyscraper and part cowboy. Each has a dancer within its structure, who is soon compelled to depart the stage by the appearance of the Chinese Conjuror, also dressed garishly. (The ballet's original production featured costume designs by Pablo Picasso.) He demonstrates his magical talents, making an egg appear from nowhere and then disappear.

He is followed by an American girl, whose various mimes depict a range of events and scenes, from driving an automobile and portraying a shipwreck (probably making reference to the Titanic, since its sinking was then a recent event) to playing a scene in a movie or dancing in a ragtime style. Next comes a ringmaster, represented by a dummy, riding in on a mechanical horse. Two acrobats then come on-stage, performing flying leaps, somersaults, and other physical stunts. There follows a grand finale, where all the performers return and beckon the crowd, generally failing, however, to entice them to come inside, most watchers feeling satisfied they witnessed a substantial portion of the performers' acts without paying an admission fee. *—Robert Cummings*

Recommended:

○ **Dorati Conducts Satie, Milhaud, Auric, Françaix & Fetler** / Dorati (cond.), London SO / 1994 / Philips 434335

ORCHESTRAL

La belle eccentrique, "serious fantasy" (1920)

La belle eccentrique is a suite for small orchestra. It numbers among Satie 's many music-hall pieces, written in what musicologists call his "café-concert idiom." This work was created in collaboration with Jean Cocteau and was first performed in 1921. It consists of four short numbers: "Grand Ritornello," "Franco-Lunar March," "Waltz of the Mysterious Kiss in the Eye," and "High-Society Cancan." It is easy to tell that this is a comic work, replete with much silliness and whimsy. Though touted as a "fantaisie serieuse" for small orchestra, it is also a work that may be staged, and Cocteau was involved in the work's original realization. Versions for piano solo and piano duet also exist.

Alan Gillmor, a Satie scholar, has noted that while many of Satie's works possess an ironic humor by virtue of their use of familiar tunes and their witty, eccentric commentary. *La belle eccentrique* is really a work whose humor lies close to the surface. It has little to offer in the way of subtlety, what with its crashing ragtime and cancan rhythms, stumbling waltzes, and grotesque, bombastic music-hall timbres. The piece is clearly, as Gillmor has noted, a return to Satie's music-hall aesthetic of the turn of the century. The opening of the work, the "Grand Ritornello," provides both an introduction to the work an interlude between the three subsequent movements, which are dances. Since the work is staged, these interludes provide time for dancers to change costumes.

La Belle eccentrique is important for two reasons. First, it shows, in Debussy's words, how "adaptable" Satie really was, composing adjacent pieces of sharply contrasting style, form, and character despite his critics' claims that he was little more than an amateur. And second, this work demonstrates the importance of melody in Satie's music, and his insistence that, even when using relatively simple popular or popular-inspired melodies, inventive, unpredictable harmonies (rather than those implied by the melodic line) may be employed to accompany them. *—Alexander Carpenter*

Recommended:

○ **Satie: Complete Solo Piano Music** / Thibaudet / 2003 / Decca 000023002

○ **L'Orchestre de Satie** / Sado (cond.), Lamoureux Concert Association Orch. / 2001 / Erato 85827

CHORAL

Messe des pauvres (Mass for the poor) (ca. 1892–1895)

Considering the life Erik Satie led, he could perhaps have dedicated the *Messe des pauvres* (Mass for the Poor) to himself; the composer lived in poverty and obscurity, his music known only to a few close friends during his lifetime. Darius Milhaud commented that "our poor Satie, who died in poverty at the Hôpital St.-Joseph in Paris, could not have imagined the irradiation and diffusion of his work on the musical world of today."

Satie was not necessary a man of religious faith, but he did have loose affiliations with *fin-de-siècle* quasi mystical cults. Immediately following his five-year appointment as the official musician of the confraternity Rose-Croix du Temple et du Graal (a splinter group of the Rosicrucian Order), which reinforced the influence of the symbolist writers, he became involved with a yet more unusual sect of his own creation. While living on the rue Cortot, in Montmartre, he founded the "The Metropolitan Church of Jesus the Leader"; he is thought to have been its only member. Contamine de Latour described the seat of the new Church as a "nondescript room, square and tile-floored, which was untimely crossed by the . . . ventilating pipe. No altar, no object which could be used for the cult, nothing that reminded one of a religious sanctuary: simply the unfinished furniture brought down from the attic where it had been rotting for months and which gave to the room an aspect both of a monk's cell and of an NCO's room." Within this "wretched" atmosphere, Satie composed his *Messe des pauvres* in 1895. This strange work for solo organ and unison voices is reminiscent of the Medieval chant and of the transcendental idealism with which the composer was fascinated. Like other works from the first phase of his career, the modal motifs of the composition were derived from plainchant and possibly from Eastern cantillation. Moving mainly stepwise or pentatonically}, the hypnotic repeated slices of melody suggest devotional liturgy, and are placed alongside meandering, sensuous harmonies. The structured patterning of phrases follows a mathematical, geometric order. The work has been compared by Edgard

Varèse to Dante's *Inferno*, and was unlike anything produced by his contemporaries, even those with similar styles such as Debussy, Massenet, Saint-Saëns, and Chausson. This disturbing, even slightly scary work takes its listeners deeper into the mind and philosophy of its composer, whose lifelong interest in the metaphysical was made manifest in his music. *—Meredith Gailey*

Recommended:

- ○ **Górecki: O Domina Nostra; Satie; Milhaud; Bryars** / Leonard,Bowers-Broadbent / 1993 / ECM 437956
- ○ **Diamond Settings** / Schwarz (cond.), Seattle SO / 1996 / Koch 7358

VOCAL

La diva de l'Empire, song (1904)

Aside from influencing the music of Claude Debussy and Maurice Ravel, Erik Satie also played a lead role in the Parisian avant-garde movement and left his mark directly on the musical world by initiating the "cult of the music hall," with works like *La Diva de l'Empire* (The Star of the Empire) (c. 1900). Known as the "cafe-concert" songs, this work and its accompanying two others, *Tendrement* and *Je te veux*, became his most popular pieces for voice. The works were written while Satie was attempting to avoid living in poverty by supporting himself as a pianist in a Montmartre cabaret. The songs were written for Paulette Darty, "Queen of the Slow Waltz." They marked a shift in his career away from the Rosicrucian idealism and his more serious works and toward a period of humor and mischief.

La Diva de l'Empire was originally written for voice and piano, but it was the transcription for solo piano by Hans Ourdine that made the work famous. *La Diva* was not a "waltz chantee," Darty's typical repertoire, but a cakewalk song, with a strutting rhythm. Using a moderate march tempo, the music depicts a diva of Napoleon's time; however, Satie later gave it the humorous subtitle, "American intermezzo." Making their way through the work's several interpretive problems, the pianist is required to maintain a strict rhythm, while the vocalist sings with her distinctive "rubato de diva." Slightly imitative of the imperial era of Offenbach's music, this brisk, cheerful song, which is touched by cynicism and filled with Anglicisms, is best summed up by one of its lines—"C'est à la fois très très innocent et très très excitant" (It is at once very, very innocent and very, very exciting).

Although *La Diva de l'Empire* was probably quite popular in its original form in the cabaret clubs, Satie chose to later create a version for beer-hall orchestra. In retrospect, the work may appear a bit dated; however, considering the fact that it was completed nearly 15 years prior to the time when serious composers began experimenting with jazz techniques, its originality is quite remarkable. In 1903, shortly after these "cafe-concert" pieces were written, Satie, nearly 40 years old, decided to work over his technique by modestly registering as a student at the Schola Cantorum, where he studied with Vincent d'Indy and Albert Roussel. After receiving his diploma, which gave him the "authority" to compose, he continued on the path he had initiated with *La Diva de l'Empire*, creating works which were slightly comic in nature, while furthering his reputation as a unique, yet bizarre man. *—Meredith Gailey*

Recommended:

- ○ **Youkali-Cabaret & Art songs by Satie, Poulnec & Weill** / O'Callaghan, Crober / 1998 / Marquis Classics 81217

Je te veux (I Want You), café-concert song (1897)

Je te veux ("I Want You") is a setting of a text by Henry Pacory. The song may be connected, according to Satie scholars, to Paulette Darty, a Parisian burlesque chanteuse. It is a "valse chantée," a "waltz song," well-suited to Darty's reputation as "Queen of the Slow Waltz." Satie composed a number of songs with her in mind and actually performed this piece with her in 1909, some 12 years after it was composed.

Like his other cabaret songs, *Je te veux* was rearranged both for solo piano and for a number of instrumental combinations, including voice with a small orchestra, full orchestra, and solo voice. The music may also appropriately be played, as musicologist Alan Gillmor notes, by a cabaret band. The song has a simple refrain/verse/refrain structure, although later reorchestrated instrumental versions included a new section (a trio) added on to the piece.

The raucousness and raunchiness of this piece made it interesting and entertaining to Parisian music-hall audiences. It is important to note, however, that the song's text was even raunchier before Satie watered it down, making it fit for public audition. *—Alexander Carpenter*

Recommended:

- ○ **Mélodies de Satie** / Barbier, Wiener / 2001 / Gallo 1003
- ○ **Jessye Norman: Les Chemins de l'amour** / Norman, Baldwin / Philips 416445

MUSICAL THEATER

Le Piège de Méduse, lyric comedy (1913)

Le Piège de Méduse is a play with dances inserted between the scenes. Satie wrote the text for this play—a "lyric comedy"—himself, and the main character, Baron Medusa, is thought to be at least semi-autobiographical. The work consists of one act divided into seven scenes, each of which is attached to one of seven "tiny dances." They are scored for a small chamber ensemble consisting of three strings (violin, cello, and double bass), three winds (clarinet, trombone, and trumpet), piano, and percussion (including bass drum, cymbals, side drum, triangle, and tambourine). The dances are quite strange in form and substance, and indeed the work itself is considered the first example of surrealist drama; as such it often borders on the bizarre. There are five important characters in the play: the wealthy Baron Medusa; his belligerent servant, Polycarpe; his foster daughter, Frisette; her fiancé, Astolfo; and Jonas the giant stuffed monkey; it is Jonas who breaks into dance between each scene, adding to the surreal elements of the drama. Typical of Satie is the use of music hall elements in his score, and the choice of dances—including a polka, a mazurka, and a two-step—reflects Satie's infatuation with popular music and dance. While the text itself is not exceptional, the play nonetheless has considerable historic importance. It should be noted, for example, that along with being the first Surrealist drama, this is the first composition requiring the use of a prepared piano, as Satie inserted paper between the hammers and strings of the instrument to create a particular timbral effect. Furthermore, as some commenators assert, this play could be considered an important precursor to the Dadaist movement. *—Alexander Carpenter*

Recommended:

- ○ **Les Inspirations Insolites D'erik Satie** / Ciccolini (cond.), Bertin, Deschamps, Falcucci, Laurence, Concerts Lamoureux. Solistes de l'Orchestre des / EMI 62877
- ○ **Satie: Socrate; Relâche; Le Piége de Meduse** / Desgraupes (cond.), Fouchecourt, Ensemble Erwartung / FNAC 592292

OPERA

Socrate, symphonic drama (1917–1918)

Composed between 1917-18, this "symphonic drama in 3 parts with voice," its text based on the *Dialogues of Plato* translated into French by Victor Cousin, is without parallel in the history of music: there was never anything like it before and has been nothing like it since. Devoid of the usual dramatic and sentimental operatic gestures, *Socrate* is nevertheless deeply moving in its simple, calm unfolding of a life moving toward a tragic end through society's injustice and misunderstanding. Constructed of simple musical patterns or cells that change very gradually and are combined or segued in "mosaics" with other patterns, the music winds about plaintively in an ancient feeling. The cellular technique was developed as early as Satie's *Uspud* (a "Christian ballet in 3 acts") of 1892, and the aesthetic of a "neutral" expression of beauty first occurred in his famous ancient Greek dance/exercises *Trois Gymnopédies* of 1888. In *Socrate*, the rhythms of basic eighth and quarter notes remain steady and plain, but have a way of immediately entering the consciousness and memory of the listener who can easily identify them as the piece progresses; these patterns seem to arbitrarily follow each other, but in fact are wedded closely in feeling to the meaning of the text. Similarly, the orchestration is "monochromatic" but also charming, pastoral, hypnotic, funereal. And the counterpoint occurs in the simplest of motions, with the harmonies recalling old church organum or the imaged pipes of ancient shepherds. In this musical context, small changes in pitch in the voice (eg., emphasis on particular tones that distinguish the mode) and subtleties of articulation and orchestration for the instruments tend to be very effective, and both are employed in a highly sophisticated manner by Satie.

As suggested by the subtitle "symphonic drama," *Socrate* hovers somewhere this side of a true operatic narrative: that is, it articulates a succession of ideas and events through music and song, but, in the spirit of French neo-Classic simplicity and emotional distance, it does so without the expectation of suspended reality, visual depiction, or representation of characters. The three acts are "Portrait de Socrate" (text from Plato's *Symposium*), "Les Bords de l'Illissus" (from the *Phaedrus*) and the devastatingly moving third act "Mort de Socrate" (from the *Phaedo*) and are related by subject matter and authorship rather than plot. They essentially are a dramatic reading of excerpts from Plato's *Dialogues*, rendered in the voice of a different male pupil—although, in further effort to dedramatize the story, a single female singer provides the voice for all of the parties represented. Satie's sense of mixed emotions, usually expressed as exquisite irony in many of his compositions, helps to reveal in this work an underlying tragedy expressed simply in actions of everyday reality—the best-known example being Socrates' last words reminding Crito that a rooster is still owed to the god Asclepius. At the end of *Socrate*, a few lines are added to this speech, then the music suddenly moves upward, making a conclusion of suspended emotion and "ineffable sweetness that lingers in the memory" (Alan Gillmor). *—"Blue Gene" Tyranny*

Synopsis:

Act One. Alcibiades provides a curious portrait of Socrates. "I propose to praise Socrates, gentlemen," he says, "by using similes. He will perhaps think that I mean to make fun of him, but my object in employing this is truth, not ridicule." He first compares him to certain statues sold in the shops that, when broken, are found to contain a cavity with a figurine of a god inside. He then compares Socrates to

Marsyus, the satyr flutist who can enthrall listeners through his music, and whose melodies long remain in the memory. Socrates, Alcibiades marvels, does the same, but without an instrument. His words alone, Alcibiades says, induce a near religious rapture.

Act Two. This act presents something more of a sequence of events, though still focused on demonstrating Socrates' wisdom. Here the singer presents both sides of a dialogue between Phaedrus and Socrates, who are walking along the banks of the Illissus looking for a place to sit and rest. Phaedrus points to a shady spot up ahead, and as they walk toward it they ponder the story of the abduction of Oreithyia by Boreas, which was said to have taken place just downstream. Socrates rationalizes the legend by proposing that the wind had blown Oreithyia onto the rocks, tragically but unmysteriously, giving rise to the more sensational myth. Upon this suggestion, they notice that they have arrived at their destination, and Socrates wonders at the beauty of the spot.

Act Three. This act is the most moving, with the clearest dramatic contour, even though it is spoken through the memory of a single character, Phaedo. He recalls his last visit to Socrates during his imprisonment, on the day of his execution by poisoning. Socrates is found released from his chains, musing on the acute similarities between pleasure and pain and manifesting a serene peace in the face of his impending death. Phaedo recalls the tender scene in which one of the guards, whom Socrates has befriended, comes to the prisoner and tearfully bids farewell. Socrates then signals to his captors to bring the poison, which he calmly drinks, then waits for its effects while Phaedo looks soberly on. *—Jeremy Grimshaw*

Recommended:

- ○ **Les inspirations insolites - Erik Satie** / Dervaux (cond.), Mesplé, Millet, Litaize, Esposito, Guiot, Paris Orch. / EMI 62877
- ○ **Satie: Socrate; Relâche; Le Piége de Medus** / Desgraupes (cond.), Fouchecourt, Ensemble Erwartung / FNAC 592292

Henri Sauguet

b. May 18, 1901, Bordeaux, France, **d.** Jun. 22, 1989, Paris, France
Composer

Henri Sauguet had a successful career in France, though he had considerably less international fame. His music is emotionally restrained, deceptively simple, and formally clear.

Born Jean Pierre Poupard, he took his mother's maiden name as his professional surname. He exhibited early interest in and skill at music and was given piano lessons. As a boy, his favorite composers were Schumann, Bizet, and Debussy. He studied organ with Paul Combes, then obtained a job in a small church near Bordeaux. He then continued his musical training by studying composition with J.P. Vaugourgin and Joseph Canteloube.

The music of Igor Stravinsky and the cool simplicity of Erik Satie's music excited him. When Jean Cocteau dubbed a group of Paris-based composers "Les Six," Sauguet started writing to one of its members, Darius Milhaud. Sauguet also began to call himself and two Bordeaux friends (another composer and a poet) "Les Trois."

The correspondence with Milhaud led to the composer asking Sauguet to send him some of his works. Sauguet wrote a piano suite called *Trois Françaises* and sent it to Milhaud. For an early effort, these tender portraits are highly worthwhile, already showing the characteristic clarity of Sauguet's musical thought. Milhaud was impressed, and recommended that the younger man should move to Paris.

Milhaud introduced Sauguet to composer Charles Koechlin, who became a teacher to Sauguet and to Satie. Although Satie was never Sauguet's teacher, he was one of the strongest influences on Sauguet's music. Sauguet and a few friends who also admired Satie (Henri Cliquet-Pleyel, Maxime Jacob, and Roger Desormière—later a famous conductor) established a group to put on a concert. They called it the "School of Arcueil," named after the location of Satie's home. Satie supported the group when they organized the concert, and introduced them at that beginning.

This led to Sauguet's first important commission when a Mme. Beriza asked him for a stage work, *Le Plumet du colonel* (*The Colonel's Helmet*). Experts on Sauguet say this bright and often comic piece has several instances of misjudged orchestration and other flaws.

Once again, the École du Arcueil gave a concert, and this led to another stage commission. Sauguet had written a ballet score called *Les Roses*, in which the marks of his inexperience and lack of conservatory training were left behind. This success led to his establishment in his chosen career when famous ballet impresario Sergei Diaghilev commissioned a new work from him. The work, *Le Chatte* (*The Cat*) was choreographed by the young George Balanchine and was an immense success. Sauguet was now able work full time at his music, although he also wrote perceptive music criticism throughout his career.

Sauguet's greatest popular success was in ballet. The best of his ballets, and the work by which he is best known outside of France, was *Les Forains* (*The Strolling Players*) (1945), about some talented, slightly tattered, but ultimately hopeful musicians.

He was a talented and important vocal composer. He worked ten years on *Le Chartreuse de Parme* (*The Charterhouse of Parma*), a number opera that had a reputation in France as his most important work. Internationally, however, operagoers find his works in that form to be short on emotion and drama.

He wrote numerous works for radio, television, stage, and film, four numbered symphonies, several charming concertos for diverse instruments, and a large quantity of chamber and other instrumental works, including solos for harmonica and musical saw. He remained a tonal composer, although at times he used an expanded form of tonality and composed some musique concrète. *—Joseph Stevenson*

Overview of Works (1921–1987)

Henri Sauguet (1901–89) was a French composer who, in his time, seemed destined to become one of the leading voices in twentieth century music. Some will assert he wrote in a neo-Classical vein, but having absorbed elements from Satie, Stravinsky, and the members of Les Six, he fashioned a style that must ultimately be described as eclectic; his music is notable for possessing a direct expressive language.

Sauguet's first breakthrough came with his opera, *Le plummet du Colonel*, when it was paired at its 1924 premiere with Stravinsky's *L'Histoire du soldat*; although a bit unrefined, the work possessed an undeniable charm. His next major stage work, the ballet *La chatte*, was lavished with a first-rate production featuring Diaghilev's ballets russes, choreography by George Ballanchine, and the dancer Serge Lifar; it was a great success at its 1927 Paris premiere.

Other stage works—the ballets *David* (1928) and *La nuit* (1929), and the opera *La contrebasse* (1930)—though well-crafted, did not make a significant mark. His 1945 ballet, *Les forains*, however, may be the greatest of his efforts for the stage. Its music is witty and light, melancholy and colorful—perfectly suited to its libretto about traveling musicians. As late as 1981, the energetic and prolific Sauguet completed a children's opera, *Tistou-les-pouces-verts*.

Sauguet wrote a significant and compelling body of instrumental and orchestral works. His *First Piano Concerto* (1934) was introduced by Clara Haskil, but despite its generally high quality it has failed to achieve the success of his somewhat mysterious *Third Piano Concerto* (1961–63), subtitled "Concert des mondes souterrains" (Concert of the underground world). His 1953 *Concerto d'Orphée for violin and orchestra* was another success and further demonstrated his instrumental versatility.

Sauguet wrote four symphonies that, in certain respects, can be compared stylistically with those of his colleague Darius Milhaud. While the latter was a bit less serious, his orchestration was similar in its muscular, sometimes neo-Classical sound. Sauguet's *First Symphony* (1945), subtitled "Expiatoire," may be his most popular. The *Third* (1956) and *Fourth* (1971) are both serious, well-crafted compositions that began receiving greater attention in the 1990s. The *Second Symphony, Allegorique, for soprano, children's chorus, and orchestra* (1949) is a very large work, and probably his least-played symphonic composition.

Sauguet also wrote many film scores, including the 1949 pair *Clochemerle* and *Les Amoureux sont seuls au monde*. In addition, he produced a host of chamber works, some for unusual combinations of instruments, like *Oriasons, for four saxophones and organ* (1976). Sauguet also wrote many songs and choral works, including the oratorio *Chant pour une vieille meurtrie* (1967). *—Robert Cummings*

Recommended:

- ○ **Sauguet: Symphony 1** / Almeida (cond.), Moscow SO / Marco Polo 8223463
- ○ **Sauguet: Les caprices de Marianne** / Rosenthal / Solstice SO 098/99
- ○ **Sauguet: Mélodies** / Abramovitz / Sonpact 93008
- ○ **Sauguet: Mélodies** / Eidi, Gardeil / 2003 / Timpani 1070
- ○ **Sauguet: Works for 2 Pianos** / G. Andranian, C. Andranian / 1995 / Arcobaleno 93732
- ○ **Parisian Ballets** / Swift (cond.), CBC Vancouver Orch. / 1996 / CBC 5152

Jordi Savall

b. Aug. 1, 1941, Igualada, Spain
Conductor, Gambist, Viol Player

Jordi Savall is among the leading instrumentalists and conductors of the European early music scene, specializing in Renaissance and Medieval music. He began studying music when he was six, learning cello and pursuing that instrument at the Barcelona Conservatory. He took an interest in early music, and began learning the viola da gamba. Savall also gained proficiency in the various members of the viola family. He studied the gamba and early music research and practice with Wieland Kuijken in Brussels and August Wenziger at the Schola Cantorum Basiliensis in Basel, obtaining a diploma as soloist and professor in 1970. In 1973 he succeeded to Wenziger's position.

In 1968 he had married the soprano Montserrat Figueras, who shared his interest in early music. With her and other musicians interested in early Spanish music, he founded in 1974 the ensemble Hespèrion XX. The ensemble took its name from an ancient name for the western European region from Italy to Iberia; Hespèrion was also a name for Venus as the Evening Star (in which aspect it appears only in the western skies).

He and Hespèrion XX quickly became well known in early music circles. They created a unique sound through the use of viols and other Medieval instruments such as the psaltery, wooden flutes, Moroccan drums, and the Afghan rebec (a double reed ancestor of the oboe). All these instrument are known to have been used by Medieval musicians, particularly in the Mediterranean region.

Savall became internationally known through his playing on the soundtrack of Alain Corneau's film *Tous les Matins du Monde* (All the Mornings of the World), concerning the French viol players of the Baroque era. Savall has extended his area of musical interest into the Baroque, leading performances of *Orfeo* by Monteverdi and *Il burbero de Buion Cuore* by Martin y Soler, and in the late 1990s conducted Beethoven's *"Eroica" Symphony* with Les Concerts des Nations (a group he founded in 1989 for Baroque music), winning praise for his well-researched and groundbreaking interpretation. He also founded La Capella Reial de Catalunya in 1987, an ensemble of instrumentalists and vocal soloists. He has recorded around 100 releases, mostly on the Astrée Auvidis label, receiving the Diapason d'Or award, among others. *—Joseph Stevenson*

Recommended:

- ○ **Marais: Pièces de Viole du Second Livre** / Savall, Hantai, Lislevand, Pierlot, Diaz-Latorre / Alia Vox 9828
- ○ **El Canto de la Sibilla I & II; El Cancionero; Cantigas** / Savall (cond.), Lawrence-King, Figueras, Estevan, Bernardini, Hespèrion XX, Capella Reial de Catalunya / 2002 / Astree 9984
- ○ **Mr. de Sainte Colombe le Fils: Pièces de Viole** / Savall, Marielle / Alia Vox 9827
- ○ **Bach: Die Kunst der Fuge** / Savall (cond.), Hespèrion XX / 2001 / Alia Vox 9818
- ○ **Purcell: Fantasias for the Viols** / Savall (cond.), Hespèrion XX / 1999 / Astree 9922
- ○ **Cabanilles: Batalles, Tientos & Passacalles** / Savall (cond.), Hespèrion XX / 1998 / Alia Vox 9801
- ○ **Tous les matins du monde** / Savall, Hantai, Biondi, Le Concert des Nations / 1991 / Valois 4640
- ○ **Alfonso X el Sabio: Cantigas de Santa Maria** / Savall (cond.), Hespèrion XX, Capella Reial de Catalunya / 2000 / Astree 9940

Wolfgang Sawallisch

b. Aug. 26, 1923, Munich, Germany
Conductor

Born in Munich in 1923, Wolfgang Sawallisch is a prominent representative of the German conducting tradition, known for his thoughtful and refined interpretations of the classical repertoire. Beginning piano studies when he was five, Sawallisch developed rapidly as a child musician. His piano teachers were Ruoff, Haas, and Sachse. In 1947, following graduation from the Munich Hochschule für Musik, Sawallisch began his professional career, working first as a repetiteur and chorus master at the Augsburg Opera Theater. In 1949, he and his recital partner, violinist Gerhard Seitz, won the Geneva International Competition as best duo. In the same year, he began obtaining guest conducting assignments. When Sawallisch conducted the Berlin Philharmonic Orchestra in 1953, he was the youngest person ever to have led that orchestra. That year, he became General Music Director at Aachen, and this appointment made him the youngest music director in Germany. He remained in Aachen until 1958, when he moved to a similar position in Wiesbaden, staying there until 1960. From 1960 to 1963, Sawallisch was in Cologne, also teaching conducting at the Conservatory. He made his first Bayreuth appearance in 1957, opening the festival with *Tristan und Isolde*. Again, he was the Festival's youngest conductor. Also in 1957 he made two debuts in London: one as pianist in a lieder recital with Elisabeth Schwarzkopf and the other as a guest conductor with the Philharmonia. He held concurrent appointments as principal conductor of the Vienna Symphony Orchestra, from 1960 to 1970, and the Hamburg State Philharmonic, from 1961 to 1973. He made his American debut conducting the Vienna Symphony Orchestra during a 1964 tour. Also in 1964, he made his first appearance guest conducting the NHK Symphony Orchestra in Japan, and has returned every year to conduct it. He held another pair of concurrent appointments through most of the 1970s: Artistic Director of L'Orchestre de la Suisse Romande, from 1972 to 1980, and General Music Director of the Bavarian State Opera in Munich, beginning in 1971. Artistic director of the Bavarian State Opera from 1976 to 1977, he became the company's director in 1982. His first appearance with the Philadelphia Orchestra was in 1984, part of his busy schedule as a guest conductor. He was appointed its Music Director in 1990, effective at the start of the 1993–94 season. In 1993, Sawallisch and the Philadelphia Orchestra toured Japan, China, and Hong Kong, the first of several acclaimed international tours. In addition to extensive touring, Sawallisch has pursued a busy recording schedule with EMI, programming an intriguing mix of the established classics, major masterworks of the twentieth century, and new music, including compositions by Druckman, Pöntinen, Rochberg, and Ullmann. He led the Philadelphia Orchestra in the first appearance by an American orchestra in Vietnam, and directed the first live Internet performance by an American symphony. Sawallisch regularly conducts Europe's greatest orchestras, including the London Philharmonic Orchestra, the Vienna Philharmonic Orchestra, and Concertgebouw Orchestra. A winner of numerous awards, Sawallisch has performed with such stars as Yefim Bronfman, Yo-Yo Ma, and Frank Peter Zimmermann. Continuing his career as a pianist, Sawallisch has accompanied some of the greatest performers of the twentieth century, including Dietrich Fischer-Dieskau and Elisabeth Schwarzkopf. Among Sawallisch's numerous acclaimed recordings is the 1998 video soundtrack of Wagner's entire Ring des Nibelungen cycle with the Bavarian State Opera. *—Joseph Stevenson*

Recommended:

- ○ **Dvořák: Symphonies 7, 8** / Sawallisch (cond.), Philadelphia Orch. / 1990 / EMI 499482
- ○ **Brahms: Symphony 4; Shicksaslied; Academic Festival Ov.** / Sawallisch (cond.), London PO, Ambrosian Singers / 1999 / EMI 73570
- ○ **Bruckner: Symphony 6** / Sawallisch (cond.), Bavarian State Orch. / Orfeo 24821
- ○ **Mendelssohn: Elias** / Sawallisch (cond.), Ameling, Schreier, Rotzsch, Adam, Gewandhaus / 1993 / Philips 438368
- ○ **Wagner: Tannhäuser** / Sawallisch (cond.), Bumbry, Silja, Greindl, Wachter, Crass, Bayreuth Festival Orch. & Chorus / 1992 / Philips 434607
- ○ **Strauss: Capriccio** / Sawallisch (cond.), Fischer-Dieskau, Schwarzkopf, Gedda, Philharmonia / EMI 49014

Bidú Sayão

b. May 11, 1902, Rio de Janeiro, Brazil, **d.** Mar. 12, 1999, Rockport, ME
Soprano

Bidú Sayão was one of the most beloved sopranos in the entire history of opera. She was known for her ethereal, silvery tone and a stage presence of delicacy and refinement.

Born to an upper-class family, she was named Balduina de Oliveira Sayão after her grandmother. Her father died when she was five years old. She wanted to be an actress, but as going on the stage was "out of the question for a girl born in a respectable family," she studied voice with the aid of an uncle. Her talent led her to one of the world's leading teachers, Elena Theodorini. Some sources say an appearance in *Lucia di Lammermoor* at Rio's Teatro Municipal, when she was 18, removed family opposition to her dream of singing. Sayão continued studies with Theodorini in Europe. In 1922, she became a pupil of Jean de Reszke, a tenor with one of history's purest vocal techniques. After he died, she returned to make a stunning second debut in Rio, in 1926, as Rosina in *The Barber of Seville*. She sang widely in Europe, with performances in Paris at La Scala and in Rome. Toscanini, hearing her in *Traviata*, engaged her for her U.S. concert debut with him at the New York Philharmonic in 1935. For the next two years she performed primarily in her native Brazil. But in 1937, she was booed outrageously as Micaela in *Carmen*, allegedly by a claque organized by the singer playing Carmen. The outraged Sayão said she would not sing in Brazil. She joined the roster of the Metropolitan Opera, debuting in 1937 as Massenet's Manon. Other favorite roles were Mimì in *La Bohème*, Debussy's Mélisande, and Susanna in *The Marriage of Figaro*.

It was Sayão who is credited with convincing Heitor Villa-Lobos to change the solo part of *Bachianas Brasileiras No. 5*, from violin to wordless soprano. The work became the composer's most famous piece, and the 1945 recording the most famous of Sayão's 35 78 rpm releases and her dozen LPs. Sayão made extensive concert tours, and endeared herself by frequently singing for wounded servicemen during World War II. She left the Met's roster in 1951 and retired from opera in 1954. She came out of retirement three years later, at the request of Villa-Lobos, to sing on his recording of his composition *Forest of the Amazon*, perhaps her only recording in stereo. It may have been the act of singing this intensely Brazilian music that prompted her to relent in her ban on singing in Brazil, for she made one farewell appearance in Rio, in 1958. After that she retired with her second husband, the well-known Italian baritone Giuseppe Danise, to their home in Lincolnville, ME, a North Atlantic seaside town (Danise died in 1963). There, she lived a quiet life caring for her cats and frequently playing cards with her local friends and visitors.

The coming of compact discs prompted reissues of many of her recordings, a fact which, she told a São Paolo newspaper, made her feel "relieved," since she had been "tormented" by the idea that all her work had been forgotten. She had a nearly fatal stroke in 1993, but recovered fairly well, considering her age of 92. In 1995, she returned to Rio for the last time, when she learned that the Beija-Flor Samba School had chosen her life story as the subject for its presentations in the great Carnival parade of that year. That was her last public appearance. She died of pneumonia, at the Penobscot Bay Medical Center in Rockport, ME, at the age of 97. *—Joseph Stevenson*

Recommended:

- ○ **Sayão sings Bachiana Brasileira 5, Arias & Brazilian Folksongs** / Sayão, etc. / 1996 / Sony 62355
- ○ **La Domoiselle elue** / Sayão, etc. / 1997 / Sony 63221
- ○ **Rarities** / Sayão, etc. / 1998 / VAI Audio 1171

Alessandro Scarlatti

b. May 2, 1660, Palermo, Italy, **d.** Oct. 22, 1725, Naples, Italy

Composer: Vocal, Opera

Alessandro Scarlatti was among the most important Italian composers of opera from the late Baroque period. He is credited with establishing the Neapolitan school of opera in the eighteenth century, rapidly improving the predominantly provincial state of music in Naples into a sophisticated and enduring tradition. He composed over 600 cantatas, more than 100 operas, many oratorios, serenatas, sonatas, and other instrumental pieces. Oddly, his historical position declined after his death and his reputation was not rehabilitated until the early twentieth century. His importance in music is further bolstered by the fact he was the father of Domenico Scarlatti (1685–1757), who in the keyboard realm was among the most individual and influential composers of his day. Another son, Pietro, also became a composer of some distinction.

Virtually nothing is known of Alessandro Scarlatti's early musical education, though he likely became a choirboy at a local church and may have studied the rudiments with the choirmaster. At the age of 12 he was sent off to a relative in Rome. He may have studied with Carissimi there until 1674, when the older composer died.

In April 1678, Scarlatti married Antonia Anzalone, who would bear him ten children, though only half would survive to adulthood. Around this time the composer became the maestro di cappella for Queen Christina of Sweden, an arts patron who had founded two academies at her palace in Rome. He served in this post until 1684, when he departed for Naples. By this time he had scored a great success in Rome with his first opera, *Gli equivoci nel sembiante* (1679), and with subsequent ones, along with many cantatas and oratorios.

At Naples, he was appointed maestro di cappella at the Viceregal Chapel, under the Viceroy of Naples, Marquis del Carpio. By the 1690s, Scarlatti was writing operas and serenatas at a prolific pace, owing mainly to the requirements of his position. One of his most successful large works during this decade was his opera *Il Pirro e Demetrio*, which was performed throughout Italy and elsewhere in Europe to critical and public acclaim.

Scarlatti took a leave of absence in June 1702, and traveled to Florence with his son, Domenico, who now exhibited his own musical talents. The elder Scarlatti had hoped for a post with Prince Ferdinando de Medici, but could not obtain one, though he would write much music for him in the coming years, including four operas. In 1703, he took on music directorship at St. Maria Maggiore in Rome, but was unhappy in the post from the first, since the Pope had forbidden theatrical performances there, thus frustrating the creative urges of any composer of opera and especially of one so prolific.

In 1707, Scarlatti was promoted to maestro di cappella at St. Maria Maggiore, but a year later, following financial difficulties, he returned to Naples to serve in his former post. He would spend another ten years there, remaining highly productive throughout, turning out many operas, including *Giunio Bruto* (1710) and the highly successful *Il Tigrane* (1715). From 1718 to 1722 Scarlatti was on leave, mostly in Rome, where his operas could now be staged. After his return to Naples in 1722, his output declined, while his financial hardships increased. He died in 1725, leaving his family in debt and ignored by those who had owed him salary. *—Robert Cummings*

Overview of Works (ca. 1677–1725)

Scarlatti was an immensely prolific composer whose output touched every genre of his day. At its heart stands some 60 operas, the majority composed before 1710 for Naples, although the earliest were first given in Rome, while he also received commissions from Venice and Florence. He shifted of the focal point of Italian Baroque opera from Venice to Naples. Scarlatti's influence as an opera composer was considerable; some developments with which he has been credited—the da capo aria and the introduction of horns into the opera orchestra—in fact predate his own adoption of them. But he was responsible for moving away from the five-act format of Venetian opera to the three-act plan that became standard in the eighteenth century and also for carrying forward the clearer division between recitative and aria that was a feature of the operas of Venetian composers such as Sartorio and Pallavicino. Although Scarlatti's earlier operas retain the comic characters who were such feature of Venetian opera, later examples, such as *Mitridate Eupatore* and *Il trionfo della libertà*, both produced in Venice in 1707, are described as being a "tragedia in musica" and contain no comic characters. They thus play an important role in the operatic reforms that led to the creation of the separate genres of opera seria and opera buffa early in the eighteenth century.

Two other groups of composition form an important corollary to Scarlatti's operas. His oratorios represent another major part of his output, the most important composed after Scarlatti was appointed maestro di cappella of Sta. Maria Maggiore in 1703. Public opera had been banned in Rome by papal decree in 1700, leaving the field open for dramatic oratorio. Many of these took Old Testament subjects and almost certainly provided an example for Handel, who met Scarlatti during his Roman sojourn (1707–08). However, *Cain, ovvero Il primo homicido* (1706), arguably Scarlatti's masterpiece in this field, was composed not for Rome, but Venice.

Late in life Scarlatti turned increasingly to the composition of chamber cantatas, mostly written for soprano and continuo, of which the final tally amounted to some 600 works. Designed for a small audience of connoisseurs, these miniature scenas, often on pastoral topics, comprise one of the most subtle and valued parts of Scarlatti's oeuvre.

As if such industry was not sufficient, Scarlatti also composed a smaller, but significant body of liturgical music that reveals his mastery of counterpoint, late examples of the madrigal, and both solo and ensemble instrumental works. *—Brian Robins*

Recommended:

- ○ **A. Scarlatti: La Folia** / Dawson, Purcell SQ / 1989 / Hyperion 66254
- ○ **A. Scarlatti: 7 Concerti con flauto** / Cologne Camerata / CPO 999619
- ○ **A. Scarlatti: La Giuditta** / McGegan (cond.), Minter, Zadori, Gregor, Mey, Gemes, Savaria Capella / 1995 / Hungaroton 12910
- ○ **A. Scarlatti: Missa di Santa Cecilia** / Abravanel (cond.), Christensen, Christensen, Preston, Utah SO / 2000 / Amadeus 7011
- ○ **A. Scarlatti: Concerti Grossi; Cello Sonatas** / Dantone (cond.), Valli, Byzantine Academy / 2001 / Arts 47616

VOCAL

Su le sponde del Tebro, chamber cantata

Many of Scarlatti's cantatas have no known date of composition, in part because he wrote so many of them. Scarlatti was the last major contributor to the genre, writing almost 800 cantatas. They were commissioned by the aristocracy and the wealthy in Italy and performed at their courts to entertain guests or for special occasions. They were also performed at *conversazioni* or academies, which were gatherings of the nobility with their friends. This cantata was probably written between the years 1690 and 1695.

Su le Sponde de Tebro is a cantata for solo voice. Its text is pastoral and contains the typical complaint of an unrequited love. The scoring features a trumpet, which is used as an obbligato instrument and in duo textures with the voice. The text and the form of the cantata are shaped by narrative passages within which are the pathetic recitatives and arias of the protagonist Aminto. This shaping is derived from the works of Monteverdi and lasted throughout the history of the cantata. It contrasts impersonal narration with personal human emotion expressed in a lyrical vein. The narration in recitative opens the cantata and intensely lyrical passages in the form of a monologue are contained within its framework. The arias in this cantata are written to contrast with one another emotionally and musically. After an orchestral ritornello the opening aria begins, featuring a trumpet obbligato with a vocal part that imitates the trumpet themes.

"Infelice miei lumi" is the only piece designated arioso. Full of chromaticism, suspensions, and diminished seventh chords, the shepherd cries out in his grief. The aria "Dite almeno" is written over an ostinato bass and it is filled with rhythmic activity. This takes the form of hemiolas, syncopations, and cross rhythms. Its only accompaniment is the basso continuo, which is made up of the harpsichord and cello. After a brief narrative, the final aria is filled with Aminto's resolve to endure. A trumpet aria, its themes are heroic and triumphal. It is in the da capo form, which means that its opening themes of victory are repeated for added emphasis. *—Rita Laurance*

Recommended:

- ○ **Scarlatti & Hasse** / King (cond.), Steele-Perkins, York, King's Consort / 1996 / Hyperion 66875
- ○ **Mozart, Scarlatti & Handel** / Schwarz (cond.), Blegen, Cooper, Columbia Chamber Ens. / 1996 / Sony 62646

OPERA

La Griselda

Griselda is Alessandro Scarlatti's last surviving complete opera. It was premiered at the Teatro Capranica in January 1721. The plot is based on the folklore tale of Patient Griselda, whose triumph is the triumph of love, fidelity, and obedience. She made her debut in literature with Boccaccio's *Decameron*, and Petrarch, Chaucer, and dozens of other authors have taken up the task of telling her tale. In the seventeenth and eighteenth centuries, her story became opera over 35 times. The original libretto was by Apostolo Zeno, who created one of the most dramatically viable libretti extant. The problem for dramatists became making Griselda a sympathetic rather than an allegorical figure, and providing motivation for the seemingly senseless cruelty of her husband, which she endures with so much fortitude.

After the opening Italian Sinfonia, the form of the opera is made up of acts consisting of the recitative plus aria combination. The ending consists mainly of recitative passages which imitate speech and leave the drama in relief. The climax of these is the accompanied recitative of Griselda, as she finally forces a confrontation with her husband Gualtiero. But Costanza, the daughter, has a final grand aria, and there is an ensemble in which all the main characters take part at the very end to close the opera. It resembles a short chorus with orchestra and is very brief, but is an effective end to a dramatic high point.

Right before its premiere, the opera went through a great deal of changes because of the addition to its cast of Carestini, a promising young castrato. Carestini had a wealthy patron, and arranged to have his debut in *Griselda* in the role of Costanza, Griselda's long lost daughter. To make his debut as spectacular as possible, Scarlatti wrote three extra arias for him, and altered the existing arias to make them more showy, adding plenty of coloratura passages. He deleted four arias of other cast members to make Carestini's performance stand out even more. Carestini apparently had a very successful debut.

Griselda is an example of the trend toward opera seria. There are no comic scenes in *Griselda* and no bass roles. There are no display scenes, or scenes given over to spectacle in this work. There are no monsters, or mythological creatures, no gods or magicians, and no bloodshed. The story revolves around a moral theme, and the musical variety comes from Scarlatti's endless supply of inventiveness within standard forms. By this time, Scarlatti was considered a grand master of the Baroque style and of operatic composition, and in this opera, he rises to his reputation. —*Rita Laurance*

Synopsis:

Act One. Under intense pressure from his subjects, King Gualtiero of Sicily has decided to renounce his wife, Griselda, despite her many years of devotion and the two children she has borne him. Though faithful, Griselda is of low birth and thus, unfit to be Queen. In fact, so angered were the people at the King's marrying a shepherdess that the first daughter of the royal household apparently had been killed years before in an act of appeasement. Now Griselda and the King have a young son, and rather than infuriate the people once more with the possibility of an heir of peasant bloodline, Gualtiero has decided to send Griselda back to her cottage in the woods and take on a new wife of noble lineage, under arrangements made by Prince Corrado of Puglia. Informed of the decision, Griselda is heartbroken, but even when the King remains unsympathetic to her pleas, she promises to take pleasure in being faithful to him—even if it means carrying out his cruel orders. Left in tears, Griselda rebuffs the consolation offered by Gualtiero's aide, Ottone, who has grown fond of the dethroned queen. Meanwhile, Corrado has arrived with Gualtiero's bride to be, Costanza; she rues her engagement, however, having fallen in love (in Isolde fashion) with Roberto, Corrado's younger brother and her escort.

Act Two. Griselda has been banished to the forest, but even the scant comfort of familiar solitude is disrupted when Ottone appears, courting her once again. His vain efforts are interrupted by Corrado, who announces that Griselda's young boy Everardo has been brought to the woods to be killed. Exploiting the situation, Ottone threatens to kill the boy himself if Griselda does not relent, but even now she remains faithful to her heartless husband. Left alone in the cottage, she sleeps fitfully until being awakened by Costanza. Thinking herself in a dream, Griselda momentarily thinks Costanza to be her long lost daughter. Even discovering her rival, however, Griselda feels a strong mutual kinship with Costanza, whose heart has likewise been broken by fate. They are startled by the arrival of Gualtiero, who reasserts his noble disdain for Griselda, but grants that she can return to the castle as Costanza's handmaiden. Corrado arrives with the news that Ottone is on his way to abduct Griselda; unexpectedly, Gualtiero has Ottone arrested.

Act Three. Despite misgivings about his treatment of Griselda, Gualtiero surprises Ottone once more by promising him that once Costanza becomes Queen, Griselda shall be his. Elsewhere in the castle, Roberto bids his final farewell to his love Costanza. They are discovered in the midst of their last amorous embrace, but again the King extends a surprising pardon, recognizing the couple's enduring love. And when, with a crowd gathered, Griselda refuses again—on pain of death—her betrothal to Ottone, Gualtiero's heart melts. He embraces Griselda as his wife, and makes a final startling announcement: Costanza is, in fact, not Griselda's rival, but her long lost daughter. —*Jeremy Grimshaw*

Recommended:

- ○ **Scarlatti: La Griselda** / Sanzogno (cond.), Freni, Panerai, Bruscantini, Alva, Luchetti, Lavani / Opera d'Oro 1308

Domenico Scarlatti

b. Oct. 26, 1685, Naples, Italy, **d.** Jul. 23, 1757, Madrid, Spain

Composer: Keyboard, Choral

Domenico Scarlatti began his compositional career following in the footsteps of his father Alessandro Scarlatti by writing operas, chamber cantatas, and other vocal music, but he is most remembered for his 555 keyboard sonatas, written between approximately 1719 and 1757.

It is believed that Domenico received most of his musical training from family members, but his father was the dominant figure in his life. It was Alessandro who arranged Domenico's first appointment, as organist and composer for Naples' Cappella Reale, and wanted him to continue with vocal music despite the enormous talent he had shown for keyboard music. Domenico was sent to Venice in 1705, where he met Handel, and in 1708 to Rome to become maestro di cappella to the exiled queen of Poland, Maria Casimira, and later, head of the *Cappella Giulia.* In these positions, he composed his operas and serenatas, and some sacred vocal works. It was also in Rome where he developed a friendship with the Portuguese ambassador, the Marquis de Fontes, which eventually led to Scarlatti's being appointed master of the royal chapel by João V of Portugal in 1719. Scarlatti was also teacher to the royal family, particularly princess Maria Barbara. Scarlatti had already written approximately 50 keyboard pieces before coming to Lisbon, but wrote many more for his students, which also included Carlos de Seixas. When Maria Barbara married Spanish prince Ferdinando, Scarlatti followed her to Spain. His first publication, 30 sonatas called "Essercizi," was issued in 1738 and sold throughout Europe. Although as King and Queen, Ferdinando and Maria Barbara introduced opera into Spain's cultural life, Scarlatti did not write any for them. However, he did assist in their private musical soirées, again writing cantatas and working with singers such as Farinelli. Scarlatti also continued to teach, and, in the last six years of his life, concentrated on organizing his sonatas in manuscripts. These one-movement sonatas are recognized as cornerstones of the keyboard repertoire, a bridge between the Baroque and the galant styles of keyboard writing. They demonstrate his facility in adapting rhythms found in contemporary Iberian popular music and his inventiveness in creating themes and developing interesting harmonies. —*Patsy Morita*

KEYBOARD

Works for Harpsichord (ca. 1699–1756)

Domenico Scarlatti was the son of one of the most famous operatic composers of the day, Alessandro Scarlatti. During the early part of his career he looked set to follow in his father's footsteps as a composer of opera and oratorio, becoming maestro di cappella of the Cappella Giulia in the Vatican in 1714. However, in 1720 Scarlatti moved to Lisbon to become master of the royal chapel and see to the musical education of the two children of King João V. One of them, the Infanta Maria Barbara would become an exceptionally talented keyboardist, and eventually Queen of Spain. Following her marriage in 1729, Scarlatti followed her to Spain on the orders of her father. He remained in her service for the rest of his life.

It was for Maria Barbara that Scarlatti composed the more than 500 keyboard sonatas upon which his reputation principally rests. Single-movement works in binary (two-part) form, they were preserved in two sets, each of 15 volumes. Typically, each follows a similar pattern, with an introductory section, a central section that includes a continuation of the theme and a final first half section that prepares and establishes a new mode. Following a repeat of the whole of this section, the sonata moves on to a modulatory passage before returning to the opening material to reestablish the original mode. This scheme has a close relationship to prototypes of Classical sonata form; it is easy to hear Scarlatti's importance in the development of that landmark musical form.

Despite their unity of design, the sonatas are astonishingly varied in mood and color. Some introduce exotic evocations of the sounds Scarlatti heard around him in Iberia, evoking such flamboyant images as whirling Spanish dances (for example K. 381 in E in the numbering of Ralph Kirkpatrick's authoritative catalog), the clicking of castanets, the strumming of guitars (K. 380 in E or K. 141 in D minor) and processions (K. 518 in F). Many of these pieces call for a high degree of virtuosity from the performer, requiring such techniques as hand crossing and the playing of powerful octaves in the bass. Other sonatas are more restrained, sometimes pastoral in character, sometimes redolent of a warm, nocturnal scene. Even when local atmosphere is not present, each sonata has a very individual character, ranging from the forward-looking Rococo pieces like K. 478 in D to fugal sonatas (K. 30 in G minor).

According to Kirkpatrick, the sonatas were designed to be played as pairs according to their original manuscript arrangement, a scheme often adhered to by modern performers. —*Brian Robins*

Recommended:

- ○ **Scarlatti: Complete Keyboard Works** / Ross, Huggett, Coin, Henry, Vallon / 1988 / Erato 45309
- ○ **Scarlatti: Sonatas** / Schiff / Hungaroton 11806
- ○ **Scarlatti: Sonatas** / Pletnev / 1995 / Virgin 45123
- ○ **Scarlatti: Sonaten** / Pogorelich / DG 435855
- ○ **Scarlatti: Fugue & 10 Sonatas** / Parmentier / 1985 / Wildboar 8501
- ○ **Scarlatti: Sonatas** / Leonhardt / 1999 / Sony 61820
- ○ **Scarlatti: 22 Sonates** / Hantai / 2001 / Astree Naive 8836
- ○ **Scarlatti: 18 Sonatas** / Tipo / 2001 / EMI 74969
- ○ **Horowitz Plays Scarlatti** / Horowitz / 2003 / Sony 90414

CHORAL

Stabat Mater, in C minor (1714)

The period from 1714–19, which Domenico Scarlatti spent in Rome employed by the Vatican as the maestro di cappella at St. Giulia, produced a considerable body of sacred and liturgical music, much of it worthy of further attention and performance. Foremost among these is his setting of the devotional *Stabat Mater* text. The work, completed in 1715, employs a choir of ten parts accompanied by organ and is rendered in a style that often seems archaic, but at moments introduces newer and powerfully expressive textures and harmonies. Despite the lush vocal sonority afforded by the large vocal forces, it is with local nuances and contours and subtle combinations of parts that Scarlatti engages the listener. At first glance, Scarlatti's *Stabat Mater* seems like a misplaced work from the sixteenth century, with its gently arching melodic lines, delicate points of imitation, and elegant surface. Occasional harmonic clues betray the piece's later date—a meditative plagal passage that frees itself of harmonic urgency, a cadence that points in an unforeseen direction. Despite the large ensemble, Scarlatti's polyphonic fabric is pulled taught and polished, with only a hint of harmonic depth added by the organ; in passages where the vocal forces are most reduced, the clarity of phrase and declamation solidly place the work in the eighteenth century, despite its seemingly antiquated style. One of this piece's most compelling characteristics is the fluidity with which it connects the words and music. The devotional poem, cast in ten stanzas of two tercets each, is not poured squarely into a corresponding series of musical passages, but rather stretched and molded into a larger and more organic form. The first four verses of the poem are bound together by a continuous musical passage and a recurring motive that is treated communally by the singers. The insistent rhetorical questions of the poem, "Quis est homo qui non fleret... Quis non posset contristari...?" (Who would not weep seeing the mother of Christ in such torment? Who would not feel compassion...?), are met first with an increasing musical urgency created by carefully wrought counterpoint, then a moment of pensive repose. In the subsequent passage, the music shifts from sheer declamation of words to expression of ideas and images, as shifting meters, variegated textures, and more angular writing enhance the poet's description of Christ's suffering. The adorations that follow, in which the poet affirms his devotion to Christ and desire to weep with Mary at the foot of the cross, eventually culminate in a masterfully crafted fugue on "Fac me cruce custodiri" (Grant that I may be protected by the cross) and a joyous chorus of "Amen." *—Jeremy Grimshaw*

Recommended:

- ○ **Scarlatti: Stabat Mater a 10 voci** / Alessandrini (cond.), Concerto Italiano / 2002 / Opus 111 30248

Giacinto Scelsi

b. Jan. 8, 1905, La Spezia, Italy, **d.** Aug. 9, 1988, Rome, Italy

Composer

Giacinto Scelsi's music was largely unknown throughout most of his life, as he refused to conduct interviews or make analytical comments about his works and rarely sought out performances. The attitudes behind his musical creations can be tied in with this reclusiveness; from the 1940s he saw music as a type of spiritual revelation. He began to compose his better known pieces at this time, works which involved static harmony with surface fluctuations of timbre and microtonal inflection. This type of harmonic minimalism was developed independently of other minimalist trends of the twentieth century, and was received with fascination by the musical world when his music finally began to receive performances and recordings in the 1980s. He wrote over 100 works, including several major pieces for orchestra, and works for chamber ensemble, string quartets, and solo and duo pieces. Many of his pieces were worked out in improvisation and subsequently written down.

Scelsi was born into a wealthy, aristocratic Italian family, a circumstance which allowed him to compose without the necessity of making a living. He played the piano from an early age, before studying composition when in his thirties with Walter Klein, a pupil of Schoenberg's, and then with the Scriabin enthusiast Egon Koehler. Scelsi absorbed the influences of his teachers in this period, using Schoenberg's techniques to write 12-tone music, but also writing in a freely atonal style. Many of the works from this time are for the piano. He traveled widely between the world wars, notably to Africa and Asia.

Around the time of the Second World War, Scelsi suffered a breakdown and was forced to spend time convalescing. His thinking began to be shaped by the eastern philosophies that he had picked up while traveling. He came to the point of view that composition was a spiritual process which had nothing to do with the individualism that had been part of most music making in Europe since the eighteenth century. Rather, he saw the composer as the creator of circumstances through which the secrets in sounds could be revealed. At this time he also became fascinated by the complex of sounds which could be produced by a single note, and reportedly played single pitches repeatedly on the piano, listening intently. These influences began to be felt in his works in the 1950s, with many pieces consisting of very slowly shifting harmony, often moving in one direction, for example in *String Quartet No. 4* (1964). This trend was at its most pronounced in the *Quattro Pezzi Su Una Nota Sola* (Four pieces each on a single note) (1959), for chamber orchestra, where refined orchestration, glissandi, trills, and microtonal movement are given prominence through the stillness of larger scale harmonic action. Other notable works from this period are *Khoom* (1962) for soprano and small ensemble and *Anahit* (1965) for violin and 18 instrumentalists. *Khoom* was part of Scelsi's early 1960s interest in the possibilities of the human voice, developed through his collaborations with the singer Michiko Hirayama. From the 1970s Scelsi's pieces became generally shorter and more succinct.

Dating Scelsi's compositions has been difficult as he redated manuscripts deliberately to confuse musicologists. He would not have his photograph taken, and preferred instead to be represented by the symbol of a horizontal line placed under a circle. *—Rachel Campbell*

Overview of Works (1929–1988)

As a young composer, Giacinto Scelsi explored various compositional schools and techniques, including neo-Classicism and the 12-tone method. This early, more conservative period in Scelsi's career is dominated by keyboard works, including four piano sonatas, seven suites, and no less than 40 preludes. Scelsi also wrote a few early chamber works, mostly for violin and piano, as well as a handful of orchestral works, such as the well-received *Rotative* from 1929. A turning point in Scelsi's career came around 1950, when he suffered from a nervous breakdown. During his recovery he discovered an unusual form of therapy: he would sit at the piano and listen to the same note, repeated over and over again, for hours on end. This led to an acute sensitivity to subtle fluctuations in tone and timbre, and, consequently, a compositional approach characterized by extended fixations on individual notes and their timbral elaborations. Among the most famous works to employ this new style are the *Quattro Pezzi su una nota sola* (Four Pieces on a Singe Note) from 1959. As suggested by the title, each piece in the work centers on a single pitch, which undergoes gradual and varied instrumental treatments and transformations, including being surrounded by broadband orchestral interference at microtonal intervals just above or below the main pitch or its octave transpositions. These ideas were explored further in Scelsi's *Fourth* (1964) and *Fifth* (1984) string quartets, *Hymnos for organ and two orchestras* (1963), and *Ohoi* (1966) and *Natura renovatur* (1967), both for string orchestra.

It should be noted that although some of the ideas encountered in these works were explored independently and/or concurrently by composers such as La Monte Young and James Tenney (see, for example, Tenney's *Critical Band*), Scelsi avoids the process-oriented methods of minimalism, choosing instead to intuitively shape his timbral explorations. In fact, in his later years, Scelsi took to a method of composing that involved the recording and transcription of his improvisations on the Ondiola (an early microtone-enabled keyboard), which he performed while in a trance-like state. This vitality and subjectivity is particularly apparent in his massive scores for orchestra and chorus, such as *Uaxuctum* (1966), *Konx-om-pax* (1960), and *Pfhat* (1974). The varied and sometimes violent surfaces that ripple across his harmonically Spartan structures thus emerge like the wildly irregular surfaces seen when seemingly smooth and congruous objects are viewed through a microscope. *—Jeremy Grimshaw*

Recommended:

- ○ **Scelsi: Quattro Illustrazioni; Suite 8; Cinque Incantesimi** / Hinterhauser / 2003 / Col Legno 20068
- ○ **Scelsi: Duo; Aitsi; Canti popolari; Wo-Ma; Sauh I & II** / Helix Ens. / Classical Sub Rosa 51
- ○ **Scelsi: The Piano Works 1** / Bessette / 2000 / Mode 92
- ○ **Scelsi: Orchestral Works 1** / Izquierdo (cond.), Vaillancourt, Carnegie Mellon Philharmonic / 2001 / Mode 95
- ○ **Scelsi: Kya** / Wyttenbach (cond.), Racine, Schmidt, Weiss, Volpe, Contrechamps Ens. / 1999 / Hat Hut 117
- ○ **Scelsi: Music for High Winds** / Robinson, Novakova / 2001 / Mode 102
- ○ **Scelsi: Pieces; Anahit; I Presagi; Yamaon; Okanagon** / Zender (cond.), Hermann, Bik, Meuge, Wien Klangforum / 1999 / Kairos 1203
- ○ **Scelsi: Khoom; Trio** / Lloyd, etc. / Salabert 8904

Christine Schäfer

b. Mar. 3, 1965, Frankfurt, Germany

Soprano

Christine Schäfer established one of the most stellar careers of any young German soprano in the 1990s and became known for her sensational acting and her mastery of a wide range of repertory and styles.

She enrolled in the Berlin Conservatory in 1984 and studied with Ingrid Figur, whom she considers her primary teacher and credits with giving her a firm technical foundation and a knack for clear projection of German words. She studied with American soprano Arleen Augér who, Schäfer said, taught her how to give total concentration to the work of understanding a musical compossition. Of composer Aribert Reimann, another of her teachers, she says, "His music is fantastic, and as a teacher he is even more so." From him she learned lieder interpretation. She also had master classes with Dietrich Fischer-Dieskau and Sena Jurinac.

After winning several prestigious prizes, she made a highly acclaimed recital debut at the Berlin Festival in 1988, singing Reimann's cycle *Nachträume*, and began to establish a promising recital and concert career. She has sung in Europe with the

Gächinger Kantorei, the Windsbacher Knabenchor, the Stuttgarter Hymnus Chorknaban, the RIAS Kammerchor, the Cologne Chamber Orchestra, the Amsterdam New Sinfonietta and Musica Antiqua of Cologne.

Her concert and recital career included a debut with the Boston Symphony Orchestra in Mahler's *Symphony No. 4* in Boston and New York with Seiji Ozawa conducting. Other conductors with whom she has worked are Sir Charles Mackerras, Uwe Gronostay, Wolfgang Schafer, Leopold Hager, Nikolaus Harnoncourt, Sir Simon Rattle, Helmuth Rilling, and Dietrich Fischer-Dieskau.

She is active on the festival circuit, with appearances at the Baroque Festival in Würzburg, the Oregon Bach Festival, the Bach Festival of Los Angeles, the Salzburg Mozart Week, and the Ansbach Bach Week.

Her operatic debut was in 1991 as Papagena in Mozart's *Magic Flute* at the Théâtre du Monnaie in Brussels. Soon she sang Pamina in the same production when it was given in Salzburg, Zerlina (*Don Giovanni*) and Gilda in Verdi's *Rigoletto* in Bern, and Berg's *Lulu* in Innsbruck, with stage direction by Brigitte Fassbaender.

Her American operatic debut was with the San Francisco Opera during their Strauss Festival of 1993, when she appeared as Sophie in *Der Rosenkavalier* and then as Zdenka in *Arabella* at the Houston Grand Opera, conducted by Christoph Eschenbach. Her debut at the Metropolitan Opera in New York was in the 2000–2001 season.

She moved into the first rank of German opera stars when she appeared in Peter Mussbach's controversial production of Lulu at the Salzburg Festival in 1995, her debut role in that Festival. When she returned two years later, it was in a drastically different role, Konstanze in Mozart's *Die Entführung aus dem Serail*. Other roles she has sung include the title role in Donizetti's *Lucia di Lamermoor* (Welsh National Opera); Elisa in Mozart's *Il Rè Pastore* (Amsterdam); Tytania in Britten's *A Midsummer Night's Dream* (Tel Aviv); Infantin in *Der Zwerg* by Zemlinsky at the Paris Opéra-Bastille; Zerbinetta in Strauss' *Ariadne auf Naxos* (Houston); and Reimann's *The House of Bernarda Alba* in Munich.

She has appeared on several discs in Graham Johnson's Hyperion Schubert series and for the label also recorded a solo recital of Robert Schumann songs, also with Johnson. *—Joseph Stevenson*

Recommended:

- ○ **Debussy & Chausson: Melodies** / Schäfer, Gage / 2000 / DG 459682
- ○ **Krenek Lieder** / Schäfer, Bauni / 1995 / Orfeo 373951
- ○ **Schubert Lieder** / Schäfer, Gage / 1997 / Orfeo 450971
- ○ **Bach: Wedding Cantatas** / Goebel (cond.), Schäfer, Cologne Musica Antiqua / DG 459621

R. Murray Schafer

b. 1933, Sarnia, Ontario, Canada

Composer

R. Murray Schafer has been established since the 1970s as Canada's premier composer, though he is known equally well outside that country for both his educational theories and for developing the idea of the "soundscape." His major compositional endeavor has been *Patria*, an as-yet-uncompleted series of 12 theatrical/operatic works begun in 1966. His music and writing reflect an omnivorous, and almost totally self-directed, education and always a concern for the human scale in music and society.

Schafer began studies rather diffidently (being unsure whether he would rather be an artist) at the University of Toronto in 1952, after earning a licentiate in piano from the Royal College of Music, London (Ontario). He was forced to leave in 1955 when he refused to apologize for laughing at his choral music professor. He did have time to acquire a strong neo-Classical compositional technique (as seen in the *Concerto for Harpsichord and Eight Wind Instruments*, 1954) from his teacher John Weinzweig, the first influential avant-garde Canadian composer. Perhaps most important to Schafer's later thinking was the contact he had at the University with Marshall McLuhan, especially with his theories of communication and the freewheeling use of evidence from widely varying sources to support them.

Schafer started an intensive course of self-education in philosophy, languages, and literature. This continued when he moved to Vienna in 1956, ostensibly to study music; in reality his two-year stay was spent studying medieval German, only one of the many obscure languages and cultures in which he would take an interest. The first composition that Schafer acknowledges as important springs from this era: the *Minnelieder*, a setting of 13 medieval German poems, for voice and chamber ensemble (1956). In 1958 Schafer moved to Great Britain, where he was a journalist, and where he prepared a performing edition of Ezra Pound's opera *Le Testament*.

Returning to Canada in 1961, Schafer organized, with other composers, a series of "Ten Centuries Concerts" in Toronto which presented rare music from all eras. Even before his return he had begun to compose more, having incorporated a flexible kind of serialism as a musical technique, and social improvement as a philosophy. Schafer became a professor at the then-recently created, and quite radical, Simon Fraser University in Burnaby, British Columbia, in 1965. During his ten-year stay there, he created the World Soundscape Project, under the auspices of which have been made many different attempts to study the sounds around us, their effects on us, and what can be done to make their quality better. Schafer applied his soundscape studies to education, which resulted in a few well-known booklets, such as *The Composer in the Classroom* (1965) and *Ear Cleaning* (1967). In all cases, Schafer's concern has been to get his readers to open up their ears and listen critically to their environment, and especially to noises caused by machines and other non-natural sources.

In 1975 Schafer moved to a farmhouse near Maynooth, Ontario, and in 1987 to another in Indian River, Ontario, to escape the "sonic sewers" of city life. The focus of Schafer's compositional career through the 1980s and 1990s was the immense opera/theater cycle *Patria*, which has grown from an initial plan for two pieces in 1966 (which were originally to be performed simultaneously) to its present plan of 12 pieces, of which most have been completed. The *Patria* cycle is intended as a practical example of Schafer's "theatre of confluence" theory, a sort of expanded Wagnerian Gesamtkunstwerk involving all the senses and in more varied settings. *—David McCarthy*

Overview of Works (1954)

Canadian composer R. Murray Schafer was largely self-taught. His musical studies at the University of Toronto in the 1950s were cut short when he was expelled for bad behavior after a year. After leaving the university, he briefly continued his compositional studies, taking private lessons; however, all of his further musical endeavors were self-directed. Consequently, Schafer's music tends to be deeply personal, highly original, and imaginative. It is also a direct reflection of the composer's personality, pushing at the boundaries of convention by employing obscure texts, musical effects at the extremes of instrumental technique, and experimental notation. Schafer's career as a composer was also combined with his work as a freelance journalist for the BBC and as a professor of music. Schafer wrote a variety of instrumental, vocal, and stage music over the course of his career. His earliest works date from the mid-1950s and include a harpsichord concerto (Schafer studied harpsichord with Greta Kraus during his brief period at the University of Toronto) and two song cycles, *Minnelieder* and *Kinderlieder*, all of which may be generally characterized as being in a neo-Classical style. His music of the 1960s reveals a turn toward serial composition (a popular trend at the time) and experimental music. Electronic elements are introduced during this period, along with indeterminacy.

In the 1970s, Schafer composed a number of parodic and irreverent orchestral works, including *North/White*, in which a snowmobile appears on stage; and *Son of Heldenleben*, a parody of Richard Strauss. At the end of the 1970s, Schafer began writing what he called "environmental music," producing an enormous cycle called *Patria*. The pieces that comprise *Patria* are either musical works that make direct use of the natural environment—as in "Princess of the Stars," which features musicians around the shore of a lake while speakers perform in canoes on the water—or works that distort or reconfigure the environment of the audience, involving them in the musical work, as in *Ra*, based on the *Egyptian Book of the Dead*, which takes the form of a musico-dramatic ritual in which the audience participates. The apotheosis of these works and the epilogue of the cycle, "And Wolf Shall Inherit the Moon," is a camping trip into the wilderness in which the audience dresses in costume and performs a ritual in the woods. *—Alexander Carpenter*

Recommended:

- ○ **Schafer: The 5 String Quartets** / Orford SQ, / 1990 / CMC 39/4090
- ○ **Schafer: Concerti** / A. Davis, Akiyama, Herbig (conds.), Aitken, Loman, Israelievitch, Vancouver SO / 1992 / CBC 5114
- ○ **Schafer: Garden of the Heart** / Bernardi (cond.), Brown, Popescu, National Arts Centre Orch. / 1997 / CBC 5173
- ○ **Schafer: Apocalypsis "Credo"; Thomas Tallis: Spem in alium** / Sund (cond.), Rao, Edwards, Ratzlaff, Edison, McGill Chamber Singers, The Calixa Lavallee Ens., The Laurier Singers, Mac / 2002 / Opening Day 9325
- ○ **Berio, Stravinsky & Schafer** / Armenian (cond.), Stilwell, Canadian CO / 1994 / Musica Viva 1073

Samuel Scheidt

b. Nov. 3, 1587, Halle, Germany, **d.** Mar. 24, 1654, Halle, Germany

Composer: Keyboard

One of the earliest German composers to forge a synthesis of traditional Germanic chorale and counterpoint with the more modern textures emerging from Italy, Samuel Scheidt was a multifaceted composer of music both sacred and secular whose fame, however, rests almost entirely on the excellence of his instrumental music.

Scheidt was born in Halle during the late 1580s, within a year of both Heinrich Schütz and Johann Hermann Schein. Both would later become friends of Scheidt, and who were engaged, like Scheidt, in the fusion of the musical idioms from northern and southern Europe. Scheidt's father was a municipal official who maintained a number of friendships with prominent local musicians, and encouraged his sons to pursue musical studies. Scheidt attended public school, and was instructed in music by the Kantor of the local Gymnasium, Matthäus Birkner, until he attained the position of organist at the Moritzkirche in Halle in 1604. After resigning the post four years later, Scheidt journeyed to Amsterdam for a period of study with well-known organist Jan Sweelinck, whose music Scheidt would later edit and publish back in Germany.

From 1609 to 1625, Scheidt served as court organist and secular keyboard composer to Christian Wilhelm of Brandenburg, the new administrator of Halle. These were prosperous years for the composer, and after 1619 Scheidt combined his duties as organist with those of Kapellmeister, strengthening the instrumental and vocal forces of the court and overseeing the rebuilding of the Mortizkirche organ. Much of Scheidt's better-known music hails from the years immediately following his appointment as Kapellmeister: three separate volumes of instrumental pieces, one collection each of motets and vocal concertos, and the *Tabulatura nova*, a massive collection of organ music, all which appeared between 1620 and 1624.

In 1625, however, Wilhelm left Halle to fight in the Thirty Years War, and Scheidt was left virtually unemployed. Despite his lack of salary and the departure of most of his musicians for more lucrative positions, Scheidt remained in Halle, earning what he could from teaching and the occasional commission from other cities' courts. He was rewarded for such loyalty in 1628, when Halle created a new and important musical post for him, that of director musices (musical director). A conflict with the Rektor of the local Gymnasium, who claimed, as did Scheidt, to have jurisdiction over the choirboys, resulted in Scheidt's dismissal from the post in 1630. The composer's personal life soon worsened when all of his children died of the plague during a 1636 outbreak.

In 1638, the return of a city administrator (now Duke August of Saxony) brought a renewed musical prosperity to Halle, and Scheidt once again assumed his duties as the city's Kapellmeister. He continued to compose music for public and private occasions until his death in 1654 at the age of 66. *—Blair Johnston*

KEYBOARD

Works for Organ (ca. 1624–1650)

Samuel Scheidt (1587–1654) was an important German composer from the early Baroque period and, without doubt, the most prominent in the realm of music for keyboard. Even his two distinguished countrymen Heinrich Schütz (1585–1672) and Johann Hermann Schein (1586–1630), giants in vocal music, did not challenge him in this genre. Scheidt's tendency to recycle his own music and that of others was not unusual for his time; Handel and Bach would likewise successfully rework older material.

Scheidt's most important keyboard effort was his *Tabulatura Nova* (1624), a three-volume collection designed primarily for organ. Scheidt himself was an organist of virtuosic skill, and many of his compositions were either for organ or involved the organ. The music in this massive collection was perhaps the most important written for keyboard up to its time, not least because it introduced staff notation, which replaced existing tablature systems and became the most widely used method of musical notation. But of course the music itself is ultimately of greater significance, and this collection is outstanding.

The first two books of the *Tabulatura Nova* contain 15 sets of variations, eight of which are based on sacred themes—specifically from Lutheran chorales—and seven on secular themes. The last volume totally excludes secular sources. What makes Scheidt's work here of such artistic consequence are his innovative use of counterpoint and his brilliantly conceived variation technique. He also adapted elements from Italian instrumental styles, but used them without appearing imitative. It is generally agreed that Scheidt's music here—and much of his output in general—divulges certain stylistic traits absorbed from his teacher, Jan Pieterszoon Sweelinck (1562–1621). The *Tabulatura Nova* exerted a crucial influence of its own, though: Bach would seize upon its contrapuntal example and develop it into one of the most sophisticated and profound bodies of technique in Baroque music.

Scheidt's next collection for solo keyboard did not appear until 1650, and was quite different from its predecessor. The *Tabulatur-Buch hundert geistlicher Lieder und Psalmen* (Tabulature Book of 100 Sacred Songs and Psalms) is a collection of settings of four-part chorales whose writing is a bit less complex than that of its predecessor but still steeped in counterpoint and other learned devices. Not only themes but also harmonies are drawn from seventeenth century Lutheran hymnals. Most of the chorales, in fact, seem modeled on those in Schein's 1627 *Cantional*, a collection of hymns for four or five singers with optional continuo. But Scheidt's chorales are native to the organ, containing inventive writing that draws the music into the keyboard realm naturally and subtly. *—Robert Cummings*

Recommended:

- ○ **Scheidt: Ludi Musici** / Savall (cond.), Hespèrion XX / 2002 / Astree 9980
- ○ **Scheidt: Tabulatura Nova Vol. 1** / Raml, Landshamer / 2003 / MDG 614115-6
- ○ **Scheidt: Concertus Sacri** / Flamig (cond.), Dresden Kreuzchor, Capella Fidicinia / 1995 / Berlin Classics 0091262

Johann Hermann Schein

b. Jan. 20, 1586, Grünhain, Germany, **d.** Nov. 19, 1630, Leipzig, Germany
Composer: Chamber Music

Johann Hermann Schein was born within a year of both Heinrich Schütz and Samuel Scheidt. Together, these three composers forged a new identity for German music during the early Baroque period, combining the traditional Germanic emphasis on contrapuntal setting of Lutheran chorales with modern stylistic innovations from Italy. In addition to his activities as a composer and poet, Schein is remembered as one of J.S. Bach's predecessors as Kantor of St. Thomas in Leipzig.

Although he was born in the small town of Grünhain in 1586, Schein spent most of his childhood years in Dresden. He showed musical promise as a child, and in 1599 was accepted into the choir of the Elector of Saxony as a boy soprano. Schein's musical education continued under the direct guidance of the court's Kapellmeister, and when his voice broke, he left the Kapelle in May of 1603 to enroll at the prestigious Schulpforta School for Music and the Humanities. After briefly returning to Dresden in 1607, he enrolled at the University of Leipzig to study music, literature, and law, remained there for four years. While a student there, he also published his first work, *Venus Kräntzlein*, a musical setting of his own poems.

Although he had always divided his attention between music and literature, in 1615 Schein was offered the post of Kapellmeister to the Duke of Weimar. However, his time at Weimar was cut short when he successfully auditioned for the job of Kantor at St. Thomas in Leipzig in late 1616. During the 1620s, Schein suffered a number of personal misfortunes, which impeded his successful professional life. His first wife died in 1624, and most or possibly all of the children born by his second wife, whom he married in 1625, died before reaching adulthood. In addition, Schein's health was declining, and, after suffering tuberculosis, scurvy and kidney stones for most of his adult life, he died in 1630, at the age of 44.

Unlike his close friend and colleague Samuel Scheidt, whose fame rests largely on the merits of his instrumental music, Schein was essentially a composer of vocal music. While his early sacred music draws heavily on the motets of Lassus and Bodenschatz—whose compilation of motets was used for musical instruction at the Schulpforta—Schein later developed a more modern style of sacred vocal concerto with basso continuo. The *Opella nova* of 1618 contains some of the earliest examples of this revolutionary new form. The texts used in his secular music are entirely his own; the music, like his work for sacred occasions, develops over time from a relatively simple, homophonic style, as in the early *Venus Kräntzlein*. More complex textures featuring greater vocal independence and basso continuo appear in *Hirten Lust*, published in 1624, the first collection of German madrigals with basso continuo. *—Blair Johnston*

CHAMBER MUSIC

Banchetto musicale (1617)

The careers of the early seventeenth century composer Johann Hermann Schein and the early eighteenth century composer J.S. Bach, though separated by a full century, are strangely parallel to one another. Schein served as Kapellmeister to the court of Weimar, and then, in 1616, moved on to take up the position of Kantor to the St. Thomas Church and School in Leipzig. Bach was similarly employed in Weimar for a long time (he eventually left Weimar specifically because he was *not* appointed Kapellmeister, or music director, when the job opened up), and, more famously, he spent almost the whole of the last half of his life with the title Thomaskantor of Leipzig. And just as Bach divided his time between composing sacred vocal music and composing secular instrumental music, so too was Schein a renowned author of vocal music (in both the German and the Italian styles, something quite remarkable for his time) and also of brilliant and widely esteemed instrumental dance suites. Indeed, it is quite appropriate to say that the long-term influence of Schein's groundbreaking *Banchetto musicale* of 1617 was such that had Schein never produced it, J.S. Bach could never possibly have written his own (much more famous) instrumental suites in quite the way that he did.

The *Banchetto musicale* is a collection of "Padouanen, Gagliarden, Courenten und Allemanden" (pavanes, galliards, courantes, and allemandes) scored for five instruments. "Violen" are asked for, by which we can assume Schein meant either viols or the more modern violins, and there is no continuo part. There are 20 separate suites in the various modes. The four individual dance movements of any one suite are all related to one another, motivically speaking: the same thematic building blocks are used for pavane, galliard, courante, and allemande. And at the end of each suite there is a "triple" in which the allemande is recast in triple meter, just as many dances are followed by "doubles" in later composers' suites. *—Blair Johnston*

Recommended:

- ○ **Schein: Banchetto Musicale** / Busca (cond.), Accademia del Ricercare / Stradivarius 33403

Hermann Scherchen

b. Jun. 21, 1891, Berlin, Germany, **d.** Jun. 12, 1966, Florence, Italy

Conductor

Scherchen was one of the leading conductors in the middle part of the twentieth century, especially valued for his pioneering performances of the contemporary music of his time. He was essentially self-taught as a musician and became a violist in the Blüthner Orchestra and the Berlin Philharmonic when he was 16. In 1911 he was an assistant to Arnold Schoenberg in the preparation of *Pierrot Lunaire* for performance. Following its Berlin premiere, the piece was taken on a tour in which Scherchen conducted. He became the conductor of the Riga Symphony Orchestra in 1914, but was soon interned by the Russians as an enemy alien when World War I started. He returned to Germany after Russia left the war to found the Neue Musikgesellschaft and the Scherchen Quartet. In 1919 he founded a militant magazine *Melos*.

He succeeded Furtwängler as the director of the Frankfurt Museum Concerts in 1922 and in the same year began a long relationship with the Winterthur Musikkollegium in Switzerland. From 1928 to 1933 he was the Generalmusikdirektor in Königsberg. He frequently conducted contemporary music festivals, especially with the International Society for Contemporary Music, with which he was connected from its founding in 1923. Among his premieres in the 1920s and 1930s were the *Three Fragments from Wozzeck* by Berg and the quarter-tone opera *Mother* by Alois Haba.

He left Germany immediately upon the rise of the Nazis to power in 1933, settling in Switzerland, where he became music director of the Zurich Radio Orchestra and also gave courses in conducting, which became a regular summer school in Switzerland in 1939. In the same year he founded the Ars Viva Orchestra. He married the Chinese composer Hsiao Shu-sien. They had a daughter, Tona Scherchen-Hsiao, born in 1937, who went back to China with her mother in 1949. She became a noted composer, especially after she moved to France in 1972.

Scherchen resumed his continent-wide activities after World War II ended. He was director of the Zürich Radio Orchestra (1944–50) and in 1950, with the support of UNESCO, opened a studio for electroacoustic research in 1954 in Gravesano, the village where he lived. He continued his writing about new music in the *Gravesano Blätter*. Unlike many conductors of his generation his "new music" was not merely the new music of his youth, but the continuing evolution of new music. In the 1950s he conducted the premieres of such works as Dallapiccola's *Il prigioniero*, Dessau's *Das Verhör des Lukullus*, and Henze's *König Hirsch*. He was the first to play any music from Schoenberg's *Aron und Moses* in Darmstadt (1951), edited it for its first performance under his colleague Hans Rosbaud, and led its first performance in Berlin. He did not appear in the United States until 1964 when he conducted the Philadelphia Orchestra.

He was the author of a leading text on conducting and of many articles supporting modern music. He suffered a heart attack while conducting Malipiero's *Orfeide* in Florence and died four days later. *—Joseph Stevenson*

Recommended:

- ○ **Hermann Scherchen** / Scherchen (cond.), Royal PO, Berlin RSO, Vienna State Opera Orch. / EMI 75956
- ○ **Scherchen conducts Bach & Schoenberg** / Scherchen (cond.) / 1998 / Tahra 245/6
- ○ **Mahler: Symphony 5** / Scherchen (cond.), Vienna State Opera Orch. / 2002 / Westminster 471268

Peter Schickele

b. Jul. 17, 1935, Ames, IA

Composer

Peter Schickele, although an accomplished composer, musicologist, performer, and radio host, is better known for "discovering" the musical works of P.D.Q. Bach, the fictional last and least son of J.S. Bach.

Schickele grew up in an amateur musical family in Washington, D.C., and in Fargo, where he became the town's only bassoonist. His composition teacher was the conductor of the Fargo-Moorhead Orchestra, Sigvald Thompson. Schickele went on to become the only music major at Swarthmore College. By the time he graduated in 1957, he had composed chamber music, songs (including rock & roll songs), and four orchestral works, and he was also arranging music for dance bands and jazz groups. He was struck by the music of Hindemith, Bartók, Elvis, and Ray Charles, but particularly by Stravinsky and the Everly Brothers.

He stopped being a loner and started studying with Roy Harris and Darius Milhaud, then William Bergsma and Vincent Persichetti at Juilliard. He received a Ford Foundation grant to compose for the Los Angeles high schools, then became a teacher himself at Juilliard from 1961 to 1965. Since then, he has dedicated himself to composing, arranging, and performing, based in New York City where he and his wife, poet Susan Sindall, make their home.

He began arranging music for Joan Baez, Buffy Sainte-Marie, and other folk singers. He created music for movies, including *Silent Running*; documentaries; and TV, including segments for *Sesame Street*. From 1968 to 1971, he and fellow composers Robert Dennis and Stanley Walden were the Open Window, a chamber rock group that played in solo and mixed media concerts and with symphony orchestras. They also wrote songs and were the pit band for the musical *Oh, Calcutta!*

After that, he concentrated on writing and performing the increasingly popular music of P.D.Q. Bach. The Bach works are a mixture of satires on, spoofs of, and homages to a whole range of classical masterpieces. The music had been heard in concerts at end-of-season events at Juilliard and the Aspen Music Festival since 1959. Public concerts of this music began in 1965 and have spawned over a dozen recordings (a few winning Grammy awards) and *The Definitive Biography of P.D.Q. Bach*, by the "discoverer" of these works, "Professor" Peter Schickele.

In 1992, he began the public radio program Schickele Mix, a musicologically educational, but entertaining, survey that draws connections between everything from the music of the ancient world to Bach to Motown. The show was given ASCAP's Deems Taylor Award in 1993.

As well as serving as composer-in-residence at schools and festivals, Schickele has received numerous commissions for new works from such varied organizations as the Saint Louis Symphony, the Minnesota Opera, the Lark and Audubon quartets, and the Chamber Music Society of Lincoln Center. He also frequently writes "personal" pieces, many of them rounds, as trinkets to commemorate friends and events. *—Patsy Morita*

Overview of Works

Peter Schickele has a triple musical identity: he not only composes under his own name and as P.D.Q. Bach (the last and least of Johann Sebastian Bach's children), but writes, lectures, and hosts the widely distributed radio show Schickele Mix, which presents a wide variety of music ranging from the most obscure classical to the most popular contemporary. Not surprisingly, then, his compositions show a wide variety of influences of all kinds, as well as a sense of humor that ranges from the wry and quirky (rather like that of his teacher Darius Milhaud) as in his *Last Tango in Bayreuth*, to the musical equivalents of pratfalls, as in a majority of the P.D.Q. Bach compositions. Schickele's compositions under his own name cover a wide variety of genres and styles, from intimate song to symphony, though among his nearly 200 compositions, chamber music and song are somewhat more numerous. They include *New Goldberg Variations for cello and piano*, a concerto for bassoon and orchestra, songs on Elizabethan lyrics, cabaret songs, folk song arrangements, and stage music, including incidental music for Sheridan's play *The Rivals*, a program of poetry (by his wife, poet Susan Sindall) and song, and both text and music in the musical *Oh! Calcutta!* He has also composed a wide variety of children's music, including arrangements for *Fantasia 2000*, the score for a film of Sendak's *Where the Wild Things Are*, and new narratives for *Peter and the Wolf* (*Sneaky Pete and the Wolf*) and *The Carnival of the Animals*. His works as P.D.Q. Bach (which he always describes as unearthed by a certain Professor Schickele) are almost entirely pastiches of classical and popular music, in about equal proportions, as are the proportions of classical and popular culture references. Despite Professor Schickele's pronouncements that P.D.Q. Bach was both ignorant and lazy, writing original music only when he couldn't remember what he was trying to steal or was so incompetent in his plagiarism that he ended up creating something new, the compositions are carefully crafted to appeal both to audiences with a thorough understanding of or only a very passing and casual acquaintance with classical music. *—Ann Feeney*

Recommended:

- ○ **Hornsmoke: Brass Music of Peter Schickele** / Schickele, Chestnut Brass Company / 1998 / Newport Classic 85638
- ○ **Peter Schickele** / Schickele, Audubon Quartet / 2000 / Centaur 2505
- ○ **Schickele: The Emperor's New Clothes** / An Die Musik / 2003 / Newport Classic 85668
- ○ **Schickele: Bestiary; Quartet** / Sherry, Shifrin, Dean, Sato, Bardo, Oei, Harms, Benz / 1984 / Vanguard 4066
- ○ **Schickele: On a Lark** / Lark Quartet / 1998 / Arabesque 6719

Works as "P.D.Q. Bach"

Given the vast musical accomplishments of both the father and his sons, it seems impossible that one of Johann Sebastian Bach's progeny could have gone completely undetected by historians until recently. Such, however, is the situation of P.D.Q. Bach, Johann's last son, whose very existence, as well as all his extant compositions, was uncovered by the modern American composer Peter Schickele in an arduous feat of scholarship beginning in the late 1950s. As Schickele reports in his definitive biography of P.D.Q. Bach (aptly titled *The Definitive Biography of P.D.Q. Bach*), P.D.Q. was the victim of a "massive cover-up conspiracy conducted by the Bach family," who did not want the world to know that the greatest master of the Baroque had managed to father a man variously described as "a one-man plague," "history's most justifiably neglected composer," and "a pimple on the face of music." The hostility from the rest of the Bachs actually began in his childhood, in which Johann Christian dubbed P.D.Q. "the noisemonger." This may have caused P.D.Q.'s hard living as an adult; one Catholic priest told contemporary music historian

Charles Burney that "in the long history of the church, P.D.Q. is the only *person* ever to have been declared a cardinal sin." Nevertheless, P.D.Q. managed to write a fair body of his own compositions, which Schickele has divided into three periods. First is the Initial Plunge, when P.D.Q. used Baroque forms in works like the *Echo Sonata for Two Groups of Unfriendly Instruments* and the *Gross Concerto*. During the Soused Period, P.D.Q. explored the influences of Haydn, Mozart, and grain spirits with works like the *Pervertimento for bagpipes, bicycle and balloons*, an opera titled *The Stoned Guest*, and the *"Erotica" Variations* for "banned instruments and piano." The third period, Contrition, finds P.D.Q. returning, "as it were, to his musical womb," with works like the cantata *Iphigenia in Brooklyn* with "bargain counter tenor" solo, the oratorio *The Seasonings*, and the *Toot Suite* for calliope, four hands. Despite the obvious diversity of influences, P.D.Q.'s works share many features. P.D.Q. was always willing to write for obscure and uninviting instruments, like the kazoo, the left-handed sewer flute, and the shower hose in D. P.D.Q. also displays a remarkable ability to anticipate future musical developments, as in the *1712 Overture*; its existence alone calls into question Tchaikovsky's intellectual honesty, but P.D.Q. also manages to conceive and interpolate the melody *"Pop Goes the Weasel"* into the structure (an interpolation removed by Tchaikovsky in his version). Finally, P.D.Q.'s oeuvre is united by its unlistenability; the only value any of these pieces could have is as unintentional humor. All in all, P.D.Q. Bach's works are more, less, and exactly what one would expect of a composer born on April 1, 1742. *—Andrew Lindemann Malone*

Recommended:

○ **The Dreaded P.D.Q. Bach** / various, Greater Hoople Area Off-Season Philharmonic / 1996 / Vanguard 159

○ **P.D.Q. Bach: 1712 Overture & Other Musical Assaults** / Walter (cond.), Greater Hoople Area Off-Season Philharmonic / 1989 / Telarc 80210

○ **Peter Schickele Presents an Evening With P.D.Q. Bach** / various, Schickele, CO / 1987 / Vanguard 79195

○ **The Ill-Conceived P.D.Q. Bach Anthology** / Wayland, Graham (conds.), various, NY Pick-Up Ens., Greater Hoople Area Off-Season Philharmonic, Okay Chorale / 1998 / Telarc 80520

András Schiff

b. Dec. 21, 1953, Budapest, Hungary
Pianist

András Schiff emerged in the last decades of the twentieth century as one of the most respected pianists of his generation. After studies with Elisabeth Vadasz, Schiff made his debut at the age of nine. At 14 Schiff began formal studies at the Franz Liszt Academy in Budapest, where he studied with Pál Kadosa, György Kurtag, and Ferenc Rados; later, he studied with British conductor and keyboard player George Malcolm in London.

Schiff came to international prominence as gold medalist in the 1974 Tchaikovsky Competition in Moscow; over the next few years, he also took top honors at the Leeds and Liszt Competitions, launching him on a successful concert and recording career. After a series of recordings for the Hungarian label Hungaroton, Schiff made a recording—as an accompanist for Hungarian soprano Sylvia Sass—for Decca. That recording's producer, Christopher Raeburn, was so impressed by Schiff's musicianship that he engaged the pianist for a project to record the Mozart piano sonatas then missing from Decca's catalogue. The results were so outstanding that Decca continued the series until Schiff produced the label's first integral set of Mozart sonatas. As a Decca/London artist, Schiff also recorded the complete Mozart piano concertos, much of the composer's chamber music, and many of the keyboard works of J.S. Bach. The last are a cornerstone of Schiffıs recorded repertory; they are uniformly excellent and especially notable for their clean delineation of Bach's contrapuntal textures. In tandem with his work in the studio, Schiff has pursued a concert career that includes appearances with the world's major orchestras and conductors. On the recital stage, he has successfully collaborated with such notables as Gidon Kremer, Yuuko Shiokawa (who became his wife), Dietrich Fischer-Dieskau, Heinz Holliger, Peter Serkin, Peter Schreier, Robert Holl, and Cecilia Bartoli. In the late 1990s, he added conducting to his list of talents, frequently conducting from the keyboard in concerto concerts. In order to perform all of Mozart's piano concertos in Salzburg over a period of seven years, he formed his own ensemble, Cappella Andrea Barca, in 1999.

Schiff's playing has been singled out for its complete technical fluency and intelligent musicality; in addition to the composers mentioned above, he is especially well known for his performances of Beethoven, Schubert, Bartók, Debussy, and Ravel. Among his post-competition honors are a Grammy Award (1989) and Hungary's highest artistic distinction, the Kossuth Prize (1996). In the 1990s he became a Teldec Artist; his recordings for the label include works by Handel, Brahms, Reger, Haydn, and Hungarian composer Sándor Veress. *—Joseph Stevenson*

Recommended:

○ **Janáček: A Recollection** / Schiff / 2001 / ECM 461660

○ **Haydn: Piano Sonatas** / Schiff / 1998 / Telarc 17141

○ **Bach: 3 Keyboard Concertos** / Malcolm (cond.), Schiff, English CO / 1984 / Denon 7236

○ **Mozart: Piano Sonatas** / Schiff / 1995 / London 443717

Aksel Schiøtz

b. Sep. 1, 1906, Roskilde, Denmark, **d.** Apr. 19, 1975, Copenhagen, Denmark
Tenor

A musician of the utmost integrity and musicality, tenor Aksel Schiøtz was a symbol of Danish resistance in the face of Nazi rule during World War II in addition to being one of Scandinavia's most accomplished lyric singers. Exemplary in opera, oratorio, and recital, he recorded extensively, preserving on disc interpretations seldom equaled since and scarcely surpassed. Before he had reached his mid-forties, however, Schiøtz was diagnosed with a brain tumor. While the operation was successful, the singer's voice suffered and his public appearances diminished. Following an early retirement, Schiøtz established himself as a singing teacher of exceptional gifts.

After graduating in 1930 from the University of Copenhagen, where he had concentrated on the study of modern languages, Schiøtz became a schoolmaster. For the next eight years, he taught languages and music in several Danish schools, pursuing his interest in music as an avocation. Denmark's most prominent choral conductor, Møgens Wöldike, offered him membership in Copenhagen's foremost male chorus and soon began to assign him solo work. In 1936, Schiøtz gave his first recital as a non-professional and, by 1939, he had decided to forego teaching and devote himself to singing full-time. Following a brief period of study with the Swedish baritone John Forsell in Stockholm, Schiøtz made his debut that same year with the Royal Opera in Copenhagen, singing Ferrando in Mozart's *Così fan tutte*. A final accomplishment in 1939 was his professional recital debut in Copenhagen.

Numerous other opera, recital, and oratorio engagements followed, notably Gounod's Faust and Sverkel in J.P.E. Hartmann's *Liden Kirsten* for the Royal Opera. One adulatory review after another followed as the tenor soared to unprecedented popularity in his native country. When the Nazis invaded Denmark, Schiøtz refused requests to sing German lieder, realizing that such performances would be used for German propaganda. He sang, instead, the music of Denmark, both art songs and folk music, his research significantly adding to the store of published Danish song. In addition to maintaining his singing career, Schiøtz became active in the Resistance, a choice which led to his being knighted by King Christian X in 1947.

In the years immediately after the war's end, Schiøtz's reputation spread abroad, largely through his many radio broadcasts. He recorded with accompanist Gerald Moore memorable performances of *Die Schöne Müllerin* and *Dichterliebe* in 1945 and 1946, respectively. In 1946, Schiøtz was engaged by the Glyndebourne Festival Chorus to alternate with Peter Pears as the Male Chorus in Benjamin Britten's *The Rape of Lucretia*.

Just as his career was achieving international scale, Schiøtz was diagnosed with the tumor whose excision left his face partially paralyzed. With intense application, he retrained, enabling himself to return to the concert stage in Copenhagen in September 1948, this time as a baritone. His New York debut a month later, however, confirmed that while his artistry was unimpaired, his voice had suffered greatly in tone and volume. Over the next few years, Schiøtz made ever fewer appearances before the public and eventually retired to devote himself to teaching in Minnesota, Toronto, Colorado, and finally, in his native Copenhagen. A 1969 text on singing, *The Singer and His Art*, reveals Schiøtz as an astute and considerate observer of singers and the vocal literature; the wise, unpretentious volume warrants a place in every singer's collection. *—Erik Eriksson*

Recommended:

○ **Schiøtz Sings Nielsen** / Schiøtz, etc. / Pearl 9140

○ **Aksel Schiøtz** / Schiøtz, etc. / Pearl 9254

○ **Schubert: Die Winterreise; Die Schöne Müllerin** / Hotter, Raucheisen; Schiøtz, Moore / 2003 / Documents 220760

Tito Schipa

b. Jan. 2, 1888, Lecce, Italy, **d.** Dec. 16, 1965, New York, NY
Tenor

Tito Schipa's recordings document the career of one of the most important lyric tenors of the twentieth century. His light, lyric voice, while smaller than most operatic tenors, was so well produced that it carried to the back of even the largest theaters, and he was greatly admired for his command of dynamics and phrasing. In recital he was known to sing in as many as five languages, always sounding like a native speaker.

Schipa's musical talents were apparent at a very young age; he studied both piano and composition before discovering his singing voice. Recognizing the young tenor's potential, the Bishop of Lecce subsidized his earliest vocal studies; the singer then went to Milan for further training. After six years of study, Schipa made his debut in Piedmont as Alfredo in *La traviata* in early 1910. On March 24 of that same year he made his debut at Messina as the Duke in *Rigoletto* with the great Claudia Muzio as Gilda. He spent the next two seasons singing in small houses in

Italy. In 1913, he traveled to Buenos Aires and then to Rio de Janeiro for his first appearances outside Italy. He was heard in *Mignon*, *La traviata*, and *Lakmé*.

In early 1914 he sang at the Teatro San Carlo in Naples, his first appearance in a major opera house in Italy. In many of his early appearances he was partnered with Amelita Galli-Curci whose voice blended perfectly with his. In December 1915, he first sang in *Prince Igor* of Borodin at la Scala and later that season also sang Des Grieux in Massenet's *Manon*. During World War I his career continued to flourish even with the travel restrictions.

In 1919, he made his U.S. debut in Chicago as the Duke in *Rigoletto* with his favored partner, Galli-Curci. For the next 20 years Schipa sang nearly all of his important roles in Chicago and also at the Ravinia Park summer performances. From 1920 to 1929 when he was not singing with the Chicago Opera Schipa could be found touring the United States and Canada giving concerts and recitals. In 1929, he returned to Italy for performances of *L'elisir d'amore* at La Scala and was later heard there in *Don Giovanni*. While in Italy he also sang in Naples, Rome, and Florence. He then began a long recital tour which was a great success.

With the monetary crisis in Chicago caused by the depression, Schipa signed a contract with the Metropolitan Opera in New York. He made his debut there in November 1932 in *L'elisir d'amore* and later in the season was heard in *Lucia di Lammermoor*, *La traviata*, *Don Giovanni*, and *Il barbiere di Siviglia*. He continued to appear at the Metropolitan Opera until 1941, but most seasons he spent the majority of his time in Italy with summers in South America. He remained in Italy during World War II and returned to Buenos Aires in 1946. In the early 1950s he began to sing less often in opera but he continued to appear in many concerts and recitals. In 1957, he sang his final performances on a recital tour in Moscow, Leningrad, and Riga. *—Richard LeSueur*

Recommended:

- ○ **Prima Voce: Schipa** / Antonicelli (cond.), Schipa, Galli-Curci, Favero / 1990 / Nimbus 7813
- ○ **Schipa Favourites** / Schipa, etc. / 1999 / ASV 5248
- ○ **Lebendige Vergangenheit: Tito Schipa** / Schipa, Galli-Curci, Bori / Preiser 89160

Thomas Schippers

b. Mar. 9, 1930, Kalamazoo, MI, **d.** Dec. 16, 1977, New York, NY
Conductor

Thomas Schippers was a talented American conductors and a particular champion of the music of Samuel Barber. He played at a public piano recital at the age of six and was a church organist when he was 14. He continued his piano studies at the Curtis Institute of Music in Philadelphia (1944–45). He also studied privately with Olga Samaroff (1946–47). He went on to Yale University, where he had some lessons in composition with Paul Hindemith.

In 1948 he took second prize in the Philadelphia Orchestra's young conductor's contest. He took a job as organist of the Greenwich Village Presbyterian Church in New York. He and group of other young musicians formed a group called the Lemonade Opera Company, which he conducted for several years.

Schippers began conducting Menotti's opera *The Consul* on Broadway shortly after its 1950 premiere. This began a strong association with Menotti and with Samuel Barber. This led to Schippers conducting the premiere performance of Menotti's short Christmas opera *Amahl and the Night Visitors*, the first opera commissioned especially for television broadcast, on the NBC network on December 24, 1951. On April 9, 1952, he conducted Menotti's *The Old Maid and the Thief* at the New York City Opera and remained on that company's conducting roster into 1954. He made his first appearances with the New York Philharmonic Orchestra, at La Scala in Milan, Italy, and at the Metropolitan Opera in 1955. When Menotti organized his new Spoleto Festival of Two Worlds he chose Schippers as its music director. He frequently guest conducted the New York Philharmonic Orchestra and made some classic recordings of music of Samuel Barber with them. When the orchestra made its historic tour of the Soviet Union under Leonard Bernstein in 1959, Schippers also went as its alternate conductor. It was he who was conducting at the Metropolitan Opera on March 4, 1960, when baritone Leonard Warren died on stage. The Metropolitan Opera often called upon him to lead newer operas, including the world premiere of Barber's *Antony and Cleopatra*, which opened its new house in Lincoln Center. In 1962 he conducted the world premiere of the late Manuel de Falla's cantata *Atlantida*. In 1964 he made his first appearance conducting at the Bayreuth Festival. In 1970 he accepted the position of music director of the Cincinnati Symphony Orchestra, becoming one of the few American-born conductors to hold such a post at a major American orchestra at the time. He also became a faculty member at the University of Cincinnati College-Conservatory of Music in 1972.

His wife died of cancer in 1973. He was himself struck by lung cancer and unable to open the Cincinnati Orchestra's season in 1977. The management gave him the title of conductor laureate. He died before the year was over, bequeathing the orchestra five million dollars. *—Joseph Stevenson*

Recommended:

- ○ **Barber & Menotti** / Schippers (cond.), Arroyo, New York PO, Columbia SO / 1996 / Sony 62837
- ○ **Menotti: Amahl & the Night Visitors** / Schippers (cond.) / 1952 / RCA 6485
- ○ **Puccini: La Bohème** / Schippers (cond.), Freni, Gedda, Sereni, Orchestra del Teatro Municipa / 1996 / EMI/Black Dog 19297
- ○ **Prokofiev: Alexander Nevsky** / Schippers (cond.), Martin, Chookasian, New York PO / 2002 / Sony 87711

Steffen Schleiermacher

b. May 3, 1960, Halle, Saxony
Pianist

Steffen Schleiermacher is active as both a composer and a pianist specializing in contemporary music. From 1980 to 1985, he studied at the Leipzig Musikhochschule under Siegfried Thiele and Friedrich Schenker (composition), Gerhard Erber (piano), and Günter Blumhagen (conducting); and at the DDR Akademie der Künste with Friedrich Goldmann (composition). He later studied piano with Aloys Kontarsky. He has performed as soloist with the Gewandhaus Orchestra of Leipzig, the Munich Philharmonic Orchestra, the German Symphony Orchestra of Berlin, and the Berlin Radio Symphony Orchestra. Schleiermacher has been the artistic director of the Ensemble Avantgarde, the *Gewandhaus Musica Nova* concert series, and an annual contemporary music festival in Leipzig. He has won an award from the Gaudeamus Competition (1985), the Hanns Eisler Prize (1989, for his *Concerto for viola and chamber ensemble*), the Schneider-Schott Music Prize (1992), and has been awarded residencies at the Villa Massimo, Rome (1992), and the Cité des Arts, Paris (1998). Schleiermacher's compositional influences include Indonesian gamelan and traditional Japanese sacred music. *—Robert Adelson*

Recommended:

- ○ **Piano Music of the Darmstadt School Vol. 1** / Schleiermacher / 2000 / MDG 6131004
- ○ **Cage: Complete Piano Music Vol. 1** / Schleiermacher / 1997 / MDG 6130781
- ○ **Glass: Early Keyboard Music** / Schleiermacher / 2001 / MDG 6131027
- ○ **Wolff: Exercises** / Schleiermacher, Blum, Williams, Dahinden / 1995 / Hat Hut 6167
- ○ **Riley: Keyboard Studies** / Schleiermacher / 2002 / MDG 6131135

Johann Heinrich Schmelzer

b. ca. 1620, Scheibbs, Austria, **d.** 1680, Prague, Bohemia (Czech Rep.)
Composer

Johann Heinrich Schmelzer (or Schmelzer von Ehrenruef) might have created considerable confusion himself over his true biography. On his sister's marriage certificate, the head of their family is identified as Daniel Schmelzer, a baker and burgher of the town of Scheibbs. But Johann Henrich applied in 1673 for documents of ennoblement and claimed his father was an officer in the army of Emperor Ferdinand II. The earliest documentation of his life is the certificate for his first marriage on June 28, 1643, which describes him as a cornettist at St. Stephen's Cathedral in Vienna. He may have been a court chapel violinist as early as 1635, and on October 1, 1649, he was appointed as a violinist in the court orchestra. There are few details of his life and career, but he wrote considerable quantities of music. Between 1659 and 1664, he published three important collections of chamber music. In 1660, composer J. Müller called him "the famous and nearly most distinguished violinist in Europe."

He enjoyed the favor of Emperor Leopold II and had been appointed to head the musicians in the retinue accompanying Leopold in 1658 to his coronation in Frankfurt am Main. The Emperor was a composer himself who frequently sought Schmelzer's professional opinion and relied on him to prepare performances of his music. As a result, he gave Schmelzer frequent gifts of money and golden chains (the latter indicated special favor).

While he wrote his share of vocal and sacred music, Schmelzer's fame and influence are primarily due to his instrumental music. He wrote nearly all of the dramatic music played at court from 1655 to 1680, including ballet music, allegorical pageants, and incidental music to spoken dramas. The court was given to lavish spectacles in which members of the royal family often took part. From this music, Schmelzer arranged dance suites, which were important to the development of the German orchestral suite. These often began with an intrada, ended with a retirada, and included a variety of dance forms (as many as nine individual numbers). He unified these suites by using shared motives, but achieved variety by being quite free in the succession of tonalities. The scoring of these suites was generally for consorts of stringed instruments, but he sometimes added cornets, clarini, trumpets, bassoons, trombones, and piffari.

Schmelzer's chamber music often includes two melody instruments and continuo. One of his most important sets of compositions was his six violin sonatas called *Sonatae unarum fidium* from 1664. Variations were typical in his sonatas and these were virtuosic. Again, his music in this genre was influential in future development of German instrumental music.

When the post of vice-imperial court Kapellmeister fell vacant on April 13, 1671, the Emperor appointed him to that position. The incumbent in that position, G.F. Sances, was an aged, ailing man, and so Schmelzer did the organizational work and most of Sances' other duties. Handling these responsibilities well, his rising fame, and Leopold's admiration, no doubt led the Emperor to grant that 1673 petition for ennoblement. At that point, Schmelzer added the noble "von Ehrenruef" to his name, and it was inherited by his sons. Sances died on November 24, 1679, and Schmelzer petitioned the Emperor on December 18 for the vacant position. The delay might be accounted for by the need to move the court to Prague while Vienna was struck by the plague. The Emperor granted it, retroactive to October 1 (Schmelzer had asked for July 1), but within three months, Schmelzer had died, probably of the plague. *—Joseph Stevenson*

Overview of Works (1657–1679)

At some time during the 1630s, Johann Heinrich Schmelzer had entered the Hapsburg Court Chapel, although he was not officially appointed to the court orchestra as a violinist until 1649. From 1655, he composed court balletti, often for insertion into the operas of court composer Antonio Draghi. He was also the founder of a new south German school of violin playing and composition whose most famous exponent was Heinrich Biber. The hallmarks of this style, developed from the music of earlier seventeenth century Italian violinist/composers, was an expansion of the technique of the instrument to include chords, high positions, and the use of what is known as scordatura, which involved tuning the instrument differently to obtain new coloristic effects. All these techniques can be heard in the collection of six violin sonatas entitled *Sonatae unarum fidium.* Four of the six use the favorite seventeenth century device of the ground bass on which to build the solo part. This enabled the composer to weave florid melodic lines that frequently take on a free, improvisatory spirit. Schmelzer was also the composer of a large body of secular and sacred vocal works, instrumental suites, and chamber works. In his court dances and the trio sonata known as *Lanterly* (a popular song), Schmelzer incorporated original folk elements, and his sonatas were frequently programmatic. Among such pieces is one of his most famous works, the moving lament composed on the death of Ferdinand III, and, in a lighter vein, *Polnische Sackpfiefer* (Polish bagpipers) and *Fechtschule* (Fencing School). Among Schmelzer's many (and mostly lost) sacred works are a number of masses, motets, and Christmas works, the last belonging to the central European "pastoral" tradition. Many works that have yet to be explored are today housed in the famous music collection of Kromeriz castle in Bohemia. *—Brian Robins*

Recommended:

- ○ **Schmelzer: Sonate unarum fidium** / Holloway, Mortensen / 1999 / ECM 465066
- ○ **Intrada Di Polcinelli** / Linden, North, Holloway, Willi / 2000 / Musicaphon 56832

Franz Schmidt

b. Dec. 22, 1874, Pressburg (Bratislava), Slovakia, **d.** Feb. 11, 1939, Perchtoldsdorf, Austria

Composer: Symphonic, Chamber Music

Like Paderewski, Gabrilowitsch, Schnabel, and Isabella Vengerova, Franz Schmidt became a piano pupil of Theodor Leschetizky at the Vienna Conservatorium in 1890, where he studied composition with Bruckner, theory with Robert Fuchs, and cello with Ferdinand Hellmesberger. Born to a German father and Slovak mother in what was then Hungary, he was declared a "musical miracle child" by a priest with whom he took organ lessons in Pressburg (Bratislava today). This encouraged his poor but hopeful parents to move to Vienna in 1888, but chronic privation forced Schmidt to play in dancehall orchestras after graduation until he was chosen in 1896 by conductor Wilhelm Jahn to be a cellist in the Vienna Hofoper Orchestra, and the Philharmoniker drawn from its ranks.

A year later, Mahler succeeded the pedestrian Jahn as artistic director and proceeded to revolutionize performance and production standards for a decade, although his Philharmonic tenure was considerably shorter. Schmidt regarded him favorably at first, but animosity developed and persisted even after Mahler's "resignation" from the Hofoper in 1907. From 1901 to 1908, Schmidt taught piano and cello at the Conservatorium in addition to his duties in the opera house. He resigned the Philharmoniker in 1911, but continued to play with the opera until 1914, when the Staatsakademie appointed him professor of piano. He became professor of counterpoint and composition in 1922, director in 1925, and head of the Musikhochschule from 1927 to 1931. His service earned him the Franz-Josef Medal and for his 60th birthday, an honorary doctorate from Vienna University. Before his retirement in 1937, his most famous pupils included pianists Friedrich Wührer and Alfred Rosé (Mahler's nephew), and composers Theodor Berger and Alfred Uhl.

Schmidt was also respected by his peers, Schreker, Marx, Krenek, and Berg, for his soloist and chamber music performances. Schoenberg particularly admired him for directing *Pierrot Lunaire* in a performance by Schmidt's students.

Although Schmidt's financial and professional fortunes stabilized, his marriages were ill-omened. His first wife went insane, was institutionalized in 1919, and was murdered by the Nazis in 1940. Their only child, Emma, died after the birth of Schmidt's grandchild (he called his *Symphony No. 4,* composed in 1933, "a Requiem for my daughter"). A second marriage to a much younger piano pupil was plagued by Schmidt's ill-health, which worsened progressively until his death.

His mature career as a composer began with *Symphony No. 1* (started in 1896, completed in 1899). The opera *Notre Dame* followed (1902–04), then three more symphonies and another opera, *Fredigundis.* Most of his piano works were composed for Paul Wittgenstein, who had lost his right arm in World War I. (Posthumously, Wührer arranged everything for two hands and as such, they were published.) Schmidt also wrote chamber music, *Variations on a Hussar's Song* for orchestra, and much organ music. However, *The Book With Seven Seals* (1935–37), an oratorio, is regarded by admirers as his masterwork, more important even than the symphonies.

After the deaths of Berg and Schreker, and the flight of Schoenberg and Zemlinsky to the U.S., Schmidt was proclaimed Austria's "most important composer of the time." He continues to be honored as the Romantic successor of Schubert and Bruckner, although his music bears a didactic resemblance to Max Reger's. Elsewhere, his music remained little-known until CD recordings in the 1990s documented several important works for non-Austrian audiences to hear. *—Roger Dettmer*

Overview of Works (1886–1939)

Franz Schmidt was the last in the great line of Austrian composers that started with Haydn and Mozart and ran through Schubert, Bruckner, and Mahler. Although an epigone and not an innovator like his exact contemporary Schoenberg, Schmidt's four symphonies, two operas, two string quartets, numerous organ works, and the massive oratorio *Das Buch mit sieben Siegln* are the final efflorescence of Austrian music before the barbarism of World War II. Schmidt's four symphonies were written over nearly four decades, starting with the melodically appealing *First* in E major (1896–99), moving through the more original three-movement *Second* in E flat major (1911–13) and the more conservative four-movement *Third* (1927–28), and reaching a peak with the deeply expressive and highly original *Fourth* in C minor (1932–33). Written as a funeral monument for his recently deceased daughter, Schmidt's *Fourth* has the four standard symphonic movements articulated as a single arching structure, with the closing movement functioning as a recapitulation of the opening movement. In technical mastery and emotional profundity, Schmidt's *Fourth* stands with Mahler's *Second* and Bruckner's *Eighth.* Schmidt's chamber music dates from the middle years of his career. In the conservative *String Quartets in A major* (1925) and *G major* (1929), Schmidt continued the line of Viennese string quartets of Haydn, Mozart, and Brahms. His three piano quintets (1926, 1932, and 1938) were composed for one-handed pianist Paul Wittgenstein and are highly attractive works. More than any other Austrian composer, Schmidt's music for organ forms a significant part of his oeuvre. His *Toccata and Fugue in E flat major* and especially his enormous *Chaccone in C sharp minor* are important additions to twentieth century organ repertoire. Of Schmidt's two operas, only the earlier *Notre Dame* (1902–04), based on Hugo, has held the stage in Austria, but orchestral excerpts still appear on concert programs. The oratorio *Das Buch mit sieben Siegln* (The Book of the Seven Seals) (1935–37), based on the *Book of Revelations,* is arguably his greatest and most characteristic work. With a prominent role for solo organ, plus soloists, chorus, and huge orchestra, *Das Buch mit Sieben Siegln* is large in scale and scope, elevated in expression and transcendental in aims. That it succeeds so well is testimony to Schmidt's technical ability and his spiritual capacities. *—James Leonard*

Recommended:

- ○ **Schmidt: Notre Dame** / Perick (cond.), Moll, Juffinger, King, Laubenthal, Berlin Radio SO / Capriccio 10248
- ○ **Schmidt: The String Quartets** / Vienna Franz Schubert Qt. / 1996 / Nimbus 5467
- ○ **Schmidt: Das Buch mit sieben Siegeln** / Dermota (cond.), Holl, Topper, Moser, Scholz, Niederösterreichisches Tonkunstlerorchester / Preiser 93263
- ○ **Schmidt: Piano Concerto; Chaconne** / Bock (cond.), Kolly, Wiener Jeunesse Orch. / 1995 / Pan 510081
- ○ **Schmidt: Piano Quintets 1 and 2** / Wachter, Hell, Ottensamer, Keuschnig, Iberer, Wallisch / 1992 / Orfeo 287921
- ○ **Schmidt: Clarinet Quintet** / Wiener Kammermusiker / Preiser 93357
- ○ **Schmidt: Organ Works I** / Juffinger / Capriccio 10261

SYMPHONIC

Symphonies (1896–1933)

Franz Schmidt's four symphonies are "after Mahler" both a stylistic and chronological sense. Composed over nearly four decades from 1896 through 1937, Schmidt's symphonies are laid out in the same large formal structures, speak the same post-Romantic melodic and harmonic language, and have the same sort of lyrical intensity of expression as Bruckner's and Mahler's symphonies, despite having been written for the most part long after their deaths. Schmidt's *Symphony No. 1 in E major* (1896–99) is in the standard four movements and is no more harmonically advanced than Dvořák's contemporary *Symphony No. 9*. A competent rather than an inspired work, the *First* is opulently scored and unfailingly tuneful. The *Symphony No. 2 in E flat major* (1911–13) is in three movements, with the standard sonata opening movement and a rondo closing movement enclosing an extended theme and variations central movement. While a more accomplished work than the *Symphony No. 1*, it is still not much more than an example of generic Austrian post-Romantic symphonism. The *Symphony No. 3 in A major* (1927–28) reverts to the four-movement model, but infuses the movements with more individuality of expression. Indeed, there are times in the slow movement when one catches a glimpse of the great work yet to come. But, taken on its own terms, the *Third* is hardly a masterpiece. Schmidt's *Symphony No. 4 in C minor* (1932–33) is his symphonic masterpiece. Fusing the four-movement form into a single, arching structure with the closing movement essentially is a recapitulation of the opening movement. But while this is hardly a formal innovation—Schubert had done as much with his *Wanderer Fantasy* more than a century before—the intensely expressive content of Schmidt's *Fourth* is what raises it to the level of great art. Conceived and executed after the death of his daughter, Schmidt's *Fourth* is a monumental funeral symphony whose central slow movement is a marcia funebre whose depth of emotion nearly equals that of Beethoven's own marcia funebre from his *"Eroica" Symphony*. Indeed, in this tombeau for his daughter, Schmidt wrote a symphony whose profundity is coupled with his technical mastery to produce a work that can stand with Mahler's *Second* or Bruckner's *Eighth*. *—James Leonard*

Recommended:

○ **Schmidt: Symphonies 1–4** / Järvi (cond.), Chicago SO, Detroit SO / 1997 / Chandos 9568

CHAMBER MUSIC

Quintet for piano (left hand) & string quartet in G major (1926)

The Austrian composer Franz Schmidt was one of a number of composers Paul Wittgenstein commissioned to write works for him. Wittgenstein, the brother of the philosopher Ludwig Wittgenstein, had lost his right arm in the First World War, and he approached Schmidt as well as Ravel and Prokofiev and other composers to provide him with repertoire. Schmidt responded with, among other things, a *Left-Hand Piano Concerto* and several chamber works for piano left-hand and various combinations of instruments. The most successful of these chamber pieces is the *Piano Quintet in G major* (1926). With lovely melodies, charming harmonies, and infectious rhythms, Schmidt's *Piano Quintet* is clearly the work of a Viennese. Composed in for movements—a brilliant opening Lebhaft, doch nicht schnell (Lively, but not too fast), a gloriously expansive Adagio, a witty Sehr ruhig (Very restful) dance movement, and an effervescent rondo finale marked Sehr lebhaft (Very lively), the piano quintet was said to be one of Wittgenstein's favorites among all the works he commissioned. *—James Leonard*

Recommended:

○ **Schmidt: Piano Quintets 1 & 2** / Wachter, Hell, Keuschnig, etc. / 1992 / Orfeo 287921

Joseph Schmidt

b. Mar. 4, 1904, Bokuwina, Romania, **d.** Nov. 16, 1942, Gyrenbad, Switzerland
Tenor

Schmidt's all too brief life and career are among the tragedies of the musical world. He was so short (under five feet) that he was all but shut out of the operatic career that his voice was born and trained for, and after fleeing the Nazis (he was of Jewish descent) in Europe, he died in an internment camp in Switzerland. He had previously been admitted to a hospital for a heart attack, but was sent back prematurely, his protests that he was unable to return taken as malingering.

Ironically enough, his most famous recordings are not the grief-stricken arias of doomed characters, but light operetta arias and movie songs that, like so many of Wunderlich's recordings, capture an effervescent romance and joie de vivre rarely equaled. His voice had an immediately distinct timbre and seemingly effortless high notes, as well as a graceful, light touch that was extremely effective for operetta and song.

He sang in the local synagogue choir, and was often called upon by the local theaters when a child's voice was needed, but it was not until after he had entered school that he decided to attempt a singing career. In 1924, he entered the Berlin State Academy for Music and Song, and after graduating, turned away from opera houses for stage roles, he began a career as a radio singer. In 1929, he sang Vasco da Gama in a radio broadcast of Meyerbeer's *L'Africaine*, and as his fame spread, performed as a concert singer worldwide, and also made a number of films, the most famous of which is *Ein Leid geht um die Welt*, whose title song, especially, was an instant hit. Returning to Europe before the war years, he attempted to leave too late, and finally ended up in the internment camp in Switzerland.

Fortunately, he left a wide recorded legacy, mostly operetta and song but also lieder and opera. Many of his best recordings have been compiled by EMI. *—Ann Feeney*

Recommended:

○ **Schmidt singt Canzonen & Unterhaltunslieder** / Schmidt, etc. / Preiser 90527

○ **Opera** / Schmidt, etc. / 1994 / Bel Age 4

Florent Schmitt

b. Sep. 28, 1870, Blâmont, France, **d.** Aug. 17, 1958, Neuilly-sur-Seine, France
Composer

Schmitt was a prolific composer for all his long life—notching 138 opus numbers, including every genre except for opera—but the works he is remembered for were written in his youth. He was difficult to pigeonhole, and has been called everything from conservative to neo-Romantic to revolutionary. His music, characterized by rhythmic energy, refined orchestration, and tonal harmony, combines his admiration for impressionism and the beginning of the reaction against it. It contains from echoes of Franck to anticipations of Stravinsky. Dutilleux wrote that Schmitt "gave back to the French school certain notions of grandeur."

Schmitt only got interested in music during his teenage years, and studied in Nancy and later in Paris with Massenet and Fauré. He won the Prix de Rome in his fifth attempt, aged 30. From Rome he sent his first masterpiece, the choral-orchestral *Psalm 47* (1904). Three years later he wrote a ballet, later rearranged as symphonic poem, *La tragédie de Salomé*, whose violence was uncommon in French music and which became his most famous piece. He was a member of the Societé Musicale Indépendante in 1908, director of the Conservatoire de Lyon (1922–24), and music critic for Le Temps (1929–39). In 1932, he appeared as soloist in his *Symphonie Concertante* for piano and orchestra in Boston. In 1938 he was appointed President of the Societé Nationale de Musique. Other important works were his *Piano Quintet* (1908), a string quartet, the *Sonata Libre en deux parts enchainées* for violin and piano, and two symphonies, the last of which was premiered only two months before his death. *—Hector Bellman*

Overview of Works (1890–1958)

Early and late, Schmitt's music mines a vein of truculence, now barbaric and garishly voluptuous, now raucously playful and cavorting. As with his contemporary d'Indy, an essential poverty of invention is helped out by overloaded scoring (used for a variety of special effects), rhythmic and harmonic audacities, exoticism, and would-be-clever conceits after the manner of Satie. The orchestral *Fonctionnaire MCMXII* (composed in 1924), subtitled "Inaction in Music" and intended as grotesque satire, for instance, may remind the hearer less of a comically incompetent bureaucrat than of Dukas' *L'Apprenti sorcier*—itself a synthetic work deeply beholden to Wagner—whose alternations of incident are mimicked and whose orchestral sleights are bodily appropriated. Dating from the 1890s, many of the many early piano pieces recall Schumann (or d'Indy recalling Schumann): for example, Schmitt's *Feuillets de voyage* (1903–13) and *Reflets d'Allemagne* (1905), for piano four-hands, owe as much to the d'Indy of *Helvetia* (three waltzes celebrating his German travels) as they do to Schumann or to Schmitt's own *Wanderjahre*. Schmitt's later piano works are less idiomatically conceived for the keyboard than as sketches for orchestral works, confirmed by subsequent orchestrations, such as *Pupazzi* (a musical conspectus of the *commedia dell'arte*), *Ombres*, *Mirages*, *Suite sans esprit de suite*, and others. Indeed, the greater the forces Schmitt works with, the more persuasive his work becomes, for he deploys his resources less like a musician than like a great tactician mounting an assault upon the listener. This is particularly true of the works upon which his reputation chiefly rests—*Psalm XLVII* for chorus, organ, and orchestra (1904) and *La tragédie de Salomé* (the symphonic poem of 1910 spun off from a successful ballet composed in 1907). The pounding syncopations of the latter, its polyrhythms, bitonality, and batteries of percussion clearly influenced Stravinsky—to whom the 1910 version is dedicated—in *Le sacre du printemps*. But where Stravinsky's work is one of the pillars of Modernism, Schmitt's is resolutely post-Romantic, reviving the Orientalism that had been such a staple of French music since Félicien David's *Le désert* of 1844, a sonic blockbuster of decadent sensuality and savage fury that seems the sounding counterpart of works by such *fin de siècle* artists as Félicien Rops, Odilon Redon, and Gustave Moreau. Even the monumental *Quintet for Piano and Strings*, whose composition occupied Schmitt from 1902 until 1908, evinces orchestral ambitions in its languishing revisitation of the erotically stricken soundscape of César Franck's piano quintet. The chamber works, numerous throughout his career, amply demonstrate Schmitt's manner of combining a verbal conceit—*Suite en rocaille*, "suite in rockwork" for flute, string trio, and harp (1934) or *Chants alizés*, "songs of the trade winds" for wind quintet (1952)—with the trick of setting off slender, melodic material in fulsomely smart-alecky busywork whose in-your-face effrontery masks an anxiety to be *au courant*. Not without charm, they etch the self-portrait of an elderly gentleman capering and playing the animated fantasist—as fantasy runs thin—and determined to be the life of the party. *—Adrian Corleonis*

Recommended:

- ○ **Schmitt: Chamber Music** / Prague Wind Quintet, Czech Nonet / 2000 / Praga 250156
- ○ **Schmitt: World Premieres** / Kaltchev / Gega 249
- ○ **Schmitt: Rapsodie Viennoise; Hasards; Violin Sonata** / Pasquier, Pidoux / Valois 4679
- ○ **Schmitt: Symphonie Concertante; Rêves; Soirs** / Robertson (cond.), Sermet, Monte Carlo PO / 2001 / Naive 4908

Artur Schnabel

b. Apr. 17, 1882, Lipnik, Austria, **d.** Aug. 15, 1951, Axenstein, Switzerland
Pianist

The present-day listener might be surprised to learn that composition was the favorite musical activity of pianist Artur Schnabel. Teaching came second in order of preference, and performance followed after that. Schnabel was reportedly uncomfortable with public performance as well as with recording, and described the years from 1919 to 1924, when he had withdrawn somewhat from active concertizing to concentrate on writing music, as the happiest of his life.

Schnabel was born in Lipnik, Poland, on April 17, 1882. When he was seven his family took him to Vienna; there he came under the tutelage of piano pedagogue Theodor Leschetizky, who spotted in the young prodigy an unusually deep musicality. It was Leschetizky who steered the boy away from virtuoso showpieces, instead encouraging him to explore the then-neglected piano sonatas of Schubert, introspective and lyrical works that needed sensitive and alert readings to come to life. Schnabel also studied theory and composition with Brahms' friend Eusebius Mandyczewski, and by the age of 19 had composed and performed a large-scale piano concerto.

In 1900 Schnabel settled in Berlin, already a growing center for new music where the forward-looking pianist-composer Ferruccio Busoni held court. Schnabel made the acquaintance of important composers and performers of the day and, through his marriage to contralto Therese Behr, immersed himself in the Romantic song literature. He joined the faculty of the Berlin State Academy in 1925.

Despite his prodigious talents as a musician, Schnabel was always more of a pianist's pianist. Eschewing the audience-pleasing blandishments of flashier soloists, he gave performances that revealed the inner significance of the music. His interpretations of the late, visionary sonatas of Beethoven were spiritual testaments, as can be heard in the landmark recordings he made in 1932 of the complete cycle of Beethoven's 32 sonatas. The company that issued the cycle, His Master's Voice, had had significant success with their subscription-funded recordings made in collaboration with the Hugo Wolf Society of that composer's complete songs, and they looked to repeat their success with Schnabel's studio performances. Although Schnabel greatly disliked the whole idea of recording, he created in HMV's studios one of the most valuable documents in the history of music, treasured not only for its technical artistry but also for the depth of Schnabel's musical insight.

In 1933, Schnabel left Berlin after the Nazi takeover of Germany. By 1939, he had settled in the United States, where he took citizenship and taught at the University of Michigan in Ann Arbor; he continued to record, but the commercial pressures of the American music industry were uncongenial for him. Though he maintained a home in New York City, he returned to Europe after World War II. In addition to his many recordings (he made far more, and with far more substantial repertoire, than such illustrious contemporaries as Rachmaninov and Busoni), Schnabel also prepared an edition of Beethoven's piano sonatas and the *Diabelli Variations*, and wrote three books: *Reflections on Music* (1933), *Music and the Line of Most Resistance* (1942), and the autobiographical *My Life and Music* (1961). As a composer, he wrote three symphonies, the aforementioned piano concerto, five string quartets, a *Rhapsody* for orchestra, piano pieces, and songs. His last work was a *Duodecimet* for strings, winds, and percussion. Most of these works remain unpublished and are only rarely heard; they demonstrate a highly original approach to the modernistic currents that flowed through Europe at mid-century. He died in Axenstein, Switzerland, on August 15, 1951. *—Mark Satola*

Recommended:

- ○ **5 Mozart Concertos** / Barbirolli, Sargent, Süsskind (conds.), Schnabel, London SO, London PO / 2002 / Archipel Records 98
- ○ **Beethoven: Complete Concertos Vol. 1** / Sargent (conds.), Schnabel, London SO, London PO / 2001 / Classica d'Oro 3032
- ○ **Beethoven: Piano Sonatas** / Schnabel / EMI 63765
- ○ **Schubert: Impromptus; Allegretto** / Schnabel / 1988 / EMI 61021

Wolfgang Schneiderhan

b. May 28, 1915, Vienna, Austria, **d.** May 18, 2002, Vienna, Austria
Violinist

Austrian violinist and sometime conductor Wolfgang Schneiderhan (born 1915) is a highly versatile artist, just as much at home in the music of Hans Werner Henze as he is in Beethoven, Mozart, and Schubert, even if he is best known for his playing of the last-named group of composers. Never a major European star, he was nevertheless active in every aspect of Austria's music scene and was widely admired for the depth of his interpretive abilities. He was married for 40 years to the legendary German soprano Irmgard Seefried.

Born in Vienna, Schneiderhan was taught violin by his mother from age 3 and gave his first concert at 5. In 1926 in Copenhagen he played Mendelssohn's violin concerto, and he subsequently toured Europe, hailed as a prodigy. But the fast-money life of a touring virtuoso demoralized the young violinist, and he turned his career in a new direction: with the help of a recommendation from an aristocratic patroness, he became, at 17, concertmaster of the new Vienna Symphony. Four years later he moved on to the same post with the Vienna Philharmonic, where he served under the great conductors Wilhelm Furtwängler and Hans Knappertsbusch. That year he also formed the Schneiderhan Quartett. In the 1940s he performed duo sonatas with Wilhelm Backhaus and other top-rank soloists, and he formed a trio with pianist Edwin Fischer and cellist Enrico Mainardi in 1948. He married Seefried that year and often performed with her as well.

Schneiderhan's solo career took off once again when he resigned his Philharmonic concertmaster post in 1949, at age 34. For many years he ruled the roost among Deutsche Grammophon's stable of violin soloists, At first he was identified with the core Viennese Classical repertoire, but he later became interested in contemporary music and explored the works of Henze, Stravinsky, and other composers. He co-founded the Lucerne Festival Strings in 1956 and also taught at the Lucerne Music Academy. In the 1970s Schneiderhan undertook yet another new career: after studying with Hans Swarowsky, he became active as a conductor. In 1975 he led a performance of Franz Schmidt's *Notre Dame* at the Vienna Volksoper. Much in demand as a teacher in his later years, Schneiderhan continued to live in Vienna. *—James Manheim*

Recommended:

- ○ **Beethoven: Sonatas for Piano & Violin** / Schneiderhan, Kempff / 2000 / DG 463605
- ○ **Bach, Mozart, Beethoven & Schubert** / Schneiderhan, Seemann / 1997 / Orfeo 971

Alfred Schnittke

b. Nov. 24, 1934, Engels, U.S.S.R., **d.** Aug. 3, 1998, Hamburg, Germany
Composer: Chamber Music, Concerto, Symphonic

Upon his emergence in the West in the early 1980s, Alfred Schnittke became one of the most talked-about, recorded, and influential composers of the last decades of the twentieth century. Schnittke was born in 1934 in the Soviet Union to German parents. After living for several years in Vienna, he returned to Moscow to attend the Conservatory from 1953–58. He returned there to teach instrumentation from 1962 through 1972. Thereafter, splitting his time between Moscow and Hamburg, he supported himself as a film composer. Schnittke composed nine symphonies, six concerti grossi, four violin concertos, two cello concertos, concertos for piano and a triple concerto for violin, viola and cello, four string quartets, ballet scores, choral and vocal works. His first opera, *Life with an Idiot*, was premiered in Amsterdam (April 1992). Two more operas, *Gesualdo* and *Historia von D. Johann Fausten* were unveiled in Vienna (May 1995) and Hamburg (June 1995) respectively. In 1985, Schnittke suffered a series of strokes, but nevertheless entered into the most creative period of his life. From 1990 until his death in 1998, he lived exclusively in Hamburg.

A Jewish-born Christian mystic, Schnittke had philosophical theories that permeated his music. According to his biographer Alexander Ivashkin, he believed a composer "should be a medium or a sensor remembering what he hears from somewhere else and whose mind acts as a translator only. Music comes from some sort of divine rather than human area." (Alfred Schnittke, Phaedon Press 1995). *—Steven Coburn*

CHAMBER MUSIC

Cello Sonata No. 1 (1978)

From the point of view of Western musicians and audiences, Soviet/Russian composer Alfred Schnittke's rise to fame was a meteoric one, beginning in the early 1990s and building steadily until the composer's death in 1998. The West was late to the Schnittke scene: he had been famous throughout Eastern Europe all throughout the 1970s and 1980s, and had long been touted as one of Dmitry Shostakovich's rightful musical heirs. Such works as the *Sonata for cello and piano* of 1978 (known after 1994 as the *Sonata No. 1 for cello and piano*) make the Shostakovich connection plain. Schnittke was and is famous for his polystylistic approach to music, and in this piece, as in many others, it is the style of Shostakovich that comes most to the fore.

The sonata is in three movements: I. Largo, II. Presto, and III. Largo. The first Largo is the shortest of the movements, lasting about three minutes. It begins with a searching passage for cello alone, to which the piano eventually adds thin, lightly dissonant counterpoint. The music comes to a complete stop, and the piano offers a calm, chorale-like thought; the cello will have none of it, however, and bursts forth with music of great passion. Just before the close of the movement the piano offers a condensed version of its calm thought, this time prompting a shady pizzicato response from the cello. In the second movement, strands of hushed notes gush forth from the cello, and the piano decides to act almost as a percussion instrument for a while. The same basic "cell" of music is repeated over and over, louder, more ornamented, and then a grotesque waltz breaks in. In the lengthy final Largo, the two players explore a grim, emotionally barren land, recalling and reshaping gestures from the first opening movement and then, at the end, during a long diminuendo towards nothingness, the Presto. *—Blair Johnston*

Recommended:

○ **Schnittke: Complete Music for Cello & Piano** / Ivashkin, Schnittke / 1998 / Chandos 9705

Piano Quintet (1972–1976)

Alfred Schnittke's *Piano Quintet* is a dark and heavy planet. Even in the midst of his bewilderingly prolific output, this extremely personal work commands a massive gravity; it seems to orient, arrange, and set in motion so many of Schnittke's works, before and after. If one wants to find the founding trauma for such a consistently agonizing body of artistic work, it can be found in the *Piano Quintet.*

This centrality may owe much to the quintet's function: conceived as a memorial to the composer's mother, who died of a stroke in September 1972, here's a composition whose substance was drawn from a real event, powerfully tangible and irrevocable. This kind of reality had not been Schnittke's basis for previous works. His *Symphony No. 1* (1972) and other contemporaneous works are brazenly extroverted stylistic carnivals, full of fantasy, denunciation, and dark humor, and are largely artistic statements on art or cultural critiques on culture itself.

In this light, the *Piano Quintet* was a radical departure into an entirely personal sphere. This shift caused the composer tremendous difficulty. After finishing the first movement very quickly, Schnittke was blocked, "unable to continue because I had to take what I wrote from an imaginary space defined in terms of sound and put it into the psychological space as defined by life, where excruciating pain seems almost unserious, and one must fight for the right to use dissonance, consonance, and assonance."

Hence the *Piano Quintet* was shelved, and Schnittke did not resume work on it for almost four years. When he did pick up the work again, his musical temperament had changed, becoming more distilled, tauter, and more unabashedly morbid. Schnittke had perfected a personal sound, a dense, claustrophobic web of chromatic clusters. This signatory sound, rich yet obscure, serves as the backdrop for much of his succeeding work, and is seamlessly crafted into this work. The second movement is a wraith-like slow waltz on the name of B-A-C-H (H in German notation is B, B is B flat). The waltz is the only "polystylistic" concession in the piece, and throughout the movement consistently descends back into torturous clusters.

The next two movements form the heart of the work, pulling it increasingly inward. Schnittke explains that they "are real experiences of grief which I would prefer not to comment on because they are of a very personal nature." Both movements bind themselves in shells of stasis; each movement suffers its own shocked outburst and epiphany. Eventually the fourth movement ruptures the thick web of chromaticism that seems to paralyze the work.

After its crushing, cathartic crisis on a single, repeated note, the movement ebbs into the work's final bars, based on a 14-measure theme repeated 14 times in the piano. Over this theme, Schubert-like in its studied rusticity, one hears blanched recollections of previous passages; everything liquefies as it materializes, swept along by the piano theme's current. Eventually a faded reconciliation emerges and the strings are silenced; the work ends on the sonic outskirts as Schnittke instructs the pianist to play *tonlos,* "without tone."

There is hypersentimentality in Schnittke's quintet, a weird excess of morose emotion that exists in few other of his works. Somehow the sentimentality works here, perhaps because of the sincerity of the utterance, perhaps because, despite wearing his heart on his sleeve, Schnittke is not merely personal but also highly idiosyncratic. The work is an uncomfortable twentieth century classic, and a key to Schnittke's music in general. *—Seth Brodsky*

Recommended:

○ **Schnittke: Klavierquintett; Shostakovich: Streichquartett 15** / Keller Qt., Lubimov / 2003 / ECM 461815

String Quartet No. 2 (1980)

In many ways, Alfred Schnittke's entire output bears the signature of tragedy. It is often a bizarre, deeply irreverent tragedy, miles from Greek antiquity. But nevertheless disaster, catastrophe, and lament are everywhere in the thousands of pages which contain Schnittke's name. So when he writes a work inspired by an actual in-the-world tragedy, it adopts a strange multi-layered hue, and offers an unremitting experience.

Schnittke's *Second Quartet* is the child of such trauma, finished in 1980 to memorialize the composer's close friend, film director Larissa Shepitko, who died from a car accident the previous year. Schnittke confesses that "for me, and for all who knew her, her death came as a severe blow." The quartet that resulted from Schnittke's reaction is a particularly intense experience, and while it employs much that is familiar Schnittke territory, it carries deeper wounds.

For example, Schnittke's hallmark "polystylism" comes through in the use of early Russian sacred music; Schnittke writes that "almost the entire tonal material of the quartet is derived from ancient Russian church song," known for its striking dissonance. But gone is any of the exhilarating funhouse irony which imprints Schnittke's other polystylistic works. Instead, the single model of Russian song is pressed and pulverized with increasingly agonized vehemence; Schnittke treats it monomaniacally as a symbol of the irreparably lost and unrecoverable. In doing so, however, he also writes a work of stunningly sustained creativity. Stravinsky's famous dictum runs that a composition can only arise as the solution to a problem. Schnittke the tragedian offers a counterdictum—that a great composition can arise out of an impossible search for a solution to an insoluble problem.

The *Quartet* opens with the cold, isolated sound of high string-harmonics in canon, and at close intervals. Sharp and pale, this music eventually erupts into outburst; Schnittke then quotes, in all its voices, the original Russian hymn on which quartet is based, forming a kind of poignantly hollow center.

Responding to this vulnerable repose, the second movement offers an outraged, depressurizing implosion, an unrelenting explosion of activity warping the Russian hymn's contour in all ways imaginable. It begins with a "refrain" in which the hymn is expanded to four-octave arpeggios in all four instruments, each instrument flying at a slightly different velocity; the remarkable effect reminds one of a globe spinning at self-destructive speed, a kind of unstable atomic delirium barely holding itself together. At various points Schnittke operates like a film director himself, splicing in contrasting scenes of distortive fury; at one brief point this hurtling sphere smolders to a stop and we once again hear the original hymn as it appeared in the first movement. Inevitably, however, the shocked refrain returns, and ends the movement in a choked mid-spin.

This torn-off end leads immediately into the catatonic third movement, marked "Mesto" ("sad"). With equal single-mindedness but a new glacial tone, this movement offers a frozen dirge around a single note, D. Schnittke infuses the sound with a frightening thickness, which eventually swells to a barbaric climax: all four instruments, each bowing quadruple-stops, hammer out seven *ffff* chords.

The fourth and last movement is a kind of broken epilogue, attempting one last time to capture the missing center. But after a traumatized return to the Quartet's opening bars, Schnittke finally turns away from centers and offers a muted, translucent coda to the whole work. This starlit firmament of string harmonics literally evaporates from sound, ringing out the Russian hymn as it fades. In such a way does the work possess a double memory, of friendship, but also of heritage and history. *—Seth Brodsky*

Recommended:

○ **Schnittke: String Quartets** / Tale Quartet / 1990 / Bis 467

○ **Kronos Quartet 25 Years** / Kronos Quartet / 1998 / Nonesuch 79504

String Quartet No. 3 (1983)

Alfred Schnittke's *Third String Quartet* from 1983 is already one of the most performed works in the post-1945 repertory. This may be due on the one hand to Schnittke's considerable reputation, and perhaps also to the *Quartet*'s use of older, more recognizable musical models. But the work's popularity may also be a result of its enormous concentration. It is one of those remarkable works that perfectly synthesizes form and content, ends and means, and in doing so rightfully earns the mantle "classic."

This achievement is particularly notable with a composer like Schnittke, so justifiably known for his "anti-classical" or "polystylistic" approach; most of Schnittke's works, this one included, depend on shattering classical norms of balance, purity, and wholeness for a multiplicity of styles. Schnittke's *Third Quartet* shatters all three within its first minute. We hear only broken pieces from other times and other works—first from Orlando de Lassus's *Stabat Mater* (later 1500's), then from Beethoven's *Grosse Fuge* for String Quartet, Op. 133 (1825), and finally from Dmitry Shostakovich's famous "musical signature" D-E flat-C-B (in German notation D-S-C-H, hence D. SCHostakovich), first used in Shostakovich's *Fifth String Quartet* of 1952. Schnittke takes these three musical modules, from disparate traditions traversing half a millennium, and puts them directly after one another, only to have the whole thread snap and fall to the ground.

Hardly "balanced, pure, and whole." And yet what Schnittke does with this historical flotsam is not only expressive, but extraordinarily resourceful, intricate, and interrelated; indeed, Schnittke eventually reveals that the Lassus, Beethoven, and Shostakovich cells are motivically intertwined, one yielding to another through fluid transformations, "developing variations." If this approach is reminiscent of Brahms, Schnittke's motivic concentration throughout the remainder of the *Quartet* is Beethovenian. In the "Agitato" second movement in particular, almost every note, figure, and expressive gesture is derived from the main motives and thus tied to the whole movement and the entire *Quartet.* And even as this "Agitato" hurls itself inevitably toward catastrophe, it follows a strict sonata-form plan of ABA (exposition of material-development-return of exposition). In its structure, compression, and expressive but controlled violence, this movement offers a striking chamber-music foil to the opening "Allegro con brio" of Beethoven's *Fifth Symphony.* Likewise, the funereal "Pesante" last movement returns to and develops the motley shards of the first movement into a single lachrymose plaint, bringing the whole Quartet to a culmination and closure. So the whole *Quartet* mirrors its middle movement's ABA-form.

And yet what makes Schnittke's *Third Quartet* most remarkable is not this "classicism," but rather this "classicism despite itself." For while the *Quartet* holds itself together so tightly, it also achieves the expressive opposite: its emotional world is constantly falling apart, by turns confused, manic, hysterical, depressed, bitter, and utterly despairing. And though the *Quartet* is so motivically unified and closed, at the same time it is referentially wide open, embracing an overwhelming number of musical and extramusical sources, including the entire string quartet tradition (from Franz Josef Haydn to Beethoven to Alban Berg and Béla Bartók) and the idea of the string quartet as artistic confession (for at the time of their respectively quoted quartets, Beethoven and Shostakovich were both consummately isolated creators, one through deafness and the other through political dissidence).

Above all, though, Schnittke's *Third Quartet* astounds though the unresolved tension of these opposites, the passage of great art into wreckage, back into great art. A work of such effective contradiction deserves the contradictory label "Classic Polystylism." *—Seth Brodsky*

Recommended:

- **Schnittke: String Quartets** / Tale Quartet / 1990 / Bis 467
- **Complete String Quartets** / Kronos Quartet / 1998 / Nonesuch 79500

String Trio (1985)

Schnittke once stated that the music of Alban Berg was dearest to him "above all others." So when the Alban Berg Foundation commissioned Schnittke in 1985 to write a work celebrating Berg's centenary, it was bound to be an especially personal work for the composer. But the sad, deeply introspective *String Trio* which materialized also marked a kind of memorial for Schnittke's own life. The work is a tribute to one of the composer's "primal scenes," as Freud called them—formative, often traumatic moments in childhood which inscribe themselves deep in the consciousness. For Schnittke, that primal scene was a three-year stay in Vienna from 1946 to 1948, when the composer was in his early teens. Along with the the sight of the bombed-out State Opera and the scene in *Everyman* in which Death himself appears, Schnittke recalled "a certain Mozart-Schubert sound which I carried around for years." Within the darkness of post-World War II Vienna, the now bombed-out cultural center where classicism and the Enlightenment had reached their pinnacles, Schnittke must have experienced this Mozart-Schubert sound with a kind of built-in irony—not the sneering irony of a skeptic, but one infused with compassion.

Schnittke used this Mozart-Schubert sound again and again in his works, though seldom with the completeness and intensity realized in the *String Trio.* Cast in two large movements, the entire work flows from a simple, six-note cadential figure straight out of a Schubert piano sonata. Freud remarks that the individual constantly returns to the "primal scene" in an imaginary space, constantly replays the scene, tries new if ineffectual solutions. In the wandering, pathologically restless opening Moderato, Schnittke seems to enact such a scenario. When the movement begins, the "Schubert" figure has already aged; it carries the weight of two centuries on its weary back and fails to actually achieve its cadence. The entire Moderato makes an obsession of this opening figure; it starts, halts, starts again, stammers in spaces tonal and atonal, fast and slow, confessional and clamorous. New, derivative themes splinter off, old ones become crushed under the attempted recovery of ultimately illusory repose. Twice, a fantastical Valkryian gallop rends the musical fabric. The movement resolves through exhaustion, spinning from the opening cadential figure a hobbled three-part minuet.

The following Adagio offers a peculiar response to the scenes of failure in the first movement. It presents no new material, but rather an alienated, reconfigured view of the opening, as if removed in both space and time. Things are slower, sparser, and more reflective. Dirge-like chorales of Russian character mix with a late Romantic lyricism; individual instruments sing out longer lines, now as laments rather than attempts. At the moment of utmost interiority, the wild gallop returns with previously unheard fury. After this final cathartic seizure, Schnittke again returns to the opening cadential figure, this time in canon above an oscillating bass. The concluding minuet from the Moderato also returns, but with a new clarity; its newly poignant nature has changed from that of a wound to that of a replica, a museum model. But the imagination, even at the extremes of its limits, still houses only images, and so this last vision sublimates into thin air. *—Seth Brodsky*

Recommended:

- **Schnittke: String Trio; Concerto for 3; Minuet; Berg: Canon** / Rostropovich, Kremer, Bashmet / 1996 / EMI 55627

Suite in the Old Style, for violin & piano (1972)

While the use of a diversity of styles provided Alfred Schnittke with an effective way to express alienation and irony in his music, the ability to write in a Baroque style was also valuable from a professional standpoint: people do not always wish to hear alienating, ironic music in film scores. But while his *Concerti grossi* made extensive use of his film music in a kind of highly charged pastiche, the *Suite in the Old Style* for violin and piano is simply a transcription of certain movements from his film scores, with no commentary from Schnittke on what it meant to compose in Baroque forms in 1973. The first two movements, a Pastorale and a Ballet, are taken from a film detailing the adventures of a dentist. Apparently, this was not a very adventurous dentist, as both these movements are cheery and inoffensive in the extreme; the Pastorale, in particular, sounds sweet enough to be salon music. The Minuet was taken from a children's animation film—which raises some questions about Soviet children's animation, for this movement is extremely slow and melancholy. The piano imitates traditional ornaments, while the violin takes the subordinate role it sometimes had in Baroque violin works; the two even play in a resigned, almost exhausted canon at one point. A Fugue taken from a film about a sportsman is resolute and accomplished, driving quickly to its emphatic coda. Fittingly, the most daring piece here was also written for a children's animation work: the final Pantomime, despite its charming melody, features bare, exposed rhythms, striking pizzicati, and even what in context feels like a searing dissonance in the violin. The Pantomime does not end so much as trail away, perhaps providing a hint that an era of musical composition was over, or at least that Schnittke's serious work would never sound quite like this again. *—Andrew Lindemann Malone*

Recommended:

- **Schnittke: Violin Sonatas; Suite in Old Style** / Gothoni, Lubotsky / Ondine 800
- **Insomnia** / Kremer, Yoshino / 1999 / Philips 456016

CONCERTO

Cello Concerto No. 2 (1989–1990)

Alfred Schnittke's *Second Cello Concerto* is a leviathan of a work, in size, length, scope, and difficulty. This may reflect the work's occasion: it realizes Schnittke's sixteen-year ambition to write a work for the great Russian cellist Mstislav Rostropovich. This ambition was of course thwarted until 1986 by Rostropovich's exile from Soviet Russia; while the cellist was not allowed back in Russia, Schnittke was not allowed to travel to Rostropovich's West.

Thus, the *Second Cello Concerto* represents a seal of friendship. However, it also carries the scar of political oppression, something Schnittke makes explicit in the work's massive fifth and final movement. This movement, a passacaglia (originally a Baroque form based on a repeating bass-pattern), uses as its ground bass a theme from Schnittke's 1974 film score to Elim Klimov's *Agony.* Schnittke's description of the film is extremely telling: it "portrays the final weeks of Russia which preceded the more than seventy-year-long night in the country's history."

Perhaps this political "sub-plot" begins to explain the *Second Cello Concerto*'s epic stature, and the nature of its sobriety. The work is constructed in five large movements; the opening Moderato serves more as prelude to the storm, announcing the soloist with a desperate but regal 12-tone line. As others have noted, the mirror-like contour of this melody invokes Alban Berg's 1935 *Violin Concerto*; both themes carry a sphinxian sense of opening and closing on themselves without letting up their mystery. Eventually the cello's line is attacked by snarling brass, and soon after the bizarre second movement begins.

Intensely difficult, the large-scale Allegro forces the soloist through an unending serpentine line; the cellist's music is not lyrical, however, but angular and gnarled—less like melody than a perpetual thread of musical litanies. Amidst this painful contortionism, the huge orchestra splits into smaller groups of garish color and texture. They antagonize the soloist much like those nasty, lovingly crafted goblins in Bosch paintings; they are embodied here in the chromatic crunchings of a harpsichord, a quivering flexatone, and a spastic contra-bassoon. Three times the orchestra quashes the cello with apoplectic eruptions based on the soloist's opening mirror motive, articulating a sensation of individual and imposter, of false-doubles and the anxiety they enforce.

This ineffable sense of catastrophe becomes more palpable in the slow third movement. This Lento moves with great lyrical introspection, its gaunt lines and ambivalent harmony lending a dark elegance to its sound. Yet musical mirrors and imposters abound; the soloist's line is consistently echoed in inversion by the orchestra, reflecting the cello's warm vocality in the steely blur of bells and glockenspiel. Likewise, the cello itself passes through reflective borders, from empty soloistic dimensions into a claustrophobic chamber of throbbing string quarter tones.

A solo recitative leads into the brutal Allegretto vivo fourth movement, where the orchestra's rage is finally given full voice. A screeching climax leads into the extraordinary last movement, based on the *Agony*-score. Schnittke calls this music a "sound-world," implying less a musical movement than a ghostly process of inhabitance and gradual change. The cello spins a line of endless, merciless transformation, like a demented singer long having forgotten the actual melody; the orchestra all the while grows like a rich, terrifying infestation, and eventually crushes the soloists with supreme density. Amidst this hysterical proliferation of musical ideas, so evocative of paranoia and madness (and thus perhaps of Rasputin himself), the cello never ceases. Even in the concerto's smoldering last bars its sings into the void, "the ever-darkening orchestral sound transforming the moment into an inaudible, eternal reverberation." *—Seth Brodsky*

Recommended:

○ **Schnittke: Cello Concerto 2; In memoriam** / Ozawa (cond.), Rostropovich, London SO / 1992 / Sony 48241

Concerto for piano & strings (1979)

Alfred Schnittke wrote his *Concerto for Piano and String Orchestra* in one extended movement. It begins with a long, slow introduction from the piano. When the strings enter, the piano joins them to play various fragments of melody. These fragments are repeated and elaborated upon, and then seem to drop out of sight. This portion of the work includes a passage that resembles a Russian Orthodox hymn and a passage reminiscent of Prokofiev. The work comes to a quasi climax, but immediately after the massed fortissimo there follows only silence. After this false climax, the piano has a cadenza reminiscent of the introduction, but which also includes echoes of the earlier music. The music moves to a frenzied climax again, and this time the climax is a true one. After it ends, however, the music becomes slower and bleaker. This section features a lamenting string quartet with occasional virtuoso figurations from the piano. The work ends in an ambiguous mood, reminiscent of what has come before, but also suggestive that there is hope for what comes after. Schnittke's piano writing is idiomatic and virtuosic, and much of the writing for the strings has a tonal character, making the *Concerto for Piano and String Orchestra* one of Schnittke's more accessible works. It is recommended for anyone wanting an introduction to this unique composer.*—Andrew Malone*

Recommended:

○ **Schnittke: Concerto Grosso I; Concerto for Oboe & Harp; Concerto for Piano & Strings** / Markiz (cond.), Pontinen, Swedrup, Jahren, Bergqvist, Lier, New Stockholm CO / 1987 / BIS 377

SYMPHONIC

Symphonies (1972–1997)

Russian composer Alfred Schnittke composed nine symphonies over the course of his career. There are a number of Schnittke's stylistic traits evident in the symphonies, in particular his "polystylism"; that is, the juxtaposing of disparate musical styles and quotations in a single work. Musicologists have remarked on the strong influence of Viennese composer Gustav Mahler in the symphonies, whose presence is most noticeably felt in the grandeur and breadth of vision of the works. Schnittke's symphonies also betray the influence of Second Viennese School composer Alban Berg, and of Schnittke's own film music.

Schnittke's earliest symphonies, especially the first and third, provide the best examples of polystylism. In the rather theatrical *First Symphony*, an amazingly wide range of musical material is employed: an array of different styles—including jazz—combines with quotations from Beethoven, Haydn, Grieg, Tchaikovsky, and Johann Strauss. The *Third Symphony* also features quotations from Classical and Romantic-era composers. The *Second* and *Fourth Symphonies* are slightly different: the *Second* is a homage to composer Anton Bruckner in six movements; the *Fourth* is polystylistic, but combines elements from Gregorian chant, Lutheran chorales, and other sacred music, set against a dense, contrapuntal orchestral background. In the *Fifth Symphony*, perhaps the apogee of his polystylism, Schnittke demonstrates how seamlessly he is able to blend disparate musical elements with his own musical language.

Schnittke's *Sixth*, *Seventh*, and *Eighth Symphonies* represent a major stylistic and esthetic shift: the dense polystylism of the earlier symphonies gives way to sparser, more transparent textures. There are echoes of the past in these symphonies, but a fundamentally new sound is heard here. Schnittke's final symphony, the *Ninth*, was completed just one year before he died. This work represents the full maturation of Schnittke's stripped-down approach to symphonic composition, a perfecting of what Ivan Moody has called the "spare style" of the last four symphonies.

Schnittke's symphonies are not merely esthetic objects, but they also function as cultural and musical critiques: the idea of the generic purity of the classical symphony and the enlightenment ideals that accompany it are deconstructed by Schnittke's complex juxtaposing of diverse musical material within the symphonic form. *—Alexander Carpenter*

Recommended:

○ **Schnittke: Symphony 1** / Segerstam (cond.), Stockholm PO / 1992 / Bis 577

○ **Schnittke: Symphony 2** / Polyansky (cond.), Veprintsev, Golub, Zdorov, Dolgov, Katsman, Russian State SO / 1997 / Chandos 9519

○ **Schnittke: Symphony 3** / Klas (cond.), Stockholm PO / 1989 / Bis 477

○ **Schnittke: Symphony 4; 3 Sacred Hymns** / Polyansky (cond.), Khlynov, Adamovich, Khudolei, Pianov, Zdorov, Russian State SO / 1996 / Chandos 9463

○ **Schnittke: Symphony 5; Concerto Grosso 4** / N. Järvi (cond.), Gothenburg SO / 1998 / Bis 427

○ **Schnittke: Symphonies 6 & 7** / Otaka (cond.), BBC National Orch. Wales / 1995 / Bis 747

○ **Schnittke: Symphony 8; Suite from "The Census List"** / Polyansky (cond.), Russian State SO / 2001 / Chandos 9885

Othmar Schoeck

b. Sep. 1, 1886, Brunnen, Switzerland, **d.** Mar. 8, 1957, Zürich, Switzerland

Composer: Vocal, Chamber Music, Concerto

Othmar Schoeck was an important Swiss composer during the first half of the twentieth century. In contrast to the more dissonant style pursued by contemporaries, Schoeck is known for his essentially tonal music and his attention to melodic values, rather than dissonant effects. As to his many works, Schoeck made major contributions to lieder with his numerous settings of song texts.

Schoeck studied formally at the Zurich Conservatory and during the period 1907–08 worked privately with Max Reger in Leipzig. When he returned to Zurich in 1908, he established a career that involved composition and conducting. Among his earliest works is a *Serenade for Orchestra* (1908) which was part of a composition festival in Baden. He quickly became recognized as a composer for orchestra and song; he held various teaching positions and performed on piano to accompany his wife, and several other singers. Schoeck remained in Switzerland throughout his career, where he was regarded as the country's foremost musician. In addition to lieder and orchestral works, Schoeck composed several operas, the most important of which is *Penthesilea* (1927), an impressive setting of Kleist's drama. Of his other works, it is notable that he composed various settings for male chorus, a medium associated with song of the choral societies of the nineteenth century.

Stylistically Schoeck's clearly tonal works involve some careful and effective use of dissonance. His music is reminiscent of Hindemith from the 1930s and 1940s. As with Hindemith, Schoeck's strong anchoring in traditional harmony and conventional forms made his music more accessible to the general public. *—James Zychowicz*

VOCAL

Songs and Song Cycles (ca. 1901–1955)

Othmar Schoeck, an eminent early twentieth century Swiss composer whose music never quite caught on in the English-speaking world, was the author of a remarkable body of songs, numbering around 350. The earliest date from 1901 and 1902—several years before he entered the Zurich Conservatory for formal training—while the last few appeared in the early-to-mid-1950s, just shortly before his death.

It is clear, listening to such early lieder as *Nachtgesang* (1901) and *Geistergruss* (1902), both settings of Goethe, that Schoeck was well aware of his Germanic predecessors in art song; Schubert and Wolf mingle together in these early songs with sometimes uncomfortable familiarity. Until entering the Conservatory in 1905, Schoeck composed only individual songs; after 1905, he more often grouped songs together as cycles, either informal (meaning that the grouping was made mostly for the sake of publication) or formal (meaning that the songs really are interconnected in a textual, musical, or story line way). As he grew older, the size of the cycles increased: *Der Sänger*, Op. 57, of 1944 contains 26 songs; *Das stille Leuchten*, Op. 60, of 1946 contains 28; and *Das holde Beschieden*, Op. 62, is built from a whopping 36 songs, all settings of poems by Mörike.

The *Drei Schilflieder*, Op. 2, to texts by Lenau are the first cycle to appear. Romantic and suave of melody, they represent Schoeck the composer in his earliest, most Romantic form. The 1920s saw a change in Schoeck's music, and by the time of *Das wandsbecker Liederbuch*, a more edgy (though still primarily tune-driven) Schoeck had come to be.

Schoeck's individual songs, as per art song tradition, are not great of length—a few pages at most. Atonality was not for him, save for the barest moment or two; but within the "limitations" of tertian (i.e., third-based) tonality, chromatically expanded when need be, he managed to capture sentiments as angst-ridden as those offered in the harsher-sounding works of his continental contemporaries. The enormous breadth of Schoeck's songwriting talents is only now being discovered generations after his heyday. *—Blair Johnston*

Recommended:

○ **Schoeck: Lebendig Begraben** / Rieger (cond.), Fischer-Dieskau, Berlin RSO / 1986 / Claves 508610

○ **Schoeck: Das hölde Bescheiden** / Fischer-Dieskau, Höll, Shirai / 1993 / Claves 509308/9

CHAMBER MUSIC

Sonata for bass clarinet & piano, Op. 41 (1928)

The clarinet sonata is something of a sport in Schoeck's work, a musical joke, a mordant drollery, a wry glimpse at the Jazz Age from the high-culture Alpine vantage of a Swiss inheritor of the great Romantic tradition of the lied. Composed between September 1927, and March 1928, it followed the Dresden Staatsoper premiere of his most radical bow to expressionism, the opera *Penthesilea*. The harshly despairing, tragic tone of *Penthesilea* and the orchestral song cycle *Lebendig Begraben* would achieve a corrosively concentrated utterance in the *Notturno*, for baritone and string quartet, composed over 1931–33, all of them dark hymns to alienation and the failure of love reflecting Schoeck's own frustrated passions and fraught with the cultural myth of the deadly enmity between the sexes fueled by such fashionably accepted writers as Nietzsche, Freud, Spengler, and Otto Weininger. Amid so much turbid, intense, impacted angst, the clarinet sonata looms as a moment of relief, if not repose. Marked Gemessen—"measured, precise," suggesting some grave formality—over slowly throbbing chords, the clarinet opens the first movement with a mellifluous theme in Schoeck's characteristic liedlike manner, but rounded with jazzily smirking innuendo, soon seconded by subtle syncopation in the piano. As new thematic material is introduced, the music always seems on the verge of confiding some frivolity even as it proceeds with stately imperturbability to its unequivocal cadence. After a brief flourish, the second movement—an interlude, really—is a briskly moving (marked Bewegt) recitative suggesting improvisation, though the interplay of clarinet and piano is actually an extended fugato with aspirations toward becoming a double fugue. Without a pause, this lifts into a tautly boogying rondo in which an engaging amalgam of rag, fox trot, and jumping syncopation alternates with chase episodes in straight time only to end too soon. Though rich in *doubles ententes*, the sonata, like all brilliant jokes, is surprisingly brief, playing for only about 15 minutes. Schoeck's faithful chronicler, Dr. Hans Corrodi, described the work, perhaps tongue-in-cheek, as "the fruit of his preoccupation with Bach." No doubt because it is unique in Schoeck's oeuvre and so far removed from his persona as "the last Romantic" and reluctant Modernist, the clarinet sonata has received little attention from either critics or performers—both, apparently, nonplussed by its sardonic humor—though it is the most substantial work in the bass clarinet repertoire and deserving of a place among the jazz-inspired compositions of Constant Lambert, Milhaud, and Stravinsky. *—Adrian Corleonis*

Recommended:

○ **Bass Clarinet** / Hagen, Rusche / MDG 6240556

CONCERTO

Concerto for horn & string orchestra, Op. 65 (1951)

A heart attack in 1944 forced Schoeck to restrict his activities and resign as conductor of the symphony concerts at St. Gall, a post he had held since 1917. This, no doubt, stimulated an ever-present strain of nostalgia—for Schoeck was, after all, the last great inheritor of the German lied tradition, which he cultivated assiduously—and his more ambitious works thereafter have a retrospective cast. Several large works testify to an autumnal, mellowed, old-master serenity—the "pastoral intermezzo," *Sommernacht*, for instance, or the cello concerto, and, pre-eminently, the *Concerto for Horn and String Orchestra*.

Through a mutual friend, August Oetiker, Schoeck had heard that Dr. Willi Aebi, a wealthy patron of the arts from Burgdorf and a gifted hornist who had, on occasion, played under Schoeck's baton, intended to approach him with a commission for a work or works for horn. When Aebi did at last write to Schoeck, May 9, 1951, the composer responded the next day: "Two movements of a horn concerto are already home and dry, and as soon as the third is ready, I will make a piano score of it and you shall receive it hot from the oven." The final movement, however, was completed only in December. The work was duly dedicated to Aebi and, with his permission, the premiere was entrusted to Hans Will, with Victor Desarzens conducting the Winterthur City Orchestra on February 6, 1952, drawing warm praise from renowned critic Willi Schuh, who was quick to appreciate its many magisterial beauties. "This quietly flowing middle movement," he noted, "is the work's heart and perhaps the most sublime instrumental piece Schoeck has written: its autumnal colors and entranced dreaming are muted as if in a transfigured backward glance at the Lenau settings of the *Elegy*...."

The first movement opens with robust swagger—a sort of sardonic *bonhomie*—soon allayed by a lingering second theme whose serrated contour seems to acknowledge a deep acceptance. A succinctly engaging contrapuntal working out keeps one's interest on the *qui vive*. The deeply affecting, lyrically eloquent second movement, suggesting suffering and serenity hand-in-hand, more than merits Schuh's praise. The third movement's spirited romp nevertheless conveys joy tried by experience—a jovial winding-up that is more than a lighthearted frolic—and skips nimbly through cyclic allusions to the first movement. Despite the fact that the concerto plays but a little more than a quarter-of-an-hour, the horn is heard almost without respite, making it both difficult and rewarding for the soloist with the stamina to meet its demands. It remains Schoeck's most popular and oft-recorded work. *—Adrian Corleonis*

Recommended:

○ **Schoek: Orchestral Works** / Albert (cond.), Schneider, Zabarella, Zurcher, Winterhur Musikkollegium / CPO 999337

Arnold Schoenberg

b. Sep. 13, 1874, Vienna, Austria, **d.** Jul. 13, 1951, Los Angeles, CA

Composer: Orchestral, Concerto, Chamber Music, Keyboard, Vocal, Choral, Opera

Arnold Schoenberg remains one of the most controversial figures in the history of music. From the final years of the nineteenth century to the period following the World War II, Schoenberg produced music of great stylistic diversity, inspiring fanatical devotion from students, admiration from peers like Mahler, Strauss, and Busoni, riotous anger from conservative Viennese audiences, and unmitigated hatred from his many detractors.

Born in Vienna on 13 September 1874, into a family that was not particularly musical, Schoenberg was largely self-taught as a musician. An amateur cellist, he demonstrated from early age a particular aptitude for composition. He received rudimentary instruction in harmony and counterpoint from Oskar Adler and studied composition briefly with Alexander Zemlinsky, his eventual brother-in-law. Early in his career, Schoenberg took jobs orchestrating operettas, but most of his life was spent teaching, both privately and at various institutions, and composing. His moves between teaching jobs were as much a result of seeking respite from the bouts of ill health which hampered him as they were due to his being offered a position.

The composer's early works bear the unmistakable stamp of high German Romanticism, perhaps nowhere more evident than in his first important composition, *Verklärte Nacht*, Op. 4 (1899). With works like the *Five Orchestral Pieces* (1909) and the epochal *Pierrot lunaire* (1912), Schoenberg embarked upon one of the most influential phases of his career. Critics reviled this "atonal" (Schoenberg preferred "pantonal") music, whose structure does not include traditional tonality. Still, the high drama and novel expressive means of Schoenberg's music also inspired a faithful and active following. Most notable among Schoenberg's disciples were Alban Berg and Anton Webern, both of whom eventually attained stature equal to that of their famous mentor. These three composers—the principal figures of the so-called Second Viennese School—were the central force in the development of atonal and 12-tone music in the first half of the twentieth century and beyond.

Schoenberg's *Suite for Piano* (1921–23) occupies a place of central importance in the composer's catalogue as his first completely 12-tone composition. Though the 12-tone technique represents only a single, and by no means predominant, aspect of the composer's style, it remains the single characteristic mostly closely associated with his music. Schoenberg made repeated, though varied, use of the technique across the spectrum of genres, from chamber works like the *String Quartet No. 4* (1936) and the *Fantasy for Violin and Piano* (1949) to orchestral works like the *Violin Concerto* (1935–36) and the *Piano Concerto* (1942), to choral works like *A Survivor from Warsaw* (1947).

Schoenberg fled the poisonous political atmosphere of Europe in 1933 and spent the remainder of his life primarily in the United States, becoming a naturalized citizen in 1941. During this phase of his career, he at times returned to frank tonality, as in the *Theme and Variations for band* (1943), reaffirming his connection to the great German musical heritage that extended back to Bach. For Schoenberg, the dissolution of tonality was a logical and inevitable step in the evolution of Western music. Despite a steady stream of critical brickbats throughout his entire career, the composer, whose life inspired one of twentieth century's great novels, Thomas Mann's *Doctor Faustus*, persisted in his aims, insisting that his music was the result of an overwhelming creative impulse. Though debate over the man and his music rages on, Schoenberg is today acknowledged as one of the most significant figures in music history. The composer, a well-known triskaidekaphobe, died in Los Angeles, California on July 13, 1951. *—AMG*

ORCHESTRAL

Accompaniment to a Film-Scene (Begleitungsmusik zu einer Lichtspielszene), Op. 34 (Oct., 1929–Feb., 1930)

Schoenberg composed *Accompaniment to a Film-Scene (Begleitungsmusik zu einer Lichtspielszene)*, Op. 34, for a silent film that existed only in his imagination. It was premiered in Berlin in 1930 with Otto Klemperer conducting. It later received its American premiere at the Hollywood Bowl on July 24, 1933, under the direction of Nicolas Slonimsky. Schoenberg's scenario moves through three parts: "Threatening Danger," "Fear," and "Catastrophe," each of which is clearly and vividly described in the music. The music itself is composed in Schoenberg's system of composing with 12 tones related only to one another, which has the effect of sounding like strictly organized chaos, surely the effect Schoenberg was aiming at. *Begleitungsmusik zu einer Lichtspielszene* is scored for a small orchestra, albeit it one with a very large percussion section. There are actually several moods within this brief, approximately eight-minute work: A soft shuddering of strings and single one-note solos from the winds, lead to fuller patterns in the strings. Engaging rhythmic variations on a restricted range of notes form the structure of these patternings. A slightly grotesque joking "pratfall" pattern leads to more lighthearted gestures. The music gains momentum and fullness, developing into complex, rushing, still dissonant 3/4 patterns until an extended melody in the strings, preceded by cymbals and gongs, makes the mood decidedly more romantic. A mysterious undercurrent reasserts itself and a midnight mystery, even horror movie seems in progress, and the music fragments quietly to a conclusion. *—James Leonard*

Recommended:

○ **Boulez Conducts Schoenberg** / Boulez (cond.), BBC SO / 1982 / Sony 48462

Chamber Symphony No. 1 in E major, Op. 9 (1906)

When Schoenberg wrote his *Chamber Symphony No. 1 in E major,* he had high hopes that this piece would establish him as a composer in Vienna and define his personal style. In the end, it did neither. Schoenberg had been and would remain an outsider in Viennese musical politics, and the style he formulated in the chamber symphony was quickly outgrown and discarded. But the work itself remains a brilliant and often beautiful example of a unique style. Scored for ten winds and five strings and written in one continuous movement in five sections, the chamber symphony is extremely terse and condensed. In just over 20 minutes, the chamber symphony moves from a very brief introduction to an exposition, a Scherzo, a development, an Adagio, and a finale that sums up all that had gone before. The writing is extremely difficult with every player a virtuoso. The language is essentially tonal, but with angular, quartal themes and lush, Wagnerian harmonies. The colors are primary, but with plangent and pungent new sonorities created by unusual doublings. The rhythm is remorseless, always moving the music forward even at moments of seeming stasis. Indeed, the overwhelming impression of the work is one of relentless busyness, of a man in a hurry with a lot to say, little time to say it, and less inclination to explain anything. The style of the chamber symphony is direct to the point of bluntness and energetic past the point of frantic. It is easy to understand why Schoenberg abandoned it: the style was difficult to sustain and impossible to duplicate. *—James Leonard*

Recommended:

○ **Boulez Conducts Schoenberg** / Boulez (cond.), InterContemporain Ens. / 1982 / Sony 48462

○ **Schoenberg: Chamber Symphonies 1 & 2; Verklärte Nacht** / Orpheus CO / 1990 / DG 429233

○ **Music of Arnold Schoenberg Vol. 3** / Craft (cond.), Philharmonia / 1999 / Koch International Classics 7463

○ **Schoenberg: Chamber Symphonies 1 & 2; Verklärte Nacht** / Holliger (cond.), CO of Europe / 2002 / Apex 44399

Chamber Symphony No. 2 in E flat minor, Op. 38 (Aug., 1906–Oct., 1939)

After Schoenberg immigrated to the United States in 1933, his compositional output slowed. In part this was due to the stress of moving itself, first from Europe to Boston in 1933, then to Los Angeles in 1934, and in part to his teaching activities. Despite his reasonably rapid acclimation to his new environment (especially to Los Angeles) his productivity did not increase, due in part to the distressing news concerning the treatment of his relatives in Austria; but also because he could find no audience for the music he wished to write. Between 1936 and 1940 he completed only two original works, the *Kol nidre,* Op. 39, and the *Chamber Symphony No. 2,* Op. 38.

In the late 1930s Schoenberg reached yet another turning point. Since the experiments of the 1920s that led to his development of the 12-tone "system" of composition, Schoenberg had been applying his ideas to models drawn from earlier periods of Western music history. As his search progressed through the Baroque and Classical eras and into the Romantic, he found himself confronted with his own early style. This may be the reason he attempted to rework his *Chamber Symphony No. 2,* begun immediately after he had finished the *Chamber Symphony No. 1,* Op. 9, in July 1906, and set down in 1916.

Described by Schoenberg himself as tonal in 1948, his *Chamber Symphony No. 2* elicited an artistic "soul search." When he picked up the sketches for the work in 1938, he found he was not the same composer he had been in 1906. Schoenberg changed little of the first movement, but nearly half of the second was newly composed, and he added what he called a "third movement" that functions more as a coda to the second.

After a hesitant introduction reminiscent of *Verklärte Nacht,* a rising string theme begins immediate development, the increased tension reaching a climax culminating in silence. Low strings enter under a flute playing an inversion of the string theme before cellos begin a new theme, which is taken up by trumpet and clarinet. The piece continues with extended development of this material, featuring a Mahlerian tendency for a melody or figure to begin in one instrument and move to another. Harmonies tend to move by step, often with all parts moving in parallel. The close of the movement revisits the earlier themes, although re-orchestrated and at a slower tempo. The rambunctious second movement, marked con fuoco, shows the influence of Schoenberg's work since 1906. Seemingly unrelated elements occur simultaneously, and the total fabric of the composition is much thicker than that of the first movement. A more aggressive overall atmosphere includes pizzicato passages and sharp brass attacks, and the orchestration in general is more representative of later Schoenberg. The slow coda takes up some of the material from the opening, while chords built on fourths make up a large part of a tonal scheme that, again, features harmonies that move by step.

Fritz Stiedry conducted the premiere of the *Chamber Symphony No. 2* in New York on December 15, 1940. Stiedry had known Schoenberg since October 1924 when he conducted the premiere of Schoenberg's *Die glückliche Hand* in Vienna. It is possible that Stiedry urged Schoenberg to complete his *Chamber Symphony No. 2,* for there exists correspondence from the composer to the conductor relating his progress on the work. *—John Palmer*

Recommended:

○ **Schoenberg: Chamber Symphonies 1 & 2; Verklärte Nacht** / Holliger (cond.), CO of Europe / 2002 / Apex 44399

○ **Schoenberg: Moses & Aron; Chamber Symphony 2** / Boulez (cond.), Inter-Contemporain Ens. / 1993 / Sony 48456

○ **Schoenberg: Chamber Symphonies 1 & 2; Verklärte Nacht** / Orpheus CO / 1990 / DG 429233

Pelleas und Melisande, symphonic poem, Op. 5 (Jul., 1902–Feb., 1903)

Only three years separate the first sketches of Arnold Schoenberg's only symphonic poem *Pelleas und Melisande,* Op. 5 from the string sextet *Verklärte Nacht* of 1899; yet in some ways the distance traveled during this brief span is greater than that traveled by many composers during an entire lifetime. While the musical roots of *Pelleas* are, by and large, the same as those of the sextet—the most immediate being debts to the underlying "Leitmotiv" techniques of Wagner and the surface-level luxuriousness of Richard Strauss' own tone-poems—the contrapuntal web that Schoenberg weaves in *Pelleas* is so dense and of such chromatic complexity that the music is transfigured into something wholly new. To be sure, *Pelleas* is not an entirely successful score: the manner in which tonal and hyper-chromatic idioms interact throughout the score is perhaps not as fluid and natural as it had been in *Verklärte Nacht,* and the piece sometimes runs the risk of collapsing under its own weight. But during the early twentieth century, Schoenberg's musical language was developing at so rapid a pace that he could scarcely keep up with himself, and it is entirely understandable that, in his effort to give birth to such a remarkably new style of musical expression, he would overstretch himself a bit; before the decade was out, the path to which *Pelleas* clearly points had been followed, with consequences that would shape an entire century of music.

In 1902, Debussy's opera based on Materlinck's *Pelleas und Melisande* was hot off the press; Schoenberg, however, had no knowledge whatsoever of the French composer's effort, and proceeded to plan his own opera after the play. He rapidly discarded this plan in favor of a purely instrumental study of the work, feeling that his emerging style would be better served if the music were allowed to shape its own course in a way that a strictly text-derived work could never do. The rich scoring of *Pelleas* reflects the same late Romantic tendency towards inflation that marks the nearly contemporaneous scoring of *Gurrelieder.* Seventeen woodwind players, 18 brass, more than a half dozen percussionists, and a reinforced contingent of strings and harps are all on call. *Pelleas und Melisande* is cast as a single large body of music, in which the four traditional symphonic movements are still vaguely discernable, but which puts more stress on the myriad structural and expressive possibilities that result from juxtaposing several levels of motivic detail than on the well-worn shadows of "arbitrary" formal outlines.

And so, after the sober, chromatic melody that begins the narrative, we are offered a tragic theme representing the beautiful Melisande and an energetic, soaring Pelleas theme. Like *Verklärte Nacht, Pelleas* draws a large-scale D minor tonality; on the local scale, however, it is even more chromatically far-flung. From time to time, more conventionally "Romantic" passages crop up, such as the love scene that appears as a kind of adagio movement. The epilogue, in which Schoenberg reflects on the death of Melisande, is a masterstroke, as is the final, resigned descent back into D minor. *—Blair Johnston*

Recommended:

○ **Schoenberg: Transfigured Night; Pelleas & Melisande** / Karajan (cond.), Berlin PO / DG 457721

○ **Music of Arnold Schoenberg Vol. 5** / Craft (cond.), Philharmonia / Koch 7471

○ **Schoenberg: Pelleas & Melisnade; Webern: Passacaglia** / Eschenbach, Houston SO / 1995 / Koch 37316

Five Pieces, Op. 16 (1909)

After breaking new musical ground with the remarkable *Three Pieces for piano,* Op. 11 of 1909, Arnold Schoenberg set out to apply the same untamed language to a larger instrumental texture. The resulting *Fünf Orchesterstücke* (Five Pieces for Orchestra), Op. 16 from later in the same year are something entirely unprecedented in the orchestral tradition; Schoenberg's dense counterpoint and extreme chromaticism demand that the ensemble be treated in a way that gives little thought to the hallowed symphonic tradition that Schoenberg knew so well and, despite his revolutionary innovations, loved so dearly.

At his publisher's request, Schoenberg added titles to each of the five pieces (later removed from most editions) in an effort to soften the blow that the works would deliver to unsuspecting audiences. A diary entry from 1912, however, attests to the great reluctance with which he did this, and reveals his effort to find the least revealing titles that he possibly could! And so we find the first work of the group labeled as "Premonitions." To say that this first piece (labeled Sehr rasch [very fast]) is tumultuous does not adequately capture the explosive effect that it had on players and listeners of the day: a series of repeated motivic shapes, including a driving bass ostinato, gradually accrete, building to an intentionally frightening climax; having arrived there, Schoenberg explores an otherworldly orchestral color built on woodwind flutter-tonguing and muted trombones.

The second piece is marked Mässige Viertel (Moderate four) and titled "The Past." Perhaps the allusion here is to the direct musical past, as hinted at by the piece's vague D minor shadows and rough ternary (ABA) form. Schoenberg's use of the orchestra is less experimental here than in the previous piece, but, if anything, even more colorful—note, for instance, the delicate interplay of the solo cello with the muted horn and bassoon counter-gesture during the opening bars.

Schoenberg removes all traditional motivic associations from the following piece, called "Chord-Colors." A single generative harmony (C-G sharp-B-E-A) is woven into a number of chromatically-altered derivatives, scored for a kaleidoscopically rotating array of instrumental colors. A light 32nd note figure in the flutes seems to rouse the group to slightly more active figurations, but Schoenberg insists that no dynamic greater than pianissimo be reached, even (indeed, especially) throughout the elaborate chromaticism of the middle portion.

The fourth piece, enigmatically titled "Peripetia," revisits the Sehr rasch world of the first piece. Wild brass and woodwind flourishes initiate the rowdiness, and the horns follow up with muted (but still fortissimo) triplets. Schoenberg keeps motivic interrelationships under heavy disguise, and, just as the music seems to be cooling down to give the audience a chance to orient itself, Schoenberg rather cruelly drives the piece home to a thrilling close.

The thick contrapuntal web of the final piece, marked Bewegte Achtel (Heavy eight) and titled "Endless Recitative," was so incomprehensible to conductors of the day that Schoenberg was forced to develop a symbol—later adopted by a large proportion of twentieth century composers—for indicating which musical material is of primary importance. As many as eight melodic voices are set to continually changing and increasingly urgent instrumental combinations. The bottom drops quickly out, however, and Schoenberg returns us to the introverted world in which we started. The scoring of the final chord for solo strings, brass in extreme register, and overlapping woodwinds is a final brilliant touch to an astounding work. *—Blair Johnston*

Recommended:

- ○ **Schoenberg: Serenade; 5 Pieces for Orchestra** / Boulez (cond.), BBC SO / 1993 / Sony 48463
- ○ **Schoenberg: Survivor from Warsaw; etc.** / Craft (cond.), London SO / 1995 / Koch 7263
- ○ **Antal Dorati; Rafael Kubelik** / Kubelik (cond.), Chicago SO / 1998 / Mercury 434397
- ○ **Schoenberg** / Dohnányi (cond.), Cleveland Orch. / 1996 / London 448279

Variations for Orchestra, Op. 31 (May, 1926–Aug., 1928)

Arnold Schoenberg's *Variations for Orchestra*, Op. 31, completed in 1928, is among a clutch of works composed from 1925–28 in his neo-Classical style. These pieces include his *Wind Quintet*, Op. 26, *Suite*, Op. 29, *String Quartet No. 3*, Op. 30, and parts of his *Suite for Piano*, Op. 25. Neo-Classicism was not a step backwards in time when handled by Schoenberg, but rather an attempt to offer listeners structural points of reference with which they could identify. His treatment of the 12-tone system is always natural and approachable. The Op. 31 shares an easygoing spirit similar to his third string quartet. Neither work is especially intense, whereas the Op. 25, Op. 26, and Op. 29 share the composer's focused, fighting spirit. Both the Op. 30 and Op. 31 were written in Berlin during Schoenberg's professorship at the Prussian Academy of Fine Arts, where he replaced the recently deceased Busoni. The professorship in composition came with more perks and privileges than Schoenberg had previously known. The better living conditions were enough to relax some of his scrappier musical instincts. In a secure enough position to write comfortably, the ferocity of his genius gave way to elegance. Schoenberg's *Variations for Orchestra include an introduction, 12 variations*, and a finale. The character of each variation is distinct and occasionally the hammer of his intense spirit does assert itself, but so do episodes of playful ease. Variation 4, marked Walzertempo, is as gentle as a Viennese waltz, while the following variation bears the mark of a stern musical champion. These diverse affects cohere seamlessly, building a holistic world of sound from a tone row constructed of two hexachords of identical intervalic properties. The famous BACH cipher (B flat, A, C, B natural) is prominent as well.

The premiere of the Op. 31 featured the illustrious Wilhelm Furtwängler conducting the Berlin Philharmonic on December 2, 1928. Never before had such an important conductor taken on a concert work by Schoenberg or any other member of the Second Viennese School. The reviews were unfavorable but they did not interfere with Schoenberg's creativity as he launched into one of the most productive periods of his career. *—John Keillor*

Recommended:

- ○ **Schoenberg: Die glückliche Hand; Variations for Orchestra; Verklärte Nacht** / Boulez (cond.), BBCSO / 1993 / Sony 48464
- ○ **Music of Arnold Schoenberg Vol. 3** / Craft (cond.), London PO / 1999 / Koch 7463
- ○ **Schoenberg: Cello Concerto; etc.** / Gielen (cond.), SWR SO, Baden-Baden / Wergo 60185

CONCERTO

Piano Concerto, Op. 42 (1942)

Arnold Schoenberg's *Piano Concerto*, Op. 42, was the composer's first work since the *Violin Concerto*, Op. 36 to employ his "method of composing with 12 tones that are related only to one another." Four of his previous works—*Kol nidre*, Op. 39, the *Second Chamber Symphony*, Op. 38, the *Variations on a Recitative for Organ*, Op. 40, and *Ode to Napoleon Buonaparte*, Op. 41 (all completed between 1938 and 1942)—retain serial principles in a relaxed form or dispense with them completely. For the first time in four years, Schoenberg would base a work on a single, ordered, 12-note series. This series appears in the opening theme of the concerto, both in the linear right hand of the piano part and in combination with the left hand (some pitch repetition does occur).

Although it is written in one movement, the concerto falls into four sections, marked Andante, Molto allegro, Adagio, and Giocoso. The division is symphonic in nature, and the rondo-like aspects of the finale reinforce this impression. The richness of the piano part is evocative of Brahms' music, as is the distribution of material between the solo and orchestra parts. Schoenberg partitions his row into two hexachords (six-note groups), each of which he tends to subdivide into trichords (three-note groups). Unlike the row Schoenberg designed for his *Ode to Napoleon Buonaparte*, Op. 41, various combinations of pitches do not result in traditional triads. However, Schoenberg's permutations of the row are sometimes very free, even from the beginning of the piece, resulting in occasional quasitonal passages. This freedom in the use of the row enables Schoenberg to write the thick, fourth-based chords at the end of the Molto allegro and the Adagio. At such moments the work seems to be moving away from the 12-tone idiom. The clear triple meter of the first section is eerily reminiscent of the Viennese waltz in both the melody and accompaniment. Entering hesitantly at first, the orchestra gradually becomes an equal participant in the proceedings. In the Molto allegro, Schoenberg employs a device he had used in his Op. 11 piano pieces—a chord in harmonics created by silently depressing four keys, then causing the strings to vibrate by striking the same notes in a lower register. The orchestra alone opens the tense, tragic Adagio, thereafter alternating with the piano's solo passages. Separation between the two forces is created in this section, in which a potential climax is averted by a moment of silence and a genuine cadenza for the piano. Oddly, the very beginning of the Giocoso returns to an F sharp far more often than would be possible in a strictly worked out 12-tone composition, reflecting Schoenberg's relaxed approach to his own method in this piece. A recurrent rhythmic motive permeates the entire section, which, in its contrasting moments and sweeping gestures, sounds at times as if it were composed in the late nineteenth century.

Sketches for the concerto suggest Schoenberg put down his first ideas on June 27, 1942; his date at the end of the finished score is December 10, 1942. The premiere of the *Piano Concerto* was given at the NBC Studios in New York with Eduard Steuermann at the piano and Leopold Stokowski conducting. Steuermann had also participated in the first performances of *Ode to Napoleon Buonaparte*, Op. 41, and *Pierrot lunaire*, Op. 21. *—John Palmer*

Recommended:

- ○ **Schoenberg: Piano Concerto; Piano Pieces, Opp. 11 & 19; Berg: Piano Sonata** / Boulez (cond.), Uchida, Cleveland Orch. / 2001 / Philips 468033
- ○ **Schoenberg: Piano Concerto; Chamber Symphonies** / Gielen (cond.), Brendel, SWF Sinfonieorchester Baden-Baden / 1996 / Philips 446683
- ○ **Schoenberg & Webern: Piano Works** / Abbado (cond.), Pollini, Berlin PO / 2001 / DG 471361

Violin Concerto, Op. 36 (1935–Sep., 1936)

Schoenberg's *Violin Concerto*, Op. 36, was first performed by the Philadelphia Orchestra under the direction of Leopold Stokowski, with Louis Krasner as soloist, on December 6, 1940. It was later recorded by Krasner with the New York Philharmonic under Dimitri Mitropoulos. Interestingly, in a letter dated December 2, 1945, to Krasner, Schoenberg asks which sections the "audience" or "music lovers" may have liked or disliked.

The *Violin Concerto* was one the first pieces Schoenberg began after immigrating to the United States. It is also one of his first 12-tone compositions since his work on the opera *Moses und Aron*, after which he began to reexplore the tonal idiom. The concerto was completed on September 23, 1936, after Schoenberg had accepted a professorship at the University of California, Los Angeles, and settled in Brentwood, CA.

In 1937, Schoenberg wrote of the concerto: "[It] is extremely difficult, just as much for the head as for the hands. I am delighted to add another 'unplayable' work to the repertoire. I want the concerto to be difficult and I want the little finger to become longer. I can wait."

Based on a single 12-tone row, the concerto is entirely dodecaphonic. The most notable general characteristics of the concerto are the autonomy of the violin part, the rigorous application of the 12-tone method, and the use of extremely wide intervallic leaps and contrasting registers.

Throughout the first movement, Schoenberg refers to Baroque-era ritornello form in the alternation of solo and orchestra sections. Unfolding slowly, the soloist begins the movement, a gradual layering of instruments occurring until the first orchestral outburst. When the soloist returns, the accompaniment becomes pizzicato strings with sustained woodwind harmonies, supporting new material and row forms. The double- and triple-stop harmonics that follow are a perfect example of the technically difficult passages that make this work infamous. An abrupt tempo change to Vivace marks a new section that is introduced by the orchestra. The soloist and orchestral strings trade figures and partitions of the rows. Schoenberg's cadenza is replete with wide leaps and harmonics, which eventually disappear as the solo violin closes the movement by reiterating its opening notes.

Vertical presentations of row forms are predominant at the beginning of the Andante grazioso second movement. In general, the orchestra plays a much larger role here, often sounding without the soloist and presenting autonomous thematic material. During the first of these orchestral passages, the cellos perform an unusual, repeated melodic third as the rest of the orchestra fills in the row form. The soloist does not become truly dominant until late in the movement, when a lengthy legato melody is accompanied only by strings. A moment before the movement closes, the soloist returns to the opening theme in a lower octave, but it is harmonized differently and trails off after two measures.

Opening with a theme that is motivic in construction, the marchlike finale is even more orchestral than the second movement. After the soloist plays the main theme, the orchestra takes over, presenting a great wealth of material. Percussion instruments such as the tambourine, snare drum, cymbal, and triangle, enter near the end of the first orchestral segment, and continue as accompaniment for the ensuing solo passage. After quoting the main theme on a different row, the soloist continues, exploring contrasting registers to an even greater degree than in the first movement. Never again does the orchestra take center stage as it has; the soloist dominates the rest of the proceedings. *—John Palmer*

Recommended:

- ○ **Berg & Schoenberg: Violin Concertos** / Mitropoulos (cond.), Krasner, West German Radio Orch. / 1991 / GM 2006
- ○ **Music of Arnold Schoenberg Vol. 4** / Craft (cond.), Schulte, Philharmonia / 2000 / Koch 7493
- ○ **Schoenberg** / Boulez (cond.), Amoyal, London SO / 1998 / Erato 24241

CHAMBER MUSIC

String Quartet No. 2 in F sharp minor, Op. 10 (1907–1908)

The *String Quartet No. 2*, Op. 10, of Arnold Schoenberg is one of the key works of musical modernism. Composed between March 1907 and August 1908, its last movement marks the decisive point at which Western art music moved from a tonally based harmonic structure to what has been called an atonal harmonic structure. Prior to the *Quartet No. 2*, Schoenberg wrote in the highly chromatic post-Wagnerian harmonic language of the fin de siècle, a language that took tonal music to the limits of its coherence by delaying the resolution of dissonances for longer and longer periods. After the *Quartet No. 2*, Schoenberg, then his pupils and then much of Western art music abandoned tonality for harmonic structures that not only allowed an extremely high level of chromatic dissonance, but which no longer required the resolution of those dissonances.

The *Quartet No. 2* itself begins tonally, and its first two movements are, in fact, in F sharp minor. The opening movement is in sonata form with the usual harmonic relation between keys. The second movement is a scherzo with trios, the second of which ends with a quotation from the plague song, *Ach, Du Liebe Augustine*. The third movement is in E flat minor, one of the most difficult keys for a string player to perform in, and sets Stefan George's poem *"Litanei"* (Litany) for soprano, the first time a vocalist had been used in a piece of chamber music. The final movement sets another poem by George, entitled *"Entruckung"* (Transport), for soprano and, although the movement ends on an F sharp major triad, it is for almost all the rest of its length, completely unconcerned with tonal harmonic relationships and structures. Instead, it relies on George's text and motivic relationships to give coherence to the music.

Interestingly, while the opening movements of the *Quartet No. 2* are anguished in tone and the third movement is one of the most harrowing pieces Schoenberg was ever to write, the closing movement is calm and even serene in tone, despite being harmonically atonal. In part, the emotional sequence of the quartet is autobiographical: while he was composing the quartet, Schoenberg's wife, Mathilda, left him and their children for the painter Richard Gerstle. Although Mathilda was later persuaded by Schoenberg's pupil Anton Webern to return to her family, her return caused the unstable Gerstle to hang himself, and this in turn caused her to lose her own sanity. Shortly after the completion of the *Quartet No. 2*, Mathilda was placed in an institution, where she remained for the rest of her life. *—James Leonard*

Recommended:

- ○ **Schoenberg: The String Quartets** / New Vienna SQ, Lear / 1999 / Philips 464046
- ○ **Schoenberg: String Quartets 1–4** / Arditti SQ, Upshaw / 2000 / Disques Montaigne 782135
- ○ **Webern, Schoenberg & Berg** / Brindisi SQ, Oelze / 1994 / Metronome 1007-01
- ○ **Arnold Schoenberg** / Schoenberg Quartet, Narucki / 2001 / Chandos 9939

String Quartets (1897–1936)

Almost entirely self-taught as a musician, Arnold Schoenberg started composing string quartets as a teenager after studying the scores of Beethoven. Schoenberg produced five or six such early works, but of these only a *Quartet in D major* from 1897 survives. He once wrote that "Mozart, Brahms, Beethoven and Dvořák were my models at this time," and Brahms and Dvořák are particularly evident in this work. Alexander Zemlinsky, Schoenberg's friend and brother-in-law (and only real music teacher) had a big influence on the *Quartet*'s final form, providing suggestions and helping to guide the writing process.

Around that time Schoenberg became aware of the large-scale works of Richard Strauss and Gustav Mahler. That influence starts to assert itself in ambitious compositions like the *Quartet No. 1 in D minor*, Op. 7 (1905)—a 40-minute work which, although in a comparatively traditional four-movement form, is quite a bit more advanced in harmony and counterpoint than its D major predecessor. The *Quartet No. 1* was booed at its premiere by the Rosé Quartet, on February 5, 1907, in Vienna.

But that response was mild compared to the jeers and laughter that greeted the first performance of the *Quartet No. 2 in F sharp minor*, Op. 10 (1907–08), by the Rosé Quartet and soprano Marie Gutheil-Schoder on December 21, 1908, in Vienna. According to newspaper reports, the music "caused elegant ladies to utter cries of pain, putting their hands to their delicate ears, and elderly gentlemen to shed tears of excitement." Schoenberg's musical language had become considerably more angular and dissonant, so much so that, as he later wrote, "... the overwhelming multitude of dissonances cannot be balanced any longer by occasional returns to such tonal triads as represent a key." By the *Quartet*'s third and fourth movements, which feature the soprano soloist in settings of Stefan George's poems *Litanei* (Litany) and *Entrückung* (Transport)—the latter featuring the famous opening line "Ich fühle Luft von anderem Planeten" ("I feel the air of another planet")—tonality's hold on the music has all but disappeared. The *Quartet No. 2* was Schoenberg's last work with a key signature for several decades.

The *Quartet No. 3*, Op. 30 was written in early 1927, and premiered in Vienna on September 19 of that year. Schoenberg had moved to the United States by the time he wrote the *Quartet No. 4*, Op. 37, in 1936. That autumn he became Professor of Music at the University of California, Los Angeles, and the *Fourth Quartet*, premiered in Los Angeles on January 9, 1937, was one of the first works he completed in California. The *Third* and *Fourth Quartets* have much in common. Both were commissioned by music patron Elizabeth Sprague Coolidge and first performed by the Kolisch Quartet, which Schoenberg called "the best string quartet I ever heard." Both are also in the customary four movements and employ the 12-tone technique (with occasional slight tonal references) in the context of traditional forms like theme-and-variations, rondo, and sonata-allegro. *—Chris Morrison*

Recommended:

- ○ **Schoenberg: String Quartets 1–4** / Arditti SQ, Upshaw / 2000 / Disques Montaigne 782135

String Trio, Op. 45 (1946)

On August 2, 1946, Schoenberg suffered a nearly fatal heart attack. Shortly afterward, almost as though in reaction, he set to work on the String Trio, Op. 45, composed between August 20 and September 23. Commissioned by Harvard University, the String Trio was partially mapped out prior to the composer's heart attack; still, Schoenberg explained to friends and students that he wrote the work with clear programmatic intent specifically related to his infirmity and recovery. The Trio is filled with extreme contrasts and what appear to be non sequiturs. Schoenberg's onetime pupil Leonard Stein later explained that "the many juxtapositions of unlike material within the Trio [are] reflections of the delirium which the composer suffered during parts of his illness.... These unusual juxtapositions also represent... the alternate phases of 'pain and suffering' and 'peace and repose' that Schoenberg experienced." In an unpublished essay, Schoenberg provided another perspective on the work: "I began the Trio, of which I have told many people that it is a 'humorous' representation of my sickness, soon after I was over the worst."

Schoenberg undoubtedly kept these comments private because of his inherent mistrust of program music.

The 12-tone Trio unfolds as a single movement in three sections; the first of these functions as an exposition, the second as a sort of development, and the last as a shortened recapitulation and coda. The first two of these parts are further divided into two sections each. Color and timbre are of the utmost importance in the Trio; in addition to normal bowing, Schoenberg draws upon an extensive palette of playing techniques, including ponticello, pizzicato, harmonics, and col legno.

The harmonic and melodic material are derived from a single primary row and its permutations. After the opening trills, Schoenberg immediately sets into relief the extreme registers of the cello and violin. A sudden change in dynamic and tempo announces the second part of the first section, which begins with a Wagnerian phrase in the violin, harmonized by the viola and cello. Throughout this lengthy slow passage, numerous attempts to reestablish the opening tempo fail. A change in pulse marks the beginning of the second section, while a canonic passage distinguishes the second part. A new melody, which also reappears in the coda, recalls a passage from Act Two of the composer's opera *Moses und Aron* (1930–32) associated with a woman healed by faith. Schoenberg described the recapitulation to Stein as "the going back and 'reliving' [the portion of his life portrayed in the first section] with the calmness and perspective of good health." Beginning note for note like the first section, the recapitulation immediately undergoes variation. Schoenberg presents some measures that exactly replicate the original while leaving others out entirely, in effect creating a shortened reprise that recalls but does not reproduce earlier events. *—John Palmer*

Recommended:

- ○ **Schoenberg: Verklärte Nacht; Trio** / Trampler, Ma, Julliard SQ / 1992 / Sony Classical 47690
- ○ **Schoenberg: Concerto for String Quartet & Orchestra; String Trio** / Lenox Quartet / 1973 / Phoenix USA 121

Verklärte Nacht, for string sextet, Op. 4 (1899)

Although Schoenberg's earliest published works were written for the voice, the composer had by then produced much other music, including a number of pieces incorporating strings. Indeed, Schoenberg had studied, at least informally, both the violin and cello, and thus was well equipped to meet the compositional challenges of his Op. 4, the substantial string sextet *Verklärte Nacht* (Transfigured Night; 1899). Its great success in Europe opened the gates of fame for the young composer, and even today, it remains one of Schoenberg's most familiar works—and certainly one of the least "difficult" for listeners.

The poetry of Richard Dehmel was a strong influence on the composer during the final years of the nineteenth century. Three of the songs from Schoenberg's Op. 2, for example, are settings of the poet's verse. Similarly, the underlying programme of *Verklärte Nacht*—the first important application of the traditionally orchestral tone poem genre to a chamber work—is taken from a poem in Dehmel's *Weib und Weit*. In later years the composer acknowledged that the compulsion he felt to express Dehmel's unique passions in music was one of the key determining factors in his early musical development.

Superficially, the programme is simple and seemingly improbable: during a brisk, moonlit evening walk, a woman confides to her lover that she is pregnant with another man's child. Before meeting her present lover, she felt that the only way to bring meaning into her life was to bring another life into the world. The man replies gently, compassionately, that the strength of their love for one another will transform the unborn babe into his own child. Schoenberg's musical structure is so entirely self-sufficient that one feels the programme to be almost nonessential. In fact, Schoenberg felt that he had so fully captured the deeper, more fundamental human drama of which Dehmel's poem is just one possible encapsulation that he was reluctant to tie his work down by its association with a literary source; consequently, he avoided public comment on the relationship between Dehmel's poem and his own musical "translation."

Verklärte Nacht is cast in a single thirty-minute D minor/D major movement for an ensemble of two violins, two violas, and two cellos. (The work also exists in Schoenberg's own arrangement for string orchestra made in the 1920s and revised in the 1940s.) Schoenberg's dual—and seemingly divergent—musical influences, Wagner and Brahms, are present throughout. Still, Schoenberg succeeds in marshalling a highly contrapuntal and chromatic language that is entirely his own for the first time in his career. After the static, quietly throbbing D minor of the opening passage, the work quickly ventures into a world of dense counterpoint, often hinting at the tonal center without making an unequivocal return. In fact, it is not until the warm D major sonority that begins the second half—corresponding to the man's loving reply—that a sense of tonal stability is restored, if only temporarily. The work comes to a close with shimmering arpeggio figures and string harmonics as the couple walks off into their new life together.*—Blair Johnston*

Recommended:

- ○ **Schoenberg: Die Glückliche Hand; Variations for Orchestra; Verklärte Nacht** / Boulez (cond.), New York PO / 1993 / Sony 48464
- ○ **Schoenberg: Pelleas & Melesande; Verklärte Nacht** / Karajan (cond.), Berlin PO / DG 457721
- ○ **Korngold: String Sextet; Schoenberg: Verklärte Nacht** / Raphael Ens. / 1990 / Hyperion 66425
- ○ **Schoenberg: Verklärte Nacht; Schubert: Quintet** / Hollywood SQ, Dinkin, Reher / 1993 / Testament 1031

Wind Quintet, Op. 26 (Apr., 1923–Aug., 1924)

Schoenberg fully knew the difficulties of his *Quintet for Winds*, Op. 26. In his sketches, he entitled the work: "Quintet for flute, oboe, intelligent clarinet, intelligent horn, bassoon." It appears more often in the classroom than in the concert hall. Nearly every measure requires maximum effort from all five players, who are charged with transmitting a tremendous wealth of ideas to the audience. Few of Schoenberg's pieces expose "how it is done" as clearly as the quintet.

The earliest sketches for Schoenberg's Wind Quintet Op. 26 date from April 14, 1923. Composition of the first movement began in earnest on April 21; the completion of the finale occurred on July 26. Only the second work Schoenberg composed using his twelve-note method, the quintet was first performed at the Viennese Festival of Music and Drama, which ran from September 14 to October 15, 1924, partly in honor of Schoenberg's birthday of September 13. The work is dedicated to Schoenberg's grandson, "Bubi Arnold."

The quintet is the first large-scale, multimovement work Schoenberg had composed in 15 years. The first movement of the *Quintet for Winds*, Op. 26, a model of economy, follows the sonata format, and its introduction would resurface in Schoenberg's *Variations for Orchestra*. The finale, a rondo, exhibits some of the light energy generally associated with Classical-era movements in rondo form.

Schoenberg's melding of innovation and tradition is most apparent in the third movement, marked Etwas langsam. The movement is cast in ternary form with the first and last section built upon the same rows and combinations of rows, creating a return not only in terms of melodic material but of harmonic content in classic recapitulatory fashion. The primary row itself bears a few links with "tradition." For instance, the two hexachords (six note groups dividing the row in half) each have the same shape and have the same intervals between all of the notes except the last. Furthermore, the first note of the second hexachord is a fifth above the first note of the first hexachord, implying a tonic-dominant relationship. The outer and inner sections of the movement are delineated in large part by their prevalent permutations of the row, and overall unity is achieved by the continuous use of particular tetrachords in either vertical or horizontal form. The movement is a perfect example of how Schoenberg felt the twelve-note method should be applied, vertically and horizontally. It is clear that the *Quintet for Winds*, Op. 26, is not a step toward a new development; rather, it embodies a totally new idiom in the history of Western music. *—John Palmer*

Recommended:

- ○ **Schoenberg, Webern, Berg** / Houston Symphony Chamber Players / 1996 / Koch 7337
- ○ **Arnold Schoenberg** / Schoenberg Quartett, Kooistra / 2001 / Chandos 9939
- ○ **Aulos Blaser Quintett Vol. 7** / Aulos Wind Quintet / 1994 / Koch 311632

KEYBOARD

Six Little Pieces, Op. 19 (1911)

At the time Schoenberg abandoned tonality—in the *Songs*, Op. 14 and the first two of the *Three Piano Pieces*, Op. 11—he found that further progress along the path of pure "expression" would lead him to a renunciation of motivic procedures as well. This left him with a choice: either construct music consisting of ideas that are complete from the outset and require no development, or create works that are continuously developmental with no clearly expository sections. Briefly, Schoenberg chose the latter method and set about composing the last two pieces in Opp. 11 and 16. About a year later, he experimented with the former possibility, writing the brief, highly compact *Six Piano Pieces, Op. 19*. For a time, Schoenberg found his path in constructing large forms around a text such as *Erwartung*, leaving the compact, non-developmental idiom to Webern. The first five pieces of Op. 19 were composed in a single day, February 19, 1911; the sixth followed on June 17. The musical equivalent of aphorisms, the longest of the set, No. 1, encompasses 18 measures while the shortest, Nos. 2 and 3, only nine each.

Leicht, zart (Light, sweet) is in many ways the most frantic and active of the set (it even boasts a trill). Descending lines in the right hand are set against rising gestures in the left, while fleeting chords contrast with single-note passages. After a brief pause, a new, songlike idea initiates the final moments of the piece.

Both form and content are derived from different types of contrast in the second piece, marked Langsam (Slow). A quiet, repeated third (G and B), played staccato in an ostinato pattern, contrasts with an angular but legato melody at a higher dynamic level. Brief pauses create the illusion of cadences constructed of minimal material. The most effective of these pauses occurs just after a vertical build-up of thirds.

Some melodic repetition and manipulation occurs in the third piece, Sehr langsam Viertel (Very slow quarter note). A bass motive appears at several pitch levels and is inverted and played in smaller note values in the treble range near the end.

Because of its tempo, Rasch, aber leicht (Fast, but light), No. 4 is the shortest of the Op. 19 pieces. It is unusual in because it features a melody distinct from an "accompaniment." Near the end, a diminution of the opening idea appears and apart from the bass line of the preceding piece, is one of the only instances of repetition. The piece closes with strident chords.

Etwas rasch (Somewhat fast) begins with a contrapuntal, linear statement, but chords built of thirds appear in a burst of activity just before its quiet close.

Revolving around two chords that actually make up a single, six-note sonority, Sehr langsam (Very slow) may be a lament on the recent death of Schoenberg's supportive elder colleague, Gustav Mahler. The dynamic never rises above *p* and falls as low as *pppp*. H.H. Stuckenschmidt has characterized the last of the set as representing "the furthest degree of dematerialization of the musical language." Some might say that it expresses the pure essence of the musical language. Two chords open and close this gloomy piece, and at only one point does anything linear intrude. *—John Palmer*

Recommended:

○ **Schoenberg & Webern: Piano Works** / Pollini / 2001 / DG 471361

○ **Schoenberg: Piano Works** / Gould / 1994 / Sony 52664

Three Pieces, Op. 11 (1909)

Arnold Schoenberg was not a pianist by training, and although in later years he developed a fluency with the instrument as both composer and player, his early efforts at writing for the piano are haunted by the luxurious nineteenth century style he had inherited. Some of his earlier song accompaniments are entirely effective on their own terms, however, and by the time of the *Drei Stücke für Klavier*, Op.11 (1909) he was finding that, as a corollary to the new, compact atonal structures he was beginning to utilize, more emotionally stringent use of the pianoforte made for fertile musical ground indeed. And so these three relatively brief pieces stand at the very gates of a revolution that was at the same time unremittingly committed to the future and, in Schoenbergs case at least, deeply rooted in the basic contrapuntal principles on which the music of his own heroes had been built.

In the first two pieces of the opus, Schoenberg's new techniques of thematic architecture—meaning that even the smallest musical gesture is intimately and directly derived from one of a handful of motivic ideas—operate in an environment in which ghosts from the tonal past still linger, including a vaguely ABA shape to Op.11 No.1. Also noteworthy are the persistent, initially tonal-sounding pedal tones F and D natural at the opening of the second piece, swiftly rebuked by the D flats, E flats, and A flats of the pianissimo upper line.

Unlike the mild-mannered first piece, the much longer second one rises to a desperately passionate climax before inevitably falling prey once again to that quiet, triplet pedal-tone figure that opened the piece. Stylistically, Op.11 No.2 owes more to Schoenberg's late Romantic heritage than do either of the other two pieces, and it is not surprising that Ferruccio Busoni chose to make an orchestral version of the piece within a year of its initial appearance.

The third piece, Bewegt, is another matter altogether. Here Schoenberg moves with fierce determination into unexplored musical territory. As its far-flung chromaticism unfolds, there is no neat three-part form or recapitulation, no clean sectional divisions (at the time, many critics labeled the work as "formless"); even the basic thematic substance of the piece is far more profuse (if just as efficient) than that of its predecessors. It comes as no surprise to learn that this forward-looking piece was composed several months after the other two, with the *Hanging Gardens*, Op.15, having been completed in the meantime. The musical distance that Schoenberg traveled in those months is truly awe inspiring. *—Blair Johnston*

Recommended:

○ **Schoenberg: Piano Works** / Gould / 1994 / Sony 52664

○ **Schoenberg & Webern: Piano Works** / Pollini / 2001 / DG 471361

Five Pieces, Op. 23 (1920–1923)

Between Schoenberg's *Six Piano Pieces*, Op. 19 and his *Five Piano Pieces*, Op. 23 lay the First World War and the ensuing depression. The period was also a compositional void for Schoenberg, whose output nearly ceased. He had reached an artistic crisis and sought a way to reach his true aim: "unity and regularity." That this was to be achieved without the procedures of tonality was of paramount importance, for Schoenberg felt that tonality had run its course. This led to his "discovery" of the "method of composing with 12 tones which are related only with one another." This did not happen overnight. Schoenberg experimented with the serialization of smaller groups of notes before applying the idea to all 12. We can find evidence of Schoenberg's experiments in the *Five Pieces for Piano*, Op. 23, a pivotal work in the composer's career.

The pieces that make up the Op. 23 set were not composed at the same time. Schoenberg wrote Nos. 1–2 and part of 4 in July 1920; the rest of Op. 23 in February 1923. By the time he began composing the 12-tone fifth movement, "Walzer" (Waltz), Schoenberg had already written works in the new idiom that would be published as part of the *Suite for Piano*, Op. 25.

The first of the *Five Pieces*, Op. 23, marked Sehr langsam (Very slow), demonstrates Schoenberg's approach to the principle of developing variation. When the opening melody reappears, the pitches are the same, but they have been moved to different octaves, changing the shape of the phrase, and are presented in a different rhythmic configuration. The retention of the pitches alone is enough to constitute a return to the theme, and through this piece we can gain insight into how Schoenberg uses pitches, not rhythms or melodic shapes, at the core of a composition. This concept lead directly to his formation of the 12-tone method.

Variation procedures continue in the second movement, Sehr rasch (Very fast), although some analysts have uncovered a sonata form structure. In this brief piece, the vertical aspect of the music is a result of the linear melodic movement.

The third piece of the set, Langsam (Slow)—sometimes referred to as a fugue because of the alternating entrances at the beginning—is again driven by variation technique. A five-note motive is put through metamorphoses so intense that at times it seems a single pitch could be considered part of any one of several forms of the motive.

Rhythmic freedom characterizes the fourth piece, Schwungvoll (Full of vitality). Here, Schoenberg juxtaposes sections of dense and sparse textures, separated by brief pauses.

Although the first four works of Op. 23 exhibit 12-tone techniques to a limited degree, these apply to smaller collections of pitches, not the entire 12 of the chromatic scale. The fifth and final work of the set (Walzer), however, is based on the repetition of a series or row of all 12 pitches. Everything that happens in this piece, both vertically and horizontally, is derived from the same series of pitches appearing in the same order. This is Schoenberg's most transparent and straightforward usage of these techniques. Schoenberg's next works, particularly the *Suite for Piano*, Op. 25, and the *Quintet for Winds*, Op. 26, would witness an expansion of the method and a greater self-assuredness on the part of the composer. *—John Palmer*

Recommended:

○ **Schoenberg & Webern: Piano Works** / Pollini / 2001 / DG 471361

○ **Arnold Schoenberg: Piano Music** / Jacobs / 1975 / Nonesuch 71309

VOCAL

The Book of the Hanging Gardens, song cycle, Op. 15 (1908–1909)

Composed during 1908 and 1909, Arnold Schoenberg's *Das Buch der hängenden Gärten* (Book of the Hanging Gardens) is the first of his many works for voice to occupy the same musical environment he had, just a few months earlier, begun to explore with the *Opus 11 piano pieces*. A few of the Hanging Gardens' numbers were actually written before Schoenberg sat down to pen Opus 11, and so the two achievements are more contemporary than their opus numbers would indicate. In these 15 songs Schoenberg moves us directly into the passionate, but wholly aristocratic world of poet Stefan George's *Hanging Gardens* collection; the same kind of doomed love affair that fuels the massive *Gurrelieder* cantata is at work here, but set instead as a set of miniature portraits that add up to a single musical utterance.

The Hanging Gardens songs are, while perhaps not so evasive of tonal references as the Op. 11 pieces or the soon-to-appear *Five Orchestral Pieces*, nevertheless quite a drastic harmonic change from such earlier settings as the Op. 2 songs or *Gurrelieder*. Throughout the cycle Schoenberg employs the piano not as an accompaniment, but rather as a completely independent observer or narrator.

This narration begins with an unaccompanied left-hand bass gesture, vague in both harmonic and rhythmic outline. As the singer (male, according to the text) goes through the painful process of striving for, and ultimately failing to keep, a woman of higher status, the piano offers its support in a number of fashions: raw chords, as in the fifth song, violent conflict (No. 8, in many ways the climax of the cycle and certainly its midpoint, both literally and in terms of psychological drama), or, frequently, dense counterpoint. In the brief No. 14 (just 11 bars), the poet's reflections on the myriad wonders of nature are supported by the kind of fragmented, shimmering arpeggio treatment that is so characteristic of Schoenberg's piano style from this time, and that would prove to be a profound influence on many later composers. The last song of the cycle is both the longest and most dramatically complex. Here all is sustained and legato; our singer has lost his love, and the garden that formerly was so beautiful to him is now a desiccated, poisonous shell. *—Blair Johnston*

Recommended:

○ **Schoenberg: Pierrot lunaire; Book of the Hanging Gardens** / de Gaetani, Kalish / 1990 / Nonesuch 79237

Brettl-Lieder (Cabaret Songs) (1901)

Arnold Schoenberg's historical significance as the father of serialism often obscures the true variety of his output. It also tends to minimize the purely musical (i.e. non-theoretical) aspects of his compositions, regardless of their style. There is perhaps no better cure for this than his eight *Brettl-Lieder* (Cabaret Songs), which showcase his most basic musical instincts and responses; these eight poems—dressed, with humor and simplicity, in a tonal language that bears no special label or distinction—give us a unique and amiable glimpse of Schoenberg's muse.

Schoenberg composed the *Brettl-Lieder* in 1901, before he moved to Berlin to work as a conductor with Überbrettl, part of Ernst von Wolzogen's Buntes Theater. Designed to use popular idioms to convey more "serious" ideas, Überbrettl (Variety Theater, or Cabaret) attracted literary luminaries of the time, including Frank Wedekind and Richard Dehmel. During the theater company's visit to Vienna in the fall of 1901, Oskar Straus had introduced Wolzogen to Schoenberg, who played some of his recently composed cabaret songs; it is certain that at least one of these, "Nachtwandler," was performed in Berlin before June 1902, when Schoenberg's association with the company ended.

The eight poems are taken in part from a collection, *Deutsche Chansons* (German Songs), published first in 1900 by Otto Julius Bierbaum. The contents of the volume were antithetical to the conservative literary trend at the end of the nineteenth century, and became an immediate success. Poets of the *Brettl-Lieder* are Frank Wedekind, Otto Julius Bierbaum, Hugo Salus, Gustav Hochstetter, Colly, Emanuel Schikaneder and Gustav Falke.

Most interesting among Schoenberg's eight settings is that of "Nachtwandler," by Gustav Falke, featuring piccolo, trumpet, and snare drum in addition to piano and soprano. The text calls for a drummer and trumpeter, who accompany the narrator on his nighttime escapes.

Other highlights include Wedekind's "Galathea," in which a narrator describes the desire to touch a young girl, Galathea. He (or she) wants to kiss, in turn, Galathea's cheeks, hair, hands, knees and feet—but not her mouth, which is reserved for the realm of fantasy. He sets the six verses in a rondo-like fashion—ABACAD—closing the song with new music that is similar to the fourth verse.

Schoenberg's setting of Bierbaum's "Gigerlette" reflects both the humor of the poem and its alternating four- and five-line verses. Fräulein Gigerlette, dressed in snow-white clothing, invites someone to tea in a room as red as wine and lit by candles. Later, the two take a carriage ride to the countryside with Cupid as their driver.

Salus' "Der genügsame Liebhaber" (Easily Satisfied Lover) is a poem begging for interpretation. A man tells us that his lady-friend has a black cat with a soft, velvety coat, and that he has a shiny, smooth bald head. The woman spends all her time caressing her cat's fur, and when he visits her, the "kitty" is in her lap, and it shivers when he strokes it. Later, he puts the kitty on his bald head and she plays with the kitty and laughs. Schoenberg's setting, strophic but with significant variation from verse to verse, is full of suggestive humor.

"Einfältiges Lied" (Simple Song) is also by Salus and tells of a king who, without scepter or crown, goes for a walk like an ordinary person. The wind then blows the hat off of his head and out of sight. Schoenberg depicts the uneven, hesitant gait of the king in the opening verse accompaniment, later portraying the wind and flying hat with aggressive, swooping melodies. *—AMG*

Recommended:

- ○ **Schoenberg: Erwartung; Brettl-Lieder** / Levine (cond.), Norman, Metropolitan Opera Orch. / 1993 / Philips 426261

Herzgewächse, song for soprano, celesta, harp & harmonium, Op. 20 (Dec., 1911)

The years 1908–09 were a prolific time for Schoenberg: he began composing in the atonal idiom and created a succession of important and deeply subjective Expressionistic works. After 1909, however, the composer suffered a prolonged dry spell, during which he composed virtually nothing and entered a depression. It was not until 1911 that Schoenberg became inspired again, producing more atonal works, but in a more accessible form. At the end of 1911, he wrote the song *Herzgewächse* (Foliage of the Heart), based on the French poem "Feuillage du coeur" by Maurice Maeterlinck. The song was composed—at Schoenberg's typical breakneck speed—for Wassily Kandinsky's journal *Der blaue Reiter* (The Blue Rider), a publication featuring the works of modern artists working in many different fields. *Herzgewächse* is an eccentric little song for soprano, harmonium, celesta, and harp, and is perhaps one of Schoenberg's most remarkable atonal compositions. Though not on the scale of his earlier atonal song cycles or operas, it nonetheless beautifully exemplifies the expressive potential of the atonal idiom.

The song's unique instrumentation is likely the result of Schoenberg's instinctive response to the poem. In a 1912 essay, published along with *Herzgewächse*, Schoenberg claimed that his text settings were the result of the immediate sonorous effect of the beginning of a poem. *Herzgewächse* is, in part, a musical example Schoenberg's theory of the relationship between text and music. The harmonium, celesta, and harp in this piece create a delicate, shimmering backdrop to the soprano line; with the instruments and high voice together, the song becomes a fragile treble soundscape. Melodically, *Herzgewächse* follows Schoenberg's earlier atonal vocal works, with which it shares a kind of athematic, fragmentary character, with small motivic figures appearing and disappearing without really being developed. Texturally, the song is pervasively polyphonic, the independent instrumental parts occasionally coming together to form contingent harmonies.

The song is comprised of four sections, each with a contrasting vocal line. As the song begins, the text describes the poet's "tired melancholy" and Schoenberg sets these verses in the lower range of the soprano. In the second section, the pathos of the text's sickly and gloomy water lilies is evoked musically through the soprano's slowly rising melody and a thickening of the otherwise sparse instrumental accompaniment. In the final two sections, the soprano line reaches remarkable heights, leaping expressively above the increasingly frenetic accompaniment. At the end of the song, the soprano is asked to sing a high F at the quietest possible dynamic level, a feat seldom accomplished convincingly on any recording. *—Alexander Carpenter*

Recommended:

- ○ **Schoenberg: Survivor from Warsaw; etc.** / Craft (cond.), Hulse, London SO / 1995 / Koch 7263
- ○ **Schoenberg: Pierrot Lunaire; etc.** / Boulex (cond.), Schäfer, Ens. InterContemporain / 1998 / DG 457630

Pierrot lunaire, melodrama for voice & chamber ensemble, Op. 21 (1912)

After the wrenching revolution Schoenberg brought to his music during the final years of the twentieth century's first decade (crystallized in such works as the *Three Pieces for piano,* Op. 11 and the *Five Orchestral Pieces,* Op. 16) the composer quickly drew back from the anguished Expressionism of these years to produce the much lighter *Dreimal sieben Gedichte aus Albert Girauds Pierrot Lunaire* (Three-times-seven Songs from Albert Giraud's Pierrot Lunaire, or, as it is known the world 'round, simply *Pierrot Lunaire*), Op. 21, of 1912—a cycle of 21 songs for voice and chamber group that, in the composer's own words, voices sentiments that are "Light, ironic, [and] satirical."

Pierrot Lunaire takes the shape of a single large melodrama in which the female voice gives the text a treatment that is midway between speech and song (the technique, called Sprechstimme, goes all the way back to Humperdinck, though it found its best use at the pens of the Second Viennese School composers). Three sections, comprised of seven songs each, showcase the five instrumentalists in all sorts of wonderfully colorful combinations as the narrator tells of the wandering Pierrot's experiences—indeed, the contrasts offered by just the piano, violin, cello, flute, and clarinet are not enough for Schoenberg, who makes the violinist, flutist, and clarinetist double on viola, piccolo, and bass clarinet, respectively. Each of the 13-line poems is a rondel, the opening lines being repeated during the middle of the poem as a kind of refrain.

Structural and motivic connections abound throughout the work, and we find such devices as the recurrence of the queasy solo flute melody of No. 7, "The Sick Moon," in the 13th song, "Decapitation" (part of *Pierrot Lunaire*'s admittedly darker second section, in which the demons of Expressionism come out to play once more), and the use of a passacaglia form in "Night," the first song of Part 2. By the time of "The Moonspot" in Part 3, Schoenberg has worked up to the level of a full double-canon (for the pair of woodwinds and the pair of strings). No. 19, "Serenade," is almost a virtuoso piece for cello and piano, while the final song of the melodrama, "O Ancient Charm of Fairy Days," is of the tender, epilogue variety. *—Blair Johnston*

Recommended:

- ○ **Schoenberg: Pierrot lunaire; etc.** / Boulez (cond.), Schäfer, Ens. InterContemporain / 1998 / DG 457630
- ○ **Schoenberg: Pierrot lunaire; Book of the Hanging Gardens** / Weisberg (cond.), de Gaetani, Contemporary Chamber Ens. / 1990 / Nonesuch 79237
- ○ **Music of Arnold Schoenberg Vol. 5** / Craft (cond.), Silja, Oldfather, Sherry, Parloff, Neidich, London PO / Koch 7471

Four Songs, Op. 2 (1899)

After the two less than entirely successful songs of Opus 1, Arnold Schoenberg engaged himself in a thorough reevaluation of both his own aesthetic direction and, more particularly, the nature of his piano writing; by the appearance of Opus 2 in late 1899, both these issues had been largely solved, at least for the time being. Here are four songs for nonspecific voice and piano, in three cases drawn from Richard Dehmel poems and in one case from the verse of Johannes Schlaf (Dehmel's work would also, in a very few years, inspire the chamber-piece *Verklärte Nacht*). While still basically concerned with the same worldly love that the impassioned Opus 1 took as its starting point, the new songs are poured into musical molds that, in both length and texture, more closely resemble the concise style Schoenberg adopted in the opening years of the twentieth century than the quasi-Brahmsian luxuriousness of his earlier works with piano.

Erwartung (Expectation), a straightforward love song in which the lover waits by a calm pond for the beloved, grants total melodic dominance to the voice, while the piano supports in E flat with rich chords and glistening arabesque figures. As the initially reserved atmosphere gives way to more extrovert passions, a new but related melody appears like an apotheosis of the beloved.

More complex in both tone and construction is the following *Schenk' mir deinen goldenen Kamb* (Give me thy Golden Comb), and like the first song, is a Richard Dehmel piece. *Schoenberg* employs a far more chromatic idiom here than he did in the previous song, effectively disfiguring the underlying F sharp minor for lengthy stretches and allowing the singer's ardent love-plea to unfold against a background of dramatic uncertainty. Also, the piano is allowed, particularly after the introduction of a gently rising motive in the second half of the song, to take a stronger role in the melodic fabric than it did in *Erwartung*.

The third song, *Erhebung* (Exaltation), though similar in some ways to *Erwartung*, is of simpler substance and setting. Here the composer reverts to a harmonic language very like that of his nineteenth century idols, but then, given the entirely traditional nature of Dehmel's love song, he could hardly have spread his newfound chromatic wings in good conscience, at least not at this stage of his career.

Opus 2 concludes with *Waldsonne* (Forest Sun), a warmly light song of summer memories and gentle love gone by. Like *Erhebung*, it is in a more conservative vein, rich with harmonic tint and drawing on a precious melody that, in keeping with the nature of the text, looks backward with great affection to Schoenberg's own musical youth. *—Blair Johnston*

Recommended:

- ○ **Schönberg & Berg: Lieder** / Fischer-Dieskau, Reimann / 1990 / EMI 63570
- ○ **Romantic Lieder Vol. 1** / Kwon, Pawassar / 1996 / Arte Nova 34049

CHORAL

Gurrelieder, oratorio (1900–1911)

In the spring of 1900, Arnold Schoenberg—having just completed the remarkable sextet *Verklärte Nacht*—began work on selected poems from Jens Peter Jacobsen's massive *Gurrelieder*, intending to enter the results in a competition. Soon, however, Schoenberg realized that a far more extensive treatment of Jacobsen's text was necessary to fulfill his musical vision; throughout the summer months, Schoenberg proceeded to sketch one of the longest and most exceedingly complex masterpieces of late Romanticism. Although composition was completed in 1901, the composer did not complete the orchestration until 1911; during the intervening years Schoenberg's musical world had been irrevocably transformed, and so we find that many portions of the work were stylistically "updated" in the process to reflect a more forward-looking perspective.

The nearly two-hour length of *Gurrelieder* is fitting, considering the sheer numbers required for its performance: the work is scored for vocal soloists, chorus and an orchestra that outdoes even Mahler at his grandest. All the well-trodden Romantic themes and anti-themes are present in Jacobsen's verse: tragic love, death, anger at and rejection of the divine will, and even a frenzied hunt scene; yet the mold into which the composer pours these dark sentiments is perhaps not so finally and irreparably doom-ridden as Jacobsen might have intended. Even the Wagnerian influence, on which Schoenberg's musical treatment draws rather heavily, is made to serve an altogether more optimistic purpose. Here is no world-ending epic, but rather a sorrowful saga that ends with the hopeful beginning of a new day.

Gurrelieder is cast into three large sections. The purely instrumental prelude is a musical evocation of the sunset. The solo trumpet gives a resigned, descending motivic outline to the elaborate orchestral texture. With the gentle first song, Waldemar (the tenor) begins to sing of his love for Tove (the soprano), after which she returns the favor. The orchestra is cut to a minimum: a handful of woodwinds and solo strings are all that Schoenberg requires to give a delightfully imitative support to the soprano. Several more love songs, concluding with the peaceful "Du wunderliche Tove," precede a lengthy orchestral passage that recapitulates and expands upon the melodic material that Schoenberg has spun up to this point. A mezzo-soprano breaks in suddenly for the famous "Song of the Forest Dove," to tell of the murder of Tove. Part I of *Gurrelieder* ends as Waldemar sinks into a passionate despair.

Part Two is both much shorter than the previous section and of far greater pathos. Schoenberg redirects the final harmonies of Part One into a sorrowful orchestral prelude into which the woodwinds, grief-stricken, sing a tune drawn from the "Song of the Forest Dove." Waldemar rants and raves against the divine injustice that took his beloved Tove from him.

Waldemar calls a massive hunt together as Part Three begins. After a grim figure on the Wagner-tubas the orchestra bursts forth in frenzied chase, soon joined by the entire chorus as Waldemar threatens Heaven itself. As the fury is spent, a dense contrapuntal passage brings us towards C major, and with it the sunrise. Perhaps significantly, the trumpet gesture that began *Gurrelieder* is given in exact inversion by the entire trumpet section to end the work as the sun comes up again in radiant splendor. *—Blair Johnston*

Recommended:

- ○ **Schoenberg: Gurrelieder** / Sinopoli (cond.), Larmore, Voigt, Weikl, Moser, Dresden Staatskapelle / 1996 / Teldec 98424
- ○ **Schoenberg: Gurrelieder** / Chailly (cond.), Hotter, Fassbaender, Jerusalem, Dunn, Berlin RSO / 1990 / London 430321

Die Jacobsleiter (Jacob's Ladder), oratorio (Jun., 1917–Jul., 1922; revised 1944)

As early as 1912, Schoenberg had begun planning some quasi-religious music, and between 1912 and 1917 worked on several pieces. *Die Jakobsleiter*, an oratorio begun in 1915 with his own text, was by far the most substantial of these, and it occupied Schoenberg for a number of years. In the summer of 1917, Schoenberg abandoned some of the smaller pieces he had been working on and turned his attention back to the oratorio. The title was taken from Balzac's *Seraphita*, which provided much of the inspiration for the oratorio. In *Seraphita*, Balzac mentions the story from *Genesis*, in which Jacob dreams of a ladder joining earth and heaven, with angels going up and down. Schoenberg, like Balzac, does not directly portray this biblical story; instead, Jacob's ladder symbolizes the theme of a connection between the earthly and the spiritual.

Die Jakobsleiter is an enormous, complex work scored for large orchestra, choruses, and soloists. It is structured much like a traditional oratorio, with clearly delineated sections devoted to aria, recitative, and chorus. The central character is the angel Gabriel, who oversees the action and comments upon it. The other characters include a number of "souls," who are called upon by Gabriel to explain how their pursuits in life were worthwhile. At the close of the first half of the libretto, the souls are found wanting and are admonished by Gabriel: they must return to earth and be reincarnated. In the second half, the imperfect souls begin their return to earth, descending from the higher level to the lower level. The character of the Chosen One, who appears in the first half to give advice to one of the souls, returns in the second half to receive Gabriel's wisdom in the form of a lecture on metaphysics and the importance of prayer. The oratorio ends with three choruses singing together, linking the souls from the high, middle, and low realms.

As with much of Schoenberg's dramatic music from his atonal period, there is some autobiographical significance to *Die Jakobsleiter*. The Chosen One, for example, like the Man in Schoenberg's 1911 opera *Die Gluckliche Hand*, is the contemporary artist called to a higher purpose, who must struggle with his peers as he looks to the art of the future. Musically, the oratorio represents a refinement of Schoenberg's earlier atonal practices, and looks ahead to the 12-tone method in its organization of chromatic structures.

Schoenberg was unable to finish the oratorio as he was called to active military service in September, 1917. Although he had completed a great deal of the music, after the war he was unable to finish the work, despite several subsequent attempts to revive it. *—Alexander Carpenter*

Recommended:

- ○ **Schoenberg: Jacob's Ladder; etc.** / Boulez (cond.), BBC Singers, BBCSO / 1982 / Sony 48462

A Survivor from Warsaw, Op. 46 (1947)

Schoenberg, a refugee from Nazi anti-Semitism, wrote this six-minute music drama expressing searing outrage over German brutality during the wartime occupation of Poland. It tells of an incident during the destruction of the Warsaw Ghetto. The text is by Schoenberg and uses both English and German, with a concluding chorus in Biblical Hebrew using the "Sh'ma Yisrael," ("Hear, O Israel," from Deuteronomy).

The work is for full orchestra, narrator, and male chorus. The work is 12-tone throughout, which works perfectly with the subject matter. In form it is cinematic, following the eyewitness account of the narrator. The survivor is found hiding in the sewers. A crowd is rounded up by the Nazi sergeant and the survivor is caught. The narrator shouts out the commands of the sergeant in German and in the present tense. From the beating and murder of the defenseless Jews arises the electrifying and defiant singing of the "Sh'ma," which is an exhortation to "love the Lord thy God with all thine heart and with all thy soul" and to pass this love on to the next generation. In this context of pure evil it becomes a radiant beacon, a triumph of belief and confidence that the faith shall endure into future generations.

The Narrator's part is written in Schoenberg's technique of "Sprechstimme," or "speaking voice." Schoenberg's text has a quality perhaps the composer did not fully appreciate. While it is in fluent and correct English, there are syntactical features that indicate the author conceived it in German and then wrote it down in English. Slightly foreign turns of phrase make the narration seem that much more authentic and immediate. *—Joseph Stevenson*

Recommended:

- ○ **Schoenberg: Survivor from Warsaw; etc.** / Craft (cond.), Callow, London SO / 1995 / Koch 7263
- ○ **Schoenberg: Survivor from Warsaw; etc.** / Abbado (cond.), Hornik, Vienna PO / 1993 / DG 431774

OPERA

Erwartung, Op. 17 (1909)

The year 1909 was an extremely important one for Schoenberg. It was at this time, immediately following the composition of the song cycle *The Book of Hanging Gardens*, Op. 15, that Schoenberg made his definitive break with tonality and began exploring alternative means of musical organization. In the *Piano Pieces*, Op. 11, and the *Five Orchestral Pieces*, Op. 16, he attempted to move toward a form more dependent on texture, dynamics, and rhetorical gesture than on pitch-oriented or motive-oriented systems of organization. His most extreme experiment in this regard was *Erwartung* (Expectation), a monodrama for soprano and orchestra on a text by Marie Pappenheim. This was a completely unique creation that attempts to portray the interior monologue of a woman waiting to meet her lover in a forest. Schoenberg himself said that the work could be understood as a nightmare scenario—the entire reality exists in the woman's mind on a purely psychological level. There is no realistic time frame—past, present, and future are blurred and the setting itself remains only suggestive and indistinct. Upon her discovery of her lover's murdered body (and there is some hint that she herself may have been the murderer), the unnamed woman proceeds through a confused and disturbed series of emotions as she remembers their love, his betrayal with another, to a strange sense of exhausted reconciliation.

In spite of a vestigial presence of D minor throughout the work, Schoenberg had by now abandoned tonality. But the treatment of such a difficult scenario required a new approach that could almost be called athematic. In his attempt to faithfully portray the hysterical, fragmentary, stream of consciousness, he created a score that mirrors and responds immediately to each of the many quixotic emotional changes in the woman's mind. In a very real sense, the score is through-composed, as there is no organized repetition except for very short fragments, generally for rhetorical effect and with no structural coherence or significance. The entire 20-minute work has no discernible musical structure outside of the general and vague sections suggested by the changing scenario of the text. Its primary effect is that of constant transformation and progression.

Erwartung is as evocative and powerful a work as anything Schoenberg composed. Its vivid scoring and invention perfectly capture the sense of psychological breakdown and impending disaster inherent in the text. The fact that Schoenberg composed the score in the astonishingly short time of 17 days may account in part for its coherence, despite the lack of formal organization. Because of its unusual format, and extraordinary difficulty, *Erwartung* had to wait until June 6, 1924, to receive its premiere, where Marie Gutheil-Schoder created the role of the woman. *—Steven Coburn*

Synopsis:

Erwartung opens on the borders of a forest. It is night and a Woman dressed in white appears. She is searching for something, but she seems anxious and confused. The scene changes as she enters the forest itself and feels her way through the dark trees. Her confusion momentarily clears as she remembers the quiet of her garden as she awaited night. It becomes clear that she is looking for her lover, who has apparently failed to make a rendezvous. The scene changes again as she comes to a clearing. Her anguish increases as she hears an unknown creature in the shadows, then calls out in despair for her lover.

Another change of scene ensues, and the Woman emerges onto a roadway where the moon shines down. There is a house in the background, and the Woman has become disheveled and exhausted. Her clothes are torn, and her hands are cut and bleeding. Her anxiety rises as she begins to fear for the life of her lover. As she is about to collapse in exhaustion and despair, she stumbles against an object. It is her lover, dead on the ground. Her sense of reality begins to dissolve, and she talks to him gently and lovingly, as if he still lived, alternating with more lucid moments of misery at his death.

Gradually she remembers that something had come between them: another woman. But then why had he promised to meet her tonight? And why had he been killed? She violently rails against the woman who had taken him from her, and then sinks into the deepest misery as she laments her own betrayed love and relives the memories now lost to her.

As morning approaches, she has a vision of her lover coming toward her. She reaches out to nothing and cries "O bist du da-Ich suchte" (Oh, is that you? I was looking for you) as the curtain falls. *—Steven Coburn*

Recommended:

- ○ **Schoenberg** / Dohnányi (cond.), Silja, Vienna PO / 1996 / London 448279
- ○ **Schoenberg Vol. 6** / Craft (cond.), Silja, Philharmonia / 2000 / Koch 7473
- ○ **Schoenberg: Erwartung; Brettl-Lieder** / Levine (cond.), Norman, Metropolitan Opera Orch. / 1993 / Philips 426261

Moses und Aron (May, 1930–Mar., 1932)

With sketches for an unfinished orchestral passacaglia in March 1920, Schoenberg began to work out the implications of the serial idea. A catch-as-catch-can life as teacher, lecturer, and conductor was relieved in 1925 by an appointment from the Prussian Academy of Arts to take over the composition masterclass formerly taught by Busoni, who had died the year before. The relative security of his new position allowed Schoenberg leisure to expand, hand-in-hand with composition, the grasp of serial procedures. In 1898 Schoenberg had become, like Mendelssohn, a convert to Lutheranism, though that did not shield him from virulent anti-Semitism, and through the 1920s he was preoccupied with his position as a Jew and an artist, eventually returning formally to Judaism in the summer of 1933. Already in 1917 he had begun the composition of *Die Jakobsleiter*, a large-scale oratorio in which a variety of religious and philosophical stances are brought before the archangel Gabriel. Tellingly, this work, like *Moses und Aron*, was to remain incomplete. Schoenberg's religious concerns became more topically focused in the drama *Der biblische Weg*, written over 1926-27, whose protagonist, Max Aruns—a composite whose dichotomy would be articulated in *Moses und Aron*—was modeled on Zionist leader Theodor Herzl. A first draft libretto of *Moses und Aron*, conceived as an oratorio, followed in 1928, with the composition of the comic opera *Von heute auf Morgen*. Composition of the first two acts of *Moses und Aron*, as an opera, occupied Schoenberg from May 1930 to March 1932. Based upon a single row, serialism attains its grandest throw, given vivacity and dramatic impetus by the astonishing array of techniques—*Sprechgesang*, *Klangfarbenmelodie*, contrapuntally rich choral writing—fashioned over a lifetime to find their ultimate expressive purpose in *Moses und Aron*. Moses' uncompromising adherence to an omnipotent, inconceivable God, for instance, is conveyed by *Sprechstimme*, while Aron's attempts to win the people to it are couched in glib arioso—an audible representation of the artist's uneasy mixture of truth and illusion, intellectual probity and charisma. The impact of *Moses und Aron*, in the hands of a great conductor, is immediate, visceral, and compelling. Hitler's rise and Schoenberg's emigration to America in 1933 put the completion of *Moses und Aron*—a third act dialogue in which Aron dies—forever out of reach. The torso received its premiere at the Zurich Stadttheater June 6, 1957, not quite six years after its composer's death. *—Adrian Corleonis*

Synopsis:

Act One, Scene One. Moses calls out to God during a journey into the desert. God orders Moses to be His prophet. Moses protests that he is old and wants to tend his sheep in peace. The voice of God reminds Moses that his people are enslaved. Moses asks how he can convince the Israelites that he brings the actual Word. God replies that he will receive instructions while his campaign is in progress, and sends Moses into the desert to meet his brother Aron.

Scene Two. Moses and Aron meet in the desert. Aron assumes he is to be God's voice before hearing his brother's instructions. The brothers discuss their plan to spread the Word, and do not see eye to eye. Moses reminds his brother that God cannot be represented because he is everything, eternal and ungraspable. Aron regards this as a problem because claims require proofs and people cannot function otherwise. Moses is being realistic about what God is, while Aron is realistic about what people need in order to believe in something. Despite their differences, both men remain on the same side of the issue; the Word of God must come from them. The Israelites must be rescued from Egyptian slavery.

Scene Three. The enslaved Israelites speak with awe of Aron in his absence. They assume he went into he desert to meet Moses, who had murdered a guard in order to leave the village. Nobody wants more trouble with the Pharaoh, or rebellion, or more gods requiring sacrifices. Some are encouraged by the idea of a god who is stronger than the others, and they have faith in Aron's abilities and intentions. There is a great argument regarding the merits of the situation and how to help the brothers shape events in favor of Israeli emancipation; they arrive at the end of the scene.

Scene Four. The people want God's Word. Immediately, Aron's translations of what Moses says are clearly reformatting the Word to appeal to the excited listeners. Still, the Israelites require further clarification about God, His wants, and his qualities. Aron attempts to be accurate, and his replies become more in keeping with Moses' vision of God. This tactic backfires and the people dismiss this new god, who cannot be seen or represented. Moses is discouraged. Aron becomes frustrated, seizes his brother's staff, and turns it into a serpent. The crowd is listening once again because the miracle demonstrated something divine. Aron wrestles with the collective ear of a now near-hysterical mob. His command that the slaves flee to the desert is met with hostility, but he is fearless and persuasive. The people assent.

Act Two, Scene One. Aron awaits Moses at the foot of the Mountain of Revelation with 70 elders. The elders have waited 40 days and are becoming impatient. Moses does not descend, and the elders see the people begin to act out of despair.

Scene Two. The Israelites are enraged at Moses' disappearance and are out for his blood and that of his elder priesthood, who are now in danger. Many people believe God has already killed Moses. Aron cannot stand the suffering any longer and allows them to worship in the old way. He promises to form an idol from the people's gold. They are overjoyed.

Scene Three. Aron fashions a golden calf at a makeshift alter, claiming that God lives in all things, including this idol, a graven image Moses would not have permitted. Touching the idol heals an invalid woman. Butchers kill animals and wine and oil are distributed. A starving youth attempts to stop the false worship and is murdered. Good humor gives way to debauchery, violence, orgies, and suicide. Priests sacrifice virgins for their blood. Total chaos ensues.

Scene Four. Moses descends from the mountain and immediately makes the golden calf vanish. The people are disheartened.

Scene Five. The brothers discuss the merits of Aron's conduct. Aron says he acted from internal comprehension of the situation and did not require instruction from his brother. Moses demands that the Israelites learn to understand the nature of God and His will. Aron counters that the people's needs must be addressed, that Moses had been gone too long, and that without an image, the Word cannot communicate. A pillar of fire appears, followed by Israelites, believing it to be the way to salvation. Aron also regards it as a sign from God. Moses cries out to God in despair of the incomprehension that surrounds him and his own inability to teach. *—John Keillor*

Recommended:

○ **Schoenberg: Moses & Aron** / Boulez (cond.), Pittman, Jennings, Merritt, Hirzel, Concertgebouw / DG 449174

Andreas Scholl

b. Nov. 10, 1967, Eltville, Germany

Countertenor

Andreas Scholl is one of the world's leading countertenors and is, naturally, one of the best-known performers of Baroque vocal music. He was born in Eltville, Germany and grew up in Kiedrich, in the Rhine region of Germany. His father was the conductor of the Kiedricher Chorbuben (Kiedrich Choir Boys), the second oldest choir in Germany, in existence for over 650 years. Andreas and his siblings Johannes and Elisabeth all sang in the choir, and Andreas therefore began his voice training there from age seven, but very little formal theory instruction.

Andreas was nearly 14 when his voice broke and settled down into a baritone speaking range. However, when the voice firmed up, he found he could still sing soprano parts in the choir. One of the vocal coaches who gave individual singing lessons to the boys soon recognized that Andreas no longer had a boy soprano voice, but a countertenor.

At that point Andreas began listening to recordings of countertenors, especially Alfred Deller and James Bowman. He and one of his school friends joined a rock group and composed music for it. They recorded two singles, neither of which made the charts. Scholl still retains an interest in composing and loves popular music.

Scholl began to think of singing as a career, and as a countertenor realized most of his opportunities would include early music. He attended the Schola Cantorum Basiliensis in Basle, Switzerland, one of the centers of older music studies, from 1987 to 1993. He soon overcame deficiencies in his theory and ear training preparation. He was a student of Richard Levitt and René Jacobs. He also had the benefit of interpretation classes with Emma Kirkby, Anthony Rooley, and Evelyn Tubb.

In 1993 his teacher René Jacobs fell ill and was unable to keep a concert commitment at the Théâtre de Grévin in France and recommended Scholl as his replacement. Scholl scored a major success in what amounted to his professional debut on an important international stage. He appeared with Jacobs in a live broadcast concert of Bach's *St. John Passion.* Going home on the train the night of the concert he met William Christie, a leading early music conductor, who had attended the concert and invited Scholl to sing on his planned recording of Handel's *Messiah.* The record was a great success and led to an extensive recording career.

He began exclusively as a concert singer, singing with the leading early music groups of Europe and elsewhere. It was not until 1998 that he first appeared in opera when he portrayed Bertarido in Handel's *Rodelinda* at the Glyndebourne Festival in England.

Along the way he won the Conseil de L'Europe and Claude Nicolas Ledoux Foundation awards in 1992. He has won numerous recording prizes, including a Gramophone Award for Vivaldi's *Stabat Mater* in 1996 and Caldara's *Maddelena ai piedi di Cristo* in 1997 for Best Baroque Vocal. In 1998 he won the Cannes Classical Award for a disc of German Baroque cantatas. He won the ECHO Classic Award in 1999, and in 1998 was the German Kultur Radio Artist of the Year. In December 1999, he sang at the Belgian royal wedding.

In addition to continuing his concert and operatic career, Andreas Scholl has returned to the Schola Cantorum Basiliensis to teach as the successor to his instructor Richard Levitt. *—Joseph Stevenson*

Recommended:

○ **Andreas Scholl: A Musical Banquet** / Scholl, Coin, Markl, Karamazov / 2001 / Decca 466917

○ **Arcadia** / Scholl, Dantone, Byzantine Academy / 2003 / Decca 000180802

○ **Vivaldi: Stabat Mater** / Banchini (cond.), Scholl, Ensemble 415 / HM 801571

Peter Schreier

b. Jul. 29, 1935, Meissen, Germany

Tenor

Peter Schreier was one of the most highly esteemed tenors of the twentieth century, particularly in German lieder, oratorio, and cantata performances as well as opera. His father was a Church Kantor and gave him his first musical training. At the age of eight Peter was entered in the preparatory class of the famous chorus the Dresdner Kreuzchor.

He made his first operatic appearance as one of the Three Boys in Mozart's *Die Zauberflöte* in 1944, which led him to consider a musical career. At the age of ten, he was admitted as a boy soprano and rapidly rose to the position of first soloist with the choir. As such he sang on some of the first German LPs ever released, of Bach cantatas on Deutsche Grammophon's Das alte Werk imprint. He traveled to France, Scandinavia, and Luxembourg, among other destinations, on tour with the Dresden choir.

He remained with the choir as a tenor after his voice changed. In 1954, he began taking private voice lessons with Polster, while working as a member of the Leipzig Radio Chorus. In 1956, he entered the Dresden Musikhochschule, where his teacher was Winkler. Schreier studied both singing and conducting. He also studied at the Dresden State Opera's training school. In 1957, he appeared in the opera studio's production of *Il matrimonio segreto* as Paolino.

He graduated from the Musikhochschule in 1959, passing the State Exam, and joined the Dresden State Opera's company as a lyric tenor. His first professional appearance was there in the small role of the First Prisoner in Beethoven's *Fidelio.* During those years he made an intriguing concert tour to India and the African nation of Mali.

He sang a guest appearance at the Berlin State Opera and in 1963 gained a contract with that company as its leading lyric tenor. He made numerous guest appearances in the Soviet Union and other countries of what was then known as the Eastern Bloc, and appeared fairly often in the West, in Vienna and the Salzburg Festival in Austria, the Bayreuth Wagner Festival House in West German, in London (debuting in 1966), the Vienna State Opera (1967), Milan's La Scala (1969), and the Teatro Colón in Buenos Aires (also 1969).

He quickly won acclaim in particular for his portrayals of Mozart's main tenor roles and as a recitalist. He was also high praised for roles as diverse as Alfred in *Die Fledermaus* and Loge in *Das Rheingold,* and appeared in the premiere of Dessau's *Einstein* as The Physicist. He also sang the role of Almaviva in Rossini's *Il barbiere di Siviglia,* Fenton in Verdi's *Otello,* and Lensky in Tchaikovsky's *Eugene Onegin,* to name a few. He regularly sang in Bach's passions, cantatas, and other choral works, and became a treasured lieder singer. His Schubert was especially regarded for its highly expressive projection and shaping of the words.

He sang primarily on East German recordings, many of which are rereleased on CD on the Berlin Classics label, and for the Philips label.

In 1970, he took up the other side of his career, conducting for the first time at a concert with the Dresden Staatskapelle. Since then he has emerged as a leading Bach and Mozart conductor.

He received numerous honors, including the National Prize (First Class) of the German Democratic Republic, the Salzburg Mozarteum's Silver Mozart Medal, and the title of Kammersänger. In 1986 he was appointed an honorary member of the Vienna Gesellschaft der Musikfreunde, the Anderson-Nexö Prize of the City of Dresden, and the Ernst con Siemans Prize of the City of Munich. *—Joseph Stevenson*

Recommended:

○ **Schreier: Arien aus Kantaten & Oratorien** / Schreier, etc. / 1995 / Berlin Classics 0091402

○ **Beethoven: Songs Vol. 1** / Schreier, Olbertz (piano) / 1993 / Berlin Classics 0020822

○ **Schubert: Die Schöne Müllerin** / Schreier, Olbertz (piano) / Brilliant 99444

Franz Schreker

b. Mar. 23, 1878, Monaco, **d.** Mar. 21, 1934, Berlin, Germany

Composer: Orchestral, Vocal, Opera

Even in Germany and Austria, where he enjoyed his greatest successes, Franz Schreker remains a shadowy figure, slowly being rediscovered as Alexander Zemlinsky (1872–1942) has been. Like several lesser eminences born in the wake of Richard Strauss, Schreker conducted and taught as well as composed. Just before World War I, and briefly after, he became a musical celebrity, but without the controversy that surrounded his lifelong friend Arnold Schoenberg. After the war, both taught in Berlin—Schreker as director of the storied Hochschule für Musik starting in 1920, Schoenberg at the Prussische Kunstakademie in 1925—until the Nazis assailed them for being Jews. Schreker was forced to resign in 1932 and given a small consolation position at the same Akademie, from which he and Schoenberg were dismissed after Hitler became Reichskanzler in 1933. Schoenberg managed to leave Germany, but Schreker suffered a heart attack and died the next year.

By that time he had been stigmatized as a creator of *Entartete Musik* (along with Mendelssohn, Mahler, Schoenberg, Berg, Weill, Eisler, and so on), and had furthermore run dry creatively. In truth, the last four of his nine operas—those after 1918—document this falling-off. He could not bring himself to exchange hyperchromanticism for Schoenberg's "free tonality." At the same time, his luridly erotic librettos—inspired by Salome of Strauss—were going out of fashion, to be replaced by Expressionism, parody, satire, Freudian Angst, and everything else that scandalized Weimar-Republicans at the same time as they were titillated.

The operas that made Schreker's reputation—*Die ferne Klang* (Distant Chiming), *Das Spielwerk und die Prinzessin* (The Music Box and the Princess), *Die Gezeichneten* (The Stigmatized), and *Der Schatzgräber* (The Treasure Digger)—were all premiered between 1912 and 1920, although he had begun the first-named as far back as 1901 without finishing it until 1910. The last two were outstandingly successful.

Professor Hans F. Redlich's lengthy entry in *Grove V* characterized Schreker's music as follows, in part:

"Its skillful blending of Teutonic and romantic elements of style forms a twentieth century parallel to Meyerbeer's eclectic type of opera.... Schreker's melodic substance as well as his iridescent harmonies are heavily indebted to French Impressionism, and to the Italian verismo of Puccini and his Anglo-German imitator [Eugène] d'Albert.... Works for the concert hall remain typical by-products of a theatrically inspired musician. As a musical colorist of great distinction... and finally as a musical mentor of a whole generation of continental composers, [he] undoubtedly made a substantial contribution to the artistic development of his time, even if his followers ultimately traveled in a quite different direction." To this add what another, more recent, unidentified German has written: "Schreker's music is strangely shimmering, capricious, seemingly diffuse, constantly shifting and flowing, not apparently disciplined... [but it] never quite loses [a] youthful glow.... *Prelude to a Drama* was in fact somewhat modified as the overture to *Die Gezeichneten*, and is a perfect example of Schreker's music as described. Strangely capricious, unable and unwilling ever to come to an end [the duration is 20 minutes, more or less], excessive yet formally circumscribed, it is the epitome of his unique, inimitable artistic achievement. He may never become world famous, but his place in German music is assured." *—Roger Dettmer*

ORCHESTRAL

Chamber Symphony for 23 instruments (1916)

Schreker's career was stifled by the Great War. After the brilliant successes of his ballet *Der Geburtstag der Infantin* in 1908 and his opera *Der ferne Klang* in 1912—leading to his appointment as professor of composition at Vienna's Imperial Music Academy—the conservatism of the war years delayed the production of his latest opera. Meanwhile, he remained quietly busy. After completing the score of *Die Gezeichneten* in June 1915, he wrote librettos—*Die tönenden Sphären*, around a vision of an early armistice and a festival of peace, and the mythic *Der Schatzgräber*. By the fall of 1916, he had set the former aside to compose *Der Schatzgräber* when a commission from the Academy prompted the composition of the *Chamber Symphony*, which incorporated music written for *Die tönenden Sphären*. The *Chamber Symphony* was first heard in a performance by the Academy's faculty on March 12, 1917. One of the faculty members, the composer Joseph Marx, left an amusing portrait of Schreker during rehearsals, leaving "the conductor's podium to savor the effect from the last row of the parquet. 'How does that sound? What do you say to that combination?' he asked repeatedly, beaming with pleasure all the while."

The *Chamber Symphony* invites that sort of response. Accustomed to employing a Wagnerian orchestra for his operas, Schreker demonstrates with a mere 23 instruments—11 strings, seven winds, harp, piano, celesta, harmonium, and percussion—that sonic witchery is not a matter of brute force but of infinite cunning. A nondeveloping nod toward sonata form—the *Chamber Symphony*'s unbroken span includes an Allegro, an Adagio, a Scherzo and a cyclic recall of the Allegro's material—provides the merest thread along which Schreker strings a shimmering aural phantasmagoria. Arresting feints, piquant harmonic shifts garbed in radiant auras of iridescent sonority, and glowing fragments of beguiling melody pass in bewildering profusion. The upshot is expansive and diffuse, suffused with an air of constant distraction as strange, hallucinatory moments yield to passionate intoxication, preternatural joy, or sudden terror. Composed between the erotically obsessed, orchestrally overloaded *Die Gezeichneten* and the straightforwardly transparent *Der Schatzgräber*, the *Chamber Symphony* represents a splendid and kaleidoscopic epitome of Schreker at the top of his bent. To the film devotee, many of these tropes—which fascinated a generation—will seem overly familiar from their recycling in the film music of Max Steiner, Franz Waxman, and Wolfgang Erich Korngold, among others. *—Adrian Corleonis*

Recommended:

- ○ **Schubert: Death & The Maiden; Schreker: Chamber Symphony** / Welser-Most (cond.), Salzburg Camerata Academica / 1999 / Angel 56813
- ○ **Schreker: Kammersinfonie; Vorspiel** / Gielen (cond.), Berlin RSO / 1986 / Koch 311078

Der Geburtstag der Infantin, suite (1923)

Austrian-German composer Franz Schreker made his first great public success with his ballet/pantomime *Der Geburtstag der Infantin* based on the novella by Oscar Wilde. Composed in ten days in 1908, *Der Geburtstag* was the centerpiece of a Gesamtkunstwerk arranged by the Jugendstil painter Gustav Klimt for the opening of the *Kunstschau Wien* (Vienna Art Show) on June 27 of that year. Combining Schreker's music with the paintings of the exhibition, plus dancing, architecture, literature, staging, and even garden design, Klimt's Gesamtkunstwerk went far beyond even Wagner's *Bayreuth*. While the ballet-pantomime was written for string orchestra, the suite Schreker drew from it is arranged for very large orchestra, including two harps and four guitars. Arranged in 1923 and dedicated to Willem Mengelberg and the Concertgebouw Orchestra Amsterdam, the piece was premiered by the dedicatees on October 23 of that year. The suite is in six movements: "Reigen" (Round Dance), "Aufzug und Kampfspiel" (Lift and War-Games), "Die Marionetten" (The Marionettes), "Minuett der Tanzerknaben—Die Tanze der Zwerg" (Minuet of the Children—The Dance of the Dwarf), "Mit dern Wind im Fruhling: In blauen Sandlen uber des Korn—Im roten Gewand im Herbst" (With the Wind in Spring: In Blue Sandals Over the Corn—In Red Robes in Autumn), and "Die Rose der Infantin—Nachklang" (The Rose of the Infanta—Postlude). A lushly beautiful score with gorgeous melodies and exquisite harmonies, *Der Geburtstag der Infantin* is one of a number of attractive *fin de siècle* works condemned by the Nazis that deserves to be revived. *—James Leonard*

Recommended:

- ○ **Schreker: Der Geburtstag der Infantin; Toch: Tanz-Suite** / Bruns (cond.), Berlin Chamber Symphony / Edition Abseits 013
- ○ **Schreker: Der Geburtstag der Infantin; Das Weib des Intaphernes** / Albrecht (cond.), BSO / 2000 / Koch 365912

Prelude to a Drama (Vorspiel) (1913)

Die Gezeichneten (Those marked by the seal) of 1913–15 was the fourth and most successful opera by Austrian-German composer Franz Schreker. A three-act grand opera to a libretto by the composer, *Die Gezeichneten* is a highly erotic, deeply pessimistic, and at least in the view of the National Socialists who later condemned it, a pathologically sick opera. It is also a profoundly beautiful work of musical art with glorious melodies, gorgeous harmonies, magnificent orchestrations, and an aesthetic unity that challenges even the best operas by Schreker's contemporary, Richard Strauss.

The *Vorspiel zu einem Drama* (Prelude to a Drama) is a work based on the Prelude to *Die Gezeichneten* that Schreker composed in 1914. The *Vorspiel* takes the opening of the opera's Prelude more or less as it appears in the opera, but transforms it into a sort of sonata form movement with an additional development and recapitulation. Thus the *Vorspiel* retains the shimmering orchestral colors, the ecstatically passionate melodies, and the sensuously erotic harmonies of the Prelude and expands them. The *Vorspiel*'s central development, however, does not so much develop the themes of the exposition as it increases their loveliness through ever more voluptuous scoring and ever more orgasmic climaxes. Similarly, the return of the opening themes at the *Vorspiel*'s recapitulation does not so much resolve the nonexistent conflicts of the development as it returns them to their original forms. *—James Leonard*

Recommended:

- ○ **Mahler: Symphony 4; Schreker: Prelude to a Drama** / Gielen (cond.), SWF Sinfonieorchester Baden-Baden / 1995 / Haenssler 93046
- ○ **Franz Schreker** / Sinaisky (cond.), BBCPO / 2000 / Chandos 9797
- ○ **Schreker: Kammersinfonie; Vorspiel** / Gielen (cond.), Berlin RSO / 1986 / Koch 311078

VOCAL

Songs and Song Cycles (1894–1927)

Schreker chose his texts not for their literary or historical value, but because he found in them sentiments and experiences that spoke to him and because the language was of the sort that prompted musical exploration. Thus, there are poems running the gamut of styles, from the folk poetry of *Des Knaben Wunderhorn* to the ponderous, lofty, love poetry of Leo Tolstoy (1828–1910). Schreker's earliest songs betray the influence of his composition teacher, Robert Fuchs (1847–1927), a devout Brahmsian who leaned toward the Viennese Classical era. Through Schreker's songs, most of which date from early in his career, one can trace the growth of his compositional powers.

"Die Rosen und der Flieder" (The Roses and Lilacs) and "Des Meeres und der liebe Wellen" (The Sea and the Sweet Waves) are among Schreker's earliest songs and contain very simple piano parts, abrupt modulations, and naïve text setting. "Des Meeres," in its faster sections, resembles some of Schubert's ballads. Clear texture and form mark the *Zwei Gesänge* (Two Songs), Op. 2. Schreker came to know Dora Leen's *Sommerfäden* (Gossamer) while he lived in the Döbling district of Vienna, where he and Leen were neighbors and, for a time, lovers. Written by another Döbling resident, Ferdinand von Saar's *Stimmen des Tages* (Voice of the Day) addresses the transience of life. Schreker's settings of these poems are built on motivic repetition and integration and contain melodies that sit well in the voice. Word painting is subtle: at the lines, "rasselnde Wagen" and "emsige Schritte" in "Stimmen des Tages", rhythmic gestures suggest the sound of busy steps and moving carriages.

Schreker's first song cycle is a setting of five poems from *Mutterliebe* (Mother's Love), by Mia Holm. Written around 1895, only two of the five songs were published, as the *Zwei Lieder auf den Tod eines Kindes* (Two Songs on a Child's Death), which demonstrate clearly Schreker's increasing skill. "O Glocken, böse Glocken" (O Bells, evil Bells) takes a Wagnerian chromatic turn at its center, while "Dass er ganz ein Engel werde" (He Becomes an Angel) suggests in its simplicity a resignation to fate.

Various moods characterize the settings of Paul Heyse's poems in Schreker's *Fünf Lieder*, Op. 3. For example, the simple, predictable "In alten Tagen" (In Olden Days) is to be sung "im Volkston," while the excellent "Es kommen Blätter" (Leaves Are Coming) features nearly free text declamation.

Schreker's harmonic language is more elaborate in the *Fünf Lieder*, Op. 4. "Frühling" (Spring), in particular, show a deft use of seventh chords, especially to suggest pain. The inspiration of Hugo Wolf appears in the chromaticism of "Wohl fühl' ich wie das Leben rinnt" (I Feel Life Running Past).

Schreker's *Fünf Gesänge* of 1909 find the composer venturing into the exotic, both in texts and the modes he uses to set them. *—John Palmer*

Recommended:

○ **Schreker: Complete Songs Vol. 1** / Kupfer, Mees, Buter, Sala / 1998 / Channel Crossings 12098

OPERA

Der ferne Klang (ca. 1903–1910)

Franz Schreker was among those composers whose works were eclipsed by the rise of National Socialism in the Germany of the 1930s. His first stage work was the one-act *Flammen*, given a concert performance in 1902. It appears that he had already begun work on *Der Ferne Klang* (The Distant Sound) at that time, but concerns (his own and those of others) over the work's highly charged eroticism resulted in hesitation and delay. The sensation surrounding the premiere of Richard Strauss' *Salome* in 1905, however, caused Schreker to gather courage and move ahead with composition, first completing the interlude separating the two scenes of Act Three. When this *Nightstück* was included in a Viennese concert in 1909, earning a warm response, Schreker resolved to move forward with the rest of the opera, completing it within a month's time in September 1910.

Additional delays occurred when the composer sought an opera house to mount the work. It was rejected by the Budapest Opera, but later accepted by Felix von Weingartner for production by the Vienna Court Opera. Following Weingartner's retirement, management delayed, feeling that they were no longer obligated to pursue bringing the work to their stage. Finally, Ludwig Rottenburg undertook a production at Frankfurt-am-Main in August 1912, and the opera enjoyed success beyond the imagination of all involved. This triumph, along with the enthusiastic reception of his later *Die Gezeichneten* (1918) and *Der Schatzgräber* (1920), would secure his reputation. This was all to be short lived: the rising influence of the Nazi party caused increasing problems for the composer, and in 1933 he was dismissed from his position at the Berlin Hochschule für Musik. His music was banned in Germany. The stress from these events led to a fatal heart attack in 1934.

Renewed interest in Schreker's music in general, and in *Der Ferne Klang* in particular, stems largely from his skillful orchestrations—an uncommon ability to manage the very large forces in his orchestra, and his genuine gift for realizing in musical terms elusive and ephemeral feelings. In *Der Ferne Klang*, Fritz pursues his distant, blessed sound, forsaking his youthful love Grete. When he finds her again, she has become a courtesan, hardened in her need to survive Fritz's having abandoned her. Reunited with her at the opera's conclusion, happiness is fleeting, for Fritz, finally hearing the music of his imagination, dies in Grete's arms. *—Erik Eriksson*

Synopsis:

Setting: Germany and Italy

Time: Early 1900s

Act One. The opera opens in the Graumann's house, where Greta is standing by the window talking to her lover, Fritz, who is outside telling her goodbye. She begs to come with him, but he refuses, fearing that the hardships they would undergo might end their love. He wants to go in search of *der ferne Klang*, a distant sound, which has entranced him with dreams of becoming a great artist ("Doch wollt'ich mich neigen"). He promises that when he comes back, rich and famous, he will marry her. When he leaves, an Old Woman comes in, asking Greta if her mother is home. When Greta goes to fetch her, the woman complains that Fritz's behavior wasn't pretty, and warns her that her father, the Innkeeper, and Dr. Vigelius are gathered at the Swan, hinting that they are up to no good, and leaves. Greta wonders what she means and cannot tell if she knows the Old Woman from before or not. Her mother comes in, muttering over Herr Graumann's drinking and gambling, which are forcing them beyond their means. The men come in with an Actor and a crowd of the inn's customers. The Actor drunkenly congratulates Greta on her upcoming wedding ("Verehrte Frau!"), telling her that her father was playing skittles, lost all his money, and staked her hand in marriage. He lost to the Innkeeper, who celebrates his luck ("Fraulein, sollten sich's uberlegen"). Greta first refuses, saying she is engaged to another, and then finally agrees to the wedding, but seizes the opportunity to run away to find Fritz. She gets lost in the woods and is ready to throw herself into the lake, but is struck by its beauty and falls asleep. The Old Woman returns and promises her "Leigt ein schones Kinchen im Moos," love, beauty, and pleasure, and Greta eagerly follows her.

Act Two. Act Two opens, after a prelude that includes an enticing love song ("Wenn er Abend kommt") in the chaos of a Venetian night club, "La casa di maschere" (The House of the Maskers). It is ten years later and Greta is the house's main attraction. The Count and the Baron come to find her. The men sing of her many charms ("Greta! Endlich!"). She flirts wildly with everyone, though she finds the pursuit of pleasure and excitement is palling, and she announces a song contest. The man whose song has the greatest effect on her and the other dancers will win her for that night. The Count sings a gloomy, gothic-style ballad ("Die gluhende Krone") about a king who wore a mysteriously glowing crown, and the Chevalier counters this with a risqué song about a girl who sells flowers in Sorrento ("Das Blumenmadchen von Sorrent"). The Count passionately urges Greta to make her choice ("Ich hab' Dich durchschaut"). Greta still thinks about Fritz, whom she calls her love, hope, or perhaps only memory. Another gondola arrives, bringing Fritz. He and Greta recognize one another and are briefly reunited. Fritz, too, is disillusioned with his life ("Schuldbeladen und reuig") and proposes marriage. She is torn between the idea of domestic happiness and the excitement of being "the beautiful Greta" of the world she knows now. However, when Fritz realizes what the surroundings and the attentions of the other men mean, when the Count challenges him for her, he says that he won't fight over a whore and leaves. Greta first calls after him and then in the finale ("Ist der Liebste fern"), dances wildly with the Count.

Act Three. Dr. Vigelius and the Actor drink and remember the old days. Vigelius is remorseful over what he and his cronies did to Greta. Fritz's opera, The Harp, is being performed in the theater. Greta, now a streetwalker, is assisted out by a policeman; her emotions overcame her during the performance. A choirister says the first two acts were well received and predicts success. A man, saying he was her last night's customer, begins to pester her, but Vigelius recognizes her and drives him away. The audience comes out, critizing the opera for its weak ending and gossiping that the author is dying. When they leave, Greta is overcome with regrets, her memories rewakened by Fritz's music ("Was sagen die Leute?"). Vigelius promises to take her to Fritz. In Fritz's study, he is overwhelmed by his sense of failure ("Wie seltsam dast ist!"), all the more so when he looks outside at nature. Rudolf comes in and tries to get him to revise the last act and also tells him about the mysterious woman who fainted during the performance. Fritz suspects that it might be Greta and asks Rudolf to find her. He begins to hear the mysterious distant sound. Vigelius arrives and tries to tell him about the woman in the theater, but Fritz can barely listen to him, and Greta comes in. They fall into one another's arms ("Hast Du mir verziehn?"), and Fritz dies in her arms, gasping that he will rewrite the last act. *—Ann Feeney*

Recommended:

○ **Schreker: Der ferne Klang** / Halasz (cond.), Harper, Grigorescu, Friess, Hagen PO / 2000 / Naxos 660074-75

Die Gezeichneten (1913–1915)

Die Gezeichneten (The Branded Ones) was Schreker's fourth opera and it, along with *Dir Ferne Klang* (completed in 1910) and *Der Schatzgräber* (1915–18), established him as one of the foremost German composers for the stage of his time, rivaling even Richard Strauss. After his death in 1934, his standing declined sharply in Germany and throughout Europe as well, and his music subsequently fell into obscurity. In the latter twentieth century, *Die Gezeichneten*—and the other two operas mentioned—were revived and are now generally recognized as masterworks. Schreker, as was his custom, fashioned his own libretto for the three-act *Die Gezeichneten*, which he originally intended for use in an opera by Zemlinsky. The complex story is set in sixteenth century Genoa, and concerns love triangle between a homely nobleman, Alviano (a sort of regal Hunchback of Notre Dame figure), the beautiful painter Carlotta, and the depraved Count Tamare. The story is actually more decadent than it sounds, as it contains orgies and a host of deliciously wicked characters. Schreker loved erotic, sensational librettos, but accompanied them, as here, with music that is lush and shimmering, especially—and surprisingly—in his use of percussion. The richly scored Overture: Prelude that opens the opera augurs the kind of sumptuous writing that predominates throughout the work, with warmly Romantic themes and a pleasant, often serene atmosphere. And when the music turns lively in this ten-minute introductory piece, it brims with optimism and joy. When the singing begins, however, sinister elements enter the fabric, though the music remains gorgeously Romantic. Its character turns stormy and heroic in the ensemble work near the end of Act One's opening number ("Lasst!—Genug!..."). The writing often seems to anticipate the lush manner in the Korngold operas, as evidenced by the vocal and orchestral music in Act One's "Ist Das Nicht—Tamare?" The music is lovely and full of emotion in Carlotta's Act One "Und Wenn's Grade Das War, Was Ich Wollt," and full of passion in the Act II closing numbers "Narr der Ihr Seid!" and "Du Susse—Du Armste—Du Schönste," dominated by the truly odd couple of Carlotta and Alviano. The second orchestral interlude in Act Three for once divulges a discordant manner in its depiction of the growing tensions in the story, but the music still does not shed its sense of glitter and almost Straussian lushness. The final number in the opera, too, "Wer schrie da?," powerfully but beautifully conveys the sense of darkness in the story's tragic ending. *—Robert Cummings*

Synopsis:

Act One. Alviano Salvago, a Genoese nobleman, is about to bequeath to his native city a marvelous gift: a beautiful island paradise he has created called Elysium. So beautiful is the island, in fact, that Alviano himself will not set foot there. He is cursed with a face and body so grotesquely deformed that he fears his presence on Elysium would ruin it. After deciding to give the island to the city, and while waiting for the Podestà (mayor) to arrive to execute the transference of the island, Alviano learns from a group of his friends that they have created a secret underground lair on the island where they hide kidnapped maidens with whom they indulge in orgies and sexual perversions. They argue against the transference, though one among them, Count Tamare, has other things on his mind: a mysterious girl with whom he has become infatuated. As fate would have it, she arrives—accompanying her father, the Podestà. She coyly rejects the amorous entreaties of Tamare, who leaves angrily. Alviano later finds himself alone with Carlotta, who divulges that she has long observed him from her window. In fact, she is painting a portrait of him and wants him to come to her studio. He finally agrees, but fears he may be the butt of a cruel joke.

Act Two. The Podestà returns from the court of Duke Adorno, who has yet to approve the transference of the island. The young deviant nobles have expressed their opposition, but the public is overwhelmingly in favor of annexing Elysium. Tamare has also sought the Duke's help, asking him to intervene in his effort to win Carlotta; he also convinces the Duke to prohibit the transference, informing him of the underground lair. In the meantime, Alviano sits in Carlotta's studio as she paints. She tells him of a painter she knew who had never acquiesced to feelings of love for fear that the ardor would overwhelm her weak heart. This same painter never painted faces or scenes, only hands. Alviano realizes that she is speaking of herself, and that she is in fact in love with him; he is bewildered by her confession. As he embraces her tenderly, they are interrupted by a messenger heralding the arrival of the Duke.

Act Three. The citizens of Genoa are gathered on the island. Alviano sets off in search of Carlotta, to whom he is now engaged. She, meanwhile, has finished her painting and subsequently lost interest in Alviano; she has likewise refused the Duke's entreaties on behalf of Tamare, who abducts her as she wanders the island. Meanwhile, the people assembled praise Alviano for his creation, but just then the Count of Justice enters (really the Duke in disguise) and accuses Alviano of the kidnapping of the maidens. Alviano reveals the lair, wherein Tamare and the nobles are discovered, along with the weakened Carlotta. Alviano rushes to her, but she rejects him cruelly and calls out for Tamare before collapsing. *—Jeremy Grimshaw*

Recommended:

○ **Schreker: Die Gezeichneten** / Albrecht (cond.), Adam, Schreckenbach, Riegel, Hopfner, Radio Symphonieorchester Wien / 2002 / Orfeo 584022

○ **Schreker: Die Gezeichneten** / Waart (cond.), Schmiege, Lang, Meens, Visser, Netherlands Radio Phil. / Marco Polo 223328

○ **Schreker: Die Gezeichneten** / Zagrosek (cond.), Goerne, Connell, Kruse, Salomaa / 1995 / London 444442

Jaap Schröder

b. Dec. 31, 1925

Violinist, Conductor

Jaap Schröder is among the most versatile of the musicians who have emerged from the historical performance movement, recording music ranging from Baroque to Romantic both as a soloist and as a chamber musician, conducting or leading a variety of top period-instrument ensembles, and enjoying a long career as a teacher in both Europe and the U.S. Born in 1925 in Amsterdam, Schröder combined violin studies in Amsterdam and Paris with musicology courses at the Sorbonne. In the 1950s and 1960s he was a member of the Netherlands String Quartet and concertmaster of the Hilversum Radio Chamber Orchestra, and in 1960 he founded his own chamber group, Concerto Amsterdam.

In the 1970s, as the movement toward historically accurate performances entered its second wave, Schröder became one of the first musicians to look toward extending its principles forward to the Classical and Romantic eras. He founded the Quartetto Esterházy in 1973 to that end, and once again he immersed himself in orchestral as well as chamber literature. From 1980 to 1984 he was concertmaster of London's Academy of Ancient Music, and he would codirect that group's recording of Mozart's complete symphonies, the first made on period instruments. He has conducted various European Baroque orchestras, as well as the Smithsonian Chamber Orchestra in Washington.

Schröder has also been active as a chamber musician and as a soloist in the U.S., as well as teaching for many years at the Yale University School of Music and holding guest appointments at several top conservatories. He founded the Smithsonian String Quartet in Washington in 1982, and his recordings have included Baroque standards like the Bach unaccompanied *Violin Sonatas* and Vivaldi's *Four Seasons*, and unfamiliar Baroque virtuoso solo literature by the likes of Biber, Veracini, and Uccellini. With chamber groups he has performed music from Mendelssohn, Gade, and both Robert and Clara Schumann, and his repertoire extends forward to Hindemith's violin concerto from *Kammermusik No. 4*. A walking compendium of expertise and performing lore, Jaap Schröder is a true jack-of-all-trades in the historical-performance investigative enterprise. *—AMG*

Recommended:

○ **Vivaldi: The Four Seasons** / Schröder, Concerto Amsterdam / HM 1955129

○ **Boccherini: Cello Concertos** / Schröder (cond.), Bylsma, Baumann, Woudenberg, Concerto Amsterdam / 1996 / Teldec 97991

Franz Schubert

b. Jan. 31, 1797, Vienna, Austria, **d.** Nov. 19, 1828, Vienna, Austria

Composer: Vocal, Keyboard, Symphonic, Orchestral, Chamber Music, Choral, Opera

Franz Peter Schubert was among the first of the Romantics, and the composer who, more than any other, brought the art song (lied) to artistic maturity. During his short but prolific career, he produced masterpieces in nearly every genre, all characterized by rich harmonies, an expansive treatment of classical forms, and a seemingly endless gift for melody. Schubert began his earliest musical training studying with his father and brothers. Having passed an audition, Schubert enrolled at the Convict school that trained young vocalists to eventually sing at the chapel of The Imperial Court. Schubert began to explore composition and wrote a song that came to the attention of the institution's director, Antonio Salieri, who along with the school's professor of harmony, hailed young Schubert as a genius. In 1813, after Schubert's voice broke, he returned to live with his father, who directed him to follow in his footsteps and become a schoolteacher. Schubert begrudgingly complied and worked miserably in that capacity by day, while composing prolifically by night. He had written more than 100 songs as well as numerous symphonic, operatic, and chamber music scores, before he reached the age of 20.

Schubert finally left his teaching position to dedicate himself completely to musical pursuits. During the summer of 1818, the young composer worked as a private music teacher to the aristocratic Esterházy family. When he left that post in the fall, Schubert lived a somewhat bohemian lifestyle, composing and spending time with a group of friends that acted as his personal support system. In 1820, Schubert was commissioned by two opera houses, the Kärthnerthor Theatre and Theater-ander-Wein, to compose a pair of operas. He wrote *Zwillingsbruden*, and *Zauberharfe*, both of which were unenthusiastically received. Schubert failed to secure a contract with a publisher, as none were willing to take a chance on a relatively unknown composer who wrote (harmonically) untraditional music. Schubert, along with the support of his artistic friends, published his own work for a collection of roughly 100 subscribers. These efforts, however, were financially unrewarding, and Schubert struggled to sustain himself. His work garnered little attention and contemporary composers dismissed his music as presumptuous and immature.

In 1823, Schubert was elected to the *Musikverein* of Graz, as an honorary member. Though this brought no financial reward and was an inconsequential appointment, Schubert relished its slight recognition, and to show his gratitude, composed his famous *Unfinished Symphony.* Five years later, Schubert's music was featured at a concert at Vienna's *Musikverein.* His work was received quite enthusiastically, and to much critical acclaim. This marked the only time during the composer's life that he enjoyed such success. This seemed to provide Schubert with a renewed sense of optimism, and despite illness, the composer continued to produce at an incredible rate. He began to organize a scheme to increase his artistic popularity, by continuing to evaluate his work and progress as a musician, perhaps even planning to study harmony privately. Schubert's health did not improve, and he soon found himself at death's door. During the composer's last moments, he instructed his brother Ferdinand to ensure that he would be buried alongside Ludwig van Beethoven's grave. Schubert revered the legendary composer, and was grateful to him, as Beethoven had praised his work after hearing a selection of songs. Schubert also highly regarded the work of both Franz Joseph Haydn and Wolfgang Amadeus Mozart. Franz Schubert died of syphilis.

Despite his short life, Schubert produced a wealth of symphonies, operas, masses, chamber music pieces, and piano sonatas, most of which are considered standard repertoire. He is known primarily for composing hundreds of songs including *Gretchen am Spinnrade*, and *Erlkönig.* He pioneered the song cycle with such works as *Die schöne Müllerin*, and *Die Winterreise*, and greatly affected the vocal writing of both Robert Schumann and Gustav Mahler. *—David Brensilver*

VOCAL

Songs (1810–1828)

Franz Schubert elevated the German art song or lied beyond its beginnings in the classically poised songs of C.P.E. Bach and Gluck, and beyond even the songs of Haydn, Mozart, and Beethoven, to a pinnacle that not even Schumann, Brahms, Strauss, Wolf, and Mahler could surpass. At the most superficial level, Schubert fused the supple bel canto of Italian melodies with the emotional and spiritual profundity of German forms and harmonies. But while no one would deny the supreme melodic beauty or extraordinary harmonic subtlety of *Gretchen am Spinnrade* (Gretchen at the Spinning Wheel) or *Du bist die Ruh* (You Are Repose), the real greatness of these songs is in their ability to universalize the specific, to turn Gretchen's melancholic desperation into all women's despair and to turn the blessed rapture of *Du bist die Ruh* into all men's bliss. Schubert's genius at finding the fullest and highest possible expression for the deepest human emotions in his lieder is his greatest accomplishment. From the early *Gretchen am Spinnrade* of his 17th year through to the late *Die Taubenpost* (The Pigeon Post) of his final year, very few of Schubert's more than 660 songs fail to touch the infinite. *Der Tod und das Mädchen* (Death and the Maiden) portrays the terror of the maiden and the majesty of death equally well. His *Mignon* songs are full of endless hope and hopeless yearning. *Auf dem Wasser zu singen* (To Be Sung on the Water) is the apotheosis of a barcarolle sung on the seas of heaven. *Heidenröslein* (The Wild Rose) is the essence of the folk song elevated to the level of great art. *Auflösung* (Dissolution) is both boundlessly exhilarating and endlessly despairing. *Der Doppelgänger* (The Ghostly Double) is possibly the most frightening song ever composed. And these are only a tiny handful of Schubert's songs. But the stand-alone solo songs are only one side of Schubert's achievement. Beginning with the long but often unsuccessful narrative ballads of his youth, Schubert came to develop an entirely new form of song: the song cycle. Although it could be said that Beethoven originated the idea of a song cycle with his *An die ferne Geliebte* (To the Distant Beloved) of 1816, no one would dispute the supremacy of Schubert's *Die schöne Müllerin* (The Miller's Beautiful Daughter) of 1823 and *Winterreise* (Winter's Journey) of 1827–1828. Each song in each cycle is magnificent, but taken together, they form a narrative greater than the sum of its parts. *Die schöne Müllerin* is a sentimental education from infatuation through love to sorrow and death. *Winterreise* is even greater: a heartbreaking journey from despair to madness traced in some of the most anguished and transcendent music ever composed. *—James Leonard*

Recommended:

- ○ **Hyperion Schubert Edition (Sampler)** / Johnson, Various artists / 1997 / Hyperion 200
- ○ **Schubert: Lieder** / Fischer-Dieskau, Moore / 2001 / EMI 74754
- ○ **Schubert: Lieder** / Ameling, Jansen, Baldwin / 1993 / Philips 438528
- ○ **An die Musik: Favorite Schubert Songs** / Terfel, Martineau / DG 445294
- ○ **Schubert: Lieder Vol. 1** / Bostridge, Drake / 1998 / EMI 56347
- ○ **Schubert: Lieder Vol. 2** / Bostridge, Drake / 2001 / EMI 57141
- ○ **Schubert: 12 Lieder & 6 Moments musicaux** / Schwarzkopf, Fischer / 2000 / EMI 67494
- ○ **Schubert: Complete Lieder Vol. 1** / Fischer-Dieskau, Moore / DG 437215
- ○ **Schubert: Complete Lieder Vol. 2** / Fischer-Dieskau, Moore / DG 437225

An die Musik ("Du holde Kunst . . ."), song, D. 547 (1817)

Between 1815 and 1827, Franz Schubert set twelve poems (and one ill-fated opera libretto) of Franz von Schober to music. The two men, roughly the same age, enjoyed a close relationship—so close, in fact, that they sometimes referred to themselves collectively as "Schobert." It was certainly this personal connection that inspired Schubert to set so many of his friend's texts, since, taken on literary merits alone, Schober's poetry was anything but outstanding.

Schober was a bit of an indulgent wanderer, his comfortable circumstances obviating the need to settle on a career (he was variously "employed" as a writer, thespian, painter, and civil servant); consequently, his ode to music may come across upon reading as a bit patronizing and pretentious. Still, Schubert's musical setting elevates what may seem to be naïve sentimentality to the level of prayer, uttered in all sincerity.

The most prominent feature of *An die Musik* is the plaintive melody, the arc of which leaps wistfully between chord tones. This gentle curve accompanies the germinal phrase of the poem: "O beloved art." Behind the lyrical melody, a simple chordal accompaniment softly undulates with rhythmic persistence, while a subtle but resolute bass line underscores the texture. The major sixth descent that gives the opening motive its characteristic reverence reappears throughout the song, lending to the otherwise restrained melody occasional moments of rhapsodic tenderness.

Early in his songwriting career, Schubert had encountered the challenge of reconciling the formal, technical, and expressive demands of music with the dramatic and/or pictorial suggestions of a text. Within a strophic (repeating) musical form this is particularly difficult, since poetic structures will align different images or thoughts with the same music in subsequent verses. In *An die Musik*, however, the simple strophic approach becomes a strength rather than a liability. Since the subject of the poem is music's inherent and independent expressive power, the music need not take its inspiration directly from the text; instead it demonstrates the poem's argument in real time—the musical landscape stands for itself.

For those who must find discrete moments of text painting, two possibilities are presented in the second half of the poem. The lush, descending sixth from the initial motive now aligns itself with what may be its textual counterpart: "So often has a sigh from your harp escaped," with the word "sigh" ("Seufzer") corresponding with the moment of descent; and the smoothly tintinnabulating triads that have characterized the accompaniment throughout could arguably be the "precious, holy chord" that grants the poet "a heavenly glimpse of a better times." *—Jeremy Grimshaw*

Recommended:

- ○ **Schumann: Dichterliebe; Schubert & Beethoven: Lieder** / Wunderlich, Giesen / DG 449747
- ○ **Schubert: Schwanengesang; Lieder** / Fischer-Dieskau, Moore / DG 415188

An Sylvia ("Was ist Sylvia, . . ."), song, D. 891 (Jul., 1826)

This is one of Schubert's three settings of Shakespeare texts from July 1826, the other two being *Ständchen* ("Hark, Hark, the Lark"), D. 889, and *Trinklied* ("Come, thou monarch of the vine"), D. 888. The composer was at the height of his powers, producing in the same year such masterpieces as the *Symphony No. 9 in C major ("Great")*, the *String Quartet No. 15*, and the four songs from Goethe's *Wilhelm Meister*, D. 877.

The text of this song is taken from Act Four, Scene Two, of Shakespeare's *The Two Gentlemen of Verona* as translated by Eduard von Bauernfeld. While Schubert had set many songs from the works of Matthisson, Goethe, Kosegarten, Schiller, and others, his interest in Shakespeare came late; not surprisingly, all three of the Shakespeare songs are of high quality. This song was first published in 1828, and the edition in which it appeared was dedicated to Maria Pachler, a patron of the composer who lived in Graz.

"An Sylvia" is a wonderful example of Schubert's adaptive approach to song writing. At this point in his career—only months from the composition of *Winterreise*, and a mere two years from death—the composer had explored nearly every approach to text setting available to him, at times pushing the boundaries of harmony, declamation, and musical form well beyond previously established limits. Yet here he created a simple strophic song—one that, in its basic materials and form, is practically indistinguishable from even his earliest works. Its elegant and self-possessed nature is perfectly suited to Shakespeare's subtle wit and poetic meter; it needed nothing more adventurous to bring out these qualities. The dialogue between the two "gentleman," who are extolling the virtues of young Sylvia, comes to life in the simple arch shaped melodies, and the structure of Schubert's verses is such that their repetition is welcome—in this way it is reminiscent of several entries from his earlier *Die schöne Müllerin*. *—AMG*

Recommended:

- ○ **Schumann: Dichterliebe; Schubert & Beethoven: Lieder** / Wunderlich, Giesen / DG 449747
- ○ **An Die Musik: Favorite Schubert Songs** / Terfel, Martineau / DG 445294

Ellens Gesang III ("Ave Maria"), song, D. 839 (Apr., 1825)

This song is a setting of text from near the closing of Canto III from Sir Walter Scott's *The Lady of The Lake*, in a translation by Adam Storck. It was composed in April, 1825, when Schubert also fashioned *Ellens Gesang I* and *Ellens Gesang II*. This third effort is probably the most successful and most popular. Even the composer spoke of its immediate widespread appeal in a letter to his parents in July, 1825, shortly after its first performances. He also indicated that he felt a certain religious devotion when he wrote it, one that came to him naturally and effortlessly. *Ellens Gesang III* was first published in 1826.

The melody of *Ellens Gesang III* (Ellen's Song) is attractive and the mood has both a secular and religious feel, at times an even operatic one. The piano accompaniment is gentle and harp-like, quite typical of the composer in this kind of music. The text begins, "Ave Maria! Maiden mild! Listen to a maiden's prayer!" Ellen prays as the clansmen are encouraged to defend their soil from the oncoming royal armies.

In the end, this is one of the composer's most successful songs, written at a time when he was at the height of his powers. Even though his life was cut short when he died before his 32nd birthday, probably of syphilis he had contracted some years before, he had already become one of the greatest masters of the lied and might have gone on, as his *"Great" C major Symphony* suggests, to become an equally great composer of orchestral music. *—Robert Cummings*

Recommended:

- ○ **Schubert: Lieder** / Otter, Forsberg, Swedish Radio Choir / DG 453481

○ **Schubert: Complete Songs Vol. 13** / McLaughlin, Johnson / 1992 / Hyperion 33013

○ **Ave Maria** / Ameling, Baldwin / Philips 420870

Erlkönig ("Wer reitet so spät"), song, D. 328 (1815)

Page after page has been written about Franz Schubert's *Erlkönig*—it is easily the most familiar single piece from the German song repertory; yet each hearing of the work seems somehow to conjure up the same spark of desperate passion in the listener that it must have conjured from those Viennese music-lovers who first encountered the song when it was published in 1821—six years after being composed—as Schubert's Opus 1.

Erlkönig the poem is a dramatic ballad, part of Johann Wolfgang von Goethe's 1782 singspiel *Der Fischerin.* It tells, in strict meter and regular four-line stanzas, the tale of a father riding through the woods late at night with his son. The evil Erl-king (the origin of the words "Erlkönig" and "Erlenkönig," both of which forms appear in Goethe's ballad, is complicated and even confused; some say they are a translation, or mistranslation, into German of the Danish word for "Elf King"), visible to the young boy, but not to his father, calls out to the lad, tempting him with thoughts of games and dances. Many times the boy cries out to his father to help him, but the father cannot see the Erl-king or his minions and writes his son's horror off as one natural phenomenon or another. Only when the boy is physically wounded does the father recognize that desperate measures are called for; though he rides with all his strength and skill, however, his boy expires before he reaches safety.

Schubert's setting of Goethe's ballad dates from sometime during Fall of 1815—a fabulously productive year during which he penned nearly 145 lieder, and countless instrumental works, while still working as a schoolteacher. The song's immense fame during the nineteenth century gave rise to many fanciful stories of its composition; some have claimed that it was composed in just a few minutes, in one fell swoop of passion, while a friend looked on, but such a genesis seems unlikely. Schubert revised his setting three times, mostly tinkering with the piano accompaniment but also altering dynamics in striking ways and inserting/deleting measures to slightly better the pacing.

And it is pacing, or motion, in a truly physical sense, that fuels both Goethe's frantic poem and Schubert's lied. There is a continuous background of repeated, triplet octaves in the piano part (very difficult and physically tiring—in one of the revisions Schubert simplified the figuration, asking for duplets instead of triplets), against which the three characters of the ballad sing their simple lines. Each persona is given his own unique tone: the child frantic and impassioned, the father noble and self-assured, Erlkönig himself relaxed and attractive as he seeks to trick the child. The result is an almost demonic fury, and as the drama unfolds and the child becomes more and more terrified and sings in a higher and higher register, the harsh dissonances of his cries, "Mein Vater, mein Vater!" become ever more bone-chilling. The racing triplets cease only at the very end of the song, as the narrator proclaims in a bit of taught recitative that "the child was dead in his [the father's] arms." *—Blair Johnston*

Recommended:

○ **An Die Musik: Favorite Schubert Songs** / Terfel, Martineau / DG 445294

○ **Schubert: Schwanengesang; 4 Lieder** / Fischer-Dieskau, Moore / 2001 / EMI 67559

○ **Schubert, Schumann & Strauss: Lieder** / Schwarzkopf, Parsons / EMI 63656

Ganymed ("Wie im Morgenglanze"), song, D. 544 (Mar., 1817)

The year 1817 saw Franz Schubert set more than 70 poems, resulting in some of his very finest songs. Of these, it may be Johann Wolfgang von Goethe's *Ganymed* that drew from him the deepest musical response.

Though Schubert's attempt in 1816 to interest Goethe in his music had resulted in a snub from the venerated poet, he continued to use his verses as the bases for lieder. Schubert also dedicated his Op. 19 collection, which includes "Ganymed," to Goethe prior to its publication (though he skipped the customary step of asking the writer's permission before committing the dedication to print).

Ganymed was the fabled Trojan youth who, called by Zeus, was carried up into Olympus to become the gods' immortal cup-bearer. Goethe's treatment of the legend avoids references to anything specifically Greek, instead focusing on the beautiful comfort of nature and the love of—and for—the divine.

Schubert's setting is marked Etwas langsam (rather slow) and falls into several broad sections, each characterized by distinctive accompanimental figuration in the piano that captures something of the unfolding poem's essence. The calm stillness of the morning saturates the opening; the singer softly intrudes on the poised, delicate seven-measure piano introduction, transforming the accompaniment into a repeating background figure that only moves forth into new territory as the poem goes on to tell of the "thousand-fold delights of love."

The composer's love of striking chromatic modulations is apparent throughout, as in the serene A flat major opening that moves into the rich land of C flat major to "languish" within a field of flowers. E major emerges from within the piano's rolling gestures ("you quench my burning thirst"); then, as the real action of the story begins to unfold and *Ganymed* begins his ascension, Schubert provides some bouncing eighth notes that gradually spin their way into F major and proceed sequentially within this final tonality. From time to time, "Ganymed" is interrupted by reflective pauses in the action, including two ecstatic salutations to the "All-loving Father," the second of which moves from a passionate fortissimo all the way down to the ethereal pianissimo that ends the song. *—Blair Johnston*

Recommended:

○ **Schubert: Goethe-Lieder** / Fischer-Dieskau, Demus / DG 457747

○ **Schubert: Die Forelle & Other Lieder** / Bostridge, Drake / 1998 / Angel 56347

○ **A Goethe Schubertiad** / Johnson, Schäfer / 1995 / Hyperion 33024

○ **Schubert: 12 Lieder & 6 Moments musicaux** / Schwarzkopf, Fischer / 2000 / EMI 67494

Gesänge aus Wilhelm Meister, 4 songs, D. 877 (Jan., 1826)

Johann Wolfgang von Goethe's *Wilhelm Meister* is full of richly drawn and compelling characterizations, but none more so than Mignon. Such is the beauty of the lyric verses that Goethe provides for her to sing in the novel that Franz Schubert was inspired to set them to music time and time again. In 1827, publisher Antonio Diabelli released four of these "Mignon Songs" as Schubert's Opus 62 (now cataloged as D. 877), calling them "Gesänge aus Wilhelm Meister von Goethe." Three of Mignon's four songs are represented in Opus 62—the first and fourth songs of D. 877 are settings of the same poem. All four of these lieder were composed during January 1826, and they represent the last settings of Goethe that the composer would craft. They are: "Nur wer die Sehnsucht kennt," "Heiss mich nicht reden," "So lasst mich scheinen," and again, "Nur wer die Sehnsucht kennt."

The first of the two "Nur wer die Sehnsucht kennt" settings is a duet, with one voice representing Mignon and one representing the Harper (each of Schubert's other settings of this text are for solo voice and piano). The duet is cast in the key of B minor, and a gently sloping melodic cell—proffered by the piano in the song's very first measure—pops up time and time again as the song unfolds. The two voices often seem isolated from one another, as the text would seem to demand, but from time to time they come together to produce gestures of the utmost expression, the most striking of which is a crystalline, pianissimo rendition of the main melodic cell in C major ("He who knows and loves me is far off," words that contrast beautifully with the closeness of the two voices at this point).

In D. 877/2, "Heiss mich nicht reden," Mignon tells of her burdensome secret. During the second, comparatively hopeful stanza, Schubert provides a chorale-like C major, voice and piano working together in total homophony.

"So lasst mich scheinen" is part of Mignon's death sequence, and, as if to mirror the great complexity of Goethe's masterful verse, Schubert crafts the song out of a tender, warm B major which a lesser composer would have wrongly thought to be irreconcilable with such bittersweet words. But how perfect it works when at two key moments Schubert brings in the briefest hint of B minor.

The final song in D. 877, another "Nur wer die Sehnsucht kennt," rolls forth in a sad 6/8 meter. There is real pang to the B flat octaves that mark both the introduction and the final instrumental postlude. Mignon tells us of her great loneliness, but it is the solo piano that seems to explore most deeply the painful, dissonant reality of solitude. *—Blair Johnston*

Recommended:

○ **An 1826 Schubertiad** / Johnson, Ainsley, Schäfer / Hyperion 13026

○ **Jan DeGaetani Sings Schubert & Wolf** / de Gaetani, Kalish / 1992 / Nonesuch 79263

Gretchen am Spinnrade ("Meine Ruh'..."), song, D. 118 (Oct. 19, 1814)

It was on October 19, 1814, that Franz Schubert composed this song, the first of 71 on poems by Johann Wolfgang von Goethe; in the opinion of some, it was upon the wings of the near-deified German Bard that Schubert was lifted to his highest musical heights. As one critic argued near the beginning of the twentieth century, "In the 30 songs that came before... Schubert had toiled, tested himself, and had his charming moments, and now and again had fumbled. This time he was transported by his genius."

The poem, taken from Part I of Goethe's monumental recasting of the *Faust* legend, finds Gretchen sitting by the window waiting for her love to return. She spins as she waits, and—though the text excerpt used in Schubert's song mentions nothing of these activities explicitly—the composer translates the rising and falling motion of her foot on the pedal, the rotation of the wheel, and the twisting of the thread into an undulating and omnipresent accompanimental figure. As Gretchen spins, her mind is racked with dread and longing; she recalls her love's endearing traits—his "noble form," his "witching words," and, most importantly, his kiss. From the outset, her prediction is not optimistic: "O, my heart is sad, my rest is o'er, / And never, alas! shall I find it, ne'er find it more."

Schubert's setting at first seems to be a simple backdrop for the poem, with the spinning wheel figure serving as sonic wallpaper. The text/tone relationship is, in fact, much more involved than that. As obvious as it may seem, what we're hearing really isn't just the spinning, we're hearing Gretchen's restlessness. Schubert enhances this tension through harmonic means, moving over the course of the verse from D minor, up to E, then F. In addition, he alters the text delivery so that the ominous opening lines reappear throughout the song, always pulling the harmony back to the original key. The most striking moment in the piece occurs as Gretchen, with an exhilarating fortissimo ascent to B flat major, thinks of her lover's kiss—at which point she can maintain the pretense of work no longer: having worked herself into a fit, she stops spinning completely, and only after several faltering efforts is she able to regain her composure and resume her task. She voices a wish for death upon his bosom, then utters once again the sorrowful refrain.

If one enjoys tracing musical genealogies, *Gretchen am Spinnrade* makes a good subject for speculation. By 1823, Schubert had turned the unbearable tension of the spinning wheel into the more subdued angst of the mill wheel, in *Die Schöne Müllerin*. Less than a century later, the anxious spinner would become the nightmarish and murderous psychopath in Schoenberg's *Erwartung*. Certainly, *Gretchen am Spinnrade* can be considered one of the prime harbingers of high Romantic expression. *—Jeremy Grimshaw*

Recommended:

- ○ **Schubert: The Complete Songs Vol. 13** / McLaughlin, Johnson / 1992 / Hyperion 33013
- ○ **Portrait of Kiri Te Kanawa** / Te Kanawa, Amner / 1983 / CBS 39208
- ○ **Elisabeth Schwarzkopf: Schubert & Mozart Lieder** / Schwarzkopf, Fischer / EMI 47326

Heidenröslein ("Sah ein Knab . . ."), song, D. 257 (Aug. 19, 1815)

Schubert's setting of Goethe's *Heidenröslein* (Wild Rose) (D. 257) from August, 1815, is one of his one-page wonders, strophic songs on one page of music which are miniature musical miracles. Like so many of Schubert's great Goethe settings, there was never a time when *Heidenröslein* did not exist: its quietly ecstatic melody has always been part of the collective memory of the human race. And like so many of Schubert's best songs, the *Heidenröslein* melody has become virtually a German folk song. Of course, it is impossible to say what exactly it is about *Heidenröslein* which makes it so great. On the page, the quietly ecstatic melody is merely a G major ditty, the piano accompaniment is a simple vamp, the rhythm is relaxed, the tempo is comfortable and the harmonies go no further from the tonic than a secondary dominant. But when sung, *Heidenröslein* becomes one of the most artlessly affecting songs in all Schubert. *—James Leonard*

Recommended:

- ○ **Schubert: Goethe-Lieder** / Fischer-Dieskau, Moore / DG 457747
- ○ **Schubert: Lieder** / von Otter, Forsberg, Swedish Radio Choir, CO of Europe / DG 453481
- ○ **Erlkönig: The Art of the Lied** / Wunderlich, Giesen / DG 445188

Der Hirt auf dem Felsen ("Wenn auf dem höchsten Fels ich steh'"), for voice, clarinet (or cello) & piano, D. 965 (Oct., 1828)

It is a truly remarkable thing that so extroverted a song as Franz Schubert's *Der Hirt auf dem Felsen*, D. 965, his second-to-last song, could have been written during the same month as the famous, gentle *Die Taubenpost*, his last song, or within just weeks of the intimate, unworldly final instrumental works. And yet *Der Hirt auf dem Felsen*'s apparent concert hall characteristics are in fact just that: the work was specifically designed for the well-known soprano Anna Milder-Hauptmann to use as a showpiece, a somewhat belated fulfillment on Schubert's part of a request she had made of him many years earlier. The song was published as Op. 129 in mid-1830, a year and a half after its composer's death.

Der Hirt auf dem Felsen is written for voice (given the work's origin, soprano is implied, but the text works equally well for a man), piano, and clarinet obbligato. The piece is an extended and very sectional one, certainly every bit as much a work of chamber music as it is a lied in the true sense of the word.

The bulk of the poem is the work of Wilhelm Müller, but some of the middle lines are the work of another poet, tentatively identified as Helmina von Chézy; the two are bound together by a certain pervasive world-weariness. There are the thoughts of a lonely lover high up on the mountaintop, listening to the echoes rise from down in the valley; grief becomes all-consuming, life no longer worth living; finally, spring, and with it rebirth, looms in the future, and the singer must make ready "for the wanderings to come." For all the superficial tendencies of the song, Schubert's feeling for the text is very genuine—he knew quite well that he was not long for this Earth; the "spring" of resurrection was to Schubert a very welcome thing, and he was indeed quite ready, even eager, for such a wandering.

This text is set up in three large, very contrasting sections of music, prefaced by just a few measures of piano introduction. The warm opening melody (Andantino, B flat major) is given a full-scale test run by the clarinet before the soprano arrives to take it over. As thoughts turn ever darker ("Deep sorrow consumes me, happiness has departed") Schubert turns to G minor and fills the bars with gently pointed eighth notes. The final B flat major Allegretto is a happy thing, riding upward on scales that each time reach a little higher than the time before as the singer celebrates the coming of spring with virtuoso fireworks that the clarinet does its best to top. *—Blair Johnston*

Recommended:

- ○ **Elly Ameling: The Early Recordings Vol. 4** / Ameling, Demus, Deinzer / 1995 / Deutsche HM 26616
- ○ **Schubert: Quintet D956; The Shepherd on the Rock** / Valente, Ma, Wright / 1990 / CBS 45901
- ○ **Schubert: The Complete Songs Vol. 9** / Auger, Johnson, King / 1990 / Hyperion 33009

Die schöne Müllerin, song cycle, D. 795 (1823)

Schubert's most recognized contribution to the musical canon was not merely his revolutionary approach to song, but his combination of vitally connected songs into cycles, as exemplified in his two cycles on texts by Wilhelm Müller, *Die Schöne Müllerin* in 1823, and *Die Winterreise* in 1827. "A frown from fortune," speculated Schubert scholar Richard Capell in 1928, "and *Die Schöne Müllerin* might have been but another of those rambling tales, extended beyond every lyrical propriety, with which Schubert now and again, as cannot be disguised, has fairly bored us. Thanks to Müller, it was something quite different—new, and endlessly engaging. The all-important advantage is that the interruptions in the recital afford a succession of new standpoints in time: a drama is revealed to us in a series of lyrical moments." One need not accept Capell's perfunctory and unforgiving generalizations of Schubert's output in order to realize that, with *Die Schöne Müllerin*, Schubert found a way to reconcile—in an extraordinary and synergistic fashion—his gift for poignant melody with the demands of large-scale form.

Still, there is something paradoxical in the last phrase of Capell's argument, which appears to admit as a plus what elsewhere seems a minus: that the moments themselves, rather than creating a finely crafted composite with a constructional integrity approaching Beethoven, are just so poignant as to make listeners oblivious to any weaknesses in the musical, poetic, and semantic macrocosm. Resonating with this view is a common reaction to Schubert's instrumental works—that the *Unfinished Symphony*, for example, is made up of a considerable variety of tunes, each of an impressive quality, disqualifying as pedantic any attempt to analyze their arrangements and relationships. Perhaps realizing that, depending on the text's level of semantic generality, his approach as a composer may lack consistency, Schubert used the recurring images in Müller's texts (the flow of the stream, the orbit of the mill wheel) to serve as a kind of unifying semantic space, within which his miraculous "lyrical moments" can occur.

The first of the song cycle's texts quickly establishes the anxiously and sometimes uneasily circular paths the 20 songs will take, and one can immediately suspect that this will not be a narrative of events so much as an exploration of certain recurring, expressive modes: "To wander is the millers joy . . . to wander, to wander, to wander. . . ." The bipartite strophic nature of the song resonates with the metaphorically circular images of the text: the water running through its eternal course; the wheel outside the mill, set in motion by the water's current; the millstones inside the mill, translating the water's endless wandering.

Strophic forms reflect these recurring symbols while allowing for a surprising range of expression. In "Die Liebe Farbe," for example, an entirely strophic (repeated) melody accompanies three verses of texts with widely varying effects. In the first, the speaker tells of the green adornments he shall don to please his love, since green is her favorite color. In the second verse, the subject is a hunter "hieing across the meadows," presumably in hunter's green. Listeners are left to assume that the hunter has stolen the speaker's love, for in the last verse, the green he shall wear is the green grass atop his grave. The once sprightly melody has now been transformed, without any apparent musical means, into the voice of irony and bitterness (underscoring Schubert's rumored opinion that there is no such thing as truly "happy music"). By looking to the text for cohesion, Schubert finds even more expressive possibilities in the music itself. *—Jeremy Grimshaw*

Recommended:

- ○ **Schubert: Die schöne Mullerin** / Fischer-Dieskau, Moore / 1997 / EMI 56240
- ○ **Schubert: Die schöne Müllerin** / Bostridge, Uchida / 2004 / EMI 57827
- ○ **Schubert: Die schöne Müllerin; 3 Lieder** / Wunderlich, Giesen / DG 447452

Schwanengesang (Swan Song), song cycle, D. 957 (1828)

Before his death in 1828, Franz Schubert had completed portions of two projected song cycles—one on poems by Ludwig Rellstab, and the other on poems of Heinrich Heine. These cycle fragments, representing a total of 13 songs, were collected after the composer's death by his brother, Ferdinand Schubert, and one of his publishers, Tobias Haslinger, who then added "Die Taubenpost" and published all fourteen as *Schwanengesang* (Swan Song) in 1829.

It is impossible to know how much thought these men gave to their hodgepodge; it is likely that their motives were entirely commercial (the Heine songs, in particular, showed promise as moneymakers). So one should not examine *Schwanengesang* in the same light as Schubert's two earlier cycles, *Die Schöne Müllerin* and *Winterreise*, both of which were conceived of as wholes by the composer. *Schwanengesang* lacks the literal sense of journey that accompanies the other cycles, and so also their sense of interpretive architecture; however, true "cycle" or not (a debatable point), it possesses enormous musical variety and emotional scope. It crystallizes the musical and literary currents present in Schubert's thinking at the time of his death, and hints at the creative paths he might have followed had he enjoyed the luxury of more time. At the very least, *Schwanengesang* showcases Schubert's flexible response to poetry and revisits the archetypes of song and sentiment that populate his output overall. Here we have "riding" songs and "wandering" songs, the friendly brook and the crashing wave, virtuosity and musical economy, all juxtaposed—as appropriate a swan song as could be for one of the greatest song composers of all time.

The seven Rellstab poems that form the first half of *Schwanengesang* were originally given to Beethoven for consideration, but Beethoven died before he had a chance to set them. The composer's secretary then passed them on to Schubert. Schubert's settings magnify the robust and conventional style of Rellstab's language; they exploit the composer's fondness for unusual modulation and active piano figurations, but they rarely challenge one's sense of the normal or expected. The joy of the Rellstab songs lies in their journey from one mood to the next in the seamless way that is so typical of Schubert.

Schubert became acquainted with Heine's *Buch der Lieder* (Book of Songs) through one of the reading groups that gradually displaced the famous "Schubertiades" (informal concerts of his works) in the last years of the composer's life. The six settings from this collection that are included in *Schwanengesang* clearly demonstrate the degree to which Schubert rethought musical structure in response to poetry. A conventional setting like "Das Fischermädchen" (The Fisher Girl)—full of tongue-in-cheek elegance—finds itself juxtaposed with "Die Stadt" (The City), in which the composer actually departs from functional tonality. These songs are entirely about mood and irony, and they leave traditional concepts of beauty and lyricism behind. In "Der Doppelgänger," Schubert weaves together the archaic technique of ostinato with vocal declamation that comes strikingly close to Sprechgesang ("speech-song")—a device that was fully a half century ahead of its time.

"Die Taubenpost" (The Carrier Pigeon) is a charming setting of Johann Gabriel Seidl, who provided texts for a number of Schubert's songs (*"Der Wanderer an den Mond"* is a well-known example). If anything, "Die Taubenpost" is an example of the way Schubert could transform a poem of modest quality into an especially memorable song. Not relating to the rest of *Schwanengesang* in any way, it was perhaps included to mitigate the very dark sentiment of the Heine settings and end the cycle on an upbeat note. *—Allen Schrott*

Recommended:

- ○ **Schubert: Schwanengesang; Lieder** / Fischer-Dieskau, Moore / DG 415188
- ○ **Schubert: Schwanengesang; 4 Lieder** / Fischer-Dieskau, Moore / 2001 / EMI 67559
- ○ **Schubert: Schwanengesang; Brahms: Vier Ernste Gesänge** / Quasthoff, Zeyen / 2001 / DG 471030
- ○ **Schubert: Schwanengesang** / Terfel, Martineau / 2000 / Marquis Classics 81257

Der Tod und das Mädchen ("Vorüber, ach vorüber"), song, D. 531 (Feb., 1817)

Schubert was a master at creating a mood in an instant and at telling a story in a constrained space of time with just the piano and voice. This very brief song is incredible in its conveying a complete drama in a very short span of time, without giving any feeling of rush or of missing parts. Rather, Schubert breaks down the story to its essentials and presents them to the listener in their most distilled form.

The song opens with quiet minor chords that immediately convey the mood of a funeral march. The mood changes to sudden near-hysteria as the maiden sees death approaching her, and begs it to leave her, she is still so young. The first theme plays again as death, in a soothing monotone for the first few bars, reassures her, saying that he has come as a friend, not to punish, and that in his arms she will sleep. The final word, "sleep" plunges down to a low D, as the song comes to an end. *—Ann Feeney*

Recommended:

- ○ **Schubert: Schwanengesang; Lieder** / Fischer-Dieskau, Moore / 2000 / DG 463503
- ○ **Schubert: The Complete Songs Vol. 11** / Fassbaender, Johnson / 1991 / Hyperion 33011
- ○ **Schubert: An Die Musik** / Terfel, Martineau / DG 445294

Die Vögel ("Wie lieblich und fröhlich"), song, D. 691 (Mar., 1820)

Schubert's setting of Friedrich von Schlegel's *Die Vögel* (The Birds) (D. 691) from March 1820 is a lighthearted dance in 3/8, a sort of avian Ländler which rarely touches a minor chord much less a minor tonality. Its lilting melody flies and glides over an easygoing peasant waltz in the piano. Schubert sets the first and last verse of Schlegel's poem to nearly the same Ländler-style music, while the central verse functions as a drone-bass trio.

Although hardly one of Schubert's weightier songs, *Die Vögel* is nevertheless one of his most delightful. *—James Leonard*

Recommended:

- ○ **Schubert & Schumann: Lieder** / Ameling, Demus / 1990 / Deutsche HM 77085
- ○ **Schubert, Schumann & Strauss: Lieder** / Schwarzkopf, Moore / EMI 63656

Winterreise, song cycle, D. 911 (1827)

The breadth of scholarly approaches to Franz Schubert's song cycle *Die Winterreise* testifies to the structural and dramatic complexity of the work; assessments range from complicated graphs, complete with interlocking axes and cryptic semantic labels, to outright sighs of resignation over the work's intractability. Perhaps this intrigue is what attracts performers and academics alike to the work; singer and scholar Michael Besack traces the ambiguous dramatic trajectory of Schubert's cycle back to antiquity. "Epic poetry and the tragic theater never produced a story with a moral," he pointed out.

A central question concerning the cycle is whether it really is one. The two dozen poems by Wilhelm Müller that Schubert took as his texts appeared piecemeal in three separate publications between 1822 and the completion of Schubert's setting in 1827; Müller's third publication, finally bearing the title Schubert would adopt, featured the newest poems along with the ones previously published (though the latter were reordered). The chronology of Schubert's setting also calls the idea of a continuous cyclical narrative into question: he set Müller's initial 12 songs early in 1827, then completed the other dozen later that year. Still, while some of the individual songs are frequently performed alone, one can easily read a composite story into the cycle. Literary scholar Cecilia Baumann describes the work as "a simple story of a rejected lover who leaves the town where his love resides and sets out in winter on an aimless journey." Schubert biographer Jacques Chailley reads a different kind of journey: "not simply that of a scorned lover—he is only a phantom—but an image behind which one can discern at each moment the journey of man toward the tomb: *Die Winterreise* is the sinister voyage of life." Such existential ideas gain support from the bleakness of *Auf dem Flusse* (At the River), in which the lover's description of the frozen stream seems to shade into one of a physical corpse, and of the melancholy hurdy-gurdy-man's lament that ends the cycle.

The songs ruminate on, rather than depict, events that have befallen the rejected lover; as the first two lines of the first song indicate ("A stranger I came hither, a stranger hence I go"), the journey has already taken place: the famous fifth song, *Der Lindenbaum*, likewise centers on symbols of remembrance. Schubert's introduction establishes a tranquil major mode with an airy, fluttering accompaniment; it becomes apparent that this figure represents the rustling of the eponymous lime tree. "Upon its bark when musing, fond words of love I made," the wanderer tells listeners, "and joy alike and sorrow still drew me to its shade." Only briefly do the mode and mood of the music change to minor, in direct correlation to the image of passing the tree in darkness. These pictorial elements lie only on the surface, however. Certain musical elements create a sense of geographical and chronological remove: the rustling figure is constantly interrupted by a leap up to a quaint stepwise descent; the echo of a "hunting horn" figure suggests distance—spatial and temporal; the wind blows off the wanderer's hat, but he trudges forward without even turning around. The cold wind listeners that it is winter; the presence of leaves is unlikely. The rustling sound is not a real, but an imagined, phenomenon: "Now many leagues I'm far from/The dear old linden tree/[But still] I ever hear it murmur/'Peace thou wouldst find with me.'" Schubert's song does not evoke images; it evokes the act of remembering images. *—Jeremy Grimshaw*

Recommended:

- ○ **Schubert: Winterreise** / Fischer-Dieskau, Moore / 2002 / EMI 67928
- ○ **Schubert: Winterreise** / Hampson, Sawallisch / 1997 / EMI 56445

KEYBOARD

Allegretto in C minor, D. 915 (May 24, 1827)

It is tempting to hear homage to Ludwig van Beethoven in Franz Schubert's little *Allegretto in C minor for piano*, D. 915, composed in late April 1827. Schubert reportedly met Beethoven for the first and only time just days before the elder composer's demise on March 26. To say that such a meeting must have been both a moment of rapture for Schubert and an occasion that carried with it a bitter sting would not be overly dramatic, for here lay dying the man whose music had probably shaped Schubert's musical persona more than any other composer save Haydn, and also the man who—more than any other in Vienna—could have lifted Schubert's all-but-ignored music from the obscurity in which it languished. If we are to believe the accounts of Beethoven's last weeks, he had on his deathbed gotten to know some of Schubert's lieder—the only genre in which the young composer knew commercial success during his lifetime—and had been more than impressed, hailing Schubert's gifts to those who came to visit him. And so it may well have been that Beethoven was in Schubert's thoughts when he sat down on April 26 to pen the *Allegretto in C minor*, D. 915 (not to be confused with D. 900, another work by the same title and in the same key composed sometime earlier); Schubert was, after all, one of the torchbearers at Beethoven's funeral.

If the Allegretto was in some way inflected by Beethoven's passing, however, it was not on the musical surface, which is typical of late Schubert in every sense save its brief duration. The key, C minor, is funereal enough, and the 6/8 meter arpeggiation of the main tune is the sort of thing that Beethoven might indeed have spun (one thinks of the scherzo to the *Fifth Symphony*, which opens in strikingly similar fashion). But there is something of Schumann or Brahms, both ardent admirers of Schubert, in the rich, pianissimo middle section of this perfectly-balanced ternary form piece; the chords come in tiny spurts, sounding something like a broken-up chorale. The opening section of the Allegretto is itself a kind of stunted three-part form sometimes called "rounded binary," but here used with a flexibility that defies textbook analysis; in the second strain Schubert throws together a devilishly clever canon between the right and left hands. After this imitation builds to a fortissimo climax, Schubert ushers the opening idea back in with a pair of gentle, pleasingly dissonant heartbeats. The entire opening section is played again, da capo. *—Blair Johnston*

Recommended:

- ○ **Sviatoslav Richter** / Richter / DG 457668
- ○ **Schubert: Impromptus; Allegretto** / Schnabel / 1988 / EMI 61021

Dances and Marches (1812–1828)

Austrian composer Franz Schubert provided dance music for parties and functioned as a sort of Biedermeyer DJ. But unlike the DJs of today's post-modernist pop music, Schubert had to compose all the music himself. More to the point, he had to be able to play it himself. This last demand required that Schubert's dances had to be relatively easy to play; after all, Schubert was a young man who was not himself entirely uninclined to imbibe, as his many drinking songs attest. In a short list of dances Schubert wrote for solo piano, Brian Newbould lists 22 sets of *Deutschers*, Minuets, *Ecossaises*, Waltzes, *Landlers*, *Valse nobles*, and *Valse sentimentales* with 291 separate dances, and that is merely a fraction of the number listed in the *New Grove*. Some of these are simply dance music with light rhythms and lighter melodies. Some of them, especially the later sets of *Valse sentimentales* (D. 779) from 1823 and the *Valse nobles* (D. 969) of 1826, with their tender melodies, poignant harmonies, and lilting rhythms, are nearly as fine as any of Schubert's short pieces for his last years. Schubert also wrote a number of dances for piano duet, but while these are often as attractive as the earlier sets of solo piano dances, they are generally less affecting. Schubert also wrote several sets of marches for duo piano, most famously the three *Marches militaries* (D. 733) from 1818, known and loved by generations of music lovers. He also composed a tragic but not altogether convincing *Grand marche funebre* (D. 859) in 1825 and a noble but not especially impressive *Grand marche heroique* (D. 885) for the coronation of Nicolas I of Russia in 1826. *—James Leonard*

Recommended:

- ○ **Schubert: Danses** / T. Leonhardt / 2002 / Cascavelle 3054

Fantasia in C major ("Wanderer"), D. 760 (Nov., 1822)

With its four-movement plan—Allegro, Adagio, Scherzo, and Finale—the *"Wanderer" Fantasy* is a sonata in all but name, though a remarkable one for its time. The work is cyclic in form and played as one continuous movement without breaks, every section having a thematic relationship, usually a distant one, to *"Der Wanderer,"* a song Schubert had composed seven years earlier. This departure from classical sonata form resembles the equally impressive and demanding Liszt piano sonata; but that is not all. The intimate nature of most of Schubert's lieder, and much of his mature piano music, is here replaced by a work on an heroic scale in which a fragmentary rhythmical pattern—long, short-short, long, short-short, long, long—heard in the first few bars of the Allegro is expanded, inverted, repeated and elaborated with dazzling effect. Schubert continues to play hide and seek with the idea throughout the opening section, returning to it in the finale so that, in many places, the effect, is more like set of variations on a rhythmic pattern than a sonata subject in its own right.

But the *"Wanderer"* is by no means a "one idea" work. Schubert did not give it the title, though it is useful for distinguishing the C major work from his other piano Fantasias. In contrast to the bravura of the first section the brooding melody of the song is revealed (slightly altered) as a lyrical interlude before further excursions. In an unfolding stream of movement come a rondo, an attempted (but soon-abandoned) fugue and, in the Scherzo, a fast waltz. Despite such contrasting elements there is a sense of continuity and integrity in the way Schubert explores each new idea before returning to the now-familiar opening and, in the final bars, releasing it from its obsessional rhythm with a whoop of joy. *—Roy Brewer*

Recommended:

- ○ **Dvořák: Piano Concerto; Schubert: Fantasy** / Richter / 1998 / EMI 66947
- ○ **Schumann: Fantasie. Op 17, Schubert: Fantasia D760** / Pollini / DG 447451

Fantasia for piano, 4 hands in F minor, D. 940 (1828)

Schubert wrote more popular works for piano, four hands and longer works for piano, four hands, but he never wrote a better work for piano, four hands than the *Fantaisie in F minor*, D. 940. Composed in January 1828, the work was premiered by Schubert and his friend, composer Franz Lachner, on May 9 of the same year at one the year's few *Schuebrtiads*. The work is in four continuous sections unified by the opening theme's melancholy tone of endless tragedy. It opens in the tonic with the sad, simple, and soulful tune Allegro molto moderato. This is followed by a stormy Largo in F sharp minor of tremendous pathos and power, then an Allegro vivace Scherzo also in F sharp minor. The tonic returns for the final section, a massive double fugue with a new subject set against the opening tune as a second subject. After an enormous polyphonic climax and a brief pause, the sad, simple, and soulful tune returns one last time, battered and beaten, but still singing its elegiac song. The work was dedicated to Karoline, the daughter of his one time patron, the Duke of Esterhazy, and bears an opus number assigned by the composer himself. *—James Leonard*

Recommended:

- ○ **Richter Plays Schubert** / Richter, Britten / Music & Arts 722
- ○ **Emil Gilels 3** / Gilels / 1999 / Philips 456799
- ○ **Mozart & Schubert: Music for Piano 4 Hands** / Perahia, Lupu / 1992 / Sony 39511

Four Impromptus, D. 899 (ca. 1827)

It really isn't fair that such weighty compositions as the four pieces contained in Franz Schubert's Op. 90 (D. 899) were given the rather inappropriate title "Impromptus" by their publisher when the first two went to press in late 1827; it wasn't until 1857 that Op. 90, Nos. 3 and 4 appeared in print. These are not just pieces of higher-grade musical meat than the average short piano piece of the 1820s. These are pieces of considerable length, three of them even spanning more than 200 bars, each a well thought-out expression of pianism that creates no sense of improvisation. The four *Impromptus*, D. 899 were probably composed at least in part during the composer's stay in Dornbach in the summer of 1827; they seem all to have been put to paper by the time Schubert arrived in Graz in September.

The first piece, in C minor, is marked Allegro molto moderato and starts off with a firm double-octave utterance, the likes of which would pop up again some five decades later at the start of Johannes Brahms' *C minor Piano Quartet*. Instantly, however, Schubert pulls this solid rug out from under our feet and proffers a limber, pianissimo melody—initially unaccompanied, but soon harmonized in march-like fashion—that, in one form or another, will saturate the entire piece, most notably in the shape of a warm A flat major melody that rides on top of triplet arpeggios in first the left and then the right hand. The piece falls into two loose halves, the second of which starts off with a reworking of the opening measures of the first—the continuous triplets now propel the music forward in dramatic fashion—and then recasts the A flat major melody in G major.

There is something etude-like about the far-flung, continuous eighth notes in Op. 90, No. 2 in E flat major/minor. During the middle section of this "da capo" piece these eighth Schubert breaks the eighth notes up a bit to set up some powerful sforzandos. Somewhat surprisingly, the piece veers into the minor mode during its ever-faster coda and never escapes back into the major mode.

If you took the Adagio cantabile of Beethoven's *Pathétique Piano Sonata* and mated it with any of a dozen Chopin Nocturnes you'd probably come up with something very like the *Andante in G flat major*, Op. 90, No. 3. In fact, Schubert lifted the cadential gesture of this lovely melody straight from that heavenly Beethoven movement.

The last impromptu of D. 899 is an Allegretto in A flat minor/major that more or less assumes the form of a scherzo and trio (Schubert even goes so far as to call the less-frantic middle section a "trio"). At the start of the piece, all attention is fixed on the cascading 16th note arpeggios, but midway through the "scherzo" portion—which is of course reprised "da capo" after the trio—Schubert inserts a delightfully swinging melody into the upper voice of the left hand. *—Blair Johnston*

Recommended:

- ○ **Schubert: Impromptus; Allegretto D915** / Schnabel / 1988 / EMI 61021
- ○ **Edwin Fischer Plays Schubert** / Fischer / 1998 / Testament 1145
- ○ **Schubert** / Schiff / 1998 / London 458139
- ○ **Maria João Pires - Le Voyage Magnifique** / Pires / 1997 / DG 457550

Four Impromptus, D. 935 (Dec., 1827)

When applied to these works of Franz Schubert, the term Impromptu is doubly misleading. None of Schubert's works in the genre (there are two sets, D. 899, and D. 935, both written in the year 1827) suggest the salonesque, extemporaneous quality that the term connotes; quite to the contrary, these are tightly knit, structurally cohesive works, often of great lyric intensity. Nor should the term be taken—again, as is often the case—to represent any diminution of scale; the longest of Schubert's examples lasts well over ten minutes! It is not surprising then to realize that the title, "Impromptu," was assigned to these works by Schubert's Viennese Publisher, Haslinger, and not the composer himself.

Schubert may, in fact, have had something much larger in mind when he composed D. 935: Robert Schumann suggested that the key sequence of the four pieces

(Nos. 1 and 4 in F minor, and Nos. 2 and 3 in A flat and B flat, respectively) formed a sonata in all but name. There is a markedly greater degree of overall unity among these Impromptus than we find in the more disparate first series, D. 899, and Schumann's observation is further strengthened by the unmistakable motivic associations between Nos. 1 and 4—a quality often associated with the opening and closing movements of a sonata. However, it is easy for this line of thought to become strained, and, whatever Schubert's intentions may have been, the urgent, driving rhythms and decorative melodic style found in these four pieces aligns them with the first popular examples of the Impromptu genre, written in Hungary during the 1820s.

The first of the set is composed in a kind of sonata-rondo form (or, perhaps more accurately in this case, a sonata-allegro form with no development), with a declamatory opening theme to which the gentler, pulsating thoughts of the two "B" sections act as the perfect foil.

The second Impromptu is a comely Allegretto, the first measures of which bear a striking resemblance to those of Beethoven's *Piano Sonata No. 12*, Op. 26 in the same key. The similarity is fleeting, however, leaving us to wonder if this ghost from the musical past was summoned by Schubert's conscious or unconscious mind. In the middle section, marked "trio" by the composer (though the movement is neither minuet nor scherzo), there is no melody per se, but rather a shapely arpeggiation in triplets.

The third impromptu of the group is a set of variations on the famous tune that Schubert had already used in both the *Rosamunde* music and the *Quartet in A minor*, D. 804. There are five variations in total, the last of which is built of sparkling virtuoso scales that finally give way to a sublime, almost chorale-like coda.

The last impromptu, Allegro scherzando, is nearly 500 measures long. A handful of rubberband-like ritardando/a tempo indications and half a dozen unexpected grand pauses help not only to make the sparkling *moto perpetuo* more exciting, but also to remind us of the pieces "scherzando" nature. *—AMG*

Recommended:

○ **Schubert: Impromptus; Allegretto D915** / Schnabel / 1988 / EMI 61021

○ **Maria João Pires - Le Voyage Magnifique** / Pires / 1997 / DG 457550

○ **Schubert: German Dances; Schubert: Grazer Galopp, etc.** / Schiff / 1998 / London 458139

○ **Edwin Fischer Plays Schubert** / Fischer / 1998 / Testament 1145

Three Marches Militaires for piano, 4 hands, D. 733 (ca. 1822)

Franz Schubert's *Trois marches militaires* (*Three Military Marches*), D. 733 are among the many works for piano, four hands that the composer produced around the time of his first summer stay at the Count of Ezterházy's summer home in Zseliz (1818). The 21-year-old Schubert accepted a job teaching music to the Count's two young daughters, probably as much to get out of his father's house for a while as for the honor of the employment, and four-hand piano music is of course superb for such instructive purposes.

Piano, four hand music was also, by and large, the only Schubert instrumental music that publishers cared to purchase during his short lifetime; the *Three Military Marches*, D. 733 were published in 1826 as Opus 51. Each is a true ternary (ABA) design; the central episode is called a trio, and the opening music is recalled, verbatim, for the closing section.

The first Military March is marked Allegro vivace and is cast in the key of D major. An unharmonized fanfare begins the affair, paving the way for a lively, pompous main theme. The trio, like the trios of the other two marches in the Opus, moves to the subdominant (here, G major). By far the best-known of the three marches, this piece contains one of Schubert's most widely performed and quoted themes. Liszt, who transcribed much of Schubert's music, wrote a masterful paraphrase of it (*Grand paraphrase de concert, S.426a*). There have also been numerous band and other arrangements of this march; perhaps less flattering to its original conception is its appearance in Igor Stravinsky's *Circus Polka*—a George Ballanchine "ballet for elephants."

Allegro molto moderato is the indication at the head of Op. 51, No. 2. In G major, it opens with a robust, full-blooded harmonic bombast, but makes room for some gentleness foreign to the previous march as it unfolds.

The most characteristically march-like of the three is probably the Military March No. 3 in E flat major. There are some colorful harmonic twists at the end of the march-proper, and a humorous bounce to the step of the trio. *—AMG*

Recommended:

○ **Schubert:Pièces for Piano 4 Hands** / Badura-Skoda, Bonatta / 1995 / Valois 4720

○ **Schubert: Piano Works for 4 Hands, Vol 2** / Jandó, Kollar / 1998 / Naxos 553441

Six Moments musicaux, D. 780 (1823–1828)

The title *Six Moments musicaux* (D. 780) was not Schubert's own and is perhaps inappropriate. One might reasonably conclude that these are not really "moments" of music at all, as some of the six pieces last more than five or six minutes. When considering that the original publisher's title was the horrible grammatical calamity *Momens musicals*, the idea that Schubert might have come up with or even approved the title becomes wholly unbelievable. However, by July 1828, when the *6 Moments musicaux* were published, Schubert was in no position to argue such matters—not only was he absolutely destitute, he was also fighting a losing battle for his very life.

The *Moments musicaux* were composed during 1827 and 1828, the third and last pieces, which were written during 1823 and 1824, excepted. Each is composed in a sectional form and many are dances of some kind. *No. 1* in C major is a minuet in the absolute abstract, meaning that, just as with a Chopin waltz, the music transcends all human footwork. The trio section rolls forward on wheels of seamless triplets.

The second *Moments musicaux* is an Andantino in A flat major, taking the shape of a gentle five-part rondo. The sparkling, dotted, homophonic, sicilienne-like rhythms in the opening music give way to pure melody and accompaniment in the form of regular left-hand arpeggiations in the F sharp minor B sections. The third piece was composed back in 1823. It has something of an Eastern European tang to it, and as a result the publisher originally tacked the label "Air Russe" to it.

There is something of Bach about the fortspinnung-like fourth piece, a Moderato in C sharp minor. It unfolds in the major mode in the middle portion, where any such reference to the minor is lost within a pianissimo dream world of richly textured syncopations that somehow seem to make reference to Johannes Brahms a decade before he was even born.

More purely Schubertian is the Allegro vivace in F minor that follows, an athletic piece of equestrian rhythms. It is composed in as textbook a rounded binary form as one might imagine.

The final piece of D. 780 is an Allegretto in A flat major that returns to the otherworldly minuet variety of the first piece. Schubert plays with listeners' harmonic expectations in the cleverest and most moving of ways. A move to E major during the second half of the minuet-proper (as opposed to the trio section) sounds somehow full of resignation; the modulation back to A flat a few measures later is absolutely heartwarming. During the codetta that precedes the trio section, Schubert teases with hints of A major/E major, but, in a startling move, snaps straight into A flat minor—and since this opening section of music is repeated verbatim after the trio, it is in this bleakest of minor modes that the piece ends. *—Blair Johnston*

Recommended:

○ **Schubert** / Schiff / 1998 / London 458139

○ **Edwin Fischer Plays Schubert** / Fischer / 1998 / Testament 1145

○ **Schubert** / Orkis / 2000 / Angel 61797

○ **Artur Schnabel Plays Schubert Vol. 2** / Schnabel / Pearl 9272

Piano Sonata No. 4 in A minor, D. 537 (Mar., 1817)

Franz Schubert spent a good part of spring 1817 and most of the following summer composing piano sonatas. The first of these 1817 sonatas, the *Piano Sonata in A minor*, D. 537, written during March and published some 35 years later as Opus 164, is also in fact the first work of its kind that Schubert managed to finish; each of the previous three piano sonatas is incomplete or fragmentary. Schubert had just turned 19 when he wrote the piece, and already he had achieved things previously unimagined in the world of German song; but success as a composer of instrumental music would elude him for some time to come. D. 537 reveals both those facets of genius that would enable him to eventually make his own mark on concert music, and those obstacles that, as a young composer, he at times found insurmountable.

Schubert's two earliest surviving piano sonatas each lacks a finale; in D. 537 Schubert does provide a finale, but it is somewhat unsure of its footing, and in retrospect it seems reasonable to ascribe the unfinished status of the first two sonatas to the fact that Schubert had not yet come to grips with the material needed to bring a piano sonata to a satisfying close. The first movement, on the other hand, follows the track of progress that we already note between the opening movements of the Sonatas Nos. 1 and 2—the First Sonata opens with a movement of quite uncertain achievement, while the Second, written about a half-year after the First, shows marked improvement.

This Fourth Sonata dates from a year-and-a-half later, and the improvement is understandably even more pronounced. Banished from this Allegro ma non troppo are the imitations of Mozart and early Beethoven that fill much those two pieces' opening movements, and in their place is a rich lyric vein all Schubert's own. The swaying opening theme, one of the gentlest "fortes" anywhere, and the swirling, buttermilk second subject are both especially pleasing. Throughout the movement Schubert uses repetition—sometimes in long-unfolding sequences—to good effect, as when, before the development, a pulsating passage of slowly descending figures taken from the second theme winds its way down to triple-piano, only to burst forth with a sudden and passionate fortissimo. The recapitulation starts in D minor rather than A minor—something not at all uncommon in Schubert's music.

The Allegretto quasi Andantino in E major that follows is highly sectionalized, with many internal repeats marked; its principal melody has a certain Haydnesque quality to it.

The finale (Allegro vivace) is a kind of sonata-allegro movement without development. Schubert's use of so many grand pauses is bold, but at times a little disconcerting—it takes a wonderful pianist to pull them all off. A pair of plastic melodies have a delightful bounce to their steps, and are a wonderful change from the dry, uncouth scales that open the movement. *—Blair Johnston*

Recommended:

- ○ **Michelangeli Plays Brahms, Schubert & Beethoven** / Michelangeli / 1999 / DG 457762
- ○ **Schubert: Complete Piano Sonatas Vol. 3** / Klien / 1996 / VoxBox 5175
- ○ **Schubert: Piano Sonatas** / Schiff / Decca 448390
- ○ **Schubert: Piano Sonatas** / Kempff / DG 463766
- ○ **Schubert: Piano Sonatas** / Badura-Skoda / Arcana 909

Piano Sonata No. 9 in B major, D. 575 (Aug., 1817)

Sonata composition did not come easily to Schubert, and throughout the works of 1817 we can follow his struggles with the genre in great detail—a triumph here, a frustration there. Schubert had not yet managed to consistently infuse his instrumental works with the individual voice that characterized his song compositions; with the *B major Piano Sonata*, however, Schubert at last succeeded in crafting a piano sonata that is, for better or worse (there are those who feel the Sonata to be disorganized and haphazard), fully and unmistakably Schubertian. That D. 575 (August, 1817—published posthumously in 1847 as Op. 147) was a step forward in his career as an instrumental composer was not lost on its composer; after a half year during which he composed almost nothing but piano sonatas, he abandoned sonata composition until well into the next year, choosing to instead direct his energies towards a series of large-scale orchestral works (including the *Sixth Symphony*).

The first movement, Allegro ma non troppo, is characterized by a lively dotted rhythm which inhabits both the ambitious and energetic first theme and the more unassuming second subject (dolce). Schubert's development is notable for harmonic trickery: he returns to the tonic key after only 19 bars, suggesting an impending recapitulation; instead, he delays for another half-dozen bars and then recapitulates in the subdominant key. The following Andante is a straightforward ternary movement that contrasts a chorale-like main melody with more active figurations; when the main theme returns, it is subtly combined with this middle-section character.

The scherzo is in G major, with a trio section in D. With the finale (Allegro giusto), Schubert moves again into the world of sonata-allegro form, but with an entirely different purpose than in the first movement. Humor abounds, beginning with the pompous D major tune that interrupts the main melody barely a dozen bars into the movement. The real second melody is graceful and sweet, a tone maintained through the exposition's close and much of the development section. During the recapitulation Schubert expands upon the D major interruption in order to reforge the exposition's tonal plan so that the movement might end, as it must, in B major. *—Blair Johnston*

Recommended:

- ○ **Schubert: Piano Sonatas** / Kempff / DG 463766
- ○ **Schubert: Piano Sonatas** / Badura-Skoda / Arcana 909
- ○ **Schubert: Complete Piano Sonatas Vol. 1** / Klien / 1996 / VoxBox 5173
- ○ **Schubert: Piano Sonatas** / Richter / 1996 / BBC 4010

Piano Sonata No. 13 in A major, D. 664 (Jul., 1819)

It was long assumed that Franz Schubert's *Piano Sonata in A major*, D. 664 (the shorter and earlier of two piano sonatas in that key) was composed during the middle months of 1825—the same period that saw the production of three other piano sonatas (D. 840, 845, and 850). The complete Schubert works' edition of the late nineteenth century—still today a prevalent and vastly influential publication—attributes the work to that year; more recent thinking, however, has relocated the piece in the summer of 1819, which Schubert spent vacationing with a close friend in Steyr, some hundred miles to the west of Vienna.

Schubert makes reference in a personal letter written during that summer to having composed a new sonata; stylistically speaking, this delightful and, compared to the other pre-1826 sonatas, well-known *A major Sonata* fits the bill quite nicely. It is composed not in the Classical four movements but rather in just three; there is no minuet/scherzo movement.

The leisurely and melodious opening movement (Allegro moderato) has several outstanding features, not the least of which is a gentle second theme that pays rhythmic homage to the Allegretto of Beethoven's *Seventh Symphony* (neither the first nor the last time Schubert would pay such tribute to that movement). The harmonies surrounding the opening theme are rich and full, but the tune itself is crafted from translucent material. Schubert calls for the entirety of the development and recapitulation to be repeated, something common in the eighteenth century but almost unheard of in Schubert's music.

The central Andante has an almost obsessive aspect to it, not reduced in any way by the absolute saturation of the movement with a single rhythmic thought; as the opening music is reprised in the second half of the movement, Schubert allows the two hands to play in canon with one another. Humor, or at least playfulness, is a key ingredient of the finale—just listen to the stop and go rhythm of the second subject, and to the way that the forzando chords of the coda briefly get lost within their own chromatic sphere. The final bars of the Sonata are as tender a recount of the opening melody, pianissimo and molto legato, as one can imagine. *—Blair Johnston*

Recommended:

- ○ **Schubert: Complete Piano Sonatas Vol. 2** / Klien / 1996 / Vox 5174
- ○ **Schubert: The Piano Sonatas** / Kempff / DG 463766
- ○ **Schubert: Piano Sonatas** / Badura-Skoda / Arcana 909

Piano Sonata No. 14 in A minor ("Grande Sonate"), D. 784 (Feb., 1823)

Franz Schubert composed his *Piano Sonata in A minor*, D. 784, in February, 1823; it was not published until 11 years after his death (as Opus 143). Four years had passed since he last turned out a work in the genre, and nearly every aspect of his life and music had changed considerably and irrevocably during the interval. Schubert had contracted syphilis in 1822, and during the early months of the following year he was largely confined to his father's house in the hope that his ravaged health might be salvaged. Musically speaking, Schubert had finally, starting with the *Quartettsatz* of 1820, found ways to pour into his instrumental music the same essence of his peculiar genius that had long animated his lieder. It is therefore in no way surprising that this *A minor Sonata* is in most ways completely unlike the charming, generally docile piano sonatas written between 1817 and 1819.

The three movements of the *Piano Sonata in A minor*, D. 784, show an almost total disregard for the conventions of Classical pianism. Harmonic figuration and melodic ornamentation as it was known to Haydn, Mozart, or even Beethoven are absent, and in their place is a kind of sparse, basic texture that has often been called "unpianistic."

The first movement is built out of large blocks of sound, often in bare octaves, that occasionally burst forth into aggressive dotted gestures or, with the arrival of the pianissimo second subject in E major, bell-like quarter notes. The rhythm throughout the movement can only be described as hyper-repetitive; behind this apparently static screen (an impression aided by the profusion of long-sustained pedal-points), however, is a very potent fury.

The following Andante is, by comparison, warm and engaging; its lovely arch-shaped melody is eventually thrown into the left hand and shadowed, two octaves above, by the triplets of the right hand.

The finale is a wild thing composed mostly in running triplets; there is a constant kinetic energy, made all the more palpable by furious imitation between the hands. A more melodious idea occasionally breaks in to dispel this demonic undercurrent (the movement is a kind of rondo). *—Blair Johnston*

Recommended:

- ○ **Schubert: Piano Sonata 13 & 14; Impromptus** / Richter / 1992 / Olympia 288
- ○ **Schubert: Piano Sonatas** / Kempff / DG 463766
- ○ **Schubert: Piano Sonatas** / Badura-Skoda / Arcana 909
- ○ **Schubert: Complete Piano Sonatas Vol. 2** / Klien / 1996 / Vox 5174

Piano Sonata No. 15 in C major ("Relique"), D. 840 (Apr., 1825)

Spring of 1825 found Schubert working, along with a number of smaller projects, on two groundbreaking sonatas for pianoforte—one eventually completed and the other abandoned midstride. The finished member of that pair is the now-famous *Sonata in A minor*, D. 845; the unfinished work, the *Piano Sonata in C major*, D. 840, begun and abandoned in April, has survived in its incomplete form and is now sometimes known as the "Relique" (the name is of course not Schubert's). Had this been a work of Brahms, the remains would surely be lost to posterity; Schubert, however, was considerably less conscious of posterity and not at all interested in "cleaning up" his musical workshop; what exists of the "Reliquie" was eventually collected and published some 30 years after his death.

Two panels of the "Relique" are complete: the first movement (Moderato) and the slow movement (Andante); the minuet and finale remain only half-baked. The first movement is striking, unconventional, and even visionary, but in the end it is not always successful; it may be that after this on-again/off-again, movement the rest of the Sonata was doomed to incompletion. Spacious gestures are set up by steady, repeating rhythms, and the kind of shocking modulations that we expect from Schubert are in full effect (he allows himself just a single jarring chromatic shift to move from the dominant of C to the dominant of B for the start of the second subject!). There is at times, however, a certain ungainliness to the music—an occasional collapse of rhythmic stride—that hinders some of the beautiful moments, and one suspects that Schubert never really got the kind of handle on the music that he might have liked.

The C minor Andante is both languid and stormy. There is a great torrent of octaves in the last ten bars that, in the end, cannot sustain its fury and subsides into an uncertain pianissimo. The minuet in A flat major is, as mentioned, incomplete, but Schubert did skip ahead to put its G sharp minor trio section to paper in full. What there is of the minuet is ridden with unusual harmonic twists and turns, and Schubert seems to have become utterly disoriented at the very point where he abandoned the movement. The finale breaks away after about 270 bars. *—Blair Johnston*

Recommended:

- ○ **Richter - Schubert** / Richter / Philips 438483
- ○ **Schubert: Piano Sonatas** / Kempff / DG 463766
- ○ **Schubert: Piano Sonatas** / Badura-Skoda / Arcana 909
- ○ **Schubert: Complete Piano Sonatas Vol. 1** / Klien / 1996 / VoxBox 5173

Piano Sonata No. 16 in A minor, D. 845 (May, 1825)

Only three of Franz Schubert's completed piano sonatas were published during his lifetime: the G major work of 1826 (D. 894) and the two sonatas composed during the spring and summer of 1825, D. 850 in D major and the *Piano Sonata in A minor*, D. 845, sometimes called No. 16. The *A minor Sonata* was the first of the three to pass through a printing press, in early 1826, and the effect of its publication was quick and pronounced. Through the mid-1820s, Schubert had been known almost exclusively as a composer of lieder since those were by and large the only pieces of his that publishers cared to purchase. With the release of the *A minor Piano Sonata*, D. 845 Schubert was suddenly the darling of many critics, and some of his fellow musicians began to think of casting him in the unenviable role of Beethoven's successor.

The *Piano Sonata in A minor*, D. 845 stands as far from the sonatas composed during Schubert's teenage years as one might imagine. Something of the terse, granite-faced quality of the previous *A minor Sonata* (D. 784 of 1823) is present in the opening movement, Moderato, of D. 845, but now there is also a hint of the starry-eyed otherworldliness—an absolute disdain for reality—that mark the final sonatas of 1828 as things truly special. The limber main theme is given right at the start in bare octaves; the second theme, presented in part before we have even arrived at the second theme key area, is really a new spin on the opening idea. Throughout the development section and, later on, the lengthy coda to the movement, the music of the opening bars reappears at length.

The following movement, Andante poco moto, is an ingenious and technically demanding set of variations (five in all) on a theme. The Scherzo (Allegro vivace) contrasts a squat, rhythmic opening with a trio section that, while retaining the same basic metric framework, remolds it into a spinning pianissimo. The finale (Allegro vivace) is a rondo built around a lean main idea; there is no contrasting lyric material, only music that either scampers around or asserts itself with dramatic forzandos. *—Blair Johnston*

Recommended:

- ○ **Schubert: Sonatas, D845 & 850** / Richter / 1995 / Melodiya 29463
- ○ **Schubert: Piano Sonatas** / Kempff / DG 463766
- ○ **Schubert: Sonatas for the Pianoforte Vol. 4** / Badura-Skoda / 1994 / Arcana 14
- ○ **Schubert: Complete Piano Sonatas Vol. 1** / Klien / 1996 / VoxBox 5173

Piano Sonata No. 17 in D major ("Gasteiner"), D. 850 (Aug., 1825)

On May 20, 1825, Schubert departed Vienna in order to tour upper Austria with the famous singer Michael Vogl, who would join him in Gmunden. As the unusually hot summer wore on, the composer found the heat nearly unbearable, though it apparently did not prevent the concert tour from achieving great success. In August, Schubert spent three weeks in the town of Gastein, located in the Austrian Alps, where, with his usual facility, he wrote this sonata and two songs. Although this so-called "Gasteiner" sonata was the composer's nineteenth keyboard sonata (including fragmentary efforts), it was only the second to be published in his lifetime.

While the heat of the 1825 summer did not encumber Schubert's inspiration, it may have stepped up his tempo indications. The composer usually tempered his Allegro markings with "moderato," but in the first and third movements he chose Allegro vivace instead. In fact, the entire sonata—the slow movement included—is swifter in pace than is typical for Schubert.

One of the two songs he wrote while in Gastein was *Das Heimweh* (Homesickness); its opening melody bears an uncanny resemblance to that of the second subject in the first movement. This lively movement—deriving its thematic material from repeated scales and chords—offers much color and excitement, but at the expense of making considerable technical demands on the performer.

The second movement (marked Con moto) has a mood of intimacy and warmth to its main theme, but this is combined with a sense of lively animation. The ensuing panel is a jaunty, rather quirky Scherzo (Allegro vivace), full of playfulness and cheer. The trio section is stately and serious, contrasting well with the other music.

The finale (a rondo marked Allegro moderato) opens in the upper register with a playful, marchlike theme. Further episodes offer color and contrast; the middle section, for example, presents a lovely lyrical theme that suddenly turns stormy. Like the first movement, the music here presents considerable challenges to the pianist throughout, both technically and interpretively. *—Robert Cummings*

Recommended:

- ○ **Schubert: Piano Sonatas, D845 & 850** / Richter / 1995 / Melodiya 29463
- ○ **Schnabel Plays Schubert** / Schnabel / EMI 64259
- ○ **Schubert: Piano Sonatas** / Kempff / DG 463766
- ○ **Schubert: Piano Sonata, Op 53; Beethoven: Piano Concerto 5** / Lupu / Seven Seas 145
- ○ **Schubert: Piano Sonatas** / Badura-Skoda / Arcana 909

Piano Sonata No. 18 in G major ("Fantasy"), D. 894 (Oct., 1826)

It was the idea of the original publisher of Franz Schubert's *Piano Sonata in G major*, D. 894, Tobias Haslinger, not to call the work a sonata. Presumably because he felt the gentle opening movement to be so far from the traditional, rigorous sonata-opener that he knew his potential customers would expect, he provided it with the rather misleading surrogate title *"Fantasie, Andante, Menuetto, and Allegretto"*; the entire Sonata has ever since been known as *"Fantasy,"* or *"Sonata-Fantasy"*. This is ironic, since the opening movement that inspired Haslinger's nomenclature is probably one of the tamest and "most perfect" (as Robert Schumann said of it) sonata-allegros Schubert ever composed.

D. 894 was written during October 1826, and is one of just three Schubert piano sonatas published during the composer's lifetime (in 1827, as Opus 78). Schubert had to take what he could get from publishers, and, however he might have felt about the work's title, his stagnant finances hardly put him in a position to bicker.

The four movements are Molto moderato e cantabile, Andante (Schubert's preferred indication for a sonata "slow" movement), Allegro moderato (the minuet and trio), and Allegretto. The first movement differs from the textbook sonata-allegro only in texture and tone, not in the basics of its actual form: the two principal subjects are both given in their traditional keys and, unlike many of Schubert's sonata-movements, the recapitulation takes place in the home key of G major. There may be no more patient melody in all of Schubert than the pianissimo opening tune, whose animation seems at times to become all but suspended. The unseen force that propels this relaxed exposition comes to the fore in the cataclysmic, triple-fortissimo climaxes of the development.

The tender, almost Schumannesque main melody of the following Andante is made to embrace some wildly contrasting sections of music, during which fortissimo sforzandos spill over into cascading figures. The Minuet is aristocratic, with a gracious, ornamented trio.

The refrain theme of the Rondo finale is nearly as unhurried as the opening theme of the first movement. The delightfully contrasting ideas include a happy peasant dance and, during the central episode, a cantabile tune in C minor. After the last reprise of the refrain idea, to which is appended a witty and wonderful coda, the four bars that opened the movement appear one last time—un poco più lento, lovingly—to draw the final cadence. *—Blair Johnston*

Recommended:

- ○ **Richter - Schubert** / Richter / Philips 438483
- ○ **Schubert: Piano Sonatas** / Kempff / DG 463766
- ○ **Schubert: Piano Sonatas** / Badura-Skoda / Arcana 909
- ○ **Schubert: Piano Sonatas, D845 & 894** / Lupu / 1987 / London 417640
- ○ **Schubert: Complete Piano Sonatas Vol. 1** / Klien / 1996 / VoxBox 5173

Piano Sonata No. 19 in C minor, D. 958 (1828)

Franz Schubert's final three piano sonatas—stunning achievements that only began to grab a place in pianists' repertoires during the latter half of the twentieth century—were all finished in September 1828, just two months before the composer died. The first of these three massive and challenging sonatas, at least as far as numbering goes, is the *Piano Sonata in C minor*, D. 958, sometimes called No. 19; like the other two piano sonatas of 1828, it is a work that Schubert dedicated to the pianist Johann Hummel. Hummel had a year earlier been present at a private evening of Schubert lieder and had expressed his admiration for the composer in the highest terms. The Sonata, however, was not published until 1839, a few years after Hummel's death, and the publisher unjustly struck Schubert's dedication from the piece and made a new one to Robert Schumann.

Schubert had, by 1828, come a long way from his days as a teenage pupil of Antonio Salieri; he still, however, cherished the traditional four-movement sonata blueprint. In the *C minor Piano Sonata* these four movements are marked Allegro, Adagio, Allegro (the minuet and trio), and Allegro.

The opening Allegro begins as a grim, stone-faced affair in punctuated chords; the first thought is soon given a new spin with an Alberti-bass style accompaniment. The second subject of this sonata-allegro movement is a tender, legato notion; most of the unusual development section is concerned with a chromatically meandering idea in the bass. Eventually the right hand adorns this mysterioso bassline with chromatic scales up and down the keyboard. There are few Schubert endings as inutterably stark as that of this first movement.

The presence of an Adagio in a Schubert piano sonata is something of a peculiarity—adagio was never one of the composer's preferred slow movement tempo indications. The movement is in the noblest kind of A flat major, and has a melody that, in both shape and treatment, hearkens back to Beethoven's serene slow movements. The triplet-ridden, unstable contrasting material is more typically Schubertian.

The minuet is full of metric witticisms, or at least rhythmic quirks, the most immediately obvious of which are the full-measure rests that mark the return of the opening tune just before the easygoing A flat major trio.

The finale is immense; its constant horse-gallop rhythm embraces a far-flung tonal plan. After the last of several tuneful efforts has been wiped clean, nearly a hundred bars of the unrelenting horse-gallop draws the movement to its terse final cadence. *—Blair Johnston*

Recommended:

- ○ **Schubert: Piano Sonatas 19 & 21** / Richter / 1993 / Olympia 335
- ○ **Schubert: Klaviersonaten, D958 & 959** / Pollini / 1987 / DG 427327
- ○ **Schubert: Piano Sonatas** / Kempff / DG 463766
- ○ **Schubert: Piano Sonatas** / Badura-Skoda / Arcana 909
- ○ **Schubert: Complete Piano Sonatas Vol. 1** / Klien / 1996 / VoxBox 5173

Piano Sonata No. 20 in A major, D. 959 (Sep., 1828)

This is Schubert's penultimate piano sonata, written in September 1828—about three months before his death. It is one of three that he wrote after the death of Beethoven (March 19, 1827), whose funeral he attended with Hummel. The passing of this great master was an important event in the life of Schubert, for though mourned the loss of the musician he greatly admired, he also perhaps felt somewhat liberated from the older composer's dominance. Appropriately, each of these last three piano sonatas contain stylistic nods to Beethoven; in the case of this A major sonata, the Rondo is based on the finale (also a Rondo) of Beethoven's *Sonata No. 16 in G major.*

The work opens with dramatic, stately chords which yield to gentler music, using the same material. The second subject is particularly lovely in its lyrical warmth and passion. The development offers both playfulness and tension, and the coda is grand and complex.

Many take the view that the ensuing Andantino, though it is not the longest or grandest of the four panels here, is the most profound. Its mesmerizing main theme is dreamy and mysterious, but often seeming on the verge of erupting into a storm. The second subject introduces a great deal of tension, eventually leading to a dramatic climax. This movement seems to pit serenity and violence, or even reason and madness, against one another.

The Scherzo is delightful in its lightness and good spirits. Yet for all the effervescence here, there is considerable craftsmanship: the arpeggiated chords appearing at the outset are a variant of the somewhat sinister ones at the end of the Andantino. The finale, as mentioned above, pays tribute to Beethoven; yet, the only truly imitative element is Schubert's borrowing of a theme from the slow movement of his own *A minor Piano Sonata,* D. 537.

This is one of Schubert's most popular piano sonatas, enjoying currency on both the recital stage and in the recording studio. Ironically, the composer could not get this masterpiece published in the remaining months of his life. It would be published in 1839, though his reputation would not begin to grow appreciably until after 1856, when he was discovered and championed by English musicologist, George Grove. *—Robert Cummings*

Recommended:

- ○ **Schnabel Plays Schubert** / Schnabel / EMI 64259
- ○ **Schubert: Klaviersonaten, D958 & 959** / Pollini / 1987 / DG 427327
- ○ **Schubert: Klaviersonate, D959; Moments musicaux, D780** / Kovacevich / 1995 / EMI 55219
- ○ **Schubert: Piano Sonatas** / Badura-Skoda / Arcana 909
- ○ **Schubert: Complete Piano Sonatas Vol. 2** / Klien / 1996 / Vox 5174

Piano Sonata No. 21 in B flat major, D. 960 (Sep., 1828)

Many of Schubert's greatest works belong to his last year, a veritable Annus Mirabilis which saw the creation of the *"Great" C major Symphony,* the *String Quintet, D. 956,* the piano trios D. 929 and D. 898, the *Mass in E flat ,D. 950,* and the *Fantasy in F minor for piano duet,* D. 940. On September 26, 1828, Schubert's *Piano Sonata in B flat major,* D. 960, his last instrumental work, was finished. The composer's last three sonatas debate limitation and leavetaking; Alfred Brendel suggests that they "lead us into romantic regions of wonderment, terror and awe." Perhaps the B flat sonata probes human mortality even more deeply than its fellows.

As Claudio Arrau once remarked, "this is a work written in the proximity of death... one feels it from the very first theme... the breaking off, and the silence after a long, mysterious trill in the bass." What Tovey described as "a sublime theme of utmost calmness and breadth" ends mysteriously with the same distant trill, returning intermittently to impart deeper anguish to music of sinister beauty. The exposition contains two other subsidiary themes, both in remote keys, and what follows also includes a remarkable self-quotation—the links between the B flat sonata's first-movement development and an insistent six-note theme taken from a setting of the cathedral scene from Goethe's *Faust,* composed in December 1814, are often overlooked. However, as John Reed suggests in *Schubert: The Final Years,* "many a recognisable variation strays much farther from its theme!"

The C sharp minor Andante sostenuto ranks alongside Schubert's finest slow movements. Sustained gravitas and sublimity of expression take us to the brink of the abyss: that remote, solitary place which T.S. Eliot knew as "the still point of the turning world." The music is dominated by a recurring figure in the accompaniment, spanning four octaves and enclosing a melody of effusive beauty. The distinctive rhythmic accompaniment recalls an Austrian folk song whose silent second beat would have enabled hammer-wielding artisans to synchronize their sledgehammer blows to maximum effect. Popular tradition maintains that Schubert observed a gang of laborers and noted down several of their work songs while on holiday at Gmunden during the summer months of 1815. The characteristic dotted-rhythm figure was used later in the *Notturno in E flat for Piano Trio (D. 897).*

A mercurial B flat major Scherzo follows, to be played "con delicatezza." But tension and incident are never absent from an overcast trio and an uneasy return to the Scherzo material via an improbable, albeit adjacent, A major. This trilogy of sonatas ends much as it began; Beethoven's influence emerges in a rondo finale whose main idea bears comparison with that of the movement written to replace the so-called *Grosse Fuge,* the original finale of Beethoven's *Quartet in B flat,* Op. 130. The rondo theme begins repeatedly in the false tonality of C minor, an ambiguity resolved as the theme appears for the last time, when, following extensive debate and development, the octave G which precedes it descends into the dominant key of F, in preparation for a brilliant final coda. "Thus Schubert ends both gaily and cheerfully," wrote Robert Schumann, "as though fully able to face another day's work." But history records otherwise: Schubert played his last three sonatas at a party held by Dr. Ignaz Menz on Saturday September 27, 1828, having finished the B flat work only the previous day. He died less than two months afterwards. *—Michael Jameson*

Recommended:

- ○ **Richter Live from Aldeburgh, 1964** / Richter / 1990 / Music & Arts 642
- ○ **Schubert: Piano Sonata in B Flat; 12 German Dances; Allegretto** / Kovacevich / 1995 / EMI 55359
- ○ **Schubert: Piano Sonatas** / Kempff / DG 463766
- ○ **Schubert: Piano Sonata, D960; Impromptus; Allegretto** / Pollini / DG 427326
- ○ **Schubert: Piano Sonatas** / Badura-Skoda / Arcana 909
- ○ **Schubert: Complete Piano Sonatas Vol. 3** / Klien / 1996 / VoxBox 5175

Three Pieces (Impromptus), D. 946 (May, 1828)

In 1827, Schubert wrote two sets of *Impromptus,* D. 899 and D. 935, each consisting of four pieces. Both collections have become staples in the keyboard repertory and are recognized as among the composer's greatest piano works. Much less well-known are these three compositions, often referred to in catalogs as the *Drei Klavierstücke,* which Schubert apparently intended to be part of yet another group of *Impromptus.* When they were completed, the composer left only tempo markings for titles. Thus, the three are titled as follows: Allegro assai (E flat minor); Allegretto (E flat major); Allegro (C major). What is difficult to explain about these pieces is their almost total neglect by pianists throughout the twentieth and into the twenty-first centuries. Their resultant lack of popularity among the public is hardly puzzling, but the relatively low opinion of them held by many musicologists is equally difficult to account for.

Most who examine these works will find they are examples of undeniably high art in the composer's keyboard output. The first two are in the rondo form of ABACA, while in the last, Schubert uses the more standard ternary form of ABA. Some musicologists have regarded the first piece primarily as a Scherzo with two trios. However one views its form, the music itself is rhythmic and lively in its main thematic material, then it turns richly Romantic in the long, slow section. After the return of the opening material, another theme is heard, also slow in contrast to the first subject and somewhat ponderous, too. After a reprise of the main themes, the piece ends.

The second item here begins in a serene, subdued mood, with the Allegretto marking sounding more like a Moderato. The theme is lovely, if somewhat wistful. Succeeding sections are lively by contrast, and offer much color and playfulness. Thus, the scheme Schubert uses here is opposite that in the first piece, with the outer sections essentially slow and the inner ones fast or lively. Overall, though, the piece serves the function of a slow movement in the set.

The third entry begins with robust good cheer, again the composer offering rhythmic drive and much color. Although the second subject is less driven and somewhat subdued, it is still lively and bright. While this is a well-crafted work, it is probably the least ambitious of the three in terms of individuality and formal complexity.

It would be difficult to compare the *Drei Klavierstücke* with its cousins, the two sets of *Impromptus*, from 1827. From a purely artistic point of view, however, all three collections can be ranked as major endeavors, with this group of three perhaps a mere rung below the other pair.

This collection was first published in 1868, at a time when the rediscovery of Schubert was beginning to take wing, owing to the efforts of English musicologist George Grove, who became a strong advocate of his music beginning in 1856. *–Robert Cummings*

Recommended:

- ○ **Maria João Pires - Le Voyage Magnifique** / Pires / 1997 / DG 457550
- ○ **Schubert: Piano Sonata, D960; Impromptus; Allegretto** / Pollini / DG 427326
- ○ **Kempff** / / 2000 / BBC 4045

Sonata for piano, 4 hands in C major ("Grand Duo"), D. 812 (Jun., 1824)

Considerable argument has taken place over this piano duet. For some time it was thought to be a "missing" Schubert symphony, composed at Bad Gastein. But modern musicological opinion is that the *"Great" C Major Symphony* was composed there, and that there is no missing work. Nevertheless, the character of this piano duet so strongly suggested symphonic form that several different orchestrations emerged during the nineteenth century; of these, Joseph Joachim's emerged victorious. The twentieth century English composer and conductor Raymond Leppard attempted his own orchestration, one that is both more imaginative and colorful and truer to Schubert's own manner or orchestration (Joachim's sounds very much like Brahms). The opening Allegro moderato is indeed symphonic in scope and drama. In the Andante con moto second movement Schubert seems to poke fun at his own stylistic habit of leaping to unexpected keys; when he does so here, the "textbook solution" key is reasserted through commonplace dominant chords, as if a schoolmaster has corrected an errant pupil. The scherzo is a strange piece, relieved by a trio which seems to strive to be as predictable as possible. The finale is predominantly humorous, despite the appearance of some noble lyrical passages. *–Joseph Stevenson*

Recommended:

- ○ **Schubert: Piano Sonata D812; Mozart: Piano Sonata K521** / Richter, Britten / Music & Arts 721
- ○ **Schubert: Music For Piano Duet II** / Eschenbach, Frantz / 1997 / EMI 69770

SYMPHONIC

Symphony No. 1 in D major, D. 82 (Oct., 1813)

Franz Schubert was 16 years old when, on October 18, 1813, he put the final touches on his first complete symphony, the *Symphony No. 1 in D major*, D. 82. An impressively polished product, it doubtlessly benefitted from the young composer's two earlier, abortive efforts in the genre (also in D major) and the handful of symphonic overtures he wrote in 1811 and 1812. Like the rest of Schubert's pre-1820 symphonies, the *Symphony No. 1* was not published until the late nineteenth century, when it was included in the original complete works edition. Schubert did, however, have the luxury of hearing it played during his lifetime; the obliging orchestra was possibly that of the seminary school from which the composer had recently disenrolled, or one of the ad-hoc ensembles put together in the house of Viennese music enthusiast Otto Hatwig.

The *Symphony No. 1* is by far the finest piece of *Schubert's* to date. Though it dates from the post-Beethoven era, the *Symphony No. 1* proudly displays Schubert's eighteenth century roots, established through his studies with Antonio Salieri (competitor of Mozart and admirer of Haydn). The grandiose Adagio introduction to the first movement and the Mozartian zip of that same movement's Allegro vivace main theme are unmistakably Classical in nature; as with many of Schubert's earliest works, there are countless superficial melodic nods to Beethoven, but the general manner of the work shows that, beyond such similarities of contour and inflection, Schubert yet had little access to the musical operations that lay at the heart of the master's symphonies.

Parts of the invigorating first movement's lengthy second subject were later deleted by the composer, presumably in the interest of structural balance, but are sometimes restored in performance. Somewhat unusually, the music of the Adagio introduction returns later in the movement to usher in the recapitulation. The Andante that follows is a light-footed movement, the graceful opening melody of which is countered by a marchlike second subject. The minuet (Allegro) returns to the boisterous D major of the first movement; its trio is an episode of great instrumental color, especially admirable for its woodwind scoring. The finale (Allegro vivace) bursts forth on a lively, much-ornamented idea in the violins; the vigorous coda that ends the Symphony is of a forcefulness and stiff harmonic fiber well outside the limits that Schubert's eighteenth century idols prescribed for themselves. *–Blair Johnston*

Recommended:

- ○ **Schubert: Symphonies 1 & 8** / Muti (cond.), Vienna PO / 1999 / Angel 73431
- ○ **Schubert: Symphonies 1 & 4** / Brueggen (cond.), Orch. of the 18th Century / 1997 / Philips 446688

Symphony No. 2 in B flat major, D. 125 (1814–1815)

The product of a brilliant 17-year-old, this symphony, while not a masterwork to rank with the Beethoven symphonies it emulated, is nevertheless a quite remarkable effort. Cast in four movements, it is already decidedly grander in scale and outlook than the 1813 *Symphony No. 1.*

The opening movement of the *Second* begins with a brief and sunny Largo introduction, after which the vigorous Allegro vivace main theme is presented by scurrying strings. The music here effervesces and brims with energy in its rising trajectory and seeming skyward flight, but soon a playful, comparatively serene melody is presented to offer brilliant contrast. The two themes are then developed imaginatively, and following a reprise, the movement ends with the same sunny, energetic character that predominated throughout.

The second movement, marked Andante, is a theme and variations whose source melody is rather simple and graceful, first played by the strings. The winds have much to say in the variations that follow and, save for one muscular variant midway through, the mood remains serene and gently playful. The ensuing Minuet, marked Allegro vivace, features a hearty, almost gruff dance tune in the outer sections and a light, playful trio at the center. The finale (Presto vivace) maintains the generally light and energetic moods of the first and third movements with a rhythmic, jaunty main theme and a carefree, somewhat playful alternate theme, which offers only mild contrast. This B flat major symphony generally lasts 30 to 35 minutes in performance. *–Robert Cummings*

Recommended:

- ○ **Schubert: Symphonies 2, 3, 5** / Brueggen (cond.), Orch. of the 18th Century / 1996 / Philips 446100
- ○ **Schubert: Symphony 2; Brahms: Symphony 2** / Böhm (cond.), London SO / 2002 / BBC 4104
- ○ **Schubert: Symphonies 2 & 6** / Harnoncourt (cond.), Concertgebouw / 1995 / Teldec 97510
- ○ **Schubert: Symphony 1–6, 8 & 9; Grand Duo; Rosamunde** / Abbado (cond.), CO of Europe / DG 423651

Symphony No. 3 in D major, D. 200 (1815)

When compared to the estimable boatload of vocal music he composed in 1815—nearly 150 lieder, three singspiels, and numerous choral works—Franz Schubert's instrumental output for the same year seems rather unimpressive. However, his second and third symphonic essays count among the total, and one might rightly conclude that these two splendid and sizeable works make up for any imbalance of musical direction. The *Symphony No. 3 in D major*, D. 200 was begun during late May and finished just under three months later, with the bulk of the work being done during July. Like each of the other early symphonies (the six written before the *"Unfinished" Symphony* of 1822), it was not published during Schubert's lifetime; only after it appeared in the first Schubert complete works edition in 1884 did it become an object of widespread attention.

Schubert places a slow introduction before the main body of the first movement. Perhaps more than any other episode of the Symphony, this shows Franz Joseph Haydn's indirect hand in the youthful Schubert's style: long-sustained octaves, complete with timpani roll, precede gradually shifting harmonies that, in true late Haydn fashion, migrate into a sullen D minor. The burst back into the major mode at the start of the Allegro con brio is a welcome one, and the fleetfooted tune that unfolds has the character of a peasant's dance to it; its infectious rhythms spread to the subsidiary melody as well. The Allegretto that follows is in ternary form; the central episode takes off on a clarinet solo, to which the strings lend a gentle "oompah" support—one of Schubert's most characteristically Viennese touches.

Filled with accented upbeats, the minuet (marked Vivace) is a particularly energetic example of its species. The oboe and bassoon get a nice duet during the German dance-like trio. The finale (Presto vivace) is a five-minute plunge headlong into the frantic (but good-naturedly so) world of the tarantella. *–Blair Johnston*

Recommended:

- ○ **Schubert: Symphonies 3 & 8** / Kleiber (cond.), Vienna PO / 1997 / DG 449745
- ○ **Schubert: Symphonies 3 & 4** / Böhm (cond.), Berlin PO / DG 453662-2
- ○ **Schubert: Symphonies 2, 3, 5** / Brueggen (cond.), Orch. of the 18th Century / 1996 / Philips 446100
- ○ **Schubert: Symphonies 3, 5 & 6** / Beecham (cond.), Royal PO / 1989 / EMI 69750
- ○ **Franz Schubert: Symphony 1–6, 8 & 9; Grand Duo; Rosamunde** / Abbado (cond.), CO of Europe / DG 423651

Symphony No. 4 in C minor ("Tragic"), D. 417 (1816)

That Franz Schubert, as a young man still learning his craft, was more influenced by the music of Haydn and Mozart than by the symphonies of Beethoven (just then reaching their stride) is readily apparent in his early orchestral works; the *Symphony No. 4 in C minor*, D. 417 (the "Tragic" Symphony, as Schubert called it), composed during the spring of 1816, is no exception. Despite the frequent comparisons made between this work and Beethoven's famous symphony in the same key, it is difficult to think of another symphonic work from the 1810s that more completely ignores Beethoven's special contributions to dramatic orchestral writing. The *"Tragic" Symphony* is the work of a teenage schoolteacher whose debt to the Viennese masters of the previous century was perhaps greater than even he realized it to be; that this journeyman work is so gripping and effective in its own right is a testimonial to Schubert's extraordinary inventive gifts—gifts that found a voice with or without the aid of structural and formal innovation.

The slow introduction to the opening movement (Adagio molto-Allegro vivace) is quite Haydnesque, with its bare fortissimo octave beginning and its almost painfully slow, searching dialogue between the upper and lower voices. However, the slippery descending sequence that lands us, to both our surprise and delight, on a G flat major harmony before ten bars have gone by is all Schubert. The Allegro vivace body of the movement takes us past all the usual sonata-allegro landmarks, but again these are given expression in a voice that is entirely Schubert's: the main theme seems more propulsive and frantic than anything Haydn might have put his name to, and even Mozart could not have written a more spirited C major close.

The keys of the two central movements—A flat major and E flat major—make clear references to the keys in which the first movement's second theme appears (A flat in the exposition, E flat in the recapitulation). The opening melody of the lovely Andante, like so many of Schubert's gentler orchestral treasures, might easily have been conceived for string quartet; a passage of considerable fury interrupts twice, but each time it is absorbed back into a loving reprise of the opening tune. The scherzo is famous for its shifty, chromatic main idea.

The finale begins with a four-bar introduction that seems to dissolve before our very eyes (or ears). After initially serving as just a background to the restless main theme, the running eighth notes begin to shape themselves into the form that will support the second theme, which is at first crafted into a duet for the first violins and clarinet. The whole of the recapitulation is recast into C major, and at the very end the C octaves that began the first movement are brought back to affirm the happy ending. *—Blair Johnston*

Recommended:

- ○ **Schubert: Symphonies 3 & 4** / Böhm (cond.), Berlin PO / DG 453662-2
- ○ **Schubert: Symphonies 1 & 4** / Brueggen (cond.), Orch. of the 18th Century / 1997 / Philips 446688
- ○ **Schubert: Symphony 4 "Tragic"; Schumann: Symphony 4** / Harnoncourt (cond.), Berlin PO / 1996 / Teldec 94543
- ○ **Franz Schubert: Symphonies 1–6, 8 & 9; Grand Duo; Rosamunde** / Abbado (cond.), Europe / DG 423651

Symphony No. 5 in B flat major, D. 485 (1816)

As a 19 year old in Vienna in 1816, Franz Schubert found his life something of a bore. His employment as an assistant master at his father's school could not have provided much fulfillment to one so talented and ambitious; further, his already plentiful compositions remained virtually unknown outside his immediate circle. Still, any personal dissatisfaction Schubert might have felt apparently had little effect on his productivity, for in that year he put to paper some 125 songs and over 50 other works for chorus, orchestra, piano, and various chamber ensembles. One of the brightest spots in this virtual avalanche of music is the *Symphony No. 5 in B flat major*, completed on October 3.

In the Fifth Symphony, Schubert takes a step back from the dramatic affect of his *"Tragic" Symphony* of a few months earlier, instead producing a work that sparkles with the clarity and ease of its obvious models, the symphonies of Haydn and especially Mozart. The distance between Schubert's early instrumental music and later works like the *"Great" Symphony in C major* (1825–28) or the *String Quintet in C major* (1828), finished just a few weeks before he died, is great; in most ways, the nonvocal works composed before 1820 are the products of an imagination still searching for the answers to questions it has posed to itself. Perhaps because it addresses a different set of challenges, the *Fifth Symphony* represents the composer's closest approach to complete mastery in the works of this period.

The usual four movements are all in place in the *Fifth Symphony*, played by an orchestra that, in keeping with the work's Classical tendencies, is rather smaller than the one called for in Schubert's previous symphony. There are no clarinets in the Fifth, no trumpets or timpani, and Schubert writes for just one flute rather than the then-customary pair. The symphony opens with an Allegro that is as lovely and streamlined a sonata-allegro as one might hope for. The first theme is preceded by a quaint, graceful four-measure introduction that reappears prominently in the development. The theme itself is a delightful notion affectionately tossed back and forth between the first violins and cellos and basses. Schubert indulges in one of his favorite sonata-form modifications in the movement: bringing the first theme back in the subdominant in the recapitulation, rather than in the expected tonic. The Andante con moto, in E flat major, grows from two contrasting (though not sharply contrasting) ideas whose back-and-forth results in a kind of rondo. The third movement is a Minuetto in G minor; its major-mode trio section is marked by an attractive lilt. The scampering main theme of the brilliant finale needs a true leggiero touch from the violins. The second theme is pure string quartet writing, a characteristic no amount of commentary from the winds can obscure. *—Blair Johnston*

Recommended:

- ○ **Schubert: Symphonies 5 & 8** / Mackerras (cond.), Orch. of the Age of Enlightenment / 1996 / Virgin 61305
- ○ **Brahms: Symphony 3; Schubert: Symphony 5; Mendelssohn: The Hebrides** / Reiner (cond.), Chicago SO / 1995 / BMG 61793
- ○ **Beethoven: Symphonie 6; Schubert: Symphony 5** / Böhm (cond.), Vienna PO / 1995 / DG 447433
- ○ **Shubert: Symphonies 3, 5 & 6** / Beecham (cond.), Royal PO / 1989 / EMI 69750
- ○ **Schubert: Symphonies 5, 8, 9; Mendelssohn: Symphonies 4 & 5** / Toscanini (cond.), NBC SO / 1999 / RCA 59480

Symphony No. 6 in C major ("Little C Major"), D. 589 (1817–1818)

Franz Peter Schubert composed this work between October 1817 and February 1818. It was first performed in 1818 by Otto Hatwig and a small orchestra in the conductor's Schottenhof apartment; the public premiere wasn't until December 14, 1828, at a *Gesellschaft der Muskfreunde* concert in Vienna. It is scored for two each of flutes, oboes, clarinets, bassoons, horns, and trumpets, plus timpani and strings.

As Salieri's pupil Schubert composed five symphonies between 1813–16, adding the *Sixth* on his own in 1817–18—the musical equivalents of May wine in recycled bottles, which is to say in forms pioneered by Haydn and perfected by Mozart that Beethoven had set about shattering when Schubert was still a nursing infant.

He paid his respects to Beethoven in the opening pages of *Symphony No. 6*, but especially in the scherzo—the first time Schubert adopted Beethoven's coinage in place of Minuet. The *Sixth* begins with a loud C major tutti that fades down, as Beethoven began his *Seventh Symphony* with the same instrumentation (but in A major) just a few years earlier. Yet Schubert's subsequent melodies prove no more heroic than his structures or harmonic bias. Although Robert Haven Schauffler wrote that his "approach to the recapitulation is Beethoven to the life," the materials themselves suggest dance tunes. By then Rossini had ensorcelled Vienna, and when Schubert wasn't being a genius he could be a blotter. The slow movement goes briskly, with a dactylic chief theme in the violins. And it does sound like Schubert on holiday in the Austrian countryside, a notable expressive advance for the 20-year-old composer.

Homage to Beethoven in the scherzo clearly derives from the deaf master's *First Symphony*—especially the use of loud-soft dynamics—but its E major Trio (Più lento) is closer to a Haydn Ländler than a Beethovenian jest.

Schubert introduces the rondo-like main theme of his Allegro moderato finale softly, as he'd done in the three previous movements. But structurally his Rossinian context is simpler than a rondo. Schauffler considered it "full of exuberant drive," despite his caveats about derivations and an abruptly harsh charge of "somewhat shoddy quality." The eminent Maurice J.E. Brown gave credit for "a great advance in technical matters over the previous five symphonies.... The use of the orchestra is masterly, its movements are expertly organized to the point of glibness, all is crisp and competent." But he concluded—as many have since—that there's little or "no heart in the work; it is all externals." Even so, Schubert was learning by doing, and proved it two years later in sketches for a *Seventh Symphony* (E minor, D. 729), followed by two movements in 1822 that posterity has christened *"the Unfinished."* *—Roger Dettmer*

Recommended:

- ○ **Schubert: Symphonies 6 & 8** / Brueggen (cond.), Orch. of the 18th Century / 1995 / Philips 442117
- ○ **Schubert: Symphonies 3, 5 & 6** / Beecham (cond.), Royal PO / 1999 / Angel 66999
- ○ **Schubert: Symphonies; Grand Duo; Rosamunde** / Abbado (cond.), CO of Europe / DG 423651

Symphony No. 8 in B minor ("Unfinished"), D. 759 (1822)

Early in 1822, Schubert was at the zenith of his career and he began writing a monumental *Symphony in B minor*. By the end of that year, he had scored the first two movements and sketched a third. He contracted syphilis late in that year and for a time was completely incapacitated, which was when he stopped work on the symphony and set it aside. By spring, he had recovered some of his strength. He was accepted for honorary membership in the Styrian Music Society at Graz in Austria. As part of his acceptance, he sent the two completed movements of the *B minor Symphony* to its director, Anselm Hüttenbrenner, who promptly stuffed them into a drawer and forgot them. It languished there until 1860, when Hüttenbrenner's younger brother Joseph came upon it and recognizing it as a lost treasure and began badgering Viennese conductor Johann Herbeck to perform the piece. The work was finally performed December 17, 1865.

The symphony itself is both large and understated. From the first, ominous opening bars, it is evident this is not the youthful Schubert who earlier crafted six lightweight symphonies. Confident and audacious, Schubert begins the 14 minute first movement by laying down a cornerstone in the basses, upon which is layered a gentle, wafting melody which gradually accumulates mass and power to a quick conclusion. This all turns out to be an introduction, and one of the composer's most brilliant melodies ensues. This, too, quickly becomes larger and more dramatic and an effective bridge leads back to the beginning. An intense, soaring center section, almost triumphant in its great chords, leads to a final reprise of the opening and the great movement ends solemnly.

The 11 minute Andante con moto movement begins with a marvelous melody, presented straightforwardly with no ornamentation, and this leads seamlessly to another marvelous woodwind melody. Great, broad shouldered strides carry the music to a new key where the themes are repeated. Tranquillity returns with the first themes and after a summation of what has passed, the movement—and the work—marches quietly to its end. *—Michael Morrison*

Recommended:

- ○ **Schubert: Symphonies 3 & 8** / Kleiber (cond.), Vienna PO / 1997 / DG 449745
- ○ **Franz Schubert** / Böhm (cond.), Berlin PO / 2000 / DG 469196
- ○ **Schubert: Unfinished Symphony; Beethoven: Symphony 5** / Walter (cond.), New York Philharmonic / 1999 / Sony 6506
- ○ **Schubert: Symphonies 7 & 8** / Weil (cond.), Classical Band / 1992 / Sony 48132
- ○ **Furtwängler: Live Recordings 1944–1953** / Furtwängler (cond.), Berlin PO / 2002 / DG 474030

Symphony No. 9 in C major ("The Great"), D. 944 (1825–1828)

This work wasn't performed in its entirety until March 21, 1839, at Leipzig, with Mendelssohn conducting. After composing six complete symphonies between 1813 and 1818 in the manner of Haydn and Mozart, Schubert completed only one more in the remaining decade of his brief life. This was *The Great C major,* written during 1825–26 (rather than 1828 as was supposed until quite recently), and thus is the allegedly lost *"Gastein" Symphony.* Although he dated a copy of the score "March 1828," it really is *No. 9,* despite an army of scholars that variously tagged it No. 7, 8, and even 10.

By 1818 the Viennese had typecast Schubert as a vocal composer, and the label stuck. His keyboard, chamber, and orchestral works were hardly known despite their excellences. Older brother Ferdinand hoarded the manuscript of *No. 9,* which Robert Schumann finally saw in 1838, and took to Leipzig. Orchestras in Vienna and Paris flatly refused to play it, however, and London musicians laughed derisively during rehearsals in 1844, when Mendelssohn tried without success to perform it there as he had in Leipzig ("with cuts"—big ones). Strings in particular hated playing its endlessly repetitive patterns: their pre-Wagner and pre-Bruckner bow arms were not ready for Schubert's "heavenly lengths." When all repeats are observed, the *Ninth* lasts over an hour, with almost no let-up in momentum. Three of Schubert's four movements employ sonata form—the first, the finale, and the song sections in an ABA scherzo. Only the slow movement is written in expanded song form (ABABA).

A soft but accented horn theme in the slow introduction foreshadows others to come in the exposition; it returns triumphantly in a long coda. The main body of the movement, marked "not too fast," is rhythmically so powerful and relentless that an unmodified Allegro tempo would have risked destroying it (and us).

Dotted rhythms characterize the A minor Andante, whose con moto qualification keeps it from dragging or sounding sentimentally sorrowful. Schubert's subsequent transition to A major is breathtaking, and his quiet writing for horns magical. As the movement began, it ends in A minor.

Beethoven-like, the Song parts of the Allegro vivace scherzo feature a miniature exposition-development-reprise (maybe Schubert knew the elder master's *Ninth* after all), full of dance melodies. C major yields to A major in the trio, with its broader tune for winds, before the song-sonata repeats.

Allegro vivace, again in C, this finale begins with a churning subject in triplet rhythm that stubbornly fights resolution (it is the grandest and most famous compositional trap in all music). Schubert finally must stop before he can introduce a new theme on clarinets and horns. Development and recapitulation follow on a titanic scale, capped by a coda in kind—a movement, altogether, just short of 1,200 measures! *—Roger Dettmer*

Recommended:

- ○ **Schubert: Symphony 9 & Incidental Music to Rosamunde** / Szell (cond.), Cleveland Orch. / 2000 / Sony 89342
- ○ **Schubert: Symphony 9; Haydn: Symphony 88** / Furtwängler (cond.), Berlin PO / DG 447439
- ○ **Schubert: Symphony 9 "The Great"; Rosamunde** / Walter (cond.), Columbia SO / 1995 / Sony 64478

ORCHESTRAL

Rosamunde, Fürstin von Cypern, incidental music, D. 797 (1823)

Romanze: Der Vollmond strahlt (Romance: The Full Moon Light Falls) (D. 797 No. 3b) is an aria extracted from incidental music Schubert provided for the stage play *Rosamunde* of 1823. Although the play was a popular and critical disaster, the music from it served Schubert well as the basis for a string quartet and an impromptu. This lovely little aria in an arrangement for voice and piano was the only extract from the score published in Schubert's lifetime. A simple strophic setting of three four-line verses, Schubert's gentle tune for the romanze moves easily over a softly rocking accompaniment in 6/8 between F minor and F major, between hope and despair, between happiness and sorrow. In the depth of Schubert's setting, one can hear the ghost of his settings of Goethe's *Mignon* lieder. *—James Leonard*

Recommended:

- ○ **Schubert: Symphony 9; Rosamunde (Excerpts)** / Walter (cond.), Columbia SO / 1995 / Sony 64478
- ○ **Furtwängler: Previously Unpublished Historic Recordings 1939–1944** / Furtwängler (cond.), Vienna PO / Tahra 1014
- ○ **Schubert: Rosamunde** / Abbado (cond.), Otter, CO of Europe / DG 431655
- ○ **Schubert: Rosamunde** / Froschauer (cond.), Georg, Westphal, Neubauer, Zoch, Cologne Radio Orch. / 2002 / Capriccio 67009/10

CHAMBER MUSIC

Arpeggione Sonata in A minor, D. 821 (Nov., 1824)

The guitarre d'amour, or *arpeggione* as it came to be known, was invented sometime during 1823 or 1824 by the respected Viennese guitar maker Johann Georg Stauffer. The instrument—a kind of enlarged guitar that could be bowed, cello-style, due to an altered fingerboard—was by no means a success; within just a few years of its birth it had for all intents and purposes suffered extinction. To music lovers, however, this short-lived instrumental curiosity will be forever remembered as the vehicle for Franz Schubert's *Sonata "per arpeggione" in A minor,* D. 821—a work now played almost exclusively by violists and cellists, although it exists in arrangements for instruments as far afield as the euphonium.

Schubert composed the *"Arpeggione" Sonata* in November 1824 shortly after returning from Zseliz, where he had spent his second summer (the first one being in 1818) teaching music to the Count of Esterházy's two daughters. The three-movement Sonata must be altered somewhat if it is to be played on cello or viola: the *arpeggione* possessed six strings, tuned to the same pitches as a guitar's, and the resulting extended range can cause problems when the piece is transcribed; in most editions, certain portions of the piece are transposed up or down an octave from their original position to avoid the extreme registers. However, Schubert by and large avoided the kind of idiosyncratic arpeggiations that earned the original instrument its nickname, focusing instead on the same focused lyricism that drives a traditional sonata for string instrument and piano; in this way, the work readily adapts to modern performance.

The opening Allegro moderato is built around a wistful melody whose fame is such that many who have never heard or heard of the *"Arpeggione" Sonata* will find that they recognize the tune. A second theme proceeds in gentle gusts of sixteenth notes; the *arpeggione* could not play fast notes with much volume at all, and so the Sonata's quicker portions are almost always marked piano or pianissimo.

The Adagio is a rich but introverted musing on an almost hymnlike subject. Schubert places great emphasis on the Neapolitan chord—a harmony also used to great effect in the opening movement—during the movement's closing measures, weakening the power of the final cadence and thus inviting the soloist to improvise a brief transition into the final, multisectioned Allegretto. *—Blair Johnston*

Recommended:

- ○ **Schubert: Arpeggione Sonata; Schumann: Fantasiestücke** / Argerich, Maisky / Philips 412230
- ○ **Rostropovich & Britten** / Rostropovich, Britten / 1999 / Decca 460974

Fantasia for violin & piano in C major ("Sei mir gegrüsst!"), D. 934 (Dec., 1827)

This easygoing, mainly lighthearted work makes it an exception to the despair and rejection that haunts many of the compositions Schubert wrote in 1828, the last year of his short life. Indeed, it can easily be imagined that in all seven movements the composer was consciously seeking the approval of the notoriously fickle Viennese musical public. Schubert's natural fluency, succulent melodies and elaborate figuration are well-displayed; nevertheless, after its first performance the work—which lasts approximately 25 minutes—earned only a sour comment from one critic: that it "occupied rather too much of the time the Viennese are prepared to devote to the pleasures of the mind."

The striking opening Adagio makes free use of the sounds and idioms of traditional gypsy music, the piano capturing the tremolando of the Hungarian cimbalom (a sort of hammered dulcimer) while the violin swoops and pirouettes around it in extravagant arabesques. The Fantasia adopts a plan remarkably similar to that of the better-known (and, let it be said, more profound) *Wanderer Fantasy* for solo piano. In the third section Schubert again makes use his own song "Sei mir gegrüsst," and its inclusion lifts the work onto an altogether higher plane. As with much of Schubert's chamber music, the harmonic scheme is complex, oscillating in strange ways around the keys of C major (in which the work begins and ends) A major, A minor, and the softly-glowing A flat major. *—Roy Brewer*

Recommended:

- ○ **Schubert: Violin Works** / Kremer, Afanassiev / DG 000001502
- ○ **Schubert: Fantasia, D934; Fantasia D760** / Schiff, Shiokawa / 2000 / ECM 464320

Octet for clarinet, horn, bassoon & strings in F major, D. 803 (1824)

By his own account, Franz Schubert set about composing his *Octet in F major for winds and strings, D. 803*, in 1824 as a means of preparing himself for the task, planned for the near future (and realized in the *Great Symphony in C major*), of composing a full-scale symphonic work. It was not the first time Schubert had done such preparatory work before proceeding to a full-scale symphony. More than a decade earlier, he had written sections of an all-wind *Octet*, D. 72 and D. 72a, before moving on to complete his very first symphony. However, in 1824 Schubert felt he was more or less starting from scratch as a symphonist. He had relatively little regard for the six symphonies of his youth and did not even include the unfinished symphonies of 1821 and 1822 in his mental catalog of works. And so, the *Octet in F* is a significant endeavor of self-betterment, as well as a wonderful chamber music achievement. The work was finished on the first day of March 1824.

Schubert opted to draw on Beethoven when composing the *Octet*, specifically Beethoven's *Septet*, Op. 20 of 1799–1800. Beethoven's work is in six movements, as is Schubert's. Beethoven's work is scored for clarinet, horn, bassoon, string trio, and contrabass; Schubert's for clarinet, horn, bassoon, string quartet, and contrabass. The choice was an apt one: Beethoven wrote his *Septet* as preparation for composing his *Symphony No. 1*.

The first movement opens with an 18-measure Adagio introduction that sets up the basic dotted-rhythm gesture (now reaching up, now reaching down) around which the Allegro body of the movement is built. The eight players should relish this zestful recollection of Mozart at his most exuberant. The second movement is an Adagio in B flat major with a silver-lined melody for the clarinet—not surprising since the *Octet* was commissioned by a clarinetist. The third movement is a scherzo and trio in all but name, the fourth a set of seven variations on a theme taken from Schubert's own *Die Freunde von Salamanka, D. 326* (1815). The fifth movement is a minuet and trio, this time in name as well as gesture and shape. The final movement's lighthearted walking-bass (or perhaps running-bass, as it is Allegro) and boisterous alla breve tune are prefaced by a slow(ish) introduction of about the same proportions as the first movement's introduction. The *Octet*'s final bars are ones of jubilant delight. *—Blair Johnston*

Recommended:

- ○ **Schubert: Violin Works** / Kremer, Zimmermann, Geringas, Brunner, Vlatkovic, Posch, Van Keulen, Thunemann / DG 000001502
- ○ **Schubert: Octet; Grand Duo** / Boskovsky (cond.), Vienna Octet / 1999 / Aura Classics 0189
- ○ **Schubert: Octet** / Linden, Griffin, Myron, McCraw, etc, / Virgin 59224
- ○ **Schubert: Octet** / Walter Boeykens Ens. / HM 1951440

Piano Quintet in A major ("Trout"), D. 667 (1819)

In the summer of 1819, Schubert traveled with the famous baritone Johann Michael Vogl to the river town of Steyr, where there was an abundance of musical activity. Schubert and Vogl's performance of the some of the composer's songs—especially *"Erlkönig"* (Schubert himself taking the part of the father!) and "Die Forelle" ("The Trout")—attracted the notice of Sylvester Paumgartner, a wealthy mining executive and an accomplished cellist, who then commissioned Schubert to write a quintet based on "The Trout" (and perhaps patterned after a work by Hummel that he had in his collection). The resulting "Trout" quintet—scored for the unusual combination of piano, viola, violoncello, and double bass—has become one of Schubert's more enduring chamber works, and it is typical of his early style. A notable feature is the integration of the piano part into the musical texture, on equal terms with those of the string players. In his own writing, Schubert referred to typical piano music as "damnable thumping" and insists in this work, as in his others, that it behave as an orderly and equal member of an ensemble.

The first movement is disproportionately long at 13 minutes, nearly a third of the length of the entire five-movement work. It is a joyful movement in sonata-allegro form, propelled forward by piano arpeggios and triplet figures in the strings.

A lyrical andante follows, sweetly expressive in the minor mode, and avoiding any sense of melancholy. It features three themes, one of which allows for an extended piano solo.

The brief third movement, a presto, begins aggressively but becomes a sort of "dance poem" containing Austrian folk tunes. The rhythmic impetus is unflagging. This leads to the work's signature movement, the theme and variations on "Die Forelle" ("The Trout"). Potentially tedious, the theme and variations form is ingenious and satisfying in Schubert's hands—each variation is both individually engaging and integral to the whole. As in the first movement, the piano is thoroughly intermingled with the strings and the resulting sound is nearly symphonic (an exception to this is the third variation, which is a swirling piano cascade with subdued string accompaniment).

The final movement is simple and light with a swirling, almost "gypsy" sound that can be reminiscent of Dvořák at times. Like the third and fourth movements, the last seems to be broken into smaller units, in the style of a set of dances.

Although he had already written 11 string quartets by the time of the "Trout" Quintet, this composition represents Schubert's first truly significant chamber work. His ability to blend and balance this combination of instruments seems instinctive and the piece is rightly considered one of his most popular and best early works. *—AMG*

Recommended:

- ○ **Scubert: Trout Quintet; Death & the Maiden** / Curzon, Vienna Quartet / 1999 / London 460650
- ○ **Schubert: Trout Quintet; Schumann: String Quartets, Op41** / Kocsis, Takacs SQ / Hungaroton 12918
- ○ **Schubert: Trout Quintet; Arpeggione; Notturno** / Immerseel, L'Archibudelli / 1998 / Sony 63361

Piano Trio No. 1 in B flat major, D. 898 (1827)

The *Piano Trio in B flat major* that Schubert began in the middle of 1827 marks his return to that particular ensemble after an interval of almost exactly 15 years. The sole earlier work for piano trio, also in B flat major but in just a single movement (D. 28), is a student work—that of the 15-year old pupil of Antonio Salieri; in marked contrast, the *B flat major Piano Trio* of 1827, Op. 99, shows Schubert nearing the very end of both career and life, fully aware of his powers' scope. It is the first of two magnificent works in the genre with which Schubert filled the void in piano trio composition that had existed since Beethoven's *"Archduke" Trio* of 1811.

The *B flat major Piano Trio*, Op.99 (D.898), is in the usual four movements, here marked Allegro moderato, Andante un poco mosso, Allegro (the scherzo), and Allegro vivace. The first movement is as happy and carefree a sonata-allegro as one might imagine; its bubbly opening theme is at first property of the strings but is soon turned over to the piano, which emulates the violin/cello octaves while the strings take over the bouncing accompaniment. A heartwarming second melody in the cello assumes an almost heroic posture when it recurs in the development.

The melody of the E flat major Andante un poco mosso is like a reflection of the famous Adagio cantabile of Beethoven's *Pathetique Sonata* (probably, knowing Schubert, the resemblance is not accidental); the direction in which Schubert heads with this little gem of a melody, however, is entirely his own. The movement falls into an ABA form, with the central C minor/major portion offering some snappy rhythms and a decorated melody that are in sharp contrast to the simple opening and closing music.

The Scherzo returns us to the good-natured B flat major of the first movement; its trio section recaptures something of the previous Andante's melodic composure. Schubert calls the last movement a Rondo, but it is far less a rondo than it is a sonata-allegro form. The violin starts things off with an ebullient tune saturated with the long/short-short rhythms that Schubert loved so dearly. During the development section we are treated to the ingenious and intricately woven counterpoint that is unique to late Schubert. *—Blair Johnston*

Recommended:

- ○ **David Oistrakh Collection Vol. 3** / Oistrakh, Oborin, Knushevitsky / 1997 / DHR 7710
- ○ **Schumann: Piano Concerto; Schubert: Trio in B flat** / Schnabel, Fournier, Szigeti / Music & Arts 1111
- ○ **Schubert: Piano Trio; Nocturne** / Beaux Arts Trio / Philips 422836
- ○ **Schubert: Piano Trios 1 & 2** / Ashkenazy, Harrell, Zukerman / London 455685

Piano Trio Movement in E flat major ("Nocturne"), D. 897 (1827)

Aside from a single movement composed during the summer of 1812 (the so-called *Sonatensatz* in B flat major, D. 28), Franz Schubert wrote nothing for piano trio until just a year before his death, when he set to work on the two trios, D. 898 and D. 929. It was probably while working on the first of those two great works, the B flat major trio, that Schubert wrote the lone movement in E flat major that has since earned sobriquet "Notturno," or Nocturne; in all likelihood, this Adagio movement was at one point intended to be the slow movement of D. 898. Dismissed from that role the movement was issued on its own as Opus 148, two decades after Schubert's death.

The rich main theme of the "Notturno" is possessed of an unusual rhythmic character—it cascades forward through the bar, either with pizzicati from the two string instruments or with the equivalent in rolled piano chords, only to suddenly halt each time; legend has it that this character comes from a folk tune Schubert heard one day while vacationing to the rural east of Salzburg. Exuberance, one might even say ecstasy, is not at all lacking in the faster contrasting sections; for the first of these Schubert moves up one half step to the key of E major, a modulation foreshadowed by a brief but passionate harmonic sequence earlier on in the piece. *—Blair Johnston*

Recommended:

○ **Schubert: String Quartet, D887; Notturno** / Takacs Quartet / 1997 / London 452854

○ **Schubert: Piano Trio; Nocturne** / Beaux Arts Trio / Philips 422836

○ **Schubert: Trout Quintet; Arpeggione; Notturno** / L'Archibudelli / 1998 / Sony 63361

Piano Trio No. 2 in E flat major, D. 929 (Nov., 1827)

The second of Franz Schubert's two full-length piano trios was begun during November 1827 and finished probably within the next few weeks. It was certainly completed by January of the following year, when Schubert held a private performance of the piece in celebration of the forthcoming marriage of his long-time friend Josef von Spaun; Spaun had encouraged the young composer at his fledgling compositional efforts while Schubert was still a preteen. The *Piano Trio No. 2 in E flat major*, Op. 100 was written almost immediately after the *Piano Trio in B flat*, Op. 99; Schubert himself felt the E flat work to be the better of the two—not at all surprising, since he had "warmed up" on the other work before writing it.

The Trio is a very different work than its B flat major sister-piece. Op. 99 is an apparently carefree work whose soaring melodies have little if any of the firmness and grit that fill the *E flat Piano Trio*; indeed, the dramatic musical battle-lines of the *E flat major Trio*, the frequent wholesale and sometimes very sudden abandonment of one mood for an absolutely contrasting one—the great swells and then deflations of confidence—would be utterly out of place in the emotionally stable Op. 99.

The diversity and placement of material throughout the opening Allegro might have baffled an eighteenth century composer. After an initial, very traditional idea, Schubert moves to the extremely distant key of B minor(!!) for an impish second subject, defined by an incessant ostinato rhythm. A third melody seems to appear in the key of the dominant B flat, but it is in fact an extension of a little pendant to the first theme. Still, it is this "third" subject that rounds off the exposition and occupies the players throughout the entire development. The Andante con moto owes its songful melody to Schubert's encounter with a Swedish folk singer shortly before, or into, the composition of the trio. There is raw passion in the movement's climax, a passion that seems unsure whether its final destination is transcendentalism or tragedy.

The Allegro moderato (Scherzo) unfolds canonically; even when the exact imitation evaporates, the spirit of friendly emulation remains intact. The trio section is physical and robust. The finale is expansive and complex; the move from the bright opening theme to the more dark-spirited second subject is made with so little transition that at first one might imagine the movement to be a rondo. After this second subject runs its course, however, we get no reprise of the opening music but rather something absolutely astonishing: a reprise of the melody from the second movement, doctored to suit the new tempo and context, that acts as an usher to the arriving development section. *—Blair Johnston*

Recommended:

○ **Schubert, Haydn: Piano Trios; Mozart: Piano Quartet, K493** / Stern, Rose, Istomin / 1995 / Sony 64516

○ **David Oistrakh Collection Vol. 3** / Oistrakh, Oborin, Knushevitsky / 1997 / DHR 7710

○ **Schubert: Piano Trios** / Beaux Arts Trio / Philips 412620

○ **Schubert: Piano Trios** / L'Archibudelli / 1996 / Sony 62695

Rondo for violin & piano in B minor ("Rondeau Brillant"), D. 895 (Oct., 1826)

Franz Schubert saw only three of his many chamber compositions put to print during his lifetime; two, the *String Quartet in A minor*, D. 804 and the *Piano Trio in E flat*, D. 929, have since attained an honored status among nineteenth century repertory warhorses. The other, the *Rondo for violin and piano*, D. 895, has not; it remains largely unknown even to violinists, and yet is at least the musical equal of the *Fantasy in C major for violin and piano* that violinists hold so dear. Schubert wrote the B minor rondo during autumn of 1826 with the hope, eventually fulfilled, that it be performed by its dedicatee, the Bohemian violinist Josef Slawjk. When published the following year as Opus 70 it was given the title "Rondo brillant" by the publisher.

The rondo is really an Introduction and Rondo: the Andante that prefaces the Allegro of the rondo proper is no mean musical appendage but in fact the source for several of the ideas that emerge in the rondo. Indeed, the very opening gesture of the Allegro—a play on the pitches B and C sharp that will return time and again in the piece—is intimately dependent on the notes of a tense violin/piano-right-hand imitation that bring the Andante to an unresolved close.

The stiff regality of the Andante's opening bars calls Handel to mind; soon a dolce melody is washed by gently flowing arpeggios in the piano right-hand, and dispelled only by the dramatic reappearance of the opening music—at first recast in B major but soon dissolved into the mysteriously-hued seventh chord that leads straight into the Allegro.

The rondo itself is in five parts (ABACA), with a barn-burning coda based on the B music. Both the B and C episodes are of far greater length and of broader tonal aspirations than the refrain theme; the B music takes off on a military-march rhythm introduced at the very end of the fiery A section, while the C music positively overflows with good-natured G major dotted rhythms. *—Blair Johnston*

Recommended:

○ **Schubert: Violin Works** / Kremer, Afanassiev / DG 000001502

○ **Schubert: Sonatinas for Violin & Piano** / Schneider, Serkin / 2000 / Vanguard 134

Rondo for violin & strings in A major, D. 438 (Jun., 1816)

Austrian composer Franz Schubert wrote no concertos for solo instrument and orchestra. Aside from obbligato instruments in some of his songs, most notably the clarinet in *Der Hirt auf dem Felsen* (The Shepherd on the Rock) (D. 965), Schubert only wrote two concerted works: the *Konzertstuck für Violine und Orchester* (Concert Piece for Violin and Orchestra) (D. 345) and the extended *Rondo für Violine und Streichorchester* (Rondo for Violin and String Orchestra) (D. 438) from June, 1816. The latter is undoubtedly Schubert's concerted masterpiece. Prefaced by an extended Adagio opening, the Rondo is both a virtuoso display piece for the soloists and a wonderful piece of music in its own right. With three themes (a cheerfully dancing opening theme, a second theme in Schubert's best faux-volkstone style, and a dramatic closing theme that moves from minor to major) deployed as an extended rondo form moving through Schubert's favorite third-related keys and climaxing in F major, Schubert's Rondo is as delightful a work as any of the closing movements of Mozart's violin concertos. *—James Leonard*

Recommended:

○ **Schubert: Violin Works** / Kremer / DG 000001502

String Quartet No. 10 in E flat major, D. 87 (Nov., 1813)

Most of Franz Schubert's mid/late childhood was spent as a choirboy at the Royal City College of Vienna; to whatever extent that Schubert was "taught" in the ordinary sense of the word, it was from the musicians resident at this institution—in particular Antonio Salieri. Schubert held Salieri in high regard, and when, in the final months of 1813, he at last gave in to his father's pressure and left the Royal College to be trained as a schoolteacher, Schubert continued to take lessons with the older composer. Schubert's *String Quartet in E flat major*, D. 87—published posthumously as Op. 125, No. 1 and sometimes referred to as the *String Quartet "No. 10"*—was written in November 1813, just after Schubert left the College. That Salieri's guidance was beneficial is clear from the outset—excepting the *Symphony in D major* composed around the same time, the Quartet is by far the most mature and altogether successful piece of instrumental music that the 16-year-old had yet produced.

The two three-measure phrases that introduce the main thought of the Quartet's first movement (Allegro moderato) show both a flexibility of timing and a kind of humor not readily apparent in Schubert's other early works. After repeating the initial 12-bar thematic idea, Schubert moves on to offer a substantial transition passage of such breadth and reluctance to leave E flat major behind that it almost seems a kind of subsidiary theme. The second main theme (dolce) makes clever use of syncopated accents while never grazing outside the sweet, graceful pasture Schubert has prescribed for it, even when the lower three instruments propel themselves forward with a rapid dotted-note accompaniment. The development is both concise and wholly traditional, and the recapitulation differs noticeably from the exposition only when changes are required to facilitate presenting the second theme in the tonic rather than the dominant.

Schubert puts the Scherzo (prestissimo) —usually the third movement in a four-movement plan—second. An Adagio in 6/8 meter follows, spinning forth calmly using the thread of one serene first violin melody and then another; sonata form is in operation, but one hardly notices.

The finale is a rambunctious Allegro in the best hybrid (Haydn-Schubert) style imaginable. The bouncing three-eighth note gesture heard at the opening of the first movement pops back up during the second theme. The accompaniment moves between electrifying 16th notes and slightly more aristocratic triplets, occasionally taking a breather to allow some chorale-like phrases to creep in. *—Blair Johnston*

Recommended:

○ **Schubert: Quatuor D87, Quatuor D804 "Rosamunde"** / Quatuor Mosaiques / 1996 / Astrée 8580

○ **Schubert: String Quartets, D87, 703 & 804** / Artis Quartet / Sony 66720

○ **Schubert: String Quartets 10 & 14** / Alban Berg Quartet / 1997 / EMI 56470

String Quartet No. 12 in C minor ("Quartettsatz"), D. 703 (Sep., 1820)

A distance of nearly half a decade separates the last string quartet composed during Franz Schubert's prentice years and the first he wrote as a fully mature composer. This is the *String Quartet in C minor*, D. 703 of December 1820, popularly known as the *"Quartettsatz"* because only a single movement of the piece was finished—putting it in the same celebrated and lengthy catalog of unfinished Schubert compositions that includes the famous *B minor Symphony* of 1822.

The *"Quartettsatz"* marks something of a coming of age for Schubert. The instrumental compositions written before the new decade all somehow lack the individuality that marks Schubert's lieder from 1815 onward; with the *"Quartettsatz,"* Schubert begins to find ways to fuse the instrumental heritage he absorbed during his years as a pupil of Salieri with those compelling dramatic aims which, for years, he had no way of corralling without a text.

The *"Quartettsatz,"* D. 703 shares something besides its unfinished status with the famous *B minor "Unfinished" Symphony*: an introduction built of fluttering, insecure string figurations. In the Symphony, these are hesitant and mysterious; in the *"Quartettsatz"* they boil with passion, beginning pianissimo with the solo first violin and then swelling to a massive fortissimo climax. In many ways, the rest of the piece is a series of similar swells from one dynamic extreme to another—the music pulsates with gritty passion, nervous fury, and soaring ecstasy, and little room is made for more temperate gestures.

That the movement is an example of some type of sonata-allegro form is clear; just what the formal boundaries of this advanced sonata design are has long been a topic of considerable discussion. If we back up and take a fresh look at the piece, however, Schubert's plan is plain to see.

We can easily follow the broad divisions of sonata form: an exposition that begins in C minor and ends in G major, a development section that eventually makes its way back to a landscape that we recognize as belonging to the exposition, a retooling of the myriad thoughts of the opening, and finally a brief reprise of the introductory "fluttering." The fact that Schubert's first substantial melodic idea—a lofty idea that spans two full octaves in the first violin—appears in A flat major rather than the tonic C minor, and reappears first in B flat major and then in E flat major as the recapitulation begins, is a matter that only a hard-boiled formalist will lose sleep over; indeed, such intentional formal obfuscation and overlapping is something that Franz Liszt would soon pick up on and transform into a whole new style. Some measure of peace is found in the repetitive, chorale-like music that acts as a coda for both the exposition and the recapitulation, but in the end, it is the nervous wreck in Schubert that wins out. *—Blair Johnston*

Recommended:

- ○ **Schubert: String Quartets, D87, 703 & 804** / Artis Quartet / Sony 66720
- ○ **Schubert: Late String Quartets** / Alban Berg Quartet / 1997 / EMI 56471

String Quartet No. 13 in A minor ("Rosamunde"), D. 804 (1824)

Sometimes referred to as the *Rosamunde Quartet* because of the second movement theme from the composer's failed stage work of the same name, this A minor work was the only one of his string quartets to be published in his lifetime. Ill and miserable with syphilis, Schubert in 1824 made the acquaintance of the renowned violinist and quartet leader Ignaz Schuppanzigh, who had just returned from a seven year visit of Russia. During their times together, Schubert resolved to return to the medium of the string quartet, which he had abjured for several years. The result was a lyrical and introspective work, almost solemn, dedicated to Schuppanzigh and premiered by him on March 14 of that year.

The work opens darkly, with low quavering in the viola and a mournful theme by the violin. Although the movement modulates to major keys and becomes more lively at points, it retreats to the pensive and downcast darkness of the opening. At over 13 minutes, the first movement is as long as any two of the other movements, and very wide in scope dramatically and emotionally. Of note, it does not contain any of Schubert's driving rhythmic vitality, but seems halting and even insistently morose, finally returning to the opening quavering and mournful theme at its end. The *Rosamunde* theme begins the second movement, but here it has been made smaller and more mournful. Simply spun out, the theme persists until an animated outburst in the middle section infuses life into it temporarily. It then returns to close out the movement. Even the third movement minuet is not immune to Schubert's despondency, as here he recalls his own setting of Schiller's *The Gods of Greece*. The text of the work is also despondent: "Beauteous world, where art thou? Come again, O lovely age of Nature's blossoming." It is not necessary to be familiar with the earlier work to realize that the movement is inordinately somber for a minuet and trio marked Allegro. Only in the Allegro Moderato finale does Schubert lift the veil of depression, and although the movement does not burst forth with the driving vitality of many of his later works, it is not gloomy. It does feature the composer's characteristic play of major against minor and arrives at a satisfying conclusion. It accurately and somewhat grimly depicts Schubert's frame of mind as he suffered through the years of his final illness. *—Michael Morrison*

Recommended:

- ○ **Schubert: Quatuor D87, Quatuor D804 "Rosamunde"** / Quatuor Mosaiques / 1996 / Astrée 8580
- ○ **Schubert: String Quartets, D887 & D804** / Amadeus Quartet / DG 459013
- ○ **Schubert: String Quartet 13 & 14** / Guarneri Quartet / 1997 / Arabesque 6687

String Quartet No. 14 in D minor ("Death and the Maiden"), D. 810 (1824)

As morbid as it may seem today, preoccupation with death was quite fashionable in the nineteenth century. The Romantic movement in music, drama, art, and literature embraced the idea of death as transcendent and fulfilling rather than fearsome. Medical science was still in its infancy, and the only real cure for many illnesses was the end of life. Death was gentle. Death was peace. Death was an end to suffering.

In this light, Franz Schubert's own fascination with death was neither unusual nor inexplicable. In March 1824, having endured the symptoms of syphilis for nearly two years, he wrote, "Each night when I go to sleep, I hope never to wake again, and each morning serves only to recall the misery of the previous day."

Since the still-youthful composer was not yet consigned to the grave, he continued to develop his musical genius, and in this same month he completed the original version of the *String Quartet in D minor, "Der Tod und das Mädchen"* (Death and the Maiden). Based on the opening theme from his song of the same name (1817), this quartet clearly illustrates Schubert's sympathy, even longing, for death. By appropriating the music of the song, Schubert also imbues the quartet with the sentiments of the original text, in which Death urges a frightened maiden to trust him: he means her no harm, and she will sleep soundly in his arms.

This work is significant for several reasons. It is considered one of Schubert's finest chamber works, and it has always occupied a favored spot in the string quartet repertory. Its frankly programmatic content connects it with later nineteenth century works, in which structural concerns yielded to extramusical and dramatic influences. Finally, the quartet is a striking reminder to those who like to pigeonhole Schubert as a miniaturist or as a "song composer": it stands alongside the *"Unfinished" Symphony* and the *Wanderer-Fantasie* as a testament to his sense of large-scale organization and to the promise unfulfilled as a result of his early death.

The work begins aggressively, with full-throated gestures that establish both the thematic and rhythmic structure of the first movement. Schubert makes use of one of his signature rhythmic devices, a quarter note followed by triplet eighths. The second theme is sweetly lyrical, joyful and upbeat, full of life and energy. The movement ends breathlessly but sweetly.

The second movement, a fourteen-minute Andante con moto, introduces the "Death" theme, which corresponds to the opening piano introduction of "*Der Tod und das Mädchen*." Five variations on the theme follow, all of which vary only slightly from the original, as if Death is insistent—not swayed or deterred.

At less than four minutes, the third-movement scherzo is abrupt and puzzling, as if its only function is to serve as prologue to the driving, almost demonic finale. It is rhythmically challenging, and features unexpected accents and cadences.

In the final movement, Schubert applies his customary momentum and drive to first establish and then build an inexorable rush. The figure of a dotted eighth note followed by a sixteenth note is used throughout as the driving force, though it is frequently interrupted. In the end, Death is relentless, and the movement swirls to a massive but abrupt conclusion. *—AMG*

Recommended:

- ○ **Schubert: "Trout" Quintet; Death & The Maiden** / Juilliard SQ / 1990 / Sony 46343
- ○ **Schubert: String Quartets 10 & 14** / Alban Berg Quartet / 1997 / EMI 56470
- ○ **David Oistrakh Collection Vol. 1** / Oistrakh, Knushevitsky, Terian, Bondarenko / 1998 / Doremi 7701

String Quartet No. 15 in G major, D. 887 (1826)

The Quartet No. 15 in G major (1826), the last of Schubert's string quartets, stands alongside the famous D minor Quartet ("Death and the Maiden") as proof that the composer was well on his way to writing large-scale works in all genres. Symphonic in organization and structure, it achieves a depth of sound that often belies the presence of only four musicians. In its scope and difficulty, it typifies Schubert's later works.

The first movement, over 23 minutes in length, features a near-symphonic introduction which substantially delays the appearance of the first theme. Characterized more by rich complexity than by the composer's characteristic rhythmic drive, this theme at several points decreases dynamically to near silence, while the rhythmic motion comes to a complete stop at least twice.

Though about half as long as the first, the second movement, Andante un poco moto, is no less richly crafted. While stylistically consistent with the previous movement, it is more lyrical and somewhat darker in character. It also makes use of the composer's distinctive "hairpin" maneuver—complete stops after which the music resumes on a different rhythmic and dynamic plane.

The Scherzo, less complex than the preceding movements, is marked by a previously absent rhythmic insistence. A driving motive in triplet rhythms assumes the fore until a contrasting lyrical center section intrudes. Eventually, the initial energy returns, and the movement ends aggressively.

The finale features an alternation between two rhythmic devices: a dotted eighth note followed by a sixteenth, and groups of triplets. Within the symphonic scope of the quartet the finale is the grandest movement of all, powerful and complex, constantly building and changing, until drawing to a surprising close. *—Michael Morrison*

Recommended:

○ **Schubert: The Last Four Quartets** / Quartetto Italiano / 1995 / Philips 446163

○ **Schubert: Late String Quartets** / Alban Berg Quartet / 1997 / EMI 56471

○ **Schubert: Quartet 15; Mozart: Adagio & Fugue In C** / Ma, Kashkashian, Kremer, Phillips / 1987 / CBS 42134

String Quintet in C major, D. 956 (1828)

Benjamin Britten once suggested that "the richest and most productive eighteen months in music history" were "the period in which Franz Schubert wrote *Winterreise*, the *C major symphony*, his last three piano sonatas, the *C Major String Quintet*, as well as a dozen other glorious pieces." The *String Quintet, D. 956* is certainly one of the pinnacles of the chamber music canon, and is often cited as a significant example of the composer's legacy.

Certainly in the period between the death of his idol, Beethoven, and his own passing, the 31-year-old Schubert achieved a breakthrough in large-scale forms the likes of which has not been seen since. But the *Quintet* strikes one more as young man's music than as a summary statement; there is a youthful ambition that is not unlike that of Beethoven's first string quartets.

For his scoring, Schubert went against the model of Mozart and Beethoven, who each added a second viola to the conventional string quartet for their quintets; Boccherini provided the only precedent for using two cellos. Schubert uses the second cello to create dense and varied textures: sometimes the cello serves as a second bass instrument under a full quartet, sometimes it's a bass-rich quartet sans violin, and sometimes there is a rich interplay between instrumental sections.

The first two movements have an expansive and deliberate buildup that seems to anticipate the sprawling structures of Anton Bruckner. But in most ways the piece remains quite conventional; it retains the standard four-movement format, and has an energetic scherzo (though a more wistful trio) and a zestful, almost Hungarian finale. Despite the bleak spaces of the slow movement, these movements suggest a youth's first steps into maturity, and the work as a whole serves as a tantalizing reminder of what might have been, had Schubert been granted more time to create and innovate. *—James Liu*

Recommended:

○ **Schubert: String Quintet** / Alban Berg Quartet, Schiff / 1998 / EMI 66942

○ **Schoenberg: Verklärte Nacht; Schubert: Quintet** / Hollywood SQ, Reher / 1993 / Testament 1031

○ **Schubert: Quintet in C; Quartettsatz in C minor** / Kavafian, Kavafian, Sherry, Neubauer, Parnas / 1990 / Omega 1015

Violin Sonata in A major ("Duo"), D. 574 (Aug., 1817)

Not published until 1851, this work of Schubert's early maturity fully deserves the designation "duo" appended by the publisher; unlike Schubert's earlier works for violin and piano, this sonata makes the keyboard a full partner and displays the composer's increasing confidence in writing for piano.

The first of the four movements is an Allegro moderato, in which a few bars of amiable piano introduction become the ambling accompaniment to a low-key, songful violin theme. Soon both instruments offer a much more animated treatment of this material and then a new idea that is essentially an elaboration of the opening piano figure. After an exposition repeat, Schubert subjects these themes to a brief development and standard recapitulation.

The Scherzo (Presto) is a rollicking piece in which a little piano fanfare launches a scurrying violin figure. The music lurches through some surprising key changes, often coming to a full stop before continuing with quite different material. Embedded between the E major outer sections of this movement is a playful C major trio, featuring highly chromatic writing for the violin.

These high spirits dissipate in time for the Andantino, a mostly lyrical dialog that drifts from C major to D flat and ultimately A flat, with a few piano trills, violin double stops (nothing to intimidate the amateur domestic players for which this sonata was probably intended), and brief, extroverted outbursts along the way.

Finally comes the Allegro vivace, in which the spirit of the earlier scherzo returns, complete with a short, leaping motif to get the movement off to a joyful start. Again, the music is full of hesitations that signal new harmonic and melodic directions; Schubert packs substantial adventure into this movement's four minutes. *—James Reel*

Recommended:

○ **Schubert: Violin Works** / Kremer, Afanassiev / DG 000001502

○ **Schubert: Trout Quintet; Sonata for Violin & Piano** / Serkin, Schneider / Vanguard 8005

○ **David Oistrakh in Prague** / Oistrakh, Bauer / Praga 256007

CHORAL

Choral Music (1812–1828)

Franz Schubert (1797–1828) composed vastly more choral settings of sacred texts than of secular texts. But sacred or secular, the majority of Schubert's choral settings were profoundly spiritual. As he wrote in a letter, "My devotion is never forced and I only compose hymns or prayers when I am involuntarily overcome by such a feeling, but when this happens it is usually true and proper devotion." While Schubert had been baptized an Austrian Catholic, he was no believer, and his own spirituality was deeply pantheistic. For Schubert, God was everywhere and in all things, and whether he is setting the text of the mass or the text of Goethe, Schubert is composing works that embody the all-embracing love of God. Almost all Schubert's choral settings were written for specific events in specific churches in Vienna and are thus essentially utilitarian works. But while all his choral works are eminently performable, they all imbibe of his spirituality. Schubert's single most important body of choral settings are his mass settings. His *Mass in F major,* D. 105, of 1814 was his first completed mass setting and his first work performed in public. It was followed the next year by the *Mass in G major,* D. 167 and the *Mass in B flat major,* D. 324, and the next year by the *Mass in C major,* D. 452. All four were short, lyrical, and altogether lovely. Schubert began the *Missa Solemnis in A flat major,* D. 678, in 1819 as a far more grandly conceived and executed work and completed it in 1826, the longest time Schubert spent on any of his works. Schubert composed his second and last *Missa Solemnis in E flat major,* D. 950, in February 1828. Even grander and more glorious than the earlier *Mass in A flat major,* Schubert's last mass ranks with the celebratory late masses of Haydn.

Schubert's partsongs and choruses have much in common with his solo songs: they cover roughly the same period, draw on similar texts, and display the same inventiveness in melody and harmony. Most of them were written for men's chorus, as a relatively new tradition of recreational singing ensembles was just beginning to spread throughout Austria and Germany. Some were written for specific occasions, some are more generic, such as the ten entitled *Trinklied.* Accompaniments, when used, range from a piano to chamber ensemble (including *Nachtegesang im Walde,* D. 913) *for male chorus and four horns* to orchestra. The *Ständchen,* D. 920 for alto, male chorus, and piano, is a fine example of Schubert's serenades. *—James Leonard*

Recommended:

○ **Schubert: Choruses** / Preinfalk (cond.), Osterreichischen Rundfunks Chor / DG 453679

○ **Schubert: Complete Part Songs for Male Voices Vol. 4** / Die Singphoniker / CPO 999400

○ **Männerchöre: Songs by Schubert for Male Voice Choir** / Viserberg (dir.), Chorus of South German Radio / Pilz Acanta 43054

○ **Schubert: Sacred Choral Music** / Knothe (cond.), Berlin Radio SO & Chorus / Capriccio 490845

Deutsche Messe (German Mass), D. 872 (1826–1827)

Franz Schubert's so-called *German Mass,* D. 872 is both one of his last works of sacred music—probably written during the autumn of 1827—and, paradoxically, the one that least bears the stamp of his musical personality. The work was initiated by a commission from Professor J. P. Neumann of the Polytechnic School of Vienna, the churchman who had, seven years earlier, provided Schubert with the libretto for the opera *Sakantala* (a project that never came to fruition). The texts of the *German Mass'* nine brief sections of music are Neumann's, and it was his idea that the work—intended for performance by amateurs—be as musically simple as possible. Schubert made good on Neumann's request: the *German Mass* is written almost entirely in a straightforward homophonic manner that one can hardly imagine Schubert to have explored on his own initiative.

Eight of the *German Mass'* nine movements correspond to equivalent portions of the Latin mass (Kyrie, Gloria, Credo, etc.). The "extra" ninth movement is an *anhang* (appendix) entitled Das Gebet des Herrn (The Lord's Prayer), added by an unidentified other in 1845; its inclusion in the mass is largely a matter of performers' discretion. There are in fact two versions of the *German Mass,* one for SATB and organ and one for SATB, organ, and wind ensemble; the version without wind ensemble may well be an adaptation made by Schubert's brother Ferdinand, who had many years earlier appropriated Schubert's *German Requiem* as his own in the interest of securing a job.

The *German Mass* sounds as much like a collection of hymns—strophically designed, harmonically simple—as something contemporaneous with the *E flat Piano Trio* or the *"Great" Symphony in C.* There is a sweetness of melody throughout, however, that cannot but draw a listener in; the scoring of the wind parts is exceptionally beautiful and efficient. Usually transparent shadows of the chorus, the instruments occasionally branch out on their own to rich effect. *—Blair Johnston*

Recommended:

- ○ **Schubert: Deutsche Messe** / Sawallisch (cond.), Popp, Fassbaender, Dallpozza, Fischer-Dieskau, Bavarian Radio Chorus & Orch. / Capitol 47407
- ○ **Schubert: Mass in A Flat Major; Deutsche Messe** / Weil (cond.), van der Kamp, Hartmann, Hering, Preyer, Weinhappel, Vienna Boys' Choir, Orch. of the Age of Enlightenment, Chorus Viennensis / 1994 / Sony 53984

Mass in G major, D. 167 (Mar., 1815)

Franz Schubert's second setting of the Latin mass—the now-famous *Mass in G major* for soloists, chorus, string orchestra, and organ, D. 167—was unpublished and all-but-unknown during Schubert's lifetime; in fact, when the mass was finally published in 1846 it was not Schubert's but rather the obscure composer Robert Führer's which appeared on the title page! History was quick to rectify this fraudulency, however, and the mass has since achieved a degree of popularity perhaps only bested in Schubert's catalog of sacred music by the final *Mass in E flat major.*

Schubert wrote the *G major Mass* between March 2 and March 7, 1815, probably to be performed at his family's church in Lichtenthal. The six sung portions of the Mass Ordinary—Kyrie, Gloria, Credo, Sanctus, Benedictus, and Agnus Dei—are all present; each is set with great brevity, but without hastiness. The mass is scored for soprano, tenor, and bass soloists, mixed chorus, strings, and organ; some years later Schubert added parts for trumpets and timpani.

The contrasting sections of the Kyrie ("Kyrie eleison" and "Christe eleison") are set apart by the composer's assigning the latter to the soprano soloist; the outer portions for choir are intensely lyrical. The Gloria is energetic and quick-footed; again in the center of the movement there are soloistic opportunities. For all its compactness, the Credo creates the impression of great weight, marching forth on a steady bassline and rising slowly from its humble, quiet beginnings to an imposing climax at the "Et resurrexit."

The Sanctus begins in a manner reminiscent of Haydn, and the ensuing fugue on "Osanna in excelsis" is similarly right out of the eighteenth century handbook. The soprano solo at the opening of the Benedictus feels very much like an aria, but the tenor soon takes over the melody; the soprano then offers a well-spun countermelody. The movement becomes a trio when the bass soloist enters with yet a third melodic strain.

Soloists (soprano and bass but no tenor) and chorus take turns in the final *Agnus Dei*, which begins in solemn E minor but moves, as during Schubert's time it must, to G major for the final "dona nobis pacem"—as truly peaceful a phrase as Schubert ever penned. —*Blair Johnston*

Recommended:

- ○ **Schubert: Deutsche Messe** / Sawallisch (cond.), Fischer-Dieskau, Popp, Schloter, Dallapozza, Bavarian Radio Chorus & Orch. / Capitol 47407
- ○ **Schubert: Mass in G; Psalm; Tantum Ergo; Schumann: Requiem** / Abbado (cond.), Bonney, Schmidt, Pita, Bryndorf, CO of Europe / DG 435486
- ○ **Schubert: Masses 2 & 6** / Shaw (cond.), Upshaw, Gordon, Stone, Atlanta SO & Chorus / 1990 / Telarc 80212

Mass in A flat major ("Missa Solemnis"), D. 678 (1819–1822)

It took Franz Schubert, a man who could throw three or four songs onto paper in a matter of hours, three full years (1819–22) to come up with a version of the *Mass No. 5 in A flat major,* D. 678 that pleased him—seven years if we include the revision of the mass that he made in 1826 when he used it to audition (unsuccessfully) for a position within the Imperial Court Chapel. At one point he chose to call the work a Missa Solemnis; he eventually decided against that title but it has nevertheless continued to appear over the years. Schubert himself felt this to be possibly the finest of his six Latin masses, and it is not difficult to understand why. Neither the most expansive or imposing of the masses (No. 6 in E flat can claim that distinction) nor the most immediately endearing of them (the simple charm of No. 2 in G seems to strike people rather faster), it is probably the finest and most perfectly balanced fusion of traditional sacred style with Schubert's own radiant songfulness and astonishing inventiveness among the composer's choral pieces.

The *A flat major Mass* may or may not have been performed during Schubert's lifetime; the records simply do not exist. It remained unpublished for decades after Schubert's death but during the last century countless listeners and musicians have come to agree with Schubert that it is a remarkable work.

The usual six portions of the Mass Ordinary are all in place: Kyrie, Gloria, Credo, Sanctus, Benedictus, and Agnus Dei. The Andante con moto Kyrie begins with mild woodwind thoughts that are soon enough duplicated by the chorus; the movement's central, "Christe eleison" portion is, as per tradition, assigned to the four vocal soloists. There is something positively symphonic about the Gloria (Allegro vivace e maestoso)—the choral writing is very frequently the poor sister of the orchestral music that "supports" it. The soloists again come out of the woodwork during the "Adoramus te" section, perhaps to prepare themselves for the more extended soloism of the central "Gratias agimus"—calm music that sounds almost as though it might have been conceived for string quartet. The Gloria culminates in a large fugue. The Credo opens in a solid and self-assured C major. There is a stunning pause and then sudden drop down to an A flat major chord for the throbbing "Et incarnatus est." The Sanctus (Andante) is absolutely stunning in its first bars, as what seems to be a confident F major pulsation in the orchestra is sharply undercut by the chorus's decision to enter in F sharp minor. The movement as a whole is one of those movements in Schubert's music where the world of Romantic harmony seems to take shape. Both soloists and chorus are given their fair share in the Benedictus, likewise in the Agnus Dei that concludes this wonderful mass; the final moments of the mass are ones of refined exultation, eventually melting down into a few lyrical woodwind twists. —*Blair Johnston*

Recommended:

- ○ **Schubert: Mass in A flat Major** / Rilling (cond.), Groop, Brown, Taylor, Volle, Oregon Bach Festival Orch. / 1997 / Haenssler 98120
- ○ **Schubert: Mass in A flat major** / Gardiner (cond.), George, York, Archer, Monteverdi Choir, Orch. Revolutionnaire et Romantique / 1999 / Philips 456578
- ○ **Schubert: 3 Masses; Tantum Ergo; Offertorium** / Sawallisch (cond.), Fischer-Dieskau, Donath, Fassbaender, Araiza, Bavarian RSO / 1999 / Angel 73365

Mass in E flat major, D. 950 (1828)

Franz Schubert was one of the torchbearers at Ludwig van Beethoven's funeral in the spring of 1827, and perhaps the effect of his passing can be heard reverberating in the *Mass No. 6 in E flat major,* D. 950, composed a year later. Indeed, the mass was dedicated to the very church where Beethoven's final rites were administered; it is difficult to imagine that Schubert would have been unaffected by the memory of an event that loomed so large in his own consciousness and in that of all Vienna. If the mass was a conscious tribute, Schubert would not live to witness its realization: he was dead by the time the work received its first performance in late 1829. The E flat Mass is an expansive work, blending ambitious Beethovenian architecture with Schubert's lyricism; it offers a worthy choral counterpart to the "heavenly length" of the composer's *Symphony No. 9* and *Piano Sonata in B flat major,* D. 960.

The *E flat Mass* is scored for an orchestra without flutes, and while there are parts for vocal soloists, they are a good deal less significant than in Schubert's earlier masses. All six sections of the Mass Ordinary are set: the Kyrie, Gloria, Credo, Sanctus, Benedictus, and Agnus Dei. Throughout the mass there is a marked infusion of calm lyricism and songfulness into the sacred music vessel, something of which earlier composers of sacred music might have avoided. There is also a great deal more vigorous counterpoint (long a hallmark of sacred music) than one finds in Schubert's only other large-scale mass, in A flat major.

Schubert's gentle blend of wind instruments at the start of the Kyrie is no less than perfect, setting quite a standard for the chorus that immediately imitates it. The *Allegro moderato e maestoso* Gloria begins a cappella. Throughout his life, Schubert had been fond of virtuosic violin writing, but seldom does he match in sheer energy the violin explosion that follows this Gloria's a cappella opening. The "Domine Deus" portion of the text is set to rather less physical music. The Credo begins Moderato, gently and quietly; with the arrival of the "Et incarnatus" text there arrives also a lovely cello melody which is soon taken over by the tenor soloist, whose refined passion seems almost too great for its slender proportions. Both the Gloria and Credo conclude with large fugues that approach those of Beethoven's *Missa Solemnis* of a few years before.

Several great examples of Schubert's unusual and thoroughly proto-Romantic modulation technique are on display at the start of the Sanctus: Schubert moves straight from E flat major to B minor, then to G minor, and finally to E flat minor. The process and even the rhythm are strikingly similar to the one employed by Schubert at the start of the Sanctus movement of the A flat Mass. Fugues appear in both the "Osanna in excelsis" portion of the Sanctus and the Agnus Dei. Midway through the Agnus Dei the firm imitation dissolves into a rich chamber music opportunity for the soloists; the fugal writing is reprised but again melts away, this time into a warm choral passage that draws the mass to a close. —*Blair Johnston*

Recommended:

- ○ **Schubert: Mass in E flat major; Tantum Ergo; Offertorium** / Sawallisch (cond.), Fischer-Dieskau, Donath, Fassbaender, Araiza, Bavarian Radio Chorus & Orch. / 1982 / EMI 692232
- ○ **Schubert: Mass in E flat major** / Rilling (cond.), Rubens, Mehnert, Genz, Stuttgart Bach Collegium / 1998 / Haenssler 98172
- ○ **Schubert: Masses 2 & 6** / Shaw (cond.), Valente, Humphrey, Simpson, Myers, Atlanta SO & Chorus / 1990 / Telarc 80212

Ständchen ("Zögernd, leise"), for alto, chorus & piano ("Notturno"), D. 920 (Jul., 1827)

Standchen (Serenade) (D. 920) is a piece d'occasion in Schubert's oeuvre. And what an occasion it must have been: a nocturnal serenade on the birthday of Louise Gosmar in July of 1827 with a text by the greatest of contemporary Viennese playwrights Franz Grillparzer. Commissioned by Louise's singing teacher Anne Frohlich who was also a friend of Schubert's, this *Standchen* was apparently supposed to be sung by soprano and a chorus of four women. But Schubert misunderstood the commission and originally set Grillparzer's poem for mezzo-soprano and four men. In the event, the song was performed with the requested performers at the appointed place and time or, rather, not quite the appointed time: Schubert himself did not arrive on time. His friends found him at his favorite coffee house where he pleaded forgetfulness and was dragged to the performance.

The work itself is slight Schubert, hardly a match for the great works of 1827—*Winterreise*, the two sets of impromptus, and the *E flat major Piano Trio*—but charming nevertheless with a graceful melody for the mezzo, a hearty chorus for the men or women of the chorus, and a perpetual motion accompaniment for the piano. *—James Leonard*

Recommended:

○ **Monica Groop: Art of the Romantic Song** / Groop, Jansen / 2001 / Ondine 986

○ **Schubert: Lieder** / von Otter, Forsberg, Swedish Radio Choir / DG 453481

OPERA

Operas, Singspiels & Incidental Music (1811–1828)

Although Austrian composer Franz Schubert wrote 18 dramatic works—including operas, singspiels, and incidental music—he never achieved success in this field. Three of the most obvious causes were the censorship prohibiting the portrayal of anything of any substance appearing on the stage, the dominance of Rossini's operas in Vienna at the time, and the astoundingly poor quality of Schubert's libretto, many by his well-meaning friends. A more significant reason might be that while Schubert was a superb composer of songs, he could not make the leap from lyrical songs to dramatic arias. While there are many beautiful melodies in Schubert's works for the stage, little of his music in this genre is dramatic. Rarely are any of the arias, duets, trios, or ensembles in Schubert's stage works dramatic: the characters can be extremely expressive in articulating their emotions, but they almost never change or grow and the action of the plot is almost never advanced by the music. Whether Schubert would have progressed beyond this had he lived longer is an open question, but none of his works for the stage have ever held the stage.

Schubert's first opera was the very Mozartean *Der Spiegelritter* from 1811–12. The proto-Romantic opera *Des Teufels Lustschloss*, which anticipates many of the harmonic innovations of Weber's *Der Freischütz*, was composed in 1814. The next year, Schubert wrote the music for four singspiels, three of them in the early summer. The first, *Der vierjährige Posten*, had a libretto by Schubert's friend, Theodor Körner; the second, *Fernando*, had a plot not dissimilar to that of Beethoven's *Fidelio*; the third, *Claudine von Villa Bella*, was in three acts, only the first of which survives; and a fourth, *Die Freunde von Salamanka*, with a libretto by Schubert's friend, Johann Mayrhofer, followed in November, 1815. Schubert's most successful stage work in his lifetime was a singspiel *Die Zwillingsbrüder* from 1819, which ran for six performances in the Karntnertortheater in 1820. This success prompted Schubert to compose and complete his first grand opera, *Alfonso und Estrella*, to a libretto by his friend, Franz Schober, in 1821–22. But Rossini-mania prevented it from being accepted by either of Vienna's houses and it was first performed in 1854 by Liszt. Schubert's last and best singspiel, *Die Verschworenen*, based on *Lysistrata*, was written in 1823, as was his last and greatest grand opera, *Fierabras*, to a libretto by his friend, Leopold Kupelwieser, and his most popular piece for the stage, the incidental music from *Rosamunde*, a four-act stage play. Although hurriedly written and with much of its music taken from works composed for other purposes—most famously the *Entr'acte No. 6*, it takes its material from the slow movement of the *String Quartet in A minor* and from the song *Der Leidende*—Schubert's music for *Rosamunde*, relieved of the necessity of advancing a plot, has the lyrical grace of his best songs. *—James Leonard*

Recommended:

○ **Schubert: Alfonso & Estrella** / Suitner (cond.), Fischer-Dieskau, Schreier, Adam, Buchner, Berlin RSO / 1994 / Berlin Classics 0021562

○ **Schubert: Fierrabras** / Muller-Kray (cond.), Wunderlich, Rohr, Wolansky, Kahmann, Bern State Orch. / Myto 89001

○ **Schubert: Rosamunde** / Abbado (cond.), Otter, Ernst, CO of Europe / DG 431655

○ **Schubert: Die Verschworenen** / Wallberg (cond.), Schmidhuber, Moll, Moser, Dallapozza, Munich Radio Orch. / CPO 999554

Erwin Schulhoff

b. Jun. 8, 1894, Prague, Bohemia (Czech Rep.), **d.** Aug. 18, 1942, Wülzburg, Bavaria, Germany

Composer: Chamber Music, Keyboard, Concerto, Orchestral

It was only 60 years after his death in the Wülzburg concentration camp that Czech composer Erwin Schulhoff began to be recognized. One of many composers whose works the Nazi regime labeled as "Entartete Musik" (degenerate music), he was effectively silenced by the stark political and social workings of fascism in the 1930s and 1940s. Schulhoff was indeed possessed of radical ideas, both political and musical, and was a founding member of the Dresden-based Werkstatt der Zeit (Workshop of the Time), but he is now known to be a composer of remarkable variety and invention whose works spanned the aesthetic void between the late romanticism of Max Reger and Scriabin and the experimental modernism of John Cage. During the 30 years of his active career he wrote sonatas, quartets, sextets, jazz piano pieces, stage music, an opera, eight symphonies, and at least one oratorio.

Schulhoff's works divide roughly into four periods that manifest wildly different stylistic and ideological principles. His early works, composed after his studies at the Prague Conservatory, betray a great debt to Reger, Dvořák, and Brahms, and are in a generally serious vein. Following his service in World War I, he found new resonance in the ideas of the Second Viennese School (Arnold Schoenberg and his pupils), but soon embraced the emerging trend of dadaism as more representative of his philosophies. This "second period" in his creative development shows a dual allegiance to these two schools of thought, resulting in rather austere serial works as well as more vigorously anti-establishment works that included experimental notation systems and an emerging sense of musical humor.

By 1923 Schulhoff had moved into yet a third creative phase that was partly inspired by his exposure (in Dresden via recordings) to American jazz. This new influence was incorporated into a maturing synthesis of European trends, combined with a renewed interest in the music of his native Czechoslovakia. During this time many of his works took on a straightforward, almost Neo-classical sound that left the complexity of serialism behind.

Schulhoff's final creative phase was precipitated by a visit to the Soviet Union in 1933, and his resulting political conversion to Stalinism. His late works betray a concerted effort to communicate in plain, unpretentious ways and to glorify the ideals of communism through the use of greatly simplified musical means. Ultimately these cannot be judged his most successful experiments. The German occupation of Czechoslovakia in 1939 resulted in Schulhoff's arrest and imprisonment in 1941. He died only months later of tuberculosis. *—Peter Bates*

CHAMBER MUSIC

Duo for violin & cello (1925)

"[Music is] never philosophy; it arises from an ecstatic condition and finds its expression in rhythmic movement."—Schulhoff

When Erwin Schulhoff dedicated his 1925 *Duo for Violin and Cello* "to Master Leoš Janáček, in deep admiration!," the composer did more than declare affections. He perhaps knew of Janáček's self-proclaimed intention to break from the burden of Schoenberg and the "new music" and do something completely different. In the eyes of its defensive opponents, the Schoenbergian school practiced an entangled idea-music, trying to conjure the distant Beethovenian spirit with a grey concoction of difficult theory and more difficult sound. At its descriptive summit was Theodor Adorno, who considered Beethoven's music as much a philosophy as Hegel's, and who demanded the same of any contemporary music as its certificate of legitimacy. Hence the precise sting and haughty pride in Schulhoff's announcement that music is "never philosophy"—a claim meant to distance himself from the New Viennese School and thought and praxis.

Schulhoff's duo is a fine exemplar of the composer's anti-philosophy. The nearly 20-minute, four-movement score looks with calculation and brilliance (much like Janáček's music did) to anti-Schoenberg sources for inspiration. It finds its roots not in an absolutist universe of "musical ideals," formal problems, and pitch-matrices, but in the soil of native musical tongues. All the duo's movements are infused with the spirit of Czech folk song, montaged in affectionately surreal ostinato objects not unlike Stravinsky's play with folk music. This quick-cutting whimsy—whereby sections do not grow argument-like out of previous ones, but playfully disorient and reorient each other—is Schulhoff's other main counter to the "new music." Where "new music" took its model from the voice, Schulhoff's duo is body-music, essentially rhythmic and ecstatic. In this perspective, it is a worthy foil to the sensuous, idyllic classicality of Ravel's *Sonata for Violin and Cello* and the arch-national posture of Kodály's own *Duo for Violin and Cello*. Of course, the root of all questing art tends to be like rather than unlike; art often recognizes that it is nothing like nature and represses this recognition. And hence, behind Schulhoff's wonderful play of folkloric patterns and effects, there is a more serious affiliation with Bach, both in the polyphonic urge and the detailed miniature craft of these distanced dances. Why would Schulhoff repress such authentic influences? Perhaps because they would steer him back to a common stream along with Schoenberg and his pupils, who worshipped Bach. *—Seth Brodsky*

Recommended:

○ **Edition Lockenhaus Vol. 4/5** / Kremer, Geringas, Hirschhorn / 1988 / ECM 1347

○ **Schulhoff: Chamber Music** / Thedeen, Krysa / 1994 / Bis 679

String Quartet No. 1 (1924)

Schulhoff's 1924 *String Quartet No. 1* was written shortly after his return to Prague, the city of his birth. He moved to Austria in 1906, at age 12, to study piano, and for most of the next two decades lived in Germany and Austria. His *String Quartet*

No. 1 came in between the periods of his experimentation with atonality and other progressive methods (1919–23), and the extreme simplification of his style that marked his compositions after 1931. This quartet is one of his finest works, exhibiting both a creative freshness and an imaginative if somewhat unusual structural plan, features that attest to Schulhoff's inventive skills in the string quartet genre. The work is cast in four movements, with a Presto con fuoco opening panel full of vigor and rhythmic poise. Its music is at once catchy in its jaunty, folk-like character. The ensuing Allegretto con moto e con malinconia grotesca deftly—and humorously—lives up to its marking with a grotesque sort of melancholy. The third movement, marked Allegro giocoso alla Slavacca, again turns folk like and also features some engaging effects, making the violin sound almost like a piccolo. The Andante molto sostenuto finale, the first truly slow movement, is charmingly gloomy in its colorfully ethereal sound world. This is one of the few early twentieth century works that can appeal to those with either conservative or adventurous tastes. *—Robert Cummings*

Recommended:

○ **Schulhoff: Chamber Works Vol.1** / Kocian Quartet / Supraphon 112166-2 131

○ **Weill, Schulhoff & Hindemith: String Quartets** / Brandis Quartet / 1994 / Nimbus 5410

KEYBOARD

Suite dansante en jazz (1931)

Erwin Schulhoff (1894–1942) was immensely fond of jazz and even more fond of dancing. As he wrote to his friend Alban Berg in 1921, "I am boundlessly fond of nightclub dancing, so much so that I have periods during which I spend whole nights dancing with one hostess or another... out of pure enjoyment of the rhythm and with my subconscious filled with sensual delight." Nor was his fondness for dancing entirely recreational. As Schulhoff continued, "thereby I acquire phenomenal inspiration for my work, as my conscious mind is incredibly earthly, even animal as it were." From his love of dancing and his love of jazz, Schulhoff wrote a series of jazz-inspired dance works between 1919 and 1931. Many of these were written for the piano, Schulhoff's own instrument, and he performed them throughout Europe and on the radio. His last major work in this style was his *Suite dansante en jazz for piano* from 1931. Set in six movements, the *Suite dansante* moves through six different dances in a little over a quarter of an hour. It begins with a short, fast Stomp, followed by a languorous Strait, a parodistic Waltz, a sensuous Tango, and a languid Slow, and ends with a fast and lascivious Fox Trot. *—James Leonard*

Recommended:

○ **Schulhoff: Jazz Inspired Piano Works** / Visek / 1993 / Supraphon 18702131

CONCERTO

Double Concerto for flute, piano & strings (1927)

While touring as assisting pianist with the Paris Wind Quintet, Schulhoff decided to write a twentieth century concerto grosso featuring his instrument and that of the quintet's flutist, René LeRoy; the two gave the first performance in Prague in 1927. It falls into the traditional three movements and is unmistakably neo-Classical in its formal clarity and reliance on burbling thematic material. The first movement, Allegro moderato, could initially pass for Paul Hindemith, although once the two soloists enter, the music generally becomes less dour and more perky in its use of ostinatos, more in the style of Schulhoff's countryman Bohuslav Martinů. It manages to use the classic sonata form even while resurrecting the Baroque practice of essentially having the two soloists play in alternation with the full orchestra (the orchestra providing only the most necessary support for the flute-and-piano passages). A nocturnal section late in the development provides momentary relief from the ostinato rhythms chugging through the rest of the movement. The soloists take a substantial cadenza near the end, first reverting to the nocturnal music, but then gradually building up speed and intensity. The melancholy Andante proceeds with a simplicity of expression, although the piano part betrays a certain restlessness. The Allegro con spirito is a rondo sporting a fast, staccato, carefree main theme that sometimes darkens, but the music never loses its momentum until a blues-tinged midpoint intermezzo for flute and piano. The energetic material ultimately returns, with the soloists and orchestra trotting all the way through to the final bars. *—James Reel*

Recommended:

○ **Schulhoff** / Hilgers (cond.), Tritonus Wimares / 2000 / MDG 6311015

ORCHESTRAL

Suite for chamber orchestra, Op. 37 (1921)

The *Suite for Chamber Orchestra* (1921) reflects Erwin Schulhoff's enchantment with artist George Grosz's collection of American jazz records. It was his first successful attempt to compose a jazz piece for orchestra. Consisting of six dances with names like "Ragtime," "Valse Boston," and "Shimmy," this bouncy, often silly work features instruments never used in the classical repertoire before, like slide whistles and car horns. "Step" is a 48-second miniature featuring only percussion instruments. Like others of his generation (Kurt Weill, Igor Stravinsky), Schulhoff loved the tango and inserts one into this piece. It is a well-scored, slinky departure from the humoresques. Sometimes the tango seethes with sex, other times it glides like a stately minuet. The suite combines bitonality and harsh dissonances with the melodic style of contemporary music. *—Peter Bates*

Recommended:

○ **Schulhoff** / Hilgers (cond.), Tritonus Wimares / 2000 / MDG 6311015

○ **Schulhoff: Ensemble Works Vol. 1** / Herbers (cond.), Ebony Band / 1994 / Channel Classics 6994

Gunther Schuller

b. Nov. 22, 1925, New York, NY

Composer: Chamber Music, Orchestral

It seems safe to say that at this stage in his life and career, Gunther Schuller represents, for countless musicians, concertgoers, and record buyers around the world, American music making at its best, almost as much as Leonard Bernstein did a half century earlier. He is composer, conductor, horn player, jazz performer, writer, administrator, publisher, and teacher, all wrapped up into one tidy bundle of seemingly endless energy. Like American music itself, however, Schuller has not always steered clear of controversy—the very masses that admire him have sometimes been baffled by his uncompromising attitudes and blunt statements.

His father played violin in the New York Philharmonic Orchestra for many decades, and it was he who oversaw Schuller's early training. Schuller mastered the French horn with remarkable speed as a student at the Manhattan School of Music (1939–41)—in 1942, aged just 16, his horn playing was heard across the country in the American radio premiere of Shostakovich's then brand-new *"Leningrad" Symphony.* A series of high-profile orchestra jobs followed: first the American Ballet Theater Orchestra, then the Cincinnati Symphony Orchestra, and then 14 seasons in the Metropolitan Opera Orchestra. During the 1950s Schuller became interested in jazz and made a name for himself as a performer in that field, playing with Miles Davis, Dizzy Gillespie and other jazz stars; in the years to come, Schuller combined jazz and traditional composition in new ways—something that he called "third stream music." After the 1958–59 season, Schuller gave up his career at the Met to build a new career as a composer.

Success in the sometimes persnickety world of American serious composition came to Schuller nearly as easily and quickly as success as a performer did, and by 1964 he was on the composition faculty of Yale University. He has also taught and administered at the Manhattan School of Music, the New England Conservatory, and Tanglewood.

In 1975 he founded his own record label and music publishing companies, GM Recordings and Margun Music (the names are drawn from the first names of Schuller and his wife Marjorie Black). He has also written several books, including the cherished manual *Horn Playing* (London and New York, 1962) and the landmark studies *Early Jazz: Its Roots and Development* (London and New York,1968) and *The Swing Era: the Development of Jazz 1930–45* (New York and Oxford, 1989). In 1997 he poured his many years' experience as a professional conductor into *The Compleat Conductor.*

As a composer, Schuller ranks among the most eclectic of his generation or any other. Schoenberg's techniques meet jazz meets Stravinskian rhythmicism meets Haydn in ways that one could never imagine without the score on the table. And his output is very large: 20-plus concertos for solo instrument(s) and orchestra, several dozen other orchestral items (including the 1965 *Symphony* and the 1994 Pulitzer Prize-winning *Of Reminiscences and Reflections*), better than 70 miscellaneous chamber pieces for ensembles and combinations of all kinds, a pair of operas, and a library of arrangements of other composers' music. *—Blair Johnston*

Overview of Works (1941)

"Gunther Schuller isn't merely a musician," critic Alan Rich famously quipped, "he's a monopoly." Indeed, after launching a highly promising career as an orchestral horn player at an incredibly early age, Schuller went on to become one of America's most successful conductors, pedagogues, and composers. And while his compositions, which number upwards of 160, comprise only a portion of his powerful influence on the musical climate of the late twentieth century (his credits include a text on conducting and important histories of jazz music), they nonetheless constitute an impressive body of work. His oeuvre likewise reflects his wide-ranging interests and comprehensive knowledge of various musical styles, not only in his famous establishment of "third stream" music, which represented a mixture of classical and jazz, but his championing of and collaborations with musicians ranging from Elliott Carter to Dizzy Gillespie to Frank Zappa. Schuller is perhaps best known for his synthesis of jazz and classical styles, as reflected in his numerous arrangements and transcriptions for jazz ensemble of works by such classical composers as Ives, Weill, Gottschalk, and even Bach, Monteverdi, Gesualdo, and Ockeghem. A number of works combine jazz and orchestral instrumental forces, such as the *Concertino for Jazz Quartet and Orchestra* (1959), *Journey Into Jazz* (1962), and the well-known *Seven Studies on Themes of Paul Klee* (1959). Despite the notoriety of Schuller's boundary-bending tendencies, however, such explicit border-crossings comprise only a portion of his output. Among his other important contributions are a series of over 20 concertos featuring "underrepresented" orchestral instruments and ensembles. These include concertos for double bass (1968), Renaissance instrumental ensemble (1970), saxophone (1983), bassoon (1985), and string quartet (1988). A number of his works pay special attention to his native instrument, the horn. Among these are two horn concertos (1944, 1976), a horn sonata (1988), and *Lines and Contrasts* (1960), a curious work for 16 horns. A number of Schuller's most successful orchestral works resulted from commissions from major symphony orchestras, including *The Past Is in the Present* (1994) and *An Arc Ascending* (1996), both for the Cincinnati Symphony, and *Of Reminiscences and Remembrances* (1993), a touching, intimate reflection on the life and then-recent passing of the composer's wife, which received a Pulitzer Prize after its premiere by the Louisville Orchestra. Schuller's oeuvre includes a number of important vocal works as well. These included a number of early devotional works and anthems; settings of classic texts by Shakespeare, Petrarch, Michelangelo, and others (in his *Six Renaissance Lyrics for Tenor and Chamber Ensemble* from 1962); renderings of later poetry by Gertrude Stein and Emily Dickinson (respectively, *Mediations* from 1960 and *Poems of Time and Eternity* from 1972); and the impressive *Mondrian's Vision* (1994) for large ensemble chorus. Schuller's work also includes a number of dance, theater, and operatic works, including a number of "television ballets," as well as a handful of film scores. *—Jeremy Grimshaw*

Recommended:

- ○ **Schuller: Sextet; Fantasy-Suite; Duologue** / Schuller (cond.), Starobin, Abramovic, Fulkerson, Finn / 1999 / Bridge 9093
- ○ **Schuller: Of Reminiscences and Reflections** / Schuller (cond.), Bernardi (cond.), Diaz, Calgary PO, Hannover Radio SO / 1995 / New World 80492
- ○ **Schuller: Orchestral Works** / Schuller (cond.) / 1998 / GM 2059
- ○ **Schuller: Three Concertos** / Rudolf (cond.), Schuller (cond.), Todd, Pasmanick, Kirstein, Cincinnati SO, Saarbrucken Radio SO / 1994 / GM 2044

CHAMBER MUSIC

Suite for wind quintet (1945)

Gunther Schuller completed his *Suite for woodwind quintet* in 1945, scoring it for bassoon, clarinet, flute, horn and oboe. Many of the numerous areas of expertise that would eventually bring to bear on his oeuvre—jazz improvisation, classical composition, and his virtuosity as a horn player—are presaged in this relatively concise work. It was first performed by an ensemble of wind players drawn from the ranks of the Metropolitan Opera Orchestra, of which Schuller was a member at that time. The oboist of this ad hoc group was Josef Marx, who would in 1957 publish the *Suite for woodwind quintet* through his firm, McGinnis & Marx Music, an important imprint in the field of woodwind music. It remains in their catalogue to this day, graded as of "medium difficulty."

In reflecting on the genesis of this youthful suite, Schuller once recalled the particular influence of then current French composers, such as those associated with Les Six. In the suite's first movement Prelude one hears casually off-kilter tonalities such as those of Milhaud or Poulenc. These sonorities, heard in the context of the nimble ostinati textures that accompany the oboe melody in the movement's outer sections, also inevitably suggest Stravinsky in Parisian mode, though the lines and textures in the Prelude's more lyrical middle section loosen up considerably. Just as Stravinsky employed stylized evocations of jazz and ragtime, Schuller's woodwind suite likewise appropriates "vernacular" styles. These ideas are most explicit in the second movement "Blues"; here Schuller enhances the sense of languor and grit through uneven phrases that lean into one another, exaggerated articulations and ornaments, and, especially, a complex, angular harmonic language that falls somewhere on the far side of Gershwin's *Rhapsody in Blue.* Schuller prefaces the score with careful instructions on how to realize the jazz rhythms and a warning to trust the "feel" of the piece as it is written. The final movement, Toccata, is the shortest in the suite. As in the first movement, Schuller uses an uneven, rather dissonant ostinato in the bassoon and clarinet as a backdrop for the oboe melody, it's angularity and context recalling the high bassoon solo in Stravinsky's *Rite of Spring.* Schuller's oboe is much less portentous than Stravinsky's bassoon, and the piece ends with a clever wink and a shrug. *—Jeremy Grimshaw*

Recommended:

- ○ **Another View** / Carter: Etudes (8) and a Fantasy, Piston: Quintet, Schuller: Suite for woodwind ensemble, Diamond: / Sierra Wind Quintet / 1992 / Cambria 1091

ORCHESTRAL

Seven Studies on Themes of Paul Klee (1959)

Although he opted for music as his career, Schuller had a youthful passion and talent for art and drew nearly 1000 pictures. This, his most famous musical work, is one of many representing paintings or photographs in music. Except for the fifth movement, it is entirely in the 12-tone system, being one of the most crowd-pleasing of all works in this technique.

The career of the Swiss artist Paul Klee was the reverse of Schuller's: he was a musically talented boy who chose art. A sense of music is nearly always present in his pictures, which repeat patterns and balance complementary colors in ways that seem related to principals of musical composition. The first, second, and seventh of the paintings Schuller depicts have musical titles. Schuller directly translates the pictorial composition (such as design, shape, and succession of colors) into musical processes. For instance, the 150 little squares in *Antique Harmonies* progress from one predominant color to another as Klee devises the composition of the painting to draw the eye across the picture and thus give it a time dimension; Schuller makes a similar phasing of one tone color to another by gradual steps.

The other four movements are mood portraits of the paintings. The cheeky "Little Blue Devil" comes on-stage with a kind of 12-tone blues harmony in orchestral jazz. The "Twittering Machine" twitters. Its spring runs down, is rewound, and it twitters some more. "Arab Village" is an aerial view. From a distance, flute and drum are heard, then a nasal dance tune in the mixed colors of oboe, harp, and viola. Actual Arab melodies are quoted, the only non-12-tone music in the suite. "An Eerie [*Unheimlich*] Moment" is tense, with an explosive release, sinking back into silence. *—Joseph Stevenson*

Recommended:

- ○ **Schuller: Orchestral Works** / Schuller (cond.) / 1998 / GM 2059
- ○ **Gershwin, Copland, Schuller & Bloch** / Dorati (cond.), Minneapolis SO / 1993 / Mercury 434329

William Schuman

b. Aug. 4, 1910, New York, NY, **d.** Feb. 15, 1992, New York, NY
Composer: Orchestral, Choral, Concerto, Opera, Ballet

William Schuman's 60-year career as a composer and an educator left an indelible mark on several generations of American musicians. Schuman began exploring jazz and popular music while attending public school, eventually forming an ensemble of his own (in which he played violin and banjo). Abandoning a career in commerce, Schuman enrolled in the Juilliard Summer School, and, in 1933, entered Columbia University's Teacher's College, eventually taking his bachelor's and master's degrees. After summer study at the Salzburg Mozarteum in 1935 and the completion of his *First Symphony* in 1936 (a work subsequently withdrawn by the composer) he received private instruction from well-known American composer Roy Harris.

Schuman found an ally in conductor Serge Koussevitsky, who, at Harris' prompting, premiered the *Symphony No. 2* in 1938 (also subsequently withdrawn). Between 1938 and 1945 Schuman served as director of publications for G. Schirmer, Inc. as well as on the faculty of Sarah Lawrence College, leaving this post to take over as president of the Juilliard School (where he remained until 1961, initiating a wide range of new projects and policies, including the complete reorganization of the theory/composition program and the creation of the Juilliard String Quartet). Other administrative positions throughout his long career include serving as president of the *Lincoln Center for the Performing Arts* (1962–69), director of the Koussevitsky Music Foundation, director of the Chamber Music Society at Lincoln Center, and director of the Walter W. Naumberg Foundation. Late in life he was awarded the National Medal of the Arts (1987), and was among those premiere American artists honored at the Kennedy Center in 1989.

Already an established composer in the early 1940s, Schuman was thrust into the national and international limelight when the very first Pulitzer Prize in music was bestowed upon him in 1943 (for his cantata *A Free Song*). His *Third Symphony,* along with Harris' and Copland's Third Symphonies, is considered by many to be the pinnacle of American symphonic achievement, with lofty aesthetic aims and rigorous contrapuntal structure. The *Violin Concerto* of 1959 (first composed in 1947, but heavily revised during the following decade) is an important American contribution to the genre, although, like most of Schuman's work, it has fallen into disuse. *—Blair Johnston*

ORCHESTRAL

New England Triptych, for orchestra or band (1956)

Based on hymn tunes by early American composer William Billings (1746–1800), William Schuman's *New England Triptych* (1956) is less a variation on its source material than a colorful impression of Billings' hardy musical spirit. The first of these three orchestral tone poems, "Be Glad Then, America," is marked by spirited forward momentum, a brief fugal section, and a concluding reference to the "shout and rejoice" passage in Billings' original. "When Jesus Wept" uses its source material as a point of departure for an extended, lyrically sad round with embellishments and melodic extensions. "Chester" is adapted from the hymn used as a marching song by the Continental Army. An appropriately hymnlike beginning changes into a texture of almost improvisatory running lines which eventually become accompaniment to a return of the march tune in the brass. The effect of the *New England Triptych* is such that it has become the most popular of Schuman's works and a signature example of the "Americana" style that pervaded American music from the 1930s to the 1950s. *—AMG*

Recommended:

- ○ **Hanson Conducts Ives, Shuman & Mennin** / Hanson (cond.), Eastman-Rochester Pops Orch. / 1991 / Mercury 432755
- ○ **Leonard Slatkin Conducts American Portraits** / Slatkin (cond.), St. Louis SO / RCA 60983

Variations on "America," arrangment of Ives' work for orchestra or band (1963)

Charles Ives wrote his cheeky set of organ variations on the patriotic hymn *America* as a teenager, in 1891. William Schuman, one of the leading American composers of the middle twentieth century, didn't discover the piece until it was played on the 1962 dedicatory organ recital of what is now called Avery Fisher Hall in Lincoln Center, of which Schuman was the president. "By the time the piece was over," Schuman wrote, "I knew that I simply had to transcribe it." So he did, on commission from Broadcast Music, Inc. Andre Kostelanetz premiered Schuman's orchestral treatment with the New York Philharmonic in 1964.

As usual for Ives, the original score had come down through the decades in a bit of a mess; Schuman adhered to E. Power Biggs' 1949 edition of the piece, so the music's polytonality and insolence are Ives' own. Schuman's own stamp comes in the extra humor he brought through his typically varied and brilliant scoring. Always a master of brass and percussion writing, he applied those instruments to the variations to excellent effect.

A brief, mock-portentous introduction based on fragments of the melody leads to a sober statement of the full theme by brass over col legno strings. The first variation keeps the melody in the strings while the woodwinds, brass, and percussion ornament it with exercise-like material. The second variation is sentimental but mildly dissonant, with satiric barbershop cadences midway and at the end. Dissonance soon comes to the fore in a slow, fierce, polytonal statement interrupted by a goofy pizzicato waltz. The fourth variation is an odd minor-mode polonaise prominently featuring the tuba, given an incongruous Spanish flair by castanets and tambourine. After a short brass chorale statement of the melody comes a perky treatment that becomes increasingly grandiose. The coda brings back material from the introduction, making it even more pompous than before. *—James Reel*

Recommended:

- ○ **Brahms: Haydn Variations; Reger: Mozart Variations; Ives/Schuman: Variations on America** / Masur (cond.), New York Philharmonic / 1992 / Teldec 174007
- ○ **William Schuman: Violin Concerto; New England Triptych; Varations on America** / Serebrier (cond.), Bournemouth Sinfonietta / 2001 / Naxos 559083

CHORAL

Carols of Death (1958)

William Schuman almost always adopted American subjects for his programmatic works, whether depicting festivals, writing a "baseball" opera, or simply setting texts from an 1897 Sears-Roebuck catalog. It is unsurprising, then, that he often turned to the works of American poets when composing for the voice. The *Carols of Death* (1958) are short a cappella settings of short poems by Walt Whitman. Schuman's artistry both serves and elevates the poetry. The first setting, "The Last Invocation," alternates crescendos and diminuendos from one line of text to the next, creating a breathing effect that begets a powerful climax at the end. In "The Unknown Region," Schuman underscores both the anxiety and peace of the text by contrasting sections in which the voices sound dispersed (as in the punchy canon on the opening words, "Darest thou now") with those in which the choir sings in unison. "To All, To Each" is the shortest of the poems, and though Schuman extends the text with frequent melismas, he never obscures the words. His handling of the phrase "lovely and soothing death"—the first three words light and ethereal, the fourth, suddenly dissonant—is particularly eloquent. *—Andrew Lindemann Malone*

Recommended:

- ○ **Darest Thou, O Soul?** / Krebill (cond.), Alexandria Choral Society, Huffman / 1995 / A Classical Record 10307

CONCERTO

Violin Concerto (1947; revised 1954)

The commission for William Schuman's *Violin Concerto* came from violinist Samuel Dushkin and conductor Sergey Koussevitzky in 1947; however, it was Isaac Stern and Charles Münch who gave the 1950 premiere. Schumann found this original version unsatisfactory, and he produced two subsequent revisions. Stern again premiered the second edition in 1954, and Roman Totenberg gave the first performance of the third and final version in 1959; it is in this version that the work is known today. The concerto is a demanding piece of symphonic writing—a real workout for both soloist and orchestra—whose passages of compact rhythmic vigor are matched by strains of the kind of long-limbed flexible melody that is one of the hallmarks of Schuman's music.

Originally the *Violin Concerto* was in three movements, but in its final form it is a two-movement composition. The first movement begins with a snappy Allegro risoluto in which the violinist plays cells of disjunct but largely legato music atop secco gestures from the orchestra. A massive orchestral climax leads to further development of these ideas and then a hushed, cantabile Molto tranquillo episode. The opening music is recalled, scherzando-style, and then Schuman provides a nicely-colored cadenza.

The second movement is even more sectionalized than the first. Brass and timpani usher in the movement's Adagio introduction, and then the soloist enters quietly. After a brief quasi cadenza, the orchestra ventures off on its own with a sharply rhythmic fugue. The violin reasserts itself over a sustained A major triad in the trumpets, and then violinist and orchestra come together for a spry Allegretto). An Adagietto offers some relaxation before the final accelerando and crescendo, in which the violinist is purposefully drowned out by the orchestra. *—Blair Johnston*

Recommended:

- ○ **Ruggles: Sun-treader; Schuman: Violin Concerto; Piston: Symphony 2** / Zukofsky, Tilson Thomas (cond.), Boston SO / 1990 / DG 429860
- ○ **Schuman: Violin Concerto** / Quint, Serebrier (cond.), Bournemouth Sinfonietta / 2001 / Naxos 559083

OPERA

The Mighty Casey (1951–1953)

Even though the subject of baseball may seem more apt for musical theater than for opera, William Schuman had such a strong interest in the sport that he based his opera *The Mighty Casey* on the game. Written between 1951 and 1953, his work was inspired by Ernest L. Thayer's poem about a legendary batsman who strikes out in his team's hour of need. Schuman was presiding over the Juilliard School and working as an editorial consultant at G. Schirmer when he wrote the opera. Even with heavy work obligations, he managed to always make time for writing music. On this matter, Schuman commented that the "continuum in my life has always been composition, I always loved education and administration, but the trick was to compose before I went to work."

Written in an eclectic style but in a traditional format, the music of *The Mighty Casey* bears suggestions of Prokofiev's *Scythian Suite* and, in spots, of Beethoven's *Ninth Symphony*. The work features athletic rhythms and is generally a crowd-pleaser, standing somewhat apart from the composer's more experimental mood of the 1950s. With the help of Jeremy Gury, Schuman expanded Thayer's poem *Casey at the Bat* into an 80-minute one-act opera. Schuman and Gury succeeded in transforming the plot from a tale that gently satirizes a showoff into a story in which the hero of little Cooperstown misses his moment of glory, leaving the audience to ponder the more profound significance of the sport. Rather than focusing on the excitement of the actual game, Schuman believed that performers "should evoke the softened feeling of recollection." Joseph W. Polisi wrote that the most significant sentiments of the opera were "expectations, anger, love, and disappointment all live on this baseball diamond. Here, successes and failures take on larger-than-life proportions which speak to issues beyond the isolated incident of an inopportune strikeout. The touching image of Casey attempting to relive his last at bat—this time with a homer as a result—reflects the hopes in all of us that the next time at bat might be the best of all."

The Mighty Casey was premiered on May 4, 1953, at the Burns School auditorium in Hartford, CT. The work was later recast as a cantata and had its premiere in this form on April 6, 1976, in Washington, D.C. *—Meredith Gailey*

Synopsis:

Scene One. As the twentieth century dawns in the town of Mudville, U.S.A., the clear blue sky provides the perfect canopy for the state baseball championship. So declares the Watchman, who engages a field worker named Merry in an appreciative conversation about the Mudville team, especially a handsome local hero named Casey, "a demon up at bat." Meanwhile, the opposing Centerville team talks strategy. Thatcher, the catcher, informs Snedeker, the pitcher, that Casey is a sucker for a pitch that's inside and high—he always swings at it, and he always misses. The two congratulate themselves that they are so well-equipped with the brains it takes to play baseball.

A while later, the Watchman passes time with the concessionaire and snack hawkers, who are waiting for the team to arrive and the game to begin. The Watchman and the chorus engage in a potted history of baseball, mainly the game's creation by Abner Doubleday. Now the chorus announces the arrival of each Mudville team member; every man pauses to introduce himself, usually with a pitch for his own local business. Finally, in a big buildup, the chorus anticipates the entrance of the Mighty Casey, idol, wonder, terror, slugger. Casey strides onto the field, in silence.

Off to the side, the Watchman notices that the usually tomboyish Merry is now wearing a pretty dress and looking grown-up; it's evident that she has a longstanding crush on Casey. Merry is distressed to hear that scouts from the big leagues are lurking in the stands, ready to offer Casey a contract; that would take Casey out of town, which Merry is desperately sure Casey would resist. Merry makes her feelings obvious in her big aria "Kiss Me Not Goodbye."

Scene Two. It's the bottom of the ninth, two men out, two on base. If Casey hits a home run, Mudville will win the championship. Problem is, two sorry hitters are up before Casey. Merry offers up a prayer to let Casey step up to the plate. Miraculously, the two poor hitters each come through, if barely. Now the bases are loaded, and to the delight of the gladdened multitude, Casey advances to the bat. The Watchman narrates the action, drawing his remarks directly from Ernest Lawrence Thayer's poem "Casey at the Bat." The catcher interrupts the proceedings by calling a timeout, and goes up to the pitcher's mound to remind his colleague to follow the strategy they plotted before the game. The pitcher lets one fly; Casey doesn't swing, and the umpire calls a strike. The crowd and the Mudville manager berate the umpire, who defends his judgment. Casey ignores the next pitch, another strike. "Hist'ry hangs on a slender thread," the crowd remarks; they and the pitcher contemplate how so much depends on the pitcher's control. Comes the third pitch, high and inside, and Casey swings furiously—but misses. There is no joy in Mudville; Casey has struck out.

Scene Three. In a brief final pantomime, Casey's failure is forgiven—and justified—as he unites with the faithful Merry. *—James Reel*

Recommended:

○ **Schuman: The Mighty Casey; A Question Of Taste** / Schwarz (cond.), Juilliard Orch. & Soloists / 1994 / Delos 1030

BALLET

Undertow (1945)

After hearing a performance of the young William Schuman's fifth symphony in 1944, Anthony Tudor had the American Ballet Theater (then called Ballet Theatre) commission a ballet score from the composer. Tudor was then the head of the contemporary English ballet section of Ballet Theatre and was a leader in the combination of modern dance techniques with those of classical ballet. His ballet *Pillar of Fire* had broken new ground in what was then termed "dramatic" or "psychological" ballet, and he continued to explore that field in *Undertow.* Tudor considered this ballet to be one of his finest ballets; it is also the summation of the choreographer's work in that category. The ballet is essentially a symbolic presentation of a psychopathic murderer's case history. Though the setting is an urban slum of the 1940s, most of the characters have names and attributes from classical mythology.

Undertow was Schuman's first important dance score. The one-act ballet is divided into three overall sections: Prologue, The Drama, and Epilogue. Schuman's score is quite descriptive, delineating characters, actions and states, adroitly bringing out the nervousness and violence of the scenario. Eclectic, it runs the gamut from ironic hymnlike passages to portions that in their explosive impact are the equal to any from Schuman's contemporaries and predecessors. Although it certainly shows the influence of Stravinsky and Roy Harris, there is a marked individuality, particularly in its driving rhythms and "apocalyptic" climax. At this climax, in addition to full orchestra, the pianist is directed to pound the black keys with the left hand and forearm.

Undertow premiered at the Metropolitan Opera House on April 10, 1945, with Antal Dorati conducting the orchestra and Hugh Laing dancing the leading role of the psychopathic Transgressor. Due to modern subject, scenario, and music, the audience reaction was mixed at best. Nonetheless, *Undertow* was in the repertory of the American Ballet Theater for a number of decades. The premiere of the concert version of *Undertow* took place on November 29, 1945, by the Los Angeles Philharmonic Orchestra with Alfred Wallenstein conducting. *—Neil Cardew-Fanning*

Recommended:

○ **Antheil: Capital of the World; Schuman: Undertow** / Levine (cond.), Ballet Theatre Orch. / 1997 / EMI 66548

○ **The NBC Broadcast Concerts, December 1950** / Cantelli (cond.), NBC SO / 2003 / Testament 1317

Clara Wieck Schumann

b. Sep. 13, 1819, Leipzig, Germany, **d.** May 20, 1896, Frankfurt am Main, Germany

Composer: Keyboard, Chamber Music, Concerto, Vocal

Clara Wieck Schumann has often been misleadingly referred to as the wife of composer Robert Schumann, and as one of the leading pianists of her day, rather than as a composer in her own right. Beginning in the last quarter of the twentieth century however, her stature as a composer finally became recognized. Still, she cannot by any reasonable measure be ranked as a major composer, owing in great part to her relatively small output. She nonetheless wrote significant compositions in both the keyboard and vocal realms. Had she been able to devote more time to composition—she was occupied by maternal matters much of the time, having given birth to eight children—she might well have risen to the artistic heights of her husband. Some of her later works—the *Six Lieder,* Op. 23, for instance—demonstrate considerable subtlety and depth.

Clara Wieck was born on September 13, 1819, in Leipzig. She began studying the piano with her domineering and difficult father, whom her mother, a talented singer, later divorced. Mr. Wieck was a piano teacher of high repute. Clara gave her debut concert in Leipzig at the age of seven playing Kalkbrenner's duet, *Variations on a March from Moses,* with him.

In 1830, Robert Schumann began study with Wieck, at which time he first met Clara. At twelve Clara toured Europe with her father, achieving great success in Paris and throughout Germany. By 1837 she was recognized as one of the leading virtuosos in Europe, and her career as a composer was blossoming as well. Her first compositions date from 1830, but her 1836 *Soirées musicales,* Op. 6, already shows considerable sophistication. In 1837 she and Schumann became engaged, with boisterous objections from her father.

Clara seems to have broken from her father's influence when she toured Paris alone in 1839. The break was made complete the following year when she married Robert Schumann. They would have eight children, and Clara would slowly watch her sensitive husband lose his sanity. The couple at first lived in Leipzig, where both taught at the University.

Clara did not write much in the early years of her marriage, though she did complete the *Six Lieder,* Op. 13 (1842–43), and some piano pieces, including the *Three Preludes and Fugue* (1845). In 1853, the Schumanns moved to Düsseldorf, and Clara had a very productive summer, producing several significant works, including her Op. 20 *Variations on a theme of Robert Schumann* and the aforementioned Op. 23. In 1854, Robert Schumann suffered a mental collapse and attempted suicide, after which he was committed to an asylum where he lived for the rest of his life. He passed away in 1856.

Johannes Brahms, who had been introduced to the Schumanns in 1853 through the violin virtuoso Joseph Joachim, became an increasingly important figure in Clara's life. To this day, their exact relationship is unclear, but it is difficult to refute claims they had an affair. Brahms was 14 years Clara's junior, and possibly felt their age difference too great an obstacle for marriage.

Clara composed little in the years following Robert's death, even after her children were grown. She lived in Berlin from 1857 to 1863, at which time she moved to Baden-Baden. After briefly returning to Berlin in 1873, she took a teaching post at the Frankfurt Hoch Conservatory (1878). She continued to concertize until 1891. She died of a stroke on May 20, 1896. *—Robert Cummings*

KEYBOARD

Soirées Musicales, Op. 6 (1834–1836)

Composed in 1835 or 1836, when she was 16 or 17 years old, Clara Wieck-Schumann's *Soirées musicales,* Op. 6, was published in 1836 by Hofmeister in Leipzig. In 1838, Hofmeister combined Wieck's *Quatre pièces caractéristiques,* Op. 5, with the six *Soirées musicales* and printed them together as the *Soirées musicales: 10 Pièces caractéristiques.* These were published, of course, under the name "Clara Wieck."

Despite her youth, Wieck had a firm command of compositional material, and it is clear from her pieces that she understood the formal and harmonic tendencies of Chopin and Mendelssohn. Her accelerated maturity was in part the result of the extended tours she had undertaken with her father.

The types of compositions in the *Soirées musicales* are typical of her previous publications, all of which are works for piano and single-movement works with titles and forms typical of the times: "Polonaise," "Caprice," "Valse," and "Mazurka," as well as sets of "Variations on a Theme" and character pieces with descriptive titles. *Soirées musicales* consists: "Toccatina," "Ballade," "Notturno," "Polonaise," "Mazurka," and "Mazurka." The set is dedicated to Henrietta Voigt.

The most individual aspects of Clara Wieck's *Soirées musicales* lie in the melodic lines and details. Her large-scale forms are clearly derived from those of other composers, alive and dead. The opening "Toccatina" is a test of digital dexterity, the central section of the piece consisting of sustained parts in the outer voices and accompanimental, moving eighth notes in between. This is framed by a leaping, frantic section in a "Presto" tempo and completely different key.

Perhaps the most inspired piece of the *Soirées musicales* is the "Notturno," in F major. The depth of feeling suggested by the long melodic line is remarkable for a 16-year-old composer. In a slow 6/8 time, the "Notturno" is in ABA form. Its first section features a rocking accompaniment in the left hand supporting a descending, single-line melody in the right. Chromatic descents in the bass add powerful pathos, while a few impressive flourishes mark the high point of the A section. In the B section a trochaic pulse begins in the left hand as the key shifts to the relative minor. The return of A is highly decorated and harmonically altered. The fourth piece, "Ballade," is harmonically rich with a dense texture. No. 5, "Mazurka," is a study in contrasts: fortissimo follows on the heels of pianissimo, and dotted-rhythm melodies give way to rapid, busy chromatic flourishes.

In his *Neue Zeitschrift für Musik* of September 12, 1837, Robert Schumann described Clara's *Soirées musicales* as boasting a "wealth of unconventional resources, an ability to entangle the secret, more deeply twisting threads and then to unravel them." Robert would later borrow the first two measures of Clara's *G major Mazurka*, Op. 6, No. 5, for the opening of the first of his 18 character pieces, *Davidsbündlertänze*, Op. 6, written in 1837. Also, Clara's Op. 6, No. 2 appears in Robert's *Novelletten*, Op. 21. *—John Palmer*

Recommended:

- ○ **Clara Schumann: Piano Music** / Iwai / 1999 / Naxos 553501
- ○ **Clara Schumann: Oeuvres de Jeunesse** / T. Laredo / Gallo 839

Variations on a Theme by Robert Schumann in F sharp minor, Op. 20 (1853)

This variations piece was given to Robert Schumann by his wife Clara upon his 43rd birthday in 1853, the year before his crippling mental breakdown. For years, the common wisdom on the dual career of Clara Wieck Schumann was that she was a much better pianist than composer. In later years, however, her art has been assessed more positively. True, her ranking will likely never reach that of her husband, but then Schumann's domestic duties as the mother of eight children most certainly detracted from her creativity as a composer, if not as a pianist. The work's theme is somber and slow, stripped down to its barest wares in the stately and simple opening statement. The first variation immediately infuses it with life, coloring it with a greater sense of Romantic warmth. The ensuing variation enlivens it even more, but takes a detour toward Chopin. The somber mood from the opening returns in the next variant and in much the same unison-like manner, but with a measure of gloom. The fourth variation is brief and lively, while the epic fifth is somewhat Brahmsian in its grandiosity and big chords. The sixth variant reverts once more to the slow and somber mood from the opening and distinguishes itself very little from that section and the third variation. The delicate and elegant manner of the seventh variation reveals more color and depth than any other and is also the longest. The theme returns to conclude the work with bits from previous variations. Brahms also wrote a work based on the same theme in 1854, dedicating it to Clara. *—Robert Cummings*

Recommended:

- ○ **Clara Schumann: Piano Music** / Iwai / 1999 / Naxos 553501
- ○ **Piano Music of Clara & Robert Schumann** / Cheng / 1996 / CBC 1087

CHAMBER MUSIC

Piano Trio in G minor, Op. 17 (1846)

Clara and Robert Schumann shared so many musical interests that after a few years of marriage, their compositions began to sound quite similar—that is, Clara's started sounding more like Robert's. In the mid-1840s, they both made a close study of Bach and Clara emerged with a fine hand at counterpoint. During the 1845–46 season, pregnant with her fourth child, Clara was unable to tour as a concert pianist and so stayed home and put her new contrapuntal skills to work in a piano trio. It is considered one of her best works and it's one of her few compositions more extended than lieder and keyboard character pieces. Like Robert, Clara here maintains a thick sound, but it's because all three instruments are playing contrapuntally much of the time, not because one is essentially doubling another's part, as was often the case with Robert. The substantial first movement, Allegro moderato, could pass for one of her husband's with its stern yet somewhat yearning, lyrical first subject, and the second subject is lighter, chordal, and syncopated. Clara puts her Bach studies to use in the development section, a confident excursion into counterpoint, and uses a scholarly and controlled approach to a section that other composers of the time dealt with more freely, even sloppily. Even so, the composer never relaxes the music's lyrical urgency. Breaking with convention, she inserts a Scherzo before the slow movement. Schumann is mindful of the Italian origin of the word "scherzo," meaning jest; this is a lighthearted piece, not the powerful, imposing fast movement preferred by Beethoven and his followers. The scherzo proper is based on a playful, dotted rhythm known as a "Scotch snap." The trio section is more lyrical, but now the Scotch snap has devolved into a rhythm that seems hesitant rather than skipping. Unexpectedly, Schumann's imagination flags somewhat in the routine harmonization of the Andante; these could be the bland chords in 3/4 time underlying any Victorian parlor song. Melodically, though, the movement has much to offer, the outer sections employing a sweet and ardent theme and the middle section slipping back into the minor mode (from the easygoing G major) for a more agitated episode. The finale, Allegretto, returns to the major mode and to sonata form. The first theme is nevertheless as dark as anything that has come earlier, whereas the second subject is more optimistic, even while alluding to the opening phrase of the slow movement. The short development section breaks into an animated fugue, but soon relaxes the fugal rules to vary the themes with greater freedom. The movement's exposition is recapitulated in full, now building to a dramatic—yet not stormy—coda that expertly releases most of its tension just before the final chords. *—James Reel*

Recommended:

- ○ **Fanny Mendelssohn & Clara Schumann: Piano Trios** / Dartington Piano Trio / 2001 / Hyperion 55078
- ○ **Clara Schumann: Piano Concerto, Piano Trio & 3 Romances** / Jochum, Silverstein, Carr / 1992 / Tudor 788

Three Romances for violin & piano, Op. 22 (1853)

After moving to Düsseldorf in early 1853, Clara and Robert Schumann finally lived in a house large enough for Clara to practice and compose without disturbing her nervous husband. During that summer, she produced several works, among them the *Three Romances for violin and piano*, Op. 22, which was published in 1855 or 1856 in Leipzig.

In nineteenth century Germany, the vague term "romance" often meant simply a short piece for piano, or for another instrument with piano accompaniment. Clara Schumann dedicated her *Three Romances* to violinist Joseph Joachim (1831–1907), who later performed the pieces for King George V of Hanover, much to the musical monarch's satisfaction.

The second of the Op. 22 set, in G minor, is representative of the three, and quite striking for its attractive lyricism. The plaintive main theme, syncopated and soaring, creates an atmosphere of melancholy that proves the perfect appetizer for the high-flying middle section. Now in the major mode, this second theme takes on an extroverted, almost majestic quality, best exemplified by its aggressive upward leaps and vigorous arpeggios. The B material alternates with sections of rapid imitation between piano and violin before giving way once again to the G minor opening tune; this time the piano plays a larger role in thematic presentation. A powerful, G minor version of the middle section's soaring theme appears just before the close, which consists of a surprising, pizzicato chord.

Nos. 1 and 3 are similarly constructed, with contrasting middle sections enclosed by reprised lyrical material. Developing variation is less important than clear delineation of form through organization of melodies; it is clear from the intricate piano writing that the composer possessed an exceptional performing technique. The violin writing is equally effective and idiomatic. *—John Palmer*

Recommended:

- ○ **Romances for Violin and Piano** / Rosand, Sung / 1995 / Vox 7505

CONCERTO

Piano Concerto in A minor, Op. 7 (1833–1836)

Young Clara Wieck's piano concerto, like that of her future husband Robert Schumann, is in A minor, but that's the only detail the two compositions share. Clara's concerto is the work of an independent-minded young piano virtuoso who, although she was only 13 when she began writing it, was fully aware of the most progressive tendencies of German music in the 1830s. It's true that Robert did have his fingers in this piece; the two were already showing their works in progress to each other and in fact, Robert orchestrated what would in two years become the finale of Clara's three-movement concerto. But it's more Chopin-esque than Schumann-esque. Originally, the Schumann-orchestrated movement stood alone under the titles *Concert-Rondo* and *Concertsatz*. The first movement, Allegro maestoso (Clara orchestrated this and the slow movement herself), begins with a serious, almost marchlike orchestral introduction interrupted by a brief piano flourish; another orchestral statement follows, then an impressive keyboard cascade that surely later inspired the opening measures of Grieg's *Concerto in A minor* (Clara's concerto, though the work of a teenager, was quite popular through the nineteenth century). The piano takes over the thematic material with minimal orchestral support; the music has a lightness, a bittersweet flavor, and a digital complexity that suggest the influence of early Chopin and, to a lesser extent, her older Leipzig colleague Felix Mendelssohn. The piano retires, allowing the orchestra to lead the movement out of its development section, but just as it seems the piano is about to launch the traditional cadenza, it instead eases directly into the slow movement, called "Romanze." This introduces a simple, graceful theme, moving upward in the manner of the main melodies of the outer movements. The piano occasionally offers a few bars of intricate filigree, and eventually it is joined by a solo cello singing the unadorned melodic line while the piano offers a more active, inventive accompaniment. (This anticipates the slow movement of Tchaikovsky's *Piano Concerto No. 2*, which is largely a trio for piano, cello, and violin.) Again, a few solo piano gestures lead directly into the final movement, the first to be composed. This is the most outgoing music so far, but it's still rather stern. It also has something of the polonaise about it, again calling Chopin to mind. (The most obvious model, though, Chopin's *Grand Polonaise Brillante*, wasn't published in its orchestral form until 1835.) This movement is almost as long as the first two combined. It's cast as a rondo, although the episodes are poorly enough differentiated (and so unified by the polonaise rhythm) that the movement could as easily be regarded as a set of grimly glittering variations. *—James Reel*

Recommended:

- ○ **Clara & Robert Schumann: Piano Concertos** / Höhenrieder, Wildner (cond.), Neue Philharmonie Westfalen / 2002 / RCA 89793

VOCAL

Songs (ca. 1830–1853)

Clara Wieck Schumann is largely known for her piano music, but increasingly for her songs as well. Her lieder style was influenced by her husband's and clearly divulges her lushly Romantic sentiments. Clara Schumann's lieder output consists of 29 works, though there are a few additional items of questionable authorship and several lost songs. She wrote two sets containing six songs each—*Sechs Lieder*, Op. 13 (1842–43), and *Sechs Lieder aus Jucunde*, Op. 23 (1853). There was another collection, *Three Songs*, Op. 12 (1840), with her remaining output consisting of singular efforts. Among her more worthwhile songs are the first two from the Op. 12 set on texts by Friedrich Rückert. The first, *Er Ist Gekommen in Sturm und Regen* (He Came in Storm and Rain) has a Robert Schumann-esque quality to its anxiety and passion and a truly memorable theme. The second, *Liebst du um Schönheit* (If You Love for Beauty), is serene and warm in its approach to love, but sounds almost too beautiful for its forlorn text. The Op. 13 set features several attractive items, including the two opening ones, *Ich Stand In dunklen Träumen* (I Stood in Dark Dreams) and *Sie Liebten Sich Beide* (They Loved Each Other), both on Heinrich Heine texts. They are sad songs of melodic distinction and feature beautiful piano accompaniment. Throughout this set, but even more so in the Op. 23 collection, the piano often takes on a nearly equal role to that of the vocalist. The later set, all on texts by Hermann Rollett, also contains its share of gems, including the middle pair, *Geheimes Flüstern hier und dort* (Soft Secret Whispers Here and There) and *Auf Einem grünen Hügel* (Upon a Green Hillock), both lovely, slow songs with quite memorable melodies. The last two in the set—*Das Ist Ein Tag, Der klingen Mag* (This Is a Day for Singing Songs) and *O Lust, O Lust* (O Joy, O Joy)—are lively and charming, full of color in their cheer with vocal lines deftly enhanced by her brilliant piano writing. *Lorelei* (1843), on texts by Heine, is one of her singular efforts, an intense love song and quite beautiful, with anxious, repeating chords on the piano that heighten the sense of passion. *Mein Stern* (My Star), from 1847, is on texts by Friederike Serre and also full of passion and tension in its outpourings of love. Again, the piano accompaniment, with its running figures, is fraught with anxiety and deftly underpins the powerful emotions in the piece. Her last song, *Das Vielchen* (The Violet; 1853) is on texts by Goethe and is light and charming, exhibiting Schumann's skill in contrasts, as the tempo and emotional thrust shift naturally throughout the piece. —*Robert Cummings*

Recommended:

○ **Lieder of Clara Schumann** / Polk, Uecker / 1992 / Arabesque 6624

Elisabeth Schumann

b. Jun. 13, 1885, Merseburg, Germany, **d.** Apr. 23, 1952, New York, NY

Soprano

The quintessential Austro-German lyric soprano, Elisabeth Schumann brought a floating, silvery (no other term will do) voice to her heartfelt, uncalculating art, endearing herself to audiences in both Europe and America. The freshness that informed her singing never failed her, even as she entered her sixties. By then, she concentrated on lieder, a field in which she had few equals. Schubert's songs found in her an ideal interpreter for all of those written from a woman's perspective. Schumann recorded extensively, also preserving her definitive Sophie in a star-studded *Rosenkavalier* captured (in slightly abridged form) on disc in the Vienna of 1933.

Born in the province of Thuringa, Schumann studied first in Dresden with Natalie Hänisch, later working with Marie Dietrich in Berlin before undergoing her final training with Alma Schadow in Hamburg. The soprano's debut took place in Hamburg in the small but exposed role of the Shepherd in *Tannhäuser* in 1909, and she soon became a valued member of the company. After a decade, Richard Strauss urged her to join the Vienna Staatsoper and she finally yielded to his importuning to become a treasured member of that house, remaining there until just before the Anschluss. In 1937, she was honored by being made an *Ehrenmitglied* of the Staatsoper, a recognition extended to only a favored few, though one she had already received from the Vienna Philharmonic. Although Schumann sang only one season at the Metropolitan Opera, her November 20, 1914, debut as Sophie was followed by 44 other performances, including such roles as Gerhilde, Gretel, Papagena, Marzelline, and—surprisingly—Musetta in *La Bohème*. Not until 1924 did London hear Schumann, but her debut as Sophie met with unrestrained praise. Ernest Newman noted, "we had a Sophie who could be trusted as a singer to see the whole great business through and rise to the top of her form in the trio." Bruno Walter conducted and among her colleagues were Lotte Lehmann, singing her very first Marschallin, and bass Richard Mayr, supreme as Baron Ochs. Schumann sang with the company until 1931, being heard also as Adele, Blondchen, and Eva, the latter role regarded as too demanding for so light a voice. Salzburg also welcomed Schumann from 1924 to 1936 in three of her finest Mozart roles—Susanna, Zerlina, and Despina—as well as Serpina in a rare production of Pergolesi's *La serva padrona*. Equally at home on the recital stage, Schumann enchanted audiences with her lovely voice and interpretive insights, always direct, never interventionist. In 1921, the soprano was invited by Richard Strauss to tour the United States in a series of lieder concerts. On November 8, 1931, Schumann returned to America to sing a Town Hall recital that drew ecstatic reviews. Olin Downes, for one, praised her phrasing, diction, and ability to re-create the composer's spirit. When the Germans swept into Austria in 1938, Schumann left for the United States, residing there for the rest of her life and becoming a citizen in 1944. She became a teacher at Philadelphia's Curtis Institute of Music while continuing to sing recitals. In 1947, she returned to England, venturing northward to participate in the first year of the Edinburgh Festival. Among Schumann's many recordings are excellent examples of her way with the songs of Schubert and her treasurable Sophie recorded in 1933 with Lehmann, Mayr, and Maria Olszewska. —*Erik Eriksson*

Recommended:

○ **Schubert Lieder** / Schumann, etc. / 2002 / Naxos 8110731

○ **Lebendige Vergangenheit: Elisabeth Schumann** / Schumann, etc. / Preiser 89031

Robert Schumann

b. Jun. 8, 1810, Zwickau, Germany, **d.** Jul. 29, 1856, Endenich, Germany

Composer: Keyboard, Vocal, Chamber Music, Concerto, Symphonic, Orchestral, Choral

One of the great composers of the nineteenth century, Schumann was the quintessential artist whose life and work embody the idea of Romanticism in music. Schumann was uncomfortable with larger musical forms, such as the symphony and the concerto (nevertheless, representative works in these genres contain moments of great beauty), expressing the full range of his lyrical genius in songs and short pieces for piano. Schumann's extraordinary ability to translate profound, delicate—and sometimes fleeting—states of the soul is exemplified by works such as the song cycle *Dichterliebe* (A Poet's Love), after Heinrich Heine, and his brilliant collections of short piano pieces, including *Phantasiestücke* (Fantastic Pieces, *Kinderszenen* (Scenes form Childhood), and *Waldszenen* (Forest Scenes). In his songs, as critics have remarked, Schumann attained the elusive union of music and poetry which Romantic poets and musicians defined as the ultimate goal of art.

Schumann's father was a bookseller who encouraged Robertıs musical and literary talents. Robert started studying piano at age ten. In 1828, he enrolled at the University of Leipzig as a law student, although he found music, philosophy, and Leipzig's taverns more interesting than the law. He also began studies with a prominent Leipzig piano teacher, Friedrich Wieck. There was serious mental illness in Schumann's family, and the composer, who most likely suffered from a manic-depressive condition, approached madness with the typical Romantic combination of fear and fascination. A compulsive womanizer and a heavy drinker, Schumann led a life that aggravated his psychological problems. His efforts to become a concert pianist failed after he developed partial paralysis of his right hand. According to a conventional story, the injury resulted from Schumann's compulsive use of a finger-strengthening device, but newer research points to mercury poisoning due to treatment for syphilis. Schumann settled on a career as a composer and musical writer, co-founding the influential *Neue Zeitschrift für Musik* and attracting attention early with his prophetic praise of Chopin. Many of his articles take the form of dialogues featuring the "League of David," young artists fighting the "Philistines," and headed by his alter egos "Florestan" and "Eusebius," intended to represent the two contrasting facets—one reserved, the other ebullient—of his personality. Schumann's music, with its sharp changes in mood, also reflects his tumultuous inner life. Wieck's highly talented pianist daughter Clara grew up and fell in love with Schumann, to her father's horror. Despite Wieck's opposition, Clara and Robert gained the legal right to marry in 1840, a day before Clara's 21st birthday. During this period Schumann composed feverishly. Spellbound by a musical thought, he would work himself to exhaustion, enthusiastically cultivating a particular genre for a period of time. (For instance, 1841 was a "year of songs" in which he brought the Romantic song cycle to its apex). He virtually invented the short, poetic, descriptive Romantic piano work, and produced such works in glorious profusion in the late 1830s. Schumann tackled larger forms in the 1840s, partly at Clara's urging; his four mature symphonies retain a place in the repertoire, but his opera *Genoveva* failed. He held several musical jobs, teaching at the newly-founded Leipzig Conservatory, eventually becoming town music director in Düsseldorf, but without much success. On February 27, 1854, he threw himself into the freezing waters of the Rhine. After his rescue, he voluntarily entered an asylum. Although he had periods of lucidity, his condition deteriorated, and he died there in 1856, probably of tertiary syphilis. —*Zoran Minderovic*

KEYBOARD

Album für die Jugend (Album for the Young), Op. 68 (1848)

Schumann's *Album for the Young* is a masterful set of 43 short, easy piano pieces in two volumes. The 25 works in the second book are somewhat more challenging and longer than those in the first, but still well within the reach of good amateur pianists. The whole set really cannot be compared with the composer's *Kinderszenen*, a collection of piano pieces about children, but from an adult perspective and requiring a substantial technique. Schumann wrote *Album for the Young* for his children, the oldest then aged seven.

The set's opening work is "Melody," a piece presenting a simple but lovely tune whose innocence and upper register writing remind one of a music box melody. "Soldier's March" follows, a cute, chipper piece brimming with childlike pride. Number four, "Choral," has an almost too somber manner, but is deftly innocent in its worshipful character. The sixth piece, "The Poor Orphan," has a touching sadness, while number eight, "The Wild Horseman," is vigorous and energetic.

Among the most popular pieces in the collection is the tenth, "The Happy Farmer Returning From Work," which exudes joy and innocence in its jaunty gait and infectious melody. The longest work in the first volume, lasting nearly three minutes, is number 15, "Spring Song," a sweetly lyrical piece whose simple but beguiling beauty will appeal, like most works in the collection, to the adult as well as child.

Little Romance, number 19, leads off the second volume with a decidedly more mature manner, the somewhat stormy character of its melody seeming to reach beyond childhood innocence almost to teenage infatuation. Still, the prevailing qualities in the second book are innocence and childlike simplicity, as demonstrated by the jaunty and rhythmic number 23, "The Horseman," or the wistful number 27, "Little Song in Canon Form."

Number 32, "Sheherazade," at about four minutes, is the longest piece in the second volume. It deftly conveys a beguiling lyrical ingenuousness, instead of the Eastern exoticism suggested by its title. "Wintertime I & II" (38 & 39) make up five minutes' worth of sweetly melancholy music, the latter piece somewhat darker in the lower register writing of the outer sections. The closing piece, "New Year's Eve," has a youthful stateliness in its almost Brahmsian melody and celebratory manner.

The original edition of the *Album* was beautifully engraved and published in the expectation that it would be Schumann's most popular work: it was, and to this day, these pieces remain a staple of the young pianist's repertoire. *—Robert Cummings*

Recommended:

- ○ **Schumann: Album für die Jugend** / Gulda / 2001 / Naxos 555711
- ○ **Great Pianists: Arturo Benedetti Michelangeli 2** / Michelangeli / 1999 / Philips 456904

Albumblätter (Album Leaves), Op. 124 (1832–1845)

The 20 small pieces that make up Robert Schumann's *Albumblätter* (Album leaves) for piano, Op. 124, were composed at varying times and under varying circumstances between around 1832 and 1845 (and thus actually predate the more famous *Album for the Young*, Op. 68, with which they have a great deal in common). By 1854, the year the *Albumblätter* were organized and published, Schumann's life, health, mind, and career were in complete disarray; the *Albumblätter*, though containing some beautiful, crystal-clear episodes, are basically uneven pieces that the composer had rejected from earlier character-piece collections, and it may be that Schumann's need to fill the void in his creative output and not a level-minded assessment of the pieces' musical merits, was the motivating factor in their eventual publication. The musical world invoked by the 20 pieces is as varied and rich as are the technical demands of these compositions. In Nos. 1 (Impromptu), 3 (Scherzino), 5 (Phantasietanz), 12 (Burla), 14 (Vision), and 17 (Elfe), we encounter something of that same rapid-tempo, quicksilver magic that marks many earlier pieces (Nos. 5 and 17, as well as No.4, one of several waltzes contained in the group, are all rejections from *Carnaval*; these three pieces are some of the collections' most attractive). The Schlummerlied (Slumber Song) at No.16 is of much greater length than most of its companion pieces—some of which, like the charming Elfe, last a bare half-minute. Schlummerlied is a touching melody in 6/8 time. The central portion of its skeletal ABA form affords just 12 short bars of G minor to break the gently rolling E flat major on either side. Save for the short Canon, No.20, Schlummerlied is the latest piece of the group, having been composed during 1841. The dense texture and intricate voicings of the penultimate piece, a Phantasiestück, require a firm technical command of the instrument. The final Canon, though only sixteen bars in length and never wavering from D major, nevertheless takes some surprising, subtle twists and turns. *—Blair Johnston*

Recommended:

- ○ **Schumann: Albumblätter; Carnaval de Vienne; Varations sur un Theme Original** / Gianoli / Ades 20324
- ○ **Schumann: Adagio & Allegro; Albumblätter; Stücke im Volkston** / Wallfisch / Chandos 8528

Arabeske, in C major, Op. 18 (1838)

Schumann's lovely *Arabesque in C major*, Op. 18, is much loved by pianists at all levels. Though it has been a specialty of virtuosi like Horowitz and Pollini, the work's technical demands are within the range of many amateurs. The piece, about seven minutes in duration, unfolds as a rondo with a light, skipping main theme underpinned by a rippling left-hand accompaniment. Though in the minor mode, the B and C sections maintain the prevailing sprightly, occasionally pastoral mood. The character of the peaceful coda is that of a lullaby tinged with whimsy and nostalgia.*—Sol Louis Siegel*

Recommended:

- ○ **Great Pianists: Maria João Pires** / Pires / 1999 / Philips 456928
- ○ **Great Pianists: Emil Gilels 3** / Gilels / 1999 / Philips 456799
- ○ **Schumann: Piano Concerto** / Kissin / 1993 / Sony 52567
- ○ **Schumann: Piano Works** / Kempff / 1975 / DG 435045

Blumenstück, in D flat major, Op. 19 (1839)

Written in Vienna the year before Schumann's marriage to Clara Wieck, this work was originally titled Guirlande (Garland) by the composer, but he eventually changed it to the arguably more appropriate *Blumenstück* (Flower Pieces). The work is made up of a series of very short, connected episodes, somewhat in the spirit of Schumann's much larger piano composition, *Carnaval*, but with each section thematically related.

The work opens with the luminescent main theme, which thrives on its arched contour and animated emotional character, conveying a sense of pulsation in the main line's trajectory as it alternates ascending and descending phrases. While it is short and repetitive as it proceeds, its music develops a sense of tension and never tires the ear. The similarly passionate and lively second episode serves as a refrain and reappears later on. Thereafter the music takes on a stormier character, its emotional pitch rising higher in the middle of the work, especially as the tempo increases for an anxious variant that erupts in a climactic episode in the latter half. Overall, this beautiful six- to seven-minute piece will likely strike the listener as being more about the courtship activities associated with flowers than about the beauty of flowers themselves. *—Robert Cummings*

Recommended:

- ○ **Schumann: Symphonische Etüden; Davidsbündlertänze; Blumenstück; Arabeske** / Schiff / 1995 / Teldec 99176
- ○ **Schumann: Toccata; Nachtstücke; Blumenstück; Four Fuges** / Richter / 1993 / London 436456

Bunte Blätter (Colored Leaves), Op. 99 (1836–1849)

This collection of mostly small piano pieces written during various periods from 1836 to 1849, was not assembled and published until 1852, two years before Schumann suffered a debilitating mental breakdown and entered a mental asylum, where he would die in 1856. *Bunte Blätter* is a unique collection, containing two small collections within it, as well as six additional separate pieces.

It opens with *Stücklein III* (Three Small Pieces), the first of which, dating to 1838, is songful and sweet in its lovely melody and sonorous harmonies. Schumann presented the piece to his wife-to-be Clara as a Christmas gift. The next two, from 1839, are each less than a minute: the first is anxious and driven, the latter, nearly as fast, but brimming with joy and sunshine in its prancing, less harried gait.

Following are the five (untitled) *Albumblätter* (Album-leaves), slightly more substantial efforts, but none longer than two-and-a-half minutes. The opening piece, from 1841, is slow and ponderous, but thematically rich enough to inspire Brahms to write a theme and variations work based on it. It is followed by a breathless, stormy dash (1838), lasting less than a minute. Another slow piece (1836) ensues, this one lyrical and melancholy, and originally designed for Schumann's popular collection *Carnaval*. An even more melancholy work (1838) follows. Its heartbreaking, almost listless manner was well served by its original title, Pain of Youth. The closing *Albumblätter* is also slow and sad, but at least shows some sunshine in its less somber musical landscape.

The chipper 1838 *Novelette* follows, with its jaunty outer sections and swirling, mysterious but light interior. The toccata-like *Praeludium* is next, filling its minute length with stormy, muscular sonorities and an ominous sense. The ensuing *Marsch* (1843), at around seven or eight minutes, is the longest piece in the set. It opens gently in its somber manner, lightens up for the Trio, and closes with the same stately seriousness with which it began. *Abendmusik* (Evening music) follows, a playful, gentle piece suggesting the evening has a little sunlight mixed with its shadows. The ensuing 1841 *Scherzo* is bright and energetic in its outer sections, while its Trio is just as lively and colorful. Colorful is also the word to describe the closing *Geschwindmarsch* (Quick march) from 1849. It brims with good-natured menace and quirky energy in its somewhat exotic sonorities. *—Robert Cummings*

Recommended:

- ○ **Richter plays Schumann, Mussorgsky & Debussy** / Richter / 2002 / BBC 4103
- ○ **Arcadi Volodos Live at Carnegie Hall** / Volodos / 1999 / Sony 60893

Carnaval, Op. 9 (1833–1835)

Though completed just eight years after the death of Beethoven, the 20 piano pieces of Robert Schumann's *Carnaval* (1833–35) occupy a musical realm which seems far removed from the older master's world. *Carnaval*'s subtitle, "Scènes mignonnes sur quatre notes," is a reference to the work's arcane, symbolic pitch structure. In 1834, Schumann was engaged to a young pianist by the name of Ernestine von Fricken, a student of his own teacher (and eventual father-in-law), Frederick Wieck. In a bit of orthographic serendipity, the composer realized that the name of his fiancée's hometown, Asch, could be translated into notes according to the German reckoning of pitch names: "A" became A natural, "S" (Es) E flat, "C" C natural, and "H" B natural. Furthermore, a reordering of the letters yielded S-C-H-A, which the young composer immediately recognized as symbolic of his own name (i.e. "SCHumAnn"). More than a striking set of character pieces and musical portraits, *Carnaval* also unfolds as a set of variations on this group of pitches; almost all of its sections incorporate a permutation of the A-S-C-H combination.

Carnaval showcases virtually all of the young Schumann's personal and musical characteristics in one form or another; a number of the pieces are musical portraits of the composer's friends and important contemporaries. The opening "Préambule," which contains music originally intended as part of a set of variations on Schubert's *Trauerwalzer*, Op. 9/2 (D. 365), is one of the few pieces in the set not explicitly organized around the A-S-C-H idea. Figures from the commedia dell' arte make appearances in "Pierrot," "Arlequin," and "Pantelon et Columbine." Schumann writes himself into the work in the guise of his two alter egos, the idealistic, dreamy Eusebius, and fiery man of action Florestan. Ernestine von Fricken is characterized in "Estrella," while Clara Wieck, Frederick Wieck's teenaged daughter, is portrayed passionato in "Chiarina." (It was eventually she, in fact, and not von Fricken, who became Schumann's wife.) Schumann includes a touching tribute to Chopin, as well as a virtuosic intermezzo whose subject is the legendary violinist Paganini. Midway through Carnaval there is a trio of four-note "Sphinxes"—probably not meant for performance—through which Schumann divulges the "secret" of the A-S-C-H pitch groupings using an archaic notation.

The final section, "Marche des Davidsbündler contre les Philistins" (March of the Davidsbünd Members Against the Philistines), is a symbolic portrayal of the members of the Davidsbünd, an imaginary group Schumann called upon in his writings and music as a confederation against the reactionary, musically dry "Philistines" of his day. Here, the Davidsbündler—Florestan, Eusebius, Estrella/Ernestine, Chiarina/Clara, Chopin, and Paganini—rout the Philistines, represented by the "Grossvalterlied," an old German song. There is humor indeed in this "conflict" as the members of the Davidsbündler are cleverly disguised behind "carnaval" masks of great musical bravado. *—Blair Johnston*

Recommended:

- ○ **Perspectives** / Uchida / 2003 / Philips 473686
- ○ **Schumann: Carnaval; Kinderszenen; Waldszenen** / Arrau / 1987 / Philips 420871
- ○ **Arturo Benedetti Michelangeli** / Michelangeli / 1996 / Testament 2088

Davidsbündlertänze, Op. 6 (1837; revised 1850)

By October 1837, Schumann completed his *Davidsbündlertänze,* Op. 6, which was printed the same year at Schumann's expense. It was the first composition Schumann undertook after reconciling with Clara Wieck. Thirteen years later, Schumann revised the set of 18 character pieces (among other early works), making numerous changes not only to the music, but to the peripheral aspects of the score, as well.

The first edition of the *Davidsbündlertänze* (Dances of the League of David) contains dances composed for a group of musical friends (both real and imagined, alive and dead) that Schumann assembled around himself in support of his ideas. Reflecting the two sides of Schumann's personality, some of the dances are marked as being composed by "E." (Eusebius) and the rest by "F." (Florestan). Florestan's pieces are the more lively and exuberant; Eusebius' are more dreamy and wandering. None of the pieces has an individual title. Franz Brendel, a contemporary of Schumann who wrote some penetrating analyses of the composer's works, notes that the juxtaposition of two disparate styles "reveal to us that humor is the principle of Schumann's early compositions." These constant and mercurial changes in humor most likely made Schumann's music less marketable, and the composer himself acknowledged that the "rascher Wechsel" (rapid changes) of mood made his music inappropriate for either public or private concerts. Perhaps to prepare the performer for the work's alternating atmospheres, Schumann prefaces the publication with the proverb: "Along the way we go are mingled weal and woe; in weal, though glad, be grave, in woe, though sad, be brave." For the second edition of the work, Schumann shorted the title to *Davidsbündler,* but still referred to the individual works as "character-pieces." Most likely, he removed the word *tänze* (dances) because none of them actually works as a dance. Also, he eliminated the initials "E." and "F." from the set.

Clara Wieck appears at the very beginning of the *Davidsbündler,* for the dances are based on the opening measures of one of her mazurkas, which is heard in the first two measures of *No. 1.* The next 17 pieces are variations on this theme, with its incremental arching and emphasis on the third and fifth scale degrees.

Schumann distorts the nature of whatever dance he may be using in a piece. For example, although the first piece feels like a mazurka, with its long notes and accents on the second beat of each 3/4 measure, it does not have the expected formal characteristics. The Ländler feel of *No. 2* is occasionally subverted by a compound duple meter in the melody, while the overall coherence of *No. 3* is threatened when the left hand seems to get ahead of the right at several points. Schumann goes further astray in *No. 6,* a lively tarantella, in which he abandons the typical accents (on beats one and four) by having the right hand emphasize the third and sixth beats, the left, beats two and five. In the trio section of the piece the rhythm becomes more traditional, but there are still accents on beat six. The seven-measure phrases of *No. 8* preclude its use as a dance, while *No. 10,* as does *No. 2,* juxtaposes a 6/8 meter in the right hand with 3/4 in the left.

The last three pieces are linked and suggest that B minor is the principal key of the set. Repeated F sharps connect *No. 16* and *No. 17,* pieces of very different personalities that tend toward B minor and the ominous. After these two profound statements, the last piece, a waltz, seems anomalous. *—John Palmer*

Recommended:

- ○ **Schumann: Davidsbündlertänze; Fantasiestücke** / Perahia / 1973 / CBS 32299
- ○ **Schumann: Davidsbündlertänze; Concert sans orchestre** / Pollini / 2001 / DG 471369
- ○ **Schumann: Piano Works** / Kempff / 1975 / DG 435045

Fantasie (Obolen auf Beethovens Monument), in C major, Op. 17 (1836)

The Phantasie in C major, Op. 17, is one of Schumann's greatest keyboard works, a completely original effort compelling in conception and design. Schumann originally composed the first movement as part of a fundraising effort for a memorial to Beethoven; indeed, it is based on a motive from Beethoven's song cycle *An die ferne Geliebte* (1816). The remaining two movements were later additions; if the work has any flaw, it is that the superiority of the first movement renders the second and third rather conventional by comparison.

The *Phantasie* differs from the more usual improvisational, single-movement cast of the keyboard fantasia in that its form is actually closer to that of a sonata; the first movement, in fact, is itself probably best described as a highly modified sonata-allegro. Here, Schumann turns his usual shortcoming—the substitution of unrelated successive musical fragments for real development—into the structural premise. Each section seems to expire, unresolved, to be followed by a new beginning; however, with the unifying element of Beethoven's motive, as well as the consistency with which each successive passage waxes and wanes, Schumann creates a unique structure that provides the appearance of unity despite the fragmentation of its content. He was never able to duplicate this feat in subsequent works, which tend to be fragmented by design into small movements, or, in the case of his large-scale efforts, lack the *Phantasie's* cohesiveness.

The second movement, a March with Trio, seems quite unremarkable despite its large scale. Still, it transcends mundaneness by the sheer brilliance of the material itself. The unremitting rhythmic drive of the principal section is utterly compelling, while the odd cross rhythms of the Trio result in a passage of exceptional lyrical beauty. The lengthy Adagio finale is of a similalry uncomplicated form that peaks in two large climaxes before the rather abbreviated coda; in the course of the movement, the tone moves from mystical to lyrical to majestic before repeating itself. Schumann originally wrote a longer ending for the *Phantasie* which quoted from the first movement, but rejected it prior to publication in favor of the extant coda. The depth and greatness of this work is such that only an artist of the very first rank can hope to do complete justice to its riches. *—Steven Coburn*

Recommended:

- ○ **Schumann: Piano Concerto; Fantasy** / Brendel / 1998 / Philips 462321
- ○ **Schumann: Fantasy in C; Faschingsschwank aus Wien; Papillons** / Richter / 2002 / EMI 75233
- ○ **Schumann: Piano Works** / Kempff / 1975 / DG 435045

Fantasiestücke, Op. 12 (1837)

Schumann's *Eight Fantasiestücke,* Op. 12 (1837) together constitute one of the composer's finest and most representative works. Intended to be played as an intact group, the set retains enough typical dance forms to be regarded as a sort of dance suite, though the pieces are longer and more complex than those of "true" dance suites like *Carnaval,* Op. 9 (1833–35) and *Davidsbündlertanze,* Op. 6 (1837). Most of the pieces are constructed in novel permutations of rounded binary and ternary forms; nearly all have contrasting, trio-like middle sections.

The first of the pieces, "Des Abends" (Evening), is a lyrical nocturne that makes interesting use of cross-rhythms. "Aufschwung" (Soaring) probably, the best-known member of the set, contrasts an aggressive opening with a fluent, lyrical "finger" passage; the central section, which employs longer rhythms, is more lyrical yet. "Warum?" (Why?) is simple and straightforward, in Schumann's most lyrical "Eusebius" style. In "Grillen" (Whims), Schumann demonstrates his ability to use rhythm to convey subtle humor; the central section employs a striking, almost archaic, chorale-like style. "In der Nacht" (In the Night), an impassioned, etude-like tone poem, is among the loveliest of the pieces. The one member of the set that eschews dance form is "Fabel" (Fable); here Schumann contrasts a slow introduction with faster episodic passages. "Traumes Wirren" (Restless Dreams) is also etude-like, but is light and buoyant in mood. The final piece, "Ende vom Lied" (End of the Song), has, despite its brevity, a certain epic quality. The coda almost seems like an afterthought, intended as an ending for the whole set rather than for this movement in particular. After the composer's death, an additional piece, "Feurigst" (Fiery), was added to the set. Though it is authentically by Schumann, it is generally considered a mismatch with the other pieces and is rarely performed with them. *—Steven Coburn*

Recommended:

○ **Schumann: Fantasiestücke; Humoreske; Novelletten** / Richter / 1995 / Melodiya 29464

○ **Schumann: Davidsbündlertänze; Fantasiestücke** / Frith / 1992 / Naxos 550493

Faschingsschwank aus Wien ("Phantasiebilder"), Op. 26 (1839)

Schumann's *Faschingschwank aus Wien*, Op. 26 (1839–40) is a rather unusual work in five movements; it is more integrated than a suite, but not quite a sonata. The first movement, an Allegro in B flat major, is very nearly a dance suite in and of itself. A principal idea in 3/4 time alternates with six contrasting episodes. The second movement is a brief Romanze in G minor, wistful and characteristic. The third movement, a Scherzino in B flat major, is a scherzo (sans trio) laid out in continuous two-bar phrases. The most distinctive movement is undoubtedly the Intermezzo in E flat minor, a passionate melody with an undulating accompaniment. The lengthy Finale in B flat major, the most technically demanding of the movements, is in a conventional sonata form. *—Steven Coburn*

Recommended:

○ **Schumann: Fantasy in C; Faschingsschwank aus Wien; Papillons** / Richter / 2002 / EMI 75233

○ **Arturo Benedetti Michelangeli** / Michelangeli / 1996 / Testament 2088

○ **Schumann: Piano Works** / Jandó / 1993 / Naxos 550783

Fünf Gesänge der Frühe, Op. 133 (1853)

By the autumn of 1853, Robert Schumann had already boarded the one-way express train to complete mental and emotional breakdown; but he had not yet actually reached the last stop on that unhappy trip, and so was still able, in October, to create and prepare for publication (the latter over several months, and with considerable difficulty—his mental focus was dissolving quickly) a set of five character pieces for piano solo that he called *Gesänge der Frühe* [Songs of Dawn], Op. 133. These five miniatures are dedicated to "the high poetess Bettina" and are Schumann's very last coherent solo piano music.

The composer's wife Clara, in her private diary, described the *Gesänge der Frühe* as, "dawn-songs, very original as always but hard to understand, their tone is so very strange." It isn't hard to hear what she meant—the Op. 133 pieces are, to a one, straightforward in appearance and outward musical form, but complex, even conflicted, in expression; touching and lovely, but always winding and twisting from one subtly-inflected psychological region to another. This sometimes unsettling character is not evidence of the composer's coming mental collapse, but is rather the crescendo of an element that had been key to his craft for a long time. This is music that at first seems straightforward but never settles down, never stops groping in its own dark (or perhaps rather than dark, it is a blinding brilliance of middle-Romantic light); Schumann simply did not compose in two dimensions, so to speak.

The five pieces in Schumann's solo piano swan song cover the tonal ground defined by the notes of the D major triad. Pieces 1, 2, and 5 are actually in D major, while 3 an 4 are in A major and F sharp minor, respectively. Op. 133, No. 1 (Im ruhigen Tempo) is a plain-textured affair, two pages long, almost chorale-like in the quality of its rhythm and its sonority. No. 2 (Belebt, nicht zu rasch) is one of those wonderful pieces that doesn't actually give us the chord of the home key in a strong, stable form until near the end of the piece. Its graceful triplets are offset by the odd intrusion here and there of pointed dotted rhythms. No. 3 (Lebhaft) is the longest and fastest of the set and never once falters from its course of constant gallop rhythms, while No. 4 (Bewegt) unfolds in downward-cascading 32nd notes. Both the chorale-like tone of No. 1 and the light-footed filigree of Nos. 2 an 4 are recaptured and then transfigured in No. 5. *—Blair Johnston*

Recommended:

○ **Schumann: Kreisleriana; Gesänge der Frühe; Allegro in B minor** / Pollini / DG 471370

Humoreske, in B flat major, Op. 20 (1839)

Originally entitled "Grosse Humoreske," this piece has been regarded by some musicologists as an ill-judged attempt by Schumann to take his formula in *Kreisleriana* a step further. This assessment is harsh, however, for these pieces, unified by their extremes ("laughing and weeping") and generally in the key of B flat major, are colorful and imaginative, full of energy and depth, and if they do not strike out new territory, they are rife with ideas and never sound tiresome.

Humoreske is comprised of five main sections, though its divisions can be reduced further by their tempo markings to 11 pieces of varying moods, each lasting three minutes or less, except for the last which has a duration of about five minutes. The introduction foreshadows the more sedate moods of the composer's *Concerto in A minor*. There follows a five-note figure that invigorates the next two sections, which often sound like a take-off on Schubert's *Marche Militaire*.

Succeeding sections offer contrasts within that fit well the "laughing and weeping" description. The fourth section is, in effect, a scherzo of great color. The fifth closes with brilliant, triumphant music. In the end, this work must be assessed as a piece in the same spirit as *Kreisleriana*, but having a distinct personality of its own, even if it must ultimately be viewed as falling short of that earlier keyboard masterpiece. *—Robert Cummings*

Recommended:

○ **An Anniversary Tribute** / Arrau / 2003 / Philips 473461

○ **Humoresque** / Golub / 1998 / Arabesque 6706

○ **Freddy Kempf plays Schumann** / Kempf / 1999 / Bis 960

Six Intermezzi (Pièces phantastiques), Op. 4 (1832)

Schumann intended his *Six Intermezzi*, Op. 4 (1832) as "longer *Papillons*." Like *Papillons* (1829–31) the *Intermezzi* resemble a dance suite in form, if not content, and were intended to be played as an intact group. Unlike *Papillons*, however, the *Intermezzi* contain neither literary allusions nor musical idiosyncrasies. Some of the individual pieces are unidentifiable as specific dances, though they retain typical ternary dance forms.

No. 1 in A major alternates a march-like section with a livelier middle section. The scherzo-like No. 2 in E minor is a depiction of Faust's and Mephistopheles' journey through the air; there is much interest in the complex rhythms that throw the underlying pulse out of sync with the melodic and harmonic rhythm. Unusual rhythms and accentuation highlight the main section of No. 3 in A minor; Schumann curiously labels the faster central section "Alternativo." Schumann constructed No. 4 in C major, the shortest of the Intermezzi, from fragments of three earlier discarded works. No. 5 in D minor is more lyrical than its partners, in spite of its fast tempo; the central section, labeled "Alternativo" as in No. 3 above, is probably the most beautiful passage in the entire set. Impetuous and virtuosic, No. 6 in B minor offers the greatest contrast between the main section and its lightly Mendelssohnian "Alternativo." *—Steven Coburn*

Recommended:

○ **Great Pianists: Christoph Eschenbach** / Eschenbach / 1999 / Philips 456763

Kinderszenen (Scenes from Childhood), Op. 15 (1838)

The 13 pieces that constitute Robert Schumann's *Kinderszenen for piano* (Scenes from Childhood), Op. 15 (1838) showcase their creator's musical imagination at the peak of its poetic clarity. As a result, the *Kinderszenen* have long been staples of the repertoire as utterly charming yet substantial miniatures, the sort of compact keyboard essays in which Schumann's genius found full expression. *Kinderszenen* was one of the projects Schumann worked on during the spring of 1838 to get through a difficult period of separation from his fiancée, Clara Wieck, who was on tour as a pianist and whose father objected to the idea of her marriage to the composer. In March of that year, Schumann wrote to Clara, "I have been waiting for your letter and have in the meantime filled several books with pieces.... You once said to me that I often seemed like a child, and I suddenly got inspired and knocked off around 30 quaint little pieces.... I selected several and titled them *Kinderszenen*. You will enjoy them, though you will need to forget that you are a virtuoso when you play them." The *Kinderszenen* are a touching tribute to the eternal, universal memories and feelings of childhood from a nostalgic adult perspective; unlike a number of Schumann's collections of piano character pieces (e.g. *Album for the Young*, Op. 68), the *Kinderszenen* are not intended to be played by children. Schumann claimed that the picturesque titles attached to the pieces were added as an afterthought in order to provide subtle suggestions to the player, a model Debussy followed decades later in his Preludes. Almost all of the Kinderszenen are miniature ternary (ABA) forms. Scene No. 1, "Von fremden Ländern und Menschen" (Of Foreign Lands and People), opens with a lovely melody whose basic motivic substance, by appearing in several vague guises throughout many of the other pieces, serves as a general unifying element. The seventh Scene, "Träumerei" (Reverie), is easily the most famous piece in the set; its charming melody and quieting power have recommended it to generations of concert pianists who wish to calm audiences after a long series of rousing encores. The *Kinderszenen* contain many delicate musical touches; Scene No. 4, "Bittendes Kind" (Pleading Child), for example, is harmonically resolved only when an unseen force (a parent?) gives in and grant the child's wish at the beginning of No. 5, "Glückes genug" (Quite Happy). In the final piece, "Der Dichter spricht" (The Poet Speaks), Schumann removes himself just a bit from the indulgent reverie to formulate a narrator's omniscient view of the child. Quietly, gently, the many moods and feelings that Schumann touched upon over the course of this remarkable 20-minute work are lovingly recalled, and the composition concludes, contentedly, in the same key of G major in which it began. *—Blair Johnston*

Recommended:

○ **Schumann: Kinderszenen; Kreisleriana** / Argerich / DG 410653

○ **Schumann: Carnaval; Kinderszenen; Waldszenen** / Arrau / 1987 / Philips 420871

○ **Great Pianists: Radu Lupu** / Lupu / 1999 / Philips 456895

○ **Schumann: Piano Works** / Kempff / 1975 / DG 435045

Kreisleriana, 8 fantasies, Op. 16 (1838)

German composer Robert Schumann described his *Kreisleriana* (1838) in the following words: 'The title is understandable only to Germans. Kreisler is a figure created by E.T.A. Hoffmann—an eccentric, wild and clever Kapellmeister." Eccentric, wild, and clever aptly sum up one aspect of the work, but *Kreisleriana* is tender, ardent, and passionate as well. This alternation between the fantastic and the lyrical, the grotesque and the loving, is one of the key characteristics of *Kreisleriana.* Written in four days in April 1838, it is dedicated to Chopin in the score, but, like most of Schumann's piano music from the late 1830s, it is really about Schumann's love for Clara Wieck. Extremely virtuosic and extremely subjective, Schumann's *Kreisleriana* is one of the high points of his compositional career.

1. Ausserst bewegt (Extremely moving) Fast and diabolical D minor outer sections flank a slow and supple B flat major central section.

2. Sehr innig und nicht zu rasch (Very inwardly and not to quickly) This is a triple time-stylized dance movement with two trios. After a tenderly musing B flat major outer section follows the fast and capricious Intermezzo I in G minor. After the return of the opening section follows the fast and passionate Intermezzo II in G minor. The second Intermezzo is followed by intensely chromatic music and darkly wends it way back to the final return of the opening.

3. Sehr aufgereg (Very agitated) Quietly creeping chromatic music in G minor, reminiscent of the first movement, flanks somewhat slower and deeply affectionate music in B flat major. The return of the G minor music is at first exact, but rises to a fortissimo climax in which the rhythm slows and the music drops down into the depths of the piano.

4. Sehr langsam (Very slowly) This meditative music in B flat major has intense lyrical music, bordering on a recitative, followed by intimately poetic music hovering between quietness and stillness.

5. Sehr lebhaft (Very lively) In this pianissimo triple-time movement in G minor that is close to a Scherzo in tone and speed are two trios: one whimsical and the other building to a dramatic climax.

6. Sehr langsam (Very slowly) The heart of *Kreisleriana* starts with a folk-like melody in B flat major, but transforms into an extremely ardent central section in C minor.

7. Sehr rasch (Very fast) A violently excited movement in C minor, the velocity and intensity increase in a central fugato until it collapses in slower, chorale-like music at its close.

8. Schnell und spielend (Fast and playful) This G minor music skulks and slinks in seemingly two tempos at once: the right hand's frisky melody moving in one tempo while the left hand's slow-moving melody in octaves is slightly out of sync. The music enigmatically ends on the bottom of the keyboard. *—James Leonard*

Recommended:

○ **Robert Schumann: Kinderszenen; Kreisleriana** / Argerich / DG 410653

○ **Schumann: Kreisleriana; Gesänge der Frühe; Nachtstücke** / Schiff / 1998 / Teldec 14566

○ **Schumann: Kreisleriana; Gesänge der Frühe; Allegro in B minor** / Pollini / DG 471370

○ **Schumann: Piano Works** / Kempff / 1975 / DG 435045

Nachtstücke (Night Pieces), Op. 23 (1839)

The origin of Schumann's *Nachtstücke* (Night Pieces; 1839) lay in a disturbing premonition the composer had between March 24 and 27, 1839. "I kept seeing funeral processions, coffins, and unhappy, distraught figures," he later wrote to his wife, Clara. Almost immediately thereafter he received the news that his brother Eduard was dying. The strangeness continued, as Schumann recounted in another letter to Clara: "Last Saturday, at half past two in the morning, while I was still on the road, I heard a chorale played by trombones." It was at that very moment, the composer later discovered, that Eduard passed on.

These events were the direct inspiration for what Schumann had originally planned to call *Leichenfantasie* (Funeral Fantasy), a set of four pieces, each of which was to bear a descriptive title: "Funeral Procession," "A Curious Society," "A Night Party," and "A Ring-Dance Song with Solo Voices." Ultimately, however, he adopted the less specific *Nachtstücke,* vaguely inspired by E.T.A. Hoffman's "Night Tales."

The opening march, despite its bright key of C major, is darkly colored and certainly nocturnal. The F major second piece, of a larger scope than its predecessor, is a characteristic representation of Schumann's symbolic twins Florestan (gentle and introspective) and Eusebius (manic and stormy) in musical conflict with one another. The third piece is a virtuosic waltz in D flat major. The final piece is tender and songlike, like a lullaby or an expression of fond parting. *—AMG*

Recommended:

○ **Schumann: Toccata; Nachtstücke; Blumenstück; Four Fuges** / Richter / 1993 / London 436456

○ **Schumann: Piano Works** / Glemser / 1994 / Naxos 550715

○ **Schumann: Piano Works** / Kempff / 1975 / DG 435045

Acht Noveletten, Op. 21 (1838)

Schumann intended the eight pieces of his *Noveletten,* Op. 21 (1838) to be performed as a group, though they are often successfully performed separately. These "tales of adventure," as the composer referred to them, provide a wholly representative example of the composer's keyboard style. No. 1 in F major alternates a staccato March with a flowing legato passage within its five sections. Technically tricky thumb repetitions provide an element of challenge for the pianist in No. 2 in D major; otherwise, this bravura piece is quite grateful and effective. A lyrical central Intermezzo provides an element of contrast. No. 3 in D major demonstrates the composer's sense of humor with rapid staccato chords; a contrasting section in B minor is passionate and wild. No. 4 in D major is a rather loosely organized but interesting Waltz that employs cross-rhythms and syncopation to good effect. No. 5 in D major is a full-blown Polonaise; its principal section, with three main ideas, is set into relief by the persistent rhythms of the Trio. Gradually increasing tempos characterize the progression of the sections in No. 6 in A major. Starting from the staccato opening, each of the subsequent, predominantly lyrical, passages is marked a few metronome beats faster until the coda, which returns to the original tempo. No. 7 in E major bookends a beautifully lyrical central section with passages featuring fast, brilliant octaves. The last member of the set, No. 8 in F sharp minor, is actually two pieces in one. The first part, a passionate Etude in 2/4, uses a jaunty dance for its first Trio. It is followed by a second Trio, similar in character but different in content. A romantic interlude connects this first large division with the second section. The marchlike nature of this section is contrasted by more lyrical passages; the melody from the romantic interlude (which Schumann calls the "Voice from Afar") returns as the climax. *—Steven Coburn*

Recommended:

○ **Sviatoslav Richter Plays Schumann** / Richter / DG 447440

Papillons (Butterflies), Op. 2 (1829–1831)

Robert Schumann's first set of character pieces for piano, *Papillons* (1829–31), may be regarded as a sort of study for the better-known *Carnaval* (1833–35). Both are musical representations of festival scenes and involve multiple characters and dance-sequences; Schumann, in fact, reworked elements of *Papillons* for use in the later work. The concept for *Papillons* was apparently suggested to the composer by Jean Paul Richter's novel *Flegeljahre* (Age of Indiscretion); originally, each of the 12 pieces had a title that made reference to that well-known literary work. The extent of the novelist's influence on Schumann is, of course, difficult to determine. Schumann removed the titles before publication, wanting, as was typical throughout his creative life, to conceal the sources of inspiration. Precisely why the work was ultimately titled *Papillons* (Butterflies) has never been explained; yet the title was obviously Schumann's invention, and the suggestion of airiness and flight is clearly borne out by the music. *Papillons,* in keeping with its origin as music for a fictitious festival or ballroom scene, is a set of dance pieces, many of them waltzes. Even at this early stage in his compositional career—*Papillons* is only the composer's second published work—Schumann's craft can hardly be called commonplace. The work draws on many external sources of inspiration, both literary and musical: witness, for instance, the canon at the octave in No. 3 that seems to make a direct allusion to a similar instance in Haydn, or the incorporation into the finale of the same old German song (the "Grossvaterlied") that the composer used to represent the Philistines in *Carnaval.* The conclusion of *Papillons* is considered by many to be the composer's first masterstroke. Atop a 26 bar pedal point on low D—an extraordinary gesture for a work written before the introduction of the modern sostenuto pedal—Schumann combines a fragment from the "Grossvaterlied" with the waltz melody that opens the work. Six accented notes represent the striking of a clock (Schumann inscribed on the score, "The clamor of the carnival dies away, the clock in the tower strikes six"), after which the pianist executes a remarkable diminuendo effected by the removal of notes, one at a time, from a sustained dominant-seventh chord. The party-goers disappear as the sound gradually vanishes into nothingness. *—Blair Johnston*

Recommended:

○ **Schumann: Fantasy in C; Faschingsschwank aus Wien; Papillons** / Richter / 2002 / EMI 75233

○ **Schumann: Carnaval; Papillons; Scenes From Childhood** / Jando / 1988 / Naxos 550076

○ **Great Pianists: Andrei Gavrilov** / Gavrilov / 1999 / Philips 456787

○ **Schumann: Piano Works** / Kempff / 1975 / DG 435045

Phantasiestücke, Op. 111 (1851)

By the time Schumann wrote this collection of three pieces, he had already been struggling with mental illness, and perhaps partially because of that growing disorder, many of his compositions were lacking the freshness and invention of his earlier ones. Although these Op. 111 *Fantasy Pieces* are without the staleness that had crept into his style, they do not quite venture into new territory, either.

All are untitled pieces, distinguished only by their tempo indication. The first is marked Molto vivace ed appassionatamente, a description that encapsulates the nature of this stormy piece. It is full of tension in its headlong rush, and the music yearns and wails, but there is never the least suggestion of pity or sorrow, only of fret and coldness.

The second piece, marked Più tosto lento—Un poco più mosso, begins serenely, but also with a somewhat disengaged emotional state and sense of hesitancy in its musical flow. The main theme is tender and sweet, but has a forced air about its mildness. Tension builds in the middle section, but when the main theme returns, the music gradually begins fading under an icy quiet.

The third of the *Fantasy Pieces* begins with a grand and triumphant theme and then goes on to an alternate playful melody of subdued character. The opening theme returns and seems to bring on the end, but the alternate material resurrects the music wittily and then closes the piece. *—Robert Cummings*

Recommended:

- ○ **Great Pianists: Vladimir Horowitz** / Horowitz / 1998 / Philips 456838

Piano Sonata No. 1 in F sharp minor ("Grosse Sonate"), Op. 11 (1833–1835)

This is an early work in Schumann's output, begun when the 23-year-old composer was engaged to marry Ernestine von Fricken and finished when he had begun romancing 15-year-old virtuoso pianist Clara Wieck, who would become his wife in 1840. Published anonymously under the names of Florestan and Eusebius (alter egos adopted for the art world by the eccentric Schumann), this sonata is cast in four movements, its large outer panels (each over 11 minutes) framing short inner movements.

The first movement opens with a lengthy but quite lovely introduction marked Un poco adagio, where the main theme from the second movement is augured in the second subject. The main section (Allegro vivace) ensues, featuring a lively, fiery theme based on Schumann's 1832 *Fandango in F sharp minor*, a piece that also provided a springboard for Clara's *Le ballet des revenants*. A richly Romantic alternate theme soon appears, its slower tempo and sensual manner offering deft contrast. After a repeat of the main materials, a stormy, brilliantly colorful development section follows, with an abbreviated, melancholy reprise then closing out the movement.

The ensuing Aria is very brief, but filled with feelings of romance and passion in the aforementioned main theme, which now flowers to utter beauty. Next comes the Scherzo, which features a jumpy, quirky melody and calmer second subject in the outer sections, surrounding a stately bright Intermezzo that exhibits the influence of Chopin.

The finale (Allegro un poco maestoso) is a rondo brimming with melodic material, the first theme a stately creation coming in rapid, repeating chords, the next having a more subdued but still lively manner. Thereafter, the movement alternates between the blustery and the reflective, moods that supposedly reflect Schumann's alter egos—Florestan (restless, disruptive) and Eusebius (contemplative). The sonata closes with a brilliantly virtuosic coda. *—Robert Cummings*

Recommended:

- ○ **Schumann: Piano Sonatas 1 & 3** / Demidenko / 1996 / Hyperion 66864
- ○ **Schumann: Fantasie Op17; Sonate Op11** / Pollini / DG 423134
- ○ **Gieseking Plays Schumann** / Gieseking / Music & Arts 1013

Piano Sonata No. 2 in G minor, Op. 22 (1833–1838)

The work now known as Robert Schumann's *Piano Sonata No. 2* in G minor, Op. 22 (1833–38) was not, in fact, the composer's second such work in order of composition. The so-called *Sonata No. 3*, really a reworking of the *Concert sans orchestre* of 1836, acquired its present identity only after Schumann revised the earlier work (including the restoration of a scherzo removed before publication) in 1853. The Second Sonata, Schumann's last large-scale work in the genre, is the most streamlined of the composer's completed piano sonatas; within its very manageable and clearly organized confines one finds some of the composer's most characteristic music for the keyboard.

A great deal has been made of the first movement's rather humorous tempo indications. Straightaway the pianist is asked to play "so rasch wie möglich" (as fast as possible), only to find in the coda the marking "schneller" (faster), and, in the concluding bars, "noch schneller" (even faster)! Capricious as such markings may seem at first glance, Schumann's musical intent is crystal clear

The first theme, which commences with no introduction, is a relentlessly forward-moving idea set atop a percolating arpeggiated texture in the left hand. The driving syncopations that Schumann forges into a transitional passage transform into a gentler second theme in the relative major. The pause in rhythmic intensity is brief; even before the development commences, the incessant sixteenth notes have reestablished themselves. Both ideas are played out in the development and the recapitulation, and, per Schumann's standard practice, are not substantially altered from their original form. The movement draws to a close with a forceful coda.

The Andantino, a melodious little ABA form in a gently rolling 6/8 meter, is one of the most charming movements Schumann ever penned. The Scherzo is so compact as to startle the listener: 64 bars suffice for its presentation, and, unusually, only eight of these are marked for repetition. The snappy rhythm of the primary idea lends the Scherzo a most witty flavor, while the brief trio section recaptures the gentle syncopations of the first movement's second theme.

Both Schumann and Clara Wieck (not yet Mrs. Schumann) felt the Sonata's original finale to be ungainly and technically recalcitrant, so in 1838 the composer provided a new, much-improved (if somewhat "square") final movement. The replacement finale is a good example of hybrid sonata-rondo form; that is, the basic "ABACA (etc.)" scheme of a rondo is organized so as to correspond to the three primary sections of a sonata-allegro. The mood and texture of the refrain theme (A) recall the first movement, while the suppleness of the secondary theme, marked "etwas langsamer" (somewhat slower), is suggested by several internal ritardandos. Schumann brings the work to an electric end by appending a prestissimo passage marked "Quasi cadenza" to the main body of the movement. *—Blair Johnston*

Recommended:

- ○ **Schumann: Fantasy in C major; Symphonic Etudes; Piano Sonata 2** / Hamelin / 2001 / Hyperion 67166
- ○ **Schumann: Piano Works** / Kempff / 1975 / DG 435045

Piano Sonata No. 3 in F minor ("Concerto without Orchestra"), Op. 14 (1835–1836)

Originally in five movements, Schumann's *Concert sans orchestre*, Op. 14, was first published with only three movements in 1836 by Haslinger in Vienna. Schumann revised the piece in 1853, publishing the work as his *Piano Sonata No. 3 in F minor* and dedicating it to German-Bohemian pianist and composer Ignaz Moscheles (1794–1870).

Haslinger persuaded Schumann to release the work in three movements, forgoing the two scherzos and retaining the slow variations as a contrasting middle movement. Also, "to whet the appetite of a more curious public," Haslinger decided on the title *Concert sans orchestre*, to which Moscheles objected. In 1853, Schumann reduced the number of variations in the slow movement from six to four and placed the second of the two rejected Scherzos between the first movement and the variations. The *Piano Sonata* did not receive its premiere until 1862, when Johannes Brahms (1833–97) gave a performance in Vienna.

The main theme of the first movement summarizes Schumann's approach to the manipulation of material. An expansive, falling theme flows in the right hand over rapid arpeggios in the left. Almost immediately, the theme dissolves into repeated sequences derived from the theme that modulate away from the tonic. Fragmentary development of material in the style of Beethoven occurs in Schumann's works in places other than in the development section, wherein entire melodic passages transposed to new harmonies are often found.

Schumann's Scherzo, marked Molto comodo (Very comfortably), brings to mind a stately minuet as opposed to a post-Beethoven scherzo. This is in part due to numerous accents on the third beat. The D major Trio moves through several harmonies, including D flat major and B flat minor, the main key areas of the Scherzo.

Entitled "Quasi variazioni," the slow movement is a set of variations on an Andantino theme by Clara Wieck, Schumann's future wife. The descending theme is strikingly similar to the main theme of the first movement and may be the seed of the whole sonata, for it appears slightly modified in the Trio of the Scherzo and in the Finale. Also, Schumann's treatment of the theme in the third variation, in which he transposes a falling chromatic gesture up a perfect fourth, resembles the opening measures of the main theme of the first movement. The beginning of the fourth variation is directly related to the opening of the Scherzo in both pitch and rhythm. The variation movement has become a favorite among pianists, and it is occasionally programmed separately from the *Piano Sonata*.

The energetic Finale is very difficult to perform and contains motivically conceived themes embedded in rapid right-hand figurations. Syncopation is a major feature of the movement and is responsible for the tremendous forward energy. Repetition, too, plays a major role in both creating forward impetus and delineating the structure. *—John Palmer*

Recommended:

- ○ **Schumann: Davidsbündlertänze; Concert sans orchestre** / Pollini / 2001 / DG 471369
- ○ **Byron Janis: Prokofiev, Rachmaninov, Schumann & Mendelssohn** / Janis / 1994 / Mercury 434333

12 Pieces for Children Big and Small, for piano, 4 hands, Op. 85 (1849)

German composer Robert Schumann was only 38 in 1848, but he was already beginning to show signs of decline as a composer and as a conductor. His creative output had slowed in recent years and his conducting of the Dresden Staatskapelle was thought to be inept and incompetent. But the combination of his friend Felix Mendelssohn's death in autumn 1847 and the revolutionary uprising of late spring 1848 seems to have inspired him as a composer and he wrote a series of works that can stand with any of his earlier works. These include many of his best Goethe songs, plus his *Szenen von Faust* and *Requiem für Mignon*, the *Introduction and Allegro for Piano and Orchestra*, the *Waldszenen* for solo piano, and the *Zwolf Vierhändige Klavierstücke für Kleine und Gross Kinder* (12 Four-Hand Piano Pieces for Small and Large Children), Op. 85.

Schumann, who loved his children and who had already written several sets of pieces for them, conceived his *Zwolf Vierhändige Klavierstücke für Kleine und Gross Kinder* as duets he would perform with his daughter, Maria. The first of the pieces—"Geburtstagsmarsch" (Birthday March)—was performed by father and daughter as a surprise for Clara Schumann on her birthday, September 13. The remaining 11 pieces were written in two batches between September 10 through 15 and between September 27 and October 1. All were written in Schumann's most charmingly childlike manner, with tender and funny melodies and simple but effective accompaniments. Tragically, the *Zwolf Vierhändige Klavierstücke für Kleine und Gross Kinder* proved to be Schumann's last great work for the piano. The pieces of piano music published afterwards—the sets of *Bunte Blätter* and *Albumblätter*—are collections of earlier works. *—James Leonard*

Recommended:

- ○ **The Art Of Alfred Brendel** / Brendel / 1996 / Philips 446920

Three Romances, Op. 28 (1839)

In the early days of his compositional career Schumann wrote almost exclusively for his own instrument, the piano. Throughout the 1830s, even after his prospects as a concert pianist were ruined by permanent damage to the fourth finger of his right hand, he continued to mostly shun the demands of chamber ensembles, the orchestra, and, the voice. During the second half of the decade, the composer's affinity for the piano can probably be largely attributed to his relationship with Clara Wieck, the extraordinary pianist who was to become his wife. Some of Schumann's piano works, like *Carnaval* Op. 9 (1833–35) and *Kreisleriana*, Op. 16 (1838), have earned a secure place in the repertoire; others, including the *Drei Romanzen*, Op. 28 (1839), remain lesser-known yet worthy examples of the composer's distinctive keyboard idiom.

Schumann himself was quite fond of these three romances, which, despite the suggestion of their title, are not lushly melodic; they are, more accurately, contrasting character pieces. The first, in B flat minor, is a breathless piece in ternary (ABA) form whose triplet rhythms never waver until the final two bars. Atop this glistening arpeggiation is a lyric melody in two strains that gives way to gentle syncopations. A passionate codetta marked by singing sforzandi and alternating piano and forte dynamics brings the work to a stern conclusion.

Of the three romances, the second, in F sharp major, has gained the most currency among pianists as an independent concert work. It is a relatively brief piece—34 bars long, including some repetition—whose thick texture led Schumann to the then-uncommon step of notating it on three staves. The 6/8 meter lends the melody the flavor of a barcarolle. The romance comes to an end as lyricism vanishes into pianissimo syncopations.

The third romance, in B major, is both the longest and, arguably, the least successful of the three. It is structured on the rondo principle, with the central digressions, themselves separated by a return of the refrain theme, titled Intermezzo I and Intermezzo II. The principal idea—sharply rhythmic, freely imitative and not at all what a later composer might think of as a "romance" theme—is attractive enough, but the piece as a whole lacks the focus of the first two. The mellow tones of the finish, however, offer the listener ample reward. *—Blair Johnston*

Recommended:

- ○ **Great Pianists: Wilhelm Kempff 3** / Kempff / 1999 / Philips 456868
- ○ **Schumann: Piano Works** / Kempff / 1975 / DG 435045

Symphonic Etudes ("Etudes in the form of variations"), Op. 13 (1834–1861)

Schumann's contributions to the literature of the piano etude, a genre just beginning to blossom in the middle nineteenth century at the hands of Chopin and Liszt, came in three isolated, extremely productive bursts, after which he abandoned the genre forever. (It is perhaps no coincidence that Schumann was also forced to abandon hopes for a performing career after permanently crippling the fourth finger of his right hand during the early 1830s.) Schumann's earliest such effort, the *Studies on Caprices of Paganini* Op. 3 (1832), is at best little more than a preliminary essay toward the later, altogether more successful *Concert Etudes on Caprices of Paganini*, Op. 10 (1833). Even this second set of Paganini-inspired works, however, cannot compare with Liszt's parallel achievement, the *Grandes études de Paganini* (1851). But with the *12 Symphonic Etudes, Op. 13* (1834, rev. 1852), Schumann achieved a remarkable level of expressivity and technical achievement that has made the work a perennial if digitally formidable recital favorite.

The 12 etudes of Op. 13 originally numbered 18; however, Schumann found the set so exhausting for the pianist that he removed five of the etudes prior to publication, both lessening the work's demands and streamlining its architecture. Johannes Brahms selected five of the additional six etudes for publication during the 1890s, and these have since joined the original 12 in many performances and recordings.

Schumann also referred to the Symphonic Etudes as "Etudes en forme de variations" (Etudes in the form of variations), and it is largely to this enhanced degree of musical connectivity that the work owes its success. The theme upon which most of the variations are based was composed by Baron von Fricken, an amateur musician and father of Ernestine von Fricken, Schumann's onetime fiancée. The third and ninth etudes bear a much weaker relationship to the theme than do their companions, while the finale is based upon different material altogether.

The theme, in C sharp minor, is infused by an atmosphere of tragedy, effectively built up into a kind of sepulchral march in the first etude-variation. The second etude is in rolling nocturne style, while the third, marked Vivace, draws upon energetic staccato textures. The fourth is a canon at the octave that uses the first measure of the Baron's theme but soon digresses. The fifth etude is also cleverly imitative, built on impish dotted rhythms (and, for a change, finishing in E major rather than in C sharp minor), while the sixth etude is a study in syncopation. The seventh etude, which like the fifth moves to E major at the end, is quick-witted and repetitive, finishing with a crescendo and a flurry of finger work. The eighth etude employs a thinner texture but is filled with intricate ornamentation. The ninth etude, a scherzo of sorts marked Presto possibile (as fast as possible), is one of the most challenging of the set; the theme is present only in the vaguest outline. The tenth etude is articulate and humorous, the eleventh the only one cast in a key other than C sharp minor; its grim key of G sharp minor and foreboding left-hand texture take the listener into the despairing depths of Schumann's craft. Etude No. 12, the finale, is cast in the altogether brighter key of D flat major, and employs a theme from an opera by Heinrich Marschner as its basic material; its joyful dotted rhythms and Allegro brillante atmosphere make for an appropriately exciting conclusion. *—Blair Johnston*

Recommended:

- ○ **Schumann: Piano Concerto; Symphonic Etudes; Arabeske** / Pollini / DG 445522
- ○ **The Art of Murray Perahia** / Perahia / Sony 48153
- ○ **Schumann: Piano Works** / Kempff / 1975 / DG 435045
- ○ **Great Pianists: Myra Hess** / Hess / 1999 / Philips 456832

Toccata in C major, Op. 7 (1829–1833)

Schumann's *Toccata*, Op. 7 is a perpetual-motion *tour de force* that calls for pianists of exceptional digital abilities. It is cast in in a sonata-allegro form; bold chords announce the main theme, which requires a continuous rocking motion in both hands even as it cascades over the keyboard. (This is likely the sort of passage that Schumann famously ruined his hands trying to master.) The second subject offers little relief for the pianist, and the development, with its unison octaves, even less. The piece finally fades away, as though from exhaustion. For all its fireworks, the *Toccata* never loses the delightful spirit of the composer at his most playful, the quality that lifts the work beyond the realm of mere technical display. *—Sol Louis Siegel*

Recommended:

- ○ **Beethoven: Sonata Op111; Schumann: Symphonic Etudes; Toccata** / Pogorelich / DG 410520
- ○ **Schumann: Symphonic Etudes; Toccata; Fantasie** / Wild / 2000 / Ivory 71001
- ○ **Schumann: Phantasiestücke; Waldszenen; Abegg Variations** / Richter / 1998 / DG 459018

Variations on the name "Abegg," in F major, Op. 1 (1830)

Robert Schumann's *Abegg Variations* (the Variations on the name "Abegg" for piano, Op. 1), despite the implications of the attached opus number, were neither his first composition nor, truth be told, his first explorations of variation form: prior to completing Op.1 in 1830 he had composed no fewer than eight polonaises, six waltzes, an incomplete piano concerto, several youthful songs, a set of variations for piano four-hands, and various other, shorter pieces. And so when he sat down to compose a group of variations for Countess Pauline von Abegg, he was certainly no mere initiate at his craft, though it would indeed be years before he reached the summit of his genius. The "Abegg" Variations remain among the composer's most frequently-played works, owing, no doubt, to a relative lack of technical challenges. Although the theme is not his strongest, and the styles of Schumann's predecessors Carl Maria von Weber and Johann Hummel at times overshadow Schumann's rather insecure voice, the variations and Finale contain ample promise of the great things yet to come.

The material of the theme is derived from the last name of the work's dedicatee, Countess von Abegg: A- B flat-E-G-G (the letter "b" being equivalent in the German nomenclature to the pitch B flat). In later years Schumann would use such letter-to-pitch derivations with more panache as in *Carnaval*, or the later fugues on the name BACH. In the opening theme of the "Abegg" Variations, however, the clumsy, repetitive three-four rhythmic motive and routine accompaniment would seem to show little promise for variational potential.

Such a judgment is immediately proven incorrect, however, as the composer provides three straight variations (in the same key, F major, and tempo, Animato) of considerable breadth and ingenuity. A lyric interlude (Cantabile) of great beauty, still derived from the same basic material but not given a variation number by the composer, dissolves to make a transition directly into the exciting Finale alla Fantasia (Vivace). *—Blair Johnston*

Recommended:

- ○ **Richter: Phantasiestücke; Waldszenen; Abegg Variations** / Richter / 1998 / DG 459018

Waldszenen (Forest Scenes), Op. 82 (1848–1849)

Schumann's *Waldszenen* (Forest Scenes), Op. 82 (1848–49) consists of nine short pieces similar in style and spirit to the composer's *Kinderszenen* (1838). "Eintritt" (Entrance) features unusual, asymmetrical phrasing. "Jäger auf der Lauer" (Hunter in Ambush) is an exciting, technically challenging piece in the cast of a typical nineteenth century hunting song. The difficulties of "Einsame Blumen" (Solitary Flowers) lie in maintaing balance between the two distinct voices in the right hand; otherwise, it is simple and melodic. "Verrufene Stelle" (Haunted Spot) evokes an air of eerie mystery with passages in slow dotted rhythms, while the fast, tricky triplets of "Freundliche Landschaft" (Friendly Landscape) create a surprisingly poetic effect. "Herbege" (At the Inn) presents a variety of material that requires great sensitivity to balance.

The best-known and most striking piece of the set is "Vogel als Prophet" (The Prophet Bird); its cross-relations, incomplete melodies, and extreme delicacy of texture create a weirdly beautiful atmosphere. "Jagdlied" (Hunting Song) is the second of the *Waldszenen* in this style and the example more typical of the genre. Rapidly repeated triplet chords both lend the piece rhythmic drive and pose a substantial technical challenge. The concluding "Abschied" (Farewell) is a touching song without words. *Waldszen* may rightly be regarded as Schumann's last really fine keyboard work. The diminishment of the composer's mental and emotional capacities in ensuing years led him to redirect his energies largely toward the compilation and revision of earlier works rather than the production of new music. *—Steven Coburn*

Recommended:

- ○ **Schumann: Carnaval de Vienne; Scènes de la forêt; Grand sonate** / Ciccolini / Cascavelle 3056
- ○ **Richter: Phantasiestücke; Waldszenen; Abegg Variations** / Richter / 1998 / DG 459018

VOCAL

Dichterliebe, song cycle, Op. 48 (1840)

Those who criticize Robert Schumann for not grasping the depths of meaning in the poems he sets perhaps could be accused of engaging in a shallow reading of the lied composer's musico-poetic sensitivities. In fact, some scholars argue that Schumann's subtlety—his ability not only to render texts, or even interpret them, but also to comment on them with tones—is the very essence of his song style. When hearing his 1840 collection, *Dichterliebe* (The Poet's Love), one must not only look for correspondences between poetic image and musical figure, but artistic incongruities, as well—moments where Schumann steps back from the verse, takes a critical stance, and engages with the poet on equal and sometimes even contradictory ground.

Widely considered his best song cycle, *Dichterliebe* was composed within a matter of days—amazingly, during the same month as Schumann's Op. 24, *Liederkreis*. *Dichterliebe* takes for its texts 16 poems from the "Lyrisches Intermezzo," a section of Heinrich Heine's *Buch der Lieder* from 1827. (Originally, Schumann's cycle included 20 songs, but four were omitted when *Dichterliebe* was published as Op. 48 in 1844.) Heine's group follows a trajectory of increasing irony. The opening poems express an innocent hope that the speaker's love will be reciprocated; the first two selections, *Im wunderschönen Monat Mai* (In the Wonderful Month of May) and *Aus meinen Tränen spriessen* (Springing From My Tears) both feature the optimistic imagery of springtime blossoms budding and birds singing. From the beginning, however, Schumann hints at a less favorable outcome. While it is not an uncommon device for Schumann to end the vocal line hanging on a dissonant chord, leaving the piano to carry out a song's conclusion, *Im wunderschönen Monat Mai* ends even more ambiguously. The song itself ends ethereally on an unresolved chord, suggesting that the singer's love may remain unrequited. By the fifth song in the cycle, the speaker's thoughts of his lover have already slipped into the past tense; the seventh song, *Ich grolle nicht*, takes on a decidedly ironic tone. A sturdy bass line supports a repeated chordal texture, while the singer's line assumes a regal, almost heroic air. The text, on the other hand, feigns austerity in order to veil its suffering: "I saw you in a dream/and saw the darkness trapped in your soul/and saw the serpent that gnaws at your heart./I saw, my love, how miserable you are." Schumann's overblown accompaniment makes it clear that it is the speaker, not his beloved, who is miserable. By the end of the collection, all pretense is gone, and the speaker's tone is jaded. Schumann's music is likewise plodding and unrelenting in its rhythm and figuration, and even more unrelenting in its dark parody. Triumphant ascending arpeggios break briefly into the major mode, only to find a sardonic answer in minor once again. Curiously, however, as the singer's final, sorrowful strains fade, a bittersweet piano postlude offers a sense of repose found nowhere in Heine's original. *—Jeremy Grimshaw*

Recommended:

- ○ **Schumann: Dichterliebe; Beethoven: An die ferne Geliebte; Lieder** / Hampson, Parsons / 1994 / EMI 55147
- ○ **Schumann: Dichterliebe; Schubert & Beethoven: Lieder** / Wunderlich, Giesen / DG 449747
- ○ **Schumann: Liederkreis Op 24; Dichterliebe** / Bostridge, Drake / 1998 / EMI 56575

Frauenliebe und -leben, song cycle, Op. 42 (1840)

Often referred to as "the year of the song" in Schumann's life, the year 1840 saw the completion of at least 137 songs, including the famous Op. 39 *Liederkreis*, *Dichterliebe* (Op. 48), and *Frauenliebe und -leben* (A Woman's Love and Life), written to poems of Adalbert von Chamisso. Schumann's impending marriage to Clara Wieck (1819–96)—hard won after a long legal battle with her father—was largely the inspiration for his burst of creativity; this seems especially clear in the case of *Frauenliebe und -leben*, which takes as its subject the earnest devotion of a wife and mother.

Schumann arranged the songs to represent something of a story, covering different stages of a woman's life. "Seit ich ihn gesehen" (Since I First Saw Him) introduces us to the focal point of the song cycle—the man whom the protagonist desires. Without having him, everything around her seems drab and lifeless, and she does not want to mingle even with her sisters. Schumann illustrates the darkness of her world by a descending seventh on "tiefstem" (deepest) near the end of the first verse. Schumann would later quote the final three measures of the song in the slow movement of his *Symphony No. 1*.

In "Er, der Herrlichste von allen" (He the most Glorious of All) we learn that the subject of her affections is kind and good, and that the woman feels unworthy of him. Constant eighth note chords, played at a lively tempo, seem to adopt the excited character of a breathless heartbeat. Beginning without introduction, "Ich kann's nicht fassen, nicht glauben" (I Cannot Grasp or Believe It) reveals that the man has chosen her; Staccato chords punctuate her excitement as the key moves from C minor to C major. By the time the woman sings the next song, "Du Ring an meinem Finger" (You, Ring on my Finger), she has become more confident and certain of her place in the world. She presses the engagement ring to her lips and, as Schumann directs that the tempo increase, says that she will "serve, him, live for him, belong to him completely."

"Helf mir, ihr Schwestern" (Help Me, Sisters), depicts wedding-day preparations; after her sisters dress her, the woman bids them farewell. In "Süsser Freund" (Sweet Friend), the woman tries to tell her new husband that she is expecting his child. As the piano conveys her excitement, she finally tells him that one day, his image will look up at her; in "An meinem Herzen, an meiner Brust" (On my Heart, on my Breast), the new mother rocks her baby to Schumann's rolling accompaniment. As she hugs the child, the arpeggios become chords.

The overwhelmingly positive and hopeful atmosphere of the cycle changes drastically in "Nun has du mir den ersten Schmerz getan" (Now You Have Hurt Me for the First Time). The D major of the previous song gives way to a somber D minor as the woman looks upon her now-dead husband, the vocal line becoming increasingly lower. The song closes with a solo piano quotation of the first song; however, the return is fittingly incomplete. The abrupt tragedy of this last song leaves the cycle somewhat poetically unbalanced, but this is clearly part of Schumann's conception. The death of her husband is sudden, unforeseen, and without cause; the end of the cycle is equally unprepared. *—John Palmer*

Recommended:

- ○ **Schumann: Frauenleibe und Leben; 5 Lieder Op 40; 15 Lieder** / von Otter, Forsberg / DG 445881
- ○ **Les Introuvables: Christa Ludwig** / Ludwig, Moore / EMI 64074

Lieder-Album für die Jugend (Song Album for the Young), Op. 79 (1849)

1848 was the great year of revolutions in Europe. Schumann had written various pieces supporting the ideals of these revolutions, such as his Opus 62, *Three Patriotic Songs for Male Chorus*, but by 1849, the aftermath had become all too real. He had written about half of the songs for this collection when he fled Dresden to avoid military conscription, and finished it while staying in the tiny village of Kreisca. He told a friend that in many ways, the turmoil in the external world drove him deeper into his art, and Clara commented that most of his works from the time had a springlike peacefulness. However, there are indications that the wars were still on his mind: he noted "revolution in Dresden" in the manuscript of the 26th song, "Des Buben Schutzenlied" (The boy's hunting song), and chose a text about a painful escape from military conscription for the seventh song.

These songs are organized by order of maturity, and the cycle ends with "Kennst du das Land" (Do you know the land), the song sung by the enigmatic half woman, half child Mignon, which he also used to begin his Opus 98, *Lieder und Gesange aus Wilhelm Meister*. The first songs are accordingly simple, drawn from poems that provide easy musical imagery, such as the fluttering of the butterfly in

"Schmetterling" (Butterfly), the second song, though he avoids the too-obvious literal imitation of a cuckoo's call in "Fruhlingsbotschaft" (Spring's herald). He also ignores the delicate irony of "Von Schlaraffenland" (From a land of plenty), giving it a hearty setting that charms even while it misses the point. (He does much the same later in the cycle, when he skips the more overtly revolutionary second verse of "Des Knaben Berglied.")

The seventh song, however, the first of the two "Zigeunerliedchen" (Little gypsy songs), is the first one in a minor key, and it introduces the harshness of human cruelty in real life, away from the world of fantasy and fairy tales; "Zigeunerliedchen II," in the same minor key, is gently resigned to unhappiness, with the story of a kidnapping. There is a brief return to the major with a song of a maturing boy who is ready to defend his home, and the moods become lighter with the next songs, including the tender return of A minor in "Der Sandmann" (The Sandman), the charming and infectious "Marienwurmchen" (Ladybug), and the warm anticipation of "Er ist's" (Spring is here), before returning to a mood of uncertainty and longing with "Kennst du das Land."

While the cycle was well-suited for family performances, consisting mostly of solos, but with a few pieces for multiple voices, it doesn't lend itself as well to a professional recital. However, most of the songs lend themselves to performance outside the cycle. "Marienwurmchen," "Kennst du das Land," and "Er ist's," in particular, have often graced the recitals of lyric sopranos such as Arleen Auger, Lucia Popp, and Elisabeth Schwartzkopf. *—Ann Feeney*

Recommended:

○ **Schumann Lieder** / Stutzmann, Sodergren / 1998 / RCA 61799

Fünf Lieder und Gesänge, Op. 127 (1840–1850)

Four of the *Fünf Lieder und Gesänge*, Op. 127, were composed in 1840—Schumann's "year of song," during which he set at least 137 poems. Among these are the 16 *Dichterliebe*, Op. 48, all settings of verses by Heinrich Heine (1797–1856). (In all, Schumann set 41 of Heine's poems.) Two of the songs of Op. 127, "Dein Angesicht" and "Es leuchtet meine Liebe," both poems by Heine, were originally intended for the *Dichterliebe* collection. The fourth selection of Op. 127, "Mein altes Ross," is from 1850, a year that saw Schumann's second greatest output of lieder. Op. 127 was published in 1854 by Heinze.

In "Sängers Trost" (Singer's Solace), by Justinus Kerner, the narrator asks the stars and moon not to forget him. A simple 16th note pattern permeates every bar of the piano accompaniment, while the voice part becomes gradually higher as the singer speaks to the stars.

Heine's "Dein Angesicht" (Your Face) considers the countenance of someone he has seen recently in a dream. He comments on how sweet and pretty she is and how red her lips are, but soon "küsst sie bleich der Tod" (the kiss of death will make them pale). In E flat major, the slow song features a voice part that hovers around repeated notes at the beginning of each line over a simple accompaniment. At "the kiss of death," Schumann moves into darker harmonies, but treats this as a central section, returning to the opening music for a repeat of the first verse.

In "Es leuchtet meine Liebe" (My Love Shines Forth), by Heine, the narrator's love manifests itself in a fairy tale in which a knight and a maiden encounter a giant in an enchanted garden. The maiden runs off, the knight is wounded and the giant stumbles home. The tale will end only with the dreamer's death. Schumann's unusually difficult accompaniment consists of chords on every beat that rise and trace a stepwise path unrelated to the intense voice part. Numerous modulations in the through-composed setting support the fantastic nature of the text, as the piano loudly conveys the maiden's flight. A piano postlude shifts the harmony from minor to major, signalling release from the frightening fairy tale.

Dotted rhythms convey the tread of a tired horse in "Mein altes Ross" (My old Steed), setting a poem by Moritz von Strachwitz.

"Schlusslied des Narren" (Final Song of the Fools) is by William Shakespeare, in a German translation by Ludwig Tieck and A. Schlegel. Schumann composed his setting of Feste's last song from *Twelfth Night* on February 1, 1840. A lively melody in 6/8 conveys the lighthearted atmosphere of Feste's speech while the shifts between major and minor express his ambivalence toward rain and wind. *—John Palmer*

Lieder und Gesänge aus Wilhelm Meister, Op. 98a (1849)

In 1849, the turbulent period after the Dresden uprising, Schumann returned to the novel *Wilhelm Meister*. He completed settings for the songs of all the characters. Both Mignon and the harper were compelling figures to Romantic-era composers. Their songs alternate, with one song from the frivolous Philene provided as momentary relief and contrast.

In the first song, *Kennst du das Land*, which was also the last of Op. 79, the scattered notes from the piano that open the song suggest Mignon's searching of her memories. Her ecstasy is indicated by soaring vocal lines, her agitation by the quick, frenzied piano chords underneath. In her second song, "Nur wer die Sehnsucht kennt," the opening is ominously intense, and the voice enters on the second chord, as if she is unable to restrain her feelings any longer. It rises to that climax as she describes the burning inside herself in a forte passage, and then retreats again, shyly and mysteriously. This passion is fully shown in her next song, with its sudden discords and emotional turmoil. Her descents into the lower vocal register also show her conflicts. Towards the end, however, after one last outburst with alarming, thunderous discords from the piano, her voice is hushed and subdued. By the last song, Mignon is already transfigured, and it is overall the calmest one. The occasional murmurs from the bass in the piano now are used to depict the earth that she is leaving. Schumann tells the entire story of Mignon concisely, with such strong characterization.

Philene's charm is felt in her lovely song, the seventh in the cycle, proclaiming the delights of the night. There could be no more effective contrast for the harper's and Mignon's depths of emotion. The accompaniment is like a dance, but with irregular rhythms that suggest dancing for the joy of it, rather than a formal dance.

The harper's first song, *Ballade des Harfners*, appears to be musically disjointed, with themes that are never fully played out, music that reflects the text then changes to seemingly meaningless patterns, and more conventional moments, such as imitations of the harp, regal chords denoting the king's speech, and gorgeous sweeps of lyricism. Schumann drew as much from the context as from the text itself, and writes as though the harper's mental condition shows through. While the harper's other two songs are more musically unified, they, too, combine a tragic dignity and mental disjointedness, as in the fourth song, "Wer nie sein Brot mit Tranen," where the imitation of the harp seems to be randomly tossed into the accompaniment, and where, despite the sense of deep gloom and guilt, the lines move upward, rather than in falling tones. Like the first, there is grandeur, emotional power, and pride, as well as anguish, expressed here. The harper's next song provides more of a clue to the source of his insanity, with the juxtaposition love and pain in the text and the music. It is also far warmer, tender, and introverted. The last follows on this growing simplicity. It also, for the first time, shows the physical actions of the harper removed from his harp; there are none of the flourishes and arpeggios, but rather, a hesitant but steady walking motif. The emotional turmoil is still hinted at in the moments of hesitancy and the quiet major chord that provides an unexpected and still ambiguous ending. Again, the entire story of this enigmatic figure is told with an almost devastating directness and power. *—Ann Feeney*

Recommended:

○ **The Songs of Robert Schumann Vol. 1** / Schäfer, Johnson / 1996 / Hyperion 33101

○ **The Songs of Robert Schumann Vol. 2** / Johnson, Keenlyside / 1998 / Hyperion 33102

○ **Goethe Lieder** / Augér, Olbertz / 1999 / Berlin Classics 0021782

Lieder und Gesänge I, 5 songs, Op. 27 (1840)

In 1840, Schumann completed at least 137 songs, including the set of five *Lieder und Gesänge*, Vol. I, published by Whistling in 1849.

The first of the Op. 27 set, "Sag' an, o lieber Vogel" (Tell Us, My Dear Bird), features a text by Friedrich Hebbel (1813–63), the German poet on whose drama *Genoveva* Schumann based his opera of the same name. Hebbel's verses are of a bird (or person?) who wishes to fly someplace, but knows not where or why, only that it is attracted by the scents of spring. Schumann's setting is strophic except for the fourth and final verse, in which he changes the shape of the melody, the rhythm of the accompaniment, and travels through new harmonies, all of which reflect the journey of the bird across the ocean.

"Dem rothen Röslein gleicht mein Lieb" (My Love is like a Red Rosebud), is by Robert Burns (1759–96), as translated by Gerhard. Again, Schumann chose a text with references to nature as the narrator compares his sweetheart to a rose and a melody. Although through-composed, the song does feature some melodic repetition.

"Was soll ich sagen?" (What Should I Say?), by Adalbert von Chamisso (1781–1838), describes the predicament of an older lover confronted with the youth and beauty of a younger lover. In E major, the through-composed song moves forcefully to the dominant at the point the narrator exclaims, "You are so young and healthy!" conveying the lover's dismay.

"Jasminenstrauch" (Jasmine Bush) is by Friedrich Rückert (1788–1866), the poet to whom Schumann turned most frequently in his search for song texts. The poem describes a jasmine bush that was completely green when it "went to sleep." In the morning, however, after being touched by sunlight and a breeze, it awakened, covered in white. In March 1840, about six months before marrying Clara Wieck, Schumann enclosed this poem in a letter to her, adding, "This lyric always makes me think of our first kiss." The gracefully rising A major arpeggio prelude is reminiscent of a song Schumann composed only weeks earlier: "Der Nussbaum" (The Nut Tree), Op. 25, No. 3, also a rumination on nature.

"Nur ein lächelnder Blick" (Only a Smiling Glance), by G.W. Zimmermann, compares the glance of a lover to a beam of light from the sun. Schumann's setting, the longest of the Op. 27 set, is varied strophic with changes mainly in the harmony and accompaniment. *—John Palmer*

Recommended:

○ **Schumann: Myrthen; Lieder und Gesänge I; Die Löwenbraut** / Partridge, Drake / 1994 / Chandos 9307

Lieder und Gesänge II, 5 songs, Op. 51 (1840–1850)

The year 1840 is considered "the year of song" in Schumann's life—not an unreasonable designation, since it saw the completion of over 130 songs. Among those produced that year were three of the five *Lieder und Gesänge*, Vol. Two, published by Whistling in 1850.

"Sehnsucht" (Yearning), setting a poem by Emanuel Geibel, indeed dates from 1840 (the date given in the Complete Edition—1842—is incorrect). Its protagonist yearns for a bucolic wonderland somewhere in the south, but is tied to his miserable existence in the north. Schumann's highly modified strophic setting sounds almost through-composed, and the refrain, "O die Schranken so eng, und die Welt so weit, und so flüchtig die Zeit" (Our boundaries are so narrow, and the world so wide, and time is fleeting), appears in several different keys.

Schumann set "Volksliedchen" (Little Folksong), by Friedrich Rückert (1788–1866), in a simple style that complements its title; the relative naivete of this song contrasts nicely with the preceding "Sehnsucht." In two verses, the narrator tells of her feelings for her lover, who is the first thing on her mind every morning when she walks into her garden.

"Ich wandre nicht" (I Do Not Wander), by C. Christern, is probably a recomposition of Schumann's *Scherzo*, Op. 39, No. 2, of 1839. Christern's narrator has no desire to travel the world because his sweetheart will not come with him, and he finds his homeland to be very beautiful. Schumann's strophic setting is built of melodic fragments, each setting a reference to a supposed attraction of the world; each of these is a transformation of the one preceding.

"Auf dem Rhein" (On the Rhine), by K.L. Immermann, dates from 1846. Immermann's subject compares her sweetheart to the Nibelungen treasure (later immortalized in Wagner's *Ring*)—hidden in the river, never to be taken away by thieves. Schumann's setting is solemn, the piano part tracing nearly every note of the melody. The range of the voice part remains narrow, low and mostly stepwise until the woman mentions her lover imbedded in her heart, at which point the melody becomes more active and slightly higher.

In 1850, Schumann set "Liebeslied" (Love Song), by Johann Wolfgang von Goethe (1749–1832). The constant, rolling-arpeggio accompaniment stands out among the songs of Op. 51, the rest of which feature either repeated chords or piano parts that move with the voice. Schumann rounds out the set of five songs by casting "Liebeslied" in the same key as that of "Sehnsucht." *—John Palmer*

Recommended:

○ **The Songs of Robert Schumann Vol. 4** / Johnson, Widmer, Doufexis / 2000 / Hyperion 33104

Lieder und Gesänge III, 5 songs, Op. 77 (1840–1850)

After a 12-year hiatus, Schumann began to produce lieder at a rapid rate, and in 1840 he completed at least 137 songs, including two of the five *Lieder und Gesänge*, Vol. III, published by Siegel & Stoll in 1851. Schumann seems to have assembled his third volume of *Lieder und Gesänge* around a particular tonal center—all the lieder are in either A major or minor except the first, "Der frohe Wandersmann," which is in D major.

"Der frohe Wandersmann" (The Happy Wanderer), by Joseph von Eichendorff (1788–1857), is a contemplation of the wonders of nature. Schumann's setting, composed in 1840, consists of four verses in a form that creates unity within variety. The ebullient melody of the first verse contrasts with the descending tune of the second, with its hints of the minor mode. For the third verse, Schumann returns to the music of the first, although there are a few rhythmic alterations and the piano chords are revoiced. The fourth verse brings with it new music that emphasizes the dominant and briefly returns to the opening of the song before a piano postlude based on the melody of the first and third verses.

"Mein Garten" (My Garden), set by Schumann in 1850, is by Hoffmann von Fallersleben and tells of a proud gardener who finds numerous flowers blooming in his garden, but does not find happiness there. Schumann's A minor setting belies the apparent joy of the first verse, in which the gardener lists his flowers. The voice part and piano accompaniment are alternately parallel and independent during the through-composed song while the plodding left-hand of the piano part conveys the sluggishness of the narrator's empty heart.

In "Geisternähe" (The Nearness of a Spirit) (1850), by F. Halm, a woman is haunted by the sense that something "spielt um meine Wangen wie süsser Rosenduft" (plays around my cheeks like the sweet smell of a rose). This turns out to be the thoughts of someone for whom she yearns. Schumann ventures through various harmonies in this through-composed song, saving the most powerful cadence on the tonic, A major, for the line, "Ich fühle deine Nähe!" (I feel you near me!), after which the already frenetic accompaniment becomes more energized.

"Stiller Vorwurf" (Quiet Reproach) is possibly by O.L. Wolff and was set by Schumann in 1840. During quiet moments, the narrator's old wounds open, and he experiences once again the pain caused by a former lover. Nevertheless, he cannot be angry with her; he can only forgive her. The through-composed setting has fleeting moments of repetition and the song remains firmly in A minor.

Schumann set C. L'Égru's "Aufträge" (Instructions) in 1850. Frantically, a man tries to convince the passing waves to bring a message to his sweetheart. The swirling accompaniment, played "lightly, sweetly," conveys the motion of the water, while the recitative-like voice part expresses the narrator's desperation. *—John Palmer*

Recommended:

○ **Songs of Robert Schumann Vol. 3** / (4 songs only) / Banse, Johnson / 1999 / Hyperion 33103

Lieder und Gesänge IV, 5 songs, Op. 96 (1850)

During July 1850, Schumann produced a spate of songs, including Op. 77 Nos. 2 and 3, Op. 125 Nos. 1, 2, 3, and 5, Op. 127 No. 4, and all five songs of the *Lieder und Gesänge, Op. 96*. Just over a month later he would leave Dresden to become the city music director of Düsseldorf, after which he would compose very few songs. Op. 96, the fourth volume of *Lieder und Gesänge*, was published in 1851 by Whistling.

"Nachtlied," (Night Song) is Schumann's setting of the famous *Wandrers Nachtlied*, (Wanderer's Night Song), by Johann Wolfgang von Goethe (1749–1832). In this sigh of the weary traveler, the setting is slow and deliberate, the melody generally diatonic. Schumann's attention to the details of the prosody is evident at the line, "kaum einen Hauch" (hardly a breath). Here, Goethe disrupts the rhythm of the poem unexpectedly to reinforce the meaning of the text, and Schumann responds to this with a sudden push towards E major. The song continues to avoid its "home" key of C major until final word of the text.

As in most of Schumann's songs, the piano part of "Schneeglöckchen" (Snowdrops) is far simpler technically than are his works for solo piano. By an anonymous poet, the text tells of the snowdrop flowers' resistance to the onslaught of winter. In ternary form, the song begins in A flat major with a light accompaniment of arpeggios. In the middle of the central section, the harmony shifts to a bright A major as winter calls. To close the song, Schumann returns to A flat and a modified version of the music for the first verse, but supporting the narrator's final question, "Wo ist mein Vaterland?" (where is my homeland?) with an unsettling C major chord. Throughout, Schumann articulates the iambic pattern of the poem.

"Ihre Stimme" (Your Voice), by Graf von Platen, tells of the special voice that one's heart understands much more than it does the meaningless babble of the rest of the world. As in most of Schumann's songs, "Ihre Stimme" has a melody and harmony that are generally diatonic. The light accompaniment continues throughout the song, which is through-composed, but with reiterated thematic units.

In "Gesungen!" (Sung!), by Wilfried von der Neun, all things—rain, passion, violence, flames—are spoken of in terms of how we hear them. A harmonically colorful setting that begins in C minor and ends, without warning, in C major, Schumann's "Gesungen!" boasts a quirky melody appropriate for the odd rhythms of the verse.

"Himmel und Erde" (Heaven and Earth), also by Neun, ends the set in A flat major. Schumann departs from the rest of the songs in Op. 96 by employing a repeated-chord accompaniment completely independent of the voice part. The majestic solemnity of the song, conveying the grandeur of heaven and earth, continues through the B major central section, which addresses the blossoms of May. *—John Palmer*

Liederkreis, 12 songs, Op. 39 (1840)

Schumann was such a quick and prolific composer that it's often difficult to draw distinct points of development in his style, but Schumann himself described these songs as "my most Romantic music ever." The Eichendorff texts are (with the exception of "Intermezzo," in which the location is not specified) all set outdoors, often with direct references to nature, and each refers to travel, whether thoughts traveling to a beloved or a physical journey, both typical Romantic concepts. They are also highly Romantic in their expressive moodiness, whether ecstatic or melancholy, and the occasional aura of mystery, whether the unexplained tears of the bride in "Auf einer Burg" or the supernatural in "Waldesgespräch." Schumann's selection of these varied poems itself creates a Romantic juxtaposition of emotions, and the passionate settings capture and emphasize those aspects.

They also show Schumann's increasing sophistication as a song composer; the piano becomes more important in its own right, and the scene painting from the piano is among Schumann's best, creating the desired effects immediately and with no excess. (The exception is the relentlessly jolly "Der frohe Wandersmann," which originally opened the cycle and which Schumann left out of the 1850 and subsequent editions.) For example, "Waldesgesprach" uses an alluring lyrical figure that quickly paints the seductive, wild figure of the Lorelei, a recitative-like dialog between the protagonists, and a hunting theme that first depicts the man as the hunter and the woman as the object of his hunt, and repeats at the end, ironically, to show the reversal of roles by the end of the song. There are quick characterizations, such as the sudden surge at "du schöne Braut" suggesting an eager lunge towards the lady, and the almost smugly seductive decrescendo on the honeyed "heim."

The cycle is atypical of Schumann in the relative lack of musical linkages between and among the songs. There is no piano postlude reprising a theme from the first song, as there is in "Frauenliebe und -leben" or "Dichterliebe," and while there are tonal connections between songs, most notably between "Auf einer Burg" and the following "In der Fremde" (which also share similar imagery), they are less closely constructed than the connections in other song cycles.

Schumann often integrated references to his and Clara's love in his songs and his instrumental and orchestral writing. In the second song, "Intermezzo," he includes the famous "Clara theme," a descending five-note pattern that in German notation spells out her name. Numerous elements of the cycle reflect events of Schumann's own life—from blissful love to the wedding procession that fills the listener with sorrow in "Im Walde," paranoia in "Zwielicht," and finally the various images of death. *—Ann Feeney*

Recommended:

- ○ **Schumann: Frauenliebe und Leben; Liederkreis Op39** / Norman, Gage / Philips 420784
- ○ **Les Introuvables de Dietrich Fischer-Dieskau** / Fischer-Dieskau, Moore / 1995 / EMI 68509
- ○ **Schumann: Liederkreis Op39; 12 Gedichte Op35** / Goerne, Schneider / 1999 / Decca 460797

Liederkreis, 9 songs, Op. 24 (1840)

Robert Schumann, the son of a book dealer, exhibited an early love for things literary. The resulting bifurcation of his artistic leanings was articulated in a letter from December 1830, in which he lamented that "If only my talent for music and poetry would so converge into a single point, the light would not be so scattered, and I could attempt a great deal." The immediate realization of this wish was the beginning of a career in music criticism (he founded a music journal in 1834); however, it would eventually see its fullest expression in the composer's outpouring of German lieder. Despite the composer's secret disclaimer from 1839—"All my life I have considered vocal music inferior to instrumental music... But don't tell anyone this!"—the following year saw Schumann compose over 125 songs, many of which now constitute some of his most famous and familiar music. Among the first of his 1840 compositions were several settings of poems from Heinrich Heine's *Buch der Lieder*, gathered under the title *Liederkreis*, and published as Opus 24.

The bouncy boom-chuck of the bass line and chords that accompany the first song, "Morgens steh' ich auf und frage," might seem to gloss over the grief of the lovelorn speaker, who finds himself unable to sleep at night, yet wanders throughout the day half-conscious. Likewise, Schumann's setting of the fourth song, "Lieb' Liebchen, leg's Händchen," might seem a little cute for the macabre scene: a contemptuous carpenter hammering away in the lover's heart, building him a casket. Both cases, however, illuminate Schumann's particular talent for understatement: his seemingly simple lyrical outpourings are the perfect compliment to Heine's often ironic touch. In the first case, as in many of his settings, slight changes in texture reveal the musical surface to be a psychological façade, beneath which stirs a tortured soul; the singer's final note lands on an unresolved chord, his love unrequited, while the piano reaches the final cadential resolution alone. In the second example, there is a recurring moment of haunting disjunction: at the end of both verses, on the phrases "Der zimmert mir einen Totensarg" ("There he builds me a coffin") and "Damit ich balde schlafen kann" ("That I may sleep"), the final three syllables are postponed by an unexpected and jarring pause; the piano proceeds with the descending minor-mode line, while the voice follows, hesitatingly out of sync, two beats later. That such subtle irony was deeply felt by the composer could be suggested by biography: at the time of his composing the *Liederkreis*, his attempts to gain the hand of his sweetheart, Clara Wieck, had theretofore been thwarted by her disapproving father. It would be several more months before Schumann's own love life would cease to so resemble the bleak romantic outlook offered by Heine.

A similarly effective song from Op. 24 is "Schöne Wiege meiner Leiden." The graceful melody and pulsing accompaniment suggest an earnest outpouring of sorrow, even resignation; however, lingering under the surface is a bitterness made even more sour by its restrained tone. Together with other charming examples, including "Ich wandelte unter den Bäumen" and "Mit Myrten und Rosen," this song exemplifies the variety of expression and succinct lyricism that are most characteristic of Schumann's songs. *—Jeremy Grimshaw*

Recommended:

- ○ **Schöne Wiege meiner Leiden** / Gura, Berner / 2004 / HM 901842
- ○ **Schumann: Dichterliebe; Liederkreis Op24** / Goerne, Ashkenazy / 1998 / London 458265
- ○ **Schumann: Dichterliebe; Liederkries Op24** / Bostridge, Drake / 1998 / EMI 56575
- ○ **Fischer-Dieskau Edition (Box Set)** / Fischer-Dieskau, Demus / 2000 / DG 463500

Myrthen, 26 songs, Op. 25 (1840)

Published in October 1840 by Kistner, *Myrthen*, Op. 25, is dedicated to the composer's wife, Clara Schumann. *Myrthen*, or myrtles, are European evergreen shrubs with white or rosy flowers that are often used to make bridal wreaths. The 26 poems included were presented to Clara on the occasion of their wedding.

Unlike *Dichterliebe* of *Frauenliebe und -leben*, the texts of *Myrthen* are not by a single poet. Among them are eight poems in translation by Robert Burns (1759–96), five by Friedrich Rückert (1788–1866), and three each by Johann Wolfgang von Goethe (1749–1832) and Heinrich Heine (1797–1856). The remaining seven are by Lord Byron, Thomas Moore, J. Mosen, and Catherine Fanshawe.

In the *Myrthen* collection of songs we find a clear contrast between Schumann's two musical personalities, "Florestan" and "Eusebius." Those in the "Florestan" style have a lively, confident character especially evident in "Freisinn," "Niemand" and the "Hochländer" lieder. Eusebius' more contemplative mood comes through in "Mein Herz ist schwer" and "Was will die einsame Träne?" Schumann also confronts numerous other emotions associated with love and marriage, such as devotion ("Lied der Saleika" and the two "Lied der Braut"), maternity ("Im Westen," "Hochländiches Wiegenlied"), loneliness ("Die Hochländer Witwe," "Weit, weit") and bravery ("Hauptmanns Weib"). A few special gems are worth discussing in detail.

Heine's "Du bist wie eine Blume" (You are like a flower) receives Schumann's most ceremonial treatment. Set in A flat major, a key associated with wedding ceremonies, the song's repeated chords provide a stately foundation for the free, almost recitative-like declamation of the brief text. A flat major is also important as the key of the first and last songs of the collection.

Schumann confronts longing and separation in two of the songs, "Der Nussbaum," by Mosen, and "Aus den östlichen Rosen," by Rückert. "Der Nussbaum" is notable particularly for Schumann's integration of the piano part into the overall rhetoric of the song. The opening piano measures later become both the completions of vocal phrases and, before "Sie flüstern von einem Mägdlein," the beginning of the phrase. In both songs the piano depicts leaves fluttering in the wind—In "Der Nussbaum" with constant arpeggios, in "Aus den östlichen Rosen," with a rapid, quiet twisting figure—while supporting a delicate, narrow-ranged voice part.

Schumann's setting of Byron's "Rätsel" is especially clever. The poem describes something without saying what it is. At the end is the question, "What is it?" Byron's answer is "a breeze," rendered in German as "Hauch." Schumann, however, omits this word from the text, leaving the piano to play the final note, a B-natural—an "H" in German. *—John Palmer*

Recommended:

- ○ **The Songs of Robert Schumann Vol. 7** / Bostridge, Johnson, Roschmann / 2002 / Hyperion 33107
- ○ **Schumann: Myrthen; Lieder und Gesänge I; Die Löwenbraut** / Dawson, Drake, Partridge / 1994 / Chandos 9307

Romanzen und Balladen II, 3 songs, Op. 49 (1840)

1840 was Schumann's first great lieder year, the one that produced the great song cycles *Myrthen*, the *Heine* and the *Eichendorff Liederkreis*, *Dichterliebe*, *Frauenliebe und -Leben*, and the *Kerner Zwolf Gedichte*. As if this was not enough, he also wrote individual songs, many of which, like these, he collected into small "Romance and Ballad Collections." He wrote *Die feindlichen Bruder* in April and *Die bieden Grenadiere* in May, both to Heine poems, and *Die Nonne* to a Frohlich poem in November. They were published, however, with *Die beiden Grenadiere* as the first, making a cyclic progression from war among nations, to war between brothers, and finally to war with one's emotions in a cloister, supposedly a place of peace.

Die beiden Grenadiere is one of Schumann's masterpieces, setting up in generally less than four minutes a drama that it might take a movie half an hour to present. The music begins dispiritedly, though still with military discipline, slowly grows in pride and resolve, bursting out with passionate energy with the famous quotation from the *Marseillaise*, and then falling back. This last stroke adds poignancy to a song that otherwise could be just bombast; the listener is left to speculate whether the soldier has fallen prey to despair or to death. Ironically, while Schumann's version is the more insightful and effective, Richard Wagner's, written only months before, was far more successful, particularly in France (doubtless Wagner's more optimistic ending, using the *Marseillaise* triumphantly, was more appealing to French sensibilities!).

While this song is certainly the best known and for the most effective, with its vivid characterization and intense drama, the other two songs have their own merits. The deliberately archaic style Heine adopted for *Die feindlichen Bruder* is reflected in the rushed, slightly breathless vocal lines and subdued piano figures suggesting the flashing of the swords; this is not an eye-witness account of either the duel or a sighting of its ghostly repetition, but rather a fireside narration, evoking a sense of spookiness rather than terror. (Some performers have even interpreted it as an ironic treatment of the craze for Gothic stories of duels, tragic loves and rivalries, and ghosts.) *Die Nonne*, with its contrasting sorrow and merriment, shows Schumann's ability to handle pathos with a delicate touch that keeps it from becoming overwrought, and so, he makes the final drooping notes a particularly striking portrayal of quiet, unexpressed grief. *—Ann Feeney*

Recommended:

- ○ **Les Introuvables de Dietrich Fischer-Dieskau** / Fischer-Dieskau, Moore / 1995 / EMI 68509
- ○ **Schumann: Lieder, Romanzen & Balladen** / Bär, Deutsch / 1997 / EMI 7243

Romanzen und Balladen III, 3 songs, Op. 53 (1840)

Schumann's third set of *Romanzen und Balladen*, Op. 53, was the last group of songs from his legendary "year of song" (1840) to be published. In the company of so many outstanding lieder, especially the song cycles *Dichterliebe* and *Frauenliebe und -leben*, the three (actually five) songs of Op. 53 have often been lost in the shuffle and are not especially familiar to listeners. But stylistically, poetically, and more importantly in their animating spirit, they are every bit as representative of Schumann the song composer. The best-known and most interesting song is the third, "Der arme Peter" (Poor Peter), which is actually three songs in one, and, therefore, a self-contained song cycle in miniature, somewhat like Beethoven's *An die ferne Geliebte*. It is often excerpted and performed on its own.

Although composed separately and to poems of three different authors, the Op. 53 songs are unified by the theme of devotion. The first song, "Blondels Lied," is by the poet Johann Gabriel Seidl, and is the tale of a medieval minstrel keeping a vigil in song for his king. At times reminiscent of "Auf einer Berg" from the Op. 39 *Liederkreis*, and even "Talismane" from *Myrthen*, it is constructed around a repeated refrain of the text "Suche treu, so findest du!" ("Seek in faith and you shall find!"). "Loreley" is among Schumann's shortest songs and usually takes less than one minute to perform. But in that brief span it manages to capture the very spirit of Romantic poetry and song writing in its evocation of a ghostly moment—the disembodied refrain, "Remember me," mingling with the sounds of the sea. Finally, Heinrich Heine's "Der arme Peter" is the unfortunate tale of a young man driven to suicide by the loss of his love. He first sees her dancing with her new groom; then avoids her for fear of saddening her with his grief; and finally determines that the grave is where he most belongs. As is typical of both Schumann and Heine, Peter's sad tale is infused with enough irony to be both sad and humorous, but never sentimental. *—Allen Schrott*

Recommended:

- ○ **Songs of Robert Schumann Vol. 3** / Banse, Johnson / 1999 / Hyperion 33103
- ○ **Schumann: Lieder, Romanzen & Balladen** / Bär, Deutsch / 1997 / EMI 7243
- ○ **Les Introuvables de Dietrich Fischer-Dieskau** / Fischer-Dieskau, Klust / 1995 / EMI 68509

Romanzen und Balladen IV, 3 songs, Op. 64 (1841–1847)

Schumann assembled his *Romazen und Balladen*, Volume IV, Op. 64, for publication in 1847 by Siegel & Stoll. Two of the songs were new, while a set of three Heine texts was composed much earlier. These works should not be confused with the later *Romanzen und Balladen* for unaccompanied mixed voices, Opp. 67, 75, 145, and 146.

"Die Soldatenbraut" (The soldier's bride) is in B flat major. In Eduard Mörike's (1804–75) poem a woman boasts about the bravery of her lover, who is a soldier. One of Schumann's simplest songs, the strophic setting contains a contrasting middle section at a slightly slower tempo that remains in B flat. A return to the text and music of the first verse leads to the end of the song, which repeats the last line.

"Das verlassne Mägdlein" (The abandoned maiden) is one of the most often set of Mörike's poems. Every morning a young woman rises very early to light the fire in her home. As she watches the flames, she remembers dreaming of her former, unfaithful lover, and hopes daybreak will banish her dreams of him. The minor mode and chromatic passages dominate the melody, but when the daylight promises to relieve the woman's woes, we hear a shift to the tonic major, on which the song ends.

Schumann's "Tragödie" (Tragedy) trilogy, to texts by Heinrich Heine (1797–1856), was the composer's first venture into choral music. Written in the fall of 1841, the pieces were set aside until their publication in the fourth volume of *Romanzen und Balladen*. These versions, however, are for soloists. In "Entflieh' mit mir und sei mein Weib" (Run off with me and be my wife) the fast tempo and repeated notes in the voice convey a sense of urgency as a man tries to convince a woman to leave with him, or else he will die where he is. In ternary form, the central section, with the man's threat of death, turns from A major to A minor. "Es fiel ein Reif in der Frühlingsnacht" (Frost on a spring night) tells of a young woman who leaves her parents' house to be with a man. Unable to find him, she wanders until she dies. Schumann's slightly varied strophic setting has a sparse accompaniment that shifts the accent within the measure, depicting the woman's aimless meandering. "Auf ihrem Grab" (At her grave) is for soprano and tenor. Next to someone's grave, a bird sings sadly and two lovers cry, not knowing why. Schumann's accompaniment generally follows the vocal lines in this through-composed setting, unified by motivic repetition. At two points, the plaintive tenor and soprano parts have imitative entrances; otherwise, they move together. *—John Palmer*

Recommended:

- ○ **Les Introuvables Dietrich Fischer-Dieskau** / Fischer-Dieskau, Klust / 1995 / EMI 68509

Four Songs, Op. 142 (1840)

Assembled from songs Schumann left unpublished at his death, the four lieder of Op. 142 were published in 1858 by Rieter-Biedermann and dedicated to Frau Livia Frege by the publisher.

"Trost im Gesang" (Solace in song), by Justinus Kerner, laments the lonely existence of the night traveler. Just as the traveler wanders off the path because it is difficult to see, Schumann moves from the opening E flat major to a distant D major at the center of this ternary-form structure. The accompaniment, plodding and nonmelodic, follows the rhythm of the melody but not the shape.

"Lehn' deine Wang'" (Rest your cheeks [against my cheeks]), by Heinrich Heine (1797–1856), was originally intended for the *Dichterliebe*, Op. 48; set aside by the composer, it remained unknown until after his death. Opening in G minor, the song's narrator asks a lover to lay her cheek against his so their tears may mingle. The second half of the song modulates to a new key as the narrator talks of the lovers' inner flames and how he will die from love's yearning. Schumann conveys the sense of "yearning" by closing the song on the dominant, with no hint of resolution.

In "Mädchen-Schwermut" (Girl's sadness), probably by Lily Bernhard, a girl weeps over her place in the joyless world. In E minor throughout, the song's melody progresses from repeated notes to a more passionate, arching shape in the second half, in which the accompaniment, too, becomes more animated. Schumann depicts the emptiness of the girl's heart by abruptly stopping the right hand flourish at the end of the song, leaving only the open chord in the bass.

"Mein Wagen rollet langsam" (My carriage rolls slowly), by Heine, was also intended for the *Dichterliebe*, Op. 48. Schumann's accompaniment depicts the slow, uneven progress of the carriage through the forest, while the constantly descending voice part creates an atmosphere of low energy. In the second verse, three "shadows" come to the carriage and nod mockingly at the passenger; when they giggle and rush away the accompaniment becomes more animated. *—John Palmer*

Recommended:

- ○ **Schumann: Liederkreis Op39; Romanzen & Balladen** / Terfel, Martineau / 2000 / DG 447042
- ○ **Schumann: Liederkreis Op24; Dichterliebe; 7 Lieder** / Bostridge, Drake / 1998 / EMI 56575
- ○ **Schumann: Liederkreis Op24; Kerner-lieder** / Prégardien, Gees / 2001 / RCA 73235

12 Songs, Op. 35 (1840)

Schumann wrote many of his first songs to Kerner's poetry when he was just 17, and in May 1840, his most prolific year, he began to think about writing settings for other Kerner texts, writing this cycle in November and December.

Even though written during a happy time in his life, its dominant emotions are longing and grief rather than contentedness. The fifth song, "Sehnsucht nach der Waldgegend," (Longing for the forests) expresses an almost aching yearning with its arching vocal phrases, which rise in longing and fall back dejected and unappeased, and with the quiet resignation of the piano chords as the vocal lines become more earth-bound, murmuring rather than exclaiming. (This song was one of Clara's favorites.) The tenth, "Stille Traneni," (Silent weeping) is one of his most passionate expressions, with its outbursts of grief shared between voice and piano. However, in the sixth song, "Auf das Trinkglas eines verstorbenen Freundes," (To the drinking glass of a dead friend) the loss is sublimated in mystical thoughts, expressed with a sonority reminiscent of Mozart's Masonic music, and the seventh, "Wanderung," is one of his most effectively jubilant pieces, comparable to "An meinem Herzen from Frauenliebe und Leben," with an easy melodiousness that shows no signs of forcing, and where there are no hints of impending grief.

In the second song, when the woman prays with the words of the title "Sterb, Lieb' und Freund" (Die, love and joy), the music uses a refrain from the final chorale from *St. John Passion*, an allusion to Schumann's attendence at a performance of Bach's work earlier in the year. The first song, "Lust der Sturmnacht," (The joy of a stormy night) is noteworthy for the masterful way that it maintains a musical consistency while remaining faithful to the text. It opens with pounding chords from the piano and an equally turbulent vocal line, vividly painting the image of the storm. When the text's mood changes to describe the joy of being indoors with a loved one, the music becomes softer and the key changes suddenly, but the rhythm continues the pounding effect. This way, the effect of the storm is maintained, emphasizing the sense of the poem. However, a similar textual transition in the third song, "Wanderlied," is less successfully carried out; the change is as sudden as that in the first song, but here it jars somewhat.

Another point of interest is in the concluding two songs, "Wer machte dic so krank?" and "Alte Laute" (Who made you so ill? and Old sounds), in which he uses the exact same melody for two different poems. This presents a challenge to performers, who must provide two different interpretations of the same music, to fit the different texts and moods. *—Ann Feeney*

Recommended:

- ○ **Schumann: Lieder** / Hampson, Parsons / Teldec 44935

○ **Schumann: Lieder** / Schreier, Shetler / 1995 / Berlin Classics 0090682

○ **Songs of Robert Schumann Vol. 2** / Keenlyside, Johnson / 1998 / Hyperion 33102

Six Songs (Reinick), Op. 36 (1840)

Schumann culled the poems of the *Sechs Gedichte*, Op. 36, from Robert Reinick's *Liederbuch eines Malers* (A Painter's Song Book). Four of the six songs were composed in June 1840, the other two later the same year. Published in 1842 by Schuberth, the *Sechs Gedichte*, Op. 36, is dedicated to Frau Dr. Livia Frege.

Reinick's poetry is far less incisive and deep than Heinrich Heine's, whose verses Schumann had set in the *Dichterliebe* only a month earlier. This relative shallowness may account for some of the lackluster settings found in the *6 Gedichte*, for Schumann's music faithfully illustrates Reinick's poetry. Also, the large-scale key structure of the set is less directed than those of the composer's other song cycles.

In *Sonntags am Rhein* (Sundays on the Rhine) the narrator reminisces about strolling along the Rhine on Sunday mornings watching the boats, hearing the organ from the nearby church, looking at the fortress on the mountain, and seeing the reflection of the "fatherland" in the waters. Schumann's constant, unrelenting eighth note motion becomes tedious, although it does suit the unchanging meter of the poem.

Ständchen (Serenade) evokes the sound of guitar music in the triplets of the left hand and the broken chords of the right. The melody is assured and stepwise, taking on the nervous character of recitative at "Liebchen, liebchen, drum eil' auch du!" (Sweetheart that's why you, too, hurry). Schumann sets the first two verses to the same music, but writes a more active melody for the third, reflecting the serenader's anticipation of being with his lover.

Like *Sonntags am Rhein, Nichts Schöneres* (Nothing More Beautiful) is repetitive. It does, however, boast more interesting harmonic material, including some harsh major sevenths in the middle of the piece as G major and its dominant sound together while the narrator recalls marrying the most beautiful sight he has ever seen.

In *An den Sonnenschein* (To the Sunshine), the narrator reproaches the sun for awakening feelings of love in his heart and making visible a beautiful world he cannot enjoy. Throughout the conservative, varied strophic setting, Schumann remains in A major and provides an accompaniment that follows the voice part nearly note for note.

Schumann directs the performers to begin *Dichters Genesung* (Poet's Convalescence) somewhat slowly and to gradually become more lively until the end. As the "Elf-queen" beckons the sick and dying poet to a blissful death, only to see him recover and stay on Earth with another beloved, Schumann vacillates between the opening key of G major and E major, in which he closes the song. The lengthy *Liebesbotschaft* (Message of Love) contains a soaring melody, with which the narrator sends his hopes on clouds. Schumann's setting is filled with arching tunes and a transparent accompaniment that traces the vocal line. *—John Palmer*

Recommended:

○ **Schumann: Lieder, Romanzen & Balladen** / Bär, Deutsch / 1997 / EMI 7243

12 Songs (from Rückert's "Liebesfrühling"), Op. 37 (1840)

Despite their occasional marital difficulties and the deeper troubles brought on by Robert's mental illness, Robert and Clara Schumann were one of the most devoted couples in musical history, and one of the few such marriages where the two partners were of roughly equal stature, though in different areas. This set contains songs written by both of them. Schumann wrote his nine songs in January, and Clara her three in June, and Schumann arranged for his publishers to release them in September as a birthday surprise for her.

Robert's songs, especially, are filled with hidden musical messages. In the first, describing a tear that Heaven wept into the sea and which was enclosed by a mussel to transform it into a pearl, the famous "Clara" theme appears in the bass, as if describing her as a pearl coming from a tear, and there is also a brief quotation from Giordani's song, "Caro mio ben" (a love song that declares, "My dear love, without you, my heart mourns"), another private message to Clara. Though perhaps not a direct message or reference, since he often skillfully used piano postludes (most notably in *Frauenliebe und -Leben*), some of his most imaginative and effective writing is in the postludes to these pieces, such as the strangely agitated ending to "Flugel! Flugel!" or the nightingale's song which ends "O ihr Herren." Like many of Schumann's later song cycles, such as the *Minnespiel aus Ruckerts Liebesfruhling* of 1849, it combines solo songs and combinations of voices: here, a modest two duets (the seventh and the last song). Again, while two vocal lines was a device Robert used often, it might have had a special meaning for the Schumanns in this set.

It is not easy to distinguish between Clara's and Robert's writing, unless the listener knows beforehand which are whose. Some scholars say that this shows that Robert must have helped her with hers, others that it shows she might have been as great a song composer as he. *—Ann Feeney*

Recommended:

○ **The Songs of Robert Schumann Vol. 4** / Johnson, Widmer, Doufexis / 2000 / Hyperion 33104

Five Songs, Op. 40 (1840)

Schumann wrote these songs to poems by Hans Christian Andersen, an author best known today for his fairy tales, and dedicated them to the poet, who had visited Robert and Clara Schumann earlier that year. The translations were by Adalbert von Chamisso, author of the texts for *Frauenliebe und -leben*, which Schumann wrote during the same period. They were in the same volume that *Frauenliebe* came from.

He noted in the letter that he sent with a presentation copy that Andersen may very well find the settings strange, as he himself found the texts strange at first. He continued to say that as he began to understand the poems and their strangeness more deeply, his music started to become increasingly strange as well.

While the situations depicted vary widely, the songs are still linked somewhat loosely by the keys, and considerably more strongly by their place in Schumann's ongoing tendency to explore changes in moods and feelings rather than to express and develop one single emotion, as well as by that element of strangeness.

Part of the strangeness lies in a certain emotional "compression"; in both "Muttertraum" and "Der Spielmann," Schumann compresses into one song the dramatic and emotional range that he unfolded over the course of a cycle in *Dichterliebe* and *Frauenliebe und -leben*, written around the same time.

Another part lies in an almost cinematic quality, such as in "Muttertraum," with its changing images: the theme suggesting the mother rocking the baby in her arms, the peaceful image in the vocal lines with the more ominous underlying piano, and the growing forcefulness of the darker mood as the song ends; in "Der Soldat," with the powerful scene painting from the imitation of the death march and the almost disturbingly vivid image in the postlude of the actual moment of death and the fall of the body; in "Der Spielmann," with the images of dancing and the "close-ups" of the fiddler's deterioration; and in "Verratene Liebe," as the gossip about the kiss spreads, at first quietly, and then thundering cheerfully all through the town. *—Ann Feeney*

Recommended:

○ **Schumann: Frauenliebe und Leben; 5 Lieder Op40; 15 Lieder** / von Otter, Forsberg / DG 445881

Six Songs (Neun), Op. 89 (1850)

Schumann's *Sechs Gesänge* (Op. 89) were composed between May 10 and May 18, 1850, and published the same year. Schumann dedicated the volume to the famed Swedish soprano, Jenny Lind (1820–87), who befriended the Schumanns in 1845 and performed with them on several occasions. The poems are all by Wielfried von der Neun—the pen name of F.W.T. Schöpff—and, in all fairness, are not the finest literary examples among the composer's song texts.

The first of the set, "Es stürmet am Abendhimmel" (The Stormy Evening Sky), equates love with changing clouds during an evening storm. At first purple and dramatic, the storm cloud eventually turns gray. Octave tremolos in the right hand suggests stormy weather, the violence of which comes out in the wide leaps in the voice part, as well as the active, yet halting, melody.

"Heimliches Verschwinden" (Secret Disappearance) describes the silent, imperceptible disappearance of spring as it gives way to the "tyranny" of summer without saying goodbye. Triplet arpeggios plummet downward around a voice part that becomes increasingly chromatic and recitative-like in the middle of the song. The rapid accompaniment, played mostly piano, lends an ephemeral atmosphere to the song.

Purple again makes an appearance in "Herbstlied" (Autumn Song), in which the narrator regrets the coming of Autumn. Again Schumann uses a tremolo pattern in the piano part to fill out the harmony and give a sense of forward motion. The song is in two parts, the second of which shifts from the minor to the major mode and features swirling arpeggios supporting the voice part, which becomes more confident as the narrator describes the distant purple mountains.

A traveler reluctantly bids farewell to the sounds of the forest in "Abschied vom Walde" (Parting from the Forest). Schumann's setting is through-composed, with a leaping, restless melody. The traveler's unsettled spirit comes through at the end of the voice part, which closes on the tonic of (B flat), but is harmonized with an inconclusive chord.

Thick, block chords propel "In's Freie" (Outdoors), a celebration of being out in open spaces away from the city. Schumann cast the song in B flat major and in ternary form with a quiet, transparent middle section. Both text and music of the opening return to close the song, which ends firmly after some text repetition.

In "Röselein, röselein" (Rosebud, Rosebud), the narrator falls asleep near a stream and has a dream of plucking and smelling a wonderful rose without thorns. When he awakes, he sees about him only thorny roses and hears the stream laugh at him, saying, "remember, all roses have thorns." Schumann's brief introduction to this A major song is in A minor, but it returns at the end in the major. The minor mode appears again as the dreamer confronts a disappointing, thorny reality. *—John Palmer*

Recommended:

○ **Schumann: Lieder** / Corneo, Stachelhaus / 1996 / MDG 6030648

Six Songs (Lenau) and "Requiem," Op. 90 (1850)

At least one ("Der schwere Abend") of these uses material from 1840 and possibly more of these songs were also written earlier than 1850, but most of them are in his later style, with frequent chromaticism and a growing sense of gloom. The last song, "Requiem," was added as a tribute to the poet, Lenau, whom Schumann believed had died. Lenau had become insane from syphilis and was dying, but not yet dead at this time. Schumann's own syphilis was exhibiting more symptoms, and he was beginning to show signs of instability. In a way, the song cycle reflects a slow collapse of earthly hopes, and the "Requiem," Schumann's own wish for peace after death. The first song is a simple one, without any secret doubts or passions, and whether the steady rhythm is the tapping of the hammer or the horse's trot as it leaves, it expresses a deep contentment. The second, however, is a love song already hinting at death and darkness. While the vocal lines have a tender, caressing tone, there is a carefully preserved ambiguity on whether the water will suffice to revive the rose; after the second verse, asking if a rebirth is possible, the song goes back to the first verse without answering the question, and the last chord, while returning to major, could as easily be the last petal dropping as the rose returns to life. The next song is clearer still in its theme of loss, with both the piano and vocal lines carrying hints of melodies that are briefly introduced but never built upon, until the brief piano postlude, by which time the loss is already established, so the sense of lost pleasure is complete. There is a brief return to an established melodic theme with the fourth song, but while the music is less gloomy, the thoughts of death and loss are still dominant in the text. For the fifth song, Schumann changed to a minor key, but this one is still a quiet, contemplative grief, silent tears falling into the moss illustrated by the soft, sinking lines. The next is almost disjointed, with sudden, heavy minor chords from the accompaniment, which is forte for the first time in the entire song cycle. The last chords after the last word, "Tod," (death), provide their own explanation for the next song, the Requiem. This last song returns to the major, but it is E flat major (the fifth and sixth were E flat minor) and still more or less subdued, as if still remembering past unhappiness. The accompaniment was originally written for a harp, rather than piano, but the effect is not completely lost. *—Ann Feeney*

Recommended:

- ○ **The Songs of Robert Schumann Vol. 1** / Schäfer, Johnson / 1996 / Hyperion 33101

Spanische Liebeslieder (10 Spanish Love Songs), Op. 138 (1849)

This opus is the second of Robert Schumann's two song cycles based on Spanish folksongs, and, like the first (*Spanisches Liederspiel*, Opus 74), it was drawn from a collection of German translations by Emanuel Geibel. Also like the first cycle, it combines songs for solo voices with duets and quartets. However, instead of solo piano this set is scored for piano duet—a device Johannes Brahms, a friend and great admirer of Schumanns, would later emulate in his sets of *Liebeslieder Waltzes*. The role of the piano is further expanded through the inclusion of two purely instrumental movements (No. 1, "Vorspiel," and No. 6, "Intermezzo")—an interesting corollary to the integral and often extended piano postludes in the composer's most significant song cycles, *Frauenliebe und -leben* and *Dichterliebe*. Whereas in those cycles the passages for piano illuminate the poetic atmosphere of the texts, here the solo movements establish the overtly Spanish flavor of the cycle. This is especially true of the "Vorspeil" which features a prominent bolero rhythm. Certain passages within the cycle itself suggest the strumming of a guitar.

Composed in 1849, Op. 138 seems an obvious model for the later and better-known Spanish cycles of Hugo Wolf. Although the Wolf settings are in the more traditional solo voice and piano format, they share a quasi-dramatic conception made especially clear in the Schumann through the use of multiple singers; texts that are not explicitly connected assume a dramatic linearity as subsequent "characters" appear with their earlier counterparts. Wolf also used a number of the same texts when compiling his cycles. *—AMG*

Recommended:

- ○ **Brahms & Schumann: Liebeslieder** / von Otter, Bonney, Bär, Streit, Deutsch, Forsberg / 1995 / EMI 55430
- ○ **The Songs of Robert Schumann Vol. 6** / Johnson, Thompson, Hough, McGreevy, Doufexis, Loges / 2002 / Hyperion 33106

Spanisches Liederspiel, 10 songs, Op. 74 (1849)

Schumann often experimented with new forms of music drama, such as his *Scenes from Goethe's Faust*, WoO 3, the choral ballads that resemble oratorios or even mini-operas, declamations such as *Schön Hedwig*, and his secular oratorio *Paradise and the Peri*. In this work, one of his earliest such experiments, he wrote a liederspiel—a combination of song cycle (Liederkreis) and singspiel—in which the poems are organized to create a semblance of a plot (Schumann also added titles to some of them to further this) and the different singers take on roles. Whereas traditional nineteenth century liederspiels were bourgeois entertainments, inserting simple songs into dramatic works and plays, Schumann's effort eliminates all elements of scenery, action, and dialogue, and so for all practical purposes amounts to a song cycle. However, Schumann's *Spanisches Liederspiel* maintains distinctly dramatic elements, using solos and duets for the exposition of the main characters, and part songs as choruses.

The texts for Op. 74 were compiled by Emanuel Geibel and are mostly adaptations of anonymous Spanish poems. However, two of them, "Intermezzo" and "Liebesgram" are taken from the writings of Gil Vicente and Christobal de Castillejo, respectively.

Schumann predicted that these songs would be among his most successful, but while they were well-received, they never caught on as he had hoped. Nonetheless, they are full of melodic invention, and their Spanish elements, such as bolero rhythms, give them a lively charm. All of the songs exhibit Schumann's trademark lyricism and his acute sense of poetic mood. The fourth piece in the cycle, "In der Nacht" (duet for soprano and tenor), is notable for its gently dissonant melancholy and elegiac melody; it is often excerpted from the cycle, perhaps more so than any other piece. The tenth song, "Der Kontrabandiste," was originally included in an appendix, judged by the composer to be musically and dramatically out of place in the cycle, but it also has become a concert favorite.

While Schumann was disappointed with its reception, he nonetheless followed something of the same pattern with his *Minnespiel* (Opus 101) to Ruckert texts, and with his *Spanische Liebeslieder* (Op. 138, also with texts by Geibel). *—Ann Feeney*

Recommended:

- ○ **The Songs of Robert Schumann Vol. 6** / Johnson, Thompson, McGreevy, Doufexis, Loges / 2002 / Hyperion 33106

CHAMBER MUSIC

Adagio and Allegro for horn & piano in A flat major, Op. 70 (1849)

1849 was Schumann's most productive year in terms of number of compositions, but it was also extremely rich in terms of the variety of works, which included choral pieces, songs, piano pieces, works for soloist(s) and orchestra, and several chamber pieces for solo instrument and piano. In a few of these works he made use of the relatively new valve horn, which had begun to show up in orchestras in the 1830s. One of Schumann's goals at the time was to create significant music that amateurs could use to further their skills on their instruments with what was called *Hausmusik*: meaningful, artistic music that they could play in private, at home. The *Adagio & Allegro for horn and piano*, Op. 70, is one of these works, but it actually takes an extremely skilled amateur to meet the technical demands of the piece. The Adagio is based on a melody that takes advantage of the valve horn's ability to play precise half-step notes. It has the demeanor of Schumann's wistful songs, requiring stamina to sustain the lyrical phrases. The rondo-form Allegro consists of a bright, vigorous main section, which utilizes the full range of horn in rapid fire figures, alternating with more poetic episodes that share melodic and rhythmic motives with the Adagio. Schumann also published versions of the piece with the violin or cello taking the solo part. The success of the horn version of *Adagio & Allegro* was a major factor in Schumann's decision to write the *Konzertstück for four horns and orchestra*, Op. 86, later that same year. *—Patsy Morita*

Recommended:

- ○ **Brain, Kell & Goossens play Schumann & Beethoven** / Brain, Moore / 1993 / Testament 1022

Märchenbilder, for viola & piano, Op. 113 (1851)

Robert Schumann's little-known *Märchenbilder* (Fairytale Pictures) for viola and piano (alternately for violin and piano, by the composer's own indication) were composed during March of 1851, during his brief and relatively unhappy tenure as conductor at Düsseldorf. Chronologically, these four fantasy pieces occupy the space between the two sonatas for violin and piano, though they can hardly be said to inhabit the same emotionally conflicted world. Instead, they draw the listener into that same glistening world of fantasy and childlike imagination that, many years earlier, drew from him some of the most beloved piano music in the repertory. However, twenty years of further experience and the first signs of approaching madness grant to these seemingly simple portraits an almost desperate sense of escapism lacking in the earlier piano works.

The first of the four *Märchenbilder*, marked Nicht schnell (Not fast), features a somber melody in D minor that recurs throughout the piece in a variety of guises. Lebhaft (spirited), which follows, is a kind of truncated rondo that contrasts its main, exuberant, theme with two much gentler digressions, while pitting the violin and piano against one another in friendly competition. Rasch (swift or brisk), a vehement moto perpetuo, follows. A secondary motive, announced by the piano in the fifth bar of the piece, is of rhythmic interest and considerable importance. The final piece of the group is set in the traditionally happy key of D major, but is nevertheless marked "Langsam, mit melancholischem Ausdruck" (Slowly, with melancholy expression). Its sonorous texture seems to presage the Adagio of Johannes Brahms' *D minor violin sonata*.*—Blair Johnston*

Recommended:

- ○ **Schumann: Chamber Music** / Argerich, Imai / 2002 / EMI 57308
- ○ **Beethoven: Notturno Op42; Mendelssohn: Viola Sonata in C minor; Schumann: Märchenbilder** / Coletti, Howard / 1997 / Hyperion 66946

○ **Schubert: Sonata In A; Schumann: Märchenbilder; Bruch: Kol Nidrei; Enesco: Konzertstück** / Bashmet, Muntian / 1990 / RCA 60112

Märchenerzählungen, for clarinet or violin, viola & piano, Op. 132 (1853)

Unlike the earlier *Märchenbilder* (Fairy Pictures), in which individual pieces evoke specific associations, the *Märchenerzählungen* (Fairy Tales) have no direct reference to any narrative or underlying program. The work was composed October 9–11, 1853, not long before Schumann's final mental breakdown and suicide attempt. Nevertheless, the music is concise and light-hearted, the four movements linked by a recurring motive. It is one of Schumann's most organically conceived works. Schumann originally wrote the piece for clarinet, viola, and piano, but the first edition, published in 1854 by Breitkopf & Härtel, offers a choice of violin or clarinet.

Throughout the highly condensed, four-movement work is a sense of increasing agitation. The most intriguing aspect of the *Märchenerzählungen* is the "kernel" of music from which much of the piece is derived. This appears early in the first movement, "Lebhaft, nicht zu schnell" (Lively, not too fast), which begins with a legato phrase in the viola that tends to move upward. A contrasting idea ensues that is detached and generally moves downward—this becomes the kernel of the rest of the piece. A song without words, the movement features an excellent blend of the instruments and intense development of the first theme. In the second movement, "Lebhaft, sehr markiert" (Lively, very accentuated), the kernel appears in numerous short outbursts in the opening segment of the movement that distort the kernel by presenting it in a fast, triplet rhythm. This movement is more clearly ternary in form, with a great change of mood in the elegant middle section. The third, slow movement, "Ruhiges tempo mit zartem Ausdruck" (Calm tempo with delicate expression), has a much more lyric, idyllic feel than the previous movements and features an important accompanimental figure in the opening measures that is an augmented version of the kernel. Furthermore, this figure, and thus the kernel, informs much of the melodic material of the movement, especially in a duet for the clarinet and viola. The Finale, "Lebhaft, sehr markiert," opens with powerful chords and seems, at first, unrelated to the previous sections. The melody, however, is a dotted-rhythm version of the kernel. The same idea also returns, augmented in the slow middle section of the Finale.

Although the movements are similar in form to the three-part character pieces found in Schumann's other works, the sections of *Märchenerzählungen* are rhapsodic in structure and tempered with an awareness of Viennese, Classical-era rhetoric. *—John Palmer*

Recommended:

○ **Mozart: Trio K498; Schumann: Märchenerzählungen Op132; Bruch: 8 Pieces** / Imai, Vignoles, Hilton / 1990 / Chandos 8776

○ **Hommage à R. Sch.** / Kashkashian, Levin, Brunner / ECM 437957

Phantasiestücke, for clarinet & piano, Op. 73 (1849)

Generally described as numbering among Schumann's least impressive works, the three *Phantasiestücke*, Op. 73 (1849) nonetheless contain moments of real interest. While each of the three pieces conveys a different mood, together they form a harmonically unified whole: the first begins in A minor and ends in A major, while the second and third are in A major. Further, at the end of each of the first two pieces, Schumann directs the performers to proceed to the next piece attacca, clearly demonstrating that the three pieces were conceived as a unified whole.

The first of the pieces, a song without words marked "Zart und mit Ausdruck" (Delicately and with expression), maintains a constant triplet-rhythm accompaniment in the piano, which supports a mostly independent clarinet line. The central section is distinguished by a move away from A minor and falling arpeggio figures in the clarinet. The return to the first section is nearly literal until the final harmonic shift to A major.

Piano and clarinet share the melody in the blithe second piece, an intermezzo marked "Lebhaft, leicht" (Lively, light). The busy central section, itself cast in two parts, is marked by a sudden change to F major. The return of the first section soon goes astray, leading to an elegant coda.

The third piece, "Rasch und mit Feuer" (Fast and with fire) begins forte and with a sense of urgency. Triplet rhythms again dominate the piano part, while the clarinet plays its most animated melody yet. The central section provides the least harmonic contrast of all, moving unobtrusively from the opening A major to A minor. Schumann writes an extended coda to confirm both the mood and key of the piece and the entire set.

Though originally intended for the clarinet, Schumann directed that the solo part could be also performed on violin or cello. *—John Palmer*

Recommended:

○ **Schumann: Chamber Music** / Argerich, Gutman / 2002 / EMI 57308

Piano Quartet in E flat major, Op. 47 (1842)

Begun on October 24, 1842, the *Piano Quartet in E flat major,* Op. 47, was completed within a month. Schumann played through the work with friends early in December, but it was not published until 1845. Although Schumann started composing the *Quartet in E flat major* only a few days after completing the *Quintet in E flat major,* Op. 44, the two works could not be more different; the (slightly) later work is actually the more traditional, especially in Schumann's use of counterpoint.

Schumann seems to have been more comfortable with the intimate instrumentation of the chamber works than he was with the full orchestra. However, the chamber works, aside from the string quartets, are piano driven, with the strings either following the keyboard part or acting in opposition to it as a unified choir. In the *Piano Quartet in E flat major,* Op. 47, thematic links between movements are heard, as well as Schumann's tendency for protracted development of material, resulting in large structures.

Schumann's arrangement of the movements (the Scherzo is second, the slow movement third) suggests a nod to Beethoven, as does the opening of the first movement, Sostenuto assai—Allegro ma non troppo. The introduction is static, non-thematic, and is reduced to its primary melodic feature—a falling/rising whole step—at the very beginning of the Allegro tempo. The second part of the introduction appears a moment later. The overall effect is similar to that of Beethoven's *String Quartet,* Op. 127, also in E flat major. The staccato scales accompanying the broad secondary theme reflect Schumann's increasing study of counterpoint, while the large-scale sonata form is extended through development in the recapitulation.

The Scherzo boasts two trio sections. The second of these features Schumann's predilection for destroying the bar line through syncopation so strong and consistent that the listener feels the downbeat in the wrong place. The piano is chiefly responsible for this "illusion," with block chords on the third beat of the measure that are tied through the first two beats of the next. The rhythm is reinforced in every other measure by a similar chord in the three string instruments, the entire passage providing an effective contrast to the nimble eighth notes of the Scherzo section.

Marked Andante cantabile and in ternary form, the third movement is notable for a passage in which Schumann directs the cellist to tune the instrument's C string down a step to B flat, enabling it to play a B flat pedal tone under staccato scales in the viola and violin. Throughout the opening section, the piano's role is chiefly accompanimental, providing repeated chords to support the melodic material shared by the cello and viola. At the shift to G flat major of the central section, however, the piano part becomes more linear. When the opening section returns, the melody appears in the viola part over a more active piano accompaniment and below a fleeting violin obbligato line that anticipates the first idea of the Finale.

Schumann's Finale, in sonata form, opens like a fugue. After an introductory outburst, the viola states the lively theme, which is next taken up by the piano on the dominant, and next by the violin. In a free rondo form, the Finale features a lengthy closing section, often referred to as a coda, that is a developmental extension of the primary material. *—John Palmer*

Recommended:

○ **Schumann: Op44 & 47** / Emerson SQ, Pressler / 1995 / DG 445848

○ **Schumann: Complete Piano Trios; Quartet Op47; Quintet Op44** / Bettelheim, Beaux Arts Trio / 1997 / Philips 456323

Piano Quintet in E flat major, Op. 44 (1842)

Robert Schumann's *Quintet for piano and strings in E flat major* has earned a place of distinction among piano quintets, one of only a handful, including Johannes Brahms' one entry in the genre and Dvořák's *Op. 81,* that are known to more than just a few performers. Although Schumann's merits as a composer of "pure" instrumental music have been debated, no astute listener can doubt that the E flat Quintet is the product of a most fertile musical imagination—fresh, buoyant, and inventive. 1842 was Schumann's year of chamber music (as 1840 was that of song): after producing three string quartets, Schumann decided to make a happy synthesis of his recently-acquired fluency with strings with the piano—his native instrument.

The first movement, marked Allegro brillante, commences with a joyous idea that rings in the ear long after the texture has taken on a gentler tone. Musings on this idea are set against characteristic pianistic figurations before the second theme, a dialogue between the cello and viola takes over. The development section begins in the key of A flat minor in the piano; fragments of melody are voiced by the other players as the music moves into distant harmonic regions. The incessant modulation and fragmentary thematic development are interrupted by a bold assertion of the previously heroic primary theme. Schumann makes little change to his exposition over the course of the recapitulation, only altering a few bars to make the necessary harmonic change, with the second theme, as expected, being re-cast in the tonic instead of dominant.

In modo d'una Marcia, Un poco largamente is the marking of the following movement, throughout which a funereal atmosphere predominates. The stark, mysterious primary melody is introduced by the first violin against a background of simple quarter notes in the lower registers of the other four instruments. The appearance of the second theme is like a welcome ray of sunlight. Schumann's rhythmic palette produces a magical feeling of stasis, as if time were standing still for a short, delicious time. It was at Felix Mendelssohn's urging that Schumann decided to throw away the A flat major section that originally served as the middle portion of this strange movement and replace it with the furious onslaught in F minor (agitato) that posterity has come to know. Perhaps the most striking moment in the movement is the remarkable, purposefully crass statement by the viola (on its C string) of the primary theme in the middle of the violent triplet activity. The movement is rounded off by a return of the initial march theme, now with a thudding pizzicato background that dies away into a quiet, otherworldly chord.

The Scherzo, molto vivace, makes a reprise of both the tonality and vivacious character of the first movement. Schumann chooses to use two separate trios in the movement, the first a lyrical canon, and the second a more robust section in A minor.

Some of Schumann's instrumental works conclude with movements that are but pale shadows of their brothers and sisters; not so with the Piano Quintet. From the opening attack in C minor (the percussiveness of which has caught many unwary listeners quite off guard) to the final glorious, contrapuntal conclusion, the composer imbues this finale with so piquant a mixture of verve, anxiety, and delicate lyricism that it must surely be considered the crowning glory of the entire work. The double-fugue that serves as a coda to the finale. Taking as its one subject the principal theme of the first movement and as its other subject the principal theme of the last movement, it forms a noble and fitting conclusion.*—Blair Johnston*

Recommended:

- ○ **Dvořák, Schumann: Piano Quintets** / Entremont, Alban Berg Quartet / 1996 / EMI 55593
- ○ **Schumann: Complete Piano Trios; Quintet Op47; Quintet Op44** / Rhodes, Bettelheim, Beaux Arts Trio / 1997 / Philips 456323

Piano Trio No. 1 in D minor, Op. 63 (1847)

For Schumann, the year 1847 was relatively "dry" in terms of composition. He revised the final scene of his *Scenes from Goethe's Faust*, which he had written three years earlier. In April, he sketched the overture to his opera, *Genoveva*, which he set aside until the next year. During the rest of 1847, he composed a few songs, the brief choral work, *Beim Abschied zu singen*, and two *Piano Trios, No. 1 in D minor*, Op. 63, and No. 2 in F major, Op. 80.

Schumann composed three trios for violin, cello and piano: in D minor, Op. 63; in F major, Op. 80 (both from 1847); and in G minor, Op. 110 (1851). The first of these, in D minor, is generally regarded as the strongest work of the three. An experimental approach to harmony in the F major Trio is usually given as a weakness when the piece measured against its Classical-era models, while the G minor Trio shows some signs of the decay that accompanied the composer's encroaching mental illness. The intimate chamber music genres allowed Schumann to indulge his preference for intricate figurations and subtle harmonic inflections that are such a salient feature of his solo piano pieces. Not surprisingly, the piano chamber works are clearly piano driven, with the strings either following the keyboard part or acting in opposition to it as a unified block.

The sonata-form first movement of the *Piano Trio in D minor* is in 4/4 meter and marked, "Mit Energie und Leidenschaft" (With energy and passion). Throughout the expansive first theme, the pianist plays rapid arpeggios outlining the harmony. During the secondary theme, however, the piano traces the melody with the strings before the closing section, which consists of a return to the first theme, now on F major and rhythmically diminished. Schumann's most ingenious stroke in the movement is the new theme in the development section.

Constrained energy marks the second movement, "Lebhaft, doch nicht zu rasch" (Lively, but not too fast) a Scherzo and Trio in F major. Its 3/4 meter is always clear in the piano part, supporting the rising, dotted melody in the strings. The rising melody appears again in the Trio, although here it is much slower and more relaxed, and rounds off with a descent.

Marked "Langsam, mit inniger Empfindungen" (Slowly, with inner feeling), the third movement is a ternary structure (ABA) with a wandering harmonic structure. Beginning on C major, the violin melody moves toward a new harmony after eight measures. After passing through C minor, a new section begins, firmly in F major, and the piano becomes clearly subservient to the violin and cello, providing repeated chords and creating a 12/8 meter. In the return of the A section, Schumann follows the opening for only seven measures; in the eighth the melody changes and the harmony heads toward A major. The movement ends with a powerful French sixth chord (in D minor) moving to an A major triad, the dominant of D major, which is the key of the Finale. The shape of the first theme of the movement is very much like that of the violin theme opening the first movement.

The Finale, marked "Mit Feuer" (With fire), begins without a break after the slow movement. Schumann links the finale to the first movement through thematic reference. The first four violin notes of the first movement appear, rhythmically altered, in the piano melody of the second and third measures of the Finale. *—John Palmer*

Recommended:

- ○ **Schumann: Complete Piano Trios** / Beaux Arts Trio / 1997 / Philips 456323
- ○ **Mendelssohn & Schumann: Trios in D minor** / Thibaud, Casals, Cortot / 2002 / Naxos 8110185
- ○ **Oleg Kagan Edition Vol. 17** / Kagan, Richter, Gutman / 1998 / Live Classics 182

Piano Trio No. 2 in F major, Op. 80 (1847)

Of his two piano trios from 1847, Schumann said the second one "makes a quicker and more ingratiating appeal" than the first one.

Marked "Sehr lebhaft" (Very lively), the first movement of the F major Piano Trio is in an ebullient 6/8 meter and cast in sonata form. The hesitant first theme is the almost entirely the property of the violin and cello, which play in parallel throughout. The unusual harmonic adventures that characterize the movement include an emphasis on D major, which becomes the dominant of G major, the harmony of the second theme group. What is unusual is that, in the key of F major, G major functions as the dominant of C major in the works of Schumann's predecessors, not as a key area of its own. The melodic role of the piano increases in the second group, which gives way to an expansive closing theme in the violin over a light accompaniment in the piano. An imitative, contrapuntal episode at the beginning of the development section provides contrast to the homophonic music played thus far, although much of the development is concerned with the lyrical closing theme, which also ends the movement.

Contrapuntal layering occurs at the beginning of the second movement, "Mit innigem Ausdruck" (With intimate expression). Dotted rhythms in the string melody contrast with the constant triplets in the piano part, the left hand of which provides yet another layer of melody. Although it begins in D flat major, the movement quickly shifts to A major for a rapid violin line. A central, "Lively" section introduces new, detached material before the highly modified return to the opening.

A scherzo with canonic tendencies, the third movement, "In mässiger Bewegung" (In a moderate movement), is in 3/8 meter and begins in B flat minor. In contrast to Schumann's first Piano Trio, Op. 63, the triple-meter movement is in third position. The brief canons appear between the violin and cello at the beginnings of the movement and the contrasting scherzo theme. In the sparse Trio, the imitative passages are between the piano and cello, just before a transformation of the main scherzo theme. A coda brings the movement to a quiet, hesitant close.

Marked "Nicht zu rasch" (Not too fast), the Finale returns to F major. The dense piano part dominates the movement as each appearance of the opening idea is further transformed. *—John Palmer*

Recommended:

- ○ **Schumann: Complete Piano Trios** / Beaux Arts Trio / 1997 / Philips 456323
- ○ **Schumann: The 3 Piano Trios; Fantasiestucke** / Borodin Trio / 1990 / Chandos 8832

Three Romances for oboe & piano, Op. 94 (1849)

Schumann wrote these three pieces in December 1849. His efforts were not tied to a commission or request by a prominent soloist of the day, unlike other examples in the genre from Weber, Spohr, and others of that era. Thus, they are not particularly challenging pieces, and may in fact be convincingly performed by good amateur oboists. Some listeners coming to this music for the first time might be surprised that compositions so clearly out of the realm of virtuosity, as this trio surely is, could achieve such a high level of art. The fact is, they are more often cited as being the greatest works for oboe from the Romantic period than any others. Of course, a violin, clarinet, or cello can replace the oboe in the score—and can deliver nearly as satisfying a result.

The first piece, marked Nicht schnell (Not quickly), presents a lovely theme on oboe, supported by imaginative accompaniment on piano. The mood is tranquil throughout. That description might also apply to the second piece, marked Einfach, innig (Simply, ardently), but for a somewhat tense middle section. All three pieces are very similar in the character of their main themes: each, in fact, is songful and might have served the voice just as well as the oboe. The third piece is the liveliest of the trio. Marked Nicht schnell, it is also the most rugged and colorful-sounding one in its main theme. There is more than a hint of Brahms here, a composer who was just beginning to make his mark. The middle section is lovely, similar in character to the opening melodies of the first two pieces. The piano accompaniment is deftly wrought throughout, never overwhelming the oboe, yet always making its supportive presence felt. These *Three Romances* were first published in 1851 and soon entered the repertory of concert oboists throughout the world. *—Robert Cummings*

Recommended:

- ○ **Schumann: Music for Clarinet & Piano** / Frost, Pontinen / 2002 / Bis 944

Three String Quartets, Op. 41 (1842)

Schumann composed his three *String Quartets*, Op. 41, very quickly in 1849. The first, in A minor, he began on June 4; the second, in F major, on June 11, before completing the first. Schumann composed the third quartet, in A major, between July 8 and 11, by which time the first two were finished. The parts were published in 1843 by Breitkopf & Härtel; the same publisher printed the score in 1849, carrying a dedication to Felix Mendelssohn (1809–47).

Schumann had attempted some string quartets in 1838 and 1839, but he abandoned them, perhaps because a chamber-music idiom without the piano was foreign to him. Even ten years later, in the Op. 41 *String Quartets*, the composer's pianistic mode of thinking clear: many melodic passages are pianistic in nature, and we find extended, homophonic segments that resemble block chords for the piano as transferred to strings. It is not surprising that Donald Taylor described the quartets as "music for string quartet but not string quartet music." After these works, Schumann would not write any chamber music that did not include the piano.

Schumann's interest in quartet composition was ignited by intense study of the quartets of Haydn, Mozart, and Beethoven; however, Schumann's works in the idiom resemble those of Mendelssohn more than those of his models.

The first movement of No. 1 features progressive tonality; the imitative slow introduction is in A minor, but leads to an "Allegro" that begins and ends in F major. Only by the end of the entire quartet can we be sure that A minor/major is the key of the piece. Schumann's scherzo is in A minor with a trio (entitled "Intermezzo") in C major that interrupts the nervous energy of the scherzo. The third movement, "Adagio," consists of three two-part sections. The second of these includes a brief development and the third provides the closure implied by, but missing from, the first. The piece closes with an innovative monothematic Finale featuring a fugal development and the introduction of new material near the end.

Quartet No. 2, in F major, is most striking for its slow movement, a set of variations with more than one theme. Both the Scherzo and Finale open with themes clearly suited to the piano.

The third Quartet, in A major, is most noteworthy for its third movement, "Adagio molto." Into three successive sections based on the same material, Schumann works some of the principles of sonata form without using the structure. The first section begins with a lengthy, meandering but self-contained melodic statement, followed by a few shorter, contrasting phrases that both modulate far from the tonic, D major, and develop the opening material. For the second section, Schumann transposes the material of the first segment and shortens both parts. Further reduction occurs in the third segment until we are left with brief, periodic melodies that close on D major. It is as if Schumann begins the movement with material in a "developed" state and ends with its "original" form. *—John Palmer*

Recommended:

○ **The Petersen Quartet** / Petersen Quartet / Capriccio 14862

Fünf Stücke im Volkston, for cello or violin & piano, Op. 102 (1849)

The *Fünf Stücke im Volkston* (Five Pieces in the Popular Style) were written by Schumann in 1849, the same year he composed the *Three Romances for oboe and piano,* Op. 94, and *Fantasiestücke, for clarinet and piano,* Op. 73. These three collections have much in common: not only did Schumann allow for substitutions for the lead instrument in all of them, but none are difficult to perform, being designed primarily for amateur musicians of good caliber. In addition, all the various pieces are tuneful and almost completely devoid of any conflict. If there is one word to best describe the character of the *Volkston* pieces, it might be mellow. All are melodically appealing and exude a tranquility throughout. The middle three may be slightly more appealing, with number three being especially lovely in its rich Romanticism, both in the cello and piano writing. The second has a pastoral sweetness, while the fourth starts off in a most lively and joyous mood, then yields to a mesmerizing melody. All these pieces are worthwhile, with Schumann's deft imagination never failing to enchant. These pieces were first published in 1851. *—Robert Cummings*

Recommended:

○ **Schubert: Sonata for Arpeggione; Schumann: Fantasiestücke** / Argerich, Maisky / Philips 412230

○ **Schumann: Cello Concerto; Adagio & Allegro; 5 Stücke im Volkston** / Oppitz, Schiff / 1993 / Philips 422414

○ **Chopin: Cello Sonata; Schumann: Works for Cello & Piano** / Thedeen, Pontinen / 1999 / Bis 1076

Violin Sonata No. 1 in A minor, Op. 105 (1851)

Both of Schumann's Sonatas for Violin and Piano (the present item and the *Sonata,* Op. 121 in D minor) were composed during his tenure as a conductor in Düsseldorf in 1851, substantially later than his chamber works—*Piano Quintet, Piano Quartet,* and the three string quartets—which have achieved a more general renown. As such, they present a different set of challenges and rewards than do those earlier works. Signs of Schumann's impending collapse are certainly evident in the *A minor Violin Sonata,* but not through any deficiency of musical value; the work's dramatic and psychological complexities speak for themselves.

The undulation of the Sonata's first movement is established by the unbroken sixteenth note figuration in the piano's right hand. The music is played out with great surges of emotion and activity; the ponderous tone of the opening bars is carried away to heights of more hopeful passion as the second theme appears. The development is concise, concerning itself almost exclusively with the opening motive. The move into the recapitulation, seamless as it is, is a masterstroke, as is the manner in which Schumann adapts the harmonic motion of the opening to achieve a sense of finality.

There could be little more contrast than that between the agitated closing bars of the first movement and the gentle tones of the second, marked Allegretto. This is a movement with virtually no dramatic motion. It is, instead, built of the same stuff that formed so many of the composer's earlier character-pieces. Witness the gentle, essentially dispassionate dialogue between contrasting musical ideas, the one built on a delicately descending, syncopated motion, the other more sprightly, with spiccato textures and trills, but no more forceful in nature than its companion. There is also a third idea, in F minor, more smoothly melodic and entirely pianissimo, which makes one appearance and then disappears forever. The frequent fermatas are by no means mere separation of phrases and sections, but are entirely necessary to the character of the movement. The agitation of the slightly quicker middle section is brief, only affording the players an opportunity to make a few more forceful statements before, inevitably, winding back down into the intimate tone of the opening. In this movement we can clearly see the myriad persona of Schumann characterized in his youthful writings by the names Florestan, Eusebius, and Master Raro in outline.

It is difficult to say whether or not the third and final movement of the Sonata, marked Lebhaft (Lively), is of lesser substance than its companions, for, in the hands of a capable duo, its perpetual motion sparkles until the final crescendo, after which the three staunch chords seem somewhat obtrusive and unnatural. More often than not, however, the movement comes across as dry and unnecessarily repetitive. But surely the movement's apparent shortcomings result from its composer's quest to explore increasingly subtle gradations of musical psychology. The feeling of irresolution at the end of the Sonata can by no means be construed as unintentional, but rather must be seen as Schumann's effort to honestly explore the depths of his own increasingly agitated and complex mind, regardless of whether or not the resulting product corresponded with preexisting musical values. *—Blair Johnston*

Recommended:

○ **Schumann: Violin Sonatas 1–3** / Faust, Avenhaus / 2000 / CPO 999597

Violin Sonata No. 2 in D minor, Op. 121 (1851)

Schumann spent most of 1851 working on pieces in minor keys. In all of these—two of the three *Phantasiestücke,* Op. 111, the *Piano Trio in G minor,* Op. 110, and the two *Violin Sonatas*—we sense an introspective, fatalistic character imbued with uncertainty and tension. The string parts have few pizzicato passages or flights of virtuosity, and in the *Violin Sonatas* the violin spends most of its time in the middle register, never given a chance to soar.

The second *Violin Sonata* was composed very quickly; Schumann began the piece on October 26, 1851, and finished it on November 2. It followed on the heels of his first *Violin Sonata,* that in A minor, Op. 105, which was composed in mid-October. One of Schumann's comments on the A minor Sonata may explain his immediate composition of another work in the genre: "I didn't like the first violin sonata, so I wrote a second, which I hope turned out better." The Violin Sonata in D minor, Op. 121, was published in 1853.

Schumann seems to have been more comfortable with the intimate instrumentation of the chamber works than he was with a large orchestra. The intimate chamber-music genres allowed the composer to indulge his preference for intricate figurations and subtle harmonic inflections that are a salient feature of his solo piano pieces. Not surprisingly, the chamber works, aside from the string quartets, are clearly piano driven, with the violin either following the keyboard part or acting in opposition to it.

Generally regarded as the superior of the two sonatas of 1851, the *Sonata for Violin and Piano in D minor,* Op. 121, begins with a stormy first movement that resembles that of the *Piano Trio in D minor,* Op. 63. Marked "Lento, con Energia," the sonata movement opens with an introduction in 3/4 based on the primary theme. Detached chords outline the theme as wild violin flourishes lead to the dominant of D minor, preparing for the beginning of the sonata-form movement. As the tempo switches to Vivace, the violin quietly presents its turning, six-measure theme that traces the tonic triad, moving in sturdy half notes over lively arpeggios in the piano. After a more active secondary theme, the first theme reappears on different harmonies to close the exposition. Schumann transforms the main theme in the development section, all the while keeping interplay between the instruments to a minimum. Aside from a few accompanimental features, the recapitulation matches the exposition until the last possible moment before the move to the secondary theme.

A Brahmsian scherzo movement follows in 6/8 and marked "Allegro di molto." More often than not, the violin follows the piano in this D major movement, taking its own path in the central trio. Thematic links with the scherzo flavor the slow movement, marked "Simplice" and set in G major. Pizzicato triple stops on the violin open the variation movement with a melody that resembles the narrow-ranged material of the scherzo. Several episodes separate the variations.

The Finale, "Con moto," moves along at a brisk pace. At the beginning, the two instruments alternate the presentation of thematic material with furious accompaniment. In the development section, Schumann shifts between fragmentary development and long stretches of thematic material while exploring "flat" keys areas.

After the main theme appears in D major, the movement remains in this new key until its rather forceful close. *—John Palmer*

Recommended:

○ **Schumann: Chamber Music** / Argerich, Schwarzberg / 1995 / EMI 555484

CONCERTO

Cello Concerto in A minor, Op. 129 (1850)

Robert Schumann wrote no fewer than seven concertante works, among which only the *Piano Concerto in A minor,* Op. 54 (1841) and the *Cello Concerto in A minor,* Op. 129 (1850) find regular representation on concert programs and recordings. The Cello Concerto, composed during the early days of Schumann's ultimately unhappy stay in Düsseldorf, has long been a favorite among performers, especially given the relative paucity of great nineteenth century concerti for that instrument.

Schumann considered calling the work a "Concert piece for cello with orchestral accompaniment"; indeed, the orchestral writing in the concerto is far more transparent and unobtrusive than is normally associated with Schumann's concert works. It is a little-known fact that the composer learned to play cello as a child, and that after damaging his right hand during the early 1830s he intended to return to the cello in an effort to better his understanding of chamber and orchestral music. Nevertheless, the unfortunate idea that the *Cello Concerto* is poorly written for the instrument persists even to the present. Such a notion may result in part from the work's lack of flashy virtuosity typically associated with instrumental concertos, a feature found in Schumann's *Piano Concerto.*

Four lean bars—three of them quiet pizzicato chords, one outlining a pianistic accompaniment figure—introduce the cello's broad opening theme. The passionate second theme, with its chromatic inflections and upward minor-seventh leaps, is almost archetypal in its use of the cello. A comparison of the concerto with both earlier and later cello concertos demonstrates Schumann's palpable influence on the way composers came to write for the instrument. The development, more Classical in tone, ventures into stormier territory and utilizes a triplet motive. Encouraged by the horn, the cello attempts a recapitulation of the initial theme; the orchestra, however, rejects the soloist's choice of F sharp minor and recommences its agitated passagework. The recapitulation proper is stunning and unexpected; characteristically, Schumann makes very little change in the exposition material as it reappears. The coda is interrupted by a recitative for the soloist that prepares a modulation to F major for the second movement.

The second movement, marked Langsam, is essentially a tender song. The soloist's rich melody floats on a sea of gently pulsating pizzicato triplets, while the passionate double-stopped outburst in the middle of the movement is a golden moment in the cellist's repertory. A brief recollection of the first movement interrupts the flow; the solo line, growing ever more excited, paves the way into the finale. While the two contrasting themes of the last movement—one rather bold, the other more intimate—are attractive enough, the level of inspiration in the finale falls short of that in the first two movements, particularly in the development. More successful, however, is the accompanied cadenza that precedes the final coda. The substitution by some players of flashier cadenzas (written by less insightful cellists) for Schumann's more musically convincing one seems, happily, to be a thing of the past. *—Blair Johnston*

Recommended:

○ **Schumann: Cello Concerto; Piano Concerto; Introduction & Allegro appassionato** / Barenboim (cond.), Du Pré, New Philharmonia Orch. / 2001 / EMI 74755

○ **Schumann: Cello Concerto; Rachmaninov: Cello Sonata** / Rostropovich, Rozhdestvensky (cond.), Leningrad PO / 1998 / DG 459022

○ **Schumann: Concertos for cello & piano** / Coin, Herreweghe (cond.), Champs Elysees Orch. / HM 1951731

Introduction and Allegro appassionato, for piano & orchestra in G major, Op. 92 (1849)

Sketched September 18–20, 1849 and orchestrated by September 26, the *Introduction and Allegro appassionato* in G major, Op. 92, was first performed on February 14, 1850, in Leipzig. The work was published by Whistling in 1852. Like the "Concerto" for four horns, Op. 86, the *Introduction and Allegro appassionato* in G major, Op. 92, received the title, "Konzertstück" (Concert Piece). Thus, Schumann recognized that such works did not fit into any of the molds brought to mind by other terms. Unfortunately, the *Introduction and Allegro appassionato,* Op. 92, has always been overshadowed by Schumann's *Piano Concerto,* Op. 54, although the later piece marks a significant stylistic departure for the composer. Schumann conceived the *Introduction and Allegro appassionato* while immersed in the works of Lord Byron. He had only recently worked on his *Manfred overture,* Op. 115, inspired by Byron, and would soon begin setting Byron in the *Hebrew Melodies,* Op. 95. Schumann translated the heroism depicted in Byron's poetry into a work for piano and orchestra.

The lengthy introduction unfolds slowly, with the pianist playing constant arpeggios, accompanied almost imperceptibly by individual instruments in the orchestra. After a dramatic pause, the Allegro begins with the orchestra performing a grand gesture, echoed by the piano, which tries to push the harmony toward E minor. Once this new key is established, a secondary theme emerges in the left hand of the piano that then shifts to the right hand for a repeat, all the while with minimal accompaniment in the orchestra.

In the adventurous development section the secondary theme receives particularly interesting treatment, appearing in the distant key of E flat minor and then dissolving into an E major rendition of the introductory material. Schumann alternates between a Beethovenian inversion and fragmentation of melodies and full statements of ideas on different harmonies in this dense, relentless development. Struggle occurs as the melodic material attempts to return to the home key. In the recapitulation we finally hear the secondary theme on the tonic, although its presentation is not literal. Schumann's grand close is not as grand as it could be.

Critics disagree concerning the importance of the *Introduction and Allegro appassionato,* some calling the work uninspired while others claim it is an important example of Schumann's mature style. Certainly, it is a unique structure in its single-movement format with multiple sections and unusual processes of development. *—John Palmer*

Recommended:

○ **Grieg & Schumann: Piano Concertos; Konzertstück** / Serkin, Ormandy (cond.), Philadelphia Orch. / 1991 / Sony 46543

○ **Sviatoslav Richter Plays Schumann** / Richter, Wislocki (cond.), Warsaw National PO / DG 447440

Konzertstück, for 4 horns & orchestra in F major, Op. 86 (1849)

Schumann's *Konzertstück in F major for four horns and orchestra,* Op. 86, is one of the composer's most neglected works. This is unfortunate because it is an inventive, compelling work that rewards repeated hearings. Unfortunately, the *Konzertstück* is generally compared to concertos by Beethoven and Brahms, works to which it bears little resemblance. Instead, it should be discussed in terms of its lyric quality and harmonic ingenuity. The *Konzertstück* was sketched February 18–20, 1849, and orchestrated by March 11. Schumann referred to 1849 as "My most fruitful year," and was truly one of his most productive, second only to 1840, his "year of song." The first performance took place in Leipzig on February 25, 1850, and the piece was published in 1851 by Schuberth.

Schumann could easily have called the *Konzertstück* a concerto, and it is difficult to understand why he did not. It is in three movements in a fast-slow-fast arrangement and the movements are thematically linked. The four solo parts are for the modern chromatic valve-horn (relatively new at the time), while the two horns in the orchestra are natural horns. Schumann calls for a large orchestra, including piccolo, two trumpets, three trombones, and two tympani. Generally, when the solo horns are playing, the orchestra horns rest.

After two chords in the orchestra, the four solo horns enter fortissimo with the aggressive first subject, and the *Lebhaft* (Lively) first movement has begun. The lack of an "orchestra exposition" makes it clear that Schumann had no intention of writing a concerto in the Viennese Classical style. Sonata form is still the structural force, however, and the movement boasts a lyric second subject and a developmental central section. Throughout the movement, the tessitura of the solo horns is high, culminating in some extremely high passages for the first horn in the recapitulation. The movement is filled with interweaving phrases in the solo horn parts and, particularly, the woodwinds.

The second movement, entitled "Romanze," begins with the cellos and oboe after a brief pause. The solo horns pick up this same idea and proceed with a lovely, lilting tune with imitative entries. More impressive is the chorale-like subject in the middle section, played first by the high strings and then by the horns, against a background of whirling arpeggios in the cellos. The opening idea returns to close the movement, which moves without pause into the finale.

Marked *Lebhaft,* the witty, vivacious finale opens with three energized measures in the orchestra before a dramatic, rising arpeggio in the first solo horn. In the ensuing moments, a conversation develops between the orchestra and soloists as virtuoso scales dominate the material. In the central section, a return of the chorale from the middle of the second movement can be heard, now in E major. At times, Schumann doubles parts excessively, but in general the texture is clear and lines are easy to follow. *—John Palmer*

Recommended:

○ **Schumann: Symphony 2; Konzertstück; Manfred Overture** / Thielemann (cond.), London Philharmonia Orch. / DG 453482

○ **The Chicago Principal: First Chair Soloists Play Famous Concertos** / Barenboim (cond.), Chicago SO / 2003 / DG 000002502

Piano Concerto in A minor, Op. 54 (1841; revised 1845)

Robert Schumann followed up his remarkable "year of song" (1840) with another compositional *annus mirabilis.* 1841 saw the creation of the composer's first works for orchestra, including the *Symphony No. 1,* Op. 38, the *Symphony No. 4,* Op. 120 (substantially revised and published a decade later), and the *Overture, Scherzo and Finale,* Op. 52. In each of these works, thematic unity among movements is of central importance, an idea widely explored in the Romantic period in guises ranging from the idée fixe of Berlioz's *Symphonie fantastique* (1830) to the leitmotives of Wagner's music dramas.

Schumann's other major work from 1841 is the Fantaisie in A minor for piano and orchestra. Though the Fantaisie as such has ultimately disappeared from the repertoire, it is only because it evolved into the first movement of the composer's Piano Concerto in A minor, completed in 1845. In this year Schumann appended two movements to the revised Fantasie; the composer's wife, the remarkable pianist Clara Wieck Schumann, premiered the result, a complete concerto, in Leipzig on New Year's Day, 1846.

The shifting moods that characterize so much of Schumann's music are clearly evident in the Piano Concerto. Still, as in the composer's contemporaneous works noted above, and despite the interval between the composition of the Concerto's first movement and the remaining two, inter-movement unity is one of the work's primary concerns. There is a quasi-symphonic character to the Concerto, in distinct contrast to the then-prevailing view of the concerto as primarily a vehicle for virtuosic display, exemplified by the concertante works of Franz Liszt and Nicolò Paganini. Indeed, Liszt showed little enthusiasm for Schumann's Concerto and tweaked the composer (who had earlier written a "Concerto Without Orchestra") by referring to it as a "concerto without piano."

Though the work's technical demands are not inconsiderable, they are almost wholly subservient to thematic interest and structural clarity. The Concerto opens with a downward-surging, darkly martial introductory gesture. The first theme, marked by a high-minded dignity, becomes the prime source of melodic material, spawning closely related themes that alternately brood and, in the major mode, provide respite from the sober atmosphere. The development caroms from one mood to the next in almost dizzying fashion, all the while exploring the ambiguities of the themes' various components. Schumann cannily uses the lengthy cadenza as a battleground for further emotional conflict before ending the movement with a decisive return of the lofty first subject.

The second movement, Intermezzo: Andantino grazioso, amply displays Schumann's immanent melodic sense within a spectrum ranging from genial to poetic to lushly yearning. The Allegro vivace finale commences without pause via an affirmative major-key return of the first movement's main theme. In various episodes, Schumann makes striking use of the finale's joyful, upward-leaping theme, as when it becomes the subject of a fugato. Metric and rhythmic ambiguities abound, coloring the dance-like spirit, and the prevailing mood is one of unfettered optimism that ultimately swells to exuberant triumph. *—Michael Rodman*

Recommended:

- ○ **Maurizio Pollini Edition: Bonus CD** / Pollini, Karajan (cond.), Vienna PO / 2001 / DG 471363
- ○ **Furtwängler: Recordings 1942–1944 Vol. 2** / Furtwängler (cond.), Gieseking, Berlin PO / 2001 / DG 471294
- ○ **Great Pianists: Artur Rubinstein 2** / Rubinstein, Krips (cond.), RCA Victor SO / 1999 / Philips 456958
- ○ **Schumann & Grieg: Piano Concertos** / Lipatti, Karajan (cond.), London Philharmonia Orch. / 1999 / Aura Classics 0229

SYMPHONIC

Symphony No. 1 in B flat major ("Spring"), Op. 38 (1841)

Schumann sketched this work between January 23 and 26, 1841, and finished scoring it February 20. Mendelssohn conducted the first performance in Leipzig five weeks later. The 24-year-old Schumann's wooing of 15-year-old Clara Wieck, the prodigy daughter of his piano teacher at Leipzig, has been as thoroughly and widely sentimentalized as Robert Browning's courtship of Elizabeth Barrett. What these contemporaneous Roberts had in common were fathers-in-law who tried but failed to block their marriages. In Papa Wieck's case, however, he was at least as worried about Schumann's neurasthenic heredity and drunkenness as he was about losing Clara's income. Over his objections, they married in September 1840, the day before her 21st birthday. Until that year Robert had composed mostly piano music, including all but two of his greatest solo works. In 1841, abruptly, he began writing reams of lieder, and, just as abruptly, switched to orchestral works. From this period come not only the *"Spring" Symphony* (sketched in a mere four days), but also a "symphonette" later reworked as the *Overture, Scherzo, and Finale*, the *D minor Symphony* revised a decade later as *No. 4*, and a *Fantasie in A minor for piano and orchestra*, later expanded into a concerto for Clara.

The *Symphony No. 1 ("Spring")* had its premiere on March 31, 1841, with Felix Mendelssohn conducting. Although the title "Spring" acquired parentheses later on, it was the fundamental inspiration behind Schumann's first completed orchestral work. In the beginning there were titles for the movements: "Spring's Awakening," "Evening," "Merry Playmates," and "Spring at its Peak." Even after their withdrawal, he asked a conductor to "instill in [his] orchestra the sense of longing for spring. This was what I felt most while writing this work. The initial trumpet passage should come…like a summons to waken. The rest of the introduction might suggest the appearance of green everywhere, and perhaps the flutter of a butterfly. In the Allegro molto vivace [that follows], everything associated with springtime gradually comes together." From the trumpet call, the main theme of the movement develops; it returns twice later on, in the recapitulation and in the coda.

The Larghetto that follows in E flat major is Schumann's portrait of Clara, although Beethoven haunts his sonorities and rhythm. A magical pianissimo passage for trombones, at the end, is reworked as the main theme of a Molto vivace scherzo that follows in B minor, which has two trios in D major (the first one derived from the opening trumpet fanfare). An exhilarating uprush launches the Allegro animato e grazioso finale, although Schumann later called it "a farewell to spring, not to be taken too frivolously." After the skittish main theme, we hear a second one in G minor; but overall a rondo spirit inhabits his sonata structure, with a coda even more exhilarating than the initial uprush. Indeed, among the works of a composer who embodied the idea of the mercurial Romantic genius, the *"Spring" Symphony* ranks as one of the happiest and most genial of all. *—Roger Dettmer*

Recommended:

- ○ **Robert Schumann** / Bernstein (cond.), Vienna PO / 2000 / DG 469199
- ○ **Schumann: Symphonies 1–4; Overture, Scherzo and Finale** / Sawallisch (cond.), Dresden Staatskapelle / 2002 / EMI 67771
- ○ **Schumann: The Four Symphonies; Manfred Overture** / Szell (cond.), Cleveland Orch. / 1996 / Sony 62349
- ○ **Schumann: Symphonies 1–4; Overture Op115; Overture Op81** / Kubelik (cond.), Berlin PO / DG 437395

Symphony No. 2 in C major, Op. 61 (1845–1846)

In the autumn of 1844 Clara moved the Schumann household to Dresden, where Robert recovered enough from a terrifying attack of nerves to complete the *A minor Piano Concerto* for her in July 1845. Soon thereafter he began thinking about a new symphony, which eventually became the third of his four, although published as *No. 2*. To fight the symptoms of syphilis, he steeped himself in Bach, out of which came several contrapuntal works for organ, pedal-piano, and conventional clavier. At last, on December 12, a sudden wave of inspiration lifted him so high that he sketched the first movement of a new *C major Symphony* in three days, had proceeded to the finale by Christmas Day, and on December 28 completed preliminary sketches. His tinnitus worsened, however, interfering with long-term concentration until February 12, 1846, when he began to orchestrate the blueprint. Schumann completed the scoring of *Symphony No. 2* only 17 days before its Leipzig premiere in November, conducted by Felix Mendelssohn, and immediately after that added three trombones to existing parts for double winds, horns, and trumpets, string choir, and timpani.

As in the *"Spring" First* and *D minor* symphonies of 1841, he created a unifying motif, and gave this new motto theme to the brass in a deeply sonorous introduction (Sostenuto assai) to the sonata-structured opening movement. A masterful segue ushers in the craggy, edgy, Allegro ma non troppo—"moody, capricious, refractory" music in Schumann's own words—this, too, derived from the motto.

The motto also underlies all three song sections of the ensuing Scherzo: Allegro vivace, which has two trio sections (as the *"Spring" Symphony* did): the first one charmingly bucolic, in G major; the other one lyrical, with an embedded theme based on Bach's name (B flat, A, C and B natural, which the Germans call H).

This is followed by a tragically expressive Adagio in C minor, whose principal subject resembles the first trio sonata of Bach's *Musical Offering*. This is the only Adagio movement in Schumann's symphonic canon, verily a *cri de coeur;* he began a fugue midway but did not complete, much less develop it. The floodtide of melody swept everything before it.

Unable to work for several weeks after completing the Adagio, a "cured" Schumann took up the finale. The principal subject of his aptly marked Allegro molto vivace quits the sickroom in order to exercise out of doors. While he borrowed its second theme from the heartsick Adagio, he expurgated all traces of melancholy. The subsequent development of both themes ends quietly in C minor, whereupon the solo oboe quotes a melodic phrase from the last song of Beethoven's *To a Distant Beloved* cycle (whose text begins, "Then accept these songs"). This and the original motto combine in the celebratory coda of what is surely Schumann's symphonic Mount Rainier. *—Roger Dettmer*

Recommended:

- ○ **Schumann: Symphonies 1 & 2** / Harnoncourt (cond.), CO of Europe / 1996 / Teldec 98320
- ○ **Schumann: Symphonies 1–4; Overture Op115; Overture Op81** / Kubelik (cond.), Berlin PO / DG 437395
- ○ **Schumann: Symphonies 1–4; Overture, Scherzo and Finale** / Sawallisch (cond.), Dresden Staatskapelle / 2002 / EMI 67771
- ○ **Schumann: The Four Symphonies; Manfred Overture** / Szell (cond.), Cleveland Orch. / 1996 / Sony 62349

Symphony No. 3 in E flat major ("Rhenish"), Op. 97 (1850)

It has often been charged that Robert Schumann's orchestral works are little more than thinly-veiled transcriptions of musical thoughts that fall more naturally on the keyboard, and that he lacked the necessary skill to realize his purely orchestral ideas effectively. Largely due to musicians' popular acceptance of these criticisms, Schumann's four mature symphonies have suffered long periods of neglect. We can freely admit Schumann's inexperience as an orchestrator, and some pianistic traits and mannerisms are bound to sneak across in the works of such an accomplished composer for the keyboard (very few composers are immune to such "seeping" effects); however, this in no way diminishes the powerful impact that his wonderfully evocative, prototypically "Romantic" (in the original, mid-nineteenth century sense of the word) symphonic compositions can have in skilled hands. A highly individual sense of formal design, strikingly beautiful thematic and harmonic substance, and a powerful influence on such later symphonists as Brahms and Tchaikovsky all recommend these musical gems to both audiences and musicians alike, who would do well to reevaluate them on their own terms, and not compare them to the works of later composers who clearly had different means and different goals.

Schumann's *"Rhenish" Symphony,* the *Symphony No.3 in E flat major,* Op.97, is so called because it was written in the fall of 1850 during the composer's tenure as conductor at Düsseldorf on the famous Rhine river. In a letter to the publisher N. Simrock in 1851 Schumann claimed that the history and spirit of that noble river and its people were running through his mind as he composed the work. The Symphony was less successful at its premiere in February 1851 (under the composer's direction) than had his two previous symphonic premieres had been. Although third in number, the "Rhenish" is actually Schumann's final entry in the genre, the forthcoming *Symphony No. 4 in D minor,* Op. 120, having been originally composed in 1841.

The heroic main theme of the opening Lebhaft is laced with hemiolas that transform its basic 3/4 time into larger bars of 3/2. A second theme in G minor is offered by the oboe and clarinet before being taken over by the violins. The astute listener will have noticed a keen similarity between the rhythmic outline of Schumann's main theme and that of the main theme to the opening movement of Johannes Brahms' *Symphony No. 3 in F major.* This similarity is enhanced even further during the transition to the second theme in the recapitulation, when the figure is played out with precisely the same intervallic content as the later Brahms melody—just one example of the deep and abiding influence Schumann's music had on his younger associate. Schumann incorporates the jovial *Rheinweinlied* (Rhine-wine Song) into the Scherzo, which, as in the *Second Symphony,* appears as the second rather than the more traditional third movement. The solid C major foundation is shaken up briefly by the A minor Trio (although, rather stubbornly, the bass continues to putter around on low C). Perhaps the most fascinating aspect of the *"Rhenish" Symphony* is the interpolation of an extra movement. Marked Feierlich (Solemn), the movement originally carried the inscription, "in the manner of an accompaniment to a solemn ceremony." The Finale is a robust outburst (marked, like the first movement, Lebhaft) which recalls some of the main theme from the fourth movement before plunging into a final burst of joyful E flat. *—Blair Johnston*

Recommended:

- ○ **Schumann: Symphonies 3 & 4** / Kubelik (cond.), SO Bayerischen Rundfunks / 1992 / Sony 48270
- ○ **Schumann: Symphonies 1 & 3; Manfred Overture** / Szell (cond.), Cleveland Orch. / 2001 / Sony 89381
- ○ **Schumann: Symphony 3; Beethoven: Egmont Overture** / Walter (cond.), New York Philharmonic / 1996 / Sony 64488
- ○ **Schumann: Symphonies 1–4; Overture, Scherzo and Finale** / Sawallisch (cond.), Dresden Staatskapelle / 2002 / EMI 67771

Symphony No. 4 in D minor, Op. 120 (1841; revised 1851)

Robert Schumann's popular appeal as one of the masters of mid-nineteenth century piano music has been injurious to his reputation in other genres. His String Quartets are frequently ignored by both public and performers due to the oft-stated but ill-informed charge that they are little better than inflated piano transcriptions, and his four mature symphonies have suffered even longer and more painful periods of neglect for similar reasons. It has become fashionable to claim that, even in those passages where Schumann's ideas are more purely orchestral in conception, he lacked enough skill at instrumentation to realize those ideas as well as a better orchestrator might have. Consequently, many conductors have taken it upon themselves to "improve" Schumann's scoring, with results that vary from the extremely effective to the indefensible, and there has hardly been a twentieth century performance or recording entirely free of such alterations.

We can freely admit Schumann's inexperience as an orchestrator, and not take offense at the subtle modifications made to his scores by such well-intentioned musicians as George Szell. On the other hand, the wholesale rewrites by Gustav Mahler have the ultimate and very unfortunate effect of removing Schumann from his element altogether (as does his similar rewrite of Beethoven's Ninth).

The first of the two charges leveled above is a different matter altogether, for these four works are by no means mere piano transcriptions. Schumann was obviously a fluent composer for the piano, and some pianistic traits and mannerisms are bound to sneak across from the one medium to the other (very few composers are immune to such "seeping" effects). This in no way, however, diminishes the impact that his wonderfully evocative, prototypically "Romantic" (in the original, mid-nineteenth century sense of the word) Symphonies can have in skilled hands. A highly individual sense of a formal design, strikingly beautiful thematic and harmonic substance, and a history of influence on such later symphonists as Brahms and Tchaikovsky all recommend these musical gems to both audiences and musicians alike, who would do well to reevaluate them on their own terms, and not compare them to the works of later composers who clearly had different means and different goals.

Schumann's *Symphony No.4 in D minor,* Op. 120, although last by number, is hardly his final effort in the genre. It was, in fact, originally composed immediately following the completion of the First Symphony in 1841, and thus predates either the Second or the Third Symphonies. Schumann, however, refrained from publishing the work until 1853, during which interval he undertook some revisions (principally in the area of orchestration, though the work's complexity would lead us to suspect that he continued to tinker with details for some time). The work is far and away the most formally innovative of the composer's four Symphonies: the four movements, each structurally incomplete, are to be played without any break. Collectively, they form a single large-scale formal design. Significantly, Schumann considered calling the piece "Symphonic Fantasia"—no doubt wondering if such a creation were still a genuine symphony. *—Blair Johnston*

Recommended:

- ○ **Schumann: The Symphonies** / Dohnányi (cond.), Cleveland Orch. / 1996 / London 452214
- ○ **Schumann: Symphonies 1–4; Overture Op115; Overture Op81** / Kubelik (cond.), Berlin PO / DG 437395
- ○ **Schumann: The Four Symphonies; Manfred Overture** / Szell (cond.), Cleveland Orch. / 1996 / Sony 62349
- ○ **Schumann: Symphonies 1–4; Overture, Scherzo and Finale** / Sawallisch (cond.), Dresden Staatskapelle / 2002 / EMI 67771
- ○ **Schumann: Symphony 4; Furtwängler: Symphony 2** / Furtwängler (cond.), Berlin PO / 1998 / DG 457722

ORCHESTRAL

Manfred, overture & incidental music, Op. 115 (1848–1849)

Schumann was possessed of a keen literary mind. His studies at the Leipzig and Heidelberg Universities and his own career as a writer, including an early attempt at a novel, helped to hone his natural insights in this direction. So, when the opportunity arose in 1848 to provide incidental music for Lord Byron's *Manfred,* he threw himself into the project with a fervor. Although only the wildly popular *Manfred Overture* has ever entered the repertory (the rest being rather difficult to program), Schumann's Opus 115 score actually includes 15 additional numbers for orchestra, choir, and various solo voices. The overture was first performed in March of 1852 with its composer at the helm, while a complete performance of the *Manfred* score was given by Franz Liszt in Weimar just three months later.

The Manfred Overture is one of Schumann's finest orchestral creations; it conveys very effectively the urgent despair of Byron's work. Three remarkable chords precede the pained, chromatic tune in the oboe and second violins. A somber texture is provided by the orchestra, here Schumann's frequently ineffective and superfluous doublings seem most appropriate, until the passion can be restrained no longer and a wild rout ensues. A few brief fragments of lyric thought in the major mode occasionally poke through—how effective are such outbursts of hope against so grim and indefatigable a background! The energy is momentarily spent as we near the midpoint of the piece; chorale-like fragments in the brass and isolated woodwind chords receive a terse commentary from the lower strings. As the anguished pursuit continues, it is easy to see the marked influence that Schumann's imitative orchestral procedures had on Tchaikovsky. The underlying E flat tonality is firmly reestablished by a long succession of E flat minor chords in the winds, against which an agitated violin figure (with that piquant raised fourth, a prominent feature throughout the work) finally runs out of energy as the initial oboe melody returns.

The remaining 15 pieces are of uneven quality, and none approaches the concentrated expression of the overture. A wide range of textures are represented. No.1, "Gesang der Geister" (Song of the Ghosts) pits a quiet, unison song (doubled by the solo violin) against an impish triplet-sixteenth note figure in the viola; while No.4, "Alpenkuhreigen," is just a single, unaccompanied folklike tune that Schumann doubles, unison, with the English horn. The purely instrumental No.5, an entr'acte to the second act that lilts forward in a charming triple-meter fashion, is perhaps the most successful of the bunch. No.7, "Hymnus der Geister Ariman's," is majestic, while No.13, which portrays the "Departure of the Sun," is quiet and spacious. The final number of Manfred, No.15 (Schluss-Scene/Closing-scene), makes effective use of dense, chromatic counterpoint. *—Blair Johnston*

Recommended:

- ○ **Schumann: Symphonies 3 & 4** / Kubelik (cond.), Bayerischen Rundfunks SO / 1992 / Sony 48270
- ○ **Schumann: Symphonies 1 & 3; Manfred Overture** / Szell (cond.), Cleveland Orch. / 2001 / Sony 89381
- ○ **The German Album: Schumann, Wagner & Liszt** / Leibowitz (cond.), Royal PO / 1993 / Chesky 96

Overture, Scherzo, & Finale in E minor/E major, Op. 52 (1841; revised 1845)

Published in 1846 by Kistner and dedicated to the Dutch violinist and conductor, J. H. Verhulst, the *Overture, Scherzo and Finale in E major,* Op. 52, was written in three weeks in 1841. The Finale was revised in 1845, shortly before publication. The *Overture, Scherzo and Finale,* Op. 52, is essentially a symphony without a slow movement; Schumann even referred to it as his "Symphony No. 2" at one time. Earlier, when Schumann offered it, unsuccessfully, to the Leipzig publisher Hofmeister, he called it a suite, pointing out that "the individual movements can be played separately." Earlier still, he referred to the piece as a Sinfonietta. Compared to Schumann's four Symphonies, the piece is smaller both in length and orchestration. Schumann's numerous ways of identifying his Op. 52 makes one wonder about any intended symphonic unity. If the movements aren't meant to be together, why arrange them that way? However, close inspection of the piece reveals that beyond their lively mood and light orchestration, the movements are related thematically. Throughout the piece, the playfulness and eloquence of Mendelssohn is never far away.

Two important motives in the slow, E minor introduction to the Overture—a graceful, leaping violin passage an aggressive, descending figure for the cellos—become important elements of the Overture proper, marked Allegro. A change to E major, as well as the increased tempo, mark the beginning of the sonata-form movement, which opens with a vivacious primary theme of falling seconds. As in many opera overtures, the development is minimal. In this case, the primary theme becomes entangled with the introductory motives for a short time before the recapitulation.

Schumann's Scherzo is in 6/8, its main theme, very narrow in range, set in the strings. The personality of the Scherzo derives from its driving, dotted figure, which becomes monotonous soon after the movement begins. In contrast, the trio section is lyrical and lovely, and on its second appearance incorporates motives from the Overture and is introduced by the descending cello line. A return of the primary theme of the Overture closes the Scherzo.

The Finale is one of Schumann's fastest movements. The main theme, a rising stepwise line in dotted rhythms played by the first violins, is presented in fugato style. An elegant secondary theme provides welcome contrast and betrays Schumann's debt to Mendelssohn in its grace and light orchestration. The Finale closes with a coda built of the main theme. *—John Palmer*

Recommended:

- ○ **Schumann: Symphony 3; Overtures** / Thielemann (cond.), London Philharmonia Orch. / DG 459680
- ○ **Schumann: Overtures** / Wildner (cond.), Polish National RSO / 1993 / Naxos 550608
- ○ **Schumann: Symphonies 1–4; Overture, Scherzo and Finale** / Sawallisch (cond.), Dresden Staatskapelle / 2002 / EMI 67771

CHORAL

Scenes from Goethe's Faust, WoO 3 (1844–1853)

Goethe had finished the second part of *Faust* only 13 years before Schumann began his setting of it, and most readers were daunted by its mysticism and abstruse symbolism. The first part, the story of Gretchen, was easy enough to comprehend and even portray in music, but the second was far less easily grasped, let alone depicted. Additionally, the author himself had declared that Mozart should have written the music for *Faust,* so any composer would not only be judged by his treatment of one of the seminal and most-widely acclaimed works in German literature, but would aslo be setting himself up to be compared to Mozart.

Schumann wrote different segments intermittently, as inspiration or opportunity struck. In fact, he worked from back to front. In 1844, he began work on the ending of Goethe's *Part Two,* with "Fausts Verklärung" (Faust's Transfiguration). In 1845, he wrote to Mendelssohn that he was hesitant to have the results published or performed, though by 1848 he had gotten up the courage to have it produced as an oratorio for a small audience, and by 1849, the year of Goethe's centenary, it was performed in Dresden, Leipzig, and Weimar. After these performances, Schumann tackled it again, adding the second and first sections, and finally, in 1853, writing the overture. It was not performed in its entirety until 1862, almost six years after Schumann's death, but then was a great success and influence.

The first of the three sections depicts the story of Gretchen 's seduction, ending with the church scene. The second shows Faust's philosophical struggles to find meaning in the face of the "vier graue Weiber"—the four gray women: Need, Guilt, Worry, and Sorrow—and ends with Faust's death. The last is Faust's transfiguration. Schumann sets these stories, growing from the relatively mundane to the philosophical to the mystical with music reflecting these focuses.

The lengthy overture is tense and tempestuous throughout, with only fleeting lyrical passages. Aside from creating a dramatic, electrifying introduction, it also suggests the conflict between good and evil as well as Faust's turbulent search for enlightenment and peace. After this, the work opens *in media res,* with Faust's courtship of Gretchen. Her story is depicted in highly operatic music, beginning with the love duet, moving to Gretchen's passionate and desperate aria, and ending with the church scene. The stage directions even include props, such as Gretchen's flower. The second part begins with a strong contrast, the lively, fresh music of Ariel and the spirits, calling to Faust to enjoy the beauties of nature, but the next scene, with the four gray women, and the last, with the lemurs digging graves, Faust's delusions of hearing a new world being created, and his ecstatic calls for this moment to stay, are prototypical Romantic music, with the combination of intense orchestration and hints of the supernatural in the music of the women and the lemurs. The last scenes contain some of Schumann's most effective choral writing, especially the majestic opening passages of the *chorus mysticus.* *—Ann Feeney*

Recommended:

- ○ **Schumann: Szenen aus Goethes Faust** / Klee (cond.), Fischer-Dieskau, Gedda, Mathis, Berry / 2002 / EMI 575667
- ○ **Schumann: Szenen aus Goethes Faust** / Abbado (cond.), Berlin PO, Terfel, Mattila, Rootering, Bonney / 1995 / Sony 66308
- ○ **Schumann: Szenen aus Goethes Faust** / Herreweghe (cond.), Dazeley, Sigmundsson, Nylund / HM 901661

Ernestine Schumann-Heink

b. Jun. 15, 1861, Lieben, Austria, **d.** Nov. 17, 1936, Hollywood, CA

Contralto

Ernestine "Tini" Schumann-Heink was born Ernestine Rössler, the daughter of an Austrian cavalry officer. Schumann-Heink made her debut in Graz at age 15, singing the alto solo in Beethoven's *Ninth Symphony.* At 17, she made her operatic debut in Dresden. While with the Dresden Opera she sang at the city's cathedral and studied voice with Franz Wuellner. She eloped with Ernst Heink, an administrator at the Dresden Opera, in 1882, causing them both to be fired. Later, Schumann-Heink managed to find a position singing bit parts at the Hamburg Opera, but her husband therafter deserted her while she was bearing their fourth child. In 1889, Schumann-Heink was asked to understudy the lead in *Carmen* in order to replace a singer who had stormed out in a fit of pique. Schumann-Heink immediately won the approval of Hamburg operagoers. Word of her artistry spread quickly, and by 1893 she had already debuted in London, Paris, and Berlin. That year she married the actor Paul Schumann, with whom she would have four more children for a total of eight. In 1896, with the hyphenated name under which she became best known, Schumann-Heink made her debut at Bayreuth; Cosima Wagner personally coached her in several Wagnerian roles. In 1897, Schumann-Heink managed to free herself from her Hamburg contract and began to tour the world under the auspices of her new company, the Berlin Opera. She made her American debut in Chicago in 1898, and first appeared at the Metropolitan in New York later that year. So happy was she with the enthusiasm of American audiences that she bought out her contract from Berlin in order to remain at the Met. Schumann-Heink's first commercial records appeared as part of Columbia's Grand Opera Series of 1903. That year, Schumann-Heink shocked the opera world by appearing in a Broadway revue, *Love's Lottery;* the show was followed by a highly profitable tour. During the tour, Paul Schumann died; Schumann-Heink then married her American manager and moved her family from "Villa Tini" in Dresden to an estate in New Jersey. She became an American citizen in 1908. Two years before, she had signed a recording contract with Victor, an agreement which would last until 1931. Her 1910 recording of *Stille Nacht, Heilige Nacht* (Silent Night) was a huge seller that stayed in the Victor catalog until she did another version in 1926. She continued to appear at the Bayreuth Festival until the outbreak of World War I. During the Great War, Schumann-Heink performed at bond rallies, visited hospitals for wounded soldiers, and sang at military encampments, finally converting her private home in Chicago into a canteen for soldiers. Enlisted men loved her so much that they called her "Mother Schumann-Heink"; few of them knew that she had sons fighting on both sides of the conflict. She resumed her professional career at the war's end. Her "Golden Jubilee" was held at the Met in 1926; that year she began to broadcast on radio, her appearances evolving into a popular weekly show that ran from 1929 to 1935. She also appeared in three Vitaphone shorts and embarked upon a relentless grind of touring and public appearences. She made her final Met appearence as Erda in Wagner's *Rheingold* in 1932 at age 71. In 1935, Schumann-Heink made an appearance in a Hollywood feature film, *Here's to Romance.* The public response was so strong that a feature starring Schumann-Heink herself was proposed, but before it could be made she died of leukemia at the age of 75. *—Uncle Dave Lewis*

Recommended:

- ○ **Arias & Songs** / Bourdon (cond.), Schumann-Heink, Farrar, Prince, Witherspoon, Schmidt, Wille / 1998 / Delos 5503
- ○ **Schumann-Heink** / Schumann-Heink, Bourdon, Witherspoon, Sammlung Kurt Hofmann / 1991 / Nimbus 7811

Heinrich Schütz

b. Oct. 9, 1585, Köstritz, Germany, **d.** Nov. 6, 1672, Dresden, Germany
Composer: Choral

Heinrich Schütz, in a way, stood as a bridge between the Renaissance and Bach. He infused his church music with a greater drama than previously heard in Germany by developing and transforming the Italian choral style he had learned in his studies with Gabrieli. Schütz's *Psalmen Davids* (1619) shows the influence of Gabrieli but also divulges his own unique voice. His melodic invention is in evidence in the *Becker Psalter* (1626), while his *Geistliche Chor-Music* (1648), a collection of motets, represents perhaps the greatest such assemblage from his century. A large number of his compositions went unpublished, most of those now lost.

Schütz was born in Köstritz (now Bad Köstritz) and raised in Weissenfels, where his father operated an inn. Young Heinrich probably studied with George Weber, a composer and the local Kantor. At 13, Schütz entered the Collegium Mauritianum in Kassel at the urging of Landgrave Moritz of Hessen, who had established it four years earlier. Schütz became a choirboy in the Landgrave's court and studied under Kapellmeister Georg Otto. Shortly after leaving the Collegium in 1608 (such lengthy study was not unusual), Schütz left for Venice to study with Giovanni Gabrieli.

In 1613, he returned to Germany and accepted a post as second organist in the Landgrave's court. Around this time he met Johann Hermann Schein, with whom he would remain close friends until Schein's death in 1631. In 1615, Schütz entered service in the Dresden court of Elector Johann Georg of Saxony and two years later became, in effect, Kapellmeister, holding the most powerful musical post in Protestant Germany.

Schütz's first sacred music publication appeared in 1619. *Psalmen Davids sampt etlichen Moteten und Concerten* comprised 26 works for various choruses and instruments. On June 1, that year, the composer married Magdalene Wildeck, 15 years his junior. Throughout the early 1620s, Schütz remained quite active in composition, perhaps finding his personal happiness a springboard for his creativity. In 1625, however, Magdalene died after a brief illness, dealing Schütz a devastating blow.

This tragedy seems to have motivated Schütz in the composition of his *Der Psalter nach Cornelius Becker*, a huge collection of partsongs, published in 1628. The composer departed Dresden for Venice on August 11, that same year, owing to economic hardship in Saxony from the ongoing Thirty Years Wars. Upon his return to Dresden in late 1629, he found economic conditions there no better. In fact, things worsened over the eight-year span (1633–41) he spent mainly in the court of Prince Christian of Denmark. Schütz served most of the period of 1642–44 in the Copenhagen court of Prince Johann Georg, though he remained officially tied to his Dresden post. The composer's *Symphoniarum sacrarum secunda pars*, a collection of sacred vocal works, appeared in 1647. After briefly taking a post in Duke Wilhelm's Weimar court in 1648, he spent several months in Weissenfels early the following year and then returned to Dresden. In 1650, Schütz published his collection, *Symphoniarum sacrarum tertia pars*.

The composer's output slowed to a trickle in his later years, but in the latter 1650s his financial situation, long precarious under Elector Johann Georg, improved when Johann Georg II succeeded his father, who died in 1656. Schütz did much traveling in his last years and lived in Weissenfels for most of his last decade. *—Robert Cummings*

CHORAL

Geistliche Chormusik, motets, SWV 369–397 (Op. 11)

By 1648, when he published his *Geistliche Chormusik* (Spiritual Choral Music), Heinrich Schütz had already been musical director of the famous Dresden court for nearly 35 years. Most of that period had been overshadowed by the calamitous 30 Years' War, which had a devastating effect on life in many parts of Europe. The war, which ended the same year as Schütz's publication appeared, had a considerable effect on musical life in Dresden, where the chapel had worked on a greatly reduced number of musicians. The 29 motets that form the *Geistliche Chormusik* reflect such economy of means. There is some dispute among scholars as to whether the collection was planned as a cycle or is simply a collection of preexisting material brought together for publication. There certainly is a coherent pattern evident in that the first 12 motets are scored in five parts, the second consisting of motets 13 to 24 in six parts, while the concluding five motets are composed in seven parts. In an important preface, Schütz makes clear that he did not necessarily intend the motets to be performed entirely with vocal forces ("this style of church music... is not always homogenous") and the works are generally performed by a mixture of voices and instruments. The texts are mainly drawn from the Old and New Testaments in Martin Luther's German translation, but some chorale texts are also included. It was noted by Bach's biographer Philipp Spitta that each of the three groups' works makes a traversal of the church's year from Advent through to Remembrance Sunday, the last Sunday before Trinity. In his preface, Schütz stresses the importance of composers being thoroughly conversant with the old "motet" or polyphonic style before attempting the influential new Italian continuo style that has become "most popular here [in Germany] and, in fact, has gained more supporters than any other style." Schütz goes on to point out he has no objections to a style he had indeed used before, but the pieces of the *Geistliche Chormusik* have the specific didactic purpose of encouraging Schütz's younger fellow composers to master the fundamentals of polyphony. This should not be taken to imply that the motets are in any way archaic, but in their eschewal of continuo bass, overt madrigalisms, or word painting, they return to the purer, non-dramatic motet style. In consequence, the music is characterized by a directness of utterance that eschews gesture in favor of a deceptive simplicity that goes directly to the heart. *—Brian Robins*

Recommended:

- ○ **Schütz: Geistliche Chormusik** / Schmidt-Gaden (cond.), Musicalische Compagney / Capriccio 10858/9
- ○ **Schütz: Geistliche Chormusik** / Suzuki (cond.), Bach Collegium Japan / 1997 / Bis 831/2

Kleine geistliche Konzerte (Little Sacred Concertos), SWV 282–337 (Opp. 8 & 9)

The Little Sacred Concertos by the seventeenth century German master Heinrich Schütz (1585–1672) were published in two volumes, the first in Leipzig in 1736, while the second which followed three years later appeared in Dresden, where Schütz spent much of his distinguished career as Kapellmeister. The use of the word "concerto" here does not conform to modern usage, implying simply that the music is designed for a small group of vocal performers in the sense first used by early Venetian Baroque composers such as Viadana (the first to use the term) and Monteverdi. Schütz himself traveled twice to Venice: on the first occasion as a young man to study with Giovanni Gabrieli, the second time in 1628–29 to Monteverdi's Venice to investigate for himself "the new manner of music which has emerged and is in practice today," as he put it.

Both sets of concertos are "little" in two senses. Firstly, in their extremely sparse scoring, which was dictated by the exigencies of the 30 Years' War, which devastated musical activity throughout central Europe. As the composer himself put it in his preface, "music was in decline and in some places discontinued altogether." All the concertos are therefore scored for between one and five solo voices with only bass continuo accompaniment. The concertos are also small in scale, the texts sometimes running to only a single sentence and rarely extending to more than four or five lines. The majority are taken from biblical sayings, but there are also extracts from Lutheran hymn texts, religious poems, and quotations from St. Augustine. About half the texts deal with penitential or somber subjects, doubtless a reflection of the dark times that witnessed the genesis of the concertos, but there also are Christmas pieces, such as the lovely "Ein Kind is uns geboren" (Unto us a child is born), SWV 302. The two books between them cover 56 concertos. Nine are for solo voice, 21 are duets, while there are nine for three voices, 11 for four voices, and six for five. Almost every kind of combination appears in the concerted works, although the most common scoring is for equal voices (e.g. two sopranos). Indeed, the most remarkable aspect of the set is the sheer variety Schütz obtains from such limited forces and brief texts. Far from being constricted by the enforced conditions that "made it impossible to play with great (large-scale) music and large choir" (Schütz), the composer shifted his emphasis to concentrate on the rhetoric of the text, a discipline that accounts for his supreme qualities as a setter of the German language. The most frequently employed musical style is a mixture of recitative and arioso, the structure of the music invariably being at the service of the words. This flexibility and freedom is particularly apparent in the solos, and, to a slightly lesser degree, in the duets, where imitative exchanges are frequent. A number of the concertos for three, four, and five voices are chorale settings. *—Brian Robins*

Recommended:

- ○ **Heinrich Schütz: Kleine geistliche Konzerte** / Cordes (cond.), Weser-Renaissance / 2000 / CPO 999675

Musikalische Exequien (Funeral Music), SWV 279–281 (Op. 7)

Heinrich Schütz's *Musicalische Exequien* was written for the funeral services of the Count Heinrich Posthumous Reuss, who died on December 3, 1635. The Count was a serious patron of music who devoted considerable resources to the court chapel. He was also a reasonably accomplished singer, and often directed the music performances at court. Having been in contact with Schütz from ca. 1617 onward (and having occasionally employed the composer to "reorganize" the music of his chapel), Reuss appears to have communicated with Schütz concerning his plans for his funeral, outlining his desires for the music in the service. Reuss chose the texts for his funeral music and had them also engraved on his coffin; these became the basis for Schütz's memorial composition, which was performed at the Count's funeral on February 4, 1636.

The first segment of Schütz's *Musikalische Exequien* is a large German motet which follows the general outline of a Lutheran "German Missa" (Kyrie and Gloria only). Its text uses citations from familiar hymns in the Lutheran liturgy grafted into a paraphrase of the Kyrie and Gloria of a normal German mass. It is scored for six-voice choir (perhaps doubled at the time by instruments) and six soloists. The second section is an eight-voice motet based on the text from Reuss' specified sermon. The third, and final, portion of the *Exequien* is a setting of the "Song of Simeon," a Biblical text also known as the "nunc dimitis." This motet is particularly interesting: one choir sings the text of the "Song of Simeon" while three other choirs sing a different text, "blessed are the dead who die in the name of the Lord. . . ." Schütz specifies in his score that the three choirs are to be placed in the distance.

Although the *Musicalische Exequien* were published shortly after the funeral, they appear not to have been performed again in their entirety during the seventeenth century. Brahms owned a copy of the work and perhaps used it as a model for his *German Requiem*. *—Andrus Madsen*

Recommended:

- ○ **Heinrich Schütz: Musikalische Exequien; Motets** / Herreweghe (cond.), Chapelle Royale / HM 2981261
- ○ **Heinrich Schütz: Motets & Concertos; Musikalische Exequien** / Gardiner (cond.), English Baroque Soloists, Monteverdi Choir / Archiv 423405
- ○ **Schütz: Musikalische Exequien; Johannes-Passion** / Ehmann (cond.), Westfalische Kantorei / 1960 / Cantate 57602

Die sieben Wortte unsers lieben Erlösers und Seeligmachers Jesu Christi, SWV 478 (1657)

Among the most famous works of the great seventeenth century German composer Heinrich Schütz (1585–1672), *The Seven Words of Jesus Christ on the Cross* is a Passiontide work based on a Renaissance tradition of gathering together the words spoken by Christ on the cross. Schütz's setting is based on Martin Luther's German translation of the Bible. The date of composition is unknown; the only clue is a copied score, the last part of which bears the date 1657. Other authorities have suggested a date around 1645, although there is no evidence to support such a claim. Whatever its date, the work is certainly a mature product of the composer's late years—a period during which the aging Schütz consistently sought to withdraw from his onerous duties as Kapellmeister at the Dresden court.

In keeping with the court's modest musical forces in the wake of the devastating 30 Years' War, *The Seven Words* is economically scored for five vocal parts (soprano, alto, two tenors, and bass), five unspecified instruments, and continuo. The choral, or turbae (crowd scenes), vocal parts are intended to be sung one-to-a-part, while the instrumental scoring is generally allotted to dark-hued instruments such as trombones or viols, who both open and close the work with instrumental sinfonias. The words of the Evangelist are mostly divided between the soprano, alto, and first tenor, although at the point of Jesus' final cry they become a four-part chorus. The soloists are accompanied only by continuo bass, thus placing the accompanied words of Jesus into strong relief. Unlike the great passion works of the eighteenth century, there is no attempt at external dramatization. Rather, this concise setting is designed as a profound and deeply moving meditation summed up in the final words: "He who respects the torment of God and often reflects on the seven words, will be cared for by God, then and in the life everlasting." *—Brian Robins*

Recommended:

- ○ **Schütz: Die sieben Worte Jesu Christi am Kreuz** / Visse (cond.), Clement Janequin Ens. / HM 1951255
- ○ **Schütz: Die sieben Worte Jesu Christi am Kreuz** / Pierlot (cond.), Ricercar Consort / 1998 / Ricercar 206412

St. John Passion, SWV 481 (1665; revised 1666)

Heinrich Schütz wrote this work in his last years, along with the other passions, the *St. Luke* and the *St. John*. These works came from the pen of a man 80 years old, a man who reached an age rarely attained by anyone in the seventeenth century, let alone by one who remained quite active in his taxing profession (kapellmeister). What is just as remarkable, though, is that all three works are fiery and full of ardor and youthful passion. They are among Schütz's finest compositions, and among the finest compositions by anyone of his time.

Schütz wrote the *St. John Passion* (History of the Life and Death of Jesus Christ according to the Evangelist *St. John*) in the Phrygian mode. It is scored for a cappella chorus and features a soprano soloist, three tenors and two basses. Schütz would likely have added instrumental accompaniment had he intended the work primarily for the concert venue, but in conformance with liturgical guidelines in Dresden, he restricted the musical scoring entirely to the vocal realm.

The work is divided into 16 sections, beginning with the spirited yet devout "Introitus: Das Leiden unsers Herren Jesu" and closing with the beautiful "O Hilf, Christie, Gottes Sohn." Schütz often has long stretches in the work of unaccompanied solo singing. In some of the earlier sections this is especially characteristic; yet, the music never turns dull, always remains vital, the lone voice typically sounding compelling and passionate, as, for example, in the third section, "Jesus antwortet," where the unaccompanied tenor part never seems barren or to yearn for choral support. The soloist takes on a chant-like quality in the sixth section, "Ware dieser nicht ein Übeltäter" and has spirited exchanges with the chorus in the eighth, "Da Schreien sie wieder allesamt."

Schütz's choral writing throughout is also effective. The tenth section, "Kreuzige Ihn" (Crucify Him), features a mood in which the composer subtly conveys both a somber anxiety and a spirit that augurs triumph. In the aforementioned final section, "O Hilf, Christie, Gottes Sohn," Schütz imparts an atmosphere of serene and angelic religiosity via the subtle coloration with which he endows the choral music. In the end, the common judgment that this work is a major masterpiece of a cappella sacred music must be affirmed. Yet, sadly, the *St. John Passion* is seldom performed and recorded. *—Robert Cummings*

Recommended:

- ○ **Schütz: St. John's Passion; Cantiones Sacrae** / Frieberger (cond.), Collegium Musicum Plagense / Christophorus 74587

St. Matthew Passion, SWV 479 (1666)

The tradition of musical settings of the events of Christ's Passion according to the accounts in the four gospels extends back to the days of chant, the plainsong later supplemented by the introduction of polyphonic choruses for the crowd (or turbae) scenes. In Lutheran Germany the use of music for didactic purposes was particularly strong, many composers producing settings of the events that lie at the heart of Christianity, the culmination being the great passions of Bach. During the first part of the seventeenth century it was customary for composers to maintain a strictly dramatic approach to their settings, eschewing the interpolation of arias and chorales commenting on the unfolding drama that would become familiar in the settings of Bach and other eighteenth century composers. It is within this context that the three passions of the greatest of Bach's German predecessors fall.

All three, one each devoted to the gospels of St. Matthew, St. John, and St. Luke, are products of the final creative years of Heinrich Schütz (1585–1672), most of whose long and distinguished career was spent as Kapellmeister at the court of Dresden. According to the court records at Dresden, they were all given during April, 1666, although only the most famous of them, the *St. Matthew Passion*, can be ascribed to that year with reasonable accuracy. Like its fellows, the *St. Matthew Passion* conforms to the spare, direct style of his later works, a style Schütz had honed of necessity during the bleak period of musical austerity occasioned by the 30 Years' War. There is no instrumental accompaniment, and the setting of the text is largely syllabic, the exceptions being invariably closely tied to special words that require special emphasis or tone-painting, a technique of which Schütz was an unexcelled master. The words of the Evangelist and other characters are set as highly flexible recitative, while most of the choruses are short terse interpolations that show the composer's great skill in articulating dramatic situations. Far from the self-imposed restraint of the setting being responsible for an underplaying of the unfolding events, it produces an immediacy of communication in which the listener is encouraged to concentrate on the spiritual meaning and message of the text. In its very economy and sparseness, the *St. Matthew Passion* represents a distillation of Schütz's art. *—Brian Robins*

Recommended:

- ○ **Schütz: St. Matthew Passion** / Kurz (cond.), Blochwitz, Heldwein, Hauptmann, Klein / 1994 / Point Classics 265017

Symphoniae Sacrae (Sacred Symphonies), motets

Heinrich Schütz made the long journey to Venice twice in his lifetime: once from 1609 to 1612, during which time he studied composition with Giovanni Gabrieli, and the second time in 1628–29, meeting both Alessandro Grandi and Claudio Monteverdi. One result of his first soujourn was the *Psalmen Davids*, Schütz's attempt to translate the Venetian polychoral style into the German liturgy. The second trip was even more momentous. Schütz found that in Venetian music, the "ancient rhythms" had by then given way to "new devices." Once again, the Dresden kapellmeister was the conduit through which Italian innovations reached German-speaking lands. During this second trip to Venice, Schütz published the first volume of his own music, entitled *Symphoniae Sacrae*.

The title acknowledges Schütz's debt to Venice; the two greatest collections of Gabrieli's music had also been called *Sacred Symphonies*. In 1629, Schütz released through the Venetian press a collection of his first 20 such pieces. Reflecting the more current styles he encountered during the second stay in Venice, Schütz's collection represents his first essays in the new concerto style of church composition. He set a variety of Latin sacred texts for one to three voices, with instruments. The voices even include bass solos (one a lament for Absalom), while the instruments comprise the new basso continuo and frequent pairs of trebles (violins, recorders, trumpets). The musical style mingles Ventian polychoral idioms and "classic" contrapuntal writing for these smaller forces; Schütz demonstrates a mastery of newer musical elements such as instrumental Ritornelli, freer handling of dissonance, and various Italian styles of vocal ornamentation.

Later in his life, Schütz published a series of volumes summing up his life's work; they included two further volumes of *Symphoniae Sacrae*. In 1647, he published the *Symphoniae Sacrae II* in Dresden (dedicated to Denmark's Catholic King). Schütz here adopted the musical style of the first volume to German liturgical texts. Its 27 pieces set German psalms and Old Testament texts (as well as a German *Magnificat*), for one to three voices, basso continuo, and pairs of treble instruments. Many individual pieces were composed much earlier and revised for this volume; parodies of Monteverdi madrigals may even be found. The 21 concerti of the third volume, printed in 1650 for the Elector Johann Georg I, present similarly madrigalian settings of German texts for the larger vocal and instrumental groups Schütz knew in Copenhagen; one of his best-known motets, *Saul, Saul, was verfolgst du mich?*, is found here. *—Timothy Dickey*

Recommended:

- ○ **Schütz: Symphoniae Sacrae; Kleine Geistliche Konzerte** / Christie, Junghanel, Kimura, Swierstra, Concerto Vocale / HM 901097
- ○ **Heinrich Schütz: Symphoniae Sacrae I - 1629** / Concerto Palatino / Accent 9178/79

Joseph Schwantner

b. Mar. 22, 1943, Chicago, IL

Composer

The career of Joseph Schwantner is perhaps as prestigious as that of any living American composer at the turn of the twenty-first century. His honors include a Pulitzer Prize (*Aftertones of Infinity*), a Guggenheim Fellowship, and no less than six Composers Fellowship Grants from the National Endowment for the Arts. His commissions include compositions for the New York Philharmonic, Boston Symphony, St. Louis Symphony, San Diego Symphony, AT&T, New York International Festival of the Arts, and Naumburg and Fromm Foundations, and his works have been performed by such ensembles as the Chicago Symphony, Boston Symphony, Cleveland Orchestra, London Philharmonic, New York Philharmonic, Philadelphia Orchestra, National Symphony, BBC Philharmonic, St. Louis Symphony, Los Angeles Philharmonic, London Sinfonietta, St. Paul Chamber Orchestra, and Los Angeles Chamber Orchestra. *New Morning for the World* (1982), composed in honor of Martin Luther King Jr., was perhaps the most oft-performed and well-known pieces for narrator and orchestra since Copland's *Lincoln Portrait*.

Such an illustrious career began humbly enough, as tuba player in his high school orchestra. But Schwantner was already composing for guitar and arranging pieces for jazz band. He attended Chicago's American Conservatory, where he studied with Bernard Dieter. After completing a bachelor's degree in 1964, Schwantner entered graduate studies at Northwestern University, where he completed master's and doctorate degrees. He held professorships at Pacific Lutheran University and Ball State before arriving at the Eastman School of Music in 1970, then becoming professor of composition at Yale.

Although trained in the high-serialist school, the mid-1970s saw Schwantner abandon that style in favor of a distinctly coloristic, harmonically rich, but solidly tonal (albeit often "pantonal") sound. His voice throughout the 1970s and 1980s is often characterized by rich, dark brass scoring, lurching polyrhythms, and mesmerizing ostinati. One favorite technique is the employment of "ringing sonorities," or sounds that are articulated loudly then suppressed and sustained. These sounds resonate with Schwantner's evocative titles like *From a Dark Millennium* (1980, for wind ensemble), *Aftertones of Infinity* (1978, for orchestra) and *Wild Angels of the Open Hills* (1978, for soprano, flute, and harp). His timbral palette is further enhanced by the use of nontraditional instruments like crystal glasses, water gongs, and bowed cymbals.

Schwantner's style in the 1990s combined occasional excursions into disorienting atonal and vaguely serialist areas with weighty and often overpowering tonal blocks, and continued to explore new timbres, as in the *Percussion Concerto* of 1994, the *Evening Land Symphony* of 1995, *In Memories Embrace* of 1996, and *Beyond Autumn*, a "poem" for horn solo and orchestra composed in 1999. *—Jeremy Grimshaw*

Overview of Works

Joseph Schwantner has established a position as one of the most important composers of orchestral music in America in the last decades of the twentieth century and the beginning of the twenty-first. His compositions, which variously and freely draw on the methods and sounds of serialism, minimalism, jazz, and neo-tonality, emphasize stark contrasts in instrumental timbre, dramatic shifts in texture and density, and extremes of dynamic and range; his often massive sounds convey a sense of danger, like a looming Richard Serra sculpture, but likewise can open onto idyllic landscapes of otherworldly serenity. Such extremes of expression often correlate with unabashedly fantastical titles—such as the Pulitzer Prize-winning orchestral work *Aftertones of Infinity* (1978). Schwantner's first works rely on 12-tone procedures, but, as seen in the early chamber works *Consortium I* and *Consortium II* (1970, 1971), Schwantner applies the method quite freely, and also lends clear emphasis to some tonal gravities through repetition, ostinati, or pedal points. Procedure remains well below the surface in wind pieces such as *From a Dark Millennium* (1981), with its ominous, lurching ostinatos and intersecting planes of sound that recall the architectonic sounds of Varèse. Also like Varèse, Schwantner takes particular interest in expanding his palette of timbres through the use of large and varied percussion batteries—the percussion concerto of 1994 being only the most extreme of several pieces notable in this regard. Other works augment the timbral possibilities of the orchestra through amplification, as in the amplified piano featured with orchestra in *Distant Runes and Incantations* (1984) or the amplified guitar with orchestra heard in *From Afar* (1987). The same concern for dramatic timbral effects and broad brush strokes of orchestral color can be heard in other symphonic works such as the Grammy-nominated *A Sudden Rainbow* (1986), *Toward Light* (1987), and *Through Interior Worlds* (1992). Though making up a small portion of his output, Schwantner's vocal works have been highly regarded, especially the orchestral song cycles *Magabunda: Four Poems of Agueda Pizarro* (nominated for a Grammy in 1984) and *Symphony "Evening Land"* (1995). Perhaps his best-known work is his tribute to Martin Luther King Jr., *New Morning for the World: "Daybreak of Freedom"* (1982), a composition for speaker and orchestra that received its premiere at the Eastman School of Music with baseball legend Willie Stargell narrating. *—Jeremy Grimshaw*

Recommended:

- ○ **The Music Of Joseph Schwantner** / Slatkin (cond.), Glennie, National SO / 1997 / BMG 68692
- ○ **Boston Musica Viva Plays: Schwantner, Ives, Berio, Davidovsky & Harris** / Boston Musica Viva / 1987 / Delos 1011

Gerard Schwarz

b. Aug. 19, 1947, Weehawken, NJ

Conductor, Trumpeter

Gerard Schwarz is one of America's top conductors, particularly noted for championing the first great age of American symphonists. He is also a gifted trumpet virtuoso. He began studying the trumpet at the age of eight. He attended the National Music Camp in Interlochen, Michigan, during the summers of 1958–60 and studied at New York's High School of Performing Arts. He studied trumpet with William Vacchiano, principal trumpeter of the New York Philharmonic Orchestra (1962–68). He received his Bachelor's Degree from the Juilliard School in 1972.

He joined the American Brass Quintet in 1965, and with it toured the United States, Europe, and Asia, remaining with the ensemble from 1965 to 1973. He was a trumpeter in the American Symphony Orchestra from 1966 to 1972, becoming its first trumpet in 1969. With that orchestra he played a considerable quantity of new and American music. During this period is was also a member of the Aspen Festival Orchestra and the Casals Festival Orchestra. He was appointed co-principal trumpet of the New York Philharmonic Orchestra from 1972 to 1975. As a trumpet player he made a number of important recordings, many of which are now in the CD catalogues. He was the first wind player to win the Ford Foundation Award for concert artists (1971–73), which enabled him to commission a trumpet concerto from Gunther Schuller, and commissioned a number of other trumpet works from composers including Dlugoszewski and Brant.

Meanwhile, he pursued a conducting career. In 1968 he began conducting for the Eliot Feld Dance Company, of which he became Music Director. He also was music director of the Waterloo Festival, and the Los Angeles Chamber Orchestra. In 1975 he was appointed music director of the 92d Street Y Chamber Symphony, which was later renamed the New York Chamber Symphony, and has maintained that position since. He became music director of New York's Mostly Mozart Festival in 1982. In 1981 he founded the Music Today contemporary music series in New York, serving as its music director through 1989.

In 1983 he was named Music Advisor of the Seattle Symphony Orchestra. In 1984 he became its Principal Conductor, and in 1985 its Music Director. With the Seattle Symphony he has become known for having one of the most innovative and wide-ranging programming of any major symphony orchestra, with a strong emphasis on music of the great American symphonic composers such as Hanson, Diamond, Creston, Copland, and their contemporaries, a large amount of which he has recorded. He has guided the orchestra to its highest artistic level, and seen it through construction and occupancy of its new venue, Benaroya Hall. He is also artistic adviser of the Tokyo Bunkamura's Orchard Hall, where he conducts the Tokyo Philharmonic in six concerts annually.*—Joseph Stevenson*

Recommended:

- ○ **Hanson: Symphony 4; Suite from Merry Mount; Lament for Beowulf** / Schwarz (cond.), Sparks, Jolles, Mendenhall, Seattle SO, NY Chamber Symphony / 1994 / Delos 3105
- ○ **Hovhaness: Mysterious Mountains** / Schwarz (cond.), Royal Liverpool Phil. / 2003 / Telarc 80604
- ○ **Piston: Symphonies 2 & 6; Sinfonietta** / Schwarz (cond.), Seattle SO, NY Chamber Symphony / 1990 / Delos 3074
- ○ **Hovhaness Treasures** / Schwarz, Hovhaness (conds.), Goff, Fujihara, Carrington, Johnson, Northwest SO / Crystal 811
- ○ **Cornet Favorites** / Schwarz, Cooper, Barron, Bolcom / 1987 / Nonesuch 79157

Elisabeth Schwarzkopf

b. Dec. 9, 1915, Jarotschin, near Posen, Germany

Soprano

The daughter of a teacher, Elisabeth Schwarzkopf began to study voice in 1934 at the Berliner Musikhochschule with Lula Mysz-Gmeiner and with Maria Ivogun. She also studied lieder interpretation with Michael Raucheisen, Ivogun's husband. In 1938, Schwarzkopf debuted in Berlin as a Flower Maid in *Parsifal.* She remained in Berlin until 1944 when she joined the Vienna State Opera making her debut as Zerbinetta in *Ariadne auf Naxos.* Her first international appearances were in 1947 at London with the Vienna State Opera on tour as Donna Elvira in *Don Giovanni* and Marzelline in *Fidelio.* She became a regular guest at Covent Garden. That same year she made her debut at the Salzburg Festival and she appeared there nearly every year until 1964. At Salzburg she was best known for her Mozart roles of Donna Elvira, Countess in *Le nozze di Figaro* and Fiordiligi in *Così fan tutte,* but also had great success as Alice Ford in *Falstaff* and the Marschallin in *Der Rosenkavalier.* Her recitals with Gerald Moore as accompanist at Salzburg were always highly regarded, but in 1953 the great conductor Wilhelm Furtwängler accompanied her in an all Wolf recital. Her Teatro alla Scala debut in 1949 as the Countess in *Le nozze di Figaro* was a great success and she sang there until 1964 in a variety of roles including Melisande, *Carmina burana, Catulli Carmina,* and *Il Trionfo* of Orff, Elisabeth in *Tannhäuser,* Elsa in *Lohengrin,* Anne in *The Rake's Progress,* Iole in Handel's *Hercules,* as well as her Mozart and Strauss roles. She made her San Francisco Opera debut in 1955, but did not sing at the Metropolitan Opera until 1964. Her belated debut there is attributed to her ties to the National Socialist regime in Germany and Austria.

As great as her reputation as an opera singer was, her work on the recital and concert stage had even higher acclaim. Her fame as a recitalist was matched only by that of Dietrich Fischer-Dieskau. Her appearances were eagerly awaited around the world. In particular, her interpretations of the songs of Schubert, Strauss, and Wolf were admired. She is one of the few singers who was able to fulfill all of the requirements of an evening devoted to the songs of Wolf. On the concert stage she was often heard in cantatas and Passions of Bach, as well as the Verdi *Requiem* and symphonies of Mahler.

The voice of Elisabeth Schwarzkopf in her very early career was a light high soprano with excellent control of fioritura and breath control. As she matured, the middle and lower registers became much stronger and she began to sing more dramatic scores while giving up the lighter roles. By the late 1950s, she concentrated her operatic appearances on five or six roles to which she devoted great energy developing her interpretations to their highest level. This attention to detail and constant probing for added interpretive depth is the reason some writers find her performances too mannered and studied. In the recording studio, where she would work for hours perfecting one phrase, she was aided by her husband, record producer Walter Legge, in finding the perfect vocal color and phrasing to illuminate each piece. Even her most vocal critics stand in awe of the hard work that she brought to bear on even the simplest of songs. It is as a Mozart, Strauss and Wolf interpreter that Elisabeth Schwarzkopf will always be remembered. *—Richard LeSueur*

Recommended:

- ○ **Strauss: 4 Last Songs** / Ackermann, Matacic (conds.), Schwarzkopf, Berry, Felbermayer, Metternich, London PO / 2004 / EMI 85825
- ○ **Wolf: Italienisches Liederbuch** / Fischer-Dieskau, Schwarzkopf, Moore / 2003 / EMI 62651
- ○ **Operetta Arias** / Ackermann (cond.), Schwarzkopf, Philharmonia Orchestra & Chorus / 1999 / Angel 67004
- ○ **Strauss: Der Rosenkavalier** / Karajan (cond.), Schwarzkopf, Ludwig, Gedda, Stich-Randall, London PO / 2001 / EMI 67609
- ○ **Mozart: Così fan tutte** / Böhm (cond.), Schwarzkopf, Ludwig, Kraus, Taddei, London PO / 2000 / Angel 67379

Albert Schweitzer

b. Jan. 14, 1875, Kayersberg, Upper Alsace, France, **d.** Sep. 4, 1965, Lambaréné, Gabon

Organist

Albert Schweitzer's towering reputation as a humanitarian and theologian has tended to overshadow his importance as organist and musicologist, especially in the study and performance of works by Johann Sebastian Bach. Schweitzer trained first as a musician and throughout his life contributed significantly to the body of critical works on Bach performance and the art of organ building. Even as he gave himself increasingly to humanitarian work in Africa, he continued to return to Europe to perform in concert.

Schweitzer's musical training began with piano lessons from his father and, later, private instruction from Eugen Münch, who introduced him to the works of Bach. During his six years at Strasbourg University, where his studies began in 1893, he pursued courses in philosophy and medicine while continuing to receive private instruction in music. In 1896, he traveled to Bayreuth where he became friends with Cosima Wagner and her then 17-year-old son, Siegfried. In 1900, Schweitzer became a Protestant curate at Saint Nikolai in Strasbourg where his responsibilities included delivering sermons and instructing confirmation classes. In 1902, he joined the University of Strasbourg as a lecturer on theology.

During this same period, Schweitzer traveled to Paris to study piano with Marie and Alfred Jaëll and to refine his organ technique in private lessons with Charles Marie Widor. He became the organist at the Société J.S. Bach in Paris, an organization he helped found. Finding contemporary organs unsuited to the performances of Bach's counterpoint, he also undertook a detailed study of organs and the art of organ building. All the while, he continued his work in medicine preparatory to his establishing a hospital in Africa.

Even while visiting equatorial Africa, and heavily engaged in the first stages of his new work as a medical missionary, Schweitzer's musical interests scarcely waned. There, he wrote his *J.S. Bach, le musicien-poète,* published first in Paris (1905) and later in Leipzig in an expanded German edition. British critic and writer Ernest Newman translated the latter into English, thereby introducing musicians in Britain and the United States to Schweitzer's important work as a musicologist. In 1909, Schweitzer assisted in drafting the *Internationales Regulativ für den Orgelbau* for a conference of the IMS. This document led to the publication of the *Orgelbewegung,* a text reflecting much of what Schweitzer had come to believe about organ construction and performance. An English language critical edition of Bach's organ works was Schweitzer's final important contribution to musicology.

Schweitzer had determined some years earlier that from the age of 30, he would dedicate himself to the service of humanity on a direct scale. To this end, he gave up his post as a cleric, finished his medical degree and, after some additional work in Paris in the specialty of tropical medicine, gathered funds to establish a modest hospital in Lambarené. Throughout the rest of his life, Schweitzer served that facility, save for periods of closure due to such exigencies as World War I, which put operations on hold for several years.

Despite unceasing commitment to his work in Africa, Schweitzer continued to spend time in Europe, presenting organ recitals and accepting engagements as a lecturer. Walter Legge, EMI producer, recorded three volumes of Bach organ works with Schweitzer, the second and third using the Silbermann instrument at Sainte Aurelie in Strasbourg, an organ whose restoration the organist himself had supervised.

For his humanitarian efforts, Schweitzer was awarded the Nobel Prize in 1952. *—Erik Eriksson*

Recommended:

- ○ **Albert Schweitzer plays Bach Vol.1** / Schweitzer / Pearl 9959

Scottish Chamber Orchestra

f. 1974, Scotland

Ensemble

The Scottish Chamber Orchestra was founded in 1974; it consists of 38 regular players, though its number can vary according to a given work's instrumental demands. The ensemble gives a regular series of concerts in Edinburgh, Glasgow, Aberdeen, St. Andrews, Dumfries, Perth and other Scottish cities, but does not claim any one location as its home. It also give regular concerts throughout the Scottish Highlands and Islands, as well as abroad, in Europe, Asia, and the U.S.

As of 2001, the orchestra's principal conductor was Joseph Swenson, who succeeded Jukka-Pekka Saraste. Serving as conductor laureate is Sir Charles Mackerras, who has made a number of highly successful recordings with the orchestra including the Brahms symphonies and five Mozart operas; the ensemble's greatest successes have come under Mackerras' baton, at least in the recording venue.

The repertory of the orchestra is quite varied, encompassing the works of Mozart and Haydn, as well as of Prokofiev and Peter Maxwell Davies. Indeed the orchestra has commissioned a number of works from the latter composer, including 10 so-called *Strathclyde Concertos.*

Conductors who have led the orchestra include Emmanuel Krivine, Andrew Litton, Nicholas McGegan, Frans Brueggen, and Jaime Laredo. The instrumental makeup of the ensemble is as follows: seven first violins and five second; four violas, four cellos, and two double basses; two flutes and one piccolo; two oboes and one English horn; two clarinets and one bass clarinet; two bassoons and one contrabassoon; two horns; two trumpets; one timpani. The SCO has recorded for Telarc, ASV, Delos and other labels. *—Robert Cummings*

Recommended:

- ○ **Mozart: Piano Concertos 22 & 27** / Mackerras (cond.), Brendel, Scottish CO / 2001 / Philips 468367
- ○ **Brahms: Serenades** / Mackerras (cond.), Scottish CO / 1999 / Telarc 80522
- ○ **Field: Piano Concertos 2 & 3** / Mackerras (cond.), O'Conor, Scottish CO / 1994 / Telarc 80370

Scottish National Orchestra

f. 1950, Glasgow, Scotland
Ensemble

In the decades since its founding, the Scottish National Orchestra has earned a reputation as a distinguished ensemble with an extensive concert schedule, wide-ranging repertoire, and a significant representation on recordings. The SNO is the direct descendant of the Scottish Orchestra, founded in Glasgow in 1890; with the establishment of the Scottish National Orchestra Society in 1950 with monies from Glasgow, Aberdeen, Edinburgh, and Dundee, the SNO became a permanent ensemble. Throughout its first 40 years, the Scottish Orchestra had no permanent principal conductor, instead relying on a series of eminent guest conductors. In 1933, John Barbirolli assumed the post of principal conductor; since that time, the orchestra has been helmed by George Szell, Warwick Braithwaite, Walter Susskind, Karl Rankl, Hans Swarowsky, Alexander Gibson (the first Scot to lead the ensemble), Neeme Järvi, Bryden Thomson, Walter Weller, and, from 1997, Alexander Lazarev.

Throughout its early years, the orchestra played its Glasgow concerts in the acoustically wonderful St. Andrew's Hall. From the time the hall was destroyed by fire in 1962, the SNO played in a series of venues of varying suitability. Finally in 1979, redesign of the Trinity Church on Claremont Street gave the SNO a permanent home of its own: the SNO Center and Sir Henry Wood Hall.

Highlights in the orchestra's history include the introduction of the Promenade concerts, under Rankl; the establishment of its longstanding partnership with the Scottish Opera, its expansion to 96 (later reduced to 89) full-time players, its first international tour (1967), and its first American tour (1975), under Gibson; and the granting of the title "Royal Scottish National Orchestra" by Queen Elizabeth II during Thomson's tenure. While the orchestra boasts a wide-ranging repertory, it has been singled out for its recordings of Bruckner, Barber, and twentieth century British composers like Bax, MacMillan, and Holst; it has also earned a particular reputation for recorded performances of film scores like *Vertigo, Titanic, Superman,* and *Star Wars: The Phantom Menace. —AMG*

Recommended:

- ○ **Elgar: Symphony 2; Crown of India Suite** / Gibson (cond.), Scottish National Orch. / 1991 / Chandos 6523
- ○ **Sibelius: Finlandia, etc.** / Gibson (cond.), Scottish National Orch. / 1990 / Chandos 6508
- ○ **Dvořák: Symphony 1; Hero's Song** / Järvi (cond.), Scottish National Orch. / 1988 / Chandos 8597
- ○ **Shostakovich: Ballet Suites** / Järvi (cond.), Scottish National Orch. / 2003 / Chandos 10088
- ○ **Dvořák: Symphony 6; Noon Witch** / Järvi (cond.), Scottish National Orch. / 1987 / Chandos 8530

Renata Scotto

b. Feb. 24, 1934, Savona, Italy
Soprano

Renata Scotto's long and successful operatic career was marked by a rare combination of dramatic intensity and vocal flexibility, which allowed her to traverse a wide variety of styles. She believed strongly in the theatrical elements of performing and always focused her energies on the meaning of a text. She also felt much of the standard verismo performing tradition to be exaggerated and vulgar, and strove to keep her performances as close to the composer's marked intentions as possible, especially with respect to subtleties of dynamics. Many speak of her as "the last of the divas."

She began vocal studies when she was fourteen, and moved to Milan when she was 16. In 1952, when she was just 19, she made her debut as Violetta (*La traviata*) at the Teatro Nuovo, followed by her La Scala debut as Walter in *La Wally.* However, only a few years later she had a vocal crisis, losing most of her upper range; she now credits her recovery to Alfredo Kraus (himself renowned for a solid technique and vocal longevity), who introducing her to his teacher, Mercedes Llopart. After completely restudying her technique, she re-began her career as a coloratura, making her London debut at the Stoll Theater as Adina in *L'elisir d'amore.* She returned to La Scala, and in 1957, replaced Maria Callas (whom she had greatly admired) as Amina in *La Sonnambula.*

In 1960, she debuted at the Chicago Opera as Mimi (*La Bohème*), followed by her Covent Garden debut in 1962 as Puccini's Cio-Cio san (*Madama Butterfly*). Her Metropolitan Opera debut was in 1965 was also as Butterfly; during the next two decades, Scotto was one of their major stars, appearing in several telecasts.

She began to add the heavier roles to her repertoire again, including Verdi's Lady Macbeth, which was to become a signature role, as well as verismo parts such as *Fedora, La Gioconda,* Francesca in Zandonai's *Paolo* and Maddalena in *Andrea Chénier.* In all of these roles she was applauded for her committed acting and stylistic fluency.

While no recording can fully recreate the impressions of a stage performance, her first recording of *Madama Butterfly,* under John Barbirolli, is one of her most vivid. *—Ann Feeney*

Recommended:

- ○ **Very Best of Renata Scotto** / Scotto, etc. / 2003 / EMI 85108
- ○ **Italian Opera Arias** / Barbirolli, Wolf-Ferrari (cond.), Scotto, London PO, Orchestra del Teatro Municipa / 2001 / EMI 74766
- ○ **Italian Opera Arias** / Scotto, etc. / 1998 / Sony 60524
- ○ **Verdi: Otello** / Levine (cond.), Domingo, McCarthy, Scotto, Milnes / 1998 / RCA 7432139501

Alexander Scriabin

b. Jan. 6, 1872, Moscow, Russia, **d.** Apr. 27, 1915, Moscow, Russia
Composer: Keyboard, Symphonic, Concerto

Mystic, visionary, virtuoso, and composer, Scriabin dedicated his life to creating musical works which would, as he believed, open the portals of the spiritual world. Scriabin took piano lessons as a child, joining, in 1884, Nikolay Zverov's class, where Rachmaninov was a fellow student. From 1888 to 1892, Scriabin studied at the Moscow Conservatory, where his teachers included Arensky, Taneyev, and Safonov. Although Scriabin's hand could not easily stretch beyond an octave, he developed into a prodigious pianist, launching an international concert career in 1894. Scriabin started composing during his Conservatory years. Mostly inspired by Chopin, his early works include nocturnes, mazurkas, preludes, and etudes for piano. Typical examples of Romantic music for the piano, these works nevertheless reveal the composer's strong individuality. Toward the end of the century, Scriabin started writing orchestral works, earning a solid reputation as a composer, and obtaining a professorship at the Moscow Conservatory in 1898. In 1903, however, Scriabin abandoned his wife and their four children and embarked on a European journey with a young admirer, Tatyana Schloezer. During his sojourn in Western Europe, which lasted six years, Scriabin started developing an original, highly personal musical idiom, experimenting with new harmonic structures and searching for new sonorities. Among the works composed during this time was the *Divine Poem.*

In 1905, Scriabin discovered the theosophical teachings of Helena Petrovna Blavatsky, which became the intellectual foundation of his musical and philosophical efforts. In true Romantic tradition, he sought to situate his work as a composer in the wider spiritual and intellectual context of his age. Previously influenced by Nietzsche's ideas about the advent of a superhuman being, Scriabin embraced theosophy as an intellectual framework for his profound feelings about humankind's quest for God. Works from this period, exemplified by the *Poem of Ecstasy* (1908) and *Prometheus* (1910), reflect Scriabin's conception of music as a bridge to mystical ecstasy. While the ideas underlying his works may seem far-fetched, Scriabin's musical language included some fascinating, and very tangible, innovations, such as chords based on fourths and unexpected chromatic effects. Lacking an inner forward-moving force, Scriabin's later works nevertheless fascinate the listener by harmonic transformations which aim to reflect certain undefinable aspects of human consciousness. In addition, the composer, who strongly believed in the synaesthetic nature of art, experimented with sounds and colors, indicating, for example, lighting specification for the performance of particular works. Indeed, Scriabin's interest in color was hardly academic, considering that , as an orchestrator, he exploited the full potential of orchestral color. While Scriabin never quite crossed the threshold to atonality, his music nevertheless replaced the traditional concept of tonality by an intricate system of chords, some of which (e.g. the "mystic chord": C-F sharp-B flat-E-A-D) had an esoteric meaning. Scriabin's gradual move into realms beyond traditional tonality can be clearly heard in his ten piano sonatas; the last five, composed during 1912–13, are without key signatures and certainly contain atonal moments. In 1915, Scriabin died in of septicemia caused by a carbuncle on his lip. Among his unfinished project was *Mysterium,* a grandiose religious synthesis of all arts which would herald the birth of a new world. *—Zoran Minderovic*

KEYBOARD

Etude in C sharp minor, Op. 2/1 (1886–1889)

This étude was the first of the *Three Pieces* from Op. 2 that are generally dated to the period between 1887–89. Scriabin was 15 years old when he wrote this étude in 1887, a time when he was already an admirer of Chopin and Liszt. The influence of the former can be heard in the harmonies and emotional tenor of the piece, but the main theme is more akin to the singing melodic creations Rachmaninov would be writing in a few years. Yet the melody divulges characteristics of Russian Gypsy music in its melancholy exoticism. This melody is really at the heart of this popular piece, one of Scriabin's earliest successes. It has an archlike contour, soaring upward in its first half, but only partially descending. Emotionally, the music is full of passion and romance, but features a sense of anxiety, too, in the end conveying some sadness or frustration in lovely simplicity. The piece lasts about three minutes and will offer appeal to most fanciers of piano music. *—Robert Cummings*

Recommended:

- ○ **Vladimir Horowitz: The Indispensable** / Horowitz / 1999 / BMG 7432163471
- ○ **Scriabin: The Complete Etudes** / Lane / Hyperion 66607

Twelve Etudes, Op. 8 (1894)

As one might surmise from the low opus number, this is early Scriabin and thus somewhat stylistically derivative. Yet while it divulges unmistakable echoes of Chopin and Liszt, it also reveals a good measure of sophistication and growing mastery of keyboard writing, pointing the way toward the later individualism of the composer. The *Etude No. 1 in C sharp minor*, with its nervously caressing thirds, is decidedly Chopin-esque, but also exhibits that quirky flow so typical of Scriabin, even in some early pieces. The *Second*, in F sharp minor, brims with passion and mystery, mixing Chopin with a kind of Rachmaninovian agitation in its cross rhythms. The *Etude No. 3 in B minor* has the same kind of tempestuous character, but challenges the soloist with a speedy mixture of octaves and single notes. *No. 4*, in B major, is relatively tranquil in its brightness and sweet nostalgia. The ensuing *Etude in E major* is more challenging than it sounds, moving consistently in and out of various octave ranges, while turning more intense as the piece progresses. The *Sixth*, in A major, is graceful and charming in its mostly upper-register sonorities and challenging sixths. The *Seventh*, in B flat minor, is full of colorful energy and virtuosic hurdles for the soloist in its Presto outer sections. *No. 8*, in A flat major, is a lovely Lento whose gentle melancholy has a characteristically Scriabin-esque broken flow to its Romantic utterances. The *Etude No. 9 in G sharp minor*, at about five minutes, is the longest and most powerful piece in the set. Octaves abound in the furor, with Liszt coming to mind in the outer sections, both in the virtuosic writing and in the sinister but dazzling nature of the music. There is a charming, mostly subdued middle section, offering imaginative contrast. The D flat major *Tenth* mixes staccato and legato writing in quirky, playful music. *No. 11*, in B flat minor, is sad in its elegance and subdued manner. The closing *Etude in D sharp minor*, lasting about four minutes, is another long effort and features a powerful sense of yearning, as if expressing some dire frustration or failure. This is probably the most famous etude in the set. *—Robert Cummings*

Recommended:

- ○ **The Great Pianists: Sviatoslav Richter 3** / Richter / 1999 / Philips 456952
- ○ **Scriabin & Glazunov: Piano Works** / Kuerti / Analekta 3044

Eight Etudes, Op. 42 (1903)

Of the 74 opus numbers in Scriabin's catalog, 13 date to 1903, probably his most productive year in keyboard composition. Not only was it a fertile period, but it also marked the appearance of his first truly mature piano works, following a two-year stretch during which the composer had mostly focused on orchestral music (*Symphony No. 2* and *No. 3*). The *Etudes*, Op. 42, are among his most rewarding piano works—works whose nascent modernity point toward the mystical and often weird compositional ideas of his final years. The music here is still post-Romantic, but sounds overripe, pushing out toward new horizons, harmonically, rhythmically, and thematically. The opening etude in D flat major has a Chopin-esque spirit but a Scriabin-esque sound. Triplets swirl and rhythms perplex as cascades of notes spin out a carefree web of light fabric and brilliant colors. The ensuing F sharp minor etude, at about a minute in duration, is one of the set's shortest entries. It is playful in its quirky melody and hushed in its brief middle section, the whole leaving a sense of capriciousness. *No. 3*, in F sharp major, is also brief, but its quivering, twittering radiance seems perfectly matched to the piece's nickname of "Mosquito." The *Etude No. 4 in F sharp major* features a lovely theme whose Romantic manner sounds a bit perfumed, as if to conceal inner decay. The piece is typical of Scriabin, reaching out beyond an expressive language not quite suited to the music. *No. 5*, in C sharp minor, has a sinister character to its roiling bass, but a sense of passion to its agitated main theme. The alternate theme is lovely and contrasts well in its more-tempered Romanticism. The *Sixth*, in D flat major, is tentative in its uncertain gait, passionate but restrained in its sudden Romantic blossomings, and intense with yearning as it confronts the soloist with challenging wide stretches and tricky rhythmic hurdles. The *Etude No. 7 in F minor*, another one-minute affair, is bright and quirky, full of sunshine, but sunshine on a misty, cool day. The closing E flat major etude features a playful nervousness in its outer sections with a start-and-stop manner in its hyperactive accompaniment. The odd, stately middle section features big chords of ambivalent emotional expression, which sound like a sobering response to Rachmaninov's sweet gloom. The whole set lasts about 16 or 17 minutes in performance. *—Robert Cummings*

Recommended:

- ○ **Scriabin: The Complete Etudes** / Lane / Hyperion 66607
- ○ **Scriabin, Myaskovsky & Prokofiev: Piano Works** / Richter / 1995 / Melodiya 29470

Fantaisie in B minor, Op. 28 (1900)

While many correctly think of Scriabin as a composer whose mature piano music reflected his mysticism and quirkiness, and whose early keyboard efforts divulged a debt to Chopin and Liszt, he also exhibited many other, sometimes elusive qualities in his compositions. In a sense, this *Fantasie*, Op. 28, is a transitional work that divulges traits not usually associated with Scriabin. It adopts a muscular manner somewhat at odds with the composer's more nuanced and subdued mature style and, being a middle-period work, divulges no obvious influence. This *Fantasie* is an immensely difficult piece, requiring fast passage work, hands that can play massive chords with heft, and a technical and interpretive grasp of keyboard coloration. Featuring big Romantic themes and rich harmonies, the work conveys a sense of spontaneity in its seemingly loose structure. Yet it is cast in a sonata-like form, with an exposition, thematic development, and reprise. The potent middle section is full of passion and explodes in climactic moments of triumph and epiphany. The reprise of the second theme is lovely and the whole piece is sprayed with powerful emotions and vivid colors. Lasting about ten minutes, most listeners, even those generally cool to Scriabin, should find this dramatic work to their liking. *—Robert Cummings*

Recommended:

- ○ **Scriabin: The Complete Piano Sonatas** / Hamelin / 1996 / Hyperion 67131
- ○ **Scriabin, Prokofiev & Shostakovich** / Richter / 1994 / Philips 438627

Ten Mazurkas, Op. 3 (1889)

These *Ten Mazurkas* are early works and thus show relatively little of the advanced compositional features that began to appear in Scriabin's piano output around the beginning of the twentieth century. Still, while they exhibit the influence of Chopin and Schumann, these *Mazurkas* divulge the composer's burgeoning musical persona, his characteristic sense of improvisation, and of quirkiness in the flow of the main line. Most are short, lasting about two or three minutes each, with the exception of the six- or seven-minute *No. 10*.

The perky but elegant *Mazurka in B minor No. 1*, marked Tempo giusto, with its stately, grand central section, exhibits that quirky but charming Scriabin-esque melodic flow. *No. 2* (Allegretto non tanto), in F sharp minor, is rife with modulations in its ebullience and charm. The ensuing *Mazurka in G minor* (Allegretto) is a melancholy, stormy piece that clearly betrays the influence of Chopin. The E major *No. 4* (Moderato) seems to serenely float along one moment, then turn jaunty and playful, if not oafish, the next.

No. 5 (Doloroso), in D sharp minor, is also melancholy and one of the more rewarding offerings in the set. It is Schumann-esque and thematically richer than most of its siblings here, reaching a considerable expressive depth in its generally meditative moods. The C sharp minor *No. 6* (Scherzando) is, as its marking indicates, a Scherzo, brilliant and playful in its outer sections—calling to mind Liszt—and relatively subdued in its middle panel. The ensuing mazurka (Con passione), in E minor, lives up to the spirit of its marking, with a strong sense of passion and yearning (or is it regret?) in its mostly descending melodic lines.

No. 8 (Con moto), in B flat minor, is elegant and Chopin-esque, and as it progresses, the sense of nostalgia grows, the hints of Chopin turning up in almost every phrase. *No. 9*, in G sharp minor, bears no tempo marking but is generally played at a moderate pacing. Its mood is melancholy, but often shifts to an agitated expressive manner. The final mazurka (Sotto voce), in the highly unusual key of E flat minor, is, as mentioned above, the longest. It is also the most complex, mixing a sense of the playful and melancholy, and exhibiting snatches of the young composer's later, more individual style, especially in the middle section. *—Robert Cummings*

Recommended:

- ○ **Konstantin Liefschitz: Debut Recording** / Lifschitz / Denon 78907
- ○ **Scriabin: Complete Piano Music (Excluding Sonatas)** / Ponti / 2002 / Vox 3606

Two Mazurkas, Op. 40 (1903)

These *Two Mazurkas* were written during a prolific period in Scriabin's career, a time when he turned out five sets of preludes (containing 19 pieces altogether), a collection of *Eight Etudes*, Op. 43, and numerous other piano pieces. Yet for the most part, the pair divulge little of that typically tortured and dark side of the composer, an area often explored in his other piano works from this period. Nor do they exhibit any substantial debt to Chopin, at least as heard in his famous mazurkas. The first of the two Op. 40 mazurkas, in D flat major and marked Allegro, has a carefree manner and conveys that quirky sense so typical of Scriabin after the turn of the century. The main theme does have a Chopin-esque quality in its graceful lightness, but is pure Scriabin in its hesitant gait and imaginative harmonies, harmonies that sometimes suggest a disturbance beneath a seemingly peaceful veneer. Some tension does emerge midway through as the theme develops, but the outer sections are quite light and cheerful. The piece lasts about a minute-and-a-half. The second mazurka is in F sharp major and carries the marking Piacevole (pleasing). Its character is similar to that of its sibling here, opening in a carefree mood, the theme graceful and full of sunshine. There is little suggestion of disturbance from the harmonies, though the music remains chipper and light throughout. The work is marginally shorter than the D flat major, lasting about a minute-and-a-quarter. Both mazurkas can fairly be judged as minor masterpieces. *—Robert Cummings*

Recommended:

- ○ **Alexander Skriabin: Mazurkas** / Deyanova / 1995 / Nimbus 5446
- ○ **Scriabin: Complete Piano Music (Excluding Sonatas)** / Ponti / 2002 / Vox 3606

Piano Sonata No. 2 in G sharp minor ("Sonata-Fantasy"), Op. 19 (1892–1897)

The final compositions of Alexander Scriabin's spectacular but relatively brief career stand at the gates of true atonality, and are representatives of a unique musical world in which traditional harmony is subjected to the more overpoweringly personal effects of an ever-deepening mystical and theosophical outlook. During the concert tour-filled 1890s, however, all these controversial things were still just shadows lurking in the corner, and such works as the *Sonata No. 2 in G sharp minor for piano,* Op. 19 continue to represent the tradition of piano music as handed down to Scriabin from Chopin and Liszt. This Sonata has always been among those works of Scriabin's most warmly received by audiences, and it is indeed a spectacularly expressive work in the hands of an insightful pianist. Scriabin was somewhat uncomfortable with calling this two-movement (slow-fast) work a sonata, and so, for a time, he let it pass as a "Sonata-Fantasy." The piece was completed during a five-month stay in Paris during 1897, but sketches date to 1892, when the composer was 20 years of age. Scriabin provided an oceanic program for the work, condensed as follows: the first section of the Andante is a calm southern night on the seashore, the movement of the deep sea is given in the development, while an illuminating E major passage offers the first rays of moonlight. The agitated Presto movement is a rendition of a terrifying ocean storm. Certainly the gently rolling arpeggiations of the Andante, and especially the deeply sonorous B major end of the exposition, call to mind something almost impossibly deep and stable—a stability soon undercut, however, by the fragmented phrases and harmonic conflicts of the development. The "moonlight" is given a treatment in the instrument's glistening upper register, occasionally recalling the same deep arpeggiations of the opening (and in doing so calling to mind Debussy's famous "moonlight" piano work *Clair de lune*); Scriabin feels no need to force his Andante into a conventional harmonic mode, and the movement ends without ever regaining the darkness of G sharp minor. The almost perpetual motion of the Presto, and its occasional outbursts of real fear, are poured back into an exuberant G sharp minor sonata allegro design. How welcome is that glowing moment before the recapitulation, when Scriabin allows us to glimpse the lyric sub-theme in D flat major, after more tragic appeals in E flat minor and B flat minor! *—Blair Johnston*

Recommended:

- ○ **Skryabin: Piano Music** / Ogdon / 1998 / Angel 72652
- ○ **Sviatoslav Richter à Prague** / Richter / Praga 356020-34

Piano Sonata No. 3 in F sharp minor ("Etats d'âme"), Op. 23 (1897)

Alexander Scriabin began composing his *Third Piano Sonata* in 1897, immediately upon completing his Second. Like that work, the Third shows only vague signs of the remarkable atonal revolution that Scriabin will, quite independently of Schoenberg or any other composer, carry out in his music during the years just prior to World War I. The *Sonata No. 3 in F sharp minor,* Op. 23 was completed in just a few months (as opposed to the nearly five years it took to finish the *Second Sonata*). Throughout this 20-minute piece, Scriabin continues to assert his own individuality over the Chopin-Liszt tradition which heavily influenced his earliest works. Although even his earliest compositions contain an ecstatic rapture entirely his own, the Third Sonata is perhaps the first truly Scriabin-esque musical statement, wholly deserving of its special little niche in the repertories of the world's pianists. Scriabin gave the Sonata several titles at various times, including "Gothic" and, from a much later period, "États d'âme (States of the Soul)," the latter an effort on the composer's part to reconcile the work with his growing interest in mystical and theosophical traditions. Happily, the programmatic outlines Scriabin indicated—from the suffering of the first movement through the respite of the second and deep feeling of the third to the final plunge into nothingness in the finale—are sufficiently vague to allow the piece to be heard as a purely musical statement. After the declamatory opening gestures of the Drammatico movement, Scriabin moves us into a soundworld richly adorned with his own unique brand of evanescent figurations and sweeping, ravishing melody. The opening statements also serve to close the movement, suitably transformed into fragments of a more tender variety. The following Allegretto is in the manner of an intermezzo—here a bass line in octaves moves around in E flat major before a central section which radiates with the gentlest simplicity. The third and fourth movements (Andante and Presto con fuoco) are fused together by a brief connecting passage that recalls the opening movement. Scriabin sings one of the most purely gorgeous melodies he had yet written (or, indeed, would ever write) in the Andante, while the Presto sets fiery chromatic gestures against nostalgic lyric passages. A triumphant restatement of the Andante's melody is made, but Scriabin pulls the rug out from under our feet and throws us back into the tumult of F sharp minor for the finish.*—Blair Johnston*

Recommended:

- ○ **Horowitz Plays Scriabin** / Horowitz / 1989 / RCA 6215
- ○ **Emil Gilels: The Giant** / Gilels / 2000 / RCA 75523
- ○ **The Great Pianists: Vladimir Sofronitsky** / Sofronitsky / 1999 / Philips 456970

Piano Sonata No. 4 in F sharp major, Op. 30 (1903)

The extramusical religious ideas which became an increasing obsession in Scriabin's last years have tended to overshadow the the composer's music and even to alienate more than a few listeners. The *Fourth Piano Sonata* was written at a time of transition for Scriabin: Musically, he was moving ever closer toward real atonality, while his personal life was marked by the deepening complexity of his theophilosophical ponderings.

The *Fourth Sonata* is divided into two closely related movements, both cast in the warm, radiant key of F sharp major. While still making use of tonal structures, Scriabin was also in the process of developing new forms into which those structures could be placed. The sonata's first movement (Andante) is built from two major motives, one reaching upward hopefully with many melodic leaps, the other moving more linearly, as though exhausted. The earlier idea eventually prevails, and the second movement (Prestissimo volande) begins without interruption. In this active movement, cast in sonata-allegro form, the upward reaching theme reappears, now with greater force and in a more tumultuous context. This gives way to the return of the movement's first theme (now abridged) and second theme (now expanded). In a glorious coda, the upward-reaching motive of the first movement reasserts itself one last time, sans the corresponding "exhaustion" motive, and the sonata ends in a truly joyful mood. *—Blair Johnston*

Recommended:

- ○ **Scriabin: 24 Preludes; Sonatas 4 & 10** / Pletnev / 1997 / Virgin 45247
- ○ **Scriabin: The Piano Sonatas** / Ashkenazy / 1997 / London 452961
- ○ **The Great Pianists: Vladimir Sofronitsky** / Sofronitsky / 1999 / Philips 456970
- ○ **Scriabin: Complete Sonatas** / Ponti / 2002 / Vox 5184

Piano Sonata No. 5 in F sharp major ("The Poem of Ecstasy"), Op. 53 (1907)

Given the general outlook of the late nineteenth century Russian musical world into which Alexander Scriabin was born, and especially the pianistic outlook inherited from the legendary Anton Rubinstein, it is not surprising that in Scriabin's very first compositions the influence of Chopin and Liszt seems more powerful than the composer's own voice. Even the first few piano sonatas, though of far greater individuality than his youthful works, still inhabit the harmonic and thematic world created by the two earlier composers. By the time of the *Fourth Sonata* in 1903, however, Scriabin was rapidly moving towards the eventual atonal revolution that he would, completely independently from Arnold Schoenberg or any other composer, carry out on his music in the years before World War I. Four years later, the *Piano Sonata No. 5,* Op. 53, by eschewing any traditional constraints of a central tonal area (the work is often described as being in F sharp minor, but this is not really the case, at least not without redefining what is meant by such a specific term—one must not be misled by key signatures, which are there for the performer's benefit) and by pouring all the music into a single unique movement, takes a vital step in the direction of this personal upheaval. The *Fifth Sonata,* one of the most frequently played of the composer's works, owes a great deal to the orchestral *Poem of Ecstasy,* and for this reason the Sonata is occasionally given that same title. Both draw on a poem by written by Scriabin, of which four lines are affixed to the beginning of the Sonata (a passage which "calls to life" the artist's "hidden longings," an example of the composer's ever-increasing obsession with his own creative powers), and, while vastly different compositions, both represent the same feverish, concentrated musical world. A deep rumbling from the very bowels of the instrument "calls to life" this restless, 12-minute excursion into the most colorful of passionate realms. Delicate, evaporative harmonies built largely of fourths (rather than the more traditional thirds) ensue, wandering about apparently aimlessly but actually working their way to a heated but not violent outburst that does, for a time, seem to be pointing towards an F sharp tonal area. But B major is just as important to the work as its myriad episodes unfold, and the strongest cadential area (implied or otherwise) is the sustained pressure on E flat during the final portion of the piece. Just as we feel a final, well-earned resolution coming, however, Scriabin thrusts his virtuoso fieldwork up into the stratosphere, where it vanishes without a trace. *—Blair Johnston*

Recommended:

- ○ **Horowitz Plays Scriabin** / Horowitz / 1989 / RCA 6215
- ○ **Scriabin: The Piano Sonatas** / Ashkenazy / 1997 / London 452961
- ○ **Sviatoslav Richter à Prague** / Richter / Praga 356020-34

Piano Sonata No. 7 in F sharp major ("White Mass"), Op. 64 (1911–1912)

Intimidated by the giant shadows cast by Beethoven and Schubert, composers in the succeeding generations of the nineteenth century were reluctant to write piano sonatas. Such keyboard masters as Schumann, Chopin, Brahms, and Liszt did not collectively produce ten. In the twentieth century, the piano sonata largely recovered on the strength of Scriabin and Prokofiev. Of Scriabin's ten numbered sonatas, the second through fifth are his most popular. Less widely performed, the *Seventh,* an imaginatively crafted work, enjoys the reputation of a rewarding work and was his own favorite. Like all of the sonatas after the 1903 *Fourth,* it is cast in a single movement. This work has been called "the world's first 12-tone composition." Serial it is not, but it is on the threshold of serialism and sounds like it. It is typical of the music Scriabin was writing in his late period in its mystical and ethereal moods and advanced harmonies. The work, dubbed "White Mass" by the composer, imparts a weirdly ceremonial air, its music evoking bell-like sonorities as well as chant and a mystical sense relating to the composer's Eastern-influenced religious ideas. In approximate sonata form with three subjects, it is full of poetic directions in French that set the mood throughout, for example: *mystérieusement sonore* (mysteriously sonorous); *avec une sombre majesté* (with sombre majesty); *avec une céleste volupté* (with heavenly delight); *très pur, avec une profonde douceur* (very pure, with profound sweetness); *avec une volupté radieuse, extatique* (with radiant, ecstatic delight); *comme des èclairs* (like flashes of lightning); and finally, *avec une joie débordante* (brimming over with joy). The sonata nervously and violently opens, tolling chords first seeming to calm the roiling, only to spur later. Whenever the music settles to reasonable calm, it turns mystical, but soon flares up again with tension always hovering, even through playful swirls and cold trills. Midway through, just before the recapitulation, the music intensifies in a brutal, bizarre buildup with dissonance and percussive chords abounding. The mood soon shifts again to a more mystical manner, subsequently suggesting various, even extreme, moods, culminating in a fortissimo 25-note arpeggiated chord. Finally, the sonata ends in a peaceful, ethereal mist. This work typically has a duration of ten minutes. *—Robert Cummings*

Recommended:

- ○ **Scriabin: The Piano Sonatas** / Ashkenazy / 1997 / London 452961
- ○ **Russian Vitruoso Piano Music** / Pontinen / 1984 / Bis 276
- ○ **Scriabin: Complete Sonatas** / Ponti / 2002 / Vox 5184

Piano Sonata No. 9 ("Black Mass"), Op. 68 (1912–1913)

Given the general outlook of the late-nineteenth century Russian musical world into which Alexander Scriabin was born, and especially the Romantic pianistic outlook inherited from the legendary Anton Rubinstein, it is not surprising that Scriabin's earliest compositions are profoundly influenced by Chopin and Liszt. Even the first few piano sonatas, though of far greater individuality than his youthful works, still the harmonic and thematic world of Chopin and Liszt. By the time of the *Fourth* (1903) and *Fifth Sonatas* (1907), however, Scriabin was rapidly moving towards the eventual atonal revolution that he would, independently from Arnold Schoenberg or any other composer, carry out on his music in the years before World War I. With the so—called *"Black Mass" Sonata* of 1913 (the Sonata No. 9, Op. 68, occasionally, but inaccurately, said to be in F major), the journey is complete. The Sonata, whose colorful subtitle is the composer's own, is a masterwork of bleak despair, a musical portrait of evil and spiritual decay whose violence and menacing harmonies are said to have shocked even the composer himself. With its antithesis, the *"White Mass" Sonata* of 1912, this work is the most infamous—if not necessarily the most frequently performed—work by Scriabin; it is a complex piece that both his champions and detractors cite evidence for their opposite views. After the *Fifth Sonata* Scriabin cast all his works in the genre into single-movement molds, and the last five (all composed over a remarkable two year span) can be heard as separate portions of one larger musical entity. Among their common features is a mutual reliance on Scriabin's much-discussed "Mystic" chord, a chromatic harmony built on the basic tones C, F sharp, B flat, E, A, and D, but rarely presented in that basic form. The *"Black Mass" Sonata* opens with a grimacing web of thin harmonies that seem to point to some not-so-distant explosion of grief; a sepulchral repeated-note gesture punctuates the otherwise lugubrious texture. A delicate second theme, more clearly drawn than is the composer's norm during these final years, appears, like a haunted vision of redemption, marked "avec une langueur naissante" (increasingly langorous). Nowhere is there any reprieve from the unbelievable harmonic tension, and, after outbursts of grim despair, the reprise of the opening bars achieves a final and utter desolation, locked in by a single low F natural. *—Blair Johnston*

Recommended:

- ○ **Scriabin: The Piano Sonatas** / Ashkenazy / 1997 / London 452961
- ○ **Scriabin: The Complete Piano Sonatas** / Hamelin / 1996 / Hyperion 67131
- ○ **Scriabin: Piano Music** / Ogdon / 1998 / EMI 72652

Piano Sonata No. 10 ("Trill"), Op. 70 (1912–1913)

Alexander Scriabin's *Tenth Sonata*, occasionally but inaccurately described as being in C major, when compared to the bleak spiritual decay and anguished harmonies of the *Ninth Sonata* (the so-called "Black Mass" whose complete desolation shocked even the composer), is an essay of brilliant, radiant light. Scriabin himself described it as a "Sonata of insects... born from the sun; they are the sun's kisses." For many years the composer had been moving further and further away from the Chopin/Liszt heritage into which he had, due to his mother's own pianistic training, been born (to be fair, Scriabin's music had always been filled with an ecstatic rapture entirely his own). With the Fourth and Fifth Sonatas he approached the gates of atonality and total thematic fragmentation, and by the time of the final five sonatas, all composed over a span of two years from 1911 to 1913, the journey was complete. The *Tenth Sonata* is not among the composer's most frequently played works, lacking either the immediate, lush appeal of his earlier compositions or the pseudo-programmatic appeal of his later ones (which are often either given poetic titles, like the "Black Mass," or are themselves musical poems, as in the case of the last orchestral works), and yet it is one of the composer's best. After a gentle, initially unaccompanied, set of melodic gestures (immediately repeated against a sonorous bass and then developed for a while) that feature the important interval of the falling third, Scriabin opens the cage in which the insects are confined: soon the music is buzzing with trills from all around—it is to this feature that the work owes its popular subtitle "Trill." Although, like all of Scriabin's later sonatas, the work is cast in a single highly individual movement, we can still see the vague shadows of traditional sonata-allegro design (or perhaps the shadows of the basic, very logical principles around which that form originally developed). Three larger sections fill roles that are essentially those of presentation, departure, and return (or exposition, development, and recapitulation). During the middle portion, the feverish buzzing rises to a climax that thrusts both hands' trills into the upper register of the instrument. The very first, single-line gesture of the piece is not given again until after the richly-varied "recapitulation" has been made; it arrives quite unexpectedly, and is punctuated by a falling fourth in the bass that ends on C natural—a pitch that, in his last music, assumes great significance for Scriabin, who came to view it as a kind of cleansing tonal focus.*—Blair Johnston*

Recommended:

- ○ **Scriabin: The Piano Sonatas** / Ashkenazy / 1997 / London 452961
- ○ **Scriabin: 24 Preludes; Sonatas 4 & 10** / Pletnev / 1997 / Virgin 45247

Three Pieces, Op. 2 (1886–1889)

Obviously this is an early effort by Scriabin, but the Op. 2 numbering is misleading: there are at least seven other works without opus numbers that preceded it, including an *E flat minor Sonata*. The composer was only 14 when he wrote the first of these pieces, the C sharp minor Etude, but it is surprisingly well crafted.

This work has a stately quality in its ascending sad theme. While the influence of Chopin is in evidence here, one already more than vaguely hears the voice of the mature Scriabin in the harmonies and in the slightly hesitant flow of the melody line. The second piece, Prelude, one minute long, is about a third the length of the Etude, but within its brief span a wistful theme is presented that has charm in its quirky gentleness. The last item here, the Impromptu alla mazurka, is Chopinesque and graceful, and features a playful, brief middle section. In sum, this trio of pieces, totaling about six minutes in performance, is not a major item in the composer's output but offers rewards to those interested in his musical language. *—Robert Cummings*

Recommended:

- ○ **Beate Berthold Plays Tchaikovsky, Rachmaninov & Scriabin** / Berthold / 1993 / EMI 7-54550
- ○ **Skryabin: Etudes; Pieces; Poèmes** / Deyanova / Nimbus 5176

Two Pieces (for left hand alone), Op. 9 (1894)

It has been conjectured that these pieces for left hand alone might have resulted from an injury to Scriabin's right shoulder, incurred in his teens. It is true that in some of his later compositions he reduced the role of the right hand. But then Scriabin was an oddball genius whose style grew increasingly radical. His focus on the left hand, both here and in later works, may have been simply an artistic quirk.

The first of this pair, the Prelude in C sharp minor, is tense and dark, featuring a sad Chopinesque theme. The music naturally has somewhat skeletal harmonies, but overall Scriabin's deft underpinnings are effective and atmospheric, at times giving the illusion that both hands are playing. The second work is a Nocturne, in D flat major. It is sweet and Lisztian, again offering an attractive melody, this one quite long-breathed. Its final appearance reaches an ecstatic climax, before gently and playfully concluding. Both these pieces enjoyed a minor vogue in the middle twentieth century, but are generally and unfairly neglected today. *—Robert Cummings*

Recommended:

- ○ **Scriabin: Complete Piano Music (Excluding Sonatas)** / Ponti / 2002 / Vox 3606
- ○ **La Nuit** / Achucarro / 1999 / Ensayo 9806
- ○ **Scriabin: Piano Concerto In F; Poèmes; Prelude & Nocturne For The Left Hand** / Neuhaus / Russian Disc 15004

Four Pieces, Op. 51 (1906)

Scriabin produced only two sets of piano pieces in the year 1906: this effort and the *Three Pieces*, Op. 52. But he was also working on one of his most important orchestral works, the *Poem of Ecstasy* (1905–08). All his compositions at this time, to one degree or other, reflected his increasing immersion in mysticism and philosophy. The music in this set exhibits his deepening expressive language and the evolution of his style toward more radical levels, a process that would culminate in *Prometheus, The Poem of Fire*, and his late piano compositions.

The first of the four works here is "Fragilité," an Allegretto rife with that Scriabinesque ethereality and otherworldly atmosphere. At the outset this piece might well convey to the uninitiated ear a sense of cocktail-lounge music gone awry, with its soothing manner and aerial sweetness all cosmically souring in such deft style. The second piece, "Prélude," carrying the marking Lugubre, is indeed lugubrious in its dark chords and glacial pacing. The obsessive, late Lisztian theme is quirky, almost pretending to be sad rather than expressing actual sadness.

The next piece, "Poème ailé," is relatively bright in its lively, somewhat chipper manner. Again, however, Scriabin shows his quirkiness in the erratic flow of the music and the disjointed jauntiness of its playful elements. The last entry here is "Danse languide," an example once more of the title being well suited to the music. Languid it is, indeed, in its January-molasses gait, but also deftly atmospheric in its ghostly mists floating above the strange dance. *—Robert Cummings*

Recommended:

- ○ **Horowitz Plays Scriabin** / Horowitz / 1989 / RCA 6215
- ○ **Scriabin: The Piano Sonatas** / Ashkenazy / 1997 / London 452961
- ○ **Scriabin: Complete Piano Music (Excluding Sonatas)** / Ponti / 2002 / Vox 3606

Two Pieces, Op. 57 (1908)

Scriabin's *Morceaux*, Op. 57 are two of his classic miniatures for piano, composed around the time he began exploring literal chromatic harmonies, the relation of colors to notes, and after his music had begun to move away from the traditional, Romantic pianistic style into a more mystical realm. These are really mood paintings, conveying ideas through a spare texture of slowly evolving harmonies. They are not atonal, but rather polytonal as they seem to pass through several keys in succession. *Désir* is less than two minutes, a misty piece that reaches upward, at first gently, then with more strength using chromatic stepping stones. However, it seems to lose that strength at the end, still reaching with an arpeggio covering much of the keyboard. *Caresse dansée*, the second piece, begins where *Désir* left off harmonically. The three-minute work also opens slowly, but it never really gains momentum. About two-thirds through, it exhibits a little more dance-like liveliness, but then it returns to its opening falling melody. It continually descends, wandering through several keys in augmented harmonies, but ending in a major chord, as if coming to a safe rest on solid ground. Both pieces have a mystical, pensive atmosphere, but still do not reach the meditative intensity of his later works, such as *Vers la flamme*. *—Patsy Morita*

Recommended:

- ○ **The Glenn Gould Silver Jubilee Album** / Gould / 1980 / Sony 60686
- ○ **Scriabin: 24 Preludes; Sonatas 4 & 10** / Pletnev / 1997 / Virgin 45247
- ○ **Scriabin: Complete Piano Music (Excluding Sonatas)** / Ponti / 2002 / Vox 3606

Two Poèmes, Op. 32 (1903)

By the time Scriabin composed the *Poèmes* (1905), he had already shaken off all significant keyboard influences, and his style had fully matured. Still, his artistic persona was still evolving; his tonal idiom would become less stable, his harmonies more daring, his sound world more ethereal.

The first of these two short *Poèmes*, marked Andante cantabile, has an airy innocence in its glistening mists and hazy images. It is impressionistic without invoking the musical language of Debussy, and is marked by bursts of passion. The second *Poème*, marked Allegro con eleganza con fiducia, is darker, a quality at once evident in its grim, nervous opening. It is typical of the composer in its fiery quality, mixing grace and thunder, hesitation and determination. Muscle and sweat yield suddenly to a quiet ending, leaving much unresolved. *—Robert Cummings*

Recommended:

- ○ **Scriabin: The Piano Sonatas** / Ashkenazy / 1997 / London 452961
- ○ **Great Pianists: Vladimir Sofronitsky** / Sofronitsky / 1999 / Philips 456970
- ○ **Scriabin: Complete Piano Music (Excluding Sonatas)** / Ponti / 2002 / Vox 3606

Twenty Four Preludes, Op. 11 (1888–1896)

This set, which covers a period of eight years and comprises Scriabin's largest collection of keyboard works, contains as wide a sampling of his art from his early years as any, and while it may not claim the musical importance of many of the later sets of *Preludes* and *Etudes*, it is nevertheless a notable collection.

These *Preludes* cover the 24 keys, running in the usual pattern, beginning with C major and A minor and ending with F major and D minor. None of the works here come close to Scriabin's mature or late style, though more than a few augur future stylistic traits, as well as divulge Scriabin's burgeoning genius at keyboard coloration and unusual harmonies. The Second, in A minor, marked Allegretto, may not quite enter the mystical world inhabiting so much of the composer's music after 1903, but its strange, wandering theme and dark harmonies are wonderfully atmospheric and advanced for their time.

The E minor Fourth (Lento) is simple and melancholy, its barren textures foreshadowing the often desolate moods in later works. The next, in D major (Andante cantabile), is more typical of his style in this period, with its hints of Chopin and Liszt and a more Romantic demeanor. The F sharp minor Eighth is among the better pieces in the set, offering a dark, profound theme whose long-breathed and angular manner attest to the composer's considerable thematic invention. No. 11, in G major (Allegro assai), is dreamy and shows hints of Impressionism, then just being developed by Debussy.

The boisterous 14th, in E flat minor (Presto), provides a break from the generally subdued moods in the surrounding *Preludes* and also features an abrupt, dramatic ending in the bass register. The very Lisztian 16th, in B flat minor, marked Misterioso, is indeed mysterious, mired in the lower ranges of the keyboard and engendering much suspense in its marchlike tread through dark terrain. The elegant E flat major 19th (Affetuoso) at times sounds like a parody of Chopin, but appears to employ a variation on the theme Scriabin used in the D sharp minor *Etude No. 12*, from Op. 8 (1894).

The robust muscularity of the C minor 20th (Appassionato) is contrasted most effectively by the mesmeric quiet and gentleness of No. 21, in B flat major (Andante). The set closes with a rousing, nervous Presto in D minor, whose big chords repeat as though stuttering in delivering its Rachmaninovish theme.

One might observe from this partial summary that the even-numbered *Preludes* appear to be the more substantial in the set. That may be the case—certainly they are longer and often of greater depth. Performance of the whole collection would last around 35 minutes. *—Robert Cummings*

Recommended:

- ○ **Scriabin: 24 Preludes; Sonatas 4 & 10** / Pletnev / 1997 / Virgin 45247
- ○ **Scriabin: Complete Piano Music (Excluding Sonatas)** / Ponti / 2002 / Vox 3606
- ○ **Scriabin: Preludes Op 11, 16, 22, 27** / Gourari / 1999 / Koch 314312

Six Preludes, Op. 13 (1895)

If one can point to a consistent characteristic in Scriabin's preludes, whose composition spanned from 1888 to 1914, it is brevity; most of the individual preludes are no longer than one and a half to two minutes. The *Six Preludes*, Op. 13 (1895) are no exception, though at nearly three minutes the first prelude of the set stretches the limits a bit. The *Six Preludes* date from a stage in the composer's career when he was still palpably under the influence of Chopin and Liszt.

Indeed, the first prelude, marked Maestoso, is certainly one of Scriabin's most Lisztian works, featuring a serene melody, rich harmonies, and a rapturous glow that recall so many of the Hungarian master's ecstatic religious pieces. The second prelude provides as stark a contrast to the first as one could imagine, the Allegro tempo and running scales combining in a spirit of nervosity and caprice. The third prelude, marked Andante, is gentle and forlorn; the fourth, marked Allegro, is elegant in its wandering theme, charming in its subdued manner. "Charming" also describes the fifth prelude, marked Allegro, which is also chipper and nonchalant . The final prelude, marked Presto, is fraught with anxiety and darkness, the main theme building from a series of descending chords and creating much tension before the prelude settles into a peaceful close. *—Robert Cummings*

Recommended:

- ○ **Scriabin: Complete Piano Music (Excluding Sonatas)** / Ponti / 2002 / Vox 3606
- ○ **Hommage à Werner Haas** / Haas / 2001 / MDG 6421086
- ○ **Skryabin: Preludes Op11; Vers la flamme Op72; Etudes Op8; Mazurkas** / Neuhaus / 1997 / Saison Russe 788032

Five Preludes, Op. 16 (1894–1895)

The Five Preludes, Op. 16 (1894–95) are among those works from the early stages of Scriabin's career that clearly demonstrate a debt to the music of Chopin and Liszt. Both Chopin and Liszt exerted a palpable influence over the young composer up to about 1900, by which time he had evolved a distinctive musical voice into which he was to soon incorporate mysticism and more radical compositional methods.

The first of the Five Preludes, marked Andante, presents a beautiful theme in the post-Romantic vein without divulging any obvious influences. There are, probably more by coincidence than by imitation, hints of Rachmaninov in the prelude's lushness and in the character of its flow. The second prelude, marked Allegro, begins with a sort of stutter-step motive that the composer cleverly converts into a theme of nervous beauty and great passion. The third prelude, marked Andante cantabile, has a Lisztian religiosity in its solemn manner, while the fourth, marked Lento, transforms the mood of the third into a more earth-bound ponderousness. The half-minute-long fifth prelude, marked Allegretto, dispels the solemnity, bringing the set to a close with a fleeting brightness. *—Robert Cummings*

Recommended:

- ○ **The Complete Preludes of Alexander Scriabin** / Lane / Hyperion 67057/8
- ○ **Horowitz Plays Scriabin** / Horowitz / 1989 / RCA 6215
- ○ **Scriabin: Complete Piano Music (Excluding Sonatas)** / Ponti / 2002 / Vox 3606
- ○ **Rare Scriabin: Music for Piano** / Nikonovich / 1996 / Olympia 550

Vers la flamme, poème, Op. 72 (1914)

Alexander Scriabin completed his *Vers la Flamme*, Op. 72 for solo piano in 1914. It is a brief work around six minutes in duration, but its epic quality is pronounced and well contoured. In keeping with its title "Towards the Flame," the music careens from a somber, burbling opening to an ecstatic vision of a cosmic rupture.

Vers la Flamme is too good to be dismissed. It is through-composed, and progresses to an epiphany of vibrant pianistic color that is not revolutionary but stunningly approached. The intermediary music (the first three minutes) builds like an especially driven opening by Chopin, which is exciting and does not overstay itself. Its destination is an echo effect of repeated notes in the high register of the piano, becoming the new focus for listeners. This build is a continuous, supercharged, romantic texture. The echo effect in the piano is something modern and could not have been produced in the nineteenth century. It does not sound like a grafting of romantic and modern techniques. Scriabin no doubt was reaching for a mystical epiphany, and the sound of such. For alert, informed listeners, the beauty of this brief movement is its apparent clawing its way into a new style, with its roots in the old. The effect, in essence, is Post-romantic in the manner of Mahler's symphonies, intensely contracted. *—John Keillor*

Recommended:

- ○ **Great Pianists of the 20th Century: Vladimir Sofronitsky** / Sofronitsky / 1999 / Philips 456970
- ○ **Horowitz Complete Masterworks Recordings 1962–1973 Vol. IX: Late Russian Romantics** / Horowitz / 1993 / Sony 53472

SYMPHONIC

Symphony No. 1 in E major, Op. 26 (1899–1900)

While it was fashionable for some at the end of the nineteenth century to defer to the weight and wisdom of history by postponing composition in so ambitious a genre as the symphony until well into one's artistic maturity, Alexander Nikolayevich Scriabin felt no such obligation. He openly conflated the roles of composer and prophet, and assumed an artistic vision virtually unmatched in its cosmic scope. This vision—which is not hard to extrapolate from the sublime transcendence sought by the Romantic symphonists, though Scriabin conveyed it in a more starry-eyed, self-assured manner than most—went hand in hand with the unflinching compositional flair that drove him to complete his first symphony at the age of 28.

The work is no trifling undertaking, either—a sprawling six movements lasting nearly an hour (longer, in fact, than both his second and third symphonies), it addresses no less a subject than the divine nature of art. In fact, in the final movement a chorus and two vocal soloists are employed to sing the praises of artistic creation. This is a gesture, of course, already loaded with meaning: ever since the baritone in the finale of Beethoven's *Ninth* interrupted the instrumental recollections with "Nay, friends, not these tones!," ushering in the exuberant choral *Ode to Joy*, the use of a chorus in a symphonic finale has been a signal of heavenly ambition, as if meeting the singing angelic hosts halfway. Scriabin utilizes other tried and true unifying techniques, as well, such as the explicit recall in the final movement of themes heard in earlier movements, and the use, albeit somewhat vestigial, of sonata structure. Some even see the work's six-movement form as a hypertrophied version of the traditional four-movement scheme, with the opening Lento acting as an extended introduction to the subsequent Allegro drammatico, the third movement's Lento positioned in the slow movement's standard inner position, the fourth movement Vivace in the scherzo's spot, and the Allegro in the penultimate, rather than ultimate slot—which is reserved for the Andante choral movement. The entire work is cast in Scriabin's characteristically lush, chromatic harmonic language, with languorous lines and thick, viscous, undulating counterpoint. This makes all the more striking the moment midway through the finale when, for the first time in the entire piece, the meter changes from flowing triple divisions to the steady, articulate 4/4 meter that carries the piece to its conclusion. *—Jeremy Grimshaw*

Recommended:

- ○ **Scriabin: Symphonies 1–3** / Muti (cond.), Philadelphia Orch., Westminster Choir / 2001 / EMI 567720
- ○ **Scriabin: Complete Symphonies** / Ashkenazy (cond.), Berlin German SO, Berlin RS Chorus / 1996 / Decca 000088102
- ○ **Scriabin: Symphony 1, Prelude, Op24; Poèms, Op32** / Golovschin (cond.), Moscow SO, Moscow Capella / 1996 / Naxos 553580

Symphony No. 2 in C minor/major, Op. 29 (1901)

The *Second Symphony* was completed in 1901, a year after the first. It is the most traditional of his symphonies in formal structure. The first two movements (Andante, Allegro) are played without a break and structurally form a classical sonata movement. In the third movement (Andante), however, he makes a remarkable advancement toward the heavily chromatic sound associated with the mature Scriabin. The movement opens with a birdsong played by the flute, another Scriabin characteristic. The rest of the movement, with its frequent evocations of birdsong and other sounds of nature, is like a long, dreamy walk through the wilderness. Even the central climax is unforced. A lovely movement, the fourth movement (Tempestuoso), a minor-key scherzo, is full of turbulent string, timpani, and brass writing, interrupted briefly in places by some more lyrical writing. Toward the end of the movement, the key modulates into the major and leads seamlessly into the final Maestoso movement with a majestic restatement of the symphony's opening theme. This generally uninspired movement lacks interesting harmonic or thematic development, and the conclusion is tepid. Even Scriabin said of the last movement, "I liked it when I wrote it, but now it doesn't please me anymore... the last part is banal." This work marks important strides in Scriabin's growth as a composer, and still shocked its initial audience somewhat when it premiered in St. Petersburg under the baton of Anatol Lyadov on January 12, 1902, but it is hard to recommend for general listening except for the true Scriabin devotee. *—John Dobson*

Recommended:

- ○ **Scriabin: Complete Symphonies** / Ashkenazy (cond.), Berlin German SO / 1996 / Decca 000088102
- ○ **Scriabin: Symphony 2; Symphonic Poem in D minor** / Golovschin (cond.), Moscow SO / 1996 / Naxos 553581

Symphony No. 3 in C minor ("Divine Poem"), Op. 43 (1902–1904)

Scriabin's Symphony No. 3 is the first of the composer's major orchestral works to bear explicit extramusical intent. The titles appended to each movement are as colorful as the music itself : "Luttes" (Struggles), "Voluptes" (Pleasures), and "Jeu divin" (Divine Play). The work's performance instructions go well beyond the traditional Allegro or Andante; here, markings such as "mysterieux," "tragique," and "sublime" appear in Scriabin's orchestral music for the first time. These indications represent far more than superficial descriptions; indeed, they demonstrate the struggle Scriabin and his contemporaries faced in trying to express the turbulent emotions of their music in conventional terms. In the program notes for the premiere, Scriabin noted that his "Divine Poem" represents the growth of the human spirit as it is freed from legends and mysteries, passes through pantheism, and ultimately affirms its liberty and unity with the universe.

"Luttes" is meant to represent the conflict between man enslaved by another God versus man himself in the role of God himself. It opens with an ominous theme in the brass; the strings soon enter with an agitated minor-mode motive that gradually migrates toward a theme in the major mode. From this point, there is no longer any solid sense of tonality, and shifts between major and minor occur suddenly and frequently. Dynamic levels are similarly in constant flux, and at times it seems as though climaxes spring up every few measures. Nevertheless, Scriabin's mastery is such that he is able to bind this long movement into a cohesive whole despite its inescapably episodic nature. "Voluptes" is pure sonic sensuality. From a quiet opening of saccharine music for winds and strings, the movement gradually builds into an expression of unbridled, powerful sensuality. This movement leads without interruption into "Jeu divin," where the spirit, freed from submission to a higher power, relinquishes itself to the supreme joy of a free existence. This is rich and richly exciting music, characterized by a torrent of unpredictable changes of mood. The work ends, with a note of gentle ecstasy, on a Brahmsian final chord. Though the work clearly lacks the maturity of later masterpieces like the *Poem of Ecstasy* (1905–08) or *Prometheus* (1908–10), it is still a highly individual and worthy effort that provides a fascinating glimpse into the development of Scriabin's singular aesthetic. *—John Dobson*

Recommended:

- ○ **Scriabin: Symphony 3; Le Poeme de l'Exstase** / Pletnev (cond.), Russian National Orch. / 1999 / DG 459681
- ○ **Scriabin: Complete Symphonies** / Ashkenazy (cond.), Berlin German SO / 1996 / Decca 000088102
- ○ **Skrjabin: Symphony 3** / Gergiev (cond.), Leningrad PO / 1995 / Leningrad Masters 1308

Symphony No. 4 in C major ("Poem of Ecstasy"), Op. 54 (1905–1908)

During the decade immediately preceding the First World War, the European musical scene was developing at an astonishing pace. Schoenberg moved from the massive, two-hour-long *Gurrelieder*, with its epic Romantic text and equally lush score, to the concise and stringent *Piano Pieces*, Op. 11 in a matter of just eight years, while by 1913 Stravinsky was ready to unveil his *Rite of Spring*. Although Scriabin stayed apart from these developments, his extraordinary innovations during the first decade of the century are at the very heart of this musical realignment. Although generally regarded as a composer for the piano, Scriabin is the author of five large-scale orchestral works (all composed between about 1900 and 1910) that showcase his revolutionary artistic genius in much the same way that the piano sonatas do. In *Le poème de l'extase* (Poem of Ecstasy), Op. 54, of 1908, the journey towards complete atonality and thematic fragmentation is by no means complete (the real musical goal would not be reached until the final few sonatas), but enough of the composer's increasingly complex mystical and theosophical views saturate the score to bring to it a density and complexity of expression denied to the three symphonies that precede it. It is a work that stands with great pride beside the massive German orchestral works of the period, both a mesmerizing portrait of those troubled years and, at the same time, a uniquely intimate picture of an artist's fascinating mind. The Poem was originally to take the shape of a fourth symphony, but Scriabin decided to cast it instead as a 20-minute orchestral poem based on his own *Poem of Ecstasy*, a 369-line poem celebrating and glorifying his own creative powers (which would, according to his vision of reality, play a crucial role in the approaching transformation of the world). The orchestra is large—twice the classical contingent of winds and brass are required—and, unlike Mahler or Schoenberg, who used even greater forces than this, by no means sparingly used. Although Scriabin's orchestral experience was limited, he was one of the early twentieth century's masters of orchestration, and throughout the *Poem of Ecstasy* his orchestral writing is brilliant. Themes are used to delineate mental and emotional states (in this way the late orchestral works are quite unlike the late piano works, which employ an almost exclusively textural and harmonic narrative structure). At the opening, the flute gesture searches longingly, the clarinet dreams, and the trumpet foretells a still-distant victory. An equestrian stride commences, only to be abruptly halted to make room for an ardent violin solo. As the many levels of expression unfold the music is highly chromatic, but not particularly dissonant. A glorious climax draws the music to an appropriately ecstatic finish in C major—a key that had, for Scriabin, a cleansing and focusing quality.—*Blair Johnston*

Recommended:

- ○ **Scriabin: Complete Symphonies** / Ashkenazy (cond.), Berlin German SO / 1996 / Decca 000088102
- ○ **Scriabin: Symphonies 1–3** / Muti (cond.), Philadelphia Orch. / 2001 / EMI 567720
- ○ **Scriabin: Symphony 3; Poem of Ecstasy** / Golovschin (cond.), Moscow State SO / 1997 / Naxos 553582
- ○ **Stokowski Conducts Berlioz & Scriabin** / Stokowski (cond.), New Philharmonia Orch. / 1999 / BBC 4018

Symphony No. 5 in F sharp major ("Prometheus, Poem of Fire"), Op. 60 (1908–1910)

This was the last orchestral work written by Scriabin, and it is widely regarded as his most radical large composition and one of his greatest masterpieces. From about 1903 onward Scriabin was drawn toward the study of theosophy, and he gradually became more daring stylistically as well. The *Symphony No. 5* reflects his increasingly eccentric artistic persona: it attempts to take the first step toward uniting all art forms, as well as to express certain religious and philosophical ideas.

The work's harmonic language is advanced—but this was only another step along the way for Scriabin, who had already fashioned a style well beyond the average listener's comprehension in his own day. The composer never realized a crucial part of his conception: in the score he specifies that certain colors should flood the concert hall during performance, projected by a "clavier à lumières," a keyboard instrument not even in existence at the time. Scriabin associated keys with colors—F major, for example, he linked with hell and saw as blood-red. At the March 15, 1911, premiere—led by Koussevitsky—the music was given without the accompanying color projections. A 1915 New York performance provided the colors for the audience, but by projecting them on a screen—a disappointing compromise for the composer.

The score also calls for a huge orchestra (eight horns, five trumpets, and other large sections), piano, organ, and chorus, whose members are instructed to wear white robes and sing with closed lips. Scriabin attempts to unify sound and color, as well as to convey his mystical and philosophical ideas via his Prometheus, a mythological character who symbolizes rebellion against God. The composer associates him with Lucifer, called the bringer of light, thereby introducing the element of bright color, infernal images, and much else into the work.

Scriabin bases the composition on a single chord of six notes, from which emerges the opening theme on muted horns and virtually all subsequent thematic material. *Prometheus* begins with music depicting Chaos, and then turns to a variety of other subjects that include joy, eroticism, human passion, and ego. Near the end, when the music reverts back to the gray mists of the opening, there is a section entitled "Dance of the Atoms of the Cosmos."

The whole work evokes ethereal and otherworldly images. The music has an aura of the surreal throughout, with thematic development taking unexpected detours and instrumental colors often brighter and more intense than the colors any machine could project in a concert hall. The expressive language of *Prometheus* lies somewhere between Stravinsky's *The Firebird*—a work written at about the same time—and some of the early 12-tone works. Still, this is tonal music, masterfully crafted and hardly offensive to the modern ear. It is also pure Scriabin from first note to last. —*Robert Cummings*

Recommended:

- ○ **Stravinsky: The Firebird; Scriabin: Prometheus** / Gergiev (cond.), Toradze, Kirov Orch. & Chorus / 1998 / Philips 446715
- ○ **Tchaikovsky: Symphony 4; Skryabin: Symphony 5** / Muti (cond.), Alexeyev, Philadelphia Orch. & Choral Arts Society / 2000 / Angel 73737
- ○ **Scriabin: Complete Symphonies** / Ashkenazy (cond.), Jablonski, Berlin German SO, Berlin RS Chorus / 1996 / Decca 000088102
- ○ **Prometheus: The Myth in Music** / (live) / Abbado (cond.), Argerich, Berlin PO & Singakademie / 1994 / Sony 53978
- ○ **Scriabin: Piano Concerto; Prometheus; Preludes** / Golovschin (cond.), Scherbakov, Moscow State SO, USSR Radio & TV Choir / 1999 / Naxos 550818

CONCERTO

Piano Concerto in F sharp minor, Op. 20 (1896)

This work was Scriabin's only true concerto and his first work that involved the orchestra. At only 24 and needing a piano concerto to show off his abilities in concert, Scriabin was still using the idiom set forth by Chopin for his piano writing, and here he took on Chopin's orchestral mannerisms, as well, although Scriabin's orchestra takes a much more active and partnerlike role than Chopin's does in his concertos. Scriabin completed the concerto in only a few days in the fall of 1896, but didn't finish the orchestration until the following May and did not premiere the work until October 23, 1897. The opening Allegro does not go to the emotional extremes that Rachmaninov does, but it does contain greatly contrasting moods and moments of tension, ending without a recapitulation in a generally dark disposition. The middle movement is a poetic Andante and four brief variations, which, even though in the major mode, still have a nostalgic feeling. Muted strings first state the theme, which then switches to the clarinet with delicate, interweaving piano accompaniment. The next variation is more like a piano scherzo; then a darker variation moves mostly into the left hand and lower registers. The fourth variation gives the theme back, inverted, to the orchestra while the pianist has a more filigree solo, including a slow cadenza before the coda. The final Allegro moderato is in sonata-rondo form and is more intensely expressive than the other movements. Its main theme features a soaring arpeggio that flies up to the high end of the keyboard, but the lyrical secondary subject, however, is the one that stays in memory. The movement ends with an extended coda that represents an ecstatic, emotional culmination, with the orchestra rising to prominence at the very end. Scriabin often performed the concerto, even after he had moved on musically and philosophically into more sophisticated areas. Also a favorite of Rachmaninov's, he conducted the composer in a 1911 performance and later performed the work himself at a memorial for Scriabin in 1915. —*Patsy Morita*

Recommended:

- ○ **Tchaikovsky & Scriabin: Piano Concertos** / Demidenko, Lazarev (cond.), BBC SO / 1994 / Hyperion 66680
- ○ **Scriabin: le Poème De L'Extase; Piano Concerto; Prometheus** / Ashkenazy, Maazel (cond.), London PO / 1989 / London 417252

Seattle Symphony Orchestra

f. Dec. 29, 1903, Seattle, WA

Ensemble

The Seattle Symphony Orchestra was founded in 1903, its first concert taking place December 29 that year at Christensen's Hall, led by violinist/conductor Harry West. The ensemble consisted of just 24 musicians that night, but expanded to 52 in 1907 when the Seattle Symphony Society was established and incorporated. That organization appointed a new conductor, Philadelphia native Michael Kegrize, and the orchestra was given a new home the following year at the newly built Moore Theatre. It had been giving performances in the Grand Opera House as of 1906. In 1909, Henry Hadley was appointed music director and by the following year, he had more than doubled the number of concerts and increased the size of the ensemble to 65. He also attracted major artists to perform with the orchestra, including Fritz Kreisler and Josef Hofmann. Despite these improvements, the orchestra often struggled to attract sufficient support and critical recognition. In 1911, John Spargur was appointed to succeed the departing Hadley and the orchestra was renamed the Seattle Philharmonic and given a new concert venue, the Metropolitan Theatre. Continued woes plagued the orchestra and it reorganized in 1919, reverting to its original name of the Seattle Symphony Orchestra. Spargur remained music director of the ensemble, now consisting of 85 musicians who performed at the University of Washington's Meany Hall. More financial and organizational problems ensued and the group lost its professional status. In 1921–23, Madame Davenport-Engberg led the SSO, which had to disband at the end of her tenure. In 1926, it reorganized once more, as Karl Krueger was appointed conductor of the now 65-member ensemble. In 1932, the orchestra began its first radio broadcasts under new director Basil Cameron, but because of the national depression and other financial concerns, the season schedule had to be reduced. Still, the orchestra rebounded and took its first West Coast tour in 1935, highlighted by a series of broadcasts over CBS radio. In the period of 1938 to 1954, the orchestra had five music directors, the second of these being one of the most prominent from the first half of the twentieth century, Sir Thomas Beecham (1941–43). Beecham's reign produced sold-out concerts, but his jesting remarks about the orchestra's abilities created much controversy. Milton Katims was appointed music director in 1954 and enjoyed the longest tenure of any conductor in the orchestra's history. He introduced many new works and attracted some of the finest artists in the world, even drawing an appearance from Igor Stravinsky in 1962. Under Katims, revenues more than quadrupled, many recordings were made, and the orchestra's reputation grew in stature. Though he remained the musical director until 1979, Katims surrendered the conductorship in 1976 to Rainer Miedél. His tenure was mostly successful, weathering a strike in 1979, and touting a highly acclaimed European tour in 1981. Following Miedél's death in 1983, Gerard Schwarz was appointed principal conductor in 1984, then music director in 1985. He is largely responsible for bringing greater recognition to the orchestra through frequent appearances on PBS and a spate of successful recordings. In the early 1990s, the SSO received a string of Grammy nominations. Gerard Schwarz has also introduced many new works: in the 2000–01 season, for example, he presented four new major compositions, including *Nanking! Nanking!* by Bright Sheng, a U.S. premiere. On September 12, 1998, the Seattle Symphony gave its first performance in its new home at Benaroya Hall. *—Robert Cummings*

Recommended:

- ○ **Piston: The Incredible Flutist** / Schwarz (cond.), Goff, Danielson, Wunrow, Seattle SO, Juilliard String Quartet / 2003 / Naxos 8559160
- ○ **Hovhaness: Symphony 22; Cello Concerto** / Davies (cond.), Starker, Seattle SO / 2003 / Naxos 8559158
- ○ **Diamond: Symphony 8; Suite from the ballet TOM; This Sacred Ground** / Schwarz (cond.), Parce, Seattle SO / 2004 / Naxos 8559156
- ○ **Western Classics** / Schwarz (cond.), Jones, LA Guitar Quartet, Seattle SO / 1996 / Delos 1603
- ○ **Music of Howard Hanson Vol. 1** / Schwarz (cond.), Rosenberger, Jolles, Mendenhall, Baunton, Johnson, Seattle SO, New York Chamber Symphony / 1998 / Delos 3705

Leif Segerstam

b. Mar. 2, 1944, Vaasa, Finland

Conductor

Leif Segerstam is primarily known as a conductor, generally ranked among the most prominent from Finland in the latter twentieth and early twenty first centuries. But he is also a composer with a massive output, making the cataloging of his music difficult. For instance, by summer 2002, he had written 81 symphonies, 18 of them having been composed or completed in that year alone. Yet that seemingly enormous body of music is not quite what it seems, since he typically writes the same piece in different scorings, using aleatoric methods involving less-complex and less-specific notation. Still, his output contains countless orchestral and choral works, concertos, songs, string quartets, and instrumental pieces.

Segerstam entered the Sibelius Academy of Music in Helsinki in his mid-teens, where he studied violin with Liisa Siikonen and conducting with Jussi Jalas. Segerstam was also an excellent pianist then and won first prize in the 1962 Maj Lind Piano Competition, held by the Sibelius Academy. The following year, he graduated with degrees in both violin and conducting and gave his first major concert as a violinist. By then, he had already written his earliest compositions, which included the brief 1960 orchestral work *A Legend* (Nils-Eric Fougstedt in Memoriam) and *Three Songs for Soprano and Piano* (1960–61). Following Segerstam's graduation, he enrolled at the Juilliard School of Music, where he studied violin with Louis Persinger, conducting with Jean Morel, and composition with Vincent Persichetti and Hall Overton. In 1965, he received his first important conducting appointment to the Finnish National Opera as director for the 1973–74 season. Segerstam held two other conducting posts at opera houses in Scandinavia and Germany, at the Royal Opera in Stockholm from 1968 to 1972, and at the Deutsche Oper in Berlin for a single season (1972–73). Segerstam turned out many compositions during these early conducting years, including several sring quartets (the *Fifth*, subtitled "Lemming," was a stylistically pivotal work in his use of aleatory methods) and the song collection *Tre plus eller fyra NNNUUUU-R*, for mezzo soprano and piano, on texts by Gunnar Björling. Segerstam successively took three conducting posts with second-tier European orchestras in the period from 1977 to 1985 (the Austrian Radio Symphony Orchestra, the Finnish Radio Symphony Orchestra, and the Rhineland-Pfalz State Philharmonic Orchestra). He was appointed chief conductor of the Danish National Radio Symphony Orchestra in 1989, a post that would allow him to record not only many classics in the repertory and modern works, but also some of his own. For the labels BIS, Ondine, and Finlandia, he turned out performances of his symphonies *No. 9, No. 11, No. 13, No. 14, No. 16, No. 17*, and *No. 18*, and violin concertos, Op. 33 and 99, with his wife Hannele Segerstam as soloist. Upon his departure from the DNRSO in 1995, he accepted the position of chief conductor for the Helsinki Philharmonic Orchestra and that same year, also returned to Stockholm's Royal Opera, once more as music director. Segerstam still held these two positions in the new century. At the Royal Opera House, Segerstam has conducted a wide range of works. In 2002, for example, he led performances of Wagner's *Tristan und Isolde*, Prokofiev's *The Fiery Angel*, and Janáček's *The Makropulos Affair*. *—Robert Cummings*

Recommended:

- ○ **Rouse: Der Gerettete Alberich; Rapture; Violin Concerto** / Segerstam (cond.), Glennie, Lin, Helsinki PO / Ondine 1016
- ○ **Langgaard: Symphony 1; Fra Dybet** / Segerstam (cond.), Danish RSO / 1994 / Chandos 9249
- ○ **Sibelius: Symphonies 2 & 6** / Segerstam (cond.), Helsinki PO / Ondine 1026
- ○ **Rautavaara: Harp Concerto; Symphony 8** / Segerstam (cond.), Nordmann, Helsinki PO / Ondine 978
- ○ **Segerstam: Symphony 16; Nocturne** / Segerstam (cond.), Danish RSO / 1992 / Bis 584
- ○ **Rautavaara: Violin Concerto; Angels & Visitations; Isle of Bliss** / Segerstam (cond.), Oliveira, Helsinki PO / Ondine 881
- ○ **Nørgard: Symphony 4 & 5** / Segerstam (cond.), Danish RSO / 1997 / Chandos 9533

Andrés Segovia

b. Feb. 21, 1893, Linares, Granada, Spain, **d.** Jun. 2, 1987, Madrid, Spain

Guitarist

Andrés Segovia, Marquis of Salobreia, was born near Jaen, Granada, Spain. He became a guitarist against the double opposition of his parents. First, they opposed his learning the guitar and got him cello and piano teachers instead. When he persisted in teaching himself guitar, they opposed his becoming a musician. He sought a guitar teacher at the Granada Institute of Music when he studied there, but found none, so continued learning the instrument on his own. He made his debut at the Centro Artística in Granada at the age of 15. He played so skillfully that he was urged to become a professional soloist. He played in Madrid in 1912, at the Paris Conservatory in 1915, and in Barcelona in 1916, and made a wildly successful tour of South America in 1919. He made his formal debut in Paris on April 7, 1924, in a program which included a new work written for him by Albert Roussel, named *Segovia*. It was the first of many works which were written for him by distinguished composers, enriching the instrument's repertory as Segovia had elevated its artistic potential. His U.S. debut was at Town Hall, New York, on January 8, 1928.

Being self-taught, his technique was unique. It was, in fact, superior to that which was being taught at the time, and extended the flexibility and expressive possibilities of the instrument. The main difference was in the method of using the right hand for strumming and picking the strings: Segovia's method paid much attention to the means of attack: whether hard parts of the fingers, fleshy parts, or the nails were used; other subtleties that affected the dynamics of the instrument; and an economy of motion that allowed longer and more sustained playing. There were classical guitarists before him, and distinguished ones even when he appeared, but it was not an instrument that was regarded as a serious vehicle for classical music. Segovia personally changed that, and not by accident. No doubt affected by his parents' attitude toward his chosen career, he had a driving desire to make it so. He wrote numerous transcriptions of older music for lute and for the Spanish vihuela. He transcribed music of Bach, Haydn, Mozart, Chopin, Handel, and others. He commissioned works by Castelnuovo-Tedesco (notably the great suite *Platero and I*), Falla, Turina, Tansman, Villa-Lobos, Torroba, Ponce, and Rodrigo, whose *Fantasia para un gentilhombre* was written for him. His reinstatement of the guitar as a solo instrument was sealed by his becoming one of the great teachers of music history. He established guitar schools or courses at the Accademia Musicale Chigiana, Siena, Santiago de Compostela, and the University of California in Berkeley. His students included Alirio Diaz, Oscar Ghiglia, and John Williams.

Segovia become one of the great names in classical music, whose mere name was enough to sell out houses worldwide. He received numerous awards and honors during his lifetime, including the Grand Cross of Isabela and Alfonso, the Gold Medal of the Royal Philharmonic Society of London, and many honorary degrees. The house where he was born had a commemorative plaque attached to it in 1969 proclaiming him the "leading son of the city." King Juan Carlos of Spain ennobled him as the Marquis of Salobreia in 1981, and in the same year a Segovia International Guitar Competition was established in his honor. He continued to give recitals and concerts until an advanced age, and had the rare opportunity, in 1984, of playing at a gala concert honoring the 75th anniversary of professional debut. *—Joseph Stevenson*

Recommended:

- ○ **The Legendary Segovia** / Segovia / 1999 / EMI 67009
- ○ **Segovia: 1927–1939 Recordings Vol. 1** / Segovia / EMI 61048
- ○ **Segovia Collection** / Segovia, etc. / 2002 / DG 471430
- ○ **Segovia: 1927–1939 Recordings Vol. 2** / Segovia / EMI 61049

- ○ **Segovia: Complete 1949 London Recordings** / Segovia, etc. / 1994 / Testament 1043
- ○ **The Art of Segovia** / Segovia, etc. / 2002 / DG 471697
- ○ **The Guitar of Andrés Segovia** / Segovia / 2004 / Dynamic 433

(José António) Carlos de Seixas

b. Jun. 11, 1704, Coimbra, Portugal, **d.** Aug. 25, 1742, Lisbon, Portugal
Composer

Carlos de Seixas was the most prominent Portuguese composer and keyboard player of his day. He mainly wrote for the keyboard, particularly toccatas (sonatas), most of which have been lost. There are differing accounts about the number Seixas produced, but it appears he composed over 700 sonatas in his short lifetime, as reported in the *Biblioteca Lusitana* by Portuguese historian Ignacio Barbosa-Machado. In any event, fewer than 100 survive and only a mere handful of choral compositions are known, though it is almost certain he wrote numerous works in the sacred choral genre. There are various theories that attempt to explain the complete absence of Seixas' original manuscripts, the most prominent being that all were lost in the earthquake that devastated Lisbon in 1755. Only copies of the composer's scores survive, probably representing only a fraction of his output.

At some point, probably in his late teens, Seixas discarded the family name of Vaz and used his first three names, José António Carlos, as several manuscripts attest. For unknown reasons, he adopted the surname (de) Seixas. He divulged talent early on, probably having been given his first music lessons by his father, the Coimbra Cathedral organist Francisco Vaz. In 1718, his father having died, Seixas was appointed organist at the cathedral. While it may involve a small measure of conjecture to conclude his talent must have been remarkable for him to attain such a prestigious position at the age of 14, it is completely safe to say that by age 16, he was one of the finest keyboard players in Portugal since he was appointed organist at the Royal Chapel in 1720. Later, while retaining the organist post, he became vice chapelmaster under chapelmaster Domenico Scarlatti. Some have suggested that the youthful Seixas was actually the more talented keyboard player of the two, citing a questionable account by J. Mazza: Seixas requested that Scarlatti give him keyboard lessons and the older master, upon seeing his young organist play, responded humbly that it was he who should receive instruction from Seixas. Little is actually known about the relationship between the two during Scarlatti's eight-year tenure at the Royal Chapel, since the older composer departed for Spain in 1728. It is generally believed, however, that the two shared a mutual respect, though one might surmise that Seixas was the more deferential, since his music did divulge an influence by Scarlatti. Still, Seixas' style had many distinctive features: his keyboard works generally featured simple harmonies and thus a greater focus on thematic content; his sonatas, unlike Scarlatti's, had multiple movements and their structures often exhibited greater complexity, somewhat auguring those of the Classical period. Seixas retained the organist post at the Royal Chapel for the remainder of his life. One outstanding event from late in his career came in 1738 when he was knighted by King João V, a further indication of his talent and prominence. *—Robert Cummings*

Overview of Works (ca. 1720–1742)

The reputation of Carlos de Seixas, Portugal's leading composer from the first half of the eighteenth century, rests on only a fraction of the compositions he wrote. Most-known for the keyboard sonata, he turned out at least 700 works in the genre according to Portuguese historian Ignacio Barbosa-Machado as he reported in the *Bibliotheca lusitana*. None of his original manuscripts survive, possibly because they were lost in the earthquake of 1755 that devastated Lisbon. Copies of a small number of his works circulated during his lifetime and it is from those that all that comprises his output is derived: about 88 keyboard sonatas (often referred to in writings of his day as toccatas), a handful of sacred choral works, and a harpsichord concerto. Amid substantial doubt, some musicologists insist on counting a harpsichord sinfonia. Also of doubtful authorship are 16 keyboard sonatas assembled in one collection.

Stylistically, Seixas is viewed as straddling the Baroque and Classical periods. One other important composer of keyboard sonatas from his time—with whom he is often compared, incidentally—was Scarlatti, most of whose sonatas were written in a single movement. Seixas, however, often cast his in two, opening with a substantive first movement typically followed by a short minuet. He also wrote them in three, four, or even five movements. Seixas is generally less given to unorthodoxy in his works than Scarlatti, but occasionally indulged in some adventuresome writing of his own. His *Harpsichord Sonata in D minor No. 7* has a lively, somewhat wild character in its lone Allegro movement, a kind of quirkiness often associated with the music of Scarlatti. The minuet in the *Sonata No. 5*, also in D minor, shows Seixas' skill at writing graceful, elegant dance music. *No. 42*, in F minor, has a deep, somewhat introspective first movement and features another attractive minuet. Seixas displays a deft sense for lyricism in *No. 46*, in G major. *No. 50*, in G minor, is another worthwhile composition and one known to offer considerable challenges to the soloist. His *Concerto for Harpsichord and String Orchestra* looks more toward the Baroque than Classical period and is formally quite conventional. Yet the music is attractive throughout, especially in the lively gigue of the finale. Cast in three movements, it is a well-crafted piece, the opening panel bringing to mind an updated Vivaldi. Too little of his choral music survived to allow for accurate assessment, though it suggests a talent perhaps on the level of that found in his keyboard works. The *Ardebat Vincentius* and *Tantum Ergo*, for example, are both finely crafted in their vocal writing and sense for the sacred realm. *—Robert Cummings*

Recommended:

- ○ **Seixas: Harpsichord Concerto; natas** / Haugsand, Norwegian Baroque Orch. / 1995 / Virgin 45114
- ○ **Seixas: Dixit Dominus, etc.** / Haugsand (cond.), Norwegian Baroque Orch. / 1994 / Virgin 45115
- ○ **Portuguese Keyboard Music Vol. 1** / Blumental / 1998 / Claudio 7279

Sequentia

f. 1977, Basel, Switzerland
Ensemble

An interest in Medieval music shared by two graduate students at the Schola Cantorum Basiliensis in Switzerland was the foundation for one of the most successful and innovative early music performing ensembles of the twentieth century. Benjamin Bagby and Barbara Thornton met in 1974 and formed the ensemble Sequentia in 1977, naming the group after the sequence, a central poetic and musical form of the High Middle Ages. Sequentia has grown into a touring and recording phenomenon, with over 20 albums to date, films for both television and independent filmmakers, tours to six continents, and awards including the International CD Prize Frankfurt, the Deutsche Shallplattenpreis, the Edison Prize (Netherlands), a Disque D'or (France), a Grammy Awards nomination, and the Innsbruck Radio Prize. The versatile ensemble is based in Cologne, Germany, and continues its established pattern of innovative research, creative programming, and sheer musical virtuosity, seeking to bring to life various musical traditions of tenth- to fourteenth century Europe.

The lineup of Sequentia changes according to the needs of each particular program. The core consisted of singer and harpist Benjamin Bagby, and singer Barbara Thornton until Thornton's untimely death in 1998; other core members have included medieval fiddlers Margriet Tindemans and Elizabeth Gaver, and singer Suzanne Norin. Groups of singers, most of them international soloists in their own right, comprise Vox Feminae and Sons of Thunder, the women's and men's ensembles of Sequentia. These two sub-groups meet intensively each year in Cologne and Boston, leading workshops and preparing for the current tour/recording project. Since their inception, Sequentia has incorporated instrumental performance, including a panoply of handcrafted replicas of stringed instruments appropriate to their repertoire.

Among the many musical repertoires brought to life by Sequentia is that of Hildegard of Bingen, who they have consistently featured. Along with Christopher Page's ensemble Gothic Voices, Sequentia can take credit for the resurgence of interest in Hildegard's music, beginning with their 1982 recording of her passionate morality play, the *Ordo Virtutem*. More recently, Sequentia produced a series of recordings encompassing Hildegard's complete works, culminating in a new production of *Ordo Virtutem* in 1998, the 900th anniversary of her birth. Other repertories in their catalog include the music of Philipe de Vitry, a series of Medieval Spanish music, and a reclamation of Medieval Nordic music, including the Icelandic Edda cycles and Benjamin Bagby's solo recitation of *Beowulf*. A recurring motif is their focus on the oral tradition underlying the music they approach; this leads to a stress on texts, linguistics, original notation, and improvisation within understood guidelines.

Each project begins with thorough and often creative scholarship, covering all aspects of linguistics, notation, musical analysis, and performance practices. For example, the *Edda* project began with Bagby's intensive study of the medieval Icelandic texts as well as current methods of Icelandic folk epic recitation, and research by Gaver into the Hardinger-fiddle tradition. At all times, their goal has been to reach and deeply internalize a contemporary understanding of the modal character of the repertoire, seeing melodies more as constellations of orally-transmitted modal gestures than as linear events. This internalization informs Sequentia's vocal performance, and, more importantly, the character of their instrumental improvisations. The ensemble is known for its characteristic full-voiced, open-throated singing, with evocative shaping of the texts. *—Timothy Dickey*

Recommended:

- ○ **Hildegard: Ordo Virtutum** / Sequentia / 1998 / Deutsche Harmonia Mundi 77394
- ○ **Hildegard: Canticles of Ecstasy** / Sequentia / 1994 / Deutsche Harmonia Mundi 77320
- ○ **Le Chancelier: School of Notre Dame** / Sequentia / 2004 / Deutsche Harmonia Mundi 60156

○ **Hildegarde: Symphoniae** / Sequentia / 2004 / Deutsche Harmonia Mundi 60152
○ **Myths from Medieval Iceland** / Sequentia / 1999 / Deutsche Harmonia Mundi 77381
○ **Hildegard: O Jerusalem** / Sequentia / 1997 / Deutsche Harmonia Mundi 77353
○ **Hildegard: Saints** / Sequentia / 1998 / Deutsche Harmonia Mundi 77378

Tullio Serafin

b. Sep. 1, 1878, Rottanova de Cavarzere, Venice, **d.** Feb. 2, 1968, Rome, Italy
Conductor

Tulio Serafin received his education at the Milan Conservatory, where he studied composition and violin. He debuted on the podium at Ferrara in 1898 and was hired by Arturo Toscanini as an assistant conductor at La Scala opera house in Milan. In 1909 he was appointed principal conductor at La Scala, serving a term interrupted during World War I (1909–14, 1917–18). He expanded the repertory away from the standard Italian operas. Notable additions to the repertory during Serafin's tenure were Italo Montemezzi's *L'Amore di tre re* (1913) and *La Nave* (1918), Richard Strauss' *Feursnot* and *Der Rosenkavalier*, Paul Dukas' *Arianne et Barbe-Bleu*, Weber's *Oberon*, and works by Humperdinck and Rimsky-Korsakov. He continued introducing new operas while he was on the conducting staff of New York's Metropolitan Opera from 1924 to 1934. He led the first American performances of Puccini's *Turandot*, Verdi's *Simon Boccanegra*, and operas of Mussorgsky, Falla, and Giordano. During his tenure at the Met he is also credited with helping develop the career of Rosa Ponselle, among many other singers he encouraged, who became one of the Met's leading stars. He conducted Ponselle in her 1931 Covent Garden appearances in two operas new to that stage, Verdi's *La forza del destino* and Romani's *Fedra*. In 1934 he became artistic director of Teatro Reale in Rome. He continued his pioneering ways, leading the first Wagner *Ring cycle* in Italian and the Italian premiere of Berg's *Wozzeck*. After the war, he premiered Britten's *Peter Grimes* in Italian when he resumed leadership at La Scala for the 1946–47 season.

He was a noted scholar of early Italian opera. His *Style, Tradition, and Conventions of Italian Melodrama of the 17th and 18th Centuries* (Milan, 1958) is a major study of its subject. Before him, only a handful of operas of the bel canto period regularly saw the stage and then in performances marred by false tradition. He edited these operas and brought back operas of Rossini, Bellini, and Donizetti. His skill as a developer of new talent (which the great singer Tito Gobbi said was "infallible") was instrumental in the careers of both Maria Callas and Joan Sutherland. He conducted Callas' greatest early performances and recordings, and he led the 1959 Covent Garden production of *Lucia di Lammermoor* that made the career of young Joan Sutherland. He was an undemonstrative conductor, using a quiet approach to urge the orchestra, turning stern only when confronting carelessness. His career was long-lived; he revived Rossini's *Otello* in Rome at the age of 84. *—Joseph Stevenson*

Recommended:

○ **Bellini: Norma** / Serafin (cond.), Callas, Stignani, Filippeschi, Cavallari, La Scala Theater Orch. & Chorus / 2003 / EMI 62642
○ **Verdi: Requiem** / Serafin (cond.), Gigli, Caniglia, Stignani, Pinza, Rome Opera House Orch. / 2001 / Naxos 110159
○ **Verdi: La traviata** / Serafin (cond.), Los Angeles, Sereni, Ercolani, Maionica, Orchestra del Teatro Municipal di Roma / 2000 / EMI 73824
○ **Verdi:Otello** / Serafin (cond.), Vickers, Rysanek, Gobbi, Carlin, Rome Opera House Orch. / 1998 / RCA 63180

Peter Serkin

b. Jul. 24, 1947, New York, NY
Pianist

Son of one of the recording era's most rigorous interpreters of piano music from the Classical age, Peter Serkin has propounded equal rigor as a pianist and musical voyageur, but in rather different directions. With a measure of integrity scarcely less than that demonstrated by his father, Rudolf, Peter Serkin has sought to serve the music of his own time while not neglecting masterworks of the past. An earlier tipping of the scales that gave the advantage to contemporary music has gradually centered itself to allow for attention to established works. Serkin has also become a respected teacher at several important institutions and continues to work in ensemble with other musicians of proven excellence. His quest for truth and adventure continues unabated.

Given the level of performance heard in his own home, Peter Serkin's early interest in music was scarcely surprising. First lessons came from his father, but later, in 1958, the young pianist was enrolled at the Curtis Institute to study with Lee Luvisi. Advanced lessons with Mieczysław Horszowski (who was still an active performer when he died at age 100) played an important part of the formation of Serkin's musical persona, as did instruction from flutist Marcel Moyse. By his early teens, the pianist had already become a veteran performer and those artists with whom he collaborated were also significant in the shaping of his interests. His performances of the Mozart *Double Piano Concerto* with George Szell, Szell's superbly prepared Cleveland Orchestra, and his father as keyboard partner are well-remembered. Once Serkin began to perform on his own, however, the repertory he performed took a pronounced turn toward the new and unusual and was offered in concerts scheduled for what he regarded as special occasions and venues. Time spent in India seemed to have both galvanized Serkin's dedication to a career and further expanded his notions of how music might be formed. The founding of the contemporary music group Tashi brought him together with violinist Ida Kavafian, cellist Fred Sherry, and Robert Marcellus-trained clarinetist Richard Stoltzman for study and performance of new works. Live performances and recordings by the ensemble only enhanced the celebrity of its players while in the process, much worthwhile music gained a new audience. Serkin's performances and recordings embrace the music of several centuries. He has recorded Bach and Mozart while a solo disc for Koch International Classics holds works by Webern, Wolpe, Messiaen, Knussen, Wuorinen, Lieberson, and Takemitsu. Lieberson's *Piano Concerto No. 1* and *No. 2* were both premiered by Serkin and the Boston Symphony Orchestra in 1983 and 1998, respectively. During the 2001–02 season, Serkin scheduled a series of concerts offering the music of Schoenberg, chamber and solo works alike, and mixing them with pieces by Haydn. During his career, Peter Serkin has performed with many of the world's most celebrated orchestras and in numerous festival venues. He serves on the faculties of the Curtis Institute, the Juilliard School of Music, and the Tanglewood Music Center. In 1983, he was honored by becoming the first pianist to have been given the outstanding achievement award granted by Siena's Accademia Musicale Chigiana. *—Erik Eriksson*

Recommended:

○ **The Ocean that has no West and no East** / Serkin / 2000 / Koch International Classics 7450
○ **Messiaen: Quartet For The End Of Time** / Tashi / 1988 / BMG 7835
○ **Messiaen: Visions de l'Amen** / Serkin, Takahashi / 1999 / BMG 68907
○ **Music for 2 Pianos** / Schiff, Serkin / 1999 / ECM 465062

Rudolf Serkin

b. Mar. 28, 1903, Eger, Austria, **d.** May 8, 1991, Guilford, VT
Pianist

Rudolf Serkin emerged from the environment of post-World War I Austria to become one of the most profound and challenging pianists of the century. Childhood studies in Vienna with Richard Robert (piano), and Joseph Marx and Arnold Schoenberg for composition, led to a 1915 debut performance with the Vienna Symphony Orchestra at the age of 12. After 1920, Serkin was associated with noted violinist Adolf Busch, both as a duo-sonata partner, and with the Busch Chamber Orchestra (and, from 1935, as Busch's son-in-law). An American debut in 1936 with the New York Philharmonic under Toscanini led to Serkin's decision to relocate to the U.S. in 1939. Invited to join the piano faculty of the Curtis Institute of Music, he quickly rose to become head of the piano department, and, from 1968, president of the Institute. He devoted his summers to cultivating several generations of young musicians at the Marlboro Festival in Vermont.

Many observers have remarked that Serkin was not a natural pianist. Indeed, he seemed rather to play by force of will alone, and the strength of his musicianship lies more in the deep insight that he brought to the music of the composers he holds dearest—traditional Austrian and German masters—than in virtuosic pianism. In the sonatas of Beethoven, Serkin finds particular inspiration. His Beethoven interpretations do not necessarily please the listener in terms of superficial "beauty," but rather convey the unique mixture of logic, violence, and spiritual transcendence that he feels is the essence of Beethoven's work. In the Brahms Concerti, Serkin's vision is nothing short of titanic. On off-nights, however, Serkin's lofty, cerebral brand of pianism sometimes failed him, and the austere, "square" approach to phrasing that makes his playing so immediately recognizable sometimes sounded unnecessarily harsh.

Rudolf Serkin's discography is impressive, spanning most of the general repertory from Bach to the early/mid-twentieth century, and includingg such relative novelties as the *F minor Concerto* of Max Reger, a composer Serkin had an abiding affinity for. His work at the Curtis Institute, and, during the summers, at the Marlboro Festival, has made him one of the most influential American teachers of the post-World War II era. Serkin's son Peter is also a pianist of considerable renown. *—Blair Johnston*

Recommended:

○ **Beethoven: Concertos 1 & 3** / Ormandy, Bernstein (conds.), Serkin, Philadelphia Orch., New York PO / 1987 / CBS 42259
○ **Serkin: The Legenday Recordings** / Szell, Ormandy, Schneider (conds.), Serkin / 1991 / Sony 47269
○ **Schubert: Sonatas D960 & 840** / Serkin / 2002 / Sony 512874
○ **Beethoven: Sonatas 8, 14, 23 & 30** / Serkin / 2003 / Sony 512868

○ **Beethoven: Diabelli, Variations; Bagatelles & Fantasy** / Serkin / 2003 / Sony 512866

○ **Beethoven: Concerto 5** / Ozawa (cond.), Serkin, BSO / 1981 / Telarc 80065

Roger Sessions

b. Dec. 28, 1896, Brooklyn, NY, **d.** Mar. 16, 1985, Princeton, NJ

Composer

One of America's musical icons, Roger Sessions had an incalculable influence on the compositional landscape of the twentieth century. A composer of rare accomplishment, deeply passionate, he attained a level of craftsmanship which nearly 75 years of work honed into profound knowledge and skill. In addition, the accomplishments of his numerous students, including such luminaries as Milton Babbitt and David Diamond, mark Sessions as a teacher of no common stature.

Born in Brooklyn during the last years of the nineteenth century, Sessions was an early bloomer. By the age of 14, he had already composed a complete opera, and entered Harvard University, where he studied music with Edward Burlingame Hill. Following graduation from Harvard in 1914, Sessions enrolled for further studies at Yale with Horatio Parker (who also counted Charles Ives among his pupils). Accepting a position at Smith College in Massachusetts, Sessions worked privately with Ernest Bloch in New York, and when Bloch was invited to become director of the newly-formed Cleveland Institute of Music, Sessions went along as his assistant, remaining there until 1925.

From 1925 to 1933 Sessions lived and worked in Europe, first in Florence, then later in Rome and Berlin. During these years the musical establishment began to take notice, and Sessions scored a marked success with his *Suite from the Black Maskers* in 1928, while his *First Symphony* had been performed to lukewarm response in Boston the previous season. Sessions' earliest music had been written in a lush, chromatic style. By the time of the *Black Maskers*, however, he had begun to favor a leaner, rather neo-Classical language.

Following his return to the States in 1933 Sessions accepted teaching positions at a number of American institutions including Boston University 1933–35, Princeton 1935–45, Berkeley 1945–51, Princeton again from 1953–65, and Juilliard from 1967 on. Beginning with the important *Violin Concerto* of 1935, Sessions' music became increasingly complex, and during the 1950s he adopted serial compositional techniques, though he used them with great flexibility, always suiting the techniques to match his own highly unique compositional voice—see, for instance, the remarkable *Third Symphony* of 1957. Sessions was awarded a special Pulitzer citation for lifetime achievement in 1974, and in 1982 received an actual Pulitzer Prize for his magnificent Concerto for Orchestra. No further works appeared after this remarkable musical achievement, and Sessions died in 1985 at the age of 88. *—Blair Johnston*

Overview of Works (1924–1981)

American composer Roger Sessions was criticized as both an "academic" composer and as more European than American. The epithet "academic" stemmed from his 62 years as a university teacher and his many awards and honors, among them two Pulitzers. The suggestion that Sessions was a de facto European composer is due to early years living in Europe and his close relationships with many important European composers, including Arnold Schoenberg, Ernst Krenek, and Darius Milhaud. Sessions' oeuvre reflects the influence of these colleagues, but also testifies to the composer's own rigorous standards of craftsmanship and uncompromising esthetic ideals.

Sessions lived in Europe from 1924 to 1935. During this time, he composed a number of significant works, including his *First Symphony*, his *Piano Sonata*, and the *Violin Concerto*, which reflect a number of contemporaneous compositional trends in Europe, neo-Classicism in particular. The works are, for the most part, tonal, but employ dissonance with considerable freedom. Texturally, they are exemplars of complex contrapuntal technique, the product of Sessions' careful, slow-paced compositional process. They are also reputed to be notoriously difficult to play.

From 1937 to the years immediately following the Second World War, Sessions completed another symphony and piano sonata, along with a string quartet and an opera, *The Trial of Lucullus*, based on a text by Bertolt Brecht. Sessions also set the verses of Walt Whitman in his choral work *Turn, O Libertad*, a move that some commentators regarded as a move toward a more Americanized style.

During the period from the end of the war to the 1960s, Sessions' style changed dramatically, due in part to his burgeoning friendship with the Viennese émigré composer Arnold Schoenberg. Sessions began to use Schoenberg's 12-tone technique, creating such important works as his *Second String Quartet*, the *Third* and *Fourth* symphonies, another piano concerto, and *Idyll of Thocritus* for soprano and orchestra. It was also during this time that Sessions completed much of his monumental opera *Montezuma*, begun in 1935 and not completed until 1963. The opera is a decidedly Romantic work, with lush orchestration and lyrical vocal lines.

Sessions composed a collection of symphonies—his *Sixth*, *Seventh*, and *Eighth*—during the mid to late 1960s in response to the Vietnam War. Other works from this period include his *Fifth Symphony*, his *Third Piano Sonata*, and a *Rhapsody for Orchestra*. The 1960s ended for Sessions with a choral setting of Whitman's "When Lilacs Last in the Dooryard Bloom'd," in memory of Martin Luther King Jr. and Robert Kennedy.

In the final decades of his life, Sessions continued to compose large-scale works, including his *Ninth Symphony* and a *Concerto for Orchestra*. In 1978, the year Sessions turned 80, he began working on another opera, *The Emperor's New Clothes*, which he would never finish. *—Alexander Carpenter*

Recommended:

○ **Sessions: When Lilacs Last In The Dooryard Bloom'd** / Ozawa (cond.), Quivar, Cossa, Hinds, Boston SO, Tanglewood Festival Chorus / 1977 / New World 80296

○ **Sessions: Symphonies 1, 2, 3** / Mitropoulos (cond.), Watanabe (cond.), Buketoff (cond.), New York Philharmonic, Royal PO, Japan Philharmonic SO / 1990 / CRI 573

○ **Sessions: Symphony 4; Symphony 5; Rhapsody** / Badea (cond.), Columbus SO / 1987 / New World 80345

○ **Sessions: Piano Sonatas; From My Diary** / Helps / 1998 / CRI 800

○ **Sessions: Quintet; Quartet** / Columbia U. Group for Contemporary Music / 1997 / Koch 7616

○ **Sessions: Divertimento; Idyll of Theocritus** / Leonard (cond.), Whitney (cond.), Nossaman, Louisville Orch. / 2003 / First Edition 12

○ **Sessions: Pieces; Duo; Sonata for violin** / Krosnick, Macomber / Koch 7153

Gil Shaham

b. Feb. 19, 1971, Champaign/Urbana, IL

Violinist

Violinist Gil Shaham entered the international spotlight in the 1990s as one of several young solo violinists vying for the attention of audiences the world over. Aided by positive publicity and an enviable recording contract with Deutsche Grammophon, Shaham proved with performances as a recitalist and through guest appearances with major orchestras that he was an artist beyond the need for public relations buildup—an artist whose musical gifts would assure him an ongoing presence among the world's leading string players.

At the age of two, Shaham moved with his parents from Illinois to Israel, where, at the age of seven, he began studies with Samuel Bernstein at the Rubin Academy of Music. Shortly thereafter, he was awarded the first of a series of annual scholarships granted through the American Israel Cultural Foundation. In 1981, he made debuts with both the Israel Philharmonic and the Jerusalem Symphony. The following year, he placed first in the Claremont Competition in Israel and left to enter the Juilliard School of Music in New York as a scholarship student and, later, to attend Columbia University. Eight years later, in 1990, Shaham was given the Avery Fisher Career Grant, preparatory to embarkining on a performing career.

His relationship with Deutsche Grammophon has produced a number of distinguished recordings, two of them Grammy nominees and another (a solo disc with pianist André Previn) a Grammy winner. In September 1998, he undertook a tour of mainland China which included performances with principal orchestras in Beijing and Shanghai.

During the 1998–99 season, Shaham participated in a two-week series of concerts by Pierre Boulez and the Chicago Symphony Orchestra devoted to the music of Béla Bartók. Resulting from this mini festival was a recording holding Bartók's *Violin Concerto No. 2* as well as the two *Rhapsodies for Violin and Orchestra*. For Deutsche Grammophon, Shaham has recorded the violin concertos of Bruch, Mendelssohn, Paganini, Saint-Saëns, Sibelius, and Tchaikovsky, with the late Giuseppe Sinopoli directing the New York Philharmonic and the Philharmonia Orchestra. His Grammy-nominated coupling of the Barber and Korngold concertos was done in collaboration with André Previn and the London Symphony Orchestra, as was a disc offering the *First* and *Second* Prokofiev concertos, also a Grammy nominee.

Among the composers represented on his solo discs are Elgar, Franck, Kreisler, Ravel, Schumann, and Strauss. Best-selling collections have included *Dvořák for Two*, recorded with accompaniment by Shaham's sister, pianist Orli Shaham, and *Paganini for Two* performed with guitarist Göran Söllscher. Also achieving remarkable sales volume was a DG recording of Vivaldi's *Four Seasons* with the Orpheus Chamber Orchestra. Shaham's Grammy-winning disc with pianist André Previn included a new sonata written by Previn for his violinist collaborator. In the summer of 2001, Deutsche Grammophon released a recording featuring Gil Shaham performing John Williams' *Violin Concerto* with the composer conducting the Boston Symphony Orchestra.

Shaham settled in New York with his wife, the violinist Adele Anthony. The instrument he has played for his recordings and public performances is a Stradivarius, the 1699 "Countess Polignac." The artist's playing is marked by a warm, flowing tone allied with a strong and comprehensive technique. Shaham has continued to prove himself a violinist more concerned with musical values than with showmanship. His seriousness as a musician has made him a favored partner for many of the world's leading conductors, and other instrumentalists have been eager to collaborate with him in chamber music performances. *—Erik Eriksson*

Recommended:

- ○ **Devil's Dance** / Shaham, Feldman / 2000 / DG 463483
- ○ **Fauré Album** / Shaham, Eguchi, Smith / 2003 / Vanguard 1239
- ○ **Paganini: Concerto 1; Saint-Saëns: Concerto 3** / Sinopoli (cond.), Shaham, New York PO / DG 29786
- ○ **Prokofiev: Concertos; Sonata for Solo Violin** / Previn (cond.), Shaham, London SO / DG 447758
- ○ **The Fiddler of the Opera** / Shaham, Eguchi / DG 447640
- ○ **Barber & Korngold** / Previn (cond.), Shaham, London SO / 1994 / DG 439886

William Sharp

b. Jun. 1, 1951, Kansas City, MO

Baritone

One of the top baritones working in classical music today is William Sharp, who is noted for his expressivity, clarity, and ability to "sell" a song in one of the most difficult and demanding realms, that of art song. He first made his bow in 1982 singing at the 92nd Street Y in New York, and Sharp's reputation grew so quickly that within two years he was singing at Lincoln Center. Sharp made his recording debut in 1989 on the New World label with a recital of American composers such as Virgil Thomson, Lee Hoiby, Paul Bowles, and others. Simply titled *William Sharp*, the album earned Sharp a Grammy nomination for Best Classical Vocal Performance. In 1990 he was one of the singers tapped to appear on the debut recording of Leonard Bernstein's valedictory work, *Arias & Barcarolles*, and this disc did take the Grammy for Best Contemporary Composition. Among his other two-dozen recordings is a disc of songs by Marc Blitzstein, in addition to recitals of works by Ernst Bacon and George Gershwin. Sharp also participated in the four-disc Albany Records series of the *Complete Songs of Charles Ives*. Sharp is in particular a strong advocate of the vocal works of American composers, and has sung their works with symphony orchestras and in recitals the world around.

Sharp is a frequent performer in various festivals all over the United States, having been heard at the Mostly Mozart Festival, the Chamber Music Society of Lincoln Center, Aspen Music Festival, the Marlboro Music Festival, and countless others. Sharp is also well known for his work as an interpreter of Baroque music, and is a member of the American Bach Soloists. In addition to all of this activity, Sharp also manages to find the time to teach voice at Boston University, a position he has held since 1993. *—Uncle Dave Lewis*

Recommended:

- ○ **William Sharp** / Sharp, Blier / 1989 / New World 80369
- ○ **He Loves and She Loves** / Kaye, Sharp, Blier / Koch 7028
- ○ **Songs And Night Songs** / Sharp, Nel, Liptak, Cameron, Inglefield, Harman / Gasparo 286

Robert Shaw

b. Apr. 30, 1916, Red Bluff, CA, **d.** Jan. 25, 1999, New Haven, CT

Conductor

Over his long career Robert Lawson Shaw became perhaps classical music's best-known choral conductor, and an important orchestral conductor as well. Born in 1916, Shaw was the son of a clergyman, and his mother sang in church choirs. As a young man he filled in as a choir leader on occasion, but did not plan a musical career, studying philosophy and comparative religion at Pomona College in suburban Los Angeles. During his freshman year, the leader of the college glee club fell ill, and he was asked by other members to substitute. After he had been at the helm for a time, a film happened to be shot on campus, and Fred Waring, the well-known pop choral director, was in the cast. Hearing Shaw's glee club, he offered him a job, and Shaw accepted after he graduated.

Shaw founded his own pop group, the Collegiate Chorale, but soon began adding classical music to its repertoire. Boston Symphony Orchestra conductor Serge Koussevitzky heard Shaw and, despite Shaw's relative inexperience, hired him to prepare his choirs. Then the great Arturo Toscanini invited Shaw and the Collegiate Chorale to join his NBC Symphony Orchestra in a performance of Beethoven's *Symphony No. 9*. The results made Shaw's reputation.

Shaw then founded the 42-voice Robert Shaw Chorale, perhaps the first full-time professional choir in the U.S. unconnected with a religious institution. Meanwhile he studied music theory, piano, and conducting technique. For eighteen years the Chorale toured incessantly and made many successful recordings, including some well-loved arrangements of Christmas favorites.

In 1953 he accepted a position conducting mainly light music with the San Diego Symphony. In 1956 George Szell invited Shaw to build a chorus to match the standards of his Cleveland Orchestra, rapidly on the rise. Shaw accepted the post, and in the process also took formal and informal lessons with Szell.

In 1966 the Atlanta Symphony Orchestra invited Shaw to become its next music director. During twenty years at its helm he built its quality and reputation to high international levels. When he took over in 1967, Atlanta was still essentially a segregated city. In his first year, Shaw established a week-long residency for the orchestra at Spelman College, one of Atlanta's historically black colleges. He also frequently conducted in the city's churches, black and white. In 1972 he gave the world premiere of Scott Joplin's opera, *Treemonisha*.

When Shaw's first five-year contract was up, the orchestra board voted not to renew his appointment because of the large quantity of twentieth century music he played, citing poor ticket sales. Within two weeks, however, 3,500 new subscribers sent in season-ticket checks, all bearing the notation that they were contingent on Shaw remaining the conductor.

Shaw was an extremely tough conductor. He raged, especially at the chorus members. He posted a formal letter after every choral rehearsal, chiding the singers and exhorting them onward. Koussevitzky once said he was "amazed that any group of adults would willingly endure such tyrannical treatment from a conductor." Shaw and the orchestra recorded for the Telarc label. He retired from the Atlanta podium in 1988 and was proclaimed conductor laureate, continuing to conduct regularly. He also made numerous guest appearances as a conductor, appearing in his signature midnight blue rather than black tails. Shaw spent four months a year in the village of Dordogne, France, where he conducted the Robert Shaw Institute and festival, sponsored by The Ohio State University.

Shaw died in 1999 of a massive stroke suffered while he attended a play directed by his youngest son. During his career he won thirteen Grammy awards and the 1991 Kennedy Center Honors. *—Joseph Stevenson*

Recommended:

- ○ **Serei Rachmaninoff: Vespers** / Shaw (cond.), Robert Shaw Festival Singers / 1990 / Telarc 80172
- ○ **Hindemith: When Lilacs Last in the Dooryard Bloom'd** / Shaw (cond.), de Gaetani, Stone, Atlanta SO & Chorus / 1987 / Telarc 80132
- ○ **Verdi: 4 Pezzi Sacri; Stravinsky: Symphony of Psalms** / Shaw (cond.), Atlanta SO & Chorus / 1991 / Telarc 80254
- ○ **Appear & Inspire** / Shaw (cond.), Bruffy, Goerke, Pittman, Ratzlaf, Robert Shaw Festival Singers / 1996 / Telarc 80408
- ○ **Barber: Prayers of Kierkegaard; Bartok: Cantata profanna; Vaughan Williams: Dona nobis pacem** / Shaw (cond.), Pelton, Clement, Gunn, Atlanta SO & Chorus / 1998 / Telarc 80479
- ○ **Amazing Grace** / Shaw (cond.), Cock, Almjeld, Bailey, Burrichter, Stalter, Robert Shaw Festival Singers / 1993 / Telarc 80325
- ○ **Choral Masterpieces** / Shaw (cond.), Baughman, Brown, Atlanta SO & Chorus / 1985 / Telarc 80119

Rodion Shchedrin

b. Dec. 16, 1932, Moscow, USSR

Composer: Keyboard, Ballet

The son of a music theorist and writer, composer Rodion Shchedrin was encouraged in his musical interests from a very young age. Initial studies at the Moscow Conservatory were interrupted by Russia's participation in World War II, but In 1948 he entered the Moscow Choral School, and three years later he returned to the Conservatory. There he studied piano with Yakov Fliyer and composition with Yuri Shaporin. At the same time, his interest in Russian folk music came to the surface; he led a 1951 trip to Belorussia to collect folk songs, some of which turn up in his early *Piano Quintet* (1952). Folk songs also play a role in his brilliant *Piano Concerto No. 1* (1954), which he wrote and premiered as his graduation composition from the Conservatory.

Not long after his graduation, Shchedrin began what has become one of his best-known works, the ballet *Konek-gorbunok* (The little humpbacked horse, 1956), which quickly became a staple of the Bolshoi ballet. Another very popular work in Russia was the opera *Not love alone* (1961). In the mid-1960s, Shchedrin started to incorporate modern sounds and techniques like tone-rows and aleatorics (chance elements) into works like his *Symphony No. 2* (1962–65) and the *Piano Concerto No. 2* (1966). Since that time, Shchedrin has consistently exhibited an eclectic taste; elements of the avant-garde, Neo-Classicism, folk, jazz, and pop music have all played roles in his music, which he has called "post-avant-garde."

In 1962, Shchedrin was recommended to succeed Tikhon Khrennikov as chairman of the Union of Soviet Composers. In the event, Khrennikov ended up staying in the post, but Shchedrin did later succeed Dmitry Shostakovich as the chairman of the Composers' Union of Russia, and remains its honorary chairman. From 1964 to 1969, Shchedrin taught composition at the Moscow Conservatory, while gaining recognition as one of the most successful Russian composers of his time. Music fans around the world have come to know *The Carmen Ballet*, his 1968 arrangement of parts of Georges Bizet's *Carmen* for strings and percussion, produced for his wife, ballerina Maya Plisetskaya. He also wrote the full-length ballet *Anna Karenina* (1972) for her.

Although elements of Russian Orthodox chants appeared in early works like *Chimes* (1967) and the Concerto for Orchestra No. 2 (written for the 125th anniversary of the New York Philharmonic), it was not until the 1980s that explicit liturgical themes found their way into works like *Stihira* (1987) and *The Sealed Angel* (1988). To date, Shchedrin has written, among many other works, five piano concertos, five concertos for orchestra, and three symphonies; the most recent of these (subtitled "*Scenes of Russian Fairy Tales*") was premiered in Berlin in June 2000. *—Chris Morrison*

KEYBOARD

In the Style of Albéniz, for piano (or various arrangements) (1952)

Shchedrin composed this Spanish-flavored morsel when he was at the Moscow Conservatory studying composition and piano. It not only has the flavor of Albéniz's piano miniatures, but almost seems to parody it, with theatrical, offbeat accents; contrasts of dynamics and tempos; scalar runs; and mordent ornaments. Its modal sound and outline are similar to the Prelude from Albéniz's *España*, while the drama of it is similar to the Malagueña from the same suite. The structure of the piece is a simple ABA form, beginning with a bravura introduction, which leads to the slow first theme. The middle section is a similarly paced melody that is more tango-like. The return of the first theme is brought to a striking end in a series of chords, a descending run, and a leap up to a fist-pounded final chord. Shchedrin dedicated the work to his future wife, ballerina Maiya Plisetskaya, for whom he would later also arrange two Albéniz tangos for her to use on-stage. *Im stil Albéniz* is a popular encore work, appearing in as varied arrangements as for cello, violin, or trumpet and piano; for xylophone; and for orchestra. *—Patsy Morita*

Recommended:

○ **Souvenir D'un Lieu Cher** / Berlinsky, Gorakhovich / 1997 / Helicon 1015

BALLET

Anna Karenina (1971)

Since Prokofiev's *Romeo and Juliet*, the authors of ballets, particularly in Russia, have not been afraid to translate great literary subjects into dance. Tolstoy's novel is another story of forbidden and doomed love: the married Anna loses everything because of her adulterous love in this tragic classic. Shchedrin, a fine composer, became a composer of ballets because of his marriage to Maya Plisetskaya, a prima ballerina for the Bolshoi. This sweeping, romantic score was written for her to portray the most touching heroine in all of Russian literature. The music darkens and becomes more dissonantly oppressive as Anna becomes more and more hopelessly trapped by her situation. It ends starkly with a tour de force of orchestration, as Shchedrin manages the most naturalistic and authentic-sounding railroad engine imitation in all of music: This train strikes Anna with a sound of almost brutal ugliness, and the train sounds recede with an indifferent mechanical soullessness which reflects how Anna has been abandoned by society. This is excellent score, in a style best described as "post-Prokofiev"; its 1972 premiere in Moscow was one of the grand musical events of the later Soviet era. There are also echoes of Tchaikovsky, the preeminent Russian ballet composer. "Although I borrowed some elements from the music of Tchaikovsky," Shchedrin has stated, "it was never my intention to fully retain its style or resort to a mere compilation. The subject of the novel, its essence and heart of the conflict are understandable to our contemporaries. What I undertook, therefore, was to synthesize the external characteristics of the times—the costumes, manners and intonations—with a modern viewpoint of Tolstoy's novel." *—Joseph Stevenson*

Recommended:

○ **Shchedrin: Anna Karenina** / Simonov (cond.), Bolshoi Theater Orch. / Russian Disc 10030

Carmen, after Bizet, for strings & percussion (1967)

Rodion Shchedrin's *Carmen* ballet score, arranged for strings, timpani, and four separate groups of percussion instruments, is without doubt his best-known work. The composer himself freely related in a press interview that the work, composed in 1967, "owed its existence to chance." Shchedrin had been asked to write the music for a *Carmen* ballet by the Cuban choreographer Alberto Alonso, "but I was highly sceptical about this idea... The very idea seemed to ignore the fact that the story had long become inseparable from Bizet's opera."

By the time he returned to the proposal, however, Shchedrin had managed to formulate a novel yet workable plan—one that would require him to co-opt material from not just one Bizet work, but three. The effort had become, he suggested, "a struggle with an overpowering musical model," so he decided to move beyond that model. Taking familiar sections from *Carmen*, and adding several more taken from other Bizet works (specifically, the incidental music for *L'Arlésienne* and the opera *La Jolie Fille de Perth*), Shchedrin compiled his so-called *Carmen Ballet*, which is in fact a suite comprising 13 separate numbers. Actually, Shchedrin leaves the somewhat tawdry tale unfinished, but provides enough groundwork for a highly effective piece of dance theatre that has entered international repertories and become a modern concert favorite.

Shchedrin also indicated that the work was not simply "a slavish obeisance to the genius of Bizet, but rather an attempt at a creative meeting of two minds." The Soviet authorities thought otherwise, however, after the world premiere, which took place at the Bolshoi Theatre in Moscow on April 20, 1967. The composer recalled that "it was banned before the second performance, on the grounds of being an insult to Bizet's masterpiece and for its sexual treatment of the character of Carmen. Thanks to the help of Dmitry Shostakovich, who intervened on my behalf with the Ministry of Culture, the ballet did eventually find its place in the repertoire." Like the other four ballets by Shchedrin, the *Carmen Ballet* was designed with the composer's wife, Bolshoi prima ballerina Maya Plisetskaya, in mind. *—Michael Jameson*

Recommended:

○ **Shchedrin: Carmen Suite; Concertos for Orchestra 1 & 2** / Pletnev (cond.), Russian National Orch. / DG 471136

○ **Shchedrin: Carmen Suite; Concerto for Orchestra "Naughty Limericks"** / Kuchar (cond.), Ukrainian State SO / 1994 / Naxos 553038

Bright Sheng

b. Dec. 6, 1955, Shanghai, China

Composer: Opera, Orchestral

Bright Sheng, Sheng Zong-Liang in Chinese, is a classical composer whose education and inspiration spanned the infamous Cultural Revolution and two continents. His first name, Bright, was adopted from an English character in a book, Mr. Bright, which seemed appropriate since his Chinese name, Liang, means "bright lights." He has developed into a successful composer in the U.S. and is the recipient of many high honors and commissions. Two of his compositions, *H'un (Lacerations): In Memoriam 1966–1976* and *Four movements for Piano Trio*, were both first runner-ups for the Pulitzer Prize in 1989 and 1991, respectively.

His musical training began when he was four years of age with piano lessons from his mother and later from a private teacher. Sheng was 11 years old when the Revolution began in 1966. Authorities confiscated his family's piano, for which he wasn't displeased, as it put an end to his lessons. Chairman Mao dictated that schooling would not proceed past junior high and these young people should enter the work force. As there were few jobs available, many young people were sent to the country to live and work with the rural peasant class. Fortunately for Sheng, Mao's wife, Jiang Quing, supported the performing arts and provided funds for performing companies to cultivate new, young talent. He was sent to Qinghai in western China and received a three-year contract with a song and dance troupe with whom he played piano. During his seven years in Qinghai, his musical education proceeded without benefit of learned teachers.

Sheng's formal musical education resumed after the end of the Cultural Revolution in 1976, with entrance into the Shanghai Conservatory of Music where he earned his undergraduate degree. Prior to coming to the U.S., Sheng's composing talents were being recognized in Chinese competitions. He won first prize in the Art Song competition in 1979 and took first and second prizes in the Chamber Music Composition Competition in 1980. After coming to the U.S. in 1982, Sheng earned a master's degree and a doctorate from Queens College and Columbia University, respectively. He studied under such eminent composers as Leonard Bernstein, Mario Davidovsky, Chou Wenchung, Hugo Weisgall, and George Perle. He continued receiving acclaim from such prestigious organizations as the National Endowment for the Arts, the Guggenheim, Rockefeller, Koussevitzky, and Naumburg Foundations, the Tanglewood Music Center, the Mary Flagler Cary Charitable Trust, and the American Academy and Institute of Arts and Letters. Sheng has held composer-in-residence positions at the Santa Fe Chamber Music Festival, the Seattle Symphony, and the Lyric Opera of Chicago. He was also the artistic director of the San Francisco Symphony's *Wet Ink 93* festival and was an artist-in-residence at the University of Washington. He has received numerous commissions from many American and foreign orchestras.

The Cultural Revolution and the time he spent in Qinghai proved to be major influences on Sheng's music. Sheng composed *H'un (Lacerations): In Memoriam 1966–1976* and *China Dreams* based on experiences from the Cultural Revolution. Other pieces, such as the opera *Song of Majnun* and *Two Folk Songs From Qinghai*, are based on folk songs learned while he was in Qinghai. Sheng is also influenced by the Hungarian composer, Béla Bartók, who himself used folk music elements in his compositions.

Bright Sheng is an associate professor of music at the University of Michigan; he contributed to Yo-Yo Ma's *Silk Road Project*, which took him back to his native China in the summer of 2000. In 2003, the Santa Fe Opera presented the world premiere of his opera, Madame Mao. *—Bruce Lundgren*

OPERA

The Song of Majnun (1992)

Shangai-born Bright Sheng settled in New York City in 1982 and has since written a number of important compositions, including this opera, *The Song of Majnun*. It has been called a Persian *Romeo and Juliet*, a fair enough description though its music is pretty far removed from that of most of the popular works associated with the Shakespearean tragedy. In the end, the music at times divulges a mixture of Chinese folk styles, Benjamin Britten (particularly from *A Midsummer Night's Dream*), and even a bit of Bernstein-tinged Broadway and Stravinsky. That said, Sheng expresses his own individual voice in the opera and his music is quite original and compelling. The libretto is by Andrew Porter and the story centers on two lovers, Majnun and Layla, whose romance is frustrated by the latter's father and ends with her suicide, leaving Majnun embracing her tomb and declaring his desire to join her. Sheng sees the story almost as a metaphor for his feelings for his native land. He uses some clever devices in the work to explain parts of the story: In Scene II, for example, village gossips rapidly chatter about the two lovers, telling of opposition to their romance and of Majnun's resultant madness (in Arabic, "Majnun" can mean "insane" or "infatuated"). Majnun's love song for Layla comes in the latter half of this scene and is heard again at the beginning of Scene Three (sung by the chorus and eventually by Layla) and elsewhere in the opera. It is ethereal and haunting, modern in its cooler lyricism and elements of tension, but quite memorable.The third scene deftly handles the theme of Majnun's love song and contains colorful excitement and brilliant vocal writing in the central part. The opera's final scene (Scene Eight—Layla's funeral and Majnun at Layla's tomb) moves from haunting to intensely powerful and finally to touchingly tragic, all moods brilliantly realized by Sheng. While Sheng's vocal music and sense for drama are excellent throughout, his orchestral writing also shows a mastery. The somewhat Stravinskyian orchestration in the long instrumental episode in the central part of Scene IV is powerfully effective in capturing the desperation of Majnun's father's attempt to persuade his son to forsake Layla and go on a holy pilgrimage. Lasting about an hour, *The Song of Majnun* is a quite approachable work and should appeal to those with a fondness for modern opera. *—Robert Cummings*

Synopsis:

Scene One. The story is set in Islamic Asia in legendary times. As a gathering of boys and girls enact a counting-out game, Layla (a young girl) and Majnun meet and fall in love. But the former's parents separate them, telling her that a husband has already been selected for her by them.

Scene Two. The Gossips recount the following events: Majnun's father takes his son's case to Layla's father, but the latter refuses to grant permission for marriage, and Majnun, devastated by the rejection, goes mad. He enters the scene with the Gossips to sing a love song.

Scene Three. The song becomes well known among the villagers and even spreads to other locales, and when Layla hears it, she realizes its words convey a message of love to her.

Scene Four. Majnun has been living in the desert. His father finds and convinces him to go to a holy shrine where he may be healed of his madness. Upon reaching the shrine, Majnun prays that his love will grow even more passionate.

Scene Five. Layla marries, and Majnun learns of the event from the Gossips. Her husband, Ibn Salam, vows to hold her in high esteem.

Scene Six. Some time later, Majnun and Layla exchange letters, hers divulging great unhappiness. They arrange a meeting in a garden, but, under a moonlit sky, cannot find each other there through the entire night. At dawn Majnun gives up and departs.

Scene Seven. Layla is dispirited and senses her life is rapidly coming to an end. She instructs her mother to look upon Majnun kindly when he visits her gravesite. Majnun has a mysterious dream: a bird resting on a high tree branch takes off and flutters toward him, dropping a jewel in his hands, a jewel that turns out to be a tear shed by Layla. She dies at the moment he catches the tear.

Scene Eight. At Layla's funeral Majnun sings a love song, hoping to join her in death. He embraces her tomb, which seems to light up brightly. *—Robert Cummings*

Recommended:

○ **The Song of Majnun** / Holmquist (cond.), Very, Grove, Lattimore, Chioldi, Martinez, Youngblood, Petro, Blackwell, Houston Grand Opera Orch. & Chorus / 1997 / Delos 3211

ORCHESTRAL

Flute Moon, for flute & orchestra (1999)

This is a brilliant and colorful concerted work for flute player and orchestra, part of a continuing line of works composed by Bright Sheng that combine aspects of Western and Chinese music.

Flute Moon represents the start of another stage in Sheng's style where Sheng finds a way to add the dynamic power of the earlier work *H'un* to the synthesis he achieved of East and West. It is a work that is nearly a concerto for flutist. It is an 18-minute piece in two movements, the second one being about twice as long as the first. It is a descriptive work, whose musical imagery stems from Chinese mythology and classic Chinese literature.

The first movement is called "Chi Lin's Dance" and calls for the flutist to use the piccolo from the first entrance (about halfway through) until the end. Chi Lin is the mythical animal called the "dragon horse," or unicorn, which looks like a monster, but symbolizes benevolence and rectitude. Chi, the male dragon horse (which has the horn while Lin, the female, does not), is represented by the string orchestra and Lin by the piccolo. The first half of the movement is dominated by the strings in forceful, driving melodies and the second half by a more gentle, but still very lively, piccolo. There is also highly dynamic and colorful writing for piano and percussion, reminiscent of the fast movements of Bartók's *Music for Strings, Percussion, and Celesta.*

Calling for the standard flute, the second movement, "Flute Moon," is a more lyrical and contemplative piece. It is based on the melody of a classical Chinese song by poet-composer Jiang Kui (1155–ca. 1235). It is, on the surface, a love song, and so the main mood is nostalgic and romantic. But the lines expressing lost youth are metaphorical allusions to China's decline at the time, when the northern half of the country had fallen to Manchurian invaders. Since the unicorns of the first movement are conventionally taken as symbols of a past Golden Age of China under the Emperor Yao, while the second movement often expresses pain and loss, *Flute Moon* itself can be taken as expressing the tragic aspects of Chinese history. *—Joseph Stevenson*

Recommended:

○ **Sheng: Flute Moon; China Dreams; Postcards** / Shui (cond.), Bezaly, Singapore SO / 2000 / Bis 1122

Postcards (1997)

Bright Sheng composed *Postcards* in 1997 on commission for Hugh Wolff and the St. Paul (Minnesota) Chamber Orchestra. The commission was funded by Ruth and John Huss, who related to Sheng reminiscences of their three-week trip throughout China in the 1980s. The four movements of Sheng's work are musical equivalents of imaginary postcards the Husses might have sent back from this trip. Each movement uses melodies and other ideas relating to the style of four different geographical regions of China. Sheng explains, "*Postcards* is a piece about nature, love, and nostalgia—they are 'love' postcards from China."

"From the Mountains" is a striking example of heterophony—the simultaneous sounding of identical themes or nearly identical themes with some time displacement. The movement begins with a folk-like melody on piccolo, oboe, English horn, and piano, played in unison. But the players' individual lines begin diverging—a note changed here, a duration changed there, as if the players don't actually count measures, or sometimes play a different note by mistake or fancy. Sheng takes these diverging lines through several instruments, and colors them with cloudy string chords, then ends the movement with the tune descending to low instruments.

The middle two movements are both fast and rhythmic. "From the River Valley" is bright, with prominent trumpet and piccolo. It is dance-like and very active, with a lyrical central section featuring woodwind solos. "From the Savage Land" is a pounding and aggressive piece built on a two-note ostinato and ends with everything condensed into a single percussive chord that hammers the rest of the music into submission.

The slow final movement, "Wish You Were Here," is a lyrical song first given to muted trumpet then given to woodwinds, especially the piccolo. The music fades to a misty mood of reminiscence. *—Joseph Stevenson*

Recommended:

○ **Sheng: Flute Moon; China Dreams; Postcards** / Shui (cond.), Singapore SO / 2000 / Bis 1122

Russell Sherman

b. Mar. 24, 1930, New York, NY

Pianist

Russell Sherman is one of the most eminent pianists in the U.S., particularly known for his recordings of Liszt piano music and Beethoven's sonatas. Sherman was raised and educated in New York City. He began playing piano at the age of six. By the time he was 11, he had progressed so rapidly that he was accepted as a student by Edward Steuermann, a great pianist who had been a pupil of Ferruccio Busoni and a friend of Arnold Schoenberg and was particularly known for his interpretations of Beethoven and music of the 12-tone school.

Sherman made his debut at New York's Town Hall at the age of 15, an acclaimed performance. He obtained his Bachelor of Arts in the Humanities from Columbia University while he was only nineteen. He studied composition with Erich Itor Kahn.

Initially he made a reputation in contemporary piano repertory and became known for a precise technique and deep insight into a variety of musical styles and performed widely in the United States. He has performed with the Chicago Symphony Orchestra, the Boston Symphony Orchestra, the Los Angeles Philharmonic, the Pittsburgh Symphony, the Philadelphia Orchestra, the New York Philharmonic, the San Francisco Symphony Orchestra, and New York's Orchestra of St. Luke's, with which he performed a cycle of the complete Beethoven piano concertos. He also performed and recorded these five concertos with the Czech Philharmonic.

In addition, he has performed in England (appearing in Queen Elizabeth Hall in London), Russia (where he played at the Tchaikovsky Hall), France, Germany, Austria, Italy, Canada, various countries in South America, and Korea. As a recitalist, he has played in the Distinguished Artists series at New York's 92nd Street Y, Carnegie Hall's Keyboard Virtuoso Series, the Mostly Mozart Festival, the Ravinia Festival, the Ambassador Foundation Series in California, and the Bank of Boston Celebrity Series.

In 1959, he joined the faculty of Pomona College (1959–62), then the University of Arizona (1962–67), and since 1969 has been on the faculty of the New England Conservatory of Music. He is now a Distinguished Artist-in-Residence there. He has published a warmly received book of anecdotes, vignettes, and insights about his life playing piano, *Piano Pieces* (1996, Farrar, Straus & Giroux). In 1973, he gained major international recognition with a recording of Liszt's *Transcendental Etudes*. In 1986, he joined the faculty of the Juilliard School, and the faculty of Harvard University in 1990 as a visiting professor.—*Joseph Stevenson*

Recommended:

- ○ **Schubert: Sonata D850 & 960** / Sherman / 1992 / Albany 084
- ○ **Premieres & Commissions** / Sherman / 2002 / GM Recordings 2071
- ○ **Beethoven: Sonatas, Vol. 1** / Sherman / 1996 / GM 2050

Mitsuko Shirai

b. May 28, 1949, Nagano, Japan

Mezzo-Soprano

Mitsuko Shirai is regarded as one of the world's great interpreters of German art song. Born and raised in Japan, Shirai studied in Stuttgart, where she came into contact with fellow student and pianist Hartmut Höll. Shirai and Höll teamed up as a duo both as artists and, shortly thereafter, in marriage. Since 1994, they have collaborated as the chief instructors in a "lied centre" for voice and piano duos at the Musikhochschule in Karlsruhe, and have conducted similar workshops in Finland, Weimar, Salzburg, at Tanglewood, and in Cincinnati, among other places. Shirai has sung with Höll in concert venues around the world, but they are especially well known in Germany and Japan, where Shirai was awarded the Great Idemitsu Music Award in 1996. Shirai is one of the most frequently recorded lieder singers of modern times; and though she has recorded for Philips, Camerata, and others, the vast majority of her recordings have appeared on the Capriccio label. She has covered a wide range of lieder running from Louis Spohr to Anton Webern, but she is not just limited to recital singing. A contralto, Shirai has also found acclaim for her performances of Gustav Mahler's orchestral songs. Shirai has also appeared in operas, most frequently in Mozart, but also in such rarities as Richard Wagner's *Das Liebesverbot*. —*Uncle Dave Lewis*

Recommended:

- ○ **Berg: Lieder** / Shirai, Höll / Capriccio 10419
- ○ **Wolf: Mörike Lieder** / Shirai, Höll / 1998 / Capriccio 10830
- ○ **Webern: Early Songs** / Shirai, Höll / Capriccio 10862
- ○ **Brahms: 21 Lieder** / Shirai, Höll / Capriccio 10204
- ○ **Songs With Viola** / Shirai, Höll, Zimmermann / Capriccio 462
- ○ **Schönberg: Ausgewählte Lieder** / Shirai, Höll / Capriccio 10514

John Shirley-Quirk

b. Aug. 28, 1931, Liverpool, England

Baritone

English baritone John Shirley-Quirk enjoyed singing and playing the violin as a child, but his true vocal talent did not become apparent until he was already studying chemistry and physics at the University of London. After several years of teaching those subjects at a British Air Force station, he began to study with the baritone Roy Henderson (1957). In 1961–62, he sang with the Cathedral Choir at St. John's in London; during the same time he made his debut at Glydebourne in 1961 as Gregor Mittenhofer in Henze's *Elegy for Young Lovers*.

In 1963, Benjamin Britten recruited him to join his English Opera Group; with that group he sang the premiere performances of Britten's *Curlew River*, *The Burning Fiery Furnace*, *The Prodigal Son*, *Owen Wingrave*, and *Death in Venice* (between 1964 and 1973). During that time, he also sang Guglielmo in *Così fan tutte* and, later, Golaud in *Pelléas et Mélisande* at the Scottish National Opera. He created the role of Lev in Tippett's *The Ice Break* at Covent Garden in 1977.

Though his career centered around British venues and the music of English composers, Shirley-Quirk's career was by no means provincial. He sang his first performances of *Wozzeck* in St. Louis, and debuted in Berlin with Bartók's *Bluebeard's Castle* in 1969. Milan's Teatro alla Scala engaged him as Rangoni in *Boris Godunov*, and in 1974 he made his Metropolitan Opera debut in Britten's *Death in Venice*. Other important roles in his career were the Speaker in *Die Zauberflöte* and the Music Master in *Ariadne auf Naxos*.

Shirley-Quirk had equal success as a recital and concert singer. He was highly regarded for his interpretation of the major choral works of Bach and Elgar and sang Mahler's *Des Knaben Wunderhorn* on many concerts in Europe, North America, and Australia. His recitals usually included songs by his mentor Benjamin Britten as well as those of Vaughan Williams and Butterworth.

John Shirley-Quirk's lyric baritone voice, while not large, commanded a wide dynamic and expressive range; he had a wonderful sense of phrasing. It was as an interpreter that he was best known; his intellectual curiousity allowed him to explore the inner world of the works he sang. His recordings, particularly of the works of Benjamin Britten, document his fine artistry. In 1975 he was named a Commander of the Order of the British Empire. —*Richard LeSueur*

Recommended:

- ○ **A Recital of English Songs** / Shirley-Quirk / Saga 3336
- ○ **Lutosławski: Symphonies 3 & 4** / Salonen (cond.), Shirley-Quirk, Los Angeles PO / 1994 / Sony 66280
- ○ **Britten: The Rape of Lucretia; Phaedra** / Britten (cond.), Baker, Pears, Luxon, Harper, English CO / 1990 / London 425666

Dmitry Shostakovich

b. Sep. 25, 1906, St. Petersburg, Russia, **d.** Aug. 9, 1975, Moscow, Russia

Composer: Symphonic, Orchestral, Concerto, Chamber Music, Keyboard, Opera, Vocal

Dmitry Shostakovich was a Russian composer whose symphonies and quartets, numbering 15 each, are among the greatest examples of these classic forms from the twentieth century. His style evolved from the brash humor and experimental character of his first period, exemplified by the operas *The Nose* and *Lady Macbeth of Mtsensk*, into both the more introverted melancholy and nationalistic fervor of his second phase (the Symphonies No. 5 and No. 7, "Leningrad"), and finally into the defiant and bleak mood of his last period (exemplified by the Symphony No. 14 and Quartet No. 15). Early in his career his music showed the influence of Prokofiev and Stravinsky, especially in his prodigious and highly successful *First Symphony*. He could effectively communicate a melancholic depth and profound sense of anguish, as one hears in many of his symphonies, concertos, and quartets. Solomon Volkov, in his controversial *Testimony: The Memoirs of Dmitry Shostakovich* explains the composer's seeming bombast as deft satire of the pomposity of the Soviet state, pointing to the "forced rejoicing" of Fifth Symphony's ending. Typical traits of Shostakovich's style include short reiterated melodic or rhythmic figures, motifs of one or two pitches or intervals, and lugubrious and manic string writing.

Dmitry Dmitrievich Shostakovich was born in St. Petersburg, in 1906, and educated at the Petrograd Conservatory. The acid style of his early *Lady Macbeth of Mtsensk* irritated Stalin, and Shostakovich was attacked in the Soviet press. Fearing imprisonment, he withdrew his already rehearsed Fourth Symphony; his Fifth Symphony (1937) carried the subtitle "A Soviet Artist's Reply to Just Criticism." It is more ingenious than most critics have fathomed, for it managed to satisfy both the backward tastes of the party censors and those of more demanding aesthetes in the West.

The 1941 German invasion of Russia inspired the composer's Seventh Symphony, subtitled "Leningrad." Impressed by the symphony's epic-heroic character, Toscanini, Koussevitsky, and Stokowski vied for the Western Hemisphere premiere; the score had to be microfilmed, flown to Teheran, driven to Cairo, and flown out. The work became an enormous success the world over, but eventually fell into obscurity. Still, the composer had for a time become a worldwide celebrity, his picture even appearing on the cover of *Time*.

Shostakovich ran afoul of the government again in 1948, when an infamous decree was issued by the Central Committee of the Communist Party accusing Shostakovich, Prokofiev, and other prominent composers of "formalist perversions." For some time he wrote mostly works glorifying Soviet life or history. Artistic repression diminished in post-Stalinist Russia, but curiously Shostakovich still drew in his modernist horns until the Thirteenth Symphony ("Babi Yar"), a 1962 work based on poems by Yevgeny Yevtushenko. The work provoked major controversy because of its first movement's subject: Russian oppression of the Jews.

In 1966 Shostakovich wrote his Second Cello Concerto, a work on an even higher level than his solid First, but one which has yet to capture as much attention from either artists or the public. That year, Shostakovich was diagnosed with a serious heart condition. He continued to compose, his works growing more sparsely scored and darker, the subject of death becoming prominent. His Fourteenth Symphony (1969), really a collection of songs on texts by Lorca, Apollinaire, Küchelbecker, and Rilke, is a death-obsessed work of considerable dissonance and showing little regard for the Socialist Realism still demanded by the state. Shostakovich died on 9 August 1975. —*AMG*

SYMPHONIC

Symphony No. 1 in F minor, Op. 10 (1926)

First symphonies are generally unsuccessful, or at least questionably successful as compositions. The Brahms First and the Prokofiev *"Classical" Symphony* are exceptions, not least because in the former instance the composer completed the work when he was 42, and in the latter because the pastiche nature of the piece reflected Prokofiev's youthful inclination toward surprises and stimulated his natural ability to write memorable melodies. Shostakovich's First Symphony is light in mood, like Prokofiev's, but is written in a thoroughly modern, if conservative vein.

Shostakovich was 19 when he completed the piece, which he used as his graduation exercise for the Leningrad Conservatory. While he was working on it, he considered calling it "Symphony—Grotesque." It was premiered on May 12, 1926, to an overwhelmingly enthusiastic reception. The symphony quickly caught on throughout the world, as Bruno Walter, Leopold Stokowski, and other noted conductors championed it. By the age of 21 Shostakovich was something of a celebrity, even mentioned in the company of the two Russian giants living abroad, Prokofiev and Stravinsky.

The symphony already shows characteristics of Shostakovich's mature style, especially in its sense—burgeoning though it was—of irony and satire, as evidenced in the mischievous second movement. Both the first and second subjects of the first movement are rather typical of the mature composer as wel; their character would be out of place in the later symphonies, though not in the ballets and film scores to come.

The work is cast in four movements, with the second lasting about five minutes and the other three having a duration of around eight to ten minutes each. The first movement begins with an introductory theme played by muted trumpet and answered by the bassoon. The main theme is marchlike and serious, while the second subject is lyrical and has an air of nonchalance and grace. There is much color in the orchestration when the themes are developed. Overall the melodies in this movement, light though they are, are as memorable as any Shostakovich would write.

As mentioned above, the second movement is satirical and a fine example of the composer's precocity. While it is colorful and imaginative, again featuring brilliant orchestration, it also divulges the influence of Prokofiev. It is no mere imitation, though. The third movement (Lento) begins with an oboe solo and leads to a threatening theme from the brass, after which a Largo brings calm but at the price of gloom. This movement also brings hints of the composer's later tragic style.

The finale is connected to the third movement by a drum roll. The finale (Allegro molto) clearly comes across as episodic, switching from fast to slow and from triple forte to triple piano, and moving from melancholy moods to irony and even playfulness. The music also has a tendency to stop and start in places. Overall, though the work is not one of Shostakovich's greatest, it is one of the finest first symphonies ever written and has remained in the standard repertory.
—Robert Cummings

Recommended:

- ○ **Shostakovich: Symphony 1; Concerto for Piano, Trumpet & Strings** / Jansons (cond.), Berlin PO / 1995 / EMI 55361
- ○ **Shostakovich: Symphonies 1, 5, 6 & 9** / Rozhdestvensky (cond.), USSR Ministry of Culture SO / 1997 / Melodiya 7432149611

Symphony No. 2 in B flat major ("To October"), Op. 14 (1927)

Composed for the tenth anniversary of the October Revolution, Shostakovich's *Symphony No. 2* (1927) is something of an historical and musical artifact. Historically, it recalls a time when people still believed in the Soviet system as the great hope for Russia and, indeed, for mankind; musically, it belongs to the period of experimentation following World War I, when old rules of form and harmony were being tossed to the winds. In the Symphony, in essence, Shostakovich simply tried out all sorts of musical ideas that interested him, hoping that the result would all be of a piece. The work's very designation as a symphony—it was originally titled "To October: A Symphonic Dedication"—appears to have been an afterthought, as though the 21-year-old composer wanted to relieve the pressure of having to follow up his spectacularly successful teenage achievement, the *Symphony No. 1* (1923–26).

The *Symphony No. 2*, cast in a single 20-minute movement, opens in a dark, ominous miasma of atonality that leads into a violent martial section. A bizarre passage for solo violin, clarinet, and bassoon introduces the work's most notorious segment, a fugue-like section with no fewer than 13 subjects. Things quiet down a bit before a blast of a factory whistle—not simulated, but the actual "instrument"—ushers in a chorus that literally sings the praises of the Revolution, culminating at the end in a shout of "October and Lenin! The new age and Lenin! The commune and Lenin!" Though embarrassingly jingoistic at times, and though a decidedly lesser accomplishment than Shostakovich's later symphonies, the work contains moments of genuine excitement and drama and provides an intriguing perspective on the evolution of one of the most-discussed composers of the twentieth century.
—Sol Louis Siegel

Recommended:

- ○ **Shostakovich: Symphonies 2 & 3** / Rostropovich (cond.), London SO, London Voices / 1994 / Teldec 90853
- ○ **Shostakovich: Symphonies 2 & 10** / Haitink (cond.), London PO, London Philharmonic Chorus / 1993 / Decca 425064

Symphony No. 3 in E flat major ("The First of May"), Op. 20 (1929)

The *Third Symphony* bears many similarities to the 1927 *Second*: each is in one movement and uses a chorus whose text celebrates Marxist or socialist ideas. Both works arose at a time when Soviet artists were generally free to create art as they saw fit. Thus, Shostakovich was not coerced or persuaded to write these "revolutionary" works, as he would later be with several other patriotic and ideological works. What has been puzzling to many observers is that the promise offered by Shostakovich's *Symphony No. 1* seems largely to have been squandered in these two works on only intermittently successful experimentalism. Apparently the composer viewed the Revolution as a signal to introduce new musical ideas, especially in the area of form. The *Third Symphony* features a most unusual form: it is cast in one movement, marked Allegretto, and has virtually no thematic development. Certain rhythmic patterns appear throughout to offer some unity, but traditional thematic transformations and relationships are absent.

The Symphony opens quietly with a theme on clarinet, establishing a pleasant, jovial mood. The music quickly turns energetic, even manic, when new thematic material appears. This work is not as densely scored, here and throughout, as are the opening passages of the *Second Symphony*, but there is a sort of density of coloration noticeable, as the direction of the music and the character of the orchestration seem ever-changing; moods shift from mischief and humor to mystery and martial sounds, from ponderousness and lyricism to bombast and drama. Taken in individual passages the music mostly works, but as a symphony, its construction becomes fragile owing to its lack of coherence. Ironically, the work's expressive language is not particularly difficult, being tonal and not particularly dissonant. In the end, the music of this symphony is quite attractive, if confusing in its structure. The choral music, which comes near the end, is a setting of a poem by S. Kirsanov ("The First of May!") that celebrates the international labor holiday.

The *Symphony No. 3* was first performed on January 21, 1930. Subsequent performances in the West, few though they were (Stokowski in 1932 and Frederick Stock in 1933), typically eliminated the pro-Soviet chorus at the end.
—Robert Cummings

Recommended:

- ○ **Shostakovich: Symphonies 1 & 3** / Haitink (cond.), London PO, London Philharmonic Chorus / 1993 / Decca 425063
- ○ **Shostakovich: Symphonies 1 & 3** / Slovak (cond.), Czecho-Slovak Radio SO, Slovak Philharmonic Chorus / 1993 / Naxos 550623
- ○ **Shostakovich: Symphonies 2–4** / Rozhdestvensky (cond.), USSR Ministry of Culture SO / 1999 / Melodiya 7432163462

Symphony No. 4 in C minor, Op. 43 (1935–1936)

Shostakovich began composing his *Symphony No. 4* in September 1935 and put it aside in January 1936 while he went on tour with his cello sonata. On January 28, he read the unsigned editorial on the front page of *Pravda* condemning him and two of his works and predicting he would come to a bad end if he didn't literally change his tune. He finished the *Fourth* in May 1936, but withdrew the work while it was still in rehearsal. The piece was premiered by Kiril Kondrashin in the U.S.S.R. in 1961 and in the West in 1962. Although Shostakovich had enough sense to withdraw the *Fourth*, he also had enough guts to finish it as he started it: as a fusion of his own archly ironic modernism with the deep emotionalism and vast scale of the Mahlerian "Romantic" symphony. The result is a gargantuan work for enormous orchestra in three movements, lasting more than an hour in performance. The opening movement is a nearly half-hour Allegretto poco moderato profligate in themes, bracing in orchestration, unfathomable in form, and unrelentingly violent in expression. With an opening theme clearly based on the opening theme of Mahler's *Symphony No. 6*, Shostakovich's *Fourth* goes its own way toward savage brutality and more savage irony. Through volcanic eruptions and tectonic disruptions, the Allegretto pushes and punches its way to a grinding conclusion. The central movement is a relatively brief Moderato con moto that slithers and sneaks through a blasted landscape, trailing themes from the Scherzo of Mahler's *Second* over ominous percussion rattling. The closing movement is as large as the opening movement, but set in several contiguous sections: an opening funeral march Largo à la Mahler, a fast and tough Allegro with a two-note ostinato, a sarcastically sentimental *Viennese Waltz*, a grandiloquent peroration for the whole massive orchestra, and a quietly ticking coda haunted by trumpet calls and a ghostly celesta.
—James Leonard

Recommended:

- ○ **Shostakovich: Symphony 4** / Haitink (cond.), London PO / 1993 / Decca 425065
- ○ **Shostakovich: Symphonies 4 & 10** / Ormandy (cond.), Philadelphia Orch. / 1996 / Sony 62409
- ○ **Shostakovich: Symphony 4; Two Pieces From Scarlatti** / Rozhdestvensky (cond.), USSR Ministry of Culture SO / 1995 / Praga 250090

○ **Shostakovich: Symphony 4** / Gergiev (cond.), Kirov Orch. / 2004 / Philips 000340602

Symphony No. 5 in D minor, Op. 47 (1937)

In 1936, the Soviet government launched an official attack against Dmitry Shostakovich's music, calling it "vulgar, formalistic, [and] neurotic." He became an example to other Soviet composers, who rightfully interpreted these events as a broad campaign against musical modernism. This constituted a crisis, both in Shostakovich's career and in Soviet music as a whole; composers had no choice but to write simple, optimistic music that spoke directly (especially through folk idioms and patriotic programs) to the people and glorified the state.

In light of these circumstances, Shostakovich's *Fifth Symphony* (first performed in 1937) is a bold composition that seems to fly in the face of his critics. Although the musical language is pared down from that of his earlier symphonies, the *Fifth* eschews any hint of a patriotic program and, instead, dwells on undeniably somber and tragic affects—wholly unacceptable public emotions at the time. According to the cellist Mstislav Rostropovich, the government would certainly have had Shostakovich executed for writing such a work had the public ovation at the first performance not lasted 40 minutes. The official story, however, is quite different. An unknown commentator dubbed the symphony "the creative reply of a Soviet artist to justified criticism," and to the work was attached an autobiographical program focusing on the composer's metamorphosis from incomprehensible formalist to standard-bearer of the communist party. Publicly, Shostakovich accepted the official interpretation of his work; however, in the controversial collection of his memoirs (*Testimony*, by Solomon Volkov) he is quoted as saying: "I think it is clear to everyone what happens in the Fifth. The rejoicing is forced, created under threat... you have to be a complete oaf not to hear that."

Regardless of its philosophical underpinnings, Shostakovich's *Symphony No. 5* is a masterpiece of the orchestral repertory, poignant and economical in its conception. There is no sign of the excess of ideas so common in the *Fourth Symphony*. Instead, Shostakovich deploys the orchestra sparingly and allows the entire work to grow naturally out of just a few motives. Given some of his earlier works, the Fifth is conservative in language. Throughout the work he allows the strings to be the dominant orchestral force, making soloistic use of the woodwinds and horn especially effective. The Moderato begins with a jagged, foreboding canon in the strings that forms the motivic basis for the entire movement. The impassioned mood is occasionally interrupted by a lyrical melody with string ostinato, later the subject of a duet for flute and horn.

The second movement (Allegretto) is a grotesque 3/4 dance which, at times, can't help but mock itself; the brass section is featured prominently. The following Largo, a sincere and personal outpouring of musical emotion, is said to have left the audience at the work's premiere in tears. Significantly, it was composed during an intensely creative period following the arrest and execution of one of Shostakovich's teachers.

The concluding Allegro non troppo has been the center of much debate: some critics consider it a poorly constructed concession to political pressure, while others have made note of its possible irony. While the prevailing mood is triumphant, there is some diversion to the somber and foreboding, and it is not until the end that it takes on the overtly "big-finishy" character for which it is so noted. *—Allen Schrott*

Recommended:

○ **Shostakovich: Symphony 5** / Mravinsky (cond.), Leningrad PO / Erato 45752

○ **Shostakovich: Symphonies 5 & 9** / Haitink (cond.), Concertgebouw / 1993 / Decca 425066

○ **Shostakovich: Symphonies 5 & 9** / Bernstein (cond.), New York Philharmonic / 1999 / Sony 61841

Symphony No. 6 in B minor, Op. 54 (1939)

When Shostakovich was writing this symphony in 1939, the artistic atmosphere in Soviet Russia was in a transitional state. Though government censorship was still pervasive, composers were encouraged to write anti-German propaganda, at least until the period of the Nazi-Soviet treaty. When Germany invaded, of course, Soviet cultural bosses were forced to turn their attention to the war, and anti-German music came back into fashion.

Shostakovich had indicated his intention to write a choral symphony about Lenin in 1938, but would not get around to it for another 22 years, until the *Symphony No. 12* (1960–61). He undoubtedly felt compelled to write patriotic music—or to promise to do so—since he had already incurred the wrath of party censors with his opera *Lady Macbeth of Mtsensk*, which was banned in 1936. His decision to abandon the idea of composing a Lenin symphony instead of his purely instrumental *Symphony No. 6* probably had something to do with fears that if such a patriotic work were greeted unenthusiastically by party arts officials, he might end up in a labor camp or cemetery with some of his less fortunate colleagues. Perhaps he sensed that Stalin may not have wanted all the glory and attention of the Revolution attributed to Lenin, and thus decided to steer clear of the idea for the time being.

In any event, Shostakovich produced a work whose gloomy and intense opening panel is counterbalanced by a pair of jovial and light movements. Put together, they are shorter than the opening Largo, and the contrast presented by their cheerfulness and wit gives the symphony a somewhat split personality. The main theme of the first movement is presented in the lower strings: it is a muscular, dark melody that is repeated in many guises during the exposition. A new theme finally appears on the English horn to launch the second subject group, and then the material is reprised, but in a much more compact way.

The second movement is marked Allegro and immediately takes on a playful character. While the music and orchestration sound like Shostakovich, the spirit of Prokofiev seems to hover above. Although there is some tension and conflict in the middle section, the impression left by this Scherzando is one of joy and good humor.

The finale, marked Presto, is exuberant, almost ecstatic throughout most of its duration. Even the subdued and brief middle section seems eager to hand the reins back to the infectious good spirits of the main material. The ending is one of the most joyous, colorful, and unpretentious the composer ever wrote. There is neither bombast here nor an extraneous note.

Shostakovich's *Symphony No. 6* was premiered on November 5, 1939, and received little notice. Coincidentally, Prokofiev's *Alexander Nevsky*, a product of the anti-German tendency then prevalent, also received its first performance at the same concert, garnering much acclaim. Some have conjectured that Shostakovich may have been fortunate that his symphony drew little attention, for Soviet censors might have singled out the tragic first movement as too cerebral and confusing. A typical performance of the work lasts just under 30 minutes. *—Robert Cummings*

Recommended:

○ **Shostakovich: Symphonies 6 & 12** / Mravinsky (cond.), Leningrad PO / Le Chant du Monde 7254017

○ **Shostakovich: Symphonies 5 & 12** / Haitink (cond.), Concertgebouw / 1993 / Philips 425067

○ **Shostakovich: Symphonies 1, 5, 6 & 9** / Rozhdestvensky (cond.), USSR Ministry of Culture SO / 1997 / Melodiya 7432149611

Symphony No. 7 in C major ("Leningrad"), Op. 60 (1941)

It is impossible to deny the overwhelming impact Shostakovich's *Symphony No. 7* had on its listeners in 1942. Written by Shostakovich after he had been transported out of his besieged hometown of Leningrad, the *Seventh* is a patriotic hymn to his city and country and a rallying cry to the foes of fascism. Its premiere in the U.S.S.R. was world news, and the securing of its first performance rights in the West was contested by Toscanini, Stokowski, and Koussevitzky. Toscanini won, and the work was rapturously received and repeatedly performed. But even before the war had ended, the exalted position of the *"Leningrad" Symphony* had slipped, and commentators in the West derided it as pompous and prosaic. The symphony, rehabilitated from being a patriotic piece to being a subversive piece based on the purported testimony of Shostakovich, only later received regular performances in the West. The truth is that Shostakovich's *Seventh* is an enormous piece for a gargantuan orchestra set in four vast movements lasting more than 70 minutes in performances. Its opening Allegretto, nearly half an hour in length, has proud and determined C major themes at its start and close and a central section that takes a theme from Offenbach and turns it into a massive ostinato that overwhelms the C major themes with its brutal banality. This is followed by a haunted Moderato of plucked strings and screeching woodwinds and by a vast Adagio with stirring strings and bold brass. The closing Allegro non troppo returns to the monumental style of the opening movement with grand and glorious themes culminating in an interminable C major climax. The truth is that the *Seventh* is a work of banal themes and bombastic climaxes, but Shostakovich's imagination and discipline have fused the banal and bombastic into an overwhelming musical work. *—James Leonard*

Recommended:

○ **Shostakovich: Symphony No. 7** / Kubelik (cond.), Concertgebouw / Audiophile 557

○ **Shostakovich: Symphonies 1 & 7** / Bernstein (cond.), Chicago SO / DG 427632

○ **Shostakovich: Symphony 7** / Mravinsky (cond.), Leningrad PO / 2000 / Omega 1030

Symphony No. 8 in C minor ("Stalingrad"), Op. 65 (1943)

Just as his countryman Prokofiev wrote a trilogy of so-called *War Sonatas* for piano, one might say that Shostakovich composed a trio of war symphonies, of which this work is the second and surely the greatest. It was preceded by the "Leningrad" symphony, a programmatic composition whose artistically dubious Bolero-like first movement buildup, now thought by some to signify the banality of evil, was originally said to represent the heroism of those defending Leningrad against the Nazi invaders. The Symphony No. 8 is surrounded by no such controversy, and is a far more profound work. Like its predecessor, it exudes an atmosphere of war and struggle, of loss and hope. But here pain and destruction become the dominant issues, replacing the Seventh's admirable but more naïve themes of heroism and triumph.

The Eighth came at a time when Soviet censors were completely occupied with the war. Shostakovich had come under attack in January 1936, for his opera *Lady Macbeth of Mtsensk* and thereafter had to modify his expressive language, even though he was hardly in the vanguard of modernism. Now the situation was changed: Prokofiev got away with writing his *Piano Sonata No. 7*, which even received a Stalin prize despite a first movement that flirted with atonality and a finale rife with dissonance. Thus Shostakovich was free to write a darker, deeper, more challenging work. But its tragic character was mainly a by-product of the war and of the composer's own often naturally pessimistic musical persona.

The massive first-movement Adagio is nearly as long as the other four combined. Its music is dark and tense throughout, consisting of an introductory theme and two long-breathed, dark melodies that form the main and secondary subjects. These two explode in the catastrophic development section, climaxed by a brutal fugal march based on the first theme. A three-note motif that appears in different guises (C-B flat-C, C-D-C, or B-C-B) serves as a motto throughout symphony and launches both of the first movement's main themes. After the explosive development section, the music seems to go into a tailspin for the remainder of the movement.

The ensuing Allegretto seems at times to suggest joviality, but quickly undercuts that feeling with an ironic twist or a turn toward desperation. The driving, neurotic Allegro non troppo that follows offers a theme that races breathlessly along, propelled, it seems, by bombs dropping in the distance. After a somewhat bombastic middle section, the theme returns and explodes in a percussive outburst, after which the Largo passacaglia begins without pause. The theme here, gloomy and profound and related to the first movement's second theme, repeats a dozen times, imparting a mood throughout of loss, if not of despair.

The finale begins with the three-note motif. While there are suggestions of relief from the oppressive strife and tragedy, the music is mostly devoid of strong emotions, as if to express a sense of numbness due to the war's terrors. The music suddenly erupts near the end of this 15-minute panel, however, with huge sustained chords that recall the catastrophic moments from the earlier movements. The three-note motif is heard repeatedly in the quiet that follows, and the symphony ends in a mood of resignation and drained emotions.

The Eighth Symphony was premiered on November 4, 1943, and Shostakovich and the work's conductor, Evgeny Mravinsky, received a half-hour ovation. Five years later, however, the composer was chastised for writing the symphony by Zhdanov and the party censors. *—Robert Cummings*

Recommended:

- ○ **Shostakovich: Symphony 8** / Haitink (cond.), Concertgebouw / 1993 / Decca 425071
- ○ **Shostakovich: Symphonies 7 & 8** / Rozhdestvensky (cond.), USSR Ministry of Culture SO / 1998 / Melodiya 7432153457

Symphony No. 9 in E flat major, Op. 70 (1945)

Shostakovich composed this work for Schumann-sized orchestra plus percussion in the summer of 1945, and Yevgeny Mravinsky led the first performance at Leningrad on November 3 of that year. Given the size of Shostakovich's war-haunted seventh and eighth symphonies, Joseph Stalin expected a *Ninth* in 1945 that "out-Mahlered Beethoven," in the late Boris Schwarz's phrase. In *Testimony*, Solomon Volkov recalled the composer's saying, "They wanted a fanfare from me, an ode, a majestic *Ninth*.... I doubt that Stalin ever questioned his own genius or greatness. But when the war against Hitler was won, he went off the deep end, like a frog puffing himself up to the size of an ox, and now I was supposed to write an apotheosis of Stalin. I simply could not.... My stubbornness cost me dearly."

Volkov called the *Ninth* a work "full of sarcasm and bitterness." Disguised as an homage to Haydn, it was Shostakovich's shortest symphony since the *Second* of 1927, despite having five movements (the last three are played without pause). In an effort to shield Shostakovich from political fallout, conductor Mravinsky called the new symphony "a joyous sigh of relief... a work directed against philistinism, which ridicules complacency and bombast, the desire to rest on one's laurels." Putting on a good face, the Soviet hierarchy echoed Mravinsky, but only temporarily.

By and large, Western critics dismissed the work as trivial. However, in his 1990 book *The New Shostakovich*, Ian MacDonald asserted that "only a dunce could have failed to realize the composer was up to something," pointing out the code-bearing nature of recurring notes and rhythms. A "Stalin motif" is frighteningly present—always two notes, one usually short, one long—from its raucous first appearance, without musical point, in the double-exposition of a giddy Allegro movement. The opening "mimic[s] the ordinary citizen's carefree relief at the victorious conclusion of the war. [But] the second subject—a crude quick-march, led by a two-note, tonic-dominant trombone—is clearly symbolic of the Vozhd [Stalin]." MacDonald hears "fights breaking out [and] for a hectic moment the music continues in two keys until the trombone wrests control," whereupon strings capitulate "and the reprise ends on sneering trills, the quick-march in control."

A Moderato movement follows, with a B minor main subject for clarinet that is "wan, sad-faced, with a telltale two-note pendant," and "a heel-dragging" second one: "a chain of two-note cells [that] subtly mock conventional grief." Horns "warn off [the] real feeling" that breaks through briefly, whereupon "happy-face clowns [usher in] a cheery scherzo... another street party [as in the first movement] that goes violently wrong."

Menacing brass octaves begin the fourth movement; then a bassoon recitative sends mixed signals, "another mask" that leaves the strings uneasy. The Allegretto finale "erupts into action.... A dark whirlwind drives the movement to a climax of teetering expectation—but all that emerges is the clownish main theme, hammered out by the entire orchestra. Shostakovich's contempt is scalding. Here are your leaders, the music jeers: circus clowns. Point made, [he] summons a helter-skelter coda and slams [the *Ninth*] shut."

For MacDonald it is "an open gesture of dissent [that] ruthlessly targeted Stalinism.... Wagnerisms, the most prominent being an allusion to Wotan's Leitmotif in the fourth movement, are probable expressions of the view, outlined in *Testimony*, of Stalin and Hitler as 'spiritual relatives.'" Shostakovich paid dearly indeed for the snub; he was damned in 1948 as a "formalist" and blacklisted, leaving him only movie scores for income. After Stalin's death in 1953 he finished a *Tenth Symphony*, in whose scherzo the Vozhd himself makes one last, unforgettably terrifying appearance. *—Roger Dettmer*

Recommended:

- ○ **Shostakovich: Symphonies 5 & 9** / Haitink (cond.), London PO / 1993 / Decca 425066
- ○ **Shostakovich: Symphonies 1, 5, 6 & 9** / Rozhdestvensky (cond.), USSR Ministry of Culture SO / 1997 / Melodiya 7432149611
- ○ **Shostakovich: Symphonies 5 & 9** / Spivakov (cond.), Russian National Orch. / 2000 / Well-Tempered Productions 5190

Symphony No. 10 in E minor, Op. 93 (1953)

This was Shostakovich's first symphony in eight years, and the gap between this and the 1945 *Ninth* owed nothing to a lack of inspiration in the genre. In 1948, Shostakovich, Prokofiev, Khachaturian, and other noted Soviet composers were censured for writing what party censors called "formalistic" music, a code word for dissonance and the expression of negative emotions or cynicism. Of course, examined against such vague and, therefore, potentially all-inclusive standards, virtually any composition could be vulnerable to attack, and many of Shostakovich's were singled out. After January 1948, most Soviet composers were simply unsure of what was safe to write. Shostakovich turned to writing patriotic bombast like the choral work *Song of the Forests* (1949), the cantata *The Sun Shines on Our Motherland* (1952), as well as vapid film scores like that for the 1950 release *The Fall of Berlin*.

On March 5, 1953, Stalin died. The stringent policies in the arts loosened somewhat in the aftermath of the dictator's passing, and Shostakovich seized the opportunity to write a large symphony, not least because he could satirize Stalin in it. In fact, the second movement is said to be a depiction of the Soviet tyrant. The music in this Allegro is angry and intense, but also quite Russian. Certainly, it can be heard as austere and hostile, sinister and threatening, thereby painting an effective and credible portrait of Stalin, but it might also express anxiety and fear, emotions hardly new to Shostakovich. Thus, the "Stalin" interpretation of this movement, while quite possibly valid, is not fully convincing, much less verifiable.

The *Symphony No. 10* opens up with a Moderato movement that is nearly as long as the ensuing three movements combined. The mood is dark and brooding and the structure is not unlike that of the *Eighth*'s opening section: there is an introductory theme, followed by two "main" themes. Here, the second of those is faster than its counterpart in the *Eighth*, and while the atmosphere is intense in the exposition and development section, there is a relaxation in intensity in the recapitulation and coda, where the *Eighth* remains mired in darkness.

As suggested above, the second movement is a biting, sinister piece. It is followed by an Allegretto of decidedly Russian character, whose mood brightens somewhat, especially in the middle section. This movement is notable because it is the first time that Shostakovich used his personal motto, D—E flat—C—B, which, via German transliteration, represents his initials, DSCH. This motif would appear in numerous subsequent works by the composer, like the *Violin Concerto No. 1* (1947–48; rev. 1955) and his popular *String Quartet No. 8* (1961).

The finale starts off with an Andante that seems mired in a slow-motion haze. Suddenly the mood turns joyous and playful, lively and colorful. An austere middle section recalls the opening gloom, but the cheerful music returns and the symphony ends in a blaze of ecstatic joy. The *Symphony No. 10* was premiered in Leningrad on December 17, 1953, under the baton of Yevgeny Mravinsky. It has become, with the *Symphony No. 5*, Shostakovich's most often performed and recorded symphony. *—Robert Cummings*

Recommended:

- ○ **Shostakovich: Symphony 10; Britten: Sinfonia da Requiem** / Rattle (cond.), London Philharmonia Orch. / 1993 / EMI 64870
- ○ **Shostakovich: Symphony 10** / Rostropovich (cond.), London SO / 1991 / Teldec 74529
- ○ **Shostakovich: Symphonies 10 & 11** / Rozhdestvensky (cond.), USSR Ministry of Culture SO / 1999 / Melodiya 7432163461
- ○ **Shostakovich: Symphony 10** / Mravinsky (cond.); Leningrad PO / 1995 / Leningrad Masters 1322

Symphony No. 11 in G minor ("The Year 1905"), Op. 103 (1957)

Shostakovich's *Symphony No. 11* ostensibly was written to commemorate the tragic events of January 9, 1905, when several hundred of about 10,000 demonstrators at the Tsar's St. Petersburg winter palace were killed on orders from government officials. The slaughter incited further demonstrations and anti-Tsarist activities, culminating in the 1917 Bolshevik Revolution. Shostakovich would later claim, in the controversial Volkov book *Testimony*, that the symphony's inspiration was actually the Hungarian Revolution of 1956. In any event, the symphony was subtitled "1905," not "1956," and most of its themes were derived from Russian revolutionary songs. Its four movements, all with subtitles, are played without pause. The first (Adagio) is subtitled "The Palace Square" and opens in a somber, dark mood built on several motifs, a crucial one on drums representing the protesters forming at the palace. Themes from two rather mournful revolutionary songs, *Listen* and *The Prisoner*, are then presented and later developed. The movement is permeated by ominous thudding drums, eerie string writing, and a growing sense of unrest. The nearly 20-minute second movement (Allegro—Adagio) is subtitled "The Ninth of January" and depicts the bloody events of that day. It is the most complex and dramatic panel, recalling motivic and thematic material from the first movement and using themes from two songs in Shostakovich's *10 Poems for chorus without orchestra*—"Comrades, the Bugles Are Sounding" and "Bare Your Heads"—the latter reappearing at climactic moments in the third and fourth movements. The most dramatic music in the second movement comes with the fugato section, which builds to a brutal, percussive climax using a variant of the demonstrators' motif to depict the slaughter. The eerie quiet from the symphony's opening follows, leading into the Adagio third movement. Subtitled "In Memoriam," it is mournful, using the melody from the popular song "You Fell As a Victim." Later, the theme from another song, "Welcome, the Free Word of Liberty," is quoted, after which comes a powerful climax. The finale (Allegro non troppo) is subtitled "The Tocsin" (alarm bell). In its feverish opening, it alludes to the music in Shostakovich's *Symphony No. 10*'s second movement, which supposedly satirizes Stalin (Volkov). Later, the melody from "Rage, You Tyrants" is used and the movement gradually takes on a defiant, triumphal air, with a bell tolling its warning at the symphony's powerful close. *—Robert Cummings*

Recommended:

- ○ **Shostakovich: Symphony 11; Jazz Suite 1; Waltz; Tahiti Trot** / Jansons (cond.), Philadelphia Orch. / 1997 / EMI 55601
- ○ **Shostakovich: Symphony 11** / DePreist (cond.), Helsinki PO / 1993 / Delos 3080
- ○ **Shostakovich: Symphony 11** / Leningrad PO, Mravinsky (cond.) / Praga 7254018

Symphony No. 12 in D minor ("The Year 1917: in Memory of Lenin"), Op. 112 (1959–1961)

There are five Shostakovich symphonies of his 15 that have political/historical programs: *Nos. 2, 3, 7, 11,* and *12.* Probably one of the strongest arguments put forth by those who support the Volkov view of the composer (i.e., that he felt constant oppression in both his professional and personal life under the Stalin and post-Stalin Soviet regimes and thus satirized his persecutors with veiled symbolism in his music), is that these five patriotic symphonies are his least effective. The *Twelfth* is probably his most approachable symphony, not least because it contains several attractive, quite memorable themes. But its expressive language is self-consciously straightforward, as if the composer were striving with every note to avoid complexity and controversy at all cost.

The *Symphony No. 12,* being rather simple and straightforward, contains nothing of the hidden symbolism one hears in other Shostakovich symphonies, like the *Fifth, Seventh,* and *Tenth.* Thus, its apparently sincere depiction of the Bolshevik Revolution as a heroic and liberating event becomes hard to reconcile with the view of Shostakovich as a dissident. Yet it is possible that the composer disapproved of the Soviet system under Stalin and the oppression that still lingered, but still harbored a positive view of Lenin and the revolutionary movement.

The *Symphony No. 12* has four continuous movements, each having subtitles relating to the Revolution: "Revolutionary Petrograd" (marked Moderato—Allegro), "Razliv" (Allegro-Adagio), "Aurora" (Allegro), and "The Dawn of Humanity" (Allegretto—Moderato). It should be mentioned here that the second-movement subtitle, "Razliv" (Overflow), refers to the locale north of St. Petersburg where Lenin hid out to conduct his revolutionary activities in safety; and Aurora was the name of the ship that fired a shot through a window of the Winter Palace, initiating the Revolution.

There are two main themes that occur throughout the symphony. The first symbolizes oppression (in the first movement introduction) and a rallying against it in the Allegro section that follows. The ensuing second theme, which is similar to the first, though more hymn-like and serene, symbolizes hope and ultimately victory over the oppressors. Both have strong appeal, and as Shostakovich develops them throughout the symphony, their metamorphoses yield music of colorful bombast, including the march near the end of the third movement and the percussion-laden coda of the finale, the drama as found in the development of the first movement, and the restlessness of the second movement.

As a populist drama, this symphony offers thematic appeal but tempers its attractive qualities with the composer's overly simplistic expressive language and blatant bombast in his apparent artistic acquiescence to Soviet authorities. Was Shostakovich a true dissident, like Solzhenitsyn, or an opportunist? *—Robert Cummings*

Recommended:

- ○ **Shostakovich: Symphonies 5 & 12** / Haitink (cond.), Concertgebouw / 1993 / Decca 425067
- ○ **Shostakovich: Symphony 12; Cello Concerto 2** / Polyansky (cond.), Russian State SO / 1998 / Chandos 9585
- ○ **Shostakovich: Symphonies 12 & 13** / Rozhdestvensky (cond.), USSR Ministry of Culture SO / 1999 / Melodiya 7432163460
- ○ **Shostakovich: Symphonies 6 & 12** / Mravinsky (cond.), Leningrad PO / Praga 254017

Symphony No. 13 in B flat minor ("Babi Yar"), Op. 113 (1962)

The death of Josef Stalin on March 5, 1953, ushered in an era of freedom for Soviet artists. But, oddly enough, for nearly a decade following the dictator's passing, Shostakovich, one of the chief targets of Soviet censors in the past, wrote nothing of a radical or adventurous nature. In 1962, however, he broke out of his conservative shell and composed his *Symphony No. 13,* whose expressive language is deeper and more uncompromising than any of his then-recent compositions. Only the unwieldy *Symphony No. 4,* whose belated premiere took place in 1961, 25 years after its completion, is as challenging and substantive.

Even before the *Symphony No. 13*'s premiere, Shostakovich was in trouble with the Khrushchev regime over it, though not because of his music, but rather because of the texts he chose to set. The work uses five poems by Evgeny Yevtushenko, and it was the first of these in particular, "Babi Yar," from which the symphony derives its subtitle, that created the controversy. It tells of oppression of the Jews in Russia, an injustice Soviets felt the need to deny.

Over the objections of government officials, the premiere of the symphony took place in December 1962. It was a success, but pressures mounted to suppress or modify the work and a second performance had to be canceled. Bowing at last to the wishes of authorities, Yevtushenko and Shostakovich allowed the texts to be attenuated. Another performance took place, with the textual changes, after which the work disappeared from Soviet concert halls for nearly three years.

The *Symphony No. 13* is made up of five movements, each having a subtitle pertaining to a Yevtushenko poem: Adagio ("Babi Yar"), Allegretto ("Humor"), Adagio ("In the store"), Largo ("Fears"), and Allegretto ("A career"). The chorus sings in unison or octaves throughout, except for a passage near the end of the third movement. The orchestral forces are sizeable, but Shostakovich's scoring tends to be sparing throughout, although there are outbursts of considerable power in several places.

The first movement is dark and dramatic, morbid and harsh. This bleak panel, with the bass soloist prominent throughout much of its duration, is an atmospheric and powerful setting of Yevtushenko's texts. The second movement is a Scherzo, and its "Humor" is often tart and brash.

The last three movements are continuous. The text of "In the store" praises the ordinary working woman. Shostakovich's music is subdued and dark throughout most of the movement, painting a bleak picture of life (which Soviet officials also could not have found much to their liking). The riveting climax in this section comes when the chorus sings (about women), "To shortchange them is shameful. . . ." The austere and dark fourth movement deals with fears, as the chorus starts off whispering the word, effectively summoning a fearful atmosphere. The last movement, which offers text praising those with integrity in their careers, begins with an attractive, slightly sad waltz, although the mood throughout is brighter than in any previous panel. The ending is quiet, with the waltz turning gossamer, almost mystical.

In the last two decades of the twentieth century, this symphony gained considerable popularity both in the concert hall and on recordings. A typical performance of it lasts from about an hour to nearly 70 minutes. *—Robert Cummings*

Recommended:

- ○ **Shostakovich: Symphony 13** / Masur (cond.), Leiferkus, New York Philharmonic, New York Choral Artists / 1994 / Teldec 90848

○ **Shostakovich: Symphony 13** / Haitink (cond.), Rintzler, Concertgebouw Orch. Amsterdam / 1993 / Decca 425073

○ **BBC Proms: Tchaikovsky & Shostakovich** / Sinaisky (cond.), Leiferkus, BBC PO, Huddersfield Choral Society, Leeds Festival Chorus / 1999 / BBC 1002

○ **Shostakovich: Symphonies 12 & 13** / Rozhdestvensky (cond.), Safiulin, USSR Ministry of Culture SO / 1999 / Melodiya 7432163460

Symphony No. 14 for soprano, bass, strings & percussion, Op. 135 (1969)

In *Testimony*, by Solomon Volkov, Shostakovich is quoted: "Fear of death may be the most intense emotion of all.... [However], death is not considered an appropriate theme for Soviet art, and writing about death is tantamount to wiping your nose on your sleeve in company....I wrote a number of works reflecting my understanding of the question, and as it seems to me, they're not particularly optimistic works. The most important of them, I feel, is the *Fourteenth Symphony*; I have special feelings for it.... [People] read this idea in the *Fourteenth*: 'Death is all-powerful.' They want the finale to be comforting, to say that death is only the beginning. But it's not a beginning, it's the real end, there will be nothing afterward, nothing...."

The musical vocabulary is his most advanced since two early and cacophonous cantata-symphonies: *No. 2 (To October)* and *No. 3 (The First of May)*. He himself chose texts in Russian translations. It is scored for vocalists, strings, and percussion. Although basically diatonic and texturally transparent, the writing in *No. 14* is recurringly atonal, with violent outbursts, and an implicit repudiation of "socialist realism." The vocal line suggests accompanied recitative or declamation, even Sprechstimme.

"De Profundis" (García Lorca) for bass. In memory of "the hundred lovers" who died in the Spanish Civil War, a bleak theme winds, while the voice declaims over a contrabass drone.

"Malagueña" (García Lorca) for soprano. A fast and frightening depiction of Death's coming and going. Castanets and a whip-crack lead without pause to—

"Loreley" (Apollinaire, "after Clemens Brentano") for soprano and baritone. A dialogue between the legendary nymph and a smitten Bishop, who seeks to save her soul, but loses it to the Rhine.

"The Suicide" (Apollinaire) for soprano. Repetitions in the text engender music that doubles back on itself hypnotically.

"Les Attentives One" (Apollinaire) for soprano. About incest and imminent death, with a macabre rhythm on tom-toms and xylophone that creates hysteria, leading to—

"Les Attentives Two" (Apollinaire) for soprano and bass. "Madame, you've lost something." "My heart, nothing important." An ostinato on xylophone accompanies the words "It is here I snap my fingers...."

"In the Santé Prison" (Apollinaire) for bass. The solitary despair of "Lazarus entering the tomb instead of coming forth as he did," with a long, eerie, pizzicato interlude.

"Reply of the Zaporozhean Cossacks to the Sultan of Constantinople" (Apollinaire) for bass. They revile a monarch "more criminal than Barabbas...fed on garbage and dirt...."

"O Delvig! Delvig!" (Küchelbecker) for bass. Addressed to poet-comrade Anton Delvig, this touchingly lyrical lament from prison contains the only ray of light in the work. There is a string epilogue before—

"The Poet's Death" (Rilke) for soprano. A winding musical line recalls "De Profundis" while the singer contemplates the corpse.

"Conclusion" (Rilke) for soprano and bass. In unison, the soloists sing over castanets and string pizzicatos of Death's immensity. It ends on a densely dissonant chord. *—Roger Dettmer*

Recommended:

○ **Shostakovich: Symphony 14** / Haitink (cond.), Fischer-Dieskau, Varady, Concertgebouw / 1993 / Decca 425074

○ **Shostakovich: Symphony 14; Britten: Nocturne** / Britten (cond.), Vishnievskaya, English CO / 1999 / BBC 8013

○ **Shostakovich: Symphonies 14 & 15** / Rozhdestvensky (cond.), USSR Ministry of Culture SO / 1998 / Melodiya 7432159057

Symphony No. 15 in A major, Op. 141 (1971)

Shostakovich's *Symphony No. 15* differs in several substantial ways from his other late symphonies. The *Eleventh* (1957), subtitled "The Year 1905," and *Twelfth* (1960), subtitled "The Year 1917," are both programmatic and relate to the political and historical events associated with the year in the title. The next two symphonies have sung texts, with the *Thirteenth* (1962), for bass, chorus, and orchestra, carrying the subtitle "Babiy Yar" (texts by Yevtushenko), and the *Symphony No. 14* (1969), for soprano and bass soloists and chamber orchestra, not really a symphony but a collection of songs based on texts by Lorca, Apollinaire, Küchelbecker, and Rilke.

With the *Symphony No. 15*, Shostakovich's last foray in the genre, the composer at last returned to the purely instrumental and non-programmatic realm, which, one could argue, he had not revisited since the 1939 *Symphony No. 6*. While it is true that the Symphonies 8, 9, and 10 carry no official program, the first two are clearly associated with the war (the Ninth is a victory celebration), and the Tenth allegedly contains a portrait of Stalin in its second movement. But the *Symphony No. 15* inhabits a purely emotional and intellectual plane, quite removed—as far as we know—from the world of politics and history. Yet it is generally agreed that the work is autobiographical, not in the sense that it depicts specific events, but rather that it expresses reflections on the past.

The Fifteenth is also unique in that it is lightly scored throughout, certainly the leanest of the composer's purely instrumental symphonies. Shostakovich had moved in this direction with the *Symphony No. 14* and had found increasing difficulty in writing in the late 1960s, owing to a nervous-system disorder—brittle-bone poliomyelitis—that gradually crippled his right hand, making simple tasks problematic and rendering the process of scoring complicated orchestral works an extremely grueling task. The *Symphony No. 15* was premiered on January 8, 1972, with the composer's son Maxim conducting. A typical performance of the work lasts from 40 to 45 minutes.

The work is divided into four movements: 1) Allegretto, 2) Adagio—Largo—Adagio, 3) Allegretto, and 4) Adagio—Allegretto. It stands apart from the composer's other symphonies in its quotations and near-quotations from compositions by others and by Shostakovich himself. The symphony is, in fact, chock full of these quotations. The first movement, for example, quotes the famous (Lone Ranger) theme from Rossini's *William Tell overture*. The Fate motif from Wagner's *Ring cycle* and themes from *Siegfried* and *Tristan und Isolde* appear in the finale. There are near-quotations from Tchaikovsky and Mahler, and Shostakovich alludes to themes in some of his earlier symphonies.

The first movement, originally subtitled "The Toyshop," has a childlike atmosphere to its playfulness, yet at times sounds under the spell of dark and cynical forces. The second movement is long and enigmatic, having a funereal mood for much of its duration and climaxing in an outburst of what is clearly anger or frustration. The third movement is the shortest in the work (about four minutes) and is bitingly satirical, even nose-thumbing. The finale contains the most cryptic and perhaps most profound music in the work. Because it, too, appears to express the composer's thoughts on death, many have concluded that the autobiographical elements in the work are expressed in a sort of cradle-to-grave story, the first movement representing childhood and the finale the composer's final years and imminent passing. *—Robert Cummings*

Recommended:

○ **Shostakovich: Symphony 15** / Rostropovich (cond.), London SO / 1991 / Teldec 74560

○ **Shostakovich: Symphony 15; Mussorgsky: Songs and Dances of Death** / Solti (cond.), Chicago SO / 1998 / Decca 458919

○ **Shostakovich: Symphony 15; Piano Sonata 2** / Ormandy (cond.), Philadelphia Orch. / 2000 / RCA 63587

○ **Shostakovich: Symphonies 14 & 15** / Rozhdestvensky (cond.), USSR Ministry of Culture SO / 1998 / Melodiya 7432159057

ORCHESTRAL

The Age of Gold, suite from the ballet, Op. 22a (1930)

Shostakovich extracted this suite from his unsuccessful 1930 so-called athletic ballet *The Age of Gold*, about the adventures of a Soviet soccer team abroad. The suite's four unnamed movements last a mere 16 or 17 minutes. The opening movement, "Introduction," derives from the work's overture. It is vigorous and colorful, sassy and sarcastic, auguring the music in the composer's 1936 *Symphony No. 5*. After a playful, mischievous opening, a parade of themes and light moods ensues, with numerous tempo shifts, the whole sounding episodic in its generally comic character. The ensuing Adagio, fully half the entire length of the suite, begins with a lovely, if slightly sour theme on soprano saxophone, representing a cabaret singer in the ballet. The middle section turns darkly intense, but the outer panels are dreamy and nocturnal. The ensuing Polka, satirizing League of Nations politicians, is humorous if a bit overdone, and the concluding rambunctious "Dance," whose music is associated with the soccer team in the ballet, clearly exhibits the influence of Stravinsky's *Petrushka*. *—Robert Cummings*

Recommended:

○ **Shostakovich Conducts Shostakovich** / M. Shostakovich (cond.), Prague SO / Supraphon 34152031

○ **Efrem Kurtz: Shostakovich: Symphony 10; The Age of Gold Suite** / Kurtz (cond.), Philharmonia Orch. / 1996 / Testament 1078

Chamber Symphony in C minor, Op. 110a (1960)

This work is an arrangement of Shostakovich's 1960 *String Quartet No. 8, Op. 110*, by the well-known conductor Rudolf Barshai. It is a quite literal transcription of a work whose original instrumentation is undoubtedly well-suited to the music. Barshai's larger arrangement then, should be regarded as an alternative version whose primary purpose is to allow greater access to Shostakovich's masterpiece.

The work is rife with quotations from Shostakovich's earlier works, including the First, Fifth and Tenth Symphonies, and *Lady Macbeth of Mtsensk*. Originally, the quartet was said by Soviet sources to be a musical exposé of Fascism, an explanation the composer did not initially challenge. Later, however, he is said to have denied the quartet was specifically associated with that idea, pointing out that the quotations from the works mentioned above would not be consistent with that interpretation. Moreover, Shostakovich quotes from the Russian song "Exhausted by the hardships of prison," whose presence in the work also cannot be reconciled with the official Soviet view of the composition.

Obviously this quartet was personal and carried much biographical significance for the composer. Indeed, the first movement Largo opens with the notes D, E flat, C and B, representing the German spelling of "DSCH," the monogram Shostakovich often used in his works. The music in this Largo is ominous and mournful, but sounds more tragic and intense in the original scoring. The savagery of the second movement, however, is conveyed quite effectively in the string orchestra arrangement. Here, Shostakovich quotes a Jewish theme that also appears in the finale of his *Trio for Piano, Violin and Cello,* Op. 67.

The third movement, marked Allegretto, fares well in Barshai's arrangement, too, though the ensuing Largo movements are more tragic-laden, their anguish coming across with greater intensity and passion in the quartet. Yet, the three-note motif in the fourth movement may have greater power in the Barshai arrangement, and the "DSCH" motto that reappears in the finale is also appropriately conveyed in the string orchestra version.

In the end, it must be said that Barshai handles all the music of this complex and tragic work with great skill. There have been many recordings of his transcription, at least as many as the quartet itself. *—Robert Cummings*

Recommended:

- **Shostakovich: Piano Concerto 1; Chamber Symphony** / Turovsky (cond.), I Musici de Montreal / 1985 / Chandos 8357
- **Written With The Heart's Blood** / Canin (cond.), New Century CO / 1996 / New Albion 088

Festive Overture, in A major, Op. 96 (1954)

The post-Stalin era in the Soviet Union was a time of great relief and increasing freedom for artists. Fearing for his welfare, Shostakovich had abandoned the symphony for nine years, finally ending the moratorium with the vastly successful *Tenth,* which he composed shortly after the March 5, 1953, death of Stalin.

With the artistic climate vastly improved, Shostakovich's expressive language ironically turned conservative and he even began to criticize the avant-garde. Shostakovich then went on to compose thoroughly unadventurous works like *The Gadfly* film score (1955), the *Piano Concerto No. 2* (1957), and the *Symphony No. 11* (1957). The *Festive Overture* came near the beginning of this period and is as conservative a composition ever to come from his pen. It is a light work written to celebrate the 37th anniversary of the Bolshevik Revolution. Its joyous mood and lack of pomp clearly suggest the composer viewed politics in a different light now and felt that political leaders no longer had to be feared.

This work lasts about five minutes and often turns up as a bonus on Shostakovich symphony recordings, thus gaining considerable currency. It is colorful and thematically appealing, sounding like typical Shostakovich in a lighter vein. While the ending flirts with bombast, it is tasteful in its brevity and understatedness. If the work is truly the composer's then-current take on the meaning of the Revolution in an encapsulated form, he must have viewed it most benignly, clearly as a happy and positive event. The freedom Shostakovich enjoyed during this time would not last long, as in the following decade he would become censured for some of his compositions again, most notably the *Symphony No. 13* (1962). *—Robert Cummings*

Recommended:

- **Shostakovich: Symphony 2; Festive Overture** / Ashkenazy (cond.), Royal PO / 1994 / London 436762
- **Shostakovich: Festive Overture & Symphony 5** / Shostakovich (cond.), London SO / 1990 / Collins 11082
- **Great Conductors of the 20th Century: Karel Ancerl** / Ancerl (cond.), Czech PO / 2002 / EMI 75091
- **Eastman Wind Ensemble Live in Osaka** / Hunsberger (cond.), Eastman Wind Ens. / 1992 / Sony 47198

The Flea (The Bedbug), suite from the incidental music, Op. 19a (1929)

After Mayakovsky's farce *The Bed Bug* closed in 1929, Shostakovich withdrew his music. Like so much of his music from the late 1920s and early 1930s, it disappeared into his drawers, then was discovered, edited, and revived by the inexhaustible Shostakovich conductor Gennady Rozhdestvensky in the late 1970s and given its second premiere shortly thereafter.

The suite which Rozhdestvensky compiled from *The Bed Bug* consists of four movements: "March," "Intermezzo," "Scene on the Boulevard," and "Final March." The opening "March" is a jaunty number for brass and winds with prominent solos for trumpet and tuba. The "Intermezzo" is a sleazy dance for orchestra featuring that bizarre musical instrument, the flexatone, aka the "singing saw." The "Scene on the Boulevard" is a slutty dance with pairs of greasy clarinets and stopped trumpet and trombone solos. The "Final March" recapitulates the opening "March," but on a larger and more vulgar level. Although clearly not Shostakovich at his tragic symphonic best, the music from *The Bed Bug Suite* is typical of his ironic light music style of the late 1920s. *—James Leonard*

Recommended:

- **Shostakovich: Orchestral Works** / Rozhdestvensky (cond.), USSR Ministry of Culture SO / 1998 / Melodiya 7432159058
- **Shostakovich: Theatre Music** / Hayroudinoff / 2001 / Chandos 9907

CONCERTO

Cello Concerto No. 1 in E flat major, Op. 107 (1959)

Shostakovich composed this music in July 1959, and Mstislav Rostropovich introduced it at Leningrad on October 4, with Yevgeny Mravinsky conducting. It is lightly scored for double winds, piccolo, contrabassoon, a single horn (no other brass), timpani, celesta, and strings.

Although a prolific composer in other forms, Shostakovich wrote only six concertos. If those for keyboard seem prevailingly saucy and sun dappled, the four string concertos are somberly serious. Where there's any laughter at all, it sounds forced and hollow. To lighten it (or try) only reinforces the "holy fool" (yurodivy) analogy that haunts Solomon Volkov's *Testimony,* the posthumously alleged *Memoirs of Dmitry Shostakovich.*

When the *First Cello Concerto* was written with almost Mozartean speed, Stalin had been dead six years but not forgotten. In 1958 Boris Pasternak was forced to decline a Nobel Prize for his anti-Stalinist novel, *Doctor Zhivago,* and then was expelled from the Writers' Union. Ian MacDonald, in *The New Shostakovich,* concluded that Pasternak's humiliation and subsequent persecution significantly influenced the *First Cello Concerto.* Volkov, on the other hand, gave no hint, nor did Elizabeth Wilson in *A Life Remembered.* Most of what she included, anent the concerto, was Rostropovich's celebration of himself, with this notable exception: "In the *First Cello Concerto* [M.R. speaking], Shostakovich alludes to Stalin's favorite song, *'Suliko.'* These allusions are undoubtedly not accidental, but... are camouflaged so craftily that even I didn't notice them to begin with. The first time Dmitry Dmitriyevich hummed this passage through to me [from the concluding rondo movement], he laughed and said, 'Slava, have you noticed?'"

Cello Concerto No. 1 is a major-key work in minor keys more often than not, recalling the mature Schubert's subtle modulations. It was his first large-scale undertaking after the *Eleventh Symphony* a year earlier and one of the works he quoted in his autobiographical *Eighth String Quartet* of 1960.

The published score has a preface, "adapted" as follows by the late Leonard Burkat:

"This four-movement concerto is divided into two large parts: the opening movement, and then three more movements played without pause. Together, they form an integral whole with unified themes and images.

"The main theme of the Allegretto first movement is a [four-note] motto that lends itself to dynamic development and reappears many times. The second theme is a rich musical image of Russian character, full of stoic grief and strength of will.

"The second movement, Moderato, has a restrained introduction, after which the cello sings a song-like theme against violas in the background. The melodious second theme is highly expressive, leading to a dramatic climax.

"The third Andantino—Allegro movement is monolog for unaccompanied cello [i.e., a long cadenza] that recalls the first-movement motto and second movement themes while preparing for—"The Allegro con moto finale in rondo form [that] sums up the whole work, with a coda [based on] the principal subject of the first movement...." The end is both harsh and abrupt. *—Roger Dettmer*

Recommended:

- **Rostropovich: The Russian Years (1950–1974)** / Rostropovich, Rozhdestvensky (cond.), Moscow Philharmonic SO / 1997 / EMI 72016
- **Shostokovich: Violin Concerto; Cello Concerto 1** / Rostropovich, Ormandy (cond.), Philadelphia Orch. / 1998 / Sony 63327

Piano Concerto No. 1 in C minor, Op. 35 (1933)

For two thirds of a century, Shostakovich's 1933 concerto for piano, virtuoso trumpeter, and string choir has lived in the shadow of Prokofiev's brittle, French-sauced *Piano Concerto No. 3* (composed between 1916 and 1921). Maybe it's the trumpet part—as difficult as any in the repertoire. Or the piano part that is difficult without always seeming to be. Or the panache as well as precision required of the strings. The bottom-line irony is that this first and finer of Shostakovich's two piano concertos is structurally superior to any of Prokofiev's five, and furthermore abundantly melodic, serious as well as satiric, and surprising throughout in the most entertaining ways.

It makes us wonder whether, during his impoverished teens when Shostakovich accompanied silent films, any of those films were by Charlie Chaplin, whose mixture of slapstick and pathos formed a visual counterpart to the composer's musical duality. Soviet musicians were expected early on to mock the decadent West, and

Shostakovich cooperated famously in the film *New Babylon*, and the ballet *The Golden Age*. At the same time, he was skewering bourgeois decadents at home in his operas *The Nose* and *Lady Macbeth of Mtsensk*. The latter, though, nearly cost him his life when Stalin saw and hated it in 1936, three years after its completion, two after huge successes in Leningrad, Moscow, and abroad.

Shostakovich completed *Lady Macbeth* in December 1932. In March 1933 he began the *First Piano Concerto*, finished in July, and introduced by him on October 15 with the Leningrad Philharmonic. If Soviet critics were puzzled, as usual, by its expressive dichotomy, the public was charmed by jokes and japery in cahoots with respectful echoes of Rachmaninov (persona non grata in the U.S.S.R. following his permanent departure in 1917). In the U.S., William Kapell became an advocate of the work until his death in 1953, but too few pianists since have followed suit. As the King of Siam sings in Rodgers and Hammerstein's Broadway evergreen, "Is a puzzlement."

The first movement, Allegro moderato, freely adapts sonata form without losing structural coherence. Plenty of melodies alternate between sweet and sour. The Lento second movement is a slow waltz with romantic tunes and overall a mood of nostalgia. The more impassioned middle section reintroduces the trumpet but then quietens for a lyrical dialogue by the soloists before a hushed conclusion.

Shostakovich marked the ensuing, very beautiful Moderato a third movement, but its purpose is to introduce the rondo-finale, an Allegro con brio as inventive as it is racy. The episodes send up Cossack dances, Parisian bistros, and brass bands. There's even a faux coda—music as Chaplinesque (in the best sense) as any, anywhere, ever. *—Roger Dettmer*

Recommended:

- ○ **Shostakovich: Piano Concerto 1; Chamber Symphony; Preludes Op 34** / Kissin, Spivakov (cond.), Moscow Virtuosi / RCA 7947
- ○ **Shostakovich: Piano Concertos 1 & 2; Symphony 1** / Rudy, Jansons (cond.), Berlin PO / 2003 / EMI 75886
- ○ **Shostakovich Plays Shostakovich** / Shostakovich, Cluytens (cond.), Vaillant, Francaise / 1993 / Capitol 54606

Piano Concerto No. 2 in F major, Op. 102 (1957)

Following the death of Stalin in 1953, the Soviet Union enjoyed a period of relative liberalization, particularly in the field of culture, which allowed many artists to express themselves more freely without fear of government rebuke. During this period, Shostakovich composed some of his most passionate, emotional works, including the *Tenth Symphony, Sixth String Quartet*, and *Second Piano Concerto*. The piece was composed in 1956 and 1957 for his son, Maxim Shostakovich, who gave the first performance on May 10, 1957, his 19th birthday. The work retains the light-hearted, almost flippant character of the *First Concerto*, but eschews its dark cynicism, overflowing with rich, firmly drawn thematic ideas. The first movement opens with a light, lively bassoon introduction before the piano solo enters with the cleverly joking main theme, giving the movement its natural sense of momentum and flow from the outset. As in many of his other piano works, Shostakovich exhibits his love for the instrument's extremes, casting the melody several times in three-octave unison while the brilliant wind orchestrations provide a contrapuntal background. The dreamy slow movement, like the rest of the concerto, is straightforward in its structure and simple in its language. The finale, more than any other movement, showcases the youthful character Shostakovich intended for his son's performance, although at no point does the work sound condescending or patronizing. As a gentle family dig, Shostakovich includes passages in the final movement quoting the well known finger-facility exercises of Hanon, saying it was the only way he could get his son to practice them. The work is enjoyable for young and old, for performer and listener, alike. *—Graham Olson*

Recommended:

- ○ **Shostakovich: Piano Concertos 1 & 2** / Bronfman, Salonen (cond.), Los Angeles Philharmonic / 1999 / Sony 60677
- ○ **Shostakovich: Piano Concertos 1 & 2; Sonata 2** / Leonskaja, Wolff (cond.), Saint Paul CO / 2001 / Erato 89092
- ○ **Shostakovich Plays Shostakovich** / Shostakovich, Cluytens (cond.), Orch. Francaise / 1993 / Capitol 54606

Violin Concerto No. 1 in A minor, Op. 77 (revised as Op. 99) (1947–1948; revised 1955)

As many know, Shostakovich wrote two violin concertos. But his work list suggests two separate versions of the First, the Op. 77 and the Op. 99. The Violin Concerto No. 1 was originally completed in 1948, but withheld for seven years by the composer, owing to the oppressive climate for artists in the Soviet Union at the time. Any new work might have drawn the wrath of Stalin and his cronies in the arts. Shostakovich returned to the score in 1955 and then assigned the higher opus number to it. Actually, the only documented change he made came not as a result of second thoughts, but as a matter of consideration for the soloist. During rehearsals in 1955, the virtuoso violinist David Oistrakh requested of Shostakovich that the opening statement of the fourth movement's main theme be given to the orchestra, so that the soloist could take a rest following the long cadenza which leads right into the finale, and Shostakovich agreed to make the change.

The *First Violin Concerto* begins as a dark work, full of that gloom and dread that pervade so many of Shostakovich's serious works. The first movement Nocturne starts off with an ominous theme that is both inwardly reflective and filled with foreboding. Midway through, a thinly veiled *Dies Irae* appears as the music becomes more tense. Yet, a climactic release never quite arrives and the suggested conflicts remain unresolved. The second movement is a rather diabolical Scherzo that contains some interesting allusions, first to the third movement of the *Tenth Symphony* (1953) and later to the first movement of the *Second Piano Concerto* (1957). The violin and woodwinds scurry about to deliver the playful yet menacing material, but gradually the character of the movement becomes more sarcastic, eventually breaking into a hallucinatory folk dance. The latter part of the Scherzo sounds less acidic, the diabolic and sarcastic elements surrender to the driving, insistent energy. The third movement is a Passacaglia that has a chorale-like quality at the outset, as the woodwinds deliver a mournful theme. The violin enters playing the main theme, one of the composer's loveliest and warmest creations. Shostakovich's 1943 *Eighth Symphony*'s fourth movement also featured a passacaglia, though of a decidedly grimmer character. Here, there is tension, but also much beauty. The latter third of the movement is taken up by a brilliant cadenza, which leads directly into the brief finale, a Burlesque of a mostly festive nature. The mood is similar to that of the faster music in the *Tenth Symphony*'s finale, though there are no clear thematic references. While the work ends triumphantly, its manic qualities suggest a discomfort by the composer, as though the happy resolution might have been disingenuous.

Shostakovich eliminated trumpets and trombones from the orchestration of this Concerto, and his writing is otherwise sensitive to the limited tone of a solo violin playing amid a large ensemble. A typical performance of this work lasts about 35 minutes. *—Robert Cummings*

Recommended:

- ○ **Prokofiev & Shostakovich: Violin Concertos** / Vengerov, Rostropovich (cond.), London SO / 1994 / Teldec 92256
- ○ **Shostakovich: Violin Concerto; Cello Concerto** / Oistrakh, Mitropoulos (cond.), New York Philharmonic / 1998 / Sony 63327

Violin Concerto No. 2 in C sharp minor, Op. 129 (1967)

As was the case with its predecessor, Shostakovich's *Second Violin Concerto* was inspired by and dedicated to David Oistrakh. Written in 1967 with the intention of being a 60th birthday present, the work was, by mistake, presented to the virtuoso a day early. Like many other works written following the composer's heart attack in 1966, this concerto exhibits the very dark, introspective tone, repeating rhythmic cells, and obscure thematic motifs so common to Shostakovich's later style. And like both of his cello concertos, the horn has a dominant role as accomplice and foil to the solo violin. Though the opening movement begins with some restraint, the first subject hurriedly reaches an agonized, dissonant climax. The beginning of the second subject eases the tension somewhat, with a segue into the development section by way of irreverent, mocking five-note figures that interchange with lyrical, imitative violin and wind passages. The ensuing development distorts the main thematic material until four vast, even chords announce the arrival of the recapitulation. The return is brief, however, as a long, unaccompanied cadenza, based upon the primary subject, gives way to an emotionally drained dissolution of thematic and rhythmic motiifs.The slow second movement, though more relaxed in tempo, offers no respite from the tension, confusion and sadness of the opening, as the violin seems to search for clarity and validation, but is repeatedly denied. The solo line responds by lashing out in frustration with a feral, recitative-like cadenza. The movement closes with an elegiac horn solo which is subsequently swept aside by the crass opening of the Finale. Opened by a brief series of imitative, sardonic exchanges between the violin and horn, the last movement soon settles into a frenetic, uncomfortably charged Allegro dominated by a chromatic, rondo-style theme which, while lively and complex, has bitter, sadistic undertones. The orchestra's momentum is then interrupted by a cadenza in which the introductory material is distorted and broken in a self-mocking fashion. The end of the piece finds major modality striving for dominance and eventually winning out, though the subsequent feeling is more dubious than triumphant. *—Graham Olson*

Recommended:

- ○ **Prokofiev & Shostakovich: Second Violin Concertos** / Vengerov, Rostropovich (cond.), London SO / 1997 / Teldec 13150
- ○ **Shostakovich: Violin Concertos 1 & 2** / Mullova, Previn (cond.), Royal PO / Philips 422364
- ○ **Shostakovich: Violin Concertos 1 & 2** / Tomasek, Mackerras (cond.), Prague Radio SO / Praga 7250052

CHAMBER MUSIC

Cello Sonata in D minor, Op. 40 (1934)

On the way to premiere his *Sonata for Cello and Piano*, Op. 40 (1934), Shostakovich reportedly first read Stalin's statement in Pravda attacking his music as "bourgeois." Indeed, the period that was to follow was a trying one for the composer, culminating in the execution of one of his most ardent supporters in the Soviet government and the withdrawal of several of his works from rehearsal and performance. The sonata, however, did not raise the ire of the state, though not because it lacked Shostakovich's characteristically problematic sarcasm. It is written very much in the style of the composer's large-scale symphonic works: four movements rife with cynicism, despair, and mockery. The opening movement is in a conventional sonata form, complete with a repeating exposition built around two resignedly lyrical themes. The main theme never truly recapitulates, though it reappears in sluggish mode following a restatement of the second subject, bringing the movement to a haunting, mysterious close.

The tactless Scherzo opens with coarse, repetitive sawing from the cello, over which the piano plays a rather heavy-handed melody in which the composer irreverently bites his thumb at those who would make his music more "accessible."

The ornamented, aria-like third movement juxtaposes slow, dragging despair with passionate hope before dying away into a heavy silence.

The rude, comically sinister finale, which builds tremendous momentum only to come to an abrupt and unceremonious end, effectively snubs those looking forward to a showy, brilliant finish. *—Graham Olson*

Recommended:

- ○ **Rostropovich: The Russian Years** / Rostropovich, Shostakovich / 1998 / EMI 72295
- ○ **Prokofiev & Shostakovich: Cello Sonatas; Stravinsky: Suite Italienne** / Moerk, Vogt / 1997 / Virgin 545274

Piano Quintet in G minor, Op. 57 (1940)

The *Quintet for piano and strings in G minor*, Op. 57, by Dmitry Shostakovich, was composed in 1940. The work was written in response to an enthusiastic request from the members of the Beethoven String Quartet, one of the former Soviet bloc's most respected chamber ensembles of the period. The group had recently programmed Shostakovich's first string quartet, and had been so impressed by the piece that the players decided unanimously to seek a new piece from the composer, which would also involve a pianist.

The new work took shape quickly, and Shostakovich completed it on September 14, 1940. Again at the request of the four quartet members, he took the difficult piano part himself at the first performance, given in November 1940 at the Moscow Conservatory. It proved an immediate popular and critical success, and many commentators agreed that the quintet was among Shostakovich's finest creations up until that point. Even the normally frosty Moscow newspapers were unstinting in their praises, with the *Literaturnaya Gazeta* describing the work in glowing terms as "a portrait of our age ... the rich-toned, perfect voice of the present." During 1941, Shostakovich's *Piano Quintet* received the inaugural Stalin Prize. In addition to the honor and artistic prestige that accompanied the award, the composer also received the coveted cash prize of 100,000 rubles, all of which Shostakovich handed over immediately for the benefit of impoverished Muscovites.

The quintet comprises (somewhat unusually for this chamber genre) five movements, each of which is in readily accessible populist style, and characterized by clearly etched and powerful melodies. The most substantial section, a fugue, follows a prelude in which the generally public mood of the work begins to be established. After the fugal second movement, there follows a brief, pithy scherzo, and an intermezzo which takes the place of the conventional slow movement, before the work ends with a brilliant finale. Virtuoso scoring and a particularly testing and soloistic piano part continue to make the piano quintet Shostakovich's most frequently played chamber work, perhaps overtaken in popularity only by his *String Quartet No. 8*. *—Michael Jameson*

Recommended:

- ○ **Shostakovich: String Quartet 3; 2 Pieces for String Octet; Piano Quintet** / Borodin Quartet, Richter / 1997 / Melodiya 40713
- ○ **Shostakovich: Piano Quintet; Piano Trio 2** / Horner, Zweig, Borodin Trio / 1983 / Chandos 8342
- ○ **Shostakovich Plays Shostakovich Vol. 2** / Shostakovich, Beethoven String Quintet / 2004 / Eclectra 2067

Piano Trio No. 1 in C minor, Op. 8 (1923)

Shostakovich wrote his *First Piano Trio* in the summer of 1923 while he was vacationing in the Crimean peninsula. Actually, "vacationing" may be too strong a word: the 17-year-old composer was sickly and anemic and had been sent to the Crimea along with his sister in order to recover his health and regain his strength. In any event, he did more than that. As his sister wrote home to their mother in Petersburg, "(he) has grown, got a suntan, is cheerful and has fallen in love." Indeed he had: the object of his affections was the vivacious and flirtatious Tatyana Glivenko, a girl two weeks his junior and the love of Shostakovich's life for nearly the next decade (only her marriage and birth of a child ultimately closed that chapter in Shostakovich's sentimental education).

But, the first fruit of that love was the *Piano Trio*, an ardent work in one quarter-hour movement which Shostakovich originally entitled "Poem." With all the work's themes derived from the opening chromatically longing motive, Shostakovich's work is a hymn to love both sacred and sensual. There is very little in the work's themes or developments which prefigure the young composer's incipient modernism and much that recalls the Romanticism which he was shortly to repudiate. But, Shostakovich was young and in love and the trio is arguably the most romantic and Romantic work he ever composed. *—James Leonard*

Recommended:

- ○ **Shostakovich: The Complete Trios & Sonatas** / Laredo, Kalichstein, Robinson / 1997 / Arabesque 6698
- ○ **Shostakovich: Piano Trios 1 & 2; Seven Romances on Verses by Alexander Blok** / Stockholm Arts Trio / 1996 / Naxos 553297

Piano Trio No. 2 in E minor, Op. 67 (1944)

Shostakovich's *Piano Trio No. 2*, Op. 67, is remarkable for a number of reasons. It was written in 1944, just after his *Symphony No. 8*, with which it shares its overall structure; it is a lamentation for both Shostakovich's close friend, musicologist Ivan Sollertinsky, and the victims of the Holocaust, the news of which horror did not reach the U.S.S.R. until the liberation of the camps began; and it is his first work to employ a "Jewish theme," a musical tribute that used the scales and rhythms of Jewish folk music as Shostakovich knew it. Shostakovich began composing the trio in December 1943. He had only completed sketches, which he was able to share with Sollertinsky before Sollertinsky's death in February 1944. Shostakovich performed the piano part in the premiere, on November 14, 1944, in Leningrad, with violinist Dmitri Tsyganov and cellist Sergei Shirinsky, both members of the Beethoven String Quartet. The first movement begins with an Andante canon, the melody played first by the cello in harmonics, which makes it the top voice, then the violin, which becomes the lower string voice, followed by the piano in the lowest register. This then breaks into a slightly faster Moderato, where the same melody is developed into a second one, and the use of canon continues. This movement is followed by a scherzo, but one with bitter humor in the key of F sharp major. It is a fast, waltz-like whirl of a movement. The B flat minor Largo third movement opens with large block chords from the piano. This chorale theme becomes the ostinato bass of a passacaglia, repeated a total of six times, while the violin and cello are again in canon with a sombre, lamenting melody full of anguished, minor second dissonances between the two parts. This moves immediately into the final Allegretto, again in E minor. Here the Jewish figurations—the Dorian mode with an augmented fourth and the iambic rhythms—are used in a macabre dance that is contrasted against a stern march and five-beat climbs up and down the scale. The strings frequently play pizzicato to add to the sharpness of the dance. The movement ends as the dance gives way to the chorale of the Largo, but this time ending in the more comforting key of E major. *—Patsy Morita*

Recommended:

- ○ **Shostakovich & Tchaikovsky: Piano Trios** / Argerich, Kremer, Maisky / 1999 / DG 459326
- ○ **Shostakovich: Trio Op 67; Sonata Op40** / Ax, Ma, Stern / 1988 / CBS 44664

String Quartet No. 1 in C major, Op. 49 (1938)

When Shostakovich composed his first string quartet, he had already written, among other things, five symphonies and incurred the rancor, often fatal, of Stalin. It was not enough for those in Shostakovich's position to be tough: they had also to be lucky. The black humor in Shostakovich's music reflects one way of coping with danger. Such humor shows in the last movement of this quartet. The quartet as a whole stands out, however, in sunny contrast to many of his later quartets. He began it as an exercise, but quickly became absorbed in his task and finished it in six weeks. He made alterations. The movements that were to be first and last switched positions. The work is brief, fewer than 15 minutes long.

Shostakovich denied that he intended the quartets to carry any meanings different from that of his other music, but this denial takes little account of the special qualities of the string quartet. In intimacy and concentration of means it becomes a more personal document than other musical forms. Although there may be a unity of meaning in Shostakovich's music, the string quartets speak more directly and on a more personal level.

The first movement (moderato) begins with a united voicing of the theme that develops under the urging of the cello. The viola sings over pulsing strings and the violin in high register enters over plucked strings. The music suggests bird songs and flight. The cello repeats the main theme while the other strings embroider. The cello underlines the theme, now played at a slower tempo. The cello goes its own way and has a brief solo. The slower pace is maintained to the end.

The viola opens the second movement (also moderato), and the opening pace is the same as that with which the first movement ended. Plucked cello accompanies the viola, but the violins enter and widely spaced sounds result. The viola's attempt to take over gives way almost immediately to the violins. The tempo becomes slightly brisker and the instruments on a basis of equality develop the dance-like theme. A soft passage for the cello produces a moment of silence, but the music resumes at a slower tempo and more ethereal sound. The movement ends gently with plucked strings.

The third movement (allegro molto) is a gentle perpetuum mobile, gentle and rocking. The viola and cello develop a theme while the violins embroider. Briefly the violins take control, but viola and cello take this short movement to its abrupt end.

The fourth movement (allegro) is only slightly longer than the third. The violins announce the main theme and all the instruments toss it about. The harmonies are acerbic and the phrasing abrupt. The violin plays the lightly skipping theme high above the other instruments. It's gay but somewhat manic. The music turns on an abrupt unison chord and goes to a quick and slightly conventional conclusion that underlines the sardonic nature of its ingredients. *—Bob Williams*

Recommended:

- ○ **Shostakovich: String Quartets 1, 2 & 4** / Borodin Quartet / 1997 / Melodiya 40712
- ○ **Shostakovich: String Quartets Vol. 2** / Eder Quartet / 1994 / Naxos 550973
- ○ **The Complete Shostakovich String Quartets Vol. 2** / Shostakovich Quartet / 1994 / Olympia 532
- ○ **Shostakovich: String Quartets 1, 2, 3** / Manhattan SQ / 1990 / ESS.A.Y. 1007

String Quartet No. 2 in A major, Op. 68 (1944)

Shostakovich wrote his *String Quartet No. 2*, Op. 68, during September 1944. It was premiered, along with the second of his piano trios, on November 9, 1944. The work opens abruptly, with a gripping, powerfully assured motif for first violin, stated in the home key of A major, with stark intervals of fifths and fourths underpinning the harmony. This idea is repeated by the cello, now in E major. Many commentators describe a neo-classical quality in this opening statement, and it's worth noting that Shostakovich gave each of the movements titles, this first being called "Overture." Its development section is much more complex, however, with the first theme now heard as kind of waltz-tune in C minor, with gentle pizzicato accompaniment, echoed by the cello. The viola, also in C minor, further explores the second subject.

The second movement, "Recitative and Romance," is enclosed by two long solo passages for first violin, supported by sustained chords, the effect being not unlike plainchants of the ancient Orthodox liturgy. Structurally, it presages the recitatives found in the *Ninth Symphony*, and offers a glimpse into the secret contemplative life of the composer. The "Romance" itself is set in slow 3/4 time, and is derived almost exclusively from ideas presented in the first movement, now argued on very different terms, however, and reaching an impressive climax.

The waltz that follows is often described as one of the most remarkable movements in Shostakovich's output, before or since, and it stands as a superb achievement. Set logically enough in the basic 3/4 rhythm that characterized the first two movements, its tonality and sound-world are unique, set in E flat minor. The voices are muted throughout, even when playing fortissimo, and the music has a sinister, ghostly atmosphere, ending mysteriously on an E flat minor chord. As Robert Matthew-Walker writes, "Shostakovich has here presented himself with an extraordinary compositional problem—which he solves with genius... The result is a concluding 'Theme and Variations,' prefaced by an introduction taking E flat minor as its starting point in powerful octaves on second violin, viola, and cello, akin to the opening statement of the *Quartet* and answered by first violin unaccompanied, thematically musing over the Waltz theme at infinitely slower tempo, but texturally recalling the Recitative and Romance." The movement continues to develop the sense of enigmatic irony that has defined the entire work, concluding (adds Matthew-Walker) "in A minor, into which deep tonal region the *Quartet* now moves, secure in its final symphonic integration of all of this undoubted masterpiece's large-scale contrasts." *—Michael Jameson*

Recommended:

- ○ **Shostakovich: String Quartets 2, 3, 4, 8 & 12** / Borodin Quartet / 1999 / Virgin 61630
- ○ **Shostakovich: String Quartets 2 & 3** / St. Petersburg Quartet / 1999 / Hyperion 67153
- ○ **Shostakovich: String Quartets Vol. 4** / Eder Quartet / 1995 / Naxos 550975

String Quartet No. 3 in F major, Op. 73 (1946)

The second string quartet by Shostakovich had marked a watershed in his developing mastery of the genre. He returned to the medium two years later, producing his next string quartet in 1946. As Robert Matthew-Walker points out, however, he had by now also "successfully tackled a formal challenge which had long fascinated Beethoven—the joining-together of movements of different character, yet done in such a way as to make their continuation both seamless and inevitable... he had not thus far attempted it in quartet writing."

Like its predecessor, the third also anticipates certain aspects found in Shostakovich's *Symphony No. 9*, both in terms of its structural mastery, but more especially for its originality of concept and deeply personal language. The work is set (following Beethoven's lead) in five movements rather than the usual four, opening rather lightheartedly with a bright F major Allegretto. Its rather simplistic first group gives way to a second idea, in C, which is actually related rhythmically to the theme which occurs at the same point in the *Ninth Symphony*. There is also a Classical double bar and repeat (as with the *Second Quartet* and *Ninth Symphony*) to close the exposition. But the development is a tersely argued double fugue, and the recapitulation is reached only after considerable harmonic wrestlings have been overcome.

Next comes a movement headed simply Moderato con moto, bringing uncomfortable memories of the biting Scherzo from *Symphony No. 5*. The key, points out Matthew-Walker, "is F minor—so near and yet so far from the clear F major which began the work." Conflict and unrestrained violence akin to the terrifying emotions unleashed in Shostakovich's *Eighth Quartet* permeate the acerbic third movement, a quasi-Mahlerian blend of Scherzo and March, with 3/4 and 2/4 time signatures exchanged in almost every measure. The music undoubtedly anticipates the shocking second movement of the *Tenth Symphony*.

There follows an extended, heart-rending Passacaglia (very suggestive of that found in Shostakovich's *Violin Concerto No. 1*, of 1947–48). It starts fortissimo, but the dynamic level declines as it runs its course, setting the scene for the finale, which brings faster-moving music and more confident ideas.

As Robert Matthew-Walker concludes, "It is sometimes claimed, not always convincingly, that there is often a hidden meaning in Shostakovich's work." In the case of his *Third String Quartet*, this notion may well have some foundation. The Borodin Quartet, who knew the composer well, insisted upon the following subtitles being appended to the movements whenever they performed this work. These were never published, and in any case, these epithets closely mirror the music itself, and are worth restating here:

I: "Calm unawareness of the future cataclysm"
II: "Rumblings of unrest and anticipation"
III: "The forces of war unleashed"
IV: "Homage to the dead"
V: "The eternal question: Why? And for what?" *—Michael Jameson*

Recommended:

- ○ **Shostakovich: String Quartets 8, 7 & 3** / Borodin Quartet / 1991 / Virgin 59041
- ○ **Shostakovich: String Quartets Vol. 3** / Eder Quartet / 1995 / Naxos 550974
- ○ **The Complete Shostakovich String Quartets Vol. 2** / Shostakovich Quartet / 1994 / Olympia 532

String Quartet No. 4 in D major, Op. 83 (1949)

Like the *Piano Trio No. 2, Op. 67* (1944), the *String Quartet No. 4* features thematic elements of Jewish inspiration. But in the postwar era and until Stalin's death in 1953, Shostakovich had become well aware he could not display any obvious sympathies with Jews and Jewish culture in his compositions and thus withheld the work from performance until after the tyrant's passing.

The first movement, marked Allegretto, begins with the viola and cello playing a drone while the violins present the main theme, with Jewish folk music figurations. The music quickly reaches an intense, ecstatic climax, and for the rest of this brief movement (typically less than four minutes' duration), the mood remains subdued. A second theme is heard, followed by a brief development, reprise, and coda, but all these sections have a deliberate sense of anticlimax in their generally dark character. The second movement (Andantino) presents a melancholy waltz, first played by the violin, then by the cello. The music intensifies as the theme is developed in the middle section, but the calmer, somewhat foreboding mood of the opening returns in the closing pages.

The third movement is a muted Scherzo (Allegretto), launched by a driving ostinato from the viola and second violin, over which the cello, then first violin play a sinister melody. A second theme provides contrast in its brighter, livelier character, but cannot dispel the generally anxious, dark mood in this four-minute panel. The finale, despite its Allegretto marking, starts slowly with a sustained viola note held from the Scherzo, over which is presented a somber melody. Soon, however, a theme of decidedly Jewish flavor is presented over a pizzicato rhythm. A second lively theme, also evidently of Jewish inspiration, is heard and both are then developed. The colorful, infectiously rhythmic, and generally bright mood prevails until the sober reappearance of the opening theme, after which the mood turns darker and the music slowly fades, the quartet pessimistically ending. *—Robert Cummings*

Recommended:

- ○ **Shostakovich: String Quartets 1, 2 & 4** / Borodin Quartet / 1997 / Melodiya 40712
- ○ **Shostakovich: String Quartets Vol. 1** / Eder Quartet / 1994 / Naxos 550972
- ○ **The Complete Shostakovich String Quartet Vol. 2** / Shostakovich Quartet / 1994 / Olympia 532

String Quartet No. 5 in B flat major, Op. 92 (1952)

While some musicologists have attempted to link Shostakovich's quartets to the character of certain of his symphonies, they have found that most often they are unrelated, independent compositions. An exception, however, is the *String Quartet*

No. 5, whose tragic demeanor and overall character resemble that of the *Symphony No. 10* (1953), at least up to the finale, where the latter work turns joyous and triumphant compared with the former's continued darkness.

At the time Shostakovich wrote this quartet, he was still living under censure from the Party czars in the arts. In 1948, the composer, along with Prokofiev, Khachaturian, and others, had received official reprimand for writing "formalistic" and "undemocratic" music. Because the attack on their music was so broad, most composers were hesitant to write anything that could be seen as adventurous. Shostakovich temporarily abandoned writing symphonies and turned to composing weak patriotic scores, like the *Song of the Forests* (1949) and the cantata *The Sun Shines on Our Motherland* (1952), as well as vapid film scores like the 1950 release, *The Fall of Berlin* and the 1950 production of *Belinsky* (released in 1953).

Still, Shostakovich could not contain his urge to write music of substance and thus produced the *String Quartet No. 4* in 1949 and the *String Quartet No. 5* in 1952. Their premieres, however, would not come until after the death of Josef Stalin, when a loosening of the stringent and vague constraints in the arts began. Had Shostakovich written the *String Quartet No. 5*, at least its finale, after the death of Stalin, the work would likely have had a happy and triumphant ending, like the post-Stalin *Symphony No. 10*. Perhaps there would have been a movement added to this quartet.

The *String Quartet No. 5* is made up of three movements: Allegro non troppo, Andante, and Moderato-Allegretto. As suggested above, the first movement is dark, with the main theme split into two often warring motifs. An attractive waltz eventually appears, and in the development section a dire struggle emerges among the thematic materials. While there had also been conflict in the exposition, the recapitulation features even more tension and skirmishing. The second movement starts without pause, and in fact begins with the same sustained F note that closes the opening movement. There are two quite lovely themes, the first songful and very Russian, and the second a beautiful theme played after the tempo increases to Andantino. The music from the second movement carries into the finale, which changes its tempo, after an introduction, to Allegretto. In the exposition and development, considerable tension is raised, though the close is peaceful with an air of resignation or departure. The work was dedicated to the Beethoven Quartet, which premiered it on November 13, 1953. *—Robert Cummings*

Recommended:

- ○ **Shostakovich: String Quartets 5–7** / Borodin Quartet / 1997 / Melodiya 40714
- ○ **Shostakovich: String Quartets 5, 7 & 9** / St. Petersburg Quartet / 2001 / Hyperion 67155
- ○ **Shostakovich: String Quartets Vol. 3** / Eder Quartet / 1995 / Naxos 550974

String Quartet No. 6 in G major, Op. 101 (1956)

With the March 5, 1953, death of Josef Stalin came a relaxation of the stringent and vague guidelines outlined for Soviet artists by the dictator's lackey in the arts, Andrei Zhdanov. Strangely enough, Shostakovich, one of the earliest victims of Stalin's attacks, consistently turned out conservative compositions in the decade that followed, like the *Festive Overture for orchestra* (1954), the film score for *The Gadfly* (1955), and the *Piano Concerto No. 2* (1957). He even criticized the avant-garde during this period and later joined the Communist Party on September 14, 1961. Beginning in 1962, however, he entered into disfavor with Soviet officials with his controversial *Symphony No. 13* and subsequent works, like the *Symphony No. 14*.

The *String Quartet No. 6* is a mostly tranquil composition that in many ways augurs the protest heard in the later symphonies and quartets. While it is a quite serious work, its expressive language is straightforward and relatively simple. Certainly, its direct style was in keeping with the composer's tendency at the time to turn out conservative, approachable music.

The *String Quartet No. 6* is made up of four movements: Allegretto, Moderato con moto, Lento, and Lento—Allegretto. The first movement begins with an innocent, happy theme. Yet, as with so many of Shostakovich's melodies in this vein, there is a hint of regret or sadness hovering around the proceedings. As the movement progresses, the music intensifies, but never fully develops into a mood of tragedy or austerity. The reprise is subdued and a feeling of suppressed frustration or anger is conveyed overall. The Moderato con moto that follows is mysterious and haunting, as depicted by the wandering opening theme and the pizzicato workings of the cello. The third movement, Lento, is solemn and hymnlike, a moving expression of sadness in a somewhat light vein, or at least light for Shostakovich. The outset of the finale carries over the same grieving mood from the previous movement, then gradually emerges from the darkness, eventually arriving at brighter music. Still, it is hardly happy or triumphant. While the writing remains fairly transparent and light throughout, the music becomes wistful and subdued as the ending approaches. There is a harnessing of emotions conveyed here, as the serenity at the close sounds detached, if not disingenuous. A typical performance of this quartet lasts about 25 minutes. *—Robert Cummings*

Recommended:

- ○ **Shostakovich: String Quartets 5–7** / Borodin Quartet / 1997 / Melodiya 40714
- ○ **Shostakovich:Complete String Quartets Vol. 3** / Shostakovich Quartet / 1994 / Olympia 533
- ○ **Shostakovich: String Quartets Vol. 1** / Eder Quartet / 1994 / Naxos 550972

String Quartet No. 7 in F sharp minor, Op. 108 (1960)

Few composers have imparted as much pain and melancholy to their compositions as Dmitry Shostakovich. It was not so much that he sought out tragedy in life as a musical inspiration—rather, tragedy and trouble seem regularly to have latched onto him. This 1960 work was dedicated to the memory of his first wife, Nina, who died in 1954. But its sadness may well be related as well to other, more current events in the composer's life. Most of his post-Stalin works were conservative and relatively upbeat, despite the greater freedom he and other artists enjoyed from 1953 (the year of Stalin's death) until 1962, when Shostakovich composed his controversial *Symphony No. 13, "Babi Yar,"* and helped set off a new era of government meddling in the arts.

The *String Quartet No. 7* was preceded by the *Cello Concerto No. 1* (1959), a work for years thought to be optimistic, but now viewed in a different light as recent interpretations by cellists and conductors have emphasized its darker side. The *Quartet No. 8*, Op. 110, would come later in the year and divulge not only the kind of bleakness and tragedy heard in the Seventh, but a brutality and harshness as well, a somewhat unusual combination in Shostakovich's works from any period.

It appears from all the evidence that Shostakovich had begun to reassess the direction of his career in the years around 1960, turning away from the less adventurous and simplistic worlds of works like the patriotic 1954 *Festive Overture* and 1957 *Piano Concerto No. 2*. Still, he would write the bombastic and relatively weak *Symphony No. 12, "The Year 1917,"* in 1961, fortunately his last major effort to kowtow to party officials.

The *Quartet No. 7* is cast in three continuous movements, each quite short; the whole has a duration of only about 12 minutes. The opening Allegretto begins with a descending three-note theme whose character is both cynical and nonchalant. As the movement progresses, the mood darkens, setting the stage for the ensuing Lento. Here the music is brooding and melancholy, with an eerie, lyrical main theme whose chilling harmonies taint the sonic fabric with perversely satisfying color. The finale begins with a rush of anxious energy which is then interrupted briefly for a return to the closing harmonies of the Lento. A nervous, driving theme appears, and now both thematic and rhythmic elements from the previous two movements are presented. The latter half of the finale is somewhat subdued in its restatements of the main theme and other materials.

The work was premiered on May 15, 1960, by the Beethoven Quartet. *—Robert Cummings*

Recommended:

- ○ **Shostakovich: String Quartets 5–7** / Borodin Quartet / 1997 / Melodiya 40714
- ○ **Shostakovich: String Quartets 7–9** / Brodsky Quartet / 2001 / Erato 89093
- ○ **Shostakovich: String Quartets Vol. 1** / Eder Quartet / 1994 / Naxos 550972

String Quartet No. 8 in C minor, Op. 110 (1960)

Along with the *Symphony No. 8*, Shostakovich's eighth string quartet is his most poignant expression of personal wartime experience, and remains one of his most popular and haunting pieces. The *Eighth* was written following a trip to Dresden, where Shostakovich saw the aftermath of German Fascism. The passionate music returns to the war by means of self-quotation: It revives a cry of personal mourning, a whirling outburst of grief (strangely, in a breakneck tempo) that he had employed in his *Second Piano Trio*. He dedicates this quartet to the "victims of Fascism" yet fills it with self-quotation, including the then-recent highly recognizable theme of his *Cello Concerto No. 1* and the barely known tune from his suppressed opera *Lady Macbeth of Mtsensk*. Since that melody, itself, lay suppressed by official Soviet condemnation, it might be said that Shostakovich is portraying himself as a victim of tyranny. The work's five contiguous movements are dominated without exception by a four-note motto based on the composer's initials, DSCH (D-Eb-C-B in German notation). The opening Largo, lush and pensive, builds up massive amounts of nervous energy which is eventually released in the furious, motoric second movement, Allegro molto, which portrays the inevitability and violence of the war machine. The demented, capering waltz that follows is where the cello concerto theme is first heard and is linked to another Largo movement by a brief quote of the *Dies irae* melody from the Catholic liturgy. In that fourth movement, the concerto theme is again used, along with a revolutionary song, "Languishing in Prison," and the tune from the opera. The final movement, also Largo, incorporates the original motto theme in the style of the first movement with the addition of a rich, almost restful countermelody.

The music of this quartet burns throughout with a passionate yearning and angry outbursts. The impact of the work, while it is technically complex and demanding, is wholly emotional, and is best heard with the composer's words kept in mind: "I feel eternal pain for those who were killed by Hitler, but I feel no less pain for those killed on Stalin's orders. I suffer for everyone who was tortured, shot, or starved to death. The majority of my symphonies are tombstones. Too many of our people died and were buried in places unknown to anyone, not even their relatives. Where do you put the tombstones? Only music can do that for them. I'm willing to write a composition for each of the victims but that's impossible, and that's only why I dedicate my music to them all."—*AMG*

Recommended:

- ○ **Shostakovich: String Quartets 8–10** / Borodin Quartet / 1997 / Melodiya 40715
- ○ **Shostakovich: String Quartet 8** / Emerson SQ / 1999 / DG 459670
- ○ **Shostakovich: String Quartets Vol. 2** / Eder Quartet / 1994 / Naxos 550973

String Quartet No. 9 in E flat major, Op. 117 (1964)

In the eyes of Soviet officials, Shostakovich had been the loyal artist of his country's people for nearly a decade following the death of Josef Stalin, in 1953. He had even become a member of the Communist Party on September 14, 1961, a status one would think hard to reconcile with the view of the composer as a dissident. However, in 1962 he created quite a stir with his *Thirteenth Symphony ("Babi Yar")*, mainly because of the controversial texts by Yevtushenko. Thereafter, Shostakovich was in and out of favor with the party censors. He wrote the *Ninth Quartet* not long after the appearance of the *Thirteenth Symphony*, and his attitude toward composition in general seemed to have permanently changed by then: there would not be another major composition associated with the Revolution or a patriotic event.

The *Ninth Quartet* is cast in five continuous movements, whose interrelationships have more to do with harmonies—notably in the accompaniment to the main theme of the first movement—and with rhythmic elements. Clearly, the structure of this work and its generally dark nature relate more to the "dissident" Shostakovich than to the loyal party member Shostakovich.

The first movement is calm, almost serene, yet cynical and ominous, too. It is a typical Shostakovich creation, with the main theme sounding philosophical and the middle section jaunty and sarcastic. The ensuing Adagio has an almost religious air in its solemnity. The third movement Allegretto is witty and rhythmic, probably the brightest panel of the five, despite hints of darkness and cynicism. Another Adagio follows, this one of a strange, brooding character, especially in the pizzicato passages in the middle section, where the music seems almost to come to a stop. The final Allegro, the longest movement by far, begins with a rush of energy and contains much material from the preceding Adagio, as well as from other movements.

If the overall character of this quartet is sometimes hard to pin down, at times sounding serious and even happy, it is due to that elusive thread that runs through much of the composer's music, where often one finds hidden meanings and deep symbolism. There is generally a feeling throughout this work of the expression of anger or tension being suppressed, although there is some release of these emotions in the finale. Shostakovich's uncertain status with Soviet officials at the time he wrote the quartet would certainly support such a view of the work. A typical performance of it lasts just under 30 minutes. —*Robert Cummings*

Recommended:

- ○ **Shostakovich: String Quartets 8–10** / Borodin Quartet / 1997 / Melodiya 40715
- ○ **Shostakovich: String Quartets Vol. 2** / Eder Quartet / 1994 / Naxos 550973
- ○ **Shostakovich: Complete String Quartets Vol. 3** / Shostakovich Quartet / 1994 / Olympia 533

String Quartet No. 10 in A flat major, Op. 118 (1964)

After the March 5, 1953, death of Stalin, there was a gradual relaxation of constraints placed on Soviet artists, thereby allowing the appearance of bolder and more daring new compositions, as well as the rehabilitation of previously banned ones. Shostakovich benefited from this liberalization in that his *Symphony No. 4* (1935–36; premiered 1961) would at last be performed and his opera *Lady Macbeth of Mtsensk*, with some changes and a new title—*Katerina Ismailova*—could return to the stage. Ironically, however, his new music was anything but adventurous: the *Festive Overture* (1954), *Piano Concerto No. 2* (1957), and *Symphonies No. 11* (1957) and *No. 12* (1960–61) are not only musically conservative, but all except the concerto are patriotic pieces, very supportive of the party ideals and its myopic view of history.

By 1962, however, it was as if Shostakovich apparently could no longer contain his desire for creative boldness and thus composed his *Symphony No. 13, "Babi Yar,"* which incurred the wrath of Soviet censors, mainly because of its text, by Yevgeny Yevtushenko, which was sympathetic to the plight of the Jews. The *String Quartet No. 10*, which came two years later, is as musically uncompromising and even has a Jewish connection, even if it is a tenuous one: it is dedicated to Warsaw-born Soviet composer Moisey Weinberg, whose music, it should be noted, sounds remarkably close in style to that of Shostakovich.

Shostakovich wrote the *String Quartet No. 10* in a mere ten days, while resident at a composer's retreat in the Armenian town of Dilizhin. Its expressive language is not as advanced as that found in his later quartets, but it is far from that of the mild-mannered and politically acquiescent world of the *Piano Concerto No. 2* and *Symphony No. 12*. The overall character of the work is dark, in some places sinister and fearful.

The quartet is made up of four movements: Andante, Allegretto furioso, Adagio, and Allegretto. The last two movements are continuous, with the finale the longest of the four and containing thematic references to the earlier movements. The quartet opens with a four-note motif that seems to pose a question or establish a sense of doubt. The mood then turns dark, but remains subdued throughout the movement. The ensuing panel, as its marking indicates, contains furious music, but it is the fury of fear and anxiety, as well as of anger.

The Adagio is a mournful passacaglia and offers a touching theme that turns darker and more ponderous as the movement progresses. The finale begins as if it is breaking away from the melancholy character of the piece, its main theme seemingly jaunty and carefree. But the music cannot escape its dark nature for long, as ghostly reminiscences of the Adagio theme and motifs from the first movement haunt the latter moments of the work. The quartet closes quietly in a somewhat detached and lonely mood.

Some have viewed this work as a statement that human feelings and emotions can overcome evil. They interpret the second movement "furioso" as that evil, and because there is no reference to its music in the closing measures, only to the serene, if melancholy, strains of the other themes, its absence signals its vanquishing. While there may be merit to this view, it might also be an overly simplistic interpretation of an enormously complex and multifaceted composition. —*Robert Cummings*

Recommended:

- ○ **Shostakovich: String Quartets 10 & 12** / St. Petersburg Quartet / 2003 / Hyperion 67156
- ○ **Shostakovich: String Quartets 8–10** / Borodin Quartet / 1997 / Melodiya 40715
- ○ **Shostakovich: String Quartets Vol. 6** / Eder Quartet / 1998 / Naxos 550977
- ○ **Shostakovich: String Quartets Vol. 4** / Shostakovich Quartet / 1994 / Olympia 534

String Quartet No. 11 in F minor, Op. 122 (1966)

It's no coincidence that Shostakovich's Quartet No. 11 shares the key of Beethoven's No. 11 (Op. 95); Shostakovich's work is dedicated to the memory of Vasily Petrovich Shirinsky, second violinist of the Beethoven Quartet, which had premiered nearly all of Shostakovich's previous quartets. Yet the Beethoven connection becomes tenuous after that point. The angry earlier work falls into four fairly conventional movements, whereas Shostakovich has produced a suite of seven short movements, the first five no longer than a minute or two each. Yet Beethoven toys with harmonic conventions, and Shostakovich, too, challenges expectations—not harmonically so much as in terms of tone. The work's mood is predominantly elegiac, but, except in one movement, hardly tragic. Indeed, an element of quiet whimsy creeps into much of this peculiar score.

The Introduction: Andantino employs a wiry, restless theme with minimal accompaniment; when the instruments all take an equal part in the voicing, the melody falls flat and static, an amplification of the chords underlying the main tune. This leads straight into the Scherzo: Allegretto, with its nagging, repetitive theme (including a big, sardonic glissando near the end) that Shostakovich sometimes treats in simple canons. This slows and disintegrates, only for listeners to be jolted awake by the intrusion of the jagged, dissonant beginning of the Recitative: Adagio. This settles into long, ominous chords under fragments of the jagged figure, soon to be interrupted by the fourth movement, Etude: Allegro. A high, waspish, perpetual-motion theme obsesses the first violin, while the other instruments play slightly menacing accompaniment; the theme is stripped down and simplified into a frantic ostinato that forms the basis of the ensuing Humoresque: Allegro.

The mood suddenly changes with the dark, grimly funereal Elegy: Adagio, a forlorn processional that makes much of concentrated two- and three-note motifs. After about four minutes—a lavish expanse, by this quartet's standards—the music segues into the Finale: Moderato. It begins with a very quiet, nattering, almost childlike tune that briefly turns into a barcarolle rhythm before reappearing as a sharp-edged pizzicato figure. Its slow, repeated-note patterns intertwine with a more sinuous melody drawn from material early in the quartet, ascending on the violin to a quiet, remote conclusion. —*James Reel*

Recommended:

- ○ **Shostakovich: String Quartets 11–13** / Borodin Quartet / 1997 / Melodiya 40716
- ○ **Shostakovich: String Quartets Vol. 4** / Shostakovich Quartet / 1994 / Olympia 534
- ○ **Shostakovich: String Quartets Vol. 6** / Eder Quartet / 1998 / Naxos 550977

String Quartet No. 12 in D flat major, Op. 133 (1968)

Shostakovich's last four quartets are generally viewed as a related group. They share a certain creative boldness in their use of various advanced compositional techniques, such as the use, or partial use, of 12-tone rows. Regarding this latter aspect, there has been some controversy about the *Quartet No. 12* in particular. Is it a composition rooted in tonality or atonality? For all its daring, especially coming from the pen of a Soviet composer from the late 1960s, it is not truly a 12-tone composition. Had it been written by a Western composer who had previously embraced serial techniques, it would have been greeted largely as a return to tonality.

The work is divided into two movements, the latter running over 20 minutes. The first movement opens with a 12-tone row stated by the cello, and the mood immediately established is dark and mournful, typical of the music of this late stage in the composer's career. He was suffering from a serious heart ailment by now and endured considerable pain from arthritis. The main theme here has a nobility to its sadness, offering consolation but little hope. The second subject, played at a faster tempo, is emotionally cold and sounds slightly Schoenbergian. After some development the movement comes to a quiet close.

The second movement opens with an angry, desperate scherzo in which tonality again becomes uncertain. Its main theme is a five-note idea—four short and one long—not far removed from the four-note motto of the Beethoven *Fifth Symphony*, though here the last two notes descend and the mood is decidedly darker. This motif dominates the first third of this long movement and serves as the stimulus, if not the agitator, behind the frantic and anxious atmosphere. There is also much colorful and virtuosic writing throughout the scherzo, including some rapid sul ponticello passages that are both chilling and thrilling. This section finally winds down on the cello, and the Adagio ensues. It is despairing in tone; even a colorful pizzicato section does not break the dark mood. A brief development section follows, wherein elements from the preceding sections and the first movement appear. Still, the mood remains rather bleak, despite the faster Moderato marking. The finale features quicker tempos and reprises material from both movements. Here the dominant motif from the scherzo section appears, but now less threateningly. Gradually it grows more exultant until it finally revels in total triumph, rejecting the implied atonality of its first appearance and settling into a very affirmative D flat. Curiously, the ending is rather Stravinsky-like; the closing chords sound similar to the ones at the end of the *Dumbarton Oaks* chamber concerto. *—Robert Cummings*

Recommended:

- ○ **Shostakovich: String Quartets 2, 3, 4, 8 & 12** / Borodin Quartet / 1999 / Virgin 61630
- ○ **Shostakovich: String Quartets Vol. 4** / Eder Quartet / 1995 / Naxos 550975
- ○ **The Complete Shostakovich String Quartets Vol. 5** / Shostakovich Quartet / 1994 / Olympia 535

String Quartet No. 13 in B flat minor, Op. 138 (1969–1970)

Shostakovich died in 1975, and in the last decade of his life, his health was not only in serious decline, but he was battling a nervous system disorder—brittle-bone poliomyelitis—that crippled his right hand. It was between stays at an orthopedic clinic that treated this condition with some success that he wrote this quartet. Shortly after completing it, he suffered another in a series of heart attacks. Some musicologists have asserted that Shostakovich's sparse scoring in his later symphonies and his propensity for turning out string quartets in his final years owes something to this frustrating and painful condition affecting his hand. This observation is probably sound, and one might further suggest that the composer's declining health and physical suffering may have contributed to the gloomy and dark moods of his late works. This work was premiered in December 1970 by the Beethoven Quartet, the group most closely identified with the composer's quartets during his lifetime.

If one could conclude with reasonable certainty that the character of the *String Quartet No. 13* is indeed connected to the physical state of the composer at the time, then one can safely declare that he must have been very ill and quite depressed, for this is a dark work full of tension and doubt, with not a hint of happiness or relief from the gloom and struggle. Yet there is no self-pity here, only a bleak sonic landscape, less a product of a nihilistic philosophy, however, than of a gentle embracing of the realities of a life coming to an end.

The work is in one long movement, marked Adagio—Doppio movimento—Tempo primo. It begins with a solemn, elegiac theme on viola. Soon the other instruments join in and impart a funereal mood, whose atmospherics depend largely on the glacial pacing and processional air of solemnity. If the *Twelfth* had seemed daring because of its opening 12-tone row on cello, as well as other flirtations with atonal techniques, this work, here and throughout, is more audacious owing to its morbid and intense sound world, a sound world Soviet leaders were uncomfortable explaining. *Leningrad Pravda* tried to put, if not a happy face on the work after its premiere, then at least a positive one, hailing the quartet as a "glorification . . . of the human spirit."

After the exposition, the music intensifies and three powerful, insistent dissonant chords bring on a Scherzo-like middle section, wherein the livelier pace of the music is supported and punctuated by percussive clacks, created by the bow striking against the torso of the instrument. This whole passage is sinister and threatening, but eventually subsides without the expected climactic outburst. The dissonant chords have a reappearance, though, before a more permanent quiet arrives.

The main material returns, but nothing like a standard reprise occurs. The mood grows, if anything, even more melancholy and darker. Yet a serenity comes as the work approaches its close. When the viola reprises the opening theme accompanied by remnants of the percussive tapping near the end of the piece, there is a haunting poignancy, as if the death-rattle effect is united peacefully with the serene sadness so as to embrace an inevitable but now bearable fate. *—Robert Cummings*

Recommended:

- ○ **Shostakovich: String Quartets 11–13** / Borodin Quartet / 1997 / Melodiya 40716
- ○ **Shostakovich: String Quartets Vol. 6** / Eder Quartet / 1998 / Naxos 550977
- ○ **Edition Lockenhaus Vol. 4/5** / Kremer, Imai, Pergamenschikow / 1988 / ECM 1347

String Quartet No. 14 in F sharp major, Op. 142 (1973)

Shostakovich composed this work for the cellist of the Beethoven Quartet, the chamber group most commonly associated with his quartets during his lifetime, having premiered 13 of the 15 (Nos. 2–14). They would have introduced the last had Sergei Shirinsky, the quartet's cellist, not died shortly before the premiere was to take place. The *String Quartet No. 14* is cast in three movements, and each features a prominent part for the cello.

The first movement is marked Allegretto and opens with a busy, somewhat menacing theme played by the cello in its lower ranges. The melody is then taken up by the first violin and then developed by the whole ensemble, whereupon the music divulges a strong sense of agitation. Another theme, a bit less animated, but otherwise of similar character, is introduced by the cello and soon the development section commences, wherein both themes are expanded upon. The ensuing reprise is only partial, with the cello playing the theme with which it opened the work.

The Adagio middle panel begins with the first violin introducing a melancholy theme in its lower ranges, after which the cello takes up the somber melody. Though the alternate theme, given by the cello to pizzicato accompaniment, divulges a somewhat brighter, even serene character, the overall mood of this movement is dark and sad.

The finale (Allegretto) begins without pause, as the first violin gently plays pizzicato, but with a sense of wandering and uncertainty. The ensemble then joins in, making a steady, soft rhythm of the notes, but soon the music intensifies with a dark theme played by the first violin. Rhythms turn anxious and the music seethes with tension until it finally relaxes for an eerie passage for cello and violin. Elements from the two previous movements are then recalled and the work ends quietly and serenely. *—Robert Cummings*

Recommended:

- ○ **Shostakovich: String Quartets 14 & 15** / Borodin Quartet / 1997 / Melodiya 40717
- ○ **Edition Lockenhaus Vol. 4/5** / Kremer, Kashkashian, Geringas, Horigome / 1988 / ECM 1347
- ○ **Shostakovich: String Quartets Vol. 5** / Eder Quartet / 1998 / Naxos 550976
- ○ **Shostakovich: String Quartets Vol. 5** / Shostakovich Quartet / 1994 / Olympia 535

String Quartet No. 15 in E flat minor, Op. 144 (1974)

The final string quartet to be composed by Dmitry Shostakovich dates from 1974. He had begun to write in this form as a personal, private exercise back in the late 1930s, when his earliest essays in the genre were as much an expression of his true personality as his massive, public declarations (such as the *Fifth Symphony*) represented aspects of his creativity that were not always truly representative of the man behind the notes. But in the 15 string quartets, it is the true Shostakovich whom we encounter; a man as shocked and revolted by the atrocities of war as he was also incensed by the madness of official proclamation and the political machinations that inevitably followed them. Such feelings of outrage found their most eloquent expression in the *Eighth Quartet*, which Shostakovich dedicated "To the Victims of War and Fascism."

The *String Quartet No. 15 in E flat minor*, Op. 144, is also one of the composer's bleakest and most profoundly introspective creations. Indeed, never before or since has there been a quartet comprising just slow movements, six in total, and all of them Adagios. There can be no question that the extreme political pressure and repressive artistic censorship to which Shostakovich, and his music, was subjected damaged his already fragile health seriously during the final decade or so of his life. Indeed, many of his late works, written in the period between 1966 and 1975, were set down in various hospitals and sanatoria, though whether he was placed in them as patient or prisoner is sometimes debatable. The *String Quartet No. 15* was written in the course of a two-week stay in a Moscow convalescent institution. It is recorded that he received visits there from his old friend Isaak Glikman, to whom he confided: "I've completed a new quartet. It is my fifteenth. I do not know if it's any good, though I have experienced a certain pleasure in writing it."

The quartet, as has been mentioned already, consists of only slow movements, each of which carries a title ("Elegy," "Serenade," "Intermezzo," "Nocturne," "Funeral March," "Epilogue"), but their solemn character rarely suggests that their composition can have been a source of genuine pleasure. The first movement evolves from just one single note, as though only partially perceived through part-closed eyes. It leads to scenes of terrifying nihilism and utter devastation, for which the only logical solution (but never full escape) must be to link a series of hopeless threnodies. Throughout the rest of the work, these sorrowful images of long-gone happiness form an enigmatic collage until the quartet finally dissolves into silence. *—Michael Jameson*

Recommended:

- **Shostakovich: String Quartets 14 & 15** / Borodin Quartet / 1997 / Melodiya 40717
- **Shostakovich: String Quartet 15; Gubaidulina: Rejoice!** / Kremer, Phillips, Kashkashian, Ma / 1989 / CBS 44924
- **Shostakovich: String Quartets Vol. 5** / Eder Quartet / 1998 / Naxos 550976
- **Shostakovich: String Quartets Vol. 4** / Shostakovich Quartet / 1994 / Olympia 534

Viola Sonata in C major, Op. 147 (1975)

This was Shostakovich's last work, completed about a month before his death. Because of his advanced and painful arthritis, as well as his unsteady hand and bad eyesight, the composer showed an increasing tendency to write sparsely scored orchestral compositions (*Symphonies No. 14* and *No. 15*, for example) and many chamber pieces in his last years, finding their reduced scoring easier to manage. Shostakovich died on August 9, 1975, of heart failure, compounded by advanced cancer of the lungs. He was also aware that he was going blind. For all the suffering he was enduring in his last days, the composer did not invest his *Sonata for viola* with nearly the morbid and gloomy moods found in most of the late quartets. He himself spoke about the work, calling the first two movements merely a "novella," and "scherzo," respectively. He was a trifle more detailed about the finale, however, describing it as "an adagio in memory of Beethoven." He also summed up the music in general as "bright and clear." This last characterization of the work is misleading, as there is a feeling of resignation throughout, even if it is, to an extent, counterbalanced by a strong sense of serenity. In the end, the work seems to be an expression of the composer coming to terms with his ineluctable and unhappy fate.

The first movement, marked Moderato, is mournful, if serene, featuring sparse textures in the piano writing. The central panel (Allegretto) is actually playful in places, though one also finds a healthy dose of acid, typical of so many of the composer's later chamber pieces. There is a Russian, slightly exotic flavor to the music here, as well. The finale is the longest and most substantive of the three movements. Its Adagio marking was a favorite of the composer at this time—indeed, his *Quartet No. 15* (1974) featured six consecutive Adagios. The mood in the finale is less gloomy than in that dark work, and the composer makes a brief reference to Beethoven's *Moonlight Sonata*.

While much of the work is subdued and uncomplicated, it does offer considerable challenges to the performers. The sonata was premiered privately on September 26, 1975, and publicly on October 1. A typical performance of the *Sonata for viola* lasts between 35 and 40 minutes. *—Robert Cummings*

Recommended:

- **Shostakovich: Viola Sonata; Chihara: Redwood; Bouchard: Pourtinade** / Kashkashian, Levin / 1991 / ECM 847538
- **Sviatoslav Richter & Yuri Bashmet** / Bashmet, Richter / 1991 / Kniga 418015

Violin Sonata, Op. 134 (1968)

The story goes that in 1967 Shostakovich presented David Oistrakh with a 60th birthday present, the *Violin Concerto No. 2*. But the composer was premature by a year, and felt obligated to write another composition for the violinist's actual 60th birthday. The work he produced was this 1968 *Sonata for Violin and Piano*, Op. 134, one of his finer late efforts.

The piece opens with an allusion to serial music: the piano presents a theme in octaves starting in the bass and rising to the upper register, playing all 12 notes of the chromatic scale before the violin enters. The tempo is Andante. The mood is grim, as is typical of the composer's late works, especially the last several quartets. A second theme appears, march-like and cynical. The two instruments exchange renditions of it, and then the main theme is reprised by the violin. Shortly thereafter another engaging idea is presented by the violin, seeming to glide eerily downward from its upper ranges, while the piano delivers chilling harmonies in both registers. There is also some ghostly sul ponticello playing in the latter pages. Not long after this work appeared, Soviet musicologists tried in vain to explain the mood of this bleak music as pastoral.

The second movement, marked Allegretto, begins with a heroic-sounding theme. But the mood quickly turns anxious, as if the composer were expressing his irony under some considerable pressure. A waltz seems to promise relief from the unbounded energy and tension, but does not manage to break the rigid mood.

The finale, marked Largo, begins with a somber introduction. Then the violin, played pizzicato, presents the dark main theme, after which come 13 variations. The piano's first rendition of the melody calls to mind the late compositions of Liszt. The music shifts moods, going from pensive to playful, from sinister to simple. An outburst on the piano just past the middle of the movement leads to a climactic episode on the violin. The eerie music from the first movement returns, as does the marchlike theme, and the work ends chillingly.

A typical performance of this sonata lasts about a half hour. Oistrakh premiered it on January 8, 1969, in a private performance before the Union of Soviet Composers. The pianist on that occasion was composer Moisei Weinberg. Sviatoslav Richter played the piano part with Oistrakh in May of that year for the first public performance.*—Robert Cummings*

Recommended:

- **Shostakovich: 19 Preludes from Op34; Violin Sonata, Op134** / Dubinsky, Edlina / 2003 / Chandos 10087
- **Shostakovich & Franck: Violin Sonatas; Khachaturian & Sibelius: Violin Concertos** / Oistrakh, Richter / 1994 / Vox 5120

KEYBOARD

Piano Sonata No. 2 in B minor, Op. 61 (1942)

Shostakovich's piano music is relatively little played, but it began to make significant inroads into the repertoire in the later years of the twentieth century. Clearly, his solo piano works are considerably different from his symphonies, lacking their epic qualities, their tragedy, and their grandiose formal designs.

The composer's *Piano Sonata No. 2* of 1942 appeared at a time when Shostakovich felt a bit safer from attacks by war-diverted party censors—yet not safe from the invading Nazis. However, there is little in the work to suggest the agonies and tumult of the war expressed in his other works from the period, such as the 1941 *Symphony No. 7 ("Leningrad")* and 1943 *Symphony No. 8*. Nor does the work in any way attempt to challenge Shostakovich's rival Prokofiev on the latter's turf: it shies away from the drama, violence, and bolder language found in his older colleague's sixth and seventh sonatas. But the Shostakovich sonata is uncompromising in its own way, featuring a mesmerizing, hallucinatory slow movement and compelling outer movements, which are, if not particularly innovative, unyielding in their adherence to a dry and somewhat detached expressive language. Still, this sonata is much more traditional than the composer's first, whose brashness and sonic mayhem conjure images of the young Shostakovich with a hammer smashing bugs.

The Sonata No. 2 consists of three movements, the first two of which are in the seven-to-eight minute range, while the finale nearly matches their combined length. The first movement (Allegretto) is fairly light, despite the tension and dissonance that come in the development. The main theme, heard at the outset against running figures in the right hand, has a tart charm. Overall, the first movement offers a mixture of mischievous delight and rowdy humor.

The aforementioned strange second movement contrasts stands in brilliant contrast to the first by presenting music that seems to come from a netherworld, owing to its haziness and dark mood. The Largo tempo at times holds the flow of the music back, threatening to bring it to the verge of stasis. Yet this movement may be the most effective of the three, not least because of the composer's deft coloration and subtle shifts in mood. At several times the music does seem to come to a halt, especially in a passage where the left hand plays a blunt chord in the bass to accompany the right as it delivers an idea in slow motion in the upper register. Everything holds together and remains wonderfully atmospheric.

The finale (Moderato) features an attractive theme that seems to wander as it slowly gains momentum. Shostakovich presents some very interesting contrapuntal writing involving this theme in the variations that follow the exposition. The tempo increases in the first two, and slower and faster passages alternate thereafter. In the slow sections the mood at times turns reflective, almost lapsing into the hypnotic quality of the Largo. The theme is transformed in colorful and beautiful ways throughout the movement.

Shostakovich himself premiered the work on November 11, 1943. Despite the championing of this sonata by Emil Gilels it never entered the standard repertory, though recent renewed interest in the entirety of this composer's output may change that status in the coming decades. *—Robert Cummings*

Recommended:

- **Shostakovich: Symphony 15; Piano Sonata 2** / Gilels / 2000 / RCA 63587
- **Youri Egorov: Prokofiev, Shostakovich & Babadjanjan** / Egorov / Canal Grande 9215

24 Preludes, Op. 34 (1932–1933)

As most are aware by now, Shostakovich is not as well known for his piano music as he is for his symphonies and quartets, but his keyboard works should certainly not be dismissed. Prior to the present set of preludes Shostakovich had not composed anything for piano since his Op. 10 *Aphorisms* of 1927. These brash works, immediately preceded by the equally brash *Piano Sonata No. 1* (1926), represent the composer at his most iconoclastic. The *24 Preludes*, however, show a somewhat mellowed composer, drawing, as Shostakovich did at his best, upon diverse eras of the musical past, but still clearly communicating his own rather melancholy personality. These are neither Bach preludes nor Chopin preludes, but contain elements of each, as well as elements resembling the character pieces of various other composers.

Keys will be given in this analysis, though the composer only barely follows them, usually beginning and ending in them only. The dreamy C major prelude (Moderato) is the leadoff piece here, and it immediately establishes an atmosphere closer to the world of Prokofiev's *Visions Fugitives* than to the composer's own earlier piano works. The next prelude (*A minor*), is playful and brash, but Shostakovich dispatches it in well under a minute, curtailing its waywardness. The third, marked Andante, in G, is also dreamy and again brings Prokofiev to mind.

The next several preludes bring marked contrasts: the E minor (No. 4) is rather philosophical and Bach-like; the half-minute D major is bristling with energy; and the ensuing B minor is humorous and full of color. No. 7, in A, is a ponderous Andante, and the next two, in F sharp minor and E, respectively, present livelier and then rambunctious music, the latter being a roller-coaster Presto. No. 10, in C sharp minor, brings color in its melancholy, and the following Allegretto, in B, bursts from the starting gate but slows down near the finish line and ends softly. The twelfth piece (G sharp minor) also begins rapidly, but its demeanor is tamer, as if to carry on the mood of its predecessor's closing bars.

If the first 12 pieces offer variety in their pacing and pianistic execution, while remaining within a limited emotional range, the latter dozen are slightly more varied. No. 13, in F sharp, is humorous but subdued, less extravagant than several counterparts in the first half, and No. 14, in E flat minor, is the most serious and morose entry, sounding like late Liszt, replete with tremolos and dark chords. Lightness returns with the D major, a playful but nervous Allegretto.

The march that ensues in No. 16 (B flat minor) is satiric and vaguely recalls Schubert. The next, in A flat, hints at sentimentality, then deftly wanders into a parody of that emotion. No. 18, in F minor, is another short, playful piece, while the next entry, in E flat, sounds similar in mood to No. 17. The Allegro furioso marking of No. 20 (C minor), continues the trend that the faster items here are the shorter. This one is less furious than its marking suggests, but quite sarcastic and brash instead. The next (B major), is also short, but emotionally cold, neither playful nor satiric.

No. 22, in G minor, is slow and gloomy, though this mood is broken in the next two pieces, in F major and D minor, respectively, the former actually divulging a genuine radiance in its eccentricity, and the latter a zany piece with much color in its march-like theme. A performance of this collection lasts about a half hour. *—Robert Cummings*

Recommended:

- ○ **Shostakovich: Three Fantastic Dances; 24 Preludes; Piano Sonata 2** / Nikolayeva / 1992 / Hyperion 66620
- ○ **Vladimir Viardo Plays Shostakovich: 24 Preludes; Piano Sonata 2** / Viardo / 1990 / Nonesuch 79234

24 Preludes & Fugues, Op. 87 (1950–1951)

Just back from a trip to Leipzig in the early autumn of 1950 where he heard Bach's *Well-Tempered Klavier* at the Bicentennial Bach Competition played by the Russian pianist Tatiana Nikolaeva, Shostakovich began his own series of *24 Preludes and Fugues*, Op. 87, based on Bach's model. He composed them quickly, starting on October 10, 1950, and finishing on February 23, 1951.

While his work would pay homage to Bach, Shostakovich's work would have several fundamental differences. First, the order of the individual pieces would be organized around the circle of fifths with a prelude and fugue in the relative minor following each major key piece rather than in ascending semi-tonal order of Bach's work. Second, Shostakovich's pieces would be composed in order—that is, C major—A minor followed by G major—E minor followed by D major—B minor—and, more significantly, this order would have a sort of subliminal narrative sub-text, taking the music from the "innocent" tonal world of the *C major Prelude and Fugue* to the profound and sublime severity of the concluding *D minor Prelude and Fugue*. Finally, Shostakovich's work, although conservative in its counterpoint and harmony—that is, there are no examples of invertible or reversible themes or counterpoint and the pieces are for the most part recognizably tonal in language—is still clearly the work of a modernist composer; his counterpoint and harmony may be conservative but the emotional and spiritual worlds of the preludes and fugues is at once sincere and ironic. The result is a work which can not only stand comparison with Bach's *Well-Tempered Klavier*, it is both Shostakovich's masterpiece for the piano and one of the contrapuntal masterpieces of the twentieth century. *—James Leonard*

Recommended:

- ○ **Shostakovich: 24 Preludes & Fugues Op 87** / Ashkenazy / 1999 / Decca 466066
- ○ **Shostakovich: 24 Preludes & Fugues Op 87** / Nikolayeva / 1991 / Hyperion 66441

OPERA

Lady Macbeth Mtsensk, Op. 29 (1930–1932)

Shostakovich loved the title character of Nikolai Leskov's *Lady Macbeth of the Mtsensk District* perhaps not wisely but too well. In writing the libretto based on Leskov's naturalistic short story with Leningrad playwright Alexander Preis, Shostakovich loved the character of Katerina Izmaylova so deeply that he could not bear to see her as Lady Macbeth, that is, as a wanton murderer who kills her father-in-law, her husband, and her husband's nephew out of boredom and lust. Instead, Shostakovich changed her from a sex-crazed fury into a heroic victim of her time and place.

Shostakovich did everything he could in fashioning *Lady Macbeth of the Mtsensk District* to make Katerina sympathetic. He not only gave her ravishingly gorgeous arias, he gave all the other characters stilted and silly arias, transforming them from characters to caricatures. He changed the plot of the story to make her more sympathetic: among other things, he eliminated the death of the child and made Katerina's lover Sergei much more of an instigator of the crimes than he was in Leskov's story. He even gave Katerina two deeply moving arias in the fourth and final act in which she sings of her love, her guilt, and her remorse. In sum, Shostakovich deliberately and purposefully altered the story to fit with his conception of love.

Yes, love. Although the subsequent history of *Lady Macbeth*—its tremendous popular success (it was playing in both Leningrad and Moscow simultaneously), its terrible denouncement on the front page of *Pravda* as "Muddle instead of Music," its withdrawal from the stage until the early 1960s—can and must be seen in political and ideological terms, Shostakovich himself seems to have imagined the opera as a work about love. While Shostakovich was composing *Lady Macbeth* from May 1930 through December 1932, he was deeply in love with Nina Vazar, whom he married in May 1932. As he wrote years later, "I dedicated *Lady Macbeth* to my bride, my future wife, so naturally the opera is about love, too, but not only love. It's also about how love could have been if the world weren't full of vile things."

There are vile things throughout the score: the awful Offenbach-style galops, the lurid music for the bestial father-in-law, the weak music for the husband, the satiric music for the police and the priests, the grinding organ interlude, the garish orchestral colors, the merciless rhythms. the hideous harmonies. But it is also filled with Shostakovich's compassionate love for Katerina in her achingly beautiful music. If Shostakovich's love for Katerina prevented him from creating an opera which was a faithful adaptation of Leskov's story or from creating an opera which would be acceptable to the cruel society in which he lived, it did enable him to create a work which can move an audience to tears. *—James Leonard*

Synopsis:

Act One. At the home of the wealthy merchant Zinovy Ismailov, his wife Katerina is intensely bored. She has no children, she's illiterate, and the house is enclosed by a high fence. When Zinovy leaves on a short business trip, the hostile stepfather Boris forces Katerina to swear her marital fidelity before the sacred icon.

Workmen are amusing themselves in the yard of the Ismailov household, pawing the fat cook Aksinya whom they've stuck into a barrel. The recently-hired worker Sergey, who has a reputation as a ladies man, is among them. When Katerina tries to intervene on Aksinya's behalf, she ends up struggling with Sergey, who quickly overpowers her.

At day's end, Katerina is in her room, preparing for bed. She expresses her feelings of loneliness and desire, when suddenly Sergey knocks at her door. He tells her that he's come to borrow a book because he's "dying of boredom." It doesn't take long for Sergey to maneuver himself past Katerina's half-hearted protests, and they become lovers.

Act Two. Boris Ismailov, suffering from insomnia, has wandered out with his lantern to inspect the darkened household, musing on his youthful adventures with the wives of absent husbands. Soon he notices that Katerina's light is on, and decides to "console" the poor woman himself. He catches Sergey escaping from Katerina's room, and flogs him 400 times in punishment.

After the flogging, Boris is hungry for replenishment. He demands that Katerina prepare him some mushrooms, and these she laces with rat poison, causing Boris to fall into horrible seizures. As he dies, he tells the workmen to summon Zinovy. A priest administers the last rites, and no one yet suspects Katerina.

In Katerina's room, she and Sergey are making love upon her gigantic bed. Sergey confesses the depth of his devotion, and Katerina vows to marry him. The ghost of Boris appears, and casts his curse upon Katerina. She hears Zinovy approaching, Sergey conceals himself. Zinovy enters demanding to know what's happened during his absence, and he begins to beat her. Sergey reveals himself. The lovers strangle Zinovy and hide his corpse in the cellar. "Now you are my husband," she says ominously as they embrace.

Act Three. A guilty compulsion draws Katerina towards the cellar, against Sergey's warnings. It is the day Sergey and Katerina are to be married. The pair exit. A peasant has meanwhile noticed the two hanging around the cellar. Thinking to find the house's choice store of liquor, he breaks in, only to discover the body of the murdered Zinovy, and runs off to fetch the police.

At the police station, there is discontent: the bribes aren't coming in, they're bored, they havn't been invited to the "hussy's" wedding feast. "I'll get even with her" the sergeant swears. To entertain themselves, they're taunting an arrested Socialist-Nihilist, who cries "Sorry, god does exist, God does exist!" in defense. When the peasant arrives with the news of the murder, they are overjoyed: at last they have something to do. They rush off, expressing hopes of "free food and liquor" and maybe to "stuff ourselves until we're sick".

The wedding reception is laid out in the garden of the Ismailov house. The guests are already drunk. "Long live the happy pair!" Even the priest encourages the newlyweds, saying "Katerina Lvovna is fairer than the sun in the sky" Suddenly, Katerina sees the broken lock on the cellar door. Before the two can escape, the police arrive, disappointed the wine is all gone, and Katerina makes a complete confession. The policemen beat Sergey with happy zeal and drag away the bound Katerina.

Act Four. Siberia. Two long chain gangs of convicts are marching, Sergey and Katerina among them, although the men are separated from the women. They stop on the bank of a forest lake to spend the night. Katerina bribes the sentry Stepanych to let her near Sergey, but Sergey has lost his love for her, blames her for everything and now dotes on a beautiful young convict named Sonyetka. Sergey weasels some stockings out of Katerina, and they taunt her to despair, while the rest of the bored convicts join in. Finally, Katerina snaps: she throws herself into the lake, dragging along Sonyetka, and both drown. The opera ends with the convicts' lament over the darkness of human fate. *—Donato Mancini*

Recommended:

- ○ **Shostakovich: Lady Macbeth of Mtsensk** / Rostropovich (cond.), Vishnievskaya, Gedda, Petkov, Finnila, Tear, Krenn / 2002 / EMI 67779B
- ○ **Shostakovich: Lady Macbeth of Mtsensk** / Chung (cond.), Ewing, Haugland, Larin, Langridge, Kotcherga, Moll, Zednik, Zaremba / DG 437511

VOCAL

Songs (1922–1974)

Like the rest of Dmitry Shostakovich's oeuvre, his songs fall into three distinct groups: songs for the general public, songs of protest, and songs written entirely for himself. The most famous of the songs of protest are the dark and brutal cycle *From Jewish Folk Poetry*, Op. 79 (1948), which, like his later *Symphony No. 13*, exposes the evils of Soviet anti-Semitism. He also wrote satires, parodies and vitriolic sarcastic protest songs. At the same time, however, Shostakovich also wrote many public songs for the Soviet government, including marching songs for the Red Army, anthems for many of the Soviet republics, and even the first song to be sung in outer space: *The Homeland Hears.* Shostakovich's most characteristic songs, however, are the ones he wrote for himself. Beginning with the *Six Romances on Texts by Japanese Poets*, Op. 21 (1928–32)—his despairing love song cycle for his soon-to-be-wife Nina—and ending with his *Four Verses of Captain Lebydkin*, Op. 146 (1974)—his hideously nihilistic setting of texts from Dostoyevsky's novel *The Devils*—Shostakovich's personal songs are his private avowal of his most profound emotions. The *Four Romances on Texts by Pushkin*, Op. 46 (1936), express his grim fatalism after his music was condemned on the front page of *Pravda.* His *Six Romances on Texts of W. Raleigh, R. Burns, and W. Shakespeare*, Op. 62 (1942), sing of the fear and terror of the early years of the Great Patriotic War. After his first heart attack in 1966 and the slow disintegration of his body until his death in 1975, Shostakovich's songs served as a musical diary for his dread of death. His *Seven Verses of A. Blok*, Op. 127 (1967), and *Six Verses of Marina Tsvetayeva*, Op. 143 (1973), mix memory with his deep love for his third wife Irina and his faith in the greatness of music in some of the most intimate and sensuous songs he ever composed. In his penultimate set of songs, the *Suite on Texts of Michelangelo Buonarroti*, Op. 145 (1975), Shostakovich even seemed to overcome morbidity through his love for his wife and his belief in the immortality of his art. But his ultimate set of songs, the *Four Verses of Captain Lebydkin*, Op. 146 (1974), renounces life, love, hope, and even art in some of the most passionately pessimistic music ever composed. Like the rest of his oeuvre, Shostakovich's songs range from the banal to the sublime. But in his best songs—the *Japanese Lyrics* and the Tsvetayeva, Blok, and Buonarroti cycles—he wrote the greatest Russian songs after Mussorgsky. *—James Leonard*

Recommended:

- ○ **Shostakovich: Complete Songs Vol. 1 (1950–1956)** / Serov, Kuznetsov, Evtodieva, Lukonin, Biryukova / 2002 / Delos 3304
- ○ **Shostakovich: Complete Songs Vol. 2 (The Last Years)** / Serov, Kuznetsov, Sokolova, Evtodieva, Molokina / 2002 / Delos 3307
- ○ **Shostakovich: Complete Songs Vol. 3 (1922–1942)** / Kuznetsov, Serov, Evtodieva, Lukonin, Shkirtil / 2003 / Delos 3309
- ○ **Shostakovich: Complete Songs Vol. 4** / Khutoretskaya (cond.), St. Petersburg Chamber Choir / 2004 / Delos 3313

From Jewish Folk Poetry, song cycle, Op. 79 (1948)

The song cycle *From Jewish Folk Poetry for soloists and piano*, Op. 79, by Soviet composer Dmitry Shostakovich is one of the central works of his compositional career. While the cycle has not attained the international celebrity of his superbly crafted and tragically ironic *Symphony No. 1*, or his artist-as-political-martyr heroism of the *Symphony No. 5*, or his "is-he-or-isn't-he a dissident" ambiguity of the *String Quartet No. 8*, *From Jewish Folk Poetry* is a deep and heartrending work. He wrote *From Jewish Folk Poetry* in 1948, 20 years after his first condemnation by the Communist government and only a few months after having been condemned a second time. In 1948, Shostakovich not only knew the horrors of Stalin, but the horrors of Nazism: He knew of the Holocaust's Final Solution for European Jewry and he knew that Stalin had conceived a similar Final Solution for Russia's Jews. Thus, Shostakovich's identification with the suffering of the Jews was total, and this song cycle is the product of his identification. The 11 songs of *From Jewish Folk Poetry* are set for soprano, mezzo-soprano, tenor, and piano (Shostakovich later composed a version of the work for chamber orchestra). The songs are impossibly tragic—"The Lament for a Dead Baby"—tremendously sad—"Before a Long Parting"—horribly ironic—"The Abandoned Father"—hideously sarcastic—"The Song of Misery"—and, finally, grotesquely ironic—"The Good Life." Set in the Jewish folk idiom that Shostakovich had first made use of in his *Piano Trio No. 2* (1944), the songs' tunes are immediately memorable, their rhythms infectious, and the harmonies both sweet and sour. Needless to say, *From Jewish Folk Poetry* was not performed in public during Stalin's lifetime, but only in private for close friends of the composer. The first public performance took place on January 15, 1955. *—James Leonard*

Recommended:

- ○ **Shostakovich: Symphony 15; From Jewish Folk Poetry** / Haitink (cond.), Söderström, Concertgebouw / 1993 / Decca 425069
- ○ **Shostakovich: Chamber Symphony; Symphony for Strings; From Jewish Folk Poetry** / Turovsky (cond.), Hart, Pelle, Nolan, I Musici de Montreal / 1997 / Chandos 7061
- ○ **Shostakovich Plays Shostakovich Vol. 2** / Maslennikov, Doloukhanova, Shostakovich, Dorliak / 2004 / Eclectra 2067

Jean Sibelius

b. Dec. 8, 1865, Hämeenlinna, Finland, **d.** Sep. 20, 1957, Järvenpää, Finland

Composer: Orchestral, Symphonic, Concerto, Chamber Music, Keyboard, Vocal

Finland's Jean Sibelius is perhaps the most important composer associated with nationalism in music and one of the most influential in the development of the symphony and symphonic poem. Sibelius was born in southern Finland, the second of three children. His physician father left the family bankrupt, owing to his financial extravagance, a trait that, along with heavy drinking, he would pass on to Jean. Jean showed talent on the violin and at age nine composed his first work for it, *Rain Drops.* In 1895 Sibelius entered the University of Helsinki to study law, but after only a year found himself drawn back to music. He took up composition studies with Martin Wegelius and violin with Mitrofan Wasiliev, then Hermann Csillag. During this time he also became a close friend of Busoni. Though Sibelius auditioned for the Vienna Philharmonic Orchestra, he would come to realize he was not suited to a career as a violinist.

In 1889 Sibelius traveled to Berlin to study counterpoint with Albert Becker, where he also was exposed to new music, particularly that of Richard Strauss. In Vienna he studied with Karl Goldmark and then Robert Fuchs, the latter said to be his most effective teacher. Now Sibelius began pondering the composition of the *Kullervo Symphony*, based on the *Kalevala* legends. Sibelius returned to Finland, taught music, and in June 1892, married Aino Järnefelt, daughter of General Alexander Järnefelt, head of one of the most influential families in Finland. The premiere of *Kullervo* in April 1893 created a veritable sensation, Sibelius thereafter being looked upon as the foremost Finnish composer. The *Lemminkäinen* suite, begun in 1895 and premiered on April 13, 1896, has come to be regarded as the most important music by Sibelius up to that time.

In 1897 the Finnish Senate voted to pay Sibelius a short-term pension, which some years later became a lifetime conferral. The honor was in lieu of his loss of an important professorship in composition at the music school, the position going to Robert Kajanus. The year 1899 saw the premiere of Sibelius' *First Symphony*, which was a tremendous success, to be sure, but not quite of the magnitude of that of *Finlandia* (1899; rev. 1900).

In the next decade Sibelius would become an international figure in the concert world. Kajanus introduced several of the composer's works abroad; Sibelius himself was invited to Heidelberg and Berlin to conduct his music. In March 1901, the *Second Symphony* was received as a statement of independence for Finland, although Sibelius always discouraged attaching programmatic ideas to his music. His only concerto, for violin, came in 1903. The next year Sibelius built a villa outside of Helsinki, named "Ainola" after his wife, where he would live for his remaining 53 years. After a 1908 operation to remove a throat tumor, Sibelius was implored to abstain from alcohol and tobacco, a sanction he followed until 1915. It is generally believed that the darkening of mood in his music during these years owes something to the health crisis.

Sibelius made frequent trips to England, having visited first in 1905 at the urging of Granville Bantock. In 1914 he traveled to Norfolk, CT, where he conducted his newest work *The Oceanides*. Sibelius spent the war years in Finland working on his *Fifth Symphony*. Sibelius traveled to England for the last time in 1921. Three years later he completed his *Seventh Symphony*, and his last work was the incidental music for *The Tempest* (1925). For his last 30 years Sibelius lived a mostly quiet life, working only on revisions and being generally regarded as the greatest living composer of symphonies. In 1955 his 90th birthday was widely celebrated throughout the world with many performances of his music. Sibelius died of a cerebral hemorrhage in 1957. *—Robert Cummings*

ORCHESTRAL

Andante Festivo, for strings (1938)

Despite the rejection of the string orchestra repertoire by several major publishers of his day, including the extremely influential Breitkopf & Härtel, Sibelius was drawn to the medium throughout his lifetime. Most of his works, however, are arrangements of works composed in other media which were more easily publishable and might be familiar to listeners in other guises. In 1922 Sibelius composed *Andante Festivo* for the 25th anniversary of the Saynatsalo plywood mill. First written for a string quartet and later arranged for a string orchestra and timpani ad libitum, it has a musical vocabulary in almost complete opposition to the prevailing trends in art and music at the time. While it would have been rather fashionable, as well as appropriate for the occasion, to capture the mechanical features of the mill, Sibelius' greatest inspiration was nature, and the work features a tone of almost sacred solemnity. Curiously, Sibelius conducted the premiere of this work, long into his retirement, in a 1939 live radio broadcast to the United States on New Year's Eve. *—Brian Wise*

Recommended:

- ○ **Sibelius: Symphonies 2, 3 & 5; The Swan of Tuonela** / Jansons (cond.), Oslo PO / 2002 / EMI 575673
- ○ **Jean Sibelius: Symphony 5; Andante Festivo; Karelia-Overture** / Järvi (cond.), Gothenburg SO / 1984 / BIS 222

The Bard (Barden), tone poem, Op. 64 (1913; revised 1914)

Lacking any detailed program, *The Bard* is the briefest of all Sibelius' orchestral tone poems. None of the usual elements of the genre are to be found in the work—drama, development, and powerful climax are all absent from this brooding, introspective essay. It is a transitional work that hints at the unique flavor of the composer's later works.

The Bard is constructed from simple, fragmentary motivic strands that remain undeveloped and ultimately unresolved. Although the piece can be divided into two sections, the distinction between the two is extremely slight. Things heat up ever so slightly in the second section, but in the end returns to the same vague melancholy that opened the work. Perhaps the only tangible musical reference to the title is the role the harp plays in defining the character and mood of *The Bard*'s musical texture. The tone poem opens with a sequence of descending chords played by the harp, with quiet sixteenth note commentary from the viola section. Throughout the piece the harp serves to demarcate key moments in the score.

From the same pivotal period of Sibelius' career as the *Symphony No. 4*, *The Dryad*, and *Oceanides*, *The Bard* reveals a composer in the process of redefining his methods, and examples of both earlier and later Sibelius can be seen. Orchestrationally, the academic, somewhat block-like methods of the composer's younger days are giving way to the thinner, more contrapuntal techniques of his later masterworks. His growing predilection for syncopation in one voice, set against a backdrop of rhythmic stability, is apparent in *The Bard*, as well.

The Bard is the type of music that always has—and likely always will—provoke heated difference of opinion from scholars and listeners alike. Of the haunting intensity of the work's atmosphere, however, there can be no doubt. *—Blair Johnston*

Recommended:

- ○ **Sibelius: En Saga; The Bard; Valse Triste** / Järvi (cond.), Gothenburg SO / 2000 / DG 457654

En Saga, tone poem, Op. 9 (1892; revised 1902)

This is one of Sibelius' earliest orchestral works, and it brims with youthful energy. It is also a highly atmospheric work, clearly evocative of the composer's beloved Finland—its people, proud history, countryside and landscapes. The title (Swedish, rather than Finnish, meaning "A Fairy Tale") suggests it is a programmatic work, and indeed there does seem to be a musical "story" present; the composer, however, never identified any specific extra-musical inspiration.

Sibelius wrote the work at the suggestion of conductor Robert Kajanus, who wanted a composition that would have wide appeal; in completing it Sibelius drew on themes from an unperformed and unpublished octet for strings and winds he had written in Berlin. At its February 16, 1893, premiere in Helsinki (led by the composer), *En Saga* was not a success, suffering as it did from a lack of formal organization. Sibelius' 1902 revision, however—coming, perhaps not insignificantly, directly after the composition of his *Symphony No. 2*—overcame these difficulties, and is now regarded as one of his finest orchestral works.

The work begins mysteriously, the music seeming to awaken and gather momentum, as strings swirl and woodwinds bark and chirp. This gives rise to a lively rhythmic theme of characteristically Sibelian character; there is something both mournful and proud in the melody—simple, yet striking. This theme is the first of three that, by development and interaction, become the de facto "characters" in this musical tale; they each struggle to maintain hold on the music as becomes more conflicted, eventually rising to a violent climax. Eventually, the musical conflict is resolved, and only the solo clarinet—accompanied by gentle strings—is left to witness the end.

Throughout *En Saga* Sibelius puts the woodwinds front and center, often using their dissonant punctuations to herald the beginning of a new section or idea. The color and character of these woodwind passages are perhaps the most identifiably Scandinavian musical feature of the score. While there are influences here of Rimsky-Korsakov and other Russian composers, *En Saga* must be regarded as one of the composer's most individual and satisfying early works. A typical performance lasts from about 17 to 20 minutes. *—AMG*

Recommended:

- ○ **Sibelius: Tone Poems** / Karajan (cond.), Berlin PO / 1992 / EMI 64331
- ○ **Sibelius: En Saga; The Bard; Valse Triste** / Järvi (cond.), Gothenburg SO / 2000 / DG 457654
- ○ **Sibelius: Tone Poems** / Vänskä (cond.), Lahti SO / 2002 / BIS 1225

Finlandia, tone poem, Op. 26 (1900)

Jean Sibelius' *Finlandia* became the composer's most enduring work in part because of the political climate in Finland at the time of its creation. Russia imposed a strict censorship policy on the small nation in 1899. In October of that year, Sibelius composed a melodrama to Finnish writer Zachria Topelius' poem *The Melting of the Ice on the Ulea River*, which is marked by a particularly patriotic fervor; "I was born free and free will I die" is typical of its sentiments, and one of which Sibelius took particular note. The following month saw a fund-raising gala organized by the Finnish press. While its ostensible purpose was to raise money for newspaper pension funds, it was in fact a front for rallying support for a free press at a time when the czarist hold on the country was tightening.

Sibelius extracted six tableaux from his melodrama for a performance intended to provide a celebratory end to the gathering on November 4. Innocuously titled *Music for Press Ceremony*, the score concluded with "Finland Awakens," which Sibelius reworked into an independent symphonic poem in the following year. Following the suggestion of his artistic confidant Axel Carpelan, he retitled this rousing patriotic essay *Finlandia*; since that time, the work has virtually become Finland's second national anthem. Because of censorship restrictions, the work was most often performed under the not-altogether-apt title Impromptu until Finland gained independence following World War I.

The work opens with a questioning, vaguely ominous brass progression that evokes the "powers of darkness" from Topelius' text, setting off a colorful drama that is at turns reflective, jubilant, and militant. Most famous, though, is a hymn-like theme which makes its first appearance in an atmosphere of quiet reverence; by the end of the work, it has become a powerful statement of triumph. Indeed, *Finlandia* is a clear precursor to the composer's symphonies, in which the orchestra so often assumes the role of an ever-strengthening, defiant juggernaut. *—AMG*

Recommended:

- ○ **Sibelius: Finlandia; Tone Poems** / Berglund (cond.), London Philharmonia Orch. / 2000 / Angel 73735
- ○ **Jean Sibelius** / Karajan (cond.), Berlin PO / 2000 / DG 469202
- ○ **Sibelius** / Segerstam (cond.), Helsinki PO / Ondine 936

Karelia Overture, Op. 10 (1893)

Sibelius was 27 and a half years old and climbing fast up the Finnish music ladder when he received a commission from a local student society (the Wiborg, or Viipuri Society of Helsinki) to compose some incidental music for an upcoming celebration of Karelian history. (Karelia was and is a geographical locale midway between Finland and Russia, an area which has been claimed by both at various times.) The occasion featured a miniature play in seven scenes, and Sibelius was asked to produce a corresponding seven items of music, plus an overture. He undertook the project with a passion, and the resulting music is both the first incidental music ever written by Sibelius—the first in a very long and distinguished series of such works, culminating in 1925's *The Tempest*—and also the first published music of his to bear the strong nationalist imprint that characterizes so much of his music from the 1890s and early 1900s.

Not all of the *Karelia* music was actually published, however. Sibelius drew up a three-movement *Suite* (Op. 11), and prepared the *Karelia Overture* for publication as Op. 10; the rest of the pieces he abandoned to their fate (which turned out to be unpublished obscurity). Once a proud and oft-heard work, the *Karelia Overture* fell into disuse during the latter half of the twentieth century—it can no longer claim a fame as great is the *Suite*'s, but it still makes a fine concert opener.

In C major, the overture is scored for an orchestra of ordinary size and build (woodwinds in pairs, brass in the customary 4-3-3-1 layout, timpani, moderate percussion, and strings). The sonata-form overture blueprint is expanded so that three rather than two themes might be offered. The first is a rising idea with some energetic triplets in Allegro moderato tempo. The second is a folkish lyric strain that first appears in E minor but later reappears in C minor; Sibelius moves briefly from duple to triple meter for this Nordic melody, which is sung by the first violins and cellos in octaves. The third theme is an intruder from the first movement of the *Karelia Suite*, Op. 11 (the Intermezzo)—a martial idea meant to represent tax collectors in the original incidental music, it is first offered in the overture by the horns and then taken up by the entire woodwind section, and then makes frequent reappearances. —*Blair Johnston*

Recommended:

- ○ **Sibelius: Symphony 1; Karelia Overture & Suite; Finlandia** / Saraste (cond.), Finnish Radio SO / 1988 / RCA 7765

Karelia Suite, Op. 11 (1893)

Sibelius' work on the incidental music to *Karelia* was borne on the rising tide of nationalism that swept through Finland in the 1890s. During this era, many considered education to be the best means of preserving cultural identity and thus opposing Russia's encroachment on Finland. Sibelius' score, composed in a frenzied rush in 1893, was a natural response to this outlook and to the Finnish people's fondness for historical tableaux.

The work was commissioned by the Viipuir Students' Association of the University of Helsinki—a student organization that was prevalent across the province of Viipuri (now part of Russia)—and was premiered at a November 1893 gala event. Proceeds from the ticket sales were to go to "improving the social and cultural life of the Eastern border districts." The work was a rousing success; as Sibelius noted in a letter to his brother Christian, "You couldn't hear a single note of the music—everyone was on their feet cheering and clapping."

Buoyed by this popular acclaim, *Karelia* got off to a promising start and was performed a handful of performances to similar acclaim. The composer, however, was less convinced of its musical value, and soon his excitement for the piece waned, likely from a belief that it was too loosely constructed and "tableaux-like" for a concert setting. He later condensed the eight scenes into the three-movement work now familiar as the *Karelia Suite*, Op. 11.

In its original form, after a patriotic overture, the work's first tableau ("Karelian Home—Runic Song, interrupted by War Music, 1293") features a stylized "Karelianist" interpretation of rune singing from the Karelia region. In the second tableau ("The Founding of Viipuri Castle, 1293"), Sibelius incorporates a fugato based on Gregorian chant, followed by a chorale-like subject intended as a reference to the blessing of the foundation stone by Bishop Petrus. Following this lofty subject matter, the third tableaux ("Narimont, the Duke of Lithuania, levying taxes in the Province of Käksim, 1333") somewhat prosaically depicts the collection of taxes; appropriately, it begins with clamorous battle music, followed by a central march section. The subject of the fourth tableau ("Ballade—Karl Knutsson in Viipuri Castle, 1446") is the famed King, who after being deposed in 1446 withdrew to Viipuri Castle to lick his wounds; in Sibelius' score, he seeks solace in the singing of a troubadour. The distinctly warlike fifth tableau ("Pontus de la Gardie at the Gates of Käkisalmi, 1580") includes several fanfares, some wildly dissonant in relation to a pedal bass, leading to a central Alla marcia. The sixth tableau ("The Siege of Viipuri, 1710") hints at Sibelius' characteristic mature style, an exciting combination of brisk motion and static, block-like harmonies. The seventh and eight tableaux ("The Reunion of Old Finland with the Rest of Finland, 1811" and "The Finnish National Anthem 'Our Land'") are allegorical renditions, the latter of which elevates the Finnish national anthem to new dramatic heights. As Jouni Kaipainen, who in 1997 edited and reconstructed parts of the original work, noted, "The nature and message of the tableau was so stunningly obvious that it is actually interesting to wonder how the Czarist censor ever managed to let it through."—*Brian Wise*

Recommended:

- ○ **Sibelius: Karelia Suite; Tapiola; Nightride & Sunrise; Finlandia** / Davis (cond.), London SO / 1999 / RCA 902668770
- ○ **Sibelius: Karelia Suite; Pohjola's Daughter; Valse Triste; Limminkäinen's Return** / Barbirolli (cond.), Halle Orch. / 1988 / EMI 769205
- ○ **Sibelius: Symphony 1; Karelia Suite** / Ashkenazy (cond.), London Philharmonia Orch. / London 50374

Kullervo, symphonic poem for vocal soloists, male chorus & orchestra, Op. 7 (1892)

Kullervo began as an Overture in E major that Sibelius wrote in 1890 as a student in Vienna. To his future wife Aino he wrote of possibly a "symphony, in three or perhaps four movements" based on the folk epic *Kalevala*, collected by Elias Lönrott in 1835, expanded in 1849 from 32 *runos* to 50, and republished in 1890. Though Sibelius later denied it, he heard a rune-singer from Karelia during the summer of 1891; inspired by her repertory of orally preserved folk music, he began to evolve a personal style. By 1892, he had completed *Kullervo*, a work in five movements of 72 minutes' total duration, which he introduced in Helsinki on April 28. He called it his Op. 7, yet never allowed another performance in his lifetime. With soprano and baritone soloists, male chorus, and orchestra, it has been identified variously as a symphony, a symphonic poem, even a cantata, but it is in fact a conflation of all three—and startlingly anticipatory in "Kullervo and his Sister," the long central movement.

The protagonist didn't materialize until 1849, as the subject of Runos 31–36: the bastard child of a pregnant housemaid, who survived a massacre by Kullervo's evil uncle. Despite attempts to destroy the child (by drowning, immolation, and finally hanging), Kullervo survives. Brain-damaged, however, he does all manner of wickedness in return to the uncle's cruel wife and properties. Hearing that his parents and three siblings survived the massacre, he finds all of them in the northland, except for a roving sister. Despite their happy reunion, Kullervo wrecks whatever he puts his hand to, and is finally sent off to pay taxes. On the journey back he encounters a maiden who resists his advances, but eventually succumbs to the warmth of his fur-lined sleigh. After they've cohabited, Kullervo discovers the woman is the missing sister, who in shame and despair drowns herself. Unbalanced by guilty rage, Kullervo declares war on his evil uncle. With a magic sword given to him by the god Ukko, he destroys everything and everyone, returns to where his sister drowned, and falls on the sword.

The opening "Introduction" is putatively a portrait of Kullervo. But while this Lisztian *mélange* in sonata form has a notable second theme, hardly anything truly Sibelian appears until the second movement, "Kullervo's Youth," with its distinctive main subject in the oral runic style. The work becomes suddenly epic in the central movement, narrated mostly by the chorus with the soloists as incestuous siblings, and which concludes starkly with the protagonist's lamentations. Next comes "Kullervo Goes the Battle," which sounds stylistically second-hand after the preceding movement. In "Kullervo's Death," the chorus sings the conclusion of Runo 36 verbatim. It doesn't quite rise to the heights of the third movement, yet is fittingly somber and ends as the work began, in E major. —*Roger Dettmer*

Recommended:

- ○ **Sibelius: Kullervo** / Salonen (cond.), Hynninen, Rorholm, Los Angeles PO, Helsinki University Chorus / 1993 / Sony 52563
- ○ **Sibelius: Kullervo** / Vänskä (cond.), Paasikivi, Laukka, Lahti SO, Helsinki University Chorus / 2000 / BIS 1215

Kuolema (Death), incidental music, Op. 44 (1903)

During the early years of the twentieth century, Jean Sibelius' reputation outside his home country of Finland rested almost exclusively on the widespread fame of just a single piece: the "Valse Triste" from his incidental music to the play *Kuolema* (Death). Sibelius was keenly interested in the theater, and when asked in 1903 by his brother-in-law Arvid Järnefelt, the author of *Kuolema*, to supply some music to support the drama, he happily responded with six numbers scored for strings and percussion. Over the next few years, two pieces were extracted from the original six and published as Op.44; two additional numbers, published as Op.62, date from 1911.

"Valse Triste," a 1904 reworking of the first musical scene, has the dubious honor of being one of the most truly overplayed pieces in musical history; yet it is still rather easy to imagine the seductive, sparkling effect that this five-minute piece must have had on European coffee-house audiences of the day. The work, cast in the traditional three-part dance form, paints a striking picture. Paavali waits at the bed-side of his dying mother, who dreams of having gone to the ball. As Paavali goes to sleep himself, Death comes to take his mother, who, believing the figure to be her own dead husband, proceeds to dance the "Valse Triste" with him; the mother has expired by the time Paavali wakes up again. The interplay of melancholy, nostalgia, and resignation in the music of the outer two sections of this miniature tone-poem remains fresh even a hundred years after it first appeared; the middle portion, admittedly somewhat less outstanding, allows for some appropriately heated dance.

In 1906 Sibelius recomposed the third and fourth musical scenes into a single number, called "Scen med tranor" (Scene with Cranes) and published as Op. 44, No. 2. For the new version Sibelius augmented the original string ensemble with two clarinets and thoroughly rewrote much of the musical material. The result is a tender portrayal of the bird-life that Sibelius loved so dearly and was so deeply influenced by in later works.

The two numbers published as Opus 62 were not put together until almost a decade after the original composition of the *Kuolema* music (added for a new production of the play in 1911). The Canzonetta, Op. 62 No.1, retains the original scoring for muted strings; it is a delicate—one might even say fragile—piece that far outshines the rather disappointing "Valse Romantique," Op. 62 No.2, the scoring of which—although supplemented by flutes, clarinet, horns and timpani—still somehow manages to come across as bland. The primary idea is promising enough, however, and in the hands of a skilled ensemble the work makes a lush impression. —*Blair Johnston*

Recommended:

- ○ **Sibelius: Symphony 7; Kuolema** / Järvi (cond.), Gothenburg SO / 1986 / Bis 311

Lemminkäinen Suite: Four Legends from the Kalevala, Op. 22 (1895; revised 1897)

Four Legends from the Kalevala is scored for an orchestra of medium size with English horn and harp in the second and bass tuba in the fourth. It was the fourth of Sibelius' orchestral works following studies at the Vienna Conservatory in 1890–91 with Karl Goldmark and Robert Fuchs. *Four Legends* was written in 1895, based on mythic events in Finland's national folk epic. The long first and third *Legends—Lemminkäinen and the Maidens of the Island (aka Saari)* and *Lemminkäinen in Tuonela*—bewildered listeners and displeased critics at the Helsinki premiere on April 13, 1896. The second Legend, however, *The Swan of Tuonela*, and the concluding one, *Lemminkäinen's Homeward Journey*, were immediately successful and were published with minor revisions in 1900. Sibelius labored over the two longer ones during 1896–97, then put them aside. They remained in a drawer until 1935, almost a decade after the composer had officially stopped composing. In 1939 he made "final" revisions, his last thoughts for orchestra. Lemminkäinen was the handsome, hereditarily randy son of Lempi, the god of erotic love. In the first musical *Legend*, based on "Runo 29," he takes refuge on a remote island from a horde of Pohjolanders whose leader he beheaded in a sword fight. The island's male population has gone to war, leaving behind 100 widows and 1,000 virgins. During the next three years, Lemminkäinen beds all but one before the men return, forcing him to flee again. The music's principal subject groups in E flat major characterize first the seducer and then the dance music of his overjoyed conquests without being specifically pictorial, as Richard Strauss had been a decade earlier in *Don Juan*. Structure here, and again in *Legend No. 3*, is organic rather than conventionally symphonic: it evolves from malleable materials heard early on, reworked with great ingenuity and expressive beauty leading to a powerfully dramatic climax. Sibelius prefaced the score of *Legend No. 2* with lines from "Runo 14": "Tuonela, the land of death, the hell of Finnish mythology, is surrounded by black waters and a rapid current, on which the Swan on Tuonela floats majestically, singing." The mood-painting is somber in A minor (anticipating the *Symphony No. 4* 16 years later), with a haunting English horn solo characterizing the black swan. In the dark-hued and gripping third *Legend*, based on "Runo 14," *Lemminkäinen* is told to kill the swan by Louhi, the cunning mistress of Pohjola, to gain the hand of a daughter. But a blind cowherd intuits his murderous intent and from a river reed fashions a poisonous serpent that kills the swan hunter. When the cowherd throws Lemminkäinen's body into the swirling river, the son of Tuonela's ruling deity angrily hacks it into 40 pieces. Lemminkäinen's supernatural mother manages, however, to retrieve the pieces and reassemble them so that her restored son in *Legend No. 4* can exultantly ride home in E flat major. *—Roger Dettmer*

Recommended:

- ○ **Sibelius: Lemminkäinen Suite** / Vänskä (cond.), Lahti SO / 1999 / Bis 1015
- ○ **Sibelius: Lemminkäinen Suite** / Järvi (cond.), Gothenburg SO / 1985 / Bis 294

Luonnotar (The Spirit of Nature), tone poem for voice & orchestra, Op. 70 (1913)

Premiered at the 1913 Gloucester Festival in England, *Luonnotar* dates to around 1910, but may have been written as late as 1912. What is unusual here is that Sibelius, the Finnish national hero, for once set text in his native Finnish language. Most of his large-scale vocal and choral works employed Swedish texts, Swedish being the composer's first language. Sibelius did, however, write a fair number of songs in Finnish. The text from *Luonnotar* is taken from the first part of the Finnish national epic the *Kalevala* and deals with the creation of the world. Sibelius wrote the work for Finnish soprano Aino Ackté, one of the few singers willing to confront the work's wide range, which encompasses B to C flat. Sibelius called *Luonnotar* a tone poem for soprano and orchestra. It opens with busy strings softly, rhythmically scurrying about. When the soprano enters, the tempo temporarily slows, but the tension remains as she sings her icy, grim music. The mood throughout the work is dark and ominous, tense and dramatic, with not a ray of sunshine anywhere. It is much like the contemporary *Symphony No. 4* (1911), in particular like that work's first and third movements. The singer and orchestra in *Luonnotar* share fairly equal roles, but the most dramatic moments are vocal. The piece lasts about nine or ten minutes. *—Robert Cummings*

Recommended:

- ○ **Sibelius: Symphony 2; Luonnotar; Pohjola's Daughter** / Bernstein (cond.), New York PO / 2000 / Sony 61848
- ○ **Sibelius: Symphony 4; Luonnatar; Finlandia** / Ashkenazy (cond.), London Philharmonia Orch. / 1982 / London 400056

Night Ride & Sunrise (Öinen ratsastus ja auringonnousu), symphonic poem, Op. 55 (1908)

Öinen ratsastus ja auringonnousu is the original Finnish title for the work known as *Night-Ride and Sunrise*, the Op. 55 orchestral tone poem composed by Jean Sibelius in 1908. As the music itself (a depiction of a wild nocturnal ride through a haunted forest, with an ensuing cathartic sunrise as a new day dawns) seems to suggest in its huge range of contrasts and emotions, it belonged to a period of changing fortunes for the composer. As his diaries of the time show, often painfully, his moods alternated between buoyant confidence and bleak despair. He was plagued by debts and his health deteriorated; he was much possessed by intimations of death, and his music became darker and the more introspective. Nor were his professional affairs much better. Self-doubt and anxiety over his ability to create the large-scale works commissioned by his publisher Lienau made it difficult increasingly difficult to fulfill the conditions of his contract. After completing his *Third Symphony*, Sibelius wrote only two other works for Lienau, neither of which was well received by the public.

The first of these was the proto-minimalist tone poem *Night-Ride and Sunrise*. It may be described as "proto-minimalist" because, although a large orchestra is employed, Sibelius created its mystical and often unearthly effects by deploying instruments in very small groups, or against the sparest of accompaniments. The work, while having obvious folkloristic connections, was nonetheless not inspired by the ancient bardic legends of Finland's *Kalevala*, as were many of Sibelius' descriptive orchestral works. Structurally, too, *Night-Ride and Sunrise* ventured decisively away from the conventions of the sonata-form tone poem. Its sparse thematic groups are often heard to recur in a series of multiple cumulative rotations, though the full resources of the orchestra are kept in check until, as the sun greets the new day, a great paean of sound erupts, so that the ending has the effect of suspending the animation of what has gone before, rather as does the conclusion of Sibelius' *Seventh Symphony*.

Many commentators have drawn attention to the fact that here, Sibelius powerfully anticipates the spare, lean textures and quasi-minimalist language of his later works, and like his somber *String Quartet in D minor*, subtitled *"Voces intimae"* (1909), this piece also prefigures the *Fourth Symphony*'s dark, brooding language to often chilling effect, as if the composer was somehow writing music which spoke of entrenched isolation, only to turn back to conscious thought at the very close. *Night-Ride and Sunrise* was premiered in St. Petersburg under Alexandre Siloti on January 21, 1909. *—Michael Jameson*

Recommended:

- ○ **Sibelius: Symphony 4; Pohjola's Daughter; Oceanides; The Bard** / Saraste (cond.), Finnish Radio SO / 1989 / RCA 7919
- ○ **Bruckner: Symphonie 4; Sibelius: Nächtlicher Ritt und Sonnenaufgang** / Jochum (cond.), Berlin PO / 1996 / DG 449718

The Oceanides (Aallottaret), tone poem, Op. 73 (1914)

The orchestral poem *The Oceanides*, one of very few programmatic Sibelius pieces not based on, or markedly influenced by, Nordic mythology, instead bears witness to another of the composer's lifelong affinities—Greco-Roman lore. The title of the work is drawn from Homer, the oceanides being a race of sea nymphs. Rich in melody and utilizing a broader palette of moods and textures than many of his earlier essays in the genre, the work was composed for the occasion of the composer's 1914 American tour.

The poem is constructed out of two small motivic ideas, with the occasional recurrence of the opening flute theme lending something of a loose rondo form to the proceedings. Remarkably "impressionist" in its aural effect, with harp harmonics and muted string effects, *The Oceanides* often ventures into a harmonic language more characteristic of Debussy than of the Finnish master. Certainly the frequent doublings (often in parallel fourths) and the striking variety of timbral blends seem quite atypical of Sibelius. Many of these scoring procedures, however, had been exploited by the composer (to a lesser degree) in earlier works—they merely reach their zenith in *The Oceanides*.

Several of the composer's usual orchestral fingerprints are in evidence: structures built on continual, "organic" development of small melodic fragments; varied and crucial use of the tympani; and a general reluctance to clarify the musical direction until the very end of the piece. The tremendous climax that develops into the conclusion of *The Oceanides* is a thing that must be witnessed to believe. The apparently uncharacteristic elements of the music vis-à-vis the composer's normal language exist on only the surface levels of textures and tone colors. In actual compositional procedure the work is typically Sibelian. *—Blair Johnston*

Recommended:

- ○ **Sibelius: Tempest; Oceanides; Nightride and Sunrise** / Segerstam (cond.), Helsinki PO / Ondine 914
- ○ **Sibelius: Symphony 4; Pohjola's Daughter; Oceanides; The Bard** / Saraste (cond.), Finnish Radio SO / 1990 / RCA 60401

Pelléas et Mélisande, incidental music, Op. 46 (1905)

In 1905, Sibelius composed music for Maurice Maeterlinck's play *Pelléas et Mélisande* (1892). Maeterlinck (1862–1949) was a Belgian symbolist poet who rose to international fame with the appearance of *Pelléas*. The story, of course, also inspired Claude Debussy to compose his masterful opera of the same name. It is interesting to compare the approaches of the two composers in dealing with the story: Debussy is more sensual and elegant, while Sibelius takes a somewhat emotionally detached, darker view of the characters and events. Some would simply described the latter's approach as typically Nordic. (It should be noted that

Gabriel Fauré wrote less distinguished incidental music for a production of *Pelléas et Melisande* in 1898.)

Maeterlinck's story, set in the medieval fantasy world of Allemonde ruled by King Arkel, deals with the affair between Pelléas and the beautiful Mélisande, who has married the former's half brother Golaud. Golaud learns of their relationship and forbids Pelléas to see Mélisande. But the two continue to have trysts—in her chamber, at the Fountain of the blind, and elsewhere. Golaud enlists the aid of his son Yniold to monitor the lovers. Meanwhile, King Arkel admires the beauty of Mélisande but becomes disturbed when Golaud speaks abusively to her. When Golaud hears Pelléas and Mélisande declare their love for each other, he slays Pelléas and wounds Mélisande. She gives birth a short while later to a baby girl, then dies.

Overall, Sibelius' music for this dark love story is subdued but generally effective in capturing the mood and spirit of Maeterlinck's sophisticated psychological drama. The composer scored it for a chamber ensemble, fully intending to create a more restrained sound world. It should be noted that the suite he derived from the incidental music closely follows the chronology of the play's action.

Sibelius imparts a stately air to the play's opening, and an orchestration that is instantly recognizable as his own. He provides immensely attractive music for Mélisande, with a somewhat forlorn theme on the lower strings and English horn. Hers may be the most poignant music in the score. Sibelius offers much brightness for Act Two, Scene One in the park, but does not fully break with the generally darker and more subdued tone of the score. For the most part, the music depicting the events in Act Three, Scene Two, which roughly correspond to those of the Three Blind Sisters in the suite, is best described by its marking of tranquillo. In the end, as incidental music for the stage, this work must be ranked with its sibling from the period, the 1906 *Belshazzar's Feast*, and with Sibelius' 1925 *The Tempest*, as his finest efforts. When this music is encountered today, it is generally heard via the suite, which is a most skillful distillation of the best moments in the original score. *—Robert Cummings*

Recommended:

- ○ **Sibelius: Karelia Suite; King Christian II, Pelléas et Mélisande** / Vänskä (cond.), Lahti SO / 1998 / Bis 918
- ○ **Smetana: The Moldau; Liszt: Les Préludes; Sibelius: Finlandia; Pelléas et Mélisande** / Karajan (cond.), Berlin PO / DG 445550

Pohjola's Daughter (Pohjolan tytär), symphonic fantasy, Op. 49 (1906)

Although Breitkopf & Härtel published the bulk of Sibelius' output until World War I, Robert Lienau in Berlin issued the orchestral music composed between 1903 and 1909. This notably fertile period included two tone poems: *Pohjola's Daughter* and *Night Ride & Sunrise*. From the very start, *Pohjola's Daughter* proved the more popular. Although Sibelius wanted to call it "Väinämöinen" (the protagonist's name) and later "The Adventure of a Hero," Lienau insisted on *Pohjola's Daughter*. And so it appeared in 1906, with a seven-stanza preface from Runo 8 of *The Kalevala*, Finland's national folk epic.

"Väinämöinen, old and truthful/Rides his sleigh and travels homeward/From the dark realm of Pohjola/From the land of gloomy chanting/"Hark! What sound?" He glances upward/Up above there on a rainbow/Sits and spins Pohjola's Daughter/In the airy blue so radiant/Thrilled and drunken with her beauty/Come down here to me, O fair one/Thus he pleads. Coy, she refuses/At his new plea, her demand is/You must conjure from my spindle/What I've long desired: a vessel. Show to me your wondrous powers/Then most gladly I will follow/Väinämöinen, old and truthful/Toils and shapes and seeks... but vainly/Ah, the proper incantation/Never will it be discovered!/Full of anger, sorely wounded/Since the fair one has renounced him/To his sleigh he springs... and onward!/But once more his head he raises/Never can the hero falter/All his grief is put behind him/Gentle tones from his remembrance/Bring him hope and lighten sorrow."

In *The Kalevala*, however, the maiden is far more demanding: she wants a horsehair evenly split by a knife without a point. Being a magician (born old, like Merlin later on), Väinämöinen does so easily. Next, as asked, he ties an egg into an invisible knot, peels birch bark from a rock, and breaks a fence rail cleanly from an iceberg. Finally, during the boat's building, a "demon" deflects the old man's ax, causing it to gash his knee. Bleeding profusely, unable to remember a healing incantation, Väinämöinen quits Pohjola to seek help.

Pohjola's Daughter is the most depictive tone poem of Sibelius' career, albeit in sonata form. The development section deals with the aged magician's frustrated efforts to build a boat from the splinters of a spindle, but doesn't include the wound. The music is thematically integrated to an extraordinary degree, evolving from a slow recitative for solo cello and a subsequent wind motif derived from that, until, as it began 12 minutes earlier, *Pohjola's Daughter* quietly ends on a unison B flat in the low strings. It bears noting that Sibelius specified two piston cornets and two trumpets, one of his rare requests for the mellower sound of cornets and one widely ignored by conductors. *—Roger Dettmer*

Recommended:

- ○ **Sibelius: Symphony 2; Luonnotar; Pohjola's Daughter** / Bernstein (cond.), New York PO / 2000 / Sony 61848
- ○ **Sibelius: Finlandia; Karelia Suite; Valse Triste; Pohjola's Daughter** / Barbirolli (cond.), Halle Orch. / 1988 / EMI 769205
- ○ **Sibelius: Symphony 2, etc.** / Ormandy (cond.), Philadelphia Orch. / 1990 / RCA 60489

Rakastava (The Beloved), suite for string orchestra, triangle & timpani, Op. 14 (1911)

Rakastava—accent on the first syllable, in English The Beloved—underwent three transformations before Sibelius arrived at the form best known ever since, when it's heard, that is. This is a neglected work of uncommon tenderness and intimacy from Sibelius' inherent reserve. The three-movement form for strings, with tympani in the outer sections and discreet triangle beats at the end of the middle one, was created in 1911 during the same period as the *Symphony No. 4*, a work of unexampled desolation in his canon. However, the listing of *Rakastava* as Op. 14 goes back to the second version, published in 1895 for men's chorus with string accompaniment. (Sibelian opus numbers can be as treacherously unreliable as the conventional numbering of Mozart's or Mendelssohn's symphonies.) In 1893, contemporaneously with the *Karelia Overture* and *Karelia Suite*, Sibelius set a text from Elias Lönnrot's 1840 collection of folk verse, *Kanteletar*, for chorus. After the 1895 revision, he made a third one in 1898 for mixed-chorus a cappella. Thirteen years passed before the brief suite for strings and percussion eventuated, whose movements are entitled "The Beloved," "The Way (or Path) of the Lover," and "Good Night, My Beloved—Farewell." The opening section has a lyrical, D minor main theme that recalls a genre commonly down-played as Scandinavian elegiac—Grieg was a prime exponent—yet transcends the genre by eschewing harmonic cliché and conventional rhythmic scansion. Sibelius' structural integration makes a whole of the three sections, while idiomatic string writing belies *Rakastava*'s choral origin. That said, the prize is a swift, brief middle movement with pulsating triplets that ends almost as soon as it has begun. This leads to a finale of remarkable sweetness that harkens back to the opening section, albeit tinged with the sweet sorrow of parting at the end. If the troubled, stripped-down, life-and-death drama of the *Symphony No. 4* plumbed the depths of private despair, it proved to be cathartic, in witness whereof *Rakastava*—-a trysting suite that might be called the garden scene in a Finnish *Romeo and Juliet*. *—Roger Dettmer*

Recommended:

- ○ **Sibelius: Pohjola's Daughter; Tapiola; Impromptu for String Orchestra** / Jarvi (cond.), Gothenburg SO / 1985 / Bis 312
- ○ **Grieg & Sibelius: Romantic Music for Strings** / Leaper (cond.), Istropolitana Capella / 1989 / Naxos 550330

Romance, for strings in C major, Op. 42 (1904)

Sibelius wrote this miniature (five-minute) composition in 1903, between two versions of a work on a much grander scale: the popular violin concerto. Unlike the concerto, or most of the composer's popular large-scale works, the charm of the Romance comes from a simple setting of a characteristic melody, with effective and straightforward use of the string orchestra.

Sibelius was going through a turbulent period of financial difficulty while writing this work, an experience which was common during the first half of his life (the introduction of certain copyright laws later would go some way to alleviating this problem). He would look back on this period, however, as a time of happiness. He was still composing in the Romantic style of his early works, partly derived from Tchaikovsky and Grieg, and it was observed at the first performance of this piece that it owed something to Tchaikovsky. In the decade following the composition of *Romance*, the composer's works became more austere, a trend especially audible from the *Fourth Symphony* onwards. It has, oddly enough, been suggested that this austerity resulted from the composer's having being forced to give up cigars and alcohol, but deeper musical and spiritual forces were no doubt at work.

Opus 42 was originally entitled "Andante," and carried that name through the first five years of its existence. The impulse for the change to "Romance" came when a review of the piece suggested that a title such as "Nocturne" or "Romance" would have been more appropriate. Sibelius evidently took the idea to heart, changing the name to Romance when he attempted to get the work published in 1908.

Romance is formed of three main sections, a slow, Andante beginning, a more rapid middle section and finally another slow section. The middle section is set apart in tempo, but melodically this little crowd-pleaser is nicely knit together. *—Rachel Campbell*

Recommended:

- ○ **Sibelius: Works for String Orchestra** / Csaba (cond.), Virtuosi di Kuhmo / Ondine 830

Tapiola, tone poem, Op. 112 (1926)

Tapio was the mythic god of Finland's northland forests and Tapiola his realm. Sibelius chose the subject for his last surviving orchestral work, commissioned in January 1926 by conductor Walter Damrosch for the New York Symphony Society Orchestra (shortly thereafter merged with the Philharmonic with Toscanini as music director). It was composed between March and May 1926, mostly on Italian holiday, was sent to his publishers in August, and was introduced by Damrosch on December 28 of that same year in New York City's Mecca Temple. If first reviews were mixed, including one by Sibelius' foremost stateside champion Olin Downes, in *The New York Times*, *Tapiola* was ranked as a crown jewel in the composer's trove within three years. It is his "last surviving orchestral work" because Sibelius did complete the first movement of an *Symphony No. 8*, which he sent to his copyist and, furthermore, wrote in 1934 that the *Eighth* was a finished work. Yet there is no surviving complete score. *Tapiola*, like the *Symphony No. 4*, is an austere work, stark in its depiction of a landmass then and since sparsely inhabited, heavily forested, and sunless for half the year. Heroes of the Kalevala never ventured that far north, stopping at Pohjola to woo daughters of Mistress Louhi. Sibelius prefaced the published score with these four lines printed in English, German, and French: "Widespread they stand, the Northland's dusky forests, Ancient, mysterious, brooding savage dreams; Within them dwells the Forest's mighty God, And wood-sprites in the gloom weave magic secrets." The principal key is B minor, and although a 20-bar introduction is marked Largamente, tempos thereafter alternate between Allegro moderato and Allegro. The music only seems to move slowly, even glacially, at moments. The work also seems monothematic, yet while several subjects derive from the main theme, Sibelius' genius produced an abundance of subtleties. No longer constricted by conventional structure, his mastery of orchestral nuance fashioned an entity of cohesion and singular coherence. Certainly one can hear wood-sprites, creatures other than humankind, but they are nonetheless thematic components of Sibelius' symphonic tapestry . The god Tapio reigns over all and all powerfully, if not happily by conventional mythic standards. When aroused for whatever reason, by whatever means, he unleashes storms of terrifying ferocity, with two of them here. Roaring brass chords in the first one are almost a tease, whereas the second, after an ominous silence, unleashes a non-accelerating crescendo that becomes a maelstrom of chromatic strings for 56 harrowing measures. *Tapiola* ends withal on three sostenuto chords in unambiguous B major, the last one a lingering decrescendo. Between 1927 and 1930, Sibelius wrote *Music for a Masonic Ritual*, Op. 113, plus a dozen salon pieces published as Opp. 114–116. In 1939, he made further (and final) revisions in the first and third of his *Four Lemminkäinen Legends*, Op. 22. But *Tapiola* remains the omega of his career as an orchestral composer, coming three decades before he died at the great age of 91. *—Roger Dettmer*

Recommended:

- ○ **Sibelius: Finlandia; Karelia Suite; Tapiola; Valse Triste, etc.** / Rosbaud (cond.), Berlin PO / DG 447453
- ○ **Sibelius: The Complete Symphonies & Tone Poems** / Berglund (cond.), Bournemouth Sinfonietta / 2001 / EMI 74485
- ○ **Sibelius: The Complete Symphonies** / Vanska (cond.), Lahti SO / 1997 / Bis 1286/8

The Tempest, incidental music, Op. 109 (1925)

The idea of providing incidental music for Shakespeare's fairy-tale play *The Tempest* is thought to have been first suggested to Sibelius by an admirer of his, Baron Axel Carpelan, as early as 1901. Two decades later, as the result of a commision from the Danish Royal Theater, Sibelius produced an astonishing hour-long score comprising graceful miniatures, austere vocal settings, earthy folklike dances, and isolated passages of raucous modernism. The work—one of the last to come from Sibelius' pen—was premiered in Copenhagen on March 15, 1926.

The 34 short pieces of Sibelius' score make varied use of a large orchestra, soloists, and choir. Along with the *Fourth Symphony* (1911), *The Tempest* represents Sibelius at his most modernistic, while at the same time it covers a wide stylistic range. In the opening movement, "The Oak Tree," a flute melody based on fragments of whole-tone and semitone scales is set against a shimmering string background. With its boisterous woodwinds, xylophone, and sudden tonal twists, "Caliban's Song" recalls contemporaneous works by Prokofiev. The tense, powerful mood painting of "The Storm" has lent it a life as an independent concert work in its own right. There is no shortage of lighter moments in the score, as in the gentle "Chorus of the Winds" and the "Dance of the Nymphs," with its gracefully twirling, pastel-tinged woodwind and string colors.

Sibelius wrote only one more major work after *The Tempest*, the tone poem *Tapiola* (1926), and lived the remainder of his life—some 30 years—in retirement. Though it may be pure coincidence, Sibelius' long compositional silence mirrors *The Tempest*'s subject matter: Like Shakespeare's Prospero, the composer chose to abjure his art, to set aside his magic craft.

Soon after its composition Sibelius arranged two concert suites from the score, in which form the work is perhaps best known today. *—Brian Wise*

Recommended:

- ○ **Sibelius: The Tempest** / Saraste (cond.), Groop, Hynninen, Silvasti, Tiilikainen, Finnish Radio SO / Ondine 813
- ○ **Sibelius** / Vanska (cond.), Lahti SO / 1999 / Bis 1125

Valse Triste, Op. 44/1 (1904)

Despite almost a century of familiarity and unsatisfactory performances by unlikely instrumental combinations, it's easy to imagine the truly magical effect that Jean Sibelius' *Valse Triste* (1904) must have had on audiences of the day. The *Valse* was extracted and published separately from the composer's incidental music to his brother-in-law's play *Kuolema* (Death). Still, the work stands quite well on its own as an orchestral poem in miniature, and it seems today as fresh, charming, and thoroughly well-crafted as it did when it single-handedly spread its composer's fame through the tea houses of Europe and America. A brief paraphrase of the *Valse* can even be found at the end of the composer's *Symphony No. 7* (1924), perhaps in acknowledgement of the tremendous effect this composition had on Sibelius' career. Cast in a ternary dance form, *Valse Triste* opens with a simple utterance, but this apparently transparent statement masterfully introduces an overwhelming mood of vast, if perhaps bittersweet, melancholy. As the music unfolds, it exhibits a remarkable ambiguity of mood, reflecting both an old woman's joy at being reunited with her dead husband and the audience's knowledge that it is in fact Death himself that the mother is dancing with. Passions rise in the middle section, and as the opening material reasserts itself at the end of the dance, it is clear that the woman has died. The work draws to a somber end with three ominous chords. *—Blair Johnston*

Recommended:

- ○ **Sibelius: Orchestral Works** / Berglund (cond.), Bournemouth Sinfonietta / 1997 / EMI 69773
- ○ **Sibelius: Karelia; Kuolema** / Vanska (cond.), Lahti SO / 1997 / Bis 915

The Wood Nymph (Skogsrået), tone poem ("Ballade"), Op. 15 (1895)

Jean Sibelius wrote four works based on the poem "The Wood Nymph" by Finnish poet Viktor Rydberg: a song with piano accompaniment (1889); a tone poem for large orchestra (1894); a melodrama for speaker, strings, two horns, and piano (1894); and a piece for solo piano (1894). Aside from the text, the song is entirely independent of the other three works, which share a common tonality and common thematic material. All four works remained unpublished and unrecorded until 1996. The tone poem and the melodrama share the same opus number of 15. The tone poem or "Ballade for Orchestra" as it is subtitled, is one of Sibelius' longest single-movement tone poems, lasting nearly 22 minutes in performance. Like his other orchestral works of the early 1890s—the *Lemminkainen* and *Karelia Suites* and the first version of the tone poem *En Saga*—*The Wood Nymph* is a powerful work of tremendous energy and power. In four sections, the work starts with a portrait of Bjorn, the hero of the work, for full brass over a pulsing string background similar to that of Marcia of the *Karelia Suite*. In the second section, the heroic music continues as Bjorn sets off into the forest, but the accompaniment changes as he encounters the jealous goblins and nymphs portrayed in a chromatic dance in the winds. The third section of the work begins Moderato with an ardent theme in the cello depicting the Wood Nymph. Her dance before Bjorn is accompanied by winds, tambourine, and triangle. The fourth section of the work is dark and weighty, with an aching violin theme over the low brass and bass drum describing the broken hero whose heart has been lost to the wood nymph. Although it is not on the same level of inspiration as *En Saga*, *The Wood Nymph*'s complete disappearance from the repertoire is inexplicable. The disappearance of the melodrama, however, is more easily explained. While the work is as attractively scored and as well-composed as the tone poem, the whole genre of the melodrama—that is, a piece of music with narrator—has disappeared from the concert hall. Like the tone poem, the melodrama is in four sections. However, the melodrama is much more compact than the tone poem, lasting a little over ten minutes in performance and is much more succinct in the thematic development. The solo piano piece based on *The Wood Nymph* is very brief and deals only with the final section of the music of the tone poem and melodrama. It has no opus number. *—James Leonard*

Recommended:

- ○ **Sibelius: The Wood-Nymph** / Vanska (cond.), Poysti, Lahti SO / 1996 / BIS 815

SYMPHONIC

Symphony No. 1 in E minor, Op. 39 (1899; revised 1900)

When, at 33, Sibelius finally composed his *Symphony No. 1*, he already had a portfolio of orchestral music. His harmonic vocabulary, technical apparatus, orchestral style, and thematic character (rooted in the Finnish language) were firmly in place and organized. If, as Beckmessers have carped from the beginning, the first symphony here and there echoes Tchaikovsky, so do contemporaneous works by Glazunov and Rachmaninov; Pyotr Il'yich's *Pathétique Symphony* was not yet six years old when Sibelius introduced his new *First* with the Helsinki Philharmonic on April 27, 1899.

Melodic substance and sonorities are voluptuous in the *First* without bursting the corset-stays of decorum or modesty. As Finnish patriotism hardened into resistance, Sibelius became emblematic both at home and abroad. His music attracted an ever-growing and appreciative following in Great Britain and the United States (but none at all in France, Italy, or Vienna). Politics aside, Russian conductors and concertgoers liked it nearly as much—especially the *First* and *Second* symphonies. While *No. 2* is technically surer and structurally tighter, *No. 1* is the more memorable melodically, and the more volatile emotionally.

The whole first movement is unified by a theme heard at the outset, played by a single clarinet over a soft timpani roll, then without accompaniment. In one way or another, the abundance of themes in a tightly argued movement derives from this opening, most ingeniously so in an episode for staccato flutes playing in thirds over strings and harp, extensively developed later on but not reprised before two E minor chords at the end.

Both the slow movement and the scherzo are free adaptations of three-part form (ABA). Instead of new material, the B section of the Andante develops the main theme of A and then reprises only that theme. Here more than anywhere else, the *Pathétique* of Pyotr Il'yich casts an occasional lugubrious shadow on isolated string and bassoon passages.

The pounding, headlong scherzo, with an A section in C, D flat, and G major, restores the timpani to prominence. The middle part, however, is slow (Lento) and sostenuto, in E major, until a transition back to the C major song section, where the previous D flat material is reprised in G flat before an accelerating coda.

The finale begins in E minor with the same theme that opened the symphony, here played throbbingly by violins, violas, and cellos before its fragmentary development by pairs or groups of winds. This is only the introduction, however, to a sonata-form Finale. Its main-theme group of fast-moving, folk-flavored segments—fragments, almost—sets up a lyrical second theme played by unison violins on the G string. Thereafter, the main-theme group is developed extensively, verging on melodrama, following which the bardic G string theme returns. It, too, is developed to a passionate climax before the ending echoes the first movement: two E minor chords—now soft, however, rather than loud, and pizzicato rather than sostenuto. *—Roger Dettmer*

Recommended:

- ○ **Sibelius: Symphony 1; Karelia Overture & Suite; Finlandia** / Saraste (cond.), Finnish Radio SO / 1988 / RCA 7765
- ○ **Sibelius: Symphonies 1, 2 & 4; Finlandia; Karelia Suite** / Ashkenazy (cond.), London Philharmonia Orch. / 1997 / London 455402
- ○ **Sibelius: The Complete Symphonies & Tone Poems** / Berglund (cond.), Helsinki PO / 2001 / EMI 74485
- ○ **Sibelius: The Complete Symphonies** / Vanska (cond.), Lahti SO / 1997 / Bis 1286/8
- ○ **Sibelius: Symphonies 1–7** / Barbirolli (cond.), Halle Orch. / 2000 / EMI 67299

Symphony No. 2 in D major, Op. 43 (1901–1902)

The genesis of the *Second Symphony* can be traced to Sibelius' trip to Italy in early 1901. The trip came about at the suggestion of his friend, the amateur musician Axel Carpelan, and it was there that he began contemplating several ambitious projects, including a four-movement tone poem based on the Don Juan story and a setting of Dante's *Divina Commedia.* While none of these plans ever came to fruition, some of the ideas sketched during this trip did find their way into the second movement of this symphony. Carpelan was also instrumental in raising money to allow Sibelius to relinquish his work at the Helsinki Conservatoire and devote himself to the composition of the *Second Symphony.* Despite his friend's help, Sibelius' return to Finland for the summer and autumn was not accompanied by any great burst of inspiration, and extensive revisions delayed the first performance, first to January 1902 and then to March 1903. But from then on, the symphony enjoyed unparalleled success in Finland and eventually led to the major breakthrough in Germany that was so craved by Scandinavian composers of this era (one which Nielsen, for instance, never achieved). The *Second Symphony* has retained an extraordinary popularity for its individualistic tonal language, dark wind coloring, muted string writing, simple folklike themes, and distinctly "national" flavor that are all Sibelian to the core.

While the opening mood is pastoral, it leads to an air of instability, in which small, short gestures seem to arise at random and then trail off. Yet there is a subtle coherence to the work that counters its seemingly shapeless quality. All of the material of the first movement emerges from either the two repeated-note subjects heard in the strings and winds at the opening, or from a brooding idea first presented in the winds and brass.

Unlike the first movement, in which the gentleness of the introduction is recaptured at the conclusion, the second movement is full of turbulence and ends without consolation. Two competing subjects seem to engage in a battle: First, a dirge-like bassoon melody in D minor, marked "lugubrious," builds to a towering culmination in winds and brass; then an ethereal, ruminative theme is played by divided strings in the key of F sharp major. The energetic scherzo, with its machine-gun figures in the strings, is built from a fragment of greatest simplicity: a repeated B flat followed by a turn around that note.

Following the precedent of Beethoven's Fifth Symphony, the Scherzo is linked directly to the finale through a grand rhetorical bridge passage. The symphony at last achieves a flowing D major melodic line that heroically shakes off the D minor preparation, in the best sense of the Romantic tradition. Also like Beethoven, Sibelius brings back the transitional material a second time so that the victory of the major key can be savored anew, after which he concludes the work with a hymn-like peroration. That said, the Second Symphony marks the end of Sibelius' early Romantic period that paid homage to his predecessors. In subsequent works, his interest rested more in pursing new formal methods based on fragmentation and recombination. *—Brian Wise*

Recommended:

- ○ **Sibelius: Symphonies 2 & 5** / Karajan (cond.), Philharmonia Orch. / 1998 / EMI 66599
- ○ **Sibelius: Symphonies 1–3** / Berglund (cond.), CO of Europe / Finlandia 23388
- ○ **Sibelius: The Complete Symphonies** / Vanska (cond.), Lahti SO / 1997 / Bis 1286/8
- ○ **Sibelius: Symphonies 1–7** / Barbirolli (cond.), Halle Orch. / 2000 / EMI 67299

Symphony No. 3 in C major, Op. 52 (1904–1907)

Jean Sibelius' reputation rests more squarely on the shoulders of his orchestral music than does that of almost any other major composer. He is certainly one of the most important symphonic composers to emerge in the post-Beethoven era, and yet one can make no sweeping statement in which all of his seven essays in the form are summed up concisely. While his highly individual techniques of motivic development and interconnection are present, to some degree, in the pair of popular and unabashedly lush symphonies with which he began his explorations of symphonic form, it is arguably with the *Symphony No. 3* in C major, Op.52, that Sibelius' powers first display themselves in full regalia.

The *Third Symphony* is occasionally referred to as the "English" Symphony, because of Sibelius' extended trip to Britain in late 1905 which seems to have affected to some degree the outlines of the still-gestating work. Completed by 1907, it is a work whose lean textures, orchestration, and dimensions continue to be disconcerting to listeners whose familiarity with the composer comes from the thicker, more epic *Second Symphony.*

The Symphony commences with a vigorously rhythmic statement by the lower strings. The primary "theme" is really an assortment of related (but at this point still disconnected) motivic fragments: the opening idea in the cellos and basses, a following sprightly woodwind tune, a dotted figure in the violins, and a noble idea in triplets first asserted by the horns and woodwinds as the opening passage reaches its climax. Sibelius makes a sudden dramatic shift to B minor to begin his secondary theme material. However, this fine cello melody soon disintegrates into running sixteenth notes that derive from the sprightly woodwind tune mentioned above. Sibelius cunningly overlaps the development and recapitulation. Now, after a slightly extended presentation of the opening motivic group, the second theme is played out in E minor against a harsh, fortissimo woodwind background. Once again the running sixteenths ensue, but before they have a chance to take over completely Sibelius makes another unusual transition, this time to a noble coda.

Even more interesting is the second movement, marked Andantino con moto, quasi allegretto and set in the key of G sharp minor. The gentle, fragmented dance tune first presented, quite shyly (pianissimo dolce), by the flutes, is perfect in its blend of gracefulness and melancholy. As this theme plays out Sibelius makes effective use of a brief connecting figure in the clarinets and of an attractive cross-rhythm. The elaborated repetition of all this material winds down to a mournful G sharp minor close to prepare the way for a schizophrenic central section.

Formally speaking, the Finale is entirely unprecedented: it cannot be described as any of the standard forms, and, indeed, it seems in many ways to defy even the very principles on which those forms were originally based. This energetic movement takes some time to get moving, first running through some scherzando string passages and a brief reprise of the second movement tune before finally arriving at the steady Allegro eighth notes that will carry the rest of the movement. After a thrilling climax in A flat major, a new and robust theme emerges in the lower strings. Soon this idea comes to dominate the proceedings, and little thought is given either to any other material or, indeed, save for two brief digressions to E minor, to any triad other than C major. The motoric drive persists to the very end. *—Blair Johnston*

Recommended:

- ○ **Sibelius: Symphonies 3 & 5** / Davis (cond.), London SO / 1994 / RCA 61963
- ○ **Sibelius: Symphonies 1–7** / Barbirolli (cond.), Halle Orch. / 2000 / EMI 67299
- ○ **Sibelius: The Complete Symphonies & Tone Poems** / Berglund (cond.), Helsinki PO / 2001 / EMI 74485
- ○ **Sibelius: The Complete Symphonies** / Vanska (cond.), Lahti SO / 1997 / Bis 1286/8

Symphony No. 4 in A minor, Op. 63 (1910–1911)

The *Fourth Symphony* has provoked much curiosity and discussion. It is certainly one of Sibelius' most enigmatic works, and the general consensus of his fans is that it is one of his best. But its austerity stands in marked contrast with the tuneful and relaxed *Symphony No. 3* (1904–07) and the heroic and extroverted *Symphony No. 5* (1914–19). Why the dramatic change in style?

The period of the *Fourth Symphony* was a difficult, traumatic time for Sibelius. His country was suffering under increasing repression from Russia. In addition, in 1907, Sibelius was diagnosed with throat cancer, for which he underwent painful surgery. Though the surgery was successful, he was forced to give up his beloved cigars and alcohol. And, as his diary of the time reflects, he came face to face with his mortality in dramatic fashion. He makes frequent note of his diminished concentration and capacity for work.

Some have sought to find in the symphony some sort of extramusical program. One of the composer's friends, music critic K.F. Wasenius, even insisted that Sibelius had told him that the Fourth was inspired by a trip to the Karelian mountain Kolivaara, and that the four movements symbolized Sibelius' impression of the mountain: the ascent, view from the top, and descent. Sibelius vehemently denied any such intent.

Around 1907, Sibelius also seems to have made a conscious decision to experiment in his work, partly motivated by his dislike of the gigantism and philosophical pretension of works like Richard Strauss' tone poems and the symphonies of Gustav Mahler. Many of Sibelius' works of this time, such as the string quartet *Voces Intimae*, Op. 56, share the Fourth Symphony's remoteness and dissonance.

The symphony was begun in early 1910, completed in April 1911, and first performed in Helsinki with Sibelius conducting, on April 3, 1911. The applause was polite only, the overall reaction one of puzzlement. Sibelius' wife Aino later recalled: "People avoided our eyes, shook their heads; their smiles were embarrassed, furtive, or ironic. Not many people came backstage to the artists' room to pay their respects." A similar response greeted the work in subsequent performances elsewhere in Europe and America.

The work is certainly slow to give up its meaning. The textures are consistently spare. Only occasionally is the entire orchestra used; much of the time we hear but a few instruments at a time. Likewise, the melodic ideas are very short, at times almost aphoristic. The first movement, for instance, seems to evolve from its querulous first four notes, a motif which recurs throughout the symphony. The music seems to drift, vague, unanchored, fragmentary, the quiet interrupted only briefly by orchestral climaxes. The movement ends abruptly and unresolved.

The second movement emerges quickly from the first. The pastoral dance of the solo oboe evokes the world of Sibelius' earlier symphonies, the movement as a whole serving as something of a light-hearted diversion. The mood darkens again in the slow third movement which, while meditative and occasionally songlike, is also haunted, with textures of an almost Webern-like spareness.

The fourth movement has many ideas and abrupt changes of mood. It opens almost cheerfully, with occasional contributions from the "Glocken" (so-named in Sibelius' score, there is still controversy over whether the composer had in mind the bright-sounding glockenspiel or the richer sound of tubular bells). A feeling of lethargy settles in, however, and the ending of the symphony is at best noncommittal, even brusque. It is a strange and haunting end to one of Sibelius' greatest compositions. *—Chris Morrison*

Recommended:

- ○ **Sibelius: Symphony 4** / Ashkenazy (cond.), London Philharmonia Orch. / 1982 / London 400056
- ○ **Sibelius: Symphonies 4 & 9; Tapiola** / Maazel (cond.), Vienna PO / 2000 / Decca 466995
- ○ **Sibelius: Symphonies 1 & 4** / Davis (cond.), London SO / 1996 / BMG 68183
- ○ **Sibelius: The Complete Symphonies & Tone Poems** / Berglund (cond.), Helsinki PO / 2001 / EMI 74485
- ○ **Sibelius: The Complete Symphonies** / Vanska (cond.), Lahti SO / 1997 / Bis 1286/8
- ○ **Sibelius: Symphonies 1–7** / Barbirolli (cond.), Halle Orch. / 2000 / EMI 67299

Symphony No. 5 in E flat major, Op. 82 (1919)

Sibelius composed three versions of this work between 1915 and 1919, and led the premiere of the last one on October 21, 1921, in Helsinki. It is abstemiously scored: double winds, brass without tuba, timpani, strings. In time for his 50th birthday, which was celebrated as a national holiday in Finland, Sibelius completed and conducted a first version of his *Fifth Symphony*, in four movements—startlingly longer than the final version and comparatively inchoate. (Persons curious to compare them may consult a recording of 5/i on the BIS label.) Only string bass parts have survived a revision begun immediately after the premiere. Still not satisfied, Sibelius rethought and reworked it over two years. What eventuated (5/iii) has become the most popular of his seven symphonies: a triumph of structural ingenuity, and a validation of non-programmatic music when Lisztians of every stripe—most notably Richard Strauss and Gustav Mahler—were deconstructing "absolute" art.

What finally evolved in the first movement is a structure that begins with the double exposition of two theme-groups, the second of them in G (where the strings enter). Sibelius didn't just restate his basic materials; his range of mood extended to a passage marked lugubre for bassoons. Through a variety of keys he reaches a long development section, which builds toward recapitulation whereupon 12/8 time, after a slow acceleration, suddenly switches to 3/4, E flat changes to B major, and Allegro moderato becomes the new basic tempo. What follows was salvaged from a separate Scherzo movement in the 1915 version—complete with Trio—but one that segues into the tonic recap of theme-groups one and two, followed by a coda that quickens to Presto.

The Andante mosso, quasi allegretto is as simple, structurally, as the first movement is complex, but hardly simplistic: in effect, there are several variations on a rhythm—two groups of five quarter notes separated by a quarter note rest. This "theme" is played first by violas and cellos after a motif for clarinets, bassoons, and horns that returns as a countermelody. Sibelius creates "six tunes" (Michael Steinberg's diction), more or less tranquil on the surface but underneath mysterious, even briefly turbulent, with a translucent passage (violins divided into eight parts) that bespeaks pure genius. Also beneath the surface is a first statement (by low strings) of the proclamative theme that will dominate the finale.

Strings play the first theme in what some Sibelians have called a rondo, but others insist is sonata-structure, a whirring, buzzing business that culminates in the heroic second theme for pairs of horns, playing whole notes, in thirds. Momentum is sustained while the two subjects pursue a complex course through various keys and mass dissonances that only the horn theme, reassigned to trumpets, can finally cut through, like a machete through jungle growth. Trombones and horns join in, until Sibelius decrees silence, followed by six chords that bring his odyssey into a safe and happy harbor. *—Roger Dettmer*

Recommended:

- ○ **Sibelius: Symphonies 3 & 5** / Davis (cond.), London SO / 1994 / RCA 61963
- ○ **Sibelius: Complete Symphonies** / Karajan (cond.), Berlin PO / 2003 / DG 000048302
- ○ **Sibelius: The Complete Symphonies** / Vanska (cond.), Lahti SO / 1997 / Bis 1286/8
- ○ **Sibelius: The Complete Symphonies & Tone Poems** / Berglund (cond.), Helsinki PO / 2001 / EMI 74485
- ○ **Sibelius: Symphonies 1–7** / Barbirolli (cond.), Halle Orch. / 2000 / EMI 67299

Symphony No. 6 in D minor, Op. 104 (1923)

Sibelius completed this work in February 1923, and conducted the premiere at Helsinki on February 19 of that same year. His first reference to the work, in 1918, described it as "wild and passionate in character. Dark with pastoral contrasts. Probably in 4 movements... intensifying in a dark orchestral swell [until] the main theme is drowned." At the same time he cautioned that his plan could change—and how it did!—"depending on the way my musical thinking develops. I am always a slave to my themes and obey their demands." Some of that "wild character" found a home in the last version of *Symphony No. 5* (1919). The *Sixth*, however, evolved as a virtual homage to Palestrina, the same Renaissance master honored in Hans Pfitzner's then young opera, *Palestrina*.

In common with the *Seventh Symphony*, his incidental music for Shakespeare's *The Tempest*, and the tone poem *Tapiola* (Sibelius' last orchestral works before he quit composing altogether in 1929), the *Symphony No. 6* is nature-painting uncluttered by "civilized" detritus. Even the fauna indigenous to subarctic Finland are absent, leaving only some birdlike motifs. It is the purest, most inward, in many ways most fascinating of his symphonies. For some of us it is also the most hypnotic, to be heard countless times without ever revealing all of its secrets.

The first movement, Allegro molto moderato, nominally in D minor, more accurately can be said to inhabit the medieval D Dorian mode (that is to say, from D to D on the white keys of the piano, whereas "natural" D minor has a flatted B, and "harmonic" D minor has a sharped C). This lends the music an archaic character that nevertheless becomes passionate as it evolves, praising the presence of God and ghosts in a cathedral of sound. Sibelius shifts into C major, however, and mostly stays there until a radiantly calm coda in D Dorian, as if there had never been C major! Nicolas Slonimsky wrote of "thematic molecules" (Cecil Gray called them "cells"), played in thirds by pairs of instruments. While these may seem random on first hearing, their development integrates everything as if by alchemy.

The second movement, Allegretto moderato serves, as in Beethoven's *Eighth*, in place of a slow movement, although Sibelius at one time thought of retitling it Andantino (lest conductors play it too briskly, as Georg Schnéevoigt did in the first recording in 1934). After a soft bid for attention on a drum tuned to F, flutes and bassoons play free-floating chords that resolve in G Dorian. Subtly, a 3/4 rhythmic pattern takes over as notes-per-measure increase from three to six to nine to 12. Scalar passages ascend only to fall partway back, while a saucy motif repeats itself until the ear is haunted for days after. The Poco vivace third movement is a brief scherzo in jig time (thus spoke Slonimsky). But it has no trio, no B section; thematic molecules from earlier movements are adapted, reorganized, and become boisterous right up to the end.

In the Allegro molto finale, Sibelius completes the C major first half of the opening motif in D Dorian. This is the symphony's densest movement texturally, the closest it comes to the 1918 promise of passion (but it is never wild). Indeed,

Sibelius here echoes the nature poems he wrote from the *Fourth Symphony* on—as well as *Tapiola* to come. In structure this comes closest to a conventional sonata-rondo, yet it is never traditional or predictable. The word concludes with quiet, undecorated D Dorian chords. *—Roger Dettmer*

Recommended:

- ○ **Sibelius: Symphonies 2 & 6** / Davis (cond.), London SO / 1995 / RCA 68218
- ○ **Sibelius: Symphonies 4–7** / Karajan (cond.), Berlin PO / DG 457748
- ○ **Sibelius: The Complete Symphonies & Tone Poems** / Berglund (cond.), Helsinki PO / 2001 / EMI 74485
- ○ **Sibelius: Symphonies 1–7** / Barbirolli (cond.), Halle Orch. / 2000 / EMI 67299
- ○ **Sibelius: The Complete Symphonies** / Vanska (cond.), Lahti SO / 1997 / Bis 1286/8

Symphony No. 7 in C major, Op. 105 (1924)

Sibelius originally intended his *Seventh Symphony* to be in three movements, but in the end fashioned it into a single movement. It is cast in four distinct sections, however: a substantial opening Adagio is followed by a scherzo-like section, and then another, larger scherzo (which may have been spawned by the "Hellenic Rondo" idea that Sibelius had originally spoken of in regard to this work), and finally a recall of materials from the Adagio section. Initially entitled "Fantasia sinfonica," the work was subsequently restored to its status of symphony by the composer and would serve as his last foray in this genre.

The *Seventh Symphony* came as the climax of a lifetime's work for Sibelius. His ongoing search for new formal procedures that began with his *Second Symphony* reaches its acme in this sweeping, motivically concentrated and highly integrated work, containing elements of both sonata form and of rondo form. While many scholars have attempted to come up with different ways to classify the Seventh, it is a futile mental exercise to fit the work into traditional formal schemes, so complete is Sibelius' mastery of transition and control of simultaneous tempos.

The Adagio begins darkly, the strings rising from their bass range but soon reaching brighter terrain as motivic bits are assembled and the main thematic material begins to unfold. Soon a somewhat somber passage begins in the lower strings, building slowly and taking on an increasingly passionate manner, culminating in a powerfully epiphanic declaration, where strings soar and then trombones gloriously resound the symphony's main theme. The Adagio section ends in a relatively subdued and bright mood.

The scherzo-like section begins almost seamlessly, evolving subtly out of the Adagio's closing material. The tempo gradually quickens and the music works up a dark intensity, but the resulting mood is generally playful and light in the first half, but menacing in the latter portion, where churning strings incite the orchestra to a torrent that culminates in a recall of the Adagio's trombone theme, now given a more somber treatment. The ensuing section is playful and lighter, but also develops some tension in its middle portion. The scoring here is fairly light and the tempo markings, Allegro molto moderato/Poco a poco meno moderato, come across as leisurely, but not brisk or driven.

Early on, the final section features another statement of the trombone theme, which is now confident and overpowering in its sense of triumph. The music thereafter moves from an angelic, almost rapturous passage for mostly unaccompanied strings toward near-stasis, before finally building from quivering strings to a resounding, all-conquering conclusion. This symphony typically has a duration of between 20 and 25 minutes. *—Robert Cummings*

Recommended:

- ○ **Sibelius: Symphony 7; Lemminkainen Suite** / Saraste (cond.), Finnish Radio SO / RCA 60575
- ○ **Sibelius: Symphony 7; Rakastava; En Saga; Kullervo** / Davis (cond.), London Symphony Chorus, London SO / 1997 / RCA 68312
- ○ **Sibelius: Symphonies 2 & 7** / Ormandy (cond.), Philadelphia Orch. / 1994 / Sony 53509
- ○ **Sibelius: The Complete Symphonies & Tone Poems** / Berglund (cond.), Helsinki PO / 2001 / EMI 74485
- ○ **Sibelius: The Complete Symphonies** / Vanska (cond.), Lahti SO / 1997 / Bis 1286/8
- ○ **Sibelius: Symphonies 1–7** / Barbirolli (cond.), Halle Orch. / 2000 / EMI 67299

CONCERTO

Six Humoresques, for violin & orchestra, Opp. 87 & 89 (1917–1918)

Jean Sibelius was a violinist by training, and it is not at all surprising that as his creative career unfolded he saw fit to produce several works that feature his own instrument in a central role. Besides the famous *Violin Concerto* there are two Serenades, a Romance (actually an orchestration of the *Romance*, Op. 78, No. 2 for violin and piano), the *Two Pieces*, Op. 77, and, most important, *Six Humoresques*.

The Humoresques, which for publication were divided into two groups, Opus 87 and Opus 89, were all composed during 1917 following the completion of the second version of the *Fifth Symphony*. World War One was difficult for Sibelius and his household, and during the two or three years on either side of 1920 the composer found it necessary to supplement his income by producing reams of commercially viable music. Much of this output, e.g. the *Marches* of Opus 91 or the *Suite champêtre*, Op. 98b, is undeniably disappointing. The Humoresques, however, are some of his best material. However sadly neglected they may have been during the last century, they should certainly be considered musical achievements on a level equal to or even surpassing the famous Concerto. By way of subtlety and charm they are virtually unrivalled in Sibelius' output.

The Opus 87 pair of Humoresques call for a chamber orchestra of strings, woodwinds, two horns, and timpani. Both require extraordinary agility on the part of its performer, but of a kind entirely different than the mid-nineteenth century gypsy outbursts that mark the *Violin Concerto*. Sibelius' ever-increasing interest in achieving a varied and colorful harmonic flavor is evident here: the consistent use of B natural within the D minor context of the First Humoresque (Commodo) seems to look forward to a similar reliance on the Dorian scale throughout the *Sixth Symphony*. Considerable agility is required to execute the pyrotechnical scale-work of the D major Humoresque within the graceful confines of the piece's cross-rhythms and hemiolas.

For Opus 89 Sibelius reduced the orchestral accompaniment considerably. The first and second Humoresques of this set call for strings alone, while the remaining pair admit only a handful of woodwinds into the arena. The first piece of the group, the Humoresque No. 3, is one of the high-points of the entire collection, and is one of Sibelius' most immediately compelling creations. An ensemble of hauntingly muted strings paves the way, Alla gavotte, for the strangely melancholy virtuoso fieldwork of the gypsy soloist. This is not a traditional dance, however, as even the lower strings eventually resign themselves to the purely textural world and sonic effect of harmonics as the violinist moves further and further away (psychologically, at least) from the ensemble.

Humoresque No. 4 (Op. 89, No. 2, that is) is perhaps the most traditional of all, recalling something of the delicate flavor of mid-nineteenth century musical miniatures. The andantino tune, however, is attractive enough within the slithering G minor context, and the soloist, for once, is afforded the opportunity to indulge in a more traditionally exhibitionistic display.

Sibelius marks the Fifth Humoresque (Op. 89, No. 3) "Commodo," a marking also used for the First. The opening bars of the Fifth Humoresque seem at first to be a continuation of the G minor tonality that dominated the previous two pieces, but the music soon slips down into a warmer E flat major. The final Humoresque (Op. 89, No. 4) resumes G minor with great melancholy. The astute violinist will find that the seemingly clear-cut contours of this delicately-framed piece are a formidable musical challenge indeed. *—Blair Johnston*

Recommended:

- ○ **Sibelius: The Complete Works for Violin** / Tetzlaff, Dausgaard (cond.), Danish National SO / 2002 / Virgin 45534
- ○ **Sibelius: Humoresques; Ghedini: Violin Concerto; Musica da Concerto** / Tenenbaum, Kapp (cond.), Czech Philharmonic CO / 2002 / ESS.A.Y. 1075

Violin Concerto in D minor, Op. 47 (1903–1904; revised 1905)

The *Violin Concerto* is not the only work Finland's Sibelius wrote for solo violin with orchestra; he wrote a variety of excellent, shorter works including *Two Serenades* (1913) and *Six Humoresques* (1917). But the Concerto is certainly the most ambitious of all these works. Despite the early enthusiasm of a few violinists—notably Maude Powell, who was the soloist in the American premiere with the New York Philharmonic in 1906 and repeated the work several times on a transcontinental tour—the Concerto was slow to catch on with audiences. Not until Jascha Heifetz took up the work and recorded it in the 1930s did the Concerto become what it is today, one of the most popular of the national Romantic concerto repertory.

Sibelius was himself a fine violinist. He took up studying the instrument at 15 with his hometown's military bandmaster, and shortly thereafter was taking part in chamber music performances and playing in his school's orchestra. He felt he had taken up the violin too late in life to become a true virtuoso, but he brought his intimate knowledge of the instrument to bear on this, his only Concerto, which he completed in 1903. The soloist at the first performance was to be the composer's friend Willy Burmeister. But when scheduling difficulties intervened, Viktor Novacek was given the honor of premiering the work in Helsinki on February 8, 1904, with Sibelius himself conducting. After this indifferently received performance, Sibelius withdrew the work for revision. Ultimately, the work was shortened, including the excision of one solo cadenza, and featured a brighter orchestral sound. The first performance of the revised score took place on October 19, 1905 in Berlin, with Richard Strauss conducting and Karl Halir, a member of Joseph Joachim's quartet, as soloist.

Sibelius had a less than high regard for virtuoso violinists or for many of the works written for them. In his Concerto, he manages to strike an ideal balance between instrumental brilliance and the more purely musical, structural, and emotional values. At one point he gave a pupil some advice about writing concertos, saying that one should be aware of the audience's patience (and the stupidity of many soloists!) and avoid long, purely orchestral passages. He certainly took his own advice, as the violinist takes up the expressive main theme of the first movement in the fourth bar, and rarely relinquishes center stage for the remainder of the Concerto's half-hour duration.

The opening movement, cast in first-movement sonata form, contrasts passages of restraint and melancholy with passages of great force and intensity. One unusual feature is the mid-movement cadenza for the soloist, which shares some qualities with like passages in the great virtuoso concertos of the nineteenth century, but is more substantial and more fully integrated into the overall form of the piece. Wind duets start the slow second movement, after which the soloist takes up the lush, almost Tchaikovskian main melody. Later in the movement the violinist is called on to play a fiendish two-part counterpoint. This is but one of the numerous technical hurdles the soloist must conquer in this work; many more arise in the brilliant, dance-like third movement, with its insistent rhythm and the folklike cast of its melodies. The excitement and momentum carry through to the very end of the work. *—Chris Morrison*

Recommended:

- **Sibelius: Violin Concerto; Serenades; Humoresque** / Mutter, Previn (cond.), Dresden Staatskapelle / DG 447895
- **Sibelius: Violin Concerto; Chausson: Poème** / Salerno-Sonnenberg, Tilson Thomas (cond.), London SO / 1993 / EMI 54855
- **Jascha Heifetz: The Supreme** / Heifetz, Hendl (cond.), Chicago SO / 2000 / RCA 63470
- **David Oistrakh Edition** / Oistrakh, Rozhdestvensky (cond.), USSR Radio & TV SO / 1997 / Melodiya 40710

CHAMBER MUSIC

String Quartet in D minor ("Voces Intimae"), Op. 56 (1908–1909)

Sibelius' *String Quartet in D minor*, Op. 56 (1908–09)—his only mature string quartet, and indeed, the only substantial chamber work he produced after the turn of the century—dates from the period between the Third and Fourth Symphonies. Like the *Fourth Symphony*, the quartet is an introspective work; however, as the subtitle, "Intimate Voices," suggests, Sibelius creates a profoundly intimate, even mysterious, atmosphere of a sort that would be impossible to realize in a symphonic work.

The quartet's five movements are thematically interrelated, each movement beginning with a motivic alteration of material from its predecessors. Such connections, however, are primarily superficial, and each of the movements has a fundamentally distinct character. The opening Andante—Allegro molto moderato is brief and enigmatic. Changes in mood can be quite sudden, and the means of presentation are subtle enough that unwary listeners may miss a great deal. The motive of the falling fourth is of particular importance: it appears early in the exposition, assumes a crucial role in a short development section, appears at the climactic moment in the coda, and figures prominently upon its reappearance in the work's finale. The Vivace, barely two minutes in length, opens with a quiet 16th note transformation of a motivic idea from the second subject of the first movement. Several unexpected measures of silence precede a volatile climax in which the opening figure is reinstated as the dominant musical idea. The passionate Adagio di molto, with its broad lines and lyrical textures, is also the most economically written of the five movements. As the music slowly unfolds, one is reminded of the spacious designs of the composer's late symphonies. The almost schizophrenic Allegretto ma pesante alternates heavy plodding with a more lighthearted spirit. A subsidiary theme takes as its point of departure the sharp outburst which ended the second movement. The motion heats up towards the end of the movement, but this new force cannot be sustained, and the music resumes the pesante character of the opening. The Allegro finale opens with a frightening flourish of activity and proceeds to the main subject, stated by the viola over bounced-bow effects in the accompanying voices. A syncopated melody follows, and these two main ideas, along with the modification of the falling fourth idea from the first movement, alternate and interact, travelling through various moods and textures and building to a rollicking climax. *—Blair Johnston*

Recommended:

- **Sibelius & Schumann: String Quartets** / Voces Intimae SQ / 1974 / Bis 10
- **Sibelius: String Quartets** / Sibelius Academy Quartet / Finlandia 95851

Suite champêtre, for string orchestra (or piano), Op. 98b (1921; revised 1921)

During the years following World War I, Jean Sibelius was faced with the arduous task of rebuilding both his career and, more urgently, his finances. As a means of accomplishing both ends, he composed a great deal of music that is both more accessible and far more commercially viable than was his norm (or probably his desire)—mostly suites, dances, and character pieces for various ensembles. On occasion Sibelius could translate his abstract musical voice into the kind of music described above with great success, producing miniatures of both great quality and widespread appeal (such as the famous *Valse Triste*). However, throughout the troubled years between the *Fifth* and *Sixth* Symphonies (from about 1919 to 1923), the results were generally less inspired, as if the composer were overextended by spinning out such quantities of music. Such is indeed the case with the *Suite champêtre for strings*, Op.98b (the second of two small orchestral suites published together as Opus 98), which exhibits very little of Sibelius' distinctive voice—although one can hardly deny that the three short pieces contained in it have a certain innocent appeal.

"Pièce caractéristique" is an old-fashioned D minor work that seems to recall Sibelius' boyhood idol, Tchaikovsky. It would be difficult, without a title-page, to assert that Sibelius is indeed the author of this very uncharacteristic little piece, though some of his flavorful melodic touches do appear in vague outline. More immediately identifiable, and also perhaps more attractive, is the flowing and warmly melancholy "Mélodie élégiaque." "Danse," which, like both of the previous pieces is cast in D minor, recalls something of the fairytale atmosphere of some of the composer's incidental music, or perhaps the *Humoresques*, which were composed just a few years before the Suite. The elfin principal idea is the most thoroughly Sibelian contained within the entire Suite. *—Blair Johnston*

Recommended:

- **Sibelius: Pelleas & Melisande; Cassazione; Presto; Suite Champétre; Suite Mignonne** / Ollila (cond.), Tapiola Sinfonietta / 2000 / Ondine 952

KEYBOARD

Works for Piano (1887–1929)

Jean Sibelius (1865–1957) wrote almost 100 works for the piano. Most of them are negligible and all of them are neglected. Most were written for the salon rather than the concert hall, few sound like they were conceived or executed for the piano, and fewer still sound at all like they might have been composed by the great Finnish master of the orchestra. Sibelius' works for piano fall into three groups. His earliest piano works include the *Six Impromptus*, Op. 5 (1893); the *Six Finnish Folksongs* (1903); the *Ten Piano Pieces*, Op. 24 (1895–1903); *Three Kyllikki Lyric Pieces for piano*, Op. 41 (1904); the *Ten Pieces for piano*, Op. 58 *(1909)*; and the *Sonata*, Op. 12 (1893). For the most part, the textures are Schumann-esque, the melodies are sentimental, the harmonies are cloying, and the only the three-movement sonata has something of the strength and passion of the young Sibelius. His late piano works include the *Ten Bagatelles*, Op. 34 (1913–16); the *Two Rondinos*, Op. 68 (1913); the *Ten Lyrical Pieces*, Op. 40 (1915–16); the *Four Lyric Pieces*, Op. 74 (1914); and the *13 Piano Pieces*, Op. 76 (1911–19). These works were composed almost exclusively to make money while Sibelius' royalty checks were held up by World War I and they are light, slight works that sound nothing at all like Sibelius. Far and away Sibelius' best works for piano are the *Three Sonatinas*, Op. 67 (1912). Written while Sibelius was working on his nihilistic *Symphony No. 4*, the *Sonatinas* are deep, dark works of restrained power and overwhelming intensity, piano works that for once sound as if Sibelius meant it. *—James Leonard*

Recommended:

- **Sibelius: Works for Piano** / Gothoni / Ondine 847
- **Mustonen Plays Sibelius** / Mustonen / Ondine 1014
- **Sibelius: Piano Music Vol. 1** / Gimse / 1999 / Naxos 553899
- **Sibelius: Piano Works Vol. 1** / Tawaststjerna / 1979 / Bis 153
- **Sibelius: The Complete Piano Transcriptions** / Tawaststjerna / 1987 / Bis 366

Six Impromptus, Op. 5 (1893)

Sibelius had a substantial output for solo piano, but is not known for his keyboard music. His interest in that genre stemmed back to his early career, as these *Six Impromptus* from 1893 attest, written around the time of his first popular orchestral works *Kullervo* (1892) and the *Karelia Suite* (1893). The *Impromptu No 1. in G minor* is marked Moderato and is somber and funereal, but utterly haunting in its gloom. The ensuing piece, in the same key, is brighter and lively (Vivace, after a brief introduction), playful and catchy, and almost childlike. *No. 3*, in A minor (Moderato), is folklike in its festive and joyful marching fashion (alla marcia). The *Impromptu No. 4 in E minor* is relaxed in its nocturnal mood and vaguely calls the music of Grieg to mind. The ensuing B minor work (Vivace) features Lisztian glitter, as if snow flakes are cascading on a wintry landscape. Its lovely theme has a Nordic stateliness searing the music into the mind's ear after just one listening. This is probably the best piece in the set. The concluding *Impromptu* (Commodo), in E major, is at about seven minutes and the longest in the set by far. It, too, is also a compelling work in its pastoral and simple charms. *—Robert Cummings*

Recommended:

- **Sibelius: Piano Pieces** / Viitasalo / Finlandia 95874
- **Sibelius: Piano Works Vol. 1** / Tawaststjerna / 1979 / Bis 153

VOCAL

Songs (1888–1954)

By far the most unusual aspect of the 93 songs of Finnish composer Jean Sibelius (1865–1957) is that, despite the fact that Sibelius was an ardent Finnish patriot, nearly every song sets Swedish poems. Only five songs are in Finnish, nine in German, one in English, one in French, and the remaining 77 are in Swedish. There are two reasons for this. Like most middle class nineteenth century Finns, Sibelius was raised speaking Swedish and learned Finnish only later in life. Also, there simply was not much lyric poetry in Finnish: the great poetry of the language was epic and Sibelius gave the epic of Finland appropriately epic settings in his *Kullervo* symphony and his symphonic poem *Lunnotar.* All but two of Sibelius' songs were composed before 1918. The earliest set, the charming songs from Op. 13, comes from the last decade of the nineteenth century, while the best of them, the songs from Op. 35 through 36, come from the first decade of the twentieth century. All but the two songs of Op. 60 are accompanied by piano (the Op. 60 pair are accompanied by guitar). Although most commentators have criticized Sibelius' piano writing as heavy and unidiomatic, the fact is that they are effective enough for the purpose of accompanying Sibelius' vocal melodies. For listeners used to Sibelius' masterfully dramatic symphonic writing, the lyricism of his songs may come as something of a shock. Indeed, Sibelius' vocal melodies are supremely lyrical: intimate, emotional, long-breathed, and wonderfully cast from the human voice. While the predominant emotions expressed range from the melancholy to the mournful, Sibelius' sensitive word settings avoid maudlin monotony. At his best in songs like *Jubal* (Op. 35, No. 1), *Teodora* (Op. 35, No. 2), *Svarta rosor* (Black Roses) (Op. 36, No. 1), and *Säv, säv, susa* (Op. 36, No. 4)—Sibelius' most popular song—Sibelius' songs are deeply affecting. *—James Leonard*

Recommended:

- ○ **Anne Sofie von Otter Sings Sibelius** / von Otter, Groop, Forsberg / 1995 / BIS 300757
- ○ **Sibelius: Songs** / Mattila, Ranta / Ondine 856
- ○ **Sibelius: Orchestral Songs** / Panula (cond.), Hynninen, Haggander, Gothenburg SO / 1985 / Bis 270

Cesare Siepi

b. Feb. 10, 1923, Milan, Italy

Bass

Bass Cesare Siepi was, as mezzo-soprano Giulietta Simionato observed in Lanfranco Rasponi's book *The Last Prima Donnas,* "the king of the bassos, a grand seigneur on the stage." For 23 seasons, he was the Metropolitan Opera's leading basso cantante, as adept in the elegance of Mozart's *Don Giovanni* and *Figaro* as he was in the long-lined, vocally demanding bass protagonists of Verdi.

His Met debut occurred when Bulgarian bass Boris Christoff was unable to receive security clearance for travel to the United States. New general manager Rudolf Bing intended his new production of Verdi's *Don Carlo* as a prototype of the beautifully sung and theatrically vivid events he wanted to make the rule rather than the exception. Siepi's brooding, superlatively sung King Phillip established the 27-year-old singer as an artist of the first rank.

Born in Milan, Siepi initially studied to become a schoolteacher and undertook courses leading toward that goal. While music had been an important element in his life and he had studied voice singly in public at the age of 15, he had no intention of pursuing music professionally. At the age of 18, however, urged by friends and knowing only two arias, he entered a national voice competition in Florence and won first prize. An impresario in the audience heard his potential and engaged the tall, handsome singer for a production of Rigoletto. Thus, Siepi, at the age of 18, made his debut as Sparafucile in Schio (near Venice) and earned reviews that made him look seriously a future in music.

The outbreak of war in Europe put his career on hold. When Italy was occupied by the Nazis, Siepi escaped to neutral Switzerland and remained there for the duration of World War II. Returning to Italy following the cessation of hostilities, he appeared at *La Fenice* as Silva in Verdi's *Ernani.* During a La Scala summer season, he sang Sparafucile once more, as well as Ramfis and Padre Guardiano. A further honor came when he was asked to sing Zaccaria in Verdi's *Nabucco* in the first production held in La Scala's reconstructed theater building. Siepi continued to appear with the company until 1950 in a series of leading roles. He also took part in Toscanini's commemoration of composer/librettist Arrigo Boito in 1948 and created the role of Nonno Innocenzo in Pizzetti's *L'oro.*

After the success of his Met debut, Siepi quickly established himself as heir to Ezio Pinza. Like Pinza, Siepi was endowed with that animal magnetism indispensable for true stardom. In roles such as Padre Guardiano, he exuded a calm authority, but as Don Giovanni, he breathed a sensuality barely concealing a core of danger and self-absorption. His suavely vocalized Don was conspicuously on display at Salzburg Festivals during the mid-1950s and is preserved on several excellent live recordings.

Siepi was also shown to advantage as bass soloist in two exceptional recordings of Verdi's *Manzoni Requiem,* first with Toscanini and his NBC Symphony in 1951 and, later, with Victor de Sabata and the La Scala Orchestra and Chorus.

Siepi's relationship with the Met resulted in a total of 379 performances over 23 seasons, all of them in leading roles (71 as Don Giovanni and 56 as Figaro). Other roles included Basilio, Ramfis, Alvise, Boris Godunov (sung in English), Silva, Zaccaria, Méphistophélès, Fiesco, Oroveso, and (in German) Gurnemanz.

Despite his close relationship with the Met, Siepi performed frequently with other houses in America and Europe. He continued to sing well into his sixties. *—Erik Eriksson*

Recommended:

- ○ **Lebendige Vergangenheit: Cesare Siepi** / Siepi, etc. / Preiser 89511
- ○ **Mozart: Don Giovanni** / Krips (cond.), Siepi, Casa, Corena, Dermota, Vienna PO / 2000 / London 466389

Beverly Sills

b. May 25, 1929, New York, NY

Soprano

With her vibrant, cheery personality, soprano Beverly Sills has always been a favorite of the general public, among the most effective spokespersons the arts have had in America. The child of immigrant parents, Sills (born Belle Miriam Silverman) discovered singing at an early age; at four she was on a morning radio program as "Bubbles" Silverman, and by age seven she had sung in a movie. At 16 she joined a touring Gilbert and Sullivan company. Her most important vocal studies were with Estelle Liebling, who had been a favored soprano of John Philip Sousa. In 1947, she made her operatic debut as Frasquita in *Carmen* at Philadelphia. She toured North America during the 1951–52 season with the Charles Wagner Opera Company, singing Violetta in *La Traviata* and Micaëla (*Carmen*). After singing in Baltimore and San Francisco, she made her debut at the New York City Opera, which was to become her artistic home for over two decades. She once again sang Violetta in that debut, but soon expanded her repertoire to include a wide range of roles. Among the twentieth century operas in which she performed were Moore's *The Ballad of Baby Doe,* Nono's *Intolleranza,* and Weisgall's *Six Characters in Three Acts.* In 1966, she reached international fame with performances as Cleopatra in Handel's *Giulio Cesare.* Her performances of Donizetti's "Tudor triology," *Roberto Devereux, Maria Stuarda,* and *Anna Bolena,* solidified her stature on the international scene. She made her Teatro alla Scala debut as Pamira in Rossini's *The Siege of Corinth* in an edition prepared by conductor Thomas Schippers. In 1975, she made her debut at the Metropolitan Opera in the same role; she had already sung Donna Anna in a concert performance there in 1966. Her Vienna debut in 1967 as the Queen of the Night (in Mozart's *Die Zauberflöte* was one of her few performances of this role. She regularly sang many other important roles in both Italian opera and in works from other countries.

She retired from performing at the age of 50, with an appearance in Menotti's *La Loca,* and accepted the position of General Manager of the New York City Opera. In 1991, she joined the board of the Metropolitan Opera, and four years later became head of New York's Lincoln Center. Sills sang regularly in concerts and recitals containing the arias from her famous roles. Her concert performance of the first version of Richard Strauss' *Ariadne auf Naxos* is justly famous, since Zerbinetta's aria in this version is much more difficult than in the revised version.

Her basic voice was a light, high soprano with excellent technique and breath control. She was best heard in roles where fragility of character was paramount, such as Marie in Donizetti's *La Fille du régiment,* Puccini's *Manon Lescaut,* and Violetta. By sheer power of character she held her own in operas normally best served by larger voices as well.

Although her artistic life was filled with great triumphs, Sills knew personal tragedy. Her daughter was born deaf and her son is mentally retarded. She has been active in the March of Dimes Mothers' March on Birth Defects and other related organizations. Her autobiography was published in 1976 with the title *Bubbles: A Self-Portrait* and was revised in 1981 as *Bubbles: An Encore*; another autobiography, *Beverly,* followed in 1987. *—Richard LeSueur*

Recommended:

- ○ **The Art of Beverly Sills** / Sills, etc. / DG 471766
- ○ **Moore: Ballad of Baby Doe** / Buckley (cond.), Sills, Bible, Cassel, New York City Opera Orch. & Chorus / 1999 / DG 465148
- ○ **The Great Recordings** / Sills, etc. / 2004 / DG 000246902
- ○ **Donizetti: Anna Bolena** / Rudel (cond.), Sills, Verrett, Plishka, Lloyd, London SO / 2000 / DG 465957
- ○ **Massenet: Manon** / Rudel (cond.), Souzay, Sills, Gedda, Bacquier, New Philharmonia / DG 000247002

Joseph Silverstein

b. Mar. 21, 1932, Detroit, MI

Violinist

One of America's most respected musicians, violinist/conductor/artistic advisor and teacher Joseph Silverstein has contributed to American musical life since his first days with the Boston Symphony Orchestra. Aside from his presence in live and recorded performances, he has been an important figure as a resource to many musical organizations, sharing expertise gained from his various responsibilities.

Silverstein's training as a violinist was exceedingly sound. After entering Philadelphia's Curtis Institute in 1945, he studied with Efrem Zimbalist, the Auer-trained virtuoso noted for his patrician taste and immaculate technique. Later, Silverstein worked with Josef Gingold and Mischa Mischakoff, two other celebrated performing pedagogues. From this period of study, Silverstein emerged with the silvery, full-bodied tone and unshakable technique that would mark his subsequent solo and ensemble work. At the time he joined the Boston Symphony Orchestra in 1955, he was its youngest member. His performance in the 1959 Concours Musical Reine Elisabeth brought the beginnings of celebrity in Europe and began a series of career-advancing events in his own country. Winning the Naumburg Foundation Award in 1960 led to a New York debut in 1961. When the BSO found its concertmaster chair open, it appointed Silverstein to that position in 1962. In his position as BSO concertmaster, Silverstein was heard not only in the violin solo moments within the orchestral repertory, but also as featured soloist both in performance and on recording. Under four BSO conductors, beginning with Charles Münch, whose tenure ran until 1963, Silverstein came to be known as one of the most able solo voices among concertmasters anywhere. With Erich Leinsdorf, who served as conductor from 1963 to 1968, Silverstein recorded impressive interpretations of the Stravinsky and Bartók concertos, and under Seiji Ozawa, his solo role in Vivaldi's *Four Seasons* was equally distinctive. In association with his BSO position, he served a chairman of the Tanglewood Music Center faculty. Other academic responsibilities followed, beginning in the 1970s with teaching appointments at Yale and Boston universities. In addition to his position as assistant conductor with the BSO, gained in 1971, Silverstein began to accept both guest engagements and appointments to other orchestras. In 1980, he accepted the musical directorship of the nearby Worcester, MA, symphony orchestra and the next year became the Baltimore Symphony Orchestra's principal guest conductor. In 1983, Silverstein was called upon to replace Varujan Kojian as conductor of the Utah Symphony Orchestra. Silverstein remained there as artistic director for 15 years, having given up his BSO concertmaster position shortly after beginning his tenure in Salt Lake City. In November 2001, Silverstein was appointed acting music director of the Florida Philharmonic following the sudden resignation of James Judd, who had led the orchestra for 14 years. The Florida orchestra was already one of ten organizations in the United States and Canada being served by Silverstein as artistic advisor. The appointment was for an 18-month period while a search would be conducted for a permanent music director. By January 2002, Silverstein was already directing performances. Silverstein is a faculty member at both the Curtis Institute and the Longy School of Music in Cambridge, MA. *—Erik Eriksson*

Recommended:

- ○ **Vivaldi: The Four Seasons** / Ozawa (cond.), Silverstein, BSO / 1982 / Telarc 80070
- ○ **Violin Encores!** / Silverstein, Zgodava (piano) / 1994 / Intersound 3517
- ○ **Achron: Violin Concerto 1, etc.** / Schwarz, Silverstein (cond.), Oliveira, Berlin RSO, Czech PO, Barcelona SO, National Orch. of Catalonia / 2003 / Naxos 8559408

Robert Simpson

b. Mar. 2, 1921, Leamington, England, **d.** Dec. 21, 1997, Tralee, Kerry, Ireland
Composer: Chamber Music, Symphonic

British composer Robert Simpson was educated at Westminster City School. His parents wanted him to be a doctor, and he did devote two years of study to medicine before the lure of music overtook him. Simpson was a lifelong pacifist and served in a mobile surgical unit during World War II as a conscientious objector. It was during this time that he began studying music with Herbert Howells and writing the first of four symphonies. For one of the works, Simpson even experimented with serial procedures. Unsatisfied with the compositions, he destroyed them and began anew, writing in his own style that often found two different tonal centers reacting against the other.

The *Piano Sonata* (1946) and his *Symphony No. 1* (1946–51) are among Simpson's earliest works. While writing his "new" *First Symphony*, Simpson discovered the music of Carl Nielsen, which had a great influence on Simpson's development as a composer.

Simpson earned his doctorate in music at the University of Durham in 1951, using his *First Symphony* as a thesis. In the same year he finished his *First String Quartet* and founded the Exploratory Concert Society, along with Donald Mitchell and Harold Truscott, which focused on little-known composers and compositions that Simpson liked. He would also go on to join the British Broadcasting Corporation as a producer and broadcaster. During his stint with the BBC, Simpson introduced the popular "Innocent Ears" program, which would reveal a composer's identity only after the duration of the recording. Simpson remained with the BBC until 1980, when a musician's strike and threat of program cuts convinced him that the ideals of the corporation were not true to his own.

Simpson moved to Ireland in 1986 and continued composing. Although left partially paralyzed by a stroke in 1991, he finished his *Second String Quintet* in 1995 and began work on his *Sixteenth String Quartet* before his death. Simpson left behind an impressive body of work, including 11 highly regarded symphonies and 15 string quartets.

He worked to revitalize public interest in composers he greatly admired and wrote of two in *The Essence of Bruckner* and *Carl Nielsen: Symphonist.* Simpson also worked tirelessly on behalf of fellow composers who suffered from lack of exposure, often devoting as much time to their promotion as his own. It was Simpson who convinced fellow British composer Havergal Brian to keep writing music, and he was instrumental in arranging for BBC performances of all 32 of Brian's symphonies. *—Tod Whitesel*

CHAMBER MUSIC

String Quartets (1952–1996)

When English composer Robert Simpson resigned from the BBC music production staff in 1980, he found himself with more time to compose than he had ever had before, and the years from 1980 until his death in 1997 were the most productive of his life. We can see it quite clearly from his catalog of string quartets: from 1952 through 1981—a span of nearly 30 years—he managed to produce eight quartets; ten years later the number was nearly double. Simpson was dedicated first and foremost to the composition of "pure" instrumental music; the symphonies may offer the truest window into his mind and soul, but the 15 string quartets present such a variety of musical ways and means, modern and traditional, all aptly mastered by the gifted Briton, that one could hardly do better than them as a first introduction to Simpson and his music.

Simpson's first three string quartets were composed from 1952 to 1954, at the start of his tenure with the BBC; he then waited nearly 20 full years before again trying his hand at the string quartet with the *Quartet No. 4* of 1973. When it rains it pours, and four more quartets appeared in the next few years (*Nos. 5* through *8*, 1975, 1975, 1977, and 1979, respectively). The mammoth *String Quartet No. 9* of 1982, along with the *Symphony No. 8* of 1981, was the first major achievement of the post-BBC years; and until the early 1990s, new string quartets appeared on a yearly or bi-yearly basis, for a grand total of 15 in 1991.

None of Robert Simpson's string quartets is much like any other one, though there are certain undeniable groups. The first three are self-contained works for the most part, whereas in later pieces Simpson often chose to stand on the shoulders of great composers of the past. *Quartets 4 and 5*, for example, were written after a "close study" of Beethoven's *Razumovsky Quartets*, and take up a pseudo-Classical manner that allows for many structural parallels between the Simpson and the Beethoven pieces. The *Ninth Quartet* is an hour-long set of variations on a theme by Haydn in which Simpson indulges in melodic and structural mirror-techniques. The four-movement *String Quartet No. 8* is an exploration of the latent possibilities of the interval of the perfect fifth.

Simpson may have been devoted to the cause of pure music, but he did not eschew a certain restrained kind of tone-painting (the scherzo of the *String Quartet No. 8*, for instance, is meant to capture the essence of the mosquito *Eretmapodites gilletti!*), nor was he an elitist who considered himself above making a humanitarian plea through his music—the inscription "For Peace" will be found at the front of the score to the *String Quartet No. 10* of 1983. *—Blair Johnston*

Recommended:

- ○ **Simpson: String Quartets 14 & 15; Two-Clarinet Quintets** / Vanbrugh Quartet / 1993 / Hyperion 66626

SYMPHONIC

Symphonies (1951–1991)

As well as being a prolific composer, Robert Simpson was a writer and, as a member of the BBC's music staff from 1951 to 1980, closely involved with the wider musical scene. The continuity and integrity of the European symphonic tradition is a recurring theme throughout his writings and goes some way toward making possible a deeper understanding of his symphonies.

With the twentieth century reaction against nineteenth century musical tastes it might seem, to say the least, unfashionable for Simpson to argue for "thematic and tonal organization" and assert that "every Symphony should fulfil one of the conditions we demand before praising any new work—that it makes quite clear the rules of its own game."

Simpson's symphonies, like those of Beethoven, Bruckner, and Nielsen, have large-scale plans, yet it would be wrong to see him as backward looking or conventional. For example, the *Fourth Symphony* quotes directly from Haydn's *Symphony No. 76 in E flat*, but is in no respect classical in concept. The composer simply said of it, "it confronts problems which do not disturb it."

Simpson's determination to deconstruct, then reconstruct, the symphonic standards of earlier composers inevitably led to allegations of pastiche; but his intentions were structural rather than imitative: each of the symphonies is original and forceful in its symphonic argument. In the three-movement *First*, Simpson is already exploring the shifting tonality that distinguishes Nielsen's symphonic style without, at the time, having heard any of the Danish composer's major works. *Symphonies Two* and *Three* make use of "tonal centers" in their overall development (as do Nielsen's), while the *Fifth* begins and ends with a soft, sustained chord reminiscent of Bruckner. Here, again, there are few other resemblances. Simpson freely acknowledged Sibelius' influence in his later symphonies but, apart from a greater economy of means and a growing use of subtle effects, it is impossible to describe them as Sibelian in sound or content.

Simpson's essays on the symphonies of Bruckner, Nielsen, and Sibelius established him as an important twentieth century critic, indeed his championship of Nielsen in the 1960s was, almost alone, responsible for consolidating the Danish composer's reputation as one of the greatest twentieth century symphonists.

It could, however, be said that he was not always able to overcome the problem of expressing musical ideas in words. His attempt to create a "psychological program" for each symphony is interesting, but not always helpful, as when he wrote of his *Fifth Symphony* that it deals "with that part of our mind which coldly observes itself no matter what disturbances, mental or physical, occur."

The most persuasive statement Simpson ever made on his own behalf was at a symposium on The Symphony in 1973, when he said, "Ultimately we can do only what we are constituted to do: whether we do it well or not is what really matters, and contact with durable human instincts is more vital than tagging on to fashions." *—Roy Brewer*

Recommended:

- ○ **Simpson: Symphonies 6 & 7** / Handley (cond.), Royal Liverpool PO / 1987 / Hyperion 66280

Giuseppe Sinopoli

b. Nov. 2, 1946, Venice, Italy, **d.** Apr. 20, 2001, Berlin, Germany

Conductor

Conductor Giuseppe Sinopoli was one of the world's great conducting stars. He gave powerful, psychologically penetrating, even expressionist, performances that were often highly controversial. At the age of 12, Sinopoli studied harmony and organ at Messina, then harmony and counterpoint at the Venice Conservatory (1965–67). At the insistence of his father he simultaneously studied medicine. From 1969 to 1973, he attended the Accademia Musicale Chigiana in Siena, studying under Franco Donatoni. He graduated with his doctorate of medicine in psychiatry and a Ph.D. in anthropology from the University of Padua in 1972. His psychiatry dissertation was on the physiology of the areas of the brain concerned with creating the sensations of sound.

After a period as Donatoni's assistant, Sinopoli was appointed to the faculty of the Venice Conservatory as Professor for Contemporary and Electronic Music. In that year he also took up conducting studies with Hans Swarowsky in Vienna. In 1975 he founded the Bruno Maderna Ensemble, an avant-garde music group, while continuing to teach and compose.

He began to make a reputation as a composer. His work, typically, was intense and followed the trend toward serial music that prevailed at the time. He received several major commissions. His largest work was an opera named *Lou Salomé*, based on the life of a nineteenth century literary figure. It was premiered at the Bavarian State Opera in Munich in 1981.

Meanwhile, his work leading the Bruno Maderna Ensemble had been noticed. He began receiving requests to conduct. In 1976 and 1977, respectively, he led highly acclaimed performances of the Verdi operas *Aïda* and *Macbeth* in Venice, then the same composer's *Macbeth* at the Deutsche Oper Berlin and *Atilla* at the Vienna State Opera. Sinopoli's London operatic debut was Puccini's *Manon Lescaut* at Covent Garden (1983) and his New York debut was at the Metropolitan with Puccini's *Tosca* (1985). As an operatic conductor, he performed frequently at the Bayreuth Festival, La Scala, and other major opera houses. He is particularly known for his electrifying performances of the Richard Strauss operas *Salome* and *Elektra*.

In addition to Bayreuth, Sinopoli was also a frequent guest at the Salzburg, Lucerne and Schlewsig-Holstein Music Festivals. From 1990 until his death, Sinopoli was Director of the Taormina Arte Festival in Sicily. He was appointed principal conductor of the Orchestra dell'Accademia di Santa Cecilia in Rome (serving there through 1987) and in 1984 became the principal conductor of the Philharmonia Orchestra in London, remaining through 1994. In 1987, his position was upgraded to that of music director of the Philharmonia, which he held until 1994. From 1992 to 2001Sinopoli was principal conductor of the Staatskapelle Dresden.

Giuseppe Sinopoli recorded exclusively for Deutsche Grammophon. His set of Maderna works won the Grand Prix International du Disque and Premio della Critica Discografia Italiana in 1981. His *Manon Lescaut* recording won both those prizes in addition to the International Record Critics Award in 1985. Further prizes were a Gramophone Award in 1987 for *La forza del destino*, the Tokyo Record Academy Prize and Stella d'Oro for *Madama Butterfly*, three prizes for *Tannhäuser*, and three for *Tosca*. Sinopoli's most honored recording was Strauss' *Salome*, which won the Orphee d'Or, the Stella d'Argento, the Grand Prix de la Nouvelle Academie du Disque, and the Edison Award. In 1994, the Italian government awarded Sinopoli its highest award, the Gran Croce al Merito, for his contribution to arts and music.

Giuseppe Sinopoli died at the Deutsche Oper Berlin of a heart attack while conducting the third act of *Aïda*. *—Joseph Stevenson*

Recommended:

- ○ **Bruckner: Symphonie 8; Strauss: Metamorphosen** / Sinopoli (cond.), Dresden Staatskapelle / 1996 / DG 447744
- ○ **Schoenberg: Pelléas & Melisande, Schoenberg: Verklärte Nacht** / Sinopoli (cond.), London PO / DG 439942
- ○ **Mussorgsky, Ravel** / Sinopoli (cond.), New York PO / DG 429785
- ○ **Webern Album** / Sinopoli (cond.), Dresden Staatskapelle / 1999 / Teldec 22902
- ○ **Strauss: Friedenstag** / Sinopoli (cond.), Voigt, Kupfer, Botha, Reiter, Dresden Staatskapelle Orch. & Chorus / DG 463494
- ○ **Mahler-Sinopoli: The Complete Recordings** / Sinopoli (cond.), Crabb, Terfel, Jo, Allen, London PO / DG 471451

Nikolaos Skalkottas

b. Mar. 21, 1904, Halkis, Greece, **d.** Sep. 20, 1949, Athens, Greece

Composer

Nikolaos Skalkottas is easily among the most important Greek composers from the first half of the twentieth century. Extremely talented from his early childhood, he mostly wrote serial and atonal music in his mature compositions and remained an almost totally unknown figure in his homeland and abroad throughout his short lifetime. His music eventually attracted some attention after his death, but still remains largely neglected.

Skalkottas' family moved to Athens when he was two, and at age five the precocious Nikolaos began studies on the violin with his father and uncle, both good amateur musicians. He entered the Athens Conservatory in 1914 and graduated six years later as a virtuoso violinist, but with relatively little knowledge of composition. In 1921, he enrolled on a scholarship at the Berlin Hochschule für Musik, where he furthered his studies on the violin with Willy Hess and also began instruction in composition. He befriended Dimitri Mitropoulos, then also a student there, who may have encouraged his interest in the more modern methods of composition. Despite his successes on the violin—Skalkottas had already given many stunning concerts, not least his rendition of the Beethoven violin concerto at his 1920 graduation from the Athens Conservatory—he decided to shift his focus to composition in 1925. He began studying that year with Philipp Jarnach, having already written several atonal compositions, including a string quartet and string trio, the scores to which are both lost. Skalkottas did not abandon the violin during this period; indeed, he earned money playing in cafés and small ensembles to support his studies. He also received funds from a Greek patron, Manolis Benakis, until 1931, when a disagreement between the two erupted. In 1926, still under Jarnach's tutelage, Skalkottas also began studying orchestration with Kurt Weill. He concluded his work with both the following year, when he enrolled at the Preussische Akademie der Künsts to commence studies with Arnold Schoenberg, who would have the most profound influence on the young composer. Skalkottas had an affair with a violin student while at the Hochshcule, Matla Temko, who gave birth to a daughter. Finances became an increasing problem for the young composer, and Skalkottas finished his studies with Schoenberg in 1932. He returned to Athens the following year, having written a number of works, both tonal and atonal, including his *Piano Concerto No. 1* (1931–32). Skalkottas suffered from nervous problems after he returned to Greece and increasingly exhibited a withdrawn, melancholic personality. His works were roundly rejected by critics and public alike and in 1934, he had to turn once more to his violin to earn a living. He played in various Athens orchestras, including the Greek Radio Symphony Orchestra. After writing little music for two years, he also returned to composing in 1934, but now did so in private. Skalkottas remained in Athens during the war, once getting arrested by the occupying Nazi forces on suspicion of resistance activity. Skalkottas married in 1946 and his wife gave birth to two children, the second of which was born on the day after the composer's premature death from a strangulated hernia on September 20, 1949. Following his death, Iohannes Papaioannou, Hans Keller, conductors Walter Goehr and Hermann Scherchen, and several other musicians began promoting Skalkottas' compositions, finally bringing recognition and a measure of fame to the neglected composer. *—Robert Cummings*

Overview of Works (1924–1949)

Greek composer Nikolaos Skalkottas was virtually unknown in his lifetime, partly because of his eccentric lack of concern about obtaining performances of his compositions, but also owing to the generally advanced nature of their expressive language. Much of his output was atonal, a fair portion of which was written in accordance with 12-tone procedures. Regardless of what style he chose, however, Skalkottas tended to use traditional classical forms, making him a structural conservative but a harmonic and melodic progressive. Some of his earliest works, dating to his student years in Berlin, are tonal and fairly approachable works, though not particularly striking or individual. The collection of piano pieces *Greek Suites*, from 1924, are such an example. But just a year later, Skalkottas produced his *Sonata for Solo Violin*, a mostly atonal work that exhibited a leap forward in his harmonic and melodic language. His style continued to rapidly evolve in the mid- and late 1920s, yielding the entirely atonal *15 Little Variations for Piano* (1927), the first work in which the composer began using 12-tone techniques, though only sparingly and with his own modifications. His *Piano Concerto No. 1* (1931–32) was among his first large atonal compositions, but after its appearance, the composer, having returned to Greece from Berlin, suffered a creative dry spell for about two years. In 1935, he began turning out works at a fairly prolific pace and his music began to divulge both a greater passion and sense of humor. The violin concerto and *Piano Concerto No. 2*, both dating to the period 1937–38, show the more passionate and epic side of the composer, while the 1943 *Sonata Concertante for Bassoon and Piano*, especially in its finale, divulges a biting humorous side. The one work that Skalkottas did score a measure of success with in Greece was his orchestral effort *36 Greek Dances* (1931–36), a tonal composition drawn on Greek folk songs. He also turned out other tonal pieces around this time, including the ballet *The Maiden and Death* (1938). Oddly, there was a spate of late scores that were also tonal, including the slightly Stravinsky-tinged chamber work *Classic Symphonia* (1947), and the piano concertino (1948) which, typical of the neglect of this composer's works, was not premiered until 1987. Skalkottas managed to mix a variety of his compositional traits in the incidental music he composed for the drama *The Spell of May*, for which he used both folk music and different atonal styles. Of course, these "different atonal styles" involved a greater freedom than used by Schoenberg and many of his disciples. Moreover, Skalkottas, like Webern, wrote many short atonal works, including the *16 Songs for Mezzo-Soprano and Piano* (1941), and the *32 Piano Pieces* (1940). But movements in sonata form like the *Piano Concertos No. 2* and *No. 3*, both from the late 1930s, and the *Overture to the Return of Ulysses* (1943–44) are quite lengthy. *—Robert Cummings*

Recommended:

- ○ **Classical Greece: The Music of Nikos Skalkottas** / Christodoulou (cond.), Demertzis, Malmo SO / 1997 / Bis 300904
- ○ **Skalkottas: Music for Violin & Piano** / Demertzis, Asteriadou / 1998 / Bis 1024
- ○ **Skalkottas: String Quartets 3 & 4** / New Hellenic Quartet / 1999 / Bis 1074
- ○ **Skalkottas: Chamber Music** / Billman, Davidsson, Andersson, New Hellenic Quartet / 2000 / Bis 1124
- ○ **Skalkottas: 32 pieces for piano** / Samaltanos / 2000 / Bis 1133/4
- ○ **Skalkottas: 36 Greek Dances; The Return of Ulysses** / Bryant, Christodoulou (cond.), BBC SO / 2002 / Bis 1333/4
- ○ **Skalkottas: Cello Works & Piano Trios** / Kitsopoulos, Asteriadou, Demertzis / 2003 / Bis 1224

Boje Skovhus

b. May 22, 1962, Ikast, Denmark
Baritone

A rising baritone star in the operatic scene of the 1990s, Boje Skovhus studied at the Aarhus Music College and the Royal Academy for Opera of Copenhagen and then went to New York for further training. After acquiring some professional experience on various stages, he had a breakout appearance at the Vienna Volksoper when he substituted at the last minute as Mozart's Don Giovanni. Since then he has enjoyed a rapidly developing career on the world's greatest opera stages.

He has been virtually adopted by the Viennese, who saw him rocket to fame on one of their stages, and regularly sings at the Volksoper and the Vienna State Opera. He regularly sings the other Mozart-Da Ponte baritone roles besides Don Giovanni, namely, the Count in *Le nozze di Figaro* and Guglielmo in *Così fan tutte*.

His good looks and a star quality make him an ideal choice for that minority of operas where the baritone part is the main or title role. Thus, he has spurred a revival of Ambroise Thomas' *Hamlet* at the Vienna Konzerthaus, Vienna Volksoper, and Royal Opera Copenhagen, as well as the little known baritone version of Massenet's *Werther*. He also has made a specialty of Britten's *Billy Budd* and Tchaikovsky's *Eugene Onegin*, including arias or scenes from them on his first opera disc under his exclusive artist contract with the Sony Classics label. Other leading baritone parts in his repertory are Berg's Wozzeck, Dallapiccola's Il Prigioniero, Peter I in *Zar und Zimmerman*, Tarquinius in Britten's *The Rape of Lucretia*, and Raimond in Othmar Schoeck's *Venus*.

Skovhus also frequently appears on the recital stage and has recorded creatively chosen recital discs. These include selections of lied settings by Hugo Wolf and Erich Wolfgang Korngold of poems by Eichendorff, a selection of songs by Robert and Clara Schumann called *The Heart of the Poet*, and the two great Schubert song cycles *Schwanengesang* and *Die schöne Müllerin*. His favored accompanist is pianist Helmut Deutsch. After his 1997 New York recital at Alice Tully Hall in Lincoln Center he was acclaimed as one of the great lieder singers of his generation.

He has appeared on many of the world's great opera stages, including the Metropolitan in New York (debuting in the 1998–99 season in *Die Fledermaus*), the Hamburg State Opera, the Houston Grand Opera, the Deutsche Oper Berlin, Opéra de Paris, Royal Opera Copenhagen, and the Bavarian State Opera.

He appears at major music festivals. Among them are Ravinia, Tanglewood, Edinburgh, the Vienna Festwochen, and the Feldkirch Schubertiade. On the orchestral concert stage, he has sung in Orff's *Carmina Burana*, Britten's *War Requiem*, Mahler's *Lieder eines fahrenden Gesellen*, Brahms' *Ein deutsche Requiem*, and Schumann's *Scenes from Faust*. *—Joseph Stevenson*

Recommended:

- ○ **Lehár: The Merry Widow** / Gardiner (cond.), Terfel, Bonney, Skovhus, Studer, Monteverdi Choir, Vienna PO / 1994 / DG 439911
- ○ **Schwanengesang: Schubert's Last Songs** / Skovhus, Deutsch (piano) / 1995 / Sony 66835
- ○ **Skovhus Sings Opera Arias** / Conlon (cond.), Skovhus, English National Opera Orch. / 1998 / Sony 60035

Leonard Slatkin

b. Sep. 1, 1944, Los Angeles, CA
Conductor

Leonard Slatkin, a fixture of the U.S. symphonic scene, is especially noted for his performances of American, Russian, and British music, and for his numerous recordings of Haydn symphonies. He was born into a famous musical family: his father was Felix Slatkin (1915–63), a St. Louis-born violinist who rose to become a film-score and light-music conductor and founded the Hollywood String Quartet. His mother was Eleanor Aller, cellist of the quartet. Thanks to their combined efforts, their son was trained in violin, viola, piano, and conducting.

Slatkin attended Indiana University (1962) and Los Angeles City College (1963), and studied with Walter Susskind, the music director of the St. Louis Symphony Orchestra, at the Aspen Music School in 1964. He then attended Juilliard School in New York, where he studied conducting with Jean Morel, graduating in 1968 with a B. Mus. degree. In that same year he became assistant conductor of the St. Louis Symphony Orchestra under Susskind, and was promoted to associate conductor in 1971, associate principal conductor in 1974, and principal guest conductor in 1974. During this period he showed his career-long commitment to musical training for young people by founding the St. Louis Youth Symphony in 1969 and serving as its conductor.

In 1974 Slatkin made his European debut as a guest conductor with the Royal Philharmonic Orchestra in London, and in 1978 he conducted the National Symphony Orchestra of Washington, D.C. for the first time. He was artistic adviser to the New Orleans Philharmonic (1977–80). In 1979 he founded the Minnesota Orchestra's Sommerfest series and served as its director for ten years.

In 1979 he was appointed music director of the St. Louis Symphony, beginning a highly successful 17-year tenure that included five triumphal international tours and many recordings for the Vox, EMI, and RCA labels. With the St. Louis orchestra he conducted a notable series of discs of music by American symphonic masters, including Bernstein, Copland, Schumann, and Piston. He also has recorded the complete Vaughan Williams and Elgar symphonies, a series of Haydn symphonies, and works of Britten, Shostakovich, and Prokofiev, among many others. He has also recorded with the National Symphony Orchestra, the Philharmonia Orchestra (London), the London Philharmonic, the London Symphony Orchestra, and the Bavarian Radio Symphony Orchestra, amassing well over a hundred releases. He has been nominated for Grammy awards more than 50 times and won four times.

In 1990 Slatkin became music director of the Great Woods Performing Arts Center in Mansfield, Massachusetts, the summer home of the Pittsburgh Symphony Orchestra. From 1992 to 1999 he served as director of the Cleveland Orchestra's Blossom Festival; the position was created so he could exercise his flair for creative and wide-ranging programming. In 1994 he was the artistic director of the Festival of American Music at London's South Bank Centre. In 1996 he took up the position of music director of the National Symphony Orchestra, and has led them in successful tours and recordings. In 2000 he was appointed chief conductor of the BBC Symphony Orchestra. He has continued his involvement with youth orchestras, and also conducts opera in many of the world's major houses and festivals. *—Joseph Stevenson*

Recommended:

- ○ **Barber: Symphony 1; Piano Concerto; Souvenirs** / Slatkin (cond.), Browning, St. Louis SO / 1991 / RCA 60732
- ○ **Tchaikovsky: The Ballets** / Slatkin (cond.), St. Louis SO / 2003 / RCA 55707
- ○ **Ravel: Piano Concertos** / Slatkin (cond.), Larrocha, St. Louis SO / 1993 / RCA 60985
- ○ **Bernstein: Kaddish; Chichester Psalms; Missa Brevis** / Slatkin (cond.), Davis, McCarthy, Murray, Benjafield, BBC Singers, BBCSO & Chorus / 2004 / Chandos 10172
- ○ **Music of Samuel Barber** / Slatkin (cond.), St. Louis SO / EMI 49463

Rolf Smedvig

b. Seattle, WA

Trumpeter

Known as the founder of the Empire Brass Quintet, Rolf Smedvig is more than a virtuoso trumpeter, with the number of his conducting appearances quickly approaching those of his soloist and chamber musician appearances.

When he was just 13, Smedvig made his debut with his hometown Seattle Symphony as a trumpet soloist. He made the metropolitan Boston area his home when he decided to study at Boston University and Tanglewood. His teachers included Armando Ghitalla, Rafael Mendez, and Maurice André. The year 1971 was an eventful one for him. He founded the Empire Brass; Leonard Bernstein asked him to be trumpet soloist in the premiere of Bernstein's *Mass* to open the Kennedy Center; and he became assistant principal trumpet of the Boston Symphony, the youngest member of the orchestra at the time, at the age of 19. He was made principal trumpet in 1979, but stayed for only two years, wanting to develop his career as a soloist and chamber musician. Since then, his career has been full and busy. As the only remaining original member and first trumpet of the Empire Brass, he makes approximately 100 concert appearances each year and has visited over 35 countries. He has appeared as a soloist with the Boston Symphony, the Cambridge Chamber Orchestra, the New World Symphony, and Japan's NHK Orchestra; toured as soloist with the Atlantic Classical Orchestra and the Scottish Orchestra and conducted the Cambridge Chamber Orchestra, the Honolulu Symphony, the Northwest Chamber Orchestra, the Zurich Tonhalle Orchestra, and the Simón Bolívar Orchestra. Smedvig has taught at Boston University, Tanglewood, and London's Royal Academy of Music, in addition to giving master classes. The 1996 Warner video *The 21st Century Band Method* features Smedvig, and he is a clinician for the instrument maker Selmer. His hundreds of arrangements for brass have been published by Schirmer, KRS Publishing, and International Music. A ballet, *Passage*, containing adapted, arranged, and original music all by Smedvig, was premiered in 1996 by the Boston Ballet. Smedvig's recordings can be found on the CBS/Sony, Angel EMI, and Telarc labels. His first Telarc CD, a 1990 release of virtuoso trumpet concertos, was nominated for a Grammy Award. 2002 saw the release of *The Glory of Gabrieli*, the 15th effort by Smedvig and the Empire Brass. Smedvig has also appeared numerous times on national television and radio programs as a soloist, conductor, and with the Empire Brass. *—Patsy Morita*

Recommended:

- ○ **Virtuoso** / Ling (cond.), Smedvig, Murray, Scottish CO, Empire Brass / 2000 / Telarc 80550
- ○ **Trumpet Concertos** / Ling (cond.), Smedvig, Scottish CO / 1990 / Telarc 80232

Bedřich Smetana

b. Mar. 2, 1824, Leitomischl, Bohemia (Czech Rep.), **d.** May 12, 1884, Prague, Bohemia (Czech Rep.)

Composer: Orchestral, Opera, Keyboard, Chamber Music

Bedřich Smetana was one of the great composers of his country's history and one of the leaders of the movement toward musical nationalism. His father was a violin teacher who gave Bedřich his first lessons and referred him to keyboard, harmony, and composition lessons when the boy requested them. His father tried to get Bedřich to apply himself in academics, but Bedřich was too focused on music to be a good student.

Bedrich Kittl, director of the Prague Conservatory, in 1844 found Smetana a job as a music teacher to the family of Count Leopold Thun while continuing music studies. He remained with the count for three and a half years, but he quit to undertake a concert tour, which turned out to be a financial failure.

Franz Liszt aided Smetana in finding a publisher for some early piano music and in 1848, Smetana founded a successful piano school.

Although he established a strong local reputation as a pianist, his piano compositions (mostly lighter works) did not earn him any special distinction as a composer.

In 1860, the Austro-Hungarian Empire granted internal political autonomy to Bohemia. A movement began to search for a genuine Czech voice in arts, including the establishment of a national theater. In 1862–63, Smetana composed *The Brandenburgers in Bohemia*, his first opera, which was a success at its premiere on January 5, 1866. His next opera was *Prodaná nevesta* (The Bartered Bride), his most famous and enduring opera today, but a failure when it premiered on May 30, 1866.

In 1866, Smetana became conductor of the Provisional Theater, re-forming its administration and attempting to raise standards. His next opera, *Dalibor* (1871), was criticized for its Wagnerian elements. He had also written *Libuse*, but could find no producer. But in 1874, he had a large success with a light, popular opera, *The Two Widows*.

However, a severe whistling in the ears (graphically depicted in his autobiographical string quartet "From My Life") led to deafness by the end of that year, symptoms of tertiary syphilis. He continued to compose and wrote his orchestral masterpiece *Ma Vlast* (My Country) from 1874 to 1879. Three more operas were premiered successfully, including *Libuse*, but the last was *The Devil's Wall* (1882). By now, Smetana was seriously ill. The brain damage from syphilis led to madness, and he was confined to an asylum where he died. National mourning was proclaimed and he was given a burial at the Vyshehrad, one of the national sites depicted in *Má Vlast*. *—Joseph Stevenson*

ORCHESTRAL

Má Vlast (My Fatherland), symphonic poems (ca. 1872–1879)

Má Vlast is made up of six tone poems all relating to Smetana's beloved Bohemia. The composer was struck deaf early in 1874, just before beginning the first piece in the set, and thus composed the entire work unable to hear a single note of it. Although its individual components are sometimes performed and recorded separately, most commonly the second in the set, *The Moldau*, the composer intended them as a single entity, to be performed like a suite or symphony. Thus played, the six parts of the work require about 75 minutes. The first, *Vysehrad*, pertains to a huge, historic rock along the Vltava River, near Prague. It opens with harps intoning a stately theme, the music growing more grandly noble as it proceeds. The mood soon turns somewhat agitated and heroic, before a reprise of the opening closes out *Vysehrad*.

The next work, *Vltava* (The Moldau), begins with pairs of swirling flutes and clarinets depicting the two springs feeding the Moldau. Soon the famous main theme, based on the Swedish folk song *Ack, Värmland du sköna*, is presented. Horns and trumpets introduce a heroic mood to portray the Forest Hunt, which is followed by folklike music in the "Peasant Wedding." Subdued, nocturnal music permeates "Moonlight: Dance of the Water Nymphs," while "the Rapids" is vigorous and stormy. The river theme returns, but soon gives way to a reprise of the main *Vysehrad* theme.

Sárka portrays the famous female rebel resentful of male authority, who takes revenge on her unfaithful lover. The tempestuous opening depicts Sárka's anger, while the ensuing march music describes her lover, Ctirad, and his soldier-companions. The lyrical section that follows expresses Ctirad's love for Sárka, while the ensuing festive gaiety enacts the drunken revelry of the soldiers. The dramatic final section brilliantly depicts Sárka's slaughter of Ctirad and his men.

The fourth, *Bohemia's Woods and Meadows*, opens busily, but as if winding down, the music representing one's arrival in the country. In the ensuing calm, the mood subtly changes from playful to gossamer and mysterious, and then to festive, the last section portraying a peasant festival.

The final two works, *Tábor* and *Blanik*, are related both musically and programmatically. The city of *Tábor* was a fifteenth century Hussite stronghold, and the music here depicts the famous rebellion there. Smetana uses the theme from the Hussite chorale *Ye Who Are God's Warriors* and fashions a defiant, stirring, often heroic portrait of the ill-fated uprising. In the final piece, the same theme is used, but now to depict the defeated Hussites, who flee to Blanik mountain. There they sleep and eventually aid in the restoration of the Czech nation. The music is mostly pastoral in the first half and colorfully triumphant in the latter portion, especially in the return of the *Vysehrad* melody. *—Robert Cummings*

Recommended:

- ○ **Smetana: Má Vlast** / Kubelik (cond.), Boston SO / 1986 / DG 429183
- ○ **Smetana: My Country** / Neumann (cond.), Czech PO / Supraphon
- ○ **Smetana: Má Vlast** / Kubelik (cond.), Czech PO / 1990 / Supraphon 111208
- ○ **Smetana: Má Vlast** / Talich (cond.), Czech PO / 1990 / Koch 37032

OPERA

Dalibor (1867–1870)

Joseph Wenzig (1807–76) wrote several plays and opera librettos derived from events in Czech history. *Dalibor* was the first of two librettos he wrote for Smetana, the second being *Libuse*. Wenzig wrote both of these in German; they were translated into Czech by Erwin Spindler. Smetana initially felt that a German text would increase the chances of performance outside his homeland. The premiere took place as part of a celebration of the laying of the cornerstone for the new National Theater in Prague.

With *Dalibor*, Smetana took a path he felt was best for Czech music by incorporating ideas from recent trends in music, as would any progressive composer in any nation. Critics, however, felt that Czech opera should be based on Czech folk songs (much as the later Soviet authorities felt about Russian opera) and perceived *Dalibor* to be Wagnerian. Bad press affected attendance and the first run saw only five performances. Revivals in 1870 and 1879 fared no better; the opera achieved real success only after the death of the embittered composer, who felt *Dalibor* to be an excellent work. One problem was that the story prompted unfortunate comparisons with *Fidelio*.

Wenzig's libretto is based on the legend of the fifteenth century knight, Dalibor, who rebelled against the Burgrave of Ploskovice, who had killed Dalibor's best friend in a humiliating manner during a battle. Dalibor attacked the Burgrave's castle and killed him. During the trial, Milada, the Burgrave's sister, testifies against Dalibor, but is so impressed by the knight's courage she becomes ashamed of her brother's actions. She disguises herself as a male musician and comes to Dalibor in his prison cell in an attempt to release him.

Dalibor opens without an overture and plunges right into Dalibor's trial scene. The brief prelude introduces the most prominent theme of the opera, a rising minor scale with dotted rhythms that refers to Dalibor and was sketched two years before Smetana began the opera. Other themes are linked to King Vladislav and Milada, but only Dalibor's goes through the thematic transformation that betrays Smetana's familiarity with the works of Liszt. Smetana's use of his themes is un-Wagnerian in that they never combine to form a web of music in the orchestra. High points include the duet closing Act Two for Dalibor and Milada and two transformations of Dalibor's theme into the major mode, the first of these when he heroically enters the room at this trial, the second at his death, when he looks forward to joining his dead friend. *—John Palmer*

Synopsis:

Act One. People gather in the castle courtyard for news of the knight Dalibor's fate. One of the crowd, Jitka, an orphan for whom Dalibor has provided care, expresses her feelings and hopes for Dalibor: she is certain he will be released. King Vladislav arrives, accompanied by fanfares, and describes Dalibor's crime. Dalibor became entangled in disputes between members of the Council of Litomeøizc and their ally, the Burgrave of Ploskovice. The Burgrave's soldiers then attacked Dalibor's home and kidnapped his friend, a violinist named Zdenìk, who then suffers a humiliating death. Dalibor, in an act of vengeance, attack's the Burgrave's castle and manages to kill the Burgrave. Milada, the Burgrave's sister, tells the King of Dalibor's crimes and the knight is imprisoned and charged with disturbing the peace of the land, attacking the cast in Ploskovice and murdering the Burgrave.

The court calls Milada as a witness, and she describes the circumstances of her brother's death and calls for retribution. Jitka enters with her plea for clemency and a duet for Milada and Jitka ensues. Afterward, Dalibor himself enters and impresses all with his noble demeanor. Vladislav reiterates the charges to Dalibor and asks the knight to respond. Dalibor does not deny his actions, but tells the king of Zdenìk and how his friend was killed by the Burgrave because of a feud. Dalibor states that he would have avenged his friend's death under any circumstances, even if the king had stood in the way. The judges, who have already decided Dalibor must die, speak with the Vladislav.

As the officials deliberate, Dalibor expresses his lack of concern about his fate, for he no longer enjoys life now that Zdenìk is dead. Milada finds this way of thinking ridiculous. One of the judges delivers the verdict: Dalibor must languish in prison until he dies. Dalibor is pleased that he will finally see Zdenìk again. All assembled are astonished at his behavior. Milada, in particular, has been swayed by Dalibor and begs Vladislav to pardon him. Vladislav, however, points out the Dalibor has threatened the king, which is inexcusable. His sentence will stand. The king, his retinue and the crowd leave, and Milada and Jitka are alone. Milada tells Jitka of her confused feelings ("Jaká, jaká to bouøce òadra mi plní"). In a duet, Jitka tells Milada her plan to help Dalibor escape from the prison.

Act Two. Near an inn, while soldiers sing inside, Jitka and her sweetheart, Vítek, sing a duet, and then Jitka tells him how Milada has dressed as a young man and has used a harp to convince people to let her into the castle and find a job. The two continue singing as the soldiers come out of the tavern.

In a room in the castle, the commander of the king's castle guard, Budivoj, asks the jailer, Benes, about his new assistant, "a poor musician." Budivoj tells Benes to keep a close watch on Dalibor and leaves. Benes sings an aria about the difficulties of being a jailer. Milada enters, bringing food for Benes, her new boss. Benes leaves to find his old violin, leaving Milada alone to ponder, in a sweeping aria, the prospect of seeing Dalibor again. When Benes returns with the violin and a lamp, he asks Milada to take it to the prisoner. They both exit.

While sleeping, Dalibor has had a dream about Zdenìk. Now awake, he sings of his desire to be near his old friend. Milada enters to give Dalibor the violin. Dalibor is ecstatic about the instrument and sings out to the dead Zdenìk. After a moment, Dalibor notices the "boy" and asks who he is, whereupon Milada reveals her true identity and begs forgiveness for her earlier behavior. She tells him she is there to rescue him. In a duet, they pledge mutual faithfulness.

Act Three. Benes and Budivoj speak with the king, Budivoj about a potential uprising of Vladislav's people and Benes about his new assistant, who has disappeared, leaving behind money and a note asking him to keep quiet. The two leave the king, who then complains of the responsibilities of being a monarch. Vladislav's advisers tell him that Dalibor must be executed that very day. Hesitantly, the king gives the orders to Budivoj.

In the prison, Dalibor is now free from his chains and sings an aria about his eventual freedom ("Ha, ky´m to kouzlem"). He is about to play a signal on the violin, but is interrupted by the arrival of Budivoj and soldiers, who march Dalibor away.

That night, Milada, accompanied by Jitka, Vitek and a groups of soldiers, awaits Dalibor's signal. Instead, she hears a group of monks, and knows something has gone wrong. She then leads the soldiers into the castle. When the group returns, Dalibor carries the wounded Milada, who soon dies. When Budivoj comes out of the castle with his soldiers, Dalibor aggressively fights them, is wounded, and welcomes death so he may again be with Zdenìk and Milada. *—John Palmer*

Recommended:

○ **Smetana: Dalibor** / Kosler (cond.), Vodicka, Urbanová, Kusnjer / Supraphon 0077

Prodaná nevesta (The Bartered Bride) (1863–1870)

Bedřich Smetana's *The Bartered Bride* dates from the happiest, most musically fulfilling period in the composer's life. Authored in the 1860s, it reflected the full flowering of his compositional skills. He had previously written the historical opera *The Brandenburgers in Bohemia* and now desired to write a work that dealt with the Czech people. In that process, he tapped into Czech melodies that bloomed as he wrote. The libretto, by Karel Sabina, reflected the composer's desire to write an authentically Czech work, though Smetana ended up reshaping the opera several times. The first version contained spoken parts, which were converted to recitative by the final version. Ironically, while it is regarded at home as the essential Czech national opera, in other countries it is treated as a lighthearted folk opera. It's Czechness is based on Smetana's use of folk dance idioms and a more colloquial language, the rhythms of which fit the dance rhythms extremely well. There are very few ensemble numbers in the opera primarily because Sabina's libretto was not written with lines suitable for ensembles. Opening with a gorgeous, briskly paced overture, the music builds through running scales on the strings to bursts of exuberant melody on the winds, reeds, and brass. Act One opens on the Feast of St. Stephen; Marenka and Jenik declare their love for each other in a tender duet. Their love, though impassioned and sincere, seems doomed as Marenka's father has brokered her in marriage to Vasek, the dullish son of landowner Tobias Micha. In Act Two, Marenka meets Vasek—who doesn't realize who she is—and dissuades him from the marriage; meanwhile, the marriage broker Kecal persuades Jenik to accept marriage to a wealthy girl; he agrees on condition that Marenka marry the son of Tobias Micha. In Act Three, the village is host to a troupe of gypsy entertainers (whose performance includes the "Dance of the Comedians"). Vasek forsakes the arranged marriage in pursuit of a dancer; Marenka remains scornful of Jenik's seeming betrayal. Jenik's plan becomes clear in the final scene, when he is revealed to be Micha's long-lost elder son. All of the mismatched couples are sorted out and a family restored in a joyous finale. *The Bartered Bride* proved to be the only Czech opera to find a significant life far beyond Czech opera companies, particularly in Germany where, as *Die verkaufte Braut*, it was widely performed in German. It even entered the repertory of such renowned conductors as Rudolf Kempe, whose specialties usually extended to Wagner and Richard Strauss. *—Bruce Eder*

Synopsis:

Act One. The story is set in a nineteenth century Bohemian Village during annual springtime festivities. Alongside tavern grounds, villagers prepare for the celebrations of the coming festival. Marenka is unhappy because she fears her parents, Krusina and Ludmila, will agree to an arranged marriage to Vasek, son of Micha and his wife Hata. Marenka is in love with Jenik, who, he tells her in explaining his mysterious past to her, was driven out of his home by a nasty stepmother.

Kecal, the marriage broker, arrives with Marenka's parents and announces that arrangements have been made. Krusina inquires about which of Micha's two sons his daughter will marry. Kecal informs him it will be Vasek, the other son being a worthless drifter that has disappeared. When Kecal informs Marenka that a husband has been chosen for her, she tells him she has a lover, Jenik. Kecal eventually decides that he will talk with Jenik and offer him money to abandon pursuit of Marenka.

Act Two. Inside a room in the tavern Jenik argues for the importance of love over alcohol, while Kecal chooses money over either. Meanwhile, Marenka, without divulging her identity, tells the bashful and naïve Vasek that the girl he is to marry is in love with another and will likely have him done away with. Swayed, Vasek vows not to marry the chosen bride but is utterly beguiled by the young woman who has just warned him about her.

Kecal finds Jenik a difficult subject to bargain with, but eventually his offer of a large sum persuades Jenik to abandon his marital intentions. The wording of the marriage contract, however, must specify Marenka will marry the son of Micha and that Micha's debt to Krusina must be forgiven when the son and Marenka are married. Kecal agrees to all terms. Krusina is favorably impressed at first that Jenik has surrendered his chance at marriage to Marenka, but when he learns that he will receive 300 crowns as payment, he is disappointed in Jenik's callousness.

Act Three. Outside the tavern grounds Vasek worries about his fate, that he could be murdered if he marries the chosen bride. A circus troupe arrives and Vasek is charmed into playing the bear by an attractive Gypsy woman, Esmeralda, when Franta, who usually dresses in the bear costume, turns up drunk. When his parents arrive, Vasek informs them he will not marry the girl they have selected for him. But when he sees it is Marenka, he happily agrees.

Marenka becomes forlorn when she learns of Jenik's rejection of her for money. Jenik soon appears, but Marenka will not allow him to explain his actions, and when Kecal arrives with the cash, things look even worse for him. After Micha enters, however, he recognizes his long-lost son, Jenik. Hata, Micha's wife, recognizes him as the stepson she treated cruelly. Jenik informs Kecal that according to the contract he is the one to marry Marenka. He also informs his father that he is entitled to a share of the family farmland. Micha agrees and Kecal acknowledges he has been taken in. When it is announced by frightened boys that the "bear" (Vasek) has escaped from the circus, Hata leads him back home. Micha blesses the marriage of Marenka and Jenik and the story ends happily. *—Robert Cummings*

Recommended:

○ **The Bartered Bride** / Kosler (cond.), Beňačková, Dvorsky, Novak / Supraphon 103511

○ **The Bartered Bride** / Chalabala (cond.), Tikalova, Zidek, Haken / Supraphon 0040

KEYBOARD

Czech Dances, Books 1–2 (1877–1879)

Smetana's *14 Czech Dances* are the major keyboard works of his later career. They were published in two books; four polkas composed in 1877 appeared as *Book One* in 1879, and ten more dances, five of them with programmatic titles, were composed in 1879 and appeared over the next two years. In these works, Smetana achieved both a new depth of immersion in Czech national rhythms and a new degree of freedom in his treatment of those rhythms. The four polkas are much freer in their treatment of the polka rhythm than Smetana's earlier compositions in the genre, bearing much the same relationship to the polka as Chopin's mazurkas do to their folk dance models. Indeed, Smetana wrote to his publisher, "My efforts are directed towards idealizing the polka in particular, as Chopin did in his day with the mazurka." Nevertheless, Smetana's engagement with Czech dance rhythms here is more specific than Chopin's was, and more specific even than that of the younger Dvořák. "Whereas Dvořák gives his pieces just a general name 'Slavic Dances'...," Smetana pointed out, "we would show which dances with real names we Czechs have." The ten dances of *Book Two* are wonderfully vivid. Some of them represent animals or rural scenes, but all have sharp rhythmic profiles that Smetana thoroughly drives home even as he creates his free "idealized" dances. The Czech dances reflect the harmonic influence of Liszt and Wagner, and they feature an abundance of contrapuntal treatment that sometimes suggests the mix of naïve material and strict counterpoint in Beethoven's late works. If Smetana's chromaticism here is less lyrical than Chopin's, less sensual than Liszt's, his contribution to the formation of a true national style is unsurpassed. *—James Manheim*

Recommended:

○ **Smetana: Czech Dances** / Leichner / Panton 811337

Polkas (1840–1883)

The polka may bring to mind images of a Midwestern beer tent, but in the 1840s it was the talk of the town, the first true dance craze. Its origins are not Polish but Bohemian (the word polka is Czech for Polish woman), and from Czech lands it spread like wildfire through all the capitals of Europe. Many of Smetana's polkas date from the early phases of his career as a would-be Bohemian piano virtuoso in the 1840s and 1850s, just as his Czech consciousness was awakening (he spoke mostly German for the first four decades of his life), Smetana wrote more than two dozen polkas for piano in all, little-known but attractive counterparts to the Polish dance pieces of Chopin. Some of them are designated "poetic polkas," a notion that might cause Weird Al Yankovic to smile, but that gives an idea of what these works are like: they are not simple dance pieces, but predominantly lyrical miniatures (mostly around two minutes long) based on the polka rhythm with its end-of-the-measure kick—which the composer treats in a variety of inventive ways. Over time, Smetana became more and more interested in Czech national rhythms, and late in life he returned to the polka with four pieces, published as *Book One* of the *Czech Dances.* "My efforts," he wrote to his publisher, "are directed towards idealizing the polka in particular, as Chopin did in his day with the mazurka." These are slightly longer and decidedly more elaborate pieces than the earlier polkas, almost short fantasias on the polka idea, and they are worthy to stand beside any other dance-based piano music of the nineteenth century. *—James Manheim*

Recommended:

○ **Smetana: Polkas** / Schiff / Teldec 21261

CHAMBER MUSIC

Piano Trio in G minor, Op. 15 (1855; revised 1857)

The death of Smetana's daughter Bedriska was the emotional impetus behind the composition of the *Trio for Piano and Strings in G minor*, Op. 15. After Bedriska succumbed to scarlet fever on September 6, 1855, Smetana was devastated; the composer immersed himself in composition, producing the trio soon enough for it to be performed later that year. Critical response was negative and may have prompted Smetana to revise the piece two years later, despite the fact that Liszt praised the work when he heard it in 1856. It was the most significant piece of chamber music he had composed up to that time, but it was not published until 1879, in Hamburg.

The work is in three movements, all of which are in G minor. The first movement is intense and lyrical, and begins with the violin alone playing a theme on the dark G string. The theme's chromatic descent through a perfect fifth evokes a Baroque-era musical symbol for grief. In nineteenth century fashion, however, Smetana extends the melody before arriving at the secondary theme of this gloomy sonata-form movement. The second theme is brighter in character than the first, and this section is further lightened by upward chromatic shifts in harmony. The development section has a central high point, followed by meandering passages that give way to the recapitulation, which brings back the tragic mood.

In the ensuing Intermezzo movement we hear references to the first movement. Its principal theme, a polka, seems to suggest the playful Bedriska, although it is derived from the main theme of the first movement. The movement is divided into two *alternativo* sections, the first of which, pastoral in atmosphere, evokes Schumann. The second of these is more mournful and includes marchlike rhythms.

For the main theme of the rondo finale, Smetana borrows nearly 100 measures from his own *Piano Sonata in G minor* of 1846. He also uses a fugato figure from his *Characteristic Variations on a Czech Folksong.* Buzzing with restless energy, the rondo theme creates a stark contrast to the preceding Intermezzo. This energy, however, is interrupted by sad, lyrical episodes for the cello. Smetana creates rhythmic drive through the simultaneous sounding of duplets and triplets through long passages in the 6/8 time movement. When the secondary theme returns near the end, it is transformed into a funeral march, with drum-like figures as accompaniment. Perhaps surprisingly, the work ends in the major mode. *—John Palmer*

Recommended:

○ **Dvořák: "Dumky" Trio; Smetana: Piano Trio in G minor** / Borodin Trio / 1986 / Chandos 8445

○ **Smetana & Tchaikovsky Piano Trios** / Golub Kaplan Carr Trio / 1995 / Arabesque 6661

String Quartet No. 2 in D minor (1882–1883)

Smetana began working on his second string quartet in the summer of 1882, when it was clear that his mental state had begun to decay. Smetana's physician forbade him to compose at all, telling him it would make blood rush to his brain and cause insanity. Smetana defied his physician's orders, noting that "if I don't commit them (his ideas) to paper immediately, I can't remember how they were even half a day later."

The *String Quartet No. 2 in D minor* was finished on March 12, 1883, written only a few measures at a time due to his constantly feeling stunned and drowsy. Like the *Quartet No. 1 in E minor*, the *Quartet in D minor* has an autobiographical impetus, but the composer left fewer clues regarding what this was. In a tortured letter to Dr. Václav Zeleny´, Smetana explains, "The new quartet continues from where the first one ended, after the catastrophe. It introduces the swirl of music of a person who has lost his hearing."

Despite his miserable state, Smetana felt confident enough about the quartet to submit it for publication, which did not take place until 1889, after the composer's death. The brief but intense work has not been as popular as its older sibling.

In the *Second String Quartet* Smetana distanced himself from the traditional Classical-era forms. The composer himself acknowledged that the first movement was unconventional, noting that "it is quite unusual in style and difficult to follow, as if the whole movement were the product of whim...." The two principal themes are related. The first is a rising D minor scale in triplet eighth notes at an Allegro tempo. This transforms into the second theme, in F major, which also rises stepwise, but at a slower tempo and with dotted rhythms. A third idea, related very closely to the second, completes the first part of the movement, which thus far roughly follows the pattern of sonata form. The central section, however, is not developmental, but acts as a contrasting episode. When the themes return in the finale section of the movement, they do so in reverse order, the first theme de-emphasized and the harmony closing on F major. Some writers consider the close in the major mode to indicate Smetana's "triumph over adversity." For the second movement, Smetana drew on a 20-measure idea he had sketched in 1848–49. In overall form, the movement resembles a scherzo: the primary section is a polka with lively syncopation and the trio is a slower, graceful section in triple meter. The third movement is more intricate and animated, containing at times a frenetic energy amplified by an unusual succession of imitative and marchlike passages. It leads, without pause, directly into the tempestuous finale, a technically difficult and harmonically dissonant movement that would later please Arnold Schoenberg. *—John Palmer*

Recommended:

○ **Dvořák, Smetana: String Quartets** / Alban Berg Quartet / 1991 / EMI 54215

○ **Smetana: String Quartets 1 & 2** / Panocha Quartet / 1999 / Supraphon 3450

Daniel Smith

b. Sep. 11, 1939, New York, NY

Bassoonist

Daniel Smith is one of the world's most prominent bassoon soloists. He studied at the Manhattan School of Music, Columbia University, and the Mannes College of Music. Smith has recorded numerous discs, with repertoire ranging from Baroque concerti to contemporary music, including jazz with a quartet under his own leadership, ragtime, and crossover.

Daniel Smith is the first bassoonist to have recorded all 37 Vivaldi bassoon concertos, in recordings made with the English Chamber Orchestra and I Solisti di Zagreb for the label ASV. Smith's Vivaldi set was selected as the Best Concerto Recording of the Year by the Music Industry Association, awarded the *Penguin Guide*'s rosette rating, and was included in *Fanfare*'s annual "Want List." Smith has also recorded with the Royal Philharmonic Orchestra and the Caravaggio Ensemble.

Smith is also noted for his support of the creation of new concerti for his chosen instrument. He gave the United States West Coast premiere of Gunther Schuller's *Concerto for Contrabassoon and Orchestra* and the world premiere of Steve Gray's *Jazz Suite for Bassoon* with the Welsh Chamber Orchestra. Daniel Smith has performed solo recitals at New York's Lincoln Center and Carnegie Recital Hall, Wigmore Hall, the BBC Concert Hall, and the Tivoli Concert Hall in Copenhagen. *—AMG*

Recommended:

- ○ **Vivaldi: Bassoon Concertos, Vol. 1** / Ledger (cond.), Smith, English CO / 1996 / ASV 971
- ○ **Bassoon Bon-Bons** / Ledger, Stratta (conds.), Smith, Vignoles, Royal PO, English CO, Coull String Quartet / 1991 / ASV 2052

Gregg Smith

b. Aug. 21, 1931, Chicago, IL

Conductor

This noted conductor and gifted composer has contributed greatly to the development of contemporary music through the formation of his chamber choir and other musical activities. Smith enrolled at the University of California at Los Angeles, where he studied composition with Leonard Stein, Lukas Foss, and Ray Moreman and conducting with Fritz Zweig. In 1956, Smith earned his master's degree. Subsequently, he taught at Ithaca College, the State University of New York (S.U.N.Y.), Stony Brook, the Peabody Conservatory, Barnard College, and at the Manhattan School of Music.

In 1955, he founded the professional chamber choir known as the Gregg Smith Singers, at first based in Los Angeles and then moving to New York in 1970. This remarkably skilled ensemble has been responsible for many premieres of contemporary works, as well as revivals of early American music. Their repertoire has included the premieres of Igor Stravinsky's *Requiem Canticles* and William Duckworth's *Southern Harmony*; the complete choral works of Arnold Schoenberg and Elliott Carter; revivals of works by Charles Ives and William Billings; as well as pieces by Edwin London, Blas Galindo, Jorge Córdoba, Harold Blumenfeld, Irving Fine, Morton Gould, William Schuman, Ned Rorem, and other moderns; and classics by Giovanni Gabrieli and Heinrich Schütz. Their recording entitled *America Sings* traced American choral music from 1620 to the present. There were also many (now out-of-print) recordings made on the group's own label, GSS. Smith also worked as an editor for G. Schirmer publishers to put out a series of contemporary American choral works under the *Gregg Smith Choral Series*.

Smith's composition interests have primarily focused on the creation of vocal music. His output to date includes two operas; about 30 choral works, including *The Continental Harmonist, Ballet on William Billings for Chorus and Small Orchestra*; the exquisite *Magnificat*; more than 50 songs, hundreds of choral arrangements; and also instrumental works for chamber ensembles. His musical language is chiefly oriented toward tonal expression, but he employs serialist procedures, speech, and extended vocal techniques to achieve certain effects. *—"Blue Gene" Tyranny*

Recommended:

- ○ **A Christmas Festival** / Smith, Kostelanetz (conds.), Biggs, Curtin, Gregg Smith Singers, Andre Kostelanetz Orch. / 1999 / Sony 64354
- ○ **La Noche** / Smith (cond.), Rees, Gregg Smith Singers / 2001 / Newport 85639
- ○ **Duckworth: Southern Harmony** / Smith (cond.), Gregg Smith Singers / 1994 / Lovely Music 2033
- ○ **Billings: The Continental Harmonist** / Smith (cond.), Gregg Smith Singers, Adirondack CO / 1991 / Premier 1008
- ○ **I Hear America Singing** / Smith (cond.), Rees, Clark, Reuter, Dorsey, Gregg Smith Singers, Adirondack CO / 1996 / Vox 3037

Hopkinson Smith

b. 1946, New York, NY

Guitarist, Lutenist

As a teenager, Hopkinson Smith played classical guitar, but then he discovered the world of early music and began teaching himself to play the lute. He graduated with honors from Harvard in 1972 with a degree in musicology, which has served him well in his research on works written for early plucked instruments, such as the vihuela, theorbo, lute, and early guitars. He studied lute with Emilio Pujol in Catalonia and Eugen Dombois in Switzerland, and then worked with viola da gambist Jordi Savall to found the ensemble Hespèrion XX in the mid-1970s. He went on to spend ten years with the group, growing creatively as a chamber musician and finding it a good balance to his solo work. Since the mid-1980s, Smith has concentrated on his research and performance of solo works for his instruments, ranging from Renaissance dances and fantasias to Baroque composers Kapsberger, the Gaultier, Mouton, Sanz, and Weiss, to name just a few. His discography includes over 20 recordings of these works on the Astrée label. He has also recorded his own transcriptions of Bach's solo violin works in addition to Bach's lute works. Smith gives master classes throughout North and South America and Europe, but is on the faculty of the Schola Cantorum in Basel, Switzerland, where he makes his home. Smith's playing is frequently noted by reviewers for its tastefulness and expertise, while also being warm and always consciously expressive no matter what type of piece he is playing. *—Patsy Morita*

Recommended:

- ○ **Bach: L'oeuvre de Luth** / Smith / 2002 / Naive 3000
- ○ **Milan: El Maestro** / Smith / 1989 / Astree 7748
- ○ **Weiss: Pieces De Luth** / Smith / 1990 / Astree 8718
- ○ **Gaultier: Pièces de Luth** / Smith / 2000 / Astree 8830
- ○ **de Navaez: Les Seys Libros del Delphín de Música** / Smith / 1989 / Astree 8706
- ○ **Sanz: Instrucción de música sobre la guitarra española** / Smith / 2000 / Astree 8828
- ○ **Kapsperger: Libro primo d'intavolatura di lauto** / Smith / 2000 / Astree 8827

Elisabeth Söderström

b. May 7, 1927, Stockholm, Sweden

Soprano

An artist of great intelligence and musical perception, Elisabeth Söderström grew from a promising young lyric soprano to a sovereign artist able to dominate a wide selection of lyric and spinto roles for three decades. Initially underrated (save by those who knew her well), she advanced to being the delight of many of her era's most distinguished conductors. Her recital repertory ranged through the great Austro-German composers, a fruitful assortment of Scandinavians, Benjamin Britten and other important English composers, substantial numbers of Czech and other Central and Eastern Europeans, and a clutch of Russians. She also had a penchant for parlor songs, sometimes slightly naughty. With a voice best described as attractive rather than ravishing, she managed to establish herself as a notable singer of Mozart and Strauss and her performances of Janáček's leading ladies were standard setting.

Söderström's father was Swedish, her mother Russian. She trained with the celebrated coloratura soprano Adelaïde von Skilondz, star of the St. Petersburg Imperial Opera. After studying at the Royal Academy of Music and Opera School in her native Stockholm, Söderström made her debut at the age of 20 at the Drottningholm Court Theatre as Bastienne. She was subsequently engaged by the Swedish Royal Opera, where she remained a member for decades, singing such roles as Louise, Violetta, Mimì, Euridice; the heroines of *Les contes d'Hoffman*, Pamina, all three soprano principals in *Rosenkavalier*, Tatiana, and the eponymous characters of Janáček. Söderström made her Salzburg debut in 1955, singing Ighino in Pfitzner's *Palestrina*. She first sang at England's Glyndebourne Festival in 1957 and remained there for more than two decades, singing roles as light as Susanna and as heroic as Leonore.

In 1959, Söderström made her first appearance at the Metropolitan Opera as Susanna. Evidence that management at the various venues she visited (the Metropolitan in particular) did not know quite what to do with her gifts was seen in the fact that in that very same year, 1959, she performed Sophie at the Metropolitan, Octavian at Glyndebourne, and the Marschallin at Stockholm. Only with later engagements did the Met understand her protean talent. In 1960, Söderström made her first appearance at Covent Garden singing Daisy Doody in Karl-Birger Blomdahl's *Aniara* with the Stockholm Opera.

If the Metropolitan failed to capitalize on Söderström's abilities until a second round of engagements from 1983 to 1987, the rest of the opera world benefited during the interim from acquaintance with a singing actress of the first rank. Söderström's Australian debut came in 1982 when she performed one of her signature Janáček roles, Emilia Marty, in *Adelaide*. In addition to her appearances in contemporary works by Henze and Ligeti, she had become a welcome guest in Vienna and continued to flourish in the ensemble atmosphere of Glyndebourne, winning special praise for her Frau Storch in Strauss' *Intermezzo* and for the Countess in the same composer's *Capriccio*.

Söderström's skills as a recitalist and concert singer were under continual refinement. Her recording of Beethoven's *Missa Solemnis* under Otto Klemperer was justly applauded, as was her role in Sir Simon Rattle's recording of Britten's *War Requiem*. Her winning presence in recital inevitably meant an evening of communicative singing. Her several volumes of Russian song recorded with Vladimir Ashkenazy added immeasurably to Western understanding of this rich, but too seldom performed repertory. Likewise, her explorations of Scandinavian song opened new vistas to those who heard her live performances and listened to her recordings. *—Erik Eriksson*

Recommended:

- ○ **Söderström sings Liszt, Schubert, Tchaikovsky, etc.** / Soderstrom, Vignoles, Isepp / BBC 4132
- ○ **Orhangen** / Soderstrom, Pehrsson, Sund, Jonsson, Von Bahr / 1981 / Bis 187
- ○ **Elisabeth Söderström & Kerstin Meyer** / Soderstrom, Eyron, Meyer / 1974 / Bis 17
- ○ **Debussy: Pelléas et Mélisande** / Boulez (cond.), Soderstrom, Minton, Wicks, McIntyr, Royal Opera House Orch. Covent Garden / 1991 / Sony 47265

Vladimir Sofronitsky

b. May 8, 1901, St. Petersburg, Russia, **d.** Aug. 29, 1961, Moscow, USSR
Pianist

Vladimir Sofronitsky was among the greatest Russian pianists of the twentieth century, and, while he had become a somewhat less prominent figure following his death, he must be still considered in the company of Richter, Gilels, and Yudina. In his time, Sofronitsky became widely recognized as the leading interpreter of and authority on the music of Scriabin in Eastern Europe. He was also highly praised for his interpretations of the piano works of Robert Schumann and he was a highly respected teacher.

His father, a successful physicist, took the family to Warsaw in 1903, where the young Sofronitsky would grow up and develop his musical skills. As a child, he showed unusual talent on the piano and his parents arranged for studies with A. Lebedeva-Getsevich and Aleksander Michalowski. At the age of 15, Sofronitsky enrolled at the St. Petersburg Conservatory, where he studied under Leonid Nikolayev. Maria Yudina was also a student at the conservatory and soon entered the same class, where she remained with Sofronitsky for a year. She would report that he was already playing with remarkable interpretive insight and virtuosic skills. Sofronitsky also took classes in composition at the conservatory from Maximilian Steinberg. In 1920, Sofronitsky married the oldest daughter of Scriabin, Elena. While he had already divulged a sympathy for the piano music of the recently deceased mystic composer—as attested by Yudina—he now had a greater intellectual and emotional connection to Scriabin's works through his wife, also a talented pianist, and through the Scriabin in-laws. Sofronitsky graduated from the conservatory in 1921, giving, among other works in his recital, a performance of the Liszt *Sonata in B minor*, which much of the faculty and student body found both thrilling and thought-provoking. Throughout most of the 1920s, Sofronitsky built up a brilliant career as a concert pianist in Russia. His first tour abroad came in 1928 and after playing in Paris, he decided to stay on. In the end, he remained two years, then returned to his Leningrad. Sofronitsky joined the faculty at the Leningrad Conservatory in 1936 and remained there until the Nazis' infamous siege of the city. He escaped by plane to Moscow in 1942 and immediately began teaching at the conservatory there. He gave many performances at the Scriabin Museum in Moscow, especially during the latter part of his career. He gradually developed alcohol and drug addictions, and in his last years his pianistic skills declined noticeably.

Sofronitsky made a fair number of recordings in the last two decades of his life, but a relatively paltry number compared with the efforts of Richter and Gilels. Not surprisingly, Sofronitsky recorded a large number of Scriabin works and also compositions by Chopin, Rachmaninov, Schumann, Prokofiev, and others. His recorded performances from the 1940s are generally more representative than those from the last decade. *—Robert Cummings*

Recommended:

- ○ **Russian Treasure** / Sofronitsky / 1993 / Multisonic 310181
- ○ **Chopin Commemoration Concert** / Sofronitsky / Arkadia 78571
- ○ **Sofronitsky, Vol. 15** / Sofronitsky / Arlecchino 132
- ○ **Scriabin: Vol. 14** / Sofronitsky / Arlecchino 119
- ○ **Sofronitsky Plays Beethoven, Prokofiev, Liszt, Chopin** / Sofronitsky / Urania 4211

Solage

b. 1300s, France (?), **d.** 1300s (?), France (?)
Composer: Vocal

Sometimes a music historian must act like an archaeologist. Absolutely no known archival documents, for instance, give any biographical information about a late fourteenth century French composer named Solage. Yet he must have been an eminent figure in French royal circles. One important music manuscript from late in the century credits him with at least a tenth of all its music. So from this fragment of an artifact, the historian makes whatever implications are possible. Something of Solage's life and circumstances may be inferred from the manuscript itself. The so-called *Chantilly Codex*, a rich presentation manuscript of 100 French songs and motets from the last decades of the century, breathes the essence of French royal and noble courtly life. Though it was copied by an expatriate Italian scribe, it probably was intended for the courts of the Counts of Foix, Gaston Fébus, and his son Mathieu, or for the fabulously wealthy court of the schismatic Popes Clement VII and Benedict XIII in Avignon. For Solage to feature so prominently in the music of these courts, he would have to move in very high circles indeed.

Further morsels of tantalizing suggestions may be found in Solage's ten or 12 pieces of music themselves. All bear traces of the late fourteenth century French high and cultured style of the *ars subtilior*. Two of them indicate Solage probably lived in Paris in the 1370s: his chanson *Plusieurs gens voy* makes fun of Parisian fashions (and of a particular lady named "Jacquete"), while his wildly chromatic *Rondeau Fumeux fume* alludes to a fashionable Parisian society of intellectuals including poet Eustache Deschamps. But by around 1380, Solage seems to have left Paris to serve Duke Jean de Berry (also known for his patronage of the *Tres Riches Heures*). Two of his ten chansons were most likely composed for the wedding of Duke Jean's son to Catherine (the sister of the King of France); a third, his *S'aincy estoit*, praises the Duke in person. A further chanson mentions the god Phoebus, perhaps a reference to Gaston Fébus, who arranged a marriage for the Duke of Berry. Solage apparently maintained his close ties with the French royal family, as well. *Joieux de cuer* contains textual allusions to Louis, the Duke of Orléans, and his wife, the daughter of Giangalleazo Visconti of Milan. *—Timothy Dickey*

VOCAL

Fumeux fume par fumée, rondeau for 3 voices (1389)

A fascinating aspect of the legend of Gaston Febus, as concerns his patronage of the arts, is that he seems to have been utterly secular in orientation. He built no churches and none of the surviving music from his court is religious in theme. The ars subtilior, the style of music that was mostly composed at Febus' court, is a quintessentially secular musical art that flowered even as news spread of the deep corruption of the clerical elite in Europe, like early twentieth century art. Its stylistic excesses seem to stem from a worldly, fatalistic despair. It is an art of decadence par excellence; an equivalent now might be anthems for aggressive corporations. Fatalistic withdrawal from the world into pleasures is certainly an attitude that proliferates in dark times. *Fumeux fume* is a remarkably myriad document in that sense. The extremely cryptic, alliterative text seems to refer the piece to the mysterious "society of smokers," a late medieval semisecret club of men who gathered to smoke tobacco and hashish, and perhaps other substances as well. Not much is known of Solage except that he worked in several of the courts where the ars subtilior was developed. His marginal position in the musical world and his extremely strange music certainly don't contradict the notion that he was one of the mysterious smokers. *Fumeux fume* is also one of the key examples of the ars subtilior, perhaps the most famous of them all. Discussions of ars subtilior come circling back to *Fumeux fume* with orbital regularity and inevitability. It is certainly a strange, mysterious piece. The salient and most noticeable feature is its blistering, relentless chromaticism. After the slightly tamed beginning, barely a note passes that isn't rubbing with some kind of evil, burning friction against another. To make it still stranger, the tessitura is all in the low tenor to bass range, causing the piece to dissolves itself into a pure, absolute expression of its edgy, harmonic conditions. *—Donato Mancini*

Recommended:

- ○ **The Renaissance in Music** / Huelgas Ens. / 1999 / Sony 60992
- ○ **Ars Magis Subtiliter: Secular Music of the Chantilly Codex** / P.A.N. Ensemble / 1989 / New Albion 021

Antonio Soler

b. Dec. 3, 1729, Olot, Gerona, Spain, **d.** Dec. 20, 1783, El Escorial, Spain
Composer: Keyboard

Antonio Francisco Javier Jose Soler was an eighteenth century Catalan composer, priest, monk, student, teacher, mathematician, inventor, and organist. His life was spent serving both the Catholic Church and music. He was a prolific composer with over 400 compositions credited to him by the time of his death at age 54. Soler spent most of his life at monasteries, particularly El Escorial, the magnificent royal palace, chapel, and monastery built by King Philip II outside of Madrid two centuries earlier.

Soler apparently came from a musical family. His brother, Mateu, played bassoon in the monastery of Las Descalzas Reales and then in the court of Carlos III, and finally in the Capilla Real. His musical training began at a very early age. In 1736, he became a student at the Benedictine monastery choir school at Montserrat where he learned organ and composition. Between 1752 and 1757, while in his early twenties, Soler studied with Domenico Scarlatti, the Italian composer who served the Spanish court of Ferdinand VI and Maria Barbara.

Prior to going to El Escorial, where he spent the rest of his life, Soler was the maestro de capilla at Lerida and was ordained subdeacon in 1752. Later that same year, he joined the Hieronymite order of monks at El Escorial monastery and professed to the order in 1753.

Soler performed many duties at El Escorial. In 1757, he became maestro de capilla. In addition, he performed as first organist, wrote much of the church music, and taught music. Perhaps his most prestigious student was the son of Carlos III, Don Gabriel de Bourbon. Soler taught the young Don Gabriel keyboard and many of the Soler's harpsichord sonatas were written for him.

It is difficult for most to grasp Soler's level of productivity, particularly in light of his many other duties and interests. His musical compositions included over 120 sonatas for harpsichord, six quintets for organ and strings, six double organ concertos, 10 masses, five requiems, 132 villancicos, and many other works. His most famous was a sonata for harpsichord entitled *Fandango.*

Soler also wrote a treatise on harmony, *Llave de la Modulación* (1762) whose concepts remain valid today. This treatise, however, caused considerable controversy and rebuke by some of his peers. These criticisms caused Soler such dismay that in 1765, he responded with a written retort, *Satisfacción a los reparos precisos*, which spanned 67 pages and was supported by such noted authorities as Morales, Palestrina, and Scarlatti. The controversy did not end until a final defense was provided in Jose Vila's *Respuestra y dictamen* in 1766.

He developed another treatise in 1771 that demonstrated his interest and skill in mathematics. This book was on Castilian and Catalan currency exchange and was published in honor of Carlos III. Soler was a man of other talents in addition to those mentioned. He invented a tuning box that was used to demonstrate differences between tones and semitones to Don Gabriel. He was also expert in organ design and construction. In 1776, he developed the specifications for an organ for the Malaga Cathedral. *—Bruce Lundgren*

KEYBOARD

Six Concertos for 2 organs (ca. 1766–1783)

Antonio Soler produced a large output that mainly consisted of sacred and keyboard compositions. In the latter genre, there are over 120 sonatas, organ works, and these *Six Concerti.* Though his keyboard compositions are usually difficult to date, much is known about the genesis and circumstances of the last: they almost certainly come from the period 1768–72, when Soler and Prince Gabriel (brother of Carlos IV) performed them at the latter's Escorial palace. The Prince began studies with the composer in 1766 and it was for him that Soler wrote these concerti, which the pair probably played on harpsichords since the two organs at the palace chapel were situated too distantly for performance. Some musicologists insist that since organos in the work's title seems to refer to keyboard instruments in general, these concerti were not necessarily intended for organ. Soler's six works share similarities: all but the three-movement *Second* are in two movements, and all feature a minuet. The *Second* in A minor also stands apart from the others in that its minuet contains a trio instead of variations, as in the other five. Though Soler could be bolder in his modulations than his mentor Scarlatti (as evidenced by the writing in *No. 4*), his harmonies throughout the set are a bit more conservative. The works, too, are not technically demanding. If the *Second* is the oddball in the group, it is also surely the jewel. Its opening Andante has a festive regality about its music and is livelier than its marking suggests. The ensuing Allegro is graceful in its busy, almost hurried manner, and the concluding minuet features colorful harmonies in its stately but slightly awkward gait. The *Third* in G major has a graceful nonchalance in its opening Andantino, while its ensuing minuet is jaunty and playful. The *Sixth* in D major features a hearty celebratory manner in its Allegro theme that subtly contrasts with pensive music, marked Andante. The *Sixth* also contains the set's most famous and most frequently recorded movement, the so-nicknamed "Emperor's Fanfare," a joyous and festive minuet with a bit of Spanish pomp. The other concerti—in C major (*No. 1*), in F major (*No. 4*), and in A major (*No. 5*)—are also worthwhile creations. Often harpsichords and clavichords, and even pianos—or sometimes combinations of these instruments—are used in performances and recordings of these works. *—Robert Cummings*

Recommended:

○ **Soler: Concertos For Two Organs** / Koopman, Mathot / Erato 45741

Fandango for keyboard in D minor (ca. 1770)

The basic question is not when the *Fandango in D minor* was written, but whether Soler was the composer. Period scholars (early Classical period, of Iberian concentration) remain divided about its authenticity, although no one disputes the work's brilliance or prodigies of invention, given that it lasts 10 to 12 minutes, depending on the performing artist. Samuel Rubio and Frederick Marvin assigned it a catalog number: S. 146 and M. 1A, respectively. But Rubio stated in his 1980 catalog that "we doubt seriously the paternity of Soler," citing as evidence "a substantially identical ostinato" by another (albeit obscure) composer, "in a *Fandango* with variations for the fortepiano."

Although pianists have and do play Padre Soler's *Fandango* (the Escorial owned at least one early fortepiano while Soler lived and worked there), the work was virtually unknown to twentieth century listeners until Rafael Puyana featured it on a Philips stereodisc of Baroque harpsichord music. Various colleagues followed suit. In 1963, furthermore, Anthony Tudor choreographed a ballet to the music that entered the American Ballet Theatre repertoire two decades later. The virtual craze subsided in time, but not the power of a work that obeys the basic rules of a quick-moving, minor-key folk dance in triple-meter, with alternating measures of tonic and dominant harmony in the bass line, above which the melody is elaborated. The nature, extent, and expressive intensification, however, are what make Soler's version singular.

The fandango first appeared in the early eighteenth century, later on with regional derivations—the malagueña, granadina, murciana, and rondeña, named for their places of origin. But flamenco was the taproot, since fandangos could be sung as well as danced. What Soler may have done was borrow or adapt an existing bass line. Pianist Santiago Rodriguez, who has played the work often as well as recorded it, remembers that it sounded "vaguely familiar" when he first studied the music—"a walking bass, similar to a street musician's, simple without being provocative." The right-hand elaboration, however, is genius. Soler stated the principal subject after a page of accompaniment that ends in a double-bar, and thereafter elaborated it at extraordinary length (not as a theme and variations, which Rubio and some others have postulated, but rather as a fantasia), with a brief F major section in the middle, before D minor returns. At this point the notation becomes a steady series of 16th notes—a developing frenzy, in effect, during the last four pages—that ends in a clearly defined coda. Rodriguez has likened this to flamenco dancers starting oppositely and finally meeting, with an implicit sexual tension expressed in both tempo and rhythm. *—Roger Dettmer*

Recommended:

○ **Soler: Fandango; 9 Sonates** / Ross / 1990 / Erato 45435

Keyboard Sonatas (ca. 1766–1783)

It is remarkable that works of such brilliance and charm as Soler's 120 keyboard sonatas were neglected for so long —and that they were conceived by a monk who rarely left the cloisters of the gloomy monastery of El Escorial near Madrid where he was maestro de capilla. Less unexpected is their debt to the sonatas of Domenico Scarlatti; Soler studied with the Italian master, who served in Spain as harpsichord teacher to King John V's daughter Maria Barbara from 1729 until his death in 1757.

Soler's life spanned the period of change and innovation that occurred between the Baroque and Classical eras. Towards the end of the eighteenth century the newly invented pianoforte was becoming established, and it was not long before it would virtually supplant the harpsichord. Most of Soler's sonatas are clearly specific to the earlier instrument, though many sound effective on the piano and some may well have been written for it. There are also a few preludes and fugues. (The frequently played *Fandango*, R. 464, is now thought to be a misattribution.) It would be a mistake, however, to think of Soler's works as mere imitations of Scarlatti's pathbreaking keyboard sonatas. His forms are more varied than those of Scarlatti's later sonatas, and his sonatas show considerable harmonic and melodic originality. Most of them are in a single movement though a few have three, or even four, movements.

Unfortunately some confusion still exists regarding the authentication of Soler's works. Some were derived from doubtful sources by the Cuban pianist and composer Joaquín Nin (1879–1949) but these, and a few others that occasionally appeared as encores, were casually accepted by both musicians and audiences until the completion between 1957 and 1972 of Fr. Samuel Rubio's four-volume *Critical Catalogue of Soler's Works.* Many still remain unpublished. It is debatable whether Soler's more formal sacred works will achieve the distinction now accorded to his keyboard sonatas, which have won a place in the virtuoso repertory of the harpsichord, and, indeed, the piano. In 1991 the Dutch harpsichordist Bob van Asperen completed a 12-CD recording of the sonatas for EMI Classics. *—Roy Brewer*

Recommended:

○ **Soler: Sonatas** / Hinrichs / 1999 / EMI 56940

Solomon (Solomon Cutner)

b. Sep. 8, 1902, London, England, **d.** Feb. 2, 1988, London, England
Pianist

The English-born Solomon (the only name he ever used in his professional life) enjoyed two separate, successful careers as a pianist. From the age of eight until his early teens, he was one of the most celebrated child prodigies of his era—a national phenomenon in England right up until the time of the First World War. However, he disappeared from the musical scene for a number of years, emerging again in the late 1920s as a mature player; this second, now international, career would last through the Second World War and into the 1950's.

Solomon was born in London, the son of an impoverished tailor from the city's East End. At the age of seven, he astonished all of the adults around him by playing his own piano arrangement of Tchaikovsky's *1812 Overture*. He began studying with Mathilde Verne, a one time student of Clara Schumann. He made his formal concert debut in 1910, playing the Tchaikovsky *Piano Concerto No. 1*, and became an overnight sensation. However, the extensive touring, concertizing, and study proved to be too much, and he found himself loathing his instrument by the age of 15. On the advice of the conductor, Sir Henry Wood, he retreated from performance and immersed himself in study, now removed from the pressures of his career; he would not return to the concert scene until the age of 21.

His playing as an adult was acclaimed for its clarity, brilliance, and overall poetic feeling. He was particularly respected by his fellow musicians for his immaculate pianism, and the easy, unobtrusive virtuosity of his work. His ego was virtually non-existent in concert, and his performances were, virtually without exception, a stunningly clear expression of the composer's intentions.

Solomon was well known for performances of the Beethoven sonatas and piano concertos, though he never did record them all. He was also renowned for his Mozart, Chopin, Brahms, and Debussy, as well as early twentieth century works such as Sir Arthur Bliss's Piano Concerto, which he premiered at the 1939 World's Fair in New York and later recorded for EMI. A plan to record the Beethoven concertos with the Philharmonia Orchestra under Wilhelm Furtwängler proved unsuccessful; the pianist objected to working with Furtwängler due to the latter's activities in Germany during the Nazi regime. In 1955, Solomon became part of a very promising piano trio with violinist Zino Francescatti and cellist Pierre Fournier, but it was not to last. In 1956, while on vacation in France, he suffered a stroke that left him paralyzed on his right side, bringing his career to an end.

His recordings, which date from the 1930s, were done for EMI and are all of interest; they have begun to appear on compact disc, either directly through EMI or under license to the Testament label. Despite the onset of his stroke in 1956, Solomon recorded a handful of works in stereo, but whether in stereo or mono, his recordings are all worth hearing, the clarity of his playing overcoming any seeming technical shortcomings in the recordings themselves. His performance of Beethoven's *Moonlight Sonata*, in particular, is notable for its poetic lyricism and natural, unforced passion. —*Bruce Eder*

Recommended:

- ○ **Piano Master: Solomon** / Solomon / Pearl 0038
- ○ **Tchaikovsky: Concerto 1; Liszt & Chopin: Piano Works** / Harty (cond.), Solomon, Halle Orch. / 2002 / Naxos 110680
- ○ **Beethoven: Concerto 3; Bliss: Concerto** / Boult (cond.), Solomon, BBCSO, Liverpool PO / 2002 / Naxos 16822
- ○ **Beethoven: Sonatas Opp 90–111** / Solomon / 1993 / EMI 64708

Georg Solti

b. Oct. 21, 1912, Budapest, Hungary, **d.** Sep. 5, 1997, Antibes, France
Conductor

Solti's interpretations held more than surface excitement. In conducting Beethoven, for example, he long held that the symphonies should be played with all their repeats to maintain their structural integrity, and he carefully rethought his approach to tempo, rhythm, and balance in those works toward the end of his life.

Solti began as a pianist, commencing his studies at age six and making his first public appearance at 12. When he was 13 he enrolled at Budapest's Franz Liszt Academy of Music, studying piano mainly with Dohnányi and, for a very short time, Bartók. He also took composition courses with Kodály. Although he aspired to be a concert pianist, upon graduating from the academy when he was 18 he took a job as répétiteur at the Budapest Opera. This practical opera experience enabled him to serve as an assistant at the Salzburg Festival to Bruno Walter in 1935 and Arturo Toscanini in 1936 and 1937. In 1938, he made his own conducting debut—by all accounts a brilliant performance—in a Budapest Opera production of Mozart's *Le nozze di Figaro*. He was Jewish, and rising anti-Semitism drove him to Switzerland in 1939, where he supported himself mainly as a concert pianist; he couldn't obtain a labor permit as a conductor. In 1942 he won the Concours International de Piano in Geneva, but it wasn't until 1944 that he had a serious chance to take up the baton again, in guest appearances with the Swiss Radio Orchestra.

In 1946, the American occupying forces invited Solti to conduct *Fidelio* at the Bavarian State Opera. Almost immediately Solti was appointed the company's general music director, a post he held until 1952; in that year he assumed the duties of general music director in Frankfurt, conducting opera productions and symphonic concerts. He also began making a name for himself in America, through appearances with the San Francisco Opera, Chicago Symphony, New York Philharmonic, and, in 1960, the Metropolitan Opera. He had made his London Covent Garden debut in 1959, and in 1961 the Royal Opera House engaged him as music director. Solti greatly improved the company's orchestral standards during his term, which lasted until 1971.

Solti made his most significant contribution during this period on LP, with the first stereo recording (for Decca) of Wagner's entire *Ring* cycle, completed in 1966. Even greater acclaim followed him as director of the Chicago Symphony, from 1969 to 1991. Yet Solti spent fairly little time in Chicago; as was becoming the norm, he held major simultaneous posts on two continents. He was music advisor to the Paris Opera 1971–73, music director of the Orchestre de Paris 1972–75 (a group he took to China in 1974), and principal conductor and artistic director of the London Philharmonic 1979–83. European guest stints included conducting the Bayreuth Festival's *Ring* cycle in 1983, marking the 100th anniversary of Wagner's death.

In 1972 he became a British subject and received his official knighthood; under the circumstances, he also sanctioned the pronunciation of his first name as "George," although he retained the German spelling.

Solti was regarded as, above all, a superb Wagnerian. His performances and countless recordings of other nineteenth century German and Austrian music were also well-regarded, as were his Verdi and his frequent forays into such twentieth century repertory as Bartók, Shostakovich, and Stravinsky. Solti served as a strong advocate for such new works as Hans Werner Henze's *Heliogabalus Imperator*, David Del Tredici's *Final Alice*, and Michael Tippett's *Symphony No. 4*, all of which he premiered in Chicago. —*James Reel*

Recommended:

- ○ **Wagner: Das Rheingold** / Solti (cond.), Flagstad, London, Kmentt, Wachter, Vienna PO / 1997 / London 455556
- ○ **Beethoven: Symphony 9** / Solti (cond.), Hillis, Lorengar, Minton, Burrows, Talvela, Chicago SO & Chorus / 1999 / London 460622
- ○ **Bach: Mass in B minor** / Solti (cond.), Hillis, Otter, Lott, Blochwitzp, Chicago SO & Chorus / 1991 / Decca 430353
- ○ **Mephisto Magic** / Solti (cond.), Kaptain, Chicago SO / 1994 / London 443444
- ○ **Haydn: The Creation** / Solti (cond.), Hillis, Morris, Burrowes, Nimsgern, Chicago SO & Chorus / 1992 / London 430739
- ○ **Bartók: Sonata for 2 Pianos & Percussion; Brahms: Variations on a Theme by Haydn** / Solti, Perahia, Corkhill, Glennie / 1988 / CBS 42625
- ○ **The Last Recording** / Solti (cond.), Agache, Daroczy, Budapest Festival Orch. / 1998 / London 458929
- ○ **Wagner: Der Ring des Nibelungen** / Solti (cond.), Flagstad, Nilsson, Sutherland, Fischer-Dieskau, Vienna PO / 1997 / Decca 455555

Fernando Sor

b. Feb. 13, 1778, Barcelona, Spain, **d.** Jul. 10, 1839, Paris, France
Composer: Chamber Music

Spanish composer Fernando Sor (originally Sors), despite having composed prolifically for various vocal and instrumental ensembles, is remembered today chiefly as a virtuoso guitarist whose hundred-plus compositions for that instrument constitute a vital part of its concert repertory. While the exact date of Sor's birth remains unknown, he is known to have been born in Barcelona and baptized on Valentine's Day in the year 1778. Of Catalan ancestry, Sor attended the choir school at Montserrat monastery and later enrolled in Barcelona's military academy. After the production of his opera *Telemaco nell'isola de Calipso* in 1797 he moved to Madrid, where he served in a number of minor administrative positions and continued to compose privately. During the French invasion of 1808 Sor's military background and patriotism roused him to fight against the invaders, though by 1810 he had resigned himself to the presence of the new regime; when the French withdrew three years later Sor opted, along with countless other Spanish artists and intellectuals, to return to Paris with them.

After two years of teaching guitar and performing in various Parisian venues, Sor moved to London and remained there for eight years (1815–23). Many of his works were published there, and his thirty-three Italian vocal ariettas (published in groups of three) made a particularly strong impact. Sor also gained fame after directing his energies toward the ballet; *Cendrillon* (1822) achieved the most favorable critical and public response and was successfully transplanted to Paris in 1822. When the Bolshoi theater in Moscow showed an interest in the work for the 1823 season, Sor accompanied the lead dancers to Moscow. He limited his compositional activities to music for the guitar while staying in Russia, and by the time he returned to Paris in 1826 he had several works for the instrument ready for publication and had completed much of the work on a *Méthode pour la guitare*, eventually published in Paris in 1830. Except for occasional trips abroad, such as a journey to London in 1828 to oversee production of a new ballet, *Hassan et le calife*, Sor remained in Paris, composing and teaching guitar, until his death in 1839.

Much of Sor's music that has survived (two symphonies, three string quartets and any number of smaller pieces have been lost since his death) has been abandoned by performers, but his music for the guitar lives on. Much of his reputation is based on the continued use of his *Méthode* by teachers and students of classical guitar. Sor's musical style derives largely from an awareness of the late eighteenth century German masters (in particular Haydn); his guitar music, with its independent voices and occasionally contrapuntal textures, shows a tendency to move away from the largely chordal textures that had been common up to that point. *—Blair Johnston*

Overview of Works

By the time he began his extensive tours throughout Europe as a famous guitar recitalist, Sor was already an international celebrity as a composer, with ballets, songs, and an opera, *Telemaco en la Isla de Calipso* (1797), to his credit; but it is mainly by over 60 solos and duets for guitar that he is now known. Though he was a Spanish composer, there is little typically Iberian about his works for guitar. As well as being a virtuoso, Sor was an eminent teacher and in 1830 wrote the first thoroughly detailed method for the guitar incorporating a new approach to the instrument. The instrument for which Sor composed was constructed on basically similar lines to those now widely known as "classical" or "Spanish" guitars, with six single strings, normally tuned to E (or D), A, d, g, b, and e'. It is played with the fingers and capable of a louder, more resonant sound than its predecessors.

Sor's output can broadly be separated into works he played in his own recitals and the shorter, easier pieces written for beginners or amateurs. The former are expressive, melodious and, for their time, remarkably original in conception. The latter, such as the polonaises, rondos, fantasias, and divertimenti, are similar in form and style to other nineteenth century guitar composers such as Carulli, Carcassi, Diabelli, and Guiliani though, since they are more adventurous, have worn better. Nevertheless Sor would probably have been quickly forgotten were it not for the nineteenth and twentieth century revival of interest in the guitar, which resulted in frequent republication. The legendary guitarist Andrés Segovia included not only Sor's more extended works in his repertory, but also many of the shorter pieces, revealing their graceful, delicate qualities to new generations of aspiring guitarists.

Sor's most durable contribution to the long history of the guitar was to show how its repertory could be developed in new directions. Earlier and more traditional playing techniques tend to concentrate mainly on chordal strumming, rapid scale passages and elaborate ornamentation which do not fully exploit the possibility of writing structured melodies in several parts or "voices." Many of Sor's finely wrought miniatures make use of this "song with accompaninment" technique, while the larger works, such as the *Variations on an aria from Mozart's "Magic Flute," Variations on the Scottish tune "Ye Banks and Braes,"* fantasias and the two sonatas are evidence that, like his contemporary the violinist Paganini, Sor was an innovative composer.

Today Sor's music may sound closer to the salon than the concert hall, yet much of it, including the cheerful pieces for beginners and more technically advanced studies, have helped to establish a solid foundation for the continuing study of the classical guitar. Sor's works are still heard, and he would have been pleased to know that even his simpler pieces would be put to such good use more than 150 years after his death. *—Roy Brewer*

Recommended:

- ○ **Sor: Complete Guitar Duets Vol. 1** / Kubica, Berkel / 1995 / Naxos 553302
- ○ **Sor: Ariette italiane; Seguidillas & Variaciones** / Figueras, Moreno / 1999 / Astree 9928
- ○ **Sor: Fortepiano Works** / Roger / 1997 / Cantus 9618
- ○ **My Careless Eyes: Songs and Guitar Music by Fernando Sor** / Tubb, Parsons / 2003 / Gaudeamus 344

CHAMBER MUSIC

Guitar Sonata No. 1 in D major ("Grand Solo"), Op. 14 (1810; revised 1822)

Three versions exist of this one-movement, classically oriented sonata: the original publication of 1810, a simplified version from 1822, and a later but undated arrangement by Sor's colleague Dionysio Aguado, who doused the music in a Romantic drama somewhat removed from Sor's more refined style. In every version, the work's structure remains the same and is beholden to the sonata-allegro movements of Mozart and especially Haydn. A slow Siciliano in the minor mode serves as an introduction; it's a procession of short phrases separated by brief pauses and soon kept on track by an ominous, thudding bass note. Romantically inclined performers can turn this into a highly effective funeral march. The movement's main matter enters with a lively theme that seems celebratory after the grim introduction. The fast tempo relaxes a bit for the second main theme, which might have emerged from a music box. Through much of the exposition, a quicker, more throbbing version of the introduction's ostinato reappears in the bass, giving the music further propulsion. The development section is brief but stormy, a reaction against the errant harmonic shifts that usher it in. The recapitulation slips in smoothly, neatly returning the movement to the main key. And even though by Sor's time a sonata conventionally consisted of three (sometimes four) movements, no slow movement or rondo round off this work. *—James Reel*

Recommended:

- ○ **Popular Guitar Music: Sor, Sojo, Lauro & Barrios** / Blanco / 1991 / Bis 133

Guitar Sonata No. 2 in C major, Op. 15b (1810; revised 1822)

Sor's *Sonata in C major, Op. 15b* is a single movement in the style of an Italian opera overture, similar to those of Paisiello and Cimarosa. The exact date of composition is unknown, but it is assumed that it is one of his early pieces, written around the time that he was in Barcelona in the late 1790s. During this period his Italianate opera *Telemaco nell'isola di Calipso* was produced at Barcelona's *Teatro de la Santa Cruz.* The overall style of the piece is similar to Sor's *Sonata,* Op. 14 and the opening Allegro of the *Grande Sonate,* Op. 22. The first part of the sonata is broken into three sections, each with its own theme. All feature short phrases and melodies moving in parallel thirds, with some dialog going on between voices. The first two themes have a repeated-note bass line supporting the melody, while the third section begins with broken chord triplets in the accompaniment line, which in turn lead into a more ornate melody, also in triplets. The second part of the sonata begins a new theme over an Alberti basslike figure, and then moves back to a recapitulation of the sonata's opening two themes and a short reference to the third before going into the coda. The rhythmic motifs that are used to transition between themes are typical of Italian operas of the late eighteenth century. Sor uses these as puctuation marks to indicate the ends of themes, rather than more sophisticated development of thematic material. The work is not especially witty, refined, or complex, but it is quite lively and good-natured. *—Patsy Morita*

Recommended:

- ○ **Sor: Divertimenti; Gran Solo** / Teicholz / 1996 / Naxos 553354

Guitar Sonata in C major ("Grande Sonate"), Op. 22 (1825)

Sor's *Grand Sonata in C major, Op. 22* is regarded as his most important concert work for guitar and part of the foundation of modern classical guitar repertoire. It is believed to be a relatively early work of his, probably written just before 1808, which was when Sor joined the fight against the French army's control of Spain. Evidence of this early date is its dedication to Manuel Godoy, the Spanish prime minister who fell from power when the royal family was exiled during that struggle. The sonata was published in 1825 in Paris, although there is some evidence of an earlier publication. It has the dimensions and something of the sound of a Haydn symphony, whereas his earlier sonatas had been single-movement works. The four movements are Allegro, Adagio, Minuetto, and Rondo allegretto. To a degree, the first movement uses the elements of the sonata-allegro form, modulating from the key of C to E flat and from C to C minor and back before the end of the exposition of the jaunty main theme. The C minor Adagio is a melancholy melody with an uncomplicated yet effective accompaniment. The Minuetto is as elegant and stately as any of Haydn's, while the final Rondo is also reminiscent of the great symphonist's spirito or spiritoso themes. In general, its sonorities are understandably not as rich as a symphony for orchestra, and it doesn't have the emotional intensity of Mozart's later symphonies or any Sturm und Drang, but the intention and pleasing nature of the Classical symphony are certainly there for the listener's enjoyment. *—Patsy Morita*

Recommended:

- ○ **Sor, Aguado, Tárrega: 19th Century Guitar Favourites** / Kraft / 1994 / Naxos 553007

Introduction, Theme, & Variations on a Theme from Mozart's "The Magic Flute," for guitar, Op. 9 (ca. 1820–1823)

Although the guitar had always enjoyed a vogue on the European continent, it truly began to emerge with the dawn of the virtuoso musician in the Romantic period, moving farther away from its common role of merely providing accompaniment. In approaching his instrument thus, Fernando Sor found himself in the august company of composer/performers like Nicolò Paganini, John Field, and others. Sor was often referred to as "the Beethoven of the guitar," not only for his skill as a performer, but also for his important body of works for the instrument. It is hardly surprising, then, that he occasionally turned to the Classical masters for inspiration.

The *Variations sur un thème de Mozart* (ca. 1820–23) draws its thematic material from the aria "Das klinget so Herrlich" from Mozart's opera *The Magic Flute* (1791). Written in E major, one of the most idiomatic keys for the guitar because of its open-string resonance, the work commences with a brooding introduction in the minor mode, curiously similar to many of Beethoven's sonata introductions. A statement of the theme is followed by the sunny first variation, which is punctuated by scale runs throughout. The second variation, in the minor mode, is solemn and stately. The third is good-natured, relaxed, and of an extemporized quality, while the prelude-like fourth, based on two alternating rhythmic figures, is more structured. The fifth variation provides a flashy conclusion, a mercurial perpetuum mobile of several dozen measures that comes to rest on a cadence of two full-textured chords. *— Wayne Reisig*

Recommended:

- ○ **Guitar Solos** / P. Romero / 1993 / Philips 434727

Kaikhosru Sorabji (Leon Dudley)

b. Aug. 14, 1892, Chingford, England, **d.** Oct. 15, 1988, Winfrith Newburgh, England

Composer: Keyboard

Kaikhosru Shapurji Sorabji was one of the most interesting figures among classical composers of the twentieth century. A fair amount of inaccurate information about his life and music has been written, largely because of his insistence on privacy and his reluctance to divulge information about himself. Sorabji was a prolific composer, turning out over 100 works, a good many of enormous length. Yet most of his compositions remain unpublished, despite an upsurge of worldwide interest in them in the last quarter of the twentieth century. Sorabji was well cared for in his childhood and teens, and his finances throughout his adult life were fixed and fully adequate to support him and his various pursuits. As a child, Sorabji showed talent on the piano and his music and general education were privately arranged by his family. His father was a Parsi and his mother is believed to have been of Spanish-Sicilian descent. Sorabji's resentment of English culture caused him to discard his own name, or most of it—he was born Leon Dudley Sorabji—in favor of the Indian names by which he became known. By 1914, he began to compose his first works. Largely self-taught and by then a brilliant pianist, he found modern music of great interest, but was attracted to the works of then-more obscure figures such as Busoni (the composer he admired most), Mahler, Schoenberg, Reger, Godowsky, and a few others. But he attached his art to no particular trend, rejecting serial composition, neo-Classicism, and the later movements in electronic and aleatoric music. After World War I, he became a music critic writing for, among other publications, the *New English Weekly* and *New Age*. In 1929–30, he wrote what would, a half century hence, become one of his better-known piano compositions, *Opus Clavicembalisticum*. It has a duration of well over four hours, but is still not his longest keyboard work: *Sonata V* (1934–35) and *Sequentia cyclica* (1948–49), among others, are even longer. Sorabji continued to compose and give infrequent concerts in the 1930s, gradually cultivating a disdain for audiences, however, and for public consumption of his music in general. By 1937, Sorabji had decided to give up public concerts altogether, though he did continue appearing in private performances. The following year, the rights to the publication of the few works of his to reach print in the postwar years were assumed by Oxford University Press. While this was good news, it was largely negated because the eccentric Sorabji had forbidden public performance of his music without his permission. Thus, little of his music would be heard over the next four decades. But Sorabji was unfazed and continued to write music, apparently unconcerned it might never be heard. True, he did play it in private concerts, but these were relatively few in number. Sorabji retired from music criticism in 1945 and largely focused on composition thereafter. It was not until 1976 that he sanctioned a major public performance of his music, that from pianist Yonty Solomon. Others followed, some from major pianists such as John Ogdon, and much later on, Marc-André Hamelin. Even a few recordings appeared in the latter twentieth century. Sorabji died at the age of 96, leaving most of his compositions in manuscript form. The bulk are for piano (or piano and orchestra), some are vocal/choral (a few with orchestra), and a handful for organ. *—Robert Cummings*

Overview of Works (1914–1984)

Kaikhosru Shapurji Sorabji composed over 100 pieces, and apart from two orchestral symphonies, three for organ, scattered works for orchestra, chamber, percussion, and a respectable body of songs, all of his works are for piano solo. They are written at an extremely high level of difficulty both rhythmically and technically, and display a chromatic language that is very dense and generally without placement in a key, yet is ethereal and otherworldly, rather than dark and clotted. Comparisons can be drawn between Sorabji's piano music and that of other archetypal modernists, including Scriabin, Liszt, Debussy, and Busoni. However Sorabji's approach is both similar to these musicians and also wholly unlike them; there is clearly only one Sorabji. Of Parsi Indian heritage and Zoroastrian in belief, Sorabji drew inspiration from eastern mysticism, shamanistic literature and other non-Western stimuli. Though he utilizes Western terminology to group his works into cycles, Sorabji's music is through-composed and makes no use of standard formal structure or thematic development.

Before considering the solo piano music, it is useful to know that Sorabji wrote eight concerti for piano and orchestra, the first in 1915 being his "opus one." The next four were written in quick succession, and the whole cycle was completed by 1924. Sorabji obviously saw no need to "start small." In 1929–30, Sorabji had completed his mammoth piano work, *Opus clavicembalisticum*, which runs more than three hours and is recognized by the *Guinness Book of World Records* as the longest nonrepetitive piano work in existence. Between 1917 and 1938, Sorabji composed five piano sonatas, each being long enough to fill up a CD. After this cycle was completed, Sorabji tackled a series of six symphonies for solo piano, starting with the *"Tantrik"* of 1938–39.

The next major cycle is the nocturnes, a form in which Sorabji demonstrated particular acumen, given his strengths in evoking faraway sounds, vague shapes and aromatic atmospheres. This group includes *In the Hothouse* (Two Pieces, 1917), *Le jardin parfumé* (1923), *Djami* (1928), and *Gulistân* (1940). Along with several occasional works, most of which are generally not "short," there is another cycle of transcriptions of non-original pieces. These range from a direct transplant of a source to another medium, such as in his arrangement of the last scene of Richard Strauss' opera *Salome* for piano four-hands (1947) to wild flights of hallucinatory fancy on a given theme (*Three Pastiches*, 1922, including "take-offs" on Chopin, Bizet, and Rimsky-Korsakov).

The initial publication of these pieces in the 1930s led to such poor readings by pianists that from 1936 Sorabji prohibited their performance without his express permission. But when approached by pianist Michael Habermann with a taped recording of several works around 1970, Sorabji happily granted his blessing for their revival. A small but growing number of keyboard artists, all endowed with superabundant technical abilities, have gradually adopted Sorabji's music into their repertoires, including John Ogden, Yonty Solomon, Kevin Bowyer, and Donna Amato. *—Uncle Dave Lewis*

Recommended:

- ○ **Sorabji: Gulistan** / Hopkins / 1995 / Altarus 9036
- ○ **Sorabji: Piano Works** / Amato / 1994 / Altarus 9025
- ○ **Sorabji: Le Jardin Parfume** / Solomon / 1992 / Altarus 9037
- ○ **Sorabji: Piano Sonata 2** / Johnson / 1999 / Altarus 9049
- ○ **Sorabji: Piano Sonata 4** / Powell / 2004 / Altarus 9069
- ○ **Sorabji: Toccata 1** / Powell / 2003 / Altarus 9068
- ○ **Michael Habermann Plays Sorabji** / Habermann / 1995 / Elan 82264
- ○ **Sorabji: The Complete Songs for Soprano** / Farnum, Kampmeier / 2002 / Centaur 2613

KEYBOARD

Opus Clavicembalisticum (1929–1930)

"With a racking head and literally my whole body shaking as with ague I write this and tell you that I have this afternoon early finished *Clavicembalisticum*.... The closing four pages are as cataclysmic and catastrophic as anything I've ever done—the harmony bites like nitric acid, the counterpoint grinds like the mills of God....," Sorabji wrote to his friend, Scottish composer Erik Chisholm, on June 25, 1930. A hearing of Ferruccio Busoni's *Fantasia Contrappuntistica*, performed by Egon Petri the previous November, prompted a critical panegyric ("The rather terrifying quality of the work, its monumental grandeur, its severe and ascetic splendour, its eerie magnificence, its utter uniqueness....") and almost certainly provoked Sorabji to match the master he most revered with a work of his own. *Opus Clavicembalisticum* was, accordingly, begun in December 1929. The composer gave its first—and very nearly last—performance in Glasgow, on December 1, 1931, at Chisholm's Active Society for the Propagation of Contemporary Music. In 1936, one John Tobin performed "Part I" of *Opus Clavicembalisticum* in London, requiring an hour and a half to get through what Sorabji considered should have taken 40 minutes, thus inciting Sorabji's notorious ban on the public performance of his works. *Opus Clavicembalisticum* was not heard publicly again in its entirety until Geoffrey Douglas Madge played it, with Sorabji's permission, in Utrecht, on November 6, 1982, after two decades of preparation.

Opus Clavicembalisticum is transparently modeled upon the *Fantasia Contrappuntistica*, but where Busoni's piece is a model of concision, playing around half an hour, Sorabji's pours forth in a gargantuan sprawl for nearly four hours. Busoni's art is Faustian, dynamic, historically aware, pressing forward with irresistible momentum; Sorabji's is Magian, static, timeless, contemplative (despite its often explosive moments), and ultimately, the impassive voice of Fate. Despite enormous contrasts, there is no development. The four fugues, for instance, are *perpetua mobiles*, their subjects and counter-subjects chasing their tails, so to speak, and tripping the contrapuntal tropes of retrograde, inversion, and retrograde inversion with a relentlessness in which more motion makes less movement.

Ostensibly, or allusively, tonal, Sorabji's astringent, constantly shifting harmony serves immediately expressive rather than formal or functional purposes. The torrential musical flow seldom, if ever, resolves. His themes are curiously faceless, having more the character of basic melodic shapes than anything resembling what is usually considered melody, even contrapuntally designed melody. Performance directions such as catastrofico, con somma forza e grandezza, quasi "mixtures," con somma strepita e furia, and many others laid on over already incredibly loaded writing seem to call for another—imaginary—instrument. The divine madness of its final pages spreads over five blackened staves. Stupendous. Menacing. Superhuman. *—Adrian Corleonis*

Recommended:

- ○ **Sorabji: Opus Clavicembalisticum** / Madge / 1983 / Bis 1062/64
- ○ **Sorabji: Opus Clavicembalisticum** / Ogdon / 1991 / Altarus 9075

John Philip Sousa

b. Nov. 6, 1854, Washington, DC, **d.** Mar. 6, 1932, Reading, PA

Composer: Band Music, Opera

American bandmaster and composer John Philip Sousa did more than anyone to elevate the status of the military wind band. Sousa's boyhood coincided with the American Civil War. The sounds of military bands were constantly in the air. His first musical training was on the violin, and his father instructed him on several wind instruments. At 13 the lure of a visiting circus was a powerful incentive for the boy to join up as a musician; however, his astute father, himself a bandsman, caught wind of the lad's intention and procured an apprenticeship in the Marine Corps Band for his son. It proved to be a happy move for all involved. The young musician sharpened his skills in that musical organization called the "President's own." He composed his first march, *Salutation*, at 16.

At 18, Sousa began to play violin in various theater orchestras. In 1880, Sousa was appointed leader of the Marine Corps Band, which he would serve for 12 years, under five presidents. He now began to hit his stride with his own marches, turning out such classics as *Semper Fidelis*, *The Washington Post*, *The Thunderer*, and *High School Cadets*. In 1892 Sousa, resigning his position with the Marine Corps, organized his own band, known simply as Sousa's Band. Through national, European, and world tours, the band's success was nothing short of a phenomenon, Sousa receiving many honors and decorations from the royal families of Great Britain and Europe.

He continued turning out his series of comic operas, including the highly successful *El capitan* (1895). From his pen flowed songs, symphonic poems, and more marches, this period seeing *The Liberty Bell* (1893), *King Cotton* (1895), *Hands Across the Sea* (1899) and, most notably, *The Stars and Stripes Forever* (1897).

With the entry of the United States into World War I, however, Sousa laid aside civilian activity and assumed command of all naval bands. In 1920, he reorganized his band and resumed touring. Sousa died while en route to conduct a high school band in Reading, PA.

Among his other achievements was his role as a founder of ASCAP. He also helped develop the sousaphone, a large tuba which features in parade bands. Ultimately, his compositions are his monument. But particularly it is the marches which endure. Sousa was not afraid to invest his marches with beautiful melody and unusual harmonies, placing them above being merely parade music. Sousa continued to explore within his chosen field until the end and many from his final decade such as *The Gridiron Club* and *Sesquicentennial Exposition* are remarkable for their inventiveness and vitality. The composer himself mused upon what constitutes the perfect march, stating that "it should make a man with a wooden leg step out." In virtually all of his creations in this field, Sousa passed this standard with flying colors. *—Wayne Gerard Reisig*

BAND MUSIC

The Fairest of the Fair, march (1908)

While Sousa's marches are often associated with patriotic subject matter, he wrote many whose inspiration came from personal experience or simply to celebrate some social event. *The Fairest of the Fair* is related to both of these categories, having been written for the 1908 Boston Food Fair, but drawing its inspiration from a young woman Sousa had met there during one of the previous Food Fairs.

In any event, its music is chipper and playful in its bright colors and pomp, and could well serve as a march for almost any celebratory or patriotic occasion. The piece opens with a jaunty theme, typical of Sousa, and features a mellow second subject that offers fine contrast in its carefree soaring quality. A variant of the main theme soon appears in much the same mellow guise of the second subject. It dominates the rest of this three-and-half-minute march, although it yields twice to colorfully bombastic outbursts and snatches of the main theme. The work closes with a grand statement of the catchy march variant. *—Robert Cummings*

Recommended:

○ **Sousa: On Wings Of Lightning** / Brion (cond.), Razumovsky SO / 1999 / Naxos 559029

Hands Across the Sea, march (1899)

Most listeners are aware that Sousa wrote much patriotic band music, often of a martial nature, but he also produced a vein of works which, while still having nationalistic and patriotic ties, are of a more idealistic cast. Such was the case with *Hands Across the Sea*, composed to buoy America's role in maintaining world peace in the post-Spanish-American War era. He prefaced the score to this march with a quotation from an English diplomat, John Hookham Frere: "A sudden thought strikes me—let us swear an eternal friendship." That said, the listener will find little in this music that varies from Sousa's more martial style, a style itself quite jovial in its triumphs, quite good-natured in its proud nationalism. *Hands Across the Sea* opens with a jaunty, carefree theme, the wind sonorities light and generally in their middle and upper ranges. An equally attractive march appears midway through, its manner initially mellow and nonchalant. It gradually turns more animated and colorful, the piccolo dancing merrily above suave wind sonorities. The work closes with this spirited theme played proudly, the brass flamboyant, the cymbals crashing, and the whole brimming with festivity and vivid color. For band music enthusiasts and Sousa mavens, this three-minute gem will have great appeal. *—Robert Cummings*

Recommended:

○ **Fennell Conducts Hands Across The Sea** / Fennell (cond.), Eastman Wind Ens. / 1994 / Mercury 434334

The Invincible Eagle, march (1901)

Premiered in Philadelphia on May 30, 1901, *Invincible Eagle* was intended for the Pan American Exposition in Buffalo, NY, where the composer eventually did lead his band in performances of it. One of Sousa's more popular marches, it did not quite achieve the success of *Stars and Stripes*, despite the composer's feeling that it would.

Many listeners often assume the instrumentation in Sousa's band compositions is somehow less complex, more an automatic kind of sound to achieve. Hearing familiar masterworks like *Invincible Eagle* and *Stars and Stripes* might especially reinforce such an errant view. But it was in compositions like these that he helped lay the foundation for the sound world of patriotic and celebratory band music. *Invincible Eagle* opens with a brief fanfare and then presents one of those typically bouncy, festive themes, suggesting little that is heroic or patriotic, but so much that is typical of Sousa's style. As the piece develops, however, it turns more dramatic, its nonchalant manner and fanfare-like episodes divulging greater heroism. Textures grow denser and the main theme transforms, taking on a more confident and less playful demeanor. In the end, this march must be assessed as on the same level with *Stars and Stripes* and Sousa's other masterful band works. *—Robert Cummings*

Recommended:

○ **Sousa Marches** / Fennell (cond.), Eastman Wind Ens. / 1992 / Philips 434300

King Cotton, march (1895)

Written the year before Sousa's most famous work, *Stars and Stripes*, the *King Cotton* march was premiered by the composer and his band in Atlanta, in 1895, at the Cotton States and International Exposition. Their many performances over a three-week period there converted what might have been financial catastrophe for the exposition's organizers to a considerable commercial success. The *King Cotton* march itself has gone on to become one of Sousa's most popular pieces.

It opens with one of those catchy Sousa tunes, its bounce and effervescence uniting with the colorful instrumentation to impart a mood of playful festivity. Gradually, as would be typical in many later works—most notably in *Stars and Stripes* and *Invincible Eagle*—the theme, and indeed the whole character of the music, turns more muscular, more dramatic in the latter half. While *King Cotton* does not quite reach for the heroism associated with the famous marches cited above, it nevertheless achieves a festive grandeur and joy that make it irresistible to band music enthusiasts. The theme itself is very similar to the one in Sousa's 1893 *Liberty Bell* march, used as the main theme to the once-popular British television comedy show, *Monty Python's Flying Circus*. In any event, the *King Cotton* march is rightly considered one of Sousa's finest band compositions. *—Robert Cummings*

Recommended:

○ **Sousa Marches** / Bashford (cond.), Grenadier Guards Band / 1996 / London 448957

The Liberty Bell, march (1893)

The Liberty Bell was one of the first marches that John Philip Sousa sent to his new publisher in 1893. Under his previous contract, the composer received $35 outright per composition with no royalties, but with the switch he became a more astute businessman. The origin of the present work, one of his most famous marches, was the rededication of the Liberty Bell in Philadelphia, which in those days was often on display at different locations around the country, a symoblic aid to the healing of the still raw wounds of the Civil War. There is also a story that Sousa was admiring the backdrop of a grade-school pageant depicting the bell and was thus inspired. Whatever the origin, it is a rousing piece that remains among the composer's dozen or so most famous. It has become even more so in recent times thanks to its having served as the theme of the madcap British television series *Monty Python's Flying Circus*.

The very introduction of this march is novel (virtually no two of Sousa's introductions even slightly resemble each other) in its downward chromatic spiral and full stop. In 6/8 time, the two skittish opening themes are linked by a common triplet figure. The soaring trio, more relaxed, is based on an ascending scale, while the grandiloquent breakstrain makes very effective use of rests. The last two sections are punctuated by chimes, providing an evocation of the great bell itself. *—Wayne Reisig*

Recommended:

○ **Hands Across The Sea: Sousa Marches** / Hills (cond.), Grenadier Guards Band / 1994 / Teldec 96061

Manhattan Beach, march (1893)

John Philip Sousa's briefest march, *Manhattan Beach*, was written in 1893 to honor the California resort of the same name. This was among the first compositions he produced for his new publisher, with royalties providing a more lucrative situation for Sousa from then on. It is among his dozen or so best-known marches.

Sousa once stated that a march must be as free from padding as a marble statue, and *Manhattan Beach* is a study in conciseness. It is simplistic in its predominantly diatonic mode and is in AABBCCDD form; when in this idiom, Sousa often hearkens back to the Austro-German band tradition and does so here. But the march is far from conventional and pure Sousa. The first theme, frisky and leap-laden, is delightfully quirky. The lyrical third theme has a folklike melody recalling, curiously, many Southern spirituals. And the closing theme, using a rhythmically insistent phrase, adds to the momentum in bringing this perky little march to a close. *—Wayne Reisig*

Recommended:

○ **Sousa Marches** / Fennell (cond.), Eastman Wind Ens. / 1992 / Philips 434300

Semper Fidelis, march (1888)

After John Philip Sousa became the conductor of the U.S. Marine Corps Band in 1880, he made headway in the public consciousness as a composer of marches. Sousa found a measure of success *Sound Off* and other works; *The Gladiator* (1886) was especially widely distributed. However, it was with *Semper Fidelis* that Sousa had his first runaway hit, in the process creating what is arguably the prototype for the great American march. Most of his earlier efforts, while very good, often harked back to British or Continental models. This march, bearing as its title the motto of the Marine Corps, "Ever Faithful," seems to speak an inherently native language, easier to perceive than describe. It is perhaps no coincidence that *Semper Fidelis* was the first musical composition to receive the official recognition of the United States Government.

The march has the form AaBbCcDd, and is in 6/8 time. The percussive, commanding intro is like a call to attention, and is followed by a galloping first theme. There is an organic link between the second and closing themes, but what comes between is a contrapuntal tour de force. After a familiar drum tattoo comes the famous "bugle call" melody accompanied by a rolling ostinato in the basses. With the reprise, swirling clarinets are layered on, and with the last reprise a trombone countermelody quite distinctive and equal to the main theme is likewise added to the texture. With this, one of the composer's "big three" marches, Sousa showed himself to be no mere commercial tunesmith, but a skillful composer within his chosen medium. *—Wayne Reisig*

Recommended:

○ **Sousa: At the Symphony Vol. 2** / Brion (cond.), Razumovsky SO / 1998 / Naxos 559013

The Stars and Stripes Forever, march (1896)

On the morning of Christmas Day, 1896, American "March King" John Philip Sousa wrote his most enduring masterwork, *The Stars and Stripes Forever,* in his New York hotel room in a couple of hours. By his own account, Sousa had been in Europe when the news reached him that his business manager had died in New York. As he hurriedly made his way back towards America aboard ship, Sousa paced up and down the deck, his mind burning with *The Stars and Stripes Forever,* born of his impatience to get back home. Sousa's march took its title from a favored toast once often proffered by Sousa's late mentor, legendary bandmaster Patrick S. Gilmore, "Here's to the Stars and Stripes forever!"

Once the band score was completed on April 26, 1897, Sousa may have tried out *The Stars and Stripes Forever* on a couple of undocumented occasions before its acknowledged premiere, which took place at a Sousa Band concert held in Philadelphia on May 14, 1897. Although the piece earned three encores at this first outing, *The Stars and Stripes Forever*'s first publication commanded no more attention in terms of sales than most other Sousa marches of the period. Sousa's publisher Church was so nonplussed by the piece that someone on the editorial staff suggested dropping the word "forever" from the title. However, Sousa refused to allow the quotation from Gilmore to be altered.

With the outbreak of the Spanish-American War in 1898, Sousa assembled a grand pageant entitled *The Trooping of the Colors* with which he toured the major American cities. The musical aspect of the show was a compilation of various numbers relating to American patriotic themes, and through careful coordination with local choral societies, Sousa managed to mount the work with voices numbering in the hundreds. In the finale, *The Stars and Stripes Forever* was trotted out as soldiers from all three branches of the military marched on-stage with flags unfurled, accented by an attractive local maid costumed as "Columbia." *The Trooping of the Colors* reached millions of Americans in a time where there was no mass media to promote it, and tapped into a public whose patriotism was enervated by the anxiety of war. Through this show, Sousa set a standard for *The Stars and Stripes Forever* as a vehicle for extravagant patriotic display, which, if anything, has only increased in intensity in the years to follow.

Sousa sought in his later work to outdo the unprecedented popularity of *The Stars and Stripes Forever,* but never succeeded. In his own programs, Sousa usually placed the piece early on, as he knew it would be requested as an encore, and repeated. In spite of the thousands of times Sousa and his band were required to play *The Stars and Stripes Forever,* they never tired of it, or of its incredible effect on audiences. *The Stars and Stripes Forever* has gone on to become the most frequently played American instrumental work of any kind. *—Uncle Dave Lewis*

Recommended:

○ **Fennell Conducts Hands Across The Sea** / Fennell (cond.), Eastman Wind Ens. / 1994 / Mercury 434334

The Thunderer, march (1889)

The origin of this march's evocative title, *The Thunderer,* is not clear; some have guessed that it refers to a celebrated orator of the time, circa 1889, or to the pyrotechnics of the drum and bugle effects in Sousa's score. Whatever the story behind its name, *The Thunderer* is one of Sousa's finest and most famous marches; it is also one of the easier Sousa marches to perform, and for this reason it was often a favorite of circus bands, who liked to take it at impressively fast tempos.

Coming the same year as the *Washington Post, The Thunderer* finds Sousa hitting his stride in developing a distinctly American-sounding march. The contrary motion of the introduction was a prototype for hundreds of similar works, and the clipped notes of the prancing first theme are (for the time) quite novel. The regimental effects first emerge in the second theme accompanied by one of Sousa's excellent countermelodies in the repeat. The trio is songlike and lyrical, so often the case in the composer's marches. Most striking is the use of rests, which alternate with the martial fanfares in the breakstrain until the powerful reprise of the trio gives full justification of the march's title. *—Wayne Reisig*

Recommended:

○ **Sousa Spectacular** / Hunsberger (cond.), Eastman Wind Ens. / 1982 / Phoenix USA 132

The Washington Post, march (1889)

The Washington Post newspaper claims in its history that this march was written as a tribute to the newspaper and performed by Sousa and his band in 1899. But of course, the work dates to 1889; moreover, *The Washington Post* in the march's title referred to the Marine contingent posted in the nation's capital at the time, not to the newspaper. It is true that Sousa performed the march at ceremonies held in 1899 by the newspaper, and the work's title was obviously fitting for the occasion.

This march has been among Sousa's most popular for years, considered by many his best known after *Stars and Stripes. The Washington Post* opens with a brief, typically Sousian fanfare, then presents one of the composer's most familiar tunes. It struts proudly upward in its first half, then steps jauntily downward in its latter portion. The second subject has a carefree spirit in its more mellow instrumentation and lively bounce. A variant of the main theme appears in the latter half and combines both the celebratory character of the opening with the more carefree temperament of the secondary material. The music grows bigger and more colorful near the close and ends with a robust sense of triumph. *—Robert Cummings*

Recommended:

○ **Sousa: Marches** / Urbanec (cond.), Czechoslovak Brass Orch. / 1972 / Nonesuch 71266

OPERA

El Capitan, operetta (1896)

In 1876, the 21-year-old John Philip Sousa was in the orchestra of the Centennial Exposition in Philadelphia, playing violin under the direction of Jacques Offenbach, who was livening the festivities with excerpts from his operettas. This could only have given a fillip to Sousa's ambition to succeed in the theater, and a stint conducting Gilbert and Sullivan's *H.M.S. Pinafore* in 1879 stoked that ambition further. Appointed leader of the U.S. Marine Band in Washington, D.C. in 1880, Sousa quickly gained a reputation as The March King. Nevertheless, his oeuvre is dotted with some 15 operettas, from the unperformed *Katherine* of 1879 to the unproduced *Irish Dragoon* of 1915, including, in between, the modest successes of *Desiree* (1883) and *The Queen of Hearts* (1885), the financial failure of *The Smugglers* (1882), and the variously successful *The Bride Elect* (1897), *The Charlatan* (1898), *Chris and the Wonderful Lamp* (1899), *The Free Lance* (1905), and *The American Maid* (1909). Among these efforts, the crown jewel is unequivocally *El Capitan,* which opened at Boston's Tremont Theatre April 13, 1896, moved to New York for a run of 112 performances, toured coast-to-coast, was revived in New York in 1897 and 1898, and played in England from July to November 1899.

In addition to Sousa's sparkling score, several matters of the moment spurred *El Capitan*'s popularity. While the Gilbert and Sullivan operettas were all the rage—often in pirated form (Sousa himself had orchestrated several from piano score)—native talent could not compete with Gilbert's verbal virtuosity and deft satire. Thus, when the young playwright Charles Klein produced a farce featuring such staples of Gilbertian comedy as mistaken identity, misplaced affections, eccentric characters, and a large military presence in chorus, Sousa seized upon it as the very thing he had sought. Moreover, the play complemented the composer's own strengths in calling for genres of which Sousa was a master—the sentimental ballad, the waltz, and (above all) martial music. Thomas Frost and Sousa supplied lyrics. For Don Medigua, the Spanish viceroy disguised as leader of the rebel troops, Sousa cobbled this introduction to the first strain of the eponymous march later extracted from the operetta:

Behold El Capitan;
Gaze on his misanthropic stare,

Notice his penetrating glare;
Come match him if you can.
He is the champion beyond compare.

Like the music, the texts are straightforward and effective. Too, the involvement of the impresario and enormously popular actor DeWolf Hopper—whose career reached its apogee in the role of *El Capitan*—virtually assured success. Finally, *El Capitan* hit the boards just as the tensions leading to the Spanish-American War of 1898 were taking shape, and Spanish despotism in a colonial Peruvian setting possessed undeniable topical interest. Indeed, aboard Admiral Dewey's flagship, as he sailed from Hong Kong to destroy the Spanish fleet in Manila, the band played the march *El Capitan*. *—Adrian Corleonis*

Synopsis:

It is sixteenth century Peru at the height of the old Spanish Empire. The King of Spain has appointed Don Medigua, his son-in-law, as viceroy to that colony, accompanied by wife Princess Marghanza and daughter Isabel. Ineffectual, Medigua manages to muddle through, letting his chamberlain Pozzo run things and appear in his stead for all public appearances. Meanwhile, Luiz Cazarro, the previous viceroy, is enraged that he has been deposed by nepotism, by a bumbler, no less, and has joined forces with insurgents who are likewise bent on overthrowing Medigua.

The leaders of the insurgents, Nevado, Scarambo, and Montalba, pay a surprise visit to the viceroy's castle in vain to meet the cowering Medigua. They inform Pozzo that they intend to oust Don Medigua and return Cazarro to the helm of the government. To do so they will employ the legendary but ruthless warrior El Capitan to lead a rebel army in storming the castle. Upon their departure, the fretful Medigua reveals to Pozzo that El Capitan, incognito as a sailor, was killed in a brawl aboard the ship that brought Medigua to Peru, his own sleuthing having uncovered El Capitan's identity and alliance with Cazarro. This he has kept secret. Then Medigua realizes that no one else in Peru can visually identify El Capitan. He, Pozzo, and Count Verrada, Isabel's suitor, concoct a plot to fight the insurgents. Medigua will pose as the dead warrior, lead a doomed rebellion, then reveal his identity and have the rebels and Cazarro hanged. If, by great odds the rebels win, his identity as El Capitan will remain.

The insurgents storm the castle and welcome back Cazarro and his daughter Estrelda. Don Medigua emerges as El Capitan while the hapless Pozzo, mistaken for the never-seen viceroy, is arrested. Estrelda, her frenzy fed by previous fantasy, has developed a crush upon seeing the "bold" new leader in the flesh. She extracts a proposal of marriage out of "El Capitan" just before his wife and daughter arrive on the scene, they benevolently having been granted limited freedom. Medigua explains his plan on the sly to them but wonders if Marghanza will be so understanding once he must assume faux conjugal duties.

The wedding day arrives, but so does word of the approach of the Spanish army. Medigua, as El Capitan, cancels plans and after getting the insurgent army drunk with wine begins to drill them into a stupor. The Spaniards arrive and defeat the rebels without shedding a drop of blood. Medigua reveals his true identity. He gives his blessing to Count Verrada and Isabel to be wed and then remembers Estrelda, now disillusioned, who begs for her father's life. Don Medigua, perhaps made more compassionate, braver, and wiser by the whole experience, grants pardons to Cazarro and the rebels if they will forgive his previous poor leadership both as viceroy and as "El Capitan." *—Wayne Reisig*

Gérard Souzay

b. Dec. 8, 1918, Angers, France, **d.** Aug. 17, 2004, Cap d'Antibes, France
Baritone

Gérard Souzay, whose real surname was Tisserand, studied philosophy in college although the family was musical (his sister was soprano Geneviève Touraine). He was a student at the Paris Conservatoire from 1940 to 1945, where he studied voice with Vanni Marcoux and Claire Croiza, but principally took master classes with the foremost French song recitalist of that period, Pierre Bernac (Poulenc's longtime companion), as well as Lotte Lehmann before and after World War II. Souzay made his first recording the same year as his professional debut, 1944. After an official Paris debut in 1945, he participated in celebrations of Fauré's centenary in London. By then 27, he was the first of his generation after World War II to give song recitals internationally, preceding his younger colleague Dietrich Fischer-Dieskau (b. 1925) by several years.

The French baritone made his U.S. debut in New York City's Town Hall in 1950, but did not sing opera until 1957, at Aix-en-Provence: Cimarosa's *Il matrimonio segreto* and Purcell's *Dido and Aeneas*. In 1960 Stokowski invited him to sing the title-role in Monteverdi's *Orfeo* with the New York City Center (later New York State) Opera. In 1962 he made his first appearance as Golaud in *Pelléas et Mélisande* at Rome under Ernest Ansermet, then repeated the role with the Paris Opéra in a performance celebrating the centenary of Debussy's birth. Eventually he sang at the Met in 1965, as Count Almaviva in *The Marriage of Figaro*, followed that same year by Glyndebourne (although illness limited him to a single performance), as well as debuts with the Vienna Staatsoper and Munich Opera. Other roles included Gluck's *Orfeo*, Méphistophélès in Berlioz's *Damnation of Faust*, Pollux in Rameau's *Castor et Pollux*, Massenet's Garrido in *La Navarraise* and Lescaut in *Manon*, even Wolfram in Wagner's *Tannhäuser*.

However, recitals and orchestral concerts remained the principal focus of Souzay's long and distinguished career, which included annual recitals at the Salzburg Festival between 1959 and 1963. Proficient in 15 languages, he introduced Baroque music before the "original instrument" era—especially music by Lully, Rameau, Handel, and Bach. He sang German as mellifluously and idiomatically as Fischer-Dieskau, his chief rival (whose intellectual word-stresses became increasingly intrusive), although Souzay's voice was lighter and smaller. His repertory embraced Russian, Spanish, Italian, even British songs. French chansons, withal, were his métier, beginning with Gounod, Fauré and their nineteenth century colleagues, but especially the Impressionist composers—Duparc, Debussy, Ravel—and the saucier Poulenc. Beginning in 1954, just as Poulenc partnered with Bernac until his death, the late Dalton Baldwin was Souzay's pianist, although not exclusively. They built an audience worldwide among audiences that had known only Italian or German opera. His presence onstage was elegantly handsome, and he sang with unforced, but nonetheless expressive, intense artistry that quietened even chronic coughers.

According to a comprehensive discography published in 1990 by Greenwood Press, he recorded over 750 titles on almost 50 labels—535 different catalog numbers—ranging from 78-rpm discs to CD reissues, and was awarded France's Grand Pix du Disque three times. Apart from operas, however, he infrequently recorded with others, only recording duets with Germaine Lubin, Elly Ameling, and his sister Geneviève. In 1985, Souzay joined the music faculty at Indiana University in Bloomington, but also taught at the University of Texas in Austin starting in 1986, where Stephen Mims made a documentary film about him, *Souzay: A Life in Art*. In addition, indefatigably, he gave master classes at the Juilliard School in New York, and in Paris, Holland, England, and Japan, where he was a special favorite of audiences in German as well as French music. *—Roger Dettmer*

Recommended:

- ○ **Lieder & Mélodies** / Souzay, etc. / Pearl 0063
- ○ **Souzay Early Recordings** / Souzay, etc. / 1999 / Dutton 7036
- ○ **Souzay Sings Ravel, Debussy, Chausson, Duparc** / Lindenberg (cond.), Souzay, Societe des Concerts du Conservatoire / 2003 / Testament 1312

Vladimir Spivakov

b. Sep. 12, 1944, Ufa, U.S.S.R.
Violinist

Vladimir Spivakov is one of the world's best-known violinists and a highly regarded conductor, and is respected for his worldwide humanitarian activities. His hometown of Ufa is in Russia's Ural Mountains, the low range traditionally regarded as the division between Europe and Asia. As often happened when children showed particularly promising musical talent, he was moved to Moscow to attend the Central School of Music. His violin teacher there was Lubov Siegal. He then attended the Leningrad Conservatory as a pupil of Veniamin (Benjamin) Sher, and then at the Tchaikovsky Conservatory in Moscow under Yuri Yankelevich.

By then, he had already won major national attention by winning, at the age of 13, the first prize for violin in the White Nights Festival in Leningrad in 1958. In 1969, he emerged on the international stage with a first prize in the International Competition for Violinists in Montreal, and the next year he was the second prize winner at the Tchaikovsky Competition in Moscow. At that point he went on the concert tour circuit throughout the U.S.S.R. and Eastern Europe.

He began appearing outside the Soviet bloc, debuting in the United States in 1975 with the New York Philharmonic, and gave a triumphant pair of recitals at Carnegie Hall in New York in 1976.

In 1977, he toured as a soloist with the Moscow State Orchestra and debuted with the London Philharmonic. He was a particular favorite in America and in the next few years appeared with the Cleveland, Dallas, Pittsburgh, and San Francisco orchestras.

Meanwhile he was studying conducting. He made his debut in that capacity at the very top rank of orchestras, leading the Chicago Symphony in 1979 at a *Ravinia Festival* summer concert. The press notices of that appearance make it clear that the occasion was a triumph, and it resulted in immediate engagements with other major symphonies around the world. Also in 1979, he founded the Moscow Virtuosi, which rapidly became known as one of the finest chamber orchestras of the world.

He maintained both his solo violin career and his conducting. He conducted such groups as the Santa Cecilia Orchestra of Rome, the Leningrad (St. Petersburg) Philharmonic, the Houston Symphony, the London Symphony, and many international chamber orchestras, such as the English, the Scottish, and major chamber groups in Rome, Dresden, and the Netherlands. In 1989, he became artistic director of the Colmar International Festival in France. In 1998 he was appointed to succeeded founder Mikhail Pletnev as the principal conductor and music director of the

Russian National Orchestra, the first privately owned orchestra in Russia since the 1917 Revolution.

He teaches at the Madrid Conservatory. He has been honored with Russia's highest prize, the National Cultural Heritage Award, and is Ambassador of the Arts of the World Economic Forum in Davos, Switzerland. He has established a Vladimir Spivakov Foundation to give creative and financial support for talented young people from around the world, and to needy children of Russia. He has also worked to raise relief for victims of Stalinism and children suffering from the Chernobyl power plant disaster. He is the founder of the European Sakharov Foundation.

He has recorded extensively for RCA Victor and conducts the Russian National Orchestra on the Well-Tempered Productions label. He plays a violin bequeathed to him by his teacher Yankelevich, a 1716 instrument made by the Venetian luthier Francesco Bogetti. —*Joseph Stevenson*

Recommended:

- **Shostakovich: Symphonies 5 & 9** / Spivakov (cond.), Russian National Orchestra / 2000 / Well-Tempered Productions 5190
- **Franck, Ravel, Strauss: Violin Sonatas** / Spivakov, Bezrodny (violin) / Capriccio 10895
- **It Ain't Necessarily So & Other Violin Miniatures** / Spivakov, Bezrodny (violin) / RCA 60861
- **Tchaikovsky: The Children's Album** / Spivakov (cond.), Moscow Virtuosi / 1994 / RCA 61964

Louis Spohr

b. Apr. 5, 1784, Braunschweig, Germany, **d.** Oct. 22, 1859, Kassel, Germany
Composer: Chamber Music, Concerto

Although virtually unknown to general audiences, the musical legacy of German composer, conductor and violinist Ludwig Spohr (1784–1859) is far-reaching indeed. Little of his own music survives in the general repertoire, but he is remembered as one of the preeminent conductors of the first half of the nineteenth century and as a seminal figure in the development of modern violin playing. Also, in addition to having invented both the violin chinrest and rehearsal numbers/letters for printed music, he was the first major conductor to use a baton.

Born in northern Germany in 1784, Spohr showed early talent for the violin, and by age 15 he was a member of the ducal orchestra at Braunschweig. At 18 he was sent by the Duke for a year of study with well-known violinist Franz Anton Eck, at the end of which time Spohr was considered ripe for a concert tour of his own. By 1805 the young virtuoso had become something of a sensation throughout Germany, where audiences adored both Spohr's playing and his compositions. Between 1805 and his death in 1859, Spohr served in a number of court positions throughout Germany and Austria. He was the leader of the orchestra at Gotha from 1805–12, leader of the orchestra at Theater an der Wien in Vienna from 1813–15, director of the Frankfurt Opera from 1817–19, and Hofkapellmeister at the city of Kassel from 1822 to 1857. He also remained a prominent figure on the international music scene, making no fewer than six tours of England throughout the years.

Over six and a half feet tall, Spohr must have been an imposing figure on the podium. His conducting repertoire was vast, including such then irregularities as J.S. Bach and Handel. A strong believer in new music, Spohr had a great impact on the careers of such progressive composers as Wagner and Berlioz. Spohr was one of the first to conduct *Der fliegende Holländer* (1842) and *Tannhäuser* (1853), though Spohr himself never fully accepted their musical aesthetic. Spohr's compositions never completely abandoned the blueprint of the Viennese masters; to the end he maintained that Mozart was the perfect composer. While his operas, such as *Jessonda* (1823), were popular during his lifetime, they have since disappeared from opera houses. Only a few of his works, notably the *Eighth Violin Concerto*—a striking work in the form of an operatic scene—and the four clarinet concertos are heard today. However, there were some signs of a growing interest in his chamber and orchestral music in the late twentieth century.

Throughout his life Spohr was famous for being as generous and warm a person as he was profound a musician. He maintained an active interest in politics and was considered a skillful painter and chess player. —*Blair Johnston*

CHAMBER MUSIC

Works for Chamber Ensemble (1797–1857)

During an article compiled in 1843 for *The Musical World*, J.W. Davison described the composer Louis Spohr as "the founder of a new feeling, if not of a new school in music." Spohr's vast output of chamber music, much of which is highly original in form, idiom, and instrumentation, seems to support Davison's conclusions. Since he was a virtuoso violinist himself, it comes as no surprise to discover that the greater portion by far of Spohr's chamber music involves strings alone. These works range in size from a set of 19 duos for two violins to music which is almost symphonic in its intentions, Spohr's four magnificent and virtually unmatched "Double Quartets."

Besides a further 36 conventionally designed string quartets, seven string quintets and the outstanding *String Sextet* (1848), these pieces comprise a significant if widely neglected grouping, in which a number of common features are apparent. Chief among these is the virtuoso complexity of the violin parts, upon which Spohr's own technical mastery was powerfully impressed. This explains why the quartets, in particular, divide into two further sub-sets. "Solo" quartets are really violin concertos with string trio accompaniment. By contrast, Spohr's conventional quartets distribute both melodic interest and virtuoso writing more evenly among the voices.

Spohr's larger string chamber works, the quintets, sextet, and double quartets contain much of his best music, since bravura aspirations were less paramount during their composition. Although the quintets often highlight first violin and first viola as duet collaborators, and the sextet reserves the most taxing parts for the first player in each pair of instruments, Spohr's "Double Quartets" explore more varied textures. Three further works, the *Octet* Op. 32, *Nonet*, Op. 31, and *"Grand" Septet*, Op. 147, required mixed strings, wind, and in the latter case, also piano. Critical consensus holds that Spohr's music attained its highest levels of originality and inspiration when such varied instrumental groupings were employed.

Spohr's first wife was an accomplished harpist, and some of the composer's most engaging chamber works are the duos for harp and violin, written between 1805 and 1819. Spohr's chamber music with piano also includes a superb *Quintet* (Op. 52) with winds, various pieces for violin and piano, and five piano trios, written 1841–49, which are widely considered to be outstanding examples of the genre. —*Michael Jameson*

Recommended:

- **Spohr: Double Quartets** / Academy of St. Martin-in-the-fields Chamber Ens. / 1998 / Hyperion 22014
- **Spohr: Octet & Nonet** / Gaudier Ens. / 1994 / Hyperion 66699
- **Spohr: Piano Trios** / New Munich Piano Trio / 1995 / Orfeo 352952
- **Spohr: Complete String Quartets Vol. 1** / New Budapest SQ / 1989 / Marco Polo 223251
- **Spohr: String Quintets, Op33/1 & 2** / Danubius SQ, Papp / 2002 / Naxos 555965
- **Spohr: Piano Chamber Music** / Pallas-Trio / 1995 / Musicaphon 56822

String Sextet in C major, Op. 140 (1848)

February 22, 1848, riots seized Paris. Two days later, the government of Louis Philippe fell. News, and violence, spread quickly—by March 13 thousands of workers filled the streets of Vienna, challenging imperial troops. Liszt, on his way back to Weimar with his new mistress Carolyne von Sayn-Wittgenstein, toured their barricades and penned a male-voice *Arbeiterchor*, which he coached the workers to sing in the open air—though he found it prudent to delay publication. In June, Wagner, Kapellmeister at Dresden, delivered an intellectually pretentious but vehement harangue before several thousand members of a group developing plans to arm the people. When fighting reached Dresden the following year, and the opera house was burnt, Wagner, fleeing to Swiss exile, was a prime suspect. Meanwhile, by the beginning of March, revolutionary fervor had brought people into the streets of Kassel, capital of Hesse—among them Louis Spohr, the Elector's Generalmusikdirektor—demanding reform. Spohr attended the insurgents' meetings, inspected their entrenchments—"You see we can make as good barricades here as in Paris!"—and led the crowd in Ernst Moritz Arndt's popular anthem for a united Germany, *Was ist des Deutschen Vaterland*. Seeking to defuse an inflammatory situation and minimize violence, the Elector acceded to all demands. For a moment, everything seemed possible—freedom of worship, of speech, an uncensored press, a German nation, utopia. A token of those heady days, Spohr entered the string *Sextet in C*, Op. 140, in his works list as "Written in March and April at the time of the glorious People's Revolution towards the Rebirth of Germany's Freedom, Unity and Greatness." To have been composed in such incendiary times, the *Sextet* breathes a curious serenity, an almost visionary aura of benediction in which the exuberant ardor of such early works as the *Nonet*, Op. 31, or the *Double Quartet*, Op. 65 (which, thanks to a classic recording featuring Heifetz and Piatigorsky among the ensemble, kept Spohr's name alive through the latter twentieth century), has mellowed. Less viscerally gripping, perhaps, the *Sextet* is immediately engaging and expressively richer—alive in every part, it possesses a tapestry-like glow. Its opening movement is a lyrically effusive hymn of thanksgiving whose themes are caressed throughout by a trilling motif. The brief, stately Larghetto is a barely restrained ode to joy that seems to pinch itself in confirmation of its dream of harmony. The final Scherzo alternates a Ländler-like promenade—the people united in a dance of freedom—with a giddily mercurial Presto. —*Adrian Corleonis*

Recommended:

- **Spohr: Octet; Sextet; Quintet** / Archibudelli, Smithsonian Chamber Players / 1993 / Sony 53370

CONCERTO

Concertos (1799–1845)

At the heart of Louis Spohr's large output of concertos is the violin, the instrument he played with virtuoso skill. He wrote several "double" concertos, One (the earliest) for violin and cello (1803), two for violin and harp (1807), and one for two violins, Op. 48 (1808), but he also produced a huge quantity for the more common combination of solo violin and orchestra; there are 15 numbered concertos, and although catalogs list either one or two others there appear to be, in fact, three unpublished concertos, bringing the total to 18.

In addition, Spohr wrote four concertos for clarinet and orchestra and the more unusual *Concerto for string quartet and orchestra in A minor* (1845), which harks back to the old sinfonia concertante of the Classical era. All four of the clarinet concertos have received some attention, though none has moved into the standard repertory or even to its fringes. Each of the four consists of three movements, and Nos. 2 (1822) and 4 (1828), which may be marginally more popular than the other two, feature finales associated with ethnic elements; the second's last movement is marked Rondo alla polacca and that of the fourth Rondo al Espagnol.

Spohr's style in virtually all his concertos feature orchestration about as advanced as that of middle-to-late Beethoven. HIs skill as an orchestrator in these works points to the most significant feature of the concertos as a whole: they are not display pieces for violin with the orchestra serving as a giant accompaniment, as in the concertos of Paganini, but works that aim toward cohesiveness of conception. For the most part their cadenzas are written out, not left to the performer to improvise. This is not to say that sheer virtuosity is absent; some of the solo parts provide considerable challenges. The "serious" central European concerto of the later Romantic period, as cultivated by Brahms and others, is often taken to be a direct outgrowth of Beethoven's violin concerto, but those of Spohr were influential as well. Spohr's music as well is of generally lighter fabric, somewhat in the vein of Mendelssohn, but with a bit less color. Among Spohr's violin concertos, No. 8 in A minor, Op. 47 (1816), has been the most popular and is perhaps his most widely performed composition. Cast in one long movement, it is dramatic, full of passion and with memorable themes.

The E minor seventh concerto, Op. 38 (1814), has also received attention over the years, and some musicologists not only consider it Spohr's finest concerto, but even compare it with Beethoven's and Mendelssohn's single efforts in the genre. While this may be inflated praise, the *Concerto No. 7* is a strong work, cast in three movements and quite serious, at times achieving profound expression in the Allegro first movement. The light-hearted Rondo finale is well-constructed and contains a jaunty and attractive main theme.

Spohr's later violin concertos tended to grow smaller, both in length and in number of movements, though his mastery remained in evidence. Nos. 12, in A major, Op. 79 (1828), and 13, in E major, Op. 92 (1835), are in two movements and among his shortest efforts. The brief A minor *Concerto No. 14*, Op. 110 (1839), is in one movement; it is noteworthy as one of the first examples of a historically oriented work, written in a deliberately antique style. These three smaller works are sometimes designated with the label "Concertino." Spohr returned to three movements with his masterful E minor *Concerto No. 15* (1844), his last effort in the genre.

Among the three unpublished and unnumbered violin concertos, the A major, WoO 12, probably from 1802–03, is a decent work, featuring a short but lovely Adagio second movement. His "double" concertos are generally well-crafted but do not rank in importance with his violin concertos. *—Robert Cummings*

Recommended:

○ **Spohr: Complete Violin Concertos** / Hoelscher, Frohlich (cond.), Berlin Radio SO / CPO 999657

○ **Spohr: Clarinet Concertos 2 & 4; Fantasia & Variations** / Wildner (cond.), Ottensamer, Slovak Radio SO Bratislava / 1994 / Naxos 550689

Clarinet Concerto No. 1 in C minor, Op. 26 (1808)

After recognition as a child prodigy and a tour as a violin virtuoso, which took him to Halle, Leipzig (where he scored a brilliant success with the prestigious Gewandhaus Orchestra), Dresden, and Berlin, the young Spohr was called to become concertmaster in Gotha, in 1805. The following year, he married virtuoso harpist Dorette Scheidler in a love match that produced a great deal of music for harp and violin, and, in quick succession, two daughters. Though he and Scheidler subsequently toured the musical capitals (Vienna, Prague, Rome, London, and Paris) together during vacations with great artistic and financial success, the post in Gotha gave him the stability to assimilate the numerous musical influences he encountered, and from this assimilation a strikingly individual voice soon began to emerge. This prolific composer's series of remarkable violin concertos (which would eventually grow to 15 works) had already been inaugurated when, in the summer of 1807, he was visited by Prince Sondershausen's concert director, the renowned clarinetist Johann Simon Hermstedt (1778–1846), who brought a commission, from Sondershausen, for a clarinet concerto. Spohr composed his *Clarinet Concerto No. 1* through fall 1808. Its premiere in Sondershausen produced the desired brilliant effect and lent a significant boost to the reputations of both Spohr and Hermstedt. When Hermstedt played the concerto in Leipzig, in November 1809, a critic noted that "it belongs to the most spirited and beautiful music which this justly famous master has ever written." At the time of this encomium, Spohr was 25 years old. As with Beethoven and Liszt, Spohr's imagination ran ahead of what was actually possible on the primitive instruments of his day. In an 1810 preface to the published work, Spohr wrote, "Since at that time [of composition] my knowledge of the clarinet was pretty nearly limited to its range and I therefore paid little attention to the weaknesses of the instrument, I have thus written much that will appear to the clarinetist at first sight as unpracticable. Herr Hermstedt, however, far from asking me to alter these passages, sought rather to perfect his instrument and soon by continuous industry arrived at the point where his clarinet had no faulty, dull, uncertain tones." Opening the first movement, a plaintive Adagio ushers in the downward leap of a sixth to an arching motif that furnishes the material of both the first and second themes in a most gracious use of what has come to be called cellular transformation gleaned from Beethoven, which was to become the basis of Liszt's thematic metamorphoses and one pillar of Franck's "cyclical" technique. As the tempo moves to Allegro and the clarinet becomes evermore effusively confiding, an initial gravity—if never entirely dispelled—is softened in florid brilliance through a substantial but always engaging development. A brief central Adagio movement spins out a mellifluously long-breathed, Romantic bel canto melody for clarinet. And the final Rondo-Vivace caps all with an exercise in garrulous *bonhommie* that Spohr would essay ever more deftly and charmingly throughout his career. *—Adrian Corleonis*

Recommended:

○ **Spohr: Clarinet Concertos 1 & 4** / Leister, Frühbeck de Burgos (cond.), Stuttgart SWR Radio-SO / 1984 / Orfeo 88101

Clarinet Concerto No. 2 in E flat major, Op. 57 (1810)

Prince Sondershausen's concert director, the renowned clarinet virtuoso Johann Simon Hermstedt (1778–1846), had scored such a resounding success with Spohr's *Clarinet Concerto No. 1* in 1808 that, for the 1810 Frankenhausen Festival, he pressed the composer for another. Featuring over 100 singers and 106 instrumentalists, the festival promised to be a trendsetting event of rare magnitude and brilliance, especially with the enormously gifted 26-year-old Spohr at the helm. Spohr set aside work on his second opera, *Der Zweikampf mit der Geliebten*, to compose the *Concerto No. 2* in a few weeks, just ahead of its premiere on June 22, 1810. Reviewing the festival, Ernst Ludwig Gerber hailed Spohr's direction of Haydn's *The Creation*—with the innovation of a roll of paper used as a primitive baton—as "the most powerful, most expressive, and in a word the most successful I have ever heard," and singled out the new clarinet concerto as "indisputably one of the most perfect artistic works of its kind." Posterity has tended to agree with Gerber: the *Concerto No. 2* continued to be played with Weber's two clarinet concertos long after most of Spohr's other work had disappeared from the concert hall. In the *Clarinet Concerto No. 1*, Spohr's manner had begun to emerge from a welter of influences. In the *Second*, he is in full stride. Of the four concertos written for Hermstedt, the *Second* is the only one in a major key, with the opening Allegro mining that eupeptic vein of effusive cheerfulness and *bürgerlich* self-satisfaction, set off by feints of chromatic delirium that was to become such an agreeable staple of his music throughout a long and amazingly prolific career. No doubt, it reflects his happy marriage to harpist Dorette Scheidler in 1806 and his growing renown as a composer and conductor. Indeed, it is remarkable for its march-like élan, which looks forward to the irresistibly driven "Ambrosian Ode" third movement of his *Symphony No. 4* (1832). A soulful second movement Adagio, yearning in its long-drawn cantilena and rapid modulations, is darkened for a moment by a mock-serious episode suggesting matters of great pith and moment before subsiding in sweetly detailed, silvery liquescence. The final, gently rollicking Rondo alla polacca, with its chirpily confiding clarinet melody and discreet chromaticisms, is Spohr in his most good-natured, bourgeois humor: a mixture of popular sentiment, rustic vigor, and scintillant musical sophistication. *—Adrian Corleonis*

Recommended:

○ **Spohr: Clarinet Concertos 2 & 4; Fantasia and Variations** / Ottensamer, Wildner (cond.), Slovak Radio SO Bratislava / 1994 / Naxos 550689

Clarinet Concerto No. 3 in F minor, WoO 19 (1821)

Although Spohr's four clarinet concertos are well-regarded—though not as highly esteemed as Weber's—the third in his series is felt to be the weakest of the lot. Here, the orchestral contribution is rudimentary and the work as a whole is less a matter of musical argument than of virtuoso display. Purely as a showpiece, however, it's quite effective. The Allegro moderato's stormy orchestral introduction quickly subsides into more reserved, expectant material with the low strings always providing an agitated undercurrent. The clarinet arrives, offers its own confident version of the tempestuous first theme, and then takes off with a fanciful treatment of the second. After a more straightforward restatement of the motifs, the soloist's part proves to be a series of trills, leaps, and runs whose relationship to the main theme is sometimes tenuous. There's no cadenza; the bulk of this flashy movement is like an accompanied cadenza with an occasional orchestral tutti. The broad Adagio casts the clarinet as a soprano in a tender opera aria in a technique familiar from Spohr's violin concertos. Eventually, the soloist repeats the long but straightforward melody, now ornamenting it with trills and fioritura. At the movement's midpoint, the orchestra revives long enough to present a stately theme that the clarinet decorates lavishly before seamlessly moving back to the original melody. The clarinet leads off the Vivace non troppo with a coy little tune over a subtle, stuttering accompaniment that hints at a waltz but rarely steps fully onto the dance floor. Although the orchestra regularly breaks in with agitated tutti passages, the clarinet maintains its serenity through most of the movement, which is a series of increasingly florid variations on the opening theme. *—James Reel*

Recommended:

○ **Spohr: Die Klarinettekonzerte 2 & 3** / Leister, Frühbeck de Burgos (cond.), Stuttgart SWR Radio-SO / 1984 / Orfeo 088201

Clarinet Concerto No. 4 in E minor, WoO 20 (1828)

At the suggestion of Carl Maria von Weber, who had declined the position, Spohr applied for and was granted the post of concertmaster in Kassel—capital of the Duchy of Hesse—which he was to hold until just before his death, 37 years later. The contract was signed February 4, 1822. The new Elector, Wilhelm II, had acceded to the throne the year before, and wanted the court opera to win renown. With security and the good will of the musicians, the public, and the court, both the Kassel musical establishment and the ever-prolific Spohr entered a new era of achievement. His friendly rivalry with Weber led not only to productions of that master's *Der Freischütz*, *Euryanthe*, and *Oberon* at Kassel, but prompted the composition of his own most viable stage work, the opera *Jessonda* (1823). In the year of his appointment, Spohr founded the Cäcilienverein, a choral society intended to "awaken the taste for fine and serious music... and unite the talented *dilettanti* of Kassel." It is not, perhaps, fortuitous that the oratorio *Die letzten Dinge*—whose enormous popularity seems incredible today—followed in 1826. In the midst of directing the opera, preparing public concerts, giving command performances at court, and participating in private soirees, work on the imposing *Symphony No. 3* was proceeding apace when Prince Sondershausen's concert director, the brilliant clarinet virtuoso Johann Simon Hermstedt (1778–1846) (for whom Spohr had composed enthusiastically received clarinet concertos in 1808, 1810, and 1821) appeared with a request for a new piece for the Nordhausen Festival. Spohr began work on his *Clarinet Concerto No. 4* in August 1828, rapidly completing it with the easy mastery of a practiced hand. It is the most substantial and least satisfying of the four, hovering throughout between taking its ostensibly dramatic minor key feints seriously and dissolving in mellifluous effusiveness. A doggedly earnest development through the first-movement Allegro vivace fails to settle the issue, and the second-movement Larghetto leaves the clarinet to pensively pursue the matter in a heavily embellished, if unmemorable, melody spun out over an alternately declamatory and march-like accompaniment that never effectively gels. With the concluding Rondo à l'espagnol, effusive melodiousness wins out, as Spohr, the *bürgerlich* purveyor of mock-serious sentiment and eupeptic entertainment, comes to the fore with rhythmic exoticism stimulating the dithering clarinet to virtuoso flourishes. The *Clarinet Concerto No. 4* is a masterpiece only in the sense that it is formally and technically executed with an enviable degree of polish. Its failure is due to the same bourgeois shallowness of feeling that renders Spohr's operas and oratorios such dead letters—they promise, but do not deliver, profundity, pathos, and tragedy. *—Adrian Corleonis*

Recommended:

○ **Spohr: Clarinet Concertos 1 & 4** / Leister, Frühbeck de Burgos (cond.), Stuttgart SWR Radio-SO / 1984 / Orfeo 88101

Gaspare Spontini

b. Nov. 14, 1774, Majolati, Ancona, Italy, **d.** Jan. 24, 1851, Majolati, Italy

Composer: Opera

That Spontini was admired by both Berlioz and Wagner is probably due to his own inspiration by Gluck, but the fact that he made an indelible impression upon such antithetical natures confirms his importance in the development of grand opera as the century of Romanticism dawned. Early evidence of musical ability delivered him from a career in the priesthood, though his studies at Naples' Conservatorio della Pietá dei Turchini were soon abandoned. Having absorbed sufficient technique to employ the facile formulas of Italian opera, Spontini set out as a freelancer, appearing in 1796 with his first opera, *Li Puntigli delle Donne*, produced during the Roman Carnival. Its success enabled him to compose comic operas for Venice, Florence, and Naples. Association with Cimarosa in the latter city in 1798 seems to have been a turning point toward more exalted ambitions, while a stint in Palermo in 1800–01, where the Bourbon court was in exile, introduced him to noble patronage. Moving on to Paris, he had the good fortune to win the interest Joséphine, wife of Napoleon I. Trivial works—including vaudevilles—vied for public favor with the more seriously striving Milton, in which the example of Gluck becomes apparent for the first time. It was only through the accident that a work by le Sueur (later to become Berlioz' teacher) was not completed in time that Spontini's *La Vestale*—composed in 1805—reached the stage of the Opéra de Paris on December 15, 1807, to overwhelming acclaim and international success. Napoleon dictated that Spontini's next opera should glorify a conquering hero, though *Fernand Cortez*, premiered on November 28, 1809, before the emperor and the King of Saxony, failed to make the point, and won enduring fame only in its 1817 revision, by which time Napoleon was vanquished and exiled. Spontini's musical command was given a fillip by his fiery presence, making him a formidable conductor. He served as director of the Théâtre Italien from 1810 to 1812. With the restoration of the Bourbon monarchy and the success of Cortez, Spontini was in favor, though his *Olympia*, in 1819, achieved but six performances. In 1820 he moved on to Berlin, where King Friedrich Wilhelm III made him Generalmusikdirektor. The success of a revised *Olympia* in 1821 was soon upstaged by Weber's *Der Freischütz*, leading to a rivalry that forced Spontini from his post in 1842. Intrigues to regain his position, a Dresden revival of *La Vestale* in 1844, and the conferring of a papal nobility in 1847 filled his final years. *—Adrian Corleonis*

OPERA

La Vestale (1807)

La Vestale was Spontini's first opera composed specifically for the Paris Opéra, and among the first great successes of his career. Having garnered only modest attention in his native Italy, Spontini established himself in Paris and quickly gained the admiration of a number of influential figures, including the composer Hector Berlioz, Napoleon, and the Empress Josephine. Their advocacy was fortunate for the composer, since the prevailing taste in French opera houses had turned toward a retrenchment of traditional French musical and dramatic styles and against increasing Italianate influence. Spontini's spacious melodies, colorful orchestrations, and modern harmonies caused the jury at the Paris Opéra to reject *La Vestale*, calling the music "bizarre" and "noisy." But, after direct intervention by the Empress, the opera was produced on December 15, 1807. It was hailed as a masterpiece by the public and critics alike, and became the biggest operatic success of the First Empire. It was revived throughout the century at the Paris Opéra and at houses abroad. It has also proved popular with modern audiences, and seems likely to remain in the repertoire.

The libretto to *La Vestale* is by Etienne de Jouy. Du Jouy asked the three greatest French composers of the era, Mehul, Boieldieu, and Cherubini, to set his libretto, but they all refused. He turned to Gasparo Spontini as a last resort, and was accepted. The libretto is exceptionally fine, and was one of Beethoven's favorites. The story, which centers around a vestal virgin torn between love and duty, gave the composer ample opportunity for dramatic exploits, spectacle, and melodrama. Supposedly taken from an historical account of an event that took place in 269 B.C., as related by J.J. Winckelmann, the libretto also bears similarities to an anonymous pantomime of 1786 inspired by a verse-tragedy of Fontanelle.

La Vestale is a true tragedie-lyrique, in the tradition of Lully, Rameau, and Gluck. There are grand divertissements at the ends of the first and third acts, and the primary dramatic arguments are carried in unadorned recitative as well as recitatif oblige in arioso style. A *deus ex macchina* in the form of a bolt of lightening results in the obligatory lieto fine, or happy ending, required in all tragedies-lyriques. The most powerful act is the second, which features Julia's aria "Impitoyables Dieux," a grand love duet, Julia's prayer, and the High Priest's sentencing of Julia to Death. *—Rita Laurance*

Synopsis:

Act One. Celebrations in honor of the heroism and bravery of the Roman general Licinius have been prepared. But as dawn breaks, we find him brooding in front of the temple of Vesta, for it is there that his true love Julia has been confined. Licinius left Rome five years ago to win her hand in marriage through deeds of valor and courage, but on his return, he finds that Julia's deceased father has given her to the Temple of Vesta as a Vestal Virgin. She has taken a vow of chastity and is responsible for keeping the sacred fire of Vesta lit and honoring the goddess with her prayers. Licinius asks his friend Cinna for aid, and the latter agrees to help the general steal Julia from the goddess's temple if necessary.

The Vestal virgins have awakened and are preparing for the day's festivities. It is the virgins who will crown General Licinius with laurels, and Julia recalls her passion for him with misgivings. She begs the high priestess to free her from her duties during the ceremony, but the high priestess advises her to take courage. She knows all about Julia's amorous feelings for Licinius. A huge triumphal procession honors Licinius. While Julia is placing laurels on his head, he leans towards her amorously and whispers to her that he will come to the temple that very night to free her. Festivities and games close the act.

Act Two. The virgins are at prayer within the temple. After the others have gone to sleep, Julia stays on to tend the fire through the night. She contemplates her love for Licinius with misery. Licinius enters the temple, and they have a joyful, lovers' reunion. But Julia quits paying attention to the Vestal fire, and the flame dies as they are speaking of their love. Crowds begin converging on the temple angrily, and Julia is forced to admit that she is guilty of having met a man in the sacred building. The high priest condemns her to death because she broke her vows, and for her negligence in letting the sacred fire go out.

Act Three. Julia is to be buried alive, and an open tomb can be seen awaiting her entrance. The lamenting Licinius resolves to rescue her. Before embarking on any drastic action, he decides to plead with the high priest and beg for mercy for his crime. But when he tells the priest that it was he who distracted Julia from her duties, the Vestal dignitary responds coldly rather than mercifully to his pleas. Julia must die. The fire has never been allowed to be extinguished, for fear of angering the goddess. A sacrificial procession begins, full of Vestal virgins and young women, and they lead in the condemned. Julia must bid farewell to all of her friends and enter the tomb of her own accord. Licinius tries to interrupt the proceedings, but is silenced by the priests and priestesses. Then he calls on his men for aid, and a drastic rescue attempt is made. Fighting erupts in the temple, and a storm breaks out overhead. At the height of the chaos and confusion, a bolt of lightening strikes the temple and rekindles the fire. The priests decide that the goddess has shown her forgiveness, and all rejoice in the outcome. Julia is freed from her tomb, and celebrations end the opera. *—Rita Laurance*

Recommended:

- ○ **Spontini: La Vestale** / Muti (cond.), Graves, Kavrakos, Sammaritano, Bramante, Raftery, Huffstodt, Prandina, Stagni, Michaels-Moore / 1995 / Sony 66357
- ○ **Spontini: La Vestale** / (Live: 1954) / Votto (cond.), Callas, Corelli, Stignani, Zaccaria, Sordello, Rossi-Lemeni / 1999 / Opera d'Oro 1227
- ○ **Spontini: La Vestale** / Previtali (cond.), Gavarini, Nicolai, Fineschi / 2001 / Warner Fonit 87472

St. John's College Choir, Cambridge

f. ca. 1670, Cambridge, England
Ensemble

The St. John's College Choir has existed since the 1670s, and even then it represented a continuation of a tradition of religious music at St. John's College, Cambridge. The Choir's 16 Choristers and four Probationers enter by passing voice trials at age seven to eight, and all receive education at St. John's College School, located on the St. John's College campus at Cambridge. The College School itself has 430 boy and girl students up to age 13.

The Choristers and Probationers sing the soprano parts in the College Choir. The rest of the singers (altos, tenors, and basses) are undergraduate students of the College, termed "Choral Students," and are, therefore also members of Cambridge University itself. They are not necessarily music students. They remain in the choir until they take their Cambridge Degrees at the end of three years, and gain their positions by auditions.

The main duty of the College Choir is to sing the daily Church of England services in the College Chapel throughout the University term, including Evensong six days a week and Sung Eucharist on Sunday mornings.

The choir travels widely, and broadcasts regularly on the BBC. Annual traditions include broadcasts of its Advent Carol Service, Passiontide Meditation, and its Ash Wednesday Choral Evensong which includes Allegri's *Miserere.*

The choir has made over 100 recordings and is one of the most respected among British choirs of its type. *—Joseph Stevenson*

Recommended:

- ○ **Tavener: Song for Athene, etc.** / Robinson (cond.), St. John's College Choir / 2000 / Naxos 555256
- ○ **Byrd & Tallis: Choral Music** / Guest (cond.), St. John's College Choir / 2000 / EMI 74002
- ○ **Duruflé: Choral Works** / Robinson (cond.), Todd, Clements, Turpin, Farrington, St. John's College Choir / 2000 / Nimbus 5599
- ○ **Charpentier & Poulenc: Motets** / Guest (cond.), City of London Sinfonia, St. John's College Choir / 1988 / Chandos 8658

St. Louis Symphony Orchestra

f. 1907, Saint Louis, MO
Ensemble

Like Cincinnati, Saint Louis benefited from an influx of German immigrants after 1848, who brought an appetite for Old World musical culture that took the form of the *Sängerbund,* supplemented after 1865 by the Theodore Thomas Orchestra's annual tour concerts. As Cincinnati's May Festivals became a regular port of call for Thomas until his death in 1905, Saint Louis created a Musical Union Orchestra in 1879, and two years later a Choral Society. These merged in 1893 and performed together until 1907, when the Saint Louis Symphony Society was formed. A violist from the Boston Symphony, Max Zach, was engaged as conductor. By the time he died in mid-season 1921, the orchestra had grown from 64 to 82 players and the season to 15 pairs of concerts in the Odeon Theater.

Saint Louis wanted Fritz Kreisler as their next conductor, but settled for Rudolph Ganz, the Swiss-born piano virtuoso from Florenz Ziegfeld's Chicago Musical College. Before their first rehearsal Ganz stated forthrightly, "Gentlemen, the orchestra is not my instrument, so please, do your best and we will learn together." They tried for the next six seasons, which included records on RCA Victor's Blue Label, national recognition for Ganz's children's concerts, and an introduction to the music of Mahler, Stravinsky, and Schoenberg. When the Odeon burned down in 1926, forcing the orchestra to play in Washington University Field House, 15 post-season pop concerts were added.

Ganz left in 1927, and Vladimir Golschmann was selected after four seasons of guest conductors. Like Sergey Koussevitzky in Boston, he was Russian-born, but made his career in Paris with eponymous concerts of new music. Under him the orchestra not only survived the Depression but flourished. In 1934, it occupied half of the new Kiel Auditorium (although one could hear basketball crowds on the other side of a steel fire-curtain when both tenants played on the same night). In 1955, however, a tired Golschmann was named emeritus. Unluckily for Saint Louis, a three-year search netted Belgian-born Edouard Van Remoortel. His contract was not extended beyond 1962, leading to another search, another unsatisfactory choice: Brazilian Eleazar Carvalho, whose appetite for avant-garde music was not matched by finesse in the standard repertory. However, before his resignation in 1966, conversion of the 40-year old Saint Louis (film) Theater into Powell Hall, one of America's acoustic showplaces, had begun.

Walter Susskind inaugurated Powell in 1968 and stayed for seven stabilizing seasons, bringing with him Leonard Slatkin as assistant conductor. Jerzy Semkow followed in 1975 for four seasons (when Thomas Peck was engaged to form a Symphony Chorus). By 1979, Slatkin was importuned to become music director, and in 17 seasons before he moved to Washington, D.C., made the orchestra one of North America's finest. After more than 20 years on Vox Records, Saint Louis returned to RCA, and added EMI. In 1996, Slatkin was succeeded by Dutch-born Hans Vonk, former Cologne Radio (1990–97) and Dresden Staatskapelle (1985–90) music director. *—Roger Dettmer*

Recommended:

- ○ **Mahler: Symphony 1** / Slatkin (cond.), St. Louis SO / 1986 / Telarc 80066
- ○ **Tchaikovsky: The Ballets** / Slatkin (cond.), St. Louis SO / 2003 / RCA 55707
- ○ **Ravel: Boléro, etc.** / Slatkin (cond.), St. Louis SO / 1980 / Telarc 80052
- ○ **Barber: Symphony 1; Piano Concerto; Souvenirs** / Slatkin (cond.), Browning, St. Louis SO / 1991 / RCA 60732

Staatskapelle Dresden

f. 1548, Dresden, Germany
Ensemble

The Dresden State Orchestra (its official name is Sächsische Staatskapelle Dresden or Saxon State Orchestra Dresden) is one of the oldest orchestras in the world and is renowned for its special, well-blended sound.

The Dresden State Opera dates its founding to 1548 when the ruler, Elector Moritz, founded a Hofkantorei (Court Chorus) and brought in foreign musicians to augment it. Dresden came to possess one of the finest royal musical establishments in Europe, under the leadership of such stellar names as Michael Praetorius and Heinrich Schütz. Johann Adolf Hasse, Kapellmeister from 1734 to 1763, brought Dresden opera to its highest level during the Baroque.

Saxony's defeat in the Seven Years' War (1756–63) required the opera to be curtailed drastically. Elector Friedrich Augustus III realized that the orchestra must be the nucleus if the opera were ever to rebuild its prestige. J.G. Naumann, director from 1776 to 1801, returned the Kapelle to the highest standards of instrumental playing. By 1810 the opera was again one of Europe's greatest.

The post-Napoleonic Congress of Vienna made Saxony a kingdom. In 1817, the director of the new Royal Kapelle founded a German Opera in addition the established Italian troupe. Under the leadership of Carl Maria von Weber from 1817–26, this company won the favor of the populace. The Italian company disbanded in 1832. Kapellmeister Karl Gottlieb Reissinger maintained high standards, assisted by Richard Wagner until the later was exiled in 1849 for revolutionary activities. Wagner premiered his *Reins, Flying Dutchman* and *Tannhäuser* in Dresden's new opera house, opened in 1841, designed by Gottfried Semper. Wagner called the orchestra a "magic harp" that stimulated his ideas of orchestration and led it often in symphony concerts.

The orchestra presented its first concert series in 1858. In 1869 the Royal Opera Theater burned down. When a new concert hall, the Gewerbehausall, opened in 1870, the orchestra gave its concerts there (along with the newly formed Dresden Philharmonic) until 1878, when a second Semper-designed opera house opened. The music director of opera and orchestra from 1882 to 1914 was Ernst von Schuch, who gave the premieres of Strauss' *Feuersnot, Salome, Elektra,* and *Der Rosenkavalier* at the Semperoper.

After World War I, the Royal Kapelle became the Sächsischer Staatsoper and the Sachsischer Staatskapelle. The orchestra remains the orchestra of the opera, which is still also called the Semperoper. In 1923, the orchestra founded its own orchestral school under Fritz Busch (later under Karl Böhm), now known as the State Academy for Music and Theater. The majority of musicians in the orchestra are natives of the region and graduates of the school, a reason for the remarkable continuity of its special sound.

The second Semper Opera House was destroyed by bombing in 1945. After the war, the orchestra and the opera performed in temporary halls until 1948, when a city theater was remodeled and opened as the Grosses Haus of a state theater complex. Joseph Keilberth brought the opera and the orchestra both to their feet as music director from 1945 to 1950. His successors with the orchestra included Rudolf Kempe, Lovro von Matacic, Othmar Suitner and Kurt Sanderling, while Rudolf Neuhaus was general music director of the opera. In 1975, Herbert Blomstedt became conductor of both the orchestra and the opera.

In 1985, the opera and orchestra again regained their own home when the replacement *Semperoper* (built on Semper's plans for the second house) finally opened with a performance of Weber's *Der Freischütz*). Under Giuseppe Sinopoli, its conductor from 1991 to 2001, the Dresden Staatskapelle continued its tradition of performance at the highest level. *—Joseph Stevenson*

Recommended:

○ **Schumann: Symphonies 1–4; Overture, Scherzo & Finale** / Sawallisch (cond.), Dresden Staatskapelle / 2002 / EMI 67771

○ **Bruckner: Symphony 8; Strauss: Metamorphosen** / Sinopoli (cond.), Dresden Staatskapelle / 1996 / DG 447744

○ **Strauss: Ein Heldenleben; Tod und Verklärung** / Kempe (cond.), Dresden Staatskapelle / 2002 / Angel 67892

Andreas Staier

b. Sep. 13, 1955, Göttingen, Germany
Fortepianist, Pianist, Harpsichordist

Andreas Staier is one of the foremost authentic-instrument keyboard players in the classical music world.

His early training was on standard piano. Courses in realizing continuo parts in Baroque music at the Hannover Conservatory led him to study harpsichord to learn the special technique of playing that instrument, which requires a considerably different technique of touch. "I fell in love with the sound of the harpsichord and became passionately enthusiastic about the repertory." He had been familiar with the Johann Sebastian Bach keyboard repertory, because so much of that is played on piano, or transcribed for it. However, study of harpsichord drew him into a repertory not frequently played on piano, going back to the English composers for the small keyboard instrument called the virginal. When he discovered that music he was, he said, "bowled over" by it. He added harpsichord studies to his courses at Hanover, and continued with it in studies in Amsterdam. His primary teachers in harpsichord and early music were Gustav Leonhardt, Nikolaus Harnoncourt, and Ton Koopman.

His interest in the fortepiano began gradually when he discovered the difference in sound and interpretation that results when that instrument is used for playing composers contemporary with it, especially Mozart and Beethoven. He added fortepiano to his studies, becoming one of the rare classical keyboard players who specializes in harpsichord and fortepiano.

In 1983 he joined Musica Antiqua Köln, a leading small Baroque ensemble, as its harpsichord player. This involved frequent touring to all parts of the world. He resigned from the ensemble in 1986 to embark on his solo career on both harpsichord and fortepiano. He also began teaching harpsichord at the Schola Cantorum Basiliensis in Basel, Switzerland, where he was on the faculty from 1987 to 1996.

He studies the keyboard repertory deeply. His recital programs and recordings include the standard Baroque composers, but also earlier music and Spanish keyboard works. His repertory extends from the English Baroque through the entire Classical period and into the Romantic era, where he plays the piano music of such composers as Mendelssohn, Schubert, Schumann, on harpsichords or pianos appropriate to the times of the music. He looks for important links among compositions of various eras. For instance, he thinks that Beethoven's *Diabelli Variations* are heard in a different light if one knows Bach's *Goldberg Variations* which, he says, are similarly illuminated by knowledge of Byrd's variations. (Apropos the *Goldberg Variations*, he says that while the work is totally suited for the harpsichord, "trying to play it on the piano is like attempting to square the circle.") He waited nearly a quarter of a century to play the *Goldberg* in public; his long-awaited first performance of it was in Montréal at the end of April, 2000.

He frequently works with other renowned artists, including Anner Bylsma, Tatiana Grindenko, René Jacobs, and various important early music ensembles. One of his closest partnerships is with the tenor Christoph Prégardien, who sings with him in the early Romantic and earlier repertory. Their recording of Schubert's *Winterreise* on Teldec won six major international recording prizes.

He has performed in major festivals and in most of the major concert halls of the world. His repertory consists nearly entirely of seventeenth, eighteenth, and early nineteenth century music, aside from a few twentieth century harpsichord pieces and is working on one twenty-first century work. It by Bryce Pauzé, a young French composer, and was especially written for the sound of the fortepiano with modern approaches to rhythm and tone color. *—Joseph Stevenson*

Recommended:

○ **Variaciones del Fandango Español** / Staier / 1999 / Teldec 21468

○ **Mozart: Sonatas** / Staier / HM 801815

○ **Domenico Scarlatti: Sonatas Vol. 1** / Staier / 1991 / Deutsche HM 77224

○ **Haydn: Concertos pour piano** / Staier, von der Goltz (cond.), Freiberger Barockorchester / HM 901854

Carl Stamitz

b. May 8, 1745, Mannheim, Germany, **d.** Nov. 9, 1801, Jena, Germany
Composer

The career of composer Carl Stamitz is closely associated with the Mannheim school, whose distinguished members included Carl's father Johann and brother Anton, and Ignaz Holzbauer, Franz Xaver Richter, and Johann Christian Cannabich. Carl Stamitz is generally considered to be the leading figure of the second generation of these composers, among which Cannabich and Stamitz's younger brother Anton are to be counted.

Born probably in early May 1745 (he was baptized on May 8), Carl Stamitz received his first music lessons from his father, then a member—but soon to be leader—of the Mannheim Orchestra, an ensemble connected with the Court of the Elector Palatine. Johann died when Carl was only 11, leaving the boy's further music education to Holzbauer, Richter, and Cannabich. In 1762, young Carl became a member of the Mannheim Orchestra, serving as a second violinist throughout his eight-year tenure there. Some of his earliest works date to this period, including the *Three Symphonies*, Op. 2. Shortly after his departure from the Mannheim Orchestra in 1770, Carl and Anton traveled to Paris, where in 1771 he accepted the dual post of court composer and conductor for the Duke Louis of Noailles. Stamitz turned out a number of works during his French years, including the *Symphony, La promenade royale*, written in Versailles in 1772; several other program symphonies; numerous quartets for various instruments; and other symphonic and chamber compositions. He also toured regularly as a violinist during the 1770s, making visits to Vienna (1772), Frankfurt (1773), and to Augsburg, Strasbourg, and back to Vienna (1774). Along with playing in concerts on these tours, he sometimes delivered manuscripts of new works, as he did on the Strasbourg visit, to satisfy a commission from Prince Kraft Ernst of Oettingen-Wallerstein. In 1777, Stamitz journeyed to London, where he lived for two years. He found less success there, though he apparently received substantial fees for the publication of numerous works, including many duos and trios for various instrumental combinations, the majority of which, however, were not published until well after his departure in 1779 or 1780. In about 1780, Stamitz settled in the Hague. There he began performing as a violist at the Court of William V of Orange, appearing in one concert with the 12-year-old Beethoven, who accompanied on fortepiano. Throughout the 1780s, Stamitz toured abroad, generally as a violist, visiting Hamburg (1785), Leipzig and Berlin (1786), and Dresden and Prague (1787). Probably in the late 1780s, Stamitz married Maria Josepha Pilz, who was 19 years his junior. The newlyweds settled in Greiz, Germany. Maria was in frail health after the birth of a son in 1790 and a daughter two years later, and Stamitz thus had to curtail his travels. He made a meager living selling his compositions to the King of Prussia and to royalty at smaller courts. He returned to Mannheim in 1795 and secured several commissions. That same year, he accepted the post of concertmaster at Jena, where he then moved his family. He also taught at the university there, but both positions yielded him only a modest income. He began to sink deeply into debt and made heroic efforts at arranging tours and concerts, but could not bring them off. Stamitz's wife died in January 1801 and he succumbed later that year. *—Robert Cummings*

Overview of Works (ca. 1770–1800)

Carl Stamitz (1745–1801) was the son of composer Johann Stamitz (1717–57) and the leading member of the Stamitz family of musicians that also included his brother Anton (b. 1750), a composer and string player. A musical conservative from the Classical period, Carl Stamitz adopted his prolific father's predilection for orchestral music, turning out 51 symphonies and 38 so-called symphonies concertantes, a genre best known through its few examples in the output of Haydn and Mozart. In addition, the younger Stamitz produced a huge output of concertos for a variety of instruments. And his chamber music output is as large, even if the quality is less consistent. Though identified with the fabled court orchestra at Mannheim in Germany, he spent much of his musical life traveling between various European capitals; his multipurpose output was thus large and varied.

In the genre of the symphony, Stamitz broke away from the influence of his father, who preferred—and became the first composer to be identified with—the four-movement structure. Carl favored the Italian approach of three movements in a fast/slow/fast pattern. The six symphonies comprising the Op. 13 set (also known as Op. 16), from 1777, have managed to attract attention over the years. The *Symphony No. 5 in C major* from that group is among his stronger efforts, while No. 4 is delightful in its vigor, offering a first movement Presto and concluding with a Prestissimo finale. The *Symphony in D major, La Chasse* (1772) is another worthy effort that has garnered praise.

Stamitz, however, is probably better known for his concertos, which offer fresh, delightful Classical-style repertory for a variety of instruments. The wind and string concertos began receiving attention toward the end of the twentieth century. The clarinet concertos, numbering 11 (some older catalogs list only ten), are quite an interesting lot. The Haydn-esque *Clarinet Concerto No. 1 in F major* (1777) already shows the composer's grasp of instrumental and orchestral writing, and stylistically divulges his ties to the Mannheim School. Stamitz's *Clarinet Concert No. 11 in E flat major* (1793) is more assured and masterful, though not significantly in advance of the *First* in expressive language.

The *Flute Concerto in D major*, Op. 27, one of his more widely played compositions, features an attractive, light opening movement and a lovely Adagio second movement. Of his 15 violin concertos, none has ever gained much currency, although his several for cello (four of six survive) and viola have gotten some attention. Stamitz's works in the symphony concertante genre have concerto-like features in their highlighting of pairs of instruments, but have also been generally neglected.

In the chamber music genre, Stamitz wrote for numerous combinations of instruments, but achieved somewhat less success. His output contains sextets, quintets, and works for larger ensembles. Quartets, trios, and duos form a large proportion, and instrumental combinations little represented in the more familiar chamber works of Haydn and Mozart. Op. 8, for example, is a set of six quartets for clarinet, violin, viola, and bassoon; Op. 2 contains six trios for two violins and bassoon. Rarely is Stamitz less than interesting in his chamber works and his scoring is aways skilled and often quite imaginative.

Stamitz wrote a small amount of vocal music, though his two largest efforts here—the singspiel *Der verliebte Vormund* and the opera *Dardanus*—were lost. His *Mass in D* and several cantatas failed to establish his reputation in the genre. *—Robert Cummings*

Recommended:

- ○ **Stamitz: 4 Symphonies** / Bamert (cond.), London Mozart Players / 1995 / Chandos 9358
- ○ **Stamitz: Cello Concertos 1–3** / Benda, Prage CO / 1993 / Naxos 550865
- ○ **Stamitz: Clarinet Concertos Vol. 1** / Berkes, Okazaki, Takashima, Budapest Nicolaus Esterhazy Sinfonia / 1997 / Naxos 553584
- ○ **Stamitz: Wind Symphonies** / Classicum Consortium / CPO 999081

CONCERTO

Flute Concerto in G major, Op. 29

Stamitz was highly adept at the galant, or early Classical, style, and his *Concerto for flute and orchestra*, Op. 29, is a perfect example of that manner: carefully crafted, tastefully entertaining, lighthearted, but not at all individual. The purpose of this music is to delight an audience, not to display arresting compositional genius.

The first movement, marked Allegro, employs the sonata form favored by the Stamitz family's Mannheim school and manipulated more famously by Haydn and Mozart. The orchestral introduction begins with a short, marchlike flourish, then continues with a succession of brief themes designed more to accommodate expressive contrast than to cling to the memory. The flute takes the lead in repeating all this material, the tunes replete with tasteful ornamentation and a few quick runs and trills. The orchestra offers a condensed review of some of the themes, whereupon the flute returns to the fore through this, the development section, inserting some fast passagework into longer, more lyrical passages. The recapitulation is interrupted by a solo cadenza that again cycles through the brief themes, but now with even greater ornamentation. A concise orchestral coda wraps up the movement.

The second movement, Andante non troppo moderato, is marked espressivo. The flute meanders through a graceful C major melody, initially over plucked strings, producing a perfumed, nocturnal effect. The middle section offers dreamy, nostalgic variations on this material, with the flute taking a brief, delicate cadenza just before the end. The concluding Rondo allegro is tied together by a busy, happy primary theme introduced by the flute and repeated by the orchestra. This alternates with a section full of rapid runs; then an extended, stately minuet; and finally a dramatic coloratura rendering of the principal theme, closing with the material with which the movement began. *—James Reel*

Recommended:

- ○ **Mannheim Flute Concertos** / J. Valek, V. Valek (cond.), Dvořák CO / 1994 / Supraphon 111872
- ○ **Stamitz & Mozart Flute Concertos** / Racine, Fournillier (cond.), English CO / 1996 / Novalis 150131

Simon Standage

b. Nov. 8, 1941, High Wycombe, England

Violinist, Conductor

As a specialist in historical violin techniques of the seventeenth and eighteenth centuries, Simon Standage has performed with many of the world's leading period instrument orchestras. After a music degree from Cambridge University in 1963, a Harkness Fellowship to study with Ivan Galamian in New York City, and, after a 1972 Wigmore Hall debut, he became a founding member of Trevor Pinnock's ensemble the English Concert. Standage served as first (solo) violinist of this ensemble from 1973 to 1991; his recording of Vivaldi's *The Four Seasons* with the English Concert received a Grammy nomination. Standage also played extensively with the English Chamber Orchestra from 1974 to 1978, led the City of London Sinfonia from 1980 to 1989, and served as associate director of the Academy of Ancient Music from 1991 to 1995. Appointed professor of Baroque violin at the Royal Academy of Music in London in 1983, he has taught at the Dresden Akademie für Alte Musik since 1993. In addition to these longtime associations, Standage has founded two ensembles devoted to historically aware string performance. The Salomon Quartet, which he founded in 1981, specializes in applying period instruments and approaches to the eighteenth century quartet and quintet repertory. In 1990, Standage and Richard Hickox founded the group Collegium Musicum 90. Under contract with Chandos Records, Collegium Musicum 90 produced more than 40 recordings in its first decade, from large-scale dramatic works to acclaimed trio sonata recordings. *—Timothy Dickey*

Recommended:

- ○ **Telemann: Music of the Nations** / Standage (cond.), Collegium Musicum 90 / 1996 / Chandos 593
- ○ **Leclair: Violin Concertos, Vol. 1** / Standage (cond. & violin), Collegium Musicum 90 / 1994 / Chandos 551
- ○ **Mozart: Violin Concertos** / Hogwood (cond.), Standage, Academy of Ancient Music / 1997 / Decca 455721
- ○ **Bach: Violin Concertos** / Standage (cond. & violin), Collegium Musicum 90 / 1996 / Chandos 0594
- ○ **Vivaldi: The Paris Concertos** / Standage (cond.), Collegium Musicum 90 / 1999 / Chandos 647

Charles Villiers Stanford

b. Sep. 30, 1852, Dublin, Ireland, **d.** Mar. 29, 1924, London, England

Composer: Choral, Orchestral

Sir Charles Stanford has been called the most important single factor in the renaissance of English music during the late nineteenth and early twentieth centuries; indeed, even if one were to overlook Stanford's own vast catalog of compositions, it would be impossible to ignore the pronounced effect Stanford's nearly 40-year teaching career had on several generations of British composers. Born in 1852 to a prominent Irish lawyer and amateur musician, Stanford manifested his musical talents early in life. Whether the stories that he was actively composing songs by age of four and giving full-length recitals by age nine are true or not, Stanford was certainly the recipient of a thorough musical and academic education, studying at Henry Tilney Bassett's school in Dublin and taking private lessons in piano, organ and composition from a number of trained musicians (including Arthur O'Leary).

At age eighteen Stanford entered Queen's College, Cambridge to pursue more serious studies in music. In 1874 he took a BA in music, having already been appointed both organist at Trinity College (a post he filled with distinction for almost 20 years) and conductor of a number of University choral societies. After graduating from Queen's College, Stanford traveled to the continent for further studies, working with composer Carl Heinrich Reinecke in Leipzig for almost two years and later (having met and impressed Joseph Joachim) with Joachim's associate Friedrich Kiel in Berlin. By the time of Stanford's return to London in the late 1870s his reputation as one of the leading British composers of the day was secure, and a number of his large compositions (such as the *Second Symphony*, 1882) were premiered during the following ten years.

Stanford was appointed to the faculty of the new Royal College of Music in 1882, and further honored when he was made a professor at Cambridge University in 1887. He was knighted in 1902, and remained a prominent feature of the musical landscape of Great Britain until his death in 1924. Stanford's lifelong service to British music earned his ashes a place of distinction next to Henry Purcell's in Westminster Abbey.

Although accounts of Stanford's life have tended to focus on his impact as a teacher (understandably, with such notables as Vaughan Williams, Holst, Samuel Coleridge-Taylor, John Ireland, Frank Bridge, and Arthur Bliss among his many pupils), his merit as a composer deserve as much mention. He is, without a doubt, the greatest British composer of sacred music since Henry Purcell: *Morning, Communion, and Evening Services in B flat*, Op.10 is almost symphonic in scope, and Stanford's many cantatas and oratorios are the preeminent British entries in the genres. His orchestral output includes seven symphonies and three piano concertos, and, although only one of his operas (*Shamus O'Brien*, 1896) achieved any kind of success, Stanford's interest in a new kind of British opera cleared a path for one of that country's most notable twentieth century composers, Benjamin Britten. *—Blair Johnston*

CHORAL

Sacred Choral Works (1868–1923)

Sit back and try to think of the first really fine British composer of sacred music after Henry Purcell (native-born, that is: Handel doesn't count); if the name Charles

Villiers Stanford, who lived a full two centuries after Purcell, came to mind, give yourself a pat on the back. There is something about the Irish-born Stanford's sacred music that raises it above the drudgery that was British church music of the eighteenth and nineteenth centuries—an honesty and a straightforward hardiness that are, by comparison to the clichéd standard of the day, so attractive that churchgoers feel a special bond with it. And there is an awful lot of it, from religious oratorios to Latin motets to English anthems to service-oriented organ music, making it even easier to understand how and why this prominent musician earned the reputation of savior of English church music.

One of Stanford's main interests was oratorio; most that he composed were secular (or at least semi-secular), but there are a few cantata-type works that deserve mention. His Opus 8, "God is our Hope and Strength," a large piece for vocal soloists (soprano, alto, tenor, baritone, and bass), chorus and orchestra, is an important early work. Closer to the other end of his life is a brilliant *Stabat Mater* that, despite its formal Latin title, is an oratorio of sorts that Stanford described as a "symphonic cantata"; it too is written for solo voices, chorus, and orchestra, but, as the composer's description indicates, it takes more the shape of a symphony than of a purely devotional work.

Other large works include a *Mass in G major*, Op. 46 (1893), a *Requiem*, Op. 63 (1897), and a *Te Deum*, Op. 66 (1898), but it is in his smaller anthems and motets, and in his complete services, that Stanford's best sacred music is to be found. Many English anthems, like "Ye Choirs of New Jerusalem," and "The Lord is my Shepherd," as well as Latin entries, such as *Justorum animae*, *Ceolus ascendit hodie* and *Beati quorum via*, have remained favorites with choirs and congregations through the years. Stanford composed five full sets of Morning, Communion, and Evening Services for chorus (sometimes with vocal soloists, sometimes without) and orchestra with organ. The earliest set, in B flat major, comes from 1879; the last, in D major—which in sharp contrast to that full and florid earliest set is scored plainly for unison voices and accompaniment—comes from 1923, just a year before the composer's death.

There is both concert and sacred organ music with Stanford's name on it, and it might be argued that the concert—which includes five organ sonatas—is the better. But church items like the *Te Deum* and *Canzona* of 1909 or thereabouts have still maintained their place in the active repertory of British organists, even if they are unknown outside British territory. —*Blair Johnston*

Recommended:

- ○ **Stanford: Sacred Choral Music Vol. 1: "The Cambridge Years"** / Hill (cond.), Winchester Cathedral Choir / 1997 / Hyperion 66964
- ○ **Stanford: Stabat Mater; Bible Songs; Te Deum laudamus** / Hickox (cond.), soloists, Leeds Philharmonic Chorus, BBC Philharmonic Brass / 1997 / Chandos 9548
- ○ **Stanford: The Complete Morning and Evening Services Vol. 1** / Lancelot (cond.), Wright, Durham Cathedral Choir / Priory 437
- ○ **Stanford: The Complete Morning and Evening Services Vol. 2** / Lancelot (cond.), Durham Cathedral Choir / Priory 514
- ○ **Stanford: The Complete Morning and Evening Services Vol. 3** / Daley (cond.), Johnstone, Oxford Christ Church Cathedral Choir / Priory 602
- ○ **Stanford: Anthems and Services** / Robinson (cond.), Whitton, St. John's College Choir / 2003 / Naxos 8555794

ORCHESTRAL

Works for Orchestra (1869–1922)

Charles Villiers Stanford, that Irish-born titan of British musical academia, was an exceedingly prolific composer who bent his facile technique to the creation of works in just about every vein—theater, sacred and secular vocal/choral, chamber, and large-scale orchestral music, without which a composer of his generation could hardly hope to build and maintain a decent reputation. Stanford's orchestral catalog, most of which wasn't published during his lifetime, is easily divided into three categories: 1) symphonies, 2) concertos or concerto-like pieces, and 3) miscellaneous fare. It is a hint of the man's musical virility that the extreme chronological ends of this orchestral catalog lie a full 54 years apart (1869–1923).

Stanford's seven symphonies cover almost 40 of those 54 years. The *Symphony No. 1 in B flat major*, without opus, is a prentice piece from 1875 that earned second prize in the Alexandra Palace Competition. After this, Stanford generally waited about five to seven years between symphonic outings. *No. 2 in D minor* ("Elegiac"), without opus, comes from 1882; *No. 3 in F minor* ("Irish"), Op. 28, from 1887. *No. 4 in F major*, Op. 31, bears the date 1889, breaking the five-to-seven year cycle; *No. 5 in D major*, Op. 56, called *"L'Allegro ed il Pensieroso,"* appeared in 1894. Stanford allowed the *Symphony No. 6 in E flat major*, Op. 94 ("In memoriam G.F. Watts"), to gestate for an unusually long time—it wasn't finished until 1905. The *Symphony No. 7 in D minor*, Op. 124, of 1911 is Stanford's final symphonic thought. His sweepingly Romantic, but thoroughly conservative, music was subject to greater neglect as musical times changed during and after the war years, and the symphonic work was first to be abandoned, difficult as it is to program.

However, Stanford kept composing works for soloist and orchestra, something which had always keenly interested him. His very first known orchestral work, in fact, is a *Rondo* for violin and orchestra composed way back in 1869. Violinists would do well to occasionally peruse the Stanford catalog: there are, in addition to that early *Rondo*, a *Suite in D*, Op. 32, composed in 1888 for Joseph Joachim, two violin concertos (Opp. 74 and 162, 1899 and 1918, respectively), a set of variations composed in 1921, and the *Irish Rhapsody No. 6*, Op. 191, of 1923—Stanford's very last orchestral piece. Cellists are also given some fine items, including the *Irish Rhapsody No. 3*, the *Irish Concertino*, Op. 161, of 1918, and an item called *Ballata and Ballabile*, Op. 160. Stanford tried his hand at piano concerto composition three times (Opp. 59, 126, 171, 1894–1919).

Paramount in the miscellaneous category are the non-solo instrument *Irish Rhapsodies* (Nos. 1, 2, 4, and 5), in which Stanford's deep love for the land of his birth and its rich musical heritage comes fully to the fore. Two early overtures, the *Concert Overture* of 1870 and the *Festival Overture* of 1877, bear witness to the bountiful creative energy of the young composer. —*Blair Johnston*

Recommended:

- ○ **Stanford: Symphonies 1–7** / Handley (cond.), Ulster Orch. / 1994 / Chandos 9279/82
- ○ **Stanford: Six Irish Rhapsodies; Piano Concerto 2; Down among the Dead Men** / Handley (cond.), Ulster Orch. / 2003 / Chandos 10116
- ○ **Stanford: Violin Concerto; Suite for Violin & Orchestra** / Marwood, Brabbins (cond.), BBC Scottish SO / 2000 / Hyperion 67208

Janos Starker

b. Jul. 5, 1924, Budapest, Hungary
Cellist

Cellist Janos Starker was born in Hungary to music-loving Russian parents. His two brothers were violinists, and he was given a cello before he was six. He made public appearances at ages six and seven. Soon he entered the Franz Liszt Academy of Music in Budapest, making his debut there at 11. He had begun teaching other children at eight, and by the time he was 12 he had five pupils. Starker regards the experience as important to his artistic development. He found himself having to articulate phenomena that students his age rarely grasp, let alone impart to others. Starker was especially influenced by Leo Weiner, a composer who taught chamber music. He has said that for more than 50 years Weiner taught every prominent Hungarian musician to learn and understand music as a language.

At 14 Starker made his professional debut playing the Dvořák concerto. He left the conservatory in 1939. After the war, when musical activities resumed, Starker became principal cellist of the Budapest Opera and the Budapest Philharmonic orchestras. Soviet Red Army forces had occupied the country, and the Communist Party was gaining dominance. Starker left the country in 1946 when relatively free travel was still possible.

He gave a successful concert in Vienna, then remained there to prepare for the Geneva Cello Competition, held in October 1946. He won only a bronze medal. "I played like a blind man," he has said. "What happens to the bird who sings and doesn't know how it sings? That's what happens to child prodigies." Starker set out to rebuild his technique. He analyzed all aspects of playing, from breathing to the physics of applying muscular force to the bow and the instrument, to phrasing, bowing, and fingering. By October of the following year he had regained his confidence. He decided to stay in the West due to the deteriorating political situation in Hungary, and headed for the United States, where Hungarian musicians had important positions.

Antal Dorati, music director of the Dallas Symphony, made Starker the orchestra's principal cellist. A year later Starker accepted Fritz Reiner's invitation to become principal cellist of the Metropolitan Opera Orchestra. In 1953 Reiner began a brilliant period as music director of the Chicago Symphony, and brought Starker with him to lead the cello section. Starker remained in Chicago until 1958, becoming a U.S. citizen in 1954 and bringing his family to the country. In 1958 he resigned his Chicago position in order to pursue his solo career. In the meantime, he had already begun making important recordings, including an early set of Bach suites. Easing the transition was an offer from Indiana University School of Music to join the faculty on a two-year trial basis. Starker quickly found Bloomington a congenial base, and attracted exceptionally talented students.

Starker's stage demeanor and public persona were rather restrained and undemonstrative. The unwary draw the same mistaken conclusion that also plagued Jascha Heifetz, charging Starker with coldness and lack of emotion. Discerning critics, however, have always tended to speak of the warmth and expressiveness of his playing. Another similarity to Heifetz lies in Starker's very focused tone, with a light, narrow, and quick vibrato. He proclaimed himself happier if, after a concert, people say "What beautiful music Schubert wrote" rather than "How well Starker plays." Similarly, he considered it at least as important to turn out the next generation of fine cello teachers as the next generation of star players. —*Joseph Stevenson*

Recommended:

- ○ **Bach: Suites for Solo Cello** / Starker / 1997 / RCA 61436

○ **Schumann, Lalo, Saint-Saëns: Concertos** / Dorati, Lawrence, Skrowaczewski (conds.), Starker, London SO / 1991 / Mercury 432010
○ **Brahms, Mendelssohn: Sonatas** / Starker, Sebok (piano) / 1996 / Mercury 434377
○ **Romantic Cello Favorites** / Starker, Neriki (piano) / 1989 / Delos 3065
○ **Schumann; Brahms; Rachmaninof** / Starker, Neriki (piano) / 1991 / BMG 60598
○ **Italian Cello Sonatas** / Starker, Sebok (piano) / 1994 / Mercury 434344
○ **Barber & Dvořák: Concertos** / Starker, etc. / RCA 60717

David Starobin

b. Sep. 27, 1951, New York, NY
Guitarist
David Starobin is a guitarist who is also a musicologist and runs Bridge Records out of New York. Through Bridge Starobin has made available many classic performances recorded at the Library of Congress, and his own playing on the Bridge releases of music by Giulio Regondi has made an indispensible contribution to the catalogue of a neglected master. David Starobin is also an expert interpreter of Contemporary guitar music. *—Uncle Dave Lewis*

Recommended:
○ **Giuliani Solo Guitar Music** / Starobin / 1991 / Bridge 9029
○ **New Music with Guitar** / Starobin, Jolles, Mason, Palma, Press, Frisch / 1988 / Bridge 9009
○ **The Great Regondi, Vol. 1** / Starobin, Rogers, Lustman / 1993 / Bridge 9039
○ **Lennon, Ruders, Crumb** / Purvis, Milnes (conds.), Starobin, Speculum Musicae / 1997 / Bridge 9071

Eleanor Steber

b. Jul. 17, 1916, Wheeling, WV, **d.** Oct. 3, 1990, Langhorn, PA
Soprano
Steber was one of the most important sopranos in the United States during the 1940s and 1950s, with a sweet and yet full voice and outstanding versatility. Her recitals were practically vocal pentathlons for their wide range of styles and vocal demands, and the day she sang Desdemona in Verdi's *Otello* for a Met matinee and Fiordiligi in Mozart's *Così fan tutte* that evening is still legendary. She is perhaps most famous for her creation of the title role in Samuel Barber's *Vanessa* (actually as a substitute for Sena Jurinac), and for commissioning his *Knoxville: Summer of 1915*. In addition to opera and recitals, she was a frequent guest on *The Voice of Firestone*'s television broadcasts. However, her career outlasted her voice, and most of her later appearances and recordings were gravely technically flawed.

Her mother was an accomplished amateur singer, and strongly encouraged her to study and to sing in school and community shows. She entered the New England Conservatory of Music, originally intending to major in piano, but her voice teacher, William Whitney, persuaded her to focus on singing, instead. Her opera debut was in 1936 in a WPA production of Wagner's *The Flying Dutchman*, a demanding role indeed for a 21-year-old. She won the 1940 Metropolitan Auditions of the Air, and made her Met debut later that year as Sophie in Strauss' *Der Rosenkavalier*. Her easy upper range, coupled with a rich, smoothly produced lower voice made her a natural for Mozart roles such as the Countess in *Le nozze di Figaro*, Pamina in *The Magic Flute*, and even Konstanze in the *Abduction from the Seraglio*, with its vocal pyrotechnics. As her voice matured, she sang some of the spinto roles in both the German and Italian repertoire, including Tosca, Desdemona, Elsa in *Lohengrin*, and the Marschallin in *Der Rosenkavalier*. She also sang Marie in the first Metropolitan production of Alban Berg's *Wozzeck* in 1959. Her relationship with the Met was not an easy one, for many reasons on both sides, and she turned her attention more and more towards recitals and concerts during the 1960s. She and her husband opened and managed a record label, ST/AND (combining their names), but when they attempted to expand, it was a dismal flop. She made some appearances on Broadway, mostly in supporting parts, and also gave one of the notorious bathhouse concerts in New York in 1973. *—Ann Feeney*

Recommended:
○ **The Early Career, 1938–1951** / Steber, etc. / 1994 / VAI 1072
○ **Eleanor Steber** / Steber, etc. / 1996 / Sony 62356
○ **Samuel Barber: Vanessa** / Mitropoulos (cond.), Gedda, Steber, Tozzi, Elias, Metropolitan Opera Orch. & Chorus / 1957 / RCA 7899
○ **Puccini: Madame Butterfly** / Rudolf (cond.), Steber, Tucker, Valdengo, Madeira, Metropolitan Opera Orch. / 1998 / Sony 62765

Crispian Steele-Perkins

b. Dec. 18, 1944, Exeter, England
Trumpeter
Crispian Steele-Perkins is one of the leading exponents of the early trumpet. His early studies were with Ernest Hall and Bernard Brown at the Guildhall School of Music. His orchestral career began with the Sadler's Wells Opera (later the English National Opera) and the Royal Philharmonic Orchestra. He soon developed an interest in the earlier repertoire for the trumpet and has since performed with many leading period instrument ensembles, including the Academy of Ancient Music, the English Baroque Soloists, Tafelmusik, the Taverner Players, Collegium Musicum 90, and the King's Consort. Steele-Perkins performs also as a concerto soloist. He was featured in the inaugural concerts of the tercentenary celebrations of both Handel and Purcell, televised from *Westminster Abbey* in 1985 and 1995, respectively. *—Robert Adelson*

Recommended:
○ **Classical Trumpet Concertos** / King (cond.), Steele-Perkins, King's Consort / 2001 / Hyperion 67266

Wilhelm Stenhammar

b. Feb. 7, 1871, Stockholm, Sweden, **d.** Nov. 20, 1927, Stockholm, Sweden
Composer: Symphonic, Concerto
Stenhammar was a Swedish pianist and self-taught composer and conductor. His compositions began as typically late Romantic fare but evolved through three periods. In the first, his primary influences were Liszt, Brahms, and Wagner, but the music is imbued with a Nordic sound without specifically quoting Swedish folk song. His early operas *Gildet på Solhaug* (1892–93) and *Tirfing* (1897–98), although unsuccessful, were the pinnacles of this period. Stenhammar's second period began as he attempted to create a more concentrated and motivically oriented style, modeled on the great classicists Beethoven, Haydn, and Mozart. In spite of this, the music of this period loses none of its Nordic color. His brilliant cantata *Ett folk* (1904–05) and the frequently played *Second Piano Concerto* are the most representative. Beginning in 1909, perhaps feeling his lack of training was detrimental to further development, Stenhammar engaged upon a nine-year course in strict counterpoint. The fruit of this study resulted in his last period, where the music becomes more contrapuntally and modally oriented, particularly in the last two of his six string quartets. Yet at the same time, his larger works, such as the orchestral *Serenade* and the *Second Symphony*, lose nothing of the earlier freshness and inspiration that make Stenhammar's music so attractive.

Stenhammar's early years were spent surrounded by culture, although he never undertook formal training except in piano. By 1900, he had established himself as a pianist, eventually giving over 1000 concerts all over Sweden. He had also debuted as a conductor in 1897 with his own overture *Excelsior!*, and eventually went on to direct the Stockholm Philharmonic Society, the Royal Opera, the New Philharmonic Society, and the Göttesborgs Orkesterförening. Stenhammar eventually became one of the most important Scandinavian musicians of his era, and his compositions, including many songs, choral works, chamber and solo pieces, and theater and orchestral works represent the best music out of turn-of-the-century Sweden. *—Steven Coburn*

Overview of Works (1888–1924)

Along with Alfvén and Peterson-Berger, Wilhelm Stenhammar was one of the three principal composers in Swedish music at the fin de siècle. Alfvén was the more structurally radical and emotional extravagant, Peterson-Berger was more typically Swedish in his elegance and sweetness, but Stenhammar was arguably the greatest. Starting with his conservative early works, which displayed tremendous technical ability, moving through his more innovative middle works with their larger forms and more advanced harmonies and culminating in his highly individual and monumental later works, Stenhammar created an oeuvre that can stand with Nielsen's and Sibelius' as the greatest Scandinavian music of its time. After the failure of his two early operas, Stenhammar never returned to the form, and aside from his songs, some choral works, and the massive final cantata *Sangen*, Stenhammar wrote little for voices. He was instead devoted to instrumental forms: two symphonies, two piano concertos, six string quartets, and a piano sonata. Of his earlier instrumental works, the *Piano Concerto No. 1 in B flat minor* (1893) is clearly based on Brahms' *Concerto in D minor*, the *Symphony No. 1 in F major* (1902–03) is obviously derived from Bruckner, and the first three string quartets (1894, 1896, 1897–1900) are rooted in Beethoven. But he began to develop his own voice in the *Piano Concerto No. 2 in D minor* (1904–07), his *Sentimental Romances* (1910), and *String Quartets No. 4* and *No. 5* (1904–09, 1910). With the *Serenade for orchestra* (1911–13), his *String Quartet No. 6* (1916), and especially his *Symphony No. 2 in G minor* (1911–15), Stenhammar created works that stand with the best of those composed in Scandinavia at the time. The *Serenade* is light and airy with textures and colors that recall those of the Impressionist, but translated into the cooler and clearer hues of Sweden. The *String Quartet No. 6* is both lyrical and contrapuntal, a combination that makes it sound simultaneously tuneful and learned. The *Symphony No. 2* is arguably Stenhammar's masterpiece: a fusion of modal polyphony and symphonic forms climaxing in a fugal Finale of tremendous strength and power. Stenhammar's magnum opus is his cantata *Sangen* (1921), a choral/orchestral work in three parts that strives to be a sort of Swedish *Ode to Joy*. Although each of its individual sections is impressive—the Sturm und Drang opening, the symphonic Interlude, and the Handelian close—the whole work does not quite hold together. *—James Leonard*

Recommended:

- ○ **Stenhammar: Piano Concerto; Suite From Incidental Music To "Chitra"** / Jarvi (cond.), Gothenburg SO / 1989 / Bis 476
- ○ **Stenhammar: Piano Concerto No. 1; Symphony No. 3** / Rozhdestvensky (cond.), Widlund, Stockholm PO / 1992 / Chandos 9074
- ○ **Stenhammar: The Complete Solo Piano Music Vol. 1** / L. Negro / 1992 / Bis 554
- ○ **Stenhammar: Songs** / Mattei, Lundin / 1994 / Bis 654
- ○ **Stenhammar: Serenade** / Jarvi (cond.), Gothenburg SO / 1985 / BIS 310
- ○ **Stenhammar: Music for the Theatre** / Volmer (cond.), Anderson, Helsingborg SO / Sterling 1045

SYMPHONIC

Symphony No. 2 in G minor, Op. 34 (1911–1915)

Swedish composer, conductor, and pianist Wilhelm Stenhammar's *Symphony No. 2 in G minor*, Op. 34, (1911–15) is his symphonic masterpiece, and one of the great Scandinavian symphonies of its time. A friend of Nielsen and Sibelius, Stenhammar wrote music that was more conservative than theirs: Stenhammar was steeped in the music of Brahms, and not for him were the harmonic or structural innovations of Nielsen, Sibelius, or his fellow Swede Hugo Alfvén. This does not mean, however, that his music lacked strength or power. Indeed, Stenhammar's *Symphony No. 2* is fully as muscular as Nielsen's *Third* or Sibelius' *Second*. But rather than write in the chromatic language of the *fin de siècle*, Stenhammar composed his *Second* in a modal language based on the almost medieval themes of the work. Using his modal language and modal themes, Stenhammar constructs huge arches and vaults of contrapuntal architecture and thereby creates a sense of monumental grandeur not unlike that of Bruckner's symphonies. The opening Allegro energico is cast in sonata form, but with the movement's expansive development balanced by an equally large coda. The following Andante sounds like a contrapuntally conceived religious procession of deep solemnity. The Scherzo switches from the sacred to the secular with a buoyant dance theme and a bucolic trio featuring the winds. The Finale is the largest movement of the four and by far the most original: after a rhapsodic, slow opening, the music unfolds as a series of fugues based on lyrical themes culminating in an impassioned slow fugue marked Tranquilemente and concluding with a massive double fugue that sounds almost choral in its lyrical beauty. *—James Leonard*

Recommended:

- ○ **Stenhammer: Symphony 2** / Jarvi (cond.), Stockholm PO / 1999 / Virgin 45244
- ○ **Stenhammar: Symphony 2; Excelsior!** / Sundkvist (cond.), Scottish National Orch. / 1996 / Naxos 55388
- ○ **Stenhammar: Symphony 2** / Westerberg (cond.), Stockholm PO / 1979 / Caprice 21151

CONCERTO

Two Sentimental Romances for violin & orchestra, Op. 28 (1910)

Swedish composer Wilhelm Stenhammar composed his *Two Sentimental Romances for Violin and Orchestra* in the summer of 1910. The two pieces have separate tempo indications—Andantino for the first and Allegro patetico for the second—and are in different and unrelated keys—A major for the first and F minor for the second—but both bear the same expressive marking of sentimental. While both pieces are very different in tone—the first is sweetly reserved and tenderly affection, while the second is much more passionately lyrical—both are defined by their expressive marking. However, Stenhammar's "sentimental" does not mean insipid or mawkish as the word has come to mean a century later, but rather "marked or governed by feeling, sensibility, or emotional idealism" as the *Merriam-Webster Dictionary* defines it. And although Stenhammar himself later repudiated the emotionalism of the *Sentimental Romances* in his more austere later string quartets and *Symphony No. 2*, the sentimentality of the two *Romances* is real and true. The *Two Sentimental Romances* also exist in versions for violin and piano and for flute and orchestra. *—James Leonard*

Recommended:

- ○ **Swedish Romantic Violin Concertos** / Ringborg, Willen (cond.), Swedish CO / 1999 / Naxos 554287
- ○ **Stenhammar: Symphonies; Piano Concertos** / Jarvi (cond.), Wallin, Malmo SO / 1983 / Bis 714

Isaac Stern

b. Jul. 21, 1920, Kremenetz, Russia, **d.** Sep. 22, 2001, New Yok City, NY, USA

Violinist

Isaac Stern was among the most distinguished of the world's violinists. He achieved a strong rapport with his audience through his own personality and his visible love for the music, with an unerring command of the proper style for each work in his exceptionally wide repertoire. His technique was impeccable, his tone strong and warm, though not rich. He performed and recorded virtually the entire standard violin repertoire, including most of the many great violin concertos of the 1930s: those of Hindemith, Berg, *Prokofiev* (No. 2), Walton, Bartok (No. 2) and other works, some quite contemporary. His repertoire extended at least from Vivaldi to Dutilleux. Stern also dubbed on-screen appearances by actors impersonating violinists; his films include *Humoresque, Tonight We Sing,* and *Fiddler on the Roof.*

Stern's family moved to the United States and settled in San Francisco when he was one year old. His mother, a professional singer, gave him his first music lessons. He began studying the violin at the San Francisco Conservatory in 1928. In 1932 he became the third immensely talented San Francisco-area boy to train with the San Francisco Symphony concertmaster Louis Persinger (the others were Menuhin and Ruggiero Ricci). However, he considered Naoum Blinder, with whom he studied until the age of 15, his only true teacher. Stern made his debut with the San Francisco Symphony on February 18, 1936, with Pierre Monteux conducting the *Third Concerto* by Saint-Saëns. After his New York debut in 1937, he returned to San Francisco for further study. He reentered concert life on February 18, 1939, again giving a recital in New York. Soon he was one of the leading American violinists, particularly noticed for his young age, and his January 8, 1943, recital at Carnegie Hall (his first solo performance there) was a smash hit.

In 1943 and 1944 Stern entertained American troops in Iceland, Greenland, and the South Pacific. After the war he toured Australia in 1947, and made his first trip to Europe in 1948. He played at Pablo Casals' Prades Festival from 1950–52, and the Edinburgh Festival in 1953. His tour of the U.S.S.R. in 1956 was an early sign of one of the recurrent thaws in the Cold War. In 1960 he formed a durable trio with pianist Eugene Istomin and cellist Leonard Rose; the group played the complete trio literature by Beethoven in bicentennial celebrations of the composer's birth. He recorded mostly for Columbia (which subsequently became CBS, then Sony Classics), with major orchestras and conductors, with the Stern-Rose-Istomin Trio, and in sonata and other duet repertory with his regular partner, Alexander Zakin. He made several appearances at the White House.

In the late 1950s, when the City of New York planned the construction of the Lincoln Center complex, it became clear that the plans as they stood would entail the destruction of the old Metropolitan Opera house and of Carnegie Hall. The latter, one of the finest concert halls in the world acoustically, was saved for posterity by the actions of a group Stern formed in 1960. Stern was chosen president of the Carnegie Hall Corporation, formed to supervise the artistic program of the great concert hall. He also was involved in the formation of the U.S. National Endowment of the Arts, and was appointed to its initial advisory board. He served as chairman of the board of the American-Israel Cultural Foundation, which aids the careers of young musicians. Stern, among other honors, was named Officer of the Légion d'honneur of France.*—Joseph Stevenson*

Recommended:

- ○ **Wieniawski & Bruch: Concertos** / Ormandy, Rostropovich, Brieff (conds.), Stern, Philadelphia Orch., Columbia SO, National SO / 1995 / Sony 66830
- ○ **Schubert, Haydn: Trios; Mozart: Piano Quartet, K493** / Stern, Rose, Istomin, Katims, Schneider / 1995 / Sony 64516
- ○ **Isaac Stern** / Kurtz, Waxman (cond.), Stern, Zakin, Levant, New York PO / Pearl 9248

Risë Stevens

b. Jun. 11, 1913, New York City, NY

Mezzo-Soprano

Mezzo-soprano Risë Stevens was one of the most prominent American opera stars during World War II and for nearly two decades afterwards. She is of Norwegian descent; her original name was Risë Steenberg. She showed early promise as a singer and studied with a teacher named Orry Prado. After graduating from high school, she landed a job with the New York Little Theater Opera Company. After that company went bankrupt, she became a dress model.

Anna Schoen-René, a voice teacher at the Juilliard School, offered her free singing lessons. Risë received a tempting job offer from the Metropolitan Opera Company but judged she was not ready and declined it. Instead, she went to Europe to hone the various crafts of an opera singer. These included classes in stagecraft with Herbert Graf and continued voice training with Marie Gutheil-Schoder at the Salzburg Mozarteum.

In 1936 she accepted conductor Georg Szell's offer of a contract with the Prague Opera, where she was listed as a contralto. There she was coached in standard contralto and mezzo repertory by Herbert Graf, and appeared in Prague, Vienna, and in Cairo, Egypt (where she traveled as part of a Viennese-based opera group. She traveled to the Teatro Colón in Buenos Aires, continuing to mature and to draw increasing attention. She finally sang with the Met in one of its appearances in Philadelphia, as Octavian in *Der Rosenkavalier*, received a contract with the company, and made her New York Met debut on December 17, 1938 as Mignon.

In 1939, she married Walter Surovy, a Czech actor, who managed her career. She debuted at Glyndebourne in 1939, and in 1940 at the San Francisco Opera. In 1941 she sang opposite Nelson Eddy in the Hollywood film *The Chocolate Soldier*, and appeared in Bing Crosby's film *Going My Way* (1944), in which she sang the *Habanera* from *Carmen*. This led to her first actual stage performance as Carmen at the Met, December 28, 1945. For some time she virtually owned the role at the Met and sang it there 75 times. She debuted at Milan's La Scala in 1954.

Stevens retired from the Metropolitan in 1961, and retired altogether from singing in 1964. Shortly after her resignation from the Met, the company went through one of the worst crises in its history. General Director Rudolf Bing cancelled the entire 1961–62 season after the company's major unions reached an impasse. Stevens sent a telegram to President John F. Kennedy outlining the importance of the Metropolitan to the United States and the world, and requested his intervention. The president honored her request, and personally persuaded the sides to accept the Secretary of Labor, Arthur Goldberg, to arbitrate their disputes. The season was saved.

Stevens' mezzo-voice quality was unusual: it was warm, light, and lyrical. This suited her to many of the important "trouser" roles. In addition to Octavian, she sang Mozart's Cherubino and Prince Orlovsky in *Fledermaus*. Other of her favorite roles were Dorabella, Delilah, Orpheus, Laura (*La Gioconda*), and Carmen, her most famous role.

After she retired from the Met stage, she became director of the company's new Metropolitan Opera National Company, a touring group providing opportunities for young singers and conductors, as well as designers and directors to participate in opera on a steady professional level. She was appointed to the faculty of the Juilliard School of Music in 1975, and was president of the Mannes College of Music in New York (1975–78). She was again associated with the Metropolitan from 1980 to 1988 as director of its National Council Auditions. *—Joseph Stevenson*

Recommended:

- ○ **Bizet: Carmen** / Stevens, etc. / 1964 / RCA 7981
- ○ **Lebendige Vergangenheit: Risë Stevens** / Stevens, etc. / Preiser 89556
- ○ **Gluck: Orfeo ed Eurdice** / Monteux (cond.), Stevens, Casa, Peters, Rome Opera House Orch. / 2000 / RCA 63534

Teresa Stich-Randall

b. Dec. 24, 1927, West Hartford, CT

Soprano

While American-born sopranos have been making waves since the days of Lillian Nordica in the early 1900s, West Hartford, CN, native Teresa Stich-Randall may have been the first American soprano whose popularity abroad outstripped her reputation at home. Stich-Randall studied voice at the Hartt School of Music, Columbia University, and finally New York University, where she made her debut in 1947 creating the role of Gertrude Stein in the premiere of Virgil Thomson's opera *The Mother of Us All*. In 1948 Stich-Randall also created the title role in Otto Luening's opera *Evangeline*. Stich-Randall's talents attracted the attention of maestro Arturo Toscanini, who cast her in a number of parts in the 1949–1950 season, fortunately so in the minor part of Nanetta in Toscanini's last performance of Verdi's opera *Falstaff*, leading to Stich-Randall's presence on one of the most celebrated recorded opera sets ever made.

In 1951 Stich-Randall made her European debut in Florence, Italy, and that same year took first prize in an international singing competition held in Lausanne. This established Stich-Randall's reputation in Europe, and although she would perform with the Chicago Lyric Opera, at the Metropolitan in New York, and on American concert tours as a soloist in the coming years, it was in Europe that most of her subsequent activity was centered. Stich-Randall was named an Austrian Kammersängen in 1962 and was the first American accorded this particular honor; afterwards, she was contracted to the Vienna State Opera and sang there primarily until her retirement around 1980. Outside of much-heralded visits home to West Hartford in 1982 and 1983, Stich-Randall has been little heard from since.

Although Teresa Stich-Randall is hardly a household name, she has many fans among those who collect vintage vocal recordings. In her concert career she frequently sang works by Handel and J.S. Bach. Stich-Randall's approach to Baroque music is signified by her light tone with no more than a subtle vibrato, clear enunciation, and an infallible sense of pitch. Stich-Randall was definitely ahead of the game in regard to latter-day period performance practice, and her best recordings generously bear this out, in particular her 1966 Vanguard recording of Pergolesi's *Stabat Mater* with alto Elisabeth Höngen. *—Uncle Dave Lewis*

Recommended:

- ○ **Haydn: Die Jahreszeiten** / Goehr (cond.), Stich-Randall, Wenk, Kretschmae, NDRSO / 1994 / FNAC 642325
- ○ **Pergolesi & Bach** / Rossi, Prohaska (conds.), Stich-Randall, Dermota, Heiller, Hongen, Vienna State Opera Orch. & Choir / 2001 / Amadeus 7014
- ○ **Bach: Cantatas 202, 209 & 51** / Heiller, Prohaska (conds.), Stich-Randall, Felbermayer, Wobisch, Nebois, Orch. & Choir of the Bach Guild / 1999 / Bach Guild 2540

Alexa Still

b. 1963

Flutist

New Zealander Alexa Still may not be a household name in the United States or Europe, but she has long been among the best-known performing artists of her native land, and her many critically acclaimed recordings have earned her a special respect from fellow performers and flute lovers alike. Ms. Still was born in 1963 and first took up the flute as an eight-year-old in New Zealand (she tells the story of how she wanted to play the saxophone but her father wouldn't hear of it!). She later attended graduate school in the United States, working under Samuel Baron at the University of New York at Stony Brook—where she took a doctorate (1987) before her 23rd birthday—and taking lessons from the well-known Thomas Nyfenger on the side. Success on the competition circuit (her victories include first prize at the East and West Artist's Competition, which included a New York debut) developed into success on the audition circuit: Still won the principal flute position with the New Zealand Symphony Orchestra in 1986. She kept the job for over a decade, and in the years since has maintained a close relationship with the organization—as a soloist she has appeared and recorded with the orchestra, and, she is married to one of the group's string bassists. Throughout her tenure with the NZSO, Still was a frequent visitor to the U.S., and in 1996 she was honored with a Fulbright Award.

Ms. Still left the orchestra in the late 1990s when named to the faculty of the University of Colorado at Boulder. She has put together nearly a dozen releases for the Koch International Classics record label, amongst which are a disc of Richard Rodney Bennett music and one of Viennese classics for flute and various chamber ensembles. Her seemingly always-growing appreciation for modern music has made her much appreciated by her composer colleagues throughout the years.

In her spare time, Alexa Still is a keen motorcyclist. *—Blair Johnston*

Recommended:

- ○ **Koechlin: The Nectaire Songs** / Still / 1997 / Koch 7394
- ○ **Alexa Still, Flute** / Braithwaite (cond.), Still, New Zealand CO / 1991 / Koch 7063

William Grant Still

b. May 11, 1895, Woodville, MS, **d.** Dec. 3, 1978, Los Angeles, CA

Composer: Symphonic, Chamber Music, Concerto

"With humble thanks to God, the Source of Inspiration." Such is the inscription to be found on the scores of the works of William Grant Still, sometimes called "The Dean of African-American Composers" and one of America's most versatile musicians.

Still was but three months old when his father, the town bandmaster, died. Shortly thereafter, his family moved to Little Rock, Arkansas. Still has written movingly of the influence his mother and grandmother had in forming his character and instilling in him a love for the arts. In addition, his new stepfather was a big music fan, and encouraged his stepson's interest by taking him to operettas and buying him recordings. Still's education continued at Wilberforce University, which he entered at age 16, and at the Oberlin Conservatory, where he studied theory and composition. He also had studies with George W. Chadwick and Edgard Varèse, all the while supporting himself by playing in orchestras and bands.

After a stint in the U.S. Navy in 1918, Still did arrangements for W. C. Handy and Paul Whiteman, played oboe in the famous Noble Sissle-Eubie Blake revue *Shuffle Along*, and began a decades-long association with radio, arranging and producing programs for the Mutual and Columbia networks. His early compositions were fairly dissonant and complex (perhaps under Varèse's influence); he made a major breakthrough when he took Chadwick's advice and started incorporating elements of African-American and popular musical styles into his works. His first big hit, and his best-known work to this day, is his first symphony, the "*Afro-American*," which was given its premiere in Rochester, New York in 1931, and was soon performed all over the world.

After moving to Los Angeles in 1934, Still turned his attention to film, providing the scores for movies like *Lost Horizon* and the original *Pennies from Heaven*. Later he also scored a number of television shows, including *Perry Mason* and *Gunsmoke*. Guggenheim and Rosenwald Fellowships allowed him to produce large-scale works like the ballet *Lenox Avenue* (1937) and the operas *Blue Steel* (1935) and *Troubled Island* (1938). The last-named work—with a libretto by Langston Hughes and based on the life of Dessalines, the first Emperor of Haiti and one of the major figures in Haiti's independence—was premiered by the New York City Opera in 1949 and was very well received.

Still continued to write politically and racially conscious works throughout his life, such as the narrated work *And They Lynched Him On A Tree* (1940) and *In Memoriam: The Colored Soldiers Who Died For Democracy* (1944). In the 1950s, he turned to writing children's works, such as *The American Scene* (1957), a set of five suites for young people based on geographic regions of the United States.

In 1981, Still's opera *A Bayou Legend* was the first by an African-American composer to be performed on national television. He was also the first African-American to conduct a major U.S. orchestra (when he led the Los Angeles Philharmonic in a Hollywood Bowl concert of his own music), and the first African American composer to have his works performed by major American orchestras and opera companies. —*Chris Morrison*

Overview of Works (1918–1971)

William Grant Still is often thought of as a single-work composer, that work being his *Symphony No. 1 "Afro-American."* Yet as most informed listeners are aware, he produced many other worthwhile compositions in most genres. His style divulged the influence of what was then known as "Negro music" and of various other folk elements, and featured generally approachable harmonies and melodies. He did, however, have a brief fling with modernist styles. Although Still served as an arranger for W.C. Handy as far back as 1916 and produced serious works in the 1920s, his first important compositions came in 1930 with the choral ballet *Sahdji* and the aforementioned *"Afro-American" Symphony*, premiered in 1931 by the Rochester Philharmonic under Howard Hanson. The event gave Still the distinction of being the first black American whose symphony was performed by a major orchestra in the United States. The work contains elements of 'Negro music', but not 'Negro Spiritual' music. The first movement has a bluesy manner and features an original main theme, one of the composer's most inventive creations. The third movement (of four) is perhaps best-known: Here, Still employs a banjo and does a clever takeoff on Gershwin's "I Got Rhythm." Still's other four symphonies have gotten far less attention, but in the latter twentieth century, *No. 2* (1937, subtitled "Song of a New Race"), and to a lesser extent *No. 3* (1958), began receiving some overdue attention. Both display a "Negro music" influence, but somewhat less so than in the "Afro-American" symphony. Still wrote nine operas, of which *Troubled Island*, about a slave rebellion in Haiti, and *A Bayou Legend*, both from 1941, are among his most important. The New York City Opera premiered the former in 1949 and PBS presented the latter on a television broadcast in 1981, both being important firsts for Still or any black American composer in his/her respective venues. *Costaso* (1950) and *Highway No. 1 USA* (1962) have also attracted some attention. In the realm of the ballet, besides the aforementioned *Sahdji*, Still wrote *Lenox Avenue* about life in Harlem and three other scores. Perhaps his most important song collection is *Songs of Separation* (1949) for soprano and piano quintet. The texts of the five songs comprising the set are mostly from black poets and Still's music is consistently absorbing and achieves considerable expressive depth. The versatile Still wrote a series of works for young listeners in the 1950s, which included *The Little Song That Wanted to be a Symphony* (1954) and *Little Red Schoolhouse* (1957). He also wrote incidental music for film and television sources. Perhaps his most-famous efforts in this genre were his scores for the *Perry Mason* television show in the 1950s and early 1960s. —*Robert Cummings*

Recommended:

- ○ **Works By William Grant Still** / Videmus / 1990 / New World 80399
- ○ **A Festive Sunday with William Grant Still** / Groh (cond.), Lipkin (cond.), Royal PO, North Arkansas SO / 1996 / Cambria 1060
- ○ **Africa: Piano Music of William Grant Still** / Oldham / 1991 / Koch 37084
- ○ **William Grant Still: The American Scene** / Clark (cond.), Astrup, Manhattan CO / 1995 / Newport Classic 85596
- ○ **More Still** / Ford (cond.) / 1999 / Cambria 1112
- ○ **Get on Board: American Music for Woodwinds by William Grant Still** / Sierra Winds / 1994 / Cambria 1083
- ○ **Oregon Festival of American Music Presents William Grant Still** / Gearhart, Steinhardt, Oregon SQ / 2002 / Koch 7546

SYMPHONIC

Symphony No. 1 ("Afro-American") (Dec. 6, 1930)

A student of George Chadwick and Edgard Varèse, William Grant Still developed an idiom that combined tonal harmonies and traditional classical structures with elements of traditional African-American music. The four-movement Afro-American Symphony (1930), the best-known of his works, remains a landmark in the history of American music as the first symphonic work by an African-American composer to be performed by a major orchestra.

The first movement, Moderato assai, opens with a plaintive theme for English horn that transforms into a bluesy muted trumpet solo. The second theme group has the clear echoes of a spiritual; like Dvořák, Still generally composed such passages in characteristic style rather than borrowing them from pre-existing sources. The second movement, Adagio, is a heartfelt meditation with melodic content derived from the opening of the first movement, a unifying element that appears throughout the entire work. The third movement is a joyous, gospel-like Animato that employs a banjo as part of its instrumental palette. The final movement, Lento con risoluzione, begins with a beautifully solemn melody for unison strings. The principal theme from the first movement makes an appearance, followed by a repeat of the string melody, now in the cellos. The symphony comes to an exuberant close among blues inflections and energetic cross-rhythms.

The symphony was premiered by the Rochester Philharmonic on October 29, 1931. —*Mona DeQuis*

Recommended:

- ○ **African Heritage Symphonic Series Vol. 1** / Freeman (cond.), Chicago Sinfonietta / 2000 / Cedille 55
- ○ **Still: Afro-American Symphony; Beach: "Gaelic" Symphony** / Krueger (cond.), Royal PO / Bridge 9086

CHAMBER MUSIC

Romance, for saxophone & piano (1954)

The classical repertoire for saxophone is small, and works for the instrument by African-American composers—strangely, given the saxophone's importance in African-American vernacular traditions—are rare indeed. Thus William Grant Still's little *Romance for saxophone and piano* was popular in recital and on recordings even prior to revivals of music by the "dean of African-American composers." It has also been arranged for saxophone and chamber orchestra. The *Romance* was published in 1966, late in Still's life, when his music had been mostly forgotten (much of his music of this period was for small chamber combinations). The work is about five minutes long and is of a lyrical cast. The opening saxophone melody, moderate in tempo and a real crowd-pleaser, speaks the Dvořák-like language of Still's early career, referring only indirectly, through its inclination toward pentatonicism and ninth harmonies, to the African-American folk and popular styles that surface more explicitly in much of Still's earlier music. A contrasting minor-key strain seems to presage a simple tripartite form, but instead the music becomes freer and less harmonically directional, punctuated by passages for piano alone. Still creates a subtle contrast with the tuneful opening material, and the transition back to that material at the end to round out the form is a pleasantly delicate surprise. The *Romance* isn't a virtuoso saxophone piece, but it demands the ability to produce a clear tone and legato phrasing over long stretches. The writing for saxophone makes no use of jazz playing techniques. —*James Manheim*

Recommended:

- ○ **Get on Board: American Music for Woodwinds by William Grant Still** / Sierra Winds / 1994 / Cambria 1083

CONCERTO

Ennanga, suite for harp & orchestra (1958)

Ennanga is the only work William Grant Still composed for the harp, and even though the harp, piano, and string quartet occupy relatively equal planes in the music, the choice of title—the Ugandan word for a miniature harp—makes the instrument's special significance clear. *Ennanga* was composed in 1956, directly after the *Serenade for cello*. Still wrote it with input from Lois Adele Craft, a harp virtuoso and friend, who also gave the premiere in Los Angeles. It was also written for violinist Louis Kaufman (and his string quartet), for whom Still composed his *Pastorale, Suite for violin and piano*, and *Lyric Suite*. *Ennanga* is in three movements: in the first, percussive textures in the harp and piano offset rhythmically charged statements from the strings; in the second, the harp sings a melancholy tune accompanied by the other instruments; and the third features the harp's characteristic glissandi. —*Allen Schrott*

Recommended:

- ○ **Works By William Grant Still** / Videmus / 1990 / New World 80399

Karlheinz Stockhausen

b. Aug. 22, 1928, Mödrath, Germany

Composer: Avant-garde, Chamber Music, Opera

Karlheinz Stockhausen emerged early on as one of the most influential and unique voices in the post-World War II European musical avant-garde and his prominence continued throughout the rest of the twentieth century and into the twenty first. Combining a keen sensitivity to the acoustical realities and possibilities of sound, rigorous and sophisticated compositional methods expanded from integral serialism, innovative theatricality, and a penchant for the mystical, Stockhausen remains one of the most innovative musical personalities to span the turn of this century.

Stockhausen was born in 1928 near Cologne. Orphaned as a teen, he immersed himself in artistic pursuits and showed promise both as a writer and a musician. He took classes at the new music school in Darmstadt with Adorno before moving to Paris, where he studied with Messiaen and met Boulez and Pierre Schaeffer. These encounters, as well as studies in phonetics and communication, proved a crucial influence on his subsequent work at the electronic music studio in Cologne; by the mid-1950s he had secured a spot in the vanguard of both electronic music and integral serialism. During the next decade he forged relationships with some of the most prominent contemporaries, including Kagel, Ligeti, and Cage, and, taking over the reins at the Darmstadt school, mentored such innovative up-and-comers as Cornelius Cardew and La Monte Young. His influence extended into popular culture, as well: he appears on the cover of the Beatles' *Sgt. Pepper's* album. Stockhausen held various appointments during the rest of the twentieth century, and continued teaching summer seminars attended by important emerging composers.

Stockhausen's most influential compositions vary widely in their style and media, and attest to the composer's far-ranging interests in science, technology, religion, cosmology, and mysticism. His various instrumental and vocal works from the 1950s, 1960s, and 1970s explore various ways of extrapolating serial methods and mathematical structures, such as the Fibonacci series, to dictate pitches, rhythms, articulations, and larger formal structures. The influential tape piece *Gesang der Jünglinge* (1955) combines the jumbled phonemes from a Biblical source text with an elaborately methodic splicing scheme. *Hymnen* (1966) mixes various national anthems with complex electronic sound structures. In *Stimmung* (1968), a group of singers intones various mystical names to the harmony of the overtone series. From the late 1970s onward, Stockhausen's efforts focused on *LICHT*, a sprawling opera cycle drawn from various religious mythologies, particularly the *Urantia Book*, a collection of writings supposedly delivered to Earth by extraterrestrials. *—Jeremy Grimshaw*

AVANT-GARDE

Gesang der Jünglinge, for electronics & taped boy's voice (1955–1956)

Karlheinz Stockhausen's *Gesang der Junglinge* (1955–56) has long been recognized as one of the touchstones in the history of electronic music. The means Stockhausen used to produce and record this work are in themselves remarkable, involving the most sophisticated studio equipment of the era. Utilizing a four-track tape recorder and four separate loudspeaker systems, the composer set out to achieve the unification of vocal and electronic sounds to generate a musical landscape in which his imagination, no less than the listener's, is "freed from the physical limitations of any one singer" or set of instruments.

The dominant technique in the production of *Gesang der Junglinge* is that of musique concrete, wherein "extramusical" occurrences are utilized as a formative or limiting context in which the actual musical event can take shape. In this case, such occurrences are electronically generated sound waves and white noise. It is within this sonic spectrum that Stockhausen arranged the electronic sounds and the sound of a boy's voice into what he has referred to as "a speech continuum," a scale between the extremes of intelligible speech and seeming nonsense.

The work's text is taken from the "Song of the Three Youths" in the Book of Daniel, in which Daniel's companions praise God for rescuing them from the fiery furnace. The symbolism of the biblical tale—the emergence from death into life—is expressed in *Gesang der Junglinge* by the dramatic formation of often incomprehensible vocal sounds into articulate words and phrases. In remarks made before the 1956 world premiere at West German Radio in Cologne, Stockhausen stated that "whenever language emerges momentarily from the sound signals of the music, it praises God."

The guiding ideal of this piece is Stockhausen's conviction that composing should not involve simply the arrangement of musical sound, but both the "composition of sounds themselves" and the "synthesizing of the individual sound." The result is more than just a musical moment or monument; it is the representation of the very emergence of music from the disorder of raw sound. *—Edward Moore*

Recommended:

○ **Stockhausen: Elektronische Musik 1952–1960** / / 2001 / Stockhausen-Verlag 003

Hymnen, for electronic & concrète sounds (1969)

It is important to note that there are three extant version of Stockhausen's *Hymnen*: the first, from 1966–67, is entitled *Hymnen* No. 22, and is a tape composition of electronic music and concrete music; the second *Hymnen* dates from the same period, but is entitled *Hymnen mit Solisten* No. 22 1/2 (Hymnen with Soloists) and features electronic and concrete music with vocal soloists; the third version is *Hymnen with Orchestra* No. 22 2/3, scored for electronic and concrete music with full orchestra, dating from 1969. The first two versions of *Hymnen* are well over 100 minutes long, while the third is less than half that length at only 38 minutes. The first version, for tape, is the principal version, though Stockhausen himself still regards the work as unfinished.

It is a monumental piece, comprised of dozens of national anthems, woven into a dense musical tapestry of electronic sounds. The work is divided into four discrete "regions," each dedicated to a different composer. The first region is dedicated to French composer and conductor Pierre Boulez, and is centered around two anthems, the *Internationale* and the *Marseillaise*. The second region is dedicated to French composer Henri Pousseur, and its structure is based on four specific musical tunes/events: the West German national anthem, part of the Russian national anthem, a number of African national hymns, and finally, a conversation recorded in the studio between Stockhausen and his assistant. The third region is dedicated to American avant-garde composer John Cage, and includes the American, Russian, and Spanish national anthems. The fourth and final region is dedicated to Italian composer Luciano Berio, and centers around the Swiss national anthem and what Stockhausen enigmatically describes as "a hymn associated with the Utopian realm of Hymunion in Harmondie unter Pluramon."

Musically, the work is a kaleidoscopic collage; anthems are presented in electronically manipulated form, or as composites of multi-layered sound. The anthems serve as points of musical reference, only to be obscured through various transformations. In the two versions of *Hymnen* with instrumentalists and vocalists, the players are expected to offer musical comments on the electronic events on tape: they use their instruments to highlight particular tones, to repeat notes, to distend or otherwise transform particular passages or groups of notes. Special effects, like string harmonics, glissandi, and extreme dynamics are also used to accompany and accentuate the tape composition.

Hymnen is at once both an homage to the 1950s French tradition of *musique concrète*—using recorded, everyday sounds from the world around as musical building blocks—and also a demonstration of formal procedures for electronic music. Stockhausen's *Hymnen* shows how disparate musical elements may be fused together into a complete and cogent musical work. *—Alexander Carpenter*

Recommended:

○ **Hymnen: Electronische Musik Mit Solisten** / / 1995 / Stockhausen-Verlag 10

Invisible Choirs, for 16-channel recording & 8- or 2-channel playback (1979)

Unsichtbare Chöre (Invisible Choirs) was conceived as a portion of Karlheinz Stockhausen's massive multimedia opera *Donnerstag aus LICHT* (Thursday from Licht). Prepared under the composer's direction as a pre-taped piece to be included in Act One ("Michael's Youth") and Act Three ("Michael's Homecoming"), the work is also presentable as an independent tape composition consisting of 35 sections and lasting just under an hour. The piece utilizes the vocal abilities of a full choir (on the prepared recording, the West German Radio Chorus), as well as clarinet in some sections, and also demands an astonishing array of extended vocal techniques, including menacing moans, haunting wails, rhythmic clucks, and eerie whispers. He also creates unique polyphonic resonances by manipulating the overtones created by different sung vowels. Stockhausen thus creates a palette of timbres and textures nearly as broad and varied as those found in his electronic works. There is an added element of intrigue to this piece, however, in that the unique moods and bizarre acoustical effects that Stockhausen achieves originally emanated from living, breathing human beings, albeit beings that are prerecorded and thus "invisible" to the listener. The importance of electronic reproduction should not be overlooked since, as in a number of Stockhausen's works, the methods of recording and playback are precisely controlled by the composer. The choir was originally recorded on 16 tracks, which in ideal performances are reduced to eight playback channels (a two-track version is also available for presentations of the piece with standard binaural stereo systems). Stockhausen suggests that audiences listening to a presentation of the tape piece should be seated concentrically, with the sound emanating from within the middle or from all sides around the perimeter. Stockhausen further indicates that "during the tape performance, the hall should be completely darkened and a starry firmament projected against the ceiling and walls." Such a setting reflects, of course, Stockhausen's famous fascination with the cosmological and the spiritual, an interest likewise manifested in the music and text of *Unischtbare Chöre*. The texts, all taken from Biblical and pseudepigraphal works (that is, not universally canonical), deal with the end of the world. The first text, taken from the *Ascension of Moses*, is used in the first seven sections of the piece and describes the day of judgment and the beginning of the Millennium. The second and third texts, which are sung during the ninth through 25th sections of the piece, are taken from the pseudepigraphal *Apocalypse of Baruch* and describe various wonders coinciding with the end of the world: that humans will "see the world that was invisible to them" and shall "live in the heavens like the stars." The final text, corresponding with the remainder of the work's 35th section, is taken from Leviticus and describes the joy of the heavens at the opening of the gates of paradise. *—Jeremy Grimshaw*

Recommended:

○ **Stockhausen: Unsichtbare Chöre** / Stephens / 1992 / Stockhausen-Verlag 031

CHAMBER MUSIC

In Freundschaft, for melody instrument (1977)

Karlheinz Stockhausen's *In Freundschaft* (In Friendship) is an occasional work composed in July 1977 as a birthday gift for the clarinetist Suzanne Stephens. Stockhausen indicates that any of several "melody" instruments—including flute, oboe, basset horn, and trombone—may be used in performances of the work. *In Freundschaft*, about 14 minutes in duration, is a clear example of Stockhausen's "formula" method of composition. The opening melody supplies the material on which the entire piece is based; its most important element is a mid-range minor second trill, which forms a kind of axis (not unlike like the drone on B in Luciano Berio's 1969 *Sequenza VII for oboe*). The "formula" is followed by three Cycles (akin to variations on a theme), then a cadenza ("Explosion I"), three more Cycles and another Explosion, and a seventh Cycle. A concluding section mirrors the opening.

In Freundschaft was first performed by flautists Lucille Goeres and Marjorie Shansky at a private birthday party for Suzanne Stephens. The piece was first performed publicly by Goeres at the Conservatoire Darius Milhaud in Aix-en-Provence. In the year following its completion, Stockhausen expanded the work; this version was premiered by clarinetist Stephens in Paris in November 1978. *—Robert Kirzinger*

Recommended:

- ○ **Stockhausen: In Freundschaft; Traum-Formel; Amour** / Stephens / 1993 / Stockhausen-Verlag 027

Kontra-Punkte, for 10 instruments (1952–1953)

Stockhausen composed *Kontra-Punkte* (1952–53) as a response to the unpublished *Punkte* (1952), a work that ultimately left him dissatisfied. He considered *Kontra-Punkte* his first mature work, assigning it No. 1 in the generally chronological numbering system of his catalogue. It is a difficult work, predicated on the idea of the resolving of timbral and temporal relationships, moving from the heterogeneous to the homogeneous. *Kontra-Punkte* is scored for ten instruments—flute, clarinet, bass clarinet, bassoon, trumpet, trombone, piano, harp, violin, and cello—and is cast in a single movement divided into two sections, further divided into 46 subsections. The instruments are grouped into six different timbral combinations, which are heard in various juxtaposition, but resolve over the course of work into a single sonority, the piano. Throughout, the instruments drop out one at a time, and the dynamic level, presented as a range of six possibilities from *sfz* to *ppp*, gradually decreases. Stockhausen also reduces the variety of possible note durations, so that by the end there are no longer very long or very short notes, but instead a middle ground of similar durations.

Kontra-Punkte follows in the tradition of the postwar serialist composers who adopted the sparse, sometimes austere esthetic of Anton Webern. However, Stockhausen here combines a colorful Webernian pointillistic tapestry with focused thematic development, creating a work that, while indeed "punctual," is not monotonous. The title suggests two of the work's most important elements: not only its contrapuntal texture, but also the composer's stance against (i.e. counter to) his own *Punkte*. *Kontra-Punkte* radically alters *Punkte*'s pointillism through the use of chords, melismas, and perceptible thematic groupings.

The piano's part, which dominates throughout, is particularly intense; indeed, Stravinsky is said to have been fond of this work, and his own *Movements* (1958–59) for piano and orchestra is alleged to have been influenced by this element of *Kontra-Punkte*. While *Kontra-Punkte* is now acknowledged as having an important place in twentieth century music, its initial reception was not favorable. Stockhausen immediately earned a reputation for being hyperintellectual, for composing music that was difficult to listen to and hard to understand. His own attempts to explain the musical and philosophical foundations for the work only served to further obscure it, and it wasn't until the 1970s that *Kontra-Punkte* was widely recognized for its intrinsic musical value. *—Alexander Carpenter*

Recommended:

- ○ **Stockhausen: Kontra-Punkte; Zeitmasze; Stop; Adieu** / Stockhausen (cond.) / 1992 / Stockhausen-Verlag 004

Zyklus, for solo percussion (1959)

Stockhausen composed *Zyklus* (1959) as part of a competition he initiated in order to find performers skilled enough to play the taxing percussion parts in his orchestral work *Gruppen*. Prospective participants complained about the lack of works available for solo percussion, so Stockhausen attempted to fill the void with *Zyklus*, a latter-day etude intended to awaken the performer to new possibilities.

Zyklus is arranged in a cycle of 17 "periods" which express nine dominant timbral groups. These periods are divided into 30 temporal units, the durations of which are decided in advance by the performer. The arrangement of the periods, in turn, is governed by nine attack cycles that correspond to the timbral groups. The nine major cycles are further divided into two semi-cycles, the arrangement of which is again left up to the discretion of the interpreter. Despite the exceptionally active role afforded—and, it is equally valid to say, demanded of—the performer in matters of organization, the overarching period structure lends the work a sense of formal coherence.

The instruments Stockhausen calls for includes only those commonly available in 1959: snare drum, hi-hat, triangle, vibraphone, tam-tam, guiro, marimba, bells, and tom-toms. However, Stockhausen also made a provision for the substitution of other instruments should the performer so choose.

Each performance is based on a random selection of any one of the 17 periods. The soloist then plays through the remaining sections; with the return of the initial section the performance ends. To allow for greater possibilities of interpretation, the score is spiral bound and written so that it is playable either upside down or right side up, though such distinctions are themselves blurred from the outset. *—AMG*

Recommended:

- ○ **Zyklus** / Yoshihara / Camerata 313
- ○ **Stockhausen: Zyklus; Refrain; Kontakte** / Wambach, Ardeleanu, Rensch / 1988 / Koch 310020

OPERA

LICHT, cycle of 7 operas (1977–2003)

"I became a human ... to bring celestial music to humans, and human music to the celestial beings, so that Man may listen to God and God may hear his children."

Though spoken by Michael, a character in Karlheinz Stockhausen's massive operatic cycle *LICHT*, these words might as well be the composer's own. Stockhausen is known not only as one of the most innovative composers of his time, but also one of the most cosmically ambitious: his works, especially the *LICHT* cycle, embody his belief in humankind's potential for spiritual evolution through music, a medium through which mortals not only approach the divine, but even communicate with our more advanced intergalactic brethren. Supplementing his own eclectic theological ideas with concepts drawn from Biblical and Apocryphal sources as well as *The Urantia Book* (an obscure text purported to have been dictated by extraterrestrials from 1928 to 1935), Stockhausen structures his opera as an epic metaphorical narrative centered on the archetypal characters Michael, Eve, and Lucifer.

Stockhausen began sketching out his plans for *LICHT* in 1977, and devoted virtually all of his compositional efforts during the next 26 years to completing the work. Each of the seven resulting operas corresponds to a day of the week, and each day corresponds to one character or an encounter between two or all three; Saturday, for example, is Lucifer's day, while Sunday depicts the mystical union of Michael and Eve. Interestingly, the operas were completed out of order, beginning with *Donnerstag* (Thursday) in 1981, then *Samstag* (Saturday) (1984), *Montag* (Monday) (1988), *Dienstag* (Tuesday) (1993), *Freitag* (Friday) (1996), *Mittwoch* (Wednesday) (1998), and *Sonntag* (Sunday) (2003). Each opera was a monumental undertaking, involving daunting orchestral forces, complex electronic enhancements, multichannel amplification systems, and, often, audacious stage effects—one scene, in fact, employs live audiovisual feed from players in helicopters flying above the venue. The music itself is comparably intricate. Stockhausen based the entire cycle on a "super-formula"—a three-stave score outlining the essential melodic identities of each of the three principal characters. The super-formula informs the cycle on every level: moment-to-moment surface features in the music draw heavily from its various elements, while on a broader level a single note within a particular figure of the formula might serve as a tonal focus for an entire scene of one of the operas. Thus, every aspect and moment of the enormous cycle is infused with the musical essence of Stockhausen's grand cosmic vision. *—Jeremy Grimshaw*

Synopsis:

LICHT presents a sweeping vision of human existence through the archetypal characters of Michael, Eve, and Lucifer. The breadth and originality of the story afford only the broadest of synopses, given below in the order in which the individual operas were composed.

The first opera in the cycle, *Donnerstag aus LICHT* (Thursday), tells the story of Michael—his tragic childhood, his seduction of Eve, his visits to seven countries of the world, his triumphant return to heaven, and his battle with Lucifer. The narrative thread is stylized, anachronous, and surreal; Lucifer is aided in his battle against Michael, for example, by a trombonist and a tap dancer. Michael's musical abilities play a central role in each of his challenges.

Samstag aus LICHT (Saturday) represents Lucifer's day through four separate scenes: Lucifer's Dream, in which he expresses his desire to halt the passage of time; Lucifer's Requiem, a dark and fantastical offering for the dead; Lucifer's Dance, featuring Satan on enormous stilts and an argument among the musicians; and Lucifer's Farewell, a bizarre exorcistic ritual.

Montag aus LICHT (Monday) is Eve's day. In the first act, she (or rather, an enormous statue of her) gives birth to seven half-beast sons, amid much clamor and celebration; Lucifer arrives and sends them back into the womb. They are reborn, under more solemn circumstances in Act Two, and in Act Three follow a piper away into the clouds.

Deinstag aus LICHT (Tuesday) depicts the war between Michael and Lucifer. In the first act, Lucifer tries to stop time by distracting the musicians from their playing; Michael must keep them going. The battle of the second act is much more violent, the explosions of the battle finally blowing a hole into a mysterious crystal world hidden in a mountain.

In *Freitag aus LICHT* (Friday), Eve's temptation by Lucifer assumes the form of three concurrent multimedia elements: electronic music, dancing, and acting. These depict Eve's giving birth to Caino, the black-skinned son of Ludon, and the eventual mixture of races.

Mittwoch aus LICHT (Wednesday) represents the day of cooperation between the three main characters—though its narrative flow is difficult to discern. In Scene One, "Welt-Parlament," a delegation is assembled to determine the meaning of love. Scene Two features a kind of instrumental competition between soloists surrounding the audience. Scene Three comprises a composition for string quartet and four helicopters (real ones, in the air above the opera venue). In the final scene, Lucifer, in the form of a dancing camel, is elected to be the "Operator" who will decode signals received from the depths of the cosmos.

Sonntag aus LICHT (Sunday), the last opera in the cycle, depicts the final union of Michael and Eve. *—Jeremy Grimshaw*

Leopold Stokowski

b. Apr. 18, 1882, London, England, **d.** Sep. 13, 1977, Nether Wallop, Hampshire, England

Conductor

Leopold Anthony Stokowski, one of the true conducting luminaries of the twentieth century, was born in London in 1882. His father was Polish, his mother Irish, but he was raised as an Englishman. His famous vaguely foreign accent somehow appeared later in his life. (It is widely believed this was an affectation, as was his name, adopted in place of the less exotic-sounding "Leo Stokes.") The young Stokowski was a precocious musician, and as a child learned to play the violin, piano, and organ with apparently little effort. At the age of 13, he became the youngest person to have been admitted to the Royal College of Music.

By 18, Stokowski had been appointed organist and choirmaster at St. James', Piccadilly. He attended Queen's College, Oxford, receiving a Bachelor of Music degree in 1903. He moved to the United States in 1905, but returned to Europe each summer for further musical studies in Berlin, Munich, and Paris. When a conductor fell ill in Paris in 1908, he made his debut as an emergency substitute. The impression he made led to a position with the Cincinnati Symphony Orchestra in which he quickly achieved notable success. However, a more tempting prospect faced him when he was asked to take over the Philadelphia Orchestra in 1912. It was during his long and fruitful association with this ensemble that Stokowski established himself as one of the leading musicians of his day.

Stokowski gave the orchestra an entirely new sound, popularly known as the "Philadelphia Sound" or the "Stokowski Sound." Its foundation was a luxuriant, sonorous tone and an exacting attention to color. He pioneered the use of "free" bowing, which produced a rich, homogenized string tone. A relentless innovator, Stokowski experimented with orchestral seating, famously lining up the string basses across the rear of the stage and, in an early instance, massing all the violins on the left side of the orchestra and the cellos on the right. He also had spotlights directed on his hands and his impressively prominent hair to enhance his dramatic, theatrical aura. One of the first modern conductors to give up the use of the baton, Stokowski employed graceful, almost hypnotic, hand gestures to work his magic.

Indeed, Stokowski was the first conductor to become a true superstar. He was regarded as something of a matinee idol, an image aided by his appearances in such films as the Deanna Durbin spectacle *One Hundred Men and a Girl* (1937) and, most famously, as the flesh-and-blood leader of the Philadelphia Orchestra in Walt Disney's animated classic Fantasia (1940). In one memorable instance, he appears to be talking to the cartoon figure of Mickey Mouse, the "star" of a sequence featuring Dukas' *The Sorcerer's Apprentice*. In a clever parody, when the slumbering apprentice dreams of himself directing the forces of Nature with the masterful sweep of his hands, Disney artists copied Stokowski's own conducting gestures.

Following his tenure in Philadelphia, Stokowski directed several other ensembles, including the All-American Youth Orchestra (which he founded), the NBC Symphony Orchestra and the New York Philharmonic (both as co-conductor), the Houston Symphony Orchestra (1955–60), and the American Symphony Orchestra, which he organized in 1962. He continued to make concert appearances and studio recordings of both standard works and unusual repertoire (including the first performance and recording of Charles Ives' decades-old *Symphony No. 4*) well into his nineties. He made his last public appearance as conductor in Venice in 1975, remaining active in the recording studio through 1977. He died on 13 September 1977 in Nether Wallop, Hampshire, England. *—AMG*

Recommended:

- ○ **Bach Transcriptions by Stokowski** / Stokowski (cond.), Philadelphia Orch. / 2002 / Archipel 56
- ○ **Debussy Album** / Stokowski (cond.), Baker, London SO, Leopold Stokowski SO / 2000 / Angel 67313
- ○ **Stokowski Fantasy** / Stokowski (cond.), Philadelphia Orch. / Pearl 9488
- ○ **Bach Transcriptions** / Stokowski (cond.), Philadelphia Orch. / Pearl 9098
- ○ **Wagner: Orchestral Works** / Stokowski (cond.), Verrett, Arroyo, Sarfaty, Ordassy, Royal PO, London SO, Symphony of the Air / 2003 / RCA 55306
- ○ **Leopold Stokowski: Conductor** / Stokowski (cond.), Barabini, Montgomery, Burg, Philadelphia Orch., All-American Youth Orch. / 2001 / Andante 2986–2989
- ○ **The Symphony Of The Air** / Stokowski (cond.), Symphony of the Air / 1994 / EMI 65427

Richard Stoltzman

b. Jul. 12, 1942, Omaha, NE

Clarinetist

Richard Stoltzman is among the world's leading clarinetists, known for his wide classical repertory and for an interest in world, jazz, and popular music that prompted him to begin making "crossover" recordings long before they became a marketing trend. His father was a railroad man who also played jazz on the alto saxophone. Richard started taking clarinet lessons when he was eight, and soon joined his father playing in local jazz clubs. While Richard was learning clarinet, he and his family sang in a choir whose inner voices were insecure. Richard would sit among the altos and tenors, playing the clarinet to give a steady pitch to the singers, and learning how to make the instrument sound like a voice. He credits this experience for his approach to tone. He does not like the standard tone-quality of the classical clarinet, having heard through his father's recordings the rich, flexible sound of the jazz greats. In addition, one of his early teachers was from India, and taught that all instrumental music should aspire to a vocal quality. He taught Richard to sing the music first, in the tone of the instrument.

Stoltzman studied mathematics and music at Ohio State University (B. Mus., 1964), then graduate music studies at Yale (M. Mus., 1967). He also studied with Robert Marseilles, Harold Wright (at the Marlboro Music School) and Kaman Opperman. His studies at Marlboro began a ten-year association that included frequent association with master musicians Rudolf Serkin, Marcel Moyse, and Pablo Casals, who deeply affected his outlook on music. Other colleagues from Marlboro, including pianist Peter Serkin, violinist Ida Kavafian, and cellist Fred Sherry joined him in founding the chamber group TASHI in 1973 (Tashi" is a Tibetan name meaning "good fortune"). Stoltzman also taught at the California Institute of the Arts (1970–71). He made his New York debut in 1974, and was the first clarinetist to ever give a solo recital in New York's Carnegie Hall. He has won both the Avery Fisher Prize in 1977 for career development, and in 1986 the Avery Fisher Artist Award, the first wind player to earn it.

In his career he has frequently played and recorded both jazz and classical music. He has appeared as soloist with many of the major symphony orchestras and conductors of the world. He plays also with chamber ensembles such as the Beaux Arts Trio and the Emerson Quartet, and has appeared in many major festivals on four continents. He has appeared with classical artists Richard Goode, Yo-Yo Ma, Raymond Leppard and the English Chamber Orchestra, Christoph Eschenbach, James Levine, and the New York Philharmonic. In addition, he has performed or recorded with popular and jazz artists Eddie Gomez, Wayne Shorter, Chick Corea, Woody Herman's Thundering Herd, Judy Collins, Mel Tormé, Gary Burton, George Shearing, and Joe Williams. *—Joseph Stevenson*

Recommended:

- ○ **Copland, Bernstein, Gershwin** / Tilson Thomas, E. Stern (conds.), Stoltzman, London SO / 1993 / RCA 617902
- ○ **Brahms: Clarinet Sonatas** / Stoltzman, Goode (piano) / 1982 / RCA 60036
- ○ **The Essential Clarinet** / Smith (cond.), Stoltzman, London SO, Woody Herman's Thundering Herd / 1992 / BMG 61360

Kathryn Stott

b. Dec. 10, 1958, Nelson, England

Pianist

Thrust into the international spotlight when she made it to the finals of the prestigious Leeds International Piano Competition in 1978 at the tender age of 20, English pianist Kathryn Stott has managed to live up to the expectations placed on her by a grateful motherland. Stott was born in Nelson, England, two weeks before Christmas 1958 and as a child attended the Yehudi Menuhin School, where, in addition to instruction from the school's regular faculty, she had the opportunity to take lessons from Nadia Boulanger. In the years leading up to her Leeds success she worked under Kendall Taylor at the Royal College of Music. During 1980s and 1990s she made her talents available to audiences around the globe, making concerto, recital, and chamber music appearances in Britain, the United States, Germany, France, Austria, Italy, Spain, Japan, Switzerland, and elsewhere.

Stott has made a special effort to include the British literature in her own repertoire; she certainly must be counted amongst the best interpreters ever of Frank Bridge's music, and also a key exponent of William Walton's piano music. Sir Peter Maxwell Davies composed his 1997 *Concerto for Piano* especially for her. She has also been a passionate champion of Gabriel Fauré's music, and in 1995 served as artistic director of an international festival in celebration of that unique French musician—an activity which earned for her the honor of being appointed *Chevalier dans l'Ordre des Arts et Lettres* by the French authorities. Recordings of Kathryn Stott are plentiful and appear under many labels, including Decca, EMI, Philips, and Hyperion. A collaboration with Yo-Yo Ma, *The Soul of the Tango*, was released in 1997 by Sony Music. *—Blair Johnston*

Recommended:

- ○ **Gabiel Fauré: Complete Music for Piano** / Stott, Roscoe / 1995 / Hyperion 66911
- ○ **Lloyd: Concerto 3** / Lloyd (cond.), Stott, BBCPO / 1989 / Albany 019
- ○ **Delius: Arrangements for Piano, 4-Hands** / Stott, Ogawa / 2003 / BIS 1347

Alessandro Stradella

b. Oct. 1, 1644, Nepi, Italy, **d.** Feb. 25, 1682, Genoa, Italy

Composer

One of the earlier members of that elite caste of composers who lived only into their mid-30s (one thinks, of course, of Mozart, Schubert and Mendelssohn), Italian Baroque composer Alessandro Stradella is considered one of the most versatile and influential musical figures of the mid-seventeenth century. Born in Rome in 1644, Stradella first appears in the historical record eleven years later when his name is among the singers listed at St. Marcello del Crocifisso Cathedral. In 1658 he became a singer at the court of Queen Christina of Sweden (stationed in Rome), who, by 1663, was sufficiently impressed with Stradella's musical skills to begin commissioning compositions from him (beginning with the motet *Chare Jesu suavissime*). Soon other Roman notables followed suit, and Stradella produced an assortment of motets, prologues and intermezzi (to be performed between the acts of other composers' operas) throughout the 1660s.

In 1669 Stradella joined the abbot Antonio Sforza and violinist Ambrogio Lonati in an unsuccessful plot to embezzle funds from the Roman Catholic Church. Stradella managed to escape imprisonment but found it advisable to flee Rome until the entire affair had been buried by the Church. By 1670 he was back in the city writing musical prologues and intermezzi for the Tordinona public theater in Rome. After 1675 (a Holy Year during which all public theater productions were forbidden) Stradella redirected his energies to sacred composition (mostly large religious-dramatic oratorios) and instrumental composition.

By 1677 Stradella had once again earned the disfavor of the Roman Church, and was forced to flee the city. Invited to the city of Venice to provide a musical education for the wealthy Alvise Contarini's mistress, Stradella instead charmed and absconded with the mistress, and a price was put on his head by the very powerful Contarini family. After an attempt on his life in October of 1677 Stradella traveled to Genoa, where a number of his operas and sacred oratorios were subsequently performed. A scandalous love affair with a Genoese noblewoman earned Stradella the wrath of the Lomellini family, and in 1681 the composer was killed by a Lomellini agent.

Stradella seems to have had plenty of money (he certainly never relied on musical commissions to survive), and it is very likely that he was born into the aristocracy. His substantial output includes 27 surviving purely instrumental works—virtually all in sonata da chiesa design, and likely a great influence on the young Arcangelo Corelli, whom we know to have had a familiarity with Stradella's music. Stradella's vocal compositions show a great musical and textual diversity. The opera *Il Trespolo tutore*, containing as it does an important, humorous bass character, is one of the earliest examples of opera buffa. While his operas all employ a relatively small orchestra (two violins and continuo), Stradella experimented with more sizeable instrumental ensembles in his cantatas and oratorios, many of which feature the kind of concerto grosso string division (i.e. concertino and tutti groups); this would soon become a prominent feature in Italian Baroque composition. *—Blair Johnston*

Overview of Works (ca. 1667–1682)

Stradella's colorful life, some heavily embellished details of which ended up in the romantic nineteenth century opera *Alessandro Stradella* by Flotow, has tended to obscure the fact that he was a highly successful and respected composer whose music has only comparatively recently started to be seriously examined. He composed in most of the major forms of his day, including opera, oratorio, both sacred and secular cantatas, and instrumental music.

As an opera composer, he is an important transitional figure who links seventeenth century Venetian opera, which was widely imported by Rome, and for which in his earlier days Stradella composed a number of prologues, intermezzos, and arias, with the operas of Alessandro Scarlatti and Handel. His own operas, four complete extant works, were composed for Genoa, where they were highly successful, the first, *La forza dell' amor paterno* (1678) immediately establishing him as a favorite of the Genoese audience. Stylistically, his operas adopt the flexibility familiar from later seventeenth century Venetian opera, a mixture of recitative, arioso, and aria. The arias, some of which show an advance on their Venetian models by employing string rather than simple continuo accompaniments, are cast in a variety of forms that includes the ABA structure that would shortly become the fully fledged da capo aria.

Six oratorios by Stradella survive, the best known of which are *San Giovanni Battista* and *La Susanna*. Both are particularly notable for displaying Stradella's powers of characterization, in the former the dignity of John the Baptist and the lasciviousness of Herodias and Salome, in *Susanna* the heroic sensitivity of the protagonist and the tawdry lewdness of the two elders who falsely accuse the heroine. As with the operas, both evince a natural gift for melody and a mastery of counterpoint. Among the sacred cantatas, the charming Christmas work "Ah, ah, troppo è ver" dramatizes the birth of Christ by contrasting the reaction of the infuriated Lucifer with the visit of the shepherds, while *L'anime del Purgatorio* also introduces Lucifer as a tragicomic figure pitted against the Angel who releases the suffering souls in purgatory. Stradella's secular cantatas still await assessment, very few having been revived to date. *—Brian Robins*

Recommended:

- ○ **Alessandro Stradella: La Susanna** / Velardi (cond.), Camerata Ligure / Bongiovanni 2121
- ○ **Stradella: Motets** / Lesne (cond.), Piau, Seminario Musicale / 1995 / Veritas 45175

Teresa Stratas

b. May 26, 1938, Toronto, Ontario

Soprano

Stratas was one of the controversial stars of the latter half of the twentieth century, and one whose personality and life, like that of Callas, another great soprano of Greek descent, are inextricably linked with her performances in the minds of many members of the public. Also like Callas, she had a special magnetism as a performer, due to her dramatic intensity and exceptional physical beauty. Her top became weak during her middle and late career and she lost some focus in the middle of her voice, which sometimes caused her to force. However, her performances on stage and on film were so riveting that most were willing to forgive those vocal flaws, and even her habit of canceling, usually due to nerves.

She grew up in Toronto and began singing in nightclubs and in her father's restaurant when she was 12. Encouraged by her successes, including radio performances, and after being given a free ticket to *La Traviata*, an experience which she said overwhelmed her with the concept of what the human voice can do, she auditioned for the Opera School at the Royal College of Music in Toronto in 1954. She had never studied voice, knew opera only from that one performance, and brought *Smoke Gets in Your Eyes* as her audition piece, but her personality and potential talent were so impressive that she was admitted, and was such a quick learner that she made her debut with the Canadian Opera as Mimì in 1958, and won the Metropolitan Opera Auditions of the Air the next year, making her debut as Pousette in *Manon* the next year. In 1960, she created the title role of Glanville-Hicks' *Nausicaa* at the Athens Festival. Her Covent Garden debut was again as Mimì in 1961, and in 1962, she made her La Scala debut as Isabella in de Falla's *Atlantida*. In 1974, she came to international fame with her appearance as Salome on a television production of *Salome*, considered one of the very few singers in living memory who could convincingly portray Salome's transformation from naive teenager to depraved woman. In 1979, she sang the title role of the first performance of the three-act version of Berg's *Lulu* at the Paris Opera.

In the 1980s, she almost completely withdrew from the operatic stage, though she made notable recordings of Weill songs, and appeared in films of *La Traviata* and *Amahl and the Night Visitors*. She also explored Broadway, earning a Tony Award for best actress for her performance in *Rags* in 1986, and recorded Julie in *Showboat*. In 1981, she backpacked through India, where among other activities, she volunteered for Mother Teresa's projects in the poorest areas of the cities. In 1988, she returned to the Met to create the role of Marie Antoinette in Corigliano's *The Ghosts of Versailles*. *—Ann Feeney*

Recommended:

- ○ **Berg: Lulu** / Stratas, Boulez (cond.), Stratas, Minton, Tear, Pludermacher, Paris Opera Orch. / 2000 / DG 463617
- ○ **Unknown Kurt Weill** / Stratas, Woitach (piano) / 1981 / Nonesuch 79019
- ○ **Verdi: La Traviata** / Patane (cond.), Wunderlich, Stratas, Fassbaender, Prey, Bavarian State Orch. & Chorus / 1993 / Orfeo 344932

Ettore Stratta

Conductor

Ettore Stratta is an Italian conductor and concert producer best known for his work in popular music and lighter classics and has had a notably successful series of "crossover" recordings.

He studied piano and composition at the Conservatory of Santa Cecilia in Rome. His conducting instructors were Tibor Serly and Eleazar de Carvalho, with whom he studied in New York and Brazil, respectively. Stratta has conducted and recorded standard classical music with the Royal Philharmonic, the English Chamber Orchestra, and the London Symphony.

However, he has gained special prominence in popular and crossover music. He has conducted the orchestra on several recordings by Barbra Streisand (including Streisand's *Greatest Hits* and *Je m'appelle Barbra*). He has also worked with Lena Horne, Stephane Grappelli, Arturo Sandoval, Yo-Yo Ma, Plácido Domingo, Samuel Ramey, and the vocal group Chanticleer.

He frequently records on the Teldec label. His releases include *Symphonic Tango*, *Symphonic Bolero*, *Symphonic Lloyd Webber*, *Symphonic Bossa Nova*, and *Symphonic Elvis*. Many of these were best-sellers on the crossover charts. In 1993 he made an acclaimed appearance at the Montreux Jazz Festival leading the world premiere of George Duke's *Muir Woods Suite*. *—Joseph Stevenson*

Recommended:

- ○ **Symphonic Tango** / Stratta (cond.), Ziegler, Console, Theodore, Federico, Royal PO / 1992 / Teldec 76997
- ○ **Boleros** / Stratta (cond.), Roditi, Calandrelli, D'Rivera / 2002 / Warner 85821
- ○ **The Symphonic Lloyd Webber** / Stratta (cond.), Royal PO / 1991 / Teldec 73742

Johann Strauss I

b. Mar. 14, 1804, Vienna, Austria, **d.** Sep. 25, 1849, Vienna, Austria
Composer: Orchestral

Johann Strauss I is one of the most important composers of nineteenth century Viennese light music. While his son, Johann Jr., has rightly surpassed him in fame and stature, he must still be assessed as an important figure in the genre, not simply because of his influence on his sons and other composers, but because of the occasional high quality of his music. His melodies tend not to flow smoothly in their brevity or in their motiflike collage structure, and his harmonies are not particularly inventive. Still, he was able to fashion attractive music in the Viennese waltz genre owing to his understanding of its nature—indeed, he was central to its evolution in the nineteenth century. Moreover, he possessed the ability to convey the best case for his works through his superior conducting skills. He had moments of genuine inspiration and created several memorable works, including the *Loreley-Rhein-Klänge* (1844) and *Radetsky-Marsch* (1848). In addition, he had a keen sense for employing popular themes from the works of other composers, as with his Op. 11 *Walzer à la Paganini.*

Although Johann Strauss had shown musical talent in his childhood, he began apprenticeship in bookbinding at age 13, while still taking lessons on the violin from Polischansky. Around this time he began playing viola for Michael Pamer in his dance orchestra. There he befriended Joseph Lanner, who would also make a name for himself as a composer in the light-music genre. Lanner formed a trio which Strauss joined at the age of 15. As the group grew to orchestra-size, young Johann took on greater responsibilities, finally becoming conductor of Lanner's second orchestra, which had splintered from the main ensemble. By this time, Strauss had studied theory with Ignaz von Seyfried, but had not yet delved into composition.

In July 1825, Strauss married Maria Anna Streim and three months later she gave birth to Johann Jr. A month before the birth, Strauss had left his post with Lanner to form his own band, comprised of some of Lanner's players. He began writing his earliest compositions not long afterward, like the Op. 1 *Täuberlin-Walzer* and the first of the *Kettenbrücken Waltzes*, Op. 4.

By the early 1830s, Strauss and his 28-piece dance orchestra had become immensely popular, owing not only to his music, but his deft conducting of it. In 1833, Strauss launched a European tour that included concerts in Germany and France. Berlioz lavished much praise on his music and performances in Paris. In 1838, he made the first of two successful trips to England, the last coming in 1849. He was even invited to play for Queen Victoria's coronation, an event for which he composed his *Queen Victoria Waltz.*

In 1842, Strauss left his wife and family, an action that freed Johann Jr., to openly study music, a profession his father had discouraged. The elder Strauss had left to live with another woman, Emilie Trampusch. He remained productive as a composer and popular as a performer throughout that decade, though Johann Jr. would form a band and become a serious, if unintended, rival.

After performing an engagement at a fashionable establishment in Vienna in September 1849, Strauss, who had contracted scarlet fever from one of the seven illegitimate children he fathered by Emilie Trampusch, became seriously ill. He died six days later, at age 45. *—Robert Cummings*

ORCHESTRAL

Radetzky-Marsch, Op. 228 (1848)

Though the music of Johann Strauss I was eclipsed by that of his more famous son, "Waltz King" Johann Strauss II, Strauss *père* wrote a number of works that have remained durable favorites, particularly on New Year's Eve and pops programs. His best-known effort is the *Radetzky March*, Op. 228 (1848), written in honor of the Austrian general Joseph Radetzky, who had rousted the Italian rebellion at Custozza earlier that year. Despite its usual military band instrumentation, the tone of the march is more elegantly celebratory than rousingly martial; indeed, it seems but a small distance removed from the dance music for which the Strauss clan was renowned. *—AMG*

Recommended:

- ○ **40 Famous Marches** / Boskovsky (cond.), Vienna PO / 1999 / Decca 466241
- ○ **Kaleidoscope** / Mackerras (cond.), London SO / 1995 / Mercury 434352

Johann Strauss II

b. Oct. 25, 1825, Vienna, Austria, **d.** Jun. 3, 1899, Vienna, Austria
Composer: Orchestral, Opera

Johann Strauss Jr. is the first truly well-known composer in those classical genres particular to his hometown, the Viennese waltz and Viennese operetta. The *Blue Danube Waltz* is not only the most popular of his works in the former category, but is among the most widely played and arranged pieces of its time, known to the most casual listener today from many radio, film and television uses of it.

Johann Strauss Jr. was born in Vienna on October 25, 1825. He showed remarkable skills early in his childhood, despite his father's opposition to any career in music for any of his three sons. Johann Sr. wanted him to become a banker, but the younger Strauss had his own ideas, taking violin lessons in secret from a player in his father's band. When Strauss was 17 his father left the family, thus allowing him to begin serious study without encumbrance. His mother, a good amateur violinist who had always encouraged him, remained supportive. Strauss now studied theory with Joseph Drechsler and took violin lessons from Anton Kohlmann. In 1844 young Johann led his first concert and a year later formed his own band, thereby competing with his father's orchestra. He was also writing his own quadrilles, mazurkas, polkas, and waltzes for performance by his ensemble, even conducting works by his father, and receiving praise from the press. He was given the honorary position of Bandmaster of the 2nd Vienna Citizens' Regiment (his father was bandmaster of the 1st regiment) in 1845, and in 1847 began composing for the Vienna Men's Choral Association.

His real success began in 1849 after Johann Strauss Sr. died. Johann Jr. merged his father's orchestra with his own and took up his father's contracts. His career moved along smoothly for the next several years, but in 1853 he became seriously ill and turned over conducting duties to his younger brother, Josef, for six months. After his recovery he resumed fully both his conducting and his composing activities, eventually gaining the respect of such composers as Brahms, Wagner, and Verdi for his seemingly unlimited imagination for using melodies.

Strauss married singer Henriette "Jetty" Treffz in August 1862, and they settled in Hietzing. Thereafter, she became his business manager and apparently a great inspiration, drawing him toward operetta, just as Viennese theater operators were becoming tired of the works of Offenbach. His first, *Indigo und die vierzig Räuber*, came in 1871, and his most famous, *Die Fledermaus*, was staged three years later with great success. *Eine Nacht in Venedig* (1883) and *Der Zigeunerbaron* (1885) were his only other international operetta hits.

In 1872, he traveled to the United States and led highly successful concerts in Boston and New York. For all the success that came in the 1870s for Strauss, there was also much grief: his mother and brother Josef died in 1870, and his wife died suddenly of a heart attack in 1878. Her death devastated him, and the suddenly helpless composer unwisely married the much-younger actress Angelika Dittrich, six weeks later. The marriage lasted only four years, though it may have saved the composer from personal disaster in the months following his wife's death.

Strauss, a Roman Catholic, left the church and had to give up his Austrian citizenship to marry Adele Deutsch in 1887, owing to the Church's unwillingness to recognize his divorce. His new wife, with whom he had lived for a long period before their marriage, seemed to inspire him much like his first wife. In his last years, Strauss remained quite productive and active. He was working on a ballet, *Cinderella*, when he developed a respiratory ailment which grew into pneumonia. He died on June 3, 1899. *—Robert Cummings*

ORCHESTRAL

Accelerationen, waltz, Op. 234 (1860)

Historians generally mark 1860 as a watershed year in Johann Strauss II's development as a composer. It was at this point in his career that he began to expand upon the Viennese waltz as handed down to him by his father, Johann Strauss I, and Joseph Lanner, and to perfect the genre of which he became the undisputed master. *Accelerationen*, Op. 234, is usually cited as Strauss' first work in his new direction. Legend has it that the composer began writing the work in the early morning hours of February 14, just after he and his orchestra had performed at a ball in Vienna's Sofiensäle. A member of the dance committee of the Technical College of Vienna, which had commissioned a new waltz from Strauss to be played that very evening, approached the composer and asked to see the new work. When Strauss replied that he hadn't had enough time to write anything, the man looked so disappointed that Strauss composed the beginning of the waltz on the spot, on the back of a menu.

Accelerationen is laid out in a traditional scheme that includes an introduction, five waltz pairs, and a coda, but the characteristics of individual sections evince a clear change in Strauss' approach to the genre. The introduction seems to imitate the sound of spinning wheels with rapid violin tremolo, while surging, accelerating brass and low strings suggest a steam locomotive—allusions which could not have escaped the faculty and students of the Technical College. Strauss' innovations in the waltz itself are evident in the structure of the melodies. Each of the 16-measure waltz tunes falls into eight-measure halves, the second of which is a variation of the first. Strauss effects these variations through changes in orchestration, dynamics, and, more significantly, the rhythms and shape of the melody; thus, what initially sounds like mere repetition is actually more like the antecedent-consequent phrasing typical of Viennese Classicism. The coda is longer and more sophisticated than most of the preceding sections. For instance, the return of the first half of the third waltz takes place within 14 measures, not the full 16, before abruptly ceding to the second half. Additionally, Strauss truncates the return of the first waltz by a measure before the work's final gesture. *—John Palmer*

Recommended:

- **Strauss Family Waltzes** / Fiedler (cond.), Boston Pops Orch. / 1994 / RCA 902661688
- **Carlos Kleiber Conducts Strauss** / Kleiber (cond.), Vienna PO / 1990 / Sony 45938

Ägyptischer (Egyptian March), Op. 335 (1869)

This wonderfully energetic piece was written in 1869 to celebrate the future opening of the Suez Canal, and was premiered in a summer concert by the composer's popular traveling orchestra in Pavlovsk, Russia, outside St. Petersburg, and then the location of Tsar Paul I's country residence. It was first played in Vienna in December of that year as a processional march for Anton Bittner's burlesque entitled *Into Egypt.*

The piece opens quietly with low drums and a distant wind section playing an exotic minorish "Egyptian" introductory melody, with the lower strings tripping along scalewise in response. On a sudden fast crescendo, three heavily accented minor chords begin the melody with the full orchestra featuring the brasses. The mood is that of an aggressive military band. The next section recasts the tune in the brighter parallel major scale with one "Arabic" alteration of the melody (a flattening of the sixth step). The mood changes to that of a spirited military parade on a sunny day. A chorus is then added singing wordlessly (on "la"s) and softly in a combination of the minor and major key melodies. The aggressive first theme then repeats with lower brass runs. This is followed by the introduction as the music slowly fades away into the distance with a repeated rhythmic figure. *—"Blue Gene" Tyranny*

Recommended:

- **Ein Straussfest II** / Kunzel (cond.), Cincinnati Pops Orch. / 1993 / Telarc 80314
- **Strauss: Waltzes** / Boskovsky (cond.), Vienna PO / 1999 / Penguin Classics 460648

An der schönen, blauen Donau (On the Beautiful, Blue Danube), waltz, Op. 314 (1867)

Johann Strauss Jr.'s status as an internationally recognized Austrian icon began with the success of his waltz, *An der schönen, blauen Donau* (The Blue Danube Waltz), at the Paris Exhibition of 1867. The Austrians, still smarting from their military defeat at the hands of the Prussians at Königgrätz in July of 1866, wholeheartedly supported Strauss's music; when the *Blue Danube* achieved a resounding success at the Paris exhibition, the Viennese felt they had shown the French that Austria, despite its recent military setback, was still an important cultural force. Writers even described Strauss's triumph with military imagery, calling Strauss a "Napoleon among composers."

Strauss's international triumph in Paris makes it easy to forget that this was neither the first performance of the *Blue Danube,* nor representative of the piece's original conception. Composed for the *Wiener Männergesang-Verein* (Vienna Men's Singing Society), the waltz was originally scored for four-part choir and orchestra or piano. Josef Weyl (1821–95) supplied the text; it was in this version that the world first heard the *Blue Danube* waltz on February 15, 1867, sung by the *Wiener Männergesang-Verein,* and accompanied by the orchestra of the Forty-Second Infantry Regiment, directed by Rudolf Weinwurm. The waltz was first performed without voices probably on March 4, 1867, and was certainly played in its familiar format on March 10, 1867, at a benefit concert for Strauss's brothers.

The title *An der schönen, blauen Donau* may have been derived from a poem by Karl Beck (1817–79) entitled, *An der Donau*; the poem, *Die feindlichen Brüder* also contains the line, "An der schönen, blauen Donau liegt mein Dörfchen still und fein." Strauss sold the *Blue Danube* for only 250fl. to Carl Anton Spina (1827–1906), who published the work in 1867. Spina realized an exceptional return on his investment.

Like most of Strauss's waltzes, the *Blue Danube* features five distinct "mini-waltzes," each with two sections. To modern listeners, the slow introduction to the *Blue Danube* is the ultimate tease, delaying what seemingly all of us know in our sleep. At the Paris exhibition, however, the opening probably produced a different effect: a heightened sense of anticipation, and curiosity about when the actual dance will begin. Even after the orchestra reaches a waltz tempo there still is no real tune, and the music seems to amble without aim.

Strauss's wealth of melodic material provides great contrast; waltz sections featuring melodies with large leaps give way to those with linear tunes within a narrow range. Quarter-note motion is juxtaposed with eight-note motion and, of course, there are contrasting keys. The D major first waltz follows an introduction on the dominant, A major, while the second half of the second is in B flat and the entire fourth waltz is in F. The coda partially summarizes the entire piece, revisiting the first part of Waltzes two and four (again in F), and then Waltz one in D. Variations of the first waltz precede the work's rousing close.*—John Palmer*

Recommended:

- **Carlos Kleiber Conducts Strauss** / Kleiber (cond.), Vienna PO / 1990 / Sony 45938
- **Johann Strauss: Waltzes** / Boskovsky (cond.), Vienna PO / Decca 467413

Annen-Polka, Op. 117 (1852)

In 1852 Strauss, at the age of 27, had achieved such success as composer and director of dance music that he was no longer looked upon as "the son of" Johann Strauss Sr. (1804–49), but as the rightful leader in his field. Strauss had merged his father's orchestra with his own shortly after his father's death, and in a few years would begin touring Europe. In May of the same year, Strauss was asked to guest conduct his *Annen-Polka,* Op. 117, at court, an appearance which led to frequent court performances and his eventual appointment to *Hofballmusikdirektor* in 1863.

Composed relatively early in Strauss' career, the *Annen-Polka* embraces none of the innovations prevalent in Strauss' later polkas such as *Vergnügungszug,* Op. 281, or *Leichtes Blut,* Op. 319. Also unlike these two particular works, *Annen-Polka* is in a moderate polka tempo, not that much faster than the *Schnell-Polka.* All four melodies of *Annen-Polka* have distinct eight-measure halves and are repeated in their entirety. Additionally, section A is rounded out by the return of its first half. Whereas the strings dominate section A, the woodwinds are prominent in B, which closes with a trill and a slow, rising figure in the brass that introduces the return of section A. Strauss does have one surprise in store: only the first melody of A returns, and this stops abruptly two measures short of completion before the flute takes over with a new tune to close the piece. *—John Palmer*

Recommended:

- **Johann Strauss: Waltzes** / Boskovsky (cond.), Vienna PO / Decca 467413
- **Johann Strauss: Waltzes and Polkas** / Ormandy (cond.), Philadelphia Orch. / 2003 / Sony 87281

Auf der Jagd (Off to the Hunt), schnellpolka, Op. 373 (1875)

Auf der Jagd (Off to the Hunt) is one of those Johann Strauss Jr. pieces that, once extracted from an operetta, has gained a life of its own. The schnellpolka comes from the 1875 operetta *Cagliostro in Wien,* a work which yielded five other dances as well as this one. The operetta revolves around the swindles of Cagliostro, who preys upon the Viennese people who are celebrating the anniversary of the expulsion of the Turks from the city.

The *Auf der Jagd* polka features two sections. Be warned: this is not for the faint-hearted. The galloping first section ends with a gunshot, one of those attention-getting sound effects Strauss was fond of using. In the second section you can hear the horns signaling the sighting of the prey. A chase and more gunshots follow. The first section is repeated and polka ends, as so many of Strauss' works do, with rapid descending scales and a dramatic cadence. *—Patsy Morita*

Recommended:

- **Strauss: The Best of Vienna** / Abbado (cond.), Vienna PO / 1998 / DG 459730
- **Ein Straussfest** / Kunzel (cond.), Cincinnati Pops Orch. / 1985 / Telarc 80098

Champagner-Polka, musical scherzo, Op. 211 (1858)

If the younger Strauss had been an American, the Southern expression "a hoot" would be a perfectly apt way to describe this joyful dance with its delightful melodies, boundless energy, dazzling orchestration, and humorous sound effects. This piece was composed during one of the Strauss' many visits to Russia, touring as a sort of musical ambassador with his orchestra.

Military trumpet tattoos make up the short introduction concluded with a smart thump from a low kettledrum. The winds begin the jolly first theme at full gallop, underscored by rhythmic string pizzicati, and punctuated by the brass and snare drum at the end of each phrase. The brass rush upward with a countersubject in the bass range. Then, just before the repeat, the winds and strings alternate trills to build the excitement, which has hardly abated in the last few moments. The first theme is repeated again. Then the winds and strings begin another frisky theme with staccato, sugarplum-fairy-type eighth notes, accompanied by a triangle which adds further sparkle to the texture. The strings stretch the theme with long notes. A brief transition is built from low tympani accents alternating with string accents providing a comic take on the bouncing and leaping motions of the dancers. Then one at a time, the sound of champagne bottle corks loudly popping are imitated by the percussionists (normally using plungers extracted quickly with force from tubes to create this sound). This leads into a recapitulation of the second trippingly staccato theme by the winds and strings and ever-present triangle with cymbals for an extra thrill. The trumpets recall the introduction, and the lilting main theme is repeated together with the brass countersubject and the transitional trills. Then, underscored by slightly more serious diminished chords resolving to the tonic major, the stereo champagne corks appear again to toast the ensemble. The orchestra flares up with two cascades of on-rushing woodwinds accented by the brass, with one especially enthusiastic cork-pop as the concluding cadence. *—"Blue Gene" Tyranny*

Recommended:

- **Ein Straussfest** / Kunzel (cond.), Cincinnati Pops Orch. / 1985 / Telarc 80098

○ **The Barbarolli Viennese Album** / Barbirolli (cond.), Halle Orch. / 2002 / Dutton 1024

Eljen a Magyar (Hail to Hungary), schnellpolka, Op. 332 (1869)

The polka was very popular in the late nineteenth century and examples were penned by nearly every major composer of dance music, performed by almost all military bands and distributed in the form of sheet music throughout the world. A French dictionary of dance terms dating from 1847 describes the polka as having a pulse rate of 104 beats per minute with an emphasis on the second beat of the measure. It exhibits a ternary (ABA) form with eight-measure subsections and sometimes include an introduction and a coda.

In 1869, Strauss had for six years been a *Hofballmusikdirektor* at the Imperial Court in Vienna. The position demanded a constant output of works suitable for Court balls, of which *Eljen a Magyar* (Hurrah for Hungary), Op. 332, stands as a typical example. Strauss' *Eljen a Magyar* is a Schnell-Polka, which was influenced by the galop, a rapid, simple dance in 2/4 meter. The polka was published in Vienna by Carl Anton Spina in 1869.

What is not typical about *Eljen a Magyar* is that the B section consists of only one melody, not the more common two or three. Furthermore, the B section does not fall into the usual eight-plus-eight pattern of repetition, but includes extensions of the melody that result in an odd sum of 28 measures. Section A contains three distinct tunes, all of which have a Viennese flavor which at Strauss' time would have been considered Hungarian. Chromatic inflections, dotted figures and cymbal crashes all evoke images of Hungary as Strauss creates variety by juxtaposing stepwise melodies with leaping ones and varying his orchestration. *—John Palmer*

Recommended:

○ **Strauss: Waltzes & Polkas** / Sandor (cond.), Gyor PO / 1999 / Hungaroton Echo 1042

○ **Johann Strauss: Waltzes** / Boskovsky (cond.), Vienna PO / Decca 467413

Frühlingsstimmen (Voices of Spring), waltz, Op. 410 (1883)

Vienna, the waltz and the Strauss family are inseparable entities. The waltzes of Johann Strauss Sr. (1804–49) evoked the air of the Viennese countryside, beer gardens and *Heurigen.* Those of his eldest son, Johann Jr., at first had the same rhythmic vitality and brief melodies. After 1860, however, this would change. The younger Strauss infused the traditional waltz format with a new vitality and sophistication that reflected the glittery, hedonistic spirit of nineteenth century imperial Vienna. He melded the rhythmic drive of his father's works with Joseph Lanner's (1801–43) lyricism, and changed the rhythmic emphasis from the beat to the measure. Strauss' seemingly unlimited melodic invention prompted him to compose melodies that did not fall into the traditional four-, eight-, or sixteen-measure patterns of earlier waltz tunes. He maintained the basic outline employed by Lanner and his father: a slow introduction, (typically) five pairs of waltzes and a coda, but increased the length of each section and the organic unity of the whole. Strauss' orchestration is often picturesque, especially in his introductions, while that of the waltzes themselves approaches a Mozartean clarity.

Strauss originally entrusted the melody of his *Frühlingsstimmen* (Voices of Spring) waltz, Op. 410, not to the violin but to the voice, specifically that of Bianca Bianchi, a coloratura soprano. Richard Genée (1823–95), librettist of *Die Fledermaus,* provided the text and the piece was composed during work on *Eine Nacht in Venedig.* The work did not please at its première at the Theater an der Wien, but proved to be a great success when Strauss brought it to Russia while on tour in 1886. Strauss later made a piano arrangement , in which form the work's popularity spread beyond Vienna. Throughout *Frühlingsstimmen* Strauss disregards ballroom traditions, producing a musically integrated concert piece with only three, not five, waltz pairs.

Forgoing a slow introduction, Strauss opens *Frühlingsstimmen* with only eight measures of prefatory material. In B flat major, the first waltz's rolling, rising and falling tune encompasses sixteen measures, but its repeat only fifteen. The second of the first waltz pair, with its detached, leaping melody, is also of an unusual length and closes with a return of the prefatory material and a complete presentation of the first waltz, this time with a repeat of a full sixteen measures. Unpredictability continues as the second waltz pair is interrupted by a six-measure bridge before the repeat of its first melody, while the second tune of the pair is extended by a couple of "extra" measures. The first half of the third waltz shows Strauss at his most experimental, clearly composing in a developmental, Beethovenian vein. After moving to A flat major, Strauss begins the new section with an eight-measure tune that begins to repeat, but this is cut off as a new melody begins. The ensuing 28 measures contain four different ideas that refuse to fall into a pattern. As if to make up for this "transgression," Strauss provides a symmetrical, sixteen-measure tune for the second half of the third waltz. Still in A flat, the opening of the coda modulates to the tonic before revisiting the waltz's prefatory material. Most of the coda is concerned with the first waltz but Strauss includes references to the bridge between the two waltzes of the second pair and an inversion of the descending chromatic line of the last waltz. *—John Palmer*

Recommended:

○ **Johann Strauss: Waltzes** / Boskovsky (cond.), Vienna PO / Decca 467413

○ **Waltzes and Arias** / Streich, Berlin Radio SO / 1998 / DG 457729

Geschichten aus dem Wienerwald (Tales from the Vienna Woods), waltz, Op. 325 (1868)

In 1860 Strauss began conceiving his waltzes with an international audience in mind, occasionally electing to "illustrate" aspects of his homeland. Arguably, the most important of these is *Geschichten aus dem Wienerwald* (Tales from the Vienna Woods), Op. 325, one of Strauss' most famous waltzes. The *Wienerwald* evokes not so much the Vienna Woods themselves as it does the Austrian *Heurigen,* small establishments outside Vienna that serve partially aged wine and food associated with the countryside. Clearly a concert piece, *Wienerwald* does not exhibit predictable patterns of repetition or 16-measure melodies, and seems nearly through-composed.

Opening with horns supporting woodwind figures that resemble bird calls, the introduction immediately places the listener outdoors and ushers in the most surprising element of the piece—a zither. The sound of the zither is generally associated with rural Austria and Southern Germany and folk music performed at country inns and homes. The tunes Strauss writes for the zither are not necessarily "folkish," although the pace of the first melody is slow enough to place the emphasis on every beat, as in a Ländler. The waltz pair performed on the zither, however, is unusual in that the second of the pair has two distinct, eight-measure melodies in two contrasting tempos. After the orchestra enters, six more pairs of waltzes follow, throughout which Strauss seems to be thinking more in terms of symphonic music rather than music for the ballroom. The repeat of the first part of Waltz, No. 1, for example, covers only 12 of the original 16 measures before shifting abruptly to the second melody of the pair, which is not repeated. The syncopation of the second half of the third waltz works against the triple meter, while the strings and trumpet share the melody of the second part of Waltz No. 4. The first half of Waltz No. 5 is not repeated but the second half is, and the second part of Waltz No. 6 is really a slow, legato variation of the first part. Syncopation is also a feature of the seventh waltz, whose first melody has a span of 20 measures. Modulations and thick orchestration create a symphonic atmosphere in the coda, which includes a literal return of the second waltz pair and part of the third before the first waltz sounds again on the zither. *—John Palmer*

Recommended:

○ **Johann Strauss: Waltzes** / Boskovsky (cond.), Vienna PO / Decca 467413

○ **Viennese Favourites** / Kempe (cond.), Vienna PO / 2002 / Testament 1275

Kaiser-Walzer (Emperor Waltz), Op. 437 (1889)

Vienna, the waltz, and the Strauss family are inseparable entities. The waltzes of Johann Strauss Sr. (1804–49) evoked the air of the Viennese countryside, beer gardens and Heurigen. Those of his eldest son, Johann Jr., at first had the same rhythmic vitality and brief melodies. After 1860, however, this would change. The younger Strauss infused the traditional waltz format and sound with a new vitality and sophistication that reflected the glittery, hedonistic spirit of nineteenth century imperial Vienna. He melded the rhythmic drive of his father's works with Joseph Lanner's (1801–43) lyricism, and changed the rhythmic emphasis from the beat to the measure. Strauss' seemingly unlimited melodic invention prompted him to compose melodies that did not fall into the traditional four, eight, or 16-measure patterns of earlier waltz tunes. He maintained the basic outline employed by Lanner and his father: a slow introduction, (typically) five pairs of waltzes and a coda, but increased the length of each section and the organic unity of the whole. Strauss's orchestration is often picturesque, especially in his introductions, while that of the waltzes themselves approaches a Mozartean clarity.

In the *Kaiser-Walzer,* Op. 437, Strauss is thinking as much in terms of the concert hall as the dance hall. It is not possible to waltz to the music of the coda, and the arrangement and patterns of repetition of the waltzes seem to be conceived to satisfy the listener as well as the dancer. The work was published in Berlin in 1889.

The duple-meter introduction to the *Kaiser-Walzer* is a mood painting conveying both the light, showy atmosphere of imperial Vienna and the martial air surrounding Kaiser Franz Joseph. A solo cello introduces the first pair of waltzes, the two of which contrast in both tempo and mood. Instead calling for a repeat of each of the two waltzes separately, Strauss directs that the entire pair be played twice. More typically, the second waltz pair features internal repeats, the second of the pair, whose melody consist of a single, repeated pitch, is again at a faster tempo than the first. A trumpet fanfare introduces Waltz No. 3 and one of Strauss's lilting, sustained melodies, while the brass appear again with an angular melody for the second part of No. 3. The fourth waltz opens with a rising, syncopated line shared between the strings and winds. The first waltz of the pair moves imperceptibly into the second and its arching string melody. Although No. 4 features internal repeats, Strauss closes the pair by returning momentarily to the rising line of the first half before moving into a modulating return to Waltz No. 1. Strauss's desire to unify the entire piece becomes evident as he next moves to not a fifth waltz but a return to the entirety of the first in the original key. A fifth waltz does follow, but only the first of the pair is new, the second is a return of the second part of Waltz No. 3. Reminiscence is the theme of the coda, which revisits the introduction as the solo cello reappears, playing the melody of the first half of Waltz No. 1 while a brief reference to the second part of the same waltz sounds in the flute. *—John Palmer*

Recommended:

○ **Johann Strauss: Waltzes** / Boskovsky (cond.), Vienna PO / Decca 467413

○ **Johann Strauss Celebration** / Meyrowitz (cond.), Berlin PO / 1999 / Teldec 28411

Künstler-Leben (Artists' Life), waltz, Op. 316 (1867)

Like *Morgenblätter*, Op. 279, and *Wiener Blut*, Op. 307, "Künstlerleben" (Artist's Life), Op. 316, was conceived with a worldwide public in mind. Strauss' expansion of the waltz continues in this work as he creates links between sections and employs harmonies only distantly related to the tonic.

Composed at roughly the same time as *An der schönen, blauen Donau*, Op. 314, *Künstlerleben*, Op. 316, also features a lengthy, slow introduction with two parts, the first of which is based on melodies from the first and fourth waltzes, while the second is in a faster, waltz tempo. The first waltz pair opens with a tune that resembles *Hail, hail the gang's all here*, and is traditional in format, with two 16-measure melodies, each repeated literally. Strauss' sense of integration becomes evident in the repeat of the first half of the second waltz, which closes not like the original, but with a rapid, leaping figure from the end of the introduction. This outburst ushers in a passage emphasizing the major mediant (E major, a key distant from the tonic C major) that also closes the second waltz of the pair. Strauss moves to F major to open the third waltz pair, which instead of a repeat of each of its two melodies features a repeat of the entire pair. Strauss returns to the typical repeat pattern for the fourth pair, whose dotted, leaping melodies contrast with those of the third and fifth waltzes. The coda, possibly Strauss' longest, revisits all five of the preceding waltzes, especially the first, which receives developmental treatment just before the close of the piece. *—John Palmer*

Recommended:

○ **Carlos Kleiber Conducts Strauss** / Kleiber (cond.), Vienna PO / 1990 / Sony 45938

○ **Fritz Reiner Conducts Johann & Josef Strauss** / Reiner (cond.), Chicago SO / 1985 / RCA 5405

Morgenblätter (Morning Papers), waltz, Op. 279 (1864)

Strauss' *Morgenblätter* (Morning Papers), Op. 279, was commissioned by the Concordia Journalists' and Writers' Association for their annual ball in 1862. The work was printed in May 1864, only a few months after the composer had been appointed Imperial *Hofballmusikdirektor* (Court Ball-Music Director). *Morgenblätter* differs from Strauss' later waltzes in its lack of new bridge material between the waltz pairs. Instead, Strauss returns to the first part of each pair to round out the structure before moving on to the next. The rhythmic ingenuity that informs his melodies is as vital as it would ever be. Groups of long and short notes open a duple-meter introduction that evokes the rhythms of a printing press. *Morgenblätter*'s best-known melody, which clearly articulates the triple meter of the waltz, opens the first pair of waltzes; for the second member of the pair, however, Strauss disguises the triple meter by employing the duple-meter pattern from the introduction. The second pair of waltzes follows the same pattern as the first, closing with a repeat of the first half and moving directly into the next pair. Waltz No. 3 follows with yet another melody that initially subverts the triple meter with its motion and pattern of accents before the piccolo takes over with a truly waltz-like tune. Pizzicato strings assume the lead in the first part of No. 4, whose rhythms resemble those of No. 1. Low brass and trumpet abruptly open the fifth pair of waltzes with an angular tune that contrasts with the sustained, static string melody of the second half. Instead of following the fifth waltz with a coda, Strauss reprises No. 2 in its entirety, varying the repeat of the second half in a manner that leads to a return of the first waltz. A coda featuring intense string tremolo bring the work to close. *—John Palmer*

Recommended:

○ **Vienna** / Reiner (cond.), Chicago SO / 1995 / RCA 68160

Perpetuum Mobile (Perpetual Motion), Ein musikalischer Scherz, Op. 257 (1861)

In September 1844, Strauss, not yet 19 years of age, began his public career as a musician directing an orchestra in performances of his own works and works of his father. Over the next 25 years, he would produce more than 300 dance pieces, most of those for his own orchestra to perform in Vienna and on tour. Among his waltzes, polkas, quadrilles, and marches the waltzes were most responsible for both his immediate success and his lasting fame. Strauss also composed the occasional Csárdás, Polonaise, Romanze, and other works that do not fit neatly into a specific category. Among these is the *Perpetuum Mobile: musikalischer Scherz* (Perpetual Motion: A Musical Joke), Op. 257.

Strauss' silly romp opens with the low brass and strings pounding out the incessant pulse before any tune begins. Nearly every instrument of the orchestra plays a "solo" during the endless progression of eight measure tunes, the first halves of which rise and the second falls. Strauss mixes instruments that play in the most disparate ranges. For example, after the bassoon hustles through its muddy melody the flute takes over and the two end up sharing a melodic passage despite the huge gap in register between them. High pitches on a glockenspiel accompany the string basses for a brief encounter, not long before the timpani takes over. Most of the tunes are intentionally silly and the overall structure leads nowhere, the piece simply fades away over the stripped-down accompaniment of the first four measures. *—John Palmer*

Recommended:

○ **Johann Strauss: Waltzes** / Boskovsky (cond.), Vienna PO / Decca 467413

Persischer (Persian March), Op. 289 (1864)

Marches are among the oldest known forms of Western music. Designed to keep large groups of people—especially soldiers—walking at the same pace, early marches were built of various drum patterns that conveyed certain meanings. By the mid-nineteenth century, the military march band had become a musical entity within itself, and many famous pieces were written for this performing format, consisting generally of wind instruments augmented by percussion borrowed from Turkish and Spanish military music. Johann Strauss II was a prolific composer of marches whose *Radetzky-Marsch*, Op. 228, inspired by the 1848 revolution in Vienna, is still performed today.

Composed and performed in 1865, the *Persischer Marsch (Persian March)*, Op. 289, was designed for one of Strauss' numerous summer seasons in the Russian town of Pavlovsk. The work was originally entitled "March of the Persian Army," but this was simplified before its publication in Vienna in 1865. Pavlovsk was an important stop on the Tsarskoye Selo Railway, the first railway line in Russia. The Vauxhall restaurant near the Pavlovsk station, financed by the railway, had fallen on hard times, and the manager felt that booking Strauss to give summer concerts there would bring back the lost customers. Strauss' summer engagements at Pavlovsk began in 1855 and continued for ten years, after which he conducted only occasionally at home and abroad. Strauss achieved great success in Russia and composed some of his more significant waltzes and polkas for his summer concerts there.

Most marches are brief, and Strauss' *Persischer Marsch* is no exception. In ABA form, the work possesses only three melodies, two of which form the A section. A tambourine punctuates every strong beat as the first melody is played on the flute. The melody itself outlines the harmonic minor scale, whose augmented second nineteenth century Europeans generally associated with music of the Middle East. As in his mature waltzes, Strauss forgoes the traditional eight- or 16-measure melodic pattern and extends the melody to his liking. Cymbal crashes provide the accents for the second tune, which is more sustained and legato than the first. Leaps figure prominently in the central section, the melody of which is eight measures long and repeated, although there is a bridge passage separating the tune and its return, while the repeat is reorchestrated and at a much louder dynamic level. Both parts of section A return in their entirety, closing the piece abruptly with no coda. *—John Palmer*

Recommended:

○ **1992 New Year's Concert** / Kleiber (cond.), Vienna PO / 1992 / Sony 48376

Pizzicato Polka, Op. 234 (1870)

Some of the characteristics of the polka appear in music performed by and written for Bohemian village musicians around 1800; aside from this, the dance's origins are obscure. A couple-dance in 2/4 meter, it seems the polka developed in Bohemia as a type of round-dance with three short, heel-and-toe half-steps on the first three half-beats and a rest on the fourth. The name may be derived from the Czech *pulka* (half) or *polska*, the Czech word for a Polish girl. Whatever its origins, it is certain that the polka first appeared in Prague in 1837. The dance was exported to Vienna in 1839 by a Bohemian regiment band, precipitating its rapid spread throughout Europe. By 1843–44 it was the favorite dance of Parisians and in May, 1844, it was first performed in the U.S. Local musicians created variants of the dance, and in the 1850s in Vienna, the elegant Polka française and the lively Schnell-Polka developed. The polka was very popular in the late nineteenth century and examples were penned by nearly every major composer of dance music, performed by almost all military bands and distributed in the form of sheet music throughout the world. A French dictionary of dance terms dating from 1847 describes the polka as having a tempo of 104 beats per minute with an emphasis on the second beat of the measure. It exhibits a ternary (ABA) form with eight-measure subsections and sometimes includes an introduction and a coda.

With his brother Josef, Johann Strauss had composed the *Pizzicato-Polka* in 1869 for one of his several visits to Russia. Scored for strings and glockenspiel, the polka was published in Vienna the next year and became very popular, especially in Italy, where Strauss included it on the program of every one of his tours. Like other works on which Strauss collaborated with one or both of his brothers, the *Pizzicato-Polka* bears no opus number.

Consisting of four melodies, the *Pizzicato-Polka* is arranged in ternary form. As the title suggests, the entirety of the piece is scored for plucked strings, although a glockenspiel appears for the first half of the central section. Possibly because of the limited instrumentation, Strauss seems to have attempted to provide as much contrast as possible in other ways, such as the rhythm and shape of melodies. After a brief introduction, the first eight-measure tune falls into two sections and outlines chords with alternating eighth and 16th note rhythms. The second melody is quite different, with its falling scales, constant eighth note pulse and occasional rests. A literal return of the first melody rounds out the A section. The central section features the glockenspiel in the first of its two melodies, which derives its identity more from color than from melodic shape. Broken chords played on all instruments open the contrasting tune, the second half of which consists of descending scales. Each melody of the B section is repeated. A full return of section A and a brief coda of descending scales closes the piece. *—John Palmer*

Recommended:

○ **Ein Straussfest** / Kunzel (cond.), Cincinnati Pops Orch. / 1985 / Telarc 80098

Rosen aus dem Süden (Roses from the South), waltz, Op. 388 (1880)

Strauss' *Das Spitzentuch der Königin*, with text by H. Bohrmann-Riegen and Richard Genée (1823–95), premiered on October 1, 1880, at the Theater an der Wien in Vienna. Originally written for Franz von Suppé (1819–95), the three-act book was based on Cervantes' *Don Quixote*. Strauss extracted the "Truffel" Couplet from *Das Spitzentuch der Königin* as the point of departure for his waltz *Rosen aus dem Süden* (Roses from the South). The waltz was published in 1880 in Hamburg, before the score of the operetta was printed.

Much of what Strauss accomplished in his transformation of the Viennese waltz from dance piece to concert piece can be heard in the opening part of the first waltz pair. The first eight-measure tune, which is strikingly similar to the opening waltz of Strauss' *Morgenblätter*, Op. 279, closes on the dominant and is answered by another eight-measure tune that returns to the tonic. This is not unusual, but during the expected "repeat" the melodies are rewritten and extended by eight measures while the harmonic progression is completely changed. Such melodic manipulation is more like the work of Brahms than of Lanner or Strauss Sr. Also like *Morgenblätter*, the second and third waltz pairs feature a repeat of their first halves (although not all conductors follow this direction), and both pairs juxtapose slow, sustained tunes in the first half with faster, active melodies in the second. The fourth waltz is another of Strauss' through-composed sections in which he develops and extends his material at the expense of the traditional waltz structure. The coda contains both new material and references to the preceding waltzes, especially the third and fourth, and of course, the first, which is fragmented and briefly developed in a Haydn-esque manner. *—John Palmer*

Recommended:

○ **Johann Strauss: Waltzes** / Boskovsky (cond.), Vienna PO / Decca 467413

Tritsch-Tratsch-Polka (Chit-Chat Polka), Op. 214 (1858)

Strauss composed the *Tritsch-Tratsch-Polka*, Op. 214 (1858) at a time when he regularly visited Russia, where he was exposed to compositional ideas that found their way into the popular Viennese forms of which he was the undisputed master. In this polka, Strauss retains the customary ternary form but tends to accent each beat equally. The A section itself consists of three parts, in turn configured in a miniature ternary scheme. Section B, containing only two melodies, is likewise rounded by a return of its first tune. Following B, the A section returns in its entirety, and the work closes with a brief coda.

With one exception, each of the polka's eight-measure melodies is repeated to create discrete 16-measure units. As in his waltzes, Strauss was not content to follow convention completely. For instance, although the third section of A consists of sixteen measures, this is not the result of an eight-measure idea merely repeated. Instead, it comprises two distinct eight-measure melodies, the first a constant eighth note pattern in the flute, the second a halting brass figure that accents the second beat of each measure. The flute and piccolo play a much larger role in this polka than they do in Strauss' waltzes, assuming a near-ubiquitous melodic role supported by pizzicato lower strings and woodwinds in contrary motion. *—John Palmer*

Recommended:

○ **1992 New Year's Concert** / Kleiber (cond.), Vienna PO / 1992 / Sony 48376

Unter Donner und Blitz (Thunder and Lightning), schnellpolka, Op. 324 (1868)

Unter Donner und Blitz (Thunder and Lightning), Op. 324, was published in 1868, just after the equally illustrative waltz, *Geschichten aus dem Wienerwald*, Op. 325.

Possibly the noisiest of Strauss' dance pieces, *Unter Donner und Blitz* evokes the sound of thunder and lightning through incessant timpani rolls and cymbal crashes. In the first half of section A, a loud timpani roll occurs every four measures, while the cymbals crash on each beat of the detached descending melody of the second half. Drum answers cymbal in the arching woodwind tune that begins section B, moving the accent to the second beat of the measure. A note-for-note return of section A completes the traditional ternary form, and a rambunctious coda creates a thunderous close. The only peculiar aspect of *Unter Donner und Blitz* is the percussive, eight-measure bridge between the two parts of section A, and the absence of any return to the first part of section A. Clearly, Strauss sought to amuse as much as compose a successful piece of music. *—John Palmer*

Recommended:

○ **1992 New Year's Concert** / Kleiber (cond.), Vienna PO / 1992 / Sony 48376

Wein, Weib und Gesang (Wine, Women and Song), waltz, Op. 333 (1869)

Published in Vienna in 1869, *Wein, Weib und Gesang* Op. 333 is a choral waltz composed for the Wiener Männergesang-Verein for a performance of February 2, 1869, with text by Josef Weyl (1821–95). Strauss would eventually complete nine works for the Society, among them *An der schönen, blauen Donau*, Op. 314. *Wein, Weib und Gesang* was very popular among Strauss' contemporaries, including Johannes Brahms (1833–97), who quoted the work in his *String Quartet*, Op. 51. *Wein, Weib und Gesang* is one of the works Strauss brought with him to Boston in 1872 to conduct at the "International Peace Jubilee," a monster affair featuring 20,000 singers and 10,000 orchestral musicians.

Encompassing three meters, four tempo markings and three key changes, Strauss' introduction approaches the realm of the symphonic poem. Opening with an idea that resembles the beginning of the second waltz, the introduction's 6/8 meter and Andantino tempo create a fluid atmosphere. Although some of the leaps and rhythms in the introduction also appear in the ensuing waltzes, the material is generally the property of the introduction, and the pause before the waltz tempo almost makes the preceding segment sound self-contained. Particularly notable is the warmth of sound, with melodies carried in inner voices and large sections of the orchestra moving in block chords.

Harmonic adventures continue in the waltzes. In the first waltz the repeat of the 16-measure melody goes astray as G major appears in the midst of the tonic, E flat major. The second tune of the pair, however, remains firmly in the tonic. The second waltz pair immediately abandons the tonic for C major, while the theme of the pair just as abruptly moves to A flat major. Each tune is a full sixteen measures long, the first returning to create an ABA structure. The second half of the third waltz features further harmonic trickery. While the first half of the 16-measure antecedent-consequent theme hovers around D minor, the second half closes on the relative F major. This is not unusual, but what is surprising is that the repeat of the entire melody begins on F major, not D minor. The first of the fourth and last waltz pair is anticipated in full at the close of the introduction, its dominant harmony (B flat major) providing the perfect route back to the tonic in the second waltz of the pair, which provides such a strong close that a lengthy coda is unnecessary. *—John Palmer*

Recommended:

○ **Strauss: The Best of Vienna** / Boskovsky (cond.), Vienna PO / 1998 / DG 459730

Wiener Blut (Vienna Blood), waltz, Op. 354 (1873)

Wiener Blut (Viennese Blood), Op. 354, is another of Strauss' mature waltzes composed with an international audience in mind. Written in June 1871, Strauss was in his 46th year and had just experienced his first success composing for the stage in *Indigo und die vierzig Räuber*. *Wiener Blut* would later become the central musical theme of the pastiche operetta by the same name. The waltz was published in 1873 in Vienna and clearly shows Strauss thinking in terms of symphonic concert works with extended melodies and developmental variations.

Strauss' introduction to *Wiener Blut* is unusual in that it begins at a fast tempo and includes a slow anticipation of the first waltz theme, set for a small string ensemble. As in many of Strauss' mature waltzes, phrase structures and repetition patterns are unpredictable; even the repeat of the very first waltz tune, one of the composer's most famous, is reorchestrated. The melodies of the second parts of waltzes Nos. 1 and 3 require extensions to fill 16 measures, and No. 5 has only one melody that fills a 38 measure span. At the same time, Strauss' melodic simplicity is at its most evident, the fourth waltz pair with its rising scalar motion in the first half and modest three-note figure bounced back and forth between flute and horn in the second. The coda consists of a literal return of the first waltz, followed by small fragments of the introduction tossed about in Beethovenian fashion. Unlike the earlier *Morgenblätter*, Op. 279, the first of each pair of waltzes does not return before moving on to the next—this only occurs after the first waltz pair, as in *Accelerationen*, Op. 234. Familiarity with the music of Liszt and Wagner may have influenced Strauss' composition of the extended, developmental tune of the fifth waltz, which is itself is introduced by a lengthy, aggressive bridge. *—John Palmer*

Recommended:

○ **Johann Strauss: Waltzes** / Boskovsky (cond.), Vienna PO / Decca 467413

OPERA

Die Fledermaus (The Bat), operetta (1874)

The Vienna State Opera has offered an annual New Year's Eve production of *Die Fledermaus* since the early 1930s, both reflecting and reinforcing the work's status as the representation of all things Viennese. It is curious then, that the piece considered the epitome of Viennese operetta is not at all representative of contemporaneous works in the genre.

Vienna in the middle nineteenth century was one of the premier cities of Europe. The capital of a vast empire, it boasted a vibrant cultural life and had long been recognized as a major musical and theatrical center. The Austrian economy was strong, and Viennese bourgeoisie spent their evenings eating, drinking, and attending the theater. However, on May 9, 1873, the Austro-Hungarian Empire suffered a debilitating stock market crash. Fortunes disappeared overnight, and businesses of all kinds suffered, including theaters. The Viennese, temporarily at least, were condemned to an austere lifestyle. It was in this atmosphere that Strauss' *Die Fledermaus* took shape.

Die Fledermaus is based on a French vaudeville, *Le Réveillon* (1872), by Henri Meilhac and Ludovic Halévy, itself based on Richard Benedix's *Das Gefängnis* of 1851. Karl Haffner created a German rendition of *Le Réveillon* and sold this to Maximillian Steiner, the director of the Theater an der Wien. Steiner gave Haffner's manuscript to Richard Genée, suggesting he develop from it a libretto. Strauss and Genée began working together, and on October 25, 1873 Strauss directed a benefit concert that included his *csárdás für Gesang*, with a text by Genée. The number was well received, and would become Rosalinde's csárdás in Act Two of *Die Fledermaus*. Spurred on by this success, Strauss reportedly completed the music for the rest of the operetta in 42 days. The premiere took place in the Theater an der Wien on April 5, 1874 (Easter Sunday).

Die Fledermaus departed in several ways from previous Viennese works. Conceived in three acts, *Die Fledermaus* requires only three stage settings, and it does not open with the customary large number for chorus. At the premiere, the characters sported contemporary public attire instead of lavish costumes, while the sets consisted of the simple interiors of people's homes and a barren jail. Furthermore, the story is set in the present and in Vienna.

While the current economic state of the empire was reflected in the production itself—there were few scene changes and a minimal group of choral numbers—the world as it "used to be" drives the story, with masked balls and freely flowing champagne. Any disappointment caused by the scaled-down production was outweighed for audiences by the chance to participate vicariously in the revelry acted out on stage. Certainly, the major element that made *Die Fledermaus* a resounding success was, and is, Strauss' music, which is more sophisticated than that of any operetta previously offered the Viennese.

Strauss' ability to characterize through music is at its finest in *Die Fledermaus*. In Act Two, Rosalinde poses as a Hungarian princess, and when asked to prove her origins, sings a Hungarian csárdás. Strauss evokes an aural image of Hungarian gypsies through the clarinet line that opens the number, the slow, rubato style of the first half, and pizzicato strings. Adele, also in Act Two, "confirms" her upper-class status with an exquisite song, during which she enumerates her fine physical qualities. Strauss produces unity through an ingenious use of melody. For instance, the melody sung by the chorus as the curtain rises on Orlofsky's party in Act Two appears earlier when Adele reads the letter inviting her to Orlofsky's party and moments later when Falke convinces Eisenstein to attend the same event. *—John Palmer*

Synopsis:

Act One. The story is set in a resort town, outside a large European city. In the Eisenstein home, Alfred, singing teacher of Russian Prince Orlofsky, serenades his one-time lover Rosalinde, who is now married to Gabriel von Eisenstein. The maid Adele enters carrying an invitation from her sister Ida to a masked ball at Prince Orlofsky's villa, scheduled for that evening. She asks Rosalinde for the night off so she can visit her supposedly sick aunt, but the request is promptly turned down. Alfred appears when Adele has left the room, and Rosalinde, enamored of his voice and his charm, convinces him to return that evening when her husband is to begin serving a two-week jail sentence for assault.

Eisenstein soon arrives with his lawyer Dr. Blind, the two arguing over the outcome of the assault charges. When the lawyer has departed, Falke, a friend of Eisenstein, enters and convinces Eisenstein to delay his appearance at the prison and attend Orlofsky's masked ball.

Rosalinde decides to give Adele a free night after all, so she can be alone with Alfred. After Adele and Eisenstein depart, Alfred returns and he and Rosalinde begin dining. Soon, however, Frank the prison warden arrives and mistakes Alfred for Eisenstein, not least because Rosalinde, not wanting to court scandal, insists that he is her husband. Alfred reluctantly plays along with the masquerade.

Act Two. At Prince Orlofsky's villa, Falke promises the Prince there will be a comical charade staged for his benefit. The players in it include Adele, who is impersonating Olga, an actress, and Eisenstein, who is called the Marquis Renard. The latter is taken by Olga's likeness to his maid, but Adele pokes fun at the comment. Soon the warden arrives, taking the identity of Chevalier Chagrin. Falke introduces him to Eisenstein, and soon Rosalinde enters, masked and posing as a Hungarian countess. Eisenstein has been flirting with women throughout the evening and even tries to charm the "countess." Recognizing him, she snatches his watch to use later as proof of his womanizing.

An attempt to make Rosalinde remove her mask by some of the guests merely results in her singing a csárdás to prove her Hungarian character. Afterward, Eisenstein relates the story of "the bat." At a masked ball he abandoned his friend Falke, who, dressed as a bat, had to walk home alone the next morning. The merriment continues until six o'clock the next morning, at which time Eisenstein departs for jail. The warden also leaves.

Act Three. Frank enters his office at the prison, with Alfred singing in the background and disturbing the other prisoners. Adele and Ida soon arrive and, believing the tipsy warden is a theatrical agent, try to impress him with their talents. Eisenstein arrives and is momentarily taken aback to see the Chevalier Chagrin there. But he is more surprised to find out that someone is serving his sentence. When Dr. Blind appears suddenly, Eisenstein borrows his wig and legal robe to find out the identity of the impostor who dined with his wife.

Rosalinde arrives to gain Alfred's release and to file for divorce from Eisenstein. She reveals her affair to the "lawyer," and then Eisenstein removes his disguise and accuses her of infidelity. She then produces his watch to prove his womanizing. The Prince, Falke, and guests from the previous night's ball arrive. Falke reveals that the whole affair had been his scheme, brought off so that "the bat" could get his revenge. *—Robert Cummings*

Recommended:

- ○ **Strauss: Die Fledermaus** / Previn (cond.), Te Kanawa, Gruberova, Fassbaender, Brendel, Leech / 1991 / Philips 432157
- ○ **Strauss: Die Fledermaus** / Karajan (cond.), Schwarzkopf, Gedda, Streich, Kunz, Christ, Krebs / 1999 / EMI 67153
- ○ **Strauss: Die Fledermaus** / Kleiber (cond.), Varady, Popp, Prey, Kollo, Weikl, Kusche / 1999 / DG 457765

Eine Nacht in Venedig (A Night in Venice), operetta (1883)

Late in 1881 Strauss began discussing a new operetta with F. Zell (pen name of Kamillo Walzel, 1829–99) and Richard Genée (1823–95). The librettists suggested two subjects: Der Bettelstudent (The Beggar-Student) and Venezianische Nächte (Venetian Nights), of which Strauss chose the latter, later changing the name to *Eine Nacht in Venedig* (A Night in Venice). Strauss may have been attracted to the subject for several reasons, not the least of which is that his father, 35 years earlier, had produced a successful gala entitled "Eine Nacht in Venedig." Also, Venice was a popular theme among the Viennese who, by 1895, had constructed a replica of the ancient seaside city in the middle of Vienna's largest public park.

Loosely basing their concept on a French comic opera, *Château Trompette*, Walzel and Genée (also the librettist of *Die Fledermaus*) together developed the characters and scenario while Walzel created the dialogue and Genée the song texts. Thus, Genée influenced the musical construction of the operetta, as he had with *Die Fledermaus*. Strauss probably began composing the operetta by late March 1882, by which time Walzel and Genée had completed the first two acts. Although Strauss preferred to introduce new works at Vienna's Theater an der Wien, private matters forced a change of plans. Strauss's second wife, Angelika Dittrich, began an affair with Franz Steiner, the director of the Theater an der Wien, inciting Strauss to sue for divorce and seek another venue for the premiere of his latest operetta.

Eine Nacht in Venedig received its première at the new Friedrich-Wilhelmstädtisches Theater in Berlin on 3 October 1883. While both public and critics cheered Strauss's music, few people were pleased with the libretto, described by one reviewer as "a hodgepodge of foolishness and tediousness." Strauss eliminated some of the offending numbers and altered the texts of others before the first performance in Vienna six days later, at the Theater an der Wien. By the end of the year, productions had been planned in New York and 16 European cities. However, the weakness of the libretto has prevented the work's lasting success.

Despite the weak libretto, *Eine Nacht in Venedig* has many brilliant moments. For example, early in Act One, the chorus introduces Caramello's multi-sectional "Willkommen, liebe Freunde" with "Evviva Caramello." The aria is interspersed with outbursts from the chorus as Caramello explains, "quietly," how much the Duke loves women. When he demonstrates a Tarantella, the meter changes from 2/4 to 6/8.

Strauss flexes his waltz muscles with the compelling "Alle maskiert," sung by Annina, Ciboletta, Caramello and Pappacoda in anticipation of the upcoming Carnival celebrations. The single waltz tune is contrasted against a rapid, recitative-like section that appears twice.

For Caramello's "Komm in die Gondel, mein Liebchen," Strauss provides one of his most lilting melodies. The sensuous tune adds to the irony of the situation, in which Caramello, crooning in a seductively slow 6/8, does not know he is indeed singing to his "Liebchen."

As Caramello watches the Duke disappear with Annina in Act III he sings the waltz, "Ach wie so herrlich zu schaun," published separately as the *Lagunen-Walzer* Op. 411. One of the most effective numbers of the operetta, it consists of a pair of waltzes, in F and B flat, the first of which returns to close the piece. The slow tempo and occasional chromatic inflections contribute to the ethereal atmosphere, marked "dreamlike" by Strauss.—*John Palmer*

Synopsis:

Act One. The story is set in late eighteenth century Venice. Amid carnival celebrations, Pappacoda, a cook, is asked to pass on a romantic note from Enrico Piselli, a naval officer and Senator Delacqua's nephew, to the Senator's young and attractive—and flirtatious—wife Barbara, so that Enrico can have a rendezvous with her. Pappacoda soon encounters his own girlfriend, Ciboletta, who expresses her view that men are naturally deceitful. The young Annina also soon appears—she is betrothed to Caramello, the Duke of Urbino's barber. Finally, Barbara comes along and Pappacoda delivers Enrico's message to her.

The Senators Delacqua and Barbaruccio soon appear to discuss their invitations to a masquerade they received from the Duke of Urbino. Delacqua wants a stewardship from the Duke, but fears for his wife owing to the Duke's womanizing ways. He thus arranges to have Barbara travel that evening by gondola to her aunt's in Murano.

Caramello soon comes along and learns from Pappacoda of Delacqua's plan to send his wife off to Murano. Knowing that the Duke would be pleased by the company of Barbara—as he was a year earlier—he decides to commandeer the gondola himself and take her to the Duke's palace. But Barbara, wanting to keep the rendezvous with Enrico, engages Annina to take the trip to Murano in her place. Caramello steers the gondola, unaware his passenger is his girlfriend. Upon arrival, he informs the Duke he has brought Barbara to him.

Act Two. All the main characters except Barbara have shown up for the masquerade. Aware now he has brought Annina instead of Barbara, Caramello strives to keep her from the Duke, though Annina herself delights in the situation. Pappacoda also worries about his sweetheart, Ciboletta, whom he cannot find.

Delacqua presents the disguised Ciboletta as his wife to the Duke; Ciboletta asks the Duke not for a stewardship, but, mindful of Pappacoda's ambitions, for the chief cook's post. The Duke makes advances to both Annina and Ciboletta, much to the consternation of the watchful Caramello and Pappacoda.

Act Three. It is midnight in St. Mark's Square, where the Duke and his party are taking part in the Carnival festivities. Delacqua learns from Ciboletta that Barbara was never taken to Murano. Ciboletta happily tells Pappacoda he has been appointed the Duke's chief cook. She also informs the Duke that Annina was posing as Barbara during the masquerade. In a thoroughly happy ending, the Duke returns Annina to Caramello and appoints him—not Delacqua—his steward. —*Robert Cummings*

Recommended:

○ **Strauss II: Operettas** / Ackermann (cond.), Schwarzkopf, Gedda, Kunz, Loose, Klein, Donch / 2001 / Angel 67532

Wiener Blut (Vienna Blood), operetta (1899)

Typically, Viennese operettas are not concerned with historical events; the generally light and farcical character of these works generally precludes plots centered around more serious topics. The model Viennese operetta, *Die Fledermaus*, by Johann Strauss II, features no historical context at all, and Strauss' first operetta, *Indigo und die vierzig Räuber*, is a fairytale.

In contrast, *Wiener Blut* is set against the Vienna of the early nineteenth century, during the Congress of Vienna. At the time, the Biedermeier city was poised to become a pulsing metropolis, a culturally sophisticated center of a modern empire. At the same time, *Wiener Blut* is an operetta about Vienna. No operetta before it (and few since) had so blatantly taken Vienna as its subject matter. Most of the characters are genuine Viennese associated with various Viennese landmarks and institutions, and whose dialect sets them apart from outsiders. Specific locations in and around the city are crucial to the drama, and the primary musical number, the waltz, *Wiener Blut*, describes what it is like to have Viennese blood coursing through one's veins.

When Franz Jauner asked Strauss in the spring of 1899 for a new operetta, he suggested using older material so the aging composer would not have to work too hard. Strauss gave his consent to the idea, but died on June 3, 1899, without giving further input. Although Strauss wanted Hermann Bahr to work on the libretto, the job fell to Victor Léon (1859–1940) and Leo Stein (1861–1921), the director of the Austrian Southern Railway. The entire work was arranged and edited by Adolph Müller Jr. *Wiener Blut* was produced as "a celebration of the 74th birthday of the eternal master Johann Strauss," and intended to be performed on October 26, 1899, the day after his 74th birthday.

Adolph Müller Jr., created the operetta from works published by the house of Cranz in Vienna, and deserves praise for arranging Strauss' melodies into genuinely effective theatrical numbers, especially the two sextets and the finale. Müller's creation of a waltz-quodlibet to close the second act, incorporating several of Strauss' waltz tunes sounding simultaneously, is truly ingenious, as is his transformation of the polka, *Freikugeln*, into a quartet to close Act I. Müller also skillfully incorporated the *Morgenblätter Waltz*, the polka *Drausst in Hietzing*, the waltz *Wein, Weib und Gesang*, *An der schönen, blauen Donau*, and the waltz *Neu Wien*.

Premiered in Vienna at the *Carltheater* on October 25, 1899, the first run of *Wiener Blut* lasted only until November 24. The director of the *Carltheater*, Franz Jauner, lamented, "The best, the very best, no longer pleases the public." A few weeks later Jauner committed suicide in his office. The "Golden Era" of Viennese operetta was at an end. On its heels followed the so-called "Silver Era," an era that would give new life to *Wiener Blut*. The management of the Theater an der Wien staged the operetta in 1905, introducing the work to a new generation that gladly embraced the pastiche of Strauss' melodies. —*John Palmer*

Synopsis:

Act One. The setting is Vienna, 1815. The first scene takes place in the villa of Count Zedlau, a philanderer who is an ambassador from a small country (the fictional Reuss-Schleiz-Greiz). His valet Josef, unable to find him anywhere, calls out to the maid. Franziska Cagliari, a ballerina, Zedlau's latest mistress, answers. Neither can find the busy Count. Franzi's father, Kagler, soon arrives to remind his daughter that she is to dance at Count Bitowski's ball later that evening.

After he departs, Zedlau finally arrives, and Franzi is suspicious that he has been with another woman. He insists he has made only a requisite appearance with his wife, Gabriele. When Franzi has departed, the Count explains to Josef that he and the Countess had met with his Prime Minister (Prince Ypsheim-Gindelbach), who mistook her for his mistress. He confides in Josef that he has developed an interest in another woman, to whom he instructs Josef to write a letter, setting up a rendezvous with her at the Heitzing fair for that evening. The Count does not know the young woman (Pepi Pleininger) is Josef's girlfriend, and, of course, Josef is unaware of who the woman is.

After the Count has departed, Pepi arrives. She is traveling to Heitzing that evening, but Josef cannot accompany her, since he'll be working. The Prime Minister soon arrives and the story's mixups begin developing: when Franzi returns he mistakes her for the Countess, and when the latter enters he takes her to be Zedlau's mistress. With both in the same room, he decides he must save the Count's reputation: he introduces Gabriele as his wife to Franzi.

Act Two. At the ball that evening, Zedlau and Gabriele agree their marriage is in trouble because of his behavior, his lack of "Vienna Blood." He then finds that he may be falling for yet another woman—his wife. He spots Pepi in the crowd, however, and hands her the letter written by Josef. She recognizes the handwriting as Josef's and assumes he will meet her at the Heitzing fair. But soon he appears and informs her he cannot go to Heitzing. At this revelation, Pepi realizes the author of the letter was Zedlau, but decides to meet him anyway.

Further comical mixups occur, the most important coming when Gabriele mistakes Pepi for Franzi, the mistress she knows about. The Countess asks her husband to take her to the Heitzing fair, but he refuses, explaining he has business with the Prime Minister. She then arranges to have the Prime Minister take her. Further comical mixups punctuate the story to close out this act.

Act Three. At the fair, three couples—Zedlau and Pepi, Josef and Franzi, and the Prime Minister and Gabriele—have separate rendevous and then meet together. The Count's philandering is uncovered, but the joyous mood allows for his reconciling with Gabriele, and Josef is reunited with Pepi, and the Prime Minister begins courting Franzi. —*Robert Cummings*

Recommended:

○ **Johann Strauss II: Wiener Blut** / Ackermann (cond.), Schwarzkopf, Gedda, Kunz / 1988 / EMI 69529

Der Zigeunerbaron (The Gypsy Baron), operetta (Oct. 24, 1885)

Der Zigeunerbaron was the first Viennese operetta set in Hungary and whose main characters were Hungarians and Gypsies. Although this may seem like a bold political gesture at a time when many Viennese felt the influx of Hungarians into Vienna threatened the city's political and financial stability, the context in which Strauss and Schnitzer frame their Hungarian characters preserves the Austrian sense of superiority. *Der Zigeunerbaron* is based on *Saffi*, a novella by the Hungarian Mór Jókai. Ignaz Schnitzer, in Vienna, developed a libretto from Jókai's scenario, while Franz Jauner, director of the Theater-an-der-Wien, secured the rights to the work and planned its production. *Der Zigeunerbaron* made its way to the stage very slowly; its premiere was on October 24, 1885, two and a half years after Strauss agreed to work on the project. Jauner traveled to Hungary to obtain Gypsy costumes, horses, and carriages for the lavish production. Both the music and libretto of *Der Zigeunerbaron* present images of Hungary and Gypsies through stereotypes that would have been recognized by contemporary Viennese. For example, Strauss aurally evokes Gypsy culture through the use of an anvil, cymbals, and gong, while Schnitzer and Jauner create Gypsy blacksmiths who wear bright clothing and can see the future.

Strauss' overture immediately transports the listener eastward with chromatic motives and unusual orchestration. The curtain rises on a chorus of gondoliers singing of marriage and partnership, but the political undertones of the text become clear as the boatmen tell nearby Gypsy women, "trust your boat without fear, although it may rock." Barinkay's return to claim his land at the opening of Act I is a representation of the wealthy Hungarians who had fled during the 1848 revolution, only to return later and rise to positions of power. Barinkay's Gypsy background becomes clear in his entrance couplet, "Als flotter Geist" ("A lively spirit"), as he describes how he befriended wild animals and told fortunes. Contemporary viewers would have immediately associated these characteristics, as well as the accompaniment by oboes and pizzicato strings, with Gypsies. However, when Barinkay pleads his sincerity, the music changes to a Viennese waltz, just as many wealthy Hungarians of the nineteenth century had shifted their allegiance from their homeland to Vienna. One of Strauss' most effective evocations of Hungarian life is Homonay's verbunkos of Act Two, a dance style derived from the method of recruiting troops in Hungary in the eighteenth century. Perhaps the ultimate expression of Austrian hegemony expressed in *Der Zigeunerbaron* is the setting of the third act. After all the fuss and fortune-telling of the first two acts, the moment of triumph and climax occurs not in Hungary but in Vienna, at the return of the victorious army from Spain. Furthermore, the army is explicitly referred to as "Austrian," despite the fact that many of its members are Hungarian Gypsies. When it becomes clear that the Gypsies Saffi and Barinkay can legally marry, the crowd sings not a Hungarian Czardas, but a Viennese waltz. *—John Palmer*

Synopsis:

Act One. The story is set in mid-eighteenth century Hungary and Austria. Having spent 20 years abroad in exile, owing to his father's bad political associations, Sandor Barinkay returns to his hometown of Temesvar and attempts to reclaim land belonging to the family. Conte Carnero, the Royal Commissioner, oversees the proposed transfer of property and enlists the aid of local farmer Zsupan to act as a witness on the deed. Having used the lands for his own farming needs, however, and since he is illiterate, Zsupan resists. But because there is said to be a treasure buried on the land, he attempts to match Barinkay with his attractive daughter Arsena. She declares she will have no part of him, however, since she has decided to marry no man below the rank of baron.

Meanwhile, Barinkay becomes attracted to a gypsy girl, Saffi. In the process he becomes recognized as leader to the band of gypsies. He returns to Arsena and now introduces himself as a "gypsy baron," but she does not fall for the ploy. Barinkay thus decides to focus his romantic attentions on Saffi.

Act Two. Barinkay is aided by Saffi and her mother Czipra in unearthing the hidden treasure on the land. Carnero, however, intervenes as a member of the morality commission, questioning Barinkay's relationship with Saffi. Barinkay claims they were married according to gypsy tradition, even though the alleged ceremony was performed and attended only by birds. Before the situation can be resolved, however, the province governor, Count Homonay, enlists both Barinkay and the unwilling Zsupan for military service in the war against Spain.

Act Three. Some time later, Zsupan arrives in Vienna with troops being demobilized. Soon Barinkay appears with another contingent of soldiers, leading them as a hero as they march along. His land back home is finally restored and he and Saffi are happily reunited. *—Robert Cummings*

Recommended:

○ **Strauss: Die Zigeunerbaron** / Ackermann (cond.), Schwarzkopf, Gedda, Prey / 1988 / EMI 69526

Josef Strauss

b. Aug. 20, 1827, Vienna, Austria, **d.** Jul. 22, 1870, Vienna, Austra

Composer: Orchestral

Josef Strauss was born into one of the most famous of Viennese musical families. His father, Johann Strauss (1804–49), was a violinist in the popular Josef Lanner dance orchestra when he married Maria Anna Streim, and then formed his own orchestra and overtook Lanner in popularity. Johann Sr. was opposed to his children going into music professionally, but he saw to it that the boys became proficient pianists. Although Johann Sr. intended him for the army, Josef studied poetry, art, and engineering. He enrolled in the Vienna Polytechnic for civil engineering and architecture degrees.

Maria Anna suggested that Josef take a position in Johann Jr.'s orchestra, but he turned down the idea, joking that he was too ugly for a career on stage. Furthermore, he was subject to fainting spells and intense headaches. Instead, he made his living as an engineer and designer. Among other things he invented a type of mechanical street-sweeper (which the city of Vienna adopted) and published two mathematical books.

In 1853, Josef conducted the orchestra for a while after Johann Jr. collapsed from overwork. He had an unexpected success and even composed a waltz set, which he hopefully called *First and Last Waltzes.* After this, too, surprised everyone by becoming highly popular, he wrote another, which he called *First Waltz after the Last.* When Johann was able to return to work in September, he found that Josef was willing to step in as an assistant at a moment's notice. The brothers were able to do this easily, since they contracted for and advertised that the orchestra would be conducted by "J. Strauss."

By 1856 was Josef ready to join the Strauss organization full-time. He took violin lessons from Franz Amon, Johann Sr.'s old teacher. Josef and Johann pretty much shared the leadership of the orchestra and its business from then until 1862, when they were joined by younger brother Eduard. In 1857 Josef married his childhood sweetheart, Karoline Pruckmayr. He spent all his spare time writing poetry, painting, and composing music, getting little sleep and continually smoking cigars. His waltzes are particularly intriguing. It is obvious that he had a poetic outlook not shared by his more down-to-earth brother. The Viennese loved his chronically pale, romantic appearance. Many of his waltzes have the greatest musical value of any the Strauss family output. He showed the influence of composers from Schubert and Chopin to Liszt and Wagner. Some of his most popular waltzes are *Love and Life, Voices of the Times, Music of the Spheres,* and *Village Swallows from Austria.* It is also known that Josef generously allowed Johann to claim as his own some waltzes actually written by Josef. He wrote a serious composition, a tone poem with orchestra called *Ode to the Night.* It received great critical acclaim, but has been lost.

In 1863 Johann was appointed Imperial and Royal Hofballmusikdirektor, which required him to largely absent himself from the family orchestra. This left Josef to take some of the orchestra's touring assignments, which he hated. He accepted an obligation to take the orchestra to Warsaw in April. There, in June, he suffered a blackout and fell from the podium. He asked to be taken to his home in Vienna, where he died within the month. *—Joseph Stevenson*

ORCHESTRAL

Auf Ferienreisen! (Off on Holiday!), schnellpolka, Op. 133 (1863)

This work is a polka, and its full title, *Auf Ferienreisen, polka schnell,* obviously divulges that fact, as well as its vigorous nature. Without doubt, it is one of Josef Strauss' most upbeat and joyous works. As Strauss family admirers know, Josef tended to be a bit introverted and generally wrote music of a less spirited and cheery nature. Often in the midst of a charming, graceful waltz, his melancholic side would seep into the music with dark, albeit subtle and well-crafted harmonies, or via some thematic mood swing. The work starts off with a vigorous rhythm, over which a trumpet call is played, which seems to incite the other instruments to join in a sonic romp. The main theme has a carefree vigor and its second subject is utterly rollicking in its stomping manner and sense of wild festivity. The middle section maintains the mood of joy and frolicsome spirit. After a return of the main materials, the trumpet call ends the music rather suddenly. Some would observe that this work's short length—about two-and-a-half minutes—is further evidence that the darker creative spirit of Josef inhibited him from writing happy music for too long. In any event, this joyous piece is well worth hearing, not least because its raucous manner is quite at odds with much Viennese light dance music. *—Robert Cummings*

Recommended:

○ **Johann, Josef & Eduard Strauss: Valses & Polkas Vols. 1 & 2** / Boskovsky (cond.), Johann Strauss Orch. / 2001 / EMI 74528

Delirien, waltz, Op. 212 (1867)

The *Delirien Waltz* starts off with a tremolo from the winds immediately creating a mood of suspense, much like a prelude to a dramatic scene in a Wagner opera. When the waltz theme is finally introduced, things lighten considerably as the world of Viennese Strauss dances comes on in heavy doses. Yet, the menace from the introduction lingers a bit before yielding to the gaiety and thereafter, the darker atmosphere from the opening makes only subtle reappearances in the harmonies and rhythms. Josef Strauss was known to have a melancholic personality, a disposition that may have contributed to his deeper harmonic sense and more subtle and imaginative handling of thematic material than the other family members. Though he was not as facile as Johann II in creating the fluff and glitter associated with the Viennese light dance music genre, he was nevertheless quite proficient at it, as the *Delirien Waltz* demonstrates. Its main theme has a relaxed, festive manner in its graceful poise. As usual, Josef deftly mixes moments of relaxation with bursts of celebration. About midway through, there is a witty section, wherein single strokes on the timpani colorfully punctuate phrases. The ensuing playful music is quite appealing, too, as is the demure return of the main theme. This waltz lasts about ten minutes and must be assessed as one of Josef Strauss' finest efforts in the genre. *—Robert Cummings*

Recommended:

○ **Johann, Josef & Eduard Strauss: Valses & Polkas Vols. 1 & 2** / Boskovsky (cond.), Johann Strauss Orch. / 2001 / EMI 74528

Dorfschwalben aus Osterreich, waltz, Op. 164 (1864)

This younger brother of Johann II and son of Johann I was himself an often-inspired composer of waltzes, polkas, and other dance forms. Moreover, a fair share of the works by Josef Strauss have become quite popular, able to stand with some of the better efforts by his older, more famous brother. This delightful effort, *Dorfschwalben Aus Osterreich* (Austrian Village Swallows), has that light, effervescent Straussian appeal, both thematically and instrumentally.

That said, the music here is no carbon copy of either his brother's works or of his father's. The piece opens with a brief pastoral introduction, a lighthearted clarinet roaming joyously about. There follows a series of waltzes, the first comical and playful, with bird chirping sounds, the whole having a delightfully carefree manner. The mood turns a bit more dignified in the next waltz, though the sense of fun and gaiety never departs. The third waltz is quite vigorous in its accented rhythms and colorful in its deft wind scoring. The mood turns more pastoral in the ensuing waltz section, owing mainly to Strauss' deft string harmonies. The opening waltz music returns to close out this splendid medley. Lasting between 12 and 15 minutes, this is one of Josef Strauss' larger waltz efforts, and certainly one of his most appealing. *—Robert Cummings*

Recommended:

○ **1992 New Year's Concert** / Kleiber (cond.), Vienna PO / 1992 / Sony 48376

Feuerfest!, polka française, Op. 269 (1869)

Strauss appended the words "Polka française" to the title of this work, though one will not necessarily hear anything particularly French in this music. It is a vigorous, colorful piece, however, from this supposedly lesser Strauss figure. Josef was not as prolific as his older brother, Johann II, and did not turn out nearly as many popular waltzes, but he demonstrated a deeper musical sense in many works with imaginative harmonies and melodic invention of great subtlety. This work, though, is light throughout and makes little attempt to achieve expressive depth. It features a joyous, bouncy theme and belled sonorities that combine to produce one of this composer's most buoyant, festive works. Lasting around three minutes, this piece begins in a playful, almost gentle manner, but swells to larger proportions as the bells punctuate strong beats and Strauss' deft scoring dresses the music in colorful instrumentation. Those bell strokes often hit with a measure of wit, as the composer occasionally has them strike a delightfully sour note. The last statement of the main theme is rollicking but outdone by the closing strokes on the bells and roaring gong. While this piece discloses no great subtleties, it will certainly offer strong appeal to those with an interest in light classical music. *—Robert Cummings*

Recommended:

○ **Ein Straussfest** / Kunzel (cond.), Cincinnati Pops Orch. / 1985 / Telarc 80098

Die Libelle, polka mazurka, Op. 204 (1866)

While Johann Strauss II was a generally upbeat extrovert, his younger brother, Josef, was rather the opposite in personality, having a somewhat withdrawn, brooding character. Not surprisingly, each brother's music often reflected his personality. True, Josef could write waltzes and polkas brimming with joy and sunshine, but beneath the surface one sometimes noticed his melancholy character seeping into the musical fabric. In *Die Libelle*, one of his more attractive polka mazurkas, the listener can hear much of that glittering Straussian sound, that deftly crafted instrumentation, but also a fair measure of emotionally disquieting music, not particularly unsettling but suggestive of gray rather than dark clouds. The work begins in a dreamy mood, then turns somewhat festive in its graceful, nonchalant main theme. Yet the music never seems to generate a lively enough tempo or a vigorous enough atmosphere to convey a sense of celebration or of merriment. The fun expressed in this dance piece sounds almost dutiful, as if its emotional aspects have been reined in—but to good effect. The music has appeal in its serene grace and in the mesmerizing character of both the opening motif and main theme. Lasting four to five minutes, *Die Libelle* will offer a more subtle appeal to those listeners interested in Viennese light music. *—Robert Cummings*

Recommended:

○ **The Strauss Family** / Boskovsky (cond.), Vienna PO / London 455254

Marien-Klänge, waltz, Op. 214 (1867)

While his older brother Johann II has fared better among audiences, Josef still had his share of successes in the waltz, polka, and other dance genres. True, he was not as facile as Johann II, but he demonstrated a deeper expressive sense in many of his compositions, both with his more advanced harmonies and more subtle melodic creations. That said, the *Marien-Klänge Waltz* only partially divulges Josef's greater artistic sensitivity, largely in the work's thematic development and in its well-constructed form. The thematic material here is generally graceful and quite deftly fashioned, two variants of the main theme presented right off, establishing playful, then slightly wistful moods before the source theme itself is heard in all its graceful color. There are stretches where Josef seems merely to want to create the Straussian family sound here, but most of his writing shows his usual skill. This waltz is often joyous and sometimes playful, but also divulges a slightly reflective, even melancholy manner at times, especially in some of the more subdued moments in string-dominated passages. Strauss deftly develops and mixes his melodic material, the moods shifting from playful to festive to delicate and graceful. In sum, this approximately eight-minute waltz offers the same kind of melodic appeal as many of the more popular works of the older Strausses, but also conveys a slightly subtler expressive manner. *—Robert Cummings*

Recommended:

○ **Wiener Bonbons** / Boskovsky (cond.), Boskovsky Ens. / Brilliant 99288

Mein Lebenslauf ist Lieb' und Lust!, waltz, Op. 263 (1869)

Josef is thought to have been one of the lesser Strausses, but musicologists and Strauss family mavens have long been aware of his considerable talent, a talent that could run deeper in expressive depth than that of his famous brother, Johann II, a more facile creator, to be sure, who found his niche and mastered it brilliantly. Josef might have been better-suited to writing more serious music, owing to his more subtle melodic and harmonic workings. *Mein Lebenslauf Ist Lieb'und Lust* clearly shows he could both write music in the lighter vein of his brother and show snatches of what might have developed into a broader, deeper art. That said, the music is quite light and festive here, but Josef masterfully mixes moods, orchestrates with a deft sense for color, and demonstrates his usual mastery of form. After a brief, playful introduction largely from the brass, the main theme is presented, a jaunty waltz tune, strongly accented and delightfully vigorous. The playful second subject adds a more subdued merriment, though cymbals and brass often punctuate the ends of phrases. Strauss manages to inject subtle surprises throughout, not least the colorful, rollicking coda. Lasting about eight minutes, this waltz will appeal to those with a preference for light classical music. *—Robert Cummings*

Recommended:

○ **Johann, Josef & Eduard Strauss: Valses & Polkas Vols. 1 & 2** / Boskovsky (cond.), Johann Strauss Orch. / 2001 / EMI 74528

Sphärenklänge (Music of the Spheres), waltz, Op. 235 (1868)

The *Sphärenklänge Waltzes* are considered one of the finest efforts of the melancholic Josef Strauss, a composer who might have developed a deeper musical language had his Strauss family heritage not constrained him to do otherwise. Still, he could turn out waltzes and other dances with nearly the craftsmanship, if not the facility, of his older brother Johann II. Josef used more inventive harmonies and understood melodic subtleties with a keenness not possessed by his older brother. The *Sphärenklänge Waltzes* here divulge his many strengths, from his mastery of form to his colorful orchestral scoring.

In the dreamy opening, Josef divulges a vague Wagnerian sense in his subtle, suggestive harmonies. The main theme is not immediately catchy, but wears on the listener on repeated hearings, exhibiting a sort of serene grace in its first subject and a playful joy in its second subject. In the middle section, Strauss imaginatively develops his thematic material, deftly retaining the air of festivity and playfulness, the dance step never missing a beat or a sense of continuity in the celebration. One can safely assess that this is one of the most sophisticated waltz works ever composed by a Strauss. Lasting about 12 minutes, it will appeal to a wide audience in and out of classical realms. *—Robert Cummings*

Recommended:

○ **1992 New Year's Concert** / Kleiber (cond.), Vienna PO / 1992 / Sony 48376

Richard Strauss

b. Jun. 11, 1864, Munich, Germany, **d.** Sep. 8, 1949, Garmisch-Partenkirchen, Germany

Composer: Opera, Orchestral, Symphonic, Concerto, Vocal, Chamber Music

Though the long career of Richard Strauss spanned one of the most chaotic periods in political, social, and cultural history of the world, the composer retained his essentially Romantic aesthetic even into the age of television, jet engines, and atom bombs. Born in Munich in 1864, Strauss was the son of Franz Joseph Strauss, the principal hornist in the Munich Court Orchestra. Strauss demonstrated musical aptitude at an early age, and extensive training in piano, violin, theory, harmony, and orchestration equipped him to produce music of extraordinary polish and maturity by the time he reached adulthood. His primary teachers had been his father, who was a musical conservative, and Ludwig Thuille, a Munich School composer and family friend. Strauss' *Serenade for 13 Winds, Op. 7* (1881), written when he was 17, led conductor Hans von Bülow to pronounce him "by far the most striking personality since Brahms." Bülow was able to give Strauss his first commission and an assistant conductor position. Through new friendships, Strauss learned to admire the writings of Schopenhauer and Nietzsche and the music of Wagner and Liszt. He embarked on a long career of conducting and composing, which take him all over Europe and the U.S.

From the beginning of Strauss' career as a composer, it was evident that the orchestra was his natural medium. With the composition of the "symphonic fantasy" *Aus Italien* in 1886, Strauss embarked on a series of works that represents both one of the pivotal phases of his career and a body of music of central importance in the late German Romantic repertoire. Though he did not invent the tone poem *per se*, he brought it to its pinnacle. In such works as *Don Juan* (1888–89), *Ein Heldenleben* (1897–98), and *Also sprach Zarathustra* (1895–96)—whose first minute or so, thanks to its use in the film *2001: A Space Odyssey*, is the composer's most readily recognizable music—Strauss displayed his abundant gift for exploiting the coloristic possibilities of the orchestra as a dramatic device like few composers ever had (or have since).

With the arrival of the twentieth century, after becoming conductor at Berlin's Hofoper, Strauss' interest turned more fully to opera, resulting in a body of unforgettable works that have long been fixtures of the repertoire: *Salome* (1903–05), *Elektra* (1906–08), and *Der Rosenkavalier* (1909–10) are just a few of his best-known efforts for the stage. In 1919, Strauss became co-director of the Vienna Staatsoper, but was forced to resign five years later by his partner, Franz Schalk, who resented being left with many of the operational duties while Strauss was frequently away guest conducting or being feted as a great composer. When the political situation in Europe became malignant in the 1930s, profound political naïveté led to Strauss' confused involvement the Nazi propaganda machine, and the composer eventually alienated both the Nazis and their opponents. With the end of World War II, however, he was permitted to resume his professional life, although it would be a mere echo of his previous fame. He began to have serious health problems, his financial situation had been compromised, and the monuments that embodied great German art for him—Goethe's Weimar house; the Dresden, Munich, and Vienna opera houses—had been destroyed. Throughout his last years, works such as the *Oboe Concerto* (1945) and the gorgeously expressive *Four Last Songs* (1948) attest to Strauss' unwavering confidence in his singular musical voice. —*AMG*

OPERA

Die Ägyptische Helena (The Egyptian Helen), Op. 75 (1923–1927; revised 1932)

This opera (*The Egyptian Helen*), Strauss' second exploration of Greek antiquity with writer Hugo von Hofmannsthal, is one of the composer's more problematic works. The searing intensity of *Elektra* was something neither artist sought to recreate, and the quicksilver ambiance Hofmannsthal was attempting to pin down proved elusive. While it is inaccurate to suggest that the composer's inspiration and creativity plummeted after *Ariadne auf Naxos* or *Die Frau ohne Schatten*, certain aspects of Hofmannsthal's libretto stretch credibility nearly to the breaking point. Still, many pages of the text are redeemed by the composer's incandescent writing for his title character, created for a soprano of spinto or dramatic caliber and claiming a luminous, soaring top register. At the Dresden premiere in June 1928, the heroine was sung by Elisabeth Rethberg and at the Metropolitan Opera's first performance in November of the same year by Maria Jeritza, both attractive singers and vocally close to ideal for the role.

In 1920 Hofmannsthal had begun to entertain the idea of a libretto based on the homeward journey of Helen and Menelaus after the sacking of Troy. Shortly before the opera's premiere, the writer considered that "... the night when the Greeks entered the burning city of Troy, Menelaus must have discovered his wife in one of the burning mansions and carried her out of the city between crumbling walls. This woman, victim of abduction, the most beautiful woman in the world, had been the cause of this awful decade of war, of this place strewn with dead, and of this fire ..." Hofmannsthal saw in this the possibility of a dramatic work and set about researching the several rather confusing versions of the legend. He wondered how all that destruction and tragedy could have presaged the resumption of a marriage of peace and conjugal blessedness.

Euripides' play *Helen* fascinated Hofmannsthal, especially with its notion of a phantom Helen—an Egyptian Helen. The mystery of the reconciliation between Helen and Menelaus so intrigued him that he concluded "only magic could have solved it." When, after several years' time, he showed the results of his work to Strauss, the composer realized that this would serve as splendid material for an opera, although he believed initially that the opera should end with the reunion at the first act's conclusion. Hofmannsthal persisted, however, with the idea that the couple should be shown in Egypt as Helen expresses her willingness to commit herself as well as her willingness to die. Thus, while the texture of the legend grew richer, the story became more complex as well.

As the collaboration progressed, both Hofmannsthal and Strauss abandoned their earlier notion of an opera with comedic overtones. Instead, the figure of Helen grew as a heroine of mystery and stature. Despite the often-convoluted libretto, the title role provides sufficient interest for a revival whenever a suitable soprano is available. —*Erik Eriksson*

Synopsis:

Act One. The opera begins at a palace entrance. An enormous Seashell is seen at mid-stage with a limitless ocean behind. Aithra emerges from the palace, impatiently awaiting the arrival of Poseidon, the ruler of the sea, for an impending banquet. Servants seek to calm her anxiety, as does the omniscient Seashell. Aithra learns that a woman is in danger of being killed by a man, the woman is none other than Helen of Troy. Summoning the spirits of the air, Aithra calls forth a storm in order to save Helen. When the ship is struck, however, Menelaus in fact saves Helen, the wife he has found after many years and brought from the ruins of Troy.

In the second scene Helen and Menelaus enter. Helen understands that her husband wishes to kill her. Confused, Menelaus beholds the palace where he is bidden by Helen to join him for a meal. He refuses, confused by her attitude of superiority. Sensing danger, Aithra calls forth her Elves of the moon whose actions distract him. He follows the ghost of the dead Paris.

As Scene Three begins, Aithra reveals herself to Helen. She assures Helen that she will save her, and sets about restoring Helen to her full beauty. Menelaus returns, believing that he has killed both Paris and Helen. Aithra hands him a draught of forgetfulness, telling him that the gods sent a spirit resembling Helen to Troy while his wife had been held at a fortress on Mount Atlas. Menelaus follows Aithra as she enters the palace to find Helen.

Scene Four opens as shafts of light fall on the bed where Helen reposes. As she awakens, Aithra informs her of her deception. When Menelaus resists embracing her, Helen asks of Aithra that they be swept away where no one knows that name of Troy. Menelaus no longer resists and, recalling his daughter Hermione, embraces Helen. Aithra spreads her magic cloak and the couple disappear.

Act Two. At their pavilion at the foot of Mount Atlas, Helen celebrates the previous evening's passion with an outpouring of joy and triumph, believing herself rid of all cares and difficulties. Menelaus awakens, still beset by dim recollections and resists Helen. She seeks for a potion given her by Aithra. In the search, the dagger once belonging to Paris falls at Menelaus' feet and, still unclear in thought, he imagines that he has killed both Paris and Helen. Turning away from her, he cries, "Siren of the air, come not near me!" In high frustration, Helen realizes that Aithra's spell is imperfect, discards the potion, and resolves to confront Menelaus with the truth.

Helen and Menelaus are interrupted by the arrival of Altair, a desert prince who pays her homage with oriental pomp and lavish gifts. Struck by her beauty, Altair desires her, as does his son Da-ud. Memories of Troy continue to trouble Menelaus, and he departs on a hunt. Accompanying him is Da-ud, now intensely jealous of Menelaus. Aithra enters with her servants, seeking to retrieve the potion of recollection. Helen, however, takes the vial, wishing to know the truth whatever the cost.

Altair interrupts, having returned to claim Helen for his own. Meanwhile, a fight has erupted between Menelaus and Da-ud, and Da-ud is killed. Altair, ignoring everything else, enters and attempts to embrace Helen, but is interrupted by a procession of mourners.

Notwithstanding Aithra's warning, Helen prepares the potion of recollection and hands it to Menelaus, who, believing it to be the death draught he has requested, drinks deeply and instantly recalls everything. He wishes to kill Helen, but she says simply, smilingly, "Aithra, he is about to kill me." Aithra has expended all her magic and calls upon Poseidon for aid. "Helen lives," she cries. "They are bringing your child." Menelaus is stunned. Dropping his sword, he declares, "I behold you as no man ever beheld his wife."

Embracing, Helen and Menelaus forgive each other and rejoice in freshly reawakened love, but Altair attacks, and once more Aithra calls upon Poseidon. His warriors disarm Altair, who is taken prisoner. Helen's daughter Hermione is brought forth by Aithra. The child turns to Menelaus and asks, "Father, where is my beautiful mother?" He escorts her to Helen, declaring, "Oh, my fortunate child, what a mother, indeed, do I now restore to you." The opera concludes with a hymn-like theme sung in unison by Helen and Menelaus. —*Erik Eriksson*

Recommended:

- ○ **Strauss: Die Ägyptische Helena** / Dorati (cond.), Jones, Hendricks, Kastu / 1991 / London 430381
- ○ **Strauss: Die Ägyptische Helena** / Botstein (cond.), Voigt, Tanner, Shafer, Grove, Robertson, Cutler / 2003 / Telarc 80605

Arabella, Op. 79 (1929–1932)

This last collaboration between Richard Strauss and the librettist Hugo von Hofmannsthal was an effort to revisit the great success of their earlier *Der Rosenkavalier.* However, the project never reached its full potential since Hofmannsthal died suddenly while preparing the libretto, leaving only the first act complete. Strauss' decision to set his departed colleague's drafts for the second and third acts stands as a tribute to him; the result is a charming and beautiful, but uneven, work, the wonderful first act of which merely hints at what could have been had their collaboration continued.

There are a number of similarities between *Arabella* and *Der Rosenkavalier.* both are period comedies set in Vienna (this time in 1860), both involve a "trouser" role (one for a female singer portraying a male character), and both have plots revolving around a proposed marriage for wealth. However, whereas the atmosphere of *Rosenkavalier* was one of opulence and high society, *Arabella* focuses in on a less auspicious slice of Viennese life. As a result its musical construction, especially with respect to moments of conversation and dramatic action, is less urbane and sophisticated, instead incorporating many elements of folk music and seeking to extract the utmost lyricism and beauty from each moment. This is especially evident in the central second act, which takes place at the Viennese coachman's ball. Yodeling and relatively simple waltz music surround a love duet of unmatched tenderness; the impression is of a series of set pieces rather than one integral scene.

Arabella is a beautiful young woman whose family intends to marry her upwards in society. For lack of money, the father has had Arabella's younger sister, Zdenka, disguised as a boy to avoid the cost of introducing them both at once. The plot revolves around Arabella's good fortune of finding true love with a wealthy Balkan landowner, and Zdenka's secret, and finally successful, efforts to snare another of her sister's suitors.

The first production of *Arabella* was complicated by interference from the Nazi government, which ousted the intended conductor, Fritz Busch (to whom Strauss dedicated the score), from his position in Dresden. However, the performance proceeded on July 1, 1933, with a new conductor and performers of Strauss' choosing. Reactions to the work have always been mixed, and so it is not performed nearly as often as Strauss' more popular works. However, the sheer beauty of much of the vocal writing and the appeal of the central characters has kept the work in the repertory, and a number of singers have made names for themselves in the central role—most notably Lotte Lehmann, and the Swiss soprano, Lisa Della Casa. *—AMG*

Synopsis:

Act One. The story is set in Vienna in the 1860s. Worried about the family's precarious finances, Countess Adelaide von Waldner seeks counsel from a fortune teller in the Waldner hotel suite. While the Waldners' daughter, Zdenka (raised as a boy, Zdenko, to save money), holds off anxious creditors, the fortune teller informs the Countess that her other daughter, Arabella, will soon marry a wealthy suitor. After the Countess and fortune teller have gone, a young suitor, Matteo, asks his friend "Zdenko" to help him in his efforts to court Arabella. He presses his case by threatening to commit suicide, unaware that Zdenka is actually in love with him.

After he departs, Arabella returns from a walk. Awaiting her are gifts from three Counts—Elemer, Dominik, and Lamoral—all suitors. Despite her feelings for Matteo, Zdenka begs her sister to marry him. Arabella dismisses her pleas, then prepares for a sleigh ride with Elemer.

Count Waldner enters complaining about his anemic finances. He informs the Countess that in desperation he sent a picture of Arabella, along with a letter, to an elderly but wealthy friend, Mandryka. Coincidentally, Mandryka's nephew, also named Mandryka, shows up just moments later. He informs the Waldners he has seen the letter and photograph of Arabella and is interested in courting her. His uncle, he reports, has recently died. He lends the Count some money and talks of his considerable real estate holdings in Slavonia.

Before departing for a sleigh ride with Zdenka, Arabella laments her lack of success in finding the right man for marriage.

Act Two. In a ballroom the Count introduces Mandryka to his wife and to Arabella. The younger pair are instantly attracted to each other and soon pledge their mutual love. Arabella is named queen of the ball and Mandryka celebrates the honor, ordering champagne and flowers. Arabella informs Elemer, Dominik, and Lamoral of her choice of Mandryka. The desperate Matteo implores Zdenka to present evidence of Arabella's love for him. She gives him the key to Arabella's bedroom, explaining it is her sister's wish to have a rendezvous with him there. Mandryka overhears the exchange and becomes enraged, thereafter drinking too much and flirting with the countess. The Count finally convinces him to return to the hotel with him.

Act Three. Arabella appears at the Waldner hotel suite a while later and confronts the departing Matteo, who has just spent the past hour in her bedroom with a woman he believed to be her. He is thus surprised to see her just entering the suite, and her coolness toward him now is further puzzling. The Count and Countess and Mandryka enter, the latter believing Matteo has made love to Arabella. He and the Count exchange harsh words over Arabella and decide to resolve their differences in a duel. Zdenka, attired in a negligee, hurries down the stairs and prevents the violent contest with her admission that she had set up the rendezvous with Matteo, then joined him in Arabella's room. Her parents forgive her, and she and Matteo declare their love for each other. Arabella and Mandryka happily reconcile and renew their plans to marry. *—Robert Cummings*

Recommended:

○ **Strauss: Arabella** / Solti (cond.), Della Casa, Gueden, Dermota, London / 1998 / Decca 460230

Ariadne auf Naxos, Op. 60–II (1916)

Richard Strauss' *Ariadne auf Naxos* (Ariadne on Naxos), an opera about a Composer who combines two contrasting acts, was created with Hugo von Hofmannsthal out of gratitude for Max Reinhardt's assistance in preparations for *Der Rosenkavalier.* It was thought that Reinhardt might use the short opera as an intermezzo in Molière's play *Le Bourgeois Gentilhomme.* The opera mixes the lofty diction of a Baroque opera seria with the low farce of the commedia dell'arte clowns, who were popular in Paris during Molière's day. Based on the same subject that Monteverdi set in 1607, the plot focused on Ariadne's abandonment by Theseus on the island of Naxos, where comedians attempted to lift her spirits until she is lovingly rescued by Bacchus. Even though its complex symbolism didn't quite please him, when Hofmannsthal offered an interpretation, the composer found inspiration and created some of his loveliest songs. After filling the work with music, dancing, and singing, that covered nearly every hue of expression; he commented, "my score—as a score—is really a masterpiece." The opera marks the definitive stage of his conversion to a Mozartean style.

Ariadne auf Naxos is best known in the revised version that Strauss and Hofmannsthal completed in 1916. It differs from the earlier version in its separation from the performance of Molière's *Le bourgeois gentilhomme,* in response to criticism of the first performance, and, more importantly, the inclusion of the newly composed and extensive prologue.

Vestiges of the Molière text remain in the prologue, which revolves around the character of the composer. This trouser role (usually sung by a mezzo-soprano) provides the frame for the ensuing one-act opera and represents Strauss' first self-reference about the nature of opera itself. (He would take up this idea later and more explicitly in his last opera, *Capriccio.*) The prologue makes Strauss' *Ariadne auf Naxos* an opera about the performance of a opera with the same name. In the prologue Strauss introduces themes that will occur more fully in the context of the following opera. In addition to presenting motives associated with Zerbinetta and her *commedia del'arte* players, Strauss also suggested the theme of the god Bacchus, who enters only in the final scene of the work.

The structure revolves around the plight of the composer in the prologue and the interplay of two stories in the following opera, making this version of the work more intricate and, in a sense, more satisfying. It is no longer the counterpart to a more or less spoken comedy, but has become a work about the nature of composition. Strauss is also able to explore the duality of comedy and tragedy, as embodied by Zerbinetta and Ariadne, in ways that had not occurred in the earlier version. When, at the end of the work, Ariadne has taken herself less seriously because of her interchange with Zerbinetta, it is made to be the result of the interaction of elements within the opera, not some motivation imposed by the librettist and dutifully set by the composer.

The work was given its premiere on October 4, 1916, in Vienna. It was received well and has remained in the repertoire in this latter version. In addition to the prologue, which is a tour de force in itself, the aria "Grossmächtige Prinzessin," in which Zerbinetta addresses Ariadne, is noteworthy for its musical content and dramatic function. The scene between Ariadne and Bacchus is also effective in conveying the apotheosis of the lovers. Near the end of the latter scene, Strauss colors the music with shimmering chords similar to those he would later use at the end of *Die Frau ohne Schatten,* when an emotional transformation also occurs. *—James Zychowicz*

Synopsis:

Prologue. A banquet is being held in the home of a fabulously wealthy Viennese man. The curtain opens behind the scenes, where the servants are making preparations for the lavish entertainments their anonymous host has ordered. The first part of the show will be a new opera called *Ariadne,* commissioned from a talented young composer. It will be his big debut. A farce will follow called *The Inconstant Zerbinetta and her Four Suitors,* followed by a grand fireworks display to conclude the evening.

The Major-domo and the Music Master get involved in a fierce exchange; it's clear that the dependence of artists on their patrons is heavy indeed; whatever their patrons' whims, they have to be accommodated. In addition, it's clear that between the two musical entertainments, there's a high level of competition for the audience's favor.

While the scenery is being erected, a lot of clowning around goes on; the tenor boxes the ears of the wigmaker, the Prima Donna mocks the singers in the opera-buffo. Yet Zerbinetta is visited by one of her many suitors, singled out as the one who will win the audience's heart, and even catches the attention of the nervous, high-strung composer. He explodes in rage about the humiliation of setting his Heroic Oeuvre being beside a trite comedy, but he calms down when a new melody pops into his head, taking his attention away from his distress.

Then, to everybody's horror, Major-domo announces yet another of the patron's outrageous whims: he wants to save time by having both operas performed simultaneously. The devastated composer, after first praying for his own death, is slowly brought back around to a relative calm and he reluctantly agrees to edit his opera. All energetically discuss the strange problem of how to bring together two such incompatible pieces. Zerbinetta lays her charms on the composer so thickly that he feels a whole new vision of life revealed before him. But then, as if on purpose, she whistles to her fellow players to get them up on-stage, which to the composer is a sacred space, and cruelly breaks the enchantment.

Opera. The curtain lifts again just as the edited version of Ariadne is beginning. The composer edited the work in such a way that there remain large gaps that the comedians are supposed to fill with their performance of sections from the opera-buffo. As the action proceeds, it becomes clear that there is strangely little friction between the two operas, and the comedians' interventions hardly disrupt Ariadne.

Awakening from a series of disturbing nightmares, Ariadne finds a reality still more distressing. She is with Dryad, Naiad, and Echo, the nymphs charged with watching over her. Theseus has recently betrayed her love cruelly, and the thought of this so completely obsesses her that she prays to the god of Death for release. This puzzles and astonishes the comedians, who can't even begin to sympathise with her feelings. Harlequin steps forth to console her with a song, which only makes Ariadne pray more fervently. Undefeated, the comedians pick up where they left off, singing and dancing for the bereaved Ariadne. Zerbinetta's aria is especially to the point, basically saying: "don't be so upset, there are plenty more good fish in the sea." Ariadne finally flees to a cave to brood, and the comedians take over, performing what's left of their play. The play is about the simultaneous courting of Zerbinetta by four different suitors, a contest that is finally won by the bold Harlequin.

Suddenly, the nymphs Naiad, Dryad, and Echo return to the stage, trumpeting the eminent arrival of the young god Bacchus. He has just recently escaped from the clutches of Circe, who uses magic potions to capture her lovers, then transforms them into animals. Bacchus, however, has been immune to her sorcery. But the impression the experience has made on him is deep enough that upon seeing Ariadne, he guesses she must be another sorceress. Ariadne, in turn, imagines that Bacchus must be Death come at last. But in the course of their interaction, the force of love quickly breaks down their barriers and both find themselves transformed by the new emotions. "I am filled with godlike joy!," Bacchus says. All the opera-buffo elements have now been banished from the stage, and even the sarcastic Zerbinetta remains silent. Bacchus becomes fully aware of Ariadne's divinity, and she of her own readiness to yield to his glorious love. The opera ends with the two lovers enfolded in a great canopy descended from above. *—Donato Mancini*

Recommended:

- ○ **Strauss: Ariadne auf Naxos** / Sinopoli (cond.), Voigt, Dessay, von Otter, Heppner, Dohmen / 2001 / DG 47132
- ○ **Strauss: Ariadne auf Naxos** / Karajan (cond.), Schwarzkopf, Streich, Seefried, Schock, Prey / Angel 67156

Capriccio, Op. 85 (1940–1941)

Capriccio (1942), the last opera Strauss completed, in some ways represents the culmination of the composer's work in this genre. *Capriccio* is sometimes described as a "conversation piece," since the plot revolves around a discussion of the nature of opera and the shifting primacy between text and music. Strauss takes up in this work ideas he had already begun to explore in the prologue to the revised version of *Ariadne auf Naxos* (1916), which opens with the character of the composer worrying about the reception to his art. In *Ariadne* the issue is not resolved, because the composer's opera is surrealistically commingled with the efforts of a commedia dell'arte group. In *Capriccio*, however, the matter receives attention as the composer and the poet explore their work and are challenged to compose an opera about that very discussion; in some ways the opera is a metaphor for operatic composition, a topic with obvious resonance and significance for Strauss.

The singer (perhaps muse) Madeleine must choose whom she favors between between Olivier and Flamand, the opera's embodiment of poetry and music, respectively. However, she can never abandon one for the other, since she needs both. This leaves the dramatic situation at the opening of the opera unresolved though perhaps better understood by the conclusion.

The libretto was written in collaboration with Clemens Krauss, the conductor who was one of Strauss' most loyal champions. Krauss based the libretto on work Strauss had earlier undertaken with Joseph Gregor and, even earlier, with Stefan Zweig. Zweig had begun to plan an opera based on Giambattista Casti's eighteenth century text *Prima la musica, poi la parole* ("First the Music, Then the Words"), the basis for Antonio Salieri's 1786 opera of the same title. In adapting the earlier libretto, Krauss maintained an eighteenth century setting and used essentially the same characters as those found in Casti's version.

Capriccio was premiered in Munich on October 28, 1942, to an enthusiastic reception and was subsequently performed in several European opera houses during World War II. It is often viewed as a particularly fitting valedictory to Strauss' work in opera and in fact includes both quotations from operas by other composers (including Gluck's *Iphigénie en Aulide*) and humorous references to Strauss' own *Ariadne* and *Daphne* (1936–37). Such references are not so much self-indulgent as self-critical, and show the composer's lighter side in the twilight of his career; at the same time, the music is more conversational, the motives and ideas more fleeting in their motion. Right from the start, from the string sextet that serves as the overture, *Capriccio* is more chamber music than grand opera. In exploring the nature of opera in *Capriccio*, Strauss relied more upon intimate gestures than upon the splashy grandeur of works like *Salome* (1904–05) or *Elektra* (1906–08); the result bears the stamp of a composer of great facility in full command of his style. *—James Zychowicz*

Synopsis:

Scene One. The action is set in the salon of a Rococo castle near Paris. It's early afternoon, and a string sextet is playing, attended by a poet, Olivier, the composer, Flammand, and the Countess Madelaine. It is her birthday. Nearby, the theatre director LaRoche is asleep in an armchair. The artists discover their rivalry for Madelaine's affections. LaRoche is roused from sleep as the music ends. They discuss art. To LaRoche, what the theatre needs is rousing music and spectacle. He announces that the great ex-actress Clairon is coming to the castle that day. Olivier once courted her, but nothing came of it. Now the Count, brother of Madelaine, is using Olivier's verse to woo the actress.

Scene Two. When the Count and his sister arrive, the artists and the director make a hasty exit. The Count complains of indifference to music, prefering poetry. Madelaine, however, loves music best. Yet she's reluctant to choose between her suitors. She assures her brother that his title alone would win Clairon; with the help of Olivier's words he has nothing to fear.

Scene Three. The artists return, announcing that all is set for the birthday entertainments. Against LaRoche's enthusiasm, the artists are complaining of the lack of substance in his shows. Clairon's arrival is announced.

Scene Four. Clairon enters, she asks Olivier if his play is ready. He declares it is, and they recite the love scene, then go off to rehearse in the adjoining room. Olivier reveals that the sonnet in the scene was addressed to Madelaine, and recites it. Flammand grabs the manuscript and rushes off.

Scene Five. Olivier declares his love to Madelaine. She's reluctant to commit her feelings, expressing a preference for music. Flammand returns with a score.

Scene Six. Flammand performs the music he's just composed for the sonnet; Madelaine is ravished. Olivier ponders aloud at the meaning of Flammand's action; who is now the author of the work? "It is mine." says Madelaine.

Scene Seven. LaRoche returns for Olivier, leaving Flammand alone with Madelaine. He declares his feelings, and presses for an answer; whom does she love? She hesitates, promising to make a decision by 11 a.m.. Flammand kisses her arm and rushes away.

Scene Eight. The Count returns, radiant at Clairon's praise of his acting. Madelaine mocks him, then reveals her terrible dilemma: will she choose words or music? "What will come of it?" the Count asks, "Perhaps an opera!" she answers.

Scene Nine. Everybody returns to the salon. While chocolate is served, a girl performs a series of dances. Olivier, Flammand, and LaRoche engage in heated discussion about dance, words and music. Two Italian singers are brought in as the next entertainment; they do a scene from an opera. The Count makes welcomed advances upon Clairon. Soon the guests press LaRoche to reveal the program of tomorrow's show. He does so, taking time to explain the myth of the birth of Pallas Athene, a staging of which will form the first half. They interject sarcastic comments. The second part of the show will be The Fall of Carthage, as he explains. Flammand and Olivier begin to attack LaRoche for creating spectacles lacking both genuine music and poetry. To the Count, the dispute is highly amusing. LaRoche, defends himself; without men like him there would be no theatre. He wins the argument; Flammand and Olivier are impressed enough to agree to write him an opera. The Count suggests that they make an opera on this day's events, a suggestion they accept. LaRoche is nervous that will be an act of indiscretion, but the artists are enthusiastic to set to work right away, and the party breaks up.

Scene Ten. Farewells are passing round. Flammand, Olivier, and Clairon are returning to Paris. The stage clears.

Scene Eleven.

Servants come into the empty salon, chatting about what they overheard, and complaining about the obscurities of opera.

Scene Twelve. The Major-Domo comes on stage, followed by M. Taupe, the prompter, who fell asleep during the rehearsal in Scene Four. He's distressed, but Major-domo promises get him back to Paris

Scene Thirteen. Madelaine enters the darkened salon in her evening gown. She is pensive. The Major-domo reappears to light the candles and announces that Olivier will arrive at 11 a.m. to find out the ending of the opera: her decision. Still unsure, she coquettishly waves at her own image in the mirror, then walks off to her supper. *—Donato Mancini*

Recommended:

- ○ **Strauss: Capriccio** / Sawallisch (cond.), Schwarzkopf, Fischer-Dieskau, Gedda, Hotter, Ludwig, Moffo, Wachter / 2000 / Angel 67391
- ○ **Strauss: Capriccio** / Schirmer (cond.), Te Kanawa, Hagegård, Hotter, Fassbaender, Heilmann / 1996 / London 444405

Daphne, Op. 82 (1936–1937)

Daphne (1936–37), Strauss' second collaboration with the librettist Joseph Gregor, marked the composer's return to classical mythology as the basis for his work. The origins of this opera date to 1935, when Strauss and Gregor were discussing their work on *Friedenstag* (1935–36). As originally conceived, *Daphne* was to be a one-act opera to be paired with Friedenstag as a double bill. The plot concerns the Greek myth of the nymph Daphne, the daughter of a river god. After catching the attention of Apollo, she flees from him; in order to keep her, Apollo changes her into a laurel tree for all eternity. The story, best known in the version presented in

Ovid's *Metamorphoses*, has served as an operatic subject since the seventeenth century; a notable instance is one of Handel's first (though now mostly lost) operas, *Daphne* (1706).

Gregor and Strauss worked through several drafts of the libretto before arriving at a final version. Earlier versions differ from the final product largely in the manner in which Strauss made use of the chorus to frame the work; most significantly, Strauss ultimately discarded the idea, which he had used in *Friedenstag*, of ending the opera with a chorus. By instead ending the opera instrumentally, Strauss arrived at an effective conclusion: Daphne's transformation into a tree is left to the imagination of the audience rather than presented in a didactic manner. In fact, the use of orchestral passages in *Daphne* is one of the most important elements of its effectiveness. The instrumental opening at once sets the stage for the fable and evokes its rustic tone. When Strauss calls for purely instrumental forces at the end of the opera, he not only underscores Daphne's transformation, but also provides a subtle framing device.

Daphne, one of Strauss' finest operatic efforts, compares favorably with his more popular works for the stage. The composer himself felt it to be the first true opera he had composed, demonstrating his capacity for self-criticism even at that advanced stage of his development. Its settings reflect a balance between declamation and the lyricism for which Strauss was so noted; solo passages give way to thicker textures, and the use of the chorus complements various scenes.

Daphne was first performed in Dresden on October 15, 1938. Since then, it has enjoyed a life independent of its pairing with *Friedenstag*. *—James Zychowicz*

Synopsis:

A group of shepherds are gathered by a stony riverbank. It is evening. The entryway to the house of the fisherman Peneios can be seen, and Mt. Olympus is in the far distance behind. Mingled sounds can be heard: herds of sheep, the barking of dogs, bells, and a powerful note from an alphorn. It is the day of the young Dionysus; the horn is calling them to the feast.

One of the older shepherds sends his son to gather the flock near the river. Soon they move off toward the house, singing, and are gone. Daphne enters, still in the height of youth, barely more than a child. She addresses the day poetically, begging that it not pass, complaining of the crude ways of humans and of her loneliness.

Leukippos suddenly reveals himself: he had been hiding behind a tree; he expresses grievance that Daphne doesn't reciprocate his love, she seems to prefer the company of trees. Even when he breaks his flute as a sign of his devotion, she remains firm and the grief-stricken Leukippos flees. In his stead, her mother Gaea appears, expressing concern about Daphne's behavior toward Leukippos; she warns her that the time for her to "awaken" draws near; she cannot escape her predestined place in nature forever.

Some maids appear with Daphne's clothing for the celebration, but she flees, followed by Gaea. The maids are left alone, lamenting that the gorgeous garments won't be worn. Leukippos' voice is heard, racked with grief; he enters soon after. The maids flirt with him wildly and advise him to disguise himself in Daphne's clothing; they all run off together, frolicking.

Peneios enters as dusk comes on. He is with shepherds and Gaea. Looking up at Olympus, which is becoming shrouded in mist, he announces to the frightened shepherds the eminent arrival of the sun god Apollo. He is boasting dangerously of his oneness with the gods, and that their feasting will make the gods envious, when an unearthly laughter is heard, accompanied by red flashes of lightning. Soon afterwards, Apollo appears, disguised as a cattleman. The shepherds and Gaea taunt Peneios: "Look what rabble came to your feast, no gods, only a humble cattleman." But Peneios is gracious and treats the cattleman with honor. They all soon drift away, leaving Apollo alone.

Daphne reappears with her maids to serve him, as per Peneios' command. Apollo is so ravished by her beauty that he kneels before her in worship. She washes the god's hands and put his weapons aside. Soon Apollo is repeating verbatim Daphne's earlier pleas that the day not end, and she seems to be swept away with emotion until Apollo kisses her—and she withdraws from his embrace in horror. "But... you called yourself: brother!"

Peneios, with all the shepherds and Gaea, soon reappears, laden with food and wine and offering praises up to Dionysus. The women bring food to the shepherds, who are dressed in ram's masks and skins. A procession of girls enters, some bearing wine and swathed in cloth, others barely dressed, whom the masked shepherds descend upon lustfully. Among the women is the disguised Leukippos.

He offers to let Daphne drink, arousing Apollo's hateful jealousy: the god steps forth and causes a storm to appear. All but Daphne and Leukippos flee in terror. The latter he now confronts, forcing him to shed his disguise. Daphne feels betrayed by both. Despite repeated warnings, Leukippos naively challenges Apollo, who finally slays him with an arrow. Only now does Daphne regret her mistreatment of Leukippos and realizes she loved him after all. "Oh my Leukippos! Why did I stay deaf to your entreaties?" She vows to remain by his graveside in mourning for the rest of her life. Apollo is so moved by her words that he grievously apologizes for interfering in their human love. He promises to carry Leukippos to heaven and has the gods fulfill Daphne's wish: she's transformed into a tree by the graveside, thereby becoming "a symbol of love never ending." *—Donato Mancini*

Recommended:

○ **Strauss: Daphne** / Bohm (cond.), Güden, Wunderlich, King, Schoffler / DG 445322

Elektra, Op. 58 (1906–1908)

Coming immediately after his one-act shocker, *Salome* (1905), *Elektra* (1909) took Richard Strauss further into a musical world that stood in bleak contrast to nineteenth century Romantic opera. This tale of multiple murder and bitter vengeance also proved crucial to Strauss' later development as a composer of opera, since it marked the beginning of his collaboration with the young Viennese poet Hugo von Hofmannsthal, whose German translation of Sophocles' Greek tragedy originally inspired Strauss to take up the subject, and with whom he would craft his most lasting masterpieces.

The story is simple. Elektra is mourning the death of her father Agamemnon, murdered by her mother, Klytemnestra. She tries to persuade her sister Chrysothemis to help her avenge his death. Their brother Orestes, whom they feared dead, returns home and is persuaded to kill both Klytemnestra and her lover, Aegisthus. ("Very unlike"—as one English nobleman is supposed to have remarked after seeing the opera—"the home life of our own dear Queen.")

As with his setting of Oscar Wilde's *Salome*, Strauss' *Elektra* is not merely an adaptation for musical purposes, but a "play set to music." As in *Sophocles'* original, the climax of the opera is not the murder of Klytemnestra and Aegisthus, but the tense relationship that develops between Elektra and Orestes as she incites him to action.

Strauss always favored the soprano voice and, in a cast of 14, indulged himself in no fewer than six, in both major and minor roles. The subliminal effect of this high tessitura, together with lavish orchestration and a certain amount of atonality, is to intensify the psychological conflicts that emerge as Elektra pursues her vengeful plan. "The struggle between words and music has been the problem of my life right from the beginning" wrote Strauss in a letter to the famous Wagner singer Ernestine Schumann-Heink, who sang Klytemnestra at the first performance. If *Elektra* wins that hidden struggle it is through the sheer power and conviction of the music.

Aside from their somewhat scandalous subject matter, there are few similarities between *Elektra* and *Salome*. As von Hofmannsthal wrote, "In *Salome* much is, so to speak, in purple and violet. In *Elektra*... it is a mixture of night and light, or black and bright." The events leading up to Orestes' deed are not matched by anything corresponding, or even faintly similar, to those in *Salome* and lead to "victory and purification—a sequence I can imagine as being much more powerful in music than in the written word."

The first night was not a success. The critic Julius Korngold sarcastically wrote "How beautiful was the Princess Salome tonight!" Strauss riposted "When a mother is slain on stage do they expect me to write a violin concerto?" Following its presentation at Covent Garden the English critic Bernard Newman wrote of "a strain of coarseness and thoughtlessness" in Strauss which persuaded him to "take up so crude a perversion of the old Greek story as that of Hugo von Hofmannsthal," and Bernard Shaw asked "Is there [anywhere] such an atmosphere of malignant and cancerous evil as we get here?" Inexplicably the first New York performance in 1932 was in French.

Yet in many ways *Elektra* is Strauss' most successful opera, though not his most popular. Its one-act structure leads to a concise, relentless and fast-developing drama of a sort not conspicuous in the composer's more Romantic works. *—Roy Brewer*

Synopsis:

In the palace courtyard, some maids are drawing water from the well under the watchful eye of a supervisor. They are wondering where Elektra is: this is normally the time when she is heard calling to her dead father, Agamemnon. They gossip about the girl's beastly behaviour. Only one young maid rises to Elektra's defence, but they shout her down and drag her back into the palace for a beating.

Enter Elektra, calling out for Agamemnon; it is the anniversary hour of his murder. She vividly describes the murder of him by Clytemnestra, and equally vividly pictures the revenge. His grave will run with the blood of his killers; Chrysothemis, her brother Orestes, the avenger, and herself will dance in triumph. Chrysothemis, her sister, arrives. She has come to warn Elektra that Clytemnestra and Aegisthus plan to imprison her in a windowless tower. Elektra doesn't care; she thinks only of vengeance, but Chrysothemis is devoured by worry; she just wants all this violence to end. Elektra spitefully tells her sister to go back to the palace with the murderers, where she belongs. As Chrysothemis flees, she warns that mother dreamt of Orestes and is deeply troubled.

Clytemnestra and servants enter, with all the paraphernalia to make a sacrifice. She recoils at the hateful look she gets from her daughter. After sending the servants away, she asks for a remedy for her terrible dreams. The double entendre of

Elektra's answer falls on deaf ears: "When the appointed victim falls under the axe, then you will dream no more." Elektra asks again that her brother Orestes be welcomed back, Clytemnestra trembles with fear: "I have forbidden you to speak of him," and threatens Elektra with torture and imprisonment if she doesn't help her in her personal plight. The enraged Elektra leaps at her mother, howling for her blood.

To Clytemnestra's relief, one of her confidantes arrives, bearing a message; an air of evil triumph comes over her and she leaves with her maids.

Chrysothemis rushes in, trumpeting Orestes' death, which Elektra won't accept as true. Servants come rushing through, the youngest one cries for a horse; he must tell Aegisthus the important news. To Elektra, who finally accepts what she's being told, the news only means that she and Chrysothemis are now charged with the revenge mission. She reveals that she posesses the weapon Agamemnon was murdered with, and had been saving it for Orestes. Her sister is horrified, but Elektra wraps herself around her to "infuse my will into your blood," and promises to prepare her wedding bed and serve her faithfully if she will only once, howl a cry as terrible as the goddess of death and use her strength to kill Clytemnestra. Chrysothemis flees.

Elektra turns again to digging up the murder weapon, whereupon a messenger arrives. As they talk, his identity is gradually revealed: Orestes. She rejoices, but refuses his embrace. Embarrassed that her obsession with revenge has worn away her beauty. Orestes proclaims his mission, as thrust upon him by the gods. Orestes' old tutor appears, and begs the excited two to quiet down, lest they give themselves away. Also, he reveals that Clytemnestra is alone; now is the time to strike! One of the confidantes appears, bearing a torch, she invites the tutor and Orestes inside, fixing the torch on a ring at the doorpost.

Elektra is savagely disappointed that she was unable to give him the axe, but, a moment later, Clytemnestra's death peals come thundering through the air. Chrysothemis appears, with an entourage of maids. Elektra presses herself against the door, savoring the screams. As it dawns on the terrified maidservants what's taking place, they announce the return of Aegisthus; they flee for fear of being implicated. Aegisthus arrives, complaining of the lack of lit torches. When Elektra reveals herself, she is so emaciated he fails to recognize her at first. She lights his torch, dancing with joy, and accompanies him to the doorway. Soon after he enters the palace, his screams are also heard. He appears at a window crying for help "Can no one hear me?" "Agamemnon can hear you!" Elektra answers.

Chrysothemis returns with the maids. Cries of "Orestes! Orestes! Orestes!" rise in the house: the many who hated the tyrant Aegisthus are celebrating their liberator. Elektra leads them in a dance of joy. Even the recalcitrant Chrysothemis rejoices, "Now our brother is here and love flows over us like oil and myrrh . . . !" Elektra's frenzied dance ends as she falls dead. *—Donato Mancini*

Recommended:

- ○ **Strauss: Elektra** / Solti (cond.), Nilsson, Resnik, Collier, Krause / Decca 417345
- ○ **Strauss: Elektra** / Böhm (cond.), Borkh, Schech, Madeira, Fischer-Dieskau / DG 445329

Die Frau ohne Schatten (The Woman without a Shadow), Op. 65 (1914–1917)

Die Frau ohne Schatten ("The Woman without a Shadow"), the third of Richard Strauss' collaborations with Hugo von Hofmannsthal, is an ambitious mixture of operatic elements, both musically and dramatically. The story is part parable, part quest, and part human drama in which love and character are put to the test; the readiest comparison is to Mozart's *The Magic Flute* (Hofmannsthal, in fact, was the first to make the connection), with its veneer of comedy removed. Based on a fairy-tale by Wilhelm Hauff, *Die Frau ohne Schatten* traces the fortunes of a childless fairy empress whose desire for a "shadow" (fertility) drives her to consider stealing the desired qualities from an unhappy mortal woman. However, she cannot bring herself to do so, and eventually gains her own shadow by developing kindness and understanding.

Hofmannsthal created a libretto of such symbolic and textual complexity that he himself had trouble keeping it straight—in fact, he wrote a concurrent prose version that allowed him to develop the themes more fully; this prose explanation sometimes accompanies the opera in performance to assist audiences. The correspondence between the librettist and Strauss shows that the composer, at times, often did not "get it" either.

The richness and complexity of Hofmannsthal's writing inspired Strauss to compose one of his densest scores, packed with intricate leitmotifs and exploiting his orchestrational talents to the fullest. In fact, it is perhaps only Strauss' ability to exploit the colors and textures of the orchestra that prevents Hofmannsthal's tale from lapsing into silliness; how many composers can pull off a chorus of unborn children that sings through the mouths of fish frying in a pan without straying into unintentional comedy?

Die Frau receives regular performances, but it has never established itself in the hearts and minds of opera-goers in the same was as Strauss' other stage works. Certainly this is partly due to the cryptic libretto, but it is also a testimony to the difficulty of the vocal writing. The role of the emperor calls for a true heldentenor, and the singers often have to compete with an orchestra of formidable size: Strauss employs quadrupled woodwinds, extensive percussion and divided strings—two sections each of violas, cellos, and basses. Having said that, however, Strauss frequently deployed the orchestra with exceptional restraint, often creating chamber-like sonorities that remind a listener of his later *Capriccio.*

Though *Die Frau* cannot rival the composer's earlier *Elektra* for sheer musical and harmonic audacity, it isn't far behind. He concocts sounds and sonorities that would seem brazen removed from their context, but which meld so well with their dramatic context as to recede into the greater musical tapestry. Whereas in *Elektra* Strauss sought to draw attention to his adventurous musical choices, here he puts them fully at the service of more subtle dramatic concerns. Highlights of the score include the passages sung by the Emperor's falcon—marvelously birdlike—and the Watchmen's hymn from the end of the first act. *—AMG*

Synopsis:

Act One. Setting: the mythical land of the Emperor of the South Eastern Islands. On a terrace of the Emperor's palace, the Spirit-Messenger delivers ominous news to the Nurse. The Emperor's wife of 12 moons and supernatural daughter of Keikobad, King of the Spirits, must cast a shadow (become pregnant) within three days or Keikobad will permanently recall her and transform the Emperor into stone.

After the Messenger has left, the Emperor announces he is departing on a three-day hunting trip. After he leaves, the Empress appears and receives her falcon, who delivers the grim news. Shocked, she seeks counsel from the nurse, who leads her away to find a shadow among humankind.

In his hut, Barak, a dyer, placates his nagging wife and makes peace among his ever-quarreling disabled brothers. Before he departs to market he expresses disappointment to his wife that they are still childless. The nurse and Empress enter, attired in peasant dress. The former entices Barak's wife to sell her shadow for great wealth. She agrees to surrender her potential for motherhood, but after the Nurse and Empress depart, she is haunted by the voices of her unborn children.

Act Two. The following day the Nurse and Empress return. The Nurse uses a seductive apparition to obtain the shadow from Barak's wife, but Barak returns, foiling the plan. In the forest at the Emperor's falcon house, the Emperor receives the falcon who bears a message for him from his wife: she and the Nurse will spend three days there. He waits for them and upon arrival detects the foul scent of the human world on them. He ponders killing his wife, but refrains.

The next day in Barak's hut, the Nurse drugs Barak's wine, and he soon passes out. When the seductive apparition appears again it seems the plan will succeed this time, but it does not: Barak's wife suddenly develops misgivings and rouses him. She soon leaves with the nurse, but the Empress stays and helps Barak. Later, at the Emperor's falcon house, the Empress, guilty she has mistreated poor Barak, has a nightmarish dream about her husband turning to stone.

Above Barak's hut the next day, a darkness hovers, as inside, the Empress, the Nurse, and Barak listen to his wife confess she has bargained away her shadow and will never have children. The Nurse magically causes a sword to appear in Barak's hands, but suddenly his wife admits the deal had not been finalized. He raises the weapon to strike her when the hut begins to quake; Barak's brothers, the Nurse, and the Empress flee, after which the structure is swallowed up by the earth.

Act Three. In a subterranean chamber, Barak and his wife, separated by a wall, lament their recent actions. Soon they hear a voice summoning them to freedom. The Nurse and Empress sail on a boat toward land, upon which is situated a temple. The latter rejects the former's contempt for mankind. The Empress enters the temple, while the Nurse maliciously frustrates the reunion of Barak and his wife, who desperately call out to each other.

Inside the Temple, the Empress refuses to drink from the golden fountain at the behest of the Guardian of the Threshold, since such action will ensnare Barak's wife's shadow. After her second refusal, however, she casts her own giant shadow and her husband suddenly appears for a joyous reunion. Barak is reunited with his wife, who also casts a shadow, and the Emperor and Empress join them for a happy ending. *—Robert Cummings*

Recommended:

- ○ **Strauss: Die Frau ohne Schatten** / Sinopoli (cond.), Voigt, Heppner, Grundheber, Hass / 1997 / Teldec 13156
- ○ **Strauss: Die Frau ohne Schatten** / Solti (cond.), Behrens, Domingo, Runkel, Jo, Van Dam, Varady / 1998 / Decca 436243

Der Rosenkavalier, Op. 59 (1909–1910)

Some regard *Der Rosenkavalier* as Strauss' finest opera, and indeed, it has remained consistently popular since its premiere in 1911. Composed during 1909 and 1910—immediately after *Elektra,* Strauss' first collaboration with dramatist

Hugo von Hofmannsthal—*Der Rosenkavalier* is an original story, conceived jointly by Hofmannsthal and Strauss through extensive correspondence. It represents an intentional departure from *Elektra* (an adaptation of Sophocles' play) in both substance and tone, and the result is one of the most sophisticated libretti ever written—full of subtle exchanges and turns of literary phrase. While the story was to have been a farce hinging upon the revelation of the character Mariandel as Octavian, Hofmannsthal developed the libretto into a more complex plot in which the primary narrative concerns the shifting relationship between the Marschallin and Octavian.

Hofmannsthal cast the drama in three acts, a more traditional scheme than *Elektra*'s extended one-act plan, and perhaps a nod to the work's eighteenth century setting. Strauss also makes use of a conspicuously conservative musical idiom, eschewing the frankly dissonant and often abrasive textures he had used in both *Elektra* and *Salome*. At the same time, the orchestration of *Der Rosenkavalier* is both richer and marked throughout by delicate and shimmering sonorities. Strauss uses waltzes throughout the score to evoke a sentimental mood and to denote the middle-class sensibilities of Baron Ochs. Waltz themes are integral to each act, and the opera's orchestral waltz sequences, along with the more formal Rosenkavalier Suite (1945), remain popular as independent concert works. The opera's most impressive music occurs in the Act Three Trio between Oktavian, Sophie, and the Marschallin. Here, Strauss uses the three women's voices to convey the emotions of a young ingenue, her youthful suitor, and the mature Marschallin to great effect, the orchestra providing a telling underscoring. The static quality of the Trio creates an elegiac mood that at once combines the expression of youthful love with mature restraint.

Der Rosenkavalier, premiered in Dresden in January 1911, was received with great enthusiasm. The opera has remained a fixture of the stage, as evidenced by new productions in every decade since. Strauss attempted to recapture *Der Rosenkavalier*'s popular appeal in his subsequent stage works; while some, like *Arabella* (1929–32), are outstanding, they never eclipsed the successful alchemy of text and music that has ensured *Der Rosenkavalier*'s permanence. —*James Zychowicz*

Synopsis:

Act One. In the Marschallin's bedroom, she and Octavian luxuriate in the afterglow of a night together. He hides when Mohammed, her page, arrives with her morning chocolate (though he clumsily leaves his sword in sight). This reminds her of a time when her husband, returning early, nearly caught her with a lover. When they hear noise outside, Octavian hides again. Her cousin Ochs comes in, assuring her that it's not too early for the nobility to visit—he once chatted for an hour with a princess as she took her bath. He tells her he is going to marry Sophie von Faninal, largely to enrich himself with her dowry, and asks the Marschallin to recommend a Rosenkavalier (knight of the rose), a young man to deliver the traditional silver rose. Octavian has emerged, dressed as a chambermaid and calling himself Mariandel, and during his conversation with the Marschallin, Ochs makes passes at "her." The Marschallin suggests none other than Octavian and shows Ochs a portrait. Ochs does notice the resemblance to Mariandel and assumes that there is an illegitimate connection, adding that he has taken on his own illegitimate son, Leopold, as his valet.

Various people come in for her morning levee, including three orphans asking for alms, a pet vendor and a hair-dresser, Valzacchi and Annina, who offer their services as spies or counter-spies as needed, and an Italian singer, who performs for her ("Di rigori armato"). Ochs corners the notary to help him draw up the wedding contract. The Italian's singing is interrupted by Och's bellowing that he, not the bride, should receive the traditional morning gift. The Marschallin tells the hairdresser he has made her look old, and she dismisses them. Alone, she remembers her own marriage as a young girl ("Da geht er hin") and imagines the day when she will be considered an old woman. When Octavian returns, he cannot understand her sudden change of mood, as she tells him that while she tries to accept the passing of time, she knows he will leave her for a woman his own age. Hurt, he leaves, and the Marschallin realizes she didn't even kiss him. She sends her lackeys in pursuit, but they return, reporting that he rode away too fast to catch. She sends Mohammed to give Octavian the rose.

Act Two. In the social-climbing von Faninal's house, the household excitedly prepares for Octavian's arrival. Sophie, accompanied by Marianne, naively anticipates bliss with her noble husband and prays to be worthy. Octavian arrives, himself dressed in silver, and formally presents her with the rose ("Mir ist die Ehre"). They are both enraptured at the beauty of the moment. Ochs interrupts their conversation with his arrival. Faninal is so excited to be marrying his daughter to the nobility that he gladly accepts Och's boorish condecension, but Sophie and Octavian are repulsed. Ochs tells her how lucky she is to be marrying a man of his charms ("Mit mir"). All except Octavian and Sophie leave, and he promises to help her escape the marriage. Valzacchi and Annina spy and leave to tell Ochs. The housemaids run in, pursued by Ochs's servants, followed by the rest. Octavian tells the company that Sophie will not marry Ochs, to Faninal's horror and Och's amusement. When Octavian demands a duel, Ochs howls in agony at a minor flesh wound. Faninal orders Octavian out and tells Sophie she will marry Ochs, no matter what. She refuses categorically, and he threatens to send her back to the convent. Ochs is bandaged and consoled with wine, and, when left alone, is delighted to receive, via Annina, a flattering request for a meeting with Mariandel.

Act Three. At an inn, Annina, Valzacchi, and Octavian, again disguised as Mariandel, set the scene for the rendez-vous. Ochs enters with Mariandel, but things do not progress as he would like. She is more interested in chattering than in drinking or being seduced and becomes maudlin, saying that wine makes her think about death. The ghostly faces that Valzacchi had prepared pop out of the shadows, alarming Ochs. Annina bursts in, dressed in mourning, followed by hotel staff and policemen, and she accuses Ochs of being her deceitful husband, while a troupe of children throw themselves at him, calling him Papa. He denies ever laying eyes on her and insists Mariandel is his fiancée Sophie von Faninal, but Mariandel wails that she has been tricked. Faninal and Sophie arrive in response to a summons, and Mariandel disappears into the bedroom, throwing out her clothes, returning as Octavian, to everybody's amusement but Ochs'. The Marschallin arrives as the scene is about to dissolve into chaos, and like a deus ex machina, sets things right. Ochs will forget about marrying Sophie. The whole scene was just a typical Viennese practical joke. Ochs accepts the situation and leaves, pursued by creditors bearing bills. Faninal leaves to recover, and Sophie, Octavian, and the Marschallin remain. Again, she smooths over the awkwardness and yields gracefully to the inevitable ("Hab' mir's gelobt"). Octavian is overwhelmed by her graciousness, and Sophie understands that something strange and wonderful has happened, though she is not sure what. Blessing the lovers, the Marschallin leaves to comfort Faninal with the thought that she will ride in his open carriage back to the city. Octavian and Sophie are lost in their bliss ("Ist ein traum"). The Marschallin and Faninal pass them, leaving, and as he remarks on the ways of young couples, she sighs ("Ja, ja"). Octavian and Sophie obliviously continue their duet. When they leave, Mohammed comes in, finds the Marschallin's handkerchief, and leaves. —*Ann Feeney*

Recommended:

- ○ **Strauss: Der Rosenkavalier** / Karajan (cond.), Schwarzkopf, Ludwig, Stich-Randall, Edelmann, Wachter / 1997 / EMI 56242
- ○ **Strauss: Der Rosenkavalier** / Haitink (cond.), Te Kanawa, Otter, Hendricks, Rydl / 1991 / EMI 54259
- ○ **Strauss: Der Rosenkavalier** / Böhm (cond.), Schech, Streich, Fischer-Dieskau, Seefried, Wagner / 2002 / DG 463668

Salome, Op. 54 (1903–1905)

Richard Strauss' third opera, *Salome*, burst like a meteor onto the early twentieth century musical scene and ushered in an era of musical modernism. When *Salome* premiered at Dresden in 1905, it was at once condemned by conservative critics for its moral decadence, and lauded by more adventuresome listeners, who heard in it signs of the avant-garde. Richard Wagner's son Siegfried emphasized *Salome*'s "perversity" and categorized it among Strauss' "dangerous works." In 1948, however, archmodernist Arnold Schoenberg singled out passages from *Salome* as examples of extended tonality. Although near the end of the nineteenth century, Strauss' tone poems had earned him accolades as *Zukunftsmusiker*, neither their philosophical programs, nor their lushly chromatic late Romantic musical languages were any match for *Salome*'s psychologically charged libretto and surprisingly dissonant score.

Strauss based his libretto for *Salome* on Hedwig Lachmann's German translation of Oscar Wilde's play, *Salomé*, of 1891. Wilde's play, written in French in and the evocative style of the symbolists, appeared in the later years of a long tradition of literary treatments of the New Testament story of Salome and John the Baptist. Mario Praz claims that Heinrich Heine's *Atta Troll* (1841) was the first literary work to portray Salome as a blatantly sexual being, an interpretation that was taken up repeatedly in later versions of the story. Indeed, the interpretation of Salome as a pathologically sexual female must have been particularly intriguing to *fin-de-siècle* writers and artists, given the contemporary fascination with the degenerate female and—influenced by the work of Sigmund Freud—with psychopathology in general. Wilde was also influenced by J.C. Heywood's dramatic poem "Salome," Mallarmé's poem "Hérodiade," and by Joris-Karl Huysmans' *À Rebours*, which portrayed Salome as the epitome of female sexual depravity.

Strauss uses orchestration, motives, key areas, and distinctions among musical languages to convey meaning in *Salome*. Strauss expands the palette of the orchestra, already fertile with timbral possibilities, giving extended solo passages to unusual instruments, and joining groups of instruments in novel and evocative combinations. The lengthy contrabassoon solo at the end of the second orchestral interlude is perhaps a singular occurrence in Western art music, and the combination of two harps playing harmonics, celesta, cymbals, and hushed woodwinds that accompany the aroused Herod after Salome's Dance of the Seven Veils paint an eerie picture of his demented world. Strauss continually weaves the clarinet's opening ascending motive (associated with the title character) into the opera's orchestral tapestry and features it as the principal musical material of Salome's frenzied, pseudo-oriental dance.

Each of the principal personages sings in a musical style that reveals aspects of his or her character: the young princess Salome sings with a flirtatious declamation style supported by delicate orchestration favoring high-pitched instruments such as flutes, violins, and celesta; later, the orchestra accompanies her final monologue with its full registral, dynamic, and timbral capabilities. Jochanaan's (John the Baptist's) music is devoutly tonal, generally favoring flat key areas—including A flat major, the key in Strauss' "system" of tonal symbolism that represents religion, and through which Strauss illustrates Jochanaan's steadfast piety. Herod's musical language is inflected with whole-tone scales; lacking a solidly tonal perfect fifth, but having instead the disorienting and dissonant tritone at its structural core, these passages conveys a sense of instability appropriate for the perverse Galilean tetrarch. *—Jennifer Hambrick*

Synopsis:

On the terrace of the palace, captain of the guard Narraboth wistfully sings of how beautiful Salome looks that night ("Wie schön ist die Prinzessin"), and a page says that the moon looks like a dead woman rising from her tomb. Narraboth instead imagines it looks like a princess with doves for feet, dancing. The soldiers comment on the Jews noisily debating religion in the banquet hall, and as Narraboth continues to rhapsodize on Salome's beauty, the page warns him that he looks at her too much, and terrible things may happen.

From a cistern, Jochanaan declares the imminent arrival of one greater than he, and one of the soldiers wants to make him be silent, the other says that he is a holy and good man. Narraboth excitedly sees that Salome is rising from the banquet table and coming out. She is agitated ("Ich will nicht bleiben"), disturbed by the way Herod looks at her. She muses that the moon is like a pure silver virgin. When she hears Jochanaan continuing to prophesy, she is curious about him and questions Narraboth and the soldiers. A slave comes to bring Herod's request for her return, and she refuses. Narraboth is perturbed by her interest in Jochanaan and tries to get her to leave, but instead, she asks him, with the promise of throwing him a flower the next day, to open the forbidden cistern. He briefly protests that he cannot but yields. Jochanaan emerges, still prophesying ("Wo ist er") and begins to speak of Salome's mother, Herodias, as a harlot who must repent of her incest. (Herodias had first been married to Herod's brother.) Salome is fascinated by him and speaks dreamily of his eyes and skin, to Narraboth's horror. Jochanaan notices her and asks who she is, and when she tells him, he orders her back, and tells her to go into the desert to seek out the Son of Man. She asks if he is as beautiful as he himself, and he again orders her back, saying he hears the wings of the angel of death in the palace. She instead tells him she desires his body, which she describes as whiter than anything in the world ("Jochanaan! Ich bin verliebt"). As he denounces her, she raves about his hair and his mouth, which she asks him to let her kiss. Narraboth is so distraught that he stabs himself and falls dead between them, but Salome ignores this completely, insisting on kissing Jochanaan's mouth. Jochanaan tells her that she must go and seek the one who can save her, and when she only reiterates her demand for a kiss, he returns to the cistern, calling her cursed.

Herod and Herodias emerge, Herod looking for Salome, to Herodias' disgust. He says the moon looks like a drunken woman searching for lovers, and Herodias responds that the moon looks only like the moon. He orders that the banquet continue outside, and slips in Narraboth's blood. Remembering that Narraboth looked longingly at Salome, he orders the body taken away. He feels a cold wind and hears the beating of wings, and then amorously asks Salome to eat and drink with him, and she refuses. Jochanaan calls from the cistern that the time he foretold has arrived, and Herodias tells him to give Jochanaan to the Jews. Five of them come forward to urge this, but Herod refuses, saying Jochanaan is a holy man. They then turn to debating the nature of visions, God, and prophecies ("Das kann nicht sein"). Jochanaan again prophesies, ("Siehe, der Tag ist nahe"), and the Jews and the Nazarenes debate whether Jesus is, as Jochanaan says, the Messiah. Herod grows nervous when they say that Jesus raised the dead, and declares that he forbids it. Jochanaan loudly denounces the daughter of Babylon and Herodias insists that he is insulting her, but Herod responds that he did not name her. He then asks Salome to dance, eventually provoking her interest by swearing to give her any reward she might name. Over Herodias' protests, she agrees. Herod suddenly feels the cold wind and hears the beating of wings, but it ceases when he rips his garland of roses from his head.

Herodias forbids Salome to dance, but she does so, in the Dance of the Seven Veils. Herod is delighted, and asks her to name her reward. She asks for a silver platter... bearing the head of Jochanaan. He is horrified but Herodias is jubilant. In a mounting frenzy, he pleads with her to ask for anything else, offering her half the kingdom, jewels, peacocks, even the veil of the temple sanctuary, but she repeats her demand for Jochanaan's head. He finally assents, and sinks back. Salome hovers over the cistern, wondering why it is taking so long and why Jochanaan is silent. An arm emerges, bearing the head. Herod and the Nazarenes are horrified, and Herodias fans herself, smiling. Salome exults, telling the head that he would not let her kiss his mouth, but now it is hers to do with as she pleases ("Ah! Du wolltest mich nicht"). She extols the beauty of his body and asks why he did not look at her, saying that if only he had, he would have loved her, and saying that nothing can quench her passion for his body. Herod is overwhelmed with fear and turns to go into the palace, ordering the torches extinguished. Salome raves that she has kissed Jochanaan's mouth, and a ray of moonlight illuminates her. Herod suddenly turns and orders the soldiers to kill her, and they rush forward and crush her between their shields. *—Ann Feeney*

Recommended:

- ○ **Strauss: Salome** / Sinopoli (cond.), Studer, Terfel, Rysanek, Hiestermann / DG 431810
- ○ **Strauss: Salome** / Solti (cond.), Nilsson, Wachter, Equiluz, Stolze, Hoffmann / London 414414
- ○ **Strauss: Salome** / Dohnányi (cond.), Malfitano, Terfel, Schwarz, Riegel, Begley / 1995 / London 444178

ORCHESTRAL

Also sprach Zarathustra (Thus Spoke Zoroaster), tone poem, Op. 30 (1896)

Like many of his contemporaries, the young Richard Strauss was enthralled with Wagner; indeed, a number of his compositions, especially the early opera *Guntram* (1887–93), reveal an intent on Strauss' part to re-create the spirit of the older composer's works. However, as evidenced by his adoption of Friedrich Nietzsche's *Also sprach Zarathustra* as the subject of a tone poem, Strauss' music soon took on a distinct identity. By this time, Nietzsche, though a former Wagner devotee, had become the most vocal and articulate critic of Wagner's philosophy and art. By aligning his artistic vision with that of Nietzsche, Strauss forever removed himself from the camp of "true" Wagnerians.

Also sprach Zarathustra (Thus Spoke Zoroaster), one of the high points of Strauss' early career, was completed in the summer of 1896 and premiered in November of the same year. Sandwiched between *Till Eulenspiegels lustige Streiche* (1894–95) and *Don Quixote* (1896–97), it was among the works that forever solidified the composer's reputation and distilled the essence of his singular orchestral language.

Also sprach Zarathustra comprises nine sections. The introduction—which has gained a peculiar immortality from its prominent use in Stanley Kubrick's film *2001: A Space Odyssey*—is followed by these distinctive episodes, each of which explores an element of Nietzsche's text, from "Von den Hinterweltlern" (From the Back-world People) to an expression of intense yearning ("Von der großen Sehnsucht") and a portrayal of joy and passion (Von den Freuden und Leidenschaften). At the center of the work is "Das Grablied" (Song of the Grave), which sets the stage for the clever and ironic "Von der Wissenschaft," in which a truncated fugue gently pokes fun at science by—perhaps prophetically—including all twelve chromatic pitches in its subject. "Der Genesende" (The Convalescent) slowly regains its strength, bursting forth into the energetic "Das Tanzlied" (Dance-Song), led by a solo fiddle.

The final section, "Nachtwandlerlied" (Song of the Night Wanderer), makes subtle use of tonal and thematic cues (most notably, a return to the tonality of the opening section) to suggest that the journey of the unnamed Night Wanderer is cyclic—eternally returning to its beginning. This lack of resolution is mirrored in the lingering dissonance, the half-step between B and C, which ends the work, capturing the questioning and unsettling nature of Nietzsche's own conclusion.

The whole of *Also sprach Zarathustra* is through-composed; though some suggest that it contains aspects of both sonata and rondo forms, no structural analysis is sustainable without reference to Nietzsche's text. Like most of Strauss' tone poems, *Also sprach Zarathustra* employs massive instrumental forces; however, it provides a contrast to Strauss' more strongly narrative works in its deployment of the orchestra in a more subtle and deft manner. Here, short, transformable motives take the place of the long, sinuous tunes that emerge in works like *Ein Heldenleben* (1898). The relative concision of its musical material suggests the composer's attempt to mirror the nature and character of his literary source. *—AMG*

Recommended:

- ○ **Strauss: Also Sprach Zarathustra; Don Juan; Four Last Songs** / Karajan (cond.), Berlin PO / 2003 / DG 000020202
- ○ **Strauss: Tone Poems** / Bohm (cond.), Berlin PO / 1988 / DG 463190
- ○ **Strauss: Also sprach Zarathustra; Ein Heldenleben** / Reiner (cond.), Chicago SO / 1993 / BMG 61494
- ○ **Strauss: Orchestral Works** / Kempe (cond.), Dresden Staatskapelle / 1999 / Angel 73614

Der Bürger als Edelmann (Le bourgeois gentilhomme), suite from the ballet, Op. 60–IIIa (1920)

By the twentieth century, the production of incidental music for preexisting dramatic works had long proven a viable creative outlet for many composers. In fact, a good deal of this "music to order" (which originally served a function akin to that of today's film scores) boasts a secure berth in the standard orchestral repertoire. Several of Beethoven's overtures, for example, fall into this category, as does Mendelssohn's music for *A Midsummer Night's Dream*. Molière's play *Le Bourgeois Gentilhomme* (1673), despite its origins over two centuries earlier, provided Richard Strauss and his collaborator, Hugo von Hofmannsthal, with a springboard for a rather novel "experiment." The idea was that not only would Strauss provide incidental music in the standard sense for the Molière comedy, but the play itself (as adapted by Hoffmannsthal) would serve as an elaborate prologue and setup for the composer's one-act opera *Ariadne auf Naxos*. Hofmannsthal introduced referential plot devices into the play (including the character of a composer) that would provide an impetus and raison d'etre for Strauss' newly composed work which would follow.

Unfortunately, this idea of "play plus opera" in practice left the opening-night audience exhausted and apparently annoyed. Aside from the audience's putative "lack of culture," in the composer's own words, one unforseen hindrance was an elaborate—and lengthy—reception sponsored by King Karl of Württemburg during the intermission between the two works. This addition of wining and dining to the evening's festivities meant that the opera, itself about an hour and a half in length, didn't even commence until two and a half hours after the beginning of the play. In this respect, at least—providing a more-than-ample evening's entertainment—Strauss' Wagnerian aspirations were certainly realized.

Reacting to the impracticality of and tepid response to this innovation, Strauss discarded the staging of the Molière work from his plan for *Ariadne*. Rather than shelve the play's incidental music, however, he fashioned nine of the numbers into a concert suite: Overture to Act One ("Jourdain the Bourgeois"), "Minuet," "The Fencing Master," "Entrance and Dance of the Tailors," "The Menuet of Lully," "Courante," "Cleonte's Entry," Prelude to Act Two ("Intermezzo"), and "The Dinner."

The suite follows the action as the play's central character, the arriviste boor Jourdain, attempts to impress the aristocracy about whose world he knows very little. The humorous intent of Molière's work is evident as Strauss vividly illustrates the empty trappings of Jourdain's ambitions: awkward (and evidently unsuccessful) dance lessons, ungainly swordplay, pompous, self-important tailors who show him how to deport himself, and, to impress his guests at an elaborate feast, a boy who springs out of a giant omelette and begins to dance.

In keeping with the original period of Molière's comedy, Strauss uses a stripped-down orchestra for the suite and incorporates into the score the music of Jean-Baptiste Lully (1632–87) as well as "baroqueries" of his own invention. *—Michael Rodman*

Recommended:

- ○ **Strauss: Orchestral Music from Stage Works** / Ormandy (cond.), Philadelphia Orch. / 1997 / Sony 62650
- ○ **Strauss: Der Bürger als Edelmann; Ariadne auf Naxos** / Nagano (cond.), Lyon Opera Orch. / 1997 / Virgin 45111
- ○ **Strauss: The Tone Poems** / Maazel (cond.), Vienna PO / 2002 / Decca 470 954

Dance Suite, for small orchestra, o.Op. 107 (1923)

German composer Richard Strauss was an old hand at classical parody by the time he was commissioned by the Vienna Staatsoper to compose a work to be performed in the Redoutensaal of the Imperial Palace in 1920. Strauss had set Molière's play *Le bourgeois gentilhomme* (1918) to faux-French music and his opera *Ariadne auf Naxos* (1911–12) is itself a highly elevated pastiche. In the *Dance Suite*, Strauss took pieces composed by the greatest of the French clavecinists, François Couperin, and orchestrated them in a stylized manner that joined Strauss' orchestral sensibility with his idiosyncratic understanding of French Baroque performance practice. The result is a work that is no longer either Couperin's nor yet wholly Strauss', but a charming mixture of both. The movements of the *Dance Suite* are as follows: "Einzug und feierlicher Reigen" (Entry and Solemn Round), a stately double-dotted French overture followed by a majestic Round dance; "Courante," a minor-keyed dance for string orchestra later joined by solo trumpet; "Carillon," a beguiling dance for celesta and harpsichord; "Sarabande," severe outer sections flanking a more serene central section; "Gavotte," a lightly scored pseudo-trio sonata movement for viola, flute, and harpsichord with a trio for oboes and bassoon; "Tourbillion" is a rushing contrapuntal piece for small string orchestra and harpsichord with a slower and more graceful trio for solo violin, solo viola, and harp; "Allemande," a festive dance for brass and strings; and "Marche," a short, quick march movement starting with strings, harpsichord, and celesta ending with the whole orchestra. *—James Leonard*

Recommended:

- ○ **Strauss: Der Bürger als Edelmann; Schlagobers Walzer; Tanz Suite nach Couperin** / Strauss (cond.), Vienna PO / L.Y.S. 120
- ○ **Strauss: Orchestral Works** / Kempe (cond.), Dresden Staatskapelle / 1999 / Angel 73614

Divertimento, for small orchestra, Op. 86 (1940–1941)

This concert suite for small orchestra—based on clavecin pieces by François Couperin "Le Grand" (1668–1733)—has an overlapping history reminiscent of Strauss' decade-long struggle to tame Molière's comedy, *Le bourgeois gentilhomme*. Despite grumbles, his research into the music of "old Lully" whetted an appetite that was not satisfied with either the opera in its final form, *Ariande auf Naxos*, or the 1920 concert suite, *Der Bürger als Edelmann*.

Finding himself at loose ends after World War I, Strauss turned to Couperin's more than 300 short works for harpsichord. The first fruit was an opulent, eight-movement setting of *19 Pièces* that he called *Tanzsuite nach Couperin*. As post-war director of the Vienna State Opera he decided this would make a charming ballet, but the premiere on February 17, 1923, became a wake. In 1938 Strauss' last podium protégé, Clemens Krauss, persuaded him to compose five more movements. These, added to the original *Tanzsuite*, formed a new ballet, *Verklungene Feste* ("Bygone festivities whose sounds have faded away" more or less). Krauss conducted this in Munich on April 5, 1941, but again success eluded Strauss-Couperin. The protégé next persuaded his Meister to compose three more movements; added to the five written for *Verklungene Feste*, they comprise *Divertimento (nach Couperin)*. This was published in 1942 as Strauss' last work with opus number and premiered by Krauss with the Vienna Philharmonic on January 31, 1943. By then, however, musical purism was on the rise throughout Europe: transcriptions of "old" music were being sneered at, ultimately cursed, leaving Strauss' candied Couperin in limbo along with Schoenberg's *Handel* and *Monn Frankensteins*, Reger's desiccated cerebrations in variation-form, Stravinsky's Tchaikovsky and Bach organ-transplants, even (for the most part today) Hindemith's *Symphonic Metamorphosis on Themes by Carl Maria von Weber*.

The Strauss *Divertimento* incorporates 17 of Couperin's *Pièces de clavecin*, meticulously listed in his score by their original, frequently obscure, sometimes archaic, French titles. The first movement contains *La Visionnaire* and eight bars of *Sarabande la Majestreuse* from the 1923 *Tanzsuite*). For the second movement, Strauss chose *La Musète de Choisi*, *La Fine Madelon*, *La Douce Janneton*, *Le Sezile*, and *Musète de Taverni*. *Le Tic-toc-choc, ou les Maillotins* and *La Lutine* (with Tic-toc coda) constitue the third movement, while the fourth is just *Les Fauvètes plaintives*. Finally, the fifth movement consists of *Le Trophée*, *L'Anguille*, *Les Jeune-Seigneurs*, *Cy-devant les Petits Maitres*, *La Linote éfarouchée*, and a grand coda based on *Le Trophée*. The three movements added in 1942 are played without pause: *Le tours de Passe-passe* (sixth), *Les ombres errantes* (seventh), and *Les Brinborions* and *La Badine* (eighth). The suite is gorgeously scored for pairs of flutes, oboes, clarinets, bassoons, and horns; English horn, trumpet, percussion; harp, celesta, harpsichord, organ; strings. *—Roger Dettmer*

Recommended:

- ○ **Strauss: Ballet Suites** / Rickenbacher (cond.), Bamberg SO / 1999 / Koch 365352

Don Juan, tone poem, Op. 20 (1888–1889)

Don Juan (1888) stands out among Strauss' early tone poems for its almost perfect structure and concise design. Taking Nikolaus Lenau's fragmentary play of the same title as his starting point, Strauss fashioned a tone poem which would convey the story of the legendary inveterate womanizer. The connection with Lenau's version of the story is confirmed by the quotation of text as an incipit in the score.

Strauss quickly captures the impetuous nature of Don Juan in the soaring theme which opens the piece. While Strauss did not allow a narrative description to be printed at the premiere (as was then often the case with program music), the story is easy enough to follow. Taking the more lyrical sections as depictions of various women, one after another, one hears the exuberant opening theme that occurs between them, and which opens the work, as Don Juan's own. This theme intensifies and becomes more ardent throughout until, near the end, it dissolves into the stormy music associated with the Commendatore, the father of a woman Don Juan had seduced. As in Mozart's similarly themed opera *Don Giovanni* (1787), the Don meets his end at the hands of the Commendatore. In Strauss' treament, however, the spirit of Don Juan emerges even after his defeat.

Strauss himself conducted the premiere of the work in fall 1889, and it was well received from the start. In its exceedingly vivid orchestration, use of short motives, and intense lyricism, *Don Juan* provides a striking and enduring encapsulation of Strauss' musical language.*—James Zychowicz*

Recommended:

- ○ **Strauss: Also Sprach Zarathustra; Don Juan; 4 Last Songs** / Tennstedt (cond.), London PO / 1999 / EMI 73560
- ○ **Strauss: Also Sprach Zarathustra; Don Juan; 4 Last Songs** / Karajan (cond.), Berlin PO / 2003 / DG 000020202
- ○ **Strauss: Tone Poems** / Böhm (cond.), Dresden Staatskapelle / 1988 / DG 463190

Ein Heldenleben (A Hero's Life), tone poem, Op. 40 (1897–1898)

Strauss completed this "tone poem for large orchestra" on December 27, 1898, and conducted the premiere on March 3, 1899, in Frankfurt. It is scored for quadrupled winds; augmented brass including eight horns, five trumpets, and two tubas; timpanist, four other percussionists, two harps, and strings (the score asks for 64). Strauss was 34 when he courted notoriety in this self-promoting musical memoir. At heart he was a Biedermeier Bürger—virtually a "family values" composer. He followed *Ein Heldenleben* with the *Sinfonia Domestica*, a home movie about himself, Frau Strauss, and their son Siegfried. Twenty years later he based an opera, *Intermezzo*, on a comic mix-up that briefly threatened his marriage. Critics complained as loudly in 1924 as they had in 1899 and 1903, but never seriously dented his reputation as Germany's leading composer after Wagner.

But Claude Debussy in 1901 reviewed (as translated by B.N. Langton Davies) a Paris concert in which Strauss conducted *A Hero's Life*. Strauss, he contended, "is practically the only original composer in Germany. His technique in the art of handling the orchestra allies him to Liszt, while his desire to base his music on literature allies him to Berlioz... *Don Quixote*, '*Also sprach Zarathustra*,' *Till Eulenspiegels lustige Streiche*. [His] characteristics reach a pitch of frenzy in *Ein Heldenleben*.... After [only] a minute or two one is captured first by the tremendous vitality of his orchestration, then by the frenzied energy that carries one along with him for as long as he chooses.... It is a book of pictures, or even a cinema. But one must admit that the man who composed a work at so continuously high a pressure is very nearly a genius [and], I say again, it is not possible to withstand his irresistible domination."

The six subsections of *Ein Heldenleben* comprise a single, massive movement in sonata form with 13 major themes (not counting quotations from seven of his previous tone poems, the opera *Guntram*, and the song "Traum durch die Dämmerung"). The work begins and ends in E flat major, with notable sorties into other keys, major and minor.

The exposition begins with "The Hero," whose bold signature tune on horns and violins leaps upward almost three octaves and is followed by several secondary subjects. "The Hero's Adversaries" (i.e., music critics) speak as nattering woodwinds, heavy-footed bass fiddles, and harrumphing tubas. They provoke an angry response in C minor until the hero regains his composure. Now "The Hero's Wife" enters—capriciously, with arabesques and furbelows, impersonated by a solo violin. All who knew henpecking Pauline de Ahna Strauss, an in-your-face soprano from a wealthy, beer-brewing, Bavarian military family, were dumbstruck. To her husband, however, "She [was] very complex, very much a woman, never twice alike." His arousal here anticipates *Der Rosenkavalier* by a decade.

But the critics won't quit. In the development the hero responds to a challenge from three offstage trumpets, and fights furiously in C minor on "The Battlefield." He wins, of course. A victory hymn based on his theme leads off the reprise, aka "The Hero's Works of Peace." This begins with a quotation from *Don Juan*, Strauss' first famous work, followed by the rest in a masterfully woven pastiche. The critics' return provokes a last discordant outburst, after which "The Hero Withdraws from the World" into peaceful E flat major, albeit with a swell of satisfaction before the work's quiet ending.

Neither before nor since has "classical" music produced anything comparable to this curriculum vitae, which Gerard Schwarz and the Seattle Symphony have recorded thrillingly on Delos DE 3094 (coupled with an early serenade for winds, and the tone poem *Macbeth*). —*Roger Dettmer*

Recommended:

- ○ **Strauss: Ein Heldenleben; Till Eulenspiegel** / Tilson Thomas (cond.), London SO / 1989 / CBS 44817
- ○ **Strauss: Tone Poems** / Bohm (cond.), Berlin PO / 1988 / DG 463190
- ○ **Richard Strauss** / Karajan (cond.), Berlin PO / 2000 / DG 469208
- ○ **Strauss: Orchestral Works** / Kempe (cond.), Dresden Staatskapelle / 1999 / Angel 73614

Macbeth, tone poem, Op. 23 (1886–1891)

Richard Strauss was a veritable fountain of music in the 1880s and 1890s, and during these years it is a rare thing indeed to find him taking the time to tinker with an already-finished piece of music. But he was sufficiently dissatisfied with the first version (1886–88) of his orchestral tone poem *Macbeth*, Op. 23, to withdraw it and completely rethink the matter of its ending. When the second version appeared some two years later and was given its Weimar premiere (October 13, 1890), all involved agreed that the changes made for a better piece. Still, however, Strauss' *Macbeth* remains the least fawned-over of his tone poem children, and one might have to wait many seasons to hear a live performance of the work.

Macbeth's unpopularity has been credited to many things over the years. It has been accused of having no memorable themes. Untrue—the themes are mostly not of the long, voluptuous variety that admittedly endear listeners to Strauss' other tone poems, but there are plenty of extraordinary and evocative motives, and their use is ingenious. There is, in fact, one gloriously self-indulgent melody that might challenge any of *Don Juan*'s famous tunes. *Macbeth* has been called too obvious an attempt to mimic the style of Liszt's symphonic poems, which is also untrue—the work is, at heart, absolutely un-Lisztian. Probably the real reason is a very simple one: Shakespeare's drama is a cold, gray one, and Strauss' 20-minute condensation of it follows suit—musicians and audiences don't seem to know what to do with a Strauss who isn't colorful, shimmering, and velvety. Strauss continued to alter the orchestration of *Macbeth* through 1891, perhaps with the idea of somewhat brightening the textures; but the work cannot escape the somberness and despondency of its subject, and there is no reason that it should. Strauss might well have created a more popular—though by no means superior—work had he never revised *Macbeth*. The original version concluded with MacDuff's triumphant entry into the castle, D major and robust. In the final version, a grim D minor ending was composed, providing the audience no light at the end of what Strauss himself sardonically described as a "horribly dissonant" tunnel. —*Blair Johnston*

Recommended:

- ○ **Strauss: Orchestral Works** / Kempe (cond.), Dresden Staatskapelle / 1999 / Angel 73614

Metamorphosen, study for 23 solo strings, Op. 142 (1945)

Toward the end of his life, Richard Strauss underwent a profound aesthetic change that resulted in some of the composer's most intensely personal and philosophical music. Among the most striking of these works from Strauss' final decade is *Metamorphosen* (1945), written in an atmosphere of devastation following World War II.

As a meditation on the bombing of Dresden (which destroyed the city and killed 130,000 of its inhabitants), *Metamorphosen* represents a significant departure from the more exuberant of Strauss' tone poems—*Til Eulenspiegel's Merry Pranks*, *Don Juan*, *Don Quixote*—by that time a half-century old. In contrast to the vivid portraiture of those works, *Metamorphosen* is wholly unrepresentational, a tragic, pessimistic reflection on a more intimate level than any of Strauss' other music.

The work unfolds in a single, long movement. Strauss sustains and develops a series of recurring, interrelated motives that, as the title indicates, are linked by their transformation into new material rather than—as in conventional variations—a common thematic identity. The work includes several direct references to the funeral march in the second movement of Beethoven's *"Eroica" Symphony*; here they sound entirely appropriate and natural within the broader structure, underlying rather than emphasizing the somber nature of the work as a whole. —*Roy Brewer*

Recommended:

- ○ **Strauss: Metamorphosen; Symphonia domestica** / Furtwängler (cond.), Berlin PO / 2001 / Classica d'Oro 1040
- ○ **The Klemperer Legacy: Mahler; Wagner; Strauss** / Klemperer (cond.), London Philharmonia Orch. / 1999 / EMI 67039
- ○ **Strauss: Orchestral Works** / Kempe (cond.), Dresden Staatskapelle / 1999 / Angel 73614

Serenade for winds in E flat major, Op. 7 (1881)

The *Serenade for 13 Wind Instruments*, Op. 7, from 1881, is the first work of the German composer Richard Strauss to have survived in the concert hall. Although a youthful work, its charm, vivacity, and technical assurance makes it a worthy successor of Mozart's *Gran Partita*, upon which it is clearly modeled. Scored for the standard double winds plus four horns and contrabassoon, the *Serenade* is a single movement work in expansive sonata form. While the essentially conservative *Serenade* is not at all indicative of the magnificent series of tone poems and operas yet to come, it is still remarkably well-composed for an 18-year-old and far superior to the reactionary works he had heretofore composed.

It was also Strauss' first composition ever to be performed outside of Munich, where he was born and raised. This premiere took place in Dresden on November 27, 1882, under the direction of Franz Wullner. This was quite an honor for the young composer, as Wullner was a well-known and highly regarded conductor, best-known for conducting the premieres of Richard Wagner's operas *Das Rheingold* (1869) and *Die Walküre* (1870). The conductor's relationship with Strauss would last much longer, with Wullner later leading the premieres of *Till Eulenspiegel* (1896) and *Don Quixote* (1898). —*James Leonard*

Recommended:

- ○ **Strauss: Music For Wind Ensemble; Oboe Concerto** / Waart (cond.), Netherlands Wind Ens. / 1993 / Philips 438733
- ○ **Mozart, Strauss & Milhaud: Music for Winds** / Fennell (cond.), Eastman Wind Ens. / 1998 / Mercury 434399

Suite for winds in B flat major, Op. 4 (1884)

Impressed by a one-movement wind serenade by the teenaged Richard Strauss, conductor Hans von Bülow asked the budding composer to write a larger-scale work for the same combination of 13 instruments (double woodwinds, four horns, contrabassoon) to be played by Bülow's famed Meiningen Orchestra. What Strauss did not initially realize was that Bülow wanted a suite employing Baroque forms—which accounts for a gavotte and fugue being appended to two more Romantic movements—and that Strauss, who had never before wielded a baton, would conduct the premiere without rehearsal. Bülow thus played a major role in launching Strauss' dual career as a composer and conductor. The *Suite in B flat* begins with a "Praeludium," marked Allegretto. The music rises up from the very bottom of the ensemble in a series of confident gestures that hint at Strauss' later, more heroic style. This theme, however, remains free of bombast and benefits from the young composer's light touch. Contrasting material includes, most prominently, a brief lyrical theme. The "Praeludium" has been called a sonata-form movement without development, which is not really true; Strauss does toy with his musical elements before moving into the recapitulation. The "Romanze" (Andante) includes short, lyrical, soaring solos for clarinet, oboe, and flute, looking ahead to the manner of Strauss' late wind concertos. Melodies unroll over sonorous horn chords and undulating woodwind figures, but wander at such length that the music can lose a sense of shape. The mischievous "Gavotte" (Allegro) features quick, burbling tunes and sudden contrasts in its outer sections; at the center is a more sinuous melody over a bagpipe-like drone, interrupted repeatedly by rhythmic interjections derived from the opening material. The final movement consists of an introduction (Andante cantabile) that initially calls to mind *Siegfried's Funeral March*, before assuming a more undulating, Italianate character and then returning to its Wagnerian inclinations. This builds up into a fugue (Allegro con brio) based on an angular theme; it's diligently structured but without particular imagination or enthusiasm until the bright, show-stopping coda. *—James Reel*

Recommended:

- ○ **Strauss: Sinfonia Domestica; Suite for Winds** / de Waart (cond.), Minnesota Orch. / 1994 / Virgin 61142
- ○ **Strauss: Music For Wind Ensemble; Oboe Concerto** / de Waart (cond.), Netherlands Wind Ens. / 1993 / Philips 438733

Till Eulenspiegels lustige Streiche (Till Eulenspiegel's Merry Pranks), tone poem, Op. 28 (1894–1895)

One of Strauss' most popular symphonic poems is *Till Eulenspiegel*, a single-movement work for orchestra. It was composed between 1894 and 1895, shortly after the premiere and critical debacle of his first opera *Guntram*. In choosing the popular tale of *Till Eulenspiegel* as the basis for the tone poem, Strauss found an effective vehicle for responding to his critics, who treated his first opera unfavorably.

The character of *Till Eulenspiegel* is a chronic prankster, whose unrelenting sense of the sardonic continually challenges his peers and lands him in trouble. Till would never learn from his mistakes and constantly thumbed his nose at convention and any criticism. The tone poem is based on a German folktale that has appeared in various versions since its first appearance in the fourteenth century. Some have found a historical basis for the character, but he is best understood as a kind of folk hero who challenges the establishment. While no single source contains all the adventures of Till Eulenspiegel, the character is recognizable in various adaptations, just as Strauss' musical depiction in the rondo theme is apparent throughout the musical compositions.

The musical form of *Till Eulenspiegel* is a large-scale rondo. By identifying the character of Till with the rondo theme, Strauss found a way to demonstrate the recalcitrant nature of the protagonist and also to unify the work. After a brief introduction, often interpreted as an expression of "once upon a time," Strauss states the theme at the very beginning in a bravura passage for horn. The theme recurs between episodes of the rondo, and it is in those episodes that Till Eulenspiegel has his adventures. In terms of musical structure, the rondo-episodes provide contrast and, as they depart further from the main idea, they also set the stage for the return of the familiar rondo theme. The subsequent episodes show Till at odds with the peasants, railing at preachers, wooing a woman and being rejected by her, and making fun of the intelligentsia. Within these sections, Strauss allowed his theme for Till to return in various guises, yet still remain recognizable. Ultimately, Till finds himself brought before judges, who review his career and sentence him to death. Even then Till cannot depart without a mocking gesture, and the piece ends with his theme fully transformed with all its permutations exhausted.

Till Eulenspiegel contains some of Strauss' most brilliant orchestration and makes use of various instruments, including the clarinet in D. Strauss approached the orchestration of this work with a kaleidoscopic hand, often abruptly shifting between instrumental groups. This gives the work its appealing color and also makes it a virtuoso piece for orchestra. In writing program music, Strauss chose a still-new approach to composition and aligned himself with the avant-garde. His brilliantly orchestrated score with its virtuosic instrumentation and colorful dissonances showed Strauss as a modernist. It remains a popular concert piece and one of Strauss' best-known compositions. *—James Zychowicz*

Recommended:

- ○ **Strauss: 5 Great Tone Poems** / Haitink (cond.), Concertgebouw / 1994 / Philips 442281
- ○ **Strauss: Tone Poems** / Bohm (cond.), Berlin PO / 1988 / DG 463190
- ○ **Strauss: Till Eulenspiegel; Tod und Verklärung** / Reiner (cond.), Vienna PO / 2000 / Decca 467122

Tod und Verklärung (Death and Transfiguration), tone poem, Op. 24 (1888–1889)

Among Strauss' tone poems, *Tod und Verklärung* ("Death and Transfiguration") stands out for its concise program of an unnamed artist's demise and the subsequent transformation of his spirit. Unlike *Ein Heldenleben*, which contained an autobiographical element, *Tod und Verklärung* is more universal in its expression of dying. Here Strauss does not present a triumphant narrative of individual accomplishment, but rather explores the fleeting images of past experience as they dissolve before a dying person's eyes. Composed in 1888–89, just after *Don Juan*, *Tod und Verklärung* departs from the kind of tone poem Strauss had written up to that time. Instead of using a literary source as the basis, he imagined his own scenario. In fact the verses by Alexander Ritter appended to the score are an afterthought Strauss added after he had completed the work. He is reputed to have said, just before his own death, that dying was just as he had depicted it in *Tod und Verklärung*.

Strauss cast the work in the form of an extended sonata form, with a structure freer than he had yet attempted in his tone poems. Several evocative motives occur at the outset, including one suggesting an irregular heartbeat that is critical to the denouement of the work. Strauss uses various other motives to depict the protagonist's respiration and suffering; he also presents, early on, a short contrasting idea, depicting an ideal state, that re-emerges the extraordinarily lovely portrayal of transfiguration later in the work. Given the relatively unspecific nature of the program, this tone poem has an open-ended quality that involves the listener in the work. The vast and varied orchestration is typical of the mature Strauss. The moment of transfiguration is brilliant: a C major chord builds from the basses up over a powerful tread that includes deep bells and gongs. *—James Zychowicz*

Recommended:

- ○ **Strauss: Till Eulenspiel; Don Juan; Death & Transfiguration** / Szell (cond.), Cleveland Orch. / 1999 / Sony 89037
- ○ **Strauss: Orchestral Works** / Kempe (cond.), Dresden Staatskapelle / 1999 / Angel 73614
- ○ **Strauss: Till Eulenspiegel; Tod und Verklärung** / Reiner (cond.), Vienna PO / 2000 / Decca 467122
- ○ **Strauss: Tone Poems** / Bohm (cond.), Berlin PO / 1988 / DG 463190
- ○ **Strauss Conducts Strauss** / Strauss (cond.), Berlin State PO / 1976 / DG 429925

SYMPHONIC

Eine Alpensinfonie (An Alpine Symphony), Op. 64 (1911–1915)

While Richard Strauss was famous as a composer of tone poems, he had, at the time of the *Alpensinfonie*, gone a dozen years without producing a major symphonic work after having shifted his focus to opera. Perhaps it was because World War I was underway and opportunities to produce new operas were fewer that he returned one last time to the tone poem.

This is a very long work (nearly an hour) of symphonic proportions. Its specific program is the succession of stages in the ascent and descent of a mountain in the Alps. This excursion, however, also stands symbolically for a Nietzschean ideal of attaining one's purpose in life through the strength of one's own will, without reliance on religious belief. Strauss begins the work with a magnificent, hushed effect: Before sunrise the bulk of the mountain becomes visible; the Night motive is heard on hushed horns against a chord that thickens itself note by note until all the notes of B minor are hanging in the air. Sunrise follows the imposing mountain theme. The "Ascent" motive starts the action. The climbers encounter a hunting party (we hear horn calls), cross a brook, go by a waterfall, pass by a meadow (cowbells are heard), get entangled in a thicket, cross the glacier (the "Waterfall" motive is harmonically "frozen" here), get through "Dangerous Moments," and enjoy a glorious feeling when they reach the summit. Now they begin the "Descent" (an inversion of the "Ascent" motive, of course), get caught in a sudden and violent thunderstorm, retrace their steps, and arrive at the foot of the mountain as the Night motive is intoned again.

The orchestration of the work is opulent. While some find it glorious, others find it puffed-up and bombastic. It uses the rarely encountered bass oboe called the Heckelphone, plus thunder sheets, a specially designed thunder machine, a wind machine, and other unusual effects as part of a 120-piece orchestra. *—Joseph Stevenson*

Recommended:

- ○ **Richard Strauss: Eine Alpensinfonie** / Karajan (cond.), Berlin PO / DG 439017
- ○ **Strauss: Eine Alpensinfonie; Rosenkavalier-Suite** / Thielemann (cond.), Vienna PO / 2003 / DG 000020726
- ○ **Strauss: Eine Alpensinfonie; Waltzes from Der Rosenkavalier** / Ashkenazy (cond.), Czech PO / Ondine 976
- ○ **Strauss: Tone Poems** / Bohm (cond.), Dresden Staatskapelle / 1988 / DG 463190

Sinfonia Domestica, Op. 53 (1902–1903)

Richard Strauss once claimed that he could translate anything into musical sounds, that he could take even the events of something so mundane as the process of eating—using one utensil and then another, sampling this dish and then that one—and craft a musical equivalent. He put his own claim to the test when composing the *Sinfonia Domestica*, Op. 53 of 1902–03; here is a tone poem (it is not strictly called such, but it is certainly not a real symphony either) whose subject is not a figure of legend, as in *Don Juan*, or the mysteries of *Death and Transfiguration*, or a portrait of the composer as hero, as in *Ein Heldenleben*, but rather a simple day in the life of a family man. The *Sinfonia Domestica* is a warm, tender, and often lightly humorous work, scored for a massive orchestra (Strauss even adds four saxophones to his orchestra). It received its world premiere all the way across the Atlantic Ocean during a 1904 festival of Strauss music in New York City.

Strauss originally wrote many programmatic indications in the score of the *Sinfonia Domestica*, but he eventually opted to take almost all of them out. Still, even without them, the "action" is easy enough to follow. An opening movement introduces us to the family as a group and then, in three sections marked Thema I, Thema Two, and Thema Three, to the father, mother, and child in turn (presumably Strauss, his wife Pauline, and their son Franz). The child's fun and games make for a fine Scherzo, but soon it is time for bed (Wiegenlied, or "lullaby"). A voluptuous Adagio contains a romantic interlude, but when morning comes the parents are found fighting with one another (Strauss appropriately provides an exhilarating double fugue, tempo Sehr Lebhaft). Peace is made, however, and the safety, coziness, and happiness of hearth and home are assured by a rousing F major. *—Blair Johnston*

Recommended:

- ○ **Fritz Reiner Conducts Richard Strauss** / Reiner (cond.), Chicago SO / 1997 / RCA 68635
- ○ **Strauss: Orchestral Works** / Kempe (cond.), Dresden Staatskapelle / 1999 / Angel 73614
- ○ **Wilhelm Furtwängler: Recordings 1942–1944 Vol. 2** / Furtwängler (cond.), Berlin PO / 2001 / DG 471294

CONCERTO

Burleske, for piano & orchestra in D minor, o.Op. 85 (1885–1886)

Strauss composed this music in 1885–86 and conducted its first performance at Eisenach on June 21, 1890, with Eugen d'Albert as soloist. Scoring is nineteenth century traditional, minus trombones and tuba. Strauss created *Burleske* during his single season as the court conductor at Meiningen, following the departure of Hans von Bülow, who had brought him there in 1884 as an assistant. Bülow, during the last part of his life, proselytized on behalf of Brahms—his candidate to inherit Beethoven's mantle. He preached the gospel so fervently that 21-year-old Strauss, like a convert at a revival meeting, was moved to shout "Amen!" His enthusiasm waned, however, once Bülow left to conduct in Hamburg and Berlin. Alexander Ritter and a coven of Wagnerites at Meiningen converted Strauss to their cause. Before that, however, Bülow's indoctrination strongly influenced two works. Strauss would write that "the results of the enthusiasm I felt for Brahms were *Wanderers Sturmlied* and *Burleske*, which Bülow indignantly criticized as unpianistic, demanding an unnatural span (his hands were so small that he could only just reach an octave)." That said, there is more of Strauss-to-come in *Burleske* than in the work which followed—his large-scale "symphonic fantasy" in four movements, called *Aus Italien* (From Italy)—or in the violin sonata of 1887–88. *Burleske* was dedicated to British-born Eugen d'Albert, a converted German composer as well as pianist, who introduced it. But Strauss, despite financial need at the time, would not give the work to a publisher ("I left [it] far behind") until he sold it in 1894 to Steingräber of Leipzig without explanation. It remains to say that *Burleske* is a sportive work in a single movement of assured craftsmanship and several piquant surprises, though seldom the antic piece its title implies.

Structurally, it combines sonata form with a variant of the rondo. A timpani motto is played straightaway. The key is D minor, the meter 3/4—already Strauss was fascinated by the endless possibilities (for him) of waltz-time. His athletic main-theme, derived from an orchestral flourish that follows the motto, is introduced by the soloist. The orchestra adds a related subtheme before a key-shift to F major for the "official" second theme, again on piano, whose opening inverts the rhythm of the main theme. The development section is dominated by the orchestra. The soloist hasn't a lot to do until the recapitulation, all of it D minor, including the second theme. After this, Strauss adds a second development—making the structure ABACA—this one starring the soloist, who gets to play a long cadenza at the end. Although a bravura flourish begins the coda, *Burleske* ends quietly with timpani and piano exchanging quiet "Wiedersehens." *—Roger Dettmer*

Recommended:

- ○ **Serkin: The Legenday Recordings** / Serkin, Ormandy (cond.) / 1991 / Sony 47269
- ○ **Strauss Concertos** / Gulda, Collins (cond.), London SO / 1999 / Decca 460296

Don Quixote, fantastic variations for cello & orchestra, Op. 35 (1897)

Strauss wrote these "Fantastic Variations on a Theme of Knightly Character" in 1897. Franz Wüllner conducted the first performance on March 8, 1898, with the Gürzenich Orchestra of Cologne. In addition to solo cello and viola, the work is scored for triple winds and contrabassoon; six horns, three trumpets, three trombones, two tubas; timpani, two percussionists, wind machine, harp, and full strings. Strauss was an omnivorous reader attracted firsthand to what Walter Starkie called "the first modern novel… a spiritual autobiography."

Strauss rearranged the novel's sequence of misadventures for purposes of structure, but otherwise put his powers of depiction at the mad Man of La Mancha's service. A myriad of marvelous touches are detailed in the first volume of *Richard Strauss: A Critical Commentary* by the late conductor Norman del Mar, who concluded that, "on the side of humor and incredible fertility of invention… Strauss at no time surpassed what [he] accomplished throughout *Don Quixote*." Amen. Let me try to condense his analysis for home-listening consultation.

A long introduction heralds ten variations and an epilogue, based on a cornucopia of themes. Three of these pertain to the Don, who is immersed in literature about chivalry until fantasy unhinges his reason. A series of dissonant chords sends him "on his adventures with the cold, quiet logic of insanity," disguised as a solo cello which iterates the Don's themes. We hear two more for his fat squire, Sancho Panza, the first one played in unison by bass clarinet and tenor tuba, the babbling second one played by the viola, which thereafter impersonates him. The deluded Don's "Ideal Lady," Dulcinea, also has a theme, introduced by the principal oboe.

In Variation One, "the Knight and his squire start their journey" by mistaking windmills for giants. When the Don attacks, he is painfully unhorsed. Variation Two, "the victorious battle against the host of the emperor Alifanfaron," turns out to be against sheep. Their orchestral bleating still astonishes a century later. Variation Three, "colloquies of the Knight and his Squire," is the first of two eloquent rhapsodies addressing honor, glory, and the "Ideal Lady." Sancho keeps interrupting. Variation Four brings "the adventure with the penitents," mistaken by the Knight of the Sorrowful Countenance for robbers; it ends when they trounce him. Variation Five, "the Knight's vigil," nobly tender music, meditates on a vision of the Ideal Woman, conjured up by a horn. Variation Six, "the meeting with Dulcinea" becomes briefly droll, one of Strauss' very best jokes (in 2+3/4 time), when Sancho's search finds only a country tart and two companions. Variation Seven is "the ride through the air," blindfolded astride a wooden horse, features a wind machine. Timpani and basses play an earthbound tremolo underneath. Variation Eight depicts "the unfortunate journey in an enchanted boat"; it floats downstream without oars until a water mill capsizes it and the intrepid duo. (Listen for the cello to shake off droplets, pizzicato.) Variation Nine brings "The combat with two magicians"—monks, actually—routed from their prayers. Variation Ten, "The duel with the Knight of the White Moon," in reality depicts a disguised townsman who has challenged Quixote. If the Don loses—and he does, ignominiously—he must renounce all further quests and return home quietly. The finale, "The Death of Don Quixote," shows the Don restored to sanity but physically depleted, meditating on his follies until "the great Creator draws/his spirit, as the sun the morning dew." When the cello slides terminally from B to B below, the orchestra offers a brief, compassionate eulogy. *—Roger Dettmer*

Recommended:

- ○ **Strauss: Don Quixote; Schoenberg: Cello Concerto** / Ma, Ozawa (cond.), Boston SO / CBS 39863
- ○ **Strauss: Don Quixote; Till Eulenspiegel** / Tortelier, Kempe (cond.), Berlin PO / 2003 / Testament 1249
- ○ **Steven Isserlis** / Isserlis, de Waart (cond.), Minnesota Orch. / 1998 / Virgin 61490

Horn Concerto No. 1 in E flat major, o.Op. 11 (1882–1883)

Strauss was only 18 and had yet to develop his own distinctive style when he completed his first horn concerto in 1883. He wrote it for his father, a professional horn player, but the elder Strauss found the work too difficult. Today's soloists, ironically, find it much easier than the horn concerto Strauss wrote at the opposite end of his life. Schumann is the dominant influence here; it's hard not to detect a bit of the earlier composer's *Konzertstück for four horns*, and other works, in some of Strauss' more declamatory passages, especially the beginning.

After the virile, Schumann-esque opening bars, which provide the soloist a bravura hunting motif, the horn offers a far more lyrical second subject. The soloist takes the lead through the development section, the orchestra merely underlining the solo part and providing a few short bridge passages, including one that gently leads straight into the second movement.

This Andante is a highly lyrical ballad for the horn over a rudimentary orchestral accompaniment built from a simple and extremely repetitive four-note figure. Halfway through, the horn takes up a more extroverted but still long-lined theme over a twittering woodwind figure; the inspiration now seems to be French opera arias.

The finale is a fast rondo featuring a bravura main theme for the horn, which gives way to more expansive but still urgent material. The scherzo-like final bars require fine control and an extremely light touch, as if Strauss were turning to Mendelssohn for a few last words. *—James Reel*

Recommended:

○ **Strauss Concertos** / Tuckwell, Kertesz (cond.), London SO / 1999 / Decca 460296

○ **Strauss & Hindemith: Horn Concertos** / Brain, Sawallisch (cond.), London Philharmonia Orch. / 2002 / EMI 67783

Horn Concerto No. 2 in E flat major, Op. 132 (1942)

Richard Strauss' *Horn Concerto No. 2* (1942) followed its predecessor by some six decades, a period during which the composer's colorful musical language came to full maturity in an exceptional body of tone poems, songs, and operas. In a manner far more evident than in the earlier work, the Second Concerto is infused with Strauss' singular lyricism, reflecting the clarity of the composer's Romantic vision amid the strengthening winds of twentieth century modernism.

Like the First Concerto, the Second is in three movements; at the same time, its Classical orientation is less pronounced than that of the First, further reflecting Strauss' evolution from gifted teenager to assured master.

The first movement, Allegro, opens with wide, dramatic leaps, requiring a soloist with excellent control of the instrument. The themes develop with rhapsodic freedom, hearkening to the expansive vocal lines of the composer's operas. The second movement, Andante con moto, exudes a calmness that is absent from the previous movement. The sonorities and scoring are more intimate here, even chamberlike; the horn's line often blends almost seamlessly with the accompaniment, lending the movement the character of a single through-composed gesture. In the Allegro molto rondo, Strauss focuses on more compact melodic units, isolating motives that become the focus of interplay between the soloist and the orchestra. Near the end the solo horn is joined by the horns in the orchestra, bringing the work to a close in bravura style. *—AMG*

Recommended:

○ **Strauss: Don Quixote; Horn Concerto 2** / Hauptmann, Karajan (cond.), Berlin PO / DG 457725

○ **Strauss & Hindemith: Horn Concertos** / Brain, Sawallisch (cond.), London Philharmonia Orch. / 2002 / EMI 67783

Oboe Concerto in D major, o.Op. 144 (1945; revised 1948)

Strauss' Oboe Concerto (1945–46) dates from the final stages of the composer's career. As a product of his lifetime of experience, it ranks as one of the finest works ever composed for the instrument. Strauss wrote the concerto at the suggestion of John De Lancie, an American soldier and professional oboist stationed near Garmisch at the end of the Second World War. (De Lancie went on to a career as principal oboist of the Philadelphia Orchestra; he also commissioned works for oboe from a number of other composers.) Though De Lancie both recorded the concerto and performed it throughout his career, the work was premiered by Marcel Saillet in Zurich on February 26, 1946.

Following the classical model, the concerto is cast in a fast-slow-fast three-movement form. The opening Allegro moderato features interplay between the oboe and solo flute and clarinet in a sort of concertato treatment. The elegiac Andante echoes the more meditative moods of the composer's later operas. While the harmonic language is essentially diatonic, Strauss makes full use of colorful chromatic inflections. The movement is remarkable for its intensity and seamlessness, in contrast to the more motivic and episodic nature of some of Strauss' music. The concluding Vivace has the playful character of the composer's incidental score to *Der Bürger aus Edelmann* (1917) or the opera *Der Rosenkavalier* (1909–10). The oboe commands center stage throughout with angular leaps and shifts of register.

The concerto is further notable for Strauss' economical scoring. This mode of relative austerity—in comparison to the expansive instrumentation of Strauss' earlier tone poems and operas—is a feature of much of the composer's late music, including the *Sonatina No. 2* for 16 winds (1943–45) and *Metamorphosen* for 23 strings (1944–45). *—James Zychowicz*

Recommended:

○ **Strauss Concertos** / Ashkenazy (cond.), Hunt, Berlin Radio SO / 1999 / Decca 460296

Violin Concerto in D minor, Op. 8 (TrV 110) (1881–1882)

Richard Strauss' *Violin Concerto in D minor, Op. 8* (1881–82), the only essay in the genre the composer ever attempted, is an interesting example of Strauss' early music. The works of this period (the *Sonata for Cello and Piano* also comes to mind) are full of warmth and melodic sentimentality: the realization of *Gemütlichkeit* carried to the extreme. Yet, at a deeper musical level, the Concerto is not entirely successful. Although Strauss, who began composing this work at the age of 17, was an extraordinarily accomplished young man, he still lacked the sort of maturity and practical experience evident in works composed just a few years hence. Indeed, in later years, Strauss himself ridiculed the Concerto. Still, it isn't fair to dismiss the Concerto out of hand as uninteresting juvenilia. The work's youthful sincerity, breadth of lyrical expression, and virtuoso fireworks retain a great deal of appeal for concertgoers, and the work does not deserve to be reduced to a mere historical curiosity. The expansive Allegro, nearly a quarter hour in length, gives the soloist a chance to demonstrate a high degree of technical skill and the full breadth of Romantic passion that the instrument is capable of expressing. The opening flourish alone is enough to frighten away many violinists. The second movement is particularly vocal in expression, sweet and pure, and provides a foretaste of the composer's magnificent operas and lieder yet to come. The concluding Rondo is the most technically demanding of the movements, at the same time presenting problems of musical coherence greater than those in the previous movements. A skillful performer, however, can transform it into a zestful display piece. The Concerto is dedicated to the composer's uncle and violin teacher, Benno Walter, who gave the premiere (with the young Strauss playing a piano reduction of the orchestral part) on December 5, 1882. *—Blair Johnston*

Recommended:

○ **Strauss: Violin Concerto; Sonata in E flat** / Chang, Sawallisch (cond.), Bavarian Radio SO / 1999 / Angel 56870

○ **Strauss Concertos** / Belkin, Ashkenazy (cond.), Berlin Radio SO / 1999 / Decca 460296

VOCAL

Enoch Arden, melodrama for speaker & piano, Op. 38 (1897)

Richard Strauss composed the melodrama *Enoch Arden* (1897) for his colleague Ernst von Possart, who had assisted Strauss in obtaining a post at the Munich Court Opera in 1896. Possart, well known for his recitations, was no doubt grateful for such a contribution to a repertory mostly eschewed by composers of Strauss' stature. Strauss and Possart performed the work together on numerous occasions, and even toured with it.

The poem, written by Alfred Lord Tennyson and published in 1864, tells the story of three children—Enoch Arden, Philip Ray, and Annie Lee—who go their separate ways upon reaching adulthood. Enoch is lost at sea; Annie, having heard nothing for years, gives up hope of seeing him again and marries Philip. Enoch eventually finds his way back but refuses to reveal himself to Annie. She learns his identity only after his quiet death years later.

As dramatic as parts of the narrative are, Strauss refrained from composing an extensive musical backdrop. Given the length of the text, Strauss' musical contribution is relatively minimal: instead of complicating the recitation with an ongoing, elaborate accompaniment, he instead provides musical punctuation and commentary. Throughout, Tennyson's spoken text is unquestionably predominant.

The work is divided into two approximately equal parts, each with a short musical prelude. Strauss assigns leitmotifs to each of the three main characters, drawing on these ideas at various points in the work. Rather than developing themes and motives, as he would in his operas, Strauss uses his musical materials more statically, recalling the "reminiscence motives" of earlier nineteenth century opera. Strauss' language here is plainer, more conservative, than that found in his other contemporaneous works. The harmonies indeed suggest an earlier style, perhaps alluding to the period in which Tennyson's poem was completed some three decades earlier.

Largely because of the very nature of the genre, *Enoch Arden* succeeds mainly on the basis of the narrator's contribution. Strauss employed a translation of the poem by Adolf Strodtmann, who effectively conveyed the drama of Tennyson's narrative in German. Performances since Strauss' own time often make use of the original English text. One of the more notable recordings of the work is that narrated by the actor Claude Rains, accompanied by Glenn Gould. *—James Zychowicz*

Recommended:

○ **Strauss: Ophelia-Lieder; Enoch Arden; Piano Sonata; 5 Piano Pieces** / Rains, Gould / 1992 / Sony 52657

Five Little Songs (Kleine Lieder), Op. 69 (1918)

After taking a 12-year vacation from song composition, Richard Strauss returned to the world of lieder in 1918 and in short order turned out four sets of them—Opp. 66, 67, 68, and 69. The last of these are the *Fünf kleine Lieder* (Five Little Songs), Op. 69, settings of poems by two important early Romantic poets: Achim von Arnim, one of two men who compiled *Des Knaben Wunderhorn* in the early nineteenth century, and Heinrich Heine. These "little songs" are really not all that short, but there is a gracefulness to them—a certain lightness of touch that can be one of the most endearing features of Strauss' music—that creates the illusion of a diminutive stature that actual measurement belies. Some of the poems, such as "Einerlei" (Sameness, the third song in the group), are, however, very brief indeed.

Strauss' sometimes irrepressible tendency to write long, voluptuous melodies is kept firmly in check throughout Op. 69: a scherzando character marks songs like "Einerlei" and "Schlechtes Wetter" (Bad Weather), the final song of the five, and the smooth legato lines of "Der Pokal" (The Goblet), Op. 69, No. 2 are more ceremonial than emotive. The final bars of "Schlechtes Wetter," and thus of Op. 69, give us Strauss at his quicksilver best: a thin thread of melody in the right hand gives in to the left hand's persistent little cascades (rain, present throughout the whole song) and everything tumbles down rapidly towards a final F major chord that, bad weather notwithstanding, seems as simple and as warm as can be. *—Blair Johnston*

Recommended:

○ **Strauss: Lieder Vol. 1** / Fischer-Dieskau, Moore / 1991 / EMI 63995

Eight Songs from "Letzte Blätter," Op. 10 (1885)

The first of Richard Strauss' many but undeservedly neglected songs to appear in print were the *Acht Gedichte aus "Letzte Blätter" von Hermann Gilm* (Eight Poems from Hermann Gilm's "Letzte Blätter"), Op. 10, of 1885 (published in 1887 by Joseph Aibl Verlag of Munich). In this remarkable octet of songs, composed when Strauss was just past 20 years old, are three of the composer's best-loved songs: "Zueignung," "Allerseen," and "Die Nacht."

The first song in the set, "Zueignung" (Dedication), is a C major setting of a poem originally titled "Habe Dank"; Strauss orchestrated and substantially altered this song in 1940 (over five decades after first composing it!). The popularity of the gorgeous E flat major "Allerseen" (All Souls' Day), Op. 10, No. 8, is shown by the fact that two very prominent contemporaries, or near-contemporaries, of Strauss loved it enough to put their own stamp on its music: Max Reger fashioned it into a version for solo piano, and Robert Heger made a version for voice and orchestra. "Die Nacht" (The Night), Op. 10, No. 3, tells its nocturnal story using hushed pulsations in the piano and a gently rotating chromatic spectrum.

The songs of Op. 10, in order, are: "Zueignung," "Nichts," "Die Nacht," "Die Georgine," "Geduld," "Die Verschwiegenen," "Die Zeitlose," and "Allerseen." *—Blair Johnston*

Recommended:

○ **Strauss: Vier letzte Lieder; 15 Lieder** / Bonney, Martineau / 1999 / London 460812

○ **Strauss: Lieder** / Popp, Sawallisch / 1988 / EMI 49318

○ **Strauss: Lieder Vol. 1** / Fischer-Dieskau, Moore / 1991 / EMI 63995

Six Songs, Op. 17 (1885–1887)

The *Songs*, Op. 17 of Richard Strauss originated during a two-year period that was a watershed for the composer. The period from 1885 to 1887 saw the gradual transformation of the Strauss from conservative to nascent progressive. Equally significant was his acquaintance with Pauline de Ahna, the willful soprano with whom he locked horns as a conductor and, according to legend, became engaged after a volatile rehearsal. The two became soul mates for life, and many of his songs, including the Op. 17 set, were created with her in mind. Strangely, no recordings exist of Strauss as accompanist to his wife in this lifelong favored medium of his.

These six songs, including the popular "Ständchen," are in the comfortable Brahmsian idiom with the occasional tinge of Wagner-Liszt chromaticism, suggesting that young Strauss was stretching out, albeit not yet into the breeze from other planets. In No. 1, "Seitdem dein Aug," the accidentals are used sparingly and appropriately for the passionate yet restrained text by Schack. "Ständchen" is firmly diatonic, sunny and happy in its unashamed "Gemütlichkeit"; here is music of a soon-to-be golden age. The following "Geheimnis" is almost Schubertian, even folklike in utterance. Contrast is provided by the brooding "Von Dunklem Schleier umsponnen" and the following "Nur Mut." However, the genial mood returns for the closing "Barcarolle." It is not surprising that this last song most likely had its genesis during the trip to Italy during which the composer also produced *Aus Italien*. If the emerging Strauss was to be the harbiniger of an age in transition, the Op. 17 set is a reflection of a still-contented and comfortable time. When an older Strauss would return to this idiom it would be from a nostalgic perspective. *— Wayne Reisig*

Recommended:

○ **Strauss: Lieder Vol. 1** / Fischer-Dieskau, Moore / 1991 / EMI 63995

Four Songs, Op. 27 (1894)

Richard Strauss' Op. 27 set of songs is one of his greatest, considered as a set. Strauss was a composer of varying inspiration, and his several dozen songs contain his share of misses among many hits. Some of his greatest songs were published alongside weaker verse settings. Perhaps the surest indication that the composer thought well of this set is that he dedicated it to "my beloved Pauline" and gave it to the singer Pauline de Ahna on their wedding day, September 10, 1894. She often performed these songs.

Strauss had become acquainted with a circle of poets in Berlin that included Kaspar Schmidt (whose real name was Max Stirner), John Henry Mackay, and Karl Henckell. All were socialists. Stirner was felt to be such a radical that he made Karl Marx seem tame, and Mackay was even more of a rabble-rouser than Stirner.

However, Strauss tended to pick the gentlest, most bourgeois, and most Romantic poetry from among the works of this group.

The opening song of the set is called "Ruhe, mein Seele!" (Calm, My Heart!) and is on a text drawn from Henckell's *Buch des Kampfes* (Book of Struggles). The name of the song comes from a recurring refrain. The song considers the past life of a person with a deeply troubled spirit, and the recurring admonition that one should calm one's heart seems to reflect the singer's passage through a stage of constant struggle.

Fine as the song is (though somewhat elusive in expression in its original form), Strauss improved it when he orchestrated it. It was 54 years after he wrote it that he provided an orchestral accompaniment, which is dated June 9, 1948. Strauss improved the timing of the song by lengthening by a measure or two some pauses between verses, and by orchestrating the blocklike chords of the original piano part.

The second song is to words by Heinrich Hart. It is a passionate expression of love. The name of the poem and song is "Cäcilie," who was Hart's wife. Her name is never stated in Hart's verses; the refrain of the song is the expression "Wenn du es wüßtest" (If you only knew), which builds in its ardent expression of love as it is repeated. Strauss orchestrated the song in 1897, partly to provide a song for Pauline to sing at his concerts as she traveled with him on his guest conducting tours. Once again the orchestration improves an already masterly piano song.

"Heimliche Aufforderung" (Secret Invitation) is the first of several songs that Strauss wrote to poems of Mackay, who also provided the text of the final song, "Morgen!" (Morning!). Much as Mackay might have wished Strauss would pick some of his socially conscious poems, these are both love poems. The first maintains the passionate tone of "Cäcilie," while "Morgen!" is serenely rapturous. Strauss made a beautiful orchestration of "Morgen!" However, he must have concluded that the highly pianistic writing of the accompaniment of "Heimliche Aufforderung" would defeat even an orchestrator of his abilities. A later orchestration by Robert Heger is lackluster. *—Joseph Stevenson*

Recommended:

○ **Strauss: Four Last Songs & 15 Lieder** / Hendricks, Sawallisch / 1996 / EMI 55594

○ **Dedication** / Heppner, Rutenberg / 1998 / BMG 63104

Five Songs, Op. 48 (1900)

1900 was a prolific year for Richard Strauss in his most consistently favored medium, lieder. That year, which also saw the opera *Feuersnot*, saw the *Ruckert* and *Uhland* cycles as well as the Opus 48. In the latter may be seen some interesting foreshadowing of the processes which would in a few years transform him from that period's most important composer into the most controversial.

Five songs make up the Opus 48 lieder, the first with text by Bierbaum and the rest by Henckell. The first, "Freundliche Vision," whose text describes an experience merging love and nature which is so intense as to seem dream-induced, penetrates the chromatic post-*Tristan* world, one which would reach fruition in *Salome* and *Elektra*; the floating vocal melody seems detached from the weighty accompaniment, as though taking leave of reality. The following "Ich schwebe" (I float), despite its title, speaks of a more earthly romance; firmly tonal save for the middle section, it speaks of youthful love and its sweet delusions; the sixths-dominated harmony and the waltz rhythm recall the Vienna of another Strauss. Yet another love, that of being alive, is espoused in the extrovert "Kling!" (Resound); here is the Richard Strauss of the tone-poems, the rapidly springing arpeggios carrying the music through abrupt modulations and equally abrupt resolutions. The last two songs are meditations upon winter, a subject to which Strauss was often drawn; as early as age seven he had made a setting of "Winterreise" (not the same text as Schubert's). No. 4, "Winterweihe," sings of the joys of a winter tryst, the warmth of the bliss indoors contrasting with the bitter outdoors; the key scheme is based on a systematic cycle of thirds, ultimately returning to the tonic. The last, "Winterliebe," speaks of a lover's journey through a wintry landscape, the thought of his beloved warming him along the way and seeing him through; appropriately, the tempo veers towards the martial, rendering the protagonist doggedly determined in his goal. The five songs are for voice and piano accompaniment. Save for "Ich schwebe," Strauss also provided alternate orchestral accompaniments as well. *— Wayne Reisig*

Recommended:

○ **Strauss: Lieder Vol. 1** / Fischer-Dieskau, Moore / 1991 / EMI 63995

Six Songs, Op. 56 (1903–1906)

After finishing the *Sechs Lieder (Six Songs), Op. 56*, of 1903–06, Richard Strauss' pen went dry for over a decade, as far as song composition is concerned, in part because of a legal action very nearly put forth against Strauss by the publishers of these very songs. It is an unfortunate thing that songs so intimate and rich as these six settings of four different poets' verses—the songs are dedicated to Strauss' wife and Strauss' mother—should be in any way connected with so sordid an affair as a narrowly avoided breach of contract suit, and, happily enough, listeners need remember only the songs themselves, all extramusical concerns having long since fallen by the wayside. Goethe, Henckell, Meyer, and Heine are the four poets represented in Op. 56, Heine being represented thrice. Very few of Strauss' many lieder are famous pieces, and these are certainly not among the best-known—no one of them can claim the popularity of, say, "Allerseelen" (from Op. 10) or "Morgen!" (from Op. 27)—but they are not at all impoverished of warm melody or well-designed harmonic treasure, and when counting up the song cycles as a whole, Op. 56 ranks high. An Andante, F major setting of Goethe's "Gefunden" (Found) opens the opus;

the piano's C octaves throb gently and then, a little later on, are transformed by the singer into a delicately rising dotted idea that eventually takes over the music altogether. Far more chromatically active, and somewhat faster, is the next song, Henckell's "Blindenklage" (Blind Man's Lament). Meyer's "Im Spätboot" (In the Late Boat) recalls, in D flat major, the kind of thick but quiet piano textures that made "Allerseen" one of Strauss' most famous songs. "Mit deinen blauen Augen" (With your Blue Eyes) is the first of the Heinrich Heine songs in Op. 56; the other two—"Frühlingsfeier" (Spring Celebration) and "Die Heiligen drei Könige aus Morgenland" (The Three Wise Men of the East)—were both orchestrated by Strauss, in 1933 and 1906, respectively. *—Blair Johnston*

Recommended:

○ **Strauss: Lieder Vol. 1** / Fischer-Dieskau, Moore / 1991 / EMI 63995

Vier letzte Lieder (Four Last Songs), for soprano & orchestra, Op. 150 (1948)

Strauss' *Vier letzte Lieder* is a set of four songs for soprano and orchestra, composed between 1946 and 1948. The texts for the songs are "Im Abendrot" by Joseph von Eichendorff, followed by three texts by Hermann Hesse, "Frühling," "Beim Schlafengehen," and "September." For many, these songs are regarded as the pinnacle of Strauss' output as a composer of lieder. For the most part, Strauss had composed his earlier lieder with piano accompaniment and refrained from writing orchestral songs, like those Gustav Mahler composed earlier in the century. In terms of style, the music itself continues in the idiom that Strauss used for his later operas, especially *Capriccio*. The melodies are long and sinuous, with subtle, chromatic harmonies which support nuances in the text. For one, "Im Abendrot," Strauss even quotes from *Tod und Verklärung* when the narrator of the poem expresses intimations of death. In all the settings of the *Vier letzte Lieder*, Strauss composed subtle music. As to the texts themselves, they deal with various subjects which interested Strauss at the time and do not necessarily have a program or single idea. If anything, they reflect poetry which attracted him strongly and inspired him to compose. The Eichendorff poem has personal connotations for Strauss, with its reflection upon death, as a couple gazes at a sunset. The remaining settings of Hesse have a similar sentiment, and suggest overtly the reflection of a composer upon his life. Strauss considered setting more of Hesse's poetry, and thus, with the possibility of more songs to be included, this set of lieder remained unperformed at the composer's death. As to the title, they were named *Vier letzte Lieder* after Strauss' death and were premiered posthumously by Wilhelm Furtwängler and Kirsten Flagstad in 1950. *—James Zychowicz*

Recommended:

○ **Strauss: Four Last Songs; 12 Orchestral Songs** / Schwarzkopf, Szell (cond.), Berlin Radio SO / 1998 / EMI 66960

○ **Strauss: Four Last Songs; operatic excerpts** / Della Casa, Bohm (cond.), Vienna PO / 2000 / Decca 467118

○ **Strauss: Orchestral Songs** / Isokoski, Janowski (cond.), Berlin Radio SO / Ondine 982

○ **Strauss: Four Last Songs; Orchestral Songs** / Fleming, Eschenbach (cond.), Houston SO / 1996 / RCA 902668539

CHAMBER MUSIC

Cello Sonata in F major, Op. 6 (1880–1883)

Though Strauss is known primarily as a composer of tone poems and operas, he nonetheless made several important contributions to the chamber literature, including the present work. Highly praised following its premiere, the *Cello Sonata* is dedicated to cellist Hans Wihan, with whose wife, Dora, Strauss fell in love prior to his own marriage to Pauline de Ahna. The Sonata is in three movements—Allegro con brio, Andante ma non troppo, and Finale: Allegro vivo—and showcases both Strauss' lyrical melodic writing for cello and his considerable understanding of the piano. Many of the formal difficulties evident in Strauss' earlier efforts, such as excessive repetition, are resolved in this piece as variation reveals itself as a burgeoning and important aspect of his compositional style. The first movement, in sonata form, features a multiplicity of themes in a kind of dialogue. Each theme is actually a group consisting of two contrasting themes: the first and second groups contrast with one another—per the typical practices of sonata form—but the themes are also internally divided, each group having one strong, declamatory theme and one of a more gentle, lyrical nature. The movement otherwise closely follows standard first-movement principles and is notable also for the incorporation of a skillful fugato. The second movement is a chorale and, as elsewhere in his music, Strauss is less comfortable with homophonic texture than with polyphony. The final movement is a humorous, canonic Allegro, marked by adventurous harmonies and a lighthearted and rhetorical use of silence that foreshadows Strauss' later works. Though the influence of Mendelssohn is clearly present, early indications of Wagner's increasing influence on Strauss are also in evidence. *—Alexander Carpenter*

Recommended:

○ **Strauss & Britten: Sonatas for Cello & Piano** / Ma, Ax / 1989 / CBS 44980

Violin Sonata in E flat major, Op. 18 (1887)

Chamber works were not of particular interest to Richard Strauss once he had passed the gates to musical maturity. The *Sonata for violin and piano in E flat major*, Op. 18, of 1887 is really the last original chamber piece to come from Strauss' pen. After the *Sonata* there are only a handful of arrangements of music from the operas, a few lost or unfinished works, and two unassuming pieces that date from many decades later: the *Allegretto for violin and piano* and the *Hochzeitspräludium* for, believe it or not, two harmoniums. The *Sonata* is a nice treat—the vast majority of late nineteenth century chamber sonatas were produced by the Brahms/Dvořák side of the great musical divide; only occasionally does one get to sample how a composer from the other "camp," in this case Strauss, felt about the genre.

The *Sonata* is roughly contemporaneous with the famous symphonic fantasy *Aus Italien* and the famous tone poem *Don Juan*, and the proximity is everywhere apparent in the music. Velvety melody and a certain refined manner of self-indulgence fill the pages of each of the work's three movements. However, in the finale the velvet is ruffled a bit, and that self-indulgence is in part replaced by self-willed urgency. The piano announces the beginning of the Allegro ma non troppo first movement with a gently heroic idea—like an echo of some triumph long past—whose basic contours will ultimately generate a fair portion of the movement's stock. A beautiful, flowing melody emerges some 20 bars later, but this is just a subsidiary to that opening idea. Another beautiful, flowing melody, this one in B flat major and marked espressivo e appassionato, serves as the proper second theme.

The second movement is called Improvisation and marked Andante cantabile. Improvised it is not: this is a very carefully crafted instrumental song. The finale begins with nine bars of sepulchral Andante introduction for the piano alone; Allegro is the tempo of the movement proper, whose initial, symphonic thrust is so compelling that it prompts the violin to explode with a frenzy of 16th notes. When everything has been said, the two instruments agree on blatant heroism for the close of the *Sonata*. *—Blair Johnston*

Recommended:

○ **Romantic Echoes: Strauss, Dvořák & Kreisler** / Kremer, Maisenberg / DG 453440

Igor Stravinsky

b. Jun. 17, 1882, Orianenbaum, Russia, **d.** Apr. 6, 1971, New York, NY

Composer: Ballet, Symphonic, Orchestral, Chamber Music, Band Music, Keyboard, Concerto, Choral, Opera, Musical Theater, Vocal

Igor Stravinsky was one of music's truly epochal innovators; no other composer of the twentieth century exerted such a pervasive influence or dominated his art in the way that Stravinsky did during his five-decade musical career. Aside from purely technical considerations such as rhythm and harmony, the most important hallmark of Stravinsky's style is, indeed, its changing face. Emerging from the spirit of late Russian nationalism and ending his career with a thorny, individual language steeped in 12-tone principles, Stravinsky assumed a number of aesthetic guises throughout the course of his development while always retaining a distinctive, essential identity.

Although he was the son of one of the Mariinsky Theater's principal basses and a talented amateur pianist, Stravinsky had no more musical training than that of any other Russian upper-class child. He entered law school, but also began private composition and orchestration studies with Nicolai Rimsky-Korsakov. By 1909, the orchestral works *Scherzo fantastique* and *Fireworks* had impressed Sergei Diaghilev enough for him to ask Stravinsky to orchestrate, and subsequently compose, ballets for his company. Stravinsky's triad of early ballets—*The Firebird* (1909–10), *Petrushka* (1910–11), and most importantly, *The Rite of Spring* (1911–13)—did more to establish his reputation than any of his other works; indeed, the riot which followed the premiere of The Rite is one of the most notorious events in music history.

Stravinsky and his family spent the war years in Switzerland, returning to France in 1920. His jazz-inflected essays of the 1910s and 1920s—notably, *Ragtime* (1918) and *The Soldier's Tale* (1918)—gave way to one of the composer's most influential aesthetic turns. The neoclassical tautness of works as diverse as the ballet *Pulcinella* (1919–20), the *Symphony of Psalms* (1930) and, decades later, the opera *The Rake's Progress* (1948–51) made a widespread impact and had an especial influence upon the fledgling school of American composers that looked to Stravinsky as its primary model. He had begun touring as a conductor and pianist, generally performing his own works. In the 1930s, he toured the Americas and wrote several pieces fulfilling American commissions, including the *Concerto in E flat, "Dumbarton Oaks"*.

After the deaths of his daughter, his wife, and his mother within a period of less than a year, Stravinsky emigrated to America, settling in California with his second wife in 1940. His works between 1940 and 1950 show a mixture of styles, but still seem centered on Russian or French traditions. Stravinsky's cultural perspective was changed after Robert Craft became his musical assistant, handling rehearsals for Stravinsky, traveling with him, and later, co-authoring his memoirs.

Craft is credited with helping Stravinsky accept 12-tone composition as one of the tools of his trade. Characteristically, though, he made novel use of such principles in his own music, producing works in a highly original vein: *Movements* (1958–59) for piano and orchestra, *Variations: Aldous Huxley in Memoriam* (1963), and the *Requiem Canticles* (1965–66) are among the most striking. Craft prepared the musicians for the exemplary series of Columbia Records LPs Stravinsky conducted through the stereo era, covering virtually all his significant works. Despite declining health in his last years, Stravinsky continued to compose until just before his death in April 1971. *—AMG*

BALLET

Agon (1953–1954)

When Igor Stravinsky's opera *The Rake's Progress* premiered in 1951, it was greeted in certain progressive musical circles as old-fashioned, proof that its composer was out of step with the times. Not surprisingly, Stravinsky was taken aback by the reaction, but quickly concluded that one way to avoid becoming irrelevant was to incorporate more modern techniques into his style. "More modern" was at that time practically synonymous with serialism, which had its roots in the 12-tone music of Arnold Schoenberg. The first major work in which Stravinsky essayed 12-tone techniques was a cantata, *Canticum Sacrum* (1955). Already, though, in the earlier *Cantata* (1951–52), Stravinsky had begun to assimilate the influence of one of Schoenberg's disciples, Anton Webern.

Stravinsky began his final ballet, *Agon*, in 1953 on a commission from Lincoln Kirstein and George Balanchine for the New York City Ballet. Because he interrupted work on *Agon*—first to compose *In Memoriam Dylan Thomas* (1954) and then the aforementioned *Canticum Sacrum*—each time he returned to the ballet, he found he had to rewrite certain parts as a result of the evolution of his style, particularly his increasing attraction to serial techniques. Thus, for example, the opening fanfare evolved over the course of three distinct versions.

The increasingly advanced nature of Stravinsky's music is matched by the plotless scenario he chose for *Agon*, which features eight female and four male dancers. As in *Canticum Sacrum*, *Agon* commences in a diatonic and fairly accessible vein, but progresses toward atonality. So, for example, as the fanfare that opens the work reappears throughout, it grows increasingly chromatic. With the tenth section, Pas-de-deux, Stravinsky makes overt use of post-Webern serial techniques. By the close of the ballet the music returns to the less complex language of its beginning, again in the manner of *Canticum Sacrum*. Even a cursory comparison with the music of Stravinsky's "Russian" and "Neo-Classic" periods strikingly demonstrates just how far the composer's musical language had evolved by the time of *Agon*.

The ballet's 12 movements are divided into four groups of three each. The first section contains Pas-de-quatre, Double pas-de-quatre, and Triple Pas-de-quatre; the second, First pas-de-trois, Saraband-Step, Gailliarde, and Coda; the third, Second pas-de-trois, Bransle simple, Bransle gay, and Bransle de Poitou; and the fourth, Pas-de-deux, Four Duos, and Four Trios. The second group is announced by a Prelude; brief Interludes precede the third and fourth groups.

There are a number of relationships between the various sections of the ballet. For instance, the music in the first set is reprised in the last number of the fourth, and the Interludes contain the same music as the Prelude. Some have contended that Stravinsky's pattern of "threes" is broken by the inclusion of the Prelude and Interludes; however, because they themselves constitute a collection of three and serve a prefatory role for the main sections, their role in the overall scheme is clearly integral rather than anomalous.

Agon was first performed in a concert version led by Robert Craft in Los Angeles on June 17, 1957. It was first performed on the stage by the New York City Ballet on December 1, 1957.*—Robert Cummings*

Synopsis:

Agon is the last of Stravinsky's ballets, and while it does not have a plot, per se, it has a very specific program that relates directly to its music. As a point of departure, Stravinsky and choreographer George Balanchine extracted moves as represented in dance diagrams found in François de la de Lauze's *Apologie de la Danse* published in 1623.

Only a plain backdrop is used for *Agon*, and the dancers wear rehearsal clothing. Twelve dancers in all are used, and the ballet is divided into three sections of four dances each, separated by a prelude and two interludes. *Agon* begins with four male dancers with their backs to the audience, facing the featureless backdrop. The first section is presented as a traditional *pas de quatre*, the first dance being performed by the four men, the second by two groups of four women, and the last by the whole company of 12 divided into three groups.

After a brief prelude, a *pas de trois* begins with two women and a man. The man breaks away from the women and dances a solo sarabande. With the galliard, the two women dance to an instrumental combination consisting of three flutes, harp, chimes, mandolin, and low strings in one of the most attractive of the musical settings. With the coda, the male dancer returns, and though the instrumentation remains the same for this dance, the music switches from a diatonic mode to gestures derived from a 12-tone series.

The first interlude is played, and a new pas de trois is begun; however, this time it is danced by two men and one woman. The woman departs after being held aloft by the two men. This leads to the "Bransle simple" danced by the pair of males to the sound of two trumpets; the entrance of trumpets throughout the score signifies the presence of male dancers. This is followed by the "Bransle gai," danced by the solo female to the clicking of castanets. When the orchestra rejoins the performance in full cry, the men return and close the section with a "Bransle double" (Bransle de Poitou).

The final interlude opens the last section, which opens with a *pas de deux* for a male and female. The male dances a series of variations, followed by another series danced by the female, and this closes with a brief coda. Next are four duos given by eight dancers in pairs, and finally, three trios danced by the whole company. With the repeat of the opening bars of the music, all but the four men who began the ballet depart, and the men return to face the backdrop, backs to the audience, just as in the start of the work. *—Uncle Dave Lewis*

Recommended:

○ **Stravinsky in America** / Tilson Thomas (cond.), London SO / 1997 / BMG 68865

Apollon musagète (1928; revised 1947)

Stravinsky composed this ballet in the latter half of 1927 and in January 1928. It is unusual in its strings-only scoring, its serene and somber moods, and lack of conflict. Stravinsky wrote the work on commission from the Elizabeth Sprague Coolidge Foundation (paying $1,000, it was his first American commission), and was allowed to select his own scenario. He had already pondered the idea of a ballet based on Greek mythology and now decided to fashion one centered on Apollo, leader of the Muses. His recently completed opera-oratorio *Œdipus Rex* might also have influenced his choice of subject, and in a more general sense the work fit the composer's Neo-Classical inclinations of the time.

In Greek mythology Apollo had nine Muses, but, probably owing to the specification in the commission that the ballet last no more than a half hour, Stravinsky reduced their number to three: Calliope, patroness of epic poetry; Polyhymnia, of mime; and Terpsichore, of the dance. The First Scene opens with "Apollo's Birth," which takes place on Delos. The music can best be described as having an epic, philosophical quality despite its serene and peaceful demeanor, though the faster tempo of the middle section, which represents the two goddesses attending the birth, offers needed contrasts and a measure of color.

Scene Two brings "Apollo's Variation," which opens with a cadenza for violin that does not break the generally somber mood. The next sections, "Pas d'action," "Calliope's Variation," "Polyhymnia's Variation," and "Terpsichore's Variation," offer a little more color and animation. Calliope's music is lithe and nonchalant, lasting about a minute-and-a-half. "Polyhymnia's Variation," shorter still, is lively and buoyant, yet even here there is a measure of restraint that serves to harness any tendency to break into joviality. "Terpsichore's Variation" is slow and emotionally detached. This is the longest variation of the last three. "Apollo's Variation" follows with new music, not repeating anything heard in the first Variation. At the outset the writing is for the full complement of strings, although a short passage for quintet eventually surfaces. Next, the adagio "Pas de deux" for Apollo and Terpsichore is elegant and serene. The "Coda," written for Apollo and the three Muses, features lively, rhythmic music. This may be the happiest music in the score, even if it is demurely so. "Apotheosis" is serene and recalls the work's opening theme. Here the music depicts Apollo leading the three Muses to Parnassus.

If the contemporaneous *Oedipus Rex* divulges Stravinsky's dark humor and tragedy in dealing with Greek mythological subjects, *Apollon musagète* is a ballet counterpart, though in an opposite way. *Apollon Musagete* shows the composer's peaceful and dignified side and features reliance on the major mode in contrast to the minor mode predilection of the former work. This is Stravinsky at his most restrained; yet within that restraint the composer finds a freedom of expression that is both appropriate to the subject matter and artistically satisfying. *—Robert Cummings*

Synopsis:

Scene One. The first scene opens on the island of Delos where Apollo is born to Leto, wife of Zeus. Soon the boy Apollo is seen standing before the huge rock edifice upon which he was born. There he casts off his swaddling garments and begins to live with more independence. A group of women on the island give him a lute to play.

Scene Two. Apollo grows toward maturity and assumes greater leadership. He is seen playing his lute and is soon honored by three of the Muses—Calliope, Terpsichore, and Polyhymnia. Apollo calls on each to state the art they represent and in response gives them an appropriate gift: Calliope (poetry) receives a tablet, Terpsichore (song and dance) a lyre, and Polyhymnia (acting) a mask. The three then dance, after which Apollo dances. When he is summoned by Zeus, he leads the trio to Mount Parnassus. There he begins ascending the huge rock (often shown with steps in later performances of the ballet). He then finishes breaking all ties of dependency with his mother and symbolically enters manhood. *—Robert Cummings*

Recommended:

- ○ **Stravinsky: Orchestral Works** / Saraste (cond.), Scottish CO, Finnish Radio SO / 2002 / Virgin 562022
- ○ **Stravinsky: The Great Ballets** / Markevitch (cond.), London SO / 1993 / Philips 438350
- ○ **Mravinsky Edition: Volume 8** / Mravinsky (cond.), Leningrad PO / 1995 / Melodiya 25197

Le baiser de la fée (The Fairy's Kiss) (1928)

Stravinsky was a longtime enthusiast of the fairy tales of Hans Christian Andersen, whose story *The Nightingale* was the inspiration for the composer's opera *Le rossignol* (1908–14). In 1928, when actress-impresario Ida Rubinstein commissioned a ballet from Stravinsky, he combined his appreciation for Andersen's work with a long-harbored notion of using melodies from the music of his compatriot Tchaikovsky as the basis for a new composition. The result was *Le baiser de la fée* (1928) or, in its full translated title, "The Fairy's Kiss, Allegorical Ballet in Four Tableaux, Inspired by the Muse of Tchaikovsky."

The ballet is based on Andersen's tale "The Ice Maiden." Stravinsky provides a compact synopsis of the story in his autobiography: "A fairy imprints her magic kiss on a child at birth and parts it from its mother. Twenty years later, when the youth has attained the very zenith of his good fortune, she repeats the fatal kiss and carries him off to live in supreme happiness with her ever afterward."

The sonic language of this ballet might be described as a combination of Tchaikovsky's opulent melodies spiked with a bit of 1920s dissonance, a characteristically colorful orchestral palette, and a hint of the emotional coolness typical of Stravinsky's neo-Classical style. Stravinsky does employ some Tchaikovskian sounds and instrumental combinations, but the textures are consistently leaner than those in Tchaikovsky's own ballets.

In 1934, Stravinsky condensed the nearly hour-long ballet into a *Divertimento* of some 25 minutes. Around the same time, he transcribed the *Divertimento* for violin and piano for his own use during concert tours with violinist Samuel Dushkin. *—Chris Morrison*

Recommended:

- ○ **Stravinsky: Symphonies; The Fairy's Kiss; Ode** / Jarvi (cond.), Scottish National Orch. / 1999 / Chandos 2408
- ○ **Mravinsky Live: Stravinsky & Tchaikovsky** / Mravinsky (cond.), Leningrad PO / 1993 / Russian Disc 11160

Jeu de cartes (Card Game) (1936)

Jeu de Cartes (The Card Game) is cleverly described as a ballet in three deals. Completed in 1936 for the newly formed American Ballet, whose choreographer was the young George Balanchine, the scenario deals with the game of poker, one of Stravinsky's favorite card games. The main character is the deceitful Joker, who fashions himself unbeatable, owing to his chameleonic ability to become any card. There are also other cards—Queens, Aces—and several card players portrayed in the ballet.

In the first two deals, the all-confident Joker dominates the proceedings, even if he does not always win. In the final deal, however, he is vanquished by a royal flush, ending his menace. Though the music is generally light, it clearly has a satirical side and the devious Joker is viewed by some to represent evil, perhaps the devil. Because of the growing tensions in Europe and the rise of Nazism during the time of its composition, many have also seen the ballet as a sort of allegory of the developing strife.

Jeu de Cartes contains several allusions to the works of other composers, a not atypical trait in much of Stravinsky's music. The second deal contains several notable instances: the first variation is related to the opening of the second movement of Beethoven's *Symphony No. 8*, and the fourth variation recalls Strauss' *Die Fledermaus*. In the Third Deal, Rossini's *The Barber of Seville Overture* is practically quoted. There are more than a few additional snippets from the music of other composers sprinkled throughout the score, including that of Tchaikovsky, Ravel, Delibes, and even from Stravinsky himself (the *Violin Concerto*, *Mavra*, and other works). But the main theme of the ballet, heard at the outset of each movement, may be the most remarkable appropriation since it appears to be a reworking or slightly veiled rendition of the famous "Fate" motto from Beethoven's *Symphony No. 5*. Near the end of the ballet, in fact, it appears almost unaltered from its form in the Beethoven symphony.

After the opening of the First Deal, the music becomes subdued and the work's episodic nature becomes apparent as a variety of inventive sequences and thematic ideas follow. Before the end of this deal the music works into a near-frenzy, then subsides once more.

After the work's main theme is stated at the outset of the Second Deal, the music retreats to a generally calm mood, then becomes more animated as the series of variations progresses. The Third Deal features the theme at the outset, after which the music never relaxes. A Ravelian waltz and the Rossini quotation suggest fun and satire, but also perhaps the deceptions of the Joker. Near the end, the "Fate" motif appears on the horns, then the oboes. The music concludes with the main theme asserting itself, but neither triumphantly nor jovially.

It should be noted that the quotations and allusions sound very much like Stravinsky, never like a reworking of the source music as the composer did in his ballet *Pulcinella*, fashioned from several works of Pergolesi. *Jeu de Cartes* is very much in the tradition of the composer's neo-Classical style, full of wit and brilliant orchestration.

A concert performance of the music typically lasts nearly 25 minutes. The composer conducted the first performance of the ballet, which took place at the *Metropolitan Opera House* in New York City on April 27, 1937. *—Robert Cummings*

Synopsis:

First Deal. The story line of this ballet is unusual since its principal characters represent playing cards in a game of poker. There are three players, who are not seen on stage, and a Master of Ceremonies. Plot development, complications, and all sense of tension center on the actions of the Joker, who confidently menaces the other cards in the belief he is invulnerable to their supposedly inferior tactics. In the first deal, one of the three players retires in defeat, the victim of the deft play of the wily and devious Joker. The two other players remain in the game, having held straights.

Second Deal. A shuffle takes place and the second deal ensues. Here the hand holding the Joker wins, with its four Aces easily trumping the opponent's four Queens.

Third Deal. Following the shuffle, the final deal takes place. Here the Joker is confident as ever of victory: he stands at the head of a hand, completing a straight flush in spades. He narrowly defeats one player holding a heart straight flush, but is himself finally vanquished by a royal flush in hearts. The Joker learns that he is, after all, not invincible and angrily hurries away from the scene. Yet the Master of Ceremonies and Joker return at the end to suggest that the game will go on. *—Robert Cummings*

Recommended:

- ○ **Stravinsky: Firebird; Jeu de Cartes** / Salonen (cond.), London Philharmonia Orch. / 1989 / CBS 44917

Les noces (The Wedding) (1923)

Les noces has an important place in Stravinsky's ballet output: it is a pivotal work, marking the end of his Russian period, and also the beginning of his Neo-Classical period. *Les noces* comes after the three main Russian-period ballets—*The Firebird*, *Petroushka*, and *The Rite of Spring*—and is the obvious result of Stravinsky's years of involvement with Russian folk music idioms. While *Les noces* has fewer direct borrowings from the folk tradition than its predecessors, it is, as musicologist Richard Taruskin has noted, the work that is perhaps most Russian: Stravinsky, so familiar with Russian folk music by the second decade of the century, was able to create his own generic folk melodies without reference to source materials. The ballet is one of Stravinsky's hybrids, a "dance cantata" that combines dance with instrumental music and solo and choral singing. There is not really a plot to the ballet; instead, it is a series of scenes depicting the ritualized preparations for a Russian peasant wedding. Stravinsky himself wrote the text, drawing on Russian popular texts and songs for his words. The piece is constructed in two parts, with four scenes. Part one consists of scene one, "At the Bride's House," scene two, "At the Bridegroom's House," and scene three, "The Bride's Departure." Part two contains the final and most elaborate scene, "The Wedding Feast." In each scene, simple melodies set texts describing the bride's anxiety, her commiserations with her bridesmaids, the parents' sorrow at the loss of their children, and the groom's anticipation of the wedding night.

Stravinsky began composing *Les noces* in 1914, and completed the short (piano) score in 1917, but took another four years to decide on the instrumentation. His original plans called for a huge orchestra, but he soon abandoned this impractical idea. He then intended to have a divided orchestra, along with folk instruments, that would perform on stage with the dancers. This plan too was abandoned. Stravinsky then began scoring the work for "mechanical" orchestra, including pianolas and cimbaloms; however, the impracticality of this scoring also became evident as Stravinsky realized the difficulties in coordinating mechanized and non-mechanized instruments, and in finding good cimbalom players. The final instrumentation consists of full percussion and four pianos. The pianos provide the pitched material, but are also blended with the copious amounts of percussion, resulting in Stravinsky's desired percussive, mechanical sound.

The music of *Les noces* is deceptively simple; Stravinsky often limits melodies to just three or four notes. *Les noces* also exemplifies Stravinsky's virtuosic manipulation of small melodic fragments or cells. These cells, or "popevki," are fragments of folk tunes—in many cases folk fragments invented by the composer—that are repeated, overlapped, juxtaposed, inverted, and reordered throughout the work, resulting in a seamless texture. Rhythms are simple, and the text setting is syllabic, but metric irregularity and shifting barlines create tension and subvert expectation pervasively. In all, *Les noces* is the apogee of Stravinsky's "Russian" period, representing his sublimation of the folk traditions that had interested him for years. Its austerity and mechanical character are forward looking, pointing towards forthcoming works in Stravinsky's "new," scaled-down Neo-Classical aesthetic. *—Alexander Carpenter*

Synopsis:

This ballet does not have a conventional story line, its subject matter dealing with the rituals and traditions associated with weddings in pre-Revolutionary Russia. This version, like the first of the three, consists of two parts and four scenes.

Part One. The first scene is subtitled "At the Bride's House," and its vocal text deals with the blessing of the bride, as well as with her aspirations and feelings about her wedding and married life. It also delves into traditions of dressing her and properly coiffing her hair. The second scene, subtitled "At the Bridegroom's House," opens with the groom's blessing and other preparations for the wedding, but also focuses on his parents' sense of loss, and expressions of support from friends and well-wishers. Scene three, "The Bride's Departure," depicts the bride's activities upon her departure for the church, as well as the ceremony itself and various festivities surrounding the event.

Part Two. The long, final scene deals with the wedding feast and its customary celebrations, which include drinking, dancing, and much other merriment. It also touches on the roles of the bride and groom, and there is a closing song celebrating love and joy in marriage. *—Robert Cummings*

Recommended:

- ○ **Stravinsky Ballets** / Ansermet (cond.), Suisse Romande Orch. / 1994 / London 443467
- ○ **The Igor Stravinsky Edition** / Craft (cond.) / Sony 46290

L'oiseau de feu (The Firebird) (1910)

The Firebird was Stravinsky's first major success, the first of his ballets to be premiered by Sergei Diaghilev's famous Ballets Russes. Its fantasy-like story tells of Prince Ivan, who befriends the Firebird and later summons the magical creature to aid him in defeating the evil magician Kastchei and his fiendish monsters.

Cast in two scenes and having 22 dance numbers, the ballet opens with the "Introduction," which is dominated by an ominous, searching ostinato, initially heard in the bass strings. The mood remains dark and mysterious in the ensuing "Kastchei's Enchanted Garden," but things brighten in the glittering instrumentation that depicts the appearance of the Firebird and in the "Dance of the Firebird," where you can almost see the creature flit and flutter. This music corresponds to the second movement in the 1919 *Suite No. 2*, the most popular of the three the composer extracted from the ballet.

After the Firebird's capture, the music turns dark and fills with yearning as the creature desperately pleads to Prince Ivan for its release, which he grants, thus gaining its favor. The music in the next four numbers deals with the enchanted princesses and is light and playful in the first two, reflective and sentimental in the latter pair.

"Daybreak" is vigorous and colorful, but conveys an ominous sense, a sense that continues when the Prince enters Kastchei's palace. The next several numbers deal with Kastchei and his retinue of monsters, and with the capture of the Prince. In these the music becomes threatening and dark, but without ever losing its fantasy-like character.

The music depicting the Firebird's reappearance to save the Prince again features a colorful, busy character. The dance of Kastchei's court and the famous Infernal dance follow, the latter a grotesque, rhythmic piece that many listeners will recognize as comprising the seventh movement of the *Suite No. 2.*

"The Lullaby" follows, featuring an exotic, lonely theme on bassoon. This section serves as the source music for the eighth movement. The brief "Kastchei Awakens" precedes the most famous music in the ballet—"Kastchei's Death"—which also comprises the *Suite No. 2*'s finale. It features a soaring, stately melody—probably the most familiar theme in any Stravinsky work—that grows grander and louder as it proceeds, crowning the ballet with an absolute sense of triumph. *—Robert Cummings*

Synopsis:

Scene One. This fairy-tale ballet is set in Tsarist Russia. Prince Ivan, son of the Tsar, is wandering through the forest one night. He comes upon the magical Firebird, who tries to hide, but is soon captured by him. She begs to be set free, but Ivan is reluctant to release the enchanting creature. The Firebird offers him one of her feathers, promising that, with it, he can summon her to his aid if ever he encounters trouble. Ivan agrees and releases the Firebird.

Later on, Ivan arrives at the courtyard of the ancient, enchanted castle of the evil magician Kastchei. There he observes 13 maidens emerging from the building to play in the garden with golden apples. One of these young girls—whom he judges all to be princesses—attracts his attention, and he soon becomes enamored of her. Stepping out from the shadows where he had been hiding, Ivan watches the maidens do a round dance, after which they reenter the castle to return to their captivity.

Disheartened by their sudden departure, the Prince decides to enter the castle to pursue the Princess he loves and the other maidens. He is quickly captured, however, by Kastchei's hideous entourage of guards, which include two-headed monsters. Kastchei appears and decides to turn his newest captive into stone. But the Prince remembers the magical feather he possesses from the Firebird. He waves it in the air and suddenly the Firebird appears. The magical creature immediately causes Kastchei and his monstrous toadies to do a frenzied dance, which leaves them completely exhausted. They are next lulled by the Firebird's magic into a deep sleep. The Firebird then leads Ivan to the source of Kastchei's power, a huge egg that contains his soul. The Prince smashes it and Kastchei dies.

Scene Two. Kastchei's castle disappears, freeing the maidens and the other victims of the evil magician—the knights who had been turned to stone. Ivan is reunited with the Princess, whom he takes to be his bride. *—Robert Cummings*

Recommended:

- ○ **Stravinsky: The Firebird; Fantaisie for Orchestra; Four Studies** / Boulez (cond.), Chicago SO / DG 437850
- ○ **Igor Stravinsky: The Great Ballets** / Haitink (cond.), London PO / 1993 / Philips 438350
- ○ **Igor Stravinsky: The Composer Vol. 9** / Craft (cond.), London Philharmonia Orch. / 1997 / MusicMasters 67177
- ○ **Stravinsky Conducts Stravinsky** / Stravinsky (cond.), Columbia SO / Sony 64136

Orpheus (1947)

Stravinsky's neo-Classical works turn to ancient Greek myth almost as often as they call upon musical styles from earlier centuries. It was perhaps inevitable that he would at some point adopt the tale of Orpheus, which had inspired so many important works from the Renaissance on, as the basis of one of his own compositions. Stravinsky wrote *his Orpheus* (1947), a ballet, while studying the music of Claudio Monteverdi. The influence of Monteverdi, composer of the first great opera based on the Orpheus myth, is indeed evident in Stravinsky's work. Still, as he always did in his neo-Classical music, Stravinsky integrated his disparate influences into his own artistic personality to produce something wholly original.

Orpheus was composed in collaboration with the choreographer George Balanchine. The two men synchronized their thoughts on music and action precisely, and when the score was complete and choreography began, Stravinsky attended rehearsals to ensure that their original vision would remain intact. Balanchine's Ballet Society premiered *Orpheus* in New York on April 28, 1948.

Opportunities for melodrama abound in the Orpheus myth; however, much in the manner of Monteverdi's treatement, Stravinsky's *Orpheus* is distinguished by nobility and restraint. The dynamic level rarely rises above mezzo-piano, and the tempi are similarly moderated. This restraint was partly dictated by the instrumentation; having assigned the role of Orpheus to the harp, Stravinsky carefully ensured that the instrument's delicate sonorities would not be overwhelmed in the texture; even the whooping string chords in the dance of the Furies are palpably tempered. At the same time, the establishment of this slow, soft atmosphere allows Stravinsky to rip the musical fabric to great effect. After a song to tame tormented souls, which has the echoes of a Bach siciliana, Hades relents and allows Eurydice and Orpheus to exit the underworld, accompanied by noble, eloquent string polyphony. A short, sharp crescendo jolts the listener to attention and is followed by a bar of silence, during which Orpheus unbinds his eyes and Eurydice falls dead. Ominous sounds from the strings lead up to the only truly fast and loud music in the score, which accompanies the dismemberment of Orpheus by the Bacchantes. This passage recalls the composer's *Rite of Spring* in its brutally shaped rhythms, stabbing accented chords, and cruel, off-center downbeats. The closing music, which depicts Apollo raising Orpheus' song heavenward, is reminiscent of the opening, lending an odd sense of peace to the work as it draws to a close. *—Andrew Lindemann Malone*

Synopsis:

Scene One. Orpheus is mourning the death of his wife, Eurydice, as he stands at her tomb. He wants to express his grieving in music and thus attempts to play his lyre, but it produces no sound. He beseeches the gods to comfort him, and the Black Angel of Death finally appears before him. Orpheus is then led across the Styx, the river bordering Hades. He is given a golden mask that blinds him and instructed not to remove it until his mission to find and return with his wife is completed.

Scene Two. This scene opens in Hades where the Black Angel leads Orpheus into the domain of the Furies, who halt the advance of the pair. The Black Angel instructs Orpheus to play the lyre, knowing the pleasant sounds of his music will calm the Furies and make them acquiescent. Although Orpheus is blinded by the mask, he manages to play the instrument and sing, the mesmerizing music not only soothing the Furies but attracting other souls consigned to the dark underworld. Pluto soon appears with Eurydice, whom he pushes toward Orpheus. At last the two are reunited and, hands joined, they depart for the world of the living.

But their journey is treacherous, rife with seemingly insurmountable challenges. Eurydice falls, and Orpheus loses his grip on her hand, and in his blindness cannot find it. His anxiety building, he removes the mask in desperation, unable to control his desire to see Eurydice. At that moment she falls to the ground, as if dying for the second time. Suddenly, Orpheus finds himself back in the normal world. He reaches for his lyre, but it vanishes. Soon he is surrounded by the Bacchantes, whom he cannot see, since he is once again blinded by the golden mask. They grasp at the mask and attack him, in the end killing him by decapitation.

Scene Three. Apollo appears at the tomb of Orpheus and holds the golden mask up high to declare Orpheus the god of music. The music heard in response to his pronouncement is but a faint echo of what Orpheus had performed. Yet, a lyre slowly ascends from his tomb toward heaven. *—Robert Cummings*

Recommended:

- ○ **Stravinsky: Petrouchka; Orpheus** / Salonen (cond.), London Philharmonia Orch. / 1993 / Sony 53274
- ○ **Stravinsky: Ballets** / Davis (cond.), London SO / 2001 / Philips 464744

Petrushka (1911; revised 1947)

Like the other two masterworks of Igor Stravinsky's early career, *The Firebird* and *The Rite of Spring*, *Petrushka* was written and produced in close collaboration with Sergei Diaghilev, producer-director of the Ballets Russes. Stravinsky wanted to refresh himself after the enormously successful *Firebird* by composing a *Konzertstück* (concert piece) for piano and orchestra. Piano *vs.* orchestra turned out to be a more accurate description, since Stravinsky eventually conceived of the piano as representing a puppet endowed with life, and contending with trumpet blasts and other violence from the orchestra. He titled it *Petrushka* after, in his words, "the immortal and unhappy hero of every fair in all countries." When Diaghilev paid a visit to Stravinsky in the summer of 1910, he immediately perceived the dramatic possibilities of the work, and they agreed on a full-length ballet exploring Petrushka's adventures, tragedy and death at the Shrovetide Fair of St. Petersburg. Alexandre Benois, an associate of Diaghilev's and a devotee of Russian puppet theater from his youth, was employed to assist in realizing the scenario. In May 1911, the score was completed and dedicated to Benois, who was also listed as co-author of the scenario.

Stravinsky borrowed folk tunes to illustrate the crowd scenes, used bitonal chords to signify Petrushka's dual existence as puppet and living being, wrote his own seductive melodies, and stitched it all together seamlessly with a genius for dramatization and flair for orchestration that could only come from Stravinsky. In 1947, Stravinsky revised the score with an eye towards concert performance, paring down the instrumentation, changing metronome markings and making other small revisions. Either version is more than adequate to get to know this marvelous work. *—Andrew Lindemann Malone*

Synopsis:

Scene One—The week before Lent, in St. Petersburg, 1830. It is Butterweek Fair, the annual celebration before Lent begins in St. Petersburg. The town square is full of celebrating people engaged in multiple activities. They are interrupted by the Showman, who presents his three puppets: the dainty Ballerina, the wealthy and sinister Moor, and sad Petrushka. They perform a short, mechanical dance in which the Moor and the Ballerina enjoy a romance at the expense of Petrushka.

Scene Two—Petrushka's dark cell. Petrushka is kicked inside by the Showman and tries to escape, but it is futile. The Ballerina enters his cell and Petrushka falls in love with her. He does tricks and generally makes a fool of himself to get her attention and, unimpressed, she takes leave of his cell. Petrushka, in a spasm of misery, pounds away at the walls of his room.

Scene Three—The Moor's room. The Moor is juggling a coconut and tries to break it with his scimitar. He fails and is convinced that the coconut is a god. He worships it. The Ballerina enters and tries to distract him with her trumpet playing and dancing. The Moor approves of her, and she is charmed by his reaction. He seduces the Ballerina to sit on his lap and get amorous.

Meanwhile, clueless Petrushka decides to "rescue" the Ballerina from the clutches of the Moor. They jump apart at his appearance. Petrushka threatens the Moor, but the Moor draws his scimitar and chases Petrushka around the room while the Ballerina politely faints. Petrushka escapes the room with his life while the Moor drags the Ballerina back to his lap and they enjoy a little more loveplay.

Scene Four—The Fair at night. The crowd is in a frenzy of varied activity. Petrushka runs out of the Showman's booth with the Moor in hot pursuit. The Moor catches Petrushka and slays him with his scimitar. The crowd is terrified. The Showman mollifies the crowd by picking up the limp gadget that was Petrushka, showing them all that he is, after all, just a puppet. The crowd disburses. Suddenly, Petrushka appears hovering above a rooftop alive, triumphant, and threatening. The Showman is terrified. *—Gerald Brennan*

Recommended:

- ○ **Stravinsky: Petrouchka; Le Sacre de printemps** / Boulez (cond.), Cleveland Orch. / DG 435769
- ○ **Stravinsky: Petrouchka; Orpheus** / Salonen (cond.), London Philharmonia Orch. / 1993 / Sony 53274
- ○ **Stravinsky: Petrouchka** / Mehta (cond.), New York PO / CBS 35823

Pulcinella (1920; revised 1965)

Before World War I, Sergei Diaghilev's ballets russes had enjoyed a tremendously rewarding relationship with Igor Stravinsky, both financially and artistically. In the aftermath of World War I, however, Stravinsky was struggling to adjust to his exile in Switzerland, and could think of nothing he wanted to compose or adapt for Diaghilev's use. Enterprisingly, Diaghilev presented Stravinsky with the work of the Baroque composer Giovanni Battista Pergolesi, with the idea that the composer could adapt the tunes into a ballet. When Stravinsky proved amenable to the idea, Diaghilev presented him with an old manuscript of Italian commedia dell'arte episodes featuring a heroine named Pulcinella, and suggested Stravinsky base the action on one of these stories. To sweeten the deal, Diaghilev assured Stravinsky that no less an artist than Pablo Picasso would design the sets, and that Léonide Massine, whom Stravinsky respected greatly, would choreograph. These inducements proved overwhelming, and Stravinsky completed *Pulcinella* in 1920; its premiere was given that May by the ballets russes in Paris, conducted by Ernest Ansermet.

The actual plot Stravinsky chose, involving jealous lovers, mistaken identities, and resuscitating magicians, is complicated and busy enough that Stravinsky himself admitted that the resulting work as more of an *action dansante* than a ballet, although it is subtitled "ballet avec chante" ("ballet with singing"). Stravinsky chose movements from numerous Pergolesi works (and works perhaps mistakenly ascribed to Pergolesi) to illustrate the action, and scored them for a small eighteenth century orchestra: no clarinets or percussion, and concerto and ripenio groups in the strings. Three vocal soloists form part of the orchestra, without portraying individual characters.

Although he distorted phrases and chord patterns in adapting Pergolesi's music, Stravinsky left much of the basic melodic and rhythmic content unaltered; Pergolesi, and his stock of bright, engaging melodies, therefore deserve much of the credit for the success of *Pulcinella.* But Stravinsky's contribution is equally engaging: *Pulcinella* is brilliantly scored, using modern string textures that would not sound out of place in Bartók, and engaging combinations like flute, oboe and pizzicato strings or (in an especially witty moment) trombone and double bass. A sense of carefree play never lets up through the score's bustlings and scurryings, and Stravinsky takes care to make sure that the instrumentation remains varied, and that the movements cohere to form a larger formal design. The result sounds characteristic of both Stravinsky and Pergolesi: eighteenth century music living in a twentieth century world.

While *Pulcinella* was a success for Diaghilev, it proved even more fruitful for Stravinsky: it eventually paved the way for his Neo-Classical style. As he was to write later, "*Pulcinella* was my discovery of the past, the epiphany through which the whole of my late work became possible. It was a backward look, of course, but it was a look in the mirror, too." *—Andrew Lindemann Malone*

Synopsis:

The story is set in eighteenth century Naples. Two young men, Coviello and Florindo, stand on opposite sides of the street outside the windows of their respective sweethearts, whom they have been attempting to court with mixed success. The former has had his eye on Rosetta, daughter of the Doctor, and the latter has focused his attentions on Prudenza, whose father is the elderly Tartaglia. But the young women are only amused by their tactics now and thus decide to douse them with water. The doctor comes outside and drives the drenched suitors away with his walking stick.

Soon Pulcinella comes along, plays his violin and dances to the music. Prudenza is captivated by him and hurries outside to wrap her arms around the handsome charmer. But Pulcinella explains he already has a sweetheart and drives her away. Next, Rosetta approaches him to make her play, and initially seems to draw little reaction from him. Soon he kisses her; unfortunately, Pimpinella, Pulcinella's betrothed, comes outside her house to witness their little intimacy. Pulcinella is able to placate his jealous, suddenly angry sweetheart. Soon Coviello and Florindo return and attack Pulcinella, who calls out desperately for help. Rosetta and Prudenza answer his cries and drive off their fumbling suitors.

After Pulcinella has composed himself, the two women begin fighting over him, but their fathers come out and take them back inside their houses. Pulcinella makes additional amends with Pimpinella, but soon confronts Coviello and Florindo again. He sees through their disguises of long cloaks but cannot escape the pair, who begin attacking him once more. Struck by a sword blow, Pulcinella falls to the ground, feigning mortal injury. The two young men are satisfied that they have avenged the spoiler of their courtships and depart with a sense of victory. Pulcinella rises to his feet and goes off, pleased his ruse has deceived the ruffians.

Four miniature Pulcinellas carry a life-size double of Pulcinella along and lay him on the ground. The lifeless figure is soon examined by the doctor and Tartaglia, their tearful daughters looking on anxiously. The doctor pronounces Pulcinella dead. A magician comes along then and informs the mourners he can raise the dead. With a confident, sweeping gesture of the hand, he commands the corpse to rise. To everyone's amazement, Pulcinella stands up, the essence of vitality. The magician then removes his disguise and reveals himself to be Pulcinella, while the other man is introduced as his cohort and lookalike, Furbo.

The tenacious Coviello and Florindo return, both disguised as Pulcinella in hopes of attracting Rosetta and Prudenza. Meanwhile, Furbo, also pretending still to be Pulcinella, attempts to make headway with Pimpinella. But Pulcinella, in a slapstick marathon, gives all the impostors a swift boot. Furbo, dressed in the magician's garb, convinces the doctor and Tartaglia that Coviello and Florindo would make fine sons-in-law, while the latter pair mend their relationships with the girls. Pulcinella, accompanied by the cap-waving four little Pulcinellas, is back with his Pimpinella, too, and the ballet ends happily. *—Robert Cummings*

Recommended:

- ○ **Stravinsky: Pulcinella; Octet; Renard; Ragtime** / Salonen (cond.), Kenny, Aler, Tomlinson, London Sinfonietta / 1991 / Sony 45965
- ○ **Stravinsky: Petrushka; Pulcinella** / Chailly (cond.), Antonacci, Shimell, Ballo, Concertgebouw Orch. / 1995 / London 443774
- ○ **Stravinsky: Le Sacre du printemps; The Firebird; Petrouchka; Pulcinella; Jeu de cartes** / C. Abbado (cond.), London SO / DG 453085

Le Sacre du printemps (The Rite of Spring) (1911–1913; revised 1947)

The day seems to have passed, thankfully, for at least one development sparked by Stravinsky's *The Rite of Spring* (1913): the concert review in ersatz, proto-Dr. Seuss-style verse, e.g.:

Who wrote this fiendish Rite of Spring
What right had he to write the thing,
Against our helpless ears to fling
Its crash, clash, cling, clang, bing, bang, bing?
And then to call it Rite of Spring,
the season when on joyous wing
The birds melodious carols sing
And harmony's in everything!
He who could write the Rite of Spring,
If I be right, by right should swing!

While lynching the composer—which the anonymous author in the *Boston Herald* of February 9, 1924 appears to advocate in his last couplet—seems a bit excessive as a pan, one must remember that such vituperations only added to the air of *succès de scandale* that had surrounded *Rite* since its Paris premiere some ten years earlier. Certainly, the impact of this legendary event (as well as similarly "colorful" receptions to the work elsewhere) expedited its recognition as an all-around seminal occurrence and achievement in the social history and art of the twentieth century. In understanding early reactions to *Rite*, it is worth considering that while Stravinsky was at a relatively early stage in his career, a cadre of older, well-known, more traditionally aligned composers—Strauss, Saint-Saëns, Sibelius, Elgar, and yes, Rachmaninov—remained active and retained a good deal of currency with audiences. At the same time, the scenario adopted by the *Rite* collaborators—Stravinsky, folklorist and artist Roerich, choreographer Nijinsky, impresario Diaghilev—was far from the usual genteel, sentimental, and romantic themes that had theretofore dominated ballet. This collection of "Scenes from Pagan Russia" (the work's subtitle) concerns itself with an exploration of nature, both human and that of the earth itself, through the rituals of renewal—ultimately, human sacrifice—of an earlier, "primitive" society.

The titles of the ballet's two main sections, "A Kiss of the Earth" and "The Exalted Sacrifice," as well as those of their internal divisions, make clear both the ritualistic, sacred, and inviolable progression of events reenacted via music and choreography, and the elements of that progression. Stravinsky skillfully sustains and continually heightens a sense of brutal inevitability over the span of the whole work while encapsulating more specific elements in individual scenes. The Introduction raises the curtain on the earth itself, the distinctive bassoon solo plaintively establishing a hushed, reverent mood. More complex colors—which Stravinsky achieves through extreme instrumental ranges (as in the above instance), special playing techniques, and endlessly changing combinations drawn from his greatly expanded orchestra—gradually emerge and expand, only to be cut off subito by a remnant of the original bassoon theme. "The Augurs of Spring" begins with one of the most famous chords in music history, a crunching bitonal sonority hammered relentlessly in a constant 2/4 meter metrically undermined by unpredictably shifting accents.

Comparable instances of such rhythmic and harmonic harshness abound throughout the work, these elements assuming, along with instrumental color, both individual and collective roles in a manner analogous to those of the characters. Like the musical elements Stravinsky uses in their portrayal, the girls, youths, and elders function together within the identity of their society, at the same time assuming and asserting individual roles in relation to one another. The action forges ahead in an increasingly frenzied trajectory, finding culmination—in a sort of primal equivalent of cold logic—in the charged, uncompromising sacrifical dance which ends both the ballet and the cycle of its ritual. *—Michael Rodman*

Synopsis:

Subtitled "Pictures of Pagan Russia," The Rite of Spring is a fantastic rendering of an alleged ritual held by tribes in prehistoric Russia, where a young maiden was selected for sacrifice to the goddess of spring. It is in a single act, divided into two parts or tableaux.

The first part, "Adoration of the Earth," opens on a barren stage whereupon several piles of loose stone are set. Male and female dancers, representing the "adolescents," sit immobile in separate groups. At the entry of the "Wise One" (usually an old man, but also sometimes an elderly woman or both together) the females rise and swarm about him. They bow as he commands quiet, and the opening oboe phrase is repeated in the orchestra. At the start of the "The augurs of Spring" with its famous pounding chords, the males rise and engage in an awkward, macho dance proclaiming their youthful virility. The females join into the dance, and pandemonium breaks out among the corps. An alarm is sounded at the start of the "Mock Abduction," and the females spilt off from the males, who become increasingly aggressive in their attempts to take possession of the females. Short of success, the males stop, and the call of spring is sounded in the flutes. Each male selects a female and lifts her over his head, and thus the corps departs, leaving four pairs of males and females behind.

The "Spring Rounds" are so executed, with the men straining under the weight of their burden, dancing low to the floor. The rest of the adolescents return, and the dance grows in intensity. However, when the spring call is sounded again, the whole company steps to the rear of the stage. The "Games of the rival tribes" break out among two groups of males in the foreground. As the Wise One returns, a stop is called to the games, which is at first ignored. But the men pay heed and the Wise One reenters ("Procession of the wise elder"). The music comes to a complete halt, the men fall to the ground, and the Wise One blesses the earth upon which the sacrifice will be held. With the return of the drum roll that opens the "Games," the whole company enjoins in a wild dance, and this brings the first part to a close.

In part two, "The Sacrifice" the females and Wise One sit at a fire underneath a scarlet moon. With the "Dance of the Mysterious Circles" the females whirl about half-consciously until a single figure is left at center stage. The men rejoin the company in the "Glorification of the chosen one," a wild dance celebrating her forthcoming sacrifice. The ancestors are summoned and perform a preparatory ritual of their own. Then the "Sacrificial Dance" begins, during which the Chosen One dances herself to exhaustion, and finally death. The men offer her body to the heavens, and surrounded by the tribe, they drop to the ground, concluding the ballet. *—Uncle Dave Lewis*

Recommended:

- ○ **Stravinsky: The Firebird (Suite); Le Sacre du Printemps** / Abbado (cond.), London SO / DG 415854
- ○ **Stravinsky: Le Sacre du Printemps; Symphony in Three Movements** / Salonen (cond.), London Philharmonia Orch. / 1990 / Sony 45796
- ○ **Stravinsky: Petrouchka; Le Sacre du printemps** / Boulez (cond.), Cleveland Orch. / DG 435769
- ○ **Igor Stravinsky: The Great Ballets** / Haitink (cond.), London PO / 1993 / Philips 438350

SYMPHONIC

Symphony in C (1940)

Just as Igor Stravinsky's 1930 *Symphony of Psalms* bears a dual dedication to God and the Boston Symphony Orchestra on its fiftieth anniversary, so does the title-page of the *Symphony in C* from ten years later, describing the work as having been "composed to the glory of God, [and] dedicated to the Chicago Symphony Orchestra on the occasion of the Fiftieth Anniversary of its existence." The commission had been offered to Stravinsky by Mrs. Robert Woods Bliss on behalf of the Chicago Symphony Orchestra in 1938, but it was not until November of 1940, with Stravinsky conducting, that the Orchestra could give the world premiere of the finished work. For, while the commission was certainly a welcome one, the actual progress of the work was interrupted first by a series of personal tragedies—the deaths of his wife, daughter and mother, during 1938 and 1939—and then, of course, by the outbreak of war in late 1939 that precipitated Stravinsky's emigration to California. The *Symphony in C*, then, is a composition whose four movements were composed in four different cities and two continents over a span of just under two years.

If the years between 1938 and 1940 were turbulent ones for both Stravinsky and the community of nations around the world, it doesn't show in the work: here is pure music, unruffled by the dynamics of personal emotion and, following Stravinsky's heartfelt beliefs on the subject, making absolutely no pretense at expressing anything except the fundamental drives of a composer struggling to come to grips, really for the first time in his life, with symphonic form. Stravinsky himself felt that there is some stylistic difference between the first half of the work, composed in Paris and Sancellmoz, and the second half, composed in Massachusetts and

California, but these distinctions of direction (or perhaps taste) are, after all is said and done, relatively minor, and in performance the Symphony comes across as essentially a very well-unified body of music.

Most of the musical narrative in the first movement, Moderato alla breve, can be traced to one use or another of a single musical idea. This cell, a rising step (either half- or whole-) followed by a falling fourth, finds expression in the very opening bars as a dramatic series of rising B natural octaves that, after a rapid crescendo, complete the motive (by rising to C and then falling back down to G) before the woodwinds take over to give, in slower note values, the whole-step form of the motive (D-E-B). Soon enough, the oboe expounds on the original form at some length over a background of constant eighths in the strings.

In the Larghetto concertante that follows, Stravinsky explores the riches of the orchestra by using a series of more or less solo textures. The Allegretto serves as the Symphony's scherzo; sharp timpani and violin strokes get the movement underway, but the woodwinds quickly take over with music of considerable wit and ingenuity.

A dreary Largo for bassoons, horns, and trombones opens the last movement. After about a minute, however, the tempo guisto alla breve body of the movement breaks in, and soon the three-note motive recurs that defined the first movement. During the coda the winds give this ur-motive a treatment in dense, slowly-moving chords, to which the strings add just one final comment. *—Blair Johnston*

Recommended:

- ○ **Stravinsky: Symphonies and Concertos** / Davis (cond.), London SO / 1994 / Philips 442583
- ○ **Stravinsky: Symphony of Psalms; Symphony in Three Movements; Symphony in C** / Tilson Thomas (cond.), London SO / 1993 / Sony 53275
- ○ **Stravinsky Conducts Stravinsky** / Stravinsky (cond.), CBC SO / Sony 64136

Symphony in Three Movements (1945)

Igor Stravinsky completed his *Symphony in Three Movements* in 1945. The first movement was begun in April of 1942, and the final work was completed a few months after the end of World War II. During this time the composer was engaged in contract negotiations to write film scores. Among the film moguls interested in commissioning Stravinsky was Louis B. Mayer, then president of MGM. Stravinsky had already written music before the projects were scrapped, and much of it found its way into *Symphony in Three Movements*. The outer movements involved wartime news footage, and the central movement was written for the appearance of the Virgin Mary in the film *The Song of Bernadette*, based on the Franz Werfel novel.

To integrate the different groups of material, Stravinsky chose to feature the piano and harp in separate, concertante roles in the first two movements, and then combined them in the third movement in an extended fugal arrangement. The symphony is a great balancing act, weaving together disparate musical ideas. The outer movements are explosive, indicative of the film score style common to American war footage. Ironic artifice, a signature sound in his music, is particularly understated in this symphony. Likewise, the middle movement, originally intended for the Virgin apparition, is suitably wrought with veneration, though perhaps not to the extent that would have pleased the film's producers. Stravinsky was not the sort of composer who gushed excessively, if at all. Any lamentations in the work are under total control. It was not in his character to express his feelings musically, and in fact, felt that music was incapable of "expressing" anything. That being the case, for him to depict Bernadette's shock and amazement at encountering the Mother of Christ would have sounded unnatural. The central movement is not rhapsodic or indicative of a human soul overwhelmed in the presence of a divine being. It is contemplative music, subtle and understated, and free of amazement. The outer movements are somewhat more successful in capturing the intended spirit of war footage. They feature tumultuous blasts of brass and driving rhythms but again the composer seems removed from the excitement and concern the music is supposed to convey, instead sounding rather bizarre and exotic. The focused intensity of a believer in either war or religion was too singular a nuance for Stravinsky to sustain for an entire film score. Ultimately, the result of this forgivable failing was an excellent and memorable symphony. *—John Keillor*

Recommended:

- ○ **Stravinsky: Symphony of Psalms; Symphony in Three Movements; Symphonies of Wind Instruments** / Boulez (cond.), Berlin PO / DG 457616
- ○ **Stravinsky: Le Sacre du Printemps; Symphony in Three Movements** / Salonen (cond.), London Philharmonia Orch. / 1990 / Sony 45796

Symphony of Psalms, for chorus & orchestra (1930; revised 1948)

Before the later stages of his career, when he began positively pouring out sacred music, settings of religious texts in Igor Stravinsky's catalog of works are relatively few and far between. There are, of course, the *Pater Noster* of 1926 and the *Credo* of 1932, but the only really sizable work in an explicitly religious vein that appeared before the *Mass* of 1947 is the famous *Symphony of Psalms* for chorus and orchestra that Stravinsky composed in 1930, to fulfill a commission offered to the composer by Serge Koussevitzky during the final days of 1929. The score of the Symphony is thus very appropriately prefaced by a dual dedication that reads, "this Symphony was composed for the glory of God and dedicated to the Boston Symphony Orchestra on the occasion of its 50th anniversary."

Like the *Symphonies of Wind Instruments* composed ten years earlier, the *Symphony of Psalms* forces us to step back and reevaluate our musical terminology. Here, symphony is used in more or less its original sense, meaning that which "sounds" or "sounds together," and without any reference to either the traditional multi-movement formal design that dominates orchestral music from Haydn's day onward, or to the overtly personal dramatic narrative that the symphony came to represent to much of the nineteenth century musical population. The somewhat contradictory title of the work reflects Stravinsky's self-proclaimed intent to achieve a kind of perfect balance between voices and instruments, neither one asserting any kind of superiority over the other. In a certain manner of speaking, we can relate this duality of expression to the same duality of sentiment indicated in the work's dedication—here is a potent realization of the idea, certainly dear to the composer's heart after the reaffirmation of his Orthodox faith in the 1920s, that man and the divine occupy two distinct areas of one and the same sphere as far as art is concerned. The three Latin psalms used in the symphony (Psalms 38, 49, and 150) are treated in a largely homophonic manner that both sharply contrasts with and, in an ineffable sense that lends a great deal to the sublime spiritual tone of the symphony, solemnly reinforces the more heavily contrapuntal texture of the instruments. On a technical level, Stravinsky sets that spiritual tone by omitting altogether some of the elements of the orchestra that we most closely associate with individual warmth and expression—the rich upper strings, the clarinets—and by recommending that the soprano and alto parts of the chorus be performed by a boys' choir.

The three movements are played without any pause. The first movement rides along on steady 16th note and eighth note figurations, on top of which the largely semitone-inflected voices offer their sober, slower-moving thoughts. The second movement is cast as a double fugue, the first for just the orchestra, the second joining all the forces together for Psalm 39. More kinetic in nature is the final movement, which contains the entirety of Psalm 150. Around the central, vibrantly energetic activity are two pillars—one introductory, one conclusive—of more serene, worshipful music. The second of these pillars is fashioned into an extensive coda that ends with an unusually spaced C major chord that, however difficult it might be to tune and balance (the first oboe, for instance, is given the E an octave plus a tenth above middle C), seems somehow to contain within it a reflection of the Symphony's ideal of superhuman clarity. *—Blair Johnston*

Recommended:

- ○ **Stravinsky: Symphony of Psalms; Symphony in Three Movements; Symphonies of Wind Instruments** / Boulez (cond.), Berlin PO, Berlin Radio Symphony Chorus / DG 457616
- ○ **Stravinsky: Symphony of Psalms; Mas; Canticum Sacrum** / O'Donnell (cond.), Roberts, Ainsley, Westminster Cathedral Choir, City of London Sinfonia / Hyperion 66437
- ○ **Stravinsky: The Composer Vol. 1** / Craft (cond.), Orchestra of St. Luke's, New York Choral Artists / 1991 / MusicMasters 67078

ORCHESTRAL

Chant du rossignol (The Song of the Nightingale), symphonic poem (1917)

Le chant du rossignol is the symphonic poem Stravinsky extracted from his opera based on a story by Hans Christian Andersen, *Le rossignol* (The Nightingale) (1914). Stravinsky began composing *Le rossignol* in early 1908 while he was still a composition pupil of Rimsky-Korsakov, and the first act of the opera was substantially completed by 1909. But the commission that led to the composition of *L'Oiseau de feu* (The Firebird) (1910), *Petrushka* (1911), and then *Le Sacre du printemps* (The Rite of Spring) (1913) delayed the composition of the second and third acts until 1914. By that time Stravinsky's style had changed nearly beyond recognition, and although Stravinsky tried to recover the thread of the composition, the music of the latter two acts of *Le rossignol* is different and far more harmonically advanced than the music from the first act.

In 1919, Stravinsky reconsidered the opera and decided to transform the musically homogenous second and third acts into a three-part symphonic poem. In order to facilitate this structural transformation, he dropped some portions of the opera's score and repeated others to achieve a symphonically balanced form. Stravinsky divided the music of the two acts into three unequal parts: the shorter "The Feast in the Emperor of China's Palace" and "The Two Nightingales," and the much longer "Illness and Recovery of the Emperor of China," with its substantial epilogue in the form of a funeral march. And in order to adjust the work to an ensemble without voices, he transferred the lines of the live Nightingale and the mechanical Nightingale to the solo flute and the solo violin. The greater ranges of these instruments in turn allowed him to expand and extend the accompaniment's textures so that they become more open and spacious.

The result is is neither a true symphonic poem—it's still far too loosely constructed for that—nor a suite from the opera—it's far too exclusive for that. *Le chant du rossignol* is a gorgeously colored, melodically extravagant, and harmonically adventurous work that sounds unlike anything else Stravinsky had ever written and anything else he was ever to compose. *—James Leonard*

Recommended:

- ○ **Boulez Conducts Stravinsky** / Boulez (cond.), Cleveland Orch. / DG 471197
- ○ **Stravinsky: The Firebird; Fireworks; Chant du rossignol; Tango** / Dorati (cond.), London SO / 1991 / Mercury 432012

Circus Polka (for a young elephant) (1944)

Most music lovers know that Igor Stravinsky was a talented composer of dance music—so talented, in fact, that he was once asked to compose music to be danced by an elephant. In 1942, Stravinsky was in America and struggling financially when the great choreographer George Balanchine came to him with such an offer. The Barnum and Bailey Circus had commissioned from Balanchine a ballet for Modoc, an elephant with outstanding talent, and gave the choreographer carte blanche in his choice of music. Balanchine knew he had his man.

Stravinsky, after verifying for some reason that the elephants in question were very young, set about composing a polka. He completed a version for piano in 1942; film composer David Raksin transcribed it for wind band so it could be played at the circus, and Stravinsky himself made a full orchestration in 1944. The polka was premiered at Madison Square Garden in the spring of 1942 in a production involving, according to the circus program, "50 Elephants and 50 Beautiful Girls in an Original Choreographic Tour de Force, Featuring MODOC, premiere ballerina." As one might expect, the *Circus Polka* is short, sweet, and playful, with bright melodies and bouncy rhythms. Stravinsky being Stravinsky, however, the work is far from a straightforward polka; there is only a single instance of the classic oom-pah polka rhythm in the work, and the tune it accompanies is not an original one, but rather, Schubert's *Marche militaire.* There are a number of little rhythmic twists and turns throughout the work; according to contemporary accounts, these posed no problems for Modoc, but baffled the remaining elephants at the premiere. Humans will no doubt find the music charming and carefree. *—Andrew Lindemann Malone*

Recommended:

- ○ **Carnival** / Batiz (cond.), Royal PO / 1994 / ASV 6124
- ○ **Stravinsky Conducts Stravinsky** / Stravinsky (cond.), New York PO / Sony 64136

Danses concertantes, for chamber orchestra (1942)

Stravinsky's *Danses concertantes* (1942) is scored for chamber orchestra, including timpani. The work is cast in five movements, and although commissioned as a concert piece, Stravinsky configured it as a ballet. Stravinsky had no particular scenario or subject in mind for this work, but its structure is such that it was probably constructed with the hope or expectation that is would be choreographed one day—an ironic circumstance, given that many of the composer's ballets were explicitly composed in a manner that facilitated their adaptation into concert works.

The music of *Danses concertantes* is characterized by syncopations, a blurred sense of downbeat, keys arranged in ascending semitones, and a certain independence in the musical lines—that is, the individual parts often sound soloistic. The *Danses concertantes* appeared in the years following the ballet *The Card Game* (1936) and the *Symphony in C* (1940), and musicologists have noted strong similarities between those two works and the *Danses.*

The work was indeed eventually choreographed, notably in 1944, 1955, and 1959. As with many of Stravinsky's ballets, the rhythmic complexity of the music makes great demands on both choreographers and dancers. *—Alexander Carpenter*

Recommended:

- ○ **Stravinsky: Apollon musagète; Concerto in D; Dumbarton Oaks** / Dutoit (cond.), Montreal Sinfonietta / 1994 / London 440327
- ○ **Ragtime: The Music of Stravinsky, McCauley and Milhaud** / Armenian (cond.), Canadian Chamber Ens. / 1996 / CBC 5159

Fireworks (Feu d'artifice), fantasy, Op. 4 (1908; revised 1930)

One of a handful of Stravinsky's early compositions with an opus number, *Fireworks* (1908) is perhaps most significant for its role in propelling the composer toward fame. Indeed, it was this work that caught the attention of the members of the ballets russes and led to the composition of the first of Stravinsky's epochal ballets, *The Firebird* (1910).

Fireworks is a short, brilliant showpiece for orchestra composed in just six weeks in late spring 1908. The work is notable for its juxtaposition of chromatic color and diatonic themes, a feature that suggests Stravinsky's debt to turn-of-the-century Russian symphonic style. In fact, Stravinsky composed *Fireworks* with the intention of showing to it Rimsky-Korsakov, his teacher and mentor, who died before Stravinsky could present the work to him.

While Stravinsky's early works are somewhat rigid and derivative, *Fireworks* is a harbinger of his compositional maturity. Among the more notable features are the masterful instrumental effects, which presage the virtuoso orchestration of *The Firebird.* The metric asymmetry and unpredictability that became a hallmarks of Stravinsky's music are present in the irregular barring, providing contrast to the regularity of the composer's earlier works. Foreshadowing another characteristic of his later style, Stravinsky develops the opening theme through the use of fugue and canon. *—Alexander Carpenter*

Recommended:

- ○ **Stravinsky: Orchestral Works** / Ashkenazy (cond.), St. Petersburg PO / 1999 / Decca 448812
- ○ **Stravinsky: The Firebird; Scherzo a la Russe; Fireworks** / Stravinsky (cond.), Columbia SO / CBS 42432

Ode, elegiacal chant (1943)

After settling in Hollywood in the early 1940s, Igor Stravinsky was offered the job of composer for Orson Welles' screen rendition of the novel *Jane Eyre.* While Stravinsky was at first enthusiastic about the project, his relations with the Hollywood moguls seem to have deteriorated and he eventually abandoned the project. During his brief period of involvement with the film, however, he composed some music for one of the novel's hunting scenes, and in 1943, feeling that the music was too good to lose, recycled it as the second movement of his *Ode for orchestra.* The *Ode* fulfilled a commission offered to him by Serge Koussevitzky. It was premiered in October 1943 with Koussevitzky himself leading the Boston Symphony Orchestra.

This "elegiacal chant," as the *Ode* is subtitled, is cast in three individual movements, the first and last of which are genuinely somber while the second is, to quote the composer, a "pleasant interlude" between the other two. The piece is written for a traditional orchestra minus the low brass. The actual scoring—at least in the outer movements—is more chamberlike than fully symphonic.

The first movement, called "Eulogy," opens with three brass chords that outline the lower neighbor-note figure of which Stravinsky was so fond. Fragments of pizzicati in the cellos and basses alternate with truncated versions of the opening horn/trumpet gesture before moving into the main body of the movement—a lush melody treated by the strings in a fugal manner against light, repeated off-beat figures in the winds. After an episode for solo strings, the winds and string section exchange their previous roles in the fugato structure. The movement comes to a gentle close as the clarinets wind toward the glistening, modified G major cadence.

Stravinsky's *Jane Eyre* hunting music takes the shape of an energetic and lightly scored scherzo that the composer calls "Eclogue." The horn section introduces the main motivic substance of the movement, including a rapid repeated-note figure that soon works its way into almost every level of the musical detail. Eventually the initial contrapuntal gesture of the horn section returns, only to dissolve away into the solo tympani and one last descending arpeggio in the lower strings.

During the third movement, "Epitaph," the sustained A naturals of the flutes are made into a fixed point against which a whole series of gestures from elsewhere in the orchestra—pungently dissonant oboes and bassoons, oscillating horns, and lush, melodic strings—are offered. When the A naturals eventually dissipate, the horns and bassoons take over in thin, two and then three-voice harmony. After a brief pause, the formerly legato strings take up a more articulated manner. Throughout *Ode,* Stravinsky focuses on his remarkable ability to bend a traditional tonal, triadic framework into a new shape; nowhere is this more plain than in the second half of "Epitaph," as the basic F major undercurrent is undercut by the insistent A flats of the bass line. Eventually, these A flats work their way up into the violins, only to slide into one last circular array of octave A naturals in the three flutes. *—Blair Johnston*

Recommended:

- ○ **Stravinsky in America** / Tilson Thomas (cond.), London SO / 1997 / BMG 68865
- ○ **Stravinsky Conducts Stravinsky** / Stravinsky (cond.), New York PO / Sony 64136
- ○ **Stravinsky Collection Vol. 2** / Atherton (cond.), Hong Kong PO / 2000 / Gmn.com 102

Scherzo à la Russe (1945)

Stravinsky originally wrote this work for jazz band on a commission from band-leader Paul Whiteman. Oddly, what the composer produced divulges little that is bona fide jazz, and perhaps that is one of the reasons for the work's failure in its initial guise. Stravinsky recast the Scherzo in this orchestral version in 1945 and found greater acceptance of it.

The work opens with a bouncy theme whose utter joy and sunny character exude a sense of Russian festivity in its lively dancing spirit. Stravinsky's orchestration is masterful here, especially in the theme's more splashy second subject, when the brass seem to overheat in their glee and threaten to turn the music sour.

In the ensuing first Trio, there is a nostalgic manner in the playful canonic theme, given by harp and piano. The melodic material here, like that in the second Trio, has been related to Russian themes in the composer's *Sonata for Two pianos* (1943–44). The main Scherzo section returns with few changes and after the reappearance of the flamboyant second subject, the second Trio follows. It is at first somewhat austere, but gradually turns more colorful and lively. The Scherzo returns to close out this buoyant, utterly charming masterwork. The composer also made a version of *Scherzo à la Russe* for two pianos in 1954, but it is the orchestral rendition of the three that is most commonly heard today. *—Robert Cummings*

Recommended:

- ○ **Stravinsky in America** / Tilson Thomas (cond.), London SO / 1997 / BMG 68865
- ○ **Stravinsky; Symphony in E flat; "The Firebird" Suite** / Pletnev (cond.), Russian National Orch. / 1997 / DG 453434

Scherzo fantastique, Op. 3 (1908; revised 1930)

It is one of those unfortunate circumstances of musical commercialism that, in order to help sell Igor Stravinsky's *Scherzo fantastique for orchestra,* Op. 3, his publisher prefaced the work with a programmatic description that, to this day, is widely considered to have actually been Stravinsky's inspiration to compose the piece. In reality, the *Scherzo fantastique* is a 12 to 15 minute work of pure music that Stravinsky composed between June 1907 and March 1908 during the final days of his apprenticeship to Nikolay Rimsky-Korsakov. The work occupies an important place in the composer's output for a couple of reasons. It is, to be fair, probably his earliest composition to really bear the unmistakable mark of a consummate craftsman. Perhaps more significantly, it was at a 1909 performance of the work that young Stravinsky first came to the attention of impresario Sergei Diaghilev, the man whose Ballet Russe carried the three theater works that thrust Stravinsky into the musical limelight (*The Firebird, Petrushka,* and *The Rite of Spring*) on its shoulders. It is worth noting that Stravinsky, who in later life came to disdain most everything he did before *The Firebird,* was never ashamed of the *Scherzo fantastique.*

It was a certain similarity between parts of the *Scherzo fantastique* and Rimsky-Korsakov's famous *Flight of the Bumblebee* that led to the *Scherzo* being used as the music for a 1917 ballet, *Les Abeilles* (The Bees), quite against the wishes of the composer. To make matters worse, Stravinsky's publisher concocted a program that describes the work as a kind of musical portrait of a day in the life of a beehive. As the program (still to be found at the head of the score) goes, the first part of the *Scherzo* portrays the buzzing and incessant, workmanlike activity of the bees, the slower middle section introduces the queen bee and the rituals of her mating, and the final section shows how, after all is said and done, the life and business of the hive continues unabated. The superimposition of any program at all is ultimately useless, as the work is far better understood as the large-scale fast-slow-fast musical form that it is.

The work begins with a gesture for muted solo trumpet that is strikingly similar to the gesture that opens the *Preludium* of 1937, after which the essential body of the *Scherzo*—brightly chromatic triple-meter figurations in the strings and woodwinds—stakes its claim. A little viola solo paves the way for the slower middle section, which features a quietly voluptuous melody that the flute (with oboe countermelody) sings against a gentle horn background. A crescendo builds as the strings take over this new music, only to dissolve away into the kind of rolling cello section accompaniment that Rimsky-Korsakov loved so much. After a rich series of unresolved pedal points that finally make their way to G major, the pace heats up. But this is no immediate reprise of the opening section, listeners have to wait until the clarinet ushers the solo trumpet of the opening back in for that. Before that can happen, the violins take off with wicked ponticello tremolandos and the woodwinds burst into a radiant kaleidoscope of sound. After the reprise, a series of leaping woodwind figures prepare a final cascade of overlapping chromatic gestures and rising arpeggios that, in turn, make way for a final cadence to B major. *—Blair Johnston*

Recommended:

- ○ **Boulez Conducts Stravinsky** / Boulez (cond.), Cleveland Orch. / DG 471197

CHAMBER MUSIC

Concerto in D, for strings ("Basel Concerto") (1946)

Paul Sacher's 1946 commission for a work to celebrate the 20th anniversary of the founding of his Basler Kammerorchester was Stravinsky's first European commission after moving to America. Stravinsky began the composition on the *Concerto in D* in early 1946 and completed it on August 8 of the same year in his home in Hollywood. The work received its first performance by Sacher and the Basler Kammerorchester on January 27, 1947, in Basel, and the work is dedicated to them. For this reason the work is sometimes referred to as the "Basle Concerto."

Written for string orchestra, the *Concerto in D* was Stravinsky's first work for string orchestra since *Apollon Musagète* (1927–28). It is approximately the same length and in approximately the same form as the *Dumbarton Oaks Concerto* (1937–38) and the *Ebony Concerto* (1945), which directly preceded the composition of the *Concerto in D.* All three works are in three movements in the fast-slow-fast order of the Baroque concerto grosso, and all three works feature the contrast of concertino and ripieno typical of the concerto grosso. In the *Concerto in D,* the movements are Vivace, Arioso: Andantino and Rondo: Allegro. The opening Vivace is roughly in sonata form; that is, the outer section functions as an exposition whose themes are repeated in approximately the same order at the movement but the central section is in a slower Moderato tempo. The central Arioso: Andantino features one of Stravinsky's few long, lyrical melodies for violins, punctuated twice by perfect cadences in unrelated keys. The concluding Rondo: Allegro is longer than the first two movements together and is in Stravinsky's typical middle-1940s spiky rhythm.

The *Concerto in D* was one of Stravinsky's last tonal works. Only *Orpheus* (1947), the *Mass* (1944/1947)and *The Rake's Progress* (1948–51) followed it. Although at the time of its composition it seemed to be another in the series of pastiche works Stravinsky had composed since *Pulcinella* (1919–20)—works that used the styles of earlier composers to furnish Stravinsky with the raw material for his compositions—the *Concerto in D* and *Orpheus* have come to be viewed retrospectively as the tired works of a composer for whom style and tonality had become a burden. *—James Leonard*

Recommended:

- ○ **Shadow Dances: Stravinsky Miniatures** / Orpheus CO / 2000 / DG 453458
- ○ **Stravinsky: Apollon Musagète; Concerto in D; Cantata** / Salonen (cond.), Stockholm CO / 1991 / Sony 46667
- ○ **Martinů: Toccata e due canzoni; Stravinsky: Concerto en Ré; Honneger: Symphony 4** / Hogwood (cond.), Kammerorchesterbasel / 2001 / Arte Nova 86236

Octet for wind instruments (1923; revised 1952)

Stravinsky's neo-Classical works in part reacted against what the composer perceived as ultra-romantic excesses in the music of German symphonic composers. However, these works must also be seen as a rejection of Stravinsky's own earlier stylistic thinking. The *Octet* was the first masterpiece in the composer's new style. Scored for flute, clarinet, two bassoons, two trumpets in A and C, and tenor and bass trombones, the *Octet* reflected Stravinsky's general reduction in instrumental forces during and after the First World War. Although the war and its dismal aftermath necessitated economical scoring, these events do not explain the composer's intriguing choice of instruments—he could have written for eight strings. It seems that Stravinsky was striving for an extreme (and un-Romantic) clarity of timbre and texture. As he explained in his 1924 article, "Some Ideas About my Octour [Octet]": "Wind instruments seem to me to be more apt to render a certain rigidity of the form I had in mind than other instruments—the stringed instruments, for example, which are less cold and more vague." Stravinsky further outlined his neo-Classical credo by stressing that the *Octet* "is not an 'emotive' work, but a musical composition based on elements which are sufficient in themselves." Accordingly, he chose classical forms commonly associated with absolute music: sonata form for the first movement, theme and variations (incorporating a fugue) for the second, and a rondo finale.

Stravinsky's application of sonata form in the first movement mostly involves surface features. A slow introduction gives way to a fanfare-like main theme, which in turn is followed by a development section featuring incessant running notes and fragments of the fanfare. The main theme then returns in full, but is performed only once, and the movement closes abruptly. A theme and five variations make up the second movement. The theme is octatonic, and does not point to any tonal center, although the harmonies under the theme strongly suggest D major. The first variation makes use of the first few notes of the *Dies irae* chant, immersed in flurries of running notes, and returns before the third and fifth variations. The second variation is march-like in character, the third a waltz, the fourth a can-can, and the last a fugue. Stravinsky closes the *Octet* with a true rondo, which opens with a constant pulsing accompaniment from one of the bassoons while the other plays the main theme. The ensuing episode opens with a brass outburst and trumpet melody, which eventually dissolves into a reappearance of the main theme. The second episode features the flute, while the final appearance of the main theme, reorchestrated and rhythmically altered, closes the movement.

The work was dedicated secretly to Vera Soudeikine (née de Bosset), whom Stravinsky had met in 1920, and with whom he had fallen in love and eventually married. Stravinsky conducted the first performance of the piece on October 18, 1923, the first time the composer had introduced one of his own works. *—John Palmer*

Recommended:

- ○ **Stravinsky: Pulcinella; Octet; Renard; Ragtime** / Salonen (cond.), London Sinfonietta / 1991 / Sony 45965
- ○ **Stravinsky: Mavra; Octet; Symphonies of Wind Instruments; Concertino** / Netherlands Wind Ens., Fischer (cond.) / 1998 / Chandos 9488

Three Pieces for solo clarinet (1919)

In the tradition of composers repaying their patrons with bits of music, Igor Stravinsky wrote his *Three Pieces for clarinet solo* (1919) as an expression of gratitude to Werner Reinhart. Reinhart had bankrolled the first production of the composer's *L'histoire du soldat* (1918) and was, furthermore, an enthusiastic amateur clarinetist. Since Stravinsky enjoyed composing for that instrument, the interests of the two men dovetailed nicely.

The first of these very brief pieces remains in the instrument's low chalumeau register. This register's cool tone proves an apt match for the meandering, introspective melody which at times seems ready to to fade into silence. It perks up just before its close, leading nicely into the second piece. Written without bar lines, this miniature opens with cascading, high arpeggios, moves into a middle section distinguished by hiccuping appoggiaturas, and brings back the arpeggios at its end. The third piece, a jazzy little essay that whizzes by at breakneck speed, recalls the "Ragtime" movement from *L'histoire*. Reinhart was no doubt pleased by Stravinsky's somewhat slight but always entertaining gift. *—Andrew Lindemann Malone*

Recommended:

- ○ **Stravinsky: Chamber Music** / Mares / HM 250073

Three Pieces for string quartet (1914; revised 1918)

Stravinsky completed his *Three Pieces for string quartet* in 1914, though they were not published until 1922. In the 1920s these pieces were not well received by critics, who were unable make sense of this fragmentary, seemingly incoherent music. Though they bear no titles, tempi, or expression markings, the pieces are actually character pieces of a sort. As musicologist Eric White notes, Stravinsky intended them as studies in "popular, fantastic, and liturgical moods." The music is difficult to play, as Stravinsky's score calls for some extreme effects from the players; the rhythmic vivacity and a certain disjunctness add a further element of challenge.

Stravinsky included orchestrations of the Three Pieces as part of the *Four Studies* for orchestra (ca. 1929), adding the titles "Dance," "Eccentric," and "Canticle." Further, Stravinsky used parts of the Three Pieces as themes or motives in other works, including the *Symphonies of Wind Instruments* (1920), the *Symphony of Psalms* (1930), and the *Symphony in C* (1939–40). *—Alexander Carpenter*

Recommended:

- ○ **Debussy, Ravel & Stravinsky: String Quartets** / Alban Berg Quartet / 2001 / EMI 67551
- ○ **Stravinsky: Etudes; L'histoire; Rossignol; Three Pieces** / Quatuor Intercontemporain / Erato 98955

Ragtime, for 11 instruments (1918)

Ragtime, *Piano-Rag-Music*, and *A Soldier's Tale* all date from roughly the same time (1918–19), and all prefigure Stravinsky's interest in jazz. *Ragtime* is a piece that grew directly out of the earlier ballet *A Soldier's Tale*, and the *Piano-Rag* for solo piano appeared less than a year after *Ragtime*. Stravinsky's *Ragtime* is scored for a small chamber orchestra of 11 instruments: flute, clarinet, two horns, trombone, bass drum, snare drum, side drum, cymbals, cimbalom, two violins, viola, and double bass. *Ragtime* is an extension of the "Ragtime" section in *A Soldier's Tale*; it is twice the length, with a larger orchestra, but retains some of the same essential features. The pervasive syncopations of ragtime music are set against an unwavering, regular 4/4 meter. Regular meter is normally an unlikely occurrence in most of Stravinsky's music, but in this piece the regularity clearly throws the syncopations into relief. Stravinsky became aware of the cimbalom in 1915 and sought to use it whenever possible. It assumes a prominent, almost soloistic role in *Ragtime*, much like in his chamber ballet *Renard*. As with numerous other Stravinsky works, *Ragtime* became a dance piece. It was choreographed in 1922 and 1960, first as a divertissement, and later as a duet. Stravinsky also created a piano arrangement of the work. *—Alexander Carpenter*

Recommended:

- ○ **Stravinsky: Pulcinella; Octet; Renard; Ragtime** / Salonen (cond.), London Sinfonietta / 1991 / Sony 45965
- ○ **Shadow Dances: Stravinsky Miniatures** / Orpheus CO / 2000 / DG 453458
- ○ **Stravinsky Conducts Stravinsky** / Stravinsky (cond.), Columbia Chamber Ens. / Sony 64136

BAND MUSIC

Symphonies of Wind Instruments (1947)

If we discount the tribute that Igor Stravinsky composed in 1908 on the occasion of the death of his beloved teacher Rimsky-Korsakov (the work was lost during the Revolution), the composer's long string of *In memoria*—by which he pays homage to some of the foremost musical, literary, and even political figures of the twentieth century—begins in 1920 with the *Symphonies of Wind Instruments*, dedicated to the memory of Claude Debussy.

Here Stravinsky consciously used the term "symphonies" in the old French meaning of a sonorous piece, as in "Symphonies and Fanfares for the King's Supper." The composition dates from 1920 and grew from a short chorale-like work he wrote in Debussy's memory; this became the last section of a work about 10 minutes in length, composed for a rather large ensemble of 23 winds. The style and melodism of the work usually results in its being listed as the last of the composer's "Russian Period" works, but because of its austerity this writer tends to regard it as being the first important indication that Stravinsky was ready to shift to an aesthetic that leaves behind sensual appeal. He would soon find the style of neo-Classicism; meantime, there is a sense that the idea behind the work is the realization of the harmonic clashes that result from Stravinsky's usual method of mixing two separate chords. The work is of more than just historical interest; Stravinsky was constantly treading new ground here, with effective even if not lovable music. The score was revised in 1947, presumably to obtain copyright for the composer in the U.S.

Obviously the sound of a piece for 23 woodwinds is something that the audience at the 1921 London premiere of the work (with Serge Koussevitzky at the helm) found quite disconcerting (many audiences today still find it so), but coincident with that textural streamlining is an even more significant and startling architectural streamlining: the entire work is based on a handful of sharply defined themes and motives that Stravinsky makes little or no attempt to connect in any way; he instead chooses to isolate them via a very careful and almost thematic use of silence. As a result of this trimming of "extraneous" detail, the work is extremely brief. *—AMG*

Recommended:

- ○ **Stravinsky: Symphony of Psalms; Symphony in Three Movements; Symphonies of Wind Instruments** / Boulez (cond.), Berlin PO / DG 457616
- ○ **Stravinsky: Symphonies and Concertos** / Waart (cond.), Netherlands Wind Ens. / 1994 / Philips 442583
- ○ **Stravinsky: Mavra; Octet; Symphonies of Wind Instruments; Concertino** / Fischer (cond.), Netherlands Wind Ens. / 1998 / Chandos 9488
- ○ **The Igor Stravinsky Edition** / Craft (cond.) / Sony 46290

KEYBOARD

Five Easy Pieces for piano, 4 hands (1917)

In November 1916, wealthy Parisian patroness Princesse Eugène Murat approached Stravinsky with an offer to engrave his *Three Pieces for String Quartet*. Stravinsky replied that the *Three Pieces* were not available for publication, but instead brokered a package deal for the publication of several short pieces, including *Renard*, the *Berceuses du chat*, and the yet unwritten *Five Easy Pieces* for piano duet. The Princesse accepted this hard bargain; publication was set up through the Geneva-based house run by the concert promoter Adolphe Henn. Stravinsky then returned to his home in Morges in order to complete the promised pieces. Work was delayed somewhat by an attack of nerves that left Stravinsky practically paralyzed. On January 4, 1917 however, Stravinsky was well enough to proceed with the Andante that opens the set. All of the pieces were written in one day, Balalaika on February 6, Napolitana on February 21, and the Galop on February 28. The Española was added on April 3, literally one day before the manuscript was shipped off to Henn in Geneva. Publication occurred later in the year, and the work was premiered in Paris on February 9, 1918.

The pieces are designed for teacher and student, the "easy" part being in the *Primo* and the more difficult texture in the *Secundo*, as in the *Three Easy Pieces* of 1914–15 that were published separately at the same time. The whole work is sufficiently easy that a single pianist can play both parts without requiring much adaptation. The opening Andante is a portrait of Erik Satie and owes something to his style; its rainy day melancholy is simply stated and directly communicative. Española may hearken back to Stravinsky's visit to Spain the previous summer. Balalaika, a fond keepsake of Russian reminiscence, is characterized by its strummed accompaniment. Napolitana was written prior to Stravinsky's first visit to Italy, and draws from surface elements of Neapolitan style. A clever, wrong-note snatch of the popular song "Funiculì, Funiculà" is heard, and just before the conclusion, Stravinsky incorporates an interesting innovation: he allows the *Primo* to drop out, leaving behind six bars of the rolling accompaniment in a "proto-minimal" texture. The concluding Galop has a prior history in that it is based on sketches made at the time of the 1914–15 set. The older sketches are signified as a can-can, and outside of its tonally wayward accompaniment, the piece is a sort of French music hall ditty with a Russian accent.

Stravinsky recast the first four of these *Easy Pieces* in orchestral garb as the *Suite No. 1 for Orchestra* (1925). Perhaps recalling the origin of the Galop, he split this orchestration off from the rest, adding it to the earlier set of *Three Easy Pieces* to form the *Suite No. 2 for Orchestra* (first performed in 1926). In their original form, however, these little works have gone on to delight several generations of piano students, teachers and amateurs, despite the rather canny circumstances behind their creation. *—Uncle Dave Lewis*

Recommended:

- ○ **Stravinsky: Music for Piano (1911–1942)** / Karis / 1994 / Bridge 9051

Piano-Rag-Music (1919)

Piano-Rag Music was composed just as the European craze for American popular music was reaching a fever peak, with the arrival of a spate of American jazz combos in Europe around 1920. Yet Stravinsky's knowledge of the jazz idiom until this point was mostly limited to printed scores brought to him from the United States by his associate, Ansermet. This three-minute solo piano work, written for Artur Rubinstein, aims at a cubist impression rather than at a direct imitation of the style.

Like the *Ragtime for Eleven Instruments* (1919) and *L'histoire du soldat*, (1918) *Piano-Rag Music* neatly reconciles the ostinati, shifting accents, and bitonal passages of Stravinsky's Russian manner with the repetitive patterns, syncopations and colorful harmonies of the jazz idiom. Indeed, the piece is remarkable for its bitonal passages (with, for example, the left hand in C and the right in F sharp major), chord clusters, a three-note basso ostinato in the middle sections, and a percussive piano style. Moreover, Stravinsky achieves an improvisatory feeling by dispensing with meters entirely during half of the piece, and employing only irregular ones in the remainder. Both light-hearted and austere, the work reveals the influence of Stravinsky's contemporary Erik Satie. *—Brian Wise*

Recommended:

- ○ **Stravinsky: The Composer Vol. 5** / Wait / 1993 / MusicMasters 67110
- ○ **Stravinsky: Music for Piano (1911–1942)** / Karis / 1994 / Bridge 9051

Tango (1940)

Soon after Stravinsky fled Europe in the 1930s and settled in sunny Hollywood, he found himself struggling for money. The royalties which had provided him a steady income in France were not forthcoming in America due to legal ambiguities, and, with his limited command of English, he was unable to find a teaching position. Faced with uncertain finances, Stravinsky wrote a number of works with the explicit intention of making a decent sum.

The *Tango* (1940) is one such example. In this work, Stravinsky seems to view the atmosphere of a tango as its essence; he virtually ignores the tango's distinctive rhythm, substituting near-constant syncopation in 4/4 time. After a terse, dark introduction, a succession of melodies tinged with blue notes and sighing cadences blossoms forth. A rumbling, dense counterpoint passage seems drawn downward; a major-mode trio section does nothing to dispel the world-weary mood. The opening melodies return, followed by a repetition of the introduction, which closes the piece. The *Tango* is slight but charming, and its commercial appeal is at once obvious. Seeking maximum return for his efforts, Stravinsky intended to transcribe the *Tango*, originally written for piano, for several different ensembles, including jazz band. Ultimately, he prepared three arrangements: two for chamber orchestra, and one for violin and piano. *—Andrew Lindemann Malone*

Recommended:

- ○ **Stravinsky: Piano Music** / Hill / 2000 / Naxos 553871
- ○ **Stravinsky: Music for Piano (1911–1942)** / Karis / 1994 / Bridge 9051

CONCERTO

Capriccio, for piano & orchestra (1929; revised 1949)

After he had premiered his *Concerto for Piano and Wind Instruments* in 1924, Stravinsky had played that work about 40 times in Europe and America. By late 1928, he decided that he needed a new solo vehicle for his piano playing and Stravinsky began composing his *Capriccio for piano and orchestra* after Christmas of that year. The work was completed in September, 1929, and premiered in Paris with Ernest Ansermet conducting the Paris Symphony Orchestra and the composer at the piano.

The *Capriccio* was composed after Stravinsky had completed his "Tchaikovsky" ballet *Le Baiser de la fée*, a work whose music is based on the songs and piano piece of Tchaikovsky, and the same spirit of melodic refinement and rhythmic gracefulness permeates the three movements of the capriccio. Having written the Allegro capriccioso ma tempo giusto, the whole work took its title from that movement. Despite being scored for three each of flutes, oboes, and clarinet, two bassoons, hour horns, two trumpets, three trombones, tuba, and timpani plus ripieno and concertino strings without second violins, the capriccio is a much lighter and more self-consciously charming work than the weighty *Piano Concerto*. It is also a more stylish work; in his writings about the capriccio, Stravinsky mentions Weber and Mendelssohn, "the two Beau Brummels" of music and his writing for the piano has some of their effervescent spirit as well.

The opening movement of the Capriccio starts with a slow-sounding introduction which is integrated the Presto body of the movement. This introduction returns at the close of the movement to give the impression of a rounded ABA form. The central movement is marked Andante rapsodico, but the expressive indication has more to do with the apparent emotionality of the themes than the structure of the music which is in a clear ABA form. The Andante capriccioso finale is the lightest and fastest of the three movements and, again, the expressive marking has more to do with the cheerful and witty quality of the themes than with the form of the music which is in rondo form.

The Capriccio is a huge step forward in Stravinsky's writing for the piano. In place of the heavy rhythms and thick textures of the *Piano Concerto*, he wrote for the piano in a manner much more in line with his manner of composing for winds and brass—that is, more gracefully and elegantly. *—James Leonard*

Recommended:

- ○ **The Music of Stravinsky** / Craft (cond.), Entremont, Columbia SO / 2000 / Sony 64085
- ○ **Ravel: Piano Concerto; Le Tombeau; Stravinsky: Capriccio for Piano & Orchestra** / Haas, Fricsay (cond.), Berlin RIAS SO / 1998 / DG 459010

Concerto for chamber orchestra in E flat major ("Dumbarton Oaks") (1938)

Considered by some to be a minor work, the *Concerto in E flat, "Dumbarton Oaks"* for chamber orchestra is representative of Stravinsky's "neo-Classic" period, which spanned the middle third of his extraordinarily creative life. The piece was commissioned in 1937 by Mr. And Mrs. Robert Woods Bliss of Dumbarton Oaks, the name of the Bliss' estate in Washington, D.C., in celebration of the couple's 30th wedding anniversary in 1938. At the time of the commission, Stravinsky had been diagnosed with tuberculosis and sent to a Swiss sanatorium to join his wife and two daughters, who were also ill. Poor health was to claim the lives of his eldest daughter, Ludmila, in 1938, and his wife, Katerina, in March 1939. While in Switzerland, Stravinsky immersed himself in the music of Bach while he wrote the *Concerto in E flat*. Because the composer's illness prevented him from traveling, the premiere performance, given on May 8, 1938, in Washington D.C., was conducted by Nadia Boulanger. As in numerous other of Stravinsky's neo-Classical works, he recapitulates forms and gestures of the Western musical tradition. Thus, the *Dumbarton Oaks Concerto* self-consciously becomes didactic music-about-music: an essay on the art of writing a concerto in the Baroque style realized in modern harmonic, rhythmic, and melodic idioms. Cast in three movements marked Tempo giusto, Allegretto, and Con moto, the *Concerto in E flat* deliberately evokes the style of J.S. Bach's *Brandenburg Concertos*. The resemblance of the beginning of Stravinsky's concerto to the first movement of Bach's *Brandenburg No. 3* is particularly striking. Concerning this close relationship, Stravinsky noted, "I do not think that Bach would have begrudged me the loan of these ideas and materials, as borrowing in this way was something he liked to do himself."

From the outset of the first movement, string outbursts frame and support the many solo woodwind excursions, and nearly every instrument has a chance to come to the foreground. The Concerto grosso contrasts of concertino and ripieno, and fugato writing permeate the movement, which ends with a slow, homophonic coda. A hesitant, repeated string figure marks the opening of the contrasting Allegretto, an ABA' structure with coda that begins with a much more sparse texture than in the first movement. More dense, the B section is built around a two-note ostinato accompaniment in the strings. A prominent flute part differentiates the return of the A section from the opening of the movement, and creates a busier atmosphere. Woodwinds punctuate a constant, slow staccato pulse in the cellos at the beginning of the third movement. In the central section, the bassoon fills a similar accompanimental role, but in a lighter and less detached manner. The cello returns, and repeated ostinato figures and stretto entrances of a short melody, both Baroque characteristics, propel the finale to its abrupt ending. *—John Palmer*

Recommended:

- ○ **Stravinsky: Ebony Concerto; Concerto in E flat; Berg: Chamber Concerto** / Boulez (cond.), InterContemporain Ens. / 1982 / DG 447405

Concerto for piano & wind instruments (1924; revised 1950)

In the early 1920s, the recent war having wreaked havoc on his personal finances, Igor Stravinsky set about ensuring the future security of his family by exploring avenues of musical life more immediately lucrative. One result of this was a rich series of works featuring the pianoforte in a solo role, designed quite specifically with Stravinsky himself as the pianist. In 1921, he fashioned three extracts from the ballet *Petrushka* into the *Trois Mouvements de Petrouchka* for Artur Rubinstein. Finding, however, that he could not successfully bring off so technically demanding a work, the composer made certain that all of his forthcoming pianoforte compositions lay well within the realm of his own technical capabilities. The *Concerto for Piano and Winds* was composed in 1923–24 for performance at one of Koussevitzky's Paris Concerts. It is the first representative in a new line of works that would eventually reach into the last decade of his active life, though by the time of *Movements* in 1959, Stravinsky was no longer in a position to give the premiere himself. In addition, the concerto is the first large-scale concert work to put to use Stravinsky's "new" neo-Classical style. Since the premiere at the Paris Opera House on May 22, 1924, it has become one of his best-known and most dearly-loved works.

Perhaps the most immediately striking aspect of the concerto, ignoring the strong affinities that the basic musical gestures have to those of the Baroque era, is the removal of the string section from the ensemble. Only the string basses remain, Stravinsky having decided that the same all-wind ensemble that he had already used in the *Symphonies of Wind Instruments*, the Octet, and, for all intents and purposes, the opera *Mavra* better complemented the timbre of the pianoforte.

The work is in three movements: 1) Largo–Allegro; 2) Larghissimo; and 3) Allegro. After the mock-grandiose, fundamentally Baroque Largo orchestral introduction, the piano enters with a rhythmically energized theme from which almost all the material of the movement is drawn in one way or another. Following the precedent set in his last few piano works, the piano is used in a very percussive manner. After a very long absence, sonata form, or something very like it, has returned to Stravinsky's bag of tricks in this movement. The Largo introduction comes back, much modified, as a coda. The piano begins the second movement alone, offering a lyric theme whose gentle steadiness is balanced by thick, ponderous chords beneath. Stravinsky makes room for two cadenzas as the movement unfolds. At the end of the final Allegro movement, the Largo introduction to the first movement is heard from again, only to this time fade away into a pause that suddenly bursts into the Vivo plunge to the final C major cadence. In 1950, Stravinsky made a revision of the concerto, making a few small changes of instrumentation and many more substantial alterations to the metronome and tempo markings; in the 1950 version, the title of the second movement has been changed from Larghissimo to Largo. *—Blair Johnston*

Recommended:

- ○ **Stephen Kovacevich 2** / Kovacevich, Davis (cond.), BBC SO / 1999 / Philips 456880

Ebony Concerto, for clarinet & jazz band (1945)

Stravinsky wrote his *Ebony Concerto* for jazz bandleader Woody Herman, who premiered it with his ensemble the Thundering Herd in March 1946. It is modeled on the Baroque concerto grosso and obviously incorporates jazz styles popular during the wartime era. Cast in three very short movements—the whole work lasting about nine minutes—it is scored for clarinet and jazz band.

Ebony Concerto opens with a lively Allegro moderato, where the themes are rhythmic and quite jerky in their unpredictability. Everything sounds Stravinskyan, though, the jazz elements fusing naturally with the composer's neo-Classical style. The most lyrical-sounding theme comes on clarinet and trombone, recalling a theme in ragtime from the composer's *L'histoire du soldat*. A reprise of the main material makes up the second half of the first movement.

The middle panel is a bluesy Andante, an almost funereal piece in its lazy, dark mists and lower-range writing for the clarinet. The brief middle section is perky and playful, but the main theme returns in all its delicious gloom to close out the movement. The finale, marked Moderato–Con moto–Moderato–Vivo, begins slowly and darkly then turns lively when a cool, bluesy theme is played by clarinet. The music from the opening returns before the playful Vivo section is presented. The work ends slowly, with the kind of tranquil mood, if not the sound of the first movement's close from the composer's contemporary *Symphony in 3 Movements*. *—Robert Cummings*

Recommended:

- ○ **Stravinsky Conducts Stravinsky** / Stravinsky (cond.), Goodman, Columbia Jazz Combo / Sony 64136
- ○ **Stravinsky: Violin Concerto; Ebony Concerto; The Flood** / Craft (cond.), Whight, London Philharmonia Orch. / 1998 / MusicMasters 67195

Violin Concerto in D major (1931)

Stravinsky composed the *Violin Concerto* (1931) at the instigation of his friend Willy Strecker, head of the music publishing house of Schotts Söhne in Mainz. Strecker and the young Russian-American violinist Samuel Dushkin approached the composer about the possibility of writing a concerto for Dushkin. Stravinsky, himself a pianist, hesitated, realizing that although he had featured the violin prominently in works like *L'histoire du soldat* (1918), it was an altogether different matter to write an extended solo work for the instrument.

Stravinsky consulted Paul Hindemith, whom he knew to be a superb string player, and asked him if he thought his lack of knowledge of violin technique would be obvious in the work. Stravinsky later noted: "Not only did he allay my doubts, but he went further and told me that it would be a very good thing, as it would make me avoid a routine technique, and would give rise to ideas which would not be suggested by the familiar movement of the fingers." Additionally, "Willy Strecker allayed my doubts by assuring me that Dushkin would place himself entirely at my disposal in order to furnish any technical details which I might require. Under such conditions the plan was very alluring."

Stravinsky then began a close collaboration with Dushkin on the solo part. Dushkin's memoirs reveal that he was quite an active partner in this endeavor. When asked about working with the young virtuoso, Stravinsky said: "When I show Sam a new passage, he is deeply moved, very excited—then a few days later he asks me to make changes." Of course, the ultimate creative decisions rested with the composer. For example, when Dushkin argued for the retention of a particularly virtuosic passage, Stravinsky said: "You remind me of a salesman at the Galeries Lafayette. You say, 'Isn't this brilliant, isn't this exquisite, look at the beautiful colours, everybody's wearing it.' I say, 'Yes, it is brilliant, it is beautiful, everyone is wearing it—I don't want it.'"

Dushkin recalled the genesis of the sonority—a wide-spanning D–E–A chord—which begins each movement of the concerto: "During the winter [1930–1931], I saw Stravinsky in Paris quite often. One day when we were lunching in a restaurant, Stravinsky took out a piece of paper and wrote down this chord and asked me if it could be played. I had never seen a chord with such an enormous stretch, from the E to the top A, and I said 'No'. Stravinsky said sadly 'What a pity.' After I got home, I tried it, and, to my astonishment, I found that in that register, the stretch of the eleventh was relatively easy to play, and the sound fascinated me. I telephoned Stravinsky at once to tell him that it could be done. When the concerto was finished, more than six months later, I understood his disappointment when I first said 'No'. This chord, in a different dress, begins each of the four movements. Stravinsky himself calls it his 'passport' to that concerto."

Although Stravinsky insisted that his Violin Concerto was not modeled after those of Mozart, Beethoven, or Brahms, he did acknowledge that "the subtitles of my concerto—Toccata, Aria, Capriccio—may suggest Bach, and so, in a superficial way, might the musical substance. I am very fond of the Bach *Concerto for Two Violins*, as the duet of the soloist with a violin from the orchestra in the last movement of my own concerto may show."

The premiere of the concerto took place on October 23, 1931 in Berlin, with Dushkin as soloist and Stravinsky conducting the Berlin Rundfunk Orchestra. *—Robert Adelson*

Recommended:

- ○ **Lutosławski: Chain 2; Partita; Stravinsky: Violin Concerto** / Mutter, Sacher (cond.), London Philharmonia Orch. / DG 423696
- ○ **Stravinsky & Rochberg: Violin Concertos** / Stern, Stravinsky (cond.), Columbia SO / 1995 / Sony 64505
- ○ **Early Concerto Recordings (1934–1943)** / Dushkin, Stravinsky (cond.), Lamoureux Concert Association Orch. / DG 459002

CHORAL

King of the Stars (Zvezdoliki), cantata (1911–1912)

The Russian title of Stravinsky's cantata *King of the Stars* (1911–12) is *Zvezdoliki*, literally "Starface." The work is scored for male chorus and full orchestra (including celesta and two harps). The text, by symbolist poet Konstantin Balmont, is in Russian; Stravinsky, as was often the case, was more interested in the text on a purely sonic level than for its content or semantic sense. "Its words are good," Stravinsky noted, "and words were what I needed, not meanings."

King of the Stars was composed at roughly the same time that Stravinsky worked on the score of his ballet masterpiece *The Rite of Spring* (1911–13). The choral writing, predominantly in four parts, is characterized by close spacing and triad-based harmonies with the addition of sevenths, ninths, 11ths, and 13ths. At times, Stravinsky sets phrases in unison to accentuate certain parts of the text.

As with many of Stravinsky's early "Russian" works, *King of the Stars* has a fundamentally bitonal harmonic structure, often employing the choral and instrumental bodies as distinct harmonic entities superimposed upon one another; the final sonority, for example, consists of two distinct chords, a C major dominant ninth chord in the orchestra and a G major seventh chord in the chorus. Debussy, to whom the work is dedicated, was among the many who deemed the work essentially unperformable, targeting its bitonality as a likely cause of serious intonation problems in performance. The work was first performed in 1939, more than a quarter century after its composition. *—Alexander Carpenter*

Recommended:

- ○ **Boulez Conducts Stravinsky** / Boulez (cond.), Cleveland Orch. & Chorus / DG 471197

Mass, for chorus & double wind quintet (1948)

After the composition of *Oedipus rex* (1926–27) it was unusual for Stravinsky to write a non-commissioned work. Also, since 1926 Stravinsky had been a communicant of the Russian Orthodox Church. Thus, it seems peculiar that the composer would write a concerted Latin mass. The motivation stems from what seems to have been a negative reaction to some masses of Mozart, which Stravinsky found in a second-hand music store in Los Angeles in 1942. The choice of the traditional Latin text of the Catholic Mass was a practical one: the Russian Orthodox Church proscribed the use of instruments in services, and Stravinsky did not want to write an unaccompanied vocal work.

The ensemble consists of a chorus of children, altos, tenors, and basses, and a double wind quintet. The opening of the Kyrie contrasts the timbres of the wind instruments, and the voices enter by imitating the instrumental introduction. Mirroring the text, the chorus intones three complete statements of "Kyrie eleison" before the central, "Christe eleison" section. After the first statement of "Christe eleison," the music takes on a clearly articulated pulse, and the children take center stage. The animated atmosphere continues through the return of the Kyrie text. Throughout the Gloria movement the vocal texture alternates between full chorus, duet, and solo. Near the middle, at "Domine Deus," a pair of voices evokes a style reminiscent of thirteenth century parallel organum, one instance in the mass that illuminates Stravinsky's familiarity with Medieval and Renaissance sacred music (although in *Expositions and Developments* Stravinsky claimed that he did not hear Machaut's mass until after he had completed his own). For the Credo, Stravinsky gave a large nod to tradition by directing that the first phrase, "Credo in unum deum," be sung by the celebrant alone. In fact, the composer specified the use of the plainchant melody listed as the "authentic" Credo intonation in the *Liber Usualis*. The harmonic organization of the movement bears a close relationship to the pitches of the plainchant intonation, and the opening and closing tonal areas (E and G) match the chant's first two pitches. The central part of the movement features a more strident sonority dominated by a major seventh chord. Like most composers of masses before him, Stravinsky set the lengthy Credo text syllabically. The composer described the movement rather succinctly: "The Credo is the longest movement. There is much to believe." The celebrant opens the Sanctus alone, and each of his florid statements of "Sanctus" is echoed by the chorus. In another nod to tradition, Stravinsky sets the Benedictus off from the rest of the movement, both by setting the text to contrasting music and by framing it with the same music for both appearances of the "Hosanna in excelsis." The Agnus Dei is built around an instrumental ritornello, which opens the movement and separates the three lines of text. *—John Palmer*

Recommended:

○ **Stravinsky: Les Noces; Mass** / Bernstein (cond.), English Bach Festival Orch. & Chorus, Trinity Boys Choir / DG 423251

○ **Stravinsky: The Composer, Vol. 7** / Craft (cond.), Orch. of St. Luke's, Gregg Smith Singers / 1995 / MusicMasters 67152

OPERA

Oedipus Rex (1927; revised 1948)

Oedipus Rex can be seen as a product of many aspects of Igor Stravinsky's development: his lifelong interest in Greek mythology and drama, his forays into what would come to be identified as neo-Classicism, and most importantly, his increasing tendency to depersonalize his music, lending it a cool, almost analytical visage. *Oedipus Rex* is one of the very first masterpieces of Stravinsky's neo-Classical period, in which he attempted to invest old forms with new vitality, and it is an impressive and absorbing musical statement.

Stravinsky's intention was to compose a lengthy, dramatic work, but he could not at first decide what language to use. He wanted something from the distant past, with an incantory tone that he could exploit musically. He eventually settled on Latin because, in his words, the language was "not dead but turned to stone and so monumentalized as to have become immune from all risk of vulgarization." (The libretto also includes narration which is to be spoken in the language of the audience.) This general theme of monumentalism extended to Stravinsky's conception of the staging, which involved as little movement as possible: Entrances and exits would be accomplished with lighting rather than actual movement, the singers would declaim from elevated platforms and move only their heads and arms, like "living statues," and the characters would remain in costumes and masks throughout. Still, Stravinsky identified the work as an "opera-oratorio" to indicate that it could be performed without staging.

The composer chose the Oedipus myth in large part because he assumed that audiences would be familiar with it, and this would, therefore, enable him to concentrate on musical dramatization rather than storytelling. He employed Jean Cocteau to write the libretto in French; after many disputes, drafts and edits, Stravinsky obtained from the writer a libretto that fit his conception, and gave it to Abbe Jean Danielou to translate into Latin. Cocteau introduced the idea of the narrator, which Stravinsky accepted only reluctantly and later regretted; still, it has the benefit of clarifying the story for those who are not familiar with it.

Oedipus Rex was performed first as an oratorio by Diaghilev's ballets russes in 1927, and premiered as an opera in the following year. The music is mostly in the minor mode; Oedipus' music in particular attempts to achieve the solace of the major mode, but is rarely successful in this regard. While the music uses elements of basic tonality, these at times seem disconnected from the drama, almost depersonalized; the C major triad in Creon's aria, sounding weirdly out of place, is an excellent example. Moreover, Stravinsky in this work abandons the shifting rhythms that characterized much of his earlier music for a steady, at times insistent pulse. All of these combine to give the listener a vivid musical depiction of an impersonal Fate pursuing Oedipus| until he must give everything up. The effect is at once chilling and mesmerizing. The general spirit of Stravinsky's interpretation is true to Sophocles' play and to ancient Greek thought, and the music, paradoxically, involves the listener by its very impersonality. *—Andrew Lindemann Malone*

Synopsis:

Act One. The action begins after Oedipus has unknowingly slain his father Laius, King of Thebes, and defeated the Sphinx, thereby becoming King of Thebes and marrying the widowed Queen, Jocasta, whom he does not realize is his mother. This work employs a speaker, who begins by announcing that Oedipus cannot escape his horrible fate, as this drama will show.

Episode One. Act One. Oedipus is beseeched by his subjects to save them from the plague ravaging the city and he promises to do so.

Episode Two. Creon, brother of Jocasta, returns from Delphi where he was sent to seek counsel from an oracle. He announces that the oracle has revealed the murderer of Laius is living in Thebes. Oedipus promises to find the guilty party.

Episode Three. The King summons Tiresias, the prophet who had forecast Oedipus' fate at birth. The seer remains silent and draws the wrath of Oedipus, who accuses him of the murder of Laius. Tiresias finally tells him that Laius' killer is himself a king. Oedipus accuses Tiresias of conspiring against him with Creon, and an argument ensues that draws the attention of Jocasta.

Act Two. Episode Four. Jocasta voices displeasure over their dispute, reminding all that they are besieged by the awful plague. She goes on, however, to mock the oracle, suggesting that he lies. She recalls the prophecy that Laius would be slain by his son, a prophecy she is convinced never came true since the King was murdered by, she believes, common thieves who attacked him at a crossroads. Hearing Jocasta say the word crossroads, Oedipus senses a chill, recalling that he did kill a man many years ago at a crossroads outside Thebes. Still, he will not accept the possibility he is Laius' killer, but summons an old shepherd, known to be a witness to the killing.

Episode Five. A messenger brings news of the death of Polybus, King of Corinth, thought by Oedipus to be his father. But the messenger reveals Polybus' deathbed admission that Oedipus was adopted. The shepherd steps forth then to give testimony and reveals knowledge of the fate of the infant Oedipus: he was found on a mountainside (not slain, as ordered by Laius and Jocasta to circumvent the awful prophecy). Jocasta flees, realizing the horrible truth about her husband. But Oedipus and the crowd of supporters revel in the belief he had divine beginnings. Their joy is short-lived as the shepherd and messenger reveal the rest: Oedipus was indeed the son of King Laius and Queen Jocasta, the son who fulfilled Tiresias' prophecy that he would murder his father and marry his mother. Oedipus accepts the bitter truth and flees in terror.

Episode Six. The messenger announces the grim fates of Oedipus and Jocasta: he has gouged out his eyes, and she, out of abject shame, has hanged herself. Still, Oedipus returns to Thebes, but is fondly turned away by its inhabitants. *—Robert Cummings*

Recommended:

○ **Stravinsky: Oedipus Rex** / Salonen (cond.), Otter, Cole, Estes, Sotin, Gedda, Chereau / 1992 / Sony 48057

○ **Stravinsky: Oedipus Rex** / Ozawa (cond.), Norman, Schreier / 1994 / Philips 438865

The Rake's Progress (1951)

Igor Stravinsky completed *The Rake's Progress* in 1951. The composer had toyed with the idea of writing an opera since he had emigrated to the United States in 1939. In 1947, his inspiration finally came to him in the form of a set of eighteenth century engravings by William Hogarth depicting the self-ruin of an Augustan rake. Stravinsky asked his publisher to contact W. H. Auden to see if he would be interested in a collaboration on the subject; Auden agreed. Their rapport was immediate, and within a week, the scenes and individual numbers had already been worked out. This was one of the few works by Stravinsky that was not commissioned; he simply wanted to do it.

Auden enlisted Chester Kallman to help hammer out the particulars of the libretto, and Robert Craft acted as the composer's personal assistant. The result is perhaps the last word in neo-Classical opera. While the musical syntax is definitively Stravinskyian, the structure is clearly reminiscent of Mozart, whose operatic touches frequently appear in *The Rake's Progress*, though morphed into the Russian composer's own harmonic language and counterpoint.

In his leading man, Stravinsky created is a sort of antipode to Mozart's violent and charismatic *Don Giovanni*. Stravinsky's hero, Tom Rakewell, is the opposite of the Don, whose courage, vigor and decisiveness might have saved the rake from his lazy, floundering self. Throughout the opera's three acts and two and a half hours, Tom always looks for the easy way out, whines, and allows himself to be led about by his late uncle's demonic manservant, Nick Shadow. While the Don is unable to back down from a challenge, Tom is unable to accept one. Even when an affluent existence is handed to him, he cannot take control of his legacy. Shadow convinces Rakewell to squander love and fortune in favor of bad business and unrelenting, tedious hedonism.

The first performance of this opera took place on September 11, at the Teatro La Fenice in Venice. Stravinsky conducted; the reviews were mixed. Many doubted the continued relevance of the composer's neo-Classical experiment, which had already seen its definitive statement in his *Symphony in C*. However, there were several conventions of eighteenth century music that Stravinsky had still left untouched until this point. Recitatives accompanied by harpsichord are a case in point; the composer's distinctive language makes the recycling of a dated convention relevant and striking. Nevertheless, *The Rake's Progress* was to be the composer's last neo-Classical work.

The Rake's Progress makes so many references to operatic history that one could spend a lifetime garnering the knowledge of opera necessary to understand them all. However, the piece's appeal rests in its effective drama and well-realized characters rather than its stylistic elements or intrinsic cleverness; it is an excellent piece that has become deservedly entrenched in the operatic canon. The best-known excerpt from the work is Ann Trulove's two-part aria, "No word from Tom." As much as any portion of the opera, it represents the freshness and vitality that Stravinsky brought to forms and ideas borrowed from eras past, and it has become a standard concert piece for sopranos. *—John Keillor*

Synopsis:

Act One. In the garden of Trulove's country house, his daughter Anne and her betrothed, Tom Rakewell, are enjoying a springtime flirtation as he looks on. He is worried about Rakewell's future because he does not have money or a job. The father generously offers Rakewell employment, but he declines, declaring that he prefers to live by his wits and awaits good fortune to come to him. When the father and daughter depart, he wishes aloud that he had money. At that moment, Nick Shadow appears, with news of Rakewell's recently departed uncle, whom he had never met or heard about. This mysterious uncle was rich and left Rakewell a fortune. The estate must be settled in London. Shadow asks for no payment until a year and a day hence, when Rakewell can determine the servant's worth and pay him accordingly. Rakewell bids the Truloves goodbye, promises to write, and makes his way to the city.

Once in London, Rakewell is led to Mother Goose's brothel. An intimidating group of regulars partake in assorted acts of leisure. Shadow has Rakewell recite, under duress, the code that he has learned, to seek beauty, however transient, and pleasure. However intimidated, he refuses to define love. Mother Goose takes advantage of his obvious discomfort and disorientation and seduces him. In the act's final scene, Anne pines after Rakewell, who has not written, and goes to the city to find him.

Act Two. Rakewell has a large house and fortune in London. With every earthly pleasure available to him, he is bored with hedonism. He is aware that his life in the city is empty, and pines for love, for Anne. He wishes aloud that he was happy, and Shadow appears with a solution. The sinister manservant proposes that Rakewell is ruled by appetite and conscience, which is responsible for his listlessness. The solution, according to Shadow, is for Rakewell to marry Baba the Turk, a bearded lady who is in the city with a traveling circus. Rakewell agrees, laughing.

In Scene Two, Anne arrives in London. Outside Rakewell's house she encounters Rakewell and his Baba, who remains in her sedan while the two talk. Rakewell tells Anne to forget him and to leave London. As she goes, a crowd gathers to catch an appreciative glance of Baba, who obliges with a lifting of her veil.

Later, Rakewell's house is cluttered with his new bride's baubles and various collectable artifacts. He is unhappy, and spurns Baba's flirtations, who then loses her temper and begins throwing knickknacks around and breaking things. Rakewell silences and stills her by covering her head and then falls asleep. He dreams about a "fantastic Baroque machine" that turns stone into bread. Rakewell awakes and tells Shadow about it, who then reveals that he has the machine that his master dreamt. Rakewell sees it as something that can be used for the common good and to redeem himself. Shadow advises that he see about drumming up investment in order to produce more of them.

Act Three. The final act opens with Rakewell's fortune ruined by the business venture. Baba still sits motionless while her husband's property is up for public auction, and the lifting of the shade reanimates her. Anne appears again. Baba tells her to go to Rakewell and then announces to the crowd that she will be returning to the stage.

In a churchyard, a year and a day after they met, Shadow demands payment of Rakewell, who is broke. The manservant, Lucifer, actually, insists that Rakewell hand over his soul, as he has nothing else to tender in exchange for services rendered. Shadow offers him a way out; if Rakewell can guess three of three cards Shadow lifts from his deck, Rakewell is free. Rakewell wins and is condemned to insanity by his enraged former employee.

In a sanatorium, Rakewell is delusional and believes he is Adonis, preparing to marry Venus. The Truloves arrive, and Anne sings Rakewell to sleep. There is nothing she can do for him and departs. No other patient believes she was ever there. Rakewell dies in grief.

Epilogue. The principals gather. Anne warns that not every man will have a woman like her to look after him. Baba says men are mad. Rakewell advises listeners to avoid self-delusion, to Trulove's agreement. Shadow says that he will always make time for men with idle hands. *—John Keillor*

Recommended:

- ○ **Stravinsky: The Rake's Progress** / Nagano (cond.), Upshaw, Ramey, Hadley, Bumbry / 1996 / Erato 12715
- ○ **Stravinsky: The Rake's Progress** / Gardiner (cond.), Terfel, Otter, Bostridge, York / 1999 / DG 459648

Renard, opera-ballet (burlesque) (1916)

Stravinsky's *Renard* (1915–16) belongs to a genre perhaps best described as "ballet hybrid." In addition to the expected dance elements, *Renard* is also a burlesque, a musical story that is sung and played. The text was written by Stravinsky himself, after stories of the Fox from the famous collection of Russian folk tales by Alexander Afanasiev. *Renard* is scored for small orchestra, percussion, timpani, cimbalom, a solo string quintet, two tenor soloists, and two bass soloists.

The story is a farmyard tale in which the Cock is twice tricked and captured by the Fox , only to be rescued each time by the Cat and the Goat. After the Cock's second rescue, the Cat and the Goat strangle the Fox, and the three friends dance and sing. Stravinsky employs the singers as part of the orchestra, and though there are exactly as many singers as characters, the vocal parts are not identified with specific characters. (The composer followed this practice in subsequent works of the same type, most notably in *Les noces* of 1914–17.)

The players remain onstage at all times, without the kind of choreography one associates with traditional ballet. Rather, as the prefatory note in the score indicates, the various characters should be played by "clowns, dancers, or acrobats" who perform in front of the curtain. Stravinsky makes prominent use of the cimbalom, a stringed instrument played with mallets, to imitate the sound of a guzla, a similar Russian folk instrument. Stravinsky knew that finding good guzla players (or even the instrument itself) would be difficult, and settled on the cimbalom after hearing it played in a nightclub in Switzerland. According to the composer, most of *Renard* was actually composed on the cimbalom rather than on the piano that was more usual for Stravinsky. The cimbalom, an instrument on which rapid repeating notes and broad arpeggios are highly idiomatic, contributes significantly to the work's linear texture. Stravinsky employs the other instruments in an almost soloistic manner, further contributing to the work's polyphonic textures. *Renard's* melodies are wide-ranging and disjunct, while the mixture of modes connects it to the polytonal/polymodal harmonic style of earlier works like *Petrushka* (1910–11). *Renard's* relative rhythmic and metric simplicity contrasts sharply with the richly complex rhythmic language of nearly contemporaneous works like *The Rite of Spring* (1911–13). *—Alexander Carpenter*

Synopsis:

Part One. Four animals are the main characters: the Cock, Fox, Cat, and Ram. The story begins with the proud Cock perched atop his roost. The Fox, dressed in clerical garb, calls out to him to repent and confess his sinful ways, charging he has taken too many wives. The Cock falls into the trap and descends contritely to confess, whereupon the Fox seizes him by the tail, preparing to dine on his gullible catch. But the Cock cries out to the Cat and Ram, who come to his rescue and drive the Fox off.

Part Two. The second part opens with the Cock sitting atop his roost once again. This time the ever-hungry Fox sports no disguise, deciding to lure his prey with his cunning and bribery, which at first fail. Eventually, the Fox's persistence pays off and the Cock descends to the ground once more only to be seized and attacked immediately. His calls for help are not immediately answered this time, but finally the Cat and Ram respond. They turn the tables on the Fox, informing him that his mate is adulterous, a revelation that stuns the attacker for a moment. His guard down, the Fox is strangled by the Cat and Ram. The story ends with the Cock, Cat, and Ram dancing and singing on-stage, asking the audience for a monetary trifle for their performance. *—Robert Cummings*

Recommended:

- ○ **Stravinsky: Pulcinella; Octet; Renard; Ragtime** / Salonen (cond.), Aler, Wilson-Johnson, Tomlinson, Robson, London Sinfonietta / 1991 / Sony 45965
- ○ **Stravinsky Conducts Stravinsky** / Stravinsky (cond.), Driscoll, Shirley, Koves, Columbia CO / Sony 64136

MUSICAL THEATER

L'histoire du soldat (The Soldier's Tale), for 3 actors, dancer & 7 instruments (1918)

Prior to embarking on his so-called "neo-Classical" period in the 1920s, Stravinsky had already pared down his style considerably from the extravagant ballet scores of the early 1910s to the economy and restraint that characterizes *L'Histoire du Soldat* (The Soldier's Tale). The forced economy of wartime influenced not only the work's modest resources, but its subject matter. Written in collaboration with the Swiss author C.F. Ramuz and based on a Russian fable about a fiddle-playing soldier (although the text is in French), *L'Histoire* was to be narrated, played and danced, but could also be performed independent of the text as a concert suite. The first performance of *L'Histoire du Soldat* took place in Lausanne Switzerland on September 28, 1918.

Stravinsky and Ramuz based their subject on a collection of Russian tales dealing with the adventures of a soldier who deserts the army and the devil who eventually possesses his soul. The soldier's desertion is somewhat glossed over, but the fiddle he carries in his knapsack and which the Devil wins from him, assumes a symbolic importance that makes the story a kind of miniature version of the Faust legend.

Despite the scenario's Russian basis, Stravinsky made the music as non-Russian as possible by using North and South American, Spanish, and German material. The score tends to mimic—and parody—standard dance styles (ragtime, waltz, and tango) as well as marches and two chorales. The unique chamber instrumentation emphasizes the high and low registers of each family (violin, double-bass, clarinet, bassoon, cornet, trombone, and percussion) that leaves room in the middle registers. The music often abstractly evokes the sound of a New Orleans jazz band, which Stravinsky had recently become acquainted with through scores imported from America by his colleague Ernest Ansermet.

The score also calls for four dramatis personae: the Soldier and the Devil (both speaking parts), the Princess (who is silent), and a Reader. Moreover, the Princess and the Devil are required to dance. The music is organized as a series of brief tableaux with the action presented mainly through mime and dancing, and continuity supplied by the narrator. The atmosphere of the entire production suggests a cabaret or an informal street entertainment, and it's portability has also been referred to as "pocket theater."

Stravinsky's harmonic language is modern, pungent and at times bitonal, yet the weight of the interest is on the high level of rhythmic complexity and intricacy. From the opening "Marche du Soldat" to the "Marche Royale," lively, unpredictable rhythms with prickly irregularities are employed in a firmly tongue-and-cheek manner. Asymmetrical phrases are juxtaposed against independent accompanimental ostinati, suggesting the uneven tread of the soldier as he ventures across the countryside. *—Brian Wise*

Recommended:

- ○ **Stravinsky: Pulcinella; Nightingale; L'Histoire du Soldat** / Boulez (cond.), Chereau, Vitez, InterContemporain Ens. / Erato 98955
- ○ **Stravinsky: The Soldier's Tale** / Jarvi (cond.), Haugland, Scottish National Orch. [members] / 1993 / Chandos 9189
- ○ **Stravinsky: L'Histoire du Soldat** / Stokowski (cond.), Singher, Aumont, Instrumental Ens. / 1999 / Vanguard 124

VOCAL

Three Japanese Lyrics, song cycle (1913)

Stravinsky's *Three Japanese Lyrics* (1912–13) were composed just as the taste for all things Oriental, from fine arts to fashion, was reaching its apex throughout Europe. Nowhere was this fad more rampant than in Paris, where the composer lived and, in 1912, had come upon an anthology of Japanese poetry translated into Russian, providing him with the texts for a group of three songs. These terse and somewhat mournful songs—"Akahito," "Mazatsumi," and "Tsaraiuki"—represent the composer's most overt adoption of Far Eastern subject matter. Like many of Stravinsky's works which draw upon elements from "exotic" sources, the songs reveal a degree of detachment, objectivity and stylization.

The *Three Japanese Lyrics* were composed some 15 to 18 months after *Le sacre du printemps* (1911–13) was completed; as in that seminal ballet, the songs' melodic material is based upon the repetition of numerous small cells. "Akahito" features a six-note ostinato comprised of slow, ornamented eighth notes that run throughout the song, while "Tsamaiuki" contains tiny refrain figures that are likewise repeated in an ostinato pattern. The *Lyrics* suggest a similarity to *Le sacre du printemps* in terms of subject matter as well. Both illustrate the dawning of spring, but while *Le sacre du printemps* expresses the death of winter through violence and elemental force, the *Lyrics* draw attention elsewhere. Here the emphasis is more upon the visual, decorative aspects of the season, symbolized by the color white—patterns of white flowers set against fresh snowfall.

Texturally, the *Lyrics* reveal another significant influence: Schoenberg's *Pierrot Lunaire* (1912). Stravinsky attended a performance of the revolutionary melodrama in Berlin in December 1912, and Schoenberg's band of flute, clarinet, violin, cello, and piano was a likely inspiration for the instrumentation of the *Lyrics* (two flutes, two clarinets, and piano quintet). Moreover, the *Lyrics*, despite their clearly tonal language, employ harsh sonorities and free chromaticism to a greater extent than in Stravinsky's previous works.

Following their first performance in 1914, many listeners were taken by the *Lyrics*' metrical freedom and ambiguity. Indeed, rather than relying upon stereotyped orientalist clichés like pentatonic scales and garish ornamentation, Stravinsky emulates Japanese speech patterns with a remarkable degree of authenticity.*—Brian Wise*

Recommended:

- ○ **The Girl With Orange Lips** / Upshaw / 1991 / Nonesuch 79262
- ○ **Stravinsky: Symphonies of Wind Instruments; Ragtime; 3 Japanese Lyrics; 2 Poems of Balmont** / Manning, Nash Ens. / 1991 / Chandos 6535

Pribaoutki, song cycle for voice & 8 instruments (1914)

Stravinsky noted that the closest English parallel of "Pribaoutki" is probably "limerick." The word refers to a kind of game, "a form of popular Russian verse" in which a short group of lines is added to word by word by the players in rapid succession. Stravinsky was very familiar with Russian folk text sources and used them in several of his compositions.

The songs are scored for voice, flute, oboe, clarinet, bassoon, violin, viola, cello, and double bass. *Pribaoutki* consists of four songs, entitled, in English: "Kornillo," "Natashka," "The Colonel," and "The Old Man and the Hare." Stravinsky insisted that a man should sing the voice part, and apparently the composer had his brother Gury, a baritone, in mind when he composed the songs. The text, as in most of Stravinsky's works with text, is set syllabically. The melodies are composed in Stravinsky's modular style; that is, they consist of short segments, with limited pitch content, that are repeated in varying patterns. Eric White also notes, significantly, that while *Pribaoutki* sounds as though Stravinsky borrowed melodies from folk music, his melodies are actually entirely original. This is the case for a number of his works composed around the same time. *Pribaoutki* prefigures the masterful *Les noces*, composed between 1914 and 1923, in which Stravinsky's profound knowledge of folk melodies inspired a large-scale work of wonderful, original folk tunes. *Pribaoutki* features mostly diatonic vocal melodies combined with a chromatically colored accompaniment from the chamber ensemble. *—Alexander Carpenter*

Recommended:

- ○ **Stravinsky: Le Noces; L'histoire du soldat; Pribaoutki; Berceuses du chat; Shakespeare Songs** / Rehak, Novak, Stros, Petrak, Czech Philharmonic Winds / Praga 250057

Cheryl Studer

b. Oct. 24, 1955, Midland, MI

Soprano

Cheryl Studer's repertoire is among the widest-ranging of those of any soprano, ranging from the Baroque to the twentieth century; her roles include Violetta (*La Traviata*), Die Kaiserin in *Die Frau ohne Schatten*, Odabella in Verdi's *Attila*, the Countess in *The Marriage of Figaro*, Floyd's *Susannah*, and nearly all of the lyric Wagner roles: Elizabeth (*Tannhäuser*), Elsa (*Lohengrin*), Freia (*Das Rheingold*), and Sieglinde (*Die Walküre*). She has also explored the art song repertory extensively; in all these things, she has applied a strong sense of musicianship and period style.

Born in Midland, Michigan, Studer took up music at an early age with piano and viola studies. She attended high school at the Interlochen Arts Academy and did her college studies at the Oberlin Conservatory and the University of Tennessee, Knoxville. She first gained recognition during three summers at the Tanglewood festival, where both Leonard Bernstein and Seiji Ozawa expressed admiration for her singing; Ozawa, in fact, engaged her for several BSO concerts during the 1978–79 season. In 1977 she also won the High Fidelity/Musical America award, and in 1978 the Metropolitan Opera Auditions.

In 1979 Studer went to Europe to continue her studies, with, among others, Hans Hotter. There she made her opera debut at the Bavarian State Opera in 1980 as the First Lady in Mozart's *The Magic Flute*. She sang with various other theaters in Germany, including Bayreuth, where she made her debut as Freia in 1985. Her United States debut was in 1984 as Micaela in *Carmen* at the Lyric Opera of Chicago. In 1987, she returned to Bayreuth to sing Elsa, which brought her to international fame. Her La Scala debut was the next year as Mathilde in Rossini's William Tell, and her Metropolitan Opera debut in 1990 was as Donna Anna in Mozart's *Don Giovanni*. During the late 1990s, she had a period of vocal problems that led to the Bavarian State Opera canceling her contracts, but after a brief time off the stage, her performances indicated a return to form.

The Sawallisch recording of Strauss' *Die Frau Ohne Schatten* shows her at her best, with a warm, lyrical tone that still has the necessary carrying power for the difficult role of the Empress.*—Ann Feeney*

Recommended:

- ○ **Franz Lehar: The Merry Widow** / Gardiner (cond.), Terfel, Bonney, Skovhus, Studer, Monteverdi Choir, Vienna PO / 1994 / DG 439911
- ○ **Strauss & Wagner Songs** / Sinopoli (cond.), Studer, Dresden Staatskapelle / 1994 / DG 439865
- ○ **Verdi: La Traviata** / Levine (cond.), Pavarotti, Studer, Pons, White, Metropolitan Opera Orch. & Chorus / DG 435797
- ○ **Wagner: Der Fliegende Holländer** / Sinopoli (cond.), Domingo, Studer, Weikl, Sotin, Berlin State Opera Orch. & Chorus / 1998 / DG 437778
- ○ **Floyd: Susannah** / Nagano (cond.), Brossmann, Erlo, Ramey, Hadley, Jones, Studer, Lyon National Opera Orch. & Chorus / 1994 / Virgin 45039

Nathalie Stutzmann

b. May 6, 1965, Paris, France
Contralto

Nathalie Stutzmann is a French contralto, especially noted as a recital and concert performer, but also seen on European opera stages. She sings a wide variety of music, including art songs of the nineteenth and twentieth centuries, Baroque opera and oratorio, and the symphonies and song cycles of Mahler. Her particular interest in German lieder is unusual for a French singer, but not surprising, since she studied with two of the finest singers of that repertory in recent memory—Hans Hotter and Christa Ludwig. Her singing is dark-hued and unmannered.

Stutzmann's musical education included not only singing, but also piano and bassoon studies; she is an accomplished chamber musician on both instruments. After vocal studies at the Ecole Nationale in Paris, she won the 1983 Brussels vocal competition, and made her concert debut in 1985, singing Bach's *Magnificat* in Paris. In 1986 she performed and recorded Magnard's opera *Guercoeur* and received positive reviews for performances of Purcell's *Dido and Aeneas* at the Opéra de Paris. A 1989 recording of Handel's *Amadigi* (with Marc Minkowski) cemented her reputation, and since that time she has enjoyed an unbroken schedule of performances and recordings. Other notable operatic roles include Gluck's *Orfeo*, Handel's *Giulio Cesare*, and Geneviève in Debussy's *Pelléas et Mélisande*. Her oratorio repertory includes all the major works of Bach, Handel, and Vivaldi. Her discography includes over 60 titles, primarily for RCA Victor, but also for Erato, EMI, Philips, Harmonia Mundi, and Sony. Her volumes of Schumann lieder, and mélodies by Chausson, Fauré, and Poulenc are representative of her best recital work. *—Allen Schrott*

Recommended:

- ○ **Poulenc: Montparnasse** / Stutzmann, Sodergren (piano) / RCA 902663137
- ○ **Faure: Melodies** / Stutzmann, Collard (piano) / 1993 / BMG 61439
- ○ **Schumann Lieder** / Stutzmann, Sodergren (piano) / 2000 / RCA 902668900

Otmar Suitner

b. May 16, 1922, Innsbruck, Austria
Conductor

Otmar Suitner is archetypical of the type of Central European conductor who comes up through the ranks (i.e., opera house, theater, or if an instrumentalist, house orchestra) and works his way up to leadership by dint of musicality. Some move on to what is essentially international "stardom," such as the case with Karajan or Klemperer. Others settle into a localized niche, but extend their reputation past national boundaries via recording prowess, often through a varied series of ensembles. In this manner, Suitner's star has ascended, the dawn of the digital era being a boon to his recognition even though he ceased conducting in the 1990s due to illness.

Otmar Suitner was born in the picturesque backdrop of the Tyrol. His father was a native and his mother was Italian, who most likely nourished his affinity for opera. In his teens, Suitner began piano studies under Weidlich at the Innsbruck Conservatory and continued the same under Ledwinka at the Salzburg Mozarteum from 1940–42, also studying conducting with Clemens Krauss at that institution. Upon completion of studies, the young man became Kapellmeister at the Innsbruck Theatre and moved through a number of both opera and orchestra positions, including Remscheid (1952), Ludwigshaven (1957), the Rhineland-Pfalz State Philharmonic Orchestra (1957) the Dresden State Opera (1960–64), and the Berlin State Opera (1964–71, continuing 1973–90). He became a fixture at Bayreuth, working closely with Wieland Wagner on the 1965 *Der fliegende Holländer* and the *Ring* cycle for 1966 and 1967. In opera, he distinguished himself in Mozart, Wagner, and Strauss, bringing to those composers a litheness and protean energy not usually associated with the Austro-German school of interpretation. His predilection for lightness can be divined from his arrangement of *Der Rosenkavalier* for small orchestra performance. No complacent traditionalist, Suitner has also been a fervent advocate of Dessau, conducting the premieres of that composer's operas *Puntila* (1966), *Einstein* (1973), and *Leonce und Lena* (1979). In 1969, he became a guest conductor with the San Francisco Opera Company and in the following decade was a frequent podium visitor in Japan, receiving honorary conductorship of the Tokyo NHK Symphony Orchestra in 1973.

The Japanese connection was to stand Suitner in good stead with the emergence of digital recording in the early 1980s. His set of the Beethoven symphonies with the Berlin Radio Symphony Orchestra for Denon was one of the very first sets of the nine to appear. Soon, Suitner was one of the digital pioneers and joined the ranks of conductors who had built a cult by dint of quality recordings, much like Rosbaud, Kegel, Wand, and others. Unfortunately, illness stayed Suitner's hand in the early 1990s and he made a premature retirement from performing and recording. Nonetheless, he retains his devotees and his 80th birthday saw the issue of an 11-CD set on the Edel label representative of his operatic and symphonic artistry. *—Wayne Reisig*

Recommended:

- ○ **Schumann: Symphonies 2 & 4** / Suitner (cond.), Staatskapelle Berlin / Denon 33CO-1967

Josef Suk (composer)

b. Jan. 4, 1874, Krecovice, Czechoslovakia, **d.** May 29, 1935, Benesov, Czechoslovakia

Composer: Symphonic, Keyboard, Orchestral, Concerto

Czech composer Josef Suk was born on January 4, 1874, in Krecovice, Bohemia, where his father was a choral director. The elder Josef Suk taught his son to play the piano, violin, and organ. In 1885, at the age of eleven, Suk entered the Prague Conservatory. By 1888, he had composed a mass, the *Krecovická mass*; he received his degree in 1891, with what became the Op. 1 piano quartet as his thesis. When Antonín Dvořák became a professor at the Conservatory, Suk stayed an extra year to study with him. Dvořák considered Suk his best student, and the two became personally close. In 1898, Suk married Dvořák's daughter Otilie.

Suk's compositional life may be divided into two periods. His early works are characterized by a late Romantic style that created a general perception of Suk as Dvořák's heir. Compared with Dvořák, Suk wrote little chamber music, but found success with the Four Pieces for violin and piano, Op. 17, written in 1900, and the *Fantasy for violin and orchestra*, Op. 24, of 1903, as well as with several solo piano works—the "Song of Love" from the six piano pieces of Op. 7 became a standard recital piece. He wrote few songs and never approached opera, concentrating mainly on orchestral music. In 1892, he wrote the *Serenade for Strings*, Op. 6, which boosted his career when Brahms promoted it, much as Dvořák himself had benefited from the Viennese giant's support years before. In 1897 and 1898, he composed incidental music for the play *Radúz a Mahulena*, one of his most popular works and one that had resonances with Suk's own happy marriage. An optimistic mood is especially evident in the piano suites *Jaro* (Spring) Op. 22 and *Letní dojmi* Op. 22b, both written in 1902. It was during this time that his son was born.

In 1904, Suk's father-in-law and mentor Dvořák died, and 14 months later, in 1905, his beloved wife Otilie passed away. Their deaths had a devastating impact, and the beginnings of a second phase of Suk's career may be discerned in the works that followed. His compositions became more introspective, complex, and infused with emotion. Completed in 1906, the symphony *Asrael*, Op. 27, exemplifies this new phase. It is a massive work, considered by many the summit of his achievement. Suk began to experiment with polytonality, notably in his symphonic poem *Zrání* (Ripening) of 1917. He expanded upon the structure and language of *Zrání* in his symphony with soloists and chorus *Epilog*, completed in 1929; these three major orchestral works form a trilogy of vast, almost Mahlerian ambition and scope. Unlike his Czech contemporaries, Suk did not incorporate folk or literary motifs into his compositions. Interestingly, however, his final composition was a Czech dance entitled *Sousedská*.

Suk made a living largely as a performer and teacher, scheduling composing time around his daily responsibilities. The lack of chamber music in his oeuvre is all the more remarkable in view of his long tenure as second violinist of the Czech Quartet. The Quartet's first concert took place in Vienna in 1893, where it received praise from Brahms, and Suk enjoyed international success with the quartet for forty years, remaining a member until he retired in 1933. In 1922 Suk assumed a professorship in composition at the Prague Conservatory, where he tutored such future Czech composers such as Martinů, Jezek and Borkovec. He was twice appointed head of the Conservatory, serving from 1924 to 1926, and from 1933 until 1935. He died in 1935, at the age of 61. *—Caroline Kovtun*

SYMPHONIC

Symphony in C minor ("Asrael"), Op. 27 (1905–1906)

Josef Suk was a pupil of the great Czech composer Dvořák. He married Dvořák's daughter Otilie (who, by the way, was also talented as a composer). Suk began this symphony after the death of his beloved mentor and father-in-law, Dvořák. Otilie died toward the end of its composition, which prompted Suk to recompose it and invest it with even deeper feeling. At that time he added the subtitle, which is the name of the legendary "Angel of Death" who attends the souls of the departed and offers them hope. The hour-long, five-movement work is a passionate outpouring of feeling. The first contrasts two themes representing, on the one hand, destiny and death and, on the other, happiness in life. The second, an Andante, is a funeral march. The third is a scherzo contrasting the dance of death and reminiscences of life. The fourth movement, a radiantly tragic Adagio, is said to be a portrait of Otilie. The fifth movement begins in a stern mood, but gradually offers hope, closing in peace and bliss. It is a deeply affecting work in a style fairly similar to that of Richard Strauss' tone poems. *—Joseph Stevenson*

Recommended:

- ○ **Suk: Asrael; Fairy Tale; Serenade** / Belohlavek (cond.), Czech PO / 1998 / Chandos 9640
- ○ **Dvořák: Stabat Mater; Suk: Asrael** / Talich (cond.), Czech PO / Supraphon 111902
- ○ **Suk: Asrael Symphony** / Pesek (cond.), Royal Liverpool PO / 1991 / Virgin 59638

○ **Suk: Symphonie Asrael; Fantastic Scherzo** / Valek (cond.), Prague Radio SO / Praga 250018

KEYBOARD

Six Pieces, Op. 7 (1891–1893)

The *Six Piano Pieces*, Op. 7, of Czech composer Josef Suk were written in the summers of 1891, 1892, and 1893. Quintessentially youthful works in the best sense of the word, the *Six Pieces* are, like Suk's *Serenade for Strings*, delightful, charming, sometimes sentimental, and often very passionate. Consisting of "Love Song," "Humoresque," "Memories," "Little Idylls," "Dumka," and "Capriccetto," the *6 Pieces* are romantic character pieces in the same mold as Schumann's or Brahms'. But Suk's *Six Pieces* are more overtly emotional than Schumann's and more obviously personal than Brahms'. Indeed, they are a virtual lover's diary of the courtship of Suk and his beloved Otilka, Dvořák's daughter: "Little Idylls" depicts two lovers caught in the rain, while "Dumka" is a lovers' quarrel and their reconciliation. The best-known of the set is the "Love Song," Suk's declaration of his love and its rapturous reception. Not only does the "Love Song" exist in many different transcriptions and arrangements, its theme often re-appeared in Suk's later work. *—James Leonard*

Recommended:

○ **Suk: Piano Works** / Fingerhut / 1992 / Chandos 9026

○ **Suk: About Mother; Moods; Song of Love** / Lauriala / 2001 / Naxos 553762

ORCHESTRAL

Fantastic Scherzo, Op. 25 (1903)

From the evidence of the *Fantastic Scherzo*, Josef Suk would seem to have been destined to follow an artistic path much like that of his father-in-law and teacher, Antonín Dvořák. It is a 15-minute work, brilliantly scored for full Romantic orchestra. Its style is not that close to that of Dvořák. Suk's harmonic language is a little more modern, something like that of the pre-Impressionist French composers such as Chabrier and Fauré. Nor was Suk as interested in evoking Czech musical folklore in his music. The work is in the typical scherzo rhythm of dotted triple-time groups, rather close in spirit to Dukas' *Sorcerer's Apprentice*. It has less of the grotesquerie, mostly being good-spirited. The closest thing to it in mood among Dvořák's works is the *Carnival Overture*, though in sound and technique it is more like the late Dvořák tone poems such as *The Wood Dove*. There are, indeed, times when the Suk work picks up something of the dark-edged mood of those Dvořák fantasies. But on the whole it is a beautifully scored, light-hearted and untroubled look at a fairy-like world.

It is also uncharacteristic of the direction Suk's work would take (and thus unlike any later works of Suk's the reader might know). The year after it was composed, Dvořák died, and soon after that Suk's own wife (Dvořák's daughter) died. The grief and the questions about death raised by these shattering losses transformed the scope and purpose of his music. But that was in the future; the listener of this work gets the last music Suk was to write untouched by the most tragic side of life. *—Joseph Stevenson*

Recommended:

○ **Marinù: Symphony 5; Janáček: SInfonietta; Suk: Fantastic Scherzo** / Bélohlávek (cond.), Czech PO / 1990 / Chandos 8897

○ **Suk: Summer Tale; Fantastic Scherzo** / Mackerras (cond.), Czech PO / 1999 / Decca 466443

Pohádka Léta (A Summer Tale), symphonic poem, Op. 29 (1907–1909)

Suk (grandfather of the great violinist of the same name who flourished in the last half of the twentieth century) was Dvořák's favorite student. By marrying Dvořák's daughter Otylka, Suk became the composer's son-in-law. Suk was a highly accomplished and serious-minded composer who wrote in a late Romantic vein. Suk's musical output is divided by an abrupt change that took place when both his beloved teacher and his wife died within about a year's time.

Summer Tale is one of a great tetralogy of orchestral compositions that represent Suk's working out the emotions and thoughts raised by the double tragedy in his life. The first was the *Asrael Symphony* (1905–06), named after the legendary angel of death. *Summer Tale*, *Ripening* (1912–17), and *Epilogue* (1920–29) are the rest. *Asrael* comes to terms with death. *Summer Tale* represents the healing power of nature. *Ripening* holds life and regeneration triumphant, and *Epilogue* is a kind of reflection on the whole cycle, tempered through the passage of time.

The work is for a very large orchestra and is a composition of a scale approaching that of Mahler's *First Symphony*, a virtual symphony of tone poems nearly 50 minutes long. It even has a movement that is analogous to the lightly scored "Blumine" movement that Mahler cut from his work.

The first movement, "Voice of light and consolation," begins with a rising theme on violins that is taken to represent Nature's promise of healing. Another important motive is a rhythmic figure borrowed from his previous work of grief, the piano suite *About Mother*, Op. 28, where it appears in the movement "About Mother's Heart." It clearly represents a heartbeat.

"Noon" is an atmospheric portrait. Violins illustrate air shimmering in the heat, while the dragging tempo of a march-like tune suggests the lethargy induced by the day's warmth. The middle movement, the rather strange "Intermezzo—Blind musicians" is the lightly scored one, using only reduced strings, two harps, and two English horns. It is a sad movement, the blind musicians endlessly playing the same tune for coins.

The fourth movement is a grotesque scherzo called "In the Power of Phantoms." The work is much like similar parts of *Asrael*. The finale, "Night," is a peaceful nocturne, only lightly disturbed at times by memories. Healing has occurred; the work ends with a lush, affirmative coda. *—Joseph Stevenson*

Recommended:

○ **Suk: Summer Tale; Fantastic Scherzo** / Mackerras (cond.), Czech PO / 1999 / Decca 466443

○ **Suk: A Summer's Tale** / Pesek (cond.), Royal Liverpool PO / 1995 / Virgin 45057

○ **Suk: A Summer Tale; Meditation on "St. Wenceslaus"; Dvořák: Husitská** / Sejna (cond.), Czech PO / Supraphon 1923

Ripening, symphonic poem, Op. 34 (1912–1917)

Although Suk's *"Asrael" Symphony* is perhaps the more deeply felt and emotionally affective work, in many ways *Ripening* is more masterful and more profound. And it is certainly the more subtly composed. The *"Asrael"* is a five-movement symphony not unlike the symphonies of Mahler in tone and structure. *Ripening* is wholly individual in tone and utterly original in structure. Called a symphonic poem by its composer, Suk's *Ripening* is based on a poem of the same title by Czech writer Antonin Sova. Suk began work on it in 1912, completed it five years later, and heard it premiered the year after that by Vaclav Talich and the newly formed Czech Philharmonic. The work's long gestation was caused in part by Suk's concert career as the second violinist of the Bohemian String Quartet and in part by the tremendous material difficulties caused by World War I, but in large part by the sheer difficulty of executing a work of such tremendous emotional range and unprecedented structural sophistication. *Ripening* could be described as being in seven large, continuous sections: Introduction, first Scherzo, Adagio, second Scherzo, "Funeral March," Fugue, and Epilogue. Each of these sections, however, partakes of motives and themes of the other sections. Thus, the slow Introduction contains the melodic seeds of Adagio and the Epilogue, the first Scherzo recalls the opening bars of the Introduction, the Adagio predicts the thematic material of the second Scherzo, the "Funeral March" recalls some of the gestures of the Adagio, the Fugue's themes are made up of motives derived from earlier themes, and the concluding Epilogue dissolves all of the themes and motives into sublime harmonies. All of this sounds tremendously complicated, but the emotional progress of *Ripening* makes its musical progress absolutely lucid. The title itself is metaphoric and might be better translated as "maturity." In the work, Suk traces a life—*his* life as it turns out—through the music. The radiant Introduction is his childhood, luminous and clear. The light-footed first Scherzo is his rambunctious youth. The ardent Adagio, marked "very expressive and passionate," is his love for his wife. The muscular second Scherzo is his early manhood. The anguished "Funeral March" is the death of his beloved wife. The Fugue is the resolution of his suffering through work. And the Epilogue is, of course, Suk's own hard-won ripening. *—James Leonard*

Recommended:

○ **Suk: Ripening; A Fairy-Tale** / Talich (cond.), Czech PO / 1956 / Supraphon 111904

○ **Suk: Ripening; Praga** / Pesek (cond.), Royal Liverpool PO / 1993 / Virgin 59318

Serenade for strings in E flat major, Op. 6 (1892)

When dismissing his Prague Conservatory composition class for the summer at the end of the 1891–92 school year, Antonín Dvořák bade 18-year-old Josef Suk, "It's summertime now, so go and make something lively for a change, to compensate for all those pomposities in minor." Suk took that advice and that summer created what is still his best-known work, a sunny and uncomplicated *Serenade* of substantial dimensions, lasting nearly a half hour. In mood and mastery it is worthy of comparison with other great nineteenth century string works such as the *Serenade* by Tchaikovsky, the *Holberg Suite* by Grieg, and the *String Serenade* by Dvořák himself. The line of sunny string works would continue with compositions by the likes of Elgar, Holst, Britten, and Diamond.

Little in the way of analysis is required to absorb and appreciate this gentle and beautiful piece, though it is worth noting that the main subject of the first movement is practically identical with part of the main theme of Brahms' violin concerto. The most substantial movement is the lyrical slow movement, at over ten minutes. One of the main pieces in the Romantic string orchestra repertory, the *Serenade* was premiered as a whole on February 25, 1895, by the Prague Conservatory Orchestra conducted by Antonín Bennewitz, to great acclaim; two movements had been heard 14 months earlier in Tabor, conducted by Suk himself. *—Joseph Stevenson*

Recommended:

- ○ **Summer Evening: Works by Kodály and Suk** / Orpheus CO / 1996 / DG 447109
- ○ **Suk: Asrael; Fairy Tale; Serenade** / Belohlavek (cond.), Czech PO / 1998 / Chandos 9640
- ○ **Great Conductors of the 20th Century: Václav Talich** / Talich (cond.), Czech PO / EMI 75483

CONCERTO

Fairy Tale (Pohádka), for violin & orchestra, Op. 16 (1899–1900)

The suite called *Fairy Tale* by Josef Suk is an arrangement and expansion of the incidental music he wrote for Julius Zeyer's *Dramatic Tale Raduzand Mahulena* in 1889. The complete incidental music included interludes, postludes, choruses, songs, and melodramas. From this, Suk extracted and then recomposed four movements that charted the destiny of the two title characters. The opening movement, "The Love of Raduz and Mahulena," is a deeply poetic depiction of their love in lushly sweet orchestral colors with the solo violin taking the lead. The following "à la Polka" second movement, despite its Polish title, is a joyous and sparkling series of Czech dances. The Funeral Music Adagio that follows is heart-numbing in its agonized power and heartrending in its palpable sense of anguished loss. And the demonic drive and cathartic release of his closing "Victory of Love" finale is, as such things would always be with Suk, the triumphant apotheosis of love. Because Suk saw himself and his own beloved Otilka as Raduz and Mahulena, the work has autobiographical implications and many of the themes and motifs of the *Fairy Tale* would reappear in Suk's later music. The solo violin of the opening and closing movements later became a symbol for the violin-playing Suk himself. "The Fate" motif of the first and third movements would become one of the two main themes of the *"Asrael" Symphony*. And, of course, the apotheosis of love finale is the overriding goal of nearly all Suk's major works. *—James Leonard*

Recommended:

- ○ **Suk: Pohadka; Praga** / Pesek (cond.), Skvor, Czech PO / Supraphon 103389
- ○ **Suk: Asrael; Fairy Tale; Serenade** / Belohlavek (cond.), Czech PO / 1998 / Chandos 9640

Josef Suk (violinist)

b. Aug. 8, 1929, Prague

Violinist

Not a virtuoso of the amaze-and-stun variety, Josef Suk has made his considerable reputation through a conscientious approach to the masters, a keen appreciation for Czech music, and a musical imagination of the first order. Grandson of Josef Suk (the composer and member of the Bohemian String Quartet) and great-grandson of Antonín Dvořák, the violinist has amassed an extensive catalog of recordings and has traveled to most of the world's major concert halls. Despite the acclaim he has achieved as a soloist, Suk has remained a devoted proponent of chamber music and has led his own chamber orchestra in distinguished performances and recordings. After private music lessons, Suk entered the Prague Conservatory, studying with violinist Jaroslav Kocian before entering the Prague Academy. During his student days, Suk had already been engaged as a member of the Prague Quartet. In 1951, he formed the Suk Trio, collaborating with two other musicians whose reputations would grow to match his own: pianist Julius Katchen and cellist Janos Starker. In 1954, his official solo debut in Prague met with spectacular success; critics rejoiced that a new artist had emerged to carry forward the tradition of great Czech violin performance. Suk has been a frequent guest artist with the Czech Philharmonic, playing concerts in Prague and touring with the orchestra to America, Japan, Australia, and other parts of Europe. He has served as artistic director of the Suk Chamber Orchestra and has appeared as a guest artist with the Smetana Quartet in concert and on recordings. Recording for EMI, Decca, and Supraphon, Suk has collaborated with Julius Katchen in the Brahms' sonatas and with Iona Brown and the Academy of St. Martin-in-the-Fields in Mozart's *Sinfonia Concertante*. In the latter project, Suk performed the viola part. To no one's surprise, Suk has recorded many works by Dvořák, including quartets, serenades, waltzes, piano quartets, trios, and string quintets. Works by Fibich, Martinů, and Janáček also figure prominently. On six occasions, Suk has won the *Grand Prix du Disque;* other awards include the *Wiener Flötenuhr* and the Edison Prize. *—Erik Eriksson*

Recommended:

- ○ **Famous Violin Encores** / Suk, Hala (piano) / Supraphon 1311
- ○ **Brahms: Violin Sonatas** / Suk, Badura-Skoda (piano) / Lotos 00472131
- ○ **Dvořák Album** / Suk, Hala (piano) / Supraphon 111466
- ○ **Dvořák: Concerto; Suk: Fantasia** / Ancerl (cond.), Suk, Czech PO / 2002 / Supraphon 3668

Sir Arthur Sullivan

b. May 13, 1842, London, England, **d.** Nov. 22, 1900, London, England

Composer: Opera, Vocal, Symphonic, Choral, Ballet

Known in his own time for his serious music as well as for the comic operas that have survived until our own day, English composer Arthur Seymour Sullivan was born in Lambeth, South London; the son of a bandmaster, he was encouraged to pursue his musical talent from an early age. He learned the wind instruments of his father's band and joined the choir of the Chapel Royal. At 14, he won the Mendelssohn Scholarship at the Royal Academy, and in 1858 he went to study in Leipzig, where his teachers included Ignaz Moscheles and Julius Rietz.

In 1861, Sullivan began to make an impact on the London music scene. His music to Shakespeare's *The Tempest* was performed at the Crystal Palace winter concerts in 1862; the following year he published six Shakespeare songs. In 1864, Sullivan became the organist at Covent Garden, where his ballet *L'île enchantée* had its premiere.

In 1867, he collaborated with F.C. Burnand on two operettas, *Cox and Box* and *The Contrabandista*. Five years later, he worked for the first time with W.S. Gilbert when they jointly created the light opera *Thespis* for the Gaiety Theatre. The piece was moderately successful, but not enough for its creators to continue working together immediately. In 1875, however, the theater manager Richard D'Oyly Carte reunited the to compose an afterpiece for a production of Offenbach's *La Périchole*. The result was *Trial By Jury*, a brief satire of the judicial process, featuring Sullivan's brother, Fred, in the lead. The afterpiece proved so successful that this time the partnership continued. In 1877, their full-length opera *The Sorcerer* premiered under Carte's auspices at the Opera Comique, followed by *H.M.S. Pinafore* in 1878. *Pinafore* proved wildly popular, solidifying a three-way partnership of Sullivan, Gilbert, and Carte that resulted in eight more operettas before a quarrel broke up the team. After a reconciliation, Gilbert and Sullivan wrote two more operas, *Utopia Ltd.* (1893) and *The Grand Duke* (1896), but these failed to catch on and the partnership ended permanently. During the run of *Patience* (1881), Carte moved his company from the Opera Comique to the Savoy; from then on, Gilbert and Sullivan's operas became collectively known as Savoy Operas. In these operas, Sullivan's unerring sense of musical parody, with targets ranging from Handel to Verdi, perfectly matched Gilbert's witty social satire.

While Sullivan is known today for his partnership with Gilbert, he was active in other compositional forms throughout his career. One of his best known compositions in his day was *The Lost Chord* (1877), a song to a text by Adelaide Proctor written at the time of Fred Sullivan's untimely death. Sullivan was acclaimed for his oratorios, including *The Prodigal Son* (1869), and hymns, of which "Onward, Christian Soldiers" (1871) was and remains particularly popular. An "Irish" *Symphony in E minor* is sometimes still performed. Sullivan also composed operettas with librettists other than Gilbert; these include *Haddon Hall* (1892) with Sydney Grundy and *The Rose of Persia* (1900) with Basil Hood. In 1883, Queen Victoria rewarded Sullivan for his contributions to English music with a knighthood.

Sullivan's dearest ambition was to compose grand opera. Carte, wishing to establish an English opera tradition, built the English Opera House, and here Sullivan's opera *Ivanhoe*, to a libretto by Julian Sturgis, premiered in 1891. The opera failed and remained Sullivan's only attempt at grand opera.

Sullivan never married, but in the 1860s or 1870s he met Mary Frances (Fanny) Ronalds, an American-born woman separated from her husband who eventually settled in London. Mrs. Ronalds, who mixed in the same aristocratic and artistic circles as Sullivan, never divorced her husband but carried on a discreet relationship with Sullivan until his death in London on November 22, 1900. *—Roberta Klarreich*

OPERA

The Gondoliers (The King of Barataria) (1889)

The Gondoliers, or The King of Barataria opened on December 7, 1889, at the Savoy Theater in London; a piano/vocal score was published in London the next year. After the grim *Ruddigore* and *Yeoman of the Guard*, *The Gondoliers* represents a return to the satirical and ebullient Gilbert and Sullivan of *The Mikado*. The team's 12th stage work together, *The Gondoliers* was an instant success with both the critics and public; one journalist remarked: "Mr. W. S. Gilbert has returned to the Gilbert of the past.... He is himself again...." The first production ran for 574 performances, second only to *The Mikado* of 1885; the sumptuous sets and costumes required by the scenario undoubtedly contributed to this success.

Deliberately distancing the plot from the British milieu and mentality, Gilbert sets his story in Venice, leaving the cloudy English sky for the sunny Mediterranean world. Gilbert's libretto mocks the idea of a democratic, or at least excessively republican, form of government, in which "everyone is somebody and no one's anybody." This is perhaps why the show has not been as successful in the United States as have Gilbert and Sullivan's others. Indeed, the first production of *The Gondoliers* in the U. S., on January 7, 1890, was a dismal failure.

The experience of foreigners in a strange land is at the heart of *The Gondoliers*, as a Spanish Duke and his family, as well as a Grand Inquisitor, arrive in Venice.

Both foreigners and natives, aristocrats and commoners, find and fuss over love along the way. Gilbert injects an element of mystery as people attempt to uncover the identity of the gondolier prince.

Gilbert's Italian setting certainly inspired some of Sullivan's expressive melodic writing, and Sullivan's skill at characterization comes to the fore in "Now Marco, dear," from the Act I finale. Parallel segments of the two verses are set in different keys and have different melodic shapes and rhythmic differences that highlight certain words, such as "And oh my pet...." The eighteenth century time frame and aristocratic characters also prompted Sullivan to compose some of his most stately numbers, especially, "Regular Royal Queen," which greatly pleased Queen Victoria. Whether sung by commoners or aristocrats, the music of *The Gondoliers* is almost all in a fast tempo. Sullivan himself commented on the near absence of slow music in the piece.

Sullivan toys with rhythm to build suspense. For instance, in the second-act quartet (No. 7), a rising melody, sung "in a contemplative fashion," halts abruptly every third measure, heightening the suspense as characters try to determine which of the gondoliers is actually a prince. The quartet is also an excellent example of Sullivan's contrapuntal writing. Three of the four women maintain the number's sweet melody as each of the four takes a turn breaking away from the groups with a more active vocal line. The result is a continuous interplay of familiar and new music. Italian and Spanish rhythms pepper the score and we even hear a tarantella as the women and girls close in on the palace.

The Gondoliers boasts one of the longest opening numbers of any of Gilbert and Sullivan's works. This roughly 20-minute segment, set in a Piazza in Venice, contains no dialogue and some text in Italian. From the entrance of the flower-bearing farm girls, Sullivan develops lively energy that sets the tone for the rest of the operetta, which a contemporary critic described as "easily the most continuously sunny and untroubled" of the team's works. *—John Palmer*

Synopsis:

Act One. The story is set in Venice and in the fictional kingdom of Barataria, in the nineteenth century. The opera opens at the Piazetta, in Venice. Gondoliers and brothers Marco and Giuseppe Palmieri marry beautiful brides, the sisters Gianetta and Tessa. Soon the four learn from the Grand Inquisitor, Don Alhambra del Bolero, that one of the brothers is actually the son of the recently deceased King of Barataria, and thus rightful claimant to the throne held by him in the small Southern European kingdom. Their identities are uncertain owing to the action of a tipsy gondolier: entrusted with the King's infant son during a revolution in Barataria, he mixed the little Prince up with his own newborn son.

It is therefore decided that both Marco and Giuseppe must sail immediately for Barataria, where they will share the throne until their true identities can be uncovered. Unfortunately, they must temporarily leave their brides in Venice. While the young women are initially saddened to be left behind, they hearten themselves to think that one of them will soon become Queen of Barataria.

The Duke and Duchess of Plaza-Toro, their daughter, Casilda, and the Duke's attendant Luiz soon arrive. The Duke has come to confer with Don Alhambra. The Duke reveals to Casilda that as a baby, she was wed to the Prince of Barataria, also a baby at the time, and, therefore, she is the Queen, but the new King's whereabouts are unknown.

Act Two. The Second Act opens with Marco and Giuseppe seated on thrones in the Baratarian Court, explaining their new republic government. Gianetta and Tessa soon arrive, and the two "Kings" order a celebration. Soon, however, Don Alhambra arrives, followed by the Duke and Duchess, Casilda, and Luiz. Don Alhambra explains that Casilda is already married to either Marco or Giuseppe. Eventually the "Kings" and all three "Queens" are left alone to discuss the situation.

Don Alhambra returns, with the Duke, et al., but most importantly, with Inez, who was foster mother to the King's son. She is the only who can explain what happened to the old King's son. She reveals to the astonishment of everyone present that neither Marco nor Giuseppe is actually the King's son. Instead, the rightful King is none other than the Duke's attendant, Luiz! Not having quite the right temperaments for ruling, Marco and Giuseppe are secretly relieved. *—Robert Cummings*

Recommended:

○ **Gilbert & Sullivan: The Gondoliers** / Godfrey (cond.), D'Oyly Carte Opera Company / 2003 / Decca 473632

H.M.S. Pinafore (The Lass that Loved a Sailor) (1878)

In April 1878, Gilbert and Sullivan toured the deck of H.M.S. Victory, taking copious notes and making drawings of everything from the riggings to the sailors' uniforms. The librettist and composer wanted the visual aspect of their new operetta, *H.M.S. Pinafore*, to be as accurate as possible. Gilbert even ordered the costumes from a naval supplier. Such attention to detail, and the procedures Gilbert used to create the scenery and rehearse the actors, would become typical of the team's working method from *H.M.S. Pinafore* on.

It was *H.M.S. Pinafore, or The Lass that Loved a Sailor* that established Gilbert and Sullivan as a creative force to be reckoned with in British comic theater. The operetta opened at the Opéra Comique Theatre in London on May 25, 1878. The first performance in the United States took place at the Boston Museum on November 25, 1878. This was pirated and modified from the British production. The vogue for *H.M.S. Pinafore* in the U.S. was unprecedented, and by March 1879, eight different theaters were running the operetta, while in Philadelphia another six houses staged the piece simultaneously; one of these was the first version translated into German. Producer Richard D'Oyly Carte brought the original, British version of *H.M.S. Pinafore* to New York in the summer of 1879. He felt the great success of pirated versions in the U.S. would prompt audiences there to attend the original production; plus, he was annoyed that he and the authors received no royalties for the American performances. Gilbert, too, was unhappy with the situation: "I will not have another libretto of mine produced if the Americans are going to steal it. It's not that I need the money so much, but it upsets my digestion." On December 1, 1879, the D'Oyly Carte production of *H.M.S. Pinafore* opened in New York to great acclaim.

Gilbert's libretto has everything necessary to create a comedy. The captain's daughter, Josephine, is being courted by two men, one a sailor (Ralph Rackstraw) and the other the Admiral of the British Navy (Sir Joseph Porter). To make things more complicated, a former nurse, Little Buttercup, exchanged two babies many years earlier.

Sullivan's music, however, was responsible for the long-term success of *H.M.S. Pinafore*. After a great first night, attendance dwindled drastically. In August, Sullivan assembled a few numbers from the show into a medley for a concert at Covent Garden that rekindled interest in the stage work. Eventually, *H.M.S. Pinafore* would run nearly 700 performances. Sullivan's melodies are what make the show memorable. From the opening sailors' chorus to Little Buttercup's simple aria, *H.M.S. Pinafore* abounds with unforgettable tunes. Sir Joseph's "When I Was Lad" is a patented Sullivan patter song that looks ahead to the Major-General's song in *The Pirates of Penzance*. In the stirring chorus, "A British Tar Is a Soaring Soul," we hear Handelian ornamental passages, and Sullivan parodies contemporary patriotic songs in "He is an Englishman." The most popular number from the show is the second-act Trio, "Never Mind the Why and Wherefore."

Gilbert's leading comic figure in *H.M.S. Pinafore*, Sir Joseph Porter, is based on Gilbert's contemporary, W.H. Smith, whom Disreali appointed First Lord of the Admiralty although Smith had never been on a ship. As Gilbert explained in 1908: "You would naturally think that the person who commanded the entire Navy would be the most accomplished sailor... but that is not the way in which such things are managed in England." *—John Palmer*

Synopsis:

Act One. The sailors of the H.M.S. Pinafore, which sits docked at Portsmouth Harbor, are readying the ship for inspection by Sir Joseph Porter, First Lord of the British Admiralty. The vessel is under the command of Captain Corcoran. Little Buttercup boards the ship and begins peddling her usual wares, which include tobacco and candy. She is the operator of a small supply boat and, despite her nickname, is a husky but still attractive woman. Though her appearance on board involves her trade, she also has an eye for the Captain.

One of the ship's sailors, Ralph Rackstraw, is madly in love with Josephine, Captain Corcoran's beautiful daughter. Unfortunately for him, she is betrothed (according to her father's wishes) to Sir Joseph. Ralph formulates a plan, however, to elope with her. But his plot, which relies on the help of fellow shipmates, is overheard by the dastardly boatswain Dick Deadeye.

Act Two. Little Buttercup finds the Captain alone on deck at night and confesses her love for him. He reacts by informing her that a relationship between them is out of the question because of his status as a Captain and her comparatively lowly position in life. But Buttercup suggests mysteriously that things could change and allow the seemingly impossible to occur.

Sir Joseph tells the Captain that Josephine is not interested in him. Corcoran advises him that his daughter views him as somewhat intimidating, owing to his high rank and distinguished social status. He encourages Sir Joseph to continue courting his daughter by declaring that love can overcome all problems of social rank. But his further efforts are futile, as Josephine believes they are speakin of her love for Ralph.

Deadeye divulges the plot he overheard to the Captain, and together the pair foil the elopement. The event draws a mild profanity from the Captain—a profanity overheard by Sir Joseph. The latter decides that the intemperate outburst cannot go unpunished and thus confines the Captain to his quarters.

Soon Little Buttercup divulges a long-kept secret: the Captain and Ralph were inadvertently switched at birth. Sir Joseph then declares that Ralph is to be Captain and Corcoran reduced to a mere seaman. Since Josephine is therefore the offspring of a less-worthy family, he happily gives his blessing to her marriage to Ralph Rackstraw. Former Captain Corcoran then takes up with Little Buttercup in an outcome fulfilling the latter's mysterious prophecy. *—Robert Cummings*

Recommended:

○ **Gilbert & Sullivan: H.M.S. Pinafore** / Godfrey (cond.), D'Oyly Carte Opera Company / 2003 / Decca 000018202

Iolanthe (The Peer and the Peri) (1882)

Billed as a "Fairy Opera," *Iolanthe; or, The Peer and the Peri* premiered on November 25, 1882 simultaneously at the Savoy Theater in London and the Standard

Theater, New York. In London, the show ran for 398 nights, a success dwarfed by that of *The Mikado* less than two and a half years later. It was the first work by Gilbert and Sullivan to premiere at the Savoy, a theater built especially for their operettas.

The audience at the Savoy on opening night of *Iolanthe* experienced the first fully electrified show on a London stage. (The Savoy had use electric light for the previous show, *Patience*, but could generate enough power to light only the auditorium.) The chorus of Fairies even had battery-powered stars in their hair.

Evidently, Gilbert originally had entitled the operetta, *Perola*, continuing the series of works featuring the letter "P" in their titles (*Pinafore*, *Pirates of Penzance*, *Patience*, and later, *Princess Ida*) At the last minute, Gilbert change the name to *Iolanthe*, although the subtitle, *The Peer and the Peri*, probably satisfied his superstitious obsession.

Critics have compared the quality of *Iolanthe* to that of Jacques Offenbach's *La Belle Hélène* (1864) and Johann Strauss Jr.'s *Die Fledermaus*. Perhaps the most impressive aspect of *Iolanthe* is its continuous dramatic impetus. Fourteen songs follow one another in rapid succession, all the while driven by a conflict between the Fairies and the Peers underpinned by Sullivan's rhythmically intoxicating setting, culminating in the march, "Young Strephon Is the Kind of Lout."

The wit of Gilbert's dialogue and sparkle of his lyrics is matched only by the energy of Sullivan's setting, imbued with his sense of both Mendelssohnian grace and simple, Victorian popular song. In two acts, *Iolanthe* presents the convergence of two worlds. Strephon, and Arcadian shepherd, the fairy Iolanthe, Strephon's mother, and choruses of Fairies interact with earthly characters such as the Lord Chancellor and the Earls of Mountararat and Tolloller, supported by choruses of all levels of British gentry—dukes, marquises, earls, viscounts and barons. Their worlds collide when Strephon interacts with members of Parliament. Fairy tale or not, *Iolanthe* focuses on contemporary issues and even makes jokes about contemporary politicians and businesses that have lost their meaning. Both Peers and Peris live "on credit," and are indebted to others for their existence. Peris owe their life on Earth to higher powers and ancient myths, while Peers are in a position of privilege stemming from politics that go back hundreds of years.

Sullivan's overture to *Iolanthe* is one of his finest, faintly resembling that of Mendelssohn's *Oberon*, and is capable of being performed successfully apart from the operetta. Sullivan developed separate musical voices for the Fairies and the Parliamentarians. The Fairies, in particularly, have music that creates a sense of floating, weightlessness and constant motion. Often, however, there is an incongruity between what they say and how they sing it, revealing that their fluidity is merely an illusion: "If you ask the special function / of our never-ceasing motion / we reply without compunction / that we haven't any notion." The choruses for the aristocratic men, however, are appropriately dignified and the bucolic solos by Strephon, Phyllis, and Iolanthe stand in stark contrast to the marked, prickly numbers for the Lord Chancellor.

In *Iolanthe*, as in other operettas, Sullivan's harmonic language is not adventurous, but there are unusual moments, such as "The Nightmare Song," in which a harmonic transition depicts the rising sun. This divergence from the rest of the consummate patter-song, with its pedal-tone accompaniment, is striking. *—John Palmer*

Synopsis:

Act One. Act One takes place in an Arcadian Landscape. Fairies attempt to persuade their Queen to pardon Iolanthe, who, 25 years ago, had married a mortal (a capital offense) and given birth to a son, Strephon. Although she was forced to abandon her husband as a condition of the commutation of her death sentence to permanent exile, Iolanthe desires to return to a normal fairy life. The Fairy Queen pardons her and also consents to aid Strephon in his plans to marry Phyllis, a ward of the Chancery Court. The marriage is opposed, however, by her guardian, the Lord Chancellor.

Before the House of Lords, Phyllis declares her intention to marry Strephon. But when Iolanthe enters and has an intimate conversation with her son, Phyllis misinterprets their interaction, believing Iolanthe, who like the other fairies has a very youthful appearance, is a rival love interest. She thus decides she will marry one of two peers: the Earl of Mountararat or the Earl of Tolloller.

Act Two. The second act takes place in a palace yard in Westminster. The other fairies take offense at Phyllis' action and cast a spell on the peers, which renders parliament acquiescent to all of Strephon's legislative proposals. The peers become fearful of his grip on Parliament and beseech the fairies to relent, but, despite the fact they have now fallen in love with the peers, they cannot rescind the effects of the spell. The Queen is dismayed that the other fairies have fallen in love with mortals, even though she herself has developed an interest in a young sentry.

The two Earls abandon their chance at marriage to Phyllis in the realization that their family tradition would require that the one who loses her hand would have to challenge the winner to a deadly duel. The Lord Chancellor, however, announces that he will marry Phyllis instead.

Strephon divulges to Phyllis that his mother is Iolanthe and that he is half-mortal and half-fairy. The two declare their intention to marry immediately. They ask Iolanthe to convince the Lord Chancellor to forswear his intentions to marry Phyllis.

She does their bidding and in the process stuns the Lord Chancellor with the revelation that she is his wife. He suddenly remembers her. Marrying a human being would normally draw a death sentence for her and for the other fairies, since they have by now all married peers, as well. But the Lord Chancellor changes the law. The Fairy Queen then weds the young Sentry. *—Robert Cummings*

Recommended:

○ **Gilbert & Sullivan: Iolanthe** / Godfrey (cond.), D'Oyly Carte Opera Company / 2003 / Decca 000018302

The Mikado (The Town of Titipu) (1884–1885)

After creating eight works for the stage, William Schwenk Gilbert and Arthur Sullivan outdid themselves with a macabre farce set in the Far East. The origins of *The Mikado* have, of course, become clouded by legends, such as the tale that Gilbert had a Japanese sword hanging from the wall in his office and when it fell to the floor one day was inspired to write the libretto (a pivotal scene in the film, *Topsy Turvy*). What is certain is that the British, by the mid-1880s, were obsessed with everything Japanese and collected kitsch ranging from fans, calendars, lacquer jewelry boxes, and screens to stationery. Gilbert did visit the popular mock-Japanese Village set up in Knightsbridge before beginning *The Mikado*. The British familiarity with aspects of Japan, superficial or otherwise, became possible only at the onset of the Meiji Era in Japan in 1867, which made Japanese culture more easily available to Western Europe and increased the West's cultural influence in Japan.

Gilbert began the book for *The Mikado* at a time of crisis for the Gilbert and Sullivan team. Earlier, Sullivan had expressed his desire to compose more interesting music, setting a libretto that addressed deep issues appropriate for more elaborate melodies and musical structures. Gilbert's affinity for the burlesque won out, however, and the result was very good for the duo's bank accounts.

The Mikado, or, The Town of Titipu opened on March 14, 1885, in the Savoy Theatre, London, with Sullivan conducting. The first production ran for 672 performances, the longest first run of any of Gilbert and Sullivan's operettas. International success came quickly and *The Mikado* received more acclaim on the European continent than did any other of their works. This was due, in part, to its "exotic" setting, but also to the universal appeal of the characters. Every culture has a bribe-hungry Pooh-Bah, giggling schoolgirls, and a pathetic, elderly Katisha. The plot, streamlined and perfectly paced, revolves around two major circumstances: the need of the Lord High Executioner to behead someone, and the flight of the Crown Prince from Imperial Palace to avoid marrying Katisha. *The Mikado* contains some of Gilbert's best dialogue and song lyrics.

Thorough to a fault, Gilbert hired a Japanese woman from the village in Knightsbridge to coach the cast in Japanese mannerisms and fan movements, as well as help with makeup. Producer Richard D'Oyly Carte ordered imported silk costumes and hired Hawes Craven to paint the sets.

Sullivan fell behind, and Hamilton Clarke had to orchestrate the overture from Sullivan's draft. Some of the numbers were not finished until right before the first performance. One stirring anecdote that is true concerns the *Mikado*'s "My Object All Sublime," which Gilbert wanted to remove after seeing the dress rehearsal. However, the members of the company convinced him to retain the number, which became a hit.

Sullivan's music is typical of his style, with little that could be construed as authentically "Japanese." The opening chorus boasts a pentatonic melody at the beginning, and the "Miya sama" march at the start of the overture and when the Emperor first appears is an actual Japanese war march. Other than these numbers, the sounds are distinctly those of Arthur Sullivan. This is particularly true of "Three Little Maids" and the men's first chorus, "If You Want to Know Who We Are," which feature music that is pure English vaudeville but present a Japanese image through gestures and movement. Sullivan is at his best in the finale to Act One, with its powerful climax. *—John Palmer*

Synopsis:

Act One. The men's chorus sets the scene in Japan ("If you want to know who we are"). Nanki-Poo enters, asking where he can find Yum-Yum, Ko-Ko's ward. He identifies himself ("A wand'ring minstrel") and gives them a sampling of his musical versatility. Questioned further, he explains that he had heard that she was freed from her engagement to her guardian, as Ko-Ko had been condemned to death for flirtation. Pish-Tush tells him that far from being executed, Ko-Ko was raised to the rank of Lord High Executioner, the highest in the town ("Our great Mikado"). His first duty as executioner is to cut his own head off. Pooh-Bah enters and explains that as an attempt to humble his inordinate family pride, when all the other ministers quit rather than serve under an ex-tailor, he deigned to take on all their roles (and salaries). He intimates that he accepts bribes for information as another self-humiliation, and when Nanki-Poo takes the hint, tells him that the wedding is planned for that very day ("Young man, despair"). Ko-Ko himself enters and tells his story ("Taken from the county jail") and then, since he may have to execute somebody, announces that he has a list of people who never would be missed ("As somebody it may happen"). He and Pooh-Bah (demanding bribes for all offices involved) go off discussing wedding plans, and when school lets out, the young ladies appear ("Comes a train of little ladies") followed by Yum-Yum, Peep-Bo, and Pitti-Sing, who introduce themselves ("Three little maids from school"). They are delighted to see Nanki-Poo, but giggle hysterically when they see Pooh-Bah, though they offer unrepentant apologies ("So please you, Sir"). Yum-Yum and Nanki-Poo are left alone, and he confides his real story. He is the son of the Mikado, who fled when the elderly Katisha insisted that he flirted with her and demanded his hand in marriage or his execution. They go into detail, with demonstrations, of how they would behave if she were not engaged to Ko-Ko ("Were you not to Ko-Ko plighted"). They leave, and Ko-Ko, Pooh-Bah, and Pish-Tush are disturbed by a letter from the Mikado, demanding to know why there have been no executions. Ko-Ko refuses to cut his own head off, as a matter of professional pride, since he can't be sure he'd do a perfect job, so another victim must be found. All have good reasons not to volunteer, ("My brain it teems"). Ko-Ko is left alone, and Nanki-Poo comes in, intent on suicide. Ko-Ko and he reach a bargain. If Nanki-Poo will let himself be beheaded in a month's time, he may marry Yum-Yum. All enjoy the reprieve, and the lovers look forward to a month of happiness ("The threatened cloud"), but Katisha arrives, threatening to reveal Nanki-Poo's identity and claim him for herself. The ensemble, however, drowns her out.

Act Two. Yum-Yum is being prepared for her wedding ("Braid the raven hair") and contemplates her own beauty ("The sun whose rays"). Her friends return, followed by Nanki-Poo and Pish-Tush, when they consider the brevity of the marriage, try to cheer themselves up with a madrigal ("Brightly dawns our wedding day"). Ko-Ko enters, with the news, confirmed by all the town officials, that the wife of a beheaded criminal is to be buried alive. Nanki-Poo and Yum-Yum are aghast, Ko-Ko somewhat less so ("Here's a how-de-do!"). Pooh-Bah announces the Mikado is on his way now, and Ko-Ko and he hatch a plan. They'll just tell the Mikado that the execution has taken place, and Nanki-Poo and Yum-Yum will disappear together. The Mikado, his troops, and Katisha enter, Katisha making it clear that as his daughter-in-law elect, she rules the roost. He explains his justice system, that the punishment must fit the crime ("My object all sublime") Ko-Ko, Pitti-Sing, and Pooh-Bah describe the execution in some detail ("The criminal cried"). However, when it becomes clear that the executionee was the son of the Mikado, it turns out those involved must die themselves, even though the Mikado himself sees the absurdity of it ("See how the Fates"). Nanki-Poo and Yum-Yum enter, on their way out of town, and they realize that if Katisha can be married to somebody else, Nanki-Poo can show himself alive, saving the others. All except Ko-Ko, the assigned bridegroom, think this a magnificent plan ("The flowers that bloom in the spring"). Katisha, alone, grieves over her beloved's death and her own continued life ("Alone, and yet alive"). Ko-Ko comes in and at first to her wrath, pleads his own love. She softens when he sings the ballad of a bird that died for love ("On a tree by a river") and they agree to marry ("There is beauty in the bellow of the blast"). All the others come on stage, but before Ko-Ko, Pitti-Sing, and Pooh-Bah can be executed, Katisha begs for mercy for all of them, saying she has just married Ko-Ko. Nanki-Poo and Yum-Yum appear, and the deception is explained. Once the Mikado orders something, it is as good as done, so Nanki-Poo was indeed dead. But now, since he is alive on the technicality, the work ends in a cheerful ensemble ("For he's gone and married Yum-Yum"). *—Ann Feeney*

Recommended:

- ○ **Gilbert & Sullivan: The Mikado** / Nash (cond.), D'Oyly Carte Opera Company / 2003 / Decca 000018402
- ○ **Gilbert & Sullivan: The Mikado** / Mackerras (cond.), Adams, Rolfe-Johnson, Suart, van Allan, Folwell, McLaughlin, Howells, Palmer / 1992 / Telarc 80284

Patience (Bunthorne's Bride) (1881)

By the late 1870s, Aestheticism had become a favored subject of parody in England's *Punch* and *Fun*—magazines specializing in comic commentary on contemporary characters. Writers for the magazines felt it their duty to mock what they saw as an "aesthetic" school of poetry and art; caricatures created by *Punch* generally had long hair, wore strange costumes and spoke in an archaic, allusive language. Early in his career, Gilbert had contributed articles to *Punch*, and so was fully in his element when he set about drafting his satirical spoof on Aesthetic poets, entitled *Patience, or Bunthorne's* Bride. Gilbert employed some of the same caricatures found in *Punch* because he knew his audience would find them familiar.

Patience opened in London at the Opéra Comique Theatre on April 23, 1881. During its 18-month run (578 performances), the production transferred to the new Savoy Theatre, constructed expressly for presenting Gilbert and Sullivan's works.

Based on Gilbert's earlier *Bab Ballad* (a type of burlesque), *The Rival Curates*, *Patience* revolves around two rival poets, Reginald Bunthorne and Archibald Grosvenor, which some contemporaries thought to be caricatures of Oscar Wilde and Algernon Swinburne. (Although Gilbert avoided clear references to any particular poet, he did write Bunthorne's verses in Swinburne's style.) Bunthorne lives in a castle with his family and enjoys adding up his receipts. He even states that if he had the Elysian Fields, he would rent them out. Grosvenor, on the other hand, is an idyllic poet and "true" aesthetic, who despises money. Conflict arises when both try to woo the same woman, who has neither money nor social standing; in the end, Grosvenor abandons his appearance of aestheticism. However, the Heavy Dragoons, the philistines of *Patience*, also depend on appearances, certain that their uniforms will attract women. When this does not work, they dress up as poets; like Bunthorne, they are phonies. Gilbert's satire was not aimed at the "aesthetics" as much as at their fawning followers, represented in *Patience* by 20 lovesick women.

Costumes and much of the set were designed by Gilbert, who wanted lush and beautiful surroundings for his characters. Much as he did with his libretto, he patterned the visual aspects of *Patience* after works of contemporary artists.

Patience was both a critical and popular success; the reviewer of the *Athenaeum* considered the libretto "as near perfection as possible." Others, however, were put off by Lady Jane's "Silvered is the raven hair." They found the lines, "There will be too much of me / In the coming by and by," when sung by the overweight Alice Barnett, to be distasteful. Sullivan asked Hugh Conway to write new lyrics (which piqued Gilbert), but the new version sold very few copies. Nonetheless, songs culled from the operetta became very popular, and the production inspired clothing, Christmas cards and tableware.

Sullivan's score, not one of his most popular, was considered by some contemporary critics as "ponderous" or "churchy," which is what the story demanded. Bounce and ebullience do appear, however, in entrance of the "Soldiers of Our Queen," and the carefree telling of "The Magnet and the Churn." Most comical is the duet, "So Go to Him and Say to Him," with its choreographed dancing and gestures. The Heavy Dragoons have appropriately manly, swaggering choruses that betray their macho emptiness. Sullivan's orchestration is brilliantly colorful in *Patience*; one of his most elegant touches is the syncopated clarinet line in the quintet, "If Saphir I choose to marry." *—John Palmer*

Synopsis:

Act One. The story is set in nineteenth century England. Twenty maidens, all once betrothed to members of the 35th Dragoon Guards, desperately seek the affections of poet Reginald Bunthorne as they roam about outside his castle. He, however, is not interested in them, since he is in love with Patience, a beautiful local milk maid. She soon appears, as do the young men of the Dragoon Guards, who are promptly rejected by their erstwhile, Bunthorne-obsessed sweethearts. Bunthorne himself finally arrives and is quickly surrounded by the adoring maidens while the Guards depart dispirited.

Bunthorne confesses to the audience that he feigns his aesthetic manner to gain attention. But when he attempts to use it on Patience, she is unmoved, declaring she understands nothing of love. She later discusses the subject of love and courtship with Lady Angela, one of the 20 maidens enthralled with Bunthorne. The result of their meeting is that Patience determines she must immediately fall in love.

Archibald Grosvenor, also a poet and a former childhood playmate of Patience, soon appears. He and Patience make known their affections for each other, but cannot ultimately admit their feelings amount to full-blown love, owing to a curious logic: since they perceive a perfection in themselves that renders mutual love a matter of selfishness, they decide they cannot develop their relationship further. Patience resolves that she will force herself to love Bunthorne instead. The latter is delighted, but is not so happy that the 20 maidens decide to pursue Grosvenor.

Act Two. Patience reveals to Bunthorne that she is actually in love with Grosvenor. Enraged, Bunthorne tells Grosvenor to curtail his charm and transform into an ordinary fellow. Under the threat of a curse, Grosvenor acquiesces to his rival's demand. When he becomes ordinary, however, the maidens adopt his manner, and worse, Patience sees that Grosvenor is now just ordinary and plain, not perfect: she judges she can now marry him. The maidens also decide they can return to their fiancées in the Dragoon Guard. The poor Bunthorne, however, has no one now and must content himself with his supposed love for flowers and poetry. *—Robert Cummings*

Recommended:

- ○ **Gilbert & Sullivan: Patience** / Godfrey (cond.), D'Oyly Carte Opera Company / 2003 / Decca 473647

The Pirates of Penzance (1879)

The very first performance of *The Pirates of Penzance* was at the Royal Bijou Theatre, Paignton, on December 30, 1879. This, however, was produced for copyright purposes. On the next night, at the New Fifth Avenue Theater in New York City, the primary production of *The Pirates of Penzance* opened, with the subtitle "Love and Duty." After some revision, the show was given in London at the Opéra Comique Theatre on April 3, 1879, with the subtitle "The Slave of Duty." This production ran for 363 nights.

Pirated productions of *H.M.S. Pinafore* had prompted producer Richard D'Oyly Carte to bring the British version of the operetta to New York. In addition, Carte, Gilbert, and Sullivan were contracted to provide a new operetta for the New Fifth Avenue Theater. This would become *The Pirates of Penzance*. When the receipts for the *Pinafore* run began to dwindle, Gilbert and Sullivan, now in New York, were asked to rush ahead with the new work, and secret rehearsals began, with the score kept in a safe to discourage pirates. Gilbert suggested lifting "Climbing Over Rocky Mountain" from the team's earlier *Thespis* to use for the entrance of General Stanley's daughters (No. 5). Sullivan composed the overture the night before the premiere, Gilbert, Alfred Cellier and Frederic Clay helping write out the orchestra parts.

To obtain British copyright, Carte sent the libretto and score to Devon, England, only days before the New York premiere. His touring company gave a matinée performance in Paignton wearing their *Pinafore* costumes and reading their parts from scripts. Thus, Carte was able to establish copyright in both England and the United States.

Gilbert continued his practice of throwing his characters into an utterly ridiculous situation and then treating the drama with great seriousness. *The Pirates of Penzance* does have its comic moments, but the portrayal of the civilized Pirates themselves seems to have endeared audiences to the show. Having pledged never to harm an orphan, as they are orphans themselves, the pirates are a well mannered bunch, so much so that Major-General Stanley's daughters want to marry them only moments after they meet. The setting, on the coast of Cornwall in the late nineteenth century, creates a romantic, not-too-exotic atmosphere.

Musically, *The Pirates of Penzance* is a more ambitious work than its predecessor, *H.M.S. Pinafore*, to which it is often compared. Aspects of serious opera, which appear briefly in the earlier work, are expanded upon in *The Pirates of Penzance*. The duet for Frederic and Ruth in Act One, for instance, sounds conspicuously like Verdi, and Mabel's soaring entrance aria is drawn from a Gounod waltz. Sullivan employs a substantial double chorus in the impressive "When the Foeman bares His Steel." Sullivan's contrapuntal skill comes to the fore in the clever accompaniment of Mabel and Frederic's duet by the group of sisters, singing about the weather to an independent melodic line, as well as in the "Paradox" trio in Act II. Most popular, however, are the simpler songs, especially "A Policeman's Lot Is Not a Happy One," and "I Am the Very Model of a Modern Major-General," a perfect patter song.

In 1980, a New York revival of *The Pirates of Penzance*, starring Linda Ronstadt as Mabel, Kevin Kline as the Pirate King, and Rex Smith as Frederic, met with great success. Originally given by the New York Shakespeare Festival during the summer, the production moved to the *Uris* on Broadway on January 8, 1981, becoming the most lucrative production of a Gilbert and Sullivan work ever undertaken. A film version followed the next year. *—John Palmer*

Synopsis:

Act One. On the shore, the pirates are celebrating Frederic's 21st birthday, which frees him from his apprenticeship and will make him a full member of their band ("Pour, oh, pour the pirate sherry"). He, however, informs them that under his indentures, he was a "slave of duty," but now he intends to leave them. Ruth explains ("When Frederic was a little lad"), she was his nursery maid, and his father instructed her to apprentice him to a pilot. However, being a little deaf, she misunderstood and signed him up to a pirate. Finding out the mistake too late, she remained with the pirate band as their maid-of-all-work. In his last deed as a pirate, Frederic explains that the reason the pirates can't make their occupation pay is that being orphans, they have vowed never do any harm to fellow orphans. Since everyone knows this, the ships they attack always declare to be completely manned by orphans. Frederic also announces his intention of leaving Ruth with them, but they refused to deprive him of the company of the one woman he has ever known, and thus must be in love with. He asks them to join him in his return to respectability, but the Pirate King declares they must live as honest pirates rather than as civilized, dishonest gentlemen ("Oh, better far to live and die"). The pirates leave, and Ruth assures a somewhat dubious Frederic that she is a beautiful woman. However, when he sees a group of young girls approaching, he compares Ruth unfavorably to them ("You told me you were fair as gold!"), and she goes off in despair. He hides as the girls enter ("Climbing over rocky mountain"), but emerges to ask if any of them would redeem a reformed pirate with her love ("Oh, is there not one maiden breast"). All refuse except for Mabel, who declares herself moved by pity ("Poor wandering one"), though her sisters speculate Frederic's handsome appearance figured in her decision. The two pledge their love while her sisters tactfully shut their eyes and talk about the weather ("How beautifully blue the sky"). The pirates return and declare their intention of immediately carrying off the girls to a parsonage and marrying them. Their father enters ("I am the model of a modern Major-General") and is able to dissuade the pirates only by declaring himself an orphan and throwing himself on their mercy. True to form, they agree, though disappointed, and declare him an honorary member of their band. Ruth returns, pleading with Frederic one last time, but he again rejects her.

Act Two. In Major-General Stanley's ancestral (by purchase) chapel, he is troubled by his conscience, as he lied to the pirates. His daughters and Frederic try to comfort him, and Frederic announces he will lead the policemen against the pirates. The policemen and their Sergeant, however, are nervous about this undertaking ("When the foeman bares his steel") and have to be urged very firmly to go. Frederic is left alone, and Ruth and the Pirate King creep in. They tell him they have to share a delightful paradox with him ("When you had left our pirate fold"). Since he was born on February 29th, he has actually just celebrated his fifth birthday. Ruth and the King point out that the letter of his contact makes him a pirate until his 21st birthday, not his 21st year of age. He reluctantly declares himself thus still a pirate. He miserably tells them that the Major-General tricked them; he is no orphan. The King and Ruth vow on bloody revenge ("Away, away!") and leave. Mabel comes and tries to dissuade Frederic from following them ("Stay, Frederic stay!"). He is adamant, and accepting this fact, they swear to be faithful. He leaves, and the Police return. They hide when the pirates enter ("With cat-like tread, upon our prey we steal"). When the Major-General comes, the pirates hide as well, and the General declares he thought he heard a noise, but it must have been the breeze. The pirates and police join in on the refrain of a sentimental ballad he sings ("Sighing softly to the river"). Both groups emerge from hiding, and the pirates rapidly disarm the police. They are about to take their revenge when the Sergeant orders them to yield ("In Queen Victoria's name"). They do so at once and are about to be taken off to trial when Ruth rushes in. She informs the police that the pirates are "all noblemen who have gone wrong," and the Major-General promptly issues a pardon for their crimes and offers them his very willing daughters as brides. *—Ann Feeney*

Recommended:

○ **Gilbert & Sullivan: The Pirates of Penzance** / Godfrey (cond.), D'Oyly Carte Opera Company / 2003 / Decca 000018702

Ruddigore (The Witch's Curse) (1887)

On November 5, 1886, William Gilbert read the complete text of a new, two-act operetta to Arthur Sullivan, over dinner. This would become *Ruddigore, or The Witch's Curse*, possibly the most controversial of Gilbert and Sullivan's works.

Sullivan did not compose the numbers in the projected performance order. Instead, he began with choruses, and within 10 days, he had finished the opening chorus and the finale of the first act; by the end of November, all the material for chorus. As usual, several numbers were not finished until days before the premiere—Sullivan completed the score at 4 a.m. on January 13. The overture was assembled by someone else.

Gilbert derived the story of *Ruddigore* from his own one-act operetta, *Ages Ago*, with music by Frederic Clay, of 1869. The plot revolves around two brothers who try to avoid succeeding to the baronetcy, because the position requires committing a crime a day to avoid death. In the second act, set in the picture gallery of the Ruddigore castle, ancestors come forth from their portraits to prompt Sir Ruthven to do his criminal duty. Ruthven realizes that, to avoid committing a crime is suicidal, and suicide itself is a crime. Logically, none of the ancestors in the paintings should have died. Thus, they all return to life and join in a chorus. Gilbert based the most interesting character, Mad Margaret, on Madge Wildfire of *The Heart of Midlothian*, by Sir Walter Scott.

Ruddigore, or The Witch's Curse opened at the Savoy Theatre on January 22, 1887. It was not immediately well received; some referred to the piece as "gloomy." It is generally considered a failure, even though it ran for 283 nights and brought its creators a large sum of money. Gilbert told a friend: "I could do with a few more such failures." Critics and the public alike enjoyed the first act, but the second failed to please. The last 20 minutes were actually hissed by the audience. Sullivan himself found the "revivification of ghosts, etc., very weak." Possibly the greatest problem with *Ruddigore* is that it followed on the heels of *The Mikado*. Public and critics alike expected the same kind of farcical romp, but received something entirely different. On March 19, 1887, a parody of *Ruddigore*, entitled *Ruddy George, or Robin Red Breast*, by H.G.F. Taylor and P. Reeve opened at Toole's Theatre in London.

"When the night wind howls" is one of the best examples of Sullivan's ability to compose "descriptive" music, with its odd text setting and swirling orchestration. The double chorus, "So welcome, gentry," of women and men betrays Sullivan's interest in writing countrapuntal numbers. Sullivan turns to folk song style in "I know a youth who loves a little maid" and Dick Dauntless' "I shipped d'ye see, in a revenue sloop," complete with a hornpipe at the end of the song. Also, "When the buds are blossoming," from the finale of the first act, reminds one of Purcell, while "Oh happy the lily," in a sprightly 9/8 meter, has a rustic flavor.

After the poor reception at the opening, Gilbert and Sullivan rewrote several parts of *Ruddigore*, abandoning the re-animation of the ghosts and changing Grossmith's song after the ghost scene. *—John Palmer*

Synopsis:

Act One. The chorus of professional bridesmaids sings in praise of Rose Maybud ("Fair is Rose"), asking her if she has any plans to marry that day. All the young men are in love with her and are unwilling to marry anybody else until they have no hopes of her. Hannah tells the story of her own doomed romance with one of the bad Baronets of Ruddigore, the late Roderic Murgatroyd, and the curse upon the line that they must commit a deadly crime a day or die in agony ("Sir Rupert Murgatroyd"). Rose confides in Hannah she could love only a man who follows all the rules of etiquette. She was a foundling, with a book of etiquette as her only possession, and she holds it sacred, so even if she did love, she could not point it out, hint, or whisper of it ("If somebody there chanced"). Hannah comments that

Robin Oakapple meets her requirements, and alone, Rose laments the shyness that keeps Robin from declaring himself. When they meet, each confides in the other about "a friend" who is too shy to admit their love ("I know a youth"). Nothing is resolved, however, and when Rose leaves, Adam greets Robin as the true Murgatroyd heir. Robin explains that he fled that title and the attendant curse. The chorus of bridesmaids hails the arrival of Richard, his foster-brother, and Richard boasts of all the ships that he has refused to fight, thus gloriously sparing many lives ("I shipped, d'ye see"). Alone with Richard, Robin confides his love and paralyzing shyness, despite his awareness of his many good qualities, which he enumerates ("My boy, you may take it from me"), and Richard offers to propose to Rose on Robin's behalf. When Rose appears, Richard so admires Robin's good taste that he proposes on his own behalf, and is accepted ("The battle's roar"). Richard explains to Robin that as they had long ago vowed to do, he has followed his heart's dictates. In their trio, "In sailing o'er life's ocean wide," Robin mentions that *his* heart tells him to settle his considerable wealth upon his bride, and Rose suddenly finds that *hers* wants to marry Robin instead. When they leave, Mad Margaret, who had been driven insane by love for Despard, enters and has an appropriately mad scene ("Cheerily carols the lark"). She suspects Rose is her rival but Rose denies it. The bridesmaids and various gentlemen from town enter and sing of the pleasures of one another's company. Despard himself appears ("Oh, why am I moody and sad") and frightens them away. Alone, he comments that while he does his one evil deed a day, enforced by the picture gallery of his ancestors, he makes up for it by doing good all the rest of the time. Richard enters, and his heart advises him to tell Despard that his older brother, the rightful heir, is still alive ("You understand?"). Both delighted, they rush out. The bridesmaids sing at the wedding, and Rose performs a madrigal ("When the buds"), but Despard interrupts the ceremony and reveals Robin's true identity. Naturally, Rose refuses to marry a bad baronet, and after Despard turns her down in favor of Margaret, whom he had loved and abandoned in true bad baronet fashion, she takes Richard as the only groom left to her. Robin is in despair, but the others look forward to weddings and wedding feasts ("Oh, happy the lily").

Act Two. In Ruddigore Castle, Robin and Adam sing of the change in his life ("I once was as weak as a new-born lamb"). They try to plan that day's evil deeds (Robin's suggestion involves making hideous faces), but Richard and Rose approach the castle ("Happily coupled are we"), though Rose is dubious about his fidelity. Nonetheless, protected by the Union Jack, which makes Robin recoil like a vampire seeing a cross, she asks Robin for permission to marry Richard ("In bygone days"). He consents, and Robin is left alone in the picture gallery. The paintings come to life ("Painted emblems") and warn Robin he is just not evil enough. Roderic demands an accounting of his crimes. Unimpressed by his catalog, which includes forging his own will, they order him to carry off a lady. When he refuses, they begin to torment him, and he finally agrees. They leave, and when Adam returns, Robin orders him to abduct a lady. He sings of his new life of crime ("Away, Remorse"), but reluctantly. Despard and Margaret, now respectable citizens ("I once was a very abandoned person") (though she frequently reverts to madness to make a point) come to persuade Robin back to virtue. He decides to do so ("My eyes are fully open").. Despard and Margaret leave, and Adam brings in the abducted Hannah, who proceeds to beat Robin up. He screams to Roderic for help, and Roderic and Hannah recognize one another. She assures him she still loves him ("There grew a little flower"). Robin, followed by all the other characters, rushes in, exclaiming that he's found the solution. Since a Ruddigore can die only by refusing to commit a crime, that refusal is suicide, which is a crime. Therefore, not only he is free of having to commit any other crimes, but Roderic is still alive. He proposes again to Rose, who agrees, Richard pairs off with one of the bridesmaids, and all the other couples and bridesmaids express their gratification ("Having been a wicked baronet"). *—Ann Feeney*

Recommended:

- ○ **Gilbert & Sullivan: Ruddigore & Cox and Box** / Godfrey (cond.), D'Oyly Carte Opera Company / 2003 / Decca 473656
- ○ **Gilbert & Sullivan: Ruddigore** / Phipps (cond.), Sadler's Wells Opera Company / 2000 / Jay 1340

Trial by Jury (1875)

In 1875, Richard D'Oyly Carte, then manager of the Royalty Theatre, commissioned Arthur Sullivan to set a one-act libretto by William Gilbert; this work, to be staged after each performance of Jacques Offenbach's (1819–80) *La Périchole*, would become *Trial by Jury*. Gilbert adapted his libretto from his single-page "operetta" written in 1868 for the satirical magazine, *Fun*. Originally, the libretto was to be set by Carl Rosa, husband of Mme. Parepa-Rosa, a childhood friend of Gilbert. In 1874, Gilbert drew up the libretto, satirizing a breach-of-promise suit, but Parepa-Rosa fell ill and eventually died, her husband subsequently pulling out of the theater business. When Gilbert first read the text to Sullivan, he became increasingly disappointed with his work after each page, while Sullivan found it increasingly funny. Sullivan required only a few weeks to compose and rehearse the work. *Trial by Jury* was published in a piano-vocal score in June 1875.

Trial by Jury opened at the Royalty Theatre on March 25, 1875, and was exceptionally well received. (Its billing as "A Dramatic Cantata" certainly aroused critical interest.) *The Times* reported: "It seems, as in the great Wagnerian operas, as though poem and music had proceeded simultaneously from one and the same brain." Running for 200 performances, the piece became so popular that impresario Richard D'Oyly Carte leased the Opéra Comique and assembled a company dedicated to the production of Gilbert and Sullivan stage works. (Six years later, the Savoy Theatre would be built with the same purpose in mind.) With *Trial by Jury*, Gilbert and Sullivan began to establish a British comic theater tradition.

Gilbert's absurd plot concerns Angelina, the Plaintiff, who sues Edwin for damages because he broke his promise to marry her. Angelina must persuade the court that her loss has been immense, but Edwin, who is now "Another's love-sick boy," tries to convince the Jury he would be a worthless husband. The Judge falls in love first with a bridesmaid, then with Angelina, whom he marries. Realistic sets and bridal costumes only amplify the farcical circumstances in which there are no romantic leads and no real love.

Trial by Jury stands out among Gilbert and Sullivan's works because there is no spoken dialogue, making it more an *opera buffa* than an operetta. *Trial by Jury* is, indeed, a succession of recitatives, arias, and ensembles, but the style of the music and satire make it pure operetta, despite the realism of the court setting.

Opening numbers in *Trial by Jury* are clearly indebted to Offenbach and Lecocq, but the atmosphere changes as the Learned Judge enters, the music taking on a Handelian tone. (In the opening run, the part of the Judge was played by Sullivan's brother, Frederic.) In his entrance number, "When I, good friends, was called to the bar," the Judge explains his rise to a high position. Sullivan was careful to set the dense text in such a way that every word is intelligible. In "He'll tell us how he came to be a judge" and "A nice dilemma we have here" we hear parodies of ensembles by Handel and the bel canto burlesque in the style of Bellini. "A nice dilemma" bears a strong relationship to the ensemble, "D'un pensiero," from the first-act finale of Bellini's *La sonnambula*. Sullivan deliberately sets the text of "A nice dilemma" awkwardly to parody the guitar-like accompaniment of the stereotypical Italian ensemble. *—John Palmer*

Synopsis:

In a court, the chorus waits for the trial to begin ("Hark, the hour of ten is sounding"). The usher informs the Jury that the trial must be impartial, despite the suffering of the plaintiff and the disgraceful behavior of the defendant ("Now, Jurymen, hear my advice"). When Edwin, the defendant, comes in, the jury threatens him with huge damages. He explains that his love for Angelina began to cloy and so he fell in love with another woman ("When first my old, old love I knew"), and because they all behaved like that as youngsters, the jury is immediately unsympathetic. The Judge comes in and describes his legal career ("When I, good friends, was called to the bar"). He was poor and unsuccessful until he married a rich attorney's "elderly, ugly daughter." This connection brought him enough cases that he became rich enough to divorce her, he concludes, and now is ready to try a breach of promise case. The jury, impressed by his qualifications, declares him a good judge and takes its oath. The chorus of bridesmaids enters ("Comes the broken flower"). The Judge promptly sends a love note to the First Bridesmaid. Angelina comes in ("O'er the season vernal") and the Judge swiftly recalls his note and gives it to her instead. Her counsel describes, in highly overwrought language Edwin's courtship and desertion of her ("With a sense of deep emotion"). She falls sobbing into the arms of first the foreman of the jury and then the judge. Edwin explains that the desire for variety is perfectly natural, but that he is perfectly willing to marry Angelina today and another lady tomorrow. The judge thinks this is a reasonable solution, but the counsel reminds him that bigamy is illegal. Both urging the jury to consider their words as they determine damages, Angelina declares her passionate love for Edwin ("I love him, I love him, with fervour unceasing") as he assures her that he has a habit of drunken violence that would make him a poor catch as a husband. The judge suggests that they get Edwin drunk and see if in fact this is true, but she and her counsel object to this plan. Annoyed ("All the legal furies seize you!") the judge comes up with another solution; he will marry Angelina himself. She is perfectly willing to marry a wealthy man ("Oh, joy unbounded") and all are delighted with the decision. *—Ann Feeney*

Recommended:

- ○ **Gilbert & Sullivan: The Yeomen of the Guard; Trial by Jury** / Mackerras (cond.), Suart, Evans, Banks, Garrett, Savidge / 1995 / Telarc 80404

Utopia Limited (The Flowers of Progress) (1893)

Even through the golden years that established Gilbert & Sullivan as a single, Janus-faced entity in such runaway successes as *H.M.S. Pinafore*, *Patience*, *The Mikado*, *Yeomen of the Guard*, or *The Gondoliers*, the collaboration of socialite, establishment composer Sir Arthur Sullivan with prickly satirist William S. Gilbert was diffident and occasionally bumpy. Matters came to a head in April 1890 in the infamous "Carpet Quarrel" as Gilbert challenged Savoy house manager and business partner Richard D'Oyly Carte over theater refurbishing expenses. Gilbert dragged the reluctant Sullivan into the escalating imbroglio and, when Sullivan sided with Carte, declared their collaboration at an end. Sullivan, moreover, had already embarked on the composition of his "English Grand Opera" *Ivanhoe* to a libretto by Julian Sturgis. *Ivanhoe* opened January 31, 1891, though its unprecedented run—then and now for opera—of 150 performances failed to cover expenses. Meanwhile, both Sullivan and Gilbert more and less successfully collaborated with others. In October of that year, reconciliation was effected, though they did not resume their collaboration until January 1893 on what would become *Utopia Limited.* Given that luridly publicized background and the fact that *Utopia* ran for only 245 performances and was not revived by the D'Oyly Carte Opera Company for more than 80 years, received opinion has been that *Utopia* lacks the scintillance of the prequarrel Savoy operas—an undistinguished score sitting heavily upon stale wit. The unprejudiced listener may well be puzzled by such a verdict, for *The Sorcerer* (1877), a comparatively lame but occasionally revived piece, ran a mere 175 performances, while *Princess Ida* (1884) achieved an initial run of 246 performances and *Ruddigore* (1887) but 288, both works remaining part of the repertoire. On the other hand, George Bernard Shaw noted, "I enjoyed the score of *Utopia* more than that of any of the previous *Savoy* operas..." and compared some of Sullivan's touches to Mozart's. *Utopia* opened October 7, 1893, to a nostalgia-rife house eager to welcome a reunited Gilbert and Sullivan. The story line of wholesale importation of English institutions to a south Pacific island kingdom afforded relentless satire, given tongue-in-cheek point by a score of unfailing resourcefulness, vivacity, and charm. *Utopia* was the most elaborate and expensive of the *Savoy* operas to mount. That, more than any intrinsic failings, must have kept it from the stage for three generations. *—Adrian Corleonis*

Synopsis:

Act One. This satirical operetta is set in the Kingdom of Utopia, in the South Sea Islands. The first act takes place in a palm grove. King Paramount, a widower, is in love with Lady Sophy, the English governess of his daughters, the Princesses Zara, Nekaya, and Kalyba. Sophy, however, resents the King because of articles she has read in a newspaper attacking his character. It turns out that they were written by the King himself, but at the insistence of Utopia's two Wise Men, Scaphio and Phantis, who serve as judges on the Utopian Supreme Court. They wield a tyrannical influence over the generally benevolent King Paramount, having the power to terminate his reign by reporting any act or omission they deem improper to Tarara, the Public Exploder, who must then "explode" the King.

Not happy with her father's vulnerable position in the kingdom, Zara conceives a plan to rescue him from the menacing Wise Men and Public Exploder. The King is already a great admirer of English culture, and thus Zara, having recently returned from England where she attends college, introduces the Flowers of Progress, six distinguished men from that country who are now directed to reform all Utopian institutions. One of them is Captain Fitzbattleaxe, with whom Zara falls in love, and another is Mr. Goldbury, who initiates a new concept in the Utopian kingdom: each citizen must become a "Company Limited," and can only be held responsible for his or her declared worth—and no one can be exploded! Other changes are also instituted to effect the most reasonable emulation of English government and society possible.

Act Two. In the palace throne room Zara and Captain Fitzbattleaxe declare their love for each other. Scaphio and Phantis express their displeasure at the changes introduced into the kingdom, not least because they have been stripped of much of their power. They attempt to incite a revolution among the Utopian people by charging that the recent changes have left the poor lawyers with no work, since there is no crime, and that doctors are struggling because of the great improvements in sanitation.

Lady Sophy soon finds that she is falling in love with the King. Zara decides that the changes introduced have not gone quite far enough and announces the formation of political parties. In one of the operetta's most imaginative satirical moments, she explains that with this final addition there will be sickness, "endless lawsuits," "crowded jails," legislative gridlock, owing to one party reflexively canceling the other's measures, but also much prosperity. Her proposal receives overwhelming approval from the people, and the King then orders the two Wise Men taken into custody to await his judgment. *—Robert Cummings*

Recommended:

○ **Gilbert & Sullivan: Utopia Limited** / Nash (cond.), Royal PO, D'Oyly Carte Opera Company / 2003 / Decca 473662

The Yeomen of the Guard (The Merryman and his Maid) (1888)

Gilbert and Sullivan followed their "dark" comedy, *Ruddigore,* with a work that is equally grim. Sentimental and realistic, *Yeomen of the Guard* has less room for Gilbert's instinctive wit and cynicism; Sullivan, however, was pleased to work on a "story of human interest" with a serious undertone, a long-time desire he would ultimately fulfill with his 1891 opera, *Ivanhoe.*

In 1888, Gilbert and Sullivan began their new project under the working title, "The Tower Warders." Their collaboration was not the most pleasant: Sullivan infuriated Gilbert by insisting that he re-construct the second act when portions of the work were already in rehearsal. Perhaps this strained collaboration took its toll on the end product, since it never attained great popularity; although *Yeomen* eventually ran for 453 performances, Sullivan wrote to Gilbert: "I must confess that the indifference of the public to *The Yeomen of the Guard* has disappointed me greatly."

The Yeomen of the Guard, or *The Merryman and his Maid* opened at the Savoy Theatre in London on October 3, 1888. Critics immediately recognized the differences between the new work and Gilbert and Sullivan's earlier, "topsy-turvy" operettas. One reviewer commented on "...the new departure they have made, exchanging the grotesque fancies and wild extravagances of the past...for an altogether soberer style of opera, approaching more closely than they have done before the old school of English opera." No doubt the sixteenth century setting prompted both this approach and people's perception of it.

Sullivan's score abounds with elements drawn from earlier music and "serious" opera. The overture to *The Yeomen of the Guard* is one of Sullivan's two best, the other being *Iolanthe.* Both of these are tightly constructed and capable of being performed apart from the rest of the score. Immediately following the overture is one of Sullivan's best descriptive pieces, Phoebe Meryll's, "When maiden loves" (often referred to as her "spinning song"). This makes *The Yeomen of the Guard* the only of Gilbert and Sullivan's works to begin without a chorus. Ever-popular is the duet, "I have a song to sing, Oh!" introducing us to the strolling musicians, Jack Point and Elsie Mayard. Here, in which a drone accompaniment and modal flavor evoke older music.

Gems from the Act Two include, Colonel Fairfax's "Free from his fetters grim," showcasing Gilbert's alliterative ability, and the trio, "A man who would woo a fair maid," a contrapuntal tour de force. The bittersweet finale of the second act is very effective, culminating in a reprise of "I have a song to sing!" Particularly ingenious and subtle is the accompaniment during Sergeant Meryll's "Is this Phoebe?" during which he looks for his daughter. The orchestra links the segments of the hesitant voice part by continuing the melody when the voice drops out. Throughout *The Yeomen of the Guard,* the instrumentation is subtle, and Sullivan calls upon the full orchestra only for the tower music. *—John Palmer*

Synopsis:

Act One. Phoebe weeps over her secret love for Fairfax ("When maiden loves"). Wilfred, the jailer, enters, and when she immediately insults him, jealously reminds her that Fairfax is to be beheaded for sorcery. The chorus of yeomen enters ("Tower Warders"). Dame Carruthers comes in and Phoebe exclaims against the injustice of the execution and the Tower itself, but Dame Carruthers reproaches her with an admiring song about its steadfastness ("When our gallant Norman foe"). All but Phoebe and her father, Sargeant. Meryll, leave, and when Leonard, her brother, returns, they conspire to save Fairfax. Nobody has seen Leonard arrive, so he will hide, letting Fairfax impersonate him to escape. They are nervous but determined ("Alas! I waver to and fro!"). Fairfax is brought in to prepare for his execution, which he faces lightly ("Is life a boon?"). When Phoebe leaves, Fairfax tells the Lieutenant that he was framed by a relative who will inherit his estate if he dies unmarried, and asks the Lieutenant to find a woman willing, for a hundred crowns (gold coins), to marry him for the hour that he has left. The Lieutenant agrees and they leave. Jack Point and Elsie enter, pursued by a mob. He and Elsie distract them with a song ("I have a song to sing, O!") telling the story of a jester who loved a woman who eventually rejected a nobleman's love for his. The crowd starts to manhandle Elsie, but the Lieutenant comes back and drives them off. Elsie and Jack explain that they need money to buy Elsie's ailing mother medicine. The Lieutenant suggests that Elsie earn the money by marrying Fairfax ("How say you, maiden?"). After receiving reassurances that she will indeed be a widow and free an hour later, she agrees and leaves, blindfolded. The Lieutenant is also looking for a jester and Jack applies ("I've jibe and joke"). When they are gone, Elsie returns upset over Fairfax's fate ("Tis done! I am a bride!"). As Wilfred enters, she leaves, and Phoebe flatters and flirts with him ("Were I thy bride") for the purpose of stealing his keys, which she passes to Meryll. When he returns them, she abruptly leaves, and he follows. Meryll returns, with the disguised Fairfax, and the Yeomen praise his daring in battle ("Didst thou not, oh, Leonard Meryll"). Phoebe enters with Wilfred, and the "brother and sister" kiss one another warmly ("To thy fraternal care"). All the others enter for the execution, and Fairfax announces the prisoner's disappearance. Jack and Elsie are horrified at thinking she is a wife, not a widow, and the Lieutenant and Yeomen sing of their rage at the escape ("All frenzied with despair I rave").

Act Two. Two days later, the Yeomen, mocked by Dame Carruthers and the women, sing of the mystery ("Night has spread her pall once more"). They leave and Jack enters, miserable, followed by an equally miserable Wilfred. Wilfred wants to change careers and be a jester, though Jack warns him it's not an amusing life ("Oh! a private buffoon"). They agree that if Wilfred will report that he shot Fairfax, making Elsie think she is a widow, Jack will teach him the trade ("Hereupon we're both agreed"). When they leave, Fairfax enters, musing that now he's chained by matrimony ("Free from his fetters grim"). Meryll enters, followed by Dame Carruthers and her niece Kate. Dame Carruthers, in love with Meryll, has guessed, from Elsie's fevered ravings, that Elsie has married Fairfax, and they speculate about the oddity ("Strange adventure! Maiden wedded"). Fairfax is pleased to learn that his mysterious bride is Elsie, but decides to test her by passionately courting her. She is attracted but refuses to listen, being married to another. A shot is heard, just as he is about to tell the truth, and the chorus, Lieutenant, Jack, and Wilfred enter. Wilfred and Jack ("Like a ghost his vigil keeping"). tell their story of how Wilfred saw Fairfax attempting to escape, and shot him as he leapt into the river. All except Elsie, Jack, Fairfax, and Phoebe leave. Jack is about to propose to Elsie, but Fairfax interrupts, chiding him for his lack of technique ("A man who would woo a fair maid"). He pretends to show Jack how to propose, but turns his proposal into a serious one, which Elsie accepts, to both Jack and Phoebe's despair ("When a wooer goes a-wooing"). All but Phoebe leave, and when Wilfred comes in, she is so agitated that she lets slip that she is jealous of Leonard's marrying Elsie, and he suddenly guesses the plot. Since Fairfax is lost to her, to save herself and the conspirators, she offers to marry him. The real Leonard enters, with Fairfax's reprieve. Meryll enters, followed covertly by Dame Carruthers, who eavesdrops, and Phoebe tells him that Wilfred has discovered the plot. Dame Carruthers emerges from hiding, and as the price of her silence, demands Meryll's hand in marriage ("Rapture, rapture, when love's votary"). He reluctantly agrees. They leave, and the chorus women enter, singing a bridal song for Elsie ("Comes the pretty young bride"). The Lieutenant comes announcing that Fairfax is alive and free, to Elsie's dismay ("Oh, day of terror, day of tears"). Crushed, she cannot even look up as Fairfax enters, finally undisguised, sternly ordering ("All thought of Leonard Meryll set aside"). When she glances up, she is delighted ("With happiness my soul is cloyed"). Jack returns, and sings his song, changing the story so the woman leaves, but with a pitying tear, the jester for the nobleman, and collapses at their feet. *—Ann Feeney*

Recommended:

○ **Gilbert & Sullivan: The Yeomen of the Guard; Trial by Jury** / Mackerras (cond.), Mellor, Archer, Suart, Stephen, Palmer, Adams, Maxwell / 1995 / Teldec 80404

VOCAL

The Lost Chord, song

Published in 1877, Arthur Sullivan's setting of *The Lost Chord*, by Adelaide Procter, is one of the very few non-theatrical works by the composer that one might hear today.

Two versions of the ballad's origins exist, both stemming from Sullivan. The first of these claims *The Lost Chord* was composed, "in sorrow at my brother's death"; the other reports that Sullivan wrote the ballad while at the bedside of his dying brother, Frederic. Whatever the case may have been, the intensity and solemnity of the piece are undeniable.

When Sullivan set Procter's poem to music, her works were very popular both in England and abroad; they were published in the United States and also translated into German. In 1877, her poems were in greater demand in England than those of any living writer except Tennyson. The theme of *The Lost Chord* is ancient, something precious and magical that may only be discovered by chance. A person seated at the organ fumbling over the keys accidentally plays a chord that feels "Like the sound of a great Amen." The poem goes on to describe the effect of this chord, which "flooded the crimson twilight," "quieted pain and sorrow," and "linked all perplexed meanings." The high point of the poem, and of Sullivan's setting, is the penultimate verse, from which the poem derives its name: "I have sought, but I seek it vainly / That one lost chord divine, / Which came from the soul of the organ / And entered into mine." In the final verse, the organist muses that he will hear this "lost chord" again "only in heaven." Sullivan's setting of *The Lost Chord* is appropriately sober. Repeated notes at the opening are similar to solemn passages in *Patience*, *The Prodigal Son*, and *In Memoriam*. Musically, *The Lost Chord* follows an AA1BA2 pattern, with the first stanza's melody (A) given a new accompaniment for its repeat (A1), which is then contrasted with new material (B). Yet another altered version of the stanza closes the ballad. Sullivan spices the piece with an unexpected harmonic change near the end of the first stanza.

The ballad became associated with Mrs. Mary Frances ("Fanny") Ronalds. Rumor has it the Prince of Wales once stated he would travel the length of Great Britain to hear Ronalds sing *The Lost Chord*. Fanny Ronalds and Arthur Sullivan carried on a clandestine relationship for over 20 years. Overexposure to *The Lost Chord* provoked parodies and earnest mockery from the public and critics alike. In 1960, a commentator wrote: "It is to be hoped that Adelaide Procter's elusive Chord has how been lost forever." Posterity has tended to look upon *The Lost Chord* and other songs such as *Sad Memories*, *Looking Back* and *Once Again*, as examples of "the depths to which Sullivan could fall" when he tried to make money. In the late 1970s, however, Nicholas Temperley was brave enough to describe the work as "Sullivan's maligned masterpiece." *—John Palmer*

Recommended:

○ **Songs My Father Taught Me** / Allen, Martineau / 2002 / Hyperion 67290

○ **Songs We Forgot to Remember** / Aler, Gershon / 1996 / Delos 3181

SYMPHONIC

Symphony in E major ("Irish") (1866)

Composing a symphony in Victorian England was a risky venture. Aside from those by Mendelssohn, the British public was not interested in symphonies, and felt more current works in the genre—for example, those of Schumann—to be eccentric. Arthur Sullivan conceived his only essay in the genre, the *Symphony in E major*, while vacationing in Northern Ireland in the summer of 1863. He had originally intended to complete the piece for the 1863–64 concert season of the Musical Society, a concert-promoting organization run by conductor Alfred Mellon. Apparently, Sullivan did not finish the work that year, since it was not premiered until 1866, and not by the Musical Society.

Reactions to the first performance were not particularly enthusiastic; after a later performance in the same year, however, a reviewer in the London *Times* described the work as "By far the most noticeable composition that has proceeded from Mr. Sullivan's pen [and] the best musical work, if judged only by the largeness of its form and the number of beautiful thoughts it contains, for a long time produced by any English composer." The score was first published after the composer's death by Novello & Co., who appended the sobriquet "Irish Symphony." The name was apparently proposed to Sullivan while he was alive, but the composer wished to avoid the inevitable comparisons with Mendelssohn's popular *Symphony No. 3 in A minor*, the "Scottish Symphony."

The first movement of the symphony in cast as a sonata-allegro. Although written in 3/4 time, the upward-leaping line in the violins and violas that characterizes introduction creates the feel of 6/8 feel through the grouping of its notes. The twelve-measure main theme begins in E minor and features downward leaps and quarter note triplets. In the development section, Sullivan extends and spins out this melody in a fashion that recalls the musical language of Schumann.

The second movement is intensely lyrical, with a simple accompaniment. Expressivity is the *raison d'être* of this movement, and this spirit continues all the way through to the lengthy oboe solo at the end. For several reasons this passage is remarkable, and not only because such long melodic stretches for the instrument are unusual. The oboe begins its lively melody in B major, the movement's prevailing key, accompanied by only a few pizzicato string chords. Within ten measures, the tune sheds its tonality and emerges in C major, and the third movement has begun. Some commentators have remarked that Sullivan's choice of C major for the third movement is "off the mark" or "unrelated," when it is simply the Neapolitan of — that is, a half step above—the dominant. Scherzo-like in its flavor, the movement has an unusual formal pattern—ABCA—that includes a brief coda based on the B section. The movement's simple, predictable melodies evoke the spirit of folk song. The finale suffers somewhat from repetitiveness, and the orchestration here is rather less imaginative than that in the rest of the work. Otherwise, the instrumentation throughout the entire symphony exhibits great variety—Sullivan's use of the bassoon is particularly notable—with moments that look forward to passages in the composer's well-known comic operas. *—John Palmer*

Recommended:

○ **Sullivan: Symphony in E major 'Irish'; Overture In Memoriam; Suite from 'The Tempest'** / Hickox (cond.), BBC PO / 2000 / Chandos 9859

CHORAL

St. Gertrude, hymn ("Onward, Christian soldiers")

On April 12, 1854, Arthur Sullivan became a chorister of the Chapel Royal, whose obligation was to sing Sundays and holidays at services at St. James Palace and to receive, in return, an exactingly thorough education. In May the following year, the precocious 12 year old had the satisfaction of hearing an anthem of his own composition, *Sing Unto the Lord and Bless His Name*, sung at services by his fellow choristers. Issued later that year by the prestigious firm of Novello, it was Sullivan's first published work. Thus, for better or worse, Sullivan was inured from the first to producing music for religious use.

Sullivan early on moved easily from royal salons to the concert hall, and from the theater to the dim purlieus where stupendously popular (and highly remunerative) hymnals were compiled. In the upshot, he produced something in the neighborhood of 100 hymns, anthems, and sacred part-songs, a number of which still linger in Protestant hymnals. Of these, *Onward, Christian Soldiers* is far and away the best-known and musically the most compelling, its banal phrases marshaled stirringly with complete conviction to the strident words of Sabine Baring-Gould. Sullivan facetiously named the tune "St. Gertrude," after the wife of his friend Ernest Clay Ker Seymer. It is one of those droll coincidences that *Onward, Christian Soldiers* should have appeared as part of an advertisement in *The Musical Times* for Novello's latest collection, *The Hymnary*, in December 1871, at just the moment that Sullivan's first collaboration with W.S. Gilbert reached the stage of London's *Gaiety Theatre. Thespis, or The Gods Grown Old*, was hissed at its opening night, December 23, and had but a short run, while *Onward, Christian Soldiers* was an immediate and enduring success. Apart from two songs and some ballet music, the score of *Thespis* has completely vanished, while *Onward, Christian Soldiers* is still being heard throughout the world. *—Adrian Corleonis*

Recommended:

○ **All Things Bright and Beautiful** / Archer (cond.), Gough, Wells Cathedral Choir / Hyperion 12104

BALLET

Pineapple Poll (1951)

Pineapple Poll is a ballet in one act and three scenes with a libretto and choreography by John Cranko commissioned by the Sadler's Wells theater, meant to coincide with the Festival of Britain. Cranko based the scenario on one of Gilbert's "Bab Ballads," entitled *The Bumboat Woman's Story.* Gilbert's "Bab Ballads" were short comic "plays" written for the British satirical magazine, *Fun.* "Bab," which is short for "Baby" (pronounced "Babby"), was Gilbert's pseudonym, originally appended to drawings and later to innumerable, brief ballads, appearing mainly in the 1860s and 1870s.

Conductor Sir Charles Mackerras gleaned excerpts of Sullivan's music from Gilbert and Sullivan operettas. This was made possible by the expiration in 1950 of the copyright on Sullivan's works. First performed at the Sadler's Wells in March 1951, *Pineapple Poll* became an immediate sensation and the production was given regularly into the late 1950s by both the Royal Ballet at Covent Garden and Sadler's Wells. In a similar manner, Mackerras has also arranged the ballet, *The Lady and the Fool,* from music by Sullivan.

The plot of *Pineapple Poll* revolves around Pineapple Poll and her colleagues, who are all madly in love with the captain of the good ship H.M.S. Hot Cross Bun. In order to board the ship, they disguise themselves in sailors' clothes, a fact that is not revealed to the audience until near the end of the ballet.

Mackerras came to know the works of Gilbert and Sullivan while he was an oboist at the *Sydney Theatre.* After playing a piano reduction of Offenbach's *Gay Parisienne* for a ballet performance, it occurred to him that an arrangement of Sullivan's music would also lend itself to a ballet setting. Mackerras describes his arrangement of Sullivan's music as "a patchwork quilt of tunes from most of the Gilbert and Sullivan operas. Every bar of *Pineapple Poll,* even the short bridge passages, is taken from some opera or other." Melodies from the various operettas intertwine in such a way that one follows the other in rapid succession. Employing a much larger ensemble than Sullivan did (three each of woodwind and trumpets, plus a large percussion section), Mackerras' orchestration is particularly lush, with many harp glissandi and warm horn passages. Most interesting is Mackerras' simultaneous scoring of the opening chorus of *Patience* and the second-act quintet from *The Gondoliers.*

The length of the complete ballet—45 minutes—prompted Mackerras to make a concert suite arrangement, which has been recorded numerous times and is easy to find. Mackerras alone has recorded the entire ballet four times. *—John Palmer*

Recommended:

○ **Sullivan: Savoy Opera Overtures; Pineapple Poll** / Mackerras (cond.), Royal PO / 1997 / EMI 66538

Franz von Suppé

b. Apr. 18, 1819, Spalato (Split), Dalmatia (Croati, **d.** May 21, 1895, Vienna, Austria

Composer: Orchestral

Composer Franz von Suppé—in full, Francesco Ezechiele Ermenegildo, Cavaliere Suppé-Demelli—was the leading light of Austrian operetta in the middle and late nineteenth century, enjoying a success that rivaled that of Frenchman Jacques Offenbach. Suppé's pedigree perhaps hinted at his promise as a composer of stage works: He was a distant relative to Italian opera luminary Gaetano Donizetti, who took an active hand in Suppé's education when the budding composer's talent became evident.

Suppé was born in Spalato, Dalmatia (now Split, Croatia); his parents, who discouraged his musical career, were Austrians of Belgian extraction. Though he demonstrated compositional aptitude at a young age—by the age of 13 he had written a Mass—Suppé studied law in Italy. After his father's death, however, he returned to Austria with his mother and made several return visits to Italy, probably resulting from his contact with Donizetti. Steeped in the music of Rossini and Verdi, he brought a lifetime's reserve of Italianate melody to Vienna.

In 1841 Suppé produced a singspiel, *Jung Lustig* (Young and Merry), which launched his career as a composer of operetta and light concert music. In 1846 he wrote his most familiar work, Dichter und Bauer (Poet and Peasant), an overture to a now-forgotten stage play; though an agreeable concert staple today, it attracted little attention at the time of its composition. Suppé enjoyed his first flush of real success with *The Country Girl* (1847), which cemented his reputation in such locales as Vienna, Baden, and Pressburg (Bratislava). His popularity remained steady for decades; in the course of his career he produced a copious quantity of lively, attractive music, emerging in the process as the virtual godfather of Viennese operetta.

That most characteristic phase of Suppé's career began with *Das Pensionat* (The Boarding School), a work designed to provide a Viennese counterpart to the phenomenally successful French operettas of Jacques Offenbach. Offenbach's works had invaded Viennese theaters, but Suppé countered their influence with such works as *Gervinus, Flotte Bursche* (Jolly Lad), and *Fatinitza,* each of which was performed more than 100 times. His fame resulted in an invitation to visit the seemingly inhospitable climes of Wagner's first Bayreuth festival in 1876.

Aside from *Poet and Peasant,* Suppé's most enduring works include the *Light Cavalry Overture* (1866) and the operetta *Boccaccio* (1879), widely regarded as the composer's finest effort. His other music includes a *Requiem,* masses, symphonies, and various choral and vocal works. *—AMG*

ORCHESTRAL

Fatinitza, overture to the operetta (1876)

The shining star of Viennese operetta in the 1860s, Suppé was temporarily eclipsed at the beginning of the next decade by the emergence of the younger Johann Strauss as a stage composer. Suppé returned to public favor in 1876 with *Fatinitza,* an operetta set during the 1854–55 Russo-Turkish war; the libretto, ironically, was one of Strauss' rejects. The overture begins sternly, with very subtle hints at both military marches and Turkish music without breaking into either. The main theme here is a little march, almost Tyrolean, that sounds like a chicken clucking. One of Suppé's typically tumultuous transitions leads to quiet but fully Turkish music, complete with triangle. The exoticism falls away almost immediately for a grand, romantic theme, although the Turkish march soon returns in full force, leading to more tumult. Another whimsical march arrives, this one sounding like a Russian folk tune. A transition of conventional operetta chugging leads to yet another march, one worthy of the Strausses; this is the work's sprightly hit tune "Vorwärts mit frischem Muth" ("Forward with renewed courage"), which is sometimes played as a separate concert piece. *—James Reel*

Recommended:

○ **Suppé: Famous Overtures** / Walter (cond.), Slovak State PO / 1996 / Naxos 553935

Light Cavalry, overture to the operetta (1866)

Franz von Suppé was already a famous composer when he completed his operetta, *Die leichte Kavallerie,* which premiered on either March 21 or 24, 1866, at the Carltheater in Vienna, where Suppé was Kapellmeister. Carlo Costa's libretto addresses issues current at that time in the Hapsburg Empire, which was about to become the Austro-Hungarian Empire.

Hungary's place in the empire, although always second to Austria's, was increasing in importance, and the Viennese were fascinated with this "exotic" land of Gypsies. Writers for the stage took advantage of this interest, and works involving Hungary or Hungarians appeared with increasing frequency. Suppé's *Die leichte Kavallerie* was one of these. One only need hear the overture to notice this characteristic. Its bravura melodies and mix of modes make it the perfect introduction to an adventure story.

Opening with a solo trumpet call, Suppé's overture to *Die leichte Kavallerie* immediately suggests a military tale. After the rest of the brass join the trumpet for a cadence, a solo horn repeats the entire gesture. In typical Suppé fashion, loud and soft segments alternate as a solo flute tries to present a theme, but is interrupted by outbursts from the orchestra before the opening trumpet melody returns, this time in several brass instruments and accompanied by an intense, repeated figure in the high strings. All this serves as an introduction to the second section of the overture, which begins with a rapid pulse in the woodwinds supporting the main theme in the violins. Out of this grows the famous, "galloping" brass theme, which is almost immediately later taken by the entire orchestra, fortissimo. A slow, quiet passage leads to a clarinet solo that introduces a plaintive string theme with a distinctly, "eastern" flavor, created through the strategic placement of half steps. This is the "Hungarian" theme of the operetta, presented here at length. The galloping returns, and after a full statement, the opening trumpet call mingles with the galloping theme to create a crashing close. *—John Palmer*

Recommended:

○ **Famous Overtures** / / 2001 / DG 469322

Ein Morgen, ein Mittag, ein Abend in Wien (Morning, Noon, and Night in Vienna), overture from the incidental music (1844)

During the first half of the 1840s, Suppé composed about 25 scores for the director of the Theater in der Josefstadt and also worked as a singer. These scores were generally for provincial theaters in and around Vienna, and in Bratislava and Sopron. Not really full-scale operettas, they are best regarded as plays with songs, usually with an overture. One of these was *Ein Morgen, ein Mittag und ein Abend in Wien* (Morning, Noon and Night in Vienna), which opened at the Theater in der Josefstadt in Vienna on February 26, 1844. The play closed after three nights, but the overture was a huge success.

As in many of Suppé's early scores, the overture to *Ein Morgen, ein Mittag und ein Abend in Wien* is infused with a lyricism developed from the composer's study with Gaetano Donizetti (1797–1848) and rhythmic manipulation learned from his perusal of works by Gioachino Rossini (1792–1868). Like Rossini, Suppé repeats eight- or 16-measure melodic ideas, adding instruments and volume each time to increase intensity. Essentially an ABA structure, this overture contrasts a slow, lyrical middle section with boisterous music that both opens and closes the piece.

An attention-grabbing bang begins the overture. The first theme then sounds quietly on pizzicato strings before a ponderous brass chorale takes over. After a seemingly random outburst from the strings, the opening bang sounds again, followed by the pizzicato string melody. Thus far, the orchestration has been very colorful, shifting from dense to thin textures before the full orchestra closes the opening section with a firm cadence.

All of the preceding music turns out to be the introduction to an extended cello solo, featuring a plaintive melody over a waltz accompaniment on pizzicato strings. The pleasantly rounded melody happens twice before the full orchestra takes over, providing a new closure to the tune in the high strings. The cello takes over once again, ending its passage with an expressive, rising line that stops abruptly when the opening bang returns. Once again, the pizzicato theme follows, but this time it is interspersed with more outbursts and leads to a moment of total silence.

Unexpectedly, a new, very active tune begins and moves along with increasing intensity. Yet another new melody, built on a dotted figure reminiscent of Rossini, enters and initiates the repetition of short melodic fragments as the dynamic and rhythmic intensity grows. Finally, a reference to the opening bang closes the piece. *—John Palmer*

Recommended:

- ○ **Suppé: Famous Overtures** / Walter (cond.), Slovak State PO / 1996 / Naxos 553935

Joan Sutherland

b. Nov. 7, 1926, Sydney, Australia

Soprano

Soprano Joan Sutherland's mother taught her the piano and singing until she was 19, well enough that Joan won several singing competitions. Her professional vocal training then began when she was admitted as a pupil of John and Aida Dickens in Sydney. The Dickenses immediately started working on her neglected soprano register (she had previously trained as a mezzo soprano).

After studies at London's Royal College of Music, Sutherland made her professional debut at the Royal Opera as First Lady in Mozart's *Die Zauberflöte* (1952). Meanwhile, she married her accompanist Richard Bonynge; theirs would become one of the most enduring of musical as well as marital partnerships. It was Bonynge's interest in the Italian style of bel canto that first led Sutherland into that repertory; he even wrote exercises for her to develop fluency and command of the style.

Sutherland began to receive leading roles in Covent Garden's general repertory in 1954, and in 1955 she sang the role of Jennifer in the world premiere of Michael Tippett's opera *The Midsummer Marriage*.

Her breakthrough into the bel canto repertory came with her *Lucia di Lammermoor* at Covent Garden on February 17, 1959. The premiere was a triumph; such a stylistically organic and natural performance of Donizetti had not been heard for generations. She quickly became the most prominent young singer exploring the neglected music of Rossini, Bellini, and Donizetti.

Her voice had a beautiful quality which bloomed above the staff, actually gaining in clarity in this high register. Her phrasing was excellent and historically informed, and projected intense emotional involvement. The voice had extraordinary agility, and could negotiate rapid ornamentation in any register with seeming ease. The major aspect of her performance that most invited criticism was her tendency to sacrifice the consonants of words to the flowing legato of her singing, resulting sometimes in the words becoming unintelligible.

Sutherland's career progressed to one of great stardom and brilliance. She debuted at La Scala in Milan in 1961 as Lucia, and made subsequent appearances at most major houses of the world. The Bonynges organized their own operatic company and took it to Australia in the 1965–66 season, a triumphant return for both. She also undertook a major recording career with the Decca (London) Record company, which preserved most of her major roles in operas of Handel, Bellini, Donizetti, and Meyerbeer. In 1976, Bonynge was appointed music director of the Australian Opera in Sydney, where he remained for ten years. Sutherland frequently appeared with the company, with stellar results. She received her knighthood as Dame Commander of the Order of the British Empire in 1979. She made her farewell operatic debut with the Sydney Opera on October 2, 1990, in *Les Huguenots* by Meyerbeer. *—Joseph Stevenson*

Recommended:

- ○ **Joan Sutherland** / Sutherland, etc. / 2001 / Decca 467914
- ○ **La Stupenda** / Sutherland, etc. / 2001 / Decca 470026
- ○ **Bellini: La Sonnambula** / Bonynge (cond.), Pavarotti, Sutherland, Ghiaurov, Jones, National PO / 1987 / London 417424
- ○ **Donizetti: La Fille Du Régiment** / Bonynge (cond.), Pavarotti, Sutherland, Sinclair, Garrett, Covent Garden Royal Opera House Chorus & Orch. / 1986 / London 414520
- ○ **Rossini: Semiramide** / Bonynge (cond.), Sutherland, Horne, Rouleau, Fyson, London SO / 1986 / Decca 425481
- ○ **Verdi: La Traviata** / Pitchard (cond.), Sutherland, Merrill, Palma, Bergonzi, Maggio Musicale Fiorentino Orch. / 2002 / Decca 470440

Johan Svendsen

b. Sep. 30, 1840, Christiana (Oslo), Norway, **d.** Jun. 14, 1911, Copenhagen, Denmark

Composer: Concerto, Orchestral, Symphonic

Johan Svendsen, along with his exact contemporary Grieg, represents Norwegian Romanticism at its apex. Outside of Norway, where his status has never been questioned, Svendsen, despite his eclipse by Grieg, has nonetheless retained a cult of admirers and it may be only a matter of time before he receives the same belated international interest accorded to Berwald and Nielsen.

Svendsen was the son of a military bandsman who instructed him on a number of wind instruments and the violin. This led him, while still a boy, to perform in both a regimental band and dance orchestras, respectively, as well as him composing music for both. His exposure to symphonic classics came with his appointment to the position of first violinist in the Norwegian Theatre Orchestra and the subsequent discovery of Beethoven's music. Further study of the masters developed through his lessons with Carl Arnold, as well as his organizing a small orchestra of his own. Procurement of a royal stipend enabled Svendsen to go the Leipzig Conservatory to study. Svendsen originally aimed for violin virtuosity, but shifted to composition due to nervous problems of the left hand. However, his musicality led to his being allowed to deputize as conductor in the conservatory orchestra. He left the conservatory with honors in 1867, having meanwhile completed his *Symphony No. 1* and string quintet. Svendsen returned to Norway where a concert of his own music drew praise from a review by Grieg. Local response, however, was tepid and Svendsen, another stipend in hand, traveled back to Leipzig and then Paris, the latter the scene of increasing performances of his works. The Franco-Prussian War in 1870 aborted a conducting position in Leipzig, but a successful performance of his *Symphony No. 1* with the Gewandhaus, as well as his betrothal to an American woman named Sara whom he had met in Paris, seemed ample compensation. Svendsen returned to Norway in 1872 to share directorship of the Christiana Music Society concerts with Grieg. The generosity of a government grant helped create a conducive atmosphere for Svendsen, these years seeing the *Symphony No. 2* and his series of *Norwegian Rhapsodies*. His star continued to ascend with him receiving directorship of the Royal Opera in Copenhagen in 1883. He traveled widely, meeting and working with Pasdeloup, Saint-Saëns, Sarasate, and even cultivating a friendship with Wagner. Sadly, his marriage had deteriorated to a point where his wife jealously flung the completed manuscript of a third symphony into a fire in 1882. Whether this was a catalyst or not, Svendsen's creativity severely tapered off at this point. He remarried in 1901. His international reputation continued until illness forced him to cease performing in 1908.

In his music, Svendsen prolifically composed in all idioms. With his bent toward classical forms, he forms a yin and yang of Norwegian Romantic music with the more overtly national Grieg. Yet there is a Nordic inflection present in the language, much as Tchaikovsky's Russian-ism shows through in his selected Western models. As such, he may rightly be placed in the august line of composers of the Nordic symphonic tradition. *—Wayne Reisig*

CONCERTO

Romance for violin & orchestra in G major, Op. 26 (1881)

Most of Svendsen's musical activities, especially later in his career, revolved around composing and conducting. However, he was also a talented violinist. He received early training on the instrument from his father, and later studied at the Leipzig Conservatory under the famous violinist Ferdinand David. Svendsen also toured extensively as a violinist, and wrote an early concerto for his instrument (the *Violin Concerto in A major*, Op. 6).

After working out of Leipzig for several years, Svendsen returned to his hometown of Christiania, Norway; he served as conductor for the Christiania Music Association from 1872 to 1877. It was in Christiania that, in 1881, Svendsen wrote his Romance in G, a work that has remained one of his most popular compositions. It is a restrained and elegant piece of about seven minutes' duration which begins in a tranquil, nostalgic vein, with the violin spinning out a sweet tune. A couple of faster interludes add a slight note of anxiety which is resolved in the quiet, touching ending. *—Chris Morrison*

Recommended:

- ○ **Svendsen: Octet; Romance; Nielsen: Quintet** / Academy of St. Martin-in-the-Fields Chamber Ens. / 1994 / Chandos 9258
- ○ **Sibelius: Violin Concerto; Svendsen: Romance; Sinding: Légende** / Leaper (cond.), Kang, Czecho-Slovak Radio SO (Bratislava) / 1990 / Naxos 550329

ORCHESTRAL

Norwegian Artists' Carnival, Op. 14 (1874)

Norwegian composer Johan Svendsen composed his *Norsk kunstnerkarneva* (Norwegian Artists' Carnival) for a specific carnival: the pre-Lenten Carnival held in Oslo by the Society of Artists in 1874. The work is in standard rondo form and has three main themes, all of them in major keys: a Norwegian folk tune, an Italian folk tune, and a popular Norwegian wedding dance. Svendsen use of these themes is apparently symbolic: the Society of Artists intended the carnival to reconcile the Norwegian festival tradition with the gaiety of Italian pre-Lenten carnival. To drive his point home, Svendsen combines all three themes contrapuntally in the work's closing section. —*James Leonard*

Recommended:

○ **Svendsen: Zorahayda; Karneval i Paris; Norsk kunstnerkarneval; Romeo og Jule** / Ruud (cond.), Trondheim SO / 1996 / Virgin 45128

SYMPHONIC

Symphony No. 1 in D major, Op. 4 (1865–1867)

The *Symphony No. 1 in D major* by Norwegian composer Johan Svendsen was written while Svendsen was a pupil at Mendelssohn's Leipzig Conservatory. It is, without question, a student work. The work is in the standard four-movement sequence of opening Allegro molto, Andante, Allegretto scherzando, and closing Finale: Allegro assai con fuoco. Its thematic and harmonic content is just as standard. The Allegro molto has an exposition with an assertive tutti main theme and a supplicating subsidiary theme for winds, a development that first states one theme then the other and then combines them both at the climax, and a recapitulation that restates both themes in the tonic key. The Andante is a lyrical mediation in the dominant. The Finale is the tonic and, starting with a noble Maestoso introduction, builds to a powerful brass-capped climax. Any of these movements could have been written by any mid-nineteenth century student composer. Only the third movement Allegretto scherzando is original in its succession of seemingly disparate themes. But even this is to be expected from a student composer who cares to show his limited independence. Svendsen's *Symphony No. 1* is a composition exercise by a talented pupil. —*James Leonard*

Recommended:

○ **Svendsen: Symphonies 1 & 2** / Jansons (cond.), Oslo PO / 1988 / EMI 749769

○ **Svendsen: The Two Symphonies** / Gothenburg SO, Jarvi (cond.) / 1987 / Bis 347

Symphony No. 2 in B flat major, Op. 15 (1874)

The *First Symphony* of the Norwegian composer Johan Svendsen was a composition exercise by a talented pupil. Svendsen's *Second*, however, is the undoubted masterpiece of nineteenth century Norwegian symphonism. It was written in 1874, during Svendsen's most creative period. This was the same year he became sole conductor of the Music Society concerts, having previously shared the podium with Grieg, and in which he began receiving an annual composer's salary from the Norwegian government.

Although like the *First Symphony* in the standard sequence of four movements, the *Second*'s thematic and harmonic content is wholly characteristic of the composer and his country. While the opening Allegro has the usual sequence of exposition with main and subsidiary themes with development and recapitulation, Svendsen's themes speak in their own voices and the harmonic relationship between the themes and its progression in the development is utterly original. The Andante sostenuto which follows goes much deeper emotionally than its predecessor in the *First Symphony*, and the Intermezzo: Allegro giusto is a stylized Norwegian folk dance. The Finale, however, is by far the most original movement. Although cast in the same slow-introduction-fast-main-movement-form as the Finale of the *First Symphony*, the Finale of the *Second* has four independent themes arranged in a wholly unique harmonic arrangement. And the climax of the movement and the symphony is more majestic and more convincing than its parallel in the *First*.—*James Leonard*

Recommended:

○ **Johan Svendsen: The Two Symphonies** / Gothenburg SO, Jarvi (cond.) / 1987 / Bis 347

○ **Johan Svendsen: Symphonies 1 & 2** / Engeset (cond.), Bournemouth Sinfonietta / 1998 / Naxos 553898

Jan Pieterszoon Sweelinck

b. May, 1562, Deventer, Netherlands, **d.** Oct. 16, 1621, Amsterdam, Netherlands
Composer

Jan Pieterszoon Sweelinck was perhaps the most important composer from the Netherlands in the late Renaissance and early Baroque eras. He is best known for his vocal compositions, typically written for five voices and possible instrumental accompaniment, and for his keyboard works, which included toccatas, chorale variations, and various fantasias. He was also one of the leading teachers in Europe during his time, numbering among his students his son Dirck Sweelinck, Hasse, Scheidt, Praetorius, plus many other notables and founders of the seventeenth century north German organ style that culminated in the music of Bach.

Sweelinck's father was the organist Peter Swybbertszoon and his mother Elske Sweeling. As a child Jan likely had his first music instruction from his father, who served as organist at Amsterdam's Oude Kerk (Old Church) from 1564 until his death in 1574. Young Sweelinck may also have studied with organist Cornelis Boskoop, who succeeded his father at the Oude Kerk for a brief tenure. For some reason Sweelinck changed his name to a variant of his mother's surname, possibly shortly after his father's death.

In any event, his keyboard talents blossomed quickly and Sweelinck succeeded Boskoop at the Oude Kerk, probably in the late 1570s. His post at the church was less a religious one and more a civil appointment, since he actually worked for the city officials of Amsterdam, not the Calvinists who controlled the church services and forbade music performance during them. Sweelinck played the organ probably in the morning and evening during periods free of official church service. He would serve in the organist post for over 40 years and be succeeded by his son, Dirck, whose tenure there was of similar length, ending upon his own death in 1652. Sweelinck's mother died in 1585, leaving the young composer to care for his younger brother and sister, which he ably did.

In 1590 Sweelinck married, and, already receiving a substantial salary, forsook an automatic increase allowed for in his contract upon marriage in favor of an alternate perquisite, that of rent-free living quarters. His wife would give birth to six children, five of whom would survive their father. By the time of his marriage, Sweelinck had already established himself as one of the finest teachers in Europe and had significant income from that activity, as well. In 1594, his first publication appeared, that of a collection of 18 chansons—works, undoubtedly, that date back to the previous decade. Additional publications came in 1597 and 1604, both collections of psalm settings. While his keyboard works rank in importance with his vocal music, none of it was published during his lifetime.

Another important vocal effort appeared in 1619, the *Cantiones sacrae*, comprised of 37 motets using Catholic liturgical texts. Because of the composition of this collection and other supporting evidence (his son would be reprimanded for inviting "papists" to a Christmas celebration in 1645), it is believed that Sweelinck and his family were Catholics.

Unlike most composers and artists, Sweelinck led a rather uneventful life, and comparatively little is known of him. He traveled outside Amsterdam only a few times, typically involving matters associated with his post at the Oude Kerk. He did return to Deventer in 1595 and 1616 for brief visits, and traveled to Antwerp (1604), Harderwijk (1608) and Rotterdam (1610). It is almost certain that Sweelinck became a close friend of British composer John Bull (1562–1628), who left England in 1613 to live in Belgium, from where he made trips to the Netherlands. —*Robert Cummings*

Overview of Works (ca. 1590–1620)

A supreme master of late-Renaissance polyphony, by the time of his death in 1621 Sweelinck had bequeathed a mighty impetus to German composers of the mid- and late seventeenth century (e.g., Weckmann, Reincken, Kuhnau, Böhm, Buxtehude, Pachelbel, Muffat, and his own pupils, the younger Jacob Praetorius, Samuel Scheidt, and Heinrich Scheidemann) in laying foundations for the towering edifice of the German Baroque, culminating in the works of Handel and J.S. Bach. As organist of Amsterdam's prestigious Oude Kirk for over 40 years, Sweelinck occupied an ambiguous position—a complete musician employed by a Calvinist institution for which any but the severest terms of praise were regarded as snares of the devil, the bulk of his surviving work was composed for private patrons, though the magistrates who employed him took pride in his international reputation as "the Orpheus of Amsterdam." Thirty-three French chansons and 19 Italian madrigals, published in 1612 in a four-volume collection of *Rimes françoises et italiennes*, document not only vivacity allied with charm but a striving for airier textures in which the number of voices, pared in the later works to three, play transparently off one another, frequently in canon. They also reveal a close acquaintance with the madrigals of Andrea Gabrieli, Marenzio, and the elder Ferrabosco. The 37 polyphonically animated Latin motets of the *Cantiones sacrae* (1619, five volumes) are drawn from Catholic liturgy, are patently designed for Catholic usage, and include the joyous Christmas perennial *Hodie Christus natus est*. His monument, the inexhaustibly resourceful 153 four- and six-voice settings of *Psalms* in the French translation of Marot and De Bèze, published between 1597 and 1621, exhibits an omnicompetent grasp of Renaissance vocal technique giving rise to expressive riches, among which Gustav Reese, in his magisterial *Music in the Renaissance*, singled out the six-voice *Or sus, serviteurs du Seigneur* and the four-voice *Il faut que de tous mes esprits* as especially fine. "With Sweelinck," Reese adds, "the great production of the Netherlanders in the field of vocal polyphony comes to an end. It does not wane ignominiously, however, but closes in a brilliant and noble sunset." If the vocal works look back, Sweelinck's keyboard pieces—fantasias, toccatas, variations—assimilate, refine, and expand the virtuosic fancies of the contemporary Elizabethan virginalists, whose works he probably came to know through John Bull, who settled in the Lowlands in 1613. Informed by Sweelinck's improvisational brilliance, they strive for a *punctus contra punctus* dynamism consummated by the High Baroque. *—Adrian Corleonis*

Recommended:

- ○ **Sweelinck: Keyboard Music** / Herrick / 2003 / Hyperion 67421/2
- ○ **Sweelinck: Organ Works** / Woolley / 2003 / Chandos 701
- ○ **Sweelinck: Organ Works** / J.D. Christie / 1994 / Naxos 550904
- ○ **Sweelinck: The Complete Keyboard Works** / Various Artists / N.M. Classics 92119
- ○ **Sweelinck: Cantiones Sacrae Vol. 1** / Marlow (cond.), Trinity College Chapel Choir / Hyperion 67103
- ○ **Choral Works of Sweelinck** / Herreweghe (cond.), Netherlands Chamber Choir / N.M. Classics 92010

Swingle Singers

f. 1962, Paris, France

Ensemble

The Swingle Singers is one of the most unique modern vocal groups, known for innovative, jazz-inflected performances of everything from Bach keyboard works to songs of the Beatles. The group formed from members of the Blue Stars, a jazz ensemble under the direction of Blossom Dearie. In 1962, Jeanette Baucomont (soprano), Anne Germain (contralto), Claudine Meunier (contralto, Claude Germain (tenor), Jean-Claude Briodin (bass-baritone), and Jean Cussac (bass-baritone) gathered in Paris under the direction of Ward Lemar Swingle (tenor) and Christine Legrand (soprano); their goal was to improve their overall musicianship and sight-reading skills by performing intricate instrumental works vocally. While making their way through Bach's *Well Tempered Clavier* the idea came to "swing" the piece; the resulting fusion gave birth to the Swingle Singers. They began performing Classical and Baroque works with a jazz rhythm section, employing a distinctive scat style in the vocal parts.

Their debut album, *Bach's Greatest Hits*, avoided the potential pitfalls of kitsch and instead proved a testament to the durability and flexibility of Bach's music, as well as to the group's vocal prowess. It also became a commercial success, appealing to a broad audience that might not otherwise have shown interest in classical music. Numerous television and radio appearances followed, as did back-to-back world tours; their music was on U.S. and U.K. Top 20 lists, and they won several Grammy awards, including Best Choral Performance and Best New Artist in 1963.

After their debut album, the Swingle Singers applied the same formula to the music of Mozart, Handel, and Vivaldi well into the 1970s. Then, in 1973, Ward Swingle traveled to England to form a smaller group called Swingle II, to perform a broader base of repertory. Swingle worked with the group until he left for the United States in 1985, where he then spent a decade lecturing and guest conducting. During that time he continued to direct the Swingle Singers as they explored the music of Dvořák, Lennon, Mancini, Bizet, Rogers/Hart, Debussy, George Butterworth, and Gerald Finzi on albums such as *Pretty Ringtime*, *Notability*, *Ticket to Ride*, and *Screen Tested*. As of 1999, Ward Swingle lives in semiretirement near Paris. *—Meredith Gailey*

Recommended:

- ○ **Anyone For Mozart, Bach, Handel, Vivaldi?** / Swingle Singers / Philips 826948
- ○ **Jazz Sebastian Bach, Vol. 1** / Swingle Singers / 1963 / Philips 4542552

Sanford Sylvan

b. New York, NY

Baritone

American baritone Sanford Sylvan is perhaps best known for his acclaimed participation in the John Adams operas *Nixon in China* and *The Death of Klinghoffer*, other operatic appearances have generally been just as well received. However, Sylvan's career has been much more intensely focused on the art song repertory—a commitment that has not gone unnoticed by recital goers and lieder/chanson-loving record buyers.

Sylvan was born in New York and as a teenager studied at the Juilliard School preparatory division; he later enrolled at the Manhattan School of Music for undergraduate work. The international spotlight first shone on him when he created the role of Chou En-Lai for the 1987 Houston Opera premiere of *Nixon in China*; the original cast recording of the work received a Grammy Award in 1989. Sylvan has since been nominated for several additional Grammys. The entire range of the repertoire has been represented in Sylvan's opera career, from Mozart (including the role of Figaro in a PBS Television broadcast of Le nozze di Figaro) through Stravinsky (*The Flood*). John Adams called on Sylvan again for the *Klinghoffer* opera in 1991, and also for a setting of Walt Whitman's *The Wound Dresser* (1988), and a number of other major contemporary composers, among them Philip Glass and John Harbison, have followed suit by employing Sylvan's considerable gifts.

When performing and recording art songs, Sanford Sylvan invariably casts David Breitman in the role of pianist; their collaborations, especially of Gabriel Fauré's chansons, are treasured. In 2000, Sanford Sylvan and David Breitman presented *The Glass Hammer*, a new song cycle by Jorge Martin, to a Carnegie Hall audience. *—Blair Johnston*

Recommended:

- ○ **L'Horizon Chimérique** / Sylvan, Breitman, Lydian String Quartet / 1996 / Nonesuch 79371
- ○ **Adams: The Wound-Dresser, etc.** / Adams, Waart (conds.), Upshaw, Sylvan, Crossley, Gekker, Orch. of St. Luke's, San Francisco SO / 1999 / Nonesuch 79453
- ○ **Jorge Martin: The Glass Hammer** / Sylvan, Breitman (piano) / 2001 / Koch 7519

George Szell

b. Jun. 7, 1897, Budapest, Hungary, **d.** Jul. 29, 1970, Cleveland, OH

Conductor

Part of the wave of great Hungarian conductors who took over American musical life just before and after World War II—the others included Fritz Reiner, Antal Dorati, and Eugene Ormandy—George Szell quickly transformed a middling Midwestern orchestra into one of the nation's Big Five. His cultivation of the Cleveland Orchestra set an example of discipline and hard work that gradually helped raise the standards of orchestras across America.

Although born in Hungary, Szell was raised in Vienna where he studied composition with Eusebius Mandyczewski, and piano with Richard Robert; he also studied composition in Prague with J.B. Foerster. Szell was a *wunderkind*, playing a Mozart piano concerto with the Vienna Symphony Orchestra when he was ten, and composing a number of solid chamber and orchestral works in a lush, late Romantic style as a child and teenager. He was 17 when he conducted the Berlin Philharmonic in a program that included one of his own compositions.

Despite these early successes, Szell rose through the conducting ranks in the traditional way of the period, with a series of opera positions: Royal Opera of Berlin (1915–17), Strasbourg (1917–18), Prague (1919–21), Darmstadt (1921–22), and Düsseldorf (1922–24). Szell's first prestigious post came to him in 1924, when he was named first conductor of the Berlin State Opera; he simultaneously served as a professor at Berlin's Hochschule für Musik. In 1929, he moved on to become general music director of the German Opera and Philharmonic in Prague, where he remained until 1937.

Szell began focusing more on orchestral repertory in the 1930s; he made his U.S. debut as guest conductor of the St. Louis Symphony in 1930, and in 1937 he was appointed conductor of the Scottish Orchestra in Glasgow, while maintaining a steady relationship with the Residentie Orkest in The Hague. Szell was in America in 1939 when war broke out in Europe; he remained in the U.S. through the war, first depending on guest engagements and then, in 1942, becoming a regular conductor at the Metropolitan Opera, where he was especially praised for his Wagner performances. In 1946 Szell took American citizenship and became music director of the Cleveland Orchestra, a post he held for 24 years. He was also the New York Philharmonic's music advisor and senior guest conductor during the last two years of his life.

Although Szell made a recordings in Europe in the 1950s and 1960s for Decca, and in Cleveland at the end of his life for EMI, the bulk of his substantial discography was the result of his long collaboration with Columbia Records in Cleveland. There, Szell had inherited an able but ordinary orchestra and, through sheer determination, molded it into one of America's finest. A Szell performance was remarkable for its textural clarity, chamber-like balances, and precision of attack and release. He drilled his orchestra mercilessly, even in works it had performed with him not long before. Szell was particularly admired for his performances of Austro-Germanic classics from Haydn to Richard Strauss, his sharp renderings of works by a select group of twentieth century composers including Bartók, Prokofiev, Janáček, and Walton), and his idiomatic way with Dvořák. Indeed, some collectors maintain that Szell's monaural, early 1950s recording of Dvořák's *Eighth Symphony* with the Concertgebouw Orchestra has never been equaled. His treatment of French composers, on the other hand, was criticized for its lack of atmosphere, and detractors maintained that he achieved precision at the expense of emotional expression. To those who demanded a warmer approach to his beloved Mozart, however, Szell is said to have retorted, "One does not pour chocolate sauce over asparagus."*—James Reel*

Recommended:

- ○ **Beethoven: Symphonies 4 & 7** / Szell (cond.), Cleveland Orch. / 1992 / Sony 48158
- ○ **Great Conductors of the 20th Century: George Szell** / Szell (cond.), Cleveland Orch., New York PO, WDRSO / EMI 75962
- ○ **Dvořák: Slavonic Dances** / Szell (cond.), Cleveland Orch. / 2002 / Legacy 89845

- ○ **Bruckner: Symphony 3** / Szell (cond.), Dresden Staatskapelle / 1995 / Sony 68448
- ○ **Mozart: Symphonies 35, 40 & 41** / Szell (cond.), Cleveland Orch. / 2002 / Sony 89834
- ○ **Dvořák: Symphony 7; Smetana: The Moldau** / Szell (cond.), Cleveland Orch. / 2000 / Sony 89412

Henryk Szeryng

b. Sep. 22, 1918, Zelazowa Wola, Poland, **d.** Mar. 8, 1988, Kassel, Germany
Violinist

Polish-born violinist Henryk Szeryng was probably the finest product of Carl Flesch's legendary teaching career. Possessing an iron technique and a musical intellect of rare insight, Szeryng established himself as one of the preeminent concert violinists of the post-World War II decades.

Szeryng was born in 1918 to a wealthy Polish industrialist whose wife had a great love of music. Studies on the piano were abandoned for the violin, though Szeryng remained skilled at the keyboard for the rest of his life. Szeryng progressed quickly on his new instrument and by age nine was sufficiently proficient to perform the Mendelssohn concerto for famed violinist Bronisław Hubermann, a friend of the family. On Hubermann's advice Szeryng was sent to Berlin to study with Carl Flesch; Szeryng would later declare that his technical prowess was solely due to that masterful teacher's influence. Two years later in 1933, Szeryng made his debut performance in Warsaw with the Beethoven concerto under Bruno Walter. That same year he embarked on a minor concert tour, soloing with orchestras in Bucharest, Vienna, and Paris.

Szeryng immediately took to the city of Paris and settled there for a period of further study and growth as a performer. There he came under the influence of legendary violinists Enescu and Thibaud, though he did not formally study with either. Szeryng also thought about pursuing composition as a career, and for six years took lessons from Nadia Boulanger.

At the outbreak of war in 1939 Szeryng enlisted with the Polish army. Being fluent in seven languages, he was assigned to General Sikorski as a translator, with whom Szeryng helped to relocate hundreds of Polish refugees in Mexico. During the war Szeryng gave hundreds of concerts for Allied troops around the globe, and in 1943, during a concert series in Mexico City, was invited to take over the string department at the University of Mexico. Szeryng accepted the offer, and assumed his duties in 1946.

He spent the next ten years in Mexico, and eventually took citizenship there. Performing infrequently, Szeryng was largely forgotten in the musical centers of Europe. A chance encounter with fellow Pole Artur Rubinstein in Mexico City convinced Szeryng to reenter the musical scene. A New York debut in 1956 immediately established Szeryng as a leading violinist of the day, and for the next 30 years Szeryng divided his time between a globe-trotting concert schedule and his teaching duties in Mexico.

As a violinist Szeryng was unique; sometimes criticized for being too restrained, he was nevertheless capable of playing with warmth and fire when he felt compelled to do so (as in his magnificent performances of the Sibelius concerto). His excellent recordings include two full sets of the Bach *Sonatas* and *Partitas*, as well as the major violin concertos in the repertory (he has also championed and recorded the work of many composers from his adopted country of Mexico). Recordings of the Beethoven and Brahms sonatas with Artur Rubinstein are particularly rewarding. Of note also is Szeryng's world-premiere recording of Paganini's *E major Violin Concerto* (No.3), which Szeryng himself reconstructed from parts held in the archives of the legendary Italian violinist's heirs.

Szeryng could at times be somewhat inconsistent. In live performances his calculated precision might turn cold, and in later years it is rumored that troubles with alcohol led to a somewhat deteriorated technical ability. Until his death in 1988 he traveled with a Mexican diplomatic passport, and was involved in various humanitarian projects through the United Nations; Szeryng never ceased believing in music as a unifying, healing power. *—Blair Johnston*

Recommended:

- ○ **Bach: Sonatas & Partitas** / Szeryng / DG 453004
- ○ **Mozart: Violin Concertos 3–5** / Gibson (cond.), Szeryng, New Philharmonia / 1995 / Philips 446231
- ○ **Early Recordings, Vol 1** / Szeryng, etc. / Arlecchino 117

Joseph Szigeti

b. Sep. 5, 1892, Budapest, Hungary, **d.** Feb. 19, 1973, Lucerne, Switzerland
Violinist

Violinist Joseph Szigeti's father and his uncle were both professional musicians and gave him music lessons. Szigeti advanced so quickly that he was soon assigned as a pupil of Jenö Hubay, later entering the celebrated virtuoso's advanced class. Szigeti began to play in public at age ten and made his formal debut in Berlin in 1905 at the age of 13. Joseph Joachim offered to teach him, but Szigeti chose to remain with Hubay.

After making his London debut was when he was 15, Szigeti remained in Britain until 1913, giving frequent concerts and becoming a favorite. Szigeti's partners in recitals included such illustrious musicians as Myra Hess and Ferruccio Busoni. Busoni, a pianist-composer and also a deep-thinking philosopher on the nature and future of music, became a formative influence on Szigeti. As with others in his line of work, Szigeti's concert career was interrupted by the outbreak of World War I. Settling in Switzerland in 1913, Szigeti accepted a position as a violin professor at the Geneva Conservatory, where he gave master classes from 1917 to 1924.

Upon returning to the concert scene in the early 1920s, Szigeti rapidly became a famous international name in classical music. He was noted for his quick understanding and advocacy of new music, and took up the cause of Prokofiev's *Violin Concerto No. 1 in D Minor Op. 19*, which he played it at the I.S.C.M. Festival in 1924. Later that same year Szigeti performed this work on his Russian tour, giving the *Concerto* its Leningrad premiere. Szigeti made his American debut in 1925, playing the Beethoven *Violin Concerto in D Major Op. 61* with the Philadelphia Orchestra under Leopold Stokowski in *Carnegie Hall*. During the 1930s Szigeti also toured in Asia, Australia, New Zealand, South America, and South Africa.

In 1938 Szigeti premiered Ernest Bloch's *Violin Concerto* in Cleveland. Among other first performances given by, or works dedicated to, Szigeti were Bartók's *Rhapsody No. 1*, Alan Rawsthorne's *Sonata*, Bloch's "Le nuit exotique," and the violin concertos of Casella and Frank Martin. Szigeti's interest in new music led him to become a persuasive advocate of many great violin works that had been premiered by others, including music by Ravel, Roussel, Milhaud, Stravinsky, and Alban Berg. With the outbreak of World War II, Szigeti settled in the United States.

Upon his arrival in America in 1940, Hungarian composer Bela Bartók renewed an earlier friendship with Szigeti, and they played some concerts together, including a famous one at the Library of Congress in Washington D.C. Szigeti also took up Bartók's new *Violin Concerto (No. 2)*, playing it widely. Through Szigeti's influence, Bartók was commissioned to write a new classical work for clarinetist Benny Goodman. Bartók responded with *Contrasts*, scored for the uniquely non-blending ensemble of piano, violin, and clarinet, thereby including Szigeti in the work's premiere. Szigeti played frequently in America during the war years, and afterward resumed his international career. He took part in the 1950 Prades Festival organized by cellist Pablo Casals. Szigeti was naturalized as an American citizen in 1951.

By 1960 Szigeti had scaled down the number of his personal appearences, and in that year he settled in Switzerland. Szigeti subsequently withdrew from the concert stage, and taught only a limited number of students. Szigeti wrote scholarly studies on great works of the violin repertory, the history of the violin and its playing styles, and made changes to his already published autobiography. Szigeti was also a welcome member of the juries on several international violin competitions, where his discerning ear and wise judgment were highly influential. *—AMG*

Recommended:

- ○ **Beethoven: Sonatas 4, 9 & 10** / Szigeti, Arrau (piano) / 2002 / Classica d'Oro 2019
- ○ **The Szigeti-Beecham Recordings** / Beecham (cond.), Szigeti, London PO / Pearl 9377
- ○ **Szigeti & Bartók** / Szigeti, Bartok (piano) / 2001 / Hungaroton 12330
- ○ **Joseph Szigeti: Violin** / Szigeti, etc. / 2001 / Andante 2991–2994
- ○ **Szigeti Plays Bach** / Stiedry (cond.), Szigeti, New Friends of Music Orch. / 2001 / Classica d'Oro 2006

Karol Szymanowski

b. Oct. 6, 1882, Timoshovka, Ukraine, **d.** Mar. 28, 1937, Lausanne, Switzerland
Composer: Keyboard, Chamber Music, Concerto, Symphonic, Opera

Composer Karol Szymanowski spent his early years in Ukraine (where many affluent Polish families still owned land at the time). An injury to the leg forced young Karol into a life of relative inactivity, and, from age seven on, attendance at school was replaced by rigorous musical studies (first under his father's tutelage, and then, from 1892 on, at Gustav Neuhaus' music school in Elisavetgrad). Although early training focused on the piano, Neuhaus was quick to observe his young student's potential as a composer. While in Elisavetgrad, Szymanowski was introduced to the German classics as well as to Chopin and Scriabin. After studies with Noskowski in Warsaw from 1903 to 1905, Szymanowski lived for a time in Berlin, helping to found that city's "Young Poland in Music" Society. During the Warsaw and Berlin years Szymanowski began absorbing the musical language of the later German masters (Richard Strauss in particular), under whose strong influence Szymanowski produced his first two symphonies (1907 and 1909, respectively).

The pre-World War I years found Szymanowski traveling extensively throughout Europe, spreading his name as a composer (among those who signed on to champion his music were fellow Poles Artur Rubinstein and violinist Paul Kochansky) and absorbing the newest trends in European art. A brief 1914 stay in Paris helped to cement a growing admiration for Debussy and the French Impressionist school. The War years themselves were spent at the family estate in Tymoszowka, where Szymanowski composed prolifically (the *Third Symphony*, First Violin Concerto, First String Quartet, as well as a number of smaller works, all date from this period). Tymoszowka suffered heavily during the Bolshevik Revolution of 1917, and the Szymanowski family was forced to relocate to nearby Elisavetgrad. Elisavetgrad, however, was soon subject to Austrian occupation, and, in late 1919, after selling all the family land (at a heavy loss), Szymanowski made a new home in Warsaw. Achieving some popular success in the new Polish capital, Szymanowski eventually became director of the Warsaw Conservatory (1926). However, tuberculosis forced him to resign this position in 1930, and the next several years were spent abroad (largely in Switzerland). Continuing health troubles forced him to enter a sanatorium, and he died in Lugano in 1937.

Szymanowski's unique brand of expressive, lyric modernism has found many admirers in the twentieth and twenty-first centuries. Though his earliest music is perhaps too closely allied to that of his childhood idol Chopin to fully stand on its own, his later work synthesizes the stylistic characteristics of a wide range of composers (Scriabin, Strauss, Reger, Debussy, Ravel) into a highly individual new language, which seems likely to bear the test of time better than many such experiments in eclecticism. *—Blair Johnston*

KEYBOARD

12 Etudes, Op. 33 (1916)

In the winter of 1914, Szymanowski made his first visit to the Tatra highland resort of Zakopane, where he would spend his final years, and in the spring embarked, with his friend Stefan Spiess, on a tour of Sicily and North Africa—Algiers, Biskra, Tunis, Constantine—returning via Italy, Paris, and London. In London he met Stravinsky—"with whom I am on the way to a perfect understanding," he wrote Spiess—and had accepted an invitation to visit Paderewski in Switzerland when the Great War broke out. Returning instead to Tymoszówka by the last train, Szymanowski entered a period of splendid isolation in which the grip of Strauss- and Reger-indebted Germanic post-Romanticism yielded before a wealth of exotic impressions, memories of the remnants of Greek and Arabic culture lit by the Mediterranean sun, and the revelation of Stravinsky's ballets. A new and renewing prehension blossomed in the spate of Dionysian works—mystical, ecstatic, hallucinatory, erotic—constituting his most opulent period. The visionary *Mythes*, coveted by all violinists; the fantastical *Violin Concerto No. 1*; and the rapt *Symphony No. 3 ("Song of the Night")* and piano triptychs—sensuously glowing *Métopes* and sardonic *Masques*—all date from the inter-war years, with the *12 Études*, Op. 33, taking shape with *Masques* in 1916.

With the longest playing under two minutes—and the entire set heard in less than 15—the *Études* possess the considerable interest of being an index to Szymanowski's expansive, rhapsodically Dionysian style in a distilled, crystallized, aphoristic form. Compact and exposed by the keyboard's black-and-white, the Dionysian oddments take on an acerbically manic mien, less scintillant or sensuous than flickering, coruscating, and frantic. A mood of *Katzenjammer* afflicts the languishing etudes (e.g., No. 2, Andantino soave, or No. 8, Lento assai mesto). Sarcasm embitters not only No. 9, Animato—marked Con brio, Burlesco—but also No. 10, Presto (Tempestoso) and No. 12, Presto. Composed in 1905, No. 5, Andante espressivo, is a misplaced curiosity. Taken together, the *12 Études, Op. 33*, look ahead to Szymanowski's laconic, harmonically acidulous last manner. *—Adrian Corleonis*

Recommended:

○ **Szymanowski: Piano Music** / Jones / 1999 / Nimbus 1750

20 Mazurkas, Op. 50 (1924–1925)

The Bolshevik Revolution of October 1917 crashed in upon Szymanowski's life of cultivated leisure with brutal force, bringing to an end his middle period and the series of fantastic masterpieces which filled it—The *Love-Songs of Hafiz*; the *Métopes* and *Masques* for piano; the *Third Symphony* ("Song of the Night"); the glowing, hallucinatory *First Violin Concerto*; and, above all, the unfinished torso of his Dionysian opera, *King Roger*. Tymoszówka, the family estate in Ukraine, was overrun and trashed, and the composer spent two traumatic years in Elisavetgrad, taking stock in a novel, *The Ephebe* (now lost), reading widely, and guarding the door against thugs. But the Revolution also brought about Polish independence the following year, and the Szymanowskis were able to return to Poland on Christmas eve 1919. A number of incomplete and unpublished works date from this period—a sort of musical stammering. Szymanowski did not again hit his stride as a composer until 1921—and in quite a different vein (indebted to Stravinsky's example)—with the song cycle *Slopiewnie*, which incorporated folk elements in an evocation of a "Lechitic" or ancestral, tribal, Polish consciousness. From 1922, he began to spend as much time as possible in Zakopane, a resort in the Tatra mountains, and to absorb the raucous, improvised, archaic music of the highlanders, which informs the works of his final period. Among these, the *20 Mazurkas*, composed over 1924-25, exhibit the sophisticated primitivism of his late style in its most etched, unequivocal form. Over the drones in open fifths and pedal points of minor seconds typical of Tatra music, he weaves a discourse of modal and bitonal inflections, with ever-varying, seemingly improvised melodic ornamentation, set off by the mazurka's characteristic rhythmic bounce. A number of them open with a tentative melodic tendril—a sort of falling highland call—before giving way to exuberance escalating to delirium. A droll garrulity, albeit astringently strutted, shimmers from pungency to piquancy, rendering this potentially hermetic idiom accessible and poised as a twentieth century Polish response to the mazurkas of Chopin. *—Adrian Corleonis*

Recommended:

○ **Szymanowski: The Complete Mazurkas** / Hamelin / 2003 / Hyperion 67399

Piano Sonata No. 1 in C major, Op. 8 (1903–1904)

Szymanowski enjoyed an enviable range of advantages: A home in which art was accepted and encouraged, private teachers, and the friendship and advice of such artists as his cousin, the distinguished pianist and teacher Heinrich Neuhaus; pianist Artur Rubinstein; the conductor Grzegorz Fitelberg; or the great violin virtuoso, Pawel Kochánski. Though Szymanowski's youth was largely passed at Tymoszówka, the comfortable family estate in Ukraine, the monotony of *le pays* was broken by frequent visits to Kiev or Vienna, where he heard the music of Wagner for the first time at age 13, a formative experience that sustained him until overlaid by the impact of Debussy, Ravel, and Stravinsky. From 1901, he studied composition in Warsaw with the distinguished Polish composer Zygmunt Noskowski, though the substance of his tuition was derived almost wholly from German Romantic models and Chopin. Szymanowski acquainted himself with the new music of Reger, Richard Strauss, and Scriabin, which would hold him in thrall until World War I. But despite an evident vocation for composition and abundant talent, his response to the stylistic riot those composers represented was uncertain, and his first steps as a composer proved halting. In 1904, as his studies with Noskowski drew to a close, his fellow student Ludomir Rózycki recalled that "When he was working on his first piano sonata, I often found him at the piano, studying meticulously the structure of Chopin's and Scriabin's piano passages. He knew how to discern in their music the secrets of piano style. Even then his every passage had a brilliant piano facture." Indeed, the writing is elaborate, pianistic, and orchestral in effect, though the handling of sonata form is rule-of-thumb and Szymanowski seems unable to think beyond the phrase, which means that his ideas fail to generate development and structure. Despite a number of brilliant moments, the ostensible drama of the first movement is curiously episodic, and fails to build convincingly. Likewise, cyclic construction—the first movement's second subject furnishes thematic material for the Adagio, as well as the Trio of the Minuet—remains a mere orthopedic device. But however hit upon, the Adagio's opening—a sort of chorale in 3/4 time—reveals the consoling lyricism of which the young composer was capable in inspired moments, though the two pages of Agitato that interrupt it have no more raison d'être than to provide crude contrast. The Minuet radiates an endearing courtliness, as of bygone times, set off by a Trio of pure charm showing Szymanowski already a master of the winning miniature. For the Finale, a portentous introduction leads to an ambitious fugue redolent of that in Franck's *Prélude, Choral et Fugue* in the large demands made on the soloist, though the lyric inspiration of the opening pages soon devolves into grandiose striving and turgid bombast. All the elements of a masterpiece are present, except the organic mastery that would come with the *Piano Sonata No. 2*. Meanwhile, the *Sonata No. 1* took first prize in a competition organized by the Chopin Birth Centenary Committee held at Lwów, in 1910. *—Adrian Corleonis*

Recommended:

○ **Szymanowski: Piano Works Vol. 3** / Roscoe / 2000 / Naxos 553867

CHAMBER MUSIC

Myths, 3 poems for violin & piano, Op. 30 (1915)

Szymanowski composed the three *Mity* (*Myths*) from March to June 1915, while he was at Jósef Jaroszyński's estate. They were written for Pawel Kochański (1887-1934), a brilliant violinist and a member of the Warsaw Philharmonic, who had composed cadenzas for Szymanowski's concertos and transcribed (for violin and piano) some of the composer's other works. Kochański's involvement with the compositional process was such that he became a collaborator, just as he was in Szymanowski's two violin concertos. *Myths* is dedicated to Zofia Kochański, the violinist's wife.

A few years before his death, Szymanowski wrote that he and Kochański had created "a new style, a new mode of expression for the violin." Some have described this new style as "impressionistic." This term makes sense when one considers Szymanowski's use of timbre as a structural element, an approach similar to Debussy's.

The violin technique required to perform *Myths* is considerable. The piece is filled with double stops, harmonics, quarter tones, and glissandi, and the composer calls for simultaneous arco bowing and left-hand pizzicato. *Myths* resembles piano music by Scriabin in its use of dense motives. Recurring sounds, as much as thematic manipulation, delineate the forms of the three movements. "La Fontaine d'Aréthuse" became the most popular of the three sections of *Myths*, most likely because it is less harmonically adventurous than its partners. It opens with a shimmering wash of sound in the piano, octave leaps in the left hand passing above and below repeated chords in the right, played *ppp* with the sustain pedal. While the rapid leaps of this "fountain" music suggest splashing water, the polytonal harmony creates anticipation. High above this colorful idea, the violin eventually enters with a soaring melodic gesture. As the piece progresses it becomes clear that the fountain music, with its irregular meter, is as much a theme as a textural gesture, and its return after a short molto agitato passage signals the approaching close of the piece, in which the violin again plays its first melody, but in a lower register.

"Narcisse," the slow central movement, is more melodic in conception than "La Fontaine d'Aréthuse." Sonata-like, it boasts two contrasting thematic ideas, but there is no development section. Instead, the middle portion of "Narcisse" presents new material.

"Dryades et Pan" opens with a quarter-tone trill depicting the summer wind. The ensuing, flashy dance of the Dryads is interrupted by Pan's flute, suggested by harmonics on the unaccompanied violin. After Pan and the Dryads dance until they drop, the wind returns to close the piece with a quiet reprise of Pan's theme. *—John Palmer*

Recommended:

○ **Enescu, Bartók & Szymanowski: Works for Violin & Piano** / Haendel, Ashkenazy / 2000 / Decca 455488

Nocturne and Tarantella, for violin & piano, Op. 28 (1915)

Szymanowski left London on the day Archduke Rudolph was assassinated in Sarajevo. On the continent, Szymanowski took the last regularly scheduled trains in a circuitous route to avoid Austria on his way to Tymoszówka, the family estate in Ukraine. Exempted from military service by a childhood knee injury, the composer refurbished a gardener's cottage there as a study amid a grove of oaks and lost himself in creative absorption of the overripe European milieu—preeminently, the impact of Debussy, Ravel, and Stravinsky—which was, at that moment, being transmogrified by political reality. The upshot was the series of works upon which his reputation largely rests—the *Symphony No. 3 "Song of the Night"*, the *Violin Concerto No. 1*, the *Métopes* and *Masques* for piano, the *Myths* for violin and piano—composed in the space of a little more than two years. Stylistically, they mark a turning away from the fulsome formality of Reger (evident in Szymanowski's *Symphony No. 2*) and the garishly riotous post-Wagnerian sound world of Richard Strauss' *Elektra* and *Salome* toward a more elaborately and luridly refined decadence colored by excursions into Stendhal, Bergson, Pater, Persian poetry, and Euripides (whose *Bacchae* would provide inspiration for Szymanowski's testamentary opera *King Roger*), as well as memories of the Mediterranean and of real excursions to Sicily and north Africa, littered with Roman remains.

The splendid isolation of Tymoszówka was broken—or enhanced—by visits to neighboring estates, such as Józef Jaroszynski's Zarudzie, where Szymanowski's friend, the great violin virtuoso Pawel Kochánski, and his wife were staying, or to Ryzawka, the estate of August Iwánski, with whom Szymanowski developed a close friendship. From March to June, 1915, the composer had been occupied with the *Myths*, completed at Zarudzie, in which the new visionary style took—with technical advice from Kochánski—flamboyant wing. By contrast, the *Nocturne & Tarantella* catch Szymanowski in the moment of transition. Composed a bit before he embarked on *Myths*, the *Nocturne* is an alternately languid and febrile exercise in exoticism. The *Tarantella*, on the other hand, was sketched during an evening of drinking with Kochánski and Iwánski at Zarudzie some time after the completion of *Myths*, and makes a labored attempt at Dionysian frenzy. Together, they are engaging but not very deeply realized, suggesting parodies of Szymanowski's most opulent period—leading a number of critics to dismiss them as kitsch—unless projected with violin wizardry and sheer visceral intensity. *—Adrian Corleonis*

Recommended:

○ **Szymanowski: Violin Concertos 1 & 2; Nocturne & Tarantella** / Kulka, Lasocki / 1996 / Naxos 553685

Three Paganini Caprices, for violin & piano, Op. 40 (1918)

"Try to imagine such a *petit maître* as myself standing guard all night with a rifle and revolver, on familiar terms with things that would have made me at least faint before, such as corpses, the wounded, some frightful bandit gangs, etc. etc. It's a miracle that we got out of this business alive," Szymanowski wrote to his friend Zdzislaw Jachimecki in 1918 from Elizavetgrad, where he and his family had taken refuge from the upheavals of the Bolshevik Revolution. Szymanowski's stranding in Elizavetgrad became a time of questioning and stock taking. To his cousin, poet Jaroslaw Iwaszkiewicz, on January 3, 1918, he complains "Can you imagine, I cannot compose now... I am writing a bit—of course without any literary aspirations—simply to get some things off my chest...." Musically he clung to his dream world of the previous few years, spent in isolation on the family estate, indulging his muse, in such things as *Songs of the Infatuated Muezzin* and the *Three Paganini Caprices*, while contemplating a specifically Polish art.

That Paganini's 1820 set of *24 Capricci for solo violin* should have appealed to composers as different as Liszt and Brahms, Blacher and Lutosławski, Rachmaninov and Szymanowski owes, perhaps, to the suggestiveness of his piquantly singing lines, which seem to cry out for harmonization and stylistic definition. With Szymanowski's piano accompaniment, Paganini's *Caprice No. 20* seems a spin-off from the former's violin sonata of 1904. In his re-arrangement of the *Caprice No. 21*—a recomposed slow first section and omission of Paganini's fast second section—the piano transports an early Romantic classic into the lushly decadent world of Szymanowski's *Violin Concerto No. 1*, explored at length in his transformation of the theme and variations of *Caprice No. 24*, which Szymanowski has made wholly his own, omitting two variations and adding one of his own. In rescoring Paganini's violin part, Szymanowski had the help of violinist Viktor Goldfeld—with whom he gave the premiere of the *Three Paganini Caprices* in Elisavetgrad on April 25, 1918, though the published recension is by Szymanowski's friend and the work's dedicatee, the great violin virtuoso Pawel Kochánski. *—Adrian Corleonis*

Recommended:

○ **Paganini's Violin** / Accardo, Manzini / 1995 / Dynamic 175

String Quartet No. 1 in C major, Op. 37 (1917)

This fine string quartet is exciting and moving in its own right. Fans of Szymanowski may find it particularly illuminating because it is a significant work of a period during which the composer was making a drastic transition of his style.

Karol Szymanowski (1882–1937) was Poland's greatest and most distinctive composer since Chopin. The earlier half of his career saw him adopt the hot-blooded, erotic romanticism of Scriabin and take an interest in music of the Near East. However, by the time World War I ended, he had shifted to a much less lush, harmonically harder-edged, yet more tonal, musical language.

Philosophically, Szymanowski during the same period lost his interest in the ego-driven Romanticism of Wagner, Richard Strauss, and Nietzsche. And personally his life changed drastically, as well: Polish independence and Communist seizure of his family property in the Ukraine required him, for the first time, to make his entire living as a musician, composer, and teacher.

The quartet is in three movements and totals a bit less than 20 minutes. Szymanowski had intended a four-movement work ending with a fully fugal final movement, but he dropped the final movement and moved the scherzo (which does have a fugato section) from second to final position.

The first and longest movement—nearly half the length of the quartet as published—is in a typical sonata-allegro form with a slow introduction. Its main expression markings are Lento assai; Allegro moderato. The opening slow section is close to the exotic, perfumed style of Szymanowski's earlier music; its melody has modal elements. The fast main body of the movement is Scriabinesque in its chromaticism, in the passionate nature of its main themes, and in the way the composer works them out. Despite the depth and passion of the music, the actual writing for quartet is entirely appropriate to the chamber ensemble: the music retains the clarity, transparency, and conversational nature of the greatest quartets.

The second movement, Andantino semplice, in modo d'una canzone, is, for a considerable stretch, in the form of a lyric melody for the first violin, with the remaining instruments forming a trio to accompany it. The last half of the expression marking means "in the style of a song," and that is an apt description of the movement up until the contrasting central section, which is sweet and mysterious at the same time. The return of the main melody does not dispel this new emotional quality, which is not resolved as the opening of the concluding movement intrudes.

This movement, Scherzando alla burlesca: vivace non troppo, begins with a quiet unison passage, then another unison—loud this time—that throws the movement into fast motion. There is a fugal passage, but this is interrupted by a sardonic waltz whose surface banality anticipates similar moments in Shostakovich's music. The music ends quietly, and perhaps just a bit anticlimactically, as the opening part of the quartet seems to set up a need for the larger-scale finale Szymanowski originally intended. *—Joseph Stevenson*

Recommended:

○ **Szymanowski: Quartets; Stravinsky: Concertino; Double Canon** / Goldner SQ / 2000 / Naxos 554315

String Quartet No. 2, Op. 56 (1927)

This masterful string quartet, notable for its variety of sound and its taut handling of material, is part of the last great flowering of Szymanowski's art. The collapse of his family fortune and profound changes in Polish society following World War I deeply affected the depression-prone composer, and resulted in a creative block. It was only with the completion of his magnum opus, the opera *Krol Roger* (King Roger), in 1924 that Szymanowski found a solid new style and could again compose with confidence.

In the meantime, he had been forced to teach at the Warsaw Conservatory and to embark on a career as a performing musician to make enough money to survive—an issue that had hardly bothered him as the scion of a wealthy family with properties in the Ukraine before World War I. Emerging from these misfortunes, he found a style that fused the neo-Classicism and rhythmic power of Stravinsky with folk music of the Tatra Mountains in southern Poland—a style that directly informed his *Second String Quartet*. Unfortunately for Szymanowski (and for those that wonder what else he might have written in this very original style), his health broke soon after the composition of the *Second Quartet*; weakness, depression, and mental deterioration soon brought a decline in his output.

The *Second Quartet* is 20 minutes long and is in three movements. The first movement begins Moderato (dolce e tranquillo) in a texture that seems borrowed from Debussy—a faint murmuring in the strings with a high violin solo that is softer than a whisper. This opening section is so quiet that its very softness creates tension. Soon the music rises above this whisper, however, and continues to an emotional exchange among the four instruments.

The second movement, Vivace, scherzando, begins with double-stop chords on all the instruments—a sonority that is shocking in its sudden loudness and violence. This movement and the middle quartets of Béla Bartók have much in common in the way of powerful rhythmic drive and interest in diversity of string colors. Here the influence of Tatra melodies is strong, though there is no direct quotation and in general the music is not as strongly infused with folk elements as Bartók's music is.

The finale is marked Lento; Moderato (tranquillo) and initially returns to the calm mood of the opening of the first movement. The main body of the movement is a fugue that begins calmly, slowly, and elegantly. But as the movement progresses it gains both speed and passion until reaching an irresistible conclusion. *—Joseph Stevenson*

Recommended:

○ **Szymanowski: Quartets; Stravinsky: Concertino; Double Canon** / Goldner SQ / 2000 / Naxos 554315

○ **Szymanowski: String Quartets; Webern: Langsamer Satz** / Carmina Quartet / Denon 79462

CONCERTO

Violin Concerto No. 1, Op. 35 (1916)

Szymanowski hit upon his own style only after a long travail through which he learned from other composers—Wagner, Strauss, and Scriabin at the beginning, then Stravinsky, Debussy, and Ravel in his mid-period—and this has been held against him. But if it is said that Wagner or Stravinsky won victories for music, for "progress," then Szymanowski is their rightful inheritor for he understood their originality, almost clairvoyantly, from the start and was able to assimilate and refine their contributions, turning them into his own highly individual purposes. This is nowhere more apparent than in the *Violin Concerto No. 1*, the apogee of his middle period works.

Exempted from military service because of a childhood leg injury, Szymanowski sat out most of World War I on the Ukrainian family estate Tymoszówka, immersed in a fabulous inner world compounded by memories of Greek, Roman, and Byzantine remains in Sicily and North Africa, nightly music making—Szymanowski's sister Stanislawa was an accomplished soprano, while the great violinist Pawel Kochanski visited frequently—and a deep absorption in literature, with Nietzsche, Goethe, and modern Polish writers preeminent. Among the latter, Tadeusz Micinski held a special place, and his surreal, seemingly hallucinogenic poem "May Night" suggested the fantastic soundscape of Szymanowski's *Violin Concerto No. 1*—"I wandered once through the colonnades that Abderrahman made for his beloved, in the amethyst night of Shéhérazade, with talismans burning in the sky ... Pan plays pipes in the oak wood, a lilting melody for dancing Ephemeredes, tangled in amorous embrace, eternally young and sacred...." Szymanowski had already dealt with Shéhérazade in the first of his piano *Masques* (1915–1916), and the literary reference is made explicit by quotation of *Shéhérazade*'s opening bars in the concerto, composed over the summer and autumn of 1916.

The concerto's single, unbroken arch opens with skittering "night music" ushering the listener immediately into an eerie, alluring psychic terrain soon dominated by the violin's entrance. The solo instrument, in its incantatory, rhapsodic, melodic profusion, is the psychopomp in this Dionysian exploration, calling up and crowning ever more rapt timbral miracles from a Promethean orchestra of virtuoso players, augmented by exotic percussion and whelmingly eloquent divisi strings. The thematic material is handled cunningly, with certain intervals prominently looming amid inversions and retrogrades, though these are always expressive—indeed, only analysts and the quickest of musicians recognize them—and never suggest the tense academicism of the same tropes employed by a Reger or a Schoenberg. Taken with the fantasticated, intoxicated atmosphere throughout, these technical devices impart unity to a constantly developing exposition that has left sonata form behind. Four great, extended episodes rise ever more climactically to an impassioned cadenza (largely supplied by Kochanski) before a fifth and grander climax tops all to vanish in a detumescently triste coda.

A scheduled performance of the concerto in St. Petersburg under Siloti, with Kochanski as soloist, was canceled amid the tumultuous events leading to the Russian Revolution. The premiere was given in Warsaw, November 1, 1922, with Józef Oziminski as soloist. *—Adrian Corleonis*

Recommended:

○ **Szymanowski: Violin Concertos 1 & 2; Nocturne & Tarantella** / Stryja (cond.), Kulka, Polish State PO & Chorus / 1996 / Naxos 553685

Violin Concerto No. 2, Op. 61 (1932–1933)

Szymanowski, the cosmopolitan wanderer and "good European," returned to a newly independent Poland on Christmas Eve 1919, followed by a change of heart and, soon after, by a radical change of style. Through the 1920s, Szymanowski shuttled between Warsaw, Paris, and Zakopane in the Tatra mountains. Of Bartek Obrochta, patriarch of a family of Zakopane musicians, writer Mieczyslaw Rytard recalls that, "Szymanowski was very much taken with that delightful, frail old mountaineer. Snow-haired, spry Bartek, always bright and witty, a marvelous teller of old folk tales, was one of the few surviving specimens of the old breed of Tatra highlanders. He had a quick wit and intelligence, but he intrigued Szymanowski mainly as a first-rate musician.... What music it was! Karol strolled around the large room, with his inevitable cigarette holder, chain smoking; he listened, he watched the players' fingers, he cocked an ear for the more interesting, original passages, he soaked in the strange, primitive melodies, dissecting them into their component parts." *Slopiewnie* (1921), the first work in the new idiom, matched poet Julian Tuwim's brilliantly imagined proto-Slavic language with Tatra-inspired music of sophisticated primitivism. Through such works as the *Mazurkas* (1924–25), the *Stabat Mater* (1925–26), and—above all—the ballet *Harnasie* (1923–31), the new style became less esoteric, if more laconic, attaining its final, most allusively polished form in the *Violin Concerto No. 2.* Sketched over August 1932 at the insistence of his friend, violinist Pawel Kochanski—who provided (as he had for the *Violin Concerto No. 1*) the cadenza—Szymanowski could not begin the orchestration until March, completing the full score on September 6, 1933. Weak from tuberculosis, Szymanowski was easily exhausted, and this was his last large-scale work.

No less cunning than the *Violin Concerto No. 1* in terms of motivic unity and continuous development, the work opens with a berceuse-like exposition of several melodic oddments evoking a sort of primal ethnic nostalgia, gyrating slowly, hypnotically within the interval of a third and alternating beguilingly between major and minor. A second, more animated thematic group enacts a *plein air* dance and march leading to an extensive cadenza ranging histrionically but brilliantly over both moods while marking the work's mid-point. The opening themes, combined with more adventurous melodic material traversing a tenth, amplify the play of dreaming wakened by raucous celebration, becoming grander and more eldritch by turns, led by bursts of something like dissonantly rustic fiddling to a high-kicking apotheosis.

If one characterizes Szymanowski's last manner as a sophisticated primitivism, it is nevertheless a curious fact that few performances embrace both aspects. In general, Polish artists respond to the folk elements with the gusto of a highland hoe-down, while Western European and American musicians play suavely to the glowing orchestral timbres familiar from Debussy and Ravel. Both are effective, but which is Szymanowski? One suspects he died undecided. The premiere was given in Warsaw on October 6, 1933, by two of the composer's closest friends, Kochanski as soloist with Grzegorz Fitelberg conducting. *—Adrian Corleonis*

Recommended:

○ **Symanowski: Violin Concertos 1 & 2; Górecki: 3 Pieces in the Old Style; Baird: Colas Breugnon** / Maksymiuk (cond.), Kulka, Polish Radio SO / 2002 / EMI 575670

SYMPHONIC

Symphony No. 4, for piano & orchestra ("Symphonie Concertante"), Op. 60 (1932)

As many listeners know, Karol Szymanowski was a brilliant pianist who wrote a large body of works for his instrument, but he also composed a substantial amount of music for orchestra, the stage, and for voice and chamber ensembles. In his *Symphony No. 4*, he included a substantial role for the piano—intending to play the first performances himself—but ensured that it contained few serious technical challenges since he was in declining health and no longer able to perform difficult music. Thus, while the symphony is a worthwhile composition, it is unlikely to attract many virtuoso pianists, though Artur Rubinstein played and recorded the piece.

Cast in three movements, the last two played without pause, the work opens with a light, exotic theme introduced by the piano. A second subject is vigorous and agitated, bringing on a change of mood, the music darkening and remaining stormy even through the cadenza near the end of this ten-minute panel. The closing pages are mostly angry and seething with tension, quite the opposite of the gentle, lovely opening. The second movement, marked Andante molto sostenuto, is mysterious and dreamy, the flute introducing an ethereal melody against running piano accompaniment. A solo violin soon takes up the theme and gives it a soothing character, a sense of flotation amid the heavens. Tension mounts in the middle section, but peace returns with a return of the flute, now joined in rendering the main theme by the piano. A bridge passage on the piano leads to the stormy finale, marked Allegro non troppo. Beginning with a rhythmic theme in the lower registers of the keyboard, the music has driving zest and color, but may strike some as being more thematically threadbare than it actually is. The latter half of the movement has a Bartókian character in its sense of motoric drive and percussive rhythms, providing a brilliant close to this powerful, 25-minute work. *—Robert Cummings*

Recommended:

○ **Szymanowski: Symphonies 2 & 4** / Sinaisky (cond.), BBC PO / 1996 / Chandos 9478

OPERA

Król Roger (King Roger), Op. 46 (1918–1924)

As Nietzsche gave up the ghost on August 25, 1900, a generation was discovering itself in his vision of the *Übermensch*—including composers Delius (*Eine Messe des Lebens*), Mahler (*Symphony No. 1, "Titan"*), Busoni (*Doktor Faust*), Richard Strauss (*Also sprach Zarathustra, Ein Heldenleben*), and Scriabin (*Symphony No. 3, "Divine Poem," Prometheus—Poem of Fire*). Though the works of Strauss and Scriabin were close models for Szymanowski's early compositions, he absorbed Nietzsche more thoroughly than either of them. Through the war years, Szymanowski explored what Nietzsche had identified as the Dionysian pole of human experience—Eros, ecstasy, intoxication, the chthonic—in such works as the *Masques for piano*, the *Symphony No. 3, "Song of the Night,"* and the *Violin Concerto No. 1*. When his cousin, poet Jaroslaw Iwaszkiewicz, proposed in June 1918 a libretto to be written around "the initiation of the hero... into the Dionysian mysteries... against the background of the ruins of the theatre at Syracuse or Segesta," Szymanowski was enthusiastic, embracing the idea as a way of making his preoccupations articulate, explicit, and testamentary. Euripides' *Bacchae* provided a point of reference, though the libretto was spun around twelfth century King Roger II of Sicily (1095–1154), both for the cultural crossroads suggested—Byzantine, Arabic, Greek, European—and scenic effect ("... the Byzantine-Arabic palace interiors would be perfect," Szymanowski wrote. "Just imagine: tarnished gold and rigid patterns of mosaics as background, or Moorish filigree...."). Despite Iwaszkiewicz's rapid loss of interest and piecemeal delivery of the libretto, Szymanowski composed the first two acts of *King Roger* between 1918 and 1923. Meanwhile, having welcomed Poland's independence and taken up residence in Warsaw at the end of 1919, he became deeply identified with the creation of an ancestrally rooted, modern, specifically Polish music, for which he found inspiration in the raucously eloquent folk music of the Tatra mountains. Subjective concerns were supplanted by responsibility, with a new emphasis on the Apollonian pole of Nietzsche's philosophy, which Szymanowski tried to incorporate in *King Roger*, rewriting the libretto of Act Three in 1921. He failed to find, in T.S. Eliot's phrase, the "objective correlative" for the new viewpoint—Roger's final monologue remains dramatically and musically unconvincing—but realizing that a large portion of his most powerful music lay in *King Roger*, he forced himself to finish it with rising irritation. To Zofia Kochanska he wrote on August 12, 1924, "I am terribly tired, because that bit of the third act which remained to be done is a real instrumental-contrapuntal hocus-pocus, so unfortunately I am not sure that I have extricated myself from it with honour!" The self-parodying third act aside, *King Roger* is Szymanowski's largest and richest score—subtle, grand, glowing, and evocative of an archetypal dimension that places it among such other testaments in music as Schoenberg's *Moses und Aron*, Berg's *Lulu*, Pfitzner's *Palestrina*, Hindemith's *Mathis der Maler*, and Busoni's *Doktor Faust*. The premiere was given at Warsaw's Teatr Wielki on June 19, 1926, conducted by Emil Mlynarski, with Szymanowski's sister, Stanislawa Szymanowska, taking the part of Roxana. *—Adrian Corleonis*

Synopsis:

Act One. The curtain rises slowly to reveal the interior of a Byzantine church. Hymns are being sung. Arrayed in gold vestments, the Archbishop stands motionless before the altar for a time before leading the worshipers in prayer. King Roger and his attendants enter. The King is greeted by the people, then addressed by the Archbishop, who complains that a strange Shepherd has been leading the people into sin. King Roger seeks an explanation from his sage, the Arab Edrisi. The sage informs him that the Shepherd has traveled throughout the King's lands, instructing the people in the ways of his own God. The Archbishop insists that the Shepherd preaches a false doctrine. Queen Roksana urges that no injurious action be taken and that the Shepherd be brought before the King to explain his religion. King Roger agrees and asks Edrisi more about the Shepherd, but other than describing his appearance, the sage tells him that he will have to learn these things from the Shepherd himself.

The Shepherd is brought before the King amidst murmurings from the crowd. He moves forthrightly to the King's throne and tells him that he worships a beautiful and youthful god. This god is a gentle shepherd who travels the land searching for lost sheep while caring for his flock. The Queen wants to learn more, even as the King cautions against being deceived. As the crowd presses ever more insistently for the Shepherd's death and the King concurs, the Queen protests that the young man utters only the truth. King Roger, perplexed, issues a call for silence and, after several moments in deep thought, declares that the man may go free to his own land. The Shepherd, his face glowing with an unfathomable understanding, leaves slowly but is halted by the King's request that he appear at the palace for judgment. Singing praise to his God, the Shepherd then leaves.

Act Two. In the interior court of the royal palace, King Roger anxiously awaits the Shepherd's arrival for he had felt the intense fire in the young man's eyes. Soon the Shepherd arrives garbed in a yellow robe, this time with four companions, each carrying musical instruments. The Shepherd tells the King that he comes in the cause of eternal love, having traveled from the Far South. Responding to the King's questioning, he tells him he has been called forth like a flower. Over the King's growing concerns about his blasphemy, the Shepherd calls for his companions to play and the Queen appears, listening, entranced, to his ecstatic utterances. The King finally calls for his soldiers to seize the Shepherd, but the shining young man pulls loose and breaks the chains that bind him, throwing them at the king's feet. He calls for those present to accompany him to his land in response to the inexplicable calling they all now hear. Queen Roksana follows him forth, leaving the King alone as he puts his hands to his face in deep puzzlement. Edrisi gazes into the dark night, but the Shepherd and his followers have disappeared. The King finally rises abruptly, casting aside his crown and sword, prepared now to be a pilgrim himself.

Act Three. The King and Edrisi arrive at the ruins of an ancient theater. The King is tired and travel-worn, a wandering beggar seeking his beloved Roksana. At that moment, her voice is heard and, as a ship draws near the shore close at hand, the Shepherd's also. Mysterious voices celebrate the awakening of the King's soul and Roksana appears cloaked in a grey mantle. The King inquires about the Shepherd's whereabouts and Roksana tells him that he is in the many wonders of nature—the stars, the stones, the altar's fire. The Shepherd's voice is heard, calling to the King. The Shepherd now appears as Dionysus surrounded by mystical figures, summoning the King to enlightenment. Roksana removes her mantle, showing herself in the garments of a maenad. She makes sacrifice before the altar as the King stands transfixed. The entire assembly then fades into darkness, leaving the King and Edrisi alone once more. With the breaking of dawn, the altar's flames expire and Edrisi wakens from the dream. King Roger stretches his arms and his heart to the rising sun, greeting Apollo just as he had given himself to Dionysus. Thus, in his new life, the two aspects, order and nature, achieve synthesis. *—Erik Eriksson*

Recommended:

- ○ **Szymanowski: King Roger; Symphony 4** / Rattle (cond.), Hampson, Szmytka, Minkiewicz, Langridge / 1999 / Angel 56823
- ○ **Szymanowski: King Roger; Prince Potemkin** / Stryja (cond.), Ochman, Zagorzanka, Grychnik / 1998 / Naxos 660062

T

Tafelmusik Baroque Orchestra

f. 1978, Toronto, Ontario, Canada

Ensemble

Tafelmusik Baroque Orchestra was formed in Toronto, Canada, in 1978. It is a period instrument orchestra; that is, the group makes use of instruments (or replicas) dating from the same period as the music they perform. The orchestra also performs according to appropriate performance practices—how the music would have been read, and how the instruments would have been played—in an effort to recreate the sounds and the esthetic of Baroque-era music (ca. 1600–1750). The name Tafelmusik is German for "table music," referring to music that would have been performed at banquets: the term comes from German Baroque composer Georg Philipp Telemann's multi-volume collection of table music. The group is based out of Trinity-St.Paul's Church in Toronto.

The orchestra had humble beginnings: in 1978, it was a small Baroque chamber ensemble, formed and led by bassoonist Susan Graves and oboist and recorder player Kenneth Solway. In its early years, Tafelmusik was a four-member chamber group, with a small yearly concert season. The core instruments the group—oboe and recorder, cello, bassoon, and harpsichord—were bolstered by soloists, guest artists, and other musicians as required. The popularity of the ensemble grew, due in part to the rise in popularity of period-instrument music in the 1980s, and Tafelmusik was able to increase its core membership to eleven over the course of the next four years. To this core of eleven players was also added the Tafelmusik Chamber Choir in 1981, thus enabling the group to add Baroque choral music to its expanding repertoire (the group is well-known for its performances of Handel's *Messiah* and of Bach's choral works).

The gradual enlargement of the ensemble, under the leadership of music director and concertmaster Jeanne Lamon, allowed for the performance of large-scale works: no longer merely a chamber ensemble, Tafelmusik, was now able to offer performances of Baroque orchestral music. Tafelmusik's burgeoning success also brought about the group's first recording in 1982, entitled *Popular Masterpieces of the Baroque*. In 1984, Tafelmusik was invited to tour in Europe, and became the first North American Baroque orchestra to do so; since then, the orchestra has visited the continent regularly, including numerous tours in Germany, France, Spain, Denmark, and England. The orchestra has been recognized in Europe as being the equal of some of the best European Baroque orchestras, and has met with great success there.

In the late 1980s and early 1990s, new international recording contracts led to wider dissemination of Tafelmusik's recordings, and the group has since received numerous Canadian and international awards and accolades for its performances and albums, including five Canadian Juno Awards, a Cannes Classical Music Award, and a "Critic's Choice" citation in *BBC Magazine*. Tafelmusik's discography comprises over fifty recordings, including recordings of Mozart's *Requiem*, Vivaldi concertos, excerpts from Handel's operas and from the *Messiah*, and of course, music by Telemann.

As of the new millennium, Tafelmusik had a core of 19 musicians, which is augmented as necessary. The concert season at Trinity-St. Paul's had grown from six concerts a year in 1978 to 45 concerts a year. The orchestra's touring schedule included visits to Europe, Asia, and frequent performances in the United States. Tafelmusik was also the orchestra in residence at the Klang und Raum Festival in Irsee, Germany. *—Alexander Carpenter*

Recommended:

- ○ **Telemann: Orchestral Suites** / Lamon (cond.), Tafelmusik Baroque Orch. / Analekta 23138
- ○ **Mozart: Overtures** / Weil (cond.), Tafelmusik Baroque Orch. / 1991 / Sony 469695
- ○ **Haydn: Symphonies 45, 46 & 47** / Weil (cond.), Tafelmusik Baroque Orch. / 1994 / Sony 53986
- ○ **W.F. Bach: Instrumental Music** / Lamon (cond.), Nediger, Tafelmusik Baroque Orch. / 1997 / Sony 62720
- ○ **Scarlatti: Salve Regina; Vivaldi: Stabat Mater; Concerti per archi** / Lamon (cond.), Lemieux, Tafelmusik Baroque Orch. / Analekta 3171

Germaine Tailleferre

b. Apr. 19, 1892, Parc-St.-Maur, France, **d.** Nov. 7, 1983, Paris, France

Composer: Chamber Music

Of significance as the sole female member of the post-World War I group of French composers known as Les Six, Germaine Tailleferre remained a prominent—if somewhat inaccessible—musician long after the disintegration of that group during the middle and late 1920s. She left behind, at her death in 1983 at the age of 91, an extensive body of work representing almost 70 years of active composition.

Tailleferre was born to a family living in the outskirts of Paris on April 19, 1892. Despite having exposed young Germaine to music from an early age, Tailleferre's parents considered music to be an inappropriate activity for a young lady, and it was not until her twelfth year that Tailleferre convinced them to allow her to pursue serious studies at the Paris Conservatoire, where she studied accompaniment, harmony, and counterpoint, eventually taking first prizes in each. During the years following her graduation she also received a few informal lessons in orchestration from Maurice Ravel.

While a student at the Conservatoire, Tailleferre met composers Auric, Milhaud and Honegger, and after the premiere of her *String Quartet* in 1918, she was invited to join the Nouveaux Jeunes, a group of young composers who identified with the aesthetic of satirical composer Erik Satie and playwright Jean Cocteau which, with the addition of Tailleferre, Durey, and Poulenc, soon became known as Les Six, though not by their own choosing. Tailleferre married twice: following a brief marriage (in 1926) to American author Ralph Barton, she married Jean Lageat, a French lawyer. In 1974, she released an autobiography, *Mémoires à l'emporte pièce*.

Tailleferre's commitment to progressive musical ideas during the early 1920s earned her a measure of notoriety throughout the Parisian musical establishment. Nevertheless, her music never abandoned its allegiance to the traditional French "voice" as passed down from Fauré through Ravel, and the seductive grace and charm of her work are perhaps best summed up by Cocteau's famous assessment of Tailleferre as the musical equivalent to painter Marie Laurencin. *The Chansons françaises* for voice and piano (1930), and the well-known *Overture for orchestra* (1932) are sparkling and quintessentially French in their lighthearted, rather humorous use of modernist techniques. In later years, she experimented with serialism; however, these works are not regarded as highly as her earlier compositions. *—Blair Johnston*

Overview of Works (1910–1979)

Tailleferre's first opera, *Zoulaina* (1931), remains unperformed, however its overture is the most frequently programmed item in her scant orchestral literature. Her next major opera, *Il était un petit navite* (1951), was written with surrealist Henri Jeanson. It was not particularly well-received, but her five radio operas of the mid-1950s, *Du style galant au style méchant*, were more lighthearted in nature and did better. Tailleferre temporarily adopted serialism in the late 1950s, and in this vein composed *Le maître* with Absurdist playwright Eugene Ionesco and *La petite sirène* with Dadaist Philippe Soupault. She also collaborated with Paul Claudel, among others.

Tailleferre's ballet *Le marchand d'oiseaux* (1923) attracted the attention of Princesse Edmond de Polignac, who subsequently became her patroness. Tailleferre's basic style, with its light touch, staccato rhythms, and lithe lyricism, was especially well-suited to ballet. It's a shame that outside of *Paris-Magie* (1949) and *Parisiana* (1953) she created nothing else in the genre, save *La Nouvelle Cythère* (1929), commissioned by Diaghilev for the ballets russes, which she abandoned at his death.

Tailleferre's highest profile may be found in her concerti, including the early *Ballade* (1920), *Piano Concerto* (1924), and *Concertino for Harp* (1925). Her masterpiece is the *Concerto Grosso for Two Pianos, Saxophone Quartet, Eight Solo Voices, and Orchestra* (1934). Needless to say, it is rarely performed due to the forces required. Her last major work was the *Concerto de la fidélité for High Soprano and Orchestra*, composed when she was 90.

Tailleferre wrote two magnificent violin sonatas, the first for Jacques Thibaud; the second being a reduction of her lost *Violin Concerto*. The *Harp Sonata* (1953) is the best known and most often played work of Tailleferre. Of her piano music, the four-hand works are worthy of especial attention. These include her *Jeux de plein air* (1917), which so impressed Satie, and the sparkling *Toccata* (1957) written in her best manner of "mouvements perpetuels." Tailleferre wrote both choral and vocal music, a number of songs being written for children. Her most important vocal work is the cycle *Six Chansons Françaises*, based on older texts dealing with the problems of women in relationships. Tailleferre also contributed scores to some 35 films and a handful of radio plays.

Most of Tailleferre's more than 300 works remain unpublished and many of them are lost, including pieces dating from her late period. In writings about Tailleferre, one often reads of the facility and ease of her music, its femininity, detachment, and, sometimes, slapdash construction. The few available recordings of her works tell a different story; the music is expertly crafted, deeply emotional, and contains far more variety than her critics are willing to acknowledge. Open-minded listeners should reap many rewards in seeking out Tailleferre, the "spiritual daughter" of Satie. *—Uncle Dave Lewis*

Recommended:

○ **Music of Germaine Tailleferre Vol. 2** / Paiement (cond.), UC Santa Cruz Orch. / 1999 / Helicon 1048

○ **Music Of Germaine Tailleferre Vol. 1** / Paiement (cond.), Porter SQ, Various Artists / 1996 / Helicon 1008

○ **Tailleferre: Music For Piano, Harp, Chant** / Art Nouveau Ens. / 2000 / Nuova Era 7341

CHAMBER MUSIC

Forlane, for flute & piano (Nov., 1972)

Germaine Tailleferre wrote this brief *Forlane* in 1972, when she was 80 years old and still working, trying to support herself and her granddaughter. It was one of several pieces written around the same time for soloist and piano, dedicated to other musicians. The *Forlane* was dedicated to flutist Jean-Pierre Bourillon. Her work, a modern take on an ancient courtly dance, immediately brings to mind Ravel's "Forlane" in *Le tombeau de Couperin*. It has the same dotted rhythm in a 6/8 meter and the same delicate and precise feel. However, Tailleferre works in a minor mode and with a four-bar phrase that ends suspended above the original key, needing a fifth bar to resolve it. The piano and flute work these phrases together, but in the modulating sections it is only the piano that carries on with the dance while the flute plays a wistful, smooth, and slower melody above it. The entire dance lasts less than three minutes, making it an enjoyable bon-bon in the modern French flute repertoire. *—Patsy Morita*

Recommended:

○ **L'Album des Six: The Complete Works for Flute and Piano** / Beynon, West / 2001 / Hyperion 67204

Harp Sonata (1953)

At the request of Spanish harpist Nicanor Zabaleta, Tailleferre wrote this sonata in 1953, issuing a revision four years later. Dedicated to Zabaleta, the work falls into three compact movements. Bobbling along with a vaguely antique air, the Allegretto is an intricately sunny march, as if for toy soldiers, that frequently veers off into complex, finger-twisting passages. The languorous Lento glides along on a habanera rhythm, a nod to Zabaleta's nationality. (The habanera was the favorite "Spanish" rhythm of such earlier composers as Bizet, Saint-Saëns, and Chabrier, even though it actually originated in Cuba.) Alternating with a little fanfare motif, the jazzy main theme of the sparkling Perpetuum mobile (Allegro gaiement) is a distant cousin of the opening melody of Ravel's *Piano Concerto in G major*. *—James Reel*

Recommended:

○ **Legende: French Music for Harp** / Ravnopolska / Gega 152

Violin Sonata No. 1 in C sharp minor (1920–Oct., 1921)

First performed by Jacques Thibaud and Alfred Cortot, this sonata has never enjoyed the advocacy of other musicians of such stature. It does have its structural weaknesses, but it is an overall engaging work in Tailleferre's early neo-Classical style and deserves wider exposure. The opening "Modéré sans lenteur" strides along confidently through its first subject, then picks up its pace and glances around nervously through the second theme. Each instrument's part could stand alone, yet they complement each other nicely and indulge in mild polytonality during the development section. The development seems to strip the first theme of its confidence by the time it returns for the recapitulation; the music here is slipping into the minor mode and is more troubled than before. The second movement is a short, witty scherzo in 5/8, just on the verge of becoming a slightly macabre waltz. The trio section, more mysterious, gets by on atmosphere rather than a memorable theme. The last two movements are joined without pause. The slow movement, "Assez lent," makes effective use of polytonality, with the violin melody wandering and trilling distractedly over the piano's unsettled, slightly out-of-kilter harmonies. A brief solo passage for the violin leads straight into the finale, "Très vite." This movement shares the troubled exuberance familiar from the music of Milhaud, indulges in some rhythmic complications, and just as it seems about to recede into the night, culminates in a little fugue that would sound jaunty were it not for a tone of desperation. *—James Reel*

Recommended:

○ **Tailleferre: Chamber Music** / Ehrlich, Eckert / 1994 / Cambria 1085

Violin Sonata No. 2 (1947–1948)

Although she was 68 when she wrote her second violin sonata, Tailleferre still had more than 20 years of composing ahead of her. Far from sounding like a work of old age, then, this sonata is particularly simple, fresh, and charming, the music of a composer experienced and confident enough to back away from complexity and harshness. For this reason, though, the sonata is definitely out of step with its time; by the mid-1950s, most leading composers were using more pungent harmonies—if they employed traditional harmony at all. The opening Allegro non troppo introduces a relaxed and carefree violin melody over a rocking piano rhythm, putting no more demands on the key of B flat major than would any composer a century earlier. The second subject is particularly broad and lyrical, and the melodies undergo development in a traditional sonata-allegro form movement utterly free of structural surprises. The Adagietto dips into D minor, achieving a poignancy safely removed from profundity. The piano plays gently throbbing material redolent of Poulenc, while the violin transforms it into a bittersweet melody in long, winding, songlike phrases. The entire movement arises from this music, contrast provided through harmonic shifts rather than significant changes in melody. Tailleferre employs two of her trademarks in this movement: a very long trill at the midpoint and a final section that sends the violin into its high range. The finale, Allegro, moves to F major for a light, playful treatment of a tune that sometimes stutters, sometimes jitters up and down the scale. A more soaring motif sometimes emerges from this, but again all the music remains closely tied to the busy primary melody. *—James Reel*

Recommended:

○ **Tailleferre: Works for Violin & Piano** / B. Mezzena, F. Mezzena / 2000 / Dynamic 223

Toru Takemitsu

b. Oct. 8, 1930, Tokyo, Japan, **d.** Feb. 20, 1996, Tokyo, Japan

Composer: Chamber Music, Keyboard, Orchestral, Concerto, Film Music

Toru Takemitsu (1930–96) was a self-taught Japanese composer who combined elements of Eastern and Western music and philosophy to create a unique sound world. Some of his early influences were the sonorities of Debussy, and Messiaen's use of nature imagery and modal scales. There is a certain influence of Webern in Takemitsu's use of silence, and Cage in his compositional philosophy, but his overall style is uniquely his own. Takemitsu believed in music as a means of ordering or contextualizing everyday sound in order to make it meaningful or comprehensible. His philosophy of "sound as life" lay behind his incorporation of natural sounds, as well as his desire to juxtapose and reconcile opposing elements such as Orient and Occident, sound and silence, and tradition and innovation. From the beginning, Takemitsu wrote highly experimental music involving improvisation, graphic notation, unusual combinations of instruments and recorded sounds. The result is music of great beauty and originality. It is usually slowly paced and quiet, but also capable of great intensity. The variety, quantity and consistency of Takemitsu's output are remarkable considering that he never worked within any kind of conventional framework or genre. In addition to the several hundred independent works of music, he scored over ninety films and published twenty books.

Takemitsu had no important teachers, and his musical career really began with the formation of the *Jikken Kobo* (Experimental Workshop) to promote and perform mixed-media art works. It was Stravinsky's acclaim of the *Requiem for strings* in 1959 that launched Takemitsu's international career. The next few years produced a wide variety of works including Takemitsu's prolific film work, and numerous new music concerts and festivals that culminated in 1967 with a commission for the 125th anniversary of the New York Philharmonic. By this time, Takemitsu had begun using traditional Japanese instruments in his music. *November Steps* is one of his most successful combinations of Eastern and Western music; Takemitsu's style was created from, and rooted in both. Takemitsu's international fame skyrocketed after this premiere, flooding him with commissions and honors that established him as one of the most influential Japanese composers of the century. *—Steven Coburn*

CHAMBER MUSIC

Eclipse, for shakuhachi & biwa (1966)

Toru Takemitsu's work is often considered as a manifestation of global culture: not only does he bring an Eastern sensibility to the Western symphonic ensemble, he also combines Japanese and European instruments. In *November Steps*, for example, the orchestra provides accompaniment for and contrast to a featured pair of Japanese instruments: the biwa, a traditional lute-like instrument with silk strings and a propensity for dramatic intonational inflections, and the shakuhachi, a bamboo recorder characterized by its variety of articulations and timbres.

Just prior to his bridging the East-West cultural gap with *November Steps*, Takemitsu's *Eclipse* emerged as his first concert work for Japanese instruments. Scored for biwa and shakuhachi as well, it served to pave the way for his subsequent intercultural efforts. The somewhat shopworn but nonetheless accurate analogy of the Japanese rock garden serves well to describe the sonic landscape of *Eclipse*. Combining two instruments whose character is so dominated by details of articulation and inflection of individual notes through intonation or texture, the piece draws attention to minute details of musical surfaces and leaves ample space between sound events to focus the ear's concentration. A note on the shakuhachi may emerge seamlessly from a long silence, or appear suddenly with explosive breath; pitches bend slowly, as if succumbing to gravity, or slowly shimmer with increasing vibrato before leaping elsewhere with unanticipated force and agility. The scrape of the plectrum against the strings of the biwa is sometimes nimble and melodic, but almost percussive in its friction at times of increased drama.

Despite the leisurely pace with which the piece unfolds and the ambiguous sense of trajectory that it conveys, the melodic contours and dramatic inflections are not left to the fancy of the performers. Rather, Takemitsu uses a special kind of notation for each instrument to indicate every nuance of sound shape. The biwa player reads from a special tablature system enhanced by graphic symbols for pitch alterations, attack qualities, and other directives, while the shakuhachi player reads lines and shapes mapped onto a time axis. There is some flexibility in the work's performance; however, portions of the piece may be repeated or juxtaposed at the performer's discretion and the spaces between some events are left unspecified. The biwa player is given additional, if ambiguous, guidance by the insertion into the score of lines of poetry by Rabindranath Tagore. Takemitsu conveys certain emotional suggestions to the performers through another method as well, one in which the image conveyed by the work's title infiltrates the very notation of the piece. Part of the score is rendered as a negative image of white notation against a black background, a visual eclipse to accompany the contrasts of sound color that comprise the essence of the music. *—Jeremy Grimshaw*

Recommended:

○ **Takemitsu: In an Autumn Garden** / Yokoyama, Tsuruta / 2002 / DG 471590

Toward the Sea I, for alto flute & guitar (1981)

Japanese composer Toru Takemitsu had a strong interest in images of water in nature. He even composed an electronic composition in 1960, *Water Music* (Mizu non kyoku), that is entirely made up of recorded sounds of water. In the early 1980s Takemitsu's style was evolving from a serial-based technique to a more linear and rhapsodic approach. His early interest in French music (particularly that of Debussy and Messiaen) was also reasserting itself in a personal adaptation of the kind of rich harmonies favored by both Frenchmen.

Toward the Sea was composed as a contribution to the "Save the Whales" campaign of Greenpeace. In Japan, historically a whale-hunting nation, this contribution was a political statement. In writing about this composition, Takemitsu said that his interest was in the sea as a "spiritual domain" and cited a passage in Herman Melville's novel *Moby Dick*: "Let the most absent-minded of men be plunged in his deepest reveries... and he will infallibly lead you to water.... Yes, as everyone knows, meditation and water are wedded together." Melville's novel also provided the form of the work, which is an 11-minute composition in three movements named "The Night," "Moby Dick," and "Cape Cod." Its tone, overall, is calm and meditative.

It is based on the motive E flat, E natural, A. In German notation these notes are "Es, E, A," spelling the English word "SEA." The original version of the composition *Toward the Sea I* is for alto flute and guitar. The music is often written in free, nonmeasured notation, although there are frequently passages in 3/16 in the more rhythmic final movement.

Takemitsu often uses unusual instrumental techniques in the alto flute part. He has devised non-traditional fingerings to produce a more "hollow sound" on the instrument. By specifying two different ways of fingering to produce the same note, then writing a "trill" using these two fingerings, he gets a fluttering effect that alternates not between different notes but by two subtly different tone colors on the same note.

After completing the first version, Takemitsu produced *Toward the Sea II*, for alto flute, harp, and string orchestra. This version retains exactly the same flute part, while the harp takes substantially the guitar part (at least where the guitar is playing figurations) and the strings make audible the harmonies outlined by the guitar part. This results in a smoother, more meditative flow of the music. In order to keep the string orchestra coordinated by a conductor's beat, Takemitsu added bar-lines throughout the piece. This makes orchestral interpretation tricky in that the conductor should strive to create the free-rhythm effect of the original.

The 1989 version, *Toward the Sea III* is for alto flute and harp. Once again Takemitsu did not change the alto flute part. The harp part here is not a transcription of the original guitar part, but is a rewriting of the guitar part to make it into an idiomatic harp part. Here Takemitsu returns to the original unmeasured notation. *—Joseph Stevenson*

Recommended:

○ **John Williams plays Takemitsu** / Williams, S. Bell / 1991 / Sony 46720

A Way a Lone, for string quartet (1981)

Although they were born on different continents and worked in different artistic disciplines, there exists an odd but indelible aesthetic affinity between writer James Joyce and composer Toru Takemitsu. Both worked within a form that develops in a linear fashion: the words, like the notes, read left to right, top to bottom, and are arranged in an order that unfolds and is perceived through time. And both Joyce and Takemitsu write in such a way as to resist that linearity: Joyce's novels are known for their skewed or slippery sense of narrative trajectory and their bending of chronological continuity, while the dramatic trajectories of Takemitsu's works are often compared to the meandering way in which one's eyes or body might navigate freely through the carefully placed objects and open spaces in a Japanese garden. In fact, Takemitsu himself gets the credit for uncovering this affinity: a number of his works incorporate elements from, or otherwise find inspiration in, Joyce's famous and enigmatic novel *Finnegan's Wake*.

Among these is Takemitsu's *A Way a Lone*, composed in 1980 on commission from the Tokyo String Quartet to commemorate that ensemble's tenth anniversary. The composer takes the title of his piece from the ending of *Finnegan's Wake*, one of the most unique and intriguing passages in literature: "The keys to. Given! A way a lone a last a loved a long the." The distant, precarious feeling of Joyce's unfinished sentence and seemingly disconnected words is reflected in the loosely ebbing structure of Takemitsu's quartet, whose harmonic wanderings and exaggerated gestures are perforated with pauses and punctuated with calculated blemishes. A solo violin might in one moment indulge in a rhapsodic melody, then, with a trepidatious breath, float into ethereally high harmonics or wax melodramatic with intoxicated glissandos and portamentos. Takemitsu's dynamic mixture of contrapuntal skill and coloristic sensibility results in dizzying textures made of variously angular lines, intricate patterns, and unimagined hues. Just as Joyce's streams of words approach music in the way they swirl into purely sonic objects, Takemitsu's music unfolds so naturally and with such spontaneity as to become a kind of surreal conversation.

While it is not difficult to read into the musical surface certain general similarities to the work from which the piece takes its title, the composer identifies Joyce's influence operating on a more technical level. Much of the musical material is constructed upon and around a three-note idea consisting of a minor second ascent followed by an upward leap of a perfect fourth. Takemitsu refers to these pitches as the "Intervals of the SEA." Here, Takemitsu reveals a subtle musical encoding of an extra-musical reference: In the traditional German terminology, the note E flat is expressed as "Es," or simply "S"; up a half step from Takemitsu's E flat is an E and a fourth up from that, the A. Takemitsu's prevalent three-note idea thus spells out "SEA" in musical letters. *—Jeremy Grimshaw*

Recommended:

○ **Chamber Music by Toru Takemitsu** / Ensemble Kaï / 1998 / Bis 920

KEYBOARD

Rain-Tree Sketch (1982)

Rain-Tree Sketch, a solo piano work composed in 1982, counts among a number of "water-themed" works Toru Takemitsu composed from the late 1970s through the subsequent decade. Many of Takemitsu's works draw on nature imagery for pictorial resonance; several pieces, for example, evoke the open space and pointillist design found in the serene traditional gardens of his native Japan. Takemitsu's water pieces, including *Rain Tree* (a percussion piece from 1981 related to the work under consideration here principally through their shared imagery), *Rain Coming* (1982), *Toward the Sea I* (1980), and *I Hear the Water Dreaming* (1987), imagine water in its various states and planes: as droplets falling from the sky, the sea resting below, or rivulets and rivers in their fluid downhill motions. Most writers associate the irregular pace and organic texture of *Rain-Tree Sketch* with Kensaburo Oe's "The Clever Rain Tree," a short story written in honor of French music critic and impresario Maurice Fleuret; Takemitsu dedicated his piece to Fleuret, as well. (There is also, however, a competing and decidedly less attractive attribution: some claim Takemitsu candidly admitted that he got the name "Rain Tree" from the label on a can of shaving cream he had seen during a trip to America, but that he endorsed the after-the-fact connection to Oe's tale because the imagery nonetheless seemed quite fitting.) Oe's story describes a tree with countless tiny leaves that collect and retain water from the morning rain shower so that throughout the day, after the storm has abated, the rain still falls from the tree. Takemitsu's piece works in a similar fashion: its precipitation falls alternately in single droplets of quiet, lone sustained notes and sudden dissonant clusters of tones, as if jostled from waterlogged branches. The composer carefully notates differentiated dynamics and accents, as well as precise pedaling techniques to lend careful nuance to these moment-to-moment contours. The piece's overall form follows an ABA structure delineated by tempo changes, but the rigidity of this form is rendered opaque by the ametrical flow of Takemitsu's gestures and the care and patience with which he releases them. *—Jeremy Grimshaw*

Recommended:

○ **Rain Tree: Complete Solo Piano Music of Toru Takemitsu** / Ogawa / 1996 / Bis 805

○ **Poésie: Yukie Nagai Plays Japanese Piano Music** / Nagai / 1995 / Bis 766

ORCHESTRAL

Dorian Horizon (Chiheisen no doria), for 17 strings (1966)

Using the metaphor of the Japanese garden to describe the music of Toru Takemitsu may sound like a Westerner's Orientalist cliché, but in fact it takes on deep and particular meanings that are deliberately woven into his works by the composer. In many pieces Takemitsu evokes a spatial rather than temporal form—often using the "garden" aesthetic as a model—in order to recast sounds as multi-dimensional, tactile entities rather than successions of functional, syntactical emblems. In other words, instead of composing tones that pass us by, Takemitsu strives to allow us to pass through them. *Dorian Horizon*, a chamber work for strings composed in 1966 on commission from the Koussevitzky Foundation, exemplifies this approach. In fact, Takemitsu once described the piece as "my mild protest against inorganic serialism." He explained further that it contains "no melodic thinking, only harmonic pitches. There is no thinking of rhythm, only pulse. It is a first sketch in my search for a new kind of polyphony." The composer applies somewhat idiosyncratic meanings to these familiar terms. By "harmonic," for example, he seems to suggest not simply sonorous chords, or even the whispered sounds of string harmonics (though they are used frequently in the piece), but rather a kind of atemporal, rather than linear sense of pitch.

The work is scored for 17 strings divided into two groups. The first, a group of eight players making up the "harmonic" element, is situated in the front of the other ensemble. The remaining nine serve what Takemitsu called an "echo" role, offering allusory and even illusory ruminations, as if presenting sonic objects from different angles or at differing distances. The piece consists of a limited number of gestures, which nonetheless convey a startling subtlety of expression: pizzicatos in some strings combined with sustained tones in others, creating a kind of bell tone; sustained pitches that are passed from instrument to instrument, changing only in octave placement, dynamic, and/or articulation; ethereal chord clusters (based on tetrachords from the E, F, and E flat Dorian scales that the piece variously employs) that move via surreal glissandos. Even the presence or absence of string vibrato plays a crucial role in altering this sparse soundscape. What better metaphor, then, than the garden: after all, says the composer, this music which "shines in the sunlight, goes grey when it is cloudy, changes color in the rain, and whose shape is mutated by the wind." *—Jeremy Grimshaw*

A Flock Descends into the Pentagonal Garden (1977)

This beautifully titled composition for orchestra was inspired by a dream in which the composer saw a flock of white birds, led by a single black bird swirling around and then descending into a pentagonal or star-shaped garden. The garden, however, turned out to be the star on the back of artist Marcel Duchamp's head in the famous photograph by Man Ray.

In Takemitsu's musical encoding or symbolism, the black bird leader is represented by the tone F sharp. The other birds are represented in pentatonic scales generated from each tone of the initial F sharp pentatonic: thus there is one five-note scale each on A flat, on B flat, C sharp, and E flat. The relationship between these scales (often presented as woodwind chords sounding like the ancient Japanese mouth organ called the sho) is original, like branches of branches on a tree, or successive ripples within ripples in a pond. The further the scale notes diverge from the initial F sharp, the greater is the activity in the writing to get them to gravitate back to that initial tone. Takemitsu described the F sharp sounding out "constantly in the manner of a drone."

A whimsical wind solo (bird theme) against a lovely sustained cluster opens the work; then a deeply ominous chord builds up to a frightening level. Lushly harmonized, lyrical melodies (bird and garden themes) float like clouds. Silvery glissandi whistle by. Booming bass tones create a surreal storm. The flight of the birds is again depicted by sensuous melodies surrounded by trilling figures and cries from the winds. Steely non-vibrato chords suggest a metallic garden, while bell-like textures and hard plucked harp strings and multiple airy glissandi are added in. The sequence of playful clarinet (bird theme) to rich strings (garden theme) to deep bass accents is repeated, and begun again; the harmonic series is reminiscent of passages in Alban Berg's opera *Lulu*. On the next repetition, the series resolves to an exquisite chord across the full range of the orchestra. *—"Blue Gene" Tyranny*

Recommended:

○ **Takemitsu: A Flock Descends** / Otaka (cond.), BBC National Orch. Wales / 1995 / Bis 760

Requiem, for strings (1957)

When Igor Stravinsky was introduced to Toru Takemitsu in 1959, he was taken aback by the young Japanese composer's frail, slight frame. "How could such severe music come have come from such a tiny man?" he is said to have wondered aloud. Just prior to their meeting, the elder composer had happened upon a recording of Takemitsu's haunting *Requiem*, a piece for string orchestra composed in 1957, when Takemitsu was just 27 years old.

The severity that so struck Stravinsky is apparent even from a cursory glance at the score: all three sections of the work are ponderously slow (Lento, Modère, Moins Lent; "I was never able to write an Allegro," the composer once quipped); likewise, the variety of orchestral color that one encounters in Takemitsu's later works (such as *From me flows what you call Time* from 1990) is absent, ceding the weight of expression to the slow, wrenching harmonies and the subtleties of the string scoring. The first section is characterized by a rich texture of chordal accompaniment, against which Takemitsu's angular melodies proceed. The middle section is punctuated by more forceful, homorhythmic passages, as well as occasional unison lines unadorned by harmonic underpinning. The last section builds in intensity, heightened by the spare use of effects like portamenti and string harmonics. The harmony ends ambiguously, underneath a violin solo that follows a twisting, ascending path into the ether. *—Jeremy Grimshaw*

Recommended:

○ **Toro Takemitsu: How Slow the Wind** / Otaka (cond.), Kioi Sinfonietta Tokyo / 2000 / BIS 301078

CONCERTO

November Steps, for shakuhachi, biwa & orchestra (1967)

At first glance Toru Takemitsu's *November Steps*, composed in 1967 for the New York Philharmonic's 125th birthday, would seem to exemplify the inevitability of Oriental/Occidental musical exchange in the age of global communication and commerce. After all, it counterpoises against the lush, booming sound of the Western orchestra two soloists playing exotic instruments from his native Japan: the shakuhachi flute and the lute-like biwa. Takemitsu presents this not as a diplomatic gesture, however, but rather a dialectical one. "Sometimes these two worlds of East and West envelope me with gentleness," the composer confided to musicologist Luciana Galliano in 1995, "but more often than not they tear me apart. What I try to do is to follow both directions. I wish not to find a resolution to this creative paradox, but to bring the two opposing sides into conflict." The concerto would seem the perfect genre to depict this tension: its connotation of the individual apart from society, the few against the many, taken to embody the position of a composer both admittedly self-conscious about his own native musical tradition and never fully at home in his adopted idiom.

This approach lends the piece a palpable energy. The two sides rarely seek to find common ground, but rather emphasize the borders of their own and each others' idiomatic profiles. Those borders, it should be noted, expand exponentially in the hands of Takemitsu, who elicits from the ensemble and soloists a seemingly unending supply of new sonorities. Throughout the piece's 11 sections (or "Steps," the term in the title corresponding roughly to a word akin to "movement" in the Japanese classical tradition), though a few structural aspects of the piece are left variable, the moment-to-moment details are deliberately conceived and notated with painstaking detail. Every sound in the composer's universe, then, is a designed and created entity. The biwa, with its pointed attack, abundant overtones, and quasi-percussive possibilities finds challenge in the orchestra's timbral agility, while one of the shakuhachi's intonational nuances might send shimmering, dissonant ripples across the strings. In performance, these reactions and interactions take on an almost theatrical element: the orchestra is distributed in an unusual fashion around the stage behind the soloists, lending a spatial aspect to the translucent layers of highly individualized elements that fill the score. They also assume a careful pace, as Takemitsu interpolates his surreal, apparitional sonorities with pensive, heavy silences. *—Jeremy Grimshaw*

Recommended:

○ **Takemitsu: In an Autumn Garden** / Yokoyama, Tsuruta / 2002 / DG 471590

riverrun, for piano & orchestra (1984)

It may seem curious that a Japanese composer with only limited facility in literary English would find himself drawn to James Joyce's novel *Finnegan's Wake*. For Toru Takemitsu, however, the linguistic barrier between him and Joyce's infamously difficult work was not a wall but a window: the author meant for the book to come across as half-formed, tied together by those twisted tendrils of logic that only hold fast in dreams and that unravel by light of day. Freed from the native speaker's inevitable impulse and vain effort to make sense of the calculatedly intractable prose, Takemitsu could listen under less duress to the surface of the text, grasping at will for discernible images, carried along by the current of words.

This adventurous undertaking was the inspiration for *riverrun*, one of a triptych of works composed in the mid-1980s as musical responses to *Finnegan's Wake*. In fact, the title, including the lowercase "R," is borrowed from the very first word of the novel. (The other two Joyce pieces, *A Way a Lone, for string quartet*, and *Far Calls, Coming, Far!, for violin and orchestra*, both take their titles from the book's final paragraph.) The work, which is scored for piano soloist and orchestra, also draws on two other prominent ideas from the book: water-related themes and "falling" imagery (rivers, after all, flow downward). If listeners adopt the composer's imagery, the river is a slow-moving one, with a gently undulating surface that is frequently rippled with eddies and, on occasion, shattered with splashes and brief rapids. Takemitsu's acute sense of instrumental color synthesizes the piano's gestures with seamless and complementary timbres from the orchestra. The soloist occasionally surfaces alone in extended cadenza-like passages, but then retreats just beneath the translucent orchestral surface. To imagine Takemitsu reading Joyce might provide a guide for how to might read—or hear—Takemitsu, not because his music is in some way intrinsically cast in a Japanese musical idiom (though certain decidedly Oriental ideas dominate his aesthetic approach to Occidental composition), but because, like Joyce's invented words and incongruous sentences, Takemitsu's gestures and textures resist being heard as musical syntax or symbols, and insist instead on being heard as veiled allusions and sheer, sonic bodies. *—Jeremy Grimshaw*

Recommended:

○ **A String Around Autumn** / Otaka (cond.), Ogawa, BBC National Orch. Wales / 2002 / Bis 1300

FILM MUSIC

Film Music (1961–1995)

Takemitsu, a lifelong movie fan who went to films in languages he didn't understand when in foreign countries ("As I watch the images... I can understand the people... it's a musical way of understanding"), wrote his first film score in 1956 for Ko Nakahira's *Kurutta Kajitsu* (*Crazed Fruit*). He went on to compose for a total of 93 pictures while also becoming internationally recognized as one of the finest composers of contemporary concert music.

One of his most influential early scores was for Hiroshi Teshigahara's *Suna no onna* (*Woman in the Dunes*) (1964). Many musique concrète techniques modified the dry, percussive sounds and hissing sounds. These modified natural sounds were combined with erotically sliding (portamento) string instruments. The results accompanied images of the stroking of skin and the sliding of the sand—"That film had three main characters: the man, the woman, and the sand."

There is a background of stillness and silence throughout the film without the usual drones or dramatic sustains to fall back on. "I don't like things that are too pure and refined... the pure is only interesting if it is contrasted with something coarse.... Though I used real instruments, these sounds were altered electronically ... raising the pitch five tones, the feeling... was totally changed." Takemitsu's approach to this film is very similar to the score for Masaki Kobayashi's *Kwaidan* (1965), three visually stunning and terrifying ghost tales by Lafacadio Hearn.

Takemitsu also employed traditional instruments in *Samurai Rebellion* (1967) and Masaki Kobayashi's *Hara Kiri* (1963); mixed sixteenth century European and Japanese instruments for Hiroshi Teshigahara's *Rikyu* (1989); made a touchingly droll electronic score for the animated romantic chase short *Love* (*Ai*) (1963); and, from his experience as a record producer and arranger, a soft rock & roll score for *Youth of Japan* (1968). Although Takemitsu longed to score comedies and love stories, he gained his reputation for dramatic and surreal works such as Masahiro Shinoda's intense black-and-white *Double Suicide* (1969); *The Pitfall* (1962); Masahiro Shinoda's exquisite *Banished Orin* (1977); the strongly anti-war films *Tokyo Trials* (1983) and *Black Rain* (1989); and Hiroshi Teshigahara's *Face of Another* (1966), for which he created both electronic atmospheres and richly tuneful music which perfectly fit the strange allegorical nature of the visuals.

The score for Nagisa Oshima's 1978 ghostly tale of obsessive love turning to violence *Empire of Passion* mixes unusual orchestral sounds—harmonic clusters, wide string portamento, cymbals upside down on tympani heads, etc.—and electronically processed original instruments—metal rods of varying lengths arranged around a metal bowl that are both struck and bowed, heavily reverberated log drum-like arrhythmic clashes, and so on.

For Akira Kurosawa's 1970 film *Dodes'ka-den*, Takemitsu created several settings of a central theme that express the innocence of its young central character whose dream is to become a trolley conductor.

For other films, Takemitsu created scores that were akin to his concert scores: *Under the Cherry Blossoms* (1975), *Ran* (1985), *Himatsuri* (1985), and *Dream Window* (1992). *—"Blue Gene" Tyranny*

Recommended:

○ **The Film Music Of Toru Takemitsu** / Adams (cond.), London Sinfonietta / Nonesuch 79404

Talich Quartet

f. 1964, Prague, Czechoslovakia
Ensemble

Formed at the Prague Conservatory in 1964, the Talich Quartet takes its name from the important conductor and founder of the Czech Philharmonic, Václav Talich (1883–1961), from whom the current first violinist is descended. Internationally recognized as one of Europe's finest quartets, the Talich performs regularly in major cities throughout the world and has made numerous recordings.

Works of Czech composers, such as Bedřich Smetana, Antonín Dvořák, Bohuslav Martinů, and Leoš Janáček, form the core of the Talich Quartet's repertoire, both in performance and on recordings. However, their extensive and varied discography also includes the complete string quartets of Mozart, Beethoven, and Bartók, which have won numerous awards including a "Golden Disc" from Czech label Supraphon and several "Grand Prix du Disque" awards as well as the French Académie du Disque Lyrique's "Diapason d'Or." Their recording history has become long and distinguished enough to merit re-releases, and in 2000 Harmonia Mundi announced the Talich Quartet's newly-repackaged Beethoven cycle on Calliope, featuring the long-time configuration of Petr Messiereur, Jan Kvapil, Jan Talich Sr. and Evzen Rattay.

After the ensemble made their 30th recording for Calliope in 1998 (Dvořák's String Quartets in G major, Op. 106, and in A flat major, Op. 105), Vladimir Bukac moved from second violin to viola (replacing founding member Jan Talich Sr.) and Petr Macecek took over the second violin spot. Jan Talich Jr., replaced Peter Messiereur on the first violin and Petr Prause took Evzen Rattay's place at the cello. By 2000, their membership was as follows: Jan Talich Jr., first violin; Petr Macecek, second violin; Vladimir Bukac, viola; and Petr Prause, cello.

Performances by the Talich are always of a high caliber and statements such as this—from a *Boston Globe* reviewer—are typical of critics' responses: "[The Talich quartet are] so serenely good that, as a listener, one has no choice but to put oneself in their hands." Comments generally point out the quartet's subtlety, elegance, and intensity in their interpretations of a wide range of styles. Annual touring schedules include Europe, Japan, and North America, and they have also toured the Middle East, Australia, and Indonesia.

The Talich Quartet made its North American debut in 1987 and received overwhelmingly positive reviews. A Vancouver critic declared, "If it isn't already a national treasure, the Talich Quartet should be.... What we had, simply, was perfection." The ensemble appears annually at the Dvořák String Quartet Festival in Prague, and in 1999 participated in the Casals Festival, the Prague Spring Music Festival and the Europalia Festival. Seemingly tireless, they also toured Japan in 1999. *—John Palmer*

Recommended:

○ **Janáček: Music for String Quartet** / Talich Quartet / Supraphon 111354
○ **Mendelssohn: Quatets Opp12 & 13** / Talich Quartet / 2001 / Calliope 9311
○ **Dvořák: "American: Quartet; Quintett Op 97** / Talich Quartet, Bukac / 2002 / Calliope 9331

Tallis Chamber Choir

f. 1982, London, England
Ensemble

The Tallis Chamber Choir is an active British choir with a broad repertory and a reputation for strongly researched programs. It was founded in 1982 by choral director Philip Simms. The chorus soon became one of the best known in England. It is a flexible organization and can provide from 12 to 60 voices for a performance, depending on the requirements of the venue and the material.

While the name of the choir suggests that it is an early music organization, its repertory in fact is generous. What the Tallis Chamber Choir shares with the early music movement is that is performances are meticulously researched and sung according to the style appropriate to the music.

The choir's flexibility is suggested by their activities in a given six-month period: They began the last half of 1999 doing a soundtrack recording for a new film called *The Criminal* and during the next week sang a concert performance of Handel's *Theodora*. A major appearance at the Wratislava Cantans Festival in Poland in September included Haydn's *The Creation* and a choral concert of music of Tallis, Byrd, Gibbons, Sheppard, Morley, Martin, and Poulenc, followed within the a month's time by performances of two Handel choral works, Mozart's *Requiem*, and Burstein's *The Gates of Time*. Then, within two weeks they sang in Scriabin's *Prometheus* and began the busy Christmas season with Handel's *Messiah*, a festive Christmas program, and Berlioz's *L'Enfance du Christ*.

In addition to soundtrack work, the choir makes backing tracks for television commercials, sings with major orchestras under some of the world's most famous conductors, and appears in music festivals throughout Europe.

Its recordings include a live recording of its *Concert for the Queen Mother's 90th Birthday*, conducted by Raymond Leppard, an appearance on a Branford Marsalis saxophone LP, Orff's *Carmina Burana*, and releases of Verdi's *Il trovatore*, Donizetti's *L'elisir d'amore*. They sang on the soundtrack of the TV documentary *Disaster at Sea*, (about the Exxon Valdez shipwreck).

Its tonal qualities are described by British critics as warm, exuberant, and technically brilliant. The Tallis Chamber Choir is not related to the Tallis Scholars, a Renaissance a cappella choral group founded in 1973 by Peter Phillips. *—Joseph Stevenson*

Recommended:

- ○ **Handel: Coronation Anthems; Silete Venti** / Summerly (cond.), Ryan, Tallis Chamber Choir, Royal Academy Consort / 2002 / Naxos 8557003
- ○ **Britten: St. Nicolas; Christ's Nativity** / Bedford (cond.), Langridge, Tallis Chamber Choir, English CO / 2003 / Naxos 8557203

Tallis Scholars

f. 1973, Oxford, England
Ensemble

The Tallis Scholars are entirely devoted to the performance of Renaissance choral music. Through scholarship, musicianship, and the careful cultivation of a distinctive vocal sound, they have established themselves as the leading exponents of that particular repertory, and they have done a great deal to increase general interest in Renaissance music through an increasing catalogue of successful recordings, as well as international concert tours.

The founder and director of The Tallis Scholars, Peter Phillips, studied Renaissance music with David Wulstan and Denis Arnold at Oxford University. In 1973 he formed The Tallis Scholars from chapel choirs at both Oxford and Cambridge, choosing from among the so-called "choral scholars," who receive tuition wavers for their full-time service to the chapel choirs of their schools. These singers represent the finest choral musicians from their respective institutions, and it is from their traditional title, as well as the name of English composer Thomas Tallis whose music has formed a central part of their repertory, that the group derives its name.

From their inception, The Tallis Scholars have maintained a reputation as one of the greatest a cappella organizations in the world. They are particularly noted for their illumination of the complex web of independent melodic lines that is characteristic of Renaissance music, which in less capable hands can lose its musical cohesion and direction.

A key part of The Tallis Scholars' success has been the dissemination of their recordings on the Gimell label which, in an innovative move, was co-founded by Phillips and Steve C. Smith in 1981 for the sole purpose of recording the group. Having at his disposal this purpose-built record company has allowed Phillips to record the music of lesser-known composers such as Cipriano de Rore, Clemens non Papa, Frei Manuel Cardoso, and Heinrich Isaac in addition to that of the more established masters such as Byrd, Palestrina, and, of course, Thomas Tallis. The selection of repertory for recordings has been carefully managed to balance the familiar with the more obscure, and a number of industry awards—including the 1987 "Record of the Year" award from *Gramophone Magazine* and two Diapason d'Or de L'Année awards—attest to the consistent quality of the results. Other awards include two more Gramophone Awards for "Best Early Music" recordings (1991 and 1994) and a Gramophone/Classic FM People's Choice Award.

Highlights of The Tallis Scholars' performing schedule have included participation in major events, such as the commemoration of the 400th anniversary of the death of *Palestrina* at the Basilica of Santa Maria Maggiore in Rome, and the celebration of the restoration of Michelangelo's The Last Judgment at the Sistine Chapel. *—AMG*

Recommended:

- ○ **Byrd: 3 Masses** / Phillips (cond.), Tallis Scholars / 2001 / Gimell 345
- ○ **Western Wind Masses by Taverner, Tye & Sheppard** / Phillips (cond.), Tallis Scholars / 2001 / Gimell 454927
- ○ **Tavener: Ikon of Light; Funeral Ikos; The Lamb** / Tavener, Phillips (conds.), Tallis Scholars, Chilingirian Qt. / 2001 / Gimell 5
- ○ **Essential Tallis Scholars** / Phillips (cond.), Tallis Scholars / 2003 / Gimell 201
- ○ **Tallis Christmas Mass** / Phillips (cond.), Tallis Scholars / 2001 / Gimell 34
- ○ **Allegri: Miserere** / Phillips (cond.), Tallis Scholars / 2001 / Gimell 339
- ○ **Tallis: Spem in Alium** / Phillips (cond.), Tallis Scholars / 2001 / Gimell 6

Thomas Tallis

b. ca. 1505, England [?], **d.** Nov. 23, 1585, Greenwich, England
Composer: Choral

The career of Thomas Tallis, Gentleman of the Chapel Royal, spanned a period of spectacular change in the English liturgical climate. Born early in the sixteenth century, his first musical appointment was as organist to a Benedictine (Catholic) Priory in Dover, two years before Henry VIII's definitive break with Rome in 1534. By 1537, Tallis was serving a London parish church as organist; in 1538 he was performing the same task for the Abbey of Holy Cross, Waltham, though this position evaporated when King Henry dissolved the monasteries in 1540. After a brief clerkship at Canterbury Cathedral, Tallis joined the Chapel Royal, where he played, sang, and composed for the remainder of his life, serving in turn Henry VIII, Edward VI, Mary Tudor, and Elizabeth I. Among the lavish rewards he eventually reaped was a famous bequest of 1575, giving him and his young pupil, William Byrd, a complete monopoly on the printing of music and ruled music paper in England.

The liturgical music in England during this time underwent great changes, not the least of which was the shift between Latin and vernacular texts. At the outset of Tallis' career, the prevailing English style of Latin music followed the soaring treble-dominated textures of the previous century, as exemplified in the *Eton Choirbook*; his early Latin motets reflect this. But by the late 1540s, Archbishop Thomas Cranmer was working toward a standard liturgical practice, built around his *Book of Common Prayer*, that would finally replace the Sarum (English Latin) rite in 1559 with exclusively vernacular worship music. The reign of the Catholic "Bloody" Mary Tudor briefly interrupted this trajectory towards the vernacular with a militant resurgence of Catholic music in an older style; Tallis' *Missa Puer natus* and the motet *Gaude gloriosa* apparently date from this time. Stylistically, the church music of England over the second half of the century was yielding to the influence of the Continental imitative style, through the music of the transplanted Italian, Ferrabosco.

Through all these changes, Tallis appears to have retained a professional steadiness and respectability, making music and composing with grace and equanimity as his situation changed. His English-language settings range from simple treatments of the psalms to anthems (such as *Hear the Voice and Prayer*) to three complete settings of the Anglican Service; this music is commonly imbued with a somber and penitential mood. His Latin-texted pieces, whether following the stylish "modern" mode of pervasive imitation or not, demonstrate restraint and even tenderness. (One of the few exceptions, though, is his best-known work today, an over-the-top and still rather mysterious experiment in polychoral writing, the forty-voiced *Spem in alium*). Surprisingly little of Tallis' instrumental music survives, despite his over 50 years of professional organ playing. *—Timothy Dickey*

CHORAL

If ye love me, anthem for 4 voices (1565)

As a staunch Catholic, Thomas Tallis wrote relatively little for the newly founded Anglican Church. The dozen anthems he composed date from either the reign of Edward VI (1547–52), the most radical period of Protestant reform, or the early years of the reign Elizabeth I. "If Ye Love Me" is the most famous of the eight anthems in four parts (alto, alto, tenor, bass). The requirements for music in the Anglican church stood diametrically opposed to the florid polyphonic style of the Tudor Catholic church. The demands for verbal clarity and simplicity were perfectly understood by Tallis, whose tiny work is a masterpiece of succinct devotional expressivity employing a juxtaposition of exquisitely wrought chordal harmony and imitative writing. "If Ye Love Me" along with other Tallis anthems, has retained its place in the Anglican church service. *—Brian Robins*

Recommended:

- ○ **Faire is the Heaven: Music of the English Church** / Rutter (cond.), Cambridge Singers / 1988 / Collegium 107
- ○ **A Tudor Collection** / Phillips (cond.), Tallis Scholars / 1995 / Gimell 454895
- ○ **Beyond Chant: Mysteries Of The Renaissance** / Keene (cond.), Voices of Ascension Chorus & Orch. / 1994 / Delos 3165

Spem in Alium, motet (ca. 1567)

In 1567, the city of London welcomed the visiting Italian musician and nobleman Alessandro Striggio. He stunned the London musical scene with a performance of his motet *Ecce beatam lucem*, written for the utterly extravagant ensemble of 40 voice parts. This rich and unique sonic world was met with great enthusiasm in London, as it had been in other European courts treated to the same piece earlier in the year. But England apparently offered a musical counterchallenge. Legend credits two of England's leading Catholic noblemen—Thomas Howard, the fourth Duke of Norfolk, and Henry Fitzalan, the twelfth Earl of Arundel—with issuing a commission to the most senior and revered English composer of the day to match Striggio's accomplishment. And that composer, Thomas Tallis, presented England with *Spem in alium*. Tallis chose an uncommon Sarum Rite text from the Book of Judith; perhaps in intended flattery to his patron, Queen Elizabeth, by comparing her to the heroic woman who saved the Israelites by killing of the chief of Nebuchadnezzar's army. This has led some commentators to suggest Elizabeth's fortieth birthday (1573) as an appropriate date of first composition. A much later anecdote (researched by Denis Stevens) relates the Duke of Norfolk's commission and a first performance at Long Gallery in the London home of the Earl of Arundel, possibly in 1471. This story imagines the Duke of Norfolk placing a gold chain upon Tallis' neck in recognition of his achievement. One other early performance venue has been suggested: the octagonal banqueting hall of Arundel Castle, providing a perfect architectural disposition for Tallis' octo-choral scoring. Tallis certainly chose his number of voices (40) and his key (G major) in response to Striggio's motet; the number 40 is further emphasized in the piece by the first arrival of all voices—on the fortieth measure. But whereas Striggio's *Ecce beatam lucem* uses a shifting kaleidoscope of vocal textures, Tallis clearly delineates his 40 voices in eight choirs of five voices each. The opening two phrases pass the melodic motifs carefully and relentlessly in imitation through all eight choirs, until the full power and majesty of the united voices arrive together on the name of the "God in Whom Israel trusts." Again, through the center of the motet, imitation wafts upward through six choirs, before a full contrapuntal response to the text for the "sins of all." A new, purer polychoral texture emerges as various choirs echo one another's block harmonies on the invocation "Domine Deus, creator coeli et terrae," and a truly arresting A major chord (on "respice") in all 40 voices demands that God consider our supplication. A second, thrilling, unison chord leads to a fantastically detailed contrapuntal tapestry in all voices until the end. *—Timothy Dickey*

Recommended:

- ○ **Tallis: Spem in Alium; Lamentations; Mass & Motets** / Magnificat / 2000 / Linn 75
- ○ **Tallis: Spem in Alium** / Phillips (cond.), Tallis Scholars / 2001 / Gimell 6

Tan Dun

b. Aug. 18, 1957, Si Mao, Hunan, China
Composer

Tan Dun is a leading Chinese-born composer and one of the most prominent in the genre of "world classical" music. He was raised by his grandmother in central Hunan, a region with distinct linguistic and folk identity, including a shamanistic culture. Tan Dun was conscripted to "reeducation" (i.e. forced labor) to the exhausting toil of rice planting as part of Mao's disastrous "Cultural Revolution" policy. To keep his mind occupied, he listened to and wrote down local folk music.

Tan made arrangements of the tunes using whatever folk instruments and other noisemakers were available (including things such as woks and agricultural implements) creating often fantastic effects. Tan played the erhu, the one-string traditional Chinese fiddle. By the time he was 17, he was the musical leader of the village, playing celebrations, weddings, and funerals. Then a riverboat carrying a Peking-style Chinese Opera troupe capsized, killing many musicians. Tan was immediately sent to join the company as a replacement.

When the Central Conservatory reopened in 1978, Tan won one of thirty slots for composition students over thousands of applicants. He was taught by Li Yinghai and Zhao Xingdao, and visiting lecturers Alexander George, Hans Werner Henze, Chou Wen-Chung, Isang Yun, George Crumb, and Toru Takemitsu. Tan became a leader in a developing "New Wave" of art when he wrote, at age 22, a symphony (*Li Sao*), based on a fourth century B.C.E. Hunan lament. The work, for western symphony orchestra, won a special "incentive" prize at the first National Symphonic Competition.

Tan received international recognition in 1983 when his String Quartet (*Feng Ya Song*) won the Weber Prize from Dresden, making Tan the first Chinese composer to win an international prize since the Communist Revolution of 1949. That same year, Party officials initiated a program attacking the New Wave as "spiritual pollution" and specifically cited Tan. But the campaign was cancelled, and Tan continued in his chosen path.

His international breakthrough was an orchestral work called *On Taoism* (1985), inspired by the death of his grandmother. It was recognized as a remarkable assertion of Chinese esthetics and musical material in the medium of the Western symphony orchestra.

Columbia University offered Tan a fellowship in 1986. Tan moved to New York (where he still makes his home) and worked on his doctorate in music. His student-period works are in an international atonal style, but his true nature reappeared in the *Eight Colors for String Quartet* (1988), using Peking Opera material. Then he wrote *Nine Songs* (1989), a revolutionary work in the form of a ritual opera using fifty newly created ceramic instruments.

Tan developed a concept of the orchestra as a form of ritual, a major feature of his subsequent work. His major prizes include the Suntory Prize Commission of 1992 and the Grawemeyer Prize for his 1996 opera *Marco Polo*. In both cases, he was the youngest composer ever to win.

He has been associated with major events of his time. He composed *Symphony 1997 (Heaven Earth Mankind)* for the transfer of Hong Kong, incorporating popular song, Chinese opera, solo cello, orchestra, and recordings of the great tomb bells of Hubei, which were cast in 433 B.C.E.

In 1999, he composed *2000 Today: A World Symphony for the Millennium* for use in the BBC's worldwide twenty-seven-hour broadcast of the arrival of the millennium.

His rapidly growing catalog and discography includes two film scores: for Denzel Washington's film, *Fallen*, and Ang Lee's martial arts epic *Crouching Tiger, Hidden Dragon*, which unites ethnic and symphonic music, cello performances by Yo-Yo Ma, and songs by Asian pop star CoCo Lee. *—Joseph Stevenson*

Overview of Works

Tan Dun bridges multiple areas of culture, particularly Asian and European music, but also that of classical and popular music. His soundtrack for the hit movie *Crouching Tiger, Hidden Dragon* was widely acclaimed by both classical and popular critics. His music is thought-provoking and often meditative, though often far removed from the traditional major harmonies and soft dynamics of music usually considered conducive to meditation. It differs, too, from new age meditative music in its strong emphasis on balance rather than on formlessness and flow. His *Yi concerti* are particularly overt as philosophical exploration, inspired by the *Book of Changes* and featuring the interaction of a static orchestral concerto (Yi0) representing what is already in existence and the solo instruments representing change. His musical influences reflect this. As a young agricultural laborer, in part of the Cultural Revolution's anti-intellectualism, he became deeply familiar with folk music and with improvising instruments and aural effects. When, after the Revolution, he joined the newly reopened Beijing Central Conservatory, he was suddenly exposed to the Western influences that had been shut out of China as decadent, such as Stravinsky and Boulez. He became prominent in the "New Wave" of the 1980s, a controversial mix of European and Asian influences, and was soon its leading composer. His first symphony, *Li Sao*, was regarded as so innovative that it couldn't be awarded first prize in the National Symphonic Competition, but also so magnificently written that it couldn't be passed over, so it was given a special award. He continued to break rules and expectations, combining influences such as serialism and traditional Asian music and European and Asian instruments, even in a time and place when this was not only musically avant-garde, but potentially politically suspect; at one time, his music was even banned from public performance or broadcast. Despite this, *On Taoism*, which he acknowledges as his most important youthful work, not only blends but synthesizes the elements; it is not a Chinese composition with Western components or vice versa, but a genuinely new style. When he came to New York to study at Columbia, he was far more exposed to Western classical music than ever before and continued to experiment with these influences, but expanding on them rather than reiterating them. His opera *Nine Songs*, for example, goes beyond atonality to combine new instruments (developed specifically for this work) and various forms of speech, from whisper to murmur to shouts to song. As his career continues, he opens his music to new influences, including multimedia, electronic music, and rock and pop music, and he also experiments with what he calls "orchestral theater," in which through placement of performers, such as surrounding the audience, the audience is called upon to think of orchestral music and the interaction between performer and audience in a new light. *—Ann Feeney*

Recommended:

- ○ **Tan Dun: Ghost Opera** / Kronos Quartet / 1997 / Nonesuch 79445
- ○ **Tan Dun: Water Passion after St. Matthew** / Tan (cond.), Soloists, Berlin RIAS-Chamber Choir / 2002 / Sony 89927
- ○ **Tan Dun: Symphony 1997** / Tan Dun (cond.), Ma, Imperial Bells Ens. (China), Yip Children's Choir / 1997 / Sony 63368
- ○ **Tan Dun: Bitter Love** / Tan Dun (cond.), Huang, New York Virtuoso Singers / 1999 / Sony 61658
- ○ **Tan Dun: 2000 Today** / Tan Dun (cond.), Various Artists / 1999 / Sony 61529
- ○ **Sharon Isbin Plays Music of Christopher Rouse & Tan Dun** / Isbin, Tang (cond.), Lisbon Gulbenkian Foundation Orch. / 2001 / Teldec 81830
- ○ **Tan Dun: Out of Peking Opera; Death & Fire; Orchestral Theatre 2** / Tang (cond.), Lin, Helsinki PO / Ondine 864

FILM MUSIC

Crouching Tiger, Hidden Dragon, film score (2000)

When the highly respected film director Ang Lee decided to make his first film set in legendary China, he turned to Tan Dun for the score. Ang Lee's film was a successful attempt to give one genre of the popular martial arts film the highest production values possible. This genre is based on a type of novel called *wu sha*, which take place in a fantasy world where sword-wielding heroes, through their mastery of spirit, have elevated themselves metaphorically and literally, leaping so high and far that they practically fly. One of the most popular *wu sha* novels is *Crouching Tiger, Hidden Dragon* by Wang Du Lu, written between the First and Second World Wars. Unlike other *wu sha* films, the story is driven by a complex web of emotions among the five main characters.

Tan Dun's music draws upon many Asian ethnic sources. The film includes virtually straight Chinese ceremonial and classical music, as well as an Eastern-flavored, but Hollywood-inflected love theme that comes to dominate the latter parts of the film. Each action sequence has its own very distinct style. The first major fight in the film, where a thief, in a spectacular aerial ballet, is pursued over the rooftops at night, is accompanied by Chinese drumming. The music accompanying a duel taking place in the tops of a bamboo forest has a haunting, floating sound.

There is a romantic flashback involving a robber chief named Lo, taking place in the Western desert that has some of the most sustained and intriguing music in the score, with a strongly Turkic style. At one point, a folk song in a Turkic dialect is sung.

The soundtrack was played by the Shanghai Symphony Orchestra (Western instruments), the Shanghai National Orchestra (Chinese), and the Shanghai Percussion Ensemble, conducted by Tan Dun. The score has a prominent solo part for cello, often played with Chinese glides and microtonal inflections. There is an especially effective track where the cello joins with the Chinese traditional fiddle, the erhu and the two instruments intertwine magically. There are additional Chinese instruments with solo parts, including the bowu, dizi, rewap, and hand drum. In its deft handling of all these musical influences, Tan Dun's score to *Crouching Tiger,*

Hidden Dragon was one of the most unusual and effective film scores of its time. *—Joseph Stevenson*

Recommended:

- **Crouching Tiger, Hidden Dragon (Original Soundtrack)** / Tan Dun (cond.), Ma, Shanghai SO / 2000 / Sony 2582

Melvyn Tan

b. Oct. 13, 1956, Singapore
Fortepianist

Singaporean-born pianist Melvyn Tan is one of the few artists who has succeeded performing on both the modern piano and the eighteenth century fortepiano. His parents noticed his ability to play back by ear the piano music his sister was practicing, and a family friend who worked as a stewardess for Australia's Qantas airline began to brag about his abilities to passengers in the first-class section. One of them agreed to finance the youngster's musical education at the Yehudi Menuhin School in Cobham, Surrey, England. Tan studied piano there, with the aging Nadia Boulanger as one of his teachers, and then moved on to the Royal College of Music in London.

Required to undertake a minor course of study in addition to his piano major, Tan tried to get into a conducting class, but found it closed. He signed up for harpsichord studies instead and became interested in early keyboard instruments. In his third year at the RCM, a friend introduced him to the fortepiano, which at the time was the province of just a few academic specialists. The college did not even own one of the instruments, but he searched around London and found places to practice. Feeling that he couldn't do both instruments justice, Tan gave up the modern piano altogether.

For a time pickings were slim, and Tan made a bare living playing harpsichord continuo parts in Baroque music ensembles. In the late 1980s, however, the historical performance movement began to move into Classical-period territory in a big way, and Tan was ready. For EMI he made a series of recordings with conductor Roger Norrington, including a complete set of Beethoven's piano concertos, and he performed widely with both historically oriented and mainstream orchestral ensembles.

In 1996, Tan returned to the modern piano almost in the way that Romantic-era musicians had come to it when it was new: as he moved forward into later repertoire (such as the piano music of Schumann), he became frustrated with the technical possibilities of older instruments. Since then Tan has been equally prominent in both mainstream and historical-practice spheres. He has recorded complete cycles of Beethoven sonatas and of Debussy and Chopin preludes in New York, London, and Tokyo; has been active in chamber ensembles; and has accompanied Anne Sofie von Otter and Angelika Kirchschlager in lieder repertory. He has ventured into contemporary music and sometimes performs a new fortepiano concerto, written for him by composer Jonathan Dove. *—James Manheim*

Recommended:

- **Mozart: Concertos 18 & 19** / McGegan (cond.), Tan, Philharmonia Baroque Orch. / 1995 / Classical Express 3957138
- **Beethoven: Complete Cello Music** / Pleeth, Tan / 1996 / Hyperion 22004
- **Beethoven: The Piano Concertos** / Norrington (cond.), Tan, LCP / 2003 / Virgin 62242

Sergey Taneyev

b. Nov. 25, 1856, Vladimir district, Russia, **d.** Jun. 19, 1915, Dyudkovo, Russia
Composer

Taneyev was an important Russian pianist, educator, and composer active at the turn of the twentieth century. Although he wrote a large quantity of keyboard, orchestral, vocal, and chamber music, he is known today primarily as the teacher of Scriabin, Rachmaninov, and Glière. As a young man, Taneyev made his first impact as a pianist, giving the first Russian performance of Tchaikovsky's *First Piano Concerto*, and the Russian premieres of all of Tchaikovsky's other works for piano and orchestra. For many years, Taneyev's teaching and administrative duties at the Moscow Conservatory prevented him from touring as a performer, but later in his life, he resumed his career as a pianist, particularly in chamber music.

Taneyev was born into a well-to-do and aristocratically connected family, and therefore had the best possible education. His most important teachers at the Moscow Conservatory were Tchaikovsky, for composition, and Nikolay Rubinstein, for piano. Taneyev received gold medals in both at his graduation in 1875. After touring as a pianist for three years, Taneyev reluctantly took a position in 1878 at the conservatory, which would eventually lead him to its directorship in 1885. After four years, he resigned, becoming once again an instructor in order to concentrate on composition. The first result of this decision was the completion and premiere of his opera *The Oresteia* in 1895. In 1905, Taneyev stopped teaching completely and resumed his career as a pianist. As a result, his compositional activities turned almost exclusively to chamber music. By the time of his death at the age of 58, Taneyev had left behind a substantial catalog of works, virtually none of which has entered the standard repertory. *—Steven Coburn*

Overview of Works (1872–1913)

Sergey Taneyev was the most technically skilled composer in late Imperial Russia. Trained under Tchaikovsky and Nikolai Rubinstein, Taneyev was a formidable pianist—he gave the premieres of all Tchaikovsky's works for piano and orchestra—a masterful contrapuntist—he wrote a textbook on fugues and left a companion book on canons incomplete at his death—and a great teacher—among his pupils were Scriabin, Rachmaninov, and Myaskovsky. But, although a tremendously gifted composer, his perfectionism prevented him from completing much more than a handful of large works. Of his four symphonies, he allowed only one to be published and performed in his lifetime and, despite arduous labor, many of his works remained torsos. Essentially a conservative composer whose orientation was cosmopolitan rather than nationalistic, Taneyev's music lacks the dramatic impact and powerful characterizations of Mussorgsky's or the epic scope and rhythmic energy of Borodin. And, unlike his teacher Tchaikovsky, Taneyev was emotionally incapable of writing a memorable lyrical theme. But unlike any other Russian composer of the time except Glazunov, Taneyev was able to develop his ideas with far more ability and, in his best works, he far exceeded any contemporary Russian composer in the strength and cogency of his structures. Of his four symphonies, the C minor (1901)—his last in order of composition but published as *Symphony No. 1*—is not only the best, it is one of the great symphonies of the Silver Age. With its fateful main theme, its supplicating second theme, its witty Scherzo (Taneyev could be quite funny when he put his mind to it), its slow movement that takes the opening movement's supplicating theme to the peak of musical passion, and a finale that brings the theme to its triumphant conclusion, Taneyev's C minor is a work fit to stand with the best symphonies of Glazunov and Rachmaninov. Taneyev wrote several choral/orchestral works, including the lofty *Saint John of Damascus* (1884) and the darkly apocalyptic *At the Reading of a Psalm* (1915). Showing his skill as a contrapuntist are his six string quartets, three string quintets, and a pair preludes and fugues for piano. Taneyev's highest achievement, however, was his opera *Oresteia* (1897–1904) after Aeschylus. An opera in three acts bearing the subtitle "Musical Trilogy," *Oresteia* is less concerned with the blood-soaked plot than with the creation of a coherent and convincing portrait of the characters. The music's dignified tone and noble sentiments are as far from Mussorgsky's grim historical operas as they are from Rimsky-Korsakov's fairy tale operas. *—James Leonard*

Recommended:

- **Taneyev: Symphonies 2 & 4** / Polyansky (cond.), Russian State SO / 2002 / Chandos 9998
- **Taneyev: Piano Quartets Opp20 &22** / Mendelssohn Piano Trio / 2001 / Centaur 2571
- **Taneyev: Concert Suite; Oresteia** / Kuusisto, Ashkenazy (cond.), Helsinki PO / 2000 / Ondine 959
- **Taneyev: Complete String Trios** / Belcanto Strings / 2000 / MDG 6341003

Alexandre Tansman

b. Jun. 12, 1897, Lodz, Poland, **d.** Nov. 15, 1986, Paris, France
Composer

Alexandre Tansman is called both a French composer of Polish birth and a Polish composer who emigrated to France. However, he likely considered France his adopted homeland; except for the war years he lived in Paris from 1919 until his death in 1986, and he chose the French spelling of his given name, Aleksander. Tansman was born in Lodz, Poland, to Jewish parents. His mother was a good amateur pianist who gave him his first piano lessons. At the age of 11, he enrolled at the Lodz Conservatory, where he studied composition and conducting in addition to piano. Among his teachers there was Wojciech Gawronski. In 1914, Tansman began studies at the Warsaw University, where he graduated with a degree in law in 1918. It is said that the exceptionally intelligent, well-rounded Tansman had learned to speak seven languages. He entered several works under two different names in the 1919 Polish National Music Competition and won three prizes.

Still, he felt his music was not sufficiently appreciated because of its modernisms and he departed for Paris in late 1919. In the French capital, he met the leading composers of the day, including Stravinsky and Ravel, whose music influenced his, particularly the neo-Classicism of the former. Tansman also developed a camaraderie with other European émigrés in Paris, including Tcherepnin and Martinů, and with Andrés Segovia, who inspired him to write several pieces for guitar. Tansman's successful concert debut in Paris in February 1920 opened inroads for his career as a pianist. He also composed many important works during his first decades in Paris, including the *Symphony No. 2* (1926) and the first two piano concertos, 1925 and 1927, respectively. As early as 1921, Vladimir Golschmann introduced his orchestral work *Impressions* to Parisian audiences and with Koussevitzky, Tansman performed his piano concertos in Paris and Boston. In 1932, Tansman launched a world tour, performing in Japan, China, Singapore, Bali, Egypt, Greece, and other exotic locations. His career as pianist and composer remained quite successful throughout the 1930s and in 1938, he was given French citizenship. But trouble was on the horizon with the growing menace of Adolf Hitler in Germany. Shortly after the occupation of France in 1941, Tansman fled with his French wife, pianist Collete Cras, and two daughters. Helped by a fund established by Charlie Chaplin, they settled in Los Angeles that same year, where Tansman met other Jewish exiles, including Arnold Schoenberg and Mario Castelnuovo-Tedesco. Tansman returned to Paris in 1946, but soon found his career would never be the same. He remained true to his largely neo-Classical style, which was quickly going out of fashion in favor of serial music and other avant-garde styles. Moreover, the music establishment in Poland, which had come under communist control, was loathe to play the works of a Jewish exile living in the West. While he continued to write much music, including operas, such as *Georges Dandin* (1973–74) and ballets, such as *Résurrection* (1961–62), as well as orchestral and instrumental works, his reputation gradually faded. *—Robert Cummings*

Overview of Works (1915–1982)

Alexandre Tansman was a Polish composer who lived most of his life in Paris but then discovered his Jewish roots with Hitler's rise to power. Thus, his music is a combination of Polish melodies, harmonies, and rhythms set in a neo-Classical style with the strong influence of the Jewish cantorial tradition, as well as the anguish of the victimized. After studying music in Poland, Tansman moved to Paris, where he met and became friends with Ravel and Stravinsky. His works from the 1920s and 1930s are informed as much by the Polishness of its origins as by the clarity of his neo-Classical forms and textures. Among the most characteristic works of this period are *Symphony No. 2* (1927) and *Piano Concerto No. 2* (1927), both essentially neo-Classical, and the *Quatre Danses polonaises* (1931) and *Rapsodie polonaise* (1940), both essentially Polish. However, with the German persecution of Jews, Tansman also incorporated Jewish elements into his music in works such as the *Rapsodie herbraique* (1933). With the help of his friend Charlie Chaplin, Tansman and his French wife were able to emigrate to the United States during the war years (1940–45) and, while living in California, he composed one of his most powerful pieces in response to the war, the choral *Symphony No. 6 "In Memoriam"* based on French texts by the composer (1944). At the end of the war, he returned to France, but because of the Communist government and its continued discrimination of Polish Jews, never to Poland. Tansman's music became increasingly preoccupied with Jewish themes in works like *Isaiah the Prophet for Chorus and Orchestra* (1950); *Prologue et Cantate*, based on texts from *Ecclesiastes* (1958); and his opera *Sabbatai Zevi, ou le faux Messie* (1958), the work he considered his masterpiece. *—James Leonard*

Recommended:

- ○ **Tansman: Cello Concerto; The Ten Commandments** / Hess, Yinon (cond.) / 2001 / Koch Schwann 36405
- ○ **Tansman: Mazurkas** / Andersen / 1997 / Talent 39
- ○ **Tansman: Works for 2 Pianos** / Blumenthal, Andersen / 1997 / Arcobaleno 9419
- ○ **Tansman: Symphony 5; Stèle in memoriam d'Igor Strawinsky; Four Movements for Orchestra** / Minsky (cond.), Czecho-Slovak State PO (Kosice) / Marco Polo 8223379
- ○ **Tansman: Complete Guitar Music** / Regnier / 1994 / Marco Polo 223690

CHAMBER MUSIC

Sonatina for bassoon & piano (1952)

Though extremely difficult to play, this sonatina poses few difficulties for listeners; as it explores the bassoon's full range, the score is generously melodic, a little flamboyant, and interestingly varied through its brief duration. It's highly typical not only of Tansman's usual style, but of the music of the so-called École de Paris, a circle of foreign-born musicians (including Bohuslav Martinů and Alexander Tcherepnin) who gathered in France and were influenced to varying degrees by the likes of Les Six and Albert Roussel. A quickly pulsing piano part generates energy in the sonatina's fast first movement, while the bassoon contends with a far-ranging line that is largely recitative. A very brief, gentler contrasting section almost immediately gives way to an abbreviated return of the opening material. A short cadenza leads straight into the slow movement, where the bassoon sweetly sings over stately piano chords. The nearly unbroken melody gently rises up the staff, then descends to the depths of the bassoon's range before a succinct piano bridge leads, as in the first movement, to the bassoon's condensed restatement of the melody. Then, attaca, comes the frantic final movement. The piano hammers out sharp little chords while the bassoon burbles and chugs in mock desperation. A canonic passage suggests that the sonatina will end in a fugue, but the instruments quickly back out of any contrapuntal commitment to each other and end the work with light, insouciant gestures. *—James Reel*

Recommended:

- ○ **The Virtuoso Bassoon** / Knardahl, Sonstevold / 1992 / Bis 122

Francisco Tárrega

b. Nov. 21, 1852, Villarreal, Castellón, Spain, **d.** Dec. 15, 1909, Barcelona, Spain
Composer

Francisco Tárrega was an important Spanish composer whose music and style of guitar playing became strongly influential in the twentieth century. He was central to reviving the guitar as a solo instrument in recital and concerts. Among his most popular compositions are *Recuerdos de la Alhambra* and *Danza mora*. He wrote nearly eighty original works for the guitar and over a hundred transcriptions, mostly of piano pieces by Chopin, Beethoven, and others.

Francisco Tárrega was born on November 21, 1852, in Villareal, Castellon, Spain. An accident in his early childhood permanently impaired his eyesight. He was taught his first lessons on guitar by Eugeni Ruiz, ironically a blind musician. In 1862, concert guitarist Julian Arcas, on tour in Castellon, heard young Francisco play and advised Tárrega's father to allow Francisco to come to Barcelona for study with him. Tárrega's father agreed, but insisted that he take piano lessons as well. His father was well aware that the guitar, as a solo vehicle, was in decline, coming increasingly to be viewed as an instrument to accompany singers, while the piano was all the rage throughout Europe.

By his early teens, Tárrega had become proficient on both instruments. For a time, he played with other musicians at local engagements to earn money, but eventually he returned home. In 1874 he enrolled at the Madrid Conservatory where he would study composition under Arrieta. He had brought along with him a recently-purchased guitar, made in Seville by Antonio Torres. Its superior sonic qualities inspired him both in his playing and in his view of the instrument's compositional potential. When Arrieta heard his student Tárrega in a guitar concert, he convinced him to focus on guitar and abandon ideas of a career involving the piano.

In about 1876, Tárrega began teaching and giving regular guitar concerts. He typically received much acclaim for his playing and began traveling to other areas of Spain to perform. By this time he was composing his first works for guitar. In 1880, he met his future wife, Maria Rizo, when he was giving a concert in Novelda. That same year he went on tour to Lyon, Paris, and London, now playing his own works in addition to those of other composers.

In 1881, he and Maria were married in Novelda. He soon began transcribing piano works of Beethoven, Chopin, Mendelssohn, and others to enlarge his guitar repertory, and, no doubt, to make use of his considerable knowledge of keyboard music. Tárrega and his wife moved to Madrid, but after the death of an infant daughter, Maria Josefa, they settled permanently in Barcelona in 1885.

On a concert tour in Valencia shortly afterward, Tárrega met a wealthy widow, Conxa Martinez, who became a valuable patron to him. She allowed him and his family use of a house in Barcelona, where he would write the bulk of his most popular works, including *Recuerdos de la Alhambra*. From the latter 1880s up to 1903, Tárrega continued composing, but limited his concerts to Spain. In about 1902, he cut his fingernails and created a sound that would become typical of those guitarists associated with his school. The following year he launched a tour of Italy, giving highly successful concerts in Rome, Naples, and Milan.

In January 1906, he was afflicted with paralysis on his right side, and though he would eventually return to the concert stage, he never completely recovered. He finished his last work, *Oremus*, on December 2, 1909. He died 13 days later. *—Robert Cummings*

Overview of Works (ca. 1875–1905)

Author of the immensely popular *Recuerdos de la Alhambra*, Francisco Tárrega (1852–1909) is one of Spain's greatest composers for the guitar. His music, exemplified by the enchantingly soulful *Recuerdos de la Alhambra*, reflects the composer's poetic imagination as well his extraordinary mastery of the instrument. A remarkable tremolo study, this work evokes the atmosphere of an imaginary, idealized Spanish-Moorish landscape redolent of magical gardens and palaces of love and Romantic dreams. Scholars have questioned the popular story, which claims that this work was inspired by the Moorish Palace in Alhambra, explaining that the true source of the composer's inspiration was his lover Doña Concepcion de Jacoby.

Known as the "Sarasate of the guitar," Tárrega was anything but a brilliant virtuoso who also composed. His repertoire included transcriptions for guitar of piano music by Mendelssohn, Thalberg, Gottschalk, Beethoven, and Chopin, and these transcriptions enabled him to develop a rich compositional idiom that was both imaginative and technically demanding.

Like his friend Isaac Albéniz, Tárrega was a leading force of Alhambrismo, the movement that sought to forge a unique form of Romanticism blending Europe's musical legacy with the rich folk traditions of Spain, including the Moorish influences. Another example of stylized Spanish-Moorish music is Tárrega's *Capricho árabe*, dedicated to another eminent Alhambrist, Tomás Bretón. Author of more than 70 original compositions and 120 transcriptions for guitar, Tárrega played a crucial role in the rebirth of the guitar as a solo instrument in the late nineteenth and early twentieth centuries. In the mid-nineteenth century, the guitar was, even in Spain, totally eclipsed by the piano, the Romantic instrument *par excellence*. By the late 1870s, however, Tárrega was working as a successful concert guitarist, starting a career that would culminate in international acclaim. His legacy was continued in the twentieth century by his students, who included Emilio Pujol. *—Zoran Minderovic*

Recommended:

- **Tárrega: Integral de Guitarra** / Russell / 1991 / Opera Tres 1003
- **Guitarra Española: Spanische Gitarrenmusik Der Jahrhundertwende** / Lieske / 1992 / Saphir 830866

Giuseppe Tartini

b. Apr. 8, 1692, Pirano, Istria, Italy, **d.** Feb. 26, 1770, Padua, Italy

Composer: Chamber Music

Despite Italian composer Giuseppe Tartini's important place in musical history, he remains known to most musicians only as the composer of the *"Devil's Trill"* violin sonata. Born on the Istrian peninsula in 1692, Tartini was the son of a minor government official in the city of Pirano (now Piran, Slovenia). Although his parents had selected a monastic life for Tartini when he was very young, in 1708 he rejected his clerical training to pursue a course of instruction in music. Soon, however, he seems to have enrolled at the University of Padua as a student of law, and was more famed during his younger days as a dueler and swordsman than as a trained musician. Despite still officially being a candidate for the priesthood, Tartini married in 1710, and, having thereby incurred the wrath of the Paduan bishop, found it necessary to hide out in the monastery at Assisi for a time. He put his time to good use: apparently he made a rigorous study of music, and by 1714 he seems to have found employment with the opera orchestra at Ancona.

Reunited with his wife in 1715, Tartini spent the next several years trying to perfect his violin technique. The legend is that he heard the virtuoso Francesco Veracini perform and resolved to live in isolation until he could accomplish the same amazing feats of dexterity. By 1720, he was engaged as soloist and leader of the orchestra at St. Anthony's in Padua. Until an arm injury in 1740 seriously limited his career, Tartini fulfilled his duties at St. Anthony's even as he built a widespread reputation as the leading violinist of his day. He made an extended visit to Prague between 1723 and 1726. Officially retiring from St. Anthony's in 1765, Tartini remained active as a teacher until a mild stroke, which he suffered in 1768, incapacitated him even further. Tartini died in 1770, the year of Beethoven's birth.

Tartini was the founder of an important school of violin playing, subsequently disseminated by such noteworthy pupils as Pietro Nardini and Johann Gottlieb Naumann. Because he did not seek fame as a composer, very little of Tartini's music was published during his lifetime. Some 135 violin concerti and over 200 violin sonatas (some of which, however, are spurious) still survive in manuscript form. A smattering of sacred vocal works (such as the Stabat Mater composed during the final year of his life) and a few sinfonias, trio sonatas, and four-part sonatas round off Tartini's considerable output. In addition to his activities as a violinist and composer, Tartini became increasingly interested in theories of acoustics and harmony as the years went by, and his 1754 theoretical treatise *Trattato di musica secondo la vera scienza dell'armonia* attempts to account for contemporary harmonic thinking in terms of the overtone series and to promote Tartini's own discovery of "sub-tones" in that series. Despite its lofty intentions (or perhaps because of them) the *Trattato* is not a particularly accurate or informative text; it does, however, provide great insight into the mind of this remarkable musician. *—Blair Johnston*

Overview of Works (ca. 1720–1760)

Tartini was a prolific composer whose works were largely written for his own instrument, the violin, although there are also some for flute. There are more than 130 violin concertos, a similar number of sonatas, and some 40 trio sonatas. Tartini's inspiration in his early days appears to have been Corelli, for whom he retained a lifelong admiration; according to historian Charles Burney (who arrived in Padua just after Tartini's death), he made his pupils learn Corelli's sonatas before allowing them to continue study. However, his earlier violin concertos owe a debt to the Venetian models of Vivaldi and Albinoni, being cast in the typical three-movement slow-fast-slow form and showing a greater interest in fire and expressive drama than those of Corelli. Around 1740, he appears to have simplified his style to a less-virtuosic style of writing that put new emphasis on expressive cantabile writing that looks forward to the Rococo or pre-Classical idiom. This new graceful style was much admired by Burney, who particularly noted the "clearness, clarity, and precision" of Tartini's basses. A number of Tartini's sonatas have programmatic titles that echo a new ambition among mid-eighteenth century composers to emulate the drama of opera. *—Brian Robins*

Recommended:

- **Tartini: The Devil's Trill & Other Violin Sonatas** / Locatelli Trio / 1991 / Hyperion 66430
- **Tartini: Concerti** / Ens. 415, Banchini (cond.), Gatti, Dieltiens / 1995 / HM 901548
- **Tartini: The Art of Bowing for Unaccompanied Violin** / Colliard / Doron 3007

CHAMBER MUSIC

Violin Sonata in G minor ("The Devil's Trill") (? 1740)

Tartini's *Le trille du diable* (The Devil's Trill) first appeared in print in 1798, 28 years after the composer's death. A legend surrounding the piece either is derived from its nickname or gave rise to it. Supposedly, Tartini took refuge in a monastery after a secret marriage to one of his students. While sleeping at the monastery, Tartini had a dream in which he asked the devil to play the violin. The devil responded by performing a sonata. When Tartini awoke, he composed a sonata for violin in imitation of that played by the devil in his dream. In one version of the legend Tartini even negotiates a contract with the devil.

Tartini was a prolific composer who wrote hundreds of trio sonatas, violin sonatas, and concertos for the violin and other instruments. In his concertos he followed the formal principles of Vivaldi but wrote music that showcased his formidable technique. In his sonatas, all movements are in the same key, and binary form is clear and predominant.

The music connected with the sonata's nickname occurs at the very end, but the full sonata is a four-movement work with fairly conventional features for the most part. As Charles Burney (1726–1814) noted, Tartini's style changed around 1744 from "extremely difficult to graceful and expressive." This is evident in the very opening of *The Devil's Trill.* Tartini stresses a falling half step in the first melody, a slow, contemplative theme in 12/8 time. The melody is periodic, moving to the dominant in the middle then back to the tonic. Variations of the theme ensue, stressing the dotted figure from the first beat of the theme. Several deceptive cadences extend the central part of the movement before a varied return to the theme. The next movement, an Allegro, begins with a jagged idea that outlines a G minor triad. In a bouncy 2/4 time, the main theme is fast and highly decorated with grace notes and trills. The entire movement is repeated. A brief slow movement provides contrast with its cantabile melody and acts more as an introduction to the Allegro finale than as a self-contained movement. Repeated notes again outline the tonic triad at the beginning of the last movement. This dissolves into a transition with a repeated, modulatory figure in the solo violin over increasingly intense accompaniment from the continuo. This leads to a new, slow theme, in which chromatic alterations touch on G major and the dominant. The rest of the movement consists of alternations between these two themes until a bravura cadenza begins with trills that outline the main theme; this cadenza is the source of the sonata's nickname. The trills are very difficult, for the performer is required to trill on one string while performing rapidly moving notes on another. After the lengthy cadenza, the continuo joins for the last few, highly dramatic measures. *—John Palmer*

Recommended:

- **Tartini: The Devil's Sonata** / Manze / 1997 / HM 907213

Violin Sonata in G minor ("Didone abbandonata"), Op. 1/10 (ca. 1731)

Giuseppe Tartini (1692–1770) was a teacher, theorist, and composer who was one of the greatest violin virtuosos of the mid-eighteenth century. The majority of works were composed for his own instrument in the form of either concertos or sonatas with basso continuo. There are comfortably over 100 examples of the latter. The *Sonata in G minor* comes from a set of 12 first published by La Cène of Amsterdam in 1732 and reprinted in London in 1746. There are three movements, the first an Affettuoso whose sighing, pathetic opening doubtlessly gives the sonata its name, the work being one of a number of sonatas given programmatic titles by Tartini. The movement also includes music in the singing, cantabile style for which he was famed. The shorter succeeding movements are a Presto requiring extremely dexterous bowing over a wide range from the performer, and an Allegro in a dance rhythm that still manages to make the odd, expressive gesture. *—Brian Robins*

Recommended:

- **Tartini: Five Sonatas for Violin & Continuo** / Biondi, Alessandrini, Naddeo, Montheilet / 1992 / Opus 111 599205

Richard Tauber

b. May 16, 1891, Linz, Austria, **d.** Jan. 8, 1948, London, England

Tenor

Richard Tauber remains, for many, the quintessential Viennese operetta tenor. As well as a performer, he was a composer, his works displaying his understanding of the operetta and song genres if not the genius of a Lehár or Johann Strauss Jr. He did not have a perfect voice; his Bs and Cs were labored and his habit of using falsetto to reach the rest of the upper range, while producing some ravishing results, could become mannered and overly applied. That said, his graceful charm of expression and lyrical warmth made him one of the most beloved singers of his time.

He was the son of an actor and theater director and an actress, and was raised by his father after the age of seven, thus increasing his exposure to music and the theater. His early studies at the Frankfurt Conservatory focused on conducting and composition, his voice studies instead taking place at Freiburg under Carl Beines. He made his opera debut at the Chemnitz Neues Stadt-Theater in March, 1913, as Tamino in Mozart's *The Magic Flute.* He was almost immediately given a five-year contract by the Dresden Opera where he became the established lyric tenor. As his career continued to develop throughout Germany, he was strongly associated with Mozart; when he appeared as Tamino, Mozart's opera was often jokingly renamed *Die Tauberflöte.* Astonishingly, however, his 1915 Berlin Opera debut was as Bacchus in Richard Strauss' *Ariadne auf Naxos* (a role that many heroic tenors find incredibly taxing), sung with 48 hours' notice and only one rehearsal! Tauber became known for his fast learning and musicianship, and was often called upon for such emergencies. He once took over as conductor for a tour with the London Philharmonic Orchestra.

In the 1920s, he began to specialize in operetta and song, and became best known for those roles and for recitals, recordings, and film work. Lehár wrote the operettas *Paganini, Der Zarewitsch, Friederike,* and *The Land of Smiles* with him in mind, and in each, made sure to include a showpiece (soon known as the Tauberlied) for his talents. In 1931, he made his debut in England at the Drury Lane Theater in Lehár's *The Land of Smiles,* and he remained in England for fear of Nazi persecution (he was of Jewish extraction), becoming a naturalized citizen in 1940. Like most singers, his career was interrupted by the war, but he made his operatic farewell in 1947 as Don Ottavio in Mozart's *Don Giovanni.* Though already seriously ill with the lung cancer that was to kill him the next year, according to critics and documented by air check recordings, it would have been a creditable performance for a singer in the best of health.

Tauber owed much of his fame to his then-prodigious 725 recordings; among tenors, only Enrico Caruso and John McCormack made more recordings. Tauber's catalog unquestionably displays the most variety, including songs by Jerome Kern and Irving Berlin, arias and duets from Verdi's *Il trovatore* and *Aida,* Offenbach's *The Tales of Hoffmann,* German lieder, and even the Neapolitan and Irish songs in which Caruso and McCormack were the main exponents. He also appeared in several movies, including a film of Leoncavallo's *Pagliacci, Blossom Time, Heart's Desire,* and *Forbidden Music.* Today, his operetta *Old Chelsea* (which he wrote to celebrate his naturalization as an English citizen) is still sometimes performed. *—Ann Feeney*

Recommended:

- ○ **My Heart's Delight** / Tauber, etc. / 1994 / ASV 5146
- ○ **Tauber in Opera** / Tauber, etc. / 1992 / Nimbus 7830
- ○ **A Programme of Lieder** / Tauber, etc. / 2002 / Naxos 8110739
- ○ **Richard Tauber Favorites Vol. 1** / Tauber, etc. / 2000 / Naxos 120513
- ○ **Old Chelsea** / Tauber, Appling, Brown / 1994 / Bel Age 103003

Sir John Tavener

b. Jan. 28, 1944, London, England
Composer: Choral, Concerto

Among the most commercially successful of living composers, John Tavener has undergone a remarkable musical and spiritual odyssey. After his conversion to the Orthodox religion, he formulated a unique new idiom, often employing a slow, almost minimalist unfolding of melodic material. Much of his music is designed for religious services. His works often require odd combinations of forces, for example *The Apocalypse* (1993), for tenor, bass, soprano, mezzo-soprano, solo saxophonists, male choir, countertenor choir, organ, brass, string quartet, and string ensemble. Overall, he may be considered a unique eclectic, part mystical and part populist.

Tavener was born in Wembley Park, near London. Long-held family beliefs to the contrary, he was probably not descended from Tudor composer John Taverner. He was raised a Protestant but as a young man converted to Catholicism. He studied piano, organ, and composition, and went on to study with Solomon, Lennox Berkeley, and Lumsdaine at the Royal Academy of Music. In 1968, after the composer's music impressed both John Lennon and Ringo Starr, Apple recorded his work *The Whale.* The next year, he became professor of composition at Trinity College.

In 1974, Tavener and Victoria Maragopoulou, a Greek ballet student, were married in an Orthodox ceremony. After eight months, however, she left for Greece, even though they remained legally married and friendly for a decade. Tavener received counsel from the Orthodox clergyman who had married them. Several works of the period, including *The Liturgy of St. John Chrysostom,* had an Orthodox or Russian bent, and in 1977 Tavener became a member of the Orthodox Church.

After recovering from a 1980 stroke, Tavener began to consider himself an Orthodox composer. In 1981 he met Mother Thekla, an Orthodox abbess in North Yorkshire. That year *Prayer for the World* appeared, and the composer described it as his most radical work. The palindromic *Ikon of Light* (1983), for chorus and string trio, was enthusiastically received, but still Tavener felt inadequate in his Russian Orthodox faith in comparison with Arvo Pärt, a member from birth and sometimes considered the more genuine of the two. After consulting with an Orthodox psychoanalyst, the composer embarked on the massive *Orthodox Vigil Service* (1984), for priests, chorus, and handbells.

In 1985 Tavener's mother died; he announced that he would cease composing, but he hardly broke stride. Among the works that followed was the heavily recorded *The Protecting Veil* (1987), for cello and strings. Shortly after finishing *Thrinos* (1990), for solo cello, Tavener had surgery to replace a defective heart valve. The composer recovered sufficiently to begin collaboration with Mother Thekla on *Let's Begin Again* (1995). With his first marriage annulled on grounds of non-consummation, Tavener and Maryanna Schaefer were married in 1991. The 1992 Virgin Classics release of *The Protecting Veil* became a best-selling classical CD, spawning further efforts by other labels. By the mid-1990s Tavener's popularity in Britain rivaled that of Benjamin Britten in his prime, and he was gaining international attention. In 1996 Tavener's father died, and the composer wrote the *Funeral Canticle* in his memory. Tavener CD releases sold consistently on both sides of the Atlantic, and in 1999 Tavener began work on *Fall And Resurrection.* His 70-minute liturgical drama *Lamentations and Praises* was commissioned by the U.S. chorus Chanticleer and released on CD in 2002. *—Robert Cummings*

CHORAL

The Lamb (1982)

John Tavener's setting of William Blake's poem "The Lamb" (from the 1789 publication *Songs of Innocence*) was performed as part of the traditional "Nine Lessons and Carols" broadcast from King's College, Cambridge, on Christmas Eve, 1982. The composer so wanted Mother Thekla—his friend, associate, and collaborator—to hear it that he urged the sagely nun to borrow a radio so she could listen to the program from the convent; he told her to listen for a signal from him that would identify his work, and so, sitting in the audience in Cambridge, he coughed loudly as a sign to Mother Thekla that his piece was about to begin. The music that followed his noisy introduction would turn out to be one of Tavener's best-known works; so commercially successful was the piece that his publisher proclaimed it "the biggest selling choral title in our catalogue, by any composer, living or dead."

The piece was originally conceived as a birthday present for the composer's nephew Simon on the occasion of his third birthday. One of Tavener's numerous occasional pieces composed for special events in the lives of family and loved ones, the music for *The Lamb* came to Tavener as an artistic revelation. As Tavener himself recalls: "I looked through the poems of William Blake and I found "The Lamb." I read the words, and immediately I heard the notes." The composer sensed the potential for success in the piece, and immediately sent it to his publisher and arranged for the performance at King's College. He also sent copies to Martin Neary, who would conduct the premiere of the work at the Winchester Cathedral, a few days before the "Nine Lessons and Carols" broadcast.

The work, scored for a cappella choir, is as gentle and meek as the title implies. Its most striking surface feature is the variation in texture that marks certain divisions in the text. The scoring alternated between three types of color: unison, contrary motion, and full harmony. The haunting melody appears alone at first, as the voices sing together; at the second line, however, the lines are set atop a mirror as a lower line follows in intervallic inversion. Retrograde iterations of the melody follow on the horizontal plane, while the vertical sonorities shimmer with crystalline dissonance. Finally, at the last quatrain of the first verse, the ensemble joins in with lush harmony—not coincidentally, on the line "Gave thee such a tender voice." The second verse of the poem is given the same musical treatment, with the inverted counterpoint symbolically setting the paradoxical line in which the Creator of the universe becomes a little child. The paradox is reconciled into doctrine with the warm cadential progression of the final four lines. *—Jeremy Grimshaw*

Recommended:

- ○ **Tavener: Ikon of Light; Funeral Ikos; The Lamb** / Tavener (cond.), Tallis Scholars / 2001 / Gimell 5
- ○ **Tavener: Song for Athene; Svyati; Other Choral Works** / Robinson (cond.), St. John's College Choir / 2000 / Naxos 555256

CONCERTO

The Protecting Veil, for cello & orchestra (1987)

Raised a Protestant, Tavener converted to the Eastern Orthodox religion in 1977 and has composed many works relating to the teachings and feast days of that faith. *The Protecting Veil* is one such composition, written for the observance of events concerning the invasion of Greece by Saracens, around 902. The Blessed Mother was said to have appeared and spread her "protecting veil" over Christians in Constantinople, sheltering them from attack and ultimately inspiring defeat of the Muslim invaders.

This one-movement, 45-minute work, is cast in eight continuous sections and is, in effect, a concerto for cello and string orchestra, written for a commission from cellist Steven Isserlis. The opening panel, called "The Protecting Veil," begins and remains throughout mainly in the upper ranges of both the cello (which represents the Blessed Mother) and strings. It features lovely meditative music of an ethereal character, based on the theme from the Russian Orthodox chant *We Magnify You.* The second section, the "Nativity of the Mother of God," like the first, is largely meditative but also exotic, featuring wavering tones and string writing that recalls the more playful side of Stravinsky.

"The Annunciation" is livelier and somewhat folklike, but becomes dark and ponderous in its latter half. In "The Incarnation," the mood brightens as sonorities rise and the cello turns busier. Here, as in the previous section, the Stravinsky-like string episode is brilliantly recalled. "The Lament of the Mother of God at the Cross" is the longest section, and features highly imaginative writing for the soloist, who performs mostly unaccompanied throughout and mainly in the lower ranges. The music is sad and anguished here, but gradually divulges a more exotic, if bleak character.

"Christ Is Risen!" is the shortest section, but also the most joyous and lively, its thematic material borrowed from the composer's Orthodox Vigil Service. The ensuing panel, "The Dormition of the Mother of God," features a lovely theme, first used in Tavener's own *Hymns to the Mother of God.* The closing section, "The Protecting Veil," consists of a reprise of the opening, as well as material to depict the sadness of the Blessed Mother. *—Robert Cummings*

Recommended:

- ○ **Tavener: The Protecting Veil; Thrinos; Britten: Cello Suite 3** / Isserlis, Rozhdestvensky (cond.), London SO / 2000 / Virgin 61849
- ○ **Tavener: Protecting Veil; In Alium** / Kliegel, Yuasa (cond.), Ulster Orch. / 1999 / Naxos 554388

John Taverner

b. ca. 1490, South Lincolnshire, England, **d.** Oct. 18, 1545, Boston, Lincolnshire, England

Composer: Choral

John Taverner is considered the most important figure in English music of his time. His compositions exist in about 30 manuscripts that were copied over about a 100-year period, beginning around the late 1520s. It is believed that many of his works were lost; a good many others survive but in partial form, such as the *Masses Mater Christi* and *Small Devotion,* and the smaller-scale antiphons *Ave Maria* and *Sub tuum praesidium.* It is generally accepted that Taverner's three (six-part) Festal Masses (*Corona spinea, Gloria tibi Trinitas,* and *O Michael*) rank with the greatest works of their kind up to that time. Taverner's contribution to the genre of the votive antiphon was also considerable, with *Ave Dei patris filia, Gaude plurimum,* and *O splendor gloriae* being among the most important.

Taverner was born most likely in south Lincolnshire, perhaps in the vicinity of Boston or Tattershall, around 1490. Nothing is known of his parents or early years. Some of his compositions—*Ave Dei patris filia* and *Gaude plurimum*—were discovered among manuscripts of Henry VIII, and there is evidence to suggest that they were written for the Chapel Royal. There is also ample reason to believe these compositions date from 1515–25, the period during which some therefore believe he lived in London. It may thus be speculated with some good reason that the composer spent some time in London in the early part of the sixteenth century.

In 1524, Taverner became a clerk-fellow of the collegiate church choir of Tattershall. In November 1526, he took on the post of Master of Choristers at Cardinal College, Oxford. The composer wrote a number of works during his Oxford years, including his three Festal Masses, the *Mass Sancti Wilhelmi,* and *Jesu Christe pastor,* a votive antiphon. In fact, during this period and the Tattershall years that immediately preceded it—that is, the period from 1520–30—it is believed that Taverner composed the bulk of his music.

In 1527, Taverner became entangled in a scandal involving the dissident religionist John Clark, who was proselytizing for Lutheran theological ideas. It is believed that Taverner was ultimately exonerated of all charges, but he left the College in April 1530 anyway, owing to its decline following the English Reformation.

Taverner's whereabouts and activities over the next six years are unknown. He is mentioned among the new members of 1537 for the Corpus Christi Gild in Boston, Lincolnshire. The Gild listed the composer as having a wife when he was admitted to membership. Her name was Rose Parrowe, a widow from Boston, with two daughters.

In 1538, Taverner took on the position as agent for the Crown when he began working for Thomas Cromwell. Many music historians have depicted the composer's role during this period as that of a fanatic bent on the demise of various religious congregations and orders, owing to their loyalty to Rome. It appears, however, that Taverner was a compassionate advocate on behalf of those targeted by Cromwell to surrender possessions to the Monarchy. In January 1539, he wrote Cromwell a letter beseeching him to forego further efforts at forcing divestiture of the holdings of many of the religious houses in Boston. In 1540, he resigned from his duties as a Crown agent. The following year, Taverner became treasurer of the Corpus Christi Gild, remaining in that role for at least three years, after which Gild records ceased. In 1545, Boston became a borough, and Taverner served as an alderman there. *—Robert Cummings*

Overview of Works (ca. 1520–1540)

Generations of English innovation culminated in the music of John Taverner. He never had the opportunity to sing in Henry VIII's Royal Chapel; he did, however, spend four years composing music and directing the richly endowed choir of Cardinal Wolsey's new "Cardinal College" (now Christ Church College, Oxford). Taverner also accepted a number of prestigious musical posts in his native Linconshire. He composed the majority of his surviving sacred music for Cardinal College in the late 1520s, though some pieces show more progressive signs. In his music can still be found the richly melismatic style of a prior generation, such as the music of the *Eton Choirbook.* Yet Taverner achieved much more rational control over his musical textures, tempering the English floridity with the application of sequences, canons, ostinato, and greater use of imitation. His melodic style is much more elegant; his rhythms, in the words of one prominent scholar, "breathe easily instead of hyperventilating." In short, John Taverner towered over his generation, and made possible the accomplishments of Tallis and Byrd.

Taverner, a lifelong Catholic, favored the sacred genres of the Roman church, even after the English reformation of the 1530s. He composed at least eight masses. Three of these, sharing a six-voiced, high-treble texture and the same vast musical scope over their Sarum Rite plainchants, likely served the great festal occasions of Cardinal College: the *Missa "Gloria tibi trinitas,"* the *Missa "Corona spinea,"* and the *Missa "O Michael."* Two other masses parody Taverner's own settings of Sarum antiphons. He also apparently composed the earliest (and one of only three) English mass settings upon a secular tune: his well-known *"Western Wind" Mass* for four voices; Sheppard and Tye emulated him in their own similar masses. Taverner also left a wealth of other polyphony for the Catholic ritual: three grandiose festal settings of the Magnificat (for six, five, and four voices); a *Te Deum laudamus*; a number of votive antiphons to Christ, the Virgin, and the Saints; and many other ritual motets (including his celebrated Easter respond, *Dum transisset sabbatum*). He did also contribute to the secular music of his time, leaving a handful of courtly love songs in English and two very important early instrumental works. First, his piece known as *Quemadmodum* may have been one of the first compositions for English viol consort. Second, the excerpt *"In nomine"* from the *Gloria tibi trinitas Mass* sparked nearly 200 years' worth of further viol consort music. *—Timothy Dickey*

Recommended:

- ○ **Taverner: Missa Gloria Tibi Trinitas** / Phillips (cond.), Tallis Scholars / 1989 / Gimell 004
- ○ **Taverner: Dum transisset sabbatum I; Kyrie "Leroy"; Missa "O Michael"** / Christophers (cond.), Sixteen / 2000 / Hyperion 55054
- ○ **Taverner: Missa "Corona Spinea"; Gaude plurimum; In pace in idipsum** / Christophers (cond.), Sixteen / 2000 / Hyperion 55051
- ○ **Taverner: Missa Mater Christi Sanctissima** / Christophers (cond.), Sixteen, Fretwork / 1993 / Hyperion 55053

CHORAL

Mass "The Western Wind," for 4 voices (ca. 1530–1540)

The best known of the eight masses by the English Tudor composer John Taverner (ca. 1490–1545), *The Western Wynde* takes its name from a secular song of unknown provenance. It is therefore what is known as a cantus firmus mass, a setting in which each section of the Ordinary takes as its root a melody heard in long notes around which is intertwined faster-moving polyphony. Often such tunes (particularly in England) had a sacred origin, and it is believed that this mass was the first by an English composer to be based on a secular melody. The setting, which as was customary with English mass settings omits the Kyrie, is scored in four vocal parts and is, of course, a cappella (unaccompanied). The melody occurs nine times in each of the four movements (Gloria, Credo, Sanctus and Benedictus, and Agnus Dei), initially in the top part and later in the contratenor or bass. Stylistically, the piece conforms to the spacious and lavish architectural polyphonic type of mass developed by English composers in the previous century; Taverner's works represent the culminating point of this style. The tunefulness of the song and its extensive and easily identifiable use almost certainly account not only for the enduring popularity of the *Western Wynde,* but also for its influence on younger Tudor composers. Both Christopher Tye and John Sheppard emulated Taverner by writing their own *Western Wynde* masses. The date of composition has not been established, but some scholars believe the mass may be a relatively early work dating from the 1520s. *—Brian Robins*

Recommended:

- ○ **Taverner: Western Wynde Mass, etc.** / Christophers (cond.), Sixteen / 2000 / Hyperion 55056
- ○ **Taverner: Missa Gloria Tibi Trinitas; Western Wind Mass** / Phillips (cond.), Tallis Scholars / 2002 / Gimell 4

Pyotr Il'yich Tchaikovsky

b. May 7, 1840, Votkinsk, Viatka district, Russia, **d.** Nov. 6, 1893, St. Petersburg, Russia

Composer: Ballet, Symphonic, Orchestral, Concerto, Opera, Vocal, Chamber Music, Keyboard, Choral

Pyotr Il'yich Tchaikovsky was the author of some of the most popular themes in all of classical music. He founded no school, struck out no new paths or compositional methods, and sought few innovations in his works. Yet the power and communicative sweep of his best music elevates it to classic status, even if it lacks the formal boldness and harmonic sophistication heard in the compositions of his contemporaries, Wagner and Bruckner. It was Tchaikovsky's unique melodic charm that could, whether in his *Piano Concerto No. 1* or in his ballet *The Nutcracker* or in his tragic last symphony, make the music sound familiar on first hearing.

Tchaikovsky was born into a family of five brothers and one sister. He began taking piano lessons at age four and showed remarkable talent, eventually surpassing his own teacher's abilities. By age nine, he exhibited severe nervous problems, not least because of his overly sensitive nature. The following year, he was sent to St. Petersburg to study at the School of Jurisprudence. The loss of his mother in 1854 dealt a crushing blow to the young Tchaikovsky. In 1859, he took a position in the Ministry of Justice, but longed for a career in music, attending concerts and operas at every opportunity. He finally began study in harmony with Zaremba in 1861, and enrolled at the St. Petersburg Conservatory the following year, eventually studying composition with Anton Rubinstein.

In 1866, the composer relocated to Moscow, accepting a professorship of harmony at the new conservatory, and shortly afterward turned out his *First Symphony*, suffering, however, a nervous breakdown during its composition. His opera *The Voyevoda* came in 1867–68 and he began another, *The Oprichnik*, in 1870, completing it two years later. Other works were appearing during this time, as well, including the *First String Quartet* (1871), the *Second Symphony* (1873), and the ballet *Swan Lake* (1875).

In 1876, Tchaikovsky traveled to Paris with his brother, Modest, and then visited Bayreuth, where he met Liszt, but was snubbed by Wagner. By 1877, Tchaikovsky was an established composer. This was the year of *Swan Lake*'s premiere and the time he began work on the *Fourth Symphony* (1877–78). It was also a time of woe: in July, Tchaikovsky, despite his homosexuality, foolishly married Antonina Ivanovna Milyukova, an obsessed admirer, their disastrous union lasting just months. The composer attempted suicide in the midst of this episode. Near the end of that year, Nadezhda von Meck, a woman he would never meet, became his patron and frequent correspondent.

Further excursions abroad came in the 1880s, along with a spate of successful compositions, including the *Serenade for Strings* (1881), *1812 Overture* (1882), and the Fifth Symphony (1888). In both 1888 and 1889, Tchaikovsky went on successful European tours as a conductor, meeting Brahms, Grieg, Dvořák, Gounod, and other notable musical figures. *Sleeping Beauty* was premiered in 1890, and *The Nutcracker* in 1892, both with success.

Throughout Tchaikovsky's last years, he was continually plagued by anxiety and depression. A trip to Paris and the United States followed one dark nervous episode in 1891. Tchaikovsky wrote his *Sixth Symphony ("Pathétique")* in 1893, and it was successfully premiered in October, that year. The composer died ten days later of cholera, or—as some now contend—from drinking poison in accordance with a death sentence conferred on him by his classmates from the School of Jurisprudence, who were fearful of shame on the institution owing to an alleged homosexual episode involving Tchaikovsky. *—Robert Cummings*

BALLET

The Nutcracker, Op. 71 (1892)

Tchaikovsky's ballet of the *Nutcracker* is based on Alexandre Dumas' translation of the original tale by E.T.A. Hoffman. Act One tells a story of how little Clara aids her magical Christmas gift (a nutcracker in the form of a soldier) defeat an army of mice. As a reward, in Act 2, he takes her to his magic kingdom and introduces her to a variety of subjects in a colorful stream of character dances. Tchaikovsky was initially displeased with the scenario for the ballet, which would be his last, because it lacked real drama. However, he reconciled himself to it and completed the *Nutcracker Suite*, Op. 71a, which was popular from its first performance, before going on to complete the entire ballet. Those seven dances—including the familiar Spanish (Chocolate), Arab (Coffee), Chinese (Tea), and Russian dances—and the overture are essentially the same as they appeared in the final, full ballet. To these he added interludes and scenes, with music and orchestrations that are just as delightful. His supply of lovely themes is endless, and he constantly provides brilliant orchestration. Unique features of his instrumentation include the Overture, which is entirely without cellos and double basses; the "Dance of the Sugar-Plum Fairy," which was inspired by the new celesta, an instrument Tchaikovsky encountered in Paris while working on the score; and the "Waltz of the Snowflakes," which uses a children's chorus. He also used toy instruments, perfectly in keeping with a story for children. The ballet was not as successful as his other stage works when it first appeared, however, now the traditional Christmas ballet is so popular that its annual performance keeps many a ballet company afloat. If all you know of this ballet is the famous suite, by all means hear the entire work. *—AMG*

Synopsis:

Act One, Scene One The curtain rises after the "Miniature Overture." It's Christmas Eve at Town Councilor Silberhaus' residence, and the children, Clara and Franz, lay asleep by the door as their parents busily finish preparations for a Christmas Party. The children are awakened, and guests, including other boys and girls, arrive just in time for the lighting of the candles on the Christmas tree. To the strains of the familiar "March," the children are presented with refreshments, and finally, their gifts. The delight of the children proves contagious, and the parents soon join in the high spirits, performing a polonaise that contrasts with the "Galop" danced by the children.

Aged Herr Drosselmeyer, Clara's godfather, arrives bearing four splendid gifts; life-size mechanical figures of a Harlequin, Columbine, a Soldier, and a Nutcracker. Clara is particularly excited about this last toy, but not Franz, who flies into a jealous rage. He throws the Nutcracker on the floor and stamps on it, breaking it. Clara is distraught and rescues the injured toy. She sings a lullaby to the Nutcracker, which is interrupted by the rowdy trumpets and drums played by the boys. Clearly the children are tired and the party is getting out of hand, so with the "Grandfather Dance" the guests depart and the children are sent off to bed. The stage lights dim so that only the candles on the tree are visible.

Clara arises from her bed and again cradles the Nutcracker. Then everything in the room begins to grow, including the Christmas Tree and the toy soldiers. All of the toys spring to life, and a toy sentinel hears the approach of the Mouse King and his band of warring mice. A battle ensues, and the Nutcracker takes charge of the toy soldiers, ordering cannon to fire loads of candy at the enemy. The battle is won when Clara throws her slipper at the Mouse King and knocks him unconscious. A spell breaks out and the homely Nutcracker is transformed into a handsome prince. The Prince then invites Clara to visit his Kingdom of Sweets.

Scene Two. En route to he Kingdom of Sweets, Clara and the Prince are travelling through the Magic Forest and it begins to snow. Under the influence of the Snow King and his Queen, the snowflakes arise and dance the "Waltz of the Snowflakes."

Act Two. Clara and the Prince arrive in the Kingdom of Sweets, which is ruled by the Sugar Plum Fairy. The Prince relates the story of how Clara rescued him from the Mouse King. The Sugar Plum Fairy declares that a grand divertissement will be given in Clara's honor. Clara and the Price are seated at a high throne to witness the following series of dances: Chocolate (Spanish Dance), Coffee (Arab Dance), Tea (Chinese Dance), Russian Dance (Trepak), the Dance of the Mirlitons (toy flutes or kazoos), Dance of the Clowns, and the Waltz of the Flowers. The Prince joins the Sugar Plum Fairy for a pas de deux and performs variations on a tarantella. The Sugar Plum Fairy takes the stage to perform. The whole company joins in the Final Waltz and Apotheosis, which is presented as a final offering to Clara in reward for her bravery. In some productions, the Prince and Clara bid farewell to the Sugar Plum Fairy and depart in a sleigh that carries them off through the sky. *—Uncle Dave Lewis*

Recommended:

- ○ **Tchaikovsky: The Nutcracker; The Sleeping Beauty (Highlights)** / Dorati (cond.), Concertgebouw / 1994 / Philips 442562
- ○ **Tchaikovsky: The Nutcracker (Motion Picture Soundtrack)** / Mackerras (cond.), London SO / 1986 / Telarc 80137

The Sleeping Beauty, Op. 66 (1888–1889)

While ballet enjoyed a golden age in the mid-nineteenth century, it is generally acknowledged that the music accompanying that medium did not flourish in tandem with the other components. Even in so celebrated a work as *Giselle*, only a balletomane would not be hard pressed to hum one of its tunes. This is by no means a criticism, for the music specified for a production was to be functional. It can be argued that Tchaikovsky is the first composer of great ballet scores, infusing them with his trademark tunefulness, emotion, and drama. Long an admirer of dance, the composer placed the same amount of effort into his three great dance scores as he would into his symphonic and operatic works. For the first time, suites from the ballets could be performed sans staging and choreography for a purely musical experience.

After the less-than-promising 1877 debut of *Swan Lake*, marred by a largely amateur production, over a decade lapsed before the composer was commissioned by the Director of the Imperial Theatres in St. Petersburg to supply music for a ballet on the Perrault fairy tale, *The Sleeping Beauty*. Tchaikovsky threw himself arms-deep into the project. Not only was the composer again on happy turf, he was currently in a state of delight by the occasional presence of the three-year old daughter of a friend's servant; despite his celebrated melancholy, children seemed to tap a joyful vein in Tchaikovsky, the feeling reciprocated in his capacity to be mischievous or silly at their level. The little girl's proximity fed a spirit of fantasy which transmitted to this most lighthearted of the composer's scores. Most musicologists and historians concede that *Sleeping Beauty* is the most perfectly wrought of Tchaikovsky's three ballet scores, classic in its restraint, especially when compared with the hyper-Romanticism of its predecessor *Swan Lake* or the seasonal whimsy of *The Nutcracker*, yet possessing the right amount of color and panache to render it pure Tchaikovsky; its waltz remains a Pops favorite.

The well-known story of the ballet opens with Princess Aurora's christening at the royal court. Rejoicing quickly fades with the uninvited appearance of the evil fairy Carabosse, who places a curse on the princess, preordaining that at 16 Aurora will prick her finger on a spindle and fall into an enchanted sleep. This comes to pass but the spell is at long last broken by Prince Charming, who forges through barriers of enchantment to kiss and awaken Aurora. The enlarged final act is a wedding celebration at which many other celebrated fairy tale characters are present. This act alone is often performed as *Aurora's Wedding*.

Sleeping Beauty was premiered to great acclaim and success, with choreography by the great Marius Petipa at the Mariinsky Theatre in St. Petersburg on January 1, 1890. In 1921, Diaghilev remounted the work for a notable London production. *– Wayne Reisig*

Synopsis:

Prologue. It is long ago at the court of King Florestan XXIV. Surrounded by an august company of nobles, ladies-in-waiting, pages, and guards is a cradle bearing the infant Princess Aurora. The mood is both solemn and festive, for the occasion is the christening of the little princess. To the strains of a stately march, the prestigious array of guests arrive, followed by a sonorous fanfare heralding the arrival of the King and Queen. Seating themselves on the thrones flanking their daughter's dais, they receive the procession of gifts, climaxed by the arrival of the Fairies, godmothers to the princess who along with their gifts bring a happy prophecy for Aurora, that she will grow beautiful physically and as a person.

At the climax of the revelry, a black carriage drawn by four huge rats rides into the great hall, from which steps the evil fairy Carabosse. She confronts Master of Ceremony Cattalabutte, incensed that she was not invited to the festivities. Cattalabutte begs forgiveness for his oversight, but the evil fairy has menacingly turned toward the infant, her progress checked by the other fairies. She will bide her time, but issues the chilling prediction that upon her 16th birthday, Aurora will prick her finger on a spindle and die. She departs, leaving the court in grief. But the Lilac Fairy, she who is the protector of Aurora, has not yet presented her gift. Her present to Aurora will be an alteration of the evil spell. The Lilac Fairy declares that while the prophecy will largely come to pass, Aurora will not die, but will be in an enchanted sleep until a prince shall awaken her with a kiss of true love.

Act One. Sixteen years pass and there is a great festival in the kingdom to honor princes from England, India, Italy, and Spain. Each young royal suitor, flowers in hand, has come to seek the hand of Aurora in marriage. Among the nearby village revelers are a group of young maids bearing spindles of fine, colorful fabric. Horrified at the specter of potential harm to his child, King Florestan demands the spindles be confiscated and is on the verge of having the maids punished. He is placated into forgiveness on the basis of their ignorance of the evil spell, so it is without too much alarm that a seemingly benign old woman presents Aurora with a colorful spindle, which the princess gladly accepts. As she capers with her new present, Aurora pricks her finger and faints into the prophesized deathlike sleep. The old woman reveals herself to be Carabosse in disguise. The four princes rush toward her, swords drawn, but the sorceress vanishes in a fiery blast of smoke. The grieving King and Queen and their court make the sad procession back to the castle, bearing the dormant princess. Once there, the Lilac Fairy appears to fulfill her amendment to Carabosse's curse. Along with Aurora, the entire court is lulled into an enchanted sleep, from which all will awaken once the princess receives the enchanted kiss.

Act Two. One hundred years later, young Prince Florimund is with a hunting party in the nearby forest. All are in high spirits but he, who for some unknown reason finds himself distracted. He then has a vision of an almost supernaturally beautiful young woman, it being Aurora. The prince dances with her, but soon his bliss fades with the vanishing vision. In its place is the Lilac Fairy, with whom Florimund senses a connection. He begs the fairy to take him to Aurora and she leads him to the castle, now overgrown with a century's foliage. Upon his approach, he is confronted by the transformed Carabosse. Bravely he does battle, vanquishes her, and enters the castle. There he finds the sleeping princess and kisses her. Not only does she awaken, but the entire court returns to the world of the living. Florimund is granted Aurora's hand in marriage by the grateful King and Queen.

Act Three. A century's layering of dust and flora must be removed from the castle to prepare for the wedding and celebration, as well as the tailoring of a sumptuous wedding dress. But all preparation is carried out in great joyousness. On the great day of celebration, the Fairies arrive, along with other notables from the realm of fairy tales. These include Puss-in-Boots, the Bluebird, and Red Riding Hood, who each contribute a dance of their own to the overall entertainment. The grand finale is the marriage of Princess Aurora and Prince Florimund, joined together, happily ever after, with the blessing of the Lilac Fairy. *– Wayne Reisig*

Recommended:

- ○ **Tchaikovsky: The Sleeping Beauty** / Gergiev (cond.), Kirov Orch. / 1993 / Philips 434922
- ○ **Tchaikovsky: The Sleeping Beauty** / Dorati (cond.), Concertgebouw / 1995 / Philips 446166
- ○ **Tchaikovsky: The Sleeping Beauty** / Pletnev (cond.), Russian National Orch. / DG 457634
- ○ **Tchaikovsky: The Sleeping Beauty** / Rozhdestvensky (cond.), BBC SO / 1987 / BBC 3003
- ○ **Tchaikovsky: The 3 Ballets** / Bonynge (cond.), National PO / 1999 / Decca 460411

Swan Lake, Op. 20 (1875–1876)

While the composition of *Swan Lake* came in the period of 1875–1876, it incorporated music from an 1871 unpublished effort entitled *The Lake of the Swans*, the composer's first attempt at ballet. In addition, a second-act waltz was said to have been adapted from his 1869 opera *Undine*. *Swan Lake* was not a success initially, but shortly after the composer's 1893 death, it began to take hold. The work was then staged in the Riccardo Drigo version, which, with many excisions, additions, and reordering of numbers, became the standard performing version for many years.

For *Swan Lake* Tchaikovsky composed an introduction and 29 dance numbers, which fall into four acts. The story, set in medieval Germany, centers on Prince Siegfried and his Princess-mother, who, reproaching her son for a lavish celebration at his chateau, commands him to take a bride from among a group of princesses invited to a ball for him the following day. Later the same evening the suddenly-bored Siegfried, at the behest of his friend Benno, gives chase with a group of hunters to a flock of swans. At a lakeside that night the Prince meets the beautiful maiden, Odette, who beseeches him to abandon the hunt for the swans, since they are her companions, cursed, like her, to adopt a winged appearance by the sorcerer Von Rotbart, except between midnight and dawn when they return to their human form. At the ball the next evening, Siegfried cannot choose a bride, but notices some strange guests, the disguised Von Rotbart and his daughter Odile, to whom the sorcerer has given the exact likeness of Odette. The unwitting Siegfried chooses her for his bride and swears to an oath of loyalty to her. In a dramatic lakeside finale, Odette throws herself into the lake and Siegfried joins her, thereby destroying Von Rotbart and his evil power. The young maidens are freed from their swan form and Siegfried and Odette are reunited when the lake vanishes.

The music associated with Odette and the swans is probably the most famous in the ballet. It first comes near the close of the first act in the "Flight of the Swans." The oboe introduces the enchanting theme with harp accompaniment, the whole creating a fantasy-like atmosphere of wonder and expectation. In the Act Four finale, this music is played faster and with agitation in preparation for the main characters' demise. There are, of course, many other famous themes in this colorful work, including the waltz in the Act One "Entrance of the Guests." It is both carefree and festive in its nonchalance and brilliant colors.

Tchaikovsky also wrote a number of dances of ethnic flavor, including an Hungarian czardas, a Spanish dance, Neapolitan dance, and mazurka, all colorfully imagined and brilliantly orchestrated. A complete performance of this ballet can range from slightly over two hours to about two hours and 20 minutes. *–Robert Cummings*

Synopsis:

Act One. The story is set is medieval Germany. In a garden outside the castle of Prince Siegfried, Siegfried's mother, courtiers, and villagers celebrate the Prince's 21st birthday. His friends are also in attendance, including Benno and his teacher Wolfgang. The Prince's mother chides him for his undisciplined lifestyle and tells him of his duty to choose a bride from among the maidens invited to the next evening's grand ball. Siegfried's mother departs, but the merriment continues, with Wolfgang fumbling at dancing and then unintentionally kissing a young man when one of the maidens eludes his puckered lips. A flock of swans flies overhead now and the Prince decides to hunt them with Benno and a group of hunters.

Act Two. At a clearing in the forest, the swans can be seen swimming in the Lake, its flock leader, Odette, wearing a magnificent crown. The hunting party arrives. Siegfried decides to stay behind while the others head into the forest. The beautiful Princess Odette soon appears and beseeches the Prince to end the swan hunt. She explains that she and her companions, constrained by a spell cast by Rothbart the evil sorcerer, can take their natural human form only from midnight to dawn, then must live as swans throughout the day. Her only escape from the spell can come when a young man pledges his love to her for all eternity. The enamored Prince immediately declares his love for her, then asks her to attend the ball on the following evening. Rothbart appears as an owl to overhear Odette tell Siegfried she will attend, but cannot appear until midnight. Her companions soon arrive and all dance until daybreak, when they once again return to their swan form.

Act Three. In the castle ballroom, six princesses are presented to Siegfried as possible brides, but he tells his mother that none are suitable. Rothbart soon appears in disguise, accompanied by his evil daughter, Odile, who bears an exact likeness to Odette. Siegfried, deceived by her appearance, happily selects her for his bride. But Rothbart now insists on a vow of eternal love for her from the Prince, and Siegfried accedes to his demand. Odette appears at the window in flight as a swan. Rothbart reveals identities, and Siegfried now realizes the trap he has fallen into.

Act Four. Odette arrives at the lakeside clearing to meet up with her companions. Rothbart summons a storm as Siegfried arrives to comfort the despairing Odette. He asks her to forgive him, but she tells him they must never see each other again. Odette attempts to depart with her companions, but Siegfried restrains her.

The lake swirls angrily as he seizes her crown and tosses it into the water. The lake rises and engulfs both Siegfried and Odette. Their drowning together breaks Rothbart's spell, and he, too, dies, finally defeated. Soon a jeweled boat appears on the lake carrying the happy lovers, alive once more. *—Robert Cummings*

Recommended:

- ○ **Tchaikovsky: Swan Lake** / Rozhdestvensky (cond.), U.S.S.R. TV & Radio SO / 1982 / Melodiya 32119
- ○ **Tchaikovsky: Swan Lake** / Dutoit (cond.), Montreal SO / 1992 / London 436212
- ○ **Tchaikovsky: Swan Lake** / Svetlanov (cond.), U.S.S.R. State SO / 2004 / Melodiya 403

SYMPHONIC

Manfred Symphony, in B minor, Op. 58 (1885)

For some time Balakirev tried to persuade Tchaikovsky to compose a work based on a program drawn by Vladimir Stasov from Byron's *Manfred*, finally succeeding in 1884. In April 1885, Tchaikovsky began work on what would become the *Manfred Symphony*, his only program work in more than one movement. Its great length—about one hour—and unwieldy structure clearly set it apart from his other orchestral compositions.

The first of the four movements deals with the tormented Manfred wandering in the Alps, pondering his past failings and his love for Astarte, all of which cause him to sink into the depths of despair. The movement opens with a dark and intense descending theme that occurs throughout the work, expressing virtually the same grim mood in subsequent appearances, typically Tchaikovskian, full of yearning and darkness, depression and gloom. In contrast, the music representing Astarte—or rather Manfred's memories of her—is lovely and gentle, consoling in its warmth. But thoughts of her only result in anguish and regret for Manfred, the music seeming to cry out and turn despairing in the closing sections.

The ensuing scherzo depicts Manfred's encounter with the Alpine fairy in a rainbow. It is marked Vivace con spirito and stands in stark contrast to the epic grimness of the preceding panel. Its main section is built upon several related short themes, all delicate and colorful, gossamer and often playful. The trio features an unforgettable theme, relaxed and joyous, full of sunshine.

The third movement, marked Andante con moto, is pastoral in mood, depicting the quiet life of Alpine hunters. The main theme seems to stroll lazily, but is not typically Tchaikovskian in its lack of warmth and passion. Still, the music is beautiful and atmospherically effective, not least because of the composer's imaginative scoring.

The finale is the longest movement and is structurally the most problematic. The music depicts the subterranean palace of Arimanes and an infernal orgy, after which Astarte's spirit foretells Manfred's release from suffering. Manfred is pardoned and then dies. The music is fairly complex throughout, first presenting two fast themes (Allegro con fuoco), then following with a brief lento section. Eventually a fugal passage using the first idea appears and development of all the material ensues. Tchaikovsky then returns to the first movement's thematic wares, which includes a beautiful restatement of Astarte's theme and a brief recapitulation of the latter part of the opening movement. While the structure of the finale is weak, its music is dramatic and powerful, compelling most of the time. *—Robert Cummings*

Recommended:

- ○ **Great Conductors of the 20th Century: Igor Markevitch** / Markevitch (cond.), London SO / 2002 / EMI 75124

Symphony No. 1 in G minor ("Winter Dreams"), Op. 13 (1866; revised 1874)

Tchaikovsky was extremely sensitive and self-critical, often revising well-crafted works or destroying or attempting to destroy them. Though he completed the *First Symphony* in August of 1866, he made a second version of it before the end of that year. Still not fully satisfied with it, he revised it once more, in 1874.

Tchaikovsky himself nicknamed the symphony "Winter Daydreams" and even gave the subtitles "Dreams Along a Wintry Wayside" to the first movement and "Land of Desolation, Land of Mists" to the second. Marked Allegro tranquillo, the opening movement does have a dreamy quality about it, despite its generally lively manner and occasionally muscular sonorities. The ensuing panel (Adagio cantabile ma non tanto) is mesmerizing in its gentleness and melodic flow, both of which invoke tranquil wintry images—no blizzards or wind here, but lots of snow outside and glowing logs in the fireplace inside. The lovely main theme, first heard on oboe, is one of the composer's most attractive creations from his early career.

In the following Scherzo (Allegro scherzando giocoso), Tchaikovsky used material from the Scherzo of his 1865 *Piano Sonata in C sharp minor*. The mood is subdued in this movement, but the music is upbeat, especially in the buoyant trio. Tchaikovsky actually foreshadows the night music of Mahler near the close of this Scherzo, when the solo cello wittily takes up the main theme. The finale, marked Andante lugubre—Allegro maestoso, has much of the winter about its glacial pacing and barren writing in the opening. The main Allegro section brings the most vigorous and colorful music in the symphony. The energetic main theme is one of the composer's most joyous creations and the orchestration throughout this movement is brilliantly realized. The first movement and the finale, as in several symphonies from the German tradition, show thematic links, and in general the work marked an auspicious beginning for a composer who would fuse Western symphonic logic with distinctively Russian subjectivity and gloom.

This work was once neglected but is now performed and recorded with much greater frequency. A typical performance of the *First Symphony* lasts between 40 and 45 minutes. *—Robert Cummings*

Recommended:

- ○ **Tchaikovsky: Symphonies 1–3** / Markevitch (cond.), London SO / 1995 / Philips 446148
- ○ **Tchaikovsky:Symphony 1; The Nutcracker** / Abbado (cond.), Chicago / Sony 48056

Symphony No. 2 in C minor ("Little Russian"), Op. 17 (1872; revised Dec., 1879)

While Tchaikovsky sometimes made use of folk themes, he rarely relied heavily on them. His *Symphony No. 2*, however, was an exception: he employed folk material in each of the work's four movements, more than in any other orchestral composition. In all, he drew on four melodies, each of Ukrainian origin (the work's nickname, "Little Russian," refers to Ukraine). Dissatisfied with the work despite its great success, Tchaikovsky revised it in 1879 and 1880, extensively reworking the outer movements. The finale, shortened considerably, emerged as one of the brightest moments in his entire output.

The work opens with the horn playing the melody from a Russian folk song called "Down Little Mother Volga," in its melancholy Ukrainian version. The Andante sostenuto tempo changes to Allegro vivo when a second lively theme of absolutely Russian character is presented. A gentle lyrical melody is then introduced by the oboe, and the ensuing development section features much tension and color. It is the opening theme, however, that dominates this movement and gives rise to its essential conflicts and tautness. The second movement is a march whose main theme the composer lifted from his opera, *Undine* (1869), the score of which he destroyed although a few fragments from it survive. This nonchalant and hardly militant march theme, Andantino marziale, is followed by two other melodies, one the tune to the folk song "Spin, My Spinner." The movement is charming and generally relaxed. The Scherzo that follows, however, is brimming with energy and good cheer, with playfulness and a deft sense for mischief. Its trio features variations on the melody to a song called "Sell, Darling, the Whip, Buy Me Boots Instead."

The finale begins with a grand brass introduction (Moderato assai). The orchestra then builds upon that music and, after several restarts, renders whole its melody, the tune to the folk song "Let the Crane Soar." This Allegro vivo music is most charming and vivacious, and the movement as a whole is colorfully orchestrated. The folk song is brilliantly varied, and a contrasting theme provides quieter interludes. The symphony concludes in unrestrained high spirits. A typical performance of the *Symphony No. 2* lasts around 35 minutes. *—Robert Cummings*

Recommended:

- ○ **Tchaikovsky: Symphonies 1–3** / Markevitch (cond.), London SO / 1995 / Philips 446148
- ○ **Tchaikovsky: Symphony 2; The Tempest** / Abbado (cond.), Chicago SO / 1985 / CBS 39359

Symphony No. 3 in D major ("Polish"), Op. 29 (1875)

The nickname of Tchaikovsky's "Polish" symphony was rather capriciously attached, and six years after the composer's death, at that. Sir August Manns led the work's London premiere and affixed this inappropriate moniker, taking a cue from Tchaikovsky's parenthetical marking for the finale, Tempo di polacca. He could just as well have focused on the second movement Alla tedesca marking, thereby calling this symphony the "German." In any event, there is nothing particularly *Polish* about the work, but much that is Russian.

This symphony is cast in five movements, the only one of the composer's symphonies with more than the standard four. The work dates from 1874, just before the creation of *Swan Lake*, and the work, with a form resembling that of a dance suite, is dancelike in many individual stretches as well. Like the *Second* symphony it has no explicit programmatic content. The first movement, marked Moderato assai, tempo di Marcia funebre (for the introduction) and Allegro brillante (for the main section), is a colorful mixture of mostly light music. After a dark opening, the mood brightens with a proud theme of martial character. A lovely, exotic melody on oboe is then presented, and when the strings enter the music sweetens in typically Tchaikovskian manner. This movement, bustling with much energy and colored with brilliant orchestration, is rhythmically one of the composer's most intriguing creations.

The second movement (Allegro moderato e semplice) is subdued and balletic; the flavor of *Swan Lake* is especially pronounced here. The ensuing Andante elegiaco offers a horn theme vaguely reminiscent of the *Fifth Symphony*'s motto. The mood remains light here, however, and features richly Romantic music that, ironically, sounds more German than anything else in the symphony, including the preceding "Alla tedesca" panel.

The Scherzo that follows is marked Allegro vivo. It is mischievous, rife with swirls and playful menace, the writing colorful and charming. The aforementioned finale (Allegro con fuoco) opens with a muscular heroic theme of typically Russian character. The music is polonaise-like (hence the "Tempo di polacca" marking referred to above), and the form is a rondo. An alternate theme is hymn-like and jubilant, and also very Russian-sounding. If the ending is a bit bombastic, even corny, it works well with this symphony whose manner is unabashedly direct and richly colorful throughout.

Typical performances of the Tchaikovsky *Third Symphony* last around 45 minutes. *—Robert Cummings*

Recommended:

○ **Tchaikovsky: Symphonies 1–3** / Markevitch (cond.), London SO / 1995 / Philips 446148

Symphony No. 4 in F minor, Op. 36 (1878)

"I should not wish for symphonic works to come from my pen which express nothing and which consist of empty playing with chords, rhythms, and modulations. Should a symphony not express those things for which there are not words but which need to be expressed?" Tchaikovsky, on his *F minor Symphony*, in a letter to Taneyev in 1878.

All of Tchaikovsky's symphonies are wrenched from deep inside him and are titanic works of love. In his writings, he speaks of many of them as if they were living things—the children he knew he otherwise would never have. The prince of these is the extroverted and wild *Fourth Symphony.*

By the end of 1876, Tchaikovsky had begun to sketch out his F minor symphony. He had also decided to marry, perhaps hoping for both social redemption and psychological catharsis. In the spring of 1877, one of his students, Antonina Milyukova, revealed herself to be hopelessly in love with him, and in July he married her. The marriage failed, and Tchaikovsky spiraled into a maelstrom of self-loathing such that he abused and then abandoned his wife, and made a half-hearted attempt at suicide. Nonetheless, Tchaikovsky continued work on the Fourth Symphony, perhaps finding escape from the misery of his life in the wonder of the music. In October of the year, his wealthy patroness, the Mme. Nadezhda von Meck, formalized a regular stipend to him. He seems to have drawn inspiration and emotional sustenance from their long-distance relationship, and by January of 1878 the work was finished.

The Fourth Symphony, although it followed the third by only three years, is suddenly decades, indeed generations ahead of the first three. Gone is Tchaikovsky's youthful naïveté, and in its place is a profound view of Man's insignificant place in a monstrous Universe. The work slams up against the boundaries of defiance, hope, resignation, and triumph and is both richly melodic and thunderously bombastic. Fate—Tchaikovsky's lifelong adversary and tormentor—suddenly has a voice, and it is heard in the blast of trombones, horns, and trumpets opening the symphony. Loud, insistent, devoid of warmth or vibrato, all of a note, it commands total attention and returns repeatedly throughout the first movement to quell even the briefest and most innocent passing thought of happiness. Among many candidates, this movement is one of Tchaikovsky's finest in terms of musical structure and emotional impact.

Still hopeful at the age of only 38, Tchaikovsky actually includes a movement of quiet contemplation and an incredibly effective pizzicato scherzo before setting free what may best be described as a great dervish of joy and celebration, which sweeps the listener away to breathtaking ecstasy. In Tchaikovsky's mind, no doubt this was how it had to be. As relentless and impersonal as is Fate, his defiance of and triumph over it had to be even greater. Advocates of a very few other great composers might argue, but the fact is Tchaikovsky, in his *Fourth Symphony*, spans Man's coming to grips with his place in the Universe as well as it has ever been done in symphonic music. The work was dedicated to von Meck but cryptically inscribed "To my best friend." The work premiered in February of 1878 in Moscow. *—Michael Morrison*

Recommended:

○ **Tchaikovsky: Symphonies 4–6** / Markevitch (cond.), London SO / 1993 / Philips 438335

○ **Tchaikovsky: Symphony 4; Romeo & Juliet** / Barenboim (cond.), Chicago SO / 1997 / Teldec 810

○ **Tchaikovsky: Symphonies 4–6** / Mravinsky (cond.), Leningrad PO / DG 419745

Symphony No. 5 in E minor, Op. 64 (1888)

Tchaikovsky composed this work between May and the end of August 1888, and conducted its premiere at St. Petersburg on November 17 of that year. Eleven years separated the "fateful" *Fourth Symphony* of 1877 from the *Fifth*, about which Tchaikovsky expressed ambivalent feelings both during its composition and later on. To his patroness, Nadezhda von Meck, he wrote in August 1888 that "it seems to me I have not failed, and that it is good." After conducting it in Prague, however, he wrote "... It is a failure; there is something repellent, something superfluous and insincere that the public instinctively recognizes." Yet by March he could write: "I like it far better now."

By no means did Tchaikovsky neglect the orchestra between 1877 (when he committed, in his words, the "rash act" of marriage) and 1888. He composed four wholly charming and fanciful suites, of which the second and third could have passed as symphonies had he chosen to call them that. Furthermore, he wrote the unnumbered but inspired *Manfred Symphony* in 1885. Yet Tchaikovsky never found symphonic structure as congenial as opera or ballet. His method was closer to Liszt's tone-poem procedure than to the Austro-German heritage, continued by Brahms and Bruckner among his contemporaries. Tchaikovsky favored sequences (in his case, the iteration and reiteration of four-bar cells) over enharmonic evolution. Listeners who've sometimes found his music as irritating as he found Brahms' tend do so because of sequence overload, finding that such repeated gestures result in an overblown effect. His greatest gifts were melody and orchestration: witness the popular songs plagiarized from his music, such as *"Moon Love,"* cribbed from the slow movement of *Symphony No. 5.*

Like the *Fourth*, the *Symphony No. 5* is unified by a six-measure "Fate" motto, heard straightaway in a darkly colored Andante introduction until, after a pause, the body of the opening 4/4 movement becomes a sonata-form Allegro con anima (with "soul" as well as spirit). It builds to a ferocious fortissimo climax before ending gloomily. Tchaikovsky marked this melodically rich slow movement Andante cantabile, con alcuna licenza (songfully unhurried, with some freedom). In D major basically, it is a 12/8 sonatina (exposition and reprise), with an elaborate three-part song structure replacing the development section. Its special glory is the solo-horn arietta looted by *"Moon Love"*, although the ominous motto theme from the first movement interrupts twice—like the Commendatore's Statue answering Don Giovanni's invitation to dinner.

The quasi-scherzo third movement is a waltz in A major out of Tchaikovsky's top balletic drawer, with a trio in F sharp minor plus a long coda that reprises the motto, now in 3/4 time. Germanic academics were scandalized by the presence of a waltz in a numbered symphony, but not Brahms, who stayed over in Hamburg to hear a rehearsal, and during a bibulous lunch with Tchaikovsky the day after praised the first three movements.

The motto launches the last movement as it did the first, but now in E major, Andante maestoso, leading to another sonata-allegro construct—this one vivace rather than moderato, with an alla breve meter that keeps it moving. At the end of the reprise, Tchaikovsky writes six B major chords—a false cadence that invariably provokes applause—before the motto, now bedecked in alb and fanon, launches a major-key coda as long as the entire development section. It quickens to a Presto dash for the double bar before broadening at the very end for a triumphantly sonorous tetrad of "end-of-file" chords. *—Roger Dettmer*

Recommended:

○ **Tchaikovsky: Symphonies 4–6** / Markevitch (cond.), London SO / 1993 / Philips 438335

○ **Tchaikovsky: Symphony 5** / Gergiev (cond.), Vienna PO / 1999 / Philips 462905

○ **Tchaikovsky: Symphony 5; March Slav** / Dorati (cond.), London SO / 1992 / Mercury 434305

○ **Tchaikovsky: Symphony 5** / Mravinsky (cond.), Leningrad PO / Erato 45755

Symphony No. 6 in B minor ("Pathétique"), Op. 74 (1893)

Tchaikovsky composed this music between February and August 1893, and conducted the first performance on October 28 of that year in St. Petersburg. Already in 1890 Tchaikovsky had written to his patroness of 13 years, Nadezhda von Meck, about a possible "program symphony." By 1893 he was ready to follow through on the idea, dedicated to his nephew Vladimir Davidov, the "Bobyk" (or "Bob") of many diary-entries and letters during the 1880s. After a successful premiere, however, he was not satisfied with *Program Symphony (No. 6)* on the title page. Several days later Modest suggested "patetichesky," which in Russian means "1, enthusiastic, passionate; 2, emotional; and 3, bombastic" (rather than "pathetic" or "arousing pity," as in English). Pyotr Il'yich was delighted by the suggestion: "Excellent, Modya, bravo, patetichesky!" He wrote this onto the score, and sent it the same day to his publisher, Jurgenson. Two days later, however, he had qualms and asked Jurgenson to suppress subtitles—to issue the work simply as *Symphony No. 6*, dedicated to Bobyk. One week later, he was dead. As for Jurgenson, he could not resist the opportunity in 1893 to publish *No. 6*, in elegant Lingua Franca, as *Symphonie pathétique.* The sobriquet has stuck ever since.

During the work's incubation Tchaikovsky was in rare good spirits, pleased with his boldness and fluency, especially in the trailblazing finale, a drawn-out Adagio of funereal character. Where others still wrote conventional slow movements, he hit on the idea of "a limping waltz" in 5/4 time. And he made the scherzo a march that builds to such a pitch of excitement that audiences ever since, everywhere, applaud at the end.

A lugubrious Adagio prologue begins with a bassoon solo in E minor that makes its way upward through the murk of divisi string basses, followed by a nervous little motif that blossoms into the main theme of an Allegro ma non troppo sonata-structure in B minor. The memorably sighing, mauve-hued melody that dominates this movement is actually its secondary subject. A crashing orchestral tutti sets up the passionately agitated development section, followed by a condensed reprise and a brief, calmed coda.

Tchaikovsky's marking for this D major "waltz" movement is Allegro con grazia—a song and trio with extended coda whose mood may be wistful, even melancholic midway, but whose spirit is balletic, to the extent of echoing *Nutcracker*'s "Waltz of the Flowers," composed a year earlier.

The March-Scherzo, Allegro molto vivace in common time, has an elfin character at the start. It is a sonatina (exposition and reprise without development) that quick-steps to an explosive climax but always returns to tonic G major.

Another sonatina (symphonic developments were Tchaikovsky's bête noire) is anchored in B minor, although the tragic second theme enters in D major. The overall mood is inconsolably grieving, but not "pathetic." Ultimately, the music returns to those murky depths in which the symphony was born some 40 minutes earlier—without, however, benediction or hope. *—Roger Dettmer*

Recommended:

- ○ **Tchaikovsky: Symphonies 4–6** / Markevitch (cond.), London SO / 1993 / Philips 438335
- ○ **Tchaikovsky: Symphonies 4–6** / Abbado (cond.), Vienna PO / 1992 / DG 437401
- ○ **Tchaikovsky: Symphonies 4–6** / Mravinsky (cond.), Leningrad Philharmonic / 1995 / DG 447423
- ○ **Tchaikovsky: Symphony 6; Romeo & Juliet** / Gergiev (cond.), Kirov Orch. / 1999 / Philips 456580
- ○ **Live Recordings 1944–1953** / (live) / Furtwängler (cond.), Berlin PO / 2002 / DG 474030

ORCHESTRAL

1812—Festival Overture, in E flat major, Op. 49 (1880)

Frequently derided as a patchwork of bombastic clichés, Tchaikovsky's *1812 Overture* is in fact a tautly crafted, brilliantly orchestrated, and immensely exciting piece for large orchestra, cathedral bells, and muzzle-loaded cannon. True enough, the work makes shameless use of Russian and French anthems and a folk hymn, and its level of sophistication as music is comparable to that of a pie in the face as humor. But, a pie in the face can be hilarious, and this can be tremendously effective music.

Opening with a gentle hymn, *God Preserve Thy People*, the work sets the scene by depicting the Russians as bucolic, peaceful folk upon whom is suddenly thrust a war of aggression at the hands of the invading conqueror, Napoleon Bonaparte. Fragments of the French anthem are heard but rather than as music, they are blunt instruments and savage thrusts, rending the peace and wounding Mother Russia. The work erupts into successive passages of angry conflict and repetition of bits of themes among shattered fragments of music suggest the random violence of war. Eventually, a stirring fanfare of horns based upon *Le Marseillaise* calls forth a monstrous cadenza of Russian fervor which swarms over the work and finally bursts into an incredibly expansive version of the original Russian hymn, which then joins with *God Preserve The Czar*, complete with cannon shots and cascading bells. The work plays out at between 15 and 20 minutes and becomes rather more effective if given a pace to build tension and energy.

Even though the work is superficial, it contains the same emotional vectors found in all of Tchaikovsky's music, and leaps to life in a properly realized and sensitive performance. Similarly, it tends to fall flat if rushed or played merely for its sonic effects. As with many of his works, Tchaikovsky at different times both praised and derided the work, and given his schizophrenic tendency to do this, his own opinion of the work may be suspect. It is effectively if conventionally orchestrated and leaves the impression that the composer enjoyed writing it. Although not among his best works, the *1812 Overture* is representative of Tchaikovsky's skills in structure and scoring, and certainly belongs in the collection of every listener at all interested in Tchaikovsky, nationalism in music, program music depicting war, or brilliant orchestration. Many otherwise serious and sophisticated listeners consider it THE premier fun piece of concert music. *—Michael Morrison*

Recommended:

- ○ **Tchaikovsky: 1812 Overture & Other Orchestral Works** / Kunzel (cond.), Cincinnati Pops Orch. / 2001 / Telarc 60541
- ○ **Tchaikovsky: 1812 Overture; Capriccio Italien; Beethoven: Wellington's Victory** / Dorati (cond.), Minnesota Orch. / 1996 / Mercury 434360

Capriccio Italien, Op. 45 (1880)

In 1880, Tchaikovsky left Russia to travel Europe, taking full advantage of the support of his sponsor, Nadezhda von Meck. Soaking up the local music while abroad, he collected souvenir melodies for later use; his favorites from the streets and music books of Rome formed the basis of his *Capriccio Italien*, a mélange that has been one his most popular orchestral works ever since. Although based on borrowed material, the *Capriccio* is vintage Tchaikovsky, easily identifiable by its distinctive orchestration and tight structure—two aspects of the composer's work that are often overlooked in favor of his own gift for melody and sentiment. *Capriccio Italien* is pure entertainment, devoid of larger expressive intent, but it is anything but simple. The tremendous variety of mood and color might remind a listener of everything from an epic tone poem to a circus calliope, and the way in which all these things are knitted together into a coherent larger structure, and the work's unfailing tunefulness, are at the heart of its appeal.

The opening trumpet fanfare was heard each morning from a barracks next to the composer's hotel; grand and solemn, and pompously harmonized, it is anything but capricious. The modally inflected string melody that follows is similarly heroic, showing no hint of a smile. But it finally gives way to the evocation of an Italian street band, heard first in the woodwinds and brass, and finally by the whole orchestra; soon the lighthearted medley takes wing, only looking back to the opening mood briefly before the final frenetic tarantella. *—Allen Schrott*

Recommended:

- ○ **Tchaikovsky: Capriccio Italien** / Gergiev (cond.), Kirov Orch. / 1994 / Philips 442775
- ○ **Tchaikovsky: 1812 Overture; Capriccio Italien; Beethoven: Wellington's Victory** / Dorati (cond.), Minneapolis SO / 1996 / Philips 434360
- ○ **Ports of Call** / Oue (cond.), Minnesota Orch. / 1997 / Reference 80

Francesca da Rimini, symphonic fantasy in E minor, Op. 32 (1876)

In 1876, Tchaikovsky was persuaded by a literary critic and friend from his conservatory days, Hermann Laroche, to write an opera based on a tale in Dante's *Divine Comedy* about Paolo and Francesca of Rimini. The story intrigued Tchaikovsky: Francesca and Paolo are lost souls in hell, owing to their adulterous affair (which was an actual historical event). The affair grew out of the latter's efforts to secure Francesca's hand in marriage, not for himself but for his unattractive hunchback brother, Gianciotto, who, after his marriage to Francesca, catches the pair in lovemaking and has them executed. Francesca narrates the circumstances of their painful afterlife in Dante's poetic account.

Plans for the opera fell through, however, and Tchaikovsky, at the behest of his brother Modest, wrote this symphonic fantasy inspired by the story. The dark opening, marked Andante lugubre, depicts the mood and scenery at the doorway to Hell, above which an inscription reads, "Abandon all hope, you who enter here." Tchaikovsky brilliantly captures the sounds and imagery associated with the whirlwind that carries lost souls, including Francesca and Paolo. The music here is agitated, with the strings swirling angrily and a sense of desperation permeating the awful feeling of ineluctable descent. The Allegro vivo marking here may well be a deliberately ironic choice by the composer, for the vivo derivatives of "spirited" and "lively" are hardly appropriate to this frenzied grimness.

After this section is presented a second time, Tchaikovsky introduces a tranquil but yearning love theme on clarinet. Why is such a lovely melody emerging from these hellish environs? Francesca's first words in her narration are, "There is no greater pain than happiness recalled in a time of misery." The strings take up the beautiful melody and the mood of sweet regret almost makes the listener forget the dark character of the preceding section.

Eventually the whirlwind music from the opening returns to depict the lovers being swept up again, perpetuating their chastisement of seeing but never communicating or touching each other. The music ends in dramatic fashion, as ten emphatic chords, punctuated by the crashing gong, bring the work to rousing, chilling conclusion. *—Robert Cummings*

Recommended:

- ○ **Great Conductors of the 20th Century: Evgeny Mravinsky** / Mravinsky (cond.), Leningrad PO / EMI 75953

Hamlet, fantasy-overture in F minor, Op. 67 (1888)

There has been some confusion concerning the identity of this *Hamlet*. Tchaikovsky was commissioned to compose incidental music for a St. Petersburg staging of Shakespeare's *Hamlet*, but failed to meet the deadline. Instead, he produced this tone poem in 1888, assigning the opus number 67. Three years later, he did compose music for the play, designating that effort Op. 67a. Some catalogs, however, have listed the fantasy overture as Op. 67a and the incidental music as Op. 67b, and both, of course, are incorrect.

This colorful tone poem differs from most of Tchaikovsky's others in that rather than portraying events, it depicts the character of Hamlet. There is a strong similarity between the opening theme here and the one that launches the composer's *Manfred Symphony* (1885). Some have also pointed out a structural similarity between *Hamlet* and Strauss' *Don Juan* (1889).

This Tchaikovsky work is powerfully dramatic and brilliantly scored, but Shakespeare's Danish Prince does not quite inspire the composer the way his teenage lovers *Romeo and Juliet* had. Still, the themes here are attractive, especially the mellow, somewhat lonely melody on oboe, and the work is generally well crafted. In the end, this is a solid but minor composition from Tchaikovsky's pen. It lasts about 17 to 18 minutes in a typical performance. *—Robert Cummings*

Recommended:

- ○ **Tchaikovsky: Orchestral Works** / Dorati (cond.), National SO / 1994 / London 443003

Nocturne, for cello & small orchestra in D minor, Op. 19/4 (1873–1888)

This *Nocturne*'s mournful principal melody works perfectly on a legato instrument such as the cello, even though it was originally intended for the piano. Tchaikovsky wrote it as the fourth of his *Six Morceaux*, Op. 19, a piano suite quickly tossed off for some ready cash. Fifteen years later, Tchaikovsky orchestrated it for a performance at a Paris concert of his music; also on the program were the *Pezzo capriccioso for cello and orchestra* and the cello version of his *Andante Cantabile*. This description applies to the version for cello and orchestra, but the transcription's musical substance doesn't differ at all from the piano original. Marked Andante sentimentale, the *Nocturne* begins with a haunting cello soliloquy interrupted by a more flowing, less crepuscular mid-section. A miniature cello cadenza leads to a reprise of the first section, the cello singing the melody as before, but now with a more ornate accompaniment, the flute providing an involved countersubject. *—James Reel*

Recommended:

- ○ **The Swan: Classic works for cello & orchestra** / Chang, Slatkin (cond.), London Philharmonia Orch. / 2000 / EMI 57052

Romeo and Juliet, fantasy-overture in B minor (1869; revised 1870)

Numerous composers have responded to Shakespeare's timeless drama of forbidden and youthful love, but Tchaikovsky's response (along with Berlioz's and Prokofiev's) is at the top of the list. It is the only one of the three to be intended as a number in a symphony concert, and, hence is by default the most famous of the lot.

Tchaikovsky, a lawyer, was still developing as a composer at age 29 when Mily Balakirev (self-appointed father figure to Russian composers) persuaded him to write an orchestral work on the subject of the "star-cross'd lovers." Balakirev outlined the form, planned the keys, and even suggested some of the actual music. After the 1870 premiere, he convinced Tchaikovsky to revise it. The work's success in this form did much to transform the composer's tendency toward crippling doubt into useful self-criticism. (Not that the transformation was ever total; Tchaikovsky suffered bouts of depression and self-doubt throughout his career.) The composer revised it again in 1880; this version is almost universally the one played. While the final version is probably the best one, the 1869 text is also a fine work and very much worth hearing. The earlier version begins with a charming tune that carries elements of the great love theme. In the first and second revisions Tchaikovsky eliminated this and replaced it with the benedictory theme representing Friar Laurence. The effect of this change on the overture's structure is large. The first version seems to begin with Juliet still in a relatively childlike state, but with the potential for the great love present in the disguised premonitions of the love theme. The focus is, therefore, on the development of the drama as it unfolds. The later versions, beginning as it were with a prayer, seem to invite the hearer to look back on a tragedy that has already happened.

Both versions proceed identically through depictions of the clashes between the houses of Montague and Capulet, and then unveil the great love music. After that, though, Tchaikovsky's original idea seems to this writer to be superior: There is a great development, fugal-sounding and allowing for contrapuntal conflict based on the overture's main rhythms and themes. It is tremendously exciting, more so than the music which replaced it. Justification for dropping it might be made along the lines that the original version has too much dramatic weight and overshadows the rest of the music. The main differences thereafter are in details of scoring, and in the finale, which in the original version is much too curt.

It is often instructive to see what a great composer has done at two different times with the same ideas and material. Whether or not it has greater musical merit, Tchaikovsky's blessing of his final version served to ensure that it is the one that prevailed, and in that form it is accepted as one of the greatest programmatic pieces in the symphonic repertoire. The yearning love theme, in particular, is universally acknowledged as one of the greatest melodies ever written, while the exciting fight music and Tchaikovsky's unfailingly clear and imaginative orchestration carry the listener through with hardly a misstep. But the original version is not far behind it in musical worth; it should be given more frequent revivals, if only for the sake of hearing the great fugato passage described above. *—Joseph Stevenson*

Recommended:

- ○ **Tchaikovsky: Symphony 6; Romeo & Juliet** / Gergiev (cond.), Kirov Orch. / 1999 / Philips 456580
- ○ **Tchaikovsky: 1812 Overture; Romeo & Juliet; Marche Slave; The Tempest** / Abbado (cond.), Berlin PO / DG 453496
- ○ **Tchaikovsky: Symphony 5; Romeo & Juliet** / Bernstein (cond.), New York PO / DG 429234
- ○ **Tchaikovsky: Swan Lake; Sleeping Beauty; Romeo and Juliet** / Stokowski (cond.) / 1996 / London 448950

Serenade for strings in C major, Op. 48 (1880)

Fresh from having completed his thunderous and shallow *1812 Overture*, Tchaikovsky set about crafting a gentle, musical work which would provide for him once again the comfort of alluding to his musical idol, Mozart, in form and spirit. This is not to say the *Serenade for String Orchestra* apes Mozart, for it does not. But it seems to have been in the composer's mind a work in the vein of a classical piece, with four sections which contrast musically, but together form a suite of contrasting but complimentary structures that do not depend upon each other as do, for example, the movements of a symphony. The second movement Waltz and, occasionally, the third movement Elégie are played alone as concert pieces. Nonetheless, taken together the four sections form a powerful and convincing work, and Tchaikovsky's consistency of form and scoring link them inexorably together.

The Serenade opens with "Piece in the form of a Sonatina" which has more passion than you would expect in a sonatina. In the furor and popularity of the second section waltz is sometimes lost the incredibly serene beauty of the lengthy third section elegy. It emerges as the longest of the four parts and contains typically wonderful, expressive writing, the type of which Tchaikovsky was a master. A perfect transition passage at the beginning of the fourth section leads to a crisp finale. Here, the composer proves yet again that he could write powerful and stirring music without resorting to sheer volume of sound or brute bombast. The objective listener realizes that the work is for string orchestra only; but the sensation is one of accumulating energy and even if there is no blazing brass, crashing cymbals, or thundering timpani, the piece nonetheless sweeps the listener to a breathless conclusion.

The work is significant in Tchaikovsky's output as an example of the composer writing from inspiration and employing the depth of his genius but without the heavy, sometimes overpowering emotional baggage which pumps up and stretches some of his work out of shape. *—Michael Morrison*

Recommended:

- ○ **Tchaikovsky: Serenade; Dvořák: Serenade** / Karajan (cond.), Berlin PO / DG 400038
- ○ **Tchaikovsky: Symphony 5; Serenade For Strings** / Ormandy (cond.); Philadelphia PO / 1991 / Sony 46538
- ○ **Tchaikovsky: The Children's Album** / Spivakov (cond.), Moscow Virtuosi / 1994 / RCA 61964

Slavonic March, Op. 31 (1876)

Marche slave (1876), one of Tchaikovsky's most popular concert works, was written for a concert to benefit soldiers wounded in the war between Serbia and Turkey. The conflict eventually escalated into all-out war between Russia and Turkey; to capitalize on the prevailing spirit of Slavic solidarity, Tchaikovsky used appropriate folk songs as the main themes in his march, incorporating the Russian national anthem, "God Save the Tsar," at key points. Still, Tchaikovsky's intent seems not to have been wholly nationalistic; his orchestration of the national anthem in its various appearances is almost satirical, though this aspect of the work is often downplayed in performance. During the Soviet era, when performances of the old Tsarist hymn were forbidden, a melody by Glinka was inserted into the *Marche slave* at appropriate points as a substitute.

The march opens as a darkly scored trudge to which an air of mystery and exoticism is added by a sinuous, quasi-Eastern melody, which gives way to a related surging string theme over a brass tattoo. A second theme group revolves around a brightly martial, rather whimsical fife-and-drum tune, which quickly builds into a hearty two-step in the brass. The Tsarist hymn bursts in over nattering woodwinds, after which Tchaikovsky, in characteristic fashion, fills out the march's second half by putting his thematic material through its paces in the various sections of the orchestra, exploiting variations in timbre and register to maximum effect. The work ends with a stirring, swirling, decidedly unmarchable coda. *—James Reel*

Recommended:

- ○ **Tchaikovsky: Capriccio Italien; Slavonic March; Lyadov: Enchanted Lake** / Gergiev (cond.), Kirov Orch. / 1994 / Philips 442775
- ○ **Tchaikovsky: 1812 Overture; Symphony 5; Violin Concerto; Orchestral Works** / Ormandy (cond.), Philadelphia Orch. / 1997 / Sony 63281

The Snow Maiden, incidental music, Op. 12 (1873)

In the repertoire of Russian Romantic music, *The Snow Maiden* is best known as an 1881 opera by Rimsky-Korsakov. Tchaikovsky would likely have converted this semi-operatic score into an opera himself had Rimsky not done so. Had Tchaikovsky written the opera—as his brother Modest said he intended—he most probably would have strengthened this score.

Tchaikovsky composed a large quantity of music to accompany Ostrovsky's play, *The Snow Maiden*, and much of it is vocal and choral, containing songs for Lel the Shepherd, and one for the peasant Brusilo, a monologue for Frost and a fair number of choruses. There are 19 numbers in all—orchestral, vocal and choral—five for the Prologue, which incorporated the introductory music to the early, un-produced opera *Undine*. That reuse was not particularly successful, its music lacking personality. Still, there is much worthwhile in the rest of the score, including the shivering birds' chorus, chorus of flowers, the carnival's choral music, and Lel's forest murmurs song.

While the dance of the clowns is rather bombastic, most of the other dance music is attractive. Tchaikovsky incorporates folk melody throughout much of the score and his colorful use of it is generally effective. In the end, though, *The Snow Maiden* is at best an uneven effort, but one that still probably deserves greater attention. *—Robert Cummings*

Recommended:

- ○ **Tchaikovsky: The Snow Maiden** / Järvi (cond.), Mishura, Grishko, Detroit SO, UMS Choral Union / 1994 / Chandos 9324

Suite No. 1 in D minor, Op. 43 (1878)

In addition to his symphonies, Tchaikovsky wrote four works of symphonic dimensions under the title suite. Because the title implies a less rigorous or serious composition, these brilliant works are unjustly neglected. All but the last of them began as a project for a symphony. But when they grew to works having more than four movements, with a predominance of dance-like music, Tchaikovsky designated them suites.

The first of these was begun at the same time the composer was writing the opera *The Maid of Orleans*. The original version was in four movements, which did not satisfy Tchaikovsky. The next year he returned to the shelved score, and added two movements.

The score is written for a large orchestra and includes some of Tchaikovsky's most striking orchestration. The first movement, "Introduzione e fuga" is an evocation of older works in this style. The formality of the fugue form might be thought to be at odds with Tchaikovsky's passionate, rhapsodic style, but when the fugue culminates, Tchaikovsky has managed to work it up into a powerful setting with horns playing a slowed-down proclamatory version of the main theme while strings and winds continue their rushing music. Then the music relaxes charmingly to conclude with clarinets and bassoons.

The second movement, "Divertissement," is based on three themes, two of which are waltz-like in mood while the middle of them is faster. Woodwind solos are plentiful in this music, strongly reminiscent of dances in Tchaikovsky ballets. The third movement, "Intermezzo," begins with a sorrowful theme, which alternates with a more radiant second theme in a lower register.

The fourth movement is entitled "Marche miniature," a title he would reuse in *The Nutcracker*. It is witty and charming, rather similar in mood to its famous ballet counterpart. Incidentally, Tchaikovsky had doubts about this movement and had to be convinced by persistent arguments to retain it. From the premiere onwards it has been one of the best-received parts of the score. The fifth movement, "Scherzo," is swift, brilliant, and folk-like, showcasing the composer's great skill at creating fine melodies. The finale is a "Gavotte." Even in the context of this restrained eighteenth century dance Tchaikovsky deploys some of his most vivid orchestration to bring the work to an effective close. *—Joseph Stevenson*

Recommended:

- ○ **Tchaikovsky: Complete Suites For Orchestra** / Dorati (cond.), New Philharmonia Orch. / 1996 / Philips 454253
- ○ **Tchaikovsky: Suite 1; The Storm; Fate** / Järvi (cond.), Detroit SO / 1997 / Chandos 9587

Suite No. 2 in C major ("Caractéristique"), Op. 53 (1883)

Tchaikovsky wrote all four of his orchestral suites in the period between the compostion of his *Fourth* (1877-78) and *Fifth* (1888) *Symphonies*. Though none of the suites has ever attained a popularity akin to that of the symphonies, the *Suite No. 2* (1883), subtitled "Caractéristique," has suffered particular neglect, likely because of its impractical requirement of four accordions in one movement. The work comprises a series of almost balletic character pieces. The main exception is the first movement, "Jeu de sons" (Game of Sounds), whose dimensions (though not its mercurial themes) suggest the opening movement of a symphony. A slow, graceful introduction evokes both the ballet stage and the opening of the composer's *Variations on a Rococo Theme* (1876). The atmosphere becomes increasingly dark; soon, however, it takes off in a more impulsive direction. Throughout the movement, Tchaikovsky relies on material of a "scurrying" character, calling to mind the *Fourth Symphony*; at one point he subjects it to fugal treatment.

The second movement, Valse, is occasionally omitted from performances and recordings. It is graceful, playful, wistful, and subject to frequent concentrated tempo shifts. A dreamier section dominated by the woodwinds de-emphasizes the 3/4 meter, but the more obviously waltzlike material repeats its way to the end. The Scherzo burlesque is almost entirely derived from a repetitive nattering figure in the first bars. This idea, sometimes reduced to a mere three-note outline, slips quickly through the orchestra. Just before the movement's midpoint the motive is assigned to the four accordions in a mocking "tribute" to the banal, repetitive music often associated with that instrument. The movement's middle section is marked by a broad, distinctively Russian theme, first sung out by the brass, which soon cedes to the accordions and their inane tune.

In the fourth movement, *Rêves d'enfant* (Child's Dreams), the woodwinds introduce a pensive theme, answered by a brighter childlike tune in the strings. These elements, as well as further folk-inspired material, alternate throughout the movement. The playful finale, *Danse baroque*, sounds more like a danse russe than a souvenir from the time of Bach. Its spirit and percussive splash immediately call to mind the *Dance of the Tumblers* from Rimsky-Korsakov's opera *The Snow Maiden*, premiered in the previous year.*—James Reel*

Recommended:

- ○ **Tchaikovsky: Complete Suites For Orchestra** / Dorati (cond.), New Philharmonia Orch. / 1996 / Philips 454253
- ○ **Tchaikovsky: Suites for Orchestra 1 & 2** / Sanderling (cond.), National SO of Ireland / 1993 / Naxos 550644

Suite No. 3 in G major, Op. 55 (1884)

Tchaikovsky wrote most four of his suites for orchestra in the period of time between his fourth and fifth symphonies. All but the last of them were, at some point in their creation, intended to be symphonies. What usually happened was that Tchaikovsky found he had assembled movements of dance-like character and lightness of mood, lacking formal sonata-allegro forms and hence without symphonic development. As a kind of substitute for development, Tchaikovsky often concluded his suites with a large-scale set of theme and variations.

This suite was premiered in 1885. It was reported that the audience was "electrified." Even so, it became customary to play the final movement by itself, particularly when it became the music for a ballet.

The first movement, "Elegie," used three themes, all of them flowing and lyrical, are in a rondo form. The second, "Valse mélancolique," actually goes beyond melancholy. It is, in fact, rather bitter and grieving in tone. The third movement, "Scherzo," is a tarantella with a rare and threatening martial air. The theme of the final variations is introduced on strings only, followed by 11 variations, most of which use a different selection of instruments. It ends with a grande polonaise in an intense and majestic mood. *—Joseph Stevenson*

Recommended:

- ○ **Tchaikovsky: Complete Suites For Orchestra** / Dorati (cond.), New Philharmonia Orch. / 1996 / Philips 454253
- ○ **Tchaikovsky: Suite 3; Francesca da Rimini** / Järvi (cond.), Detroit SO / 1996 / Chandos 9419

Suite No. 4 in G major ("Mozartiana"), Op. 61 (1887)

This is the only one of Tchaikovsky's four fine orchestral suites that did not begin as a projected symphony. It is also the only one with as few as four movements. He was a lifelong admirer of Mozart and sought here to pay tribute to his favorite composer. He started thinking about the music in 1884, but did not actually turn to its composition until 1887.

The four movements are based on a number of lesser-known pieces by Mozart, but strikingly recomposed to the extent that they are wholly consistent with Tchaikovsky's own style and temperament. (Some 25 years after Tchaikovsky's death, his countryman Stravinsky did a similar exercise with Tchaikovsky's music to produce the ballet *The Fairy's Kiss*, mainly transforming the sound of the older composer's scores into his own.)

The first movement, "Gigue," is based on Mozart's *Gigue in C*, K. 574. The second, "Minuet," is based on the *Minuet in D*, K. 355. These are brief, rather straightforward arrangements, rather lightly scored, and retain more of the quality of their originals than is true of the remaining two movements. The third movement, "Preghiera," is an orchestration of Liszt's piano transcription of Mozart's motet *Ave verum corpus*, K. 618. It is a sonorous and majestic sounding version, notable for its remarkably effective harp part.

The final part, "Theme & Variations," is notably longer than the other three movements combined. It is based on Mozart's *Theme and Variations*, K. 455, on a theme from Gluck's opera *The Pilgrimage to Mecca*. The orchestration is again brilliant, a distinct orchestral sound being given to each of the ten variations, chosen in such a way that the orchestration possesses its own dramatic progression. *—Joseph Stevenson*

Recommended:

- ○ **Tchaikovsky: Complete Suites For Orchestra** / Dorati (cond.), New Philharmonia Orch. / 1996 / Philips 454253
- ○ **Tchaikovsky: Serenade for Strings; Suite 4** / Serebrier (cond.), Scottish CO / 1990 / ASV 719

The Tempest, fantasy-overture in F minor, Op. 18 (1873)

There are two pairs of works in Tchaikovsky's oeuvre that are often confused, the first couple being the Op. 3 opera *Voyevoda* (1867-68) and *Voyevoda*, the symphonic ballad for orchestra, Op. 78. The other confusable pair of siblings are the 1864 overture for orchestra *The Storm*, Op. 76, and the work under examination here, *The Tempest*, from 1873, a later composition, despite the higher opus number of the first work. *The Tempest* is a fantasia inspired by the Shakespeare play of the same name. It is not as well known as Tchaikovsky's other orchestral work after Shakespeare, the *Romeo and Juliet Overture-Fantasy*, but is nearly on the artistic level on that powerfully dramatic work. Like *Romeo and Juliet* it followed a written-out program; *The Tempest* is less complex than *Romeo and Juliet* partly because that program is itself simpler in structure. The *Romeo and Juliet* program was written by the composer Balakirev and specified a complex correspondence of themes with the characters in the play, but the program for *The Tempest*, written by an art historian named Stasov, specified only a loose sequence of scenes.

The Tempest begins quietly with an air of calm and expectation, the music depicting a placid sea and Ferdinand's ship sailing along confidently. Soon the mood becomes intense and violent as Ariel, at the behest of the magician Prospero, summons a tempest. The music rages on; Tchaikovsky's orchestration is masterful in color and atmospheric splendor as the ship wrecks.

The music depicting the happenings on Shakespeare's fantasy island is finely imagined and intelligently structured throughout. The love theme used to express the burgeoning and then blossoming feelings between Miranda and Ferdinand is beautiful and convincing, if not quite as memorable as that in *Romeo and Juliet*. Ariel comes across quite colorfully here, too, with an air of fantasy always seeming to hover above the proceedings. In the closing section, the music reverts back to the calm, seafaring mood of the opening.

A typical performance of *The Tempest* lasts about 20 minutes. *—Robert Cummings*

Recommended:

- ○ **Tchaikovsky: Orchestral Works** / Dorati (cond.), National SO / 1994 / London 443003
- ○ **Tchaikovsky: Romeo & Juliet; Marche Slave; The Tempest** / Abbado (cond.), Berlin PO / DG 453496

The Voyevoda—Symphonic Ballad, Op. post. 78 (1890–1891)

Tchaikovsky's symphonic ballad *The Voyevoda* is the least familiar amongst his series of free-standing descriptive orchestral works. It is also the shortest, by a margin of some five or six minutes, and although the conciseness of its two principal thematic groups and its resourceful orchestration have attracted interest from scholars and musicologists, *The Voyevoda* is hardly ever performed in public.

Tchaikovsky began to sketch out the work in the latter part of 1890, and completed the score in the following year. The "Voyevoda" of the title was a Polish landowner, and the subject of a novel by Mickiewicz. A dedicated patriot, he had answered the call to arms in the cause of national freedom. Now, having returned home after defending his country in battle, he finds his wife in the embrace of a former lover. The Voyevoda thus decides to kill them both himself, but at the critical moment, it is he who is tragically killed by a bullet from his own gun.

The morbid subject matter undoubtedly fascinated Tchaikovsky, and indeed, the omnipresent strand of malignant fate controlling human destiny is a familiar theme in a large number of his works, and one made more poignant, perhaps, given the facts concerning Tchaikovsky's own death.

The Voyevoda, Op. 78, is cast for conventional orchestral resources, with the addition of harp and English horn. The work opens quietly, with a restless ostinato for cellos and basses heard above a throbbing tympani beat, all the while developing in volume and intensity, suggesting the Voyevoda's torment. A cascading second theme, later punctuated by stabbing unison chords, depicts his plan of action. Shimmering harp writing and an expansive wind melody part way through suggest moments of earlier happiness, but the obsessive ostinato figures return to haunt the Voyevoda, who pledges to complete his task. Trombones and tympani are employed to depict the fatal shot, before the work ends ominously. *—Michael Jameson*

Recommended:

- ○ **Tchaikovsky: Orchestral Works** / Dorati (cond.), National SO / 1994 / London 443003

CONCERTO

Andante cantabile, for cello and string orchestra in D major (1888)

Like most composers, Tchaikovsky often arranged or reworked earlier compositions. This *Andante Cantabile* is an arrangement for cello and string orchestra of the second movement of his *String Quartet No. 1*, the most popular of his chamber works.

The character of the music remains essentially the same in this version, though, naturally, the focus shifts more heavily to the solo cello. Of course, anyone familiar with the *Quartet* will know that much of the writing is in the middle ranges of the violins and viola and would thus adapt reasonably well to the cello. The piece opens with a lovely, if somewhat solemn theme, whose pacing may seem slower than the Andante marking given in the score. The brighter alternate melody works up some tension in its two brief appearances, but the piece is dominated by the sweet main theme, which, upon its final return, turns more gentle and reflective.

A typical performance of the *Andante Cantabile* lasts from six to seven minutes. *—Robert Cummings*

Recommended:

- ○ **Tchaikovsky: Rococo Variations; Andante cantabile** / Maisky, Orpheus CO / DG 453460
- ○ **Elgar and Saint-Saëns: Cello Concertos** / Rolston, Bernardi (cond.), Calgary PO / 1995 / CBC 5153

Pezzo capriccioso, for cello & orchestra in B minor, Op. 62 (1887)

Tchaikovsky wrote this piece during a summertime visit to Germany and dedicated it to Anatoly Brandukov, a pupil of the cellist who premiered (and drastically revised) the composer's *Variations on a Rococo Theme*. Brandukov, too, saw fit to toy with the *Pezzo Capriccioso* after its 1888 publication, and it is heard today in both his version and Tchaikovsky's original; the following description refers to Tchaikovsky's conception.

The piece is capricious—not in a lighthearted way, but in its manner of toying with various aspects of a mood. That mood is initially rather dark; the work begins with a dramatic declamation from the soloist, a theme that ascends the scale at the beginning of each phrase, even though the phrase itself falls. This gives way to a rising, impulsive melody that would be eminently singable if it didn't devolve to instrumental passagework. About halfway through, a mercurial scherzo briefly takes over, but soon gives way to the main theme it had interrupted. Soon, though, the scherzo material succinctly provides the last word. This was the last completed work for solo instrument and orchestra that Tchaikovsky wrote. *—James Reel*

Recommended:

- ○ **Tchaikovsky: Music for Cello & Orchestra** / Wallfisch, Simon (cond.), English CO / 1983 / Chandos 8347

Piano Concerto No. 1 in B flat minor, Op. 23 (1874)

Although Tchaikovsky was already an accomplished composer (having already produced his first two symphonies, a string quartet, and two notable tone poems, all of these successful and enduring works), he still sought the approval of mentors such as Balakirev and Nicolas Rubinstein. On Christmas Eve 1874 he played the concerto for Rubinstein (its intended soloist) in an empty classroom. Rubinstein responded with a torrent of castigation, made famous by Tchaikovsky's own recollection. Tchaikovsky slunk off in despair. Later Rubinstein called him back and detailed a list of changes that must be made by a certain date if Rubinstein were to perform it. Tchaikovsky wrote that he responded, "I shall not change a single note, and I shall publish the concerto as it is now." He continued in his reminiscence, "And this, indeed, I did." Well, not entirely. Although there are no really substantial changes, he did subject the concerto to some minor revision before it was printed, as happens with most compositions. The premiere fell to Hans von Bülow, who played it first in Boston, October 15, 1875. The audience was enraptured and demanded a repeat of the entire final movement. Von Bülow took the concerto back to Europe, where it was quickly added to the repertoire of other leading pianists; even Rubinstein started playing it in 1878. It has been a giant success, virtually the epitome of the romantic piano concerto, ever since.

The form of the concerto is lopsided: possessing a notably large scale introduction, the broad melodies of the first movement run its length out to nearly 25 minutes, more than the length of the two remaining movements combined. Its arresting opening horn call, with bold orchestral chords interrupting, leads immediately to one of the most recognizable and beloved of classical melodies, played by strings with rich harmonic support from the piano solo. Tchaikovsky initiates a great formal surprise by going straightway into a full-fledged cadenza for the piano solo, a powerful treatment of the theme. The strings then reassert the melody in its original form—and all this is only the introduction to the first movement proper. A lengthy introduction to be sure (106 measures), but once it ends, that's the last time in the concerto this music is used in any way. The movement proper is a full-scale sonata-allegro treatment of two themes, one reputedly a Ukrainian folk theme, the other a gentle romantic theme. There is great drama and passion in its working out; when it is all over one realizes that there is also a minimum (for Tchaikovsky) of angst and pathos.

The second movement is tender, beginning with pizzicato chords so quiet as to be almost whispers. A flute melody of young adolescent tenderness is the main theme of the movement. There is a central section with a delicate waltz.

The finale opens with a rushing string figure and a powerful drum stroke. The main theme is an arresting, galloping dance made up of many short phrases. Yet another romantic theme provides contrast. *—Joseph Stevenson*

Recommended:

- ○ **Tchaikovsky: Concerto 1; Rachmaninoff: Concerto 2** / Cliburn, Kondrashin (cond.), RCA Victor SO / RCA 0786355912
- ○ **Tchaikovsky: Concerto 1; Beethoven: Concerto 5** / Horowitz, Toscanini (cond.), NBC SO / 1990 / RCA 7992
- ○ **Tchaikovsky Vol. 2** / Richter, Karajan (cond.), Vienna SO / 2001 / DG 469271
- ○ **Mravinsky Live: Tchaikovsky** / Gilels, Mravinsky (cond.), Leningrad PO / Russian Disc 11170

Piano Concerto No. 2 in G major, Op. 44 (1880)

In some circles, Tchaikovsky's *Piano Concerto No. 2* is thought to be superior to his ever-popular *First*, one of the most played and recorded concertos ever written. Still, defenders of the *Second* must concede to certain imperfections; the first two movements, for example, are rather long for their material. The latter, in fact, was heavily abridged by Rachmaninov's cousin, Alexander Siloti. The concerto was actually published in this cut edition, which was for a time quite popular.

This mammoth three-movement work, performances of which typically exceed three-quarters of an hour begins with a proud theme first stated in the orchestra, then by the piano in big chords. A warm, romantic alternate theme, introduced partially by the clarinet, is taken up by the piano. Eventually Tchaikovsky introduces a brief cadenza, and soon afterward a massive cadenza appears, the main theme permeating it, often in subtle guises. A reprise initiated by the orchestra follows, with a brilliant coda closing the movement.

The second movement features lengthy solo appearances by the cello and violin, the former instrument introducing the main theme at the outset, soon joined by the violin, with the piano silent for the first four minutes or so. The lovely melody is at last taken up by the piano, and the mood seems to swim in serenity and beauty. Tension develops in the middle section in a long orchestral passage. The cello and violin return again, with the piano eventually reentering, but in an accompanimental role, and thereafter not really seizing center stage. While the piano has a limited role in this central panel, the music is imaginative and finely crafted.

The final begins with the piano playing an ebullient theme whose joyous ascending chords at the outset are followed by a playful descent. A busy second theme of strong Russian flavor quickly follows. The piano then delivers a lyrical variation on it that bleaches its ethnicity out and imparts a carefree, infectious joy. The whole movement bustles with energy and happiness, with brilliant piano writing and Tchaikovsky's typically imaginative orchestration. *—Robert Cummings*

Recommended:

- ○ **Tchaikovsky: Piano Concertos 1 & 2** / Cherkassky, Ludwig (cond.), Berlin PO / DG 457751
- ○ **Tchaikovsky, Prokofiev & Bartók: Piano Concertos** / Gilels, Maazel (cond.) / 1999 / EMI 68637
- ○ **Tchaikovsky: Piano Concerto 2; Concert Fantasy** / Glemser, Wit (cond.), Polish RTSO / 1996 / Naxos 550820

Piano Concerto No. 3 in E flat major, Op. post. 75 (1893)

The Tchaikovsky *Piano Concerto No. 3* is rarely heard, though it is a finely crafted work worth greater attention. It has suffered alongside the magnificent and superior *Second* and the ever-popular *First*. Moreover, it is not a bona fide concerto at all, the composer having completed only the first movement before his sudden death in 1893. Contrary to the suggestion of a few, it is highly unlikely he intended to produce a one-movement concerto.

Tchaikovsky wrote two other piano pieces the same year bearing the titles "Andante" and "Finale," respectively. Following his death, Taneyev orchestrated these and attached them to the *Concerto*, though Tchaikovsky had left no indication they were to be a part of it. But the pair did share something in common with the completed first movement: a theme source—the incomplete *Symphony No. 7*.

In any event, the opening movement of this *Concerto* is the most compelling, featuring an exuberant main theme whose first two notes are the central melodic element. An attractive slow melody is soon presented, followed by a theme of great vivacity and rhythmic drive. The large cadenza is not entirely successful, but the movement as a whole works well. The slow movement and finale fashioned by Taneyev also have considerable appeal, even if the orchestration is not a good match for Tchaikovsky's. Still, the *Piano Concerto No. 3* is probably strongest in its incomplete, single-movement form. *—Robert Cummings*

Recommended:

- ○ **Tchaikovsky, Prokofiev & Bartók: Piano Concertos** / Gilels, Maazel (cond.) / 1999 / EMI 68637
- ○ **Tchaikovsky: Piano Concertos 2 & 3** / Pletnev, Fedoseyev (cond.), London Philharmonia Orch. / 1991 / Virgin 59631
- ○ **Tchaikovsky: Piano Concertos 1 & 3; Concert Fantasy** / Gavrilov, Ashkenazy (cond.), Berlin PO / 1996 / EMI 89484

Sérénade mélancolique, for violin & orchestra in B minor, Op. 26 (1875)

It is safe to say that without the help of Russian violinist Adolph Brodsky, Pyotr Il'yich Tchaikovsky's *Violin Concerto* would not be held in nearly the popular esteem that it is today held, or at least to say that without Brodsky the work would have had to wait much longer for its day in the sun to arrive. For upon seeing the *Concerto*, Leopold Auer, the violinist for whom Tchaikovsky had actually composed the work and who was to have given the premiere, decreed it both unplayable and aesthetically questionable, just as Nikolai Rubinstein had done with the composer's *Piano Concerto* a few years earlier. It was only because Brodsky generously offered to take Auer's place as soloist that the work was heard at all. The grateful composer immediately struck Auer's name from the dedication and replaced it with Adolph Brodsky's. Most critics of the day, however, agreed with Auer's verdict; though, as it happened, Auer himself later reversed his judgment and became, through his brilliant students, the *Concerto*'s greatest champion.

This was not the first time that Brodsky had used his immense skills in Tchaikovsky's aid when an association with Auer proved unfruitful. On January 28, 1876, Brodsky had given the premiere of another work Tchaikovsky wrote with Auer in mind, the *Sérénade mélancolique for violin and orchestra*, Op. 26, composed almost exactly one year earlier. In the case of the *Sérénade*, the dedication to Leopold Auer survives; perhaps it was only when Auer had failed him for the second time, and Brodsky had bailed him out for the second time, that Tchaikovsky grew angry enough at Auer to strike out the *Concerto*'s dedication.

The single-movement *Sérénade mélancolique* is of diminutive proportions compared to the *Violin Concerto*. A large three-part (ABA) form is at work in the piece. In the opening strains of the first section (Andante) the violin sings a quiet tune entirely on the G string. A second theme appears (Pochissimo più mosso), related to the woodwind introduction and hinting at the realm of D flat major, but never actually manages to make a cadence to that key before the middle section proper takes off with its agitato-running eighth notes. Two massive Largamente outbursts in E and B flat major make for a rousing climax, but soon things dissolve away into a brief and very subdued violin cadenza, which in turn moves without break of any kind into the reprise of the opening section, now played with the addition of shimmering flute tremolandos. The opening bars of the piece come back at the end of the brief coda, just before the violin reflects once more, almost despondently, upon the melancholy theme of the first section, and draws the whole affair to a triple pianissimo close. *—Blair Johnston*

Recommended:

- ○ **Tchaikovsky: Violin Concerto; Mendelssohn: Concerto for Violin, Piano & String Orchestra** / Kremer, Maazel (cond.), Berlin PO / 1998 / DG 459043
- ○ **Tchaikovsky & Mendelssohn: Violin Concertos** / Heifetz, Reiner (cond.) / 1995 / RCA 61743
- ○ **David Oistrakh Collection Vol. 6** / Oistrakh, Kondrashin (cond.), U.S.S.R. SO / 2000 / Doremi 7742

Souvenir d'un lieu cher, for violin & piano, Op. 42 (1878)

This charming violin work owes its generation to the unique relationship between Tchaikovsky and his wealthy patroness, Nadezhda von Meck. Effectively freeing the composer from any financial burden in life, this patronage carried with it the unusual "rider" that the two parties were never to meet. This stipulation did not, however, prevent Tchaikovsky from enjoying the amenities of Mme. von Meck's lovely Ukrainian estate when the mistress herself was away; during just such a stay in the spring of 1878 Tchaikovsky found the quiet grounds and comfortable home so much to his liking that he immediately set about commemorating the vacation by putting together the *Souvenir d'un lieu cher*, Op. 42 for violin and piano. The dedication of this three-movement musical truffle, the musical cousin of the *Violin Concerto* the composer had completed just one month earlier, is in fact made not to Mme. von Meck, but instead to the estate itself: Braïlov.

The first piece of the *Souvenir*, "Méditation," was actually penned while the composer was writing his *Violin Concerto* and originally served as that work's central movement. Tchaikovsky eventually chose to replace the "Méditation" with the now-famous "Canzonetta," but, ever loathe to waste material, he immediate recycled it as the opening number of Op. 42. It is cast in a large ABA form; the reprise of the repetitive and rather melancholy D minor opening, with its dark violin melody in the lowest register, incorporates some of the glistening triplet arabesques that fill the dolce middle portion. A little coda makes a very delicate move to D major, disappearing into the violin's high E string. In retrospect, it may have been the impassioned climaxes of the two outer sections, whose robust virtuoso outbursts and thick accompaniment are too similar to the Concerto's first movement, that led Tchaikovsky to remove the "Méditation" from the *Violin Concerto*.

A Scherzo in C minor follows, again outlining a compound ternary form. In the opening and closing sections—Presto giocoso—Tchaikovsky returns again and again to the quiet but tension-filled rising idea in running eighth notes that begins the piece; although there are some digressions, it is only when we arrive at the middle section (Con molto espressione e un poco agitato) that a real shift of gears takes place. Here, all is song, with a wave-like accompaniment in the piano right hand and an impassioned tune in the violin that pauses for breath only as the transition back to the reprise of the opening music starts to unfold.

Perhaps the strongest piece of the three, and certainly the only one to have achieved any real fame of its own, is the "Mélodie" in E flat major that concludes the group. It has a gorgeous violin melody that moves along in arch-shaped eighth note groupings, sometimes lovingly imitated by the piano, to which a very brief central portion in grazioso scherzando 16ths provides some contrast. The little codetta at the end is as tender as music can be. *—Blair Johnston*

Recommended:

- ○ **Virtuoso Vengerov** / Vengerov, Golan / 1993 / Teldec 77351

Valse-scherzo, for violin & orchestra in C major, Op. 34 (1877)

Tchaikovsky's light *Valse-scherzo* (1877) has been recorded surprisingly frequently, especially in the latter part of the twentieth century. Its prominence in the recorded repertoire is certainly due in large part to its useful role as filler on recordings featuring the composer's *Violin Concerto in D major*, a work it immediately preceded in the chronology of the composer's works. The *Valse-scherzo* is thus often, and accurately, regarded as an exercise in preparation for the more substantial concerto; indeed, it may even have originally been intended as part of the larger work.

The colorful *Valse-scherzo* features much attractive writing for the violin, appealing, if not particularly memorable tunes, and scoring that showcases the composer's deft orchestration skills. While it lacks the more distinctive character of Tchaikovsky's other short work for violin and orchestra, the *Sérénade mélancolique*, Op. 26 (1875), the vibrant, joyous *Valse-scherzo* must be judged one of the composer's lesser—but not negligible—efforts. *—Robert Cummings*

Recommended:

○ **Glazunov & Kabalevsky: Violin Concertos** / Shaham, Pletnev (cond.), Russian National Orch. / DG 457064

Variations on a Rococo Theme, for cello & orchestra in A major, Op. 33 (1876)

Three of the most brilliant virtuoso display pieces in the symphonic literature all came from the tormented pen of Pyotr Tchaikovsky. These are his *First Piano Concerto*, his *Violin Concerto*, and this work for cello and orchestra. Done in the potentially tedious theme and variations format, the work begins with a simple theme and plumbs the depths and streaks to the heights of the capabilities of what is arguably the most beautiful and wide ranging of the stringed instruments of the orchestra.

The rococo theme itself is a simple one and if it tips its hat to the eighteenth century—and Tchaikovsky's musical idol, Mozart—it is thoroughly Tchaikovskyian and utterly Romantic. Each of the seven variations is skillfully crafted and none sounds contrived or forced—always a potential trap in this form. Two expressive cadenzas further push the performance envelope of the cello and at least one variation is as powerfully mournful and expressive as anything the morose Russian ever composed. The work finally bursts forth into a joyous final variation and concludes with satisfying enthusiasm, but without overly produced bombast.

Rococo Variations were composed in short score near the end of 1876 for Wilhelm Fitzhagen, who was principal cellist at the Moscow Conservatory. Fitzhagen got a short score of the new variations so he could make the cello part idiomatic while Tchaikovsky was orchestrating the rest. This was introduced at a Moscow concert on November 30, 1877, when the composer was "recuperating" in Switzerland from the debacle of his one and only marriage earlier that year. He didn't know of revisions Fitzhagen made and presented to the publisher Jurgenson as "authorized." Tchaikovsky's own version had a brief introduction for strings before the theme itself, in two parts, then eight variations, and a coda. Fitzhagen added repeat marks to both halves of the theme, killed variation 8, rearranged the original order (to 1, 2, 7, 5, 6, 3, 4), and truncated the coda. Although biographer David Brown has damned this version as "deplorably corrupt," it remains charming, albeit less effective than the original, finally published in a 1956 Soviet edition of Tchaikovsky's complete works.

The genius in the work is the manner in which Tchaikovsky transforms the original theme into numerous and different personalities, each logical and effective. There is never a sense of stalling or contrivance, nor, in spite of the ferocious virtuoso demands in certain of the variations, of mere pyrotechnic display. It is the work of Tchaikovsky the musician and composer, not of the tormented and overwrought soul who could sometimes pound the listener into submission with emotional extremes. Those interested in beautiful and challenging works for cello and in hearing Tchaikovsky at his musical best should enjoy this piece immensely. *—Michael Morrison*

Recommended:

○ **Dvořák: Cellokonzert; Tchaikovsky: Rokoko-Variationen** / Karajan (cond.), Rostropovich, Berlin PO / DG 447413

○ **Dvořák: Cello Concerto; Bruch: Kol Nidre; Tchaikovsky: Rococo Variations** / Starker, Dorati (cond.), London SO / 1990 / Mercury 432001

Violin Concerto in D major, Op. 35 (1878)

Tchaikovsky composed this work in 1878. At Clarens, near Geneva, following both his mistake of a marriage and his suicide attempt, Tchaikovsky completed both *Onegin* and the *Fourth Symphony* early in 1878. After a round trip to Moscow in February for the symphony's premiere, he was visited at Clarens by the violinist Yosif Kotek. Tchaikovsky, in fondness for Kotek, sketched out a violin concerto in just 11 days and had finished scoring it two weeks later, including a new slow movement in place of one that both Kotek and Tchaikovsky's younger brother, Modest, considered to be weak.

Pyotr Il'yich dedicated the new concerto to Leopold Auer, the fabled Hungarian émigré who would teach two generations of Russian virtuosi. However, just as Nikolai Rubinstein had vilified the *B flat minor Piano Concerto* four years earlier, Auer declared this new one "unplayable" (though he too recanted, and became one of the work's champions). It was, therefore, a Viennese audience that heard the first performance with Adolf Brodsky and conductor Hans Richter on December 4, 1881. It was an insufficiently rehearsed and poorly accompanied performance, about which Eduard Hanslick wrote, "It brings to us the revolting thought that there may be music that 'stinks in the ear.'" Yet he also wrote in same review that "the concerto has proportion, is musical, and is not without genius."

In addition to its structural soundness, the concerto fairly teems with melodies, in such abundance that the orchestra's gorgeous opening tune never returns! Thereafter the soloist gets first crack at the rest of them, beginning with the "very moderate" principal theme. The second one is marked molto espressivo, after which the main theme returns, before the development section that ends in a showy solo cadenza, followed by the reprise and coda.

The andante Canzonetta ("little song") in 3/4 time with ABA form features a G minor main theme (additionally marked molto espressivo) and a contrastingly quicker, Chopinesque second theme in E flat major. Without pause the next movement lifts off like an SST from the tarmac. It is a Trepak in rondo form, with two extroverted themes of folkloric character, capped by an extended coda that concludes the piece dervishly. No Russian composer before or since Tchaikovsky has ended a concerto with greater finesse or panache, not even Rachmaninov (who learned wherefrom to take his cue early on, with Tchaikovsky's blessing). *—Roger Dettmer*

Recommended:

○ **Tchaikovsky & Glazunov: Violin Concertos** / Vengerov, Abbado (cond.), Berlin PO / 1995 / Teldec 90881

○ **Tchaikovsky & Brahms: Violin Concertos** / Oistrakh, Mar (cond.), Royal PO / 2002 / BBC 4102

OPERA

Eugene Onegin, Op. 24 (1877–1878)

Tchaikovsky wrote *Eugene Onegin* in 1878, using a libretto by Konstantin Shilovsky and himself, based on the epic poem by Pushkin. The composer was first drawn to the project by the famous "letter scene" (Act One, Scene Two), in which Tatyana declares her affections for Onegin. Tchaikovsky provided music for this scene—at least the latter part of it—first and built the rest of the work around it, ultimately producing his most popular opera.

If the libretto supplies many opportunities for dramatic scenes, Tchaikovsky's music certainly rises to almost every occasion. As Tatyana writes the letter, for instance, the music suggests her innocence, and seems to convey the act of writing, as well: the oboe singing an animated and typically Tchaikovskian motif, with the clarinet, flute, and horn providing subtle commentary, invokes a feeling of both intimacy and action, a private venting of one's thoughts and passions. Tatyana is given a beautiful and moving theme here, and the whole scene is set afire emotionally. Near the end a horn motif appears, which permeates much of the opera, serving as a sort of motto theme.

Lensky's aria preceding the duel is another highlight of the opera. In fact, his music is probably more attractive than that of Onegin, a character Tchaikovsky rather despised. That is one reason he made Tatyana the central figure in the opera, despite Onegin's protagonist status in Pushkin's poem. There is a fair amount of excellent folk-inspired music here, all, however, in the first act. The first chorus and chorus of the girls collecting berries, as well as the Dance of the Reapers, are all fine examples. It should be noted that Tchaikovsky added an ecossaise for the penultimate scene in the opera in 1885. *—Robert Cummings*

Synopsis:

Act One. In the garden on Madame Larina's country estate, Tatyana and Olga are signing a romantic song ("Slikhali l vi za") indoors while their mother, Madame Larina, and Filipyevna are making jam outside. The song reminds their mother of her own youth and how her romantic dreams ended with an arranged marriage. She and Filipyevna conclude that routine is the substitute for happiness that Heaven sends. Peasants come in, singing, and present her with a ceremonial sheaf marking the end of the harvest season. At her request, they sing again, when Tatyana and Olga come in. The song has made Tatyana dreamy, but Olga instead wants to dance. She sings of the pleasures of being young and carefree ("Ya ne sposobna k grusti"). Madame Larina gently cautions Tatyana against taking books and romantic notions too seriously. Lensky comes to pay a visit and introduces his friend Eugene Onegin. Tatyana is immediately smitten with the sophisticated stranger, while Onegin is puzzled that the poetic Lensky is in love with blandly pretty Olga. He, however, greets an amused Olga ecstatically, since they have been separated for a whole day ("Ya lyublyu vas"), while Onegin asks Tatyana about her life. She tells him she spends her time reading and daydreaming. When it is time to go in to eat, Filipyevna wonders if Tatyana has fallen for Onegin. In her room, late that night, Tatyana is restless and asks Filipyevna to tell the story of her own marriage. Filipyevna describes her fright at being thrust into a family of strangers, but Tatyana stops listening and asks for pen and paper. In the famous letter scene ("Puskai pogibnu ya"), she pours out her infatuation with Onegin, whom she perceives as the man God destined for her and whom she has dreamt of all her life. When Filipyevna comes back in the morning, Tatyana, who has not slept, asks her to deliver the letter. In another part of the garden, servant girls are singing. Tatyana enters, aghast at her reckless behavior and at Onegin's approach. He tells her that if he had been in search of a wife, he could have chosen no better ("Kogda bi zhisn"), but he has no interest in marriage. To her deep humiliation, he tells her such girlish outpourings could lead her to disaster, and leads her out.

Act Two. At the ball given for Tatyana's name day, Onegin is bored and is annoyed by the gossip about him, and decides to punish Lensky for bringing him. He flirts with a receptive Olga and claims every dance with her, even the ones she had promised an increasingly unhappy Lensky. Monsieur Triquet, a French tutor, sings some old-fashioned couplets in praise of Tatyana. After yet another rejection by Olga, Lensky erupts in reproaches for them both and insults Onegin as a would-be seducer. Madame Larina begs him not to cause a scene in her house, and he bitterly responds that her house is where his dreams were shattered. Onegin is secretly ashamed of his heartless behavior, being truly fond of Lensky, but when Lensky, completely out of control, challenges him to a duel, he has to accept. The guests and Larina family comment in horror, some ruing the impulsiveness of young men, Tatyana afraid for their lives, Olga insisting the scene is not *her fault.*

In scene two, Lensky and his second are waiting for Onegin. Lensky wonders where the peaceful days of his youth have gone ("Kuda, kuda") and what will happen. He resigns himself to death, if that is what fate demands. He hopes that Olga will not forget him and calls to her to come to his grave and remember his love. Onegin and his second (his valet) arrive, Onegin carelessly apologizing for the delay. Zaretsky, Lensky's second, pompously lays out the customary rules. Both Onegin and Lensky secretly want to reconcile and laugh off the quarrel, but neither is willing to back down. Onegin shoots before Lensky has fully taken aim, and when his friend falls dead, buries his face in his hands.

Act Three. Into an elegant St. Petersburg salon, years later, Onegin enters. His life is meaningless, as travel does not ease his restlessness, and at home, he is haunted by the image of Lensky's bloodied corpse. The guests comment on the serene beauty of Prince Gremin's wife, and Onegin is astounded to recognize her as Tatyana. She herself is disturbed to see him. Gremin, an old acquaintance and distant relation of Onegin's, tells him with great dignity of his love for Tatyana, who renewed his long-lost youth and brought him happiness. For him, she shines like a pure star amidst the vacuous and self-seeking fashionable crowds. He presents Onegin to her and they chat briefly before Tatyana says she is tired and leaves on her husband's arm. Onegin realizes that now he is as infatuated with this sophisticated beauty as she once was with him ("Uzhel ta samaya"). In scene two, at her home, Tatyana is weeping over the love letters he has sent. When Onegin appears, she asks him why he is pursuing her now, after once rejecting her. Is it because she has become wealthy and prominent in society? He passionately avows his love, and they both regret that they were once so close to being happy together. She tells him to leave her, as her duty is to her husband, but he falls to his knees declaring she is his sole happiness. She admits that she loves him but when he tells her she must come with him, their love gives her no other choice, she firmly refuses, and leaves the room, as he exclaims in despair. —Ann Feeney

Recommended:

○ **Tchaikovsky: Eugene Onegin** / Bychkov (cond.), Hvorostovsky, Focile, Shicoff, Borodina / 1993 / Philips 438235

○ **Tchaikovsky: Eugene Onegin** / Levine (cond.), Allen, Freni, Otter, Shicoff, Burchuladze / DG 423959

Pique Dame (The Queen of Spades), Op. 68 (1890)

Based on a short story by Pushkin and fashioned into a libretto by the composer's brother Modest, *The Queen of Spades* was composed two years Tchaikovsky originally rejected the subject as uninspiring. A commission by the director of the Imperial Theaters, Vsevolozhsky, stirred his creative juices, however, and he finished the opera's three acts and five scenes in five months, making some changes to the libretto along the way.

The story is set in eighteenth century St. Petersburg and focuses on the young officer Gherman, who, in a public garden, confides to his gambler friend Tomsky his love for a strange young woman. Prince Yeletsky enters their company and receives congratulations on his recent engagement. The elderly Countess and her granddaughter, Liza, then enter the garden. It turns out she is the fiancée of the Prince—and also the young woman Gherman is in love with.

Tomsky tells Gherman of the Countess' secret method of gambling, using a certain sequence of three cards that always wins. Gherman is fascinated by the story. In a meeting in Liza's room, Gherman and Liza declare their love for each other. But it is not just love that occupies the young officer's mind subsequently—he becomes obsessed with finding out the winning three-card secret from the Countess. He goes to her quarters, but instead of learning the sequence, he frightens the elderly woman to death. Liza learns of his deed and obsession, but forgives him. In a rendezvous later by a canal, Gherman rejects her and she jumps into the canal.

The Countess' ghost reveals the gambling secret to Gherman, who then goes to the casino and wins twice with it, betting first on three, then on seven. Playing now against Prince Yeletsky, he intends to select the ace, the third of the three cards. But in his anxiety he chooses the queen of spades instead. He loses everything and stabs himself to death.

Tchaikovsky's music is interesting throughout the opera, often thoroughly absorbing. The work was written between the *Fifth* (1888) and *Sixth* (1893) symphonies, and is stylistically related to their intense emotional expressiveness and epic demeanor. The love theme here, first appearing in the second scene and again in the last, is attractive enough but does not sear into the memory like so many others by Tchaikovsky. There is a haunting melancholy theme with a descending contour associated with Gherman (in his first-scene entrance and arioso) that also seems partially to appear at the mention of the three-card sequence.

Tchaikovsky uses eighteenth century pastiche in the opera, probably more than in any other work: consider Liza and Pauline's duet, Tomsky's number in the final scene, and the Countess' "Je crains de lui," snatched from Grétry's *Richard the Lionhearted.* The opera is unusually dramatic and, for a Russian opera, direct and dramatic in its telling. Tchaikovsky portrays the inner lives of all the characters, including some fascinating subsidiary ones encountered on the gambling floor, with deft quick musical strokes. Although not one of the inevitably recurring operas, this fine musical drama has a secure place in the repertoire. In sum, while this opera has flaws that have kept it from the top rank of frequency of performance on opera stages outside Russia, it is rightly regarded as Tchaikovsky's best effort after *Evgeny Onegin.* —*Robert Cummings*

Synopsis:

Act One. The story is set in late eighteenth century St. Petersburg, Russia. Amid a playful springtime scene in Summer Garden, officers Chekalinsky and Surin discuss the melancholy manner of their colleague Hermann (Gherman). When the latter enters, he reveals to Count Tomsky that his recent dispirited state is the result of his falling in love with a beautiful woman, whose name he does not know and whose social rank is likely beyond his reach. Hermann and Tomsky later offer congratulations to Prince Yeletsky on his betrothal.

When Lisa appears with her grandmother, the Countess, Yeletsky identifies her as his betrothed, much to the horror of Hermann, who recognizes her as the woman with whom he is in love. Tomsky then recounts the mysterious past of the Countess: after a terrible losing streak at a casino, she recovered her losses using a secret three-card series given her by the Count of St. Germain. The Countess subsequently divulged the secret combination twice, but cannot for a third time or will die. Hermann overhears the story and determines to learn the secret as a way to steal Lisa from Yeletsky.

Lisa and her confidante Pauline party and sing with friends in Lisa's quarters. Lisa's Governess soon enters to scold them for their uncouth manner of celebration. When all have departed, Lisa wanders out onto the balcony. Below, Hermann attempts to win her over with his romantic outpourings. The Countess calls Lisa to bed, abruptly ending the encounter.

Act Two. At a masked ball, most of the guests go outside to observe the colorful fireworks. Yeletsky and Lisa remain inside, however, the former romancing his betrothed. Hermann appears soon, perusing a message from Lisa requesting a tryst. Surin and Chekalinsky sneak up behind Hermann and taunt him about being the third one to learn the "three-card" secret.

Guests reappear and the Master of Ceremonies announces the staging of a play, *The Faithful Shepherdess.* When it is over, Hermann meets briefly with Lisa, who gives him a key and directions to the Countess' bedroom.

Hermann enters her room and soon the Countess arrives with several attendants. When she is left alone, she goes to bed. Hermann awakens her and begs to learn the "three-card" combination. She remains silent and when he threatens her with his revolver, she dies in terror. Lisa enters and turns aghast both at the sight of the lifeless Countess and in the realization that Hermann had used her. She commands him to leave.

Act Three. In his barracks the tormented Hermann mulls over a letter from the now-forgiving Lisa, who asks for a midnight rendezvous with him. The Countess' ghost suddenly appears, urges Hermann to marry Lisa, then divulges the three-card combination: "three, seven, Ace."

Lisa anxiously awaits Hermann near the Neva river. He arrives there at midnight, but reveals he has learned the three-card secret and must go to the casino. He departs and the suddenly distraught Lisa jumps into the river and drowns.

At the casino, Yeletsky declares he will find luck at cards if he cannot have it at love. Hermann arrives and wagers heavily, beating Chekalinsky first on the "three," then on the "seven." Only Yeletsky will accept his challenge for the final card. It is revealed to be not an ace, but the Queen of Spades, which Hermann sees as the face of the Countess, now mocking in her victory. Overcome with madness, he stabs himself to death. —*Robert Cummings*

Recommended:

○ **Tchaikovsky: Pique Dame** / Gergiev (cond.), Kirov Chorus & Orch. / 1993 / Philips 438141

VOCAL

Six Songs, Op. 6 (1869)

By 1869, Tchaikovsky was off to a good start in what was traditionally a difficult profession. Thanks to the intercession of the Rubinstein brothers and by dint of Tchaikovsky's own late developed but conspicuous talent, the young man had achieved the post of professor of harmony at the newly established Moscow Conservatory. Owing to this security, however modest, almost from the start he began to compose with considerable ease and, even then, striking technique. Among the most notable of Tchaikovsky's works from this year, which also saw the first version of the *Romeo and Juliet Overture*, were the Opus 6 songs, his first cycle which he deemed worthy of an opus number.

In them can be heard the work of a sensitive young person; they share a yearning, anxious character, yet in some cases possess an almost Mendelssohnian restraint. Together they reflect on the melancholy facets of love. The first, "Do not believe, my friend" (Tolstoy) is brooding and fragile, with inflections of Russian folk song. Less restrained is the following "Not a word, O my friend" (Hartmann), already showing the anguished expression of the mature Tchaikovsky. No. 3, "Painfully and sweetly" (Rostopchina) is restrained and cryptic. "A tear trembles," again with Tolstoy text, is more animated, owing to a mercurial accompaniment, yet avoids excessive pathos, as does the serene yet questing "Why?" (Heine). The final song of the set, "None but the lonely heart" (Goethe), unabashedly wears its heart on its sleeve and is one of Tchaikovsky's best-known melodies. It is a compendium of almost all of the composer's salient features and could have been created at almost any point in his life. The soaring passion as the song reaches its final climax is indicative of the command that the composer would have of dramatic effect, even in nonvocal or nontheatrical music. *—Wayne Reisig*

Recommended:

- ○ **Tchaikovsky Romances** / Borodina, Gergieva / 1994 / Philips 442013
- ○ **Tchaikovsky: Songs** / Rodgers, Vignoles / 1992 / Hyperion 66617

Six Songs, Op. 38 (1878)

The Opus 38 Songs of Tchaikovsky came from the period immediately following his brief disastrous marriage, ensuing nervous breakdown, and remarkable quick rebound. The latter was surely helped along by his trip abroad with his brother and the arrival in his life of patroness Nadezhda von Meck, providing for him one of the most curious relationships two human beings have ever shared. Created with renewed fervor and skill, each of the six songs examines a specific aspect of love, yet none with the sarcasm or bitterness one would have expected from a man fresh from the said experience. The passion at times is as deeply felt as that of the contemporary *Fourth Symphony*. It could be that the surfacing intensity, present in so much of Tchaikovsky's music, is the sublimation of lifelong feelings that the composer concealed in a less understanding age.

In each of the songs (the first four of which utilize text by Tolstoy), the music is most convincingly married to text. The first, "Don Juan's Serenade," is striking for its rhythmic pyrotechnics, the effect of rapidly alternating meters ingeniously achieved by displaced accents and bar overlaps. Fiery in temperament, here is the unashamed, hedonistic Don of legend, not the complex figure of Lenau's. The second song, "'Twas in Early Spring," again is rhythmically striking, with 2/4 vocal against 6/8 accompaniment. The mood, however, is very different, being a shared autumnal remembrance of young love. No. 3, "At the Ball," is a deft yet languid waltz, the protagonist in the throes of a love sparked by mere glances exchanged across the dance-floor. This is followed by the animated "Oh, If Only You Could," an earnest enticement to forget a past love and start fresh. The fifth, "A Dead Man's Love" (with lyrics by Lermontov), is macabre even by Romantic Russian standards. After a series of funereal chords with which the song commences, the music becomes as agitated as a lost soul in its depiction of an earthly love so strong that even the glories of the afterlife yields no balm for the pain of departure. The last in the cycle, "Florentine Song" (sometimes called "Pimpinella") bears a text by Tchaikovsky and is in his Italian mode, a lifelong favorite haunt in musical expression as well as his travels. Lyrical and sunny, yet slightly wry, the song finds the suitor unfurling an eloquent overture to his beloved, the song ending with him awaiting her reply. *—Wayne Reisig*

Recommended:

- ○ **Tchaikovsky: Complete Songs Vol. 3** / Kazarnovskaya, Orfenova / 2001 / Naxos 555371
- ○ **My Restless Soul** / Hvorostovsky, Arkadiev / Philips 442536
- ○ **Russian Romances** / Hvorostovsky, Boshnyakovich / 1991 / Philips 432119

Six Songs, Op. 73 (1893)

This was the last song collection by Tchaikovsky, written in his final year while he was working on his tragic *Symphony No. 6*, the *Pathétique*. This Op. 73 group is viewed as one of his more important sets, owing to the composer's advancing expressive language in some of the songs. For example, the second item, "Night," has been viewed as Impressionistic, having elements of a style that Debussy was just then forming. All six works are settings of poems by Danil Maximovich Rathaus (1868–1937), whose mostly sentimental emotions and direct manner worked well with Tchaikovsky's similar musical temperament.

The first of these songs—or Romances, as they are often called—is "We Sat Together." The text tells of a couple who cannot talk to each other to resolve their personal differences. The music is melancholy and slow-paced, although the middle section features much passion and animation. The close returns to the sad mood of the opening. The character of the second song is similar to that of its predecessor, but the emotional pitch here is both more intense and colder—colder because of its starkness and gloom. The text describes a woman's dying, and Tchaikovsky's music perfectly matches its dark emotional thrust.

"This Moonlit Night," No. 3, is brighter and livelier than the preceding songs, but its subject of frustrated love brings a sad close, though the lingering piano accompaniment continues in an upbeat mood. The fourth item, "The Sun Has Set," is a love song full of yearning and passion, and reaching an ecstatic outburst at the end. "On Gloomy Day," despite its title, continues the generally brighter moods heard in the last few songs. Here, in another outpouring of love, the music is effervescent and joyous, if tinged with anxiety. The ebullient melody soars, while the accompaniment is vivacious and colorful throughout.

The last song, "Once More, As Before," offers music returning to the mood in the first two. Gloom pervades and the pacing is slow as the music builds in intensity, finally arriving at a sense of serenity, a sense of resignation, effectively matching those sentiments in the text.

It is the first two and last songs in this group which are probably the most important. A performance of the entire set would last about 15 minutes. *—Robert Cummings*

Recommended:

- ○ **Tchaikovsky: Songs** / Larin, Bekova Sisters / 1995 / Chandos 9428
- ○ **In The Silence Of The Night** / Mishura, Ryvkin / 1996 / VAI Audio 2003

CHAMBER MUSIC

Piano Trio in A minor ("In Memory of a Great Artist"), Op. 50 (1882)

Bearing the inscription "To the memory of a great artist," this trio was dedicated to the recently deceased pianist Nikolai Rubinstein, with whom Tchaikovsky had maintained a difficult friendship. Fittingly, the trio's piano part is quite challenging and often overwhelms the material for violin and cello. Tchaikovsky was not much of a pianist and never realized how difficult his keyboard music could be.

The first movement, "Pezzo elegiaco" (elegiac piece), opens with an expansive motto that will recur throughout the work; the intense, soulful theme is introduced by the cello over a stewing piano accompaniment. The theme then is taken by the violin, soon rejoined in counterpoint by the cello. At length, the piano makes its own statement of the theme. The motto is subsequently fragmented and glued back together with fresh material of a striving, Russian nature. More important new material enters floridly in the piano, offering a slightly brighter outlook but with no less fervor. All this is developed in Tchaikovsky's standard manner, relying on obsessive repetition of thematic elements rather than real transformation of them, although one section offers an extended nostalgic reverie for the strings. The recapitulation is a verbatim repetition of the exposition, except that a second little development section is appended near the end.

The second movement consists of a theme followed by eleven variations. The piano states the theme, an appealingly naive folklike tune, and it is then picked up by the strings. The variations are said to have recalled unspecified scenes from Rubinstein's life; they constitute a series of genre pieces that sometimes freely depart from the theme, although the first variation is essentially a restatement of the theme by the strings. In the second variation, the cello plays the melody again, over nimble counterpoint from the violin and piano. The third is a scherzo for piano, with pizzicato accompaniment. The fourth is a soulful, highly Slavic treatment. In the fifth, the piano evokes a music box or possibly sleigh bells. Sixth comes a light but lengthy waltz, initially led by the cello, although the piano aggressively cuts in at the middle. The seventh variation keeps the theme at home in the piano, while the strings take meandering excursions. The eighth variation is a big, gruff fugue; the ninth, in sharp contrast, is a slow meditation full of gloomy arpeggios. Cheer returns with the tenth variation, a playful mazurka. The eleventh variation actually constitutes the final movement. It is in strict sonata form, and takes off from a treatment of the melody that owes much to the last of Schumann's *Symphonic Etudes* (which Tchaikovsky had orchestrated as a student). All the motifs in this movement are, one way or another, derived from the same theme until the extended coda, where the motto from the first movement bursts onto the scene and carries the trio to a despairing conclusion. *—James Reel*

Recommended:

- ○ **Tchaikovsky: Piano Trio in Am; Mendelssohn: Piano Trio Op49** / Heifetz, Rubinstein, Piatigorsky / RCA 7768
- ○ **David Oistrakh Collection Vol. 6** / Oistrakh, Oborin, Knushevitsky / 2000 / Doremi 7742

Souvenir de Florence, for string sextet in D major, Op. 70 (1887–1890; revised Dec., 1891)

As this work's dates show, Tchaikovsky took awhile to compose this music. It was requested by the St. Petersburg Chamber Music Society for performance in the 1889–1890 season. Tchaikovsky accepted the commission despite his general lack of interest in chamber music. It is scored for string sextet (two each of violins, violas, and cellos). He did not complete it on time because he turned to composition of his opera *Queen of Spades*. An avid traveler, he spent part of winter 1890 in Florence, Italy, to which he had already paid six happy visits. Leaving Russia in

January 1890, he made fast progress on the opera. Having completed it, he finally turned back his string sextet in June 1890, and completed the score by the end of July. His trip to Florence seems to have provided the focus of the work and accounts for its title. The work was premiered in November 1892, following some revisions made due to balance problems.

The music is a bit at odds with the expectations aroused by its title; although there is a sunny mood to it, it is not a musical travelogue. The first movement is a happy and lyrical one, with particularly effective contrast of the main themes of the work in its development section. In its recapitulation Tchaikovsky holds back the first subject until after second subject, using the initial theme to propel the music to a bubbly conclusion. The second movement is in a three-part form following an introduction. It is lyrical in mood, with a particularly haunting effect of shimmering triplets played at the tip of the bows occurring in the middle part. Although in form a scherzo, the moderately-paced third movement has a Brahmsian sense of melancholy which is only relieved by the contrasting trio section. The finale is a rondo-sonata with folk-type melodies and highly interesting contrapuntal treatment of the recurring rondo episode. It has been observed that the final movement, in particular, is orchestrally conceived, rather than in the style of chamber music. The work is, fittingly, often performed by string orchestras, and is actually more effective in that format. *—Joseph Stevenson*

Recommended:

- ○ **Tchaikovsky: Souvenir de Florence; Arensky: Quartet in A minor** / Raphael Ens. / 1993 / Hyperion 66648
- ○ **Tchaikovsky: Serenade for Strings; Souvenir de Florence** / Entremont (cond.), Vienna CO / 1991 / Naxos 550404

String Quartet No. 1 in D major, Op. 11 (1871)

The young Tchaikovsky, barely surviving on his meager salary from the Moscow Conservatory, decided to raise a little money and call attention to his work in early 1871 by presenting a concert of recent compositions. The program was a great success; it consisted of several songs and piano pieces, and, written especially for the occasion, the *String Quartet No. 1.*

The first movement, Moderato e semplice, takes traditional sonata form and features a fuller, richer development than Tchaikovsky generally had managed. The two songlike main themes are similar rhythmically and atmospherically, although the first is more anticipatory and the second is more of an outright serenade.

The second movement, Andante cantabile, is one of this composer's most beloved creations and is often heard arranged for string orchestra as well as for any number of instrumental combinations. The first melody is a simple, melancholy folk song that Tchaikovsky is said to have learned from a carpenter in Kamenka. The second is original, very much a ballad initially sung by the first violin over the cello's descending, chromatic pizzicato notes.

The scherzo, Allegro non tanto e con fuoco, is launched with a forceful theme that nevertheless skips to an almost dancelike rhythm. The movement's trio section is more frolicsome, but carries a harmonic tension that keeps it in line with the earlier material. The finale, Allegro giusto, unravels and reweaves two themes. The first is much brighter and more celebratory than anything that has come before; the second, introduced by the viola, is lyrical and Russian, and its B flat tonality makes an arresting contrast with the D major material it follows.

Tchaikovsky would write two further string quartets (and a one-movement student piece has also survived), but for most music lovers this Opus 11 work is *the* Tchaikovsky quartet, as melodic and emotive as the composer's popular orchestral scores. *—James Reel*

Recommended:

- ○ **Tchaikovsky: String Quartets 1–3; Souvenir de Florence** / Borodin Quartet / 1993 / Teldec 90422
- ○ **Tchaikovsky: Complete String Quartets** / Borodin Quartet / 2000 / Chandos 9871

String Quartet No. 2 in F major, Op. 22 (1874)

On the whole, Tchaikovsky's *String Quartet No. 2* (1874) is a darker work than its popular predecessor. The first movement begins with a melancholy, faintly dissonant Adagio introduction, through which weaves an elaborate violin filigree. The music shifts into Moderato assai, and though the pace picks up, the mood never lifts. The themes could almost double as arias of love and fury (the composer had recently completed his opera *The Oprichnik*); they are generally declaimed by a single instrument, with the other three providing nervous accompaniment. The second movement, Allegro giusto, is a gentle scherzo hobbling along in an irregular 7/4 rhythm (two bars in 6/8 followed by one in 9/8), characteristic of much Russian folk music. The central trio provides a charming waltz episode, with a strong accent on the second beat. The opening material returns, now marked con fuoco, concluding the movement at a slightly higher dramatic pitch.

The Andante ma non tanto is a rondo that begins with a lament (which will return to unify the movement), summons the courage for a more vigorous second section, and ultimately fades into a wistful ending. The Allegro con moto finale is happier stuff, six minutes crammed with a cornucopia of themes and variants, most of them bouncing over a galloping rhythm. The movement includes a little fugue derived from the opening theme, builds excitement with every new episode, and concludes with an exultant coda. *—James Reel*

Recommended:

- ○ **Tchaikovsky: Complete String Quartets** / Borodin Quartet / 2000 / Chandos 9871

String Quartet No. 3 in E flat minor, Op. 30 (1876)

Though Tchaikovsky wrote his *String Quartet No. 3* (1876) at about the same time as his *Piano Concerto No. 1* (1874–75) and the ballet *Swan Lake* (1875–16), the chamber work never achieved the popularity of those beloved compositions. Perhaps this is because the quartet is particularly grim music, written in memory of the composer's friend Ferdinand Laub, a violinist who had participated in the premieres of Tchaikovsky's two earlier string quartets.

The elegiac tone is set from the very beginning of the huge first movement, in the two funereal themes of the Andante sostenuto introduction. After this outpouring of grief, the movement's main Allegro moderato is marked by conflict between an impetuous first theme and a more lullaby-like second theme that looks forward to an aria in the last act of *Eugene Onegin* (1877–78). The movement is rounded out by a return of the introductory material.

The second movement, Allegretto vivo e scherzando, is a miniature by comparison. The outer sections are anxious and restive, but the middle section smooths things out a bit, with the viola taking a prominent role.

The third movement, a grief-laden Andante funebre e doloroso, is the quartet's heart. The commanding initial chords are followed by a mournful dirge. The repetition of this theme is followed in turn by a bridge passage evoking Russian Orthodox chant, and then a somber second subject. After a brief reappearance of the first theme comes a new tune that is quickly nudged aside by the chant material. This uncharacteristically Russian music dominates the movement until its end.

The bold, invigorating finale eases the tension without recourse to optimism. Both main themes echo the folk music of southern Russia, maintaining a determinedly vigorous pace to the end, save for a brief and shattering reminiscence of the slow movement. *—James Reel*

Recommended:

- ○ **Tchaikovsky: String Quartets 1 & 2** / Kontra Quartet / 1992 / Bis 642
- ○ **Tchaikovsky: Complete String Quartets** / Borodin Quartet / 2000 / Chandos 9871

KEYBOARD

Children's Album: 24 Easy Pieces, Op. 39 (1878)

Tchaikovsky intended these 24 easy pieces to be played "by" children, rather than "for" them. They're extremely short, all but two clocking in at well under a minute.

No. 1 is a slow, tender "Morning Prayer" in 3/4 time. Things pick up with the second item, a moderately-paced but stimulating "Winter Morning." No. 3 is a brisk, highly staccato 3/8 picture of a "Little Horseman." No. 4 is "Mama," an expressive, lingering portrait. A balance for such feminine material comes with No. 5, a sprightly "March of the Wooden Soldiers." All may be quiet on the battle front, but there's trouble back home. The sixth piece, "The Sick Doll," is a languishing Lento in G minor. The unfortunate sequel is "Dolly's Funeral," a C minor march marked, appropriately, Grave. Something of a wake comes with No. 8, a lively waltz. Then, the nursery being a fickle place, "The New Doll" arrives in a charming Andantino movement.

A series of folk-inspired pieces begins with No. 10, a D minor Mazurka. No. 11 is a simple, extremely short (ten bars) "Russian Folksong," one that Tchaikovsky had included in the 50 Russian folk songs he'd arranged for piano duet in 1869. No. 12 is a sentimental "Peasant's Song," in which Tchaikovsky evokes a concertina wheezing back and forth between two chords. No. 13 is called, generically, "Folk Song" (Russian Dance), and employs the same tune Glinka used in his orchestral *Kamarinskaya.* No. 14 is a rousing little polka. The next piece heads south; it's a lively "Italian Ditty" with the staccato oom-pah-pah accompaniment one hears in many early and middle Verdi arias. No. 16 swings northwest for a placid, antique-sounding, G minor "French Melody." No. 17 is a "German Song" with a hint of yodeling, and for No. 18 it's back to Italy for a "Neapolitan Dance Tune," a stripped-down version of part of the "Neapolitan Dance" in *Swan Lake.*

No. 19 returns to the nursery at bedtime with an evocative C major "Old Nurse's Song." When the lights go out, the witch "Baba-Yaga" appears in E minor—yet she seems to have arrived from Liadov's quirky little orchestral piece of the same name rather than from the terrifying penultimate movement of Mussorgsky's *Pictures at an Exhibition.* No. 21 brings lovely, melodic "Sweet Dreams," the set's longest piece. Soon it's time to wake up to the "Song of the Lark," a relatively bravura piece full of right-hand arabesques. It's Sunday morning, as we'll soon discover, and upon leaving the house we encounter "The Organ-Grinder," Tchaikovsky picked up this Moderato 3/4 tune from a Venetian street singer and would soon incorporate it into the middle section of the *"Rêverie interrompue"* closing his Opus 40 set of piano pieces. Finally, No. 24 finds us "In Church"—Russian Orthodox, of course, as we can tell from the E minor chanting and low pedal-point tolling of a bell toward the end.—*James Reel*

Recommended:

○ **Schumann: Kinderszenen; Tchaikovsky: Album for the Young; Debussy: Children's Corner Suite** / Biret / 1993 / Naxos 550885

○ **Tchaikovsky: Children's Album; Piano Sonata in G** / Pletnev / Melodiya 1000005

Dumka, in C minor, Op. 59 (1886)

Though only a fraction as long as the composer's ambitious *Sonata in G major,* Tchaikovsky's *Dumka in C minor,* Op. 59 (1886) is one of the composer's most successful piano works. The dumka, a narrative Slavic folk song that veers abruptly from melancholy to exhilaration, was a source of inspiration for a number of composers; its best-known incarnation is probably that in Dvořák's popular *"Dumky" Trio,* Op. 65 (1890–91). Despite its subtitle, "Russian rustic scene," Tchaikovsky's version of the dumka lacks a detailed program. It begins with an Andantino cantabile ballad that may derive from a Russian folk song. The theme undergoes some rudimentary development before giving way to an eccentric, exciting con anima section, followed by a more relaxed passage, a bravura cadenza, and a hammering Moderato con fuoco. Relief arrives with two broader passages, Andante meno mosso and Adagio, diminuendo. The opening ballad sneaks back in, very quietly at first but marking its departure with three loud, abrupt chords. The work's virtuosic demands have attracted flamboyant pianists through the years, but the work has never quite achieved repertory status; still, the *Dumka* remains Tchaikovsky's most outstanding solo work for concert rather than salon use. —*James Reel*

Recommended:

○ **Stephen Hough's New Piano Album** / Hough / 1999 / Hyperion 67043

Morceaux, Op. 19 (1873)

This odd collection brings together five innocuous genre pieces with a substantial theme-and-variations set. The first item, known bilingually as "Abend-Träumerei" and "Rêverie du Soir," is a slow, G minor arabesque in 3/4 time, with a lyrical middle section. Next comes a "Scherzo humoristique" in D major, an effervescent piece in 3/8 with a more serious yet improvised-sounding middle section, full of short, obsessively repeated melody fragments that seem to want to burst into a folk song. The third piece, "Feuillet d'Album," is an abbreviated, highly lyrical item simple enough for student pianists; it's in standard ABA form, but the B section is barely discernible from the rest. Fourth is a Nocturne marked Andante sentimentale, a haunting, hesitant soliloquy interrupted by a more flowing midsection. A miniature cadenza leads to a reprise of the first section, now given a much more ornate treatment. Next is a B flat Capriccioso in 2/4 time, which Tchaikovsky originally thought to work into a symphony. The main material is quite poignant, but contrast arrives with the middle section, a jaunty Allegro vivacissimo in D minor.

The sixth piece consists of a modest, expressive 16-bar theme in 3/4 time, followed by 12 variations and a coda. The first variation nudges the theme forward only slightly. The second flows more smoothly under triplets in the right hand. Variation 3 brings outright brilliance to the proceedings, intensified with the bravura staccato chords in Variation 4. The fifth variation is an amorous Andante, but the sixth brings back a staccato snap. The seventh could be the chordal outline of a hymn, while the eighth is an unexpectedly exultant waltz in D minor. Variation 9 turns the theme into a mazurka, complete with miniature cadenza. Variation 10 brings back the theme pretty much intact under florid passagework. The next variation is an exuberant Allegro brillante in the style of Schumann. Variation 12 features a tonic pedal-point in the bass all the way through (looking ahead to a technique Tchaikovsky would employ in a movement of his *"Polish" Symphony*). The whole thing ends with a virtuosic presto coda, driving toward a final crowd-pleasing crescendo. —*James Reel*

Recommended:

○ **Great Pianists: Andrei Gavrilov** / Gavrilov / 1999 / Philips 456787

Morceaux, Op. 51 (1882)

These lighthearted salon pieces were the first piano music to enter Tchaikovsky's catalog since 1878. Half are waltzes, and all are dedicated to women.

No. 1 is a flashy "Valse de salon," with rippling outer sections; the middle portion is a halting, mainly chordal sequence that returns to the main matter with a little cadenza. The overall effect is quite brilliant.

No. 2 is titled "Polka peu dansant." This B minor piece has a hesitant, Chopinesque quality in its A section, but the B section features a surging melody with restless accompaniment that is echt-Tchaikovsky. The A section returns, followed by a coda in which the B section's broken-chord accompaniment underlies a different melody.

No. 3 is a chromatic, improvisatory "Menuetto scherzo," extremely tangled and frisky. This sandwiches a trio section of right-hand phrase fragments over abbreviated left-hand runs.

No. 4, "Natha Valse," seems to be a musical portrait of its dedicatee, Natha Plesskaya. The outer sections are gentle, sentimental, yet playful; the middle section is more outgoing, marked Animato.

The fifth piece, "Romance," apparently portrays Tchaikovsky's niece Vera. More flowing and graceful than its predecessor, the piece begins with one of the composer's favorite designations, Andante cantabile. The middle section is more ornate and assertive, with the melody constantly whipping around on itself in a quick five-note turn. A miniature recitative leads back to the A section.

No. 6 is a "Valse sentimentale," highly Chopinesque in its sweet melancholy; the middle section is faster and more brusque. The repeat of the first part now leaves room for a short improvised cadenza just before the end. —*James Reel*

Recommended:

○ **Tchaikovsky: Piano Music Vol. 1** / Yablonskaya / 1995 / Naxos 553063

Piano Sonata in G major, Op. 37 (1878)

The "Grande Sonate" (1878) is Tchaikovsky's only "official" piano sonata; he never intended to publish his student *Sonata in C sharp minor* (1865), though that work was posthumously issued as the composer's Op. 80. The *Sonata in G major,* however, is a fully mature work written during the same period as masterpieces like the *Fourth Symphony* (1877–78) and the *Violin Concerto* (1878). Still, the sonata is somewhat less successful than a work like the Violin Concerto, principally because in aspiring to produce a highly pianistic, virtuoso showpiece, Tchaikovsky failed to capitalize on his greatest strength, a singular sense of melody.

The main theme of the first movement, Moderato e risoluto, is an undeniably flashy and heroic statement characterized by bold hammered chords. The second subject, marked Tranquillo, offers some lyrical relief. These two subjects pass through several unusual modulations and meager elaborations in the long development section. The slightly truncated recapitulation is dominated to the end by the forceful, obsessive first theme.

The second movement, Andante non troppo, quasi moderato, again begins chordally, but this time the theme is far more meditative. It alternates, quasi-rondo-style, with two other sections; one, a highly Schumannesque episode in dotted rhythms, is more radiant, the other, ardently lyrical in Tchaikovsky's distinctive fashion.

The brief Scherzo begins with a robust if somewhat gangly subject marked by animated passagework. The more nimble trio section features a melody atop a series of deft runs in the left hand.

The finale, a bravura rondo, hearkens to the hectoring manner of the first movement. Marked Allegro vivace, it launches with declamatory, syncopated chords and swirling runs, while a lighter staccato-chord motif tries to insinuate itself into the texture. After a lyrical episode, the first section, now stripped down, returns, only to give way to the lyrical material, this time presented more floridly and expansively. It builds to a climax, whereupon massive octaves thrust toward a recapitulation of the main theme. As the music to all appearances rushes headlong toward an extroverted conclusion, it unexpectedly pulls back to briefly recall briefly the quieter material, and the sonata ends rather abruptly with a short sequence of chords. —*James Reel*

Recommended:

○ **Tchaikovsky: Piano Sonatas** / Howard / 1997 / Hyperion 16939

○ **Sviatoslav Richter: Tchaikovsky & Mussorgsky** / Richter / 1995 / Melodiya 29469

The Seasons, Op. 37b (1875–1876)

The suffix "bis" at the end of an opus number often means the piece is an arrangement or adaptation of another work. In this case it was appended by Tchaikovsky's publisher, linking it to the then-recently published *Grand Sonata in G Major for piano,* Op. 37, although no sound musical relation exists between the two works. Here, Tchaikovsky wrote 12 separate pieces as part of a commission from Nikolai Bernard, publisher of the monthly music magazine, *Novelliste.* The composer was to provide an appropriate piece for each of the 12 issues of the magazine, a work reflecting feelings or images associated with the month in the title.

January, subtitled "At the Fireside," has an intimate mood, tinged with regret and gentle playfulness, and featuring an attractive Schumann-esque main theme. February ("Carnival") is festive and joyous, the music jaunty and hardly divulging images of snow and dark nights. March ("The Song of the Lark") reverts to a mood similar to that heard in January, but featuring sparser textures and a greater sense of melancholy, as though a feeling hovers that winter will not soon end. April ("Snowdrop") is bright and seems to usher in spring, albeit a spring with a few clouds and rain storms.

The fifth piece here, May ("Starlit nights"), is sweet in its ascending arpeggios, though its theme turns stately on the lower register of the keyboard. The brief middle section is lively but does not break the generally intimate feeling. June ("Barcarolle") has become one of the most popular pieces from the set: its melody is memorable, sounding Chopin-esque in its sweet gloom and mixture of happiness and sadness. July ("The Song of the Reapers") is the briefest of the 12 pieces, but manages several mood swings, moving from the proud to the industrious, then to the playful, maintaining a joyous demeanor throughout.

August ("Harvest") is busy and a bit hectic in the outer sections, but the central portion is simple and lyrical, unhurried and calm. September ("The Hunt") is regal in the fanfare-like music of the first part, but then turns demure for a time while the more garish elements from the opening gradually infiltrate to retake center stage. October ("Autumn Song") is another popular piece, with a life of its own apart from this set. Its slow main theme is melancholy, featuring a refrainlike phrase of mostly ascending notes that is the heart of its sad nature.

November ("Troika") is hardly less popular than June or October. It is bright in mood and direct in its expressive language, and offers a playful, mischievous middle section. December ("Christmas") is almost childlike in its charming waltz, the music seeming to yearn for orchestral dress and placement in one of the composer's ballets. Typical performances of this whole set can range from 35 to 45 minutes. *—Robert Cummings*

Recommended:

○ **Tchaikovsky: The Seasons** / Ashkenazy / Decca 466562

○ **Tchaikovsky: The Seasons; 6 Pieces Op21** / Pletnev / 1994 / Virgin 45042

○ **Sergei Rachmaninoff: In Concert 2** / Rachmaninov / 1990 / Klavier 11027

Souvenir de Hapsal, Op. 2 (1867)

Tchaikovsky's *Souvenir de Hapsal,* Op. 2 (1867) is a set of three pieces that takes its title from the Baltic seaside town where Tchaikovsky completed the music during a summer holiday. The first piece, "Ruines d'un chateau" (Ruins of a Castle), opens nostalgically in E minor, Adagio mysterioso, and closes with the same material after a blithe central Allegro section. The second piece is a rather Schumannesque Scherzo in F major with a florid, lyrical middle section. The final piece, in F major, is Tchaikovsky's earliest "hit tune," "Song without Words." Its first section is marked grazioso e cantabile, but the music seems to want to dance rather than sing. A brief, more declamatory section follows before the earlier material returns in wisps rather than in a full reprise.*—James Reel*

Recommended:

○ **Tea Time** / Nel / 1995 / ESS.A.Y. 1042

CHORAL

Liturgy of St. John Chrysostom, Op. 41 (1878)

In Russian Orthodox ceremony, the accepted rite is that compiled by St. John Chrysostom (344–407) which is written and sung in "Old," or "Church," Slavonic. As with its Latin counterpart in the Western church, the mass, the St. John Liturgy provides opportunites for fresh settings by professional composers for use in the Russian Orthodox Church. Pyotr Tchaikovsky's turn came in 1878, although the commission came through his publisher, Juergenson, rather than through the Russian Orthodox Church itself. Tchaikovsky was very pleased to undertake this commission, as in his own words "the liturgy of St. John Chrysostom is one of the most exalted works of art. Anyone following the liturgy of the service attentively, trying to comprehend the meaning of each ceremony, will be stirred to the very depth of his being." Tchaikovsky completed his setting in 1880, and, after a trial run-through with a chorus from the Moscow Conservatory (which the composer regarded as "one of the happiest moments of my career as an artist"), the work was given a concert performance in Moscow in December 1880.

Tchaikovsky's *St. John Liturgy* was a resounding success with the Russian public, but not so with the Russian Orthodox Church. The Church hierarchy rejected it not on musical grounds, but on its initial place of venue, since they deemed it inappropriate for the liturgy to be given in a public concert and subject to applause. Tchaikovsky was deeply pained by the official condemnation of his work by the Church, but in 1883 the newly crowned Tsar of Russia, Alexander III, asked Tchaikovsky for more sacred music, a request that the composer happily complied with a handful of hymns and other settings. Tchaikovsky's attitude in his sacred music was to "preserve these old chants in their original form" and to "help restore the original character and style of our Church music." His relatively conservative approach resulted in music which was built to last, and happily, they have prevailed, as pieces from the Tchaikovsky liturgy have in time become some of the most frequently performed liturgical music in Russia. Its lasting appeal stems, in part, from the aspect of purely musical personality that Tchaikovsky was unable to subserve to the liturgical text, and in individual pieces, such as the lovely "We Sing Thee," the unmistakable personal stamp of Tchaikovsky ultimately wins out. *—Uncle Dave Lewis*

Recommended:

○ **Tchaikovsky: Liturgy of St. John Chrysostom** / Hobdych (cond.), Mezhulin, Ovdiy, Kiev Chamber Chorus / 1997 / Naxos 553854

Alexander Tcherepnin

b. Jan. 20, 1899, St. Petersburg, Russia, **d.** Sep. 29, 1977, Paris, France

Composer

Alexander Tcherepnin was a Russian-born composer, pianist and conductor known for his cosmopolitan style that included influences from France and the Far East. Tcherepnin's father, Nikolay Tcherepnin, was an important composer and conductor, and it was his influence and teaching that formed Alexander's early training. In 1921 Tcherepnin's family fled the aftermath of the Bolshevik revolution, and the young composer began his career in their adopted home of Paris. From the beginning he favored new and experimental techniques, and during the 1920s he fomulated his own 9-tone scale (now called the Tcherepnin Scale), consisting of three overlapping major and minor tetrachords; this allowed for the simultaneous sounding of major and minor sonorities, which the composer found particularly satisfying. He also developed a new form of counterpoint—called "interpoint"—which allows for the combination of several self-contained contrapuntal structures. These musical devices were not so much abstract concepts as attempts on the part of the emerging composer to codify his very instinctive and individual approaches to sound and rhythm. These tendencies had already been expressed in early works, such as the bitonal *Pièces sans titres,* Op. 7, from 1913.

From 1934 through 1937, he toured the Far East, using Tokyo, Shanghai and Peking alternately as bases of operation; he would have considerable influence as a teacher of both Japanese and Chinese composers of the period. He also met his wife, the pianist Lee Hsien Ming while in China. The newly-married couple returned to Paris in 1938, but the turmoil of World War II put a stop to musical activities. Immediately following the war, however, he resumed his creative output, eventually relocating to Chicago in 1950, and finally settling in New York in 1964.

Although Tcherepnin's style was Russian at heart, it lacked much of the Romantic melancholy and overt nationalism seen in other Russian-born composers. Instead, his earlier works are characterized by a French leanness and clarity and an emphasis on the clean articulation of form. Some, such as in the *Second Piano Concerto* (1923), bear a similarity to the works of Prokofiev in their motoric rhythms. Tcherepnin himself considered his style to be "Eurasian." Notable works include the *Piano Concerto 4* (1947), the *Cinq études de concert* and his opera *The Farmer and the Nymph* (1952)—all of which have a distinctly oriental sound—and the *Fifth Piano Concerto* (1963) and *Serenade for Strings* (1964), both of which suggest aggressive exploration of new concepts at the end of his life. Tcherepnin produced a wide variety of works in every genre, eventually even incorporating electronic elements in his radio score *The Story of Ivan the Fool.* *—AMG*

Overview of Works (1918–1977)

Born in St. Petersburg, composer and pianist Alexander Tcherepnin (1899–1977) spent the majority of his life abroad, becoming a United States citizen in 1958. The son of pianist Nikolay Tcherepnin, he moved with his family after the Russian Revolution to Tbilisi, then to Paris in 1921. Taught first by his father and then by a succession of Russian pedagogues, he demonstrated a gift for composing even at a very early age. While in Tbilisi, he became keenly interested in Georgian folk music and, later, chose to describe himself as a "Eurasian" composer. His first works, written for piano, were published before he emigrated. Upon arrival in Paris, Tcherepnin entered the Conservatoire to study both performance and composition.

Initial modeling on the music of Prokofiev gave way to other influences. As early as 1918, in his *Sonatine Romantique,* Tcherepnin fashioned a nine-step scale based on hexachords that could be reshaped into some 36 variations. Winning the Schott competition in 1925 with his *Concerto de camera* significantly broadened his reputation. The bold and ethnic music-based *Magna Mater* for orchestra (1926), demonstrated Tcherepnin's ability to create spectacular effects on a larger scale. His *Symphony No. 1* (1927) employs conspicuous percussive effects. Completed in 1932, his *Third Piano Concerto* reflects use of what he called "interpoint," the weaving together of countermelodies.

In 1923, the famed ballerina Anna Pavlova commissioned from him a ballet, *Ajanta's Frescoes,* performed in London later that same year. Subsequent ballets were *Training* (premiered in Vienna in 1934), *Trepak* (New York, 1938), *La légende de Razine* (Paris, 1941), and *Le déjeuner sur l'herbe,* an adaptation from music by Lanner (Paris, 1945).

Trips to the Near East in 1931 and to China in 1934 resulted in a further enrichment of Tcherepnin's musical language. He remained in China from 1934 to 1937 to study classical Chinese music and in 1938 married pianist Lee Hsien Ming shortly before returning to Paris. There, the composer set about assembling his *Anthology of Russian Music* and also experimented with different instrumentation in smaller forms, such as his *Sonatine Sportive for saxophone and piano* (1938).

In 1949, Tcherepnin accepted an offer to teach at DePaul University in Chicago. His *Second Symphony* was premiered by Raphael Kubelik and the Chicago Symphony Orchestra in 1952. Examples of Tcherepnin's continuing experimentation in composition may be found in his *Divertimento* (1957), his *Third* and *Fourth Symphonies* (the latter finished in 1957), his *Piano Concerto No. 5* (1963), and within the diamond-point textures of his *Serenade for Strings,* completed in 1963.

Tcherepnin also wrote several operas, the first of which, *01-01,* had its premiere in Weimar in 1928. *Die Hochzeit der Sobeide* featured a libretto based on the work of the esteemed Austrian writer Hugo von Hofmannsthal and was first presented in Vienna in 1933. His final opera, *The Farmer and the Nymph* (1952), reflects Tcherepnin's affection for Chinese music. *—Erik Eriksson*

Recommended:

- ○ **Tcherepnin: Concert Etudes; Message; Sonatas; Ten Bagatelles** / Braden / Newport Classic 85521
- ○ **Tcherepnin: Complete Music for Cello and Piano** / Tozer, Ivashkin / 1999 / Chandos 9770
- ○ **Tcherepnin: Symphonies 1 & 2; Piano Concerto 5** / Shui (cond.), Ogawa, Singapore SO / 1999 / Bis 1017
- ○ **Tcherepnin: Symphonies 3 & 4; Piano Concerto 6** / Shui (cond.), Ogawa, Singapore SO / 1999 / Bis 1018
- ○ **Tcherepnin: Narcisse et Echo** / Rozhdestvensky (cond.), Hague Residentie Orch. / 1998 / Chandos 9670

Dame Kiri Te Kanawa

b. Mar. 6, 1944, Gisborne, New Zealand
Soprano

New Zealand born soprano Kiri Te Kanawa is of Maori descent. Her earliest vocal studies were with Sister Maria Leo in Auckland. She won the *Melbourne Sun* contest and went to London where she studied with Vera Rozsa at the London Opera Center. It was there that she first appeared on stage as the second lady in *Die Zauberflöte* of Mozart. In 1969, she sang Elena in Rossini's *La donna del lago* at the Camden Festival. In 1970, she made her debut at the Royal Opera, Covent Garden as Xenia in *Boris Godunov* and the following year she captured the public attention as the Countess in *Le nozze di Figaro*, a role for which she became world famous. Her American debut came that summer at the Santa Fe Opera, again as the Countess, as she was for her San Francisco Opera debut in 1972. She was soon singing at all of the major opera houses of Europe adding roles in *Don Giovanni*, *Cosi fan tutte*, and *Die Zauberflöte* to her Mozart repertoire. Her Metropolitan Opera debut in 1974 as Desdemona in *Otello* came on only a few hours notice when she substituted for the ailing Teresa Stratas. Her other Verdi roles include Amelia in *Simon Boccanegra* and Violetta in *La Traviata*. Her primary roles in the French repertoire were Micaëla in *Carmen* and Marguerite in *Faust*. The Houston Grand Opera was the site of her first *Arabella* in 1977 and since then she has made a specialty of Strauss' aristocratic ladies including the Marschallin in *Der Rosenkavalier* and the Countess in *Capriccio*. She was able to display her comic side with performances of Johann Strauss' *Die Fledermaus*. Her appearances in the operas of Puccini have been infrequent but she was a lovely Mimì. Many critics found her *Tosca* lacking the dramatic edge the role requires, but she always sang the role beautifully. Her appearances at the festivals at Salzburg and Glyndebourne are always highlights of the season.

Te Kanawa has earned fame also as a recitalist. Her programs included songs of Purcell, Schubert, Fauré, Canteloube, Liszt, and, of course, Strauss. She often included Maori folk songs as part of these programs or as encores. In concert she sang the *Vier Letzte Lieder* of Strauss and Mozart's *Exsultate jubilate*. Perhaps her most famous appearance was at the wedding of Prince Charles and Lady Diana Spencer at Westminster Abbey in 1981 singing "Let the bright seraphim" from Handel's *Samson*. The following year she was made a Dame Commander of the Order of the British Empire.

The voice of Kiri Te Kanawa is a lovely bright soprano, with great ease and beauty in the upper register. The wonderful legato phrasing and good technique have served her well in in many Mozart roles. She displays a wonderful expansive style which is required by the Strauss roles she performs. She has rarely tried to move her voice beyond its natural limits and this has provided her with a long, successful career. Her many recordings give an excellent indication of the finer points of her performances and she has recorded most of her important interpretations. Several of her important roles have been documented on video which allows the public to remember the totality of her performances. Kiri Te Kanawa will have a special place in the hearts of Mozart and Strauss enthusiasts as long her recordings and videos exist. *—Richard LeSueur*

Recommended:

- ○ **Canteloube: Chants D'Auvergne; Villa-Lobos: Bachianas brasileiras 5** / Tate (cond.), Te Kanawa, English CO / 1995 / London 444995
- ○ **Kiri: A Portrait** / Te Kanawa, etc. / 2004 / Decca 000186302
- ○ **Mozart: Mass in C minor; Ave Verum Corpus** / Marriner (cond.), Te Kanawa, Otter, Johnson, Lloyd, Academy of St. Martin-in-the-Fields / 1994 / Philips 438999
- ○ **Classics** / Te Kanawa, etc. / 1993 / Philips 434725
- ○ **Strauss: Die Fledermaus** / Previn (cond.), Te Kanawa, Krause, Fassbaender, Leech Vienna PO / 1991 / Philips 432157

Renata Tebaldi

b. Feb. 1, 1922, Pesaro, Italy, **d.** Dec. 19, 2004
Soprano

Renata Tebaldi faced great physical difficulties when she contracted polio at the age of three. Overcoming her disability, she later studied voice at the Arrigo Boito Conservatory in Parma with the great soprano Carmen Melis. Her first public appearance came in 1944 as Elena in Boito's *Mefistofele* at the *Teatro Municipale* in Rovigo. That same year she repeated the role in Parma and Venice. Arturo Toscanini heard her and asked her to participate in the reopening of the Teatro alla Scala in Milan in 1946. She also sang the Verdi *Requiem* there that year, as well as Mimì in *La bohème* and Eva in *Die Meistersinger* (in Italian). From 1949 to 1954, she sang frequently at La Scala, but she left over bitter feelings regarding Maria Callas, her only real rival as prima donna of the company. During this time, she also sang regularly in many of the important opera houses in Italy. She was also heard in South America and was a favorite in Buenos Aires and Rio de Janeiro. In 1950, she debuted at the Royal Opera, Covent Garden in London as Desdemona in *Otello* and at the San Francisco Opera as Aida. She was a regular guest at the Lyric Opera of Chicago. In 1955, she made her Metropolitan Opera debut as Desdemona and remained a favorite of the New York public for the next 20 years. She sang most her important roles in New York including Mimì in *La bohème*, Maddalena in *Andrea Chenier*, *Tosca*, *Aida*, Violetta in *La Traviata*, Manon in *Manon Lescaut*, *Adriana Lecouvreur*, *La Gioconda*, and Alice Ford in *Falstaff*. These are the same roles that she sang at opera houses in Vienna, Berlin, Paris, Barcelona, and Amsterdam. In the early years of her career, Tebaldi sang in many operas which she was not to repeat later including Handel's *Giulio Cesare*, Rossini's *L'Assedio di Corinto*, Verdi's *Giovanna d'Arco*, Wagner's *Lohengrin* and *Tannhäuser*, Mozart's *Don Giovanni* (Donna Elvira), and Spontini's *Olympia* and *Agnes di Hohenstaufen*.

Besides her work in opera, Tebaldi appeared in recital and in concerts. Her recital programs consisted primarily of Italian songs and operatic arias. On the concert stage, besides the Verdi *Requiem* she also sang Mozart's *Requiem*, Rossini's *Stabat Mater* and Bach's *St. Matthew Passion*.

Tebaldi's voice was a very powerful spinto soprano of great beauty. She was able to sustain a long lyric line with little trouble and in the early years of her career she exhibited good control of florid passages. The extreme top of the range was lovely when singing softly, but tended to lose pitch when sung at full volume. Toscanini considered her voice one of the most beautiful in the twentieth century, and early in her career some critics felt that she was slighting the drama. She went through a vocal crisis in the early 1960s, but returned having restudied her voice and added more dramatic roles such as Gioconda and Minnie in *La fanciulla del west* to her repertoire and at the same time becoming a more intense actress. She was very careful about the roles she sang and how often she would sing. Rudolf Bing, manager of the Metropolitan Opera is quoted saying that "Tebaldi has dimples of steel," a sentiment echoed by many other managers. Her many recordings document the range of repertoire she sang and the great artistry she displayed. *—Richard LeSueur*

Recommended:

- ○ **A Tebaldi Fesival** / Tebaldi, etc. / 1997 / London 452456
- ○ **Grandi Voci: Renata Tebaldi** / Tebaldi, etc. / 1993 / London 440408
- ○ **Puccini: La Bohème** / Erede (cond.), Tebaldi, Corena, Palma, Guden, Chorus & Orch. of St. Cecilia Academy / 1993 / London 440233
- ○ **Puccini: Madama Butterfly** / Serafin (cond.), Tebaldi, Bergonzi, Cossotto, Mercuriali, Chorus & Orch. of St. Cecilia Academy / 1999 / London 452594

Georg Philipp Telemann

b. Mar. 14, 1681, Magdeburg, Germany, **d.** Jun. 25, 1767, Hamburg, Germany
Composer: Chamber Music, Concerto, Orchestral, Vocal

Georg Philipp Telemann was generally considered the most important German composer of his day, but his reputation faded soon after his death. His enormous output included at least 31 cantata cycles, numerous operas, concertos for various instruments, oratorios, songs, countless works for civic occasions and church services, passions, serenades, suites, and abundant keyboard and chamber music. Unfortunately, many of these works have been lost. Telemann's inevitable revival did not come until the 1920s, but it would continue into the new millennium. There are similarities in his works to the melodic styles of Bach, and Handel.

Telemann was born in 1681, in Magdeburg. His father was a Lutheran deacon who died in 1685, leaving his wife to care for their three children. As a boy growing up in Magdeburg, the youth showed remarkable talent in music. He studied under the highly-respected Kantor Benedict Christiani, at the Old City School. Telemann, who would remain largely self-taught throughout life, quickly learned to play the flute, violin, and various keyboard instruments. He began to write music well before he reached his teens, turning out short instrumental works and arias, and working on an opera, *Sigismundus*, at age 12.

Telemann was sent away to Zellerfeld in 1694 to study under the guidance of Caspar Calvoer, who encouraged the youth in composition and musical performance. Telemann would eventually become proficient on the viola da gamba, transverse flute, oboe, trombone, double bass, and other instruments.

At the age of 20, the composer resolved to study law in Leipzig, but a chance meeting in Halle with the 16-year-old Georg Friedrich Handel appears to have drawn him back to music. Telemann soon began writing cantatas for a church service in Leipzig and quickly became a local celebrity. In 1702, he assumed directorship of the Leipzig Opera. Over the next three years he wrote four operas specifically for performance there.

Telemann exhibited a certain restlessness in his career. He was Kapellmeister in Sorau, now part of Poland (1705–08), and served at the court in Eisenach (1708–12). In 1712, he accepted the appointments in Frankfurt of Kapellmeister at the Church of the Barefoot Friars and director of municipal music. His personal life was hardly less settled: in 1709 he married Amalie Eberlin, who died just two years later in childbirth, and in 1714 he married Maria Katharina Textor, who would abandon him for a Swedish officer.

In 1721 Telemann's opera, *Der geduldige Socrates* was performed in Hamburg. That same year, Hamburg's officials offered Telemann the positions of Kantor of the Johanneum and musical director of the city's principal churches. Telemann accepted knowing he was obliged to write two cantatas every Sunday, a new Passion every year, various other religious works, and music for civic events. He not only met his obligations, but in 1722 also accepted the appointment of director of the Hamburg Opera, serving until its 1738 closure.

In the 1740s, and until about 1755, Telemann focused less on composition, turning instead toward the study of music theory. He wrote many oratorios in the mid-1750s, including *Donnerode* (1756), *Das befreite Israel* (1759), and *Die Auferstehung und Himmelfahrt Jesu* (1760). Telemann died at the age of 86 on June 25, 1767. *—Robert Cummings*

CHAMBER MUSIC

Six Concerts and Six Suites, for flute, violin, cello & continuo (1734)

Georg Philipp Telemann worked as his own publisher for most of his music from 1715 to 1740, producing 47 known printed editions of his music; Telemann was practically unique in this respect among composers of his time. In Telemann's day one was required to apply for permission from the state to publish anything, and composers were seldom paid for editions of their works—the preponderance of "bootleg" musical publications by firms such as John Walsh in London or La Céne in Amsterdam was the rule rather than the exception. Yet Telemann remained in control of the dissemination of his work for most of his long life and in many cases reorganized compositions to fit the requirements of publication of a particular set of works.

Perhaps no published Telemann set was more radical in this regard than *Six Concerts et Six Suites*, printed in Hamburg in 1734. This consisted of four separate part books containing 12 works, six being chamber concertos, and the rest dance suites in the French style. The parts are for flute, violin, figured bass, and harpsichord and can be used in this original configuration or shuffled to yield new combinations—take out the violin part and you have a trio for flute, cello, and harpsichord. Or take out the flute and you have a different trio for violin, cello, and harpsichord. Finally, use only the parts for flute and harpsichord and you have a sonata for harpsichord with flute accompaniment, an arrangement that looks forward to the accompanied solo setting common to keyboard music of the mid- to late eighteenth century, but practically unknown in Telemann's time. If one were to take all of Telemann's suggestions for realization, the *Six Concerts et Six Suites* would produce 48 works—played end to end all of this would add up to more than ten hours of music. It seems the idea of "more bang for your buck" is not limited to the twentieth century!

No matter what the configuration, the music is of outstanding quality, containing some of Telemann's most inspired contributions to French-styled Baroque chamber music. *—Uncle Dave Lewis*

Recommended:

○ **Telemann: Concerts & Suites 1734** / Cologne Camerata / CPO 999690

Essercizii Musici, collection of sonatas and trios for various instruments (1740)

The full title of this collection, in English translation, is "Musical Diversions, Consisting of 12 Solo and 12 Trio Sonatas for Various Instruments." It's practical music in more ways than one; Telemann self-published the *Essercizii Musici* to help pay off his wife's debts. Beyond that, it's music aimed at the lucrative market of bourgeois, amateur musicians, who passed their evenings playing music in their homes.

For this set, Telemann wrote something for each instrument commonly found in the eighteenth century German household: keyboard (harpsichord works better than its softer-voiced cousins in the ensemble pieces), violin, recorder, transverse flute, oboe, and viola da gamba. Each of those instruments is provided a pair of solo sonatas, which in most cases means that it is the featured melody instrument against continuo accompaniment (at least harpsichord and sometimes gamba as well). Only the harpsichord truly plays alone in its two sonatas, which are actually suites: a slow, singing introduction followed by a handful of dance movements, such as bourée, sarabande, gavotte, passepied, and gigue. The other solo sonatas are generally cast in the four-movement church sonata format, a series of movements with only tempo designations rather than dance titles. The first and third movements are slow and often sweet; the second and fourth movements are fast, but not virtuosic.

To achieve the greatest commercial appeal, Telemann wrote trio sonatas to accommodate almost every imaginable combination of the instruments mentioned. The Baroque trio sonata requires two melody instruments and bass accompaniment, and that accompaniment often falls to not one but two instruments: harpsichord and gamba. But Telemann does not relegate the harpsichord to an exclusively accompanimental role; several of these trio sonatas call for a standard melody instrument (flute, recorder, oboe, even gamba) with obbligato harpsichord as the second melody instrument; the continuo part then presumably falls solely to a gamba or Baroque cello, rather than a second harpsichord (a bourgeois home was not likely to have two). Most of the trio sonatas fall into the standard slow-fast-slow-fast church sonata pattern, although Telemann occasionally deviates from this, as in the three-movement *Trio in F major for recorder, gamba, and continuo.* Intended as it is for good amateur players, the music offers no great technical difficulties, and emphasizes charm and grace over pathos and depth of expression. Still, these are not throwaway scores; they are well crafted and cannily designed for a carefully targeted group of eager consumers. *—James Reel*

Recommended:

○ **Telemann: Essercizii Musici** / Hantai, Marq, Francais / 2003 / Naïve 8890

○ **Telemann in Paris: Trios & Quartets** / Ens. le petit bruit / 1999 / Cantate 56834

12 Fantasias for flute, TWV 40:2–13 (1732–1733)

Though modern listeners generally relegate Georg Philipp Telemann to the periphery of historical importance, his consummate skill (which was highly esteemed by both Bach and Mozart) gained him considerable notoriety in his time. Not only was Telemann astonishingly prolific in virtually every genre, he also invested considerable effort in learning to play the various instruments for which he would compose. As a result, his smooth musical style is complemented by a deep sensitivity for idiom: he seems to know intuitively which musical gestures will best articulate a particular instrument's inherent nature.

This is certainly the case with the *12 Fantasies for Flute*, composed from 1732 to 1733. Though diverse in character, each of the dozen fantasies variously exploits the wide variety of expressive and technical possibilities of the instrument. The contrasting movements and sections in each fantasy alternately demand technical dexterity and expressive nuance. Because Telemann employs no continuo accompaniment, the flute's single line assumes various roles simultaneously—sometimes soaring to a high note before quickly dipping down to provide a closing cadential figure, or spreading itself pointillistically across several layers of foreground and background texture. A prime example can be found in the middle section of the opening Vivace of Fantasy No. 1, where Telemann created the illusion of a fugal texture by rapidly sending the flute across registers to intermittently execute quasi-contrapuntal figurations. Likewise, as the initial Presto of the C major Fantasy (No. 5) begins, the flutist seems to play both the melody and a pedal tone. The composer exhibits a variety of stylistic moods to match his various modes of gestural expression, from the regal dotted rhythms and French Overture attitude of the Fantasy in D major (No. 7), to the Baroque flourishes of the F sharp minor Fantasy (No. 10), to the various characters of the six movements that comprise the G minor Fantasy which closes the series. *—Jeremy Grimshaw*

Recommended:

○ **Telemann: Fantasias TWV40:2–13** / Guimond / 1995 / Analekta 28053

12 Fantasias for violin, TWV 40:14–25 (1735)

Georg Philipp Telemann (1681–1767) composed his *12 Fantasien für Violine ohne Bass* (12 Fantasias for violin without basso continuo) in 1735 for Panton Hebestreit, the director of music at Eisenach. Unlike the other great Baroque works for solo violin, the sonatas and partitas of Bach, or the *Rosary Sonatas* of Biber, Telemann's *Fantasien* are extremely diverse works in three or four movements written in 12 different keys with all the movements distinctly different from each other. The element of fantasy is central to their conception and execution and the music often seems unpremeditated and even improvised. And yet Telemann's imagination never falters and each work is a masterpiece of its kind. *—James Leonard*

Recommended:

○ **Telemann: Twelve Fantasias For Solo Violin** / DuBeau / Fleurs de Lys 23048

Der getreue Music-Meister, collection of vocal and chamber instrumental pieces (1728)

Like Telemann's later *Essercizii Musici, The Faithful Music-Master* was intended for purchase by bourgeois amateurs who amused themselves by playing music at home. This collection, however, is explicitly didactic. Telemann issued it in the form of a serial, or music journal, broken into 25 lessons issued every two weeks between November 13, 1728, and November 1, 1729. Each issue contained one large-scale composition, usually a sonata for solo instrument and continuo, but sometimes a trio sonata, a suite for a single instrument such as harpsichord or lute, or even a vocal cantata. Alongside this were vocal arias, small character pieces, canons, and exercises in counterpoint to be completed by the purchaser. The amount of this "extra" material depended solely on how much space remained in each four-page issue after inclusion of the principal piece.

Daringly, Telemann wrote selections not only for such common household instruments as violin, recorder, and harpsichord, but also for such specialty items as trumpet, horn, and chalumeau. In most cases, this music could easily be adapted for other instruments. Even so, Telemann did not anticipate his subscribers would be forming their own orchestras; no piece calls for more than five or six performers, although some require rather unusual combinations (in one case, two sopranos, two violins, and continuo).

Despite the pedagogical nature of *The Faithful Music-Master,* many of these compositions require—or help develop in the player—fairly high skill. The solo violin, gamba, and harpsichord works are particularly advanced, though not of insurmountable difficulty, and the arias are taken from operas Telemann had written for professional singers (*Emma und Eginhard, Calypso, Belsazar,* and *Sancio und Aesop,* now otherwise lost). Telemann invited other composers to contribute to the series. Many of these guests were obscure workaday musicians from the Hamburg area, but a few rather famous names also pop up: Bonporti, Zelenka, Pisendel, Weiss, and even J.S. Bach, who supplied a "riddle canon" (BWV 1074). *—James Reel*

Recommended:

○ **Telemann: Der Getreue Music-Meister** / Kohnen, Fabbriciani, Denti, Ceglar / 1997 / Arts 47317

Paris Quartets, for flute, violin, viola da gamba & continuo (1730–1737)

As Georg Philipp Telemann (1681–1767) wrote in his autobiography of 1739, "my long-planned journey to Paris, where I had had a standing invitation from various virtuosi there who had taken a liking to several of my printed works, took place at Michaelmas in 1737. It lasted eight months. There, on receipt of a royal publishing privilege extending for 20 years, I had several new quartets printed by subscription. They made the ears of the Court and the whole city most remarkably attentive, and these quartets rapidly won for me almost universal acclaim, accompanied by exceeding courtesy." Entitled *Six Nouveaux Quatuors en Suites a une flute transviere, un violin, une basse de viole, ou violoncel et basse continue* (Six New Quartets or Suites for transverse flute, violin, bass viol or violincello and basso continuo) and published in Paris in 1738, Telemann's so-called *Paris Quartets* contained elements of the not only the French style, with its grand overture and feminine melodies, but also the Italian style with its virtuoso writing and extravagant melodies, the German style with its severe counterpoint and grave slow movements, and even the Polish style, which Telemann characterized as "barbaric." The *Paris Quartets* were among Telemann's most popular works during his lifetime and remain among his most frequently performed chamber music. *—James Leonard*

Recommended:

○ **Telemann: Paris Quartets 1–12** / B. Kuijken, S. Kuijken, W. Kuijken, Leonhardt / Sony 63115

Septet (Concerto), for 3 oboes, 3 violins & continuo in B flat major, TWV 44:43 (before 1768)

This *Septet* is often called a concerto and has also been arranged as a concerto for three trumpets and orchestra. The first movement is a jaunty, duple meter Allegro with the violins and oboes calling and echoing each other as separate concertino groups. In the middle of the movement, the first violin and first oboe get to do more florid solo work. The G minor Largo middle movement is something like a funeral march. The instruments come in one after another until they are all playing solid, block chords, with some solo melody work for the first violin and first oboe. The movement ends with an uncertain-sounding seventh chord, to lead back to the major mode of the final Allegro, a cheerful, bouncy movement in triple meter with constant running eighth notes switching from the continuo line to the soloists. Again, there is much echoing between the concertino groups, but even more between individual instruments. The septet is a charming example of Telemann's Italianate works for chamber ensemble. *—Patsy Morita*

Recommended:

○ **Telemann: Admiralitätsmusik; Trumpet Concert** / Thom (cond.), Telemann CO / 1998 / Berlin Classics 0030492

○ **Telemann: Wind Concertos** / Goebel (cond.), Musica Antiqua Köln / Archiv 419633

Tafelmusik (Musique de table), 18 chamber pieces for various ensembles organized into 3 "productions" (1733)

No Baroque composer showed greater flair when it came to marketing his own works than Telemann. Numerous publications, many serving a didactic purpose, were seen into print by this astonishingly industrious composer. Two large-scale publications in particular stand out for their range and diversity, *Der getreue Music-Meister* ("The Faithful Music Master") (1727–29), and *Musique de Table* (Table Music), published in 1733 under its French title, but more frequently refered to by the German name of *Tafelmusik.* As was his custom when having his music published, he himself oversaw the publication down to editing and engraving. The contents are unlikely to have been written especially for the publication, more probably being drawn from the composer's existing stock of works. The name chosen for the collection reflects a long tradition of publishing works under such titles as "a music banquet" or something similar, and does not necessarily imply that the three "productions" into which Telemann divided the publication were literally intended to form the accompaniment to a meal. The suggestion that the music was culled from preexisting works is underlined by the fact that there is no attempt to provide unity of key, although each set does have a principal key (E minor, D major, and B flat major respectively).

The format of each part consists of six works that include both orchestral and chamber music. An opening orchestral suite, consisting of a French overture followed either by the usual stylized dances or by Telemann's piquantly named character pieces, is followed by a quartet. Then comes a concerto for two or three instruments: transverse flute and violin in Production One, three violins in Production Two, and two horns in Production Three. Two chamber works follow: the first a trio sonata in all three cases, the second a solo sonata for transverse flute and basso continuo (One), violin and basso continuo (Two), or oboe and continuo (Three). Finally, Telemann rounds off each Production with a short orchestral conclusion. Production One is the most chamberlike, with the Concerto in A for flute and violin a particular highlight. The second Production is more extroverted, with the inclusion of trumpet and oboe in the opening Suite in D introducing a note of ceremony absent in its predecessor. The final Production opens with a Suite in B flat distinguished by a splendid Ouverture and several picturesque movements such as the rustic Bergerie. Its resplendent concerto for two horns in E flat is also worthy of particular notice. *—Brian Robins*

Recommended:

○ **Telemann: Tafelmusik** / Goebel (cond.), Musica Antiqua Köln / Archiv 427619

CONCERTO

Concerto for horn, violin, 2 violas & continuo in D major, TWV 51:D8 (1708–1714)

The highly prolific Georg Philipp Telemann composed only this one work for horn among his many concertos for one or more instruments and orchestra.

The dates given for its composition are from the period when he was working either as court composer for Eisenach (beginning around 1708) or as city music director in Frankfurt-am-Main, after 1712. The lack of hard information about its composition means that there also are no clues as to which horn player Telemann had in mind when he wrote the concerto, but it can be inferred from the difficult writing that the performer was an advanced master of the instrument.

The work has pretty much the same layout and proportions of the typical Italian concerto of the time as exemplified by those of Antonio Vivaldi. That is, the concerto runs about nine minutes and is in the fast-slow-fast pattern. The title page says it is for "corno da caccia" and orchestra. That name literally means "hunting horn," but Telemann probably had in mind a standard concert horn, with crooks inserted to tune it in the high key of D.

The writing in the opening movement does suggest the instrument's origin as a means of giving signals during the hunt or on the arrival of post-carriages. Although the main theme is full of figurations with that suggestion, it is a fluent and melodic work, well advanced in musical imagination over simple horn calls. The second movement uses the horn in a slow, song-form piece with qualities of vocal music of the time, not excluding decorative touches in the melody. The finale is a minuet in the slowish regal tempo that was still standard for that courtly dance at the time. *—Joseph Stevenson*

Recommended:

○ **Horn Concertos** / Tuckwell, Marriner (cond.), Academy of St. Martin-in-the-Fields / 1996 / EMI 69395

Trumpet Concerto in D major, TWV 51:D7 (ca. 1708–1714)

Composed sometime between 1710 and 1720, certainly before the composer moved to Hamburg in 1721 to take up the duties of music director of the latter city's five largest churches, Georg Philipp Telemann's only concerto for trumpet, the *Concerto in D major for trumpet, violins, and basso continuo,* is a sparkling, seven- or eight-minute piece. It is among the first solo trumpet concertos penned by a German composer—indeed, some scholars believe that it may even be the very first such work.

The sonata da chiesa, with its four-movement, slow-fast-slow-fast plan, is the blueprint that Telemann uses for the concerto. By comparison with some of the music written for solo trumpet nowadays, the Telemann concerto might not sound particularly demanding or flashy; but we must bear in mind that Telemann's solo instrument was not the facile modern valved trumpet but rather the longer valveless Baroque trumpet—an instrument with a comparatively limited selection of pitches at the ready (essentially the overtone series). So, while the trumpet truly takes center stage in the opening Adagio, not even allowing the violins to take up anything even remotely resembling a melody, it is forced to make frequent pauses during the following Allegro, in which the music grows faster and more exhausting (happily, these pauses fit in well with the general ritornello form of the movement); the violins leap on these opportunities to grab the theme. The third movement, a Grave in B minor, is for the violins and basso continuo alone. Having rested a movement, the trumpet returns, brightly and joyously, in the Allegro finale. *—Blair Johnston*

Recommended:

- ○ **Trumpet Voluntary** / Andre, Marriner (cond.) / 1993 / Erato 92123
- ○ **Telemann: Trumpet Concertos** / Hardenberger, Brown (cond.), Academy of St. Martin-in-the-Fields / Philips 420954

ORCHESTRAL

Overture: Alster Echo, for 4 horns, 2 oboes, bassoon, strings & continuo in F major, TWV 55:F11 (1725)

This work, described by conductor and composer Gunther Schuller as "a tour de force of orchestration and ingenuity," was written around 1725 for the unusual combination of four horns, two oboes, bassoon, and two violins; it has also been performed by larger Baroque orchestral ensembles. As the title suggests, the work is a programmatic depiction of Alster Lake and its surroundings, near Hamburg. The nine movements of this suite contain quite a variety of imaginative sound effects. One depicts swans floating on the lake's surface; another uses the horns to evoke cannon fire. There are echo effects, suggestions of mythological themes associated with the area, and imitations of frogs and crows that will raise a smile from an audience every time. Especially notable is the movement entitled "Village Music of the Alster Shepherds," which contains a panoply of wrong notes and other forms of musical noise. A forerunner of Mozart's *Ein musikalischer Spass* (A Musical Joke), it likewise depicts the musical malfeasance of an ill-trained band of small-town players. Given that Telemann's music remained well known into the 1770s, it is tempting to wonder whether Mozart might have modeled his own parody on this work. Although not one of Telemann's best-known pieces, the *Alster Echo* holds considerable appeal both for specialists interested in the nature of Baroque musical allusion and for general audiences interested in having a good time. *—James Manheim*

Recommended:

- ○ **Telemann: Water Music; Alster Overture; "The Frogs" Concerto** / Pickett (cond.), New London Consort / 1998 / Decca 455621

Overture: Burlesque de Quichotte, for strings & continuo in G major, TWV 55:G10 (1761)

Telemann wrote several freestanding orchestral suites of character pieces, along the lines of what Rameau and Couperin did on the harpsichord, but his *Don Quixote* suite is actually drawn from an opera, *Don Quixote der Löwenritter*, inspired by the famous Cervantes novel. The first movement is a not-quite-conventional French overture. Its opening Largo section, complete with the standard dotted rhythms, includes some comically swooping figures and the ornaments have a strong shuddering effect. The ensuing Allegro fugal section is playful and hyperactive, but hardly engages in serious counterpoint.

Now ensues a series of short movements either illustrating certain Don Quixote adventures or setting particular scenes. The Andantino, "Awakening of Don Quixote," is a brief pastoral piece with light Spanish inflections. Now awake and modestly armed, the Knight of the Mournful Countenance launches a Moderato assault: "His Attack on the Windmills," a spirited rendition of the famous scene in which Quixote believes himself to be charging on a gang of giants.

"Sighs of Love for Princess Aline" is an Andante in which Quixote turns his thoughts to the princess known as Dulcinea, who is actually a peasant girl. Almost every measure of this movement features a two-note, descending "sighing" figure. The next movement introduces the knight's squire; it's an allegro moderato called "Sancho Panza Swindled," an inverse of the Aline movement in that here the principal motif is a humorously rising two-note figure.

Two brief equestrian movements follow: an allegretto called "Rosinante Galloping," a surprisingly graceful but by no means fast minuet depicting Quixote's old steed; the next movement, "The Gallop of Sancho Panza's Mule," is actually the minuet's measured, hesitant trio, followed by a brief repeat of the "Rosinante" music. Finally comes a vivace movement counter-intuitively titled "Don Quixote at Rest," far more of a gallop than what was just heard, and presumably music to accompany Quixote's dreams of great adventure. *—James Reel*

Recommended:

- ○ **Telemann: Orchestral Suites** / Lamon (cond.), Tafelmusik Baroque Orch. / Analekta 23138

VOCAL

Vocal Works (1718–1768)

Even by the prolific standards of the eighteenth century, the industry of Georg Philipp Telemann (1681–1767) was extraordinary. In addition to a huge number of chamber and orchestral works, many of them published by the composer himself and distributed by subscription throughout Europe, Telemann composed an enormous body of both sacred and secular vocal works.

Many of these date from after 1721, the year in which Telemann was invited to take up the position of Kantor of the Johanneum in Hamburg, a position that also involved the musical directorship of the city's five principal churches. In this capacity Telemann produced a staggering number of cantatas for weekly liturgical use, publishing no less than four complete cycles for the church's year (a requirement that amounted to over 70 works for each year). Mostly scored in four parts for soloists and choir with strings and wind instruments (to which were added brass and timpani on feast days), they are more "worldly" works than Bach's more familiar cantatas. Their strength lies in Telemann's ability to dramatize a text, often with the employment of vivid word-painting and colorful orchestral writing. These same assets are put to even more potent use in Telemann's passions and oratorios, among the latter being a remarkable series of works composed in his seventies that show his ever-fertile mind readily embracing new Enlightenment concepts. The passions, which include settings taken from all four evangelists, also trace his development as a composer, Telemann having composed one for each year between 1722 and 1767 (although nearly half are now lost). Again Telemann differs from Bach in these works, being more interested in the human drama of Christ's death than contemplative spiritual meditation upon it.

Telemann's post in Hamburg, a free mercantile city, was a civic appointment that, in addition to carrying responsibilities to the church, involved providing music for important events in the life of the city, including annual celebrations held by the commandant of Hamburg's militia. For these he provided celebratory odes and secular cantatas. Additionally, Telemann became involved with Hamburg's famous Gänsemarkt opera house, the first public opera house established in Germany (at the end of the seventeenth century). The year after arriving in the Hanseatic city, Telemann was appointed director (an appointment that brought him into some conflict with the city fathers). Telemann, who had composed operas from as early as 1703, himself claimed to have composed 35 works for the Gänsemarkt, although only 18 are known. Among them are a number of comic operas that suggest that Telemann's importance in the development of the genre has yet to be recognized, his buffo intermezzo *Pimpinone* (1725), for example, having appeared eight years before Pergolesi's famously seminal *La serva padrona*. *—Brian Robins*

Recommended:

- ○ **Telemann: Trauer-Actus Canatas** / Junghanel (cond.), Cantus Cölln / HM 901768
- ○ **Telemann: Chamber Cantatas & Trio Sonatas** / Brandes, Lane, Musica Pacifica / 2001 / Dorian 93239
- ○ **Telemann: Danziger Cantatas** / Max (cond.), Mertens, Crook, Schubert, Schmithusen / Capriccio 10853
- ○ **Telemann: Cantatas** / Max (cond.), Stotzel (cond.), Varcoe, Schlick, Pregardien, etc. / Brilliant 99996/1-3
- ○ **Telemann: Solo Cantatas** / Malina (cond.), Lax, Affetti Musicali / Hungaroton 31597
- ○ **Telemann: Cantatas** / Schlick, Gwilt, Fortino, Harras, Franklin / Cantate 58003

MISCELLANEOUS

Instrumental Works (1708–1767)

Extraordinarily prolific in every field in which he worked, Georg Philipp Telemann (1681–1767) was one of the leading German composers of the later or high Baroque period. Unlike his friend Bach, Telemann was a truly cosmopolitan figure who maintained contacts with other composers and theorists over a wide area. He also showed considerable business acumen, preparing, publishing, and promoting his own works with considerable success. It was this reason that his instrumental music, much of it designed for amateurs or published with a didactic purpose, was widely distributed throughout Europe. It established for Telemann an international reputation enjoyed by few of his contemporaries.

Telemann's instrumental music can be divided into three categories: orchestral works, chamber works, and solo works for harpsichord or organ. The latter can be considered briefly, since the keyboard works in general occupy a position of lesser importance than that of the other genres. Much of it, which includes suites, fugues, fantasias, and sonatas, was written for teaching purposes and was included in the mammoth publication *Der getreue Music-Meister*, published in Hamburg in 1728 and 1729. In addition to solo pieces, it also includes songs and chamber works featuring an astonishing range of wind and string instruments. Another huge collection to encompass a diverse selection of solos, chamber works, and orchestral works is the *Musique de Table* (Tafelmusik), which Telemann published in 1733, also in Hamburg. The majority of the orchestral works, well over 200 extant works, are either concertos or suites, the two standard forms of the late Baroque. The concertos are scored for anything between one and four solo instruments and are normally cast in the standard three movements. They frequently display the influence of the Venetian concertos of Vivaldi, whereas the suites (or overtures—the two terms are synonymous) often have a strong French flavor. They consist of an overture in the standard French style, opening with a strongly accented dotted-rhythm section in moderate tempo. That is followed by an allegro, often employing fugal writing, and a return to the opening. The overture, generally by far the most extended movement, is followed by a number of movements, primarily stylized dances (minuet, gigue, bourrée, etc.). However, Telemann is unusual among his contemporaries in including genre pieces, often given whimsical titles, in some of the suites' movements, which show the influence of Polish folk music. This propensity to assume, chameleon-like, a variety of national styles is a further indication of Telemann's cosmopolitan outlook. While his music rarely attempts the profundity of Bach, almost all Telemann's instrumental music bears witness to an extraordinarily fertile and creative musical mind that was capable of deploying any combination of instruments colorfully, and with the utmost craftsmanship and skill. In its general avoidance of more complex counterpoint in favor of simpler, more open textures, Telemann's music frequently points forward to the changing styles that lead to the Rococo and, ultimately, the Classical era of Haydn and Mozart. *—Brian Robins*

Recommended:

- ○ **Telemann: Oboe Sonatas** / Goodwin, Toll, North, Sheppard, Cranham / 1996 / HM 907152
- ○ **Telemann: Chamber Music** / Chandos Baroque Players / 2002 / Hyperion 55108
- ○ **Telemann: Six Trios 1718** / Cologne Camerata / CPO 999957
- ○ **Chamber Music with Viola Da Gamba** / Coin (cond.), Limoges Baroque Ens. / 1998 / Astree 8632
- ○ **Telemann: Triple Concertos** / Standage, Collegium Musicum 90 / 1995 / Chandos 580
- ○ **Die Kleine Kammermusik** / Winschermann, Linde, Lautenbacher / Musicaphon 51539
- ○ **Telemann: Quartets** / Cunningham, Hazelzet, Meyerson / Virgin 59049

Yuri Temirkanov

b. Dec. 10, 1938, Nal'chik, USSR
Conductor

Despite extravagant podium demeanor and a dry, quirky sense of humor, Russian conductor Yuri Temirkanov has established himself as one of the twenty-first century's most accomplished and challenging conductors. With two important orchestras under his care, he is a world figure and persuasive in the music of his own country, but artistically curious and increasingly interested in other areas of the repertory. After having sharpened the ensemble within his venerable St. Petersburg Philharmonic Orchestra, he wrought a similar advance within the Baltimore Symphony Orchestra. Accomplished without a single firing, his uplift in the accuracy of performance took place in an orchestra many regarded as already near world class. His brilliant notions of orchestral color have likewise been in evidence, stretching the B.S.O. in new directions. Born in the Caucasus, Temirkanov began his musical training at age nine before studying the violin and viola at the Leningrad Conservatory's School for Talented Children when he was 13. Later, he completed his studies in viola and began training as a conductor at the conservatory itself. After graduation in 1965, he made his professional conducting debut at the Maliy Opera Theatre in Leningrad, directing a performance of *La Traviata.* Upon winning the celebrated All-Soviet National Conducting Competition in 1966, Temirkanov was invited by Kiril Kondrashin to undertake a tour of Europe and America with the Moscow Chamber Orchestra and violinist David Oistrakh. In early 1967, the conductor made his debut with the Leningrad Philharmonic and was thereupon invited to become the orchestra's assistant conductor under Yevgeny Mravinsky. In 1968, Temirkanov was appointed principal conductor of the Leningrad Symphony Orchestra, continuing there until his engagement as music director of the Kirov Opera and Ballet in 1976. In 1987, he made his debut at Covent Garden leading his opera company in Kirov productions of *Yevgeny Onegin, Pique Dame,* and *Boris Godunov.* In 1980, he was appointed principal guest conductor of the Royal Philharmonic Orchestra and in 1988, he succeeded Mravinsky as principal conductor of the Leningrad Philharmonic. That year, he became the first Soviet artist granted permission to perform in the United States after cultural relations were resumed in the aftermath of the war in Afghanistan. After serving as principal conductor of the Royal Philharmonic Orchestra from 1992, Temirkanov assumed the title of conductor laureate. He also serves as principal guest conductor of the Danish National Radio Symphony Orchestra. In Baltimore, Temirkanov's assumption of authority manifested itself with his dismissal of the orchestra's chorus, a move that rankled many, but that failed to cripple his involvement with the orchestra. Temirkanov, who had been direct in deeming the B.S.O. not of the first rank even before his tenure began in January 2000, nonetheless insisted the orchestra was a very good one and could be improved. Distinct improvements have been apparent to critics and public alike. Among Temirkanov's many recordings are exemplary ones of the Russian repertory, especially of works by Tchaikovsky, Rachmaninov, Prokofiev, Stravinsky, and Khachaturian. *—Erik Eriksson*

Recommended:

- ○ **Rachmaninoff: Symphony 2; Vocalise** / Temirkanov (cond.), St. Petersburg PO / 1994 / RCA 61281
- ○ **Prokofiev: Symphony 1; Romeo & Juliet Suite 2; Love for 3 Oranges Suite** / Temirkanov (cond.), St. Petersburg PO / 2003 / RCA 68408
- ○ **Rachmaninov: Symphonic Dances** / Temirkanov (cond.), Alexeyev, St. Petersburg PO / 1995 / BMG 62710

Klaus Tennstedt

b. Jun. 6, 1926, Merseburg, Germany, **d.** Jan. 11, 1998, Kiel, Germany
Conductor

A man who had thought life held no greater challenge than could be provided by a smaller theater or second-tier orchestra somewhere in Central Europe, conductor Klaus Tennstedt found himself propelled into the celebrity spotlight following several acclaimed guest appearances. His frail psyche and unstable health eventually broke under the weight of these responsibilities and he was obliged to all but retire from active conducting. Nonetheless, those all-too-few years of international productivity revealed an intense, revelatory approach to familiar Romantic period scores and the rapturous applause he received from audiences and players alike was entirely deserved.

Tennstedt began his musical training with his father, violinist Hermann Tennstedt. After studies in violin and conducting at the Leipzig Hochschule für Musik, young Tennstedt was engaged as orchestra leader at the Halle Stadttheater in 1948. Forced by a growth on his left hand to abandon the violin, Tennstedt redirected his energies to piano and conducting and he made his debut as conductor at Halle in 1952. Beginning in 1954, he was appointed a concertmaster at the opera in Chemnitz and in 1958, he became general music director at the Dresden Staatsoper, a position he held until 1962. From 1962 to 1971, Tennstedt was general music director at the Mecklenburg Staatsoper in Schwerin, a period that afforded him time for guest appearances with the Dresden Staatskapelle and Leipzig Gewandhaus orchestras, among other ensembles in Eastern European and Soviet bloc cities. When directing a 1971 concert in Sweden, Tennstedt elected to defect and thereafter began a period of work with the Swedish Radio Orchestra. Another position as general music director opened for him in 1972, this time at Kiel, and he remained in that post until 1976.

Meanwhile, a life-altering event for Tennstedt occurred in 1974. Invited to Canada to conduct the Toronto Symphony Orchestra in Bruckner's *Symphony No. 7,* the conductor's performance was greeted with such thunderous acclamation that word began to travel around the world. A Boston Symphony Orchestra appearance shortly thereafter brought international interest and Tennstedt's direction of Bruckner's *Symphony No. 8* was the stuff from which legends are born. Invitations came from New York, Cleveland, Chicago, and Philadelphia, the other "big five" American orchestras. The amazed conductor made his British debut with the London Symphony Orchestra in 1976, prompting additional engagements with the Berlin Philharmonic, the Vienna Philharmonic, and the Paris Orchestra. Tennstedt was honored by becoming the first German conductor to conduct the Israel Philharmonic in 1978 and a year later was engaged by Hamburg's NDR Symphony Orchestra as principal conductor, a position he held until 1981. In 1979, he also became principal guest conductor with the Minnesota Orchestra and, from 1980, he held the same title with the London Philharmonic Orchestra. In 1983, Tennstedt was appointed music director of the London Philharmonic, leading the orchestra in recordings and on tours abroad that won adulatory reviews. In 1983, he made his debut with the Metropolitan Opera, leading impressive performances of *Fidelio* despite less than fully satisfactory singers.

Eventually, the burdens of celebrity exacted an immense toll. Two hip replacements, radiation treatment for throat cancer, and increasing numbers of cancellations hounded his work. Self-doubt crippled his ability to continue working at the level that had brought him fame. Doctors ordered extended periods of rest, but to little lasting benefit. When he collapsed at a rehearsal in 1987, Tennstedt resigned his post with the LPO, conducting the orchestra infrequently thereafter as conductor laureate. *—Erik Eriksson*

Recommended:

- ○ **Mahler: Symphony 4** / Tennstedt (cond.), Popp / 2000 / EMI 73706
- ○ **Mahler: Complete Symphonies** / Tennstedt (cond.), Popp, Hill, Mathis, Wiens, London PO / 1998 / EMI 72941
- ○ **Beethoven: Symphony 9** / Tennstedt (cond.), Tear, Hodgson, Howell, Haggander, London PO / BBC 4131

Bryn Terfel

b. Nov. 9, 1965, Pantglas, Wales, England
Baritone

The Welsh baritone Bryn Terfel rose with astonishing speed to the top ranks of international operatic stardom in the 1990s. He is known for a big, warm voice, intelligent and dramatically apt portrayals, a six-foot-three-inch frame and those intangibles that add up to star presence.

He was born Bryn Terfel Jones and was brought up in a small village near Snowdonia, speaking Welsh. Even as a small child he was busy singing; he went to various *eisteddfods* (singing competitions) throughout Wales, his supportive mother, Nesta, chauffeuring him around. He used the money he won to buy soccer shoes. The *eisteddfods* taught him to face the stage calmly. "When I went to college I was streets ahead of others because I was used to facing the public," he says. He was awarded a scholarship when he applied to London's Guildhall School of Music and Drama. His teachers there were Arthur Reckless and Rudolf Piernay. Since there was already a professional singer named Bryn Jones, he adopted his middle name, for his stage billing.

He won two of the main prizes for Guildhall singers: the Kathleen Ferrier Scholarship in 1988 and the 1989 Gold Medal Award. Also in 1989, he won the Lieder Prize at the Cardiff Singer of the World Competition and second prize all-around in that competition. This competition is broadcast Europe-wide, and he immediately began getting requests to sing from the leading conductors. Sir Georg Solti called him "one of the great talents of the last ten years."

Although he got offers for all sorts of repertory, he weighed them with care, with a view to preserving the voice through a long career. Although he was already being offered the role of Wotan in three of Wagner's *Ring* operas, he started singing such roles as Figaro, and Leporello (lighter and more lyrical roles) and Jokanaan in Strauss' *Salome* (a heavier, though still lyrical, one, but relatively short). He edged into Wagnerian territory in the lyrical part of Wolfram in *Tannhäusser*, a part known for the lovely "Song to the Evening Star." In 1992, he won the *Gramophone Magazine* "Young Singer of the Year" citation and the "Newcomer of the Year" award at the inaugural International Classical Music Awards in 1993.

He has added Dr. Miracle and Captain Balstrode (Britten's *Peter Grimes*) to his roles, moved over from Leporello to Don Giovanni, sung Nick Shadow in Stravinsky's *The Rake's Progress*, and has triumphed in Verdi's *Falstaff*, which he plays with notable humanity and restraint; his *Falstaff* is a braggart who overrates himself, but not the buffoon some other singers make him. He also sings the evil Scarpia in *Tosca*.

He is active on the recital and concert stage. Mendelssohn's *Elijah* is one of his mainstays. Songs of Handel, Vaughan Williams, Schubert, and Richard Rodgers figure in his recitals and recordings.

He remains a passionate fan of football (both soccer and rugby) and enjoys opening major international matches such as the Bledisloe Cup in Australia. When the Rugby World Cup was held in Cardiff, Wales, he opened it with a memorable duet with pop singing star Shirley Bassey of the Rugby theme song, "World In Union."

In 1999, the small Welsh island of Bardsey revived an ancient tradition (which died out in 1927) by inviting Terfel to become their honorary monarch. Even though he has conquered the world of opera—even overcoming the dismal acoustics of the Sydney Opera House—he remains centered on Wales, where, whenever he can, he still helps his father with the farming chores. *—Joseph Stevenson*

Recommended:

○ **Verdi: Falstaff** / Abbado (cond.), Terfel, Hampson, Roschmann, Pieczonka, Berlin PO / 2001 / DG 471194

○ **Schubert: An Die Musik** / Terfel, Martineau / DG 445294

○ **The Vagabond** / Terfel, Martineau / 1995 / DG 445946

○ **Mozart: Nozze di Figaro** / Gardiner (cond.), Terfel, Martinpelto, Mason, Clarkson, Monteverdi Choir, EBS / Archiv 439871

Maggie Teyte

b. Apr. 17, 1888, Wolverhampton, England, **d.** May 26, 1976, London, England
Soprano

The daughter of a British midlands pub keeper, Maggie Tate changed the spelling of her surname when she went to Paris in 1903 to study with the storied tenor Jean de Reszke. First, though, she trained at the Royal Musical College as a light lyric soprano, and made her London debut in 1906 singing excerpts from Mozart's *The Marriage of Figaro* and *Don Giovanni*. Her professional debut came a year later in concert at Monte Carlo, followed by her stage debut there as Zerlina. In 1907, the Paris Opéra-Comique engaged her for two seasons. On 12 June 1908, she succeeded Mary Garden as Debussy's Mélisande, who had sung the role sixty times since the opera's premiere in 1902. The composer coached Teyte, as he had Garden, and later accompanied her as pianist *and* conductor—the only singer he ever performed with publicly—despite writing in 1908 that she "was more than a distant princess," and "showed barely as much emotion as a prison door." Before the manager replaced her in 1910 with his own wife, Teyte had sung Mélisande 19 times. (Of her successor Debussy would write, "she brings a furious zeal... portraying [her] as a kind of melancholy washerwoman," whereas "the good Miss Teyte" had a "charming voice and a true feeling for the character.")

Returning to London, she made her Covent Garden debut in d'Albert's *Tiefland* with the Beecham Opera Company, and later sang Mélisande, Cherubino, Blonde (in Mozart's *Abduction from the Seraglio*), Gounod's Marguerite, Antonia in *The Tales of Hoffmann*, Humperdinck's Hänsel, and Madama Butterfly. In 1911, she joined the Chicago Grand Opera Company, debuting as Cherubino, then sang Massenet's Cendrillon opposite Mary Garden's Prince Charming, followed by Marguerite, Antonia, and Lygie in Jean Nouguès' novelty, *Quo vadis?* After the Chicago season ended, Teyte captivated New York on tour as Cendrillon, a role she repeated in 1912–13, along with starring roles in *La bohème* and Goldmark's *The Cricket on the Hearth* (repeated in 1913–14). Teyte's final Chicago season also featured Butterfly and Hänsel.

She charmed Boston Opera audiences in January 1914, and returned for three seasons as Mimì, Zerlina, and Butterfly; she added Verdi's *A Masked Ball*, and Wolf-Ferrari's *The Secret of Suzanne* for a two-month Boston visit to Paris before the outbreak of World War I. After a dark year, Boston heard her in 1915–16 as Nedda in *Pagliacci*, Mimì, and Hänsel, but the company collapsed in January 1917 after a single week, despite Teyte's Marguerite and Mimì. She went home to England in 1919, co-starred in Messager's final opera, *Monsieur Beaucaire*, at Birmingham, and, in 1923, created the Princess in Holst's *The Perfect Fool*. Her subsequent operatic appearances were random, however: Hänsel and Mélisande at Covent Garden in 1930, Hänsel in 1936, Euridice in Gluck's *Orfeo* in 1937, and her Covent Garden farewell as Butterfly in 1938. She appeared, though, in operettas throughout the 1930s, and in recitals and recordings of French music with pianists Alfred Cortot and Gerald Moore. During World War II, Teyte sang for Allied troops, and then in 1948 (at age sixty), her first U.S. Mélisande with the New York City Opera. She made her final operatic appearance as Belinda opposite Kirsten Flagstad in Purcell's *Dido and Aeneas* in 1951. Her last public appearances came in 1955—at London's Royal Festival Hall on her 67th birthday, and five months later at Wigmore Hall.

Subsequently she wrote an autobiography, *Star on the Door*, and in 1958 was made a Dame of the British Empire for her services to music. *—Roger Dettmer*

Recommended:

○ **Maggie Teyte** / Teyte, etc. / 2001 / Decca 467916

○ **Maggie Teyte in Concert** / Teyte, etc. / 1994 / VAI Audio 1063

○ **A Vocal Portrait** / Teyte, etc. / 2002 / Naxos 6

Jean-Yves Thibaudet

b. Sep. 7, 1961, Lyon, France
Pianist

Thibaudet was born in Lyon to a French father and a German mother. The mother provided Thibaudet with his first piano lessons at age five, and later his father taught him to play the violin. Thibaudet's skill at the keyboard developed rapidly, and he gave his first recital at the age of seven, following with his first concerto appearance at age nine. At 12, Thibaudet was awarded a gold medal upon graduating from the Conservatory of Music in Lyon, and he continued his studies at the Paris Conservatoire with Madame Lucette Descaves, who had known Ravel personally and was on intimate terms with both Ravel's scores and those of Debussy. Thibaudet completed his studies with Aldo Ciccolini, whom Thibaudet himself credits for helping to shape his own style and technique.

Thibaudet won the Prix du Conservatoire at age 15, and then took the competition circuit by storm, winning prizes at the Viotti, Casadesus, and Busoni competitions. When Thibaudet took first prize at the International Piano Competition in Japan in 1980, he made his first recordings for Denon. Upon winning the Young Concert Artists International Auditions in New York in 1981, Thibaudet's career as a touring artist began in earnest. Thibaudet signed a recording contract with Decca/London, and has since recorded more than 20 CDs for them. These include the complete piano works of Ravel (a Deutsche Schallplattenpreis winner and Grammy nominee) and Debussy; the Grieg, Ravel, Liszt, and Rachmaninov Concerti, concertinos of Honegger and Françaix, and D'Indy's *Symphony On a French Mountain Air*. He has also recorded transcriptions of Liszt, the Addinsell *"Warsaw" Concerto*, and works of Gershwin, Brahms, Schumann, Messiaen, and Chopin. Thibaudet has played concerts at symphony halls and music festivals throughout the world, and has worked in tandem with artists such as the violinist Joshua Bell, cellist Truls Mork, and singers Matthias Goerne, Dmitri Hvorostovsky, Cecilia Bartoli and Reneé Fleming.

Thibaudet has also turned his attention to popular music, notably in his acclaimed *Conversations with Bill Evans* and *Reflections on Duke*. His warm, rich tone and Apollonian approach to jazz music exposes the strong Classical underpinnings of Evans and Ellington without resorting to schmaltz, cheekiness, or other typical pitfalls of Classical "crossover" recordings. In classical repertoire, Thibaudet is both technically solid and on intimate terms with the music he plays, yet sometimes takes adventurous turns in interpretation. A good example of this is found in his recording of Liszt's transcription of the Wagner *Tristan and Isolde* "Libestod." At one point, Liszt transcribes Wagner's inner voices in a syncopated, "funky" manner, and rather than attempting to flatten these out through use of rubato, Thibaudet plays them "funky," in tempo, as written.

Thibaudet dresses impeccably, and was a friend of the late designer Gianni Versace. The bright red socks he wore at early recitals raised a fair number of eyebrows, but Thibaudet has cited the need for a splash of color in the usual monochromatic settings employed in concert appearances. In addition to his interest in high fashion, Thibaudet enjoys sports such as tennis and water skiing, good conversation, tango music and opera. In 1997 Thibaudet made his Metropolitan Opera debut in the minor role of Boleslao in Giordano's *Fedora*; not that he plans to abandon his keyboard in favor of a singing career, but just for the experience it provided.

As he once asked in an interview, "How can you play the piano without understanding opera, or art, sculpture, or literature for that matter?"

In June 2000, Thibaudet's recording of Debussy's *Images and Etudes* was picked as an "Editor's Choice" in *Gramophone*. *—Uncle Dave Lewis*

Recommended:

- ○ **Ravel & Francaix: Concertos** / Dutoit (cond.), Thibaudet, Montreal SO / 1996 / London 452448
- ○ **Magic of Satie** / Thibaudet / 2002 / Decca 470290
- ○ **Chopin I Love** / Thibaudet / 1999 / Decca 466357
- ○ **Ravel: L'Oeuvre pour Piano Seul** / Thibaudet / 1992 / London 433515
- ○ **Debussy: Piano Works Vol. 1** / Thibaudet / 1996 / London 452022

Ambroise Thomas

b. Aug. 5, 1811, Metz, France, **d.** Feb. 12, 1896, Paris, France

Composer: Opera

One of the leading opera composers of nineteenth century France, Ambroise Thomas was a successor to Meyerbeer, Auber, and Offenbach. He was responsible for *Mignon*, one of the most popular operas ever written, and the hauntingly beautiful *Hamlet*.

Born into a musical family, Thomas entered the Paris Conservatory in 1828. He won the Prix de Rome for a cantata he wrote there, and studied in Italy and Germany for several years. Returning to Paris in 1835, he turned his attention to composing for the stage. As with much light opera of the period, their wild plot turns and characterizations today seem ludicrous; *Le Songe d'une nuit d'été* (A Midsummer Night's Dream), for example, includes in its "cast" of characters William Shakespeare (who is drunk for a major part of the action), Queen Elizabeth (as a seductive muse), and Sir John Falstaff. Few of these early operatic works remain in the modern repertory, even in France, apart from some choruses and the very Rossinian overture to his 1851 opera *Raymond*.

Thomas assumed a professorship at the Paris Conservatory in 1856, but ceased composing following the failure of *Le roman d'Elvire* (The Story of Elvira) in 1860. Then, in 1866, newly inspired and with a fresher, simpler approach to both melody and plot, he re-emerged with *Mignon*; it was an immediate hit, going on to receive over 1,000 performances at the Opéra-Comique alone between 1866 and 1894.

Thomas next offered the public his adaptation of *Hamlet* (1868), hailed at the *Opéra-Comique* as a masterpiece of even greater proportions than *Mignon*; even Verdi abandoned his own intention of composing a *Hamlet* in deference to Thomas. Though the score contains a great deal of exceptionally beautiful music—not to mention the first use of a saxophone in an opera—*Hamlet* has not weathered the test of time as well as *Mignon*; this is largely due to its libretto, which is regarded as a severe corruption of its source—among other major alterations, Thomas's *Hamlet* had a happy ending!

Astonishingly, in the midst of this period of fierce activity, Thomas found time and strength to volunteer for service in the Franco-Prussian War of 1870. Afterwards he became director of the Paris Conservatory; in this post, which he held for the remainder of his life, he proved at first to be an innovative music educator. In later years, however, he came to display resentment toward a new generation of composers, including Fauré and Debussy—as his last opera, *Françoise de Rimini* (1882), failed to find success—and became a far more rigid, conservative figure.

Thomas was not entirely eclipsed in his own time, however: in 1894, following the thousandth performance of *Mignon*, he became the first composer ever to be awarded the *Grand Croix* of the Legion of Honor.

In 1943, nearly 50 years after his death, the English film producer-directors Michael Powell and Emeric Pressburger used a portion of *Mignon* as a key plot device in their epic film *The Life and Death of Colonel Blimp*, knowing that audiences would recognize and appreciate it. Both *Mignon* and *Hamlet* are represented in the CD catalog, and EMI has even released a version of *Hamlet* with both the original (i.e. happy) ending and the revised "unhappy" ending (written for the *Covent Garden* premiere).*—Bruce Eder*

OPERA

Hamlet (1868)

Ambroise Thomas' *Hamlet* was one of many attempts during the nineteenth century to adapt a Shakespearean play into a dramatic opera. Most efforts to this end met with little or no success, but Thomas' work endured at the Paris Opera until the early twentieth century. The work's premiere on March 9, 1868, was met with critical and public acclaim; audiences particularly loved Ophelia's mad scene, which Thomas had specifically adapted to the talents of the Swedish soprano Christine Nilsson. Critics hailed the opera as a masterpiece, and it was viewed as the composer's greatest work to that point. *Hamlet*'s success came on the heels of acclaim for Thomas' *Mignon*, and this one-two musical punch catapulted the composer into the first ranks of French opera.

Hamlet's libretto was written by M. Carré and J. Barbier, who used as a source an 1847 stage adaptation by Alexandre Dumas *père* and Paul Maurice. The Dumas-Maurice libretto changes the ending of the play: Hamlet lives to be crowned king. Carre and Barbier followed this formula, which was roundly criticized—most vociferously, and none too surprisingly, by the British. To appease his critics at Covent Garden, Thomas composed an alternative ending which makes use of Shakespeare's original scenario. Although the "happy" ending may seem a sacrilegeous departure from Shakespeare, such elements were a tradition in French opera and fully expected by the public.

The rest of the opera conforms to the spirit of the original play. Thomas especially captures Shakespeare's dramatic intensity in the recitatives; Hamlet's speeches, the king's musings, and Ophelia's grief are all amplified by their spare musical treatment. Emotions and texts are set to a speechlike declamation entirely within French operatic tradition. The opera is further noteworthy for the experimental spirit of its orchestration, which introduces saxophones, cannon, and bass saxhorn into the ensemble.

Several moments in the libretto provide Thomas ample opportunity for effective scene painting. The ghost's appearance on the ramparts, Ophelia's funeral procession, and the coronation of Gertrude all allow for plenty of action, atmosphere, and pageantry. The device of a play within a play, during which Hamlet tries to trap his uncle into revealing his guilt, is an especial dramatic centerpiece. *—Rita Laurance*

Synopsis:

Act One. The curtain rises on the coronation of Gertrude, queen and consort of Claudius, the King of Denmark, in progress at the castle of Elsinore. Prince Hamlet is despondent at the recent death of his father and what he feels is the too-hasty remarriage of his mother. With Ophelia, he sings a duet ("Doute de la lumière"). Ophelia and her father, Polonius, say goodbye to her brother, Laertes, who is soon to leave Denmark. While walking on the ramparts of the castle Hamlet sees the ghost of his father, who tells Hamlet he was murdered by his brother Claudius (the King). Hamlet then swears revenge on Claudius for the death of his father.

Act Two. Ophelia complains that Hamlet is no longer in love with her. She asks Gertrude's permission to join a convent, but Gertrude refuses, worried that such an event would intensify her son's already odd behavior. Claudius attempts, unsuccessfully, to assuage Gertrude's fears concerning her son. Later, Hamlet suggests a little entertainment: a play staged by a wandering troupe of actors. The play, opening with a chorus and a drinking song, is about the murder of King Gonzago during his sleep. The actors mime to Hamlet's recitation. As he watches, Claudius becomes ill, betraying his guilt, at which Hamlet becomes enraged. A septet closes the act.

Act Three. The act opens with a version of Hamlet's monologue, "To be or not to be." Hiding behind a tapestry, Hamlet watches Claudius while he tries to pray, but is unable to concentrate. Polonius enters and begins to speak with Claudius. What Hamlet overhears confirms his suspicion that Claudius murdered his father and also reveals that Polonius knew of the plot. Dismayed by this new knowledge, Hamlet rejects Ophelia and dismisses her love for him. At the close of the act there is a duet between Gertrude and Hamlet, who, bearing a knife, intends to kill his mother. The Ghost intervenes and stops Hamlet.

Act Four. Based on Ophelia's mad scene, it opens with a *ballet-divertissement*, ("La fête du printemps"). Ophelia asks the gentlemen at court if she may join in their games. She begins to imagine that she is married to Hamlet and is afraid he will betray her. She distributes flowers before singing a ballad about the Wilis, the spirits who drown unfaithful lovers ("Pâle et blonde, dort sous l'eau profonde"). Ophelia gradually loses touch with reality, goes mad, and drowns herself. An off-stage chorus hums the tune of the ballad.

Act Five. The act begins with an abbreviated presentation of Shakespeare's graveyard scene. After this, the plot diverges from the original. When Hamlet learns of Ophelia's death he sings ("Comme une pâle fleur éclose au souffle de la tombe"). A funeral procession, accompanied by a march and a chorus of girls signals the arrival of Ophelia's coffin. Another visit from the Ghost encourages Hamlet to kill Claudius, after which he is proclaimed King of Denmark ("Vive le roi Hamlet"). *—John Palmer*

Recommended:

- ○ **Thomas: Hamlet** / Almeida (cond.), Hampson, Anderson, Ramey, Graves, Kunde / 1993 / EMI 754820

Mignon (1866)

The dismal failure of Ambroise Thomas' Le roma d'Elvire in 1860, combined with the success of Gounod's *Faust* the year before, prompted Thomas to quit composing opera for the next six years. However, when Jules Barbier and Michel Carré—the librettists for Gounod's masterpiece, and the future authors of Thomas' *Hamlet* (1868)—approached Thomas with the *Mignon* story, they found the composer eager to eclipse his rival's earlier triumph. Barbier and Carré based the libretto on Goethe's *Wilhelm Meister Lehrjahre*.

Predictably, Thomas imitated aspects of Gounod's style in his new work, and he further insured success by delaying the premiere until the management of the Opéra-Comique could assemble a strong cast. With this accomplished, *Mignon* was first performed on November 17, 1866. It was an immediate success, and was performed 100 times at the Opéra-Comique in the eight months after the premiere. In 1870, it was given in London and in 1871 it was staged in New York.

Barbier and Carré made fundamental changes to the character of *Mignon* as drawn by Goethe. In the novel, she is not the main character, but by extracting her trials and tribulations from the context of the work as a whole, Barbier and Carré made *Mignon* the focal point of the opera. Furthermore, the librettists created a happy ending (Mignon lives, whereas she dies in the novel), obligatory for works written for the Opéra-Comique stage at the time. Nevertheless, Barbier and Carré manage to maintain the spirit of Goethe's story.

Thomas was eager to please, and made adjustments to his score when necessary. For the London performance, the composer replaced the spoken dialogue with recitatives and adapted the role of Frédéric for a contralto, composing the famous Act II rondo-gavotte, "In veder l'amata stanza," based on material from the preceding entr'acte. Philine also received a new aria: "Alerta, Filina." Furthermore, the work was sung in Italian. For German stages, Thomas was willing to completely change the end of the work, having *Mignon* die in Wilhelm's arms when she hears Philine's voice from offstage. Undoubtedly, this made the opera more palatable to German audiences, who knew and identified with Goethe's masterpiece.

Thomas' eclecticism proved a hindrance to his success in his early years. Composing in various styles with numerous, and obvious, models (Auber, Hérold, Rossini), Thomas did not find his own voice until *Le caïd* of 1849, which still owes much to Rossini. It was not until *Mignon* that the aspects of Thomas' eclectic musical personality coalesced to create an impressively unified work.

Mignon draws its strength from Thomas' careful musical representation of the characters. *Mignon*'s music alternately illustrates her jealousy, love, and affection in no uncertain terms. Her complexity is unmatched in any other of Thomas' operas. Philine's superficial personality comes across in her predictable music, especially the polonaise aria, "Je suis Titania." Wilhelm's youthful but sensible character comes through in vivacious, yet studied music, especially in the first part of Act II, in which we hear clearly the contrast between his music and that for Frédéric and the uncontrollably jealous *Mignon*. Wilhelm's sincerity comes to the fore near the end of the second act, when he greets *Mignon* after their earlier confrontation. Lothario's amnesia becomes apparent not only through his change of clothes and description of his past in the final act, but also through his music, which takes on a more noble character when his memory returns. *—John Palmer*

Synopsis:

Act One. The courtyard of an inn in a small German town. The wandering minstrel Lothario accompanies himself on the harp and sings ("Fugitif et tremblant") to drinking townsfolk and travelers. A troupe of actors, among them Philine and Laerte, watch as gypsies dance. Jarno, the gypsy chief, threatens Mignon with a beating if she does not dance, but Lothario and a student, Wilhelm Meister, intervene and help her. She is grateful, and to thank them she divides her collected wildflowers between the two men. Wilhelm reveals to Laerte, one of the actors, that his is twenty years old and has left his home in Vienna to travel and find adventure. Wilhelm allows Laerte to take his flowers and present them to Philine, another member of the troupe, because he, too, is impressed with her beauty. Laerte leaves with Philine. Wilhelm and Mignon speak of Mignon's childhood, of which she has only a few memories because she was kidnapped by foreign gypsies from a country warmer than Germany ("Connais-tu le pays?"). Wilhelm decides to buy Mignon's freedom and makes a bargain with Jarno. Lothario returns and informs Mignon he is travelling south and must say goodbye ("Légères hirondelles"). Lothario asks Mignon to go with him, but she tells him she wishes to stay with Wilhelm. Philine enters, and although she is being followed by her young admirer, Frédéric, she only has eyes for Wilhelm. Baron de Rosenberg, Frédéric's uncle, has invited the troupe of actors to play at his castle. As the actors leave for Rosenberg's castle, Mignon sees the flowers she gave Wilhelm in Philine's hands and becomes very upset, because she has fallen in love with Wilhelm.

Act Two. Philine delights in her luxurious surroundings at the Rosenberg castle. Outside, Laerte sings of Philine's beauty. Entering the room, he brings with him Mignon and Wilhelm, who the sing a duet ("Je crois entendre les doux compliments"), while Mignon pretends to be asleep. After the three others leave, Mignon, extremely jealous, tries on one of Philine's costumes and applies some of the actress's makeup. Frédéric enters and sings his famous rondo-gavotte. Looking for Mignon, Wilhelm returns and is challenged by Frédéric, but Mignon moves between them as they are about to fight. The sight of Mignon in one of Philine's costumes makes Frédéric laugh and Wilhelm concerned; he decides he and Mignon cannot be together and bids her farewell. As Wilhelm leaves with Philine, the actress mocks Mignon and the way she looks.

The scene shifts to the park of the castle.

Mignon has been made crazy by jealousy ("Elle est là, près de lui?"). She intends to jump into the river, but the sound of a harp stops her. She realizes it is Lothario, who consoles her ("As-tu souffert? As-tu pleuré?"). The acting troupe is performing *A Midsummer Night's Dream* in Rosenberg's conservatory, and at this moment applause for Philine comes forth from the building. Mignon screams that she wishes the building were hit by lightning and set on fire, the runs off. Lothario walks toward the conservatory while saying "Fire, fire," to himself. Philine, spurred on by the applause, sings a polonaise ("Je suis Titania"), while the actors and audience members come out into the park. Mignon returns and is welcomed affectionately by Wilhelm. Philine notices this and sends Mignon into the conservatory for the flowers Mignon had earlier given to Wilhelm. When Wilhelm sees flames shooting from the building, which Lothario has set on fire, he runs inside and returns with Mignon, who is unconscious and clutches a bunch of charred flowers.

Act Three. The gallery of a castle in Italy. Mignon and Lothario have come to Italy with Wilhelm, where Mignon rests, tended to by Lothario, who prays for her to recover. One of the servants, Antonio, tells them the story of the previous owners of the castle, the Ciprianis: Their young daughter disappeared and was believed to have drowned. As a result the mother died of grief, and both of these events drove the father mad and into exile. Antonio tells Wilhelm that the castle is now available at a very good price. Wilhelm then pledges that, because the Cipriani castle has played a significant part in Mignon's recovery, he will buy it for her. When Lothario hears the name, "Cipriani," he turns and leaves the gallery. Although Wilhelm finds this behavior odd, his attention is drawn to Mignon. Wilhelm receives a letter from Laerte informing him that Philine is on her way. When Mignon wakes up she expresses her attraction to her strangely familiar surroundings ("Je suis heureuse! l'air m'enivre"), and Wilhelm tells Mignon of his love for her. When Mignon hears Philine's voice from outside she faints. When she regains consciousness she sees Lothario, in extravagant clothing, walking toward her and Wilhelm. Lothario welcomes them to his palace and gives Mignon a little box. Inside, she finds a book that belongs to one Sperata, the daughter of the house, presumed to be dead. When she starts to read the prayer inside the book she realizes she knows it by heart. Mignon is Sperata and Lothario, now in his right mind, is her father. With Wilhelm they celebrate their reunion. *—John Palmer*

Recommended:

○ **Mignon** / Almeida (cond.), Horne, Welting, Zaccaria, Von Stade / 1998 / Sony 34590

Randall Thompson

b. Apr. 21, 1899, New York, NY, **d.** Jul. 9, 1984, Boston, MA

Composer: Choral, Symphonic

American composer Randall Thompson, best known for his choral *Alleluia*, was born Ira Randall Thompson in New York City. Thompson's father was an English teacher, and he was reared in an environment that emphasized excellence in matters of academics. One refuge from this routine was the family's summer vacation home in Vienna, MA, where Thompson took interest in an old parlor reed organ. At this instrument Thompson wrote his earliest musical works around 1915. In 1916, Thompson entered Harvard University where he applied for membership in the Glee Club, but was rejected. Thompson would spend much of his future career composing choral music, which he once stated was "an attempt to strike back" at the forces that turned him away. At Harvard, Thompson studied with Edward Burlingame Hill, among others.

In 1922 Thompson won a scholarship to the American Academy at Rome, where his studied with Gian Francesco Malipiero, who helped deepen Thompson's interest in the polyphonic choral music of the Renaissance. Back in America by the end of the 1920s, Thompson utilized a Guggenheim Foundation grant to examine the state of college level music education in America. The results were published in book form as *College Music*, a text that helped reset the collegiate agenda in music education nationwide. In 1936 Thompson's cantata *The Peaceable Kingdom*, inspired by the work of American primitive painter Edward Hicks, was premiered in Cambridge and helped establish Thompson's popularity as a composer.

No work of Thompson's, however, earned in equal measure the incredible celebrity accorded to his *Alleluia* (1940). It was written in four days at the request of maestro Sergey Koussevitzky for a work to celebrate the opening of the new Berkshire Music Center at Tanglewood. It was an immediate success and has been performed countless times by choruses large and small, professional and amateur. Among Thompson's other well-known choral works are his *The Testament of Freedom* (1943) based on texts of Thomas Jefferson and *Frostiana* (1959) on the texts of poet Robert Frost.

Thompson was also a significant American symphonist, producing three symphonies that are of high quality. Thompson's *Symphony No. 2* (1931) had a strong advocate in a student from the Curtis Institute, Leonard Bernstein, who made his first appearance as conductor when he led the Berkshire Music Center Orchestra through this work on July 12, 1939; Bernstein later recorded it with the New York Philharmonic in 1968. Thompson also produced a small amount of chamber and piano music and one short opera, *Solomon and Balkis* (1942). Thompson's career as an educator was substantive, as in addition to acting as head of Curtis he held professorships at Wellesley, University of California in Berkeley, University of Virginia in Charlottesville, Princeton, and finally Harvard itself, from whence he retired from teaching in 1965. He continued to compose until long afterward, and was still writing music up to within a few months of his death at the age of 85.

Randall Thompson is often confused with his Harvard colleague and friend Virgil Thomson, who spelled his name without the "p." *—Uncle Dave Lewis*

CHORAL

Alleluia (1940)

Although American composer Randall Thompson wrote two operas, three symphonies, and many other choral works, he is far and away best known for his *Alleluia for chorus.* Since its premiere in 1940, Thompson's *Alleluia* has been performed countless times by amateur and professional choirs, giving Thompson a fair shot at being the most frequently performed of all American serious composers. Commissioned by Sergey Koussevitzky for the opening exercises of the Berkshire (now the Tanglewood) Music Festival. Thompson received the commission in spring 1940, but was occupied with other commissions until June 30 of that year. He wrote the work from July 1 through 5, but the music didn't reach choral director G. Wallace "Woody" Woodworth until 45 minutes before the concert was to start on July 8. Woodworth reassured the students that "Well, text is at least one thing we won't have to worry about"—Thompson's text sets only the work *Alleluia*—and amazingly, the performance went off splendidly. Since that time, Thompson's *Alleluia* has been performed at the start of each Tanglewood Festival season. Thompson's *Alleluia* is anything but joyous. Marked Lento, the music moves slowly and pensively toward its climax in waves of choral sound. As Thompson later remarked, "The music in my particular *Alleluia* cannot be made to sound joyous... here it is comparable to the Book of Job where it is written The Lord gave and the Lord has taken away. Blessed be the name of the Lord." *—James Leonard*

Recommended:

- ○ **Choral Music of Amy Beach and Randall Thompson** / M. F. Somerville (cond.), Harvard University Choir / 2002 / ASV 1125
- ○ **A Robert Shaw Christmas: Angels on High** / Shaw (cond.), Robert Shaw Chamber Singers / 1997 / Telarc 80461

Frostiana, cycle for chorus & piano (1959)

In 1958, preparing for the commemoration of the bicentennial anniversary of its incorporation, the town of Amherst, MA, commissioned composer Randall Thompson to set a group of texts by Robert Frost, a poet distinguished even in a town famous for its writers. Thompson was, at the time, professor of music at Harvard, one of the schools at which Frost had taught before finally returning to Amherst College. The product of the "collaboration" of these two naturalized New Englanders was a seven-song sequence for accompanied mixed chorus, *Frostiana.*

The first piece is a bold attempt to set perhaps the most famous poem in American literary history, *The Road Not Taken.* The result, however, somehow lands squarely in the English choral tradition, moving nobly along, but with a feel reminiscent of Vaughan Williams. The second and third songs are for men's and women's chorus, respectively. "The Pasture," for a TBB grouping, is so plaintively lilting that one wishes Frost had written more than two verses. For an SAA combination, "Come In" depicts orchestrally the call of a thrush, which grows more impassioned. Though the chorus is in turn moved by the birdsong, it ultimately resists, and the song dies away.

The central song of the cycle, "The Telephone," is a charming dialogue between men's and women's choruses, though the men almost monopolize the conversation. "A Girl's Garden," the fifth song, is a brisk, mostly unison, folk song-like setting for women's chorus. Another hugely famous Frost poem, *Stopping By the Woods On a Snowy Evening,* for men's chorus, follows. The simple poem is made more mysterious by enigmatic harmonic changes.

The final song of the cycle, mirroring the first, is a measured, stirring setting of "Choose Something Like a Star." Soprano voices soar for extended periods, while the lower voices declaim the text. In keeping with Thompson's general desire to set clearly the texts of the only poet ever to win four Pulitzer Prizes, the choral writing moves almost exclusively in homophonic fashion, occasionally even in unison. Each song starts simply and builds to a climax, with parts dividing further along the way.

Frostiana, composed over the course of a summer month in Switzerland, was premiered on October 18, 1959, in Amherst, with the composer conducting and the poet in the audience. An interesting, although likely apocryphal, anecdote has Frost leaping up at the conclusion, begging the performers to "sing it again." More probable, however, is the version that maintains that the poet had no public reaction, and likely did not hold it in high regard. Nevertheless, *Frostiana,* in whole or in part, has secured a place in the choral repertoire for moderately advanced groups due to its direct, highly singable melodic lines. *—Thomas Oram*

Recommended:

- ○ **Thompson: Frostiana; Testament of Freedom** / Clark (cond.), Manhattan CO, New York Choral Society / 1995 / Koch 37206

The Testament of Freedom, for chorus & orchestra (1943)

Certainly it is tempting to dismiss Randall Thompson's *The Testament of Freedom,* a series of choral settings from the writings of Thomas Jefferson, as a piece of World War II propaganda. Many critics have derided it as simple and jingoistic. Yet parts of the work are undoubtedly stirring, and it has received performances worldwide.

Thompson selected four passages from Jefferson's collected works for the four parts of *The Testament of Freedom.* These include excerpts from "A Summary View of the Rights of British America" (1774), the "Declaration of Causes and Necessity of Taking up Arms" (July 6, 1775), and a letter to John Adams (September 12, 1821). The resulting text is something like a religious cantata, although it is intended to praise the ideal of nationhood.

The first movement, "The God who gave us life," begins as a rousing unison hymn which grows stronger and fuller with each repetition of text, culminating in a bombastic final cadence. "We have counted the cost," the second movement, is slower and foreboding with much text declaimed in unison in what amounts to an inflexible recitative. Like its predecessor, it expands and contracts to a climax at the end. The third movement, "We fight not for glory or conquest," is a quick, bold march which gets gradually faster as it progresses to a cry of "We have taken up arms," and then subsides before returning to the original tempo. "I shall not die without a hope," the finale, begins in a quiet lento. Fugue-like counterpoint develops between the tenors and basses in the only extended polyphonic passage in the entire work. An instrumental passage then soars into a stringendo return of the first-movement text and music, swelling the hymn to the close, a stirring final cadence with dual emphasis on "life" and "liberty."

Composed for the 200th anniversary of Jefferson's birthday, *The Testament of Freedom* had its premiere, appropriately, at the University of Virginia on its Founder's Day, April 13, 1943, with the composer at the keyboard, as part of a nationwide radio broadcast. It was then rebroadcast to the Armed Forces serving overseas. In 1944, Thompson responded to strong demand for the piece, arranging the accompaniment for orchestra.

It is the text which keeps *The Testament of Freedom* from becoming a grandiose display of flag-waving American pride. Too profound to be merely patriotic, Jefferson's words are brought out consistently by Thompson's homophonic settings. The repetitively static declamation of text can, it is true, drag the work down. Indeed, if anything sounds dated in the work, it might well be the music, always tonal and set in a heavy-handed four to the bar. Thompson may also go to the well once too often with his crescendos and accelerandos up to the climax. Nevertheless, the work remains in the choral repertoire thanks to the powerful male sound it requires (it has since been edited for mixed chorus)—and thanks to the inescapable rush of patriotic fervor that it engenders, something largely missing from American art music of the twentieth century. *—Thomas Oram*

Recommended:

- ○ **Thompson: Frostiana; Testament of Freedom** / Clark (cond.), Manhattan CO, New York Choral Society / 1995 / Koch 37206

SYMPHONIC

Symphony No. 2 in E minor (1931)

Randall Thompson (1899–1984) was quite a popular American composer in the 1940s and 1950s. Best known for his choral music, he also wrote three symphonies, the second of which is probably the best remembered. For a time it fell into general neglect, but it occasionally turns up on a concert program; the several recordings of the work that appeared in the 1990s were perhaps signs of a revival in its fortunes.

The *Second Symphony,* cast in four movements, is quite direct and simple in its expressive language. The first movement (Allegro) is muscular and heroic, but also has a playful manner about it. Overall, the music here abounds in excitement and rhythmic appeal; it is full of the bright colors and naïve charm that any high-school chorister who has sung Thompson's music will know. The ensuing Largo is lovely and sentimental, with the character, in places, of a score for a lavish 1930s big-screen love story. Some passages sound like a mixture of Hanson and Korngold, although the latter was probably unknown to Thompson at the time.

The heroic vigor of the Vivace third movement charms, and the Finale, which opens with an attractive Andante moderato, then moves on to an upbeat and rhythmically driven Allegro con spirito and provides a colorful and exciting close. In the end, one is prompted to wonder why this charming work is not more popular. *—Robert Cummings*

Recommended:

- ○ **American Masters: Harris, Thompson, Diamond** / Bernstein (cond.), New York PO / 1998 / Sony 60594

Virgil Thomson

b. Nov. 25, 1896, Kansas City, MO, **d.** Sep. 30, 1989, New York, NY

Composer: Opera, Keyboard, Symphonic, Film Music

Perhaps best known for his collaborations with author Gertrude Stein, American composer and music critic Virgil Thomson was born in Kansas City. He began playing piano at the age of five and began taking lessons with local teachers at age 12. He studied organ from 1909 until 1917, and again in 1919. As a young man, Thomson worked as an organist in his family's church of Calvary Baptist, as well as in other churches throughout Kansas City. After attending Central High School from 1908 to 1913, Thomson enrolled at a local junior college, where he studied from 1915 to 1917, and again in 1919. During World War I, Thomson enrolled in the Army, where he served in a field artillery unit. He also received training in radio telephony at Columbia University and in aviation in Texas. The war ended shortly before Thomson was to leave for France.

In the fall of 1919, Thomson enrolled at Harvard University, where he met three individuals who would come to have a profound influence on the young musician. The first of these was Edward Burlingame Hill, with whom Thomson studied orchestration and modern French music. Archibald T. Davison was the conductor of the Harvard Glee Club, a group with which Thomson spent three years as assistant and accompanist. Thomson also came into contact with S. Foster Damon, a Blake Scholar who introduced him to the music of Satie and the writings of Gertrude Stein. Thomson began to compose in 1920, while still a student at Harvard.

Thomson spent the summer of 1921 touring Europe with the Glee Club. As the tour wound down, Thomson decided to remain, and under a John Knowles Paine Traveling Fellowship, he studied organ with Nadia Boulanger and counterpoint privately. During this time, he continued to compose and had his first critical writings published by the *Boston Transcript*. Upon his return the U.S., Thomson returned to Harvard and became organist/choirmaster at King's Chapel in Boston. After his graduation from Harvard in 1923, a grant from the Juilliard School allowed him to go to New York, where he studied conducting with Chalmers Clifton and counterpoint with Rosario Scalero.

From 1925 to 1940, aside from occasional visits to the U.S., Thomson resided in Paris. It was there, in 1926, that he met Stein. The two began to plan an opera, the result of which is *Four Saints in Three Acts*, perhaps Thomson's most famous work. For a period of approximately seven years after the composition of *Four Saints in Three Acts*, Thomson explored the problems of "pure" music as he worked on expanding his technical facility as a composer, especially in regards to writing for string instruments. During the late 1930s, Thomson returned to a more nationalistic vein with the scores to two films, *The Plow That Broke the Plain* and *The River*, and a ballet, *Filling Station*.

In October of 1940, Thomson became music critic for *The New York Herald Tribune*. Although he continued to compose during his 14 years at the post, Thomson established himself as one of the foremost critical writers of the era. His writings, which are characterized by a brilliant and at times deeply provocative, but always highly opinionated whit, furnished material for three anthologies; *The Musical Scene*, *The Art of Judging Music and Music*, and *Right and Left*. Throughout the 1950s and 1960s, Thomson traveled extensively as a guest lecturer, or a conference participant, all the while continuing to conduct, write articles, and compose. *—Stephen Kingsbury*

Overview of Works (1920–1985)

Virgil Thomson wrote music in several styles, leaving much of his work difficult to categorize. He was mostly tonal, but dabbled in quasi-serial techniques, as in his 1949 *A Solemn Music* for band (arranged for orchestra in 1961). And in works like his film score (and suite) *The Plow That Broke the Plains* (1936), he could write both cowboy Americana and catchy blues music. Erik Satie was both an idol and a stylistic influence, yet Impressionist elements also appear in his compositions and Thomson acknowledged a debt to Debussy. In the end, he must be viewed as an eclectic whose music was generally approachable and boldly individual.

Thomson's first serious composition was his *Sonata da chiesa* (1926, revised in 1973), a rather dissonant piece full of humor and mischief, the music, in its brilliant and unusual instrumentation (clarinet, horn, trumpet, trombone, and viola), deftly parodies its own initial seriousness. Shortly after finishing it, Thomson began work on the first of his three operas, *Four Saints in Three Acts* (1927-33). The puzzling and rather plotless libretto by Gertrude Stein and Thomson's unexceptional but still imaginative score have conspired against the work's acceptance. Better are his other two operas, the 1947 *The Mother of Us All* (another Stein collaboration) and *Lord Byron* (1961-68, libretto by Jack Larson). The former, a mostly humorous piece supposedly about Susan B. Anthony, features energetic, witty music and colorful orchestration, while the latter, probably Thomson's greatest opera, offers both deeper music and a stronger libretto, which together yield a true sense of passion, something the composer often avoided—or could not achieve—in other works. Thomson wrote a large series of pieces for piano, many later orchestrated, called *Portraits*, the first coming in 1927 and the last in 1985. In all, there are more than 150 and their subjects include Picasso, Gertrude Stein, Aaron Copland, and Eugene Ormandy. Their music is typically witty and colorful and includes waltzes, hymns (Baptist hymns were often a source of quotation for Thomson), canonic writing, simple scales, and other various forms and elements. Thomson's songs are among his finest creations and he must rank among the very best American composers in this vocal genre. The *Four Songs to Poems of Thomas Campion* (1951), *Shakespeare Songs* (1956–57), and *Praises and Prayers* (1963) are just three of his better sets. His choral music significantly divulges his Baptist background only in his arrangements (*My Shepherd Will Supply My Need*), but his other works in the genre show his generally eclectic style, from his 1960 requiem mass *Missa pro defunctis*, which occasionally employs jazzy elements, to *The Nativity as Sung by the Shepherds* (1966-67). Thomson's other film scores include the outstanding *The River* (1937) and *Louisiana Story* (1948). His *Three Pictures for Orchestra—The Seine at Night* (1947), *Sea Piece With Birds* (1952), and *Wheat Field at Noon* (1948) are among his finest orchestral works. *—Robert Cummings*

Recommended:

- ○ **Thomson: Symphony on a Hymn Tune; Symphonies 2 & 3; Pilgrims & Pioneers** / J. Sedares (cond.), New Zealand SO / 2000 / Naxos 559022
- ○ **Nothing Devine is Mundane: The Songs of Virgil Thomson** / Ohrenstein, Sharp, Siebert, Bush / 1997 / Albany 272
- ○ **Virgil Thomson** / Frohnmayer, McCracken, Lyman, Cassin, Cohen, Voorhees, Skelton / 1994 / Centaur 2180
- ○ **Early and as Remembered** / Mikhashoff, Herr, Boudler, Kuehn / 1991 / New Albion 034

OPERA

Four Saints in Three Acts (1927–1928)

By joining the army in 1917 Virgil Thomson freed himself from years of organ-loft drudgery in Protestant churches throughout his hometown of Kansas City, Missouri. But his European "debut" was delayed until 1921, as a member of the touring Harvard Glee Club. Although most of his comrades returned to school, Thomson stayed on to study with the renowned pedagogue Nadia Boulanger: organ officially, counterpoint privately. When their association became confrontational, he too returned home, graduated from Harvard in 1923, then studied traditional counterpoint for two more years in New York City.

Returning to Paris in 1925, he met all the right avant-garde people, and was courted as a protégé by Ezra Pound (already George Antheil's sponsor). But Thomson joined Gertrude Stein's circle instead after meeting her in 1926. By then he'd already made a setting of her poem *Susie Asado* (1926), adding *Preciosilla* (1927) and *Capital Capitals* (1927) later on. Their major collaboration, however, was a Dada-ish confection called *Four Saints in Three Acts*, which Stein began writing in 1927. By then Thomson had completed the first three movements of *Symphony on a Hymn Tune*, and in the same vein—drawing upon his organ-loft immersion in Southern Baptist hymnody—he began to compose music for the expatriate poet's semi-surreal, plotless "libretto" (set in Spain because she loved it there).

Thomson's contribution was free-associative—music both simplistic and sophisticated—but the two shared a wavelength nonetheless. In the autobiography to celebrate his 70th birthday, Thomson took credit for many of the ideas that gave Stein's characters shape as well as context. He also made textual cuts later on, when the money was eventually found to premiere *Four Saints*—in Hartford, Connecticut, on February 8, 1934, six years after its completion. Because he prized their diction, Thomson insisted on Afro-American singers for the "more than 30 saints" in four acts (and scenes galore), who surround St. Teresa of Avila —there are two of her, so she can sing duets with herself—and St. Ignatius Loyola.

It was his idea to have a Compère and Commère (implicitly himself and Stein), who serve as traffic cops and docents. To create a semblance of coherent theater within Frances Stettheimer's fanciful cellophane sets, however, Thomson needed to recruit Maurice Grosser, who contrived a "scenario." John Houseman agreed to direct (and was a frequent collaborator later on, notably in Orson Welles' Mercury Theatre productions). Frederick Ashton, then at the beginning of his career, choreographed.

The production got widespread coverage, moved to Broadway for 60 performances, and went on tour—including Chicago, where Stein finally saw it—but has rarely been remounted since. *Four Saints* works fine in concert, without staged "events" to distract from Stein's eremitic text and Thomson's slyly homespun music, which includes a harmonium and an accordion. More successful onstage is their second operatic collaboration (and Stein's last work), *The Mother of Us All*, begun in 1946 and completed a year later. *—Roger Dettmer*

Synopsis:

When Gertrude Stein gave Thomson her "libretto" titled *Four Saints in Three Acts*, it consisted of a prologue and four acts. Her only other indications regarding setting and subject matter are found below (in italics). The following "synopsis" (for want of a more suitable term) is based on a scenario that Thomson asked Maurice Grosser to concoct (after the fact) for the first production. Stein provided no plot—just words, many of them puns, many free-associative, most of them surreal. She gave names (both invented and historically accurate) to 16 saints—17 if you count St. Teresas I and II, the bifurcated heroine. But everyone in the double chorus is also a saint: not even Thomson was sure of the exact number. He suggested the inclusion of two nonecclesiastics, Compère and Commère, who mainly try to keep track of the number of acts and scenes. Presumably the setting is sixteenth century Spain—Avila and, later on, Barcelona—as certain as one can be in this protracted example of *Dadaïsme*. Oh, and Heaven, too, in the brief last act, where all the saints are joyfully reunited.

Prologue. A narrative of prepare for saints amounts to a roll call after Compère and Commère talk of "four benches separately," three in the sun, one not in the sun. Subsequently Chorus I breaks into "My country 'tis of thee sweet land of liberty of thee I sing" (unpunctuated) before naming of a slew of saints, leading into the first act.

Act One. Saint Teresa half indoors and half out of doors at Avila—"A pleasure April Fool's Day a pleasure Saint Theresa seated." Grosser had her painting flowers on outsized eggs, after which her fictional acolyte, Saint Settlement, photographed Teresa II with a dove. Next, St. Ignatius Loyola serenades Teresa II with a guitar. He presents her with flowers, and shows her a model of the Heavenly Mansion. Grosser ended the act with Saint Theresa II "in ecstasy" as the Spanish spring prompts her to prepare for summer, and finally, wearing a halo, "pretending to hold a baby in her arms."

Act Two. Might it be mountains if it were not Barcelona is St. Ignatius' territory, and that of *his* fictive acolyte, St. Chavez. Grosser decided it should be a garden party, which included "Dance of Angels" and a love scene between Compère and Commère that is almost entirely a recitation of scene numbers. Saint Teresa overhears them, and both I and II approve; "they" are given a telescope through which to see the Heavenly Mansion, and speculate on its architecture.

Act Three. Saint Ignatius and one of two literally are in a monastery garden mending fish nets. They are joined by Saints Teresa and Settlement. To them and to his fellow friars St. Ignatius recounts his *Vision of the Holy Ghost*: "Pigeons on the grass alas [and] a magpie in the sky," while offstage the full chorus sings "Let Lucy Lily Lily Lucy Lucy..." over and over. After "a dance in the Spanish style" there is a "Storm in miniature without rain," and St. Ignatius' prediction of the Last Judgment. The Saints parade, singing "in wed in dead/in dead led wed/in led wed dead. ..." An orchestral Intermezzo recalls the Prelude, followed by the Prologue to Act Four (Compère and Commère, still counting the number of saints and acts).

Act Four. The sisters and saints reassembled and reënacting why they went away to stay in Heaven. The opera ends apace with "Last Act. Which is a fact." And a crescendo roll on a snare drum for punctuation. *—Roger Dettmer*

Recommended:

○ **Thomson: Four Saints In Three Acts** / Orchestra of Our Time; various soloists / 1982 / Nonesuch 79035

○ **Thomson: Four Saints In Three Acts; The Plow That Broke The Plains** / (abridged) / Thomson (cond.), various soloists / 1996 / RCA 68163

The Mother of Us All (1947)

Based on the life and struggles of suffragette Susan B. Anthony (1820-1906), this "pageant" has as its theme "the winning in the United States of political rights for women." We hear gentle arias expressing her weariness at leading a totally public life in the seemingly endless fight for equal rights for women. There are also deep reflections about the meaning of "family," and the humanistic actions versus a blind obedience towards the law. There are magnificent marches and chorus sections as well as atmospheric passages beautiful and engaging in their simplicity. In fleeting reference, Thomson sometimes quotes tunes that have become imbedded in American life, such as Gertrude S.'s brief charming song set to a slightly transformed "London Bridge Is Falling Down" in Act One, Scene Two, "My father's name was Daniel, he had a black beard, he was not tall at all...."

Largely through the structural influence of Stein's text, Thomson achieves a unique flexibility in this opera that was to greatly inform his later works like the *Third Symphony* and the film scores. There are several methods through which Thomson achieves this, chief of which are the unusual rhythmic turns which displace the habitual sense of symmetrical resolution. Avoiding traditional modulations and recitatives, Thomson also constantly refreshes our interest by patching one song right to another with minimal break. And then he will recall a song in the orchestra to underscore a completely new vocal, such as Susan B. Anthony's moving and lyrical theme, between a hymn and a trumpet call, that first appears in G major and C major, compassionately describing an existential state of humanity, only to reappear in C minor and then C major at the finale to underscore the famous line "Do you know because I tell you so, or do you know." The curtain then descends in silence followed by the most gentle of major chords.

The list of Americana characters include both historical personages, some widely separated in time, and imaginary figures. Besides the dramatic soprano Susan B. Anthony, the cast includes Anne, Susan's devoted friend; the writer Gertrude S., and composer Virgil T., both costumed as in life; the politicos and political V.I.P.s Daniel Webster, Andrew Johnson, John Adams, Ulysses S. Grant, and Thaddeus Stevens; Civil War veterans Jo the Loiterer and Chris the Citizen; contralto Indiana Elliott; part angel, part ghost, part ingenue Angel More, the former sweetheart of Daniel Webster; feminists Henrietta M., Jenny Reefer (with her outspoken sense of humor), and Anna Hope; Henry B.; Victorian capitalist Anthony Comstock; peacemaker Constance Fletcher; intellectuals Gloster Heming and Isabel Wentworth; lyric soprano Lillian Russell; French painter Herman Atlan; college professor Donald Gallup; multiple page boys or postillions called A.A. and T.T.; a Negro Man and a Negro Woman, rural laborers of the 1860s-1870s; and Indiana Elliott's brother, a Midwestern farmer. *—"Blue Gene" Tyranny*

Synopsis:

Act One. Most of this episodic opera is set in nineteenth century America, around 1870. Composer Thomson and librettist Gertrude Stein serve as adjunct characters, occasionally narrating from their positions downstage. The opening scene gives the audience a glimpse of life at home for Susan B. Anthony and her ever-present companion, her sister Anne, who are shown conversing. The following scene takes place at a political rally under a tent, attended by Daniel Webster and other politicians (Andrew Johnson, Ulysses S. Grant, John Adams, etc.) whose pompous manner is derided by two young men, Jo (the Loiterer) and Chris (the Citizen). Before a crowd that also includes Lillian Russell, Angel More, and Constance Fletcher, Susan engages Webster in a debate (a fictional incident—like much else in the opera—since, as far as it is known, the two never met), their texts mostly drawn from actual quotations.

The ensuing scene happens in a public place outside Susan's house, where Andrew Johnson and Thaddeus Stevens argue politics and Constance Fletcher and John Adams appear as lovers. Jo and Chris are cast as philosophers, but with a satirical bent. Susan, in the following scene, sees difficulties ahead for her cause of women's suffrage, and she later explains her ideas to Chris and Jo.

At the wedding of Jo and Indiana Elliot, officiated by Daniel Webster, the latter's brother attempts to stop the proceedings. Indiana repudiates him, and Susan then expounds on the institution of marriage, not standing in opposition to it. When the ceremony ends, she predicts that the female children of Jo and Elliot will have the right to vote in their adulthood.

Act Two. Susan, in her drawing room, rejects offers by her supporters to give a speech, while Jo worries over the refusal by Indiana to adopt his surname. Finally, Susan acquiesces and decides to deliver the speech. Afterwards, Susan and Anne discuss her ideas on men. The former remains optimistic about her cause, undeterred by male politicians who have recently set a precedent (to counter her influence) by inserting the word "men" into a Constitutional amendment. Lillian Russell, now a supporter of women's suffrage, John Adams, Constance Fletcher, Daniel Webster, and others enter. Adams expresses his preference for the beauty of Fletcher over that of Russell, and Webster chides Susan for her interest in women's suffrage, a movement he dismisses as unimportant. Indiana has decided she will adopt the name "Indiana Loiterer" if her husband reciprocates by taking Elliot as his surname. The scene ends with most of those present offering praise to Susan for her great leadership.

Epilogue. The Epilogue takes place at a later, unspecified time, in the halls of Congress as a ceremony is being conducted at the unveiling of a statue of Susan B. Anthony. Anne arrives alone, and following soon are John Adams, Constance Fletcher, U.S. Grant, Indiana, and others. Virgil Thomson unveils the Anthony statue, and Susan herself then steps forth to expound on her life and work. *—Robert Cummings*

Recommended:

○ **The Mother of Us All** / Leppard (cond.), Santa Fe Opera / 1977 / New World 80288

KEYBOARD

Portraits (1929–1985)

The practice of painting musical "portraits" of people was not a new one in the mid-twentieth century. Couperin and Schumann claimed to have done so. Anton Rubinstein did so overtly in his *Kamenniy-ostrov*, and Elgar subtly and namelessly embedded a portrait in the renowned *Enigma Variations*. American composer Virgil Thomson took the practice further, however, making a lifelong habit of sketching others in musical notation.

Early in his career Thomson became part of the salon of noted author Gertrude Stein, who exerted a complex influence on the composer. Stein made a habit of rendering people she met in poetry or prose, an approach which struck Thomson as novel. While suffering through a period of composer's block in southern France in 1928, Thomson thought to dash off a piece for solo violin entitled *Portrait of Señorita Juanita de Medina Accompanied by Her Mother*. Excited by the compositional possibilities, Thomson next produced a portrait of a soprano friend, *Madame Marthe-Marthine*; more were to follow, including one, appropriately enough, of *Miss Gertrude Stein as a Young Girl*.

Thomson was setting a pattern that would continue for the remaining 60 years of his life; he produced nearly 300 such portraits. Though no two were alike, his method in making them varied little. During a time between the composition of two monumental works (for example, after the opera *Four Saints in Three Acts* and before the *Symphony on a Hymn Tune*), Thomson found these pieces (most just a minute or two in length) a refreshing change, using them as both mental exercise and leisure pursuit. Beginning with fellow composer Henri Sauguet, Thomson asked subjects to "sit" for him, as if they were to be painted. Thomson would go into deep concentration, and quickly sketch out, in a single sitting lasting as long as an hour and a half, a piece based largely on the aura or feeling created by the subject. The resulting piece could be simple and melodic or atonal and fiery, depending on the person and especially on Thomson's impression of him or her.

Orchestration might come, but only later. The majority of the portraits are for piano solo; notable ones are the tempestuous *Bugles and Birds: A Portrait of Pablo Picasso* and the dodecaphonic *Portrait of Alice Branlière*. Other portraits are for violin solo, or for any number of combinations: brass quintet, four clarinets (*Five Portraits for Four Clarinets*), or even the most elaborate, the orchestral *Concerto for Flute, Strings, Harp and Percussion*, a representation of Thomson's close friend, painter Roger Baker. Portraits may be found singly (*Portrait of Jamie Campbell*), in collections (*A Family Portrait*, consisting of five portraits for brass quintet), or scattered throughout his other works (as in *Ten Etudes for Piano*, which include the *Portrait of Briggs Buchanan*).

Thomson's portraits distinguish him from his twentieth century American colleagues, although many have yet to receive publication. In creating and exploiting an original genre of composition, Thomson refracted many friends and colleagues through his own inimitably clever compositional lens. *—Thomas Oram*

Recommended:

○ **Early and as Remembered** / Mikhashoff, Herr, Boudler, Kuehn / 1991 / New Albion 034

SYMPHONIC

Symphony No. 1 ("Symphony on a Hymn Tune") (1926–1928)

Thomson composed this first of his three symphonies in Europe between 1926 and 1928. After orchestrating it for standard-size orchestra (double winds, brass, timpani, strings, and three percussionists), he brought the finished work with him to the U.S. on a visit in 1929. During the same gestating period he wrote the opera *Four Saints in Three Acts* to a text by Gertrude Stein. Thomson had not yet heard any music by Charles Ives (most of which was composed between 1900 and 1918), which likewise featured hymn tunes, parlor songs, marches, and the like. Most other persons hadn't heard it either, even privately, before Nicolas Slonimsky led a chamber-orchestra version of *Three Places in New England* (ca. 1908–14) in 1931–32 for avant-garde audiences in New York, Havana, and Paris.

During his four-month stateside visit, Thomson played *Symphony on a Hymn Tune* for Serge Koussevitzky, then in his fifth year as conductor of the Boston Symphony Orchestra (a post Thomson's student reportage from Paris in 1921 had helped the Russian-born maestro to secure). Koussevitzky praised the first three movements, but after the last one "threw up his hands" and said "I could never play my audience that," urging Thomson to write a new, presumably more "serious" finale. Although hurt by the rebuff, Thomson did not; instead, he put the work in a drawer where it remained until 1945. By then he was in his fifth year as chief music critic of *The New York Herald Tribune*. Artur Rodzinski, then music director of the New York Philharmonic, asked Thomson to conduct the symphony himself, which the composer did on February 22, 1945. "The press," he wrote, "was almost wholly disapproving," especially his *New York Times* counterpart (and beleagured rival), who dismissed it as "trivial and inconsequential."

Oddly, not even Ives' belated recognition a year later (when New York's tastemakers discovered the Third Symphony) encouraged a revival of Thomson's kindred work, until Howard Hanson conducted it for Mercury Records in 1965. Erich Leinsdorf championed it in his terminal seasons as a global guest conductor, before and after Thomson's death in 1989. In 2000, Naxos released an outstandingly insightful recording of all three Thomson symphonies by James Sedares and the New Zealand Symphony, resulting in worldwide recognition.

Thomson himself described the work as "a set of variations on the hymn '*How Firm a Foundation*.' Each movement consists of a further set of variations tightened up in various ways, the first in the manner of a sonata, the second as a Bach chorale prelude, the third as a passacaglia. The fourth is twice tightened-up, once as a fugato, once as a rondo." He also included a second hymn, "Yes, Jesus Loves Me," plus the secular "For He's a Jolly Good Fellow." Composer John Cage, in pointing out a wealth of sly parodies and irreverent puns, suggested that the work be subtitled "Musique concrète: Four Adventures in Collage 20 Years Ahead of Their Time." *—Roger Dettmer*

Recommended:

○ **Thomson: Symphony on a Hymn Tune; Symphonies 2 & 3; Pilgrims & Pioneers** / Sedares (cond.), New Zealand SO / 2000 / Naxos 559022

FILM MUSIC

The Plow That Broke the Plains, film score and suite (1936)

Aaron Copland declared Thomson's score for *The Plow That Broke the Plains* to be "a lesson in how to treat Americana," and this music strongly influenced such later Copland American pieces as *Rodeo* and *Appalachian Spring*. The music originated on the soundtrack of a short Pare Lorentz documentary commissioned by the U.S. Department of Agriculture's Farm Security Administration. It's a curious film, honest in its depiction of the devastation wrought upon America's farmland during the Dustbowl years, but concluding with a call for confidence in the government's efforts to reclaim the land for future agricultural use. Thomson's music closely follows the tone of each scene, incorporating at one point a bluesy jazz band sound and at another some orchestrated cowboy tunes, all amid a more standard "classical" orchestral approach. The concert suite Thomson prepared in 1942 does not substantially differ from the music heard in the film. The bleak Prelude opposes a mildly dissonant string motif with a woodwind setting of the "Doxology"; the use of this chorale may remind some listeners of Thomson's *Symphony on a Hymn Tune*. "Pastorale (Grass)" is a sweet little movement employing the woodwinds (and later, brass and strings) in canonic polyphony that builds to a substantial climax. "Cattle" employs guitar and woodwinds and later, strings and brass, in a deft medley of cowboy waltzes, primarily "I Ride an Old Paint" with splashes of "Streets of Laredo" and "Git Along Little Dogies." "Blues (Speculation)" takes on alto and tenor saxophones and banjo for a 1920s-style jazz lament more comic-acerbic than pathetic. The main tune shares a subtle kinship with the Prelude's third theme. "Drought" is a haunting 16-bar canon, followed by the concluding movement "Devastation." This returns to the motif that opened the suite, touches again on the "Doxology," and then reworks the Prelude's third theme into a new, gradually more confident melody. Incongruously, a tango beat arrives, as if this were a film about the struggles of Latin American farm workers, but this helps build the music to a defiant climax in the face of natural disaster. *—James Reel*

Recommended:

○ **Thomson: Suites from The River & The Plow That Broke The Plains; Stravinsky: L'histoire du Soldat** / Stokowski (cond.), Symphony of the Air / 1994 / Vanguard 1

The Three Tenors

f. 1990, Rome, Italy
Ensemble

The list of performances by the Three Tenors—Luciano Pavarotti, Plácido Domingo, and José Carreras—is not long, and they have recorded only a few albums. Yet they rank among the most successful performers the world of classical music has ever experienced. Their debut concert, held in Rome on July 7, 1990, drew an international television viewership of over one billion people.

Individually, the three tenors were arguably the world's top opera stars of the 1970s and 1980s; often considered rivals, they weren't particularly close. What brought them together was the devastating illness of Carreras, who was diagnosed with leukemia in the summer of 1987 and given a 10 percent chance of survival. A friendship sprang up as Pavarotti and Domingo visited him in the hospital, and after Carreras recovered he suggested that the three join to perform a benefit concert for a leukemia foundation he had created. Held at the end of the World Cup soccer competition, an event with maximum television visibility, the concert succeeded beyond anything Carreras might have imagined. An important behind-the-scenes presence was composer Lalo Schifrin, who arranged favorite operatic selections for the trio; a group consisting of three male singers was a novelty at the time.

The dimensions of the Three Tenors' success became clear when the album *Carreras, Domingo, Pavarotti: The Three Tenors in Concert* sold over ten million copies and became the best-selling classical album of all time. The tenors reunited for another concert and album at the next World Cup, held in Los Angeles in 1994. Although they had performed together only once in the interim, they repeated their 1990 success at Dodger Stadium on July 16, 1994. Among the audience of 60,000 were California royalty such as future governor Arnold Schwarzenegger, and the concert extended the Tenors' reach into segments of the American music-buying public that otherwise had little contact with classical music. The Three Tenors were now international superstars.

The tenors reunited for a third mega-spectacle at the Paris World Cup in 1998, performing at the Champ de Mars near the Eiffel Tower. Between 1994 and 2003 they performed about 30 concerts at large stadiums around the world, but Pavarotti's stated intention to retire from performing in 2004 seemed likely to put an end to the trio's reign atop classical sales charts. Growth in opera audiences, even as other forms of classical music declined, seemed at least partly attributable to their efforts. *—James Manheim*

Recommended:

○ **The Three Tenors in Concert** / Mehta (cond.), Carreras, Domingo, Pavarotti, Maggio Musicale Fiorentino Orch. / 1990 / Decca 430433

Lawrence Tibbett

b. Nov. 16, 1896, Bakersfield, CA, **d.** Jul. 15, 1960, New York
Baritone

Baritone Lawrence Tibbett was one of the glamor figures of opera in the 1930s and 1940s—a strikingly handsome man with a virile voice and plenty of dramatic talent. He began his career balancing between drama and music, at one point acting in a Shakespeare company directed by Tyrone Power Sr., appearing in musicals, and singing in various churches. Tenor Joseph Dupuy heard him and took him on as a pupil, and later Basil Ruysdael gave him several lessons, including the natural technique of delivering text and music that greatly contributed to his success.

Through various connections, he met Frances Alda, a soprano and wife of Gatti-Casazza, the general manager of the Metropolitan Opera. She arranged for him to audition, and he made his Met debut in 1923 in the small part of Lewicki in *Boris Godunov*; his debut in a lead role (Valentin in Gounod's *Faust*) came quickly. His first great career success was in 1925, in an all-star tribute to Antonio Scotti, in which he substituted as Ford in Verdi's *Othello* for Vincente Ballester. After Ford's monologue, the house went wild, applauding and shouting for 16 minutes, and Tibbett's future as the Met's leading baritone lay clearly ahead. (This future seemed in doubt after Tibbett became too violent in an onstage confrontation in *La cena delle beffe* and threw his leading lady to the ground; after the performance, Beniamino Gigli whistled Chopin's famous *Funeral March* outside Tibbett's dressing room door, but no long-term harm was done.)

Tibbett became a passionate champion of American opera, and in the late 1920s and 1930s he sang in the world premieres of many notable American works, the best known of which are *The King's Henchman* and *Peter Ibbetson* (Deems Taylor), *The Emperor Jones* (Louis Gruenberg), *Merry Mount* (Howard Hanson), *In the Pasha's Garden* (John Seymour), and *Caponsacchi* (Richard Hageman). Additionally, he was a major figure on radio, was the first president of the American Guild of Musical Artists, and was one of the first "serious" opera singers to appear in full-length films, starting with Lionel Barrymore's 1929 *The Rogue Song*. He followed this with *New Moon* (1930), *The Prodigal* (1931), *Cuban Love Song* (1931), *Metropolitan* (1935), and *Under Your Spell* (1936).

He did not, however, sing outside the United States until 1937, when he debuted as Scarpia in Puccini's *Tosca* at Covent Garden; this led to his creation of the role of Don Juan in Eugene Goossens' *Don Juan de Mañara*. In 1940, he was ill for several months with a throat problem, and this and his growing alcoholism led to serious vocal difficulties; many of his subsequent performances were deeply criticized. He began to move back to drama and musicals towards the end of his career, appearing in the Broadway opera *The Barrier*, by Jan Meyerowitz and Langston Hughes, and making his stage farewell in *Fanny* in 1956. He died in an automobile accident. *—Ann Feeney*

Recommended:

- ○ **Stanford Archive Series** / Tibbett, etc. / 1997 / Delos 5500
- ○ **From Broadway to Hollywood** / Tibbett, etc. / 1996 / Nimbus 7881
- ○ **The RCA Victor Vocal Series** / Tibbett, etc. / 1989 / RCA 7808

Colin Tilney

b. Oct. 31, 1933, London, England
Harpsichordist

Colin Tilney is an English early music keyboard player, an unusually active survivor of the first generation of musicians who brought the idea of historically informed performance to the general concertgoer's consciousness. Tilney's repertoire stretches from the sixteenth century to the late eighteenth, and he has played the fortepiano, the virginal, and even an occasional continuo organ in addition to his main instrument, the harpsichord. Further, he has often attempted to match specific instruments with appropriate repertoire. Born in London, Tilney studied music and languages at Cambridge and then sought out harpsichord lessons with several teachers, Gustav Leonhardt among them. He began performing and recording, at first mostly in ensembles devoted to English music, in the early 1960s. His U.S. debut came in 1971. Tilney has taught at the University of Toronto and at Toronto's Royal Conservatory of Music since 1979 and has edited several printed collections of specialized Baroque repertoire, including *The Art of the Unmeasured Prelude* (1991). He has made an acclaimed recording of Bach's *Well-Tempered Clavier* and has recorded the complete keyboard works of Matthew Locke. A good example of Tilney's work on disc is the 1996 album *Scarlatti High and Low*, which presented Domenico Scarlatti harpsichord sonatas that lay at the extremes of the instrument's range. Here and elsewhere, Tilney not only presents unusual music engagingly, but also embodies expertise on the historical development of keyboard instruments. His interests also extend to contemporary music, and he has commissioned works for harpsichord from various Canadian composers and from the British quasi-serialist Elisabeth Lutyens. *—James Manheim*

Recommended:

- ○ **Tilney Plays Mozart** / Tilney / 2000 / Doremi 71137
- ○ **Harpsichord Music of Frescobaldi** / Tilney / 1990 / Dorian 90124
- ○ **Ladders to Heaven** / Tilney / 2003 / Dorian 93253
- ○ **Songs of Mozart** / Baird, Tilney / 1993 / Dorian 90173

Michael Tilson Thomas

b. Dec. 21, 1944, Los Angeles, CA
Conductor

Michael Tilson Thomas is among the most famous American-born conductors, with a bright, extroverted personality and a wide-ranging repertoire that has allowed him to take a place at the forefront of experimenation with the form and content of symphonic concerts. His grandparents were Boris and Bessie Thomaschevsky, founders of New York's Yiddish Theater, and his father Ted Thomas was an avid amateur pianist and worked in films and television.

Tilson Thomas attended the University of Southern California. where his composition and conducting teacher was Ingolf Dahl. At the age of 19 he was named music director of the Young Musicians Foundation Orchestra, and was selected as accompanist for master classes by Jascha Heifetz and Gregor Piatigorsky. In 1969 he won the Koussevitzky Prize at the Tanglewood festival in Massachusetts, which carried with it an appointment as assistant conductor of the festival's parent, the Boston Symphony Orchestra.

On October 22, 1969, he was called to replace William Steinberg in a Carnegie Hall concert at the last minute, repeating the circumstances of Leonard Bernstein's sensational emergency debut 26 years earlier. The results were nearly identical: Tilson Thomas was catapulted into the top ranks of American conductors. In 1970 he was appointed associate conductor of the BSO. He has served as music director of the Buffalo Philharmonic Orchestra, (1971–79), principal guest conductor of the Los Angeles Philharmonic (1981–85), principal conductor of the London Symphony Orchestra (1988–95), and was appointed music director of the San Francisco Symphony Orchestra in 1995.

He is the founder of the Florida-based New World Symphony Orchestra, which comprises a group of young and promising professional symphonic musicians. Membership in that ensemble is now considered a desirable first step in an orchestral career. Tilson Thomas remains its music director and has recorded notable CDs with the group, including a highly popular Villa-Lobos compilation.

Also a composer, Tilson Thomas wrote *From the Diary of Anne Frank* on commission from UNICEF in 1990 (actress Audrey Hepburn was the narrator at the premiere). The work has been performed in several countries and languages. He has also written *Showa/Shoáh* for the city of Hiroshima's memorial services on the fiftieth anniversary of its nuclear bombing. *—Joseph Stevenson*

Recommended:

- ○ **Tilson Thomas Performs & Conducts Gershwin** / Tilson Thomas (cond. & piano), Levee, Los Angeles PO / 1985 / CBS 39699
- ○ **Mahler: Symphony 4** / Tilson Thomas (cond.), Claycomb, San Francisco SO / San Francisco Symphony 4
- ○ **Ives: A Symphony, New England Holidays** / Tilson Thomas (cond.), Chicago SO / 1992 / Sony 42381
- ○ **Ives: Symphonies 2 & 3** / Tilson Thomas (cond.), Concertgebouw / 1982 / Sony 46440
- ○ **Barber & Copland** / Tilson Thomas (cond.), Hendricks, London SO / 1995 / EMI 55358
- ○ **Prokofiev: Romeo and Juliet** / Tilson Thomas (cond.), San Francisco SO / 2004 / RCA 59424
- ○ **Mahler: Symphony 3** / Tilson Thomas (cond.), George, DeYoung, San Francisco SO / 2002 / San Francisco Symphony 3

Georg Tintner

b. May 22, 1917, Vienna, Austria, **d.** Oct. 2, 1999, Halifax, Nova Scotia, Canada
Conductor

Born in Vienna, conductor Georg Tintner was a direct heir to the great tradition of nineteenth century musicianship, studying conducting in the 1930s with Felix Weingartner and music composition with Joseph Marx. Beginning his professional career at 12 as a member of the Vienna Boys Choir, Tintner accepted his first job as a conductor at the Vienna Volksoper at the tender age of 19. Tintner's career was barely underway when Hitler annexed Austria, displacing the 20-year-old rising star and making him a refugee from his homeland—he would never return to live in Vienna.

Tintner doesn't turn up until 1945, and then in Auckland, New Zealand, where he led the Auckland String Players until the mid-1950s. From there he moved to Australia, where he was based for the next 30 years, conducting the National Opera and Australian Opera and leading the first televised operas in Australian history. In the 1966–67 season Tintner served as resident conductor of the Cape Town Municipal Orchestra in South Africa. In the late 1960s Tintner made his first appearances in London with the Sadler's Wells Opera. Tintner's command of operatic repertory was enormous, and he conducted two-thirds of the works he undertook from memory.

In 1987 Tintner moved to Canada in order to accept the position of leader of the Nova Scotia Symphony Orchestra, beginning the last, and greatest, chapter of his life. His concerts were now regularly being broadcast by the CBC and Tintner began to record prolifically for CBC Records and for Naxos. This established interest anew in the now 70-something conductor, and in 1993 Tintner was awarded the Silver Cross of Honor by the city and province of Vienna, one of many awards and distinctions accorded to Tintner late in life. Tintner also conducted in the United States for the first time, leading the Michigan Opera Theater in Detroit. The pain and infirmity brought on by a lengthy bout with cancer ultimately proved too much for the conductor, who at age 82 managed to propel himself from the 11th story of his apartment building in Halifax, ending his life.

Tintner's complete cycle of the symphonies of Bruckner for Naxos are magnificent; combining a sense of experience, control, authority, and seemingly endless patience. Although known for his success in big classical works, Tintner was able to establish a sense of intimacy in his music making that was unique, and often spoke from the podium, one on one, to his audiences. For its part, Naxos has established a Georg Tintner Memorial Edition, rereleasing his recordings from both their catalog and that of CBC in addition to some live concerts taken from broadcasts; so far it has totaled 12 volumes, containing many truly great and worthwhile performances. *—Uncle Dave Lewis*

Recommended:

- ○ **Mozart: Symphonies 31, 35 & 40** / Tintner (cond.), Nova Scotia Symphony / 2003 / Naxos 8557233
- ○ **Mozart: Symphonies 34 & 41** / Tintner (cond.), Nova Scotia Symphony / 2003 / Naxos 8557239
- ○ **Bruckner: Symphony 4** / Tintner (cond.), Royal Scottish National Orch. / 1998 / Naxos 554128
- ○ **Bruckner: Symphony 7** / Tintner (cond.), Royal Scottish National Orch. / 1999 / Naxos 554269
- ○ **Bruckner: Symphonies 8 & 0** / Tintner (cond.), Irish National SO / 1998 / Naxos 554215-16
- ○ **Bruckner: Symphony 9** / Tintner (cond.), Royal Scottish National Orch. / 1999 / Naxos 554268

Michael Tippett

b. Jan. 2, 1905, London, England, **d.** Jan. 8, 1998, London, England

Composer: Choral, Chamber Music, Orchestral

A composer who came to music relatively late in life, Sir Michael Tippett has come to be regarded as one of the most original and important British composers of the twentieth century. Tippett brought a highly individual interpretation to twentieth century neo-Classicism, writing in all the principal genres. His compositions are characterized by a strong rhythmic vitality and a complexity of the basically tonal harmonic language, and were a vehicle for the articulation of his personal views of philosophical, social, and personal issues.

Tippett spent his childhood in Wetherden, a small village in Suffolk where his parents moved shortly after he was born. At the age of 13, he won a scholarship to Fettes College in Edinburgh. However, he disliked Fettes, and in 1920 transferred to Stamford Grammar School in Lincolnshire. Aside from piano lessons, Tippett received no musical training in his childhood. Despite this, after leaving Stamford, he expressed an interest in becoming a composer. At first, he decided to train as a professional pianist, staying on at Stamford so that he could continue to study with Frances Tinkler. However, in the summer of 1923 he left to begin study at London's Royal College of Music. While at the RCM, he studied composition with Charles Wood and C.H. Kitson, as well as piano with Aubin Raymar and conducting with Sargent and Boult.

When he left the RCM in 1928, Tippett settled in Oxted, Surrey. In 1929, he asked to teach French part-time at the local preparatory school. Thus began a series of occupations, which gave him money to live on, as well as some freedom to compose. In 1930, he gave a concert of his own works, which he felt highlighted the relative immaturity of his technique. With this in mind, Tippett began to study counterpoint and free composition with R.O. Morris. Soon after completing his lessons with Morris, in July 1932, Tippett was asked to run the music at an annual work-camp in north Yorkshire. Musically, these experiences were positive; however, for Tippett, a political leftist, the miserable conditions encountered at the work camps inspired an even more radical commitment. Eventually, Tippett came to espouse a strictly pacifist viewpoint. He centered his activities for the unemployed in London at Morley College, where in 1933 he was asked to conduct what later became the South London Orchestra, a group formed specifically to give unemployed musicians the opportunity to continue playing. A year later he also began conducting two choirs which were run by the Royal Arsenal Cooperative Society. In the summer of 1940 the South London Orchestra was disbanded. In October, after Morley College was almost destroyed in an air raid and the director of music was evacuated from London, Tippett was asked to become director of music. In November 1940, Tippett joined the Peace Pledge Union. After he received his call-up papers he registered as a conscientious objector. His case was heard in 1942, and he was ordered to non-combatant military duties. Tippett refused to comply, believing that he could best serve his country as a musician. He was sentenced to three months imprisonment, but qualified for a one-third remission.

In 1951 Tippett resigned from Morley College. Aside from working as a broadcaster at the BBC, he devoted himself entirely to composition. Tippett was knighted in 1966, and in 1979 he was made a Companion of Honour. He died peacefully at home on January 8, 1998. *—Stephen Kingsbury*

Overview of Works (1926–1995)

Michael Tippett was a true original among twentieth century English composers. Influenced by the angular rhythms of Stravinsky, the linear yet lyrical counterpoint of the English Renaissance madrigalists, the expressive vocal writing of Purcell, and above all by the visionary music and humanist personality of Beethoven, Tippett's music has nothing about it of the pastoral nationalism of Holst or Vaughan Williams, much less the wistful nostalgia and nervous splendor of Elgar. He wrote important works in all the major genres—five operas, four symphonies, five string quartets, four piano sonatas—plus significant works beyond easy categorization. In all of these works, Tippett's powerful character—humanitarian, physical, pacifistic, visionary, open to diverse styles of music but unified by his strong individuality—is immediately audible.

It is possible to divide Tippett's career into four phases. A late starter as a composer, his first representative work is the *Double Concerto for String Orchestra* (1938-39), a work whose soaring string writing and complex but infectious rhythms immediately established his voice. The masterpiece of his first period was the deeply affecting *A Child of Our Time* (1939–41), a work of topical political significance that marks the first use in Tippett's music of the blues as a musical symbol of suffering humanity. Tippett's second period started with his gorgeously lyrical first opera *The Midsummer Marriage* (1946–52) and includes the modernist but highly personal works of the late 1940s and 1950s: the lightly dancing *Symphony No. 1* (1944–45), the ebullient *Birthday Suite for Prince Charles* (1948), the neo-Baroque *Fantasia on a Theme of Corelli for String Orchestra* (1953), and the potently scored *Symphony No. 2* (1956–57), culminating in his second opera, the monumental tragedy *King Priam* (1958–61). Tippett's third period started with the knotty and gnarly *The Vision of St. Augustine for baritone, chorus, and orchestra* (1963–65) and includes some of his most complex and powerful works, the psychological opera *The Knot Garden* (1966–70) and the furiously concentrated two-movement *Symphony No. 3* (1970–72) for soprano and orchestra, which includes quotations from both the blues and Beethoven's *Symphony No. 9*. Tippett's fourth period is almost impossible to define: The range of his musical allusions grew to include a rock band in his fourth opera, *The Ice Break* (1973–76), and rap in his fifth and final opera, *New Year* (1986–88). The depth of his vision included everything from pre-history to post-history in his strange and majestic *The Mask of Time* (1980–82) for soloists, chorus, and orchestra, and the complexity of his structures generated the birth-through-death life story of the one-movement *Symphony No. 4* (1976–77). Lastly, the power of his musical imagination created the elusive shapes and luminous lights of his final orchestral work, *The Rose Lake* (1991–93). *—James Leonard*

Recommended:

- ○ **Tippett: Choral Works** / Darlington (cond.), Christ Church Cathedral Choir / 1990 / Nimbus 5266
- ○ **Tippett: A Child of our Time** / Hickox (cond.), White, Clarey, Haymon, Evans, London SO & Chorus / 1992 / Chandos 9123
- ○ **Tippett: King Priam** / Atherton (cond.), Langridge, Allen, Harper, Murray, Minton, Tear / 1995 / Chandos 9406/7
- ○ **Tippett: Symphony 1; Piano Concerto** / Hickox (cond.), Shelley, Bournemouth Sinfonietta / 1995 / Chandos 9333
- ○ **Tippett: Symphony 2; Suite from New Year** / Hickox (cond.), Bournemouth Sinfonietta / 1994 / Chandos 9299
- ○ **Tippett: Symphony 3; Praeludium** / Hickox (cond.), Robinson, Bournemouth Sinfonietta / 1994 / Chandos 9276
- ○ **Tippett: Symphony 4; Fantasia Concertante on a Theme of Corelli; Fantasia on a Theme of Handel** / Hickox (cond.), O'Brien, Shelley, Koos, Verrall, Bournemouth Sinfonietta / 1993 / Chandos 9233
- ○ **Tippett: Triple Concerto; Concerto for Orchestra** / Hickox (cond.), Chilingirian, Groote, Rowland-Jones, Walden, Bournemouth Sinfonietta / 1995 / Chandos 9384
- ○ **Tippett: The 5 String Quartets** / Lindsay SQ / 1996 / ASV 231

CHORAL

A Child of Our Time, oratorio (1939–1941)

A Child of our Time is an oratorio, scored for soloists, chorus, and orchestra. The history of its genesis is both fascinating and complex. As early as the years following World War I, Tippett had begun to plan out a musical work that would give voice to his empathy for the exploited and downtrodden. Further inspired by the terrible effects of unemployment in England in the 1930s, Tippett planned to write an opera on the theme of rejection. He considered the Easter Rising in 1916 in Dublin for his subject, but quickly abandoned the idea as too difficult to dramatize. By the mid-1930s, Tippett had decided to write an oratorio rather than an opera, but it was not until 1938 that he found the subject for his drama: the Nazi pogroms in Germany and Austria precipitated by the assassination of a German diplomat by a young Jew. The title of the oratorio was taken from German author Odon von Horvath's novel that recounts the bleak misfortunes of a young Nazi soldier who suffers for his compassion and idealism. While Tippett's inspiration for the text of the oratorio was derived from specific events in history, the work avoids direct reference to any particular historical moment: Tippett sought to create a drama that was timeless, rather than political—a work that spoke more generally to the harshness of human oppression.

After conceiving of the basic idea, Tippett asked T.S. Eliot to write a suitable libretto; Eliot refused, and so Tippett resolved to write the text himself. In its final form, the libretto contains a mixture of Jungian themes (inspired by Tippett's study of Jungian psychoanalysis) and Negro spirituals, whose emotional power and universality the composer found perfectly suited to the oratorio's theme.

Tippett studied the oratorios of Handel and Bach for inspiration, and he in fact borrowed one of Bach's chorales to form the backbone of his own oratorio. Primarily, however, *A Child of our Time* represents Tippett's desire to blend the essential qualities of Negro spirituals with features of his own style. The music, then, reflects the rhythmic and melodic style of the spirituals, but also Tippett's own complex harmonic language. In order to blend the contrasting idioms—the simple diatonic harmonies of the spirituals and Tippett's more chromatic, contrapuntal writing—Tippett chose a single melodic interval—the minor third—found frequently in the chosen spirituals, and used it as the motivic basis for the oratorio. In terms of overarching form, the work is in three parts, with an introductory orchestral prelude. Tippett follows the model of Bach and Handel by alternating sections of narrative recitative with more expansive choral pieces and solo arias. *—Alexander Carpenter*

Recommended:

○ **Tippett: A Child of our Time** / Hickox (cond.), White, Clarey, Haymon, Evans, London SO & Chorus / 1992 / Chandos 9123

CHAMBER MUSIC

The Blue Guitar, for guitar (1982–1983)

English composer Michael Tippett (1905–98) only composed one work for solo guitar, *The Blue Guitar.* Written for Julian Bream in 1983 and premiered in June of that year, *The Blue Guitar* was inspired by the poem of the same name by American poet Wallace Stevens, which was in turn inspired by the painting by Pablo Picasso entitled *The Man With the Blue Guitar.* Tippett described the origin of the work as follows: "In 1934, a Picasso exhibition came to Hertford, CT. The poet Wallace Stevens went to see it. He was struck by a painting with a guitar player. The impact stimulated him to write a poem with the title: *The Man With a Blue Guitar.* He set down the matter of the poem in the first stanza, which begins:

The man bent over his guitar,
A shearsman of sorts. The day was green.
They said, 'You have a blue guitar,
You do not play things as they are.'
The man replied, 'Things as they are
Are changed upon the blue guitar.'

Stevens explores the paradox of outer reality and artistic reality in a further 32 stanzas. Reading the poem acted for me roughly as the sight of Picasso's picture did for the poet. But of course all the words and concepts have disappeared and this piece for guitar is essentially music..."

The Blue Guitar, described as a sonata for guitar, is in three short movements: medium slow, fast, and very slow. Although its music is not overtly inspired by the blues, *The Blue Guitar* still has elements of the blues: flattened thirds, sixths, and sevenths in its melody and harmony, as well as slow tempos in its two outer movements. The style of the work is typically late Tippett, if anything in Tippett's late style could be said to be typical. The melodic shapes are elliptical, the harmonies are vaguely tonal but more often simply evocative, and the forms are oblique. Nevertheless, *The Blue Guitar* is a strangely lovely work and surely one of the major additions to the solo guitar repertoire. *—James Leonard*

Recommended:

○ **Sir Michael Tippett: Orchestral & Instrumental Works** / Ogden / 1998 / Nimbus 1759

ORCHESTRAL

Fantasia Concertante on a Theme of Corelli, for strings (1953)

In 1953, the Edinburgh Festival commissioned Michael Tippett to compose a piece for the tercentenary of the birth of Arcangelo Corelli (1653–1713). Some 12 years earlier, Tippett had completed a *Fantasia on a Theme of Handel for piano and orchestra,* but the youthful work (youthful, at least in terms of Tippett's career) is less successful than this more mature *Fantasia Concertante on a Theme of Corelli.* Also, for the *Corelli Fantasia,* Tippett calls for only strings, forgoing the percussive sound of the piano. Tippett completed the piece in three weeks, shortly after finishing his opera, *The Midsummer Marriage.* Tippett bases his *Fantasia Concertante* on two disparate melodic ideas from Corelli's *Concerto Grosso in F major,* Op. 6, No. 2, taking the Adagio theme and splicing it to a later, Vivace passage. Tippett maintains the divisions that are an important feature of Corelli's *Concerto*: the concertino, consisting of two violins and cello; the concerto grosso, which is the larger part of the orchestra; and a concerto terzo, representing the part of the sound performed in Corelli's orchestra by the basso continuo. The person slated to conduct the piece, Malcolm Sargent, gave a press conference before the performance and denounced the work, saying he wished to "get the intellectuals out of music." Tippett conducted the premiere himself, and it was left to the next generation of conductors to champion the work.

Although Tippett does not construct the *Fantasia Concertante,* in its entirety, in the style of Corelli, he does develop an Italian baroque flavor when he wishes. The *Fantasia's* opening moments suspend a sustained, singing melody over pizzicato strings in a style that is clearly modeled on Corelli. This and the second of Corelli's melodies are then put through seven variations, the lines becoming decorated to a greater extent than in the composer's completely original orchestra works. At one point, Tippett extracts Corelli's bass line, which has been transformed to F major, and transposes it to A flat major to create, as the composer once put it, "a melody of pure Puccini!" After the seventh variation, the real fantasia section begins and takes as its point of departure a transcription by Corelli of the subject from an *Organ Fugue in G minor,* BWV 578 by Bach, which is itself based on a tune by Corelli. To this historical layering Tippett adds several layers of counterpoint, creating an increasingly thick, fugal texture that reaches a powerful climax. The energy of this climax dissipates through a coda that is based on music from the closing *Dawn Chorus* of Tippett's *The Midsummer Marriage.* Throughout the *Fantasia Concertante,* the lush string orchestration and sweet solo violin passages remind the listener that the world of Vaughan Williams' fantasias is never very far away. *—John Palmer*

Recommended:

○ **Tippett: Piano Concerto; Praeludium; Fantasia on a Theme of Handel** / Hickox (cond.), O'Brien, Verrall, Koos, Bournemouth Sinfonietta / 2001 / Chandos 9934

Tokyo String Quartet

f. 1969, Tokyo, Japan
Ensemble

Shortly after its inception, the Tokyo Quartet became one of the most prominent string quartets in the world; since then, they have continued to uphold their reputation for insightful interpretations and a beautiful tonal blend. The quartet's original members—Koichiro Harada (first violin), Yoshiko Nakura (second violin), Kazuhide Isomura (viola), and Sadao Harada (cello)—all attened the Toho Gakuen (School of Music) during the 1960s, coming under the tutelage of the legendarily skilled and tyrannical pedagogue Hideo Saito. Another influence on the Tokyo's early development—perhaps even more important—was the Juilliard Quartet, which gave a series of workshops at Nikko during 1966; Harada, Isomura and Harada were all in attendance. It was, in fact, the members of the Juilliard Quartet who pointed out to the young players that there was then no permanent quartet in Japan, and that they might be the right musicians to form one. This led to arrangements for the group to study at the Juilliard School of Music; there the Tokyo Quartet was born.

The quartet was at first a casual endeavor—a "study quartet"—but it got serious quickly. In 1970, the Tokyo won the Coleman String Quartet Competition (judged by the members of the Amadeus Quartet), the Young Concert Artists International Auditions, and the Munich International Chamber Music Competition. From Munich, the quartet received a guarantee of a hundred concerts and an instant contract with Deutsche Grammophon; soon, the quartet had concertized around the world and won a Grand Prix du Disque. In 1974 the Corcoran Gallery in Washington D.C. lent them a group of priceless Amati instruments; they used these in concert until 1988.

Also in 1974, Kikuei Ikeda replaced Nakura as second violinist, making the quartet all-male; the quartet said at the time that Nakura wished to pursue a solo career, but in a 1975 interview with the Associated Press, Juilliard's Robert Mann said, "They always had it in mind to get rid of their girl player." In 1981 there was a further—and more surprising—shift in personnel when the departing Koichiro Harada was replaced with the group's first non-Japanese member, the Canadian-English-Armenian violinist Peter Oundjian. The quartet's playing, if anything, improved with Oundjian as leader; interpretations were freer and more passionate, while the playing maintained its beautiful blend. This happy association ended in 1996 when a hand injury prompted Oundjian's replacement—temporarily at first by the Orford String Quartet's first violinist, Andrew Dawes, and then permanently (1997) by the Borodin Quartet's Mikhail Kopelman. In 2000, Sadao Harada was replaced by Clive Greensmith, former principal cellist of the Royal Philharmonic Orchestra in London, making the Tokyo quartet truly international in membership.

Tokyo's interpretations are primarily distinguished by their determination to serve the music, rather than to display virtuosity. Their tone has shifted somewhat with the changes in personnel, but the quartet has always managed to make the adjustment successfully without sacrificing the quality of their blend. *—Andrew Lindemann Malone*

Recommended:

- ○ **Beethoven: Middle Quartets** / Tokyo SQ / 1993 / RCA 60462
- ○ **Bartok & Janáček: Complete String Quartets** / Tokyo SQ / 1996 / RCA 68286

Thomas Tomkins

b. 1572, St. David's, England, **d.** Jun. 9, 1656, Martin Hussingtree, England
Composer: Vocal

Thomas Tomkins was a Renaissance English composer known primarily for his virginal music and sacred music. A somewhat conservative composer, his substantial surviving music includes liturgical music, Anglican anthems, madrigals, and varied keyboard and consort works.

Tomkins was born into a musical family. His father, also named Thomas, was a vicar-choral of the Cathedral of St. David's, and his siblings became, variously, a composer (John), an organist (Giles) and a consort musician (Robert). He was, like Robert Morley, a student of Byrd and his master's style of music continued to influence his music all his life. Around 1596, he succeeded Nathaniel Patrick as organist to Worcester Cathedral, a post that he retained for most of his life. By 1620, he was full member of the Chapel Royal, and it appears that he divided his time between Worcester and London. In 1621, he became organist to the Chapel Royal, a very prestigious post, which he held jointly with Orlando Gibbons. He was nominated for the position of Composer of the Kings Music in 1628, but lost out to Alfonso Ferrabosco.

After 1628, he appears to have spent more time in Worcester. With the pre-civil war unrest, clashes between the radical Worcesterians and the more conservative Cathedral clergy grew nasty. Upon the outbreak of active civil war, roundheads attached the Cathedral and the organ dismantled in 1646. Tomkins, however, stayed in Worcester near the cathedral for another eight years before moving to the town of Martin Hussingtree, where his son Nathaniel lived. He died two years later.

Tomkins was the last of the school of English composers in the mold of Byrd. He continued to write in this style long after it was outdated and (relatively) unfashionable. His great collection of madrigals, for example, was his *Songs of 3, 4, 5, and 6 Parts* published in 1622. This collection comprised madrigals of a surprisingly outdated style, all of them belonging to the era *prima prattica* rather than the newer *seconda*. His large number of anthems fared somewhat better. His instrumental music, while also old-fashioned for the time, is compositionally sound and contains some very inventive work.

This clinging to older practices perhaps accounts for Tomkins' rather confused position in music history. Some scholars praise him as a genius. Some damn him as a dilettante. The truth, however, lies between these two extremes. He was simply a talented, if highly conservative composer, who wrote in a style that obviously pleased himself rather than the dictates of fashion. *—David Cashman*

Overview of Works (1601–1654)

A pupil of William Byrd's, Thomas Tomkins (1572–1656) lived a long life that took him from the twilight of the great Elizabethan era to near the end of Cromwell's Commonwealth. Born in Wales, Tomkins was appointed choirmaster of Worcester Cathedral in 1596, later becoming an organist at the Chapel Royal while maintaining close contact with Worcester throughout his life. While Tomkins is best remembered for his music written for the Anglican liturgy, he was a versatile composer whose output also includes secular songs and madrigals, consort music, and solo keyboard works.

Tomkins' works for the Anglican liturgy fall into two groups: anthems and services (the settings of the canticles for the morning and evening services). These may again be subdivided into two. In the instance of services, there are three so-called "short" services, and three verse services. The former are traditional works that show the influence of Tomkins' master Byrd, particularly evident in the instance of the *Third Service*, which appears to have been modeled on Byrd's well-known *"Great" Service*. The three verse services, so-called because they include passages for one or more soloists, are more individual. The finest is probably the *Fourth Service*, which in the rich diversity of vocal combinations displays Tomkins' flair for vocal color at its best. In the *Fifth Service*, the composer extends the solo vocal writing to new limits. The anthems can similarly be divided between the verse type and full choral anthems. While the unaccompanied full anthems, often composed in madrigalian style, outnumber verse anthems, it is again in the latter that Tomkins displays his greatest mastery and flexibility. Particularly notable are two outstanding anthems in six parts, "Above the stars," and "Give sentence with me, O God."

Most of Tomkins' extant secular vocal music appeared in his publication, *Songs* (1622), which was dedicated to Byrd; it also includes a few sacred works, among which is the full anthem *When David heard*, one of his most remarkable compositions. In all there are 28 pieces for three, four, five, or six voices—works that conform to the conservative madrigalian idiom of better known English madrigalist such as John Wilbye or Thomas Weelkes. Equally as conservative in style is Tomkins' consort music, which looks back to the forms and contrapuntal structures of earlier composers rather than embracing the newly emergent Baroque style. Scored for viol consort comprising three to six instruments with or without organ, they restrict themselves to the stylized dances and fantasias familiar from the works of Byrd. Much the same might be said of his keyboard works, composed for virginals, harpsichord, clavichord, and organ, which similarly maintain the English tradition of composing finely wrought sets of contrapuntal variations, freely composed fantasies, dances, and pieces based on a cantus firmus, or preexistent melody. *—Brian Robins*

Recommended:

- ○ **Tomkins: The Great Service** / Phillips (cond.), Tallis Scholars / 2002 / Gimell 24
- ○ **Tomkins: Songs of 4, 5 & 6 Parts** / Dobra (cond.), Tomkins Vocal Ens. Budapest / Hungaroton 31514
- ○ **Tomkins: Consort Music for Viols and Voices; Keyboard Music** / Roberts, Red Byrd, Rose Consort of Viols / 1995 / Naxos 550602
- ○ **Tomkins: Keyboard Music Vol. 1** / Klapprott / MDG 0563

VOCAL

When David Heard That Absalom Was Slain, for 5 voices (before 1622)

One of the major composers of music for the Anglican church during the seventeenth century, Thomas Tomkins (1572–1656) was a master of the verse anthem, a form alternating sections for one or more soloists with full choral writing. However, *When David Heard*, one of Tomkins' masterpieces, falls into the category of full anthem. Scored in five parts (mean, or treble, two altos, tenor, and bass), it was published in Tomkins' *Songs* (1622), a volume that bears a dedication to his master, William Byrd. The text is the well-known story of David's grief at the death of his son Absalom as related in 2 Samuel 18:33. Tomkins' madrigalian setting falls into two sections, the first narrative, the second a profound exposition on the words "O my son Absalom, would God I had died for thee," the anguish building to the last searing outburst. *—Brian Robins*

Recommended:

- ○ **Thomas Tomkins: The Great Service** / Phillips (cond.), Tallis Scholars / 2002 / Gimell 24
- ○ **Thomas Tomkins: Choral & Organ Music** / Summerly (cond.), Cummings, Oxford Camerata / 1999 / Naxos 553794

Dubravka Tomšič

b. 1940, Dubrovnik, Croatia
Pianist

Slovenia's Dubravka Tomšič is something of a connoisseur's pianist, not a marquee name widely known outside of classical music circles, but often listed among the finest players in the world by those in the know. Only now becoming well known in the West, she was a marquee name in the former Yugoslavia and in other Eastern European countries. Born in 1940 in the Croatian city of Dubrovnik, she gave her first piano recital at age five. She grew up in the Slovenian capital of Ljubljana and studied at the Ljubljana Academy of Music during her childhood. Her talents were noticed by the great Chilean-American pianist Claudio Arrau, who encouraged her to come to the U.S. to study. So, when she was 12, Tomšič moved to New York and enrolled at the Juilliard School, where her primary teacher was Katherine Bacon. The teenaged pianist gave recitals around New York, including one in Carnegie Hall that attracted the attention of Artur Rubinstein. Tomšič studied for two years with Rubinstein, and he called her "a perfect and marvelous pianist." She graduated from Juilliard with two special awards, by which time she had an appearance with the New York Philharmonic under her belt.

After these high-flying beginnings, however, Tomšič chose to return home to Ljubljana. From the late 1950s until the late 1980s she taught at the Ljubljana Academy of Music (where she is still a professor), raised a family, and built a considerable reputation in southeastern Europe. Her return to the U.S. spotlight came in 1989 with an acclaimed performance at the Newport Music Festival in Rhode Island, and since then she has played recitals in over a dozen U.S. cities (often finding herself immediately asked back afterward) and around Europe. She has also made concerto appearances with orchestras and performed at several major music festivals. Since 1987 she has released over 60 recordings, including most of the major Romantic concertos and solo piano music from Bach and Scarlatti to Debussy and Rachmaninov.

At the keyboard, Tomšič's reserved demeanor belies the expressivity of her playing. Noted for the variety of tone colors she can coax from the piano and for the power and smoothness of her trills, Tomšič offered performances that often evoked the adjective "seamless." Her "dazzling technique," noted the *Boston Phoenix* after a Tomšič concert that finally ended after five encores, "is never an end but a means of achieving emotional directness and poetic insinuation." *—James Manheim*

Recommended:

- ○ **Debussy Recital** / Tomšič / Stradivari 6078
- ○ **Chopin: Waltzes** / Tomšič / 1994 / Point Classics 267130

Giuseppe Torelli

b. Apr. 22, 1658, Verona, Italy, **d.** Feb. 8, 1709, Bologna, Italy

Composer

Giuseppe Torelli was a Baroque composer whose music served as an essential link in the evolution of the concerto grosso and solo concerto forms. His works were published in seven collections of concertos, sinfonias, and sonatas, all appearing chronologically. Thus, one can trace his progress from the rather conventional style of the early chamber-oriented concertos and sonatas to the more expansive and stronger efforts of the middle sets. The last two of his collections, 12 *Concerti musicali* and 12 *Concerti grossi con una pastorale* are the flowering of his efforts in the these genres. The *Concerti musicali* are more deftly written than his previous efforts, with ritornellos taking a more prominent role, while the *Concerti grossi* show his full grasp of structure and a crucial balancing of the roles of the soloist and the orchestral players.

Torelli was born in Verona, Italy, on April 22, 1658. Not much is known about his early years, though it has been suggested that Giuliano Massaroti was one of Torelli's earliest teachers, owing to his close proximity in Verona. Torelli departed Verona in the early 1680s and shortly afterward may have taken the post as Maestro di Cappella at the Imola Cathedral in the Bologna province. An accomplished string player, he also began studying composition with G. A. Perti around this time. Torelli's first published works were the ten *Sonate a 3*, for violin and basso continuo, and twelve *Concerto da camera* for two violins and basso continuo. Both appeared in 1686, and were probably written shortly after his arrival in Bologna.

In 1687, Torelli published his third collection of works, this one a set of twelve Sinfonie, for two to four instruments. His next (1688) was the 12 *Concertino per camera*, for violin and cello. Around 1690 Torelli began writing his first trumpet works, the *Suonata con stromenti e tromba*. The composer's growing interest in the trumpet, unusual for a string player, likely owed something to the virtuoso trumpeter Giovanni Pellegrino Brandi, who occasionally performed with the San Petronio orchestra, of which Torelli was a member.

In 1692 Torelli published another collection of works, the *Sinfonie a 3 e concerti a 4*. Four years later he departed Bologna, eventually reaching Ansbach, Germany, where he engaged in some joint musical ventures with his friend, Pistocchi, the famous *castrato* and composer. There are accounts that during this time, Torelli toured Germany with Pistocchi.

Torelli was appointed maestro di concerto in Ansbach, probably in 1697. It appears that during his tenure there, he wrote very little music, apparently finding the duties demanding. The composer was known to suffer from hypochondria in his later years, and the condition may well have been worsening for him while away from home.

Torelli spent some time in Vienna but was back in Bologna in 1701, quickly landing a position with the newly-formed San Petronio cappella musicale. Torelli and Pistocchi seem to have appeared in a number of concerts together in the early 1700s, most likely earning substantial fees. Relatively little is known about Torelli in his final years, except that he composed little music. His only significant effort was the twelve *Concerti grossi con una pastorale*, Op. 8, which features one of his more popular pieces, the so-called *Christmas Eve Concerto* (No. 6). Torelli died on February 8, 1709. *—Robert Cummings*

Overview of Works (ca. 1685–1709)

Baroque composer Giuseppe Torelli (1658–1709) is generally associated with the development of the solo concerto and concerto grosso forms. While he did not single-handedly create them, he was an essential part of their evolution. He also composed a significant body of works for trumpet and strings.

Although most of Torelli's compositions are difficult to date exactly, many were published chronologically over a period of 23 years, thus allowing one to observe his stylistic progress. The first two collections to appear were both from 1686, the Op. 1 *Sonate a 3*, a set of ten trio sonatas, and 12 *Concerto da camera*, Op. 2, for two violins and basso continuo. The latter is really a suite of dance pieces and does not display much progress from the rather indistinct style of Op. 1.

His next three efforts were the 12 "symphonies" (*Sinfonie*), Op. 3 (1687), for two to four instruments, 12 chamber concertos, Op. 4 (1688), for violin and cello (perhaps one of the earliest duet collections for those two instruments) and 12 *Sinfonie a 3 e concerti a 4*, Op. 5 (1692), which consists of six trio sonatas and six concertos, with the composer calling for the doubling of both the three players in the sonatas and the four in the concertos, thus requiring relatively large forces for that time. This expansion of the ensemble was a key step in the development of the concerto form, for it allowed the composer to specify a contrast between solo passages and those for full ensemble. In these early works Torelli also groped toward the organizing principle of the ritornello, the refrain for full ensemble that might appear in the various keys through which a movement passed. The Opp. 4 and 5 works are unusual in their instrumentation and divulge some development in the composer's style, but are not watershed efforts like the collections in Opp. 6 and 8.

Unfortunately, Op. 7 was lost. The remaining two sets here, the *Concerti musicali* (1698), consisting of two violin concertos and ten other works with concerto-like features, and the Op. 8 *Concerti grossi con una pastorale per il SS Natale* (Concerti Grossi with a Pastoral for the Church of Ss. Natale) (1709), comprised of both concertos and concerti grossi, are masterful. This last collection may include Torelli's most brilliant compositions, for here the composer deftly shapes structures and imaginatively balances the roles of the concerto soloist and the accompanying ensemble players.

Torelli's trumpet works divulge his considerable skills in what was a rather alien genre for a string-playing composer. He wrote sonatas, concertos, and sinfonias for trumpet and various accompanying ensembles. His works include the 1690 *Suonata con stromenti e tromba* (Sonata for Trumpet and Strings), *Sonata a 5, due trombe, e violini unisoni* (Sonata for Five Players, with Two Trumpets and Unison Violins) (1692), *Sinfonia con 2 trombe et altri strumenti* (Sinfonia for TwoTrumpets and Other Instruments), and *Sinfonia con 2 trombe e instromenti* (Sinfonia for Two Trumpets and Ensemble), the latter two likely dating to the early 1690s. Most of the trumpet works were written in the late 1680s to the mid-1690s, probably for the virtuoso trumpeter Giovanni Pellegrino Brandi. Although Handel's music has given rise to connotations of outdoors performance for trumpet music of the Baroque, Torelli's trumpet pieces were ecclesiastical works. In sum, Torelli must be assessed as one of the seminal figures in the development of the concerto form, and the author of at least a handful of genuine masterpieces. *—Robert Cummings*

Recommended:

- ○ **Torelli: Sonate, Sinfonie e Concerti** / Colusso (cond.), Verzari, Seicentonovecento Ens. / Bongiovanni 10008
- ○ **Torelli: Sinfonie e Concerti Op5** / Sasso (cond.), Rome Instrumental Ens. / 1997 / Stradivarius 33461
- ○ **Torelli: Works for trumpets and orchestra** / Vartolo (cond.), various soloists & orchestra / Bongiovanni 5523

Michael Torke

b. Sep. 22, 1961, Milwaukee, WI

Composer

Michael Torke, born in Milwaukee in 1961, has emerged as a contemporary composer whose music has been received with uncharacteristic warmth by traditional classical audiences and newcomers to "serious" music alike. Torke's music is characterized by a fusion of styles that range from lush Romanticism to pop- and jazz-influenced idioms. Typically, the composer makes use of colorful timbres, minimalism-influenced repetition, and dance rhythms. A number of his works have proven especially adaptable as dance scores; a number were specifically commissioned by dance ensembles.

Torke pursued formal musical studies at the Eastman School of Music, where he earned degrees in piano performance and composition; his principal teachers there included Christopher Rouse and Joseph Schwantner (composition) and David Burge (piano). His subsequent period of study with Jacob Druckman at Yale yielded two of his earliest successes, both of which demonstrate the composer's penchant for combining classical form and technique with "popular" content: *Bright Blue Music* (1985), commissioned by the New York Youth Orchestra, and *The Yellow Pages* (1985). The former was the earliest entry in an extensive series of color-themed works that eventually came to include *Ecstatic Orange* (1985), *Green* (1986), *Purple* (1987), *Copper* (1988), *Red* (1991), and others.

Torke has explored vocal idioms in such works as *Mass* (1990), for baritone, chorus and chamber orchestra, and *King of Hearts* (1993), a television opera commissioned by the United Kingdom's Channel 4. Torke's music is sometimes described as "post-minimalist," and this characteristic is at once apparent in his *Four Proverbs* (1993) for female voice and instrumental ensemble. In this work he intricately blends melodic cells with series of syllables to produce a distinctively textured work based on a handful of basic ideas.

Torke's *Javelin* (1994), commissioned by the 1994 Olympic Commission to commemorate the fiftieth anniversary of the Atlanta Symphony Orchestra, has proven to be one of the composer's most popular works. One measure of *Javelin*'s success was its simultaneous release on two different recording s— one with Yoel Levi and the Atlanta Symphony, the other with John Williams and the Boston Pops—in 1996, a rare distinction for a contemporary concert work. Torke was the recipient of one of the more high-profile commissions in the 1990s, a choral symphony in celebration of the new millennium commissioned by the Walt Disney Corporation. The much-acclaimed result, *Four Seasons*, was premiered by Kurt Masur and the New York Philharmonic on October 8, 1999; it was also prominently featured as part of the Y2K festivities at Disney's Epcot Center in Florida on New Year's Eve, 1999. *—AMG*

Overview of Works

By the time of his graduation from the Eastman School of Music, Michael Torke (b. 1961) was fast becoming a spearhead of the post-minimalist movement; yet as he moved ahead, his stylistic frame widened. Torke's music can have the fiery glint of early Stravinsky, the opulence of Richard Strauss, or the infectious insistence of a rock progression—any or all set against a virile, constantly pulsing rhythmic background. As is so often the case, eclecticism gave birth to a highly individual compositional language.

Torke's auspicious debut on the world music stage came in 1984 with his *Vanada*, a striking chamber work which utilized elements of popular music. The following year saw the first of his celebrated "color" works for orchestra, *Ecstatic Orange*, followed by *The Yellow Pages*, the Les Six-like *Green*, *Purple*, the Straussian *Bright Blue Music*, and finally *Ash*, which has been described as "Beethovenian," especially in its orchestration. In these, the young composer picks up the thread of Scriabin and Sir Arthur Bliss in exploring the relation between visual and aural color. There is something impressionistic in Torke's respondse to the subjective feelings evoked by each of the colors; but this is only one aspect of his work. Torke's own description of the reminiscence which influenced his orchestral work *December*, that of observing the mingling of large snowflakes with the glow of Christmas lights while on his paper route in his boyhood Milwaukee, would seem to represent a certain modern suburban Romanticism.

Torke's *Javelin* (1994), written for the Atlanta Symphony, later became inextricably linked to the 1996 Olympics, but it would seem that the nucleus was the composer's simple fondness for the titular word and the shape of its letters. But the composer does not preclude the delight in taking a more workbench-like approach. This may be seen in the contemporary choral work *Book of Proverbs*, in which he shows himself to be no mean hand at writing for the human voice. After the striking Coplandesque instrumental opening and the Bernstein-flavored "The Door Turns," Torke derives melodic variation by rearranging the words of the text in "Better a Dry Crust" while retaining the same corresponding note of each word, a kaleidoscopic approach to development. Together, Michael Torke's imagination and honesty of response fuse to produce one of contemporary music's freshest and happiest voices. *—Wayne Reisig*

Recommended:

- ○ **Torke: Book of Proverbs** / Waart (cond.), Torke (cond.), Bott, Ollmann, Anderson, Netherlands Radio PO, Argo Band / 1999 / Decca 466721
- ○ **Torke: Rapture; An American Abroad; Jasper** / Alsop (cond.), Currie, Scottish National Orch. / 2002 / Naxos 8559167
- ○ **Michael Torke: Chamber Works** / Miller (cond.), Nagano (cond.), London Sinfonietta / 1990 / Argo 430209
- ○ **Javelin: The Music of Michael Torke** / Nagano (cond.), Zinman (cond.), Levi (cond.), Zagrosek (cond.), Torke (cond.), Atlanta SO, London Philharmonia Orch., London Sinfonietta, Baltimore SO / 1996 / Argo 452101

Toronto Symphony Orchestra

f. 1906, Toronto, Ontario, Canada
Ensemble

The Toronto Symphony Orchestra is generally ranked among the finest Canadian orchestras. In 1906, Frank Welsman established the ensemble, giving it the name Toronto Conservatory Symphony Orchestra. Two years later, it was simply renamed the Toronto Symphony Orchestra. It presented concerts in Massey Music Hall and soon began attracting some of the world's most important artists, including composer/performers Rachmaninov and Elgar, the latter appearing in 1911 to lead the TSO in a performance of his oratorio *The Dream of Gerontius*. World War I drained the orchestra of its younger personnel and shortly after the 1918 armistice, the TSO disbanded. In 1922, it was re-formed by local musicians and Austrian musician Luigi von Kunits, who had been an assistant conductor of the Pittsburgh Symphony Orchestra. Named the New Symphony Orchestra, the ensemble gave its first concert in Massey Hall in April, 1923, under the baton of its music director, von Kunits. In 1927, the orchestra reverted to its previous name, the Toronto Symphony Orchestra, and two years later began broadcasting concerts over CBC radio on a weekly basis. Von Kunits died in 1931 and Sir Ernest MacMillan was appointed his successor that year. A native Canadian, he would have the longest tenure of any of the ensemble's music directors, stepping down in 1956. MacMillan expanded the number of concerts and included children's concerts, broadened the repertory, made regular radio broadcasts (which had become sporadic under von Kunits), and the TSO cut its first recordings, among which was Holst's *The Planets* issued on RCA. By the end of his tenure, MacMillan had built the orchestra into a major ensemble, even if it remained a rank or so below world-class orchestras. Walter Süsskind succeeded him in 1956 and would expand the number of concert weeks in the season, which by the time he resigned in 1965 numbered 30. Süsskind introduced works by some of the rising stars of the avant-garde, such as Luciano Berio. He also led an enthusiastically received concert at Carnegie in 1963, which further enhanced the TSO's growing stature in North America. Thirty-year-old Seiji Ozawa was appointed music director in 1965, following Süsskind's resignation earlier that year. His energetic manner and tours abroad—England and France (1966) and Japan (1969)—gave the orchestra both much-needed exposure and considerable acclaim, but also helped the young Ozawa in his meteoric rise. Czech conductor Karel Ancerl was appointed music director in 1969. He introduced outdoor concerts and led hugely successful Beethoven and Brahms festivals in 1970 and 1971, respectively, yet overall was received with less enthusiasm by the Toronto public than his youthful predecessor. Ancerl died unexpectedly in 1973 and Victor Feldbrill, resident conductor from 1973–77, led the orchestra with guest conductors until British maestro Andrew Davis was appointed music director in 1975. Davis made many successful tours with the TSO and several critically acclaimed recordings, including one for Columbia Records of Janáček's *The Cunning Little Vixen Suite* and *Taras Bulba*. When he stepped down in 1988, German-born Gunther Herbig succeeded him, serving five years. Finnish conductor Jukka-Pekka Saraste was appointed music director in 1994 and left at the end of the 2001–02 season. He made several well-received recordings with the TSO, including one for the Finlandia label of excerpts from Prokofiev's *Romeo and Juliet Ballet* and suite from *The Love for Three Oranges*. Since 1982, the TSO has presented its concerts in Roy Thomson Hall. *—Robert Cummings*

Recommended:

- ○ **Holst: Planets, etc.** / A. Davis, del Mar (cond.), Toronto SO, Bournemouth Sinfonietta / 2000 / Angel 73733
- ○ **Symphonic Spectaculars** / A. Davis, Toronto SO / 1988 / CBC 5068
- ○ **Messiaen: Turangalîla Symphony** / Ozawa (cond.), Loriod, Toronto SO / 2004 / RCA 59418

Paul Tortelier

b. Mar. 21, 1914, Paris, France, **d.** Dec. 18, 1990, Villacreaux, France
Cellist

A consummate artist whose approach to the cello was directed toward breathing life into the music, Paul Tortelier earned the respect and affection of countless colleagues. An enduring friendship with Pablo Casals found him playing, in the words of a French critic, Apollo to Casals' Jupiter. Like Casals, Tortelier emphasized using but one finger at a time on the string to allow free vibration. Fantasy and emotional freedom marked his performances and attracted numerous young players.

Given a cello by his mother at age six, Tortelier was prompted toward a career from the beginning. His first teacher, Beatrice Bluhm, exposed young Paul to the flexible wrist and free bowing arm favored by the Franco-Belgian School. At ten, Tortelier entered the Paris Conservatoire, where his studied with Gérard Hekking, who encouraged a sense of rhythmic freedom and instilled in his pupil an abiding love for Bach. While his lessons continued, he performed in Paris cafés and cinemas; at 16, he graduated from the Conservatoire with a first prize.

After joining the Paris Radio Orchestra as assistant principal, Tortelier made a debut with Lamoureux Concert Association, all the while studying harmony with Jean Gallon at the Conservatoire. Completion of those courses brought another first prize, this time in composition. As a member of the Monte Carlo Symphony Orchestra, Tortelier played under the direction of Toscanini and Walter and performed as soloist in Richard Strauss' *Don Quixote* under the composer's direction.

Though his career advanced in the late 1930s, taking him to Asia and Africa, as well as North and South America, World War II curtailed his activities. After the war, he resumed his concert appearances. Impressed by efforts to establish Israeli statehood, Tortelier (a Catholic) moved his family to Mabaroth, a kibbutz only several hundred yards from the enemy border. The first Prades Festival, celebrating the 200th anniversary of Bach's death in 1950, drew an invitation from Casals to be principal cellist. From 1956 to 1969, Tortelier was a professor at the Paris Conservatoire; from 1969 to 1975, he taught at the Folkwang Hochschule in Essen, Germany. Conducting occupied more of his time in later years, as did composition (two concertos included). His book, *How I Play, How I Teach*, has become a standard text for performance of modern cello works. *—Erik Eriksson*

Recommended:

- ○ **Fauré & Debussy: Sonatas** / Tortelier, Hubeau / Erato 45660
- ○ **Beethoven: Cello Sonatas** / Tortelier, Heidsieck / 1994 / EMI 569422
- ○ **Vivaldi: Six Sonatas, Op14** / Tortelier, Veyron-Lacroix / Erato 45658
- ○ **Dvořák: Concerto; Brahms: Double Concerto** / Previn, Berglund (conds.), Menuhin, Tortelier, London SO, London PO / 2003 / EMI 75865

Yan Pascal Tortelier

b. Apr. 19, 1947, Paris, France
Conductor

Yan-Pascal Tortelier is among the finest conductors emerging in the last quarter of the twentieth century.

He comes from an eminent musical family: His father was cellist Paul Tortelier (1914–90). Yan-Pascal studied violin and piano and began studying harmony and counterpoint with Nadia Boulanger. Of his violin studies at the Paris Conservatoire he says he "thinks he reached a high standard" but "couldn't quite make it." In fact, he won First Prize in violin at the Conservatory at age 14 and at the same age made his debut as a soloist with the London Philharmonic in Brahms' *Double Concerto* (1962).

He took conducting studies with Franco Ferrara in the Accademia Chigiana in Siena in 1973. He began guest conducting and in 1974 was appointed associate conductor of the Orchestre du Capitole de Toulouse, remaining in that position through the season ending in 1983. He also conducted opera performances in Toulouse. He was principal conductor and artistic director of the Ulster Orchestra (Belfast, Northern Ireland, 1989–92). In 1990 he was named principal conductor of the BBC Philharmonic, effective at the start of the 1992 season, remaining in that position until 2002. As such, he frequently appeared leading live concerts on the BBC from that orchestra's home at Bridgewater Hall in Manchester, as well as at annual performances at the Henry Woods "Proms" Concerts. In 1995, he took it on a very successful tour of the U.S. to celebrate the orchestra's 60th anniversary season.

Tortelier also guest conducts widely, appearing at some of the world's leading orchestras. His first appearance in the U.S. was in 1985, with the Seattle Symphony Orchestra. In the early part of 2000 his scheduled guest appearances included concerts with Amsterdam's *Royal Concertgebouw,* the St. Petersburg Philharmonic Orchestra, the Czech Philharmonic, and the San Francisco Symphony.

He records exclusively for Chandos Records, which has released performances with the BBC Philharmonic and the Ulster Orchestra, included complete orchestral works of Debussy and Ravel. The later series included Tortelier's own orchestration of Ravel's *Trio.* With the BBC Philharmonic Tortelier has worked on complete cycles of music by Roussel and Dutilleux, and has also recorded works by Lutosławski, Fauré, and Dukas, including two discs that won the prestigious Diapason d'Or award. *—Joseph Stevenson*

Recommended:

- ○ **Dutilleux: L'arbre des songs; Timbres, espace, mouvement; etc.** / Tortelier (cond.), Hill, Davies, Charlier, BBCPO / 1996 / Chandos 9504
- ○ **Milhaud, Poulenc, Ibert: Orchestral Works** / Tortelier (cond.), Ulster Orch. / 1992 / Chandos 9023
- ○ **Roussel: Bacchus & Ariane; Le Festin de l'Araignée** / Tortelier (cond.), BBCPO / 1996 / Chandos 9494
- ○ **Dukas: La Péri; Chabrier: Suite Pastorale** / Tortelier (cond.), Ulster Orch. / 1990 / Chandos 8852

Arturo Toscanini

b. Mar. 25, 1867, Parma, Italy, **d.** Jan. 16, 1957, New York, NY

Conductor

Few orchestral conductors have attained the public recognition accorded Arturo Toscanini, due in part to his many recordings and frequent broadcast performances, but also to his dedication to the art of music-making. In a career spanning 68 years, he did more than anyone to revive the popular image of the all-powerful maestro.

In 1885, at age 19, he graduated from the Parma Conservatory as a cellist, and joined an opera company for a tour of South America. When in Rio de Janeiro, the incompetence of the Brazilian conductor engaged for the tour so incensed the Italian singers and players that he was forced to resign, and the 20-year-old cellist was asked to take the baton for Verdi's *Aida.* By the end of the tour he had led 26 performances of 11 operas, all from memory.

Between 1887 and 1895, Toscanini conducted in many Italian opera houses, and in 1896 became the principal conductor of Turin's Regio Opera House, leading the first Italian performances of Wagner's *Götterdämmerung, Tristan and Isolde* and *Die Walküre,* and the première of Puccini's *La Bohème,* as well as a series of highly successful orchestral concerts. He was the principal conductor at La Scala, Milan, from 1800 to 1908, and first appeared at New York's Metropolitan Opera in 1915, where he conducted the première of Puccini's *La fanciulla del West.* In the same year he made his debut in the U.S. as a symphonic conductor.

Recalled to La Scala in 1919, he reformed the orchestra and took it on a triumphant tour of the U.S., conducting 67 concerts in 77 days, followed by an Italian tour in which he led 38 concerts in 56 days. From 1926–27, he was a guest conductor with the New York Philharmonic Orchestra, and in 1929 left *La Scala* to become its permanent conductor, a post he filled until 1939.

In 1937 Toscanini was invited by NBC to conduct broadcast concerts in America with a new symphony orchestra specifically created for the purpose. He then toured with that orchestra to South America in 1940 and throughout the United States in 1950. He also conducted a memorable series of concerts with the BBC Symphony Orchestra in London between 1935 and 1939.

Toscanini's opposition to Fascism and Nazism was implacable. In 1931, he was attacked for refusing to play the *Giovanezza,* a Fascist anthem. In the same year he was the first non-German conductor to appear at the Wagner Festspielhaus in Bayreuth, but refused to return in 1933 in protest of the Nazi's treatment of Jewish musicians. He also turned his back on the Salzburg Festival because the Jewish conductor Bruno Walter's performances there were not broadcast in Germany. In 1938–39, he conducted without fee at a festival in Lucerne, Switzerland, where the orchestra was composed entirely of musicians who had fled German persecution.

Toscanini's conducting style featured a precise, vigorous beat and vivid body-language, which orchestras understood and responded to with dramatic results. By the end of his career he had memorized 250 symphonic works, and over 100 operas. Though he enthusiastically embraced post-Romantic, twentieth century music, he virtually ignored the Second Viennese School and the new breed of American composers that were making their mark by the 1950s. It was not false modesty, but genuine humility that led him to say in an interview "I am no genius. I have created nothing. I play the music of other men. I am just a musician." *—Roy Brewer*

Recommended:

- ○ **Beethoven: 9 Symphonies** / Toscanini (cond.), Shaw, Farrell, Peerce, Merriman, Scott, Robert Shaw Chorale, NBCSO / 2003 / RCA 55702
- ○ **Toscanini: First Recordings** / Toscanini (cond.), New York PO, La Scala Theater Orchestra & Chorus / 1996 / Symposium 1189
- ○ **Beethoven: Missa Solemnis** / Toscanini (cond.), Williamson, Bjoerling, Milanov, Kipnis, NBCSO / Music & Arts 4259
- ○ **Rossini Overtures** / Toscanini (cond.), BBCSO, NBCSO / 2000 / Aura Classics 0233
- ○ **Schubert: Symphonies 5, 8 & 9; Mendelssohn: Symphonies 4 & 5** / Toscanini (cond.), NBCSO / 1999 / RCA 59480
- ○ **Wagner: Preludes** / Toscanini (cond.), NBCSO / 1992 / BMG 60305

Jennie Tourel

b. Jun. 22, 1900, Vitebsk, Belarus, **d.** Nov. 23, 1973, New York, NY

Mezzo-Soprano

Jennie Tourel was born Bella or Jennie Davidovich in the city of Vitebsk, now in Belarus. In childhood, Tourel studied the flute and then piano. Tourel and her family were forced to flee during the Russian Revolution; they settled first in Gdansk, Poland and then in Paris.

Tourel continued her piano studies in Paris, but switched to singing under the tutelage of Reynaldo Hahn and Anna El-Tour. Sources differ as to when Tourel made her debut and where; some say the Chicago Civic Opera in 1930, others the Opéra Russe (in Paris) in 1931. Tourel made her debut with the Metropolitan Opera in New York on May 15, 1937 in *Mignon*; a recording survives of this performance. Tourel's earliest recordings are all live opera "bootlegs"; a 1944 Met performance of Bellini's *Norma,* in which Tourel appears opposite Zinka Milanov, is particularly prized by collectors.

As Paris fell before the Nazis in 1940, Tourel fled to Lisbon to board one of the last ships heading to the United States. Tourel rejoined the Met, remaining there until 1947, and became established as the reigning mezzo in New York City, extraordinarily popular as well in performances with the New York Philharmonic. In 1945, she premiered the vocal/orchestral versions of several Samuel Barber songs, including *Sure, on this Shining Night,* in a CBS broadcast led by the composer. Tourel also worked with Villa-Lobos, Poulenc, Virgil Thomson, Lukas Foss (the *Song of Songs*), and others. In Venice in 1951, Tourel created the role of Baba the Turk in Stravinsky's opera *The Rake's Progress.* The sheer number of works Tourel introduced in one way or another is in itself impressive.

But it was Tourel's association with Leonard Bernstein that proved most fruitful. The partnership began in 1942 with Bernstein taking the role of piano accompanist to Tourel in recitals, and lasted until she died. Their connection went beyond music; they shared many common interests, and greatly enjoyed hosting loud parties with hundreds in attendance. Tourel premiered Bernstein's *Jeremiah Symphony* under the composer in Pittsburgh in 1944, and also sang at the premiere of his third symphony, "*Kaddish,*" in Tel Aviv in 1963. Several of Bernstein's songs were written for her, including "I Hate Music" (1943). Among the many recordings Tourel made with Bernstein functioning both as piano accompanist and conductor were those of Mussorgsky's *Songs and Dances of Death,* Berlioz's *La Mort de Cléopâtre,* Ravel's *Shéhérazade,* and their 1962 recording of the Mahler *"Resurrection" Symphony.*

Tourel was an eccentric who delighted in befuddling critics with conflicting information on her background. She tried to reduce her age by ten years, relocated her birthplace to Toronto, and in later years emphatically denied having created her stage name by modifying that of her teacher. Tourel taught at Juilliard and at the Aspen Music School; her impact on younger musicians was considerable and not necessarily limited to singers. Among Tourel's protégés were mezzo-soprano Barbara Hendricks, pianist James Levine, bassist Gary Karr, and, to a certain extent, Bernstein himself. She made her last major appearance in 1972 in Seattle in Thomas Pastieri's opera *Black Widow,* and died the following year at the age of 73.

Tourel's reputation as a difficult and uncooperative subject has followed her in her afterlife, and her name rarely appears on critical short lists of great singers. However, her recordings are well established with the public and Tourel is still frequently heard on NPR and other classical radio outlets three decades after her death. *—Uncle Dave Lewis*

Recommended:

- ○ **Jennie Tourel** / Tourel, etc. / 2001 / Decca 467907
- ○ **Art of Jennie Tourel** / Tourel, etc. / 2003 / VAI Audio 1213
- ○ **Ravel, Berlioz, Offenbach** / Tourel, etc. / Pearl 198
- ○ **Bernstein: Jeremiah's Symphony; Age Of Anxiety** / Bernstein (cond.), Tourel, Entremont, New York PO / 1999 / Sony 60697

Charles Tournemire

b. Jan. 22, 1870, Bordeaux, France, **d.** Nov. 4, 1939, Arcachon, France

Composer: Keyboard

Composer and organist Tournemire was an enormously gifted and prolific composer whose work remained mostly unknown through much of the late twentieth century. He wrote most of his colossal output without any expectations of performance or publication, and indeed, the majority of his compositions have never been published. His musical language began in a post-Franckian style, adopted impressionistic harmonies as well as modal and polytonal influences, but rejected Stravinsky. He could have been France's response to Gustav Mahler.

A precocious child, he was appointed organist of the church of St. Pierre in Bordeaux at the age of 11. He studied at the Conservatoire de Paris with Franck and Widor, winning in 1891 the first prize in organ. He continued his studies with d'Indy at the Schola Cantorum. In 1898 he succeeded Pierné as organist in St. Clotilde, where he remained until his death. As organist, he toured Germany, Holland, and Russia, before the Great War. Although he had written a substantial number of works, he destroyed all his compositions previous to 1900. Four years later, his cantata *Le sang de la sirène* won the prize City of Paris. Between 1900 and 1914 he composed his first five symphonies—which are, thus, exact contemporaries of the first five of Sibelius—all of which were performed. In the year 1910 he composed his *Poème* for organ and orchestra and the *Triple Choral* for organ. An opera, *Les Dieux sont morts* (1912) was staged in Paris in 1924. The War caused a break in Tournemire's creative life. He was mobilized and, although he had projected the *Sixth Symphony* in 1915, he could only start to work on it in 1917. This symphony as well as the two that followed it were never performed in his lifetime. In 1919 he was appointed professor in the Conservatoire, but the War had brought about a cultural and musical change of ambience and Tournemire found himself out of step with the times of Les Six and Stravinsky.

From 1921 he devoted his best compositional efforts to the church. His great oratorios came after his last symphony: *La Quête du Saint-Graal* (1926–27), *l'Apocalypse de Saint-Jean* (1932–36), and *La douloureuse Passion du Christ* (1936–37). The last 12 years of his life were mostly devoted to organ music. Between 1927 and 1932 he worked on the colossal *l'Orgue mystique.* This work comprises 51 Offices, sets of five pieces for the Holy Mass, for every Sunday of the year. The complete work would last about 15 hours of music, longer than the complete organ works of J.S. Bach. Other organ works are the *Fantaisie symphonique* (1933–34), the *Sept Chorals-Poèmes* on the last seven words of Christ (1935), the *Symphonie-Choral* (1935), and the *Symphonie sacrée* (1936). Among the works unpublished and unperformed there are three other operas and a trilogy of oratorios (*Faust—Don Quichotte—Saint François d'Assise*). During the first weeks of the Second World War, he was in Arcachon, near his birthplace, when he died in unknown circumstances. His body was found lying in the street. *—Hector Bellman*

KEYBOARD

Works for Organ (1894–1939)

Although Charles Tournemire composed operas, orchestral music (eight symphonies), and vocal, choral, and chamber works, he is best known for his organ compositions. These are stylistically quite distinctive in their serious demeanor, often exotic sonorities, modal writing (including use of even Asian modalities), hints of Impressionism à la Debussy, and occasional use of harmonies associated with German composers of his day. Without doubt, Tournemire's most important and widely known effort in organ literature is his cycle of 51 suites, or offices, entitled *L'orgue mystique* (1927–32), written for the Roman Catholic liturgy. Each office typically contains music to accompany the Introit (Prelude), Offertory, Elevation, and Communion, with a fifth piece used as a closing work. For example, *Office No. 13,* for Sexagesima Sunday, consists of a Prelude, Offertory, Elevation, Communion and *Pièce fresque,* while *Office No. 35 "In Assumptione"* concludes with a Paraphrase-Carillon. It is the last piece here that is the longest, most virtuosic, and most colorful, sharply contrasting with the four shorter, slower, and mostly contemplative and celestial previous movements. This pattern is generally followed throughout *L'orgue mystique,* with the character of the music tending to be serious, often solemn, then turning a bit more colorful for the finale. The writing is modal, but the composer's harmonies are unusual, imparting an atmosphere that often anticipates the mystical style of Messiaen. Tournemire's music here never descends into mere generic-sounding church music. Nor do his other mature solo organ works suggest a less-distinctive musical persona. The *Fantasie symphonique* (1933–34) and the four so-called organ symphonies—*Symphonie-Choral* (1935), *Symphonie Sacrée* (1936), and the *Fresques Symphoniques Sacrées,* Opp. 75 & 76 (1938–39)—all display his mastery in the latter stages of his career. Even the early *Sortie,* Op. 3 (1894), though it divulges a Franckian influence in its well-behaved cheer, already divulges a high level of creativity for its color and thematic appeal. Tournemire was a master of improvisation and gave many astonishing performances of music in this genre. Thus, several compositions credited to him are not to be found on his numbered works list since they are transcriptions of these improvisatory efforts. The *Five Improvisations* (1931) are brilliant examples of his creative genius, as evidenced by the Duruflé transcription of them. The *Choral Victimae Paschali* and *Petite rapsodie improvisé,* both from this set, demonstrate Tournemire's facile manner in producing music of such finished mastery that the casual listener would not likely suspect their origin was in improvisation. In larger realms, Tournemire's *Symphony No. 6* (1915–18) is scored for vocal soloist, chorus, orchestra, and organ. It is a powerful, often exotic work, employing many motifs that are developed and expanded to symbolize an evolution of spirituality. The organ's role here, however, is less prominent than in a concerto. *—Robert Cummings*

Recommended:

- ○ **Tournemire: Chorale Poèmes Op67; L'Orgue Mystique** / Delvallée / Arion 68158
- ○ **Tournemire: L'Orgue Mystique; Le Cycle de Pâques Op56** / Delvallée / Accord 206002
- ○ **Tournemire: Symphony 6** / Bartholomee (cond.), Galvez-Vallejo, Liège PO / 1995 / Valois 4757

Joan Tower

b. Sep. 6, 1938, New Rochelle, NY

Composer: Chamber Music, Concerto, Orchestral

Joan Tower is one of the most prominent American composers from the latter part of the twentieth century. Still active and very much an important artist in the twenty-first century, she initially made her mark as a pianist. She first began composing in the 1960s with little notice, her music then incorporating serial techniques. In the 1970s, however, she turned to a more approachable style, offering works with quite graspable melodies, strong and powerful rhythms (the rhythmic character of her 1993 ballet *Stepping Stones* has been compared to that of Stravinsky's *The Rite of Spring*) and, in orchestral pieces, masterfully conceived instrumentation, often evoking vivid imagery. Among her more significant works are her five *Fanfares for the Uncommon Woman* and *Silver Ladders,* all for orchestra, as well as the chamber works *Turning Points* and *Night Fields. The Last Dance* was premiered in February 2000 by the Orchestra of St. Luke's with success.

When she was nine, her family moved to Bolivia. For the next decade, her talent in music, particularly on the piano, grew rapidly, portending formidable skills. She returned to the United States to study piano at Bennington College. She also took instruction in composition from Calabro and Brant. Her most important study in this area, however, came at Columbia University with Luening, Beeson, and Ussachevsky, who undoubtedly influenced her to compose in her less approachable early style. She earned a doctorate degree from Columbia in 1968.

The following year, she helped found the New York-based Da Capo Chamber Players and served as the group's pianist. She also took on a faculty post in composition at Bard College in 1972 and remains there in that capacity today. Tower would write a number of successful works for the Da Capo Players over the years, including *Platinum Spirals* (1976), *Amazon I* (1977), and *Wings* (1981). The group received several awards in its early years, including a 1973 Naumberg Award. Up to the 1980s, all of Tower's works were scored for solo instruments or chamber ensembles. Her first orchestral composition, *Sequoia,* came at the relatively late date in her career of 1981. Not surprisingly, it was an immense success, taken up shortly after its premiere by many American and foreign orchestras.

Buoyed by her first effort, Tower began writing many more works for orchestra in the 1980s and left the Da Capo Players in 1984. The following year, she became composer-in-residence for the St. Louis Symphony Orchestra, holding that post until 1988. Two significant works emerged from this period, *Silver Ladders* and the first *Fanfare for the Uncommon Woman.*

On a commission from the Milwaukee Ballet, Tower wrote *Stepping Stones* in 1993. Later, the composer, who often conducts, led a performance of *Celebration* from this ballet at the *White House.* Among her compositions are the 1996 *Rapids* (*Piano Concerto No. 2*), which she wrote for her friend, the pianist Ursula Oppens; and *Tambor* (1998), written for the Pittsburgh Symphony Orchestra.

Beginning with the 1999–2000 season, Tower launched a three-year stint as composer-in-residence with the Orchestra of St. Luke's. She lives in Annandale-on-Hudson, New York. *—Robert Cummings*

Overview of Works

"... the overall shape and contour of the tree are really very simple."—Joan Tower

The awe that arises from the simple is a paradoxical awe. In its light, the simple is changed, inverted: it blooms into an overwhelming complexity and that complexity in turn reflects great light. Composer Joan Tower seems to understand this; to construct simple things that want to inspire awe is her signature move. And her pieces, each built from the most basic materials, gestures, and ideas, often accomplish this goal. Since here first major orchestral commission *Sequoia* in 1981, her works have awed audiences with a towering sense of simplicity, whose luminescence reveals a wealth of sub-surface details. But rooting her works is Tower's unshakable conviction that the basic and even the generic can be developed into inextricably specific objects with all the labyrinthine folds and temporal sophistication of any organic entity: "With each work, I try to go beyond matters of 'style'... to carve out a piece's identity and soul so that it emerges as an individual personality and makes a strong statement." This conviction is more striking than it at first appears. Style, after all, is often the most effective way of "carving" out the individuality of a piece and of severing and saving it from the madding crowd of other musics. Tower's wish to go "beyond matters of style" would seem to catapult her works back into the mire of the anonymous. And her most steadfast building blocks can easily be identified as "anonymous." She often constructs works out of nothing more than a rising scale, a balancing of oppositions, a speeding or slowing propulsion, or a rhythmic rift between duple and triple pulses. Likewise, her harmonic thinking, remarkably resilient since the early 1980s, is based on octatonic scales—peculiar for their lack of tonic—hence many scores seem to spiral in a non-Euclidean harmonic universe where normal, individuating principles disintegrate. But in fact, this impulse toward a transcendence of style is very close to Tower's opposite impulse not to flee or escape, but to move toward and capture. Here, Tower's model is perhaps Beethoven, in whom the language of seventeenth and eighteenth century music reached at once a point of greatest objectivity and subjectivity. Works like the *Symphony No. 9* seem to hold forth as wonders of nature herself, while crying out as the emotional fingerprints of a specific ego. In feeling attracted to the same simultaneity, Tower appears to receive Beethoven's influence through the hands of Shostakovich. Through his rhythmic velocity, motivic patterning, harmonic pungency, and dramatic timing, Tower appears to have found a core model to revise and transform. In her abstraction of the Shostakovich style, she has cooled a musical archetype of its morbidity and infused it with a new and vital-nature mysticism. It can be heard in larger works such as the Grawemeyer and Freidheim award-winning orchestra piece *Silver Ladders*, but also in virtuoso solo scores like *Clocks for guitar*. *—Seth Brodsky*

Recommended:

- ○ **Joan Tower: Black Topaz** / Isbin, Wincenc, Emelianoff, Double Edge the Muir SQ / 1995 / New World 80470
- ○ **Joan Tower: Concertos** / Silverstein (cond.), Oliveira, Wincenc, Oppens, Shifrin, Louisville Orch. / 1997 / D'Note 1016
- ○ **Fanfares for the Uncommon Woman** / Alsop (cond.), Colorado SO / 1999 / Koch 7469
- ○ **Meet the Composer: Joan Tower** / Slatkin (cond.), Smith (cond.), Harrell, Bowman, St. Louis SO, Louisville Orch. / 2004 / First Edition 25

CHAMBER MUSIC

Hexachords, for flute (1972)

Joan Tower broke with academic serialism completely in 1976, but there were signs of the coming break long before then. *Hexachords*, written for flutist Patricia Spencer, illustrates one step of Tower's departure. This piece uses six pitches exclusively (thus the title), but uses them without a specific order; its methods and effects stray from the serial ideal. This piece is by no means tonal but it has, nevertheless, an appealing fluidity and organic feeling. Rather than manipulate the pitches as a tone row, Tower concentrates on exploring the capabilities of the flute in relation to these six pitches. She varies the length of vibrato, contrasts the upper and lower extremes of the flute's register, and changes dynamics, rhythm, and tempo with assured quickness. All these changes create a volatile atmosphere in which the music seems about to shift even when it is still. This feeling is emphasized by her division of the piece into five sections, which, she has written, "are most easily differentiated by a sense of either going somewhere or staying somewhere." Yet there always seems to be a musical logic to the movement, a feeling that the music is developing from itself rather than from an abstract principle—a sensation absent from much academic serial music but almost always present in Tower's work. The rhythms succeed each other in interesting ways; snatches of tunes are taken up repeatedly, and the different registers sometimes seem to assume distinct characters. Tower writes that the "counterpoint of tunes…[in *Hexachords*]…hopefully keeps the listener's attention," and the hope is well placed. *—Andrew Lindemann Malone*

Recommended:

- ○ **American Flute Works** / Maurer / 1995 / Albany 167
- ○ **Joan Tower: Chamber & Solo Works** / Spencer / 1990 / CRI 582

Petroushkates, for flute, violin, clarinet, cello & piano (1980)

In 1969, Joan Tower founded the Da Capo Players, a group of musicians based in New York and dedicated to the performance of new music. For their tenth anniversary, the Da Capo Players, in conjunction with the New York State Council on the Arts, commissioned from Tower a new piece that was first performed in 1980 in New York's Alice Tully Hall.

Entitled *Petroushskates*, the piece is scored for flute, clarinet, violin, cello, and piano, a chamber ensemble that became something of a standard in the later twentieth century. Tower drew on two disparate sources of inspiration: Stravinsky's ballet *Petrushka*, and the visual imagery of figure skating. Tower herself best explains the musical impact of ice skating: "In an attempt to understand why figure skating, especially pair skating, was so beautiful and moving to me I discovered a musical corollary I had been working on for a while—the idea of seamless action." Tower had always revered and respected Stravinsky, in particular *Petrushka*, and had wanted to created an homage to him for some time. Just as Stravinsky parodied and quoted Pergolesi, Bach, Tchaikovsky and others, Tower followed a similar path in her use of material from Stravinsky's *Petrushka*. In her mind, the pair of skaters she initially intended to illustrate grew into a "whole company of skaters, thereby creating a sort of musical carnival on ice."

At the opening of *Petroushskates*, trills in the flute and clarinet, harmonics in the cello, and rapidly rocking chords in the piano evoke the opening and several other portions of Stravinsky's *Petrushka*. The piano part, in particular, reminds us of Stravinsky's ballet, although it does not contain Stravinsky's famous juxtaposition of chords a tritone apart. Trills and bits of melody come and go as the meter changes frequently and instruments play in the extremes of their registers. All of these elements suggest Stravinsky from the beginning of the piece.

After the tumultuous start, the instruments in *Petroushskates* rise to a very high register before suddenly dropping both in pitch and dynamic level as the tempo slows. The flute and clarinet introduce the "skating theme," in which the clarinet has rhythmically irregular groups of notes while the flute presents material focused on a minor second with angular figurations that again point to Stravinsky. The intensity builds as the section becomes more dissonant and the flute and clarinet begin a conversation of fast scales.

The tension breaks abruptly with the onset of a slow tempo, the dissonance continuing in the clarinet and flute. This brief section gives way to a return of the opening, *Petrushka*-based rhythms, but this time we hear thick, rumbling chords in the lower register of the piano, accented in a manner reminiscent of *The Rite of Spring*. To close the piece Tower repeats the opening material, although many of the trills are now in the piano; other gestures are redistributed among the instruments. *—John Palmer*

Recommended:

- ○ **The Composer-Performer: 40th Anniversary** / Da Capo Chamber Players / 1994 / CRI 670

Wings, for clarinet (1981)

Accustomed to close interactions with a small chamber group, Joan Tower wrote many works for the Da Capo Chamber Players, the performance ensemble she founded in 1969. Of these works, which include *Hexachords* (1972), *Amazon* (1977), *Petroushskates* (1980), *Platinum Spirals* (1976), and *Wings* (1981), the last became the most popular after its original release through CRI. Known for her many commissions, Tower often wrote with a particular performer in mind, reflecting the closeness she had to those who worked with and for her. "In an ideal musical world, a composer has a friendly, creative and ongoing working relationship with performers for whom s/he writes. It is a special world full of wonderful music making between both parties," she commented.

Wings was written in 1981and dedicated to her friend and colleague Laura Flax (a member of the Da Capo Chamber Players), who premiered the piece at a recital in Merkin Hall, New York City, on December 14, 1981. The composition, with clearly focused expression and daunting performance requirements that fully display the capacity of the solo instrument, quickly became a part of clarinetists' solo repertories.

The composer wrote, "The image behind the piece is one of a large bird—perhaps a falcon—at times flying very high gliding along the thermal currents, barely moving. At other moments, the bird goes into elaborate flight patterns that loop around, diving downwards, gaining tremendous speeds." The overall feel of the composition is a surging upward thrust, which appears after a quiet beginning and closes in a most dramatic way. The first of Tower's glides is heard when the hushed sustained pitch opens the piece. It is also formed when the music pauses around one pitch then the next, contemplating the departure and arrival of each moment, musically and symbolically. Loops and dives are formed as turbulent arpeggios and trills precede legato calms. Emphasis on each twist and turn is found as motion and speed accelerate. At the close of the composition rising fourths recur, prior to the reemergence of the initial pitch, which sends the finale into a heavenly ascent. The *Quartet for the End of Time* by Olivier Messiaen was a direct influence on the composition of *Wings*. *—Meredith Gailey*

Recommended:

- ○ **Joan Tower: Chamber & Solo Works** / Flax / 1990 / CRI 582

CONCERTO

Breakfast Rhythms I & II, for clarinet & chamber orchestra (1974–1975)

Joan Tower wrote *Breakfast Rhythms I & II, for clarinet and chamber orchestra* in 1974 and 1975, after she had started to move away from the serial influences of Babbitt and Wuorinen and toward the styles of Messiaen and Crumb. It is typical of her works from the 1970s that were influenced by, as Mary Lou Humphrey explained, "a more fluid organic technique." Tower stated that *Breakfast Rhythms I & II* "is influenced by Beethoven's use of textural and rhythmic contrast. In both movements, there is a sense of large and small-scale balancing. Pitch patterns form the basis of the harmonic structure and melodic activity as they are isolated, completed or combined with other patterns. Orderly yet angular ensemble writing regularly gives way to more lyrical passages for the clarinet which lend at-home and away-from-home feelings." The piece was commissioned by the National Endowment for the Arts and was dedicated to the talented clarinetist Allen Blustine.

In *Breakfast Rhythms I* the conventional solo/ensemble relationship is replaced with something of greater freedom. The clarinet engages in a variety of fluctuating relationships with the piano, cello, flute/piccolo, violin, and vibraphone/unpitched percussion. The fundamental material for this first movement is a six-note chromatic group, which is either completed, isolated, or combined with another hexachord to define the harmonies and contents of each section. The constantly changing pitches, dynamics, and timbres create an obsessive mood, while the frequent revisitation of earlier gestures forms a network of melodies, textures, rhythms, and sonorities.

The frequent occurrence of pentatonic sonorities gives *Breakfast Rhythms II* a brighter, more chordal sound than the first. The first melody of the clarinet is a slow moving line marked by dynamic fluctuation, accompanied by a few chords from the ensemble. The second melody is made of jagged staccato passages, accompanied by contrapuntal contrasts. The final melody is composed of quieter legato barcarolle rhythms that are passed between the soloist and the ensemble. *—Meredith Gailey*

Recommended:

○ **Joan Tower: Chamber & Solo Works** / Shulman (cond.), Blustine, Da Capo Chamber Players / 1990 / CRI 582

ORCHESTRAL

Sequoia (1981)

In composing her orchestral work *Sequoia*, composer Joan Tower sought not only to evoke the awe experienced in the shadow of the looming tree, but to mimic its elegant and organic structure in the structure of the music. "The achievement of such great heights by the giant, majestic sequoia seems to me an incredible feat of balance," Tower explained. "Yet in spite of its power and grandeur, its leaves are tiny, no larger than a thumbnail." Thus, her composition traces the contour of the tree on both the large and small scale and in its overall shape and minute details.

In fact, the piece seems to proceed slowly across the sequoia's surface, in a spiral fashion, moving from the ground up. The work begins with low, soft, chthonic rumblings in the percussion that grow to a roar, from which a G pedal tone emerges. This sustained tone serves as a central column from which the rest of the composition branches out. The composer describes the unfolding of the piece as a constant balancing, affected by shifts in tempo, rhythm, texture, and timbre. The work's three continuous sections juxtapose passages of hushed repose with bursts of rhythmic intensity and orchestral color. Tower creates an almost cinematic tension through her use of driving metrical inertia, violent syncopations, and vivid instrumental combinations, as well as the softer passages in which she slowly gathers energy through the carefully paced deployment of dissonances and timbral nuances. The diversity of the musical surface in the faster passages serves to propel Tower's rather straightforward melodic lines, which are often articulated in heavy, punctuated unisons. The imagery of "branches" emerges in passages that seem to divert off into tangents from a central thread, itself an outgrowth of a larger musical idea.

Composed between 1979 and 1981 on commission from the Jerome Foundation and the American Composers Orchestra, *Sequoia* was Tower's first composition for full orchestral forces. It marked an auspicious beginning for her career as a mature orchestral composer, and was received warmly by the numerous orchestras that subsequently performed it. *—Jeremy Grimshaw*

Recommended:

○ **Tower: Silver Ladders; Island Prelude; Music for Cello & Orchestra; Sequoia** / Slatkin (cond.), St. Louis SO / 1990 / Meet The Composer 79245

Pete Townshend

b. May 19, 1945, London, England

Composer: Opera

Pete Townshend is a composer, guitarist, and musical director of the British rock group the Who. He grew up in Shepherd's Bush, a middle-class suburb of London, and attended art school as a youth. At age 13 Townshend began gigging with guitarist (and later bassist) John Entwistle, who in early 1962 encouraged Townshend to join him in the Detours, a group led by singer Roger Daltrey. Two years later the group changed its name to the Who. The first recording contract the Who signed restricted them from "cover" songs, and Townshend quickly fell into the role of the group's principal songwriter, a position he'd seldom relinquish for the next 30 years of the Who's history. It was the Who's manager Kit Lambert who first suggested that Townshend write a rock opera in 1966. Townshend's first operatic effort, *Quads*, was quickly abandoned, but yielded the hit song "I'm a Boy." Later that year, Townshend delivered a ten-minute mini-opera in the form of *A Quick One While He's Away*.

Throughout 1968 Townshend worked on *Tommy*, a rock opera about a deaf, dumb, and blind kid who is declared a messiah when cured of his afflictions. Upon its release in May 1969, *Tommy* wasn't an immediate success, but once afloat, *Tommy* stayed on the U.S. album charts for more than two years and transformed the Who from cult favorites to superstars. *Tommy* was made into a popular movie in 1975, and in 1993 was adapted into a musical, *The Who's Tommy*, winning a Tony Award. Townshend embarked on his next rock opera, *Lifehouse*, in late 1970, but this plan was scuttled with a single-disc of the leftovers issued as *Who's Next* in 1971.

By mid-1973, Townshend was at it again with the rock opera *Quadrophenia* about the early history of the Who as seen through the eyes of one of its "mod" fans of the mid-1960s. *Quadrophenia* is widely admired and regarded as Townshend's most challenging rock opera; it was made into a film in 1979, and the group toured with a technologically revamped version of the work in 1996 and into 1997. Since 1983's breakup of the Who, Townshend has issued albums on his own, a couple of them being close to the idea of the rock opera, but actually being more in the vein of concept albums. *—Uncle Dave Lewis*

OPERA

Tommy, a rock opera (1969)

Throughout 1968 Pete Townshend, chief songwriter of the rock group the Who, composed *Tommy*, a rock opera inspired by the example of Indian avatar Meher Baba. In his youth Meher Baba had become temporarily unable to respond to the outside world owing to a kiss on the forehead received from a Perfect Master, sending him into a mystical trance. A couple of years later Baba was painfully revived when hit on the head with a stone thrown by another Perfect Master; from that time his work as an avatar began. Townshend adapted the basic idea behind this story and updated it to his own time and circumstance, locating it in the context of "Swinging London" and the drug-fueled popular culture adherent to this era. Townshend had composed "mini-operas" before, but *Tommy* was a fairly full-length work running over an hour, resulting in a rather complicated and expensive recording project that was completed in March 1969.

Upon the initial release of the album in May 1969, sales figures were disappointing. The Who realized that their fortunes rested on how well *Tommy* performed, and began to play the whole work through consistently in live shows. The Who managed to slowly build a following for *Tommy*, and the band's manager Kit Lambert helped by booking performances of *Tommy* into regular classical concert venues, thus enhancing its reputation as a serious work. The stratagem paid off, particularly in the United States, where the burgeoning phenomenon of album-oriented rock radio adopted *Tommy* wholesale, sometimes airing the entire piece without commercials.

With *Tommy* the form of the "rock opera," which some critics argued was oxymoronic in its very conception, was truly born. In creating *Tommy*, the Who were very careful not to take into the work any additional elements that they themselves couldn't perform on-stage. Although *Tommy* is rightly recognized as Townshend's creation, two of its numbers were composed by the Who's bassist, John Entwistle, who also contributed the distinctive horn parts to the "Overture." Many more rock-oriented fans have complained about the short snatches of recitative in the work, such as "Tommy Can You Hear Me?" and "There's a Doctor," although as in a traditional opera these devices are needed to help propel the story forward. In retrospect it is clear that the original *Tommy* could've used a bit more continuity than it had, and this is addressed in subsequent versions of the work, which add lines of dialogue and additional music to fill the story out. Among these later incarnations have been Ken Russell's motion picture adaptation, made in 1975, and a Tony Award-winning musical, *The Who's Tommy*, which opened in 1993. In 1996 *Tommy* was developed into an interactive CD-ROM for personal computers.

Tommy did not altogether eliminate the notion that rock musicians were incapable of creating musical works on the ambitious scale of opera, oratorio, or a large symphonies, nor did it launch in the "rock opera" a formula that would be successfully followed by many. Nonetheless, *Tommy* certainly put the age-old prejudice against rock musicians creating "serious" music to a significant and compelling test, and it remains the best-known and most enduring extended work of any kind produced in the turbulent decade of the 1960s. *—Uncle Dave Lewis*

Synopsis:

It is England, 1940, and the island nation has been bearing the brunt on both fronts to uphold democracy. Dashing RAF Captain Walker meets an attractive young welder at the hangar. He courts her; they date, fall in love, and are married. Soon the captain is called into action. His plane is shot down, he is captured by the Germans, and held prisoner, although he is believed missing in action by the RAF. It is this tragic news that is brought to the home front to Mrs. Walker, who is with child by the Captain.

The war ends and former POW Walker heads home to resume life, unaware that he is presumed dead. Meanwhile his wife, believing herself widowed, has resumed dating. The Captain arrives to find her having a late dinner with her lover. Not aware of their ignorance of his situation and believing it to be flagrant adultery, the enraged officer barges in and kills the Suitor in front of his wife and 4-year-old son Tommy, who has witnessed this act in the reflection of a mirror. When the realization of the consequences of this tragic misunderstanding sinks in, Tommy's parents tell him that he has neither heard nor seen what has happened, and that he will not breathe a word of it to anyone. Tommy enters a traumatized state of being deaf, dumb, and blind. At this point, the adult Tommy anachronistically appears from a distance, to act as narrator for the lad throughout the action. Despite this ultimate handicap, Tommy's inner experiences are far from pathetic, but constitute an amazing spiritual journey, at odds with the glum and often cruel external world of the boy. Meanwhile, Captain Walker has been found not guilty of murder by the British court on the basis of extenuating circumstances. However, to his and Mrs. Walker's surprise and horror, Tommy remains in his present state. Subsequent medical intervention fails to relieve the symptoms.

It is Christmas 1950. Tommy's extended family has come to visit. Unfortunately, this includes perverted Uncle Ernie, who molests the boy, and sadistic Cousin Kevin, who abuses him. When finished, the latter hauls him to the neighborhood hangout with the intent of making sport of Tommy until the boy amazes all present with an astonishing ability to play record-breaking pinball despite his seeming absence of sight and hearing. This fact is shared with the Walkers, who now sense a glimmer of hope for their son.

It is 1960. Tommy has become a local hero due to his pinball prowess, but repeated cures (including the projected employment of a prostitute) have failed to roust the boy from his psychosomatic shell. The anxious parents are at their wits' end until Mrs. Walker finds Tommy staring into the same mirror in which he witnessed the murder 15 years prior. Frustrated she smashes it, resulting in the instant return of Tommy's senses. Amid the astonishment and joy, Tommy proclaims himself free and leaves home, the celebration dampened by his curt rejection of his family.

News of the "miracle cure" spreads and Tommy's local celebrity becomes national. He draws mass crowds, filling stadiums. At one event, a teenage girl, Sally Simpson, attempts to reach Tommy but is pulled aside and brutalized by security guards. A shocked Tommy intervenes and tends to the girl. He realizes that there is a negative side to the adulation. In sympathy he invites Simpson and those present to his house. Once there he tells Simpson that who she is in the world is important enough and that there is no need to pattern herself after him. The throng overhears this and is disillusioned by this philosophy. They leave the premises, word of this self-iconoclasm sure to spread. The adult Tommy, now one with the narrator, feels his old isolation haunting, encroaching. With mighty resolve, he shakes it off and returns to his family. The scene of so much outward pain of his younger years has been purged by understanding, forgiveness, and love. He accepts his family... mother, father, even Uncle Ernie and Cousin Kevin... and they him. The long healing and the amazing journey are now complete. *—Wayne Reisig*

Recommended:

○ **Tommy** / The Who / 1996 / MCA 11417

Giorgio Tozzi

b. Jan. 8, 1923, Chicago, IL
Bass

An eminent opera singer, Giorgio Tozzi is also thoroughly at home in American musical theater. He began to study singing at the age of 13. Entering Chicago's DePaul University with the intention of becoming a biologist, he changed his mind and studied voice with Rosa Raisa, Giacomo Rimini, and John Daggett Howell. His operatic debut was in the American premiere of Benjamin Britten's chamber opera *The Rape of Lucretia*, as Tarquinius, which was a 1948 Broadway production rather than an opera presentation. In 1949, he went to London to sing in a musical, *Tough at the Top*. He remained in Europe to study in Milan with Giulio Lorandi. Tozzi's Italian debut was at Milan's Teatro Nuovo as Rodolfo in *La sonnambula*; his La Scala debut was in 1953, in Catalani's *La Wally*. He returned to the United States, where his first appearance at the Metropolitan Opera was in 1955, in *La Gioconda*. Tozzi then joined the Metropolitan company, staying there until 1973. As his operatic career developed, Tozzi maintained a keen interest in musicals, starring in several acclaimed productions. His performance in the Broadway revival of *Most Happy Fella* brought him a Tony Award nomination for Best Actor in a Musical. In 1957, Tozzi won the Critics' Award for Best Actor in a Musical for the production of *South Pacific* in San Francisco, opposite Mary Martin. He was also on the sound track of the film *South Pacific* as the voice of Emile Debeque, acted by Rosanno Brazzi. The soundtrack of that film brought Tozzi a gold record from RCA Victor, and he also won three Grammy Awards. In 1958, he created the role of The Doctor in the world premiere of Samuel Barber's *Vanessa* at the Met. Other roles in his repertoire were the title role in Musorgsky's *Boris Godunov*, King Philip in *Don Carlo*, Mephistopheles in Gounod's *Faust*, the title role of *Don Giovanni*, Gremin in Tchaikovsky's *Eugene Onegin*, Don Basilio in Rossini's *Barber of Seville*, Gurnemanz in *Parsifal*, Arkel in Debussy's *Pélleas et Mélisande*, Figaro in *The Marriage of Figaro*, King Marke in *Tristan und Isolde*, and Hans Pogner in *Die Meistersinger*. Tozzi's appearance in the Hamburg Opera's film *Die Meistersinger*, as Hans Sachs, is, he says, his proudest professional achievement. He also filmed his roles as Boris Godunov and as King Melchior in Menotti's *Amahl and the Night Visitors*. Tozzi has sung in all the great opera houses. In his 20 years with the Metropolitan, he sang 400 performances. In addition to his work in operas in musicals, Tozzi has often appeared on film and television in singing and non-singing roles. Throughout his career, Tozzi has been an enthusiastic teacher, always eager to encourage younger musicians. During his tenure at the Met, Tozzi taught at the Juilliard School in New York City. In 1991, became a professor at the Indiana University School of Music. *—Joseph Stevenson*

Recommended:

○ **Puccini: La Fanciulla del West** / Capuana (cond.), Tebaldi, Tozzi, Del Monaco, Palma, St. Cecilia Academy Orch. / 1989 / Decca 421595

○ **Barber: Vanessa** / Mitropoulos (cond.), Gedda, Steber, Tozzi, Elias, Metropolitan Opera Orch. & Chorus / 1957 / RCA 7899

○ **Puccini: La bohème** / Beecham (cond.), Bjoerling, Los Angeles, Merrill, Tozzi, RCA. Victor Orch. & Chorus / 2002 / Angel 67753

Walter Trampler

b. Aug. 25, 1915, Munich, Germany, **d.** Sep. 27, 1997, Nova Scotia, Canada
Violist

Walter Trampler was a fixture in the viola world for very nearly three-quarters of a century, serving that rich but often underappreciated kingdom both as a soloist of the top rank and as a teacher. Trampler was born in Munich in 1915 and lived in Germany for the first 24 years of his life; but, like so many of his countrymen, he emigrated to the United States in 1939 when he could simply no longer bear the domestic pressure cooker that was Germany at that time.

Trampler's first music lessons were provided by his violinist father, and his earliest significant public appearance was made not playing the viola, but rather its higher-strung sister instrument in a 1933 performance of the Beethoven *Violin Concerto*. Meanwhile he had taken to the viola as a parallel means of musical expression: he played that instrument in the German Radio Orchestra from the mid-1930s until the time of his emigration (he was in fact the principal violist), and also played it in the now-forgotten Strub Quartet. Trampler's activities during the first few years of his American residency were many and varied. He served with the American Army during World War II; he taught at Mills College in California for a short time; he played violin in the Boston Symphony Orchestra for a time (1942–44); he served as principal violist of the New York City Opera Orchestra, and then in 1947 he founded the New Music String Quartet—a godsend ensemble to contemporary composers up until its dissolution in the late 1950s—and played viola in it. The attention this brought him led to an appointment, in 1962, to the faculty of the Juilliard School. He would go on to teach also at the New England Conservatory, the Boston University School of the Arts, and Yale University. He was, in addition, a founding member of the Chamber Music Society of Lincoln Center.

Trampler's elegant, sonorous viola playing was well-suited both to the standard repertoire, of which he recorded a great deal, and new music; a number of prominent twentieth century composers, including Luciano Berio and Hans Werner Henze, fashioned works specifically for him. He also devoted a portion of his skill and time to the viola d'amore and its representative works. *—Blair Johnston*

Recommended:

○ **Brahms: String Quintets** / Trampler, Juilliard SQ / 2001 / Sony 89737

○ **Brahms: Piano Quartets** / Trampler, Schneider, Parnas, Brown / 2003 / Artemis Classics 1228

Tatiana Troyanos

b. Sep. 12, 1938, New York, NY, **d.** Aug. 21, 1993, New York, NY
Mezzo-Soprano

The dynamic mezzo-soprano Tatiana Troyanos was born into a singing family; her Greek father was a tenor, and her German mother a soprano. Born in New York, Troyanos studied at the Juilliard School with Hans J. Heinz, while singing occasionally in the New York area (she was a member of the original chorus for the Broadway production of *The Sound of Music*). In April 1963 she made her operatic debut with the New York City Opera, in the New York premiere of Benjamin Britten's *A Midsummer Night's Dream*. She remained with the City Opera for two years.

Julius Rudel, then musical director of the City Opera, helped Troyanos get a Rockefeller Foundation scholarship to allow her to travel to Europe. She signed on with the Hamburg State Opera, making her debut with that company as Suzuki in *Madame Butterfly* in 1966. Later that same year she played the Composer in Strauss' *Ariadne auf Naxos*, a role she continued to sing frequently. Troyanos remained with the Hamburg Opera for a decade, while also making frequent appearances worldwide. She made her Covent Garden debut in 1968 as Octavian in *Der Rosenkavalier*, another role she repeated often. Some international attention came her way in 1969 when she sang in the world premiere of Penderecki's opera *The Devils of Loudun*.

In the 1970s and 1980s she continued to expand her repertoire. She sang the title role in Handel's *Ariodante* in the 1971 inaugural performance at Washington D.C.'s Kennedy Center, and made her Metropolitan Opera debut in 1976. She took on bel canto roles in works by the likes of Donizetti and Bellini, and began performing regularly in Wagner's music dramas. Dramatic roles such as Dido in Berlioz's *Les Troyens* and Countess Geschwitz in Berg's *Lulu* also became staples in her performing schedule. In 1992 she created the role of Queen Isabella in Philip Glass' *The Voyage.*

Over the years she made many significant recordings, including a renowned *Carmen* under Sir Georg Solti's direction, as well as Leonard Bernstein's 1987 re-recording of his own *West Side Story.* Troyanos was diagnosed with cancer in July 1993, and died a month later. *—Chris Morrison*

Recommended:

- ○ **In Recital** / Troyanos, Levine / 1999 / VAI Audio 1187
- ○ **Purcell: Dido & Aeneas** / Leppard (cond.), Troyanos, Langridge, Hodgson, Maxwell, English CO / 2001 / Elektra 89242
- ○ **Bizet: Carmen** / Solti (cond.), Domingo, Te Kanawa, Allen, Van Dam, Troyanos, London PO / 1985 / London 414489
- ○ **Strauss: Ariadne auf Naxos** / Solti (cond.), Price, Troyanos, Parsons, Kunz, London PO / 1992 / London 430384

Evelyn Tubb

b. England

Soprano

English singer Evelyn Tubb studied at the Guildhall School of Music in London. She later joined the Consort of Musicke with which she has made dozens of recordings and appeared in several television presentations. She is also a frequent collaborator with guitarist and lutenist Michael Fields. Tubb has performed oratorio, opera, and music-theater repertoire that runs the gamut from Hildegard von Bingen to Peter Maxwell Davies. She created the title role in John Eccles's *Semele* (1707) for the Mayfield Chamber Opera. She has taught worldwide, including at the Scola Cantorum Basiliensis and the Dartington International Summer School.

She is noted for her performances which strive for drama and presence as well as historical accuracy. She credits her interest in all kinds of music, not just classical, and in dance and even T'ai chi with helping her make her performances true characterizations and not just well-sung music. *—Robert Adelson*

Recommended:

- ○ **The Mad Lover** / Tubb, etc. / Musica Oscura 70987
- ○ **My Careless Eyes** / Tubb, Parsons / 2003 / Gaudeamus 344
- ○ **The Mantle of Orpheus** / Rooley (cond.), Kirkby, Tubb, Boothby, Miller, Consort of Musicke / 1995 / Musica Oscura 070977

Richard Tucker

b. Aug. 28, 1913, New York, NY, **d.** Jan. 8, 1975, Kalamazoo, MI

Tenor

The 1950s and 1960s were an unusual time for tenors—on one hand, Kraus, Gedda, and Bergonzi were faithful re-creators, on the other, there were such individualists as Franco Corelli and Richard Tucker (1913–75), who rejoiced in their vocal idiosyncrasies, and sang in a manner that best displayed their vocal strengths. For some listeners, with his open, powerful, and seemingly tireless voice, Richard Tucker was not only the supreme Verdi tenor of his time, but of the entire twentieth century. For others, his interpolated sobs and gulps, his perceived lack of sensitivity to textual or musical nuances, and tendency to sing everything at full forte, regardless of the score's indications, was both vulgar and unstylish, nearly the opposite of what Verdi singing should be.

He first sang professionally at the age of six as an alto in a local synagogue, and continued to sing at weddings and bar mitzvahs while he was growing up. In his teens, he studied with Paul Althouse, sang as a professional cantor, and made his operatic debut as Alfredo in *La Traviata* at the Jolson Theater in New York in 1943. In 1944, Althouse invited Edward Johnson, general director of the Metropolitan Opera, to hear his pupil sing services at the Brooklyn Jewish Temple, and Johnson was impressed enough to offer him a contract. Tucker made his Met debut as Enzo in Ponchielli's *La Gioconda* in early 1945, the first of over 600 performances for the Met (499 in the house, 225 on tour). He made his Italian debut at the *Arena di Verona* in the same role in 1947, opposite debuting soprano Maria Callas, and made his Covent Garden debut in 1957, his Vienna debut in 1958, and his La Scala debut in 1969. However, the Met was his home base, and where he was a favorite. While his voice had the power of a spinto, its basic timbre was lyrical, enough so that Rudolf Bing was able to convince him to sing Ferrando in the now-famous English-language production of *Cosi fan tutte,* with Eleanor Steber and Blanche Thebom.

Tucker was a devout believer, and proud of his Judaic heritage, and he also made several recordings, now classics, of Jewish sacred music. During the Vietnam War, he even went overseas to serve as cantor for Seder services for the United States troops. He also performed Cesar Franck's *Panis angelicus* at the funeral services of Robert Kennedy.

He died in Kalamazoo, Michigan. Due to his close ties with the Met and its audiences, his funeral service was held on the Met's stage. His family established the Richard Tucker Foundation, which awards a prize to a rising opera star each year. Some of the past winners include Renée Fleming, Dwayne Croft, and Paul Groves. Tucker's recording of *Cosi fan tutte,* based on the Met production, captures his voice in its prime as he sings with uncommon elegance and grace. Sony has also re-released a representative album of his Verdi arias with Eileen Farrell.*—Ann Feeney*

Recommended:

- ○ **Lebendige Vergangenheit: Richard Tucker** / Tucker, etc. / Preiser 89552
- ○ **Passover Seder Festival** / Secunda (cond.), Tucker, Richardson, Cohen, Sholom Secunda Chorus / 1992 / Sony 48304
- ○ **Puccini: Bohème** / Leinsdorf (cond.), Moffo, Merrill, Tucker, Tozz, Rome Opera House Orch. / 1998 / RCA 63179
- ○ **Verdi: La Traviata** / Previtali (cond.), Merrill, Moffo, Palma, Tucker, Rome Opera House Orch. & Chorus / 1997 / RCA 902668885

Barry Tuckwell

b. Mar. 5, 1931, Melbourne, Australia

French Horn Player

Barry Tuckwell is perhaps the world's most renowned French horn player, and is believed to have made more recordings than any other hornist in history. As a child, he studied violin and piano, as taught by his father and older brother. He was a chorister at St. Andrew's Cathedral in Sydney, and also served as organist there. He began to study the horn at 13 with Alan Mann of the Sydney Conservatory. He made such rapid progress that he became a member of the Sydney Symphony Orchestra at the age of 15, remaining in the orchestra from 1947 to 1950. By that time he had publicly performed nearly every major concerto in the standard repertory.

He went to England at 19, in part because of Britain's wider career opportunities but also to study informally with the great horn virtuoso Dennis Brain. Tuckwell also credits listening to the recordings of jazz trombonist Tommy Dorsey with shaping his idea of brass sound.

Tuckwell's professional career blossomed first as the Assistant First Horn in the Hallé Orchestra in Manchester, then with the Scottish National Orchestra, and eventually the First Horn of the Bournemouth Symphony Orchestra. In 1955, at the age of 24, he became Principal Horn of the London Symphony Orchestra. He became regarded as one of the most able and respected members of the orchestra, which elected him to its Board of Directors, and ultimately to its Chairmanship

During his LSO years he appeared regularly as a soloist, and in 1968 he left the orchestra to pursue a career exclusively as a horn soloist. He toured and taught widely all over the world, and is responsible for the commissioning of works that have become important addition to the horn repertory, including compositions by Gunther Schuller, Oliver Knussen, Richard Rodney Bennett, Thea Musgrave, and Ian Hamilton.

He was the first President of the International Horn Society (1970–76) and served another term from 1992–94, and is now a member of its Advisory Committee. He has worked diligently to advance horn playing, and has worked on instrument design with makers such as Holton and Lawson. He was Professor of Horn at the Royal Academy of Music in London (1962–72), Artist-in-residence at New Hampshire's Dartmouth College, Pomona College in California, and the Stratford Festival in Ontario. Tuckwell is also a noted editor of horn music, and has authored two books on the techniques of horn playing.

In 1982 he helped found the Maryland Symphony Orchestra, serving as its music director into 1998. He was also Music Director of the Tasmanian Symphony Orchestra in Hobart, Australia. He also frequently appears as a guest conductor, and has recorded an album of Wagner overtures. In 1992 Tuckwell was granted permanent U.S. residency under the new "Extraordinary Ability" immigration category, and became a U.S. Citizen in 1997. He retired from professional horn playing in 1996, at the age of 65. He continues to conduct and teach, and works with promising youngsters at the Kendall Betts Horn Camp, Lyman, New Hampshire. *—Joseph Stevenson*

Recommended:

- ○ **Mozart: Concertos** / Marriner (cond.), Tuckwell, Academy of St. Martin-in-the-Fields / 2001 / EMI 74967
- ○ **Knussen: Concerto, etc.** / Knussen (cond.), Tuckwell, Constable, Shelton, Collins, London Sinfonietta / 2003 / DG 000141002

Rosalyn Tureck

b. Dec. 14, 1914, Chicago, IL, **d.** Jul. 17, 2003, Bronx, NY

Pianist

After childhood keyboard lessons with various teachers in Chicago, Rosalyn Tureck went to Juilliard to study with the famed Olga Samaroff. Though she had performed in recitals and concerts as a child in Chicago, Tureck attracted particular attention with her New York debut shortly after her graduation in 1935. Over the next ten years, she narrowed her repertoire, eventually becoming most closely associated with the music of J.S. Bach. After her European debut in 1947, she began a successful international career that eventually took her to Africa, Asia, Latin America, and Israel. In the early 1960s she took up the harpsichord and clavichord, though the piano remained her primary vehicle for performance; she also occasionally took the podium as conductor. In tandem with a well-regarded concert and recording career, Tureck held numerous teaching posts as such institutions as Juilliard, Columbia University, and Oxford University; and published articles and books on pedagogical and performance-related topics, particularly in relation to the music of Bach. As a performer she was singled out for her intensity of feeling and clear contrapuntal sense; no less a luminary than Glenn Gould spoke highly of her considerable gifts. *—Steven Coburn*

Recommended:

- ○ **Bach: Goldberg Variations** / Tureck / DG 459599
- ○ **Bach: The Great Solo Works** / Tureck / 1990 / VAI Audio 1041
- ○ **The Young Firebrand** / Tureck / 1994 / VAI Audio 1058
- ○ **Rosalyn Tureck** / Tureck / 1998 / Philips 456976
- ○ **Bach: The Well-Tempered Clavier, Book 1** / Tureck / 2002 / BBC 4109

Joaquín Turina

b. Dec. 9, 1882, Seville, Spain, **d.** Jan. 14, 1949, Madrid, Spain
Composer: Chamber Music, Keyboard, Orchestral, Concerto

When he was a small boy, one of Joaquín Turina's favorite toys was a small accordion, and music was always his favorite subject at school. He studied piano and theory in his hometown of Seville and made his debut there as a pianist at age 14. His success led him to Madrid, where he tried to get his opera *La sulamita* (c. 1900) and his zarzuela *Fea y con gracia* (1904) performed. The latter was staged to no great success, but Turina showed his music to many prominent musicians and struck up a friendship with Manuel de Falla.

After studying piano at the Madrid Conservatory with José Tragó, Turina went to Paris, where he worked with Vincent d'Indy at the Schola Cantorum from 1905 to 1914. He also took some piano lessons with Moritz Moszkowski. During his years in Paris he was encouraged by the great French composers of that time—Claude Debussy, Maurice Ravel, Paul Dukas, and his teacher d'Indy—and wrote a few works in the French style of the day. After the premiere of his *Piano Quintet*, Op. 1 in 1907, Turina went to a café with *Isaac Albéniz* and de Falla. They convinced Turina to write in a more consciously Spanish style. As Turina put it, "[w]e were three Spaniards gathered together in that corner of Paris and it was our duty to fight bravely for the national music of our country."

One of his first truly Spanish works was *La procesión del Rocío*, written in France in 1912 and premiered by the Madrid Symphony the following year. This portrait of a religious festival helped establish Turina's reputation, and by the time he returned to Spain with Falla in 1914, he was already recognized as a leading Spanish composer. Turina took a post as choirmaster at the Teatro Real, a position he held until the theater closed in 1925. He continued to be very active in Spain's musical life, serving as pianist of the Quinteto de Madrid, conducting opera and orchestral performances, and writing musical criticism for *El Debate* and other publications. He also composed works like the two books of *Mujeres Españolas* for piano (1917, 1932), a series of portraits of Spanish women, and *La oración del torero* (The Bullfighter's Prayer, 1925). In 1920 he wrote two of his most popular pieces, the *Danzas Fantásticas* for orchestra or piano, and the *Sinfonía Sevillana*, which won first prize in a competition for a musical picture of life in Seville.

In 1930 he was appointed professor of composition at the Madrid Conservatory. He and his family suffered a certain amount of persecution by the Republicans during the Spanish Civil War, but Turina was able to carry on with his musical activities both during and after the war. He founded the General Music Commission of the Ministry of Education, of which he served as commissioner in 1941. He became a member of the Spanish Academy of Arts, was awarded the Grand Cross of Alfonso X the Wise, and died in early 1949 after a long struggle with cancer. *—Chris Morrison*

CHAMBER MUSIC

Fandanguillo, for guitar, Op. 36 (1926)

The *Fandanguillo* was one of the many products of the emergence of Andrés Segovia as a guitar virtuoso. In the 1920s, early in his career, Segovia asked Joaquín Turina to compose some solo guitar works for him. In 1926, Turina produced the *Fandanguillo*, which he said was derived in part from some of the traditional music of his homeland. The rhythmic qualities of flamenco music are never far away in this work, and the zapateado—the percussive sounds produced by the heels of a dancer's shoes hitting the floor—are called to mind in the percussive sounds drawn from the the guitar strings. This short work is for the most part an extroverted one, with a more mellow central section providing contrast. A run of harmonics toward the end of the piece leads into its quiet chordal ending. *—Chris Morrison*

Recommended:

- ○ **Andrés Segovia: The Complete 1949 London Recordings** / Segovia / 1994 / Testament 1043

Homenaje a Tárrega, for guitar, Op. 69 (1932)

While playing the guitar had been an Iberian pastime for centuries before, Francisco Tárrega, who died in 1909, is generally considered the founder of modern guitar technique. This means that many people are deeply in his debt. One was Joaquin Turina, who wrote a number of short works for guitar and allowed the native music of Spain to influence many of his other works. Thus, it is fitting that Turina composed the *Homenaje a Tárrega*, published as Op. 69 and consisting of two short, tricky, thoroughly idiomatic flamenco pieces for solo guitar. The two pieces that make up the *Homenaje a Tárrega*, Turina's last music for solo guitar, were written for Andrés Segovia, who had approached Turina, as well as many other composers, in the 1920s for new guitar works. The first piece is a garrotín in 2/4 time, with an opening full of large gestures that soon yields to music which is less public but no less demanding. It trails off ambiguously at the end, finally settling dreamily into the major mode, which until then has gone unused. The second flamenco is a soleares in 3/4 time, quicker and more demanding than its predecessor, as Turina basically presents a series of variations on the contrasting quick runs and forceful strums characteristic of the flamenco style. This is slight but charming music, written with care to serve a noble purpose. *—Andrew Lindemann Malone*

Recommended:

- ○ **Julian Bream Plays Spanish Guitar Music** / Bream / 2001 / Westminster 471236

La Oración del torero, for lute quartet, Op. 34 (1925)

La oración del torero (The Bullfighter's Prayer), mixing the tried-and-true Spanish themes of religion and bullfighting, was a key work in cementing Turina's national recognition in Spain. An unassuming miniature, the work was composed in 1925 for, and dedicated to, the Aguilar Lute Quartet. Inspired by the work's popularity, Turina quickly rescored it for string quartet and, eventually, for string orchestra. The rescorings became the most popular versions of the work, and the composition in whatever form became one of Turina's most widely recorded chamber selections. Those who have recorded the work include the Mexico City Philharmonic Orchestra, the Manhattan Quartet, the Hamburg Symphony Orchestra, and the Hollywood Quartet. One of the attractive features of Turina's music in general is that among the composers of the Spanish nationalist movement, he was the only one to write a significant amount of chamber music. Despite the plethora of Spanish scenes and themes mentioned in the titles of his pieces, he kept one foot in the French tradition and tended more than his compatriots to compose in traditional pan-national forms. About eight or nine minutes long, *La oración del torero* offers a variety of colors and energy levels appropriate to its subject. The work begins calmly, passing through episodes of propulsive rhythm and temperamental outbursts to reach a high-powered climax. The prayerful opening material returns to round things out. Despite all the Spanish character on display, the work shows the influence of Debussy, as Turina's music so often does, in its profusion of parallel ninth chords. Even in the bullring, Turina shows his typical grace and subtlety. *—James Manheim*

Recommended:

- ○ **Spanish Works for String Orchestra** / Claret (cond.), Orquestra Nacional de Cambra d'Andorra / 1998 / Nimbus 5570

Piano Trio No. 1, Op. 35 (1926)

Despite its title, the *Trio No. 1 in D major* was not actually Turina's first trio. In 1904, he wrote a substantial but little-known *Trio in F major*. But by 1926, the year he produced the D major trio, Turina had developed a more personal style, having assimilated a variety of early influences and given more prominent expression to his Spanish heritage (as recommended by his countryman Isaac Albéniz). Published with a dedication to the Infanta Isabel de Borbón, the *Trio in D major* won the 1926 Spanish National Competition. The work is in three movements; the opening Prelude and Fugue begins with a rather moody descending line from the violin and cello. A second, more peaceful theme is introduced by the piano and all three instruments join in a continued meditation on that theme. The Fugue follows, based on a sweet theme related to the piano idea. After further contrapuntal development that turns forceful and passionate, the movement quietly ends. The second movement is a Theme and Variations; the sinuous theme, initially announced by the cello over mellow piano chords, leads into a sequence of five variations, featuring lively Spanish rhythms, not a little humor, and a hint of Impressionism. The theme in its original form closes the movement, with the cello's statement of the tune answered by the violin. An energetic passage for cello and violin opens the lively Sonata finale, which is largely based on the Spanish-sounding opening theme. After the theme is contrapuntally developed, the first movement's fugue and opening themes make brief return appearances before the forceful piano chords close the work. *—Chris Morrison*

Recommended:

- ○ **Pasión** / Eroica Trio / 2000 / Angel 57033B

KEYBOARD

Album de viaje, Op. 15 (1916)

A Spaniard of Italian descent from Andalucía, Joaquín Turina went to Paris to study with d'Indy and came under Debussy's spell. In the course of a 1907 café meeting with Falla and Albéniz, he swore allegiance to the ideal of Spanish nationalism. But French impressionism continued to color his music, which more often fell into conventional pan-European forms than did the productions of his more individualistically Spanish contemporaries. Especially in his works for his own instrument, the piano, Turina's music offers grace and an appealing warmth that sometimes verges on the popular, suggesting what might have happened if Debussy had taken an extended southern vacation (or if a Spanish zarzuela composer had been bitten by the modernist bug). Examples of all these strands in his output are offered by the *Album de viaje* (Travel Album), Op. 15, which the composer undertook after a 1916 tour around the Mediterranean shore. The travel album was by then a time-honored and even hoary Romantic form, and Turina's five little descriptive pieces, totaling perhaps 20 minutes in performance, offer little in the way of a distinctively modern psychology. But they're lovely, evocative pieces that would make a perfect gift for anyone headed to this part of the world. A special highlight is the third piece in the set, "Gibraltar," which pokes fun at that British-ruled island's population by skewering "God Save the King [Queen]" with Ivesian dissonances amid a colorful bustle of town streets. Three movements are slow and quiet: the opening "Retrato" (Portrait), the following "El casino de Algeciras," and the fourth piece, "Paseo nocturno," which features a brisker evening promenade in the middle, sandwiched by almost bluesy outer sections. Tonally, Turina often relies in these pieces on a gentle pentatonic sound that can be sharpened into quartal harmonies at times, and the vaguely Bartók-like finale, the vigorous "Fiesta mora en Tanger" (Moorish Fiesta in Tangier), features a sharp contrast of major third and perfect fourth. Colorful and thoroughly accessible, this is one set of musical postcards that anyone would be happy to receive in the mail. *—James Manheim*

Recommended:

○ **Spanish Piano Music** / M. Jones / 1999 / Nimbus 5619/23

El Castillo de Almodóvar, suite, Op. 65 (1931)

The Castle of Almodóvar del Rio stands on a 333-foot-high hill outside the city of Cordoba in Andalusia. It was built in about 740 by the Arabic Moors of Spain and was considered by them impregnable. Nonetheless, in the thirteenth century Almodóvar fell into the hands of the Castilian king Ferdinand III after he had laid siege to it for a period of some four years. Philip IV turned it into a monastery in the early seventeenth century, but by the end of the nineteenth, the castle was uninhabitable and beginning to fall apart. In 1916, a full-time restoration project was undertaken by the Spanish government to reclaim the Castle of Almodóvar del Rio, which was completed in 1930. A year later, Spanish composer Joaquín Turina composed a piano suite, no doubt inspired by the castle shortly after it reopened, *El Castillo de Almodóvar*, which Turina numbered as his Op. 65. The suite lasts about 15 minutes and consists of three movements, "Silueta nocturna" (Nocturnal Silhouette), "Evocación medieval" (Medieval Evocation), and "A plena luz" (In Total Sunlight). The style of the music is Spanish-flavored, but rooted in French impressionism, and although the castle itself was Arabic, there is very little of that type of tonal coloring in Turina's music. The Castle of Almodóvar del Rio is located on a wide, flat plain and is the only structure that stands within miles of itself; the opening movement, "Silueta nocturna," represents the imposing relief in which the castle is seen at night. The "Evocación medieval" may have been intended as reflecting the sound of medieval music as early twentieth composers imagined it (as in Fritz Kreisler's *Aucassin et Nicolette*), and as such, even harkens back to the sound of nineteenth century salon music in some passages. "A plena luz" is more direct and captures the towering grandeur of the castle as it is seen on a hot, cloudless summer's day. The popularity of the suite *El Castillo de Almodóvar* was immediate, in spite of the troubles Turina was then having with the Spanish Republicans attacking his reputation. In 1933, Turina expanded the suite into a full orchestration, producing what ultimately proved his final work in the symphonic genre. Though while the orchestral version of *El Castillo de Almodóvar* remains an obscurity, the popularity of the original piano pieces have only increased with the passage of time. *—Uncle Dave Lewis*

Recommended:

○ **Turina: Sinfonia Sevillana; Ritmos; Evangelio; El Castillo de Almodóvar** / Leaper (cond.), Williams, Gran Canaria PO / 1999 / ASV 1066

Danzas gitanas, Set 1, Op. 55 (1930)

Joaquín Turina was nearing his 50th year when he composed the first set of the charming piano miniatures *Danzas gitanas*, Op. 55, in 1930—the same year he was appointed to the faculty of the Madrid Conservatory. But there is nothing "middle-aged" about the *Danzas gitanas*, unless it be the experienced suavity of their textures and tunes: the music seems on the contrary quite young, quite vivacious.

The first of the five dances of Op. 55, Set 1, depicts a "Zambra," which is a traditional party complete with dancing and flamenco music. An eight-measure Adagio introduction sets the stage for the Allegretto quasi andantino body of the movement and its incessant gallop rhythm. No. 2 is a "Danza de la seducción"; bearing the title in mind, the reader is invited to draw his/her own conclusions about the way the lithe, sizzling melody spins around hot A major chords during the central portion. "Danza ritual," No. 3, is an Andante that shares many basic musical elements with the previous dance: again there is an opening treble melody, developing a soft harmonic cushion, a throbbing, pulsing broken-chord passage in the middle, and again the traditional three-part song form. But the feel of the music is altogether different; tempered, stoic tradition, not sweet seduction, is offered here. The first set of *Danzas gitanas* also features a number called "Generalife"—a molto vivo, 3/8 time moto perpetuo that is punctuated by a crashing, hemiola-filled "polo gitano" idea. *—Blair Johnston*

Recommended:

○ **Turina: Complete Piano Works Vol. 3: Danzas** / Soria / Edicions Albert Moraleda 6403

Mujeres españolas, Set 1, Op. 17 (1917)

Turina is generally regarded as one of the four or five great Spanish composers from the twentieth century. He perhaps strove more diligently than his contemporaries to absorb cosmopolitan elements into his approach to composition. That said, he never turned away from nationalist styles and his piano music is usually instantly recognizable for its Spanish rhythms and sonorities. This set of three pieces, as its title suggests (Spanish Women), brims with the colors of Spain in these attractive portraits. The first of the three pieces, *La madrileña clásica* (The Classical Madrilenan), is full of glitter and color from its opening notes: trills and runs and splashy chords fill the air, the music finally settling down to a subdued, subtly captivating theme. The second piece, *La andaluza sentimental* (The Sentimental Andalucian), offers a slow, ponderous theme in deftly crafted piano writing. For all the subtle beauties this piece yields, however, there is not much that is overtly sentimental in its character. But the next work, *La morena coqueta* (The Coquettish Brunette), with more than a few hints of Debussy, vividly depicts its titled persona in music of many moods, from leisurely to almost frenzied, from mysterious to provocative. *—Robert Cummings*

Recommended:

○ **Turina: Mujeres Españolas** / Buechner / 1992 / Connoisseur Society 4186

Mujeres españolas, Set 2, Op. 73 (1932)

This is the second and final set in Turina's output bearing the title *Mujeres españolas*, the earlier one (Op. 17) having just three pieces and dating to 1917. There are other similarly titled collections in his oeuvre, however, such as *Mujeres de Sevilla* (1935). Turina loved to do musical portraits and generally chose the piano as his means of expression for them. In this later set of Spanish Women, he produced some of his finest and most-appealing music in the genre. The first piece, "La gitana enamorada" (The Infatuated Gypsy), is exotic in its catchy, rhythmic themes and mixture of Spanish and Gypsy elements, a blend decidedly favoring the former ethnic flavors. "La florista" (The Florist) follows, a Debussy-tinged piece whose slightly dry capriciousness is balanced by its bursts of bubbly joy. The ensuing "La Senorita Que Baila" (The Dancing Girl) is demure and nonchalant: this clever dancer is graceful and balletic, lithe, and alluring. The fourth, "La Murciana guapa" (The Pretty Woman From Murcia) is subdued and light, emotionally cool and subtle in its lovely, slightly wistful theme. The closing piece, "La alegre Sevillana" (The Happy Sevillian), alternates festive and colorful moods with more subdued but still sunny music. This masterful collection will appeal to twentieth century piano aficionados, as well as admirers of Spanish piano music. *—Robert Cummings*

Recommended:

○ **Turina: Mujeres Españolas** / Buechner / 1992 / Connoisseur Society 4186

ORCHESTRAL

Danzas fantásticas, Op. 22 (1920)

In contrast to his friend and fellow composer Manuel de Falla (six years older), Turina was less interested in mainstream European music and continued to write in the rich, colorful Andalusian style which most often is associated with Spanish music. *Danzas fantásticas* is a brilliant, wholly Spanish piece and Turina's best-known work (there is also a piano version).

It is inspired by the novel *La orgía* by José Mas. The three movements have the following sentences from the book printed above them: (1) "It seemed as if the figures in that incomparable picture were moving inside the claice of a flower." (2) "The guitar's strings sounded the lament of a soul helpless under the weight of bitterness." (3) "The perfume of the flowers merged with the odor of manzanilla, and from the bottom of raised glasses, full of wine incomparable as incense, joy flowed." Each of the dances is in a different style from a different Spanish tradition. The first is a jota from Aragón, the second is a Basque zortziko, and the third is an Andalusian farruca. *—Joseph Stevenson*

Recommended:

○ **Turina: Danzas Fantasticas; Sinfonia Sevillana; Debussy: Iberia** / Lopez-Cobos (cond.), Cincinnati SO / 2001 / Telarc 60574

La procesión del Rocio, symphonic poem, Op. 9 (1913)

This was the first orchestral work by Joaquin Turina. At its premiere in Madrid under the baton of Enrique Fernández Arbós in March 1913, it proved so popular that it had to be repeated on the spot. It is an exotic and colorful portrait of a fiesta in the composer's native Seville, equal in brilliance and orchestral magic to similar works by Ravel or Debussy.

The first movement quickly shows scenes from the festival, opening with a seguidilla, then a coplas (oboe) and soleares (viola), before closing with a rather tipsy fandango. The other movement is the religious procession itself, a ceremonial march with interruptions for religious hymns. At the end, church bells peal out and trumpets play the Spanish royal anthem. Conductor Antonio de Almeida has pointed out that after the work was published the composer wrote some changes in the percussion parts, which have not been incorporated into the published edition. *—Joseph Stevenson*

Recommended:

- ○ **Turina: Danzas Fantasticas; Sinfonia Sevillana; Debussy: Iberia** / Lopez-Cobos (cond.), Cincinnati SO / 2001 / Telarc 60574

CONCERTO

Rapsodia sinfónica, for piano & strings, Op. 66 (1931)

This compact work is not quite the lush extravaganza the term "symphonic rhapsody" may imply; the orchestra is limited to strings and the piano sometimes falls back into an accompaniment role. Yet it's full of Iberian atmosphere, particularly in the second half, and like Falla's *Nights in the Gardens of Spain*, it sensitively evokes a nocturnal scene in Andalusia, the gypsy-dominated area of southern Spain. The rhapsody begins with a slow but assertive statement by the strings, punctuated by a couple piano notes; the keyboard makes its true entrance with a vaguely oriental cascade of notes, similar to the piano's appearance in Ravel's *Left-Hand Concerto* (which was premiered the same year Turina wrote this rhapsody). This Andante section continues with the piano and orchestra uttering and answering each other's richly harmonized phrases. Occasionally, a solo violin comes forward with its own brief commentary, slick with portamento. A long passage for strings alone ultimately leads to the rhapsody's Allegro vivo section, a scherzo in which the piano takes a more prominent, flashy role. The excitement eases after a few moments, allowing a more romantic interlude, but soon the scherzo material returns with its rondeña rhythms and quickly alternating 3/4 and 6/8 passages to exciting effect. Even so, Turina moves the rhapsody toward its conclusion with a restatement of the broader, romantic material, giving the piano almost the last word with a flamenco-like flourish. *—James Reel*

Recommended:

- ○ **The San Diego Chamber Orchestra: Turina & Rodrigo** / Barra (cond.), G. Romero, San Diego CO / 1992 / Koch 37160
- ○ **Ivory Classics 5th Anniversary** / Freccia (cond.), Wild, Royal PO / 2002 / Ivory Classics 72010

Yuli Turovsky

b. Jun. 7, 1937, Moscow, U.S.S.R.

Conductor

Yuli Turovsky is one of many Russian émigré musicians who has established a career in the West as a conductor and soloist. Like Mstislav Rostropovich, he was trained as a cellist who gradually became attracted to conducting, often splitting his career evenly between the podium and instrumental performance. He is probably best-known as the conductor of I Musici de Montréal, the Canadian chamber ensemble he founded and with which he has appeared on over 40 recordings.

Turovsky started lessons on the cello at seven; two years later, in 1946, he began studies at Moscow's Central School of Music. After graduating in 1957, he enrolled at the Tchaikovsky Conservatory, where he studied cello with Galina Kozolupova. He graduated in 1962 with high honors and received a doctorate degree from the conservatory in 1969, by which time he had already established a career both as a soloist and chamber music collaborator. He was a member of the Moscow Chamber Orchestra, led by Rudolf Barshai, serving as principal cellist and often performing as a soloist. He had also tried his hand at conducting by this time, leading a group formed at Moscow's Gnessin Music School. In 1969, he captured first prize at the prestigious U.S.S.R. Cello Competition, after which his career rapidly advanced. He made a number of recordings with the Soviet label Melodiya and began gaining international recognition from their issue, as well as from his tours abroad with the MCO In 1976, he emigrated from the Soviet Union to Canada with his wife, Eleonora Turovsky, a violinist with whom he often concertized. Settling in Montreal, Turovsky founded the Borodin Trio in 1977 and, with his wife, also formed the Turovsky Duo. The other members of the Borodin Trio were Luba Edlina on piano and Rostislav Dubinsky on violin. Turovsky also joined the faculty of the Montreal Conservatory in 1977, serving until 1985. In 1980, Turovsky was granted Canadian citizenship and the following year began teaching at the University of Montreal. He founded the Montreal-based chamber ensemble I Musici de Montréal in 1983, but the group would not give its first public concert until November 1984. The ensemble consists of only 15 players—nine violinists, three violists, two cellists, and one double-bass player. Eleonora Turovsky was appointed concertmaster. (It should be noted that she is also a well-known painter, her work having attracted attention at exhibitions in both Moscow and Montreal.) In 1983, Turovsky and his I Musici group began making recordings for the Chandos label. Their more successful efforts included the Shostakovich *Symphony No. 14*, the Tchaikovsky *Souvenir de Florence*, and Schoenberg's *Verklärte Nachte*. In 1993, Turovsky departed the Borodin Trio as his activities both in the concert hall and recording studio were growing more demanding. He had made about 25 recordings with the group, which included performances of piano trios by Hummel, Mozart, Mendelssohn, and many other works. *—Robert Cummings*

Recommended:

- ○ **Shchedrin: Carmen Suite** / Y. Turovsky (cond.), I Musici de Montreal, Repercussion Ensemble / 1994 / Chandos 9288
- ○ **Shostakovich: Chamber Symphony, etc.** / Y. Turovsky (cond.), Hart, Pelle, Nolan, I Musici de Montreal / 2000 / Chandos 6617
- ○ **Schnittke: Concerto Grosso 1; Pärt: Tabula Rasa; Görecki: Concerto** / Y. Turovsky (cond.), E. Turovsky, N. Turovsky, Perrin, I Musici de Montreal / 1997 / Chandos 9590

Turtle Island String Quartet

f. 1986, Oakland, CA

Ensemble

One of the most recognized facets of postmodern culture is the blurring of boundaries between high art and low art, between "popular" and "cultured" traditions. All too often, this combination assumes an air of disassociation or cold observation—what Fredric Jameson has called "blank parody." Nonetheless, while the Turtle Island String Quartet certainly represents in music the dissolution of genre, race, and/or class distinctions, the variety of influences and sources from which the ensemble draws inspiration are combined into a sonic collage that is celebratory, rather than cynical. While we get a sense of this demolition of boundaries from groups like the Kronos or Brodsky Quartets, Turtle Island seems to pretend that these boundaries never existed—their performances of Dizzie Gillespie or Cole Porter make the music of these men sound as native to the string quartet idiom as that of Vivaldi. "A standard beyond reach of its few contemporaries," one critic has written. "In the multifarious idiom they have all but invented, Turtle Island remains the *ne plus ultra*."

The idea for the group initially came about while violinist and founding member David Balakrishnan was pondering subjects related to his master's thesis at Antioch University. The ensemble was formed three years later in Oakland, California, with the intention of giving voice to an eclectic, intergeneric, and intergenerational swath of music. Such an outlook invariably draws comparison (like the one above) to the Kronos Quartet, who caught the public eye around the same time. Curiously enough, however, Kronos had formed a decade earlier, in Oakland as well. Still, the Kronos Quartet, with their austere publicity photos and air of sternly hip progressivism, transmit a kind of intimidating East Coast attitude, while Turtle Island's loud shirts and more playfully transgressive programs seem to more tellingly reflect the cultural tone of their native California. Both groups undertake an adventurously varied repertoire, one that has valuably enhanced the scope of "classical" music; still, Turtle Island seems to infuse their performances with a bit more mirth and popular appeal—though arguably at the cost of excluding some of the particularly challenging works—for players and audiences alike—that Kronos champions.

A Turtle Island concert is a fairly laid-back event, and draws a crowd that is as ecumenical as the music itself. Likewise, the group's discography reflects their virtuosic polymath tendencies. Projects like their tribute to the swing music of Ellington and Gershwin, or their approach to more recent jazz masters like Miles Davis and Chick Corea, are complemented by their full-circle embrace, around the turn of the twenty-first century, of more "traditional" string quartet repertoire.

Whatever the genre, however, the thread that connects virtually all of their undertakings is an emphasis on improvisation. Sound reason supports this approach, since during the period that saw Haydn compose his first string quartets, the musicians involved were more or less the equivalent of today's gigging jazz musician; the disappearance of improvisation from the classical music realm is, in fact, a relatively recent trend—one that Turtle Island hopes to reverse. By doing so, all music and music making are seen as various shapes cut from the same fabric—a kind of musical postmodernism with a distinctly optimistic outlook toward music's future. *—Jeremy Grimshaw*

Recommended:

- ○ **The Hamburg Concert** / Turtle Island SQ / 1998 / CCn'C 282
- ○ **Danzón** / Turtle Island SQ / 2001 / Turtle Island 7529
- ○ **By the Fireside** / Turtle Island SQ / 1995 / Windham Hill 11175

U

Mitsuko Uchida

b. Dec. 20, 1948, Tokyo, Japan

Pianist

Mitsuko Uchida, a thoughtful and iconoclastic pianist, was born in Tokyo in 1948. She began her studies in piano during childhood. Her parents, who were diplomats, moved to Austria when Uchida was 12, and she enrolled at the Vienna Academy of Music. Even at this young age, Uchida rebelled against the conventional wisdom her teachers tried to impart. She wished to exercise her own judgment in performance, and the Academy did not want to let her. Judges at competitions, on the other hand, liked her judgment, giving her the second prize at the Beethoven Competition in 1968 and another second prize at the prestigous Chopin Competition in 1970. Uchida, however, was dissatisfied with her playing and retired from the competition circuit. Her career built up mostly through word of mouth during the 1970s. During the 1980s, Uchida built up a particular reputation as a Mozart interpreter—ironic for someone who did not like Mozart's music when studying it at the Vienna Academy. She received notice for outstanding performances of the Mozart sonatas in London and Tokyo in 1982, and recorded a universally acclaimed set of the complete sonatas for Philips. Uchida also appeared as soloist and conductor with the English Chamber Orchestra in a cycle of the complete Mozart concerti during 1985–86. She eventually recorded these for Philips as well, with the ECO conducted by Jeffrey Tate. Uchida, never one to rest on her laurels, moved into different repertoire during the 1990s, winning particular notice for her Debussy and Schubert solo piano recordings and her Beethoven concerti. She has also been a champion of the music of Schoenberg, Bartók and Berg, and often seeks to draw parallels between standard repertoire works and these modern masters. Like Martha Argerich, to whom she is sometimes compared, Uchida does not record or concertize prolifically (although she does both more than Argerich). Uchida does not like to be pigeonholed, and often strikes out on her own path; for example, she and a piano technician spent two years transforming a piano into something she felt she could use for Schubert. Uchida then insisted that Philips put the technician's name on the back of the CD—an unusual gesture. While Uchida's interpretations generally sound fresh and spontaneous, these characteristics arise from reasoned and deliberate musical choices. Far from prolific, she is always thought-provoking. Uchida currently resides in London. *—Andrew Lindemann Malone*

Recommended:

- ○ **Perspectives** / Tate (cond.), Uchida, English CO / 2003 / Philips 473686
- ○ **Schoenberg, Berg & Webern** / Boulez (cond.), Uchida, Cleveland Orch. / 2001 / Philips 468033
- ○ **Schubert: Impromptus** / Uchida / 1997 / Philips 456245
- ○ **Mozart:Concertos** / Tate (cond.), Uchida, English CO / 1993 / Philips 438207
- ○ **Mozart: Sonatas** / Uchida / 1991 / Philips 422719
- ○ **Mitsuko Uchida** / Tate (cond.), Uchida, English CO / 1999 / Philips 456982

Dawn Upshaw

b. Jul. 17, 1960, Nashville, TN

Soprano

Dawn Upshaw is a leading American soprano, known for her exceptional interest in contemporary music, and is highly active as a recitalist. She was raised in Park Forest, Illinois, and attended college at Illinois Wesleyan University, graduating with a Bachelor of Arts in 1982. She went to New York to study voice with Ellen Faull at Manhattan School of Music, earning her Masters Degree there in 1984. Success came very quickly. She won 1984's Young Concert Artists Auditions, after which James Levine, Music Director of the Metropolitan Opera, invited her to join the Metropolitan Opera Studio. In 1985 she was co-winner of the Naumburg Competition in New York. Her initial operatic appearances there were as minor characters. Her first professional recital was in Alice Tully Hall in New York in 1986. The recital drew acclaim not only for the quality and intelligence of her singing, but for the uniquely informed and adventurous choice of repertoire.

Soon she was receiving leading roles in opera, and has appeared in many of the world's major operatic venues. Her leading roles include all leading roles in all the major Mozart operas, Sophie in Massenet's *Werther*, both Constance and Blanche in Poulenc's *Dialogues des Carmelites*, Mélisande in Debussy's *Pelléas et Mélisande*; the Angel in Messiaen's *St. Françoise d'Assise*, and Ann Trulove in Stravinsky's *The Rake's Progress*. She created the role of Daisy Buchanan in John Harbison's *The Great Gatsby* in its world premiere at the Met, and the title role in Kaija Saariaho's *Clemence* at the Salzburg Festival. Her portrayal of Handel's *Theodora* in 1996 at the Glyndebourne Festival Opera, a production directed by Peter Sellars, was a triumph.

Even so, it is on the recital stage that she has gained her greatest stardom. She reserves two-thirds of her time for recitals. On the concert stage she has a natural charm and lack of pretension that engages the audience, qualities that are said to carry over offstage where she is called a "diva who doesn't act like one." She has sung on many of the main recital stages of the world, including the Theatre Champs Elysées in Paris, London's Wigmore Hall, and the Amsterdam Concertgebouw. She is prized for her work in French chanson and American art song, and she has strongly supported the work of John Harbison. She has appeared in stagings of Bach's *Cantata* BWV 199 (directed by Sellars) and George Crumb's *Ancient Voices of Children* (staged by Bill T. Jones). Her orchestral song repertoire includes works by Mahler, Canteloube, and Ravel, Lukas Foss's *Time Cycle*, and Henryk Górecki's *Symphony of Sorrowful Songs*.

She records for Nonesuch Records. Her release of the Gorecki Symphony is an international hit, with over half a million copies sold, a phenomenal total in classical music. Her discs have won several Grammy awards. On television she appeared in "Christmas at the White House" in the USA, and on a live telecast on the BBC of her London Proms Concert appearance, "Dawn at Dusk." She sings American popular and musical theater songs with freedom and understanding of the style. She sings this repertoire in concerts to benefit Classical Action, which promotes AIDS research. She frequently appears with pianists Richard Goode, Margo Garrett, and Jerome Duclos, the Kronos and Arditti Quartets, and the Chamber Music Society of Lincoln Center. *—Joseph Stevenson*

Recommended:

- ○ **Messiaen: Saint François d'Assise** / Nagano (cond.), Ortner, Upshaw, Van Dam, Aler, Halle Orch. / 1999 / DG 445176
- ○ **Gorecki: Symphony 3** / Zinman (cond.), Upshaw, London Sinfonietta / 1992 / Nonesuch 79282
- ○ **The Girl With Orange Lips** / Upshaw, Smith, Bartlett, Allen / 1991 / Nonesuch 79262
- ○ **White Moon: Songs To Morpheus** / Upshaw, Starobin, Garrett, Assad, Orpheus CO / 1996 / Nonesuch 79364

Utah Symphony Orchestra

f. 1940, Salt Lake City, UT

Ensemble

Salt Lake City, Utah was settled by members of the Latter-Day Saints (or Mormon) church who traveled there by wagon train in the 1840s in search of a livable, isolated location where they could pursue their religion in peace. Singing their music of faith sustained them on the trip, and one of their first actions upon settling in the Great Salt Lake Valley was to form a choral group, which became the Mormon Tabernacle Chorus. While many of the settlers had musical instruments, they did not have a local orchestra until 1892, when the Salt Lake symphony gave its one and only concert. In 1902, a Salt Lake Symphony Orchestra Association was formed, lasting for nine years. The next group, the Salt Lake Philharmonic, formed by an autonomous group of musicians, survived from 1913 to 1925.

The Great Depression forced many musicians out of work. The Federal Music Project of the Works Progress Administration appointed Reginald Beals to form an organization to employ indigent musicians. He started with a core of five players to form the Utah State Sinfonietta in 1935. It grew in size, and in five years gave over a thousand concerts to a combined audience of nearly 350,000. When the temporary Depression project was phasing out, Salt Lake leaders decided to keep the orchestra in existence, and formed the Utah State Symphony Orchestra Association on April 4, 1940. The USSO gave its first concert five weeks later, with Hans Heniot as the first music director. The name was changed to the Utah Symphony in 1946. Werner Janssen was hired as conductor, but lasted only a year. Maurice Abravanel, a pupil of Gustav Mahler, was hired to a one-year contract in 1947; he remained for 32 years.

Despite periodic funding crises, the orchestra survived and grew. It made history when it became the first orchestra to record a complete Mahler symphony cycle, accomplishing that feat in just one year. This was part of the Utah Symphony's treasured series of nearly 120 recordings for Vanguard Records. The orchestra also recorded a remarkable range of music, including works by Milhaud, Varése, Honegger, Satie, Gottschalk, and many other lesser-known works.

Abravanel was succeeded by Varujan Kojian (1979–84), then by Joseph Silverstein (1983–98). In 1998 Keith Lockhart became music director. From 1946 to 1979 the orchestra performed in the Mormon Tabernacle. Seeking a venue to call its own, the orchestra succeeded in building a new Symphony Hall, completed for the 1979-80 season. The acoustically superb building was renamed Abravanel Hall in 1993. *—Joseph Stevenson*

Recommended:

- ○ **Berlioz: Requiem; Mahler: Symphony 1** / Abravanel (cond.), Bressler, Utah SO / 2004 / Artemis 1506
- ○ **Brahms: Symphony 4; Overtures** / Abravanel (cond.), Utah SO / 2004 / Silverline 288257
- ○ **Sibelius: Symphonies 1 & 4** / Abravanel (cond.), Utah SO / 2004 / Silverline 288245

V

José Van Dam

b. Aug. 25, 1940
Bass

José van Dam has recorded nearly 150 roles, appeared in multiple world premieres, received most of the awards given to singers, is one of the most respected musicians of his generation—and almost nobody outside the world of classical music has even heard his name. His presence is rather austere, and his singing is notable for subtlety and attention to detail. His bass-baritone voice is rich, and his phrasing is impeccable in nearly every musical style, from Baroque to contemporary. He is an intense though introverted actor, and even starred in *Le Maitre de Musique*, a film about a reclusive singer who retires from the operatic stage to teach. While his somewhat limited bottom range makes the lowest notes of the bass roles problematic, his musicianship and sense of drama more than suffice to win him critical acclaim as Philip II and as Boris.

Unusually for an opera singer, his family was not a musical one. When he was 11, a family friend encouraged him to join the church choir. He began to study sight-singing and piano, and at 13 he became the pupil of Frederic Anspach of the Brussels Conservatory. He entered the Conservatory at the age of 17; won the first prize of the Conservatory the next year; at 20 won first prizes at the Liege and Toulouse competitions; and was engaged by the Paris Opera in 1962, where he made his operatic debut in Berlioz's *Les Troyens*, as Priam and the Voice of Mercury. In 1964 he sang the role of Escamillo for the first time, appearing in this role countless times in the future and recording it no fewer than four times. In 1965, he joined the Geneva Opera, where he sang the role of Maitre Fal in the world premiere of Milhaud's *La Mère Coupable*. Lorin Maazel engaged him to sing in his recording of Ravel's *L'heure Espagnol* on Deutsche Grammophon and invited him to become a member of the Deutsche Oper. He made his La Scala and Covent Garden debuts in 1973; in 1974, was named a Berliner Kammersänger and won the German Music Critics' Prize; and in 1975, made his Metropolitan Opera debut.

During the 1970s and 1980s, he continued to add new roles to his repertoire and began his long-standing partnership with Herbert von Karajan and with the Salzburg Festival. As he and his voice matured, he dropped certain roles, such as Escamillo and Figaro, and added roles such as Philip II, the Flying Dutchman, and Simon Boccanegra. In 1983, he sang the title role in the world premiere of Messiaen's Saint François d'Assise. He also continued to perform and record oratorio repertoire and became a noted interpreter of German lieder and French song, particularly the music of Henri Duparc. In the mid-1990s, he began again to explore new operatic repertoire, portraying Scarpia for the first time in 1995. He fared well in the inevitable comparisons to Gobbi. Both took a similar approach to roles—studying the historical and literary sources for the character, but regarding them as supplementary to what the composer and librettist created.

He recorded widely for many labels. His aria recital CD on Forlane displays his versatility as an opera singer and his dramatic power. In the Wagner repertoire, his Amfortas in Karajan's recording on DG is a vivid depiction of that tormented king. In French opera, his Don Quichotte (EMI) under Plasson, brings out the humor, nobility, and pathos of the title role. He also was an admirable Leporello in the Losey film of *Don Giovanni*. *—Ann Feeney*

Recommended:

- ○ **José van Dam** / Nagano (cond.), Van Dam, Lyon Opera Orch. / 1992 / Virgin 59236
- ○ **Le Chant d'un Maître** / Van Dam, etc. / Forlane 302270
- ○ **Wagner: Der fliegende Holländer** / Karajan (cond.), Van Dam, Moll, Moser, Hofmann, Berlin PO / EMI 47054
- ○ **Debussy: Pelléas et Mélisande** / Karajan (cond.), Von Stade, Van Dam, Raimondi, Stilwell, Berlin PO / 1999 / EMI 67168

Jos van Immerseel

b. Nov. 9, 1945, Antwerp, Belgium
Fortepianist

Jos van Immerseel is an outstanding period keyboard player who has been heard on the clavicembalo and fortepiano. Eugene Tracy, Flor Peeters, and Kenneth Gilbert were his instructors at the Royal Conservatory in Antwerp, where he won first prizes in piano, organ, and harpsichord between 1961 and 1971. During that period, he also won a number of competitions, culminating with the winning of the inaugural *Paris Forum International de Clavecin* in 1973. He is in demand as a soloist around the world, traveling with his own fortepiano at times, known for his musical receptiveness and responsiveness and his improvisational skills. He founded the Collegium Musicum in Antwerp, conducting that ensemble and the Collegium Vocale to expand his interest in Renaissance and Baroque music. In 1985, he found the orchestra Anima Eterna, also a period instrument group, which he has conducted from the keyboard. Much of his performing is focused on music of the Classical and early Romantic eras, although he has also recorded songs of Fauré with Max van Egmond, and of Debussy with Sandrine Plau, and the music of César Franck. Vera Beths and Anner Bylsma regularly perform and record with him, as well, most notably in Schubert's chamber works.

In addition to his performing and recording, van Immerseel keeps busy with writing articles and reviews, producing radio programs, and teaching. He has taught at the Antwerp Conservatory and Amsterdam's Sweelinck Conservatory; used the instruments in Antwerp's Vleeshuis Museum to give classes for its academy; and since 1992 has been on the faculty of the Paris Conservatoire.

Van Immerseel records for Channel Classics and Sony, among other labels. His Beethoven piano concerto recordings with Tafelmusik were noted for the cadenzas, which he wrote in keeping with the capabilities of the period instrument. However, one of his finest achievements is his recording of the fortepiano version of Haydn's *The Seven Last Words of Christ*. *—Patsy Morita*

Recommended:

- ○ **Haydn: The Seven Last Words** / Immerseel / 1995 / Channel Classics 6894
- ○ **Clementi: Piano Sonatas** / Immerseel / Accent 67911
- ○ **Schubert: Trout Quintet; Arpeggione & Notturno** / Immerseel, L'Archibudelli / 1998 / Sony 63361
- ○ **Liszt: Pièces Tardives** / Immerseel, Istomin / 2004 / Zig Zag 40902

Vanessa-Mae

b. Oct. 27, 1978, Singapore
Violinist

Crossover violinist Vanessa-Mae's full name is Vanessa-Mae Vanakom Nicholson, and she was born in Singapore to an English father and a Chinese mother. At age three she took up the piano; at four her parents divorced, and she and her mother moved to England. At five, she switched from piano to violin, studying with Lin Yao Ji at the Central Conservatory in Beijing and Felix Andrievsky at the Royal College of Music in London. At nine, Vanessa-Mae made her concert debut with the Philharmonia Orchestra and toured England playing the Tchaikovsky concerto, with her mother, Pamela Nicholson, acting as co-manager. At 12 she toured with the London Mozart Players, and at 13, she began her recording career. Her early recordings have been repackaged by Angel as *The Classical Collection 1*.

Her breakthrough disc, *The Violin Player*, bowed on the charts in fall 1995, featuring a "Toccata and Fugue" based on Bach's *Toccata and Fugue in D minor* and incorporating wailing electric guitar and a pumping, synthetic dance beat. *The Violin Player* was made with entirely commercial intentions, and the promotional material circulating at the time did nothing to understate the extraordinary allure of the young artist. The notorious "wet T-shirt" poses that appeared in the CD booklet and video raised eyebrows among commentators in the U.S., who published articles roundly condemning the classical music industry for exploiting children and flirting with obscenity. Despite the negative publicity, several of the tracks on *The Violin Player* were adopted into the mainstream of the dance club scene in Europe and Asia, and the disc went on to sell in excess of three million copies worldwide. In 1996, Vanessa-Mae won the Best New Female Artist distinction at the BRIT Awards; she was the first classical artist to do so.

Since the release of *The Violin Player*, Vanessa-Mae has gone on to amass an international legion of admirers through touring, recording and television appearances; her popularity is especially strong in Asia. She has just as easily inspired hostility and outright rejection on the part of her colleagues in the world of classical music. Many complain that she is a half-developed talent who is using her good looks and the pop promotional machine to make her a star at the expense of the classical tradition. Vanessa-Mae claims that she doesn't listen to critics and has opined that "to have an ordinary Classical career would have been just a bit too lazy." However, her releases after *The Violin Player* have been a mixed bag, as she attempts to find a niche somewhere between the classical repertoire and her natural acumen for club dance mixes, others of which have circulated widely in Asia. There is one standout among her later recordings; the *China Girl* disc, in which she gets to the heart of the Gang Chen *Butterfly Lovers* violin concerto. *Gramophone*, a magazine usually known for its harsh treatment of crossover artists, allowed that "this whole collection makes agreeably easy listening."

In 1998, Vanessa-Mae made her acting debut in the Hallmark Television movie *Arabian Nights*. In 1999, Vanessa-Mae and her mother, Pamela Nicholson, had a parting of the ways over issues relating to her management, and the following year Vanessa-Mae revealed to a reporter that she was being harassed by a stalker. Among the first classical artists to utilize MIDI programming technology in works for public consumption, Vanessa-Mae has added a lively new aspect to the debate about the relevance of classical music in an era dominated by the pop music marketplace. *—Uncle Dave Lewis*

Recommended:

○ **Ultimate Vanessa-Mae** / Vanessa-Mae, etc. / 2003 / EMI 592500
○ **China Girl** / Vanessa-Mae, etc. / 1997 / EMI 56483
○ **The Violin Player** / Vanessa-Mae, etc. / 1995 / EMI 55089

Edgard Varèse

b. Dec. 22, 1883, Paris, France, **d.** Nov. 6, 1965, New York, NY
Composer: Avant-garde, Chamber Music, Orchestral, Vocal

Despite his output of only slightly more than a dozen compositions, Edgard Varèse is regarded as one of the most influential musicians of the twentieth century. His concept of "organized sound" led to many experiments in form and texture. He was constantly on the lookout for new sound sources (working throughout his life with engineers, scientists and instrument builders), and was one of the first to extensively explore percussion, electronics, and taped sounds. He was, as Henry Miller called him, "The stratospheric Colossus of Sound."

Varèse spent his early childhood in Paris and Burgundy. His father wanted him to study math and engineering in preparation for a career in business. However, Varèse pursued music, studying at the Schola Cantorum with Albert Roussel and Vincent d'Indy and at the Paris Conservatoire with Charles Marie Widor. Varèse moved to Berlin in 1907, in part to meet Ferruccio Busoni; Varèse had been impressed with Busoni's *Sketch for a New Aesthetic in Music* (1907), which anticipated many of Varèse's own later explorations. Unfortunately, of the music Varèse wrote during that time, only one song survives. The other manuscripts were destroyed in a warehouse fire.

Unable to find regular work, Varèse moved to the United States in 1915, becoming a U.S. citizen in 1926. The first work he completed after the emigration is in fact titled *Amériques*, an extroverted celebration of his new life. In addition to composing, Varèse promoted new music through the establishment of his New Symphony Orchestra in 1919, the International Composers' Guild in 1921, and the Pan American Society in 1926. He continued to have difficulty making money, though, and spent some time as a piano salesman; he also made a brief appearance in a 1918 John Barrymore film.

Varèse maintained his connection with Europe, and had an extended stay in Paris between 1928 and 1933 during which he continued his sonic explorations and heard many of his works performed. In 1931 he completed *Ionisation*, a notorious piece for thirteen percussionists playing about forty different instruments. Back in the U.S., he attempted to get Bell Telephone and others interested in creating a center for electric instrument research. The failure of that project led to an extended depression. Over the next ten-plus years, Varèse completed only one work, *Density 21.5* for solo flute, spending the time teaching (at Santa Fe's Arsuna School of Fine Arts, Columbia University, and Darmstadt) and thinking about what new direction his music should take.

The anonymous gift of an Ampex tape recorder in 1953 was the motivation Varèse needed. He set to work on the tape portion of his work *Déserts*, which was premiered in Paris in 1954 in a concert which was broadcast live in stereo, the first stereo music broadcast ever in France. He was involved with several film projects, writing music for documentaries on Léger and Joan Miró. He also wrote the *Poème électronique* for tape for Le Corbusier's pavilion at the 1958 Brussels exhibition, where Varèse's music was heard through more than 400 loudspeakers, accompanied by Le Corbusier's visuals.

Varèse and his music received much attention in the 1960s. His works were widely performed, recorded and published, and he received honors from the National Institute of Arts and Letters and the Royal Swedish Academy. He also won the first Koussevitzky International Recording Award in 1963. But Varèse wrote little music during these last years. His final work, the unfinished *Nocturnal* (with text by Anaïs Nin), was performed at a tribute concert in 1961 and completed years later by composer Chou Wen-chung. *—Chris Morrison*

AVANT-GARDE

Déserts (1950–1954)

This powerfully moving work, created between 1950 and 1954, was the first piece for magnetic tape—two-tracks of "organized sound"—and orchestra. Possibly first conceived when Varèse lived in the deserts of New Mexico in the mid-1930s, it was imagined to be a score to which a film would have been subsequently made—a film consisting of images of the deserts of Earth, of the sea (vast distances under the water), of outer space (galaxies, etc.), but above all, the deserts in the mind of humankind—especially a memory of the terrors and agonies from the world wars of the first half of the twentieth century, including concentration camps, atomic warfare, and their continuing resonances. The taped music (originally planned for an unrealized work called "Trinum") primarily presents those images in three interpolations that separate the music for the acoustic orchestra—winds, brass, a resonant piano, and five groups of percussion. This orchestra part expresses the gradual advance of mankind toward spiritual sunlight. The orchestra music is built from intense aggregates of sound, rather than scales for melody, and rhythm is treated not as a continuous pulse, but as a support for the soundform, rhythm as a vibration of intensity. Of course, this highly dramatic work, in touch with the deeper, repressed emotions of world society at the time it was created (and powerful still), caused protest and violent reactions in many concert halls. It is now recognized as an exceptional example of truly humanistic music. *—"Blue Gene" Tyranny*

Recommended:

○ **Boulez Conducts Varèse** / Boulez (cond.), Chicago SO / 2001 / DG 471137
○ **L'oeuvre de Edgar Varèse Vol. 2** / Nagano (cond.), Orchestre National de France / 1996 / Erato 14332
○ **Varèse: The Complete Works** / Chailly (cond.), Concertgebouw / 1998 / London 460208

Poème électronique, for tape (1957–1958)

Poème électronique, part of a multi-media presentation created for the 1958 Brussels World's Fair, was one of the earliest compositions fully realized through electronics. Even though many of its sounds are easily modulated today, the work's dramatic conception has helped it to retain its vitality through the years.

Its creation began in 1956, when Louis C. Kalff, the artistic director of the Philips Corporation, approached the famed architect Le Corbusier to design their pavilion at the Fair. Le Corbusier replied with his concept for an "Electronic Poem"—an audiovisual presentation that would transcend the usual bounds of architecture. Le Corbusier sought out Edgard Varèse immediately as his collaborator. There was some corporate resistance to this choice, but Le Corbusier was adamant, and further insisted that Varèse be paid handsomely for the work. Le Corbusier gave Varèse leave to do anything he wanted musically; the rapport between the two artists was instant and very supportive.

The composition of *Poème électronique* was very slow, beginning on September 2, 1957. Much to the credit of the Philips Corporation, which had strong reservations about the degree to which their pavilion had become an avant-garde affair, they generously put at the composer's disposal an enormous laboratory and technical support team. Because Le Corbusier was constantly globe-hopping and working on several projects at once, the composer often communicated instead with the architect's assistant, Iannis Xénakis, himself a gifted composer. It was he who, on December 21, played for the Philips representatives an excerpt of *Poème électronique*, much to their displeasure; they wanted something more consonant and conventional. When Le Corbusier was finally contacted in Chandigarh and told of the deadlock between the composer and the company, he told them that he would withdraw from the pavilion project if there were any more talk of replacing his colleague.

Varèse heard his completed work for the first time on May 2, 1958; it was projected through 400 loudspeakers scattered strategically throughout the pavilion. Some of the (difficult to describe) sounds from which it is made were conceived either as (1) "verticalities"—short, mostly sharp sounds such as a huge church chime, small, imaginary grotesque creatures, percussion and machine-like sounds (complex spectral noise)—or (2) horizontalities—sustained, slowly modulated sounds such as primitive chant, sudden screaming, long tones, voices with impossible ranges singing from afar, a church in a jungle (modulated organ chords), and rocketship launch sounds. The piece's internal structure was based on classical Golden Section proportions and the Fibonacci series. Xénakis also contributed some musical material to be heard during intermission periods, and Varèse approved of this enthusiastically.

The completed pavilion combined Varèse's musical tape with an elaborate Le Corbusier-designed visual presentation, which was projected on the side of the building. It was a lukewarm success at the World's Fair; some critics preferred the music without the visuals; others were not fond of either element. The structure itself—now thought to have been substantially designed by Xénakis—was considered inadequate and poorly designed. However, the outpouring of admiration from artists of all media was impressive. On November 9, the piece was heard in New

York, but its effect was much diminished because of limitations in the sound system used, and it did not hold up well outside of its intended context. Nevertheless, the work remains a hallmark of electronic composition. *—AMG*

Recommended:

○ **Varèse: Poème électronique; Babbitt: Philomel; Phonemena; Xenakis: Mycènes Alpha** / Sollberger, Bettina / 1990 / Neuma 450

CHAMBER MUSIC

Density 21.5, for flute (1936)

The only example of Edgard Varèse's mature music that doesn't require electronics or substantial performing forces, *Density 21.5* is one of the very few true masterpieces among the limited repertory for unaccompanied flute. The work's title refers to the specific gravity of platinum; Varèse wrote *Density 21.5* as an "inaugural" piece for French flutist Georges Barrère's new instrument, which was made of this precious metal.

Density 21.5 immediately predated a period during which Varèse produced little music; it was, in fact, the last work of any consequence the composer wrote until after World War II. The composer's energies during this interval were directed primarily toward the development of his ideas regarding the spatialization of sound, which reached their culmination in the seminal electronic work *Poème electronique* (1957–1958).

According to the composer, *Density 21.5* is based on two melodic ideas—one modal, one atonal—and all of the subsequent material is generated from these two themes. Despite the inherent limitations of writing for an unaccompanied melodic instrument, Varèse expertly explores new areas of space and time, utilizing registral contrasts to effect polyphonic continuity. An important work whose principles proved highly influential, *Density 21.5* aptly demonstrates both the singular creative powers of its creator and the expressive and technical possibilities of the instrument. *—Sean Hickey*

Recommended:

○ **Varèse: The Complete Works** / Zoon / 1998 / London 460208

○ **Incantation** / Zukerman / 1996 / Delos 3184

Hyperprisme, for winds & percussion (1922–1923)

In 1923, crucial points were marked in the development of Western music: Schoenberg's Op. 25 presented the beginnings of his 12-tone theory; Stravinsky's octet launched his neo-Classicist phase; Milhaud's *La creation du monde* integrated French "new simplicity" with American jazz. Despite the distinction of these various currents, they each concerned either a desire to innovate structure or revolutionize style. On the other hand, Edgard Varèse attempted a revolution not of style or structure, but of pure sound. "I refuse to submit myself only to sounds that have already been heard," Varèse had complained a few years earlier. "What I am looking for are new technical mediums that lend themselves to every expression of thought and can keep up with thought."

It was in this spirit that Varèse completed his groundbreaking work for wind ensemble and percussion, *Hyperprisme*. Varèse's search for new sounds led him to utilize the percussion section to a greater extent than any composer before him. The sensitive ear for previously unimagined timbral combinations of non-pitched percussion instruments that one finds in *Ionisation* (1929) was first fully established with *Hyperprisme* (and further developed in the wind/percussion piece *Intégrales* from 1926). One of the distinguishing features of *Hyperprisme* was that it entirely eliminated the string section (the orchestrational role of which had already been diminished in his *Offrandes* from 1921) because Varèse thought strings evoked outmoded Romantic modes of expression. Instead, *Hyperprisme* highlighted the blocky, strident character of the brass, the shrillness of the winds, and the endless variety of sounds afforded by a greatly expanded percussion battery; in addition to the flute, clarinet, and full orchestral brass section, Varèse scored the piece for nearly 20 different percussion instruments played with a variety of techniques. Of course, Varèse's skill is not measured by the sheer number of different sounds he assembles, but the way in which he assembles them. His approach to orchestration involves an extreme fluidity of texture so that instruments might follow distinct paths in one moment and assemble to create a complex composite gesture or color in the next. He often articulates the attack of a note or shape of a melodic gesture in the winds by punctuating it with percussion; in a sense, the winds act as vowels, the percussion instruments as consonants. At the same time, resonant instruments like cymbals and gongs—which offer less rhythmic agility than, say, Chinese wood blocks or a snare drum—provide a washed broadband sound that throws melodic and rhythmic elements into greater relief. Furthermore, the greater attention to non-pitched percussion demands a greater exploration of rhythmic possibilities; Varèse's ability to convey musical emotion through purely rhythmic means rivals that of any composer of the twentieth century. *—Jeremy Grimshaw*

Recommended:

○ **L'oevre de Edgar Varèse Vol. 1** / Nagano (cond.), Orchestre National de France / Erato 92137

○ **Varèse: The Complete Works** / Chailly (cond.), Concertgebouw / 1998 / London 460208

Intégrales for winds & percussion (1924–1925)

At some time during the early 1920s, Varèse found the right metaphor to express what he was after in sound. His idea of "spatial music" is notably like that of the younger Giacinto Scelsi in that it intuits a fantastical music based on the three-dimensional physical properties of sound. He said he became aware of this dimension of sound while listening to the Scherzo of Beethoven's *Symphony No. 7*. Probably because the hall was over-resonant, this familiar music seemed to detach and project itself in space. This anecdote, among others, reminds listeners that Varèse's ideas are all traceable back to moments in other composers' work. But he developed from those epiphanic episodes of estrangement or touches of cleverness in another's music a wholly original mode of musical thought. The very intense *Intégrales* is one of his most enthralling pieces. It's written for an ensemble that allowed him the widest pitch range, with piccolo and screeching clarinet on the high end, trombone and double bass on the other, filled out with other brass, woodwinds, and 17 marvelous percussion instruments. The highly sculptural music moves forward through rhythmic variation and by his ever-changing orchestrations. It's built up in short sections that internally develop with tense expansion and contraction of smaller rhythmic cells. These variations grow ever more ambiguous and more complex until they reach, at the end of a section, a degree of unintelligibility by saturation. The process repeats over and over again, on conflicting planes, while wizardly orchestrations (especially the percussion) prismatically refract the rhythms and pitches so that almost every sound reaches listeners as glowingly colorful and novel. *Intégrales* is a living musical architecture reduced to the bold purity of planes and angles. Each moment of the music crashes in upon the last, smashing it brutally out of the way and insisting on its presence as spatial and not temporal music that projects itself, as Varèse would have said, like "a beam of light sent forth by a powerful searchlight." *—Donato Mancini*

Recommended:

○ **Varese: Arcana; Ameriques; Ionization; Density 21.5; Offrandes; Integrales; Octandre** / Boulez (cond.), InterContemporain Ens. / 1990 / Sony 45844

○ **Varèse: Arcana; Intégrales; Déserts** / Lyndon-Gee (cond.), Polish National RSO / 2001 / Naxos 554820

○ **Varèse: The Complete Works** / Chailly (cond.) / 1998 / London 460208

Ionisation, for 13 percussion instruments (1929–1931)

In 1917, Varèse boldly announced that he longed "for instruments which are obedient to my thought and whim, with their contribution of a whole new world of unsuspected sounds, which will lend themselves to the exigencies of my inner rhythm." From 1918 to 1936, Varèse abandoned tradition almost completely. *Hyperprism* of 1923, for example, provoked a riot at its premiere. During his quest for new sonorities and effects, which climaxed in *Ionisation*, Varèse incorporated new musical instruments wherever possible. *Ionisation*, composed between 1929 and 1931, attracted the greatest interest and divergent critical opinions of all his works. The score introduced the electrical siren as a musical instrument for the very first time, and denoted the start of Varèse' increasing interest in electronic music. Nicolas Slonimsky conducted it at Carnegie Hall, on March 6, 1933, and the composer later dedicated the work to him. Carlos Salzedo, Henry Cowell, Paul Creston, and William Schuman performed as some of the 13 instrumentalists required. Its effect was likened by a critic at the time to receiving "a sock in the jaw." Varèse argued in his defence that "in music we composers are forced to use instruments that have not changed for two centuries.... Composers like anyone else today are delighted to use the many gadgets continually put on the market for our daily comfort. But when they hear sounds that no violins, wind instruments, or percussion of the orchestra can produce, it does not occur to them to demand those sounds for science. Yet science is even now equipped to give them everything they may require."

The title is derived from the ionization of molecules, as electrons are dispersed through the process of atomic change. In *Ionisation*, rhythmic cells are expanded, varied, and contrasted against one another. Their timbre keeps them identifiable as each cell becomes more involved and larger, and these cells grow in such a way that renders them independent of one another. The dramatic contour is in the degrees to which these rhythmic cells, which evolve into recognizable blocks of sound, seem to not be working together, continually growing and expanding the soundscape with the friction of their coexistence. Occasional relief is found in rhythmic unisons, that bind the separate blocks of sound into a single, propulsive rush, but there are not many. Varèse loved the unmanageable aspects of nature, the things that humans have no control over, and reveled in the way that, from our perspective, nature does not run smoothly. *—AMG*

Recommended:

○ **Boulez Conducts Varèse** / Boulez (cond.), Chicago SO / 2001 / DG 471137

○ **Percussion Music** / Desroches (cond.), New Jersey Percussion Ens. / Nonesuch 79150

○ **Varèse: The Complete Works** / Chailly (cond.); Concertgebouw / 1998 / London 460208

Octandre, for winds, brass & double bass (1923)

Varèse often insisted that music is both a science and an art. With his ingeniously inventive orchestration in mind, through which he put many sounds into the world that had never existed before, perhaps he should have summed it up as "alchemy"; he certainly did love the symbolism of arcane religions. *Octandre* is a brilliant, purely technical study of the inexplicable abracadabra of sound that Carlos Chávez rightly called gold. With this accomplishment, Varèse moved significantly closer to his ideal of a purely material music of "spatial projection." But although *Octandre* could be by no other composer, it is unlike Varèse's other works in a couple of significant ways. The piece is in three movements, labeled according to tempo—Assez lent, Très vif et nerveux, Grave-Animé et jubilatoire. Each opens with a different instrument to announce its particular character—oboe, piccolo, and bassoon—and is essentially a revisitation of the same structural concepts from a unique angle. More significant, however, is the absence of percussion, which usually forms the very core of his sound. Anyone familiar with his other pieces so feels the absence that their ears prick up every couple of beats expecting percussion noise, as if the violent drums are only waiting in ambush. By the time of *Octandre*, 1923, he'd already composed several pieces—*Amériques*, *Offrandes*, *Hyperprism*—that extensively used percussion. Sonic researcher that he was, he perhaps wanted to test his ability to work without his favorite tools and so, deliberately limited himself. He knew such an exercise could only increase his knowledge and bring him that much closer to realizing the mysterious, unheard-of music of his waking visions. And so it did. Varèse did not, however, abandon his usual aesthetic in *Octandre*: the winds, brass, and double bass are conspicuously made to fill in, against their instrumental natures, for the absent percussion. They're often used only to articulate nervous rhythmic motifs that unexpectedly accumulate from solo passages into massive, weapon-like pounding in shattering, prismatic colors. Wherever somewhat extraneous melodic lines surface, usually in lonely solo passages, they get pureed before long in the blades of emphatic rhythm, especially in the clamor of the shimmering brass that comes in like the attacking sword of an imaginary sun god. *—Donato Mancini*

Recommended:

○ **Varèse: Arcana; Ameriques; Ionization; Density 21.5; Offrandes; Integrales; Octandre** / Boulez (cond.), InterContemporain Ens. / 1990 / Sony 45844

○ **The Medinah Sessions** / Chicago Pro Musica / 2001 / Reference 2102

○ **Varèse: The Complete Works** / Chailly (cond.), Concertgebouw / 1998 / London 460208

ORCHESTRAL

Amériques (1918–1921)

Written shortly after Varèse settled in the U.S. from Europe, *Amériques* is a work with no specific program, though it does depict the sounds (rather than the sights) of New York, particularly of its activities associated with the Hudson River. In Varèse's own words, it evoked for him "... all discoveries, all adventures. (America) meant the unknown. And in this symbolical sense—new worlds on this planet, in outer space, and in the minds of men—I gave the title signifying 'Americas' to the first work I wrote in America." Scored for a huge orchestra with a heavily augmented percussion section (ten performers playing 21 instruments!), the piece opens exotically with a flute in its lower ranges playing a lonely theme over a motoric but subdued rhythm by harp. Here the work more than vaguely resembles the opening of *The Rite of Spring*. Soon the orchestra lights up with percussion clacking and hissing and brass roaring. A recurring moaning effect depicts the ubiquitous river foghorns, but a high C sharp whistle represents a sound that haunted Varèse throughout his childhood. The music juxtaposes colorful, percussion-laden outbursts with passages of mysterious calm and sonorities generally dominated by brass, flutes, oboes, and other wind instruments. First-time listeners may hear the music as episodic and chaotic, with snatches of Bartókian menace and Debussyian darkness, but as the work progresses, tension imaginatively accrues, with each climax surpassing the last, the orchestration revealing ever more colorful textures, the river turning into a tidal wave awash in conflict, exoticism, and pure excitement. The frenzied ending is astonishing, leaving the listener breathless and drained. *—Robert Cummings*

Recommended:

○ **Boulez Conducts Varèse** / Boulez (cond.), Chicago SO / 2001 / DG 471137

○ **Varèse; Honegger** / Abravanel (cond.), Utah SO / 1996 / Vanguard 40

○ **Varèse: The Complete Works** / Chailly (cond.), Concertgebouw / 1998 / London 460208

Arcana (1925–1927; revised 1960)

Varèse's passionate views concerning composition and the physicality of sound are expressed coherently in *Arcana*. In this work, a kind of a freely extended passacaglia, a basic 11-note musical idea is subjected to all kinds of permutations and variations, eventually returning in an echo of its original shape just before a coda. The musical continuity provided by this scheme allowed Varèse great freedom in orchestration, enabling him to frequently change instrumental combinations without much fear of confusing the listener behind. The works repetetiveness, revealing certain obvious patterns, also allows the listeners to better appreciate the painstakingly chosen and constructed timbres. The orchestra required for *Arcana* is enormous: 120 players on a greater number of instruments, including 40 different percussions that are a constant presence in the overall sound. Disliking the lack of pitch-precision in the strings, Varèse uses the string section quite idiosyncratically. While Varèse described *Arcana* as a symphonic poem, his critics, perhaps more astutely, have relied on visual analogies to describe the work, evoking such objects as paintings and frescoes. The harmonic stasis of the piece and its emphasis on color—it is a kind of visualized music—do invite such analogies. In their efforts to describe the music vividness, writers have reached for extreme images. describig, for example, describing *Arcana* as Mount Etna blazing in the night. Not quite volcanic, however, *Arcana* is nevertheless something like a series of orchestral eruptions, as a result of melodic continuity, exciting rhythmic displacements, and novel coloristic choices. This is easily one of Varèse's most approachanble pieces. The title points to to the arcane writings of Paracelsus (1493–1541). While Paracelsus didn't inspire *Arcana*, Varèse has compared his dream world to the mystical insights found in the works of Paracelsus. Thus, the symphonic poem is named *Arcana* not after Paracelsus, but in homage to him, of whom Varèse once remarked: "You can count Paracelsus among my friends." *—Donato Mancini*

Recommended:

○ **Boulez Conducts Varèse** / Boulez (cond.), Chicago SO / 2001 / DG 471137

○ **Varèse: Arcana; Intégrales; Ionisation; Kraft: Concerto; Contextures** / Mehta (cond.), Los Angeles PO / 1995 / Decca 448580

○ **Varèse: The Complete Works** / Chailly (cond.), Concertgebouw / 1998 / London 460208

VOCAL

Ecuatorial (1932–1934)

In the late 1920s, Varèse began seriously collecting ideas for an opera, possibly to be called "L'astronome." He initially made overtures toward a collaboration with Robert Desnos and Alejo Carpentier. When that didn't work out, he instinctively turned to perhaps the one then-living French writer whose aesthetic ideals mirrored his own: Antonin Artaud. Artaud's descriptions of his imagined theater sound like one of Varèse's afternoon wet dreams: "I wanted... a work in which we feel the whole nervous system burning like an incandescent lamp... new, strange, and radiant Epiphany in the sky." According to Varèse's descriptions, the Varèse/Artaud opera would have aimed to inflict terror in the audience, as if in a musical theater of cruelty, with violently loud music, terrifying noises, and blinding spotlights turned directly at the helpless spectators. "L'astronome" was never composed, but it is in *Ecuatorial* for bass solo (or bass choir), trumpets, trombones, piano, pipe organ, two Ondes Martenots, and a battery of percussion, where Varèse perhaps came closest to the primitive soul of the opera he'd imagined. Artaud's ideas about theater had flared when he witnessed a performance of ancient Balinese masked dance. Likewise, Varèse, and like so many other twentieth century artists, found release in things non-European and primitive. *Ecuatorial* presents the text that inspired it—a guttural Mayan prayer to the God of Life in all his aspects, nurturing (green pastures, procreation) and violent (the lightning that shatters the night sky). The "elemental, rude intensity" of the music, as Varèse described it, is perfectly matched to the text, with normal Varèsian rhythmic pounding and brassy eruptions. Each instrumental group has such a distinct color that they never really blend. Rather, they intersect, touch, clash, and send brilliant sparks off each other. Not a note in all of *Ecuatorial* is arrived at by pedestrian means; every step is a dangerous jump to the next spot, where the instruments battle for aural space. One possibly regrettable point is that there isn't more writing for the Ondes Martenots in *Ecuatorial*. The all-too-brief passages of Ondes/piano and Ondes/organ, in their very science fiction sublimity, are among the most memorable in all of Varèse's music. *—Donato Mancini*

Recommended:

○ **Varèse: Offrandes; Intégrales; Octandre; Ecuatorial** / Weisberg (cond.), Paul, Contemporary Chamber Ens. / 1972 / Nonesuch 71269

○ **Varèse: The Complete Works** / Chailly (cond.), Concertgebouw / 1998 / London 460208

Nocturnal (1961)

Nocturnal was Edgard Varèse's last work, which was edited and completed by his former student, Chou Wen-chung. It was commissioned by and dedicated to the Koussevitzky Music Foundation. The work is scored for soprano, men's chorus, small orchestra, piano, an extended percussion section and two Ondes Martenots. The text includes phrases taken from Anaïs Nin's *The House of Incest*, as well as phonetic syllables of the composer's own devising. Dark and haunting, *Nocturnal* implies a tryst among siblings that captures the French novelist's alarming, mixed feelings towards unconventional and potentially damaging erotic scenarios.

The music derives some conventions from the Medieval Catholic church. Responsorial chant, the practice of alternating between a soloist and choir, is utilized to generate a perversely holy scenario. The evening union between brother and sister is clear, and the soprano clearly sings in first person while the male choir is ambiguous; its role is that of a standard chorus, commenting on the proceedings half in syllables and half in textual declarations of the dramatic impact the moment is generating. Nin's ability to make even horrifying sexual situations seem adventurous for the subject (herself) is coupled with a tone of sacrifice. This sort of writing works admirably with Varèse's understanding of nature as an uncontrollable force; both siblings are in the grip of improper desires, but the power of youthful, erotic energy is illustrated here with a largeness of emotional scope that is a testament to human vitality's propensity for spinning out of morality's orbit. Nothing is condoned in the music; *Nocturnal* combines the brother and sister's situation with that of the surrender of Christ; incest is a betrayal just as Christ was betrayed, who begged for the forgiveness for all who had betrayed him. No blame is assigned and no coercion is implied.

Nocturnal was composed for a Composers' Showcase concert in his honor. Its premiere took place at the Town Hall in New York on May 1, 1961, with Robert Craft conducting. It is the one work of Varèse's that did not "crystallize," which is how he described music that was finished to his satisfaction. Illness and indecision kept him from finishing the job. The score for the first performance had been completed only two days before the premiere, and there was only one rehearsal, except that Carlos Salzedo had done some preliminary work with the chorus. The following autumn, the composer went to work on a second version of the piece and it is difficult to discern drafts from the second version, *Nocturnal II*, from revisions of the first work. To make matters more difficult for historians, Varèse then began another work, *Night*, for a near-identical ensemble and more excerpts from Nin's *The House of Incest*. This work never neared completion. *—John Keillor*

Recommended:

○ **Varese & Honegger** / Abravanel (cond.), Bybee, Utah SO / 1996 / Vanguard 40

○ **Varèse: The Complete Works** / Chailly (cond.), Leonard, Concertgebouw / 1998 / London 460208

Offrandes, for soprano & chamber orchestra (1921)

The mesmerizing two-part *Offrandes* is possibly the most direct statement of his tormented inner world Edgard Varèse ever made. It's that tremor of personal pain pulsating through all the vividly colored din that Stravinsky was reacting to when he said that the first harp attack in part two nearly gives him a heart attack. He called it "the most extraordinary noise in all of Varèse." *Offrandes* is for soprano and a representative chamber orchestra, with harp and eight percussion instruments. These are used in ever-changing combinations (emphasizing percussion, winds, and brass) and with a constantly varied dynamic. Except for the vocal part, there's no melody as such. The accompaniment is all built on flinty little rhythmic gestures that sometimes mutate into a fragment of a tune. The stormy instrumental parts could almost make up a Varèse piece by themselves. They often go into a howl or die down to nervous mutterings of percussion—ominous rattles of snare drum, woodblocks, castanets—under the heavily chromatic vocal line. In part one, "The Song From Above," it seems as if he is suppressing a wish that the voice was a more flexible instrument, reaching so high he strains her range. In part two, "The Southern Cross," however, on a dreamlike, apocalyptic poem by José Tablada, he's in complete control and makes the precariousness of her top notes into a potent source of dramatic tension. The point, as in all of Varèse's mature music, is color, intensity, and instrumental attack, which here evoke a vivid, haunted internal world. As Tablada says in his Apocalyptic text: "... the murdered women are awakening." Although listeners always feel that Varèse's music is poetically composed from his subjective center, his instrumental aesthetic is more mechanical (or machine-like) than organic. The lyricism that the soprano brings to *Offrandes* illuminates the organic/mechanic dialectic of struggle that powers Varèse's music: the diminishing scale of the human individual in relation to humanity's rigid bureaucracies and its machines. Varèse certainly looked forward to the future, especially the musical freedoms it would bring, but the tragic sense of humanity in retreat before the brutal steamroller of conformity was a source of great spiritual suffering to him, which he movingly expressed in *Offrandes*. *—Donato Mancini*

Recommended:

○ **Varèse: Arcana; Ameriques; Ionization; Density 21.5; Offrandes; Integrales; Octandre** / Boulez (cond.), Yakar, InterContemporain Ens. / 1990 / Sony 45844

○ **L'oevre de Edgar Varèse Vol. 1** / Nagano (cond.), Bryn-Julson, Orchestre National de France / Erato 92137

○ **Varèse: The Complete Works** / Chailly (cond.), Concertgebouw / 1998 / London 460208

Ralph Vaughan Williams

b. Oct. 12, 1872, Down Ampney, England, **d.** Aug. 26, 1958, London, England
Composer: Orchestral, Band Music, Symphonic, Choral, Vocal, Concerto, Chamber Music, Ballet

Ralph Vaughan Williams left a varied oeuvre that includes orchestral works, songs, operas, and various choral compositions. While primarily drawing on the rich tradition of English folksong and hymnody, Vaughan Williams produced well-loved works that fit into larger European traditions and gained worldwide popularity.

Vaughan Williams, who lost his father early in life, was cared for by his mother. Related, through his mother, to both Charles Darwin and the Wedgwoods of pottery fame, he grew up without financial worries. He studied history and music at Trinity College, Cambridge, and finished up at the Royal College of Music, where he worked with Parry, Wood, and Stanford. In 1897, the year he married Adeline Fisher, Vaughan Williams traveled to Berlin to study with Max Bruch, also seeking Maurice Ravel as a teacher several years later, despite the fact that the French composer was three years his junior. In 1903, he started collecting English folksongs; certain characteristics of English folk music, particularly its modal tonalities, in many ways informed his approach to composition. Vaughan Williams further developed his style while working as editor of the *English Hymnal*, which was completed in 1906. His work on the *English Hymnal* went beyond editing, for he contributed several new hymn tunes, most notably the *Sine nomine*, the tune for the hymn *For All the Saints*. The composer's interest in and knowledge of traditional English music is reflected in his song cycle *On Wenlock Edge* (1909), based on selections from A.E. Housman's immensely popular volume of poetry *A Shropshire Lad*. In his *Fantasia on a Theme of Thomas Tallis*, composed in 1910, Vaughan Williams introduced antiphonal effects within the context of modal tonality, juxtaposing consonant, but unrelated, triads. Composed in 1914, his *Symphony No. 2, "A London Symphony"* brings to life, with great charm, the sounds of London from dawn to dusk. That year, Vaughan Williams also wrote his pastoral *The Lark Ascending*, for violin and orchestra. When World War I broke out, the 41-year-old composer enlisted as an orderly in the medical corps, becoming famous for organizing choral singing and other entertainment in the trenches. He was commissioned from the ranks, ending his war service as an artillery officer. The war interrupted the composer's work but did not, it seems, disrupt the inner continuity of his creative development. The *Symphony No. 3 ("Pastoral")*, composed in 1922, conjures up a familiar world, effectively incorporating folksong motives into sonorities created by sequential chords. While critics detected pessimistic moods and themes in the later symphonies, ascribing a shift to a darker vision to the composer's alleged general pessimism about the world, Vaughan Williams refused to attach any programmatic content to these works. However, the composer created a convincing musical description of a desolate world in his *Symphony No. 7 "Sinfonia Antarctica"* (1952), which was inspired by the request to write the music for the film *Scott of the Antarctic*. In addition to his symphonies, Vaughan Williams composed highly acclaimed religious music, as well as works inspired by English spiritual literature, culminating in his 1951 opera *The Pilgrim's Progress*, based on the spiritual classic by John Bunyan. An artist of extraordinary creative energy, Vaughan Williams continued composing with undiminished powers until his death at 87. *—AMG*

ORCHESTRAL

Fantasia on a Theme by Thomas Tallis, for 2 string orchestras (1910; revised 1919)

The first performance of Vaughan Williams' *Fantasia on a Theme by Thomas Tallis* took place at the Three Choirs Festival in Gloucester Cathedral on September 6, 1910. The program was primarily devoted to Sir Edward Elgar's oratorio *The Dream of Gerontius*, which may partly account for its relatively cool reception. But its treatment, unusual for its day, of the unusual source material may also have puzzled the audience.

Vaughan Williams encountered Tallis' hymn while editing *The English Hymnal* in 1906; it had first appeared in Archbishop Parker's *Metrical Psalter* in 1567, set to the words, "Why fumeth in fight?" The peculiar modal qualities of the tune, with its prominent flatted seventh, not only allowed the composer considerable harmonic freedom from the prevailing strictures of diatonicism and chromaticism, but also made possible the simultaneous sense of the ancient and the modern that is the work's hallmark.

The *Tallis Fantasia* is scored for two string orchestras, one functioning as a "distant" choir, and a solo string quartet. After five widely spaced chords and a few bars in which the theme is fragmentarily mused upon by pizzicato basses, cellos, and swaying middle strings, arco, Tallis' hymntune is stated in its original harmony by violas and celli with tremolando accompaniment by the high strings, and is then repeated in a setting that exploits all of the harmonic and contrapuntal facilities of a large string section.

The string choirs then separate for a short section in which fragments of Tallis' theme in the first string orchestra are answered by distant chordal musings from the second orchestra. This serves not only as a brief development section but also introduces the solo string quartet, whose masterly counterpoint demonstrates

Vaughan Williams' affinity for stringed instruments. As the rhapsodic meditation increases in intensity, the more modern aspects of the composition come into focus, with vaguely impressionistic harmonies mingling with the modal, leading to an impressive climax in which the two orchestras are unleashed in their full chordal power. The string quartet leads a final, luminous musing on Tallis' tune, and the Fantasia ends with a short coda in which the solo violin pronounces a brief benediction as the orchestra falls away. *—Mark Satola*

Recommended:

- ○ **Vaughan Williams: Tallis Fantasia; Barber: Adagio for Strings; Grainger: Irish Tune** / Slatkin (cond.), St. Louis SO / 1981 / Telarc 80059
- ○ **Elgar & Vaughan Williams: Orchestral Works** / Barbirolli (cond.), City of London Sinfonia / 2000 / Angel 67264
- ○ **Vaughan Williams: Dona Nobis Pacem and Other Works** / Sargent (cond.), London Philharmonia Orch. / 2001 / EMI 574782

Fantasia on Greensleeves, for harp, flute & strings (1934)

This well-known concert hall arrangement of *Fantasia on Greensleeves* appeared five years after the premiere of Vaughan Williams' Shakespearean opera *Sir John in Love*, wherein the short piece served as an entr'acte. Greaves' arrangement for strings, harp and two flutes expanded the intermezzo by adding a middle section based on the Norfolk folk song "Lovely Joan," which Vaughan Williams had collected in 1908 and which he used elsewhere in the 1929 opera. A wistful descending cadence from solo flute with harp arpeggio introduces the well-known melody, with strummed chords from the harp, suggesting a lute accompaniment, and high strings tremolando above the tune. In the middle section, the two flutes play an intertwining duet on "Lovely Joan" before the return of *Greensleeves*. A shimmering cadence from the strings and harp brings the work to a glowing conclusion. *—Mark Satola*

Recommended:

- ○ **Vaughan Williams: Serenade; English Folk Song Suite; Fantasia on Greensleeves, etc.** / Boult (cond.), London SO / 1991 / EMI 64022

Norfolk Rhapsody No. 1 in E minor (1905–1906; revised 1914)

Vaughan Williams composed this work in 1905 and 1906 but revised it considerably in 1914. Sir Henry Wood introduced the original version in Queen's Hall, London, on August 23, 1906. Vaughan Williams was already past 30 when he found—in English folk music first, then in early hymnody—the keys to a personal style that served him nobly over several periods for the next half century. He was still composing when, just short of his 87th birthday, death reprieved him from the attrition of aging. No major composer of any nationality started later; few matched his perseverance or durability; even fewer felt the need—not even the beleaguered Bruckner—to revise as much or as often. As late as 1951, his 80th year, Vaughan Williams made new editions of Symphonies One through Six (*No. 7, the Antarctic*, was in progress, and the *Eighth* and *Ninth* were as yet unborn).

Four short works for orchestra preceded the first *Norfolk Rhapsody*, but the composer published only one of these—*In the Fen Country* of 1904 (albeit in a 1935 revision). Actually, there were three *Norfolk Rhapsodies*, but Vaughan Williams withdrew *Nos. 2* and *3* after conducting them at Cardiff in 1907. The lone survivor is considered the composer's first "official" folk song work, for it followed a January 1905 collecting expedition "in the King's Lynn neighbourhood," according to Hugh Ross' 1950 study of the composer for Oxford University Press.

Three of his discoveries at fishing villages in fog-shrouded Norfolk, north of London, are quoted in this E minor rhapsody, which Hugh Ottaway characterizes in the *New Grove Twentieth-Century English Masters* as having "a distinctive tone poetry, atmospheric and pure in expression, that points clearly to the next period [1909–1914]."

Ross further described the work as follows: "the adagio opening is as tenuous as a misty dawn, and there is a suggestion of the chilly vapours fluttered by a breeze from the [North] Sea. The viola sings to us 'The Captain's Apprentice'—one of the noblest and possibly the most directly tragic of English folk-songs. . . . 'A bold young sailor courted me' rather shyly intrudes, and then 'On board on a '98' [identified by the composer's widow Ursula as "a type of warship, designated by the number of guns she carried"]. . . . The ending section never rises above *piano*, and closes in the sea mist of the beginning . . . a deeply considered work . . . a moving piece of music which inspires and retains affection as well as admiration." The quiet ending of the revised version was the first of a series of poetic sonic "dissolves" that would become a trademark of the composer's music. *—Roger Dettmer*

Recommended:

- ○ **Vaughan Williams: English Folk Song Suite; Fantasia on Greensleeves; Norfolk Rhapsody, etc.** / Boult (cond.), New Philharmonia Orch. / 1991 / EMI 64022
- ○ **Vaughan Williams: Pastoral Symphony; Norfolk Rhapsodies** / Hickox (cond.), London SO / 2003 / Chandos 5002

Partita for double string orchestra (1946–1948)

In 1938, Vaughan Williams wrote a piece called *Double Trio*, but shelved it for nearly a decade. After the war, he picked the score of the work back up and decided its music would be better-suited to a larger instrumentation. He fashioned the piece for two string orchestras of disproportionate size, neither featuring second violins. The mood is light throughout and Vaughan Williams avoids using the two string bodies for contrast, choosing instead to alternate their roles, with one playing in the foreground and one in the background. The *Partita* is comprised of four movements with the first, a Prelude, marked Andante tranquillo. It is a pleasant, thoroughly enjoyable creation whose thematic charm and subtle scoring reveal this multifaceted composer's more genial side while setting the general tone of the work. The second movement is a Scherzo, or as Vaughan Williams calls it here, Scherzo Ostinato. Marked Presto, it is a catchy piece whose menacing elements are really good-natured and colorful, having much the spirit of the Scherzo in the composer's largely serene *Symphony No. 5* (completed in 1943). The third movement is an Intermezzo, marked Andante con moto and carrying the subtitle "Homage to Henry Hall." Hall (1898–1989) was a prominent British band conductor who for years led the BBC Dance Orchestra. The Intermezzo's main theme is haunting and somewhat nocturnal, and even though it nearly turns funereal, its music remains light and subtly colorful. The finale, "Fantasia," is marked Allegro and is lively and brilliant in its scoring with rhythmic aspects that are imaginatively developed. The *Partita* lasts around 20 minutes in a typical performance and should have wide appeal, especially to fanciers of music for string ensembles. *—Robert Cummings*

Recommended:

- ○ **Vaughan Williams: Dona Nobis Pacem and Other Works** / Boult (cond.), London PO / 2001 / EMI 574782

Five Variants of "Dives and Lazarus," for string orchestra & harp (1939)

The folk song *Dives and Lazarus* was the source of inspiration for this lovely work for string orchestra and harp(s). With a text based on the Biblical characters Dives (pronounced Dy-vess), the rich man, and Lazarus, the poor man (from Luke 16:19–31), it caught the attention of Vaughan Williams, who had a keen interest in collecting and arranging folk music, like his Hungarian counterparts Bartók and Kodály. The English master first acquainted himself with the *Dives and Lazarus* folk tune in 1893.

The *Five Variants* opens with a simple statement of the folk song melody, a stately, slightly wistful creation that soars with a disarming warmth and beauty in the mellow, middle-range scoring here. It mostly ascends in its seeming heavenward trajectory, curling downward, however, in its closing bars to form an arched contour.

The first variant begins in the strings' upper ranges and has a slightly ethereal glaze to its sweeter treatment of the melody. The ensuing variation is livelier, but its animation produces a more fervent sense rather than greater rhythmic drive. Still, it provides fine contrast as it stands between two slower variants.

That said, the third variation does not lack a feeling of animation: it begins sweetly on solo violin and harp, but yields a vitality not of swift movement but in the buoyancy of its soaring character and vibrant beauty. The attractive brief coda to this section might almost be counted as an additional variation. The fourth variant is lively, though eschewing, once again, any sense of fleetness or impetuosity, instead brimming with a vivacious and colorful folkish character.

Vaughan Williams collected the last variation in 1905, on a visit to Norfolk, England. It is stately and triumphant in its first appearance, but turns serene and slightly wistful when taken up by the solo cello. The work concludes quietly amid a feeling of great tranquility. A typical performance of this composition lasts around 12 minutes. *—Robert Cummings*

Recommended:

- ○ **Hickox Conducts Vaughan Williams** / Hickox (cond.), Northern Sinfonia of England / 2000 / EMI 73986

The Wasps, Aristophanic Suite (1909)

As had his teachers Sir Hubert Parry and Sir Charles Villiers Stanford before him, in 1909 Vaughan Williams was asked by the Greek Play Committee at Cambridge to write incidental music for their annual performance, which that year featured Aristophanes' satirical play *The Wasps*. Originally constituting an overture and 17 other items scored for tenor and baritone soloists, male chorus and orchestra, the music was heard for the first time at the performance of the play on November 26, 1909. The music was a huge hit, and a couple of years later Vaughan Williams extracted what he called an *Aristophanic Suite* from his incidental music; the Suite was first performed on July 23, 1912, with Vaughan Williams himself conducting the New Symphony Orchestra.

While the play itself is strongly satirical, Vaughan Williams' music is consistently good-natured. The music is also among his first to reflect the sound and spirit of English folk song, even though no actual folk songs are heard. Neither are heard any ancient Greek scales or quotations from Greek music; authenticity was not the composer's aim.

The overture to *The Wasps* was one of Vaughan Williams' first works to enter the fringes of the standard repertory, and has remained a concert and recording staple. We hear the buzzing of the wasps at the beginning of the overture, followed by a sequence of jolly melodies. More restrained and lyrical music temporarily takes over. Then suddenly the wasps return and the tempo picks up again. After a brief dramatic interlude, the tunes of the opening return, closing the overture in lively style. It might be noted that one of Vaughan Williams' first recordings as a conductor was of this overture, made with the Aeolian Orchestra in 1925.

The *Aristophanic Suite* also includes "The March Past of the Kitchen Utensils," a fine comic march, and a couple of Entr'actes. The Suite concludes with an exotic Ballet which, after a return of the buzzing wasps, leads into the rambunctious Final Tableau and a whirlwind coda. *—Chris Morrison*

Recommended:

○ **Vaughan Williams: Tallis Fantasia & Orchestral Works** / Marriner (cond.), Academy of St. Martin-in-the-Fields / 1995 / Philips 442427

○ **Unforgettable Classics: Great British Music** / Silvestri (cond.), Bournemouth Sinfonietta / 1997 / EMI 72433

○ **Vaughan Williams: Job; The Wasps** / Boult (cond.), London PO / 1994 / Everest 9006

BAND MUSIC

English Folk Song Suite for military band (1923)

Ralph Vaughan Williams (1872–1958) composed his *English Folk Song Suite* for military band at the invitation of the band of the Royal Military School of Music. He completed it in 1923 and it was premiered in 1924. The work is scored for large military band including piccolo, flutes, oboes, clarinets, bass clarinet, bassoon, horn, trumpets, bass trumpet, cornets, saxophones, trombones, bass tubas, euphonium, and percussion. The following year Vaughan Williams asked his student at the Royal College of Music, Gordon Jacob, to reorchestrate the work for full orchestra, and Jacob also did an arrangement for conventional brass band. The work is arranged in three movements and incorporates nine folk songs. The opening March includes "Seventeen Come Sunday," "Pretty Caroline," and "Dives and Lazarus." The central Intermezzo includes "My Bonny Boy" and "Green Bushes." The closing March—Folksongs From Somerset includes "Blow Away the Morning Dew," "High Germany," "The Tree So High," and "John Barleycorn." As befits Vaughan Williams at his most robust and cheerful, the *English Folk Song Suite* is one of his happiest and most attractive works. *—James Leonard*

Recommended:

○ **Frederick Fennell conducts Holst, Vaughan Williams, Mennin & Persichetti** / Fennell (cond.), Eastman Wind Ens. / 1999 / Mercury 462960

Toccata Marziale, for military band in B flat major (1924)

This is yet another band work by Vaughan Williams, a composer whose style adapted well to almost any medium, save for the keyboard. Here, he fashioned a work of neo-Classical character and wit, auguring the offbeat world of his 1954 *Concerto for Tuba and Orchestra*, and, to a lesser extent, the exotic realm of his *Eighth Symphony* (1953–1955; rev. 1958). Much has been made by certain musicologists of the *Toccata Marziale*'s supposed advanced compositional features, but in fact they are rather typical of the composer in their thematic, harmonic and instrumental characteristics—Vaughan Williams would have been the first to admit he blazed no theoretical trails or established no school.

The piece is jolly and somewhat Stravinskian in character, featuring lean scoring, vibrant colors, and deft wit. The music augurs the scherzo movements from several of the composer's later symphonies, including the *Fifth* and *Ninth*. Any similarity to style of Stravinsky, as noted above, is probably coincidental, since that Russian composer's neo-Classical manner is far removed from the normally Romantic and often gruff style of Vaughan Williams. The *Toccata Marziale*, marked Allegro maestoso, lasts about four minutes and is full of color and energy. It is not an important work in the composer's oeuvre, but is nevertheless an attractive, well-crafted diversion. *—Robert Cummings*

Recommended:

○ **Frederick Fennell conducts Holst, Vaughan Williams, etc.** / Fennell (cond.), Eastman Wind Ens. / 1999 / Mercury 462960

Variations for brass band (1957)

The great British brass band tradition has been fostered since 1860 by an annual competition for bands. Held in the Crystal Palace until that edifice burned in the 1930s, it is a major event at the Royal Albert Hall in London. Each year there is a new test piece, required of all bands and in 1957 Ralph Vaughan Williams (by then a revered, grandfatherly figure in British music) was finally persuaded to write a composition for that purpose.

The 12-minute composition comprises a theme and 11 variations. The brief variations are in a variety of moods and styles, including a waltz, a polonaise, a chorale, a canon, an arabesque, and a fugue. It tests ensemble coordination, command of and flexibility concerning styles, and richness of sound. It does not, however, have much in the way of solo passages, nor does it give the band challenging new sound contrasts to deal with. These aspects caused the brass band players who played it and the band mavens who heard it some disappointment, and this was especially keen considering that display of the prowess of a band's solo players was always considered a key ingredient in a contest piece. As a result, these variations, one of the composer's last works, have been rarely played. It has actually been heard more often in Vaughan Williams' transcription for full orchestra, and in a version for symphonic band (what the British call a "military band," i.e., with woodwinds). *—Joseph Stevenson*

Recommended:

○ **Eastman Wind Ensemble: Husa, Copland, Vaughan Williams & Hindemith** / Hunsberger (cond.), Eastman Wind Ens. / 1989 / CBS 44916

SYMPHONIC

Symphony No. 1 ("A Sea Symphony") (1903–1909; revised 1923)

The poetry of Walt Whitman was a rallying point for Vaughan Williams and his fellow students at Cambridge in the 1890's; for the composer, Whitman remained a lifelong source of inspiration. His largest Whitman setting is *A Sea Symphony*, which Vaughan Williams began writing in 1903, when he was 31 years old, and which he completed, only after much revision in 1909. Whitman's decidedly non-ecclesiastical vision of the soul's journey through life as a sea voyage into uncharted regions certainly appealed to Vaughan Williams, a declared agnostic who once exclaimed "Who believes in God nowadays, I should like to know?" according to fellow Trinity scholar Betrand Russell. Drawing inspiration from the cantatas of Parry and the operettas of Sullivan, as well as the English folk songs he had recently begun to collect, Vaughan Williams fashioned a huge score that contains some of the finest choral writing of its era. In the first movement, "A Song for All Seas, All Ships," a stern brass flourish is answered by full chorus, "Behold the sea itself." Thematic motives that will inform the rest of the work are immediately sounded: the words "and on its limitless, heaving breast, the ships" are set to a noble, arching theme that appeared more than once in Vaughan Williams' music, from the early unpublished tone-poem The Solent to the Symphony No. 9 of 1958. A quicker, shanty-like section ensues, making use of the folk song "Tarry Trowsers," in which the baritone soloist sings "a rude, brief recitative of ships sailing the seas." The dramatic entry of the soprano is heralded by the opening brass flourish; her cavatina extends the imagery into the spiritual: "... for the soul of man one flag above all the rest ... emblem of man elate above death [.]" The second movement is a nocturne, "On the Beach at Night, Alone," for baritone and chorus, in which, to a dark, rocking accompaniment the soloist muses on "the clef of the universes" and, over a soft marchlike tread in the bass (the legacy of Parry), envisions how "A vast similitude interlocks all." The chorus unleashes a forthright and powerful declamation after which the initial mystery of the opening returns, this time with orchestra alone. A sprightly version of the opening fanfare, with pizzicato strings, launches the scherzo "The Waves" for chorus alone. The quick and lightly scored counterpoint in the orchestral accompaniment underscores the interplay of "whistling winds ... undulating waves ... that whirling current" through which a ship plies its way. The trio is a broad, Parryesque melody to the words "Where the great vessel sailing and tacking displaced the surface." The movement concludes with alternating fanfares for both brass and chorus. "The Explorers" is fully half an hour in length, a finale containing some of Vaughan Williams' most noble music. Here the metaphor of the soul as a ship voyaging through the seas of life is most forthrightly expressed. A quiet introduction for hushed chorus ("O vast Rondure, swimming in space") is followed by a slow march describing the "restless" soul of man from its origins in Adam and Eve, climaxing in a vision of the poet, "the true son of God" who will guide mankind through his songs. The soprano and baritone soloists sing of the Soul "taking ship" to "launch out on trackless seas" in a duet of operatic fervor. A faster section ("Away O Soul!") launches the Soul's journey, with a final note of benediction ("O daring joy, but safe! are they not all the seas of God?") before the symphony sinks from sight in the lowest strings. *—Mark Satola*

Recommended:

○ **Vaughan Williams: A Sea Symphony** / Boult (cond.), Armstrong, Case, London PO / 1991 / EMI 64016

○ **Vaughan Williams: A Sea Symphony** / Thomson (cond.), Joly (cond.), Kenny, Cook, London SO / 1989 / Chandos 8764

Symphony No. 2 in G major ("A London Symphony") (1911–1913; revised 1918)

Geoffrey Toye, with the Queen's Hall Orchestra, led the first performance of Vaughan Wiliams *"London" Symphony* in London on March 27, 1914. As late as 1951, Vaughan Williams made new editions of symphonies Nos. 1–6. He wrote to Sir John Barbirolli that "The *London Symphony* is past mending—though with all its faults I love it still; indeed it is my favourite of my family of six." His favorite had a checkered history. His friend George Butterworth said, "You know, you ought to write a symphony." Vaughan Williams duly wrote and heard performed *A London Symphony*, then sent the score to Germany in 1914, for publication. It got lost, but from the parts was reconstructed; Vaughan Williams made cuts and adjustments in 1918, again in 1920, before publishing the work with a dedication to Butterworth's memory. But he wasn't finished: Vaughan Williams made trims in 1934 and still more in 1936 for another published edition that remains definitive. The pleas to restore certain passages fell on deaf ears: "It's much too long, much too long, and there was some horrid modern music in the middle—awful stuff. I cut that out—couldn't stand it," this to Bernard Herrmann, who'd performed the 1920 version in New York.

In four movements, it is more like four related tone poems in the style of Sibelius' *Lemminkäinen Legends*. Vaughan Williams tended to downplay their programmatic character, especially in later years, but he did write the following, interleaved with observations by Michael Kennedy and Butterworth in square-brackets:

"There are four movements. The first begins with a slow prelude [just before dawn as Wordsworth described it—'all that mighty heart is lying still'—harp and clarinet intone the Westminster chimes]. This leads to a vigorous allegro—which may perhaps suggest the noise and hurry of London, with its always underlying calm [two solo cellos, two solo violins and harp begin a reverie in one of London's green spaces, or churches, which merges into the recapitulation of the main themes...].

"The second (slow) movement has been called 'Bloomsbury Square on a November afternoon.' This may serve as a clue to the music, but it is not a necessary 'explanation' of it. [For Butterworth, 'an idyll of grey skies and secluded by-ways.' Kennedy heard 'a lavender-seller's cry, which Vaughan Williams noted in Chelsea ... a hansom cab's jingle'].

"The third movement is a nocturne in the form of a scherzo. If the hearer will imagine himself standing on Westminster Embankment at night, surrounded by the distant sounds of the Strand, with its great hotels on the one side and the 'New Cut' on the other, with its crowded streets and flaring lights [Cockney conviviality, to the simulated sounds of a mouth-organ], it may serve as a mood in which to listen....

"The last movement consists of an agitated theme in three-time, alternating with a march movement, at first solemn [not all in London are occasions of pageantry] and later on energetic. At the end of the finale comes a suggestion of the noise and fever of the first movement—this time much subdued—then the 'Westminster Chimes' once more. An 'Epilogue' follows in which the slow prelude is developed into a movement of some length [Clearly the rippling figures on flutes, violins, and violas represent the Thames.... The coda was suggested by a passage in H.G. Welles' novel, *Tono Bungay*: 'To run down the Thames so is to run one's hand over the pages in the book of England from end to end.... The river passes—London passes, England passes....']." *—Roger Dettmer*

Recommended:

- **Vaughan Williams: A London Symphony** / Hickox (cond.), London SO / 2001 / Chandos 9902
- **Vaughan Williams: A London Symphony; Fantasia on a Theme by Thomas Tallis** / Boult (cond.), London PO / 1991 / EMI 64017
- **Barbirolli Conducts Vaughan Williams** / Barbirolli (cond.), Halle Orch. / Dutton 1021

Symphony No. 3 ("Pastoral") (1921)

Vaughan Williams' Third Symphony, *A Pastoral Symphony*, puzzled more than a few hearers at its premiere on January 26, 1922. Here was a symphony in four movements, three of which were meditative and slow and which remained at a soft dynamic level, rarely rising to anything resembling a fortissimo climax until the third movement, a Moderato pesante functioning as a scherzo. The quiet modal themes, developing organically instead of according to classical form, the melismatic writing for section principals throughout, and the evocation through folklike material of the English occasioned Peter Warlock's famous quip that it was like "a cow looking over a gate." In reality, *A Pastoral Symphony* can be heard as Vaughan Williams' "War Requiem," one of three works written in the early 1920s that employ an otherworldly atmosphere to express the dark reality of the war just finished. (Its companions are the one-act opera *The Shepherds of the Delectable Mountains, after Bunyan*, and the Mass in G minor for unaccompanied double chorus.) Vaughan Williams drove an ambulance in France during the Great War, and some of his experiences made their way into the score, notably a bugler heard practicing at sunset.

The first movement, Molto moderato, opens with woodwinds in undulating consecutive triads, over which the solo violin sounds out its first folk-like theme, joined by other soloists in counterpoint that develops like the interweaving tendrils of plants. The overall mood is of great harmonic beauty, at once diatonic and modal, with an undercurrent of sadness. Subtle dissonance reigns as the second movement (Lento moderato) opens, though the gentle treatment impresses the listener more with the music's implied shadow than with the clash of notes. The solo horn sounds its call of A, G, E, and D against a string chord of F minor, which swirls upward into a theme of genuine sadness on middle strings, with solo oboe prominent. The distant bugler haunts the glowing middle section, an accompanied cadenza for trumpet that climaxes in an anguished tutti on the horn's initial call. As the movement subsides, the horn and trumpet themes, now on clarinet and horn respectively, intertwine. The scherzo uses sketches from a scene of *Falstaff* and the fairies, and is the only untroubled movement of the symphony. A heavy, dance-like tread on low strings is answered by horns and trombones in triple time, leading to a quicker section in which the trumpet is prominent. The themes are plainly folk-influenced and are presented in a straightforward manner, with the trumpet tune of the trio returning grandly at the conclusion, only to give way to a remarkable coda, very quiet and fast, in which new themes rush through in riotous counterpoint before disappearing with a soft and magical chord from the celesta. In the finale, a wordless soprano intones a plaintive, pentatonic melody over soft timpani, followed by a warm and consoling melody, the most fully developed of the symphony. The orchestration here is rich and glowing, though shadows darken a quicker section in which fragments of the soprano's theme protest against troubled harmonies, climaxing in a full-throated cry from the high strings, alone and unison, of the singer's tune. The consoling theme returns and the movement dies away to a high shimmering note on the upper strings, against which the soprano intones her distant vocalise. *—Mark Satola*

Recommended:

- **Vaughan Williams: Pastoral Symphony; Norfolk Rhapsody 2** / Hickox (cond.), Evans, London SO / 2002 / Chandos 10001
- **Vaughan Williams: Symphonies 3 & 5** / Boult (cond.), Price, New Philharmonia Orch. / 1991 / EMI 64018

Symphony No. 4 in F minor (1931–1934)

"I don't know whether I like it, but it's what I meant." Vaughan Williams referred in these famous words to his *Symphony No. 4*, which was sketched out over the years 1931 and 1932, completed in 1934, and first performed in London on April 10, 1935, by the BBC Symphony Orchestra under Sir Adrian Boult. The dissonance and power of the *Symphony No. 4* were not new elements in Vaughan Williams' music; some of the same can be heard, for instance, in the ballet *Job* (1930). But the unrelenting vision of the *Fourth* was new and surprising.

What does the *Fourth* mean? Interestingly and not very helpfully, it was the first of Vaughan Williams' symphonies not to have a descriptive title attached to it. Many thought that the symphony was a commentary on world events, in particular the rise of totalitarianism and the eventual outbreak of World War II. Sir Adrian Boult thought so: "He foresaw the whole thing." As usual, Vaughan Williams rejected such specificity, although he did admit in a letter to a friend that the "beauty" of the symphony reflected "unbeautiful times—because we know that beauty can come from unbeautiful things (e.g. King Lear, Rembrandt's School of Anatomy, Wagner's *Niebelungs*, etc.)" As Vaughan Williams was completing the *Fourth*, he was also starting on the oratorio *Dona Nobis Pacem*, which does make direct reference to war. But the composer's widow Ursula saw the symphony as autobiographical, a reflection of her husband's character: "The towering furies of which he was capable, his fire, pride, and strength are all revealed and so are his imagination and lyricism."

The symphony begins with an imperious theme that frequently recurs later in the work. The tone is one of anger and aggression. Even the more restrained second theme has a pulsating energy lurking beneath it, and the movement's occasional moments of humor are acid tinged. After its driving energy and frequent brass outbursts, the quiet coda of the movement comes as a surprise. But the feeling is more of enervation than calm. Next is the slow movement, marked Andante moderato, which opens with a wandering melody related to material from the first movement over a strong pizzicato accompaniment. Much is made of the contrast between the remorseless tread of the accompaniment versus the rather forlorn quality of the melodic material. The movement exudes a sense of weariness. A lonely flute solo acts as a coda. The Scherzo, marked Allegro molto, is dance-like, but rhythmically unpredictable and mercurial. After a fugal interlude, the dance opening returns. A strange and mysterious passage in which a quiet recollection of the first movement's main theme sounds over a pounding drum rhythm, leads without break into the vigorous Finale, which one might see as the resolution of the conflict of the first three movements. The final movement strides purposely forward, with frequent brass eruptions. The mood is one of excitement, but of agitation, as well. A peaceful theme emerges in the strings and is developed for a time. Then the initial music breaks out again, leading into a fugal development that whips up a lot of energy and leads to a brass-drenched peroration derived from the symphony's opening pages. *—Chris Morrison*

Recommended:

- **Vaughan Williams: Symphony No. 4; Mass in G minor; Choral Songs** / Hickox (cond.), London SO / 2002 / Chandos 9984
- **Vaughan Williams: Symphonies 4 & 5; Tallis Fantasia** / Vaughan Williams (cond.), BBC SO / Pearl 0062
- **Vaughan Williams: Symphonies 4 & 6** / Boult (cond.), New Philharmonia Orch. / 1991 / EMI 64019

Symphony No. 5 in D major (1938–1943; revised 1951)

During the late 1930s and early 1940s, Vaughan Williams was occupied with a wide variety of musical projects. His earliest film scores date from this time, such as those for *The 49th Parallel* (1940) and *Coastal Command* (1942). He also contributed to the war effort with works like the *Five Wartime Hymns* (1942) and the pageant *England's Pleasant Land* (1938); the latter work incorporates early sketches for the *Symphony No. 5*. There was also the ongoing labor on the opera/morality play *The Pilgrim's Progress*. Some incidental commissions also came his way, like the *Serenade to Music* written for Sir Henry Wood's golden jubilee as a conductor (1938).

And there was the *Symphony No. 5*, largely written over the years 1938 to 1943. Vaughan Williams himself conducted the London Philharmonic in the work's first performance at a Royal Albert Hall Promenade concert on June 24, 1943. A decade separates this symphony and its predecessor, and a work more unlike the violent and tumultuous *Symphony No. 4* would be hard to imagine. Vaughan Williams scholar Michael Kennedy has called the *Fifth* the "symphony of the celestial city," which perhaps gives some indication of the work's radiance and lyricism.

The *Symphony No. 5* was dedicated to Jean Sibelius, and the latter's own *Symphony No. 5* is evoked in the serene and mysterious opening Preludio. French horns sound out in D major over a low C in the strings, an ambiguity that is partly resolved when a radiant E major emerges in the strings. There are some darker moments during the more animated development section, but the opening horn calls return, and the main melody is heroically sounded out with brass and tympani. The epilogue is more ambivalent, wandering sadly toward a haunting and uncertain ending. The second movement, Scherzo, is a sardonic little dance that emerges out of swirling strings. Blasts from the brass section occasionally interrupt the tune. As turbulent as the music gets, the scoring is light and nimble throughout. The music relaxes toward the end of the movement, perhaps in anticipation of what is to follow.

The *Symphony No. 5* derives some of its thematic content from the opera *The Pilgrim's Progress*, but only in the third movement "Romanza" is the connection between opera and symphony dramatically apparent. In the manuscript score, Vaughan Williams included a brief quotation from Bunyan's work: "Upon this place stood a cross, and a little below a sepulchre. Then he said: 'He hath given me rest by his sorrow, and life by his death.'" The movement begins mysteriously, as a stately chorale-like theme is presented. Woodwinds, particularly English horn and oboe, introduce a new theme (taken from Act One, Scene Two of the opera). The music becomes temporarily blustery, but the chorale theme returns and builds to a noble climax. A solo violin leads into the hushed and poignant coda. Like the Brahms *Symphony No. 4*, the Vaughan Williams *Fifth* ends with a Passacaglia; the stately theme is heard in the low strings at first, and is developed by the rest of the orchestra. Variations on the passacaglia theme range from the playful to the jubilant to the restive. A big, brass-laden climax leads to a return of the symphony's opening French horn call, this time in a more assertive guise. The strings reflect on motifs from the first movement, with the passacaglia theme lurking nearby, and fade into a very peaceful and beautiful ending to what some have called Vaughan Williams' greatest symphony. *—Chris Morrison*

Recommended:

- ○ **Vaughan Williams: Symphonies 3 & 5** / Boult (cond.), London PO / 1991 / EMI 64018
- ○ **Vaughan Williams: Symphony 5; Valiant-for-truth, etc.** / Hickox (cond.), London SO / 1999 / Chandos 9666
- ○ **Vaughan Williams: Symphony 5; Bax: Tintagel** / Barbirolli (cond.), London SO / 1994 / EMI 65110
- ○ **Vaughan Williams: Symphony 5; Norwalk Rhapsody, etc.** / Haitink (cond.), London PO / 1995 / EMI 55487

Symphony No. 6 in E minor (1944–1947; revised 1950)

With the lyrical *Symphony No. 5* (1938–43), many figured that Vaughan Williams—who was, after all, in his early seventies by this time—was in essence saying farewell to the symphonic idiom. So the surprise and interest was that much greater when the *Symphony No. 6* was announced in 1947. Beginning with some sketches from the score for the film *The Flemish Farm* (1943), Vaughan Williams worked on the *Symphony No. 6* over the years 1944–47. It was given its first performance at the *Royal Albert Hall* on April 21, 1948, by the BBC Symphony Orchestra conducted by Sir Adrian Boult. The work was received with tremendous acclaim, and in its first year of existence it was performed nearly 100 times.

The unusual tone of the work, particularly the utter desolation of the final movement, has led many commentators to seek out some kind of extramusical program. Vaughan Williams, as usual, strongly rejected any such interpretations. The first movement, simply marked Allegro, opens tempestuously. After a brief respite, a swaggering, syncopated marchlike section breaks out. Its jazzy gait leads into a stately melody, which is presented first by the strings and then, boldly, by the brass, with heavy percussive accents. After further episodes, the stately tune ultimately returns in a more expressive guise, with flowing strings and strumming harp, gradually building into a final return of the stormy opening music. A single held note from the cellos and basses directly leads into the Moderato second movement. It is eerie and menacing, a chilly landscape that builds to a big, monolithic climax, as a martial three-note figure is hammered out over 90 times by trumpet, brass, and percussion, dominating everything around it. As the crescendo spends itself, a lonely English horn solo over wisps of strings leads into the third movement, a Scherzo marked Allegro vivace. This third movement has some of the sardonic quality of Shostakovich as it generates a considerable amount of undirected energy. A surprising and rather sleazy saxophone solo takes over, with the snare drum tapping away behind it. The saxophone melody is transformed into a noisy, stentorian climax that dies away to some woodwind chatter.

That leads into the ghostly Epilogue: Moderato, which drifts about purposelessly for some ten minutes at a consistently quiet dynamic. Small fragments of melody try to coalesce, but consistently fail. This movement, and to some extent the second, evokes the chilly, featureless landscapes of Vaughan Williams' score for the film *Scott of the Antarctic* (1948), and the attendant *Sinfonia antartica* (*Symphony No. 7*, 1949–52). The music continues to drift among muted strings and brass, the former bringing the work to an uneasy end as they rock back and forth, almost inaudibly, between E flat major and E minor chords. This movement's evanescent texture and emotional blankness, not to mention its sheer quietness, are very disturbing, and led some commentators to think that Vaughan Williams was imagining some kind of postwar or post-atomic devastation. The composer rejected such literalism; the only clue he provided was a reference to Prospero's famous speech from *The Tempest*: "We are such stuff/As dreams are made on, and our little life/Is rounded with a sleep." Perhaps coincidentally, in 1951 Vaughan Williams set these very words to music for chorus as one of his *Three Shakespearean Songs*. *—Chris Morrison*

Recommended:

- ○ **Vaughan Williams: Symphonies 4 & 6** / Boult (cond.), New Philharmonia Orch. / 1991 / EMI 64019
- ○ **Vaughan Williams: Symphony 6; Tuba Concerto** / Thomson (cond.), London SO / 1989 / Chandos 8740

Symphony No. 7 ("Sinfonia Antartica") (1949–1952)

Of Vaughan Williams' 11 film scores, the best known is his music for Ealing Studios' 1948 production *Scott of the Antarctic*, the story of the failed South Pole expedition of Robert Falcon Scott. His imagination fired by the subject, Vaughan Williams raced well ahead of studio production, composing most of the music without any visual references to the movie. The resulting music was thereby of unusual independent strength and lent itself particularly well to programmatic symphonic treatment. Vaughan Williams undertook that process between 1949 and 1952, and Sir John Barbirolli conducted the premiere of the new symphony (Vaughan Williams' Seventh) in Manchester on January 21, 1953. In five movements, the *Sinfonia Antartica* is more of a large concert suite than a classically developed symphony. In the score, each movement is given a superscription which the composer preferred be read silently, but which are sometimes spoken in performance (words of Shelley, Coleridge, and Donne are quoted, as well as the psalms and Scott's journals). In addition, atmospheric use is made throughout of a wordless soprano soloist and women's chorus, and the orchestra is augmented by vibraphone, organ, and wind machine, marking a new interest in unusual orchestral sonorities by the 80-year-old composer.

The opening tune, grim and striving, calls up the theme of man's stubble against implacable nature. After its dark harmonies, with their undercurrent of inevitable tragedy, we are introduced to the Antarctic continent itself by a shimmering mosaic of tone-painting, in which vibraphone, women's eerie, keening voices and wind machine make explicit the hostile environment. Into this cold landscape intrudes a heraldic trumpet call, the challenge of man to the unknown region, bringing the movement to a fine, optimistic climax, propelled by crisp rolls from the side drum. The voyage to Antarctica is portrayed in the Scherzo, sea spray and cold winds delineated in Debussy-like pointillism. Encounters with whales (a deep groaning theme in the basses) and penguins (a comic, loping episode for trumpet) are set forth before the movement ends suddenly and enigmatically, without a return of the scherzo. The most impressive sound-painting occurs in the third movement, "Landscape," originally accompanying the film's sequence on the awesome Beardmore glacier. A bare, chromatic theme, in canon in the trombones and tuba, is accompanied by icy and glittering fragments from percussion. The weight of this inexorable tune carries the movement forward to an astonishing climax in which the utter inhumanity of the southernmost land is given voice with an all-stops outburst from the organ, after which the music seems to collapse exhausted. A moment of warmth follows in the brief Intermezzo, in the composer's late lyrical style, the main theme given by solo oboe above a piquant mix of major and minor harmonies. Music originally for the apparent suicide of Captain Oates (who left the tent during a fierce blizzard) sounds an ominous note that is more fully developed in the fifth movement. "Epilogue" opens with a minor-key transformation of the first movement's trumpet call. The striving motto theme is now a resolute march, but the music of Antarctica slices into its determined optimism, with chorus and wind machine enveloping the music in a cold storm of defeat. The motto returns elegiacally, and then the wind, snow and wordless voices have the last word. *—Mark Satola*

Recommended:

- ○ **Vaughan Williams: Sinfonia Antartica; A Pastoral Symphony** / Davis (cond.), Rozario, BBC SO / 1997 / Teldec 13139

- ○ **Vaughan Williams: Sinfonia Antartica; Toward the Unknown Region** / Thomson (cond.), London SO / 1989 / Chandos 8796
- ○ **Vaughan Williams: Symphonies 7 & 8** / Previn (cond.), Harper, Richardson, London SO, Ambrosian Singers / RCA 60590

Symphony No. 8 in D minor (1953–1956)

The shortest and probably the most lighthearted of his nine symphonies, Vaughan Williams' *Symphony No. 8* was first performed on May 2, 1956, at the Free Trade Hall, Manchester, by the Hallé Orchestra conducted by Sir John Barbirolli, to whom the work is dedicated. Vaughan Williams was 83 years old at this point, and the variety and quality of his musical output showed no signs of flagging. Indeed, the composer was bringing new elements, new textures, and emotions into his work. A seemingly uncomplicated work, the *Symphony No. 8* exhibits a slightly dark undercurrent, and an enigmatic quality that was made even more manifest in the *Symphony No. 9* of the composer's final year, 1958.

The first movement of the *Eighth* is a Fantasia, subtitled "Variazioni senza thema" (Variations without a Theme). Vaughan Williams perhaps more accurately, described the movement as "Seven variations in search of a theme." It opens with one of the main elements of the movement, a querulous four-note phrase on which the flute elaborates, accompanied by glistening percussion. The music is restless, by turns stormy and lyrical. A jaunty, sardonic episode leads into the coda, in which flute, bassoon, and trumpet dance around the "theme," with harp and vibraphone providing a shimmering backdrop.

The woodwinds and brass are highlighted in the second movement, marked Scherzo alla marcia. It is a curious and slightly creepy march, with a more reflective, waltzlike central section, calling Stravinsky to mind in the combinations of textures and the not-quite-serious attitude. The third movement, Cavatina, is for strings only, unfolding itself in a rich polyphonic fabric. It sounds superficially like the more familiar Vaughan Williams works for string orchestra (such as the *Fantasia on a Theme of Thomas Tallis* or *The Lark Ascending*), but here there is a slight pall of anxiety and restlessness over even the most mellifluous passages.

Much the same might be said of the final movement, Toccata, in which the orchestra is joined by five percussionists playing, as Vaughan Williams put it, "all the 'phones and 'spiels known to the composer." One can hear preliminary evidence of this interest in percussion instruments in the Christmas cantata *Hodie* (1948), and it is said that Vaughan Williams was inspired by a performance of Puccini's *Turandot* to include percussion in the finale of the *Symphony No. 8*. The percussion by no means dominates the texture, however, but supports the diverse goings-on in the rest of the orchestra. The movement is certainly extroverted, but once again there is a darker presence in the music. Perhaps the composer had it right when he called the Toccata "a rather sinister exordium." A grand and noisy climax brings the work to a close. *—Chris Morrison*

Recommended:

- ○ **Vaughan Williams: Symphonies 8 & 9** / Boult (cond.), London PO / 1991 / EMI 64021
- ○ **Vaughan Williams: Symphonies 7 & 8** / Previn (cond.), London SO / RCA 60590
- ○ **Barbirolli Conducts Vaughan Williams** / Barbirolli (cond.), Halle Orch. / Dutton 1021

Symphony No. 9 in E minor (1956–1958)

Even in his mid-eighties, Vaughan Williams led an unusually active life. He traveled to Majorca, Austria, Italy, and, when at home in England, he had a busy round of concerts, festival appearances, and composing. His last symphony, the *Ninth*, was begun during his stay in Majorca, and completed back in England in 1957. It was given its premiere at London's Royal Albert Hall, with Sir Malcolm Sargent conducting the Royal Philharmonic Orchestra on April 2, 1958. Coincidentally, Vaughan Williams' last public appearance was at another Royal Albert Hall performance of the *Ninth* four months later. And on August 26, 1958, three weeks after that appearance, Sir Adrian Boult was to have recorded the *Ninth* with the BBC Symphony. Those plans were abandoned as news was received of Vaughan Williams' death that morning at age 86.

The *Symphony No. 9* has at best a mixed reputation. Some see in it evidence of Vaughan Williams' failing powers late in his career, of a reliance on the same old tricks, so to speak. Certainly the work is an enigmatic one. There are many abrupt changes of mood and texture, and those textures are enlivened by the presence of a trio of saxophones and, for the first time in a Vaughan Williams symphony, a flügelhorn. Two significant influences on the tone of the *Ninth* should be noted. One is Vaughan Williams' own *Symphony No. 6* of about a decade earlier. The other important influence is Thomas Hardy, specifically the novel *Tess of the D'Urbervilles*. The opening movement of the *Ninth* was, in fact, originally called "Wessex Prelude," a reference to a location in many of Hardy's novels.

The first movement, marked Moderato maestoso, opens mysteriously but turbulently. A trio of saxophones later blares away in a reminiscence of the *Symphony No. 6*. Tension increases, and the climax of the movement is followed by a more songful variant of the turbulent opening, with solo violin and strumming harp. A flügelhorn (once described by Vaughan Williams as "this beautiful and neglected instrument") sings briefly, and a strange, hushed coda features the return of the saxophones.

The flügelhorn becomes more prominent in the second movement, Andante sostenuto. Its song is threatened by a slightly sardonic martial figure that keeps attempting to break through. A more poignant section, thought by some to be a reference to Tess, is brought to a halt by the tolling of a bell and the return of the martial music. This beautifully scored and mercurial movement ends poignantly, but the spell is abruptly broken by the onset of the third-movement Scherzo. A jaunty but dark little tune, first presented and later elaborated on by the three saxophones, is eventually elaborated and polyphonically developed by the full orchestra. After several magical little interludes, the three saxophones return at the close.

This leads into the remarkable final movement, Andante tranquillo, with its variety of themes, moods, and passing references to the first three movements. Delicately scored, the movement begins polyphonically in the strings, and develops in a rhapsodic fashion with many sparse, chamberlike textures. The counterpoint in the strings becomes stormy and builds to a grandiose peroration, and after three loud and quickly fading E major chords, harp glissandos and a hint of saxophone are heard as the strings fade to silence. *—Chris Morrison*

Recommended:

- ○ **Vaughan Williams: Symphonies 8 & 9** / Boult (cond.), London PO / 1991 / EMI 64021
- ○ **Vaughan Williams: Symphony 9; Piano Concerto** / Thomson (cond.), London SO / 1991 / Chandos 8941
- ○ **Vaughan Williams: Symphonies 5 & 9** / Bakels (cond.), Bournemouth Sinfonietta / 1998 / Naxos 550738
- ○ **Vaughan Williams: Symphony 9; Arnold: Symphony 3** / Boult (cond.), London PO / 1994 / Everest 9001

CHORAL

Church and Choral Music (ca. 1900–1956)

After his symphonic works, the English composer Ralph Vaughan Williams is best-known for his choral works. This is particularly true in his native country, with its strong tradition of choral singing where most of his choral music has been continuously performed by amateur and church choirs since its premiere. His first great choral work was his setting of Whitman's "Toward the Unknown Region" (1906), a short but awe-inspiring work for chorus and orchestra. The greatest of his early choral works is undoubtedly *A Sea Symphony* (1910), also setting a text of Whitman for soprano and baritone soloists with chorus and orchestra, the grand and glorious apotheosis of the English choral tradition. After the intervention of World War I, Vaughan Williams composed the austerely spiritual *Mass in G minor* (1921), the most deliberately modal work written in England in 300 years. *Sancta civitas* (The Sacred City) (1925), his setting of the *Book of Revelations* for tenor and baritone soloists with semi-chorus, chorus, and orchestra, is one of Vaughan Williams' noblest and loftiest works, a serene contemplation of the intersection of the celestial and the mundane. This serenity was shattered by the rise of fascism in the 1930s and his *Dona nobis pacem* (Grant us peace) (1936) sets texts drawn from the *Bible* and the *Angelican Liturgy*, as well as poems by Whitman, to form a deeply moving work railing against war and the terror of war. Three years later, Vaughan Williams composed a setting of Shakespeare's *The Merchant of Venice*, Act Five, Scene One, as a tribute to conductor Henry J. Woods in the form of an orchestral serenade (*Serenade to Music*) with 16 solo singers (more often performed in an alternate version for chorus) that is at once sublimely lyrical and sensually supple. To celebrate the end of World War II, Vaughan Williams was commissioned by the BBC to compose a *Song of Thanksgiving* (originally entitled Song of Victory). Composed in 1944 to texts he drew from the Bible, Shakespeare, and Kipling, Vaughan Williams' work is written in his best, expansive, and public mode. Still active as a composer even in his eighties, Vaughan Williams wrote *Hodie* (This Day) (1954) for soprano, tenor, and baritone soloists with chorus, organ, and orchestra as a Christmas piece. Although a lifelong agnostic, Vaughan Williams' church music was supposedly written more in a spirit of community rather than in the spirit of the specifically spiritual. Nevertheless, the music of *Hodie* is suffused with a passionate spirituality that transcends the traditional and social intents of the work to make it a great piece of religious art. *—James Leonard*

Recommended:

- ○ **Vaughan Williams: Hodie; Fantasia on Christmas Carols** / Hickox (cond.); London SO & Chorus / 1990 / EMI 754128
- ○ **Vaughan Williams: Over hill, over dale** / Layton (cond.), George, Bostridge, Holst Singers / 1995 / Hyperion 66777
- ○ **Hymns of Vaughan Williams** / Somerville (cond.), Swann, Choir of First Church LA, / Gothic 49121

Dona Nobis Pacem, cantata (1936)

Intended as a plea to avert war at a time when tensions in Europe were rising sharply, *Dona Nobis Pacem* (Give Us Peace) takes it texts from four different sources, the mass, the Bible, poet Walt Whitman, and the British pacifist Quaker John Bright. The cantata is divided into six sections and lasts about 40 minutes. Its music is fairly eclectic in style, like much of Vaughan Williams' output, and was perhaps designed as an English counterpart to Verdi's *Requiem*, as suggested by the composer in his essay "A Musical Autobiography."

The first section, "Agnus Dei," marked Lento, is based on texts from the mass, and opens with the soprano soloist making a desperate plea for peace. Tension accrues thereafter in this short movement and is vented in the percussion-laden opening of the following section, "Beat, beat, drums!" Marked Allegro moderato, the music here is quite muscular and sometimes violent, featuring colorful writing for the brass, with many fanfare-like passages. This and the next two sections use texts by Whitman.

The second movement finally subsides for the gentle arrival of the next section, "Reconciliation." Here, Vaughan Williams offers a tender lullaby (Allegro moderato) for those lost in war. The latter part, however, conveys a more desolate, darker take on its sense of grief. The melancholy mood is mostly retained in the next section, "Dirge for Two Veterans," which was originally written in 1914. Partially because of the eclecticism of the work's style, the dirge's insertion in *Dona Nobis Pacem* is relatively seamless. Here, Vaughan Williams presents a symphonic march movement of stately melancholy.

The next section, on texts from John Bright and the Bible, opens darkly with the baritone soloist singing parts of Bright's well-known 1855 speech, "The Angel of Death," after which this movement is titled. The music then erupts fiercely when the chorus enters, and the mood remains unsettling throughout the remainder of this movement. The composer, however, offers plentiful hope in the final section, "O Man Greatly Beloved," on texts from seven books of the Bible. It opens in a pastoral mood and features some imaginative contrapuntal writing. Soon the mood turns glorious and brims with a sense of hope, perhaps even of triumph over conflict. The music then takes on a serene manner when the soprano soloist sings her hopeful prayer of peace. *—Robert Cummings*

Recommended:

- ○ **Vaughan Williams: Sancta Civitas; Dona Nobis Pacem** / Hickox (cond.), Terfel, Kenny, London SO & Chorus / 1993 / EMI 54788
- ○ **Vaughan Williams: Dona Nobis Pacem and Other Works** / Boult (cond.), Armstrong, Case, London PO & Chorus / 2001 / EMI 574782
- ○ **Vaughan Williams: Toward the Unknown Region; Dona Nobis Pacem, etc.** / Best (cond.), Allen, Howarth, Corydon Orch. & Singers / 1993 / Hyperion 66655

Shakespeare Songs (1951)

In early 1951, Vaughan Williams was asked to write a special test piece for unaccompanied mixed chorus for the National Competitive Festival of the British Federation of Music Festivals, to be held in June of that year. Despite the fact that Vaughan Williams was president of the Federation, he was not overly enthusiastic about the commission. But after much prodding, he created the *Three Shakespearean Songs*, which were premiered on June 23, 1951, by the combined choirs of the Federation under the direction of C. Armstrong Gibbs.

All three of the Songs maintain a pretty consistently quiet dynamic. Rather than create a series of brash, virtuoso showpieces, Vaughan Williams went in the direction of subtlety and restraint. The first song, *Full Fathom Five* (from *The Tempest*), imitates the sounds of bells; the tonality is not quite stable at first, but becomes more so in the contrasting, melodic middle section. *The cloud-capp'd towers* from Prospero's farewell speech in *The Tempest*, is largely homophonic in texture and quite haunting. Vaughan Williams cited a portion of this text ("We are such stuff as dreams are made on...") in relation to the eerie and desolate final movement of his *Symphony No. 6* (1948), and this song shares in some of that atmosphere. A brief and lively *Over hill, over dale* (from A Midsummer Night's Dream) closes the set. *—Chris Morrison*

Recommended:

- ○ **There is Sweet Music: English Choral Song 1890–1950** / Rutter (cond.), Cambridge Singers / 2002 / Collegium 505
- ○ **British Choral Music of the 20th Century** / Darlington (cond.), Oxford Christ Church Cathedral Choir / 2001 / Nimbus 5691-5

VOCAL

Folk Songs (ca. 1900–1935)

To say that English composer Ralph Vaughan Williams loved English folk music is to understate the intensity and duration of his relationship to the folk music of his country. From the time he "discovered" English folk music in his twenties until his death almost 70 years later, the melodies, harmonies, and rhythms of English folk songs permeated his music. Indeed, it is impossible to imagine Vaughan Williams' music without English folk music. His orchestral music from the *Norfolk Rhapsody* (1905); his choral music from the *Fantasia on Christmas Carols* (1912), his symphonies from *A London Symphony* (1920), his operas from *Hugh the Drover* (1924): all of these are suffused with English folk songs. When it came to actual folk songs, Vaughan Williams not only used them as bases forhis own compositions, as in his *English Folk Song Suite* (1923) or *Five Variants of Dives and Lazarus* (1939), but he also made numerous arrangements and harmonizations of them for solo voices, combinations of solo voices, part songs, and chorus. Among the best-known of these are *Bushes and Briers*, *Sweet William's Ghost*, *Seventeen Come Sunday*, *The Coventry Carol*, *Rolling in the Dew*, *John Barleycorn*, and, of course, *Greensleeves*, arguably Vaughan Williams' most popular work. *—James Leonard*

Recommended:

- ○ **Vaughan Williams: Folk Songs Of Britain** / Deller, Dupre, Deller Consort / 1997 / Vanguard 8109

Songs (ca. 1894–1958)

Although English composer Ralph Vaughan Williams composed 164 songs, these are frequently considered among the least of his output. And yet among those songs are not only some of his most characteristic works of his early maturity, but also include his many arrangements of his beloved English folk songs. Vaughan Williams four greatest sets of songs are *The House of Life* (1903), the *Songs of Travel* (1901–1904), the *Five Mystical Songs* (1911), and *On Wenlock Edge* (1908–1909). *The House of Life* is a setting of *Dante Gabriel Rossetti's* sonnet sequence of the same name for voice and piano. The six songs of *The House of Life* are written in a more complex and self-consciously "artsy" lyrical style than most of his later works. The *Songs of Travel* setting the poetry of Robert Louis Stevenson were published song by song starting from 1902 and were collected and published together in 1907, except the ninth and last song, which was found among Vaughan Williams' papers after his death and first published in 1960. Slightly less self-consciously "artsy" and rather more self-consciously "folksy" than *The House of Life*, the *Songs of Travel* reveal more of the mature composer. But in neither set of these early songs does the piano accompaniment add anything to the vocal melody except harmonic underpinning, and all their musical interest lies in their tunes.

The graceful and glorious vocal melodies *Five Mystical Songs*, which Vaughan Williams wrote in three different versions, solves the problem of piano accompaniment by having one version accompanied by piano, a second version accompanied by organ with optional chorus, and a third version accompanied by orchestra and optional chorus. The songs, set to texts by metaphysical poet George Herbert, are in Vaughan Williams' agnostic-mystic manner, with spiritually passionate vocal melodies soaring over robustly radiant accompaniments. Then there are his settings of A.E. Houseman's *On Wenlock Edge*. Like the *Five Mystical Songs*, *On Wenlock Edge* exists in two versions, one for voice, piano, and string quartet, and one for orchestra. In both, the accompaniments are clearly influenced by Vaughan Williams' studies in orchestration with Ravel: The music shines with a pellucid luminosity that was to become the hallmark of Vaughan Williams' music for the rest of his life. The vocal melodies are suffused with Vaughan Williams' love of the English folk song, but his love transfigures the idiom of folk song into something more elevated and universal. After *On Wenlock Edge*, Vaughan Williams' interest in song writing diminished, and the remaining 56 years of his life have far fewer songs until the final blissfully ecstatic settings for voice and piano culled from William Blake's *Songs of Innocence* and *Songs of Experience* (1956). *—James Leonard*

Recommended:

- ○ **Vaughan Williams: Along the Field and other songs** / Ainsley, Nash Ens. / Hyperion 67168
- ○ **Vaughan Williams: On Wenlock Edge; Five Mystical Songs** / Johnson, Keenlyside, Duke Quartet / 2003 / Naxos 8557114
- ○ **Silent Noon: Songs of Ralph Vaughan Williams** / Golden, Woodman, Bean / 1993 / Koch 7168

Linden Lea, song for voice & orchestra ("In Linden Lea" / "A Dorset Song") (1901)

Linden Lea is the most popular of Vaughan Williams' songs, and probably the one piece of music that made him the most money over the course of his life. He wrote it in 1901 while he was working on his Doctor of Music degree at Cambridge, to a text (in Dorsetshire dialect) by the cleric and poet William Barnes (1800–1886). Vaughan Williams had lately become involved with a new journal on songs and singing called *The Vocalist*; appropriately, its first edition, which appeared in April 1902, featured an article by Vaughan Williams called "A School of English Music" along with the sheet music for *Linden Lea*.

Among his friends at Cambridge were the brothers Nicholas and Ivor Gatty, both musicians, who came from the quiet Yorkshire village of Hooton Roberts. Vaughan Williams often visited the Gatty brothers there, and it was there that *Linden Lea* received its first performance on September 4, 1902. Within a few years the song had become enormously well known, so much so that Vaughan Williams could refer in a 1925 letter to "such sins of my youth as *Linden Lea*, which becomes every year more horribly popular." Over a dozen arrangements exist of the song, which begins with the poet reminiscing about the sights and sounds of *Linden Lea*, particularly the apple tree which "do lean down low." The mood becomes temporarily agitated as the poet reflects on the money making possibilities in "dark-room'd towns." But, in contemplation of the return trip home, the song ends softly and reflectively. *—Chris Morrison*

Recommended:

- **The Very Best of Janet Baker** / Baker, Moore / 2002 / EMI 75069
- **On the Idle Hill of Summer: Song Cycles & Songs by Vaughan Williams, Butterworth, Quilter, Peel** / T. Allen, Parsons / 2001 / EMI 67428

On Wenlock Edge, song cycle for tenor, piano, & string quartet (1908–1909)

The song cycle *On Wenlock Edge*, settings of poetry by A.E. Housman, was composed for the most part in 1909. The year before, Vaughan Williams had traveled to France to study with Maurice Ravel. Although they were only together for three months and concentrated primarily on orchestration studies, Vaughan Williams found it an immensely valuable experience. On his return to England, Vaughan Williams set to work on his *String Quartet in G minor* and *On Wenlock Edge*. The song cycle, scored for the somewhat unusual combination of voice, piano, and string quartet, was premiered on November 15, 1909, with tenor Gervase Elwes, pianist Frederick Kiddle, and the Schwiller Quartet. In the early 1920s Vaughan Williams arranged the cycle for voice and orchestra. This later version, which perhaps evokes more of the poems' atmospherics, was premiered in January 1924.

The poems are drawn from Housman's *A Shropshire Lad* of 1896. Housman didn't much care for musical settings of his poetry, and apparently particularly disliked *On Wenlock Edge*. There is some argument about how well Vaughan Williams captured the bleakness and disillusionment of Housman's poetry. As attractive as *On Wenlock Edge* is, Vaughan Williams' much later and more angular Housman settings of *Along the Field* (1927) are probably closer to what Housman would have admired.

In the first song, "On Wenlock Edge," the imagery of "the old wind in the old anger" gives Vaughan Williams the chance to engage in some tone painting. This opener's historical perspective turns in subsequent songs to more personal emotions. "From Far, From Eve and Morning" is brief and comparatively simple but beautiful; the very gradual entry of the strings in the second verse (in the original chamber setting) is particularly memorable. "Is My Team Ploughing?" is more complex and despairing; Ravel's influence on Vaughan Williams is particularly clear here, in a song that was called by one early critic "a miniature tragedy." The very short interlude "Oh, When I Was in Love with You" is followed by the most ambitious of these songs, "Bredon Hill." The instruments imitate the bells of Bredon, which sound in the summer and at other times summon the folk to church, weddings, and funerals. The very still opening almost suspends time, which is most appropriate given how past, present, and future are fused in Housman's verse. Finally, "Clun" is gentle and melancholy. It misses perhaps some of the despair of Housman's poem, but the setting of the poem's final words is quite touching, and the very spare instrumental epilogue is very effective indeed. *—Chris Morrison*

Recommended:

- **Vaughan Williams: Symphony 6; In the Fen Country; On Wenlock Edge** / Bostridge, Haitink (cond.), London PO / 1999 / EMI 56762
- **Vaughan Williams: Along the Field and other songs** / Ainsley, Nash Ens. / Hyperion 67168

Serenade to Music ("How sweet the moonlight sleeps upon this bank!") for 16 soloists & orchestra (1938)

One of the finest of all musical settings of Shakespeare, the *Serenade to Music* was written for and dedicated to Henry Wood on the occasion of his golden jubilee as a conductor, "in grateful recognition of his services to music." Wood, who for decades had been associated with the enormously popular *Promenade Concerts* in London, had participated in many premieres of Vaughan Williams' compositions and was much admired by the composer. For his tribute, Vaughan Williams had the splendid idea of creating a work that would incorporate the talents of 16 well-known British singers who had had long associations with Wood, for each of whom Vaughan Williams would create a characteristic phrase to sing. These 16 singers took part in the premiere of the *Serenade* at Wood's Golden Jubilee concert at the Royal Albert Hall, London, on October 5, 1938, with Wood himself conducting a large orchestra of musicians drawn from the London Symphony, London Philharmonic, BBC Symphony, and Queen's Hall orchestras. It was an emotional performance that, it is said, reduced Sergey Rachmaninov, who was in attendance, to tears. Thankfully these same performers recorded the work a few days later, so listeners today can share in the moving quality of the event.

Vaughan Williams chose for his text Lorenzo's speech on music in Portia's garden from Act Five, Scene One of *The Merchant of Venice*. The opening gesture of the *Serenade* is unusually beautiful, and a solo violin helps establish the languorous mood of a Mediterranean garden. The voices enter, and one of the sopranos sings a rapturous ascending phrase at the first mention of "sweet harmony." Men's voices take over to describe the "floor of heaven ... thick inlaid with patines of bright gold," and a brief note of anxiety enters. Fanfares then sound the wakening of Diana, followed by a more melancholy passage contemplating "the man that hath no music in himself." Diana's fanfares briefly return and lead back to the peaceful opening melody, which also concludes the work in hushed fashion. The singers collectively intone the final words, "sweet harmony," and the piece ends in utter tranquillity. *—Chris Morrison*

Recommended:

- **Vaughan Williams: Serenade; English Folk Song Suite; Fantasia on Greensleeves, etc.** / Boult (cond.), London PO / 1991 / EMI 64022
- **Vaughan Williams: Te Deum; Serenade; Dona Nobis Pacem** / Wood (cond.), BBC SO / Pearl 9342

Songs of Travel, song cycle (1901–1904)

In 1904, Vaughan Williams started work as music editor of *The English Hymnal*. Partly as a consequence of that editorial work, he also spent a good portion of that year traveling widely in England collecting folk songs, a pursuit he had begun only the year before. These efforts, as well as his love for the songs of Schubert and Schumann, combine in the *Songs of Travel*, settings of nine poems by Robert Louis Stevenson. It was one of two song cycles Vaughan Williams completed in 1904, the other being the Rossetti cycle *The House of Life*.

Only in recent years have listeners been able to experience this set of songs as the cycle it was intended to be. The first eight of the nine songs were given their premieres at Bechstein Hall, London, on December 2, 1904, by baritone Walter Creighton and pianist Hamilton Harty (who also made a Romantic-sized arrangement of Handel's *Water Music* for orchestra). The following year, three of the livelier songs were published as Book I; this was followed in 1907 by Book II, consisting of four darker, more restrained songs. Only in 1960 was the complete cycle first performed, after the ninth and final song of the set, "I Have Trod the Upward and the Downward Slope," was rediscovered amongst Vaughan Williams' papers after his death. Vaughan Williams had orchestrated the original Book I in 1905; his assistant Roy Douglas arranged the rest of the cycle for orchestra in 1961 and 1962.

The *Winterreise*-like theme of the wanderer encountering and dealing with life's challenges seems to have been an appealing one for Vaughan Williams, and he responded with what were arguably his finest songs up to this time. The opening song, "The Vagabond," sets the tone with its purposeful tread, interrupted only by a darker current in the third verse as the vagabond contemplates the winds and cold of autumn. The wistful tone and lyrical arpeggios of "Let Beauty Awake" are followed by "The Roadside Fire," with its memorable tune and rhapsodic reference to the "fine song for singing, the rare song to hear!" "Youth and Love" is peaceful, with a light chordal accompaniment, becoming agitated only when the youth cries "a wayside word" to his beloved. "In Dreams" and "The Infinite Shining Heavens" share a certain melancholy; one hears in the latter song some unusual turns of melody and rhythm that foreshadow the later and more mature Vaughan Williams style. "Whither Must I Wander?" was the earliest of these songs, published separately in the third issue of the journal *The Vocalist* in 1902; it is probably the most folklike song of the set. The reflective "Bright is the Ring of Words" is followed by the brief and fitting epilogue "I Have Trod the Upward and the Downward Slope." Its quiet piano postlude closes the cycle. *—Chris Morrison*

Recommended:

- **The Vagabond & Other Songs by Vaughan Williams, Butterworth, Finzi & Ireland** / Terfel, Martineau / 1995 / DG 445946
- **Vaughan Williams, Elgar, Butterworth: Orchestral Songs** / Allen, Rattle (cond.), Birmingham SO / 1993 / EMI 64731
- **Song Cycles and Songs by Vaughan Williams, Warlock, Butterworth and Gurney** / Johnson, Willison / 2001 / EMI 574785

CONCERTO

Flos Campi, suite for viola, small chorus & small orchestra (1925)

Vaughan Williams played the viola, and frequently professed it was his favorite instrument. Along with the *Suite for viola and orchestra* of 1934, his most significant work for the instrument is the unusual *Flos Campi* (Flower of the Field), which combines the viola with a spare orchestral backing of strings, winds, tabor, and celesta, along with a mixed choir that sings wordlessly. It was first performed on October 10, 1925, in London, with violist Lionel Tertis, voices from the Royal College of Music, and the Queen's Hall Orchestra conducted by Sir Henry Wood. The reaction was mixed, and even such close friends of the composer as Gustav Holst admitted themselves puzzled by this subtle and voluptuous work.

In a program note for a 1927 performance, Vaughan Williams admitted "The title *Flos Campi* was taken by some to connote an atmosphere of 'buttercups and daisies....'" This is, in fact, far from the atmosphere of this work. Each of its six movements is headed by a quotation from the Old Testament's Song of Solomon, and it is the passionate quality of that text which informs *Flos Campi*. The work opens with the juxtaposition of viola and oboe, both playing melodically but in different keys, creating palpable tension. This opening movement is languorous and mysterious, its associated text speaking of the sickness of love, of how it is a "lily among thorns." Nature springs to life in the second movement, with the "singing of birds" and the "voice of the turtle." But the beloved is not present, and the third movement is passionate and agitated, with the viola accompanied mostly by the women of the choir. Men "expert in war" are at Solomon's bed in the vigorous fourth-movement march, in which the violist has an opportunity for some virtuoso display. The music builds to a rather tense climax, at which point we hear the murmuring of voices, over which the viola soars longingly. The orchestra takes up this music in a more peaceful strain, and the choir sings in sweet polyphony. The opening viola-oboe duet returns, but its ambivalence is resolved as the melodic material of the fifth movement is taken up again in a quiet and magical coda. *—Chris Morrison*

Recommended:

- ○ **Vaughan Williams: Serenade to Music; Flos Campi; Five Mystical Songs; Fantasia on Christmas Carols** / Best (cond.), Imai, English CO, Corydon Singers / 1990 / Hyperion 66420
- ○ **Walton: Viola Concerto; Vaughan Williams: Flos Campi** / Primrose, Boult (cond.), London Philharmonia Orch., BBC Theatre Orch. & Chorus / Pearl 9252

The Lark Ascending, romance for violin & orchestra (1914; revised 1920)

The Lark Ascending is a relatively simple piece—its musical discourse is plainly and easily perceived; yet at its heart is an emotional profundity that links it with other works by Vaughan Williams from the same period, in which a calm, almost detached pastoral approach is used to convey great feeling. Vaughan Williams completed *The Lark Ascending* in 1914 for violinist Marie Hall, with whom he consulted on the solo part. After a thorough revision in 1920, she first played it in a violin-piano arrangement in Shirehampton Public Hall in December 1920. The first performance of the orchestral version was in London, at a Queen's Hall concert in June, 1921, during the second Congress of British Music Society.

Verses from George Meredith's poem "The Lark Ascending" precede this evocative tone painting, describing the unique circling ascent of the lark, accompanied by its long-breathed, rhapsodic song. The writing for the violin mimics the "silver chain of sound...In chirrup, whistle, slur and shake" described by Meredith, though of course it also carries the main melodic argument. A brief cadence of soft chords from winds and strings discreetly usher in the first flight of the soloist, who rhapsodizes without accompaniment on a folklike theme of considerable plasticity. The orchestra then quietly enters, and the first theme is developed organically until the section closes with a reprise of the solo cadenza.

A more straightforward folk theme on woodwinds begins the middle section, which has been likened to the pastoral countryside over which the lark soars; the violin's free descant over the orchestra certainly underscores that impression. A magical moment ensues when solo woodwinds evoke a panoply of birdsong under the busy rustling of the violin; the effect is like a choir of birds led by the virtuoso lark. Vaughan Williams would achieve a similar effect in *Jane Scroop: Her Lament for Philip Sparrow* from his 1935 choral suite *Five Tudor Portraits*. A note of sadness and nostalgia informs the reprise of the first section, and the piece ends with one more cadenza from the violin, whose song circles ever higher into the upper reaches of the instrument until it more disappears than ends; as quoted from Meredith, "Till lost on his aerial rings / In light, and then the fancy sings." *—Mark Satola*

Recommended:

- ○ **Vaughan Williams: English Folk Song Suite; Fantasia on Greensleeves; The Lark Ascending, etc.** / Boult (cond.), Bean, New Philharmonia Orch. / 1991 / EMI 64022
- ○ **Vaughan Williams: Orchestral Works** / Marriner (cond.), Brown, Academy of St. Martin-in-the-Fields / 1999 / Decca 460357
- ○ **Vaughan Williams: Symphony 5; Norfolk Rhapsody 1; The Lark Ascending** / Haitink (cond.), Chang, London PO / 1995 / EMI 55487

Oboe Concerto in A minor (1944)

Vaughan Williams began work on his Oboe Concerto immediately upon completion of his Symphony No. 5 in D major. The concerto in fact uses themes originally intended for the Symphony. Leon Goossens, for whom it was written, gave the first performance in Liverpool on September 30, 1944. Pastoral in tone and expansively modal in expression, the Oboe Concerto is deceptively easy to listen to, given the considerable difficulties that Vaughan Williams sets for the accompanying string orchestra, which in the space of the concerto's eighteen minutes must navigate a host of technical challenges, all at dynamic levels that don't overwhelm the soft timbres of the solo instrument.

The first movement, Rondo Pastorale, opens with three soft chords from the strings, over which the oboe sounds a supple and pensive modal theme, which is developed in linear fashion over thoughtful commentary from the strings. From the outset, the oboe seems curiously alone with its thoughts—a solitary shepherd piping on a hillside? A livelier second theme, dance-like but rhythmically uneven, is introduced by the oboe and then taken up by the strings in canon. A return of the first theme brings about a moment of lovely contemplation, a short accompanied cadenza and a brief, somewhat sad conclusion. There is only a superficial nod to eighteenth century dance forms in the second movement, Minuet and Musette. The Minuet is indeed in three-quarter time, and the Musette makes use of a strong pedal point, but beyond that, the writing is plainly modern. Further, the two dances are seamlessly integrated, testament to Vaughan Williams' often overlooked subtlety. The movement is brief and leads directly to the finale, Scherzo. In the last movement, the writing for strings is supremely difficult, full of quick figurations and tricky counterpoint, over which the oboe sounds a chattering theme that quickly resolves into a feather-light waltz. A broader, more nostalgic melody serves as the second theme and recalls the shapes of themes already heard. There is a chromatic working out of the opening theme, quietly dissonant and in complex rhythm, before an aching, wistful passage in which the harmonies recall such neo-classicists as Wiren and Larsson, before a return of the quick waltz with the second theme in tow, and a richly harmonized slow coda. The three chords which began the work end it as well.*—Mark Satola*

Recommended:

- ○ **Hickox Conducts Vaughan Williams** / Hickox (cond.), Northern Sinfonia of England / 2000 / EMI 73986

Piano Concerto in C major (1926–1931; revised 1946)

Vaughan Williams wrote the first two movements of this *Piano Concerto* in 1926, and the last in 1930–1931, which contradicts the composer's program note for the first performances, which suggest the finale was written entirely in the year 1930. He composed the work for pianist Harriet Cohen; it was not a success, coming under criticism for its supposed excess of ferocity and grimness. True, the work has a measure of these qualities, but it also contains much wit and many lighthearted passages.

Vaughan Williams scored the concerto for a large orchestra and much of the writing demands the soloist hold his/her own against huge washes of sound. Adrian Boult, who was the conductor at the premiere, and several others suggested to the composer that he might provide a two piano version of the work to create what they perceived as a greater sonic balance between the keyboard and orchestra. In 1946, Joseph Cooper, in collaboration with Vaughan Williams, fashioned a two piano and orchestra rendition which, apart from a few small changes, is largely a faithful arrangement. The original version was neglected for a time, but when this concerto is played today, it is usually heard in the single-piano rendition.

The concerto is cast in three movements: Toccata (Allegro moderato); Romanza (Lento); and Fuga Chromatica con Finale alla Tedesca. The first movement is a hard-driving, somewhat grim movement and accounts for the concerto's tough and violent reputation. The piano begins the work with a series of brilliant chords, and soon the orchestra introduces a jovial, folk-like theme. A shorter theme on piano soon appears and there follows some imaginative development of the materials. The movement ends with a brief Ravellian cadenza which connects to the Romanza middle panel. Oddly, the Toccata's music sounds more than remotely like Bartók's, especially as heard in his first two piano concertos, the earliest of which did not appear until a year after Vaughan Williams had written this. The opening movement may strike some as diffuse in structure and emotionally cold, but its rewards are considerable for the patient listener.

That said, it may be that the Romanza is the most attractive and finely-conceived movement in the work. It is unusual for Vaughan Williams in that it has an almost bluesy atmosphere. The main theme, first played by the piano and then taken up by the flute, is lovely, again suggesting the influence of Ravel, with whom Vaughan Williams studied in 1908. A warm theme in the middle section is more typical of the composer's post-Romantic style, but it is actually a variation on a theme from Bax's *Third Symphony*. The finale begins without pause after the lovely, quiet ending of the Romanza. The first part is devoted to a rhythmic fugue of great color. A brilliant cadenza bridges this section with the finale proper, which uses the same material from the fugue, but underpins it harmonically rather than fugally. *—Robert Cummings*

Recommended:

- ○ **Vaughan Williams & Delius: Piano Concertos; Finzi: Eclouge** / Lane, Handley (cond.), Royal Liverpool PO / 2003 / EMI 575983
- ○ **Vaughan Williams: Symphony 9; Piano Concerto** / Shelley, Thomson (cond.), London SO / 1991 / Chandos 8941

Tuba Concerto in F minor (1954)

Vaughan Williams wrote his *Concerto for Bass Tuba* in F minor for Philip Catelinet, the principal tuba player of the London Symphony Orchestra, on the occasion of the LSO's golden jubilee. It was given its premiere by Catelinet, with the LSO under the direction of Sir John Barbirolli, at London's Royal Festival Hall on June 13, 1954.

Vaughan Williams's professed aim was to "give a show" for the tuba, and that he certainly did, exploring the entirety of the bass tuba's range of expression. In size and form the work is not unlike one of Mozart's bigger horn concertos, with major cadenzas coming at the ends of both fast movements. The moods of the solo part vary from a kind of genial rumbustiousness, to an ardent lyricism, and considerable virtuosity is required of the soloist.

The Allegro moderato first movement is tuneful and has an easygoing gait. The central Romanza features a graceful, lovely tune of a folkish cast, on which the tuba rhapsodizes. The final movement is a jaunty and virtuosic Finale (marked Rondo alla tedesca). The Bass Tuba Concerto may not be one of Vaughan Williams' most substantial pieces, but he takes the instrument seriously and provides it an attractive showcase. *—AMG*

Recommended:

○ **The Chicago Principal: First Chair Soloists Play Famous Concertos** / Jacobs, Barenboim (cond.), Chicago SO / 2003 / DG 000002502

CHAMBER MUSIC

Studies in English Folk Song, for cello & piano (1926)

Written for cellist May Mukle, the *Six Studies in English Folk Song* also exist in alternate versions for clarinet, violin and viola, and have further been effectively played on bassoon. These pensive studies (only the last one is in a lively tempo) go beyond simple harmonization of a melody. Vaughan Williams employs his usual effective writing for stringed instruments to create miniature rhapsodies on the folk songs *Lovely on the Water, Spurn Point, Van Diemen's Land, She Borrowed Some of Her Mother's Gold, The Lady and the Dragoon* and the jaunty *As I walked Over London Bridge.* No great virtuosic demands are made on the cellist, who must nevertheless play with insight and a touch of self-effacement, allowing the poignant songs to reveal their own considerable beauties.*—Mark Satola*

Recommended:

○ **Vaughan Williams: Violin Sonata; String Quartet in A minor; Phantasy Quintet** / Parkhouse, Croxford / 1994 / EMI 65100

BALLET

Job, A Masque for Dancing (1927–1930)

Vaughan Williams wrote only one work that he called a ballet—*Old King Cole* (1923)—but turned out several masques, including *Job*, which is really a ballet. While it is not a repertory item with the world's ballet companies, it has received a fair measure of attention, especially in England.

The work is cast in nine scenes, with an epilogue (the last scene). The scenario is by Geoffrey Keynes and Gwendolyn Raverat, after William Blake's *Illustrations of the Book of Job.* Oddly, Vaughan Williams' own synopsis, which was printed in the music score, differs slightly from the one issued by Keynes. The composer's splits the fifth scene in two, thus accounting for nine scenes, whereas Keynes' scenario uses eight scenes. The story centers on Satan's menacing of Job, eventually provoking him to curse God. In the end, it is Satan, however, who is defeated, and Job, now humbled and stronger, triumphant.

The first scene, Introduction: "Pastoral Dance—Satan's Appeal to God," features a gentle, serene opening, followed by the darker music of Satan. The next scene, "Satan's Triumphal Dance," begins menacingly and then presents a witty, diabolical dance, whose music augurs that in the colorful scherzo of Vaughan Williams' *Symphony No. 9* (1958), both works featuring imaginative writing for the xylophone. "Minuet of Job's Sons and Their Wives" follows, an exotic and subdued piece, which exhibits deliciously atmospheric music, in large part from the oboe and winds.

"Job's Dream—Dance of Plague, Pestilence, Famine and Battle" begins in a subdued, but ominous mood, then powerfully fulfills that wary feeling. "Dance of the Messengers" follows, which is largely subdued and again features imaginative writing for the winds. The ensuing scene, "Dance of Job's Comforters—Job's Curse—A Vision of Satan," features, as one might expect, a colorful mixture of music. The opening is witty and highlights the saxophone (if used, as a bass clarinet may be substituted), whose diabolically slithering notes perfectly depict the Comforters, who are really "three wily hypocrites."

The seventh scene, "Elihu's Dance of Youth and Beauty—Pavane of the Sons of the Morning," begins with a lovely viola solo and later features an attractive dance of rather solemn character. The next scene, "Galliard of the Sons of Morning—Altar Dance and Heavenly Pavane," is full of drama and color, from the hopeful opening to the more celestial and triumphant music thereafter. The last scene, "Epilogue," follows without break. It is serene and gently triumphant in mood, and recalls music from the opening scene: in both scenes Job sits contentedly with his wife, though he is noticeably older in the latter.

Job has been viewed as auguring the *Symphony No. 4* (1931-1934), a violent and dramatic work of profound character. While there are stylistic similarities between the two compositions, *Job* features less anxiety and a greater sense of repose and serenity. *—Robert Cummings*

Recommended:

○ **Vaughan Williams: Symphony 9; Job** / Davis (cond.), BBC SO / 1997 / Teldec 98463

○ **Vaughan Williams: Job; The Wasps** / Boult (cond.), London PO / 1994 / Everest 9006

Sandor Végh

b. May 17, 1912, Kolosvár, Hungary, **d.** Jan. 7, 1997, Freilassing, Germany

Conductor

Sándor Végh was best known as one of the great chamber music violinists of the twentieth century. He began studying piano at the age of six. He entered the Budapest Conservatory in 1924, taking violin studies with Jeno Hubay and composition under Zoltán Kodály. He began a career as a solo violinist, and in 1927 played a Richard Strauss composition under the composer's baton. He graduated from the Conservatory in 1930, having won the Hubay Prize and the Reményi Prize from the institution in 1927. As his solo career was developing, he joined the Hungarian Trio, with Ilonka Krauss and Laszlo Vencze.

In 1934 he became one of the founder-members of the Hungarian String Quartet. He was initially the first violin, but gave that position to Zoltán Szekeley and took second chair. He participated with the Hungarian String Quartet in the first performance of Béla Bartók's *String Quartet No. 5* (1936).

Végh left the Hungarian Quartet in 1940 to found his own quartet, the Végh String Quartet. During the same season he became a professor at the Liszt Academy of Music in Budapest. He and the quartet left Hungary in 1946. The quartet continued to give concerts until the mid-1970s; Végh also made solo appearances as a violinist. He took French citizenship in 1953.

In 1952 he met cellist Pablo Casals, who invited Végh to join him in giving summer classes in Zermatt, Switzerland (1952–62), and to appear annually in Casals' Prades Festival (1953–69). He found teaching rewarding, and thereafter taught in Basle Conservatory (1953–63), the Conservatory of Freiburg im Breigau (1954–62), the Düsseldorf Conservatory (1962–69) and the Mozarteum in Salzburg (1971–97, becoming a professor there in 1978).

In the meanwhile he began conducting. He founded the Cervo (Italy) Chamber Music Festival in 1962 and often conducted there. He founded the Sándor Végh Chamber Orchestra and conducted it for a term lasting from 1968 to 1971, and conducted the Marlboro Festival Orchestra (1974–77). In 1979 he became conductor of the Camerata Academica at the Mozarteum. With them he made a recording of Mozart's divertimentos and serenades that won the Grand Prix du Disque of 1989.

He was awarded an honorary appointment as Commander of the British Empire in 1988 and the Gold Medal of Salzburg in 1987. After a long illness, he died at a hospital in Freilassing, just across the border from Salzburg. *—Joseph Stevenson*

Recommended:

○ **Haydn: Symphonies 85, 88 & 96** / Végh (cond.), Salzburg Camerata Academica / 1997 / Orfeo 468971

○ **Stravinsky, Berg, Bartok** / Végh (cond.), Salzburg Camerata Academica / Capriccio 10300

○ **Mozart: Serenades & Divertimenti** / Végh (cond.), Salzburg Camerata Academica / Capriccio 10185

Maxim Vengerov

b. Aug. 15, 1974, Novosibirsk, USSR

Violinist

In an age where bright, attractive, and talented young violinists seem to emerge as often as new hybrid roses, Maxim Vengerov is a remarkable standout. He took to violin naturally. His family was musical—his mother was the conductor of a 500-voice choir. As a four-year-old he would begin practice after dinner and keep going until he was too tired, then go outside and ride his tricycle to wind down, usually at 3 a.m. His father decided to find the best available teacher, and took him, without appointment, to Galina Turchaninova who, oddly, greeted them by saying, "Oh, I've been expecting you." She took him as a student. Before the first lesson Turchaninova realized a case of mistaken identity had occurred: she thought Maxim was a boy the director of the Conservatory had sent over, who never showed up. Turchaninova was a very strict teacher, and the boy at one point refused to play a note for five straight lessons. She called Maxim's mother in to inform her she was dismissing him as her student. When his mother broke down in tears, Maxim realized he had done wrong, picked up his violin, and played 17 assigned pieces from memory; he had been practicing them even though he had not been playing them. "Very well," said Turchaninova, and agreed to continue his lessons. "A violinist like Maxim is born only once in a hundred years."

When Maxim was seven the government gave permission for the family to move to Moscow where he could be enrolled in the State's top school for talented musical children. His technique was fully polished before he was ten; from them on he needed only to study musical and interpretive issues.

He studied with Zakhar Bron, another great teacher, and at ten won the Junior Wieniawski Competition in Poland. He immediately had concert engagements in Russia and even with western European orchestras such as the Amsterdam Royal Concertgebouw and the BBC Philharmonic. His Moscow debut was in 1985, he first appeared in Germany in 1987, and in London in 1989. He won the prestigious Carl Flesch Competition (named after one of the great violin pedagogues) in 1990, and first appeared in New York with the Philharmonic in 1991.

In 1995, he released his recordings of the Shostakovich and Prokofiev *First Violin Concertos* on the Teldec label. This disc was Best Concerto Recording and Best Record of the Year in the Gramophone Awards, was nominated for two Grammy Awards, and represented an early collaboration with his favorite conductor, Mstislav Rostropovich. He has followed that success with many other recordings, including sequel to his prize winning release, the *Second Violin Concertos* of

Shostakovich and Prokofiev, which won the equally prestigious Edison Award in 1997. He has also won awards as Gramophone Young Artist of the Year and the Ritmo Artist of the Year in Spain.

Maxim Vengerov was named in 1997 as the Envoy for Music of the United Nations' Children's Emergency Fund (UNICEF), the first classical musician to be so appointed. In 1997, he was asked by conductor Kurt Masur to play the season's opening concert of the New York Philharmonic.

In 2000, after a ten-year exclusive contract with Teldec, he signed with EMI, releasing Shchedrin's *Concerto Cantabile* (which was written for him) with Rostropovich conducting. He has played Baroque violin in recitals with harpsichordist Trevor Pinnock, and made his conducting debut with the English Chamber Orchestra.

Maxim Vengerov played the 1727 "Reynier" Stradivarius and, in 2000, with the aid of Mrs. Yoko Nagae Ceschina was able to purchase the famous "ex-Kreutzer" Stradivarius. He uses Jascha Heifetz's bow. He now makes his home in Israel. *—Joseph Stevenson*

Recommended:

- ○ **Brahms: Concerto** / Barenboim (cond.), Vengerov, Chicago SO / 1999 / Teldec 17144
- ○ **Beethoven: Sonatas "Spring" & "Kreutzer"** / Vengerov, Golan (piano) / 2001 / Teldec 89079
- ○ **Prokofiev & Shostakovich: Concertos** / Rostropovich (cond.), Vengerov, London SO / 1997 / Teldec 13150
- ○ **Lalo, Saint-Saëns, Ravel** / Pappano (cond.), Vengerov, Philharmonia / 2003 / EMI 57593
- ○ **Tchaikovsky & Glazunov: Concertos** / Abbado (cond.), Vengerov, Berlin PO / 1995 / Teldec 90881

Marion Verbruggen

b. 1950, Amsterdam, Netherlands

Recorder Player

Marion Verbruggen is known for her magnetic performances, which demonstrate not only her skills as a recorder player, but also her understanding of the repertoire. She makes playing the recorder look effortless, switching easily between the tenor, alto-, and soprano-voiced instruments during any recital or concert. She can also play florid ornaments, crisp accents, and smoothly liquid passages while maintaining ideal breath control. Verbruggen adds subtlety of shading and vibrancy to her music, having what one reviewer called a "flip sense of articulation." After taking up the recorder as a child, Verbruggen studied at the Royal Conservatory in The Hague with Frans Brueggen, graduating cum laude. She was a prizewinner at the first International Recorder Competition in Bruges, and has also received the Erwin Bodky Award for early music and the Nicolai Prize for contemporary Dutch music, showing her appreciation for new music as well as traditional works for the recorder. Verbruggen has even made her own recorder transcription of Bach's *Cello Suites*. Her performing and teaching tours, and her festival appearances, have taken her to Japan and Australia, as well as all over North America and Europe. Tafelmusik, the Orchestra of the Age of Enlightenment, and Akademie für alte Musik Berlin are just a few of the ensembles with which she has appeared as soloist. She has also recorded early chamber music with Gustav Leonhardt, Bob van Asperen, Wieland Kuijken, and Lucy van Dael. Her recordings, primarily on the Harmonia Mundi label, include Vivaldi's recorder concertos; Bach's trio sonatas; *Ay Amor!*, a collection of seventeenth century Spanish music; and two discs of selections from Jacob van Eyck's *Der Fluyten Lust-hof*. *—Patsy Morita*

Recommended:

- ○ **Vivaldi: 7 Concertos** / Goodwin, Toll, Verbruggen, Godburn, Comberti, Holloway / 2001 / Classical Express 3957046
- ○ **Les Plaisirs** / Verbruggen, Cunningham / HM 907093
- ○ **Handel: Sonatas for Recorder** / Koopman, Linden, Verbruggen / 1995 / HM 907151

Giuseppe Verdi

b. Oct. 9, 1813, Le Roncole, Italy, **d.** Jan. 27, 1901, Milan, Italy

Composer: Opera, Choral, Chamber Music

Giuseppe Verdi was to opera in the Italian tradition what Beethoven was to the symphony. When he arrived on the scene some had suggested that effective opera after Rossini was not possible. Verdi, however, took the form to new heights of drama and musical expression. Partisans see him as at least the equal of Wagner, even though his style and musical persona were of an entirely different cast. In the end, both Verdi's popular vein—as heard in the operas *Rigoletto*, *Il trovatore*, and *La traviata*—and his deeper side—found in *Aida*, *Otello*, and *Falstaff*—demonstrate his mastery and far-reaching development of Italian opera.

Verdi showed talent by the age of seven and even played organ at a local church. Around this time he was given an old piano, which he quickly learned to play with proficiency. He moved to Busseto in 1823 and began study the following year with Ferdinando Provesi. By age 15 he had become an assistant church organist and had already started composing. Beginning in 1832, he studied privately with Vincenzo Lavigna in Milan, after the Conservatory there turned him away.

He returned to Busseto and married Margherita Barezzi in 1836. Having achieved publication of some songs, he moved to Milan in 1839 and composed his first opera, *Oberto*. It was a success, though his next effort, *Un giorno di regno*, was an abject failure. Worse, Verdi's wife died during its composition. (Their two children had died in the previous two years.) Stunned and depressed, the composer struggled on to rebound with *Nabucco* (1842) and *I lombardi* (1843). *Macbeth*, *Luisa Miller*, and other operas came in the 1840s, most with great success.

Around 1847, Verdi developed a relationship with soprano Giuseppina Strepponi and the two lived together for many years on Verdi's farm, Sant'Agata, before finally marrying in 1859. In the period 1851–53, the composer wrote three of his most popular operas. *Rigoletto* (1851) and *Il trovatore* (1853) were instant successes, but *La traviata* (1853) was a disappointment at its premiere, though a year later, with minor revisions, it was warmly received. After an extended excursion to Paris in 1853, Verdi returned to Busseto and turned out *Simon Boccanegra* (1857) and *Un ballo in maschera* (1859), both embroiling him in politics, an activity he was already immersed in, since he served in the local parliament and later in national parliament as senator. In St. Petersburg, Verdi's *La forza del destino* premiered in 1862 and *Don Carlos* in Paris in 1867.

Having relocated to Genoa, Verdi composed *Aida* in the years 1870–71. Its Cairo premiere in 1871 was a success, but the composer then gave up opera, at least for a time. His *String Quartet* (1873) and *Requiem* (1874) showed his creative juices were still very much alive. His next opera, *Otello*, came finally in 1886, Verdi working slowly and getting sidetracked revising earlier operas. One more opera came from his pen, *Falstaff*, in 1893, which scored a stunning success. Critical opinion has it that his last three operas are his finest, that the elderly composer became bolder and more imaginative in his later years.

In these later years, Verdi also worked to found a hospital and, in Milan, a home for retired musicians. In 1897, Giuseppina Verdi died and the composer thereafter lived at the Grand Hotel in Milan, finding companionship with retired soprano Teresa Stolz. A year later, his *Quatro pezzi sacri* premiered in Paris. This would be the composer's last work. On January 21, 1901, Verdi suffered a stroke and died six days later. *—Robert Cummings*

OPERA

Aida (1871)

In 1869, a new opera house opened in Cairo with Verdi's *Rigoletto*. The Khedive wanted a more spectacular opera done there, so he commissioned a new work from Verdi. A libretto was prepared by Antonio Ghislanzoni based on a French synopsis by Camille du Locle. Verdi worked very closely with Ghislanzoni on the form and the exact text of the libretto, and at all times urged that conventional forms be abandoned if they did not serve any dramatic purpose. The premiere in Cairo was delayed from January until December 1871 because the set designs and costumes were trapped in Paris during the Franco-Prussian War. The opera was an immediate success, but Verdi continued to revise the score. He composed a full overture for the Teatro alla Scala premiere, but discarded it before the performances took place; however, the extension of the ballet music for the Paris premiere was incorporated into the printed score.

The score to *Aida* is the culmination of all of Verdi's earlier struggle to let the music advance the plot. The Triumphal March and ballet from Act Two are not just display pieces, but an integral part of the celebrations of a victorious army. Except for this scene, *Aida* is really a very intimate opera with most scenes requiring only a couple of characters; in fact, a great deal of the choral singing comes from offstage. The tenor's entrance aria ("Celeste Aida") is a dreamy romance about his beloved Aida, showing the tender side of the warrior. Coming before the tenor has a chance to warm up his voice, it is one of the most difficult entrances in opera. The role of Aida is one of the most gratifying found in any of the Verdi operas. With two important arias plus duets with each of the major characters, the soprano is given the opportunity to display all aspects of her talents. The jealous Amneris joins a long list of important mezzo-soprano roles Verdi created. She is the one who brings various dramatic elements together, and her duet with Radames is one of the great confrontation scenes in opera. Amonasro has the shortest baritone role in any of the late Verdi operas, appearing in only two scenes. He is also the only father in Verdi to put his child in a secondary position; he wants only to win the war with Egypt. The sweep of the score to *Aida* led many early critics to complain that Verdi had given in to the influence of Wagner, but it really is the culmination of the stylistic experiments which were first heard in *La forza del destino*, *Simon Boccanegra*, and *Don Carlo*. With its famous arias and ensembles, *Aida* has become one of the most popular operas ever written, and familiarity only brings new details to the listener's attention. *—Richard LeSueur*

Synopsis:

Act One. The high priest Ramfis tells General Radames that Isis will announce the warrior chosen to lead the Egyptian army against the Ethiopian invading army.

Left alone, Radames dreams that it will be he and also dreams of his beloved Aida ("Celeste Aida"), a slave who is also daughter of the Ethiopian King. Egyptian Princess Amneris, in love with Radames, enters and coyly asks why he is looking so enraptured. When Aida enters, though, Amneris greets her tenderly saying she is neither slave nor servant, but a sister, she becomes suspicious that Aida is her rival. The Pharaoh enters and a messenger brings news of the approaching enemy army. Ramfis announces Radames is the chosen leader, and all, even Aida, tell him to come back a victor. Alone, Aida laments her fate ("Ritorna vincitor") that she must hope for the defeat of either her beloved or her country. In the next scene, Radames is given his armor in a sacred ceremony.

Act Two. In Amneris' apartment, while dancers entertain her, she awaits Radames' triumphant return. Aida enters, and Amneris tricks her (by pretending Radames was killed) into admitting her love, and then turns on her in a fury for presuming that she, a slave, can rival a princess. Aida nearly bursts out that she herself is a princess, but instead pleads in vain for mercy. In the triumphal march, the spoils and captives are brought in; among the captives is Amonasro, Aida's father, who pretends to be a common soldier and says he saw the king's corpse. He pleads for mercy for the defeated Ethiopians, but the priests demand their deaths. Radames, whom the Pharaoh promised anything he might wish for, asks for mercy for the captives and a compromise is reached: Aida and her father will remain prisoners, the rest are set free. Amonasro plots his revenge as, in the final ensemble, Radames is also promised Amneris' hand and, thus, eventually the throne of Egypt. He and Aida are in despair, and Amneris is jubilant.

Act Three. Amneris and Ramfis go to the temple to prepare for the wedding. Aida waits for Radames and longs for her homeland, which she will never see again ("O patria mia"). Amonasro appears and tells her that he is already preparing a counterattack and orders her to find out from Radames which route the Egyptian troops will take. She refuses to betray her beloved, but when he denounces her as no longer his daughter, but the obedient slave of the Pharaohs, she sadly agrees. He promises her she will be restored to her rightful rank, with Radames at her side, if she persuades him to flee with her. Radames enters, and Aida persuades him their only hope of happiness is to flee together to Ethiopia. She asks which route the Egyptians will take, so they can avoid it, and when he answers, Amonasro reveals himself and his true identity. Amneris and Ramfis overhear, and Radames blocks Aida's and Amonasro's capture, but himself surrenders.

Act Four. Amneris determines to save Radames, whom she still loves, and has him brought to her. She offers her help if he will denounce his love for Aida, which he refuses, though rejoicing at the news that though Amonasro was killed in his flight, Aida escaped. Enraged, she sends him back to his prison, but is immediately repentant and cries out in agony for the gods to have pity as she hears the trial taking place. As Radames is condemned to be buried alive in the temple vaults, she launches into a bitter tirade against the priests' cruelty, as they repeat, unmoved, that he will die.

In a double scene, the bottom half is the vault where Radames is buried alive, the upper half the temple. He hopes that Aida will escape to her homeland and be happy, and is amazed to hear her voice. She had a presentiment of his sentence and has come to die with him. The two of them sing of the eternal day they will enjoy together in death, while Amneris tearfully prays above in the temple for Isis to welcome Radames to the peace of paradise. *—Ann Feeney*

Recommended:

- ○ **Verdi: Aida** / Solti (cond.), Price, Vickers, Gorr, Merrill, Tozzi / 1987 / London 417416
- ○ **Verdi: Aida** / Muti (cond.), Caballé, Domingo, Cossotto, Ghiaurov, Cappuccilli / EMI 47271
- ○ **Verdi: Aida** / Perlea (cond.), Milanov, Bjoerling, Barbieri, Warren, Christoff / 1968 / RCA 6652

Attila (1846)

Verdi's *Atilla* dates from what the composer dismissively called his "galley period"; nonetheless, like so many of his early works, the opera is interesting both in its own right and as an early indication of Verdi's mature style. *Atilla* is marked by a steady and rousing energy. While many moments lack elegance, there are also elements of more subtle beauty; the heroine's "Liberamente or piangi" is outstanding, and the "Rome" ensemble is powerful enough to stand with those in Verdi's later works. Odabella's fiery aria and cabaletta in which she determines to kill Attila with his own sword, Foresto's aria lamenting her capture by the Huns, and Attila's own aria describing a vision of an old man barring him from Rome also demonstrate a strong creativity and musical power. While Ezio's music is rather pedestrian, it can be dramatic and effective in the care of the right singer.

The opera is very loosely based on the story of Attila the Hun, and depicts his death at the hands of Odabella, an enemy woman with whom he had fallen in love. Nearly all of the characters, with the exception of the rather bland tenor role, Foresto, present a challenging mix of contradictions. Odabella is bloodthirsty, yet feminine and vulnerable; Attila is a mix of cruelty and generosity; Ezio, the Roman general, is both treacherous and deeply patriotic. Attila's death arouses a mixture of feelings, a sympathy for the treachery surrounding his death, and at the same time a sharing in the sense of victory his demise brings to Odabella, Ezio, and Foresto. *—Ann Feeney*

Synopsis:

Prologue. Attila's forces have conquered and razed Aquileia, and sing in praise of plunder, rape, and their leader. Attila enters and they kneel. He tells them to rise as proud victors, as only the vanquished should be in the dust, and to sing a song of victory. Uldino brings in a group of women, to Attila's surprise and anger, as he had ordered all the inhabitants killed. Uldino explains that their bravery was worthy; they fought alongside their men. Attila asks Odabella, their leader, what could make women so brave, and she proudly answers that Italian women love their country and when it is threatened, will fight to defend it, unlike the barbarian women who remain behind the lines to weep. He admires her response and offers her anything in his power. When she demands her sword back, he gives her his own, and she privately exults at the thought that she will use his own sword to avenge her people upon him.

Attila warmly greets the Roman envoy Ezio as a worthy enemy, who once even defeated his forces, and Ezio asks to speak with him alone. He offers Attila a private pact. The Byzantine emperor is a weak old man, the Roman emperor an untried boy. Attila may have the rest of the universe, but Italy must be Ezio's. Attila refuses and Ezio attempts to resume his role as Roman envoy, but Attila announces he will have nothing to do with such treacherous behavior and he will next conquer Rome. Ezio reminds him of his own previous victory and that he defends Rome.

The next scene is on the Adriatic, in the spot that will become Venice. A group of Christian penitents sing hymns. Foresto leads the survivors from Aquileia and declares they will build another mighty city there. He is distraught, though, at the knowledge that Odabella is in Attila's power ("Ella in poter del barbaro" and says it would be less painful to know she were dead, though he consoles himself with the thought that their new city will be the marvel of both land and sea.

Act One. Outside Attila's camp, Odabella has left the celebrations and weeps for her father and Foresto, whose faces she imagines in the clouds ("Oh, nel fuggente nuvolo"). Foresto appears, in disguise as a Hun, and rebukes her for attending the celebrations of her father's death and destruction of her home, sharing the Huns' feasts and smiling at Attila. She retorts that she has a Biblical precedent, specifically, Judith, who used her wiles on Holofernes and killed him to save her people, and she intends just the same.

In Attila's tent, he awakens from a nightmare ("Mentre gonfiarsi") in which he was at the gates of Rome, ready to enter and conquer, but an old man, dressed in white, blocked the way and threw him to the ground, saying Attila may be the scourge of the world, but this is the dwelling place of God. He shakes off his fears and summons his soldiers and priests. They sing a hymn to Wotan, but Attila freezes at the sound of Christian hymns which he hears approaching. Young children appear, followed by an old man (Bishop Leo, later Pope Leo) whom Attila recognizes as the old man in his dream. When Leo warns Attila away in the same words from the dream, Attila sees this as a divine sign and kneels in submission.

Act Two. Ezio's encampment outside Rome. He angrily reads a letter from the Emperor Valentinian, declaring that Attila and the Romans have concluded a peace treaty and ordering his return. He sadly compares the former glory of Rome with its current state ("Dagli immortali vertici"), but resolves to fight and if necessary, die as the last true Roman, mourned by all Italy ("E gettata la mia sorte"). A band of Huns brings him an invitation from Attila to join the feast celebrating the truce, and when Foresto, still disguised, remains behind and suggests that they take that chance to kill Attila, Ezio agrees.

At the banquet, his Druids warn Attila of impending disaster but he ignores them. Foresto has bribed Uldino to poison Attila's drink and tells Odabella so. Odabella wants to kill Attila herself, and so keeps him from drinking the poison. Foresto reveals that he was the one who did it, and Attila threatens him with dire punishment. Odabella asks that Foresto be made her prisoner. Attila declares his intention of marrying her and making her his queen, and of attacking Rome after all. Odabella persuades Foresto to flee, though he is outraged at her apparent treachery, and the Huns happily anticipate the coming battle.

Act Three. Foresto thinks that Odabella has betrayed him and their revenge ("Che non avrebe il misero"). He and Ezio plan to ambush the Huns. Odabella enters, distraught at the thought of the wedding, but when Foresto sees and reproaches her, she tries to assure him she still loves only him ("Te sol quest'anima"). Attila follows her and seeing her plotting with them, and hearing the approaching Roman soldiers, realizes he has been duped. Odabella stabs him with his own sword, and he dies, asking, "You, too, Odabella?". Ezio, Foresto, and Odabella declare they have been avenged. *—Ann Feeney*

Recommended:

- ○ **Verdi: Attila** / (live) / Sinopoli (cond.), Ghiaurov, Cappuccilli, Zampieri, Visconti, Sramek, Hopferweiser / 2003 / Orfeo 601032

Un ballo in maschera (1859)

Antonio Somma based the libretto of *Un ballo in maschera* on Eugène Scribe's libretto, *Gustave III, ou Le bal masque*, written for Daniel-François-Esprit Auber and first performed in 1833. Although Somma was a skillful poet, Verdi found it necessary to instruct him in the art of developing a libretto. Verdi and Somma first worked together on *Re Lear*, but this was never completed. Facing a deadline for the Teatro San Carlo in Naples, Verdi and Somma forged ahead with *Un ballo in maschera* (at first entitled *Una Vendetta in Domino*), but the Neapolitan censors demanded so many significant changes Verdi withdrew the piece and offered it to the Teatro Apollo in Rome. The Roman censors required, among other things, a change of locale, thus the action of *Un ballo in maschera* takes place in and around Boston, Massachusetts, near the end of the seventeenth century. (In protest to this and other changes, Somma asked that his name be omitted from the program.) It was first performed on February 17, 1859, achieving a great success and within three years playing throughout Europe and in New York. Some modern settings restore Scribe's eighteenth century Swedish setting and characters, a practice Verdi never approved. Scribe's libretto, based in part on historical fact, concerns the 1792 assassination of King Gustave III of Sweden at a masked ball. Although the real murder was most likely politically motivated, Scribe adds the element of jealousy by creating an affair between the King and the assassin's wife. Much of the opera is a straightforward translation of Scribe's libretto.

Verdi's *Un ballo in maschera* is often discussed as an example of his "middle period" and shows the infusing of French elements into Verdi's intense approach to Italian serious opera. Contrapuntal writing permeates the orchestral prelude, which introduces us to the "sympathy" motive we hear in the opening chorus, the conspirator's motive and the melody of Riccardo's first aria, "La revidrà nell'estasi." Throughout the opera the orchestra continues to speak conspicuously, especially in the English horn obbligato in Amelia's first aria and similar passages for the cello in her second. An excellent example of the orchestral colors Verdi achieves is the fortune teller Ulrica's first scene (the second scene of Act One), featuring dark, low woodwinds playing unsettling tritones. Verdi applies old forms to Ulrica's ensuing aria, "Re dell'abisso," which begins in the minor and moves to the major for the cabaletta portion. Later in the scene, Verdi illustrates Ulrica's mysterious powers through her highly chromatic, "Della città all'occaso." *Un ballo in maschera* contains only one duet, one of Verdi's greatest. Occurring in Act II between Riccardo and Amelia, the duet is a succession of declamatory outbursts that create a dialogue, held together by melodic material in the orchestra. A second section further contrasts the characters' melodic personalities and the duet closes with a lively cabaletta, "Oh qual soave brivido." This became a model for Verdi's soprano-tenor duets. *—John Palmer*

Synopsis:

The opera was originally written about King Gustavus of Sweden but, due to censorship, was changed to the story of a colonial governor of Boston. Productions often change the setting back to the original. This synopsis uses the Boston names.

Act One. Riccardo's courtiers wait for him to enter, some of them muttering threats among themselves. He comes in, greets them, and is presented with the list of guests for a masked ball. Seeing Amelia's name, he falls into an amorous reverie: "La rivedro nell'estasi." The crowd leaves and Renato enters to warn Riccardo of plots against his life ("Alla vita") and to urge him to take them seriously. A judge enters, requesting a sentence of banishment against the fortune teller Ulrica, whom Oscar defends as a powerful seeress. Riccardo decides to have some fun and invites the courtiers to join him that night at her hut, in disguise, to determine the truth.

In her hut, Ulrica summons the devil ("Re dell'abisso"), impressing the crowd of onlookers. Riccardo, disguised as a fisherman, is the first of his court to arrive. A sailor, Silvano, asks Ulrica when he will be rewarded for his faithful service to Riccardo. She tells him that soon he will receive money and a promotion. Riccardo scrawls a commission on a piece of paper and slips it and some money into Silvano's pocket. When he reaches for money to pay Ulrica, he discovers both, and he and the crowd are amazed. A servant of Amelia's arrives and asks Ulrica to see her privately. Riccardo remains hidden and is delighted when Amelia confesses to Ulrica her love for him and asks for help in ending it. Ulrica tells her to gather a certain herb at the foot of the gallows at midnight and she leaves. As the rest of the court enters, all disguised, Riccardo, still pretending to be a fisherman and singing a barcarolle, "Di' tu se fedele," asks for his fortune. After telling him not to ask, she finally reveals that he will die soon, killed by the next man to shake his hand. He declares this is a joke or madness. Renato comes in and grasps his hand, and Silvano and the others recognize him and sing his praises.

Act Two. Amelia, heavily veiled, is at the gallows, unhappily gathering the herb ("Ma dell'arido"). Riccardo appears and in their dramatic duet, "Teci io sto," she finally confesses her love, but pleads for his help to remain faithful to Renato. Renato follows Riccardo to warn him of an ambush, but does not recognize the veiled woman. Riccardo agrees to exchange cloaks and flee only if Renato will escort the woman back to the city without trying to find out who she is. The conspirators enter a moment later and, in their confrontation with Renato, Amelia is forced to remove her veil, to their amusement and Renato's heartbroken fury. He tells Sam and Tom to come to his house the next morning.

Act Three. The act opens in their home, where Amelia is trying to claim her innocence. When Renato will not listen, she asks to embrace her son before Renato kills her: "Morro, ma prima." He agrees and, when she leaves, resolves to kill Riccardo, the more guilty party, instead ("Eri tu") because he has broken his trust and their friendship. Sam and Tom arrive and Renato, offering his son as a hostage if necessary, asks to join them. The quarrel over who shall actually kill Riccardo and Renato forces Amelia to draw lots from a vase. She draws his and suspects a plot. Oscar appears with an invitation to the masked ball, and the conspirators agree that that is the time and place.

In the next scene, Riccardo painfully decides to do his duty and send Renato and Amelia away: "Forse la soglia attinse." Oscar arrives with an anonymous letter warning him not to go to the ball, but he decides to do so anyway to see Amelia one last time. At the ball, Renato tricks Oscar into describing Riccardo's disguise. As Amelia and Riccardo are saying farewell, he kills Riccardo. With his dying breath, Riccardo assures the now repentant Renato that Amelia remained chaste, that he was going to send them away, and that he pardons all who took part in the plot. *—Ann Feeney*

Recommended:

- ○ **Verdi: Un Ballo in Maschera** / Leinsdorf (cond.), Price, Bergonzi, Verrett, Merrill, Grist, Flagello / 1967 / RCA 86645
- ○ **Verdi: Un Ballo In Maschera** / Votto (cond.), Callas, di Stefano, Gobbi, Barbieri, Ratti / 1997 / EMI 56320

Don Carlo (1884)

Schiller's *Don Carlos* was first suggested to Verdi in 1850 by the Paris Opéra. Verdi rejected the idea, but continued negotiations led to the composition and production of *Les vêpres siciliennes* in 1855. When the new director of the Paris Opéra, Auguste Perrin, approached Verdi in 1865 concerning a new work for Napoleon III's Universal Exhibition of 1867, Verdi had become tired of the intolerance of Italian theatergoers. Paris seemed to offer more creative potential, a stable company of singers and players, and a large budget. Verdi accepted Perrin's proposition, hoping to score a major success in grand opera.

After considering several librettos, Verdi decided on one by Joseph Méry and Camille du Locle that adapted the dramatic poem *Don Carlos, Infant von Spanien*, by Friedrich Schiller (1759–1805). However, Verdi felt that the story lacked the spectacle necessary for grand opera, and suggested the addition of the immense and colorful coronation scene in Act III. No one has yet successfully explained why Philip should be crowned in the middle of his reign.

Such additions made the work run beyond the maximum time allowed by the Opéra, and numerous cuts were made during the eight months of rehearsals. (These sections remained unknown until 1969.) Finally, the original, five-act, French version of *Don Carlos* was performed at the Académie Impériale de Musique in Paris on March 11, 1867. A revised version in Italian was first staged on January 10, 1884, at the Teatro alla Scala in Milan.

Throughout the composition process, Verdi shaped the libretto to his liking, suggesting meters and occasionally writing lines and drafting scenes such the final one, in which Elizabeth makes her fateful decision. He also added the Philip-Inquisitor duet that is part of Schiller's play. In general the work, especially through the character of the Marquis de Posa, advocates freedom of thought; Verdi may have been reacting in part to Pope Pius IX's "Syllabus of Errors" of 1864, which denounces this very idea.

Conflicts of a political sort abound in *Don Carlos*, in which the titular hero is in love with Elizabeth de Valois, who has become the wife of his father, King Philip II, as the result of a political marriage. Furthermore, the Marquis de Posa, Don Carlos's best friend, is wanted by the Grand Inquisitor because he is a "freethinker." Philip discovers his wife's infidelity and must decide what to do about his son while the Grand Inquisitor asserts his power over him. According to Verdi, the climax of the opera is the auto-da-fé scene in Act Three.

The revised version sets an Italian translation by Angelo Zanardini of the revised libretto by Camille du Locle. Verdi and Zanardini dropped the entire first act, placing all of the action in Spain. One problem that results is that when we hear the "love theme" for Don Carlos and Elizabeth, returning in leitmotiv fashion, we have no context from which to make sense of it; it originally appeared in the abandoned first act. Also, the opening Prelude and Introduction of the original Act One provide important links to the beginning of Act Four. *—John Palmer*

Synopsis:

Act One. French woodcutters and peasants hope for an end to the war between Spain and France. Don Carlos, who has covertly come to France, enters and watches Elizabeth, his fiancée, offer them hope of peace. He sings of her beauty and his hopes for their love ("Io la vidi"). Elizabeth and her page return, lost. Carlos introduces himself as a Spanish nobleman, and Tebaldo goes to find help. Carlos and Elizabeth talk, and he gives her a gift from Carlos, a portrait, which of course is of himself. Both sing blissfully of their future together, but when Tebaldo and French and Spanish courtiers enter, Lerma officially asks Elizabeth for her hand, but for King Philip, not Carlos. She sadly agrees, for the sake of peace.

Act Two. In the cloister of San Juste, a monk prays for the soul of Charles V, Philip's father, who abdicated to die there. Carlos enters and mourns the loss of

Elizabeth to his own father. He thinks he sees in the monk Charles V's ghost, reputed to haunt the cloister. His best friend Rodrigo enters and urges him to help the oppressed people of Flanders. Carlos admits his love for Elizabeth, which Rodrigo urges him to forget in a noble cause, and the two swear loyalty to one another and the cause of freedom ("Dio, che nell'alma"). Carlos wavers momentarily when Philip and Elizabeth enter, but Rodrigo tells him to keep his resolve.

In the palace garden, Eboli amuses the ladies with the Veil Song, about mistaken identities. Rodrigo urges Elizabeth to see Carlos, who is desperately in need of the affection he never received from his father. Eboli thinks Rodrigo is also pleading with her on Carlos' behalf for a non-maternal love. Elizabeth agrees to see Carlos and has her ladies leave them completely alone. Carlos at first calmly asks her to intervene with the king to have him sent to Flanders as viceroy, but soon passionately declares his love, even falling in a faint as she reminds him of her duty. Eventually, he becomes so unbalanced she sarcastically tells him to go kill his father and with bloodied hands, lead his mother to the altar, and he rushes off. Philip enters and is angered to see her unattended. He banishes her lady-in-waiting, the Countess Aremberg, and Elizabeth bids her an affectionate farewell, also indirectly rebuking Philip. The court leaves, but Philip orders Rodrigo to stay, asking why he has not requested, after loyal service, any favors. Rodrigo describes the horrors of martial law in Flanders and passionately pleads for freedom. Philip, though moved by his idealism and bravery in speaking so openly, defends his harsh policies and says Rodrigo will think differently when he knows human nature better. He in turn confides his suspicions of Carlos and Elizabeth, and rejoices that at last he has found a loyal and honest man.

Act Three. Carlos reads a note requesting an assignation, and when a veiled lady appears, greets her with rapture. However, it is Eboli, who realizing his feelings, threatens him. Rodrigo, who has been watching, is ready to kill her, but Carlos stops him. Rodrigo asks Carlos for any potentially incriminating papers he might have, and Carlos, after a moment's suspicion, agrees.

At an *auto-da-fe*, heretics are being burnt. Carlos leads in a group of Flemish deputies who plead for mercy for their country. Philip refuses and Carlos draws his sword, but is disarmed by Rodrigo. Philip creates him a Duke for this service. A voice from Heaven welcomes the heretics' souls.

Act Four. Alone, Philip broods about his loveless marriage and empty life ("Ella giammai m'amo"). The Inquisitor appears and recommends that Carlos be killed. He goes on to demand Rodrigo's life, as well, and Philip at first angrily refuses, but is worn down. After the Inquisitor leaves, Elizabeth bursts in, saying her jewel case has been stolen. Philip has it and opens it to reveal a portrait of Carlos. He accuses her of adultery and she faints. Eboli and Rodrigo rush in to help her at his calls, and when Rodrigo and Philip leave, Eboli remorsefully confesses to Elizabeth that it was she who stole the case and that she herself has been Philip's mistress. Elizabeth orders her to choose exile or a convent, and Eboli curses her own beauty ("O don fatale"), but swears to save Carlos before entering the convent.

Rodrigo visits the imprisoned Carlos and tells him that he has sacrificed his own life to save his friend's ("Per me giunto") by incriminating himself with Carlos' papers. He is shot by an assassin and dies in Carlos' arms. Philip enters to free Carlos, who, almost insane with grief, reveals the truth to the stricken Philip. Eboli appears, having instigated a riot to help save Carlos, and leads him to safety, although the Inquisitor appears to disperse the crowd, which implores God and Philip's forgiveness.

Act Five. At the cloister, Elizabeth sings a farewell to her youth ("Tu che la vanita") and asks the soul of the Emperor to carry her tears to the feet of God. Carlos appears, and they bid one another farewell. Now he only lives to carry out Rodrigo's dreams. They imagine their reunion in Heaven. As he leaves, calling her "mother," Philip, the Inquisitor, and guards appear to arrest him, but the monk from before appears, this time in the Emperor's regalia, and as all exclaim that it is the ghost of Charles V, he leads Carlos inside the cloister. *—Ann Feeney*

Recommended:

○ **Verdi: Don Carlo** / (Italian Version) / Giulini (cond.), Domingo, Caballé, Raimondi, Verrett, Milnes, Estes / 2000 / EMI 67397

○ **Verdi: Don Carlo** / (French Version) / Pappano (cond.), Alagna, Van Dam, Hampson, Mattila, Meier, Halfvarson / 1996 / EMI 56152

Ernani (1844)

In June, 1843, Verdi signed a contract with the Teatro La Fenice, Venice, for a new opera; it would be his fifth work for the stage and his first for a theater other than Milan's La Scala. Verdi persuaded the young poet Francesco Maria Piave to write a libretto based on Victor Hugo's play, *Hernani*, of 1830. *Ernani* would be the first of Verdi and Piave's many collaborations, and was very popular from its first performance on March 9, 1844. *Ernani* represents a turning point in Verdi's career. Because his previous operas had been composed for La Scala, he had grown accustomed to writing works for a large stage appropriate for immense choral scenes. For the significantly smaller La Fenice, Verdi had to develop a more intimate drama focusing on personal conflict and confrontation. To do this, he had to compose in a different way, leading him to alter the traditional set "numbers" of Italian opera.

One of Verdi's innovative strokes happens early in *Ernani*. In the first scene of Act One, Ernani describes his love for Elvira, whom he wants to steal from Don de Silva, her fiancé. The cavatina is organized in the traditional double-aria format, but Verdi extends the first half, "Come rugiada al cespite," distorting its proportions in order to convey Ernani's obsession with Silva. Elvira's cavatina in the next scene is similarly expanded. The later duet between Elvira and Don Carlos is one of the first examples of what would become a common formula for Verdi's duets: the first half is recitative-like in its quick text declamation, with melodic continuity provided by the orchestra. In the second part the characters have contrasting melodies—Carlos' lyrical and Elvira's aggressive—representing their dissimilar feelings. Most impressive is the "Recitative e Terzo" in the middle of Act Two. A disguised Ernani confronts Elvira and Silva; the resulting trio is primarily a combination of solos by Ernani and a duet for Elvira and Ernani. Later in the act, when Ernani makes his foolish, deadly deal with Silva, brass instruments intone a passage that first appeared in the overture and will sound again, at the close of the drama. The high point of the third act is Carlos' aria, "O de' verd'anni miei," in which he, waiting to learn if he has been elected Holy Roman Emperor, tells himself he must change and become an upright person. As the aria progresses, the florid style of Carlos' previous music gives way to broader, more confident expression. Verdi comes full circle in the finale of Act Four, in which Ernani must commit suicide in accordance with his pact with Silva. As Silva reminds him of the deal, the solemn brass chords return to prod Ernani toward his death. *—John Palmer*

Synopsis:

Act One. "Il bandito" ("The Bandit") The act opens in the mountains of Aragon in Ernani's camp of bandits and rebels. They sing a lively drinking song and, when Ernani enters, ask him why he is so pensive. He responds in the aria "Come ruggiada al cespite" that he is in love with Elvira, who is to marry her uncle tomorrow. He asks them to help him carry her off and, at their agreement, sings the cabaletta "Oh, tu che l'alma adora," declaring that their love will make him forget his sorrows.

In Silva's castle, Elvira waits for Ernani and yearns for him to rescue her ("Ernani, involami"). Her ladies bring her gifts from Silva, but she is unimpressed, singing in the cabaletta "Tutto disprezzo" that she disdains anything that does not speak to her of Ernani, while they wonder why a bride should look so sad. They all leave and Carlos enters. He muses on his love for her and, when she orders him to leave, passionately protests his love: "Da quel di." She refuses to leave with him. When he threatens to use force, she seizes his dagger and threatens to kill them both. Ernani enters and he and Carlos confront one another while Elvira begs them both to respect her reputation. Silva and the chorus enter and he pours out his shame at seeing his bride-to-be with two other men: "Infelice, e tu credevi." (Often this is followed by the cabaletta "Alfin che un brando," which Verdi added later.) He challenges both men to a duel. Elvira's bedroom becomes still more crowded when Riccardo enters and reveals the king's identity. In the subsequent ensemble, Silva begs forgiveness for having doubted the king's intentions, and Carlos reveals that he wants Silva's advice in campaigning for the throne of the Holy Roman Emperor. He invites himself to stay and save Ernani (presumably for his own revenge later), dismissing him as "a faithful man of mine." In the following ensemble, Ernani darkly comments that he faithfully follows the king to avenge his father, killed by Carlos' father.

Act Two. "L'ospite" (The Guest) The chorus celebrates the impending marriage. Ernani enters, disguised as a pilgrim, and Silva offers him hospitality. Seeing Elvira enter in her bridal finery, Ernani offers Silva a wedding gift: the king's price on his own head. Silva assures Ernani that as his guest he has the rights of a brother and leads his people out to prepare to defend the castle. Elvira rushes back in, and when she tells Ernani she intended to kill herself at the altar, they fall into one another's arms. Silva returns and is furious, but still hides Ernani. Carlos enters, and when Silva refuses to dishonor his family name by giving up his guest, Carlos takes Elvira with him as a hostage, singing insinuatingly that he wishes her to be happy: "Vieni meco." Silva pleads with Carlos not to take her ("Io l'amo, al vecchio misero") but when Carlos demands Ernani instead, Silva still refuses. When they leave, he brings Ernani (who has heard nothing) out of his hiding place and demands a duel. Ernani will not fight but offers his life freely instead. Pleading to be allowed to see Elvira first, after hearing Carlos has taken her away, he tells Silva that the king wants Elvira for himself. He begs to be allowed to help rescue her before dying. Whenever Silva should blow the hunting horn Ernani gives him, then he, Ernani, will die. Silva, Ernani, and his men swear revenge.

Act Three. "La clemenza" (The Clemency) Carlos and Riccardo are waiting in the tomb of Charlemagne, the first Holy Roman Emperor, for the results of the election. Carlos tells Riccardo to leave and asks that a cannon sound three times if he is elected. Alone, he resolves in the aria "Oh, de verd'anni" that if elected, he will rise on the wings of virtue and his name will conquer the ages. He hides as the conspirators, Silva, and Ernani enter. Ernani's name is drawn as the one to kill the king. Silva offers Ernani the horn back if Ernani gives the task to him, but Ernani refuses. The conspirators sing the stirring "Si ridesti il leon," and the cannon sounds. Carlos emerges and the electors and crowd enter to acclaim him as Emperor. He sentences the conspirators, but Elvira's pleas for mercy remind him of his vow;

instead, he restores Ernani's titles and lands and gives him Elvira's hand. All praise this act of clemency, except Silva, who declares his intent of revenge.

Act Four. "La maschera" (The Masquerader) The guests at Ernani's castle rejoice after the wedding at a masked ball, but are perturbed when a sinister masked figure enters. They leave as Ernani and Elvira enter and sing tenderly of their newfound happiness. Ernani hears the horn and desperately sends Elvira away, feigning pain from an old wound. After a moment, he tells himself the sound was a delusion, but as he turns to follow Elvira, Silva appears and demands Ernani's life. Ernani pleads for mercy ("Solingo, errante, misero") but Silva is implacable, offering Ernani the choice of either a dagger or poison. Ernani hesitates on the brink of refusal, but when Silva calls him a dishonored perjurer, he seizes the dagger. Elvira rushes in, first threatening and then pleading with Silva. In the final trio, "Quel pianto, Elvira, ascondimi," Elvira and Ernani express their desperation, and Silva repeats that he will have no mercy. Ernani stabs himself, but when Elvira seizes the dagger to kill herself, he tells her to love him and to live. Silva gloats as Ernani dies and Elvira collapses. —Ann Feeney

Recommended:

○ **Verdi: Ernani** / Muti (cond.), Domingo, Freni, Ghiaurov, Bruson / 1993 / EMI 47083

Falstaff (1893)

Verdi's last opera, *Falstaff,* was his first comic opera in over 50 years. Verdi and his librettist, Boito, kept the composition secret since Verdi was somewhat less comfortable with comic opera, and he wanted to have the option of canceling the production—even after the dress rehearsal. Boito's libretto has its basis in Shakespeare's *The Merry Wives of Windsor* with additional material from *Henry VI,* parts 1 and 2. The premiere at the Teatro alla Scala was a triumph, but, as always, Verdi continued to make adjustments to the score for both the Rome and Paris premieres; these changes were incorporated into the final version of the score.

A mercurial work, *Falstaff* is an opera that breaks with earlier operatic convention in many ways. While the title character has few moments for vocal display, his two important monologues are marvelous examples of comedy in music. The leading soprano, Alice Ford, has no arias at all. The jealous husband Ford's monologue is a brilliant display piece—but it loses its dramatic punch when removed from the integral and brilliantly paced dramatic whole. Only the two lovers, Nannetta and Fenton, have lyric moments which remind the listener of the younger Verdi; their music is in a simpler style than that for the other characters, perhaps reflecting their relative innocence.

Falstaff sounds musically simple, largely due to the skill with which the composer matched his score to the natural pace of the comedy; yet it is by far Verdi's most complex score—even more so than *Othello,* which sounds on its surface to be far more daunting. The last act finale is the only formal fugue Verdi ever put into an opera (although he had used the form in his *Messa da Requiem*). His use of different meters for the women and the men singing at the same time in the second scene of Act One creates a feeling of controlled mass confusion—exactly what the plot requires at that time. The music for the fairies in Act Three is almost Mendelssohnian in character. Early audiences were often puzzled by this complexity but nearly always gave in to the charm and originality of the score; Verdi's by-then-unassailable reputation was no doubt helpful in opening uncertain ears to his innovations.

The orchestral writing is especially gratifying—and difficult; the amount of nuance required from the ensemble is staggering. The orchestral trills which show the wine warming *Falstaff* after being dunked into the Thames River is one of the finest examples. Another innovative feature of the score is the numerous passages which are sung without any accompaniment; Verdi had done this before, for example in *Luisa Miller,* but it is a much more prominent feature in *Falstaff.*

Falstaff will probably never be performed with the regularity enjoyed by Verdi's other works, largely due to the enormous rehearsal demands required to sufficiently prepare an ensemble cast. However, it is universally recognized as one of opera's finest masterpieces, and the composer's crowning achievement. *—Richard LeSueur*

Synopsis:

Act One, Scene One. At a room in the Garter Inn, Sir John Falstaff carefully seals two letters and starts drinking sherry as Bardolph, Pistol, and Dr Caius come in. A quarrel between Falstaff and Caius ensues over Falstaff's raucous behavior. After ejecting Caius, Falstaff tells the others of his plans to make lucrative liaisons with one of two wives of rich burghers, Mistress Meg Page or Mistress Alice Ford. With only pennies left to his name, he has little choice but to set the dishonorable scheme in motion; honor won't fill his large belly, his "kingdom" as he calls it. When the two refuse to help him, a page is sent out to deliver the letters.

Scene Two. In the garden of Ford, Meg, and Alice compare the love letters each has received; they are identical but for the name of the addressee. They plan to amuse themselves by taking a comic revenge on that "King of paunches." The men, Caius, Bardolph, Ford, Fenton, and Pistol, all range themselves to join in the revenge scheme; all have suffered Falstaff's impetuous gibes. Fenton and Nannetta, Ford's daughter, show their love for one another when the others leave, although Nannetta has been promised, against her will, to Dr Caius.

Act Two, Scene One. At the Garter Inn again Mistress Quickly delivers a message to Falstaff inviting him to meet with Mistress Ford, smothers him with flattery, and leaves. Disguised as Signor Fontana, Ford approaches Falstaff through Bardolph, asking him to intercede with Mistress Ford on his behalf, offering gold as payment. Only too happy to help, Falstaff goes off to bedeck himself in his greatest finery while Ford muses jealously over the faithlessness of women. After some comical bumbling, they go out arm in arm.

Scene Two. In a room at Ford's house, Alice, Meg, and Nannetta confirm their plans for Falstaff. The interview is just beginning, with an outpouring of high flattery, when the sound of the men approaching forces the women to hide him behind a screen. Ford bursts in with the rest of the men. They search unsuccessfully for "the secret lover," and go out to search the rest of the house, while the women hide him in a laundry basket and cover him in dirty clothes. Ford returns to check behind the screen, and discovers instead Fenton and Nannetta embracing. When he again leaves in a fury, Alice has the servants empty the laundry basket into the Thames running below.

Act Three, Scene One. Outside the inn, a gloomy Falstaff, after thoroughly reviling the world, starts to regain his courage with the help of ample wine. Dame Quickly arrives, and, after restoring his confidence in her, arranges for Falstaff to again meet Alice Ford. This time the plan is that he should dress himself as the Black Huntsman and await the Mistress at midnight in Windsor Park. The others come forward as Falstaff retires to the inn, sorting out their own parts in the tragicomedy to come.

Scene Two. By Herne's great oak in Windsor Park, all the conspirators assemble, each in a different fantastical disguise, then hide themselves. Falstaff arrives and Alice presents herself to him "O shining love!," but as they come together, Meg's voice is heard crying out; the witches are coming! In terror, Falstaff throws himself at the ground, afraid that he'll die if he sees the supernatural beings. The "fairies" stumble upon him, and a horde of children disguised as elves and imps set about tormenting him with little kicks, pinches, pokes, jabs, and bites until he fully repents his wicked ways. To quicken the love between Nannetta and Fenton, the women confuse Caius and Fenton in their disguises. Caius is shocked when the masks come off to discover that he's been fooling around with Bardolph. The witty shock of this finally makes Ford agree to the union of Fenton and Nannetta. Only Falstaff is excluded from the happy ending, although he can at least proclaim: "Everything in the world's a jest; We are all figures of fun." —*Donato Mancini*

Recommended:

○ **Verdi: Falstaff** / Karajan (cond.), Gobbi, Schwarzkopf, Merriman, Panerai, Barbieri, Moffo, Alva / 1999 / Angel 67162

○ **Verdi: Falstaff** / Abbado (cond.), Terfel, Pieczonka, Hampson, Röschmann, Diadkova / 2001 / DG 471194

○ **Verdi: Falstaff** / Solti (cond.), Evans, Freni, Simionato, Merrill, Kraus / 1989 / Decca 417168

La forza del destino (1862)

For nearly two years after the premiere of *Un ballo in maschera,* Verdi seemed uninterested in composing. No doubt his mind was occupied with other duties, both domestic (he married Giuseppina Strepponi) and political (he was nominated, in 1861, as a deputy in the new Italian parliament). In late 1860, a commission from the Imperial Theater of St. Petersburg prompted Verdi to break his silence as an artist.

Francesco Maria Piave based his four-act libretto on the 1835 Spanish play, *Don Alvaro, o La fuerza del sino,* by Angel di Saavedra (1791–1865), who was influenced by Victor Hugo. Into this, Verdi inserted a scene from Friedrich Schiller's (1759–1805) *Wallenstein's Camp,* as translated by Andrea Maffei, which the composer had long wished to set. By November 1861, *La forza del destino* was complete except for the orchestration, which Verdi usually finished after experiencing the acoustics of the proposed theater. The final product is Verdi's most sprawling, dramatically intricate opera.

The premiere of *La forza del destino* (The Force of Destiny) was planned for the first part of the 1861–1862 season, but the prima donna became ill and the production was postponed. The premiere, on November 10, 1862, was not as successful as Verdi had wished, and the next year he began altering the score. On February 27, 1869, a revised version with additions by Antonio Ghislanzoni, was first performed at the Teatro alla Scala in Milan.

Verdi and Piave create a tangled tale in which the characters come together through coincidence. Melitone and Preziosilla provide asides and comic elements as the three main characters, Donna Leonora, Don Carlo, and Don Alvaro play out their tragic parts. The chorus, appearing in nearly every scene, is of greater importance than in any other of Verdi's operas and has some of the most famous numbers in the opera, including, "Compagni, sostiamo" (new for 1869) and "Rataplan, rataplan," both in Act Three.

One of the major differences between the 1862 and 1869 versions is the overture. In the first version, we find a concise prelude. Verdi expanded this in 1869 to a lengthy assemblage of melodies from the opera, stressing a three-note motive that is often called the "fate" motive, and a rising, four-note scale associated with Leonora. Verdi was not concerned with overall structure in this potpourri of tunes. The finale of the last act underwent the greatest changes between versions. In the first, Alvaro kills Carlo in a duel, Leonora enters to be reunited with Alvaro only to be stabbed by the dying Carlo, and Alvaro throws himself from a mountaintop (this was not the "lighthearted" Italian opera the St. Petersburg audience expected). In the revised version (more likely to be staged today), the duel occurs offstage, as does Carlos' stabbing of Leonora, who returns to the stage for the trio, "Non imprecare, umiliati." As the mode shifts from minor to major, Alvaro exclaims that he is redeemed. *—John Palmer*

Synopsis:

Act One. The Marchese affectionately says good night to his daughter, Leonora, but is concerned that she seems so unhappy, despite the fact that he has given her time to forget Alvaro, whose mixed Indian-Spanish ancestry makes him unworthy in the Marchese's eyes. After he leaves, she is troubled by her conscience, as she plans to elope with Alvaro that night. Alvaro arrives and, after a moment's vacillation, she decides to go through with the elopement. However, the Marchese appears and denounces them both. Alvaro swears that Leonora is innocent and throws down his pistol to surrender. It goes off, killing the Marchese, who curses Leonora as he dies.

Act Two. Carlo is pursuing Leonora and Alvaro (who have been separated and believe each other dead). He has arrived in an inn disguised as Pereda, a student: "Son Pereda, son ricco d'onore." Leonora has hidden in the same inn and overhears him telling the story as though it happened to a friend, and he says that Alvaro returned to the Americas. Preziosilla, the gypsy, who secretly tells him that she has seen through his disguise, sings of the glory of war.

Act Three. Leonora travels to a monastery where she hopes to take refuge ("Son giunta"). At first barred by Fra Melitone, she convinces the Padre Guardiano to let her stay, dressed in a monk's habit, in the abandoned hermit's cave. She will see nobody until she herself is near death, when she may ring the bell to summon him. She prays to the Virgin, "La Vergine degli Angeli," and the monks utter a curse on anyone who disturbs the hermit's refuge.

Act Four. Alvaro (in disguise) fights in the Spanish army and prays for death to end his suffering: "O tu che in seno." He's had bad luck before the opera even began, too, as he now reveals: his mother was the last of the royal Incan line, and she and his father were executed for trying to regain her throne. He himself lives only because his true lineage is unknown. He rescues Carlo (also in disguise) from a gambling fight and they swear friendship. In battle, Alvaro is wounded and entrusts his papers to Carlo to burn: "Solemne in quest'ora." Carlo's suspicions are aroused, and after fighting his conscience ("Urna fatale") doesn't open the papers but searches Alvaro's other belongings. He finds Leonora's portrait and is delighted to hear that Alvaro will recover from his injuries, so that he may kill him himself. He challenges Alvaro to a duel, but Alvaro protests that he had no intention of harming Carlo's father and that he did not seduce Leonora. Carlo reveals that she is still alive, but sardonically rejects Alvaro's joyous proposal that together they find her and that Carlo bless their marriage. He plans to find her, but to kill her. Alvaro then draws his sword, but they are separated by a patrol. Alvaro decides to enter a monastery. After he has left, soldiers and peasants enter and Preziosilla leads a lively song and dance. Fra Melitone preaches against such revelry instead of repentance, angering some of the soldiers, but Preziosilla distracts them with another song.

Act Five. The final act takes place at the monastery, which should look familiar, as it's the one Leonora entered. Alvaro is regarded as a saint by the local beggars, but not by Melitone, who considers him insane and describes his strange, brooding behavior. Carlo appears and insists on fighting Alvaro, who begs to be left in peace. He meant no harm to anyone and now is a priest: what good would bloodshed do? Carlo accuses him of cowardice and insults his ancestry, but Alvaro even kneels to ask to be left alone. Carlo slaps him and Alvaro, finally aroused to lasting anger, seizes a sword and they rush out to fight. Meanwhile, Leonora is praying for peace ("Pace, pace, mio Dio") when she hears the sound of fighting, and she reenters her cave, repeating the curse on any disturbing that refuge. Alvaro comes in, raving to himself that he has again unwillingly killed one of Leonora's family. Carlo is heard off-stage shouting for a priest to hear his confession and save his soul. Alvaro considers himself no longer sanctified and runs to the cave to ask the hermit to hear the dying man's confession. Leonora, without entering, says she cannot summon the hermit, but when Alvaro insists that a man's soul is at stake, she at last rings the bell. Emerging a moment later, she and Alvaro recognize one another, and he tells her that her brother is dying. She runs to find him and Alvaro rails against the destiny that let him find Leonora again only when he has just killed her brother. She screams off-stage and is supported by Padre Guardiano. Carlo was unforgiving and stabbed her as she knelt to embrace him. Alvaro (with some justification) curses fate, but Leonora and the Padre tell him instead to kneel and pray: "Non imprecare." Unable to resist her wish, he does so, but as Leonora dies, he murmurs, "Dead," as the Padre insists she has "Ascended to God." (In the earlier Moscow version, Leonora dies before the Padre Guardiano arrives, and Alvaro, cursing himself as nothing but destruction, calls for Hell to swallow him and for the world to be destroyed as he throws himself over a conveniently placed cliff.) *—Ann Feeney*

Recommended:

- ○ **Verdi: La Forza del Destino** / Levine (cond.), Price, Domingo, Milnes, Cossotto, Bacquer / 1998 / RCA 39502
- ○ **Verdi: La Forza del Destino** / Serafin (cond.), Callas, Tucker, Tagliabue, Rossi-Lemeni, Nicolai, Capecchi / 1997 / EMI 56323

I Vespri siciliani (Les vêpres siciliennes) (1855)

In February 1852, Verdi signed a contract to provide Paris with a grand opera to be staged in 1855, during the Universal Exhibition. It is clear from the contract that the composer knew himself to be a valuable commodity. He laid out a strict timetable for delivery of libretto and music and stipulated there would be three months rehearsal time allotted to his pieces and no other new work that season. Verdi requested a text by Eugène Scribe (1791–1861), Giacomo Meyerbeer's chief librettist. Verdi and Scribe elected to adapt an old libretto, entitled *La Duc d'Albe*, written in 1838 by Scribe and Charles Duveyrier (1803–1866) for Jacques Halévy (1799–1862). Halévy never set the text, and Gaetano Donizetti (1797–1848) began working on it in 1839, but failed to finish. Verdi accepted the scenario but wanted some changes, including moving the action from the Netherlands to Palermo, Sicily, at the time of the 1282 revolt against the French. Verdi fashioned the libretto to his liking, especially the fourth act. He was intent on having scenes of great spectacle, such as those in some of Meyerbeer's operas, but he did not get them.

Les vêpres siciliennes was first performed at the Académie Impériale de Musique in Paris on June 13, 1855, to critical acclaim. The first Italian version, translated by Eugenio Caimi, was distorted by the requirements of the Italian censors and entitled *Giovanna de Guzman.* Subsequent performances as *I vespri siciliani* retained most of Caimi's text and this is the Italian version performed today.

Consisting of themes from the opera, Verdi's overture, occasionally performed in concert, is his longest and has elements of sonata form. It is in two parts, the first focusing on "death" motives and Hélène's first aria, and the second on the duet for Henri and Montfort in Act Three. Verdi opens the drama with a stirring double chorus contrasting the occupying French soldiers with the Sicilian people through their disparate music. Other highlights include the unusual duet for Montfort and Henri that forms the finale of Act One. Montfort's opening melody is "conversational" in that it does not fall into short segments, but extends to 30 measures while modulating. The characters' mutual hatred comes through in their themes. Verdi exploits "local color" in the music beginning Act Two, which evokes the movement of the boat on which Procida arrives, and a barcarolle later in the act, depicting a boat full of French soldiers. Procida's entrance aria, "Et toi, Palerme," is the most famous number from the opera and features exquisite orchestration. In the central section, as Procida describes his travels from country to country, the harmony migrates from place to place. The Trio for Hélène, Henri, and Procida in Act Five is a high point. The huge choral finale of Act Three is typical of French grand opera. *—John Palmer*

Synopsis:

Act One. In the public square, French soldiers are drinking, watched sullenly by Sicilians. Elena, in mourning for her brother whom Monforte had executed, appears on her way from church and is forced to sing for the soldiers. She uses the opportunity to sing about a ship in a storm, where the sailors' fate is in their own hands, a line she repeats to incite an uprising. Monforte ends it merely by appearing, and disperses the crowd. Arrigo, who has been tried for treason but unexpectedly freed, appears and loudly tells Elena that the French were too cowardly to punish his unabashedly rebellious acts. Monforte calmly says it was his own clemency that saved Arrigo, sends Elena and the others away, and questions Arrigo about his family. Arrigo answers, albeit defiantly, that he never knew his father, but was raised by his mother and Elena's brother, whom he calls a hero. Monforte urges him to join the French army; Arrigo refuses and defies Monforte's orders not to associate with Elena.

Act Two. Outside Palermo, Procida sings of his oppressed country ("O tu Palermo") and his attempts to raise foreign aid. Arrigo and Elena meet him and they plan a revolt. Arrigo declares his love for Elena, who says she will marry him when he has avenged her brother. An officer comes with an invitation for Arrigo to attend Monforte's masked ball, and when he refuses, he is arrested. Procida stirs more Sicilian anger by covertly encouraging French soldiers to abduct some Sicilian girls. A boat of guests to the ball goes by, including French officers and Sicilian women.

Act Three. Monforte reads a letter from a woman he himself had abducted. She tells him that after she fled, she bore a son, Arrigo, whom she raised to hate him. Monforte sings of his loneliness and yearning for his son's love: "In braccio alle dovizie." When Arrigo is brought in, he is still defiant, but surprised at his treatment; Monforte's men act as though they were his servants. In a dramatic duet, "Mentre contemplo," Monforte tries, without mentioning their relationship, to earn Arrigo's affection by reminding him that he, Monforte, saved Arrigo from a rebel's fate, and finally shows him the letter. Arrigo realizes that he has lost his chance of marrying Elena, and though he admits he is drawn to Monforte, declares he cannot give his mother's persecutor a son's love. Monforte pleads in vain for Arrigo to accept a sacred paternal love. At the ball after a ballet, Arrigo discovers that the conspirators plan to kill Monforte, and tries to persuade Monforte to leave without explaining why. Unsuccessful, when Elena prepares to stab Monforte, Arrigo shields him with his own body, saving him. His fellow Sicilians denounce him.

Act Four. Imprisoned, Elena and Procida await execution. Arrigo is permitted to see them, and as Elena is brought to him, he speaks of his desolation at having lost her love: "Giorno di pianto." She mocks his frenzied declaration that he is innocent, but when he explains that while he saved his father's life, he considers any filial duty paid and will now rejoin their efforts, she admits her renewed love: "Arrigo, ah parli." Monforte appears and orders their immediate executions, unless Arrigo acknowledges him by calling him "Father." Procida is secretly told that the weapons for the revolt have arrived. Elena exhorts Arrigo to remain firm, but seeing the scaffold and hearing monks pray for those about to die, he gives in. Monforte not only releases the prisoners, but announces that Arrigo and Elena will marry to mark the amnesty. Procida tells her to agree, saying it will bring them victory.

Act Five. Elena sings of her happiness ("Merce, dilette amiche") and hopes for peace as she accepts gifts of flowers, and she and Arrigo sing of their love. Procida whispers to her that the wedding bells will signal a massacre of the French. She tries to call off the marriage without explaining, but Monforte overrides her and himself orders the bells rung. The Sicilians advance on him and the rest of the unarmed French as the curtain falls. *—Ann Feeney*

Recommended:

○ **Verdi: I Vespri Siciliani** / Levine (cond.), Arroyo, Domingo, Milnes, Raimondi / 1999 / RCA 63492

Luisa Miller (1849)

The last important opera before Verdi's great middle period, *Luisa Miller* highlights the composer's efforts to move beyond the strict operatic conventions of the 1840s. It dates from a time in Verdi's career during which the public was less receptive to his work—a period which saw the premiers of *Il Corsaro, La battaglia di Legnano* and *Stiffelio,* none of which have any significant performance history. However, *Luisa Miller* has managed to remain on the perimeter of the repertoire since its premiere in Naples on December 8, 1949.

As was typical at the time, Verdi's librettist, Salvadore Cammarano, based *Luisa Miller* on a preexisting dramatic work, namely Schiller's play, *Kabale und Liebe* (Schiller's plays were a very popular source for opera librettos, and Verdi had already used his *Die Rauber* as the basis for *I Masnadieri*). The plot revolves around a pair of lovers, Rodolfo and Luisa, whose desire to marry is in conflict with the political and personal aspirations of Rodolfo's father, the somewhat nefarious Count Walter.

The overture to *Luisa Miller* is of interest. Except for a slight quickening of the tempo at the very end, the entire piece is in one tempo and based on single theme from the third act; the thematic development Verdi brings to this single theme is rare at this time. The grander overtures to *I vespri siciliani* and *La Forza del destino* cannot match the concentrated intensity of this masterpiece.

Verdi begins to depart from tradition in other ways as well. In most operas of the period, the curtain opens to a chorus and then a two-part (slow-fast) aria sung by a major character. However, in *Luisa Miller,* the introduction leads directly into the first aria which, although in the traditional two parts, contains numerous choral interjections. Aside from condensing what would have traditionally been two set pieces into one more compact statement, this device serves to embed the aria itself more firmly into the texture of the work, and harder to excerpt. Similarly, Rodolfo's great Act Two aria, "Quando le sere al placido," is actually a portion of the Act Two finale and, though it is easy to pull the slow section out of context, the cabaletta (the faster, contrasting section) is harder to remove. This style of embedding the arias into the entire fabric of the opera will reach its zenith in the operas of Puccini.

Verdi followed convention in casting the important roles; the soprano and tenor are the young lovers, and the father is a baritone. The role of Miller is in that great line of baritone fathers which brought out Verdi's best writing, beginning with *Nabucco* and continuing through *Rigoletto,* Germont (*La traviata*), and ending with Ford (*Falstaff*). The "other woman" is, of course, a mezzo-soprano.

The vocal writing of the opera does not make unusal demands on the singers, but they must all have some degree of flexibility and good dynamic control. There is also a long unaccompanied quartet preceding the Act Two finale which can prove very difficult if any of the performers have pitch problems. Although first heard at the Metropolitan Opera in 1929, it was the 1967 production there which brought the beauties of this score to public attention and established it as a permanent repertoire work. *—Richard LeSueur*

Synopsis:

Act One. Outside Miller's home, on Luisa's birthday, her friends greet her, and she is impatient for "Carlo," her beloved, to appear. He does so and they pledge their love as Miller expresses his unease. Everyone leaves for church, and Miller is stopped by Wurm. Wurm had asked Miller before for Luisa's hand, but Miller agreed to the match only if Luisa consented, and he retierates his belief that the choice of a spouse is sacred, and he is her father, not her tyrant ("Sacra e la scelta"). Wurm angrily informs him that "Carlo" is the son of Count Walter, and can hardly have honorable intentions towards a peasant girl, and Miller vents his fears ("Ah, fu giusto").

Inside the castle, the Count broods that God has punished him with an ungrateful son, though he would give his life to see Rodolfo happy and powerful. He sends for Rodolfo and orders him to marry his cousin Federica, the well-connected young widow that he has chosen. Federica is in love with Rodolfo and alone together, they share happy childhood memories, but he tells her that he loves another. She is grieved and angry, and he begs her forgiveness for hurting her.

In Miller's house, Miller tells Luisa of her lover's true identity, but Rodolfo comes in and declares that Luisa is his wife. The Count and his retinue come in, and he insults Luisa, causing Miller to respond in kind ("Fra mortali non opressa"). Miller and Luisa are placed under arrest, despite Rodolfo's pleas, and it is not until he threatens to reveal how the Count came to power that they are released.

Act Two. At home, Luisa is told that Miller has just been covertly taken away to the castle. She is about to follow when Wurm enters and tells her she can save her father's life only by writing a letter to him, Wurm, saying that she never loved Rodolfo, only his position, and asking Wurm to elope with her. She prays for help, but finally writes at his dictation. He tells her to come with him to the castle to tell Federica the same story.

The Count tells Wurm that their crime, killing his cousin, the former Count, before he could marry and father an heir, was witnessed by Rodolfo. The Count declares the deed, which he committed only for his son's sake, has brought him no happiness, only fear and guilt. Federica comes in, and Wurm makes Luisa repeat that she never loved Rodolfo. Luisa burns with jealousy to see her rival's relief and joy, while Wurm and the Count resolve to pursue this good fortune.

Rodolfo receives the letter Luisa wrote, and he sadly recalls their love, which he believes to have been an illusion ("Quando le sere al placido"). He sends for Wurm, who evades the duel Rodolfo demands. The Count pretends to yield and tells Rodolfo he is free to marry Luisa. At Rodolfo's story of betrayal, the Count suggests that Rodolfo show his contempt by marrying Federica. Rodolfo, in despair, agrees.

Act Three. In Miller's house again, Luisa and Miller are reunited. She shows her father a letter she has written to Rodolfo, saying she has sworn not to tell the truth, but death will release her from that vow. She is confident of God's forgiveness, but her father is horrified by this suicide note and tells her it would kill him, too. She agrees to leave the village with him, instead, and they sing of how even as homeless beggars, they will have each other ("Andrem, raminghi e poveri"). He leaves to sleep, and she prays. Rodolfo enters, telling the servant who accompanies him that he will await his father there. He poisons a glass of water, and after Luisa admits, without defending herself, that she did write the letter to Wurm, he drinks some, giving her the rest. He then tells her they will die together, and she, freed of her oath, tells the truth. He curses the day he was born and his father, and she pleads with him not to blaspheme. Miller comes in and Luisa bids him a tender farewell as she dies. The Count, with Wurm and the rest of his followers, enters, and as he dies, Rodolfo kills Wurm, and exclaims "Now see your punishment" as he falls dead at his father's feet. *—Ann Feeney*

Recommended:

○ **Verdi: Luisa Miller** / Maag (cond.), Pavarotti, Caballé, Milnes / Decca 000064612

○ **Verdi: Luisa Miller** / Cleva (cond.), Bergonzi, Moffo, Verrett, Tozzi / 1965 / RCA 6646

Macbeth (1847)

Giuseppe Verdi was always fascinated by the plays of Shakespeare; he wrote three operas based on them, and contemplated a fourth (based on *King Lear*) but was never able to find the proper libretto. *Macbeth* was the earliest of these Shakespeare adaptations, and a work which never quite satisfied the composer. The first version of the opera premiered in 1847 in Florence, but the version best known today is the revision the composer made for the 1865 Parisian revival. The changes include a new aria for Lady Macbeth in Act Two, the addition of a ballet scene for the witches, and the removal of Macbeth's death scene. In nearly every scene, there are at least some minor changes.

There is a famous letter in which Verdi states that Lady Macbeth must not have a beautiful voice, but must portray the evil of her character. It is difficult to reconcile this statement with the music he composed for her, which is some of the most florid, difficult, and dramatic of his career. Her entrance begins with a spoken reading of the letter from Macbeth, followed by a recitative. In her Sleepwalking scene, we find Verdi at his most dramatic, with the vocal line being more spoken than sung, yet at the end she is required to rise to a high D flat as softly as possible. The title role, while not as complex, requires considerable dramatic flair, as well as the bel canto line to bring off his aria, "Pietà, rispetto, amore." Of the secondary characters, Macduff and Banquo are most notable, and both have lovely arias.

Shakespeare's three witches become a three-part chorus whose music inspires more laughter than fear in this setting. Choruses denouncing tyranny often brought out the best in Verdi, and so it is not surprising that the patriotic choral outcry before Macduff's aria is among the strongest pieces in the work. The ballet music written for the premiere of the revised version in Paris is usually omitted today without much harm to the score.

The performance history of *Macbeth* was relatively sparse until it was revived in German in the 1930s; since that time the opera has had continued success, although it did not reach the Metropolitan Opera until 1959. Part of the problem was the casting of Lady Macbeth. Although it asks for high Cs, and even a D flat, in the Sleepwalking scene, the role lies very low for most sopranos. The early German revivals often cast the role with a mezzo-soprano; today the role is entrusted to any singer who feels that she can adequately portray the role. Two of the greatest singing actresses of the twentieth century had a great success with the role: Maria Callas (although she only sang it five times) and Leonie Rysanek (who sang the Metropolitan Opera premiere). In its best moments, *Macbeth* conveys all of the drama of Shakespeare and melds it with some of Verdi's finest music. *—Richard LeSueur*

Synopsis:

Act One. Witches congregate on a heath and boast of their recent deeds. They disappear when Macbeth and Banquo enter after successfully quelling a rebellion. The witches reappear, greeting Banquo as the father of kings, and Macbeth as Thane of Glamis and Cawdor, and future king. They vanish again as a troop of messengers enters to tell Macbeth that he is now named the Thane of Cawdor. Banquo fears a hellish influence and Macbeth tells himself he will not yield to his thoughts of bloody conquest to the throne.

In Macbeth's castle, his wife reads his news of the witches' prophecy, and expresses her impatient ambition ("Vieni, t'affretta"). At the news that the king will stay in the castle that very night, she calls on hell's powers to help her ("Or tutti sorgete"). Macbeth arrives and though daunted, finally agrees to kill the king, who arrives with his cortege. Macbeth returns to the stage alone, and after hesitating again ("Mi si affaccia"), goes to commit the crime. Lady Macbeth waits for him, and after the murder, he is tormented by his conscience, though she chides this as cowardice, and goes to smear the guards with the king's blood to incriminate them before leading him back to bed. Macduff and Banquo enter and Macduff goes into the king's room to awaken him, and the murder is discovered. In the dramatic ensemble, "Schiudi, inferno, la bocca," all unite in cursing the murderer.

Act Two. Macbeth, now king, is troubled by the thoughts that Banquo's sons will reign after him, and he and Lady Macbeth decide that family must die. She sings of the darkening night and the voluptuous joy of power ("La luce langue"). In a wood outside the castle, a group of assassins wait for Banquo and his son. They enter, Banquo troubled by thoughts of impending doom and remembers the night of Duncan's murder ("Come dal ciel"). He is killed but his son escapes. At that evening's banquet, Lady Macbeth sings a toast. One of the assassins brings Macbeth news of Banquo's death and the son's escape. Macbeth, to the company, feigns ignorance of Banquo's whereabouts, but suddenly sees Banquo's ghost, and recoils in horror, raving about the bloody corpse he sees. The guests and his wife see nothing, and while she rebukes him again for cowardice, they voice their suspicions, and Macduff determines to leave Scotland.

Act Three. The witches, in their cave, prepare a spell and dance. Macbeth arrives and demands to know the future. The visions they show him warn him of Macduff, though they tell him no man born of a woman can harm him and that he will be undefeated until Birnam Wood moves against him. They then show him a procession of kings, Banquo's descendants, and he faints. Lady Macbeth arrives, and they resolve to kill Macduff and his entire family.

Act Four. On the border between Scotland and England, refugees are gathered and sing of their oppressed country ("Patria opressa"). Among them is Macduff, who mourns the death of his family and the fact that he was not present to protect them ("Ah, la paterno mano"). Malcolm appears with his army and he and Macduff prepare to invade Scotland to overthrow Macbeth, Malcolm ordering his men to cover themselves with tree boughs as camouflage.

In the castle, Lady Macbeth relives their crimes as she sleepwalks ("Una macchia"). Macbeth is alone, brooding that his only legacy is hate ("Pieta, rispetto, amore"). He is told of Lady Macbeth's death, which he calls as meaningless as life itself. His retainers rush in to tell him that Birnam Wood is moving and they vow to win or die in battle. In the battle, Macduff and Macbeth fight, and Macduff reveals that he was not born from his mother, but torn from her womb. They exit, fighting and Macbeth is killed. (In some versions, he dies onstage ("Mal per me"). Malcolm is acclaimed as king and Macduff as Scotland's savior. *—Ann Feeney*

Recommended:

- ○ **Verdi: Macbeth** / Leinsdorf (cond.), Warren, Rysanek, Bergonzi / 1959 / RCA 4516
- ○ **Verdi: Macbeth** / Schippers (cond.), Nilsson, Taddei, Prevedi / 1991 / Decca 433039

Nabucco (Nabucodonosor) (1842)

Nabucco was Verdi's first great success. It is linked not only with the composer's history but also with the history of Italy. The "hit tune," the chorus "Va, pensiero," (Fly, my thoughts) became the unofficial hymn of Italian national liberation and reunification, and even today almost holds the status of national anthem. It was so strongly associated with Verdi that the crowds at his funeral procession spontaneously began to sing it as the cortege passed through the crowded streets of Rome.

Verdi at this time in his life was deeply discouraged and unhappy, due both to personal tragedy and to a lack of musical success, and it was the impresario Merelli who forced the libretto upon him. When Verdi tossed the text on a table, intending to have nothing to do with it, it opened at the words "Va, pensiero," and he read it, and then read the rest; at their next meeting, Merelli was able to persuade Verdi to continue his musical career with a setting of this libretto. So it's not that surprising that this one section has somewhat overshadowed the rest of the work, but the whole has as much to offer as this one part.

Abigaille is notorious as a killer role for the soprano daring enough to take it on—the voices it is said to have ruined include that of Giuseppina Strepponi, Verdi's lover and later his wife—but the rewards it offers are enough to tempt many a singer. The role has one of opera's most dramatic entrances, a beautiful aria and stunningly forceful cabaletta, a striking duet with Nabucco, and a death scene that can steal the show. Even Abigaille's recitatives are full of energy and virtuosic effect; one contains a two-octave leap to a high C. The role of Nabucco runs the gamut of emotions, from haughty belligerence to tender paternal love to insanity to humble faith in the God of the Hebrews, expressed in highly effective, if not yet completely individualized music. Zachary is the musical and dramatic predecessor to Procida in *I Vespri Siciliani.* Driven by patriotic fervor, he emerges in music that alternates between stirring exhortation, religious reflection, and hints of the single-minded ferocity that was to emerge again still later in *Ernani* and in the Inquisitor in *Don Carlo.* *—Ann Feeney*

Synopsis:

Act One: Jerusalem. At the Temple of Solomon, the Hebrews lament their recent defeat by Nabucco and pray for protection. Zaccaria exhorts them to hope ("Sperate... d'Egitto la"), recalls God's deliverance in the past, and reminds them that they have a hostage, Fenena. Zaccaria and the crowd leave and Ismaele and Fenena express their love. When he had been in Babylon as an ambassador, both Fenena and Abigaille had fallen in love with him, but it was Fenena whose love he returned and who rescued him when he was imprisoned. He promises to help her escape, but Abigaille appears, in armor, at the head of a troop of Babylonian soldiers. She taunts Ismaele but then promises him and his people safety in return for his love, which he refuses. The priests and Hebrew soldiers rush in with the news that Nabucco is approaching, and Nabucco rides on horseback into the temple itself. He contemptuously dismisses Zaccaria's warning that he is in the house of God, and orders his soldiers onward, but when Zaccaria seizes a dagger to kill Fenena, he halts them and dismounts, though ordering the Hebrews to kneel before him. Zaccaria is ready to kill Fenena, but Ismaele disarms him and frees her. As the Hebrews curse Ismaele, Nabucco orders his men to sack and raze the Temple.

Act Two: L'Empio" (The Sinner). The Hebrews are enslaved and Fenena is ruling as regent in Nabucco's absence. Abigaille has discovered that she is not Nabucco's daughter, but a slave's. In her aria "Anch'io dischiuso" she remembers the days when she was compassionate to the woes of others, but now is only capable of feeling rage, which will descend upon everyone, even herself. The High Priest of Baal tells her that Fenena has freed the captives and that if she, Abigaille, will seize power, the priests and nobles will back her, having already spread the rumor that Nabucco has been killed in battle. In the cabaletta "Salgo gia del trono aurato," Abigaille exults.

In another part of the palace, Zaccaria prays for guidance ("Tu che sul labbro") as he plans to convert Fenena. The rest of the Hebrews appear, at first cursing Ismaele, who begs for death, but then Anna and Zaccaria appear with Fenena, declaring it was a Hebrew woman he saved as Fenena has converted. Abdallo rushes in to warn Fenena that Nabucco has been killed and the people are calling for Abigaille. When Abigaille appears and demands the crown from Fenena, she refuses. Nabucco suddenly returns, and himself takes it, raging against both Abigaille and his people. Their god led them to betray their king, but now, there is no god but Nabucco himself. Zaccaria warns him against blaspheming against Jehovah and Nabucco condemns the Hebrews to death. When Fenena says that she is now a Hebrew, Nabucco repeats that he himself is God, and a thunderbolt is heard. The crown falls from Nabucco's head and he collapses, insane. Zaccaria declares that Jehovah has punished him, but Abigaille seizes the crown, declaring that Baal's glory is not dead.

Act Three: La profezia" (The Prophecy). Abigaille is about to sign the death sentence for the Hebrews and Fenena when Nabucco, still half-insane, appears. Abigaille at first pretends that she is merely acting for him until he recovers, and tells him to sign the sentence himself. He is reluctant until she tells him he is a coward, at which he immediately signs. As Abigaille orders it carried out, Nabucco remembers Fenena, but Abigaille declares she is a traitor and will die. Nabucco recovers for a moment and tells Abigaille she is not of royal blood, but a slave. She, in return, shows him the paper that discloses her identity and triumphantly destroys it. He, hearing the trumpets announcing the death sentence, at first calls for his guards, but Abigaille tells him that he is now her prisoner, kept by those same guards. He laments that now he is only the shadow of a king and begs Abigaille to remain queen and spare Fenena, but she rejects him.

In the second scene, the chained Hebrews are laboring and sing the famous chorus "Va, pensiero," thinking of their beloved, lost homeland. Zaccaria exhorts them not to lament but to hope for God's justice in the scene "Oh, chi piange," and they are encouraged.

Act Four: L'idolo infranto (The Shattered Idol). Imprisoned in his room, Nabucco is disturbed by a nightmare. He awakens to hear shouts, which he first imagines to be a call to arms, but then realizes is the sound of the crowd awaiting Fenena's public execution. He tries to rush to her rescue, but realizes he is a helpless prisoner. In the aria "Ah, prigioniero io son... Dio di Giuda," he prays to the God of the Jews for help and forgiveness, swearing that if his mind and freedom are restored, he will worship only Jehovah. Abdallo and the remaining loyal soldiers enter, and he declares that he is now sane again, and demands his sword to lead them to save his daughter.

In the second scene, the Hebrews are waiting to be killed upon the altar of Baal. Zaccaria comforts Fenena, telling her that she will be rewarded in heaven. Outside, there are cries of "Long live Nabucco," and he enters at the head of his troops. He orders the figure of Baal to be destroyed, but before anyone can touch it, it miraculously explodes. Nabucco orders the Hebrews to be released and the Temple of Solomon to be rebuilt. Abigaille, defeated, has taken poison, and as they all pray, she is brought in. She repents, prays for forgiveness, and dies. *—Ann Feeney*

Recommended:

○ **Verdi: Nabucco** / Sinopoli (cond.), Cappuccilli, Domingo, Nesterenko, Dimitrova, Terrani / DG 410512

○ **Verdi: Nabucco** / Muti (cond.), Manuguerra, Lucchetti, Ghiaurov, Scotto, Obraztsova / 1986 / EMI 47488

Otello (1887)

Verdi's second Shakespearean opera was to be his last dramatic (in the descriptive sense) work, followed only by his sublimely comedic *Falstaff.* He began to think about an operatic setting of *Otello* in 1879, and he asked Arrigo Boito to draft a libretto. However, Verdi was not sure that he had the energy to work and fight for what he felt was needed to bring this tragedy to the stage. Boito and Ricordi, Verdi's publisher, gently prodded the composer, and finally, in 1886, Verdi completed the score. Except for the omission of the first act of the play, the libretto follows very closely the plot of Shakepeare's play. The only major addition is the "Credo" for Iago in Act II. There is no equivalent passage in the original and yet this aria sums up Iago's philosophy. Boito and Verdi considered using the title "Iago" instead of "Otello," but in time felt that the change would not be for the best. The premiere was a great success not only for Verdi and Boito, but also for the entire cast. For the first performances in France, Verdi rewrote part of Act Three, adding a ballet and condensing the finale of the act. The ballet music is played on concerts occasionally, but the other changes are forgotten.

The score to *Otello* is extremely dramatic and complex. The curtain rises to a tremendous storm, and Otello's entrance, though less than a minute long, sets the tone for this dramatic role. Otello is the heaviest role Verdi wrote, and only in the love duet is he allowed a chance to show his tender side. The second act duet with Iago has the excitement found in the cabalettas of Verdi's earlier operas, but remains an integral part of the dramatic context. Although Iago has several important solo scenes, it is as the manipulator of others that he is most important. He has no extended scene with long lyric phrases with which to show off his vocal talents. He is almost like a narrator keeping the action moving. Desdemona is one of the most placid of Verdi's heroines, but she does try to stand up to Otello in Act Three. The "Willow song" and "Ave Maria" in Act Four are part of one of the great lyric scenes for soprano. The choral and orchestral writing is among of the most complex that Verdi had yet composed. The repeated use of the "kiss motif" to bind together the opera has been likened to a Wagnerian Leitmotiv, but Verdi uses this device only when Otello is thinking of the kiss, not to foreshadow what will be happening. *Otello* will continue to be a popular opera as long as a great dramatic tenor is available to sing Otello and a great baritone singing-actor is available to portray Iago. *—Richard LeSueur*

Synopsis:

Act One. In a plaza overlooking the harbor, the anxious Cypriots watch as Otello's ship is battered by the storm, but it finally comes to port safely, despite Iago's muttered wish. Otello disembarks, praising God for their triumph over the Turks: "Esultate." Roderigo confesses to Iago his hopeless love for Desdemona, and Iago declares his hatred for Otello, who had promoted Cassio instead of himself, and promises to help. The crowd celebrates the victory and Iago starts a drinking song, "Inaffia l'ugola," telling Roderigo they need to get Cassio drunk. They succeed, and when Montano summons the now belligerent Cassio for guard duty, Cassio turns on him, wounding him. This starts a general fight, and Otello appears to quell it. He strips Cassio of his rank and orders all to leave. Desdemona, who had followed him, remains, and they kiss and sing the ecstatic love duet "Gia nella notte densa," recalling past sorrows in the face of this joy.

Act Two. Iago comforts Cassio and tells him that if Desdemona intercedes for him, Otello will surely pardon him. When Cassio leaves, he sings his Credo, iterating his belief in God's and man's malignancy. Otello enters and Iago arouses his suspicions, which momentarily disperse as he watches Desdemona serenaded by sailors and Cypriot women and children, but arise again when she insists that he forgive Cassio. Growing angry, he throws down the handkerchief that she offers when he complains of a headache. Iago then forces Emilia to give him the handkerchief. When Emilia and Desdemona leave, Otello sings of his shattered dreams: "Ora e per sempre." Iago further plays on Otello's suspicions, saying he has seen Cassio with the handkerchief that was Otello's own first love token to Desdemona. Otello and he swear revenge in the fiery duet "Si pel ciel."

Act Three. Iago and Otello are waiting for the Venetian ambassador. Iago leaves at Desdemona's entrance and Otello, who at first feigns calm, is infuriated by her again pleading for Cassio. He accuses her of infidelity. As she asserts her innocence, he assumes a dangerous calm, but breaks down completely after she leaves ("Dio! mi potevi"), mourning that the one thing he treasured most is lost. Iago tells him Cassio is approaching and makes him hide. As Iago and Cassio converse, Iago manipulates the conversation to make it sound as though Cassio is boasting of his affair with Desdemona, and when Cassio shows Iago the handkerchief he has found in his home, Otello is driven into a frenzy. Cassio leaves at the sound of the ambassador's approach. Iago tells Otello that he himself will kill Cassio and that Otello should kill Desdemona in the marriage bed she has sullied. Otello agrees. When the crowd appears to see the ambassador, with Desdemona among them, Otello manages to receive the ambassador and his recall to Venice calmly; but at Desdemona's innocent conversation, he loses his temper and throws her to the ground, to the shocked dismay of all. He orders everyone to leave and falls in a faint as Iago laughs at the collapsed "lion of Venice."

In Desdemona's bedroom, Emilia brushes her hair as Desdemona sings the sad "Willow Song." She has a premonition of disaster and bids Emilia an emotional farewell. Alone, she sings the Ave Maria and goes to bed. Otello enters and wakes her with a kiss. He resumes his accusations and, despite her denials, tells her that Cassio is dead and that she too will die. Refusing even her plea to be allowed to say one last Ave, he strangles her. Emilia pounds on the door and, when he lets her in, says that Cassio has killed Roderigo. Desdemona revives and claims that she dies innocent, but she protects Otello by claiming that she has killed herself. As she dies (for real this time), Emilia calls Otello a murderer. Otello tells her Iago himself showed that Desdemona was unfaithful, and Emilia, calling him a fool for believing Iago, cries for help. Montano, Lodovico, Cassio, and Iago enter, and Iago's treachery is quickly revealed. He flees, and Otello, kissing Desdemona one last time, kills himself. *—Ann Feeney*

Recommended:

○ **Verdi: Otello** / Levine (cond.), Domingo, Scotto, Milnes / 1998 / RCA 7432139501

○ **Verdi: Otello** / Serafin (cond.), Vickers, Rysanek, Gobbi / 1998 / RCA 63180

Rigoletto (1851)

After the difficulty with censors that Verdi encountered while composing *Stiffelio,* the easy track for his next work would have been to pick a subject much less controversial. However Verdi turned to Victor Hugo's play *Le roi s'amuse* which had been banned in Paris after one performance. But by turning the play's King into a duke and moving the action from France to Mantua, the librettist Piave was able to satisfy both the composer and the censors. This tragic tale inspired Verdi like none since *Macbeth*; the premiere was a triumph and it immediately became a hit around the world. However, local censors often banned the original text, and so the music was occasionally heard set to a substantially changed libretto; in some versions, the unfortunate Gilda was even revived to live happily ever after. Fortunately, though some of them were truly abysmal, none of these temporary changes altered the success of what is still recognized as one of Verdi's finest scores.

Rigoletto provided an important break with earlier operatic convention; only the Duke has the conventional two-part (slow-fast) aria that had been the steadfast building block of scenes for many years (until the 1960s, most opera lovers did not know the second section of this aria ("Possente amor") because it was nearly always omitted from performances). The other two arias for the Duke are more like canzonettas, sounding like something anyone could toss off in a light hearted moment. Gilda's only aria is a dreamy reflection on the young man with whom she has fallen in love; it lacks the expected bravura conclusion. Rigoletto's arias do not follow the expected formal styles of this period at all; they are more like through-composed monologues, but they still command impressive vocal resources.

The role of Rigoletto is the first fully developed character found in Verdi's operas; his changes of mood and emotion seem naturally wedded to the dramatic situation, and his music has an inevitable quality, seemingly driving the story to its tragic conclusion. The duets between Gilda and Rigoletto play an important role in the style of the opera: in the second scene of Act One, the mood created is one of the tender loving care of a father for his daughter, but by the end of Act II, the listener can sense his anger during "Tutte le feste al tempio" only to explode at "Si, vendetta." The tragic consequences of this anger become the focal point of the plot.

The opening of the final act contains two of the most famous pieces in all opera: the Duke's "La donna e mobile" (which needs no introduction), and the famous quartet, "Bella figlia dell'amore," in which each character is expressing a different emotion. An interesting element of the quartet is that all four characters are not in the same place, nor directly interacting with one another; while the Duke flirts with a woman inside Sparafucile's Inn , Rigoletto and Gilda peer through the window and comment on their own feelings.

While the music for both Gilda and the Duke looks back in form and content to earlier operas, that for *Rigoletto* shows Verdi starting down the path of dramatic characterization that would eventually culminate in *Otello.* With its wealth of famous arias and ensembles, *Rigoletto* will continue to be performed as long as there are singers capable of fulfilling the music's demands. *—Richard LeSueur*

Synopsis:

Act One. At a party in the Duke of Mantua's palace, while chatting of a mysterious bourgeois beauty he is pursuing, he eyes the women, especially the Countess Ceprano. When one of his courtiers warns him to be discreet or the Count might get in the way, the Duke laughingly sings that one woman or another, it's all the same to him ("Questa o quella"). He overtly courts the Countess and leads her out, under the eye of the fuming Count, whom Rigoletto, the Duke's hunchbacked jester, mocks. After Rigoletto has left, Marullo excitedly tells the other courtiers that Rigoletto, as laughable as it is, has a mistress, whom he visits every night. The Duke returns, vexed by the nuisance of the Count, but while he agrees with Rigoletto that kidnapping the Countess is an excellent idea, he doesn't like the other suggestions of exiling or killing the Count. The Count overhears, but the Duke laughs the situation off, telling Rigoletto not to carry his jokes too far. The Count and the other courtiers decide Rigoletto has to be punished for his cruel jokes. Monterone comes in and insists on addressing the Duke, who has dishonored his daughter. Rigoletto makes fun of him, in turn, and Monterone curses them both. The Duke simply orders Monterone arrested, but Rigoletto is terrified.

On the way home, still frightened by the curse, Rigoletto is stopped by a sinister figure, Sparafucile, who introduces himself as a sword for hire, should Rigoletto ever need one. His beautiful sister is the bait he uses. Rigoletto bitterly reflects on how his deformity and the court have warped him to the point where he is just like the assassin, but with his tongue as his weapon. He enters his home, where his daughter Gilda happily greets him. She asks him about himself, his home, his family, and he evades the questions, saying that she is his home, family, religion, and entire universe. He does tell her of her mother, who pitied and loved him, and then died, leaving him only with Gilda. He is highly protective and reiterates his order that she is never to leave the house, except to go to church. The Duke slips into the garden and is astonished to learn that his target is Rigoletto's daughter. After warning Giovanna to watch over her charge and keep her unsullied, Rigoletto leaves. Gilda admits to Giovanna that she feels guilty, she has said nothing of the handsome young stranger she sees in church and has fallen in love with. The Duke, that selfsame stranger, appears and declares his love ("E il sol dell'anima"), and Gilda quickly responds. He leaves after they exchange vows of eternal love, and she reflects on her love for Gualtier Malde, the name he has assumed ("Caro nome"). The courtiers appear, and when Rigoletto comes by, they convince him they intend to kidnap the Countess for the Duke. Blindfolding him while pretending to put just a mask on him, they have him hold the ladder against his own wall, which he thinks is Ceprano's, and they carry off the terrified Gilda. Rigoletto realizes he has been tricked and cries out "La maledizione" (the curse).

Act Two. The Duke anxiously wonders where Gilda is; he had gone back, only to find the house deserted. He tenderly sings that he thinks he sees her frightened tears ("Parmi veder le lagrime"). The courtiers tell him they've brought him Rigoletto's mistress, whom the Duke knows is Gilda, and he rushes off to her ("Possente amor mi chiama"). Rigoletto appears, feigning unconcern, but soon breaks down and demands that they return his daughter, eventually breaking down in sobbing pleas ("Cortigani... miei signori"). Gilda rushes in, having been with the Duke, and tearfully tells her father she is dishonored. He tries to console her in their duet ("Piangi, fanciulla"). Monterone is brought in on his way to prison and bitterly sings that his curse has been unavailing. Rigoletto declares the old man mistaken, that he will punish the offense ("Si, vendetta"), while Gilda pleads for mercy for the man she still loves.

Act Three. Rigoletto has contracted with Sparafucile to kill the Duke, who comes to Sparafucile's inn to meet Maddalena, the sister. He cheerfully sings that women are fickle ("La donna e mobile"), but no man who hasn't known her love can be happy. Rigoletto brings Gilda to see the Duke's true nature. The Duke makes love to Maddalena inside, Rigoletto and Gilda watch from outside, and the four sing the famous quartet "Bella figlia dell'amore." Rigoletto orders Gilda to leave for Verona disguised as a man for safety, and he pays Sparafucile the advance on his fee. Maddalena has fallen for the charming young man, and pleads with her brother to spare him. Sparafucile finally agrees that if another person can be found so they will have a body to present to Rigoletto, the handsome stranger can live. Gilda, who has crept back, hears this and determines to die for the Duke. She pretends to be a beggar asking for shelter and enters to be murdered in his place. Rigoletto returns, and Sparafucile gives him a sack with a corpse. Rigoletto insists on throwing the body in the river himself, but as he is about to do so, he hears the Duke's voice. Tearing open the sack, he realizes his revenge has struck Gilda instead. She is not yet dead and tells him, as he begs her not to die, that in heaven, with her mother, she will pray for him. She dies and Rigoletto falls over her body, again crying, "La maledizione!" *—Ann Feeney*

Recommended:

- ○ **Verdi: Rigoletto** / Bonynge (cond.), Milnes, Pavarotti, Sutherland / 1985 / London 414269
- ○ **Verdi: Rigoletto** / Cellini (cond.), Warren, Peerce, Berger / Preiser 90452

Simon Boccanegra (1857)

In 1856, Verdi agreed to write a new opera for Teatro la Fenice in Venice. Although his thoughts again turned to Shakespeare's *King Lear,* Verdi finally decided that Antonio Gutierrez's *Simon Bocanegra* would be a better subject for the Venitian public. Francesco Piave wrote the basic libretto, but becuase Verdi was in Paris at the time, Giuseppe Montanelli provided the changes which Verdi required. At the premiere on March 12, 1857, the libretto was universally criticized as being nearly unintelligible. The music also failed to please the public: they found it too declamatory and without melody. In 1880, Verdi began to work on a total revision of the opera with Arrigo Boito providing the new text. Every scene except the second act has many minor changes to the score, but the primary change was the addition of the council chamber scene in Act One. Boito wanted to make more changes, but Verdi stood firm in his decision not to rewrite the entire work despite his admiration for Boito's new text. Because of this, Boito requested that his name not be placed on the title page. The opera was certainly more successful at the March 24, 1881, premiere of the revised version, but the public still found the opera gloomy, and it has never found its way into the central repertoire.

The music of *Simon Boccanegra* is very different from most of Verdi's other operas. This is his first opera without a prelude or overture (although the 1857 version did have a prelude). The curtain rises immediately on the prologue with the action taking place 25 years before the rest of the opera. The first scene of Act One is dominated by an aria for Amelia and one of Verdi's great father-daughter duets. The entire scene in the council chamber is of the highest order. Remember that this section was entirely new and was written just before *Otello.* The second act is not nearly up to this level, as can be expected since it was left nearly intact as first composed. The tenor in this opera is really of secondary importance, although he does have a lovely aria in "Senyo avvampar nell'anima." It is interesting to note that the title character does not have an aria which is easily pulled from the opera for concert and recital use, yet Boccanegra appears in nearly every scene of the opera. By this time, Verdi had completely dispensed with the two-part aria with cabaletta style, and all of the arias are used to move the action forward rather than comment on what has happened. The recitative preceeding Fiesco's "Il lacerato spirito" sounds unconvincing within the context of the whole opera because this is the only remaining example of recitative in the older style. All other such passages were revised in 1881. Given the proper cast of singing-actors, *Simon Boccanegra* is one of Verdi's most dramatic operas. At its best, this opera can stand comparison with its predecessor, *Aida,* and its follower, *Otello.* *—Richard LeSueur*

Synopsis:

Prologue. Paolo and Pietro, two plebians, determine to have Boccanegra elected Doge. Boccanegra arrives in response to Paolo's message, and is uninterested in the power, but Paolo tells him if elected, he would be able to marry Maria Fiesco, with whom he has had a child, and who is now kept a virtual prisoner by her father. He leaves, and when other plebians enter, Paolo works on their emotions by reminding them of Maria's fate. As they disperse, Fiesco, her father, emerges. Maria has just died. He curses Boccanegra and in his lament, asks Fiesco to pray for him ("Il lacerato spirito"). Boccanegra returns, still unaware of her death, and pleads for Fiesco's forgiveness, even offering to let Fiesco kill him to appease his hate. Fiesco offers his forgiveness on one condition, that Boccanegra give him the daughter Maria bore, swearing to make the child happy. Boccanegra says that in his absence, the child's nurse died, the child disappeared, and he has been unable to locate her. Fiesco coldly refuses any forgiveness and withdraws into the shadows. Thinking he has gone, Boccanegra enters the palace, only to find Maria's corpse. He staggers out as the crowd returns, acclaiming him as Doge, to Fiesco's fury.

Act One. Twenty-five years later, in the Grimaldi palace, a young woman known as Amelia Grimaldi sings of the beauty of the sea and recalls a childhood far away from such splendors ("Come in quest'ora"). Her lover, Gabriele Adorno, sings to her from off-stage, and as he enters, she asks him to end his plots against the Doge, fearing that he and her guardian, Andrea (actually Fiesco), also a conspirator, will be killed. She also asks him to ask Andrea for her hand immediately, as she thinks the Doge will order her to marry Paolo. When he does so, Andrea informs him that Amelia is not a Grimaldi, but a foundling, secretly adopted to prevent seizure of the estate when the heirs were exiled by Boccanegra. Adorno says he still adores her, and Andrea solemnly pronounces his blessing.

The Doge, with Paolo in his retinue, arrives, and he dismisses them to speak with Amelia alone. He offers her a pardon for her "brothers," but she forestalls his request for her hand on Paolo's behalf by declaring she loves another and hates Paolo as a fortune-hunter. Feeling a strange sympathy with Boccanegra, she confides what little she knows of her history, that she was raised by an old nurse who died, but she remembers visits from a seafarer. He can hardly believe that she might be his long-lost daughter, but shows her a locket with a picture that exactly matches one in her own locket, and the reunited father and daughter blissfully fall into one another's arms ("Figlia a tal nome"). She leaves, and Boccanegra curtly tells the expectant Paolo to renounce his hopes. Paolo, angry, orders Pietro to have her kidnapped.

In the Doge's Council Chamber, Boccanegra urges peace with Venice, as Genoa and Venice are both Italy, but Paolo leads the Council in refusing. They hear a riot outside, and Adorno and Fiesco are driven inside by a mob that accuses Adorno of murdering Lorenzini. He declares that he was protecting Amelia Grimaldi from Lorenzini's kidnapping attempt. Amelia herself enters and describes the attempted abduction, which she foiled by threatening to tell the Doge who was behind the plot, though now she refuses to do so. Patricians and plebians accuse one another, and Boccanegra passionately urges peace ("Plebe, patrizi") restoring calm. Adorno gives himself up as the Doge's prisoner, and Boccanegra tells him to keep his sword, he wants only his word as surety. Guessing the kidnapper's identity, he calls upon Paolo to curse the evildoer. Paolo, terrified, does so.

Act Two. Paolo, haunted by having had to curse himself, poisons the Doge's water goblet, but also offers Fiesco the chance to kill Boccanegra when he comes in to sleep. Fiesco refuses such a vile act, but when Paolo tells Adorno that Boccanegra intends to keep Amelia for himself and leaves, Adorno remains behind, furious at the thought. Boccanegra had had Adorno's father executed for treason and now is stealing his beloved. He prays ("Cielo, pietoso") that Amelia is still guiltless. She enters and refuses to explain what she is doing in Boccanegra's bedroom, just telling Adorno to trust her. He remains suspicious and hides when Boccanegra enters. At Amelia's pleas, the Doge says he will forgive Adorno's own plotting, and when she leaves, he drinks the poisoned water and falls asleep. Adorno emerges from hiding, hesitates to kill a sleeping man, but reminds himself he is avenging his father. Amelia saves Boccanegra, and when he awakens, the two men angrily confront one another until Boccanegra says that Amelia is his daughter. Adorno is shocked, begs her forgiveness for his suspicions, and confesses the attempted murder to Boccanegra, who, for the sake of building peace, forgives him and offers him Amelia's hand. Adorno vows to defend Boccanegra in the brewing rebellion.

Act Four. The uprising has been defeated, and Fiesco is set free. Paolo is condemned to die, but gloats that he has already ensured Boccanegra's death, though he is tortured by the sound of Amelia's wedding to Adorno, being celebrated offstage. Fiesco hides as he hears the Doge enter and emerges to confront him. Boccanegra recognizes his old enemy Fiesco, but tells him Amelia is the daughter he had mourned for as lost. Fiesco weeps over Boccanegra's impending death as the two men are reconciled. Adorno and Amelia enter, and Boccanegra names Adorno as his successor and dies in her arms, murmuring "Maria," her name and that of her mother. *—Ann Feeney*

Recommended:

○ **Verdi: Simon Boccanegra** / Abbado (cond.), Carreras, Freni, Van Dam, Ghiaurov / DG 449752

La Traviata (1853)

The last of the three great operas of Giuseppe Verdi's middle period, *La Traviata* is now one of his most popular works. Written for the Teatro la Fenice in Venice, it was first heard on March 6, 1853. The libretto, by Francesco Maria Piave, details the ill-fated love affair between a young gentleman named Alfredo Germont and a terminally ill courtesan named Violetta. It is based on the play *La dame aux camélias* by Alexander Dumas Jr., which premiered the previous year.

Perhaps surprisingly, *La Traviata*'s opening night was a fiasco. Legend gives two reasons for the failure: the generous size of the soprano (supposedly dying of consumption!) and the use of a contemporary stage setting, which was considered distasteful at the time (subsequent performances were re-set in the 1700s; the reinstatement of Verdi's original conception did not occur until the 1880s). Verdi withdrew the opera and, after making significant changes in the second and third acts, premiered the new version at the Teatro Gallo di San Benedetto in 1854. It is in this version that the opera has enjoyed its continued success.

In many ways, *La Traviata* follows the established operatic traditions of the 1850s. Each act is composed of smaller dramatic units made up of traditional set pieces in clearly identifiable forms (a structure known as la solita forma), and each of the three major characters is given a two-part aria (slow-fast) which displays a change of the character's mood. (For many years the cabalettas for Alfredo and Giorgio Germont were omitted not only in the theater but also on recording. By the 1980s, one verse of the cabaletta for Alfredo began to be heard in the theater on a more regular basis but Giorgio Germont's cabaletta has not made its way to most stages.) Also, like its predecessor, *Rigoletto*, *La Traviata* has a full overture—a device that would make only rare appearances in Verdi's later works.

However, in other ways *La Traviata* begins to stretch, and expand upon, the mid-nineteenth century Italian norms. This is especially evident in the depth of characterization written into the role of Violetta. Formal musical concerns, while still evident, begin to take a backseat to more immediate dramatic issues. In the first act alone, Verdi takes the character of Violetta from the gregarious hostess of the opening drinking song to the intimate lover of "Un di felice" and "Ah, fors' e lui" to the wild abandon of the courtesan in "Sempre libera." In the final act—as she succumbs to her disease and dies—she sings only a few gasped lines, rather than the full double aria which would be found in most operas of Verdi's predecessors. The other roles are not as well defined, but Alfredo and Giorgio Germont far outstrip the one-dimensional characters encountered in most operas of this period. Although there are opportunities for pure vocal display in their arias, even these displays are tied to the character. For example, Alfredo's "O mio rimorso" shows the impetuosity of youth as he runs off to save the good name of his beloved.

Verdi's use of the traditional forms in combination with a new dramatic conviction would lead to the more dramatic style of his later operas. This delicate blend of old and new styles is perhaps what has kept *La Traviata* ever fresh and appealing in modern opera houses.*—Richard LeSueur*

Synopsis:

Act One. Violetta is throwing a party. Gastone introduces Alfredo Germont to Violetta, declaring him another admirer. Baron Douphol, Violetta's current lover and financial supporter, takes a dislike to Alfredo, compounded when she teasingly compares his behavior during her last illness to Alfredo's, who came each day to ask about her health, without ever having even met her. Alfredo is called upon for a toast after Douphol declines, and after some hesitation, he launches into a sparkling song praising love ("Libiamo, libiamo"). Violetta follows with a verse saying that life is meaningless without pleasure, as fleeting as it is. Violetta invites the guests to dance, but has a fainting spell. She tells them to go on anyway. Alfredo stays behind, and declares he is the only one in the world who loves her, and he wants to take care of her. She laughs, but is moved when he tells her he has loved her for a year ("Un di, felice"). She tells him to look for someone capable of love and then they are interrupted by guests curious about her absence. Embarrassed, she tells Alfredo not to talk to her again of love, but does give him a flower, telling him to bring it back when it has faded. The guests all leave, and she wonders if Alfredo is the love she had dreamt of ("Ah, forse' lui"). After her pensive mood passes, she determines to continue her life of pleasure ("Sempre libera"), but hesitates at the sound of his voice outside.

Act Two. Violetta and Alfredo are living together outside Paris. Alfredo reflects on his happiness ("De miei bollenti spiriti"), but when he asks the maid Annina where she has been, she tells him she has been arranging the sale of Violetta's possessions. He realizes his naivete and resolves to get money and rushes off. Violetta enters and tells Annina she is waiting for a business visit. When a man comes in, she is surprised and affronted when he introduces himself as Giorgio Germont, Alfredo's father, come to extricate his son. She tells him that Alfredo is not ruining himself for her, and reveals their circumstances. He sees she is not the gold-digger he had imagined, but tells her the affair must stop ("Pura siccome un angelo") for the sake of his daughter's impending marriage. Violetta offers to leave Alfredo for a while, but Germont says that it must be for good. She protests that she is mortally ill and Alfredo is all she has, but at his adamant warning that such a love cannot outlast her beauty and pleas to save the happiness of an innocent girl and his entire family, she finally agrees, asking him only to embrace her as a daughter and, after she is dead, to tell Alfredo of her sacrifice. He leaves, and she starts to write to Alfredo, who enters a moment later. He is confused and momentarily suspicious, and she begs him to love her as much as she loves him, as she leaves. A messenger brings him her letter of farewell and Germont comes in to comfort him and urge him to come home ("Di Provenza il mar il suol"), but Alfredo is bent on revenge.

Act Three. At Flora's gambling party, guests are dressed as gypsies and matadors. Violetta and Douphol arrive, followed a moment later by Alfredo, who gambles with Douphol and wins, all the while hurling barely veiled insults at Violetta, arousing Douphol's anger. When the guests leave for supper, Violetta asks Alfredo to meet her. He at first taunts her and then insists that she leave with him, but she begs him to leave before Douphol can challenge him, saying she has sworn never to see him again. Lying to protect Germont, she says she loves Douphol. Alfredo calls in the other guests and denounces her, throwing his winnings at her feet. She collapses, and the guests order Alfredo out. Germont appears, and rebukes his son. Violetta revives, and tells him she still loves him ("Alfredo, Alfredo"). Douphol challenges him, and Alfredo is overwhelmed with remorse.

Act Four. Annina watches over her the dying Violetta as she sleeps, and when she wakes up, the doctor arrives. He tells her she will recover soon, but whispers to Annina it is a matter of hours. Violetta tells Annina to keep half of her remaining money for herself and give half to the poor. She reads a letter from Germont, telling her Alfredo and Douphol fought, the Baron was wounded but will recover, and Alfredo will come back from abroad to ask her forgiveness. She says it is too late, and prays God to forgive her past ("Addio, del passato"). Outside, a carnival procession passes, and Annina rushes in, telling Violetta to remain calm. Alfredo enters, and they sing of leaving Paris together ("Parigi, o cara"). She wants to dress and go to church, but is too weak and realizes nothing, not even Alfredo's love, can save her. Germont and the doctor arrive, and she bids Alfredo a tender farewell, giving him a portrait of herself and telling him that should an innocent girl give him her heart, he should marry her and give her the portrait "of one who prays for her, for you." For a moment, she feels her strength returning, and exclaims she is coming back to life, but collapses, dead. *—Ann Feeney*

Recommended:

- ○ **Verdi: La Traviata** / Kleiber (cond.), Cotrubas, Domingo, Milnes / 1977 / DG 4770772
- ○ **Verdi: La Traviata** / Bonynge (cond.), Sutherland, Pavarotti, Manuguerra / 1991 / London 430491
- ○ **Verdi: La Traviata** / Previtali (cond.), Moffo, Tucker, Merrill / 1997 / RCA 902668885
- ○ **Verdi: La Traviata** / Ceccato (cond.), Sills, Gedda, Panerai / 1988 / EMI 69827
- ○ **Verdi: La Traviata** / (live: 1966) / Giulini (cond.), Callas, di Stefano, Bastianini / 1997 / EMI 66450

Il Trovatore (1853)

The second of the three great middle period operas that solidified Verdi's fame, *Il Trovatore* is the work that is most based in the traditions of the first half of the nineteenth century. Based on a play by Gutierrez, the plot is filled with the twists and unlikely coincidences that, over the years, have made the opera the butt of many jokes. However, Verdi was stirred to the height of his inspiration by this work, and from its premiere it was an even greater success than its predecessor, *Rigoletto.*

The original text was by one of the composer's favorite librettists Salvatore Cammarano, but Cammarano died soon after the initial draft was completed, forcing Verdi to turn to Leone Bardare for revisions. Verdi initially contemplated naming the opera after its Gypsy character, Azucena, but in the end the tenor ruled the day.

In 1856, Verdi was commissioned to revise the opera slightly for a French version at the Paris Opéra; he added a ballet to the third act, rewrote the ending of the final scene, and made other minor revisions. None of these revisions have been incorporated into the standard performance version of the opera.

The importance of *Il Trovatore* lies in its music; it displays some of the most ingratiating melodies Verdi ever wrote. It has been said that in order to mount a successful performance of this opera, all you need (!) are the four greatest Verdi voices available. From the soaring phrases of Leonora's opening aria to the martial excitement of Manrico's "Di quella pira," all of the conventional operatic forms are used to give the singers a chance to shine. Only Azucena does not have the traditional two-part aria, but she has some of the most memorable solos and duets in the entire opera. From her entrance with the drama of "Stride la vampa" to the tenderness of her Act Four duet with Manrico, she displays a full range of emotion. Di Luna, the baritone villain, is more one dimensional. The role of Manrico is one of the most difficult that Verdi wrote; he needs the grace of a lyric tenor for "Ah si, ben mio" and a full dramatic tenor sound for the following "Di quella pira" (which contains two unwritten high Cs that add considerably to its difficulty). Most tenors find it safer to have this aria transposed down in performance and some even do this on recordings.

Verdi's *Il Trovatore* is among the last of the "stand and sing" operas: those that give their best effect when well sung, regardless of dramatic portrayals. With its wealth of great music, *Il Trovatore* will always be an audience favorite, while the critics will complain about its lack of subtlety. *—Richard LeSueur*

Synopsis:

Act One "Il duello" (The duel). Ferrando tells his men to be alert, while the Count di Luna waits to discover his rival for Leonora. To keep them awake, he tells the story of how his brother, as a baby, was apparently bewitched by an old gypsy, who was then burned at the stake. The gypsy's daughter kidnapped the child and in revenge, burned him in the same spot. The old father died of grief, but clung to the belief that his son was not dead, and urged his remaining son always to look for him.

Leonora in the next scene tells Inez of how she fell in love with a mysterious contestant at a tournament, who now comes to serenade her ("Tacea la notte"). Inez is uneasy, but Leonora declares her undying love. Di Luna appears, and is infuriated to hear the troubadour singing to Leonora. She rushes out, right into di Luna's arms, but recognizes her mistake and declares her love for Manrico. The Count is even more annoyed by this whole situation when he recognizes Manrico as an enemy leader, and the two men rush off to fight.

Act Two "La gitana" (The gypsy). In the gypsy camp, Manrico is recovering from wounds received in battle with the Count's forces. The gypsies sing the Anvil chorus. Azucena relives the burning of her mother ("Stride la vampa"), and how in her haste for revenge, she killed her own child. Manrico is confused, but she assures him he is her real son. He tells her of the mysterious force that kept him from killing the Count in their duel. A message comes for Manrico, that Leonora thinks he died and is entering a convent. He leaves, despite Azucena's entreaties.

Outside the convent, di Luna sings of his love for Leonora ("Il balen del suo sorriso") and that she must be his. He and his men interrupt the ceremony before she takes vows, but she is rescued by Manrico and his forces.

Act Three "Il figlio della zingara" (The gypsy's son). Di Luna and his men are preparing to attack the castle where Manrico has taken Leonora, and the men confidently sing of their coming victory. Azucena is discovered wandering around near the camp, and when di Luna and Ferrando question her, Ferrando recognizes her as the woman who burnt the child. She calls for her son Manrico to help her, and di Luna realizes he has his enemy's mother in his hands.

Inside, Manrico and Leonora are waiting to be married, and he reassures her that even if he is killed, death will be just waiting for her in Heaven("Ah si, ben mio"). Ruiz rushes in to tell Manrico that Azucena will be burned at the stake, and Manrico prepares his men to rescue her ("Di quella pira")

Act Four "Il supplizio" (The penalty). Manrico has been defeated. Ruiz brings Leonora, who had escaped, back. She hopes that thoughts of love comfort Manrico ("D'amor sull'ali"). She hears priests singing a Miserere, and Manrico's voice singing of his love, and she declares her determination to save him or die trying ("Tu vedrai che amor"). Di Luna emerges, giving the order for Manrico's beheading and Azucena's burning, and when her pleas for Manrico's life are useless, she offers him herself in exchange. He agrees, overjoyed at the thought, and she secretly drinks poison.

In the prison, Manrico tries to soothe Azucena with the thought of their homeland ("Ai nostri monti"). She falls asleep, and Leonora enters, telling Manrico he is free. When she says, however, that she must stay, he refuses to leave, even though she pleads with him, and he angrily denounces her for selling herself to di Luna for any price. She falls to the ground, and tells him she has taken poison. As he remorsefully exclaims that he dared curse such an angel, di Luna enters and realizes what she has done. The moment she dies, he orders Manrico to be taken outside and killed. Azucena wakes up, the Count tells her Manrico is being executed now, and she tells him to stop. Gloatingly, he tells her Manrico is already dead, and she tells him that he has executed his own lost brother, and she has thus avenged her mother, as he cries out in horror. *—Ann Feeney*

Recommended:

- ○ **Verdi: Il Trovatore** / Mehta (cond.), Price, Domingo, Milnes, Cossotto / 1998 / RCA 7432139504
- ○ **Verdi: Il Trovatore** / Cellini (cond.), Bjoerling, Milanov, Warren, Barbieri / RCA Victor 6643
- ○ **Verdi: Il Trovatore** / Serafin (cond.), Bergonzi, Stella, Bastianini, Cossotto / DG 453118

CHORAL

Quattro pezzi sacri (4 Sacred Pieces), for chorus & orchestra (1889–1897)

In the twilight of his life, Giuseppe Verdi published a heterogeneous collection of four pieces entitled the *Quattro pezzi sacri.* Composed over perhaps eight years prior to their publication, they reveal the eyes of Italy's most famous opera composer looking toward the afterlife through the sacred texts of the Catholic church. Much of the music is quite progressive: the style reflects the great tonal expansion of the latter nineteenth century, as well as his own advances in operatic composition. At the same time, the *Quattro pezzi* provide Verdi's retrospective view of some highlights of his pan-Italian cultural heritage, making references as far back in history as Dante and Palestrina.

Two of the *Quattro pezzi,* in fact, borrow the traditional texture of *stile antico* church compositions, a cappella choral writing. In the *Laudi alla Vergine Maria* (composed around 1890), Verdi used only a quartet of solo women's voices to set his Italian text from the final Canto of Dante's *Paradiso.* He deliberately evoked the music of the Italian Renaissance in the thin vocal texture, with its clear cadences and imitative writing; the voice-leading, on the other hand, is often richly chromatic and wanders far from the home key. Verdi's *Ave Maria* similarly translates a severe, four-voiced unaccompanied choral texture into a thoroughly "modern" harmonic idiom. The piece took life as Verdi's response to an editorial challenge in a Milanese periodical (1888) for any composer to write music based upon a *scala enigamtica.* Verdi places this challenging scale in each voice in turn as an archaic cantus firmus. The other voices weave often extremely chromatic harmonies about it; almost every note of the 12-tone scale appears in the first four measures alone.

The final two pieces deploy the full range of choral and orchestral forces. *Stabat mater* (1896–1897) sets the complete drama of the Passion as seen through Mary's eyes; it does so in a series of pointillistic images from the ancient Latin text. In preparation for the winter 1895 composition of the *Te Deum*, Verdi studied the music of both Victoria and Purcell, though he ultimately created something quite different. His intention was a musically adventuresome portrayal of his own emotional responses to the traditional text. The "immense father" is also the "king of glory" (seen in brass fanfares), born in human flesh of a Virgin, and will return as "Judge." Mankind trembles before this judge; Verdi asked to have this personally expressive score buried with him. *—Timothy Dickey*

Recommended:

- ○ **Verdi: Quattro Pezzi Sacri; Stravinsky: Symphony of Psalms** / Shaw (cond.), Atlanta SO & Chorus / 1991 / Telarc 80254
- ○ **Verdi: Requiem; Quattro Pezzi Sacri** / Reiner (cond.), Vienna PO, Singverein der Gesellschaft der Musikfreunde / 2000 / Decca 467119

Requiem Mass (Manzoni Requiem) (1874)

That Verdi's *Messa da Requiem* should be infused with the dramatic power of the his operas is no surprise. The text of the requiem is the most dramatic Verdi ever set, allowing him to explore his new ability to compose large sections of music on a "symphonic" scale with powerful passages for chorus and orchestra.

As much as Verdi lamented the death of Gioachino Rossini (1792–1868), he was more moved by the death of novelist Alessandro Manzoni in 1873. When Rossini died, Verdi felt that only Manzoni remained of Italy's great tradition. After Manzoni died, Verdi wrote to Contessa Maffei, "Now all is over! And with him ends... the greatest of our glories." When Verdi and Manzoni met in 1848, Verdi described the experience as one of being in the presence "of a saint." It was for Manzoni that Verdi composed his requiem.

From the very beginning, Verdi's Requiem was intended for the concert hall, not the church. This gave the composer some freedom when setting the text, although he remained much more faithful to the standard liturgy than did Berlioz in his setting. Verdi's Requiem was first performed on May 22, 1874, in Milan, on the first anniversary of Manzoni's death.

Verdi conveys the solemnity of the *Requiem Mass* through the opening cello line, a muted, descending phrase. The orchestra has the thematic material in the first part of the Introit, "Requiem aeternam," as the chorus sings the text in snatches. To balance this, the central part of the movement, "Te decet hymnus," is for unaccompanied chorus. After the return of the "Requiem aeternam" the Kyrie begins, introducing the soloists.

The "Dies irae," opening the Sequence, is the most famous part of Verdi's *Requiem.* Brass and bass drum make their first appearance in this tumultuous outburst depicting the "day of wrath." Distant trumpets sound and are joined by the rest of the brass before the "Tuba mirum." Quietly, the solo bass begins the "Mors stupebit" (Death is struck), accompanied by pizzicato basses and bass drum. After the solo mezzo-soprano delivers the "liber scriptus proferetur," the chorus bursts in with a reprise of the "Dies irae," an event dictated by musical considerations that has nothing to do with the requiem mass text. For the "Lacrimosa," Verdi extended and rewrote a duet for Don Carlos and King Philip he had cut from *Don Carlos* before its premiere. Like Cherubini, Verdi unites the Sanctus and Benedictus.

Verdi composed the concluding "Libera me," for soprano, chorus, and orchestra in 1868–1869 as his part of a collaborative requiem for Rossini, the remaining sections of which were to be set by other Italian composers. The project came to nothing, but Verdi kept his "Libera me" and eagerly seized the opportunity to use it as part of a complete requiem. After the solo soprano begins the movement, the chorus again intercedes with the "Dies irae," which is followed by a beautiful reprise of the "Requiem aeternam" and a closing, fugal setting of the "Libera me." *—John Palmer*

Recommended:

- ○ **Verdi: Requiem** / Reiner (cond.), Price, Bjoerling, Tozzi, Elias, Vienna PO, Singverein der Gesellschaft der Musikfreunde / 2000 / Decca 467119
- ○ **Verdi: Requiem** / Solti (cond.), Price, Baker, Van Dam, Lucchetti, Chicago SO & Chorus / 1993 / RCA 61403

CHAMBER MUSIC

String Quartet in E minor (1873)

It would be fair to suggest that Giuseppe Verdi, creator of many of the world's greatest operatic dramas, exhibited little interest in any other non-vocal musical forms, and thus it must have surprised his contemporaries greatly to discover that he had produced a very fine quartet for strings in 1873, which he subsequently published three years later. During the winter months of 1872–1873, the composer was living in Naples, where he undertook a detailed overhaul of the opera *Don Carlos*, and conducted several new revivals of other works, (including one of *Aida*) at the city's opera house. It was during this period that Verdi began to sketch his string quartet, which he seems to have commenced purely as a study at first, and only began to take the project seriously when he realized that a substantial work was beginning to emerge.

The Verdi biographer and scholar Julian Budden details events surrounding its first performance as follows: "on the evening of 1 April friends of the composer were bidden to the Hotel delle Crocelle. There, in the foyer, they found four chairs and four music-stands of an eighteenth century design with candle attached. Four players entered and without a word of explanation began to play Verdi's *String Quartet in E minor.* To begin with Verdi seems to have regarded it as a private diversion... later he agreed to its publication."

The work comprises four substantial and technically demanding movements, and has been widely admired for the forcefulness of its musical ideas and its structural cohesion. It opens with a powerful Allegro, with an urgently sculpted first group giving way to a somewhat more relaxed second subject. The slow movement, marked Andantino, brings the most vocally expansive and lyrical material, though even here one would hardly credit the work to a master of the opera stage with little prior experience of writing chamber music. Next comes a Prestissimo movement, unsettled and vehement in mood, while the finale contains a massive fugue illustrating Verdi's mastery of contrapuntal techniques. Although infrequently performed, Verdi's sole chamber work occupies a unique position in the history of the quartet genre. *—Michael Jameson*

Recommended:

- ○ **Verdi, Strauss: String Quartets** / Delme SQ / 1988 / Hyperion 55012

Blandine Verlet

Harpsichordist

Blandine Verlet, a noted French harpsichordist, studied with Ruggiero Gerlin and Ralph Kirkpatrick. She began recording in the late 1970s for Philips, switching to the Astree label in the 1990s. Her recordings range from J.S. Bach's keyboard works to Froberger to lesser known composers such as Louis Couperin and Elisabeth-Claude Jacquet de la Guerre. Her second recording of the *Goldberg Variations*, in 1992, has been called "one of the finest harpsichord versions in the catalog." With violinist Gerard Poulet she has recorded early violin sonatas by Mozart, using the older Baroque keyboard instruments rather than a fortepiano or modern piano. Verlet has also worked with flutist Stephen Preston and viola da gambist Jordi Savall. Her playing is noted for her control and restraint in not letting emotion carry her away. *—Patsy Morita*

Recommended:

- ○ **L. Couperin: Les piéces de clavessin** / Verlet / 1992 / Astrée 8819
- ○ **Bach: Goldberg Variations** / Verlet / 1999 / Astrée 128745
- ○ **Handel: Suites** / Verlet / 1998 / Astrée 8655
- ○ **Couperin: Barricades Mystérieuses, Pièces de Clavecin** / Verlet / 2003 / Naïve 3003
- ○ **Harpsichord Works, Vol. 1** / Verlet / Astrée 8731

Matthijs Vermeulen

b. Feb. 8, 1888, Helmond, Netherlands, **d.** Jul. 26, 1967, Laren, Netherlands

Composer

Matthijs Vermeulen was born the son of a blacksmith in the Noord-Brabant province of the Netherlands. At age 14 he entered the Abbey of Berne at Heeswijk with the intention of becoming a priest; there he received thorough instruction in sixteenth century harmony. In 1907, Vermeulen left the monastery and enrolled into the Amsterdam Conservatory. After two years' study, Vermeulen took his first job as music critic on the Amsterdam daily *De Tijd*; his work as a perceptive and provocative writer placed his name in circulation long before his compositions were known.

The composer Alphons Diepenbrock played an important role in Vermeulen's early life, offering encouragement, advice and assistance. At the opposite end of Vermeulen's spectrum was the powerful music director of the Amsterdam Concertgebouw, Willem Mengelberg, frequently the target of Vermeulen's most pointed criticism. Upon completing his *Symphony No. 1 ("Symphonia Carminum")* in 1914, Vermeulen mailed the score to Mengelberg for possible performance. More than a year later, Mengelberg mailed it back with the advice that Vermeulen should study with composer Cornelis Dopper, a highly popular, if not terribly original, composer. Vermeulen was deeply offended. As World War I raged in greater Europe, Vermeulen's criticism increasingly focused attention on Mengelberg and his relentlessly pro-German programming at the Concertgebouw. In 1920, Vermeulen greeted the Concertgebouw premiere of Dopper's *Seventh Symphony* with the shouted comment "Long live Sousa!" Vermeulen was subsequently barred from the Concertgebouw, and Mengelberg refused to consider the score of Vermeulen's newly completed *Symphony No. 2 ("Prélude à la nouvelle journée")* (1919–20).

As a music critic prohibited from attending public concerts, Vermeulen was without hope of employment in Amsterdam, and he relocated to Paris with the intention of making it as a composer. With his *Cello Sonata No. 1* (1918) Vermeulen turned his back on Romanticism, adopting an ultramodern idiom based on systems of his own devising, but also heavily influenced by the symphonies of Gustav Mahler. Despite the active interest of influential figures such as Serge Koussevitzky and Nadia Boulanger, only occasional performances of Vermeulen's music occurred in Paris. In order to make ends meet, in 1926 Vermeulen signed on as the Paris correspondent for a newspaper based in the Dutch East Indies. Outside of retouching or orchestrating older works, the decade of the 1930s was largely unproductive musically for Vermeulen.

In 1939, conductor Eduard van Beinum defied Mengelberg's 1920 ban on Vermeulen, premiering the composer's *Third Symphony ("Thrène et peán")* (1921–22) in Amsterdam. This rekindled Vermeulen's interest in his own work, and as World War II and the occupation of Paris raged about him, Vermeulen produced two major symphonies, *No. 4 ("Les Victoires")* (1940–41) and *No. 5 "Les lendemains chantants"* (1941–45). In 1944, Vermeulen's wife died, and one of his sons was killed fighting on the side of the French.

After the War, Vermeulen returned to Amsterdam, accepting a position as critic on a prominent weekly. After a long silence, Vermeulen reinitiated his compositional activity when his 30-year-old *Symphony No. 2* won the Queen Elizabeth Prize in a competition in Belgium in 1953. Vermeulen retired from journalism in 1956, afterward composing his last two symphonies, a string quartet, and several other works, although increasing deafness and his fragile health made it difficult for him to enjoy the fruits of these later labors. Today Matthijs Vermeulen is recognized as the major Dutch composer of symphonies, and is remembered both as a modernist pioneer and a descendant of the symphonic legacy of Mahler and Richard Strauss. *—Uncle Dave Lewis*

Overview of Works (1912–1965)

The music of Dutch composer Matthijs Vermeulen is nearly impossible to describe. Essentially self-taught as a composer, Vermeulen as a mature composer wrote music has almost nothing in common with any of the other music of the same period. It is clearly not tonal; neither is it conclusively atonal. Nor does it adhere to any discernible preconceived harmonic system, but rather creates its own coherent and cohesive system in each new work. It is profoundly melodic—indeed, one could fairly say that his works are essentially melodic in conception—but there are rarely less than three or four and sometimes as many as 100 separate melodies sounding at the same time. It is deeply rhythmic, but the rhythm has little to do with the bar line or the time signature and is rooted in more fundamental pulses that are layered, thereby giving rise to astounding complexities. It is intensely colorful, but the colors are strange and uncanny with extraordinary combinations of instruments frequently at the distant edges of their range. The composers closest to Vermeulen in spirit might be the English eccentric Havergal Brian or American transcendentalist Charles Ives. Vermeulen's oeuvre exclusively consists of songs, chamber music, and orchestral music. Of these, the orchestral music is by far the most significant: There are seven symphonies from the early Brahmsian *Symphonia carminum* (1912–1914) through to the otherworldly *Dithyrambes pour les temps à veni* (Dithyrambes for the time to come) (1963–1967). Although each of the symphonies creates its own sound world, each is obviously the work of Vermeulen: the convoluted primitivism, the relentlessly aggressive rhythms, the weirdly luminous colors, the insistent but almost incomprehensible melodies. While Vermeulen's music is clearly not for all but the hardiest listener, it is extraordinarily compelling and deeply affecting. *—James Leonard*

Recommended:

- ○ **Vermeulen: Chamber Music** / Bylsma, Leeuw, Schoenberg Quartett, etc. / Donemus 39
- ○ **Vermeulen: Orchestral Music** / various artists / Donemus 36
- ○ **Vermeulen: Symphonies 2, 6 & 7** / Rozhdestvensky (cond.), Hague Residentie Orch. / 2002 / Chandos 9735

Shirley Verrett

b. May 31, 1931, New Orleans, LA

Mezzo-Soprano

Shirley Verrett (accent on the last syllable, VerrETT) is one of America's finest opera stars and recital singers, and is one of the remarkable generation of great African-American singers who came to international prominence in the 1950s and 1960s.

She studied voice in Los Angeles with Anna Fitziu and Hall Johnson. In 1955, she won the nationally broadcast CBS program *Arthur Godfrey's Talent Scouts*, leading her to join the Juilliard School. While still a student, she appeared in professional engagements of exceptional importance, including a performance of Falla's *El amor brujo* conducted by Leopold Stokowski, and an operatic debut as Lucretia in Britten's *The Rape of Lucretia*. In 1958 (billed as Shirley Carter), she portrayed Irina in Kurt Weill's *Lost in the Stars* at the New York City Opera. She made her European debut in Nicholas Nabokov's opera *Rasputins Tod* at Cologne in 1959.

Her powerful, dark voice initially characterized her as a mezzo-soprano. She sang such roles as Eboli, Dalila, Amneris, Azucena, and Gluck's Orpheus, as well as Carmen. It soon became clear that she was more properly classed as a dramatic soprano with an exceptional range. She has outstanding evenness across a range well exceeding two octaves.

Verrett also is an outstanding dramatic actress, who joined stage gesture to the musical phrase and to the word with exceptional understanding. She became known early in her career for her blazing portrayal of Bizet's *Carmen*, which she first sang at the Spoleto Festival in 1962. She used it for her debuts at the Bol'shoy (1963), La Scala (1964), Metropolitan Opera (1968), and Covent Garden (1973). (New York had already seen her in the role at the City Opera in 1964.) She sang at the Metropolitan for over 20 years, and also appeared often at La Scala, Covent Garden, the Bolshoi, the Paris Opéra, the San Francisco Opera, the Staatsoper in Vienna, and the Lyric Opera of Chicago, and has appeared at many other of the great opera houses of the world, frequently being asked by them to participate in season-opening productions.

She made operatic history on October 23, 1973, at the first Metropolitan Opera performance of Berlioz's five-act opera *Les Troyens* when her co-star Christa Ludwig took ill and she sang both of the opera's heroines, Cassandra and Dido. *Les Troyens* has also been an important item in her repertory; she was invited to sing in it in the 1990 opening of the new Bastille Opéra in Paris, an event that was, moreover, a commemoration of the 200th anniversary of the French Revolution.

She sang with virtually every great conductor, including Abbado, Leinsdorf, Colin Davis, Krips, Karajan, Giulini, Prêtre, Ozawa, Haitink, Maazel, Levine, Schippers, Solti, Kubelik, and Ormandy, both on the operatic stage and in numerous concert performances. She is an ardent recitalist, singing the great German lieder repertory from Schubert to Mahler, French mélodies, and modern composers such as Ned Rorem, Darius Milhaud, and Falla.

She frequently appeared on the PBS television series *Live from Lincoln Center*. She joined the University of Michigan faculty in 1996, and is the James Earl Jones Distinguished University Professor of Music there. In addition, she teaches each summer at the Accademia Musicale Chigiana in Siena, Italy.

Verrett has received numerous awards including honorary doctorates from Holy Cross College and Northeastern University; the Marian Anderson, Naumburg, and Sullivan Awards; and fellowships from the Ford, Martha Baird Rockefeller, and John Hay Whitney Foundations. In 1970, the French government appointed her *Chevalier des Arts et des Lettres* and in 1984 *Commandeur des Arts et des Lettres*.

She has made numerous operatic, song, and spiritual recordings. *—Joseph Stevenson*

Recommended:

- ○ **Shirley Verrett in Opera** / Verrett, etc. / 1968 / RCA 61457
- ○ **Portraits: Shirley Verrett** / Verrett, Ferro (cond.) / 2002 / Warner Fonit 43341
- ○ **Verdi: Don Carlo** / Giulini (cond.), Domingo, Caballe, Verrett, Milnes, Royal Opera House Orch. Covent Garden / 2000 / Angel 67397
- ○ **Donizetti: Anna Bolena** / Rudel (cond.), Sills, Verrett, Plishka, Lloyd, Tear, London SO / 2000 / DG 465957

Jon Vickers

b. Oct. 29, 1926, Prince Albert, Sask., Canada

Tenor

While Jon Vickers was best known as a Wagnerian heldentenor, he was also capable of singing lieder, baroque opera, spinto Italian roles, and even the comic role of Vasek in *The Bartered Bride*. His voice and physique both radiated power, and his stage presence was one of the most impressive of his era. Like many singers with huge voices, he sometimes resorted to crooning soft passages, but the effect of such a voice scaled down was still highly impressive. He was a man of equally powerful convictions, and refused to sing roles which he considered to be lacking in morality, or whose lack of morality did not carry a lesson.

His father was a lay preacher, and the young Vickers often sang for services. As his vocal gifts became more and more evident, he began to reconsider his aspirations for a career in business; his inclination towards music was confirmed in 1950, when he received a Royal Conservatory scholarship to study voice in Toronto. There he learned technique (founded in Baroque rather than Wagnerian music) from George Lambert and interpretation from Herman Geiger-Torel. He made his operatic debut as the Duke in *Rigoletto* at the Toronto Opera in 1952, and continued to sing in local houses and for Canadian radio in a wide variety of roles, from Ferrando in *Cosi fan tutte* to Alfredo in *La Traviata* to a few excerpts from *Die Walküre* and *Parsifal*.

In 1956, frustrated with what appeared to be a limited career and unsure whether he wanted the pressures of an operatic lifestyle, he was considering leaving music, but within a month of the deadline he gave himself to decide, Covent Garden invited him to make his debut as Riccardo in *Un Ballo in Maschera* in 1957. Other roles and debuts quickly followed: his Bayreuth debut as Siegmund in 1958, his Vienna State Opera debut in 1959 in the same role, his Met debut as Canio in 1960, and his La Scala debut the same year as Florestan in *Fidelio*. His first *Peter Grimes* was at the Met in 1967. By that time, he was one of the world's major heldentenors, and in 1969 he was made a Companion of the Order of Canada. He made his Salzburg Festival debut the next year, as Verdi's *Otello* (a role he filmed with von Karajan). In 1976, he took on the title role of Handel's Samson at the work's United States premiere in Dallas, and followed that with performances in other major U.S. houses. He retired in 1988.

Vickers was known for having a prickly temperament, and was famous for once interrupting the last act of *Tristan und Isolde* to shout at the audience, "Stop your damned coughing!" In other ways, he was deeply modest—he refused to call himself an "artist," insisting that he was merely the interpreter of the real artists, the composers, and refused to make recital pieces or recordings of arias outside of the context of the complete work, saying that this practice inappropriately elevated the performer above the music.

His *Peter Grimes* is one of the most memorable renditions of the role (despite the fact that Britten found the thought of Vickers singing it so far from the original spirit that he refused to attend his performances or hear the recording), and his *Tristan und Isolde* is magnificent, with one of the most moving death scenes on record. In the Italian repertoire, he made a powerful Radames on the Solti recording with Leontyne Price. *—Ann Feeney*

Recommended:

- ○ **My Song Resounds** / Vickers, Woitach / 2001 / CBC 2024
- ○ **Britten: Peter Grimes** / Davis (cond.), Allen, Vickers, Harper, Allan, Royal Opera House Orch. / 1999 / Philips 462847
- ○ **Wagner: Die Walküre** / Leinsdorf (cond.), Nilsson, Vickers, London, Brouwenstijn London SO / 2002 / Decca 470443
- ○ **Beethoven: Fidelio** / Klemperer (cond.), Ludwig, Vickers, Berry, Frick, London PO / 2000 / Angel 67361

Tomás Luis de Victoria

b. 1548, Avila, Spain, **d.** Aug. 20, 1611, Madrid, Spain

Composer: Choral

The dominating figure of sixteenth century Spanish music, Tomás Luis de Victoria was born in Avila. He was sent to Rome to study, possibly for a time under Palestrina during the latter's years at the Roman Seminary. In 1571 he succeeded Palestrina there as choirmaster, a post he also subsequently occupied at the Jesuit Order's German College. Later he became active as a priest, working at St. Girolamo della Carità. Following his return to Spain in 1585, Victoria served the Empress Maria and her daughter as teacher, organist, and choirmaster until his death in 1611.

By the time Victoria arrived in Rome, the conservative ecclesiastical establishment and the Council of Trent had ensured that any musical hint of the "lascivious or the impure" was largely banished (Palestrina was even moved to dismiss his publication of secular madrigals as a youthful peccadillo). It is therefore not surprising to find that Victoria's output consists solely of religious music that eschews even the use of secular cantus firmus, and that displays the formal perfection and the well-smoothed vocal writing of the Palestrina style. What *is* surprising is that despite his Roman training and years of service in the city, Victoria so strongly retained his Spanish roots. Some of his finest works were composed after his return home, and many of them contain features that seem to epitomize the deeply mystical approach of so much Spanish Renaissance music. Comparison with Palestrina reveals a greater emphasis on chromatic color and use of dynamic contrast; Victoria's block harmonies and multiple choirs look forward to the Baroque. His response to words is acute and highly personal, a characteristic particularly suited to the comparatively dynamic and plastic form of the motet and to other texts which allow full rein to subjective treatment. Of Victoria's 44 motets, the early four-part *O quam gloriosum* can perhaps be allowed a special mention, since it is pervaded by a youthful vigor and joyous radiance that gives lie to the understandable impression that Spanish Renaissance composers were preoccupied with somber religious subjects. His widely performed Christmas motet, *O magnum mysterium*, exudes a quiet sense of wonder. Victoria's fame as a motet composer has tended to overshadow his masses, yet at their finest, as in the lovely *Missa Ave maris stella*, they are not inferior to those of Palestrina.

To discover Victoria at his greatest, however, one must ultimately return to the darker side, and in particular to the two works by which he is best known, the *Tenebrae Responsories* (first published in 1585) and the *Requiem* of 1605, a work of timeless serenity. The former is a setting of 18 pieces that adhere to the traditional form of the responsory, with its alternation of verse and refrain. The work takes us through the Passion story in music that relies not so much on the drama of the events themselves as on a quite extraordinarily direct and profound response to the text, a response frequently achieved by means of the greatest simplicity, or, perhaps more accurately, apparent simplicity. *—Brian Robins*

CHORAL

Overview of Works (ca. 1570–1605)

The composers of the height of the musical Renaissance typically exhibit an international style with personal accents: Palestrina was the consummate and reserved Roman church musician, Lassus the utter cosmopolitan, and Byrd the courtier and closet Catholic. Victoria, the austere Spanish Jesuit, is seen as fervent, mystical, and quintessentially imbued with the spirit of the Counter Reformation. It is true that he did add a characteristic stamp of passion to the classical polyphonic style of the "Roman School," and he did compose sacred music exclusively. But the familiar image of Victoria generated by a small number of plangent motets demands revision. His masses and motets contain hallmark chromatic alterations, diminished melodic intervals, and tonal fluctuations, but these features are deployed in both laments and jubilation. He was constantly revising his own work, and considered himself a progressive in composition for double choir and organ. Though only Latin-texted works survive, the affects of madrigalian word painting abound in them; the tenderness of *Quam pulchri sunt gressus tui*, for instance, absolutely pulsates with a more worldly sensuality.

Victoria was fortunate enough to publish nearly all of his compositions during his lifetime; the masses were printed in 1576, 1583, 1594 (a collection containing reworked pieces, intended to cover the entire liturgical year), and 1600. Over half of them parody model pieces of exultant, solemn character, selected from among his own compositions (eight motets, three Marian antiphons, and a psalm) intended for high festal occasions. The *Missa Ascendens Christus*, for instance, though in minor mode, displays a completely uplifting affect; the slightly later *Missa Vidi speciosam* (six-voiced), borrows from its Song of Songs motet a shimmering, radiant texture. Later mass settings (and revisions of earlier ones) are freer in quoting their models, are more concise, and tend to recycle large blocks of material. One apparent anomaly in the late masses is the *Missa Pro victoria*, the "battle mass" on Janequin's *La Guerre*; in addition to its secular model (unique within Victoria's output), this polychoral mass adopts rapid concertante declamation, suggesting the (victorious) battle of faith itself. Four masses, two of them requiems (a four-voiced mass and his "swan song" Office of the Dead for six), paraphrase plainchant models.

A varied but relatively small number of other liturgical pieces complete Victoria's surviving corpus. Around 45 motets betray both his conservative Roman training and his personal chromatic fingerprints (such as *O magnum mysterium*, with its spacious opening in paired imitation, and the stark and powerful opening chords of *O quam gloriosum*). A 1585 publication of motetlike Holy Week music (dedicated not to any worldly potentate or patron, but to the triune God Himself!) contains three passionate sets of *Tenebrae Responsories*, three of Lamentations, two dramatic Passions, and other liturgically specified items, all rich in text painting and plangent harmonies. In addition, he left his beloved Church a series of polychoral psalm settings, a complete set of 16 Magnificats in all tones (two of which were later reworked for double choir), and a set of 32 responsorial hymns for the entire church year. *—Timothy Dickey*

Recommended:

- ○ **Victoria: Cantica Beatae Virginis** / Savall (cond.), Hespèrion XX, Capella Reial de Catalunya / 2002 / Astree 9975
- ○ **Victoria: Tenebrae Responsories** / Phillips (cond.), Tallis Scholars / 2001 / Gimell 22
- ○ **Victoria: Missa Gaudeamus; Missa Pro Victoria; Motets** / Carwood (cond.), Cardinall's Musick / 2000 / ASV 198
- ○ **Victoria: Ave Maris Stella; O Quam Gloriosum** / Hill (cond.), Westminster Cathedral Chr. / 2003 / Hyperion 21114
- ○ **Victoria: Missa Dum Complerentur** / O'Donnell (cond.), Westminster Cathedral Chr. / 1996 / Hyperion 66886
- ○ **Victoria: Missa 'Vidi Speciosam'** / Hill (cond.), Westminster Cathedral Chr. / 1988 / Hyperion 66129
- ○ **Victoria: Missa Trahe Me Post Te** / O'Donnell (cond.), Westminster Cathedral Chr. / 1994 / Hyperion 66738

O magnum mysterium, mass for 4 voices

A 1613 description of the "rules" of parody mass composition by Pietro Cerone describes the common practice of composers when unifying the five movements of an Ordinary of the Mass setting around a model composition. Each movement (Kyrie, Gloria, etc.) should begin with the opening motif of the model and end with the closing; internal motivic material may be further woven into the fabric of the movements. But Tomas Luis de Victoria gradually divested himself of dependence on these classical rules. In a mass setting such as this one, based on his own 1572 Christmas motet *O magnum mysterium*, (as in his 1583 *Mass O quam gloriosum)* the analyst's impression is that Victoria's understanding of his own model was so subtle that only subliminal echoes of the model reach the musical surface. Though the motet model is quite extensive, reflecting on the mystery of the Incarnation at Christmas, the mass which Victoria writes upon it adopts a generally more energetic and celebratory ethos. Only two movements of this Mass—Kyrie and Sanctus—allude to the motet's memorable opening, wherein pairs of voices imitate a motif of a falling fifth. Some sectional closings borrow music which closes a section of the motet (on text "jacentem in presepio"). No direct reference to either jubilant "Alleluia" with which the motet model closes appears, nor is there a wisp of the lovely middle section from the motet at "O beata Virgo." Rather, large tracts of the Mass seem freely composed and quite compactly at that. Only in the so-called "Battle Mass," the *Missa pro Victoria*, does this composer ask his singers to spit out the text out as rapidly and exuberantly (witness the joyous musical surge at the text "Et resurrexit"). Victoria published the *Missa O magnum* himself in 1592, in his third collection of masses; he published this volume in Rome, while on leave from his position as convent chaplain to the Dowager Empress Maria in Madrid. The very publication is unique, as musicologist Robert Stevenson has noted, in that Victoria appears to intended a series of masses for the entire liturgical year—Christmastide *(O magnum mysterium)*, Lent *(Quarti toni)*, Easter *(Trahe me post te)*, Ascension *(Ascendens Christus)*, Assumption *(Vidi speciosam)*, and Trinity *(Salve regina)*, with a Requiem Mass (in four voices) appended. *—Timothy Dickey*

Recommended:

○ **Victoria: O Magnum Mysterium; Ascendens Christus in altum** / Hill (cond.), Westminster Cathedral Chr. / 1986 / Hyperion 66190

O magnum mysterium, motet for 4 voices (1572)

Two upper voices begin a duet in reverential awe, imitating a "great" fall of a melodic fifth, and an intense half-step—thus opens one of the most famous motets of the entire sixteenth century, Tomas Luis de Victoria's *O magnum mysterium*. And yet the young Spanish composer offers nothing truly revolutionary in the work; rather he demonstrates his traditional musical training in conservative Counter-Reformation Rome, which resulted in a characteristically intense attention to each minute detail of his composition. An overused, but still apt, comparison to the painting of the Spanish artist El Greco notes the similar attention both men placed on the emotional content of each brushstroke and how the totality of these individual strokes creates the complete affect. Victoria published this motet in his first musical anthology (the *Motecta* of 1572, published by Gardano in Venice), when he was only 24. Its inscription assigns it to the Feast of the Circumcision of Christ, though the text actually comes from a responsory of the Christmas Matins service, and more appropriately matches the Christmas celebration. What a great mystery, cries the text, that the lowly animals may view the Messiah born in a manger and the blessed Virgin who bore Him. Alleluia. Victoria's setting moves from its long-breathed and reverential opening into a suave series of imitative passages, concluding with the text "laid in a manger." For the exclamation "O beata Virgo" ("O Blessed Virgin!"), a general pause sets up a hushed and mystical passage of homophony: the outer voices move in parallel, with relative immobility in the center blurring the rhythmic lines. This passage proved too extraordinary to feature at all in the mass which Victoria based upon this motet, though he did quote the gesture in a later motet, *Vere languores*. Two jubilant "Alleluia" sections (one in a dance-like triple time) close the motet and suggest necessary revision of the popular image of Victoria as merely a pale, brooding kind of Catholic. *—Timothy Dickey*

Recommended:

○ **Victoria: Cantica Beatae Virginis** / Savall (cond.), Hespèrion XX, Capella Reial de Catalunya / 2002 / Astree 9975

Officium Hebdomadae Sanctae, for 3–8 voices

A well-worn analogy compares the music of the High Renaissance composer Palestrina to the graceful and balanced painting of Raphael; the music of his contemporary Tomas Luis de Victoria evokes the more intense brushwork of El Greco. Born in Avila in Castile, the same Spanish Counter-Reformation town as the mystic St. Teresa, Victoria spent the central 20 years of his career in Rome, studying for the priesthood at the Jesuit Collegio Germanico and serving the Roman musical establishment. The majority of his music (all on sacred texts) was published during this time. But he vivified the reserved and "classical" style of Willaert and Palestrina's church polyphony with his close attention to the local affect of his texts. Victoria's spirituality, at the same time highly orthodox and deeply passionate, bleeds through the pages of his Holy Week music. The rites for the High feast days between Palm Sunday and Easter, known as the *Officium Hebdomadae Sanctae*, memorialize the Triumphal Entry of Christ into Jerusalem, and the events of His Passion and death. This same title appeared on one of the last volumes Victoria published in 1585 before returning permanently to Spain; its official dedication not to a worldly prince or pope, but rather directly to the Trinity may reflect its personal importance to him. The lavishly printed folio collection includes two settings of the Passion narratives, three sets of Lamentations of Jeremiah, three sets of Tenebrae Responsories, and miscellaneous other pieces (such as settings of two motets for Palm Sunday and the *Vere languores* for Good Friday). The Lamentations and the Responsories serve the special "Tenebrae" liturgies of Matins for the *Triduum Sacrum*—Maundy Thursday, Good Friday, and Holy Saturday—night-time services involving ritual darkening of the church. Fifteen candles—symbolizing Christ, the 12 Apostles, and the two Marys—provide the lighting for these services, and all are extinguished one at a time as the liturgy progresses. The deep symbolism in the liturgical structure also prescribes three divisions ("Nocturnes"), each comprising in alternation three Psalms, three Lessons, and three Responsories, thus embedding a series of interlocking Trinitarian symbols in the very fabric of the liturgy. Victoria provides polyphonic music for the second and third Nocturne of each service, following the proper liturgical structure perfectly. The 18 motets, in three groups of [3+3], each follow the "Responsory" form of aBcB, while the third of each group adds a concluding repeat: aBcBaB. The composer calls attention to his structural fidelity by lightening the vocal texture each time in the "c" section (the Versicle). The middle Responsory of each trio, furthermore, invariably uses a higher group of voices. This utter regularity of structure does not, however, constrict the composer's florid imagination. He deploys all his compositional resources to enhance the pathos and dramatic effect of his settings. Different groups of voices may dialogue antiphonally, or otherwise paint the text (as in a cascade at "fons aquae" in "Recessit pater noster"); homophonic textures alternate with imitation (which may pictorialize the lamb "led to the slaughter" in "Eram quasi agnus," or the physical leading of Jesus to his trial in "Iesum tradidit"). And everywhere, Victoria's plangent use of chromatic alterations and surprising harmonic progressions (such as those which dominate the openings of "Tenebrae factae sunt" and "Caligaverunt") enrich the music with aural potency. The music and text of each piece must be considered carefully together; as in the painting of El Greco, the emotional affect of the image seen from a distance depends on the intense emotional energy of each brushstroke. *—Timothy Dickey*

Recommended:

○ **Victoria: Tenebrae Responsories** / Phillips (cond.), Tallis Scholars / 2001 / Gimell 22

Pro defunctis, mass for 6 voices

With the promulgation of the Catholic doctrine of Purgatory in the later Middle Ages, the regular performance of obituary masses for the benefit of departed souls took on great urgency. Yearly, on All Souls' Day (November 2), the Catholic Church says a solemn mass and Office for all the departed; the same liturgy applies to all Christian burials, and to memorial prayer services for deceased individuals. By the sixteenth century, polyphonic composition of some selected movements of the requiem mass became quite common; even during the tumult of the Reformation, Catholic-nationality composers such as Spaniards Francisco Guerrero and Cristóbal de Morales contributed to the tradition. It should come as no surprise that their younger colleague Tomás Luis de Victoria wrote two requiems, the first appearing in print as early as his first *Book of Masses* (Rome, 1583). Moreover, he reissued the same piece of music in his second book (1592, also published in Rome, though Victoria was back in Madrid), in which he attempted an ambitious program of a complete series of masses for the seasons of the liturgical year, ending with the four-voiced *Requiem*. The better-known 1605 *Officium defunctorum*, containing a six-voiced *Requiem* mass (SSATTB), builds upon this first composition. The entire *Officium defunctorum* was a set of works intended for the funeral of Empress Maria of Austria; Victoria called it a *cygneam cantionem* or swan song.

Victoria spent most of the first half of his career serving as both priest and musician in Rome, possibly even studying composition under Palestrina (who also wrote an austere requiem). But while the classicizing influence of the Roman style always shows in his music, Victoria's deeply emotional spirituality imbues it with passion. The 1605 Requiem is no exception. Structurally, he fulfills all liturgical propriety, setting the Introit "Requiem aeternam" (from which the requiem mass itself derives its name), the Kyrie, Gradual, Offertory ("Domine Jesu Christe"), Sanctus, Agnus Dei One–Three, and Communion ("Lux aeterna"). To this he adds a Matins lesson setting (*Taedet animam meam"*, a motet (*Versa est in luctum*), and the responsory *Libera me*, a solemn prayer from the burial service that follows the mass. The deliberate, carefully smoothed surface of Palestrina's music is very much in evidence here, but Victoria is deeper-hued, with more distinctive profiles for each section and a richer palette of (still very strictly controlled) dissonances.

The 1605 *Missa pro defunctis* is what scholars of Renaissance music call a paraphrase mass. Each section is built on a preexisting melody (in this case the chants of the traditional requiem mass) that is fully woven into the texture and thus has symbolic value more than special musical prominence. The chants of a paraphrase mass may migrate from voice to voice, but in Victoria's mass the chant opens each section, solo, in the lower of the two soprano lines and remains there as the music continues. *—AMG*

Recommended:

○ **Victoria: Requiem** / Phillips (cond.), Tallis Scholars / 2001 / Gimell 12

Vienna Boys' Choir

f. Jul. 7, 1498, Vienna, Austria

Ensemble

The Wiener Sängerknaben or Vienna Boys' Choir (sometimes translated Vienna Choir Boys) is the world's foremost children's choral group. It is also among the oldest of all musical organizations, having been founded pursuant to an Imperial decree of Holy Roman Emperor Maximilian I on July 7, 1498; the Emperor wished boys' voices to be added to the choir of the Imperial Chapel, or Hofkapelle. This established a tradition of having the boys sing in weekly Sunday masses in the Imperial Chapel of the Hofburg Palace in Vienna, a tradition that continues today.

Over the centuries, illustrious composers have written masterpieces for the Boys' Choir of the Imperial Chapel, including Mozart, Bruckner, Gluck, and

Schubert. Many great musicians got their start as members of the Boys' Choir; among them were the great conductors Hans Richter, Clemens Krauss, and Lovro von Matacic. During the days of the Austro-Hungarian Empire, the choir became renowned for its secular performances as well, appearing in colorful Imperial-style military uniforms, each complete with a dagger. After World War I, wide popular and governmental disfavor of all things Imperial resulted in the dissolution of many long-standing institutions, including the Imperial Chapel Choir. However, Chaplain Joseph Schnitt remained in his position at the chapel and regathered the choir. Sparing no personal expense, he reestablished a boarding school for the choristers. He replaced the imperial uniforms with a distinctive sailor-style uniform.

The Vienna Boys' Choir has the most stringent training and admittance policy in the world. Boys wishing to join must first gain entrance to a preparatory school where they receive a complete elementary education. Their instruction includes elements of musical theory, sight-singing, and the practice of singing, and instruction on at least one instrument; at the age of nine, they have to pass an examination based strictly on musical ability and vocal quality. There is no religious requirement. The teaching is purposely intensive in order that their education not be slighted due to the frequent touring. There are usually two choirs away on a tour at any given time, most frequently for three months. They are accompanied by their choirmaster, their tutor, and a nurse. Vienna Choir Boys have visited the United States well in excess of 50 times since 1932 and have traveled to all six inhabited continents. They are beloved the world over for their lively singing style and beautiful tone and have commissioned a number of new works, including Britten's *The Golden Vanity*. *—Joseph Stevenson*

Recommended:

- ○ **Angelic Voices** / Vienna Boys' Choir, VSO, Vienna State Opera CO / 1998 / Philips 462778
- ○ **Edelweiss** / Vienna Boys' Choir / 1998 / Laserlight 14312
- ○ **Portrait** / Harrer (cond.), Equiluz, Scharinger, Jelosits, Cencic, Vienna Boys' Choir / 1993 / Philips 434726

Vienna Philharmonic Orchestra

f. 1842, Vienna, Austria

Ensemble

Since its inception in 1842, the Vienna Philharmonic Orchestra has represented the best in the Central European orchestral tradition. Before the VPO was founded, in fact, there was no permanent, professional orchestra to be found outside the opera halls in the city of Mozart, Haydn, and Beethoven. In 1833, Franz Lachner, conductor at the Hofoper, had formed a musicians' association from the ranks of the opera orchestras to play symphonic music, but this was a temporary endeavor. Nine years later, a group of music critics and other interested parties persuaded Otto Nicolai, principal conductor of the Kärntertortheater, to conduct the first Wiener Philharmoniker concert at the Grosser Redoutensaal (Great Ballroom) on March 28, 1842. The VPO was founded as the first completely self-governing orchestra, and it has remained so ever since.

Although until 1860 concerts were irregular, the orchestra quickly built up a reputation. From 1860 to 1875, Otto Dessoff was permanent conductor, bringing the music of Johannes Brahms, Richard Wagner, and Franz Liszt into the concert halls. Hans Richter succeeded Dessoff and conducted the orchestra until 1898, introducing Anton Bruckner and Antonín Dvořák to Viennese audiences. Both of these conductors played major roles in establishing the VPO as one of the finest orchestras in the world. During this time, the VPO had numerous premieres of now-classic works such as Brahms' *Second Symphony* and Bruckner's *Eighth*; sometimes, as in the case of Bruckner's *Third*, the premiere was conducted by the composer himself. The great Gustav Mahler conducted from 1898 to 1901, but his tenure was marked by dissension within the orchestra.

The longest-term conductor of the post-Mahler era was Felix Weingartner, from 1908 to 1927. He was beloved by the orchestra for his measured, classical style and in particular for his Beethoven interpretations. From 1933 to 1938, the revered conductors Bruno Walter and Wilhelm Furtwängler shared the subscription concerts; after Hitler's annexation of Austria in 1938, the Nazi Party dissolved the Philharmonic, but the decision was reversed after Furtwängler intervened. The VPO led an uneasy life during the war, but afterwards reclaimed its place in the world's orchestral pantheon. The list of conductors who have led VPO subscription concerts reads like an honor roll of maestros; besides the men already mentioned, composer Richard Strauss, Arturo Toscanini, Dmitri Mitropoulos, Hans Knappertsbusch, Herbert von Karajan, and Leonard Bernstein have each taken turns at the podium.

The VPO is one of the most traditional orchestras in the world today. Some of its traditions are much-beloved, like the annual New Year's concerts of waltzes by the Strauss family; others have come under fire in recent years. While the VPO premiered a lot of music in its early days, it now prefers to play mostly music written before 1900, which created a controversy at the Salzburg Festival during the 1990s. The orchestra also refused until 1997 to accept a female musician as a full member, threatening to disband rather than cave in to political pressure. The only woman in the VPO is harpist Anna Lelkes, who was granted full membership after 26 years of service. It seems that Lelkes is viewed as the exception which confirms the rule. Generally, the VPO opposes hiring musicians who are not Central European men, in order to preserve what is perceived as a unique quality of sound. While the orchestra's policies may be controversial, it cannot be disputed ithat the VPO is one of the world's finest orchestras, performing with exceptional finesse and clarity, with a beautifully blended woodwind and brass sound that meshes perfectly with its subtle, lush strings. *—Andrew Lindemann Malone*

Recommended:

- ○ **Best of New Year's Concert** / VPO, etc. / DG 000166302
- ○ **Wiener Philharmoniker 150th Anniversary** / VPO, etc. / 1991 / London 433330
- ○ **20th Century Masters** / VPO, etc. / 2003 / Andante 4080
- ○ **Anton Bruckner** / VPO, etc. / 2003 / Andante 4070
- ○ **(1948–1955): Mahler** / VPO, etc. / 2002 / Andante 4973
- ○ **1952–1957): Beethoven** / VPO, etc. / 2002 / Andante 4988
- ○ **(1957–1963)** / VPO, etc. / 2001 / Andante 4997-5000

Vienna Symphony Orchestra

f. 1900, Vienna, Austria

Ensemble

The Vienna Symphony Orchestra was founded in 1900 and consolidated in 1921 from the ranks of another Viennese orchestra. The group's first permanent conductor was Ferdinand Löwe, a noted pupil of Anton Bruckner who conducted the premiere of Bruckner's *Symphony No. 9*. He led the orchestra for its first 24 years.

Although it never aspired to the reputation of the Vienna Philharmonic, the Vienna Symphony's guest conductors during the early twentieth century included many names more commonly associated with the better known orchestra, among them Felix Weingartner, Gustav Mahler, Bruno Walter, Richard Strauss, and Arnold Schoenberg.

The Vienna Symphony was taken over by the city of Vienna in 1938 as a municipal orchestra. After World War II, with the resumption of artistic life in Vienna, the orchestra came under the direction of Herbert von Karajan, who was kept from working with the more prestigious Philharmonic by his rival Wilhelm Furtwängler.

The Vienna Symphony also became the orchestra of choice for early recordings by such noted conductors as Otto Klemperer and Jascha Horenstein, and also served as host to such figures as Ferenc Fricsay and even Karl Böhm, who recorded Richard Strauss' *Daphne*, a notably beautiful though little known opera, the premiere of which he had conducted with the orchestra in the 1930s. *—Bruce Eder*

Recommended:

- ○ **Mahler Symphony 1; Bruckner Symphony 9** / Horenstein (cond.), VSO / 1992 / Vox 5508
- ○ **The 1950s Haydn Symphonies Recordings** / Scherchen (cond.), Vienna State Opera Orch., VSO / DG 000185402

Louis Vierne

b. Oct. 8, 1870, Poitiers, France, **d.** Jun. 2, 1937, Paris, France

Composer: Keyboard

Born blind, Vierne partially regained sight at age six. Obvious talent was rewarded with piano and solfège studies, to which were added harmony, violin, and a general course when he entered the Institution National des Jeunes Aveugles in Paris in 1880. There he was befriended by César Franck who, from 1886, gave him private tuition in harmony while including Vierne in his organ class at the Paris Conservatoire. The lessons of the master were not lost on him—Franck possessed perhaps the richest harmonic palette in Western music and Vierne effortlessly absorbed many of its features. Vierne entered the Conservatoire as a full-time student in 1890. Franck died in November, succeeded by Charles-Marie Widor as professor of organ. Vierne soon became Widor's assistant, a post he continued to hold under Guilmant—where he taught Dupré and Nadia Boulanger—and deputized for Widor at St. Sulpice. Vierne took the Conservatoire's first prize for organ in 1894, though his career waited until 1900 to be spectacularly launched when, on May 21, he triumphed over four other organists in a competition for the prestigious post of titular organist at Notre Dame de Paris (its magnificent instrument reconditioned by Cavaillé-Coll) where his audience came to include such luminaries as Clémenceau and Rodin. The *Symphony No. 1 for organ* (1898–99) forecasts the succession of moods—grand and assertively virile, searchingly contrapuntal, effusive, and distressingly confessional—which would deepen anguishingly in succeeding works, reflecting an unhappy marriage and divorce, professional disappointments, the loss of a son and a brother in the Great War, and a continual battle to retain minimal sight. After being passed over for professorship of the Conservatoire's organ class in 1911, Vierne taught at the Schola Cantorum. His *Symphony No. 2 for organ*, completed in 1903, drew from no less a critic than Debussy the stunning accolade, "M. Vierne's symphony is truly remarkable. It combines rich musicality with ingenious discoveries in the special sonority of the organ. J.S. Bach, the father of us all, would have been well pleased...." The spate of disturbingly eloquent compositions—*mélodies*, piano pieces, chamber works, mass settings, the *Symphony in A*, and numerous works for organ (including, at last, six symphonies)—continued to pour forth until his death. Concert tours took him to England in 1924 and 1925, and on to a three-month visit to the U.S. and Canada in 1927. Vierne died of a heart attack at the organ of Notre Dame during a public concert on June 2, 1937. *—Adrian Corleonis*

KEYBOARD

Pièces de fantaisie, Suites 1–4, Opp. 51, 53, 54 & 55 (1926–1927)

This grand tour of the major and minor keys requires a mighty ocean liner of an instrument; unlike this series, Vierne's earlier *Pieces in Free Style* didn't require pedal tones or a terribly wide variety of registrations. The 24 pieces are grouped into four books of six, but their sequence follows no harmonic scheme. In each suite, though, the opening movement is some sort of introduction and the final movement is always a processional. Each suite could be a Low Mass sequence in secular garb, the standard Prelude, Introit, Offertory, Elevation, Communion, and Recessional here taking more fanciful titles. A few movements, particularly in the first suite, carry generic indications, like Andantino and Intermezzo. Sometimes the movements are mood pieces ("Résignation," even "Requiem Aeternam"), but they are mostly impressionistic nature paintings (*Hymne au soleil, Claire de lune, Etoile du soir, Sur le Rhin*) and evocations of the fantastic (*Naïades, Gargouilles et Chimères, Fantômes*). Vierne suggested registrations for each piece, but in his foreword to each volume he gave performers permission to alter them according to the nature of the instrument on which the music would be played. Vierne did not allow organists free rein, though: "It goes without saying," he wrote, "that players should take care to avoid disparate, picturesque, or eccentric effects not justified by the nature of the music." A few of Vierne's more popular works are found in these suites, such as the "Impromptu" and "Carillon de Westminster" from the third suite and "Naïades" from the fourth. The "Carillon de Westminster" was dedicated to organ builder Henry Willis III. Similarly, "Clair de lune" in the second suite was dedicated to organ builder Ernest M. Skinner. The suites were written to be used on his 1927 tour of America, undertaken to raise funds to repair the organ of Notre Dame in Paris. As such, the pieces are not as serious as his *Organ Symphonies* and display more of the pianistic possibilities of the instrument along with its colorful elegance. There is a sense of appropriateness that such fanciful, impressionistic, feeling works should be written by a man who was practically blind, therefore relying on his other senses and imagination to make his way in the world.*—James Reel*

Recommended:

○ **André Marchal: First Recordings, Paris: 1936–1948** / Marchal / 2003 / Arbiter 135

Symphony No. 2 in E minor, Op. 20 (1902–1903)

Vierne's *Second Symphony* for organ captures him on the threshold of his maturity—despite partial blindness, a commanding, even swashbuckling, figure of passionate eloquence and cunning technical competence. Having competed for and won the post of titular organist at the prestigious Notre Dame de Paris on May 21, 1900, by the time he came to compose the *Second Symphony*, between July 1902 and April 1903, the rich timbres and sheer power of Notre Dame's splendid Cavaillé-Coll instrument had become an extension of himself. If the *First Symphony* for organ seemed less a symphony than a suite, the *Second* measures up to the form with an initial Allegro of virile assertiveness whose contrasting themes, in good Franckist cyclic fashion, are pressed to supply melodic material for succeeding movements. Before the symphony was completed, Vierne's preview performance of the ruminative second movement Choral and blithe third movement Scherzo drew from no less a critic than Debussy a stunning notice in *Gil Blas*—"M. Vierne's symphony is truly remarkable. It combines rich musicality with ingenious discoveries in the special sonority of the organ. J.S. Bach, the father of us all, would have been well pleased with M. Vierne." Vierne, himself, thought highly enough of the scherzo that he later transcribed it for organ and orchestra. The following cantabile is a pithy meditation escalating in intensity to a sort of tormented rapture—a notable instance of the chromatically inflected morbidity which often besets Vierne's most searching expressions—before subsiding in eloquent disquiet. The virtuoso Final whips the previous movement's uneasiness to an ever more tortured Sturm und Drang, intense and powerful, which achieves resolution only through a bravura flourish. *—Adrian Corleonis*

Recommended:

○ **Vierne: Symphony 2; Les Angélus** / Hill / 1999 / Hyperion 55044

Symphony No. 6 in B minor, Op. 59 (1930)

The *Sixth Symphony* was Vierne's last large-scale composition for organ. A six-part *Messe basse pour les défunts* would follow in 1934, but that is muted, minor, functional. Composed between July 15 and September 15, 1930, at Roquebrune on the Mediterranean, as he approached his 60th birthday, the *Sixth Symphony*, on the other hand, is testamentary, if not confessional. Among other things, it is a testament of his triumphant career as organist, inspired improviser, and acclaimed composer. But it is also the tormented confession to a lifetime of disappointment, professional frustration, failing health, blindness, loss (of friends, family, wife, lovers), betrayal, and despair. To this work Vierne brought the full range of chromatic writing that had increasingly marked his later music; the first and second movements both have tone row-like themes that use all 12 notes of the chromatic scale.

The extended first movement Introduction et Allegro is a pilgrim's progress from distressed darkness to defiant acceptance. Though its agony of spirit is palpable, it is not without grandeur. The mournfully pleading Aria which follows wanders in the Slough of Despond—the voice of one crying in the wilderness. The Scherzo is one of Vierne's grotesqueries, a brief but disturbingly bizarre exercise in grim playfulness. Beginning in and returning to the organ's lowest register, a long Adagio traces a progress from profound depression, through despairing regret, to resignation. The remarkable Final makes tormented play of two themes—the first of grim cheer and a second which seems to smile through tears—which are less combined than juxtaposed in a determined tour-de-force coda to make Vierne's last and somewhat frenetic show of virile assertiveness. The intensely personal nature of the *Sixth Symphony*, and the fact that Vierne's keyboard technique had begun to slip with age, no doubt account for the fact that it was left to Vierne's pupil, Maurice Duruflé, to give the work its delayed premiere, at Notre Dame, in 1935. *—Adrian Corleonis*

Recommended:

○ **Vierne: Organ Symphonies 3 & 6** / Mathieu / 1996 / Naxos 553524

○ **Complete Organ Symphonies of Louis Vierne Vol. 4** / Simcock / Priory 425

Works for Organ (1894–1934)

Louis Vierne, successor to Charles-Marie Widor as professor of organ at the Paris Conservatoire, followed in Widor's footsteps by channeling much of his musical energy into the composition of organ symphonies. Vierne did not live nearly as long as Widor, however—both died in 1937, when Vierne was just under 67 and Widor was well over 90—and so his list of important works is considerably shorter.

First and foremost are the six organ symphonies composed between 1898 and 1930. Grandiose, massive music composed to exploit the immense capacities of the organ at the Notre Dame Cathedral (where Vierne worked from 1900 until his death), these are not, as one might at first suspect, symphonies for orchestra and organ such as Saint-Saëns' famous *Organ Symphony*; they are multimovement works for organ alone, symphonic in nature but cast in forms that allow qualities of the symphony, sonata, and suite to join together. Vierne's organ symphonies may be more respected and oft-played than even Widor's ten works in the genre.

Vierne composed many shorter organ pieces; he sometimes bundled many together into volumes—there are the 24 *pièces en style libre* of 1913, and then four volumes' worth of *Pièces de fantasie* dating from the late 1920s. Vierne's orchestral music, which includes a *Symphony* (1908), a tone poem, and some works for piano or organ and orchestra, is not so plentiful nor today so well-remembered as his organ music. Just as thoroughly forgotten (perhaps because it was never well-known in the first place) is Vierne's chamber music, the centerpieces of which are a *Violin Sonata* (1906), a *Cello Sonata* (1910) and a *String Quartet*.

Today, Vierne is considered more important as a teacher than a composer (Marcel Dupré and Nadia Boulanger are among those that studied with him), but his music exudes the rich, peculiarly French sense of harmony and fluidity that many musicians find irresistible. *—Blair Johnston*

Recommended:

○ **Vierne: Complete Organ Symphonies** / Oosten / 1996 / MDG 3160732

○ **Vierne: Works for Piano** / Gardon / 1995 / Timpani 2023

○ **Vierne: Mélodies** / Delunsch, Icart, Kerdoncuff / 1997 / Timpani 1040

○ **Vierne: L'œuvre d'orgue Intégral Vol. 1** / Cochereau, Baker / Solstice SO 811

○ **Vierne: Piano Quintet Op42; String Quartet Op12** / Tacchino, Athenaeum Enesco SQ / 2000 / Disques Pierre Verany 700011

Henri Vieuxtemps

b. Feb. 17, 1820, Verviers, Belgium, **d.** Jun. 6, 1881, Mustapha, Algiers, Algeria

Composer: Concerto

Henri Vieuxtemps was a child prodigy and one of the most important composers of violin music in the latter nineteenth century. He was an innovator within the Romantic movement, though he was not always successful in that role. Vieuxtemps' melodies are generally attractive, and if they are a bit saccharine at times, they nevertheless have strong appeal. Almost all his music involves the violin, whether in orchestral, chamber, or solo genres. He may have left an equally lasting legacy in the realm of violin performance, having been central to the development of the Russian School and influential throughout Europe, as well.

Henri Vieuxtemps was musically precocious, taking his first violin lessons at the age of four from his father, an amateur violinist, who by trade was a weaver. He later studied with Lecloux-Dejonc and, incredibly, performed a violin concerto by Rode at age six! He went on concert tour at eight years of age, appearing in Liege, Brussels, and other nearby cities. He caught the notice of Charles de Bériot, who subsequently took him on as a student. In 1829, de Bériot introduced him to Parisian audiences, who were strongly enthusiastic at the youth's debut concert.

Bériot's marriage and concert obligations forced him to end his private lessons with Vieuxtemps in 1831. Young Henri then traveled to Brussels and worked with Pauline Garcia, Bériot's sister-in-law. While she did not instruct him, she was of great assistance in the performance of duets. Two years later Vieuxtemps went on a concert tour of Germany and Austria, accompanied by his father. He performed Beethoven's violin concerto in Vienna, and decided to settle there temporarily and take instruction in composition from Sechter. At his London debut in mid-1834, he met Paganini, and the two were mutually impressed. Vieuxtemps then went on to study composition in Paris with Antonin Reicha.

By 1836, Vieuxtemps he had composed his first violin concerto, published later as No. 2, in F sharp. Further concert tours ensued, including two to Russia, in 1837 and 1840, respectively. In between, he suffered from an illness that required a long period of recuperation. During his last tour of Russia, Vieuxtemps wrote his Second Violin Concerto, which received much acclaim, especially in Paris.

Vieuxtemps made his first of three concert tours of the United States in 1843–44. In the latter year, he married Viennese pianist Josephine Eder. Having had much success in Russia, he accepted a post in St. Petersburg as Court violinist in 1846. During this period he composed his most popular violin concerto, No. 4 in D minor, Op. 31.

He left Russia in 1851 and resumed his career as a virtuoso performer. His second American tour occurred in 1857–58, Vieuxtemps again achieving great success with critics and public alike. His Fifth Violin Concerto came in 1861. The composer and his wife and family moved to Paris five years later, owing to the unstable political situation in Frankfurt, where they had been living since 1855. His wife died suddenly in 1868, after which he resumed foreign concert tours for a time. He took a teaching post at the Brussels Conservatory in 1871, where his students included Ysaye, and two years later suffered a stroke resulting in paralysis of his right arm. This episode effectively ended his career as a soloist, though he eventually regained enough ability to perform chamber music in private concerts. He was also able to compose in his last decade.

In 1879, he moved to Algeria where his daughter lived. His inability to play with proficiency in his final years was a source of great frustration for him. *—Robert Cummings*

CONCERTO

Violin Concertos (1840–1879)

Henri Vieuxtemps (1820–81) wrote seven violin concertos, though only the *Fourth* and *Fifth* have been concertized and recorded with any regularity. In the case of the former work, it is played by many, perhaps most, violin virtuosos today, while the latter remains on the fringes of the repertory, not least because of the attention given it by Jascha Heifetz, who recorded it twice.

Vieuxtemps, one of the leading virtuoso violinists of the mid-nineteenth century, was also widely admired as a composer for his concertos and chamber works. Berlioz heaped lavish praise on his 1840 *First Violin Concerto* (in E major, Op. 10). He came along at an auspicious time, when Paganini's works were beginning to be seen as the virtuoso vehicles they were, when Spohr's concertos were waning in popularity, and when the compositions of Rode, Viotti and others were still mired in traditional and conservative styles. Thus, his fresher voice was greeted with enthusiasm.

The *First Concerto* is attractive and well-constructed, consisting of three movements, with the first (Allegro moderato) lasting about 25 minutes. Here, the orchestra has much to say and the violin writing is brilliant. The middle panel (Adagio) is very brief and the Rondo finale substantial, containing some virtuosic hurdles for the soloist.

The *Second Concerto*, in F sharp minor, Op. 19, is really his first, being written in 1836. Its three movements are not as substantial as the first concerto's, though they feature attractive themes and brilliant writing.

Ysaÿe declared that the A minor *Third Concerto*, Op. 25, showed the influence of Beethoven's *Violin Concerto*. Again, the first movement (Allegro) is large and features a lengthy orchestral introduction, in which the voice of Beethoven can be noticed. The Adagio second movement is lovely and the Rondo finale also attractive.

The *Fourth*, in D minor, Op. 31, is probably the most subtle and well-balanced work of the seven. Consisting of four movements, it is dramatic in the first, even profound, lovely and serene in the second, and buoyant and colorful in the third. The finale offers a main theme which bears a close resemblance to that in the finale of the Beethoven *Fifth Symphony*, but the music here never sounds stale or imitative.

The *Fifth Concerto* ("Grétry"), in A minor, Op. 37, features a second movement taken up by a difficult and compelling cadenza—which must have attracted Heifetz—followed by a short Adagio and Allegro con fuoco finale. The first movement (Allegro non troppo) is probably the best of the four.

The four-movement *Sixth Concerto*, in G major, Op. 47, features a lovely second movement, marked Pastorale: Andante con moto, and a brilliant Rondo finale.

The *Seventh*, cast in three movements, has an attractive opening panel, but the atmospheric middle movement (Melancolie: Andante Sostenuto) is also compelling in its wistful and sad manner. *—Robert Cummings*

Recommended:

- ○ **Vieuxtemps: Violin Concertos 1 & 4** / Keylin, Burkh (cond.), Janáček PO, Yuasa (cond.), Arnhem PO / 2000 / Naxos 554506
- ○ **Vieuxtemps: Violin Concertos 2 & 3** / Keylin, Burkh (cond.), Janáček PO / 1997 / Naxos 554114
- ○ **Vieuxtemps: Violin Concertos 5, 6 & 7** / Keylin, Mogrelia (cond.), Slovak RSO, Yuasa (cond.), Arnhem PO / 2003 / Naxos 8557016

Violin Concerto No. 4 in D minor, Op. 31 (ca. 1850)

The orchestral writing in this, Vieuxtemps' own favorite among his concertos, is sensitive and makes particularly good use of the woodwinds. But aside from the substantial introduction and various tutti passages, the violinist is clearly the center of attention. The first movement, Andante, begins with a lengthy, weighty introduction that opens like a quiet chorale and then gradually builds speed, loudness, and intensity, with brass and tympani providing extra heft. As all of this recedes, a downward-swirling figure in the strings suggests water flowing away into the murk. The soloist finally enters with a declamatory line, spitting out double-stop notes, but this almost immediately melts into more lyrical, yet still ardent material. This, with its recitative-like material, seems like a second introduction, but it is indeed the movement's main thematic substance. A lengthy, tempestuous cadenza eventually surrenders to a stern orchestral passage; this fades into a long-held horn note that serves as a bridge to the second movement. This Adagio religioso begins with a woodwind chorale; the violin soon enters, serenely trilling above the orchestra, and sings a long, ardent prayer that gradually builds to a state of ecstasy. As the music calms, harp arpeggios grace another passage of violin trills. Some contemporary listeners may find this movement's pretty pieties off-putting, but religious sentimentality was a major element of much Franco-Belgian music of the mid-nineteenth century, and this Vieuxtemps slow movement is an important example of the style. The Scherzo, marked Vivace, brings a welcome impishness to the concerto and has much in common with the vibrant, assertive violin works of Saint-Saëns. The movement's central trio section slows down and stretches out with grand, sweeping orchestral support for the violin's happily quivering line. Before the Finale marziale fully gets underway, the strings and woodwinds revisit material from the concerto's beginning. This time, the Andante introduction is succinct and the full orchestra soon presents a festive march, again resembling the style of Saint-Saëns. After a full tour around the parade ground, the soloist finally joins in, first with a recitative and then with the main march tune. Rapid passagework and harrowing double-stops prevent the movement from falling into pomposity; at one point, the violin plays an ardent, decidedly non-military melody. And later, the soloist even gives the march tune a remarkably lyrical treatment. Midway through this movement, the music kicks into the major mode and the concerto ends in heady victory. *—James Reel*

Recommended:

- ○ **Vieuxtemps: Violin Concertos 1 & 4** / Keylin, Yuasa (cond.), Arnhem PO / 2000 / Naxos 554506
- ○ **Great Violinists: Heifetz** / Heifetz, Barbirolli (cond.), London PO / 2000 / Naxos 110943

Violin Concerto No. 5 in A minor ("Grétry"), Op. 37 (1861)

Although the *Violin Concerto No. 4* is "the" Vieuxtemps concerto, No. 5 in A minor is also relatively familiar and has been championed by the likes of Leopold Auer, Jascha Heifetz, and Itzhak Perlman. Vieuxtemps wrote it in 1858–1859 as a competition piece for Hubert Léonard at the Brussels Conservatory. The work originally held only two movements, but Vieuxtemps later added a third; they are played without interruption.

The first movement, Allegro non troppo, announces its main themes through the orchestra without soloist. The opening motif is suspenseful and tragic; soon the music becomes grander with the orchestra playing at full blast, and eventually the thematic material spreads out with longer note values, and subsides. The violin finally enters with rising, searching phrases, which quickly morph into complex passagework, a preview of coming attractions. Soon the soloist picks up the orchestra's themes, punctuating their lyricism with flurries of virtuosity. Vieuxtemps provided two cadenzas; one is fairly contrapuntal, and the other is full of double stops and other splashy techniques.

A brief Moderato passage leads to the Adagio movement, an effusion of A minor lyricism. Toward the end, the music modulates to C major to quote a melody from André Grétry's opera *Lucile*, here highly romanticized (hence the concerto's sometime nickname, "Grétry"). After the violin plays the final ornamented measure of this older material, the music swoops back into A minor for the concluding Allegro con fuoco, a final burst of virtuosity so brief that it is little more than a coda to the preceding two movements. *—James Reel*

Recommended:

- ○ **Mendelssohn: Concerto Op 64; Vieuxtemps: Concerto Op37** / Chee-Yun, Lopez-Cobos (cond.), London PO / Denon 78913

Roger Vignoles

b. Jul. 12, 1945, Cheltenham, England
Pianist

Older than several others among the superbly schooled and stylistically sensitive group of accompanists to have come from the United Kingdom in the last quarter of the twentieth century, Roger Vignoles ranks with the finest. Originally inspired by Gerald Moore, who advanced piano accompanying from subordination to full partnership, Vignoles has shown from the beginning a canny grasp of differing schools of songwriting and the gift for putting his singers at ease. Moreover, his own interests stretch to wide horizons; he is as on the mark with songs from the cabaret as with the rarefied atmospheres found in the songs of Duparc. Following studies at Magdalene College in Cambridge, England, Vignoles resolved that he would pursue a career as a piano accompanist. Further studies at the Royal College of Music and in private classes with Paul Hamburger (himself a noted accompanist) prepared him for his 1967 debut at London's *Purcell Room.* From 1969 to 1971, Vignoles worked as a coach and répétiteur at the Royal Opera House. One of his first regular collaborators was Swedish soprano Elisabeth Söderström. Pleased with her young accompanist's work and personality, the singer frequently reengaged him during the 1970s and 1980s. During this period, other singers took note of his work and began to engage him for recitals. Three of the most prominent were Sarah Walker, Thomas Allan, and Kiri Te Kanawa (the latter two before their respective knighthoods). With both Allan and Walker, the association was long lasting, leaving some memorable recordings as evidence. The Walker/Vignoles partnership resulted in concerts and recordings exploring German lieder, French mélodie, and even an eclectic and intriguing assortment of cabaret songs. From 1974 to 1981, Vignoles taught the art of accompaniment at the Royal College of Music. A regular presence at many of the world's leading festivals, Vignoles has become an important part of the Schubertiade at Feldkirch. At Queen Elizabeth Hall in London, he created a week-long series in 1997 billed as "Landscape into Song." The following year, he initiated the Nagaoka Winter Festival in Japan, returning each year since as artistic director to conduct master classes and perform in recital. He contributed to the 2001 Schumann Festival in London and has accompanied Benjamin Britten's *Canticles* on several occasions, including a staged version given in Barcelona. Master-class experiences have given Vignoles a perspective more sympathetic to terrified young singers than is often accorded by former star singers conducting the affairs. He has urged allowing the participants time to sing a few phrases before being pounced on and corrected. His own ability to make singers comfortable and able to give of their best has made him a valued ally. Vignoles continues to be one of the most sought-after collaborators for singers. Among his many outstanding recordings are a disc devoted to the complete songs of Duparc with Walker and Allan. With French soprano Véronique Gens, he has recorded a disc devoted to mélodies by Fauré, Debussy, and Poulenc. First recital recordings by Swedish mezzo Katarina Karnéus and Samoan bass-baritone Jonathan Lemalu have also greatly benefited from Vignoles' presence, both stabilizing and enlivening. A recording of Schumann songs, including *Frauenliebe und -leben* with mezzo-soprano Bernarda Fink, has also won admiring reviews. *—Erik Eriksson*

Recommended:

- ○ **Beethoven Songs** / Genz, Vignoles / 2003 / Hyperion 21055
- ○ **Brahms: Violin Sonatas** / Pauk, Vignoles / Brilliant 99800/8
- ○ **Schubert: 19 Lieder** / Walker, Vignoles / Brilliant 99449
- ○ **French & English Songs** / Allen, Parsons, Vignoles / 2002 / Virgin 562059

Heitor Villa-Lobos

b. Mar. 5, 1887, Rio de Janeiro, Brazil, **d.** Nov. 17, 1959, Rio de Janeiro, Brazil
Composer: Chamber Music, Vocal, Keyboard, Orchestral, Symphonic, Concerto

The music of Heitor Villa-Lobos is known for its characteristic nationalism, driving rhythms, and original instrumentation. He was trained as an autodidact opposed to academic instruction, his music grew in a completely independent and individual fashion.

Villa-Lobos began studying music at an early age, when his father, a worker at the National Library and an amateur musician, taught him to play cello, viola, and guitar. These early influences later became evident in the orchestration of some of his more prominent works. Although he intended to enter school to study medicine, Villa-Lobos soon found that he preferred spending time with the local popular musicians, becoming familiar with the various musical styles native to Rio de Janeiro's street and night life. Among other skills, he learned to improvise guitar melodies over the "choro," a popular instrumental genre of the time, which lent Villa-Lobos the effortless Latin nationality so strongly present in his music.

From the ages of 18 to 25 he traveled extensively throughout Brazil and the African-influenced Caribbean nations, collecting themes and assessing the major style characteristics of the local musics. It was also during this time that Villa-Lobos composed his first major compositions, most notably his *Piano Trio No. 1.*

When he returned to Rio de Janeiro in 1912, Villa-Lobos briefly attempted to receive a more formalized education, but his personality and musical practice proved ill-matched with the academic establishment and, although he made important connections with the faculty, he soon left classes. He spent the next ten years composing and playing freelance cello in cafes and cinemas to earn a living. He eventually gained national recognition and a fair sum of government funding with the premiere of his *Third Symphony, "A guerra,"* the first part of a symphonic trilogy commissioned by the Brazilian government to commemorate World War I.

From 1923 to 1930, Villa-Lobos found himself centered in Paris, where he was a huge success, his music being widely published and frequently performed. He eventually returned to Brazil, however, becoming one of the most esteemed artists of the new Nationalist regime, which lasted until 1945. During the 1930s, Villa-Lobos involved himself deeply and enthusiastically with public music education, once again traveling throughout Brazil to offer his services as a teacher and school coordinator. In 1945, his passion reached the ultimate fruition when he founded the Brazilian Academy of Music. He spent the last ten years of his life traveling and conducting, primarily in New York and Paris. *—Graham Olson*

CHAMBER MUSIC

Bachianas Brasileiras No. 1, for 8 cellos (1930)

The 1930s brought an increased consciousness among many composers of the need to reduce the complexity of their music in a bid to make their music more appealing to the common people. It was also an era of nationalistic regimes. When Villa-Lobos returned to Brazil in 1930, after several years in Paris, his music was immediately affected by both these trends. Seeking to influence the wide-ranging social policy of Vargas' "Estado Nova" (New State) to include national music education, Heitor Villa-Lobos began two major projects: the *Guia Prático* (Practical Guide), a music curriculum using Brazilian materials; and the nine *Bachianas Brasileiras,* dedicated to demonstrating a link between Brazilian music and the themes of Johann Sebastian Bach.

Appealing to Brazilian national pride, he announced that he saw great similarities between Brazilian national melody and the melody-style of Johann Sebastian Bach, and began to write his series of works called *Bachianas Brasileiras,* meant to display this dual nature of Brazilian music.

The first of these works was for a new form of chamber ensemble: a group of eight cellos. Villa-Lobos also used this ensemble for some transcriptions of Bach works, so by including this work on programs with these transcriptions he could reinforce his contention about Brazilian music.

Bachiana Brasileira No. 1 is in three movements. In accordance with what would become his usual practice Villa-Lobos gave each movement two titles, a "Bachian" one and a Brazilian one.

"Introdução (Introduction); Embolada." An embolada is a kind of perpetuum mobile from northeastern Brazilian traveling musicians. It is a rapid and rhythmic invention with a two-section melody.

"Prelúdio; Modinha." This section has the most Bachian melody of the work, a flowing and lovely tune. Formally, it serves as the first part of a "prelude and fugue" pair. A "Modinha" is a type of Brazilian song.

"Fuga; Conversa." The Brazilian title, "Conversation" denotes the flavor of the work, which is a fugue written so that the interchanges between parts resemble the improvised musical "conversation" of a chôros ensemble. *—Joseph Stevenson*

Recommended:

- ○ **Rondo Violoncello** / Buck (cond.), Cello-Ensemble Peter Buck / HM 905240

Chôros No. 1, for guitar ("Tipico brasileiro") (1920)

As a young man in Rio de Janeiro, Heitor Villa-Lobos frequently played with street musicians, improvising on popular songs and dances of the day. One of the musical forms with which he was well familiar was the chôro, the origin of which is rather obscure. Villa-Lobos himself saw the chôro as a popular dance in which, in his words, "are synthesized the different modalities of Brazilian, Indian, and popular music." Starting in 1920, Villa-Lobos began composing his own chôros (he designated each of those works with the plural form of the word), eventually producing 14 such works. They range in size from solo miniatures (*No. 1 for guitar, No. 5 for piano*) to sizable works for large forces (*No. 10 for orchestra and chorus*). The *Chôros No. 1 for guitar,* dedicated to Ernesto Nazareth, is an insouciant five-minute piece in rondo form featuring a sequence of memorable melodies, spiced by a few expressive dissonances and a hint of the swinging rhythm of the tango. *—Chris Morrison*

Recommended:

- ○ **La Paloma: Spanish & Latin American Favourites** / Romero / 1991 / Philips 432102
- ○ **Julian Bream: The Ultimate Guitar Collection** / Bream / 1996 / RCA 33705

Doze Estudios, for guitar (1928)

This collection of etudes has an interesting twist or two in its history, which has only recently been unearthed. For decades this collection was listed as having been composed in 1929. The published edition and other circumstances surrounding the composition give no obvious clue concerning the existence of an earlier version. In 1996, however, it was revealed by Eduardo Fernandez in the magazine *Guitar*

Review that another manuscript of these etudes was in existence, carrying the date of 1928. It turned out that this version had been filed away unnoticed for many years in the Villa-Lobos museum in Rio de Janeiro. The question several scholars have asked in recent times is whether the later version amounts to a revision by the composer, or is a touching-up by another hand.

The changes are not substantial though; in *No. 10* and *No. 11* of the 1928 set, there are some sections not found in the later versions. It should be noted that either version is a good representation of the composer's musical ideas, but the original may be slightly more substantial. How did the changes come about? There is no definitive answer, but it seems that Andrés Segovia may have suggested some or perhaps all of them to Villa-Lobos, who, perhaps out of deference to the judgment of the great guitarist or due to doubts in his own abilities, incorporated them into the score.

Most of the etudes are in the one-and-a-half to three-minute range. The original *Eleventh* is the longest, at around four minutes, while the *Second*, at about a minute, is the shortest. The first two (E minor and A, respectively) are charming and light, while the *Third* (D major) and *Fourth* (G major) are more substantial, with more color and stronger interpretive demands. The *Fifth* (C major) is dreamy and gentle, with the *Sixth* (E minor) offering stormy contrast and the *Seventh* (E major) presenting lively, light music. The C sharp minor *Eighth* is slow and, with the *Eleventh* (E minor), offers the deepest music in the collection. The *Ninth* (F sharp minor) is delightful in its wistful lightness and the *Tenth* (B minor) is dark and mysterious. Without a doubt, the *Twelfth* (A minor) offers the most fireworks of any of the etudes here and is the perfect virtuoso showpiece to close the set. *—Robert Cummings*

Recommended:

○ **Villa-Lobos: Complete Music for Solo Guitar** / Kraft / 2000 / Naxos 553987

O canto do cisne negro (Song of the Black Swan), for cello & piano (1917)

O canto do cisne negro (Song of the Black Swan) is extracted from Villa-Lobos' symphonic poem *Naufragio de Kleônicos*. It is a flowing, impressionistic duet for cello and piano that reveals Villa-Lobos' affection for the string instrument his father taught him as a child, and which he lavished with attention throughout his life; the piece occupies a fittingly melancholy space, given its swan-song title. *O canto* was excerpted from *Naufragio* in 1917, a year after the source work's composition, along with a version for violin and piano; it has since become a concert favorite for cellist/pianist duos. The music itself is very simple in conception: the piano arpeggiates an endless series of chords—some sweet, some spicy, always favoring the upper registers—while the cello sings plaintively, also without interruption. The resulting texture is reminiscent of Ravel and Debussy, especially in harmonic vocabulary, but it also readily announces itself as a work of Villa-Lobos, especially in its fusion of lyricism and sensuality. *—Allen Schrott*

Recommended:

○ **Cello Song** / J. Lloyd Webber, Lenehan / 1993 / Philips 434917

Cinco Prelúdios, for guitar (1940)

Written in 1940, in Rio de Janeiro for the famed guitarist Andrés Segovia, the *Five Preludes* contain the same fusion of Brazilian popular music and European classical traditions that marks so many of Heitor Villa-Lobos' guitar works. Perhaps the only difference between these works and his much earlier guitar compositions, like the *Suite populaire brésilienne* of 1908 to 1912, is a slight darkening and mellowing of mood. All of this music betrays Villa-Lobos' formidable firsthand knowledge of the guitar, which he had been playing for some 40 years prior to the composition of the *Preludes*.

The *Prelude No. 1 in E minor* is restrained, mildly sad, and quite evocative of Brazilian music. The carnivals of Rio de Janeiro inspired the *Prelude No. 2 in E major*, it is more of a virtuoso exercise, full fast-paced arpeggios. The melancholic *Prelude No. 3 in A minor* seems to have been, like Villa-Lobos' extensive series of *Bachianas brasileiras*, something of an homage to Johann Sebastian Bach. The *Prelude No. 4 in E minor*, said by some to be Villa-Lobos' impression of Brazil's Indians, is the most serious-minded work of the set; it is dark and dramatic, and makes expressive use of the guitar's harmonics. Rio's social life, particularly among the youth of the city, was the inspiration for the final *Prelude in D major*, a graceful waltz in a moderately slow tempo. *—Chris Morrison*

Recommended:

○ **Manuel Barrueco: Brouwer, Villa-Lobos & Orbon** / Barrueco / 1997 / EMI 66576

○ **Rodrigo & Villa-Lobos** / Bream / 1991 / RCA 6525

Quinteto em forme de choros, for flute, oboe, clarinet, englsh horn & bassoon (1928)

Through the 1920s, Villa-Lobos wrote 14 numbered works ranging from a guitar miniature to massive pieces for orchestra, band, and chorus that all bore the title "Chôros." The chôro (Villa-Lobos always used the word's plural form) is popular Brazilian street music played by itinerant musicians; it's sentimental, improvisatory, draws from any number of musical traditions (usually dance-related), and is characterized by unpredictable bass lines and unexpected modulations. While he was at it, Villa-Lobos wrote a handful of further pieces in this vein that he did not include in his formal series; the most musically substantial of these is the wind quintet "in chôros form." Its single movement subdivides into several short episodes, as if the musicians were improvising according to their own whims. It begins with a lugubrious growl in the low winds, answered by very brief interjections from the higher instruments. These soon take over with dissonant, melodically wayward material. After a while, the ensemble introduces the percolating rhythm typical of Villa-Lobos' chôros series, but this is almost immediately overcome by plaintive material that the various instruments utter almost independently of one another. There's a tangled duet for oboe and clarinet, followed by a more extended section with a melody growing out of a chugging rhythm that sounds rather like Morse code. A free flute cadenza leads to a long, mournful passage involving most of the ensemble. The music continues to evolve, with special melodic attention given to the flute and a chattering figure eventually flits through the ensemble, attempting without complete success to transform the score into a dance piece. The quintet ends with shrill chords; such dissonance, as well as thematic vagueness, sets this work apart from the more heavily folkloric chôros pieces in the main series. *—James Reel*

Recommended:

○ **Villa-Lobos: Music for Flute** / Bennett, Black, King, O'Neill, Knight / 1989 / Hyperion 55057

○ **Best Of The New York Woodwind Quintet Vol. 2** / New York Woodwind Quintet / 1996 / Boston Skyline 139

Suite populaire brésilienne (Brazilian Folk Suite), for guitar (1908–1912)

In his teens and early twenties, Heitor Villa-Lobos attempted several times to pursue formal musical studies. But each time he found himself frustrated by the rigidity of the academic approach and inevitably returned to the folk and popular music (and musicians) of his native Brazil. He often performed and improvised with amateur street musicians, and he supported himself financially by playing in the cinemas, nightclubs, and cafés of Rio de Janeiro. At that time, Brazilian music drew on both popular and classical European styles and forms, and the same combination quickly became second nature for Villa-Lobos when he started composing his own music. The five pieces that make up the *Suite populaire brésilienne* were written over the years 1908 to 1912. They were selected from among Villa-Lobos' many early guitar pieces and assembled into a suite by his French publisher, Max Eschig.

The titles of these pieces, each of which combines a European form with a Brazilian dance, the chôro, reflect the composer's approach. (Such hybrids were characteristic of Brazilian popular dance music at the time.) The opening Mazurka-Chôros, with its somewhat nostalgic tone, is followed by a Schottisch-Chôros (the schottisch was a kind of polka-like dance popular in the nineteenth century), a bittersweet Valsa-Chôros, and a lovely, almost classically styled Gavota-Chôros. The concluding *Chôrinho*, a miniature chôros, is a bit darker-hued and dramatic than the previous four pieces. But all are tuneful and easygoing works that one can easily imagine being played and improvised upon by Brazilian street musicians. *—Chris Morrison*

Recommended:

○ **Villa-Lobos: Complete Solo Guitar Works** / Leisner / 2000 / Azica 71211

String Quartets (1915–1959)

In 1958, near the end of his life, Villa-Lobos declared, "I love to write quartets. One could say that it is a mania." Indeed, he composed 17 string quartets over the long course of his career, from a folkloric suite in 1915 to the severe final work of 1957. Yet this was not exactly a steady preoccupation throughout his life; the last eleven quartets poured fourth between 1942 and 1957. Villa-Lobos' quartet output is divided into three phases, although this has more to do with chronology than style. The varied works of that late 15-year period are all clumped together, as are the first four quartets, which have little in common other than having been written in the World War I years. The middle period, such as it is, consists of nothing more than the two quartets from the 1930s isolated between the early and late bursts of quartet activity.

Although almost all the Villa-Lobos quartets follow the standard four-movement pattern, the internal structure of these movements is only tenuously related to the European traditions established by Haydn. Villa-Lobos generally avoided sonata-allegro form, with its rigorous key relationships and central development section; instead, he preferred a freer variation form with sudden, dramatic contrasts. His main lessons from the past came from Renaissance polyphony (which Villa-Lobos sometimes gave a modern, polytonal, or atonal twist) and fugal writing inspired by Bach. One other major characteristic of these works is that, more often than not, the cello is the group's anchoring and leading voice. Villa-Lobos himself was a cellist; he wrote several works for cello ensemble and lavished some of his most expressive passages on the instrument he knew best. Villa-Lobos' *First* is his least characteristic, a six-movement suite alluding to Brazilian folk music. The *Second* is more traditional, but the *Third* is a fully Impressionistic work modeled after the quartets of Debussy and Ravel, right down to the pizzicato movement. The *Fourth* quartet gives the first hint of the composer's later *Bachianas Brasileiras* style. The *Fifth* and *Sixth* quartets from the 1930s are even more overtly nationalistic than the first; the *Fifth* quotes folk melodies. The later quartets are much more technically intricate and often abstract. The *Seventh* is particularly complex; the *Eighth* abandons tonality except at the end of each movement; the *Ninth* is completely atonal and expressionistic; the *Tenth* edges back toward tonality, but ignores folklore; and the *Eleventh* fully embraces tonality again while emphasizing complex thematic relations over local color. The *Twelfth* quartet is a bridge from severity back toward folklore; the *Thirteenth* employs Brazilian elements so stylized that they are hard to recognize; the *Fourteenth* is chromatic and disturbing; the *Fifteenth* is tonal and bright; the *Sixteenth* is something of a Brazilian carnival; and the *Seventeenth* is more abstract and universal. —*James Reel*

Recommended:

○ **Villa-Lobos: String Quartets Vol. 1** / Cuarteto LatinoAmericano / 1995 / Dorian 90205

○ **Villa-Lobos: String Quartets Vol. 2** / Cuarteto LatinoAmericano / 196 / Dorian 90220

VOCAL

Bachianas Brasileiras No. 5, for voice & 8 cellos (1938–1945)

Villa-Lobos' series of nine works titled *Bachianas Brasileiras* reflects both the composer's Brazilian heritage and his lifelong admiration for the music of Johann Sebastian Bach. The fifth entry in the series (1938–1945), which has emerged as the most popular of the composer's works, further suggests the scope of his sonic imagination in its unusual scoring for soprano and eight solo cellos. Like most of its companion works, *Bachianas Brasileiras No. 5* exhibits characteristics of the Baroque suite, and those of Bach in particular. The first movement, an adagio Aria, is marked by a particular lyrical expansiveness. The more spirited Danza, noted the composer, "represents a persistent and characteristic rhythm much like the emboladas, those strange melodies of the Brazilian hinterland. The melody suggests the birds of Brazil." —*AMG*

Recommended:

○ **Bidú Sayão sings Bachiana brasileira No. 5, Arias & Brazilian Folksongs** / Sayão, Villa-Lobos (cond.) / 1996 / Sony 62355

Serestas, song cycle (1925)

These dozen pieces qualify as pseudofolk music and are wholly original works, stylized and slightly ironic, and inspired by the Brazilian folk style. Villa-Lobos made more of their indigenous nature than perhaps is justified, going out of his way to define *Seresta* as "a new form of vocal composition reminiscent of all kinds of traditional serenades, all [tunes] of our . . . wandering minstrels, of various songs and calls of our wagoners, cowherds . . . [who come from] the hinterland, and also from the Brazilian capital." The texts are not traditional, but are the work of various then-living Brazilian poets, including Alvaro Moreyra, Manuel Bandeira, and Olegario Marianno. What most of these songs have in common are straightforward but folkish melodies, fairly simple accompaniment, and an air of sadness or nostalgia. Eleven of them are for solo voice and piano, but, perversely, the third is for chorus and piano, making performances of the complete cycle impractical. "Pobre céga" (Poor Blind Woman) modally wavers over a spare ostinato, and "O anjo da guarda" (The Guardian Angel) keeps the simple accompaniment in the piano's singing middle register, with the voice an octave above. "Canção da folha morta" (Song of a Dead Leaf), the choral number, is one of the most folklorish pieces, with a catchy, syncopated refrain. "Saudades da minha vida" (Longing of My Life) is a highlight of the set, with its broad, expressive melodies arising from a simple chordal accompaniment. "Modinha" is a stylized version of the Brazilian folk song of that name, with a guitarlike accompaniment. "Na paz do outono" (In the Peace of Autumn) dangles a simple, triad-based tune over a syncopated accompaniment. "Cantigua do viuvo" (Song of a Widow) is another song with the piano imitating the plucked guitar. "Canção do carreiro" (Song of the Wagonman) arises from two motifs heard first in the accompaniment; Villa-Lobos claimed it was based on the "wild themes" of Brazil's cowboys and indigenous peoples. His setting of Ribeiro Couto's poetry was so free and full of repetitions and glissandi that the poet insisted the song be revised. "Abril" is a nature scene in April. "Desejo" (I Desire) is a humorous Rio street scene. "Redondilha" (roughly, Ring-o'-Roses) is another witty song, this time employing extensive vocal glissandi. "Realejo" is a waltz that parodies the inexpressive music of the hand organ of the title. —*James Reel*

Recommended:

○ **Modinha: Brazilian Songs** / Castro / 2001 / Ensayo 9807

Tu passaste por este jardim, song (Canções típicas brasileiras No. 9) (1919–1935)

This is the ninth of 13 songs comprising Villa-Lobos' cycle entitled *Canções típicas brasileiras* (Typical Brazilian Folk Songs). As its title suggests, each is an arrangement of a folk song, but its writing probably divulges as much about the composer's individual style as it does about the folk source it was drawn on. Villa-Lobos had an abiding interest in folk music and, like Bartók, often collected folk tunes and songs. True, he never developed this undertaking into quite the elaborate avocation of his Hungarian counterpart, but he nevertheless devoted a significant amount of energy to this realm. *Tu passaste por este jardim* (You Have Been in This Garden) is a charming, salonstyle song, light in mood and featuring playful accompaniment on the piano. The melody sounds familiar, with each successive phrase seeming to mirror the preceding one: the first swoops down and then ends on the ascent, while the next has an archlike shape, closing on the descent. It is all quite charming in its simplicity and carefree manner, but comes across as more cosmopolitan than Brazilian. Nevertheless, this is a delightful song that will appeal to varied tastes. —*Robert Cummings*

Recommended:

○ **Villa-Lobos: Songs** / Alexander, Heller, Chaplin / 1994 / Etcetera 1165

KEYBOARD

Carnaval das crianças brasilieras, suite (1919–1920)

Many twentieth century composers wrote music for children, the more prominent examples being Prokofiev (*Peter and the Wolf*) and Britten (*Young Person's Guide to the Orchestra*). But the keyboard literature is rich in works of this type as well and from some of the same composers: Prokofiev produced the charming *Music for Children*, Bartók the collection of folk transcriptions *For Children*, and Villa-Lobos' colorful *Carnaval das criancas brasileiras*, commonly translated as "Children's Carnival." The eight pieces in this collection are all tuneful and fairly uncomplicated, but like the Prokofiev and Bartók sets, they can be enjoyed by adults. The first piece here, "The Toy Horse of Little Pierrot," seems to vigorously gallop along, its giddyup rhythmic manner conveying much playfulness despite a fair measure of dissonance. The second, "The Little Devil's Whip," has a childlike glitter in its rapid opening chords and thereafter becomes mischievous in its sense of chasing up and down the keyboard. "The Morning Pierrette" follows, a playful, relatively relaxed piece that turns sassy and innocent by turns. The fourth item, "The Little Bells of Little Domino," delivers the bell-like sounds suggested in the title alright, but often in sonorities that can harass the ear when they ring with a bad boy vehemence from the piano's upper register. The fifth is "The Adventures of the Little Ragpicker," which presents the portrait of a busy, not always neat or patient child, as notes can clumsily tumble down the keyboard with a seemingly deliberate recklessness. The next piece, "Mischievousness of the Masked Darling," brims with impish energy at the outset, but turns sweeter in the playful menace of its upper-register sonorities. The seventh, "The Harmonica of a Precocious Daydreamer," has a dreamy nonchalance in its sometimes wayward manner, the harmonica player seeming at times to haphazardly toss notes about. The concluding piece, "The Revelry of a Group of Children," is a joyous romp, full of color and zest. In the end, these eight works are notable more for their depiction of scenes and moods than for their catchy themes. —*Robert Cummings*

Recommended:

○ **Villa-Lobos: Complete Solo Piano Music Vol. 1** / Halász / 1995 / Bis 712

Chôros No. 5 ("Alma brasiliera") (1925)

"Brazilian Soul" is the subtitle Villa-Lobos gave to this short and perhaps most popular installment in his *Chôros* series for various instruments, inspired by Brazilian street music. It's a quiet, highly expressive piano piece in which a slow, yearning melody expands over a syncopated, stretched-out ostinato figure in the bass. Melody and accompaniment become more intertwined in the second section without introducing new material. In the middle, the bass figure breaks out into a sparkling folk dance. This gives way to a more gruff, stomping dance based on the earlier material, and in the end the introspective opening passage returns in its original form. —*James Reel*

Recommended:

○ **Villa-Lobos: Instrumental & Orchestral Works** / Ortiz / 1998 / EMI 72670

Ciclo brasileiro, suite (1936–1937)

The *Ciclo Brasileiro* (Brazilian Cycle) is comprised of four pieces that are among the composer's more compelling efforts in the piano genre. Villa-Lobos felt strongly enough about the second to reuse its material in his charming opera *Magdalena* (1947). The four works are *Plantio do Caboclo* (Pioneer's Song), *Impressões seresteiras* (Impressions of the Minstrels), *Festa no sertão* (Festival in the Sagebrush), and *Dança do índio branco* (Dance of the White Indian), each of which poses problems in translation, though the parenthetical titles provided approximate their meanings well enough. The set's opening piece is an atmospheric work that suggests a lament in its lovely rocking theme and gentle rhythmic swirling in the upper register. Some translations of the title, in fact, indicate the serene, almost dreamy music here is a lamentation. The second work is the most popular in the set, mainly owing to its catchy melancholy melody, a deft creation that brings to mind a sort of Latin Rachmaninov. In contrast to the slower character of the preceding works, the third presents lively, somewhat motoric music of a cheerful nature, again with hints of Rachmaninov. The last of the four pieces provides an extraordinary finale to the set: it can be played as though two conflicting tempos are vying for rhythmic control. A fast, ferocious rhythm is heard from the bass regions, over which a grandiose slower theme is played. These opposing elements unite, so to speak, to convey a colorful struggle in bravura writing that suggests a Latin Liszt. Most piano music aficionados will enjoy these four pieces; hardly neglected fare, but works that have not achieved the popularity they deserve. *—Robert Cummings*

Recommended:

○ **Villa-Lobos: Piano Music Vol. 3** / Rubinsky / 2003 / Naxos 8555286

Cirandas (1926)

A "ciranda" is a Portuguese circle or round dance originally performed by adults, but in Brazil, it mostly became the pastime of children. One participant stands inside the circle and sings while the others hold hands and sing around him or her. In these piano pieces, Villa-Lobos created an atmosphere guided by the spirit and feeling of each simple melody, as he had in the previous year's *Cirandinhas* or "little cirandas."

"Terezinha de Jesus" is built on an unabashedly celebratory rhythm, with an introspective, romantic melody for the midsection. (Most of the "cirandas" have an ABA structure). Terezinha is a small municipality in Pernambuco.

"A Condessa" (The Countess) has a touching, nostalgic melody and a suddenly on-rushing midsection, all of which clearly shows the influence of the Schumann and Chopin compositions beloved by the composer's wife, pianist Lucília Guimarães.

"Senhore Dona Sancha" is depicted in a bravado melody with pulsating dissonant accompaniment in the midsection.

"O cravo brigou com a rósa" (The Carnation Fought with the Rose) opens with furiously energetic tremolos, but proceeds on to a childlike major tune.

"Pobre céga" (Poor Blind Woman) depicts the lady slowly finding her way by probing (short grace note stabs) and making sudden confident movements that come to a halt.

"Passa, passa, gavião" (Go away, go away, Hawk) has a protesting little melody and rapidly rotating figures throughout that, depending on your point of view, depict either the flight of the bird or the fleeing victim.

"Xô, xô, passarinho" (Shoo, shoo, Little Bird) begins with a pesky figure repeated in the deep bass; this may be a little bird but a big annoyance. A lazy, calm feeling pervades the middle section.

"Vamos atraz da sérra calunga" (Let's go to the mountain, Calunga) features an adventurous rhythm and complex harmonies suggesting a strenuous climb, and a jazzy section depicting the joy of sightseeing.

The swift arpeggios of "Fui no Tóróró" (I went to Tororó) against a slower, peaceful melodic line seem to indicate a journey by air or sea, and the anticipation of a warm greeting.

"O pintor de Cannahy" (The Painter of Canai) interweaves a comic accompaniment against a slightly heartbroken lyrical melody in a three-against-four rhythm.

Something tragic and angry must have occurred in "Nesta rua, nesta rua" (In this street, in this street) for the chords are strident and dissonant, but later contrast with a sad tune.

"Ohla o passarinho, Dominé" (Look at the Little Bird, Dominé) flies along delicately at a dizzying rate.

"A procura de uma agulha" (Looking for a Needle) has a slowly exploring modal tune, accompanied by rich Satie-like chords. Sudden excitations reveal mistaken discoveries.

"A canôa virou" (The Canoe Capsized) opens with a happy traveling theme that soon becomes immersed in watery whole-tone harmonies.

"Que lindas olhos" (What Beautiful Eyes) has a rich impressionist and romantic melody surrounded by intimations of strangeness and tragedy.

"Có-có-có" (Chip, chip, chip) contrasts a melody played with little chippy grace notes against fast chord tremolos. *—"Blue Gene" Tyranny*

Recommended:

○ **Piano Music of Villa-Lobos Vol. 2** / Petchersky / 1996 / ASV 959

Danças características africanas (1914–1915)

The three dances comprising this collection were originally written for piano, but there are two other versions of them: Villa-Lobos fashioned a rendition for chamber ensemble and piano (1914–1916) and for full orchestra (1916). Attractive as the later pair are, it is the piano original here that seems to be the preferred version, the music is more often encountered in the concert hall and on record in that form than in the others. Like Bartók and Vaughan Williams, Villa-Lobos had an abiding interest in folk music, mainly that from his native Brazil. The three pieces are drawn on music from the Caripunas Indians of Mato Grosso, which at times displays African flavors, not least because that Southwestern Brazilian tribe's roots can be partially traced to Africa. The titles of the three pieces are as exotic-sounding as their music: *Farrapós, Kankukús,* and *Kankikís.* The first opens with a fanfare-like motif that sounds more primitive than exotic. A lively rhythmic theme is then presented whose ethnic traits are as much Latin as Brazilian-Indian. The ensuing *Kankukús* is relatively moderately paced in its jaunty mix of cultures, again with Villa-Lobos blending Latin elements with the rhythmic, rawer sounds of the Indians. While *Kankikís* has a measure of exoticism, it could almost pass for folk-inspired music from Eastern Europe. It eventually divulges more Latin and exotic elements and provides a colorful finale to this charming set of short piano pieces. Together, the three works have a duration of about 10 to 12 minutes. *—Robert Cummings*

Recommended:

○ **Villa-Lobos: Piano Music Vol. 3** / Rubinsky / 2003 / Naxos 8555286

A lenda do caboclo (1920)

The brief ballad *A lenda do Caboclo* (The Legend of the Native) is one of Villa-Lobos' most popular piano pieces. Its most notable feature is the slow tango-like, syncopated bass line. The work switches between the minor and major modes, opening with an introduction made up of just the accompaniment before the swaying, light melody begins. A duple meter interlude in the major appears, with a new melodic line in the left hand while the right hand provides an impelling, dotted-rhythm accompaniment. The main theme returns in a lighter version, leading to a dramatic section that develops and transforms the theme. The introduction and opening melody are quietly revisited, with an added coda of small chords lifting off into the clouds. *—Patsy Morita*

Recommended:

○ **Villa-Lobos: Mômo Precoce and solo piano works** / Fernandez / 2002 / Centaur 2576

A Prole do Bebê, 3 suites (1918–1926)

Despite their titles and Villa-Lobos' long-standing interest in music for young people, the short piano works that make up the suites *A prole do Bebê* weren't written for children to play, but were the composer's reflections on aspects and memories of childhood. The first suite, "The Dolls," was written in 1918 and dedicated to Villa-Lobos' wife Lucilia, whom he had married half a dozen years before. The less well-known, more advanced, and pianistically complex second suite, "The Little Animals," followed three years later and was dedicated to the American pianist Aline von Bärentzen, who was noted for her interest in Latin American music. The third suite, which was supposedly a set of nine pieces dealing with sports and games (like "Football" and "Lead Soldiers"), is a bit of a mystery. Written as early as 1916 or as late as 1926, depending on the source, the suite is now lost. Legendary pianist Artur Rubinstein played parts of the first suite of *A prole do Bebê* in a July 1922 concert in Rio de Janeiro that helped Villa-Lobos make a name as a composer. Rubinstein frequently returned to these pieces in later years and the seventh and penultimate piece in the suite, "Punch," was the final work he played in public. The suite contrasts lyrical pieces like the sixth, "The Poor Little Rag Doll," with more extroverted, impetuous pieces like the second, "The Little Brunette Papier-Mâché Doll," and the fifth, "The Little Black Wooden Doll." Unlike many of his other compositions of the time, Villa-Lobos seldom makes reference to Brazilian folk music in this suite; just a hint of such music appears in the lively third, "The Little Mestiza Clay Doll," with its unusual 3-3-2 rhythmic structure. One significant influence on the first suite seems to be the Impressionism of composers like Claude Debussy, evident in the opening "The Little White Porcelain Doll." The Brazilian influence is rather more evident in the second suite; at least four of its nine pieces make allusions to popular and children's songs native to the country. Due to its technical complexity, one commentator has likened the suite to a set of transcendental études. Not only are there virtuoso sections, like the tour-de-force final piece, "The Little Glass Wolf," and the swirling, toccata-like third, "The Little Papier-Mâché Mouse," Villa-Lobos also tosses in the occasional advanced performance techniques, such as the tone cluster that ends the first, "The Little Paper Cockroach." Jazzy rhythms underlie the sixth, "The Little Tin Ox," and eighth, "The Little Cotton Bear." The bird songs of the seventh, "The Little Cloth Bird," anticipates Olivier Messiaen's many bird song-inspired pieces and Villa-Lobos evokes other sound effects elsewhere in the suite, such as dogs barking, cats meowing, and the sound of glass breaking. *—Chris Morrison*

Recommended:

○ **For Children** / Rév / Hyperion 66185

Rudepoêma (1921–1926)

Rudepoêma is Villa-Lobos' most extended work for solo piano, begun while he was working in Brazilian movie houses, but finished after he had gone to study composition in Paris. He intended it to be a musical portrait of Artur Rubinstein, whom he had met in the late 1910s. Rubinstein is said to have been taken aback when he learned this, as the piece is often described as primitive, and most of it is marked with the performance direction Tres sauvage. However, it is a high-energy, virtuosic work well suited to Rubinstein's skills, and he did perform it often. The nearly 20-minute work shows the influence of the composers Villa-Lobos studied and met while in Paris, being particularly reminiscent of Milhaud's and Stravinsky's styles. Besides the virtuosic technical demands made on the performer, *Rudepoêma* includes polytonalities and polyrhythms in its complexities and much less of the Brazilian folk music characteristics that are found in most of Villa-Lobos' compositions, although there are glimpses of Brazilian dance rhythms and Amerindian melodic figures. The sectional, quasi-sonata form composition begins with a double exposition. The first subject is a four-note motive, simply played with a tango-like sway, but which quickly explodes into thicker textures and a more wild nature. This is followed by a six-note idea and one built of rapidly repeated notes that combine to form the second subject, in a slightly calmer demeanor. The so-called development section makes up the majority of the composition, wherein the two subjects are transfigured and transmuted in various tempos, keys, and rhythms, using such devices as ostinato, pedal points, and huge chords played with the fist in the process. The latter part of the development is more measured and deliberate, more hypnotic than the intense, vivid, rapidly changing scherzo-like first part. Something of a recapitulation is presented before a coda, in which the pianist is required to cross hands, scrambling down the whole keyboard and concluding with four fist-pounded chords. *—Patsy Morita*

Recommended:

○ **Villa-Lobos: Piano Music** / Hamelin / Hyperion 67176

ORCHESTRAL

Bachianas Brasileiras No. 2 (1930)

The *Bachianas Brasileiras No. 2* was one of the first in the series of works that Villa-Lobos composed quickly after he announced the link between Bach and Brazilian music. It is scored for a small orchestra of ten wind instruments, a standard string section, piano and celesta, and a percussion section of standard instruments and four native Brazilian rattles (ganzá, chocalhos, matraca, and recoreco). It is the most popular of all the eight purely instrumental *Bachianas Brasileiras* and is one of the rare pieces in the series that includes descriptive music. Here Villa-Lobos describes scenes of the Brazilian countryside and its people. (As usual in the *Bachianas* series, Villa-Lobos provided dual titles, one stating the name of a form known to Bach and the other identifying its Brazilian characteristic.)

"Prelúdio; O Canto do Capadocio." The first movement is a lovely and insinuating Adagio with a somewhat faster (Andantino mosso) central dance-like section. The Brazilian title means "The Song of a Capadocio." "Capadocio" is the name of a popular published guitar method that was widely taught in Brazil. It also meant a musician, a kind of slacker who would sing, woo the women, and generally float through life with his music and love. Villa-Lobos transcribed this movement for cello and piano (A. 251 in Appleby's catalog).

"Aria; O Canto da Nossa Terra." Not unexpectedly, a Bachian melody that some have compared to the aria sections of Bach's cantatas dominates this movement. The Brazilian title means "The Song of Our Land." It opens in the tempo "Lento assai." It is in a three-part form, with a "Tempo di marcia" in the middle. This has a pulsing rhythm driven by the piano and melody primarily given to the saxophone.

"Dansa; Lembrança do Sertão." Villa-Lobos, who loved the mid-range instruments of the orchestra, gives the flowing dance melody to the trombone over a fluent rhythm in the strings. There is a more assertive dance rhythm in the central section. The title means "Memories of the Sertão," the hot, dry northeastern region of the country.

"Toccata; O trenzinho do Caipira." This is the famous "Little Train of the Caipira," and the composer's full array of percussion is held back until this concluding movement to portray the creaking and puffing of this stalwart back-country "little engine that could." It is irresistible, fun music. While its bright rhythms attract attention, the listener soon realizes that the train's melody is extraordinarily beautiful. *—Joseph Stevenson*

Recommended:

○ **Latin American Masters: Orbon, Villa-Lobos, Estevez & Chavez:** / Mata (cond.), Simon Bolivar SO of Venezuela / 1994 / Dorian 90179

Bachianas Brasileiras No. 9, for chorus or string orchestra (1945)

As the other *Bachianas Brasileiras* were written during the 1930s, the period of Gétulio Vargas' regime, *No. 9* was the last one, written in the same year Vargas was deposed. Villa-Lobos had become associated with Vargas's government when it appointed Villa-Lobos music education superintendent for Rio de Janeiro.

Bachiana Brasileira No. 9 is the only one that does not have double titles (one title based on classical music forms and the other relating to Brazil in some manner). Instead, this eight-minute work (the shortest in the series) is in quintessentially Bachian form of the prelude and fugue.

The work is scored for string orchestra (Villa-Lobos also wrote a version of it for wordless choir, but this is rarely performed). The opening, marked with the Italian direction "vague and mystical" begins with a striking sonority using high strings. A very Bachian aria melody unfolds, with harmonization that is often bitonal.

The concluding fugue (this *Bachiana* being one of four in the series that end in a fugue) has a typical quick subject. It rises to a strong and calm conclusion that is a fitting end to one of the most famous series of classical compositions ever written in South America.*—Joseph Stevenson*

Recommended:

○ **Ginastera, Villa-Lobos & Evangelista** / Turovsky (cond.), I Musici de Montreal / 1996 / Chandos 9434

SYMPHONIC

Symphonies (1916–1957)

Heitor Villa-Lobos is generally regarded as Brazil's greatest composer, and certain of his orchestral works, namely *Uirpurú*, the *Bachianas Brasilieras No. 2* containing "The Little Train of the Caipira," and *Floresta do Amazonas*, are among his most celebrated creations. So it is more than a little surprising that Villa-Lobos' 12 symphonies are among his least-known works. Some of Villa-Lobos' most eminent scholars have disparaged these pieces, stating that his basic style was at odds with symphonic form. But this opinion is based on examination of unedited manuscript scores rather than from hearing the works played, and typically the manuscript sources are riddled with hundreds of errors and variant readings. Since 1997, conductor Carl St. Clair has been working with the Stuttgart Radio Symphony Orchestra, which Villa-Lobos himself once led in 1953, in producing a recorded edition of the Villa-Lobos symphonies for the CPO label in Germany. Villa-Lobos' symphonies are a mixed bag, but some are a good deal better than their reputation would suggest.

The first five of Villa-Lobos' symphonies were composed in only a four-year period between 1916 and 1920, and all five bear some relation to contemporary events. *Symphony No. 1* is subtitled "O Imprevisto" (The Unexpected); in it Villa-Lobos strikes out into the symphonic medium forging his own way, playfully combining Brazilian folk forms with concepts derived from post-Romantic, French music. The score of *Symphony No. 2, "Ascensaõ"* (The Ascension; 1917), still awaits, although it was once recorded by conductor Werner Janssen back in the 1940s. The next three symphonies form a trilogy that is directly addressed to the war in Europe: *Symphony No. 3, "A Guerra"* (The War, 1919); *Symphony No. 4, "A Vitória"* (The Victory, 1919); and *Symphony No. 5, "A Paz"* (The Peace, 1920). *Symphony No. 4* is the only one of Villa-Lobos' symphonies that the composer recorded himself. Unfortunately, no trace of the score of Villa-Lobos' *Symphony No. 5* has been located; it was already known to be missing in the composer's lifetime and is yet the subject of a worldwide search.

More than two decades were to pass before Villa-Lobos elected to return to writing symphonies. In 1944 Villa-Lobos composed his *Symphony No. 6, "Sobre a linhas das montanhas do Brasil"* (The Mountains of Brazil), in which he employed a technique similar to that used in his piano piece *New York Skyline*. Working from aerial photographs of the mountain peaks of Pao de Aucar and Corcovado, Villa-Lobos traced his melodic line from their topographical outline. The next work in the canon, *Symphony No. 7, "Odissèia de uma raça"* (Odyssey of a Race, 1945), is one of the longest and most complex of the symphonies; it is not to be confused with his symphonic poem of the same name, which followed in 1953.

Villa-Lobos' final five symphonies belong to the 1950s. *Symphonies No. 8* (1950) and *No. 9* (1952) were both composed on commission from the Philadelphia Orchestra and its maestro, Eugene Ormandy. *Symphony No. 10, "Sinfonia amerìndia"* (1954), was commissioned by the city of São Paulo to commemorate the opening of its fourth century. This is the largest of Villa-Lobos' symphonies, scored for three soloists, chorus, and orchestra on a sixteenth century poem by José de Anchieta; it lasts well over an hour. Villa-Lobos' final two symphonies are less ambitious and contain some of the most immediately appealing music found among his efforts in symphonic form. *Symphony No. 11* (1955) was composed in observance of the 75th anniversary of the Boston Symphony Orchestra and premiered under Charles Münch. *Symphony No. 12* (1957) was first heard on a concert by the then newly formed American Symphony Orchestra of Washington, D.C. *—Uncle Dave Lewis*

Recommended:

○ **Villa-Lobos: Symphonies 1 & 11** / St. Clair (cond.), Stuttgart SWR RSO / CPO 999568

○ **Villa-Lobos: Symphonies 3 & 9** / St. Clair (cond.), Stuttgart SWR RSO / 2002 / CPO 999712

○ **Villa-Lobos: Symphonies 4 & 12** / St. Clair (cond.), Stuttgart SWR RSO / 2000 / CPO 999525

○ **Villa-Lobos: Symphonies 6 & 8** / St. Clair (cond.), Stuttgart SWR RSO / CPO 999517

○ **Villa-Lobos: Symphony 7; Sinfonietta 1** / St. Clair (cond.), Stuttgart SWR RSO / 2002 / CPO 999713

○ **Villa-Lobos: Sinfonía 10 ("Amerindia")** / Pérez (cond.), Tenerife SO / HM 987041

CONCERTO

Bachianas Brasileiras No. 4, for piano or orchestra (1941)

In 1930 Villa-Lobos produced three pieces for the *Bachianas Brasileiras*, including the eventual fourth movement of this *Bachiana*, for piano solo. Over the next few years he added three additional movements to make a four-movement suite. In 1941 he orchestrated them for a full symphony orchestra with two flutes plus piccolo, two oboes plus English horn, two clarinets, two bassoons, seven trumpets, three trombones, tuba, strings, and a percussion section of timpani, bombo, tamtam, xylophone, and celesta. The piano version of this *Bachiana* premiered in

November 1939 with Viera Brandao at the keyboard. The composer conducted the world premiere of the orchestral version in 1942.

As is the usual case with *Bachianas Brasileiras*, Villa-Lobos stressed the conjunction of Bach and Brazil by giving dual titles in Portuguese to each movement, one reflecting a Bach form, the other suggesting the Brazilian nature of the music.

The first movement is called, somewhat redundantly, "Prelúdio; Introduçao." It is a monothematic movement in B minor with a theme whose Bachian quality is the first aspect to strike the listener. Later rhythmic development adds Brazilian elements to it, but the movement never departs from working with the single theme.

The second movement is also notable for a smooth and graceful melody. "Coral; Canto do sertão" (Chorale; Song of the Sertão) is also in a slow tempo, being marked "largo," with a faster middle section. The Sertão is the dry brushland country of the northeastern part of Brazil, which has its own distinct folk music.

Unusually in this series Villa-Lobos uses a genuine folk tune in the third movement, "Aria; Cantiga." (Both the Bachian word and the Brazilian mean, essentially, "song"). The folk song is from the northeast and is called "O mana, Deix'eu ir" (Oh, sister, let me go). Villa-Lobos uses his favorite form for a *Bachiana* movement, a slowish (Moderato) opening and closing section contrasting with a fast (Vivace) central section. Brilliant Brazilian rhythms add a festive tone.

The final movement, "Dansa; Miudinho," uses the samba-like rhythms of the dance called the miudinho. This movement is rhythmically insistent and remains in the fast tempo of Molto animato. Villa-Lobos used the same theme in "Vamos, Maruca" ("Let's go, Maruca"), No. 128 of the *Guia Prático*. *—Joseph Stevenson*

Recommended:

○ **Villa-Lobos: Bachianas Brasileiras 2, 4 & 8** / Lopez-Cobos (cond.), Cincinnati SO / 1995 / Telarc 80393

Fantasia for saxophone, 2 horns & strings, Op. 630 (1948)

This dance-driven saxophone concerto in miniature demonstrates how Villa-Lobos could integrate nearly any instrument into a Brazilian sound world while still composing a fully "classical" piece. Of the three short movements, the first, "Animé," is the longest, clocking in at about four minutes. An agitated, downward cascade for the strings ushers in the soloist, playing an angular, strongly rhythmic theme relying on quickly repeated notes. A second melody is much broader and more luxurious and spreads across half the movement before the opening rat-a-tat theme begins to insinuate itself very subtly into the proceedings again. Even then, the more lyrical melody remains in control to the movement's end. The second movement, "Lent," relies on a sexy, chromatic melody that lingers in the soprano saxophone's high register. After only the briefest pause, the finale, 'Très animé," arrives with an impulsive, sometimes jittery theme over a firm beat. The solo part wanders off into trills while the small orchestra stretches out in long, voluptuous chords. But soon, the dance rhythm returns stronger than ever, bouncing toward a conclusion in which the saxophone departs with an upward flourish, seeming to vanish from the movement without providing a harmonic resolution. *—James Reel*

Recommended:

○ **Music for Saxophone and Orchestra** / Kerkezos, Brabbins (cond.), London Philharmonia Orch. / 2002 / Naxos 8557063

Guitar Concerto (1951)

Heitor Villa-Lobos' *Concerto for guitar and orchestra* is the late capstone to a revolutionary body of guitar works by the composer that began with his *Études* in 1929. Written for Andrés Segovia in 1951, the concerto itself bears the mark of an old composer looking back on earlier, more severe styles and recuperating them into sentimental fantasy. The opening Allegro precioso perfectly displays the synthesizing fecundity of Villa-Lobos' melting-pot imagination. After the strings initiate a Bartók-like head-motto of folk-derived rigid declamation, the guitar immediately enters with a figuration characteristic of Villa-Lobos' earlier guitar works: the guitarist repeats a motive while traveling down the neck of the instrument. It's a simple gesture, but releases in its executive ease a delightful wealth of weird harmonies. Soon enough, the guitar and orchestra are confidently dialoguing and begin a magically continuous string of stylizations: one minute a ritornello of Bach-like polyphony and shape, the next a movie soundtrack vista. The argument passes through all manner of Villa-Lobosian masks, from the learned to the folk, from Beethovenian motivic development through modal sequences right out of Debussy's later work. The following Andantino e andante is even more infused with the wistful remembrance of Debussy, though suffused with Villa-Lobos' inextricable confidence and native tone. The movement is a multi-sectioned rhapsody singing through its tempo and style changes with an ever-intoxicating harmonic brew. Instead of Debussy's sentimentalized French folklore, Villa-Lobos' "Brazilian sentimental" inflected with the sound of northeast Brazilian folk melodies can be heard, yet without quite quoting anything specific. The cadenza is a feat: a fond look back by the composer to his back-breaking, beastly, beating guitar *Études* of 1929, in which the instrument is taken through its gauntlet of technical effects (harmonics, arpeggios, scales, madly repeated chords, and whimsical neck-sliding sequences) with suavity and bluster. Villa-Lobos originally wrote the concerto without a cadenza, but Segovia, ever the calculating (if reserved) showman, demanded the composer write him one. Villa-Lobos composed a veritable movement in itself for guitar alone and the cadenza is now known almost as much as an unaccompanied recital item as it is in its original context. The final Allegretto non troppo is announced by a declamatory sweep of the guitar's 12th-fret harmonics, after which the winds play out a groovy unison figure. This is quickly swept aside by further rhapsodizing, only to come back harmonized by the guitar itself. A parade of themes and thematic transformations ensue, each passage hinting at some type of popular dance (the Baroque gigue, the waltz, duple dances, etc.), simultaneously swathing it in a harmonic ambience of modal mixtures. The most structurally "liberated" of the movements, it spins through its luxurious guises until an abrupt bare-octave close. *—Seth Brodsky*

Recommended:

○ **Villa-Lobos: Instrumental and Orchestral Works** / Romero, Lopez-Cobos (cond.), London PO / 1998 / EMI 72670

○ **Rodrigo & Villa-Lobos** / Bream, Previn (cond.), London SO / 1991 / RCA 6525

○ **The Great Guitar Concertos** / Williams, Barenboim (cond.) / 1989 / CBS 44791

Piano Concertos (1945–1957)

Although he had composed works for piano and orchestra earlier in his career—including a *Suite* (1913) for his pianist wife Lucília Guimarães as well as the rhapsodic *Momoprecoce* (1929)—Heitor Villa-Lobos was nearly 60 by the time he wrote the first of his five piano concertos in 1945.

All five of the piano concertos were written for pianist friends and acquaintances. While there are references to his Brazilian heritage scattered throughout the works—for instance, the slow movement of the *Piano Concerto No. 2*, which makes use of an Amerindian song—for the most part they reflect the more conservative musical mainstream of the day. Amidst the lush orchestration and virtuosic writing for the pianist, hints of the styles of Rachmaninov, Bartók, Shostakovich, even Gershwin are not hard to find. The five concertos are all in four movements, the third of which is dominated by a cadenza for the soloist.

The big, cinematic *Concerto No. 1* (1945), generally regarded as the best of the five, was written for Ellen Ballon, who premiered it on October 11, 1946, in Rio de Janeiro, as part of a "Festival Villa-Lobos." Each movement is in a mosaic form akin to Villa-Lobos' *Chôros* series, where one fairly self-contained episode follows another. The composer's long-time friend João de Souza Lima was the dedicatee of the *Piano Concerto No. 2* (1948); their mutual Brazilian heritage is reflected not only in the folk song used in the second movement, but is also hinted at in the second theme of the final movement, which is something of a modinha.

Two other Brazilian pianist friends, Arnaldo Estrella and Bernardo Segall, inspired the *Concerto Nos. 3* and *4*. *No. 4* was written in 1952 in both Paris and New York, while *No. 3* was begun in 1952 in Rio de Janeiro and only completed in 1957 in New York. These works haven't had much currency since their premieres, although they contain some colorful moments and noteworthy effects, notably the use of vibraphone and celesta in the *Concerto No. 3*.

The *Concerto No. 5* of 1954 is probably the most popular of the set, due in large part to the efforts of Polish pianist Felicia Blumenthal. She premiered the concerto at London's Royal Festival Hall on May 8, 1955, recorded it the following month under Villa-Lobos' direction, and championed the work for years thereafter. One critic at the London premiere referred to the work as "a piano tuner's orgy," but audiences have continued to respond to its high spirits. *—Chris Morrison*

Giovanni Battista Viotti

b. May 12, 1755, Fontanetto da Po, Italy, **d.** Mar. 3, 1824, London, England

Composer: Concerto

Italian violinist and composer G.B. Viotti was one of the seminal figures in the development of the modern school of violin playing. Although his career as a composer was rather overshadowed by his prestige as a virtuoso, Viotti's music was held in very high regard by his contemporaries, and several later composers show his influence.

Viotti was born into a lower-class household in the year 1755. As a result of his impressive musical talent, the boy received an education—musical and otherwise—in the household of Prince Alfonso of Turin, and, by 1770, was considered ripe for apprenticeship to the legendary violinist Gaetano Pugnani. After serving as a violinist in the orchestra of the royal chapel in Turin from 1775 to 1780, Viotti accompanied Pugnani on an extensive concert tour of Switzerland, Germany, Poland and Russia. By 1781, however, Viotti had grown uncomfortable with being billed as Pugnani's pupil and he journeyed to Paris alone, making his professional début there the following year.

Although he quickly established himself as one of Europe's pre-eminent violinists, Viotti retired from active concertizing in 1783 to accept a position with the court of Marie Antoinette at Versailles. After 1788 his interests turned increasingly towards opera, and he served for four seasons as director of the newly formed Théâtre de Monsieur. Although the new company was a success, by 1792 the Revolution had made further productions impossible, and Viotti relocated to London.

Reestablishing himself as an active violinist, Viotti served as both soloist and director of a number of British ensembles (including acting as opera manager at King's Theatre from 1794–95) until the British government began to suspect him of political treachery, and he was forced to flee to Hamburg in 1798.

By 1801 Viotti's name had been cleared, but upon his return to London he retired from concertizing to devote himself to the administration of a wine business. By 1818 the business had gone bankrupt and Viotti was forced to take over as director of the Paris Opéra to pay off his debts. His tenure, however, was an unhappy one and he retired from the post, still deeply in debt, in 1821. He died in 1824 while visiting some friends in London.

While the number of violin pupils Viotti actually taught is rather small, several of the most influential players of the day, including Kreutzer and Baillot, considered themselves to be his disciples. The 29 violin concertos remain Viotti's most significant contribution as a composer, and it is in these works that his true compositional prowess is revealed (the many chamber works and vocal arias being, by comparison, relatively uninspired). The last ten concertos, in particular, begin to approach the Romantic idiom, and it is clear that Viotti's idiomatic figurations and noble lyricism made an impact on Beethoven's conception of the violin concerto. Of particular note is the *Concerto No.22 in A minor*, which Brahms hailed as a masterpiece and used as a model in the composition of his own concerto for the instrument. *—Blair Johnston*

CONCERTO

Violin Concertos (ca. 1780–1800)

These days, the name Giovanni Battista Viotti is for the most part remembered only by teachers of the violin, who grab at one or perhaps two of his pieces to use as instructional works for their intermediate students. But between 1782, when the Italian Viotti made his debut at the Concerts Spirituels in Paris, and 1802, when he retired as an active performer, there was hardly a more famous musician in Europe—and, until Paganini's rise in the second and third decades of the nineteenth century, Europe certainly knew no more famous violinist. He is rightly considered the father of nineteenth century violin playing, and it is safe to say that neither Vieuxtemps nor Wieniawski, neither Ysaÿe nor Kreisler, could have played in quite the way that they did had not Viotti come before them and written new kinds of violin music to show the way. Viotti composed 29 violin concertos between 1781 and about 1805.

Viotti began writing concertos when the Parisian "galant" style of the mid-Classical era was in vogue. Thus, the earliest of his concertos are brief, charming, and unambitious (especially No. 3 in A major, which predates Nos. 1 and 2 by about a year). Viotti, like Tartini before him, maintained that the violin must sing if it is to make good music, and "singing" is the almost exclusive focus here. The work is, like all of the other concertos, in three movements. Viotti soon began to expand the premise of his concerto-writing, however, to include the diverse, pan-European influences of symphony and opera, and the concertos grew ever less dependent on the Classical model of the day. They became freer and of broader dramatic scope.

The virtuoso fireworks contained in Viotti's concertos are not of the type that will exhilarate an audience used to hearing the fireworks of post-Paganini violinist-composers, but the pieces are by no means easy to play. Viotti took the "passage"—those parts of a concerto during which the themes are abandoned (or at least disguised) and virtuoso display of one kind or another takes over—to a new level, both in terms of technical difficulty and of the degree to which such "passages" are connected to the main stream of the music. It is this connectedness, coupled with truly inspired melodic courses, that raises Viotti's concertos above the violinist-composer norm. Certainly Mozart, who knew and loved many Viotti works and even transcribed the *Concerto No. 16 in E minor* for a different orchestra (he added brass and timpani), thought well of them. And Johannes Brahms, who was first introduced to Viotti's music when his friend Joseph Joachim rescued the *Concerto No. 22 in A minor* from oblivion, also thought so: he actually quoted strands of the Viotti work in his own *Double Concerto for violin and cello*, Op. 102, of 1887. That concerto is perhaps the most frequently performed of Viotti's works today. *—Blair Johnston*

Recommended:

- ○ **Viotti: Violin Concertos Vol. 3** / Mezzena, Symphonia Perusina / 1996 / Dynamic 103
- ○ **Viotti: Violin Concertos Vol. 5** / Mezzena, Symphonia Perusina / 1998 / Dynamic 206
- ○ **Viotti: Violin Concertos Vol. 9** / Mezzena, Symphonia Perusina / 2003 / Dynamic 425
- ○ **Viotti: Violin Concertos 8–11, 12** / Borin (cond.), Mezzena, Viotti CO / 1994 / Dynamic 63

Galina Vishnievskaya

b. Oct. 25, 1926, Leningrad (St. Petersburg), U.S.S.R.

Soprano

Galina Pavolovna Vishnievskaya became the most exciting soprano to emerge in the Soviet Union after World War II. She had a major career on the Bolshoi stage, cruelly cut short due to the political beliefs of her and her husband.

She had a strong and attractive natural voice and was originally taken to be a mezzo-soprano. During World War II, she sang incessantly for the troops while studying privately with Vera Garina in Leningrad. She began singing in operetta in 1944 and was, in general, regarded as a light music specialist. When her true vocal range was discovered, however, she developed a powerful, highly dramatic voice with unique personal coloration and the capability of the most intense expression. She was appointed a soloist for the Leningrad Philharmonic and then joined Moscow's Bolshoi Theater in 1952. Her dramatic voice, strikingly beautiful appearance, and wide range as an actress made her the house's leading star in very short order. On a tour in Czechoslovakia, she was intensely wooed by the young cellist Mstislav Rostropovich, as recounted in her autobiography *Galina: A Russian Story* (New York, 1984).

She sang in all the major dramatic soprano parts of the standard Western repertoire (Butterfly, Tosca, Violetta, Aida, Leonore, and Liu), in addition to Russian roles like Tatyana (*Yevgeny Onegin*), Kupava (*Snegurochka*), Natasha (*War and Peace*), Sofiya (*Semyon Kotko*), and Marfa (*Khovanshchina*). Many of these were recorded by the Soviet state recording and broadcasting companies. Some of her roles were preserved on television and in films. She made international debuts (the Met, La Scala, Covent Garden, etc.) between 1961 and 1964. At the same time, English composer Benjamin Britten wrote the soprano part in his *War Requiem* specifically for her. However, Soviet authorities withheld permission for her to leave the country. She was permitted to go to London a few months later to participate in the classic composer-led performance of the work. Later, Britten wrote a Russian-language Pushkin song cycle, *The Poet's Echo*, for her and her husband in Rostropovich's largely unrecognized capacity as a recital pianist.

Meanwhile, she also showed herself as a great recitalist, particularly in the songs of the Russian masters, including Shostakovich, who wrote his *Seven Romances* for her. In 1966, she appeared on film in the title role of Shostakovich's opera *Katerina Ismailova*, one of her greatest performances. Shostakovich wrote the soprano part of his *Symphony No. 14* for her, and she sang at its premiere in 1969. Her recording of it is a gramophone classic.

She and Rostropovich supported the Nobel Prize-winning author Alexander Solzhenitsyn in his struggles with Soviet officialdom, even sheltering him in their summer house. Once again, official pressure against them tightened and ultimately, both musicians found their bookings canceled, and Vishnievskaya was expelled from the Bolshoi. Vishnievskaya lost valuable years of her artistic prime in this dispute before they left the U.S.S.R. in 1974. In 1978, the U.S.S.R. proclaimed them "ideological renegades" and stripped them of Soviet citizenship.

Vishnievskaya had a few years during which she successfully appeared as a guest artist in leading international opera houses. The highlight of her Western career was the recording she made with Rostropovich conducting the original version of *Lady Macbeth of Mtsensk*, a performance of breathtaking passion and intensity that is a treasure of the recording art.

In one of the last acts of the Soviet Union, Mikhail Gorbachev restored the couple's citizenship in 1990. They made a triumphal return to Russia, documented in the television film *Soldiers of Music*. Since then, they have devoted much effort to improving the lot of musical life in their homeland. *—Joseph Stevenson*

Recommended:

- ○ **Shostakovich & Mussorgsky** / Rostropovich (cond.), Vishnievskaya, Geddai, London PO / 2004 / EMI 62830
- ○ **Russian Songs & Arias** / Rostropovich (cond.), Vishnievskaya, London PO / 2003 / EMI 62654
- ○ **Mussorgsky: Boris Godunov** / Karajan (cond.), Ghiaurov, Talvela, Cvejic, Spiess, Vienna PO / 1988 / Decca 411862
- ○ **Shostakovich: Lady Macbeth of Mtsensk** / Rostropovich (cond.), Gedda, Tear, Krenn, Byers, Vishnievskaya, London PO / 2002 / EMI 67779B

Dominique Visse

b. Aug. 30, 1955, Lisieux, France

Countertenor

French countertenor Dominique Visse has participated in the early music revival in France since its inception. Although he became a chorister at the Cathedral of Notre Dame in Paris at the age of 13, he pursued studies on organ and flute at the Versailles Conservatory. As an instrumentalist, he developed an interest in medieval and Renaissance repertories, only occasionally singing as a countertenor. It was only after studies with Alfred Deller and René Jacobs between 1976 and 1978 that he decided to specialize in singing. In 1978, he founded the Ensemble Clément Janequin and joined the newly formed period-instrument group Les Arts Florissants under William Christie. In 1982, he made his opera debut at Tourcoing in Monteverdi's *L'incoronazione di Poppea*. Other notable performances included the title role of Charpentier's *Actéon* at Edinburgh (1985), Annius in Gluck's *La clemenza di Tito* at Tourcoing (1987) and at Lausanne (1991), Cupid in Charpentier's *Orphée aux enfers* at the Paris Opera (1987), and Delfa in Cavalli's *Giasone at Innsbruck* (1988). He created the role of Geronimo in Claude Prey's *Le rouge et le noir* at Aix-en-Provence in 1989. Visse has recorded Cavalli's *Xerse* and

Giasone; Charpentier's *Actéon*, *Les arts florissants*, *David et Jonathas*, and *Le malade imaginaire*; Campra's *Tancrède*; Rameau's *Anacréon*; and Hasse's *Cleofide*. He is married to the soprano Agnès Mellon. *—Robert Adelson*

Recommended:

- ○ **Janequin: La Bataille Chanson & Mass** / Clement Janequin Ens., Visse / HM 926012
- ○ **Songs for 7 Centuries** / Visse, Bellocq / Seven Seas 135
- ○ **Les Plaisirs du Palais** / Clement Janequin Ens., Visse / HM 901729
- ○ **Portrait** / Clement Janequin Ens., Visse / 1998 / HM 290868

Philippe de Vitry

b. Oct. 31, 1291, Vitry, Champagne, France, **d.** Jun. 9, 1361, Paris, France
Composer: Vocal

Philippe de Vitry, poet and musician, philosopher and intellectual, councilor to three kings, began his stellar career with a master of arts degree from the Sorbonne. Pope John XXII conferred upon him the first of many ecclesiastical revenues in 1321. By this point, Vitry may have already been serving as a notary to the Royal Court; his documented service to French royalty spanned three reigns, Charles le Bel, Philippe VI, and Jean II. In 1346, Vitry accompanied Jean to war as a "companion in arms," and he served as an ambassador to the Papal court in Avignon starting in 1350. In that year, he was named Bishop of Meaux, a post he retained until his death in 1361. During his life, Vitry was commended by no less a writer than Francesco Petrarch as "the one true poet of France," and by numerous professional musicians as the "flower and jewel of singers"; he was said to have discovered the very means of composing music in his time.

Philippe de Vitry has long been erroneously thought to have codified his new theories of music composition some time around 1320 in a revolutionary treatise called the *Ars Nova*, or "New Art" (setting its teaching in contrast to the compositional styles in the previous century). Musicologists now doubt that such a single work existed. Nevertheless, vestiges of his teachings on music have survived in a number of smaller treatises and tracts by his pupils. His expansions of musical practice largely deal with rhythmic features: the codification of different mensurations (or musical time signatures), specifically duple time; the use of red notation to indicate new proportional rhythmic values; and the standardization of a new shorter note value, the minim. In each of these cases, it seems he influenced his peers and pupils more in codification than in revolutionary invention.

Though a contemporary musical treatise suggests Vitry "discovered" the means of composition for secular verse forms such as the ballade, the lay, and the rondeau, virtually none of his secular music survives. Almost all his extant music is in the form of the fourteenth century motet, not to be confused with the Renaissance musical form by this name. The motets display a dramatically hierarchical ordering of voices, with a slow-moving tenor voice based upon a plainchant melody (often subject to rhythmic manipulations), complemented by one or more upper voices, moving in shorter note values and set to different texts. The added texts, assumed to be the work of the composer himself, most often add an ironic level of commentary to the chant text, enhancing the rational pungency of the piece's affect. The most famous of the motets attributed to Vitry appear in the provocative and sumptuous illuminated manuscript, dated 1316, of the *Roman de Fauvel*, in which the corrupt government of France is personified as an ass. *—Timothy Dickey*

VOCAL

Overview of Works (ca. 1320–1360)

Philippe de Vitry's contemporaries saw in him a consummate intellectual. His literary and scholarly works alone cemented his reputation for over 100 years. His lengthy verse allegory *Le chapel des trois fleurs de lis* of 1335, for instance, lauded the crusading efforts of the French Bourbon monarchs; his shorter pastoral *Le dit du franc Gontier* enjoyed wide circulation into the fifteenth century. Vitry's expertise as a teacher and scholar of music theory led to the misconception that he himself invented the revolutionary rhythmic and notational system known as the ars nova, and that he wrote the musical treatise of that name. Vitry apparently was well-versed in the mathematical sciences as well, though no treatises of his survive in this field.

Vitry's crowning achievement in musical composition was his isorhythmic motets. Unfortunately, only two such motets carry his name in their fourteenth century manuscript sources; music historians and performers vividly debate which other anonymous pieces were composed by Vitry. The list of motets acknowledged to be his ranges from five motets to more than 20; attributions are made on the basis of musical style, of quotation in the ars nova treatise and other literary works, and even by correlating motet texts with Vitry's marginal notes in books he owned. Vitry may have written many motet texts himself, and many take on richly political overtones. Of the four or more of his motets interpolated into the 1316 illuminated manuscript copy of the *Roman de Fauvel*, for instance, all offer scathing criticisms of corruption in contemporary French politics. Often the motets are polytextual, juxtaposing as many as three different texts (even in different languages) between various voice parts, in a witty dialogue. Vitry's upper voice melodies often display an astounding rhythmic facility. They can contain supple combinations of every conceivable rhythmic value, in alternating groups of twos and threes, yet often a rigorous periodic phrase structure regulates them. Most often Vitry disposes the lowest (tenor) voice in a motet according to the systematic application of isorhythm: a simple melody, often chant-based, repeats several times, subject to identical rhythmic values. Here, too, the composer shows his great skill, sometimes fashioning the rhythms in completely symmetric (and even palindromic) patterns.

Some fourteenth century observers credited Vitry with inventing one of the secular *formes fixes*, the ballade. Though he probably did not create it, he certainly wrote a large number of such chansons, both monophonic and polyphonic. Unfortunately, all are now lost. *—Timothy Dickey*

Recommended:

- ○ **Le Roman de Fauvel** / Cohen (cond.), Visse, Azéma, Boston Camerata / 1995 / Erato 96392
- ○ **Philippe De Vitry: Motets & Chansons** / Sequentia / 1991 / DG 77095

Antonio Vivaldi

b. Mar. 4, 1678, Venice, Italy, **d.** Jul. 28, 1741, Vienna, Austria
Composer: Concerto, Chamber Music, Choral, Vocal, Orchestral, Opera

The creator of hundreds of spirited, extroverted instrumental works, Italian composer Antonio Vivaldi is widely recognized as the master of the Baroque instrumental concerto, which he perfected and popularized more than any of his contemporaries. Vivaldi's kinetic rhythms, fluid melodies, bright instrumental effects, and extensions of instrumental technique make his some of the most enjoyable of Baroque music. He was highly influential among his contemporaries and successors: even as esteemed a figure as Johann Sebastian Bach adapted some of Vivaldi's music. Vivaldi's variable textures and dramatic effects initiated the shift toward what became the Classical style; a deeper understanding of his music begins with the realization that, compared with Bach and even Handel, he was Baroque music's archprogressive. Though not as familiar as his concerti, Vivaldi's stage and choral music is still of value; his sometimes bouncy, sometimes lyrical *Gloria in D major* (1708) has remained a perennial favorite. His operas were widely performed in his own time.

Details regarding Vivaldi's early life are few. His father was a violinist in the Catherdral of Venice's orchestra and probably Antonio's first teacher. There is much speculation about other teachers, such as Corelli, but no evidence to support this. Vivaldi studied for the priesthood as a young man and was ordained in 1703. He was known for much of his career as "il prete rosso" (the red-haired priest), but soon after his ordination he declined to take on his ecclesiastical duties. Later in life he cited ill health as the reason, but other motivations have been proposed; perhaps Vivaldi simply wanted to explore new opportunties as a composer. It didn't take him long. Landing a job as a violin teacher at a girls' orphanage in Venice (where he would work in one capacity or another during several stretches of his life), he published a set of trio sonatas and another of violin sonatas. Word of his abilities spread around Europe, and in 1711 an Amsterdam publisher brought out, under the title *L'estro armonico* (Harmonic Inspiration), a set of Vivaldi's concertos for one or more violins with orchestra. These were best sellers (it was this group of concertos that spurred Bach's transcriptions), and Vivaldi followed them up with several more equally successful concerto sets. Perhaps the most prolific of all the great European composers, he once boasted that he could compose a concerto faster than a copyist could ready the individual parts for the players in the orchestra. He began to compose operas, worked from 1718 to 1720 in the court of the German principality of Hessen-Darmstadt, and traveled in Austria and perhaps Bohemia. Throughout his career, he had his choice of commissions from nobility and the highest members of society, the ability to use the best performers, and enough business savvy to try to control the publication of his works, although due to his popularity, many were published without his consent. Later in life Vivaldi was plagued by rumors of a sexual liaison with one of his vocal students, and he was censured by ecclesiastical authorities. His Italian career on the rocks, he headed for Vienna. He died there and was buried as a pauper in 1741, although at the height of his career his publications had earned a comfortable living. *—AMG*

CONCERTO

Il cimento dell'Armonia e dell'Invenzione, 12 concertos, Op. 8 (1725)

It was common in Vivaldi's time to gather up a set of six or 12 works in similar form and for the same forces and publish them under an umbrella title. The 12 violin concertos of this lot were mostly composed at different times, and their original manuscripts, which differ in some respects from the published versions, are scattered among several libraries in different countries. Their collective Italian title, which graced their publication in 1725 in Amsterdam (Vivaldi was both controversial and popular all over Europe), means "The Trial of Harmony and Invention." That title, although not out of line with the conventions of Vivaldi's time, does suggest something of the particular tension between form and fantasy in his works in general and in these concertos in particular.

Concealed within the larger set are the most famous of all Baroque solo concertos, for numbers one through four were indeed composed as a group—none other than the ubiquitous *Four Seasons*, "Spring," "Summer," "Fall," and "Winter." These are pure program music. Each one is headed by a sonnet probably written by Vivaldi himself, describing with precision just what happens in the four concertos. If you follow the sonnets while listening, you can see just how detailed Vivaldi's description is, right down to someone losing footing on the ice and falling on his or her rear—unlike in other titled Baroque pieces where the title connotes little more than a general mood. The overexposure of these concertos should not make us forget what fine masterpieces they actually are; part of their genius lies in the way they reconcile vivid pictorial description with the requirements of Baroque concerto form, which even in Vivaldi's hands was a rather rigid thing.

Several of the other concertos in the Op. 8 set are likewise programmatic in nature, which might have suggested to Vivaldi or another compiler that the works belonged together. Anyone who enjoys the *Four Seasons* will find the "La caccia" (The Hunt) or "La tempesta di mare" (The Storm at Sea) concertos to be cut from the same cloth, equally rewarding, and much less familiar. The entire set has been recorded by several of the most daring Baroque performers of the day, including conductor Nikolaus Harnoncourt and violinist Fabio Biondi. *—James Manheim*

Recommended:

○ **Vivaldi: Le quattro stagioni** / Marriner (cond.), Academy of St. Martin-in-the-Fields, various soloists / 2000 / Decca 466232

Concerto alla rustica, for strings & continuo in G major, RV 151 (1729–1730)

Antonio Vivaldi's concerti without soloists are generally included among the antecedents of the Classical-period symphony. Probably written for highly skilled professional orchestras, these works, mostly written in a contrapuntal style, show what the orchestra can do when it is not in any way subordinated to a soloist. All of these features manifest themselves in the *Concerto alla rustica for strings in G major*, RV 151. Despite the idea of provincialism implied in the title, this work is a brilliant, sophisticated example of late-Baroque style. The first movement Presto is a virtuoso showpiece for Baroque orchestra, with a bouncy melody that never stops moving. However, the high spirits are quickly and dramatically countered by an unexpected juxtaposition of the same material in a fierce minor, which ends the movement. Ornamental runs from a solo violin decorate the simple melody of the brief Adagio that follows, while the final movement, in dance rhythm, has a busy cello line to support its graceful violin melody. In this exciting work, Vivaldi packs much musical content into a brief time interval. *—Andrew Lindemann Malone*

Recommended:

○ **Vivaldi: Four Seasons; Concerti; Sinfonia** / Parrott (cond.), Taverner Players / 1995 / Capitol 45117

○ **Vivaldi: 14 Concertos** / Bylsma, MacIntosh, Pleeth, Higgett / 1997 / L'Oiseau-Lyre 455703

Concerto for 3 violins, strings & continuo in F major, RV 551 (before 1742)

The *Concerto for 3 violins, strings, and continuo in F major* is often counted among Antonio Vivaldi's more striking concerti; the profusion of his favorite solo instrument apparently inspired him to find fresh ways for the violins to interact and create exceptionally colorful textures using the interactions. The appeal of Vivaldi's invention is evident in the very first episode of the ritornello-form first movement: The three violins each solo in sequence, the first two with the same exuberant line, the third with different material that eventually draws the first two back into the fray for some high-spirited harmonizing. Similar antics inform the remainder of the episodes in the first movement: unexpected entries and exits creating ear-catching textures and are spiced by Vivaldian virtuoso runs and arpeggios. The second movement drops the orchestra altogether, as one violin plays a graceful, sad melody above busy, quiet ostinato accompaniment from the other two violins, one playing arpeggios and the other plucking out a rhythm; the effect is luminous, especially when a few bars of the bare accompaniment close the movement. In the third movement, the first violin also gets more prominence, but the three violins as a unit are still a formidable force. During the last episode, they unleash an avalanche of minor mode notes to lead into the last ritornello, but Vivaldi nevertheless manages to snatch major mode victory from the jaws of defeat—an imaginative ending to a highly imaginative concerto. *—Andrew Lindemann Malone*

Recommended:

○ **Vivaldi: Il Proteo** / Antonini (cond.), Coin, Giardino Armonico / 1995 / Teldec 94552

Concerto for flute, oboe, violin, bassoon & continuo in F major, RV 99 (before 1742)

This concerto, one of about 20 Vivaldi wrote for a small group of instruments without string orchestra, clearly looks forward to the Classical era, although its exact date of composition is unknown. In the ritornello structures of the first and third movements, the role of the orchestral tutti is filled by the four solo instruments playing in unison or octaves. The central slow movement is a quartet for the soloists, with the continuo silent; with a few changes it could have gone almost unnoticed as a movement of an early Classical divertimento or Feldparthie. Vivaldi is more apt throughout to explore varied combinations possible within the solo group than to exploit the contrast between solo and tutti passages. The brief ritornellos rarely even get a chance to finish before the individual instruments go their separate ways. There is great artistry in the way the ritornello is cut off and in the harmonic twists and turns the music takes after this happens. The flute (whose part is also performable on a recorder) dominates the little ensemble of solo instruments, getting the opportunity, especially in the finale, to show off some virtuoso playing. Yet the oboe and bassoon, quite novel in concertos in Vivaldi's time, are not slighted; the bassoon does not simply double the continuo bass line but enriches the texture with delightful runs of its own. The concerto is thematically related to another, RV 571, for violin, two oboes, two horns, and bassoon. Despite the roller coaster ride of variety it contains, it's all over in less than ten minutes. *—James Manheim*

Recommended:

○ **Vivaldi: Concerti da camera** / L'Astrée / 2004 / Opus 111 30394

○ **Vivaldi: Seven Concertos** / Goodwin, Toll, Verbruggen, Godburn, Comberti, Holloway / 2001 / Classical Express 3957046

Concerto for strings & continuo in C major, RV 114 (1729–1730)

This short two-movement piece is one of Vivaldi's so-called "Paris Concertos," so called because their original manuscripts reside in the library of the Paris Conservatory. It is one of about 60 concertos Vivaldi wrote for string orchestra alone, with no solo part; these were sometimes called ripieno concertos, but they were very close to the emerging genre of the orchestral sinfonia and may have influenced it. In the dotted rhythms that populate its opening movement, the concerto does show the influence of French Baroque music, but in other ways it looks forward to the Classical style. The first movement is built around the contrast between the dotted-rhythm figure and a group of running 16th notes in the violins, and this contrast is neatly harnessed to shifts in the rate of harmonic motion; the dotted figure is stolid and harmonically almost immobile, while the 16th notes veer around the circle of fifths. The effect is almost one of a historical dialogue of styles. The 16th note figure includes a number of quasi-fugal passages, a hallmark of Vivaldi's ripieno concertos. The first movement ends with a two-bar violin solo leading to a dominant chord, and thence into the second movement—which against all expectations is a set of variations. These are based on a brief and distinctive syncopated arpeggio theme, and they offer all kinds of variety; several variations right before the end are in C minor, and the final reprise of the opening theme has the character of a recapitulation after all that minor. The opening syncopation is treated with extraordinary invention in the variations, and the structure of the group of variations as a whole is subtle. In all, for a piece of music that lasts no more than six minutes in performance, this little concerto holds extraordinary interest. *—James Manheim*

Recommended:

○ **Vivaldi: Concerti for Strings** / Labadie (cond.), Les Violons du Roy / 1999 / Dorian 90255

Double Cello Concerto in G minor, RV 531 (before 1742)

Vivaldi's only concerto for the unusual combination of two cellos was probably, like so many of his concertos, written for the all-girl orchestra of the Ospedale della Pietà in Venice, with which he was associated for some four decades. The tone color of the paired cellos and the minor key help to account for the relatively somber sound of the work. The cellos announce their presence at the very beginning of the energetic opening Allegro, which also features a particularly attractive interlude in the major mode. The solo instruments sometimes harmonize with one another, at other times respond to one another in canonic imitation. After a songful Largo of rather grave beauty, the work concludes with an extroverted Allegro. *—Chris Morrison*

Recommended:

○ **Vivaldi: Concerti** / Biondi (cond.), Naddeo, Fantinuoli, Europa Galante / 1993 / Opus 111 3086

○ **Vivaldi: 14 Concertos** / Hogwood (cond.), Bylsma, Pleeth / 1997 / L'Oiseau-Lyre 455703

Double Concerto, for viola d'amore, lute, strings & continuo in D minor, RV 540 (1740)

In March 1738 composer Antonio Vivaldi did not survive the annual review given for confirmation of his job as master of music at the Ospedale della Pietà in Venice. Vivaldi had enjoyed this position on and off since 1713, but the powers that made the decision in 1738 were of a different mind, possibly due to the rumor that Vivaldi had taken a mistress who had been his former student at the Ospedale. Nonetheless, they did not cut Vivaldi off completely, and when Prince Frederick Christian, Elector of Saxony and King of Poland, was slated to arrive, Vivaldi was engaged to lead a special concert at the Ospedale in his honor. The concert was held at the Ospedale on March 21, 1740, and it would prove Vivaldi's last hurrah in Venice.

Vivaldi composed three concerti and one Sinfonia for this gala event, presented on a program with a number of other works, now forgotten or lost. One of the Vivaldi pieces, the *Double Concerto for viola d'amore & lute, strings & continuo in D minor,* RV 540, has become an audience favorite in modern times; it has folk dance-like qualities and the interplay between the viola d'amore and lute vaguely resembles a country hoedown. At the original concert, the viola d'amore part may have been played by 21-year-old virtuoso Chiaretta (1718–1796), then regarded as the top string player at the Ospedale, supplanting the part once played by Vivaldi's alleged paramour, Anna Maria Girò (1696–1782).

The work must have been well received, as the Prince accepted the manuscript of it, along with the other Vivaldi pieces played on that occasion, and took them home to Dresden, depositing the precious scores in the Sächsische Landesbibliothek where they still reside. For Vivaldi himself, his position in Venice vis-à-vis 1740 was at best a hollow victory. As his friend Charles de Brosses wrote, "(Vivaldi) is not as appreciated here (in Venice) as he deserves. Here, everything follows current fashion and music from days gone by does not reap any reward; Vivaldi's music has been heard here for too long." In the fall of 1740, Vivaldi left Venice for the last time, and by the end of June the following year, he was dead, buried in a pauper's grave in Vienna. *—Uncle Dave Lewis*

Recommended:

- ○ **Vivaldi: Concert for the Prince of Poland** / Manze (cond.), Academy of Ancient Music (UK) / 2002 / HM 2907230

Double Flute Concerto in C major, RV 533 (before 1742)

Of the nearly 50 concertos that Vivaldi wrote for two soloists, strings, and continuo, the *Concerto in C major,* RV 533, is the only one for two flutes, specifically transverse flutes, not recorders, which are more frequently found in Baroque music. There is the belief that the transverse flute was a more acceptable instrument for use in a religious institution, such as the orphanage where Vivaldi taught, because in the eyes of the Church, the recorder had been associated with lasciviousness in ancient writings. It was most likely that Vivaldi began writing for the flute in the late 1720s, after the talented flutist Johann Joachim Quantz had toured in 1726 and Ignazio Sieber was reappointed as flute master at the orphanage in 1728. In most aspects, this concerto is typical of Vivaldi's non-descriptive concerto style. It is in the fast-slow-fast, three-movement structure; makes use of the ritornello form; and has a generally lighthearted temperament. The opening Allegro molto begins with an extended exposition of the main figures, and as the concerto progresses, each ritornello statement of those figures is briefer than the last. The four episodes between the ritornellos make extensive use of echoing and parallel movement between the two flutes, even at one point using the two flutes together to echo themselves. The gentle Largo contrasts with the fast movements in that it is scored just for the two flutes and continuo, without the string complement. An Allegro completes the concerto, again in the ritornello form. Its main melodic figures are similar to the first movement's in that they are repeated, then used to modulate downward to a second figure, then restated before the first episode for the soloists. Although echoing and parallel motion are again used between the soloists, the episodes in this movement have much more melodic interplay of the two flutes and more ornamentation. *—Patsy Morita*

Recommended:

- ○ **Vivaldio: Wind Concerti** / Kraemer (cond.), Dobing, Wilson, Jeffrey, City of London Sinfonia / 1995 / Naxos 553204
- ○ **Vivaldi: 14 Concertos** / Hogwood (cond.), McGegan, Preston, Academy of Ancient Music / 1997 / L'Oiseau-Lyre 455703

Double Mandolin Concerto in G major, RV 532 (before 1742)

The exact date of composition for this thoroughly enjoyable concerto is unknown, but it is assumed that Vivaldi wrote it for the students at the Ospedale della Pietà. Given the range of notes used by him for the solo parts, the concerto was probably intended for the mandolino, a six-string, high-pitched instrument tuned in fourths, popular in Venice during Vivaldi's life. The fact that the solo parts contain no chords suggests that the instruments were to be played finger-style, that is with the fingers plucking the strings rather than a plectrum. Given the quiet sound of the mandolin, the concerto is most effective when performed with a chamber orchestra, and it also sounds well performed on guitars. The opening and closing Allegro movements are built with the same ritornello structure, ABACADA, with Vivaldi's usual construction of themes from repeating rhythmic motives. Both are light, crisp, and in a 2/4 meter, giving them an almost quickstep nature. The strings are played détaché throughout these movements, to more closely match the plucking of the mandolins. The solo parts use both echoing and parallel movement in the episodes, with trills and other ornaments thrown in to give them a little more texture. The middle Andante is perhaps the most famous movement of the concerto. It is in D minor, with the two mandolins performing throughout over just violins and violas played pizzicato and in unison. The graceful melody is built mostly of overlapping, echoing phrases with the two coming together only to intensify the emotion at certain points through the harmony of the parts. The opening section is repeated in an ornamented fashion, followed by a contrasting, more developmental section that moves through several keys before returning to home and the same ending as the opening section. Given the appeal of the two pleasant outer movements and the delicacy of the middle movement, it's easy to see why this is one of Vivaldi's most popular concertos. *—Patsy Morita*

Recommended:

- ○ **Vivaldi: Music for Lute & Mandolin** / O'Dette, Holman, Jeffrey, Parley of Instruments / 1987 / Hyperion 66160

Double Trumpet Concerto in C major, RV 537 (before 1742)

Antonio Vivaldi's popular *Double Trumpet Concerto in C Major,* RV 537 is remarkable in that the work itself is among Vivaldi's best-known creations and yet we know practically nothing about it. The source of this concerto is a single manuscript located in the Renzo Giordano Collection at the National Library of Turin, a large gathering of manuscripts believed to preserve what is left of the ones Vivaldi himself accumulated during his lifetime. This served as the source used by Gian Francesco Malipiero, who first edited this concerto for publication in 1950. The second movement also appears in Vivaldi's *Violin Concerto in C major,* RV 110, another undated manuscript found in the same collection.

The material is appropriately flashy and fanfare-like in the outer movements, both of which are marked Allegro and propelled by vigorous rhythmic support from the strings. The trumpets usually play together in the solo passages and add some interesting color to the strings when playing along in the tutti. In the first movement the strings take a turn toward the minor mode, which the trumpets turn back to the major. The central Largo is basically serves as a short bridge between the two outer movements; the soloists are not heard, and the strings tread through a series of nonmelodic repeated chords. The third movement dashes forward vigorously and emphatically in triple meter. When the strings turn to the minor mode this time the trumpets respond in kind.

This is Vivaldi's only concerto featuring trumpets; the *Double Concerto in D major,* RV 781 (formerly RV 563) was believed at one time to be a second Vivaldi two trumpet concerto, but more recent scholarly investigation has revealed that it is a double oboe concerto. *—AMG*

Recommended:

- ○ **The Fam'd Italian masters** / Steele-Perkins, Balsom, Parley of Instruments / 2003 / Hyperion 67359

L'estro armonico, 12 concertos, Op. 3 (1711)

The place of Venetian-born Antonio Vivaldi (1678–1741) as a concerto composer is today firmly established, largely thanks to the ubiquitous *Four Seasons.* What is perhaps less fully appreciated is Vivaldi's importance in the development of the concerto genre as a whole. When his groundbreaking set of concertos was published by the Amsterdam publisher Etienne Roger as opus 3 in 1711, the form was no more than about 30 years old.

L'estro armonico, the rubric that heads Vivaldi's first published set of concertos (a group including works that may date back as far as the final years of the seventeenth century), does not translate easily, but is generally rendered as something like "The Harmonic Fancy." It is apt in the sense that it conveys some sense of the unusual or bizarre that features so strongly in Vivaldi's musical make-up. All 12 concertos are concertino works scored for strings and continuo, which is to say that they call for one or more players who both form part of the ensemble (the ripieno) and function as soloists. This division is generally articulated in quicker movements by the contrasts of weight and texture between recurring full tutti sections and those episodes in which the soloists develop and expand the thematic material. Known as ritornello form, it was to become the standard form for the quicker movements of the Venetian concerto, a form that would exert a powerful influence throughout Europe. Slow movements adopt a more varied form, but are lyrical pieces, sometimes a tutti unison (*No. 1* in D) or gentle repeated chords (*No. 5* in A, *No. 11* in D minor) that are distinguished overall by their cantabile writing. Nine of the 12 concertos adopt the three-movement form in a fast (allegro)-slow (largo)-fast (allegro, or, in the instance of No. 6 in A minor, presto) scheme that would also become the paradigmatic format for the Italian concerto. In two concertos, Nos. *4* in E minor, which has four short movements, and *7* in F, which has five equally brief sections, Vivaldi adopted the multi-sectional form of the Corellian concerto grosso, a type he thereafter abandoned. Significantly, these are two of the four works in *L'estro armonico* (the others are *No. 1,* and *No. 10* in B minor) to be scored for four violins and strings (the latter also including a solo part for cello). They are thus in general closer to the concerto grosso than the remaining works, all of which are scored for either one or two violins, with the addition of a cello part in *No. 11.* Here the solo parts attain a greater degree of the brilliance and flamboyance typically associated with the composer. *—Brian Robins*

Recommended:

- ○ **Vivaldi: Concertos** / Pinnock (cond.), English Concert, various soloists / Archiv 471317
- ○ **Vivaldi: 12 Concertos for 1, 2 & 4 Violins** / Hogwood (cond.), Academy of Ancient Music, various soloists / L'Oiseau-Lyre 414554

The Four Seasons (Le quattro stagioni), 4 violin concertos, Op. 8/1–4 (1725)

Having produced hundreds of examples, Antonio Vivaldi must be regarded as the indisputable king of the Baroque instrumental concerto. In writing such works for a multitude of different instruments—violin, viola d'amore, cello, mandolin, flute, oboe, bassoon, trumpet, horn, and others—both alone and in various combinations, Vivaldi was a seminal figure in the development of a genre that attained Classical perfection in the works of Mozart and Beethoven, reached its pinnacle in the Romantic works of Paganini, Brahms, and Tchaikovsky, and enjoyed continued currency throughout the twentieth century in the works of composers diverse as Berg, Prokofiev, and Ligeti. Given the sheer quantity of Vivaldi's concertos for violin—he wrote at least 35 in the key of D major alone—it's not surprising that many have lapsed into near-total obscurity. On the other hand, it is a grouping of four concertos from Vivaldi's Op. 8 (1725)—known collectively as *The Four Seasons*—that remains the composer's best-known and most characteristic work. Aside from the features that have come to be associated with most of Vivaldi's music—grace, virtuosity, energetic motoric rhythms—the concertos of *The Four Seasons* are remarkable for their extraordinary programmatic imagination, which is counterbalanced by close attention to formal structure. Each concerto is accompanied by a descriptive poem whose imagery becomes an essential element of the musical fabric. The birds that greet the season "with their joyful song" in *La primavera* (Spring), for example, are colorfully depicted in the work's elaborately ornamented figuration. *L'estate* (Summer) is painted in similarly vivid colors that portray both the piping of a shepherd and a gathering storm. *L'autunno* (Autumn) is marked by a folksy harvest celebration and the galloping of a hunting party on horseback. The bleakness and dissonance of *L'inverno* (Winter) create a severe but expressive portrait that provides a striking summation of Vivaldi's pictorial ingenuity in these four works. *—AMG*

Recommended:

- ○ **Vivaldi: Le Quattro Stagioni** / Pinnock (cond.), Standage, English Concert / Archiv 400045
- ○ **Vivaldi: The Four Seasons** / Antonini (cond.), Onofri, Grazzi, Giardino Armonico / Teldec 97671

Lute (Chamber) Concerto in D major, RV 93 (1716)

One of four works composed by Vivaldi to feature the lute, RV 93 is a chamber concerto scored for solo strings and lute. During Vivaldi's lifetime, the lute was nearing the end of a long and distinguished career as a solo instrument, its final glory achieved in the suites of Bach and his fellow German, Sylvius Weiss. The *D major Concerto*, along with the Trios for violin and lute in G minor, RV63 and C major, RV 85 was composed in Bohemia during the 1730s. In this short, attractive three-movement work, Vivaldi exploits the instrument's timbres and ability to play arpeggios to appealing affect. It opens with an Allegro giusto whose ritornello contrasts a tuneful opening theme with a more lyrical motif in the minor mode. The soloist enters to the same material, which is worked out with typical alternation between soloists and strings. The central Largo is a reflective meditation by the soloist over sustained violin accompaniment and pizzicato bass, with an exquisitely simple shift from triple to duple meter, while the final Allegro brings a return to the high spirits of the first subject of the opening movement and has a bit of tarantella-like feel with its 6/8 rhythms. As with Vivaldi's other lute works, the Concerto in D was not published during Vivaldi's lifetime. The autograph manuscript is preserved in the Biblioteca Nazionale, Turin. *—Brian Robins*

Recommended:

- ○ **Vivaldi: Music for Lute & Mandolin** / O'Dette, Holman, Parley of Instruments / 1987 / Hyperion 66160
- ○ **The Ultimate Guitar Collection** / Bream, Gardiner (cond.), Monteverdi Orch. / 1996 / RCA 33705
- ○ **Vivaldi: Complete Works for Lute** / Lislevand / 1999 / Astree 128587

Mandolin Concerto in C major, RV 425 (before 1742)

This work, the only solo mandolin concerto out of the hundreds of concertos Vivaldi composed, was featured in the film *Kramer vs. Kramer.* It shows that Vivaldi was as capable of instrumentally idiomatic writing in this special case as he was in his more common violin concertos, which often call for unusual techniques and effects. The mandolin part in this concerto is not technically difficult, but it rests attractively beneath the player's fingers, and the work has often been recorded. Vivaldi effectively uses melodic profile to draw a contrast between the strings and the serenading mandolin; the orchestral ritornello of the first movement consists of little more than open octaves and fifths, while the mandolin has sprightly melodic material. In one of those clever touches with which Vivaldi's concertos are replete, however, the two textures are linked together: the ritornello ends with a short cadence in broken thirds, and the soloist begins by repeating the same music, as if a relay runner were receiving the baton from a teammate. The minor-key central movement is a fine example of Vivaldi's minimalist melancholy, and the finale is a deceptively simple Allegro that lets the soloist unpack the rudimentary melodic inversion upon which the ritornello is based. One of the solo passages seems to refer back to the concerto's opening movement—an instance of cyclical technique that, if intentional, would place Vivaldi well ahead of his time in this as in so many other things. There also exists a Vivaldi concerto for two mandolins, and mandolinists also sometimes appropriate the more numerous Vivaldi pieces for guitar or lute. *—James Manheim*

Recommended:

- ○ **Vivaldi: Concerti per liuto e mandolino** / Antonini (cond.), Galfetti, Giardino Armonico / 1993 / Teldec 91182
- ○ **Vivaldi: Music for Lute and Mandolin** / O'Dette, Holman, Parley of Instruments / 1987 / Hyperion 66160

Piccolo (Flautino) Concerto in C major, RV 444 (before 1742)

This is the second of Vivaldi's three concertos for "flautino," a term that has been interpreted to mean different instruments. Most commonly it is now assumed that Vivaldi intended these for the Baroque equivalent of the smallest sized recorder, the sopranino, an F scale instrument, although he might have also intended them for the French flageolet, a G scale instrument. However, these concertos are usually performed on the sopranino or the piccolo. The *Concerto in C major*, RV 444, is not unlike the 12 concertos of his *Il cimento dell'Armonia e dell'Invenzione*, Op. 8, in both structure and character. The concerto features a virtuosic solo part, with thirty-second notes, trills, and arpeggios for the recorder throughout the piece. In each solo episode of the opening Allegro non molto movement, rhythmic mottos are repeated and developed to explore different harmonic possibilities, while testing the performer's ability to play both legato and détaché rapidly. The Largo in A minor is typical of Vivaldi's middle movement construction, using mottos to create an aria-like melody over a simple accompaniment. The brief, final Allegro molto begins with a bouncy orchestral statement that returns to reestablish the home key of C major in each ritornello. The soloist is again tested in the intervening episodes with trills and arpeggios. The understated virtuosity of the concerto adds to the appeal of its charming character to make it the most famous of the three flautino concertos. *—Patsy Morita*

Recommended:

- ○ **Vivaldi: 7 Concerti** / Pinnock (cond.), Holtslag, English Concert / 1995 / Archiv 445839
- ○ **Vivaldi: Flute Concetos; Recorder Concertos** / McGegan (cond.), Verbruggen, Philharmonia Baroque Orch. / 2002 / HM 2907340/41

Recorder Concerto in C minor, RV 441 (before 1742)

Antonio Vivaldi only wrote two concerti specifically for the recorder ("flauto"), one of which is the RV 441 concerto in C minor. By contrast, 13 of Vivaldi's concerti specify the transverse flute ("flauto traverso"), but the fact that two of the flute concerti in his Op. 10 of 1728 were adapted from works originally written for recorder shows that the two can be easily substituted for one another in concert. The recorder certainly had to have been popular when Vivaldi wrote RV 441, for it demands a real recorder virtuoso.

Structurally, each movement follows standard ritornello form, with typically Vivaldian touches like modulation within ritornello sections in the outer movements. The minor mode is almost unrelieved throughout, with only a few momentary major moments. But the first movement is remarkable for the leaping arpeggios it demands of the recorder player, derived from violin playing and much more difficult on the recorder. In the Largo slow movement a simple ritornello provides a frame for the short, sad, generously embellished solo. This seems a momentary respite compared to the Allegro finale; the ritornello music here is dramatically slower than the recorder's solos, which are again rife with treacherous runs and arpeggios that most performers wouldn't want to try on the flute, either. *—Andrew Lindemann Malone*

Recommended:

- ○ **Vivaldi: Wind Concertos** / Marriner (cond.), Bennett, Academy of St. Martin-in-the-Fields / 1999 / Decca 460645
- ○ **Vivaldi: Flute Concetos; Recorder Concertos** / McGegan (cond.), Verbruggen, Philharmonia Baroque Orch. / 2002 / HM 2907340/41
- ○ **Vivaldi: Recorder Concertos** / Laurin, Drottningholm Court Baroque Ens. / 1991 / BIS 635
- ○ **Vivaldi: La Notte; La Tempesta di Mare; Il Gardellino** / Marq, Spinosi, Matheus Ensemble / 2002 / Opus 111 30371

CHAMBER MUSIC

Chamber Concerto, for flute or violin, 2 violins, bassoon & continuo in G minor ("La notte"), RV 104 (1716)

Vivaldi's "La notte" concerto tosses, turns, and eventually sleepwalks into his Op. 10 collection of concertos, the instrumentation there stripped down to a mere flute and strings in perhaps the musical equivalent of dreaming that you're naked in public. The original version, though designed for a chamber ensemble, is more richly scored; calling for either flute or violin as soloist, the chamber concerto yanks the bassoon out of its continuo role to become nearly a full co-soloist in the last movement with all of this backed by strings and continuo. Vivaldi appended descriptive titles not only to the concerto as a whole, but also to two of its movements; with nothing more than this to go on, though, the nocturnal program remains vague. Unusually for Vivaldi, this concerto falls into four movements rather than three, yet it's not quite the slow-fast-slow-fast pattern Vivaldi favored in his sonatas. The first movement progresses from a Largo introduction to a Presto called "Fantasmi" (Phantasms). The Largo creeps along in short, dotted phrases separated by substantial rests. After several hesitant utterances, the flute falls into long, vertiginous trills and then leaps into the Presto section, which is replete with creepy, abrupt arpeggios jumping out of nowhere. The music returns to the mood and tempo of the beginning and is interrupted by the brief second movement, another Presto. This frenzied, shivering interlude gives way to the third movement, another Largo, this one marked "Il sonno" (The Dream). Neither pleasant nor nightmarish, this dream is at least slightly disturbing, the strings providing one long moan while the flute wanders through uncertain harmonies, employing a melody also found in Vivaldi's "Autumn" concerto. The concluding Allegro is every bit as jittery as the second Presto, with the bassoon assuming new prominence, sometimes providing limited counterpoint to the flute's frantic part, sometimes doubling it. *—James Reel*

Recommended:

- ○ **Famosi Concerti da Camera** / Antonini (cond.), Giardino Armonico / 1993 / Teldec 91852

Chamber Concerto, for recorder, 2 violins & continuo in A minor, RV 108 (1716)

Though called a concerto, this composition is actually a chamber work for three melody instruments and continuo (usually played by harpsichord and cello or gamba), a format far more popular in Germany than in Vivaldi's Italy. Furthermore, the recorder (or sometimes flute) is not treated precisely like a virtuoso solo instrument; rather, it leads a dialog with the two violins, supported by the continuo.

The opening Allegro features a dance-like figure for the recorder that is often echoed bar-by-bar by the violins, although otherwise the strings largely chug along playing fast arpeggiated versions of the music's basic chord sequence. Between restatements of the main theme, which sometimes comes in the minor mode, the recorder indulges in rapid runs and flourishes.

The Largo again finds the violins playing melodic sequences that are little more than arpeggios on the music's chord sequence, while the recorder plays a languid, sometimes melancholy aria-like melody that invites increasing ornamentation. The final Allegro is unusual for Vivaldi in that it's a giga; the composer usually employed dances only in his sonatas, not his concertos. When the violins are occasionally prominent, the movement sounds less Scottish than Italian as it takes on the character of a tarantella. *—James Reel*

Recommended:

- ○ **Famosi Concerti da Camera** / Antonini (cond.), Giardino Armonico / 1993 / Teldec 91852

Trio Sonata for violin, lute & continuo in C major, RV 82 (1730)

Antonio Vivaldi's two trio sonatas for lute, violin, and continuo, catalogued as RV 82 and 85 respectively, were both commissioned by and dedicated to Count Johann Joseph von Wrtby of Bohemia, as far as historians can determine. This has led some to conclude that these sonatas were composed during the early 1730s, because Vivaldi was probably present at Czech revivals of his operas during that period and Wrtby died in 1734.

Wrtby had chosen an excellent man to carry out his commission; Vivaldi wrote for solo lute at many times during his life, and the very fact that he would elevate the lute from continuo to solo instrument speaks to both his confidence in and his mastery of its resources. The RV 82 work, in C major, in particular shows a canny understanding of both the lute's limitations and its gifts. In the first movement, the lute leads the way in developing the sunny, gently rhythmic melody, while the violin generally plays a simplified version of the lute's line. The contrasting, combined timbres interact well, especially when Vivaldi occasionally sustains a note in the violin and lets the lute shower it with ornaments of various elaborate kinds. The second movement is in the minor mode, hushed and quiet, with a melody built on small, accumulating descents. In this movement, the lute proves especially eloquent, as its plucking emphasizes the broken feel of the melody. The third movement brings a theme more vigorous than that of the first movement, but no less cheerful, and the thematic development is once again entrusted to the combination of lute and violin. Here the violin gets to play staccato occasionally, thus complementing the lute's quick, athletic ornaments with its own sharp notes. Vivaldi's work in general shows an awareness of tone color that few other Baroque composers had, and the *Trio Sonata*, RV 82, is an excellent example. *—Andrew Lindemann Malone*

Recommended:

- ○ **Vivaldi: Music for Lute and Mandolin** / O'Dette, Holman, Parley of Instruments / 1987 / Hyperion 66160
- ○ **Vivaldi: Complete Works for Italian Lute** / Lindberg, Huggett, Sparf / 1985 / Bis 290
- ○ **Vivaldi: L'Oeuvre Complet Pour Luth** / Lislevand, Morini, Kraemer / 1996 / Astree 8587
- ○ **John Williams Plays Vivaldi Concertos** / Williams, Pertis, Frank / 1991 / Sony 46556

CHORAL

Beatus vir (Psalm 112), in C major, RV 597 (before 1742)

This work is the better known and earlier version of the *Beatus vir*, RV 795. The later one is an even larger-scale effort incorporating some changes in the score. There are two other *Beatus virs* in Vivaldi's catalog, the entirely different RV 598 and the probably similar RV 599, a lost effort that is believed to have been an earlier version of this RV 597 *Beatus vir* and, therefore, of the later RV 795 as well.

In any event, this RV 597 rendition is more often performed and recorded than the later version. It is comprised of nine movements and opens with "Beatus vir qui timet Dominum," a lovely choral piece for female voices that features a lengthy introduction on strings. There are five other "Beatus vir" sections scattered throughout the work, all very brief and serving as a refrain, each repeating the main choral theme from the opening movement, an angelic creation of ecstatic character. If these repeats are counted as separate sections, then the work can be broken down into 14 separate movements. "Potens in terra" follows, a more muscular piece in contrast, scored for male chorus. Following the first "Beatus vir" repeat is the lively "Gloriae et divitiae," which features fine vocal writing for female soloists. After another "Beatus vir" comes "Exortum est in tenebris" and "Jucundus homo," the former mixing male and female choruses in ecstatic music and the latter featuring an almost playful introduction on organ and a lovely solo for soprano ensuing. "In Memoria eternal" (No. 9) is framed by two more "Beatus vir" movements. It is among the deeper and more probing sections, beginning with a pensive introduction on strings, after which the choruses touchingly sing mournful music. "Paratum cor eius" follows, a vigorous triumphant movement that is deftly contrasted by the ensuing "Peccator videbit," which begins with slow but lovely music and then alternates that material with lively and jubilant music. The final "Beatus vir" appears, after which comes the concluding "Gloria Patri," a triumphant movement in which the choruses sing with vigor and convey a sense of angelic majesty. *—Robert Cummings*

Recommended:

- ○ **Vivaldi: Gloria; Beatus Vir; Magnificat** / Corboz (cond.), Lausanne Ensemble Vocal / Erato 17919

Gloria, in D major, RV 589 (1715)

During the year 1713 there was a shift in Antonio Vivaldi's responsibilities as maestro di violino of Venice's Pio Ospedale della Pietà. Up until that point secular music had been his bread and butter, but he then turned his attention to the composition of sacred choral works, some of which became the finest treasures of his vast musical output. It was sometime during the next few years that Vivaldi put to paper the now-famous *Gloria in D major* for vocal soloists, chorus and orchestra (RV 589). It is remarkable to think that for two centuries after Vivaldi's death the very existence of this beloved work was unknown even to Baroque scholars, and that it was only rediscovered in the late 1920s. Having been long buried—with a host of other unknown pieces in a pile of forgotten Vivaldi manuscripts—the Gloria had its first modern performance in the fall of 1939. The rest, as they say, is history.

In composing, Vivaldi broke the standard Gloria text into 11 sections, each of which is given a discrete musical setting. All the vocal parts, from the two soprano and alto soloists right down to the tenor and bass, were originally written for women's voices, as no men were allowed at the all-female Pio Ospedale della Pietà (Vivaldi and the few other male staff were, of course, members of the priesthood); occasionally the bass part moves so low that even the remarkable female basses of the Pietà must have had to transpose up an octave. Just two wind instruments—an oboe and a trumpet—are added to the usual Baroque contingent of strings, and the basso continuo would probably have been played by organ.

A joyous tone is set at the very start of the Gloria, with jubilant shouts of "Gloria in excelsis Deo" from the chorus. "Et in terra pax hominibus bonae voluntatis" (section two) is sung in imitation to a less exuberant B minor backdrop; the violins add some pointed rapid-note gestures, quite similar in kind to those found in Vivaldi's many string concertos.

Vivaldi moves back to a rambunctious allegro, this time in G major, for the solo soprano duet of section three ("Laudamus te"); the start of section four ("Gratias agimus te") is slow, dignified, and entirely homophonic, but as the chorus moves on to sing "propter magnam gloriam" it becomes a fugal Allegro.

A wonderful Largo duet between the solo soprano and the solo violin follows ("Domine Deus, Rex coelestis"); the chorus joins again for the very joyful F major section six ("Domine Fili unigente").

The spacious Adagio of section seven ("Domine Deus, Agnus Dei") features both chorus and the alto soloist, who takes the spotlight once again, this time more gregariously, in section nine ("Qui sedes ad dexteram Patris"). Between these sections is the interlude "Qui tollis peccata mundi".

The penultimate portion of the *Gloria* (section ten, "Quoniam tu solus sanctus") takes the shape of a brief reprise of the broken-octave music from section one, while the stunning double fugue that ends the *Gloria* (section eleven, "Cum Sancto Spiritu") is in fact an arrangement by Vivaldi of a piece composed in 1708 by Giovanni Maria Ruggieri—a piece also adapted by Vivaldi for use in his other, lesser-known *Gloria* RV 588. —*Blair Johnston*

Recommended:

- ○ **Vivaldi: Gloria; Magnificat** / Alessandrini (cond.), York, Mingardo, Biccire, Italiano Concerto / 1997 / Opus 111 195
- ○ **Vivaldi: Gloria; Motets; Cantatas** / Preston (cond.), Kirkby, Nelson, Watkinson, Academy of Ancient Music (UK), Oxford Christ Church Cathedral Chr. / 1997 / L'Oiseau-Lyre 455727
- ○ **Vivaldi: Gloria** / Darlington (cond.), Kwella, Carwood, Priday, Wyn-Rogers, Hanover Band, Christ Church Cathedral Chr. / 1990 / Nimbus 5278
- ○ **Vivaldi: Glorias; Dixit Dominus; Magnificat; Beatus Vir** / Guest (cond.), Kwella, Russell, Bowen, Wilkens, St. John's College Choir / 1994 / London 443455

Magnificat in G minor, RV 610 (1713–1719)

Eighteenth century tourists flocked to the Sunday services at Venice's wealthy religious establishments. Jean-Jacques Rousseau himself wrote a glowing report of the music sung in the Scuole grandi, or confraternal churches, of the city; he specifically claimed that the music at the Venetian Pio Spedale della Pietá was far superior to Venetian opera singing, and might rival any musical performance in the world. The "hospital" of the Pietá maintained a large (female) choir and a professional maestro di cappella; in addition, for nearly 40 years they were in the habit of commissioning music from Venice's own Antonio Vivaldi. Many of his more splendid choral works for the church received their first performances at the Pietá, including the single best-known piece in his lifetime, Vivaldi's *Magnificat in G minor.*

In its best-known form, RV 610, Vivaldi's *Magnificat* disposes the canticle text (Luke 1:46–55) across nine movements. It serves the festal celebrations of the evening Vespers service. In this version, a full string ensemble supports a mixed choir—either four or eight voices plus soloists. The very beginning features a homophonic wall of sound, praising God in a highly chromatic idiom; Vivaldi used the same lush progression in at least four other pieces of music, two mass movements and two concerti. The second movement resembles a brief instrumental concerto, with an active violin Ritornello, three successive vocal solos, and a "punning" interruption by the full choir that echoes the word *omnes* (everyone). A central trio of choral movements each display Vivaldi's witty sense of text-painting: an affective chromatic passage with seventh leaps for *Et misericordia* (and His mercy), a stormy string accompaniment for *Fecit potentiam* (He has showed strength with His arm), and a wild orchestral unison for the *Deposuit* (He has cast down the proud). Two further soli movements (one of which suddenly introduces two oboes) and a choral hymn lead to the final chorus. Vivaldi once again presents a musical pun, as the text "As it was in the beginning" refers to the very chromatic opening music; a jubilant fugue brings the piece to a close.

This version of Vivaldi's *Magnificat* dates from the late 1720s and represents a mixed-choir revision of his first composition (for the women of the Pietá around 1715). It may have been written for the choir of Cardinal Ottoboni. Vivaldi also made a much later version (known as RV 611) for the Pietá in 1739, with new versions of several movements. —*Timothy Dickey*

Recommended:

- ○ **Vivaldi: Glorias; Dixit Dominus; Magnificat; Beatus Vir** / Ledger (cond.), King, Cockerham, Castle, Academy of St. Martin-in-the-Fields, King's College Choir / 1994 / London 443455
- ○ **Vivaldi: Gloria; Beatus Vir; Magnificat** / Corboz (cond.), Schaer, Schweizer, Spreckelsen, Lausanne Ens. Vocal / Erato 17919
- ○ **Vivaldi: Cantatas, Concertos & Magnificat** / Lamon (cond.), Kirkby, Ingram, LeBlanc, Forget, Cunningham, Tafelmusik / 2004 / Hyperion 55190

VOCAL

Cantatas (before 1742)

Though Antonio Vivaldi's fame principally rests upon his prodigious output of concertos and other instrumental music, he also composed heavily for voices. During his career, he wrote over 45 operas, some 60 sacred vocal works, four oratorios, and several dozen cantatas. Much of the non-operatic literature was the product of Vivaldi's three-and-a-half decades of service as music director for Venice's Ospedale della Pietá, a women's orphanage and musical conservatory. The Pietá's sacred music and concerts attracted an enthusiastic audience both of native Venetians and travelers from abroad; the better singers also may have given private concerts out in the homes of the Venetian aristocracy. Despite a complete lack of historical data about the composition and performance of Vivaldi's many cantatas, such highbrow concerts seem the most likely context for them.

A majority of Vivaldi's roughly 37 cantatas survive in one of two manuscript volumes now in the library of Turin. Diligent efforts by music historians have garnered just one concrete source for Vivaldi's cantata texts; part of one cantata text be found in the works of Metastasio. Either the remaining texts were the work of an unknown (and less than competent) local Venetian poet, or Vivaldi may have written them himself. The texts almost all treat in highly conventional language with the theme of "love." Their over-sentimentalized imagery presents syrupy versions of the old Petrarchan antitheses: joy and despair, love and torment.

Despite the poor literary quality of the texts, however, Vivaldi's cantatas provide charming, and often highly challenging vocal diversions. The texts afford Vivaldi opportunities for highly inventive, and often virtuosic, melodies as well as dynamic effects in the accompaniments. Their music reflects in many ways his experience of contemporary Venetian opera. Most of his cantatas involve a solo singer accompanied by basso continuo and sometimes an obbligato solo instrument; this was the most common scoring throughout the chamber performance history of this genre. All, furthermore, present the female voice (even those with male protagonists). The form of each piece revolves around a pair (rarely a trio) of vocal arias set off by recitatives: either Aria–Recit–Aria or Recit–Aria–Recit–Aria. In the recitatives, the composer cherishes every opportunity for radical harmonic shifts and vocal flourishes to reflect local features of the text; in the arias, most frequently a single *Affekt* from the aria text provides a musical concept for the entire movement. —*Timothy Dickey*

Recommended:

- ○ **Vivaldi: Cantate, Opera Omnia Vol. 1** / Anfuso, Baiano / 1991 / Stilnovo 8807

Nisi Dominus (Psalm 127), for voice, viola d'amore, strings & continuo in G minor, RV 608 (before 1742)

Vivaldi's *Nisi Dominus*, RV 608, is in G minor and is scored for solo voice, viola d'amore, a small string group, and continuo. It is one of two settings by Vivaldi of the *Nisi dominus* (Psalm 126 or 127) text. The other, RV 803, only recently authenticated, dates from the late 1730s, but RV 608 is an early work, perhaps composed for the Venetian girls' orphanage that employed the composer in the 1710s. In nine short sections, the work is remarkable for its variety; it supports the conclusion that the obscurity of Vivaldi's vocal music is due more to historical accident than to any lack of quality. Though it has been sung by male countertenors, the vocal part would probably have been composed for a female alto if the work indeed originated during Vivaldi's tenure at the orphanage.

It is the variety of instrumental accompaniments, as vivid as those of any Baroque opera, that bring the work to life. The third section, "Surgite" ("It is vain for you to rise up early, to sit up late, to eat the bread of sorrows") is an accompanied recitative with vigorous illustrations of both the early riser and the bread of sorrows in the orchestral strings. The following "Cum dederit" ("When He shall give sleep...") is a masterful chromatic siciliana that ranks among the most alluring Baroque depictions of sleep, complete with string mutes. "Sicut sagittae" ("Like arrows in the hand of a mighty man...") offers more operatic text-painting, with stabbing unisons dominating the texture. The "Gloria" section replaces the usual festive mood with a meditative, dark setting, and the other movements are similarly original. Some have simple continuo accompaniment, while others have a viola d'amore part (perhaps written for Vivaldi's own use, for he was a virtuoso player on the instrument) taking on a concerto-like role. It is perhaps only the presence of that unusual instrument that has kept this lovely work from the pinnacles of popularity where some of Vivaldi's other compositions reside. —*James Manheim*

Recommended:

- ○ **Vivaldi: Stabat Mater; Nisi Dominus; Longe mala** / Daniels, Biondi (cond.), Europa Galante / 2001 / Virgin 45474
- ○ **Vivaldi: Vespri per l'Assunzione di Maria Vergine** / Alessandrini (cond.), Mingardo, Belli, Italiano Concerto / 2003 / Opus 111 30383
- ○ **Vivaldi: Gloria; Motets; Cantatas** / Hogwood (cond.), Bowman / 1997 / L'Oiseau-Lyre 455727

Stabat Mater, hymn for voice, strings & continuo in F minor, RV 621 (before 1742)

Antonio Vivaldi had no outlet for composing sacred vocal music at the Ospedale della Pieta, where such music was the responsibility of the choirmaster, until 1713 when the reigning choirmaster quit and was not replaced until 1719. A man of Vivaldi's faith, however, could be expected to seek out opportunities to write such music. He evidently found one in 1711 at the Feast of the Purification of the Blessed Virgin at the Chiesa della Pace in Brescia, where he and his father had been invited to play the violin. Following persuasions unknown, the church's music expenditures book details payment for a *Stabat Mater* composed by Vivaldi" in 1712. The Chiesa della Pace rarely commissioned new music and the *Stabat Mater* was not even a standard text at the time (it was added to the Roman Missal and Breviary in 1727), but Vivaldi's skill as a composer evidently won the day, as one would expect when considering this masterpiece. Vivaldi set 10 of the 20 verses of the *Stabat Mater*, marking it as a hymn for Vespers, but while every other hymn Vivaldi composed used strict strophic form, here Vivaldi repeated the music from movements 1–3 in movements 4–6, and ended with three movements with new music. However, many of the movements contain thematic resemblances. All nine movements are also cast in F minor except the second and fifth, which are in C minor, and until the "Amen," the fastest tempo in the piece is an Andante. All of these techniques work to sustain an unrelievedly bleak atmosphere suitable to a depiction of Mary's anguish while watching Jesus suffer on the cross. Vivaldi brings out the dark coloring of the male alto voice with spare, sustained accompaniments, falling melodies, and in the C minor movements, extended, almost desperate closing melismas. "Eja Mater," the seventh movement, illustrates Mary's suffering with a whiplike string figure that sounds especially dramatic coming after the repeated music. The cumulative effect is shattering and the sorrowful atmosphere dominates right up to the final chords of the "Amen": a picardy third perhaps suggesting the light that followed the crucifixion. The light here, however, only makes the darkness that has come before seem all the more oppressive. —*Andrew Lindemann Malone*

Recommended:

○ **Vivaldi: Stabat Mater; Nisi Dominus; Longe mala** / Daniels, Biondi (cond.), Europa Galante / 2001 / Virgin 45474

ORCHESTRAL

Sinfonia al Santo Sepolcro, sonata for 2 violins, viola & continuo in B minor, RV 169 (1728)

Antonio Vivaldi's *Sinfonia al Santo Sepolcro in B minor,* RV 169, is one of two pieces he composed bearing the subtitle "al Santo Sepolcro," the other being a *Sonata in E flat major,* RV 130. Both works are scored for two violins, viola, and continuo, although it is generally accepted that the Sinfonia may be played by either orchestral or chamber forces. There are many chapels in Italy that are called "al Santo Sepolcro" (of the Holy Sepulchre), but given the provenance of the undated Vivaldi manuscript in Turin, it may have been written for a chapel incorporated as part of the Sacro Monte complex in nearby Varallo, Italy. Built in 1491 by Franciscan monk Bernardo Calmì, this chapel is a scaled-down replica of the Church of the Holy Sepulchre in Jerusalem that sits on top of the place where it is believed that Christ was entombed. Italian Pilgrims hoping to travel to the Holy Land in the late fifteenth century were discouraged by war raging with the Turks; the Varallo chapel was built with the intention of providing a reasonable substitute for the real thing. Ultimately the chapel was joined by 43 other buildings forming a "new Jerusalem" and signifying the history of salvation; many of these were decorated by Renaissance master painter Gaudenzio Ferrari. The final chapel at Sacro Monte was not completed and opened until 1728; perhaps this provides the occasion for Vivaldi's compositions "al Santo Sepolcro."

The *Sinfonia al Santo Sepolcro* is couched in a harmonic language that is thorny even for Vivaldi—in the opening measures of the Adagio molto the music passes through a unison pitch, a minor second, and a tri-tone to arrive at its first B minor chord. The rest of the opening is harmonically unstable in the extreme, but is not out of character for what was known as "passion music" in the Baroque—a highly chromatic idiom reserved for representing Christ's pain and suffering. The concluding Allegro ma pocco passes through similar territory with rapid-fire figures wending their way in a call and response-type pattern. Though it's all over in only three or four minutes, the *Sinfonia al Santo Sepolcro* represents Vivaldi at his most intense and dramatic, which explains why it is becoming among the most popular of Vivaldi's works outside of his major opus numbered sets. —*Uncle Dave Lewis*

Recommended:

○ **Festa Italiana** / Europa Galante / 1996 / Opus 111 1996

○ **From Monteverdi to Vivaldi** / Parrott, Taverner Consort / 2003 / Virgin 562167

○ **Vivaldi: Musica da camera e da chiesa** / Medlam, London Baroque / 1994 / Virgin 61171

OPERA

Operas (1731–1741)

Vivaldi is remembered as a composer of instrumental music, and many regard him as the master of the Baroque concerto. It is less widely known that Vivaldi was also one of the most popular and successful opera composers of his time. No one knows exactly how many operas Vivaldi wrote: a conservative estimate would be between 30 and 40, though Vivaldi himself claimed to have written nearly 100 (he was likely exaggerating). As it stands, about 20 opera scores survive, not all of them complete. His first opera, *Ottone in villa,* premiered in Vicenza in 1713, some years after he had firmly established himself as a composer of instrumental music. In 1714, Vivaldi made his operatic debut in Venice with his opera *Orlando finto pazzo.* As his reputation as an opera composer grew, Vivaldi began to receive commissions from other cities, including Mantua, Milan, Rome, and Florence. Some of his most successful operas included *Impermestra, La fida ninfa,* and *Griselda,* the last of which featured a libretto by the famed Carlo Goldoni. Vivaldi continued writing operas until his death in 1741, shortly after which his final opera *L'oracolo in Messenia* was premiered in Vienna.

Vivaldi's operas closely follow the traditions of eighteenth century Italian opera. They are predominantly in three acts and reflect the dramatic and musical conventions of opera seria. The operas begin with an instrumental overture, a sinfonia that is usually not related musically to the opera it precedes. Each opera is comprised primarily of alternating secco recitative (i.e., "dry" recitative, accompanied solely by continuo) and da capo arias, with occasional vocal duets and ensembles. While the recitative is generally secco, the arias often feature complex obbligato accompaniment and contrapuntal textures. Melodically, Vivaldi favors unusual intervals, used for dramatic effect; harmonically, the operas' numbers tend towards relatively simple tonic-dominant structures, with chromatic chords also used dramatically. Most of the arias are in major keys, standard for the time and genre. Some of his later operas reflect the influence of other regions—they include dances and choral ensembles—and some are set in exotic locations, such as the Orient.

Like many Baroque composers—Handel especially—Vivaldi's operas feature copious borrowing. Vivaldi borrowed themes not only from his own instrumental works, but sometimes entire arias from earlier operas. He also borrowed freely from other composers' operas. Vivaldi was criticized by his contemporaries for a certain lack of inventiveness in his operas, and in truth his contributions to the development of opera are, in the end, negligible; however, the music is good and strongly reflects Vivaldi's skill as an instrumental composer. —*Alexander Carpenter*

Recommended:

○ **Vivaldi: Orlando Furioso (Highlights)** / Scimone (cond.), Horne, Los Angeles, Bruscantini, Terrani, Zaccaria, Kozma / Erato 98523

○ **Vivaldi: Farnace (Favourite Aires)** / Savall (cond.), Mingardo, Fernandez, Le Concert des Nations / 2003 / Alia Vox 9830

○ **The Vivaldi Album** / Bartoli, Antonini (cond.), Giardino Armonico / 1999 / Decca 466569

Deborah Voigt

b. Apr. 8, 1960, Chicago, IL

Soprano

Deborah Voigt is a leading dramatic soprano, particularly noted for singing Germanic repertory. The raw power and beauty of her voice, combined with unusually fine musicianship and interpretive genius, have made her one of the most sought-after singers of the 1990s and 2000s.

Voigt had little contact with classical music growing up. She was always musical, however, and while attending the University of California, Fullerton, she enjoyed singing with guitar for elementary school children (she calls this her "Julie Andrews/Sound of Music phase"). After graduation she was accepted into the San Francisco Opera's young artist program, where she received intensive coaching and small roles. From that experience, Voigt began carving out a respectable young career, and the magnitude of her talents soon became evident: while she was singing a small role in Richard Strauss' *Elektra* at the Theatre de la Monnaie in Brussels in 1987, an assistant conductor predicted that "someday [she would] make a wonderful Chrysothemis," referring to the major role of Elektra's sister, which has since become one of Voigt's signatures.

The next year she gained international fame as the winner of the Luciano Pavarotti Voice Competition; in 1990 she won the Gold Medal at the Tchaikovsky International Competition in Moscow; and in 1992 she won the Richard Tucker Award, which provides a generous award each year to an American artist showing exceptional promise for an outstanding career.

Starring as Ariadne in Strauss' *Ariadne auf Naxos* with the Boston Lyric Opera became Voigt's breakthrough performance. She repeated the role in her debuts in Munich and Vienna, and later that year she debuted at New York's Metropolitan Opera House as Amelia in Verdi's *Un ballo in maschera.* In 1992 the prediction of that assistant conductor in Belgium came true when she sang Chrysothemis in a cast that included Hildegard Behrens and Leonie Rysanek and was conducted by James Levine. She rapidly became recognized as one of the most powerful dramatic voices in the world. David Patrick Stearns wrote in *USA Today* in August, 1996, "There comes a point in a Deborah Voigt opera performance, at the end of a difficult aria, when you think she has given her all. Suddenly, the voice hits overdrive—and a whole new level of vocal power. Audiences go wild."

Voigt has been most closely associated with the works of Strauss (Chrysothemis, Ariadne, the Empress in *Die Frau ohne Schatten,* The Egyptian Helen) and Verdi (Lady Macbeth, Amelia, *Aida,* Leonora in *La forza del destino*). But later in the 1990s she began branching out into Wagnerian roles (Senta, Elsa, Sieglinde, Elisabeth). She is also famous for the part of Cassandra in Berlioz's *Les Troyens,* Mathilde in Rossini's *William Tell* and Leonore in Beethoven's *Fidelio.* Her concert hall repertory includes Schoenberg's *Guerrelieder,* Zemlinsky's *Lyric Symphony,* the Verdi *Requiem,* Mahler's *Klagende Lied* and *Second* and *Eighth Symphonies,* Rossini's *Stabat Mater,* and Strauss' *Four Last Songs.*

The early 2000s brought Voigt's career to a new level. In 2003 she sang the prized role of Isolde in Wagner's *Tristan und Isolde* at the Vienna State Opera and was rewarded with a 23-minute ovation at the production's premiere on May 25. She sang four roles at the Met in New York in the 2003–04 season and also made her Carnegie Hall recital debut in April of 2004, with James Levine accompanying her. (She has also been known to commandeer the keyboard herself at times.) She was named 2003 Vocalist of the Year by *Musical America*, and as of the mid-2000s she was one of the world's most active and critically acclaimed sopranos. *—Joseph Stevenson*

Recommended:

- ○ **Obsessions** / Voigt, Armstrong (cond.), Bavarian Radio SO / 2004 / EMI Classics 57681
- ○ **Strauss: Die Ägyptische Helena** / Botstein (cond.), Voigt, Tanner, Shafer, Grove, Robertson, Cutler / 2003 / Telarc 80605
- ○ **Strauss: Ariadne auf Naxos** / Sinopoli (cond.), Voigt, Dessay, Von Otter, Heppner, Dohmen / 2001 / DG 47132

Kevin Volans

b. Jul. 26, 1949, Pietermaritzburg, South Africa

Composer

As a white man born in South Africa in 1949, trained largely in Europe in the 1970s, and eventually patriated in Ireland in the 1980s, Kevin Volans has often confronted in his music the issue of identity. "Like many white South Africans of my generation, I was brought up to think I was European," Volans wrote in 1986. "I went to live in Europe and found this was not true. I returned to Africa and was disappointed to find I could not really regard myself as African." It is this struggle with identity, however, that has contributed to his popular success as a composer. As multiculturalism spread into the mainstream consciousness via the world music boom during the last two decades of the twentieth century, Volans' mixture of African and European music styles (or often, stylizations) found resonance with classical music consumers eager to embrace the sounds of a "global community."

Volans received his initial musical education in South Africa, where he received a bachelor's degree from the University of Witwatersrand, Johannesburg, before leaving for Europe to undertake graduate studies. Volans spent the better part of a decade in Europe, studying composition with Karlheinz Stockhausen and music theater with Mauricio Kagel. During the late 1970s, Volans returned to South Africa several times to conduct field recordings and he returned again from 1981 to 1985 to take a teaching position and complete a doctoral degree at the University of Natal before returning to Europe. Having established himself as an important figure in the Neue Einfachkeit (New Simplicity) movement during the 1970s and early 1980s, Volans became increasingly interested in traditional African musics during his extended return to South Africa in the 1980s. A series of "African paraphrase" pieces (a term he invented but would later reject) reflected his interest in native African styles. The first of these, *Mbira* and *Matepe* (both from 1980) realized borrowed African musical ideas through four-hand harpsichord arrangements in an effort to "set up an African colonization of Western music and instruments." Another piece, *White Man Sleeps* (1982), augmented the harpsichord duo with a bass viol and percussion. The work, which drew on the sounds of Venda panpipes, San bow music, and Bosotho concertina playing, later met with remarkable popular acclaim when an arrangement for string quartet was released by the Kronos Quartet in 1987; subsequent projects with Kronos, *Hunting and Gathering* (1987) and *The Songlines* (1988), met with similar success. Volans began to distance himself in the 1990s from the kind of explicit multiculturalism that had brought him such broad recognition and most of his works from the last decade of the twentieth century, such as his piano concerto *One Hundred Frames* (1991) and his opera *Man With Footsoles of the Wind* (1993), avoided dealing with issues of "Africanism" in any overt musical way. The 1990s also found Volans devoting considerable attention to collaborations with choreographers and dance groups, resulting in such projects as *Chevron* (1990), *Wanting to Tell Stories* (1993), *Blue, Yellow* (1995), and *Duetti* (1995). *—Jeremy Grimshaw*

Overview of Works (1980)

Even though his later works address more abstract compositional concerns, Kevin Volans is best known for his works based on or inspired by African music and culture. A white South African who studied in Europe and eventually settled in Ireland, Volans initially emphasized his connections to Africa, mixing European and indigenous styles in an act of "reverse colonialism," but later deemphasized (and even all but denied) the influence of African styles on his development. This ongoing crisis of identity has in fact lent his works much of their tension and energy, even when direct allusion gives way to more abstract and subtle influences. Aside from some early tape experiments, Volans' first surviving works are a pair of "African paraphrases" for two harpsichords and rattles, *Mbira* and *Matepe* (both 1980). A subsequent work for two harpsichords, bass viol, and percussion, *White Man Sleeps* (1982) was later arranged for string quartet (1986). The popular 1993 recording of this work by the Kronos Quartet made Volans internationally famous, and his subsequent series of string quartets (six of them in total were completed by the turn of the century) likewise enjoyed wide distribution. After *White Man Sleeps* and despite evocative titles accompanying each quartet (No. 2 *"Hunting: Gathering"*; No. 4 *"The Ramanjuan Notebooks"*; etc.), the fifth quartet (1994) is the only one to return to explicitly African-derived musical ideas. Volans has actively composed in a variety of genres. He was perhaps most prolific during the 1990s in music for dance, providing scores for nine dance productions, including *Chevron* (1990), *Blue, Yellow* (1995), *Things I Don't Know* (1998), and *Zeno at 4am* (2001). His chamber compositions (aside from the quartets) include works for percussion (*She Who Sleeps With a Small Blanket*, 1985; *Asanga*, 1997; *Akrodha*, 1998), winds (*This Is How It Is*, 1995; an arrangement of Debussy's *L'isle joyuese*, 1995), and various mixed ensembles often using harpsichord and combinations of winds and percussion. Volans has composed a limited number of solo piano pieces, but seems rather inclined to composing for two pianos (*Leaping Dance*, 1984; *Striding Dance*, 1992; and *Cicada*, 1994; and others). His most ambitious projects include the orchestral work *One Hundred Frames* (1991); concertos for piano, cello, and violin duo; a work for three choruses, *One Fine Day* (2000); and a chamber opera, *The Man With Footsoles of Wind* (1993). *—Jeremy Grimshaw*

Recommended:

- ○ **Volans: Hunting; Gathering** / Duke Quartet / 2002 / Black Box 1069
- ○ **Volans: Concerto for Piano & Winds, etc.** / Donohoe, Volans, Netherlands Wind Ens., Harding (cond.), Steinmann (cond.), / 1997 / Chandos 9563
- ○ **Volans: White Man Sleeps** / Volans, Smith Quartet / 1994 / United 88034

Frederica Von Stade

b. Jun. 1, 1945, Somerville, NJ

Mezzo-Soprano

While Von Stade's sweet, lyrical timbre is eminently suitable for the more gentle heroines, she was also delightfully coltish yet still aristocratic as Cherubino, her most famous role, and other trouser roles such as Massenet's Cherubin, Hansel, and Octavian, a spunky Rosina, and she even created the role of the utterly villainous Marquise de Merteuil in Conrad Susa and Philip Littell's *The Dangerous Liaisons*. She specializes in Mozart, Rossini, and nineteenth century French repertoire, but she also sings Monteverdi, Rameau, and Richard Strauss, the mezzo version of Bellini's *La Sonnambula*, French chanson, and German lieder, as well as jazz and musical theater songs.

While her family had produced a few professional and amateur musicians, including a great-aunt who sang at the Opera Comique, Von Stade became an opera singer almost by chance, when in 1966, she enrolled in the Mannes School of Music as a part-time student, to learn to read music for her own enjoyment. Recognizing her potential talent, the faculty encouraged her to enroll full-time, and during her second year, she began studies with Sebastian Engelberg, who taught her technique and taught her how to open an upper range she hadn't even known she possessed. In 1969, she auditioned for the Metropolitan Opera, though still uncertain that opera was the career for her, and was immediately offered a three-year contract. While most of her roles were small parts, including her 1970 debut role as the Third Boy in *Die Zauberflöte*, she did sing the occasional lead. One of those lead roles was Cherubino, and Rolf Liebermann, who was in attendance that night, offered her the role for the Paris Opera for a 1973 performance that began a long-standing association with the Paris Opera and French music. Cherubino was also her debut role at the Glyndebourne Festival the same year, and at Salzburg the next year. In 1976, she and her then-husband and voice teacher Peter Elkus, moved to Paris, and she also made her La Scala debut as Berlioz's Marguerite in *La Damnation de Faust*. In 1985, she encountered personal and some vocal problems when she and Elkus stopped working together, and in 1990 divorced.

She was always careful in building her repertoire, never pushing her voice further than Octavian in *Rosenkavalier*, which she added to her repertoire in 1976, or Charlotte in *Werther*, which she took on in 1980. Some of the roles she added were ones written for her, such as Tina in Dominick Argento's *The Aspern Papers*. She also dropped some of her most beloved roles, including Cherubino in 1992 and Rosina in *Il Barbiere di Siviglia* in 1994, when she felt that she was no longer the youngster that the roles demanded, and that there were plenty of other mezzos to take on those roles.

While she never recorded Rosina, one of her finer roles, she made a number of excellent recordings. Her *Songs of the Auvergne* (Sony) are a model of grace and simplicity, and while her physical portrayal of the adolescent aristocrat Cherubino of course cannot be captured on a sound-only medium, her recording of *Le Nozze di Figaro* with Solti (Decca) is a delight, and for many, her Mélisande with Karajan (EMI) is the best on record. *—Ann Feeney*

Recommended:

- ○ **Voyage à Paris** / Von Stade, Katz / 1995 / RCA 902662711
- ○ **Massenet: Werther** / Davis (cond.), Von Stade, Carreras, Allen, Lloyd, Buchanan / 2004 / Philips 000338302
- ○ **Offenbach: Arias & Overtures** / Von Stade, Almeida (cond.), Scottish CO / 1995 / RCA 68116
- ○ **R. Strauss: Der Rosenkavalier** / Waart (cond.), Von Stade, Carreras, Lear, Bastin / 2003 / Decca 000064512
- ○ **Debussy: Pelléas et Mélisande** / Karajan (cond.), Von Stade, Van Dam, Raimondi, Stilwell, Berlin PO / 1999 / EMI 67168

W

Edo de Waart

b. Jun. 1, 1941, Amsterdam, Netherlands

Conductor

Edo de Waart established a notable conducting career in the last third of the twentieth century, becoming known for clear, exciting performances in a wide range of repertory. He came from a musical family, being the son of a choral singer. He studied oboe with Haakon Stotijn and also conducting at the Music Lyceum in Amsterdam. He became co-principal oboe of the Amsterdam Philharmonic in 1961 and associate principal of the Concertgebouw Orchestra in 1963. Meanwhile, he studied conducting, including a course with Franco Ferrara at Hilversum in 1964. This led to a debut with the Netherlands Radio Philharmonic in 1964. That same year he won the prestigious Dimitri Mitropoulos Conductors' Competition in New York, which resulted in a year-long appointment as an assistant conductor of the New York Philharmonic (1965–66). He became assistant conductor of the Amsterdam Concertgebouw under Bernard Haitink in 1966. He made an impressive recorded debut with the Netherlands Wind Ensemble, which he founded in 1967, including classic recordings of Mozart wind music. He was also appointed co-music director of the Rotterdam Philharmonic with Jean Fournet, becoming sole music director when Fournet vacated his appointment in 1973. His association with the Rotterdam Philharmonic, which lasted until 1979, became noted for firm, exciting orchestral performances and intriguing choices of repertory. In 1975 he became principal guest conductor of the San Francisco Symphony Orchestra, and was elevated to music director in 1977. Although the orchestra was often capable of fine performances, it was variable and had weaknesses. De Waart lifted its standards, turning it into a consistently fine orchestra. In 1985 he conducted an acclaimed series of the complete Wagner *Ring* operas in San Francisco.

Over the years he has made many appearances as an opera conductor, including Bayreuth, Covent Garden, the Santa Fe Opera, Paris' Bastille Opera, and the Metropolitan. In 1996 he debuted at *the Salzburg Festival* with Mozart's *The Marriage of Figaro.*

In 1993 he was appointed chief conductor and artistic director of the Sydney (Australia) Symphony Orchestra, and in August 1995 led it on its first European tour in 20 years. In 1996 he took it on its first tours of Japan and Taiwan, and in 1998, on an American tour. He has been appointed artistic director of the Netherlands Dutch Radio and Television Organization, and chief conductor of the Netherlands Radio Philharmonic. At the beginning of the 1999–2000 season he began his tenure as chief conductor of the Netherlands Opera. *—Joseph Stevenson*

Recommended:

- ○ **R. Strauss Album** / de Waart ((cond.), Minnesota Orch. / 1994 / Virgin 61142
- ○ **Adams: Harmonium** / de Waart ((cond.), George, San Francisco SO & Chorus / 1984 / ECM 821465
- ○ **Mahler: Symphony 1** / de Waart (cond.), Minnesota Orch. / 1990 / Virgin 61258
- ○ **Adams: Nixon in China (Highlights)** / de Waart (cond.), Sylvan, Friedman, Maddalena, Opatz, Orch. of St. Luke's / 1999 / Nonesuch 79453

Richard Wagner

b. May 22, 1813, Leipzig, Germany, **d.** Feb. 13, 1883, Venice, Italy

Composer: Opera, Orchestral, Vocal

Richard Wagner was one of the most revolutionary figures in the history of music, a composer who made pivotal contributions to the development of harmony and musical drama that reverberate even today. Indeed, though Wagner occasionally produced successful music written on a relatively modest scale, opera—the bigger, the better—was clearly his milieu, and his aesthetic is perhaps the most grandiose that Western music has ever known. Early in his career, Wagner learned both the elements and the practical, political realities of his craft by writing a handful of operas which were unenthusiastically, even angrily, received. Beginning with *Rienzi* (1838–40) and *The Flying Dutchman* (1841), however, he enjoyed a string of successes that propelled him to immortality and changed the face of music. His monumental Ring cycle of four operas—*Das Rheingold* (1853–54), *Die Walküre* (1854–56), *Siegfried* (1856–71) and *Götterdämmerung* (1869–74)—remains the most ambitious and influential contribution by any composer to the opera literature. *Tristan and Isolde* (1857–59) is perhaps the most representative example of Wagner's musical style, which is characterized by a high degree of chromaticism, a restless, searching tonal instability, lush harmonies, and the association of specific musical elements (known as leitmotifs, the flexible manipulation of which is one of the glories of Wagner's music) with certain characters and plot points. Wagner wrote text as well as music for all his operas, which he preferred to call "music dramas."

Wagner's life matched his music for sheer drama. Born in Leipzig on May 22, 1813, he began in the early 1830s to write prolifically on music and the arts in general; over his whole career, his music would to some degree serve to demonstrate his aesthetic theories. He often worked as a conductor in his early years; a conducting engagement took him to Riga, Latvia, in 1837, but he fled the country in the middle of the night two years later to elude creditors. Wagner as a young man had some sympathy with the revolutionary movements of the middle nineteenth century (and even the Ring cycle contains a distinct anti-materialist and vaguely socialist drift); in the Dresden uprisings of 1849 he apparently took up arms, and he had to leave Germany when the police restored order. Settling in Zurich, Switzerland, he wrote little for some years but evolved the intellectual framework for his towering mature masterpieces. Wagner returned to Germany in 1864 under the protection and patronage of King Ludwig II of Bavaria; it was in Bayreuth, near Munich, that he undertook the construction of an opera house (completed in 1876) built to his personal specifications and suited to the massive fusion of music, staging, text, and scene design that his later operas entailed. Bayreuth became something of a shrine for the fanatical Wagnerites who carried the torch after his death; it remains the goal of many a pilgrimage today. His attitude toward Jews was deeply ambivalent (he believed, mistakenly, that his stepfather was Jewish), but some of his writings contain anti-Semitic elements that have aroused considerable controversy among opera lovers, especially in view of Adolf Hitler's apparent predilection for the composer's music. *—AMG*

OPERA

Der fliegende Holländer (The Flying Dutchman) (1841; revised 1846)

This legend of a Dutch sea captain cursed to sail the earth unendingly, only coming ashore once every seven years to seek the selfless love of a woman, featured themes that would be of enduring interest to Wagner: the theme of a wanderer in search of redemption reappears several times in his later *Ring des Nibelungen*; that of redemption through a woman's act of self-sacrifice appears both in *Tannhäuser* and the *Ring*; and that of a pre-destined and unbreakable love is central to both the *Ring* and *Tristan and Isolde*. In this and several other ways the composition of *Der fliegende Holländer* foreshadowed the events of the composer's development as a mature composer.

Wagner's principal source for his opera about the *Flying Dutchman* was Heinrich Heine's version of the legend in his *Aus den Memoiren des Herren von Schnabelewopski*, published in 1834; but while Heine's retelling of the legend is ironic, Wagner stripped it of these elements and instead focused on the elements of love and redemption. The composer claimed that the work's inspiration was a stormy crossing from Riga to London in August 1839; however, Wagner's original prose sketch was set not in Norway, but Scotland, and Senta was originally "Anna." Wagner changed the setting to Norway just a few weeks before the opera's premiere (in Dresden, January 2, 1843) in order to distance it from a production of Pierre-Louis Dietsch's *Le vaisseau fantôme*, which was also a setting of Wagner's libretto (he had sold it to the Paris Opéra in 1841, hoping to gain the commission for himself).

It is likewise not true, as Wagner claimed, that the entire work grew from the "thematic seed" of Senta's Act Two ballad, although elements of the song do appear in the Dutchman's monologue and in Erik's dream. This claim was most likely Wagner's attempt to align this relatively early work with the thematic construction of his later music dramas. However, *Der fliegende Holländer* does show Wagner's early moves towards large-scale form, and the blurring of divisions between musical sections.

In many ways, *Dutchman* resembles its predecessors in German Romantic opera, especially those with supernatural plots. Senta's portentous ballad in Act Two, for example, resembles the prophetic song sung by the heroine of Marschner's *Der*

Vampyr, which Wagner helped prepare for performance in Wurzburg in 1833. Wagner also uses dramatic devices such as the seemingly hypnotic state in which the Dutchman and Senta first encounter each other, to emphasize the unearthly nature and fatedness of the bond between them.

The Dresden premiere of *Dutchman* was not the success that Wagner had hoped. Having bathed in the exaggerated splendor and grandeur of his Meyerbeerian *Rienzi*, those in the audience expected a similar spectacle and were somewhat disappointed. However, *Der fliegende Holländer* quickly gained in popularity and has remained a favorite. Perhaps the most familiar excerpts from the score are the "Sailor's chorus" from Act Three and the "Spinning chorus" from Act Two, which precedes Senta's ballad (which foretells of the Dutchman's presence), but the Dutchman's joyful aria "Wie aus der Ferne längst vergang'ner Zeiten" and Daland's "Mögst du mein Kind" are also memorable. *—AMG*

Synopsis:

Act One. Daland's ship has just arrived and dropped anchor at a Norwegian harbor. The young steersman on watch falls asleep, and the Flying Dutchman's ghostly ship, with blood-red sails, appears alongside Daland's vessel. The Dutchman relates that he can only come to land every seven years to seek redemption from a curse. Daland returns to deck, and the Dutchman offers him a huge reward for a single night's shelter. Thrilled with his luck, Daland also mentions his unmarried daughter, and is pleased at the Dutchman's evident interest.

Act Two. In a large room in Daland's house, a number of women are spinning for their sweethearts who are away at sea. Daland's daughter Senta is preoccupied with a portrait of a bearded man in seafaring dress, and sings the ballad of the Flying Dutchman, which explains that he is under a curse for a blasphemous oath. Although she has never seen the man himself, Senta is certain that she will be the instrument of his redemption.

Erik, a huntsman in love with Senta, enters and worriedly tells her that he has dreamed that her father brings home a seaman who resembles the portrait. When he realizes that he cannot get Senta's attention, he rushes away in agitation, while she continues to gaze at the picture.

Senta's father enters with the Dutchman, whom Senta recognizes as the man in the picture. Daland leaves the two alone, and their mutual fascination is made obvious by a long, silent gaze. Senta finally confides to him her resolve to save him from his curse, and the Dutchman warns her of the difficulty of the task. She must prove absolutely constant and faithful, or she will share his curse. Senta eagerly promises him fidelity to death. When Daland returns, she tells him that the homecoming festivities may also celebrate her betrothal to the Dutchman.

Act Three. After dark, the Norwegian ship at the harbor is illuminated for a party; the crew sings, dances, and drinks on deck, while the Dutch ship beside remains dark and silent. The seamen's wives and sweethearts call to the Dutch crew to come out and join their festivities, but are answered with an eerie silence. The Norwegians, reminded of the legend of the Flying Dutchman, become ill at ease and drink and carouse more rowdily to dispel their fears. A storm blows up around the Dutch ship, and its ghostly crew finally reveals itself with a strange, forbidding song.

Senta and Erik emerge from the house; Erik distractedly reminds her that she had once promised to be faithful to him. The Dutchman overhears, and stricken, releases Senta from her vow. He tells her that it is just as well that she will not share his terrible fate, and leaves to board his ship. Senta, desperate to prove her saving fidelity, throws herself into the sea. The Dutchman's ship disappears beneath the waves, and the receding waters reveal the transfigured pair ascending to heaven. *—Theresa Muir*

Recommended:

- ○ **Der fliegende Holländer** / Klemperer (cond.), Adam, Silja, Talvela / 2000 / Angel 67405B
- ○ **Der fliegende Holländer** / Konwitschny (cond.), Fischer-Dieskau, Wunderlich, Frick, Schech / 1994 / Berlin Classics 0020972
- ○ **Der fliegende Holländer** / Dorati (cond.), London, Rysanek, Tozzi, Elias, Liebl / 1990 / London 417319
- ○ **Der fliegende Holländer** / Barenboim (cond.), Eaglen, Mewes, Struckmann, Holl, Palmer, Villazon / 2002 / Teldec 88063
- ○ **Der fliegende Holländer** / Krauss (cond.), Hotter, Hann, Ursuleac, Willer, Klarwein, Ostertag / Preiser 90250

Die Götterdämmerung (Twilight of the Gods) (1869–1874)

Wagner completed the first draft of *Siegfrieds Tod*, later renamed *Götterdämmerung* in October 1848. Realizing that much knowledge of the situation was preassumed, he added a Prologue, and eventually turned the project into a cycle of four operas. He changed the dramatic focus from Siegfried to Wotan, and consequently had to revise *Siegfrieds Tod*. In 1852, he changed the end so that Walhall and the gods were destroyed. In 1856, more changes were made in light of his reading of Schopenhauer and interest in Buddhism. The first complete draft of the score was completed in April 1872, and the entire opera finally completed on November 21, 1874.

Götterdämmerung is a colossal work, one of the longest evenings of opera in the standard repertory. The Prologue and Act I, connected by the orchestral "Siegfried's Rhine Journey" probably comprise the longest continuous stretch of music heard in any operatic work. Despite this, the drama is so compressed that events seem almost to race to their cataclysmic end. *Götterdämmerung*'s structure echoes that of the entire cycle, with a prologue and three acts reflecting the large-scale plan of the prologue and three evenings.

Musically, Wagner has gained such mastery of his drama and musical motives, that he treats both with superb fluidity. At the same time, there seem to be regressive moments. For example, the Act Two chorus of the Gibichung vassals seems like an artifact of the old grand opera, as does the revenge trio in the same act, with its ensemble singing, and duplications of text. These events are partially explained by the libretto having preceded the music by more than 20 years, from a time when Wagner's music-dramatic theories had not been fully realized.

Wagner's use of his Leitmotives produces uncannily powerful psychological effects. For example, in Act Three, at the moment of Siegfried's death, the audience sees what he sees, by the use of Brünnhilde's awakening music from *Siegfried* Act Three, which then fades with his consciousness. It has been observed that the audience's memory for dramatic narrative have been stretched almost to their limits by the arc between these two moments; but an even longer stretch comes when the Funeral Music begins with the timpani strokes from Brünnhilde's annunciation of Siegmund's death in *Die Walküre*.

The music following Brünnhilde's immolation, even if it does not "explain" anything, is hugely consoling after the multiple tragedies, and that consoling effect again lies in Wagner's masterful manipulation of memory. Over a simmering stew of Leitmotives—those of the Rhine, Walhall, and Siegfried—the violins sing an arching melody first heard in *Die Walküre*, when Sieglinde burst out with this melody after Brünnhilde told her that she was bearing Siegmund's child. The label traditionally attached to this melody, "Redemption by Love," has misled audiences; in fact, Wagner considered it a song of praise to his heroine, Brünnhilde. His choice to end the entire vast work with this melody is indeed explanatory. *—Theresa Muir*

Synopsis:

Prologue. The three Norns (fate-weaving daughters of Wotan and Erda) recall how Wotan gave an eye to drink from the fountain of wisdom, then broke a branch from the great ash tree and made himself a spear. The tree withered and the fountain dried. Wotan engraved the spear with runes that gave him power over the world, but Siegfried broke the spear. Wotan returned to Valhalla and had the ash tree cut down and piled around the castle, where he and the gods now sit and wait for it and the world to be destroyed by fire. The rock frays the thread they are weaving, and they return to Erda within the Earth. Outside their home in a cave on the mountain, Brunhilde bids Siegfried farewell as he travels to seek adventure. He promises to be faithful and perform great deeds in her honor, and as a sign of his fidelity, gives her the ring. She gives him Grane, her horse, as a parting gift and watches him ride away.

Act One. Hagen says that Gunther and Gutrune must marry to continue their lineage. He suggests that Gunther marry Brunhilde and that Gutrune marry Siegfried. He tells Gunther that if they give Siegfried a magic potion, he will fall in love with Gutrune and forget Brunhilde, and will brave the magic fire that protects Brunhilde and bring her back for Gunther. Siegfried arrives and Gutrune leaves. The men talk, and Siegfried shows them the tarnhelm, explaining that he doesn't know what its use is. Hagen explains its powers and further questions Siegfried, who reveals that he gave the ring to Brunhilde. Gutrune returns with the magic drink, and Siegfried drinks, forgets Brunhilde, and falls in love with Gutrune. She leaves in confusion and Siegfried offers to bring Gunther Brunhilde as his bride, saying he will use the tarnhelm to assume Gunther's appearance. Gunther promises him Gutrune in return. The two swear blood brotherhood ("Blühenden Lebens") on their life's blood. They leave, and Gutrune anticipates Siegfried's love, Hagen the power of the ring ("Hier sitz ich"). On Brunhilde's mountain, Waltraute begs her to return the ring to the Rhinemaidens ("Seit er von dir") to save the gods from destruction. She refuses, as it was Siegfried's love gift to her. Waltraute leaves, predicting doom. Siegfried enters, appearing as Gunther, and seizes the ring, forcing her into the cave. As he is about to enter, he unsheathes his sword, saying it will lie between them as she is Gunther's.

Act Two. Hagen is motionless outside the castle. Alberich mysteriously appears, and reminding him of how the ring was stolen from him ("Schlafst du, Hagen") makes him swear to take it. Siegfried enters and announces that Gunther and Brunhilde are following. He goes inside with Gutrune. Hagen calls to the vassals to gather ("Hoiho! Hoiho!)" as they are being invaded—by brides. Gunther leads Brunhilde in, and when she sees Gutrune with Siegfried, who is wearing the ring, she accuses him of betraying her. Siegfried does not understand and at Hagen's demand, swears on Hagen's spear that he was never Brunhilde's husband ("Helle Wehr!"). She swears her own oath to destroy him. He laughs off her anger and leaves with Gutrune. Alone, Brunhilde, Hagen, and Gunther plot revenge. Brunhilde says that she used her magic powers to make Siegfried invulnerable, but she did not protect his back, which he would never turn to an enemy. Gunther has qualms, but Hagen promises they can make it look like a hunting accident, reminding him that that way they will have all Siegfried's treasure, including the ring. The vassals return, celebrating the wedding.

Act Three. Siegfried, who has gotten lost during the hunt, encounters the Rhinemaidens, who ask him to return the ring. He almost does so, but refuses when they threaten him, and they tell him he will die before the day ends. Hagen and Gunther find him, and he recounts their warning. Hagen gives him a drink that restores his memory, and at Hagen's urging, he tells of his life, including learning the language of birds, finding Brunhilde, and making her his wife ("Mime hiess ein mürrischer Zwerg"). Hagen asks Siegfried what the two ravens are saying, and as Siegfried turns to look at them, Hagen says they tell him to avenge Gunther, and stabs him in the back. Dying, Siegfried sings passionately to Brunhilde ("Brunhilde! Heilige Braut"). Vassals carry his body to the castle. Gutrune has sensed disaster and watches them return from the hunt. When she sees Siegfried, she faints, then accuses Gunther of killing him. He says it was Hagen, and Hagen says he avenged Siegfried's false oath, then kills Gunther to keep him from claiming the ring. He tries to snatch it from Siegfried's hand, but to the crowd's horror, the dead hand closes over it in warning. Brunhilde emerges and contemptuously says they are like children crying over spilt milk, and says Gutrune was never Siegfried's true wife. She orders them to build a funeral pyre, and in the Immolation Scene, laments his death and says the ring will return to the Rhinemaidens. She sends his ravens to Wotan with the message that the gods are finished, and orders Loge to join them. She lights the fire, and then mounts Grane and rides the horse into the fire. The fire ignites the hall, and the Rhine rises. Hagen orders the Rhinemaidens away from the ring, but they seize him, as well, and drag him under the water as they hold the ring in triumph. In the distance, Wotan and the gods impassively watch the flames approach Valhalla. *—Ann Feeney*

Recommended:

- ○ **Götterdämmerung** / Solti (cond.), Nilsson, Fischer-Dieskau, Ludwig, Popp, Frick, Windgassen / 1997 / Decca 455569
- ○ **Der Ring Des Nibelungen** / Furtwängler (cond.), Jurinac, Klose, Greindl, Poell, Pernerstorfer / 1990 / EMI 67123
- ○ **Der Ring Des Nibelungen** / Levine (cond.), Behrens, Salminen, Studer, Schwarz, Weikl / DG 445354
- ○ **Der Ring Des Nibelungen** / Solti (cond.), Nilsson, Fischer-Dieskau, Ludwig, Popp, Frick, Windgassen / 1997 / Decca 455555

Lohengrin (1848)

Lohengrin stands as a pivotal work in the career of Richard Wagner. In terms of its structure and approach, it is usually grouped at the end of his early operas; at the same time, it demonstrates many of the ideas and techniques that would achieve full fruition in his later music dramas. Indeed, at the same time as Wagner was drafting the work, many of the ideas for his later works, such as *Tristan* and the *Ring* cycle, were already percolating (an even put to paper in some preliminary form). On the other hand, the stylistic division usually placed just after *Lohengrin* corresponds with a biographical one: having fled to Zurich as a political exile before the opera's Weimar premiere (in 1850, with Franz Liszt conducting), Wagner would spend the next decade articulating his aesthetic philosophies through a series of important essays. These would transform many of the ideas hinted at in *Lohengrin* into a full-fledged musical paradigm shift.

The story for the opera was nearly a decade in gestation. Wagner first encountered the *Lohengrin* myth in 1841, and within five years had outlined a scenario for an opera on the subject. The score followed a few years later, in 1848. The story is set in Antwerp, in the tenth century, where Elsa, sister to the would-be duke, Gottfried, is accused of his murder. A mysterious figure arrives to defend her and even take her as his bride, but he commands her to not inquire about his name or his unknown provenance. A count, Telramund, and his sorcerer wife, Ortrud, are Elsa's accusers, and in fact, the real culprits in Gottfried's disappearance. They lay a series of intrigues to convince Elsa to ask her mysterious hero his identity, and in so doing, bring about a sad ending to the love story but an unexpectedly happy conclusion: the return of Gottfried.

In articulating this plot through musical means, Wagner demonstrates a number of his hallmark techniques as well as his keen sense of multilayered drama. The tension between Elsa's love for her mysterious hero and her uneasy curiosity about his background is embodied by the semitone relationship of the key areas associated with each of them (A flat and A natural, respectively). Ortrud's sinister machinations cast an eerie shadow of diminished chord sonorities whenever she appears or her plans fall into place (especially effective when, in the third act, as Elsa succumbs to Ortrud's deception she also adopts a version of her theme). Likewise, the F minor sonority that consistently stands for the "forbidden question" clashes forebodingly with the C major harmonies that characterize the wedding procession at the end of Act Two. These type of dramatic conceits combine with the most obvious one: as the opera centers on the utterance of the unknown name, the audience, who has been unceremoniously provided with the secret identity of the hero in the very title of the work, is in constant tension with the opera's protagonists. *—Jeremy Grimshaw*

Synopsis:

Act One. The opera opens in a meadow beside the Scheldt River, near Antwerp. Heinrich (King Henry the Fowler) has arrived to call the Brabantines to help him defend Germany against the invading Hungarians. A Herald summons the Brabantines, but one noble, Friedrich von Telramund, accuses Elsa of murdering her brother, Gottfried, the heir to the dukedom of Brabant. He claims the succession for himself.

Elsa does not defend herself, but reports a vision of a knightly champion who will defend her. The king and the others are moved, but Telramund demands combat. The Heralds twice trumpet a call for someone to defend Elsa's claim, but nobody appears. Elsa kneels in prayer, and Lohengrin appears, in a boat drawn by a swan. He offers himself as Elsa's champion, but makes her promise that she will never ask his name or origin. They pledge themselves to each other.

Lohengrin defeats Telramund, but spares his life. Telramund's wife, Ortrud, is a pagan witch, who has used sorcery to protect Telramund. She wonders about the stranger who can overcome her powers. Telramund, humiliated, falls at her feet.

Act Two. At the Fortress at Antwerp. Telramund reproaches Ortrud for his disgrace. She tells him that Lohengrin would lose his power if Elsa were to ask his name and origin. Ortrud calls to Elsa on the balcony and falsely appeals to her generosity. Ortrud calls upon her gods and ingratiates herself with Elsa, but also plants in her mind doubts and suspicions about Lohengrin.

The Herald announces that Telramund is banished, and that the stranger will wed Elsa today and assume the title of Protector, not Gottfried's title of Duke. Tomorrow he will lead them into battle. The wedding procession is interrupted first by Telramund, who accuses Lohengrin of sorcery. He demands that Lohengrin reveal his name and Lohengrin refuses. Only Elsa can command him, he says. Whe he looks at Elsa, however, he can see she is troubled. As they reach top step of cathedral, Elsa fearfully sees Ortrud making a threatening gesture.

Act Three. In Elsa's bridal chamber, Elsa pleads with Lohengrin to reveal himself to her. He refuses, first with reassurances of love, and then with warnings. Telramund bursts into the bridal chamber with his henchmen. Lohengrin slays Telramund, and orders the body brought before Heinrich. He declares that he will reveal all there.

Back on the bank of the Scheldt, Telramund's covered body is brought before Heinrich. Elsa and Lohengrin enter. Lohengrin announces he can no longer lead the army into battle. He killed Telramund in self-defense, and Elsa has broken her vow. He reveals himself as son of Parsifal and Knight of the Holy Grail. Now he must return to Monsalvat. The swan reappears with boat. Lohengrin tells Elsa if they had lived together a year without her questioning him, her brother would have been returned to her. He gives her his sword, ring and horn, to keep for Gottfried should he return. Ortrud reveals that she herself bewitched Gottfried, and that Gottfried is actually the swan drawing Lohengrin's boat. Now, she taunts, he can never be restored. Lohengrin kneels to pray, and a dove descends, hovering over the boat. The swan vanishes, and in his place appears Gottfried. Lohengrin proclaims him Duke of Brabant, and vanishes. Elsa falls lifeless to the ground. *—Theresa Muir*

Recommended:

- ○ **Wagner: Lohengrin** / Kempe (cond.), Thomas, Grummer, Ludwig, Fischer-Dieskau, Frick, Wiener / 2000 / Angel 67411
- ○ **Wagner: Lohengrin** / Solti (cond.), Domingo, Fischer-Dieskau, Norman, Scharinger, Nimsgern / 2002 / Decca 470795

Die Meistersinger von Nürnberg (1862–1867)

In 1845, having already completed his fifth opera, *Tannhäuser*, and contemplating a new one on the story of *Lohengrin*, Richard Wagner was inspired to take up the subject of the medieval "Mastersingers" by his reading of Georg Gottfried Gervinus' *Geschichte der poetischen National-Literatur der Deutschen.* However, although he composed a prose draft of a libretto in the same year, it would take him more than 20 years to bring the project to completion. After further researching the subject in Jakob Grimm's *Über den altdeutschen Meistergesang* of 1811 and Wagenseil's 1697 history of Nuremberg, entitled *Nuremberg Chronicle*, Wagner finally penned a verse libretto for *Die Meistersinger* in the winter of 1861–1862. He then broke off work on *Siegfried* (which he had also lain aside to complete *Tristan und Isolde* in 1859) in order to compose the score.

Fortunately for Wagner, much of this work took place under the patronage of Ludwig II, King of Bavaria, who called the composer to his court in May 1864, to offer his support. Wagner set up house in a country estate outside Lucerne, Switzerland, with his future second wife, Cosima von Bülow (née Liszt) (then wife of the conductor Hans von Bülow), and completed the score in relative peace. For Wagner, this was a change of pace, since he spent much of his early career fleeing from debtors. Finally completed, *Die Meistersinger von Nürnberg* premiered to great acclaim at the Munich Court Opera on June 21, 1868—with the cuckolded von Bülow conducting.

Wagner used the traditions of the German Mastersingers as the basis for the musical conception of his opera. Through his frequent use of bar form (AAB, or Stollen,

Stollen, Abgesang), for example, Wagner pays musical homage to these early composers, whose preserved output overwhelmingly favors this formal arrangement. One of the underlying themes of *Die Meistersinger*—that rules, while necessary for the tempering of inspiration, cannot create great art—is illustrated musically in Act One, Scene Three, when the character Kothner sings mechanical, etude-like music while reading the rules for composing a Mastersong. In stark contrast to Kothner's pedantry is Walther's trial song, which consists of a ravishing wash of chromatic exuberance contained within the boundaries of no prescribed formal plan. If Walther, the naturally great musician, represents Wagner himself, then it is equally true that the obtuse and curmudgeonly Sixtus Beckmesser represents Wagner's artistic and aesthetic nemesis, Eduard Hanslick. Beckmesser's music makes this association sardonically clear, making frequent use of artless staccato notes that seem to bite, rather than sing.

Seen in its most favorable light, *Meistersinger* is a good natured comic parable about the relationship between art and those that create it. However, the work also harbors elements of Wagner's growing anti-semitism and his desire to eliminate non-Germanic elements from his music. The characterization of Beckmesser, as well as being a jab at the composer's rival critic, also clearly establishes that character as a Jew through references to the Grimm fairy tale "The Jew in the Thorn Bush." For some listeners, this association coupled with the unfavorable caricature, taints the overall geniality of the work with an element of menace; but, by any purely artistic assessment *Die Meistersinger* is a finely crafted drama, rich with dramatic and musical textures that showcase Wagner's creative gifts at their best. *—AMG*

Synopsis:

Act One. St. Katharine's church. While the congregation sings a chorale tune, Walther, a young nobleman, hides behind a pillar and tries to get Eva's attention. After the service, he approaches her and asks if she is betrothed, and although she tries various ruses to get rid of her nurse Magdalene, she is unable to answer. Magdalene explains that Eva will marry the winner of the next day's song contest. To enter the contest, Walther needs to be initiated into the mastersingers' rules, and arranges to be instructed by Magdalene's sweetheart, David, Hans Sach's apprentice.

David takes some joking from his fellow apprentices, and tries to explain the rules to Walther, who is overwhelmed with their complexity. Eva's father, Pogner, enters with Beckmesser the clerk. Pogner welcomes Walther to the guild, although he is surprised that the young man wants to enter. Kothner calls the roll and Pogner announces the prizes for the song contest, including Eva's hand, with the injunction that Eva must agree. Not all the mastersingers are happy about this proviso. Sachs proposes that the winner be chosen by the people, a suggestion which is rejected.

Walther is introduced and asked about his teacher. He explains ("Am stillen Herd") that he leaned from the poems of Master Walther von der Vogelweide and from nature itself. His trial song is unsuccessful; Walther loses his temper at Beckmesser's constant scratching on his slate. Beckmesser leads a chorus opposing Walther, but Sachs finds the song original. Walther aggravates the uproar by finishing his song from the singer's chair, and the masters reject his application. The young man stomps out in a huff, while Sachs watches thoughtfully.

Act Two. A narrow street in Nuremberg; Pogner's and Sach's houses are visible. The apprentices tease David again. He tells Magdalene of Walther's misfortune at the Song School. Sachs arrives and puts David to work; Pogner and Eva sit on a bench under the lime tree by their house. Eva questions her father about Walther.

As they go inside, Sachs sets about work under his elder tree. Eva approaches and tries to get him to reveal a likely winner of the next day's contest. Magdalene calls her home, telling her that Beckmesser is going to serenade her.

Walther arrives, and encounters Eva; they sing an ardent duet. He suggest eloping, and gets carried away with his anger at the Mastersingers, until he is interrupted by the Nightwatchman's horn. Eva and Magdalene go into the house and change clothing with each other. Sachs, realizing what is happening, lights the alley for the young lovers' escape. They are about to make their escape when Beckmesser arrives and tunes his lute. Walther immediately wants to confront the clerk and is dissuaded by Eva. Sachs, under his lime tree, begins his own loud song while he hammers at his shoes. Beckmesser, thinking Magdalene at the window is Eva, pleads with Sachs to stop the noise. The commotion eventually rises to a level that brings the neighbors out onto the streets. The scene disintegrates into a riot. David attacks Beckmesser, believing him to be serenading Magdalene. The Nightwatchman's horn interrupts the chaos, and everyone quickly flees. On his return to the street, he finds everything as placid as before.

Act Three. Sach's workshop. David enters and finds Sachs deep in contemplation. Sachs asks David to sing the song he has learned for St. Johns' Day; but David, thinking of the previous evening, sings the tune of Beckmesser's serenade. David remembers that it is his master's name day. The apprentice leaves and Sachs resumes his reflection on humanity's foolishness ("Wahn! Wahn!").

Walther enters and relates a dream to Sachs. Under the master's guidance, Walther uses the dream's inspiration to compose a new Prize Song, but cannot yet complete it.

In the third scene, Beckmesser is seen alone in Sach's workshop, still stinging and angry from his beating the previous evening. He finds Walther's new song and pockets it, believing it to be Sach's entry in the contest for Eva's hand. Sachs reenters and Beckmesser confronts him, but Sachs offers him the song. Beckmesser takes the song and withdraws to learn it.

Eva enters, complaining about the new shoes Sachs has made her, but eventually expresses her worries about Walther and the contest. Sachs pretends not to understand, and ignores Walther's return (despite Eva's joyful cry). Walther presents the last verse of his song, and Eva weeps on Sach's shoulder; Sachs. embarrassed, tries to withdraw. Eva, torn between her new young sweetheart and her trusted old friend, draws Sachs back. Sachs reminds her of the story of Tristan and Isolde, and gently tells her he has no desire to play the role of King Mark. Magdalene and David enter, and Sachs greets David with a blow on the ear—his initiation as a journeyman. He also announces a new "child"—Walther's song. Each character reflects separately in a quintet.

The setting changes to a meadow. The guilds process in with pomp and ceremony, followed by maidens and apprentices. Sachs is hailed by the townspeople. The contest begins, and Beckmesser, who is first, makes a grotesque mess of Walther's song, which he sings to the tune of his serenade. He rushes off in humiliation, but blaming Sachs for the song.

Sachs denies the song is his, and introduces Walther to make sense of the song. Walther sings his song and is awarded the prize. He refuses the Master's chain that Pogner offers him. Sachs presents a stirring address about German art's enduring qualities , and the chorus hail him and "holy German art."*—Theresa Muir*

Recommended:

- ○ **Die Meistersinger von Nürnberg** / Karajan (cond.), Kollo, Donath, Adam, Schreier, Hesse, Ridderbusch / 1999 / EMI 67148
- ○ **Die Meistersinger Von Nürnberg** / Jochum (cond.), Fischer-Dieskau, Ligendza, Ludwig, Domingo, Laubenthal, Hermann / DG 415278
- ○ **Die Meistersinger von Nürnberg** / Toscanini (cond.), Nissen, Reining, Wiedemann, Noort, Thorborg / 2003 / Andante 3040
- ○ **Die Meistersinger von Nürnberg** / Solti (cond.), Wolfe, Heppner, Vermillion, Mattila, Opie, Lippert, Pape / 2002 / Decca 470800

Parsifal (1878–1882)

According to his autobiography, Wagner conceived of his *Parsifal* as early as 1857; however, it would be his last completed work, premiered in 1882, the year before his death. His major sources were the epic poem, *Parzival*, by the thirteenth century poet Wolfram von Eschenbach (who incidentally, appears as a character in *Tannhäuser*), and the medieval romance, *Perceval, ou li Contes de Graal*, by Wolfram's near-contemporary, Chrétien de Troyes.

Parsifal is the story of a young man whose virtue and compassion become the salvation of the Knights of the Holy Grail. He wards off temptation and danger to regain the spear with which Christ's side was pierced on the cross; in the process he heals the king, Amfortas, of a cursed wound, and relieves the fallen woman, Kundry, from her eternal wandering.

The medieval literature about the Holy Grail is complex and varied, with roots in Celtic paganism; the identification of the Holy Grail as the cup of the Last Supper or as a vessel that caught Christ's blood at the Crucifixion did not appear until work the thirteenth century Burgundian poet, Robert de Boron. While on the surface a Christian drama (reinforced for modern audiences by its frequent adoption as a Easter-season feature), *Parsifal* still resonates with paganism, especially through the figure of Kundry. Perhaps the strongest philosophical influence, however, came from Buddhism by way of Schopenhauer, for whom compassion and renunciation of the will, or appetites, were central concepts.

Parsifal was Wagner's only work specifically composed for the special acoustics of his Bayreuth theater (where the orchestra pit is hidden under the stage), and its particular sound-world is distinct from all of its predecessors. One of the most extraordinary aspects of the work is Wagner's orchestrally delineated sense of space distinct to each of his locations (the Grail castle of Acts One and Three; Klingsor's magic realm).

Musically, the work reaches both backwards and forward. The extraordinary music of the first act Transformation scene combines a triadic ground bass with progressively chromatic harmonies, creating an almost tangible sense of movement from the outside world to a hidden place of awe. The haunting milieu of the Grail castle in Act I is conjured by the tolling bells, the deliberately archaic a cappella choruses (Wagner studied Palestrina for these), and Titurel's offstage voice, punctuated by timpani. Kundry's raging solo passages in Act Three are almost Expressionistic in nature, with their wide, dissonant leaps, laughs, cries, and groans. The Transformation of Act Three (Titurel's funeral march) and the knights' double chorus, is constructed on harrowing dissonances, and swerves closer to atonality than any previous Wagnerian work. *—Theresa Muir*

Synopsis:

Act One. The Realm of the Grail, dawn in a forest clearing. Gurnemanz, a knight of the Holy Grail, awakens two young esquires. He bids them prepare a bath for

Amfortas, the guardian of the Grail, who suffers from a mysterious wound. Suddenly, Kundry, a wild-looking woman, appears with balsam from Arabia for Amfortas, who also arrives, carried on a litter. Amfortas accepts Kundry's balsam, but reminds them that his only hope is a prophesied healer, "a pure fool" and goes to his bath.

Gurnemanz narrates the story of how Amfortas obtained his terrible wound, and lost the sacred spear to the magician Klingsor. Amfortas' father Titurel had assembled a brotherhood of knights to help him protect the Grail. Klingsor was barred because he had castrated himself in order to attain chastity. To avenge himself, he created a magic garden full of beautiful women to corrupt the knights. Amfortas set out with the sacred spear to defeat him, but encountered a "fearfully beautiful woman." While Amfortas was occupied with her, Klingsor wounded him with the spear, and snatched it away.

A group of knights enters, dragging a young man with a bow. He has shot down one of the swans who live on the holy lake. Gurnemanz reprimands him, and ashamed, the boy breaks his bow. He cannot answer questions about himself, except that his mother's name was Herzeleide (Heart's sorrow). Kundry announces that his mother died after he left home. The enraged boy attacks her, and must be restrained.

Amfortas is taken back toward the castle, and Gurnemanz offers to take the boy with them. The scene changes to the Grail Castle. The boy watches as Amfortas is carried in. Titurel's voice is heard commanding Amfortas to uncover the Grail, but Amfortas shrinks back in dread. Titurel insists; he and the community depend on the ritual. Amfortas takes the Grail from its shrine and consecrates the bread and wine. The boy clutches his heart when he hears Amfortas' cry of pain. Amfortas is removed, and the knights recess from the room. Gurnemanz asks the boy if he understands what he has seen, but he cannot answer. Gurnemanz angrily dismisses him.

Act Two. From his castle, Klingsor watches a young knight approaching, and calls out for Kundry, who is bound in service to him. She spits insults at him, but must obey his command to seduce the knight. They watch him defeat Klingsor's guards. Suddenly, the tower sinks, and is replaced by a garden filled with magic flowers.

Flower maidens rush in and compete for the new young man's attention. He becomes uneasy, and tries to extricate himself, as the girls press him. All are halted by the sound of Kundry's voice calling, "Parsifal!," which the young man recognizes as his forgotten name. She appears, transformed into a gorgeous siren, and banishes the flower maidens.

Kundry describes his mother's death of a broken heart when he left without returning. Parsifal is grieved and guilty. Subtly combining maternal and sexual imagery, Kundry suggests that he atone for his mother's death by making love to her. She finishes with a long kiss on Parsifal's lips. Clutching his side, he breaks away, crying out "Amfortas! The wound!"

Kundry tells him of her curse, how she laughed at Christ on the day of the Crucifixion, and how she has been condemned to wander since then. She appeals to Parsifal to use his new enlightenment to save her, and insists that "one hour together" would bring her salvation. Parsifal continues to resist. He asks if she will help him find Amfortas, and in a fury of frustration, she curses him to wander for years. She calls Klingsor, who appears with the spear and hurls it at Parsifal, who miraculously catches it. He makes the sign of the Cross with it; the castle falls, and the magic garden vanishes.

Act Three. In an open meadow in the land of the Grail, is the hut of Gurnemanz, who has aged many years. Hearing groans, he emerges from his hut, and discovers Kundry lying on the ground. He revives her, but she will say only "Dienen... dienen (To serve... to serve)." The two see a stranger in black armor approaching, carrying a spear. Gurnemanz requests he put down his weapon, as it is Good Friday. Parsifal places the spear in the ground, and kneels to pray before it. Watching, Gurnemanz and Kundry recognize him and the spear. Gurnemanz tells Parsifal that the knights of the Grail are in disarray. Longing for death, Amfortas refuses to uncover the Grail, and Titurel has just died. Kundry washes Parsifal's feet, and Gurnemanz anoints him the new Grail King.

Reminded of Good Friday, Parsifal is overcome by sadness, but Gurnemanz, showing him the beauty of the meadow, tells him that nature rejoices at the redemption of sinners. The three depart for the Grail Castle, and there is a corresponding Transformation to the one in Act I. Two groups of knights enter the hall, one carrying Titurel's coffin, and the other carrying Amfortas' litter. Titurel's casket is opened, and the knights all cry out in grief. They insist that Amfortas uncover the Grail. Amfortas refuses, and when the knights press him, he bids them to kill him and end his suffering. Parsifal, watching unobserved, steps forward with the spear and touches its point to Amfortas' wound. Amfortas is healed, and yields the Grail to Parsifal, who takes it from the shrine. Kundry sinks lifeless to the ground. Parsifal gestures a blessing with the Grail. The hall fills with light, and a white dove descends and hovers above the scene. *—Theresa Muir*

Recommended:

○ **Parsifal** / Knappertsbusch (cond.), Windgassen, Mödl, Weber, London, Uhde, Mill / 1993 / Teldec 76047

○ **Parsifal** / Knappertsbusch (cond.), Thomas, Dalis, Hotter, London, Janowitz, Silja, Talvela / 2001 / Philips 464756

○ **Parsifal** / Solti (cond.), Kollo, Ludwig, Fischer-Dieskau, Te Kanawa, Hotter, Popp / 2002 / Decca 470805

○ **Parsifal** / Karajan (cond.), Hofmann, Vejzovic, Van Dam, Nimsgern, Moll / DG 413347

Das Rheingold (The Rhine Gold) (1853–1854)

Das Rheingold introduces a primeval collection of gods, nymphs, giants, and dwarves who instigate the situations inherited by Wotan's children, the humans Siegmund and Sieglinde, and the Valkyrie, Brünnhilde. It is a brief glimpse of an Edenic world, already beginning to be corrupted by greed and lust for power. Musically, *Das Rheingold* introduces many of the motives associated with objects and ideas of importance in the drama. Among these are the Rheingold, the Ring, Walhall, Wotan's spear, and the renunciation of love. *Das Rheingold* also introduces Wagner's huge Ring orchestra, its versatility, and at times, Wagner's sheer audacity with sound. At one astonishing moment in the transition to scene three, the orchestra falls silent, leaving the enslaved Nibelungs' forging rhythm to ring out on 18 tuned anvils. *Rheingold* requires six harps for its conclusion, accompanying the forlorn cries of the betrayed Rhine Daughters. The extraordinary prelude, which is in essence the prelude to the entire cycle, should also be mentioned. The first sound the listener hears is a low E flat, played on the double basses, which seems to appear out of nowhere. This single thread of sound slowly becomes a remarkable extension of the single key of E flat, layering arpeggio upon arpeggio and figuration upon figuration, adding different orchestral voices with their different colors to suggest the growth of a mighty river from its source to an overwhelming torrent. Wagner wrote in his autobiography that the sound came to him in a trancelike state in which he felt almost drowned. Although there is no evidence to contradict this account, Wagner often used fanciful accounts of unmediated inspiration to explain his compositions. Against Wagner's wishes, *Das Rheingold* was premiered in 1869 for Wagner's patron, King Ludwig II, in Munich. Wagner had intended to introduce the complete cycle at his new *Festival Theater* in Bayreuth, and neither the work nor the opera house had yet been completed. Ludwig did not want to wait to hear the completed operas. *—Theresa Muir*

Synopsis:

Setting: Unspecified Nordic country

Time: Legendary

Scene One. The opera begins with the Rhinemaidens (Woglinde, Wellgunde, Flosshilde) swimming in the Rhine, laughing and playing ("Weia! Waga!"). The Nibelung Alberich tries to make love to them, but they slip away, teasing him. Light flashes off the gold on top of one of the rocks, and the Rhinemaidens say that a ring forged from the gold would give its owner absolute power, but it cannot be taken except by someone who renounces love. Alberich climbs to the rock, shouts a renunciation, and steals it. The Rhinemaidens exclaim in anger and dismay.

Scene Two. Wotan, king of the gods, exclaims that now Valhalla is complete. Fricka reminds him that in return for their building it, he offered Freia, the goddess of youth, to the giants Fasolt and Fafner ("Vollendet das ewige Werk"). Fricka adds that the castle has not satisfied his desire for glory, but has sharpened it. Freia runs in, fleeing the giants. Wotan impatiently wonders where the fire god Loge is, as Loge (moonlighting as the god of crooked attorneys) said he has a plan for getting out of the bargain. When the giants enter and demand Freia, Wotan asks what other payment they would accept. Fasolt responds that they want Freia and that Wotan swore on his sacred spear that he would give her to them. To break such an oath would illegitimize his power. The thunder god Donner and Froh, Friea's brothers, move to attack them, but Wotan stops them. Loge returns and reports that he unsuccessfully searched the Earth for a greater treasure, but there is nothing worth more than youth and beauty ("So weit Leben und Weben"). Only one being has ever chosen wealth over love, the dwarf Alberich. The other gods urge Wotan to seize Alberich's treasure and offer it to the giants. Wotan refuses, at which the giants drag Freia away. As she disappears, the gods suddenly realize that without Freia and her golden apples of eternal youth, they are aging as mortals. Wotan takes Loge to steal the treasure.

Scene Three. In the underworld Nibelung kingdom, Alberich abuses his brother Mime for not finishing his work. As he is being beaten, he drops his work, the tarnhelm, which lets the wearer take any desired shape or become invisible. Mime whimpers it wasn't ready yet, but Alberich accuses him of trying to steal it for himself. He puts it on, becomes invisible, and resumes beating Mime. He leaves, and Mime crouches in the corner. Loge and Wotan find him, and he tells the gods Alberich is using the ring to enslave the Nibelungs and make them mine gold for him, and made Mime create the tarnhelm. Alberich returns, beating Nibelungs who bring in gold, and then sends them back with Mime. The gods flatter him, and he boasts of his power, saying that he will be master of the gods and their wives will be his. They ask him to demonstrate his great powers, and he turns himself into a huge serpent. Loge asks if he can also transform himself into something tiny, such as a toad. He does so, and as Wotan traps him, Loge grabs the tarnhelm. They tie him up and drag him to the upperworld.

Scene Four. Loge taunts him and Wotan tells him that he will let Alberich ransom himself in exchange for the gold. Alberich agrees, and he uses the ring to make his Nibelung slaves bring it. Loge takes the tarnhelm, as well. While he protests loudly, Alberich consoles himself with the thought that with the ring, he can regain everything. Wotan now demands the ring itself. Alberich accuses him of breaking faith; the ring was not part of the bargain, and warns him that the ring will bring him a curse. Wotan impatiently yanks it off his finger and puts it on his own. When Loge unties him, Alberich pronounces the curse: the ring will bring doom to anyone who owns it ("Wie durch Fluch"). Alberich leaves as Fasolt and Fafner return with Freia. Wotan offers them the gold. They say that they will accept a pile the same size as Freia, and the gods pile up the gold in front of her. Fafner says that he can still see her hair, and the tarnhelm is added to the heap. Fasolt demands the ring to close the space through which he can still see one of Freia's eyes. Wotan refuses, and they start to take her away again. Erda rises from the Earth and warns him that with her knowledge of the future, she has foreseen the doom of the gods ("Weiche, Wotan, weiche"). Wotan must relinquish the ring, she says, and sinks back into the ground. Wotan calls to the giants to release Freia, and adds the ring to the pile. The giants immediately quarrel over how to divide it, with Loge adding fuel to the flames. Fasolt grabs the ring, and Fafner kills him and takes it. Wotan realizes that the curse is already working. Fafner drags the corpse and treasure away. At Wotan's order, Donner and Froh summon a thunderstorm to clear the mists ("Heda! Hedo!"), and Wotan sings of their new abode ("Abendlich strahlt der Sonne Augen"). The gods cross the rainbow bridge that appears, and Loge muses that they are deceiving themselves into thinking all is well. He'll make up his mind later about remaining with them and follows them. The Rhinemaidens, below, sing of their lost gold, and Wotan shouts to Loge to silence them. He laughs at them, and the gods continue to enter Valhalla. *—Ann Feeney*

Recommended:

- ○ **Das Rheingold** / Solti (cond.), Flagstad, London, Kmentt, Wachter / 1997 / London 455556
- ○ **Das Rheingold** / Karajan (cond.), Fischer-Dieskau, Donath, Moser, Kerns, Talvela / DG 457781
- ○ **Der Ring des Nibelungen** / Furtwängler (cond.), Frick, Jurinac, Greindl, Poell / 1990 / EMI 67123

Rienzi, der Letzte der Tribunen (1838–1840)

Richard Wagner composed his third opera, *Rienzi, der Letzte der Tribunen* (Rienzi, the Last of the Roman Tribunes) under dire financial, professional, and personal circumstances. The failure of his second opera, *Das Liebesverbot,* at its only performance in 1836 in Magdeburg, set Wagner in flight from his creditors. He went first to Berlin in an unsuccessful effort to arrange performances of *Das Liebesverbot,* and later joined his lover Minna Planer in Königsberg. There Wagner and Minna married, but promises of a conductorship did not materialize, and pressure from Wagner's creditors forced Minna to flee in desperation to her parents' Dresden home. Wagner finally accepted a position at the opera house at Riga, where Minna returned to him in October 1837. It was in Riga, amidst the French and Italian operas he was charged with conducting, that Wagner began composing *Rienzi.* However, further attempts to avoid his debts halted his compositional work; it was not until his term in a Parisian debtor's prison in 1840 that he was able to complete the project.

Rienzi was Wagner's musical response to G.N. Baermann's German translation of Bulwer-Lytton's 1835 novel on the fourteenth century Cola di Rienzi, and possibly also to Mary Russell Mitford's 1828 play on the same theme. It was first premiered in Dresden on October 20, 1842. Modern audiences cannot now hear performances of this "original" *Rienzi*: Wagner made many cuts in his lengthy opera for the 1845 edition of the score and the autograph score has fallen into oblivion. It is possible that Adolf Hitler, to whom the autograph was presented by the President of the Reichsarbeitskammer in 1839, was the last person to know its whereabouts. John Deathridge has noted that most of the twentieth century performances of *Rienzi* have been based on a score (published in 1898–99) which Cosima Wagner and Julius Kniese manufactured—by making numerous unauthorized cuts and stylistic alterations to the music and drama—with the intention of converting it from a French opera and into a Wagnerian music-drama.

The music of *Rienzi* reveals, at every turn, Wagner's efforts to compose a fashionable "Parisian" opera. Wagner relied heavily on closed forms (most notably the ternary aria form) in structuring individual numbers, and often extended the closed-form idea to a larger-scale level to include whole sections of scenes. The influence of French grand opera is also evident in the scope of the work, which is extraordinarily large. Impossible to stage in anything but the largest of theaters, it includes huge military processions and crowd scenes that would have made Meyerbeer proud. *—Jennifer Hambrick*

Synopsis:

Act One. In Rome Paolo Orsini and a group of his henchmen are attempting to abduct Rienzi's sister, Irene. They are stopped by their rivals, Adriano Colonna, and his kinsmen. Adriano is the son of Stefano Colonna, the head of the Colonna family, who is also feuding with Rienzi; but Adriano is in love with Irene. A fight ensues, and is interrupted by the arrival of Rienzi, who is urged to take power and bring law and order to the city. Adriano makes amends by pledging loyalty to Rienzi, who promises him his sister in marriage. Rienzi declines kingship, but accepts the title of tribune.

Act Two. In a great hall in the Capitol. Patrician youths are celebrating a peace mission throughout the cities of Italy. The Colonnas and the Orsini conspire together against Rienzi, who receives a group of foreign ambassadors and claims for the Roman people the right to vote for the Holy Roman Emperor.

A ballet, representing the unity of ancient and modern Rome, is performed. Orsini attacks Rienzi and stabs him, but his knife is blunted against Rienzi's steel breastplate. Meanwhile, the Colonna faction has attempted to seize the Capitol. Senators and the people clamor for the death of the traitors, but Adriano and Irene plead for Stefano's life. Rienzi pardons the rebels.

Act Three. In the old Roman Forum the nobles are plotting again. Adriano is torn between his divided loyalties. Rienzi appears on horseback at the head of a procession. The bodies of Paolo Orsini and Stefano Colonna are brought in and displayed. Adriano curses Rienzi and swears revenge.

Act Four. Before the church of St. John Lateran, a citizen, Baroncelli, accuses Rienzi of offering his sister Irene in exchange for an alliance with the nobles. Adriano, in disguise, reveals himself and supports the charge. Rienzi enters, but Adriano cannot bring himself to assassinate him in Irene's presence. The nobles excommunicate Rienzi, who is abandoned by his followers.

Act Five. In the Capitol Rienzi prays for strength and leaves to arm himself. Adriano tries to take Irene away by force, but she resists. Outside, the people riot. They throw stones at Rienzi and set fire to the Capitol. Amidst the fire, Rienzi and Irene are seen on a balcony. Adriano attempts to rescue Irene, but the building collapses, burying the three of them. *—Theresa Muir*

Recommended:

- ○ **Rienzi** / Hollreiser (cond.), Schreier, Kollo, Vogel, Adam, Springer, Leib, Hillebrand / 1999 / EMI 67131
- ○ **Rienzi** / Krips (cond.), Ludwig, Berry, Stich-Randall, Svanholm, Schoffler / Golden Melodram 10039

Siegfried (1856–1871)

It has been much discussed that Wagner halted composition of *Siegfried* partway through Act Two (leaving Siegfried under a linden tree) in 1857, and did not begin work on Act Two until 1869, finally reaching completion in 1871. The *Ring* project had reached a financial crisis, and having moved on mentally to *Tristan,* Wagner was eager to tackle its different musical and dramatic problems. The intervening years also saw the completion and performance of *Die Meistersinger.*

Wagner's sense of what he wanted to do with the Ring drama changed by the time he returned to *Siegfried.* When he began the Ring, he had clearly seen Siegfried as the hero of the drama, but the desire to more fully explore Wotan's predicament impelled him to expand the project. Wagner's readings of the philosopher Schopenhauer also had altered his conception to a more pessimistic one, in which the power of love alone would not be sufficient to conquer the curse of greed and corruption.

An unusual aspect of this work is that the dramatic action consists almost exclusively of confrontations: in Act One, Mime and Siegfried, and the Wanderer and Mime; Act Two, the Wanderer and Alberich, Siegfried and Fafner, Mime and Alberich, Siegfried and Mime again; then Act Three, the Wanderer and Erda, the Wanderer and Siegfried, and Siegfried and Brünnhilde. In *Siegfried,* Wotan has resolved to desist from controlling events and calls himself the Wanderer. He is very much present throughout this drama, however, which introduces his new motive, a unique, compact creation. It is at once descending, chromatic, sequential, and cyclic, and neatly conveys the god's renunciation and his ceaseless wandering through the realm of earth.

Siegfried has many elements of a folk or fairy tale: a dark, menacing forest as a setting; a naive, but heroic foundling, a dwarf, a pet bear who makes a brief appearance, a ferocious dragon and a talking bird. The dragon (Fafner) and bird are actually given voices with which to communicate: the dragon is an offstage bass projected through a speaking tube, and the bird is a coloratura soprano. *Siegfried*'s colorful orchestration also reflects its fairy tale milieu, with its anvil, stage horn, and double-reed effects. The *"Forest Murmurs"* interlude in Act Two features solo woodwinds in a delightfully tremulous imitation of nature. The addition of a high, bright, penetrating soprano voice as the Wood Bird is almost an instrumental effect as well. The essential fairy tale confrontation between Siegfried and the dragon is preceded and accompanied by a fanciful clash of motives and timbres as Siegfried's horn does vivid battle with Fafner's contrabassoon.

Inevitably, the first two acts of *Siegfried* are stylistically closer to *Das Rheingold* and *Die Walküre*, where the motivic material was generally concise. Act Three introduces more expansive motives associated with the Wanderer's dialogue with Erda, and Siegfried and Brünnhilde's grand concluding love duet. The use of motives looks towards the freedom and fluidity of *Götterdämmerung*, and they are combined in denser polyphonic textures, reflecting the technique developed in *Tristan*. *—Theresa Muir*

Synopsis:

Act One. Act One opens in Mime's cave. Mime works at an anvil, muttering that his foundling, Siegfried, breaks every sword that he makes ("Zwangvolle Plage!"). He is unable to reforge the shattered sword Nothung (Needful), with which Siegfried would be able to kill Fafner and take his treasure. Mime, then, would be able to take the ring and rule the world. Siegfried comes in and shows that Mime has some family discipline problems—he sets a bear on Mime, smashes the new sword, throws food on the ground, and grabs him by the throat to find out about his true parentage. Mime tells him of how he found a dying woman in the forest and brought her to his cave ("Als sullendes Kind"). She gave birth to a child before she died, telling her own name, Sieglinde, saying that the child's father died in combat, and telling Mime to name the child Siegfried. As proof, Mime shows Siegfried the broken sword blade that the woman had been carrying. Siegfried orders Mime to repair the sword, threatening to beat him unless he does so, and leaves. Mime knows he does not have the skill and huddles in a bundle of misery. The Wanderer (Wotan in disguise), comes in wearing a cloak and a hat that hides his missing eye and carrying a huge spear. Mime orders him off, but is doomed to be ignored. The Wanderer says that there is little wisdom in the world, and when Mime says he has as much as he needs, suggests a riddle game, the loser to forfeit his head. Mime asks first, and the Wanderer answers his questions about the inhabitants of the Earth (the Nibelung, whom Alberich ruled with the ring), the rulers of the Earth (the giants Fasolt and Fafner, now Fafner alone, after he killed his brother and transformed himself into a dragon), and the ruler of the heavens (Wotan). Mime answers Wotan's first two questions, about those Wotan has treated the most harshly but loves the most (the Walsungs: Siegmund, Sieglinde, and Siegfried), the sword Siegfried must use to defeat Fafner (Nothung), but fails when the Wanderer asks who will reforge the sword. Instead of demanding Mime's head, he answers that the one without fear will reforge it, and he will leave Mime's head as a prize. Siegfried returns and when he asks about this "fear" concept that Mime keeps talking about, Mime says that he will teach him fear at Fafner's lair. Siegfried, in an exalted mood, himself forges the sword ("Nothung! Nothung!") and when he is done, triumphantly breaks the anvil with it.

Act Two. Outside Fafner's cave, Alberich and Wotan encounter one another. Alberich is bitter, Wotan seemingly unmoved, even calling to Fafner to give up the ring, which Fafner refuses. They both leave. Mime and Siegfried come in, and Mime warns Siegfried about Fafner's poisonous breath and saliva. Siegfried doesn't see much chance of learning about fear here, and Mime goes off. Siegfried muses on the beauty of nature and wonders about his unknown family. He tries to imitate a bird's call with a reed, but fails. He instead blows his horn, awakening Fafner, who emerges. He is still unafraid of the huge dragon, and they fight. After Siegfried delivers a deathblow, Fafner realizes that the curse has finally destroyed him, and he warns Siegfried against Mime, then dies without answering Siegfried's question about his own birth. When he pulls his sword out, Siegfried is splashed with some blood, which burns his hand. When he raises it to his mouth, instinctively, the taste of the blood lets him understand the Forest Bird's song. The bird tells him of the tarnhelm and ring inside the cave, and Siegfried goes to find them. Alberich and Mime return and fight over the treasure. When Siegfried remerges, the blood also lets him understand Mime's intentions behind his flattery, and when Mime inadvertantly thus says that he will drug and kill Siegfried and take the treasure, he kills Mime. Alberich laughs mockingly. The bird tells Siegfried of Brunhilde, who can be awakened only by one who knows no fear. Siegfried vows to do so, and the bird's voice leads him away.

Act Three. Wotan summons Erda, asking to know how he can avert the impending doom. Erda tells him first to ask the Norns and then suggests the wise Brunhilde. She rebukes him for unjustly punishing her so harshly for her disobedience. Erda offers no help or consolation, and Wotan resigns himself to the gods' fate, as Siegfried and Brunhilde will, with the power of love, redeem the world. He sits to wait for Siegfried. When Siegfried comes, Wotan questions him, and Siegfried becomes annoyed, eventually ordering him out of the way. Wotan blocks his way with the spear, and angry at this defiance, tells him this is the spear shattered his father's sword. Siegfried shatters the spear with his sword, shouting that he is avenging his father, and Wotan disappears. Siegfried plunges into the flames that surround Brunhilde's rock. On the rock, Siegfried sees only a figure in armor. He cautiously approaches, and as he undoes the armor, realizes, with sudden fright, the first fear in his life, that the figure is not a man, but a woman. She awakens and greets the sunlight and then Siegfried as the hero son of Sieglinde, whom she loved even before his birth ("Heil, dir Sonne!"). She herself is suddenly afraid of mortal love, but then are soon passionately drawn to one another, singing of the love that laughs at death, and embrace ("Leuchtende Liebe!"). *—Ann Feeney*

Recommended:

- ○ **Siegfried** / Solti (cond.), Sutherland, Nilsson, Hotter, Neidlinger, Windgassen, Hoffgen / 1997 / London 455564
- ○ **Siegfried** / Karajan (cond.), Stewart, Dernesch, Ridderbusch, Dominguez, Thomas / DG 457790
- ○ **Der Ring des Nibelungen** / Furtwängler (cond.), Klose, Streich, Greindl, Frantz, Pernerstorfer / 1990 / EMI 67123

Tannhäuser (1843–1865)

On January 23, 1883, Cosima Wagner wrote in her diary that her husband believed he still owed *Tannhäuser* to the world. Wagner completed the first version of the opera in 1845 during his tenure as Kapellmeister at the royal court of Dresden. No other work in his oeuvre would receive as much constant attention. It seems that Wagner, who considered *Tannhäuser* a watershed work in his output, was never satisfied with any single version of it.

Tannhäuser, the medieval legend of the knight from Thannhausen, was premièred in Dresden in October 1845. Wagner began the process of revising the work immediately. Dresden audiences saw performances of at least three different incarnations of the opera, and the version of the score Wagner published in 1860 was yet again different. Wagner subjected *Tannhäuser* to further emendations, including the translation of the libretto into French, for each of the three performances of the work at the Paris Opéra in 1861, and the version first performed in Vienna in 1875 was of a still different score. The early Parisian performances of *Tannhäuser* have lived in infamy and illustrate the circumstances in which Wagner made the most significant changes to the opera. The Jockey Club had demanded, in keeping with French tradition, that the opera contain a ballet in Act Three. Wagner extended the Venusberg scene at the opening of the opera to include a ballet. Objecting to the early placement of the ballet, the Jockey Club organized a clangorous display of disapproval. Performances of *Tannhäuser* today generally draw on either the "Dresden" or the "Paris" version.

The orchestra introduces the drama's most important themes in the *Tannhäuser* prelude. Act I begins at the Venusberg, chromatic swirls and robust orchestration forming the musical backdrop for frolicking fauna at the grotto of the love goddess. The master singer Tannhäuser sings three appeals for Venus to release him to the world beyond her mountain, each appeal one semitone higher than the one preceding, revealing Tannhäuser's heightening intensity. In the valley before the Wartburg resound a shepherd's song and a chorus of older pilgrims making their way to Rome. Wagner constructs the chorus of the pious pilgrims in a four-part chorale setting reminiscent of the Lutheran chorales of J.S. Bach. In the Act Two song contest, Wolfram, Tannhäuser, and Biterolf sing artful songs on the nature of love. Having returned unsuccessfully from his pilgrimage to Rome, Tannhäuser sings to Wolfram of his experiences there, his musical manner alternating between willful expanses in his previous songful vein and recitative utterances. The chromatic Venusberg music returns when Tannhäuser realizes that he has no choice but to live out his destiny of damnation in the service of Venus herself. On learning that Elisabeth has died so that his own sins may be forgiven, Tannhäuser hears the devoutly diatonic music of Elisabeth's funeral procession, which, having purified the Venusberg music of its excessive chromaticism, invites the final triumphal statement of the theme from the pilgrims' chorus as the opera draws to a close. *—Jennifer Hambrick*

Synopsis:

Act One. In the foreground of the Venusberg—the Arcadian realm of the love goddess—Tannhäuser sits motionless at the feet of the reclining Venus, his head on her knee, his harp by his side. Sirens, Naiads, Nymphs, Fauns, Satyrs, and Bacchantes cavort in the background, their erotic gestures culminating in an orgy of unrestrained partnering. Fearing complete chaos, the three Graces attempt unsuccessfully to restore order, eventually waking the sleeping Cupids to assist them. The Cupids shower arrows upon the revelers, whom the Graces disperse. The entire background disappears into a heavy mist, leaving visible only Tannhäuser, Venus, and the Graces. The Graces exit in the direction of a grotto. Tannhäuser moves with a start and sings of the daylight and spring he has not seen since joining Venus, who admonishes him to give thanks for the love she has given him. Singing that Venus' love is too powerful for a mortal, Tannhäuser begs Venus to free him so that he may again commune with humankind. Venus, confused, is loath to release Tannhäuser, and attempts to seduce him into staying. Tannhäuser promises to be a staunch advocate of love in the world of mortals and again begs Venus to set him free. She relents, acrimoniously predicting that Tannhäuser will return to her, begging for mercy. Tannhäuser claims he will never return to her and that he seeks only penance for his sins and death.

Tannhäuser takes his leave from the Venusberg, seeking the redemption from sin from the Virgin Mary. En route to the Wartburg, Tannhäuser hears from afar the song of a procession of pilgrims venturing to Rome for absolution and bewails his sins. Hermann, the Landgrave of Thuringia, notices the penitential figure. Upon recognizing him as Tannhäuser, who had previously left the Wartburg, Hermann and his retinue of knights and minstrels welcome him, demanding that he never again leave their company. Not revealing where his travels had taken him, Tannhäuser tells the men that he will not find the peace he seeks by staying with them. Tannhäuser agrees to stay only when Wolfram tells him that the virtuous Elisabeth had fallen in love with him.

Act Two. In the Wartburg's Hall of Song, Elisabeth joyfully awaits the return of Tannhäuser's music in the singers' festival. Elisabeth thanks God for the miracle that led Tannhäuser back to her. Tannhäuser and Elisabeth praise the power of love. Wolfram, in the background, reveals his love for Elisabeth, lamenting his hopelessness. Hermann opens the song contest, instructing the singers to sing of the nature of love. Wolfram sings of a beautiful fountain that is the source of purest love. Tannhäuser responds to Wolfram's song, admitting that the fountain of which Wolfram speaks brings about wild longing in him. Walter sings next, claiming that Tannhäuser has misunderstood the true nature of the fountain, which is chastity itself. Tannhäuser responds in disagreement with Walter, claiming that if chastity were the noblest of human love, then the human race would wither away. (Walter's song and Tannhäuser's preceding response to Wolfram were omitted from the Paris version.) Biterolf sings of love's power to inspire man to take up arms in defense of it and woman's honor. Tannhäuser mocks Biterolf, claiming that the love he describes, so far removed from human pleasure, is not worth strife. Wolfram sings a paean to pure, holy love, in response to which Tannhäuser sings of the fleshly pleasures of love, inviting all who have never experienced them to accompany him to the Venusberg. Horror descends upon the Hall of Song. Elisabeth is the sole noble lady who does not flee. Taking up arms, Hermann and his minstrels and knights disavow their allegiance to Tannhäuser. Elisabeth intervenes, begging for Tannhäuser's salvation. At Hermann's instruction Tannhäuser sets forth for Rome, joining the band of young pilgrims seeking absolution from the Pope.

Act Three. Several months later, the pilgrims, their sins forgiven, return to the Wartburg. Elisabeth seeks Tannhäuser among the pilgrims returning from Rome; despondent, she sings a prayer for the Virgin to receive her soul and departs. Wolfram, who has followed her, sings his Hymn to the Evening Star to guide her. Tannhäuser finally appears after nightfall. The Pope having refused his supplication, Tannhäuser tells Wolfram that he wishes to return to the Venusberg and invokes the aid of the love goddess herself to show him the way. Venus appears, forgiving Tannhäuser's earlier pridefulness. Wolfram struggles to keep Tannhäuser from joining Venus by telling him that he has been redeemed through Elisabeth. Venus vanishes, defeated, as Elisabeth's funeral procession approaches. Tannhäuser dies upon Elisabeth's body and morning illuminates the scene of pilgrims and minstrels as a chorus of young pilgrims sing praises to the redeeming God. *—Jennifer Hambrick*

Recommended:

- ○ **Tannhäuser** / Solti (cond.), Ludwig, Kollo, Equiluz, Hollweg, Dernesch / 2002 / Decca 470810
- ○ **Tannhäuser** / Konwitschny (cond.), Grummer, Hopf, Frick, Fischer-Dieskau, Wunderlich / 1990 / EMI 63214

Tristan und Isolde (1857–1859)

Wagner's stated intention to write an opera based on the legend of Tristan and Isold, of whom he had read in the thirteenth century narrative poem by Gottfried von Strassburg, first appears in a letter to Franz Liszt of December 16, 1854. The earliest musical sketches date from December 1856, by which date Wagner had already completed the text for *Der Ring des Nibelungen*, as well as the music for *Das Rheingold* and *Die Walküre*, and through Act Two of *Siegfried*. Wagner had also completed three of his most important writings on the aesthetics of drama.

The composition of *Tristan und Isolde* is entwined in a nexus of Wagner's personal and theoretical concerns. In August 1857, Wagner stopped work on the music for *Siegfried*, in order to set to work full time on *Tristan* because, as stated in his 1860 essay *The Music of the Future*, he wanted to compose an opera of more modest scale with a chance of being produced. The music-drama was completed in Lucerne in March 1859. Wagner's had also composed five songs to poems by Mathilde Wesendonck, his patron's wife, with whom he had become deeply infatuated, two of which he designated as studies for *Tristan und Isolde*.

Wagner himself acknowledged that with the composition of *Tristan*, he transcended the musical and dramaturgical theories he set out in his earlier treatises. Indeed, the musical language of *Tristan* has long been acknowledged as the beginning of musical modernism. The harmonic language of *Tristan*, heaving as it does with prolonged courses of unresolved dissonances, not only enacts musically the sexual tension between the opera's two central characters, but also points to the liberation of dissonance from the constraints of tonality that Arnold Schoenberg and others in the twentieth century would champion. The Prelude to *Tristan* fully exemplifies Wagner's forward-looking approach to both harmony and the issue of musical form—or, some would say, formlessness—that operates centrally in his music-dramas. Alfred Lorenz argued in his 1924 study, *The Musical Form of Richard Wagner*'s "Tristan und Isolde", that the opera's prelude and three acts consist of large-scale Bogen ("arch," e.g., ABA; Prelude-Act One, and Act Two) and Bar (e.g., AAB; Act Three) forms, and that the entire opera-prelude and all acts combined falls into a giant Bogen form. In 2000, Robert Bailey argued that the form of the Prelude to *Tristan* can be understood to unfold in cycles of repeating phrase units. The Prelude also unfolds Wagner's Leitmotif technique, in which instrumental music introduces central motives which correspond with characters and ideas. Wagner seems to have explored the implications of one of *Tristan*'s central Leitmotif—that consisting of four ascending chromatic pitches and introduced by the oboe in the opening measures of the Prelude—in his song "Im Treibhaus," which was one of the five Wesendonck songs. Additionally, a strong connection exists between the music of the Act Two love scene of *Tristan* and that of another study for *Tristan*, Wagner's earlier Wesendonck song, "Träume." *—Jennifer Hambrick*

Synopsis:

Act One. Tristan's ship is bringing Isolde from Ireland to Cornwall. A young sailor sings of an Irish maiden he left behind ("Westwarts schweift der Blick"), and Isolde fumes, thinking it an insult. She watches Tristan standing in the stern and tells her maid Brangäne to summon him. Tristan courteously refuses, but his servant Kurwenal laughs at the thought that Tristan would obey her summons and mocks her by retelling the story of Tristan's killing the Irish champion Morold, Isolde's fiancé, and sending his head back instead of the demanded tribute. When Brangäne reports this to Isolde, Isolde launches her narrative and curse ("Wie lachend sie"). Tristan was wounded in the fight with Morold and knowing her gift for healing, came to her, calling himself Tantris. She recognized Tristan's sword from a fragment still embedded in Morold's head and raised it to kill him, but when she looked in his eyes, she was unable to. He repaid this by returning to demand her as a bride for his aged uncle Mark. Brangäne tries to comfort her by reminding Isolde that she has love potions from her mother, but Isolde prepares a poison. Kurwenal gruffly orders the women to prepare for landing, but she insists on seeing Tristan first. She bids Brangäne farewell, telling her to bring her last greetings home. Tristan enters and greets her courteously. She reminds him of his deception, and he offers her his sword again. She ironically declines, saying she will drink a cup of peace with her husband's nephew and signals to Brangäne to bring the potion. Brangäne brings a cup forward and Tristan, feeling a sudden premonition, nearly drinks it all, but she seizes it from his hand and finishes it. They immediately embrace in ecstasy as Brangäne is horrified at the results of her rash action, substituting the love potion for the poison. They are only partially brought back to reality by the shouts announcing the ship's landing.

Act Two. The act takes place at night in Mark's castle's garden. Isolde and Brangäne listen to the sounds of horns from Mark's hunting party, receding into the distance. Brangäne tries to warn Isolde that she suspects the knight Melot, jealous of Tristan's position, has set a trap, but Isolde impatiently tells her to extinguish the torch, a signal to Tristan to come. Brangäne again laments her substitution of the love potion, but Isolde tells her it was the power of love, and when Brangäne hesitates, extinguishes the torch itself. Tristan rushes into her arms ("Isolde! Geliebte!") and they sing of the day that keeps them apart and the darkness that joins them. They imagine fusing into one being ("O sink hernieder, Nacht der Liebe"). Brangäne, keeping watch, sings from the tower. The duet is cut short by Mark's return; Melot has set a trap. Mark sadly asks how his beloved Tristan could betray him so ("Mir dies?"), and Tristan responds that he cannot answer ("O Konig, das kann ich dir nicht sagen"). He asks Isolde if she will follow him into eternal night and at her assent, kisses her on the brow. Melot attacks him and Tristan lets himself be wounded and falls to the ground.

Act Three. In his castle in Brittany, Tristan lies unconscious under a tree as Kurwenal watches over him. Kurwenal asks a shepherd to change his melancholy song to a joyful one if he sees the ship bringing Isolde. Tristan revives and asks where he is, and Kurwenal tells him that he carried him to his home. Tristan thanks him with grateful affection for his loyalty and sings that he and Isolde are still held in day, but will be united in night. At Kurwenal's telling him that Isolde is coming, he deliriously imagines that he sees her. He then relives moments from his childhood and the deaths of his parents. Reflecting on all his sufferings, he curses the love potion and falls back. Kurwenal thinks he is dead, but detects signs of life, and Tristan again imagines Isolde approaching ("Wie sie selig"). The shepherd's tune changes, and Kurwenal runs to bring Isolde in. Tristan feverishly tears the bandage from his wound and laughs at the sight of his blood. Isolde enters, and he sinks dying in her arms, to her agonized disbelief. The shepherd says another ship is arriving, and he and Kurwenal barricade the door. When Melot appears, Kurwenal strikes him dead, and not listening to Brangäne or Mark, furiously attacks. Wounded, he drags himself back to Tristan and dies. Mark, whom Brangäne had told everything, is aghast; he had come to unite Tristan and Isolde, but instead faces these needless deaths. Isolde sings the Liebestod (Lovedeath) ("Mild und leise"), imagining Tristan smiling at her and being eternally united to him, and slowly falls onto his body, dead. *—Ann Feeney*

Recommended:

○ **Tristan und Isolde** / Furtwängler (cond.), Flagstad, Suthaus, Thebom, Fischer-Dieskau, Schock, Greindl / 2001 / EMI 67626

○ **Tristan und Isolde** / Kleiber (cond.), Price, Kollo, Fassbaender, Fischer-Dieskau, Moll / DG 413315

○ **Tristan und Isolde** / Böhm (cond.), Nilsson, Windgassen, Ludwig, Talvela, Waechter, Schreier / 1997 / DG 449772

○ **Tristan und Isolde** / Bernstein (cond.), Hofmann, Behrens, Minton, Weikl, Zednik, Moser / 1993 / Philips 438241

Die Walküre (The Valkyrie) (1854–1856)

Of the four episodes of *Der Ring des Nibelungen, Die Walküre* is most often performed separately, and arguably may be Wagner's best-loved work. The source of this affection is certainly Wagner's sensitive depictions of Siegmund and Sieglinde's love, and the father-daughter relationship of Wotan and Brünnhilde. The work was first criticized for Siegmund and Sieglinde's incestuous love, but Wagner made them appealing, rendered their story with tenderness, and bestowed on them some of his most glorious music. In *Die Walküre*, Wagner achieved equality of music and words with flexible ease. Act I, in particular, is a masterpiece of rhapsodic melody joined to a tight plan of steadily rising tension released in successive climaxes as the two are drawn to each other and reveal their pasts.

Act Two, Scene Two has one of the work's epic narrations ("Als junger Liebe Lust mir verblich"), as Wotan confesses his dilemma to his daughter Brünnhilde. These narrations in Wagner's dramas provide an opportunity to stop and reflect on events and to see them from the perspective of other characters. The device also allows Wagner to bring Leitmotifs strongly into play to represent the relationships of different characters, objects and ideas through their transformation, and thus he furnishes some of the most powerful psychological moments in the drama. As Wotan recalls the theft of the gold, the building of Valhalla, and the ring, each of their leitmotifs are heard; the motifs of the curse and the sword join the texture, and their accumulation drives the narration to its climax as Wotan confesses to his horrified daughter that he only desires one thing—"das Ende, das Ende."

Act Three opens with the well known "Ride of the Valkyries," in which Wotan's daughters, the Valkyries, assemble on their mountaintop after scouting a battlefield for dead warriors. Listeners acquainted with only the concert version may be surprised to hear the eight voices of the Valkyries over the orchestral texure, and one can understand the tremendous impact originally made in the theater by this curtain-raiser. In Wagner's Bayreuth theater, with the orchestra under the stage, the voices are much more prominent.

The opera concludes with Wotan's impressive and moving farewell to Brünnhilde, as he leaves her to sleep, surrounded by a ring of fire. Much of this episode's material is new and unique, including the powerful melody with which Wotan exclaims his farewell; but it is punctuated by important motives such as Loge's fire, and introduces ones that will be important later in the drama, such as the sleep motive (closely related to Erda's characteristic music) and that of the downfall of the gods. The orchestral texture here is rich and full, with brass supporting Wotan's song, and a sweeping countermelody in unison cellos. Wotan's allusion to one "who does not fear the point of my spear," is set to the Wälsung motive, and strongly echoed in the brass, while rippling harps accompany a lilting lullaby-like motive in the upper woodwinds. *—Theresa Muir*

Synopsis:

Act One. Siegmund staggers into Hunding's hut, gasping that he must rest, and collapses. Sieglinde enters and bends over him, and when he recovers, gives him water. He asks who she is, and she says that she and the house belong to Hunding. He explains that his sword and shield were broken and he is fleeing his enemies. When she invites him to stay to rest, he says that he will only bring misfortune, and she responds that misfortune itself lives in the house. Hunding enters and though gruffly, follows the rule of hospitality and offers him food and shelter. He asks his guest's story, and Siegmund says that his name is Wehwalt (Woeful), and he is one of the Walsungs. He, his parents, and his twin sister lived in the woods, but one day he and his father came back from hunting to find the house burnt, his mother killed, and his sister gone. After that, his father died in battle. He himself had recently tried to save a woman from a forced marriage, but in the battle, he was forced to flee, weaponless. Hunding exclaims that he is one of the family that Siegmund attacked, and though tonight he may claim shelter, tomorrow he will have to fight. He orders Sieglinde to prepare his night drink and follow him. She silently tries to draw Siegmund's attention to the sword embedded in a tree trunk, but he doesn't notice. Siegmund, alone, desperately remembers that his father promised him a sword in his time of need, but now he has none ("Ein Schwert verhiess mir"). He then thinks about how beautiful Sieglinde is, and she returns. She says she drugged Hunding's drink and describes how she was kidnapped and forced to marry him. At the wedding feast, a one-eyed stranger appeared and thrust a sword into the tree, saying it would belong to the man who could remove it. None of the guests could, and she hopes the man who can will avenge her. The doors mysteriously swing open, flooding the room with moonlight. Siegmund sings blissfully of the beautiful spring night that has vanquished winter's storms ("Wintersturme"), and she responds that he is the spring itself ("Du bist der Lenz"). They recognize one another as the lost twin, and Siegmund realizes their father was the mysterious guest. She now names him Siegmund (guardian of victory), and he names the sword "Nothung," (Needful), draws it from the tree, and they rush out together.

Act Two. Wotan orders Brunhilde to gather the Valkyries, his warrior daughters by Erda, who gather the bodies of heroes after battle and restore them to life in Valhalla, to assist Siegmund, and she sings her famous battle cry "Hojotoho!" but quickly departs as Fricka approaches. Fricka demands that he instead aid Hunding, who demanded her help to punish the adulterous pair Siegmund and Sieglinde, and reminding Wotan his power rests on his laws, forces an increasingly desperate Wotan to agree. Brunhilde returns and Wotan pours out the story of how he had fathered Siegmund to break the ring's curse, but now must kill him. He bitterly foresees the doom of the gods ("O heilige Schmach... Als junger Liebe"), which he now welcomes. Brunhilde pleads for Siegmund, arousing Wotan's anger, and he orders her to obey and leaves. Siegmund and Sieglinde come in, exhausted. She begs Siegmund to leave her to die, and imagines his being beset by Hunding's dogs and faints. He cradles her in his arms. Brunhilde emerges, calling to him ("Siegmund, sich' auf mich"), and tells him he must die, but promises him glory in Valhalla. He asks if Sieglinde may accompany him, and when she says she cannot, he refuses to go. She tells him he is doomed to die, and he vows to kill Sieglinde and then himself. Moved, she promises to help him. When he hears Hunding's horn, Siegmund goes to fight him, but just as he is about to strike a killing blow, Wotan shatters Nothung with his spear, and Hunding kills the defenseless Siegmund. Brunhilde flees with Sieglinde and the shattered sword. Wotan looks at his dead son and then with a gesture, kills Hunding, telling him to go to Fricka. In a rage, he vows to punish the disobedient Brunhilde.

Act Three. The act opens with the Ride of the Valkyries, who enter with the bodies of heroes who died in battle, to be brought to life again in Valhalla. They are amazed when Brunhilde enters with Sieglinde, and she begs for their help, which they refuse, afraid of Wotan, but they do tell Sieglinde to flee to a place near Fafner's cave, where Wotan never goes. Brunhilde gives her the shattered sword and tells her that she is bearing Siegmund's child, who will be the hero Siegfried. She exclaims in wonder ("O herstes Wunder") and leaves. Wotan enters and despite her sisters' pleas, takes her Valkyrie powers away from her, saying she will be made to sleep until any man finds and claims her. He orders her sisters never to see her again, under pain of the same fate. They flee in dismay and she falls at his feet. She pleads that she was obeying his will, if not his orders, reminding him of his love for Siegmund, and he agrees to protect her with a ring of fire so only the bravest hero may awaken her. He sadly bids her farewell ("Leb' wohl, du kuhnes, herrliches Kind") and kisses her eyes, beginning the spell. He puts her in her armor and summons Loge to create the fire, then declares that no man who fears his spear may enter the flames, and leaves. *—Ann Feeney*

Recommended:

○ **Die Walküre** / Solti (cond.), Nilsson, Hotter, Ludwig, Crespin, Frick, Watts, Fassbaender / London 455559

○ **Die Walküre** / Levine (cond.), Norman, Morris, Ludwig, Moll, Behrens, Lakes, Runkel / DG 423389

○ **Der Ring des Nibelungen** / Furtwängler (cond.), Frick, Konetzni, Frantz, Malaniuk, Cavelti, Schmedes / 1990 / EMI 67123

ORCHESTRAL

Siegfried Idyll, for small orchestra in E major (1870)

The full title on the original manuscript of Wagner's *Siegfried Idyll* reads, "Tribschen-Idyll, with Fidi-Birdsong and Orange Sunrise, presented as a symphonic birthday greeting to his Cosima by her Richard, 1870." The "Siegfried" in the title does not refer to the composer's opera of the same name, as is often supposed, but to his infant son, whose pet name was "Fidi." The "orange sunrise" refers to the color of Cosima's bedroom wallpaper, which brightly reflected the morning light. Though the work is sometimes heard in an arrangement for full orchestra, Wagner originally wrote it for an ensemble of 15 players. Having prepared and rehearsed the work in secret, Wagner gathered his small orchestra on the stairway on Christmas morning, 1870, and awakened Cosima with its first performance (Cosima's birthday was December 24; the Wagner family celebrated that day and the Christmas holiday together). Afterward, Wagner and Cosima's five children presented her with the score.

As is reflected in the uncharacteristically (for Wagner) modest scoring, the *Siegfried Idyll* is a particularly intimate work, meant to acknowledge and celebrate the year that Wagner and Cosima could finally legitimize their union. Several stressful years had passed since Cosima had left her first husband, the conductor Hans von Bülow, in 1866. The divorce was finalized at last in 1870, and in August of that year Cosima and Wagner wed.

Wagner wrote *Siegfried Idyll* while he was occupied with the completing and intial staging of *Der Ring des Nibelungen.* The music for *Siegfried* (1856–71), the third part of the cycle, had caused the composer great difficulty; he had set it aside in frustration in 1857, returning to it only in 1869. Wagner borrowed *Siegfried Idyll's* principal themes from *Siegfried* and *Die Walküre* (1854–56), where they have specific meanings within the cycle's system of leitmotives. Within the context in *Siegfried Idyll,* however, these themes are take on a more general nature as expressions of triumphant love and affection. Wagner had never intended to publish the work, but financial problems forced him to make it public in 1877. *—Theresa Muir*

Recommended:

- ○ **Wagner: Orchestral Music** / Klemperer (cond.), London PO / 2002 / EMI 67896
- ○ **Wagner: Tannhäuser; Siegfried-Idyll; Tristan und Isolde** / Karajan (cond.), Vienna PO / 1988 / DG 423613
- ○ **Glenn Gould Conducts & Plays Richard Wagner** / Gould (cond.), Toronto SO / 1994 / Sony 52650

VOCAL

Wesendonk Lieder (1857–1858)

Richard Wagner's settings of Mathilde Wesendonck's *Fünf Gedichte,* which date from November 1857 to May 1858, are not merely by-products of the composer's predilection for uniting words and music; they are documentation of an intimate friendship between the married poet, whose husband more than once kept the financial wolf from Wagner's door, and the composer. The *Wesendonk-Lieder* have their origins in Wagner's period of intense work on *Tristan und Isolde* (1857–60). Indeed, Wagner designated two of the *Wesendonk-Lieder,* "Im Treibhaus" and "Träume," as "studies" for *Tristan.* Although the exact nature of the Wagner-Wesendonk friendship will likely remain unclear, it is tempting, especially in view of Wagner's usual romantic modus operandi, to view the love story of *Tristan* and the serenely metaphysical textual and musical union in the *Wesendonk-Lieder* as reflections of a real-life love story.

Wagner's sensitivity to Wesendonk's poetry manifests itself musically in symbolic harmonic progressions, progressive tonality, and mimetic text-painting. In "Der Engel," the piano accompaniment depicts the contrast between heavenly angels and earthly cares: series of ascending arpeggiated chords reach upwards at the mention of angels, and repeated eighth note chords plod earth bound when the singer sings of fear, worry, and floods of tears. The plagal harmonic gesture Wagner weaves into the harmonic fabric of the song, and which he states most clearly in the piano postlude, underscores the religious implications of the idea of heavenly redemption in Wesendonk's text. If the imagery of "Der Engel" suggests infinity, in "Stehe still!" time, always in motion, is the "measure of eternity." Wagner's piano writing appeals to the tradition of work-music in the vein of Schubert's *Gretchen am Spinnrade,* in which driving rhythmic activity depicts the toils of labor. The large-scale tonal shift from C minor to C major underscores the mood shift in the text: joy, not time, is measured when two souls unite. The mutual understanding of the united souls transcends words. Wagner composes music that represents silence by gradually reducing the activity of the piano part to a recitative texture of sustained chords beneath speech-like declamation. A greenhouse is the backdrop for "Im Treibhaus," in which Wesendonk paints the image of palm branches reaching longingly into thin air only to grasp a desolate emptiness. One recognizes the melodic motive that permeates this song in even the opening measures of *Tristan.* Wagner's skill as tone poet is also apparent in his use of tremolo in the piano part to depict the whispering that "anxiously fills the dark room," and in his use of repeated D-E flat dyads to represent drops of water falling on leaves. In "Schmerzen," the sorrows and joys of life are allegorized in the image of the daily setting and rising of the sun. Again, a large-scale shift from C minor to C major tracks the psychological progression from sorrow to bliss: indeed, the text tells us that sorrow is the source of joy. Wagner divides the two eight-line sections of text in his setting by a brief fanfare gesture—an arpeggiated B flat major triad, which returns, transposed to the final tonic C major, to close the song. In a letter of September 28, 1861, to Mathilde Wesendonck, Wagner wrote that his musical setting of "Träume" was "finer than all I have made!" He indicates that this song was the source of the night scene from the second act of *Tristan.* Indeed, the kinship is unmistakable. The descending whole-tone motive that hovers above ethereal harmonies is a sigh released as one abandons worldly concerns in spirit-redeeming dreams before taking permanent leave through death. The intersection of death and otherworldly bliss will resound most famously in *Tristan.* *—Jennifer Hambrick*

Recommended:

- ○ **Mahler & Wagner: Orchestral Song Cycles** / Flagstad, Knappertsbusch (cond.), Vienna PO / 2001 / Decca 468486
- ○ **Strauss: Four Last Songs; Wagner: Wesendonck-Lieder** / Norman, Davis (cond.), London SO / 2001 / Philips 464742

John Wallace

b. May 14, 1949, Methihil, Fife, Scotland
Trumpeter

Scottish trumpeter John Wallace studied at King's College, Cambridge (1967–70), the Royal Academy of Music (1970–72), and York University (1972–74). His principal teachers included Alan Bush and David Blake. From 1976 until 1995, Wallace was principal trumpeter with the Philharmonia Orchestra and in 1988, he joined the London Sinfonietta. In 1986, he founded the Wallace Collection, a brass ensemble of flexible instrumentation, with which he has made numerous recordings. He has given the world premieres of solo works by Tim Souster, Peter Maxwell Davies, Malcolm Arnold, Dominic Muldowney, Robert Saxton, James MacMillan, and Mark-Anthony Turnage. Wallace teaches at the Royal Academy of Music and was made an Order of the British Empire in 1995. *—Robert Adelson*

Recommended:

- ○ **Virtuoso Trumpet Concertos** / Wright (cond.), Wallace, Philharmonia, Wallace Collection / 1999 / Wallace Collection 2006
- ○ **Vivaldi Concerti; Baroque Trumpet Music** / Wallace, Wallace Collection / 1994 / Nimbus 7012

Elizabeth Wallfisch

b. Jan. 28, 1952, Melbourne, Australia
Violinist

Ever since her emergence in the early 1970s, Elizabeth Wallfisch has pursued a triple-threat career as a violinist with a range of repertory from the Baroque to the contemporary, and as a conductor/leader of various period music ensembles. She was a natural musician from early childhood and made her debut as a concerto soloist at age 12. She also performed with the Melbourne Symphony Orchestra in the final of the ABC Concerto Competition and later studied under Fredericke Grinke at the Royal Academy of Music in London, where she distinguished herself with the President's Prize and other awards. Her other early awards include the Franco Gulli Senior Prize for violin at the Accademica Chigiana at age 20 and a shared win of the Mozart Memorial Prize later that year. She distinguished herself as a Baroque specialist in 1974 when she won the prize for most outstanding performance of Bach in the Carl Flesch Competition. Wallfisch emerged as a recitalist in the mid-1970s, as well as performing as a guest soloist with various orchestras in her native Australia and in England. After establishing herself as a concert artist in England with the London Mozart Players and the Royal Liverpool Philharmonic Orchestra, Wallfisch turned her attention and skills toward the Baroque violin and began developing her reputation and technique in that highly specialized area, as a conductor and leader, as well as a soloist. Her broadcasts and early recordings led Wallfisch to found the Locatelli Trio in 1989 in collaboration with Paul Nicholson and Richard Tunnicliffe, through which she began giving recitals of Baroque music, and she has regularly led the Orchestra of the Age of Enlightenment. Wallfisch's most notable recordings have been in conjunction with the latter group, with which she has done the complete violin concerto works of Johann Sebastian Bach and Franz Josef Haydn. She has also performed the works of C.P.E. Bach, J.M. Kraus, and Josef Myslivecek, and such English composers as Thomas Arne. Although most closely identified with Baroque repertory, Wallfisch has also performed such works as Johannes Brahms' *Double Concerto for Violin and Cello* and *Concerto for Violin and Orchestra.* Her repertory extends up to such late Romantics as Richard Strauss, post-Romantics including Igor Stravinsky, modernists including Dmitry Shostakovich, and to the works of contemporary Australian composers Peter Sculthorpe and Esther Rofe. Wallfisch has held academic positions, including artist-in-residence at Melbourne University, but is primarily a performing musician. Her engagements have included tours with the Hanover Band under Roy Goodman during the 2000–01 season. She is married to cellist Raphael Wallfisch, with whom she has also performed. *—Bruce Eder*

Recommended:

- ○ **Locatelli: L'Arte del Violino** / Kraemer (cond.), Wallfisch, Raglan Baroque Players / 1994 / Hyperion 66721
- ○ **Tartini: Violin Concertos** / Draemer (cond.), Wallfisch, Raglan Baroque Players / 2003 / Hyperion 67345
- ○ **Bach: Violin Concertos** / Wallfisch, MacIntosh, Bury, Beznosiuk, Orch. of the Age of Enlightenment / 1993 / Virgin 59319
- ○ **Haydn: Violin Concertos** / Wallfisch, Robson, Watkin, Warnock, Orch. of the Age of Enlightenment / 1996 / Virgin 61301
- ○ **Leclair: Sonatas II** / Wallfisch, Nicholson, Tunnicliffe / 1999 / Hyperion 67068

Bruno Walter

b. Sep. 15, 1876, Berlin, Germany, **d.** Feb. 17, 1962, Beverly Hills, CA
Conductor

Bruno Walter helped to shape the very essence of interpretive style among conductors. He was born Bruno Schlesinger to an average, middle-class Jewish family.

His talent was discovered early, and at age nine he entered the Stern Conservatory to study piano, making his debut at 13 with the Berlin Philharmonic. Impressed with Hans von Bülow's handling of the orchestra at the Bayreuth Festival, the boy decided to take up conducting. At age 17 in 1893, Schlesinger made his conducting debut with the Cologne Opera. In 1894, Schlesinger moved to Hamburg and worked under Gustav Mahler, whose influence would prove central to the development of his approach and ideals. After leaving Hamburg, the young conductor worked a succession of provincial European opera houses; in Breslau Schlesinger changed his name to Walter, Schlesinger being too common a surname in Silesia.

In 1900, Walter succeeded Schalk at the Berlin State Opera and made his first recordings, beginning a career that would stretch into the era of stereo and number in the hundreds of titles. He also conducted his first orchestral concert, the featured work being Berlioz's *Symphonie fantastique*. In 1901, Walter decided he was ready to take advantage of Mahler's open invitation to join the Vienna Court Opera as an assistant. Walter stayed in Vienna until 1913, taking Austrian citizenship in 1911. After Mahler died, Walter mounted the premieres of *Das Lied von der Erde* (Munich, 1911) and the Mahler *Ninth* (Vienna, 1912).

In 1913, Walter moved to Munich to lead the Bavarian Court Opera, and this is where his conducting career took wing. He revived the long-neglected Mozart operas, attracted worldwide attention for his careful handling of operas by Wagner and Verdi, and premiered significant new operas by Korngold and Pfitzner. Walter abruptly left Munich in 1923, embarking upon a variety of destinations, including the United States, Great Britain, Paris, Rome, and the U.S.S.R. In 1925, he helped institute the Salzburg Festival and was named musical director of the Berlin State Opera. In 1929, Walter had a falling out with the Berlin management, and departed to succeed Wilhelm Furtwängler at the *Leipzig Gewandhaus*. When the National Socialists came to power under Hitler in 1933, Bruno Walter was stripped of his post in Leipzig and took refuge in Vienna. He was a guest conductor with the Vienna State Opera and was named musical director of the Vienna Philharmonic in 1935; during this time he also frequently appeared with the Amsterdam Concertgebouw. When the Nazis took Austria without firing a shot in 1938, Walter was on the run again, this time to France and the Paris Conservatoire. His stay in France proved brief, as in 1939 Walter escaped to the United States.

Walter settled in Los Angeles, and remained based out of Southern California for the rest of his long life. While Walter's American period is most readily associated with the New York Philharmonic, he conducted a number of American orchestras in these years, especially the Los Angeles Philharmonic, but also the Minneapolis Symphony, the NBC Symphony, and at the Metropolitan Opera in New York. After the war, Walter made a number of return visits to Vienna and other European cities, and in London recorded Mahler's lieder with Kathleen Ferrier, his own favorites among his recordings. A heart attack in 1957 caused Walter to curtail his engagements, and he made his farewell appearance in Vienna in 1960 conducting Mahler's *Fourth*.

Walter's catalog of original works contains two symphonies, choral works, and a violin sonata; however, all of his endeavors as a composer were completed before 1911. *—Uncle Dave Lewis*

Recommended:

- ○ **Beethoven: Symphonies 1 & 2** / Walter (cond.), Columbia SO / 1995 / Sony 64460
- ○ **Mahler: Symphonies 1 & 2; Lieder eines fahrenden Gesellen** / Walter (cond.), Forrester, Miller, Cundari, Columbia SO, New York PO / 1994 / Sony 64447
- ○ **Mozart: Symphonies 39–41** / Walter (cond.), New York PO / 1995 / Sony 64477
- ○ **Bruno Walter** / Walter (cond.), Lehmann, Melchior, Ferrier, Jerger, Vienna PO, New York PO, Société des Concerts du Conservatoire, British SO / EMI 75133
- ○ **Walter: Maestro Generoso** / Walter (cond.), Vienna PO, Paris Conservatory Orch., NBCSO / 2000 / History 205242
- ○ **Early Electrical Recordings (1925–1931)** / Walter (cond.), etc. / 1994 / VAI Audio 1059
- ○ **Brahms: Symphonies 2 & 3** / Walter (cond.), Chicago SO / 1995 / Sony 64471
- ○ **Mahler: Das Lied von der Erde** / Walter (cond.), Ferrier, Patzak, Vienna PO / 2000 / Decca 466576

William Walton

b. Mar. 29, 1902, Oldham, Lancashire, England, **d.** Mar. 8, 1983, Ischia, Italy
Composer: Orchestral, Choral, Musical Theater, Vocal, Film Music, Chamber Music, Symphonic, Concerto

Occupying an important historical position between his better-known colleagues Ralph Vaughan Williams and Benjamin Britten, William Walton is seen by many as the first modern British composer to approach the brilliance and vitality which characterized English music during Handel's day.

Born in northwest England during the first years of the twentieth century, Walton was the son of a choirmaster, and appropriately, served as a chorister at Christ Church Cathedral at Oxford from 1912 to 1918. Studies at the University itself proved unsatisfying, and William left Oxford without a degree in 1920, relying instead upon the patronage of the Sitwell family, who had befriended the young composer. Through the influence of this affluent and well-known family, Walton was able to break into the London music scene, and by 1922 his chamber piece *Façade* had achieved some popularity with the concert-going public. A performance of his comic overture *Portsmouth Point* in Zurich in 1926, and Paul Hindemith's championing of his Viola Concerto in 1929 helped introduce Walton music into the European music scene. The famous *Belshazzar's Feast* for chorus and orchestra soon followed, and the 1930s brought with commissions from well-known musical figures, including Jascha Heifetz, who asked the composer to write him a Violin Concerto in 1939.

Walton spent much of World War II composing music for films, including *Next of Kin* and *The Foreman Went to France*. In 1948, he moved to Ischia, a small island off of Naples, and he was knighted in 1951. In 1954, after many years of effort, his grand opera *Troilus and Cressida* was produced at Covent Garden; unfortunately, the work has not received the attention it deserves. Walton composed prolifically until the end of his life, fulfilling commissions for such notables as George Szell, Gregor Piatigorsky and Mstislav Rostropovich. In 1973, he conducted a fiftieth anniversary performance of *Facade*. While never again achieving the degree of public and critical acclaim which he enjoyed before the World War II, he was nevertheless able to live comfortably on Ischia, where he died in 1983.

Although he was overshadowed in the latter half of his career by Benjamin Britten, Walton was never the old-fashioned reactionary (a frequent, but unjust, accusation). Much like his contemporaries Poulenc and Prokofiev, Walton was at heart an expressive, lyric composer who refused to subjugate this natural ability to the "modernist" tendencies that the press berated him for not embracing. His music is a sparkling synthesis of old and new, the greatest examples of which can be found in the two Symphonies (1935 and 1960), and the Viola (1929), Violin (1939) and Cello (1956) Concertos. *—Blair Johnston*

ORCHESTRAL

Crown Imperial, coronation march (1937; revised 1963)

Walton was confident when composing in the grand manner; as an admirer of Elgar's *Pomp and Circumstance* marches, he did not resent comparisons between this splendid march, written for the coronation of King George VI and Queen Elizabeth, and the older composer's popular patriotic flourishes.

The commission by the BBC called for "a symphonic march for Coronation Week," for which the composer would receive a fee of 40 guineas (about $58 at present-day exchange rates). Walton agreed enthusiastically and completed the work in a fortnight.

The march was played in Westminster Abbey immediately before the ceremony, for the entrance of Queen Mary, the Queen Mother. It must have made an impressive effect indeed in that historic setting. The royal family was popular and the British Empire still an imperial power. The broad cantabile melody exudes confidence, rising to an impressive brass climax to which even the most dedicated republican can thrill. This was no time for subtlety and introspection, and Walton's music is both majestic and imperious. *—Roy Brewer*

Recommended:

- ○ **Vaughan Williams: Symphony 8; Bax: Oboe Quintet, etc.** / Barbirolli (cond.), Halle Orch. / 2002 / BBC 4100

Orb and Scepter, coronation march (1952–1953)

As the composer of the splendid march *Crown Imperial* for the coronation of King George VI and Queen Elizabeth 18 years earlier, Walton was an obvious choice to write another for the coronation of Elizabeth II in 1953. The title incorporates the two symbols of royal power carried by the Queen at her coronation. The composer wanted to dedicate it to the Elizabeth II, but this was an unusual request since it had been granted on only four royal occasions in the preceding 15 years. Following a formal approach by the Arts Council of Great Britain, Her Majesty accepted.

The march formed part of the music played before the ceremony in Westminster Abbey on June 2, and was repeated five days later under the baton of Sir John Barbirolli at the Royal Festival Hall, when the music critic of the *London Times* reported "It makes a joyful noise in the march proper, and it is in the trio that majesty comes to the fore with a sweeping diatonic tune in C major reminiscent of Parry as well as Elgar."

A *Coronation Te Deum*, which Walton wrote at the request of Sir William McKie, director of music for the Coronation Service (which Walton and his wife attended at the invitation of the Earl Marshal of England, the Duke of Gloucester), was also performed during the Abbey ceremony.

There is no doubt that Walton relished writing stirring music, and did so brilliantly. The march is more complex than *Crown Imperial*, yet has an engaging and festive freshness. The opening two-bar fanfare is followed by a trio section and that "sweeping" tune in C major restated in an elaborate coda and ends with a final brass fanfare. More manageable arrangements of this large and rhythmically complex score include one for military band, one for organ, one for small orchestra by

McKie, and two by Roy Douglas, one for piano and one for small orchestra, all made in 1953. *—Roy Brewer*

Recommended:

○ **Walton: Symphony 1; Belshazzar's Feast; Orchestral Works** / Willcocks (cond.), London PO / 1999 / Chandos 2410

Scapino, comedy overture (1940; revised 1950)

William Walton's *Scapino: A Comedy Overture* took as its inspiration a series of engravings from 1622 by Jacques Callot of the *Balli di sfessania*—specifically Callot's depiction of the jaunty and mischievous Scapino, a character related to those of the *commedia dell'arte*. This was not the first time Walton had been inspired by a scene from the visual arts; his *Portsmouth Point Overture*, a work for orchestra composed in 1925 when the composer was 23, emerged as a musical reflection on a famous caricature by Thomas Rowlandson (1756–1827) of the busy docks of Portsmouth. In that earlier work, as in the *Scapino Overture*, Walton's score stands as more of a character study than a pictorialization; furthermore, by the time he composed *Scapino*, Walton's sense of expressive balance had been refined and his orchestrational and figurational palette had been expanded, resulting in a work with the same kind of energy and programmatic engagement as the *Portsmouth Point Overture*, but one whose contrasting sections and structural play form a more cohesive musical character.

Callot's Scapino, the hero of Molière's *Les Fourberies de Scapin* and a perhaps a distant cousin to the Figaro character archetype, is a kind of henchman or servant—a sneaky sidekick to the *commedia's* more familiar Harlequin. His role was to arrange for his master's amorous adventures—in fact, as several writers have observed, his name suggests an etymological connection to the word "escapade." In commenting on Walton's musical realization of the character, scholar David Drew describes Scapino as "something between Leporello and Till Eulenspiegel." Certainly, his meddling mirth finds voice in the opening gesture of the piece, a rather saucy trumpet fanfare made of dotted rhythms and melodic leaps, set against snickeringly dissonant staccato chords in the strings. His role as romantic go-between is expressed by the stepwise melodic contours and espressivo articulation of a subsequent theme, given over to the viola and English horn. Such recombinations of moods characterize the rest of the piece—giocoso dotted figures appear intermittently, most prominently in ostentatious brass exclamations, while at one point the second theme from the beginning (heard originally in the viola and English horn) is stretched durationally and rendered with guitarlike strummings in the strings, who are instructed to play their parts come una serenata ("As a serenade").

Scapino was composed on commission from Frederick Stock and the Chicago Symphony on the occasion of the group's 50th anniversary, and received its world premiere by that ensemble, conducted by Stock, in 1941. As it originally appeared, the score called for triple winds and a brass section augmented by coronets. Walton later withdrew this arrangement, and in 1951 published the version for standard orchestral forces that appears on programs and recordings today. *—Jeremy Grimshaw*

Recommended:

○ **Walton: Symphonies, Concertos & Overtures** / Previn (cond.), London SO / 1999 / Angel 73371

CHORAL

Belshazzar's Feast, for baritone, double chorus & orchestra (1930–1931; revised 1931)

In 1929, Walton received the first commission ever offered by the BBC to a British composer, for a work "scored for small chorus, small orchestra not exceeding fifteen [players], and soloist." For the work's subject, Walton chose the biblical fall of Belshazzar (better known as Nebuchadnezzar, King of Babylon, the despotic conqueror of Jerusalem), as dramatized by his friend and benefactor, Sir Osbert Sitwell. By the end of 1930, a member of the BBC's music staff nervously reported that Walton's effort had "grown to such proportions that it cannot be considered a work specially written for broadcasting."

Nevertheless, the composer completed it, and on a grand scale, including two brass bands. Before the premiere in October 1931, the chorus called a strike, saying that the work was impossibly difficult to perform. The composer deflected the complaint thus: "I *know* it is difficult... but naturally it isn't written for a church choir." The sweep and drama of the work, which was described by the critic Compton Mackenzie as "like a great explosive sunset," has since proved irresistible to audiences. The eminent British conductor Henry Wood considered it "truly marvelous, like the world coming to an end."

The scene is set with a description of the material wealth of Babylon (a substantial section which Thomas Beecham irreverently called "the shopping list"), including "the souls of men." The raw energy as the oppressors praise their gods of silver, brass, gold and other precious possessions is followed by a chorus of profound lamentation as the Israelites contemplate their fate and affirm their belief in God. As the feasting at Belshazzar's palace becomes wilder and more abandoned, a mysterious Hebrew message appears on the wall: "mene mene tekel uparsin" (You have been weighed in the balance and found wanting). Nemesis is swift: "that night was the king Belshazzar slain and his kingdom divided."

Walton worte music in the grand manner with utmost confidence, and his orchestration, brilliant and evocative, stands in sharp contrast to that of the works that, from Handel onward, formed the major part of the English choral tradition. *—Roy Brewer*

Recommended:

○ **Walton: Belshazzar's Feast; Portsmouth Point; Scapino; Symphony 2** / Previn (cond.), Shirley-Quirk, London SO & Chorus / 2001 / EMI 4924029

MUSICAL THEATER

Façade, for reciter & ensemble (1922–1977)

Just as with Weill in Weimar and Milhaud in France, the interwar years in England saw the emergence of an aesthetic characterized by a surreal detachment and alienation—not only between audience and work, but between elements of works themselves. In the early 1920s, poet Edith Sitwell noticed trends towards abstraction in sculpture and painting, and sought to pursue similar ideas in English verse. As her brother Osbert described, Edith "had lately—in 1920 and 21—written various dance measures and abstract poems of transcendent technical skill.... A young musician, William Walton, was then sharing a house with us, and we decided together that he should set the poems to music, and that they should be presented in as abstract a manner as possible."

So abstract was the product of their collaboration, in fact, that the premiere given on June 12, 1923, under the title *Façade*, places it within that elite canon of musical works that provoked their opening-night audiences to riot. Osbert again recalls the scene: "...seldom has there been such an outburst of critical rage and hysteria in an audience.... At the end my sister was warned not to leave the shelter of her dressing room until the crowd had dispersed, or she might meet with injury."

Perhaps most challenging were Sitwell's nonsensical texts, which wander with semantic abandon through fields of disconnected imagery and syntactical dead ends. Anything serves as linguistic glue here: meaning, rhyme, assonance, association. This kind of poetry seems to sit just this side of the fence, on the other side of which Hugo Ball's indecipherable Dadaist syllable collections reside. By retaining words and stringing them together in such a sonorous way, Sitwell lends the work a rather distinct level of meaning—or perhaps more accurately, a unique level of meaninglessness. All the components of speech are there, and in the right positions (subjects, objects, modifiers, etc.) but they combine into a delightfully dysfunctional train of thought.

That description is apt when applied to the music as well. Just as the ambiguity of the text subverts its own construction, Walton's music occupies a strange place of parody and allusion: most of the numerous pieces (ranging in number from ten to thirty, depending on which version of the work is performed) are caricatures of geographically-specific styles, as reflected in titles like "Swiss Yodelling Song," "Scotch Rhapsody," "Noche Espagnole," and "Tango-Pasodoble." The various chamber combinations within the ensemble are purposely inelegant, with extroverted fanfare and *oompah*. Within the context of Walton's score, one can almost think of the reciter's part as yet another instrument, one separated from the others only by the articulatory breadth of speech. The words are delivered in a kind of self-conscious public-address monotone, but in strict and often lively rhythm. The speaker is hidden from the audience, and speaks through a megaphone placed in the mouth of a large and rather grotesque face painted on a scrim.

Walton extracted an orchestral suite from *Façade* in 1926, and then another in 1938. In 1977, he produced a sequel, *Façade II*, which returned to the original chamber ensemble and narration format. Also a setting of Edith Sitwell's poetry, this second suite has seen performances by such esteemed performers of new music as Peter Pears and Cathy Berberian, to whom it is dedicated. *—Jeremy Grimshaw*

Recommended:

○ **Walton: Façade 1 & 2 (complete)** / Hickox (cond.), S. Walton, Baker, City of London Sinfonia / 1990 / Chandos 8869

○ **Walton: Façade, Books I & II** / Silverstein (cond.), Redgrave, Lincoln Center Chamber Music Society / 1997 / Arabesque 6699

VOCAL

Anon in Love, song cycle for tenor & guitar or orchestra (1959)

Walton's *Anon in Love* (1959) comprises nine settings of anonymous sixteenth- and seventeenth century lyrics on the subject of "man in love." While linked by this central theme, the songs are otherwise contrasting in style and treatment. Walton's choice of a guitar accompaniment is typical of his penchant for exploring new sonorities; at the time, certainly, the vocal/guitar combination was rarely used by composers. From a technical standpoint, the songs are challenging for singer and guitarist alike.

The first three settings have an Elizabethan flavor, recalling the word painting and decorous lyrics of many sixteenth century English madrigals. In the first, "Fain would I change that note," a lute air from Hume's *Musicall Humors* (1605), the voice ranges over an octave and a half, with bright harmonics on the guitar. In the second, "Stay sweet love" from John Farmer's first set of madrigals (1599), the guitar part is marked by graceful repeated sixteenth note chords and descending arpeggios. In the third song, "Lady, when I behold the roses sprouting," from Wilbye's first book of madrigals (1598), the range of the voice grows in wider and wider leaps to eventually encompass a twelfth, complemented by a pleasingly arpeggiated guitar accompaniment.

The remaining three songs strike an earthier note. "My love in her attire" and "I gave her cakes and ale" reflect the saucy character of many English popular songs. The latter is marked by lively commentary from the guitar, with brilliant chords, ornamentation, and swift arpeggios. The final song, "To couple is a custom," has a diatonic, four-square Medieval character, yet is the most genuinely Romantic of the whole cycle. In the last verse the words "Come fiddler scrape the crowd" refer not to the fiddle but the Welsh crwth, a bowed lyre that preceded the more aristocratic viol. *—Roy Brewer*

Recommended:

○ **Walton: Violin Sonata; Piano Quartet; Anon in Love** / Ainsley, Ogden / Hyperion 67340

○ **Music For Voice & Guitar** / Pears, Bream / 1993 / RCA 902661601

FILM MUSIC

Hamlet (1947)

The English composer William Walton (1902–1983) was not only a distinguished composer of opera, oratorios, symphonies, and chamber music, he was arguably England's greatest film composer of the middle years of the twentieth century. Starting with *Escape Me Never* (1934) and concluding with *The Sisters* (1970), Walton wrote the scores for 14 films.

The undoubted climax of his film work was the series of scores he wrote for Laurence Olivier's three Shakespeare films, *Henry V* (1943–1944), *Hamlet* (1947), and *Richard III* (1955). Of these, the music from *Hamlet* is, except for the "Funeral March," the least frequently heard in the concert hall. However, this is primarily because Walton's music for *Hamlet* is the most fully integrated into the action of the film and he thus declined to form it into a separate concert suite. Nevertheless, the music is fits superbly with the action of the film, tracing its dramatic and psychological elements with lyrical themes and brilliant scoring. *—James Leonard*

Recommended:

○ **Walton: Film Music Vol. 1** / Marriner (cond.), Gielgud, Academy of St. Martin-in-the-Fields / 1990 / Chandos 8842

Henry V (1943–1944)

Walton's earliest film scores were modest affairs, mainly composed for public information and propaganda shorts made by the wartime Ministry of Information and the BBC. In 1943, at the height of World War II, a production of Shakespeare's *Henry V* was conceived in a collaboration between the British filmmaker Dallas Bower, the actor Laurence Olivier and the producer Filippo de Giudice. Walton was commissioned to write the music, which turned out to be far from "incidental." The composer planned almost everything with Olivier, who, when the film was released in 1944, said that the music had "more guts, more spunk, more attack, more venom than one would have thought was hidden in Walton's personality."

The score subtly captures the contrast between the troubled times of Henry V and the relative calm of the early Elizabethan period. The opening scenes at Shakespeare's Globe Theatre contain evocative, but never imitative, echoes of Elizabethan theater music. In some parts plainchant is used to create an atmosphere, but in general the style is very much of the twentieth century. A beautiful Passacaglia accompanies the death of Falstaff, and Mistress Quickly sings a sad song of farewell to the old knight. Throughout the film, the clichés so often associated with screen epics are absent. The French scenes use an adaptation of an Auvergne song called "Baliëro," and the Battle of Agincourt is a tour de force combining natural noises with a truly terrifying sound picture of the onslaught. Even when the music is at its most intense, Shakespeare's text is always given room to reach its full stature. Unusually, the battle music was written before the shooting of the film, and the action was tailored to fit it. The Duke of Burgundy's despairing speech after the battle is accompanied by pastoral music.

Such characteristic music stands easily on its own merits. A suite containing concert versions of four numbers appeared in 1945, another was put together by the conductor Malcolm Sargent, and a third was arranged by Muir Matheson (who conducted the film score) for the 1964 Shakespeare birthday celebrations. All are representative of the high standard of the original pieces, and all contain the overture "The Globe Playhouse," "The Death of Falstaff," the song "Touch her Soft Lips and Part," and the "Agincourt Song."

It may fairly be said that no film score has earned such praise and enjoyed such durability; indeed, Lord Olivier once remarked in a radio interview, "I have always said that if it wasn't for the music *Henry V* would not have been the success that it was." *—Roy Brewer*

Recommended:

○ **Walton: Film Music Vol. 3** / Marriner (cond.), Plummer, Academy of St. Martin-in-the-Fields / 1990 / Chandos 8892

Richard III (1955)

Having netted a big success with his film score for Shakespeare's *Henry V* in 1954, Walton received a commission, from Alexander Korda, for another film starring Laurence Olivier—this time a production of the Bard's *Richard III*. The composer labored under the dual pressures of high expectations and short preparation time (although he did have the opportunity to discuss the project with Olivier), but in the end he produced a wholly satisfying score that functioned well both within the context of the film, and as an independent orchestral suite (entitled *A Shakespeare Suite*—prepared in 1964 on Walton's authority).

The pageantry of the play presents golden opportunities for Walton's expansive ceremonial style; these include numerous fanfares, a stirring section called "With drums and colors," and the Finale, "Trumpets sound." There are also more atmospheric passages, as in the Prelude, where solo trumpets answer one another antiphonally across the battlefield on the night before Bosworth. Military exuberance is tempered by moments of quiet beauty, as in the brief Elizabethan dance "Music plays" and the poignant Andante doloroso for strings and harp—a lament for the doomed "Princes in the Tower." Walton makes nods to the period flavor of the production, but these are merely hints, as heard in the modally inflected "I would I knew my heart."

The complex plot of the play seems to have persuaded Walton to keep his musical profile low; as a result, there are relatively few extended or fully developed passages—very much unlike his score for the somewhat slower-moving *Henry V*. N. Richardson prepared an arrangement of the score for military band, published in 1973. *—Roy Brewer*

Recommended:

○ **Walton: Film Music Vol. 4** / Marriner (cond.), Gielgud, Academy of St. Martin-in-the-Field / 1991 / Chandos 8841

CHAMBER MUSIC

Five Bagatelles for guitar (1971)

By the 1970s, the "classical" guitar was enjoying immense popularity, largely through the efforts of Andrés Segovia, yet little important music for the instrument was then being written. Walton's song cycle with guitar *Anon in Love* (1959), commissioned by the tenor Peter Pears and the English guitarist Julian Bream, had demonstrated the composer's confident and imaginative approach to the instrument, and in 1971 Bream commissioned from Walton a set of solo works.

While Bream's interpretations were an artistic success, the Five Bagatelles have never been prominent in the twentieth century guitar repertory. In addition to their considerable technical difficulties, they lack the traditional Latin/Spanish associations that were integral to the spread of the guitar's popularity from the 1960s onwards. (The third, however, is a study in a slow Cuban rhythm.)

After their first performance at the Bath Festival in 1972, a critic cautiously observed that the bagatelles "showed Walton's professionalism in writing for solo guitar while yet retaining his own personality." Walton later transcribed them for piano and, in 1976, as a suite for orchestra titled *Varii Cappricci*. After playing the bagatelles during a visit to Walton, Bream was surprised to learn that the composer had forgotten he had originally written them for guitar!

As the title implies, the bagatelles are modestly scaled and playful in style, with wayward harmonies, quirky rhythms, and an elusive tunefulness. The fourth contains battente effects—a rapid thrumming of the player's hand across all six strings—and the final Waltz avoids sentimentality at the last moment by ending with a sharp knock on the body of the instrument. *—Roy Brewer*

Recommended:

○ **Twentieth-Century Guitar I** / Bream / 1993 / BMG 902661595

○ **Guitar for Relaxation** / Bream / 2000 / RCA 63675

String Quartet No. 2 in A minor (1945–1947)

Aside from an early and unfortunate venture into the string quartet realm which the composer quickly withdrew from public performance, the *Quartet in A minor* stands as William Walton's only effort in the medium. Walton began work on the piece in 1945. The return to the string quartet genre did not come easily to Walton. As he wrote to a friend in 1945, "I'm in a suicidal struggle with four strings and am making no headway whatever. Brick walls, slit trenches... I'm afraid I've done film music for too long." Despite his initial difficulty, however the work gradually took shape—he wrote to the same friend a short time later that he had "captured a trench" and "overcome some barbed wire entanglements"—and Walton finished it in time for its premiere in 1947 by the Blech Quartet.

The work assumes largely traditional forms, to the point that thereafter many of Walton's critics, impatient with the composer's accessibility, familiarity, and unassuming expressive nuance, began to complain that his music was unadventurous, that it broke no new ground, that it merely comprised "the mixture as before." True, the musical language employed by Walton in this work offers little by way of technical or conceptual innovation, and occasionally entire passages go by that could pass for the work of a late Beethovenian contemporary or a would-be Brahms. Still, for most audiences historiography holds only so much sway when it comes down to an actual encounter with the music in concert or on recording, and what Walton's quartet may lack in innovation or surprises it makes up for in skill of construction and sincerity of expression.

The first of the quartet's four movements is cast in a fairly traditional sonata form, the thematic constituency of the exposition being first, a soft and lyrical line presented by the viola and adopted with subtle variations by the violins; and second, a jarring sforzando figure introduced by the first violin in terse staccato notes, which gradually cedes to an equally agitated passage set in quintuple meter. The expository material is reworked in the development section until finally settling into a lively fugato texture, followed by a transition into a condensed recapitulation. The second movement, marked Presto, takes on a scherzando character. Its form is an irregular combination of two closely related sections in a playful triple meter, the second section distinguished by its employment of a drone bass. The third movement, cast, like the first, in a sonata form, begins slow and stark, with an elegiac melody in the viola that wanders gracefully through various harmonic areas. As the viola moves into a new thematic area, the rest of the ensemble provides quaint pizzicato accompaniment. The development and recapitulation are less transparent than those of the first movement, as Walton takes greater liberties in revisiting and revising the initial material. The rondo finale adopts one of Walton's characteristically punchy rhythmic attitudes, the refrain material counterposed with various episodic figurations. *—Jeremy Grimshaw*

Recommended:

- **Walton: String Quartet 1; Quartet in A minor** / Gabrieli SQ / 1991 / Chandos 8944

SYMPHONIC

Symphony No. 1 in B flat minor (1931–1935)

Walton composed this work from 1931 to 1935. Sir Hamilton Harty conducted movements 1–3 on December 3, 1934, and the completed work on November 6, 1935.

If *Façade* gained Walton notoriety at 22, and *Belshazzar* won him respectable acclaim at 29, *Symphony No. 1* sealed his fame at age 33. Urged by Sir Hamilton Harty (who was then conductor of the Hallé Orchestra at Manchester), he began the symphony in 1931 and by the end of the next year had movements 1 and 2 in short score. During this time, however, a Swiss liaison with Imma von Doernberg, daughter of a prince and princess, was souring, and she left him. Between the "malicious" scherzo (Presto con malizia) and the lyrically "melancholy" slow movement that follows (Andante con malinconia, misspelled "malincolia" in Walton's score), he met Viscountess Alice Wimborne who, although married at the time, became his lover until her death in 1948.

The symphony still had only three movements in 1934, which Harty insisted on premiering with his newly acquired London Symphony. Despite the composer's misgivings, they had a great public and critical success, and were in fact given two more performances; these resolved him to finish the work. He had planned in his head how most of the finale would go, but hung himself up partway in. When he asked his friend and colleague Constant Lambert how to proceed, the answer was: Write a fugue. To Walton's plaint, "But I don't know how to write one," Lambert replied, "There are a couple of pages on the subject in *Grove's Dictionary*." The result was a dam-breaking fugue three minutes into the movement before the pace switched from Brioso ed ardentemente (spiritedly, ardently) to Vivacissimo, leading to a return of the Maestoso materials that began it. The finale provided a powerful culmination of this implicit tribute to Sibelius. When the work was new, much was made of "jazz influences," especially in the first two movements. But the music's rhythmic energy is characteristically Waltonian, just as motivic themes and their organic growth from tiny cells echo Sibelius. The opening movement (Allegro assai)—after a horn call that simultaneously suggests Strauss' *Zarathustra* and one of Holst's *Planets*—builds from a three-note motif played by the oboe to a sonata structure of impressive size and contrapuntal complexity, in which B flat major succeeds B flat minor. The scherzo is chiefly (though not exclusively) in E minor as it hurtles forward in 3/4 time, one beat to the bar, with a false ending followed by five silent bars, then a cursory codetta. This is Walton's "Imma" movement, just as the ensuing slow movement reflects an emotional void, and grows thematically out of a single C sharp that haunts its duration. The finale finds Walton's sanguinity restored with its marchlike Maestoso. Throughout the work he achieved signature sonorities with a standard Brahms orchestra to which only two percussionists and a second timpanist in the finale were added. *—Roger Dettmer*

Recommended:

- **Walton: Belshazzar's Feast; Symphony 1** / Walton (cond.), Royal PO / 2002 / BBC 4097
- **Walton: Symphonies 1 & 2** / Mackerras (cond.), London PO / EMI 64766
- **Walton: Collected Works** / Previn (cond.), London SO / 2002 / RCA Red Seal 92575
- **Walton: Symphonies, Concertos & Overtures** / Haitink (cond.), London PO / 1999 / Angel 73371

Symphony No. 2 (1957–1960)

William Walton's *Second Symphony* was premiered in 1960 by the Royal Liverpool Philharmonic. The work's initial reception was lukewarm. Having long established a compositional style that avoided the technical trends of high modernism, his tonally-grounded music was dismissed by more academically-minded audiences; at the same time, more casual listeners failed to penetrate the friendly surface of his music to find its subtle nuances and innovations, and several critics complained that the *Second Symphony* offered nothing new. The renewed interest in tonality (and/or reaction against atonality) at the end of the twentieth century, however, resulted in a reassessment of Walton's musical language and a reengagement with nearly forgotten works like the *Symphony No. 2*. This trend has facilitated the sort of reaction promised by one of a handful of this work's early fans. "The *Second Symphony*," wrote a critic speaking for the minority, "is curiously reluctant to yield its secrets and inner meanings through a few hearings. Not that it is difficult music, but it does need concentrated and frequent listening before the veil parts and one is admitted to the inner circle of its highly distinctive sound-world."

The work is scored for substantial orchestral forces, will full strings and brass, triple winds, two harps, piano, and a large percussion battery. Its three movements, lasting a combined half-hour, assume fairly standard structures. The first movement (marked Allegro molto) follows an audible sonata form with the expected first and second theme areas, transitions, developments, and modulations, though it reverses the recapitulation so that it mirrors, rather than repeats, the theme areas of the exposition. The opening motive, comprised most predominantly of a tense half step followed by a stark leap of a sharp seventh, establishes the tense and mysterious mood of the movement, which undoubtedly owes some of its orchestrational and melodic drama to Walton's film work during the war years. A close listening reveals a high level of motivic unity embedded within the musical special effects, as the initial figure makes a presence in nearly every phrase.

The inner movement, Lento assai, finds Walton alternately at his most evasive and his most lyrical. The arching, rhapsodic melodies in the violins and upper winds are some of his most beautiful, but find themselves challenged at every turn by pensive harmonic shifts and textural effects. Walton demonstrates a masterful management of tension when, in the minutes before the movement's denouement, a dominant pedal underscores a seemingly endless approach to an elusive cadence (a cliché à la Wagner's "Liebestod"); however, as the tension begins to settle, the basses, rather than resolving upwards by leap to the tonic, wind their way slowly and chromatically downward, creating a rather disoriented sense of repose. The finale takes the form of a passacaglia, with a 14-bar theme that is introduced forcefully by the orchestra in unison. The theme (which, interestingly, exhausts all 12 chromatic tones) undergoes several contrasting variations before a scherzando coda draws the work to a close. *—Jeremy Grimshaw*

Recommended:

- **Walton: Symphonies, Concertos & Overtures** / Haitink (cond.), London PO / 1999 / Angel 73371
- **Walton: Symphonies 1 & 2** / Mackerras (cond.), London SO / EMI 64766
- **Walton: Belshazzar's Feast; Symphony 2, etc.** / Previn (cond.), London SO / 2001 / EMI 4924029

CONCERTO

Cello Concerto (1955–1956; revised 1975)

In 1956, the cellist Piatigorsky commissioned Walton to write a cello concerto. Although he did not play the instrument, the composer agreed, flippantly adding "I'm a professional composer. I'll write for anybody if he pays me." After meeting Walton, Piatigorsky told the pianist Ivor Newton, through whom the commission had been forwarded, "I have never encountered such a rare combination of greatness and simplicity. A great composer like Walton needs no suggestions from me." The concerto was completed in eight months and exploits the cello's rich sound and expressive cantabile, with exciting accompanied and unaccompanied cadenzas. The orchestra is fairly small and the solo part is clearly heard throughout. The work is basically in two substantial movements linked by a fully worked out scherzo creating a balanced whole. In the first movement, (Moderato), which has no cadenza, the principal theme, a broad, meditative melody, is first given to the cello, then developed by soloist and orchestra, often featuring the wind section. The Scherzo, marked Allegro appassionato, opens in rapid triple time followed by a more relaxed section and a marchlike interlude with a snappy coda. The final movement, featuring a colorful theme with two variations for orchestra alone and two (variations two and four) for unaccompanied cello, clearly establishes the underlying thematic coherence of the concerto, which has considerable rhythmic freedom and melodic variety throughout. This movement ends with a short Adagio recalling motifs from earlier movements. The concerto is one of Walton's most accessible works and provides an excellent introduction to his occasionally quirky, but always and inventive, style of writing. —*Roy Brewer*

Recommended:

- ○ **Walton: Collected Works** / Munch (cond.), Piatigorsky, Boston SO / 2002 / RCA Red Seal 92575
- ○ **Walton: Cello Concerto; Coronation Te Deum** / Walton (cond.), Fournier, Royal PO / 2002 / BBC 4098

Viola Concerto (1928–1929; revised 1936)

In 1928, the conductor Sir Thomas Beecham suggested to Walton that he write a concerto for the eminent violist Lionel Tertis. The composer agreed and started work on it almost immediately; on completion he sent it to Tertis who, much to Walton's disappointment, rejected it. In his biography, *My Viola and I* (Elek, 1974) Tertis relented: "I had not learnt to appreciate Walton's style. The innovations in his musical language which now seem so logical and so truly in the mainstream of music then struck me as far-fetched." The composer and violist Paul Hindemith gave the first performance in London in October 1929, when the *Sunday Times* critic Ernest Newman wrote, somewhat unenthusiastically, "The composer has a grasp of musical logic, a sense of fitness and a command of craftsmanship that is very unusual in a young man." In 1960, and again in 1961, Walton—ever the perfectionist—extensively revised the work, but it has never been among his most-admired compositions.

Tertis' original reservations may well have had something to do with the fact that the concerto is not, in any obvious sense, a showpiece for the viola. It certainly makes virtuosic demands on the soloist, but its strengths lie in the intimate dialogues between viola and orchestra and the intricate, almost casual, way in which the themes are crafted.

In the first movement, Andante commodo, the music, though lyrical, is haunted by feelings of restlessness, with frequent time changes and shifts of harmony. There is even a trace of impatience in the way, rising to its highest register, the viola delivers its own version of the second subject.

The second movement, Vivo con molto preciso, has three main thematic ideas. It opens with fast, rhythmic figures tossed between orchestra and soloist, abruptly cut short by quiet chords in the brass and followed by lively explorations by the soloist. The movement closes with a more contemplative version of the opening theme, and ends quietly.

The final movement, Allegro moderato, the longest of the three, starts with a rather unpromising melody for bassoon, soon to be expanded, enriched, and brought to a climax by the viola before being passed to the orchestra. The poetic sincerity with which Walton returns to earlier themes as the movement draws to a close is among the concerto's finest moments.—*Roy Brewer*

Recommended:

- ○ **Walton: Violin & Viola Concertos** / Kennedy, Previn (cond.), Royal PO / 1987 / EMI 49628
- ○ **Britten: Violin Concerto; Walton: Viola Concerto** / Vengerov, Rostropovich (cond.), London SO / 2003 / EMI 57510

Violin Concerto (1936–1939; revised 1943)

Walton first met Jascha Heifetz in 1936, and in 1938 the virtuoso violinist commissioned him to write a concerto. In the same year, the British Council for the Arts asked Walton for a work to be performed at the New York Fair in June 1939, and the prospect of an early premiere looked likely. However, Walton was dissatisfied with the last movement, which he suspected was "not difficult enough for Heifetz," and withdrew the concerto from the New York concert. At the invitation of Heifetz he sailed to the United States in 1939 to discuss it with the soloist, who made a few suggestions for changes; but war broke out in Europe, so the premiere took place in Cleveland, OH, in December 1939 with Heifetz and Artur Rodzinski conducting. The concerto was not heard in New York until 1941, when critic Virgil Thompson wrote, "Its material is inoffensive but extremely vague. Its violin writing is glittery, its texture is continuous. The whole surface of it is dainty and luxurious [but] there is very little substance beneath." Today's listeners might well feel that, on closer acquaintance, the concerto has many hidden depths. It is among the most lyrical of Walton's major works, free from the tensions that mark his *Symphony No. 1* and full of quirky, seemingly improvisatory surprises. Its tonality is precarious and rhythms complex; yet in many respects it is one of Walton's most romantic works.

The first movement (Andante tranquillo) is the slowest of the three and highly demanding on the soloist. The second movement (Presto capriccioso alla Napolitana) is mostly very fast, with a songlike middle section in waltz time marked Cantelina. The finale (Vivace), marked Tema con improvazione, starts in a lively 3/4 tempo and contains some of Walton's most eloquent inventions, with much thematic interweaving ending in a spectacular flourish. Two of the variations are for full orchestra, and two for solo violin.

There is no sign of the doubt and indecision that preceded the work in its final form. Delicate and full-blooded by turns, its most attractive qualities lie in the ways in which Walton's lively imagination spreads a sunny, Mediterranean glow over what is, by any standards, a challenge to both players and listeners. —*Roy Brewer*

Recommended:

- ○ **Walton: Violin & Viola Concertos** / Kennedy, Previn (cond.), Royal PO / 1987 / EMI 49628
- ○ **Elgar & Walton: Violin Concertos** / Heifetz, Goossens (cond.), Cincinnati SO / 2000 / Naxos 110939

Günter Wand

b. Jan. 7, 1912, Elberfeld, Germany, **d.** Feb. 14, 2002, Ulmiz, Switzerland

Conductor

Conductor Günter Wand was one of a handful of musicians who were working before World War II and whose career remained viable at the end of the twentieth century. In contrast to the best known of his peers, Sir Georg Solti and Rafael Kubelik, he was the opposite of the jet set, international conductor, and limited the number and scope of his engagements, primarily in Europe. Although Wand composed a small number of works, including ballet music, orchestral songs, and one cantata, he was known by most listeners as a conductor. His performances were noted for their precise attention to detail and special care in matters of stylistic propriety.

Wand studied at the Cologne Conservatory, initially as a composition and piano student. His conducting technique was almost entirely self-taught. He began his career in Wuppertal and Allenstein as a repetiteur and conductor, and was later made chief conductor in Detmold. In 1939, he was appointed a conductor, and subsequently first conductor, with the Cologne Opera, where he remained until the opera house was destroyed by Allied bombing raids in 1944. He then became conductor of the Salzburg Mozarteum Orchestra for the remainder of the war, until April 1945. With the end of fighting, he returned to Cologne to begin reconstructing the city's musical life, first as music director of the Cologne Opera, where he remained for three years (1945–48), and as director of concerts, initially a 10-year appointment that was later extended for life. He taught music in the city, and became a professor at the Hochschule für Musik in 1948. He also became head of the Gürzenich Orchestra, a post he held until 1974.

Wand began making appearances as a guest conductor throughout Europe during the early 1950s, including his British debut with the London Symphony Orchestra in 1951. His guest appearances included concerts in the Soviet Union and Japan. His professional life, however, remained centered in Cologne, where he was at the center of the revived city's musical life. In addition to his performances of the mainstream German-Austrian repertory—Beethoven, Schubert, Brahms, and Bruckner—he was a major advocate of the works of such contemporary composers as Ligeti, Varèse, and Zimmermann, and recorded the music of Frank Martin and Anton Webern.

Wand resigned his Cologne positions in 1974 and moved to Switzerland, where he became a regular guest conductor of the Berne Symphony Orchestra. After 1974, he began working more closely with the various broadcast orchestras in Germany and elsewhere in Europe, and was also hailed for his performances of the operas of Mozart and Verdi. Wand recorded exclusively for RCA/BMG, including all of Bruckner's symphonies—a major feat at the time—with the Cologne Radio Symphony Orchestra, as well as Schubert's extant eight symphonies; and he later recorded the Schubert symphonies with the NDR symphony and the Berlin Philharmonic. From 1982 until 1991, he also took over the post of music director of the Radio Symphony Orchestra of Hamburg. Among his recordings are the complete Brahms and Beethoven symphonies. These recordings have attracted a substantial international following, acclaimed for their attention to the details of the written score and the spirituality of the playing. —*Bruce Eder*

Recommended:

- ○ **Schubert: Symphony 5; Rosamunde (excerpts)** / Wand (cond.), Kolner RSO / 2002 / RCA 63944
- ○ **Bruckner: Symphony 8** / Wand (cond.), Berlin PO / 2001 / RCA 82866
- ○ **Brahms: Symphonies 2 & 4** / Wand (cond.), North German RSO / 2001 / RCA 89101
- ○ **Bruckner: Symphony 4** / Wand (cond.), Berlin PO / 1998 / RCA 902668839
- ○ **Beethoven: Symphonies 1 & 6** / Wand (cond.), North German RSO / 2001 / RCA 89108

William Warfield

b. Jan. 22, 1920, West Helena, AR, **d.** Aug. 25, 2002, Chicago, IL

Baritone

William Warfield was one of the great baritones of the twentieth century, known for a voice of exceptional richness. With the exception of Paul Robeson, he is the singer most closely identified with Jerome Kern's song *Ol' Man River* and is the best-known singer of George Gershwin's Porgy.

He was born in the Mississippi River town of West Helena, Arkansas. He was the first of five sons. His father moved the family to Rochester, New York, when the children were still quite young, seeking greater opportunities there, eventually becoming the pastor of Mount Vernon Baptist Church.

All five boys sang in the church choir. William sang in high school. He says that a classmate of his brought him a program from 1936, showing that his first public performance of *Ol' Man River* was at the age of 16. (This was the year of the release of the original film of *Show Boat*, in which Paul Robeson sang the song.) William's high school music teacher, Elsa Miller, recognized his talents. In his senior year, he won the national Music Educators League Competition, giving him a scholarship to the U.S. music school of his choice. He picked the Eastman School of Music, intending a career as a music teacher.

World War II interrupted his education after he obtained his bachelor's degree. He served four years in military intelligence, then returned to Eastman to study for his masters. There, he was encouraged to consider a professional singing career by Robeson and another great pioneer black classical singer, Marian Anderson.

His first professional appearances were in theater, including a stint with the national touring company of the musical *Call Me Mister*, Dorothy Heyward's play *Set My People Free*, and Marc Blitzstein's opera *Regina*. He sang in churches and synagnogues, and developed a night club act, singing and playing piano. When he played at a Toronto nightclub, a Canadian stockbroker named Walter Carr heard him and gave him the financial backing for a New York City debut, a recital at Town Hall on March 19, 1950. His recital, comprising religious music of the Renaissance and Baroque, German songs of Schubert and Loewe, and a diverse group of American songs, was one of the most memorable in years and launched him on a solid performing career.

He easily became the baritone of choice for black-oriented roles, such as Porgy and Joe in the color film remake of *Show Boat*, and he made memorable non-singing performances on the *Hallmark Hall of Fame* as De Lawd in Marc Connelly's *Green Pastures* in 1957 and 1959. One of his most important productions of *Porgy and Bess* was undertaken at the request of the U.S. State Department, where he sang it for ten weeks on a European tour with Leontyne Price as Bess. He married Miss Price in 1952. They separated a few years later and were formally divorced in 1972.

As time passed, Warfield was able to devote more of his time to the standard repertory, particularly in concert performances where he sang with many great conductors and orchestras in such major works as the Bach *Passions*, Handel's *Messiah*, Mendelssohn's *Elijah*, the Mozart and Verdi requiems, the Brahms *German Requiem* and *Vier Ernste Gesänge*, Mussorgsky's *Songs and Dances of Death*, and one of his favorite works, Aaron Copland's *Old American Songs* (which he recorded in both the piano version and the orchestration, with Copland as conductor).

In 1974, he joined the faculty of the University of Illinois, remaining there through 1990. In 1994, he was appointed a professor at Northwestern University in Evanston, Illinois. William Warfield died on August 25, 2002, from injuries sustained during a fall. *—Joseph Stevenson*

Recommended:

- ○ **Gershwin: Porgy & Bess** / Henderson (cond.), Price, Warfield, Boatwright, Bubblesb, RCA Victor Orch. / 1963 / RCA 5234
- ○ **Copland Conducts Copland** / Copland (cond.), Warfield, London SO, Chicago SO / 2003 / Sony 90403

Dale Warland

b. Apr. 14, 1932, Badger, IA

Conductor

The man behind the celebrated Dale Warland Singers has distinguished himself not only as a choral director, but also as an arranger, composer, guest conductor, and festival adjudicator. Through his uncanny ability to draw from choristers a tonal sophistication in which a tensile inner core is always warmly, softly sheathed, he has achieved sounds envied by fellow choral conductors. The accuracy of intonation he obtains from his singers is another source of wonder, whether from his own ensemble or chorales he periodically guest conducts.

Warland chose St. Olaf College in Northfield, MN, for his university training, thereby placing himself in a school with an honored choral tradition. After graduating from St. Olaf in 1954, Warland served as a first lieutenant in the United States Air Force and founded the Scott Male Chorus at Illinois' Scott Air Force base. Following his two years of active duty, Warland enrolled at the University of Minnesota to begin work on his master's degree, also serving as the minister of music for University Lutheran Church in Hope, MN. In 1960, master's degree in hand, Warland entered the University of Southern California School of Music to pursue his doctorate in music. In 1963, he joined the faculty at California's Humboldt State College and in 1965, doctorate completed, he became chairman of the music department at Keuka College in Keuka, NY. By the time he had reached his mid-thirties, Warland had begun to make a name for himself. He was called back to the Twin Cities to become director of choral activities at Macalester College in St. Paul. That same year, he served as an assistant to Robert Shaw at the celebrated Meadowbrook School of Music and was engaged to prepare the chorus for Krzysztof Penderecki's *Passion According to St. Luke*, which was having its American premiere in a Twin Cities production led by the composer himself. In 1971, Warland was awarded a Ford Foundation grant to study with two of the world's finest choral directors. He traveled to Sweden to work with Eric Ericson and to England to train with David Willcocks, then-director of music at Kings College, Cambridge. The following year saw the birth of the Dale Warland Singers in a June 12 concert at the Walker Art Center. In 1976 and 1977, Warland worked with another famous choral conductor, Norman Luboff, to produce two recordings with his new ensemble and, in 1977, he took his singers on a tour of Scandinavia. By 1980, Warland was able to initiate a subscription series with his Singers. The same year, he was appointed to the choral panel of the National Endowment for the Arts. Although Warland resigned from Macalester College in 1985 to devote himself to his ensemble, he nonetheless brought the college's concert choir with his own group to perform in Germany during J.S. Bach's 300th anniversary celebrations. A grant from the Major Jerome Foundation in 1987 enabled Warland to inaugurate the Dale Warland Singers' New Choral Music Program for Emerging Composers, a venture that led to significant additions to the choral literature. Given the St. Olaf College Distinguished Alumnus Award in 1988, Warland gained still more celebrity when his Singers performed with the Mormon Tabernacle Choir. Honors have accrued, among them the very first Margaret Hillis Award for Choral Excellence. Guest engagements, meanwhile, have taken Warland from Estonia to Japan. The Dale Warland Singers disbanded in 2004. *—Erik Eriksson*

Recommended:

- ○ **Argento: Walden Pond** / Warland (cond.), , Dale Warland Singers, Lark Quartet / 2003 / Gothic 49217
- ○ **Bernstein & Britten** / Warland (cond.), Dale Warland Singers / 1999 / American Choral 123
- ○ **Cathedral Classics** / Warland (cond.), Dale Warland Singers / 1994 / American Choral 120

Peter Warlock

b. Oct. 30, 1894, London, England, **d.** Dec. 17, 1930, London, England

Composer: Vocal, Chamber Music, Orchestral

Peter Warlock was born Philip Heseltine in the Savoy Hotel, the only son of a London solicitor. His father died when he was two, and Heseltine was raised by his mother. He was educated in the English public schools, and was encouraged in his passion for music by a teacher at Eton, Colin Taylor. Outside of that, he had little or no significant musical training. In 1908, Heseltine discovered the music of Frederick Delius and was enraptured by his work; upon meeting Delius in 1911, a lifelong friendship ensued. Heseltine entered Oxford in 1913, but soon dropped out, relocating to London to work as music critic for the *Daily Mail*. With the outbreak of war, Heseltine was deemed unfit for military duty. In 1916 adopted the pen name "Peter Warlock" amid a host of others used in his criticism. When he began to compose seriously around 1918, this was the pseudonym that Heseltine favored for his original work.

In 1918, Warlock and composer Cecil Gray undertook publication of *The Sackbut*, a periodical dedicated to informed and lively discussion of the contemporary music world. Warlock held this post until the magazine was absorbed into the house of publisher J.C. Curwen in 1921. Warlock also turned his attention to English music of past eras, particularly that of the Elizabethan age. He would edit a great deal of this "ancient" music for modern publication, and Warlock's editions are of such a high standard that generations of subsequent research have failed to unseat many of them. In 1923, he composed his song cycle to poems of Yeats, *The Curlew*, which represented Britain in the 1924 ISCM Festival in Salzburg. That same year, he scored three Christmas carols for the Bach Choir; this set contained the ethereal and mystic *Balulalow*, since becoming a choral staple of the Yuletide season. Warlock's *Capriol Suite*, his best known orchestral work, was completed in 1926. Another famous Christmas carol, *Bethlehem Down*, made its bow in *The London Daily Telegraph*'s Christmas Eve edition of 1927. He published book length essays on Delius, Gesualdo, and Thomas Whythorne.

In early 1929, Thomas Beecham named Warlock editor of *MILO* (*The Magazine of the Imperial League of Opera*). Only three issues appeared before the magazine folded. Warlock fell into a deep depression, unable to find work and drinking heavily. On December 17, 1930, Warlock's landlady phoned her utility company as there was a strong smell of gas coming from Warlock's flat. Once inside, the police found Warlock dead from asphyxiation at the age of 36.

Warlock's main output consists of songs, written in a modern style, characterized by extroverted ebulliance on one hand and serene, transparent calm on the other. Critics who deal with Warlock sometimes attempt to present him as a kind of schizophrenic, transporting good qualities to "Heseltine" and bad to "Warlock." From reminiscences of his friends, it seems a more complex situation. Heseltine/Warlock was an alcoholic, a naughty limericks writer, and a sadist who often lashed out in the press against bad performances and the opinions of writers, particularly Edwin Newman, whose views offended him. Warlock's music was of its own special category; as conductor/composer Constant Lambert noted in 1938, "It would be an easy matter for me to write down the names of at least 30 of [Warlock's] songs which are flawless in inspiration and workmanship. It is no exaggeration to say that this achievement entitles him to be classed with Dowland, Mussorgsky, and Debussy as one of the greatest song writers that music has known." —*Uncle Dave Lewis*

Overview of Works (1911–1930)

The enigmatic and somewhat eccentric British composer Peter Warlock (born Philip Heseltine) wrote relatively little music in his short lifetime, but is remembered as an important composer of song. Indeed, most of his compositions are solo songs with piano accompaniment, including settings of poems by Shakespeare, Yeats, Shelley, and Marlowe. He also wrote piano music, choral works, and a handful of orchestral pieces. Warlock has been described as a miniaturist, because of his concentration on solo songs, but otherwise virtually defies categorization. His musical language is unique, due in part to the fact that his musical training—abortive piano studies in his youth—was deficient.

Ultimately, Warlock's output is a somewhat bewildering blend of Edwardian and Elizabethan music, English folk songs, Delius, and Bartók. In his œuvre, riotous pub songs stand side by side with medieval-style songs and gentle choral settings of English carols. Warlock's experience as an editor of early music contributed greatly to his own harmonic language and style. He wrote books about the composers Frederick Delius and Gesualdo, whose compositional practices may be heard in his music. Béla Bartók's influence is also present in Warlock's work. Warlock's earliest music consists largely of simple, harmonic text settings; as his style evolved, his music became more contrapuntal. Interpretations of Warlock's music are often colored by the Warlock myth; namely that he was a schizophrenic who adopted the persona of "Peter Warlock" to compose his idiosyncratic tunes. It is more likely that Warlock's difficult upbringing and frustration with his own musical shortcomings contributed to his compositional quirks, rather than any real mental illness. —*Alexander Carpenter*

Recommended:

- ○ **A Warlock Centenary Album** / The Curlew; Songs & Carols; Capriol Suite / (various) / 1994 / EMI 65101
- ○ **Songs by Peter Warlock** / Ainsley, Vignoles / 1994 / Hyperion 66736
- ○ **The British Music Collection: Peter Warlock** / Marriner (cond.), Hill, Kraemer, Parsons, Bailey, Academy of St. Martin-in-the-Fields / 2001 / Decca 000200702

VOCAL

The Curlew, song cycle for tenor, flute, english horn & string quartet (1920–1922)

The curlew's cry is the symbol of unrequited love in Peter Warlock's dolorous masterpiece, which sets poems by W.B. Yeats. Warlock makes excellent use of his unusual accompanying ensemble of flute, English horn, and strings (either as a quartet or orchestra). At the very beginning, the English horn utters the curlew's song in rising sevenths. This is taken up and embellished by the viola(s). The long, haunting instrumental introduction continues with violin arabesques; a desolate, repeated-note flute solo said to imitate the call of the peewit; a return of the English horn; and finally, a cello passage that leads into the late arrival of the tenor with "O curlew, cry no more in the air... because your crying brings to my mind the passion-dimm'd eyes and long heavy hair that was shaken out over my breast. There is enough evil in the crying of wind." This is "He reproves the curlew" from Yeats' *The Wind Among the Reeds* (the source of most of the texts here) and is initially sung to the English horn theme, which recurs throughout the song cycle and ends the first song. An extended, hushed instrumental interlude leads to the brief second song, "The Lover Mourns for the Loss of Love," where the tenor recalls his dream—only a dream—that "the old despair would end in love," to the accompaniment of muted strings. "The Withering of the Boughs," from *In the Seven Woods*, is the longest song in the set and each of its three verses is echoed—and, in the first section, foreshadowed—instrumentally. The first is unsettled but still quite slow, culminating in the words "The boughs have withered because I have told them my dreams." (Each verse ends this way, the last with the words spoken, not sung, in a near whisper.) The second verse briefly rides with the witches and "their crowns of pearl and their spindles of wool and their secret smile," but the tenor maintains that they are not the ones who have not withered the boughs; the withering is, again, the fault of his dreams. The third section is a serene depiction of "the sleepy country where swans fly round coupled with golden chains and sing as they fly," until the English horn and pizzicato strings return the tenor to his self-obsessed reality. A long, Moderato instrumental section with distant-seeming solos by violin and flute drifts through half-formed recitative phrases and general despondency, fading away to allow the tenor to sing his last song, "He Hears the Cry of the Sedge." This lacks accompaniment until the very end. The singer finally acknowledges that "your breast will not lie by the breast of your beloved in sleep," and the lower strings provide the final, accepting cadence. —*James Reel*

Recommended:

- ○ **Warlock: The Curlew; Capriol Suite; Serenade; Songs** / Ainsley, Nash Ensemble / 1997 / Hyperion 66938
- ○ **A Warlock Centenary Album** / Partridge, London Music Group / 1994 / EMI 65101

CHAMBER MUSIC

Capriol Suite, for piano, 4 hands or string orchestra (1926)

The *Capriol Suite* is quintessential Peter Warlock—the pseudonym by which Philip Heseltine is known to all lovers of English song. Composed for string orchestra in 1926, five of its six movements are loosely based on ancient tunes drawn from *Orchésographie*, a treatise on dance published in 1589 and ascribed to one Thoinot Arbeau, an anagrammatic pseudonym of French priest and savant Jéhan Tabourot (1519–1595). Arbeau is engaged in dialogue with Capriol, a lawyer who wishes to learn to dance; hence, the title. Critic and composer Cecil Gray noted that, "if one compares these tunes with what the composer has made of them it will be seen that to all intents and purposes it can be regarded as an original work." The charm of the *Capriol Suite* is its ineffable manner of summoning an aura of the archaic within a modern aural frame, so to speak—that is, with the accelerated pace of contemporary urban life. The stately opening "Basse Danse" might almost be a transcription, while the following grave and gracious "Pavane," in fact, is an arrangement of Arbeau's four-part "Belle qui tiens ma vie." "Tordion" skips briskly into airy pizzicato nothingness, followed by the rustic "Bransle"—brawl, in English—becoming ever more spirited to end in a boisterous melee. The gently exquisite "Pieds-en-l'air" is pure Warlock, calling to mind the clutch of songs scattered throughout his oeuvre. For instance, "Chopcherry" or "Passing By" or "My Own Country," a pristine spring of feeling, undistorted by mockery, flows, though the cadence takes a syrupy Edwardian turn. The final vivacious "Mattachins" is a sword dance ending in a cross-rhythmic riot. The upshot of these cunningly distilled miniatures, playing together about ten minutes, is not only a drolly modern take on Elizabethan music but an unconscious self-portrait through which Heseltine is now glimpsed, the retiring scholar nursing a vein of urbane poetry, now the bibulous, roistering Warlock.

In this connection, Gray, the boon companion, keenest observer, and first biographer, said, "No account of Peter Warlock would be complete without reference to his harlequinesque propensity for suddenly indulging in extravagant displays of acrobatic dancing and *pas seuls* in all places and on all occasions, whenever he happened to be in a state of elation... the most vivid... recollection... that I retain was that of his departure one afternoon from Charing Cross Station.... On emerging from the booking-hall, instead of going straight to his train, he suddenly began to execute the most astonishing dance I have ever seen... worthy of Nijinsky himself.... Gradually the normal activities of the station came to a standstill... on the faces of the onlookers amusement quickly gave way to sheer astonishment, and astonishment to a kind of awestruck, spellbound admiration, as this strange, bearded, faunlike creature danced there all by himself.... Then, suddenly, the spell was broken. A whistle sounded, and Peter's train began slowly to move out of the station. With one final prodigious bound into the air he dashed to the barrier, brushed aside the protesting ticket-collector, clambered on to the footboard of the last carriage... and waved a courtly and dignified farewell to the assembled crowd...."

In 1928, the composer re-scored the *Capriol Suite* for full orchestra, augmenting the raucousness of the more extroverted numbers, though it is the deftly wrought original version for strings that is most often heard. Arrangements by others, for guitar quartet, winds, and even for a consort of recorders, are a tribute to its indelible charms and enduring appeal. —*Adrian Corleonis*

Recommended:

- ○ **English String Music** / Studt (cond.), Bournemouth Sinfonietta / 1994 / Naxos 550823
- ○ **Elgar, Ravel, Fauré & Warlock** / Groves (cond.), English Sinfonia / Carlton 2017

ORCHESTRAL

Serenade for string orchestra (1921–1922)

As a schoolboy of 15 at Eton, Philip Heseltine—known to all lovers of English song as Peter Warlock—developed an interest in the music of Delius that was soon to become a consuming passion, without having heard a note of it in performance. "And although I have heard nothing of his music," he writes to his mother, "yet from what I can discover at the piano, I may say that so far as I have yet found, Delius comes nearest to my own imperfect ideal of music...." By chance, his mother, a society lady, was to meet Delius on the occasion of the London premiere of his *Songs of Sunset* conducted by Thomas Beecham. Heseltine attended on June 16, 1911, and was introduced to the composer during intermission. An intense and ever more personal correspondence followed, through which Delius gradually assumed the role of father figure.

By 1923, in full swagger as Peter Warlock, Heseltine wrote the first book on Delius, perfervid, polemical, and poetic by turns, full of inaccuracies (though he was born in 1862, the composer's birth date is given as 1863), but highly readable and useful in helping define Delius' style while divining the shape of a career still in progress.

In the same year, Heseltine completed the *Serenade for String Orchestra*, dedicated "To Frederick Delius on his 60th birthday"—as noted, Delius was actually turning 61—in which the fluently dreaming style of Delius at his most ecstatic graciously melds with the more angular gait of Peter Warlock. Already in the grip of the syphilitic paralysis that would leave him blind and unable to compose, on February 26, 1923, Delius dictated this missive: "My dear Phil, Forgive me for not answering your kind letter of congratulations and acknowledging your charming serenade, which I received early in the morning on my birthday to my greatest surprise and pleasure. I like it very much indeed; it is a very delicate composition of a fine harmonist... Percy Grainger and Alexander Lippay played me the *Serenade* several times from the score and they all liked it." *—Adrian Corleonis*

Recommended:

○ **A Warlock Centenary Album** / del Mar (cond.) / 1994 / EMI 65101

○ **Fantasia on Greensleeves** / Marriner, Academy of St. Martin-in-the-Fields / 1997 / London 452707

Leonard Warren

b. Apr. 21, 1911, New York, NY, **d.** Mar. 4, 1960, New York, NY
Baritone

Baritone Leonard Warren had a remarkably well-produced voice, with a naturally wide range, with secure high notes, and smooth, rich timbre throughout. He was most associated with Verdi, which he sang with a good deal of artistry and feel for the natural line, though he also excelled in Puccini (especially Scarpia) and verismo.

He first planned on a business career and studied for a year at Columbia College, but in 1933 decided to quit that to pursue a singing career. He first studied at the Greenwich House Music School, and in 1935, auditioned at the Radio City Music Hall. He had hoped to become a lead singer, but Robert Weede was the reigning baritone there, and Warren was just offered a place in the choir. He sang there for the next three years, augmenting his income with the occasional radio program, wedding, or funeral, and studied with Sidney Dietch, and eventually made it to the Metropolitan Auditions of the Air in 1938. When the Radio City Music Hall refused his request for a few weeks off to prepare (he knew only a few arias and had never sung on the opera stage before), he quit, and threw himself into preparations on his own. Legend has it that at the audition, the conductor Wilfrid Pelletier rushed backstage, convinced that they were playing a prank on him, and Warren was lip-synching to a Ruffo or De Luca recording. He won, rather to his own surprise, not only the auditions, but a stipend to study in Italy with, among others, Giuseppe de Luca and Riccardo Picozzi. There, he learned five complete roles in less than seven months, despite having seen just one complete opera in his life. He made his Met debut, which was also his staged opera debut, as Paolo in Verdi's *Simon Boccanegra* in January 1939 (Tibbett sang Boccanegra), and soon became a favorite baritone at that house, singing all the major Verdi baritone roles. At first awkward on stage, he studied acting, and while never a great operatic actor, became more at ease on stage and put a good deal of thought into his interpretations. Like many opera stars of the time he was offered film contracts, and made his film debut in 1949 in *When Irish Eyes are Smiling*. He created the role of Ilo in Menotti's *The Island God* (which Menotti withdrew shortly after the premiere).

Like his successor, Robert Merrill, and to a lesser extent Sherrill Milnes, as well as his predecessor, Lawrence Tibbett, his artistic home was the Met, though he did perform in other countries, making his Teatro Colón debut as Rigoletto in 1942, appearing in *Il trovatore* in Mexico City in 1948, and making his La Scala debut in 1953 as Iago. In 1958, he also made a tour of the Soviet Union. He had been suffering from high blood pressure and died on stage at the Metropolitan during a 1960 performance of *La forza del destino*.

His Macbeth under Erich Leinsdorf, with Leonie Rysanek (BMG/RCA), is excellent, and he and Bjoerling are both at their best on a recording, also with Leinsdorf, of *Tosca* (BMG/RCA). *—Ann Feeney*

Recommended:

○ **Arias & Concert Songs** / Warren, etc. / 2000 / BMG 1/2

○ **On Tour in Russia** / Warren etc. / RCA 7807

○ **Verdi: Rigoletto** / Cellini (cond.), Warren, Peerce, Berger, Varnay, Robert Shaw Chorale, RCA Victor Orch. & Chorus / Preiser 90452

○ **Verdi: Macbeth** / Leinsdorf (cond.), Warren, Bergonzi, Rysanek, Marsh, Metropolitan Opera Orch. & Chorus / 1959 / RCA 4516

○ **Verdi: Il Trovatore** / Cellini (cond.), Bjoerling, Milanov, Warren, Barbieri, Robert Shaw Chorale, RCA. Victor Orch. / RCA 6643

André Watts

b. Jun. 20, 1946, Nuremberg, Germany
Pianist

André Watts has successfully extended an initial burst of publicity into decades of popular success and critical acclaim. He brings a marked lyrical quality to the standard piano repertory. Born on a United States Army base in Nuremberg, part of the U.S. Occupied Zone of Germany in the years following World War II, he was the son of an American soldier who had married a Hungarian woman. His mother gave André his first piano lessons.

When the family returned to the U.S. they settled in Philadelphia, and Watts continued his piano studies. At the age of nine he made his public debut in a children's concert, playing Haydn's *D Major Piano Concerto* with the Philadelphia Orchestra. He continued studies at the Philadelphia Music Academy ,where his teachers were Doris Bawden and Clement Petrillo.

Watts was 14 when he made his official Philadelphia Orchestra debut, in César Franck's *Symphonic Variations*. His real breakthrough came two years later when Leonard Bernstein asked him to appear on a New York Philharmonic Young People's Concert that was broadcast nationwide. Watts became a national sensation in the Liszt E flat concerto, which he played with complete technical mastery and self-assurance. Two weeks later, Glenn Gould was forced to cancel a regular subscription concert due to illness. Bernstein called on Watts as a last-minute replacement, and he reprised the Liszt concerto to the approval of New York's tough critics and audiences. Watts then settled on the great teacher and pianist Leon Fleisher as his mentor, emerging as a complete pianist and artist, with his technique polished of any insecurities and his own personal interpretations of familiar music in place. Watts began to build an international reputation with appearances in London and at the Amsterdam Concertgebouw, all the while completing a degree at the Peabody Conservatory in Baltimore.

After making his Carnegie Hall solo debut in New York at the age of 20, Watts celebrated his 21st birthday by playing Brahms' *Piano Concerto No. 2* with the Berlin Philharmonic Orchestra. He returned to Nuremberg for a recital in 1970 and was hailed as a returning native son. Watts has often been selected to perform at important commemorative events, playing for example at a concert in honor of Richard Nixon's first inauguration as President in 1969. In 1976 a Watts recital was featured on the U.S. PBS network's *Live from Lincoln Center* program; it was the first full-length piano recital ever broadcast on television, and, with his telegenic looks, he remained a favorite of broadcast audiences. In 2000 he appeared internationally on television in a program celebrating the Philadelphia Orchestra's centennial.

Watts specializes in the standard repertory from Beethoven through Rachmaninov, often performing Mozart and Scarlatti as well. He has been an unusually frequent recipient of prestigious prizes, becoming (at 26) the youngest person ever to receive an honorary doctorate from Yale University and winning the Avery Fisher Prize in 1988. Watts remains active as a performer, recording artist, and teacher; beginning in 2000 he served as Artist-in-Residence at the University of Maryland. He has recorded in recent years primarily for the Telarc and Angel/EMI labels, and a double-CD release in the Philips "Great Pianists of the 20th Century" series, featuring music by composers ranging from Beethoven to Gershwin, serves as a good introduction to his work and retrospective appreciation of his stature. *—Joseph Stevenson*

Recommended:

○ **André Watts** / Bernstein (cond.), Watts, New York PO, London SO / 1999 / Philips 456985

○ **Tchaikovsky: Concerto 1; Saint-Saëns: Concerto 2** / Levi (cond.), Watts, Atlanta SO / 1995 / Telarc 80386

○ **MacDowell: Concerto 2; Liszt: Concertos** / Litton (cond.), Watts, Dallas SO / Telarc 80429

Franz Waxman

b. Dec. 24, 1906, Königshütte, Upper Silesia, **d.** Feb. 24, 1967, Los Angeles, CA
Composer: Concerto

Franz Waxman (Wachsmann) was one of the most prolific and respected twentieth century composers of film music. He also produced a large output of concert music, including orchestral, choral, chamber, and instrumental works. In addition, Waxman was a noted conductor and impresario.

Franz Waxman was born in Konigshutte, Germany (now Chorzow, Poland), the last of six children. Persuaded to prepare for a career in banking by his industrialist father, young Franz, who had studied piano from the age of seven, reluctantly worked as a teller for over two years. After leaving his banking career, he began advanced studies in piano and composition, first in Dresden, then in Berlin. He earned money as a pianist performing in nightclubs and with jazz ensembles. He began doing band arrangements while working with the Weintraub Syncopaters and eventually started doing orchestral arrangements for filmmakers, his first major effort being Frederick Hollander's score for the 1930 film *Blue Angel*. His first original film score was *Kabinett de Dr. Larifari* (1930) and by the end of 1933, he had 11 scores to his credit. The 1934 production of Fritz Lang's *Liliom* was his first major triumph. Lang engaged Waxman to travel to the United States with him to do arrangements for the 1934 film version of Jerome Kern's *Music in the Air*. Waxman's first original score of the 144 he would do in Hollywood was for the 1935 film *The Bride of Frankenstein*. That same year, he signed a two-year contract with Universal Pictures to both compose scores and act as the studio's music department director. His efforts during this period include *The Invisible Ray* (1936) and Fritz Lang's *Fury* (1936). In 1937, MGM signed Waxman to a seven-year contract, initiating a relationship that would yield scores for such major efforts as *Captains Courageous* (1937), *The Adventures of Huckleberry Finn* (1939), *Dr. Jekyll and Mr. Hyde* (1941), *Suspicion* (1941), and *Woman of the Year* (1942). Waxman's services were occasionally subcontracted to other filmmakers during this period, twice resulting in Academy Award nominations for him, *The Young in Heart* (1938) and *Rebecca* (1940), both for David O. Selznick. Meanwhile, Waxman was also turning out scores for the concert stage, most notably the *Souvenirs de Paris Waltzes* (1939) and the suite from *Rebecca* (1940). His next studio affiliation came in 1943 with Warner Bros., which also resulted in numerous major scores, including *Mr. Skeffington* (1944), and *Objective, Burma!* (1945). Waxman established the Los Angeles International Music Festival in 1947, which premiered works by Stravinsky, Shostakovich, Vaughan Williams, and many other major composers. He also worked as conductor and administered many of the festival's events. Waxman's now-popular *Carmen Fantasie* (1947), written for *Humoresque* (with Isaac Stern brilliantly captured on the soundtrack), was recorded for RCA by Jascha Heifetz. In 1950 and 1951, Waxman won Academy Awards for Best Film Score for *Sunset Boulevard* and *A Place in the Sun*, respectively, becoming the first composer to win in successive years. More famous scores followed in the decade ahead, including those for *Prince Valiant* (1954), *The Spirit of St. Louis* (1957), *The Nun's Story* (1959), and *Taras Bulba* (1962). He continued turning out fine orchestral works too, like *Reminiscences* (1953) and *Ruth* (1960). Beginning in the late 1950s, Waxman wrote music for numerous well-known television series, including *The Twilight Zone* (1959), *The Fugitive* (1963), and *Peyton Place* (1964). Waxman remained active composing film scores and concert music in his last years. *—Robert Cummings*

CONCERTO

Carmen Fantasy (after Bizet), for violin & orchestra (1947)

This 12-minute display piece was one of several works Waxman wrote for a 1945 film, *Humoresque*, starring John Garfield as a struggling violinist. Waxman's friend Jascha Heifetz agreed to record the violin part for the soundtrack, and together he and Waxman selected familiar classical works to be adapted for violin and orchestra, with the violin parts tailor-made for Heifetz. Unfortunately, Warner Bros. would not agree to Heifetz' contract terms, and so Heifetz did not play it in the film; that job fell to Isaac Stern. Heifetz did finally recorded it in 1947, however, and this now-classic recording has never been out of print. Waxman wanted to arrange the *Fantasy* as a trumpet solo for Manny Klein, but never completed this version. When producer Friedmann Engelbrecht was producing a recording with trumpeter Sergei Nakariakov he asked Aleksandr Markovich to finish Waxman's sketches; the success of that recording has led to the work becoming a trumpet favorite, which in turn has stimulated new interest in the violin original. The *Carmen Fantasy* is based on themes from Georges Bizet's famous opera, *Carmen*, and is among the most brilliant of the many existing adaptations of this favorite. *—Joseph Stevenson*

Recommended:

○ **Humoresque** / Salerno-Sonnenberg, Litton (cond.), London SO / Nonesuch 79464

Carl Maria von Weber

b. Nov. 18, 1786, Eutin, Oldenburg, Germany, **d.** Jun. 5, 1826, London, England
Composer: Opera, Concerto, Chamber Music, Keyboard

Composer, conductor, virtuoso, novelist, and essayist, Carl Maria von Weber is one of the great figures of German Romanticism. Known for his opera *Der Freischütz*, a work which expresses the spirit and aspirations of German Romanticism, Weber was the quintessential Romantic artist, turning to poetry, history, folklore, and myths for inspiration and striving to create a convincing synthesis of fantastic literature and music. Resembling the Faust legend, *Der Freischütz* (the term suggests the idea of an marksman relying on magic) is a story of two lovers whose ultimate fate is decided by supernatural forces, a story which Weber brings to life by masterfully translating into music the otherworldly, particularly sinister, aspects of the narrative. Weber's additional claim to fame are his works for woodwind instruments, which include two concertos and a concertino for clarinet, a concerto for bassoon, and a superb quintet for clarinet and string quartet. Born in 1786, Weber studied with Michael Haydn and Abbé Vogler. Appointed Kappelmeister at Breslau in 1804, he gained fame as an opera composer with the production, in 1811, of *Abu Hassan*. In 1813, he became director of the Prague Opera. In Prague, where he remained until 1816, Weber developed a mostly French repertoire, taking an active, and highly creative, part in the practical aspects of opera production. Underlying his often controversial efforts to reform opera production was his ardent desire to create a German operatic tradition. Although there were, indeed, capable composers in the German-speaking lands, the idea of a German opera provoked much opposition, as the public, trained to perceive opera as an exclusively Italian art form, regarded the concept of German opera as a contradiction in terms, despite the existence of a singspiel tradition, brilliantly exemplified by the Magic Flute by Mozart. While Weber's appointment as Royal Kappelmeister at Dresden, not to mention the triumphant production of Der *Freischütz* (1821), certainly strengthened his position as champion of German opera, his opponents remained unconvinced. Weber's next opera, *Euryanthe* (1823), failed to repeat the success of *Der Freischütz*. In *Euryanthe*, his only opera without spoken dialogue, Weber introduced the device of recurrent themes throughout the entire opera, thus anticipating Wagner. Although Weber brilliantly adapted a variety of harmonic styles and textures to the dramatic narrative, the overall effect was seriously hampered by a rambling libretto, an inept adaptation of a medieval romance already used by Shakespeare in *Cymbeline*. In 1825, Weber was invited to London. Among the works he was expected to conduct was *Oberon*, another opera with a Shakespearean theme. The librettist, who took the story from Shakespeare's *Midsummer Night's Dream*, created, in a misguided effort to please the public, an incredible hodgepodge, even more convoluted than *Euryanthe*, that not even Weber's genius could salvage. Nevertheless, *Oberon*, which the English public received with admiration, contains much gorgeous music, including examples of lush orchestration and exquisite tone painting. Often performed in concert, the overture is a true Romantic gem. Already in poor health before his London tour, Weber died in the English capital in 1826, shortly after the premiere of *Oberon* at Covent Garden. *—Zoran Minderovic*

OPERA

Euryanthe, Op. 81 (1822–1823)

Euryanthe is Carl Maria von Weber's "would have been, could have been, should have been" masterpiece. Premiered at the Vienna *Kärntnertortheater* on October 25, 1823, it was conceived as a follow-up to the composer's highly successful *Der Freischütz*. However, Weber was not content to write his new work in a similar vein; rather, he attempted to create a genuinely through-composed music drama that left behind all elements of popular German theater (such as spoken dialogue). From a purely musical standpoint, the experiment was a success; Weber managed to blend musical sections together with a fluidity that was ahead of its time, and his vivid orchestrations and use of dense chromaticism made for evocative dramatic music. However, the libretto was of such poor quality that even the composer's fine music could not shape it into satisfying theater, and the work sank under the weight of its own flaws. At best, *Euryanthe* has retained a tenuous place in the operatic repertory.

The libretto in question was by Helmina von Chezy, who took as her source a semihistorical account—from the time of King Louis VI ("The Fat")—of a wager made by the Count de Nevers about the fidelity of his wife, Euryanthe (Chezy herself published a German translation of the work, called *L'Histoire du très-noble et chevalereaux prince Gérard, comte de Nevers, et de la très-vertueuse et très chaste princesse Euriant de Savoye, sa mye*, in 1823). Weber accepted the basic outline of the story, but insisted on the addition of many supernatural and fantastic elements, such as the purgatorial ghost that plagues Euryanthe, and whose salvation finally redeems her in the eyes of her husband. It is arguably these elements that burden the libretto more than any other, and so the composer bears considerable responsibility for the complicated and implausible final draft. However, it is also the supernatural elements of the story that give rise to Weber's most original and satisfying music.

Weber made extensive use of recurring motives in *Euryanthe*. Representing specific characters and situations, these motives add cohesiveness to the score and give the orchestra added prominence. The "ghost" music is especially distinctive. Derived from material in the work's overture, it features a thin chorus of violins over a lower-string tremolo that creates an insubstantial, restless quality. Lysiart and Eglantine—the two villains who conspire to falsely accuse Euryanthe in the eyes of her husband—are portrayed in highly chromatic music that at times stretches the boundaries of tonality. This places them in direct contrast to the story's protagonists, whose much more stable, prevailingly diatonic, music combats, and eventually defeats, that of the conspirators.

Euryanthe exerted a strong influence on such diverse composers as Schumann, Wagner, Marschner, Mahler, Berlioz, Liszt, and Spohr. While not nearly successful as its better-known predecessor, *Der Freischütz*, it nevertheless represents a more fully realized conception of music drama as it would emerge in the later nineteenth century, and perhaps the conclusive break between German Romantic opera and the tradition of the singspiel. *—AMG*

Synopsis:

Act One. The opera opens at the palace of King Louis VI where a group of ladies, nobles, and knights have gathered for a festivity. The king sees that Adolar, the Count of Nevers, is preoccupied, and asks him to sing a song in praise of his beautiful wife Euryanthe. After he has sung, all praise Euryanthe with him. But Lysiart, the Count of the Forest, is extremely jealous of Adolar, and bets Adolar that Euryanthe is not as faithful as she appears nor as happy. Adolar takes up the bet, asserting that she is as true as she is beautiful.

Euryanthe, at the palace at Nevers, misses Adolar as he misses her. Eglantine of Puiset enters. She is suspicious of Euryanthe, for Euryanthe has undertaken some strange nocturnal wanderings of late, for which Eglantine would like an explanation. Eglantine also secretly hates Euryanthe and is looking for a way to betray her. Euryanthe finally confesses that she has been praying at the tomb of Adolar's dead sister, who committed suicide with some poison contained in her ring. Adolar wished to join her lover Udo in death, but now her soul can find no rest until the ring is washed clean by the tears of an innocent girl in despair. Shocked that she has betrayed Adolar's secret to Eglantine, Euryanthe begs the other to keep the story to herself. Although Eglantine reassures Euryanthe of her friendship, she is a rival for the love of Adolar, and is only looking for a reason to denounce her. Lysiart arrives just then, and is welcomed to the palace by Euryanthe. His knights all join in her praises, and Lysiart is filled with uncontrollable passion for her.

Act Two. Night has fallen and the scene opens on Lysiart. He is tortured by thoughts of Euryanthe. He cannot bear the thought that she belongs to the Count of Nevers, but he loves her, and already feel guilt and remorse for his wicked intentions towards Adolar. Eglantine also has been plotting. At the tomb of Adolar's sister Emma, she has removed the poisoned ring from the corpse, and now emerges into the night. She plans to use it to discredit Euryanthe. Not seeing Lysiart standing in the darkness, she begins to rant out loud of her hatred and jealousy of Euryanthe. Lysiart comes forward, and proposes marriage to her. They form an evil alliance, and call on the powers of the night to aid them in the defeat of the Count and his beloved wife.

Back at the King's Hall, Adolar longs for Euryanthe. She is not long in coming, and the two have a loving reunion. They sing of their adoration for one another, and all welcome her to the court. However, Count Lysiart enters and announces to those assembled that it is he who has won the wager, and that Euryanthe has been unfaithful to Adolar. Adolar, although shaken, affirms his faith in Euryanthe. Nevertheless, Lysiart produces the ring of Emma and tells the story of the dead girl. Euryanthe guiltily confesses that she broke her vow of silence. All of the court judges that Euryanthe has completely betrayed her husband, and that Lysiart has won the wager. The price of the bet was all of the lands of the Count of Never, and Adolar forfeits them to Lysiart immediately. He takes Euryanthe by the hand, and the two set off to be exiles in the wilderness.

Act Three. Adolar and Euryanthe are wandering in the mountains. Completely disillusioned, he plans to kill her. Although she protests her innocence to him, he refuses to give her even a look or kind word. When a snake approaches the two, she tries to protect him, and risks her life in doing so. After he has killed the snake, he decides to leave Euryanthe alone in the wilderness, on her own, but alive. After he has gone, she sings of her despair, and of her longing for death. Her reveries are interrupted by the arrival of a hunting party from the king's court. When he recognizes her, King Louis asks her if she would like to do penance for her sin, but she protests her innocence. She tells him that it was Eglantine who told the Count of the Forest the story of Adolar's sister, and the King is overjoyed. He offers to return the lands that Lysiart stole from the Count of Nevers, and to reunite her with Adolar. Although happy, she collapses from exhaustion. The king and his men carry her off.

In a clearing in front of the castle at Nevers, Adolar is extremely bitter, but the townsfolk assure him that it was all Eglantine's doing, and that the two who now live in his castle were traitorous. They promise to help him win back his lands in battle. Eglantine and Lysiart approach to the sound of wedding music. Eglantine is pale and ashen, and beset by visions of Emma's ghost. Lysiart commands his men to capture Adolar and imprison him, but when they recognize Adolar, they welcome him with joy. A conflict between Lysiart and Adolar is only prevented by the arrival of the king, who tells them that Euryanthe's heart is completely broken. Eglantine vents her triumphant rage on Lysiart, and he in turn stabs her repeatedly until she is dead. Euryanthe is brought in, and peaceful music is heard. All become aware that the ghost of Emma is now at rest, and that innocent tears have washed her poisoned ring clean. Lysiart is led off to prison, and the rest of the company rejoices. *—Rita Laurance*

Recommended:

○ **Weber: Euryanthe** / Zallinger (cond.), Reining, Rossel-Majdan, Delorka, Kamann, Berry, Austrian RSO / Gala 703

Der Freischütz, Op. 77 (1817–1821)

Ten years after Weber composed the highly successful *Abu Hassan*, he found a libretto he felt he could use effectively. He had always been attracted to the common Central European tale of the "free-shooter." It concerns the man who makes a pact with the devil in order to obtain magic bullets or arrows that will always find their target. No one is safe from them, not even the evil one from whom they came. The free-shooter is a damned soul, avoided by his fellows, unhappy, and his end is always violent. There were many versions of the Freischütz story, most based on the historical account of Georg Schmidt, a clerk who in 1710 was tried and convicted of trying to obtain magic bullets by bargaining with the devil. Johann Apel and Friedrich Laun had turned the story into the opening tale of their *Gespensterbuch* of 1810. The librettist for Weber's opera was Johann Friedrich Kind. From Apel and Laun he borrowed many innovations to the historical story. A love motive was added for the misguided hero, who wishes to earn the hand of his beloved Agathe, a virtuous and pious woman, by becoming the most skilled huntsman in the area. Also in Kind's cast are Samiel and Caspar, two representatives of Satan; Aennchen, an innocent girl and comic element, derived from the French opera-comique; and Ottokar, the benevolent Prince, standard Romantic opera fare. Hunters, villagers, and bridesmaids make up the choruses that bring to life the surrounding countryside. Kind was also invented of the Wolf's Glen scene, famous for bringing to life, through nature, all the evil forces of the universe and in the psychology of man.

Weber himself saw this opera as a battle between the forces of good and evil and planned the structure around a downward curve into darkness, which is suddenly brought back up into the light. He writes in his notes that many of the scenes take place in the evening or at night, including Agathe's big scena that takes place in the moonlight. He planned his orchestrations around two elements: the forces of evil and the huntsmen's music. The forces of evil he orchestrated in the lowest registers of the various instruments, bringing out qualities and timbres never before known in the history of the orchestra. Berlioz, Beethoven, and others admired his handling of the orchestra. The two main threads that form the background for Weber's opera are the German singspiel and French opera. It was common in German singspiel to use folk elements and melodies, but Weber takes this tendency one step further. Many of his melodies are derived from actual folk melodies, and others imitate folk melodies to such a degree that they became popular folk tunes after the opera became well known. The entr'acte was introduced from French opera. In addition, from French compositional practices Weber developed the "reminiscence motive," which reuses material to emphasize a mood or character. This eventually developed into the German leitmotiv.*—Rita Laurance*

Synopsis:

Act One. The opera opens in the Bohemian forest, in a clearing in front of an inn. Killian has just won a shooting match and is congratulated by the villagers. They laugh at Max, one of the foresters, for his inability to come even close to his target. The teasing is about to erupt into a fight when Cuno and the other foresters of Prince Ottokar arrive. Among them is Caspar, a forester who is in league with the devil's assistant Samiel. He tells Max that perhaps his gun is bewitched. He suggests that Max go to the crossroads on Friday next, draw a circle around him, and call forth the Great Huntsman. Cuno scolds Caspar to silence, but warns Max that he mustn't fail on the morrow, for in order to win the hand of Agathe and become the next chief forester, he must win the shooting match. Agathe is the beautiful and virtuous daughter of Cuno. At the thought of his probable failure, Max becomes despondent. Finally, all the huntsmen join in a chorus in praise of hunting, and a dance ends the festivities. Max is left alone in the night.

Alone, Max ponders his fate. Caspar comes out of the inn and joins him. He orders some wine, but offends Max with a raucous drinking song. He insists that he can help Max win the trial. He gives Max his gun and tells him to shoot. When Max fires, the bullet hits an eagle, bringing it down. The astounded Max returns the gun to its owner, who says that the bullet was a magic bullet. However, that was his last magic bullet, and in order to obtain more, Max must meet him at the Wolf's Glen at midnight, to bargain with the Great Huntsman. After Max has gone, Caspar gloats over his impending victory. He plans to give Max's soul to Samiel, and then he will be free to go on living.

Act Two. Agathe worries over Max's absence, and is beset by unhappy thoughts. She visited the hermit in the morning and he gave her a bunch of roses, but they don't cheer her up. She offers a prayer for Max's return and contemplates her coming wedding to him. When he arrives, he tells her that he must go into the forest to retrieve a stag which he has shot, but he mentions that the stag is near the Wolf's Glen, and Agathe becomes upset. Both she and Aennchen are horrified that he is even thinking of going near the place. Max blithely replies that a hunter cannot be afraid of the forest and goes off.

At the Wolf's Glen, Caspar makes a circle of boulders in which he places a skull, a crucible, a bullet mold, and an eagle's wing. A chorus of spirits shrieks in the night and Caspar calls up the evil Samiel as the clock strikes twelve. In return for Max's soul, Samiel agrees to allow Caspar to live for three more years. Caspar asks for seven bullets, the last of which will belong to Samiel. This bullet, Caspar suggests, should be directed at the innocent Agathe. When Max arrives, he is disturbed by visions of his dead mother and of Agathe. But he agrees to help Caspar in the casting of the bullets, and the spells begin. Into the crucible Caspar places three bullets that have found their mark, a shard of glass from the window of a church, quicksilver, and the eyes of a hoopoe and a lynx. As each bullet is cast, apparitions appear, until the seventh conjures up Samiel himself.

Act Three. Hunting horns introduce the forest scene. The weather is fine, and Max is being congratulated on his flawless shooting. But he has already fired three of the four bullets which Caspar gave him from the night before. Caspar has secretly used up the other bullets, and Max's final bullet belongs to Samiel.

Agathe is already dressed in her wedding gown, and is at prayer in her room. The night before she had a strange and troubling dream. She dreamt that she was a white dove, but that Max shot her, and she fell dead. When the dove disappeared, she returned to being herself, and a black bird lay dead in her place. Aennchen tries to comfort her but when instead of a bridal wreath, a funeral wreath is delivered to the inn, both women become thoroughly shaken.

Prince Ottokar and his retinue have gathered for the shooting match. He commands Max to shoot at a white dove on the bough of a tree nearby. Agathe cries out as she is struck instead of the dove, but her bridal wreath has caught the bullet, and she is not harmed. Because the bullet failed, Samiel arrives to claim Caspar. Caspar dies, cursing all.

Max confesses that he was using magic bullets cast by Caspar in the Wolf's Glen. Although Cuno and Agathe beg for clemency for him, he is banished from the forest. The hermit convinces the Prince to mitigate his sentence to a one-year probation, and all agree to look forward to the wedding in one year. *—Rita Laurance*

Recommended:

- ○ **Weber: Der Freischütz** / Kleiber (cond.), Schreier, Janowitz, Mathis, Adam, Dresden Staatskapelle / 1998 / DG 457736
- ○ **Weber: Der Freischütz** / Keilberth (cond.), Schock, Prey, Otto, Grümmer, Berlin PO / 1988 / EMI 769342

Oberon (1825–1826)

Oberon is Weber's final opera and one of his most impressive works. He composed the work between 1825 and 1826 on commission for Covent Garden, and it premiered there in April 1826.

Weber found a rich and evocative story for the stage. *Oberon* has settings in medieval France, at the legendary Arabian court of Haroun al-Raschid and in the fairy world. Oberon refuses to return to Titania until he has proof that at least one pair of lovers can remain faithful. The fairy Puck procures a magic horn, which he gives to one of Charlemagne's knights, Huon, so that Huon can rescue his lady Reiza from the Arabian court and thus become living testimony to faithfulness. The combination of elements alone allowed Weber much opportunity to compose music suggestive of locale and emotion. While the libretto is often regarded as extremely weak, the music surpasses those constraints.

Weber learned English to work more closely with his librettist, James Robinson Planché. Performances in German, as usually occur, reflect a translation from the original form of the opera. The first translation was by Weber's sometime collaborator Theodore Hell. Other German versions were made to bring it effectively to the stage and to make the music more continuous than in the original, which was written to suit English tastes for spectacle and for dialogue rather than recitative. Gustav Mahler not only adjusted several numbers, but also rewrote some of the opera to arrive at a consistent performing score.

With *Der Freischütz* and *Euryanthe*, Weber had composed two successful operas that set the standard for the German stage. *Oberon* shows not only Weber's mature style, but also reflects an intensified—almost bel canto—lyricism. He avoided the menacing naturalism of *Der Freischütz* or the more formal elegance of *Euryanthe*. Instead, he arrived at a light and deft approach to the work, which anticipates the "elfin" sounds Mendelssohn created in his music for Shakespeare's *A Midsummer Night's Dream*. In doing so, Weber used exposed wind passages and made the string textures more transparent. The unifying theme of the magic horn brought a different color to the work and contributed a musical cue to the dramaturgy. Even though *Oberon* involves spoken dialogue, the musical numbers are nonetheless operatic and many of them are sustained scenes. The famous soprano aria for Reiza, "Ocean! Thou mighty monster," is comparable to the kind of music Bellini would take up in *Norma* and other works in the 1830s. At the same time, the orchestra plays an important role in the work and functions as more than mere accompaniment. The aria cited above is effective because of the interaction that occurs between the solo voice and the orchestra. Without burying the voice under a symphonic texture, Weber creates a blend between the media. This kind of intense musical interplay is typical of Weber's work late in his career, and his influence on succeeding generations is notable for it. *—James Zychowicz*

Synopsis:

Act One. Oberon the Elf king lies asleep in his bower, while fairies hover over him and sing softly while he rests. Puck arrives and disperses the group, saying that Oberon has separated from his wife Titania, Queen of the fairies. They have disagreed on which are the more inconstant, men or women, and they have sworn not to become reunited until they have found a constant pair of lovers. As Oberon wakes he utters regrets over his "fatal" vow.

Puck brings Oberon the news that Charlemagne has sent Huon of Bordeaux to Baghdad. Huon is to become betrothed to the daughter of the Caliph by killing his right hand man. Huon and Sherasmin, his esquire, lie sleeping in the forest as Oberon and Puck come upon them. Oberon gives Huon a dream of Reiza in a Persian Kiosk, and she cries out to him to rescue her. When the two men wake, Oberon gives them gifts for the journey; a hunting horn that when blown brings help to the one in need or causes men to dance with joy, and a golden cup that fills with wine by itself, but only for an honest man. If a villain were to put the cup to his lips, they would be scorched and burnt. Oberon magically whisks them away to the banks of the Tigris, near Baghdad. There they see Prince Babekan being attacked by a lion. They come to his aid and he is grateful. But when they attempt to drink a drink of friendship out of Huon's magic cup, the Prince's lips are seared and burnt. He turns on the two, but is easily defeated. The grandmother of Reiza's maid Fatima welcomes the two heroes into her cottage. Reiza is to be married to Prince Babekan the very next day. But she has dreamt that she will be rescued by a noble knight, whom she will then marry. In her dream Reiza saw Huon and Sherasmin, and so closely described them to the old woman that the woman recognizes them almost immediately. She hurries to the palace to tell the princess that her rescuer is near.

Back in Baghdad at the Prince's harem, Reiza confesses to Fatima her horror at the prospect of marrying the Prince. She would prefer death. Fatima's grandmother brings the news that the knight has really arrived. And as all go to rest, Reiza awaits her rescuer.

Act Two. In the great hall, the Caliph announces that the time for the wedding of the Prince has arrived, and Reiza is brought in. Just as the ceremony is about to take place, Huon and Sherasmin enter. Huon blows his magic horn, which freezes his enemies to the floor, and the two take Reiza and escape from the palace. Then Oberon appears to transport the three to a ship, which is waiting to take them to Greece. Sherasmin, meanwhile, has been wooing Fatima, Reiza's maid. He convinces her to join them, and the four leave together.

They are not long at sea, however, before Puck calls up a storm that wrecks the boat on some rocks. Reiza drinks of the magic cup and is refreshed, and Huon goes to look for help. Reiza sees a ship approaching and waves to it, but it is pirates, and they kidnap her and take her away. They threaten to kill Huon when he returns, but relent and just tie him up. Oberon appears in the sky and summons Puck to him. Puck is to take Huon to Ibrahim the gardener after one week has passed. In the meantime, Huon lies asleep in an arbor, surrounded by singing spirits and mermaids.

Act Three. In Tunis at the home of Ibrahim, the gardener of the Emir, Fatima and Sherasmin have been washed ashore and taken as slaves into his household. They have been married and are extremely happy, although they miss Huon and Reiza. Just then Huon magically appears. And a boat appears in the harbor which is said to be carrying a beautiful woman as a gift for the Emir. Sherasmin and Fatima surmise that it must be Reiza, and all three hope for a reunion. But their magic horn has been lost in the shipwreck, and they don't know how they will rescue Fatima, or escape the palace.

Reiza arrives at the harem of the Emir Almanzor, who welcomes her warmly. Huon, meanwhile, enters the service of the Emir's gardener along with his two other companions. Roshana, the wife of the Emir, becomes jealous of Reiza and all the attention the Emir is showing her. She offers to make Huon Emir if only he will murder Almanzor. When he refuses, she pretends that he tried to attack her. The Emir throws both him and his wife in prison as a result, intending to have them both burned alive.

Sherasmin is deeply angered by the bad turn of their fortunes, and cries out loud that Oberon has betrayed them. But when he does so, he is pricked by a rose bush, and finds the magic horn hanging from one of its branches. He takes the horn and he and Fatima set off to rescue Huon and Reiza. Reiza has told the Emir that she is Huon's wife, and that she will not marry the Emir. So she, too, is to be burned alive.

Just as they are about to go up in flames, Sherasmin sounds the horn, and all of the people begin to dance. He blows the horn again and the funeral pyre disappears. Oberon and Titania magically appear and express their gratitude for the constancy that Huon and Reiza have shown to one another. They will now be reunited in love, and Huon and Reiza will be returned to the court of Charlemagne. *—Rita Laurance*

Recommended:

- ○ **Weber: Oberon** / Janowski (cond.), Van der Walt, Nielsen, Seiffert, Kasarova, Skovhus, Paulsen, Berlin SO / 1997 / RCA 68505

CONCERTO

Andante and Rondo Ungarese, for bassoon & orchestra in C minor, Op. 35 (1813)

Weber wrote the first version of this work in 1809 for his brother Fritz, a violist, not a bassoonist. Violists still play the *Andante and Hungarian Rondo* from time to time, but the piece is more commonly heard in its bassoon incarnation from 1813, arranged on request from bassoonist Georg Friedrich Brandt (for whom Weber had already written a full-length concerto). The bassoon version recasts the solo part a bit and expands two of the tuttis, but there are no substantial differences between the two editions. The Andante introduces a cautious, simple tune, entering as if on tiptoe (complete with pizzicato strings), then spins out three variations. In the first, the orchestra plays the theme unchanged, while the bassoon weaves around it. The soloist develops the second variation into more of a romance, but the third returns to the pattern of the first variation, with the bassoon now given an even more intricate part. The rondo takes off from a whimsical, skipping tune; this is interwoven with a series of episodes that play with rhythmic accents and, in the second, trills. At the end, the bassoon indulges in a long flurry of triplets leaving hardly a pause for breath, one of the few obviously virtuosic effects in a particularly amiable piece. *—James Reel*

Recommended:

- ○ **Mozart, Weber, Hummel: Bassoon Concertos** / Popov, Polyansky (cond.), Russian State SO / 1998 / Chandos 9656

Bassoon Concerto in F major, Op. 75 (1811; revised 1822)

Weber was only 25 when Munich court bassoonist Georg Friedrich Brandt asked him for a concerto, and he produced one of the two most significant works in the instrument's limited concerto repertoire (the other being Mozart's). Eleven years later, in 1822, Weber prepared the concerto for publication, making a few alterations along the way. Most of the changes were small, affecting details of the solo part and string scoring and expanding a couple of tutti passages. More significantly, though, Weber decided not to introduce the first movement's second theme in a minor key. Some bassoonists feel that this brightening to a major mode deprives the music of necessary atmosphere and a few have revived the original version. Otherwise, few listeners will notice much difference between the two editions.

The first movement, Allegro ma non troppo, follows the period's usual template. The orchestra succinctly lays out two highly contrasting themes—a martial statement soothed by a much more lyrical melody—whereupon the bassoonist appropriates them, with minimal orchestral accompaniment. Weber gets down to the business of development with alacrity, lavishing bravura passagework upon the soloist, and emphasizing the march tune. He recapitulates the themes and efficiently moves into the coda without offering the soloist a real cadenza. The highly lyrical Adagio could be an aria lifted from one of Weber's operas, complete with a horn-accompanied middle section that calls *Der Freischütz* to mind. The soloist takes the briefest of cadenzas, lingering in its high register just before the end. The concluding Rondo (Allegro) finds the bassoon itself introducing the insouciant main theme, then pursuing it and commenting on it through the intervening episodes that either are splattered with rapid-fire notes or send the bassoon bumping up and down its range. *—James Reel*

Recommended:

○ **Bassoon Concertos** / Perkins, Boyd (cond.), Manchester Camerata / 2002 / Hyperion 67288

Clarinet Concerto No. 1 in F minor, Op. 73 (1811)

Carl Maria von Weber (1786–1826) composed his *Clarinet Concerto No. 1 in F minor, Op. 73*, in 1811 after his *Concertino for Clarinet and Orchester in E flat major, Op. 26*, and before his *Clarinet Concerto No. 2 in E flat major, Op. 74*. All three works were written for and dedicated to the clarinetist Heinrich Joseph Baermann, and all three show a complete understanding of the capabilities of the instrument. Weber's *Clarinet Concerto No. 1* is distinctly different from the earlier concertino: where the earlier work is lightly playful and lyrically expressive, the *Concerto No. 1* is deeply serious and dramatically, almost operatically, expressive. The concerto is in three movements: a forceful opening Allegro, an intensely expressive central Adagio, and an energetic closing Rondo Allegretto. Weber is clearly a master of the Romantic orchestra, and his writing for the soloists is supremely skillful throughout. *—James Leonard*

Recommended:

○ **Weber: Clarinet Concertos 1 & 2; Concertino; Clarinet Quintet** / Meyer, Blomstedt (cond.), Dresden Staatskapelle / 2003 / EMI 67989

Clarinet Concerto No. 2 in E flat major, Op. 74 (1811)

Carl Maria von Weber (1786–1826) composed his *Clarinet Concerto No. 2 in E flat major, Op. 74*, in 1811 immediately after his *Clarinet Concerto No. 1 in F minor, Op. 73*, and his *Concertino for Clarinet and Orchestra in E flat major, Op. 26*. Like the earlier works, Weber wrote his *Concerto No. 2* for clarinet virtuoso Heinrich Joseph Baermann and the work displays a thorough knowledge of the capacities of the instrument. After the most dramatic *Concerto in F minor*, the *Concerto in E flat major* revisits the more lighter and more lyrical world of the *Concertino in E flat*. Set in three movements, the *Concerto in E flat* opens with a virtuosic Allegro, moves through a gloriously bel canto Andante Romanza, and closes with a playful Alla Polacca. As in all his orchestral works, Weber's mastery of color and tone is complete, and his writing for the soloist is breathtakingly difficult but wholly idiomatic. *—James Leonard*

Recommended:

○ **Weber: Clarinet Concertos 1 & 2; Concertino; Clarinet Quintet** / Meyer, Blomstedt (cond.), Dresden Staatskapelle / 2003 / EMI 67989

Concertino for clarinet & orchestra in E flat major, Op. 26 (1811)

Weber wrote his *Concertino for clarinet and orchestra in E flat major* (1811) for Heinrich Bärmann, one of the most accomplished clarinetists of the day. As the instrument was relatively new, Weber's works for the clarinet broke new ground by affording it a new measure of prominence and displaying its wide-ranging capabilties for both expressivity and virtuosic display.

The Concertino consists of three short movements that conform to the traditional organization of the solo concerto: Adagio ma non troppo, Andante, and Allegro. It opens with a tragic song for the clarinet that resembles nothing so much as an opera aria; indeed, the most notable aspect of the work is perhaps the distinctively vocal manner in which Weber uses the clarinet. From this starting point Weber spins increasingly elaborate variations that eventually make their way back to the original gloomy mood.

The success of the premiere, given in the presence (and at the request) of the King of Bavaria, was such that the king commissioned from Weber two full-scale clarinet concerti; these works, together with the Concertino, remain pioneering efforts in the history of the instrument as well as cornerstones of its repertoire. *—AMG*

Recommended:

○ **Weber: Clarinet Concertos 1 & 2; Concertino; Clarinet Quintet** / Meyer, Blomstedt (cond.), Dresden Staatskapelle / 2003 / EMI 67989

Konzertstück for piano & orchestra in F minor, Op. 79 (1821)

Weber composed this *Concert Piece* in 1821 and played the first performance at Berlin on June 28 of that year. The *Konzertstück*, third and last of Weber's works for piano and orchestra, was created while he rehearsed the first performance of *Der Freischütz* in Berlin, and was premiered by him just ten days after a triumphant first performance of his best opera. The *Concert Piece* is unlike the two piano concertos that preceded it, for Weber wrote all four sections of this volatile work (complete with "plot") in a single movement. As he played it through for his wife and his young English pupil, Julius Benedict, the composer told them the following scenario:

"A châtelaine sits alone on her balcony, gazing off in the distance. Her knight has gone on a Crusade to the Holy Land. Years have passed, battles have been fought; is he still alive? Will she ever see him again?" The music, in F minor, is marked Larghetto affetuoso and colored plaintively by clarinets and bassoons, very much in the spirit of Weber's new Romanticism.

Then, Allegro passionato but still in F minor, "her excited imagination summons a vision of her noble husband lying wounded and forsaken on the battlefield. Could she not fly to his side and die with him? She falls back, unconscious. Then from the distance comes the sound of a trumpet. There in the forest something flashes in the sunlight as it comes nearer and nearer." First from the clarinet, then in the full orchestra a Tempo di marcia bursts forth in C major, with echoes of Beethoven and, as it quickens, *Fidelio* especially.

"Knights and squires, with the Crusaders' cross and banners waving, are acclaimed by the crowd. And there her husband is among them!" An octave glissando signals the lady's joyful recognition before "she sinks into his arms." An impassioned bridge passage for solo piano brings on a Presto giocoso in F major, depicting "happiness without end! The woods and waves sing a song of love, while a thousand voices proclaim its victory" as Weber emerges from the keyboard era of Hummel and Czerny to light the way for Liszt. *—Roger Dettmer*

Recommended:

○ **Weber: Piano Concertos 1 & 2; Koncertstück** / Demidenko, Mackerras (cond.), Scottish CO / 1995 / Hyperion 66729

Piano Concerto No. 1 in C major, Op. 11 (1810)

Carl Maria von Weber (1786–1826) composed his *Piano Concerto No. 1 in C major* in 1810 and gave the work its premiere in Mannheim the same year. Stylistically, the work's overall structure is clearly based on the model of Mozart's concertos, and many of the work's details are drawn from Beethoven's own *Piano Concerto in C major*. The double exposition in the opening Allegro is Mozartean, while the descending double octaves at the end of the development are Beethovenian. But while the work's antecedents are easy to spot, Weber's own identity is apparent in every bar. One of the great piano virtuosos of the early nineteenth century, Weber's tremendous technique and enormous sonorities inform every movement of the work, especially the brilliantly rhythmic closing Presto. And the central Adagio in A flat major is pure Weber: lyrical Romantic melodies of deep expressivity for the piano set against a delicately colorful chamber orchestra of viola, two solo cellos, and bass with two horns. *—James Leonard*

Recommended:

○ **Weber: Piano Concertos 1 & 2; Koncertstück** / Demidenko, Mackerras (cond.), Scottish CO / 1995 / Hyperion 66729

Piano Concerto No. 2 in E flat major, Op. 32 (1811–1812)

Carl Maria von Weber (1786–1826) composed his *Piano Concerto in E flat major* in 1812 and gave the work its premiere in Gotha the same year. The work is clearly and directly modeled on Beethoven's *Piano Concerto in E flat major*, a work Weber purchased in 1810. Both works are in three movements, with the opening and closing movements in E flat major and the central movement in B major. Like Beethoven's *Concerto*, Weber's opening Allegro maestoso is athletic and virtuosic, albeit Weber fit his to suit his own brilliant technique. Like Beethoven's *Concerto*, Weber's central Adagio is full of elevated pathos and heartrending lyricism, albeit Weber's melodies are far more overtly Romantic than Beethoven's. And like Beethoven's *Concerto*, Weber's closing Rondo Presto is in 6/8 time and features unexpected modulations and transitions, albeit Weber's orchestration is far more colorful and unusual than Beethoven's. *—James Leonard*

Recommended:

○ **Weber: Piano Concertos 1 & 2; Koncertstück** / Demidenko, Mackerras (cond.), Scottish CO / 1995 / Hyperion 66729

CHAMBER MUSIC

Clarinet Quintet in B flat major, Op. 34 (1811–1815)

It is doubtful whether Weber's sparkling *Quintet for clarinet and strings* would have come into existence had the composer had not counted among his friends Frederick Baermann, one of the preeminent clarinet virtuosi of the day. No doubt inspired by Baermann's extraordinary skill on the instrument, Weber produced in the Quintet one of his most charismatic works for the clarinet, and one of the most technically demanding. The Quintet is far more than a mere vehicle for virtuosic exhibitionism; the clarinet, in fact, provides a sort of intricate embroidery for the ensemble rather than assuming a truly leading role. Still, in terms of its prominence, the instrument must be regarded as first among equals in this fancifully Romantic work.

After a meditative opening the mood quickly lightens. The slow movement, a Fantasia, wanders pensively through shadowy groves of melody, at last fading away with a poetic dimineuendo al fine. The Minuetto capriccio is full of good humor, ending with a jokey phrase that somehow forgets to bring the movement to a close. The final movement, a Rondo and galop full of dancing gaiety, returns again and again to a devilish little phrase marked by a breathless flurry of notes. *—Roy Brewer*

Recommended:

- ○ **Chamber Music of Carl Maria von Weber** / Shifrin, Kavafian, Sherry, Neubauer, Bachmann / 1997 / Delos 3194

Grand Duo Concertante, for clarinet & piano in B flat major, Op. 48 (1815–1816)

The 28-year-old Carl Maria von Weber began composing this piece in July 1815, working first on the Rondo finale, then turning to the Andante con moto middle panel. He completed the first movement last, in November 1816, around his thirtieth birthday. This reverse process of composition seemed to hamper neither the work's structural fabric nor its final, rather imposing musical worth.

While the piano gets second billing in this work, its role is nearly equal to that of the clarinet. Weber himself was a virtuoso pianist and this composition was one of several he wrote for clarinetist Heinrich Baermann, equally gifted in his instrumental realm.

The first movement begins vigorously, with many utterly enchanting exchanges between clarinet and piano. A serene and lovely theme is then introduced on clarinet, with the piano initially serving in an accompaniment role, but then later prodding the music into playfulness. A development section ensues, where Weber's writing is masterful and colorful throughout. A recapitulation and coda close out this sonata-allegro movement in deft style.

The second movement begins with a mournful theme on clarinet. The piano follows with an extended solo section, after which the two instruments reunite and eventually deliver a lovely, if gloomy, close. The finale dispels the darkness from the previous movement with the clarinet's joyful main theme. The music is gentle at first, but then bursts forth with greater energy and merriment. The ending is fast and brilliant, and features colorful writing for both instruments. The *Grand Duo Concertante* usually lasts just over 20 minutes. *—Robert Cummings*

Recommended:

- ○ **Chamber Music of Carl Maria von Weber** / Shifrin, Golub / 1997 / Delos 3194

Introduction, Theme and Variations for clarinet & strings in B flat major (1811–1815)

Weber is fairly well-known for his chamber music for clarinet, having produced works like the *Quintet for Clarinet and Strings*, Op. 34; the *Grand Duo Concertant*, Op. 48; and *Seven Variations*, Op. 33, both for clarinet and piano. The *Introduction, Theme and Variations* here, which suspiciously carries an Op. Posth. tag, is a piece whose authorship has been called into question. For years it had been attributed to Weber, but later scholarship suggests it might be the work of Joseph Küffner. Naturally, its date of composition is also uncertain. In any event, the piece is a worthwhile composition that fanciers of clarinet music should find quite appealing. The work is short, lasting about nine or ten minutes, with the "Introduction" presenting a lovely Mozartean dreaminess in the clarinet melody and rather simple string accompaniment. In the main section, the clarinet plays a chipper, innocent theme several times, after which the strings are finally given a chance to step to the fore. The variations are attractive, the second an especially perky creation, wherein the first violin is given a charming solo. Most of the music is playful or dreamy and also somewhat childlike in its utter obliviousness to the world's woes. The writing for the clarinet is finely imagined, especially in the closing variation, where the music rushes headlong through a gauntlet of technical challenges for the soloist. *—Robert Cummings*

Recommended:

- ○ **Chamber Music of Carl Maria von Weber** / Shifrin, Lin, Neubauer, Hoffman / 1997 / Delos 3194

Trio for flute, cello & piano in G minor, Op. 63 (1818–1819)

The flute figures in nearly half of Weber's small catalog of chamber music and the most substantial of these items (though not quite as extended as his more popular clarinet quintet) is the *Flute Trio* with the flute replacing the violin in the usual trio configuration. It's unclear why Weber chose this instrumentation; he designed his clarinet and bassoon works for specific soloists, but no court flutist seems to have inspired this trio, which is dedicated to Philipp Jungh, Weber's friend and doctor. (Weber's flute sonatas are merely alternate versions of his violin sonatas, fairly easy pieces intended for domestic consumption.) The somber first movement (Allegro moderato) begins with long cello and flute lines over a throbbing piano accompaniment and is full of dramatic outbursts. The second theme abounds in more conventional, Classical-style twittering and this tension between dark Romanticism and bright Classicism drives the movement's development with Romanticism having the last word. The Scherzo begins with a rugged, offbeat figure reminiscent of the out-of-kilter scherzo from Beethoven's *"Spring" Sonata*, though lacking Beethoven's humor. This alternates with a flighty waltz melody, a strong contrast that allows Weber to leave out the scherzo's customary trio section. The third movement, Andante espressivo, bears the title "Schäfers Klage" or "Shepherd's Lament." The simple flute tune creeps along, seemingly unsure of itself, gradually elaborated by all three instruments except for a strange, chromatic interruption similar to the spot where Weber's *Oberon Overture* harmonically falls apart. The long finale (Allegro) is more conventional, a loose assemblage of chipper tunes, some lyrical and some of the sewing-machine variety. Weber gives the instruments free rein, allowing each to come to prominence through the movement's course and then recede into the general trio texture. *—James Reel*

Recommended:

- ○ **Weber: Trio In G Minor; 6 Sonatas For Flute & Piano Op10** / Canino, Nicolet, Filippini / 1990 / Novalis 150065
- ○ **Haydn, Hummel, Gyrowetz, Weber: Flute Trios** / Haupt, Zenziper, Teutsch / Capriccio 10398

Variations on a theme from "Silvana," for clarinet & piano, Op. 33 (1811)

Weber whipped this piece out during a concert tour with his clarinetist friend Heinrich Joseph Bärmann. The two were to give a concert in Prague, where Weber hoped to have his opera *Silvana* produced. To advertise the opera's felicities to Prague's audiences, Weber wrote, rehearsed, and performed all in a single day a quarter-hour's worth of variations on the aria *Warum musst' ich dich je erblikken*. Weber had already worked variants on this tune into the fifth of his six "progressive" sonatas for violin and piano. The stately melody moves smoothly and gradually up the scale, pauses at a little trill, continues its ascent, and gently descends like a feather. It repeats its course around a couple of mildly contrasting little sections, then embarks on a series of flashy variations, or so one assumes upon hearing the first. The second is given entirely to the piano; upon its return, the clarinet is in a more thoughtful mood and offers a slow, highly expressive third variation. This approach holds steady well into the work's central portion, the clarinetist displaying virtuosity only in a brief passage of trills and wide leaps. The piano again takes a variation for itself, returning us to the realm of pure showmanship. Aside from one long, ominous detour, the ensuing variations are florid and stretch widely through the clarinet's range. Surprisingly, the set ends not with fireworks, but with a demure restatement of the original theme. *—James Reel*

Recommended:

- ○ **A Tribute to Gerald Moore** / Moore, de Peyer / 2003 / EMI 67994

KEYBOARD

Invitation to the Dance (Aufforderung zum Tanze), rondo brillant for piano, Op. 65 (1819)

Dance aficionados know this as the score for Michel Fokine's *Le spectre de la rose* using Hector Berlioz's orchestration of Weber's piano score. (Interestingly, the dance piece is inspired by Théophile Gautier's poem of the same name, which Berlioz had set as part of his song cycle *Les nuits d'été*, but Berlioz himself made no connection between his song and Weber's score.) In the ballet, a girl dreams that the rose she'd worn to the ball comes to her in the form of a man, waltzing with her through the wee hours. The program, such as it is, for Weber's piano piece is similar but more straightforward: A young man approaches a young woman and graciously asks her to dance; they do so through a series of waltzes, and then, in slow music mirroring the introduction, they bid each other adieu. Weber's score requires great dexterity from the pianist, but its sequence of generous, hummable waltz tunes makes no demands on the audience (except that they must refrain from applauding over the beginning of the quiet coda). The introduction/conclusion is delicate and poetic, a gently rising and then wandering motif answered by a few gracefully falling phrases. The main waltz-rondo sequence begins and keeps returning to an exuberant little tune that leaps up, swirls down, and repeats (Weber's liberal use of repeats can make this piece sound tedious in the hands of a dull pianist). Most of the rest of the material keeps the pianist's hands whirling up and down the keyboard in 3/4 time, creating music even more effervescent than that of Josef Lanner and Johann Strauss I, who hadn't even begun to popularize the waltz when Weber wrote this piece. *—James Reel*

Recommended:

○ **Great Pianists: Ignacy Friedman** / Friedman / 1999 / Philips 456784

○ **Romantic Piano Favourites Vol. 1** / Szokolay / 1995 / Naxos 8.550052

Piano Sonata No. 1 in C major ("Perpetuum Mobile"), Op. 24 (1812)

While Carl Maria von Weber's importance is largely tied to opera and to his role in establishing the Romantic movement, his piano compositions are also important, as both Liszt and Chopin attested. The four sonatas must stand at the core of his solo output and although the *Fourth* (1819–22) is generally acknowledged as the finest, the *First* here is quite an imaginative, powerful composition in its own right. Cast in four movements, the sonata already divulges the composer's quite distinctive style, which augurs Chopin and often features a singing line of great beauty. The opening panel, marked Allegro, clearly has a Chopin-esque quality. Its playful, colorful main theme and imaginative virtuosic writing—not to mention the opening downward scale, which eerily anticipates the opening of the "Revolutionary Etude"—delightfully call Chopin to mind and deftly engage the listener. The singing quality mentioned above can be found in the dramatic Adagio second movement, whose middle section is particularly lovely. Again, the music here augurs Chopin. The third movement, Minuetto: Allegro, is delightful in its splashy colors and vigorous playfulness. Weber nicknamed the finale "L'infatigable," an appropriate tag for this Rondo. Marked Presto, it brims with energy and wit, its happy notes speeding by like feline patter until the approaching ending, when the music turns muscular and rollicking. —*Robert Cummings*

Recommended:

○ **Weber: Complete Piano Sonatas** / Keene / 2001 / Newport Classic 60165

Piano Sonata No. 2 in A flat major, Op. 39 (1814–1816)

Carl Maria von Weber (1786–1826) composed his *Piano Sonata No. 2 in A flat major* in 1816, four years after his *Piano Sonata No. 1 in C major* and just before his *Piano Sonata No. 3 in D minor.* Like Weber's other piano works, his *Sonata in A flat major* is a virtuoso work with singing melodies and dramatic structures. The opening Allegro moderato, Con spirito ed assai legato is a large-scale sonata with lyrical themes and stormy developments. The following Andante is a weird graceful theme with a set of spooky variations. The following Menuetto capriccioso/ Presto assai is a fast and witty virtuoso scherzo and a grandly lyrical trio. The closing Rondo (Moderato e molto grazioso) is warmly lyrical and expansively dramatic. And like Weber's other piano works, his *Piano Sonata in A flat major* is pretty much ignored by most pianists. —*James Leonard*

Recommended:

○ **Piano Masters: Noel Mewton-Wood** / Mewton-Wood / Pearl 0031

Anton Webern

b. Dec. 3, 1883, Vienna, Austria, **d.** Sep. 15, 1945, Mittersill, Austria

Composer: Symphonic, Orchestral, Chamber Music, Keyboard, Vocal, Concerto, Choral

Anton (von) Webern was one of the key figures in the so-called Second Viennese School. A pupil of Schoenberg, he became known for his concise and highly individual atonal and serial compositions. In many ways he was more influential than his teacher: in the postwar years leading figures in the avant-garde like Boulez, Stockhausen, and Dallapiccola, found more substance in his music and forms than in those of Schoenberg. Hence, one often heard—and still hears—the term "post-Webern serialism." His mature style was relatively straightforward, featuring simple harmonies and transparent textures, silent pauses, and brevity of expression. While his influence and stature are acknowledged and his music often played, Webern has landed no work in the standard repertory. Much of his music is viewed as difficult and intellectual by the public, though it is in fact comparatively quite approachable, much less challenging than the works of Boulez, Cage, and others.

Webern's family moved to Graz in 1890, then four years later to Klagenfurt, where he would attend the gymnasium for his general education. He showed talent early on and studied both piano and cello with Edwin Komauer during his early years in Klagenfurt. He graduated from the gymnasium in 1902 and enrolled at the University of Vienna. There he studied under Graedener, Adler, and Navratil. In 1904, however, he began his most serious period of study, when he became a pupil of Schoenberg.

Schoenberg was then, and remained for some time to come, one of the most progressive figures in musical composition, being among the first to write entirely atonal music, and then finalizing his serial technique in the 1920s. Webern now became a close friend of Alban Berg, also one of Schoenberg's pupils. During these years of study, Webern began to focus on vocal composition, turning out several sets of songs. He also wrote some important chamber works, including the *String Quartet* (1905).

In 1908, Webern launched a career as a conductor, taking a position at Bad Ischl. He was not particularly successful in this new endeavor, but acquired subsequent posts at Teplitz, Danzig, Stettin, and Prague, this last assignment ending in 1918, when he returned to Vienna. During these years Webern had continued to write song collections (for example, *Four Songs*, Op. 13; 1917), as well as chamber music (*Sonata for Cello and Piano*; 1914).

After the war, Webern, along with Berg, took part in Schoenberg's Society for Private Musical Performances, an organization dedicated to the performance of modern works. After this, he returned to conducting, but for the most part garnered only secondary posts, such as director of the Vienna Workers' Chorus (1922–34), which he fulfilled concurrently with other positions. He did manage, however, to obtain regular conducting appearances on Austrian Radio. In 1926, he took on a teaching post at the Jewish Cultural Institute for the Blind.

After the Nazis came to power, Webern's work with the Vienna Workers' Chorus was ended, and four years later, his relationship with Austrian Radio was terminated. He composed three important choral works—the *Cantatas* Nos. 1, 2, and 3—in the period 1938–44, and in 1940 he produced his orchestral composition *Variations*, Op. 30. Webern's death nearly a half year after the end of the war in Europe occurred in a freak incident in Mittersill (near Salzburg) when an American soldier mistakenly shot him while he was on an extended excursion to visit his daughter. —*Robert Cummings*

SYMPHONIC

Symphony, Op. 21 (1927–1928)

The *Symphony*, Op. 21, was the first large-scale orchestral work Webern had written since the *Five Pieces*, Op. 10, 15 years earlier. The work marks the beginning of a period of extreme compression in Webern's music. Dedicated to his daughter Christine, the *Symphony* is a work of severe economy and restrained expression. Its symmetrical structure and pointillistic texture are quintessential hallmarks of Webern's mature compositional style.

Scored for clarinet, bass clarinet, two horns, harp, first and second violins, viola, and cello, the *Symphony* is widely regarded as a masterpiece in miniature: Webern's teacher and mentor Arnold Schoenberg was astounded and moved by the work's concision. Like most of Webern's 12-tone works, the *Symphony* is based on a single series dominated by semitones. The work consists of two short movements. The first is in two parts—statement and development—and begins with a double canon in four parts; the second movement is a theme with seven variations and a coda, and also includes the use of canon.

The *Symphony* is perhaps most remarkable for its use of symmetry, which in some quarters has stirred accusations against Webern of a certain excessive pedantry. That symmetry takes several forms, from the work's palindromic series to the canonic variations that work in both directions from the exact center of the piece outwards. The astute listener can spend a lifetime hearing an intricate web of such structural correlations within the *Symphony*, which is a sort of superpalindrome. —*Alexander Carpenter*

Recommended:

○ **Webern 2** / Boulez (cond.), Berlin PO / DG 457639

○ **Webern: Passacaglia; Symphony; Five Pieces** / Yuasa (cond.), Ulster Orch. / 2001 / Naxos 554841

ORCHESTRAL

Im Sommerwind, idyll (1904)

Im Sommerwind, an "idyll" for large orchestra composed in 1904, is not the very first Anton Webern orchestral piece, as some lists of works and just as many authors seem to indicate. 1903 and 1904 saw the issue of six small items for orchestra (some for full, some just for strings, some more finished than others), items that go by the rather generic title *Movement* today. But *Im Sommerwind* was Webern's most ambitious project to date, orchestral and otherwise: except for the above-mentioned *Movements*, Webern's pre-1904 work consists almost wholly of short songs for voice and piano. The degree to which the ambition that fueled its composition was realized, artistically speaking, is open to some debate. *Im Sommerwind* was never performed during Webern's lifetime, not for lack of opportunity, but because Webern decided that it, like the rest of the pieces composed before the *Passacaglia*, Op. 1 (1908), was not worthy of performance. The piece seems, on the other hand, to really have meant something to Webern, and as an effusive imitation of late-Romantic tone-poem style it is not altogether unimpressive. Webern didn't, at any rate, destroy the manuscript, which was unearthed in the post-War years and tidied up for a world premiere performance by Eugene Ormandy and the Philadelphia Orchestra in 1962.

The generic but velvety late-Romantic manner of *Im Sommerwind* is, then, something almost unique in Webern's catalog. Most the songs written between 1899 and 1904 have significantly more "bite" to them—an individual, if largely untrained and somewhat clumsy Webern is to be heard. By contrast, Webern is obviously standing on the shoulders of the nearest available musical giant—Richard Strauss—in *Im Sommerwind*, very probably because the lush orchestral idiom he felt called to draw upon was a fairly new and unfamiliar one to him. As it happened, the idiom would never grow more familiar to him, save through other composer's works—when Schoenberg, with whom Webern studied from late 1904 on, began to summarily dismiss everything Strauss and Strauss-like, Webern was not far behind.

Im Sommerwind, idyll though it be called, is in fact a tone poem; its model is a poem of the same name by Bruno Wille. The work lasts around 12 or 13 minutes, and is scored for a fairly sizeable orchestra: 13 woodwind players, six horns, a pair of trumpets (but no trombones), percussion, two harps, and, of course, strings. —*Blair Johnston*

Recommended:

- **Webern: Orchestral Music** / Dohnányi (cond.), Cleveland Orch. / 1995 / London 444593
- **Complete Webern** / Boulez (cond.), Berlin PO / DG 457637
- **Great Conductors of the 20th Century: Eugene Ormandy** / Ormandy (cond.), Philadelphia Orch. / EMI 75127

Passacaglia, Op. 1 (1908)

There has hardly been a composer who didn't disown some of his works. Some, like Johannes Brahms, simply destroyed the unworthy pieces and leave posterity to wonder what treasures might have been lost to painstaking perfectionism. Others, not finding it within themselves to physically obliterate what they toiled so hard to produce, bury the offending manuscripts in their personal libraries or attics, leaving open the possibility that someday the "lost" may be found. Anton Webern was of the second type—dozens and dozens of previously unknown works by him trickled onto the field in the decades following his death in 1945, some early student works, some finished mature compositions that never saw the light of day, and some pieces caught halfway between draft and finished product. His Opus 1, the *Passacaglia for orchestra* is, as is known well today, hardly his first effort at the craft; many, many pieces predate it. The label Opus 1 is thus a touch misleading: the *Passacaglia* is not so much the beginning of Webern's journey as it is the first waystation at which he stopped to say, "aha—here we have something." Each of the pieces that preceded it is to some degree irreparably flawed, technically and often aesthetically; by contrast, the *Passacaglia* is the first piece that might truly and proudly be reckoned a "Webern"—hence, Opus 1.

The *Passacaglia* dates from spring 1908, a time during which its composer was caught in an uncomfortable limbo between student life and life as a professional conductor; Webern found his first real job, assistant conductor and chorus coach at the theater of the posh resort town of Bad Ischl, during the summer of 1908. His first conducting experiences were not apparently everything Webern had hoped them to be, but he remained relatively undaunted, and in November conducted the premiere of the *Passacaglia* back in Vienna. The piece was and would always remain the most welcome of Webern's works so far as concert promoters and ticket sellers were concerned, and in 1918, partly as a response to the work's relative popularity, Webern made a version for piano six-hands (yes, six, not four!); this arrangement has since, however, been lost.

Opus 1 is a proper passacaglia; it has an eight-bar ground bass in D minor, which is repeated over and over again as new music unfolds around it. The individual "variations" are not explicitly identified and marked as such, but for most of the piece they are simple enough to follow, even after Webern surrounds the ground bass with chromatic gusts and torrents that put a real strain on D minor and tosses the ground bass out of the actual bass up into the upper voices. A great deal of the latter portion of Webern's *Passacaglia* is, however, more freely composed; here the eight-bar theme disappears for large spans, and the rigid, repetitive structure is disguised as music that sounds, curiously, a little like a sonata-form development and recapitulation. —*Blair Johnston*

Recommended:

- **Complete Webern** / Boulez (cond.), Berlin PO / DG 457637
- **Webern: Orchestral Music** / Dohnányi (cond.), Cleveland Orch. / 1995 / London 444593
- **Schoenberg: A Survivor from Warsaw; Webern: Orchestral Works** / Abbado (cond.), Vienna PO / 1993 / DG 431774

Six Pieces, Op. 6 (1909; revised 1928)

In 1909, Anton Webern wrote his *Six Pieces for Orchestra,* Op. 6, as his first attempt to apply the atonal musical language to a large ensemble. It was a productive year for the 26-year-old composer, who had made startling progress in his compositional technique. Listening to his orchestral *Passacaglia,* Op. 1, from the previous year, reveals an unprecedented degree of musical growth. In terms of syntax and orchestration, his teacher Arnold Schoenberg was the trailblazer. Fate handed Webern the will and ability to uniquely realize his former teacher's compositional discoveries.

Op. 6 plumbed the depths of Schoenberg's notion of Klangfarbenmelodie (tone-color melody) which fashions the different tone colors available in the orchestra with melodic shapes. Schoenberg created a famous example with his *Five Pieces for Orchestra,* Op. 16, in the previous year. The third movement, named "Farben" (Colors), caused an enormous amount of speculation and study in attempt to discern a system that apparently does not exist. For Webern, the idea suited his need for pure expression, so that instruments and timbres recur quasi thematically at key points in the same manner of tempo, pitches, rhythm, etc., to create coherence out of music's raw components. While Webern's Op. 1 was Brahmsian in style, his Op. 6 was Mahlerian. Gustav Mahler's symphonies had grappled with the nuances of orchestral color to an unprecedented degree, constantly recombining groups of instruments to heighten the nuances of late-Romantic expression. Webern's Op. 6 follows through with six different explorations of Klangfarbenmelodie that, while not revealing a codified system, uses sparse textures to clearly reveal the idea at work. Webern's orchestral movements come across as meditations of regret presented with great self-control. When the entire orchestra plays, which is rare, it is not an expressively wild gesticulation, but a swelling of emotion that is heartfelt, yet never released without extended anticipation. This represents a great inner intensity that never brushes shoulders with despair or madness. In this way, the spirit of Brahms' cool exterior and simmering undercurrent still held Webern fast and would continue to do so throughout his writing career. In spite of this, the Op. 6 premiere on March 31, 1913, ended in a full-scale riot. One uncharitable critic wrote that its instrumentation "can only be described in terms of a barnyard." Webern, traumatized by the event, fled to a spa near Trieste to recuperate.—*John Keillor*

Recommended:

- **Complete Webern** / Boulez (cond.), Berlin PO / DG 457637
- **Webern: Orchestral Music** / Dohnányi (cond.), Cleveland Orch. / 1995 / London 444593
- **Schoenberg, Webern, Berg: Orchestral Works** / Rattle (cond.), City of Birmingham SO / 2003 / EMI 75880

Five Pieces, Op. 10 (1911–1913)

Anton Webern's *Five Pieces for Orchestra,* Op. 10 require less than five minutes to perform. The movements are not thematically connected, nor do they include traditional formal plans or tonal relationships. What they do contain is probably the most convincing utilization of Klangfarbenmelodie (tone-color melody) ever and apply an aphoristic approach to composition for orchestra for the first time.

These pieces are the last orchestral works Webern published before his adoption of the 12-tone method. His Op. 1 *Passacaglia for Orchestra* was post-Brahmsian and his Op. 5 orchestral works were atonal, sectional, and hint at the initial implications of the new musical language. Op. 10 expresses only the raw components of musical sound: notes, intervals, scraps of ostinato, rhythms, attack, volume, and tone color. While Op. 5 was written in brief enough sections and durations to be considered miniatures, Op. 10 does away with the conventions of a traditional orchestral narrative. The result is an aphoristic approach that condenses the sound into one, hyper-expressive text. The result is a spilling over of artistic idea that is undeniable, immediate, and difficult to articulate.

What can be discerned is a flow of tone-color that is continually associative. For example, a plucked violin relates to the harp heard earlier. A horn can function as color conduit between a flute and a trumpet. This is in addition to tempos changing and recurring and many other basic, identifiable materials, such as register. With so much going on in a very brief period, the spirit of the movements harness a precariousness that might be the closest to the Expressionist oeuvre among Webern's instrumental works. The function of each musical signpost is always fluctuating, further abstracting the surface and underlying structure. A painstaking order is obviously at work in these movements. This music pushes the traditional limits of perception and yet exhibits strikingly lucid, even candid intentions. Webern's mastery of this language is palpable, but this is hardly a comfort. Webern was primarily concerned with the contours of natural phenomena, which follow a logic separate from the world humanity has created for itself.

The premiere of Op. 10 was on June 22, 1924, over ten years after its completion. Webern conducted the five movements himself, in Zurich, during the fourth festival of the International Society for Contemporary Composers. Critics had time to absorb Webern's approach to music by then, and wrote favorably, even glowingly, of the work. Music reporters from Berlin, who had lambasted him in the past, described the composer as "a true musical poet," and provided many similar accolades as well. The concert catapulted the composer to international fame. In terms of winning respect from the music world, this concert may have been the most successful evening of Anton Webern's career. —*John Keillor*

Recommended:

- **Complete Webern** / Boulez (cond.), InterContemporain Ens. / DG 457637
- **Webern: Orchestral Music** / Dohnányi (cond.), Cleveland Orch. / 1995 / London 444593
- **Webern: Complete Works Opp1–31** / Boulez (cond.), London SO / 1991 / Sony 45845

CHAMBER MUSIC

Six Bagatelles for string quartet, Op. 9 (1911–1913)

Webern's *Six Bagatelles for string quartet,* Op. 9 (1911–13) represent a critical step for the evolution of atonal musical techniques. They also mark a critical step for the composer, who in his attempt to realize the ideas of his mentor, Arnold Schoenberg, emerged as a true original. For several years, Webern had doted on Schoenberg personally and artistically. When Schoenberg wrote his *Six Little Piano Pieces,* Op. 19, in 1911, Webern noted that some of the movements lacked contrast. While Schoenberg apparently gave little thought to the implications of his new work, Webern wrangled with this problem of contrast in the still-emerging language of atonality. Later that year, Webern wrote the internal movements of Op. 9, considering the result as his second string quartet.

In the following year Webern followed Schoenberg to Berlin, where the revered master composed his epochal *Pierrot Lunaire*, which featuring the Sprechstimme (song-speech) technique. Webern presently composed three movements for string quartet, the second of which featured a Sprechstimme setting of his own poetry. Schoenberg, who had composed a string quartet with the addition of soprano in 1908, was no doubt painfully aware that Webern was in danger of becoming a faceless copycat. Schoenberg's response was to not comment on Webern's new work at all. Hurt and dismayed, Webern eliminated the Sprechstimme movement and used the two remaining movements to bookend his second string quartet. Schoenberg was very pleased with the result and even provided a glowing preface for its publication.

The Six Bagatelles require about five minutes to perform. One difference between Op. 9 and Webern's previous quartet, Op. 5, is that the earlier work contains movements built from sections and contrasts—in that sense, much in the spirit of Haydn. However, the movements of its successor are through-composed, not sectional, and there are no contrasts that require resolution. The level of musical tension is, nonetheless, very high; the work achieves this effect because the material in the first two measures provides ample opportunity to highlight and juxtapose individual musical gestures, and the dramatic envelope is controlled by the density of such activity.

Alban Berg attempted a similar approach in his *Four Pieces for clarinet and piano*, Op. 4, but Schoenberg felt that Webern was more suited to this particular challenge and persuaded Berg not to pursue this compositional direction. Even Webern himself managed to carve out only two more works in this manner (Opp. 10 and 11) before he exhausted its possibilities. With this trio of works, however, he made a lasting impression upon the keener listeners of his day, and the Six Bagatelles remain among the strangest and most compelling aphorisms in the string quartet repertoire. *—John Keillor*

Recommended:

○ **Webern: Works for String Quartet; String Trio Op20** / Emerson SQ / DG 445828

○ **Webern: Complete String Trios & Quartets** / Arditti SQ / 2000 / Disques Montaigne 782136

Langsamer Satz (Slow Movement), for string quartet (1905)

Webern composed this work for string quartet in June 1905, but it wasn't publicly performed until May 27, 1962, in Seattle. The *Langsamer Satz* (literally "Slow Movement") originated during a hiking trip in Lower Austria that Webern took with his cousin, Wilhelmine Mörtl, who later became his wife. It is love music, as Webern diarized ecstatically—an outpouring by the 21-year-old composer, whose studies with Arnold Schoenberg had begun the previous autumn.

"To walk forever like this among the flowers, with my dearest one beside me, to feel oneself so entirely at one with the Universe, without care, free as the lark in the sky above—Oh what splendor... when night fell (after the rain) the sky shed bitter tears but I wandered with her along a road," wrote Webern in language reminiscent of the poet Richard Dehmel, who had inspired Schoenberg's *Verklärte Nacht*—a work not without influence on the present composition. "A coat protected the two of us. Our love rose to infinite heights and filled the Universe. Two souls were enraptured." The *Langsamer Satz* is tonal music, albeit chromatic, firmly ensconsed in a tradition stretching from Liszt through Wagner to Hugo Wolf, Richard Strauss, and Mahler. The last named had not as yet entranced Webern, but during the 1930s he led Vienna's Workingmen Symphony Orchestra in readings of Mahler's music allegedly as insightful as Bruno Walter's, and certainly more comprehensive.

Webern wrote tonal music for several more years after 1905—until, as Schoenberg's most intuitive pupil, he became "more Catholic than the Pope," to borrow an apposite aphorism (it nettled the Master when Webern anticipated his serial dicta, especially as regards rhythm). At 13 minutes plus, the *Langsamer Satz* is marginally the lengthiest of all Webern works, longer even than *In Sommerwind* that preceded it, or the *Passacaglia*, Op. 1, both orchestral, that followed. (With his radical renunciation of tonality came a new minimalism.) It has a root key, C minor, and a traditional sonata-form structure.

After the leading Webern scholar, Hans Moldenhauer, settled in Spokane in 1939, Washington state became the world center for Webern's music. Seattle hosted the first of six International festivals, held between 1962 and 1978, in May 1962. It was there, at that time, the University of Washington String Quartet gave the world premiere of the *Langsamer Satz* in its original form. In 1992 Gerard Schwarz recorded his arrangement of the work for string choir with the Seattle Symphony (Delos 3121, *Transformations for Strings*). This arrangement for string choir is surely as valid as Schoenberg's of his own *Verklärte Nacht*, originally for string sextet, dating from the same period. *—Roger Dettmer*

Recommended:

○ **Brindisi String Quartet Plays Webern, Schoenberg & Berg** / Brindisi SQ / 1994 / Metronome 1007-01

Five Movements for string quartet, Op. 5 (1909)

Webern wrote the Op. 5 *Five Movements* (or *Five Pieces*, as they are sometimes called) in the spring of 1909, the year after he had been given his first official musical post, as a conductor of operettas at the Austrian spa of Bad Ischl. A pick-up group gave the *Movements* their first performance on February 8, 1910.

His compositions of this time betray barely a hint of the light operettas that he so disliked conducting. Webern was continuing his explorations of the atonality also being employed by his compatriots Alban Berg and Arnold Schoenberg, while beginning to incorporate the spare gestures and concision of thought which became so pronounced in his works of the early 1910s. A talented cellist, Webern also had a full knowledge of the techniques available to string players, and the Op. 5 *Movements* feature all manner of pizzicati, harmonics, tremolos, and other textures.

The first of the *Movements*—in sonata form, with a pair of themes followed by their development and a reprise—is the most expansive of the five, moving quickly from a bittersweet theme to harsh pizzicati and quiet, ghostly gestures. The brusque, occasionally playful third movement shares some of the energy of the first. The hushed second movement, the lyrical and spare fourth, and the spectral fifth (with its almost despairing cello line and the play between the high and low extremes of register) are all quiet and almost aphoristic in their briefness.

In the summer of 1928 Webern revisited the *Five Movements*, arranging them for string orchestra. Aside from a few octave doublings, solo and tutti markings, and some redistribution of notes between the cellos and basses, the actual changes in the score were fairly minimal, although the increased body of strings (Webern felt that an orchestra of 80 players was desirable) lent a more dramatic, even melodramatic, air to some of the music. After working on his *Quartet*, Op. 22, Webern decided he was unsatisfied with the orchestral arrangement of Op. 5 and made a new one, with more extensive changes, in the early months of 1929. This arrangement was introduced in Philadelphia on March 26, 1930, by the Philadelphia Chamber String Sinfonietta under the direction of Fabien Sevitzky. *—Chris Morrison*

Recommended:

○ **Webern: Complete String Trios & String Quartets Vol. 3** / Arditti SQ / 1994 / Disques Montaigne 789008

○ **Neue Wiener Schule** / LaSalle Quartet / DG 419994

○ **Webern: Works for String Quartet; String Trio Op20** / Emerson SQ / DG 445828

○ **Brindisi String Quartet Plays Webern, Schoenberg & Berg** / Brindisi SQ / 1994 / Metronome 1007-01

Quartet for clarinet, saxophone, piano & violin, Op. 22 (1928–1930)

Webern wrote his Quartet for violin, clarinet, tenor saxophone, and piano, Op. 22 (1928–30) for the 60th birthday of architect Adolf Loos. As happened during the composition of his *String Trio*, Op. 20 (1926–27), Webern discarded sketches for a projected third movement after deeming the first two movements a complete entity. Another connection the Quartet shares with the String Trio is an opaque structure Stravinsky described as "scatty."

The Quartet was originally intended as a sort of reflection of nature, depicting landscapes and flora. After Webern had sketched themes according to this intent, the work gradually morphed into its completely different final form. The canons that had by this time begun to permeate Webern's music are more loosely realized in the Quartet than in the composer's previous works. In the first movement, for example, their most conspicuous feature is a two-note "limping" motive, a short-long rhythm that is later reversed; in the middle of the movement, the motive is sounded both in its original rhythmic values and in augmentation.

The second movement alludes to techniques Webern more fully developed in his Concerto, Op. 24 (1931–34). Most prominent is the splintering of notes within a phrase among the various instruments in the sort of intricate pointillistic texture that became one of the most identifiable hallmarks of the composer's style.

When uniformly unfavorable reviews poured in after the Quartet's premiere in Vienna on April 13, 1931, Webern was unworried. Though the performance must have been superb—the personnel included violinist Rudolf Kolisch and pianist Eduard Steuermann—one critic wrote that the work displayed "amazing similarity to certain basic human utterances of an indecent nature." *—John Keillor*

Recommended:

○ **Chambersax** / Horch, Barton, Payne / 1999 / Clarinet Classics 29

String Quartet, Op. 28 (1936–1938)

The Nazi seizure of the power in Austria in 1934 brought Webern's conducting career to an end. While the resulting loss of income sent him to the edge of destitution, it gave him the time he needed to work on his own compositions. He took full advantage of the freedom, and music flowed from his pen in a slow, steady stream until about 1940. The Op. 28 string quartet, completed in April, 1938, arrived near the end of this period of intense concentration. It brings together in instrumental music the structural rigor of his Op. 27 *Variations for piano*, with the lyrical mode he'd been developing in his lieder.

Webern himself described Op. 28 as "purely lyrical," stating that the concern of the work is "not epic breadth, but lyrical conciseness." Indeed, the rather terse,

12-tone Op. 28 could scarcely be further from the soaring, strident influence of Mahler. Webern emphasized that the quartet is akin to the two-movement sonatas of Beethoven. The effort to hear (and perform) his music within the continuum of tradition is like an "open sesame" at the gates of his mystery; all the forbidding difficulties of the style politely move out of the way. It's surprisingly easy to hear the Beethoven and song-like qualities in Op. 28 when you try.

The tone row is based on B flat-A-C-B, or the German notes B-A-C-H, which are then inverted and, finally, transposed. The row is perfectly audible in the opening gesture of the first movement, and if it isn't exactly easy to follow all the subsequent permutations without the score, the signature of the row is clearly inscribed all over the piece. The presence of so many semi-tones allows the desired lyricism to emerge (a melodic semi-tone is inherently lyrical) and creates a total tonal ambiguity that he wanted.

The first movement has the most fragmented surface of the three. Because the melodic gestures are divided across the instruments, and across pizzicato or bowing techniques, it is initially somewhat difficult to follow. In fact, it often sounds like Webern is using the quartet as a four-fingered piano. Movements two and three are consistently more idiomatic and, hence, easier to grasp. Number two, a kind of mad little ballet, is made up mostly of brief lyrical statements over a walking pizzicato accompaniment. It's unemotional, slightly kooky, and so flawless it's bizarre. Number three is the most varied in tone and texture, punctuated with so many silences that we wonder if it's experiencing a mechanical crisis. The kind of beauty this all achieves, the kind of poetry it reaches—for it's impossible to appreciate Webern's music without a sympathetic and poetic ear—is an external, cerebral one. Each carefully weighted note, like words in a work by Raymond Roussel, "reveals music as the unexpected meeting place of the most distant figures of reality." —*Donato Mancini*

Recommended:

○ **Webern: Works for String Quartet; String Trio** / Emerson SQ / DG 445828

○ **Webern: Complete Works for String Quartet** / New Leipzig SQ / MDG 3070589

String Trio, Op. 20 (1926–1927)

The chamber works of Anton Webern, especially those written after his adoption of the 12-tone technique in the late 1920s, present the listener with an enigmatic combination of austere structural integrity and intense, koan-like expressivity. In the *Trio for Strings*, which Webern began writing in 1926, completed in 1927, and premiered in 1928, the composer seems at first glance to be at his most rarefied. The piece is made of the most tenuous of musical materials; indeed, it is characterized by what scholar Julian Johnson has described as an "ungraspability of surface." Its occasional fits of restless melodic energy are separated by veils of sustained notes and static harmonies that presage minimalist ruminations (indeed, minimalist pioneer La Monte Young's groundbreaking *Trio for Strings* was composed under the influence of heavy doses of Webern's chamber music). Webern's signature symmetries and palindromes unfold and spin in eccentric motivic orbits, while frequent changes in timbre and articulation add an additional plane of discourse to Webern's contrapuntal shapes.

The first of the *Trio*'s two movements (which was actually composed second) creates a finely wrought pointillistic surface, with angular glyphs set against sustained harmonies that have elicited comparisons to Debussy. The sense of temporal pause is enhanced by the use of another of Webern's signature techniques: some notes appear only in a specific register when they are encountered in their serial order, thus lending an analogous sense of deliberate spatiality and acoustic consistency to the piece's overall sound field—a technique also used quite famously in the elaborate canons of his next numbered work, the *Symphony*, Op. 21. The second movement weaves a denser, less diaphanous texture, its semi-contrapuntal substructures and thematic interconnections flowing in more rapid succession and floating nearer to the surface. Themes expand and contrast, widen and narrow in their arcs, and extend in opposite directions around a moving axis. The momentarily held chords serve as suspense rather than repose, while wide intervallic leaps and looser rhythmic divisions resist alighting comfortably on the ear. Of particular interest is the middle portion of the movement, which Webern referred to unassumingly as the development section. Here Webern articulates contours in various positions and durational proportions, in a kind of cubist fashion, while further disrupting the temporal geometry with repeated notes and held harmonies. The drastic contrasts in line and timbre unfold analogously in the movement's dynamics as well, from suddenly proximate sforzandos to distant, whispering harmonics. —*Jeremy Grimshaw*

Recommended:

○ **Webern: Complete String Trios and Quartets** / Arditti SQ / 2000 / Disques Montaigne 782136

KEYBOARD

Variations, Op. 27 (1935–1936)

As "modern" as it is in other respects, Webern's *Variations for Piano, Op. 27* (1935–36), the composer's only important work for piano solo, is written in the tradition of the recital piece, and even provides the performer ample opportunity for virtuoso display. In just under five minutes, Webern presents a flurry of information, presented with new types of articulation and writing for the piano. There are no crescendo or diminuendo markings—the dynamic contrasts are all stark juxtapositions of piano and forte passages. It seems Webern is exploring the Baroque-era characteristic of terraced dynamics.

Webern's *Variations for Piano*, Op. 27 are constructed according to strict 12-tone procedures. The theme is really a collection of short groups of motives. These are altered in accordance with the combinatorial procedures of the 12-tone method, using various permutations of the primary row. It is organized into three movements, the first of which is organized around symmetrical pitch schemes.

Most intriguing is the second movement, in which a strict canon is obscured by Webern's registral and rhythmic changes. This procedure—using a musical device to create structure then making that structure nearly imperceptible—is at work in other of Webern's pieces, particularly the *Symphony, Op. 21* (1928). One reason the canon is difficult to detect is that the very complex procedure passes by rapidly in this very compressed movement. Webern explores great extremes of register and sudden changes in dynamic and articulation, all happening at lightning speed and related to the primary tone row.

Variations, Op. 27 received its premiere performance on October 26, 1936, in Vienna at a concert sponsored by the Vienna chapter of the International Society for Contemporary Music. A few days later, Webern heard a second performance of the *Variations* at the Verein für neue Musik (Society for New Music). This was the last time Webern heard one of his compositions performed in Vienna. —*John Palmer*

Recommended:

○ **Schoenberg & Webern: Piano Works** / Pollini / 2001 / DG 471361

VOCAL

Five Canons on Latin Texts, for voice, clarinet & bass clarinet, Op. 16 (1923–1924)

The *Five Canons on Latin Texts, Op. 16*, count among a handful of vocal works composed by Anton Webern in the 1910s and 1920s, and exemplify the manner in which his seemingly austere, constructivist methods serve as means to what ultimately are deeply expressive ends. They present listeners with a composer possessing a keen poetic sensitivity, as well as an almost microscopically calibrated emotional precision. The Op. 16 pieces are striking in their Spartan instrumentation: a lone soprano is joined only by a B flat clarinet and a bass clarinet, instruments arguably as approximate to the human voice as any, separated from the singer primarily in the inability to deliver text. They also emphasize Webern's penchant for canonical structures—indeed, the entire collection is rife with echoed contours of lines in counterpoint and complementary motivic shapes as melodies unfolding in mirror images, like the angular peaks of a mountain range reflected in inversion on the surface of a lake. Despite the spare and homogeneous forces used, the often strict canonical writing, and, indeed, the use of highly religious texts sung in arcane Latin (taken from the Catholic Breviary), the pieces reveal subtle and profound expressive details to those with an ear to listen closely.

In the first piece, "Christus factus est pro nobis," the vocal and clarinet lines intertwine contrapuntally as well as timbrally—as Christiane Oelze's recording on Deutsche Grammophon expertly brings out by matching the initial voice quality with the clarinet's opening trills. Webern even indulges in a bit of tone painting, with an unexpectedly high leap on "nomen quod est *super* omne nomen" (name above all other names). In a similar fashion, the upward gestures in the clarinet that begin the second movement, "Dormi Jesu," contrapuntally set up their descending inversions in the voice in the opening words ("Sleep, Jesus"). The clarinet ominously shadows the vocal line at a moment's delay in the third movement ("Crux fidelis"), then foreshadows in the fourth ("Asperges me"). Perhaps due to its invocational nature, the fifth and final movement, "Crucem tuam adoramus, Domine" (We Worship Thy Cross, Lord), is the most ardent and active. Its intensity derives from shifts of articulation, from low, nimble staccatos to full-voiced, adulatory ascents—and here again a telling word picture: a high C sharp on "guadium" (joy). That all these expressive elements occur within the rigors of canonical forms speaks to the transcendence Webern sought in these pieces. —*Jeremy Grimshaw*

Recommended:

○ **Boulez Conducts Webern** / Oelze, InterContemporain Ens. / DG 437786

Lieder nach Gedichten von Stefan George, Op. 4 (1908–1909)

Together with the five songs of Op. 3 and four unpublished items, all of them settings of poems by Stefan George, Webern renounced his allegiance to late Romanticism's dalliance with chromaticism and definitively followed Schoenberg into full atonality. Compared to the Op. 3 songs, those of Op. 4 are longer and feature more chordal (and therefore, more dissonant-sounding) accompaniment. Even so, the music retains some vestige of a tonal system, the songs anchored by recurring chords or chord patterns. As in the companion set, these songs inhabit, so to speak, a very low, mysterious dynamic level. The texts allude in many ways to death (and perhaps resurrection) and Webern's music is appropriately mournful and haunted.

"Eingang" (Entrance) bids goodbye to the world of humans and finds the singer entering the "shivering coolness" and "expectant silence" of the forest. In "Noch zwingt mich treue," the singer is compelled by faithfulness to watch over a lover and share "the beauty of your suffering"; this is a particularly anguished setting, with the piano and soprano actually producing a few, fleeting forte notes. "Ja Heil und Dank" (Yes, Hail and Thanks) expresses appreciation for a beloved who "calmed the constant, loud heartbeat with that anticipation of you . . . during these radiance-filled weeks of dying." In "So ich traurig bin," the singer declares that when she is sad, she need only imagine herself with her beloved. "Ihr tratet zu dem Herde" finds the person addressed by the poem stepping toward a cold hearth, dipping his fingers into the ashes ("searching, touching, grasping"), thereby bringing the hearth aglow again. *—James Reel*

Recommended:

- ○ **Fischer-Dieskau sings Schoenberg, Berg & Webern** / Fischer-Dieskau, Reimann / 2002 / Classica d'Oro 4015
- ○ **Webern: Early Songs, Opp 3, 4 & 12** / Shirai, Höll / Capriccio 10862

Five Sacred Songs for soprano & ensemble, Op. 15 (1917–1922)

Along with the *Six Songs, Op. 14*, the *Five Canons*, Op. 16, and a handful of other vocal works in the mid-1920s, the *Five Sacred Songs*, Op. 15, are situated with Anton Webern's oeuvre at a crucial juncture. After this cluster of text settings, Webern's emphasis on instrumental music would underscore his adoption of the 12-tone method of composition only recently presented to the world by his mentor Arnold Schoenberg. And while scholars observe an extreme angularity in Webern's vocal writing that resists any inclination toward lyricism in the traditional sense, his text settings have an acute and often poignant expressivity all their own.

The fifth song in the set, "Fahr hin, o Seel" (Pass on, My Soul), was actually the first to be composed, in 1917. Its lucid canonic structure, its relatively restrained melodic contours, its longer length, and its use of the full instrumental ensemble (voice, clarinet/bass clarinet, trumpet, harp, and violin/viola) lend it a sense of repose and arrival that befit the quasi-narrative constituted by the five texts as a whole: a journey from mortality through death toward redemption and heavenly rest. The angularity of the first movement, then, points up the transcendent distance to be traversed over the cycle as a whole. Comprising a description of Jesus' arrival at the cross and his words of comfort to his mother, it follows a melodic thread built of wide, motivically interrelated leaps, tenuously set against a viscous, rhythmically fluid chordal background. Still, even in this opening song a foreshadow of redemption is offered: in a moment of pictorialism that starkly contrasts Webern's reputation as the most austere of composers, the soprano leaps to a breathtakingly high and crystalline C sharp on the word "heaven." The second and fourth movements, both written during a summer vacation in 1922, shimmer with an anxiousness appropriate to the devout, forward-looking optimism of their texts: the former projects a "morning"-themed text from *Das Knaben Wunderhorn* as the dawn of immortality, with exaggeratedly wide melodic arcs; the latter, which was composed last of all five songs, uses more reduced instrumentation and more selective melodic leaps (such as the heavenward ascent on "God's peace") to depict the expectation of immortality. The third and central movement is a spiritual call to arms, one that also ties specific elements of Webern's spare linear forms to images in the text: each of the "three little angels" mentioned in the text gets its own motive. *—Jeremy Grimshaw*

Recommended:

- ○ **Boulez Conducts Webern** / Boulez (cond.), Oelze, InterContemporain Ensemble / DG 437786

Five Songs from "Der siebente Ring," Op. 3 (1908–1909)

Webern's Op. 3 is a set of five lieder for soprano with texts from Stephan George's *The Seventh Ring*. They are the composer's first published atonal works. The Op. 3 songs also show Webern asserting himself as more artistically independent of his teacher, Arnold Schoenberg.

Viennese intellectualism was deeply swayed by Freud's writings on psychoanalysis. The reaction among artists was to challenge the public to explore its own unconscious reactions to the modern world. In spite of this necessary cultural exploration, Webern remained interested in a spiritual investigation that focused on humanity and nature as miraculous creations to be treated with the utmost tenderness.

Stefan George, a contemporary of Webern from the previous generation, was of enough like mind to excite the young composer to action. Though Schoenberg had used George's texts as well during this period, Webern would gravitate towards comparable poetry for the rest of his life. The themes of love for others and for life, regarded intimately, were the glue of his spiritual outlook.

The songs themselves sound intimate, almost to a painful degree. They are brief and require an almost whispering style of diction for the singer. The atonality is strictly enforced, with little recurrence of earlier material. Of course, this cannot be done to the letter because, without any recurring sound, there would be no coherence. The solution was to transform the aural recurrence in protracted or diminished forms, or to conceal the obvious qualities of the previously heard section in different high/low registers. Webern was fond of quoting his friend Berg on this compositional topic: "Never offer a literal restatement. Think of what the music has lived through."

Webern was also being subtly influenced by French symbolism and its musical manifestation, Debussy's *Pelléas et Mélisande*, which Webern had heard twice while job hunting in Berlin in 1908. The non-declamatory, recitative style heard in the opera suited the quiet elation he had to offer. George was responding to something similar in contemporary French poetry, but from a more urbane perspective. The lack of explosions, the absence of climax or rhetoric appealed to both Webern and George. Without these tools, the ambiguity left behind, the wonder, was part of the intended result. In Webern's music, the crispness of distinguishing sections is eschewed in favor of something more flora-like; moments of a specific musical character overgrew one another. The potential rhythms were deliberately clouded with non-metric melodies and accompaniments that did not clarify any beat.

Op. 3 is the first of Webern's works to include his signature use of long, dissonant intervals, sevenths and ninths, in his vocal lines. However, there are also melodic arabesques, brief moments of narrow-ranged vocal lines that twist like vines and vegetable matter. The dissonance of these lieder is not enforced, as heard in Schoenberg's and Berg's works. There are no audibly conscious, expressionist shocks planted in the songs. Rather, they follow the consequences of Webern's creed "to render oneself intelligible."

The first item, "Dies ist ein Lied für dich allein," is a song "of childish longing . . . meant to move but you alone." The second, "Im Windwsweben," declares that the singer's romantic quest was a mere dream "in the wind's murmur"; "now I must live all day in longing for your eyes and hair." The third, "An Bachesranft," observes the first clues to the arrival of spring beside a stream. The fourth, "Im Morgentaun," recounts a visit in morning dew to see a cherry tree in bud. The final song, "Kahl reckt der Baum," likens a bare tree's straining for life through the winter to a dream rising with grace: "in pain . . . in ice it still hopes for spring." *—John Keillor*

Recommended:

- ○ **Complete Webern** / Oelze, Schneider / DG 457637
- ○ **Anton Webern: Complete Works, Opp1–31** / Harper, Rosen / 1991 / Sony 45845
- ○ **Webern: Early Songs, Opp3, 4 & 12** / Shirai, Holl / Capriccio 10862

Three Songs for soprano, clarinet & guitar, Op. 18 (1925)

Anton Webern's *Three Songs, Op. 18*, are, in character, siblings to his *Three Traditional Rhymes*, Op. 17, of the previous year; both sets exude a self-assured intimacy and clarity of expressive purpose. The combination of the composer's characteristically sparse textures and an unconventional scoring (soprano voice, E flat clarinet, and guitar) presents a number of special performance challenges, not the least of which is managing to bring out dynamic variety without ever exceeding the volume constraints of the guitar. The rhythmic difficulty of the score and the intervallically challenging voice part risk, in less than fully capable hands, sounding like modernistic pretension; however, a faithful performance reveals the composer's lighthearted approach, and an undercurrent of depth that somehow affirms the goodhearted, free breaths that constitute these minute-long songs.

The texts illustrate a flirtation with one's betrothed and the Mother Mary. It is a strange romance to contemporary sensibilities, but it has a prevailing sweetness that affirms both love and faith in a holistic way.

Expressionism, which pervaded the Austrian avant-garde as recently as ten years earlier, had more or less been exhausted in the imaginations of most composers. Among Webern's most immediate peers, the Second Viennese School, only Alban Berg's opera *Wozzeck*, completed in 1925, adhered to the psycho-dramatic conventions of Expressionism to any lasting effect. At that time, Schoenberg was working with loosely classical forms, and Webern was drawing inspiration from Dutch music of the Renaissance. With Expressionism past, there was no movement to replace it the way Romanticism seamlessly replaced Classicism. Webern's newly independent outlook was free to accommodate his own worldview and musical outlook, which were inextricable from a need to celebrate God's creations. A large part of this investigation took the form of botanical research. The natural lines of development that he found in flora would translate to him as methods of manipulating the tone row. The musical compositions that resulted from Webern's enquiries took the form of a constant recombination of basic elements that never transform their beginnings, but constantly rearticulate the initial music in new ways. Webern's atonal investigations had taught him how to use the most basic elements of music to glean their maximum expressive power. His use of the tone row in these songs is still fairly simple, perhaps because he could make so much out of comparatively little. It would be a few years down the road before he would break down the row into mirror forms, cells, and other, more complex 12-tone innovations.

Like his Op. 17, Webern's *Three Songs*, Op. 18 was not heard publicly during the composer's lifetime. Robert Craft conducted the songs' premiere on February 8, 1954, in Los Angeles. The soloist was Grace-Lynne Martin. *—John Keillor*

Recommended:

- ○ **Boulez Conducts Webern** / Oelze, Boulez (cond.), InterContemporain Ensemble / DG 437786
- ○ **Nuits: Weiß wie Lilien** / Nussbaum (cond.), Aisthesis Ensemble / 2000 / Bis 1090

Three Traditional Rhymes, for soprano, clarinet, bass clarinet, violin & viola, Op. 17 (1924–1925)

Webern composed these three songs in 1924, but they were not performed until 1953, eight years after his death. They were the first pieces he wrote using the then-new 12-tone method of composition created by his mentor, Arnold Schoenberg. Songs make up much of Webern's oeuvre, and it is interesting to note that despite the new technique employed in the *Traditional Rhymes*, they actually differ very little from his earlier songs in terms of their overall sonorous effect.

The *Three Traditional Rhymes* are scored for soprano soloist and three instruments and rather neatly exemplify Webern's compositional style: they feature extremely wide leaps in the vocal line, disjunct and angular instrumental writing, and are pervasively linear in texture. Like many of Webern's songs, they are very expressive and evocative, but also notoriously difficult to sing. The rhymes themselves are short, quasi-religious poems: the first is an admonishment of sinners, the second a kind of prayer to the Virgin, the third a plea to Jesus for salvation. Webern's next work, his Op. 18 songs of 1925, would be three more settings of folk texts. *—Alexander Carpenter*

Recommended:

- ○ **Complete Webern** / Boulez (cond.), Oelze, InterContemporain Ensemble / DG 457637
- ○ **Anton Webern: Complete Works Opp1–31** / Kolbe (cond.), Lukomska / 1991 / Sony 45845

CONCERTO

Concerto for 9 instruments, Op. 24 (1931–1934)

In the early 1930s, while the world economy was disintegrating and German politics were descending into barbarism, Anton Webern retreated into his world of strictly organized sounds. Webern first sketched the work that would become his *Konzert*, Op. 24, on January, 16, 1931; it began life as a single-movement orchestral piece inspired by his visit to his parents' graves, and based on a 12-tone row so tightly organized that the standard 48 permutations were reduced to only 12. As the work grew into three movements, Webern continued distilling its essence and concentrating its form. In the final version, Webern reduced the number of instruments to nine—flute, oboe, and clarinet; horn, trumpet, and trombone; violin, viola, and piano. The *Konzert* was completed on September 13, 1934, and dedicated to Webern's teacher and friend Arnold Schoenberg.

The opening movement (in duple time, marked Etwas lebhaft), is in three parts with an introduction and postlude; each section is clearly articulated by tempo markings. Each section is more intensely worked out then the one before it, culminating in a fortissimo stringendo climax at the end of the third section. The central movement is a brief, gentle waltz for muted instruments in two sections; the closing movement is a quick dance for winds, strings, and muted brass above the piano, rushing headlong toward a climactic chord in the winds, brass, and piano in the final bars. *—James Leonard*

Recommended:

- ○ **Complete Webern** / InterContemporain Ens. / DG 457637
- ○ **Webern: Im Sommerwind; Orchestral Pieces; Variations** / Sinopoli (cond.), Dresden Staatskapelle / 1999 / Teldec 22902

CHORAL

Cantata No. 2 for soprano, bass, chorus & orchestra, Op. 31 (1941–1943)

Webern began work on what would become his *Cantata No. 2* in spring 1941 and completed it in winter 1943. In it, he set six poems by Hildegard Jone that fuse the two great loves of Webern's spiritual life: pantheism and Christianity. Webern's largest work, the *Cantata No. 2* is scored for soprano and bass soloists plus mixed choir and a delicately colored orchestra consisting of piccolo, flute, oboe, English horn, clarinet, bass clarinet, saxophone, bassoon, horn, trumpet, trombone, tuba, bells, glockenspiel, celesta, and strings. Cast in six movements and lasting more than a quarter of an hour, the cantata is Webern's longest work. It was also his last work: Webern was accidentally shot and killed at the end of World War II. The cantata received its posthumous premiere under Hans Rosbaud in 1950. The cantata opens with a powerful strophic setting of "Schweigt auch die Welt" (Silent Is the World) for heroic bass and brass-led orchestra in fast triple time. The second movement is "Sehr tief verhalten innerst Leben singt" (Very Deep Innermost Life Sings), a pastoral song for lyrical bass and shimmering orchestra in gently shuddering duple time. The third movement is "Schöpfen aus Brunnen des Himmels" (Created From the Springs of Heaven), a joyfully ringing, four-part work in lilting triple time scored for ecstatic soprano, blissful women's chorus, and glittering orchestra. The fourth movement, the first to be composed, is "Leichteste Burden der Baume" (Lightest Burden of Trees), a short aria in quick duple time for stratospheric soprano and very lightly scored orchestra. The fifth movement, the heart of the work, is "Freundselig ist das Wort" (Compassionate Is the Word), a three-part song with the expressive soprano alternating with the full chorus in the outer sections and then singing alone in the central section, with an evanescent orchestra made up of solo strings and winds against celesta and harp. The sixth and final movement is "Gelockert aus dem Schosse" (Delivered From the Womb), a canonic chorale for full chorus doubled by the warmly colored orchestra. *—James Leonard*

Recommended:

- ○ **Boulez Conducts Webern Vol. 3** / Boulez (cond.), Oelze, Finley, Berlin PO, BBC Singers / DG 447765

Entflieht auf leichten Kähnen, Op. 2 (1908)

Anton Webern met his mentor Arnold Schoenberg for the first time in the fall of 1904. Webern had only started composing about five years before that and, impressed by *Verklärte Nacht* and other Schoenberg works, he sought the older musician out and became Schoenberg's first private pupil in Vienna. While working on his dissertation on Heinrich Isaac's *Choralis Constantinus*, Webern worked on several compositions under Schoenberg's supervision, the last of which was the short work for unaccompanied chorus *Entflieht auf leichten Kähnen*, completed in September, 1908. The poem is by Stefan George, who quickly became a Webern favorite, as he set over a dozen of George's other poems over the next few years (George also provided the texts for Schoenberg's notorious *String Quartet No. 2*).

As George's poem falls into three four-line verses, so Webern's setting is in three connected sections. The quiet ascending melodic line that opens the work mirrors George's invitation to "take flight in light barks." Gradually the polyphony becomes more chromatic and dense, in four parts with canonic interaction between the men's and women's voices. A moving hush descends at the mention of the "new sorrow" that ensues once one leaves these "tipsy, sunny worlds." Then, after a pause, the setting of the final two lines acts as a sort of reprise of the first section as the chorus sings of the "stille Trauer" (silent sadness) of spring. To help support the chorus' intonation, Webern prepared a spare instrumental backing of violin, viola, cello, harmonium, and piano for the work in 1914. Despite this, and although the work was published in 1921, it wasn't given its first performance until April 10, 1927, and was performed seldom if ever during the remainder of Webern's lifetime. *—Chris Morrison*

Recommended:

- ○ **Boulez Conducts Webern** / Boulez (cond.), BBC Singers / DG 437786
- ○ **Webern: Complete Vocal Chamber Works** / Leeuw (cond.), Netherlands Chamb. Choir / Koch 314005

Two Songs for chorus, clarinet, bass clarinet, celesta, guitar & violin, Op. 19 (1925–1926)

Webern's *Two Songs*, Op. 19, of January 1926 are his first fully serial published compositions. They had been preceded by an unpublished children's piece for piano and the first song of two songs in Op. 17 from late 1924, but Webern spent a year working on his compositional technique before releasing Op. 19. The poems for the songs are taken from Goethe's *Chinese-German Book of Hours and Seasons* and both are two-verse, pantheistic hymns to nature, one of Webern's favorite subjects. Scored for mixed chorus accompanied by a small instrumental ensemble consisting of clarinet, bass clarinet, violin, guitar, and celesta, both songs are very brief; the first lasts less than a minute and a half, the second barely a minute. The first, "Weiss wie Lilien" (White as Lilies), starts with a short instrumental prelude followed by the countrapuntal singing of the chorus and ending with an emphatic cadence. The second, "Ziehn die Schafe," starts with a quick flourish for clarinet and violin accompanied by guitar, followed by the more homophonic singing of the chorus and ending with the whole ensemble slipping upwards into the ether. *—James Leonard*

Recommended:

- ○ **Boulez Conducts Webern** / Boulez (cond.), BBC Singers, Aimard, InterContemporain Ensemble / DG 437786

Thomas Weelkes

b. ca. 1575, England [?], **d.** Dec. 1, 1623, London, England

Composer: Vocal, Choral

Thomas Weelkes has been known as one of the great names in the flowering of the Elizabethan madrigal, in a class with Morley, Wilbye, and Gibbons. Unlike many of his famous contemporaries, however, Weelkes never seems to have served the royal household in London, rather eking out a living as a provincial church musician. He first privately served noble patrons George Phillpot, and then Edward Darcye, following this with an uneasy tenure as Winchester College organist from 1598 to 1602. He then took the appointment as organist and choirmaster at Chichester Cathedral, with a lucrative clerkship on the side. Unfortunately, he spent the greater part of his church career being reprimanded by the ecclesiastical authorities; he was "noted and famed for a common drunkard and notorious swearer and blasphemer," and was dismissed from his musical duties at least once. After the death of his wife in 1622, Weelkes left all his responsibilities, and spent his last year in London.

His first (and best-known) compositions fed the tremendous vogue for Italianate music in Elizabethan England. In comparison to the then-recent publications of Morley, Weelkes lacked the elder madrigalist's graceful simplicity in the form; his resounding sonorities and imaginative contrasts, however, were already present in the *First Book of Madrigals* (3–6 voices, 1597). The volumes of 1598 (5 voiced) and 1600 (5 and 6 voiced) present Weelkes' best work, and some of the best English madrigals of all time. Weelkes' style in this music coalesces his understanding of the tradition of Flemish polyphony through the Englishman William Byrd, with Weelkes' own fascination with Italian music, especially the rich text-painting and daring chromaticism of Marenzio. Other characteristic traits include embedded musical contrasts, such as those in *O care, thou wilt despatch me*, the brilliant sonorities of *Thule*, the period of *Cosmography*, and the careful structural constructs found in his contribution to Morley's volume of Orianna madrigals: *As Vesta was from Latmos hill descending*.

Weelkes' long tenure serving the Church yielded a rich (though lesser-known) harvest of liturgical compositions. He produced both "Full" and "Verse" anthems, the latter involving passages written for soloists. The Verse Anthems afforded him more room for text-sensitivity, in addition to being more practically suited to a smaller, provincial choir. However, the fullness of his textures brings a note of brilliance and grandeur to the Full Anthems, such as his Hosanna to the Son of David. He also wrote ten complete Anglican Services, more restrained (and again practical) in style—the mark of a conscientious, if sometimes ill-behaved, church musician. These Services often demonstrate deep structural relationships between the various canticles, and even contain motivic ties to related anthems. *—Timothy Dickey*

VOCAL

Madrigals (ca. 1597–1608)

Along with Thomas Morley, Orlando Gibbons, William Byrd, and John Wilbye, Thomas Weelkes counts among the most prominent English composers to contribute to the madrigal genre. Although his professional career was cut rather short, due in part to his complementary bad habits of drinking and swearing, he managed to produce four volumes of madrigals by the time he was 35. The fourth remained his last, as the last years before his death at 49 were occupied variously with obligations for church music and struggles with personal problems. Composed within a decade, the four madrigal books represent a turning point in English music, as the influence of the Italian madrigal began to overshadow the lingering presence of Flemish polyphony.

Weelkes' madrigals are characterized by an acute attention to emotional content manifesting as dramatic chromaticism and poignant utilization of dissonance. While some scholars have criticized the sometimes unwieldy manner in which he juggles with large ensembles and his tendency to convey depths of expression at the expense of word declamation, accentuation, and poetic flow, most nonetheless recognize his ability to milk meaning from his texts and his skill and moving smoothly between vivid pictorialism and carefully crafted counterpoint.

His first collection, published in 1597 under the title *Madrigals to 3, 4, 5, & 6 Voyces*, already demonstrates Weelkes' concern for structure as articulated by lucid repetition schemes and structural divisions clearly articulated through texture and changes in meter. Perhaps the most striking and notable piece from this collection is *Cease Sorrows Now*, a four-voice work whose strange mixture of optimism of mourning finds voice in masterful chromatic work, particularly in the ominous rising lines that ascend—from the grave, as it were—on the words "Before I die, I'll sing my faint farewell." This piece finds a counterpart in *Cease Now Delight*, from Weelkes' subsequent collection from 1598 (*Balletts and Madrigals to Five Voyces*). Composed to commemorate the death of Irish military leader Thomas Lord Borough, the piece lays down layer upon layer of counterpoint, saturated with dissonant expression with such evocative phrases as "give Sorrow leave to speak" and "floods of tears bewailing his decease." Lighter spirits are represented in the collection as well, as in the "fa-la-las" that punctuate the ballett "Harke all ye lovely saints above."

Weelkes' third collection, *Madrigals of 5 & 6 Part*, appeared in 1600. Weelkes' skill at counterpoint is most apparent here, in the dense imitative textures of *As Vesta was from Latmos Hill Descending*. Again, structure is balanced with image, as when a string of nimbly descending scales appears when "Diana's darlings came running down the hill." The most memorable piece from Weelkes' final collection (*Ayeres or Phantasticke Spirites for Three Voices*, 1608) is the moving ode to Thomas Morley, *Death Hath Deprived Me of My Dearest Friend*. *—Jeremy Grimshaw*

Recommended:

- ○ **Weelkes: Madrigals and Anthems** / Rooley (cond.), Consort of Musicke / 1999 / ASV 195

CHORAL

Anthems (ca. 1602–1608)

Weelkes' early years were devoted almost exclusively to his astonishingly varied and creative madrigal compositions, but after 1608, he stopped publishing these in favor of sacred compositions. Weelkes was appointed organist and choir master of Chichester Cathedral sometime around 1602. While his relationship with his employers deteriorated to the point where he was dismissed in 1619, his long tenure at the cathedral argues that his employers were fully aware of his extraordinary musical talents. Certainly, his work did not appear to diminish in quality; though his madrigals are generally considered his effective works, his sacred music shows steady levels of musical quality, despite being far less innovative (particularly when compared with his groundbreaking secular compositions, such as *Thule*). This could be an effect of a more conservative audience, and it is also possible that some of his more creative efforts were lost. (Typically, church music was far less widely published and copied than secular music; churches tended to retain pieces for their own performances while patrons and composers both tried to diffuse secular compositions as widely as possible to enhance their fame.)

Strictly speaking, he wrote two "crossover" works between madrigals and church music: two sacred madrigals based on laments by David: *O Jonathan* and *When David Heard*. These, particularly the latter, are tremendously powerful works, both for their emotional impact and for their technique. *When David Heard*, written for seven voices, displays one of the most striking uses of counterpoint in all the English madrigal tradition and was also a significant influence upon later composers, particularly Tompkins. Unfortunately, while he wrote at least ten complete church services, of all his sacred music, only about 40 anthems and the two sacred madrigals have survived in a complete form. Some of the services have been partially reconstructed from Batten's transcriptions for organ, including the *Short Service for Five Voices*. Assuming the transcription did not exaggerate its use, this service features a daring display of almost constant imitation and repetition; aside from being striking in its own right, the effect ensures that much of the music remains in the listener's mind long after the conclusion.

His anthems display many of the consistent features of his madrigal writing, including dramatically sensitive use of repetition, occasional use of Italianate chromaticism, and a masterful use of polyphony. His six-voice *Hosanna to the Son of David* is remarkable for its brilliance of color and deftness of touch, creating a piece that seems to sparkle with its own jubilance without losing the sense of being a sacred piece. *—Ann Feeney*

Recommended:

- ○ **Weelkes: Ninth Service & Anthems** / Darlington (cond.), Christ Church Cathedral Choir / 1988 / Nimbus 5125

Kurt Weill

b. Mar. 2, 1900, Dessau, Germany, **d.** Apr. 3, 1950, New York, NY

Composer: Opera, Vocal, Musical Theater, Symphonic, Concerto

The son of a cantor, Kurt Weill was born in Dessau into a family that took in operatic performances as a main form of entertainment. When Weill was in his teens the director of the Dessau Hoftheater, Albert Bing, encouraged him in the study of music. Weill briefly studied composition with Engelbert Humperdinck and was already working professionally as a conductor when he attended composer Ferruccio Busoni's master classes in Berlin. Delighted to see the positive responses of an audience to his first collaboration with playwright Georg Kaiser, *Der Protagonist* (1926), he thereafter resolved to work toward accessibility in his music. In 1926 Weill married actress Lotte Lenya, whose reedy, quavering singing voice he called "the one I hear in my head when I am writing my songs."

In 1927 Weill began his collaboration with leftist playwright and poet Bertolt Brecht; their first joint venture, *Mahagonny-Songspiel* (1927), launched the number "Alabama Song," which, to their surprise, became a minor pop hit in Europe. The next show, *Die Dreigroschenoper* (The Three-Penny Opera, 1928) was a monstrous success, in particular the song "Moritat" (Mack the Knife). Nonetheless, strain in their association was already being felt, and after the completion of their magnificent "school opera" *Der Jasager* (1930), the two parted company. Brecht and Weill were brought together once more in Paris to create *Die Sieben Todsünden* (The Seven Deadly Sins) (1934). In the meantime, Weill collaborated with Caspar Neher on the opera *Die Bürgschaft* (1931) and Georg Kaiser again on *Der Silbersee* (1933), works that garnered the hostile attention of the then-emerging Nazi party. With the rise to power of Hitler, Weill and Lenya were forced to dissolve their union and flee continental Europe. Weill found his way to New York in 1935; rejoining Lenya, Weill became a citizen and devoted himself to American democracy with a vengeance, preferring his name pronounced like "wile" rather than "vile." After a series of frustrating flops, Weill hit his stride with playwright Maxwell Anderson, producing his first hit, *Knickerbocker Holiday* (1938). In the dozen years left to him, Weill's stature on Broadway grew with a series of hit shows, including *Lady in the Dark* (1941), *One Touch of Venus* (1943), *Love Life* (1948), and *Lost in the Stars* (1949). Weill had ambitions to create what he regarded as "the first American folk opera"; the closest of his American works to reach that goal is *Street Scene* (1946), a sort of "urban folk opera" based on a play by Elmer Rice with lyrics by Langston Hughes.

On April 3, 1950, Weill unexpectedly suffered a massive coronary and died in Lenya's arms. Weill's estate was valued at less than 1,000 dollars, and Lenya realized that his contribution to musical theater was likewise undervalued. She commissioned composer Marc Blitzstein to adapt an English-language version of *Die Dreigroschenoper*, it opened off-Broadway in 1954 and ran for three years, touching off a Weill revival that continues. *—Uncle Dave Lewis*

OPERA

Aufstieg und Fall der Stadt Mahagonny (Rise and Fall of the City of Mahagonny) (1929)

A collaboration between composer Kurt Weill and librettist Bertolt Brecht, *Aufstieg und Fall der Stadt Mahagonny* conveys the sense of alienation and disillusionment that characterized the interwar period in Germany, and stands as a harrowing example of the darkly apocalyptic wit of its creators. Though its musical materials—which borrow freely from jazz and cabaret styles—demonstrate a palpable sense of parody, Weill was careful to note that irony should not be read into the piece itself, but observed firsthand in the kind of world the piece portrays. "It is not advisable to shift presentation of the work to the side of the ironic or the grotesque," Weill pointed out in the foreword to the production book. "Since the incidents are not symbolic but typical, economy in the scenic means and in the expression of the individual actor commends itself most strongly." It is the directness, the eerie familiarity of the sights and sounds, that lend the piece its power. As philosopher and critic T.W. Adorno observed in 1931, Weill's music demonstrates "a circumspect sharpness which by means of its leaps and sidesteps makes articulate something which the song public would prefer not to know about."

Set rather tenuously in the United States (according to a surreal geography, somewhere between Pensacola and the Gold Coast), the story follows a group of fugitive criminals who set up a resort town in hopes of attracting newly rich customers returning with full pockets from the Gold Rush. Among those who arrive are a group of young girls in search of whisky, men, and money. Their carnal desires alternate with nostalgic lyricism in the famous "Alabama Song." The awkward dissonances and clunky melodies of the verses are so overshadowed by the wistfully arching line of the chorus that the real dramatic intention of this popular song is perhaps lost on many listeners, who likely never hear it in context or in its entirety. Other visitors to the town include a group of men returning from seven years' labor in Alaska, eager to spend their hard-earned cash on Mahagonny's pleasures—which include the girls, who have found employment of the most ancient kind in this city of sin. A romance develops between Jimmy and Jenny, though this relationship is like every other interpersonal exchange in Mahagonny: sentiments seem to fall on half-deaf ears, the characters talk past each other. There is a sense that everyone on-stage is oblivious to everyone else, except when self interest prompts interaction—a disjunction that finds voice in Weill's dialectical juxtapositions of musical materials. In the end, several of the men suffer ignominious demises (one eats so much he dies, another is executed for his inability to pay a bar tab), the citizens divide into arbitrarily opposing political factions, and God himself condemns the residents to hell. They refuse to go, however, insisting that hell can be no worse than Mahagonny. *—Jeremy Grimshaw*

Synopsis:

Act One. As *Aufstieg und Fall der Stadt Mahagonny* (Rise and Fall of the City of Mahagonny) begins, two titles preface the rise of the curtain. One is an alert that says Leokadja Begbick, Trinity Moses, and Fatty the Bookkeeper are all on the run from the police, who seek their arrest for bank fraud and white slave trading. The other, in red letters, reads "HOW THE CITY OF MAHAGONNY WAS FOUNDED." The fugitives enter in a decrepit truck, and, after assessing the state of their vehicle, abandon their plans to head for the Gold Coast. Instead, they decide to indirectly cash in on the gold rush by catering to the wants and lusts of those who strike it rich, and set out to establish a resort town. After all, says Begbick, "It's a lot easier to get gold out of men than out of rivers!" As the scene ends, titles projected onto the scrim tell that their city has grown quickly and drawn its first customers. Jenny and her group of young female colleagues appear in front of the curtain, wearily singing of their need for booze, men, and money ("Alabama Song"). As they exit, a new title tells that news of Mahagonny's pleasures has reached major cities. An off-stage chorus of metropolites complains about the drudgery of urban living, while Fatty and Moses urge them to visit Mahagonny. As the next scene begins, Jimmy Mahoney, Jacob Schmidt, Alaska Wolf Joe, and Pennybank Bill are introduced. The four are returning from seven years' labor in Alaska and are ready to spend their hard-earned cash on liquor and women. Begbick welcomes them to Mahagonny and introduces them to the group of girls seen earlier. After haggling over the prices for her services with Schmidt, Jenny takes a liking to Mahoney. As the whole group heads for town, they pass another group of tourists heading in the opposite direction. Begbick dismisses the disgruntled customers' complaints and calms her new clients by lowering her prices. Nonetheless, an unhappy Mahoney, with suitcase in hand, agrees to return to Mahagonny only after numerous entreaties by his friends. As a new scene begins, the men are among a crowd in a restaurant, languorously drinking and smoking. An on-stage pianist executes a painfully schmaltzy version of Badarzewska's *A Maiden's Prayer*, which Schmidt reverently identifies to the other diners as "eternal art." Mahoney sings as he stews about the state of Mahagonny, which, though prosperous by all appearances, has adopted numerous proscriptive policies: signs posted around the stage, for example, read "No rough stuff" and "Avoid Offensive Songs." His temper gets the better of him, and he fires his gun in the air and brandishes a knife. An altercation seems immanent, when suddenly the news arrives that a hurricane is headed toward Mahagonny. During the confusion that ensues, Mahoney has an epiphany: the secret to pure human happiness, he concludes, is absolute self-indulgence. His song converts his companions and the entrepreneurs alike: "Lie down and get kicked if you want to. As for me, I will stand up and kick!"

Act Two. A crowd nervously awaits a hurricane, while a news reporter's voice provides updates over a loudspeaker. The storm demolishes several nearby towns and is only a minute away from hitting Mahagonny, when it suddenly makes an unlikely half-circle detour around the town before continuing on its course. In the wake of their miraculous deliverance and Mahoney's persuasive pronouncement, a new policy is instituted in Mahagonny: whatever it is that you want to do, "DO IT." A chorus of men announces four particular emphases of overindulgence: gluttony, sex, violence, and drinking—each of which is played out in subsequent scenes. First, Schmidt gorges himself to death in an effort to down the flesh of three cows. Then the three men are offered the quick and cold company of prostitutes. Next comes a boxing match between Alaska Wolf Joe and Moses. As Joe flounders, Mahoney prods him with the self-serving encouragement that all of his money is riding on Joe's win; Bill, on the other hand, confesses that he has bet on his friend's opponent. After an ugly bout, Moses emerges the champion, while Alaska Wolf Joe fails to emerge at all. Moses has pummeled him to death. The next scene finds Jenny, Mahoney, Bill, and a group of men drinking heavily, all on Mahoney's tab. Mahoney decides to construct a boat out of the pool table and a curtain rod, and he and Jenny pretend to sail the South Seas. When the tab becomes due, however, Mahoney desperately tries to navigate his *imaginary* ship to the *real* Alaska. When his escape fails, he reveals that he is out of cash. He begs Jenny for help, but she coldly refuses with classic Brechtian irony: "The things they ask us girls to do!" Mahoney is taken away in chains.

Act Three. The act subsequently begins in the courtroom, where an accused murderer wordlessly and successfully negotiating a bribe, leading the judge to suddenly "condemn him...given the circumstances...to freedom!" As the murderer leaves, Mahoney is brought to the bench. He entreats his friend Bill for help with bribe money. "You know how much I care," insists Bill, "but with cash it's quite another matter." Begbick reads the charges, which all return a guilty verdict: solicitation of prostitution from one Jenny Smith; the singing of a happy song; and most damagingly, failure to pay his bar tab (plus the cost of the curtain rod). Mahoney is sentenced to death and taken to the gallows. As gruesome as this situation is, a projected title insists that no one in the audience would have paid Mahoney's tab either, so no one should be too shocked. In the final surreal scenes, Moses, acting the part of God, visits Mahagonny and condemns its feuding residents to Hell. They refuse, insisting that they are already there. *—Jeremy Grimshaw*

Recommended:

○ **Weill: Aufstieg und Fall der Stadt Mahagonny** / Latham-Koenig (cond.), Silja, Schlemm, Hirte, Lehrberger, Cologne RO / Capriccio 10160/1

Die Dreigroschenoper (The Threepenny Opera) (1928)

Kurt Weill and Bertolt Brecht's *Die Dreigroschenoper* (The Threepenny Opera) was far and away the greatest commercial success in either of their careers, enjoying thousands of performances in Germany alone. In many ways it was a revolutionary work, turning its back on traditional operatic practices and unabashedly reverting to the tradition of the number opera, as well as forming a viable synthesis between "highbrow" and "lowbrow" musical traditions. It has endured as Weill's most recognizable work, and the popularity of excerpted songs, such as "Mack the Knife" will ensure its reputation for years to come.

In 1920 a revival of John Gay's *The Beggar's Opera* (1728) opened in London and proceeded to break the record for the longest-running production—a record previously held by Gay's 1728 original (*The Beggar's Opera* was in fact so popular in the 1920s that it spawned a line of product tie-ins, including fans, figurines, and illustrations). Music publisher B. Schott Söhne tried to cash in on that show's popularity by contracting an adaptation with Paul Hindemith in 1925, but the composer refused, leaving the way clear for others to try. Weill and Brecht, who were in the midst of work on their *Aufstieg und Fall der Stadt Mahagonny* (The Rise and Fall of the City of Mahagonny), interrupted that project and set to work on their own adaptation, which became *The Threepenny Opera*.

The first production, in 1928, was fraught with difficulties. Days before the premier, revisions were still being made, cast members were being replaced and fighting amongst themselves, and the director was threatening to quit. The production was expected to fail dismally. Everyone involved was then caught off guard when, within a week of the premiere, "Threepenny fever" had spread across Germany, and theaters throughout the country were announcing productions of *Die Dreigroschenoper.* Noted musicologist and arch-modernist Theodore Adorno insisted that the public liked *Threepenny* only because they didn't understand it—that Weill had embedded an ironic statement in a false gesture towards popular musical styles—a gesture which the public had misinterpreted as sincere. This was nonsense to Weill, who made no apologies for the work's popularity.

Die Dreigroschenoper differed from the original *Beggar's Opera* in some important aspects. While 51 of the 69 songs in Gay's work are traceable to European folk or popular tunes, Weill composed an entirely original score (save the "Morgenchoral," which is retained from Gay's original). Also, while Gay's work contained pointed, and specific, social commentary, the 1928 *Dreigroschenoper* contained no such explicit references, though it often took a satirical or farcical tone. When Brecht released a "literary" version of the work in 1933, he awkwardly interpolated several dogmatic discourses, betraying his increasingly Marxist views, but this version has never gained the popularity of the original. In both, the gangster Macheath, facing execution, is suddenly granted a reprieve because, as a character in Gay's opera states, "an opera must end happily!" *—AMG*

Synopsis:

Prologue. The story, based on John Gay's *The Beggar's Opera,* is set in and around London in 1830. At the beginning of the Prologue, and preceding certain subsequent scenes, a caption is displayed on screens for the audience. The opening caption announces the fair in the Soho section of London, and proclaims the aggressive tactics of the beggars, thieves, and whores.

Act One. The ensuing caption declares that businessman Jonathan Jeremiah Peachum has opened a shop whose goods are affordable to the poor, making him popular among London's many beggars. Peachum's wife informs him of their daughter Polly's interest in the young man known as Macheath, but Peachum later reveals that the man is none other than the notorious womanizer and criminal Mack the Knife.

Mack the Knife marries Polly the next day and celebrates the event that afternoon. Polly sings a song to cheer up her new husband, who is disappointed in the trappings stolen by his men for the celebration. Police Chief Brown, a close friend of Mack, who always turns a blind eye to his criminality, pays him a brief visit. Mack's men soon depart, leaving Mack and Polly to their romance. At his shop Peachum ponders his likely ruination over his daughter's marriage to Mack the Knife.

Act Two. Peachum pursues Mack, intent on turning him over to the authorities. Mack flees, while Mrs. Peachum surmises he has gone to Turnbridge with his prostitutes. Polly comes to his aid, warning him of her mother's plan to bribe the girls to turn him in. While Mack is away, Polly takes over as head of his criminal gang.

The following scene bears a caption divulging the whores' betrayal of him in Turnbridge. While Mack sings, Jenny the whore goes to the window to alert the Constable outside to make his arrest.

Mack is in prison and Police Chief Brown laments that he could have helped his friend. His daughter Lucy, who is secretly also married to Mack, meets with Polly outside the prison and a fight breaks out between them. After Mrs. Peachum arrives and takes Polly with her, Lucy helps Mack escape. He rushes away to his whores again, while Peachum enters the prison to discover Mack gone. He chides Brown for allowing the criminal to escape.

Act Three. Peachum plots to disrupt the Coronation of the Queen by exposing the misery among the poor in London. After he delivers a rousing address to the beggars, he is arrested by Brown. He is soon released, however, having blackmailed Brown, who is also forced to seek out Mack. Once more Mack is double-crossed by the whores. This time he is sentenced to be hanged, but when he is taken to the gallows, a messenger from the King brings word that Mack is to be spared. *—Robert Cummings*

Recommended:

- ○ **Weill: The Threepenny Opera** / Mauceri (cond.), Lemper, Kollo, Milva, Berlin RIAS Sinfonietta / 1989 / Decca 430075
- ○ **Die Dreigroschenoper: Berlin 1930** / Mackeben (cond.), Lenya, M. Dietrich / 2002 / Teldec 42663

Die sieben Todsünden (The Seven Deadly Sins), ballet-opera (1933)

Premiered in Paris in the summer of 1933, *Die sieben Todsünden* (The Seven Deadly Sins) was the first work Weill wrote after fleeing Germany. The composer once again collaborated with Bertolt Brecht to create this "sung ballet," which portrays the lead character, Anna, with two different performers: a singer (Anna I), representing Anna's outward attitudes, and a dancer (Anna II) who conveys the character's inner turmoil. Though not as well known as *Aufstieg und Fall der Stadt Mahagonny* (1927), *Die sieben Todsünden* nevertheless stands as prime example of the sort of deeply and darkly ironic social critique that characterizes the fruits of the Weill/Brecht collaboration.

The conflict represented by the unique double-persona lead character seems somehow connected to several interpersonal conflicts between the individuals involved in the work's conception. Only a year before premiering the role of Anna I, and six years after marrying Weill, Lotte Lenya had separated from her composer husband. Likewise Tilly Losch, whose dancing skills and striking physical resemblance to Lenya made her the prime candidate to play the role of Anna II would divorce impresario Edward James soon after their joint work on the production. And, of course, librettist Brecht had angrily threatened litigation—and even physical violence—against Weill after a disagreement surrounding the Berlin staging of *Aufstieg und Fall der Stadt Mahagonny.* These rifts find odd resonance in the double portrayal of Anna, who navigates several dilemmas via two diametrically opposed selves: a recklessly ambitious outer personality (Anna I) which conceals a tragically unhappy inner soul (Anna II).

The work tells the story of a girl who leaves home to find work in various big American cities, hoping to earn enough money for her family to build a house on the banks of the Mississippi River. On the way, she is "tempted" by each of the seven Biblical sins. Brecht inverts these, however, treating them not as moral transgressions, but rather as episodic commentaries on the conflicts between morals and money that inevitably emerge in a capitalist society. For example, it is not Anna's prostitution that transgresses the prohibition against Lust. Rather, her sin is falling in love: her real romance threatens business and drives away paying clients. Throughout the work, each time Anna wavers in trading dignity for dollars she is reproved by her family, whom Weill and Brecht set off musically and dramaturgically as an omniscient male quartet. Their observations accompany Anna as she passes from city to city and sin to sin, and their prayer is always the same: "Lord, enlighten our children that they may find the path to Prosperity, that they may not transgress the Laws that make us rich and happy!" Weill's hauntingly sardonic mixture of cabaret sounds and complexly dissonant contrapuntal techniques provides the perfect counterpoint to Brecht's text, utilizing various degrees of irony and alienation to create a highly austere, yet deeply expressive work. *—Jeremy Grimshaw*

Synopsis:

Prologue. The main character(s) are introduced: Anna I and Anna I; the former takes a singing role while the latter is the dancer. Although they introduce themselves as sisters with different personalities ("My sister is pretty," Anna I explains. "I am practical. She's a bit crazy, but I have my head on straight..."), they are really the same person, with "one past and one future, one heart and one bank account." (Nonetheless, because they execute different actions on-stage, this double-persona entity will be referred to hereafter in the plural, even though their actions represent those of a single person.) The Annas have been sent by their family in Louisiana to the city to earn money, with which the family hopes to build a little house on the banks of the Mississippi River. In their attempts to make good on their errand, the two Annas engage in inverted versions of the seven deadly sins from the *Bible*: Sloth, Pride, Anger, Gluttony, Lust, Avarice, and Envy. In doing so, they enact a commentary not on personal morality, but on the danger of hypocrisy within the context of middle-class capitalist society, in which morals and money frequently find themselves at odds.

Scene One. The Annas have come up with a money-making scheme. They go to a park, where Anna II makes romantic gestures toward unknown men as a form of blackmail. Anna I offers to get rid of her pesky "sister" for a price. They successfully complete this ruse several times, but Anna II grows tired and takes a nap on a park bench. The family, represented by a men's quartet, omnisciently observes the scene and offers their own commentary: "If you didn't drag her out of bed in the morning, the lazy lump wouldn't ever get up.... Idleness is the beginning of vice!" They then intone the sardonic words that will become their repeated prayer: "Lord enlighten our children, that they may find the path to Prosperity," adding their hopes that the Annas "do not transgress the Laws that make us rich and happy!" The sin of Sloth, then, is not committed in performing the scam, but in resting from it.

Scene Two. Anna I tells us that they have gone on to Memphis and found work as cabaret dancers. Anna II, however, has overstepped the bounds of her job: she has sensed in herself a certain talent and has displeased her audiences by trying to be artistic instead of sexy. In doing so, Anna II has fallen to the temptation of Pride. "Those people pay good money to see something," Anna I complains, "and when one hides one's nakedness like a rotten fish, you can't expect much applause.... So I told my sister Anna: Pride is for rich people!" The family concurs: "Only one who can overcome Self will obtain the Reward."

Scene Three. The sisters are in Los Angeles working as film extras. Problems arise, however, when Anna II commits the sin of Anger by taking issue with the maltreatment of a horse on the set. Her actions lead to her dismissal from the job. The family is heard complaining about the pittance they receive from the girls, and Anna I warns her sister to get control of her temper. "He who gets angry at cruelty," she advises, "is digging his own grave."

Scene Four. The next scene addresses the sin of Gluttony. The girls are in Philadelphia making decent money as solo dancers. In order to keep the job, however, they have to watch their weight carefully. "They don't want a hippopotamus in Philadelphia!" They are weighed every day, and if their slight 110-pound frame gains an ounce the contract is broken. "Stick with it," the family insists, "Gluttony doesn't do anyone any good!"

Scene Five. The girls move on to Boston, where they grapple with the sin of Lust. Anna II is once again spoiling their money-making scheme: while Anna I "faithfully" offers a steady customer sexual favors in exchange for cash, Anna II becomes romantically involved with someone else. Such dependence, Anna I warns, diminishes their value as a sexual commodity. Anna I convinces her sister to break it off with her lover and apologize to the customer. "This is how it must be," Anna II sobs. "But it is so hard!" Meanwhile, the family again intones their unholy prayer.

Scene Six. Baltimore is next, where the Annas are tempted by Avarice. "Already in Baltimore," the family reads in the newspaper, "all kinds of people are shooting themselves over Anna!" They worry, however, that if she gets too greedy her fans will abandon her. "We hope our Anna will have the wits to not take the shirt off everyone's back and steal every last penny," the family sings. "Pure avarice is not the best plan."

Scene Seven. The sisters finally find themselves in San Francisco. They have had success, but Anna II finds herself envious of those who "spend their days at leisure, not for sale, proud, protesting every cruelty... loving only the lover...." This Envy is her final sin, which her sister urges her to renounce along with the others. "Only one who can overcome Self," the family reminds her, "will obtain the Reward."

Epilogue. The epilogue marks the sisters' return to Louisiana at the end of their seven-year errand. Anna I rejoices at their accomplishments and at the little house on the banks of the Mississippi. By this time, however, it is known that Anna I is the façade concealing the true inner self represented by Anna II. Anna I continues to celebrate, and attempts to get her sister's endorsement. Anna II wearily and unconvincingly acquiesces. *—Jeremy Grimshaw*

Recommended:

○ **Weill: The Seven Deadly Sins; Symphony 2** / Nagano (cond.), Stratas, Lyon Opera Orch. / 1997 / Erato 063017068

○ **Weill: The Seven Deadly Sins; Little Threepenny Music** / Tilson Thomas (cond.), Migenes, Tear, Opie, London SO / 1988 / Sony 44529

Street Scene (1946)

Weill saw a production of Elmer Rice's Pulitzer-Prize-winning play *Street Scene* in 1929, before leaving Berlin; he would return to it 18 years later, after his move to the United States, as the source for one of his most successful stage works. Weill enlisted the author himself to revise the text, and the noted poet Langston Hughes to write song lyrics; the resulting work, variously called an "American Opera," a "Broadway Opera," and a "Broadway Musical," was a critical success: Olin Downes, the often reserved music critic for the *New York Times*, called it "the most important step toward significantly American opera that the writer has yet encountered in musical theater."

The story of *Street Scene* centers around Anna Maurrant and her family—residents of a New York City brownstone. The conflicts between Anna, her husband Frank, and their daughter, Rose, become the focal point in the drama. This family drama set within the larger context of the brownstone and its residents, making the work feel like a sort of "day in the life" in its lighter moments. In order to capture the flavor of city life, Weill conducted extensive "field research"; he sought to make everything from the children's games and schoolgirls' songs to the dance numbers more authentic. As Weill himself noted, "the play lends itself to a variety of music, just as the streets of New York themselves embrace the music of many lands and many people."

Street Scene incorporated several timely issues in its dramatic progression: racial tensions, questions of poverty and social justice, and domestic issues, including infidelity and violence. The weight of all of these maladies is symbolized by the opening number, "Ain't it awful the heat"—the scorching weather is a tangible incarnation of the oppressive circumstances under which the tenants live. In this sense, *Street Scene* hearkens back to the psychological tension of Weill's earlier one-act opera, *Der Protagonist* (1925); in that work also, it's just a matter of time before unfortunate circumstances bring underlying tensions to the surface, with tragic consequences. In both cases, the outcome is apparent well ahead of time, and part of Weill's genius is letting the audience carry the weight of that knowledge without losing dramatic purpose or musical interest.

Weill saw *Street Scene* as his greatest achievement, a perfectly balanced integration of music and drama. As Weill wrote in a memo to his collaborators, "Ever since Elmer and I started talking about this show, we thought in terms of... a show that flows naturally from dialogue into music and back... It is no accident that the emotional parts are the high spots of the show because we have achieved a complete blending of music and words and action."

Memorable excerpts from the score include the comical "Wouldn't You Like to Be on Broadway?"; Frank Maurrant's family values polemic, "Let things be like they always was"; the light-hearted "Ice Cream Sextet"; and Sam Kaplan's "Lonely House." In every case, the engagement between Rice's carefully pruned drama, Weill's music, and Hughes' song texts is made clear; the work jells into an engaging and stylistically interesting piece of musical theater. *—Jeremy Grimshaw*

Synopsis:

Act One. It is a summer evening on a poor street in New York City, and a few of the residents of brownstone #364 are sitting in stoops and windows, gossiping about absent neighbors and complaining about the awful heat. Henry the janitor appears, singing the blues to himself. The women continue chatting, particularly about the love life of their neighbor, Mrs. Maurrant, whom they suspect has been cheating on her rather thuggish husband with Sankey, the milk man. Mrs. Maurrant appears, bemoaning her troubles and expressing her secret desires in song. Sam Kaplan, a bookish youth from a Jewish family, appears, pausing on his way to the library. While Mrs. Maurrant is troubled over the gross insensitivity of her husband, Sam is troubled by adolescence in general and his unrequited love for Mrs. Maurrant's daughter Rose in particular. Mr. Buchanan, whose wife is in labor, to the amusement of the women present, seems to overestimate his own paternal stress while remaining rather ignorant of his wife's brunt of the parental burden. As Buchanan steps inside to answer his wife's cries, Mr. Maurrant, whose mean, swaggering personality has driven his wife into the arms of another man, appears. Arriving home from a log day at work he goes inside, leaving his unhappy wife to sing again of her longing for compassion. Her optimistic words betray her inner hopelessness: in insisting that "I always will believe there'll be a brighter day!" she admits that such a day will perpetually be sought and never found. For the time being though, as luck would have it, the milk man conspicuously passes by. Pretending to look for her tardy son Willie, Mrs. Maurrant follows after him, eliciting another round of gossip from her nosy neighbors. Next comes a bit of comic relief in the form of Lippo, the bubbly Italian violin teacher from the first floor, who sings an ode to the ice cream cone as he passes one out to everyone present. During this lighthearted passage, however, Maurrant has decided to look for his wife, whom he saw from his second-story window. Deciding to buy her unlikely explanation for leaving, Maurrant redirects his anger toward Sam's father, Abraham Kaplan, and his leftist political sentiments.

At this point a group of school children enter, including Jenny, Charlie, and Mary Hildebrand. They are singing their school song and celebrating graduation day. Jenny is particularly lauded by her mother and the neighbors for having won a scholarship; this cheerful scene is undercut, however, by the pending eviction facing the Hildebrands the following day. Lippo once again breaks the gloom by initiating a dance. Mrs. Maurrant goes inside, Mr. Maurrant leaves to get drunk, and the neighbors gossip a bit more until Sam scolds them for their insensitivity. They retire to their apartments, leaving Sam to sing once more of his loneliness. Just as he goes inside for the evening his beloved Rose appears, though in the company of another suitor. Easter, a friend from her work, makes a pass at her, promising that he could make her a star if she would be his mistress. He finally leaves after his efforts prove unsuccessful. In the mean time, Mrs. Buchanan is on the verge of delivery. As Rose runs to get the doctor, Mae Jones and Dick McGann enter for the first time, drinking heavily and happily. Despite their intoxicated state they manage a song and dance number, which concludes as Rose returns from the doctor. She is met by Mae's brutish brother Vincent, who not only harasses Rose, but also handily floors Sam when he tries to intercede. Rose, well aware of the fate she would face in the arms of a man like Vincent, assures Sam of her devotion and admiration. They exchange tender sentiments before saying goodnight.

Act Two. The second act begins with the sound of morning in the city and a sing-song children's sidewalk game. The Buchanan baby has entered the world happy and healthy, and the new father thanks Mrs. Maurrant for her invaluable help during the night. Mr. Maurrant heads off for work, indicating that he will be gone until the next day. Before he leaves, Rose begs him to treat her mother with more kindness. Instead, he angrily implies that rather than being up all night with new mother and baby, Mrs. Maurrant was out on less virtuous errands. After he leaves, Rose voices her worry that her mother is not being discreet enough about her affair. "If you have nobody who understands," replies Mrs. Maurrant, "you might as well be dead." When Sam appears, Rose tells her of Easter's promises. They engage in an impassioned duet, during which they decide to run away together. In the mean time, the Hildebrands are being turned out into the streets and Mrs. Maurrant has invited Sankey up to her apartment. A suspicious Mr. Maurrant comes home unexpectedly and, finding his wife's lover in his apartment, shoots them both in a fit of rage. As he is being carried away by the police he spies his daughter and affirms with anguish his love for the wife he murdered. Rose tells her father goodbye, and realizes that she must say goodbye to Sam also, in hopes that by leaving the brownstone behind and leaving him to pursue his studies, they both will find better lives. The opera ends with the ensemble once again absentmindedly chatting, gossiping, and bemoaning the oppressive heat. *—Jeremy Grimshaw*

Recommended:

○ **Weill: Street Scene (Original Broadway Cast)** / Abravanel (cond.), Jeffreys, Stoska, Sullivan / CBS 44668

○ **Weill: Street Scene (Original London Cast)** / Carl Davis (cond.), Ciesinski, Kelly, van Allan, ENO Chorus & Orch. / Jay 1232

VOCAL

Mahagonny Songspiel, for soloists & orchestra (1927)

The *Mahagonny-Gesänge* were five texts Bertolt Brecht published in 1926. Brecht and Weill were busy enlarging their idea of the City of Mahagonny—a mythic, wide-open frontier city in America—into an opera when they were asked to contribute to an evening of short chamber operas. They decided to use the "Gesänge" as a "style study" for the opera project and Weill set the Brecht texts, adding an epilogue. The resulting "Songspiel" was given a simple staging. It is in Weill's cabaret-like style, including two English-language songs, somehow capturing the decadence of late 1920s Berlin. The original version has a remarkable formal cogency. This and the full-length opera (*The Rise and Fall of the City of Mahagonny*) are the only authentic versions. In 1932 Weill sanctioned an extended version of the *Songspiel* devised by Maurice de Abravanel, which added a few numbers from the opera. He probably did so as a stopgap because any prospect for staging the opera had by that time disappeared. A 1960 mushing together of the *Songspiel* and texts and music from the opera into a kind of theater piece with incidental music, called *Das kleine Mahagonny* should be considered inauthentic. *—Joseph Stevenson*

Recommended:

- ○ **Weill: The Seven Deadly Sins; Mahagonny Songspiel** / Mauceri (cond.), Lemper, Berlin RIAS Sinfonietta / 1990 / London 430168
- ○ **Weill: Kleine Dreigroschenmusik; Mahagonny Songspiel; Happy End, Berliner Requiem** / Atherton (cond.), London Sinfonietta / 1976 / DG 459442

MUSICAL THEATER

Works for Musical Theater (1929–1948)

Musical theater works dominate Weill's oeuvre. As a young composer in Germany, studying with Alban Berg and later Engelbert Humperdinck, Weill composed mainly instrumental works, including orchestral and chamber music; however, Weill also began writing songs in the early decades of the twentieth century and his interest in vocal music would soon lead him to a career as a composer of opera and musicals.

Weill's first work for musical theater was *Die Zaubernacht* (The Magic Night), composed in 1922. It is a children's ballet pantomime in one act. Scored for nine instruments and soprano soloist, *Die Zaubernacht* tells the story of a fairy that brings toys to life. While the work's simple and direct music was criticized by members of the German press as unmelodious, *Die Zaubernacht* proved an important work for Weill's development as a composer of musicals: he remarked that "the stage has its own musical form, which develops organically out of the flow of the plot."

Weill's next major work for the theater was the singspiel *Mahagonny*, written in collaboration with Bertolt Brecht in 1927. The work deals with the subject of the decay of moral life in a big American city. Musically, *Mahagonny* is important because it is an early instance of Weill using popular idioms in his work, including elements of jazz and pop tunes; his choice of instruments for the work includes two saxophones, also a reflection of his burgeoning attraction to popular music. *Mahagonny* would later become the opera *Aufstieg und Fall der Stadt Mahagonny*, whose 1930 premiere in Berlin was disrupted by Nazi sympathizers.

In Vienna 1929, Weill and Brecht's major work, *Die Dreigroschenoper* (The Three Penny Opera), was premiered. It is work of "epic theater," based on John Gay's ballad opera *The Beggar's Opera*. It is from *Die Dreigroschenoper* that we get the classic song "Mack the Knife." We also see Weill adopting an even more austere, popular style, though his harmonies are still colored with dissonance.

Most of Weill's major contributions to music theater were made on Broadway, after the composer had fled Nazi Germany for Paris, then New York. In New York Weill composed a number of classic musicals, including *Johnny Johnson*, *Knickerbocker Holiday*, *Lady in the Dark*, *Street Scene*, and *Love Life*. *Lady in the Dark*, premiered in 1941, dramatizes the psychoanalytic treatment of a young woman, reflecting the contemporary fascination with Freudian psychoanalysis. *Street Scene*, a tale of life in a New York apartment building on two hot summer days, premiered in 1947 and was Weill's last major success on Broadway. *Street Scene* represents the full maturation of Weill as a composer of musical theater, fluidly combining jazzy songs, choral music, and instrumental music in an evocative, moody score. *—Alexander Carpenter*

Recommended:

- ○ **Lady in The Dark** / Abravanel (cond.), Engel, Reardon, Green, Kaye / Sony 62869
- ○ **September Songs** / Stratas, Lenya, Costello, Cave, Harvey, etc. / 1997 / Sony 63046
- ○ **Weill: Berlin & American Theater Songs** / Lenya, Bean (cond.) / 1988 / Sony 42658
- ○ **Der Silbersee** / Stenz (cond.), London Sinfonietta / 1999 / RCA 63447
- ○ **Lady In The Dark** / Dorrell (cond.), Original London Cast / 1998 / Jay 1278
- ○ **Ute Lemper Sings Kurt Weill** / Lemper, Meyer, Rautenberg / 1988 / London 425204
- ○ **Happy End** / Latham-Koenig (cond.), Raffeiner, Ploog, Ramm, Kimbrough, Cologne Pro Musica, Konig Ens. / Capriccio 60015
- ○ **Weill: Songs** / Farley, Vignoles / 1992 / ASV 790
- ○ **Speak Low: Songs By Kurt Weill** / von Otter, Gardiner (cond.), Forsberg / 1994 / DG 439894

SYMPHONIC

Symphony No. 2 (1933–1934)

Weill began work on this symphony in January 1933, mere months before he was to leave Nazi Germany for Paris. While composing this work, he sometimes referred to it as his first symphony, since his actual *First Symphony* of 1921 had not yet been performed. It was also his last symphony: after completing it in Paris in 1934, he would focus almost exclusively on theater and vocal music, never writing another piece of "absolute" orchestral music again.

The *Second Symphony*, which Weill alternately called *Symphonic Fantasy* or *Three Night Scenes*, is cast in three movements: Sonata, Largo, Rondo. The work opens with a funeral march in which the main thematic material is presented. The march is followed by a Classical allegro in sonata form. The opening march is heard again in the slow second movement. In the third movement, thematic material from the preceding movements is carefully interwoven in a high-spirited finale. Stylistically, the *Second Symphony* represents a seamless blending of traditions, with clear, Classical-inspired formal structures enmeshed with bold and expressive Romantic gestures. Though Weill insisted that this work was not a programmatic piece, a number of commentators have noted that the symphony seems to reflect the upheaval in Weill's life—his exile and divorce—and the contemporary political situation as dark clouds began gathering over Germany and Europe.

The *Second Symphony* received its premiere in Amsterdam in October 1934, conducted by Bruno Walter. *—Alexander Carpenter*

Recommended:

- ○ **Weill: The Seven Deadly Sins; Symphony 2** / Nagano (cond.), Lyon Opera Orch. / 1997 / Erato 063017068
- ○ **Goldschmidt: Suite Op 5; Gerhard: Concertino Op12; Weill: Symphony 2** / J. Bruns (cond.), Kammersymphonie Berlin / 2002 / EDA 18
- ○ **Honegger & Weill: Orchestral Works** / Jansons (cond.), Berlin PO / 2002 / EMI 575658

CONCERTO

Concerto for violin and wind orchestra, Op. 12 (1924)

The frenzied earnestness of German musical life between the end of the Great War and Hitler's rise to power—the Jazz Age—looms as at once fantastic and touching. The intense rivalries and jealous watchfulness, manifestoes and critical infighting, performance politics and machinations—satirically reflected in the gamey knockabout of Berlin cabaret—and, above all, the very different musics of Schoenberg, Stravinsky, Hindemith, Schreker, Pfitzner, and Toch, to name but a few, were full of megalomania. Young composers responded to this bewildering plurality by becoming camp followers or avant-garde faddists according to type—one recognizes in Krenek, for instance, the eternal opportunist, in Jarnach the organization man, and in Weill the idealist.

In this carnival atmosphere, Ferruccio Busoni's return to Berlin in the fall of 1920 must have made him an Apollonius of Tyana—a revered sage and miracle worker to some, a mystagogical charlatan to others. Kurt Weill was among the initial members of Busoni's composition master class, sponsored by the Prussian State Academy, and remained to become less a student than a disciple and confidant. Looking back, he wrote that "We young musicians had clung to a distorted image of beauty. But we could not shape the new that we longed for—we could not find the form for our content. We burst the bonds of tradition, but we stammered where we wanted to thunder. Then Busoni returned to Berlin."

That this is no exaggeration is confirmed by Weill's *Sonata for Cello and Piano*, completed in the summer of 1920—a work awash in the surging, billowing gestures of Strauss and Schreker, spiced with an acerb harmonic vocabulary, and pedantically developed beyond the point of diminishing returns. Indeed, Weill continued to "stammer" during the master class period, July 1921 to October 1923, in such works as the lugubrious *First Symphony* and the involved, overlong a cappella *Recordare*, and did not absorb the lessons of the master until Busoni was on his deathbed. Then, suddenly, it came together in the *Concerto for Violin and Wind instruments*, composed over April-May 1924, with its "objective" coolness, its formal concision, its nod to his mentor's *Italianità*; it is Weill's first masterpiece, whose curious musical Esperanto becomes a living language. Composed for Joseph Szigeti—who eventually performed it all over Europe—the *Concerto* was given its premiere in Paris on June 11, 1925, by Marcel Darrieux with Walther Straram conducting the Straram Orchestra.

Weill's choice of instrumentation for his concerto was innovative; indeed, there had been no violin concerto like it before. The orchestration—an orchestral wind section with percussion plus a single double bass—sets the voice of the violin apart entirely from the sound world of the ensemble. His use of the winds, especially, is characteristic of the "socially-conscious" works he wrote in the 1920s (from *Der Protagonist* and *The Rise and Fall of the City of Mahagonny* to *The Threepenny Opera*).

The first movement occupies a surreal sound world in which ghostly tranquillo episodes alternate with distant alarums and excursions coming closer and fading away in pseudo-Baroque business. The succeeding Notturno—with its prominent xylophone, conjures a spectrally brittle pantomime; this is interrupted by a pleading, protesting central Cadenza, again awakening martial fanfares. The piquant and eerie Serenata's Allegretto can only be the love song of Pierrot to Columbine. The final agitato tarantella passes like a haunted dreamscape impassively observed. *—Adrian Corleonis*

Recommended:

○ **Weill: Berliner Requiem; Vom Tod im Wald; Violinkonzert** / Herreweghe (cond.), Glab, Ensemble Musique Oblique / Harmonia Mundi 901422

Felix Weingartner

b. Feb. 6, 1863, Zara, Yugoslavia, **d.** Jul. 5, 1942, Winterthun, Switzerland
Conductor

Felix Weingartner, who did much to shape the modern art of conducting, studied piano and composition in Graz, Austria with the composer W.A. Remy. On the recommendation of Hanslick, he received a stipend from the state, and in 1881 he went on to study philosophy at Leipzig University, later attending the Leipzig Conservatory where he made the acquaintance of Liszt. Liszt persuaded him to become a conductor and helped to produce Weingartner's first opera, *Sakuntala*, at Weimar in 1884. In the same year he began his conducting career in Königsberg.

Thereafter, Weingartner was constantly on the move: Danzig (1885–87); as Hans von Bülow's assistant in Hamburg (1887–89); Mannheim (1889–91); Berlin's Kaim Royal Opera Orchestra (1891–98); the Vienna Opera, where he succeeded Mahler (1898–1903); Hamburg again (1912–14); Darmstadt (1914–19); Vienna Volksoper and the Vienna Philharmonic Orchestra (1919–27). Over the same period, he toured Europe, making his first visits to London in 1898 and to the U.S. in 1905, where he conducted the Boston Opera Company for its 1912–13 season. From 1927 to 1933, he was director of the Conservatory and Symphony Orchestra in Basel, Switzerland, and returned tp the Vienna State Opera from 1935–36. In his second period with the Vienna Opera he appeared tired, and resigned at the end of the season. In 1939, Weingartner was awarded the Gold Medal of the Royal Philharmonic Society in London.

Nor were Weingartner's activities confined to conducting: he was also a prolific composer. His output includes eight operas, six symphonies, two concertos, chamber music and songs, though none of his works had more than a brief success. Together with Charles Malherbe, he edited the complete works of Berlioz and was one of the first to bring that composer's works back into public favor. Weingartner's arrangement of Weber's *Invitation to the Dance* was recorded four times by him, and he also recorded his own orchestral arrangement of Beethoven's *"Hammerklavier" piano sonata* (Op. 106) with the Royal Philharmonic Orchestra.

Weingartner was among the first great conductors to insist on a meticulous interpretation of the composer's score and steady, moderate tempi. While in Hamburg, he clashed with Hans von Bülow, whom he criticized for romantic exaggeration and wayward performances. In 1895, Weingartner wrote a book, *On Conducting*, in which he accused von Bülow of "wanting to divert the attention of the audience from the music to himself."

His baton technique was refined and simple. The English critic Neville Cardus wrote this of his podium style: "Weingartner does not use the familiar gestures of the modern 'dictator' conductors; he retains the old fashioned belief that an instrumentalist understands how to play his notes correctly, and does not need illumination in the form of arts that scarcely belong to a conductor—the arts of Terpsichore and declamation. His gestures are quiet; he is always dignified.... He belongs to the cultured epoch of music, the epoch of good manners, good taste and scholarship."

Weingartner made his first recordings in 1910 with the American soprano Lucille Marvel, who became the third of his five wives. He recorded all the Beethoven symphonies, some several times, most famously with the Vienna Philharmonic Orchestra in the 1930s. In Japan, his Beethoven *"Choral" Symphony* sold over 100,000 copies, a remarkable achievement. Weingartner's immense reputation was obscured by the rise of the high-profile, much-recorded conductors of the 1950s and 1960s. However, CD transfers have been made of some of his finest Beethoven performances. *—Roy Brewer*

Recommended:

○ **Beethoven: Symphony 9** / Weingartner (cond.), Vienna PO / 2003 / Naxos 8110863

○ **Beethoven: Symphonies 5 & 6** / Weingartner (cond.), Royal PO, London PO, British SO / 2003 / Naxos 8110861

○ **Beethoven: Symphonies 1 & 2; Fidelio Overture; Leonore Overture 2** / Weingartner (cond.), Vienna PO, London SO, London PO / 2002 / Naxos 8110856

○ **Beethoven, Berlioz, Weber** / Weingartner (cond.), Vienna PO, London SO, London PO / EMI 75965

Sylvius Leopold Weiss

b. Oct. 12, 1686, Breslau, Germany, **d.** Oct. 16, 1750, Dresden, Germany
Composer

The master lutenist of the eighteenth century, Weiss was born in Breslau (now Wroclaw in Poland) into a lute-playing family, and first learned the instrument from his father, Johann Jacob Weiss. In 1706, Weiss made his professional debut in the Breslau court, in which his family served. Weiss' extraordinary talent gained the attention of Elector Johann Wilhelm, dedicatee of Corelli's Op. 6 and an intelligent patron of music. Weiss served in Wilhelm's court in Dusseldorf for the next two years, and his earliest known compositions date from this time.

In 1708, Weiss left Dusseldorf for Rome in the retinue of Prince Alexander Sobieski, heir to the exiled Queen of Poland. Weiss resided in the Zuccari palazzo until 1714, absorbing new Italian styles firsthand and touring with the Prince to various courts. By the time of the Prince's death, Weiss' reputation was already well established, and he spent the next several years touring the continent and taking fixed employment only briefly. In Prague he met the prominent Bohemian lutenist Count Johann Anton Losy, whose work had a considerable impact. After Losy's death, Weiss would write a memorial Tombeau that remains one of most eloquent works.

In 1718, Weiss grew weary of wandering and decided to settle into a lucrative post offered him at the court of Dresden. Though this did not prevent him from traveling on occasion, Dresden would serve him as home base for the rest of his life. Attempts to dislodge Weiss from Dresden made by representatives of the Vienna Court, including princely sums of money offered, went ignored. Weiss is known to have met with the violinist Franz Benda in 1738. His only documented meeting with Johann Sebastian Bach took place the following year in Leipzig, although the composers were in all probability well known to one another by this time. Bach's personal secretary, Johann Elias Bach, wrote that "we heard some very fine music when my cousin from Dresden [Wilhelm Friedmann Bach] came to stay for four weeks, together with the famous lute-player Mr. Weiss." Bach, no slouch at the lute himself and an enthusiast of the hybrid lute-harpsichord, may have written his lute suites with Weiss in mind.

At his death in 1750, Weiss was 66 years of age. He was, and still is, regarded as the greatest of all lutenists, and the instrument fell into decline within two decades of his death. An evaluation by the Markgrafin Wilhelmine de Bayreuth, sister of Frederick II of Prussia and herself a composer, would serve well as epitaph; "(Weiss) excels so much in playing the Lute that no one has ever matched him, and those who will come after him will only be left with the glory of imitating him."

Some of his "Suonate" are missing their preludes, which were usually improvised. Seventy suites, however, are known in their entirety; most last about 20 to 25 minutes in performance. As a composer, Weiss shows extraordinary originality; his suites stand comparison with those of J.S. Bach. Only one of the suites, No. 49 in B flat minor, appeared in print during Weiss' own lifetime; his work was not intended for amateur players but for virtuosi whose skills approached his own. A modern printed edition of Weiss' complete works has been underway since 1980. *—Uncle Dave Lewis*

Overview of Works (1706–1750)

One of the last great composer/lute players, Sylvius Weiss was renowned for his powers of extemporization (he is said to have entered into friendly competition with Bach, who played the harpsichord while Weiss played the lute), his playing eliciting praise from all who heard him. He is said to have been "incomparable in expressing music's affects," had a rare control over dynamics, and that he was "master of his instrument, and could do with it whatever he wanted." Although Weiss is known to have written concertos for his instrument, none of these survive, and his known output today consists of the chamber works featuring the lute, and, above all, a body of some 600 manuscript pieces arranged into suites or sonatas. Unlike Bach, Weiss makes little differentiation between the two genres, works under both names consisting of a prelude or some other kind of introductory movement followed by a succession of stylized dances in the French mode. The instrument Weiss composed for was a large Baroque instrument, which had 13 courses of strings rather than the 11 of the Renaissance lute. It plays a major role in dictating the sound of his music, which, although including such techniques as the style brisé ("broken" or arpeggiated chords) associated with the great seventeenth century school of French lutenists, is far more robust than French music. To an even greater degree than is the case with Bach, Weiss' style represents a synthesis between the Italian music he had experienced during his long sojourn in Italy and his German contrapuntal heritage. His music is also written totally idiomatically for the lute; it would be difficult to imagine it being played on any other instrument. In extended pieces such as the Passacaille that concludes the *Suite in D* (No. 13), Weiss shows an outstanding grasp of structure, while the sheer exuberance of some of his quicker dances disguises the demands made by Weiss on his performers. Particularly notable among the slower dances are Weiss' Allemandes, pieces one of his performers has described playing as being the equivalent "to the making of a crystal sculpture, in which each note must be carefully chiseled with the appropriate tone color." *—Brian Robins*

Recommended:

- ○ **Weiss: Sonatas for Lute Vol. 1** / Barto / 1997 / Naxos 553773
- ○ **Weiss: Pièces de Luth** / Smith / 1990 / Astrée 8718
- ○ **Weiss: Sonatas for Two Lutes** / Schroder, Barto / 1998 / Symphonia 98159
- ○ **Weiss: The Dresden Manuscript Vol. 1** / Schneiderman / 2001 / Centaur 2526
- ○ **Weiss: Lute Concerti** / Stone, Tempesta di Mare / 2004 / Chandos 707

Alexis Weissenberg

b. Jul. 26, 1929, Sofia, Bulgaria
Pianist

If one wanted to make a biographical feature film about a classical musician, the life of the Bulgarian-American-French pianist Alexis Weissenberg would furnish ideal subject material. Born in Sofia in 1929, Weissenberg was taught to play the piano by his mother. Several members of her family were Vienna Conservatory–trained musicians, and Weissenberg grew up in an environment where the sight-reading of chamber music was as common as watching television is for most children today. His second piano teacher was a disciplinarian dentist, his third Bulgaria's top composer and pedagogue, Pancho Vladigerov, at whose house Weissenberg heard Dinu Lipatti perform.

At age 10, Weissenberg gave his first recital, performing, among other works, an etude of his own composition. Shortly thereafter, Weissenberg and his mother attempted to flee Bulgaria for Turkey as fascist terror deepened. They were caught and thrown in a concentration camp. "Only three elements remained constant," Weissenberg recalled. "Silence, singing, and crying." What saved the pair was an accordion Weissenberg had been given as a gift by an aunt. A German guard who liked music let Weissenberg play and after three months put the Weissenbergs on a train to Istanbul, throwing the accordion into their compartment through an open window as they left.

They made their way to Turkey and then to Israel, where Weissenberg studied at the Jerusalem Academy of Music and performed with the Israel Philharmonic under the baton of Leonard Bernstein. He left his accordion with a group of children after playing an outdoor concert and departed for the U.S. in 1946. Weissenberg enrolled at the Juilliard School of Music, studying with Olga Samaroff and at times with Artur Schnabel, and making contact with Vladimir Horowitz, who urged Weissenberg to enter the Leventritt Award competition. Weissenberg won the award in 1947, and his career was launched. His U.S. debut came with the New York Philharmonic, conducted by George Szell, and for the next ten years he toured the U.S. and Europe.

In 1956 Weissenberg moved to Paris, eventually becoming a French citizen. For a decade beginning around that time, he took a hiatus from performing, subjecting himself to a reconstruction of his keyboard technique. His performances of Chopin, Rachmaninov, and Prokofiev were especially notable, and the Bach *Chromatic Fantasy and Fugue* was a staple of his recital programming. His recordings of the 1960s and 1970s remained well represented in reissues on the EMI label as of the early 2000s, and he remained active into old age. *—James Manheim*

Recommended:

- ○ **Rachmaninoff: Preludes** / Weissenberg / 1990 / RCA 60568
- ○ **Bach, Chopin, Brahms** / Weissenberg / 2000 / Aura 0117
- ○ **Les Introuvables d'Alexis Weissenberg** / Weissenberg, etc. / 2004 / EMI 5858372
- ○ **Les Bis de Alexis Weissenberg** / Weissenberg / EMI 7691142
- ○ **Alexis Weissenberg** / Weissenberg / 1998 / Philips 456988

Franz Welser-Möst

b. Aug. 16, 1960, Linz, Austria
Conductor

Franz Welser-Möst first made a splash in the classical music scene while still in his twenties. After conducting a number of European youth orchestras, Welser-Möst gained favorable attention and worldwide notice as a conductor with the London Philharmonic (1986), which he led during a successful European tour. From that point, he found himself in constant demand as a guest conductor; among the more notable of his engagements were his operatic debut (conducting Rossini's *L'Italiana in Algeri* at the Vienna State Opera in 1987) and his American debut (conducting the St. Louis Symphony in 1989).

Welser-Möst's first important permanent position was director of the *London Philharmonic*, a post he assumed in 1990; in 1995 he became music director of the Zürich Opera. In 1999, Welser-Möst received the most lucrative and prestigious appointment of his career to date: directorship of the Cleveland Symphony (beginning in 2002), replacing the departing Christoph von Dohnányi.

Welser-Möst boasts an extensive discography, which is highlighted by notable recordings of Bruckner, Stravinsky, and Franz Schmidt; his recording of Schmidt's *Symphony No. 4* and *Variations on a Hussar's Song* won the Gramophone Orchestral Award in 1996. *—AMG*

Recommended:

- ○ **Bruckner: Symphony 5** / Welser-Most (cond.), London PO / 2003 / EMI 75862
- ○ **Mendelssohn: Symphonies 3 & 4** / Welser-Most (cond.), London SO / 2001 / EMI 74965
- ○ **Orff: Carmina Burana** / Welser-Most (cond.), Chance, Hendricks, Black, London PO / 1992 / EMI 54054

Westminster Abbey Choir

f. ca. 1065, London, England
Ensemble

The modern Westminster Abbey Choir is an institution with a history at least 500 years long. Westminster Abbey, founded by Edward the Confessor, was consecrated on December 28, 1065, and William the Conqueror became the first British monarch crowned there the following year. Every British ruler since has assumed power there as well, but beyond pomp and circumstance the Abbey has offered daily worship services for nearly a millennium. Integral to those services over much of that period has been the music of the Westminster Abbey Choir. Records of the choir date to the 1479 appointment of William Cornysh as "Master of the Song Scole." By 1540, Henry VIII had fixed the choir's membership at a size of 12 adult male singers (known as Lay Vicars) and ten boy choristers, and these proportions remain in force today.

The choir may be augmented by students of the Westminster Abbey Choir School, the only choir-based educational institution in England; its 36 students either are choir members or are studying in preparation for membership. These young students sing at Evensong six days a week and at three Sunday services. Auditions for boy singers are held when they are eight years old; when they reach age 14, they leave the choir. Some go on to become Lay Vicars, and the demanding musical training the choristers receive has generated illustrious English musical careers ranging from those of Orlando Gibbons and Henry Purcell to that of David Willcocks.

Royal wedding enthusiasts will have noted the choir's presence at events pertaining to the British monarchy, and in recent years, the choir has undertaken concert tours and recording sessions in addition to its official duties. The Westminster Abbey Choir has toured the U.S. four times and has made perhaps two dozen recordings. They are quite a varied lot, some of them (such as *The Royal Golden Wedding*) capitalizing on public fascination with English pageantry, while others offer a traditionalist sound in the early music repertory (the choir's recording of Palestrina's *Pope Marcellus Mass* is a standard) or expertly fill the need for a Christmas tradition that seems to have existed since time immemorial. What the second millennium will bring musically for the Westminster Abbey Choir remains to be seen. *—James Manheim*

Recommended:

- ○ **Palestrina: Missa Papae Marcelli; Allegri: Miserere** / Preston (cond.), Westminster Abbey Choir / Archiv 415517
- ○ **Innocence** / Neary (cond.), Nixon, Rozario, Fullbrook, Titus, Newry, Westminster Abbey Choir, English CO / 1995 / Sony 66613
- ○ **Favourite Hymns** / Neary (cond.), Baker, Westminster Abbey Choir / 1997 / Griffin 4018
- ○ **Music For Queen Mary** / Neary (cond.), Bostridge, Chance, Kirkby, Tubb, Westminster Abbey Choir, New London Consort / 1995 / Sony 66243

Westminster Cathedral Choir

f. 1910, London, England
Ensemble

London's Westminster Cathedral is the leading Catholic church in England. The Benedictine monks who built and owned Westminster Abbey reclaimed part of the marsh around Westminster. The Abbey (by that time property of the Church of England) sold the land for use as a prison. When the prison was retired, the Roman Catholic Church acquired the land in 1884 for a new cathedral. It is actually one of the newest churches in London. Its foundation stone was laid in 1895, and the Cathedral was consecrated in 1910.

From the initial planning of the Cathedral by Cardinal Herbert Vaughan, music was given great weight in the church's activities. Cardinal Vaughan had been inspired by the Solesmes Abbey's revival of Gregorian chant and by the accomplishments of the Anglican Church's choral tradition. Music is the largest single item in the Cathedral's budget. It operates a full-time choral school for its choristers, where each child is required to learn two instruments in addition to vocal studies. Westminster Cathedral is the only church in the world that celebrates a fully sung mass every day.

The Westminster Cathedral Choir, among just a few others, can credibly be called the best choir in Europe. Sir Richard Terry, the church's first Master of Music, was a devoted scholar of pre-Baroque polyphonic church music and revived choral masterpieces of Tudor-era English composers and their contemporaries on the Continent. He also vigorously championed new composition. Over the years composers of the stature of Ralph Vaughan Williams, Lennox Berkeley, Gustav Holst, Benjamin Britten, Herbert Howells, William Mathias, and David Sanger have composed for the Cathedral Choir.

It made one of the earliest British choral recordings, an acoustic disc cut in 1908. In the compact disc age, it has made a highly acclaimed series of recordings for the British label Hyperion, ranging in repertory from Renaissance polyphony to music of Britten, Poulenc, Langlais, and Stravinsky. It sings concerts and tours as its church service schedule permits, and frequently broadcasts. It joined the Choir of St. Paul's Cathedral (the largest Anglican Church) in 1992 to inaugurate that church's newly restored organ. *—Joseph Stevenson*

Recommended:

- ○ **Britten: Ceremony of Carols** / O'Donnell (cond.), Westminster Cathedral Choir / 1986 / Hyperion 66220
- ○ **Palestrina: Missa Ecce ego Johannes** / O'Donnell (cond.), Westminster Cathedral Choir / 1999 / Hyperion 67099
- ○ **Martin: Mass for Double Choir; Pizzetti: Messa di Requiem** / O'Donnell (cond.), Westminster Cathedral Choir / 2003 / Hyperion 21017
- ○ **Music of the Westminster Cathedral Choir** / Westminster Cathedral Choir / Hyperion 100

Charles-Marie Widor

b. Feb. 21, 1844, Lyon, France, **d.** Mar. 12, 1937, Paris, France

Composer: Keyboard, Orchestral

With an active performing career spanning eight decades, and an impressive class of students that included Darius Milhaud, Albert Schweitzer, and Marcel Dupré, French organist and composer Charles-Marie Widor maintained a lifelong position as one of the country's most prominent and influential musicians. Born in 1844, Widor was given his first lessons by his father, a well-known organ-builder and amateur performer. By age 11, Widor's skill had manifest itself so strongly that he was able to successfully compete for the job of organist at the lycée in his hometown of Lyons. A few years later the young musician traveled to Brussels, where he came under the tutelage of organist J.-N. Lemmens, a well-known teacher at the Brussels Conservatory, whose own teacher could boast of having studied with a student of J.S. Bach. Therefore, the venerable German tradition of Bach interpretation formed the backbone of Widor's work with Lemmens. By 1870 Widor had earned a one-year position as replacement organist at St. Sulpice Cathedral in Paris; the appointment was such a success that Widor held on to the position until just four years before his death 67 years later.

During the 1870s Widor's career as a composer for media other than the organ began to take shape. Between the time of appointment at St. Sulpice in 1870 and the turn of the century, he produced three full symphonies, two ballets, a number of chamber works, and some sacred vocal music. Widor joined the organ faculty of the Paris Conservatoire in 1890 (replacing César Franck), and by 1896 had also been appointed professor of composition. During the early years of the twentieth century, Widor divided his time between his work at St. Sulpice, his duties with the Conservatoire, and activities on the administrative staff of the Académie des Beaux-Arts. Widor's strength and dexterity on the organ remained basically unimpaired until his retirement from St. Sulpice in 1933, at which time his student Marcel Dupré took over. Widor died four years later at the age of 93.

Widor was, by all accounts, one of the most formidable organists of the nineteenth and twentieth centuries. His dedication to the music of Bach in particular, earned him the respect of several generations of musicians worldwide. Widor's student Albert Schweitzer, who helped Widor edit Bach's complete organ works, did much to publicize Widor's ideals. Widor was considered by many to be the greatest improviser after César Franck, and Gabriel Faure, another gifted improviser and friend of Widor's, is known to have challenged Widor to improvisational "duels" on a number of occasions. Not surprisingly, Widor's compositions for organ have outlasted his other works. The ten Symphonies for organ are particularly powerful, especially the *Symphonie Gothique* (1895) and the *Symphonie Romaine* (1900), in which the composer's knowledge of plainchant, and his penchant for delicate contrapuntal textures come to the fore in a most rewarding way.*—Blair Johnston*

KEYBOARD

Symphony No. 1 in C minor, Op. 13/1 (1872)

Charles-Marie Widor (1844–1937) composed his *Symphony No. 1 in C minor* in 1872. It is, in fact, more of a symphonic suite for organ in seven short movements: Prelude (Moderato), Allegretto, Adagio, Intermezzo, Marche Pontificale, Meditation (Lento), and Finale (Allegro). A work of extreme virtuosity and extraordinary sonorities, Widor's C minor is extravagantly colored and massively scored. Except for its central Marche Pontificale, Widor's *Symphony in C minor* is hardly as popular as his later organ symphonies. But it is the first of the great French organ symphonies and requires at least academic acknowledgement. *—James Leonard*

Recommended:

- ○ **Widor: Complete Organ Works Vol. 1** / Oosten / 1993 / MDG 3160401

Symphony No. 2 in D major, Op. 13/2 (1872)

Charles-Marie Widor (1844–1937) composed his *Organ Symphony No. 2 in D major* in 1872. Like his *Symphony No. 1*, it is less a symphony than a suite, in this case, six short movements Prelude Circulare (Andantino), Pastorale (Moderato), Andante, Salve Regina (Allegro), Adagio, and Finale (Allegro), to which Widor added a Scherzo (Allegro) in 1887. And like his *Symphony No. 1*, Widor's *Second* is an extremely difficult work demanding an organist of supreme technique and no inhibitions about displaying it. Unlike his *First*, however, Widor's *Second* has no movements that are frequently excerpted to grant the work a degree of familiarity to concert audiences, and it remains known almost exclusively among organists. *—James Leonard*

Recommended:

- ○ **Widor: Organ Symphonies 2 & 8** / Fagius / 1998 / Bis 1007

Symphony No. 5 in F minor, Op. 42/1 (1880)

In terms of tonal architecture, Charles-Marie Widor began his second set of organ symphonies, the four works of Op. 42, published in or around 1880, precisely where he left off with the previous set. The keynotes of the four organ symphonies of that first set (Op. 13) are C—D—E—F, and the *Symphony No. 5* for organ, Op. 42, No. 1, is set in the same key as the last of those symphonies: F minor (and, significantly, the four works of Op. 42 outline a keynote scheme parallel to that of Op. 13: F—G—A—B). In the *Symphony No. 5*, which today may be the most frequently played of Widor's organ symphonies (and certainly contains his most famous movement), we can hear the composer beginning to explore, tentatively and just a little bit at a time, a more chromatically-involved musical palette than he allowed himself in Op. 13.

The *Organ Symphony No. 5* is in five movements, making it the most compact—in terms of movement-total, not duration or musical language—organ symphony yet. Compared to the slim, quasi-improvisatory Toccata that opens the *Symphony No. 4 in F minor*, the opening Allegro vivo of the *Symphony No. 5* is a massive, solidly built movement whose arch-shaped main idea is put through many changes of timbre and character, including a scherzando central episode, over the course of 15 pages of music. With the next movement, the somewhat unusual layout of the Symphony makes itself plain: two quick movements and then two slower movements and a finale. If the goal is to find a traditional symphonic layout in the work, the Allegro cantabile second movement can be considered a kind of scherzo, and the two slower movements, Andantino quasi allegretto and Adagio, might be thought of as a kind of conglomerate slow movement. The energetic Toccata that ends the Symphony, with its repeating, ever-modulating subject, is easily Widor's most famous piece. It is often performed by church organists as a stand-alone composition. *—Blair Johnston*

Recommended:

- ○ **Widor: Symphonies 5 & 10** / Chorzempa / Philips 410054

Symphony No. 6 in G minor, Op. 42/2 (1878)

Early on in its existence, Charles-Marie Widor's *Symphony No. 6 in G minor for organ, Op. 42, No. 2*—or at least two movements of the work—led a kind of dual musical life. This "symphony" (Widor used the word in its general sense of "concordant sound" to designate a series of solo organ pieces) was published along with the other three works of Op. 42, in or around 1880. Widor extracted two of Op. 42, No. 2's movements, arranged them for organ and orchestra, added an arrangement of a movement from the second of the Op. 13 organ symphonies, and called the resulting hodgepodge work a *Symphony for organ and orchestra*; it was first performed in 1882 by the London Philharmonic Orchestra and then, save for the odd performance here or there, essentially forgotten. The original organ work, however, remains a favorite among organists.

Like its immediate predecessor (*No. 5 in F minor*), the *Organ Symphony No. 6 in G minor* is in five movements. The immense power of the Cavaillé-Coll organ at the church of St. Sulpice is invoked at the opening of the Allegro first movement, while its capacity for lyricism and devout (though in this case not specifically religious) introspection comes to the fore in the following Adagio, a movement in which Widor's increasing interest in chromaticism is very much evident. A scherzo-like intermezzo and a cantabile of great fluidity make up the third and fourth movements. After the ruffled D flat major sonority at the end of the fourth movement, the G major plagal gestures—triple-forte, no less—at the opening of the Vivace finale have a near-primal power. *—Blair Johnston*

Recommended:

- ○ **Organ Works; Organ Transcriptions** / Marshall / 2000 / Virgin 562173

ORCHESTRAL

Symphony No. 3 for organ & orchestra, Op. 69 (1895)

Charles-Marie Widor (1884–1937) wrote two purely orchestral symphonies and eight purely organ symphonies before composing his *Symphony No. 3 for orchestra and organ* in 1895. Although technically it is a work divided into two movements, both of the movements are in fact shorter movements grouped together. The opening movement starts with an Adagio then moves through an Andante to end with an Allegro, and the closing movement starts with a Vivace then moves through a Tranquillamente and an Allegro to end with a Largo. The organ takes a leading role throughout the work, with the orchestra performing more of an accompanimental role. As in virtually all of Widor's works for organ, the solo part is extremely demanding and extraordinarily colorful. *—James Leonard*

Recommended:

○ **Guilmant: Symphony 2; Widor: Symphony 3; Franck: Choral 2** / Tracey, Tortelier (cond.), BBC PO / 2000 / Chandos 9785

Henryk Wieniawski

b. Jul. 10, 1835, Lublin, Poland, **d.** Mar. 31, 1880, Moscow, Russia

Composer: Chamber Music, Concerto

Often compared to Paganini, Wieniawski was one of the greatest violinists of the Romantic era. As a performer, he dazzled audiences with his stupendous technique, expressive phrasing, and rich tone. As a composer, he succeeded in blending brilliant virtuosity with true Romantic inspiration. Like his compatriot Chopin, Wieniawski wrote music which celebrated the spirit of Poland, with his popular *Polonaise in D major* serving as a sterling example. Wieniawski's talent as a composer came to the fore in his extraordinary *Violin Concerto No. 2*, regarded as one of the great works of the Romantic violin repertoire.

Born in Poland while the country was under foreign rule, Wieniawski was a member of a family which produced several remarkable musicians. Recognized as a prodigy, Wieniawski auditioned for the Paris Conservatoire at the age of nine. In 1846, he received first prize in violin. Two years later, Wieniawski embarked on a career as a concert violinist, performing first in Paris and then in St. Petersburg. After achieving great success in St. Petersburg, Wieniawski returned to Paris to study composition.

Between 1851 and 1853, Wieniawski lived in Russia, giving concerts with his younger brother Joseph. In many ways the typical Romantic virtuoso, Wieniawski was also developing into a serious composer. The works published by the time he was 18 included the *Polonaise in D major* and the *Violin Concerto No. 1 in F sharp minor*. A work in which musical inspiration may have been, as critics later maintained, subordinated to the virtuoso's need to demonstrate his sheer technical prowess, the *Violin Concerto No. 1* nevertheless hugely impressed European audiences, launching Wieniawski's international career as a violinist-composer.

Wieniawski's career entered a new phase in 1860, when he moved to St. Petersburg. Wieniawski immediately became one of the country's principal musical figures. First violinist to the Tsar and professor of violin at the newly-founded Conservatory, he also led the Russian Musical Society's orchestra and string quartet. He exerted a tremendous influence on the Russian violin tradition; his unusual bowing style, with a stiff wrist and raised elbow, later became a trademark of Russian violinists, who, despite the seeming discomfort of the technique, kept rising to the pinnacle of violin performance. Wieniawski also matured as a composer. The *Violin Concerto No. 2*, composed in Russia in 1862, supports the violin with an orchestral part which, going beyond mere accompaniment, fully participates in the composition's thematic development. Also, anticipating cyclical compositional forms, Wieniawski reiterates the soulful second theme of the first movement in the final movement.

Wieniawski's Russian period ended in 1872, when he resumed his career as an international virtuoso. Following a grueling, two-year North American tour, Wieniawski returned to Europe to succeed Vieuxtemps as professor at the Brussels Conservatory. He kept that post until 1877 while maintaining his busy concert schedule. In 1878, although weakened by a serious heart condition, Wieniawski played in Paris, Berlin, and Moscow. In Berlin, on November 11, 1878, Wieniawski collapsed while performing his second violin concerto; in Moscow, on December 17, he was unable to complete his performance of Beethoven's "Kreutzer" sonata. Undaunted, Wieniawski started a Russian tour in 1879, but was taken to the hospital in Odessa. On February 14, 1880, Wieniawski was brought to the house of Tchaikovsky's patroness Nadezhda von Meck. The dying Wieniawski was also in a desperate financial situation, and friends had to raise money for a life insurance payment in order to secure the future of his family. Two months after Wieniawski's death, his youngest daughter, Irene, was born. *—Zoran Minderovic*

CHAMBER MUSIC

Eight Etudes-caprices for 2 violins, Op. 18 (1862)

The *Eight Études-Caprices*, Op. 18, of Henryk Wieniawski are unusual in the genre of instructive works in that he wrote them for violin "with the accompaniment of a second violin." And for most of the eight, it isn't necessarily what is traditionally thought of as an accompaniment either. The first violin parts are what you would expect, each focusing on a different playing technique, here meant for the most advanced performers. Each one has its own musical line and could be played alone, sounding perfectly natural by itself. (*Nos. 4* and *5* are sometimes heard in recital, with a piano replacing the second violin.) The second violin, instead of providing a harmony to the first violin—what would be a normal function of an accompaniment—provides a melody to which the etude becomes more of a harmony. *Etude No. 1* starts out as a duet, both violins playing similar figures, then the first violin works on trills while the second carries on with the original melody. *No. 2* also has the second violin playing a lyrical melody with the first violin's accompaniment, although there is an "agitated and vigorous" central section. The second violin has more of a harmonizing role in the third etude, against the smooth runs of the first violin. The same is true in *No. 4*, a saltarello, and in No. *5*, entitled "Praeludium," where the first violin practices its double-stops. In *No. 6*, the melody is first stated in the first violin, but then switches to the second while the first goes up and down scales in series of intervallic jumps. Detached bowing is the subject of *Etude No. 7*, while the second violin carries its melody all the way through it. The lively final etude is really a duet and a challenge to both violinists, as the second copies some of the first's figures and chords. The *Etudes-Caprices* were written in the same period as Wieniawski's *Violin Concerto No. 2*, while he was in St. Petersburg, and, along with his etudes in *L'école moderne*, Op. 10, are often ranked with Paganini's *Caprices* as more than just challenging technical exercises. *—Patsy Morita*

Recommended:

○ **David & Igor Oistrach: Bach, Handel, Vivaldi, Benda, Wieniawski & Sarasate** / D. Oistrakh, I. Oistrakh / 2000 / DG 463616

Two Mazurkas for violin & piano, Op. 19 (ca. 1860)

It has probably been said before, but in many ways Henryk Wieniawski (1835–80) was the Chopin of the violin. He was Polish and spent some time in Paris, though not as a political refugee like Chopin. Both men were attracted to the dance forms from their country, too; the mazurka crops up in the oeuvre of each. This Op. 19 pair dates from about 1860, by which year the violin virtuoso Wieniawski had already become a seasoned composer.

These two pieces are scored for violin and piano. The first, *Obertass*, is colorful, featuring an ebullient, jaunty theme and Wieniawski's typically brilliant writing for the violin. The melody's memorable character and the work's charming elegance make it attractive for both violinists and audience. The second piece, *Le ménétrier*, begins with gentle pizzicato chords, after which the violin delivers a hearty, jovial main theme whose peasant character flavors the mood with infectious spice. The alternate material is elegant and subdued, providing nice contrast to the boisterousness of the stomping main dance tune. A third theme, restrained and elegant, comprises an attractive middle section. This piece is almost twice the roughly two-minute length of *Obertass*.

These mazurkas are well-crafted light compositions, as thematically memorable as most by Chopin, with violin writing that is masterful and consistently colorful throughout. *—Robert Cummings*

Recommended:

○ **Wieniawski: Violin Showpieces** / Bisengaliev, Lenehan / 1994 / Naxos 550744

Scherzo-tarantelle, for violin & piano in G minor, Op. 16 (1855)

Listening to a performance of Henryk Wieniawski's *Scherzo-tarantelle* Op. 16 for violin and piano—an electrifying, virtuosic walk on a tight-rope—it is not hard to believe the stories of hard drinking and heavy gambling that have always surrounded the brilliant Polish-born violinist-composer: here is a piece of music whose every measure fully lives up to Wieniawski's personal motto, "Il faut risquer" (I must risk it). Life by that motto was not always kind to Wieniawski, and the rise and fall of both his career and his health were just about as rapid as the left-hand fireworks contained within this four-and-a-half-minute showpiece. Just 21 when *Scherzo-tarantelle* was first published (1856), Wieniawski was already the well-known author of over a dozen charming salon pieces for violin and piano, and very possibly the most famous violinist of the post-Paganini generation. But just six years later he would peak as both performer and composer (with the fabulous *Concerto No. 2 in D minor*, Op. 22), thereafter starting a long decline towards his premature death.

With *Scherzo-tarantelle*, Wieniawski proves himself a master of miniature. Neither profundity of thought nor musical innovation were of any real concern to the composer (though with the Second Concerto he managed to achieve a good bit of both); he instead put his considerable skill towards impeccable craftsmanship and, most importantly, potent, immediate expression of all the violin's myriad characters.

After the violinist has plowed his or her way through an opening Presto filled—as one expects in the traditional Italian tarantella—with hectic, running eighth notes, there is an immediate change to the major mode for a Tranquillo whose sweeping, voluptuous violin melody is immediately restated by the piano, now accompanied by the violin. After a brief reunion with the music of the opening section, the composer reaches once again into his well-stocked bag of melody for a graceful cantabile. *Scherzo-tarantelle* is rounded off with a reprise of the Presto, now truncated and reshaped at the very end to hint, tantalizingly but insincerely, at a change to G major. *—Blair Johnston*

Recommended:

○ **Enescu, Bartók & Szymanowski: Works for Violin & Piano** / Haendel, Ashkenazy / 2000 / Decca 455488

CONCERTO

Violin Concerto No. 1 in F sharp minor, Op. 14 (1852)

This is a youthful work by Wieniawski, written when he was just 18. He had begun his brilliant career as a touring virtuoso two years before and composed this concerto for his own purposes, as would be the case with the more popular *Concerto No. 2* from 1862. The *Concerto No. 1* is cast in three movements, with the first being greater in length than the remaining two combined. It is marked Allegro moderato and opens with the clarinet presenting the stormy, heroic main theme, which is then taken up by the orchestra. A lovely, romantic melody is introduced by the cellos and soon the exposition concludes with abruptness. The violin enters dramatically, then gives its account of the themes, finding much drama in the first and both sweetness and passion in the slower one. The development section features brilliant writing for the violin and orchestral scoring that underscores the heroic aspects of the main theme. A dramatic and effective cadenza precedes the recapitulation. The second movement, "Preghira: Larghetto," is short—about five minutes—and features a solemn, somewhat sad theme whose manner sweetens a bit when the violin takes it up after the orchestral presentation. Yet there remains a sense of melancholy here, but a melancholy of yearning, not of loss. The Rondo finale, marked Allegro giocoso, features a folkish main theme playfully rendered by the violin. A lovely, alternate melody of romantic character offers contrast to the vigor of the faster sections and a chance for the violin to sing in its lower ranges. The ending is brilliant and colorful, featuring deftly imagined virtuosic writing for the violin. *—Robert Cummings*

Recommended:

○ **Wieniawski: Violin Concertos 1 & 2; Sarasate: Zigeunerweisen** / Shaham, Foster (cond.), London SO / 1991 / DG 431815

Violin Concerto No. 2 in D minor, Op. 22 (1862)

Henryk Wieniawski might have thought twice about dedicating his last and greatest work for violin and orchestra, the *Violin Concerto No. 2 in D minor*, Op. 22 of 1862, to the famous Spanish violinist Pablo de Sarasate had he known that a quarter century after he wrote the piece he and Sarasate would be rivals in a very real and commercially measurable way; the two were certainly the foremost violinist-composers of their day (at least after Vieuxtemps' career-ending illness). Composing a virtuoso concerto in the nineteenth century was not an enviable task, especially if one was to play it oneself: the virtuoso drew audiences by exploiting technical excellence and by indulging that audience in a perhaps inordinate amount of sweet, syrupy melody, and usually that meant intentionally writing music that would have little durability. Wieniawski's own *Violin Concerto No. 1 in F sharp minor*, Op. 14 was a big hit that made his name throughout Europe; but today, forced to stand or stumble on its lasting merits as a work of music, it is largely ignored. When Wieniawski set about composing his *Second Concerto*, he took a different approach; while still ensuring that the work had its quota of flash-and-dazzle and sweet song, Wieniawski made certain to provide his new child with the kind of dramatic backbone and excellent musical structure that are usually lacking in such works. It is no *"Emperor" Concerto*, to be sure, but Wieniawski's *Second* can hold its own in some pretty imposing company; in fact, most critics and musicians of the day were far more bowled over by the piece itself than by Wieniawski's renditions of it.

The concerto is in three movements: Allegro moderato, Andante non troppo (Romance), and Allegro con fuoco-Allegro moderato. An urgent melody opens the orchestral exposition of the first movement, and when the violin enters it takes over this lyrical weave. It is inevitable that showy finger-work takes over the movement at some point, but, rather unusually, there is no cadenza to the movement. Instead, the movement builds to a fine virtuoso climax and then makes its way, via a closing passage for the orchestra alone, straight to the following Romance, which surely must count among the most straightforwardly beautiful instrumental songs ever composed. The finale is marked "à la Zingara"—and gypsy it is, from the frantic moto perpetuo that is the movement's main theme to the robust, earthy dance in D major that breaks in twice, the second time to draw a clamorous, show-stopping close. *—Blair Johnston*

Recommended:

○ **Gil Shaham Plays Wieniawski, Saint-Saëns & Sarasate** / Shaham, Foster (cond.), London SO / 1998 / DG 459056

Fantaisie brillante on Themes from Gounod's "Faust," for violin & orchestra, Op. 20 (1865)

Operas served as a source of inspiration and thematic plunder to many of the great composers from the eighteenth and nineteenth centuries, including Beethoven, Chopin, and Liszt. Wieniawski would write several works based on operatic themes, including *Fantasia on a Theme from Meyerbeer's Le Prophéte* and *Fantasia on a Theme from Grétry's Richard the Lionhearted*. The 1859 Gounod opera *Faust* was making its way across European stages in the early 1860s and after Wieniawski attended a performance of it, he was moved to fashion this colorful work, which, at around 15 minutes, is among his largest compositions for violin and orchestra, with only the two concertos of significantly greater length. The work opens with the orchestra playing the dark theme heard at the outset of the first scene following the introduction. The violin enters and soon plays a lovely rendition of the famous theme from the Valentin's aria, *O sainte medaille*. In the opera, of course, this is sung by a baritone, but Wieniawski deftly adapts the melody to the lower and middle ranges of the violin, imparting a sweeter sense to the music. Other *Faust* themes appear throughout this work, including that of the violin solo in the "Garden Scene." As is generally the case with most fantasy pieces based on stage works, there is a good measure of virtuosic writing here. The most demanding passages come in the latter part, where Wieniawski imparts color and grace to the bravura, crowning this minor gem with a dazzling ending. *—Robert Cummings*

Recommended:

○ **Vanessa-Mae: The Classical Collection, Part 1** / Vanessa-Mae, Inglis (cond.), London Mozart Players / 2000 / EMI 67456

Légende, for violin & orchestra in G minor, Op. 17 (1859)

It was near the end of his first stint as a wandering virtuoso (1851–60) that Henryk Wieniawski composed what is probably his most famous work, *Légende* for violin and orchestra, Op. 17 (though it has long since been more popular in its arrangement for violin and piano). The year 1860 has two important bookmarks as far as Wieniawski fans are concerned: Wieniawski's marriage to British society's Isabella Hampton and his acceptance of Anton Rubinstein's offer to settle in St. Petersburg and help establish a conservatory in the city. *Légende* was composed with the first of those bookmarks in mind, and Wieniawski dedicated it to his new bride. It is a wonderful representative of a long-dead species—the sentimental salon-ballad; it is technically undemanding enough to yield its treasures to student violinists, yet rich enough in melody to interest virtuosos the world around.

Légende is a simple, three-part song for violin, unassuming but well-crafted in its soon-to-be-outdated, cream-puff way. A melancholy rustling in the piano (or orchestra) spurs the violin to produce a lovely, wistful G minor tune. In the middle section (G major), syrupy parallel thirds argue in favor of life's brighter side; but a passionate mini-cadenza leads us back into the opening music, whose reprise the violin caps off by annexing the piano rustling of the opening and transforming it into a sparkling little coda. *—Blair Johnston*

Recommended:

○ **Romance** / Mutter, Levine (cond.), Vienna PO / 1995 / DG 447070

Polonaise (No. 1) de concert, for violin & orchestra in D major, Op. 4 (1852)

Of Henryk Wieniawski's two concert polonaises for violin and orchestra (or piano), the earlier—the *Polonaise de concert in D major*, Op. 4—is probably the better known. Wieniawski was himself, of course, a Pole, and that he should—in 1852, during his first attempts to secure international recognition—put together a show-stopping, virtuosic example of his country's most famous dance form is hardly surprising. What might surprise some (at least those who hold Wieniawski in the low esteem awarded to nearly all virtuoso performer/composers) is the fact that, Chopin's polonaises aside, Wieniawski's first polonaise is among the finest examples of its breed to visit concert halls with any frequency. The energetic rhythmic ideas have backbone (as at the very opening: has ever an eight-bar phrase moved with such speed through so many individual characters without losing sight of its musical goal?), the less robust melodies suppleness and grace; and the polonaise's tendency to hover in a near-schizophrenic fashion on the border between heroism and deep melancholy is given full play. There is plenty of ear-candy for those that demand instant gratification: the piece is not easy to play, and Wieniawski has made sure that nobody in the audience could possibly miss the fact—he had a reputation and a career to build, after all. *—Blair Johnston*

Recommended:

○ **The Legendary Jascha Heifetz** / Heifetz, Bay / 1999 / EMI 67005

Polonaise (No. 2) brillante, for violin & orchestra in A major, Op. 21 (1870)

Although the great virtuoso would live another ten years after composing it, Henryk Wieniawski's second concert polonaise for violin and orchestra (or piano), the *Polonaise brillante* in A major, Op. 21, was one of the last works he wrote. Only the *Reminiscences of San Francisco*, Op. 24 seems to have been composed after this polonaise, though a couple of works, including the famous *Violin Concerto No. 2*, bear higher opus numbers. The *Polonaise brillante* is rather less famous than its sister piece of 18 years earlier, the *Polonaise de concert in D*, Op. 4). The later polonaise is a longer and more difficult piece, making it less accessible to violinists of lower rank and less suitable as a quick concert finale. But while the A major polonaise lilves up to its title with a brilliance far beyond that of the earlier D major piece, it is a also a less flexible and less tightly crafted piece. Perhaps the years have simply aged it more than the D major. Still, if refined violinistic fireworks are the goal, one can hardly do better than the *Polonaise brillante*, and there is genuine salon charm to the F major, dolce e tranquillo melody that carries the work's middle portion. *—Blair Johnston*

Recommended:

○ **Leonidas Kavakos Plays Debussy, Kreisler, Paganini, Schubert, Tchaikovsky & Wieniawski** / Kavakos, Nagy / 1992 / Delos 3116

John Wilbye

b. Mar. 1574, Diss, Norfolk, England, **d.** Sep. 1638, Colchester, England

Composer: Choral

John Wilbye was a prominent exponent of the English madrigal. Born the third son of an English tanner in Diss, Norfolk, Wilbye attracted the notice of a nearby wealthy landowner, Sir Thomas Cornwallis. Cornwallis' daughter Elizabeth married the son of another local wealthy landowner, Sir Thomas Kytson, who subsequently employed Wilbye as resident musician of Hengrave, his magnificent estate. The Kytsons were patrons of all the arts, and Wilbye was continually encouraged to provide madrigals and musical instruction. He remained in this position until the death of Lady Kytson in 1628, at which point he retired to the home of her younger daughter, Lady Rivers, until his death in 1638. Perhaps as a result of his having been permitted to rent a profitable sheep farm, Wilbye died a wealthy man. As of the end of the twentieth century, both the magnificent house at Hengrave and the "Great brick house opposite Holy Trinity Church" of Lady Rivers still stand, and Wilbye's living quarters, furnishings, and some of his effects may be seen. He was never married.

Considered by many the finest of all English madrigal composers, Wilbye was prolific in the form. In 1598, his first set of madrigals was published under the title *The First Set of English Madrigals to 3, 4, 5, and 6 Voices*; it was dedicated to Sir Charles Cavendish, who had married the elder daughter of Sir Thomas Kytson, Wilbye's patron. The set contains 30 works, six each of which are for three and four voices, ten of which are for five voices, and eight for six voices. The set is considered early—some of the works came from Wilbye's teen years and early twenties—but the works range from fetching to masterful and the young composer already asserts his mastery of the form.

Ten years later, a second set was published, "both for Voyals [viols] and Voyces." It was dedicated to Lady Arabella Stuart, whose mother, Lady Lennox, was Elizabeth Cavendish, sister of Sir Charles, the patron and sponsor of the first set. Of these there are 34, eight each of which are for three, four, and six voices and the remaining ten for five voices. This set is considered more mature and masterful than the first set and is thought of by many scholars as the pinnacle of madrigal writing. Of particular note among these are "Draw on, sweet night," "Stay Corydon," and "Softly, O softly drop." Among the most popular works in this collection is "Sweet honey sucking bees," possibly because of its peculiar title but also because of its contrasting sections and superb vocal counterpoint.

These two sets include most of Wilbye's surviving music. He composed a work as part of Morley's "The Triumphes of Oriana" entitled "The Lady Oriana," for six voices, and a pair of motets, "I am quite tired with groans" and "O God, the rock of my whole strength" for four and five voices, respectively. He is supposed to have written a book of lessons for lute, but this, having been sold in the library of the Reverend William Gostling of Canterbury in 1777, seems to have vanished. The decline in popularity of the madrigal coincides almost exactly with Wilbye's death in 1638, although many of his madrigals are commonly heard to this day. *—Michael Morrison*

CHORAL

Madrigals (ca. 1598–1609)

John Wilbye is thought of by many as the finest of all English madrigalists of the Elizabethan and Jacobean era, a period that witnessed an astonishing flowering of the form after it arrived from Italy very late in the genre's history. Wilbye's career represents a typical example of the enlightened patronage of the arts that flourished in England at this time. For many years, he was in the service of the wealthy Kytson family, at whose country seat Hengrave the composer was employed as a domestic musician. Wilbye is unusual in that, save for very few sacred works and instrumental pieces, he is known only for his madrigals. These were published in two books, the first of which appeared in 1598. Its contents, 30 pieces in all, include settings for three, four, five, and six voices. It was followed 11 years later by a second selection of 34 works, divided in similar fashion to the earlier book. While there are pieces of outstanding quality in the 1598 book (the exquisite *Adieu, sweet Amaryllis* might be cited as an example), Wilbye's reputation rests almost entirely on the contents of the second book. This includes the most famous of his madrigals, the six-part *Draw on, Sweet Night*, with its contrast between the minor modes expressive of the poet's deep emotions and the D major employed in the references to the balm of night ("best friend unto those cares"). The five-part *Weep, Weep Mine Eyes*, which draws on Dowland's famously influential *Lachrimae* in its opening bars, shows Wilbye as one of the few English composers who sought to match the Italian madrigalists for expressive depth of emotion, although like his fellow Englishmen he rarely indulges in the kind of dramatic outburst or explicit word-painting that is such a feature of the work of composers like Rore or Marenzio. Elsewhere, Wilbye was content to express less-intense emotions and a number of his madrigals explore the pastoral themes so popular among his fellow Englishmen. *—Brian Robins*

Recommended:

○ **Flora Gave Me Fairest Flowers** / Rutter (cond.), Cambridge Singers / 1987 / Collegium 105

Earl Wild

b. Nov. 26, 1915, Pittsburgh, PA

Pianist

Liszt was often called a "piano-centaur," so at one was he with the instrument. Earl Wild could be described in similar terms. The gift of absolute pitch revealed itself at age three as his avidity for the keyboard took prodigious strides. At six he read music fluently, and before he was 12 he was studying piano with Selmar Janson, a pupil of d'Albert and Scharwenka (both students of Liszt). Busoni's "disciple," Egon Petri; Paul Doguereau, a student of Paderewski and Ravel; and Elena Barère, wife of the phenomenal Russian pianist Simon Barère, provided later tuition. With his superb *mécanique* and enormous hands, Wild was predestined to take his place among the great pianists, while his training and place in time spread before him the riches, traditions, and secrets of Romantic pianism. In his early teens, Wild was already composing, arranging, and transcribing music for radio station KDKA in Pittsburgh while playing piano and celesta in the Pittsburgh Symphony under Otto Klemperer. NBC hired him as a staff pianist in 1937, a stint that included playing under Toscanini in the NBC Symphony and with whom Wild gave a legendary broadcast performance of Gershwin's *Rhapsody in Blue* in 1942, thereby coming to national notice as a major artist. During World War II, Wild served in the U.S. Navy playing fourth flute in the Navy Band, performing recitals at the White House, and frequently accompanying Eleanor Roosevelt to play "The Star Spangled Banner" on her speaking tours. From 1945 to 1968, Wild was employed by ABC as staff pianist, conductor, and composer—his oratorio, *Revelations*, was broadcast to popular acclaim in 1962 and again in 1964. His *"Doo-Dah" Variations for piano and orchestra*, on Stephen Foster's "Camptown Races," was premiered by Wild with the Des Moines Symphony Orchestra on September 26, 1992. He has also given world-premiere performances of Paul Creston's *Piano Concerto No. 1* and Marvin David Levy's *Piano Concerto No. 1*, a work composed for him. But it is as an interpreter of Romantic literature, especially Liszt—and such neglected figures as Thalberg, Herz, Scharwenka, Balakirev, Paderewski, Godowsky, and Medtner—that Wild is most notable. And, like them, he has cultivated the art of piano transcription, recreating the songs of Rachmaninov and Gershwin in his own omnicompetent style. Since his first recording in 1939, Wild has compiled an imposing legacy of recorded performances combining scholarly savoir faire with the flair and visceral impact of the born showman. He is internationally in demand as a teacher. *—Adrian Corleonis*

Recommended:

○ **20th & 21st Century Sonatas** / Wild / 2000 / Ivory 71005
○ **Piano Masters: Earl Wild** / Wild / 2000 / Pearl 0091
○ **Earl Wild** / Wild / 1999 / Philips 456991
○ **Gershwin Album** / Wild / RCA 61727
○ **Hahn: Le Rossignol Éperdu** / Wild / 2001 / Ivory 72006
○ **Earl Wild plays Rachmaninov** / Wild / 1991 / Chesky 58
○ **Earl Wild—The Romantic Master** / Wild / 1995 / Sony 62036

Adrian Willaert

b. ca. 1490, Flanders [Belgium], **d.** Dec. 7, 1562, Venice, Italy

Composer

The most influential Franco-Flemish composer of the so-called "Post-Josquin" generation, and the founder of the Venetian school at San Marco that would shine well into the next century, Adrian Willaert was born in historical obscurity, somewhere near the end of the fifteenth century. Even the location of his birth remains uncertain, with conflicting information given by two contemporary witnesses. His pupil, the music theorist Giuseffo Zarlino, claims Willaert went from the Netherlands to Paris as a young man to enroll in a course of law at the famed University, but instead began musical training under the composer Jean Mouton, member of the French Royal Chapel. Zarlino relates another charming anecdote about Adrian's precocious talent: apparently on the occasion of Willaert's first visit to the Papal Chapel (possibly in 1514 or 1515), the singers were performing a motet of Willaert's, and assuming it to be the work of the great Josquin Desprez.

As early as October 1514, an agent of Cardinal Ippolito I d'Este, brother of Alfonso the Duke of Ferrara, hired the young Willaert in Rome. He entered service to the Ferrarese ruling family by July 1515 at the latest, and received formal appointment to the Este Cardinal's household in April 1516. In addition to singing in the Cardinal's private chapel, Willaert ably plied his compositional talents—his music appears in several early Italian manuscripts of the 1510s and 1520s, as well as in printed anthologies by Andrea Antico and Ottaviano Petrucci. Willaert's service to the well-traveled Cardinal also provided him with international contacts. He followed Ippolito on a trip to Hungary in 1517 and may have visited as far as Kraków on this voyage; a later motet may have been intended to honor the coronation of the Emperor Ferdinand I as King of Hungary. After Cardinal Ippolito's death in 1520, Willaert entered the service of his brother the Duke. His patronage by the powerful Este family seems to have cemented the foundations of Willaert's Italian career. This relationship lasted even after his departure for Venice; Duke Alfonso is said to have personally visited Willaert's bed of convalescence (likely from his later chronic attacks of gout) while on a state visit.

Andrea Gritti, the Doge of Venice, intervened in the deliberations at San Marco, urging that Willaert be hired as maestro di capella for the Venetian cathedral. Adrian served in this capacity from December 1527 through the remainder of his life. He encountered there a strong choral establishment of some 16 singers, and built San Marco's music program to one famous throughout Christendom. Among those who came to Venice to learn from Willaert are the eminent theoreticians Zarlino and Nicola Vicentino, and a host of famous composers, including Cipriano de Rore, Constanzo Porta, and Andrea Gabrieli (uncle of Giovanni). Correnspondence written to Willaert by other Italian theorists, important new publication releases, and even cathedral decrees appointing choirboys to the specific tasks of copying and maintaining his compositions for San Marco attest to his continuing compositional life. His salary was significantly increased several times, and his will left the considerable sum of 1,600 ducats to his wife. Contrary to popular myth (fed by Zarlino's adoration of his master, the "Divine Adriano"), Willaert did not "invent" the Venetian antiphonal practice of *cori spezzati*. He did, however, by the consistent exercise of his musical brilliance in this rich state for 35 years, set the stage for the splendor of Venetian music from Gabrieli to Monteverdi. *—Timothy Dickey*

Overview of Works (ca. 1520–1550)

The "Divine Adriano," as Willaert was known to his fellow Venetian Gioseffo Zarlino, was one the most versatile and accomplished composers between Josquin and Orlando di Lasso. The influence of his teacher Jean Mouton may be seen in his early mastery of counterpoint, as well as his selection of motets by Mouton and other French royal composers as models for his 14 surviving masses. His early chansons, both three-voiced arrangements of popular tunes, and four-voiced motet-like pieces, also shadow Mouton. But in his numerous motets (about 175), Willaert found a personal style which would resonate with later composers through the century. Willaert shared with Clemens non Papa and Nicolas Gombert, other prominent members of the post-Josquin generation, a fluid and continuous contrapuntal style in equal voices; he added impeccable declamation and deep sensitivity to textual nuance. In this, his music embodied the humanist ideal of marriage between word and tone.

The plenary example of his mature style is the 27 motets and 25 madrigals collected into his *Musica Nova* of 1559. The revolutionary pairing of motets and madrigals in the same publication itself mirrors Bembo's theoretical setting of the Latin and Italian languages on equal par. Willaert's musical collection for four to seven voices (with emphasis on the thicker textures) places the genres on equal footing, with text-presentation in the foreground. The motets are primarily multi-sectional works and present their texts, taken from the Old Testament and from liturgical sequences, in careful and often syllabic motives that are woven into a continuous fabric of counterpoint. They favor low and dense textures, and sometimes feature complex canonic procedures. All but one of the madrigals set sonnets from Petrarch's *Canzoniere*, in two *partes* filled with similarly dense counterpoint. Willaert's thoughtful musical exegeses of Petrarch's elusive texts mark his characteristic antitheses with clever though restrained text-painting, and articulate their structure by cadences which follow the sense and syntax of the poetry, not merely the rhymed lines.

Willaert's influence upon the sixteenth century extended even beyond this central publication. The 1542 *Hymnorum musica* offered hymns for the entire church year; *I salmi* of 1550 included polychoral psalms for the highest feasts at Venice's San Marco (those marked by the *Pala d'Oro*). Though this collection does not actually represent the first essays in the genre, Willaert expanded it to broaden the relationship between the two choirs and laid the importance of the genre for generations to come. He was a powerful force in the Northern acceptance of the Neapolitan Canzone Villanesca after da Nola, and pioneered the lute intabulation of madrigals with his arrangements of Verdelot. His highly contrapuntal *Ricercare* (possibly based in style upon his motets) paved the way for an important instrumental genre. His experimental duo (hidden quartet), *Quid non ebrietas* of 1529, expanded the possibilities of the entire hexachordal system, enabling the chromatic art of his pupil Cipriano da Rore. *—Timothy Dickey*

Recommended:

- ○ **Willaert: Le Villanesche** / Negri (cond.), Milan "Euterpe" Ensemble / 1993 / Stradivarius 33311
- ○ **Willaert: Missa Christus resurgens; Magnificat sexti toni; Ave Maria** / Summerly (cond.), Oxford Camerata / 1998 / Naxos 553211
- ○ **Willaert: Intavolature dei Madrigali di Verdelot** / Zambon, Nasillo, Piccollo, Balestracci, Desiderio / 1995 / Stradivarius 33325
- ○ **Willaert: Madrigali, Chansons, Villanelle** / Romanesca / Ricercar 151145
- ○ **Willaert: Mottetti et Ricercari** / Collarile (cond.), Accademia della Selva / 2003 / Stradivarius 33656

David Willcocks

b. Dec. 30, 1919, Newquay, England

Conductor

There are few conductors of choral music who have achieved higher levels of recognition or acclaim than Sir David Willcocks. For over 30 years, as conductor of the Bach Choir and director of the Royal College of Music, he has achieved a standard of performing and teaching second to none in the musical world.

Willcocks was a chorister at Westminster Abbey from ages 10 through 14, and later studied at Clifton College, before becoming an organ scholar at King's College, Cambridge, in 1939. His studies were interrupted by the outbreak of World War II, during which he served in the British Infantry, winning the Military Cross in 1944. He returned to King's College in 1945 to complete his studies, and became a Fellow of King's College in 1947, and conductor of the Cambridge Philharmonic Society that same year, as well as conductor of the Salisbury Musical Society and organist at Salisbury Cathedral. In 1950, he took the post of organist at Worcester Cathedral, and became conductor of the Worcester Festival Choral Society and the City of Birmingham Choir, a position he kept for seven years.

By the end of the decade, he was the director of music at King's College Cambridge, the organist of Cambridge University, and conductor of the Cambridge University Music Society, posts that he held into the 1970s, when he accepted the post of director at the Royal College of Music. In 1960, he also became music director of the Bach Choir. Willcocks has conducted in most European countries, as well as Japan and the United States, and edited several collections of choral music.

Willcocks has made relatively few recordings since the end of the 1950s, probably less than 150, principally with the King's College Choir and the Bach Choir, the English Chamber Orchestra, the Academy of St. Martin-in-the-Fields, the Jacques Orchestra, the Philharmonia Orchestra, and the London Symphony Orchestra. His repertory ranges from England's Tudor era—especially the music of John Taverner—to such twentieth century composers as Ralph Vaughan Williams. In addition to such works as Haydn's *The Creation* and the *Nelson Mass*, masses by Palestrina and Charpentier, and Taverner's *The Western Wind*, he has conducted such modern music as Britten's *War Requiem* and *Hymn To St. Cecilia*, Vaughan Williams' *Mass In G*, *Hodie*, and *Sancta Civitas*, and a relative handful of pure orchestral works, such as Vaughan Williams' gorgeous *Five Variants On Dives and Lazarus* (of which he has made the definitive recording). Willcocks' 1962 recording of Haydn's *Mass No. 9* almost single-handedly began the restoration of the composer's choral music before the modern listening public. His crowning achievement, however, could be his recording of Handel's *Messiah*, featuring a contingent of all male singers (with counter-tenor replacing the alto) with the King's College Choir and the Academy of St. Martin-in-the-Fields for EMI, a superbly paced, exquisitely textured recording. *—Bruce Eder*

Recommended:

- ○ **Byrd: Masses; Magnificat & Nunc dimittis; Taverner: Mass "The Western Wind"** / Willcocks (cond.), King's College Choir / 1996 / London 452170
- ○ **Noël: Christmas at King's** / Willcocks (cond.), King's College Choir, London SO / 1995 / London 444848
- ○ **Britten: Choral Works** / Willcocks, Ledger (conds.), Corkhill, Lancelot, Bowman, Ellis, King's College Choir / 2004 / EMI 62797

John Williams (composer and conductor)

b. Feb. 8, 1932, New York. NY

Composer: Film Music

Conductor

Quick, who's the one person who has been nominated for an Oscar more often than anyone else in any category? That would be composer John Williams, nominated over 40 times for his original film scores and orchestrations. He received his first Oscar nomination in 1969 for the score to *Valley of the Dolls*, and since then he has become the most recognized film composer in history, not just because of his scores, but also because he has successfully followed in Arthur Fiedler's footsteps as conductor of the Boston Pops Orchestra.

Williams grew up in New York, where his father was drummer in the Raymond Scott Quintette and other bands. All four children in the family naturally took music lessons. Williams studied piano as a child, and later trumpet, trombone, and clarinet. He did some work as a teenager with pianist and arranger Bobby van Epps, and also enrolled in composition classes at UCLA before joining the U.S. Air Force in 1951, where he arranged band music and took up conducting. Williams studied piano with Rosina Lhevinne at Juilliard and worked as a jazz pianist. He then returned to

California and studied composition with Mario Castelnuovo-Tedesco. His compositional career began in the early 1960s with television series such as *Peter Gunn, Wagon Train, Gilligan's Island,* and *Lost in Space.* He was able to work as an orchestrator and arranger with industry giants Bernard Herrmann, Franz Waxman, Alfred Newman, Henry Mancini, and André Previn. In 1972 he received his first Academy Award for his adaptation of Jerry Bock's music for *Fiddler on the Roof,* but it was his scores for Steven Spielberg's *Jaws* (1975) and George Lucas' *Star Wars* (1977) that brought him real notice. Those full, orchestral scores lead some to claim that he alone was responsible for reviving the symphonic style of film music and were the beginning of two long-standing composer/director partnerships. A public face appeared to go with the name when Williams was chosen to conduct the Boston Pops after Fiedler's death. Under his leadership, the orchestra maintained its popularity, toured America several times, and made concert versions of his movie themes regular pops fare. Although maintaining close ties to Boston after leaving the Pops in 1993 and continuing to guest conduct a number of orchestras, Williams has spent more of his time since the mid-1990s composing concert music, such as 1995's bassoon concerto *The Five Sacred Trees,* and 2000's violin concerto *TreeSong,* while still charming cinema audiences with music that, while fully rooted in traditional Romantic idioms, easily expresses the emotion and action of the film's story. *—Patsy Morita*

Recommended:

○ **Summon the Heroes** / Williams (cond.), Oliver, Kerber, Boston Pops Orch. / 1996 / Sony 62592

○ **Best of John Williams & Boston Pops** / Williams (cond.), Boston Pops Orch. / 1987 / Philips 420178

Overview of Works

John Williams' most widely heard and recognized music is his 80 or so film scores, which include *Jaws,* the *Star Wars* saga, and the *Harry Potter* films. From some of these he has arranged concert suites and excerpts that are frequently heard on the pops programs of ensembles ranging from professional orchestras to high school bands. These include *Three Pieces from Schindler's List* for violin and orchestra and *Devil's Dance* from the *Witches of Eastwick,* also for violin. However, Williams has also written a fair amount of occasional music and instrumental music, as well. His occasional music is much in the same style (i.e. traditional Romantic) as his film music, utilizing representational themes that can be developed in a primarily tonal, popularist American sound, akin to works of Howard Hanson and Aaron Copland. Among these works are the *Liberty Fanfare,* written for the 100th anniversary of the Statue of Liberty; the *Olympic Fanfare,* for the 1980 Los Angeles Olympics; and 1996's *Summon the Heroes* for the Atlanta Summer Olympics. In 2002 Williams composed *Soundings* for the opening of the Walt Disney Hall, the new home of the Los Angeles Philharmonic, which employed taped sounds created by hitting the building's various metal surfaces—which were in turn imitated by orchestra instruments—and the hall's carillon. Williams' instrumental pieces include eight concertos; a piano sonata (1951); *Prelude and Fugue for winds and percussion* (1968); *A Nostalgic Jazz Odyssey* (1971); and *Essay for strings,* a symphony, and a *Sinfonietta for winds* all from 1968. His works from the 1960s are more dissonant, but later works use more straightforward expressions. The concertos—which include those for flute, violin, tuba, clarinet, cello, bassoon, trumpet, and horn—were all written for specific performers, such as Gil Shaham, Yo-Yo Ma, and Dale Clevenger. They are more personal in nature, often being inspired by poetry as well as the particular artist, yet all still extremely expressive. *—Patsy Morita*

Recommended:

○ **Best of John Williams and Boston Pops Orchestra** / Williams (cond.), Boston Pops / 1987 / Philips 420178

○ **Yo-Yo Ma Plays Music of John Williams** / Ma, Williams (cond.) / 2002 / Sony 89670

FILM MUSIC

Jaws (1975)

Jaws was the film that introduced the name of John Williams to the wider moviegoing public. He had been working in television and film for 15 years or so and had already received the admiration of colleagues within the industry with two Academy Award nominations and one Oscar. It also wasn't the first time he had worked with director Steven Spielberg. However, that now familiar, two-note "Shark Theme" is permanently embedded in the public consciousness as an authentic piece of American pop culture. The two notes increase in speed and intensity, until the theme bursts into full, menacing power in the strings, similar to Mussorgsky's darker music, and using the French horn in the opposite of its typical nineteenth century idiom, the hunting call. Instead of inviting you to chase after the beast, it's encouraging you to run away. In a way, Williams' music makes up for the fact that, due to technical difficulties, there is not much of the shark to see in the film. The remainder of his music for the film is typical of his film scores, rooted in the Romantic tradition with themes that are developed to match the emotion and action on the screen. Although it is not as notable as his music for later films, the score for *Jaws* is what earned Williams his second Oscar. *—Patsy Morita*

Recommended:

○ **Jaws (Original Soundtrack)** / Williams (cond.) / 1975 / MCA 1660

Schindler's List (1993)

In composing the music for *Schindler's List,* for which he won his fifth Academy Award, John Williams created what many see as his most affecting film score. The work is different from his other film scores in that, although complementing the action and emotion of the film, it is somehow separate, not following each scene's action in detail through many themes that each represent a different idea or person. There is one main theme, simply called "Theme from Schindler's List," written specifically for violinist Itzhak Perlman, accompanied by orchestra, which is a haunting, simple melody that, while deeply expressive, in no way exploits the emotion of the story. It expands to incorporate some rhythmic and harmonic idioms of Eastern European Jewish music. This theme reappears in different cues in the score, each cue, as it appears on the soundtrack release, seeming like a self-contained mini tone poem or variation of the theme. "Schindler's Workforce" not only adds more Jewish musical idioms, but also uses the clarinet and cimbalom in a piece that is built out of an essential, repeated figure, only shifting harmony to create some sense of animation to describe the monotony of the factory workers' day. The score is not as broad in harmonic exploration (although there are atonal moments) or large in expression as his other scores, which is in keeping with the nature of the story. What makes the score so successful is its emotional directness that addresses, but maintains a distance from, the narrative. *—Patsy Morita*

Recommended:

○ **Schindler's List** / Williams (cond.), Perlman / MCA MCAD10969

Star Wars Saga

John Williams' scores for George Lucas' *Star Wars* saga have been compared to Wagner's *Ring Cycle* for the imaginative use of themes and leitmotifs to tell an epic story. After the success of his score for Steven Spielberg's *Jaws,* Spielberg recommended Williams to his friend Lucas for scoring the first *Star Wars* film in 1976–1977. Lucas, in turn, suggested doing something akin to Korngold's *Captain Blood* music (i.e., something richly orchestral with swashbuckling, heroic themes). Williams' resulting music was credited with reviving the tradition of using symphonic music to accompany a film.

The same main and end titles frame each film, a reference to the serialized short films of the 1930s and a promise of an exciting tale to follow. And what follows is music that complements and enhances the storytelling. His music is, as Lucas wanted, tonal, orchestral, acoustic, and organic, underscoring the emotional context of each scene. There are many places throughout the score where the original themes are underpinned by harmonies and progressions that are similar to (some would say directly quoting) those used by composers ranging from Howard Hanson to Béla Bartók, but that is also following in the footsteps of Korngold.

Williams' themes most obviously represent specific characters, but they also represent traits of the characters, such as altruism, justice, or cruelty. These motifs are developed into new themes to represent groups of people. Themes from the first series of three films reappear in the second series, linking them musically, but also linking the major ideas of the story.

Williams is adept at using a full palette of instrumental and vocal timbres to illustrate the action on the screen. In the first film, he uses pizzicato strings to steadily accompany the work of the industrious Jawas, and spiky percussion to describe the brief attack of the Sand People. In *Attack of the Clones,* an electric guitar blends in with the sounds of flying ships in "The Chase Through Coruscant." Less literally descriptive is the choral "Duel of the Fates" in *The Phantom Menace,* which uses a Sanskrit text to emphasize the duel between the Jedi and Darth Maul over the destiny of Anakin Skywalker.

In addition, Williams composed incidental music—music heard within the context of the stories—in a variety of styles. The Cantina scene in *Star Wars* is rooted in jazz, but with a bit of discordant harmony used to indicate its foreignness; "Lapti Nek" is a disco song sung by the band in Jabba's palace in *Return of the Jedi;* and there's the piece for the Gungan band to play in the parade at the end of *The Phantom Menace,* full of bright brass and percussion.

The popularity of the soundtrack recordings and the number of performances of excerpts at concerts is a compliment to Williams' ability to combine musical ideas, sounds, and styles into a set of film scores that seem so naturally a part of the saga. *—Patsy Morita*

Recommended:

○ **Music from the Star Wars Saga** / Williams (cond.), Boston Pops / Philips 432050

John Williams (guitar)

b. Apr. 24, 1941, Melbourne, Australia

Guitarist

John Williams, classical guitar virtuoso, is known for his wide-ranging approach to repertory, which includes appearances playing electric rock guitar and international music. John's father Leonard (Len) Williams was an accomplished guitarist who emigrated from Britain to Australia, married a Melbourne woman of Chinese-British descent, and was best known there for his jazz playing. As he taught John to play guitar, it soon became apparent that the boy was a gifted guitarist, and the family planned to move back to London so that he could pursue further studies. To afford the trip, Len Williams took an additional job as a hippo-keeper at the Melbourne Zoo.

They eventually moved to London in 1952. John performed at Conway Hall in London in 1955, making enough of an impression that the famous guitarist Andrés Segovia invited John to study at his courses at the Accademia Chigiana in Siena, Italy. John accepted and became a student of the pioneering guitar soloist from 1957 to 1959.

Williams made his official debut at London's Wigmore Hall in 1958, and received reviews that noted a strong, clean tone and a polished though undemonstrative technique. However, Williams does not give Segovia or his other official teachers a large share of the credit for his technique. He says that most of these teachers were too "authoritarian" in their approach, not excluding Segovia who, he says, had a tendency to expect his pupils to adopt his interpretive "mannerisms," and would get quite angry when they didn't. The guitarist with whom he formed the closest association is Julian Bream, a fellow student of Segovia. Bream has often appeared in concert and on recordings as a guitar duo with Williams.

Williams has toured throughout the world. He has performed and recorded nearly the entire standard guitar repertory, plus a large quantity of transcriptions. Several of these transcriptions are by his own hand. He was a professor of guitar at the Royal College of Music in London from 1960 to 1973. However, he also has a strong tendency to explore music outside the classical tradition. He does session work on film soundtracks, has arranged Beatles songs, and plays electric guitar in Sky, a classical-rock fusion band. He has also formed his own ensembles, John Williams and Friends and Attacca, to explore other music. On a CD release called *The Guitarist*, he uses Turkish and Greek rhythms and harmonies to support Medieval music. The 2002 album, *The Magic Box*, examines African music. *—Joseph Stevenson*

Recommended:

- ○ **Harvey & Gray: Concertos** / Daniel (cond.), Williams, London SO / 1996 / Sony 68337
- ○ **The Guitarist** / Goodchild (cond.), Williams / 1998 / Sony 90399
- ○ **Great Guitar Concertos** / Williams, etc. / 1989 / CBS 44791
- ○ **Guitar Recital** / Williams / 1996 / London 452173
- ○ **The Magic Box** / Williams, Pleeth, Harvey, Clarvis, Etheridge, Loveday, Laurence, Kegg, Bebey / 2002 / Sony 89483
- ○ **Brouwer: The Black Decameron** / Mercurio (cond.), Williams, London Sinfonietta / 1997 / Sony 63173
- ○ **Takemitsu Album** / Salonen (cond.), Williams, Bell, Hulse, London Sinfonietta / 1991 / Sony 46720

Christopher Wilson

b. May 23, 1951, Redhill, Surrey, England

Lutenist

English lutenist Christopher Wilson studied with Diana Poulton at the Royal College of Music from 1970 to 1972, and performed his debut recital at Wigmore Hall in 1977. He has performed and recorded a remarkable range of sixteenth- and seventeenth century music for solo lute. He is also a frequent collaborator with singers Paul Agnew, Rufus Müller, Michael Chance, and Shirley Rumsey (with whom he formed the duo Kithara). He founded the Lute Group and has played with such ensembles as the Consort of Musicke, Fretwork, English Baroque Soloists, and Gothic Voices. He teaches the lute at Trinity College of Music in London. *—Robert Adelson*

Recommended:

- ○ **Elizabethan Lute Music** / Wilson / 1991 / Virgin 91216
- ○ **Milán, Narváez: Music for Vihuela** / Wilson / 1996 / Naxos 553523
- ○ **Byrd: Complete Consort Music** / Wilson, Fretwork / 1994 / Virgin 45031

Dag Wirén

b. Oct. 15, 1905, Stridsberg, Sweden, **d.** Apr. 19, 1986, Stockholm, Sweden

Composer: Chamber Music

Dag Wirén is not widely known outside his native Sweden, though his music began gaining notice internationally on recordings in the decade following his death. His first serious compositions date to the 1930s and divulge a neo-Classicism tinged by a Romantic warmth. By the middle of the following decade, his style had settled into a kind of early form of minimalism, but with themes, usually short, motto-like creations divulging a more complex and subtle form of evolution, relying on little repetition and thus achieving an entirely different kind of effect from that of the minimalists. While in the end, he must still be assessed as a secondary figure, he may yet generate a reevaluation and reach front-rank, or nearly front-rank, status.

Dag Wirén showed musical talent at an early age, but did not enroll at the Swedish Royal Academy of Music in Stockholm until 1926. There he studied composition with the conservative composer Ernst Ellberg. Wirén's own conservative style in the 1930s must be accounted for in part by Ellberg's influence. The young composer also studied organ at the academy, becoming quite proficient on the instrument, but never developing enough interest to write for the instrument as he would the piano, for which he wrote several solo pieces (*Ironic Small Pieces*, Op. 19; *Sonatina*, Op. 25, etc.) and which appear in compositions throughout his chamber works list. Wirén graduated from the academy in 1931 and then departed for Paris, where he would study composition from 1932–34 with Leonid Sabaneyev. There he also developed a camaraderie with fellow Swedish composers Gunnar de Frumerie and Gösta Nystroem. Wirén acknowledged that his exposure to the music of Prokofiev, Stravinsky, and Honegger had a great influence on him, though he still considered Bach, Mozart, and Nielsen his idols. He produced his *Symphony No. 1* in 1932 and the *Second* in 1939, neither making much of a mark, the former being withdrawn by the composer and the latter often looked upon by musicologists as light, Sibelius-like fare. While his style was still evolving in the 1930s and often not successful, Wirén did produce his most popular composition then, the 1937 *Serenade for Strings*, whose marchlike fourth movement has become familiar to listeners the world over. In 1938, Wirén became music critic of the Stockholm newspaper *Svenska Morgenbladet*, serving in that capacity until 1946. During the war years, Wirén composed some of his most important compositions, including the *Symphony No. 3* (1942–43). In 1943, he composed incidental music for a stage production of *The Merchant of Venice* and by the end of the war, he finished his *String Quartet No. 2*, Op. 28 (1941–45). In 1947, Wirén became the vice-chair for the Swedish Composers Association, a post he would hold until 1963. By that time, he was working on his fifth (and last) symphony, which he completed the following year. Wirén produced a fairly sizable output, but after the early 1970s, he wrote virtually nothing of significance and his later compositions—those from the latter 1960s—often divulged a lightness of expressive language. *—Robert Cummings*

Overview of Works (1931–1972)

Although the Swedish composer Dag Wirén composed operas, symphonies, string quartets, and many other serious works, he is best known—indeed, often only known—for his *Serenade for Strings* (1937). This endlessly charming work, especially its final March movement, which brilliantly parodies military music, is one of the most popular pieces of Swedish music after Alfvén's *Swedish Rhapsodies* and has given Wirén a worldwide fame he might not otherwise enjoy. However, the *Serenade* is atypically light for Wirén, who composed in the clear and powerful neo-Classical language he learned while studying in France in the 1930s where Stravinsky, Prokofiev, and Honegger were his models. His series of symphonies and string quartets, especially the *Fifth* in each genre, are composed in his "metamorphosis technique," the creation of large works based on the development of single melodic, harmonic, and rhythmic cells. *—James Leonard*

Recommended:

- ○ **Wirén: Symphonies & Overtures** / Dausgaard (cond.), Norrkoping SO / CPO 999677
- ○ **Wirén: Chamber Music** / Riska (cond.), Hogman, Bojsten, Jubilate Choir / 1996 / Bis 797
- ○ **Wirén: Chamber Music** / Stockholm Arts Trio / 1992 / BIS 582
- ○ **Wirén: Gyckeldans** / Karpe (cond.), Bengtson, Dala Sinfoniettan / Nosag 41
- ○ **Wirén: Serenade Op 11; Sinfonietta Op 7; Symphony 4; Music Op40** / Westerberg (cond.), Ehrling (cond.), Hedwall (cond.), Stockholm SO, Swedish RSO, Örebro CO / Swedish Society 1035

CHAMBER MUSIC

Serenade for strings, Op 11 (1937)

Wirén, whose credo was "I believe in God, Mozart, and Carl Nielsen," seems to have been especially moved by the holy spirit of Mozart when he wrote his *Serenade for Strings*, the work that would become his one international success. Like Mozart's entertainment pieces for string ensemble, particularly *Eine kleine Nachtmusik* and the K. 136–138 divertimenti, Wirén's *Serenade* is breezy, spontaneous, optimistic, and compact. The first movement, "Preludium," is an Allegro molto in which a long-lined melody seems to fly over a burbling rhythm, with contrast provided by a witty, marchlike tune. The Andante espressivo offers a moment of repose and an occasionally darker tone, with a serene melody stretching over a lighthearted pizzicato accompaniment. Third comes a Scherzo, Allegro vivace, that merrily skips around a central trio that seems slightly tense; again, there's a constant pizzicato undercurrent. The concluding "Marcia" was used many years ago as the theme of the BBC cultural show *Monitor*, and its popularity spread from there. This begins with a fast, childlike march, predominantly happy, but deflecting a couple of threatening intrusions. The middle section is a march of a more German parade-ground nature. *—James Reel*

Recommended:

- ○ **A Swedish Serenade** / Salonen (cond.), Stockholm Sinfonietta / 1984 / BIS 285

Pieter Wispelwey

b. 1962, Haarlem, Netherlands
Cellist
Usually it takes many years for an artist to build up a reputation that will allow him or her to take liberties in where and what they perform, and even then, there are few who are willing to perform as many diverse works in one season as cellist Pieter Wispelwey does. Wispelwey's first encounters with music were through his violinist father and his father's amateur string quartet. Wispelwey studied in Amsterdam with Dicky Boeke and Anner Bylsma, and then in the U.S. with Paul Katz and in England with William Pleeth. Boeke encouraged him to listen to as many things as possible, and growing up during the height of the period performance movement in Amsterdam in the 1960s and 1970s also gave him ample opportunity to learn a variety of styles. In fact, because of his ability to play the Baroque cello, the piccolo cello, and the modern cello, and because his first recording was of the Bach *Cello Suites* on period instruments, he was labeled a Baroque cellist. However, since then he has shattered that image through his concerts and recordings. Wispelwey is well-versed in the primary repertoire, able to play a couple of different concertos and different recital programs all in one week. He has performed at the Concertgebouw, Wigmore Hall, Teatro Colon, the Sydney Opera House, and Walt Disney Hall. He has worked with the Rotterdam Philharmonic, the BBC Symphony, the Camerata Academica Salzburg, and the Deutsche Kammerphilharmonie Bremen, among other orchestras. He toured and recorded with the Australian Chamber Orchestra without a conductor. His chamber music partners include pianists Dejan Lazic and Paolo Giacometti and the Emerson String Quartet. Channel Classics has allowed Wispelwey great freedom, not only in choosing a recording repertoire that includes mainstream works (Beethoven's sonatas), lesser known works (Lutosławski's concerto, Crumb's sonata), and transcriptions (Chopin waltzes and mazurkas), but also in the production process from editing to liner notes. This allows him to control what he wants to communicate, because what is important to him is communicating the original ideas and sounds the composer intended to the listener. Wispelwey sometimes views concerto performances as "combat" between the soloist and orchestra or soloist and conductor, but for the most part believes that a performance is all about communication between musicians and between musicians and the audience. *—Patsy Morita*

Recommended:

- ○ **Shostakovich, Prokofiev, Britten: Sonatas** / Wispelwey, Lazic (piano) / 2003 / Channel Classics 20098
- ○ **Britten: Cello Suites** / Wispelwey / 2001 / Channel Classics 17198
- ○ **Bach: Cello Suites** / Wispelwey / 1998 / Channel Classics 12298
- ○ **Tchaikovsky, Saint-Saëns, Bruch** / Wispelwey, etc. / 2001 / Channel Classics 16598
- ○ **Shostakovich: Concerto 1; Kodály: Sonata for Cello Solo** / Wispelwey, Australian CO / 1999 / Channel Crossings 15398

Hugo Wolf

b. Mar. 13, 1860, Windischgraz, Austria, **d.** Feb. 22, 1903, Vienna, Austria
Composer: Vocal, Chamber Music
Hugo Wolf, a native of Windischgraz (now Slovenjgradec, Slovenia), in the Austro-Hungarian province of Styria, was born on March 13, 1860 and died on February 22, 1903, three weeks before his 43rd birthday—like Schubert, German music's first great lieder composer, of tertiary syphilis. Like Schumann, the other great lieder composer (also syphilitic), Wolf died in an insane asylum after trying to drown himself in October 1898. (He had committed himself a year earlier, but was discharged after four months.) Also like Schumann, he composed in manic bursts between periods of depression, once the disease entered its second stage, and like two predecessors, was an unsuccessful composer of stage music.

Wolf completed only one opera, *Der Corregidor* (1895–96), based on the same Spanish comedy Falla later used in *The Three-Cornered Hat*. Indifferently and with difficulty he also composed incidental music for two plays long forgotten. As a teenager, he began but never finished a violin concerto and two symphonies (in 1879 he lost the manuscript of a third symphony while traveling). His orchestral repertory amounts to *Penthesilea* (after Kleist; 1883–85), a turbidly scored, Liszt-Wagnerian symphonic poem; *Christnacht*, a choral work both naive and sublime (1886–89), and the *Italian Serenade* (a 1892 arrangement of his charming 1887 *Serenade in G for String Quartet*).

Despite haphazard education that ended in a series of expulsions, Wolf the lieder composer was possessed of (and by) a psychological insight that revealed as early as 1878 what poured forth later between arid stretches—some 300 songs, the finest of them both emotionally penetrating and musically profound. Mörike, Goethe (the *Mignon—Lieder* are incomparable), Kleist, Lenau, and Heine were his favorite German poets, plus Eichendorff when Wolf reached the expressive summit in 1887. For three years prior he had been an outspoken critic—the only job he ever held—in Vienna's weekly *Salonblatt*. Pro-Wagner and anti-Brahms, he was as honest as Berlioz had been, and thus made powerful enemies who took revenge later on. Wolf habitually lived hand to mouth, supported by a circle of friends who provided shelter and sustenance for ten years, and finally in 1896 gave him his own apartment. By then, however, the disease had entered its third stage, and his mood swings alienated many who cared deeply. On 19 September 1897, he cracked—blaming Mahler, his friend of 20 years and onetime roommate, of sabotaging *Der Corregidor* at the *Hofoper*.

In October 1889, Wolf had turned his attention from German poetry to translations of Spanish poets. Between Halloween and the following May, he composed forty-four songs called the *Spanish Songbook*. Then, between September 1890 and December 1891, he composed 22 song translations comprising Part I of an *Italian Songbook*. Thereafter he didn't write a note of original music until March 1895, when he undertook *Der Corregidor*, completing all four acts in piano score within twelve weeks. After laboriously scoring it, he wrote twenty-four songs in isolation between 25 March and 30 April 1896—Part II of the *Italian Songbook*. He spent the next months revising *Der Corregidor*. After setting his last songs in March 1897, three somber sonnets by Michelangelo, Wolf worked tirelessly on another Spanish opera, *Manuel Venegas*, which amounted to sixty pages of piano score, before his breakdown. Following his death, he was buried alongside Beethoven and Schubert in Vienna's Central Cemetery, impoverished to the end but officially a cultural hero. *—Roger Dettmer*

VOCAL

Drei Gedichte von Michelangelo (1897)
Throughout his career, Wolf was obsessed with attaining success composing in large forms, and was continually dismayed by his label as a "songwriter"; he wrote that "... such recognition ... disturbs me down to the very depths of my soul." (Wolf's obsession with success in the large-scale genre of opera would be the final expression of his madness.) Probably because of this urge to compose on a vast scale, Wolf compiled songs into volumes, each with enough variety to create a lengthy recital with contrasting sections. Also, Wolf linked songs within each book to produce a greater whole. The songbook became Wolf's large-scale form.

Hugo Wolf finished his three *Michelangelo Lieder*, for bass voice and piano, only six months before his mental breakdown and lengthy terminal illness—the result of syphilis. In December 1896, Paul Müller, the founder of the Berlin Hugo-Wolf Verein (Hugo Wolf Society), had given Wolf a gift of Michelangelo's sonnets in German translations by Walter Robert-Tornow. Wolf's three settings from the volume were published in Mannheim in 1898. A fourth song from the collection, entitled "Irdische und himmlische Liebe" and written at about the same time, was destroyed by the composer. Composition of the songs coincided with Wolf's perusal of Hermann Grimm's biography of Michelangelo. They would be the composer's last completed songs.

Wolf completed "Wohl denk' ich oft an mein vergang'nes Leben" (I often think on my past life), in G minor/major, on March 18, 1897. The composer described the song in a letter to a friend: "[It] begins with a melancholy introduction and holds fast to this tone until the line before the last, ... [then] takes on unexpectedly a vigorous character (developed from the previous motive) and closes festively with triumphal fanfares, like a flourish of trumpets sounded for [Michelangelo] by his contemporaries in homage." In the process, G minor changes to G major for a firm and triumphant close. The clarity of the melody is superb, as is its support by the harmonically captivating countermelody in the piano.

"Alles endet, was entstehet" (Everything ends that begins), in C sharp minor, is dated March 20, 1897. Wolf originally entitled the song, "Vanitas Vanitatum." Michelangelo's poem is a canzona in the style of Petrarch that speaks in no uncertain terms of death and the transitoriness of earthly things. Similarly, Wolf gives a stark, streamlined setting. He thought the song "truly enough to drive one crazy.... Such perilous things I am now producing to the public danger." In "Alles endet, was entstehet" we find Wolf using harmony to accentuate single words in the text. For example, at "Menschen waren wir ja auch / Froh und traurig, so wie ihr" (We, too, were once people / Happy and sad, like you), he switches between major and minor inflections to convey the difference between the "Froh und traurig" (happy and sad).

Melancholy marks "Fühlt meine Seele das ersehnte Lied von Gott" (My soul feels the yearning song of God), in E minor/major and composed in March 1897. Perhaps because the text is concerned with the present human condition, Wolf creates a more lush setting than for the first two songs. Opening slowly and reservedly, the vocal line becomes increasingly agitated and the harmony more colorful. At "ist es ein Klang, ein Traumgesicht," we hear a chromatically descending motive that recurs through the rest of the song, suggesting resignation. In this case, it is the submission of a man's heart to his mistress. The postlude of "Fühlt meine Seele" is similar to those of "Peregrina I" and "Peregrina II," both settings of poems by Eduard Mörike (1804–75) composed in 1888. *—John Palmer*

Recommended:

- ○ **Alexander Kipnis sings Brahms & Wolf** / Kipnis, Moore, Bos, Wolff / Preiser 89204

Gedichte von Eduard Mörike (1888–1891)

Wolf composed the 53 *Mörike Lieder* between February 16 and November 26, 1888. The *Mörike Lieder* were strikingly original, as contemporary critics noted, despite Wolf's contention that he was continuing the tradition of Schubert and Schumann.

Eduard Mörike (1804–75), a Swabian poet, was a favorite among late nineteenth century German composers. A Protestant pastor with leaning toward Catholicism, Mörike had, while young, encountered a woman he called, "Peregrina" (wanderer), who was apparently unstable and had wandered into his town. The exact nature of their relationship is uncertain, but he wrote numerous poems about her that are filled with emotional and erotic tension.

Several aspects of Wolf's songs are traditional, such as the repeated phrases in "Er ist's," or the occasional selection of texts for their musical potential as opposed to their poetic greatness. Most of the songs, however, are original in conception, featuring Wolf's unfailing instincts for text setting and his ability to portray the meaning of both single words and an entire poem through rhythm and harmony. Also, Wolf's predilection for reading through piano reductions of Wagner's operas comes through in many of his piano parts.

"Das verlassene Mägdlein" (The forsaken girl) had been set over fifty times when Wolf completed his on March 24. Every morning, a young woman rises very early to light the fire in her home. As she watches the flames, she remembers dreaming of her former, unfaithful lover, and hopes daybreak will banish her dreams of him. In A minor, the simple, transparent piano part portrays the stillness of early morning, while a shift to A major conveys the brightness of the flames. Also, unsettling augmented chords support her mention of the unfaithful lover. The lively triplet accompaniment of "Er ist's" (It's spring), of May 5, is sometimes juxtaposed with duplets in the voice. An extended, energetic piano conclusion makes the work a great concert piece that is very unlike Schumann's introspective setting of the same poem.

Variation technique appears in "Storchenbotschaft" (The storks' message) (March 27), in which two storks try to tell a man he has twins. Unable to speak, the birds must gesture while the man tries to guess what they mean. The music becomes increasingly animated until the final outburst when the man realizes the truth. Wolf alters the melody of his strophic "Um Mitternacht" (At midnight) (April 20) in order to emphasize certain words, particularly "süsser" (sweet). Rhythm is often the unifying factor of a song, such as the 5/4 meter of "Jägerlied" (Hunter's song) (February 22), which reflects the trochaic pentameter of the poem, while the pace and rhythm of "Fussreise" (Walking-tour) (March 21) evokes walking.

Wolf set two of Mörike's poems concerning the mysterious "Peregrina." The poem of "Peregrina I" (April 28) concerns Mörike's earliest feelings of physical desire for the woman, while Wolf's "Peregrina II" (April 30) sets the fourth of Mörike's five poems on the subject, in which the image of the woman haunts the poet after he has rejected her. Both of Wolf's songs build erotic tension through the same descending chromatic motive.

Homesick wanderers appear frequently in German lieder, and Wolf's idyllic "Heimweh" (homesickness) (April 1) is a perfect example, in which the lethargic accompaniment matches the unenthusiastic gait of the traveler.

The profound "Der Genesene an die Hoffnung," which Wolf placed at the head of the *Mörike Lieder*, was completed on March 6. As the subject of the poem gradually overcomes his illness, the music becomes more triumphant, climaxing with fanfare-like passages. *—John Palmer*

Recommended:

- ○ **Wolf: Mörike Lieder** / Rodgers, Genz, Vignoles / 2001 / Hyperion 67311/12
- ○ **Wolf: Mörike Lieder** / Fischer-Dieskau, Moore / Orfeo 140401

Gedichte von J.W. von Goethe (1888–1889)

Wolf's fondness for the "liederbuch" (book of songs) betrayed his desire to broaden the scope of his output; he spent most of his career trying to shed his image as a mere "songwriter"—a miniaturist. His compilation of songs into large volumes, each with a sense of poetic and dramatic unity, yet enough variety to allow for the performance of the whole in recital without risk of monotony, was his only real success at large-scale composition.

Wolf composed his *Gedichte von J. W. v. Goethe* in a volcanic eruption of creativity (many days saw the completion of two songs) between October 27, 1888 and February 12, 1889 ("Die Spröde" would be recomposed on October 21, 1889). The book, containing 51 settings in all, was published in Vienna in 1890.

Wolf extends musical boundaries in his *Goethe Gedichte* even further than in his settings of Eichendorff and Mörike poems. The piano parts are exceptionally expansive in "Prometheus" and "Mignon II"; melodies are intensely lyrical in "Blumengrass" and "Gleich und Gleich."

Ten of the pieces, including the four "Mignon" songs, are from Goethe's *Wilhelm Meister*. Of the Goethe settings these are by far the best known; they are of special interest because Wolf was at times confronted with the task of conveying the poem's context within a larger drama. In particular, he wished to bring into relief the pathological aspects of Mignon's character, as well as the borderline insanity of the Harpist (another character from the novel). It was bold for Wolf to set the *Wilhelm Meister* poems and to place them first in his collection; this was sure to invite comparison of his settings with those of numerous composers, including Beethoven, Schubert, and Schumann. Wolf noted that in some cases, particularly Schubert's, some of Goethe's poems had already been given their consummate settings, but in others his predecessors had not fully understood the poetic text.

The Harpist's "Wer nie sein Brot mit Thränen aß" (He who has never eaten his bread with tears) receives an especially emotional setting—alluding to the surrounding dramatic circumstances: the Harpist's incestuous love has produced Mignon, but he does not yet know this. Like his predecessor, Schubert, Wolf evokes the Harpist's plodding footsteps in "An die Türen will ich schleichen" (I want to creep to the doors); unlike his predecessors (Beethoven, Schubert, Schumann), all of whose settings were strophic, Wolf addresses the increasing intensity of the verses of Mignon's "Kennst du das Land?" (Do you know that place?) by changing the music from verse to verse; his setting of this poem is generally considered among his finest achievements. Similarly, Mignon's "Nur wer die Sehnsucht kennt" (Only he who knows yearning) has been set many times, but Wolf's interpretation stands out because of its nervous, agitated atmosphere.

Among the poems not drawn from *Wilhelm Meister*, "Anakreons Grab" (Anacreon's Grave) is a gem; chromaticism pervades the piece (about standing at a poet's grave), which occasionally evokes Wagner's *Tristan*. Nos. 39 and 40, "Nicht Gelegenheit macht Diebe" and "Hochbeglückt in deiner Liebe," are musically linked; the key of the former (F major) is the dominant of the latter (B flat major).

The book closes with three of Wolf's most powerful songs. In "Prometheus," the hero mocks the gods, requiring a tumultuous, orchestrally conceived piano part; this is perhaps why it is one of the few of his songs that Wolf transcribed for orchestra. The pastoral, mythical "Ganymed" (also orchestrated by Wolf) stands in stark contrast with its fluid movement and calm atmosphere. In "Grenzen der Menschheit" (Boundaries of humanity) humankind's pointless reaching for the stars is conveyed in the restless, inconclusive setting. *—John Palmer*

Recommended:

- ○ **Elisabeth Schwarzkopf Songbook** / Schwarzkopf, Moore, Parsons / 1995 / EMI 65860
- ○ **The Hugo Wolf Society Complete Edition** / (various) / 1998 / EMI 66640
- ○ **Wolf: Goethe Lieder** / Johnson, McGreevy / 2001 / Hyperion 67130

Gedichte von Joseph v. Eichendorff (1880–1888)

Hugo Wolf was perennially obsessed with composing in large-scale forms, and was dismayed when critics referred to him as a "songwriter," writing that "... such recognition... disturbs me down to the very depths of my soul." (Wolf's obsession with success in the large-scale genre of opera would be the final expression of his madness.) Probably because of this urge, Wolf compiled songs into large volumes, each with enough variety to create a lengthy recital with contrasting sections; these songbooks would become his large-scale works.

Though he later found the writer's work somewhat superficial, instead preferring the more detailed supernatural imagery of Eduard Möricke, Joseph von Eichendorff (1788–1857) was arguably Wolf's first poetic inspiration. He especially responded to the poet's realistic, humorous texts with well developed characters or scenes, by and large eschewing the pastoral- or love-poems favored by Robert Schumann. Two of his settings, "Erwartung" and "Die Nacht," date from early 1880, and five more from late 1886 and the spring of 1887. Aside from "Verschwiegene Liebe," which Wolf set on August 31, 1888, Wolf composed the rest of the *Eichendorff Lieder* in September 1888.

The 20 *Eichendorff Lieder* were published in 1889 by Lacom in Vienna. For a revised edition of 1898 Wolf removed "Erwartung, "Die Nacht" and "Waldmädchen," but these were later restored in a posthumous edition of 1904 (by Heckel). Wolf did not orchestrate any of his *Eichendorff Lieder*.

With glissandos and other flourishes, Wolf depicts the extravagant gestures, swaggering gait and braggartism of the protagonist in "Der Schreckenberger"—composed on September 14, 1888 while on a walk in Ischl. Wolf composed the less impressive "Der Glücksritter," which is musically linked to "Der Schreckenberger," while traveling between Ischl and Weissenbach two days later. "Der Musikant" draws a picture of an amiable fellow who evidently is not a very good melodist. Composed on March 19, 1887 in Vienna, "Die Zigeunerin" is downright brilliant; today, it appears on recital programs as often as any other of Wolf's lieder. It is a masterpiece of form, delineated in part by imaginative use of harmony, and is driven by infectious rhythms.

In "Der Scholar" Wolf illustrates the pedantry of the students and the monotony of rainy weather through a staccato accompaniment while drawing a gentle, affectionate caricature of the old professor. "Der Verzweifelte Liebhaber" has the characteristics of an improvised recitative. "Der Freund," dedicated to Joseph Schalk, is self-consciously heroic and often disparaged even by fans of Wolf's music, while "Heimweh" depicts a traveler's sentimental longing for his home and heartfelt patriotism, conveyed most intensely in Wolf's piano postlude. In "Liebesglück" we hear a contradiction between Wolf's fiery rhythms and his conventional, song-like melody, which is well suited to the poem's simple message and language. Despite its early date, "Die Nacht" must be ranked with the most important of Wolf's lieder; its effect is only apparent when performers observe the recommended, very slow tempo.

"Das Ständchen" is perhaps the most artfully composed of the set, with masterful counterpoint throughout. Here, the voice is that of an old man remembering his nights spent serenading a sweetheart. The right hand of the piano part represents the melody of his long-past song, while in the left hand we hear the louder sound of the present serenader and his lute, which the old man hears. One of Wolf's most original songs, its melody is completely free, expressing every word in the text. *—John Palmer*

Recommended:

- ○ **Wolf: Eichendorff-Leider** / Fink, Genz, Vignoles / 1998 / Hyperion 66909
- ○ **Wolf & Korngold: Eichendorff-Lieder** / Skovhus, Deutsch / 1994 / Sony 57969

Italienisches Liederbuch, Books 1–2 (1891–1896)

Wolf composed the first volume of the *Italienisches Liederbuch* (Italian Songbook) between September 25, 1890, and December 23, 1891, writing more than half the songs in December after many months of inactivity. Those of Volume II appeared between March 25 and August 1, 1896. The composer culled the poems of both volumes from a collection of anonymous Italian verse in German translation by Paul Heyse, the translator of many of the songs in Wolf's *Spanisches Liederbuch*. The *Italienisches Liederbuch* is Wolf's most unified and integrated collection. This may be due, in part, to the anonymity of the poets, eliminating the need for the composer to confront a particular poetic personality. Also, all of the songs, to one degree or another, are love songs; aside from "Gesegnet sei, durch den die Welt entstund," none is religious. The consistently compressed nature of the verses promoted concise settings, in which Wolf's oscillation between orchestral, Wagnerian arrangements and Schumannesque intimacy has boiled down to a uniform style.

The 22 lieder of Volume I were published in Mainz in 1892. "Mir ward gesagt, du reisest in die Ferne" (I was told you were leaving), the first lied Wolf composed for the *Italienisches Liederbuch*, is about the unhappy parting of lovers. Wolf shows the disparity between the desires of the two people in the contrast between the rising phrases of the voice part and the descending bass line in the piano, mediated by almost constant chords in the right hand. The opposing movement creates a "duet" of sorts with a Wagnerian, chromatic course that, in its frequent dissonance, expresses the pain of the poem's subject. In "Gesegnet sei, durch den die Welt entstund" (Praised be the one through whom the world arose), one of his most sparse creations, Wolf emphasizes the climax by arriving at a sudden pianissimo when the narrator mentions "die Schönheit und dein Angesicht" (Beauty and your face). "Du denkst mit einem Fädchen mich zu fangen" (You think you can catch me with a little thread) is a diminutive song of 17 measures in which the nearly autonomous piano part provides a rhythmic and melodic counterpoint to the almost spoken voice part.

Despite the four-year hiatus between Volume I and the 24 lieder of Volume II, Wolf was able to resume composing in the lyrical manner. "Nicht länger kann ich singen" (I can no longer sing) and "Schweig' einmal still" (Be still) are musically linked. Both are in A minor and both employ the same melodic intervals. In the distressing "Nicht länger," Wolf conveys the anguish of the protagonist by creating a setting that seems detached from the poem. Quite the opposite, "Schweig' einmal still" clearly illustrates the awful voice of the serenader by imitating donkey sounds. Other illustrative moments occur in "Ich liess mir sagen" (I must say) and, especially, "Mein Liebster hat zu Tische mich geladen" (My beloved invited me to dinner), in which the chopping of the very stale bread is clear in the accents of the accompaniment. *—John Palmer*

Recommended:

- ○ **Wolf: Italienisches Liederbuch** / Fischer-Dieskau, Schwarzkopf, Moore / 1990 / EMI 63732
- ○ **Wolf: Italienisches Liederbuch** / Lott, Schreier, Johnson / 1994 / Hyperion 66760

Sechs Lieder für eine Frauenstimme (1877–1882)

Wolf's first published songs were his *Sechs Lieder für eine Frauenstimme*, collected and printed in 1888. Like those of *Sechs Gedichte von Scheffel, Mörike, Goethe und Kerner*, these songs were not composed as a set, but were assembled from the numerous lieder Wolf had written up to that point. Thereafter, the composer would begin to conceive of large groups of interrelated songs, either by the same poet or drawn from the same source.

Composed between June 6–19, 1877, "Morgentau" (Morning Dew) is possibly to a text by Albert Reinhold. Although not an ambitious song, the melody is sweet, simple and entrancing, and the overall structure and atmosphere remind one of Schumann's lyrical bent. The song's accompaniment seems to capture the mood of the poem—full of the sights and scents of early morning. Wolf set "Das Vöglein" (Little Bird), by Friedrich Hebbel, on May 2, 1878. Already we find the composers distinctive voice emerging in the clarity of the piano part, which is a humorous representation of the fluttering and chirping of birds.

Imagery of spring permeates "Die Spinnerin" (The Spinster), by Friedrich Rückert (1788–1866), which Wolf composed on April 5–12, 1878. A young woman cannot bring herself to spin thread because she sees through her window the stirrings of spring; more distracting, however, are the stirrings of spring within her heart. Rapidly alternating notes between the hands in the accompaniment evoke the motion of a spinning wheel. Robert Reinick's "Wiegenlied im Sommer" (Cradle-song in Summer), was composed on December 17, 1882. Cast in Wolf's "idyllic" key—F major—the song is an example of the composer's "soft" side, as seen in the gentle melody and easily rolling accompaniment. Its sister-song, "Wiegenlied im Winter" (Cradle-song in Winter), also by Reinick, is dated December 20, 1882. In a darker A flat major, the setting conveys some of the harshness of winter months.

"Mausfallensprüchlein" (Mousetrap Rhyme), set on June 18, 1882, is a poem by Eduard Mörike (1804–75). In an effort to catch a mouse, a small child "walks around the mousetrap and says: "Kleine Gäste, kleines Haus / Liebe Mäusin oder Maus..." (Tiny guests, tiny house / Dear girl or boy mouse...). The right hand of Wolf's piano part imitates the scurrying of little creatures as the child sings the rhyme to attract a mouse. "Mausfallensprüchlein" is one of the composer's most genuinely humorous lieder; the text is set to produce the utmost clarity, the melodic leaps becoming larger as the child commands the mouse to dance. *—John Palmer*

Spanisches Liederbuch, nach Heyse und Geibel (1889–1890)

Hugo Wolf began working on the *Spanisches Liederbuch* on October 28, 1889, with his setting of the anonymous poem, "Wer sein holdes Lieb verloren." Wolf's completion of Gil Vincente's "Wehe der, die mich verstrickte," on April 27, 1890, brought his work on the *Spanisches Liederbuch* to a close. The entire set was composed in Perchtoldsdorf and published in Mainz in 1891.

The *Spanisches Liederbuch* is drawn from a collection of Spanish poems of the sixteenth and seventeenth centuries, translated into German by Emanuel Geibel and Paul Heyse. Only seventeen of the poems have known authors; these include Lope de Vega, Luis de Camões (Portuguese), Miguel de Cervantes, Juan Ruiz, Nicolas Nuñez, Lopez de Ubeda, Don Manuel del Rio, José de Valdivielso, Alvaro Fernandez de Almeida, Rodrigo de Cota, Cristobal de Castillejo, Gil Vincente, Don Luis el Chico, and Maria Doceo. The collection contains ten religious and 34 secular songs.

Wolf had reached a level of compositional maturity that enabled him to work from the underlying ideas in the poems instead of responding to details in them. Thus, we find a greater use of recurrent rhythmic motives and accompaniment figures than in earlier works, and a more vivid use of harmony to convey the overall sense of a poem.

Of the 13 "geistliche," or religious, poems translated by Geibel and Heyse, Wolf chose ten and placed them first in his *Spanisches Liederbuch*. Wolf opens the *Spanisches Liederbuch* with the oldest poem of the collection, "Nun bin ich dein," by Ruiz. An unusual meter of 4/2 and the plodding rhythm of the piece convey the anguish of the sinner who asks forgiveness. "Ach, wie lang die Seele schlummert" has a similar theme and setting, but is more an inward, personal meditation in which bold modulations nearly obliterate the tonality. The slow tempo and trudging repeated notes of "Mühvoll komm' ich und beladen" (I come troubled and heavily laden) communicate the weight of guilt.

The rest of the *Spanisches Liederbuch* consists of "weltliche" (worldly, or secular) songs, most of which have an erotic theme. A prime example of these is "In dem Schatten meiner Locken" (In the shade of my tresses), one of Wolf's finest songs that has been a standard part of the lied repertoire almost since its publication. The poem tells of a woman and her lover, who sleeps in the shade cast by her hair. The woman laments that her efforts at brushing her hair are in vain, for it always becomes disheveled. She wonders if she should wake her lover, but decides not to. Shifts in metric feel between 3/4 and 6/8 create a sense of indecision. Set in B flat major, the song traces the woman's thoughts through changes in harmony. Wolf moves quickly to D major before the woman asks, "Weck' ich ihn nun auf?" (Do I wake him?), giving the impression that the thought just occurred to her. She hesitates, then answers, "Ach nein!" (Ah, no!) on a G flat major chord, suggesting the affection the woman has for her lover.

"Klinge, klinge, mein Pandero" (Ring ring my tambourine)—another notable favorite from the songbook—is filled with dance rhythms and trills imitating the jingling of a tambourine. Wolf's setting of "Auf dem grünen Balkon" (On the green balcony) combines a Spanish-inflected, guitar-like accompaniment with a flexible voice part. A woman beckons her suitor to her balcony only to reject him with a wave of her finger. The vocal line rises in intensity until the woman says, "No," where the dynamic immediately drops to pianissimo and the harmony moves to the dominant. *—John Palmer*

Recommended:

- ○ **Wolf: Spanisches Liederbuch** / Fischer-Dieskau, Schwarzkopf, Moore / DG 457726
- ○ **Wolf: Spanisches Liederbuch** / Bar, von Otter, Parsons / 1995 / EMI 55325

CHAMBER MUSIC

Italian Serenade, for string quartet in G major (1887)

Among nineteenth century chamber works, we find an unusual subcategory of pieces by composers more often associated with other genres. One example might be Verdi's *String Quartet in E minor*, and Hugo Wolf's *Italian Serenade* is yet another. The original string quartet version of the serenade was written with astonishing speed, in fact between May 2 and 4, 1887, when Wolf was largely preoccupied in creating vocal settings of Eichendorff's poems. Indeed, the work does seems quite closely related to one of these—"Der Soldat I"—dated March 7, 1887. And like another Eichendorff setting "Das Ständchen," of September 1888, the *Italian Serenade* actually begins with some preliminary strummings on open fifths and repeated notes as if to check tuning, rather like a band readying itself before the music actually gets under way.

It is reasonable to suggest that Wolf created a new genre of "comic" serenades with the work. The comic atmosphere is established with the mock-tuning at the beginning for eight whole measures. The key here is the tonic G major, but the passages end with "wrong" repeated E flats! The inner voices (second violin and viola) put matters to rights, in a pizzicato passage that restores the correct key, before the real entertainment starts.

The movement is in rondo form, cleverly adapted so that the players seem like personalities in an amorous comedy. The entire first episode could almost be the lover preparing his declaration, climaxing with a bold outburst in 6/8 time. In the development section, there are elaborate new countermelodies (second violin), and a recitative-like idea for cello, answered (at first mockingly, then more compliantly) by the instruments. After more dance-like digressions, and a return of the rondo theme, the *Serenade* ends as it began, amid the thrumming of imaginary guitars.

Most critics agree that the original string quartet version is superior to the later revision (1892) for string orchestra. There is also some evidence that Wolf considered adding two extra movements, but never did so. —*Michael Jameson*

Recommended:

- ○ **Great Conductors of the 20th Century: Rudolf Kempe** / Kempe (cond.), Munich PO / EMI 75950

Ermanno Wolf-Ferrari

b. Jan. 12, 1876, Venice, Italy, **d.** Jan. 21, 1948, Venice, Italy

Composer

Ermanno Wolf-Ferrari was an important Italian composer of the late nineteenth and early twentieth centuries. His comic operas may be his best-known works, but none have endured in the standard repertory. Toward the latter twentieth century his Op. 26 *Violin Concerto* (1901) began gaining some currency, as well as chamber works like *Piano Trios*, Opp. 5 and 7, and the *Idillio-concertino*, Op. 15.

Wolf-Ferrari was born in Venice on January 12, 1876, to a Bavarian father and an Italian mother. He showed unusual talent on the piano in his childhood, but gradually felt drawn toward painting, the art world of his father. He enrolled at the Academia di Belle Arti when he was 15 and two years later relocated to Munich to pursue further art instruction. However, he soon began composition studies with Rheinberger at the Munich Akademie der Tonkunst. His first works date to 1893, with his *E flat Serenade* for strings possibly being the earliest serious effort.

In 1895, the young composer, previously known Ermanno Wolf, became Ermanno Wolf-Ferrari, attaching his mother's maiden name to the family surname. Apparently, he desired renewed connection to the Italian side of his heritage. Indeed, he returned to Venice that year in a vain attempt to launch his composing career. He would fail to interest the famous publisher Giulio Ricordi in his early operas, *Irene* (1895–96) and the incomplete *La Camargo* (1897).

However, his first serious effort at opera, *Cenerentola* (1900), did reach the stage in Venice on February 22, 1900. Though it failed, the composer's 1902 revision achieved great success in Bremen, Germany. His 1901 cantata *La vita nuova* was also greeted enthusiastically. Wolf-Ferrari's next operas met with general acceptance as well; *Le donne curiose* (1903), *I quattro rusteghi* (1906), and *Il segreto di Susanna* (1909), all comedies, were staged in Munich. The latter two became quite popular on the world's operatic stages for a time. During this period Wolf-Ferrari served in his native Venice as director of the *Liceo Musicale*.

After 1909 he made his living largely from his compositions. The First World War forced Wolf-Ferrari to abandon Munich for Zurich, where he wrote little. Ironically, the one major work he did turn out was another comedy, *Gli amanti sposi* (1916; originally begun in 1904). After the war he moved back to Munich, but still regularly visited Venice and maintained influential musical contacts.

His output remained meager until the mid-1920s when he completed *Das Himmelsklied* (1917–25). His next operatic effort was *Sly* (1927), perhaps his most complex and most underrated. (The U.S. premiere of the work did not take place until 1999, when the Washington Opera, with José Carreras in the lead, introduced it.)

Wolf-Ferrari has generally been described as a gentle man with a childlike manner, whose music always reflected a conservative bent. Many have speculated the wartime woes he suffered in watching the two countries of his heritage divided by conflict, left indelible scars that altered his compositional style and focus.

Indeed, after three decades away from the instrumental realm, Wolf-Ferrari returned to the genre with the 1933 *Idillio-concertino*, for oboe, two horns, and strings, Op. 15. By the mid-1940s his opus number had reached above 30, largely on the strength of his renewed efforts in instrumental music—only four operas followed *Sly*. Yet, outside of the 1946 *Violin Concerto*, most of these works were subsequently ignored, despite their generally solid features.

Wolf-Ferrari died in Venice on January 21, 1948, his reputation already fading. —*Robert Cummings*

Overview of Works (1895–1947)

Ermanno Wolf-Ferrari was a composer of contradictions. An Italian whose greatest successes were in Germany, a composer of post-Mascagni verismo operas who wrote the funniest comic operas of the first half of the twentieth century, a composer of chamber music that is sometimes in the conservative Mendelssohn-Schumann mold and sometimes clearly based on Wagner's *Tristan*, a composer who could as easily write in a pastiche of eighteenth century operatic conventions and in a neo-Bachian oratorio style, Wolf-Ferrari seemed capable of almost anything except long-lasting success. His verisimo opera *I gioielli della Madonna* (The Jewels of the Madonna) (1911) was a huge success, but in Berlin, not Italy. His neo-Baroque oratorio *La vita nuova* (1901) received more than 500 hundred performances before 1937, but only two of these were in Italy. His *Sinfonia da camera* for 11 instruments (1901) is part Mendelssohn, part Schumann, and distinctly a work of parts held together only by the strength of Wolf-Ferrari's melodic imagination. His *Violin Sonata in A minor* (1901) infuses a Brahmsian work with the intense chromaticism of Wagner. Best known for his comic operas based on the comedies of Goldoni, he wrote works that are to a greater or lesser degree pastiches of eighteenth century Italian forms, and nearly all of them received their premieres in Munich. If ultimately an unsuccessful composer in all the genres in which he wrote, Wolf-Ferrari will live in his series of comic operas. —*James Leonard*

Recommended:

- ○ **Sly** / Maxym (cond.), Polaski, Bader, Haertel, Reeh, Niedersächsischen Staatsoper Hannover / 1999 / Arts 47549
- ○ **Das Himmelskleid** / Markson (cond.), Ruzzafante, Basa, Adam, Gómez, Hagen PO & Opera Chorus / 1997 / Marco Polo 223261
- ○ **I Quattro Rusteghi** / Gracis (cond.), Olivero, Barbieri, Lazzari, Rossi-Lemeni / 2003 / Opera d'Oro 1385
- ○ **The Jewels of the Madonna** / Serebrier (cond.), Royal PO / 1993 / ASV 861
- ○ **Wolf-Ferrari: Italian Song Book** / Canino, Janicke / CPO 999270
- ○ **Wolf-Ferrari: Cello Concerto; Sinfonia Brevis** / Francis (cond.), Rivinius, Frankfurt Radio SO / CPO 999278

Christian Wolff

b. Mar. 8, 1934, Nice, France

Composer

Alongside John Cage, Morton Feldman, and Earle Brown, composer Christian Wolff emerged in the 1950s on the New York experimental music scene and became a prominent champion of the aesthetics of musical indeterminism. His works, which became increasingly explicit in their political content as his career progressed, stress choice, artistic cooperation and interdependence, and an accommodating attitude toward the potential relationships between music, sound, and silence.

Wolff was born in Nice, France, but moved to the United States during his childhood. He took a rather indirect route to composition, studying classics and comparative literature at Harvard University, where he also taught, before taking positions in both music and literature at Mills College and later Dartmouth. Though active as a pianist and electric guitarist throughout his career, he was largely self-taught as a composer, and from the beginning his works relied more on careful aesthetic design than compositional "craft" in the traditional sense. This is not to say, however, that his compositions lack depth or complexity; indeed, they point up some of the most crucial philosophical issues of his time, and do so in a way that engages and invites close listening and careful consideration.

Although his works of the 1950s already conveyed a decidedly "democratic" subtext, with their reliance on freedom and reaction ("parliamentary participation"), they did so through traditional notation and sometimes invoked, however obscurely, traditional forms. The flexibility of their realizations owed to Cage's influence, while their sparse surfaces recalled Webern, and in some cases resonated with La Monte Young's early works. Wolff's compositions from the late 1950s and 1960s placed increased effort on real-time cooperation between performers, who worked somewhat freely, within certain set parameters (set durations with unspecified pitches, for example), but were required to alter their performative decisions consequent to each other's actions.

Wolff explicitly drew analogies between his compositional methods and political views, and during the 1970s even set texts related to his democratic socialist positions. This effort coincided with similar artistic endeavors espoused by Cornelius Cardew and Frederic Rzewski, both of whom Wolff interacted with during this period. Later works turned inwards to more specifically musical topics, perhaps due in part to Wolff's somewhat self-effacing assessment of the composer's role. As he observed in a 1991 interview: "Most political music, paradoxically enough, is for the converted; it's an instrument of cohesion for a group that already knows what it wants...." —*Jeremy Grimshaw*

Overview of Works

Wolff's first compositions appear to be serialist but were in fact not written following those procedures. Pitches, separated by long silences, are repeated and reoriented, creating a static universe without forward motion. For example, Wolff's remarkable *Serenade* (1950) is a mobile employing only two open fifths to produce a plaintive, elegant sensation of eternal time, very modern and very ancient.

From 1957 to 1964, Wolff created pieces in which performers freely choose from graphic notations ("outlines"). Employing a game-like "cueing" technique, they respond to each other: "...precise actions under...indeterminate conditions" (Wolff, *On Form*). These interdependent actions give a lively social aspect to Wolff's work, like a small temporarily closed society. For example, the *Duo for Violinist and Pianist* (1961) is a "duo" between time continuity arising from cues and fine measurements of duration. In Wolff's *For 1, 2 or 3 People and a Conductor* (1964) for any instruments, "the players constantly have options of what to play...It's as though you take a walk with a friend or friends, going by whatever way you like, agreeing on the way...or getting lost or going nowhere in particular...the landscape in which they walk is what is given."

From 1965 to 1973, Wolff opened up the scores even more, engaging performers in "parliamentary participation," eliminating the conductor's "monarchical authority": e.g., *Electric Spring* series (1966–70), *Burdocks* for one or more orchestras (1970–71), and *Edges* (1969) for any number of players, with 25 signs that stand for musical and extramusical characteristics. *Snowdrop* (1970), notated in unbarred staves, is composed of gently ascending scales with charming, droll pauses.

Beginning in the 1970s, Wolff created works with overt political content: e.g., *Changing the System* (1972–73); *String Bass Exercise out of 'Bandiera rossa'* (1975); *Piano Song (I Am a Dangerous Woman)* (1983) with Joan Cavanagh's brilliant anti-war poem; *I Like to Think of Harriet Tubman* (1984); *Piano Trio (Greenham—Seneca—Camiso)* (1985) named after three women's peace encampments; *Malvina* (1989), a tribute to singer/songwriter Malvina Reynolds who championed the causes of oppressed people; the *Eisler Ensemble Pieces* (1983) used material from Cornelius Cardew's *Revolution is the Main Trend in the World Today* and the Appalachian tune "Dig a Hole in a Meadow" about a local woman killed in a shooting match between moonshiners and government agents. Wolff said this work "expresses cheerful defiance and resilience in the face of an oppressive authority."

Works from the 1990s include *Stardust Pieces* written for Wolff's third child whose middle name is Starbuck, its movements like a friendly family conversation; *Ruth* (1991), evocative of innovative composer Ruth Crawford Seeger, is written in standard notation with microtonal intervals, striking (drumming on) the body of the instruments, whistling, freedom of timbres, little jazzy breaks, etc.; *Peggy* (1993) for folksinger Peggy Seeger is built on fragments from familiar folk songs. —*"Blue Gene" Tyranny*

Recommended:

- ○ **Bread and Roses: Piano Works, 1976–1983** / Pinkas / 1995 / Mode 43
- ○ **Wolff, Vol. 2: Chamber Works** / Fulkerson (cond.), Anderson, Denyer / 1998 / Mode 69
- ○ **Wolff: Exercises** / Schleiermacher, Blum, Williams, Dahinden / 1995 / Hat Hut 6167
- ○ **Wolff: Look She Said (Complete Works for Bass)** / Black, Lorentz, Josephson / 2002 / Mode 109
- ○ **Wolff: Tilbury; Snowdrop** / Kleeb, Dahinden, Polisoidis / 1999 / Mode 74
- ○ **Wolff: Complete Music for Violin & Piano** / Clarke, Sabat / 2003 / Mode 126
- ○ **Wolff: Early Piano Music (1951–1961)** / Tilbury, Wolff, Prevost / 2002 / Matchless Recordings 51
- ○ **Wolff: (Re:) Making Music - Works 1962–1999** / Fulkerson (cond.), Barton Workshop / 2004 / Mode 133

Hugh Wolff

b. Oct. 21, 1953, Paris, France

Conductor

Hugh Wolff, one of the few American conductors to enjoy a truly international reputation, has become especially renowned for his advocacy of contemporary music. Wolff, born in Paris to American parents, received a thorough musical training; he pursued formal studies in piano, composition, and conducting, earning degrees from Harvard University and the Peabody Institute. He also had the opportunity to study composition with Olivier Messiaen and conducting with Charles Bruch in Paris.

Wolff's conducting career began in 1979, when he was appointed Exxon/Arts Endowment Conductor of the National Symphony Orchestra; he served as associate conductor of that ensemble, then led by Mstislav Rostropovich, from 1982 to 1985. During that period he also served as music director of the Northeastern Pennsylvania Philharmonic (1981–86), his first such appointment. In 1985 became music director of the New Jersey Symphony Orchestra, a post he retained until 1992. From the 1980s to the present he has also appeared frequently as a guest conductor throughout the United States and Europe, including appearances with the Czech Philharmonic, the Royal Stockholm Philharmonic, the London Philharmonic, the English Chamber Orchestra, and the Israel Philharmonic.

Wolff came into new prominence through his association with the St. Paul Chamber Orchestra, which he led as principal conductor (1988–91) and music director (1991–2000). During his tenure there, he recorded over 20 compact discs—more than those of any other conductor of the SPCO—of repertoire ranging from Vivaldi to Dvořák to Ravel to new works by young composers like Edgar Meyer. He also led the ensemble on a well-received European tour.

Since 1997 Wolff has served as chief conductor of the Radio Orchestra of Frankfurt. In 2001, his recordings of Antheil's *Symphonies Nos. 1 & 6* and of Barber's and Meyer's violin concertos, with Hilary Hahn, won Cannes Classical awards. —*Joseph Stevenson*

Recommended:

- ○ **Haydn: Symphonies 82 & 84** / Wolff (cond.), St. Paul CO / 2002 / Apex 48746
- ○ **Antheil: Symphonies 4 & 5** / Wolff (cond.), Frankfurt RSO / CPO 999706

Stefan Wolpe

b. Aug. 25, 1902, Berlin, Germany, **d.** Apr. 4, 1972, New York, NY

Composer: Chamber Music

Stefan Wolpe was a composer notable for providing a fresh perspective on atonality. Despite excursions into popular, folk and jazz idioms, Wolpe continued to compose in atonal styles throughout his career. His works are often characterized by cross-cutting and discontinuity between different musical gestures and textures, quite possibly an influence he gathered from Dadaism. Wolpe was an influential teacher in the United States, where his pupils included Morton Feldman, Ralph Shapey and Charles Wuorinen.

Wolpe spent the early part of his life in Berlin, a stimulating artistic milieu in the 1920s and 1930s. He associated there with the Bauhaus, studied composition with the expressionist composer Schreker, and became a devotee of Busoni. He supported himself as a jazz pianist in cabaret and cinemas.

Wolpe's early compositions use the 12-tone techniques of Schoenberg and the Second Viennese School. From the outset he favored irregular rhythms and contrapuntal textures, and his music is notable for avoiding the isolated points of sound (pointillism) which was common to Schoenberg and his followers. He was also influenced by jazz and popular dance music in such pieces as *Tango* (1927), and his socialist convictions led him to reflect on the function of music in society. At this time he believed that music should be socially useful; he wrote worker's songs and pieces that satirized society. He also simplified his dense, atonal writing, making it more accessible to people without musical training.

When the Nazis rose to power in Germany, Wolpe fled from the country, traveling through Russia and Rumania before landing in Vienna in 1933–1934, and studied there with Webern. From Vienna he moved to Palestine, where he became interested in his Jewish musical heritage. He absorbed traits of the local music, which found their way into such works as *Songs From the Hebrew* (1938) for soprano and piano, and the ballet suite *Man From Midian* (1942). He also wrote songs and choruses for the Kibbutz movement, several of which have become folk songs in Israel.

In 1938 Wolpe moved to New York, where his mature style crystallized. Important works from this period are *Enactments* (1950–53) for three pianos, *Battle Piece* (1947) for solo piano, and the notorious Symphony (1956). Wolpe's association with influential artists and musicians continued in America, where he had connections with New York jazz musicians and Abstract Expressionist painters. From 1952–1956 he taught at Black Mountain College with John Cage, David Tudor and Lou Harrison. In the 1950s and early 1960s he regularly lectured at the Darmstadt Summer School. He contracted Parkinson's Disease in 1964, which proved fatal. —*Rachel Campbell*

Overview of Works (1920–1971)

Stefan Wolpe was one of the first composers who saw a need for building a bridge between the modern artist and the increasingly alienated audience. Socialism of all varieties was repelled by both the formalism of serial and atonal music, as well as the "depravity" of jazz and popular idioms, two idioms that, on the surface, would seem irreconcilable. Ironically, some ethical reconciliation was needed; one need but recall Schoenberg's observation that "it's not for everybody if it's art" to understand the tapping of jazz and popular idioms by Wolpe in order to reach a wider audience and be in step with the ethic of utopian socialism espoused by the Bauhaus movement, the ideals of which were anathema to a particular then-ascendant party in Germany. These sundry elements may all be found at play in Wolpe's mature works. Already a noted virtuoso pianist at 18, Wolpe took to the aesthetics of the Second Viennese school, particularly the serial or 12-tone field. Although he would largely destroy most of his early work, the combined influence of the sharp, crisp tone of his preferred instrument, as well as the importance of the isolated individual note, would lead to the texture that was to predominate his work throughout his short life. The austerity of this was leavened by his involvement with the Bauhaus movement and attraction to current popular dance music. The result, in 1928, was his satirical opera *Zeus und Elida* (libretto by Wickerhauser and Hahn), which drew a bead on the then emerging Adolf Hitler. This led to Wolpe's position as music director with the experimental theater Die Truppe, the 1933 banning of which by the now-entrenched Nazi party forced the composer to flee to Vienna. This setback was assuaged by a brief period of study with Anton Webern and a reinvestigation and rethinking of the 12-tone technique. Predominant among the results were the *Two Studies for Orchestra*, which utilizes tone rows based upon thirds and augmented fourths, revealing Wolpe's inclination to tonality. Shortly after this watershed period, Wolpe would be forced to flee again, this time to Palestine to accept a teaching position. Here, he was drawn to Jewish and Arabic music and their distinctive scales, further diversifying the composer's makeup. In 1938, Wolpe came to the United States, where he held teaching posts until the end of his life. His musical vision then became focused and nourished by many sources as he produced his ballet scores *Zemach* and *Man From Midian*, *Enactments* for three pianos, a 1956 symphony, and *Broken Sequences*. In his mature style, Wolpe was able to fuse the modern Viennese, jazz, popular, and Middle Eastern influences into an organic whole, the flavor of the fusion coloring his output. *—Wayne Reisig*

Recommended:

- ○ **Wolpe: Compositions for Piano (1920–1952)** / Holzman / 2002 / Bridge 9116
- ○ **Wolpe: Piano Music** / Madge / CPO 999055
- ○ **Wolpe: Piece in 3 Parts; Suite im Hexachord for oboe & clarinet; etc.** / Purvis (cond.), Knussen (cond.), Speculum Musicae, Chamber Music Society of Lincoln Center / 1993 / Bridge 9043
- ○ **Wolpe: Wild Roses** / Berendsen, Bloch / 1997 / Symposium 1216

CHAMBER MUSIC

String Quartet (1968–1969)

Serialist in orientation, the *String Quartet* of 1969 in two movements features Wolpe's trademark outbursts of energy separated by silences, and interludes of rich contrapuntal melodies. In the approximately eight-minute first movement, there is much imitative crosstalk between the strings—sweeping and scooping gestures and glissandi, emphatically marked statements, and nervous trilling and tremolo, all of which have a dialogue-like quality. The close interweaving of contrapuntal lines often creates tense tone clusters. The second movement, approximately nine and a half minutes long, opens with a steady emphatic row that maintains the tensions from the first movement. The row soon breaks apart into quickly rushing gestures that have only very brief resting points of a second or so. Some fleeting, beautifully composed passages containing harmonics and pizzicati seem to squeeze out harmonic sounds like a bubble bursting on top of flowing water. Swelling tone clusters underscore flying solos. Toward the end, the music seems to briefly settle into a series of contemplative movements surrounded by silences, and then to evolve into a grotesque dance. A single sustained note ends the work.

Wolpe was, throughout the 1960s, determined to continue work in spite of the developing effects of Parkinson's disease. Still, by late in the decade, his manual skills had deteriorated to a point that extended, multi-instrument works were very nearly beyond his scope. So the *String Quartet*—his only work in the genre—seems a truly mighty achievement, even if it has only two movements and lasts under 20 minutes; the effort could not have been a painless one for either mind or body. *—AMG*

Recommended:

- ○ **American String Quartets, 1950–1970** / Concord SQ / 1995 / VoxBox 5143

Fritz Wunderlich

b. Sep. 26, 1930, Kusel, Germany, **d.** Sep. 17, 1966, Heidelberg, Germany

Tenor

Fritz Wunderlich could be considered the James Dean of the singing world—a young, charismatic performer who suffered a tragic death at the height of his career and abilities, and whose posthumous reputation has grown beyond that which he was able to enjoy during his short life. Considered among the finest Mozartean tenors of his day, Wunderlich embraced a wide repertory that expanded to included the works of Strauss, Schubert, Bach, and Mahler, and he left behind many excellent recordings that have been the primary source of his legacy.

Wunderlich (Friedrich Karl Otto) was born in Kusel, Rheinland-Pfalz, Germany. His life included music from the very beginning, since his father was the director of a local choir and his mother was a violinist. The young tenor gained mild local celebrity for his singing in Kusel, and in 1950 he departed for the Freiburg Musikhochschule with partial financing from the town; he met the remainder of his study-related expenses by directing a small dance band in Breisgau. Wunderlich's first operatic appearance was, appropriately enough, as Tamino in a student production of Mozart's *Die Zauberflöte*—a role with which he would remain associated for the rest of his career. In fact, he made his professional debut with the very same piece just a year later (1955) at the Stuttgart Opera. He remained with Stuttgart until he was hired by the Frankfurt Opera company, staying there from 1958 to 1960. He first appeared in the *Salzburg Festival* in 1959, where he sang the part of Henry in Richard Strauss's *Die schweigsame Frau*. He became a member of the Munich Opera in 1960 and from 1962 also was a regular at the Vienna State Opera.

Wunderlich quickly earned a reputation as the leading lyric tenor in Germany. His clear, strong voice easily filled an operatic hall, but he always retained a purity of sound and line that was equally well suited to more intimate settings. In international appearances he essayed mostly Mozart roles, for which he was especially celebrated and which did not tax the dramatic limits of his voice; however in the smaller houses of his native Germany he explored slightly more adventurous repertory, including Alfredo in *La Traviata* and Lensky in *Eugene Onegin*. All of his performances were marked by an unflappable lyricism and an associated control of phrasing and breath—both of which have remained his most lauded qualities. Wunderlich created the role of Tiresias in the first performance of Carl Orff's *Oedipus der Tyrann* in Stuttgart in 1959, and sang the part of Christoph in Werner Egk's *Die Verlobung in San Domingo* in Munich in 1962. He contemplated expanding further, into the lyrical Wagnerian roles. This was not to be, as he died in an accidental fall at a friend's home. *—AMG*

Recommended:

- ○ **Very Best of Fritz Wunderlich** / Wunderlich, etc. / 2003 / EMI 75915
- ○ **Schumann, Schubert & Beethoven** / Wunderlich, Giesen (piano) / DG 449747
- ○ **Léhar: Das Land des Lächelns** / Marszalek (cons.). Wunderlich, Fahberg, Cologne Radio Orch. / Gala 329
- ○ **Mozart: Die Zauberflöte** / Keilberth (cond.), Wunderlich, Frick, Koth, Berry, Vienna PO / Golden Melodram 50044

Charles Wuorinen

b. Jun. 9, 1938, New York, NY

Composer

With over 200 compositions to his credit, Charles Wuorinen is one of the most prolific contemporary American composers. Born in 1938, he studied at Columbia University, where he worked with Otto Luening, Vladimir Ussachevsky, and Jack Beeson. A major presence in American music for over four decades, Wuorienen has taught at numerous schools, including Columbia, Princeton, the New England Conservatory, the Manhattan School of Music, Yale, and SUNY Buffalo. He has been on the faculty of Rutgers University since 1984. He has won numerous awards, such as the Lili Boulanger Memorial Award, the 1970 Pulitzer Prize (for Time's Encomium), and a McArthur Fellowship, to name a few.

Wuorinen's music is uniquely serial, and primarily 12-tone in nature. His major influences are the modernist European school, namely Schoenberg, though the influence of late Stravinsky and Babbitt are also unmistakable. Much of his music requires extreme virtuosity on the part of the performer, such as his Chamber Concertos, which typically include wide leaps, extreme dynamic contrasts, and a rapid exchange of pitches. Fractal geometry and the mathematical theories of Benoit Mandelbrot have influenced works such as *Bamboula Squared* and the *Natural Fantasy* for organ.

However, Wuorinen's later music begins to demonstrate tonal relationships, though to a limited degree, such as pitch-centered openings and conclusions, octave doublings, and timbral transpositions of thematic ideas. His music also evolved to include clear rhythmic relationships—his earlier works avoided this characteristic—and his melodies also became more conjunct in nature.

Wuorinen's music continues to evolve, with later works such as the Rhapsody for Violin and Orchestra and New York Notes containing further rhythmic clarity, more recognizable melodic structures and clearer orchestration. Clearly this is not the style of the same composer as was found in his earlier works. His most recent works include Symphony Seven, a Piano Quintet for Ursula Oppens, and a Percussion Quartet.

Wuorinen is also the author of *Simple Composition* a useful text for composers who are beginning to use 12-tone techniques. Wuorinen has also been active as a pianist and has conducted his own works, as well as those of other contemporary composers, with many of major orchestras in the United States. In 1962, Wuorinen co-founded The Group for Contemporary Music, an ensemble dedicated to the performance of new chamber music. With his already impressive resume, extremely prolific output, and evolving but unique style, it is sure that Charles Wuorinen will be remembered for his numerous contributions to music, serialism and beyond. *—Michael Blostein*

Overview of Works

Charles Wuorinen has produced a large body of compositions, slightly over 200 by 2002. Most of the early works were written in a modernist expressive language, but those coming after the mid-1970s typically divulge greater melodic content.

Wuorinen's music is rarely revolutionary, generally well-constructed and imaginatively conceived, and fairly approachable, especially in relation to post-Webern serial music and other modern styles. Wuorinen began composing in his childhood, but his earliest surviving effort is an arrangement of two lute songs by Thomas Campion for male voices, dating to 1956. Other works soon appeared, but his most significant early compositions came in the early 1960s, mainly in the chamber music genre. His 1964 *Chamber Concerto for Flute and Ten Players*, one of his earliest masterpieces, has the soloist deftly bringing order to the work amid initial recalcitrance from the accompanying players. There are two other chamber concertos from this period, the *Chamber Concerto for Cello and Ten Players* (1963) and the *Chamber Concerto for Oboe and Ten Players* (1965). Perhaps his most important work from the 1960s was *Time's Encomium* (1968–69), a striking electronic composition that was awarded the Pulitzer Prize in 1970. The opening may now sound dated and the sonorities quaint in general, but in this purely electronic work Wuorinen ingeniously allows for interpretation of prepared materials during performance. But it was not just works in the chamber arena from his early years that achieved success, as the 1966 *Piano Concerto* attests. Still, its scoring is chamber-like and the piano writing finely imagined and not plagued by ineffective bouts of virtuosity. *Speculum speculi* (1972), for six players, is another successful chamber work. Here, Wuorinen explores pitch centers and partially rehabilitates tonality in his music, as he also does in the *Concerto for Amplified Violin and Orchestra* (written for Paul Zukofsky) from the same year. Wuorinen has admired the works of Stravinsky and in 1974, when Stravinsky's widow offered him the opportunity to use materials her husband had planned for a composition, he seized it and produced *A Reliquary for Igor Stravinsky* (1975). Wuorinen's *Two Part Symphony* (1978) divulges traces of Stravinsky; the composer halfheartedly suggested the work should have been entitled "Symphony in C." Wuorinen's other symphonies—if they can be called that—are also interesting works. They include the 1976 *Percussion Symphony*, for 24 players; *Microsymphony* (1992); and *Symphony Seven* (1997). There is also another composition called *Ecclesiastical Symphonies* (1981), consisting of the four purely orchestral movements from his 1980 oratorio for chorus and orchestra, *The Celestial Sphere*, one of his largest works. Another choral work of significance is *Genesis* (1989), composed on a joint commission from the San Francisco Symphony and Minnesota Orchestra. In 2001, Wuorinen finished his opera *Haroun and the Sea of Stories*, based on the 1990 children's novel of the same title by Salman Rushdie. *—Robert Cummings*

Recommended:

- ○ **Wuorinen: A Winter's Tale; Horn Trio; Horn Trio Continued; etc.** / Schmidt (cond.), Bryn-Julson, Karlin, Blankenburg, Atkinson, Edmondson, Ginstling, Gottschewski, Sims / 2000 / Cambria 8802
- ○ **Wuorinen: Lepton** / Wuorinen (cond.), Sherry, Schulte, Gekker, Palmer, Kennedy, Gould, Winn, Avery, Fedele, Milarsky, Kiebler, Tarrete / 2002 / Tzadik 7077
- ○ **Wuorinen: Works For Violin & Piano, 1969–1983** / Ohlsson, Hudson, Speculum Musicae / 1988 / Bridge 9008
- ○ **Wuorinen: Chamber Works** / Ohlsson, Group for Contemporary Music / 1990 / New World 80385
- ○ **Wuorinen: Concerto for amplified violin; Archangel; Arch'opteryx** / Wuorinen (cond.), Sherry, Taylor, Orch. of St. Luke's / Koch 7110
- ○ **Wuorinen: Horn Trio; Horn Trio Continued; Double Solo; Trombone Trio** / Koch 7123
- ○ **The Haroun Songbook** / Bush, Chioldi, Golden, Farnum, Schaffner / 2004 / Albany 664

X

Iannis Xenakis

b. May 29, 1922, Braila, Rumania, **d.** Feb. 4, 2001, Paris, France

Composer: Chamber Music, Orchestral, Avant-garde, Keyboard

Iannis Xenakis was a French composer of Greek heritage and Romanian birth, known for his revolutionary ideas regarding the systematic, mathematical organization of music and its structural parallels with architecture, and for his pioneering work in electronic music. Xenakis' initial exposure to music came in the first ten years of his life, when he was surrounded by the folk music of the Romanian countryside and the liturgy of the Byzantine Orthodox Church. In 1942, when his family moved to Greece, he was exposed to the music of Beethoven and Brahms for the first time.

His life grew turbulent when he entered Athens Polytechnic with the intent of becoming an engineer. When Greece was invaded during the World War II, Xenakis became passionately involved with resistance and liberation groups, first protesting against Nazi rule and, later, opposing the British, who, in 1944, drove out the Germans but sided with right-wing politicians against the Greek National Liberation Front. Xenakis was seriously wounded, his face disfigured, when he was hit by a British shell; he also lost vision in one eye. As a member of the resistance, he was eventually arrested and sentenced to death. He escaped in 1947, hoping to reach the United States. He ended up settling in Paris, however, and taking French nationality. In Paris, Xenakis made numerous important contacts, befriending Messiaen, Honegger, Mihaud, and the celebrated architect Le Corbusier, who were all impressed by his innovative and brilliantly intellectual approach to music. Working with Le Corbusier, Xenakis was highly involved with civil planning and architecture, designing some landmark sites throughout the world. For him, architecture was musical, and music was architectural. He frequently used one to inspire the other, basing pieces on computer programs and complex mathematical equations. This approach resulted in highly theoretical, systematic music characterized by intricately calculated rhythms, dense and often explosive textural fields, extended timbral effects, and "clouds" of sound that contain countless "particles." Some of his most important works include the orchestral *Metastaseis* (1954), *Pithoprakta* (1956), *Nomos Alpha* for solo cello, and groundbreaking electronic works such as *Bohor I*, and *Concert P-H*. Xenakis was the founder of the EMAMu in Paris and its American counterpart, the Center for Musical Mathematics and Automation in Bloomington, Indiana. *—Graham Olson*

CHAMBER MUSIC

Eonta, for 2 trumpets, 3 trombones & piano (1963)

Xenakis' first solo piece, *Herma* (1961), for piano, combines sets of pitches with a statistical rhythmic distribution. In 1962, the composer developed a computer program that generated musical sequences based on probability functions. After producing a family of computer-generated pieces, Xenakis moved on to developing richer sets of relationships among musical elements. *Eonta* (1963) represents a crucial step in that direction.

By the early 1960s Xenakis had, in spite of being outside the Parisian musical establishment, developed an impressive international reputation. Cognizant of his talents, Pierre Boulez, who directed the elite Domaine Musicale, commissioned from Xenakis a work for piano, two trumpets, and three trombones. Xenakis had at this time written little for instruments other than strings and piano, so *Eonta* posed an interesting challenge. When presented with the score, Boulez deemed it unplayable and took the step of doubling the brass parts. (To Xenakis' credit, *Eonta* has been played countless times in its original form.) The piano part was written for the extraordinary Yuji Takahashi, who had had commissioned *Herma*. Indeed, the two works are quite similar, proceeding by means of shifting densities, dynamics, registers, and pitch collections.

Eonta opens with a long piano solo, statistical in origin and athletic in character, that races and jumps all over the keyboard. The brass are treated much differently, entering with a long crescendo on a single chord, which moves to a second chord then a third, expanding outward in register and creating a sense of harmonic identity. Xenakis develops dynamics and articulations, and even includes directions regarding the players' placement and movement. (This last aspect would become increasingly important in the composer's music.) Throughout the introduction of the brass, the piano continues its frenetic activity, until its music is suddenly cut off, leaving only the resonance to blend with the brass, the first point of real conjunction in the work.

Having assumed the fore, the brass carry on with new material. After the previous registral expansion, they converge on a narrow span, introducing microtonal alterations which provide a strong contrast to the piano's fixed pitches. The brass extend their range again, interrupted by another conjunction, a series of tutti two-chord rhythmic gestures that stand out as a focal point. A succession of textures follow, including a long passage in which the piano is mostly silent and the brass imitate the piano's figurations. A passage of polyphonic scalar contours expands then fractures, finally landing on a five-note diatonic chord. *Eonta* finishes with the brass sounding a repeated two-note chord (trumpets high, trombones low) that drops a half step to finish. *—Jim Harley*

Recommended:

- ○ **Xenakis: Ensemble Music 1** / Bornstein (cond.), ST-X Ensemble / 1996 / Mode 53

Pléïades, for 6 percussionists (1978)

Xenakis' reputation as one of the twentieth century's foremost composers of hard-driving music for percussion is no doubt a result of his long association with the outstanding six-member Percussions de Strasbourg. *Pléïades* (1978) is one of three works (including *Persephassa* (1969) and *Idmen B* (1985)) that Xenakis wrote expressly for this ensemble.

Named after the constellation of the daughter of Atlas, *Pléïades* is indeed a work of cosmic proportions. Written in four movements of some 45 minutes' total duration, it is Xenakis' most ambitious instrumental work aside from the full-length ballet *Kraanerg*. Three of the four movements utilize an instrumentation derived from a single family of instruments—mallet ("keyboard"), skin, or metallic instruments—while the fourth is a combination of the other three. This work is fiercely difficult for the performers, presenting densely layered polyrhythms and intricate patterns and requiring enormous strength and concentration. For the listener, the music is an exotic dance full of powerful rhythms and evocative sonorities; the movement for mallet instruments, for example, makes use of a pitch formation that resembles the pelog scale of the Javanese gamelan. Xenakis adds his own twist by reconfiguring the scale so that it does not repeat at the octave. In this way, different melodic patterns and harmonic tensions are generated in each register.

The composer makes much of the timbral distinction between the wooden instruments (marimba and xylophone) and the metallic vibraphones, posing the groups against one another. In the movement for metallic instruments, Xenakis calls for an instrument constructed specifically for this piece. The sixxen is configured like a keyboard, but is fashioned from metallic bars that are less pure in tone than those of the vibraphone. Heard in a live setting, they are piercingly loud; on recordings, they sound like a gamelan, their "exotic" tuning adding much in the way of color.

Xenakis proposes two orders for the presentation of the four movements: One begins with the "mélange" movement, while the other ends with it. Both options are plausible, since this movement is comprised of the materials used elsewhere in the piece, and it can therefore aptly serve as either introduction or summation. In either case, *Pléïades* is a true tour de force. The performance challenges it poses has granted it the status of a benchmark work which readily measures the skill of percussion ensembles.*—James Harley*

Recommended:

- ○ **Xenakis: Pléiades; Psappha** / Kroumata Percussion Ens. / 1981 / Bis 482
- ○ **Xénakis: Pléïdes** / Strasbourg Percussionists / HM 905185

Waarg, for 13 musicians (1988)

Xenakis enjoyed a long and fruitful relationship with the London Sinfonietta. He composed *Phlegra* for the ensemble in 1975, and completed his fourth commission for them in 1997 with *O-Mega*. *Waarg* (1988) was a follow-up to the highly successful *Thalleïn*, premiered in 1985. While the earlier piece is characterized by a particular brilliance, *Waarg* is dense and rather sombre; the title itself means "work," perhaps an indication of its serious tone. While certainly challenging from a technical standpoint, *Waarg* is more orchestral than chamberlike, indicating an aesthetic shift in the years following *Thalleïn*.

Waarg's opening features the winds in a sustained expansion from a single pitch to a chord. The emphasis on tone color is striking as the central note is passed from one instrument to another. The focus thereafter is on harmonic color, though instrumental timbre continues to play a role as Xenakis often treats the woodwind, brass, and string instruments as distinct entities. Xenakis sculpts and orchestrates the sonorities with great subtlety, fleshing out melodic passages with the addition of close-voiced parallel harmonies or clusters. The tempo is generally quite slow, but ostinato figures, often comprised of just two notes, provide rhythmic propulsion.

Waarg takes shape in a quite fluid manner, various strands of material flowing over, under, and into one other. Gradually, the activity accumulates, with more and more frequent intrusions of faster elements. At *Waarg*'s high point, there is an extraordinary passage in which each instrument pursues its own intricate path, creating a brisk contrapuntal texture of great density. A slow and chorale-like—though fitful—section for woodwinds and strings brings the work to a close. *—James Harley*

Recommended:

○ **Xenakis: Eonta; Échange; Waarg; Palimpsest** / ASKO Ensemble / 1990 / Attaca 9054

ORCHESTRAL

Metastaseis, for 60 musicians (Anastenaria, Part 3) (1953–1954)

Metastaseis is widely considered Iannis Xenakis' first mature work. It is also one of just a few pieces, like Beethoven's *Symphony No. 9* and Stravinsky's *Le Sacre du Printemps*, that irrevocably changed history. *Metastaseis* treats the orchestra as if it were material for architectural construction. (Xenakis was working at the time for famed architect, Le Corbusier.) The textures, featuring the orchestral strings, are shaped according to global concerns and proportions rather than motivic development or contrapuntal combinations. Never before had the sliding sounds of the glissando been treated as a primary element; never before had each player been required to play an independent part, the 46 glissandi interlocking to create textures of incredible intensity and dynamism. For the audience at its first performance at the 1955 Donaueschingen Festival in Germany, it was as if this composer had arrived from another planet (to paraphrase one critic); the cheering and booing carried on far longer than the piece itself.

The opening of *Metastaseis* has come to seem archetypal. The full complement of strings enter in succession, sustaining a single note. Gradually, individuals pull away, sliding slowly toward new notes. The listener, whose ear has been drawn into the rich inner energy of this opening unison, finds the sound expanding in continuous fashion, with no points of stability along the way for orientation. Eventually, the texture fills out the full range of the strings, arriving on a massive cluster of 46 notes. This sonority, also never heard before in the history of music, carries on, being articulated by changes of dynamics and mode of playing, the durations governed by the Fibonacci series (1, 2, 3, 5, 8, 13, etc.), which, coincidentally, is closely related to Le Corbusier's modular proportions.

The second section is more "traditional." Most of the orchestra drops away, leaving a group of strings playing an angular, contrapuntal passage that is strongly reminiscent of Webern and his serialist successors. In a sense, this section makes explicit how far removed the rest of the score is from the concerns of other composers. This section is followed by a third, in which the global glissando texture of the opening is fragmented, creating a succession of short gestures, usually fanning out from a single pitch. The winds and percussion have a more prominent role here, too, though always subjugated to the strings. *Metastaseis* closes with a shortened version of the opening, reversed so that the strings, beginning on a large cluster, gradually close in on a single mid-register unison. At the end, it's apparent that Xenakis has taken us on an incredible journey, voyaging through sonorities strange and new, bursting with energy but carefully organized. *—Jim Harley*

Recommended:

○ **Donaueschinger Musiktage 40 Jahre 1945–1995** / Holliger, Pears, Dietrich / Col Legno 31800

Pithoprakta, for 49 musicians (1955–1956)

After his riotous debut as a composer the previous year, Xenakis followed the novelty of massed string glissandi in *Metastaseis* with an even more iconoclastic work. *Pithoprakta*, Greek for "actions through probability," treats the orchestra in a completely new way. One inspiration was the movement of molecules, and as the music opens with individual string players tapping out irregular rhythms on the body of their instruments, the knocking sounds bounce unpredictably around the orchestra in illustration of the model. The whole piece, in fact, contains nothing but successions of similarly complex textures, ranging from the percussive opening to clouds of plucked notes, teeming masses of short glissandi, or sliding sounds, sparking effusions of staccato notes, and seemingly countless combinations of these.

As with *Metastaseis*, the large, subdivided string section receives most of the composer's attention. Xenakis colors the strings with sparing touches of percussion and trombones. *Pithoprakta* was completed in 1956 and premiered in Munich in 1957. It is important to realize that while many composers embraced a "sonoristic" approach to the orchestra soon thereafter (such as Ligeti and Penderecki), this piece, along with *Metastaseis*, came first. The compositional finesse by which the textures are deployed and varied is masterful. Xenakis unrolled a full arsenal of mathematical procedures based primarily on statistics and probability theory, in order to create and control the thousands and thousands of individual notes and attacks that he produced to achieve the massive textures upon which the piece is built. The music is continually evolving, and exists on several levels simultaneously. These include the density of events, ambits, register, sonority, speed of events, and overall dynamic levels. The fluidity of form is remarkable, and the intensity of energy is extremely captivating. *Pithoprakta* is written for an orchestral ensemble of strings, trombones, and woodblock; this is bold music of an originality and force rarely experienced. *—James Harley*

Recommended:

○ **Xenakis: Metastaseis; Pithoprakta; Eonta** / Le Roux (cond.), ORTF / 2001 / Le Chant du Monde 278368

AVANT-GARDE

Bohor, for electro-acoustic sounds (1962)

Iannis Xenakis, who had been working as an engineering and architectural assistant to the famed Le Corbusier from 1947, was drawn to the electronic music studio, and its capacity for scientific experimentation. He began working at the *Groupe de Recherches Musicales* (GRM) studio in Paris in 1955, and continued to produce tape works there until 1962. Studio founder Pierre Schaeffer had developed an approach to the discipline of electroacoustic music based on the classification and recombination of recorded sounds recognizably taken from the real world. He termed this approach "musique concrète," and it remains an important facet of the new compositional genre of pre-recorded or synthesized sounds. Xenakis, on the other hand, was primarily interested in studying the phenomenon of density, and the creation of noisy textures that were often quite nebulous in terms of semantic identity. *Bohor*, produced and premiered in 1962, was his most extreme work in this vein, and it marked the end of his association with the GRM studio (Pierre Schaeffer is reported to have hated it!).

At over 20 minutes in length, *Bohor* is a substantial piece, and would have been all the more impressive in its original eight-channel form. It is a radical study in formal construction, shaped from an absolutely continuous texture—always loud, always noisy, and always unsettling. The shifts of density and introduction of new layers of sonority as the piece goes along keep the listener's interest, but the music is primarily concerned with maintaining a maximum level of energy and sustaining it for the duration of the piece. The intensity only increases, amazingly, right until the end, when the sound seems to be torn away, leaving a silence of released tension and ringing ears (Xenakis has always preferred to present his electroacoustic music at extremely high dynamic levels). Relentless intensity will soon cause the listener to tire and tune out (or run out of the room!), so one can only admire the subtle variation of texture and density Xenakis deploys in order to balance the violent energy of the noisy sonorities. This combination of expressive directness and formal integrity is a hall-mark of this composer's distinctive style. His later electroacoustic works, like *Persepolis* and *Le Légende d'Eer*, are even more ambitious. *—James Harley*

Recommended:

○ **Xenakis: Electronic Music** / / 1997 / Electronic Music Foundation 3

Diamorphoses, for 2-track tape & at least 4 loudspeakers (1957)

The studio at Radio France dedicated to the creation of new sounds was launched in 1948 by electroacoustic pioneer Pierre Schaeffer. Iannis Xenakis was quickly fascinated by the expanded possibilities of musique concrète, and by 1955 had begun working there, as part of what became known as the *Groupe de Recherches Musicales* (GRM). Between 1957 and 1962, he completed a number of pieces, the first being *Diamorphoses*. The sound-world Xenakis designed for this work combines the violent noises of jet engines, trains, and an earthquake with high bell-like sounds. The contrasting character of these sonic layers interacts with shifting densities and successions of events to produce a complex, yet balanced form. The equilibrium of high, sharply defined sounds and low, continuous ones is made manifest in the overall architecture; the outer passages are dominated by the roaring, sustained sounds framing a central section of more discontinuous, shifting textures of bells and many other sonorities. Xenakis has never been considered one of the major figures associated with GRM, but *Diamorphoses* remains an influential piece of musique concrète from the first decade of this new genre. *—James Harley*

Recommended:

○ **Xenakis: Electronic Music** / / 1997 / Electronic Music Foundation 3

ST/4, for string quartet (1956–1962)

In the works of Iannis Xenakis, terms like "form" and "structure" are not merely metaphors for comparing a time-based art (music) to a material-based one (sculpture, architecture, etc.). Trained as an architect as well as a composer, Xenakis thought of "structure" in literal terms and many of his works are devised to manifest a mathematical idea rather than convey a mood (although, as he might argue, numbers made audible have their own potential for a special kind of expressivity). Reaching his maturity as a composer during the 1950s, Xenakis rejected both the imperceptibility of the processes at work in the serialist music of composers like Pierre Boulez and Milton Babbitt and the arbitrariness of John Cage's emerging aleatoricism. In his works from this period, Xenakis developed a number of methods for realizing numeric principles through musical forms. These principles can be seen at work in the piece under consideration here, *ST/4*, composed between 1955 and 1962. Scored for string quartet, *ST/4* is one of a number of pieces in Xenakis' "ST" series. The title given here is actually an abbreviation of the piece's full name: *ST/4-1, 080262.* The ST in the title stands for "stochastic," the term used to describe the probability formulas that generate the tone, timbre, and timing of each musical event. The subsequent numeral 4 indicates the number of performers involved and the numeral 1 indicates that this is the first piece to use a particular generative method. The string of numbers that follow give the date of the piece's completion (February 8, 1962). Other pieces in the "ST" series include *ST/10* and *ST/48*, also from 1962, as well as a handful of pieces that apply similar stochastic principles but forego the unwieldy utilitarian titles (such as *Morsima-Amorsima* from the same year).

By the time Xenakis began composing *ST/4*, his generative formulas for creating structures had become complex enough and computers readily available enough that he delegated to a computer the generation of the specific note-to-note events within the larger stochastic structures delineated by his calculations. The composer thus identified the parameters within which probability calculations would be made for various musical aspects: instrumentation, pitch, note duration, timbre, attack, and others (And Xenakis was sure to make a wide variety of possibilities available, such as percussive sounds on the body of the instrument, intonational inflections, and other extended techniques). The computer was instructed to generate sound events within the parameters given; the music thus does not delineate a structure, per se, but rather laregely operates at random within a structure. The "boundaries" of the form are not perceived, but rather are the "space" the form contains. This seemingly mechanical process thus has a kind of organic quality in the same way that trees have a given general shape but are infinitely varied in their details of form. *—Jeremy Grimshaw*

Recommended:

○ **Xenakis: Chamber Music, 1955–1990** / Arditti SQ / 2000 / Disques Montaigne 782137

KEYBOARD

Mists (1981)

Following the roiling, oceanic energy of *Evryali* (1973), Xenakis turned again to a watery image for his third piano solo, *Mists* (1980). Composed for Australian virtuoso Roger Woodward, *Mists* builds on principles from *Evryali*, adding a few new twists along the way. "Arborescences," dense, polyphonic bundles of melodies, are again prominent, here grouped into two different types. One is a "thicker" version of the sweeping waves of *Evryali*, with two or more layers shaping the contour rather than just one. The other opens out from the instrument's middle register, the contours taking shape in more sinewy and dendritic form. In both instances, Xenakis makes generous use of polyrhythms to distinguish the different strands within the texture: in certain passages, in fact, the pianist is asked to simultaneously manage four distinct rhythmic/temporal schemes. The other main texture Xenakis employs in *Mists* is a pointillistic one in which single notes are played in "haphazard" fashion to create a cloud of sounds; the range may either encompass the full register of the piano or be quite restricted, giving rise to recognizable motifs.

Xenakis' notation, devised for this piece and employed extensively thereafter, provides a temporal/spatial grid within which the stemless notes are placed geometrically, the aim being to achieve a high degree of rhythmic accuracy without encumbering the performer with overly complex metric notation. Given that the temporal placement is generated from stochastic (probabilistic functions on a computer, absolute precision is not necessary (nor possible, in most cases).

The piece is organized into three sections. The first contains the two kinds of arborescences; the second is entirely stochastic, employing the aforementioned "note clouds"; and the third is a sequence of alternations between the two types of material. There are also a number of silences that serve as a striking repose for the relentless onslaught of densely voiced musical gestures. These are not impressionistic "mists," but wind-driven, penetrating needles of urgent musical expression. *—James Harley*

Recommended:

○ **Xenakis: Chamber Music, 1955–1990** / Helffer / 2000 / Disques Montaigne 782137

Y

Sophie Yates

Harpsichordist

One of the world's preeminent harpsichordists, Sophie Yates is known for her critically acclaimed performances of Baroque music. Universally praised for her profound understanding of Baroque style, Yates is also admired for her refined touch and discreet virtuosity. Indeed, critics have often lauded Yates for subordinating her enormous virtuosity to stylistic and aesthetic concerns. As a specialist in French Baroque music, Yates masterfully captures the elusive style of French Baroque keyboard performance, perfectly conjuring up the enigmatic atmosphere of distant intimacy heard in pieces by Couperin and Rameau. Commenting on her album *French Baroque Harpsichord*, critic Robert Haskins admired Yates' subtle renditions of Couperin's music. "In her readings of *Les Idées heureuses*, she savors the melodic quality of the ornamentation and the stately but fluid rhythms to marvelous effect." From the vantage point of the French Baroque, Yates has also explored Italian, German, and Iberian repertoires, bringing to light many forgotten harpsichord pieces. Her exploration of Spanish and Portuguese music has been particularly successful, yielding the album *Spanish and Portuguese Harpsichord*, in which, as Haskins observed, she "combines her ability to project a profound inner intensity with scintillant technique." Yates studied harpsichord at the Royal College of Music in London. Her career was launched when she won the International Erwin Bodky Competition at the Boston Early Music Festival. Invited to tour the eastern United States, Yates subsequently received offers from other parts of the world. In fact, Yates could be described as a true globetrotting harpsichordist, having played in Syria, Morocco, Australia, and Japan. With her home base in London, she regularly tours Europe. A teacher at the Royal College of Music, Yates is also a virginals specialist, searching for old instruments and exploring the repertoire. Her highly praised albums, released by Chandos, include *Rameau: Pièces de clavecin*, *Romanesca: Italian Music for the Harpsichord*, and *Fandango: Scarlatti in Iberia*. In 1999, Yates released her first album devoted to Handel's harpsichord music. In the liner notes for her second Handel album, Yates remarked that Handel's harpsichord pieces not only exhibit such typicially Handelian features as rhythmic vitality and melodic inventiveness, but also "give us a fascinating insight into the composer's more private world." *—Zoran Minderovic*

Recommended:

- ○ **Handel: Harpsichord Works, Vol. 3** / Yates / 2002 / Chandos 688
- ○ **Handel: Harpsichord Works, Vol. 2** / Yates / 2001 / Chandos 669
- ○ **Rameau: Harpsichord Pieces** / Yates / 2000 / Chandos 659
- ○ **French Baroque Harpsichord** / Yates / 1993 / Chandos 545
- ○ **La Sophie** / Yates / 1996 / Chandos 598

Narciso Yepes

b. Nov. 14, 1927, Marchena, Spain, **d.** May 3, 1997, Murcia, Spain

Guitarist

Narciso Yepes was one of the finest virtuoso classical guitarists of the twentieth century, generally ranked second after Andrés Segovia. Despite a strong interest in music from the Baroque period, his overwhelming preference was for the serious compositions of Spanish composers from the early twentieth century, though he also showed interest in flamenco music. He displayed a special fondness for the works of Joaquín Rodrigo and was instrumental in the rediscovery of many previously neglected Baroque compositions. He also achieved distinction as a composer, especially in the realm of film music.

Narciso Yepes was born in the small town of Marchena, Spain, located near Lorca. He showed musical talent in his pre-school years, prompting his peasant father to give him his first guitar when he was only four. He soon played with great proficiency and his father arranged for young Narciso to take lessons in guitar and solfeggio in Lorca from Jesús Guevara. Yepes enrolled at the Valencia Conservatory at age 13 and was instructed (though not in guitar) by composer/pianist Vicente Asencio. He gave his first public performance in Valencia at the Teatro Serrano, then returned with his family to Lorca. There he played for Ataulfo Argenta, conductor of the Spanish National Orchestra, who was so impressed by his skills that he convinced Yepes to travel to Madrid to launch his career. There, the young guitarist met some of the most influential musicians in the country, including Joaquín Rodrigo, who had completed his guitar masterpiece, the *Concierto de Aranjuez*, several years earlier. Yepes found the work most attractive and decided to play it for his official concert debut in 1947, for which he was partnered with Argenta, who led the Orquesta de Cámara. His further performances of the work during the early years of his career are now seen as crucial to the current popularity of the Rodrigo concerto. Yepes' concerts were well-received and he quickly became one of the most highly regarded guitarists in Spain. He gave a successful tour of Europe in 1948—with notable success in Geneva, Switzerland—then two years later relocated to Paris for further study with George Enescu and Walter Gieseking. He also spent time with Nadia Boulanger, though apparently never became a student. Yepes wrote and performed the music for the 1952 film *Jeux interdits*, which garnered awards at Cannes, Venice, and Hollywood. Yepes met his wife—who was of Polish origin—in Paris, and they were married in 1958. Their union produced three children, one of whom, Ignacio, became a conductor, and another, Ana, a choreographer with the Paris Opera. In the 1960s, Yepes was especially active as both a guitar soloist and composer. He achieved acclaim for his score of the 1961 film *La fille aux yeux d'or*. In 1964, Yepes developed and thereafter played a ten-string guitar, which he asserted was superior to the six-stringed guitar especially in the realm of the transcription. In the 1970s and 1980s, Yepes remained active in all facets of his career, but made fewer concert appearances. He received many awards during this period, including an honorary doctorate degree from the University of Murcia, and various artistic, radio, and television citations. In 1980, he made his highly praised recording of the Rodrigo *Concierto de Aranjuez* with the Philharmonia Orchestra conducted by García Navarro. In 1993, Yepes was forced to sharply curtail his concert activity owing to his declining health. He gave his final concert in Santander, Spain, in 1996. *—Robert Cummings*

Recommended:

- ○ **Spanish Guitar Music** / Yepes / 2003 / DG 474437
- ○ **Rodrigo: Concierto de Aranjuez; Fantasia para un gentilhombre** / Alonso (cond.), Yepes, Orquesta Sinfonica R.T.V. Espanola / DG 469629
- ○ **Vivaldi: Lute Concertos** / Kuentz (cond.), Yepes, T & S Ochi / DG 429528
- ○ **Asturias: The Art Of The Guitar** / Yepes / 1989 / DG 459613
- ○ **Malagueña: Spanish Guitar Music** / Yepes / DG 469649

La Monte Young

b. Oct. 14, 1935, Bern, Idaho

Composer: Chamber Music, Keyboard

La Monte Young's place near the center of the 1960s New York art community—a circle that included such icons as Yoko Ono and Andy Warhol, starkly contrasts with his rustic beginnings. Young was born on October 14, 1935, in a small log cabin in Bern, Idaho. His father, destitute and in search of work, moved the family several times between Idaho, Utah, and California. Finally settling in Los Angeles, Young enrolled at John Marshall High, a school well known in the area for its superior music programs. By the time he entered Los Angeles City College in 1953, his saxophone skills were such that in an audition for a coveted spot in the school's acclaimed jazz band he beat out Eric Dolphy, who would later become famous as a sideman for John Coltrane.

The next three years would see Young's interests shift however, and by the time he transferred to UCLA in 1957, he had all but given up the saxophone in favor of composition. At UCLA, the influence of Webern was combined with heavy doses of chant and organum, Japanese gagaku, Indonesian gamelan, and Indian music. As he listened for hours to the ragas of Ali Akbar Kahn or the reverent tenor of the ancient liturgy, he became fascinated with long, sustained tones; consequently, minimalism as a twentieth century musical genre can arguably be traced to Young's groundbreaking composition of 1958, *Trio for Strings*.

A 1959 summer course in Darmstadt with Stockhausen exposed Young to John Cage's philosophies on indeterminacy and found sounds. Around the time of Young's return to Berkeley, he approached Terry Riley and, as Riley recalls, exclaimed "If they thought I was wild before, wait 'til they see what I'm going to do now!" Young's new aesthetic was made apparent in a noontime concert at Berkeley's Hertz hall, which featured *Poem for Chairs, Tables, Benches, etc.* The work called for novel sounds such as the friction of furniture sliding across the floor, executed within certain controlled parameters. The following year, Young composed what would become some of his most infamous works: the conceptual series entitled *Compositions 1960*. Perhaps the most outlandish work of this period however, is *Piano Piece for David Tudor #1*, in which the performer provides his piano with a bale of hay to eat and a bucket of water to drink.

During this period, Young received a grant from the University to study in New York. Soon he was organizing a series of performances in the Chambers Street loft of Yoko Ono. At each of these, the evening's events were outlined on concert programs that also featured the bold disclaimer, "THE PURPOSE OF THIS SERIES IS NOT ENTERTAINMENT."

In 1962 ,Young married visual artist Marian Zazeela, and the two moved into a large apartment/studio/rehearsal space in Lower Manhattan. He formed an ensemble that included his wife Marian and, for a time, John Cale, Angus MacLise, and Tony Conrad—all original members of the rock band the Velvet Underground. Young's group eventually took on the name The Theater of Eternal Music, and began executing their complex harmonic improvisations in coordination with electronically-produced drones determined by Young, and a series of colored projections created by Zazeela. This multi-sensory experience was dubbed "Dream House." Subsequent works, such as *The Tortoise, His Dreams and Journeys*, and *The Well-Tuned Piano*, further developed the idea of improvisation and drones. *—Jeremy Grimshaw*

Overview of Works

La Monte Young is considered by many to be the founding father of the American minimalist movement (Brian Eno has called him "the granddaddy of us all"), and his compositions draw upon styles as widely varied as serialism, electronic music, and concept art. Though a seminal figure, most of his works are experienced directly by only a handful of listeners. His scores are not available through traditional publishing houses, his recordings are few and of limited distribution, and the parameters of pieces often demand rarely realized performance conditions. The unique circumstances of his career thus make him one of the most talked about and least understood composers of his day.

Young's earliest surviving works reflect his study of 12-tone methods (he was a student of Leonard Stein, one of Arnold Schoenberg's star pupils) while at the same time suggesting future directions. A significant portion of *for Brass* from 1957 utilized, for the first time, extremely long sustained tones; this idea was expanded even further in the groundbreaking *Trio for Strings* from 1958. Composed during his last year at UCLA, the trio followed a carefully plotted serial procedure in its pitch content and dynamics, but took Webernian focus to an extreme: the piece is comprised entirely of long sustained chords and pitches as well as gaping rests.

Young's early serial works are followed chronologically by a brief period during which he explored various conceptual possibilities. The most infamous of these is *Compositions 1960*, a collection of pieces ranging from the totally borrowed (one of them instructs the performer to play some other piece) to the utterly unperformable (such as the one instructing a player to feed hay to a piano, or another that simply ruminates, without any instruction, on an imagined whirlpool somewhere in the ocean). The piece most connected stylistically to the rest of his output, however, is certainly *Compositions 1960 #7*, which provides the player with two notes a perfect fifth apart and the simple rubric: "to be held for a long time."

Beginning in the 1960s, Young began to make a name for himself for his hours-long improvisations on sustained harmonies, as in the various manifestations of the piece *Four Dreams of China* that he realized with his ensemble, the Theater of Eternal Music. His harmonically static improvisational style also emerged in *The Well-Tuned Piano*, which he began conceiving in 1964 and continued to develop during the subsequent decades. Comprising up to six hours of improvisations on ethereal harmonies created by its unique tuning system, *The Well-Tuned Piano* stands as one of the most monumental keyboard works from the latter half of the twentieth century. Other of Young's most important works are not "works" in the traditional sense, however, but sound and light "environments" created with his wife, the visual artist Marian Zazeela. The most prominent of these is the *Dream House* installation in lower Manhattan, which opened in 1993 and continued for the next several years. *—Jeremy Grimshaw*

Recommended:

- ○ **The Well-Tuned Piano** / 1987 / Gramavision 79452
- ○ **The Second Dream of the High-Tension Line** / Neill (cond.), Burns, Kelley, Trosclair, Clymer, Donato, Fleming, O'Connor, Theatre of Eternal Music / 1991 / Gramavision 79467

CHAMBER MUSIC

Trio for Strings (1958)

The *Trio for Strings* was composed while La Monte Young was completing his undergraduate degree at UCLA, and preparing for graduate studies at Berkeley. Raised under rustic and extremely poor circumstances in rural Idaho and Utah, Young's first real exposure to the wide variety of the world's music—ranging from Webern, to Indian ragas, to Japanese Gagaku, to the medieval polyphony of the Notre Dame school—had a potent alchemical effect. It was from this milieu that the *Trio* emerged. The finished work was so extreme that when he presented it to Seymour Shifrin, his new professor at Berkeley, the latter arranged for a special performance of the work in his home—for the sole purpose of demonstrating its failure.

Despite the initially cold reception of the composer and his work, one writer some 40 years later would call the *Trio for Strings* the "fountainhead of minimalism," and pop minimalist Brian Eno would call Young "The granddaddy of us all." Because his musical conceptions are stubbornly esoteric, and because his style of minimalism never evolved into the more marketable sounds that lent a measure of fame to successors like Reich, Glass, Riley, and Adams, La Monte Young is often overlooked. Nonetheless, his works represent minimalism at its most minimal, and the *Trio for Strings* stands of one of the earliest extended concentrations on a limited number of musical events.

Though linked with minimalism, the *Trio for Strings* is actually a serial work. The pitches used are derived from a 12-tone process; the durations of the notes are precisely calculated. Likewise, though the piece is mostly on the quiet side, the dynamic markings comprise a very deliberate system of eleven gradations of volume, ranging from *pppppp* to *fff*. Still, despite these serial procedures, the contour and character of the piece establish its historical importance as a forerunner of 1960s minimalism.

The Trio begins with the viola on a lone C sharp; this note, like every other in the piece, is played in as plain and faceless a fashion as possible. Low dynamics predominate throughout, and the score demands that "Vibrato should not be used at any time, *ever*!" About 40 seconds into the piece, the violin adds an E flat, which is also sustained. A minute after the entrance of this second note, the cello intones a D. All three tones are sustained for an extended period, before they drop out in a piecemeal fashion—one that is chronologically symmetrical to the way in which they entered. The initial C sharp is thus the last note to disappear into the chasmic rest that follows. The pattern is thus set for the rest of the piece: chords are built note by note at a glacial pace, before being dismantled in the same way; the chords are separated by gaping pauses, of the kind Terry Riley was probably thinking when he said that "[Young's rests] are like being on a space station and waiting for lunch."

Despite its rather experimental nature, the *Trio for Strings* is perhaps Young's most "performable" piece. The extremes of process found in the *Trio* soon became extremes of means, as Young turned to much more conceptual compositional methods in the 1960s. *—Jeremy Grimshaw*

KEYBOARD

The Well-Tuned Piano, for prepared piano (1964)

While his disciples might call La Monte Young the emperor of minimalism, his critics might counter that the emperor wears no clothes. Though his musical experiments are similar to some of John Cage's more notorious works—in one of Cage's pieces the performer sits at a piano silently for four minutes and 33 seconds; one of Young's involves bringing the piano a bale of hay to eat and a bucket of water to drink—Cage's works of that nature seem clearly more conceptual and less performative, while Young speaks *and performs* with a very straight face.

Such is the case with *The Well-Tuned Piano*. Adapting its name from Bach's milestone *The Well-Tempered Clavier*, Young's magnum opus reflects his devotion to the system of "just intonation." While Bach's *Well-Tempered Clavier* marked the adoption of the equal-tempered tuning system in Western music—the system, familiar to our ears, that skews the intervals of the scale slightly to allow transposition to any key without having to retune the instrument—Young's five-hour work (give or take an hour, since large portions of it are improvised) utilizes mathematically perfect, Pythagorean intervals that sound slightly out-of-tune to our well-tempered ears, but that create shimmering resonances and clouds of overtones not possible with equal tuning. As each theme or melody unfolds, it slowly accelerates, until the notes are repeated so rapidly that their overtones blend and resonate, hovering, as it were, like a cloud above the piano. Even if the listener is not committed to taking in an entire uninterrupted performance, the moment-to-moment musical events can be quite engaging and often beautiful. Like Philip Glass and Steve Reich, members of the next minimalist generation, Young was heavily influenced by non-Western music, as well as non-Western ideas. The just intonation system espoused in *The Well-Tuned Piano* is found frequently in the music of other cultures, and some have compared the slowly unfolding ideas in the *The Well-Tuned Piano*, in spirit if not in sound, to an Indian raga. Young speaks both in spiritual and scientific terms about the piece, frequently citing psychoacoustical research on the effects of sustained or repeated resonances—resonances, which he says, are "illuminated before me as if emanating from the Universal Source of the Eternal Sound." The various sections of the piece are given appropriately mystical names, including "The Goddess of the Caverns Underneath the Pool," "The Theme of the Lyre of Orpheus," and "The Homage to Brahms Variation of the Theme of the Dawn of Eternal Time in the Deepest Pool." While such extramusical accoutrements might stir up suspicions, judgment should be suspended until the work can be experienced or at least sampled. There is something otherworldly, if not as astrally ennobling as Young might claim, about the sonic fields created by "true" intervals, and Young's deliberations upon these sounds are artfully constructed. *—Jeremy Grimshaw*

Recommended:

○ **The Well-Tuned Piano** / 1987 / Gramavision 79452

Eugene-Auguste Ysaÿe

b. Jul. 16, 1858, Liège, Belgium, **d.** May 12, 1931, Liège, Belgium
Composer: Chamber Music

Eugène Ysaÿe was one of the greatest violinists who ever lived. He coupled beauty of tone and remarkable technical ability with a depth of musical expression that few violinists before or since can be said to have equalled, or even approached. Ysaÿe succeeded in breathing new life into an art that had become polarized by two divergent styles and personalities: the austere temperament of Joseph Joachim (1831–1907), and the flashy virtuosity of Pablo de Sarasate (1844–1908). Ysaÿe achieved a grand synthesis of these two approaches by imbuing the "serious" music of Mozart, Brahms, and Beethoven, so dear to Joachim, with the flashy yet never superficial brilliance that Sarasate had been wont to apply to "lesser" works in the repertoire. Ysaÿe became the leading violinist of his time, spawning many illustrious pupils and proteges, among them Josef Gingold and Fritz Kreisler. Ysaÿe was also an accomplished composer, whose *Six Sonatas for Solo Violin*, Opus 27 (1924) are recognized masterpieces of the genre.

Eugène Ysaÿe was born on July 16, 1858 in Liege, Belgium. He received his first violin lessons from his father when he was five years old. After this he studied with Rodolphe Massart, making his first public appearance at age seven. Ysaÿe was not, however, a prodigy; he was later kicked out of the Liege Conservatory due to poor performance! But he persisted, and went on to study with the famous violinist and composer Henryk Wieniawski (1835–80) with whom he made considerable progress; he was soon accepted as a student by the legendary Belgian violinist-composer Henri Vieuxtemps (1820–81).

In 1879, Ysaÿe made the acquaintance of Joseph Joachim, and performed with Clara Schumann. He soon began touring, visiting Norway in 1881, and playing at the Paris Conservatory in 1883. In Paris, he befriended the composer Cesar Franck, who wrote his beautiful *Sonata for Piano and Violin in A Major* (1886) as a wedding present for Ysaÿe. This work soon became a signature piece for the violinist, who stamped it with his own inimitable style.

During this period, Ysaÿe founded the Concerts in Brussels that bore his name, as well as his own string quartet, which included his pupil Mathieu Crickboom, to whom Ysaÿe later dedicated the fifth of his *Six Sonatas for Solo Violin*. This ensemble premiered Claude Debussy's *String Quartet No. 1 in G Minor, Opus 10* in 1893. A year later Ysaÿe made his first appearance in America, where he met with tremendous sucess, finally returning in 1918 to take over the post of conductor for the Cincinnati Symphony Orchestra which he held until 1922.

After his retirement from conducting, Ysaÿe devoted himself fully to composing, and the teaching of a select group of pupils, including Josef Gingold, who later went on to achieve international fame. By this time, Ysaÿe's performance technique had declined, due to a rapid deterioration of his right-arm stability—a condition known to violinists as "bow tremor." This was probably the result of diabetes, with which he had been struggling for some time. Despite the fact that his performance career lasted for only 25 years, Ysaÿe exercised a tremendous influence on violinsts—an influence still being felt today. His personal aura and grand musical sensibility were only two aspects of a complex personality that not only "played" but also lived the music he held dear. He was an authentic performer, an artist of immense stature and unmatched musical ability. Eugène Ysaÿe died on May 12, 1931, at the age of 72. *—Edward Moore*

CHAMBER MUSIC

Rêve d'enfant, for violin & piano, Op. 14 (ca. 1895–1900)

Composed in the mid-1890s and dedicated to Ysaÿe's youngest son Antoine—later to become his father's biographer and publisher—the *Rêve d'enfant* mines a familiar vein of sentiment after the manner of Fauré's *Berceuse*, Brahms' *Lullaby*, and countless other encore effusions. Over an engagingly tugging accompaniment, the violin sings a suavely rocking melody—an archetypal cradle song—which becomes melodically involved and, for a moment, impassioned before a reprise of the opening and a diminuendo fadeout. The harmonic idiom and dreamy aura recall the more quietly ecstatic moments of Franck's violin sonata, composed in 1886 as a wedding present for Ysaÿe and dedicated to him. Ysaÿe was undoubtedly the greatest violinist after Paganini—an artist who, like Busoni and Godowsky at the piano, bridged the Romantic and Modern manners of playing. Thus, his revealing, if primitive, acoustic recording of the *Rève d'enfant* made in 1913 is of supreme interest. Dwelling lovingly over the piece at a slower tempo than any contemporary violinist would allow himself, he softens the melody in discreetly crooning portamenti while unfolding it with a subtle rhythmic flexibility—or rubato—and sweetness of tone that invests every note with meaning and beside which the flawless precision of today's best violinists seems deadpan, generic, and empty. With the challenging but eloquent *Six Sonatas for Solo Violin* and the ambitiously substantial *Poème élégiaque*, the *Rève d'enfant* has remained at the fringe of the repertoire largely thanks to the *pietas* of violinists, while Ysaÿe's some 60 other compositions, ranging from chamber works, concertos, and an opera, have been forgotten. The *Rêve d'enfant* also exists in a scoring for violin and orchestra. *—Adrian Corleonis*

Recommended:

○ **Encore!** / Midori, McDonald / 1992 / Sony 52568

Six Sonatas for solo violin, Op. 27 (1923)

Despite the fact that Ysaÿe had no formal training as a composer, his works are not only masterfully crafted, demonstrating various dimensions of violinistic expressiveness and sonority, but also provide the listener with a remarkable aesthetic experience. As a peerless virtuoso, Ysaÿe writes with a profound understanding of the violin's soul; as a performer deeply immersed in the music of his time, he evinces a familiarity with many styles; yet Ysaÿe's music, despite many recognizable echoes of other composers, clearly exhibits an unmistakable artistic individuality.

Inspired by a Bach recital by Joseph Szigeti, Ysaÿe's outlined these six sonatas in a day. The six works are dedicated to, respectively, Szigeti, Jacques Thibaud, George Enescu, Fritz Kreisler, Mathieu Crickboom (a member of the Ysaÿe Quartet), and Manuel Quiroga. Because each sonata is dedicated to a violinist, or, in some cases, a violinist-composer, every work has a distinct individuality. For example, *Sonata No. 6* has a subtle, but unmistakable, Iberian flavor. Predictably, the sonata dedicated to George Enescu conjures up a truly Central European atmosphere. Like Fritz Kreisler, Ysaÿe in *Sonata No. 4* re-creates the Baroque style with remarkable charm; this is a Baroque, or quasi-Baroque, sound which seduces the listener by its unpretentious spontaneity and freshness. Significantly, while exploring a variety of musical styles, Ysaÿe never lapses into sterile eclecticism; after all, these works are marked by his powerful individuality. Underlying his tasteful stylistic explorations is Ysaÿe's boundless interest in, and fascination by, his instrument. Containing an array of extreme, even breathtaking, technical challenges, these sonatas also explore the rich sonorities of the violin, with particular emphasis on original, and perhaps surprising, harmonic effects. *—Joseph Stevenson*

Recommended:

○ **Ysaye: Sonatas for violin Op27** / Kremer / Mobile Fidelity Sound 921

○ **Ysaye: Sonatas for violin Op27** / Shumsky / 1996 / Nimbus 7715

Z

Nicanor Zabaleta

b. Jan. 7, 1907, San Sebastian, Spain, **d.** Mar. 31, 1993, San Juan, Puerto Rico
Harpist
Nicanor Zabaleta was one of the foremost harpists of the twentieth century, as important to the advancement of the harp as Segovia was to the guitar. At the age of seven, Zabaleta's father, an amateur musician, bought him a harp from an antique shop. The young Nicanor soon began taking lessons from Vincenta Tormo de Calvo, who was on the Madrid Conservatory faculty, and with Luisa Menarguez. At 17, he began studies in Paris; among his teachers there were Marcel Tournier and Jacqueline Borot. He made his official concert debut in the French capital in 1926. After a brief stint in the military, he traveled to the United States, where he made his North American debut in 1934 and remained a resident for the next two decades. Two years later, he began concert tours of Cuba and Mexico, where he achieved enough critical acclaim to command substantial fees for his concert appearances. His association with Australian-born American composer/critic Peggy Glanville-Hicks, who was active in organizing concerts of contemporary music in the 1940s and 1950s, further advanced his career in the United States. At a 1950 concert in Puerto Rico, Zabaleta met his future wife Graziela, and they were married two years later. They relocated to Spain and Zabaleta thereafter began touring the major cities of Europe, including Paris, Amsterdam, London, Munich, Copenhagen, and Zurich. Joaquín Rodrigo arranged his *Concierto de Aranjuez* as the *Concierto Serenata* for him in 1952, and Argentinian composer Alberto Ginastera composed a concerto (1956–64) for him, which Zabaleta premiered with Eugene Ormandy and the Philadelphia Orchestra in 1965. Nearly 30 other composers from throughout Europe and the Americas wrote works for him, as well. But his repertory was often more traditional and included works by Bach, Handel, Mozart, Debussy, and Ravel. Along with giving numerous solo and orchestral concerts, Zabaleta made many recordings, mostly in the 1960s and the decades following. It is estimated that he sold as many as three million records. His later concerts included critical successes at the Theatre Champs Élysées in Paris on March 21, 1981, and in San Jose, CA, on March 12 and 13, where he played concertos by Mozart and Villa-Lobos. His final concert, on June 16, 1992, in Madrid, was given when he was already in seriously declining health. *—Robert Cummings*

Recommended:

○ **Great Works for Harp** / Zabaleta, etc. / 1993 / DG 439693

Gheorghe Zamfir

b. May 6, 1941, Gaesti, Romania
Pan Flute Player
Gheorghe Zamfir is without a doubt the world's best-known pan flute player. He has made numerous recordings and became widely popular in the latter decades of the twentieth century.

Zamfir studied music first at the Bucharest Academy of Music, then at the Bucharest Conservatory. While he must be credited to a large extent with being self-taught on the pan flute, he did take lessons on his chosen instrument from Fanica Luca, his most influential teacher. By the late 1960s, he had become a virtuoso pan flute player, with a few recordings to his credit. Still, he remained little-known in his native Romania and was a virtual unknown outside its borders. His lack of recognition at that time owes much to the limited appeal of the pan flute even in his homeland, where there was a reluctance to manufacture the ancient instrument. In 1969, Zamfir met with Swiss musicologist Marcel Cellier, who would be largely responsible for the pan flutist's discovery. Cellier was an organist and engaged Zamfir to join him in a series of concerts in Switzerland, Europe, and elsewhere that eventually resulted in several recordings featuring the pair playing their chosen instruments. One of their more successful collaborations was the album *Flute de Pan et Orgue*, which was taped from a live concert in Australia. In 1984, the two were given a Grand Prix Award by the Academie du Disque Français for that recording. In 1971, Zamfir met Joeri Murk, a fledgling manufacturer of pan flutes whom he inspired in the years following to produce more instruments. (Murk would also go on to found a pan flute school in 1976 in Zurich.) In 1974, the president of Philips had come to Cellier's Swiss residence, where he met Zamfir and immediately signed him to a contract. This yielded worldwide issue of a number of highly successful recordings. Shortly after signing the contract with Philips, Zamfir moved to Switzerland with his wife, Marie-Noele. Zamfir gave his Carnegie Hall debut in 1981, after which his career continued with increasing success both on the concert stage and in the recording studio. In 1993, he began teaching at the Dajoeri Pan Flute School in Zurich and five years later, established his own pan flute school, also located in the Swiss capital. The following year, he took Swiss citizenship.

Zamfir's unique style of playing is characterized by the bending of pitches and imaginative improvisation. He toured Europe with his own ensemble, the Florian Econonu Orchestra, with which he released several recordings. He has been featured on the soundtracks of numerous films, including *Picnic at Hanging Rock* and *The Karate Kid*. Zamfir continues to concertize and record a wide variety of music. Sales of Zamfir's LPs and CDs have generally been strong, owing to their purchase by many buyers who previously had little or no exposure to the pan flute, but who found its exotic, soothing sonorities of great appeal. His albums for Philips have included *Music by Candlelight* (1983), *Romance* (1984), *A Return to Romance* (1988), and *Magic of the Panpipes* (2001). *—Robert Cummings*

Recommended:

○ **Zamfir Gold: Greatest Hits** / Zamfir, etc. / 2003 / Universal 981014
○ **Magic of the Panpipes** / Zamfir, etc. / Philips 468138
○ **Songs of Romance Vol. 1** / Zamfir / 1997 / Ranwood 8263

Benjamin Zander

b. Mar. 9, 1939, Gerrard Cross, England
Conductor
Benjamin Zander is one of those rare musicians who gained celebrity only in the later stages of their careers. A virtual unknown, Zander began to receive considerable critical attention in the mid-1990s, mainly for his recordings with the then-obscure Boston Philharmonic Orchestra; this led to great interest from concert promoters and impresarios. On the merits of his imaginative interpretive ideas and solid podium technique, he became practically an overnight sensation—as he was nearing the age of 60!

Benjamin Zander was born on March 9, 1939, in Gerrards Cross, Buckinghampshire, England. He demonstrated remarkable musical talent in his early childhood and even began composing at the age of nine; his burgeoning artistry on the cello was also of a rare caliber. Eventually he attracted the notice of Benjamin Britten and Imogen Holst, daughter of composer Gustav Holst, both of whom began teaching young Benjamin. At the age of 15, Zander left England, eventually to take up studies on the cello with Gaspar Cassado. He then toured Europe giving many highly successful concerts before finally deciding to return to England to enroll at the University College London. After graduation, he traveled to the U.S. for post-graduate studies at Harvard University.

Zander has lived in Boston since the mid-1960s and he began teaching there at the New England Conservatory in 1967. Five years later, he became conductor of the NEC Youth Philharmonic Orchestra. In 1979 the Boston Philharmonic Orchestra was founded and Zander appointed its music director, a post he still holds in the 2000–01 season. While both he and the orchestra remained in relative obscurity for their first fifteen or so years, together they began to garner considerable recognition in the 1990s, both in the concert hall and on recordings. Their account of the massive Mahler *Eighth Symphony*, performed in the 1998–99 season and repeated in 2000 at Symphony Hall in Boston and at Carnegie Hall in New York, received much critical acclaim.

Because of his successes in the recording venue, Zander has moved near to superstar status, owing mostly to his recordings of several Mahler symphonies with the Boston Philharmonic and the Philharmonia Orchestra. He has established a relationship with this latter group, and in 1998 began a cycle of Beethoven symphonies with them for Telarc Records that will reach completion in the early 2000s.

In 2000, Zander was nominated for a Grammy award in the "Best Orchestral Performance" category for his recording of the Mahler *Ninth Symphony* with the Philharmonia Orchestra. Zander is unusual in that he also has a career as a motivational speaker in management development. He appears regularly before groups from various corporations and organizations, and works in this endeavor with his wife Rosamund Stone Zander, a noted psychotherapist. Together they wrote the book *The Art of Possibility*, published in September 2000 by Harvard Business School Press.

In January 2000, Zander was featured on a *60 Minutes* segment, which dealt with both his musical and speaking careers. He has also appeared on the ABC News program *Nightline*, on BBC television and on PBS television with a program entitled, *Living on One Buttock*. Zander has recorded for several labels including Telarc, Carlton Classics, and CPI. Besides his continuing involvement with the New England Conservatory of Music, he also teaches gifted students at the well known Walnut Hill School. Like many important artists today, Zander has his own website, accessible at www.benjaminzander.com. *—Robert Cummings*

Recommended:

- ○ **Mahler: Symphony 6** / Zander (cond.), Philharmonia / 2002 / Telarc 80586
- ○ **Mahler: Symphony 3** / Zander (cond.), Toyne, Paasikivi, Mackie, Fulcher, Philharmonia / 2004 / Telarc 80599

Frank Zappa

b. Dec. 21, 1940, Baltimore, MD, **d.** Dec. 4, 1993, Los Angeles, CA
Composer

Frank Zappa was one of the most accomplished composers of the rock era. His music shows an affinity for such classical figures as Stockhausen and Varèse, an affection for late 1950s doo wop, and a facility with the guitar-heavy sounds that dominated popular music in the 1970s. But Zappa was also a satirist whose scorn seemed bottomless and whose sense of absurd humor delighted his fans, even when he crossed over the broadest bounds of good taste. Finally, Zappa was perhaps the most prolific record-maker of his time, turning out massive amounts of music on his own Barking Pumpkin label and through distribution deals with Rykodisc and Rhino after long, unhappy associations with industry giants like Warner Brothers and the now-defunct MGM.

Frank Zappa was born in Baltimore on December 21, 1940; his father, a meteorologist, later moved the family to California. In his teens, young Frank played guitar and studied music, largely on his own; but at the age of 14 he read an article about the avant-garde composer Edgard Varèse, sparking a lifelong interest in both Varèse and the composition of contemporary classical music.

By age 18, Zappa had formed and performed in many musical groups. In 1960, he composed the soundtrack to the forgettable film, *The World's Greatest Sinner*. Two years later, he acquired his own recording studio in San Bernardino. His innate mistrust of authority received a boost when he spent ten days in jail, having produced a pornographic audio tape for an undercover vice cop.

Zappa composed another film score for *Run Home Slow* in 1965. That same year he joined the band Soul Giants, which was soon reconstituted as the Mothers (then further renamed the Mothers of Invention at the time of their first record deal). They released their debut, *Freak Out!*, in 1966; following efforts included *Absolutely Free* (1967), *We're Only in It for the Money* (1968), and *Cruising with Reuben and the Jets* (1968). The first and last of these are in Zappa's doo wop style.

After these initial recordings, Zappa initiated the first of many personnel shakeups within the Mothers of Invention. In 1970, he released four albums, including *Hot Rats*, which divulged a mixture of jazz and rock styles. While he had some success, Zappa's first big hit did not come until the 1974 *"Don't Eat The Yellow Snow."* Others would come slowly, like *"Dancin' Fool"* (1979) and *"Valley Girl"* (1982). This last effort featured his 14-year-old daughter, Moon Unit.

Best known of Zappa's classical works are his *Bob in Dacron and Sad Jane and Mo' 'n Herb's Vacation*, for full orchestra, and *Penis Dimension*, a rather explicit scatological work for chorus, soloists, and orchestra. They show a remarkable degree of fluency with musical materials absorbed from his self-studies of scores, especially those of Varèse.

The names of Zappa's four children (besides Moon Unit, they are Dweezil—also a musician—Ahmet Rodan, and Diva) once caused the composer to remark wryly that their surname would give them more trouble. In the 1980s, such groups as Parents Music Resource Center, led by wives of U.S. Senators, including Tipper Gore, lobbied for, among other things, the labeling of recordings. Zappa, his career experiencing a lull, became active in opposing these attempts at censorship, writing President Reagan and testifying in 1985 before a Senate Committee.

By the early 1990s Zappa's career was in full swing once again, but he was diagnosed with incurable prostate cancer. It is an irony that a decade before, one of his typically nose-thumbing songs was entitled "Why Does It Hurt When I Pee." Zappa died on December 4, 1993, in Los Angeles. *—Robert Cummings*

Overview of Works (1964–1993)

Frank Zappa's many accomplishments as a musician are difficult to summarize in brief: Zappa was not only an influential rock/jazz guitarist and band leader, but also a producer, studio engineer, a champion of avant-garde music, a conductor, and a composer of contemporary art music. His life work includes dozens of stylistically diverse albums that blur the borders between rock, pop, and classical music. Zappa's music has always been, in a sense, marginal; however, he accumulated a legion of devotees—including both rock fans and major figures in contemporary art music—over the course of three decades of musicmaking. Zappa's music is important insofar as it represents an attempt to synthesize rock music with techniques derived from the avant-garde.

Zappa's formal musical training was limited; thus, it is somewhat remarkable that he was able to comprehend the complex ideas and techniques of modern art music and replicate them in his own compositions. Zappa began composing in the early 1960s, writing soundtracks for B movies. In 1966, with the group The Mothers of Invention, Zappa released the album *Freak Out*, a seminal work whose improvisational character presages subsequent forays into the realm of the avant-garde. Zappa's works, when performed, always retained something of an improvised character through his dual roles of guitarist and conductor, directing the band/orchestra through composed pieces but with sudden changes in tempo and rhythm.

His music of the later 1960s and the 1970s is a complex blend of disparate styles and influences, from the music of modern composers like Varèse, Stravinsky, and Stockhausen, to blues, rock, and film and television music. On albums like 1973's *Over-Nite Sensation*, classical music and snippets of popular music—TV commercials, bubble gum pop, etc.—are juxtaposed in musical collages reminiscent of Charles Ives' combinations of simple hymns and folk melodies with complex, "high art" music. Most of Zappa's compositions reflect his desire to explore and deconstruct the opposition of popular and art music: his music serves as an ongoing critique of both traditions.

In the 1980s, Zappa recorded some of his works with both the London Symphony and Pierre Boulez's famous Ensemble Intercontemporain. His later compositions included a number of synthesizer pieces, including his own arrangements of the music of eighteenth century composer Francesco Zappa, a distant relative. In 1986, Zappa composed the album *Jazz from Hell*, written and performed entirely on a Synclavier synthesizer in his home studio.

Two of Zappa's other major contributions to classical music include his advocacy—together with Boulez—of the music of "noise" composer Edgard Varèse, and his harsh criticism of American orchestral musicians and their unions for their exorbitant rehearsal and recording fees, responsible, according to Zappa, for the decline of classical music in the United States. *—Alexander Carpenter*

Recommended:

- ○ **The Zappa Album** / Ensemble Ambrosius / Bis 5013
- ○ **Ensemble Modern Plays Frank Zappa** / Ensemble Modern / 2004 / RCA Red Seal 59842
- ○ **Zappa: The Yellow Shark** / Rundel (cond.), Ensemble Modern / Rykodisc 40560
- ○ **Boulez Conducts Zappa: The Perfect Stranger** / Boulez (cond.), InterContemporain Ensemble, Barking Pumpkin Digital Gratification Consort / 1995 / Vack 1253
- ○ **Zappa: The London Symphony Orchestra, Vols. 1 & 2** / Nagano (cond.), London SO, Ocker, Mann, Wackerman / 1995 / Vack 1252

Jan Dismas Zelenka

b. Oct. 16, 1679, Lounovice, Bohemia (Czech Rep.), **d.** Dec. 22, 1745, Dresden, Germany
Composer: Chamber Music, Orchestral

An innovative Baroque composer whose reputation was steadily on the rise during the anything-goes years of the waning twentieth century, Jan Dismas Zelenka was born in Lounovice, Bohemia (now part of the Czech Republic). He was a court musician in Dresden for most of his career, and both J. S. Bach and Georg Philipp Telemann knew and admired his music. Except for brief periods of travel, during which he refined his craft (he took lessons from Fux and Lotti even after his own technique had been perfected), he served as a double bass player in the court orchestra and later aided the ailing court music director Heinichen in his duties. Upon Heinichen's death, the position was awarded to another musician, which greatly disappointed Zelenka, who felt that his accomplishments as a composer had not been recognized. He died in Dresden, on December 22, 1745. Zelenka was best known, in his own time as in ours, for his harmonic and dynamic daring. An indefatigable experimentalist, he pushed the often conventional harmonic language of the Baroque to its limits, frequently using chromaticism in general and unresolved chains of suspensions in particular. Zelenka's dynamic markings, quite unusual for the Baroque, bring to mind a composer of the Romantic era. It is to his credit that the unusual devices he employed were woven into a composition's basic concept, and not treated as mere tricks. Zelenka was also known for his pioneering use of Czech folk rhythms, anticipating Haydn's use of central European folk music by half a century. Many of his innovations appear in his trio sonatas and other instrumental works (one of which bears the witty—and enigmatic—name of "Hipocondrie à 7"). It should noted that Zelenka also wrote a great deal of choral music of a more conventional character, including some in the stile antico—the strict polyphonic style of the Renaissance. *—AMG*

Overview of Works (1711–1744)

Unlike many of his late Baroque musical contemporaries, Jan Dismas Zelenka did not undertake early compositional training. He began life as a double bass player, only producing his first known composition (the *Missa Sanctae Ceciliae*) around 30 years of age. He did immediately try to improve himself, seeking study abroad in Italy and France. Only in 1716, at age 37, was Zelenka able to travel, studying composition for four years in Vienna with the renowned Johann Joseph Fux. Apart from this journey and a 1723 visit to Prague, Zelenka spent his life serving the court chapel in Dresden, though perversely never achieving the position of chapelmaster. As such, he produced a large output of mostly church music, and contributed in his rough-hewn and delightfully idiosyncratic manner to the development of the Dresden musical establishment. His works were known and admired by numerous of his contemporaries, not the least of which being Telemann and J.S. Bach.

Zelenka's innovative and often unorthodox style reveals a number of general stylistic influences. From his study with Fux, Zelenka learned highly polished contrapuntal writing and the older Italianate church style. Yet he continually spiced his rhythms with syncopation, irregular phrasing, and asymmetrical structures, vestiges of his native Czech folk music. In addition, Zelenka's music displays a richly imaginative use of orchestration, both in innovative scorings for rare instruments such as the soprano chalumeau, and in scintillating and virtuosic instrumental writing. To this quirky scoring, he adds sometimes surprising harmonic twists to give further bite to his musical goulash.

Most of Zelenka's surviving music dates from three distinct periods later in his life. While in Vienna, he produced almost all of his orchestral works; the two exceptions are one later *Capriccio* and the S. Wenceslaus music for the 1723 coronation of the King of Bohemia. Upon returning to the Dresden court, Zelenka set about composing church music in earnest. In addition to a large number of concerted masses, he composed no fewer than six sets of requiem music, Lamentations and other Holy Week pieces, 18 settings of the Marian antiphons, and a vast amount of music for the Vespers liturgy: 39 festal psalms, two Magnificats, and ten Vesper hymns. Many of these works unite full choral, orchestral, and solo vocal forces, often in several "numbers"; a few of the ritual pieces adopt more intimate scorings. His later masses and litanies (from the 1730s) are acknowledged among the finest of the era. *—Timothy Dickey*

Recommended:

- ○ **Zelenka: Composizione per Orchestra** / Collegium 1704 / 1995 / Supraphon 0009
- ○ **Zelenka: Orchestral Works & Trio Sonatas** / Bern Camerata, Wijnkoop / Archiv 000001702
- ○ **Sacred Music by Jan Dismas Zelenka** / King (cond.), George, Harvey, Blaze, Outram, Gilchrist, Sampson, King's Consort / 2003 / Hyperion 67350
- ○ **Zelenka: Magnificat** / Kuhn (cond.), Prague CO, Czech PO, Kuhn Mixed Choir, Prague PC / 1997 / Supraphon 3315
- ○ **Zelenka: I Penitenti al Sepolcro del Redentore** / Hugo (cond.), Kozena, Pospisil, Prokes, Regia Musicalis Capella / 2004 / Supraphon 3785

CHAMBER MUSIC

Capriccios, ZWV 182-185, 190 (ca. 1717–1729)

Zelenka wrote but a handful of works for orchestra, most of them between the years 1717 and 1723. At the time he was serving as double bassist in the orchestra of Prince Elector Friedrich August of Saxony. Four of the five *Capriccios* came about as a result of the Prince's desire to wed the Habsburg princess Maria Josepha. After the marriage negotiations were complete, the Prince traveled from his home court in Dresden to Vienna in the summer of 1717, staying until the summer of the following year. Zelenka and many of his fellow musicians at the Dresden court were ordered to Vienna to entertain the Prince during his stay there. Zelenka wrote the first four of the *Capriccios* during that year spent in Vienna. The *Capriccio No. 5* followed in 1729, when Zelenka and the rest of the court were back in Dresden. It is not known for what occasion Zelenka produced this last *Capriccio*, but in sound and style it is consistent with its predecessors.

One of the Prince Elector's favorite entertainments was the hunt, and it is thought that Zelenka wrote the first four *Capriccios*—among his first instrumental compositions—to accompany the Prince's hunting parties; the music would be performed either out-of-doors or at the meal after the hunt was completed. The hunting horns used during such hunting parties were a fascination for the Prince, who went so far as to obtain two of these natural horns (that is, non-valved horns which could primarily produce natural tones and overtones, with other notes available through the use of special playing techniques) for his orchestra. Zelenka employed these horns in his *Capriccios*, and these works have become infamous for their wide-ranging, elaborate, and ferociously difficult horn parts. The *Capriccios* are also remembered for some of Zelenka's compositional eccentricities—unusual rhythms and phrase lengths, surprising twists of harmony, and the composer's keen ear for tone color.

The *Capriccios* are all scored similarly—for the two hunting horns, along with a pair of oboes, strings, and basso continuo—and follow the typical format for instrumental suites of the time, with an introductory overture followed by a sequence of short dances or character pieces. Some of the dances Zelenka incorporated were a bit unusual, such as the "Paysan" in the *Capriccio No. 1*, the "Canarie" (a fast gigue-like dance which may have originated in the Canary Islands) in *No. 2*, and the "Villanella" in *No. 5*. One also finds character pieces, such as the "Il contento" and "Il furibondo" movements in *No. 5*. Zelenka shows his skills in counterpoint in movements like the opening movement of *No. 1*. Given the melodic charm and color of the five *Capriccios*, it seems almost a shame that Zelenka wrote so little instrumental music. After the early 1720s, he concentrated almost exclusively on sacred music, and the *Capriccio No. 5* was the only independent instrumental work he produced between 1723 and his death in 1745. *—Chris Morrison*

Recommended:

- ○ **Zelenka: Concerto ZWV186; Capriccios ZWV182-185** / Panton 811235

Six Trio Sonatas for 2 oboes, bassoon & continuo, ZWV 181 (ca. 1721–1722)

The music of Jan Dismas Zelenka is one of the great finds of twentieth century musicology, and the six trio sonatas for two oboes and bassoon (or other continuo instruments), Z 181, represent some of the best of this newly rediscovered treasure trove. During his lifetime (which was roughly contemporaneous with Bach's), Zelenka was well known as a string bass player and well admired, especially by those in the musical "know" like J.S. Bach, as a composer. But after his death most of his works were buried deep within hard-to-access European archives, all but forgotten and banned from publication on the orders of the Dresden court (as a result of some involved and unpleasant circumstances). They remained in this unhappy condition until the years following World War I. The six duo oboe sonatas probably date from sometime between 1714 and 1716, and in any event no later than 1723 (when Zelenka took them to Prague). During these years Zelenka divided his time between Vienna and his adopted home city of Dresden. Their modern-day reintroduction into the repertory may be credited in large part to the advocacy of the brilliant oboist Heinz Holliger.

Zelenka's style is among the most fascinating of all late Baroque composers'; it is easy to understand Bach's appreciation of a composer able to toss rich chromaticism around without sacrificing purity of line, to expand the harmonic domain without resorting to eccentricity, a composer not afraid to create instrumental parts of almost absurd difficulty—players of Zelenka's time were not all that used to dealing with polyrhythms and multiple stacked dissonances, to say nothing of the sheer technical demands made on the performers in music like the six Z 181 sonatas. Five of the six sonatas take the then-venerable four-movement sonata da chiesa form: slow-fast-slow-fast. No. 5, the odd man out, is instead a three-movement, fast-slow-fast work modeled somewhat after the newer Italian concerto shape. The sonatas are: No. 1 in F major, No. 2 in G minor, No. 3 in B flat major, No. 4 in G minor, No. 5 in F major, and No. 6 in C minor. *—Blair Johnston*

Recommended:

- ○ **Zelenka: 6 Sonatas for 2 Oboes & Bassoon** / Banchini, Kohnen, Dombrecht, Ponseele, Van Der Meer, Bond, Ebbinge / Accent 8848

ORCHESTRAL

Hipocondrie à 7 Concertanti, in A major, ZWV 187 (1723)

Surely one of the most oddly titled of all classical compositions, the *Hipocondrie* was one of "six concerti written in a hurry in Prague in 1723," according to a note on the original manuscript. It is scored for two oboes, bassoon, two violins, viola, and continuo. Although it is an instrumental work (the bulk of Zelenka's compositions were choral), the nine-minute *Hipocondrie* offers a good introduction to the music of this extremely unorthodox Czech composer. The French word *hipocondrie* meant much the same thing as its cognate "hypochondria" means today: early editions of the *Dictionnaire de L'Académie Française* defined the word as "a kind of malady, usually of long duration, that makes one strange and morose, and in which one complains of various pains and of excessive suffering, in spite of an appearance of good health. Deep sorrow, sedentary habits, etc., predispose one to *hipocondrie*." Difficult as it might seem to represent this concept musically, Zelenka pulls it off. Formally the *Hipocondrie* is a three-section French overture, opening with a processional dotted rhythm, moving into a faster stretch with contrapuntal elements, and finally broadening out into slow, chordal music once again. Zelenka's opening section begins conventionally in the major but makes a bizarre shift to the parallel minor in the consequent (answering) half of its first phrase. The music twists back to major again, but the entire opening section vacillates between major and minor in a way that suggests nothing so much as lack of confidence. The quicker second section, which offers a display of the contrapuntal prowess that gained Zelenka admiration from Bach and other composers, has the effect of a burst of nervous energy. After a striking false conclusion comes the return to the slow tempo, now swathed in a profusion of diminished harmonies that impart an air of profound gloom. The only missing Zelenka trademark is his bent toward irregular rhythms, but if ever there was Baroque music for a neurotic age, this is it, and the *Hipocondrie* might well inspire the listener to check out other works of Zelenka that are filled with similar marvels. *—James Manheim*

Recommended:

- ○ **Zelenka: Hipocondrie; Trio Sonata; Overture** / Harnoncourt (cond.), Vienna Concentus Musicus / 1997 / Teldec 17386

Alexander von Zemlinsky

b. Oct. 14, 1871, Vienna, Austria, **d.** Mar. 15, 1942, Larchmont, NY

Composer: Vocal, Chamber Music, Orchestral

Although he himself was a highly gifted composer, Austrian-born Alexander Zemlinsky is today better remembered as the man who taught both Arnold Schoenberg and Erich Wolfgang Korngold than for his own creations. Zemlinsky was born to a Vienna-based Polish family in 1871. After attending the Vienna Conservatory from 1887 to 1892 (first studying piano with Anton Door and later composition with J.N. Fuchs) he joined the Wiener Tonkünstlerverein (Vienna Composer's Society) in 1893. He made the acquaintance of Arnold Schoenberg in 1895, teaching him counterpoint for many months, and thus becoming that remarkable musician's only formal teacher.

Zemlinsky's *Piano Trio, Op. 3* had already received the approval of Johannes Brahms (to whose music the work bears a strong resemblance), who recommended the work to Simrock for publication, and his Viennese reputation was furthered by the successful premiere of his *Symphony No. 2* in 1897 and by Mahler's presentation of his opera *Es war einmal* in 1900.

Zemlinsky served as Kapellmeister at the Carltheater in Vienna from 1899 until his appointment as Kapellmeister at the Volksoper in 1906. From 1911 until 1927 he worked in Prague as opera conductor of the Deutsches Landestheater, where he gave the premiere of Schoenberg's *Erwartung* in 1924. Moving from Prague to Berlin at the end of his tenure with the Landestheater, Zemlinsky served first as Kapellmeister at the Kroll Opera where he worked under Otto Klemperer, and later as professor at the city's Hochschule für Musik. Fearful of the frightening state of politics in Berlin, Zemlinsky returned to Vienna in 1933, devoting himself to composition full-time (while still making occasional appearances as a conductor), before relocating to the United States in 1938. He died in Larchmont, New York four years later.

Zemlinsky's music, highly regarded by the Viennese circle which he did a great deal to help create, has since fallen into disuse. While his early music owes a great deal to Brahms, by the turn of the century Zemlinsky had adopted a more progressive Wagnerian chromaticism. As the Schoenberg circle's innovations during the early decades of the twentieth century grew more and more daring, however, Zemlinsky responded with an increased belief in the value of tonality. Of particular value is the *Lyrische Symphony,* Op.18 of 1923, which set the precedent for (and was quoted in) Alban Berg's *Lyric Suite* of 1926. *—Blair Johnston*

VOCAL

Songs (1889–1939)

Along with his eight operas, the 117 songs of Austrian composer Alexander von Zemlinsky form the heart of his oeuvre. From the warmly late Romantic early songs of the fin de siècle that join the melodic language of Brahms and Richard Strauss to Zemlinsky's own darkly toned harmonic language; through the orchestral songs of the postwar decades, which, while reminiscent of the late orchestral songs of Mahler, have a passionate sensuality all Zemlinsky's own; to his late, piano-accompanied songs that join his European art song orientation with the poetry of the Harlem Renaissance; Zemlinsky's songs chart his career as a composer. Of the *fin de siècle* songs, the *Sechs Gesänge (Six Songs) on poems of Maeterlinck* (1910–13) are the most representative of Zemlinsky's exquisite harmonic language and nostalgic sexuality. Of the postwar songs, the *Lyrische Symphonie* (Lyric Symphony) for soprano, baritone, and orchestra (1923) is undoubtedly Zemlinsky's masterpiece. Setting world-weary poems by Rabindranath Tagore, the *Lyrische Symphonie* takes Mahler's earlier song cycle symphony *Das Lied von der Erde* as the starting point for his own profoundly expressive symphonic song cycle on life, love, and death. The two sets of lieder, Op. 22 and 27, (1934 and 1936), mix the poetry of eighteenth and nineteenth century Germans with the poetry of twentieth century African Americans in a music that is still deeply rooted in the art music of fin de siècle Austria. *—James Leonard*

Recommended:

- ○ **Zemlinsky: Lieder** / Bonney, Otter, Blochwitz, Garben, Schmidt / DG 427348
- ○ **Zemlinsky: Posthumous Songs** / Ziesak, Schmidt, Vermillion, Blochwitz, Garben / 1995 / Sony 57960

Lyrische Symphonie, for soprano, baritone & orchestra, Op. 18 (1922–1923)

Alexander Zemlinsky wrote to his publisher in September 1922, "This summer I've written something along the lines of *The Song of the Earth.* I haven't got a name for it yet. It consists of seven related songs for baritone, soprano, and orchestra to be played without a break." After receiving the name *Lyrische Symphonie,* it was premiered under Zemlinsky in 1924 at the *German Theater* in Prague, where Zemlinsky had been the music director since 1911. The work sets seven poems by Bengali writer Rabindranath Tagore that record the course of a love affair from conception to fulfillment and dissolution. The harmonic language is highly erotic, lushly decadent, and sometimes almost atonal. The melodies are extremely expressive and often intensely sensual. The orchestration is richly oriental and exquisitely colorful. Although clearly a work *after The Song of the Earth,* Zemlinsky's *Lyrische Symphonie* is still an extremely affecting piece of post-fin de siècle passionate, sexual pessimism. *—James Leonard*

Recommended:

- ○ **Zemlinsky: Lyrische Symphonie** / Conlon (cond.), Skovhus, Isokoski / 2002 / EMI 557307
- ○ **Zemlinsky: Lyrische Symphonie; Symphonische Gesänge** / Chailly (cond.), Hagegård, Marc, Concertgebouw / 1994 / London 443569

CHAMBER MUSIC

String Quartet No. 1 in A major, Op. 4 (1896)

The *String Quartet No. 1 in A major,* Op. 4, from 1896 was the first work that the young Alexander von Zemlinsky showed the elderly Brahms. Brahms was so impressed by the quartet that he recommended it to his publisher Simrock. One can understand why Brahms was impressed. Not only is Zemlinsky's first quartet a remarkably self-assured piece of work for a 25-year-old composer, but it is written in a style that Brahms would have found highly congenial, the conservative Romanticism he himself espoused. The formal structures of the outer movements are clearly based on Schubert and middle-period Beethoven while the inner movements are intermezzos in the manner of Brahms. The opening Allegro con fuoco is laid out in sonata form with three themes; a development builds to a stormy climax; and a recapitulation restates the three themes in transposition. The following Allegretto is modeled on the third movement of Brahms' *Symphony No. 2* with the outer sections marked Im volkston (In the style of a folksong) and the central section a rushing Presto. The following slow movement echoes the pomp of Wagner's *Die Meistersinger* in its stately progress. The closing movement is the most overtly Brahmsian both in melodic shapes and its rhythmic intricacies. *—James Leonard*

Recommended:

- ○ **Music from Vienna, Vol. 1** / Brodsky Quartet / 2001 / Challenge 72040

String Quartet No. 4, Op. 25 (1936)

The *String Quartet No. 4* of Alexander von Zemlinsky was composed in 1936 and dedicated to the memory of Zemlinsky's friend Alban Berg who had died on Christmas Eve 1935. Like Berg's *Lyric Suite for string quartet,* Zemlinsky's *Fourth* is a suite of six movements consisting of an alternation of fast and slow tempos. The opening Prelude is marked senza expressione and quotes the main theme of Zemlinsky's second quartet, the theme that is a musical symbol for Zemlinsky himself. The second movement is a brutal rondo Burlesque like the closing movement of Zemlinsky's *Third.* The third movement is the lyrical heart of the work, a brief but deeply emotional Adagietto. The fourth movement is called Intermezzo, but it is actually the pivotal dramatic moment in the quartet: after energetic and heroic striving, the music seems to expire in the upper air of the violins. The penultimate movement is a Theme and Variations subtitled Barcarole, a comforting and consoling interlude before the fury of the Finale-Doppelfuge (Finale–Double Fugue). Recalling the themes, rhythms, and particularly the frenzied energy of the Burlesque and the Intermezzo in its themes and their working out, the Finale takes the *Fourth* to a thrilling and terrifying conclusion. *—James Leonard*

Recommended:

- ○ **Zemlinsky: String Quartets 3 & 4; Müller-Hermann: String Quartet Op. 6** / Artis Quartett / 1999 / Nimbus 5604

Trio for piano, clarinet & cello in D minor, Op. 3 (1895–1896)

The *Trio* for piano, clarinet & cello in D minor, Op. 3, from 1896, of the Austrian composer Alexander von Zemlinsky is a work of conservative Romanticism modeled on Brahms' own trio scored for the same instruments of 1892. Indeed, the closing Allegro in D minor of Zemlinsky's *Trio* takes its main theme directly from the main theme of the parallel movement in Brahms' *Trio.* Nor is Brahms the only influence apparent in Zemlinsky's work: the opening Allegro ma no troppo in D minor sounds distinctly Slavic with echoes of Tchaikovsky and Dvořák in its themes and the central Andante's big sentimental tune in D major recalls the gestures of the passionate second theme of the closing movement of Mahler's *First Symphony.* Despite these imitations, Zemlinsky's *Trio* is an appealing and well-made work by a minor master of the *fin de siècle.* *—James Leonard*

Recommended:

- ○ **Zemlinsky & Korngold: Piano Trios** / Beaux Arts Trio / 1994 / Philips 434072

ORCHESTRAL

Die Seejungfrau (The Mermaid), symphonic fantasy (1902–1903)

This richly orchestrated and envisioned, sweepingly Romantic symphonic poem is based on Hans Christian Andersen's fairy tale. "The Mermaid" received one performance on January 25, 1905, at a concert that also premiered (Zemlinsky's brother-in-law) Arnold Schoenberg's well-known symphonic poem *Pelleas und Melisande.* The two composers are reported to have had many conversations about the possibilities of uniting the aesthetics of so-called "pure music" (Brahms, Busoni, Chopin, and others) with the narrative Romanticism of Wagner, Liszt, Berlioz, and others through the symphonic poem format. Zemlinsky withdrew his composition from further performance, and it wasn't until 1984 that the scores of the various movements (separated in America and Vienna) were correctly identified and a full performance was again staged.

Zemlinsky does not provide a clear programme for the three movements, but musical analogues can generally be inferred by the listener. The first movement's tempo is "Sehr mässig bewegt (Very moderate in movement)" and opens with a depiction of the depths of the sea bed alternating with the playfulness of the mermaid and other sea creatures. The initially playful theme is turned into a furious sea storm, depicting the shipwreck (briefly interrupted by a lyrical theme of concern) and eventual rescue of the Prince.

The second movement, "Sehr bewegt, rauschend (Much movement, thunderous)," opens with a marvelous effect: a roll on a suspended cymbal grows into a tremendous crescendo with the gradual accumulation of trilling winds and tremulous strings. The longing of the Mermaid for the Prince is depicted in lyrical and playful lines. The Prince receives some hunting call-type grandeur, but the main attention is paid to the Mermaid's feelings.

The third movement is "Sehr gedehnt, mit schmerzvollem Ausdruck" (Very flexible, with sorrowful expression). The visit to the Sea Witch seems to be depicted in the opening of this movement as one hears oddly chromatic passages in the high winds, which alternate with the love theme given to a solo violin in the first movement. This is followed by the Prince's wedding, surrounded by great bursts of passionate, unresolved emotion (the overwhelming feelings of the Mermaid as she watches this spectacle, rather than music for the wedding itself). This is some of the composer's finest and most original writing from his early period. The beginning music describing the depths of the sea is heard again, and gentle music describes the Mermaid's transformation into an eternal spirit of the air. *—"Blue Gene" Tyranny*

Recommended:

- ○ **Zemlinsky: Die Seejungfrau; Symphonic Songs Op20** / Neumann (cond.), Wenkel / Wergo 62092
- ○ **Zemlinsky: Choral & Orchestral Works** / Conlon (cond.), Voigt, Albert, Kuebler, Cologne PO / 2002 / EMI 5751842

Krystian Zimerman

b. Dec. 5, 1956, Zabrce, Poland
Pianist

Krystian Zimerman stands as one of the most sensitive and controversial concert pianists to emerge in the latter half of the twentieth century. His extensive recordings with Deutsche Grammaphon cover a broad range of repertoire from the classical period to modernity, including the complete piano concertos of Beethoven and Brahms, important works by Schubert, Liszt, Grieg, Bartók, and Szymanowski, and all of Debussy's preludes. At the same time, early in his career Zimerman established a reputation for maintaining dauntingly high personal artistic standards, being very selective in undertaking projects, and limiting himself to only a small number of concert engagements each year.

Initially a student of his pianist father, and later, Andrzej Jasinski and Artur Rubinstein, Zimerman demonstrated his nuanced and distinctive technique at a young age. He was already concertizing as a very young boy, and was not yet 20 years old when he took first prize in the 1975 International Chopin Competition in Warsaw. During the 1980s and 1990s, Zimerman performed concertos with the world's finest orchestras and conductors, including the premiere of Lutosławski's *Piano Concerto* (which was composed for and dedicated to the pianist).

Zimerman's creation of the Polish Festival Orchestra in 1999 remains one of his greatest accomplishments. To commemorate the 150th anniversary of the death of Chopin, Zimerman personally selected an ensemble of young musicians, which he then led in unusually numerous and rigorous rehearsals of Chopin's two piano concertos. The orchestra developed a highly idiomatic sound, one that brought out intricate subtleties from Chopin's oft-maligned orchestral scores and illuminated a new level of interplay between soloist and orchestra in these works. Once they had fully developed their unique approach, Zimerman and the PFO undertook extensive world tours, performing Chopin's piano concertos for audiences the world over. They also released a recording that sold out quickly and caused a noted division among critics, who, as is has often been the case with Zimerman's work, were sharply divided between engaged enthusiasts and appalled traditionalists. *—Jeremy Grimshaw*

Recommended:

- ○ **Debussy: Préludes** / Zimerman / DG 435773
- ○ **Liszt & Chopin** / Ozawa (cond.), Zimerman, BSO / 1998 / DG 459053
- ○ **Ravel: Concertos** / Boulez (cond.), Zimerman, Cleveland Orch., London SO / DG 449213
- ○ **Beethoven: Concertos** / Bernstein (cond.), Zimerman, Vienna PO / DG 435467
- ○ **Schubert: Impromptus** / Zimerman / 1991 / DG 423612

Bernd Alois Zimmermann

b. Mar. 20, 1918, Bliesheim, Germany, **d.** Aug. 10, 1970, Königsdorf, Germany
Composer

One of the most important German composers to emerge during the post-World War II era, Bernd Alois Zimmermann was born in the outskirts of Cologne in 1918. His schooling at the Cologne Musikhochschule was interrupted when he was drafted for military service in the early days of the Second World War. Discharged in 1942, Zimmermann resumed his academic training with Jarnach and Lemacher, and between 1948 and 1950 enrolled in the summer courses at Darmstadt. He was engaged as a lecturer in music theory at Cologne University in the early years of the 1950s, and, from 1957 on, taught composition at the Cologne Musikhochschule.

Until his untimely death in 1970 Zimmermann produced a steady stream of music for both concert and radio (having been director of not only composition at the Musikhochschule but also radio, film, and stage music as well). In 1965 his "pluralistic" opera (so called because it incorporates elements of many different musical styles, juxtaposing live orchestra with electronic sounds and utilizing a fair amount quotation as well) *Die Soldaten* was successfully premiered in Cologne. The work, perhaps Zimmermann's most eloquent musical statement, has since been hailed as the greatest operatic achievement since Alban Berg's *Lulu*.

Zimmermann's music frequently borders on unplayability, and it is only through the exceptional gifts of a handful of players and conductors (including cellist Siegfried Palm and conductor Hans Rosbaud) that his powerful musical creations escaped oblivion. His work reveals a deeply religious sentiment (as in the second volume, sub-titled "devotional exercises" of the solo piano work *Enchiridion*, or the viola concerto *Antiphonen* from 1962), and in later years Zimmermann, increasingly withdrawn from the musical establishment (indeed, from the rest of the world as well), came to view his music as a personal act of communication with the Divine. His final work, an "ecclesiastical action" for two speakers, bass, and orchestra, completed just five days before his death, concludes with a quotation of J.S. Bach's chorale *Es ist genug.—Blair Johnston*

Overview of Works (1937–1970)

Bernd Alois Zimmermann was a pioneer in collage technique, that being the incorporation of pre-existing material into an original musical composition. Like Anton Webern, Zimmermann had a keen interest in musicology and history, going back to the Middle Ages. He was also exceedingly well read in literature from the ancients to the contemporary. Thus, with such a catholic range of interest, the composer was well prepared to tread a different path. Early on, the composer's mature style crystallized. His earliest works, such as the *Sinfonia Prosodica* and the *Concerto for Orchestra*, reveal a serialism leavened by tonal inclination for expressive purposes, eliciting a cross section of acclaim from all camps. Added to this treatment of the 12-tone technique was his first major foray into quotation in the *Trumpet Concerto* in which a tone row is called into play with the famous American spiritual "Nobody Knows the Trouble I've Seen." Looking back to the high Baroque era, the gospel tune is used as a chorale would be in a chorale prelude, the composer's active mind drawing on jazz technique in the development of the work. All the salient features were in place when Zimmermann, only 39, commenced upon his masterwork, the opera *Die Soldaten*. It would take seven years before it saw completion and performance a year later in 1965. Nonetheless, it met with immediate acclaim and to this day has been cited as the most important German opera since those of Alban Berg four decades prior. Undoubtedly the summit of his output, *Die Soldaten* reveals all of Zimmermann's interests and inspirations. The grim libretto will undoubtedly recall the military backdrop of *Wozzeck*. Each of the scenes in its four acts is structured on a smaller musical form, some distinctly ancient (ricercare, toccata, etc.). Gregorian chant and Bach chorales are woven into an Expressionist musical fabric, Zimmermann looking back to Webern more than Berg in his use of glinting flecks of color. At his death in 1970, Zimmermann's had been working on his second opera *Medea*. Zimmermann's interest in music of the distant past may be divined by his numerous arrangements of folk and Renaissance music for various media, as well as his music for stage, radio, and television. While his output was substantial, it marks a mere 52-year life span and joins the considerable body of musical "what ifs?" *—Wayne Reisig*

Recommended:

- ○ **Zimmermann: Dialogue; Monologue; Perspektiven; Photopsis** / B. Kontarsky (cond.), Grau, Schumacher / 1997 / Col Legno 20002
- ○ **Zimmerman: Présence; Perspektiven; Intercomunicazione** / Palm, Gawriloff, The Kontarskys / DG 437725

OPERA

Die Soldaten (1957–1965)

The tragic drama of Bernd Alois Zimmermann's first and only opera, *Die Soldaten* (The Soldiers) (1957–60), is undoubtedly linked to the time he spent in military service, which interrupted his studies at the Cologne Musikhochschule and the universities of Cologne and Bonn. This work has been proclaimed the most significant German opera since Berg's *Lulu*, and is ranked as one of the musical landmarks of the twentieth century. When Zimmermann began the piece in 1957, he had just started as professor of composition and as chair of the department of radio, film, and stage music at the Cologne Musikhochschule. The following year *Die Soldaten* was formally commissioned by the Cologne Opera, where it eventually had its premiere nearly ten years later.

Conceptually, *Die Soldaten* was born in the middle of the 1950s, when Zimmerman was considering writing an opera setting of Ben Jonson's *Volpone*; however, this text was discarded and attention was given to J.M.R. Lenz's *Soldaten*, which Manfred Gurlitt had explored in the earlier part of the twentieth century. Zimmermann found himself respectfully drawn to the way the text explored how fundamentally honest, ordinary people could be destroyed by certain situations and the strength of others. Essentially, it was a drama of social criticism and class conflict, which made a disturbing statement about the entire postwar generation, while offering a metaphor for the modern world. In his own libretto, Zimmermann condensed the lengthy text into four acts and poured in his hatred of the culture of militarism as he depicted the atrocities of the Second World War. In this well planned, formally structured, pluralist "collage," scenes are staged at different levels or angles simultaneously; the original concept had involved 12 acting areas, each with its own instrumental ensemble. In addition, several layers of multi-media, including video and electronic tape, merged together at once, within a combination of jazz, music, language, dance, pantomime, and circus. The work incorporates 40 roles, but the focus is on Marie, a young girl who is degraded in the hands of a corrupt and egotistical military aristocracy. It reflects the influence of Berg, Bach, Mozart, Debussy, Dante, Dostoevsky, Aeschylus, Joyce, Pound, Mayakovsky, and the medieval Catholic philosophy.

Despite its title, Zimmermann's *Die Soldaten* centers not around the soldiers in the story, but the young woman, Marie. Over the course of four acts—deployed, after the manner of Berg's *Wozzeck*, as a series of traditional instrumental forms (ciacona, ricercare, toccata, etc.)—Marie transforms from a lovestruck girl to a woman of tarnished reputation, to a prostitute, and, finally, a beggar.

When Zimmerman first presented *Die Soldaten* to the Cologne Opera, it was rejected as technically impossible. Between 1963 and 1964, the composer reduced the dramatic dimensions and trimmed the forces to create an acceptable simplified version. The first appearance of the opera took place in Cologne on February 15, 1965, conducted by Michael Gielen and directed by Hans Neugebauer. It was performed for the first time in America, in Boston, in 1982, where it was conducted by Sarah Caldwell, and in 1991 it was staged by the New York City Opera under Christopher Keene and Rhoda Levine. In *Die Soldaten*, Zimmermann succeeded in showing how separate and synchronous dramatic strands could effectively portray the monstrous dehumanizing effects of war. *—Meredith Gailey*

Synopsis:

Act One. In Lille, in the house of Marie's father, Wesener, Marie writes a letter to the family Stolzius of Armentières. She had fallen in love with the young man of the house during a recent visit; Stolzius likewise has fallen for her, but his mother forbids the relationship. Despite this infatuation, Marie accepts an invitation to the theater from a soldier, Desportes, but, concerned for her reputation, Wesener prohibits Marie from going. Later, Marie shows her father a love poem from Desportes; the father is swayed somewhat by Desportes' social status, but urges Marie not to write off Stolzius yet. Elsewhere, a group of officers discuss female virtue; a whore, they conclude, will be a whore regardless, so why concern oneself with a woman's virtue?

Act Two. In a café in Armentières, a group of rowdy soldiers mocks Stolzius over rumors of Marie's infidelity. Stolzius writes an angry letter to Marie, which she reads to Desportes; amused at the challenge, Desportes lures her into her bedroom. In a simultaneous staging, Stolzius is seen reading with grief Marie's subsequent letter and vowing revenge.

Act Three. Stolzius joins the ranks of the military, hoping to gain access to Desportes; he finds employ as a servant to Desportes' colleague, Major Mary—who, by this time has curried Marie's favor while Desportes is away. Stolzius accompanies Mary to the Wesener house, where Marie notices a resemblance but fails to recognize her former love. Apparently, Mary is not Marie's only interest; the Count de la Roche fancies her as well. His mother, the Countess, forbids the relationship on grounds of social standing, but out of concern for the girl, offers to take her on as a servant.

Act Four. Scene One unfolds at a dizzying pace, with a dream sequence and several plot developments represented in multiple simultaneous scenes on-stage and projected film. Marie flees the Countess' house. A guard, sent by Desportes to find Marie, captures and rapes her. Stolzius buys poison with which to kill Desportes. Marie, broken, becomes a streetwalker. The subsequent scene finds Stolzius serving dinner to Desportes and Mary. Desportes disparages Marie, surmising that she had been a whore all along, indulging him only for the gifts he gave her; his cruel commentary is interrupted when, downing his poisoned soup, he collapses dead. Stolzius receives the sword of Mary's retribution without resistance. The opera ends tragically as Wesener, walking along a dreary road, grudgingly gives some coins to a beggar woman—not recognizing her as his long-lost daughter. *—Jeremy Grimshaw*

CHORAL

Requiem für einen jungen Dichter (1967–1969)

After the success of the long-delayed premiere of his opera *Die Soldaten* in 1966, German composer Bernd Alois Zimmermann turned his attention to what would become his boldest musical statement, the *Requiem für einen jungen Dichter* (Requiem for a young poet). It is a 65-minute score for huge forces, including a narrator, two vocal soloists, three choruses, full orchestra (minus the high strings), two pianos, Hammond organ, and a jazz combo. Sprinkled throughout the piece are taped recordings of speeches by historical figures Winston Churchill, Josef Stalin, Alexander Dubcek, Joseph Gobbels, Joachim von Ribbentrop, and others. The text of the work combines a fragmentary Latin mass setting with words of poets who committed suicide: Vladimir Mayakovsky, Sergei Esenin, and Konrad Bayer among them. The music is also heavily invested in collage technique, making use of strains borrowed from a wide range of music from Richard Wagner's *Tristan und Isolde* to the Beatles' song "Hey Jude." The choral parts are difficult in the extreme; in the concluding "Dona nobis pacem," there is a point where they are required to sing cluster chords containing all of the notes in the chromatic scale.

The *Requiem für einen jungen Dichter* is a very serious, dark, bleak, and pessimistic piece. It is sort of like the Beethoven *"Choral" Symphony* for a postmodern world, with the "joy" of Beethoven's creation transformed into despair. In continental Europe it has been reserved for special occasions, much as the Beethoven *Ninth* itself once was, although toward the end of the twentieth century performances of Zimmermann's *Requiem* have become more frequent. In the United States, the *Requiem* is still little known; its Carnegie Hall premiere wasn't given until April 20, 1999, under Michael Gielen, who led the original Dusseldorf premiere of the work in 1969 and has proved its main proponent over the years. While Zimmermann survived long enough to complete a few more pieces, he was found dead by his own hand not much more than a year after the original premiere of the *Requiem*. "Zimmermann was a manic depressive," conductor Michael Gielen once told the author, "he was manic when he was composing and depressive once he finished (a composition). After he was done with the *Requiem für einen jungen Dichter* everyone who knew him also knew he wouldn't be able to come out of that final depression." *—Uncle Dave Lewis*

David Zinman

b. Jul. 9, 1936, New York, NY

Conductor

David Zinman is an American conductor, well known for his broad repertoire with large emphasis on recent music both in North America and Europe. His own instrument was the violin, which he studied at Oberlin College Conservatory of Music in Ohio. He took a Masters in composition at the University of Minnesota in 1963. During the same period he attended the Berkshire Music Center at Tanglewood. French conductor Pierre Monteux noticed him, leading to Zinman's enrolling in Monteux's conducting school in Maine. From 1961 to 1963 Zinman served as Monteux's assistant, and he considers Monteux his primary mentor.

He appeared as a guest conductor at the Nederlands Kammerorkest, after which the organization engaged him as its conductor. He held that position from 1965 to 1977. His success in Holland led one of the country's leading full-size orchestras, the Rotterdam Philharmonic, to invite him to be its music director (1979–82). He also conducted at the Holland Festival. In the meantime he had been music adviser (1972–74) and music director (1974–85) of the Rochester (NY) Philharmonic. In 1983 he became principal guest conductor of the Baltimore Symphony Orchestra. This association was elevated to the position of music director in 1985.

Zinman has been known for a very broad repertoire and innovative programming. In Baltimore he added a summer music festival, a discovery series of contemporary music, and Saturday morning "Casual Concerts," with commentary by the conductor. His highly acclaimed recordings on such labels as Telarc, Argo, and Sony Classics include music as traditional as the Elgar symphonies and overtures and as unusual as Michael Daugherty's *Metropolis Symphony*, based on characters and situations from the Superman comic books. He has helped spark interest in a new type of American symphonic music. Turning its back on the abstruse, international sound of the 12-tone music that was current around the world between 1950 and 1980, Zinman had helped promote an type of tonal music featuring the driving rhythms that characterize American popular and jazz music. Although the music is often controversial, the presence of such elements in this music thrills much of the established audience and attracts a new one.

In 1998 Zinman stepped down from his Baltimore position, but continued as music director and chief conductor of the Zurich Tonhalle Orchestra (since 1995), and as music director of the *Aspen Music Festival*. *—Joseph Stevenson*

Recommended:

- ○ **Danielpour: Concerto for Orchestra; Anima Mundi** / Zinman (cond.), Pittsburgh SO / 1997 / Sony 62822
- ○ **Rouse: Symphony 1; Phantasmata** / Zinman (cond.), Baltimore SO / 1989 / Nonesuch 79230

- ○ **Daugherty: Metropolis Symphony; Bizarro** / Zinman (cond.), Greenberg, Controulis, Sparks, Baltimore SO / 1996 / Argo 452103
- ○ **Gorecki: Symphony 3** / Zinman (cond.), Upshaw, London Sinfonietta / 1992 / Nonesuch 79282
- ○ **Barber: Adagio For Strings, etc.** / Zinman (cond.), Baltimore SO / 1992 / Argo 436288
- ○ **Berlioz: Symphonie Fantastique, etc.** / Zinman (cond.), Baltimore SO / 1991 / Telarc 80271

Eugenia Zukerman

b. Sep. 25, 1944, Cambridge, MA

Flutist

Eugenia Zuckerman is one of the world's best-known flutists, known for her particular interest in innovative ways of bringing classical music to new audiences and in musical education. She is also an author of novels and nonfiction books.

She was born Eugenia Rich in the Boston suburb that is the home of Harvard University. A flute student since childhood, she began her higher education as an English major at Barnard College. Soon her interest in music asserted itself and transferred to the Juilliard School of Music in New York, where from 1964 to 1966 she was a pupil of the leading flutist Julius Baker, soloist with the New York Philharmonic.

In 1970, she won the Young Concert Artists Concert Audition, which earned her as a prize her debut recital at New York's Town Hall in 1971. The recital won rave reviews, and initiated a major worldwide concert and recital career. She has performed with some of the major orchestras of North America, Europe, Asia, and the Middle East. These include the Los Angeles Philharmonic, the Minnesota Orchestra, the English Chamber Orchestra, the Israel Chamber Orchestra, and the National Symphony Orchestra of Washington, D.C.

She is very active on the international music festival scene, with appearances at the Aspen Music Festival, the Angel-Fire Festival, Mostly Mozart, the OK Mozart International Festival, the Ravinia Festival, Tanglewood, Edinburgh, the South Bank Festival in London, the Spoleto Festival in Italy, the Yehudi Menuhin Gstaad Festival in Switzerland, and the Schleswig-Holstein Festival. She became the Music Director of the Vail Valley Music Festival in Colorado in 1998.

In 1968, she married the famous violinist Pinchas Zukerman and frequently appeared with him in concert. They were divorced in 1985.

In 1980, she became the arts correspondent for the *CBS Sunday Morning* news program and, over the course of that association, has done over 300 artist profiles. In 1988, she began a regular lecture-performance series with keyboard player Anthony Newman at the New York Public Library's Celeste Bartos Forum. These concerts combine musical performance with readings from letters and other historical documents shedding light on the music. The concert-lectures are short, given just after the end of a working day and are the prototype for the increasingly popular American concept of rush-hour concerts.

Eugenia has recorded for the CBS Masterworks, ProArte, Vox Cum Laude, and Newport Classics labels, followed by an exclusive contract with Delos Records.

As an author, she has written two published novels, *Deceptive Cadence* (Viking, 1981) and *Taking the Heat* (Simon and Schuster, 1991), and a non-fiction book. The latter is the result of being diagnosed with a career-threatening, rare lung disease that required her to take the cortisone-based medication Prednisone. Concerned with the problems of potential side effects, she joined with her sister, physician Julie R. Inglefinger, to write *Coping with Prednisone (and Other Cortisone-Related Medicines): It May Work Miracles but How Do You Handle the Side Effects* (St. Martin's Press, 1997). She has also sold three screen plays, one each to 20th Century Fox, MGM, and Universal Pictures, and has been published in *Esquire*, *Vogue*, and the *New York Times* magazines, among others. *—Joseph Stevenson*

Recommended:

- ○ **Mozart: 7 Sonatas** / Zukerman, Newman (piano) / 1992 / Newport 60120
- ○ **Incantation** / Zukerman / 1996 / Delos 3184

Pinchas Zukerman

b. Jul. 46, 1948, Tel Aviv, Israel

Violinist, Violist

Israeli-born Pinchas Zukerman has kept his face and music before the public for more than four decades with his wide range of activities: he is a world-class violinist, violist, conductor, and administrator. Zukerman's first instrument was the recorder, his second the clarinet. But soon he took after his father, a violinist of Polish background. By the time he was eight, Zukerman was studying at the Tel Aviv Academy of Music, and when he was 12 he moved to New York to matriculate at the Juilliard School. Isaac Stern signed papers to become his legal guardian. Zukerman studied with Ivan Galamian, the Juilliard's avatar of hardcore Russian-school playing, and was also encouraged by cellist Pablo Casals.

After jointly winning the Leventritt Competition with Kyung-Wha Chung in 1966, Zukerman began performing widely. His career as a top-flight international soloist began with his New York debut at Lincoln Center in 1969. Zukerman performed on both violin and viola, taking full advantage of the various repertoires his versatility opened up to him. He played duo sonatas and music for larger chamber ensembles, recorded the Mozart *Sinfonia Concertante for violin, viola, and orchestra* with Stern, and also began building a career as a conductor. Zukerman performed music from the Baroque era to premieres of new works by Lutosławski and others. By the early 2000s, Zukerman had made over 100 recordings as a soloist, covering the entire standard violin and viola repertoire.

In 1980, Zukerman was named music director of the St. Paul Chamber Orchestra. He restored the group's financial health, oversaw a move into a new 2,000-seat theater, and made a series of recordings, both as conductor and soloist, that became mainstays of radio programming. In 1998, as his marriage to Hollywood starlet Tuesday Weld dissolved, Zukerman accepted the music directorship of Canada's National Arts Centre Orchestra in Ottawa. His efforts there encompassed unusual levels of community and educational outreach; he became a pioneer in the use of videoconferencing and webcasting technology to communicate the immediacy of classical music making. He helped launch the career of the young Russian violin sensation Ilya Gringolts; after seeing a video of Gringolts' playing that his parents had sent from Russia, Zukerman arranged for Gringolts to study at Juilliard with Itzhak Perlman and conducted Gringolts' North American debut with the NAC Orchestra. He remains internationally active as a soloist and guest conductor. *—James Manheim*

Recommended:

- ○ **Beethoven: Sonatas 5, 8 & 9** / Zukerman, Barenboim (piano) / 1992 / EMI 64631
- ○ **Mozart: Concertos 1–3** / Zukerman, St. Paul CO / 2002 / Sony 89840
- ○ **Bach & Vivaldi: Concertos** / Zukerman, Garcia, English CO / 2001 / RCA 68002
- ○ **Brahms: Concerto; Bruch: Concerto 1** / Mehta (cond.), Zukerman, Los Angeles PO, London PO / 1999 / BMG 68046
- ○ **Franck, Debussy, Faure** / Zukerman, Neikrug (piano) / RCA 62697

Paul Zukofsky

b. Oct. 22, 1943, Brooklyn, NY

Violinist

Paul Zukofsky is a violinist, conductor, and chamber musician. He is generally associated with the advancement and performance of modern music, having premiered and recorded works by Wuorinen, Glass, Carter, Babbitt, and numerous other twentieth century composers. But he has also divulged a sympathy for the music of Bach in his well-received recordings of the solo sonatas and partitas.

Zukofsky showed interest in music before the age of three and started taking his first lessons on the violin at four. His skills advanced so rapidly that he began studies with Ivan Galamian when he was just seven. His resumé as a child performer is equally impressive, having given his first public concert at six and his first with an orchestra, the New Haven Symphony Orchestra, when he was ten. Three years later, he gave a recital at Carnegie Hall. By the mid-1960s, Zukofsky had become well known in both solo and chamber repertory. In the latter genre, he would team up with Gilbert Kalish for many concert appearances and recordings over the years. He also began conducting orchestras, often chamber-sized ensembles and usually in modern repertory. He served as music director for one season (1978–79) of the Colonial Symphony Orchestra, a Madison, NJ–based ensemble. In this post, however, he also conducted works by Beethoven, Mozart, and other mainstream composers. Zukofsky has also led the Contemporary Chamber Ensemble since the 1970s, becoming its conductor in 1984. Beginning in the 1970s, Zukofsky developed a relationship with the Reykjavik College of Music in Iceland, regularly appearing in concerts and conducting seminars there. He also appeared in many concerts as conductor at the Lincoln Center for the Performing Arts in the last two decades of the twentieth century, often leading the Contemporary Chamber Ensemble and the Juilliard Orchestra. Zukofsky became a close friend of composer Philip Glass in the early 1970s and even appeared as Einstein in his opera *Einstein on the Beach* (1976). The character Zukofsky portrayed, of course, does not sing, but plays the violin instead. Zukofsky inspired Glass to write his *Violin Concerto* (1986–87) and gave the work's premiere on April 5, 1987, with the American Composers Orchestra under the direction of Dennis Russell Davies. From 1992–96, Zukofsky was director of the Arnold Schoenberg Institute at the University of Southern California. As both a conductor and violinist, he remains active in the new century and has made over 60 recordings for a number of labels, including Sony, Camerata, CRI, and one of his own, CP2, of whose parent company, Musical Observations, Inc., he is president. He has extensively recorded for this label since the early 1990s, issuing performances of works, often in premiere issues, by Cage, Feldman, Xenakis, Glass, and several other modern composers. *—Robert Cummings*

Recommended:

- ○ **Shapey, Riegger, Piston, Crumb, Sollberger, Berger** / Sollberger (cond.), Zukofsky, Kalish, Jolley, Desroches, Brehm, Blustine, Sollberger / 2002 / CP2 114

○ **Cage Album** / Zukofsky / CP2 103

○ **Schnabel Album** / Zukofsky (cond. & violin), Gregg Smith Singers / 1996 / CP2 110

Ellen Taaffe Zwilich

b. Apr. 30, 1939, Miami, FL

Composer

Ellen Taaffe Zwilich emerged in the last two decades of the twentieth century as one of the most recognized and sought after composers in the classical music world. Her success reflects the firm foothold of so-called neo-Romanticism in contemporary orchestral repertoire and a move among many composers to find an expressive, intuitive musical language more resonant with universal human emotion than earlier, more fractious and detached twentieth century trends.

Zwilich did not begin her composing career writing in this vein. Her earliest works, such as the *Symposium for Orchestra* (which Pierre Boulez conducted in 1975) or the *String Quartet* 1974, featured the angular contours and difficult harmonic language that one might expect from a student of Elliott Carter and Roger Sessions (both professors at Juilliard). Her music took a decidedly more accessible and emotional turn as the composer approached maturity—due, in part, to the deep introspection that followed the death in 1979 of her husband, violinist Joseph Zwilich. Her career quickly took off during the subsequent decade. After the premiere of her *Symphony No. 1* by Gunther Schuller and the American Composers Orchestra in 1982, she received a nearly continuous string of symphonic commissions from various orchestras, including the New York Philharmonic, the Chicago Symphony, and the Boston Symphony. These commissions resulted in three subsequent symphonies, the orchestral work *Symbolon* (1988), and an impressive collection of over a dozen concertos during the 1980s and 1990s. Zwilich also composed a number of well-received chamber works during this period, including a *Concerto for trumpet and small ensemble* (1984), as well as the *String Quartet No. 2* (1998), commissioned by the Emerson Quartet. In the 1990s, Zwilich also undertook significant audience outreach projects, such as the Making Music concert and lecture series, which she organized, and, for Carnegie Hall's family concert series, the charming *Peanuts Gallery* (1997), a composition for piano and orchestra inspired by the beloved Charles Schulz comics.

Although to describe Zwilich as an outstanding *woman* composer would unjustly confine her success, she does deserve credit for opening a number of doors for female composers. She was the first woman to receive a doctoral degree in composition from the Juilliard School, the first woman to receive the Pulitzer Prize in music (for her *Symphony No. 1*), and was named the inaugural holder of the Composer's Chair at Carnegie Hall. *—Jeremy Grimshaw*

Overview of Works

That Zwilich is a female composer and works in a largely tonal idiom takes a back seat to her being one of America's foremost and best-liked composers of classical music. Her versatility may be divined by perusing an output that runs the gamut from the venerable traditional forms to a work based on Charles Schulz's "Peanuts" characters. As with so many of the composers of the second half of the twentieth century, Zwilich's earlier works represented the drier academic ethic of earlier decades, in her case the influence of her teachers Sessions and Carter. Her style started to change around the time of the passing of her husband, noted violinist Joseph Zwilich, in 1979. In 1983, her *Symphony No. 1*, which was awarded a Pulitzer Prize for music (the first for a woman composer), shows the first ruminations of this tendency. Although tonal, it is far from a white-key, diatonic language ranging through a brooding, ambiguous first movement, a central long-breathed one that may recall Shostakovich's slow movements, and a merry third in which "highlights" of more pronounced traditional tonality color the overall palette. Also, an inclination toward motivic development in lieu of sonata or rondo forms may be seen to emerge here and became more pronounced as her music evolved. This may recall Sibelius' processes; in fact, Zwilich's approach to this method is streamlined, relying on greater economy and simplicity. Also reminiscent of the Finn are her insistent ostinatos and long-held, almost grinding appoggiaturas used to great dramatic effect. These salient features may be heard in her four symphonies, with *Symphony No. 4*, from 1999, using a children's chorus to join the orchestra. If Zwilich elects for a more traditional approach to musical building blocks, there is an abundance of inventiveness, even fun, with her concepts and approaches. Her 1981 *Passages* is scored for soprano and an eclectic chamber orchestra; in the finale of this, the vocalist takes on wordless syllables and joins the ensemble as a fellow instrumentalist. Zwilich's other works have included concerti for lesser-tapped instruments, among them a trombone concerto in 1988 and a bassoon concerto in 1992, as well as numerous choral and vocal works. One of her most conspicuous works is the 1997 concerto for piano and chamber orchestra, *Peanuts Gallery*, based on the characters from Schultz's comic strip, which takes its place with Carpenter's *Krazy Kat* ballet among "serious" music cum the Sunday funnies. *— Wayne Reisig*

Recommended:

○ **Zwilich: Piano Concerto; Double Concerto; Triple Concerto** / M. Stern (cond.), Laredo, Robinson, Kalichstein / 2002 / Koch 7537

○ **Zwilich: Concerto Grosso; Symphony 3; Oboe Concerto** / Sedares (cond.), Mack, Louisville Orch. / 1995 / Koch 7278

○ **Zwilich: Symphony 4; Bass Trombone Concerto; Horn Concerto** / L. Gregorian (cond.), Jolley, Johnson / 2000 / Koch 7487

○ **Zwilich: Symphony 1; Celebration; Prologue & Variations** / J. Nelson (cond.), Indianapolis SO / 1986 / New World 80336

Essays

Classical Music for Newcomers

"Do you like classical music?" It may be that you're a little embarrassed by the question. "Yes," some people answer—"but I don't know anything about music." Well, if you've encountered a piece of classical music that you loved, then you know more than you think you do. Maybe you've heard Andrea Bocelli sing the aria "Che gelida manina" from Puccini's opera *La Bohème*, or maybe you've had your attention snared by a lush orchestral piece like Pachelbel's *Canon* or Samuel Barber's *Adagio for Strings*. Maybe you've played the piano or participated in a school orchestra or band. Classical music is everywhere around us—in movies, in television commercials, in schools, in the memories of our parents and grandparents. Anywhere that it's caught your attention is a good place to start.

Classical vs. Popular Music

Whether you sit down to master classical harmony or rock guitar, you'll study chords and how they fit together either way. If you learn to play an instrument, you'll most likely learn both classical and popular selections—and you'll find that musicians don't tend to worry much about categories. Classical music and popular music, both part of the cultural frame of reference of most Americans and Europeans, share many aspects of musical language. Yet there are some prominent differences as well. Coming to classical music from popular music is less of a leap than you might think, but there are a few ways in which you have to retune your ears.

One important difference comes in regard to duration. Popular songs are usually brief; most of them are under five minutes long. Classical compositions, on the other hand, range from 20-second pieces to works that last several hours. The average symphonic concert work lasts perhaps half an hour, and this requires a change of perspective for those accustomed to listening to popular songs. How does a composer make such a large piece of music hang together? It's a question worth asking of any piece of music, but for classical compositions it's one of critical importance.

Another difference is that popular music is mostly vocal music. Be it rock, country, R&B, or pop, ballads or dance music, there is usually a singer, and a text that carries a major share of a composition's meaning. But vocal music is only a province, and not even the most extended province, of the territory of classical music. Even in the realms of opera and art song, the music is the message.

Though classical music is very much a living tradition today—listen to John Adams' *Harmonielehre* for a work that draws on historical traditions and yet is entirely of our own time—it also has a thousand-year history of having been preserved for posterity by musical notation. Popular music, sometimes notated but often including spontaneous elements, has a deep history of its own, of course. Yet our definite knowledge of music that was never written down is limited to a period beginning just over a century ago, when the first recordings were made. Notation allows, if not greater complexity, at least a greater degree of control over musical events on the part of a composer external to a given performance of a piece. Whereas a pop recording, very broadly speaking, depends on an interaction between performer and song, classical music rests on a triad: composer, work, and performer.

And generally speaking, the dynamic range, the difference in volume between the loudest and the softest moments, is greater in classical music than in pop. Some pieces are very loud, some are very soft, and some vary widely within a single piece, sometimes so extremely as to have made it nearly impossible to capture the full range in recordings before the arrival of digital techniques. The distinction here is not a hard and fast one, but it's no accident that the salesperson at a high-end stereo shop will bring out a classical CD to demonstrate what a fine pair of speakers can do.

What to Listen For in Classical Music

Quite a few books have been written on this very subject, so there's no way we can give you a complete overview here. But don't let that unnerve you! Too many people have the idea that classical works consist of an arcane set of codes, known only to an elite group of lifetime concertgoers. Nothing could be further from the truth. There are plenty of places to get a foothold.

Just like any other music, classical music is full of tunes. And a tune is often a piece's central "idea"—if you hear a melody that catches your ear, it's both fun and instructive to listen for it again. How does the composer prepare you for its return? And how does the melody change, if at all, when it returns? Does the composer use little bits of the melody in combination with other material in the piece? As you luxuriate in that beautiful tune, pay attention to what happens to it along the way—and all of a sudden, all the discussions of "form" that you read in classical concert program notes won't seem so mysterious. Many factors work together to make the famous first movement of Beethoven's *Symphony No. 5* such a powerful piece of music, but the single most important one is the way the dramatic short-short-short-LONG motif heard at the beginning is worked and reworked and reworked again.

Another good place to start is simply to ask yourself what instruments (or voices) you're hearing and how they're used. One of the joys of classical music is its endlessly varied instrumental combinations—classical works are written for everything from one gentle instrument (Bach's *Suite for Solo Cello No. 4*) to Mahler's so-called *Symphony of a Thousand*, which does indeed approach four figures in the orchestral and choral forces required. Some classical listeners prefer music written for small groups such as a string quartet—"chamber music," as it's called. And nearly everybody who has tried sitting down at a piano keyboard has had a brush with some of the classics for solo piano. Try Robert Schumann's *Kinderszenen* (Scenes of Childhood) for a taste of what Romantic-era (nineteenth century) piano music is all about.

And it may help you grasp the spirit of a classical piece to know where and when it was composed. Classical music represents a thousand years of the cultural history of Europe, America, and the rest of the world. If you gain enough familiarity, it is possible to place an unknown work in time and be accurate to within a few years. Most of the music heard on recordings and concert programs dates from between 1700 and the present day, but in recent years more and more performers have explored the music of the Medieval and Renaissance eras. Of course the relationship between the sound of music and the culture that surrounds it is a complicated one. But the soaring spaces of a Gothic cathedral in Paris seem to come alive in memory when you hear the vast four-part *organum* of Pérotin—as do the devotional spirit of German Lutheranism in the cantatas of Bach and the American worship of landscape in Copland's *Appalachian Spring*.

Why each person develops a particular attachment to certain pieces of music is a question shrouded in obscurity. No matter what the experts tell you, no matter how many courses on musical appreciation you take, no matter how "great" or important a piece is, if after listening to it intently several times its language does not say anything to you, then it may simply not be your kind of music. All that said, there is something objective about the relative difficulty of some composers. There is little doubt that the tune-filled works of, say, Vivaldi (such as *The Four Seasons*) and Mozart make for comparatively easy listening, whereas five hours of Wagner opera may not be every listener's chosen cup of tea.

An extra dose of patience may be required when listening to certain music of the twentieth century as well, but little is accomplished if you run away from any music without trying it. Every epoch brings innovations that are resisted by traditionalists, but soon become normal and accepted. Who knows? If you find new music that makes sense to you, you may find yourself out in front of a trend.

But above all, trust your feelings. The greatest composer is the one whose music touches you most effectively.

—*James Manheim*

Form in Classical Music

Sometimes, discussions of musical form can seem like fences put up by the classical music in-crowd to keep outsiders away. The words used to describe common forms and their sections tend to be long and Latinate, and some are flat-out offenses against the English language—whoever came up with "retransition" ought to be drawn and quartered. But be not afraid, new classical listener! As with most kinds of professional jargon, there's less to this set of words than first meets the ear.

No composer worth his or her salt ever cared much about the terminology of musical form. Sonata-allegro form, ritornello form, rondo form, and all the rest aren't rules for composing music; they're shorthand notations, devised after the fact, to describe solutions that worked for some large group of composers, somewhere, at some time. They don't work very well at all as descriptions of individual pieces of music, because more often than not the interest of a composition resides in how it departs from common procedures rather than in how it follows those procedures. Nevertheless, it will help you appreciate classical compositions if you know a little bit about the common forms of classical music. Why? Because if you have a feel for the form of a piece, you'll know what the composer is expecting you to be expecting!

Form, to put it in the simplest terms, is the way a piece of music is organized. And all of the tens of thousands of ways a piece of music might be organized boil down to two simple possibilities: two stretches of music may be similar, or they may be different. If you're here because the court sent you to music school instead of traffic school by mistake, you now have the key point and can go home. But for the rest of us, let's take things a little bit farther—let's say you're a composer. You sit down with your piano, your guitar, your pen and music paper. How are you going to organize your piece?

Say you've come up with a pretty good tune—what's the next step? Well, you can just repeat it several times and be done with it. That might seem pretty simple, but if you're putting music to the words of a poem that moves along in nice, regular verses, it can be just the ticket. In fact, some of the best-known "art songs" in classical music—works like Schubert's "An die Musik"—take the form of a series of verses, each with the same music. We call this strophic form, and though it usually refers to vocal pieces, an instrumental dance from the Renaissance era can have exactly the same structure. The word "strophe," in fact, referred originally not to poetry, but to the movements of the chorus across the stage in ancient Greek drama. Another simple possibility is to come up with a second good tune that makes some kind of effective contrast with the first one, and then to bookend that second tune with statements of the first one. That gives you what we might call an ABA form, also known as ternary form or song form even though not all songs work this way.

Maybe you're playing an instrument and want to show off your skills. This gives you another option for what to do when you repeat your tune—you can elaborate it and throw in some technical challenges. Maybe you want to repeat the tune six or eight or 33 times, with the variations getting progressively more difficult or introducing little bits of drama along the way. What we call variation form might seem to be a simple thing, but in fact it offers a composer limitless possibilities—which might explain why variation form is one of the oldest construction blueprints in classical music even as new sets of variations are being written every year.

Now, suppose you want to vary your repetitive structure a bit, either because you're setting poem with a block of text that repeats, or because you decide that to drive home the poet's meaning you want to repeat some of the text and back it up with especially powerful music. If your repeated block of text is just a few lines long, you've got yourself a refrain. Nonsense texts like the "fa la la la la" in a Christmas carol are usually refrains. If your repeated block forms a whole little self-contained statement, we call it a chorus, whether it's actually sung by a chorus or not (see what we mean about confusing terminology?). The resulting form, reasonably enough, is referred to as verse-chorus form. All over the world, this form is an effective way of bringing people together in groups to make music, but in the hands of a skilled composer it can take on great subtleties indeed—do you want to make your chorus music similar to the verse but especially intense? subtly different from it as a kind of commentary? quasi-dramatic, in order to reveal an emotion that lurks submerged during the verse (think about the way Chuck Berry's "Maybelline" is structured)?

It's all up to you. Composers down through the ages have made their own decisions and have come up with infinite variations on these basic song-inspired forms. In the numbers-and-mathematics-obsessed medieval era, song composers in France devised complex refrain structures called formes fixes (fixed forms) in which repetitions of parallel stretches of text and music would sometimes but not always coincide. The golden age of the Broadway musical in the first half of the twentieth century brought a different kind of complexity: composers like George Gershwin, Jerome Kern, and Irving Berlin shrank the verse in size and importance (and eventually got rid of it completely), but expanded the chorus and began to elaborate *it* into interesting subdivisions and contrasts. A chorus with four distinct sections or long phrases is often designated with letter shorthand like AABA (listen to Berlin's "Blue Skies") or ABAC ("All of Me").

Now let's suppose you're an instrumentalist, and you want a way of organizing your composition that doesn't follow a vocal model. When the concerto, a composition for one or more soloists and orchestra, got started in the early 1700s, a natural way to organize it was to employ the alternation principle we have already encountered: you can assign your orchestra a good, solid chunk of music and have the soloist really take off with new music in between. In this case we call the orchestral refrain a ritornello and the whole structure a ritornello form. Or, for a short piece, there's binary form. As the name implies, this involves dividing your piece into two halves, either or both of which may be repeated. Listen to many of the small dance pieces that together make up Handel's masterpiece, the *Water Music*. You'll notice that they start out in a certain key—the harmonic "home base" of the piece—and then move into another key area in which you feel that you've departed from that home base. At the end of its first half, the piece comes to rest in that new key, and over the course of the second half it makes its way back to the place where it started.

Over the course of the eighteenth century, composers expanded this little scheme. If you're composing a piece of music, a good way to make it more effective is to use several musical parameters to mark off a significant event—if you're changing keys, for example, you might mark that event with a new melody or some kind of new musical texture or instrumentation. This is what Mozart, Haydn, and their contemporaries did to the little binary-form pieces they inherited from the Baroque era. They stretched out this binary form and marked out its sigificant events—like the return of the home key, say—by parceling out melodic material effectively and by manipulating the dramatic ebb and flow of the music, the speed at which things were happening.

Listen if you can to the first movement of Mozart's *Symphony No. 40 in G minor*, K. 550 (a movement is a section of a work with multiple separate sections—a symphony often has four of them). At the beginning we move from the stormy music of the opening to a more tranquil section in a new key, and this more tranquil music is announced by a new melody. This part of the movement, where Mozart lays out his musical materials, is called the exposition. Eventually he comes to rest in the new key with a flourish, and there is a strong feeling of a temporary stopping place. Then Mozart vigorously reworks the material he has introduced, combining the two melodies, moving rapidly through several keys, and generally stirring things up to a higher level of drama. This section of the movement is called the development, for the composer develops the music introduced in the exposition. Finally Mozart seems to be working up to a high point of excitement, and simultaneously you realize that you're about to return to the home key, to harmonic home base (this is the passage some call the retransition. Finally you hear the opening material of the movement, in its home key, and the composer runs through much of the remaining material of the beginning, this time without departing from the home key. This section is called the recapitulation, and if there's some final little detail at the end of the movement, that's called the coda (Italian for "tail").

Put this whole scheme together, and we call it sonata form or sonata-allegro form. Both terms are needlessly confusing—it occurs just as often in symphonies as in instrumental sonatas, and is also quite common in slow movements, not just in quick allegro ones—but they're the terms history has stuck us with. Sonata form is one of the central achievements of classical music, for it enabled composers to tie together a movement 20 minutes long or even longer with a variegated but powerful internal logic. It appears in works with all kinds of instrumentation, from solo works to string quartets to symphonies. The concerto for soloist and orchestra has its own special version of sonata form, with a so-called double exposition—first the orchestra lays out the music, then the soloist varies it and and gets the chance to display his or her technique. Some writers have even suggested that sonata form was the musical analogue for the imperial ambitions of Europe as it colonized the globe—it was a musical way of making strong long-range connections. If you still feel overwhelmed, here's the first step, the Idiot's Guide to Classical Music version: if you're at a classical concert and you're hearing a piece called Symphony No. Something, listen closely to the music you hear at the beginning of the first movement, and see if you can determine not just when it appears again, but how the composer sets up its return.

The last movement of a symphony might be cast in sonata form, but the composer might also decide on something more lighthearted and less rigorous. One common form for symphonic movements expands upon our basic idea of alternating familiar material with something new: rondo form, as its name implies, is "rounded" by the periodic return of the opening material of the movement, yielding a structure like ABACA or even ABACADA. If the composer ventured far afield from the opening material and introduced some drama into a rondo movement, the result might be a hybrid form sometimes called a sonata-rondo form.

Beethoven was at once the king of sonata-form composers and the one who started to break the form's hegemony—in the first movement of the *Symphony No. 7* you'll find the logic of sonata form, but you'll also hear an intensity that seems to spill over the neat boundaries of its various parts. The progressive composers of the Romantic nineteenth century had no use for such well-ordered layouts. For them, the form of a piece followed the sequence of emotions a composer was trying to express. Often, Romantic composers used a recurring melody or other musical idea that might symbolize a memory, a scene, a hidden emotion. If this recurring idea is worked into the basic material of several movements of a piece but treated differently as it appears anew, we call this cyclic form. Another common way the Romantics structured their music was to follow the form of an extramusical work, most often a novel, poem, or play. This wasn't just a matter of vague inspiration; audiences might be provided with a little booklet recounting the story the music was telling. Liszt's symphonic poem *Hamlet* provides a good example of what we call program music; such music is often described as programmatic.

All of the forms we have described so far have endured into the twentieth and twenty-first centuries, along with a host of new ways of putting a piece of music together. In recent years, we might argue, the sonata-form aesthetic of home, departure, conflict, and return has been partially displaced by conceptions of form that emphasize ultimately Eastern-inspired visions (or auditions) of life as a series of cycles. In classical music and in the popular dance scene alike, modern audiences prize not goal-directed motion but intensive explorations of the moment. No doubt, at some time in the future, writers will create majestic polysyllabic names for certain forms that have recurred unusually often. In the meantime, those who listen to classical music will continue to find understanding and delight by asking the same questions as ever: how is this piece of music put together? how is the composer highlighting that structure, or departing from it? and what does it all mean?

—*James Manheim*

Music of the Middle Ages

The medieval era is a temporal division even more vague than the other major time periods of European history, covering perhaps a thousand years from the decline and fall of the Western Roman Empire in the fifth century C.E. to the rise of what we call Renaissance ideas around 1450. We do not know all the music that flourished over this vast span of time, but we can glimpse its variety. So-called Gregorian chant is an important part of medieval music, but far from the whole story: medieval music was secular as well as sacred, lively as well as somber, earthy as well as mystical. Medieval musicians established the fundamental building blocks of the European musical tradition that followed: they created and refined systems of musical notation, and they developed what we call polyphony, the simultaneous combination of independent lines of music.

Medieval Music and Ancient Music

Like many other aspects of medieval European society, medieval music depended in its general outlines on practices inherited from antiquity. Although our knowledge of music prior to the earliest notated chant is sparse, we believe that the medieval world inherited general musical ideas and features from ancient Greece, Rome, and Byzantium. Medieval Christian musicians took from their predecessors an idea of music as a single melody line, and they classified melodies by "mode"—a collection of pitches similar to what we would call a scale, but also encompassing voice ranges and certain melodic formulas. Very little actual music came down to medieval Europe from the ancient world, but ancient theoretical writings were comparatively abundant. Partly as a result, medieval thinking about music had a scientific and mathematical tinge interwoven with its religious significance: music was seen as linked to other arts and sciences and to the deeper order of the universe as a whole.

Chant and Secular Monophony

The liturgical melodies of medieval Christian churches and monasteries, which to modern ears epitomize pure faith and a static timelessness, actually reflect centuries of musical development and even political change. This body of music is popularly referred to as Gregorian chant, after Pope Gregory the Great (ca. 540–604), who according to legend composed it himself under divine inspiration. Modern research has shown that chants originated in many different places and evolved over the centuries, yet Gregory still deserves part of the credit for the way the tradition developed: he, more than most of the other early popes, worked to centralize church authority in Rome —and an ultimate result of that centralization was that chants were written down in musical notation in order to bring consistency to the music of Christian institutions spread out over most of a continent. Chant lies between the oral and the written, the local and the administratively standardized, the improvised and the compositionally specified.

Music was integral to every aspect of medieval Christian worship; specific chants were linked to different parts of individual services, to services held at specific times of the day and night (the Mass and the daily Offices or Hours had their own chants), and to the various phases of the liturgical year. Texts might come from the Bible or from non-biblical sources within Christian liturgy—or they might be newly composed. The repertoire of an individual monk or chorister might consist of hundreds of chants, but as notation took hold, innovation began to supplant the importance of memory and oral tradition. The notation of the chant, dating from roughly the ninth century, not only preserved the music but changed it, prompting a new spirit of creativity and elaboration that eventually resulted in the emergence of polyphony. New chants were composed, and some, such as those of the German abbess Hildegard of Bingen, bore the strong imprint of an individual creative personality. Chants are often classified as *syllabic* (having mostly one note per syllable of text), *neumatic* (with several notes per syllable), or *melismatic* (featuring long efflorescences of melody on single text syllables).

Not all medieval monophonic (single-line) music was sacred. The French troubadors and trouvères and their counterparts in other lands, poet-composers associated with noble courts, created sophisticated fusions of poetry and monophonic song, often on themes of a perfect, unattainable love. The music of these bards was notated only sporadically, but modern performers have extrapolated new music to fit the large body of existing texts. Several groups of songs that have come down to us, both secular and sacred, constitute little dramas; such works as *The Play of Herod* and the French *Play of Robin and Marian* were among the first examples of musical theater in the European tradition. The large body of *Cantigas de Santa Maria* (Songs in Praise of the Virgin Mary) compiled under the supervision of King Alfonso the Wise in thirteenth century Spain have come down to us in a manuscript with illustrations showing how these monophonic pieces might have been accompanied on a variety of instruments.

Early Polyphony

It was medieval musicians who first pursued harmony and polyphony as systematic arts. Writers of the ninth century documented an existing improvised practice, termed organum, whereby singers would add a second vocal line parallel to a line of chant. Over time the two lines might become more independent of one another, and singers began to codify rules that specified how to create consonant (pleasing) or dissonant combinations. Thus, over several centuries, the art and discipline of polyphony (music with several parts) was born. One hotbed of experimentation was the Abbey of St. Martial near Limoges, in west-central France, but slowly notation, and the new music it made possible, spread around Western Europe. By the twelfth century, various textures were available to makers of organum; there were "florid" pieces, with many notes in the added voice for each note of the chant or tenor, as opposed to note-against-note discant pieces. A lengthier composition, with added texts explicating the message of the original chant, might contain sections of both kinds.

In late twelfth century Paris, composers defined vast realms of musical space by alternating plainchant with highly elaborated florid organum and discant sections that might have three and even four voices. From this period come the first composers who were individually recognized by their contemporaries: manuscripts refer to a Léonin and Pérotin who were active at Notre Dame cathedral in Paris, and it is hard to hear the soaring *Viderunt omnes* organum of the latter without thinking of that soaring Gothic structure. Freely composed multipart pieces, called conductus, also began to appear.

The Motet and the Ars Nova

Early in the thirteenth century, discant sections of organum began to take on life as independent motets (the term is derived from the French "mot," or word, and signfies simply a newly texted piece). These pieces featured texts for the upper voices in addition to that of the tenor—often a different, and not necessarily sacred, text for each voice. Secular texts, and texts in the French language, were freely combined with sacred and Latin texts. Motets of the late thirteenth century, such as those by Petrus de Cruce, often combined a rapidly moving, speechlike top voice, a slower middle voice, and a very slow tenor. The Ars Nova motet of the early fourteenth century moved further in the direction of rhythmic complexity, with new "imperfect" (i.e., duple) divisions of long note values and intricate isorhythmic organization of the tenor itself in which repetitions of tune and rhythmic pattern might overlap rather than coincide.

Here the mathematical qualities of medieval music came to the fore. The new rhythms of the Ars Nova were notated in a series of evolving systems that continue to pose challenges to scholars who have studied them for years. The isorhythm idea was elaborated over the fourteenth and much of the fifteenth centuries, eventually reaching levels of extreme complexity. Yet fourteenth century music was not just a mathematical exercise. Even as Europeans' lives were plague-shadowed and short, much of their music was secular and could be described above all as fun. Texts became more stylistically accomplished, and many included satirical elements. The early fourteenth century *Roman de Fauvel*, featuring isorhythmic motets by Philippe de Vitry, told the story of an ass named Fauvel whose name was made up of the first letters of six terrible character flaws. The work was well enough known to leave its traces even on the English language: the expression "to curry favor" is derived from "to curry (comb the hair of) Fauvel."

Machaut and Late Fourteenth Century Song

The major trends of fourteenth century music reached their fullest development in the music of Guillaume de Machaut (1300–1377). Machaut composed music in all the major genres of the day: motets in which all the parts were organized in isorhythms, monophonic songs, the first complete setting of the Ordinary of the Mass, and polyphonic songs that embedded structural complexity and musical puzzles in a framework of elegant courtly love poetry, with a new spirit of lyricism. Machaut might be thought of as the first composer in the European tradition who was conscious of himself as an artist. His polyphonic songs fall into the so-called formes fixes (fixed forms) of French medieval poetry—the rondeau, ballade, and virelai, which feature interlocking musical and textual refrains that might be elegantly manipulated or commented upon in the text; for a well-known example consider the rondeau *Ma fin est mon commencement* (My End Is My Beginning). Machaut was a poet-musician who wrote his own texts, and late in life he wrote a sort of autobiographical poem, the *Voir dit*, which also contains a number of musical compositions.

In southern France in the late fourteenth century, polyphonic song reached an unparalleled level of rhythmic complexity in the hothouse atmosphere of the papal power center of Avignon. The famous chanson *Belle, Bonne, Sage* of Baude Cordier was notated in the shape of a heart, with shifts between red and black noteheads indicating changes in the rhythmic grouping in force. Whereas traditional music history focused primarily on developments in France during the medieval era, modern performers have investigated other national traditions, several of which were in full flower by the end of the fourteenth century. In Italy, Francesco Landini (ca. 1325–1397) cultivated a smooth, lyrical melodic and harmonic style, and several of his compatriots, such as Johannes Ciconia and Jacopo da Bologna, wrote songs whose charm and grace seems undiminshed by the centuries.

New Trends in England and Burgundy

England had a national musical tradition during the medieval era, spawning tunes such as the *Boar's Head Carol* that have survived until the present day. Even in its own time English music was recognized as distinct; Continental writers identified a "contenance angloise" around the middle of the fifteenth century that was distinguished primarily by what we today would call familiar harmonies. They sound familiar because they feature the intervals of a third and a sixth between voices—common in the chords you may have learned on the piano or guitar, but rarer in the music of Machaut and earlier French composers, for in that music these intervals were considered dissonant.

English music had a direct influence on composers in the powerful French region of Burgundy. The Burgundian composer Guillaume Dufay (1400–1474) incorporated English influences into a progressive song style. Dufay's music seems poised between medieval and Renaissance. Some of his works, such as the massive isorhythmic motet *Nuper rosarum flores*, seem rooted in the medieval era, but in much of his religious music Dufay pioneered the characteristic texture of Renaissance music: music with four voices of equal importance.

Medieval Music and the Modern Scene

Twenty years ago the average music lover, if he or she had any mental picture of medieval music at all, might have imagined a procession of monks intoning chant melodies that seemed the very essence of timelessness—the perfect example of a spiritual music that held itself apart from the affairs of the world and remained a rock of permanence in the midst of change. Today, on the rise in popularity even beyond classical music's usual listenership, medieval music seems instead to reflect the long pageant of vibrant and rapidly changing cultures of which it was a part. Performers constantly unearth new repertories and devise new ways of approaching music that is already well known. Medieval music blazed paths followed by later composers; viewed a certain way, it foreshadows the future of European art music. It is no mere forerunner, however, but a tradition with diverse joys to offer in its own right.

—*James Manheim*

Music of the Renaissance

The educated elite of Europe in the fifteenth and sixteenth centuries boasted of living in an age of exciting rebirth. Historians and chroniclers such as Leonardo Bruni, Filippo Villani, and Giorgio Vasari saw their own time as one of great cultural expansion, one which had emerged from the long "Dark Ages" of Catholic Europe and one which rivalled the very heights of Classical antiquity. Writers and poets from Petrarch on studied ancient Greek and Latin. A new generation of literary scholars sought to emulate directly the style and rhetorical power of the ancient languages. Generations of painters and sculptors, from Cimabue and Giotto to the theorist Leon Battista Alberti, likewise pursued the "realism" and moral affect of antique models. In many cases, such "humanist" (the term comes from *studiae humanitatis*, the first liberal arts) zeal for Classical models first appeared in Florence and other Italian city-states, but rapidly was felt throughout the Western world.

In a similar way, musicians and music theorists saw the emergence of a distinctly fresh musical style in their own time. The poet Martin le Franc in the 1440s famously described the music of Guillaume Dufay and Gilles de Bins (Binchois) as adopting from the English a "new way of making sweet consonance." By the 1470s, the prolific music theorist Johannes Tinctoris could claim that in the face of a completely "new art," music merely decades old was utterly unlistenable. He wrote on the ancient division of musical melodies into eight modes, linked the proper manner of composition to the rhetorical structure of a Ciceronian oration, and praised the manifold moral affects of music upon the human body. He further classified the music of his time into three style heights (mirroring the venerable *Rota Virgiliana*): Masses (*cantus magnus*), motets (*cantus mediocris*), and songs (*cantus parvus*). His threefold hierarchy still serves to categorize the music which emerged in the cathedrals, princely courts, and urban centers of Renaissance Europe.

Among the kaleidoscopic spectrum of fifteenth century musical developments, the first genre to produce distinctly new fruit was the secular French chanson. Early generations of composers inheirited a rich tradition of courtly poetic *formes fixes* from the fourteenth century and grafted a new "sweetness" onto it. Dufay, Binchois, Ockeghem, and Busnois, all wrote polyphonic French songs with fuller (triadic) harmonic textures and an increasingly rich sense for archlike melodic shapes. At first, the new sound seemed linked to English-occupied France after Agincourt. These chansons, however, spread quickly to the Italian states; much of the music survives in manuscripts either associated with the Loire valley or larger Italian centers. By the late-fifteenth century generation of Josquin Desprez, Loyset Compère, and Alexander Agricola, incursions by more popular French secular musics and by the new imitative style of counterpoint were quietly but firmly dismantling the courtly chanson. Other European cultures by the turn of the sixteenth century had similarly thriving styles of secular polyphony: the German tenorlied of Heinrich Isaac and Ludwig Senfl, the Italian frottola and canti carnascialeschi of Bartolomeo Tromboncino.

Meanwhile, musicians employed by both cathedrals and princely court chapels began to forge an entirely new genre of musical composition: the cyclic Mass ordinary. Early English influence is evident. The first complete polyphonic settings of the Mass in the century were composed by Englishmen such as John Dunstaple and Leonel Power. Working first in pairs of musically linked Mass movements, the English apparently then conceived a series of five Mass movements all based upon the same unifying cantus firmus. The early unifying melodies came from the chant liturgy and often were associated with royal and papal ceremonies. In the 1460s, Masses based entirely upon *secular* melodies began to overtake those based on liturgical chant; two of Dufay's four late Masses and several of the Masses of Ockeghem use French chansons as *cantus firmus*. Composers competing on an increasingly international musical stage paid one another homage by writing Masses on the same chanson; such Mass families include the related pair of *Fortuna desperata* Masses by Josquin and Jacob Obrecht, larger groups based on French chansons from the international "hit parade" such as *De tous biens playne* and *Malheur me bat*, and a famous and extensive series of Masses (over 30 of them) based upon the tune *L'homme armé*. Canonic Masses and Masses based upon plainchants for the Blessed Virgin Mary and for the Requiem Mass continued their own vibrant traditions.

Though fifteenth century composers directed their greatest artifice onto polyphony for the Mass, the century's greatest stylistic upheavals may have transpired among the wide variety of compositions known as motets. Continental composers such as Dufay had a long tradition of polytextual motets, involving isorhythm in one or more voices, for high ceremonial occasions; Dufay's *Nuper rosarum flores*, written for the 1436 dedication of Florence Cathedral, provides a richly symbolic example. Johannes Regis and Jacob Obrecht extended the tradition of the polytextual motet, though a much wider array of Latin-texted polyphonic composition was growing alongside it. Intense late medieval devotion to the Virgin Mary helped fuel a distinct subgenre which adorned the liturgical Office with polyphonic settings of her canticle (the Magnificat) and the Marian antiphons. Other popular and liturgically-specific subgroups of the Latin motet include settings of Office Psalms and hymns, Mass Proper cycles, Lamentations of Jeremiah, and Passion narratives. In addition, "motets" survive from the time which set para-liturgical texts such as the sensual imagery of the Song of Songs, the populist worship music of the confraternities and even Classical and humanistic texts. Groups of motets could apparently even replace elements of the official Catholic liturgy, as in the Milanese "motetti missales" cycles.

By the turn of the sixteenth century, then, the baseline of all European musical styles was undergoing a complete transformation. The motet in the hands of Josquin and the somewhat later generation of Johannes Mouton, Pierre de la Rue, Adrian Willaert, and Nicolas Gombert strived for an ever more direct mode of text-expression. Vocal compass in their polyphony had expanded. This led to more distinction between voice parts, yet more equality of function among them. The contrapuntal device of imitation was becoming more and more common; "pervasive imitation," where all voices begin a musical/textual phrase with the same melodic motive, describes an integral part of the style. Musical genres did tend to interbreed, with motet-chansons mingling in the same piece, motets substituting into Mass movements, and Masses increasingly borrowing complete musical passages from motet or chanson models. In addition, after the turn of the century, the advent of music printing from movable type led to much wider musical dissemination and interchange. Ottaviano Petrucci first printed his large collection of secular songs the *Odhecaton* in 1501, following it quite closely with a series of printed anthologies of Masses (by Josquin, Obrecht, and many others), motets, Laude, and frottole. While earlier music required highly-paid professional scribes to prepare single manuscript copies, the sixteenth century first enjoyed the benefits of mass production.

In music for the sixteenth century Catholic church, some level of stylistic unanimity remained. Mass composition witnessed the triumph of the "parody," or "imitation" Mass. Rather than using a single borrowed voice as *cantus firmus*, the new technique involved the borrowing of many voices from a chanson or motet, intact in their contrapuntal relationships. It was first used as early as the 1470s by Johannes Martini. Later composers such as Clemens non Papa, Cristobal de Morales, and Francisco Guerrero created "imitation" Masses which so carefully echoed the sound of their models that sixteenth century theorists could distill "rules" for Mass composition. The style of pervading imitation thrived in both Mass and motet. One famous musicologist concluded this was the "Central Musical Language" for all of Christendom; certainly there exists some level of commonality in motet composition throughout the century. The motet genre did benefit, however, from an ever-increasing tendency towards close musical reflection of the text; melodic "madrigalisms," chromatic harmonies, and other overt attempts to mirror textual imagery frequently bled over into motet writing. This tendency towards expressionistic gestures continued into some of the later motet cycles of Orlandus Lassus.

The Protestant Reformation and the Catholic Church's own self-reformation later in the century spurred the development of several related yet contrasting genres of music composition. While sixteenth century Catholic composers continued to write settings of the Latin Psalms (including some spectacular pieces for divided choirs in Ferrara and then Venice), Protestant doctrine dictated the singing of Psalms in the vernacular. Thus emerged polyphonic Psalters in German (including important translations by Martin Luther himself), French (by Clement Marot and Claude Goudimel), and Dutch (the *Souterliedekens*). Henry VIII's England made a reasonably smooth transition from the Masses and motets of the *Eton Choirbook* to polyphonic settings of the English Service (morning and evening prayers); the English anthem filled the same liturgically ambiguous yet musically important function as the Latin motet. Thomas Tallis, Christoper Tye, and Thomas Weelkes contributed to each genre.

In addition, the various national secular styles continued rich new developments to the century's end. Alongside the many imitative-style chansons of Crequillon, Gombert, and Clemens, a new Parisian style of chanson emerged in the 1520s. In an effort to recast the moral effects of ancient poetic feet in the French language, Claudin de Sermisy and others evolved a simpler and more direct style of chanson declamation. Clement Jannequin extended his efforts, but also contributed to a more evocative and "programmatic" style involving onomotopoeia. The Italian madrigal enjoyed an even richer tradition across the sixteenth century, from the popular compositions of Philippe Verdelot and Jacques Arcadelt in the 1520s and 1530s, to the more adventuresome efforts of Willaert and Cipriano de Rore. Virtuoso singers in the city of Mantua helped make possible the often more extroverted text-settings of Claudio Marenzio and Giaches de Wert; Carlo Gesualdo's chromaticism travelled famously over a stylistic cliff. Instrumental music also continued to press forward. The fifteenth century's simpler chanson arrangements and lute and organ tablatures gave way to the more substantial surviving repertories by organists such as Cabezon and Cavazzoni, lutenists such as Francesco da Milano, and the newer concerted compositions of Andrea and Giovanni Gabrieli.

Each stylistic and repertorial thread tends to culminate in one or more of a quartet of composers writing towards the end of the century: Giovanni Pierluigi da Palestrina, Tomás Luis de Victoria, William Byrd, and Orlandus Lassus. The music of each represents a highly personal synthesis of the "High Renaissance" style. In Palestrina's over 100 Masses and nearly 300 motets, the balance and utterly careful dissonant treatment of his century reaches an apogee in service to the Catholic liturgy. Victoria learned the same refined style in Rome, yet applied his own passionate and almost ascetic intensity to the harmonic and melodic language; a common but apt analogy compares Palestrina to Raphael, and Victoria to El Greco. William Byrd served both the Anglican communion and the underground English Catholics with a wealth of excellent music for services, in addition to an extensive repertory for keyboard. Orlandus Lassus composed well and prolifically in nearly every genre known to the sixteenth century, composing music fluently for texts in at least five separate languages; in every measure, his command of the musical language reflects his sensitivity to the nuances of his text.

It could be said that the seeds for the dissolution of this musical style were already sown in the midst of these fruitful lives. The age which knew a new "sweetness" in its song and flexed its muscles to bend that sweetness in ever more powerful and intimate service to words, quickly discovered the limits of its own potency. Madrigalists, already stretching the stylistic envelope, would soon stumble upon new practices which would render their own gains obsolete. Already in 1600, musicians were experimenting with radically new devices such as monody, chromatic madrigal techniques, and extended instrumentation, to seek the same end: the rhetorical power of ancient melody.

—Timothy Dickey

Music of the Baroque Period

In the second half of the eighteenth century, intellectuals dismissed Baroque art and music (which modern historians place in the 1600–1750 time frame) as an aberration, a necessary, if embarrassing, step toward the developing Classical style. Indeed, Classicism is beauty, balance, and formal perfection, a condition, to paraphrase Walter Pater, to which all art should aspire. We unconsciously accept this point of view when we call Western music itself, as manifested throughout its 1,500-year history, "classical." Is Baroque music essentially primitive, a diamond in the rough, a block of marble, which is only potentially a work of art? Is the term "baroque" really derived, as critics believed for more than two centuries, from the Portuguese word for "deformed pearl"? While scholars still argue about the semantics and etymologies of "baroque," with some suggesting a derivation of a name used as a mnemonic device by students of logic, the music speaks for itself, calling all these intellectual constructs into question. For example, the music of J.S. Bach (1685–1750), particularly works such as the *Art of the Fugue*, not only attain an unsurpassed level of formal integrity but also transcend, paradoxically, traditional modes of musical expression (voice or instruments), revealing the metaphysical essence of music itself: pure movement.

If music is pure movement, inspired by profound spiritual and metaphysical impulses, then all Baroque art is quintessentially musical. Having lost the coordinates of a unified mental world view that existed in the Middle Ages and the Renaissance, the Baroque spirit is restless; passionate, innovative, and spacious, it indefatigably strives to grasp the Absolute, which, in the seventeenth century, came either from irrefutable scientific knowledge or from the ineffable mystery of God. These contradictory aspirations truly constitute the mental background of Baroque art and music. To the chiaroscuro of Descartes' (1596–1650) rationalism and Pascal's (1623–1662) mysticism correspond the contrasting realms of darkness and light in the paintings of Caravaggio (1573–1610), as well as the sharply contrasting sonorities of Baroque music. And to the distinct religious visions of Catholicism and Protestantism correspond, for example, the Marian motets of Marc-Antoine Charpentier (1643–1704) and Bach's biblical narratives, inspired by Protestantism's emphasis on the Scriptures and exemplified by Bach's monumental *St. Matthew Passion*.

Baroque art and music, in their complex grandeur, provided a human response to the paradoxical uncertainties of the new age. Caravaggio, who introduced chiaroscuro to Western art, exemplified this response. As Sister Wendy Beckett wrote in her *Story of Painting*: "For the first time, as it were, an artist looked at the full reality of human existence, its highs and lows, its glories and its sordid materiality." In his seminal painting *The Supper at Emmaus* (1601), which depicts the moment when the Disciples recognize the resurrected Christ, Caravaggio attained the eminently Baroque synthesis of the three fundamental manifestations of reality: divine, human, and natural, with nature being represented in the basket of fruit on the table. These realms were presented, with equal evocative power, in Baroque music. For example, the art of French harpsichordists, which reached its summit in the works of François Couperin (1668–1733) and Jean-Philippe Rameau (1683–1764), brilliantly captured fugitive moods, feeling, and impressions, sometimes yielding unforgettable vignettes of individual character types. Couperin's "Ame-en-peine" ("Suffering Soul," from his *Pièces de clavecin, Book II* is the very essence of dolor, while Rameau's "Fanfarinette" ("Little Fanfare," from his *Nouvelles suites de pièces de clavecin*) conjures up an atmosphere of elegant nonchalance and exquisite charm. With equally skillful suggestiveness, Catholic and Protestant composers, faithful to their respective traditions, contemplated the divine, creating music of extraordinary power and enduring popularity in such works as the *Gloria* of Antonio Vivaldi (1678–1741), Bach's *Magnificat*, and the *Messiah* of George Frideric Handel (1685–1759). Finally, Baroque musicians also found inspiration in nature, enriching the chiaroscuro tonal palette with the spectrum of colors provided by instrumental sounds. The pinnacle of descriptive art in Baroque music came with Vivaldi's four concertos known as the *Four Seasons*, which brilliantly evoke the particular atmosphere, flavor, and spirit of each season, creating an eternally fresh musical calendar.

While Baroque painting reached its summit immediately, with the appearance of Caravaggio, music developed in its own way. The earliest stirrings of the Baroque spirit can be heard in the late Renaissance madrigal (poetry set to music, usually for four voices), when expressions of strong emotions started disturbing the delicate balance of voices typical of Renaissance music. Representative of this new expressiveness were Carlo Gesualdo (ca. 1561–1613), the Italian prince who murdered his wife, and Claudio Monteverdi (1567–1643), whose madrigals introduces dissonances which undermine the harmonic texture defined by Renaissance style. Strong emotions, represented by dissonance, eventually destroyed the homogenous, balanced structure of Renaissance polyphony when composers started using a solo voice as the dominant expressive medium, breaking the Renaissance equilibrium of voices into a dynamic of foreground voices and vocal or instrumental accompaniment. Then, in true Baroque spirit, this change in structure led eventually to a new polarity in which the solo and the bass voices came to define a given musical composition. The melody exists in relation to the continuous bass, the *basso continuo,* which for many theorists defines the musical Baroque.

However, this fundamental polarity by itself fails to account for the immense richness of Baroque music. Other basic technical factors were at work. First, Baroque composers founded modern tonality, the system of keys, when they replaced the ancient modes—established patterns of tones and semitones—with the modern scale. The next step was equal temperament, a tuning system in which the distance between two adjacent tones became immutable. With the equally tempered scale, music entered a realm of mathematically defined quantities. While music lost its archaic patina, scientifically defined tonality open a whole new, seeming inexhaustible, harmonic universe, which Bach brilliantly explored in his two-volume *Well-Tempered Clavier* (1722 and ca. 1740), each book of which contained 24 preludes and fugues (representing the 12 major and 12 minor keys that define the modern tonal universe).

Having inherited a predominantly vocal tradition with a set of strongly characteristic textures, Baroque composers followed an impulse to create an entirely new sound. The foundation of this new sound was a radical expansion of sonic space, begun by the late Renaissance practice of divided choirs. Flourishing in Venice, and exemplified by the polychoral compositions of Giovanni Gabrieli (ca. 1557–1612), this practice, which implied the idea of infinite sonic space, included contrasting juxtapositions of pitch and vocal mass, echo effects, and variations of volume and timbre. In essence, polychorality, as an idea, underlies the instrumental concerto, an eminently Baroque genre, which juxtaposes a solo instrumentalist (concerto), or a small group of soloists (concerto grosso), with a larger ensemble. Appearing around 1700, the concerto predominantly featured the violin, the Baroque instrument par excellence. The genius of Antonio Vivaldi towers among the masters of the violin concerto: the violin is a perfect vehicle for his tremendous energy, boundless imagination, and captivating themes. Interestingly, Vivaldi also composed extraordinary concertos for other instruments, including bassoon and flute. While the trio sonatas (for two violins and continuo) and concerti grossi of Arcangelo Corelli (1653–1713) established the Baroque standard for these genres, it was Vivaldi's particular genius that inspired Bach to bring the concerto, in his magnificent six Brandenburg Concertos, to the level of universal genius.

In the sixteenth century, as the enthusiasm experienced by the early Humanists waned, a spirit of melancholy introspection entered European literature. Embodied in the brilliant essays of Montaigne (1533–1592), this spirit appeared, in authentic Baroque form, in the *Anatomy of Melancholy* of Robert Burton (1577–1640), a monumental, labyrinthine, dizzying meditation on just about everything, with particular emphasis on remedies, spiritual or otherwise, for melancholy. Also prominent in the plays of Shakespeare (1564–1616) and Pedro Calderón de la Barca (1600–1681), the motif of melancholy points to the "solitary voice" topos, easily recognized in Pascal's anguished realization that he is imprisoned by "the terrifying expanses of the universe." Caravaggio poignantly depicted the solitary musician's melancholy gaze in his extraordinary painting The Lute Player (1596), which brings to mind the soulful music of John Dowland (ca. 1563– ca.1626) and other great lutenists. Indeed, the Baroque of contemplative solitude can be heard in music written for string instruments: the lute, a medieval instrument, the viola da gamba, which originated in the Renaissance, and the violin, the quintessence of the Baroque. If the origin of an instrument determines, to an extent, the character of its repertoire, traces of late Renaissance melancholy in Marin Marais' (1656–1728) *Pièces de viole* need not be viewed as anachronistic. The protean beauty of Marais' pieces for viola da gamba is imaginatively described in Pascal Quignard's novel *Tous les matins du monde* (1991), which inspired an enormously popular film. Yet Marais, whose ethereally mournful viola da gamba music evokes the feeling of lost time, also created the shocking masterpiece of Baroque realism, *Le tableau de l'opération de la taille* (Pieces de viole, Book V), in which he musically depicts his own gall bladder surgery.

There is less passion and more introspection in music for solo violin, which follows a deep metaphysical impulse. Consider the *Mystery Sonatas* of Heinrich Biber (1644–1704), a prayerful musical meditation on the Mysteries of the Rosary. Because the Mystery Sonatas include accompaniment, scholars have singled out the Passacaglia for unaccompanied violin as the work anticipating Bach's great Chaconne in D minor. Perhaps the pinnacle of Bach's six sonatas and partitas for unaccompanied violin, the Chaconne (from the Partita in D minor) not only stretches the violin technique to create an impression of harmonic richness and contrapuntal intricacy, but also, attaining tremendous metaphysical depth and narrative authenticity, introduces the listener to an illuminating and inexhaustible meditation on the mysteries of life, death, and eternity.

Solo music by definition, compositions for keyboard (harpsichord and organ) in many ways reflect the physical experience of exploring a keyboard, which naturally leads the performer to the pleasures of free improvisation. From this experience of improvisation sprang such composition types as the ricercar (from the Italian "ricercare," "to seek") and toccatas (from the Italian "toccare," "to touch"). Another source of inspiration for keyboard composers was dance music. In Bach's hands, suites of dances, such as his six English and six French suites, attained an extraordinary level of formal sophistication, elegance, and musical suggestiveness. Quite different in spirit from the intimate familiarity of Couperin's harpsichord music (to which one may compare the brilliant familiarity of the amazingly concise keyboard sonatas of Domenico Scarlatti [1685–1757]), Bach's keyboard music not only explores the newly discovered space of equally tempered tonality but also creates an astonishing synthesis of formal perfection and improvisatory inventiveness. Complex contrapuntal pieces were paired or joined with quasi-improvisatory procedures. Examples of this synthesis include the famous Toccata and Fugue for organ in D minor, the Goldberg Variations, and the astonishing Chromatic Fantasia and Fugue in D minor, regarded as perhaps the highest expression of Bach's genius as a composer for keyboard.

While opera is often perceived as a Romantic and modern genre, Baroque masterpieces such as Rameau's *Hippolyte et Aricie* (1733) and Handel's *Serse* (1735) established an aesthetic standard that many now as unsurpassed; more and more Baroque operas are unearthed and performed every year. As a genre, opera was unwittingly created, around 1600, by a group of intellectuals who wished to revive ancient Greek drama. Imagining that a dramatic work with soloists, a chorus, and instrumental accompaniment might replicate the authentic experience of Greek drama (which certainly included music), opera's creators, not knowing what ancient Greek music sounded like, had to obtain new music of their own. Opera was, from its very beginnings, an eminently Baroque genre, and it was here that the fundamental contrast of melody line and accompaniment took shape. Created by Italian scholars, poets, and musicians, the genre was dominated by Italian masters, attaining greatness in the hands of Claudio Monteverdi (1567–1643), whose *L'incoronazione di Poppea* (The Coronation of Poppea) was a masterful depiction of extreme passions. Rameau's *Hippolyte* is perhaps the finest manifestation of Baroque operatic art. With its carefully constructed dramatic narrative, resplendent harmonies, finely crafted melodies, and opulent instrumentation, Rameau's opera is among the greatest examples of Baroque music.

The Baroque is the first period in music to have started with two distinct traditions of church music: until the Protestant Reformation, all European sacred music was by definition Catholic. During the Baroque period, Catholic composers still used genres, such as the mass and the motet, which had originated in the Middle Ages. However, Charpentier's masses and motets are not medieval music: relying on the vocal and instrumental resources available to Baroque composers, these works fully expressed a new, passionate, mystical spirituality, which, while ultimately stemming from a medieval world view, asserted itself with extraordinary vigor and suggestiveness.

Church composers found an appropriate dramatic genre in the oratorio, in which biblical and other devotional narrative was set to music. Initially dominated by Catholic composers, the genre eventually became a powerful vehicle of Protestant spirituality, as exemplified by Handel's great works, which include *Saul*, *Israel in Egypt*, *Judas Maccabaeus*, and *Messiah*. But the greatest monuments of Baroque church music came from the pen of Bach, a pious Lutheran and one of greatest composers of all time, who grasped and expressed the immense depth of the mystery of faith in his *Magnificat*, *Christmas Oratorio*, St. Matthew Passion, and the stupendous *Mass in B minor*, for which he used the text of the Catholic liturgy in order to emphasize the universality of the Christian faith.

—Zoran Minderovic

Music of the Classical Period

The Classical era within "classical music" begins in perhaps 1735 and ends around 1825, encompassing some overlap with the surrounding periods of Baroque and Romantic. What does the word "Classical" mean here? The music has little to do with the Classical civilizations of ancient Greece and Rome. The key to understanding the early development of Classicism in music lies with the appearance of a new style in the early eighteenth century, one that attracted the term *galant* and other adjectives. This approach emphasized elegance and clarity of melody over the rugged counterpoint favored in the Baroque. Mozart and other Classical-era composers seem now to embody the height of elegance—but in their own day they were part of a movement that prized naturalness and simplicity over intellect and elaboration. And, just as they did when they were adopted by the 1960s counterculture, ideals of naturalness and simplicity carried political overtones.

Thanks to its mighty Viennese triad of Mozart, Haydn, and Beethoven, listeners tend of think of Classical-era music as Austrian in essence. But its origins were Italian. The beginnings of true classical style around 1730 may be traced to Bologna, where teacher and composer Francesco Durante began to impart to his students an aesthetic of radical simplification. One of Durante's pupils, Giovanni Pergolesi, arrived at a clear-cut and then highly controversial style that stripped away practically all the expected counterpoint (music with several independent lines, like a round) in favor of thin textures and sprightly melodies. Pergolesi's *Stabat Mater* of 1736 replaced the version written in 1710 by Domenico Scarlatti in Bologna Cathedral; and while Pergolesi's *Stabat Mater* sounded naked in comparison to Scarlatti's setting, its simplicity and emotional impact marked something wholly new.

Soon Italian composers and the Germans who closely observed them devised a new form that allowed them to expand their ideas: the symphony. Originally conceived as a brief prelude to a vocal cantata or opera, the symphony began to take on a life of its own as a type of concert entertainment played by a court orchestra. Although Giovanni Battista Sammartini is generally credited as the first composer to write true symphonies, the Viennese composer Georg Matthais Monn may have beaten him by a couple of years.

Reflected even in the work of older composers such as Georg Philipp Telemann, who adapted to it late in life, the new Classical style finally moved to center stage in European music around 1750. Several of its most celebrated early practitioners were sons of the king of Baroque composers, Johann Sebastian Bach. Carl Phillip Emanuel Bach spent many years working for the music-loving King of Prussia, Frederick the Great. C.P.E. Bach, as he is known, seems to have assimilated the Italian innovations very early on, at least by 1738. He inherited a certain bent toward drama and complexity from his father, and when these qualities encountered the new styles, highly unusual combinations resulted. C.P.E Bach associated with writers such as Friedrich Klopstock, who developed the overheated literary style known as Sturm und Drang (storm and stress), and he created a musical style to match: the *empfindsamer Stil*, or expressive style, exerted a strong influence over Franz Joseph Haydn.

Haydn, a student of the Italian Nicola Popora, joined the service of the powerful Austro-Hungarian Eszterházy family in 1759. Polite and industrious, Haydn worked hard for three decades, creating, rehearsing, and performing high-quality music for his patrons. As he turned out symphony after symphony (108 in all), Haydn developed procedures that coalesced into what became known sonata-allegro form. Put simply, this meant that a movement often consisted of a series of large sections—a primary theme area, secondary theme area, development section, recapitulation, and coda—marked off by harmonic shifts. Haydn revolutionized the symphony by applying the sonata-allegro principle to it, setting the number of movements at four and making individual movements longer and more complex. Haydn is also credited with standardizing the string quartet: two violins, a viola, and a cello. Isolated at the Eszterházy estate for much of his career, Haydn hardly realized what a celebrity he was: his works were played everywhere and were eagerly studied by other composers—perhaps most eagerly of all by Mozart.

Why did Classical-era music take the shape it did? Perhaps it was attractive to the landed aristocracy of Europe, with their liking for the predictable and their disdain for jarring effects. But it also found favor with intellectuals such as Rousseau, Diderot, and Voltaire, who tied music to the ancient Classical notion of order and balance in all the arts and believed that that access to higher forms of learning for all citizens would usher in an Age of Reason, eliminating ignorance and creating worldwide peace and democracy. The landed gentry would have to go—but they would not go easy.

The European courts would survive to witness the greatest exponent of melody ever to seek work at their doors, Wolfgang Amadeus Mozart. Mozart began as a child prodigy, tutored in composition at his father's knee. Strongly affected early on by the work of the Bolognese teacher Padre Martini's most brilliant student, Johann Christian Bach, Mozart combined several talents into a popular and moving style that was musically so sound it had the much-prized quality of seeming effortlessness. Perhaps Mozart's greatest contributions came in opera; he also made lasting contributions to the symphony, chamber music, keyboard music, and choral music. Mozart's reputation does not rest on formal innovations of the kind that Haydn introduced; rather it is the mastery, effectiveness, and sheer beauty of his work that place it in a class by itself. Contrary to popular accounts, his early death in 1791 was widely noted, observed and mourned—and it stirred speculation that musical change was in the wind.

Indeed, Ludwig van Beethoven was coming of age as the horrors of the French Revolution and its Reign of Terror challenged the notion that the quest for democracy would lead to a halcyon the Age of Reason. In 1792 Beethoven moved to Vienna from Bonn and soon established himself as the natural heir to Mozart and the aging Haydn. By the end of the decade, however, Beethoven was steamrollering the neat boundaries of Classical forms. Broadly speaking, Beethoven united Classical ideals of abstract form and balance with the concerns that would dominate the Romantic century to come: human nature and experience, the social contract, the power of the natural world. When Beethoven's 50-minute *"Eroica" Symphony* was premiered in 1803, critics and composers alike thought that he had lost his mind. Long or short, his works took on a scope and intensity that seemed at odds with Classical style even as they maintained its logic. Beethoven redefined the piano sonata as a powerful form of individual expression, wrote string quartets of unparalleled complexity, and turned the concerto into a virtuoso essay on the theme of the individual versus the crowd. With the group of songs called *An die ferne Geliebte*, he created the song cycle, a genre that was the very essence of emotional subjectivity.

By the end of the 1810s, younger composers such as Franz Schubert and Franz Berwald began to take the hint that Beethoven was on the right track. In 1824, Beethoven's *Ninth Symphony*, more than an hour in length, became the new model of what a symphony could be, embracing a chorus, vocal soloists, and a vision of a new world. The following year, an audience member at a Paris performance of Rousseau's 1752 opera *Le devin du village* tossed a powdered wig onto the stage. The point was made; only magistrates were wearing powdered wigs anymore, and the opera, once a symbol of the revolutionary spirit, was withdrawn from the repertory as too old-fashioned. This simple event may be viewed as a death knell for the Classical style.

Classical Instruments and Genres

During the Classical era, composers began to exert a new influence over how the music they wrote was performed. Haydn suggested at the start of the published score of his "Oxford" symphony that if the work were given even one rehearsal, it would be better served than if it were read cold at the concert. No composer had made such a specification before. Gradually, expression marks and specified tempos in both written and published scores grew more prominent. Percussion and certain wind parts, previously indicated sketchily if present at all, now were written out. The clarinet, the bassoon, and eventually the trombone emerged as important instruments during the Classical era.

The symphony, the string quartet, and the solo concerto came to full maturity, while the multiple-instrument concertos of the Baroque and the early Classical periods declined in importance. Johann Sebastian Bach had arranged his keyboard concertos from violin works, and Vivaldi never wrote any keyboard concertos at all. In comparison, by 1765 Bach's sons Carl Phillip Emanuel and Johann Christian had each already written dozens of them. The pianoforte (or piano) was invented by Bartolomeo Cristofori in 1729, was refined, and became readily available by about 1770. Soon the harpsichord would seem a quaint relic.

One defining feature of Classical music was the rise of comic opera—and opera would have been central to an eighteenth century music enthusiast's concertgoing experiences. Giovanni Pergolesi's intermezzo *La serva padrona* (1733) was the pioneering work in this style, and its central story of a servant outwitting a master would set a dangerous precedent for works to come—most importantly Mozart's *The Marriage of Figaro*. Early comic operas portrayed realistic characters in familiar situations and did away with the old Greco-Roman pantheon of mythic figures (Baroque composers actually turned to the Greek and Roman classics more often than Classical composers did!).

Serious opera continued to use mythological and antique settings, but change came to that genre as well. The music of Christoph Willibald Gluck's 1761 opera *Orfeo ed Euridice* was simple and clear-textured, and for the first time arias and recitatives were married into one harmonious unit. The libretto was structured for dramatic effect, avoiding heavy metaphorical allusions and references to obscure mythic figures having nothing to do with the story at hand. Gluck's "reforms" were not to everyone's taste, but in time they took hold. Mozart's operas were prime examples of the new directness the reforms made possible; *Don Giovanni, his tale of Don Juan's* carousing ways and grim finale, would have been unthinkable at the dawn of the Classical era.

Major Composers and the Wider Scene

Very few operas from the Classical period beyond those of Gluck and Mozart are now performed, and in general the modern view of Classical-era music suffers from too strong a focus on too few composers. Haydn, Mozart, Beethoven are cited as the Father, Son, and Holy Ghost of Classical style. Such a view unnecessarily limits the understanding of this crucial phase of Western music. Detailed scholarly investigation of Classicism beyond this trio mostly got underway only toward the end of the twentieth century, and much Classical-era music has never been performed, recorded, or published.

True, getting a grip on even the basic works of Haydn, Mozart, and Beethoven probably provides more than enough listening for any one lifetime. And some of the "second rank," such as Karl Ditters von Dittersdorf or Georg Matthias Monn, may not set your soul on fire. But if you explore a little deeper, you find composers from all over Europe who were touched by the new currents and made something distinctive from them: Juan Arriaga and Carlos Baguer from Spain; the Franco-German Franz Ignaz Beck; the keyboard virtuosos Muzio Clementi (from Italy) and Jan Ladislav Dussek (a well-traveled Czech), both of whom heavily influenced Beethoven; the German-born Swede Joseph Martin Kraus; the Czech symphonist Jan Vanhal; the operatic and church composer Luigi Cherubini (Beethoven's own favorite among his contemporaries); the composers of the Mannheim School; early North American and Spanish-American composers; and countless others. All these composers belong to the Classical era, all are interesting and enjoyable on their own terms, and all are unique in approach.

Indeed, an understanding of the big picture of the Classical era can deepen one's appreciation of its leading lights. Haydn, Mozart, and Beethoven did not create their works in a vacuum. Rather, they lived in a time of rapid, fundamental changes—contributing, at some level, to those changes but also swimming in currents stirred by others. The discovery of the many treasures that wait to be heard and enjoyed from this era is at the same time a journey of inquiry into a fascinating period of history that underlies many of the most basic assumptions of contemporary societies.

—Uncle Dave Lewis

Music of the Romantic Period

Musical Romanticism is rooted in the cultural ferment of the late eighteenth century, and grew out of the intense individualism of Rousseau, the extreme emotionalism of Schiller and early Goethe, and the rational idealism of the Enlightenment. But Romanticism is also rooted in the burgeoning spiritual crisis of the late eighteenth century. With the advancement of science, Enlightenment philosophers had begun to doubt that traditional religions had a hegemony on revelation. As importantly, they had begun to believe that poets, artists, and composers were inspired and that their works touched the infinite. Together with individualism, emotionalism, and idealism, this belief in inspired creators defined Romanticism.

The history of Romanticism is also the history of the nineteenth century. Both began with the cataclysm of the French Revolution, declined with the fall of Napoleon, grew introspective during Restoration, reached their first peak before the Revolutions of 1848, declined again after the Revolutions' failure, reached their apex in the years after the Franco-Prussian War, and finally collapsed with the apocalypse of the First World War. Intimations of the new movement can be heard in Joseph Haydn's Sturm und Drang symphonies and string quartets of the 1770s, but the first truly Romantic music was music of the French Revolution. In François Gossec's *Hymne a l'Etre Suprème* (1794) for massed choruses, enormous orchestra, and brass bands, in Etienne Méhul's powerful *G minor Symphony* (1808), and in

Gaspare Spontini's tragic opera *La vestale* (1807), Romanticism first found its voice by turning the music of Revolution into the music of Empire.

Early Romanticism found its highest expression in the music of the German-Austrian composer Ludwig van Beethoven. Taught in the high Classical style by Haydn, Beethoven transformed himself from Haydn's heir into an artistic hero. His works from the "Heroic Decade," the enormous *Eroica Symphony* (1803), the dramatic *Egmont* incidental music (1809-1810), his only opera *Fidelio* (1804-1806), and especially his archetypal *per aspera ad astra* C minor *Symphony No. 5* (1808), are revolutionary in their size, their intensity, their cogency, and their power. After the final defeat of Napoleon, the return of the old order, and the rise of police states, Beethoven's music became both more public and transcendent in his works for soloists, chorus and orchestra—the *Missa Solemnis* (1823) and *D minor Symphony No. 9* (1824)—and more private and sublime in his final piano sonatas (1816-1822) and string quartets (1823-1826).

In the Europe of the 1820s, both Beethoven's public and private works were beyond the comprehension of his contemporaries who were enthralled by the comic operas of Rossini and the virtuosity of Paganini. In post-Imperial France, Hector Berlioz's deliriously passionate *Symphonie fantastique* (1830) was considered *outré*. In Germany, Carl Maria von Weber's frightening supernatural opera *Der Freischütz* (1817-1821) was considered *unglaublich*. In Austria, Franz Schubert's song cycle *Die Winterreise* (1827) was heard only by the composer's closest friends, who considered it unbearably terrifying. With the deaths of Weber in 1826, of Beethoven in 1827, and Schubert in 1828, the first generation of German Romantic composers effectively ended. Berlioz continued to write wildly passionate music in his colossal *Grande Messe de Morts* (1837), his passionate *symphonie dramatique Romeo et Juliet* (1839), and his spectacular *légende dramatique Damnation de Faust* (1845 -1846), but the Paris of the Restoration continued to ignore them in favor of the bel canto operas of Bellini and the spectacle operas of Meyerbeer. Only in the virtuoso piano works of Frederic Chopin and Franz Liszt did the French find a Romanticism to their taste. But while works like Chopin's *G minor Ballade* (1831) and *B flat minor Piano Sonata* (1837) and Liszt's *Années de Pèlerinage* (1838-1861) and *Hungarian Rhapsodies* (1846-1885) were brilliantly virtuostic, they were also intensely individualistic, extremely emotional and quintessentially Romantic.

Most second-generation German Romantic composers were less ambitious than Beethoven or Berlioz. Robert Schumann's ardent *Fantaisie* for solo piano (1836) and his poetic *Dichterliebe* song cycle (1840) expressed his personal feelings, and his later *Faust* oratorio (1844-1853) and *Rhenish Symphony* (1850) were imperfect attempts at grand public statements in the manner of Beethoven's heroic decade. Felix Mendelssohn's youthful *Overture to A Midsummer Night's Dream* (1826) reimagines Weber's supernatural world as the realm of dainty fairies, his later *Scottish Symphony* (1842) reimagines the land of Scott as a postcard, and his *Elijah* oratorio (1846) reimagines Handel's Imperial English oratorios as a hymn to Victorian piety.

The early operas of Richard Wagner, however, were enormously ambitious expansions of the first generation of Romantics. In *Der fliegende Hollander* (1841), Wagner transforms Weber's supernatural world into a haunted mystical seascape. In *Tannhauser* (1843-1865), he transforms a German medieval legend into a sexual morality play. In *Lohengrin* (1848), he transforms a tenth century myth into a psychological study of faith and trust. In all three operas, Wagner's drama centers on a transcendental love story expressed through music as passionate as Berlioz's and as heroic as Beethoven's, but imbued with Wagner's gigiantic personality. With Mendelssohn's death in 1847, Schumann's madness in 1854, and Wagner's exile from Germany for his participation in the Revolution of 1848, the second generation of German Romantic composers effectively ended.

The failure of revolution did nothing to quell Wagner's ambitions. In Switzerland, Wagner transformed himself from a composer of German Romantic operas into the composer of idealistic music dramas, of *Gesamtkunstwerk*, which would combine all the arts into grandiose works of such transcendental power that they would transform all who heard them. Wagner spent nearly a decade formulating his ideas, and the works he composed in his Swiss exile were not premiered until decades later. Nor did the Revolutions' failure stop Liszt's transformation of himself from a French piano virtuoso into a German symphonic composer. In his symphonic poems, works for orchestra based on myths, as in *Prometheus* (1850-1855), or on philosophical notion, as in *Die Ideale* (1856), and in his two symphonies based on the *Divine Comedy* of Dante (1855-1856) and Goethe's *Faust* (1854-1857), Liszt re-created himself in Weimar as the Aaron to Wagner's Moses, whose music inspired a third generation of German Romantics.

Opposed to Liszt and Wagner was Johannes Brahms, a protégé of Schumann's and an admirer of Schubert's, whose works neither attempted to fuse music with other arts nor to infuse music with extra-musical elements, but rather were suffused with the music of his German forefathers. After the passionate piano works of his youth like his four *Ballades* (1854) and the *D minor Concerto* (1854-1859), Brahms grew both more musically conservative and more emotionally reserved. His *Ein deutsches Requiem* (1857-1868) sublimates his own personal emotions into a massive work for soloists, chorus, and orchestra in the monumental style of the German baroque. His C minor *Symphony No. 1* (1855-1876) fuses the *per aspera ad astra* structure of Beethoven's *Symphony No. 5* with Brahms' own compositional manner. Brahms' *Symphony No. 2* (1877) fuses the pastorals of Beethoven's *Symphony No. 6* with his own emotional melancholy. His F major *Symphony No. 3* (1883) fuses the artistic heroism of Beethoven's *Eroica* with his own heroic stoicism. His E minor *Symphony No. 4* (1884-1885) fuses the Baroque form of the passacaglia with his own passionate pessimism.

The same year that Brahms premiered his *C minor Symphony*, Wagner premiered his *Der Ring der Nibelungen*. A tetralogy of music dramas starting with creation and ending with apocalypse, Wagner's *Ring* is by far the most ambitious work of musical Romanticism. In it, Wagner not only transformed Germanic mythology into an enormous metaphor for everything from the most intimate human relationships to the largest economic, social and political systems, he composed music of utmost beauty and overwhelming power. Nor was the *Ring* all of Wagner's achievement. In his *Die Meistersinger von Nürnberg* (1862-1867), he wrote a work which combined a innate understanding of humanity with music of tremendous expressivity. In his *Tristan und Isolde* (1859), he wrote a work whose sexual passion is embodied in the most advanced, the most chromatic and the most intense music of German Romanticism. In *Parsifal* (1878-1882), he wrote a mystery play of compassion and renunciation, a work which replaces traditional religious myths with the myth of the divinely inspired creator.

The fourth and final generation of German Romantic composers, indeed, the almost the entire final generation of European Romantic composers, is rooted in Wagner. Aside from composers like Charles Gounod (*Faust*, 1856-1859) and Jules Massenet (*Werther*, 1892), nearly every French composer of the last quarter of the nineteenth century was heavily influenced by Wagner. French operas from Ernest Chausson's *Le roi Arthus* (1886-1895), Claude Debussy's *Pelleas et Melisande* (1893-1902), Paul Dukas' *Ariane et Barbe-Bleue* (1899-1907), through Gabriel Faure's *Penelope* (1913) were all composed using Wagner's ideas about music and drama. French symphonies from Lalo's *G minor Symphony* (1886), Franck's *D minor Symphony* (1886-1888), Chausson's *B flat major Symphony* (1889-1890), Dukas' *C major Symphony* (1895-1896) through Magnard's *C sharp minor Symphony* (1913) were composed using Wagner's chromatic musical language.

Nor were French composers the only nationality influenced by Wagner. Czech composer Bedřich Smetana's cycle of symphonic poems *Ma Vlast* (1872-1879) was shaped Wagner's formal structures. Russian composer Nicolai Rimsky-Korsakov's fairy-tale opera *The Tale of Tsar Sultan* (1900-1901) was illuminated by Wagner's extraordinary colors. Alexander Scriabin's orgasmic *Le Poeme de l'Extase* (1907) and his self-deifying symphony *Promethée, le Poeme du feu* (1908-1910) caricatured Wagner's myth of the divinely inspired creator. Only overtly nationalist composers like the Czech Antonín Dvořák and the Russian Modest Mussorgsky and Italian opera composers like Verdi and Puccini escaped Wagner's influence for the most part. Yet even in the earliest works of Dvořák and the last works of Verdi, it is possible to hear echoes of Wagner's music.

Wagner's greatest influence was on German and Austrian composers of the *fin de siècle*. The symphonies of Anton Bruckner are highly individualistic works based on his exhaustive studies of counterpoint and profoundly spiritual character, but their enormous sonorities and massive structures are indebted to Wagner. Although the early works of Richard Strauss were influenced by Mendelssohn and Brahms, his tone poems—from *Don Juan* (1888-1889) through *Also sprach Zarathustra* (1896) to *Eine Alpensinfonie* (1911-1915)—are based on Liszt's model and composed with Wagner's chromaticism and power, and Strauss' early operas *Guntram* (1892-1893) and *Feuersnot* (1900-1901) are clearly cast in the Wagnerian mold. The songs of Hugo Wolf rarely last more than a few minutes, but their intense chromaticism and extreme expressivity derive directly from Wagner.

Even Gustav Mahler, the greatest of the last generation of Romantic composers, is deeply beholden to Wagner's music. Starting with the *Inferno dal' Paradiso* which closes his *First Symphony* (1884-1896) and the monumental funeral march which opens his *Second Symphony* (1888-1903), Mahler's music is modeled on Wagner's. But with the apocalypse and transfiguration that closes his *Second*, the fusion of Pantheism and Christianity that runs through his *Third* (1893-1906), and the blissful view of heaven that closes his *Fourth* (1899-1910), Mahler transformed himself from Wagner's heir into his reincarnation as a divinely inspired creator. But even in his astringent *Fifth Symphony* (1901-1902), his severe and tragic *Sixth Symphony* (1903-1906), and his the shimmering *Seventh Symphony* (1904-1905), there are echoes of Wagner's *Tristan* in their sensual slow movements. At his peak in the monumental *Eighth Symphony* (1806), a work which sets a medieval Pentecostal hymn and the conclusion of Faust for the largest choral-orchestral ensemble ever assembled, a work which embodies the highest ideals of German Romanticism at its most passionately idealistic, Mahler's music still recalls the deep humanity of *Meistersinger* fused with the transcendent spirituality of the *Missa Solemnis*. Only after confronting his own mortality in his endlessly sorrowful but ultimately luminous *Das Lied von der Erde* (1908-1909), his infinitely terrifying and ultimately terminal *Ninth Symphony* (1908–1909), and his excruciatingly painful and ultimately beatific unfinished *Tenth* (1910) does Mahler become himself.

The rest of the final generation of Romantics were twisted and distorted versions of Romanticism. Sibelius' nihilistic A minor *Symphony No. 4* (1911), Schoenberg's tortured *Erwartung* (1909), Stravinsky's violent *Le Sacre du printemps*, and Berg's monstrous Marsch from *Three Pieces for Orchestra* (1913) were the music of the inevitably impending apocalypse.

—James Leonard

Post-Romantic Music

The Post-Romantic period in European art music could as easily and perhaps more accurately be defined as the Post-Wagner Era. Even before his death in 1883, nearly every composer in Europe defined himself either in allegiance with or in opposition to Wagner's music. With his four final monumental music-dramas—the mythic apocalypse of *Der Ring des Nibelungen*, the tonal nationalism of *Die Meistersinger von Nurnberg*, the sensually chromatic love-death of *Tristan und Isolde*, the redemption through suffering of the pseudo-spiriutal *Parsifal*—Wagner essentially set the limits of European art music until the First World War.

The direct heirs of Wagner were the German and Austrian composers of central Europe. The two most eminent of these were Gustav Mahler (1860–1911) and Richard Strauss (1864–1949). Mahler was a Bohemian Jew whose adulation of Wagner influenced both the style and substance of his early composition. In the love-death of *Lieder eines fahrenden Gesellen* (Songs of a Traveling Wayfarer) (1883–1896) and his *First Symphony* (1884), the apocalyptic visions of the *Second Symphony* (1888–1903) and the evolutionary mythology of the *Third Symphony* (1893–1906), Mahler was clearly a disciple of Wagner. Only with the sharp-edged *Fifth Symphony* (1901–1902) and the darkly tragic *Sixth Symphony* (1903–1906) did Mahler establish a more linear and personal style of composition. With his massive choral-orchestral *Eighth Symphony* (1906), however, Mahler took the tonal nationalism of *Meistersinger* and infused it with his own lyrical counterpoint to create one of the greatest works of German Romanticism's highest ideals. In his death-haunted final works, Mahler adapted Wagner's notion of redemption-through-suffering to his own pantheistic world view in the transfiguring despair of *Das Lied von der Erde* (The Song of the Earth) (1908–1909) and the transcendent nihilism of the *Ninth Symphony* (1909–1909).

Strauss, on the other hand, was uninterested in Wagner's morals and metaphysics and concerned himself solely with Wagner's chromaticism and characterization. In his early symphonic poems, Strauss created characters and dramatic situations which were almost devoid of metaphysics: his *Don Juan* (1888–1889) is an chromatic sensualist; his *Tod und Verklärung* (Death and Transfiguration) (1888–1889) is more convincing when depicting the agonized atmosphere of the death scene than when evoking the soul's idealistic transfiguration; and his *Also sprach Zarathustra* (1896) takes its title from Nietzsche's philosophy but takes its musical characterization from a picaresque novel. Given Strauss' dramatic proclivities, it was inevitable that he would turn to opera, and although his first two attempts failed to keep the stage, *Salome* (1903–1905) and *Elektra* (1906–1908) were extraordinarily successful. Both take the excruciating chromatic tonality of *Tristan* to the borders of atonality, and both end with a sort of love-death, but neither is concerned with metaphysics and are instead musical characterizations of sexual pathologies. In his final pre-War operas, *Der Rosenkavalier* (1909–1910) and *Ariadne auf Naxos* (1911–1912), Strauss retreated from the borders of both atonality and sexual pathology to dwell instead in a neo-classical tonal world of deeply human characters.

Of the other German and Austrian composers active during this period, Max Reger (1873–1916) was a Brahmsian contrapuntal reactionary; Hans Pfitzner (1869–1949) was a Wagnerian epigone who became a reactionary; and Arnold Schoenberg (1874–1951) was a Wagnerian epigone in *Verklärte Nacht* (Transfigured Night) (1899) who became an atonal radical in works like the one-act Expressionist opera *Erwartung* (Expectation) (1909).

Like Mahler and Strauss, Claude Debussy (1862–1918) started his compositional career as a devoted Wagnerian; his earliest extant works like *Demoiselle élue* (The Blessed Damoiselle) (1887–1888) are soaked in the lush orchestral chromaticism of *Tristan*. Even his first truly individual works like the gorgeously sensual *Prelude à l'après-midi d'un faune* (1894) and the pellucidly passionate opera *Pelleas et Mélisande* (1893–1902) are indebted to *Tristan* in their fusion of love and death. Debussy's highly personal mature works from after the *fin de siècle*—the monumental orchestral heroics of *La Mer* (1903–1905), the diaphanous lucidity of *Images* (1905–1912) and the transparent sonorities of *Jeux* (1912–1913)—are all pieces whose evocative clarity could have come from no other composer. Yet even after having established his own style, Debussy was still able to summon up the ghost of Wagner's *gesamtkunstwerke* in his *Le martyre de Saint Sébastien* (1911), incidental music for D'Annunzio's mystery play for soloists, chorus and orchestra. Other French composers of the time were more obviously indebted to Wagner: Ernest Chausson (1855–1899) in his chromatic love-death *Poème de l'amour et de la mer;* Vincent d'Indy (1851–1931) in mythic operas like *L'Etranger;* and Alberic Magnard (1865–1914) in his moral-metaphysical opera *Guercoeur*. Even the young Maurice Ravel (1875–1937) wrote in a Tristanesque manner in his orchestral song cycle *Sheherazade* (1903).

In England, Edward Elgar (1857–1934) and Frederick Delius (1862–1934) each embraced different aspects of the Wagnerian legacy. Elgar had his first success in *The Dream of Gerontius* (1900) by injecting Wagnerian chromatic anguish into the English oratorio tradition. But in his trio of mature works—the massive Kiplingesque *First Symphony* (1907–1908), the intimately passionate *Violin Concerto* (1909–1910), and the monumental but inward *Second Symphony* (1909–1911)—Elgar created his own grandly anxious musical style. Delius rejected England for the Continent and Wagner's monumentality for his sensuality. At his best, as in the opera *A Village Romeo and Juliet (1899–1901),* Delius' music could effectively evoke a chromatic world of sensual nostalgia. Even the early works of the English nationalist Ralph Vaughan Williams (1872–1958), like the *Fantasia on a Theme by Thomas Tallis* (1910), were Wagnerian in their lush string writing à la *Parsifal*.

In Scandinavia, the major composers of each country reacted to different aspects of Wagner. Edvard Grieg (1843–1907) belongs chronologically to an earlier generation, but his later music combines his innate love of the lyricism of Norwegian folk songs with a Wagnerian chromatic passion in works like *Two Elegiac Melodies* (1880) and with Wagnerian monumentality in his incidental music to *Peer Gynt* (1874–1875). Carl Nielsen's (1865–1931) music is both a reaction to Danish sentimentality and to Wagnerian monumentality. In works like the *Third Symphony* (1910–1911) and the *Fourth Symphony* (1914–1916) Nielsen created a nationalist music which is rhythmically athletic and harmonically adventurous. Jean Sibelius (1865–1957) began his career as a composer of Wagnerian orchestral monumentalities based on Finnish myths as in his symphonic poems *En Saga* (1892) and *Lemminkainen* (1895). But with his tragic *First Symphony* (1899) and his heroic *Second Symphony* (1901–1902), Sibelius moved beyond Finnish myths to extol Finnish nationalism. Sibelius' greatest pre-War work was his *Fourth Symphony* (1910–1911), a work as nihilistic as Mahler's *Ninth*, but written in a gnomic and almost atonal language. Sweden's Wilhelm Stenhammar (1871–1927) reacted against his youthful enthusiasm for Wagner by turning to a conservative Brahmsian style in works like his hard-muscled *Second Symphony* (1911–1915).

Russia of the Silver Age had an enormous number of composers, all of whom were to a degree nationalists and all of whom were to a degree indebted to Wagner. Alexander Scriabin (1872–1915), took Wagner's chromatic tonality over the edge of atonality and Wagner's mythic monumentality past myth to the narcissistic egotism of works like *The Poem of Ecstasy* (1907). Sergey Rachmaninov (1873–1943) took Wagner's equation of love and death, but eliminated the notion of transfiguration in works like the despairing tone-poem *The Isle of the Dead* (1909). Even Igor Stravinsky (1882–1971) started life as a Wagnerian, albeit a Wagnerian derived from his teacher Rimsky-Korsakov, in the Russian fairy tale ballet *The Firebird* (1909–1910). But he quickly moved past Wagner in the Russian verisimo ballet *Petrushka* (1911) and the atonal harmonies and the explosive rhythms of *Le Sacre du printemps* (1911–1913).

In the other European countries, Hungary's Béla Bartók (1881–1945) suffused his nationalism with Wagnerian sensual chromaticism in his opera *Bluebeard's Castle* (1911); Poland's Karol Szymanowski (1882–1937) moved through a number of styles during his career, but he started as a Wagnerian-cum-Straussian composer in his *First Symphony* (1906–1907). Bohemia's Josef Suk (1874–1935) joined the Wagernian ideas of sensual love-death and redemption-though-suffering in his passionately tragic *Asrael Symphony* (1905); Moravia's Leoš Janáček (1854–1928) deliberately cultivated a folk-song based style in reaction against the German-Austrian Wagnerian style in work's like his opera *Jenufa* (1894–1903). Spain's Enrique Granados (1867–1916) grew out of the indigenous tradition of zarzuelas, but in his late opera *Goyescas* (1913–1915) he infused that tradition with the rich chromaticism of *Tristan*. In the United States, even Charles Ives (1874–1954) could be said to derive the American nationalism of his *Third Symphony* (The Camp Meeting) (1904–1911) from Wagner's *Meistersinger* via Dvořák's Symphony from the New World and the transcendental idealism of his Emersonian *Fourth Symphony* (1910–1916) from Wagner's metaphysical myths.

Of all the European countries, only Italy seemed capable of escaping Wagner's influence because Italian composers had their own highly developed operatic traditions and their own great operatic composer in Giuseppi Verdi (1813–1901). But even Verdi's late through-composed operas *Otello* (1887) and Falstaff (1893) are indebted, to a certain extent, to Wagner's motific compositional methods. Giacomo Puccini (1858–1924) owes far more to Verdi than to any other composer in his dramatic style, but in the voluptuousness of his chromatic orchestral language one can still hear echoes of Wagner's *Tristan*.

—James Leonard

Modern Music (1900–1950)

In many ways the dramatic shifts that occurred in the realm of music in the first half of the twentieth century simply reflect the political, cultural, scientific, and technological changes of times. Freud plumbed the depths of the subconscious to uncover our secret motivations and compulsions. The development of recorded sound revolutionized the way music could be disseminated and perceived. Political upheavals compelled some composers to alter their styles, or conform to particular expectations, and others to flee their native countries altogether and to spread their influence, and to be influenced, abroad.

This is not to say that the musical world erupted into chaos overnight. Echoes of Romanticism lingered well into the new century. Claude Debussy continued to expand the tonal palette through modal explorations and textural experimentation (*La mer*, 1905; *The Sunken Cathedral*, 1910); later works, such as the curious ballet *Jeux* and the *Images III* for piano, abandon symbolism's already tenuous grasp on narrative, taking as their "subject" the mere *notion* of an image. Gustav Mahler's monumental symphonies resonate with Romantic grandeur, while at the same time foreshadowing the minute orchestrational detail and psychological angst of Expressionism. Richard Strauss' operas *Salome* and *Elektra* stretch tonality, and emotional tractability, to their ultimate limits.

The early works of Austrian composer Arnold Schoenberg likewise contain the emotionally-charged embers of high Romanticism, transformed into the psychological conflict of Expressionism. Early works, including *Verklärte Nacht* (1899) and *Pelléas et Mélisande* (1903) demonstrate a strong Wagnerian influence in their use of leitmotif and extreme chromaticism, while subsequent compositions, such as the *Chamber Symphony* (1906), maintain only a vestigial sense of tonality or "key." By the time Schoenberg composed the haunting Expressionist song cycle *Pierrot Lunaire* (1912), he had succeeded in "emancipating the dissonance" by abandoning tonal expectations altogether.

While the Freudian subconscious fed Schoenberg's innovations, other composers approached the outer edges of harmonic language from different directions, often with an ear to inherited musical traditions. In Eastern Europe, Hungarians Bela Bartók and Zoltán Kodály found inspiration in folksongs, which they recorded, notated, and sometimes wove into entirely new compositions; even in later, more formalist works, such as Bartók's *Music for Strings, Percussion, and Celeste* and the *Concerto for Orchestra*, a discernible Hungarian flavor underscores the strident chromaticism, polytonal modalities, and complex thematic, contrapuntal, and numerological structures. In America, Charles Ives layered patriotic songs, hymns, and folk tunes into rowdy, bumptious collages; works such as the *Concord Sonata*, the *Symphony No. 4*, and his numerous solo songs paint over familiar melodies or fragments in bold, dissonant strokes. The complex chords at the heart of Russian composer Alexander Scriabin's monumental orchestral works (such as the *Poem of Ecstasy*, 1908; and *Prometheus: Poem of Fire*, 1910), build upon the harmonic developments of Mussorgsky, Rimsky-Korsakov, and other members of the "Mighty Handful," as well as Scriabin's own eclectic, synesthetic brand of musical mysticism.

Igor Stravinsky, the most prominent figure in the subsequent generation of Russian composers, looked even more deeply into his national identity for musical inspiration (even though he spent most of his life as an expatriate), and the three ballets from his so-called "Russian Period"—*The Firebird* (1910), *Petrushka* (1911), and *The Rite of Spring* (1913)—caused even more of a stir. Stravinsky drew heavily from Russian folklore and folksong in these works, while presenting folk elements within the context of a harmonically dense and rhythmically innovative musical language. The relentless ostinati, percussive chords, and angular, uneven rhythms heard in the Rite, combined with the unusual choreography of the premiere performance, actually incited the first audience, so the story goes, to riot.

During the late 1910s, Schoenberg entered a period of intense study and experimentation, having found the highly intuitive and unmethodical approach of his Expressionist pieces difficult to sustain. Finally, in the early 1920s, he presented the fruits of his labors: a new method of composing, in which all twelve pitches of the chromatic scale would be organized "democratically" rather than hierarchized according to function within a tonal system. Schoenberg used the 12-Tone method, as it came to be called, in almost all of his subsequent works, such as the *Piano Suite*, Op. 25 (1923), the *Variations for Orchestra* (1928), and the opera *Moses und Aron*.

Schoenberg and his pupils, Anton Webern and Alban Berg, comprised the "Second Viennese School." All three eventually embraced the 12-tone method, but to varying degrees and in drastically different ways. Webern's style underwent the least obvious change after the adoption of 12-tone method; although earlier works such as the *Four Pieces for Violin and Piano* (1910) and the *Five Pieces for Small Orchestra* (1913) predate 12-tone technique, they share with those pieces (such as *Symphony*, 1928, and *Variations for Piano*, 1936) an emphasis on very wide and very narrow intervals (seconds, sevenths, ninths), an acute concern for changes in timbre or tone color (*klangfarbenmelodie*), and a preference for concise, symmetrical structures. Whereas Schoenberg used 12-tone rows to create thematic material, Webern abandoned the idea of "theme" altogether, in favor of sparse, translucent textures and rigorous palindromes.

Berg strayed from Schoenberg's model in the opposite direction: in moving from late atonal works such as the hauntingly dark opera *Wozzeck* (1922) to 12-tone works such as the *Violin Concerto* (1935), Berg retained hints of tonality. The Concerto's tone row, for example, contains several triadic adjacencies with tonal implications. Berg also infused his compositions with symbolic content: melodies in the Concerto refer to an abandoned love and a deceased friend; virtually every structural parameter of the *Lyric Suite* (1926), a private manuscript found after the composer's death, was devised to convey coded numerological messages to a secret lover.

Not a member of Schoenberg's group, the French composer Olivier Messiaen nonetheless expanded the organizational rigor of serialism into the realms of pitch, dynamics, and articulation, combining new resources with the architectonic devices of the Medieval isorhythmic motet, rhythms from India, melodies borrowed from bird calls, and his own highly religious sense of expression (*Quartet for the End of Time*, 1941)

Stravinsky, whom music historians have traditionally (if somewhat perfunctorily) positioned as the representative of neoclassicism (opposite 12-tone music and Second Viennese School), developed his neoclassic style roughly coincidentally with the end of World War I. Not only were huge works such as the Rite financially infeasible during the strapped interwar years, but the gravity of the postwar condition seems to have imposed an aesthetic of restraint, while the purity of forms offered by the "classic" ideal promised an antidote to the self-indulgent decadence of Romanticism and Expressionism. Works such as *L'Histoire du Soldat* (1918), *Three Small Pieces for String Quartet* (1914), and *Symphony of Psalms* (1930) exhibit a streamlined approach to texture and a clarity of form, a certain "rigidity," as Stravinsky described it, that seeks total objectivity. Often Stravinsky took a stylistic model, such as Baroque music (*Pulcinella*, 1920) or jazz (*Ragtime*, 1918), and held it "at arms length" as he examined its musical possibilities.

Neoclassicism, understood as a return to expressive and conceptual transparency, was perhaps the dominant theme in France during the early twentieth century. A whole group of composers, known as "Les Six," found inspiration in the revolutionary musings of Erik Satie, whose straightforward keyboard works (*Gymnopedie*, *Gnossiennes*) and bemused stage works (*Relâche*, *Parade*) offered a model for skilled but not over-serious composition, as well as in the consummate craftsmanship and historical awareness of Ravel (*Le Tombeau de Couperin*) and the rhythmic vitality of American jazz. Of the six—Francis Poulenc, Darius Milhaud, Arthur Honegger, Georges Auric, Germaine Tailleferre, and Louis Durey—Milhaud and Poulenc are the most well-known: the former for his numerous concertos and stage works, including the jazz-inspired, primitivist-futurist ballet *La Creation du Monde* (1923); the latter for his vocal works, including a number of solo songs, as well as sacred works such as the famous *Gloria* (1960).

Neoclassic tendencies took hold in Germany as well. Ferruccio Busoni, a prominent composer and teacher in Berlin around the turn of the century, detected in music an underlying "oneness of expression" shared by music of all periods, and espoused combining a comprehensive, all-inclusive but noncommittal attitude towards music of the past with an openness to musical innovation on the most fundamental levels. His own works, from his superb transcriptions of Bach and Brahms to operas such as *Doktor Faust* (1925) and *Arlecchino* (1916), reflect these ideals. One of Busoni's students, Kurt Weill, became a prominent figure in the Weimar Republic, composing politically and musically trenchant stage works, such as the *Threepenny Opera* (1928), *The Rise and Fall of the City of Mahagonny* (1929), and *Der Silbersee* (1933), that enjoyed international popularity. Weill combined the emotionally detached nature of Busoni's broad but unsentimental neoclassicism with a deeply subversive and ironic use of jazz and popular idioms. The sounds stuck, even when the irony was tempered, and upon fleeing to America after the rise of Hitler, Weill enjoyed a successful career on Broadway.

Another Weimar composer, Paul Hindemith, embraced a kind of neoclassicism that removed music from the overarching sweep of history and lent it more immediacy as *gebrauchsmusik*, or "music for use." The *Piano Suite 1922*, for example, emphasizes the physicality of the instrument and the player's movements, while the *Kammermusik* series likewise emphasizes craft, construction, and performance, invoking historical models as gestures.

The historical predominance granted to 12-tone music and neoclassicism during the first decades of the twentieth century overshadows a number of other, more disparate—but nonetheless influential—trends in music, many of them developing from earlier traditions without the deliberate rupture with the past implied by twelve-tone music and neo-classicism alike. The careers of Sergei Prokofiev and Dmitry Shostakovich in Russia, and Carl Orff in Germany, were influenced indelibly by their efforts to avoid censure by oppressive political regimes; their efforts to innovate within their imposed strictures often uncovered new untapped possibilities. A number of British composers, including Elgar, Vaughn Williams, Holst, and Walton, as well as Scandinavian symphonists Sibelius and Nielsen, retained a firm tonal foundation while developing their own harmonic and melodic idioms. Later British composers, such as Tippett and Britten, developed highly complex harmonic languages; Britten's *Peter Grimes* (1945), with its combination of compelling lyricism and dense intertextuality, ushered in a new age of the opera in England. New England composer Amy Beach (*Gaelic Symphony*, *Piano Quintet*) picked up where Brahms left off, and Aaron Copland's endearing ballets and orchestral pieces, became the virtual cultural soundtrack of middle America, while Puccini enthralled audiences worldwide with tunes from his Italian *verismo* operas (*Madame Butterfly, Turandot*).

At the same time, particularly in America, some composers began to deconstruct music into its most basic elements, then rearrange them in previously unimagined ways. The massive ensemble works of Edgard Varèse (*Equatorial, Ionisation*), with their colliding tectonic shapes and innovative timbres, focused attention on musical shapes and surfaces, and presaged the advent of electronic music. Following the lead of Ives, aggressive pianist/performers like Leo Ornstein (*Sonata Sauvage*) and John Alden Carpenter (*Suicide in an Airplane*) embraced extreme dissonance and untempered physicality. Henry Cowell's experiments with new sounds of all kinds—from the vernacular (hymn and Fuging tunes) to the esoteric (the inside of the piano, as in *The Banshee* and *Tides of Menaunaun*)—paved the way for John Cage's experiments. Harry Partch composed new pieces built upon entirely new scales and played upon curious and beautiful instruments of his own invention.

Countless other composers, too isolated in style or location to fit conveniently into surveys such as this, nonetheless contributed to the immense diversity of musical possibility that composers in the second half of the twentieth century inherited. Still, a number of prominent strands are clearly discernible: 12-tone music was taken in various directions by the integral serialists; the various manifestations of neoclassicism informed later composers' postmodern plunder of music history; the quest for new sound resources was taken up by electronic composers and electronic instrument engineers. And of course, for the first time in history, the widespread availability of sound recordings made virtually all of it available to virtually everyone.

—Jeremy Grimshaw

Music from 1950 to 1975

A synthesis of historical consciousness and explorational zeitgeist elicited a panoply of musical responses during the third quarter of the twentieth century, from deliberate ruptures with the past, to determined efforts to expand and innovate within inherited traditions, to taking the very concept of "musical tradition" itself as the subject for new musical discourse.

Many prominent figures from the early twentieth century continued to produce new works at the century's midpoint; Paul Hindemith's final operas date from this period, as do a number of works by Milhaud and Shostakovich. Following the conservative idiom of William Walton, the next generation of British composers, including Benjamin Britten and Michael Tippett extended the borders of tonality into highly complex and expressively flexible languages. A number of American composers, such as Aaron Copland, Howard Hanson, and Walter Piston, followed even more conservative, tonally-oriented paths, though not without establishing their own highly individualized styles. Still others incorporated jazz and vernacular music and American culture in sophisticated ways, as in the "Third Stream" music of Gunther Schuller, the stage works of Marc Blitzstein and Virgil Thomson, or, among the next generation, the series of adventurously neo-tonal works in David Del Tradici's *Alice in Wonderland* series.

Many composers, however, saw tonality as a tired holdover with little room left for innovation. Serialism, a more recent inheritance, became one of the most dominant forces at mid-century. Luigi Dallapiccola (*Il Prigionero*, 1948; *Parole di San Paolo*, 1964), in Italy, and Ernst Krenek (*Sestina*, 1957), in Austria, to name only two of many, both adopted and innovated Schoenberg's dodecaphonic method. Such seemingly unlikely figures as Copland and Stravinsky even composed serial music near the end of their careers. American composer Milton Babbitt (*Three Compositions for Piano*, 1947; *String Quartet No. 2*, 1954), introduced the concept of expanding serial procedures to dictate rhythms, articulations, and even text phonemes, as well as pitches. Babbitt and other American serialists sought to make music as structurally complex, logical, and scientifically oriented as theoretical physics.

This multifaceted approach to precompositional procedure emerged in Europe as well, but followed a decidedly different tack. Olivier Messiaen had paved the way for European serialism, with his ascetic craftsmanship and use of austere structural devices such as isorhythms (*Quatuor pout la fin du temps*, 1940). He also introduced the idea of associating pitches in a series with concordant series of duration, dynamics, and articulation, in the third of his *Quatre Etudes de rhythme* (1949), "Mode de valeurs et d'intensités." Pierre Boulez saw in this the possibility of creating music based entirely on abstract logic rather than intuition and gesture; his two-piano work *Structures I* (1952) extrapolates from the precompositional materials of Messiaen's "Mode de valeurs" a rigorous system of musical control. Boulez's goal was not to continue the tradition of the Second Viennese School, but to rebel against it; he saw Schoenberg's use of dodecaphony as short-sighted, in that by applying 12-tone procedures to traditional paradigms like "themes" and "melodies," it simply put new wine in old bottles. Later (in the works *Le Marteau sans maitre*, 1955; *Pli selon pli*, 1962), Boulez recognized a certain impracticality and imperceptibility in the rigor of his earlier methods, and applied his philosophy of objective compositional control to the broader structures and shapes of his music while allowing more flexibility in note-to-note details.

The German composer Karlheinz Stockhausen, having encountered Messiaen's work at the summer composition seminar at Darmstadt (which he himself would later oversee), developed an approach to serialism that placed a greater emphasis on architectonic control than moment-to-moment order. *Gruppen*, from 1957, orders the music played by three distinct orchestras according to statistical contours such as overall pitch content and event densities. Similar ideas emerge later in the works of Iannis Xenakis, who literally mapped principles of architecture onto his compositions. In fact, a number of composers after mid-century took a "sculptural" or "architectural" approach to sound organization. Edgard Varése's orchestral works since the 1920s had treated sound masses as material, spatial entities; in his *Threnody for the Victims of Hiroshima* (1961), Krzysztof Penderecki used chromatic clusters of varying widths to create broadband contours of sound; Gyorgy Ligeti composed pieces made of dense contrapuntal lines like girders, tapering and widening to create temporal shapes; Conlon Nancarrow composed works with such mathematically complex relationships that they could only be performed on a player piano.

The emergence of electronic music afforded composers expanded measures of control over their sonic resources. In groundbreaking works such as *Gesang der Jünglinge* (1956), Stockhausen annexed the design of musical sounds and timbres themselves into the creative domain of the composer. Milton Babbitt founded a state-of-the-art studio at Princeton, where he composed groundbreaking acoustic and electroacoustic works (such as *Philomel*, 1964), while Boulez established the world famous IRCAM studio. By this time Morton Subotnick and others had already written some of the earliest works for console synthesizers. Another branch of electronic music, known as "Musique Concrète," used recording, editing, and filtering technologies to create music from assemblages of sounds from the everyday world; pioneers in this field included Otto Leuning and Vladimir Ussachevsky.

While many composers sought new ways of exerting control over their musical materials, the American composer John Cage sought to relinquish it. His early works combined percussion, "found sounds," and invented sonorities with highly organized structural schemes, as in his *Constructions for percussion ensemble* (1939–1941) and the *Sonatas and Interludes for prepared piano* (1948). In the 1950s Cage began introducing elements of indeterminacy into his compositions; his *Music of Changes* (1951) for piano derived all of its compositional parameters from the chance methods of the Chinese *I Ching*, or Book of Changes. Paradoxically, the work's entirely randomized method produced a musical surface rather similar in its effect to early serial works for piano by Babbitt and Boulez from around the same period. And in fact, both approaches had a similar goal: to create a musical language that could be objective (i.e., structured according to its own terms) rather than expressive (based on human emotion). The serialists sought this through heightened control, while Cage sought it by listening to and accepting the world of sound itself.

Not only did Cage utilize chance methods as precompositional procedures, but also allowed degrees of variability in the execution of many of his works. His *Concerto for Piano and Orchestra* (1958) calls for substantial shuffling of its components, which themselves include highly unconventional and imprecise notation. In Cage's infamous *4'33"*, the silence of the performer compels the audience to focus on the otherwise unnoticed sounds surrounding them. Other composers also created works that could vary widely from performance to performance. In Morton Feldman's *King of Denmark* (1964), the composer achieves his characteristically pointillistic texture by indicating graphically only the overall parameters—general range, number of notes, etc.—of each sound constellation in the piece.

While such compositions relied on the real-time intuition of the performers, the early minimalist movement in music that took hold in the late 1950s and early 1960s initially sought to remove the element of directional time all together, positioning the element of variability within the realm of music perception rather than performance. Inspired by the procedural rigor of serialism as well as Cage's interest in "sound itself," *La Monte Young*'s early works, such as the glacially static 12-tone work, the *Trio for Strings* (1958), allowed listeners ample time to "get inside" of each dissonant, drawn-out chord. Later, Young's interest in the psychological effects of long sustained tones and intervals eventually led him to reject equal temperament and adopt highly specialized tunings based on the overtone series, as heard in his monumental keyboard work *The Well-Tuned Piano* (1964) and the static and complex sonic environments of his *Dream House* installations. Young's disciple, Terry Riley, introduced minimalist repetition to a broad audience with the popularity of his groundbreaking work *In C*. Philip Glass' works from the late 1960s and early 1970s methodically exploited the possibilities of composing through the gradual expansion and contraction of tiny melodic cells. Steve Reich's early tape pieces, such as *Come Out* and *It's Gonna Rain*, and his subsequent instrumental works of the until the mid-1970s, comprised elaborate canons made of a single musical idea looped and thrown out of sync with itself; these works used repetition to open up the universe of acoustical diversity that exists, microscopically, on seemingly unbroken musical surfaces.

Within a few years, both Reich and Glass had retreated from the rigor of their earlier works and were composing with more lyricism and harmonic direction. Later composers, especially John Adams, steered this more palatable kind of minimalism towards the realm of neo-tonality. Several composers, on the other hand, remained interested in the artistic implications of sound as an acoustical phenomenon, zooming the microscope in further rather than expanding its frame outward. James Tenney's *For Ann, Rising* (1969) layers ever-ascending glissandi into a kind of acoustical barber pole; Alvin Lucier's *I Am Sitting in a Room* (1969) ping-pongs a recording of the performer's voice back into the performance space over and over again, each rerecording accruing more of the room's resonance until all that remains of the speech are ethereal hums and whistles.

While the minimalists and their acoustically oriented contemporaries burrowed into the sonic matter of music as deeply as possible, a number of composers in Europe and America around the same time did quite the opposite, stepping outside of music and music history, holding musical traditions at arms length through stylization and passing them through intricate layers of collage, allusion, and parody. The third movement of Luciano Berio's *Sinfonia* (1969), for example, takes as its skeleton the whole of the Scherzo from Mahler's *Second Symphony*, adorning it with layers of quotations from Schoenberg, Monteverdi, Samuel Beckett, and countless others. Berio's *Sequenzas* methodically deconstruct the performance histories and expectations of various solo instruments. Mauricio Kagel's multimedia work *Ludwig van* (1970) is made entirely of borrowed Beethoven. B.A. Zimmermann, Peter Maxwell Davies, and Hans Werner Henze saturated many of their operas and theatrical works with quotations, allusions, and imitations; Maxwell Davies' trenchant use of Handel, for example, provides one of the most haunting moments in psychologically taut monodrama *Eight Songs for a Mad King* (1969).

While a number of prominent threads can be discerned in the web of musical directions during the 1950s and 1960s, rarely did these constitute clearly divided camps with loyal adherents. Rather, they represent the multiplicity of avenues available to all composers—and indeed, any categorization of composers should not suggest impermeable boundaries between styles. Cage collaborated with electronic composer Lejaren Hiller on the event-piece *HPSCHD*; studying at the Princeton studio, Paul Lansky took electronic music to realms far removed from Babbitt's serialism; the raucous collages that dominate Peter Maxwell Davies' œuvre are tempered by his substantial, if lesser-known body of serenely neotonal works; minimalist pioneer La Monte Young formed an eclectic microtonal blues band. Many composers from this period defy categorization altogether, even allowing for divided allegiances. Elliot Carter, in an oeuvre that spans virtually the entire century, exhibits a gestural precision and rhythmic inventiveness that match the level of control suggested by serialism, but without adherence to particular precompositional procedures. George Crumb's highly virtuosic and lyrical works, such as Ancient Voices of Children (1970) and Lux aeternae (1971), use exotic instruments and historical quotations, but primarily for their sheer sonic effects rather than their referential possibilities.

Music in the twentieth century is often defined as a series of crises—the coup against tonality, the lack of consensus on a universal musical syntax, the infiltration of non-Western and vernacular styles, the ambiguous attitudes towards music history. These conflicts did not dissipate during the period immediately following World War II. Rather, the multiplicity of trends during this period served to change the status of musical diveristy: from a temporary state of affairs waiting in vain for resolution, to an ongoing and vital condition of music in the postmodern age.

—Jeremy Grimshaw

Music since 1975

Since 1900 such a diversity of musical styles has emerged that music historians have been helpless to find a term that encompasses it all (in a manner comparable to designations like "Baroque" or "Romantic," for example), assigning the period a number ("Twentieth century music") rather than a name. As the century progressed, the various and sometimes contradictory strands of musical development, each with its own set of aesthetic doctrines, seemed to suggest something of a cultural identity crisis; there was no longer a "universal" or "shared" musical language to replace the common tongue of the tonal system that had dominated Western music for hundreds of years. By the end of the twentieth century, as the world itself became more interconnected, this multiplicity of musical style came to be embraced as a reflection of the world in which it exists. Listening to music of the last quarter of the last century and the first years of this one, one encounters virtually every conceivable boundary being tested and transgressed. Geographical distances are traversed through stylistic synthesis, the traditional divisions between "high" art and "low" art, or classical and popular music, becomes increasingly fuzzy, and even the once-discrete elements from which music of previous eras was made—melody, harmony, form—blend into a more fluid continuum of texture and sound.

In fact, one of the most prominent musical movements since 1975, minimalism, sought precisely to draw attention away from where the music was "going," focusing instead on the immediate surface of the sound. The earliest experiments in minimalism, such as Philip Glass' relentlessly austere *Music in Similar Motion* or Steve Reich's *Four Organs*, refused to ripple their surfaces with drama or emotion, using repetition to defamiliarize the sonority of basic musical materials and draw attention to microscopic fluctuations in a continuous musical fabric. Gradually, however, these composers began to employ long periods of stasis to heighten the intensity of dramatic arcs by contrasting them more sharply. Glass' monumental opera *Einstein on the Beach* (1976), for example, builds slowly and gradually, through a series of internally static plateaus, towards a breathtakingly forceful finale. Likewise, in works such as the large ensemble piece *The Desert Music*, Steve Reich alternately draws one in to observe the minute details of his intricate canonic structures, then propels one forward with his undulating rhythms and spiraling chord progressions towards ecstatic climaxes. In both of these works, and numerous others in the minimalist genre, the infectious rhythms and sense of constant kinetic energy reflect the excitement and anxiety of modernity and technological advances. (This is perhaps why music imitative of Reich and Glass is so often heard in advertisements for cars, computers, and telecommunications companies.)

Curiously, minimalism's resonance with the modern Western world often converges with influences from distant places. In his study of African drumming, Reich developed a taste for metrical ambiguity; in listening to his *Music for Eighteen Musicians* from 1976, for example, one hears a 12-beat pattern (based on West African rhythm) that continually shifts shape from three groups of four to four groups of three. Another minimalist, Terry Riley, infuses much of his music with the melodic shapes and mythological overtones of Indian music. Riley's *Shri Camel* (1976), for example, comprises a delightfully incongruous and sonically stunning set of electric keyboard improvisations, the figurations flavored by Indian-influenced melodic contours and ornamentation.

Other composers have combined Eastern and Western styles in much more explicit ways. The works of Lou Harrison often combine traditional Western ensembles with instruments from Java, Taiwan, Japan, and numerous other regions. South African composer Kevin Volans, whose string quartet *White Man Sleeps* was made famous by the Kronos Quartet, combines Western and African sounds as a gesture of "reverse colonialism." Japanese composer Toru Takemitsu applied a distinctly Eastern aesthetic to his works for Western orchestra; the delicate textures of works such as *From Me Flows What You Call Time* are often compared to Japanese rock gardens. Crossing boundaries of time as well as distance, Chinese composer Tan Dun's *Symphony 1997* utilizes large orchestral and choral forces, as well as an ancient set of 64 tuned bells dating back 2,400 years.

The multicultural leanings of recent music may derive from the same postmodern mentality that draws together music from "serious" and "popular" traditions. This is, of course, a common trope in the twentieth century (consider Milhaud, Gershwin, or Gunther Schuller), one that reaches full integration in the century's last decades. William Bolcom's epic three-hour cycle from 1984, *Songs of Innocence and Experience*, features an enormous ensemble that includes among its 300 performers an orchestra, a madrigal group, and a rock band. John Adams sends up Arnold Schoenberg's famous *Chamber Symphony* from 1907 with his own work by the same name; Adams' *Chamber Symphony*, however, combines Schoenberg's atonality with the punchy, slapstick dissonance of cartoon music. Likewise, Adams, Peter Maxwell Davies, Christopher Rouse, and others have incorporated live rock musicians into their stage and concert works, while the generation after them, represented by composers such as Aaron Jay Kernis and Thomas Adés, integrates elements of popular music into their compositions in an almost casual manner, as if by this time such crossings are unremarkable. Outside of the traditional orchestral concert hall the borders become even more ambiguous. The performance art of Laurie Anderson seems a cross between the incisive social commentary of Kurt Weill, the absurdity of Dada, and the stage presence of Cyndi Lauper; in fact, the meditative ballad "O Superman," from her extended stage work *United States*, surged unexpectedly up the pop charts in 1981. Other artists straddle the high/low border even more explicitly. Glenn Branca's symphonies call for ensembles of hyperamplified and specially retuned electric guitars. British musician Brian Eno works both as a minimalist composer (see *Music for Airports*) and as a rock music producer (of albums by Talking Heads and U2), and also collaborated in the 1970s on a rather artsy series of albums with David Bowie (which later served as the inspiration for Philip Glass' *First* and *Fourth Symphonies*). The influence flows in the other direction as well: an excerpt from *Mild und Leise*, an electronic piece by composer and Princeton professor Paul Lansky, appears in a song by the rock band Radiohead, while several of Steve Reich's minimalist works have been subjected to reinterpretation by a cadre of dance club DJs and released by Nonesuch as *Reich Remixed*.

Not all composers have turned their ears outward in this manner, however. Many have looked within the conventions, traditions, and history of Western music for inspiration, and in fact there is a whole strand of contemporary art music, particularly in Europe, that takes as its subject matter the act of composition itself. Louis Andriessen's quasi-minimalist work *Hoketus* (1977) takes a rhythmic principle borrowed from the middle ages and extrapolates it into a dizzyingly complex chamber piece. Wolfgang Rihm describes the slow unfolding of materials in his stunning violin concerto, *Gesungene Zeit*, as a search for a musical idea: the violin, high in its register, slowly turns and glimmers in an attempt to build resonance and energize the orchestra. Russian composer Alfred Schnittke dismantled, reassembled, and caricaturized various archaic forms, as in the mind-boggling Toccata from his *Concerto Grosso No. 1*, which features an imitative texture that begins reasonably enough in two violins, but metastasizes into an unwieldy mass of simultaneous lines following after each other in rapid succession. British composer Harrison Birtwistle similarly sets up forms and structures that are self-consciously off-kilter; in works such as *Carmen Arcadiae Mechanicae Perpetuum* (1977), one hears not only the mechanical hum, but the hiccups too.

Similarly, the physicality of performing serves as the subject for a number of works by contemporary European composers. Helmut Lachenmann is well known for his use of "extended techniques"—often his works contain long stretches in which the performer makes noise with the instrument in all the "wrong" ways, in an ironic gesture of failed music-making (see, for example, the bumbling, stuttering speakers and disoriented orchestra in *Zwei Gefühle…, Musik für Leonard* from 1992). Luciano Berio's famous series of *Sequenzas* present virtual catalogs of the myriad sound possibilities of each featured instrument. Still others utilize these sorts of unusual sound possibilities in a more integrated, expressive fashion. Listening to George Crumb's ensemble piece such as *Ancient Voices of Children* or the piano duo *Zeitgeist (Tableau Vivant)*, one is struck not only by the sheer variety of sounds encountered, but the way they flow into each other in a kind of intuitive logic of tone color.

Still other composers explore new sonorities through the use of scientific principles. Composers like Milton Babbitt and Bryan Ferneyhough create musical analogies to mathematical principles, subjecting collections and orderings of notes and rhythms to various formulaic transformations generally too complex to perceive audibly (which is not to say, however, that their effects cannot be engaging). Although the "scores" of works by Iannis Xenakis often consist of intimidating mathematical formulas and graphs to indicate things like pitch range or textural density, the composer insisted that, because the sound reflected "universal principles" of number, anyone with an attentive and sympathetic ear can understand the music. His final work, for example, *O-Mega*, might be heard not so much in terms of its local details, but rather the overall shapes and contours that the sound masses fill out over time. Still others deal with the science of sound itself. James Tenney's music draws on extensive research in psychoacoustics to create unexpected physical vibrational phenomena, while Alvin Lucier, in pieces such as *I Am Sitting in a Room*, explores the acoustical properties of the spaces in which his music is performed. La Monte Young, considered the father of the minimalist movement in music, creates sound environments made entirely of static sine waves whose relative frequencies (based on a complex, symmetrical array of prime numbers) create a shimmering sound spectrum that changes continually as one moves through the sound space. Similarly complex principles inform Young's monumental keyboard work, the *Well-Tuned Piano*, with its radically unique tuning system based on the harmonic series; as one becomes accustomed to the unusual vibrancy of the pitches (which stray far from the arrangement found on a standard piano), one detects nuances of emotion and gesture never encountered before in music confined to normal tunings. Others use microtonality in a more dynamic fashion, applying it variably as an expressive or intensifying device, as in Ben Johnston's moving string quartet arrangement of *Amazing Grace*.

In addition to new developments in the last decades of the twentieth century, a number of important and highly influential composers who first established their reputations in the middle of the century continued producing new works and exerting influence on the musical landscape. Karlheinz Stockhausen, a pioneer in electronic music and serialism from as early as the 1950s, continued work on his opera cycle, *Licht*, well into the twenty-first century. Influential composer John Cage, who died in 1992, composed a number of important works in the years before his death, some of them in a relatively traditional vein. Elliot Carter, as late as *Night Fantasies* from 1980, continued to use dense, rhythmically complex layers of highly differentiated lines. Here the complexity of the notation distracts from the clarity of gesture, which is straightforward and expressive, though of complex rather than sentimental moods.

The variety of musical styles encountered in the years approaching the end of the twentieth century can indeed be intimidating; it seems that each composer operates according to an entirely unique set of rules, let alone according to differing personal styles. Still, listening to contemporary music requires not so much a knowledge of particular musical grammars or conventions—there are so many, and indeed, listening to new music as if trying to decipher a spoken language one hasn't yet learned can be a very frustrating enterprise—rather, it requires an ability and willingness to abandon presuppositions and listen both attentively and intuitively to the sound *as such*.

—Jeremy Grimshaw

Avant-Garde Music

The term "avant-garde" was used during the First World War in the French military to describe a line of troops that would advance first into battle. Many would be killed, but they would clear a path for the main regiment. "Avant-garde" was first applied off the battlefield to visual artists, often to the passionately antiwar and avowedly anti-art Dadaists and their works that disregarded normal aesthetic values. This usage helped establish the idea that an artist might be on the cutting edge of developments in culture and technology. Musicians rose to the occasion, if in many cases to the dismay of their audiences.

The Chrysalis: Futurism, Dada, and American Experimentalism

To get a sense of the European musical avant-garde's beginnings, one must look not only at the Dadaists but also at the Italian Futurist movement. Though they worshiped technology and tended to favor the war, Futurists shared with the Dadaists an interest in developing, from the ground up, new forms of expression. In his 1913 manifesto *The Art of Noise*, painter Luigi Russolo proposed an orchestra of "noise intoners" (*intonarumori*) that would play music consisting of "pure sound"—and he actually built a few, resembling hand-cranked phonographs. Musicians were also active in the various Dada cells located in Zurich, Berlin, Paris, Hannover and New York. Painter Marcel Duchamp composed only two musical works, but these were compiled by chance methods in anticipation of John Cage's work in the 1950s. Sound Poetry, the art of building recitations out vowels and fragments of words, was a particularly favored Dadaist device; Hanover-based collagist Kurt Schwitters developed it extensively in his *Ur-Sonate* (1925), a multi-movement solo voice work for which a typographical layout provides the score.

Among the New York Dadaists in 1917 was a French émigré named Edgar Varése, a trained composer who had studied with d'Indy, Roussel, and Widor. He became interested in instrumental combinations that could create sounds never before heard and was strongly enthusiastic about the possibilities of electronics, having conducted experiments with a helmholtz siren starting in 1905. In the 1920s, Varése produced short compositions, including *Hyperprism*, *Octandre*, and *Offrandes*, that explored the extremes of instrumental ranges and techniques. In 1929 he composed *Ionisation*, one of the first works written for percussion ensemble. Varése's work, small as his output was (only about a dozen mature works), proved immensely influential.

The term "Futurist" was applied by the music press to artists unrelated to the Italian or Russian movements. American pianist Leo Ornstein around 1913 became the first concert artist to tour as a "futurist pianist," playing scurrilously dissonant, loud, cold, and mechanical music. Audience members hissed, booed, and sometimes got into fistfights. George Antheil, the self-styled "Bad Boy of Music," incorporated into his *Ballet mécanique* two airplane propellers, bells, buzzers, an alarm clock, siren, and several additional pianists and mallet percussionists. At the premiere in Paris in 1926 the wind from the propellers blew the wigs off women in the audience, and its Carnegie Hall premiere in 1927 was a scandal that Antheil later admitted did irreparable damage to his career. Nonetheless, *Ballet mécanique* is the defining avant-garde work of the 1920s, a piece that made use of every bit of technology and audacity available to its composer.

Another American "futurist pianist" who had toured Europe in the 1920s would catalyze a new phase of avant-garde development. Henry Cowell coined the term "tone cluster" to describe the chords made up of adjacent notes that he had been playing since 1912. Ignoring detractors who felt that merely sitting down on the piano's keys would produce similar results, Cowell made a theoretical case for his discovery. Cowell co-invented the Rhythmicon (the first electronic rhythm machine) and founded the periodical *New Music Quarterly* in 1927, publishing important early avant-garde scores. Cowell's interest in indigenous music worldwide proved as influential as his avant-garde experiments and sowed the seeds of musical multiculturalism long before the term existed.

Harry Partch was a California composer who had written scores for a number of conventional classical works, including a piano concerto, by 1928, when he shoved them all into a potbellied stove in a New Orleans hotel to demonstrate his dissatisfaction with the standard equal-tempered Western scale. Living for a time as a hobo during the 1930s, he would devote the rest of his life to exploring the possibilities between the "cracks of the keys"; he built an entire orchestra of special instruments to play the notes and created a body of compositions for it. What Partch did for pitch, Conlon Nancarrow did for rhythm—but it is much easier to train a musician on a set of microtonally tuned "cloud-chamber bowls" than it is to get a pair of violinists to play a pattern like 13 notes against 14 in strict time, as Nancarrow discovered after his earliest works were published in 1935. Nancarrow settled in Mexico City, where he concentrated on building player pianos in order to hear his hyper-complex music played correctly.

Nikolai Roslavets, Sergei Protopopov, and Alexander Mosolov were among a school of Russian composers who developed their own brand of Futurism; Mosolov was a Futurist in the Italian sense, a composer whose loud, propulsive, and harshly dissonant music sought to send the machine age trundling like a runaway freight train into the very lap of his audience. Initially the Soviet regime embraced the Futurists' works, but in 1930, as Stalin began his totalitarian transformation of Russian society, the avant-garde movement came to an end as swiftly as a bullet reached writer Vladimir Mayakovsky's brain. In Germany, the Nazis' chilling opposition to anything they considered "Entartete Kunst" (Degenerate Art) became known, and many prominent avant-gardists left the continent—if they were lucky.

After World War II: Systems, Graphic Notation, Improvisation, and Chance Procedures

The 12-tone system devised by Arnold Schoenberg and elaborated by his students Alban Berg and Anton Webern was not in itself avant-garde; compositions by all three used the technique in the service of traditional aesthetic norms. But in the 1950s two major experimentally minded figures emerged from the serialist background: French composer/conductor Pierre Boulez, a student of Messiaen, composed thick, highly complex pieces that sounded like the musical equivalent of atomic particles blasting apart, and the German Karlheinz Stockhausen, a source of controversy into the next century, was responsible for the huge, mega-complex multi-orchestral *Gruppen* and the chilling electronic *Gesang der Jünglige* (1958), which appeared to come to grips with Germany's legacy of the Holocaust.

American composer John Cage was an early convert to serialism but abandoned the technique in 1938 in favor of new quests. He toured as leader of a percussion ensemble in support of a dance troupe, and in 1940 he discovered he could create his own percussion ensemble by inserting various objects into the strings of a grand piano, thus bringing into being the "prepared piano." In the 1940s Cage often organized his compositions in haiku-like sections using a predetermined number of measures; this principle underlies his prepared-piano masterwork, the *Sonatas and Interludes* (1946–1948). Cage discovered the I Ching oracle and devised ways of organizing music using the tosses of the tablets, and later other chance procedures. In 1952 Cage composed *4'33"* for any combination of instruments, an "empty" composition which provided only the durations of three movements without additional instruction. The debate over the work, which served Cage well in terms of publicity, rages on. One side accepts Cage's own argument that the piece was designed to make us stop and take notice of the world of sounds around us; others contend that *4'33"* is a fascist exercise forcing an audience to listen to nothing for no good reason.

"Graphic" scores, in visual designs that suggested general outlines but not specific music, were developed by New York composers under the influence of jazz and flourished in Europe as well. Polish composer Kryzstof Penderecki gained fame for his *Threnody for the Victims of Hiroshima* (1963), literally drawn out in the score as a huge expanding wedge signifying an atomic explosion. More generally, composers sought to share the decision-making process with performers in various ways. Stockhausen's solo percussion piece *Zyklus* (1959) permits a player to start and stop at any point in the work, and by the late 1960s Stockhausen was composing scores consisting only of verbal instructions. German composer Bernd Alois Zimmermann mapped out strategies for "free jazz"-type improvisation intended for classically trained musicians. Neo-Dadaist avant-garde movements such as the U.S. Fluxus group, with its associated composers George Brecht, Nam June Paik (whose works sometimes entailed physical danger for audiences), and LaMonte Young, created works consisting of little more than instructions written on cards, blurring the boundary between musical performance and other kinds of action.

Electronic Composition

With the availability of electronics in the post-World War II period, studios sprang up all over the world. There were radio-backed studios in Europe such as ORTF (1946), RAI (1949), and WDR-Köln (1951), collegiate labs at McGill University in Montreal (1948) and Columbia-Princeton (1951), and commercial ventures such as the studio at IBM (1955) and Raymond Scott's Manhattan Research Inc. (1948). Practically all the music produced by the electronic music studios was avant-garde in the sense that it was creating wholly new sounds and new kinds of performance to go with them. Early concerts, such as that given by Luening and Ussachevsky at the Museum of Modern Art in 1952, induced audiences to applaud a tape recorder. Iannis Xenakis, an avant-garde composer whose works straddled the serial/controlled-improvisation fence, succeeded in coaxing a string quartet score, *ST/4* (1964), from an ILLIAC II computer at Indiana University, and performance ensembles such as the ONCE Group in Ann Arbor, Michigan and the British group AMM worked to make real-time public performance of electronic music a reality.

Minimalism: The Avant-Garde and the Return to Tonality

By the end of the 1960s the spirit of challenge and a positive attitude towards change had put the avant-garde, paradoxically, in the driver's seat in Western art music. The avant-garde was split into two distinct camps; the fussy, control-freakish serialists headed by Boulez and the shaggy-dog, do-your-own-thing school associated with Cage, but both groups gained traction on college campuses and even in concert halls. Even electronic music enjoyed popular success as a Nonesuch Records release of Morton Subotnick's *Silver Apples of the Moon* became an essential record-collection item for progressive American listeners. In 1965 critic Henry Pleasants wrote a book entitled *The Agony of Modern Music*, warning that the unrelieved dominance of avant-garde styles would lead to a disintegration of concert life. Most avant-garde composers on both sides of the aisle laughed the book off as the empty ravings of a conservative.

The 1970s marked the rise of a new music at once innovative and newly appealing to audiences, however. Minimalist composition, a broad term incorporating the efforts of such disparate figures as Steve Reich, Philip Glass, John Adams, and the Dutch composer Louis Andriessen, exploited in various ways a predilection for repetition of short musical phrases. Though minimalism was regarded as a fresh development in the avant-garde of the day, it emerged in hindsight as a reaction against the complexities of the serial avant-garde that enabled composers to readopt some aspects of tonality. In Eastern Europe a similar wind was blowing in the music of the Estonian Arvo Pärt, Polish composer Henryk Górecki, and the Russian Valentin Silvestrov.

The Avant-Garde in a Conservative Era

In 1980s America, cultural attitudes shifted rightward and government arts funding was sharply cut. Academic serialists managed to circle their wagons and retain their jobs, but non-serial experimental and electronic composers were cut loose to try their luck. Many of the latter group would abandon the whole notion of continuing the avant-garde or experimental tradition. By the 1990s, audiences in the concert hall began to shun programs that featured the premieres of new works, and by the turn of the century many were staying away from any type of classical concert. This precipitated a crisis in classical music, and many critics blamed the avant-garde for causing a decline in musical life.

Avant-garde jazz continues to thrive, particularly in Europe, and experimental music in a popular context may be found in nightclubs, art galleries, and parties. But classical composers are largely avoiding avant-garde experimentation. The New York "Downtown" school of composers, influenced in equal parts by jazz, classical, rock, and electronic elements, dismisses the whole idea of carrying on the avant-garde classical music tradition as irrelevant. Their serialist "uptown" counterparts, still ensconced in university professorships, are viewed as throwbacks to an era that has run its course. Indeed, it does appear that serialism and atonal composition in general are "dead." What the twenty-first century retains of the twentieth's avant-garde tradition, if anything, remains to be seen.

—Uncle Dave Lewis

Ballet Music

Twentieth century choreographer George Balanchine proclaimed that music was the basis and guiding force of dance, but truly great scores came relatively late in the evolution of great dance. The initial emphasis was on visual spectacle, athletic grace, and storytelling; music was a necessary support for all this, but not an aesthetic priority. Only in the middle to late nineteenth century did great ballet become linked to superb music; indeed, some of that period's finest ballet scores, by Léo Delibes and Pyotr Ilyich Tchaikovsky, have proven more durable than the original choreography. As the twentieth century began, choreographers and impresarios began commissioning scores from the trendiest composers of the day; the most popular works of Igor Stravinsky and Aaron Copland, for instance, are dance music. By the late twentieth century, choreographers were beginning to adapt concert scores – and pop songs and even silence – to their purposes, and now the time of great original ballet music has waned. Yet the finest works from ballet music's 100-year heyday are now staples of the orchestral concert repertory, and music for the dance is assured of a long, independent existence.

Classical ballet emerged from the tradition of Medieval and Renaissance court spectacles. Dancing was an integral part of all this, particularly during the great flowering of the spectacle in northern Italy in the sixteenth century, and the practice became equally popular in the French court just a bit later. By the 1630s these grand entertainments were available to any paying customer, nobleman or commoner. In the 1650s, French King Louis XIV brought to his court a dancing partner named Jean Baptiste Lully, who soon became the most powerful and wealthy composer in France. Among Lully's duties was the composition of music for stylized court ballets; eventually he collaborated with the playwright Molière on a new form, the comédie-ballet, which included dialog. Through the course of his career, Lully wrote dance music increasingly attuned to the dramatic or comic characters it accompanied, but even by the standards of his own time his music was stiff, stuffy, and harmonically thin, and today it holds interest primarily for aficionados of French Baroque music. A somewhat more interesting score in the Lully manner is André Campra's 1697 opera-ballet *L'Europe galante*.

The opera-ballet hybrid made an enormous leap in quality with the arrival in the 1730s of Jean-Philippe Rameau. In his works, such as *Les Indes galantes*, lovely vocal passages give way to extensive dance sequences. In contrast to the staid music of Lully, Rameau's ballet sequences are energetic, harmonically inventive, and imaginatively scored. While Rameau could write his share of stately, measured dance pieces, he was best in his more unfettered dances – those written for primitive, exotic characters, or those imitating storms or battles. Rameau's harmony was always orderly; he was, after all, a grand theorist. But he did sometimes modulate to new keys in ways that were so swift and expressive that the music seems a century ahead of its time. This sort of effect would not be achieved so regularly again until the Romantic era of Delibes and Tchaikovsky. Rameau was similarly forward-thinking in his approach to orchestration. His use of percussion and independent woodwinds (in other words, the flutes didn't merely play the violin music) made his musical tempests and earthquakes the most evocative of the period.

Ballet masters in the mid to late eighteenth century began to assert their primacy over composers, and even as dancing was becoming on one hand more virtuosic (among the Italians) and on the other hand more subtly character-centered (among the French), music was relegated to a secondary role and no significant composers wrote primarily for the ballet. In 1778, W.A. Mozart cranked out *Les petits riens*, but that is a negligible entry in his catalog. Gluck's *Don Juan* and Beethoven's *The Creatures of Prometheus* are the only two significant ballet scores from the Classical era to survive. As dance productions, both have gone extinct, but the music is occasionally recorded, and the overture to Beethoven's score remains secure in the concert hall.

In the early nineteenth century, ballet's most able composers were opera specialists incorporating dance sequences into their works; one notable example is the ballet-divertissement in Giacomo Meyerbeer's 1831 opera *Robert le Diable*. A ballet scene became de rigeur in operas presented in Paris through the nineteenth century; foreign composers were required to insert a dance sequence in the third acts of their works, even if they made little dramatic sense. Not even Giuseppe Verdi could escape this requirement, which led, among other things, to the 30-minute ballet "The Four Seasons" in the French version of his *I Vespri Siciliani*. (Richard Wagner rebelled by inserting the "Venusburg Music" for dancing immediately after the overture in Tannhäuser, so it wouldn't disrupt the opera's action.)

Otherwise, ballet composing through the first half of the nineteenth century was a pastime for musical hacks. The role of the score was merely decorative, and little more important than the footlights; as long as it was there, nobody in the audience needed to pay any attention to it. It was the functional work of insipid composers whose main duty was to keep a good, clear, danceable beat. In fact, many ballet scores were simply cobbled together from popular tunes of the time.

A significant advance came in 1841, with Adolphe Adam's score for *Giselle*, the earliest full-length ballet still in the international repertory. Adam's score has its flimsy moments, but it's not altogether negligible. Instead of just tossing together silly tunes that more or less reflected the stage action, Adam pioneered the use of leitmotif, using certain melodies several times throughout the work, each melody representing a specific character, emotion, or situation. A well-used leitmotif heightens the music's drama.

After Adam, Tchaikovsky and Delibes wrote the first major ballet scores that were truly integral to the production. The scores consisted of well-crafted pieces that propelled the story but were strong enough to stand on their own. Delibes' two major works are *Coppélia* of 1870, still widely danced, and *Sylvia* of 1876, now known mainly through orchestral excerpts.

Tchaikovsky heard *Coppélia* soon after he'd finished his first ballet, *Swan Lake*. He exclaimed that if he'd known what glorious music Delibes had written, he'd have been too intimidated to complete his own score. Tchaikovsky was much more adept at melody and orchestral color than at musical architecture, so he was a more natural composer of ballets, with their sequences of brief, evocative items, than of symphonies, which require more than translating emotions into vivid music without concern for proper modulation sequences. Tchaikovsky began *Swan Lake* around 1871 as a fairly modest entertainment for his sister's household. In 1875–1876 he expanded the score for a full-fledged four-act ballet that was first performed in Moscow in 1877. Perhaps for the first time in dance history, here was a ballet with music far stronger than its choreography. The introduction sets the tone with a haunting woodwind theme that represents the fate of Odette, a beautiful woman by night who is transformed into a swan during daylight hours until a prince swears his eternal devotion to her. Tchaikovsky brings back this swan theme at several points in the story, intensifying the work's dramatic effect. But the nearly three-hour score is not all tragedy; there are graceful waltzes, a famous bumptious scene for a group of cygnets, and passionately lyrical passages danced by Odette and the prince who loves her.

The Sleeping Beauty of 1890 is Tchaikovsky's most highly regarded ballet score, with its complex use of leitmotifs and smooth integration of character dances. Its reputation has been boosted by the choreography of Marius Petipa; it's perhaps the best work of that gifted, influential late nineteenth-century choreographer. But *The Nutcracker*, first performed in 1892, is certainly Tchaikovsky's most popular ballet. The famous story is gotten out of the way in the first act, and the second is devoted almost entirely to sparkling character dances. Yet a dark streak runs through portions of this score, too. Especially in the Act Two passages for Clara and her nutcracker prince, the music can express a poignance and yearning that wouldn't be heard again in ballet music until Sergei Prokofiev's World War II-era *Romeo and Juliet* and *Cinderella*.

From the 1890s on, ballet (and, later, modern dance) showcased some of the most progressive and innovative composers of the day. The two seminal orchestral works of the Impressionist movement, Claude Debussy's *Prelude to the Afternoon of a Faun* and Maurice Ravel's *Daphnis and Chloe*, are both dance scores. Igor Stravinsky's first act of riot-inducing primitivism was *The Rite of Spring*, now a standard orchestral showpiece. The two other early works that made Stravinsky's reputation, *The Firebird* and *Petrushka*, were also devised for Serge Diaghilev's ballets russes. Stravinsky would maintain ties to the dance stage through most of his career; in partnership with George Balanchine, he later produced such works as *Apollon Musagète*, *Orpheus*, *Jeu de Cartes*, and the serial *Agon*.

Ballet flourished in the early decades of the Soviet Union, and many of the most important dance scores of the first half of the twentieth century were composed there and in France by Prokofiev. His ballet music ranges from the dissonant, primitivist-industrialist *Chout* and *Le Pas d'Acier* to the effusively Romantic, evening-length *Romeo and Juliet* and *Cinderella*. Prokofiev's *Romeo and Juliet* score is particularly notable for capturing every psychological and emotional element of Shakespeare's play: the passion, the hormonal exuberance, the violence, the yearning, even the humor. The bittersweet *Cinderella* is almost as varied, its fairy-tale innocence and funny business mingling with loneliness and even dread.

Around mid-century, the United States came into its own as a center of dance and dance music. Not only was Balanchine doing important work with Stravinsky and other composers in the classical ballet style, but the new "modern dance" form was employing some of the most prominent American-based composers. Aaron Copland became a full-fledged populist with his cowboy ballets *Rodeo* and *Billy the Kid*, the former work incorporating a number of old Western melodies. More sober but no less popular is his *Appalachian Spring*, written for modern-dance pioneer Martha Graham. (A suite from *Appalachian Spring*, arranged for full orchestra rather than the initial 13 instruments, garnered Copland a Pulitzer Prize.) In the 1940s and '50s, Graham was especially adept at recruiting significant composers, some of them at the beginning of their careers, to score her psychologically intense, dramatically inscrutable dances. Besides *Appalachian Spring*, the other great musical success from this source is Samuel Barber's *Cave of the Heart*, also known as *Medea*, a portion of which is now an American classic. Not every score for a Graham dance entered the standard orchestral repertory, but not for lack of celebrity composers; the Graham legacy includes Paul Hindemith's *Herodiade*, William Schuman's *Night Journey*, Gian Carlo Menotti's *Errand into the Maze*, and Norman Dello Joio's *Seraphic Dialogue* (later transformed into his *Triumph of St. Joan Symphony*).

Dance music followed many styles during the twentieth century, from the Spanish and Latin-American nationalism of Manuel de Falla's *Three-Cornered Hat* and Alberto Ginastera's *Estancia* to John Cage's indeterminate and highly theorized *The Seasons*, as well as several collaborations Cage undertook with avant-garde choreographer Merce Cunningham. In recent decades, dance music has returned to its roots in interdisciplinary multimedia extravaganzas in the theater works of performance artist Meredith Monk, among others.

Today, dance companies rely heavily on revivals of old favorites like *The Nutcracker*, and choreographers of every ilk are beginning to prefer to work with recorded music they already know, music predictable in its content, cueing, and pacing. Existing classical concert music, Frank Sinatra recordings, and 1990s alternative rock are kicking contemporary composers off the dance stage, and budgetary constraints tend to limit newly composed dance music to whatever can be produced electronically, or by one or two instrumentalists. The era of great orchestral dance scores may be over.

—James Reel

Band Music

The word "band" can refer to almost any group of instruments, but in the context of Western concert music it generally means a brass band, military band, wind band, mixed band, or symphonic band. These groups are made up primarily of brass or wind instruments (or both) as opposed to a symphony orchestra, which has a large string section combined with the foregoing instruments in smaller numbers. Unlike a symphony orchestra, which has a standardized number of players to a part (unless otherwise prescribed by the work which is being played), wind and brass bands are more flexible in this regard. Relatively few musicians, and usually only those of top quality, can hope to gain a position in a symphony orchestra. But bands are accessible to most able players in the civilized world - many high schools, most colleges and even small communities have bands where even unexceptional musicians can play for fun and to learn.

The history of Western band music actually predates that of the symphony orchestra by quite some time. Small bands, usually made up of trumpets, shawms, and drums, begin to appear in European iconography towards the end of the thirteenth century and may have been around for some time before that. The distinction between early bands and the consort style groups that played at court was that the band instruments were designated for use outdoors, whereas the stringed consorts performed inside. The first extensive use of bands in the military was on the battlefields of the French/Swedish phase of the Thirty Year's War (1618–1648). During this time the shawms were replaced by the French "Hautbois" or oboe.

Another major seventeenth century development in Western band music was the arrival on the scene of Turkish Janissary bands or the "Mehter Band," with their distinctive cymbals, kettledrums, and the big bass drum, known as "davul" by the Turks. Conventional wisdom places the introduction of the Mehter instruments into Europe during the Siege of Vienna in September 1683, when a combined Polish, German, and Austrian offensive forced the Turks out of Vienna, leaving their instruments behind. Other sources disagree, citing that the earliest group of Mehter in Europe on record appearing at Württemberg as early as 1617. In any event, by 1700 European wind bands had adopted the noisy percussion instruments of the Mehter, although not their music, which was not written down and is lost to time.

The eighteenth century witnessed a quantum leap in the development of band music worldwide. Military bands became common in England, Germany, and France, and by mid-century a new wind instrument, the clarinet, took its place beside the oboes. The Turkish percussion instruments were much louder than the simple frame drums used by earlier European bands, and for that reason regimental bands began to increase in size. From about 1720 the concept of Harmoniemusik, wind music written for indoor entertainment minus percussion, was introduced. In the eighteenth century repertoire written by major composers specifically for band and/or wind ensembles appears for the first time in the form of pieces written by George Frederick Handel (*Royal Fireworks Music*), Johann Christian Bach, Joseph Haydn, Michael Haydn, Ludwig van Beethoven, and in the famous wind serenades of Wolfgang Mozart.

Not long after the French Revolution ground to its bloody end in 1794, yet a new type of band was established in France, the forerunner of the modern symphonic band as personified by the band of the Republican Guard. Parisian instrument builder Adolphe Sax worked on improving both the flexibility of tone and portability of band instruments. While few of the brass "Saxhorns" that Sax built, which proved so popular in the nineteenth century that they are still in use at present, his 1841 invention of the saxophone ultimately revolutionized band music, although its initial reception was cool and acceptance somewhat delayed. Ill-fated Frenchman Louis Jullien helped to popularize bands of massive size worldwide in the first half of the nineteenth century through his "monster concerts," some of which were promoted by P.T. Barnum. In Europe different families of instruments tended to dominate the sounds of regional bands—in Germany the Prussian military bands placed the emphasis on the brass, with a rank of saxhorns in addition to the regular trumpets, trombones, and tubas. In Italy the clarinets were considered the primary melodic voice in the band, and the brass was used in a comparatively smaller number. It is believed that Irish bandmaster Patrick S. Gilmore was the first to lead a band which had winds and brass in roughly equal amounts and to devise a wind section whose instruments covered the whole range normally expected from an orchestral body of strings.

Wind bands in the United States were already fairly common by the time Moravian composer David Moritz Michael wrote his suite *The Water Journey* in 1813, but military style bands really took hold in the United States around 1850. By the time of the American Civil War more than 500 bands were amassed on the Union side alone. In the midst of this harsh struggle was born a golden age in American band music that to date has not been surpassed in America, nor anywhere. Although a march was already formally identifiable as "foot lifter" that consisted of two or three strains, composer John Philip Sousa helped refine the lowly march into a form of high musical art, adding complex transitions, lengthening the customary unison introductory tags, introducing breakdown strains and other devices to give the March a greater fluidity and a sense of musical purpose.

Sousa's Band was only one of a number of professional touring groups of the late nineteenth and early twentieth centuries, including those of Gilmore, Giuseppe Creatore, Marco Vessela, Patrick Conway, Edwin Franko Goldman, Frank Simon, and many others. These bands provided the soundtrack to life in American public parks during the summertime, when families were most likely to gather for outdoor entertainment. Southern American bands made up of mixed-race creoles and African-American musicians played a pivotal role in the development of jazz music slightly before the turn of the twentieth century. The bright and clear sound of wind and brass instruments were ideal for recording in the acoustic era, whereas a conventional symphony orchestra or string group made records that sounded muddy in this slightly deaf technology, first marketed to the public in 1889. As a result military bands made up the majority of phonograph records in the years before 1920, accompanying singers and providing every imaginable type of musical fare for early record companies.

Although bands usually performed some opera arias and other pieces borrowed from the concert hall in their live engagements, the music they played was considered popular in its time, and band music had more than its share of detractors, particularly Boston-based critic John Sullivan Dwight, who was constantly railing against what he saw as a lack of culture in band music and decried its association with war-making. Despite Dwight's objections, bands became so common in America by the end of the nineteenth century that they were even heard playing between the breaks of sporting events, a function marching bands still perform today at football halftimes.

In the early twentieth century the respectability issue was finally taken seriously by some composers, particularly in England, where Gustav Holst, Ralph Vaughan Williams, and Percy Grainger wrote large, multi-movement suites in a modern style especially for wind band. English composer Kenneth Alford helped carry on the tradition of Sousa but adopted a snappier, more contemporary profile in works such as his *Colonel Bogey March*; others would find yet more ways to update the basic march, including former dance bandleader Glenn Miller who found a way to inject Swing into military music during World War II. Likewise Iowa-based composer Karl L. King did for the circus march what Sousa had done for military marches.

By 1920 the American Bandmasters' Association was formed and its members began to push for an increased role for band music in education. In 1932 Albert Austin Harding of the University of Illinois devised the symphonic band, a non-marching, sit-down orchestra of wind instruments, and this became the model for concert bands at the university level. By the 1950s most American high schools had a band of some kind, and community bands were still thriving. By the end of the twentieth century, when symphony orchestras found themselves straining to the breaking point in order just to survive, bands are still going strong, although some of the high school and community groups have fallen on hard times or have been eliminated. Contemporary composers pay more attention to bands than ever, with figures such as John Adams, Christopher Rouse, and Louis Andriessen writing specifically for symphonic bands and some composers, such as H. Owen Reed and Ron Nelson, making a name mainly in the composition of band music of a serious kind.

Bands continue to play popular music, as well as the "classics," marches and nearly anything else you can imagine. Wherever people get together to have fun, or for an event such as a picnic, a game, or even a neighborhood festival, bands are welcome and usually found. The tremendous flexibility of the basic wind and brass band model makes it possible for almost anyone to participate, have fun and enjoy playing music. It doesn't matter if you're "good" at it, although it helps, but even if not, most listeners will still enjoy the effort.

—Uncle Dave Lewis

Chamber Music

The term chamber music may reasonably be applied to concert music that is performed by small groups of instrumentalists made up of nine or fewer players, as opposed to orchestral or band music, which is played by larger forces. Chamber music gets its designation from the practice of playing such music indoors, in a "chamber" or room, rather than outdoors, as one would expect from a wind band. When the term was coined in about the middle of the sixteenth century, the specific chambers being referred to were the drawing rooms belonging to wealthy European aristocracy, where private concerts were described as *musique de chambre*, *musica da camera*, or "Kammermusik." At this early stage of the game, much chamber music was played from parts written for voices or semi-improvised. String consorts, small orchestras made up of string players written in anywhere from five to 21 parts, were common in England and Spain well into the seventeenth century.

It wasn't until the dawning of the "second practice" in the Baroque era around 1600 that composers began to construct a musical repertoire specific to the needs of chamber ensembles. The introduction of the figured bass accompaniment, plus that of solo instrumental works, two-voice canzonettas, and solo cantatas with continuo helped make chamber music into a common enterprise. Toward the beginning of the eighteenth century, publishers began to wise up to this trend; the *Sonata da chiesa a tre, Op. 1*, of Arcangelo Corelli (1681) is often cited as the first major milestone in the publication of chamber music. The popularity of this edition was widespread throughout continental Europe, and helped establish the trio sonata as a major form of chamber music within the late-Baroque period. Most composers of any value active from 1700 to 1750 (for example Antonio Vivaldi and Johann Sebastian Bach) composed sets of sonatas for publication in order to feed a growing and lucrative market. Certain works of Georg Philip Telemann, such as *Tafelmusik* (1733), stand out as excellent examples of this trend, in addition to placing the specific purpose of the pieces within the context of domestic music-making.

As music moved into the Classical era, chamber combinations proved well suited to the projection of the emerging *style galant*, which emphasized a clear-cut approach to melody and simple, elegant accompaniment. The next major development in chamber music would occur around 1758 when Austrian composer Franz Josef Haydn began to compose string quartets. Although Georg Philip Telemann and a few others developed works from about 1730 that could be seen as consisting of the basic instrumentation of two violins, viola, and cello, the six *Quartets*, Op. 1, of Haydn, published by Bremner in 1766, were widely disseminated throughout Europe and helped fuel the string quartet craze of the later eighteenth century. Initially, the first violin part carried the majority of the melodic material while the other parts followed along, filling in the harmony. French quartet composers of the 1770s began to favor a more independent treatment of the individual voices; both Haydn and his ardent admirer Wolfgang Amadeus Mozart followed suit. Although the string quartet remained the primary chamber ensemble of the Classical era, some wind bands began to shrink in size and come indoors, as well. Dubbed "Harmoniemusik," these small five- and six-piece bands were the first chamber-sized woodwind groups, often playing medleys of arias from popular operatic music of the day, or in divertimenti, suites of short pieces designed to be played during dinnertime. Some of Haydn's early quartets were likewise entitled *cassations* (another term meaning divertimenti) upon their initial publication.

As the Classical era gave way to the Romantic around 1810, the quartet held its ground as chamber works became longer and more serious in tone than their predecessors. Ludwig van Beethoven chose the quartet medium in which to execute his latest and most advanced musical ideas, and this helped elevate the quartet in the minds of composers as an important challenge that needed to be met with everything one had. This became particularly important as chamber music by this time was finally growing away from its established base as a private or courtly type of music-making. The Müller Brothers Quartet, founded in 1835, was the first professional string quartet, and throughout Europe societies were formed to foster the public performance of chamber music. At this time chamber music cast in larger instrumental groups and began to become more common, such as in Franz Schubert's *Quintets*, Felix Mendelssohn's *Octet*, and the *Nonet*, Op. 31, of Louis Spohr.

The late Romantic period was heavily invested in the forms of opera and symphony, and in a sense this was a threat to the continued relevance of chamber music, along with the gradual disappearance of the European court that had supported its initial development. Some composers held out against the tide, in particular Johannes Brahms, who was most comfortable expressing his grandest conceptions in chamber forms. Brahms' close friend, violinist Joseph Joachim, was in accord with Brahms on this point, and the former led the Joachim Quartet, likely the greatest string quartet of the nineteenth century. Among other key composers of chamber music in the late nineteenth century included Antonín Dvořák and César Franck; the violin and piano duo of Eugen Ysaÿe and Raoul Pugno also helped establish the duet format as a force to be reckoned with in recitals. Schubert's magnificent quartets and quintets gradually become known after 1860, and seemed "new" at the time. Nonetheless, the late-Romantic period was a time of eclipse for chamber music, apart from the popularity of domestic music-making among amateurs. Much of the music composed and published to support such activity was mass-produced and was neither challenging to the players nor terribly imaginative musically.

With the dawn of the twentieth century there was an explosion of interest in chamber music among serious composers. Modernist musicians sought to react against the emotional overabundance of Romantic music and its reliance on large instrumental forms; thus, chamber music provided an ideal outlet for modernist expression. Many of the core repertory works for string quartet, including Debussy and Ravel's quartets, Béla Bartók's quartets, Charles Ives' *Quartet No. 2*, Stravinsky's *Three Pieces*, and Anton Webern's *Five Quartets*, Op. 5, were all written between 1900 and 1940. These works are all far too difficult for amateur players and were obviously meant for concert performance only. Arnold Schoenberg introduced the modern concept of a chamber orchestra with his *Chamber Symphony No. 1 in E major*, Op. 9 (1906). Even theatrical works got a dressing-down in terms of scale, witness Stravinsky's *L'histoire du Soldat* (1917), Busoni's *Arlecchino* (1917), or Darius Milhaud's *Opéras-minutes*—short theatrical pieces written for only a few performers. Professional chamber groups flourished in the early part of the twentieth century, among them the Léner Quartet, Flonzaley Quartet, Budapest Quartet, and the trio of Thibault/Casals/Cortot. Recording of such professional groups began around 1927 and greatly expanded the general public's understanding of chamber music, as did regular broadcasts of professional chamber groups on radio given in the 1930s.

Uncommon combinations of instruments into chamber groups, for example violin, clarinet, and piano (Ives' *Largo*, Bartók's *Contrasts*) or clarinet, saxophone, violin, and piano (Anton Webern's *Quartet*, Op. 22) became more frequently employed after 1900. In the mid-'30s composer Paul Hindemith instituted a series of solo sonatas for each major instrument in the orchestra, including the bassoon, tuba, and other secondary types of Western instruments. By the 1940s some Western composers, such as Alan Hovhaness and Henry Cowell, began to write pieces where non-Western instruments can be used in place of familiar instruments. The 1950s witnessed the rise of international serialism, and the so-called "Darmstadt trio" (usually a combination of instruments like flute, harpsichord, and oboe) became regarded as a cliché in playing hyper-atonal, sparsely textured music derived from serial procedures. The instrumental duo consisting of a live player accompanied by an electronic part on tape likewise emerged mid-century. Domestic chamber music-making, which had continued up to the start of World War II, began to decline sharply afterward; during the war even many of the best professional European ensembles were forced to flee to America in order to escape Nazi oppression. As opportunities for practicing domestic chamber music declined, specialized workshops and festivals, such as the Marlboro Music Festival and the Cabrillo Music Festival, and participation of young musicians in master classes held by professional groups became more commonplace. The aspiring chamber musician of 1970 had better "chops" and was more competitive than his/her counterpart in 1920, but had considerably less experience sharing music played with friends or relatives.

In the present day, professional ensembles playing core repertoire, such as the Juilliard, Emerson, and Tokyo quartets and Beaux Arts Trio, still hold a significant place in the concert world. But as general interest in contemporary music began to decline in the 1980s, record companies specializing in new music began to rely heavily on pieces written for chamber ensembles, as these could be recorded cheaply. New music specialists such as the Kronos Quartet began to delve into playing rock music once in awhile to help build an audience. In time this has indirectly led to groups as Bond, an all-female string quartet that plays mostly rock music and dresses in fetching outfits. Later years also witnessed the rise of superstar performances of core classics, chamber arrangements of classic rock and the bluegrass-styled chamber performances of Yo-Yo Ma, Edgar Meyer, and Mark O'Connor. None of this extracurricular activity is harmful to chamber music as a whole, and in the big picture it is clear that chamber music is more important to the continuation of the classical tradition than ever. For composers, however, the marketing of star performers is a double-edged sword, as postmodern chamber groups and instrumentalists tend to be better known than the composers whose works that they play. Likewise, one is left to wonder if the rock group-inspired efforts of loud "downtown" ensembles such as Bang on a Can are representative of a new wave of chamber music or something else entirely. Only time will tell.

—Uncle Dave Lewis

Choral Music

"Choral music" is not the same kind of classification as "Baroque music," or even "symphonic music;" it is broader. A chorus of singers is, at some level, an elemental human musical grouping, and choruses in Western culture go back to the ancient Greek stage and beyond. Thus an overview of choral music must ask not only what music is being sung, but also who is doing the singing—for there have been many kinds of choruses in the history of Western music. Some have been made up of professional specialists, like most other classical ensembles. Some choristers have been churchgoers or even people who have devoted their entire lives to living and worshipping within the walls of religious institutions. Some have been community members interested both in making music and in making friends. And a few (don't tell the pursed-lips types who shush you at concerts!) have been groups of drinking companions.

Though not thoroughgoing, the link between choral music and the church is strong. The tradition of choral music in Europe and the Americas extends in an unbroken line back to the so-called Gregorian chant of medieval monasteries. Although this body of liturgical song was probably not composed by Pope Gregory the Great (ca. 540—604) as legend has it, his administrative skills are credited with spreading the Roman church's influence and the chant along with it. Many listeners enjoy listening to modern-day recordings of chant by such groups as the Santo Domingo de Silos Abbey Monks' Choir and prize them for their contemplative quality. But for a medieval monk, chant was all in a day's work. Chants were sung many times each day and night, as integral parts of a specified sequence of liturgical events, and the chants that have come down to us differ greatly one from another. Some are long and ornate, with many notes per syllable and a structure that evokes chant's ultimately Middle Eastern origins; others are short proclamations or bearers of lengthy texts. The key to enjoying chant is not just to enter a meditative frame of mind, but also to imagine a kind of worship into which music was inextricably woven.

Chant was, in one well-known formulation, the chrysalis from which Western music grew. Once it was written down in musical notation (a phenomenon originally related to an attempt on the part of the Carolingian dynasty to standardize what was sung around its far-flung holdings), chants began to be elaborated—and the medieval mind was all about elaboration! Monks inserted elaborate glosses, known as tropes, into existing chants. And by the middle of the ninth century or so, some were experimenting with singing in multiple lines of music instead of in unison. From modest beginnings in southwestern France, choral polyphony—multipart music—became more and more ambitious. One high-water mark came in the late twelfth and early thirteenth centuries at Notre Dame Cathedral in Paris, where the first composers known by name in the European tradition, Léonin and Pérotin, created vast works in a style called organum that today seem perfect sonic analogues to the Gothic cathedral's physical spaces. Organum featured two or three voices in rapid motion over a single syllable of chant that might be held for as long as several minutes.

The slow line of music in such pieces was known as the tenor, deriving from a Latin word meaning "to hold," and well into the Renaissance era choral pieces were often organized around the tenor line—which might or might not be a chant. Many Renaissance masses were based on a little folk song called *L'homme armé* (The Armed Man); it might be stretched out, compressed, or otherwise mathematically manipulated. Josquin Desprez, the greatest composer of the Renaissance, wrote two so-called *L'homme armé* masses that provide excellent illustrations of this "cantus firmus mass" technique. Beginning in the late fifteenth century, however, a new texture came to the fore in choral music: choral pieces, typically unaccompanied or a cappella ("in the manner of the chapel"), were often written in four voices, with each voice having an activity level similar to the others. From this period come the familiar designations of the four voice parts in classical and religious music: soprano (originally superius, or "highest voice"), alto, tenor, and bass. In a sixteenth century mass or motet (a multipart setting of a sacred text other than the mass), the voices often enter in imitation, following one another with identical material in the manner of a round. For the casual listener, the result of this equality of voices is a smooth musical surface and a quality often described as sweet. The ultimate expression of the homogeneous Renaissance texture was accomplished by Giovanni Pierluigi da Palestrina, the leading composer of the Catholic Counter Reformation in the late sixteenth century; in works such as the *Pope Marcellus Mass* (1567), every melodic curve is graceful, every rough edge smoothed down, every note part of a profoundly serene musical countenance. The choral music of the Renaissance is most often exposed to the general public in concerts by collegiate glee clubs, which often begin with a segment devoted to such composers as the Englishman Thomas Tallis and the Spaniard Tomás Luis de Victoria.

Just as Gregorian chant served as the underpinning for centuries of polyphonic choral music, so too have other traditions grown from religious cornerstones. The most important of these was the German Lutheran chorale, a single-line congregational melody of which *A Mighty Fortress Is Our God* is a familiar example. Some of these may have been composed by the founder of Protestantism himself, Martin Luther (1483–1546); although they drew on earlier Catholic Latin hymns, the chorales were written in German and gave rise to an entire genre of sacred choral music in vernacular languages. Simply harmonizing a chorale in four parts was the least of what a composer might do with it—even if the harmonized chorale in the hands of the masterly Johann Sebastian Bach seems to contain an infinitude of possibilities. Bach's over 200 church cantatas, works written for a chorus, soloists, and small orchestra, and intended for liturgical use on specific Sundays of the year, are mostly built on chorales, in any number of different ways.

The Baroque era of Bach and Handel also saw the composition of choral works on a much larger scale. Bach's towering interpretation of the Passion story, the *St. Matthew Passion*, stood at the apex of a tradition of settings of the biblical narrative; the early Baroque composer Heinrich Schütz, who transplanted the resplendent multichoral style of Venice's St. Mark's Cathedral to Germany, was another composer who tackled the Passion story. One important genre was the oratorio, a semi-dramatic work, usually on a sacred subject, without staged action, but with soloists depicting the speeches of individuals. Handel's *Messiah* (1741) is the most famous of all oratorios, but the music of the seventeenth and eighteenth centuries offers the enterprising listener (or community choir) a range of powerful and colorful works, from Giacomo Carissimi's *Jephthe* (1650) to the two oratorio masterpieces of Haydn's old age, *The Creation* (1798), with its wonderful images-in-sound of oceans, mountains, and animal life taking shape, and the secular *The Seasons* (1801).

Catholic church services were still a major generator of choral compositions by the time of Haydn and Mozart (and remain one today). Mozart was employed by the Archbishop of Salzburg for the first part of his career, resulting in such sunny choral works as the *"Coronation" Mass in C major, K. 337*, and even Haydn's last six masses, big pieces heavily shaped by the language of his orchestral music, were written for the private use of his longtime employer, the Esterházy family. Gradually, however, church music took on an increasingly ceremonial function. Beethoven's *Missa solemnis*, the major all-choral composition of his late years, was a concert work, not one intended for liturgical use, and musically it is very much of a piece with his better-known *Symphony No. 9*.

Audiences of the nineteenth century loved big choral works, but they heard them for the most part in the concert hall rather than in church. One important choral composer among the early Romantics was Mendelssohn, who in terms of public exposure rediscovered and repopularized the choral music of Bach (although cognoscenti had known about it all along). Mendelssohn's oratorio *Elijah* would have been familiar indeed to a nineteenth century English audience—more so than the masses of Franz Schubert, which breathe the same incredible lyrical spirit as his better-known songs. Liszt and especially Berlioz exploited the Romantic desire to break the mold of existing choral music in terms of sheer size; Berlioz's *Requiem* mass of 1837 is outsized in every way, featuring four separate brass bands distributed around the auditorium in addition to a massive chorus.

As grand as choral spectacles might become, however, choral music never lost its status as a community music in which interested, musically educated, nonprofessional singers might become involved. The ancestors of today's community choirs were nineteenth century amateur ensembles like Boston's Handel and Haydn Society, which still exists today (albeit in a professionalized form). The range of choral music written in the nineteenth century, from Beethoven onward, remains one of that era's least appreciated aspects. Schubert and other nineteenth century composers wrote a great deal of music for small, often all-male vocal ensembles which doubled as social gatherings. The perfect counterpart to the Berlioz requiem mass is the *German Requiem* by Brahms, a work well within the reach of ordinary choirs and one with a direct and empathetic appeal. Much of today's sacred choral music treats traditional texts freely, and Brahms kicked off this trend in a way by replacing the traditional words of the Mass for the Dead with texts he selected from Martin Luther's German translation of the Bible.

In the largely rural United States of the late eighteenth and early nineteenth centuries, the first job involved in presenting choral music was teaching the choristers to read music—if they couldn't, their only recourse in church was to have a minister or song leader "line out" a hymn by singing it to them phrase by phrase. Many early American choral composers, including William Billings (the author of the great New England hymn *Chester*) doubled as singing teachers, and from their efforts grew the characteristically American tradition of shape-note hymnody or fasola singing, which migrated down the Appalachian spine and survives today in the South. Meanwhile, several waves of religious revivalism each contributed new hymns to the repertoire of American churches and those around the world.

Choral music thus has a ready-made market in the many choirs that dot the landscape of every Western country, and it has retained its general popularity even as other classical genres have suffered. During the rehearsal process a chorus gets to know a piece in such a way that even difficult music becomes accessible, with the result that performances of even a dense short work like Schoenberg's *Friede auf Erden* (Peace on Earth) have been fairly frequently heard. Stravinsky was a twentieth century composer who favored the chorus with both the Dionysian wedding piece *Les noces* and the coolly Neo-Classical *Symphony of Psalms*, and nearly every other modern composer has written works that have entered the choral repertory and even, like Benjamin Britten's *Ceremony of Carols*, become well-loved favorites. An entire sacred branch of the recent minimalist movement, sometimes dubbed "holy minimalism," is centered on choral works by such composers as John Tavener and Arvo Pärt, who use choral sonorities in a mystical way, and crowd-pleasing choral works by the likes of Britain's John Rutter compete with crossover albums atop the classical bestseller lists. The chorus remains what it has been for a thousand years or more—an ensemble at the center of music's appeal.

—James Manheim

The Concerto

The term "concerto" has been used to describe several different kinds of composition throughout the centuries. In the late sixteenth and early seventeenth centuries the word was used to describe a sacred composition for voices and instruments—pieces which might require either very large performing forces, as in the case of many Monteverdi and Gabrieli examples, or just a handful of singers and players, as best typified in collections by Michael Praetorius, Monteverdi again, and in Heinrich Schütz's well-known *Kleine geistliche Concerte* (Small Sacred Concerti) from the late 1730s. However, as the Baroque period unfolded, and secular instrumental music grew in importance, the word concerto came to refer to a new family of purely instrumental compositional forms. During the late Baroque three distinct but related types of concerto were in use: the ripieno concerto, the concerto grosso, and the early solo concerto.

The ripieno concerto, which began to flourish at the very end of the seventeenth century, is a throwback to the original meaning of concerto: an ensemble piece. Most ripieno concerti do not contain passages for soloist.

The concerto grosso is little more than an expansion of the trio sonata principle (a work built of three fundamental voices: two solo instruments, usually violins, and basso continuo) to fit a larger ensemble. In the Baroque concerto grosso, two contrasting groups of players are employed, setting up the dramatic opposition between soloist(s) and orchestra which is such an integral part of the concerto's development. The concerto grosso group (literally, "large ensemble") comprises a substantial body of string players, and is written largely in a four-voice texture, while the concertino ("small ensemble") is a group of soloists, often two violins and a cello (and thus is rather like a trio sonata embedded in a larger group). By the turn of the eighteenth century the concerto grosso had become the most influential, and to the Italian audiences of the day, the most modern musical genre around, largely due to the sweeping success of Arcangelo Corelli. Usually following the normal sequence of slow-fast-slow-fast movements prescribed by trio sonata tradition, Corelli uses the tutti group (sections played by the tutti group are often called the "ripieno" sections) to mark cadences, and to provide stark contrasts in texture. The concertino writing is not virtuosic by later standards, and the players were expected to indulge in a great deal of ornamentation.

The transition from concerto grosso to modern solo concerto is a murky one. Giuseppe Torelli, who, like his almost exact contemporary Corelli, was an accomplished violinist as well as composer, deserves as much credit as any. In the preface to his *Concerti musicali*, Op.6 (1698), Torelli indicates that violin passages marked "solo" are to be performed by just one virtuosic player, while the remainder of the music is to be played with three or four on a part; the result is a modified ripieno concerto. It is Torelli's new structural design, as well as his idiomatic, soloistic figurations and homophonic textures, which most directly paved the way towards the later Classical concerto. In addition, many of Torelli's concerti employ the three-movement scheme (fast-slow-fast) common to later concertos.

Italian violinist-composer Antonio Vivaldi fully developed the Baroque concerto along these lines. Vivaldi was responsible for nearly 425 concertos with soloist(s), typically a violinist. In his works the technical difficulty of the violin writing increases dramatically, even as the general texture of the pieces becomes quite a bit simpler. Vivaldi's concertos use what is known as ritornello form, a somewhat predictable alternation between passages for soloist (with basso continuo) and tutti (meaning "everyone," sometimes called ritornelli). Vivaldi usually employs a scheme of four or five regularly recurring tutti sections (ritornelli), though he could be quite flexible in such matters.

During Vivaldi's lifetime the first concertos for instruments other then the violin began to appear. Handel's oboe concertos, as well as works for cello, flute, bassoon, and oboe by Vivaldi himself, are among the very first such pieces.

J.S. Bach's concerto output includes 14 concertos for harpsichord, which are the earliest extant harpsichord concertos by any composer and mostly transcriptions or arrangements of earlier works (his own or otherwise); and three violin concertos (the third being for two violins). However, it is the six *Brandenburg Concertos* which remain Bach's most significant contribution to the genre. These pieces effectively fuse Bach's own highly evolved sense of German contrapuntalism with the more traditional Italian concerto style. All but two of the works are concerti grossi (the third and sixth have no soloists, and therefore must be considered ripieno concertos). The allegro movements of the concertos employ a ritornello structure clearly derived from Bach's intimate knowledge of Vivaldi.

During the Classical period there are two important concerto-oriented developments: the gradual synthesis of traditional ritornello design with the increasingly influential sonata-allegro form, and an increasing emphasis on individual instrumental virtuosity, which, while not damaging the popularity of the traditional violin concerto (carried through the period by such virtuoso violinist-composers as Nardini, Pugnani, Viotti, and Paganini), helped to raise the solo keyboard concerto to equal status. At least two of Bach's sons deserve mention for their important contributions to the keyboard concerto literature during the early-Classical period: Carl Philipp Emanuel and Johann Christian. Like their father, these composers were also highly gifted keyboardists, and their concertos provide ample evidence of the increasing demand for virtuosic display.

Although Franz Joseph Haydn's violin, cello, and trumpet concertos contain much fine music, one must look to Mozart to really see the classical concerto at its peak. In Mozart's 23 original piano concertos you clearly see the outlines of the combination ritornello/sonata-allegro structure (this hybrid form is sometimes called ritornello-sonata form or Classical first movement concerto form). This pattern would serve as the basic blueprint for the first movement, and sometimes the last as well, of virtually all concertos throughout the nineteenth and early twentieth centuries. The movement opens with an orchestral exposition, or ritornello, followed by a solo exposition which modulates to a related key. A second ritornello in this new key leads into a development section by the soloist. A tutti section, both the soloist and orchestra together, recapitulates the main theme(s) in the original key. The soloist then plays a cadenza, and the movement ends with a tutti coda.

Of course, this design does not take into consideration the vast flexibility a composer might employ in distributing his thematic material throughout the movement. The orchestral and solo expositions might be virtually identical except in instrumentation and the modulation that occurs near the end of the soloist's exposition, or they might be built of entirely different thematic material. By the mid- to late-Classical period, composers had assimilated the idea of contrasting theme groups from sonata-allegro design into first movement concerto form, and within the expositions and the tutti recapitulation one can expect to find two themes which contrast in both character and key area.

In the Classical concerto, the third movement will sometimes be in ritornello-sonata design, though more often in a kind of rondo form (which itself has a great deal in common with Baroque ritornello form), while the second movement is often found to be in ternary design or occasionally a kind of sonata form with little or no development.

Beethoven contributed to concerto form in much the same way that he contributed to symphonic and chamber music forms: first, he increased both the breadth of thematic and tonal contrast within the movement, as well as the actual length of the movement, and, second, he significantly raised the technical demands upon the performer. A great deal has often been made of Beethoven's use of the piano in the very opening measures of his Fourth and Fifth Concertos, but it should be noted that Mozart himself had experimented with this same idea in his *E flat Concerto*, K. 271, from 1771. Beethoven's violin concerto is the first major work for the instrument to employ fully developed Classical ritornello-sonata design. Being itself influenced by the difficult concertos of violinist-composer G.B. Viotti (as indeed was Brahms' violin concerto many years later), it is quite technically challenging.

During the nineteenth century there are two distinct lineages of concertos: the first follows the Classical pattern as laid out by Mozart and Beethoven, while the other represents the more progressive element of nineteenth century music.

During the 1830s Mendelssohn composed two concertos for piano and orchestra, both of which imitate Beethoven in the introduction of soloist before the end of the opening tutti. In his 1844 *Violin Concerto in E minor*, Mendelssohn introduces the soloist at the very beginning of the movement, thus completely eliminating the need for the repeated exposition structure of ritornello-sonata form. Composers immediately caught on to the idea, and during the nineteenth century the synthesis of concerto form with sonata design is so complete that differences between the two are few and far between (save the obvious differences in instrumentation and, of course, the insertion of a cadenza). Mendelssohn's *Violin Concerto* also includes a written-out cadenza located not near the end of the movement, as one would expect, but rather in the very heart of the structure. In addition, each movement is connected to its neighbors via a brief transitional passage. The concertos of Schumann (cello, piano, and a somewhat unfinished violin concerto), Brahms (two for piano, one for violin), and Dvořák (cello and violin) carry on the Mozart/Beethoven tradition more exactly, employing the dual exposition and placing the cadenza at its expected location.

The more progressive strand of nineteenth century concerto can be traced back to virtuoso Italian violinist Niccolo Paganini, though not because he himself had anything to do with such progressive composition. The man himself made such an impression on the young Franz Liszt that a whole new arena of virtuoso composition was opened up. Both of Liszt's piano concertos are highly individual in form. The *E flat concerto* in particular is fascinating, being a group of five connected movements, thematically cyclical (to a degree), which collectively form a large, unified structure that leads up to the final movement, itself a kind of peroration to the whole entity. It need not be said that the technical demands of these pieces are fearsome.

More conservative in form, though hardly less challenging to the performer, are the two piano concertos by Frederic Chopin. Edvard Grieg's sole *Piano Concerto*, itself having been warmly approved of by Liszt, is now one of the most frequently played works in the standard repertory. Tchaikovsky's violin and piano concertos are among the most frequently recorded of all classical works.

Also during the Romantic period, works developed that are often classified as concertos, but are similar only in that they feature a soloist and orchestra. These are typically fantasies, such as Sarasate's *Carmen Fantasy* or Bruch's *Scottish Fantasy* (both for violin and orchestra), or tone poems, such as Richard Strauss' *Don Quixote* (for cello and orchestra), but could also be dances, variations, or other forms. These works are found in one movement, a series of connected movements, or even separate movements. Milhaud's *Scaramouche* (for saxophone), Gershwin's *Rhapsody in Blue*, and Takemitsu's *November Steps* (for shakuhachi and biwa) are a twentieth century examples of these "concerted" works.

As the nineteenth century gave way to the twentieth, it must be said that the concerto lost some ground to other instrumental forms. Nevertheless, several monuments of the post-Romantic period should be noted. The famous Sibelius *Violin Concerto* of 1903 (later substantially revised) follows closely in the Mendelssohn tradition, though certainly its blend of Scandinavian atmosphere with southern European warmth has no precedent. Both Elgar and Nielsen produced important violin concertos; Elgar's is a particularly long, difficult, but ultimately rewarding piece.

Prokofiev's five piano concertos reflect the composer's constantly changing attitudes towards his art. The first concerto (D flat) is a bright, youthful piece in several connected sections. The second, however, is a massive four movement piece in G minor, dark, forbidding, and eminently masterful. The third, and best known, has a regular, pulse-driven, somewhat neo-classical character. Prokofiev also contributed two important (and vastly dissimilar) violin concertos, and the *Sinfonia Concertante* for cello and orchestra.

Shostakovich is responsible for two concertos each for violin, piano, and cello. The cello pieces are by far the most frequently played (owing in part to the somewhat limited cello repertory). Alban Berg composed a well known *Violin Concerto* (1935) which uses 12-tone techniques with great flexibility (the tone row is disposed so as to make use of traditional triadic structures). Samuel Barber's three concertos (violin, cello, and an important piano concerto of 1962) remain both accessible and rewarding.

Among the most significant twentieth century concertos are those of Béla Bartók. Three piano concertos (the third slightly unfinished) and a violin concerto from 1938 (now known as the *Violin Concerto No.2* due to the discovery of a youthful, unsatisfying work for violin and orchestra) and an extremely unfinished viola concerto all reflect the composer's formal and contrapuntal mastery, as well as his inimitable blend of Western style with Hungarian folk nuances. In addition, Bartók composed a striking Concerto for Orchestra in 1943, a genre already introduced by Hindemith in 1925, and which would be further explored by Elliott Carter in 1969 and by Roger Sessions in the early 1980s. Such pieces, rather than employing any specific soloists, instead seek to display the virtuosic potential of the entire orchestra.

As the twentieth century came to a close, composers continued to find new and interesting uses for the venerable old concerto form. Penderecki's *Violin Concerto No.1* and Elliott Carter's *Violin Concerto* of the early 1990s are two of the better known late-twentieth century examples. The concerto remains today one of the most accessible, popular forms to concertgoers, who find something refreshingly mysterious and heroic about the virtuoso soloist.

—AMG

Film Music

Film music has existed almost as long as film itself has been a popular entertainment medium. From the first time that movies broke the two-to-three-minute running time and the sheer novelty of watching movement on a screen had worn off, producers and exhibitors (i.e. theater owners) recognized that they worked better with audio accompaniment of some sort. In the early days, it was often left to individual theater owners and managers, hiring a solo pianist or organist, or piano-and-violin duo, and later, small orchestras. In 1908 Camille Saint-Saëns became the first composer of any note to write a piece of music to accompany a movie when he was commissioned to write the score for *The Assassination of the Duke de Guise*, the first release of the Parisian-based Film d'Art, a production company set up to bring high quality theatrical performers and works to the new medium. More typically during the first two decades of the twentieth century, the better producers and distributors offered lead sheets, printed scores with basic thematic material, keyed to specific scenes, and arrangements for everything from a single piano to an orchestra of 10 to 15 instruments. In other instances, there were books of music cues, designed by publishers—sometimes by composers under contract, sometimes from their existing library of music, or based on out-of-copyright tunes—to accompany movies.

Producer-director D.W. Griffith broke fresh ground in music when he commissioned original, full-length, fully orchestrated scores to accompany showings of his *Birth of a Nation* (1915) and *Intolerance* (1916) in the largest theaters. Another breakthrough came in 1916 with Thomas Ince's release of *Civilization*, an epic for which violinist-turned-composer (and future director) Victor Schertzinger (1880–1941) composed a full orchestral score with chorus—all hidden from the view of the audience on the movie's initial run, prompting them to believe that they were seeing sound-on-picture.

And then the talkies came along in 1927. The arrival of synchronized sound presented exhibitors with a huge new expense: refitting their theaters. Even among those large theaters that presented variety shows around their films, the talkies eliminated the need to have an orchestra accompany movies.

The first successful talkie, *The Jazz Singer* (1927), was essentially a silent with talking sequences. The talkies were supposed to reflect real life, and it was believed that music, other than a few bars over the opening or closing credits, had no place in anything but musicals. After all, the thinking went, we don't have musical accompaniment in real life, unless someone is playing a radio or record, or a band is performing. So music disappeared, except in musicals.

Hollywood did bring musical talent—performers, composers, arrangers, and conductors—from the East Coast. In 1929, RKO licensed the rights to a Broadway musical called *Rio Rita*, and asked for additional songs, which brought the composer out west with his resident conductor-arranger, Max Steiner (1888–1971). That same year, Irving Berlin was commissioned to write the songs for a movie musical called *Jubilee*, being made at MGM. He recommended a conductor, Alfred Newman (1901–1970).

Steiner and Newman began to show studio executives what music could do for movies. By 1932 Steiner was composing wall-to-wall scores for movies like *Bird of Paradise*, and with *King Kong* (1933) he wrote the first film music of the sound era that was impressive in its own right; equally important, audiences loved it. Newman established himself initially as a conductor and arranger. In 1931, however, he wrote an orchestral introduction to King Vidor's film adaptation of the Elmer Rice play *Street Scene*, that caught the ear of much of Hollywood. Steiner and Newman were the two most influential and trusted names in movie music for the next 20 years, and both remained active into the 1960's. Steiner favored a "leitmotif" approach to scoring, similar in nature to Wagnerian opera, and music, keyed to the action on the screen; Newman, by contrast, favored "mood" scoring, in which the tone of a scene is suggested, rather than the action.

Arriving a little later in Hollywood was Erich Wolfgang Korngold of Vienna, a former child-prodigy musician and composer whose opera *Die tote Stadt* was a genuinely successful and widely performed piece of twentieth century composition. He arrived in Hollywood as the music director for Max Reinhardt's 1934 Warner Bros. production of *A Midsummer Night's Dream*. At their best, Korngold's scores, starting with *Captain Blood* and running through *Anthony Adverse* to *The Sea Hawk* and *The Constant Nymph*, exhibited a level of sophistication akin to Beethoven, Brahms, Mendelssohn, and Wagner.

Steiner, Newman, and Korngold were soon joined by such figures as Franz Waxman at MGM, Frank Skinner (and, later, Hans J. Salter) at Universal, Victor Young at Paramount; and freelancers such as Dimitri Tiomkin (1899–1979), a former student of Glazunov and concert pianist who started out writing heavily Russian-influenced scores (*Lost Horizon*), but made his real mark in westerns (*High Noon*, *Red River*, etc.), and the young David Raksin (b. 1912) (who started out as an arranger for Charles Chaplin and later wrote two of Hollywood's most popular orchestral scores, *Laura* and *Forever Amber*). It was the heyday for melodic music in movies, which was wonderful for the box office, although it also left film music locked in a Romantic mode, far removed from developments that were taking place in serious music.

The British studios were more pressed financially, and most movie music was the product of bandleaders subbing as composers. The exceptions were the more ambitious works of better producers and directors, who took the time to worry about their scores. Alfred Hitchcock's 1934 version of *The Man Who Knew Too Much* was highlighted by the presence of the extraordinary, Elgar-like *Storm Cloud Cantata*, written by Australian composer Arthur Benjamin for an extended climactic scene. Sir Alexander Korda, the founder-head of London Films, commissioned a score from Sir Arthur Bliss for the 1936 epic science fiction film *Things To Come*, which took on a separate life in the concert hall as a five-movement suite. Sir William Walton wrote some of his most celebrated music for movies, including the scores for Laurence Olivier's *Henry V*, *Hamlet*, and *Richard III*. Ralph Vaughan Williams came to film music at the age of 69, in 1941, with Michael Powell's *Forty-Ninth Parallel*, and went on to compose the music to a half-dozen movies during the final 17 years of his life.

In Soviet Russia, Dmitri Shostakovich also wrote a celebrated score for a film version of *Hamlet*, but the most successful Soviet-based film composer of all was Sergei Prokofiev. Indeed, two of his most popular works, the *Lt. Kije Suite* and the cantata *Alexander Nevsky*, both originated as film projects. "Lt. Kije" was written for a long-forgotten, savagely satirical film, released in the west as *The Czar Wants To Sleep* (1930). *Alexander Nevsky* was written for Eisenstein's 1937 patriotic movie of the same title.

In America, only Aaron Copland, among established figures in the concert hall, ever followed the lead of Prokofiev and Shostakovich, with music for *Of Mice And Men* (1939) and *Our Town* (1940), and later *The Red Pony* (1948), *The Heiress* (1949), and *Something Wild* (1961). Leonard Bernstein and George Antheil dabbled in film scoring, without lingering very long.

Their reticence aside, however, Steiner, Newman, and Korngold had opened the door in Hollywood for serious composers. Bernard Herrmann (1911–1975), a New York-based conductor-composer, and Hungarian-born Miklós Rózsa, both arrived in Hollywood in 1940 and brought new sounds with them: Herrmann the modern dissonances of early twentieth century music and Rozsa the odd, vaguely eastern, and very exotic timbres inspired by the folk music of Hungary. Both men attracted new waves of listeners who enjoyed their scores as music, although Rozsa was the one with a following in the concert hall, with conductor Bruno Walter and Richard Strauss counted among his fans.

By the 1950s, they'd been joined by the new generation of composers, trained in classical music, but also comfortable with jazz and other mid-twentieth century musical genres. Alex North, Jerome Moross, Leonard Rosenman, and Juilliard-trained Elmer Bernstein were multi-lingual composers, capable of writing in numerous idioms and "voices." Rosenman moved freely between feature films and television, writing music for such diverse vehicles as the James Dean movie *Rebel Without a Cause* and episodes of *The Twilight Zone*. The most popular score of Moross' career, for William Wyler's epic western *The Big Country*, came late in the decade. Bernstein, after making his mark with the jazz-based *Man with the Golden Arm*, wrote the most popular western movie score of all time, *The Magnificent Seven*. Alex North scored pictures as important as *A Streetcar Named Desire* and *Spartacus*, but the single most successful piece of music he ever wrote was the theme written for an obscure, low-budget movie called *Unchained* (1955). "Unchained Melody" was recorded by dozens of singers, becoming a hit in the hands of the Righteous Brothers, whose 1965 recording carried the composition full circle 25 years later, as the principal theme of the fantasy film *Ghost* (1990).

The advent of the long-playing record at the dawn of the 1950s helped movie music finally start to achieve some direct presence in people's homes, an event that had both positive and negative aspects. The most popular scores of Steiner (*Gone With the Wind*, etc.) and Korngold (*The Sea Hawk*, etc.) found places in record stores, as did many of Rozsa's more accessible soundtracks (most notably *Ben-Hur*, for which he won his third Oscar, and became the first Hollywood soundtrack to prove so popular that a "Volume 2" album was issued in its wake with more music), and even a small handful of Herrmann's scores (*Vertigo*, etc.).

As the economics of filmmaking changed for the worse with the penetration of television into American homes, the income derived from selling soundtrack albums, and the hit songs derived from soundtracks, took on a higher priority. The turning point came in 1965 with the release of David Lean's *Dr. Zhivago*. The movie was a massive success, and so was its soundtrack, the work of a former military band percussionist named Maurice Jarre, who'd previously scored *Lawrence of Arabia* and several dozen French-made films. The popularity of the soundtrack was driven by "Lara's Theme," a romantic theme set to words as "Somewhere My Love." Most producers and every studio now sought out music for their films that could be turned into hit singles. In 1966, producer-bandleader Bert Kaempfert and his music for Ronald Neame's comedy-thriller *A Man Could Get Killed* yielded a huge pop hit with "Strangers in the Night."

The result of this pop-chart activity was another generation shift in the writing of movie scores. Kaempfert and veteran bandleader-arrangers like Frank DeVol, and jazz-oriented figures such as Quincy Jones and Lalo Schifrin began dominating the film work of the middle-late 1960's. In Europe, Ennio Morricone (b. 1928) brought the depth and richness of opera to the western and the gangster film, and became the dominant figure on that continent.

They were joined by one composer who'd taken a long time to come into his own: Jerry Goldsmith (b. 1929). He'd emerged in the mid-1960's as a distinctive new voice in film music, his music for war-related subjects such as *In Harm's Way* (1965) and *The Sand Pebbles* (1966), and gentle, character-driven dramas like *Lillies of the Field* (1963) and *A Patch of Blue* (1966), Goldsmith showed himself capable of writing inventive, uplifting, inspiring music, while his music for *Planet of the Apes* (1968) was daringly experimental and atonal. Even his television work of the 1960's showed distinction, his scores for *The Twilight Zone*, his title music for such series as *Dr. Kildare* and *The Man from U.N.C.L.E.* all standing out in the memory of those who heard them.

The big studios hired or commissioned Goldsmith, Schifrin et al, while Rozsa and Herrmann hung on, writing for more artistically engaged producers and directors, including Alain Resnais (*Providence*), Brian De Palma (*Sisters*, *Obsession*), and Martin Scorsese (*Taxi Driver*).

All of the contemporary leaders in the field of soundtrack music were swept aside—at least, in the public's consciousness—at the end of the 1970's by the rise of one composer: John Williams (b. 1932), also Juilliard-trained. Williams, gradually had gotten noticed in Hollywood, winning an Oscar for adapting the score of the Broadway hit *Fiddler on the Roof* in Norman Jewison's 1971 film. In 1973, his music for *Jaws*, proved inextricably associated with the action for the movie. *Jaws* was the first of Hollywood's $100 million-plus grossing summer hits—a pure pop culture phenomenon that gave Williams his first successful soundtrack album. Four years later, he became a household name with his music for George Lucas' *Star Wars*. The irony was that the *Star Wars* music was a pure stylistic throwback to the 1940s: a rich, sumptuous Romantic-style melodic score. Williams suddenly became the most in-demand composer seen in Hollywood since Steiner.

Yet a newer generation of film composers arrived in the 1980s and 1990s, with backgrounds in rock music, including Danny Elfman (ex-Oingo Boingo, b. 1954), Howard Shore (b. 1947), Peter Gabriel (ex-Genesis, and an ethnic music expert also), Andy Summers (ex-Police and Animals), Brian May, and Ryuichi Sakamoto (ex-Yellow Magic Orchestra), among many others. They're more accustomed to working with synthesizers than orchestras, and their musical language is based more in pop and rock than opera, symphony, and concerto. Shore and Elfman are among the busiest representatives of this generation.

At the same time, ironically, Hollywood has come almost full circle, back to notions of assembling soundtracks that go back to 1930. Since the end of the 1970s, the studios have increasingly preferred (especially where comedies, action films, and youth films are concerned) to license established hits and new songs by current popular artists, with far less attention paid to instrumental scoring. It started at Universal, whose success with the soundtracks of *Animal House*, which relied on classic hits by Sam Cooke and Paul & Paula between the Elmer Bernstein music, and *Fast Times at Ridgemont High* (1982), with its array of contemporary rock hits by Jackson Browne et al., showed the movie industry what songs, as opposed to musical scores, could do for profits.

—Bruce Eder

Keyboard Music

Pre-Baroque

Music specifically for keyboard appeared after the invention of moveable type and was usually settings of songs or variations. The organ is the oldest of keyboard instruments; early versions, regulated by water, existed in the third century B.C. Pipe organs, with air bellows, were in use by the sixth century AD, primarily for large public events and ceremonies. By the ninth century, it was used for accompanying church services, as its design became less unwieldy, and its sound less raucous. Organs had pedal keyboards by the end of the fourteenth century; stops and a second manual were added in the early fifteenth century. Until the early sixteenth century, the organ just accompanied the choir or alternated verses with it. Merulo, whose ideas of keyboard playing technique became the foundation of modern technique, developed the ricercar, a form of imitative variation, which led to the toccata. The improvisational work was used to precede other church music, hence its also being known as a prelude or fantasia. Organ canzonas were the forerunners of the fugue.

The harpsichord was likely invented in the fourteenth century, but not widely used until the fifteenth century. The *Fitzwilliam Virginal Book* contains song settings and variations, written by Elizabethan composers John Bull, William Byrd, Orlando Gibbons, Giles Farnaby, and many others for an English instrument related to the harpsichord. Additional melody lines were added to both sacred and secular songs to make them polyphonic. Variations were worked on songs and on dances, usually with the original melody in the bass line. They involved contrasting accompaniments using figurative ornamentation, passage work punctuated by chords, or small motives. Variations on dances were called partitas; other types of variation were the chaconne and the passacaglia, which differed in style from country to country.

Baroque

Frescobaldi's ricercars and toccatas for organ and harpsichord show a shift from modal harmonies to major/minor tonal harmonies and a reliance on improvisation, which displayed contrapuntal drama rather than technical virtuosity. The toccata was transformed into the prelude of the prelude and fugue.

Many of the harpsichord works of the era were dance-based. Usually these were grouped together as a suite or partita, with the order of the dances varying from country to country. Preludes were later added to suites. François Couperin, although an organist, is well known for his four volumes of *Pièces de Clavecin*, suites comprised of dances with a few character pieces mixed in. His treatise, *L'art de toucher de clavecin*, compares the imagination and rhythmic freedom of preludes to prose, while the pieces with a more regular meter are poetry.

Bach's four volume *Clavier-Übung*, which contained partitas, the *Italian Concerto*, toccatas, and the *Goldberg Variations*, was his only keyboard collection published during his lifetime. His organ works—the chorale preludes, toccatas, preludes, and fugues—were based on fugal ideas. The *Goldberg Variations* are like other Baroque variations, built on a ground, a melody or motive of the bass line. His *Well-Tempered Clavier*, like his two-part inventions, was meant to teach the keyboard performer how to play clean contrapuntal lines. The prelude and fugue pairs show all the color possibilities of the newly discovered 'equal' temperament.

The keyboard sonata developed in the last decade of the 1600s. Kuhnau's show specifically contrasting key, tempo, theme, and affect between movements. Domenico Scarlatti's over 550 sonatas are typically one movement, binary form, and rely on arresting themes, often with repeated rhythmic patterns.

Classical

Between 1760 and 1790 most keyboard works were published as being for either harpsichord or the new fortepiano, although they were written for one or the other. Piano music, with its notation of varying dynamics, was obviously not suited to being played on the harpsichord. Antonio Soler, a student of Scarlatti, wrote some of the last harpsichord sonatas.

Jan Ladislav Dussek was the first real touring virtuoso pianist; Hummel was another. Both wrote sonatas in the galant style, satisfying to the amateur musician, with an emphasis on melody. The style was soon superseded by emotional qualities and character within a single piece, as seen in the sonatas of C.P.E. Bach. Haydn's sonatas show development from the "galant" to the new Empfindsamkeit. His later sonatas show some of the Sturm und Drang of his symphonies and chamber music.

Mozart's piano sonatas, with their easy range and straightforward construction are obviously meant for the amateur or student. Mozart's other important solo keyboard works are his sets of variations, crowd pleasers he used at concerts. Their popularity meant that more of these were published during his life than his sonatas. The last sets often take on the character of Baroque fantasias with arpeggios, recitative-like solos, and sudden changes of texture and harmony.

Clementi understood piano technique and the instrument's capabilities better than others. In addition to several sonatas, he wrote two exercise books to demonstrate to people that they too could become skilled players with practice.

The mature Classical sonatas of Beethoven's early period move toward a more colorful use of the piano; some have a fourth movement, suggesting he might have been working out forms for string quartets or symphonies. His middle period sonatas are more dramatic concert pieces. His sets of variations from this period show dramatic change of key and character with each variation. The large form, grandness, and lyricism of his last sonatas anticipate the Romantic era.

As the piano began to evolve, evolution in the organ stagnated somewhat. Organ works written in the Classical period continued in the functional tradition of Bach. Choral preludes, voluntaries, and other liturgical pieces dominate the repertoire. Soler's organ sonatas and concertos for two organs are exceptions to this.

Romantic

In the Romantic era, programmatic and character pieces became the major forms for piano music, as the instrument became richer and more resonant after the invention of the iron frame and cross-stringing. Most pieces had a simple ABA structure, with lyrical melodies and colorful harmonies, utilizing the sostenuto and una corda pedals which had become standard. The pieces went by such names as impromptu, album leaf, fantasy, nocturne, humoresque, song without words, intermezzo, scherzo, caprice, or lyric piece. Pioneers of these forms included the Bohemians Vaclav Jan Krtitel Tomasek and Jan Václav Vorísek, whose impromptus may have influenced Schubert, and the Anglo-Irish composer John Field is credited with inventing the "nocturne" form that was then taken up by Chopin. Schumann's character pieces are definitive for the era. Brahms carried on the traditional styles of Beethoven, Schubert, and Schumann.

Attendees of concerts by Sigismund Thalberg, Liszt, and Anton Rubinstein, expected to hear rhapsodic medleys of themes from popular orchestral, opera, and ballet scores past and present, which demonstrated the piano's range of dynamics and dramatics and the technical power needed to draw them out. Liszt in particular wrote with thick chords, rapid figurations, and quick harmonic changes to show off his skills as a pianist. His later pieces, although less virtuosic, are no less difficult as he explored more progressive harmonies and coloristic possibilities.

Folk music idioms are found in Liszt's *Hungarian Rhapsodies*, Dvořák's *Slavonic Dances*, Grieg's Norwegian dances, and Albeniz's and Granados' Spanish dances. In the United States, Gottschalk's music frequently employed sounds of black, Creole, Caribbean, and South American music. Ragtime, best represented by

Joplin, Lamb, and Scott, would influence French and American composers of the twentieth century.

Although Mendelssohn did write organ sonatas, most of his works were in the same forms Bach had used, but with the Romantic sensibility. Around the 1830s, organs builders started using more expressive reed and imitative stops, which led to installations of organs in secular halls and secular recitals. Liszt and Franck created large scale, symphonic sounding works. However, Charles Widor warned against the organ being used as a "pseudo-orchestra." Max Reger's works took advantage of the innovations in stops, soundboards, and action that went into the German Romantic organs. Other important organ composers for the period, of both secular and sacred works, include Saint-Saëns, Elgar, and Karg-Elert.

Modern and Contemporary

During the twentieth century, nationalistic trends and more individualized styles were obvious. Debussy's coloristic effects are distinctive; Ravel's music, while closely associated with Debussy, also looked back to eighteenth century forms, such as the harpsichord suite and the toccata. Milhaud and Poulenc reacted against Impressionism with polytonality and dissonance, using lyrical or witty melodies, and Satie reacted satirically against Germanic Romanticism with irreverent performance instructions. Primitive and naturalistic folk sounds speak through Bartok's economic and percussive writing. Rachmaninoff carried on the Romantic traditions of character, melody, and virtuosity. Prokofiev worked in classical forms with repeated rhythmic patterns and melodies supported by harmonies with controlled dissonances. Scriabin's etudes and preludes experiment with scales, harmonies, and polytonality. Ives wrote complex sonatas and pieces for both piano and organ, juxtaposing seemingly incompatible musical ideas. Schoenberg's use of quartal harmonies and 12-tone chromaticism would lead to serialism.

The organ was relieved of any limitations in size and location of pipes, thanks to mechanical, pneumatic, and electric advances. The French organ tradition with its hallmarks of emotion, expressivity, and improvisation, was passed on from Franck and Widor to Guilmant, then Duruflé. Students of these included Pierné, Tournemire, Vierne, and Dupré. In America, the separate genre of theater organ music developed, while in Germany (and Scandinavia to some extent), a neo-Baroque style developed among Ernst Pepping, Hugo Distler, Flor Peeters, and Carl Nielsen.

Chromatic-dissonant/serialist techniques are represented in the keyboard works of Messiaen (using imitations of birdsong), then later, Babbitt (extreme serialism); Ligeti; Virgil Thomson and Walter Piston, whose expressive works descend from Satie; and Peter Maxwell Davies (non-tonal, but with clarity and simplicity). Ligeti, for one, has written for harpsichord. (There is little new music for the instrument alone, although its ability to produce overtones and its percussive possibilities blend well with other instruments, modern and electronic.) Leo Sowerby and William Albright mixed a wide variety of styles, including jazz styles, in their piano and organ music. New sounds were created by America's Henry Cowell, with his tone clusters and direct manipulation the piano strings, and by John Cage with his "prepared" pianos. His pieces also employ knocks on the casing and sound broad. Regardless of any popular appeal of these types of innovations, they are limited somewhat by the lack of a standard notation and by variances in piano design from one manufacturer to another.

The late twentieth and early twenty-first centuries found Alfred Schnittke, Morton Feldman, Pierre Boulez, John Tavener, Philip Glass, Terry Riley, Arvo Pärt, Sofia Gubaydulina, and Frederic Rzewski writing for keyboard. A few pianists, such as Olli Mustonen, Stephen Hough, and Fazil Say perform their own works alongside the works of Beethoven and Liszt, while harpsichordist Sophie Yates regularly commissions new works for solo virginal. However, there are few current, major composers of "classical" music for whom the keyboard is fundamental to or represents a majority of his or her catalog, and technical innovations in keyboard instruments, including synthesizers and electric pianos and organs, are more often used in popular music.

—Patsy Morita

Opera

Opera: sung drama or comedy with set pieces for solo voice, vocal ensembles, often with chorus and/or ballet and accompanied by an instrumental ensemble. Born in Italy, opera took its name from the Italian word for "works." Most scholars and musicologists agree that Jacopo Corsi and Florentine-based composer Jacopo Peri were the authors of the first opera, *Dafne*, set to pastoral verse by Ottavio Rinuccini. The first published opera was *Euridice*, by Peri's rival, Giulio Caccini. The Florentine school sought to sidestep the polyphony of their age to provide greater emphasis on words. In centuries since, drama, comedy, allegory, and historical novels have provided the basis for sung text, or libretti. Initially, solos and ensembles were connected by recitative (recitativo), a form of heightened speech pitched on specific notes and accompanied by a leaner complement of instruments. By the late nineteenth century, opera had become largely through-composed, in which plot-forwarding dialogue was fully sung.

In the earliest years, operas were based primarily on tragic or heroic subjects. Claudio Monteverdi (1567–1643), the first composer whose operas endured as viable stage works, set to music such figures as Orpheus, Ulysses, and Nero. Monteverdi used a larger, more imaginatively deployed orchestra, calling on it to intensify the drama. His particular gift was to humanize his protagonists through musical means. Venetian composer Francesco Cavalli (1602–1676) rejected the view that melody was inferior and wrote some attractive ones; he also presaged the form in which solo pieces would be written, da capo, in which the first section of an aria is repeated following the introduction of a middle portion.

Alessandro Scarlatti (1660–1725) shifted the drama/music balance to give greater importance to the music and advanced the cause of the da capo aria. The beauty of his music revealed new expressive possibilities. Opera in its dramatic form was, by now, referred to as opera seria. Unfortunately, the form calcified in the hands of lesser composers who followed Scarlatti. Arias developed into virtuosic display pieces and texts became so formalized that dramatic interest was much diminished.

In contrast to opera seria, opera buffa (comic opera) developed in the mid-eighteenth century, growing from the interludes presented as leavening items between acts of serious operas and of spoken theatre. Characters of simple, but lively invention populated these works. Giovanni Pergolesi (1710–1736) was acclaimed in numerous European cities for his 1733 intermezzo, *La serva padrona*.

The formalism of opera seria begged for reform; Christoph Willibald Gluck (1714–1787) provided it. German born, but well-known in both Vienna and Paris, Gluck released serious opera from stilted libretti and set sequences of recitative and aria. Simpler and more dramatically vivid works such as *Orfeo ed Euridice* (1762) touched audience sensibilities directly.

With the bel canto composers of the early nineteenth century, larger orchestras prevailed. While Gioacchino Rossini (1792–1868) wrote numerous comic operas in which the effervescent vocal display characteristic of the bel canto style is still much in evidence, his serious works owe something to Gluck. Vincenzo Bellini (1801–1835) composed long, graceful melodies for both serious and lighter works. Gaetano Donizetti (1797–1848) wrote dozens of operas ranging from comic masterpieces (*L'elisir d'amore* and *Don Pasquale*) to works of grim dramatic power (*Lucia di Lammermoor*, *Maria Stuarda*, and *La favorite*). His stronger, more sinewy orchestrations presaged those of Giuseppe Verdi (1813–1901). Verdi, like Donizetti, was pressured into writing quickly to satisfy the Italian public's insatiable demand for new operas. While his orchestrations initially were crude, his fecund middle period demonstrated a greater technical proficiency (*La traviata*, *Rigoletto*, and *Il trovatore*). In his full maturity, his sophistication in scoring rivaled Wagner's (*Otello* and *Falstaff*). With orchestras of growing size and better, more powerful instruments, voices were obliged to cope with daunting volume. Virtuosic display essentially disappeared, replaced by more forceful voice production for soaring climaxes.

A new Italian school emerged in the late nineteenth century. Verismo, manifest in *Cavalleria Rusticana* by Pietro Mascagni (1863–1945), was embraced by Ruggiero Leoncavallo (1857–1919), Umberto Giordano (1867–1948), Francesco Cilea (1866–1950), and the master of the form, Giaccomo Puccini (1858–1924). Verismo, the Italian word for realism, applied itself to raw, naturalistic stories. Orchestras reached maximum size, taxing singers whose instruments often lost flexibility as they strained for volume. Even Puccini's delicate Mimi had to cope with heavy orchestration in *La Bohème*.

In the twentieth century, Italian opera was dominated by the Veristi, later producing a few modernists of international note such as Ildebrando Pizzetti (1880–1968), Luigi Dallapiccola (1904–1975), and Luciano Berio (1925–2003). These composers utilized a variety of techniques for voice and orchestra, including atonality, Sprechstimme (speech/song) and various electronic devices.

German Opera

In Germany and Austria, opera derived from the Italian school, especially as it was represented in Vienna. With Haydn and Mozart, Austro-German opera moved from purely Italian to something distinct. Haydn's operas, however delightful and well-crafted, are seldom performed in modern times, save under festival circumstances. Mozart's, though, are cornerstones of the repertory in opera houses worldwide. In his singspiels, with spoken dialogue, he began the process that would later result in a truly German opera, presaging Beethoven and Weber. His facility in melody and orchestration were gifts of genius. In *Die Entführung aus dem Serail* (Abduction from the Seraglio), Mozart provided the "Turkish music" (side drums and cymbals) adored by the Viennese public. In *Die Zauberflöte*, he melded low comedy and high purpose to create an enduring masterwork.

Ludwig van Beethoven is a sidebar in opera history, albeit an important one. His much-revised *Fidelio* is flawed, but glorious in its loftiest, most heroic moments. It was left to Carl Maria von Weber (1786–1826) to formalize the German school. *Der Freischütz* became an international success in 1821. *Euryanthe* and *Oberon*, though both burdened by inadequate libretti, were significant works.

The earliest operas of Richard Wagner (1813–1883) were clearly derived from Weber's (with some Meyerbeer evident in *Rienzi*), but by *Der fliegende Holländer* (1841), Wagner had begun to reveal his own distinct persona, one distinctly German in temperament. By the time he began his *Ring der Nibelungen* cycle of operas, Wagner was employing a very large orchestra to achieve what he called a Gesamtkunstwerk, a work fusing all the fine arts. Composition of the Ring was interrupted by exile and the birthing of *Tristan und Isolde* and *Die Meistersinger.* Two works of greater contrast can scarcely be imagined: unquenchable love that can lead only to annihilation and a comedy of richest humanity. When Wagner resumed the Ring in 1869, it was with a still higher level of understanding and craft. *Parsifal,* from 1882, joined Wagner's mature works, establishing the composer as the most influential composer of his age.

After Wagner, Richard Strauss (1864–1949) brought opera back to earth with his disturbing *Salome,* terrifying *Elektra,* knowing *Der Rosenkavalier,* sophisticated *Ariadne auf Naxos,* and other works alternating the historical/allegorical with subjects of domestic intimacy. Strauss' orchestras grew even larger, reaching a magnitude beyond which further growth was impractical. One of the most accomplished orchestrators ever, Strauss knew no boundaries in what he could achieve in symphonic sound; his love of the human voice likewise yielded memorable scenes, especially for sopranos.

Many composers, such as Alexander von Zemlinsky (1871–1942), Franz Schmidt (1874–1939), and Erich Korngold (1897–1957), continued to compose as late Romantics, applying increased complexities to orchestral timbre and harmonic language, but remaining within the tradition. Others, however, felt that the Romantic Movement had reached a terminus; the orchestral excesses had to be broken apart and a new beginning made. Arnold Schoenberg (1874–1951), whose oratorio Gurrelieder was a swollen example of late Romanticism, devised a method of composition that eliminated traditional tonality. The 12-tone method was applied to his four operas, from the monodrama *Erwartung* (1909) to his unfinished *Moses und Aron* (begun in 1930). His disciple, Alban Berg (1885–1935) achieved even more in *Wozzeck* (1922) and *Lulu* (left incomplete at the time of his death). Both were harrowing works, but ones with affecting lyric moments.

In post-war Germany, Hans Werner Henze (born 1926) continued in the 12-tone school in such works as König Hirsch (premiered 1956) and *Elegy for Young Lovers* (premiered 1961). The more radical Karlheinz Stockhausen (born 1928) employed electronic and aleatoric devices in his works.

Opera in France may be said to have emerged from the ballet. It developed with Jean-Baptiste Lully (1632–1687) and was enriched in harmony by Jean-Phillipe Rameau (1683–1764). As these composers of formal works established themselves, opéra comique was emerging from the realm of popular plays with songs. André Grétry (1741–1813) was among the most noteworthy composers of these, injecting his works with brilliance and high spirits.

Paris benefited from Gluck's presence, and his was the dominant voice in serious opera, though not without challenge from Niccolà Piccinni (1728–1800). Another composer of foreign birth, Gasparo Spontini (1774–1851), assumed importance in Paris with his *La vestale.* Fromental Halévy (1799–1862) followed, achieving success with *La Juive.* German-born Giacomo Meyerbeer won the preeminent position in nineteenth century Paris with his grand operas, such as *Les Huguenots* and *Le Prophéte,* combining resplendent principals, orchestra, chorus, ballet, and unquestioned spectacle. Gradually, heroic works were supplanted by the operas of Gounod (1818–1893), Bizet (1838–1875), Massenet (1842–1912), works whose protagonists show more human dimension. Claude Debussy (1862–1918) completed only one opera, *Pelléas et Mélisande,* an Impressionistic masterpiece. In the mid-twentieth century, Francis Poulenc (1899–1963) wrote *Dialogues des Carmélites,* which joined the standard repertory.

England celebrated its Henry Purcell (1659–1695) for his *Dido and Aeneas, King Arthur,* and *The Fairy Queen,* but it was German-born George Frideric Handel (1685–1759) who was most celebrated for his Italian-language operas which offered London music of radiance and strength. Not until the twentieth century were there other British composers of redoubtable excellence. Lord Benjamin Britten (1913–1976) was the most celebrated, recognized as a stage composer first for his *Peter Grimes* in 1945. A succession of other operas confirmed his mastery of the form. The musically challenging stage works of Sir Michael Tippett (1905–1998) earned high marks despite the composer's own, over-dense libretti. Earlier, Ralph Vaughan Williams (1872–1958) wrote *Sir John in Love* and *The Pilgrim's Progress* in an English pastoral style. Frederick Delius (1862–1934), always the iconoclast, created great beauty in *A Village Romeo and Juliet* and *Fennimore and Gerda,* works now seldom produced. Among post-World War II composers, Harrison Birtwistle (born 1934) met with critical approval for his incisive, intricately-orchestrated *Gawain.*

In Russia, Mikhail Glinka (1804–1857) was regarded as the founder of his country's national opera. *A Life for the Tsar* and *Russlan and Ludmila* owe much to the Italian lyric tradition and other composers of Western Europe, but focus on Russian themes. His successors, Alexander Borodin (1833–1887), Nikolai Rimsky-Korsakov (1844–1908), Modest Mussorgsky (1839–1881), and Pioter Ilyich Tchaikovsky (1840–1893) were all in his debt. In the twentieth century, Igor Stravinsky (1882–1971) began as a nationalistic colorist, then redirected himself to neo-classicism (*The Rake's Progress*). Sergei Prokofiev (1891–1953) and Dmitri Shostakovich (1906–1975) both wrote trenchant, gripping operas of enduring value.

Scandinavia produced little of interest until the twentieth century. Danes Carl Nielsen (1865–1931) and Poul Ruders (born 1949) both achieved distinction, Nielsen for *Saul og David* and *Maskarade* (a ripely comic work), Ruders for his chilling *The Handmaid's Tale* (1998).

In America, opera grew largely from European models, though George Gershwin's *Porgy and Bess* (1935) proved distinctly of its time and setting. In the second half of the twentieth century, Carlisle Floyd (born 1926) became popular with *Susannah* (1956) and *Of Mice and Men* (1970) and other well-crafted, though eclectic, works. In the final quarter of the twentieth century, Americans such as William Bolcom and John Corigliano, both born in 1938, fashioned stageworthy operas from stylistically diverse elements, musically interesting and dramatically cohesive for American audiences grown more eager to hear new works.

—Erik Eriksson

Orchestral Music

Nobody has yet defined precisely where chamber music ends and orchestral music begins. Is it where we run out of terms to describe an ensemble by number (octet, nonet, decet)? Is it when the music becomes so complex that it requires a conductor? But some modern septets require direction, while the Orpheus Chamber Orchestra plays beautifully without a musical traffic cop. Wherever we draw the line, it's safe to generalize that orchestral music enjoys great potential—sometimes unrealized—of color, contrast, volume, and texture. Because of the orchestra's internal variety, even repeated material can change character merely through a change of instrumentation.

Despite the great variety of instruments available two millennia ago, an orchestra was not really necessary as long as music remained monodic, based on single lines and not involving any real harmony. Through the Middle Ages and Renaissance, music for the court and countryside was primarily for dancing, or for single-voice minstrels, and these uses were well satisfied by modest instrumental resources. Church music, fixated on text, didn't really require more than voices, and indeed the church authorities periodically discouraged instrumental accompaniment.

Another consideration is the unsuitability of early instruments for aggregate playing. Instrumental tone was too raucous to blend well in large groups, even assuming large groups of able musicians could be assembled. With the emergence in the fifteenth and sixteenth centuries of consorts—small groups of similar instruments in different ranges, such as viols, or recorders—and the increasing sophistication of harmonic thinking, both composers and players began to appreciate the potential of larger ensembles.

More than anything, it was the rise of opera that spurred the development of the modern orchestra. Early opera—basically, that of the seventeenth and early eighteenth centuries—dramatized ancient myths and heroic exploits and required a flexible, varied accompaniment equally capable of setting a simple, pastoral mood and intensifying the drama through special effects. One of the earliest examples of what we would almost recognize as a modern orchestra is the ensemble demanded by Monteverdi's 1607 opera *Orfeo.* The score calls for 36 instruments (some musicians may have played more than one): 17 assorted strings; a harp; pairs of archlutes, harpsichords, and cornetti; three organs; four trombones; four trumpets; and a flute. Obviously, this did not become the standard orchestral format, and Monteverdi didn't bother to specify which instruments played what lines except when he deployed just a few at a time. But it was a start.

The development and spreading popularity of the violin family from the middle sixteenth century provided what would soon become the core of the orchestra. String instruments (and players) were soon plentiful, and although the technical skills of most non-soloists were fairly limited, groups of violins, violas, cellos, and basses could produce pleasing and varied sounds.

Orchestral music began to come into its own as a self-sufficient entity with the Baroque concerto form, most often a showcase for a dazzling soloist set against a more routine body of strings. A related type of music, the concerto grosso, set small groups of instruments within the orchestra against each other. Eventually the dance suite also became a popular orchestral vehicle; this was usually an introductory movement followed by a series of minuets, sarabandes, gavottes, and other popular forms of the day. An extension of this was the suite that depicted animals, places, or personalities; Georg Philipp Telemann was particularly adept at this. Such composers as Arcangelo Corelli and George Frideric Handel excelled with the concerto grosso format; Antonio Vivaldi, J.S. Bach, and Telemann each produced many solo concertos; Bach's four *Orchestral Suites* are prime examples of the dance suite unrelated to some theatrical work. Keep in mind, though, that most of this music could be and often was played by only one or two musicians per part, and, strictly speaking, the resulting ensemble of only eight to a dozen players is usually counted as chamber rather than orchestral music.

On occasion, when available, woodwind, brass, and percussion instruments found their way into these ensembles, and the orchestra began to take shape as a palette of tone colors. One of the most popular early works to assemble this diversity of instruments is Bach's *Brandenburg Concerto No. 1,* which calls for strings, two horns, three oboes, bassoon, and harpsichord.

In the mid to late eighteenth century, many composers contributed to the development of what we now regard as the Classical symphony; W.A. Mozart and Joseph Haydn stood in the forefront of this group. Their most mature symphonies required the basic modern orchestra: a body of strings (a dozen or two, varying from town to town), supplemented by pairs of flutes, oboes, bassoons, and horns. Trumpets and drums were added for festive music, and toward the end of the century clarinets were also finding their way into the mix. Nothing was standardized, though; in the 1770s, the *Concert Spirituel* orchestra in Paris boasted 13 first violins, eleven second violins, four violas, ten cellos, four basses, two flutes, three oboes, two clarinets, four bassoons, two horns, two trumpets, and timpani. Orchestras elsewhere held as many as four horns and six bassoons, if the string body was large enough to stand up to them.

Music of the second half of the eighteenth century was becoming somewhat simpler, even while it was growing more sonically dense. The importance of counterpoint faded, and composers of the Classical era placed greater emphasis on accompanied melody. At any given time, strings or woodwinds might be playing the main tune, while the rest of the orchestra provided the harmonic support. (At this point the woodwinds were used primarily to carry snatches of melody when they weren't fleshing out the harmony; within a hundred years, their role would greatly expand.) Meanwhile, orchestral musicians were mastering more and more special effects that within a few decades would be part of any ensemble's basic vocabulary. From the 1760s, for example, the superb orchestra at Mannheim was celebrated for its ability to play softly with good tone, and to glide smoothly through crescendos and diminuendos.

Venues for orchestral music began to change during this period, as well. Initially an orchestra was a status symbol for aristocrats; staff musicians were classified as servants, and they would give private performances for the noble family and its guests. Haydn came up through such a system. Toward the end of the eighteenth century, public concerts became more common. Often they were presented as fashionable events for high society; sometimes they were organized by composers wishing to publicize their newest works. A typical orchestral concert of this era included a concerto, some concert arias, perhaps a chamber piece, and a symphony, although its movements may have been scattered through the concert.

In the nineteenth century, technical advances made almost every instrument either more powerful, more reliable, or more versatile in the number and quality of notes available to it. In the first quarter of the century, the trombone and tuba became more common in the orchestra, and the string complement grew in order to avoid being overpowered by these instruments. Composers eagerly exploited the new possibilities; Ludwig van Beethoven's music began to thunder mightily, but it also took advantage of the increasingly lithe woodwinds. The works of Beethoven and his principle Austro-Germanic successors (Robert Schumann, Johannes Brahms, Anton Bruckner) tended to favor a firm bass foundation and thickly scored harmony within abstract structures, mainly the symphony and concerto. Meanwhile, French composers more often than not strove for a lighter sound even while piling as many instruments as possible into the orchestra, and began seeking inspiration in works of art and literature. Hector Berlioz was most notorious in this regard; his *Symphonie fantastique* not only purported to recount an opium dream in music, but did so with the addition of piccolo, cornets, an extra timpani player, tubular bells, bass drum, and cymbals to the standard orchestra.

The Romantic movement had finally come to music, a few decades after it flowered in literature and art, and many composers were now using the orchestra as a vehicle for deeply personal expression (and, sometimes, ego inflation). With its tremendous dynamic range and variety of tone colors, the orchestra could express anything from delicate, poetic musings on love to the violence of war. Program music—scores dealing less with traditional structural principles than with pictorial narrative and kaleidoscopic emotion—contended with the symphony and concerto for dominance in orchestral concerts. Even the Germans got in on the act, led by Franz Liszt, who was ethnically Hungarian but culturally Teutonic. He advanced the cause of the symphonic poem, availing himself of a French freedom of imagination even while continuing to orchestrate thickly, like a German.

The master of orchestration in the late nineteenth century was a Russian, Nikolay Rimsky-Korsakov, who could draw effects that were sometimes lush, sometimes exotic, from common instruments used in uncommon ranges or combinations. His successor in this regard was Richard Strauss, a master of lavishly orchestrated symphonic poems. Yet as the nineteenth century bled into the twentieth, the French retained a felicitous touch with orchestral color, best exemplified by the works of Claude Debussy and Maurice Ravel.

Toward the end of the nineteenth century the orchestral concert had begun to settle into its modern format: first, a concert overture, symphonic poem, ballet suite, or some other light fare; next, a concerto; and after intermission, a symphony. This, even as the symphony as a form began to decline. Symphonic poems, dance-inspired pieces, suites drawn from theater works, bursts of abstract expression adhering to new form—this was the music propelling the cultural advance of the twentieth century.

Timbre became as critical a component of orchestral composition as form; sound began to shape a work almost as much as patterns of pitch, rhythm, and harmony. This can be heard in music of composers as tenuously related as Claude Debussy, Anton Webern, Olivier Messiaen, and Pierre Boulez.

Whereas Baroque composers had been careful not to write beyond the abilities of their orchestral players and simply ignored instruments that were unreliable or hard to find, composers of the twentieth century eagerly pushed musicians to their limits and freely dropped in whatever odd instruments, usually percussion, corresponded to the sounds in their heads. Consequently, new music of the century was initially played quite poorly. But as conductors and composers persevered, musicians became steadily more adept at making sense of polyrhythms, irregular meters, overlapping or nonexistent tonality, and extended techniques. As the players' ability increased, the music sounded more musical—even that which was intentionally dissonant or haphazardly organized. By the turn of the twenty-first century, provincial American and European orchestras that had been unbearably scrappy a few decades before were approaching the standards of the world's top ensembles and were playing new music with tremendous confidence and skill.

Unfortunately, as the twenty-first century begins, they rarely have a chance to apply this ability to new scores of any scope or sustained complexity. Few composers undertake a major orchestral score without a commission—a full payment and promise of performance. So they write what they're asked to write, and except in the major music centers, that means five- to ten-minute concert openers. Orchestras commission short pieces for three main reasons: an increasingly unfounded fear that audiences will reject anything new, a lack of funds to support the composition of lengthy works, and a lack of rehearsal time to master potentially complex, unfamiliar music. This comes at a time of unprecedented stylistic variety, including—to mention only composers active in America—the strenuous adventures in pitch, rhythm, and texture of Elliott Carter; the stripped-down, vigorous pulsation of Philip Glass; the dense layerings of Jewish, Latin American, and academic influences of Osvaldo Golijov; the bittersweet Romanticism of Lowell Liebermann; and the pop-culture exuberance of Michael Daugherty. The tenuous financial situation of orchestras and record companies is calling the further development and dissemination of orchestral music into question. Whether the orchestra and its repertoire will go the way of the viol consort remains to be seen.

—James Reel

The Symphony

The symphony has its roots in the orchestral weight of the overtures of the French High Baroque, in the rhythmic propulsion of the sinfonias of the Italian early Classical period, and in the unity in diversity of suites of the German late Baroque. The first multi-movement orchestral works to be called symphonies were written by Germans living in Mannheim in the mid-eighteenth century. Their usual sequence of movements was fast-slow-fast with an occasional dance movements added either before or after the central movement. Written in the burgeoning early Classical style, symphonies by the Mannheim composers featured arpeggiated, diatonic tunes over simple accompaniments with rapid harmonic progression in their quick outer movements, expansive lyrical melodies over graceful accompaniments with broader harmonic changes and stylized but still recognizable minutes in their central slow movements. As a form, the Mannheim symphony was not only innovative, it was easily imitated and as easily improved upon.

The first great composer of symphonies was the Austrian Joseph Haydn (1732–1809). From his sprightly early cycle of Symphonies Nos. 6 through 8 (1761) through his passionate *Sturm und Drang* Symphonies Nos. 44 through 52 (1768–1772) the elegant Symphonies Nos. 82 through 87 written for Paris (1785–1786) to the monumental Symphonies Nos. 93 through 104 written for London (1791–1795), Haydn brought the form to its first maturity. In his hands, the symphony became a strong but supple four movements capable of expressing a wide range of thoughts and emotions within carefully wrought forms with memorable themes, inventive developments, soulful slow movements, vivacious dances, and exciting finales embodied in the brilliant colors of the High Classical orchestra and imbued with Haydn's brilliant wit and deep humanity.

While there were many other great symphonists in the High Classical period—Karl Ditters von Dittersdorf, Joseph Martin Krauss, Antonio Rossetti, François Gossec, and Michael Haydn, the greatest was Austrian Wolfgang Amadeus Mozart (1756–1791). Although most of his earliest symphonies are light works written to entertain, Mozart's later symphonies are as fine as Haydn's. The *G minor Symphony,* K. 183 (1773) is as powerful a work as any of Haydn's *Sturm und Drang* symphonies, and his *A major Symphony,* K. 201 from (1774) is as lively as his best piano concertos from the same period. His single movement *G major Symphony* K. 318 (1779) is a superbly realized work despite its unconventional form. But Mozart's supreme achievement as a symphonist is his last six symphonies. The *D major "Haffner,"* K. 385 (1782), the *C major "Linz,"* K. 425 (1783), and the three movement *D major "Prague,"* K. 504 (1786) are all extraordinary works, but the best are Mozart's final triptych of symphonies (1788), the lyrical *E flat major,* K. 543, the tragic *G minor,* K. 550, and the contrapuntal *C major "Jupiter,"* K. 551.

The greatest of the post-Haydn generation of symphonists was the German-Austrian composer Ludwig van Beethoven (1770–1827). Beethoven began in his elegantly witty *C major Symphony,* Op. 21 (1800) and powerfully argued *D major Symphony,* Op. 36 (1802) by imitating the monumental form of Haydn*'s London Symphonies* fused with the elegant content of Mozart's final triptych. But in his massive and muscular *E flat major "Eroica" Symphony* (1803), Beethoven went far beyond the High Classical style of Haydn and Mozart. With huge themes and enormous developments, incredible intensity and overwhelming energy, Beethoven's Eroica irrevocably enlarged symphonic form. After the graceful *B flat major Symphony,* Op. 60 (1807), Beethoven composed the archetypal *per aspera ad astra C minor Symphony,* Op. 67 (1808). As intense but much more concentrated that the Eroica, the Symphony's trajectory from the fuliginous darkness of the opening movement's C minor to the triumphal brightness of the closing movement's C major made it the model for the Romantic symphony of the nineteenth century. After the lyrical *F major "Pastoral,"* Op. 68 (1808) and the Dionysiac A major, Op. 92) and hilarious *F major,* Op. 93 (both 1812), Beethoven stopped writing symphonies for more than a decade. When he returned to the form with the *D minor Symphony,* Op. 125 (1824), Beethoven wrote the grandest and most transcendental symphony ever composed. With the tragedy of the opening movement, the strength of its Scherzo, the beauty of its slow movement and the glory of its closing movement scored for soloist, chorus, and enormous orchestra, Beethoven's final symphony was far beyond the comprehension of his contemporaries.

Beethoven*'s* D minor Symphony was also incomprehensible to the next generation of German composers who modeled their symphonies after works from his Eroica decade. The nine symphonies of the Austrian Franz Schubert (1797–1828) are at first more Mozartean than Beethovenian. Only in the lyrical and tragic two movement unfinished *B minor* D. 759 (1822) and in the colossal energy and gargantuan scale of the *C major,* D. 944 (1825–1828) did Schubert find himself as a symphonic composer on parity with Beethoven. The five orchestral symphonies of the German Felix Mendelssohn (1809–1847) are superbly composed neo-Mozartean works at their best, in the bright *A major "Italian"* (1833) and the glowering *A Minor "Scottish"* of 1842, and pseudo-Handel at their worst, in the *Lobgesang* of 1840. Three of the four symphonies of Robert Schumann (1810–1856)—the bucolic *B flat "Spring"* (1841), the Biedermeier Eroica of the *E flat "Rhenish"* (1850) and especially the *D minor Symphony* (1841)—were all clearly based on Beethoven. The extravagant orchestral works of Frenchman Hector Berlioz (1803–1869) are based as much on the works of the composers of the Revolution and the Empire as on Beethoven. His *Symphonie fantastique* (1830) is a passionate five movement phantasmagoria; his *Sinfonie funèbre et triumphale* (1840) is grandiose work scored for gargantuan military band. His *symphonie dramatique Romeo et Juliette* (1839) is Shakespeare's love story scored for chorus and orchestra. But all of them have the heightened dramatic expression of Beethoven's *Eroica and C minor* symphonies as their ideal. The two symphonies of Franz Liszt (1811–1886)—the striving, sentimental and sardonic Faust (1854) and the *per aspera ad astra* Dante (1855)—are as much derived from Berlioz as from Beethoven. The four symphonies of the German-Austrian composer Johannes Brahms (1833–1897) are clearly based on Beethoven from the *per aspera ad astra* C minor (1876) through the bucolic *D major* (1877) to the heroic *F major* (1883) to the tragic *E minor* (1885), but all of them express Brahms' passionate pessimism. Of the nine symphonies of the Bohemian composer Antonín Dvořák (1841–1904), the last five—starting from the heroic *F major* (1875) through the bucolic *D major* (1880), the tragic *D minor* (1884), the radiant *G major* (1888) to the nostalgic *E minor* "From the New World" (1893)—are instantly memorable. Of the 11 symphonies by the Austrian Anton Bruckner (1824–1896), the last six—starting with heroically Romantic *E flat major* (1874) through the contrapuntally fantastic *B-flat major* (1875), the rugged *A major* (1879), the luminous *E major* (1883), the *per aspera ad astra C minor* (1890) to the tragic and transcendental unfinished *D minor* (1896)—are infinitely magnificent.

The first generation of Russian symphonists were either ardent nationalists like Mily Balakirev (1837–1910) in his muscular *C major* (1864), Alexander Borodin (1833–1887) in his heroic *B minor Symphony* (1876), and Nicolay Rimsky-Korsakov (1844–1908) in his colorful *Antar* (1875), or passionate Westernizers like Pyotr Tchaikovsky (1840–1893) in his tragically suicidal *B minor* (1893). The second generation of Russian symphonists were all epigone's like Alexander Glazunov (1865–1936) in his bucolic *F major* (1902), Sergey Rachmaninov (1873–1943) in his *per aspera ad astra E minor* (1907), or Alexander Scriabin in his megalomaniac *Promethée, le Poème du feu* (1910). The only kind of symphonies the last generation of French symphonists wrote were *per aspera ad astra* symphonies starting with Cesar Franck's *D minor* (1888) and ending with Albéric Magnard's (1865–1914) *C sharp minor* (1913).

Gustav Mahler (1860–1911), the greatest of the last generation of Romantic symphonists, only wrote *per aspera ad astra* symphonies, but his path to the stars was always different. The first four end in Paradise, but the *D major* (1888) suffers through Inferno, the *C minor* (1892) witnesses the apocalypse and the resurrection, the *D minor* (1893) ascends through the Great Chain of Being, and the *G major* (1899) sees Heaven through the eyes of a dead child. The central three symphonies end in affirmation (the *C sharp minor,* 1902), in nihilism (the *A minor,* 1906), or in ecstasy (the *E minor,* 1905), but they all pass the shadow of the valley of death. The monumental *E-flat major* (1906) embodies the highest ideals of German Romanticism at its most passionately idealistic and stands with its head in the stars. All of the last three stand face to face with death: *Das Lied von der Erde* (1908) accepts it through luminous lyricism, the *D major* (1909) succumbs to it with excruciating agony, and the unfinished *F sharp minor* (1910) transcends it with infinite love.

After the First World War, all the Modernist symphonists composed were *per aspera ad astra* symphonies but although they struggled mightily, they rarely reached the stars. Denmark's Carl Nielsen (1865–1931) fights the First War to victory in his *Fifth* (1922). Finland's Jean Sibelius (1865–1957) exiles himself to the great north in his *Seventh* (1924). England's Ralph Vaughan Williams (1872–1958) and William Walton (1902–1983) predict the Second War in their violent *Fourth* (1934) and malignant *First* (1935), respectively. Igor Stravinsky (1882–1971) depicts the Second War in his *Symphony in Three Movements* (1945). Sergey Prokofiev (1891–1953) fights the Second War to victory in his *Fifth* (1944).

The greatest of the Modernist symphonists was the U.S.S.R.'s Dmitry Shostakovich (1906–1975), a composer who embodied the whole of the twentieth century in his 15 symphonies. The first four are ironic parodies: the brilliant *First* (1923) of *per aspera ad astra* symphonies; the Revolutionary *Second* (1927) and *Third* (1929) of choral symphonies and patriotic hymns; and the massive *Fourth* (1935) of Mahler's whole symphonic style. The *Fifth* (1937) is a deadly serious inversion of the *per aspera ad astra* symphony which sinks from ironic tragedy through immobilizing fear to banal brutality. The next four are about the Great Terror and the Great Patriotic War: the schizophrenic *Sixth* (1939) about the anxious dread, the relentless *Seventh* (1941) about the inexorable horror, the pitiless *Eighth* (1943) about the infinite suffering, and the sarcastic *Ninth* (1945) about the awful victory of the lesser of the two greatest evils of the Century. The next four are ironic parodies about life and death in the Soviet State: the massive and malevolent *Tenth* (1953) about the death of Stalin, the monumental and murderous *Eleventh* (1957) about the Revolution of 1905, the extraordinarily banal *Twelfth* (1961) about the life of Lenin, and the grim and gloomy choral-orchestral *Thirteenth* (1962) about life in the U.S.S.R. The last two drop the pretences but not the irony and face mortality and the void. *The Fourteenth* (1969), a song cycle for soloists, strings and percussion, sings only of the terror and the bitterness of death, and the *Fifteenth* (1971), a parody four-movement symphony based on themes from Rossini's heroic *Guillaume Tell,* Wagner's apocalyptic *Gotterdammerung,* and Shostakovich's own relentless, inexorable *Leningrad Symphony,* ends clinking off into emptiness.

—James Leonard

Vocal Music

Broadly speaking, vocal music is any music for the voice. Opera and choral music are often broken out into categories of their own, however, leaving solo songs and small-group music with one voice to a part under the term's umbrella. Audiences raised on popular music may find the sound of classical vocal music unfamiliar, but it's worth making the effort to get past any initial disorientation: "art songs," as classical songs are often called, are still songs, and a song in any tradition is usually a direct, straightforward expression of a familiar emotion. Vocal music, therefore, offers an ideal path into the whole world of classical music for any newcomer.

The Art Song

The vocal category encompasses a great deal of music, but it was the Romantics of the nineteenth century, with their strong appreciation for the connection between poetry and music, who brought the art song to its highest point of development. The most important pioneers in this regard came from Germany, where composers on the forefront of general stylistic developments had a strongly philosophical poetic tradition on which they could draw. Some of the texts of German art songs were classics of German poetry by the likes of Johann Wolfgang von Goethe and Heinrich Heine, while others were by authors who today are little known. Art songs from German-speaking lands are called lieder, from the German word for "songs."

German composers pioneered the song cycle, a setting of a group of related poems that might tell a story or explore a single idea. A song cycle might be compared to the album in the era of recorded music; it is a set of songs unified by a single idea. Franz Schubert wrote several great song cycles, of which the disillusioned and downbeat *Winterreise* (A Winter Journey) is perhaps the most powerful. Ludwig van Beethoven, with his comparatively rarely heard *An die ferne Geliebte* (To the Distant Beloved), blazed the way for the song cycle as he did for so many other new developments. Robert Schumann, with the song cycle *Dichterliebe* (A Poet's Love) among many other works, showed himself an ideal interpreter of the rather bipolar love poetry of Heine. Later in the century the Austrian composer Hugo Wolf was another noted composers of song cycles; his *Spanisches Liederbuch* (Spanish Songbook) and *Italienisches Liederbuch* (Italian Songbook), settings of poems translated from the languages in their respective titles, are intricate creations prized by lovers of art song for their subtle inflections of feeling.

Many individual songs that were not part of song cycles have also become well known. Schubert, who once wrote eight songs in a single day, seemed to have a profound understanding of Goethe's poetry; his setting of the song *Gretchen am Spinnrade* (Gretchen at the Spinning Wheel), from Goethe's play *Faust*, brings the restless obsession of Goethe's wronged young heroine to life. Schubert's *Der Tod und das Mädchen* (Death and the Maiden) is one of several songs by this greatest of all song composers that portrays death's approach with a gripping simplicity. One of the greatest of all song composers was Johannes Brahms, whose individual songs ranged from folk-influenced ditties to densely worked-out creations that paralleled the complexities of the composer's chamber music. His 1878 song *Feldeinsamkeit* (Solitude in the Field) comes close to the essence of the Romantic impulse in its lovely depiction of a young person lying in tall grass at night, listening to the sounds of nature and gazing at the heavens. The song's harmonically lush accompaniment conspires with its deceptively simple vocal line to open a tremendous vista of spiritual freedom and peace.

Although the songs of Schubert and Schumann might be considered the classics of the art song literature, many connoisseurs of the genre are especially enthusiastic about songs of the late nineteenth century. This was the era of nationalism in music, and national schools of art song flourished in every country. The profusion of music for voice and piano around this time had roots that were partly economic: the piano was as essential a piece of household equipment, in both Europe and America, as a television and DVD are today, and since there were many singers around to team up with pianists, printed editions of songs enjoyed strong sales. But songs also made ideal expressions of the nationalist impulse. Composers made settings of the best poetry their countries had to offer, and in some places the emergence of an art song literature was bound up with the reemergence of formerly suppressed national languages. The few Finnish-language songs of Jean Sibelius and the Czech-language songs of Antonín Dvořák, both enjoying revivals in recent years, featured languages that had only recently come into use among educated listeners in their respective countries.

Some national song traditions had names in their own language. The French art song, probably the most important tradition after Germany's, was called a *mélodie*, for example. Important French song composers of the late nineteenth and early twentieth centuries included Gabriel Fauré, Claude Debussy, and Maurice Ravel. The ineffable French quality of the songs of this group can be partially pinned down by considering their restrained, classic feel; they often have a serene mood and introduce intense drama only by degrees. Fauré's songs are notable for their free treatment of harmony, not aimed toward rule-breaking chromaticism but at a range of shades of effect. It was Fauré's harmonies that helped shape Debussy's "impressionistic" style (a term that the composer himself rejected). Debussy's songs are every bit as evocative of Parisian scenes and natural surroundings as are his better-known orchestral tone poems, and, as in the *Fêtes galantes* song cycle written to texts by Paul Verlaine, he favored poetry by the most innovative French writers of the day.

As distinctive as French *mélodies* are the songs of Russia, always a staple of recitals by touring Russian opera singers and increasingly popular among singers of all nationalities. Among the most prolific Russian song composers was Sergey Rachmaninov, whose vocally demanding works feature especially dynamic interplay between the vocal and piano lines—the composer, after all, made his living as a piano virtuoso. One of Rachmaninov's most famous vocal works, the *Vocalise* (1912), has no text at all, just a single continuing vowel sound from the hard-working vocal soloist. Modest Mussorgsky's grim *Songs and Dances of Death* (1882) are another landmark of Russian song repertoire.

Both the *Vocalise* and the *Songs and Dances of Death* are often performed in arrangements for voice and orchestra, and the orchestral song is another important subdivision of the vocal repertoire. France's Hector Berlioz, with his orchestral version of his song cycle *Les nuits d'été* (Summer Nights, completed in 1856), was an important figure in the history of the orchestral song, but it was the German Post-Romantics, Gustav Mahler and Richard Strauss above all, who brought the form to its full maturity. Mahler's *Lieder eines fahrenden Gesellen* (Songs of a Traveling Young Man, completed in 1896), with its combination of naïve simplicity and treacherous psychological terrain, shares many qualities with his symphonies, and the sublime beauties of Strauss's *Four Last Songs* (1948) seemed a transcendent summing-up of their composer's entire career.

Songs Ancient and Modern

Although if you attend a concert or purchase a recording billed as a song recital you will likely hear music of the nineteenth century and beyond, solo songs and those for small groups have constituted an important genre through the entire history of classical music, from the medieval courtly love songs of Guillaume de Machaut onward. The lute song of sixteenth century England is a lovely species of melancholy song, with John Dowland as its greatest practitioner. For many music fans and participants in college singing groups, however, the madrigal was the quintessential genre of Renaissance-era vocal music. The madrigal was a multipart song, often with a text on a romantic theme, that married a sprightly lyricism to subtle contrapuntal art. English madrigal composers such as Thomas Morley, Thomas Weelkes, and Orlando Gibbons (composer of the beautiful "The Silver Swan," a madrigal with a lovely elegiac tone), are the best-known madrigal composers in English-speaking countries, but the English madrigal evolved from an Italian form with a tradition extending over much of the sixteenth century. Italian madrigalists such as Cipriano de Rore, Luca Marenzio, and the bizarrely experimental Carlo Gesualdo have all shown up frequently in concerts and recording catalogues of Renaissance music in recent years.

The solo voice was the foundation stone of Baroque music, and vocal compositions of that era extended well beyond the operas that stood at the center of Baroque concert life. Although the word "cantata" (whose Italian meaning is "something sung") for modern listeners brings to mind the choral church compositions of Johann Sebastian Bach, the cantata was originally a solo genre (sometimes known, confusingly, as a "concerto"). The solo cantata was primarily identified with Italy, the fountainhead of seventeenth century stylistic innovation. Bach wrote solo cantatas of his own, and the genre extended forward to such Classical-era works as Mozart's *Exsultate jubilate* and beyond.

Just as some singers take the earlier eras of the classical tradition for a specialty, others focus on music of the twentieth century and beyond. The category of vocal music in the twentieth century includes a good deal of what is usually considered popular song, and in general the art song recital is a place where the division between popular and classical music, problematical to begin with, becomes especially blurred. Vocalists often program music by George Gershwin, Harold Arlen, Richard Rodgers, and other composers of the Broadway tradition side by side with songs of Schubert, Schumann, and Brahms, and many of the stars of the genre, including Renée Fleming, Bryn Terfel, and Dawn Upshaw, have released top-selling albums of show tunes and their descendants in the world of popular song. One reason for the ease with which these artists can "cross over" is that the Broadway stage in the era prior to electronic amplification demanded singers who had, through classical training, developed the ability to be heard throughout a large theater—an art different in kind from those styles that involve a singer making use of an electronic medium like a microphone. Another is that the Broadway musical, especially in its earlier eras, had strong connections with the European light opera tradition.

At the other end of the spectrum, many modernist composers of the twentieth century favored the art song because the direct appeal of the human voice and the compact size and structure of most songs helped listeners grasp unfamiliar material. Several composers who wrote art songs in English make good places to start with modern vocal music, for example the iconoclastic New Englander Charles Ives, whose songs quote a whole range of American music in clever and philosophically interesting ways (and who also set the *Feldeinsamkeit* text, in both English and German), his fellow American Samuel Barber, whose songs are masterpieces of lyric beauty, and the English composer Benjamin Britten, whose works offer an intelligently conducted tour through the best of English poetry, old and new.

The song in classical music, then, has flourished in fundamentally diverse eras, surviving changes in musical language, in structures of patronage, in the relationship between music and poetry. It is durable precisely because vocal music is a basic form of human expression, because classical musicians, like others, are drawn naturally to song.

—James Manheim

Index

B

C

D

G

L

M

N

O

T